Silent Film Necrology

SECOND EDITION

To Michele Austerlitz,
with great love and affection,
and to my beloved brother, Anthony James Vazzana,
both of whom helped me in my time of need.

Silent Film Necrology

SECOND EDITION

Eugene Michael Vazzana

Foreword by Annette D'Agostino Lloyd

McFarland & Company, Inc., Publishers
Jefferson, North Carolina, and London

The present work is a reprint of the illustrated case bound edition of Silent Film Necrology, 2d ed. *first published in 2001 by McFarland.*

LIBRARY OF CONGRESS CATALOGUING-IN-PUBLICATION DATA

Vazzana, Eugene Michael, 1940–2001.
Silent film necrology / Eugene Michael Vazzana;
foreword by Annette D'Agostino Lloyd.—2d ed.
p. cm.

ISBN 978-0-7864-4515-8
softcover : 50# alkaline paper ♾

1. Motion picture actors and actresses—United States—Obituaries—Indexes. 2. Silent films—United States—History and criticism. 3. Motion pictures—United States—Biography—Indexes.
I. Title.
PN1998.2.V38 2011 016.79143'028'092273—dc21 2001031608

BRITISH LIBRARY CATALOGUING DATA ARE AVAILABLE

Manufactured in the United States of America

Front cover: Blanche Sweet in *Judith of Bethulia* (1913).

McFarland & Company, Inc., Publishers
Box 611, Jefferson, North Carolina 28640
www.mcfarlandpub.com

Contents

Foreword

The many aspects of Gene Vazzana can be glimpsed in his writings, and what and who he wrote about. His *Silent Film Newsletter*, which graduated to *The Silent Film Monthly* and, ultimately, *The Silent Film Annual*, introduced scores of eager minds to the beauty and elegance of the roots of cinema, and its practitioners. In many ways, these opuses were love songs, as well.

With a vivid shock of white hair, a constant companion cigarette dangling from his mouth, and a perennial notebook in his jacket pocket, Vazzana would scout memorabilia shows in Manhattan, seeking out magazines, stills, books, and whatever ephemera would assist him in his ultimate goal: comprehensively chronicling the silent film era. That is the environment in which I first met Gene, in 1993, when I was in my infancy as a researcher. What a fortunate meeting, for someone like me, for this man would soon become what he still is for me: a prime role model.

When the first edition of the *Silent Film Necrology* was first published in 1995, Gene autographed my copy, and immediately voiced his intent to start work on a second edition, and to have it ready for release in five years. He began this quest as he accomplished the first: gathering obituaries from far and near, scouring magazines for helpful complementary citations, dissecting piles of death certificates, and consulting with specialists for help in verifying facts. His greatest strength (but there were many) was his ability to unselfishly conduct research, nitpicking and scrutinizing each and every detail—Minutia should have been his middle name—all with an end towards a significant contribution to film scholarship. This Vazzana did, day in process. For years, I watched Gene work in the library. I talked shop (i.e., silent film) with him for endless hours, both on the phone and in person. I'd joke with him about how each strand of white hair that made up his prized coif was resultant from too many nights up, working. I think Gene knew that I out and out copy his technique to this day; I admire his work ethic greatly, and I love the fact that, like him, I represent the period of film that he so adored.

Duplicating perfection is not a simple task—those who try are, usually, doomed to being branded either a failure or an imitator. In the case of Gene Vazzana, however, this edition of the *Silent Film Necrology* will, in more than the obvious ways, accomplish its hefty goal, to the point of being *more* helpful than its predecessor. In the years since the publication of the first edition, Gene continued to learn—and the lessons he absorbed, the new facts he unearthed, and the enhancements he added, all represent the finest in film scholarship. His goal extended further than that—towards memorialization—and he prided himself in not only shaping a helpful necrology, but also complementing the birth and death credentials with article and book citations and whatever facts he could provide. He *always* strove for perfection; those of us he called friends were so fortunate to be around such a person.

Successfully completing this book was goal number one to Gene, particularly after he was diagnosed with stomach cancer, the disease that tragically took his life on January 1, 2001. Finish, he did, and in the amount of time he predicted in 1995; I take comfort in that fact, as well as in knowing the extreme relief Gene must have felt in this achievement.

I have hardly begun to fill in the dash between the dates that made up the life of Eugene Michael Vazzana, but I feel better knowing that I have put to paper what a great man this author was, and what a sparkling part of my life he was. And, I am not alone: each recipient of his work, ultimately, will become, and will remain, one of his legions of grateful friends.

Annette D'Agostino Lloyd

Abbreviation Key

AMD Annette M. D'Agostino, comp., *Filmmakers in* The Moving Picture World; *An Index of Articles, 1907–1927* (Jefferson NC: McFarland, 1997)

AMPAS Academy of Motion Picture Arts and Sciences, Margaret Herrick Library, 8949 Wilshire Blvd., Beverly Hills CA 90211

AS André Siscot, *Les gens du cinéma* [*The People of the Movie World*] (Brussels, Belgium: Éditions Memor, 1998)

ASC American Society of Cinematographers (ASC), P.O. Box 2230, Hollywood CA 90078

Ball Robert Hamilton Ball, *Shakespeare on Silent Film; A Strange Eventful History* (London: George Allen and Unwin, Ltd., 1968)

BHD Billy H. Doyle, *The Ultimate Directory of the Silent Screen Performers; A Necrology of Births and Deaths and Essays on 50 Lost Players,* ed. Anthony Slide (Metuchen NJ: Scarecrow Press, 1995); "BHD, addendum" refers to additions and revisions sent by Doyle to the author

BHD1 Billy H. Doyle, *The Ultimate Directory of Silent and Sound Era Performers; A Necrology of Actors and Actresses,* ed. Anthony Slide (Lanham MD: Scarecrow Press, 1999)

BHD2 Billy H. Doyle, *The Ultimate Directory of Film Technicians; A Necrology of Dates and Places of Births and Deaths of More than 9,000 Producers, Screenwriters, Composers, Cinematographers, Art Directors, Costume Designers, Choreographers, Executives, and Publicists* (Lanham MD: Scarecrow Press, 1999)

Blum Daniel Blum, *A Pictorial History of the Silent Screen* (New York: Grosset & Dunlap, 1953). Daniel Blum, *A Pictorial History of the American Theatre, 1860–1970,* 3rd ed. (New York NY: Crown Publishers, Inc., 1972)

BR Buck Rainey, *Sweethearts of the Sage: Biographies and Filmographies of 258 Actresses Appearing in Western Movies* (Jefferson NC: McFarland, 1992)

Brownlow Kevin Brownlow, *The Parade's Gone By...* (Berkeley: University of California Press, 1968)

BS Michael G. Ankerich, *Broken Silence; Conversations with 23 Silent Film Stars* (Jefferson NC: McFarland, 1993)

CCN *Century Cyclopedia of Names*

CEPMJ *The Complete Encyclopedia of Popular Music and Jazz 1900–1950,* 4 Vols. (Arlington House, 1974)

CFC *Classic Film Collector* (renamed *Classic Images*)

CH Clive Hirschhorn, *The Universal Story* (New York: Crown, 1983)

CI *Classic Images,* P.O. Box 809, Muscatine IA 52761 (numbered by issue; there is no volume number)

Cinema Arts Published by Cinema Magazine, Inc., 250 Park Avenue, New York NY (Vol. I, No. 1, June 1937)

CNW Kalton C. Lahue, *Continued Next Week: A History of the Moving Picture Serial* (Norman: University of Oklahoma Press, 1964)

CP Ken D. Jones, Arthur F. McClure, and Alfred F. Twomey, *Character People* (South Brunswick NJ: A.S. Barnes, 1976)

DAB *Dictionary of American Biography*

EK Ephraim Katz, *The Film Encyclopedia* (New York: Perigee Books, 1982)

EK 1994 Ephraim Katz, Melina Corey and George Ochoa, *The Film Encyclopedia* (New York: Harper Collins, 1994)

FDY "Work of Scenarists," pp. 417 *et passim*; "Cameramen's Work," pp. 455 *et passim, Film Daily Yearbook, 1929*

FFF Charles Donald Fox, *Famous Film Folk; A Gallery of Life Portraits and Biographies* (New York: George H. Doran Company, 1925)

Finch John Richard Finch, *Close-Ups from the Golden Age of the Silent Cinema* (New York: A.S. Barnes, 1978)

FIR *Films in Review,* P.O. Box 589, New York NY 10021

FR Data supplied by Frank Reichelt, Troisdorf, Germany

FSFM Elinor Hughes, *Famous Stars of Filmdom (Men)* (Boston: L.C. Page & Co., 1932)

FSFW Elinor Hughes, *Famous Stars of Filmdom (Women)* (Boston: L.C. Page & Co., 1931)

FSS Roy Liebman, *From Silents to Sound; A Biographical Encyclopedia of Performers Who Made the Transition to Talking Pictures* (Jefferson NC: McFarland, 1998)

GK George Katchmer, *Eighty Silent Film Stars; Biographies and Filmographies of the Obscure to the Well Known* (Jefferson NC: McFarland, 1991)

GSS Sheridan Morley, *The Great Stage Stars; Distinguished Theatrical Careers of the Past and Present* (New York: Facts on File Publication, 1986)

Halliwell's Filmgoer's Companion ed. John Walker, 12th ed. (New York: Harper Collins, 1989)

HCH Hal C. Herman, *How I Broke into the Movies; Signed Autobiographies; by Sixty Famous Screen Stars* (rpt., Sandy Hook CT: Yesteryear Press, 1984)

IFN William T. Stewart, Arthur F. McClure and Ken D. Jones, *International Film Necrology* (New York: Garland, 1981)

JCD Data supplied by Juan Carlos Dominguez, Córdoba, Argentina

JCL John C. Lahue, *Gentlemen to the Rescue; The Heroes of the Silent Screen* (Cranbury NJ: A.S. Barnes, 1972)

JS John Stewart, *Italian Film: A Who's Who* (Jefferson NC: McFarland, 1994)

Jura Jean-Jacques Jura and Rodney Norman Bardin II, *Balboa Films; A History and Filmography of the Silent Film Studio* (Jefferson NC: McFarland, 1999)

KOM Anthony Slide, *The Kindergarten of the Movies: A History of the Fine Arts Company* (Metuchen NJ: Scarecrow Press, 1980)

LACD Extracts from the Los Angeles CA City Directory, 1920 (r = residence; h = home)

LD Kalton C. Lahue, *Ladies in Distress* (New York: A.S. Barnes, 1971)

Lowrey Carolyn Lowrey, *The First One Hundred Noted Men and Women of the Screen* (New York: Moffat, Yard, 1920)

MH Charles Donald Fox, *Mirrors of Hollywood; with Brief Biographies of Favorite Film Folk* (New York: Charles Renard, 1925)

MM *Movie Magazine,* 1926 Broadway, New York NY

MoMA Museum of Modern Art, 11 West 53rd Street, New York NY 10019

MPA *Motion Picture Almanac* (Chicago: Quigley, 1929–1931)

MPC *Motion Picture Classic,* Brewster Publications, Inc., 18410 Jamaica Avenue, Jamaica NY

MPM *Motion Picture Magazine*

MPN *Moving Picture News,* ed. Alfred H. Saunders (New York: Cinematographer Publishing Co.)

MPS *Moving Picture Stories* (early fan magazine)

MPSM *Motion Picture Story Magazine*

MPW *Motion Picture World* (early trade paper)

MSBB "Mirror Studio Blue Book," *Dramatic Mirror,* 28 Dec 1918, pp. 1018–54

Musser Charles Musser, *Before the Nickelodeon; Edwin S. Porter and the Edison Manufacturing Company* (Berkeley: University of California Press, 1991)

MVRB Commonwealth of Massachusetts, Department of Health, Registrar of Vital Records and Statistics, 470 Atlantic Avenue, 2nd flr., Boston MA 02210-2224 (617-753-8600)

MW *Movie Weekly* (early fan magazine)

NEAB *National Encyclopedia of American Biography*

1921 Directory *Motion Picture Studio Directory and Trade Annual, 1921* (New York: Motion Picture News, 1921)

NNAT *Notable Names in the American Theatre* (Clifton NJ: James T. White and Co., 1976), "Necrology," pp. 343–488

NYDM *The New York Dramatic Mirror* (established 1879)

NYFHC New York Family History Center, 2 Lincoln Square, New York NY 10023 (212-873-1690)

NYMPC or **NYMP Co** New York Motion Picture Co.

NYT *The New York Times*

O&W Ted Okuda, with Edward Watz, *The Columbia Comedy Shorts; Two-Reel Hollywood Film Comedies, 1933–1958* (Jefferson NC: McFarland, 1986)

Ontario Office of the Registrar General, PO Box 4600, 189 Red River Road, Thunder Bay, Ontario, Canada P7B 6L8 (In Ontario 1-800-461-2156; 1-807-343-7420)

Paris and Hollywood Paris Publishing Co., Broadway at Eleventh Street, Louisville KY (25¢ a copy; $2.50 per year; later titled *Paris and Hollywood Screen Secrets Magazine*)

Parish James Robert Parish, *Hollywood Character Actors* (New Rochelle NY: Arlington House, 1978)

Photoplay Arts Portfolio *Photoplay Arts Portfolio of Eclair [Kalem, Thanhouser] Moving-Picture Stars with Biographies and Autographs* (New York: Photoplay Arts Co., 1914; unpaginated) [at MoMA Library]

PNI Byron A. Falk, Jr., and Valerie R. Falk, *Personal Name Index to "The New York Times Index, 1851–1974"* (Succasunna NJ: Roxbury Data Interface, 1976)

Quinlan David Quinlan, *Illustrated Directory of Film Stars* (New York: Hippocrene Books, 1986)

Ragan David Ragan, *Who's Who in Hollywood, 1900–1976* (New Rochelle NY: Facts on File, 1976)

Ragan 2 David Ragan, *Who's Who in Hollywood* (New York: Facts on File, 1992; revised edition)

Ramsaye Terry Ramsaye, *A Thousand and One Nights; A History of the Motion Picture Through 1925* (rpt. 1986; New York: Simon & Schuster, 1926)

RL Data supplied by Richard E. Levinson, Toronto, Canada

Screen Book; Love Stories from the Movies. Novel Magazine Corporation, 225 Varick Street, New York NY (bimonthly, 25¢ a copy, $1.50 a year. B.A. Mackinnon, President)

SD *Stage Deaths: A Biographical Guide to International Theatrical Obituaries, 1850 to 1990* (Westport CT: Greenwood Press, 1991), 2 vols., compiled by George B. Bryan

The Silent Film Annual 501 Maryland Avenue #J, Oakmont PA 15139; Gene Vazzana, editor

Singer Michael Singer, ed., *Film Directors; A Complete Guide; Eighth Annual International Edition* (n.p.: Long Eagle, 1990)

Slide Anthony Slide, *The Big V: A History of the Vitagraph Company* (Metuchen NJ: Scarecrow Press, 1987)

Slide, *Aspects* Anthony Slide, *Aspects of American Film Prior to 1920* (Metuchen NJ: Scarecrow Press, 1978)

SOS William M. Drew, *Speaking of Silents; First Ladies of the Screen* (Vestal NY: Vestal Press, 1989)

Spehr Paul C. Spehr, *The Movies Begin; Making Movies in New Jersey 1887–1920* (Newark: Newark Museum, 1977)

SW *Screen World,* ed. John Willis (Crown Publishers)

Truitt Evelyn Mack Truitt, *Who Was Who on Screen* (New York: R.R. Bowker, 1974), revised ed., 1984

Variety *Variety Obituaries, 1905–1986* (New York: Garland, 1988) and supplement to 1988 [unpaginated]. Also *see* Jeb H. Perry, *Variety Obits: An Index to Obituaries in Variety, 1905–1978* (Metuchen NJ: Scarecrow Press, 1980)

VB Data supplied by Victor Berch, Marlborough MA

Vinson James Vinson, ed., *The International Dictionary of Films and Filmmakers: Volume III* (Chicago: St. James Press, 1986)

Waldman Harry Waldman, *Hollywood and the Foreign Touch: A Dictionary of Foreign Filmmakers and Their Films from America, 1910–1995* (Lanham MD: Scarecrow Press, 1996)

Wampas Star Western Association of Motion Picture Advertisers; each year 1922–1929 it voted for 13 actresses as the most promising stars of the future, based on past performances.

WBO1, WBO2 Richard Lamparski, (1) *Whatever Became of...?* (New York: Crown, 1967); (2) Second Series, 1968), etc.

WFE Clarence Winchester, *The World Film Encyclopedia* (London: Amalgamated Press, 1933)

Woodland Hills CA The Motion Picture Country Hospital

WWIT *Who's Who in the Theater* (various publishing data)

WWS Charles Fox and Milton L. Silver, eds., *Who's Who on the Screen* (New York: Ross Publishing Co., 1920)

WWVC Stephen Herbert and Luke McKernan, eds., *Who's Who of Victorian Cinema* (London: British Film Institute, 1996)

WWWA *Who Was Who in America,* various volumes (A.N. Marquis Co.)

Introduction

The silent film era in the United States began in the East, in New York and New Jersey. Once silent film took hold as regular entertainment for the masses, it was bound to spread to every city across the nation and to every nation on the globe. Legitimate actors avoided the flickers until it was clear that when they were "at liberty" they could obtain employment, and enough of it, to keep them occupied during the summer months and between engagements. As salaries rose, actors were accepting work in films more readily, so much so that by 1915 theatrical managers were in an uproar when their actors defected to the films. This was a time when many actresses had three names; when you could walk into the grounds of a studio in Fort Lee, New Jersey, and get hired on the spot; when film work became an option because you had to support a mother and siblings, with no father; when part of your biography as reported in the magazines included a stay in a convent; when you saw someone you knew in a film and you went to Hollywood, found your friend, and ended up in films yourself, as did John Gilbert with Herschel Mayall in 1915. The rewards were great if success was attained: the most popular stars were rewarded beyond anyone's imagination. The ascent to success was often arduous; the descent was often unexpected and abrupt.

They are mostly gone now, those talented people who worked so hard to provide entertainment on a regular basis. They deserve to be remembered and a necrology is, in a way, a book of remembrance.

This volume is far from exhaustive. There is still much research to do with *The New York Dramatic Mirror, Motography, Billboard, The Hollywood Reporter,* and other publications. Time is the culprit,

> But at my back I always hear
> Time's wingèd chariot hurrying near...

My original book was published in June 1995, and since that time I have continued research on the material. Many corrections have been made and more importantly, many new entries have been included in the present volume. A spectacular book was published by André Siscot, *Les Gens du Cinéma* (*The People of the Movie World*) (Brussels, Belgium: Éditions Memor, 1998), which contains 1,185 pages of entries, many of them from countries difficult to research in the United States Mr. Siscot promises a revision of his text in the future and this will be a real boon to researchers.

Research on individuals grows apace and new books are appearing more frequently. Some of the latest ones are those volumes on Florence Lawrence (Kelly R. Brown), H. Rider Haggard (Phil Leibfried), Ramon Novarro (Allan R. Ellenberger), Ben Hecht (Florice Whyte-Kovan), and Carl Th. Dreyer (Jean and Dale D. Drum), to name a few of the best.

Many people volunteered to help me with citations, foremost among them Victor A. Berch of Marlborough, Massachusetts, who sent me hundreds of photocopies from his research, some from obscure publications. I owe him a debt of gratitude for his unstinting dedication to film research and his sharing it with me.

Others who helped were William C. Clogston of Chicago, Illinois; Mrs. Janice Healey of London, England, who sent me obituaries from England and Asia; Philip Leibfried of New York, New York, who sent me obituaries from *The New York Times;* Rick Levinson of Montreal, Canada, who sent me a number of birth certificates from Canada; Madeline Matz of the Library of Congress, Motion Picture, Broadcasting and Recorded Sound Division, Washington, D.C.; and Miss Lillian Tudiver of Brooklyn, New York, who gave me her data on many entries. Others, cited in the text, also gave me their help and I thank them all for their generous assistance.

This is a necrology and annotated bibliography of silent era film industry personnel. It includes actors, actresses, directors, executives, producers, cinematographers, stunt performers, publicists, composers, inventors, and many more.

Volume numbers have been omitted from most publications, especially from *Variety* and *The New York Times* citations because all that is needed to find the data on microfilm is the date. Most deaths that occurred in Hollywood have been changed to Los Angeles CA, because Hollywood is in Los Angeles County. I have retained NB for Nebraska instead of the curious change to NE made by the Post Office. *Né* (masculine) and *née* (feminine) both mean "born" in French; these terms are used for the birth name, while b. ("born") is used for the place and date of birth. I have omitted d. ("died") to save space, using a dash instead.

Names in **bold** have an entry of their own.

While I have used "scenarist" instead of screenwriter, I have avoided neologisms that didn't take, such as "scenarioist," or "chauffing" for riding in a car. In magazines, "luncheon" was used more often than "lunch"; this gave a formal aspect to the occasion as befit the interviewing of a film star (or "photoplayer"). Cameraman and cinematographer are synonymous, although the former is the older word used.

There are several entries for animals and one cartoon character, Mickey Mouse; the latter is included to remind everyone that a number of cartoon characters (Farmer Alfalfa, Krazy Kat, etc.) were regular features on the silent screen.

Some characters herein are so fascinating as to deserve a biography, among them Corse Payton. The early silent era in Turin, Italy—note in this text how many Italian silent film players were born in Turin—roughly equivalent to what was happening in New York City in the 1910s, also deserves a book in English.

This volume should remain an inducement to further research.

Gene Vazzana
Pittsburgh, Pennsylvania
October 31, 2000

Silent Film Necrology

A

Aasen, John [circus giant/actor] (*né* Johan Aasen, b. Minneapolis MN, 1887?–1 Aug 1938 [51], Mendocino CA). "Ex-Circus Giant Dies; John Aasen, 8 Ft. 9 In. in Height, Had Appeared in Film Comedies," *NYT,* 3 Aug 1938. AMD, p. 15. IFN, p. 3. "'Why Worry,' Lloyd's Next Comedy[,] Is Listed for Premiere," *MPW,* 28 Jul 1923, 320.

Abbas, Hector [actor] (b. Amsterdam, Holland, 9 Nov 1884–11 Nov 1942 [58], London, England). BHD1, p. 1. IFN, p. 1.

Abbe, Charles S[mith] [actor] (b. South Windham CT, 23 May 1859–16 Jun 1932 [73], Darien CT; blood poisoning from infected tooth). m. Emily A. Bruce. "Charles S. Abbe," *Variety,* 21 Jun 1932. BHD, p. 88 (b. 1860). IFN, p. 3. NNAT, p. 343. SD. Truitt, p. 1.

Abbe, Jack Yutaka [actor] (b. Japan, 1895–3 Jan 1977 [81], Tokyo, Japan). BHD, p. 88. IFN, p. 3. LACD, "photoplayer," r 1904 Argyle Avenue.

Abbe, James [actor/cinematographer] (b. Alfred ME, 17 Jul 1883–11 Nov 1973 [90], San Francisco CA). "James Abbe, 91, Dies; A Photo Journalist," *NYT,* 13 Nov 1973, 48:2. BHD, p. 88; BHD2, p. 1.

Abbe, John [photographer]. No data found. AMD, p. 15. "Director Storn Engages Well Known Photographer," *MPW,* 27 Nov 1920, 488.

Abbey, May Evers [actress] (b. Hartford CT, 1872–20 Aug 1952 [80], New York NY [Death Certificate No. 18165: Mary Lessey; age 82]; jumped or fell from window). m. **George Lessey** (d. 1947). (Edison, 1912.) "Mrs. May A. Lessey," *Variety,* 27 Aug 1952. AMD, p. 15. BHD, p. 88. IFN, p. 3. "Miss May Abbey," *MPW,* 31 May 1913, 905.

Abbot, Harold P. [actor] (b. 1890?–17 Apr 1922 [32], Albuquerque NM; tuberculosis). "Harold P. Abbot," *Variety,* 5 May 1922.

Abbott, Albert [musician] (b. IA, 28 Mar 1884–4 Sep 1962 [78], Reseda CA; heart attack). "Al Abbott," *Variety,* 12 Sep 1962. IFN, p. 3. SA. Truitt, p. 1.

Abbott, Mrs. Dorothy [scenarist]. No data found. LACD, "filmwriter," h 628 1/2 W. Vernon Avenue.

Abbott, Frank[lin] **H.** [actor] (b. CA, 16 Jul 1878–2 Feb 1957 [78], Los Angeles CA). BHD, p. 88. IFN, p. 3. SA. Truitt, p. 1.

Abbott, Fred [writer/director]. No data found. AMD, p. 15. "Edison Company in Detroit," *MPW,* 30 Oct 1915, 769.

Abbott, George Francis [playwright/director/actor/producer/scenarist] (b. Forestville NY, 25 Jun 1887–31 Jan 1995 [107], Miami Beach FL; stroke). m. (1) Ednah Levis, 1913 (d. 1930); (2) Mary Sinclair, 1946–1951; (3) Joy Valderrama, 1983. *Mister Abbott* (1963). (Broadway debut: *The Misleading Lady,* Nov 1913.) Marilyn Berger, "George Abbott, Broadway Giant With Hit After Hit, Dead at 107," *NYT,* 1 Feb 1995, A1, D20 (reprinted on 2 Feb). Jeremy Gerard, "George Abbott," *Variety,* 6 Feb 1995, 84:1. "George Abbott Memorial," *NYT,* 23 May 1995, B11:1 (to be held on 5 June). Mel Gussow, "Abbott Is Remembered in the Colorful Spirit of Broadway; Fond, funny memories and strains of 'Hey There,'" *NYT,* 6 Jun 1995, B18:1 (speakers included Natalia Makarova, Kitty Carlisle Hart, Eli Wallach, John Raitt, and Jerome Robbins). BHD2, p. 1.

Abbott, Gypsy [vaudeville/film actress] (b. Atlanta GA, 31 Jan 1897–25 Jul 1952 [55], Los Angeles CA). m. **Henry King**, ca. 1914 (d. 1982). (Balboa, 1914.) "Mrs. Gypsy Abbott King," *Variety,* 30 Jul 1952. BHD, p. 88. IFN, p. 3. Billy H. Doyle, "Lost Players," *CI,* 153 (Mar 1988), 53–54.

Abbott, James Francis [actor] (b. 1872?–19 Jan 1954 [81], No. Hollywood CA). "James Francis Abbott," *Variety,* 27 Jan 1954. IFN, p. 3. Truitt, p. 1.

Abbott, L[enwood] **B**[allard] [special effects cinematographer] (b. Pasadena CA, 13 Jun 1908–28 Sep 1985 [77], Los Angeles CA). m. Muriel. *Special Effects—Wire, Tape and Rubber Band Style* (1960's). (Began 1926.) "L.B. Abbott," *Variety,* 9 Oct 1985. "L.B. Abbot [sic]; Oscar Winning Cinematographer," *LA Times,* 4 Oct 1985, II, p. 2. BHD2, p. 1. Katz 1994.

Abbott, Marion [stage/film actress] (b. Danville KY, 27 Jan 1865?–15 Jan 1937 [71], Philadelphia PA; pneumonia). "Miss Marion Abbott, Retired Actress, Dies; Had Roles in Plays with Maude Adams and E.H. Sothern—37 Years on the Stage," *NYT,* 17 Jan 1937, B8:7. AMD, p. 15. BHD, p. 88 (b. 1867). IFN, p. 3. SA (b. 1866). "Distinctive Engages Marion Abbott," *MPW,* 30 Dec 1922, 883.

Abdullah, Achmed [scenarist] (*né?,* b. Yalta, Crimea, 12 May 1881–12 May 1945 [64], New York NY). m. (1) Jean Wick; (2) Rosemary A. Doland, 1940. *The Cat Had Nine Lives* (1933). "Achmed Abdullah," *Variety,* 16 May 1945. BHD2, p. 1. SD.

Abel, Alfred [actor/director] (b. Leipzig, Germany, 12 Mar 1879–12 Dec 1937 [58], Berlin, Germany). BHD1, p. 2; BHD2, p. 1. IFN, p. 3. Vittorio Martinelli, "Kino-Lieblinge," *Griffithiana,* 38/39 (Oct 1990), 41.

Abel, David [cinematographer] (b. Amsterdam, Holland, 15 Dec 1883–12 Nov 1973 [89], Los Angeles CA). BHD2, p. 1. FDY, p. 455. KOM, p. 127.

Abel, Walter Charles [stage/film actor] (b. St. Paul MN, 6 Jun 1898–26 Mar 1987 [88], Ivoryton, Middlesex CT; heart attack). m. Marietta Bitter. Jeremy Gerard, "Walter Abel, 88, Actor in Theater and Films," *NYT,* 28 Mar 1987, 32:1. "Walter Abel Dies at 88; Vet Actor on Stage, in Films," *Variety,* 1 Apr 1987. BHD1, p. 2. IFN, p. 3. SA. SD.

Abeles, Edward S. [actor/director] (b. St. Louis MO, 4 Nov 1869–10 Jul 1919 [49], New York NY; pneumonia). "Edward Abeles," *Variety,* 18 Jul 1919. BHD, p. 88. IFN, p. 3. SA.

Abingdon, William L[epper] (father of **William Abingdon**) [actor] (*né* William Lepper Abington, b. Tewcesterherthcontes, England, 2 May 1859–17 May 1918 [59], New York NY; suicide). m. (2 sons). "Actor Brooded Over War; Abingdon's Notes Told Suicide Motive—Cohan to Deliver Eulogy," *NYT,* 19 May 1918, 23 (eulogies to be delivered by George M. Cohan and De Wolf Hopper; to be buried in Woodlawn Cemetery. "'For some time I have been suffering from neurasthenia, melancholia, a desire to avoid people, and a lack of interest in anything and everything,' one of the notes read. 'Haven't been near the club in three weeks. Hiding away in cheap picture shows or staying at home....'"). "Funeral of W.L. Abingdon; More Than 400 Friends of Dead Actor Attend Services," *NYT,* 20 May 1918, 11:4 ("George M. Cohan and De Wolf Hopper, who were to have made addresses at the services[,] were unable to attend." Burial was in Evergreen Cemetery, Brooklyn NY. Two of the pallbearers were William Courtleigh and Joseph Kilgour.). AS, p. 31.

Abingdon, William (son of **William L. Abingdon**) [actor/director] (*née* William Benjamin Pilgrim, b. London, England, 1 Jul 1888–13 Dec 1959 [71], Esther, Surrey, England). m. **Bijou Fernandez** (d. 1961); Cecilia Elen. "William Abingdon," *Variety,* 23 Dec 1959. AS, p. 31. SD.

Abrams, Charles [executive] (b. 1874–5 May 1930 [56?], New York NY). AMD, p. 15. BHD2, p. 1. "Breaking Records," *MPW,* 13 Apr 1912, 131. "Charles Abrams Back from the West," *MPW,* 20 Jul 1912, 256.

Abrams, Hiram [President of Paramount, 1916–19; United Artists Corp., 1919–26] (b. Portland ME, 1878?–15 Nov 1926 [48], New York NY [Death Certificate No. 28260]; heart attack). "Hiram Abrams Dead; United Artists' Head; Was Associate of Mary Pickford, Fairbanks, Chaplin and Griffith," *NYT,* 6 Nov 1926, 27:2. "Hiram Abrams," *Variety,* 17 Nov 1926. AMD, p. 15. BHD2, p. 1. SA. "Abrams Head of Paramount," *MPW,* 24 Jun 1916, 2214.

Abrams, Leon [scenarist/director] (b. Granville NY, 28 Jul 1892–5 Jul 1977 [84], Moraga, Contra Costa CA). "Leon Abrams," *Variety,* 27 Jul 1977. BHD2, p. 1 (b. 16 Apr 1895; d. Walnut Creek CA). FDY, p. 417.

Abramson, Ivan [playwright/director/scenarist/composer/Ivan Film Company] (b. Vilna, Russia, 1869?–15 Sep 1934 [65], New York NY [Death Certificate No. 20537]). m. **Lizzie Einhorn** (d. 1945). "Ivan Abramson," *Variety,* 18 Sep 1934. AMD, p. 16. BHD2, p. 1 (b. Vilnius, Lithuania). IFN, p. 3. MSBB, p. 1044. "Ivan Abramson Master Craftsman," *MPW,* 4 Mar 1916, 1455.

Abramson, Mrs. Ivan *see* **Einhorn, Lizzie**

Abramson, Max [silent title writer/publicist] (b. New York NY, 1890?–11 Apr 1956 [66], New York NY [Death Certificate No. 8041]). m. Rose Alden. "Max Abramson Dies; Publicist of Movies," *NYT,* 12 Apr 1956, 31:3. "Max Abramson," *Variety,* 18 Apr 1956. BHD2, p. 1.

Abranches, Adelina [stage/film actress] (*née* Margarita Adelina Abranches, b. Lisbon, Portugal, 15 Aug 1865–21 Nov 1945 [80], Lisbon, Portugal). m. actor Luis Ruas (daughter Aura, d. 23 Mar 1962; son Alfredo Ruas). "Adelina Abranches," *NYT,* 23 Nov 1945, 23:2. AS, p. 31 (b. 1866).

Abril, Dorothy [actress] (b. Paterson NJ, 10 Jun 1897–28 Apr 1977 [79], Los Angeles CA). BHD1, p. 88. IFN, p. 3. Robert A. Evans, "Evans' 1977 Chronicle," *FIR,* XXIX, Mar 1978, 149 (age 80).

Achard, Marcel [actor/playwright/scenarist] (b. Sainte-Foy-les-Lyon, France, 5 Jul 1899–4 Sep 1974 [75], Paris, France; diabetes). m. Lily. "Marcel Achard," *Variety,* 25 Sep 1974, 62:2. BHD2, p. 2 (d. 1975).

Acheson, Frank [actor]. No data found. LACD, "actor," r 307 Wall.

Achterberg, Frtiz [actor] (b. Berlin, Germany, 2 Nov 1888–Oct 1971 [82]). IFN, p. 3. BHD, p. 88.

Acker, Edward [scenarist]. No data found. AMD, p. 16. "Edward Acker," *MPW,* 30 Sep 1916, 2114.

Acker, Eugene [actor] (b. Stockholm, Sweden, 13 May 1889–26 Jun 1971 [82], San Francisco CA). (Essanay). BHD, p. 88.

Acker, Jean [actress] (b. Trenton NJ, 23 Oct 1892–16 Aug 1978 [85], Los Angeles CA). m. **Rudolph Valentino**, 5 Nov 1919 (d. 1926). "Jean Acker," *Variety,* 23 Aug 1978. AMD, p. 16. BHD1, p. 2 (b. 1893). IFN, p. 3. LACD, "photoplayer," h 1954 Pinehurst Road. MH, p. 93. SA. "Jean Acker Weds Rodolpho Valentino," *MPW,* 22 Nov 1919, 435. "'Rodolph Couldn't Have Treated Me Worse,' Cries Jean Acker; Her Story of Romance, Illness and Divorce Brings to Light Sensational Revelations of Valentino's Intimate Life," *MW,* II, 28 Oct 1922, 11, 28. "Jean Acker Remarrying," *Variety,* 7 Jun 1923, p. 20 (to marry Marquis Luis de Sazany Sandoval, a Spanish grandee).

Ackerman, Walter [actor] (b. New York NY, 28 Jun 1881–12 Dec 1938 [57], Bishop CA). "Walter Ackerman ... had been in pictures since 1907," *Variety,* 21 Dec 1938. BHD1, p. 2. IFN, p. 3. SA. Slide, p. 156. Truitt, p. 1.

Ackland, Victor L. [cameraman] (b. 6 Nov 1882–Jun 1967 [84], CA).

Acord, Art [stage/film actor] (*né* Artemus Ward Acord, b. Glenwood [Prattsville], Sevier UT, 17 Apr 1890–4 Jan 1931 [40], Chihuahua, Mexico; overdose of potassium cyanide). m. **Edythe Sterling**, 1913–16—div. 1919, NV (d. 1962); Edna Mae Nores, 1919–25—div. 1926, Los Angeles Superior Court (d. 1984); **Louise Lorraine**—interlocutory decree, 1928—div. 1929, Los Angeles Superior Court (d. 1981). Grange B. McKinney, *Art Acord and the Movies* (Capistrano Beach CA: Western Classics, 2000). (Began Bison, 1909; Selig; Universal; American; FP-L; Fox.) "Art Acord Suicide," *Variety,* 7 Jan 1931. AMD, p. 16. BHD, p. 88. MSBB, p. 1021 (b. OK). GK, pp. 1–8. IFN, p. 3. MH, p. 93 (b. Stillwater OK). Truitt, p. 1. "Rode 'em Cowboy, That's How," *MPW,* 2 Oct 1915, 81. "Art Acord's Idea of Married Life; Wife in Divorce Action, Tells It—Enter Home Drunk or Not at All," *Variety,* 26 Mar 1924, p. 17 (Noyes claimed that Acord deserted her Christmas day, 1922, and that he frequently entertained Louise Lorraine; she filed suit for divorce on grounds of desertion.). "Double Divorce; Acords and Brays in Court—Theory Mrs. Bray and Acord in Chili," *Variety,* 9 Jul 1924, p. 19 (Noyes named Louise Lorraine [Mrs. Joseph Bray] correspondent in divorce suit). "On the Set and Off," *MW,* 6 Jun 1925, 41:3 (in a divorce settlement, Mrs. Acord [Nores] had to choose between Rex, Acord's dog, and $125 a month alimony. Louise Lorraine was named as co-respondent in the pending divorce suit. She later won $50 a week for 50 weeks). Eldon K. Everett, "The Tragic Cowpuncher ... Art Acord," *CFC,* 44 (Fall, 1974), 43. George A. Katchmer, "Art Acord; The Holy Terror," *CI,* 80 (Feb 1982), 34–35, 55; "Art Acord Filmography," *CI,* 81 (Mar 1982), 8. George Katchmer, "Art Acord," *CI,* 255 (Sep 1996), 37–38. That Acord was half Ute Indian is pure Hollywood fiction. He was Danish on his maternal side and Pennsylvania Dutch on his father's side. *See* his genealogical file at the Mormon Temple (Ancestral File No. AFN:1VBS-D7). Grange B. McKinney of San Clemente CA kindly provided data for this entry.

Acosta, Enrique [actor] (b. Mexico, 26 Feb 1870–22 May 1949 [79], Los Angeles CA). BHD1, p. 2. IFN, p. 3. George Katchmer, "Forgotten Cowboys and Cowgirls—Part XVII," *CI,* 194 (Aug 1991), 42.

Acres, Birt [photographer/director] (b. Richmond VA, 23 Jul 1854–1918 [64?]). *The Illustrated History of the Cinema,* consultant ed., David Robinson; ed., Ann Lloyd (NY: Macmillan, 1986), p. 14. BHD2, p. 2.

Adair, Belle [actress] (b. NYC?, 1890?). AMD, p. 16. *Photoplay Arts Portfolio* [Eclair]). "Belle Adair for Eclair Leads," *MPW,* 10 Jan 1914, 154. "Belle Adair," *MPW,* 7 Mar 1914, 1224.

Adair, Janice [actress] (b. Morpeth, England, 1904–13 Jul 1948 [44?]). BHD1, p. 2 (d. 1996).

Adair, Jean [actress] (*née* Violet McNaughton, b. Hamilton, Ontario, Canada, 13 Jun 1873–11 May 1953 [80], New York NY [Death Certificate No. 10945; age 79]). "Miss Jean Adair, Noted Actress, 80; Veteran of 25 Productions on Broadway Dies—Appeared in 'Arsenic' and 'Crucible,'" *NYT,* 12 May 1953, 27:5. "Jean Adair," *Variety,* 13 May 1953. BHD, p. 2. IFN, p. 3. SA. SD. Truitt, p. 1.

Adair, Robert [actor] (b. San Francisco CA, 3 Jan 1900–10 Aug 1954 [54], London, England). "Robert Adair," *Variety,* 18 Aug 1954 (spent 17 years in Hollywood prior to WWII). BHD1, p. 2. IFN, p. 3. Truitt, p. 1.

Adair, Robin [actress] (b. Miles City MT, 11 Feb 1884–Feb 1965 [81?]). BHD, p. 88 (b. 1885).

Adair, Virginia [actress]. No data found. LACD, "photoplayer," r 1712 Whitley Avenue.

Adalbert, Max [actor] (*né* Maximilian Adalbert Krampf, b. Dantzig, Germany, 19 Dec 1874–7 Sep 1933 [58], Munich, Germany; heart attack). BHD1, p. 2 (b. Gdansk, Poland; d. Berlin, Germany). IFN, p. 4. SA.

Adams, Allen [actor] (d. 1918). BHD, p. 88.

Adams, Barton [actor/assistant director] (b. 1900?–9 Jul 1970 [70], Los Angeles CA; peritonitis). (At Paramount for 35 years.) "Barton Adams," *Variety,* 22 Jul 1970. BHD, p. 88; BHD2, p. 2.

Adams, Blake [actor] (b. Scotland–d. 17 Aug 1913, London, England). IFN, p. 4. BHD, p. 88.

Adams, Claire [actress] (b. Winnipeg, Canada, 24 Sep 1898–25 Sep 1978 [80], Melbourne, Australia). m. (1) **Benjamin B. Hampton** (d. 1932); (2) Donald Mackinnon, London, 1938. "Claire Adams," *Variety,* 18 Oct 1978. BHD, p. 88. FFF, p. 145. IFN, p. 4. MH, p. 94. WWS, p. 239. George A. Katchmer, "Forgotten Cowboys/Girls—Part VII," *CI,* 179 (May 1990), 44.

Adams, Constance [actress] (b. East Orange NJ, 27 Apr 1873–17 Jul 1960 [87], Los Angeles CA). m. **Cecil B. De Mille** (d. 1959). BHD, p. 89 (b. 1874). SA.

Adams, Dora Mills [actress] (b. Lowville NJ). (Vitagraph; FP-L.)

Adams, Eddie [title writer]. No data found. FDY, 1929 (*The Racket,* 1928), p. 441.

Adams, Edith [film/stage actress/wardrobe mistress/dancer] (b. 1878?–10 Jan 1957 [78], Queens, New York NY [Death Certificate No. 503; M.E. Case No. 129; age 71]). "Edith Adams," *Variety,* 23 Jan 1957. BHD, p. 89. IFN, p. 4. Truitt, p. 1.

Adams, Ernest S. [actor] (b. San Francisco CA, 18 Jun 1885–26 Nov 1947 [62], Los Angeles CA). "Ernest Adams," *Variety,* 3 Dec 1947. BHD1, p. 3. IFN, p. 4. Truitt, p. 2. Mario DeMarco, "Ernie Adams," *CI,* 205 (Jul 1992), 39.

Adams, Frances Sale [actress] (b. 8 Aug 1892–6 Aug 1969 [77], Los Angeles CA). (Griffith; American.) "Frances Sale Adams," *Variety,* 13 Aug 1969. AS, p. 34 (Frances Sale Adams). BHD, p. 294 (Frances Sale). IFN, p. 262. Truitt, p. 295.

Adams, Frank R[amsey] [playwright/scenarist] (b. Morrison IL, 7 Jul 1883–8 Oct 1963 [80], White Lakes MI). m. (1) Hazel L. Judd; (2) Lorna Margrave. "Frank R. Adams," *Variety,* 16 Oct 1963. BHD2, p. 2. SD.

Adams, George F. [circus clown/stage/film actor] (b. 1853?–26 May 1935 [82], Brooklyn NY; cerebral hemorrhage). "George F. Adams," *Variety,* 118, 29 May 1935, 62:1. AMD, p. 16. "George Adams in 'Humpty Dumpty' Pictures," *MPW,* 1 Jun 1912, 820.

Adams, James B. [actor] (b. Paterson NJ, 4 Oct 1888–19 Dec 1933 [45], Glendale CA). "James B. Adams," *Variety,* 26 Dec 1933 (age 43). AMD, p. 16. BHD1, p. 3. FFF, p. 129. IFN, p. 4. "Jimmie Adams Is Featured in Third Mermaid Comedy," *MPW,* 31 Jul 1920, 621.

Adams, John Wolcott [actor] (b. Worcester MA, 1874–3 Jun 1925 [51?], New York NY). BHD, p. 89. SA.

Adams, Kathryn [actress] (*née* Kathryn Colson, b. St. Louis MO, 25 May 1893–17 Feb 1959 [65], Los Angeles CA). m. Jacques Magnin. "Kathryn Adams [Mrs. J. Magnin]," *NYT,* 19 Feb 1959, 31:1 (age 63). "Kathryn Adams," *Variety,* 25 Feb 1959. AMD, p. 16. BHD, p. 89 (b. 1895). IFN, p. 4. LACD, "photoplayer," h 1553 N. Mariposa. SD. Truitt, p. 2. WWS, p. 241. "Kathryn Adams—Thanhouser Leading Woman," *MPW,* 25 Nov 1916, 1178.

Adams, Lionel [actor] (b. New Orleans LA, 1866?–10 Aug 1952 [86], New York NY [Death Certificate No. 17451]). "Lionel Adams," *Variety,* 13 Aug 1952. BHD, p. 89. IFN, p. 4. "Lionel Adams," *MPW,* 14 Jun 1913, 1114. "Lionel Adams," *MPW,* 28 Nov 1914, 1243.

Adams, Mary [actress] (b. 1860?–28 Oct 1916 [56], New York NY). "Mary Adams," *Variety,* 3 Nov 1916 (no mention of films).

Adams, Maude [stage/film actress/producer] (*née* Maude Ewing Kiskadden, b. Salt Lake City UT, 11 Nov 1872–17 Jul 1953 [80], Columbia MO; heart attack). "Maude Adams Is Dead at 80; Won Fame in Peter Pan Role; 'Winsome, Lonely Dreamer of Dreams' Captivated Audiences of 3 Decades," *NYT,* 18 Jul 1953, 1:3, 13:2. "Maude Adams," *Variety,* 22 Jul 1953 (d. Tannersville NY). AMD, p. 16. GSS, p. 2. SA. SD. "Miss Adams Well Now; Completely Recovered from Appendicitis Operation, Mr. [Alf] Hayman [Frohman representative] Says," *NYT,* 8 Jun 1905, 9:5 (operation on 23 May at home, 33 E. 41st Street, NYC). Hugh F. Hoffman, "The Moving Picture and the Actor," *MPW,* 26 Feb 1910, 291. "Maude Adams's Mother," *NYDM,* 3 Jun 1914, 7:3 ("The Life Story of Maude Adams and Her Mother," by Annie Adams Kiskadden [Adams's actress mother], to be published in the Jun 1914 *Green Book Magazine* for several issues. Mrs. Kiskadden's parents "aided Brigham Young in the founding of Salt Lake City."). "Maude Adams Enters Films as Producer, Not Actress," *MPW,* 14 Mar 1921, 154. "On the Set and Off," *MW,* IV, 22 Nov 1924, 31:1.

Adams, May (or **Mae**) [actress] (*née* Mary Gruppe, b. 1860?–28 Oct 1916 [56], New York NY). "May Adams (Mary Gruppe)," *Variety,* 3 Nov 1916. BHD1, p. 603. SA.

Adams, Mildred B. [actress]. No data found. AMD, p. 16. LACD, "actress," h 112 N. Serrano Avenue. "Mildred Adams with Universal," *MPW,* 10 Apr 1915, 218.

Adams, Peggy [actress]. No data found. AMD, p. 17. "Peggy Adams New Lead for Victor Moore," *MPW,* 13 Oct 1917, 219.

Adams, Ray A. [filmmaker]. No data found. LACD, "filmmaker," r 2213 Dayton Avenue.

Adams, Samuel Hopkins [novelist/scenarist] (b. Dunkirk NY, 1871?–15 Nov 1958 [87], Beaufort SC). m. (1) Elizabeth R. Noyes (d. 1957)—div. (daughters Mrs. Cecil C. Ardell and Hester Hopkins Adams; (2) actress Jane Peyton Van Norman, 11 Mar 1915, NYC (d. 8 Sep 1946; her 4th marriage). (Wrote *Flaming Youth, It Happened One Night* and *The Gorgeous Hussy.*) "Samuel Hopkins Adams Is Dead; Novelist and Biographer Was 87; Chronicler of Erie Canal Also Wrote Crusading Magazine Articles," *NYT,* 17 Nov 1958, 31:2. "Mrs. Samuel H. Adams; Wife of Writer Was Known on the Stage as Jane Peyton," *NYT,* 9 Sep 1946, 9:2. "Samuel Hopkins Adams," *Variety,* 212, 19 Nov 1958, 79:3. AMD, p. 17. "Writer Weds Actress," *NYDM,* 17 Mar 1915, 7:1. "F.P. Signs Adams," *MPW,* 6 Nov 1926, 4.

Adams, Stella [actress] (b. Sherman TX, 24 Apr 1883–17 Sep 1961 [78], Woodland Hills CA). BHD1, p. 3. IFN, p. 4.

Adams, Victoria [actress] (b. MO, 17 Jun 1897–13 May 1961 [63], Los Angeles CA). BHD, p. 89. IFN, p. 4.

Adams, William P[erry] [stage/radio/film actor] (b. Tiffin OH, 8 May 1887–29 Sep 1972 [85], New York NY). m. actress Eleanor Wells. "William Perry Adams," *Variety,* 4 Oct 1972, p. 62. BHD1, p. 4. IFN, p. 4 (d. 30 Sep).

Adams, William Stuart [cinematographer] (b. New York NY, 2 Jun 1892–3 Dec 1930 [38], Hollywood CA; from fever contracted in Borneo on location for Universal's *White Captive*). "William Stuart Adams," *Variety,* 10 Dec 1930. BHD2, p. 2. FDY, p. 455.

Adamson, Evelyn S. [actress] (b. 1901?–29 Oct 1958 [57], Los Angeles CA). BHD, p. 89. IFN, p. 4. LACD, "photoplayer," r 1916 N. St. Andrews Place. SA.

Adamson, Ewart [scenarist] (b. Dundee, Scotland, 23 Oct 1882–28 Nov 1945 [63], No. Hollywood CA). "Ewart Adamson," *Variety,* 5 Dec 1945. AMD, p. 17. BHD2, p. 2. FDY, p. 417. IFN, p. 4. SA. "Ewart Adamson Added to Realart Editorial Staff," *MPW,* 30 Apr 1921, 953. "Ewart Adamson," *MPW,* 30 Jul 1927, 318.

Adamson, Victor *see* **Mix, Art**

Addams, Jane [suffragette/actress]. No data found. AMD, p. 17. "Anna Shaw and Jane Addams in Pictures," *MPW,* 18 May 1912, 617.

Ade, George [writer/scenarist] (b. Kentland IN, 9 Feb 1866–16 May 1944 [78], Kentland IN; following three heart attacks). (Essanay.) "George Ade Dies; Indiana Humorist; Author, Who Won Fame with 'Fables in Slang'; Had Been Ill Since Last June; Satire Marked Wisdom; Began as Newspaper Reporter—Successful Playwright—Adopted Style of Aesop," *NYT,* 17 May 1944, 19:1. "George Ade," *Variety,* 24 May 1944. AMD, p. 17. BHD2, p. 2 (d. Brook IN). IFN, p. 4. SA. "Film Famous Authors; Vitagraph Company Prepares Novel Series for Authors' League Benefit," *NYDM,* 28 Jan 1914, 30:4. "Ade to Write Scripts; Humorist Will Write Series for Essanay Company's Pictures," *NYDM,* 15 Apr 1914, 38:4. "Essanay Will Do More Ade Fables," *MPW,* 29 Apr 1916, 779. Kunitz & Haycraft, *Twentieth Century Authors* (Wilson, 1942).

Adler, Bertram [publicist] (b. 1891?–18 Mar 1939 [48], New York NY). (Thanhouser.) "Bert Adler," *Variety,* 134, 22 Mar 1939, 62:1. AMD, p. 17. Bertram Adler, "The 'Free Usher' Evil," *MPW,* 26 Mar 1910, 463. F.J. Beecroft, "Publicity Men I Have Met…," *NYDM,* 14 Jan 1914, 48 (*see Beefroft, Chester,* for full citation). "Bert Adler on Studio Wasteage," *NYDM,* 8 Sep 1915, 24:2 (cannot blame studio managers because the waster "jumps the fence into the camp of the opposition. For, no matter what his trouble has been, the opposition will take him." *See* Heffron and Reichenbach for more on the same topic.).

Adler, Charles [member of Yacht Club Boys: vaudeville and cafe act] (b. 1895?–22 Jun 1955 [60], New York NY; heart attack). "Charles Adler," *Variety,* 29 Jun 1955.

Adler, Felix [actor/producer/writer] (b. 22 Jan 1884–25 Mar 1963 [79], Los Angeles CA; pneumonia). "Felix Adler," *Variety,* 27 Mar 1963 ("He was a noted gagster during the silent screen era and was called upon to write titles as well as beef up plot development.") AMD, p. 17. BHD2, p. 2. "Felix Adler Is 'Home Again' on Sennett Lot," *MPW,* 2 May 1927, 835. "Dame Rumor Still Chases Felix Adler," *MPW,* 14 May 1927, 97.

Adler, Jacob P[avlovitch] [stage/film actor/producer] (b. Odessa, Russia, 12 Feb 1855–31 Mar 1926 [71], New York NY [Death Certificate No. 10367; age 72]). m. Sarah Levitzka (actress Sarah Adler; d. 29 Apr 1953); Dinah Shtettin. "Jacob Adler, Actor and Producer, Dies; Tragedian, Called Founder of Yiddish Theatre, Succumbs to Old Age and Stroke at 71; King Lear Favorite Role; His Best Known Art Was Shylock—Was Connected with Grant St., Kessler and Thalia Theatres," *NYT,* 1 Apr 1926, 25:3. "Jacob P. Adler," *Variety,* 7 Apr 1926. AMD, p. 17. BHD, p. 89 (d. 1 Apr). IFN, p. 4. SA. "Yiddish Theater Becomes Picture House," *MPW,* 18 Sep 1909, 376. "Jacob P. Adler in Their First Production," *MPW,* 30 May 1914, 1267. "Jacob P. Adler," *MPW,* 20 Jun 1914, 1706. "Sarah Adler," *MPW,* 22 Aug 1914, 1086.

Adler, Louis B. [executive] (d. 10 Dec 1921). BHD2, p. 2.

Adler, Robert [actor] (b. Hoboken NJ, 24 Mar 1906–19 Dec 1987 [81], Glendale CA). BHD1, p. 4.

Adolfi, John G. [stage/film actor/director] (b. New York NY, 19 Feb 1888–11 May 1933 [45], Canoe River [102 miles north of Revelstoke, British Columbia], Canada; paralytic stroke). (Vitagraph; Reliance; Universal; Fox.) "John G. Adolfi; Movie Director Guided Arliss in Several of His Films," *NYT,* 15 May 1933, 15:3. "John G. Adolfi Dies While on Hunting Trip," *Variety,* 16 May 1933. AMD, p. 17. BHD2, p. 2. IFN, p. 4 (age 44). Katz, p. 12. MSBB, p. 1044. WWS, p. 353. "John Adolfi on Way Home," *MPW,* 18 Mar 1916, 1828. "John G. Adolfi," *MPW,* 15 Jul 1916, 464 (b. 1885).

Adorée, Renée [stage/film actress] (*née* Jeanne Renée de la Fonté, b. Lille, France, 30 Sep 1898–5 Oct 1933 [35], Sunland CA; tuberculosis). m. **Tom Moore**, 1921–27 (d. 1955); LA merchant William Sherman Gill, 28 Jun 1927—div. 1929. (Film debut: *The Strongest.*) "Renee Adoree, 31, Film Player, Dead; Born in Circus Tent in France, She Was Toe Dancer, Horsewoman and Acrobat at 10," *NYT,* 6 Oct 1933, 17:4. "Renee Adoree," *Variety,* 10 Oct 1933 (d. Tujunga CA, age 31). AMD, p. 17. BHD1, p. 4. FFF, p. 215. HCH, p. 121. IFN, p. 4. MH, p. 94. SA. Truitt, p. 2. Harry Carr, "The Girl Who Couldn't Stop Crying," *Classic,* XVIII, Sep 1923, 39, 76. Dorothy Donnell, "The Child of the Circus Vans; Renée Adorée Was a Child Rider in France," *MPC,* XXII, Oct 1925, 32–33, 79, 80. Carol White, "Renée Makes Good; The Girl Who Became the Talk of Hollywood with One Role," *MPC,* XXIII, Apr 1926, 38–39, 88. Henry Wilson, "The Genius Enchanting; Her name is Renee de la Fointe—the French named her Adoree and she is here rechristened Amoreuse," *Photoplay Magazine,* XXX, Jun 1926, 63, 134–35. June Lee, "Dan Cupid's Bulletin Board," *Paris and Hollywood,* 2 (Sep 1926), 21 (granted her final decree of divorce from Moore). "The Girl on the Cover," *Cinema Arts,* V (Oct 1926), 46. Charles Paton, "No Sugar Coat for Renée; Renée Adorée Is Honest 'Cause She Won['']t Pretend. She Faces Things by Their True Value—and Ends by Laughing 'Em Off," *MPC,* XXIV, Dec 1926, 58–59. "Wedding Bliss Ousts Divorce in Film Mecca," *MPW,* 9 Jul 1927, 81. June Lee, "Dan Cupid's Bulletin Board," *Paris and Hollywood Screen Secrets,* III (Oct 1927), 35 (wed Gill). Katherine Albert, "A Daughter of the Sawdust," *Screenland,* XVI, Dec 1927, 29, 82, 84. FSS, p. 1.

Adrian, Gilbert A. [costume designer] (*né* Adrian Adolph Greenberg, b. Naugatuck CT, 3 Mar 1903–13 Sep 1959 [56], Los Angeles CA; suicide). m. **Janet Gaynor**, 1939, Yuma AZ (d. 1984). (De Mille; MGM.) "Adrian Designer, Is Dead on Coast; Husband of Janet Gaynor Made Gowns for Top Film Stars—Served M-G-M," *NYT,* 14 Sep 1959, 29:3. "Adrian's Estate to Widow," *NYT,* 28 Oct 1959, 42:3. "Adrian," *Variety,* 16 Sep 1959. AMD, p. 17. BHD2, p. 2. SA. "Engages Adrian," *MPW,* 16 Dec 1922, 640 (19 years old). Pamela Pratt Forbes, "The Men Behind the Gowns," *Cinema Arts,* I, Jun 1937, 74–75 ("His first job was with Irving Berlin in the Music Box Revue. Rudolph Valentino stole him for Hollywood and put him on the screen."). Jimmy Bangley, "The Adrian Adventure," *CI,* 248 (Feb 1996), 32, C2.

Adrian, Paul [actor] (b. Berlin, Germany, 21 Nov 1850–25 Mar 1908 [57], Darmstadt, Germany). SA.

Agar, Jane [actress] (b. Sharon Township OH, 2 Mar 1889–10 Jun 1948 [59], Lakewood OH). "Jane Agar," *Variety,* 16 Jun 1948. BHD, p. 89. IFN, p. 4. Truitt, p. 2.

Agate, May [actress] (b. Manchester, England, 29 Dec 1892–1960 [68]). BHD1, p. 4.

Aggerholm, Ellen [actress]. No data found. AMD, p. 17. "Ellen Aggerholm," *MPW,* 23 Aug 1913, 850.

Agnew, Frances [scenarist]. No data found. AMD, p. 17. FDY, p. 417. "Agnew Joins Paramount," *MPW,* 1 Nov 1924, 31. "Frances Agnew: Her Fox Titles," *MPW,* 18 Dec 1926, 506.

Agnew, Robert (Bobby) Dean [actor] (b. Dayton KY, 4 Jun 1899–8 Nov 1983 [84], 1000 Palms CA; kidney ailment). (Universal; Fox.) "Robert (Bobby) Agnew," *Variety,* 25 Jan 1984. BHD1, p. 5. FFF, p. 444. Katz, pp. 13–14 (b. Louisville KY). MH, p. 94. SA (b. 4 Nov). FSS, p. 1.

Aguglia, Mimi Gerolama [stage/film actress] (b. Palermo, Italy, 21 Dec 1884–30 Jul 1970 [85], Woodland Hills CA). "Mimi Aguglia," *Variety,* 12 Aug 1970 (d. 31 Jul). BHD1, p. 5. IFN, p. 5. SA. Truitt, p. 2. "Newsy Notes from Filmland," *NYDM,* 18 Nov 1914, 25:3 (at Genesee Film Co., Rochester NY).

Ahearn, George [vaudevillian/actor] (b. 1885?–5 Jun 1935 [50], Watervliet NY). "George Ahearn," *Variety,* 12 Jun 1935.

Aherne, Brian de Lacy (brother of **Patrick Aherne**) [actor] (b. King's Norton, Worcestershire, England, 2 May 1902–10 Feb 1986 [83], Boca Grande FL, heart attack). (In silents in England; U.S. film debut: *Song of Songs,* Paramount, 1933). *A Proper Job* (Boston: Houghton Mifflin, 1969). m. (1) Joan Fontaine, 1939 (marriage dissolved in 1943); (2) Eleanor de Liagre Labrot, 1946. David Bird, "Brian Aherne, 83; Stage and Film Star Admired for Suavity," *NYT,* 11 Feb 1986, D30:4. "Brian Ahearn," *Variety,* 12 Feb 1986. BHD1, p. 5. SA. SD.

Aherne, Patrick (brother of **Brian Aherne**) [stage/film actor] (b. King's Norton, Worcestershire, England, 6 Jan 1901–30 Sep 1970 [69], Woodland Hills CA; cancer). m. (4 sons, 2 daughters). "Patrick Aherne," *Variety,* 14 Oct 1970, 71:2. BHD1, p. 5. IFN, p. 5.

Aicken, Eilnor [actress] (b. England, 1834–5 May 1914 [80?]). BHD, p. 89.

Aiken, Sol *see* **Stein, Abe M.**

Aimos, Raymond [actor] (b. La Fere, France, 1889–22 Aug 1944 [55], Paris, France). BHD1, p. 6. IFN, p. 5.

Ainley, Henry H[inchcliffe] (father of Richard Ainley) [actor] (b. Leeds, England, 21 Aug 1879–31 Oct 1945 [66], London, England). m. Suzanne Sheldon; Elaine Fearon. "Henry Ainley, Long on English Stage; Noted Shakespearean Actor Dies at 66—Voice Considered One of the Finest," *NYT,* 1 Nov 1945. "Henry H. Ainley," *Variety,* 7 Nov 1945. BHD1, p. 5. GSS, p. 4. IFN, p. 5. Katz, pp. 14–15 (b. Morley, England). Truitt, p. 2.

Ainslee, Marion [scenarist/title writer]. No data found. AMD, p. 17. FDY, pp. 417, 441. "Writing Titles," *MPW,* 22 Aug 1925, 848.

Ainsley, Norman [actor] (*né* Norman Ainsley Blume, b. Edinburgh, Scotland, 4 May 1881–23 Jan 1948 [67], Hollywood CA; private sanitarium). "Norman Ainsley," *Variety,* 28 Jan 1948. BHD1, p. 5. SD.

Ainsworth, Phil [actor]. No data found. m. **Barbara LaMarr**—separated 1923 (d. 1926). "Phil Ainsworth Released," *Variety,* 22 Feb 1923, p. 44 (…"released in San Francisco of bogus check charges preferred against him. He is the husband of Barbara La Marr. They recently separated.").

Ainsworth, Sidney [actor] (*né* Charles Sydney Ainsworth, b. Manchester, England, 21 Dec 1871–21 May 1922 [50], Madison WI). "Sidney Ainsworth," *Variety,* 26 May 1922. AMD, p. 17. BHD, p. 89 (b. 1872). IFN, p. 5. Truitt, p. 2. WWS, p. 203. "Sydney Ainsworth," *MPW,* 15 Apr 1916, 449.

Aiston, Arthur C. [stage/film actor/playwright/producer] (b. So. Lee MA, 30 Aug 1868–26 Feb 1924 [55]). m. Jane Cochrane. "Arthur C. Aiston," *Variety,* 28 Feb 1924 (age 58; buried in Holyoke MA). NNAT. SD. "Mohawk Film Co. Sued; Arthur C. Aiston Sues for Failure to Produce His Play, 'Tennessee's Pardner,'" *NYDM,* 7 Oct 1914, 28:3 (for breach of contract against Mohawk which "agreed to forfeit a certain sum of money if the company failed to produce his play before 5 Jun 1914.").

Aitken, Harry E. (brother of **Roy E. Aitken**) [producer] (b. Waukesha WI, 1870 or 1877–1 Aug 1956 [79?], Chicago IL; heart attack). (Majestic; Mutual; Triangle.) Al P. Nelson and Roy E. Aitken, *The Birth of a Nation Story.* "Harry E. Aitken, 79, a Movie Executive," *NYT,* 2 Aug 1956, 25:6. "Harry E. Aitken," *Variety,* 8 Aug 1956. AMD, p. 17. BHD2, p. 3 (b. 1879). SA. "Another Independent Manufacturer, *MPW,* 30 Sep 1911, 983 [Majestic]. "A Successful Organizer; Resume of the Activities of H.E. Aitken, Recently Elected President and General Manager of the Mutual Film Corporation," *MPW,* 26 Apr 1913, 357. David A. Balch, "Why the Movies of Six Years Ago Were Better Than Now," *MW,* 12 May 1923, 10 (was to reissue old Triangle films such as *The Good Bad Man* and *The Half Breed*).

Aitken, Roy E. (brother of **Harry E. Aitken**) [managing director] (b. 13 Jun 1882–28 Oct 1976 [94], Waukesha WI). AMD, p. 18. BHD2, p. 3. "Roy Aitken in Charge of Majestic," *MPW,* 8 Jun 1912, 936.

Aitken, Spottiswoode [stage/film actor] (*né* Frank Spottiswoode Aitken, b. Edinburgh, Scotland, 16 Apr 1868–24 Feb 1933 [64], Los Angeles CA). (Griffith; Reliance; American.) "Frank S. Aitken," *Variety,* 28 Feb 1933. AMD, p. 18. BHD, p. 89. IFN, p. 5. MH, p. 94. MSBB, p. 1021. Spehr, p. 112. Truitt, p. 3. "Births," *NYDM,* 1 Sep 1915, 15:1 (son b. 12 Aug, LA CA). "A Lead, Director, and Two Heavies Join Universal," *MPW,* 26 Jul 1919, 512. George Katchmer, "Spottiswoode Aiken [sic]," *CI,* 255 (Sep 1996), 38.

Aked, Muriel [actress] (b. Bingley, England, 9 Nov 1887–21 Mar 1955 [67], Seattle, Yorkshire, England). "Muriel Aked," *Variety,* 13 Apr 1955 (d. 23 Mar). BHD1, p. 6. IFN, p. 5. Truitt, p. 3.

Akins, Zoë [scenarist] (b. Humansville MO, 30 Oct 1883?–29 Oct 1958 [74], Los Angeles CA; cancer). m. Hugo Rumbold, 1932. "Zoe Akins Is Dead; Pulitzer Winner; Playwright Was Cited in 1935 for 'The Old Maid'—Wrote Novels, Poetry," *NYT,* 30 Oct 1958, 31:1 (age 72). "Zoe Akins," *Variety,* 5 Nov 1958 (age 74). BHD2, p. 3 (b. 1885). SA (b. 1886). WWWA (b. 1886).

Alba, María [actress] (*née* Maria Casajuana, b. Barcelona, Spain, 19 Mar 1910–25 Oct 1999 [89], San Diego CA; complications from Alzheimer's disease). (Made Spanish-language films in Hollywood, 1930–31; Fox.) Waldman, p. 4 (b. 1905). Harris Lentz III, "Maria Alba, 89," *CI,* 299 (May 2000), p. 56.

Albanesi, Meggie [actress] (*née* Margherita Cecilia Brigida Marie Albanesi, b. London, England, 8 Oct 1899–9 Dec 1923 [24], Broadstairs, Kent, England; pneumonia following throat operation). "Meggie Albanesi Dead," *Variety,* 13 Dec 1923 and "Meggie Albanesi," 20 Dec 1923. AMD, p. 18 (Albonesi, Meggie). BHD, p. 90. IFN, p. 5. SD. "Meggie Albonese in 'Great Day,'" *MPW,* 14 Aug 1920, 903.

Albani, Marcella [actress] (b. Rome, Italy, 7 Dec 1901). m. Mario Franchini. JS, p. 4 (in Italian silents from1919).

Alberini, Filoteo [inventor/director/producer] (b. Turin, Italy, 14 Mar 1865–12 Apr 1937 [72], Rome, Italy). AMD, p. 18. BHD2, p. 3. SA. JS, p. 4 (in Italian silents from 1905; invented the Alberini Cinetografo in 1895 and the Autostereoscopio in 1911). "Enters American Field," *MPW,* 10 May 1924, 198.

Alberni, Luis (or **Louis**) [actor] (b. Barcelona, Spain, 4 Oct 1886–23 Dec 1962 [76], Hollywood CA). (d. Jan 1963). "Luis Alberni," *Variety,* 2 Jan 1963 (age 75). BHD1, p. 6. IFN, p. 5. SA. Truitt, p. 3.

Albers, Hans [actor/writer] (b. Hamburg, Germany, 22 Sep 1892–24 Jul 1960 [67], Munich, Germany). m. Hansl Burg. (Film debut: *Das Spitzentuch der Fürstin Wolkowska,* Deutsche Bioscop-Film, 1917). "Hans Albers," *Variety,* 27 Jul 1960. BHD1, p. 6 (b. 1893). IFN, p. 5. Eberhard Spiess, *Hans Albers; Eine Filmographie* (Frankfurt, Germany: Kommunales Kino, 1977).

Albert, Dan [actor/assistant director] (b. Nashville TN, 1890–17 Aug 1919 [29], Nashville TN). (Keystone.) AMD, p. 18. BHD, p. 90; BHD2, p. 3. IFN, p. 5. SA. "Obituary," *MPW,* 23 Aug 1919, 1119.

Albert, Elsie (aunt of **Baby Early**) [actress] (b. North Caldwell NJ, 20 Nov 1897–7 Oct 1981 [83], OR). m. Harold Clarke Mathews, 1914. (Edison; Kalem; Yankee Films.) BHD, p. 90 (b. 1888). John E. Thayer, "Elsie Albert; A Reel Yankee Film Star," *CFC,* 50 (Spring 1976), 35–36; "Elsie Albert," *CFC,* 56 (Fall 1977), 56 (b. 20 Nov 1897). Luther Hathcock, "Baby Early [letter]," *CI,* 92 (Feb 1983), 11, 15 (cites death in Nov 1981 [95], Corona CA). Truitt, 1983 (b. 1888).

Albert, Katherine [actress] (b. 1902–26 Jul 1970 [68?], Santa Monica CA). BHD, p. 90.

Alberti, Fritz [actor] (b. Hanau, Germany, 22 Oct 1877–Sep 1954 [76]). BHD1, p. 6. IFN, p. 5.

Alberti, Viola [actress] (b. Lewiston PA, 1874). BHD, p. 90.

Albertini, Alberto [actor] (*né* Goucko Giuseppe Germani, b. Cogoleto, Italy, 31 Aug 1898–22 Oct 1957 [59], Genoa, Italy). m. Maddalena Colla. JS, p. 6 (in Italian silents from 1915).

Albertini, Luciano [actor] (b. Lugo di Romagna, Italy, 30 Nov 1891–Nov 1941 [49?], Lugo di Romagna, Italy). BHD1, p. 603 (d. Bologna, Italy). JS, p. 6 (in Italian silents from 1913).

Albertson, Albert [actor]. No data found. AMD, p. 18. "Albert Albertson," *MPW,* 10 Nov 1917, 845.

Albertson, Arthur W. [actor] (b. Waycross GA, 6 Jan 1891–20 Oct 1926 [35], New York NY). (Kalem.) BHD, p. 90 (d. 19 Oct). SA. Truitt, 1983. "In the Picture Studios," *NYDM,* 11 Dec 1915, 34:4 (after playing leads in the Kalem Jacksonville company, "has been transferred to the New York studios and joined the 'Ventures of Marguerite' company.).

Albertson, E. Coit [actor] (b. Reading PA, 14 Oct 1880–13 Dec 1953 [73], Los Angeles CA). (Fox; Curtiss Pictures Corp.; Grossman Pictures.) BHD, p. 90.

Albertson, Frank [film/stage/TV actor] (b. Fergus Falls MN, 2 Feb 1909–29 Feb 1964 [55], Santa Monica CA). m. Grace. (1st major film: *Prep and Pep,* 1928.) "Frank Albertson Is Dead at 55; Film, Broadway and TV Actor," *NYT,* 4 Mar 1964. BHD1, p. 6. FSS, p. 2. IFN, p. 5. Katz, p. 16 (began 1922). Truitt, p. 3.

Albertson, Mabel [actress] (b. Haverhill MA, 27 Jul 1901–28 Sep 1982 [81], Santa Monica CA). BHD1, p. 6.

Albin, Emmy [actress] (b. 1873–1959 [86?]). BHD1, p. 603.

Albes, Emil F[riedrich] [actor] (b. Pyrmont, Germany, 30 Oct 1861–22 Mar 1923 [61], Berlin, Germany). BHD, p. 90; BHD2, p. 3.

Albright, Hardie [stage/film/TV actor/writer] (*né* Hardy Albrecht, b. Charleroi PA, 16 Dec 1903–7 Dec 1975 [71], Mission Community Hospital, Mission Viejo CA). m. (1) **Martha Sleeper** (d. 1983; daughter Victoria); (2) Arnita Wallace. (Began on stage in 1926; Fox; final film: *Angel on My Shoulder,* 1946.) "Hardie Albright," *Variety,* 24 Dec 1975, 46:4. AS, p. 43.

Alcovar, Pierre [actor] (b. France, 14 Mar 1893–1954 [61]). BHD, p. 90.

Alda, Frances [opera/radio singer/actress] (*née* Frances Jean Davies, b. Christchurch, New Zealand, 31 May 1883–18 Sep 1952 [68], Venice, Italy). m. (1) Giulio Gatti-Casazza—div. 1928; (2) Ray Vir Den. *Men, Woman and Tenors,* 1937. "Frances Alda," *Variety,* 24 Sep 1952, 63:1. BHD1, p. 7.

Alden, Joan [actress] (*née* Marion Balaban, b. 1909–15 Jun 1997 [87], Rancho Mirage CA). (Appeared as Molly O'Day in *The Call of the Heart,* 1928, with Edmund Cobb). BHD1, p. 603. Don Juan, "So This Is Hollywood," *Paris and Hollywood,* 2 (Oct 1926), 79 (won a Chicago beauty contest and a Universal contract, where she is playing leads in the Sweet Sixteen comedies.). "Joan Alden [obituary]," *CI,* 266 (Aug 1997), p. 51:1.

Alden, Mary [actress] (b. New York NY, 18 Jun 1883–2 Jul 1946 [63], Woodland Hills CA). (Griffith.) "Mary Maguire Alden," *Variety,* 10 Jul 1946. AMD, p. 18. BHD1, p. 7. FFF, p. 134. FSS, p. 2. IFN, p. 6. Katz, pp. 17–18 (b. New Orleans LA). Truitt, p. 3. W.E. Wing, "On the Pacific Coast; Business of Shocking Society," *NYDM,* 2 Dec 1914, 23:1 (Alden was a former tight-rope walker). "Mary Alden Is Not Middle-Aged Woman," *MPW,* 23 Jul 1921, 426. Hazel Shelley, "The Young Old Lady," *MPC,* Dec 1921, 46–47, 97. Faith Service, "In Order to Be Happy," *Classic,* Aug 1923, 40, 76–77. Gladys Hall, "A New Secret About Women," *MW,* 5 Jan 1924, 7.

Alden, Robert [member of The Two Bobs with Bob Adams] [actor] (b. 1882?–23 Mar 1932 [50], London, England). "Robert Alden," *Variety,* 5 Apr 1932.

Alder, William F. [cinematographer]. (Metro.) "Mrs. Wm. F. Alder," *Variety,* 2 Sep 1925 (d. 25 Aug 1925 [38], Los Angeles CA). Kenneth Macgowan, *Behind the Screen* (New York, 1965), p. 436.

Alderson, Erville [actor] (b. Kansas City, MO, 11 Sep 1882–4 Aug 1957 [74], Glendale CA). "Erville Anderson [sic]," *Variety,* 14 Aug 1957. BHD1, p. 7. IFN, p. 6. SA. Truitt, p. 4.

Alderson, Floyd T[aliaferro] [actor] (aka Wally Wales and Hal Taliaferro, b. Sheridan WY, 13 Nov 1895–12 Feb 1980 [84], Sheridan WY; pneumonia). m. Mary Bell Towers; Gwendolyn Costello. (Began in 1915; Universal.) "Floyd T. Alderson," *Variety,* 12 May 1980 (b. MT). AMD, p. 353 (Wally Wales). AS, p. 1123 (Wally Wales, b. 1891); p. 1053 (Hal Taliaferro, b. 1895). BHD, p. 328 (Wally Wales). FSS, p. 285 (Wally Wales). IFN, p. 288. Katz, p. 1118 (Alperson). "Wally Wales," *MPW,* 18 Dec 1926, 509. Ed Wyatt, "In Search of a Boyhood Hero," *CI,* 209 (Nov 1992), 42–44. George Katchmer, "Wally Wales," *CI,* 228 (Jun 1994), 41.

Aldine, James [actor] (b. Pearl River NY, 17 Nov 1902–27 Jan 1985 [82], Long Beach CA). BHD1, p. 7.

Aldini, Carlo [actor] (b. Bologna, Italy). JSj, p. 7 (in Italian silents from 1919).

Aldis, "Duke" [assistant director]. No data found. AMD, p. 18. "'Duke' Aldis Joins Pallas," *MPW,* 27 Nov 1915, 1639.

Aldor, Bernd [actor] (b. Constantinople, Turkey, 23 Mar 1887). BHD, p. 90.

Aldrich, Charles T. [actor]. No data found. AMD, p. 18. "Charles T. Aldrich," *MPW,* 4 Sep 1915, 1626.

Aldrich, Elizabeth [stage/film actress]. No data found. "In the Picture Studios," *NYDM,* 29 Sep 1915, 26:3 (to debut in *The Cowardly Way* for Equitable).

Aldrich, Mariska [Mika] [actress] (*née* Mariska Horvath, b. Boston, MA?, 27 Mar 1881–28 Sep 1965 [84], Los Angeles CA; intestinal obstuction). m. James Francis Aldrich, Apr 1901—div. 1914. IFN, p. 6. SA.

Aldrich, William F. [producer]. No data found. AMD, p. 18. "Bill Aldrich to Make Automobile Picture," *MPW,* 24 Feb 1917, 1198.

Aldridge, Alfred [actor] (b. New Orleans LA, 1876?–4 May 1934 [58], Los Angeles CA). "Alfred Aldridge," *Variety,* 15 May 1934. BHD, p. 90. IFN, p. 6. Truitt, p. 4.

Aldwin, Irene [actress]. No data found. LACD, "photoplayer," r 1724 Winona Blvd.

Alessandrini, Goffredo [director] (b. Cairo, Egypt, 9 Sep 1904–16 May 1978 [73], Rome, Italy). m. **Anna Magnani**, 1935—annulled 1950 (d. 1973). BHD2, p. 4. JS, p. 7 (in U.S., 1930–31, dubbing films into Italian).

Alexander, Ben [actor] (*né* Nicholas Benton Alexander, b. Goldfield NY, 26 May 1911–5 Jul 1969 [58], Hollywood CA; died of natural causes). (Nicholas Alexander). (De Mille; Griffith.) "Ben Alexander Is Dead at 58; Co-Starred in Dragnet Series," *NYT,* 6 Jul 1969, 45:1. "Ben Alexander," *Variety,* 9 Jul 1969. AMD, p. 18. BHD1, p. 8. FFF, p. 214. FSS, p. 3. IFN, p. 6. LACD, "photoplayer," r 1812 Winona Blvd. MH, p. 94. Truitt, p. 4. "Signs 'Little Ben,'" *MPW,* 21 Oct 1922, 707. "With 1st National," *MPW,* 15 Sep 1923, 279. "Bennie to Attend Premiere," *MPW,* 14 Feb 1925, 718.

Alexander, Claire [actress: Sennett Bathing Beauty] (b. New York NY, 1898–16 Nov 1927 [29?], Alhambra CA; double pneumonia). "Claire Alexander," *Variety,* 30 Nov 1927. AMD, p. 18. BHD, p. 90. Truitt, p. 4. "Claire Alexander," *MPW,* 3 Jun 1916, 1703. "Claire Alexander Ill," *MPW,* 9 Dec 1916, 1480. "Claire Alexander Recovered," *MPW,* 20 Jan 1917, 384.

Alexander, Clifford [actor] (b. San Jose CA, 17 Jan 1891–2 Mar 1965 [74], San Francisco CA). BHD, p. 90.

Alexander, Edward [actor] (b. Ogdensburg NY, 2 May 1886–15 Aug 1964 [78], Dearborn MI; heart attack). (Fox; Universal; Horsley.) "Edward Alexander," *Variety,* 16 Sep 1954. AMD, p. 18. IFN, p. 6 (age 76). SA. Truitt, p. 4 (d. Dearborn OH). "Edward Alexander," *MPW,* 6 Mar 1915, 1458.

Alexander, Frank D. "Fatty" [actor] (b. Olympia WA, 24 May 1866?–8 Sep 1937 [71], No. Hollywood CA). (Keystone, 1913; Roach; Sennett.) "Frank (Fatty) Alexander," *NYT,* 9 Sep 1937, 23:5 (age 58; weighed 465 lbs. at his death). "Frank Alexander," *Variety,* 15 Sep 1937 (age 58). AMD, p. 18. BHD, p. 90 (b. 1879). IFN, p. 6 (age 58). Slide, *The Big V,* p. 157 (b. 1866). Truitt, p. 4. "'Fatty' Alexander Marries," *MPW,* 2 Jan 1926, 75.

Alexander, Georg [actor] (*né* Werner Lüddeckens, b. Hanover, Germany, 3 Apr 1889–30 Oct 1943 [54], Berlin, Germany). BHD1, p. 8 (d. 1945). IFN, p. 6 (d. 1946). Vittorio Martinelli, "Kino-Lieblinge," *Griffithiana,* 38/39 (Oct 1990), 42.

Alexander, Sir George [actor] (b. Reading, England, 19 Jun 1858–16 Mar 1918 [59]). BHD, p. 90 (d. 15 Mar). IFN, p. 6.

Alexander, Gerard (or **Girrard**) [actress] (b. 1877?–6 Apr 1962 [85], Los Angeles CA). m. **Bertram Grassby**, 1916 (d. 1953). (Universal.) "Mrs. Gerard A. Grassby," *Variety,* 18 Apr 1962 ("former motion picture actress"). AMD, p. 18. AS, p. 459 (Mrs. Gerard A. Grassby). BHD, p. 90 (d. 8 Apr); p. 184. IFN, p. 6. LACD, "photoplayer," r 1632 Vista. "Universal Players Marry," *MPW,* 12 Feb 1916, 936.

Alexander, Gus "Shorty" [actor]. No data found. AMD, p. 18. "Gus Alexander in Moon Comedies," *MPW,* 22 Jun 1918, 1742. "Blackton Signs Dunn and Alexander," *MPW,* 14 Jun 1919, 1640. "Gus Alexander in Red Seal Series," *MPW,* 17 Jul 1926, 168.

Alexander, Janet [actress] (b. Ewell, Surrey, England-d. 28 Jun 1961). BHD1, p. 8.

Alexander, J[oseph] **Grubb** [vaudeville actor/playwright/scenarist/composer] (b. Scranton PA, 25 Dec 1887–11 Jan 1932 [44], Los Angeles CA; pneumonia). m. vaudeville actress Elinor Ernest. "Joseph G. Alexander, Actor, Dies on Coast; Adapted 'Trilby' to Screen [from the original novel]—John Barrymore Took Role of Svengali," *NYT,* 12 Jan 1932, 23:4. BHD2, p. 4. FDY, p. 417. LACD, "screenwriter," r 6510 Sunset Blvd.

Alexander, John [actor] (b. 1865?–5 Apr 1951 [86], Ontario CA). m. Genevieve Hamper. "John Alexander," *Variety,* 11 Apr 1951. IFN, p. 6. Truitt, p. 4.

Alexander, Lois A. [actress] (b. Warsaw IN, 16 Aug 1890–3 May 1968 [77], Washington DC). "Lois A. Alexander," *Variety,* 8 May 1968.

Alexander, Muriel [stage actress/film director] (b. Cape Town, South Africa, 1884–Mar 1975 [90?]). "Muriel Alexander," *Variety,* 26 Mar 1975 (age 91). BHD, p. 90.

Alexander, Richard [actor] (b. Dallas TX, 18 Nov 1902–9 Aug 1989 [86], Woodland Hills CA; pulmonary illness). (Film debut: *Leopard*

Lady, 1924.) "Richard Alexander," *Variety,* 6 Sep 1989. BHD1, p. 8. SA. George A. Katchmer, "Remembering the Great Silents," *CI,* 178 (Apr 1990), 40.

Alexander, Sara [actress] (b. Wheeling WV, 1839–24 Dec 1926 [87], New York NY). "Sara Alexander," *Variety,* 5 Jan 1927. BHD, p. 91. SA. Truitt, p. 4.

Alexanderscu, Sicu [actor] (b. 1896–1973 [77?]). BHD1, p. 603.

Alexandersson, Gösta [actor] (b. Stockholm, Sweden, 16 Oct 1909–17 Mar 1988 [78]). BHD1, p. 603.

Alexandre, Rene [stage/film actor] (d. Dec 1914, Belgium). m. actress Gabrielle Robinne. (Pathé.) "Film Actor War Victim," *Variety,* 5 Dec 1914. AMD, p. 18. BHD, p. 91. IFN, p. 6 has d. 19 Aug 1946 (61). "Pathe Star Killed; Rene Alexandre a Victim of the Severe Fighting in Belgium," *NYDM,* 2 Dec 1914, 24:4 ("Alexandre was to the Pathe French drama what Max Linder (who was recently wounded) is to the Pathe French comedy." Pathe had just released his film, *More than a Queen.*). "Obituary," *MPW,* 12 Dec 1914, 1503.

Alexandresco [actress]. No data found. AMD, p. 18. "Noted European Actors in Rex Ingram's 'The Arab,'" *MPW,* 9 Feb 1924, 466.

Alexandria, Gladys [actress]. No data found. AMD, p. 18. "Gladys Alexandria with Metro," *MPW,* 21 Oct 1916, 413.

Alexandrov, Grigori V. [scenarist/actor/director] (*né* Grigori Mormonenko, b. Yekaterinburg, Russia, 23 Feb 1903–20 Dec 1983 [80], Moscow, Russia). BHD2, p. 4. FDY, p. 417 (Aleksandrov, G.V.). Katz 1994.

Alexianne, Mlle. [actress in Italian silents]. No data found.

Alexis, Demetrius [actor] (b. Greece, 1 Dec 1895–12 Mar 1973 [77], Beverly Hills CA). BHD1, p. 8 (b. 1905). IFN, p. 6 (b. 1905).

Algier, Sidney H. [actor/director/scenarist] (b. Examokin PA, 5 Dec 1885–25 Apr 1945 [59], West Los Angeles CA; heart attack). "Sidney Alexander," *Variety,* 2 May 1945 (d. Sawtelle CA, 24 Apr; age 52). BHD, p. 91 (b. Shamokin PA); BHD2, p. 4. IFN, p. 6.. SA. Truitt, p. 4 (b. Shamokin PA, 1889).

Ali, George [stage/film actor] (*né* George Bolingbroke, b. 1866?–26 Apr 1947 [81], Freeport, LI NY). m. Helen Jerome (d. 1958). "George Ali," *Variety,* 7 May 1947. BHD, p. 91. IFN, p. 6. SD. "Buster Brown's Pup Sure Cure for Blues; Outcault Cartoons Transferred to the Stage; Two Chief Figures Funny...," *NYT,* 25 Jan 1905, 9:3 (Ali, as Tige, received a rave review for his acting.).

Alison, George [actor] (b. London, England, 1865–14 Jan 1936 [70], Norwalk CT). BHD, p. 91.

Alkire, Walter H. [executive]. No data found. LACD, h 5632 Fountain Avenue; Alkire Photo Play Co. (National Academy of Photo Play Arts), E.C. Tompkins, vice-president, 405 S. Hill, room 308.

Allah, Ben [scenarist]. No data found. FDY, p. 417.

Allaire, Josiah [actor] (b. 1865–8 Oct 1935 [70?]). BHD, p. 91.

Allan, Hugh [actor] (*né* Allan Abram Hughes, b. near Oakland CA, 5 Nov 1903–12 Feb 1997 [93], Memphis TN; self-inflicted gunshot wound). (Film debut: *What Fools Men,* 1925; 1st National.) m. Lou Williamson, Apr 1932. AS, p. 47 (b. NY NY). BHD1, p. 603. Ragan, *Who's Who in Hollywood,* p. 21. "Hugh Allan," *MPW,* 28 May 1927, 256. Nancy Pryor, "The Sheik Is Out; Hugh Allen Says It Leaves Him Cold," *MPC,* Jun 1928, 26, 87. Michael Ankerich, "Hugh Allan: The Actor Who Should Have Been a Star," *CI,* 215 (May 1993), C4 *et passim* (includes filmography).

Allanby, Thomas W. *see* **Allenby, Thomas W.**

Allardt, Arthur [actor] (b. New York NY, 7 Apr 1883). (Frontier Co.) BHD, p. 91. LACD, "actor," h 5519 Sierra Vista Avenue (Allard). "Gossip of the Studios," *NYDM,* 5 Aug 1914, 23:2 (left the Frontier Co.).

Allegretti, Aurelio [cinematographer]. No data found. JS, p. 8 (in Italian silents from 1914).

Allen, A. Hylton [actor] (b. Pulborough, England, 25 Oct 1879–6 Feb 1975 [95]). BHD1, p. 8.

Allen, Alfred [actor/director] (b. Alfred NY, 8 Apr 1866–18 Jun 1947 [81], New York NY). BHD1, p. 9. IFN, p. 6. LACD, "director, Universal Film Co.," r University Club. SA. George A. Katchmer, "Forgotten Cowboys and Cowgirls—Part XVII," *CI,* 194 (Aug 1991), 42 (d. 18 Jan).

Allen, Alta [actress] (*née* Alta Crowin). m. **Hampton Del Ruth**, 1920 (d. 1958). No data found. AMD, p. 18. "Hampton Del Ruth Weds," *MPW,* 18 Dec 1920, 889.

Allen, Bert [cinematographer] (b. 1886?–1915 [29], Los Angeles CA). AMD, p. 19. "Obituary," *MPW,* 25 Sep 1915, 2182.

Allen, Bob [film/stage/TV actor] (*né* Irvine E. Theodore Baehr, b. Mt. Vernon NY, 9 Aug 1906–9 Oct 1998 [92], Oyster Bay NY). m. Evelyn Peirce, 1934 (son, Dr. Theodore Baehr; daughter, Katherine). (Extra at Paramount, 1926; Columbia; TC-F; AA nomination for *The Life of Lafayette,* 1936.) Andy Newman, "Robert Allen, 92, Texas Ranger in Westerns," *NYT,* 14 Oct 1998, A21. Kara Blond, "Bob Allen; Good-guy Hollywood cowboy in 1930s," *PP-G,* 13 Oct 1998, B-5:1. Bobby J. Copeland, "Ranger Bob Allen," *CI* (Nov 1996), C-4.

Allen, Christopher C. [actor] (b. 1869–7 Nov 1955 [86], Los Angeles CA). BHD, p. 91. IFN, p. 6.

Allen, Dave [actor/assistant director/founded Central Casting Corp., 1926] (b. Albany NY, 15 Aug 1885–3 Jan 1955 [69], Los Angeles CA). (Columbia.) "Dave Allen," *NYT,* 5 Jan 1955, 23:2. "Dave Allen," *Variety,* 12 Jan 1955 (age 68). BHD, p. 91; BHD2, p. 4. IFN, p. 6.

Allen, Diana [actress] (b. Gotland, Sweden). (Film debut: *Woman,* 1918.) m. Samuel P. Booth. (Maurice Tourneur Productions.) AMD, p. 19. "Diana Allen Scores in Victor Kremer's 'Voices,'" *MPW,* 14 Aug 1920, 885. "Blond[e] Swedish Maiden Plays Lead in 'The Kentuckians,'" *MPW,* 25 Sep 1920, 480.

Allen, Dorothy [actress] (Houston TX, b. 23 Oct 1896–30 Sep 1970 [73], New York NY). "Dorothy Allen," *NYT,* 2 Oct 1970, 38:1. "Dorothy Allen," *Variety,* 7 Oct 1970. BHD, p. 91. IFN, p. 7 (age 74). Truitt, p. 4.

Allen, Edith [actress]. No data found. "*Virtuous Liars* [review]," *MW,* 26 Apr 1924, 26 (her 2nd and last film).

Allen, E[dwin] **H**[ampton] [actor/assistant director/general manager of Inceville] (b. Canton Lewis Co. MO, 15 Nov 1885–13 Aug 1942 [56], Los Angeles CA). m. Margaret Thompson, 1914. BHD, p. 91; BHD2, p. 4. IFN, p. 7. W.E. Wing, "On the Pacific Coast," *NYDM,* 25 Nov 1914, 28:3.

Allen, Eileen [actress] (b. 1891?–24 May 1957 [66], Washington DC). m. Charles Dillingham. AS, p. 48. BHD1, p. 603. "Eileen Allen (Mrs. Charles Dillingham)," *Variety,* 12 Jun 1957.

Allen, Estelle [actress] (aka Estelle Whitman, b. Portland OR, 5 Jan 1892–14 Jul 1970 [78], Los Angeles CA). m. **Gayne Whitman** (d. 1958). (Vitagraph; NYMP Co.; American; Triangle.) AMD, p. 19. BHD, p. 91. IFN, p. 7. "New Domino Lead," *NYDM,* 5 May 1915, 22:4. "Alfred Vosburgh and Estelle Allen with Morosco," *MPW,* 14 Oct 1916, 217. "Estelle Whitman," *CFC,* 28 (Fall, 1970), X3. AS, p. 1148 (Estelle Whitman). IFN, p. 317. Truitt, p. 350.

Allen, Ethan H. [actor/scenarist/director] (b. MO, 11 May 1882–21 Aug 1940 [58], Los Angeles CA). (Bison.) "Ethan Allen," *Variety,* 28 Aug 1940. BHD2, p. 4. IFN, p. 7. Truitt, p. 4.

Allen, Eugene H. [assistant director] (b. Philadelphia PA, 4 Mar 1882–26 Jan 1965 [82], Los Angeles CA). (Ince; FP-L; Educational.) "Eugene H. Allen," *Variety,* 28 Aug 1940. BHD2, p. 5. IFN, p. 7.

Allen, Florence [member of DeCoy, Wagner & Thiess] [actress] (b. 1889?–15 May 1924 [35], Chicago IL; acute appendicitis). m. Norman J. Thiess. "Florence Allen," *Variety,* 21 May 1924 (interred at Catholic Cemetery, Chicago).

Allen, Fred [actor] (*né* John Florence Sullivan, b. Boston MA, 31 May 1894–17 Mar 1956 [61], New York NY [Death Certificate No. 6101, M.E. Case No. 2166]; heart attack). m. Portland Hoffa, 1927. "Fred Allen Dies While on Stroll; Won Fame as Wit on Radio After a Stage Career," *NYT,* 18 Mar 1956, 1:1, 88:6 (b. Cambridge MA). "Rites for Allen to Be Held Here; St. Malachy's Will Be Scene Tomorrow of Funeral for Radio and TV Humorist," *NYT,* 19 Mar 1956, 31:1. "Allen Is Mourned by Show Business; 2,000 Persons Throng Rites at St. Malachy's Church for Noted Humorist," *NYT,* 21 Mar 1956, 37:4. Robert J. Landry, "Fred Allen Parlayed His Deadpan Wit into International Renown," *Variety,* 21 Mar 1956 (b. Lynn MA). BHD1, p.9 (b. Cambridge). IFN, p. 7. SA. Truitt, p. 4.

Allen, Harry R. [actor] (b. Sydney, Australia, 10 Jul 1883–4 Dec 1951 [68], Los Angeles CA). BHD1, p. 9. IFN, p. 7. SA.

Allen, Ida Coggswell Bailey [scenarist]. No data found. AMD, p. 19. "Mrs. Allen Joins Universal Staff," *MPW,* 20 Apr 1918, 397.

Allen, Jack [producer]. No data found. AMD, p. 19. LACD, "photoplayer," h 803 S. Figueroa. "Major Jack Allen to Make Animal Films for Universal," *MPW,* 1 Mar 1919, 1194. "Jack Allen, Animal Filmer, Again Signed by Universal," *MPW,* 6 Sep 1919, 1478.

Allen, Joseph [actor] (b. Bristol, England, 2 Jan 1840–12 Jan 1917 [77], Chicago IL). BHD, p. 91. IFN, p. 7.

Allen, Joseph A., Sr. (father of Joseph Allen, Jr.) [actor] (b. Worcester MA, 23 Feb 1873 [MVRB, vol. 252, p. 383]–9 Sep 1952 [79], Newton MA). "Joseph Allen, 80, Character Actor; Veteran of Stage Is Dead—Was Associated with George M. Cohan for 18 Years," *NYT,* 10 Sep 1952, 29:6. "Joseph Allen," *Variety,* 17 Sep 1952. BHD1, p. 9 (b. 1872). IFN, p. 7. LACD, "photoplayer," h 133 W. 21st Street. Truitt, p. 5.

Allen, Kenneth [stuntman] (b. 26 Apr 1904–15 Jan 1976 [71], Alameda CA). BHD, p. 91 (b. 1903). IFN, p. 7.

Allen, Lex [actor]. No data found. LACD, "photoplayer, Vitagraph Co." (no address).

Allen, Lloyd [assistant director]. No data found. "Wife of Lloyd Allen," *Variety,* 2 Oct 1963, Hollywood CA).

Allen, Maud[e] [actress] (*née* Maude Allen Giannone, b. Toronto, Canada, 27 Aug 1880–7 Nov 1956 [76], WA). "Maude Allen [Giannone]," *Variety,* 21 Nov 1956 (in silents with Norma Talmadge). AMD, p. 18. IFN, p. 7. SA. "Maud Allan [sic] on Screen; Bosworth-Morosco Production to Present Famous Dancer in Film Debut [*The Rugmaker's Daughter*]," *NYDM,* 2 Jun 1915, 21:1 ("Recently Miss Allan is said to have refused a $5,000 offer to appear in one of her dances before the camera.") "Maud Allan with Bosworth-Morosco," *MPW,* 5 Jun 1915, 1619. "Special Music for Maud Allan," *MPW,* 24 Jul 1915, 627.

Allen, Nita (or Anita) [actress] (d. 3 Jul 1915, Los Angeles CA; after an operation for appendicitis). "Nita Allen," *Variety,* 9 Jul 1915. AS, p. 48. BHD1, p. 603.

Allen, Paul [cinematographer] (b, 1895–15 Aug 1956 [61?], Los Angeles CA). BHD2, p. 5. FDY, p. 455.

Allen, Paul B. [actor] (b. 1886?–3 Apr 1956 [70]). "Paul B. Allen," *Variety,* 11 Apr 1956.

Allen, Phyllis [actress] (b. Staten Island NY, 25 Nov 1861–26 Mar 1938 [76], Los Angeles CA). (Sennett; Chaplin.) "Phyllis Allen," *Variety,* 30 Mar 1938. BHD, p. 91. IFN, p. 7. LACD, "photoplayer," r 230 S. Beaudry Avenue. Truitt, p. 5.

Allen, Ricca [actress] (b. Victoria, B.C., Canada, 9 Jun 1863–13 Sep 1949 [86], Los Angeles CA). (World.) BHD1, p. 10. IFN, p. 7. SA.

Allen, Robert (Bob) [actor] (*né* Irving Theodore Baehr, b. Mt. Vernon NY, 29 Mar 1906–9 Jun 1992 [86], Rexville NY). m. Evelyn Pierce. Katz, p. 22 (began 1926).

Allen, Ruth [scenarist]. No data found. AMD, p. 19. "Ruth Allen a Free Lance," *MPW,* 28 Jun 1919, 1928.

Allen, Sam E. [actor] (b. Baltimore MD, 25 Dec 1861–13 Sep 1934 [72], Los Angeles CA). "Sam Allen," *Variety,* 18 Sep 1934). BHD1, p. 10. IFN, p. 7. Truitt, p. 7. George A. Katchmer, "Forgotten Cowboys and Cowgirls—Part XVII," *CI,* 194 (Aug 1991), 42.

Allen, Victor [actor]. George A. Katchmer, "Forgotten Cowboys and Cowgirls—Part XVII," *CI,* 194 (Aug 1991), 42.

Allen, Viola [actress] (b. Huntsville AL, 27 Oct 1867–9 May 1948 [80], New York NY [Death Certificate No. 11138 (Viola Duryea)]). m. Peter Duryea. (Film debut: *The White Sister,* Essanay, 1915.) "Viola Allen Dead; Once Stage Star; Leading Lady at 15, in 1884, She Played Variety of Roles After Success in Classics," *NYT,* 10 May 1948, 21:1. "Viola Allen," *Variety,* 12 May 1948. AMD, p. 19. BHD, p. 91. IFN, p. 7 (b. 1869). SD. Felice Levy, *Obituaries on File,* Vol. I (New York: Facts on File, 1979). "Viola Allen Signed; Will Make Screen Debut in Essanay Adaptation of 'The White Sister,'" *NYDM,* 31 Mar 1915, 24:2. "Viola Allen with Essanay," *MPW,* 10 Apr 1915, 216. "Miss Allen's Reasons; Liking for 'The White Sister' Moved Star to Consider Appearance on Screen," *NYDM,* 5 May 1915, 24:4 ("...because of her warm admiration for the author [the late F. Marion Crawford] and his family"; she had done the play version). "A New Essanay Star," *Pictures and the Picturegoer,* 8 May 1915, 92.

Allen, Winifred [actress] (b. New Rochelle NY, 26 Jun 1896–3 Jan 1943 [46], New Rochelle NY). m. Lawrence Sperry, 20 Feb 1918. (FP-L.) AMD, p. 19. BHD1, p. 603. "Winifred Allen Featured by Triangle," *MPW,* 28 Apr 1917, 591. Cal York, "Plays and Players," *Photoplay,* Jul 1917, 114 (to be made a Triangle star). "Cupid Slides from a Cloud," *MPW,* 9 Mar 1918, 1356.

Allenby, Thomas W. [actor] (b. Tasmania, Australia, 15 Jul 1861–19 Dec 1933 [72], Hollywood CA; killed in a car accident). "Thomas Allenby," *Variety,* 26 Dec 1933. AS, p. 49. BHD1, p. 603. IFN, p. 7. LACD, "photoplayer," r 1415 Vine. SA. Truitt, p. 5.

Aller, Joseph L. (b. Russia, 5 Dec 1882–19 Feb 1950 [67], Los Angeles CA). (Griffith, 1909; Rothacker-Aller Co.; Triangle.) "Joseph L. Aller," *Variety,* 1 Mar 1950 (film processor). BHD2, p. 5.

Allerton, Helen [actress] (aka Little Helen Allerton, *né* Helen Schweisthal, b. 1888–4 Nov 1959 [71], Golf IL). "Helen Kilduff," *Variety,* 11 Nov 1959. BHD, p. 91. IFN, p. 7. Truitt, p. 5.

Alley, Alfred W. [art director]. No data found. AMD, p. 19. "Alley Appointed Art Director," *MPW,* 24 Jul 1920, 493.

Allgood, Sara [actress] (b. Dublin, Ireland, 15 Oct 1879–13 Sep 1950 [70], Woodland Hills CA; heart attack). m. Leslie Henson (d. 1957). (Stage debut: London, 1904.) "Sara Allgood Dies; Stage, Screen Star; Character Actress Had Noted Career with Abbey Players Before Turning to Films," *NYT,* 14 Sep 1950, 31:1 (age 66; b. 1883). "Sara Allgood," *Variety,* 20 Sep 1950 (age 66; began 1929). BHD1, p. 10. GSS, p. 7. IFN, p. 7. Katz, p. 23. SA. SD.

Allibert, Jean-Louis [actor] (b. Paris, France, 14 Dec 1897–Jan 1980 [82], Paris, France). BHD1, p. 10.

Allison, May [singer/stage/film actress] (b. Rising Fawn CA, 14 Jun 1890–27 Mar 1989 [98], Bratenahl [Cleveland] OH; respiratory ailment). (May Osborne; b. 1897). m. (1) **Robert Ellis** (d. 1935); (2) **James R. Quirk**, 15 Nov 1926 (d. 1932); (3) Carl N. Osborne (b. 13 Apr 1885–d. May 1982). (American; FP-L; Metro; film debut: *A Fool There Was,* 1915.) "May Allison," *Variety,* 12 Apr 1989 (b. Rising Fawn GA). AMD, p. 19. BHD, p. 91. FFF, p. 131 (b. 1897). LACD, "photoplayer," r Hotel Hollywood. Lowrey, p. 2. MH, p. 94. MSBB, p. 1030 (b. GA). SA. WWS, p. 109. "Miss May Allison," *NYDM,* 5 Aug 1914, 5:2 (photo; appearing in *Apartment 12-K,* Maxine Elliott Theatre). "May Allison Now a Screen Artist," *MPW,* 30 Jan 1915, 688. "Briefs of Biography; From Gawgia, Suh!," *NYDM,* 29 Sep 1915, 36:3 (b. GA). "New Metro Stars," *MPW,* 25 Mar 1916, 2013. "Metro Stars Not Married [Allison and Harold Lockwood]," *MPW,* 20 May 1916, 1348. Ruth Mabrey, "'Vacations in Married Life Are Necessary!,' Says May Allison; Screen star who was rumored separating from her husband, tells why occasional vacations are needed in matrimony," *MW,* 19 Apr 1924, 17. Regina Cannon, "'Marriage Was Not Enough to Make Me Happy!,' Says May Allison," *MW,* 7 Jun 1924, 7. "Thumbnail Sketches No. 2; May Allison and Sex Appeal," *MPC,* Jan 1925, 63. Sarah Edmonton, "The Many May Allisons," *MPC,* Aug 1925, 58, 87, 89. "Marriages," *MPW,* 27 Nov 1926, 3. DeWitt Bodeen, "Lockwood & Allison; Their Love Affairs Were Once as Popular as Bush & Baynes," *FIR,* May 1971, 275–98.

Allister, Claude [stage/film actor] (*né* Claud Palmer, b. London, England, 3 Oct 1888–26 Jul 1970 [81], Santa Barbara CA; cancer). m. Gwen Dowling (d. 1981). (MGM.) "Claud Allister, 76, Actor of Stage and Movies, Dies," *NYT,* 31 Jul 1970, 30:6 (age 76). "Claud Allister," *Variety,* 5 Aug 1970 (age 76). BHD1, p. 10. IFN, p. 7. SA.

Allworth, Frank [stage/film actor] (b. 1900–2 Sep 1935 [35], Philadelphia PA; dropped dead during stage performance of *Portuguese Gal* with Lenore Ulric). "Frank Allworth," *Variety,* 4 Sep 1935. BHD, p. 91. IFN, p. 7.

Allyn, Freda [scenarist]. No data found. LACD, "scenario wrioter," r 851 S. Flower Street.

Allyn, Lilly [actress] (b. 1886–5 May 1944 [58?], Philadelphia PA). BHD, p. 92. IFN, p. 7 (age 78).

Almirante, Italia Manzini (cousin of **Luigi Almirante**) [actress] (b. Taranto, Italy, 1890–Oct 1941 [51?], São Paolo, Brazil). JS, p. 9 (in Italian silents from 1906).

Almirante, Luigi (cousin of **Italia Manzini Almirante**) [actor] (b. Tunisia, North AFrica, 30 Sep 1886–6 May 1963 [76]). IFN, p. 7. JS, p. 8 (in Italian silents from 1926).

Almirante, Mario [director] (b. Molfetta, Italy, 18 Feb 1890). JS, p. 9 (in Italian silents from 1920).

Almirante, Nunzio [actor] (b. Collesano, Italy, 3 Dec 1837–1906 [68?], Dell'Aquila, Italy). SA.

Alperson, Edward L. [actor/producer] (b. Omaha NB, 13 Nov 1895–3 Jul 1969 [73], Beverly Hills CA). m. (1) Lillian (d. 1963); (2) Sara. (Preferred Pictures, 1919; WB, 1924; TC-F; Grand National Pictures, 1936–39.) "Edward L. Alperson," *Variety,* 9 Jul 1969. BHD2, p. 5 (b. 1896).

Alsop, Martin Luther [actor] (Equitable.) No data found. m. (2) Alvinia—div. in SF CA; (3) Hazel Louise Robbins, 30 Dec 1916, West Newton MA. "Married," *NYDM,* 13 Jan 1917, p. 11.

Alston, Arthur [actor] (b. 1880?–31 May 1919 [39], London, England). m. (1 son). "Arthur Alston Dead," *Variety,* 13 Jun 1919, 4:3.

Alston, George [scenic artist]. No data found. (Sennett.) LACD, "scenic artist," Mack Sennett Comedies.

Alston, Howard [scenic artist]. No data found. (Sennett.) LACD, "scenic artist," Mack Sennett Comedies.

Alstrup, Carl [actor] (b. Copenhagen, Denmark, 11 Apr 1877–2 Oct 1942 [65]). AMD, p. 19. BHD, p. 92. IFN, p. 8. "New Great Northern Star," *MPW,* 11 Nov 1911, 461.

Alt, Al[exander] [actor] (b. New York NY, 8 Oct 1897–8 Feb 1992 [94], Santa Monica CA). AMD, p. 19. BHD, addendum; BHD2, p. 5. "Julius and Abe Stern Pick Four Century Comedy Stars," *MPW,* 13 Dec 1924, 652.

Altemus, Charlotte Jane [stage/film actress]. No data found. AMD, p. 19. "Miss Altemus in Transition, Stage to Screen," *MPW,* 25 Jun 1927, 591.

Alter, Lottie [actress] (b. La Crosse WI, 16 Jan 1879–25 Dec 1924 [45], Beecherst NY). BHD, p. 92.

Althouse, Earl F. [actor] (b. 16 Aug 1892–6 Feb 1971 [78], Gladwyne PA). (Lubin.) "Earl F. Althouse," *Variety*, 17 Feb 1971. BHD, p. 92 (b. 1893). IFN, p. 8. Truitt, p. 5.

Alton, John [cinematographer] (b. Sopron, Hungary, 5 Oct 1901–2 Jun 1996 [94], Santa Monica CA; complications from hip replacement surgery). m. Rozalia Kiss (d. 1987). (Began at MGM, 1924; Joinville [Paris]; Columbia; RKO; Republic; Paramount; Monogram; AA with Alfred Gilks for *An American in Paris*, MGM, 1951.) *Painting with Light* (1995). "John Alton," *Variety*, 10 Jun 1996, 48:1. BHD2, p. 5.

Alton, Maxine [scenarist]. No data found. FDY, p. 417.

Altschuler, Modest (b. Mahilyow, Belraus, 15 Feb 1873–12 Sep 1963 [90], Los Angeles CA). BHD1, p. 603.

Alvarado, Don [actor] (*né* José Paige, b. Albuquerque NM, 4 Nov 1904–31 Mar 1967 [62], Los Angeles CA; cancer). "Don Alvarado," *Variety*, 12 Apr 1967. AMD, p. 19. BHD1, p. 11 (b. 1900). FSS, p. 3. IFN, p. 8. SA. Truitt, p. 5; Truitt 1983 (b. 1900). "Don Alvarado," *MPW*, 4 Jun 1927, 333. "Don Alvarado with D.W. Griffith," *MPW*, 20 Aug 1927, 529.

Alvarez Rubio, Pablo [stage/film actor] (b. Madrid, Spain, 1896–1983 [87?]). (Began 1923; made two Spanish-language films in Hollywood). Waldman, p. 7.

Alves da Cunha, Jose Maria [actor] (b. 1889–25 Sep 1956 [67?], Lisbon, Portugal). BHD1, p. 11.

Alw, Gabriel [actor] (b. Eskilstuma, Sweden, 25 Dec 1889–9 Nov 1946 [56], Stockholm, Sweden). AS, p. 52. BHD1, p. 603.

Amador, Charles Edward [actor/scenarist] (b. Mexico, 5 Mar 1896–7 Apr 1974 [78], Chula Vista CA). BHD, p. 92; BHD2, p. 5. LACD, "photoplayer," r 1811 Rodney Drive.

Amann, Betty [actress] (b. Pirmasens, Germany, 10 Mar 1905–3 Aug 1990 [85]). BHD1, p. 11.

Amato, Giuseppe [founded Film Abrrosio, 1905/actor/writer/director/producer] (*né* Giuseppe Vasaturo, b. Turin, Italy, 1869–3 Feb 1964 [94?], Rome, Italy; heart attack). "Giuseppe Amato," *Variety*, 12 Feb 1964 (age 64), p. 86. BHD2, p. 6 (b. Naples, Italy, 24 Aug 1899). IFN, p. 8 (b. Naples). JS, p. 10 (b. Naples, Italy, 24 Aug 1899).

Amato, Pasquale [actor/opera singer] (b. Naples, Italy, 21 Mar 1878–12 Aug 1942 [64], Jackson Heights, Queens NY; died after dinner [Death Certificate No. 5923]). "Pasquale Amato, Baritone, Was 63; Teacher of Voice Culture at Louisiana State University Dies in Jackson Heights [while visiting friends]; Made His Debut in Naples [1900]; Heard at the Metropolitan in 'Traviata' in 1908, 8 Years After First Performance," *NYT*, 13 Aug 1942, 19:6. "Pasquale Amato," *Variety*, 19 Aug 1942. BHD1, p. 11. IFN, p. 8. SA. Oscar Thompson, *International Encyclopedia of Music and Musicians*, 9th ed., ed. Robin Sabin (NY: Dodd, Mead, 1964).

Amazar, Elaine [actress]. No data found. (1st U.S. film: *As a Man Thinks*, Artco, 1919.)

Amazar, Elvira "Vera" [actress]. No data found; may be Vera Amazar, (b. 16 Feb 1899–Feb 1971 [72?], NY). AMD, p. 19. "Mme. Vera Amazar Must Have 'Ze Hand Claps,'" *MPW*, 17 May 1919, 1060. "Mme. Amazar Likes Picture Work," *MPW*, 24 May 1919, 1238.

Amberg, Hugo [publicist]. No data found. AMD, p. 19. "Hugo Amberg Goes to Germany," *MPW*, 14 Mar 1914, 1367.

Ambrosio, Arturo [producer/director] (b. Turin, Italy, 1869–1960 [91?]). m. (son, **Paolo**). AMD, p. 19. JS, p. 11 (said to have produced over 1,500 films). Katz, p. 26. "Important Interview with Mr. Arturo Ambrosio," *MPW*, 6 Nov 1909, 640. "The Founder of 'Ambrosio [1905],'" *MPW*, 9 Aug 1913, 615.

Ambrosio, Paolo (son of **Arturo Ambrosio**) [actor/director] (b. Turin, Italy). JS, p. 11 ("As a child he acted in some of his father's films," from 1919 or earlier).

Ames, Bert [title writer]. No data found. FDY, p. 441.

Ames, Gerald [actor] (*né* Percy Gerald Ames, b. Lewisham, London, England, 12 Sep 1880–2 Jul 1933 [52], London, England; from fall in an underground subway). m. actress Mary Dibley. "Gerald Ames," *Variety*, 18 Jul 1933 (d. 4 Jul). BHD, p. 92 (b. 1881). IFN, p. 8. SD. Truitt, p. 6.

Ames, Percy F. [actor] (b. Brighton, Sussex, England, 1874–28 Mar 1936 [62], New York NY [Death Certificate No. 8254]). m. Sybil Comins. "Percy Ames," *Variety*, 1 Apr 1936. BHD1, p. 12. SD.

Ames, Robert D. [actor] (b. Hartford CT, 23 Mar 1889–27 Nov 1931 [42], New York NY [Death Certificate No. 27387]). m. (2?) Frances Goodrich—div. 1923; (3) Vivienne Segal, 30 Jul 1923, Newark NJ–div. May 1926; (4) Muriel Oakes, 10 Feb 1927, Waukegan IL—div. 10 Nov 1930. "Robert Ames, Actor, Found Dead in Hotel; Body Discovered on Floor of Room in the Delmonico by a Chambermaid; Came Here to Make Film; Physician Says Star of Many Stage and Screen Successes Had a Hemorrhage," *NYT*, 28 Nov 1931, 15:3. "Robt. Ames Found Dead in His Hotel Room," *Variety*, 1 Dec 1931. AMD, p. 19. BHD1, p. 12. FSS, p. 3. IFN, p. 8. "DeMille Signs Robert Ames," *MPW*, 2 May 1925, 74. June Lee, "Dan Cupid's Bulletin Board," *Paris and Hollywood*, Oct 1926, 88 (according to Vivienne Segal, after her marriage to Ames he refused to work, "even compelling her to pay alimony of $100 a week to Mrs. Francis Goodrich, his divorced wife. At various times, the actress claims, the amount of money owned by her film husband totalled $15,000. She charged desertion."). June Lee, "Dan Cupid's Bulletin Board," *Paris and Hollywood Screen Secrets Magazine*, May 1927, 53 (wed Oakes).

Amy, George J. [director/editor] (b. Brooklyn NY, Oct 15 Oct 1900–18 Dec 1986 [86], Van Nuys CA). (b. 9 Sep 1903). (WB; FP-L.) "George J. Amy," *Variety*, 31 Dec 1986. BHD2, p. 6 (d. LA CA). Katz, pp. 27–28 (b. 1903). SA (b. 1903).

Ander, Charlotte [actress] (b. Berlin, Germany, 14 Aug 1902–5 Aug 1969 [66]). BHD, p. 92.

Anders, Glenn [actor] (b. Los Angeles CA, 1 Sep 1889–26 Oct 1981 [92], Edgewood NJ. BHD1, p. 12.

Andersen, Robert Christian [actor/director] (b. Odense [Copenhagen], Denmark, 22 Jul 1890–14 May 1988 [97], Burton MI). (Griffith.) AMD, p. 19. BHD1, p. 13 and BHD2, p. 6 (d. 25 Jun 1963, Woodland Hills CA). "Robert Christian Andersen Has Signed with Universal," *MPW*, 1 Mar 1919, 1206. "Robert Andersen on 'Mental Make-Up,'" *Theatre Magazine*, Mar 1919, 187. "Has Prominent Role," *MPW*, 16 Jun 1923, 595. "Anderson a Disciple of Labor," *MPW*, 3 Nov 1923, 92.

Anderson, Augusta [stage/film actress]. No data found. (Biograph.) AMD, p. 19. "Augusta Anderson," *MPW*, 5 Sep 1914, 1379. "Augusta Anderson," *MPW*, 6 Nov 1915, 1149. Appeared in *A Good Little Devil*, 27 Jan 1913, at the Republic Theatre, NY.

Anderson, Burt "Bo" [actor] (b. New York NY, 23 Nov 1920–29 Mar 1986 [65], Los Angeles CA). BHD1, p. 13.

Anderson, Carl [executive]. AMD, p. 20. "Anderson a Motion Picture Pioneer," *MPW*, XXXII, 9 Jun 1917, 1586. "Anderson Goes to Coast," *MPW*, 8 Sep 1917, 1518. "Anderson Back from the Coast," *MPW*, 29 Sep 1917, 1975. "Carl Anderson Promises Splendid Plays," *MPW*, 6 Apr 1918, 69. "Anderson Contracts with Hollywood Enterprises," *MPW*, 6 Oct 1923, 479. "Anderson Establishes Units in 3 Leading English Cities," *MPW*, 13 Oct 1923, 562. "Anderson Buys from Hampton Great Authors Productions," *MPW*, 27 Oct 1923, 725.

Anderson, Charles E. (Cap) [actor] (b. Stockholm, Sweden, 27 Oct 1882–24 Mar 1956 [73], Los Angeles CA). BHD1, p. 13. IFN, p. 8. George Katchmer, "Forgotten Cowboys and Cowgirls—Part XVII," *CI*, 194 (Aug 1991), 42–43.

Anderson, Claire Mathis [Sennett Bathing Beauty] (b. Detroit MI, 8 May 1895–23 Mar 1964 [68], Venice CA). (Reliance-Majestic; Keystone.) "Claire Mathes Anderson, Silent-Film Actress, 68," *NYT*, 27 Mar 1964, 27:1. "Claire M. Anderson," *Variety*, 8 Apr 1964. BHD, p. 92. IFN, p. 8. Truitt, p. 6. George Katchmer, "Remembering the Great Silents," *CI*, 220 (Oct 1993), 40.

Anderson, Dallas [actor] (b. Grieff, Scotland, 12 Jul 1874–16 Nov 1934 [60], Richmond VA; from injuries in a car accident on 13 Nov). "Dallas Anderson," *Variety*, 20 Nov 1934. BHD, p. 92. IFN, p. 8.

Anderson, Doris [scenarist]. No data found. FDY, p. 417.

Anderson, Edyth Stroud [actress]. No data found. (Lubin.) AMD, p. 20. "Lubin Players to Wed Before Camera," *MPW*, 30 Jan 1915, 662.

Anderson, Erville *see* **Alderson, Erville**

Anderson, F. [title writer]. No data found. FDY, p. 441.

Anderson, Florence [dancer/actress/wardrobe mistress of Radio City Music Hall] (*née?*, b. Liverpool, England, 1882?–25 Nov 1962 [80], New York NY). m. **Gus Anderson** (d. 1947). "Florence Anderson, Wardrobe Mistress," *NYT*, 27 Nov 1962, 37:2 ("In between appearances at the Hippodrome [as a dancer] she took small parts in silent films."). BHD, p. 92.

Anderson, Frank (father of **Mignon Anderson**) [opera/vaudeville/stage/film actor] (b. Baltimore MD-d. Sep? 1914, New York NY). m. Hallie Howard. "Frank Anderson Dies," *NYDM*, 7 Oct 1914, 32:2.

Anderson, G.M. "Broncho Billy" (*né* Gilbert Maxwell Aronson, b. Little Rock AR, 21 Mar 1880–20 Jan 1971 [90], Woodland Hills CA). m. Mollie Louise Schabbleman. (Began 1903; Edison; Vitagraph; Selig; Essanay.) "Broncho Billy Anderson Is Dead at 88," *NYT,* 21 Jan 1971, 38:1. "Broncho Billy Anderson," *Variety,* 27 Jan 1971. AMD, p. 20. BHD, p. 92 and BHD2, p. 6 (b. 1884). FSS, p. 4. IFN, p. 8 (b. 1884). Truitt, p. 6 (in films from 1902). "Trade Notes," *MPW,* 3 Aug 1907, 342. "Will Make Pictures in Mexico," *MPW,* 18 Sep 1909, 381. "Essanay Producers in Texas and Mexico; To Install Temporary Studio in El Paso—Essanay Western Pictures in Great Demand," *MPW,* 4 Dec 1909, 801:1 (left Denver for El Paso the previous week. *The Best Man Wins,* Essanay's first Western, 20 Nov 1909, "is reported to have been a winner. The pohotography in the picture is excellent, while the subject, a sparkling little comedy, is a choice one."). "The Essanay Company Out West," *MPW,* 4 Dec 1909, 801–02 (in Denver for six weeks, then on to Las Vegas abnd Catalina Island. His troupe included J.J. Robbins, expert photographer; Jack O'Brien, "a handsome young actor, who does the 'heavies'"; Arthur Smith, character actor, and W.K. Russell, "property man and assistant hero and villain." Leading ladies, soubrettes, ingenues, mobs, and posses to be "secured from the stock companies and vaudeville houses of the various cities that serve as a base for operations.... Last Tuesday ... *The Heart of a Cowboy* was put on at Mt. Morrison..." [A synopsis of the film is provided in this article.] "Miss Loma Besserer, the 'girl' on the occasion, has played leads in many stock companies, but it was her first experience with 'moving pictures,' and started off with true 'leading lady' refinement and reserve. ¶'No, no,' cried Mr. Anderson. 'Charming in a theater, Miss Besserer, and you certainly look a picture. BNut you've got to ACT a picture! This is practically pantomime, you know. Turn loose!'.... Leading ladies and leading men, according to their professional standing, are paid from $15 to $100 a day, and the Essanay Company even offered George and Josephine Cohan $2,000 for one dance." No actor managed by Klaw & Erlanger is allowed to make films. "And as for the 'plays' themselves $100 is paid for a good one, and many of the country's famous authors are turning their attention to this new source of income.")." "The 'Acting' Member of Essanay," *MPW,* 6 Jan 1912, 27–28. "Some Prominent Essanay Photoplayers," *MPW,* 11 Jul 1914, 234–35. "Brief Biographies of Popular Players," *MPC,* Mar 1916, 41–42. "'Broncho' Anderson Sues Essanay Films," *MPW,* 10 Dec 1927, 24. Gunnar Lundquist, "The Father Figure of the Western Film; Broncho Billy Anderson; They All Rode in His Tracks," *CI,* 144 (Jun 1987), 21–23, C1; Part II (Jul 1987), 41–45. Gunnar Lundquist, "Broncho Billy's Filmography," *CI,* 147 (Sep 1987), 47–50; 148 (Oct 1987), C1–C2. George Katchmer, "Broncho Billy Anderson," *CI,* 255 (Sep 1996), 38–39 (b. 1884).

Anderson, George M. [stage/film actor] (b. New York NY, 6 Mar 1886–26 Aug 1948 [62], Los Angeles CA). "George Anderson," *Variety,* 1 Sep 1948 (age 57; "He had been in pictures 15 years following an earlier stage career."). BHD1, p. 13. IFN, p. 8.

Anderson, Gertrude H. [stage/film actress] (*née* Gertrude Hoffman, b. Montreal, Canada, 7 May 1898–3 Jun 1955 [57], Washington DC). (Vitagraph.) "Gertrude Hoffman," *Variety,* 8 Jun 1955. AS, p. 532 (Gertrude Hoffman). BHD, p. 201 (Hoffman). IFN, p. 143 (Hoffman). "In Favor of Gaby; Cleveland Court Enjoins Gertrude Hoffman from Giving Imitation of Deslys," *NYDM,* 4 Feb 1914, 6:2 (imitations described as "improper, unbecoming burlesque").

Anderson, Gus [actor] (d. 1947). m. **Florence** (d. 1962).

Anderson, Helen (*née* Helen Morris, d. 2 May 1958, Greensboro NC). m. Larry Anderson. "Helen Anderson [Mrs. Larry Anderson]," *Variety,* 14 May 1958.

Anderson, James [actor] (b. Scotland, 1872?–22 Mar 1953 [81], Glasgow, Scotland; from burns). "James Anderson," *Variety,* 1 Apr 1953. BHD1, p. 13. IFN, p. 8. Truitt, p. 7.

Anderson, Lawrence [actor] (b. Hampstead, England, 1893–28 Mar 1939 [46], London, England). BHD1, p. 13. IFN, p. 8.

Anderson, Leona B. [singer/dancer in vaudeville] (b. Philadelphia PA, 23 Nov 1897–29 Mar 1985 [87], Columbus OH). "Lena Mendoza," *Variety,* 10 Apr 1985 ("Mendoza" was her stage name). BHD1, p. 13.

Anderson, Louis F[rancis] [cameraman] (b. Denver CO, 28 May 1903–10 Nov 1991 [88], Woodland Hills CA). (RKO.) "Louis F. Anderson," *Variety,* 20 Apr 1992, p. 60. BHD2, p. 6.

Anderson, M.A. [cinematographer]. No data found. FDY, p. 455.

Anderson, Margaret [actress] (b. New York NY, 1884–22 Apr 1922 [38?], New York NY). BHD, p. 92. IFN, p. 8.

Anderson, Mary [stage actress] (*née* Mary Antoinette Anderson, b. Sacramento CA, 28 Jul 1859–29 May 1940 [80], Court Farm, Broadway, Worcestershire, England). m. Antonio F. de Navarro, 1890 (d. 11 Oct 1932). *A Few Memories* (NY: Harper, 1896). J.M. Farrar, *Mary Anderson; The Story of Her Life and Professional Career* (London: D. Bogue, 1884). Albert R. Frey, *Mary Anderson in Her Dramatic Roles* (NY: W.J. Kelly, 1892). Henry L. Williams, *The "Queen of the Drama," Mary Anderson; Her Life On and Off the Stage* (NY: Williams, 1885). William Winter, *Stage Life of Mary Anderson* (NY: G.J. Coombes, 1896). Mary Anderson de Navarro, *A Few More Memories* (London: Hutchinson & Co., 1936). (Stage debut: 27 Nov 1875, Louisville KY; NYC debut: 12 Nov 1877, Fifth Avenue Theatre, as Pauline in *The Lady of Lyons;* London debut: 3 Sep 1883, as Parthenia in *Ingomar;* Ince). "Mary Anderson, 80, Noted Actress, Dies; She Had Brilliant Career [14 years; collapsed 7 Mar 1889, Washington DC, onstage in *Perdita*] on American Stage—Widow of Antonio de Navarro; Scored a Success at 16; Lived on Farm in England Since Retirement—Hostess to Many Notables," *NYT,* 30 May 1940, 17:1 (acted onstage 1916–17). "Mary Anderson," *Variety,* 5 Jun 1940. IFN, p. 8. "Mary Anderson for Screen," *NYDM,* 6 Nov 1915, 24:1 (to appear in films after almost 20 years' absence from the stage). George Katchmer, "Remembering the Great Silents," *CI,* 243 (Sep 1995), 40.

Anderson, Mary "Sunshine" (daughter of **Mrs. Nellie Anderson**) [actress] (b. Brooklyn NY, 28 Jun 1897). m. **Pliny Goodfriend** (d. 1981). (Ince; Vitagraph.) AMD, p. 20. MH, p. 94. 1921 Directory, p. 210. MSBB, p. 1030. Slide, p. 134. "Mary Anderson," *MPW,* 17 Mar 1917, 1778. Grace Kingsley, "Mary Anderson of the Films," *Photoplay Magazine,* Jun 1917, 80–81, 152–53. Mary Anderson, "How I Got It," *Motion Picture Magazine,* Dec 1917, p. 78. "Mary Anderson Joins Fred Stone's Company," *MPW,* 28 Sep 1918, 1856. "Burr Engages Mary Anderson to Appear in His Series of All-Star Comedies," *MPW,* 30 Sep 1922, 399.

Anderson, Mignon (daughter of stage actors **Frank Anderson** and Hallie Howard) [stage/film actress] (b. Baltimore MD, 15 Mar 1891–25 Feb 1983 [91], Los Angeles CA). (b. 31 Mar 1892; Mignon Foster). m. **J. Morris Foster,** 13 Apr 1915 (d. 1966). "Mignon Anderson," *Variety,* 23 Mar 1983. (Began as an extra in 1910 at Thanhouser [New Rochelle NY]; Exclusive; Universal; Paramount; TC-F; last film: *Kisses,* Metro, 1922.) AMD, p. 20. BHD, p. 92 (b. 31 Mar 1892). LACD, "photoplayer," r 6128 Salem Place. SA. "Mignon Anderson—Her Secret," *MPW,* 8 Jun 1912, 921. Harriet Holmes, "Winsome Mignon Anderson, the Little 'Dresden China Girl,'" *Photoplay* (Nov 1913), 59–60. "Frank Anderson Dies," *NYDM,* 7 Oct 1914, 32:2 (father, an opera, stage and vaudeville actor, born in Baltimore, died in NYC). "Honeymooners Surprised," *MPW,* 15 May 1915, 1092. "Mignon Anderson Joins Ivan," *MPW,* 25 Mar 1916, 2016. "Mignon Anderson Joins Universal," *MPW,* 13 Jan 1917, 222. John E. Thayer, "Mignon and Thanhouser," *CFC,* 40 (Fall, 1973), 7 *et passim.* Murray Summers, "Mignon Anderson: Bio- and Autobiographical Notes," *Filmograph,* IV, No. 1 (1973), 40. George Katchmer, "Remembering the Great Silents," *CI,* 222 (Dec 1993), C15.

Anderson, Nancy Ellen [scenarist]. No data found. m. **Frank Woods** (d. 1939). Edward Azlant, "Screenwriting for the early silent film: forgotten pioneers, 1897–1911," *Film History,* 1997) 244.

Anderson, Mrs. Nellie (mother of **Mary Anderson**) [stage/film actress] (*née?,* b. Brooklyn NY, Jun 1874). (Metro; World; Vitagraph.) BHD, p. 92 (Helen Relya Anderson). MSBB, p. 1030.

Anderson, Robert *see* **Andersen, Robert Christian**

Anderson, Warner [actor] (b. Brooklyn NY, 10 Mar 1911–26 Aug 1976 [65], Santa Monica CA; cancer). m. Leeta. "Warner Anderson," *Variety,* 1 Sep 1976. BHD1, p. 14. IFN, p. 8. SA. SD. Truitt 1983.

Anderson, William (b. 1871?–Sep? 1940 [69], Melbourne, Australia). m. [Miss] Eugene Duggan. "William Anderson," *Variety,* 18 Sep 1940.

Anderton, Edith Stout [actress]. No data found. (Lubin.) "Gossip of the Studios," *NYDM,* 20 Jan 1915, 33:1 (to marry Clarence Jay Elner on 13 Feb).

Andlauer, William A. [newsreel cameraman for Paramount] (b. 1881?–1 Aug 1953 [72], Kansas City KS). "William A. Andlauer," *Variety,* 5 Aug 1953 ("During the early days of silents Andlauer operated the Bonaventure Theatre which financed the founding of Andlauer & Sims Film Co., which filmed and projected pix for churches, clubs and businesses.").

Andor, Paul [actor] (b. Cincinnati OH, 20 Jan 1901–26 Jun 1991 [90], Berlin, Germany). BHD1, p. 14.

Andra, Fern [stage/film actress] (*née* Vernal Andrews, b. Watseka IL, 24 Nov 1893–8 Feb 1974 [80], Aiken SC; cancer). m. **Ian Keith,** 1932 and 15 Feb 1934, Tia Juana, Mexico (d. 1960); Brig. Gen. Samuel E. Dockrell (d. 19 Sep 1973). (1st film made in Vienna.) "Fern Andra," *Variety,* 20 Feb 1974, p. 55. BHD1, p. 14. IFN, p. 9. JS, p. 13 (made films in Italy, 1923–24). SA. "Marriages," *Variety,* 20 Feb 1934, 52:5 (m. Keith "to insure the legality of their first ceremony in 1932."). Vittorio Martinelli, "Kino-Lieblinge," *Griffithiana,* Oct 1990, 9.

Andrada, David DeCosta [actor] (b. Brooklyn NY, 27 Dec 1865–3 Jan 1941 [75], Long Branch NJ). BHD, p. 92.

André, Marcel [actor] (b. 1885–1974 [89?]). (MGM.) Waldman, p. 10.

Andre, Monya [actress] (b. 12 Apr 1897–5 Jan 1981 [83], Los Angeles CA). BHD1, p. 14.

Andre, Victor [sculptor]. No data found. LACD, "sculptor," Metro Pictures Corp., h. 443 W. 49th Street.

Andreani, Henri [director] (b. Corsica, France, 1872–3 Apr 1936 [64?], Paris, France). BHD2, p. 7.

Andrew, Sylvia [actress] (b. London, England, 1895–31 Mar 1959 [64?], Santa Monica CA). BHD, p. 92.

Andrews, Ann [actress] (b. Los Angeles CA, 13 Oct 1886–23 Jan 1986 [99], New York NY). BHD, p. 92 (b. 1890).

Andrews, Bobbie (b. England, 20 Feb 1896–11 Nov 1976 [80]). BHD, p. 92.

Andrews, Frank B. [actor, *fl.* 1914–25). No data found.

Andrews, Udell Sylvester "Del" [director/scenarist/film editor/cameraman/costumer] (*né* Udell Endrows, b. 1894?–27 Oct 1942 [48], Tonopah NV; after heart attack). m. Edith E., 1921 (1 son, Del, Jr.). (Ince, 1912.) "Del Andrews," *Variety,* 4 Nov 1942 (age 48). AMD, p. 20. FDY, p. 417. IFN, p. 9. SA. "Hunt Stromberg Signs Andrews," *MPW,* 29 Apr 1922, 933. "Andrews to Direct Thomson," *MPW,* 14 Feb 1925, 715. "Andrews to Direct 'Gumps,'" *MPW,* 17 Oct 1925, 568. "Udell Sylvester Andrews to Direct," *MPW,* 25 Dec 1926, 585. June Lee, "Dan Cupid's Bulletin Board," *Paris and Hollywood Screen Secrets,* Oct 1927, 37 ("Complaining that her husband, Del Andrews, well-known director, went out to a party in dress clothes and returned wearing a blanket, Mrs. Edith E. Andrews is asking for a divorce. Mrs. Andrews charges that this has not been the first mysterious absence of her husband, and that furthermore he was frequently intoxicated, and insulted her in the presence of friends." Del, Jr., was three years old.).

Andreyor, Yvette [actress] (b. Paris, France, 1892–1962 [70], Paris, France). (Gaumont.) BHD1, p. 15. IFN, p. 9. Photo, *MPSM,* Sep 1912, 13.

Andriot, Josette [actress] (*née* Camille Andriot, b. France, 1886–1942 [56?]). AS, p. 60. BHD1, p. 603.

Andriot, Lucien [cinematographer] (b. Paris, France, 19 Nov 1892–Mar 1979 [86], Riverside CA). AMD, p. 20. BHD2, p. 7. FDY, p. 455. Spehr, p. 112. "Lucien Andriot with Capellani," *MPW,* 17 May 1919, 1040. "Lucien Andriot Signed," *MPW,* 9 Jan 1926, 158. "Lucien Andriot," *MPW,* 5 Mar 1927, 27. "Lucien Andriot at Camera on Fox's 'Carmen,'" *MPW,* 2 Apr 1927, 488. W.G.C. Bosco, "Aces of the Camera: Lucien Andriot, A.S.C.," *American Cinematographer,* Feb 1947, 43, 72–73.

Andriot, Poupee (b. New York NY, 29 Oct 1899–13 Nov 1988 [89], Northridge CA). BHD1, p. 15.

Andrus, Marguerite [actress]. (Christie.) b. 11 Jan 1890–May 1984 (94), Ault Field WA.

Angel, Harold [actor]. No data found. LACD, "photoplayer," r 4810 S. Normandie.

Angeles, Bert [director] (b. London, England, 1875?–30 May 1950 [74], New York NY [Death Certificate Index No. 5480]). (Vitagraph.) "Bert Angeles," *NYT,* 1 Jun 1950, 27:6. "Bert Angeles," *Variety,* 7 Jun 1950. BHD2, p. 7. IFN, p. 9 (age 75). "With the Film Men," *NYDM,* 11 Mar 1914, 30:2.

Angelini, Giacomo [cinematographer]. No data found. JS, p. 15 (in Italian silents from 1914).

Angelo, Jean [actor] (*né* Jean Jacques Barthelemy, b. Paris, France, 17 May 1875–26 Nov 1933 [58], Paris, France; pneumonia). "Jean Angelo," *Variety,* 12 Dec 1933 (age 45). BHD1, p. 14. IFN, p. 9. SA.

Anger, Lou [stage/film actor/producer] (b. 1880–21 May 1946 [65?], The Talmadge Apts., Hollywood CA; pneumonia). m. musical comedy actress Sophys Bernhard. "Lou Anger," *Variety,* 29 May 1946, p. 58. SA.

Angle, Milton [scenarist]. No data found. FDY, p. 417.

Anglin, Margaret [stage/film actress] (b. Ottawa, Canada, 1876?–7 Jan 1958 [81], Toronto, Canada). m. Howard Hull. "Margaret Anglin," *Variety,* 209, 15 Jan 1958, 70:2. AMD, p. 20. "Miss Anglin's New Play; Actress Made Debut as Star in 'A Wife's Strategy,'" *NYT,* 17 Jan 1905, 5:1 (Harmanus Bleecker Hall, Albany NY with John E. Kellerd, in a "badly constructed play"). "Margaret Anglin for the Screen," *MPW,* 8 Jul 1916, 256. "Margaret Anglin's First Picture," *MPW,* 16 Sep 1916, 1834. "Movie History in the Making Ten Years Ago," *Paris and Hollywood,* Sep 1926, 86 (in 1916 she organized the Margaret Anglin Pictures Corp. and purchased a twenty-acre plot near Detroit MI, where a studio was erected).

Anker, William [actor] (b. France, 1860). BHD, p. 93.

Annabella [dancer/actress] (*née* Suzanne Georgette Charpentier, b. La Varenne-Saint-Hillaire, France, 14 Jul 1909–18 Sep 1996 [86], Neuilly-sur-Seine, Paris, France; heart attack). m. (1) actor Jean Murat, 1932–38; (2) Tyrone Power, 1939–48. (Film debut: *Napoleon,* 1926; sole U.S. film, *Suez,* 1938; last film *Le Plus Bel Amour de Don Juan* [*The Most Beautiful Love of Don Juan,* 1952].) Eric Pace, "Annabella, 86, Film Actress Known for Playing Gamines," *NYT,* 21 Sep 1996, p. 23. Doug Galloway, "Suzanne (Annabella) Charpentier," *Variety,* 30 Sep 1996, p. 178:2. BHD1, p. 15. Waldman, p. 11. "Suzanne Charpentier; French actress known as Annabella," *PP-G,* 20 Sep 1996, B-6:3. "Annabella," *The Independent,* 21 Sep 1996, p. 18.

Annabelle (Mrs. Annabelle Whitford Buchanan) [actress/dancer] (*née* Annabelle Moore, b. 6 Jul 1878–30 Nov 1961 [83], Chicago IL). m. 1912. (Edison; Bioscope; appeared in an 1895 film for Edison for $15.00; Ziegfeld Follies as Peerless Annabelle, 1907 [Gibson Bathing Girl]–1910.) "Annabelle W. Buchan [sic]," *Variety,* 6 Dec 1961 ("was dancing at the Iroquois Theatre in Chicago in 1903 when 575 persons lost their lives in the historic fire."). AS, p. 180 (Annabelle W. Buchan). BHD, p. 336 (Annabelle Whitford). IFN, p. 317 (Annabelle Whitford). SA. Truitt, p. 264 (Peerless Annabelle). "Annabelle," *Who's Who of Victorian Cinema,* pp. 15–16 (appeared in Edison films, 1894–97; featured in the first Kinetoscope showing in London in Oct 1894. "The sale of her films was further boosted in December 1896 when it was revealed that she had been approached to appear naked at a private dinner party at Sherry's Restaurant, New York.").

Annerley, Frederick [actor] (b. England, 18 Oct 1887–13 Nov 1967 [80]). BHD, p. 93.

Anry, Barat [actor] (b. 1871–4 Jan 1929 [57?], Versailles, France). BHD, p. 93. IFN, p. 9.

Anschutz, Ottomar [cinematographer] (b. Lejzno, Poland, 16 May 1846–30 May 1907 [61], Berlin, Germany). BHD2, p. 7 (b. Leszno, Poland). SA.

Anson, George W. [actor] (b. Montrose, Scotland, 25 Nov 1847–2 Aug 1920 [72], London, England). BHD, p. 93.

Anson, James [actor] (aka Yakima Jim, b. 1883–Aug 1925 [42?], Los Angeles CA). BHD, p. 93. IFN, p. 9.

Anson, Laura [actress] (b. Omaha NB, 2 Jan 1892–15 Jul 1968 [76], Woodland Hills CA). m. **Philo McCullough** (d. 1981). "Laura Anson McCullough," *Variety,* 24 Jul 1968. BHD, p. 93. IFN, p. 9. Truitt, p. 8.

Anspacher, Dr. Louis K. [playwright] (b. Cincinnati OH, 1878?–10 May 1947 [69], Nashville TN; heart attack). m. (1) actress Kathryn Kidder, 1905 (d. 1939); (2) Florence Sutro. "Dr. Louis K. Anspacher," *Variety,* 166, 14 May 1947, 55:1. AMD, p. 20. "Louis K. Anspacher," *MPW,* 22 Jun 1918, 1741.

Antamoro, Giulio Cesare [director] (b. Rome, Italy, 1 Jul 1877–8 Dec 1945 [68], Rome, Italy). AS, p. 62; p. 428 (Gant). JS, p. 15 (in Italian silents from 1910).

Anthony, Clairette [artist/actress]. No data found. m. Howard Chesebrough Okio, 15 Jan 1919, NYC. AMD, p. 20. "Miss Anthony Weds Army Man," *MPW,* 1 Feb 1919, 613.

Anthony, DeLeon [film editor/title writer] (b. 28 Sep 1901–12 Jun 1979 [78], Westminster CA). (Paramount; WB from 1929–67.) "DeLeon Anthony," *Variety,* 27 Jun 1979. FDY, p. 441.

Anthony, Jack [actor] (*né* John Anthony Herbertson, b. Pennistown, Glasgow, Scotland, b. 1900?–28 Feb 1962 [61], Dunbar, Scotland). "Jack Anthony," *Variety,* 14 Mar 1962. BHD, p. 93. IFN, p. 9. George A. Katchmer, "Forgotten Cowboys and Cowgirls—Part XVII," *CI,* 194 (Aug 1991), 43.

Anthony, Lee [title writer]. No data found. FDY, p. 441.

Anthony, Stuart [scenarist] (b. Tattnal County GA, 1886?–28 Apr 1942 [56], Beverly Hills CA). "Stuart Anthony," *NYT,* 30 Apr 1942, 19:5. "Stuart Anthony," *Variety,* 6 May 1942. BHD2, p. 7 (b. 1891). FDY, p. 417. IFN, p. 9.

Anthony, Walter [title writer/scenarist] (b. Stockton CA, 13 Feb 1872?–1 May 1945 [73], Los Angeles CA). "Walter Anthony," *Variety,* 9 May 1945. AMD, p. 20. BHD2, p. 7 (b. 1876). FDY, p. 441. "Sign Walter Anthony," *MPW,* 6 Sep 1924, 65. "To Title 'Les Miserables,'" *MPW,* 16 Apr 1927, 630.

Antibus, Pearl Iva [actress] (aka Pearl Chappelle, b. Phoenix AZ, 10 May 1890–17 Jun 1976 [86], Windsor CA 95492). (Kalem; Fox.) "Pearl Antibus," *The Press Democrat* [Santa Rosa CA], 28 Jun 1976, p. 25.

Antoine, Andre [director] (b. Limoges, France, 31 Jan 1858–19 Oct 1943 [85]). BHD2, p. 7.

Antonov, Aleksandr P. [actor] (b. Russia,

13 Feb 1898–26 Nov 1962 [64]). BHD, p. 93. IFN, p. 9.

Antwerp, A. Van *see* **Van Antwerp, Albert**

Aoki, Tsuru [actress] (b. Tokyo, Japan, 9 Sep 1892–18 Oct 1961 [69], Tokyo, Japan; peritonitis). m. **Sessue Hayakawa,** 1 May 1914 (d. 1973). (Ince.) "Mrs. Sessue Hayakawa," *NYT,* 19 Oct 1961, 35:3. "Tsuru Aoki," *Variety,* 8 Nov 1961 (age 68). AMD, p. 21. BHD1, p. 16. IFN, p. 9. MH, p. 94. Truitt, p. 8; Truitt 1983. WWS, p. 234. "Japanese Girl Is New Film Star," *MPW,* 27 Dec 1913, 1528 (signed with Ince). "Aoki Tsuru," *MPW,* 14 Feb 1914, 825. "Mrs. Sessue Hayakawa Is Newest of Universal Stars," *MPW,* 2 Aug 1919, 687. "To Star Tsuru Aoki in Film Verson of McCall Novel," *MPW,* 16 Aug 1919, 969.

Aoyama, Yukio, "The Japanese Julian Eltinge" [stage/film actor/playwright] (b. Nagoya City, Japan, 1888). AMD, p. 21. BHD, p. 93. MSBB, p. 1021. "Ruth Roland Engages Aoyama," *MPW,* 22 Nov 1919, 452.

Apfel, Edward [director]. No data found. AMD, p. 21. "Apfel with Majestic," *MPW,* 3 Aug 1912, 455.

Apfel, Oscar C. [stage/film actor/scenarist/producer/director] (b. Cleveland OH, 17 Jan 1879–21 Mar 1938 [59], Los Angeles CA; heart attack). m. Marion. (Edison; Reliance; Pathé; Selig; FP-L; Morosco; Paramount; Fox; Paralta.) "Oscar C. Apfel; Movie Director and Character Actor Dies in Hollywood," *NYT,* 23 Mar 1938, 23:4. "Oscar C. Apfel," *Variety,* 30 Mar 1938. AMD, p. 21. BHD1, p. 16; BHD2, p. 7. FDY, p. 417. IFN, p. 9. Lowrey, p. 4. MSBB, p. 1044. SA. SD. Truitt, p. 8. "Oscar C. Apfel," *MPW,* 7 Sep 1912, 969. "Apfel Has a Patent," *MPW,* 26 Sep 1914, 1760. "Oscar Apfel 'Does a Brodie,'" *MPW,* 30 Sep 1916, 2121–22. "Oscar Apfel Goes to the Yorke-Metro," *MPW,* 30 Dec 1916, 1963. "Capellani Engages Oscar Apfel," *MPW,* 20 Dec 1919, 9689. "Apfel to Direct," *MPW,* 29 Sep 1923, 435.

Apolloni, Camillo [actor/director]). No data found. JS, p. 16 (in Italian silents from 1914).

Appel, Anna [stage/film actress] (*née?,* b. Bucharest, Romania, 1 May 1887?–19 Nov 1963 [76], New York NY [Death Certificate Index No. 24877]). m. (1) Isadore Appel (d. 1909); (2) Sigmund Ben Avi (d. 1924). "Anna Appel Dead; Yiddish Actress; Character Player Also Had Many Broadway Roles," *NYT,* 21 Nov 1963, 39:3. "Anna Appel," *Variety,* 27 Nov 1963 (age 75). BHD1, p. 16. IFN, p. 9. SA (b. 1888). Truitt, p. 8.

Appel, Samuel [actor] (b. Magdalina, Mexico, 8 Aug 1871–18 Jun 1947 [75], Los Angeles CA). BHD1, p. 16. IFN, p. 9.

Appleby, Dorothy [actress] (b. Portland ME, 6 Jan 1908–9 Aug 1990 [82], Long Island NY). BHD1, p. 16.

Applegate, Hazel [actress] (b. 1886–30 Oct 1959 [73], Chicago IL). "Hazel Applegate," *Variety,* 4 Nov 1959. BHD, p. 93. IFN, p. 10.

Applegate, Roy [actor/director]. No data found. AMD, p. 21. "Applegate Heavyweight Cast," *MPW,* 6 Apr 1912, 32. "Roy Applegate with Lubin," *MPW,* 15 Jun 1912, 1023. "Roy Applegate with Equitable," *MPW,* 11 Sep 1915, 1813. "Roy Applegate," *MPW,* 30 Oct 1915, 801.

Appling, Bert [actor] (b. Madera CA, 6 Dec 1871–14 Jan 1960 [88], Downey CA). (Triangle.) BHD, p. 93. George A. Katchmer, "Remembering the Great Silents," *CI,* 183 (Sep 1990), 44; 203 (May 1992), 41.

Aquilanti, Pacifico "Cocó" [actor]. No data found. JS, pp. 16–17 (in Italian silents from 1910. "He left movies for *avanspettacolo* (the live variety act preceding a film).").

Arata, Ubaldo [cinematographer] (b. Ovada, Italy, 23 Mar 1895–Dec 1947 [52?], Rome, Italy). JS, p. 17 (in Italian silents from 1911 or earlier).

Arbenina, Stella [actress] (b. St. Petersburg, Russia, 27 Sep 1885–26 Apr 1976 [90], London, England). BHD1, p. 16. IFN, p. 10 (age 91).

Arbó, Manuel (cousin of Virginia Fábregas) [stage/film actor] (*né* Manuel Arbó de Val, b. Madrid, Spain, 1898). (Spain, 1915; Spanish-language films in Hollywood, 1930–31; 200 films in the next 35 years.) Waldman, p. 14.

Arbuckle, Andrew (brother of **Macklyn Arbuckle**; cousin of **Roscoe "Fatty" Arbuckle**) [vaudeville/film actor] (b. Galveston TX, 5 Sep 1887–21 Sep 1939 [52], Los Angeles CA). m. Blanche Duquesne, Oct 1915, Gretna Green CA. (Griffith; Lasky; Balboa; Metro.) AMD, p. 21. BHD, p. 93. IFN, p. 10. J. Van Cartmell, "Along the Pacific Coast," *NYDM,* 30 Oct 1915, 27:1 (midnight elopement with Duquesne). "Andrew Arbuckle Marries," *MPW,* 30 Oct 1915, 952. Al Ray, "Before the Stars Shone," *Picture-Play Magazine,* Sep 1917, 92. "Jack White Signs Andrew Arbuckle," *MPW,* 25 Aug 1923, 671.

Arbuckle, Macklyn N. (brother of **Andrew Arbuckle**; cousin of **Roscoe "Fatty" Arbuckle**) [actor] (b. San Antonio TX, 9 Jul 1863?–31 Mar 1931 [67], Waddington NY; brain hemorrhage). m. Elizabeth S. Carlisle. "Macklyn Arbuckle," *Variety,* 8 Apr 1931 (President of San Antonio Pictures Corporation, 1918; age 68). AMD, p. 21. BHD, p. 93. IFN, p. 10 (b. 1866). SD. "Famous Players Secure Macklyn Arbuckle," *MPW,* 6 Jun 1914, 1412. "Securing Arbuckle's Wardrobe No Laughing Matter," *MPW,* 27 Feb 1915, 1290. "Macklyn Arbuckle Selects Studio Site in San Antonio," *MPW,* 31 May 1919, 1312. "Macklyn Arbuckle All Set," *MPW,* 7 Oct 1922, 483. "Rockefeller Aids Equity Players; John D. Jr. Becomes 'Founder' on Pledging to Give $1,000 Toward Permanent Theatre; Plans Told at Dinner; Organization Aims to Open Houses Also in Chicago and San Francisco," *NYT,* 28 Jan 1924, 17:3 (Arbuckle was toastmaster; Harry O. Stubbs was master of ceremonies). "Mrs. Macklyn Arbuckle in 'Janice [Meredith],'" *Variety,* 28 May 1924, p. 30 (believed to be her film debut).

Arbuckle, Roscoe "Fatty" (cousin of **Andrew** and **Macklyn Arbuckle**) [film/stage actor/scenarist/director] (aka William Goodrich and Will B. Good, *né* Roscoe Conkling Arbuckle, b. Smith Center KS, 24 Mar 1887–29 Jun 1933 [46], New York NY). Andy Edmonds, *Frame-Up!; The Untold Story of Roscoe "Fatty" Arbuckle* (New York: William Morrow and Co., Inc., 1991); Stuart Oderman, *Roscoe "Fatty" Arbuckle: A Biography of the Silent Film Comedian, 1887–1933* (Jefferson NC: McFarland, 1994); Robert Young, Jr., *Roscoe "Fatty" Arbuckle; A Bio-Bibliography* (Westport CT: Greenwood Press, 1994). m. **Minta Durfee,** 5 Aug 1908, Long Beach CA, onstage at the Byde a Whyle theatre—div. 31 Dec 1923 (d. 1975). (Selig; Sennett; Paramount; WB.) "Fatty Arbuckle Dies in His Sleep; Film Comedian, Central Figure in Coast Tragedy in 1921, Long Barred from Screen; On Eve of His 'Come-Back,'" *NYT,* 30 Jun 1933, 17:4. "Roscoe (Fatty) Arbuckle," *Variety,* 4 Jul 1933. AMD, pp. 21–22 (Arbuckle); p. 141 (Goodrich). BHD1, p. 16; BHD2, p. 8. FSS, p. 4. IFN, p. 10 (b. San Jose CA). Lowrey, p. 6. MSBB, p. 1021. Truitt, p. 9 (b. 24 May). WWS, p. 30 (b. Galveston TX). "Arbuckle Honorary Member of Frisco's Screen Club," *MPW,* 12 Dec 1914, 1496. Cover, *NYDM,* 6 Nov 1915 (with Flora Zabelle and Raymond Hitchcock, "Triangle-Keystone Stars at the Knickerbocker"). Robert F. Moore, "Feeding with Fatty Arbuckle," *MPC,* Nov 1916, 45–46, 67. "Fatty and Mabel's New Year," *MPW,* 8 Jan 1916, 251. "Arbuckle a Venetian," *MPW,* 26 Aug 1916, 1415. "'Fatty' Arbuckle Allied with Paramount," *MPW,* 27 Jan 1917, 500. "Roscoe 'Fatty' Arbuckle," *MPW,* 10 Mar 1917, 1550. "Arbuckle Finishes Transcontinental Trip," *MPW,* 24 Mar 1917, 1930–31. "Arbuckle to Be Screeners' Guest," *MPW,* 7 Apr 1917, 105. "Screen Club Holds a Beefsteak," *MPW,* 14 Apr 1917, 243. "Arbuckle to Return to Pacific Coast," *MPW,* 13 Oct 1917, 220. "Why Not Try a Number on the Screen?," *MPW,* 9 Mar 1918, 1361. "Arbuckle Taboos Pies—Except as Props," *MPW,* 9 Mar 1918, 1390. "How Fatty Arbuckle Makes 'Love,'" *MPW,* 8 Mar 1919, 1319. "Arbuckle Signs to Appear Exclusively in Five Reelers," *MPW,* 27 Mar 1920, 2171. "'Fatty' Arbuckle Lauds Keaton Comedy, Boosting 'Buster' as His Successor," *MPW,* 23 Oct 1920, 1133. "Arbuckle Works Day and Night on Paramount Films," *MPW,* 6 Nov 1920, 38. "Exhibitors Withdraw Arbuckle Comedies, Awaiting Court Action on Murder Charge," *MPW,* 24 Sep 1921, 382, 384. Arthur James, "The Sordid Arbuckle Tragedy," *MPW,* 24 Sep 1921, 383. "It Is Not for Us to Pass Judgment on Roscoe Arbuckle, Says M.P.T.O.A.," *MPW,* 24 Sep 1921, 395. "Damage to Our Business," *MPW,* 22 Oct 1921, 888. "Arbuckle Acquitted," *MPW,* 22 Apr 1922, 833 (acquitted on 12 Apr). "Hays Gives Arbuckle Chance to Come Back; Protests Raised," *MPW,* 30 Dec 1922, 840. "[Durfee] Divorces 'Fatty' Arbuckle; Wife Says He Earns $25,000 a Year as Movie Director," *NYT,* 1 Jan 1924, 25:8 (desertion/no support. "Arbuckle did not appeal and made no contest. She asked neither alimony nor the right to resume her maiden name." Her petition "referred to the charges brought against him following the death of VIrginia Rapp [sic] by saying she went to his support because she believed him inncocent. Arbuckle deserted her in 1917, she said."). "Roscoe Arbuckle May Return to the Screen," *MW,* 21 Jun 1924, 21 (to use the moniker "Will B. Good"). "Cantor's Next Film to Launch New Year," *MPW,* 25 Dec 1926, 580. "Carlos Signs Arbuckle," *MPW,* 19 Mar 1927, 163. "'Fatty' May Return," *MPW,* 26 Mar 1927, 267. "Arbuckle Wins Much Applause," *MPW,* 2 May 1927, 787. "Roscoe Arbuckle in a Broadway Revival," *MPW,* 4 Jun 1927, 327. Dorothy Calhoun, "Not a Sob-Story; Fatty Arbuckle Figures It Out," *MPC,* Jul 1927, 45, 76, 79. "Agitation on Arbuckle Flops in Washington," *MPW,* 27 Aug 1927, 583. Mrs. Al St. John, "About the 'Arbuckle Affair,'" *CFC,* 22 (Fall, 1968), 29. Jay Rozgonyi, "Fatty Arbuckle: Lost and Found," *CI,* 210 (Dec 1992), 16–17, 20, C20. Richard M. Roberts, "Fatty Arbuckle Re-examined," *CI,* 213 (Mar 1993), 50–53. Richard M. Roberts, "Fatty After the Fall," *CI,* 214 (Apr 1993), 42, 44, 56 (includes filmography). Henry Jenkins, "Hey, Pop! Credits and Synopses of the Six Fatty Arbuckle Vitaphones," *Griffithiana,* 48/49 (Oct 1993), 54–61. James Neibaur, "Roscoe Arbuckle at Vitaphone," *CI,* 268 (Oct 1997), C12–13 (hired by Warner in Feb 1932).

Arcaro, Flavia [stage singer/film actress] (b. Mejico TX, 22 Jun 1876–8 Apr 1937 [61], New York NY). "Flavia Arcaro, Singer and Actress; She Had Appeared in Important Roles on Broadway—Dies in Bronx at 61," *NYT,* 9 Apr 1937, 21:2. "Flavia Arcaro," *Variety,* 14 Apr 1937. AMD, p. 22 (Arcoria). BHD, p. 93. IFN, p. 10. "Flavia Arcoria," *MPW,* 5 Jun 1915, 1590.

Arch, Robert [scenarist/title writer]. No data found. FDY, pp. 417, 441.

Archainbaud, George [actor/film and TV director] (b. Paris, France, 7 May 1890–20 Feb 1959 [69], Beverly Hills CA; heart attack). m. **Katherine Johnston**, 18 May 1921, Mamaroneck NY. (Fort Lee NJ, 1915; World; Selznick; RKO; Paramount; UA; Columbia.) "George Archainbaud," *NYT,* 21 Feb 1959, 21:6. "George Archainbaud," *Variety,* 25 Feb 1959, p. 63 (age 68). AMD, p. 22. BHD2, p. 8. IFN, p. 10. Katz, p. 41. Spehr, p. 112. Truitt, p. 9. "Archainbaud Engaged by Capellani," *MPW,* 3 May 1919, 651. "George Archainbaud, Director, Weds Katherine Johnston," *MPW,* 4 Jun 1921, 503.

Archer, Fred R[obert] [pioneer cinematographer] (b. GA, 3 Dec 1889–29 Apr 1963 [73], Los Angeles CA). "Fred R. Archer," *Variety,* 15 May 1963 (age 75). BHD2, p. 8.

Archer, Harry [actor/composer] (*né* Harry Auracher, b. Creston IA, 21 Feb 1886?–23 Apr 1960 [74], New York NY [Death Certificate Index No. 9185]). m. Ruth Gillette. "Harry Archer," *Variety,* 27 Apr 1960 (age 72). NNAT (b. 1888). CEPMJ, 1900–1950, Vol. 2, pp. 506–07 (b. 1881).

Archer, Henry [actor]. No data found. LACD, "photoplayer," h 1322 Ardath Avenue.

Archer, Louis A. [stage/film actor] (b. 1874?–Aug 1922 [48], Los Angeles CA). AMD, p. 22. BHD, p. 93. IFN, p. 10. LACD, "actor," r 2107 1/2 E. 1st Street. "Lew Archer in Pictures; Quits Vaudeville Stage," *MPW,* 17 Apr 1926, 537.

Archer, Polly [actress]. No data found. AMD, p. 22. "Polly Archer in Leading Role," *MPW,* 1 Sep 1923, 64.

Archer, Stella [actress]. No data found. AMD, p. 22. "Stella Archer," *MPW,* 29 May 1915, 1411.

Archer, William [writer] (b. Perth, Scotland, 23 Sep 1856–27 Dec 1924 [68], London, England; heart disease). m. Frances Elizabeth Trickett, 1884. "William Archer Dies; Critic and Author of 'The Green Goddess' Succumbs to Heart Failure," *Variety,* 14 Jan 1925. BHD1, p. 8. Kunitz & Haycraft, *Twentieth Century Authors,* pp. 37–38. NNAT. SD.

Archibald, William [playwright/scenarist/actor/dancer] (*né* John William Wharton Archibald, b. Trinidad, British West Indies, 7 Mar 1917–27 Dec 1970 [53], New York NY; infectious hepatitis). "William Archibald, Playwright, Actor and Dancer, Is Dead at 53," *NYT,* 29 Dec 1970, 32:1. "William Archibald," *Variety,* 30 Dec 1970. BHD2, p. 8.

Archie, Will [midget actor]. No data found. (Headline Amusement Co.) "First Headline Comedy [*Pee-Wee's Courtship*]," *NYDM,* 23 Jun 1915, 21:2 (Archie was to be supported by "all the stars of the lilliputian world, including Louis Merkel, Herbert Rice, Jimmie Rosen, Leila Coutna, Violet Howard, the original Mrs. Tom Thumb, and her second husband, Count Magri.").

Ardath, Fred [stage/film actor] (b. 1883–11 Mar 1955 [72?], New York NY). AMD, p. 22. BHD1, p. 17. "Fred Ardath, Vaudeville Comedian, Starred in New Arrow Series of Two-Reel Comedies," *MPW,* 26 Jun 1920, 1751.

Ardea, Liliana [actress]). No data found. JS, p. 17 (in Italian silents from 1920).

Ardell, Franklyn [actor] (b. NJ, 1 May 1885–17 Apr 1960 [74], Los Angeles Co. CA). BHD1, p. 17.

Ardell, John E. [actor] (b. Ontario, Canada, 24 Mar 1880–26 Apr 1949 [69], Hollywood CA; found dead in car from carbon monoxide gas). "John E. Ardell," *Variety,* 4 May 1949. BHD1, p. 17. IFN, p. 10. Truitt, p. 9.

Ardell, Lillian [actress] (d. 15 Mar 1950, New York NY). BHD1, p. 17. IFN, p. 10.

Arden, Edwin Hunter Pendleton [playwright/stage/film actor] (b. St. Louis MO, 13 Feb 1864–2 Oct 1918 [54], Forest Hills, New York NY [Death Certificate No. 27416; age 58]). m. Agnes A.E. Keene. (Film debut: *Eagle's Nest,* Lubin 5-reeler; World; Pathé.) "Edwin Arden Drops Dead; Actor of Many Leading Roles Is Stricken After a Rehearsal," *NYT,* 3 Oct 1918, 13:2 (stage debut: Chicago, 1882). "Edwin Hunter Pendleton Arden," *Variety,* 11 Oct 1918. AMD, p. 22. BHD, p. 93. IFN, p. 10. SD. "Two Plays Well Staged; Rich Productions Is [sic] Which Proctor Players Score," *NYT,* 23 Feb 1905, 9:3 (in *The Helmet of Navarro*). "Arden Joins Pathe; Famous Player Will Be Seen in Second Series of 'Elaine,'" *NYDM,* 17 Mar 1915, 21:4 (his 2nd film). "Edwin Arden with Pathe," *MPW,* 27 Mar 1915, 1914d. "Edwin Arden Tells Why Pictures Help Him," *MPW,* 5 Jun 1915, 1624. "Edwin Arden in World Film," *MPW,* 16 Oct 1915, 457. Edwin Arden, "A New Angle on 'Waste,'" *NYDM,* 30 Oct 1915, 24:3 (The actor, full of inspiration, must wait until a scene is ready to be filmed. Or he may be interrupted during filming. The answer is more preparation before photography begins. "It is the quiver of an eyelash, the almost imperceptible twitch of a muscle, the composition of the lips which interpret the same shades of different emotions that they, combined with the voice, do on the speaking stage." The director must provide "inspired" acting to his public.). "Obituary," *MPW,* 19 Oct 1918, 392. *Theatre Magazine,* Nov 1918, 320.

Arden, Jane [actress] (b. Canada, 20 Oct 1904–21 Mar 1981 [76], Studio City CA). AMD, p. 22. BHD1, p. 17. "Jane Arden," *MPW,* 23 Jan 1926, 317.

Arehn, Nils [actor] (b. 30 Dec 1877–1 Apr 1928 [50], Stockholm, Sweden). BHD1, p. 603.

Arendt, Ekkehard [actor] (b. Vienna, Austria, 10 Jun 1892–10 May 1954 [61]). BHD, p. 93.

Arenz, Rollin [actor]. No data found. LACD, "photoplayer," h 2002 Sunset Blvd.

Arey, Wayne [actor] (b. Rock Falls IL, 12 Apr 1880–2 Jul 1937 [57], New York NY). (Thanhouser.) "Wayne Arey; Veteran Actor Was in the Federal Projects' 'Professor Mamlock,'" *NYT,* 3 Jul 1937, 15:2. AMD, p. 22. BHD, p. 93. IFN, p. 10. "Wayne Arey, Thanhouser Star," *MPW,* 7 Oct 1916, 90.

Ari, Carina [actress] (b. Stockholm, Sweden, 14 Apr 1897–24 Dec 1970 [73], Buenos Aires, Argentina). BHD1, p. 603.

Arians, Elizabeth [actress] (d. 28 Feb 1922). BHD, p. 93.

Arlen, Betty [actress: Wampas Star, 1925] (b. Providence KY, 9 Nov 1904–4 Aug 1966 [61], Farmington NM). BHD1, p. 17.

Arlen, Michael [novelist/dramatist/scenarist] (*né* Dikran Kouyoumdjian, b. Rustchuk, Bulgaria, 16 Nov 1895–23 Jun 1956 [60], New York NY). m. Countess Atalanta Mercati, 1928. "Michael Arlen," *Variety,* 203, 27 Jun 1956, 63:1 (wrote *The Green Hat* [1924], filmed as *A Woman of Affairs,* 1929 [Greta Garbo], and *Outcast Lady,* 1934 [Constance Bennettt]). AMD, p. 22. BHD2, p. 8 (b. 1896). Kunitz & Haycraft, *Twentieth Century Authors,* p. 39. "Paramount Signs Arlen," *MPW,* 11 Apr 1925, 597. "Michael Arlen Coming," *MPW,* 5 Sep 1925, 82. "Arlen Coming East," *MPW,* 12 Dec 1925, 544.

Arlen, Richard [actor] (*né* Cornelius Van Mattimore, b. Charlottesville VA, 1 Sep 1898–28 Mar 1976 [77], Sherman Oaks CA; emphysema). (b. 1899). m. (1) Ruth Austin; (2) **Jobyna Ralston**, 28 Jan 1927 (d. 1967); (3) Margaret Kinsella. (Began 1920.) "Richard Arlen, Actor, Dies; Star of First Oscar Film"; Robert E. Tomasson, "Won Coveted Role [in *Wings,* 1927]," *NYT,* 29 Mar 1976, 32:5. "Richard Arlen, Actor 52 Years, Dies at 75 from Emphysema," *Variety,* 31 Mar 1976 (age 75). Jerry Belcher, "Actor Richard Arlen Dies; Swashbuckled to Stardom," *LA Times,* 29 Mar 1976. "300 Stars Attend Arlen Rites," *LA Herald-Examiner,* 1 Apr 1976. AMD, p. 22. BHD1, p. 18 (b. 1899). FSS, p. 5. IFN, p. 10. Truitt 1983. "Richard Arlen," WBO1, pp. 202–203. "Miss Ralston to Wed," *MPW,* 9 Oct 1926, 343. "Arlen—Ralston," *MPW,* 12 Feb 1927, 475. "Richard Arlen," *MPW,* 21 May 1927, 196. "Arlen Signed by Columbia," *MPW,* 23 Jul 1927, 256. Mary Spencer, "Richard the Lion-Hearted; The Arlen Ship Comes In After Seven Years' Hard Luck," *MPC,* Oct 1927, 55, 78, 88. Blake McVeigh, "Arlen," *Screenland,* Dec 1927, 30–31, 76. Jobyna Ralston, "How Real Are Those Love Scenes?," *Screenland,* Jan 1929, 18–19. Christopher Finch and Linda Rosenkrantz, *Gone Hollywood* (Garden City NY: Doubleday & Co., Inc., 1979), p. 85 ("Occasionally, people were discovered on the lot.... Richard Arlen was making a delivery, by motorcycle, at Paramount when he collided with a truck and broke his leg. The studio doctor apparently thought it might be diplomatic if Arlen were offered extra work and passed the word on to the casting director."). "Buck Rainey's Filmographies," *CI,* 181 (Jul 1990), 30–32; Part II, 182 (Aug 1990), 34–36.

Arley, Cecile [actress] (*née* Cecile Arnole, b. Louisville KY–d. 1931). (Sennett.) IFN, p. 11.

Arling, Charles [stage/film actor] (b. Toronto, Canada, 22 Aug 1880?). (Pathé; Keystone; Fox; Artcraft; last film in 1922.) AMD, p. 22. BHD, p. 93. LACD, "photoplayer," h 1835 Argyle Ave. MSBB, p. 1021. "Charles Arling," *MPW,* 17 Mar 1917, 1778. George Katchmer, "Remembering the Great Silents," *CI,* 243 (Sep 1995), 40.

Arlington, Paul [director] (d. 23 Dec 1917). AMD, p. 22. "Obituary," *MPW,* 19 Jan 1918, 346.

Arliss, Florence M[ontgomery] [actress] (*née* Florence Montgomery, b. 1873?–11 Mar 1950 [77], London, England). m. **George Arliss** (d. 1946). "Mrs. George Arliss," *Variety,* 22 Mar 1950. BHD1, p. 18. IFN, p. 10. SD. Truitt, p. 9.

Arliss, George Augustus [stage/film actor] (*né* Augustus George Arliss-Andrews, b. London, England, 10 Apr 1868–5 Feb 1946 [77], London, England; bronchopneumonia). m. **Florence Mont-**

gomery (d. 1950). *Up the Years from Bloomsbury* (1927); *My Ten Years in the Studios* (1940). "George Arliss, 77, Noted Actor, Dead; 60-Year Veteran of British and American Stage and Screen—'Disraeli' Among His Hits; Monocle His Trademark; Series of Successes in Plays Led to Film Bid in 1920—'Dr. Syn' Last Picture," *NYT,* 6 Feb 1946, 23:1. "George Arliss," *Variety,* 6 Feb 1946. AMD, pp. 22–23. BHD1, p. 18. FSFM, p. 6. FSS, p. 6. GSS, p. 9 (d. NY NY). IFN, p. 10. Katz, p. 44 (*né* Andrews). SD. Truitt, p. 9. "Charles Chaplin Is His Picture Model, George Arliss Says at Pathé Luncheon," *MPW,* 29 Jan 1921, 558. "Said Mr. Arliss to Faith Service," *Classic,* Oct 1922, 22–23, 85. "King George May Dub George Arliss a 'Sir,'" *MPW,* 27 Oct 1923, 755.

Armand, Aida [actress]. No data found. AMD, p. 23. "Aida Armand," *MPW,* 29 Sep 1917, 1994.

Armand, Teddy V. [actor] (*né* Edwin C. Winscott, b. 1874–12 Jul 1947 [73], Los Angeles CA). "Edwin C. Winscott," *Variety,* 16 Jul 1947. IFN, p. 10. Truitt, p. 9.

Armandis, Gigi [director] (*né* Luigi Armandis). No data found. JS, p. 18 (in Italian silents from 1916).

Armat, Thomas J. [inventor] (b. Fredericksburg VA, 26 Oct 1866–30 Sep 1948 [81], Washington DC). "Thomas Armat, 81, A Pioneer in Films; Inventor in '90s of Vitascope Projector, Long Attributed to Edison, Dies in Capital," *NYT,* 1 Oct 1948, 25:4. "Thomas Armat," *Variety,* 6 Oct 1948. BHD2, p. 8. WWVC, p. 18.

Armelle, Suzanne [actress in Italian silents]. No data found.

Armenise, Vittorio [cinematographer] (*né* Victor Armenise, b. Bari, Italy, 4 Jan 1896). JS, p. 19 (in Italian silents from 1919).

Armetta, Henry [stage/film actor] (b. Palermo, Sicily, Italy, 4 Jul 1888–21 Oct 1945 [57], San Diego CA; heart attack). "Henry Armetta, 57, Character Actor; Specialist in Stage and Screen Comedy Roles Dies During a Performance in New Play," *NYT,* 23 Oct 1945, 17:3 (began 1923). "Henry Armetta," *Variety,* 24 Oct 1945. BHD1, p. 18. IFN, p. 10. Truitt, p. 9.

Armitage, Pauline [actress] (b. 1898–16 Feb 1926 [27?], New York NY). BHD, p. 94.

Armoud, Keith *see* **Binder, Raymond Jerome**

Arms, Louis L. [publicist]. No data found. AMD, p. 23. "Arms to Direct Goldwyn Publicity," *MPW,* 23 Jun 1917, 1945.

Armstrong, Billy [actor] (b. Bristol, England, 14 Jan 1891–1 Mar 1924 [33], Sunland CA). m. **Marion Parker** (d. 1920). AMD, p. 23. BHD, p. 94. IFN, p. 11. "Armstrong Makes Bow in Cub Comedies," *MPW,* 12 Feb 1916, 955. "Former Film Actress Dies," *MPW,* 20 Nov 1920, 318.

Armstrong, Clyde [stage/film actor] (b. Wales, 1879–30 Sep 1937 [58], New York NY). m. Juliet Goodwin. "Clyde Armstrong, Stage Veteran, 58; He Also Had Appeared in Many Films and Coached Students of Theatre—Dies Here," *NYT,* 1 Oct 1937, 22:2. "Clyde Armstrong," *Variety,* 6 Oct 1937. BHD, p. 94. IFN, p. 11. Truitt, p. 10.

Armstrong, Edward [executive] (d. 11 Jul 1924). BHD2, p. 8.

Armstrong, Frank [set dresser at Paramount for 5 years] (b. 1883?–11 Jan 1928 [44], Los Angeles CA; acute indigestion). (Began ca. 1913.) "Frank Armstrong," *Variety,* 18 Jan 1928. BHD2, p. 8.

Armstrong, Helen [actress]. (American). No data found. AMD, p. 23. "Trouble in the 'Infantry,'" *MPW,* 28 Jun 1913, 1364.

Armstrong, Leroy [Universal research department] (b. Plymouth IN, 13 May 1854–29 Mar 1927 [73], Lankershim CA; apoplexy). (Universal.) "Leroy Armstrong," *Variety,* 6 Apr 1927. WWWA.

Armstrong, Margaret or Marguerite *see* **Miss du Pont**

Armstrong, Paul [playwright] (b. Kidder [St. Joseph] MO, 25 Apr 1869–30 Aug 1915 [46], 829 Park Avenue, New York NY; heart failure). m. (1) Bella Abell, 24 Jul 1899, London (3 daughters: Annabel, Murrel, and Elizabeth)—div. 10 Dec 1913; (2) **Catherine Calvert**, New Haven CT, 12 Dec 1913 (d. 1971; 1 son). "Paul Armstrong, Playwright, Dies; Author of 'Alias Jimmy Valentine' [produced Jan 1910] Stricken Suddenly After a Ride in Central Park; Once a Sporting Writer [*nom de plume* of 'Right Cross']; His Plays [beginning in 1904] Include 'Salomy Jane [1908],' 'The Heir to the Hoorah,' and 'The Deep Purple [with Wilson Mizner, 1910],'" *NYT,* 31 Aug 1915, 9:5. "Paul Armstrong," *Variety,* 3 Sep 1915. "Paul Armstrong's Funeral," *NYT,* 2 Sep 1915, 9:3 (held in the Armstrong apartment at 829 Park Avenue. Body cremated at Fresh Pond, LI NY). "Paul Armstrong," *Variety,* 3 Sep 1915 (age 47). AMD, p. 23. "Equitable Acquires Three Armstrong Plays," *MPW,* 14 Aug 1915, 1149. "When Applegate Met Armstrong," *MPW,* 2 Oct 1915, 67. "Death of Paul Armstrong," *NYDM,* 8 Sep 1915, 7:2 (wrote *Via Wireless, Going Some,* with Rex Beach. Wilson Mizner, Rex Beach, Robert Keene, Mike Donlin, and others attended his funeral services). Charles W. Collins, *Green Book,* XI, 651–66. J.L.H., *Dictionary of American Biography,* Vol. I (1928), pp. 358–59 ("At a time when the American stage gave promise of better things he devoted his talent mainly to melodrama and was one of the last writers to compete successfully in this field with the moving-picture theatre.").

Armstrong, R[oger] Dale [cameraman/director] (b. Mechanicsville IA, 1881?–24 Jul 1934 [53], Sierra Madre CA). "R. Dale Armstrong," *Variety,* 31 Jul 1934. BHD2, p. 8.

Armstrong, Robert [actor] (b. Saginaw MI, 20 Nov 1890–20 Apr 1973 [82], Santa Monica CA; heart attack). m. Ethel Kent [Jones?]; Louise; Gladys Dubois. (RKO-Pathé.) "Robert Armstrong, Actor, Dies; Played Director in 'King Kong'"; Steven R. Weisman, "A 50-Year Career," *NYT,* 22 Apr 1973, 55:1. "Robert Armstrong," *Variety,* 25 Apr 1973 (d. 1 day before Merian C. Cooper). BHD, p. 94. IFN, p. 11. Katz, pp. 45–46 (began 1927). SD. Herbert Cruikshank, "He'll Be a BIG Star in a Year; Yes, *Zat's* Unquestionably True of Robert Armstrong with Success Before and a Love-Life Behind Him," *MPC,* Jan 1929, 43, 74, 87 (married to Ethel Jones). Sydney Valentine, "His Double Life; All About a Good Bad Man; The Cause of a New Crime Rave," *Screenland,* Jan 1929, 51, 111.

Armstrong, Sam [Armstrong & Phelps; agent] (*né* Samuel Henry Piles, b. Seattle WA, 1899?–1 Nov 1974 [75], Santa Monica CA). "Sam Armstrong," *Variety,* 13 Nov 1974. BHD2, p. 8.

Armstrong, Will H. (b. Peoria IL, 18 Dec 1868–29 Jul 1943 [74], Los Angeles CA). "Will Armstrong," *Variety,* 4 Aug 1943 (d. 28 Jul). BHD, p. 94. IFN, p. 11. Truitt, p. 10.

Arna, Lissy [film/stage/TV actress] (*née* Elisabeth Arndt, b. Berlin, Germany, 1897–22 Jan 1964 [66?], Berlin, Germany; cancer). m. **Hanns Schwarz** (d. 1946). (Began 1919; First National.) "Lissy Arna," *Variety,* 12 Feb 1964, p. 86 (age 64). BHD, p. 94. IFN, p. 12 (age 64). Waldman, p. 16 (b. 1904).

Arnaud, Etienne [director] (b. 1879–1955 [76?]). (Eclair.) AMD, p. 23. BHD2, p. 8. "Famous Director for the Independents," *MPW,* 30 Dec 1911, 1079 (M[onsieur?] Arnaud).

Arnaud, Pierre [title writer]. No data found. FDY, p. 441.

Arnaud, Yvonne [stage/film actress] (b. Bordeaux, France, 20 Dec 1892–20 Sep 1958 [65], London, England). m. actor Hugh McLellan, 1920. "Yvonne Arnaud," *Variety,* 24 Sep 1958, p. 63. BHD1, p. 19. IFN, p. 11.

Arnheim, Valy [actor] (*né* Valentin Appel, b. Waldau/Riga, Germany, 8 Jun 1883–11 Aug 1950 [67], Berlin, Germany). IFN, p. 11 (d. Nov 1950). Vittorio Martinelli, "Kino-Lieblinge," *Griffithiana,* Oct 1990, 43.

Arno, Sig [stage/film actor] (b. Hamburg, Germany, 27 Dec 1895–17 Aug 1975 [79], Woodland Hills CA; complications of Parkinson's disease). "Sig Arno," *Variety,* 20 Aug 1975, p. 78. BHD1, p. 19. IFN, p. 11.

Arnold, Betty [actress]. No data found. AMD, p. 23. "C.B.C. Will Star Chicago Girl," *MPW,* 16 Jun 1923, 590.

Arnold, Cecile *see* **Arley, Cecile**

Arnold, Edward [stage/film/radio/TV actor] (*né* Guenther Edward Schneider, b. New York NY, 18 Feb 1890–26 Apr 1956 [66], Encino CA; brain hemorhhage). m. (1) Harriet Marshall, 20 Apr 1916—div. 1927 (children, Elizabeth and Edward, Jr.); (2) singer Olive Emerson, 1929—div. 1948; (3) Cleo McClain. With Frances Fisher Dubue, *Lorenzo Goes to Hollywood; The Autobiography of Edward Arnold* (NY: Liveright Publishing Corp., 1940). (Essanay in Chicago, 1915, at $125 a week; World Film Pictures; MGM.) "Edward Arnold, Actor, Dies at 66; Star Performer of Character Roles in Many Movies Began Career in '05," *NYT,* 27 Apr 1956, 27:1. "Edward Arnold," *Variety,* 2 May 1956. AMD, p. 23. BHD1, p. 19. IFN, p. 11. Katz, pp. 46–47 (*né* Arnold). Truitt, p. 10. "Edward Arnold," *MPW,* 15 Apr 1916, 451. "Essanay Leading Man Marries," *MPW,* 13 May 1916, 1155. Ernest Corneau, "The Edward Arnold Story," *CFC,* 46 (Spring, 1975), 34–35. Joe Collura, "Edward Arnold; The Early Years," *CI,* 123 (Sep 1985), 48–50, 63. John Roberts, "Diamond Eddie: The Edward Arnold Story," *CI,* 304 (Oct 2000), 12–14, 67–68 (includes filmography).

Arnold, Gertrud [actress] (b. Stolp, Poland, 3 Mar 1873–11 Jan 1931 [57], Berlin, Germany). BHD1, p. 19 (b. Slupsk, Poland). IFN, p. 11.

Arnold, Grace [actress] (b. London, England, 19 Sep 1894–26 Feb 1979 [84]). IFN, p. 11.

Arnold, Helen Prettyman [actress] (b. Louisville KY). (Frohman Amusement Corp.) AMD, p. 23. "Helen Arnold, Prize Winner," *MPW,* 7 Oct 1916, 92 (she was a finalist in Photoplay Magazine's Beauty and Brains Contest; "Slender, graceful and dignified, Miss Arnold's future is almost an assured fact."). "Helen Prettyman Arnold," *MPW,* 24 Feb 1917, 1183.

Arnold, Jessie [actress] (b. Lyons MI, 3 Dec 1884–5 May 1955 [70], Los Angeles CA). AMD, p. 23. BHD1, p. 19. IFN, p. 11. Truitt 1983 (b. 29 Jun 1877–10 Jun 1971). "Jessie Arnold with Universal," *MPW,* 29 Apr 1916, 813.

Arnold, John [cinematographer] (b. New York NY, 16 Nov 1887–11 Jan 1964 [76], Palm Springs CA). (b. 1889). (Edison; Biograph; Vitagraph; Rex; World; Metro.) "John Arnold," *Variety,* 22 Jan 1964. AMD, p. 23. BHD2, p. 9 (b. 1888). FDY, p. 455. Katz, p. 47 (b. 1889). "The Life Photo Engages John Arnold," *MPW,* 14 Nov 1914, 939. "John Arnold," *MPW,* 8 Jan 1927, 113.

Arnold, Lois [actress] (b. St. Augustine FL, 1862?–26 Jan 1947 [84], Philadelphia PA). "Lois Arnold," *Variety,* 29 Jan 1947 (actress for more than 60 years). BHD, p. 94 (b. 1877). IFN, p. 11.

Arnold, Mabel [actress] (b. TX, 25 Apr 1888–6 Jan 1964 [75], Hollywood CA). "Mabel Arnold," *Variety,* 15 Jan 1964 (d. 7 Jan). BHD, p. 619 (under Wiles, Mabel). IFN, p. 11. LACD, "photoplayer," r 427 S. Figueroa. Truitt, p. 10.

Arnold, Marcella [actress/stuntwoman] (b. Chicago IL, 26 Sep 1906–3 Mar 1937 [39], Pasadena CA). "Two Killed [Arnold and George Daly] on Coast in Pix Within Week," *Variety,* 10 Mar 1937. BHD1, p. 19. IFN, p. 11.

Arnold, Sylvia [actress]. No data found. AMD, p. 23. "Sylvia Arnold, Newcomer," *MPW,* 13 Apr 1918, 230.

Arnst, Bobbe [actor] (b. New York NY, 11 Oct 1903–25 Nov 1980 [77], Los Angeles CA). m. Johnny Weismuller. (In *The Perils of Pauline,* 1914.) "Bobby Arnst," *CI,* 76 (Jul 1981), 50. BHD1, p. 19 (b. 1909).

Aronsson, Gustaf [actor] (b. 1872–1930 [58?]). BHD1, p. 604.

Arquillieres, Alexandre Claudius [actor] (b. Boen-sur-Lignon, France, 18 Apr 1870–9 Jun 1953 [83], St. Etienne, France). AS, p. 71. BHD1, p. 604.

Arras, Harry L. [actor] (b. Buffalo NY, 31 May 1881–29 Jan 1942 [60], Hollywood CA; heart attack). "Harry Arras," *Variety,* 4 Feb 1942 (d. 28 Jan). BHD1, p. 20. IFN, p. 11. Truitt, p. 10.

Artaud, Antonin [stage/film actor/writer/scenarist] (b. Marseilles, France, 4 Sep 1896–4 Mar 1948 [51], Ivry-sur-Seine, France). BHD1, p. 20. IFN, p. 11. Albert Bermel, "A Portrait of Artaud Recalls a Stage Rebel and Movie Matinee Idol," *NYT,* 16 Jul 1995, 15:1 (review of Gérard Mordillat's *My Life and Times with Antonin Artaud,* 1993; age 52).

Arthur, Daniel V. [producer] (b. 1867?–6 Dec 1939 [72], New York NY; apoplexy). m. **Marie Cahill**, 18 Jun 1903 (d. 1933). "Daniel V. Arthur, Theatre Veteran; Husband of Marie Cahill, Long Active as Producer and Manager, Dies at 73; Started in Grand Rapids; Presented 'Nancy Brown' by Broadhurst and Rankin, in the Season of 1902–03," *NYT,* 7 Dec 1939, 27:6. "Daniel V. Arthur," *Variety,* 13 Dec 1939. AMD, p. 23. "Daniel V. Arthur Comes In," *MPW,* 7 Mar 1914, 1251.

Arthur, George K. [actor] (*né* Arthur George Brest, b. Brentford, Middlesex, England, 27 Apr 1889–30 May 1985 [96], London, England). m. (1) Melba Lloyd (sister of Doris Lloyd); (2) Elaine, 1940. AMD, p. 23. BHD1, p. 20; BHD2, p. 9 (b. 1899, London; d. NY NY). FSS, p. 8. Katz, p. 49. "George K. Arthur Signed by M-G-M," *MPW,* 25 Jul 1925, 443. "Arthur Signs New Contract," *MPW,* 13 Feb 1926, 611. Dorothy Donnell, "He Got into Pictures by the Tradesman's Entrance; George Arthur Couldn't Get a Film Job So He Sold Groceries," *MPC,* Dec 1925, 36–37, 74, 76. "Flashes from Filmland," *Paris and Hollywood Screen Secrets Magazine,* Aug 1927, 10 (Arthur "scrawled his name on the dotted line of a Metro contract renewing his services as a featured player with the studios."). Dunham Thorp, "The Mutt and Jeff of the Movies," *MPC,* Sep 1927, 41, 85, 91.

Arthur, George M[ilton] [title writer/assistant director and film supervisor for Sam Bischoff] (b. Brooklyn NY, 6 Apr 1898–8 Mar 1949 [50], Los Angeles CA; heart attack). (Vitagraph.) "George M. Arthur," *NYT,* 9 Mar 1949, 25:2 ("He came to Hollywood at 17 and worked for the Vitagraph Company, first in laboratory and then as a camera man."). BHD2, p. 9. FDY, p. 441.

Arthur, Jean [film/stage actress: Wampas Star, 1929] (*née* Gladys Georgianna Greene, b. Plattsburgh NY, 17 Oct 1900–19 Jun 1991 [90], Carmel CA). m. (1) Julian Ancker, 1928 (annulled); (2) Frank Ross. Arthur Pierce and Douglas Swarthout, *Jean Arthur; A Bio-Bibliography* (New York: Greenwood Press, 1990) (b. 1905); John Oller, *Jean Arthur: The Actress Nobody Knew* (Edison NJ: Limelight Editions, 1997). Peter B. Flint, "Jean Arthur, Actress Who Starred in Films by Capra, Is Dead at 90," *NYT,* 20 Jun 1991, D24:1. "Jean Arthur," *Variety,* 24 Jun 1991 (b. NYC). AMD, p. 23. BHD1, p. 20. BR, pp. 247–52. FSS, p. 8. "Jean Arthur's Debut," *MPW,* 30 Jun 1923, 759. "Jean Arthur Again Monty Banks' Lead," *MPW,* 13 Aug 1927, 469. Buck Rainey, "Jean Arthur; Beautiful and Determined She Fought Her Way Out of Poverty," *CI,* 105 (Mar 1984), 17–19 (b. NYC); 106 (Apr 1984), 42–43 (with filmography). Eve Golden, "Jean Arthur; One Terrific Actress," *CI,* 205 (Jul 1992), 16, 18, 61. Lee Israel, "The Freaking Out of Jean Arthur," *CI,* 221 (Nov 1993), C10, C16.

Arthur, John [scenarist] (b. 1872?–21 Jul 1916 [44], New York NY; intestinal trouble). AMD, p. 23. BHD2, p. 9. "Obituary," *MPW,* 5 Aug 1916, 917.

Arthur, Johnny [actor] (*né* John Lennox Arthur Williams, b. Scottsdale PA, 20 May 1883–31 Dec 1951 [68], Woodland Hills CA; heart attack). (Christie; MGM.) "Johnny Arthur," *Variety,* 9 Jan 1952. AMD, p. 23. BHD1, p. 20. FSS, p. 10. IFN, p. 11. Truitt, p. 11. "Johnny Arthur Signed," *MPW,* 22 May 1926, 2. "Arthur Convalescent," *MPW,* 5 Mar 1927, 12. "Johnny Arthur," *MPW,* 11 Jun 1927, 409. "Johnny Arthur," *MPW,* 17 Dec 1927, 17.

Arthur, Julia [stage/film actress] (*née* Julia Lewis, b. Hamilton, Ontario, Canada, 3 May 1868–28 Mar 1950 [81], Boston MA). m. Benjamin Pierce Cheney, 1897 (d. 1942). (Film debut: *The Woman the Germans Shot,* Select, 1918.) "Julia Arthur, 81, Retired Actress; Shakespearean Star at Turn of Century Dies—Widow of Pierce Cheney, Financier," *NYT,* 30 Mar 1950, 29:5. "Julia Arthur," *Variety,* 5 Apr 1950 (age 81). AMD, p. 23. BHD, p. 94 (b. 1869). IFN, p. 11. Truitt, p. 11. "Julia Arthur Is Featured in Edith Cavell Picture," *MPW,* 28 Sep 1918, 1905. "Julia Arthur Sees Herself as Screen Edith Cavell," *MPW,* 2 Nov 1918, 610. "Julia Arthur Touring Canada," *MPW,* 19 Apr 1919, 369. "Julia Arthur Praises the Movies," *MPW,* 19 Apr 1919, 374.

Arthur, Lee [playwright] (b. Shreveport LA, 1877?–10 Dec 1917 [40], Los Angeles CA; pneumonia after injuries from auto accident 10 weeks earlier). m. Alice Brown. "Lee Arthur, Playwright," *NYT,* 11 Dec 1917, 15:6. "Lee Arthur," *Variety,* 14 Dec 1917. AMD, p. 23. BHD2, p. 9 (b. 1870; d. 9 Dec). SD. "Lee Arthur," *MPW,* 12 Dec 1914, 1496. "Lee Arthur with Edison," *MPW,* 3 Apr 1915, 47. "Obituary," *MPW,* 29 Dec 1917, 1948 (d. 8 Dec).

Arthur, Louise [actress] (b. 1900–9 Jun 1925 [25], Los Angeles CA). BHD, p. 94. IFN, p. 11.

Arthur, Paul [stage/film actor] (*né* Paul A. McDonough, b. London, England, 19 Jul 1859–12 May 1928 [68], London, England). "Paul Arthur Dies Abroad," *Variety,* 16 May 1928, p. 56 (b. U.S.; age 69). BHD, p. 94.

Artigue, Pierre [animator[(b. New Iberia LA, 1872–6 Nov 1934 [62?], Los Angeles CA). BHD2, p. 9.

Arto, Florence *see* **Vidor, Florence**

Arundale, Sybil [stage/film actress] (b. London, England, 20 Jun 1882–5 Sep 1965 [83], London, England). "Sybil Arundale," *Variety,* 15 Sep 1965, p. 94. BHD1, p. 20. IFN, p. 12.

Arundell, Teddy (b. Devonshire, England–d. 5 Nov 1922, London, England). BHD, p. 94.

Arvidson, Linda [stage/screen actress] (*née* Linda Johnson, b. San Francisco CA, 1876?–26 Jul 1949 [73], New York NY [Death Certificate No. 16014 (Linda Griffith)]). m. **D.W. Griffith**, 14 May 1906, Boston MA (d. 1948). *When the Movies Were Young* (NY: E.P. Dutton & Co., 1925). (Biograph; K&E; Kinemacolor.) "Mrs. Linda Griffith," *Variety,* 3 Aug 1949. BHD, p. 94 (b. 1884). IFN, p. 12 (age 65). MSBB, p. 1034. Truitt, p. 11. "Lives of the Players; Linda A. Griffith," *MPS,* 11 Jul 1913, 29. "Linda Griffith's Career," *NYDM,* 22 Jul 1916, p. 27. "Linda Arvidson Griffith," *MPW,* 29 Jul 1916, 774 (Linda Arvidson Griffith). Faith Service, "When the Movies Were Young," *Pictures,* Sep 1926, 32–33, 81.

Arzner, Dorothy [scenarist/film editor/director] (b. San Francisco CA, 3 Jan 1897–1 Oct 1979 [82], La Quinta CA). (FP-L; MGM.) "Dorothy Arzner," *Variety,* 10 Oct 1979. AMD, p. 23. BHD2, p. 9. FDY, p. 417. IFN, p. 12. LACD, "script reader," r 617 Shatto Pl. "Paramount's First Woman Director Signs," *MPW,* 18 Dec 1926, 493. "First Woman Director at Paramount Studios," *MPW,* 18 Dec 1926, 497. "Woman Director to Start Second," *MPW,* 23 Apr 1927, 712. "Dorothy Arzner Will Direct Clara Bow," *MPW,* 24 Sep 1927, 223. Julie Lang, "Directed by Dorothy Arzner!; The Story of the Only Woman to Achieve Consistent Success as a Motion Picture Director," *Screenland,* Aug 1929, 70 71, 112.

Asberry, Richard W. [actor]. No data found. LACD, "photoplayer," r 216 N. Bonnie Brae.

Asche, Oscar [actor/writer] (b. Geelong, Victoria, Australia, 26 Jan 1871–23 Mar 1936 [65], Marlow, Bucks, England). m. **Lily Brayton** (d. 1953). BHD1, p. 20; BHD2, p. 9. IFN, p. 12.

Ascher, Anton [actor] (b. 1868?–30 Sep 1928 [60], New York NY). "Anton Ascher," *Variety,* 3 Oct 1928. BHD, p. 94. IFN, p. 12.

Ash, Gordon [actor] (b. England, 1877?–20 Apr 1929 [52], New York NY; acute alcoholism). m. actress Eva Leonard Boyne. "Gordon Ash," *Variety,* 24 Apr 1929 (interred at Kensico). BHD, p. 94.

Ash, Jerome H. "Jerry" [actor/cinematographer] (b. 1892?–5 Jan 1953 [60], San Francisco CA). (U-I.) "Jerome H. Ash," *NYT,* 6 Jan 1953, 29:2. "Jerome H. Ash," *Variety,* 14 Jan 1953. BHD, p. 94; BHD2, p. 9. FDY, p. 455. IFN, p. 12.

Asher, Ephraim M. "Eph" [publicist/producer] (b. Susanville CA, 1888?–29 Oct 1937 [49], Los Angeles CA; stroke of paralysis). m. actress Lillian Bonner. (Began 1920; Sennett.) "Ephraim M. Asher, Film Producer, 49; Universal Executive Who Made Several Major Pictures Stricken in Hollywood," *NYT,* 30 Oct 1937, 19:2. "Eph Ascher," *Variety,* 3 Nov 1937. AMD, pp. 23–24. BHD2, p. 9. "E.M. Asher in New York to Direct Sennett Publicity," *MPW,* 21 Feb 1920, 1271. "Comedies Will Continue the Vogue, Asher Says," *MPW,* 4 Dec 1926, 343.

Asher, Irving [executive/producer] (b. San Francisco CA, 16 Sep 1903–17 Mar 1985 [81], Indio CA). m. **Laura LaPlante**, 19 Jun 1932, Paris, France (d. 1996). (Began 1919; London Films; MGM.) "Irving Asher," *Variety,* 27 Mar 1985. BHD2, p. 9.

Asher, Max, "The Funniest Dutch Comedian in Pictures" [actor/makeup artist] (*né* Max Ascher?, b. Oakland CA, 5 May 1879–15 Apr 1957 [77], Hollywood CA). (Sennett, 1912; Universal-Joker; Vitagraph; Powers.) "Max Asher, 77, former actor in silent pictures and a makeup man in various studios since 1939, died in Hollywood April 15. Wife survives," *Variety,* 1 May 1957 (age 77). AMD, p. 24. BHD1, p. 21 (b. 1885). FSS, p. 10. IFN, p. 12 (age 71). Katz, pp. 50–51 (b. 1880). Truitt, p. 11 (b. 1880). "Max Asher," *MPW,* 15 Nov 1913, 717. "Max Asher," *MPW,* 24 Oct 1914, 505. George A. Katchmer, "Remembering the Great Silents," *CI,* 184 (Oct 1990), 58.

Asher, Roland H. [scenarist/assistant director] (brother of scenarist Jerry Asher) (b. Los Angeles CA, 2 Aug 1895–18 Apr 1953 [58], Woodland Hills CA). "Rollie Asher," *Variety,* 22 Apr 1953. BHD2, p. 9. FDY, p. 417. IFN, p. 12.

Ashley, Arthur H. [actor/director] (b. New York NY, 6 Oct 1885–28 Dec 1970 [85], East Islip, LI NY). m. Helen. "Arthur Ashley," *NYT,* 30 Dec 1970, 28:2. "Arthur Ashley," *Variety,* 13 Jan 1971 (managed the Percy Williams Home, a haven for aging actors, in East Islip). AMD, p. 24. BHD, p. 94; BHD2, p. 10 (b. 1886). IFN, p. 12. Spehr, p. 112. "Arthur Ashley in Vaudeville," *MPW,* 16 Jan 1915, 371. "Blackwell and Ashley with World Film," *MPW,* 1 Apr 1916, 62. "Ashley to Continue with World," *MPW,* 6 Oct 1917, 82. "Arthur Ashley with Goldwyn," *MPW,* 8 Dec 1917, 1493. "Arthur Ashley Engaged by World," *MPW,* 31 May 1919, 1322.

Ashley, Beulah [actress/script supervisor] (b. MS, 24 Jan 1899–6 Jul 1965 [66], Los Angeles CA; cancer). "Beulah Ashley," *Variety,* 14 Jul 1965. BHD, p. 94. IFN, p. 12.

Ashley, Charles [director] (b. London, England, 1872). m. Gretchen Frase, 24 Sep 1917. AMD, p. 24. BHD2, p. 10. "Ashley—Frase," *MPW,* 20 Oct 1917, 377.

Ashton, Dorrit (b. 1873?–25 Jul 1936 [63], Los Angeles CA). m. **Charles Newton** (d. 1926). "Dorrit Ashton," *Variety,* 5 Aug 1936. BHD, p. 94. IFN, p. 12. Truitt, p. 11.

Ashton, H.D. [film editor]. No data found. AMD, p. 24. "H.D. Ashton," *MPW,* 1 Dec 1917, 1331.

Ashton, Herbert, Jr. [actor/scenarist/director] (b. San Francisco CA, 25 Sep 1902–13 Aug 1960 [57], San Francisco CA). BHD1, p. 21; BHD2, p. 10. IFN, p. 12.

Ashton, Iris [actress]. No data found. m. William Albert Badger. "Iris Ashton Deceived," *Variety,* 21 Jun 1923, p. 19 (she thought she was marrying a millionaire).

Ashton, Rosalie [scenarist]. No data found. AMD, p. 24. "Scenario Writers Join World Film," *MPW,* 9 Mar 1918, 1349. "World Signs Scenario Expert as Reader," *MPW,* 6 Jul 1918, 81. "Rosalie Ashton Writing for Spitz," *MPW,* 5 Jun 1920, 1305.

Ashton, Sylvia [actress] (*née?,* b. Denver CO, 26 Jan 1880–18 Nov 1940 [60], Los Angeles CA). (Sennett.) "Sylvia Ashton," *NYT,* 19 Nov 1940, 24:2 (retired 1928). "Mrs. Sylvia Ashton," *Variety,* 20 Nov 1940 (d. 17 Jan). BHD, p. 95. IFN, p. 12. Truitt, p. 11.

Ashton, Vera [actress] (*née?,* b. MO, 28 Feb 1900–27 Apr 1965 [65], Los Angeles CA). m. Thomas Ashton. "Vera Ashton [Mrs. Thomas Ashton]," *Variety,* 5 May 1965 (d. 28 Apr). BHD, p. 95. IFN, p. 12. Truitt, p. 11.

Ashwell, Lena [actress] (b. Wellesley Training Ship, England, 25 Sep 1871–13 Mar 1957 [85], London, England). BHD, p. 95.

Aslin, Edna [actress]. George Katchmer, "Remembering the Great Silents," *CI,* 220 (Oct 1993), 40 (appeared in *The Cowboy and the Outlaw,* 1929; *The Invaders,* 1929; *Riders of the Rio Grande,* 1929; *Breezy Bill,* 1930).

Asquith, Anthony [scenarist/director/producer] (b. London, England, 9 Nov 1902–20 Feb 1968 [65], London, England; cancer). Bachelor. (1st film: *Shooting Stars,* 1928). "Anthony Asquith," *Variety,* 28 Feb 1968, p. 63 ("An early escapade that brought him his first publicity, was doubling [in a blond wig] for silent film actress Phyllis Neilson Terry, in some chariot stunt scenes in the 1926 *Boadicia.*"). John Roberts, "Anthony Asquith," *CI,* 231 (Sep 1994), C2, 56. BHD2, p. 10. IFN, p. 23.

Asquith, Mary [actress] (b. 1873?–22 Dec 1942 [69], Brooklyn NY). (Fox.) "Mary Asquith; Former Actress, Author, Play Broker, Dies in Brooklyn at 69," *NYT,* 24 Dec 1942, 15:4. "Mary Asquith," *Variety,* 30 Dec 1942. BHD, p. 95.

Astaire, Adele (sister of **Fred Astaire**) [stage/film dancer/actress] (b. Omaha NB, 10 Sep 1898–25 Jan 1981 [82], Scottsdale AZ). m. Lord Charles Cavendish. BHD1, p. 21 (b. 1896).

Astaire, Fred (brother of **Adele Astaire**) [stage/film/TV dancer/actor/singer] (*né* Frederick Austerlitz, b. Omaha NB, 10 May 1899–22 Jun 1987 [88], Los Angeles CA; pneumonia). m. Phyllis Baker, Jul 1933 (d. 1954); Robyn Smith, 1980. *Steps in Time.* Richard F. Shepard, "Fred Astaire, the Ultimate Dancer, Dies," *NYT,* 23 Jun 1987, A1, D31:1. "Fred Astaire Succumbs at 88; World's Greatest Pop Dancer," *Variety,* 327, 24 Jun 1987, 2:1, 106. "Mrs. Fred Astaire Dies; Wife of the Dancing Star Is Victim of Cancer at 46," *NYT,* 14 Sep 1954, 27:4 (d. 13 Sep 1954 [46], Beverly Hills CA; cancer. Survived by Fred, Jr., Ava, and Peter Potter, son by her 1st marriage). BHD1, p. 21.

Asther, Nils [stage/film actor] (*né* Nilsen Asther, b. Hellerup [near Copenhagen], Denmark, 17 Jan 1897–13 Oct 1981 (84), near Stockholm, Sweden). m. (2) **Vivian Duncan**, 1930–div. 1932. "Nils Asther, 84, Silent Leading Man to Garbo, Dies in Sweden," *Variety,* 21 Oct 1981 (with Garbo in *Wild Orchids,* MGM, 1929; last film, *Gudrun,* Denmark, 1963). AMD, p. 24. BHD1, p. 21. FSS, p. 10. "Nils Asther," *MPW,* 9 Jul 1927, 87. Frances Breedlove, "Nils Asther Discovers America," *Cinema Arts,* VI (Oct 1927), 15, 49 ("now only twenty-six years old"). "Asther Returns to M-G-M," *MPW,* 24 Dec 1927, 21.

Astor, Camille [actress] (b. Warsaw, Poland, 1 Sep 1896–16 Sep 1944 [48], Los Angeles CA). BHD, p. 95.

Astor, Gertrude [stage/film actress] (b. Lakewood OH, 9 Nov 1889–9 Nov 1977 [88], Woodland Hills CA; stroke). (b. 1889). (Universal.) "Gertrude Astor, 90, an Actress in Silent Films and the Talkies," *NYT,* 12 Nov 1977, 24:2. "Gertrude Astor," *Variety,* 16 Nov 1977. BHD1, p. 22. FSS, p. 11. IFN, p. 12. LACD, "photoplayer," h 1762 Vine. Buck Rainey, "Films of Gertrude Astor," *CI,* 192 (May 1991), C9-C10, C12; Part II, 192 (Jun 1991), 24, 30. George Katchmer, "Remembering the Great Silents, *CI,* 243 (Sep 1995), 40, 42.

Astor, Mary [film/stage/radio/TV actress: Wampas Star, 1926] (*née* Lucile Vasconcellos Langhanke, b. Quincy IL, 3 May 1906–25 Sep 1987 [81], Woodland Hills CA; emphysema; interred at Holy Cross Cemetery, LA CA). m. (1) **Kenneth Hawks**, 24 Feb 1928 (d. 2 Jan 1930); (2) Franklyn Thorpe, Jun 1931 (daughter, Marylyn Huoli Thorpe, b. 16 Jun 1932)—div. 1935; (3) Manuel del Campo, Feb 1937 (son, Anthony, b. 1939); (4) Thomas Wheelock, 25 Dec 1945—div. 1955. *My Story; An Autobiography* (Garden City NY: Doubleday, 1959); *A Life on Film* (NY: Delacorte Press, 1971). (Film debut: *Sentimental Tommy,* Paramount 1921 [sequence cut].) Peter B. Flint, "Mary Astor, 81, Is Dead; Star of 'Maltese Falcon,'" *NYT,* 26 Sep 1987, 34:1. "Mary Astor Dies on Coast at 81; Versatile Star Bridged Silent Era," *Variety,* 30 Sep 1987. AMD, p. 24. BHD1, p. 22. FFF, p. 236. FSS, p. 12. SD. "Brewster Magazines Announce Winners of 'The Fame and Fortune Contest,'" *MPW,* 20 Nov 1920, 329. "Can't Break Contract," *MPW,* 14 Oct 1922, 556 (17 years old). Gladys Hall, "'What I Think of the Men of Today,' by Mary Astor," *MW,* 12 May 1923, 7. Alma Talley, "'I Don't Want to Play a Luring Lady,'" *MW,* 4 Jul 1925, 25–26. June Lee, "Dan Cupid's Bulletin Board," *Paris and Hollywood,* Oct 1926, 32 (announced her engagement to Irving Asher). "Starke-White Wed; Mary Astor Next," *MPW,* 10 Sep 1927, 89. Barrie Roberts, "Mary Astor: Reluctant Legend," *CI,* 302 (Aug 2000), 6–14, 59–60 (includes filmography).

Astrea [actress] (b. Venice, Italy). JS, p. 20 (in films from 1919 [*Astrea*]).

Atasheva, Pera (sister of cameraman Julius Fogelman) [scenarist] (b. 1900?–24 Sep 1965 [65], Moscow, Russia). m. **Sergei M. Eisenstein**, 1929 (d. 1948). "Pera Atasheva," *Variety,* 13 Oct 1965, 86:1.

Atherton, Gertrude [actress/scenarist] (*née* Gertrude Franklin Horn, b. San Francisco CA, 30 Oct 1857–14 Jun 1948 [90], San Francisco CA; "ailments connected with her advanced age"). m. George H. Bowen Atherton (d. 1887). *Adventures of a Novelist* (1932). "Mrs. Atherton, 90, Novelist, Is Dead; Author of 'Black Oxen' [1923] and 'The Conqueror' Among Sixty Books Published Since '92," *NYT,* 15 Jun 1948, 27:1. AMD, p. 24. BHD2, p. 10. SD. "Gertrude Atherton Leaves to Assist with Production," *MPW,* 2 Aug 1919, 694. "Gertrude Atherton Arrives on Coast," *MPW,* 9 Aug 1919, 851.

Atherton, Venie [actress] (b. 1862?–3 Oct 1927 [65], New York NY; heart and kidney complications [interred at Greenwood Cemetery]). m. John Mackay. "Venie Atherton (Mrs. John Mackay)," *Variety,* 12 Oct 1927. BHD, p. 95.

Atkins, Robert [stage/film actor/director] (b. Dulwich, England, 10 Aug 1886–9 Feb 1972 [85], London, England). "Robert Atkins," *Variety,* 23 Feb 1972, 71:3. BHD1, p. 22.

Atkins, Thomas C. [actor/director/producer/writer] (b. Springfield MA, 18 Jul 1887–18 Jun 1968 [80], Los Angeles CA; heart attack). m. Dorothy. "Thomas C. Atkins," *Variety,* 26 Jun 1968 (began with Selznick, 1919). BHD2, p. 10.

Atkinson, Evelyn [actress] (b. 1900?–16 Dec 1954 [54], Seattle WA). m. Leroy M. Dehan. "Mrs. Leroy M. Dehan [Evelyn Atkinson]," *Variety,* 22 Dec 1954. BHD, p. 95. IFN, p. 12. Truitt, p. 12.

Atkinson, Florence [actress]. No data found. AMD, p. 24. "Miss Atkinson Badly Burned," *MPW,* 5 Jan 1918, 107. "Little Whisperings from Everywhere in Playerdom," *Motion Picture Magazine,* Feb 1918, 142 ("...was badly burned while playing the vampire in 'The Marionettes' with Clara Kimball Young. Her hair became ignited from an alcohol lamp and she was badly burned about the arms and shoulders.").

Atkinson, Frank [actor/writer] (b. Oldham, Lancashire, England, 19 Mar 1890–23 Feb 1963 [72], Pinner, England). m. Jeanne D'Arcy. "Frank Atkinson," *Variety,* 13 Mar 1963. BHD, p. 95. IFN, p. 12 (b. 1890). SD. Truitt, p. 12 (b. Blackpool, England, 1893).

Atkinson, George A. [actor/scenarist] (b. Liverpool, England, 15 Dec 1877–1 May 1968 [90], Woodland Hills CA; arterio-sclerosis). BHD1, p. 22; BHD2, p. 10. IFN, p. 13. LACD, "photoplayer," r 3910 Sunset Blvd.

Atkinson, Josephine [actress] (d. 6 Jan 1954, Los Angeles CA). BHD, p. 95.

Atkinson, Marguerite [actress]. No data found. LACD, r 144 S. Virgil Ave.

Atkinson, Maude [actress] (b. England, 1885–7 Mar 1944 [59], No. Hollywood CA). BHD1, p. 22. IFN, p. 13.

Atkinson, William E. [sales manager for Kinemacolor Co./executive/V-P of MGM] (b. Cheshire, England, 22 Mar 1880–18 May 1940 [60], Charlottesville VA; heart attack; interred at Monticello Memorial Park). m. Ethel (2 sons, Wilson and William B.; daughter Marian). "William E. Atkinson," *Variety,* 22 May 1940, 62:1. BHD2, p. 10.

Attenburg, Carl [cinematographer]. No data found. FDY, p. 455.

Attic, Joseph M. [actor] (b. France, 13 Jun 1892–17 Mar 1971 [78], Redondo Beach CA). m. **Gladys Hoffman**, Aug 1923 (d. 1962). (Eclair; Pathé [France]; Universal; Fox; World; Reliance; Palace Players.) BHD, p. 95 (b. 14 Jun). "Gladys Hoffman Weds," *Variety,* 23 Aug 1923, p. 18. BHD2, p. 10 (b. 14 Jun).

Atwell, Ben H. [opera/legit publicist] (b. Syracuse NY, 1876?–21 Feb 1951 [74], Los Angeles CA). m. soprano Marcella Albus (d. 1937). "Ben H. Atwell," *Variety,* 181, 28 Feb 1951, 63:1 (member of The Lambs and The Silurians). AMD, p. 24. B.H. Atwell, "Pity the Poor Press Agent," *MPW,* 20 Jul 1918, 341–42.

Atwell, Grace [actress] (b. Boston MA, 13 Jul 1872–2 Nov 1952 [80], Los Angeles CA). m. **Edwin Mordant** (d. 1942). "Mrs. Grace Atwell," *Variety,* 12 Nov 1952. AS, p. 784 (Grace Mordant). BHD, p. 95; addendum (Grace Mordant). IFN, p. 13. Truitt, p. 238.

Atwell, Roy [actor] (b. Syracuse NY, 2 May 1878?–6 Feb 1962 [83], New York NY [Death Certificate No. 2988; age 82]). m. (1) Blanche Meoredy (Blanche West), 1907; (2) Dorothy Young–1916; (3) Ethel Smith, 1916–1936. "Roy Atwell Dies; Stage Comedian; Ex-Star of Musicals, Radio and Vaudeville Was 83," *NYT,* 7 Feb 1962, 34:3. "Roy Atwell," *Variety,* 14 Feb 1962 (cites extensive theater work). BHD1, p. 23. IFN, p. 13. Truitt, p. 12.

Atwill, Lionel [actor] (*né* Lionel Alfred William Atwill, b. Croydon, Surrey, England, 1 Mar 1885–22 Apr 1946 [61], Pacific Palisades CA; pneumonia). m. (1) Phyllis Ralph; (2) Elsie McKay; (3) Louise Cromwell Stotesburg, 1930, MD; (4) Paula Pruter, 1944, Las Vegas NV. "Lionel Atwill, 61, Noted Actor, Dies; Veteran of Stage and Screen Made London Debut in 1904—Star in Shaw, Pinero," *NYT,* 23 Apr 1946, 21:1 (began in films in 1932). "Lionel Atwill," *Variety,* 24 Apr 1946. BHD1, p. 23. IFN, p. 13. SD. Truitt, p. 12.

Aubrey, James [actor] (b. Liverpool, England, 23 Oct 1887–2 Sep 1983 [95], Woodland Hills CA). AMD, p. 24. BHD1, p. 22. Slide, p. 134. WWS, p. 105. "Jimmy Aubrey," *CI,* 102 (Dec 1983), 10. "'Heine and Louie' Comedies Going Well," *MPW,* 11 Sep 1915, 1840. "Aubrey Forms Own Company, to Make Two-Reel Comedies," *MPW,* 9 Jun 1923, 523. "Jimmy Aubrey Under Contract with Vitagraph for Two Years," *MPW,* 22 May 1920, 1060. George A. Katchmer, "Forgotten Cowboys and Cowgirls—Pt. XVI," *CI,* 19 (Jul 1991), 34 (b. 2 Sep 1883).

Auburn, Joy *see* **McCormick, Alyce**

Auen, Carl [actor] (b. Düsseldorf, Germany, 16 Feb 1892–23 Jun 1972 [80], Berlin, Germany). BHD1, p. 23.

Auer, Anna [actress] (b. 1860?–2 Apr 1944 [84], Ft. Lee NJ). m. William Baker (d. 1932). "Mrs. Willis Baker," *Variety,* 5 Apr 1944. BHD, p. 97. IFN, p. 15 (Anna Auer Baker). SD.

Auer, Florence [stage/film actress] (b. Albany NY, 3 Mar 1880–14 May 1962 [82], New York NY [Death Certificate No. 10657]). "Florence Auer, Acted in Stage and Films," *NYT,* 15 May 1962, 39:3. BHD1, p. 23. IFN, p. 13.

Auer, John H. [director/producer/actor] (b. Budapest, Hungary, 3 Aug 1906–15 Mar 1975 [68], Riverside CA). BHD, p. 95; BHD2, p. 10. IFN, p. 13.

Auer, Mischa [actor] (*né* Mischa Ounkowski, b. St. Petersburg, Russia, 17 Mar 1905–5 Mar 1967 [61], Rome, Italy; heart attack). (Film debut: *Something Always Happens,* 1928). "Mischa Auer, Comedian in Scores of Movies, Dies," *NYT,* 6 Mar 1967, 29:2 (age 63). "Mischa Auer," *Variety,* 8 Mar 1967 (age 62). BHD1, p. 23. IFN, p. 13. JS, p. 20 (made films in Italy from 1949 to 1968. "His mother's father was violinist Leopold Auer, who took him to the U.S.A. in 1920.").

Auerbach, Henry L. [actor] (d. 22 Aug 1916, Oakland CA). BHD, p. 95.

Aug, Edna [stage/film actress] (b. Cincinnati OH, 1878?–30 Nov 1938 [60], Willow NY). (Universal.) "Edna Aug, Favorite on Pre-War Stage; Former Vaudeville Comedienne and Character Actress Dies in Seclusion on Farm; Made 17 Foreign Tours; She Refused Play [*Madame Sunshine*] Written by Tarkington to Induce Her to Return to Theatre," *NYT,* 2 Dec 1938, 23:5. "Edna Aug," *Variety,* 7 Dec 1938. BHD, p. 95. IFN, p. 13. "In the Picture Studios," *NYDM,* 8 Sep 1915, 36:4 (one of the stage stars at Universal).

Auger, Edward [executive]. No data found. AMD, p. 24. "Edward Auger Succeeds Kane," *MPW,* 7 Nov 1914, 791.

August, Edwin [actor/producer/director/writer] (*né* Edwin August Phillip von der Butz, b. St. Louis MO, 20 Nov 1883–4 Mar 1964 [80], Los Angeles CA). (Edison; Biograph; Eaco Films; Lubin.) "Edwin August," *Variety,* 11 Mar 1964. AMD, p. 24. BHD1, p. 23; BHD2, p. 10 (b. 10 Nov). FSS, p. 13. IFN, p. 13. Truitt, p. 12. "Edwin August Makes Change; Now a Member of the Power's Picture Players in the Stock Company," *MPN,* 6 Jul 1912, 9. "Joins Powers Players," *MPW,* 13 Jul 1912, 153. "Lives of the Players; Edwin August," *MPS,* 31 Jan 1913, 31. "Lives of the Players; Edwin August, Powers Star, Tells of Career," *MPS,* 28 Mar 1913, 29. "August a Free Lance; Has Strong Backing in Organizing 'Edwin August Feature Films Company,'" *NYDM,* 8 Apr 1914, 32:2. "Edwin August Now a Composer of Music," *MPW,* 20 May 1916, 1308 (wrote *Honey, Teach Me How to Fox Trot*). "August Directing Film in Colors," *MPW,* 3 Dec 1927, 21.

August, Hal [actor] (*né* Frank T. Halleck, b. 1890?–21 Sep 1918 [28], Chicago IL; pneumonia). "Frank Halleck," *Variety,* 11 Oct 1918. AMD, p. 25. BHD, p. 95. IFN, p. 13. "Hal August," *MPW,* 2 Jan 1915, 56. "Obituary," *MPW,* 19 Oct 1918, 363 (age 26).

August, Joseph H. [cinematographer] (b. Idaho Springs CO, 26 Apr 1890–25 Sep 1947 [57], Culver City CA; heart attack). "Joseph August," *NYT,* 26 Sep 1947, 23:3. "Joseph August," *Variety,* 1 Oct 1947. BHD2, p. 10 (b. Lawson CO). FDY, p. 455. IFN, p. 13. Katz, pp. 57–58. LACD, "cameraman," h 1151 Sanborn Ave.

Ault, Marie [actress] (*née* Marie Cragg, b. Wigan, England, 2 Sep 1870–9 May 1951 [80], London, England). m. James A. Patterson. "Marie Ault," *NYT,* 10 May 1951, 31:1. "Marie Ault," *Variety,* 16 May 1951. BHD1, p. 24. IFN, p. 13. SD. Truitt, p. 12.

Aultman, O.A. [cinematographer]. No data found. AMD, p. 25. "Pathé Cameraman Defies Death in Mexico and Brings Out Pictures of Revolution," *MPW,* 12 Jun 1920, 1489. "Pathé Cameraman Has Thrilling Time Getting exclusive 'Shots' of Villa," *MPW,* 11 Sep 1920, 241.

Austen, Leslie [actor] (b. London, England, 1888–16 Aug 1924 [36]). (Metro; U.S. Amusement Co.; Fox.) BHD, p. 95 (b. 1886). IFN, p. 13. MSBB, p. 1021. "Wife of Leslie Austin," *Variety,* 24 Apr 1940 (d. 17 Apr 1940, NY NY).

Austin, Albert [vaudeville/film actor/director/writer] (b. Birmingham, England, 1882–17 Aug 1953 [71], No. Hollywood CA). (Metro.) "Albert Austin," *NYT,* 19 Aug 1953, 29:2 (age 70). "Albert Austin," *Variety,* 26 Aug 1953. AMD, p. 25. BHD, p. 95; BHD2, p. 11 (b. 1885; d. LA CA). IFN, p. 13. LACD, "photoplayer," h 1010 N. Oxford Ave. Truitt, p. 13. "Austin to Play with Chaplin," *MPW,* 28 Dec 1918, 1488. "Austin Is Directing Bull Montana," *MPW,* 27 Jan 1923, 385:4.

Austin, Blanche [actress]. No data found. AMD, p. 25. "Blanche Austin," *MPW,* 14 Nov 1914, 921.

Austin, Charles [actor] (b. 1878–14 Jan 1944 [65?], London, England). BHD, p. 95. IFN, p. 13 (age 63).

Austin, Frank [actor] (*né* George Francis Austin, b. Mound City MO, 9 Oct 1877–13 May 1954 [76], Los Angeles CA). m. Katheryne—div. 1924. BHD1, p. 24. IFN, p. 13. "G.F. Austin Gets Divorce," *Variety,* 28 May 1924, p. 19 (grounds of desertion). George A. Katchmer, "Forgotten Cowboys and Cowgirls—Part XIII," *CI,* 190 (Apr 1991), C4.

Austin, Harold [actor] (b. 1890?–5 Mar 1931 [41], Liberty NY). "Harry Austin," *Variety,* 11 Mar 1931.

Austin, Jere [stage/film actor/director] (b. Minneapolis MN, 24 Mar 1876–12 Nov 1927 [51], Los Angeles CA; cancer). (Vitagraph; Selig; Kalem; Goldwyn.) "Jere Austin," *Variety,* 16 Nov 1927. BHD, p. 96; BHD2, p. 11. IFN, p. 13. MSBB, p. 1021. Truitt, p. 13.

Austin, Johanna [actress] (*né* Anna R. Austin, b. 1853?–1 Jun 1944 [91], Los Angeles CA). BHD, p. 96. IFN, p. 13. Truitt, p. 13.

Austin, William Crosby Piercy [actor/film editor] (b. Georgetown, British Guyana, 18 Jun 1884–15 Jun 1975 [91], Los Angeles CA). (b. 18 Jun). (MGM.) BHD1, p. 24 (b. 12 Jun). IFN, p. 13. George Katchmer, "Remembering the Great Silents," *CI,* 222 (Dec 1993), C15–C16.

Autant-Lara, Claude [director] (*né* Claude Autant, b. Luzarches, France, 5 Aug 1901–5 Feb 2000 [98], Nice, France). m. Ghislaine Auboin. Suzanne Daley, (First feature: *Ciboulette,* 1932; last film: *Gloria,* 1977.) "Claude Autant-Lrra, 98, a Film Director," *NYT,* 9 Feb 2000, B10. Harris Lentz, III, "Claude Autant-Lara, 98," *CI,* 297 (Mar 2000), 53. (MGM.) Waldman, p. 19 (b. 1903; directed two French-language films with Buster Keaton, *Buster Se Marie* [1931], and *Le Plombier Amoureux* [1932]; last film: *Gloria* [USA], 1977).

Auten, Harold [title writer/scenarist/producer] (b. England, 1891–3 Oct 1964 [73?], East Stroudsburg PA). BHD2, p. 11. FDY, p. 441.

Auzinger, Max [actor] (aka Ben Ali Bey, b. 26 Jul 1839–11 May 1928 [88]). BHD, p. 96.

Avare, Adrien [colorist]. No data found. AMD, p. 25. "Adrien Avare, Colorist," *MPW,* 8 Jan 1916, 224.

Avery, Charles *see* **Bradford, Charles Avery**

Avery, Patricia (third cousin of John D. Rockefeller) [actress: Wampas Star, 1927] (b. Boston MA, 19 Nov 1902–21 Aug 1973 [70], La Crescenta CA). (Possible screen debut: bit in *A Certain Young Man;* MGM.) AMD, p. 25. AS, p. 80. BHD1, p. 604. "Patricia Avery Signs New Contract," *MPW,* 11 Sep 1926, 119. Gertrude Sinclair, "Patricia Avery; The Screen's Newest Cinderella; A Fairy Tale Comes True in Hollywood—and Patricia Avery Jumps From Studio Typist to Screen Player," *Cinema Arts,* Sep 1926, 24–25, 56.

Avery, Suzanne [scenarist]. No data found. FDY, p. 417.

Avon, Violet *see* **La Plante, Violet**

Axelsson, Einar [actor] (b. Lund, Sweden, 25 Feb 1895–30 Oct 1971 [76]). BHD1, p. 24.

Axt, William L. [composer] (b. New York NY, 18 Apr 1887?–13 Feb 1959 [71], Ukiah CA). (MGM Studio Music Dept.) "William L. Axt," *NYT,* 15 Feb 1959, 86:6. "William L. Axt," *Variety,* 18 Feb 1959. BHD2, p. 11. *ASCAP Biographical Dictionary,* p. 18 (b. 1888).

Axzelle, Carl [actor] (b. Sweden, 11 Apr 1881–30 Oct 1958 [76], Malibu CA). BHD1, p. 604; BHD2, p. 11.

Axzell, Evelyn [actress] (b. England, 22 Dec 1880–11 May 1977 [96], Palm Springs CA). BHD1, p. 604 (b. 1890).

Aye, Maryon [actress: Sennett Bathing Beauty/Wampas Star, 1922] (*née* Marion Forrester?, b. Chicago IL, 5 Apr 1903–20 Jul 1951 [48], Los Angeles CA; ten days after poisoning herself). m. actor Harry D. Wilson, Feb 1920, NYC. "Maryon Aye," *NYT,* 22 Jul 1951, 61:2 (d. Los Angeles CA). "Marion Aye," *Variety,* 25 Jul 1951 (age 45). AMD, p. 25. BHD, p. 96. BR, p. 98. IFN, p. 14. LACD, "photoplayer," r 1755 Ivar St. (Marian M. Aye). MH, p. 94. Truitt, p. 13 (b. 1906). "Sennett Beauty Weds," *LA Times,* 27 Feb 1920, III, p. 4 (if Harry Wilson is the same as Harold Wilson, see entry for the latter). "Signs Morality Clause," *MPW,* 29 Oct 1921, 1026. "Maryon Aye Is Put Under Contract," *MPW,* 3 Mar 1923, 78. "On the Set and Off," *MW,* 11 Oct 1924, 20 (sued husband for divorce). George A. Katchmer, "Remembering the Great Silents," *CI,* 183 (Sep 1990), 44.

Ayers, Dudley [actor] (d. Sep 1930, San Francisco CA). BHD, p. 96.

Ayers, E.G. [actor]. No data found. LACD, "photoplayer," r 344 S. Olive.

Ayerton, Robert [actor] (d. 18 May 1924). BHD, p. 96. IFN, p. 14.

Aylesworth, Arthur [actor] (b. Apponaug RI, 12 Aug 1883–26 Jun 1946 [62], Los Angeles CA). IFN, p. 14.

Ayling, Robert [actor] (d. 28 Aug 1919, New York NY). BHD, p. 96. IFN, p. 14.

Aylmer, Mimi [actress] (b. London, England, 1895). JS. p. 22 (in Italian silents from 1914).

Aylott, Dave [actor/director] (b. London, England, 1885–31 Oct 1969 [84?], England). BHD, p. 96; BHD2, p. 11.

Aynesworth, Allan [actor] (b. Sandhurst, Berkshire, England, 14 Apr 1864–22 Aug 1959 [95], Camberley, Surrey, England). BHD1, p. 24. IFN, p. 14.

Ayres, Agnes [actress] (aka Agnes Eyre, *née* Agnes Hinkle, b. Carbondale IL, 4 Apr 1898–25 Dec 1940 [42], Los Angeles CA; stroke). m. Frank P. Schuker, 1921; S. Manuel Reachi—div. 1927 (1 child). (Began 1915; Vitagraph; Paramount; Essanay.) "Agnes Ayres, Star of Silent Pictures; Actress Who Played Opposite Rudolph Valentino in 'Sheik' Dies in Hollywood, Calif.; Lost Her Fortune in 1929; Tried to Make Comeback in the Talkies—Had Small Role in Cooper-Raft Film in '37," *NYT,* 26 Dec 1940, 19:5. "Agnes Ayres," *Variety,* 1 Jan 1941. AMD, p. 25. BHD1, p. 24. FFF, p. 136 (b. 1901). FSS, p. 13. IFN, p. 14. Katz, p. 63 (b. 4 Sep 1896). MH, p. 94 (b. Chicago IL). MSBB, p. 1030 (b. 1896). SD. Spehr, p. 114 (b. Chicago, 1896). Truitt, p. 13 (b. 4 Sep 1898). WWS, p. 40 (b. Chicago). "Leaves Law for Screen," *MPW,* 26 Aug 1916, 1415. "Agnes Ayres Deserted the Law," *MPW,* 27 Sep 1919, 1951. "Agnes Ayres, New Fox Star, Seen in 'Sacred Silents,'" *MPW,* 27 Sep 1919, 1970. "Agnes Ayres Is Promoted to Star," *MPW,* 9 Jul 1921, 225. "Sues for Divorce," *MPW,* 23 Jul 1921, 413. "Agnes Ayres to Be Featured Opposite Rudolph Valentino," *MPW,* 23 Jul 1921, 425. Ruth Mary Harris, "Springtime—and Romance," *Picture-Play Magazine,* Jun 1923, 48–49, 88. "Loot; Bandit Robs Agnes Ayres' Home," *MW,* 11 Jul 1925, 35 ("$10,000 in gems, clothing and government bonds."). "On the Set and Off," *MW,* 22 Aug 1925, 31–32 (sued PDC for $25,000 because only 1 of 3 films she contracted for were made). "On the Set and Off," *MW,* 19 Sep 1925, 44 (Ayres asked for $50,000 more in her suit against PDC. She claimed that the defendant concern did not make two pictures on her contract, "and that this idle period has damaged her future earning capacity."). "Roach Signs to Star Agnes Ayres," *MPW,* 13 Nov 1926, 87. Don Juan, "So This Is Hollywood," *Paris and Hollywood Screen Secrets Magazine,* May 1927, 32 (appearing in a comedy short with Anna May Wong on the Roach lot). June Lee, "Dan Cupid's Bulletin Board," *Paris and Hollywood Screen Secrets,* Oct 1927, 36 (divorced Reachi. "Under the terms of the property settlement each relinquishes any claim to property of the other, and their one child is to remain in \the custody of the mother—at the latter's expense.").

Ayres, Arthur P. [director]. No data found. LACD, h 1809 W. 27th St.

Ayres, Dudley [actor] (d. 1930, San Francisco CA; suicide by shooting). m. (1) Isabel Fletcher; (2) Wilkes; (3) Marjorie. "Dudley Ayres," *Variety,* 10 Sep 1930.

Ayres, Lew [musician/film and TV actor/writer] (*né* Lewis Frederick Ayre III, b. Minneapolis MN, 28 Dec 1908–30 Dec 1996 [88], Los Angeles CA; after being in a coma for several days). m. (1) Lola Lane, 14 Sep 1931, Las Vegas NV—div. 1933; (2) Ginger Rogers, 1934–41; (3) Diana Hall, 1964. *Altars of the East.* (Film debut: *The Sophomore,* Pathé 1929; MGM; AA nomination for *Johnny Belinda,* 1948.) Mel Gussow, "Lew Ayres, Actor, Dies at 88; Conscience Bound His Career," *NYT,* 1 Jan 1997, 47:1 ("A fellow's never through till he quits trying."). "Lew Ayres," *Variety,* 20 Jan 1997, 50:3. Minerva Canto, "Lew Ayres; Actor who was original Dr. Kildare [1938]," *Pittsburgh Post-Gazette,* 70, 1 Jan 1997, B-8:3. Katz, pp. 63–64. BHD1 p. 25. Joan Standish, "Lew Ayres and Lola Lane Make Up and Marry," *Movie Classic,* Dec 1931, 40. Herbert G. Luft, "Lew Ayres"; Richard E. Braff, "Lew Ayres Filmography," *FIR,* Jun/Jul 1978, 345–55. Michael G. Ankerich, "Lew Ayres: A Life of Self-Education," *CI,* 175 (Jan 1990), 6, 8, 57. Nadine Brozan, "Chronicle; A lawyer finds a movie star, and his long-standing wish comes true," *NYT,* 6 Oct 1993, B9:1. Chapter 1, "Lew Ayres," *BS,* pp. 1–14 (includes filmography). Laura Wagner, "Lew Ayres: The Unpretentious Star," *CI,* 260 (Feb 1997), p. 5.

Ayres, Ruby [actress] (b. London, England, 1883?–14 Nov 1955 [72], Weybridge, Surrey, England; pneumonia). m. Reginald William Pocock, 1909. "Ruby Ayres Dies; A British Author; Writer of Romantic Novels Sold 8,000,000 Copies—Produced Play in 1932," *NYT,* 15 Nov 1955, 29:1 (1st novel: *Richard Chatterton V.C.,* 1916).

Ayres, Sydney [actor/director] (*né* David Sidney Ayres, b. New York NY, 28 Aug 1879–9 Sep 1916 [37], Oakland CA). (Selig; Nestor; American; Powers.) "Sydney Ayres," *Variety,* 22 Sep 1916. AMD, p. 25. BHD, p. 96. IFN, p. 14. "New Leading Man for 'Flying A,'" *MPW,* 18 Oct 1913, 272. "Sydney Ayres Leaves American," *MPW,* 3 Oct 1914, 76. "Sydney Ayres," *MPW,* 29 Nov 1913,

990. Billy H. Doyle, "Lost Players," *CI*, 152 (Feb 1988), C12.

Ayrton, Randle [actor/producer] (b. Chester, England, 9 Aug 1869–28 May 1940 [70], Stratford-on-Avon, England). "Randle Ayrton," *Variety*, 26 Jun 1940. BHD1, p. 25. IFN, p. 14.

Azzuri, Paolo [actor] (b. 6 Oct 1878). JS, p. 22 (in Italian silents from 1907).

B

Babbitt, Orrin [actor] (b. 1883–5 Jul 1941 [58], Warwick RI). BHD, p. 96. IFN, p. 14.

Babcock, Theodore [actor] (b. Brooklyn NY, 14 Feb 1868–7 Sep 1930 [62], New York NY). BHD, p. 96. IFN, p. 14.

Baber, Sidney [actor]. No data found. AMD, p. 25. "Sidney Baber," *MPW*, 6 Feb 1915, 810.

Babette, Nilde [actress]. No data found. AMD, p. 25. "Jester Comedies Sign Nilde Babette," *MPW*, 16 Feb 1918, 981.

Baby Early (niece of **Elsie Albert**) ["Matty and Baby Early" team/child actress] (*née* Gorman, b. 1906?–20 May 1982 [76], Lake Hopatcong [Dover] NJ; emphysema). m. Earle E. Gehrig. (Universal, 1912; retired 1919.). J. Van CArtmell, "Along the Pacific Coast," *NYDM*, 4 Aug 1915, 26:2 (she and Master Frank Butterworth called by their director, H.C. Matthews, "the coming Mary Pickfords and Henry Walthalls."). AS, p. 83. BHD1, p. 609. Luther Hathcock, "Baby Early [letter]," *CI*, 92 (Feb 1983), 11, 55.

Baby Twinkles (niece of painter Charles Edward Perugini) [child actress] (*née* Florence Hunter, b. Chiswick, w. London, England, 12 Aug 1914–9 Aug 2000 [85], Ripon, North Yorkshire, England). m. Eric Kenyon, 1943 (2 daughters). (Film debut: *A Fallen Star*, 1916; Ideal Film Company; final film: *God on the Rocks*, Channel 4, 1990.) Howard Mutti-Mewse, "Baby Twinkles," *Independent Review*, 25 Aug 2000, p. 6 ("Her mother had photographs taken of her and sent them to film and stage agents which resulted in a screen test by the London Film Company and Gaumont British.... The film tests were successful, and from the age of two to seven and a half Baby Twinkles became one of the industry's first and brightest child actors.... By 1921, Twinkles was in such demand that it was not unusual for two studios to telephone in the same day offering her work. Her salary was increased to one guinea per day." By the time she appeared in *Carnival*, 1921, "the London County Council stepped in. This meant school, and she could only accept small parts during the holidays. Unfortunately, the work dried up, and by 1922 her film career was virtually over." Around this time Charlie Chaplin wrote to her mother. "Chaplin was adamant. My mother wrote and thanked him for his interest in me, but explained that I was to return to my school studies. Perhaps she had some kind of insight into what he was to be like with the girls. After all, I was only seven years old and there was never any mention of my mother joining me.").

Baccani, Ettore [actor] (d. 26 Oct 1919, Rome Italy). JS, p. 23 (in Italian silents from 1912).

Bach, Olaf [actor] (b. Hamburg, Germany, 7 Apr 1892–1 Nov 1963 [71]). BHD1, p. 25.

Bach, Reginald [stage director/actor] (b. Shepperton, England, 3 Sep 1886–6 Jan 1941 [54], New York NY). "Reginald Bach," *Variety*, 15 Jan 1941, p. 54. BHD1, p. 25. IFN, p. 14.

Bachmann, J[ohn] **G.** [producer/President of Preferred Pictures Corporation] (b. 1889?–10 Jun 1952 [63], Hollywood CA; heart attack). m. Fay. "Jack G. Bachmann," *NYT*, 12 Jun 1952, 34:4. "John Bachmann," *Variety*, 18 Jun 1952 ("Starting in N.Y. 36 years ago, he was associated with B.P. Schulberg in the production of silent pictures."). AMD, p. 25. BHD2, p. 12. "Schulberg and Bachmann Discuss 1925 Productions," *MPW*, 27 Dec 1924, 867. "Preferred to Continue Under Bachmann," *MPW*, 26 Dec 1925, 754. "Bachmann Rates High as Successful Producer," *MPW*, 4 Dec 1926, 343. "Bachmann Supervisor of Paramount Units," *MPW*, 13 Aug 1927, 445.

Bachmann, Max [art designer]. No data found. AMD, p. 26. "Sculptor Who Designed 'The Burning of Rome' Defends His Work," *MPW*, 5 Dec 1908, 445.

Bachwitz, Hans [scenarist]. No data found. FDY, p. 417.

Backer, Franklyn E. [producer] (b. 1877?–3 Aug 1949 [72], Suffern NY). m. Louise. "Franklyn E. Backer," *NYT*, 4 Aug 1949, 23:2 (Bergen City NJ photographer; no mention of his connection with films).

Backer, George [executive]. No data found. AMD, p. 26. "George Backer," *MPW*, 22 Dec 1917, 1795.

Backus, Frank [actor] (d. 14 Jan 1923, Buffalo NY). BHD, p. 96.

Backus, George [actor] (b. Columbus OH, 1858?–21 May 1939 [81], Merrick, LI NY). m. Louise Salather (d. 1938). "George Backus," *Variety*, 24 May 1939 (d. 22 May). BHD, p. 96. IFN, p. 14. SD. Truitt, p. 14.

Backus, Lionel C. [actor/casting director] (b. NY, 28 Dec 1901–10 Jun 1981 [79], Woodland Hills CA). BHD1, p. 25; BHD2, p. 12.

Baclanova, Olga [film/stage actress] (*née* Olga Petrovna Baklanova, b. Moscow, Russia, 19 Aug 1896–6 Sep 1974 [78], Vevey, Switzerland). (Olga Davis). m. (1) Vlademar Zoppi, ca. 1922, Russia (1 son); (2) **Nicholas Soussanin**, 1929 (d. 1975); (3) Richard Davis. "Film debut: *Symphony of Love and Death*, Russia, 1914; American film debut: *The Dove*, 1928; Paramount; Fox; MGM.) "Olga Baclanova," *Variety*, 18 Sep 1974 (age 74). BHD1, p. 25 (b. 1899). IFN, p. 14. Katz, p. 66. FSS, p. 13. Charles Stumpf, "Olga Baclanova: Miscast Legend," *CI*, 276 (Jun 1998), 32, C1-C3. Paul Meienberg, "More About Baclanova [letter]," *CI*, 277 (Jul 1998), 17–18 (probably b. 1896 and not 1899).

Bacon, Frank (father of **Lloyd Bacon**) [stage/film actor] (b. Marysville CA, 16 Jan 1864–19 Nov 1922 [58], Chicago IL). m. Jennie Weidman (d. 1956). "Frank Bacon," *Variety*, 24 Nov 1922. AMD, p. 26. BHD, p. 96. IFN, p. 14. SD. Truitt, p. 14. "Frank Bacon," *MPW*, 20 Feb 1915, 1468. "In the Picture Studios," *NYDM*, 11 Aug 1915, 27:1 (to debut in *The Silent Voice*, Metro).

Bacon, Gerald [producer]. No data found. AMD, p. 26. "Gerald Bacon Is Signed for Big Hall Productions," *MPW*, 10 May 1919, 837.

Bacon, Irving [actor] (b. St. Joseph MO, 6 Sep 1893–5 Feb 1965 [71], Hollywood CA). "Irving, Bacon," *Variety*, 10 Feb 1965. BHD1, p. 25. IFN, p. 14. Truitt, p. 14.

Bacon, Lloyd F. (son of **Frank Bacon**) [actor/director] b. San Jose CA, 4 Dec 1889–15 Nov 1955 [65], Burbank CA). (b. 4 Dec 1889). m. Margaret Adele (d. 1989). "Lloyd Bacon Dies; Film Director, 65," *NYT*, 16 Nov 1955, 35:4. "Lloyd Bacon," *Variety*, 23 Nov 1955. "Margaret Adele Bacon," *Variety*, 1 Feb 1989 (d. 19 Jan 1989 [81], Encino CA). AMD, p. 26. BHD, p. 96; BHD2, p. 12. IFN, p. 14. LACD, "actor," r 2632 Newell. Truitt, p. 14. "Bacon's Son in National Film," *MPW*, 4 Sep 1920, 48. "Bacon Signed to Direct for Warner," *MPW*, 22 May 1926, 300. "Lloyd Bacon," *MPW*, 6 Aug 1927, 384. George Katchmer, "Forgotten Cowboys and Cowgirls—Part XV," *CI*, 192 (Jun 1991), 42–43.

Bacon, Mai [actress] (b. Ilkley, England, 3 Apr 1898–3 Jun 1981 [83]). BHD1, p. 25.

Bacon, Walter Scott (father of WB art director Arch Bacon) [actor/assistant director] (b. 13 May 1891–7 Nov 1973 [82], Los Angeles CA; heart attack). m. Sybil. (Universal.) "Walter Scott Bacon," *Variety*, 5 Dec 1973, p. 62. BHD, p. 97; BHD2, p. 12. IFN, p. 14.

Badaracco, Jacob A. [cinematographer] (b. Hoboken NJ, 20 Dec 1882–4 Jan 1969 [86], Burbank CA). BHD2, p. 12. FDY, p. 455.

Baddeley, Hermione [actress] (b. Broseley, Shropshire, England, 12 Nov 1906–19 Aug 1986 [79], Los Angeles CA). BHD1, p. 26 (b. 13 Nov 1908).

Badet, Regina [actress] (b. 1876-Nov 1949 [73?], Bordeaux, France). BHD, p. 97. Cal York, "Plays and Players," *Photoplay*, Jul 1917, 113 (William A. Brady was to use her in World films).

Badger, Clarence G. [scenarist/director] (b. San Francisco CA, 8 Jun 1880–17 Jun 1964 [84], Sydney, Australia). m. Lillian Schoene, 16 Jul 1914. (Triangle-Keystone; Universal; Goldwyn.) "Clarence Badger," *NYT*, 20 Jun 1964, 25:2. "Clarence Badger," *Variety*, 24 Jun 1964. AMD, p. 26. BHD2, p. 12 (d. New South Wales, Australia). IFN, p. 14. Lowrey, p. 8. WWS, p. 347. "Gossip of the Studios," *NYDM*, 12 Aug 1914, 27:1. "Badger Now Goldwyn Director," *MPW*, 16 Feb 1918, 987. "Goldwyn Proud of Its Quintet of Directors," *MPW*, 27 Jul 1918, 547. "Given Loving Cup," *MPW*, 7 Jul 1923, 53.

Badger, Clarence, Jr. [actor] (b. 8 Mar 1904–21 Apr 1992 [88], Los Angeles Co. CA). BHD1, p. 26.

Badgley, Frank C. [actor/scenarist] (b. Ottawa, Ontario, Canada, 1 Jan 1893–9 Sep 1955 [62], Ottawa, Canada). "Frank C. Badgley," *Variety*,

14 Sep 1955 (age 62; "He once was with D.W. Griffith's scenario department and also did some acting as a heavy in the silent screen days"). AMD, p. 26. BHD, p. 97; BHD2, p. 12 (b. 1895). IFN, p. 14. Truitt 1983 (b. 1895). "War Hero Makes Screen Debut," *MPW,* 25 Sep 1920, 515. "Badgley to Have Prominent Part in Dorothy Gish Film," *MPW,* 2 Oct 1920, 612.

Badgley, Gerald [actor] (b. Saginaw MI, 8 Aug 1885-Mar 1983 [97], District Heights MD?). BHD1, p. 604.

Badgley, Helen "The Thanhouser Kidlet" [child actress] (b. Saratoga Springs NY, 1 Dec 1908–25 Oct 1977 [68], Phoeniz AZ). m. R.J. Coar. AMD, p. 26. BHD, p. 96. IFN, p. 14. *Photoplay Arts Portfolio* [Thanhouser]. "Hail the 'Thanhouser Kidlet!,'" *MPW,* 24 Feb 1912, 693. "Helen Badgley," *MPW,* 11 Jan 1913, 145. "Mayor Mitchel and the Kidlet Co-Stars," *MPW,* 4 Dec 1915, 1857. "Helen Badgley Back in Pictures," *MPW,* 9 Jun 1917, 1638. Thomas Fulbright, "The Thanhouser Kidlet," *CFC,* 19 (Fall, 1967), 14 ff.

Baer, Arthur (Bugs) [actor] (b. Philadelphia PA, 9 Jan 1886–17 May 1969 [83], New York NY). BHD1, p. 26.

Baer, Fred E. [publicist]. No data found. AMD, p. 26. "Fred E. Baer," *MPW,* 26 Mar 1927, 310.

Baggot, King [stage/film actor/director] (b. St. Louis MO, 7 Nov 1879–11 Jul 1948 [68], Los Angeles CA). (IMP, 1909; Universal.) m. Ruth Constantine (b. 1889), 3 Dec 1912, Ft. Lee NJ (1 son, King Robert Baggot, b. 11 Jul 1914)—div. 1930; Dorothea. (Stage, 1901; first documented film, *The Awakening of Bess,* 27 Dec 1909; Imp; UA.) "King Baggot, 58, Early Film Star; Leading Man of Silent Era Dies; In Industry Since '09, He Also Was a Director," *NYT,* 13 Jul 1948, 27:4. "King Baggot," *Variety,* 14 Jul 1948. AMD, p. 26. BHD1, p. 26; BHD2, p. 12. FSS, p. 15. IFN, p. 15 (b. 7 Nov 1879). Katz, p. 68 (b. 1874). MSBB, p. 1021. Spehr, p. 114 (b. 1879). Truitt, p. 14 (b. 1874). WWS, p. 261. "King Baggot as Author-Actor," *MPW,* 24 Aug 1912, 776. "Screen Club Elects Officers," *MPW,* 12 Oct 1912, 131. "Baggot-Constantine," *MPW,* 14 Dec 1912, 1058 (re marriage to Constantine). King Baggot, "The Director's Work," *NYDM,* 10 Jun 1914, 28:1, 40:4. "An Heir to the Throne," *NYDM,* 15 Jul 1914, 25:1 (son b. 7 Jul 1914, NYC, 10 lbs.). "King Baggot, Jr., Comes to Town," *MPW,* 18 Jul 1914, 439. "Director Baggot," *MPW,* 5 Feb 1916, 791. Sue Roberts, "Where Have They Gone?," *Motion Picture Magazine,* Feb 1918, 134 (left films "definitely" about a year ago, but just signed to play in a serial written by William J. Flynn, chief of the United States Secret Service.). "King Baggot Returns to Stage," *MPW,* 15 Mar 1919, 1468. Hazel Simpson Naylor, "Cabbages and Kings," *MPC,* Oct 1921, 26, 85. "King Baggot to Direct Next Sam E. Rork Film," *MPW,* 29 Nov 1926, 284. Anthony Slide, *Silent Portraits; Stars of the Silent Screen in Historic Photographs* (Vestal NY: The Vestal Press, Ltd., 1989), p. 12, has b. 1874. Sally Dumaux, "King Baggot and the Mystery of 'The Lost Mirror,'" *CI,* 269 (Nov 1997), C10-C12 (King was his mother's maiden name). *Note:* the birthdate on Baggot's tombstone is incorrect.

Bagley, Frank Burnham [scenarist] (b. 1876–25 Aug 1917 [41?], East Orange NJ). BHD2, p. 12.

Bai, Gohar [actor] (b. 1910–28 Sep 1985 [75?], Bombay, India). BHD1, p. 26.

Bail, Benjamin [cinematographer]. No data found. AMD, p. 26. LACD, "cameraman," r 422 Central. "Benjamin Bail Promoted to Cameraman," *MPW,* 29 Nov 1919, 555.

Bailey, Buck (Orlo) [actor] (d. Clevelend OH, 18 Jun 1923). BHD, p. 97.

Bailey, Consuelo (b. 10 Oct 1899-Sep 1976 [76]). (the sole entry for Bailey, Consuelo, in the Social Security Death Index).

Bailey, Edwin D. [actor] (b. Oakland CA, 1873–22 Jul 1950 [77?], Santa Monica CA). BHD, p. 97. IFN, p. 15 ("Edwin B").

Bailey, Frankie, "The Girl with the Million Dollar Legs" [actress] (*née* Frankie Walters, b. New Orleans LA, 29 May 1859–8 Jul 1953 [94], Los Angeles CA). m. Frank Robinson. "Frankie Bailey," *Variety,* 15 Jul 1953. BHD, p. 97. NNAT. SD. Truitt, p. 14.

Bailey, Harry A. [actor] (b. 1880?–9 Aug 1954 [74], Los Angeles CA). BHD1, p. 27. IFN, p. 15.

Bailey, Mildred Ethelyn [actress] (b. Deep Water CT, 1899). m. L.S. Tobias. "Mildred Rinker," *Variety,* 19 Dec 1951, 63. (Metro.) MSBB, p. 1030.

Bailey, Oliver D. [actor/director/producer/writer] (b. OH, 1877?–12 Jul 1932 [55], Long Lake, Harrison ME). "Oliver D. Bailey," *Variety,* 19 Jul 1932. BHD, p. 97; BHD2, p. 12.

Bailey, Temple [writer]. No data found. AMD, p. 26. "Temple Bailey Signs Contract with F.B.O. for Five Years," *MPW,* 2 Apr 1927, 486.

Bailey, William H. [minstrel producer] (b. 1862?–16 Dec 1934 [72], New Lexington OH). "William H. Bailey," *Variety,* 1 Jan 1935. "William H. Bailey," *MPW,* 27 Dec 1913, 1549.

Bailey, William J. [actor]. No data found. LACD, "photoplayer," r 529 Wall.

Bailey, William Norton [actor/director] (*né* Gordon Reineck, b. Omaha NB, 26 Sep 1886–8 Nov 1962 [76], Los Angeles CA). (Began 1912; Cosmopolitan.) "William Bailey," *Variety,* 14 Nov 1962. AMD, p. 26. BHD1, p. 27; BHD2, p. 12. IFN, p. 15. 1921 Directory, p. 155. Truitt, p. 14. "William Norton 'Bill' Bailey," *MPW,* 27 Dec 1913, 1549. "William Bailey Closes with Essanay," *MPW,* 28 Feb 1914, 1094. "Bill Bailey on United Program," *MPW,* 1 May 1915, 731. "William Norton Bailey," *MPW,* 15 Jun 1918, 1585. Regina Cannon, "Can a Woman Marry Any Man She Wants? 'No!,' Says William Bailey," *MW,* 22 Sep 1923, 8.

Baily, George Donald [actor] (b. 1863?–11 Dec 1927 [64], Los Angeles CA; from poison "under mysterious circumstances"). "Mysterious Death," *Variety,* 14 Dec 1927. BHD, p. 97.

Bain, Agnes Fletcher [scenarist]. No data found. AMD, p. 27. "Agnes Bain Scenarizes Hope's 'Sophia,'" *MPW,* 9 Oct 1920, 801.

Bain, Fred [film editor] (d. 26 Jun 1965, near Del Mar CA; auto accident). "Fred Bain," *Variety,* 7 Jul 1965. BHD2, p. 12.

Bainbridge, Rolinda [actress]. (Edison; FP-L; Metro.) AMD, p. 27. "Rolinda Bainbridge Again with Brabin," *MPW,* 4 May 1918, 717.

Bainbridge, Sherman [actor/scenarist] (b. New York NY, 25 Feb 1880–14 Jan 1950 [69], Los Angeles CA). BHD1, p. 604; BHD2, p. 13.

Bainbridge, William H. [actor] (b. England, 21 Mar 1853–24 Oct 1931 [78]). BHD, p. 97. IFN, p. 15. George Katchmer, "Remembering the Great Silents," *CI,* 222 (Dec 1993), C16 (in films from at least 1917).

Baine, Beverly *see* **Bayne, Beverly**

Baines, Beulah [actress] (b. 1905–16 Aug 1930 [25?], Banning CA). "Beulah Baines," *Variety,* 27 Aug 1930. BHD, p. 97. IFN, p. 15. Truitt, p. 14.

Baird, Dorothea [actress] (b. Teddington, England, 20 May 1875–24 Sep 1933 [58], Broadstairs, Kent, England). BHD, p. 97.

Baird, Leah [stage/film actress/scenarist/producer] (b. Chicago IL, 20 Jun 1883–3 Oct 1971 [88], Los Angeles CA). m. Arthur F. Beck, 25 Nov 1914. (Morton Snow Stock Co., Troy NY; Arthur Byron Stock Co.; Vitagraph, 1911; Universal-Imp; Pathé; Artcraft; Associated Exhibitors; Arrow; WB; UA; film debut: *Wooing Winifred.*) "Leah Baird," *Variety,* 13 Oct 1971. AMD, p. 27. BHD1, p. 27. FDY, p. 417. FSS, p. 15. IFN, p. 15. Lowrey, p. 10. MH, p. 95. MSBB, p. 1030 (b. 1887). Slide, pp. 134–35. Truitt, p. 14. WWS, p. 265. "Miss Leah Baird," *MPW,* 30 Mar 1912, 1175 (with Vitagraph). E.M.L.. "Chats with the Players; Leah Baird, of the Vitagraph Company," *MPSM,* Sep 1912, 133–34 (film debut given as *Chumps*). "Miss Leah Baird with Imp English Company," *MPW,* 14 Jun 1913, 1143. "Leah Baird; Leading Woman with the Imp Company," *MPS,* 19 Dec 1913, 26. "Two Players Wed," *NYDM,* 2 Dec 1914, 24:1 (m. non-professional). "Leah Baird," *MPW,* 25 Mar 1916, 2013. "Leah Baird Goes to Universal City," *MPW,* 9 Sep 1916, 1670. "Leah Baird to Be Starred," *MPW,* 10 Nov 1917, 864. "Baird Special Has Big Appeal for Women," *MPW,* 24 Mar 1923, 461. "Star Turns Scenarist," *MPW,* 27 Nov 1926, 3. Billy H. Doyle, "Lost Players," *CI,* 193 (Jul 1991), 36. BHD, pp. 1–3.

Baird, Stewart [author/singer/stage/vaudeville/film actor] (b. Jamaica Plain [Boston] MA, 18 Nov 1880 [MVRB, Vol. 315, p. 220]–28 Oct 1947 [66], New York NY [Death Certificate Index No. 23196]). m. Ann Dews. (FP-L; Kalem; Metro.) "Stewart Baird," *Variety,* 5 Nov 1947. BHD, p. 97 (b. 1881). IFN, p. 15. MSBB, p. 1021. SD. Harvard College—Class of 1903, "Records of the Class," (Twenty-Fifth Anniversary Report), pp. 46–49. "Stewart Baird—Actor, Critic and Playwright; Star of 'The Beauties' Is a Young Artist of Ideas and Ideals," *NYDM,* 11 Mar 1914, 22:1.

Baker, C[harles] **Graham** [cartoonist/journalist/scenarist/dialogue writer/producer] (b. Evansville IN, 16 Jul 1887–15 May 1950 [62], Los Angeles CA). "C. Graham Baker," *Variety,* 24 May 1950. (Vitagraph.) AMD, p. 27. BHD2, p. 13. FDY, p. 417; p. 441 (dialogue writer on *The Singing Fool,* 1928). IFN, p. 15. "New Vitagraph Comedies," *NYDM,* 30 Oct 1915, 27:3 (introduced a new comedy character at Vitagraph called Itsky, the Inventor). "Graham Baker Many Sided," *MPW,* 15 Sep 1917, 1672. "C. Graham Baker Succeeds Chester as Vitagraph's Chief Scenario Editor," *MPW,* 3 Dec 1921, 557. "Baker Finishes Script," *MPW,* 2 Feb 1924, 377. "C. Graham Baker with Inspiration," *MPW,* 1 Aug 1925, 555.

Baker, Charles [scenic artist]. No data found. (Griffith.) LACD, "scenic artist."

Baker, Daniel E. [actor/minstrel] (b. New York NY, 1861?–6 Dec 1939 [78], Englewood NJ). m. Nellie Buckley Baker. "Daniel E. Baker," *Variety,* 13 Dec 1939. NNAT.

Baker, (Baby) Doris [child actress] (b. 1908).

Baker, Eddie [actor: Keystone Cop/assistant director/first Secretary/Treasurer of the Screen Actors Guild] (*né* Edward King, b. Davis WV, 17 Nov 1894–4 Feb 1968 [73], Los Angeles CA; emphysema). (Biograph; Selig; Clune; Keystone; Kalem; Univ.) "Eddie Baker," *Variety,* 14 Feb 1968. AMD, p. 27. BHD1, p. 28; BHD2, p. 13 (b. 1897). IFN, p. 15. LACD, "photoplayer," r 538 S. Fremont Ave. Truitt, p. 15. *MPN Studio Directory,* 21 Oct 1916. "Eddie Baker Poisoned by Oak," *MPW,* 13 Jun 1925, 785. "Eddie Baker Is Co-Directing," *MPW,* 21 Aug 1926, 489.

Baker, Elsie [actress] (b. Chicago IL, 13 Jul 1893–16 Aug 1971 [78]). BHD, p. 97. IFN, p. 15.

Baker, Frank [actor] (b. Melbourne, Australia, 11 Oct 1892–30 Dec 1980 [88], Woodland Hills CA). (b. 1894). "Frank Baker," *Variety,* 28 Jan 1981. BHD1, p. 28 (b. 1894). George Katchmer, "Forgotten Cowboys and Cowgirls—Part XVI," *CI,* 193 (Jul 1991), 34.

Baker, Friend F. [cinematographer]. No data found. LACD, "cameraman," h 1538 Morningside Ct.

Baker, George D[uane] [stock/vaudeville/film director/scenarist] (b. Champaign IL, 22 Apr 1868–2 Jun 1933 [65], Los Angeles CA). (Vitagraph; Metro; MGM.) "George D. Baker," *Variety,* 6 Jun 1933. AMD, p. 27. BHD2, p. 13. Lowrey, p. 12. MSBB, p. 1044. Slide, p. 135. "George Duane Baker," *MPW,* 14 Aug 1915, 1138. "George Duane Baker Joins Metro," *MPW,* 15 Jul 1916, 463. "Director Baker Appears as Actor," *MPW,* 21 Apr 1917, 465 (in *Sowers and Reapers*). "Baker Leaves Cosmopolitan; to Produce Independently," *MPW,* 25 Sep 1920, 504. "George Baker Believes in Writing Own Continuities," *MPW,* 27 Nov 1920, 495. "George Duane Baker Renews S-L Contract; Will Make New Gareth Hughes Series," *MPW,* 10 Sep 1921, 166.

Baker, Hettie Gray [film aide] (b. Hartford CT, 1881?–14 Nov 1957 [76], Porters Corners NY). "Miss Hettie Baker, ex-Fox Films Aide," *NYT,* 15 Nov 1957, 28:3. "Hettie Gray Baker," *Variety,* 20 Nov 1957. BHD2, p. 13 (Hettie Grey Baker). 1921 Directory, p. 283.

Baker, J. Frank (Home Run) [actor] (b. Trappe MD, 13 Mar 1886–28 Jun 1963 [77], Trappe MD). BHD, p. 97.

Baker, Josephine [film editor]. No data found. AMD, p. 27. "Dr. Baker to Edit 'Better Babies' for Fox News," *MPW,* 22 Nov 1919, 417.

Baker, Josephine [stage/film dancer/singer/actress] (b. St. Louis MO, 3 Jun 1903–12 Apr 1975 [71], Paris, France; after stroke on 10 Apr). m. Count Heno Abatino—div.; Jo Bouillon—div. (To France in 1925.) "Josephine Baker, 68, Led Parade of U.S. Artists to France," *Variety,* 16 Apr 1975, p. 95 (age 68). BHD1, p. 28 (b. 1906). IFN, p. 15 (b. 1901).

Baker, Lee [actor] (b. Ovid MI, 12 May 1875–24 Feb 1948 [72], Los Angeles CA). m. (1) Edith Evelyn (d. 1933); (2) Zoe Arthur. "Lee Baker," *Variety,* 3 Mar 1948. BHD1, p. 28 (b. 16 May). IFN, p. 16. SD. Truitt, p. 15.

Baker, Melville P[ratt] (son of **Robert M. Baker**) [scenarist] (b. Wellesley Hills MA, 24 Apr 1901–10 Apr 1958 [56], Nice, France; heart attack). m. (1) Gladys Franklin Gould, 1924; (2) Mary, 1931–45; (3) Dorothy Gilliam, 1946. "Melville Baker, a Screen Writer; Adapter of Molnar Plays for Stage Is Dead—Wrote Several Film Scripts," *NYT,* 12 Apr 1958, 19:3. "Melville Baker," *Variety,* 16 Apr 1958 ("From 1930 to 1940 he lived in Hollywood, writing numerous screenplays."). BHD2, p. 13. FDY, p. 417.

Baker, Nellie Bly [switchboard operator/actress]. No data found. Dorothy Donnell, "Getting in by the Back Door," *MPS,* 26 Aug 1924, 20–21, 31 (Chaplin wanted her for *A Woman of Paris,* and "so the little drab-looking, far from beautiful telephone girl took of her headpiece and put on some greasepaint and did the best she could.").

Baker, Robert M. (father of **Melville P. Baker**) [playwright/scenarist] (b. 1869?–6 May 1929 [60], New York NY [Death Certificate Index No. 13015); fall from 12th floor hotel window. "Robert M. Baker," *Variety,* 8 May 1929 (becoming blind, he "staggered to the window for relief and lost his balance"; age 55). BHD2, p. 13 (b. 1873).

Baker, Snowy (or **Rex**) [actor] (*né* Reg. L. Baker, b. Sydney, Australia, 8 Feb 1894–2 Dec 1953 [59]). (Carroll Brothers; Phil Goldstone Productions.) AMD, p. 27. BHD, p. 97. "Snowy Baker to Star," *MPW,* 1 Jan 1921, 44. Edgar M. Wyatt, "Snowy Baker Galloped Across the Silver Screen Down Under," *CI,* 199 (Jan 1992), 34.

Baker, Tarkington (cousin of **Booth Tarkington**) [producer/publicist/President of Visugraphic Pictures Corp.] (b. Vincennes IN, 6 Aug 1878–1 Jan 1924 [45], New York NY [Death Certificate Index No. 274]). m. Myla J. Closser. "Tarkington Baker," *Variety,* 10 Jan 1924. WWWA (d. 1 Jan 1924). AMD, p. 27. BHD2, p. 13. Walter K. Hill, "Publicity Man Gets a Valentine," *MPW,* 15 Mar 1919, 1457. "Tarkington Booth to Produce," *MPW,* 27 Mar 1920, 2107. "Booth Tarkington to Write Scenarios for His Cousin," *MPW,* 10 Apr 1920, 215. "Tarkington Baker Sees Growing Demand for Stories Written Solely for the Screen," *MPW,* 8 May 1920, 852.

Baker, William [actor] (b. 1888–21 Dec 1916 [28], New York NY). BHD, p. 97. IFN, p. 16.

Baker, Willis [actor] (b. Circleville OH, 1851–20 Apr 1932 [80?], Hackensack NJ). BHD, p. 97.

Bakewell, William [film/stage actor] (b. Los Angeles CA, 2 May 1908–15 Apr 1993 [84], Los Angeles CA; leukemia). *Hollywood Be Thy Name; Random Recollections of a Movie Veteran from Silents to Talkies to TV* (Metuchen NJ: Scarecrow Press, 1991). (Film debut: *He's a Prince* [aka *A Regular Fellow,* Paramount, 1925]; Fox; FBO.) m. Jennifer Holt. "Billy Bakewell," *Variety,* 26 Apr 1993, p. 84:1 (in 23 silents). BHD1, p. 28. FSS, p. 15. Katz, p. 71. Dorothy Manners, "The Native Son Also Rises; William Bakewell of Hollywood Will Always Remember Himself as the Young Man Who Knew Coolidge," *MPC,* Jan 1929, 55, 84 (met Coolidge in Baltimore while filming *Annapolis*). Ruth Biery, "If I Were President; William Bakewell, Now of Voting Age, Gives Some Hard Thought to Mr. Hoover's Problems," *MPC,* Mar 1930, 41, 80, 95. Michael G. Ankerich, "Reel Stars; Some Things Never Change," *CI,* 173 (Nov 1989), 8–9. Margarita Lorenz Shelps, "William Bakewell," *FIR,* Nov/Dec 1990, 514–23. Chapter 2, "William Bakewell," *BS,* pp. 15–30 (includes filmography).

Balboni, Silvano [director/cinematographer]. No data found. m. **June Mathis**, 6 Dec 1924, Mission of St. Cecilia, Riverside CA (d. 1927). AMD, p. 27. FDY, p. 455. "June Mathis Weds Balboni," *MPW,* 20 Dec 1924, 712. "Rowland Gives Balboni Long Term Contract," *MPW,* 30 Jan 1926, 444.

Baldridge, Bert [cinematographer]. No data found. FDY, p. 455.

Baldridge, Sidney A. [cinematographer] (b. Dallas TX, 28 Nov 1887–14 Jul 1979 [91], Los Angeles Co. CA). BHD2, p. 13.

Baldwin, Curley [actor] (b. 18 May 1898–Feb 1983 [84]). (Curlie Baldwin). George A. Katchmer, "Remembering the Great Silents," *CI,* 231 (Sep 1994), 49.

Baldwin, Earl W. [scenarist] (b. Newark NJ, 11 Jan 1901–9 Oct 1970 [69], Los Angeles CA). (WB.) "Earl Baldwin," *Variety,* 4 Nov 1970 (first script: *Man Crazy,* 1st National, 1928). BHD2, p. 13. FDY, p. 417.

Baldwin, George V. [actor] (b. England–d. 28 Feb 1923, Manila, Philippine Islands; suicide with poison). "George Baldwin," *Variety,* 8 Mar 1923. BHD. p. 98.

Baldwin, [Mr.] **Ivy** [trapeze artist/parachutist/wirewalker from ca. 1881] (b. Houston TX, 31 Jul 1866–8 Oct 1953 [87], Eldorado Springs CO). "Ivy Baldwin, Risked Death on High Wires," *NYT,* 10 Oct 1953, 17:4. "Ivy Baldwin," *Variety,* 14 Oct 1953. AMD, p. 28. "Baldwin on Wire in Storm," *MPW,* 27 Jun 1908, 541.

Baldwin, Jesse [actor]. No data found. LACD, "photoplayer," h 800 Sunset Blvd.

Baldwin, Kitty [actress] (b. 1853–27 Jul 1934 [81], Buffalo NY). (Life Photo Film Corp.) "Kitty Baldwin," *Variety,* 31 Jul 1934. BHD, p. 98. IFN, p. 16. Truitt, p. 15.

Baldwin, Ruth Ann [scenarist]. No data found. LACD. "scenario writer," r 3048 W. 12th.

Baldwin, Winnie [actress]. (Ince.) No data found.

Balfour, Augustus [actor] (b. Philadelphia PA, 1866). BHD, p. 98.

Balfour, Betty [actress/producer] (b. London, England, 27 Mar 1902–4 Nov 1978 [76], Weybridge, Surrey, England). BHD1, p. 29; BHD2, p. 13 (b. 1903–d. 1977). Garth Pedler, "Betty Balfour in 'The Vagabond Queen' (1929)," *CI,* 108 (Jun 1984), 29–30, 50.

Balfour, Charles [actor] (b. Rayville LA, 1888?–10 May 1912 [24], CA). (Bison.) "Bison Actor Killed," *MPW,* 1 Jun 1912, 810. BHD, p. 98 (d. 9 May).

Balfour, Eve [actress]. No data found. AMD, p. 28. "Eve Baldwin Now on Way to the United States," *MPW,* 20 Dec 1919, 944.

Balfour, Lorna [actress] (b. London, England, 26 Nov 1912–2 Mar 1932 [19], Hollywood CA; after appendicitis operation). "Lorna Balfour," *Variety,* 8 Mar 1932. BHD1, p. 29. IFN, p. 16.

Balfour, Michael [vaudeville/film/stage/TV actor/circus clown/ sculptor/painter] (b. Kent, England, 11 Feb 1918–24 Oct 1997 [79], England). m. Kathleen Stuart (2 sons, Shane and Perry); 2 adopted daughters (Nicola and Miranda Gooch) from his companion, Daphne Gooch. (Sennett, 1924; English film debut: *Just William's Luck,* 1947; last film: *The Holcroft Covenant,* 1985.) BHD, p. 604 (b. Detroit MI). "Michael Balfour; Character actor who ugly face brought him parts in more than 250 films," *The Daily Telegraph,* 27 Oct 1997, p. 23 (appeared in his first film with the Keystone Cops. "Although good-natured and gentle in character, Balfour had a strong streak of melancholy, which manifested itself in overfondness for drink. It was a failing to which his wife, the actress Kathleen Stuart, also succumbed."). *The Daily Telegraph*, 27 Oct 1997. "Michael Balfour," *The London Times*, 8 Nov 1997, p. 25 (in 1947 Laurence Oliver wanted an American actor for *Born Yesterday* and Balfour auditioned with a Detroit accent and a new past. Thus began the myth that he was born in the U.S. In 1953 a car accident left him with 98 stitches in his face. He remarked that there was no difference before and after. He was diagnosed with cancer of the sinus in 1992.). Nicola Gooch, *Stage*, 13 Nov 1997, p. 34 (when *Stage* printed his premature obituary in 1989, he said, "Death is something I can live without."). Ragan, *Who's Who in Hollywood*, p. 79.

Balfour, Mrs. Susan [actress]. (Edison; Lubin; Imp; Reliance.) AMD, p. 28. Hugh Hoffman, "In the Catskills with Reliance," *MPW*, 24 Aug 1912, 751.

Balfour, William [actor] (b. 14 Oct 1874–12 Apr 1964 [89], New York NY). BHD, p. 98.

Balistrieri, Virginia [actress] (b. Trapani, Italy, 15 Jan 1888). JS, p. 26 (in Italian silents from 1914).

Ball, Arthur [executive at Technicolor] (b. 1895?–27 Aug 1951 [56]; suicide by inhaling carbon monoxide from his car's exhaust). "Arthur Ball," *Variety*, 29 Aug 1951 ("He was first cameraman for Technicolor when it was formed 30 years ago.... The present three-color Technicolor camera reportedly was his original idea.").

Ball, Ernest [composer] (b. Cleveland OH, 1877–3 May 1927 [50?], Santa Ana CA). BHD2, p. 13.

Ball, Eustace Hale [writer/director/artist] (b. Gallipolis OH, 4 Nov 1881–20 Apr 1931 [49], Laguna Beach CA). m. Mary, 26 Oct 1917, NYC. Eustace Hale Ball, *Photoplay Scenarios; How to Write and Sell Them* (NY: Hearst's International Library Co., 1915). (Reliance; Solax, Majestic; Eclair.) BHD2, p. 13. *The National Cyclopædia of American Biography*, pp. 266–67 (Ball's stories were filmed and he wrote two books on the technique of motion pictures: *The Art of the Photo Play* and *Cinema Tales, How to Write and Sell Them*). "New Film Enterprise; Eustace Hale Ball Heads Company to Produce Historical Plays," *NYDM*, 2 Apr 1913, 27:1. "The Historical Film Company," *MPW*, 12 Apr 1913, 177.

Ball, Eva Lewis [actress] (b. 1881–6 May 1939 [58?], Los Angeles CA). BHD, p. 98.

Ballance, Harry G. [branch manager]. No data found. (FP-L.) LACD, "branch manager," h 1036 Beacon Ave.

Ballard, Gladys [actress] (aka Gladys Gentry). No data found. AMD, p. 28. "Gladys Gentry Is Stage Name of Gladys Ballard," *MPW*, 5 Mar 1921, 75.

Ballerino, Melvin [casting director]. No data found. AMD, p. 28. "Is New Metro Casting Director," *MPW*, 20 Sep 1919, 1811.

Ballin, Hugo [art director/director/producer] (b. New York NY, 7 Mar 1879–27 Nov 1956 [77], Santa Monica CA). m. **Mabel** Croft, CT (d. 1958). "Hugo Ballin, 76, Noted Muralist; West Coast Artist Dies—Had Produced 100 Movies, Including 'East Lynne,'" *NYT*, 28 Nov 1956, 35:6. "Hugo Ballin," *Variety*, 5 Dec 1956. AMD, p. 28. BHD, p. 98; BHD2, p. 14. IFN, p. 16. LACD, "art director," r Hotel Hollywood. 1921 Directory, p. 257. "Hugo Ballin Joins Goldwyn" *MPW*, 10 Mar 1917, 1584. "Hugo Ballin Writes a Script," *MPW*, 25 Jan 1919, 464. Kenneth MacGowan, "The New Studio Art," *MPC*, Mar 1919, 16–18, 65–66, 74. "Ballin and Lynch Added to F.P.-L's Production Staff," *MPW*, 25 Jul 1925, 443. Madeline Matzen, "The Disillusioned Director; Hugo Ballin has become discouraged in his effort to make beautiful pictures...," *MPC*, Aug 1926, 30, 74.

Ballin, Mabel [actress] (*née* Mabel Croft, b. Philadelphia PA, 1885–24 Jul 1958 [73], Santa Monica CA). m. **Hugo Ballin**, CT (d. 1956). (Vitagraph; Triangle; Goldwyn; Universal; World; Ballin Independent Co.; Encore.) "Mrs. Mabel Ballin," *NYT*, 28 Jul 1958, 23:5. "Mrs. Mabel Ballin," *Variety*, 30 Jul 1958. AMD, p. 28. BHD, p. 98. FFF, p. 210. IFN, p. 16 (age 71). LACD, r Hotel Hollywood. MH, p. 95. Truitt, p. 15. "Ballin to Direct in East," *MPW*, 9 Aug 1919, 807. "Mabel Ballin Is Star in Film 'East Lynne,'" *MPW*, 11 Dec 1920, 749. Adele Whitely Fletcher, "Romance, Unwrapped," *MPC*, Oct 1921, 20–21, 81. Billy Doyle, "Lost Players," *CI*, 201 (Mar 1992), 20, 22. BHD, pp. 3–5.

Ballmain, Rollo [actor] (b. Scotland, 1857–5 Dec 1920 [63?], Weston-Super-Mare, Somerset, England). BHD, p. 98.

Ballou, Marion [actress] (b. 1871?–25 Mar 1939 [68], Hollywood CA). m. Mr. Pouncefort. "Marion Ballou," *Variety*, 29 Mar 1939 (was to have been in *GWTW*). IFN, p. 16.

Balshofer, Fred J. [producer] (b. New York NY, 2 Nov 1877–21 Jun 1969 [91], Calabasas Park CA). m. Cecil Weston. With Arthur C. Miller, *One Reel a Week* (Berkeley CA: University of California Press, 1967). Wife's obituary: "Cecil Weston," *Variety*, 18 Aug 1976. AMD, p. 28. BHD2, p. 14. LACD, Balschofer, "motion picture director," h 7067 Hawthorn Ave. Spehr, p. 114 (1878–1968). "'Bison' Company Lost," *MPW*, 12 Nov 1910, 1113. "Lost Bison Company Turns Up," *MPW*, 26 Nov 1910, 1235. "Cup Presentation by the Bison Stock Co. to Mr. J. Fred Balshofer [sic], at Los Angeles," *MPW*, 23 Dec 1911, 987 (cites birthday of 2 Nov). "Quality Pictures Corporation," *MPW*, 10 Jul 1915, 240–41. "Success of Screened Novels," *MPW*, 21 Jul 1917, 398.

Bamattre, Martha [actress] (b. 19 Nov 1891–12 Jul 1970 [78], Glendale CA). "Martha Bamattre," *Variety*, 22 Jul 1970 (began 1927). BHD, p. 98. IFN, p. 16. Truitt, p. 15.

Bambrick, Gertrude [actress] (b. 1889). m. (1) **Marshall Neilan**, 21 Dec 1913, Hoboken NJ—div. Mar 1921 (d. 1958); (2) Jack Alicoate. (K&E; Biograph.) "Newsy Week on the Coast; Marshall Neilan and Gertrude Bambrick Wed...," *NYDM*, 27 May 1914, 27:1 (kept marriage a secret for six months). "Mrs. Neilan Gets Divorce; Blanche Sweet 'Other Woman'; Mother of Movie Star's Estranged Wife Blames the Husband for Causing Break," *Toledo Blade*, 18 Mar 1921.

Bamester, Katherine [actress] (d. 16 Oct 1919, Chicago IL; auto accident). "Katherine Bamester," *Variety*, 24 Oct 1919, p. 16. AS, p. 92. BHD1, p. 604.

Bancroft, George [stage/film actor] (b. Philadelphia PA, 30 Sep 1882–2 Oct 1956 [74], Santa Monica CA). m. prima donna Octavia Broske, 1913. (Began 1924; Lubin; Paramount.) "George Bancroft, A Movie Actor, 74; Former Broadway Performer Dies—Won Screen Fame for Portrayal of Villains," *NYT*, 4 Oct 1956, 33:4; "George Bancroft Rites Today," *NYT*, 5 Oct 1956, 25:4. "George Bancroft," *Variety*, 10 Oct 1956. AMD, p. 28. BHD1, p. 30. FSS, p. 16. GK, pp. 8–15. IFN, p. 16. Truitt, p. 15. Hal K. Wells, "A New Sort of Bad Man; He Became Famous Overnight for His *Slade*, Smiling Killer, of 'The Pony Express,'" *MPC*, Jan 1926, 35, 71. "George Bancroft," *MPW*, 23 Jul 1927, 239:2 ("Bancroft was on the stage in his early childhood and was one of the matinee idols of his day."). "Paramount Signs Bancroft," *MPW*, 27 Aug 1927, 582. George A. Katchmer, "George Bancroft; Portrayal of a Gangster," *CI*, 126 (Dec 1985), 16–17, 63.

Bandini, Augusto [actor] (b. Rome, Italy, 1 Apr 1889). JS, p. 26 (in Italian silents from 1916).

Bando, Tsumasaburo [actor] (b. Japan, 1898–7 Jul 1953 [55], Kyoto, Japan). "Tsumasaburo Bando," *Variety*, 15 Jul 1953. IFN, p. 16. Truitt, p. 16.

Bangs, Frank C. [cinematographer] (b. 1863–29 Aug 1928 [65?], Clearwater FL). BHD2, p. 14.

Banker, Bill [actor] (b. 1907–22 Sep 1985 [78?]). BHD, p. 98.

Bankhead, Tallulah [fillm/stage actress] (b. Huntsville AL, 31 Jan 1902–12 Dec 1968 [66], New York NY; pneumonia and emphysema). m. John Emery. *Tallulah; My Autobiography* (NY: Harper, 1952). Murray Schumach, "Tallulah Bankhead Dead at 65; Vibrant Stage and Screen Star," *NYT*, 13 Dec 1968, 1:3, 42:1; "Tallulah Bankhead Buried in Maryland," *NYT*, 15 Dec 1968, 86:1. Hobe Morrison, "Power Personality Marked Tallulah, Late Star Might Have (with Some Discipline) Been One of All-Time Great Actresses," *Variety*, 18 Dec 1968. AMD, p. 28. BHD1, p. 30. IFN, p. 16 (b. 31 Jan 1903). Truitt, p. 16 (b. 31 Jan). "Moore's Leading Woman Is an Alabama Bankhead," *MPW*, 7 Sep 1918, 1406. "Miss Bankhead in Films," *MPW*, 22 Oct 1927, 484.

Banks, Charles E. [scenarist]. No data found. FDY, p. 417.

Banks, Mrs. Estar [stage/film actress] (b. Boston MA). (Biograph; Edison; FP-L; Universal; Popular Plays and Players; Vitagraph; World.) MSBB, p. 1030.

Banks, Monty [actor/scenarist] (*né* Mario Bianchi, b. Nice, France, 18 Jul 1897–7 Jan 1950 [52], Arona, Italy). m. Gladys Frazin; Gracie Fields. "Monty Banks, 52, Screen Director; Comedy Star of Silent Movies, Husband of Gracie Fields, Dies on Trip in Italy," *NYT*, 9 Jan 1950, 25:3; "Gracie Fields Inherits $200,000," *NYT*, 25 Feb 1950, 10:3. "Monty Banks," *Variety*, 11 Jan 1950. AMD, p. 28. BHD1, p. 30; BHD2, p. 14 (b. Cesena, Italy). FDY, p. 417. IFN, p. 17. Katz, p. 75 (b. Cesena, Italy). LACD, "actor," r 1401 N. Western Ave. MH, p. 95. Truitt, p. 16 (b. Casene, Italy). WWS, p. 225. "Warner Describes Full-Dress Comedies Starring Actor Met Wholly by Chance," *MPW*, 19 Jun 1920, 1603. "Monty in His Tenth Year," *MPW*, 28 May 1927, 256. "Monty Banks, Screen Comedian, Sued by a Business Associate," *MPW*, 8 Oct 1927, 360.

Banks, Perry [actor] (b. Victoria, B.C., Canada, 24 Apr 1877–10 Oct 1934 [57], Santa Barbara CA). (American.) BHD, p. 98. IFN, p. 17.

Banky, Vilma, "The Hungarian Rhapsody" and "Europe's Mary Pickford" [film/stage actress] (*née* Banky Vilma Baulsey or Vilma Concit, b. Nagydorog [Budapest], Hungary, 9 Jan 1898–18 Mar 1991 [92], Los Angeles CA; cardiorespiratory arrest). m. **Rod La Rocque**, 26 Jun 1927, Beverly Hills CA (d. 1969). (Last film: *Der Rebell* [*The Rebel*], Austria, 1932.) Mryna Oliver, "Vilma Banky; Silent Screen Star Died in 1991," *LA Times*, 12 Dec 1992, A32 ("Embittered because none of her friends visited her during her later years of poor health, she specified that no notice of her death be made."). "Vilma Banky," *Variety*, 19 Oct 1992, p. 176. AMD, p. 28. BHD1, p. 30. FSS, p. 16. Katz, p. 75. Faith Service, "Miss Banky from Budapest," *MW*, V, 18 Apr 1925, 4–5. "Vilma Banky Cast," *MPW*, 11 Jul 1925, 201. Doris Curran, "Filmdom Snubs Her; Why Women Will Always Be Jealous of Vilma Banky," *MPC*, Dec 1925, 30–31, 82–83. "The Screen Boulevardier; Inside Gossip of the Picture Studios," *MPC*, Feb 1926, 61 (Julius Banky-Koncsics, Banky's younger brother, signed by Goldwyn). Lucille Arms, "American Men, Marriage and Hollywood," *MM*, Mar 1926, 41–42, 100–01. "Vilma Banky," *MPW*, 3 Apr 1926, 344. Doris Denbo, "The Hungarian Rhapsody Is Blue," *MPC*, Jan 1927, 58, 91. Mary Sharon, "Vilma Banky Speads of Love!; A Personal Chat About Marriage with a Beloved Blonde," *Paris and Hollywood Screen Secrets Magazine*, Aug 1927, 16–18 (her engagement to La Rocque was announced on 10 Apr 1927 at a tea given her by Mrs. Samuel Goldwyn. "This thing love is shust terrible...I say, not for the Vilma is this so terrible thing and then I find I do so much love my Rod and I too cannot get away."). Paul Paige, "Close-Ups and Fade-Outs," *Paris and Hollywood Screen Secrets Magazine*, Aug 1927, 42 (her parents were so proud of her screen success that her father, John Concit, was granted permission to change the family name to Banky. Vilma's brother and sister also adopted the name.). Grace Kingsley, "'No Foolin'; One marriage ceremony in Hollywood that was 'For Keeps'; The love match of Vilma Banky and Rod LaRoque," *Screenland*, Oct 1927, 22–23, 90, 92, 94–95. Dorothy Donnell, "Not That They Mind, But—Being the Imaginary Thoughts of Ronald Colman and Vilma Banky on Seeing Each Other Make Love to a New Co-Star," *MPC*, Feb 1929, 58. Dorothy Manners, "Lessons in Love; I—Vilma Banky Teaches the Art of Being Happy with Both a Husband and a Career," *MPC*, Aug 1929, 18–19, 87. DeWitt Bodeen, "LaRocque/Banky [letter]," *FIR*, Oct 1977, 511. "Letters," *FIR*, Feb 1978, 123 (b. 1902). Michael Ankerich, "Vilma Banky: Gone But Not Forgotten," *CI*, 208 (Oct 1992), 40, 58 (b. 1903). Michael Ankerich, "Pondering the Banky Story," *CI*, 212 (Feb 1993), 33, 56.

Bannerman, Margaret [actress] (b. Toronto, Canada, 15 Dec 1895–25 Apr 1976 [80], Englewood NJ). "Margaret Bannerman," *Variety*, 5 May 1976, p. 191. BHD1, p. 31 (b. 1896). IFN, p. 17.

Bannister, Harry [actor] (b. Holland MI, 29 Sep 1889–26 Feb 1961 [72], New York NY [Death Certificate Index No. 4574; age 77]). m. **Ann Harding** (d. 1981); (2) Leah M. Welt. "Harry Bannister," *Variety*, 1 Mar 1961. BHD1, p. 31 (b. 1888). IFN, p. 17. SD. Truitt, p. 16.

Bannon, Frank [publicist]. No data found. AMD, p. 28. "Bannon Resigns from Edison," *MPW*, 9 Oct 1915, 237.

Bannon, W. Earl [scenic artist]. No data found. LACD, "scenic artist," r 6046 Eleanor Ave.

Bantock, Leedham [director] (b. 1870–15 Oct 1928 [58?], Catalina Island CA). BHD2, p. 14.

Banton, Travis [costumer] (b. TX, 18 Aug 1874?–2 Feb 1958 [84], Los Angeles CA; throat cancer). (Paramount.) "Travis Banton Dies; Coast Dress Designer Worked on Gowns for 'Auntie Mame,'" *NYT*, 3 Feb 1958, 23:4. "Travis Banton," *Variety*, 5 Feb 1958. BHD2, p. 14 (b. 1894). Dorothy Donnell, "From Hollywood to You," *MPS*, 24 Feb 1925, 8–9 ("...a businesslike young man named Travis Banton imported for the purpose of creating ravishing gowns for this film [*The Dressmaker of Paris*]."). Helen Carlisle, "Have Your Costume Match Your Hair; Travis Banton, Noted Designer, Gives Style Suggestions to Movie Weekly Readers," *MW*, 14 Mar 1925, 4–5, 33. Pamela Pratt Forbes, "The Men Behind the Gowns," *Cinema Arts*, Jun 1937, 74–75 ("...Walter Wanger became interested in his work and sent the young designer to Hollywood to design the clothes for 'The Dressmaker of Paris.'"). David Chierichetti, "There Will Never Be Another Like Travis Banton," *Films of the Golden Age*, Winter 1997/1998, 64–73.

Banvard, Fifi [actress] (b. 1901–24 Jun 1962 [61], Sydney, Australia). BHD, p. 98. IFN, p. 17.

Bara, Lori (sister of **Theda Bara**) [actress/scenarist] (*née* Lori Goodman, b. Cincinnati OH, Oct 1897–4 Aug 1965 [67], Los Angeles CA). m. (2) **Ward Wing**, Nov 1927—div. AMD, p. 369 (under Wing, Ward). BHD, p. 98; BHD2, p. 14. "Wedding March," *MPW*, 3 Dec 1927, 23.

Bara, Theda, "The Vamp" (sister of **Lori Bara**) [film/stage actress] (*née* Theodosia Goodman, b. Cincinnati OH, 20 Jul ca. 1885–7 Apr 1955 [69?], Los Angeles CA; cancer; cremated). m. (1) stage manager Tom Bodkin, Pittsburgh PA, 1920; (2) **Charles J. Brabin**, 2 Jul 1921, Greenwich CT. (Stage debut: *The Devil*, 18 Aug 1908, NYC; Fox; film debut: *The Stain;* last film: *Madame Mystery*, Roach, 1926.) Ronald Genini, *Theda Bara; A Biography of the Silent Screen Vamp, with a Filmography* (Jefferson NC: McFarland & Co., Inc., 1996); Eve Golden, *Vamp: The Rise and Fall of Theda Bara* (Emprise Publishing, Inc., 1996). "Theda Bara Dies; Screen Star, 65; 'Siren' of Silent Films Was Top Box-Office Attraction During the Twenties; Denounced in Churches," *NYT*, 8 Apr 1955, 21:1; "Rites for Theda Bara Today," *NYT*, 9 Apr 1955, 13:4; "Theda Bara Rites Held on Coast," *NYT*, 10 Apr 1955, 88:1. "Theda Bara," *Variety*, 13 Apr 1955. AMD, p. 29. BHD, p. 98. FFF, p. 211 (b. 1890). IFN, p. 17 (b. 22 Jul 1892; age 62). MH, p. 95 (b. 1890). MSBB, p. 1030 (b. 1890). Truitt, p. 16. "Some 500,000 Spectators Follow Her Every Day; This Is the Amazing Public Assembled in One Year by Theda Bara, the Flaming Comet of the Cinema Firmament," *NYT*, 20 Feb 1916, 8:2. Roberta Courtlandt, "Theda, Misunderstood Vampire; Theda Bara's Greatest Wish Is to Play the Part of a Sweet, Essentially Feminine Woman," *MPC*, Oct 1916, 25–28. "Bara's First 'Vampire' Role in Months," *MPW*, 16 Dec 1916, 1664. "Theda Bara Goes to Broadway," *MPW*, 20 Oct 1917, 414. "Theda Makes 'Em All Baras; Actress's Family Join Her in Dropping Name of Goodman," *NYT Film Reviews*, 17 Nov 1917. "Bara Suffers from Prostration," *MPW*, 5 Oct 1918, 62. Frederick James Smith, "Keeping That Appointment with Theda Bara," *MPC*, Jan 1919, 16–17, 78. Grace Kingsley, "Flashes; Theda Bara Marries; World's Champ Vamp Weds Theatrical Manager," *LA Times*, 4 Feb 1920, II, p. 9 (m. Bodkin while rehearsing for the stage play *The Blue Flame.*). "Theda Bara's Life Romance," *MW*, 7 Jan 1922, 25–26. Lewis F. Levenson, "'I'm Going Back to Vamping,' Says Theda Bara," *MW*, 28 Oct 1922, 7, 23. "Theda Bara to Star in 'The Easiest Way,'" *MPW*, 25 Nov 1922, 334. David A. Balch, "Famous Movie Vamp Plays New Role—That of Editor; Theda Bara, world renowned creator of the screen vampire, visits the editorial office of *Movie Weekly* and is editor for a day," *MW*, 2 Jun 1923, 3. Gladys Hall, "The Real Theda Bara—at Home," *MW*, 2 Jun 1923, 9. Grace Kingsley, "Why I Don't Want Theda Bara to Return to the Screen—by Her Husband," *MW*, 2 Jun 1923, 13, 31. Vincent de Sola, "Theda Bara's Face Tells Why She Was a Vampire," *MW*, 2 Jun 1923, 18, 30. John W. Vandercook, "Theda Bara Returns to the Screen; Famous movie vamp signs contract to appear again in movies, after retirement of several years—First picture to be *Declassee*," *MW*, 21 Jun 1924, 7, 28. "Theda Bara," *MPW*, 22 May 1926, 326. "Movie History in the Making Ten Years Ago," *Paris and Hollywood Screen Secrets Magazine*, Aug 1927, 84 ("...shortly after her siren-venture, she dickered with Adolph Zukor for a two-year contract for $1,000,000, and got it."). Alan Brock, "The Unfilled Dream of a Star," *CFC*, Fall, 1970, 6–8, 11. DeWitt Bodeen, "Theda Bara; The Screen's First Publicity-Made Star Was a Woman of Sensibility," *FIR*, May 1968, 266–87. Robert Hamilton Ball, *Shakespeare on Silent Film; A Strange Eventful History* (George Allen and Unwin, Ltd., 1968), p. 365 (the Italian name Di Bara came from her maternal Swiss grandfather, Francis Bara de Coppet).

Barale, Matteo [cinematographer]). No data found. JS, p. 27 (in Italian silents from 1914).

Barbat, Percy D. [actor] (b. 23 May 1882–20 Jun 1965 [83], San Antonio TX). "Percy D. Barbat," *Variety*, 7 Jul 1965. BHD1, p. 31. IFN, p. 17.

Barbee, John [actor] (b. 30 Jul 1892–20 Apr 1981 [88], Los Angeles CA). BHD1, p. 31 (b. 1893).

Barbee, Richard [actor] (b. Lafayette IN, 30 Mar 1885–26 Oct 1965 [80], Santa Monica CA). BHD1, p. 31.

Barberis, Rene [director/scenarist] (b. Nice, French Riviera, 11 Mar 1886–11 Aug 1959 [73]). Garth Pedler, "Rolla Norman and Sandra Milowanoff in *Just Luck* (1928)," *CI*, 220 (Oct 1993), 44–47.

Barbier, George W. [stage/actor] (b. Philadelphia PA, 19 Nov 1864–19 Jul 1945 [80], Los Angeles CA). m. Caroline Thatcher. "George Barbier," *Variety*, 25 Jul 1945 (age 79). BHD1, p. 31. IFN, p. 17. Truitt, p. 16.

Barbour, Edwin Wilbur [stage/film actor/playwright/scenarist] (b. Philadelphia PA-d. 14 Sep 1914, Philadelphia PA). (Lubin.) "Edwin Wilbur Barbour," *Variety*, 18 Sep 1914. AMD, p. 29. BHD, p. 98; BHD2, p. 14. IFN, p. 17. "Barbour Takes Vacation," *MPW*, 15 Nov 1913, 743. "Edwin Wilbur Barbour," *MPW*, 12 Sep 1914, 1522. "Edwin Barbour Dead; Prominent Actor and Playwright Had Been with Lubin Past Three Years," *NYDM*, 23 Sep 1914, 25:1. "Obituary," *MPW*, 26 Sep 1914, 1790.

Barbour, Joyce [actress] (b. Birmingham, England, 22 Mar 1901–14 Mar 1977 [75]). BHD1, p. 31.

Barclay, Delancey [stage/film actor] (b. New York NY-d. 10 Dec 1917, New York NY). "Delancey Barclay," *Variety*, 14 Dec 1917, p. 21 (d. 11 Dec). BHD, p. 98.

Barclay, Don Van Tassel [actor] (b. Astoria

OR, 26 Dec 1892–16 Oct 1975 [82], Palm Springs CA). (Sennett.) "Don Barclay," *Variety,* 22 Oct 1975 (age 83). AMD, p. 29. BHD1, p. 31 (b. Ashland OR). IFN, p. 17. "Don Barclay," *MPW,* 2 Mar 1918, 1255. "Barclay to Co-Star with [Lige] Conley," *MPW,* 16 Sep 1922, 188.

Barclay, Eric [actor] (b. Sweden, 17 Nov 1894–1938 [44?]). BHD1, p. 31.

Barclay, L[eo] **W.** [press agent/publicist] (b. 1893?–19 Aug 1949 [56], Los Angeles CA; following operation). (Began work in Hollywood in 1922 for Sam Goldwyn.) "Leo W. Barclay," *Variety,* 175, 24 Aug 1949, 63:4. AMD, p. 29. L.W. Barclay, "Speaking of Service," *MPW,* 20 Jul 1918, 354–56.

Bard, Ben [actor] (*né* Ben Greenberg, b. Milwaukee WI, 26 Jan 1893–17 May 1974 [81], Los Angeles CA). m. Martha Pryor, 24 Dec 1915, New Orleans LA—div. Aug 1926, Los Angeles CA; **Ruth Roland** (d. 1937). (Fox.) AMD, p. 29. BHD1, p. 33 (b. 23 Jan). IFN, p. 17. "Ben Bard Seeks to Divorce Wife After Ten Years," 11 Aug 1926 (MoMA clipping). "Fox Signs Again," *MPW,* 16 Oct 1926, 3. Dorothy Manners, "Three Heroes Make a Heavy; Ben Bard, a Composite of Rudolpoh Valentino, Conway Tearle and Ricardo Cortez," *MPC,* Nov 1926, 56, 83 (on the stage with Jack Pearl).

Bard, Maria [stage/film actress] (*né* Migo Bard, b. Switzerland, 7 Jul 1901–6 Apr 1944 [42], Germany). m. **Werner Krauss** (d. 1959). "Maria Bard," *Variety,* 12 Apr 1944, p. 38 (age 43). BHD, p. 99 (known in silents as Migo Bard).

Bardine, Mabel [casting director/actress]. No data found. Charles E. Dexter, "Girls Who Come to Me to Get in the Movies," *MW,* 23 Jun 1923, 8, 29.

Bardo, Frank G. [actor]. No data found. LACD, "photoplayer," r 717 Wall.

Bardou, Camille Ernest Joseph [actor] (b. Fresnay-sur-Sarthe, France, 24 Aug 1872–1941 [69?], Orly, France). AS, p. 96. BHD1, p. 604 (b. 1870).

Baremore, R.W. "Barry" [publicist]. No data found. AMD, p. 29. "Barry Joins Metro," *MPW,* 4 Aug 1923, 360.

Baren, L. Lawrence [publicist]. No data found. AMD, p. 29. "New Ivan Publicity Man," *MPW,* 18 Nov 1916, 1014.

Baring, Mrs. Mathilde (mother of **Isabel Lamon**) [actress] (*née?,* b. New Orleans LA, 18 Sep 1879). BHD, p. 99. (Edison; Eclair.)

Barker, Adella (or Adelaide) [actress] (b. 1857?–29 Sep 1930 [73?], Amityville, LI NY). "Adella Barker," *Variety,* 1 Oct 1930. BHD, p. 99. IFN, p. 17.

Barker, Al [director]. No data found. (Garson Studios, Inc.) LACD, "director," r Hotel Hollywood.

Barker, Bradley [stock/vaudeville/legit stage/film actor/director/original screen voice of Leo, the Metro Lion] (b. Hempstead, LI NY, 1883–29 Sep 1951 [68], New York NY [Death Certificate Index No. 20057]). (Fox; FP-L; Kalem; Popular Players; World; Alco.) "Bradley Barker," *Variety,* 3 Oct 1951. AMD, p. 29. BHD, p. 99; BHD2, p. 14. IFN, p. 17. MSBB, p. 1021. Truitt, p. 16. "Bardley Barker with Kalem," *NYDM,* 6 Nov 1915, 24:2. "Bradley Barker with Kalem," *MPW,* 6 Nov 1915, 1150. "Bradley Barker Returns to Fox Forces," *MPW,* 26 Jan 1918, 503. "Bradley Barker Returns to Universal," *MPW,* 29 Jun 1918, 1829.

Barker, Corinne [actress] (b. 1893?–6 Aug 1928 [35], New York NY). m. **Hobart Henley**, Jul 1920 (d. 1928) (Goldwyn.) AMD, p. 29. BHD, p. 99. IFN, p. 17. "Hobart Henley Weds Suddenly Before Sailing for Europe," *MPW,* 7 Aug 1920, 706.

Barker, Eric L. [actor] (b. Thornton Heath, England, 20 Feb 1912–1 Jun 1990 [88], Faversham, England). BHD1, p. 32.

Barker, Florence [actress] (b. Los Angeles CA, 22 Nov 1891–15 Feb 1913 [21], Los Angeles CA; pneumonia). "Los Angeles, Feb. 27. Florence Barker, an actress, died in this city (her home) of pneumonia," *Variety,* 28 Feb 1913. AMD, p. 29. BHD, p. 99. IFN, p. 17. "New Powers Star; Florence Barker Joins the Producing Company of the Powers Picture Players as Leading Woman," *MPW,* 20 Jul 1912, 254.

Barker, Mary E. [stage/film actress] (b. 1848?–30 Jul 1913 [65], Ossining NY; accident in a one-horse surrey; nterred in Calvary Cemetery). "Drove in Front of a Train; Two Women Passengers Killed, But Driver Was Uninjured," *NYT,* 31 Jul 1913, 1:6 (age 60). "Mrs. Barker and Daughter [Gertrude M.] Killed," *NYDM,* 6 Aug 1913, 11:2. "Mary Barker, Actress," *NYDM,* 24 Sep 1913, p. 12:2 (she died before her film, *Tess of the D'Urbervilles,* with Mrs. Fiske, was released that year).

Barker, Reginald Charles [actor/director] (b. Bothwell, Scotland, 2 Apr 1886–23 Feb 1945 [59], Los Angeles CA). m. **Clara Williams**, 1920 (d. 1928); (2) Nona Claridge; (3) Kathleen McHugh. "Reginald Barker; Veteran Director of Silent Films Once Acted on the Stage," *NYT,* 24 Feb 1945, 11:3. "Reginald Charles Barker," *Variety,* 28 Feb 1945. AMD, p. 29. BHD, p. 99; BHD2, p. 14 (b. Winnipeg, Manitoba, Canada). FDY, p. 417. IFN, p. 17. Lowrey, p. 14. 1921 Directory, p. 257 (b. Winnipeg, Canada). SD. Truitt, p. 16. George Blaisdell, "New York Motion Picture Company," *MPW,* 10 Jul 1915, 233. "Director and Star Wed," *MPW,* 28 Feb 1920, 1480 (wed Clara Williams). "Barker Returns to M-G-M," *MPW,* 6 Feb 1926, 545.

Barks, Carl [cartoonist] (b. 1901?–26 Aug 2000 [99], so. OR; leukemia). "Carl Barks; Cartoonist raised Donald Duck," *PP-G,* 27 Aug 2000, E-5.

Barlatier, André [cameraman] (b. France, 1882?–7 Nov 1943 [61], Los Angeles CA). (Universal; Columbia.) "Andre Barlatier," *Variety,* 10 Nov 1943. AMD, p. 29. BHD2, p. 14. FDY, p. 455. "Andre Barlatier," *MPW,* 11 Dec 1926, 407.

Barleon, Amelia [actress] (b. Chicago IL, 1 Apr 1878–17 Jun 1969 [91], Jamaica NY). (Amelie Barleon). BHD1, p. 32.

Barlow, Reginald [actor] (b. Cambridge MA, 17 Jun 1866–6 Jul 1943 [77], Los Angeles CA). m. **Selma Rose** (d. 1933). "Reginald Barlow," *Variety,* 14 Jul 1943 (b. Springfield MA; age 76). BHD1, p. 32. IFN, p. 17. Truitt, p. 16.

Barlow, William [Barlow Brothers' Minstrels] (b. Paducah KY, 1852?–23 Jul 1937 [85], San Pedro CA). "William Barlow," *NYT,* 25 Jul 1937, II, 7:4. "William Barlow," *Variety,* 28 Jul 1937.

Barnabó, Guglielmo [actor) (b. Ancona, Italy, 11 May 1888–31 May 1954 [66], Ancona, Italy). JS, p. 29 (in Italian silents from 1926).

Barnard, Ivor [actor] (b. London, England, 13 Jun 1887–30 Jun 1953 [66]). BHD1, p. 32. IFN, p. 17.

Barnell, Nora Ely [actress/casting director] (b. 1882–10 Jul 1933 [51], Los Angeles CA). "Nora Ely Barnell," *Variety,* 18 Jul 1933. BHD, p. 99. IFN, p. 17. Truitt, p. 16.

Barnes, Frank [actor] (*né* Richard Allen, b. 1875?–1 Nov 1940 [65], Bronx NY [Death Certificate Index No. 10163]). "Frank Barnes," *Variety,* 13 Nov 1940. BHD, pp. 91, 99 (Richard Allen). IFN, p. 18. Truitt, p. 17.

Barnes, Freeman [actor] (b. New York NY). (Reliance; Pathé; Kalem; FP-L; Kleine.)

Barnes, George [actor] (b. 1890–18 Nov 1949 [59?], Los Angeles CA). BHD, p. 99.

Barnes, George E. [actor] (b. 1879–3 Mar 1926 [46?], Honolulu HI). BHD, p. 99.

Barnes, George S. [cinematographer] (b. CA, 16 Oct 1892–30 May 1953 [60], Los Angeles CA). m. 7 times: Joan Blondell, 1932–36. "George Barnes, Won Photography 'Oscar,'" *NYT,* 1 Jun 1953, 23:5. "George Barnes," *Variety,* 3 Jun 1953. BHD, p. 99; BHD2, p. 15. FDY, p. 455. IFN, p. 18.

Barnes, Hattie Delaro *see* **Delaro, Hattie**

Barnes, J[ohn] **H**[enry] [actor] (Watlington, Oxfordshire, England, 26 Feb 1850–10 Nov 1925 [75], London, England). BHD. p. 99.

Barnes, Justus D. [gunman in *The Great Train Robbery,* Edison, 1903] (b. Little Falls NY, 1861?–6 Feb 1946 [84], Weedsport NY). "Justus D. Barnes; Stage and Screen Actor, 84, Dies in Weedsport, N.Y.," *NYT,* 8 Feb 1946, 19:2. "Justus D. Barnes," *Variety,* 13 Feb 1946. BHD, p. 99. IFN, p. 18. Truitt, p. 17. Musser, p. 525, n. 59.

Barnes, Mac M. [actor] (d. 10 Jan 1923, Los Angeles CA). BHD, p. 99.

Barnes, Robert E. [production manager and assistant director of Desilu] (b. 1890?–23 Jun 1959 [69], Hollywood CA; heart attack). "Robert E. Barnes," *Variety,* 1 Jul 1959.

Barnes, T. Roy [actor] (b. Lincolnshire, England, 11 Aug 1879–30 Mar 1937 [57], Los Angeles CA). m. Bessie Crawford. "T. Roy Barnes," *Variety,* 31 Mar 1937. AMD, p. 29. BHD1, p. 33 (b. 1880). FSS, p. 17. IFN, p. 18 (b. 1880). MH, p. 95. Truitt, p. 17 (b. 1880). "Goldwyn Signs Popular Comedian," *MPW,* 7 Feb 1920, 922. "T. Roy Barnes," *MPW,* 12 Jul 1924, insert.

Barnes, V.L. [actor] (b. IN, 1870?–9 Aug 1949 [79], Los Angeles CA). "V.L. Barnes," *Variety,* 17 Aug 1949. BHD, p. 99. IFN, p. 18. Truitt, p. 17.

Barnet, Boris V. [director/actor] (b. Moscow, Russia, 16 Jun 1902–8 Jan 1965 [62], Riga, Latvia). BHD1, p. 33; BHD2, p. 15. IFN, p. 18.

Barnett, Carrie (mother of **Ann Doran**) [actress]. No data found.

Barnett, Chester A. [stage/film actor] (b. Piedmont MO, 29 Feb 1885–22 Sep 1947 [62], Jefferson City MO; pneumonia). (World-Equitable.) "Chester A. Barnett," *NYT,* 24 Sep 1947, 23:3. "Chester A. Barnett," *Variety,* 1 Oct 1947. AMD, p. 30. BHD, p. 99. IFN, p. 18. Spehr, p. 114. Truitt, p. 17. "'Crystal' Gets Another Well-Known Actor," *MPW,* 26 Oct 1912, 352. Peter Wade, "The Waking Dreamer; Poet, Priest and Musician, with a Knotty Biceps, Make Up a Remarkable Man," *MPC,* Oct 1916, 56–57, 70.

Barnett, Vincent [actor] (b. Pittsburgh PA, 4 Jul 1902–10 Aug 1977 [75], Encino CA; heart ailment). "Vince Barnett," *Variety,* 17 Aug 1977.

Barney, Jay [actor] (*né* John B. Kleinschmidt, b. Chicago IL, 14 Mar 1913–19 May 1985 [72], PA). (John Kleinschmidt). "Jay Barney, Actor, Dies at 72; Appeared Often on Broadway," *NYT,* 14 Jun 1985, D18:6. "Jay Barney," *Variety,* 29 May 1985.

Barni, Ruggero [actor]). No data found. JS, pp. 29–30 (in Italian silents from 1914).

Barnstead, B.M. [scenarist]. No data found. LACD, "writer," r 1307 S. Flower.

Baron, Louis [actor] (*né* Louis Bouchene, b. Alencon, France, 20 Sep 1837–1 Mar 1920 [82], Asnieres-sur-Seine, France). AS, p. 98.

Barr, Arturo [cinematographer]). No data found. JSj, p. 30 (in Italian silents from 1919).

Barr, Clarence [actor] (b. Omaha NB, 8 Jun 1876-Jun 1968 [92?]). (Klaw & Erlanger.) BHD, p. 99.

Barr, Natli [actress] (*née* Nathalie Barrache, b. Russia). AMD, p. 30. "Natli Barr to Go West for Picture," *MPW,* 8 Jan 1927, 126. Renee Van Dyke, "Paragraphs Pertaining to Players and Pictures," *Cinema Arts,* V (Jan 1927), 49 ("...She is well born, highly cultured and has family connections with some of the most famous members of the Old Russian nobility, a sister having married a prince..."). "From Foreign Lands," *Picture-Play,* April 1927, 30:1 (in French films).

Barrache, Natalie *see* **Barr, Natli**

Barrat, Robert H[arriot] [actor] (b. New York NY, 10 Jul 1889–7 Jan 1970 [80], Los Angeles CA). m. Mary Dean. BHD1, p. 33 (b. 1891). IFN, p. 18. SD. Truitt, p. 17 (age 78).

Barrell, Dona [scenarist] (b. 1891?–5 Apr 1941 [50], Los Angeles CA). "Dona Barrell," *Variety,* 16 Apr 1941. AMD, p. 30. BHD2, p. 15. FDY, p. 417. "Miss Barrell Re-signs," *MPW,* 3 Jul 1926, 42.

Barrett, Charles C. [actor] (b. Baltimore MD, 1871–11 Feb 1929 [57?], Baltimore MD). BHD, p. 99.

Barrett, Dorothy [actress]. No data found. (Lubin.) "Additions to Lubin Western," *NYDM,* 26 May 1915, 22:3 (she and C.C. Miller were signed by Capt. Wilbert Melville at Lubin).

Barrett, Ivy Rice [actress: Sennett Bathing Beauty from 1915] (aka Ivy Crosthwaite, b. San Diego CA, 1898?–8 Nov 1962 [64], Los Angeles CA). m. Adolph Linkof, 10 Jul 1915 (d. Dec 1970). (Keystone.) "Ivy R. Barrett," *Variety,* 14 Nov 1962. AS, p. 99; p. 270 (Ivy Crosthwaite). BHD, p. 140. IFN, p. 68. Truitt 1983. J. Van Cartmell, "Along the Pacific Coast," *NYDM,* 21 Jul 1915, 22:1 ("Ivy Crothwaite who has the reputation as a high diver and swimmer and is a member of the Keystone Company was married July 10 to Adolph Linkof...").

Barrett, Minnette "Minnie" [actress] (b. Gainesville GA, 25 Mar 1880–20 Jun 1964 [84], Whitestone [Queens] NY [Death Certificate Index No. 8120]). "Minnette Barrett," *Variety,* 24 Jun 1964. AMD, p. 30. AS, p. 99. BHD, p. 99 (b. 1884). IFN, p. 18. "Minnette Barrett, a Lasky Star," *MPW,* 30 Oct 1915, 808.

Barrett, Patrick J. [actor] (b. Holden MO, 1889?–25 Mar 1959 [70]). AS, p. 99 (b. 1887). IFN, p. 18.

Barrie, Sir James M. [playwright/actor/scenarist] (b. Kirriemuir, Scotland, 9 May 1860–19 Jun 1937 [77], London, England; pneumonia). AMD, p. 30. AS, p. 100. BHD, p. 99; BHD2j, p. 15. "Barrie Visits Studio; Distinguished Playwright an Interested Guest at Famous Players' Forces," *NYDM,* 21 Oct 1914, 28:1 (he termed his experience "a peep into fairyland."). "Barrie to Write Story for Famous," *MPW,* 18 Jul 1925, 359.

Barrie, Nigel [dancer/comic opera/stage/film actor] (*né* Roynon Cholmondeley Nigel-Jones, b. Calcutta, India, 5 Feb 1889–8 Oct 1971 [82], England). m. (1) Helen Lee, 1919–25; Gertrude Poklington, 1925. (Wharton Bros.; FP-L; CKY; Cosmopolitan; Robertson-Cole; B.B. Features; Hampton Equity; PDC; Chadwick; FBO.) AMD, p. 30. AS, p. 100 (d. LA CA). BHD1, p. 34. "Madame Critic," *NYDM,* 15 Jul 1914, 4:1 (dancing with Joan Sawyer. "Miss Sawyer has solved the problem of a not-so-handsome dancing partner, and her dances have taken on a new interest because the women all rave over Barrie."). "Nigel Barrie: Master of the Modern Dance; He Has Played Everything from Classic and Dramatic Roles to Foremost Parts in Musical Comedy," *NYDM,* 12 Aug 1914, 18:2 (25 years old; arrived in America from England on 4 Jul 1914). "Nigel Barrie Supporting Miss Clark," *MPW,* 18 Aug 1917, 1078. "Barrie Began Career in Comic Opera," *MPW,* 29 Mar 1919, 1828. Billy H. Doyle, "Lost Players," *CI,* 145 (Jul 1987), 48.

Barringer, A.B. "Barry" [actor/scenarist] (b. Mobile AL, 25 Jun 1888–21 May 1938 [49], Los Angeles CA; heart attack). (Monogram.) "Barry Barringer," *NYT,* 23 May 1938, 17:3. "Barry Barringer," *Variety,* 25 May 1938 ("He was an actor in the silent days...later turning to scripting."). AS, p. 100 (b. 22 Jun). BHD, p. 99; BHD2, p. 15. FDY, p. 417. IFN, p. 18. Truitt 1983.

Barringer, Ned [actor/scenarist] (*né* Spencer Edward Barringer, b. 1888–13 Feb 1976 [87], Leavenworth KS; cancer). "Ned Barringer," *Variety,* 18 Feb 1976, p. 126. AS, p. 100. BHD, p. 99; BHD2, p. 15.

Barrington, Herbert [actor] (*né* Herbert Barrington Hollingsworth, b. England, 1872–26 Oct 1933 [61], Tarrytown NY). m. Julia von Schultes. (Pilot Films.) "Herbert Barrington," *Variety,* 31 Oct 1933. AS, p. 100. BHD, p. 99. IFN, p. 18. SD. Truitt, p. 18.

Barrington, Rutland [actor] (*né* George Rutland Barrington-Fleet, b. Penge, England, 15 Jan 1853–1 Jun 1922 [69], London, England). "George Rutland Barrington-Fleet," *Variety,* 9 Jun 1922, p. 7. BHD, p. 99.

Barrington, Sidney [actor] (b. 1869?–11 Jan 1913 (43], New York NY; found dead). m. Minnie Belle (d. 1911). (Reliance; FP-L.) "Find Actor a Suicide; Sidney Barrington Will Be Buried by the Actors' Fund," *NYT,* 12 Jan 1913, II, 2:7 ("The gas in the room was turned on full. In a letter, which was marked 'To be opened in case of accident,' the actor wrote: 'I buried my wife, Minnie Belle, one year ago February in San Francisco. We had been in the show business for fourteen years and were well known as Mr. and Mrs. Sidney Barrington.'"). "Actor Found Dead; Sidney Barrington, Slugged by Thugs During Holidays, Succumbs," *NYDM,* 22 Jan 1913, 12 ("A letter found stating his identity and saying he was despondent and without funds, gave rise to the theory of suicide.").

Barriscale, Bessie [stage/film actress] (*née* Elizabeth Barry Scale, b. Hoboken NJ, 30 Sep 1884–30 Jun 1965 [81], Kentfield CA). (Ince; Paralta.) m. **Howard C. Hickman** (d. 1949). "Bessie Barriscale," *Variety,* 14 Jul 1965. AMD, p. 30. AS, p. 100. BHD1, p. 34 (b. NY NY, 8 Dec). FSS, p. 17. IFN, p. 18. LACD, "actor," r 673 S. Oxford Ave. Lowrey, p. 16. MSBB, p. 1032. Truitt, p. 18. WWS, p. 129 (b. NY NY). "Miss Bessie Barriscale in Belasco Play," *MPW,* 8 Aug 1914, 847. "Briefs of Biography; From Stardom to Picture Stock," *NYDM,* 29 Sep 1915, 36:3. "Bessie Barriscale," *MPW,* 17 Mar 1917, 1778. "Manager Frothingham Pays Bessie Barriscale Tribute," *MPW,* 6 Dec 1919, 663.

Barroero, Olimpia [actress]). No data found. JS, p. 30 (in Italian silents from 1918).

Barron, Frederick C. [actor] (b. Melbourne, Australia, 1888?–9 Oct 1955 [67], Central Islip, LI NY). "Frederick C. Barron," *Variety,* 12 Oct 1955 (began 1898). BHD, p. 100. IFN, p. 18. Truitt, p. 18.

Barrows, Henry A. [actor] (b. Saco ME, 29 Apr 1875–25 Mar 1945 [69], Los Angeles CA). (Vitagraph.) BHD1, p. 34. IFN, p. 18. George Katchmer, "Remembering the Great Silents," *CI,* 234 (Dec 1994), 42–43.

Barrows, James O. [actor] (b. Copperopolis CA, 29 Mar 1855–7 Dec 1925 [70], Los Angeles CA; heart attack). (Universal.) "James O. Barrows," *Variety,* 16 Dec 1925 (age 72). AS, p. 100 (b. SF CA). BHD, p. 100. IFN, p. 18. Truitt, p. 18 (b. 1853). George Katchmer, "Remembering the Great Silents," *CI,* 234 (Dec 1994), 43.

Barrows, Nicholas T. [scenarist]. No data found. FDY, p. 417.

Barrows, Willard [treasurer]. No data found. (Brentwood Film Corp.) LACD, "treasurer," h 1942 Holly Drive.

Barry, Arthur [actor] (*né* Alfred Booty, b. England, 1868?–21 Dec 1938 [70], Flushing NY; pneumonia). m. Grace C. "Arthur Barry," *Variety,* 28 Dec 1938. AS, p. 100.

Barry, Eddie [actor] (*né* Edward Miles, b. Philadelphia PA, Oct 1886–22 Jan 1967 [80], Newquay, England). (Christie.) "Edward Barrie," *Variety,* 8 Feb 1967. AMD, p. 30. BHD, p. 100. "Film Men Saved; Ed. Barry and Edgar Hounsell [a London film man] Cable Screeners of Escape from 'Lusitania,'" *NYDM,* 12 May 1915, 21:1. "Christie Star Is Some Astronomer," *MPW,* 5 Jul 1919, 48. In *Her Bridal Night-Mare* (Christie, 1920). Film ad, *Save Me Sadie* (Christie), *LA Times,* 22 Feb 1920, III, p. 16.

Barry, Eleanor [actress]. (Lubin.) No data found.

Barry, George [scenarist] (b. 1873–Nov 1930 [57?], Los Angeles CA). "George Barry," *Variety,* 10 Dec 1930, 68. BHD2, p. 15.

Barry, Jack [actor] (b. Meriden CT, 26 Apr 1887–23 Apr 1961 [73], Shrewsbury MA). BHD, p. 100.

Barry, Joan [actress] (b. London, England, 5 Nov 1901–10 Apr 1989 [87], Marbella, Spain). AS, p. 101. BHD1, p. 34.

Barry, Joseph [assistant director] (b. CA, 18 Feb 1924–9 Jul 1974 [50]). AS, p. 101. IFN, p. 19.

Barry, Margaret [actress]. No data found. AMD, p. 30. "Blackton Signs Mme. Margaret Barry," *MPW,* 17 May 1919, 1038.

Barry, Richard [writer]. No data found. AMD, p. 30. "The Author Winds," *MPW,* 27 May 1916, 1493. "Mutual Settles with Barry," *MPW,* 4 Nov 1916, 679.

Barry, Robert [actor] (b. 1901?–21 Mar 1931 [30], Santa Monica CA; from injuries sustained in an auto accident). "Robert Barry," *Variety,* 25 Mar 1931. AS, p. 101. IFN, p. 19.

Barry, Tom [actor/scenarist] (b. Kansas City MO, 31 Jul 1884–7 Nov 1931 [47], Los Angeles CA). "Tom Barry," *Variety,* 10 Nov 1931, 63. BHD2, p. 16.

Barry, Viola [stage/film actress] (aka Peggy Pearce, b. Evanston IL, 4 Jun 1894–2 Apr 1964 [69], Los Angeles CA). m. **Jack Conway** (d. 1952); (2) **F. McGrew Willis** (d. 1957). (Griffith; Keystone.) "Viola Barry," *Variety,* 15 Apr 1964. BHD, p. 100; 272 (Peggy Pearce, b. Long Beach CA-26 Feb 1975, Burbank CA). IFN, p. 19. SD. Truitt, p. 18.

Barry, William [publicist]. No data found. (Nicholas Power Co.) *See* Beecroft, Chester, for citation.

Barry, Wesley E. [stage/film actor] (b. Los Angeles CA, 10 Aug 1907–11 Apr 1994 [86], Fresno CA). m. Julia A. Wood, 1926, Newark NJ. (Began ca. 1918.) AMD, p. 30. AS, p. 101 (d. LA CA). BHD1, p. 34; BHD2, p. 16 (b. 1906). FFF, p. 59. FSS, p. 18. MH, p. 95. WWS, p. 65. *The Los Angeles Times,* 14 Apr 1994. "Neilan Signs Wesley Barry," *MPW,* 5 Jul 1919, 54. "Neilan to Star Wesley Barry in an Original Boy Story," *MPW,* 1 May 1920, 680. Dorothy Donnell, "From Hollywood to You," *MPS,* 28 Jul 1925, 15–16, 28 (his mother sued Russell Productions, a Poverty Row concern, for $1,000 for back pay due her son, now on a vaudeville tour). "Marriage," *MPW,* 26 Jun 1926, 4. June Lee, "Dan Cupid's Bulletin Board," *Paris and Hollywood,* Oct 1926, 86–87 (married Wood. "We hear that Barry is trying to enter the United States Naval Academy, and, if he is successful, will desert the films."). Billy Doyle, "Lost Players," *CI,* 234 (Dec 1994), 26, 32.

Barrye, Emily [actress/scenarist] (b. IL, 24 Jan 1895–15 Dec 1957 [62], Los Angeles CA). (Universal.) "Emily Barrye," *Variety,* 18 Dec 1957. AS, p. 101. BHD1, p. 34; BHD2, p. 16. IFN, p. 19. Truitt, p. 18. George Katchmer, "Remembering the Great Silents," *CI,* 222 (Dec 1993), C16.

Barrymore, Ethel (daughter of Maurice Barrymore and Georgiana Drew; sister of **Lionel** and **John Barrymore**) [stage/film actress] (*née* Ethel Mae Blythe, b. Philadelphia PA, 15 Aug 1879–18 Jun 1959 [79], Beverly Hills CA). m. Russell Griswold Colt. (Metro.) *Memories; An Autobiography* (NY: Harper, 1955); Margot Peters, *The House of Barrymore* (New York: Alfred A. Knopf, 1990). "Ethel Barrymore Is Dead at 79; One of Stage's 'Royal Family'; Famed Actress Began Career at 14, Captivating Audiences with Voice and Manner," *NYT,* 19 Jun 1959, 1:5, 25:2. "Ethel Barrymore, '1st Lady of the American Theatre,' Passes at 79," *Variety,* 24 Jun 1959. AMD, p. 30. BHD1, p. 34. FSS, p. 18. GSS, pp. 23–26. IFN, p. 19. MSBB, p. 1030. SD. Spehr, p. 114. Truitt, p. 18. "Denies Miss Barrymore Is Ill," *NYT,* 6 Feb 1905, 7;1 (supposed to be "on the verge of physical collapse"; "She is playing on the road in 'Sunday,' and never missed a performance, according to Mr. [Charles] Frohman [her manager].") "The Musical Side of Ethel Barrymore; Popular Young Actress Has Taken Up the Violin—Never Travels Without Her Nebraska 'Strad'—How Near She Came to Being a Concert Pianiste," *NYT,* 19 Feb 1905, Sec. III, 7:1 (with 3 drawings of her). "News Kept from Daughter; Ethel Barrymore Plays While Her Father Lies Dead," *NYT,* 26 Mar 1905, 9:5 (25 Mar, Philadelphia PA, Garrick Theatre. "Miss Barrymore's manager, Horace McVickar, had received a message for the young actress, but he decided to keep it from her until the matinée performance was over, in accordance with a generally accepted rule of the stage never to carry a message to a member of the company, particularly a leading member, while a play is on. The message, besides, contained instructions from the Frohman offices not to inform Miss Barrymore until the play had ended.... The night performance was canceled, of course."). "Frohman Names More Stars for Pictures," *MPW,* XV, 18 Jan 1913, 275. "$10,000 to Pose," *Variety,* 23 Jan 1914, 23:3 (to be in *Captain Jinks,* All Star Film Co.). "Drew and Barrymore; Ethel and Uncle John Brought Together for May Revival of 'Scrap of Paper,'" *NYDM,* 1 Apr 1914, 13 (Barrymore painting on cover). "Ethel Barrymore for All-Star," *MPW,* 4 Apr 1914, 79. "Ethel Barrymore with Metro," *MPW,* 15 May 1915, 1056. "From Screen to Stage," *MPW,* 8 Dec 1917, 1522. "Actors Name Ethel Barrymore for A.E.A. Vice-Presidency," *MPW,* 15 May 1920, 970.

Barrymore, John, "The Great Profile" (son of Maurice Barrymore; brother of **Lionel** and **Ethel Barrymore**) [stage/film actor] (*né* John Sidney Blythe, b. Philadelphia PA, 14 Feb 1882–29 May 1942 [60], Los Angeles CA). m. (1) Katherine Corri Harris (b. ca. 1891), 1 Sep 1910 (d. 1927); (2) Michael Strange (*née* Blanche Oelrichs, 15 Aug 1920, NYC [d. 5 Nov 1950]; (3) **Dolores Costello**, 24 Nov 1928—div. 24 Aug 1934 (d. 1979); (4) Elaine J[acobs] Barrie. *Confessions of an Actor* (Indianapolis IN: Bobbs-Merrill Co., 1926). Diana Barrymore [daughter] and Gerold Frank, *Too Much, Too Soon* (NY: Henry Holt & Co., 1957). Martin F. Norden, *John Barrymore; A Bio-Bibliography* (Westport CT: Greenwood Press, 1995). (Film debut: *An American Citizen,* FP-L, 1914.) "John Barrymore Dies in Hollywood; Actor, 60, in Stage and Screen Career, Kept the Tradition of Famous Theatre Family," *NYT,* 30 May 1942, 1:3; "Barrymore's Death Ends Brilliant Stage Career," 6:2. "Barrymore Reburied in Philly Family Plot," *NYT,* 18 Dec 1980. "John Barrymore's Many Friends Compel Larger Turnout at Services," *Variety,* 3 Jun 1942. "Maurice Barrymore Dies in Sanitarium; Noted Actor Had Been in Long Island Home Four Years; Had a Brilliant Career; Came Here from England Thirty Years Ago—Was Associated with Many of the Best Actors," *NYT,* 26 Mar 1905, 9:5 ([actor/playwright] *né* Herbert Blythe, b. India, 1846?–25 Mar 1905 [58], Long Island Home, Amityville NY. Married Georgiana Drew [daughter of Mrs. John Drew], Philadelphia PA, 31 Dec 1876 [d. 1895 or before]. Came to U.S.A. in 1875. A boxer, he won the Queensberry Cup in England in 1872. Went insane on 27 Mar 1901 "at a Harlem Theatre when he suddenly dropped his lines and began to rave. The following day he became violent and was taken to Bellevue insane ward by his son John."). "Barrymore's Body Here; Funeral to Be Private—Burial Will Take Place in Philadelphia To-Day," *NYT,* 27 Mar 1905, 9:2 (26 Mar. Body brought from Amityville NY to the Stephen Merritt Burial Co. at 19th Street and 8th Avenue. "Frederick Gebhard drove down from New York in an automobile yesterday and brought flowers with him to place on the actor's body.") "Funeral for Barrymore [29 Mar]; Dr. [George C.] Houghton Officiates at Private Ceremony—Buried at Philadelphia," *NYT,* 30 Mar 1905, 9:6 (Rev. Houghton, of the Little Church Around the Corner, read the service of the Episcopal Church. The few present included Ethel Barrymore, John Drew, Benjamin J. Fagin, and one or two close friends of the family. The body was interred in the Drew plot at Glenwood Cemetery beside Mrs. Barrymore.). AMD, p. 31. BHD1, p. 34. FFF, p. 237 (b. 15 Feb). FSFM, p. 26 (b. 15 Feb). FSS, p. 19. GSS, pp. 26–28 (b. 15 Feb). IFN, p. 19. MH, p. 95 (b. 15 Feb). MSBB, p. 1021. Truitt, p. 18. WWS, p. 28. "John Barrymore Stars in Double Role," *MPW,* 15 Jan 1916, 447. "Al Woods Extols John Barrymore," *MPW,* 16 Mar 1918, 1530. "John Barrymore Added to Warner Staff of Distinguished Stars for 1923 Films," *MPW,* 3 Mar 1923, 73. "John Speaks for Himself," *MPC,* Aug 1925, 59. Catharine Brody, "The Youngest of the Barrymores," *MW,* 26 Sep 1925, 13, 38 (filming *The Sea Beast*). Helen Carlisle, "A Bird of Strange Plumage," *MM,* Nov 1925, 32–33, 72–74. Hugh Miller [stage actor], "The Flame and the Lamp [Jannings and Barrymore]," *MPC,* Sep 1927, 33, 81, 88. Paul Paige, "Close-Ups and Fade-Outs," *Paris and Hollywood Screen Secrets Magazine,* Aug 1927, 98 (in 1910, Harris's father "made a hasty trip from Europe in an unsuccessful attempt to prevent her wedding to Barrymore. Later she married Alfred D.B. Pratt; divorced 1923. She then married Leon Orlowski, secretary of the Polish Legation, in 1925.). "The Man on the Cover," *Cinema Arts,* Oct 1927, 25. "Favor Barrymore, Shearer," *MPW,* 10 Dec 1927, 14. Cedric Belfrage, "Filming *Tempest* with Unrehearsed Effects; John Barrymore Started a Tempest in a Russian Teacup—With Lemon and Several Lumps," *MPC,* Apr 1928, 25, 70–71. Charles Darnton, "'There's Actin' Going on Here; All men, says John Barrymore, boast of their work. It's their way of dramatizing themselves," *The New Movie Magazine,* Oct 1934, 38, 75–77. John Finch and Linda Rosenkrantz, *Gone Hollywood* (Garden City NY: Doubleday & Co. Inc., 1979), p. 250 ("At his hilltop home, Bella Vista, John Barrymore housed an opossum, a kinkajou, a mouse deer, scores of Siamese cats, and numerous dogs... Clementine, a gift from English actress Gladys Cooper, was a monkey who bit everyone else in the house, but unutterably adored Barrymore. She would sit opposite him for hours, staring with absolute devotion. After his family forced him to give her to a zoo, Barrymore was told by the vet that she had been fascinated not by his divine looks or sterling personality, but by the alcohol fumes he emitted. Thereafter, he would make special visits to the zoo, just to breathe on Clementine."). Ben Brantley, "Bizarre Behavior, but It's in the Script," *NYT,* 25 Apr 1996, C13, C20 (review of *Jack: A Night on the Town with John Barrymore,* starring Nicol Williamson).

Barrymore, Lionel (son of Maurice Barrymore; brother of **John** and **Ethel Barrymore**) [stage/film/radio actor/director] (*né* Lionel Blythe, b. Philadelphia PA, 28 Apr 1878–15 Nov 1954 [76], Van Nuys CA; heart attack). m. **Doris Rankin**, 19 June 1904 NYC (d. ca. 1946); **Irene Fenwick**, 16 Jul 1923, Rome, Italy (d. 1936). With Cameron Shipp, *We Barrymores* (New York: Appleton-Century-Crofts, 1951). (AA, 1930–31.) "Lionel Barrymore Is Dead at 76; Actor's Career Spanned 61 Years; Veteran Screen and Stage Star Also Gained Fame as Scrooge on Radio," *NYT,* 16

Nov 1954, 1:3, 29:3. "A Man in His Life Plays Many Parts; Lionel Barrymore Dead at 76, Had Been Painter, Etcher, Musician and Star of Stage and Screen," *Variety,* 17 Nov 1954. AMD, p. 31. AS, p. 101. BHD1, p. 35; BHD2, p. 16. FFF, p. 212. FSS, p. 20. GSS, pp. 28–29 (d. 16 Nov). IFN, p. 19. Truitt, pp. 18–19. WWS, p. 72. "Lionel Barrymore Quits?; Report of Quarrel with [Charles] Frohman Denied in This City," *NYT,* 2 May 1905, 9:2 (he was allegedly denied a $1,000 advance in Denver CO. Alf Hayman, Frohman's representative, denied this.). "Lionel Barrymore Signs with Pathé," *MPW,* 15 May 1915, 1095. "Metro Signs Three New Stars," *NYDM,* 22 Sep 1915, 35:1 (Martha Hedman, Barrymore, and Hamilton Revelle). "Lionel Barrymore with Metro," *MPW,* 18 Dec 1915, 2211. "Court Won't Stop Lionel Barrymore's Picture Work," *MPW,* 26 Feb 1921, 1085. "Lionel Barrymore Signs Long M-G-M Contract," *MPW,* 3 Apr 1926, 3. Cedric Belfrage, "He's in Pictures for the Money; Lionel Barrymore Is Frankly Uninterested in the *Art* of the Movies," *MPC,* Nov 1928, 58, 87 ("The movies had the misfortune to come along in the twentieth century, and because they appeal to the masses there can be no sincerity in them.").

Barrymore, William [actor] (aka Kit Carson and Boris Bullock, b. Russia, 17 Aug 1899–23 Apr 1979 [79], San Diego CA). BHD1, p. 35. IFN, p. 19.

Barsha, Leon [editor/director/producer] (b. New York NY, 26 Dec 1905–13 Nov 1964 [58], Los Angeles CA). (Universal.) "Leon Barsha," *Variety,* 18 Nov 1964. BHD2, p. 16.

Barskaya, Margarita [director] (*née* Margarita Aleksandrovna Tsjardynina-Barskaja, b. Baku, Russia [Azerbaijan], 1901–1937 [36?], Moscow, Russia). AS, p. 102. BHD2, p. 16.

Barsky, I[sador] **J. Bud** [publicist/writer/producer/general manager of Columbia Pictures] (b. Odessa, Russia, 19 Jun 1891–18 Dec 1967 [76], Los Angeles CA; cancer). "Bud Barsky," *NYT,* 21 Dec 1967, 37:4 ("He built some of the first Hollywood sound stages…"). "Bud Barsky," *Variety,* 27 Dec 1967 (made half-reelers at Fort Lee NJ; to Hollywood in 1922. "He merged with late John M. Stahl to form Tiffany-Stahl Productions."). AMD, p. 31. AS, p. 102. BHD2, p. 16. "Barsky Goes with Ford Exhibition," *MPW,* 11 Dec 1915, 2035. "Barsky Writes Comedy War Pictures," *MPW,* 8 Jan 1916, 232.

Bartels, Louis John [actor] (b. Bunker Hill IL, 19 Oct 1895–4 Mar 1932 [36], Los Angeles CA). m. Martha Wood. (Pathé.) "Louis John Bartels," *Variety,* 8 Mar 1932. BHD1, p. 35. IFN, p. 19. SD.

Barter, H.H. [technical director]. No data found. AMD, p. 31. "Universal Has New Technical Director," *MPW,* 26 Feb 1916, 1304.

Bartet, Julia [actress] (b. Paris, France, 1854-Nov 1941 [87?], Paris, France). BHD, p. 100.

Barthelmess, Richard Semler [actor] (b. New York NY, 9 May 1895 [Birth Certificate No. 24547]–17 Aug 1963 [68], Southampton, LI NY [Death Certificate Index No. 33); cancer). m. (1) **Mary Hay,** 18 Jun 1920, NYC—div. (d. 1957); (2) Mrs. Jessica Sargent, Reno NV. (Began as an extra in *Romeo and Juliet,* with Bushman and Bayne.) "Richard Barthelmess, 68, Dies; Boyish Idol of Silent Film Era," *NYT,* 18 Aug 1963, 80:2; "Rites Held in Southampton for Richard Barthelmess," *NYT,* 21 Aug 1963, 33:3. "Richard Barthelmess," *Variety,* 21 Aug 1963. AMD, p. 31. BHD1, p. 35. FFF, p. 32. FSFM, p. 49. FSS, p. 22. GK, pp. 15–24. HCH, p. 27. IFN, p. 19. MH, p. 95. Truitt, p. 19 (b. 1897). WWS, p. 55. "Griffith Engages Barthelmess," *MPW,* 1 Feb 1919, 602. Mary Keane Taylor, "And He Wants to Be a Playwright!; Dick Barthelmess Disdains Stars and Longs to Dash Off the Big American Drama," *MPC,* Feb 1919, 39–40, 70. "Barthelmess Becomes a Star; Others to Head Own Companies," *MPW,* 12 Jun 1920, 1424. "Cupid Clinched Job in 'Way Down East' and Now 'Dick' Barthelmess Is Married," *MPW,* 26 Jun 1920, 1758. "The Actor on the Cover," *MPS,* 13 May 1921, 29 (b. 1896; member of the Lambs, NYC, and the LA Athletic Club). Faith Service, "Pre-Griffith Days," *Classic,* Dec 1922, 18–19, 84 (extensive pre-Griffith work). "Barthelmess Coming Back," *Variety,* 26 Mar 1924, 23:5 (from vacation in Bermuda. He breached his contract with Inspiration Pictures "with the likelihood the latter will bring legal action. The question of royalties due Barthelmess has been settled.".). John England, "A Day in the Studio with Richard Barthelmess," *MW,* 29 Mar 1924. Beatrice Wilson, "A Terribly Intimate Portrait," *Classic,* Aug 1924, 38–40, 75. David A. Balch, "Did Jealousy, the Green-Eyed Monster, Cause Break Between Gish and Barthelmess?; Reported rupture of popular screen star with president of Inspiration Pictures [Charles H. Duell], gives rise to belief that split arose out of professional jealousy—Dick sails for Bermuda," *MW,* 12 Apr 1924, 4–5. Gladys Hall and Adele Whitely Fletcher, "We Interview Dick Barthelmess," *MV,* 17 Jan 1925, 16–18, 34. Richard Barthelmess, "The True Story of My Life," *MW,* 14 Mar 1925, 6–8, 28; 21 Mar 1925, 12–13, 34; 28 Mar 1925, 15–16, 32; 4 Apr 1925, 1516, 31; 11 Apr 1925, 14–15, 33; 18 Apr 1925, 13–14, 33; 25 Apr 1925, 13–14, 33; 2 May 1925, 15–16, 32; 9 May 1925, 15–16, 31, 16 May 1925, 15–16, 32. "Rowland Signs Barthelmess for Eight Big Productions," *MPW,* 27 Feb 1926, 792. "Beatrice Wilson, "For Richard, for Poorer; The New Mrs. Barthelmess Is a Meet Helpmeet for Dick," *MPC,* May 1929, 51, 76. George Katchmer, "Richard Barthelmess," *CI,* 119 (May 1985), 23–24, 34, 60. Richard E. Braff, "The Films of Richard Barthelmess," *CI,* 167 (May 1989), 52, 54; "Additional Films," *CI,* 228 (Jun 1994), 51.

Bartholomae, Philip H. [scenarist] (b. Chicago IL, 1879?–5 Jan 1947 [67], Winnetka IL). "Philip H. Bartholomae," *Variety,* 15 Jan 1947. AMD, p. 31. AS, p. 102. BHD2, p. 16. NNAT. "Philip Bartholomae with Pathé," *MPW,* 24 Feb 1917, 1199. "Philip Bartholomae Signed by Ziegfeld Company to Write Story for First Florence Reed Film," *MPW,* 6 Nov 1920, 65. "Philip Bartholomae Pays Tribute to Ziegfeld for Using Stage Players in Pictures," *MPW,* 25 Dec 1920, 1075. Tom Waller, "Philip Bartholomae," *MPW,* 26 Nov 1927, 20–21.

Bartholomew, Lee O. [cameraman] (b. 1876–2 Oct 1950 [74?], St. Louis MO). AMD, p. 31. AS, p. 102. "Lee Bartholomew Promoted," *MPW,* 27 Mar 1915, 1914g.

Bartlett, Donald W. [journalist/title writer/scenarist] (b. 1886?–20 Jun 1941 [55], New York NY [Death Certificate Index No. 13430]). m. Edna. (Paramount; WB; Universal.) "Donald W. Bartlett," *Variety,* 25 Jun 1941. AMD, p. 31. "Don Bartlett, of Vitagraph, Established Great Record," *MPW,* 3 Apr 1920, 116.

Bartlett, Elsie [stage/film actress] (d. 1944, Daytona Beach FL). m. **Joseph Schildkraut,** 1923 (d. 1964). AMD, pp. 31–32. BHD1, p. 35. IFN, p. 19. "Elsie Bartlett to Appear in Series of Feature Films," *MPW,* 14 Jun 1919, 1639. "Playing with Leatrice Joy," *MPW,* 16 Jul 1927, 188:1. "Elsie Bartlett in a DeMille Picture," *MPW,* 16 Jul 1927, 188:4.

Bartlett, Harry W. [vaudeville/stage/film actor] (b. Pittsburgh PA, 1862–14 Feb 1933 [71], New York NY). m. Lethe Collins. "Harry W. Bartlett," *Variety,* 28 Feb 1933, p. 70. BHD, p. 100.

Bartlett, Lanier [scenarist] (b. Oakland CA, 1879). AMD, p. 32. BHD2, p. 16. "Lanier Bartlett Joins Triangle Staff," *MPW,* 2 Mar 1918, 1213.

Bartlett, Randolph I. [publicist/title writer/scenarist/producer] (b. Glencoe, Ontario, Canada, 1881?–30 Sep 1943 [62], New York NY [Death Certificate Index No. 21417]; heart attack). m. Frances Leonor Bermudez; Rose. (Paramount.) "Randolph I. Bartlett; Copy Editor on New York Sun Had Been in Film Business," *NYT,* 2 Oct 1943, 13:5 ("After [WWI] he returned to California and entered the motion-picture industry. He was sent to France by Paramount Pictures to make French films, later leaving the company to supervise productions for French film firms."). "Randolph Bartlett," *Variety,* 6 Oct 1943. AMD, p. 32. AS, p. 102. BHD2, p. 16. FDY, pp. 417, 441. "Bartlett Back in Pictures, Deserting Literary Work," *MPW,* 25 Jan 1919, 478. "Randolph Bartlett Back with Selznick," *MPW,* 14 Feb 1920, 1091. "Bartlett Goes Over to Famous Players," *MPW,* 11 Feb 1922, 611. "Randolph Bartlett Titling Two New Gothic Pictures," *MPW,* 11 Jul 1925, 193. "New F.B.O. Editor," *MPW,* 28 May 1927, 250. "Wedding March," *MPW,* 3 Dec 1927, 23 (m. Bermudez).

Bartlett, Sy [scenarist/producer] (*né* Sydney Sacha Bartlett, b. Nikolaiev, Ukraine, Russia, 10 Jul 1900?–29 May 1978 [78], Los Angeles CA; cancer). (b. 1902). m. Ellen Drew; **Alice White** (d. 1983). (TC-F.) "Sy Bartlett," *Variety,* 7 Jun 1978. AS, p. 103 (b. 1909). BHD2, p. 16. IFN, p. 19. SD (*né* Sadra Baranier).

Barton, Bruce [writer] (b. Robbins TN, 5 Aug 1886–5 Jul 1967 [80], New York NY). m. Esther M. Randall, 1913 (d. 1951). "Bruce Barton, Ad Man, Is Dead; Author, Former Representative; A Founder of B.B.D.O., Was Denounced by Roosevelt as Foe of New Deal," *NYT,* 6 Jul 1967, 1:3 35:3 ("I think it's almost a disgrace for a man to die rich."); "Bruce Barton Left $2.8-Million Estate," 25 Jul 1967, 16:8. "Bruce Barton," *Variety,* 12 Jul 1967. AMD, p. 32. AS, p. 103. "Barton to Write for F.P.-L.," *MPW,* 28 Aug 1926, 529.

Barton, Buzz [actor] (*né* William Andrew Lamoreaux, aka Red Lennox, b. Galletin MO, 3 Sep 1913–20 Nov 1980 [67], Sylmar CA). m. Thelma Doyle, 22 Jun 1947. (Began ca. 1924; FBO.) AMD, p. 32. AS, p. 103 (d. 20 Sep 1990, St. Louis MO). BHD1, p. 35 (d. Reseda CA). FSS, p. 23. Truitt 1983. "Buzz Barton at Work on Second for F.B.O.," *MPW,* 6 Aug 1927, 399. Nick Nicholls, "Buzz Barton," *CI,* 125 (Nov 1985), 27; *CI,* 191 (May 1991).

Barton, Charles T. [actor] (b. Sacramento CA, 25 May 1902–5 Dec 1981 [79], Burbank CA; heart attack). AS, p. 103. BHD, p. 100; BHD2, p. 16 (b. SF CA).

Barton, James Edward [actor] (b. Gloucester

NJ, 1 Nov 1890–19 Feb 1962 [71], Mineola, LI NY). m. (1) Ottile R. Kleinert; Kathryn Penman. "James Barton" and "Jim Barton, 71, A Vaude Great," *Variety*, 21 Feb 1962. AS, p. 103. BHD1, p. 35. IFN, p. 19. SD. Truitt, p. 19.

Barton, Joe [actor] (b. 1883–5 Jul 1937 [54], Los Angeles CA). AS, p. 103. BHD, p. 100. IFN, p. 100.

Barton, John [actor] (b. Germantown PA, 1 May 1870?–23 Dec 1946 [76], New York NY [Death Certificate Index No. 27339; age 70]). m. Anne Ashley (d. 1947). "John Barton," *Variety*, 25 Dec 1946. AS, p. 103 (b. 1872). BHD, p. 100 (b. 1872). SD. Truitt, 1983 (b. 1872).

Barton, Steve [assistant director]. No data found. AMD, p. 32. "Steve Barton Engaged by Balshofer," *MPW*, 28 Oct 1916, 563.

Bary (or **Bery**), **Jean** *see* **Laverty, Jean**

Bary, Leon [actor] (b. Paris, France, 1880–1954 [74], France). m. Marie F. Crousaz, 28 May 1917. (Sennett.) AMD, p. 32. BHD1, p. 36. IFN, p. 19. "Bary Saw Service in France," *MPW*, 23 Jun 1917, 1965. "Leon Bary Weds Marie F. Crousaz," *MPW*, 14 Jul 1917, 225. George A. Katchmer, "More Forgotten Cowboys and Cowgirls—Chapter 6," *CI*, 172 (Oct 1889), C12.

Barzini, Luigi (father of Luigi Barzini, Jr. [1908–1984], the author of *The Italians*) [journalist/scenarist] (b. Orvieto, Italy, 7 Feb 1874–6 Sep 1947 [ ], Milan, Italy). JS, p. 31 (in Italian silents from 1919).

Basch, Felix [actor/director] (b. Vienna, Austria, 16 Sep 1882–17 May 1944 [61], Los Angeles CA). "Felix Basch," *Variety*, 24 May 1944, 39. AS, p. 103 (b. 1885; d. 1943). BHD2, p. 16.

Bashford, Herbert [playwright/novelist/historian/poet/actor] (b. Sioux City IA, , 4 Mar 1871–13 Jul 1928 [57], Piedmont CA; pneumonia). "Herbert Bashford," *Variety*, 18 Jul 1928, p. 58 (wrote *Woman He Married* and *Light in the Dark*). AS, p. 104. WWWA.

Baskcomb, A.W. [actor] (b. London, England, 5 Jul 1880–10 Dec 1939 [59], London, England). AS, p. 104. BHD, p. 100. IFN, p. 19.

Basquette, Lina [actress: Wampas Star, 1928] (half-sister of Marge Champion [*née* Marjorie Celeste Belcher]) (*née* Lena Copeland Baskette [originally, Bosquet], b. San Mateo CA, 19 Apr 1907–30 Sep 1994 [87], Wheeling WV; cancer). m. 9 times to 7 men: (1) **Sam L. Warner**, 4 Jul 1925 (d. 1927); (2) **J. Peverell Marley**, Jan 1929–11 Sep 1930 (d. 1964); (3–4) Theodore "Teddy" Hayes, 19 Oct 1931, Newark NJ—Sep 1932, Nogales, Mexico (remarried twice: 27 Dec 1932); (5) Henry Mollinson—Apr 1947; (6) Warren Gilmore; (7) Frank Mancuso. (Film debut: *The Juvenile Dancer Supreme*, Lena Baskette's Featurettes, Universal, 1916.) *Lina; DeMille's Godless Girl* (Fairfax VA: Denlingers Pub., Ltd., 1990). "Lina Basquette, Silent-Film Star and Dog Breeder, Is Dead at 87," *NYT*, 6 Oct 1994, D23:1. AMD, p. 32. AS, p. 104. BHD1, p. 36. BR, pp. 256–59. FSS, p. 24. Katz, p. 88. 1921 Directory, p. 246. "Eight-Year-Old Child Dancer Signed by 'U' for 6 Years," *MPW*, 25 Mar 1916, 1736. "Lina Basquette," *MPW*, 30 Jun 1917, 2081. "Lina Basquette," *MPW*, 11 Aug 1917, 951. "Lina Basquette Returns to Screen in F.B.O. Picture," *MPW*, 13 Aug 1927, 467. "Sam L. Warner Dies in Hollywood Hospital," *MPW*, 8 Oct 1927, 337, 343. "Warner Gives Whole Estate to Relatives," *MPW*, 29 Oct 1927, 543. "Lina Basquette to Work Five Years for DeMille," *MPW*, 19 Nov 1927, 25. Dorothy Manners, "High Hats for Sale; Slightly—but No Longer—Used by Lina Basquette, Janet Gaynor, and Olive Borden," *MPC*, Feb 1929, 26, 82. Buck Rainey, "Lina Basquette; Every Man's Dream of a Fiery Latin Sunset," *CI*, 95 (May 1983), 23–24; II, 96 (Jun 1983), 7. Michael G. Ankerich, "Reel Stars," *CI*, 166 (Apr 1989), 9, 18. George A. Katchmer, "Remembering the Great Silents," *CI*, 17 (Oct 1989), C12. Ray Formanek, Jr., "Silent Film Star Returns in Movie [*Paradise Park*] About Aging Grandmother's Dreams," *Las Vegas Review-Journal*, 29 Sep 1991, B8:1. Farm: Honey Hallow (Lahaska PA). Chapter 3, "Lina Basquette," *BS*, pp. 31–44 (includes filmography).

Basserman, Albert Eugene [actor] (b. Mannheim, Germany, 7 Sep 1867–15 May 1952 [84], Oceano Atlantico; heart attack). m. Elsie Schiff, 1908. "Albert Basserman," *Variety*, 21 May 1952, p. 63 (d. Zurich, Switzerland, age 85). AS, p. 104 (d. Zurich, Switzerland; at the airport). BHD1, p. 36 (d. Zurich, Switzerland). Vittorio Martinelli, "Kino-Lieblinge," *Griffithiana*, Oct 1990, 44.

Bassett, Albert Anthony [actor] (b. 1885–5 Aug 1955 [70?], Los Angeles CA). AMD, p. 32. AS, p. 104 (Tony Bassett). "The Roll of Honor," *MPW*, 21 Jul 1917, 433.

Bassett, Roy [film salesman] (b. 1899?–27 Jul 1961 [62], Los Angeles CA). (Allied Artists; Republic.) "Roy Bassett," *Variety*, 9 Aug 1961 ("a salesman for 40 years with Allied Artists and Republic").

Bassett, Russell [actor] (b. Milwaukee WI, 24 Oct 1845–8 May 1918 [72], New York NY [Death Certificate No. 15589]; cerebral hemorrhage). "Russell Bassett," *NYT*, 9 May 1918, 13:5. "Russell Bassett," *Variety*, 17 May 1918. AMD, p. 32. AS. p. 104. BHD, p. 100 (d. 7 May). IFN, p. 20. P.M. Powell, "Doings at Los Angeles," *MPW*, 12 Apr 1913, 152. Richard Willis, "Russell Bassett, Grand Old Man of Moving Pictures," *MPS*, 16 May 1913, 27, 32. "Russell Bassett," *MPW*, 7 Nov 1914, 766. "Obituary," *MPW*, 25 May 1918, 1126 (age 74).

Bassi, Parsifal [actor/director/producer]) (b. Bologna, Italy, 15 Dec 1892–10 Jan 1960 [67], Bologna, Italy). AS, p. 104. BHD, p. 17. JS, p. 31 (in Italian silents from 1920).

Baston, J[ack] **Thornton** [actor] (b. San Francisco CA, 6 Aug 1892–3 May 1970 [77], Los Angeles CA). AS, p. 105. BHD1, p. 36. IFN, p. 20. George Katchmer, "Forgotten Cowboys and Cowgirls—Part XVI," *CI*, 193 (Jul 1991), 34.

Batalov, Nikolai P[etrovich] (uncle of Aleksei Vladimirovich Batalov, b. 1928) [actor] (b. Moscow, Russia, 6 Dec 1899–10 Nov 1937 [37], Moscow, Russia). AS, p. 105. BHD1, p. 36. IFN, p. 20.

Batcheff, Pierre [actor] (*né* Piotr Bacev, b. Kharbin, Siberia, Russia, 1901–13 Apr 1932 [31], Paris, France; suicide with overdose of Veronal). AS, p. 105 (b. 1906). BHD1, p. 36. IFN, p. 20.

Batcheller, George R. [President of Chesterfield Motion Pictures Corp.] (b. Providence RI, 1892?–28 Sep 1938 [46], Pelham NY). m. Mildred. "George R. Batcheller," *NYT*, 29 Sep 1938, 25:5.

Batchelor, Charles [actor] (b. London, England, 1845–1910 [64] [Death Certificate No. 384? (illegible microfilm)]).

Bate, Henry Clay [publicist]. No data found. AMD, p. 32. "Bate a Benedict," *MPW*, 23 Aug 1924, 637.

Bateman, Helen [actress] (*née* Helen Reaume). No data found. AMD, p. 32. "Actress Changes Name," *MPW*, 7 Apr 1917, 107.

Bateman, Victory [stage/film actress] (b. Philadelphia PA, 6 Apr 1865–2 Mar 1926 [60], Los Angeles CA; bronchial asthma). m. Edward Compton. "Victory Bateman," *Variety*, 10 Mar 1926. AMD, p. 32. BHD, p. 101. IFN, p. 20 (b. NY NY). MH, p. 95. Truitt, p. 20. "Victoria Bateman Burned in Hotel; Actress Nearly Lost Her Life in Hotel Fire; Her Condition Serious; Unconscious, She Was Dragged from Her Room by the Hotel Proprietor," *NYT*, 7 Mar 1905, 9:3 (On 6 Mar in Edwardsville IL, Bateman was visiting friends appearing in *Dr. Jekyll and Mr. Hyde*. At the Leland Hotel she took a nap. At 3 p.m. the proprietor broke down her door, crawled under the smoke on his hands and knees, and dragged the unconscious woman, lying on the floor, out.). "Bigger Majestic Company," *MPW*, 15 Nov 1913, 741. "Morosco-Bosworth Secures Virginia Bateman," *MPW*, 5 Jun 1915, 1615. "Virginia Bateman with Metro," *MPW*, 16 Oct 1920, 914. "Virginia Bateman Signed," *MPW*, 26 Sep 1925, 344.

Bates, Arthur W. [actor]. No data found. AMD, p. 32. "Arthur Bates Joins Colors," *MPW*, 22 Jun 1918, 1701.

Bates, Blanche [stage/film actress] (b. Portland OR, 25 Aug 1873–25 Dec 1941 [68], San Francisco CA). m. (1) Milton F. Davis; playwright George Creel, 1912. (Film debut: *The Border Legion*, Goldwyn, 1918.) "Blanche Bates, 69, Dies on the Coast; Noted Actress Stricken After Christmas Reception—Last Appeared Here in 1933; Spent 36 Years on Stage; She Won Acclaim in Belasco's 'Girl of the Golden West'—Wife of George Creel," *NYT*, 26 Dec 1941, XCI, 13:1. "Blanche Bates," *Variety*, 31 Dec 1941 (age 69). AMD, p. 32. BHD, p. 101. IFN, p. 20. SD. Truitt, p. 20. "Blanche Bates Pours Tea Following Screen Debut," *MPW*, 25 Jan 1919, 476.

Bates, Frank [executive]. No data found. AMD, p. 32. "Frank Bates," *MPW*, 23 May 1914, 1097.

Bates, Granville [stage/film actor] (b. Harvard IL, 7 Jan 1882–9 Jul 1940 [58], Hollywood CA; heart attack). m. Josephine Weller, 1930. (Essanay, Chicago; WB.) "Granville Bates Is Dead at 58, 40 Years on Stage and Screen; Character Actor Was to Have Begun Biggest Role of Career [the Judge in *My Favorite Wife*] Within 2 Days," *The New York Herald Tribune*, 10 Jul 1940, 18:2 (b. Chicago). "Granville Bates," *Variety*, 10 Jul 1940. *New York Sun*, 10 Jul 1940, p. 21; *Newsweek*, 22 Jul 1940, p. 16:6. BHD1, p. 37 (d. 8 Jul). IFN, p. 20.

Bates, Harry G. [actor] (b. 1870?–29 Dec 1932 [62], E. Islip, LI NY). (Stage debut, 1889.) "Harry G. Bates," *Variety*, 10 Jan 1933.

Bates, Kathryn [actress] (b. RI, 23 Sep 1877–1 Jan 1964 [86], Los Angeles Co. CA). BHD1, p. 37. IFN, p. 20.

Bates, Leslie A. [actor] (b. Waukegan IL, 6 Jun 1877–8 Aug 1930 [53], Hollywood CA; from injuries sustained in auto collision). "Leslie A. Bates," *Variety*, 13 Aug 1930. BHD1, p. 37. IFN, p. 20. Truitt, p. 20. George Katchmer, "More Forgotten Cowboys and Cowgirls, Chap. 6," *CI*, 172 (Oct 1989), C12; "Update," 179 (May 1990), 43.

Bates, Louise Emerald [actress] (b. MA, 28 Dec 1886–11 Jun 1972 [85], Los Angeles CA). : Louise Mortimer, b. 27 Nov). (Thanhouser.) AMD, p. 32. BHD1, p. 37. IFN, p. 215 (Louise Bates Mortimer). "Louise Bates Now 'Falstaff Girl,'" *MPW,* 16 Oct 1915, 455.

Bates, Marie [actress] (*née* Helen Marie Melvin, b. Boston MA, 1853?–12 Mar 1923 [70], Glenbrook CT). m. Marius Bates. "Marie Bates," *Variety,* 15 Mar 1923. SD.

Bates, Tom [actor] (b. 1864?–11 Apr 1930 [66]). BHD, p. 101. IFN, p. 20.

Bates, Wilbur M. [publicist]. No data found. AMD, p. 32. "Wilbur Bates Gets in the Game," *MPW,* 3 Mar 1917, 1338. "Wilbur Bates," *MPW,* 28 Jul 1917, 620. "Bates Resigns from Paralta," *MPW,* 17 Nov 1917, 1002.

Batley, Dorothy [actress] (b. London, England, 18 Jan 1902–8 Dec 1983 [81], London, England). BHD1, p. 37.

Batley, Ernest G. [actor/director/producer] (b. England, 1873–20 Feb 1965 [92?], Westbourne, England). AS, p. 105 (d. 1917). BHD, p. 101; BHD2, p. 17.

Batley, Ethyle [actress/scenarist/director] (b. 1879–22 Apr 1917 [37?], London, England). BHD, p. 100' BHD2, p. 17.

Batten, John [actor] (b. Rotorua, New Zealand, 3 Apr 1903–10 Aug 1993 [90], Colchester, England). BHD1, p. 37.

Battiferri, Fernanda [actress] (b. Rome, Italy, 4 Sep 1896). m. **Gastone Monaldi** (d. 1932). AS, p. 106. JS, p. 32 (in Italian silents from 1915).

Battinelli, Joseph [actor] (b. Naples, Italy). David A. Balch, "From East Side Gangster to Movie Actor," *MW,* 7 Jun 1924, 9 (also played in Italian films).

Battista, Miriam [actress] (*née* Miriam C.J. Battista, b. New York NY, 14 Jul 1912 [Birth Certificate Index No. 37143]–25 Dec 1980 [68], New York NY). "Miriam Battista, Actress in the Theater and Films," *NYT,* 27 Dec 1980, 26. AMD, p. 32. AS, p. 106. BHD1, p. 37 (b. 1914). FFF, p. 164. MH, p. 95. "Miriam Battista Returns to Films," *MPW,* 2 Jul 1921, 66.

Batty, Stephen [actor] (b. Budapest, Hungary, 1882–6 Dec 1938 [56?], Patton CA). BHD, p. 101.

Bauchens, Anne [film editor/script supervisor/assistant director] (b. St. Louis MO, 2 Feb 1882–7 May 1967 [85], Woodland Hills CA). (FP-L.) "Anne Bauchens," *Variety,* 17 May 1967. BHD, p. 17. IFN, p. 20.

Bauer, Arthur Richard [actor] (b. Vienna, Austria, 30 Mar 1878). BHD, p. 101. *Photoplay Arts Portfolio* [Thanhouser] (b. 1897).

Bauer, Inez [actress] (b. CA, 21 Jan 1888–15 May 1975 [87], Millbrae CA). BHD, p. 101.

Bauer, Myrtle C. [actress]. No data found. AMD, p. 32. "Myrtle C. Bauer," *MPW,* 7 Jul 1917, 99.

Bauer, Yevgeni (Eugene) [director] (b. Russia, 1880–1917 [37?]). BHD2, p. 17.

Baum, Mrs. H. William *see* **Doscher, Doris**

Baum, Harry [actor] (b. 27 Dec 1915–31 Jan 1974 [58], Los Angeles CA). BHD1, p. 38. IFN, p. 20.

Baum, L[yman] **Frank** [author] (b. Chittenango NY, 15 May 1856–6 May 1919 [62], Hollywood CA). "L. Frank Baum," *Variety,* 16 May 1919. AMD, p. 33. "L. Frank Baum," *MPW,* 25 Jul 1914, 579. "L. Frank Baum," *MPW,* 10 Oct 1914, 201. *Twentieth Century Authors,* p. 89.

Bauman, William J. [actor/director/producer]. No data found. (Vitagraph.) AMD, p. 33. LACD, "director," h 105 E. 49th. "Metro Secures Two New Directors," *MPW,* 22 May 1915, 1277.

Baumann, Charles O. [producer] (b. Brooklyn NY, 6 Jul 1876-Apr 1964 [87]). AMD, p. 33. "Manufacturers Balk at Sales Company," *MPW,* 28 May 1910, 893. "Charles Baumann Goes West," *MPW,* 13 Aug 1910, 344. "Races Across Country, But Beaten by Death," *MPW,* 3 Sep 1910, 517 (son Frank d. 21 Aug 1910 [14]). "Independent Factions Organize," *MPW,* 1 Jun 1912, 807–08. "Another 'Independent' Split," *MPW,* 6 Jul 1912, 129. "Another Big Programme; Charles O. Baumann Heads New Popular Corporation, Which Will Release Regular Service," *NYDM,* 26 Aug 1914, 24:4. George Blaisdell, "Charles O. Baumann Talks of Plans," *MPW,* 5 Sep 1914, 1349. "Kessel-Baumann-Aitken," *MPW,* 3 Jul 1915, 42. G. Blaisdell, "Mecca of the Motion Picture," *MPW,* 10 Jul 1915, 215–20.

Baumer, N.J. [executive]. No data found. AMD, p. 33. "N.J. Baumer," *MPW,* 7 Oct 1916, 91.

Baur, Harry [actor] (b. Montrouge, France, 12 Apr 1880–8 Apr 1943 [62], Paris, France). (Edison; Kleine-Eclipse.) "Harry Baur," *Variety,* 14 Apr 1943. BHD1, p. 38. IFN, p. 20. Truitt, p. 20.

Baxley, Jack [actor] (*né* Andrew J. Baxley, b. TX, 4 Jul 1884–10 Dec 1950 [66], Los Angeles CA). BHD1, p. 38.

Baxter, Barry [actor] (b. Winchester, England, 5 Aug 1894–27 May 1922 [27], New York NY; pneumonia after operation). "Barry Baxter," *Variety,* 2 Jun 1922 (age 25). BHD, p. 101. SD.

Baxter, Billy [actor] (b. 1873–7 Jun 1936 [63?]). IFN, p. 20.

Baxter, George [cameraman] (b. 6 Apr 1881–27 Dec 1975 [94], Woodland Hills CA; cerebral vascular accident). m. Vera. (Began 1922.) "George Baxter," *Variety,* 28 Jan 1976. AS, p. 108. BHD2, p. 17.

Baxter, Leeds L. [studio manager] (b. Brooklyn NY, 1883?–9 Jun 1933 [50], Los Angeles CA; hear attack). m. (Accountant with Jesse L. Lasky films, 1911; business manager with Fairbanks; general manager of Marshall Neilan productions for 5 years; assistant manager, MGM, 8 years.) "Leeds Baxter," *Variety,* 111, 13 Jun 1933, 54:2. BHD2, p. 17. LACD, "studio mgr," 809 Green Ave.

Baxter, Mae [May?] [actress] (*née?,* b. 1885?–8 Dec 1934 [49], San Francisco CA). m. Lincoln Leeds Baxter (d. 1933). "Mrs. Mae Baxter," *Variety,* 11 Dec 1934 (in *Penrod?*).

Baxter, Marian *see* **Montgomery, Peggy**

Baxter, Thuma Jadee [actress] (b. Milton KY, 15 Jun 1890–11 Jan 1974 [83], Los Angeles CA). BHD, p. 101.

Baxter, Warner Leroy [actor] (b. Columbus OH, 29 Mar 1889–7 May 1951 [62], Beverly Hills CA; bronchial pneumonia). m. (1) Viola Caldwell; (2) **Winifred Bryson,** 29 Jan 1918 (d. 1987). (Ince; Paramount.) "Warner Baxter, 59, Film Star, Is Dead; Winner of 'Oscar' in 1929—Best Known for Cisco Kid and 'Crime Doctor' Portrayals," *NYT,* 8 May 1951, 31:1 (b. 1893). "Warner Baxter," *Variety,* 9 May 1951 (age 59). AMD, p. 33. BHD1, p. 38. FFF, p. 133. FSFM, p. 69. FSS, p. 25. GK, pp. 24–34. IFN, p. 21. MH, p. 96. Truitt, p. 20. "F.B.O. Signs Baxter to Contract," *MPW,* 16 Dec 1922, 646. Maude Cheatham, "The Endless Honeymoon of the Warner Baxters," *Classic,* Jul 1923, 24–25, 78. "His Early Bend Told in Long Run," *MPW,* 3 Nov 1923, 90. "Warner Baxter Signed," *MPW,* 11 Jul 1925, 190. George A. Katchmer, "Warner (Cisco Kid) Baxter," *CI,* 114 (Dec 1984), 31 *et passim.* "Buck Rainey's Filmographies; Warner Baxter, Heartthrob of the Thirties, Part I," *CI,* 171 (Sep 1989), 49–50; Part II, 172 (Oct 1989), 40–43; 231 (Sep 1994), 43. Eve Golden, "Warner Baxter: The Thinking Woman's Gable," *CI,* 243 (Sep 1995), C10-C11.

Bay, Maria [actress]. No data found. JS, p. 33 (in Italian silents from 1911).

Bay, Tom [actor] (*né* William T. Bay, b. San Antonio TX, 22 Feb 1901–11 Oct 1933 [32], Burbank CA; killed by shooting). *Tim McCoy Remembers the West* (NY: Double-day & Co., 1977). "Tom Bay," *Variety,* 17 Oct 1933. BHD1, p. 38. IFN, p. 21. Truitt, p. 21. George A. Katchmer, "Remembering the Great Silents," *CI,* 183 (Sep 1990), 44.

Bay, Vivian [actress] (aka Vivian Ray). George A. Katchmer, "Remembering the Great Silents," *CI,* 184 (Oct 1990), 58.

Bayer, Charles W. [actor] (b. 1893–28 Nov 1953 [60?], Los Angeles CA). BHD, p. 101.

Bayes, Nora [stage/film actress] (*née* Eleanor Goldberg, b. 1878?–19 Mar 1928 [50?], Brooklyn NY). m. (1) Otto Gressing; (2) Jack Norworth; (3) Harry Clarke; (4) Arthur Goldoni; (5) Benjamin Friedland, 1925. "Nora Bayes," *Variety,* 21 Mar 1928, 73:1 (b. in Milwaukee, Chicago or Los Angeles; recorded with Victor and Columbia Records). AMD, p. 33. "Nora Bayes in Pictures," *MPW,* 30 Mar 1918, 1803.

Bayfield, Harry [actor] (b. Denver CO, 29 Nov 1889–16 Feb 1946 [56], Los Angeles CA). BHD1, p. 38.

Bayley, Audre [actress]. No data found. (Sennett.) "Six Reasons Why Mack Sennett Comedies Are Popular," *Cinema Arts,* Aug 1926, 23 (photo).

Bayley, Hilda [actress] (b. London, England, 1 Sep 1888–25 May 1971 [82], London, England). BHD1, p. 38. IFN, p. 21.

Bayliff, W. Lane [actor] (b. London, England, 6 Apr 1870-Feb 1938 [67], Australia). BHD, p. 101. IFN, p. 21.

Bayma-Riva, Mary [actrress]. No data found. JS, p. 33 (in Italian silents from 1913).

Bayne, Beverly [actress] (*née* Beverly Pearl von Name, b. Minneapolis MN, 22 Nov 1892–18 Aug 1982 [89], Scottsdale AZ; heart attack). (b. 1893). m. **Francis X. Bushman,** 29 Jul 1918, Baltimore MD—div. 1932 (d. 1966); (2) Charles T. Hvass. (Film debut, *The Loan Shark;* Essanay; Metro.) "Beverly Bain," *Variety,* 8 Sep 1982. AMD, p. 33. BHD1, p. 39 (b. 1893; d. 29 Aug). FFF, p. 146 (b. 1895). Finch, p. 255 (b. 22 Nov 1892). MH, p. 96 (b. 1895). MSBB, p. 1030 (b. 1885; in 500 photoplays). SD. Slide, p. 157 (b. 1893). WWS, p. 262. "Beverly Bayne Hurt," *MPW,* 14 Dec 1912, 1064. "Some Prominent Essanay Photoplayers," *MPW,* 11 Jul 1914, 234–35. "How I Became a Photoplayer," *Motion Picture Magazine,*

Feb 1915, 113. "Beverly Bayne Signs with Metro," *NYDM,* 1 Sep 1915, 26:1 (she was Bushman's leading lady at Essanay "and it is very probable that she will alternate in that capacity with Marguerite Snow for the Quality Pictures Corporation."). "Beverly Bayne Signs with Quality," *MPW,* 4 Sep 1915, 1623. "Bushman and Bayne at San Diego," *MPW,* 25 Sep 1915, 2182. "Bushman and Bayne Re-Sign," *MPW,* 16 Jun 1917, 1800. "Al Ray, "Before the Stars Shone," *Picture-Play Masgazine,* Sep 1917, 93 (caught the eye of a director during a tour of the Chicago Essanay Studios and "was invited to act before the camera."). Roberta Courtland, "Beverly the Beautiful," *Motion Picture Magazine,* Feb 1918, 88–90 (during the interview, Bushman entered the little sitting-room. "'We have been asked to sample—and endorse—this new brand of chocolates, Bevs,' he remarked, with a delightfully boyish grin," leaving when he realized an interview was in progress.). "Bushman Marries Beverly Bayne," *MPW,* 17 Aug 1918, 967. "Beverly Bayne Signs," *MPW,* 13 Sep 1924, 126. "On the Set and Off," *MW,* 28 Feb 1925, 34 (separated from Bushman). Tom Fullbright, "Presenting Miss Beverly Ba[y]ne," *CFC,* 29 (Winter, 1970), 6–7; Part II, 30, 8–9; Part III, 31 (Summer, 1971), 9–11, 60; Part IV (Fall, 1971), 6–7.

Baynton, Henry [actor/manager] (b. Warwick, England, 23 Sep 1892–2 Jan 1951 [58], London, England). "Henry Baynton," *Variety,* 10 Jan 1951, p. 63. BHD, p. 101.

Bazzichelli, Giacomo [cinematographer]. No data found. JS, pp. 33–34 (in Italian silents from 1916).

Beach, Corra [actress/scenarist] (b. Toledo OH, 19 Dec 1880–5 Oct 1963 [82], No. Hollwyood CA). AS, p. 108. BHD, p., 101; BHD2, p. 17. IFN, p. 21.

Beach, Rex Ellingwood [writer/scenarist/director/producer] (brother-in-law of **Fred Stone**) (b. Atwood, Antrim Co., MI, 1 Sep 1877–7 Dec 1949 [72], Sebring FL; throat cancer and failing eyesight/suicide). m. Edith Greta Crater, 1907, NYC (d. 15 Apr 1947, Sebring FL). *Personal Exposures* (1941). *NYT,* 8 Dec 1949. "Died," *Time, The Weekly Magazine,* 19 Dec 1949, 71:1. "Rex Beach," *Variety,* 14 Dec 1949. AMD, p. 33. AS, p. 109. BHD2, p. 17. *Twentieth Century Authors,* pp. 91–92. WWWA. "Beach, Rex Ellingwood," *The National Cyclopœdia of American Biography,* Vol. 14 (1910), pp. 58–59. "Another Literary Work Filmed," *MPW,* 8 Jan 1910, 9. "Film Famous Authors; Vitagraph Company Prepares Novel Series for Authors' League Benefit," *NYDM,* 28 Jan 1914, 30:4. James S. McQuade, "Rex E. Beach," *MPW,* 21 Mar 1914, 1506. "Rex Beach Writing His Own Titles," *MPW,* 25 Aug 1917, 1205. "Rex Beach Exercises Author's New Prerogative," *MPW,* 23 Nov 1918, 847. "Beach Defined Director's Status," *MPW,* 21 Jun 1919, 1791. "Rex Beach Says Insufficient Time Is Given to Preparation of Continuities," *MPW,* 30 Aug 1919, 1290. "Joins Paramount," *MPW,* 11 Nov 1922, 156. "Buy Rex Beach Stories," *MPW,* 20 Aug 1927, 509. "Beach, Rex," *Dictionary of American Biography,* Supp. 4 (1974), pp. 59–61 (first story, *The Mule Driver and the Garrulous Mute, McClure's Magazine;* first book, *Pardners* [1905]. Also wrote *The Spoilers* [1906]. "Beach was the first American author to insert a clause about movie rights in his contracts, securing for himself a footnote in film history and a great deal of additional revenue." Fourteen novels and sixteen scenarios of Beach's were filmed; participated as a swimmer in the Olympic Games at St. Louis MO in 1904. His papers are at Rollins College, Winter Park FL; additional material at Syracuse University). "Wife of Rex Beach Dead," *NYT,* 15 Apr 1947, 25:5.

Beahan, Charles [scenarist] (b. 11 Feb 1903–18 Aug 1968 [65], Los Angeles CA; following surgery). "Charles Beahan," *Variety,* 21 Aug 1968. AS, p. 109. BHD2, p. 17.

Beal, Dolly [actress: Sennett Bathing Beauty]. No data found.

Beal, Frank G. [actor/director] (father of **Scott Beal**) (b. Cleveland OH, 11 Sep 1862–20 Dec 1934 [72], Los Angeles CA). m. **Louise Lester** (d. 1952). (Fox.) "Frank Beal," *Variety,* 25 Dec 1934. AMD, p. 33. AS, p. 109. BHD1, p. 39; BHD2, p. 18. IFN, p. 21. LACD, "director," h 1348 Vista. Truitt, p. 21 (b. 1864). "Gossip of the Studios," *NYDM,* 5 Aug 1914, 23:1 (photo). "History of Indiana," *MPW,* 22 Apr 1916, 632. "Frank Beal Now Fox Director," *MPW,* 26 Oct 1918, 500. George Katchmer, "Forgotten Cowboys/Girls—Part VII," *CI,* 179 (May 1990), 44.

Beal, Mrs. Louise Lester *see* **Lester, Louise**

Beal, Mary Egan [actress] (b. 1878?–10 Mar 1929 [50], Los Angeles CA; pneumonia). "Mary Egan Beal," *Variety,* 20 Mar 1929.

Beal, Scott Rathbone (son of **Frank Beal** and **Louise Lester**) [actor/assistant director] (b. Quinnesec MI, 14 Apr 1890–10 Jul 1973 [83], Los Angeles CA; cancer). m. Wilhelmina Eichert (nonprofessional), at SF CA, Nov? 1916. (Ross Photo Plays Co.) "Scott Beal," *Variety,* 24 Jul 1973. AS, p. 109. BHD, p. 101; BHD2, p. 18. IFN, p. 21. "Scott Beal," *Variety,* 8 Dec 1916, 7:3.

Beaman, Renee [scenarist]. No data found. LACD, "scenario writer," r 6129 Carl Ave.

Beamish, Frank [actor] (b. Memphis TN, 1881–3 Oct 1921 [40], New York NY). "Frank Beamish," *Variety,* 14 Oct 1921. BHD, p. 101. IFN, p. 21. Truitt, p. 21.

Beard, Matthew "Stymie" [actor] (b. Los Angeles CA, 1 Jan 1925–8 Jan 1981 [56], Los Angeles CA). BHD1, p. 39.

Bearnard, Armand [actor] (b. Paris, France, 21 May 1894–1968 [74?], Paris, France). BHD, p. 101.

Beasley, Barney [actor]. No data found. LACD, "photoplayer," r 6427 Sunset Blvd.

Beaton, Mary Louise (niece of **Richard Rowland**) [actress] (b. Philadelphia PA-d. 25 Jan 1961, Los Angeles CA). AMD, p. 33. BHD, p. 101. IFN, p. 21. "School Girl in Films," *LA Times,* 6 Feb 1920, II, p. 9 (signed with Metro). "Mary Beaton Makes Her Screen Debut with Metro," *MPW,* 28 Feb 1920, 1498. "Mary Louise Beaton's Work in Lytell Film Proves Her a 'Find,' Says Metro," *MPW,* 19 Feb 1921, 949. "Rowland's Niece a Bride," *MPW,* 8 Sep 1923, 131.

Beatty, George [actor] (b. 1888–21 Feb 1955 [66?], So. Stroudsburg NY). BHD, p. 102.

Beatty, Jerome [publicist/scenarist] ()b. Lawrence KS, 14 Nov 1886–8 May 1967 [80], Newton CT. AMD, p. 34. BHD2, p. 18. "Jerome Beatty with Thanhauser," *MPW,* 29 Jul 1916, 772. "Beatty Goes to McClures," *MPW,* 23 Dec 1916, 1794. "John C. Flinn Moves Higher Up with FP-L as J.B. Succeeds Him," *MPW,* 21 Feb 1920, 1204. "Jerome Beatty," *MPW,* 26 Mar 1927, 310. "Jerome Beatty Is F.N. Adv. Director," *MPW,* 3 Dec 1927, 7. 14.

Beatty, May [actress] (b. Christchurch, New Zealand, 4 Jun 1880–1 Apr 1945 [64], Covina CA). "May Beatty," *Variety,* 11 Apr 1945, p. 50. BHD1, p. 39.

Beaubien, Julien [actress] (*née* Julien A. Dolenzai, b. 1896?–18 Oct 1947 [51], Long Branch NJ). "Mrs. J.A. Dolenzai Murray," *Variety,* 22 Oct 1947. BHD, p. 102. IFN, p. 21. Truitt, p. 21.

Beauchamp, Clement H. [actor/director] (aka Jerry Drew, b. Bloomfield IA, 26 Aug 1898–14 Nov 1992 [94], Santa Rosa CA). AMD, p. 34. AS, p. 338 (Jerry Drew). BHD1, p. 163 (Jerry Drew). "Actor Injured in Auto Accident," *MPW,* 28 Feb 1920, 1480. "Beauchamp Acting and Directing," *MPW,* 2 Oct 1926, 290. "Clement Beauchamp Gone; No Police Aid Asked," *MPW,* 5 Nov 1927, 16 (changed name to Jerry Drew).

Beaudet, Louise [comic opera/film actress] (b. St. Emilie, Quebec, Canada, 1861–31 Dec 1947 [86], New York NY [Death Certificate Index No. 28431; age 87]). "Louise Beaudet," *Variety,* 7 Jan 1948. AMD, p. 34. BHD, p. 102. IFN, p. 21. Robert Grau, "The Film Studio; A Gold Laden Haven for the Patriarchs of the Stage," *NYDM,* 8 Sep 1915, 3:1 ("a new vogue for the old-time actor, who in the evening of life is firmly intrenched in the film studio, enjoying a change of environment replete with the comforts so rarely meted out to stage folk before the days of scientific visualization of their artistry." Their homes were near the studio and they could own a car. "For the first time in their prolonged careers they know the sensation of salaries paid with clock-like regularity for fifty-two weeks in the year. Not one [stage actor] has been with he Vitagraph less than three years." J. Stuart Blackton's weekly payroll for actors at Vitagraph was $20,000: 175 actors, $25 to $1,000 a week pay. Grau mentions Charles Kent, Beaudet, Cissy Fitzgerald, Sidney Drew, S. Rankin Drew, William Humphries, Van Dyke Brooke, and Harry Davenport, all from the stage. "Altogether, there is much to indicate that, while youth is a great asset in seeking conquest on the screen, there is always a welcome for that matured artistry so surely possessed by the old-time actor."). "Louise Beaudet," *MPW,* 20 Nov 1915, 1470. Louise Beaudet, Poem, *NYDM,* 11 Dec 1915, 24:1 (re the mispronunciation of her surname—it rhymes with "okay"). "Louise Beaudet," *MPW,* 9 Jun 1917, 1592.

Beaudine, Harold (brother of **William Beaudine**) [director] (b. New York NY, 29 Nov 1894–9 May 1949 [55], Los Angeles CA). m. Stephanie Tappe, 1924. (Christie.) "Harold Beaudine," *Variety,* 11 May 1949 ("retired motion picture director, who supervised some of the early day Christie comedies"). AMD, p. 34. AS, p. 110. BHD, p. 102; BHD2, p. 18. "Director Beaudine Weds," *MPW,* 17 May 1924, 304. "Harold Beaudine," *MPW,* 29 Nov 1926, 275.

Beaudine, William M. (brother of **Harold Beaudine**) [director] (b. New York NY, 15 Jan 1892–18 Mar 1970 [78], Canoga Park CA). "William Beaudine," *Variety,* 25 Mar 1970. AS, p. 110. BHD, p. 102; BHD2, p. 18. LACD, "moving picture director," h 8021 Fountain Ave. "Beaudine to Direct," *MPW,* 8 Mar 1924, 114. "Beaudine Back with Warners," *MPW,* 26 Dec 1925, 760.

Beaumont, Diana [actress] (b. London, England, 8 May 1909–21 Jun 1964 [55], London, England). BHD1, p. 40.

Beaumont, Gerald [journalist/writer] (b. London, England, 1880?–29 Jun 1926 [46], Los Angeles CA; pneumonia). "Gerald Beaumont," *Variety*, 30 Jun 1926. AS, p. 110. BHD2, . 18.

Beaumont, Harry [director] (b. Abilene KS, 10 Feb 1888–22 Dec 1966 [78], Santa Monica CA). (Selig-Polyscope Co.; Vitagraph; Edison; Essanay.) AMD, p. 34. AS, p. 110. BHD p. 102; BHD2, p. 18. IFN, p. 21. Spehr, p. 116 (b. 1893). Truitt, p. 21. "Three New Edison Directors," *MPW*, 24 Jul 1915, 632. "Harry Beaumont with Essanay," *MPW*, 22 Jan 1916, 607. "Harry Beaumont," *MPW*, 27 Oct 1917, 544 (b. 1883). "Warners Sign Harry Beaumont," *MPW*, 14 Apr 1923, 762.

Beaumont, Lucy [stage/film actress] (b. Bristol, England, 18 May 1873–24 Apr 1937 [63], New York NY [Death Certificate Index No. 10549; age 62]). m. Capt. Douglas Begora; Douglas A. Harris. (MGM.) "Lucy Beaumont," *Variety*, 28 Apr 1937. BHD1, p. 40. IFN, p. 21. SD. Truitt, p. 21. George Katchmer, "Remembering the Great Silents," *CI*, 243 (Sep 1995), 42 (b. 1863).

Beaumont, Nellie [actress] (b. Ramsgate, Kent, England, 1870–26 Oct 1938 [68?], Concord NH). BHD, p. 102.

Beavers, Louise [actress] (b. Cincinnati OH, 8 Mar 1902–26 Oct 1962 [60], Los Angeles CA; heart attack). m. LeRoy Moore. (Began 1924.) "Louise Beavers, Actress, 60; Starred in 'Beulah' TV Series," *NYT*, 27 Oct 1962, 25:2. "Louise Beavers," *Variety*, 31 Oct 1962. BHD1, p. 40 (b. 1898). IFN, p. 21.

Beban, George, Jr. (son of **George Beban, Sr.**) [actor] (b. New York NY, 16 Jun 1914–28 Sep 1977 [63], Burbank CA). BHD, p. 102.

Beban, George, Sr. (father of **George Beban, Jr.**) [stage/film actor/scenarist] (b. San Francisco CA, 5 Nov 1873–5 Oct 1928 [54], Los Angeles CA; thrown from a horse on 29 Sep 1928). m. Edith E. MacBride (d. 1926). (Ince; NYMP Co.; World; Morosco.) "George Beban Dies After Riding Accident; Actor, Kicked by Horse, Succumbs in Los Angeles Hospital of Complications," *NYT*, 6 Oct 1928, 19:4. "George Beban," *Variety*, 10 Oct 1928 (age 55). AMD, p. 34. AS, p. 110. BHD, p. 102; BHD2, p. 18. FDY, p. 417. IFN, p. 21 (age 55). MH, p. 96. SD. MSBB, p. 1021 ("greatest portrayer of Italian character parts in America."). Spehr, p. 116. Truitt, p. 22. WWS, p. 51. "George Beban an Originating Genius," *MPW*, 9 Oct 1915, 278. "Beban's Bit," *MPW*, 18 Dec 1915, 2205. "George Beban with Pallas," *MPW*, 18 Mar 1916, 1817. "Beban Now Heads His Own Company," *MPW*, 16 Mar 1918, 1497–98. "Mrs. George Beban Dies," *MPW*, 18 Dec 1926, p. 4 (d. 10 Dec 1926, NY). Merton, "He'll Help You Get in the Movies!, George Beban, Renowned Stage and Screen Actor, to Retire from Public Life to Develop Young Talent for the Screen," *Paris and Hollywood Screen Secrets Magazine*, III (May 1927), 22–25 (touring in *The Loves of Ricardo*. To institute of motion picture school of acting. "Financially able to undertake the project he intends leaving nothing undone in the way of finding and schooling potential stars." His current find was Amille Milanne. Claims that he married Helen Jerome Eddy.).

Becci, Franco [actor] (b. Rome, Italy, 1 Dec [1880's]-5 Nov 1951 [ca. 66?], Rome, Italy). JS, p. 34 (in Italian silents from 1919).

Bech (or Beck), Lily [actress] (*née* Lily Beck Magnussen, b. Denmark, 29 Dec 1885–1939 [53]). m. **Victor Seastrom**—div. 1916 (d. 1960). BHD, p. 102. IFN, p. 21. Katz, p. 96. "Lily Beck; One of Great Northern's Charming Players," *MPW*, 13 Sep 1913, 1165 (photograph only).

Bechdolt, Fred R. [writer]. No data found. AMD, p. 34. "Kalem Signs Another Big Author," *MPW*, 6 Jan 1917, 62.

Bechtel, William A. "Billy" [actor] (b. Berlin, Germany, 12 Jun 1867–27 Oct 1930 [63], Los Angeles CA). m. **Jenny**. (Edison, 1908.) "William A. Bechtel," *Variety*, 5 Nov 1930. BHD1, p. 40. IFN, p. 21. Truitt, p. 22. "Bechtels Leave Edison," *NYDM*, 10 Mar 1915, 29:1 (had 500 roles in Edison films). "Gossip of the Studios," *NYDM*, 5 May 1915, 29:1–2 (with photos of Bechtel and wife. He took "a couple of months' vacation from the clicking shutter.").

Bechtel, Mrs. William (Jenny) [actress] (*née*?, b. New York, NY, 12 Jun 1861–21 Oct 1938 [77], Los Angeles CA). (Edison, 1908.) BHD, p. 102.

Beck, Arthur F. [executive]. No data found. AMD, p. 34. "Arthur F. Beck Heads Sterling," *MPW*, 29 Dec 1917, 1963.

Beck, Cornish (or Cornice) [actor] (b. 2 Jan 1907–Jan 1970 [63]). AMD, p. 34. "Beck Made Debut Early in Life," *MPW*, 11 Sep 1920, 198.

Beck, Fred [executive[. No data found. AMD, p. 34. "Fred Beck Returns to 20th Century Co.," *MPW*, 19 Feb 1916, 1139.

Beck, Ludwig [actor] (b. 1887-Jan 1962 [74?]). BHD, p. 102; BHD2, p. 18.

Becker, Bruno C. [director] (b. 1890–9 Feb 1926 [35?], Hollywood CA; acute bronchitis). m. **Gail Henry** (d. 1972). "Bruno C. Becker," *Variety*, 17 Feb 1926. AS, p. 111. BHD2, p. 18. Cal York, "Plays and Players," *Photoplay Magazine*, Feb 1917, 86 (married Henry).

Becker, Frederick G. [actor] (b. Chicago IL, 8 Sep 1882–28 Mar 1966 [83], Glendale CA). BHD, p. 102; BHD2, p. 18.

Beckman, John [art director] (b. Astoria OR, 1898-Los Angeles Co. CA, 26 Oct 1989 [91?], Sherman Oaks CA; heart attack in his sleep). AS, p. 111. BHD2, p. 18.

Beckway, William T. [cinematographer]. No data found. AMD, p. 35. "Beckway Engaged by Metro," *MPW*, 13 Dec 1919, 778.

Beckwith, Brainerd [actor] (b. 11 Dec 1902–20 Jan 1981 [78], Pasadena CA). BHD1, p. 604.

Beckwith, Walter [actor]. No data found. LACD, "actor," r 1401 N. Western Ave.

Bedding, Thomas [publicist/director/writer]. No data found. AMD, p. 35. Thomas Bedding, "Moving Pictures in Natural Colors," *MPW*, IV, 9 Jan 1909, 30–31. Thomas Bedding, "The Largest Manufacturer of Films for Moving Pictures in the World," *MPW*, V, 7 Agu 1909, 186. Thomas Bedding, "Edison: His Life and Inventions," *MPW*, 3 Dec 1910, 1280–81. "Bedding with I.M.P.," *MPW*, 9 Dec 1911, 812. "Thomas Bedding," *MPW*, 9 Oct 1915, 280. "Thomas Bedding Resigns from World Film," *MPW*, 4 Dec 1915, 1811. "General Film to Release Subject Starring Edna Mayo," *MPW*, 23 Nov 1918, 846.

Bedells, Phyllis [actress] (b. Bristol, Gloucester, England, 2 Aug 1894–2 May 1985 [90], London, England). BHD, p. 102.

Bedford, Barbara [actress] (*née* Violet May Rose, b. Eastman, near Prairie du Chiene WI, 19 Jul 1903–25 Oct 1981 [78], Jacksonville FL). m. **Albert Roscoe**, 26 Aug 1922–30; remarried (d. 1933); **Irvin V. Willat** (d. 1976); actor Terry Spencer, 1940 (d. 3 Oct 1954). (Began as an extra, 1919.) AMD, p. 35. BHD1, p. 41. BR, pp. 98–101. FFF, p. 148. FSS, p. 26. Katz, p. 97. MH, p. 96. "Beautiful New Fox Star Began Career in an Unusual Fashion," *MPW*, 3 Sep 1921, 82. "Ince Signs Bedford," *MPW*, 1 Nov 1924, 57. "Barbara Bedford," *MPW*, 22 Aug 1925, 846. Tom Walter, "Barbara Bedford," *MPW*, 23 Apr 1927, 710–11. "Barbara Bedford Scorns Reduction," *MPW*, 24 Sep 1927, 227. "Buck Rainey's Filmographies; Barbara Bedford; Dependable, Talented and Personable, She Adapted Easily to Her Many Roles," *CI*, 113 (Nov 1984), 37–38; *CI*, 114 (Dec 1984), 19 *et passim*. George A. Katchmer, "More Forgotten Cowboys and Cowgirls—Chapter 6," *CI*, 172 (Oct 1989), C12. Billy Doyle, "Barbara Bedford," *CI*, 253 (Jul 1996), C2-C3.

Bedford, Louis R. [actor]. No data found. LACD, "photoplayer," r 1760 New Hampshire Ave.

Bee, Richard [scenarist]. No data found. FDY, p. 417.

Beebe, Ford I., Sr. [publicist/title writer/scenarist/actor] (b. Grand Rapids MI, 26 Nov 1888–26 Nov 1978 [90], Lake Elsinore CA, CA). AMD, p. 35. AS, p. 112. BHD2, p. 18. FDY, pp. 417, 441. Katz, p. 97 (began 1920). LACD, "reporter, *Motion Picture News*," h 2025 Cambridge. "Ford Beebe with Signal," *MPW*, 6 May 1916, 995.

Beebe, Marjorie [actress] (b. Kansas City MO, 1908?). (FBO; Fox.) AMD, p. 35. Erle Hampton, "Margie's Magic," *Screenland*, *XV*, Sep 1927, 28–29, 100–01. "Marjorie Beebe," *MPW*, 17 Dec 1927, 32.

Beecher, Ada [actress] (b. 1862?–30 Mar 1935 [73], Los Angeles CA). BHD, p. 102. IFN, p. 22. Truitt, p. 22.

Beecher, Janet (sister of Olive Wyndham) [actress] (*née* Martha Mysenburg, b. Jefferson City MO, 21 Oct 1884–6 Aug 1955 [70], Washington CT; heart attack). m. (1) Henry R. Guggenheimer; (2) Richard H. Hoffman. (In *Fine Feathers*, Cosmos Feature Film Corp., 1915). "Janet Beecher," *Variety*, 10 Aug 1955 (age 69; began in films in 1932). AMD, p. 35. BHD1, p. 41. IFN, p. 22. SD. Truitt, p. 22. "Janet Beecher," *MPW*, 5 Jun 1915, 1619.

Beecher, Margaret (granddaughter of Henry Ward Beecher; grand-niece of Harriet B. Stowe) [actress]. No data found. (Hemmer Superior Productions, Inc.; in *Birthright*, 1920.) AMD, p. 35. "Margaret Beecher Makes Her Screen Debut in Hemmer Film," *MPW*, 7 Aug 1920, 760. "Margaret Beecher in Playgoer's Film," *MPW*, 18 Mar 1922, 264.

Beecroft, Arthur [producer] (b. 1878–8 Jul 1934 [56?], Mamaroneck NY). BHD2, p. 19.

Beecroft, Chester [publicist/writer/manager] (b. New York NY, 1881–7 Jan 1959 [77?]). AMD, p. 35. BHD2, p. 19. "Chester Beecroft with General Films," *MPW*, 6 Sep 1913, 1051. "Flickers," *MPW*, 22 Nov 1913, 871. F.J. Beecroft, "Publicity Men I Have Met; F.J.B. Gives a Chatty Account of the Deadly Enemies of the Anvil Chorus and Their Important Work," *NYDM*, 14 Jan 1914, 48 (other publicists named here are Philip Mindil, Joe

Brandt, Joseph White Farnham, Samuel Hopkins Hadley, R.R. Nehles, Don Meaney, Sam Spedon, Omer F. Doud, John B. Clymer, Charles Nixon, William Barry, Lloyd Robinson, H. Antoine D'Arcy, P. Allen Parsons, Bert Ennis, Willard Holcomb, B.P. Schulberg, Victor Johnson, H.Z. Levine, and Bert Adler). "Chester Beecroft," *MPW,* 28 Mar 1914, 1691. Merritt Crawford, "The First Big Time Movie Press Agent," *MPW,* 26 Feb 1927, 623, 652.

Beecroft, Victor R. [stage/film actor] (b. London, England, 1887?–25 Mar 1958 [71], Newport News VA). "Victor R. Beecroft," *Variety,* 2 Apr 1958 ("Beecroft, who preferred the stage to the screen, nevertheless appeared in several silents"). AS, p. 112. BHD, p. 102. IFN, p. 22. Truitt, p. 22.

Beers, Fred C. [casting director/actor] (b. Wilkes-Barre PA, 8 Oct 1895–16 Nov 1946 [51]). (Service Bureau Motion Picture Producers.) IFN, p. 22. LACD, "casting director," r 1526 S. Hope.

Beery, Noah W.L., Jr. (son of **Noah Beery, Sr.**; nephew of **Wallace** and **William C. Beery**) (b. New York NY, 10 Aug 1913 [Birth Certificate Index No. 40334]-1 Nov 1994 [81], near Tehachapi CA, cerebral thrombosis). m. Maxine Jones (daughter of Buck Jones), 1940–66; Lisa. (Film debut: *The Mark of Zorro,* 1920.) "Noah Beery Jr., 81, an Actor Known for Playing Sidekicks," *NYT,* 3 Nov 1994, B15:4 (brain surgery on Sept. 18th; on TV in *Riverboat, Circus Boy* and *The Rockford Files* [1974–80]). "Noah Beery Jr.," *Variety,* 7 Nov 1994, p. 52:1. "'Rockford's Noah Beery Jr. Dies at 81," *NY Post,* 2 Nov 1994, 74:4. BHD1, p. 41. Katz, p. 98.

Beery, Noah N., Sr. (brother of **Wallace** and **William C. Beery**; father of **Noah Beery, Jr.**) [actor] (b. Kansas City MO, 17 Jan 1882–1 Apr 1946 [64], Los Angeles CA; heart attack). m. Margaret Lindsay (d. 1955). "Noah Beery Sr., 62, Film Veteran, Dies; Villain on Screen for Many Years, Star of Todd Stage Show, Succumbs on Coast," *NYT,* 2 Apr 1946, 28:2. "Noah Beery, Sr.," *Variety,* 3 Apr 1946 (age 62). AMD, p. 35. BHD, p. 102 (b. Smithville MO). FFF, p. 63 (b. 17 Jan 1882). FSS, p. 26. GK, pp. 34–49. HCH, p. 123. IFN, p. 22 (b. Smithville MO). LACD, "actor," h 6421 Ivarene Ave. MH, p. 96. SD. Truitt, p. 22 (b. 1884). "Mayer Engages Noah Beery," *MPW,* 20 Dec 1919, 962. Grace Kingsley, "Strange to Say the Stars Adore Him Even Though He Steals the Picture," *MW,* 2 Aug 1924, 16–17, 29. "Beery Signs with Paramount," *MPW,* 4 Apr 1925, 490. Helen Fulton, "The Heart of a Bad Man; The Stethoscope Is Applied to Noah Beery," *MM,* Jan 1926, 67, 114. "Noah Beery Signed by Samuel Goldwyn," *MPW,* 26 Nov 1927, 23. George A. Katchmer, "Noah Beery, Sr.; The Villain's Villain!," *CI,* 71 (Sep 1980), 40–41.

Beery, Wallace T. Webster (brother of **Noah Beery, Sr.**, and **William C. Beery**) [Forepaugh-Sells Circus/ stage/film actor/director] (b. Kansas City MO, 1 Apr 1885–15 Apr 1949 [64], Beverly Hills CA; heart attack). m. (1) **Gloria Swanson**, 27 Mar 1916—div. 13 Dec 1918; Areta (Rita) Gillman, 1930. (Essanay, 1913; Keystone; Universal; MGM.) "Wallace Beery, 64, Screen Star, Dies; Leading Performer 30 Years Won 'Oscar' in 1931 for His Role in 'The Champ,'" *NYT,* 17 Apr 1949, 77:1. "Wallace Beery," *Variety,* 20 Apr 1949 (age 60). AMD, p. 35. BHD1, p. 41. FFF, p. 21 (b. 1886). FSS, p. 27. GK, pp. 49–67. HCH, p. 95. IFN, p. 22. LACD, "actor," r 6732 Hollywood Blvd. MH, p. 96 (b. 1886). SD. Truitt, p. 23. "Studio Gossip," *NYDM,* 23 Jun 1915, 30:4 (he shot a diminutive squirrel; the kick of the gun threw him out of his canoe, "thus adding a bit of business not called for in the 'script."). "Wallace Beery to Direct Carter DeHaven," *MPW,* 27 May 1916, 1524. "Wallace Beery to Wed," *MPW,* 9 Aug 1924, 436 (did not marry). Harry Carr, "He Learned About Villains from Topsy; A Surprising Chapter in Wallace Beery's Life...," *MPC,* Nov 1924, 35, 77–78. Geoffrey Shurlock, "For Men Only! A Few Chapters in the Life of Wallace Beery, the Greatest Champion of the Homely Man, Who Started His Screen Career as a Female Impersonator," *Paris and Hollywood,* Sep 1926, 24–27, 86 ("My first job in pictures would have been as a cowboy—if I had got the job. Ford Sterling and I were loafing between musical comedy engagements in New York, and heard that there was an engagement open at the old Thanhouser Studio." He couldn't ride, but signed up for the next day—but it rained. He then went to Essanay in Chicago and met and directed Swanson and married her. "...I got her the first job she had with Sennett as a bathing beauty." Beery's "ferocious ugliness beats the delighted female into ecstatic adoration; and the men all root for him wildly because his popularity lifts the curse from their own unprepossessing countenences."). "Beery Patches Up Differences with Famous," *MPW,* 12 Feb 1927, 491. "Beery Denies Knowing Girl Accuser," *MPW,* 1 Oct 1927, 291. Helen Louise Walker, "Just Plane Crazy; Because He Is, Wallace Beery Keeps Everyone He Knows Up in the Air," *MPC,* Nov 1928, 55, 86, 88 ("Way back in the early days when he and Gloria Swanson were still man and wife, he had the first automobile in the picture colony."). Earl Anderson, "Wallace Beery," *FIR,* Jun/Jul 1973, 330–57; Aug/Sep, 415–22. George A. Katchmer, "Aw, Shucks!; Wallace Beery," *CI,* 135 (Sep 1986), 13–14, 16; 136 (Oct 1986), 15–18. Richard E. Braff, "The Films of Wallace Beery," *CI,* 149 (Nov 1987), C18, 56; 150 (Dec 1987), 45–47, 61; #231, 43.

Beery, William C. [Keystone Cop] (brother of **Noah Beery, Sr.**, and **Wallace Beery**) (b. Clay Co. MO, 5 Apr 1879–25 Dec 1949 [70], Beverly Hills CA). (Sennett; Essanay.) "W.C. Beery, Aided Brothers' Film Start," *NYT,* 26 Dec 1949, 29:4. "William C. Beery," *Variety,* 28 Dec 1949. BHD, p. 102. IFN, p. 22.

Begeman, Dwight [cameraman]. No data found. AMD, p. 35. "More Metro Men Enlist," *MPW,* 22 Dec 1917, 1770.

Begg, Gordon [actor] (*né* Alexander Gordon Begg, b. Aberdeen, Scotland, 14 Jan 1868–Feb 1954 [86]). BHD1, p. 41. IFN, p. 22.

Beggs, Lee "Larry" [stage/film actor/director] (b. New York NY, 1871?–17 Nov 1943 [72], New York NY [Death Certificate Index No. 25042; age 73]). (Vitagraph; Solax.) "Lee Beggs," *Variety,* 24 Nov 1943. AMD, p. 35. AS, p. 112 (d. 18 Nov). BHD1, p. 41; BHD2, p. 19 (b. Omaha NB; d. 18 Nov). IFN, p. 22 (Lee Beggs). SD. "What's in a Face?," *MPW,* 23 Dec 1911, 993. Lester Sweyd, "What They Are Doing Now," *Motion Picture Magazine,* Feb 1918, 12 ("Appearing in vaudeville in a sketch called 'Old Folks at Home,' we find Lee Beggs...who was one of the original members of the old Solax Company.").

Beggs, William [actor] (b. Belfast, Ireland, 1893?–11 Sep 1925 [32], Phoenix AZ; punctured lung from auto accident). m. "William Beggs," *Variety,* 23 Sep 1925.

Begley, Ed [actor] (*né* Edward James Begley, b. Hartford CT, 25 Mar 1901–28 Apr 1970 [69], Los Angeles CA; heart attack). m. (1) Amanda Huff; (2) Dorothy Reeves; (3) Helen Jordan. "Ed Begley," *Variety,* 6 May 1970. BHD1, p. 41. IFN, p. 22. SD.

Behmer, Ernst [actor] (b. Konigsberg, Germany, 22 Dec 1875–26 Feb 1938 [62]). BHD, p. 102.

Behn, Harry [scenarist]. No data found. AMD, p. 35. FDY, p. 417. Tom Waller, "Harry Behn," *MPW,* 23 Jul 1927, 234–35.

Behrens, Ben [film editor] (b. 1891?–21 Feb 1962 [71], Los Angeles CA). "Ben Behrens," *Variety,* 28 Feb 1962. BHD2, p. 19.

Behrens, Frederick [actor] (b. 1853?–5 Jan 1938 [84], Los Angeles CA). "Frederick Behrens," *Variety,* 12 Jan 1938. AS, p/ 113. IFN, p. 22.

Behrle, Fred F. [actor] (b. San Diego CA, 8 Jul 1891–20 May 1941 [49], San Fernando CA; heart attack). (Vitagraph.) "Fred Behrle," *Variety,* 28 May 1941. AS, p. 113. BHD1, p. 41. IFN, p. 22. Truitt, p. 23.

Beierle, Alfred [actor] (b. Berlin, Germany, 4 Jun 1885–16 Mar 1950 [64]). BHD, p. 102.

Bela, Nicholas [stage/film actor/writer] (b. Budapest, Hungary, 18 Jul 1900–18 Nov 1963 [63], New York NY; heart attack). m. Katherine Davis—div. 1947. "Nicholas Bela, Playwright, Dies; Testified on Communist Links," *NYT,* 24 Nov 1963, 23:1 ("Mr. Bela came to this country in 1928 upon being hired by a European talent scout of First National Studios in Burbank, Calif. He had been an actor and director with the Budapest Comedy Theater. He was in Hollywood as a production assistant, writer and character actor until 1943, when he became a free-lance writer in New York."). "Nicholas Bela," *Variety,* 27 Nov 1963. AS, p. 113 (d. 19 Nov). BHD1, p. 42; BHD2, p. 19 (d. 19 Nov). IFN, p. 22.

Belasco, Arthur J.B. [actor] (b. 14 May 1888–8 Nov 1979 [91], Los Angeles CA). AS, p. 113. BHD1, p. 42.

Belasco, David (brother of **Walter Belasco**; 3rd cousin of **Genevieve** and **Jay Belasco**) [scenarist/producer] (b. San Francisco CA, 25 Jul 1853–14 May 1931 [77], New York NY [Death Certificate Index No. 13409]). m. Cecilia Loverich (d. 1926). "David Belasco," *Variety,* 20 May 1931. AMD, p. 35. AS, p. 113. BHD, p. 103; BHD2, p. 19 (b. 1854). IFN, p. 22. SD. "David Belasco Earns $5.00," *MPW,* 7 Jun 1913, 1013. "Belasco on Motion Pictures," *MPW,* 13 Jun 1914, 1513–14. "A New Outlet for Genius; That Is David Belasco's Impression of the Picture Art—An Exclusive Interview with the Wizard of the Stage," *NYDM,* 17 Feb 1915, 23:1. "David Belasco Welcomed Into Picture Industry by Will Hays," *MPW,* 31 Mar 1923, 560. Kenneth MacGowan, "The Equity Tangle and the Actors' Strike," *MPC,* Sep 1924, 46, 88. Gwen MacDougall of Berkshire, England, supplied data on the Belascos.

Belasco, Genevieve (daughter of Selina and Isaac Doloro Belasco of England; 3rd cousin of **David** and **Jay Belasco**) [actress] (b. London, England, aka Genevieve Dolaro, 1872–17 Nov 1956 [84], New York NY [Death Certificate Index No. 24302; age 84]). "Genevieve Belasco," *Variety,* 21 Nov 1956. BHD, p. 103. IFN, p. 22. Truitt, p. 23.

Belasco, Jay (3rd cousin of **David** and

Genevieve Belasco) [actor] (*né* Reginald James Belasco, b. Guisbrough, County of York, England, 11 Jan 1889–May 1949 [60], Santa Monica CA; coronary occlusion). (Keystone, 1915; Strand-Mutual; Marine, Universal; Christie; Realart; Selznick; Pathé; Educational.) AMD, p. 35. BHD1, p. 42 (b. Brooklyn, 1888). MH, p. 96. "Jay Belasco in 'The Rivals,'" *MPW,* 4 Nov 1916, 676. Billy H. Doyle, "Jay Belasco," *The Silent Film Newsletter,* Jun 1993, 64.

Belasco, Walter (brother of **David Belasco**) [actor] (b. Vancouver, Canada, 1864?–21 Jun 1939 [75], San Francisco CA). (NYMPC, 1913; Bluebird; Universal.) AS, p. 113. BHD, p. 103. IFN, p. 22. 1918 Studio Directory (b. 1876).

Belcher, Alice [actress] (b. 1880?–9 May 1939 [59], Los Angeles CA). "Alice Belcher," *Variety,* 17 May 1939. BHD, p. 103 (b. 1869). IFN, p. 22. Truitt, p. 23.

Belcher, Charles M. [actor] (b. San Francisco CA, 27 Jul 1872–10 Dec 1943 [71], Los Angeles CA). "Charles Belcher," *Variety,* 15 Dec 1943 (age 65). AS, pp. 113–14. BHD1, p. 42. IFN, p. 22.

Belcher, Ernest, "Dance Director to Movieland" (father of Marge Champion; step-father of **Lina Basquette**) (b. 8 Jun 1882–24 Feb 1973 [90], Los Angeles CA). "Ernest Belcher," *Variety,* 7 Mar 1973 ("Belcher launched his career with D.W. Griffith when he taught Carol Dempster her dance numbers in 'Broken Blossoms,' in 1918. In 1919, he moved to Mack Sennett studio and it was estimated he did more than one-half of all dance sequences in films during the next 10 years"; worked to the late 1960's). BHD2, p. 19. Nellie B. Parker, "Dancing for the Screen," *MPC,* Sep 1927, 39, 84, 87 (discusses Belcher and Theodore Kosloff).

Belcher, Frank H. [actor/opera singer] (b. San Francisco CA, 1868?–27 Feb 1947 [78], Brentwood, LI NY). m. Nan. "Frank Belcher; Retired Actor and Singer Was Member of Lambs 43 Years," *NYT,* 28 Feb 1947, 24:3. "Frank H. Belcher," *Variety,* 5 Mar 1947 (in vaudeville with James J. Corbett). AMD, p. 36. AS, p. 114. BHD, p. 103. "Frank Belcher with George Kleine," *MPW,* 11 Dec 1915, 2002.

Belfield, Richard [actor] (b. Philadelphia PA, 23 Jul 1873–2 Jan 1940 [66], Los Angeles CA). BHD, p. 103. IFN, p. 23.

Bel Geddes, Norman (father of Barbara Bel Geddes) [director/art director/writer/stage producer] (b. 1899?–8 May 1958 [59], New York NY). m. Edith Lutyens. AMD, p. 36. "Norman Bel Geddes," *Variety,* 210, 14 May 1958, 63:1 (age 65; directed *Nathan Hale,* Universal, 1916). "Joins Paramount," *MPW,* 7 Jun 1924, 538.

Bell, Adelaide [vaudeville dancer] (d. 9 Jun 1942, Brooklyn NY). "Adelaide Bell," *Variety,* 17 Jun 1942 (with Harry Lauder and Ziegfeld).

Bell, Arnold "Jimmy" [actor] (d. 12 Mar 1988). BHD1, p. 42.

Bell, Digby Valentine [stage/vaudeville/film actor] (b. Milwaukee WI, 1851?–20 Jun 1917 [66], New York NY [Death Certificate Index No. 19759; age 67]). m. (1) Lillian Dunton (d. 1902); (2) Laura Joyce (*née* Hannah Joyce Maskell, d. 1904). (Film debut: *Father and the Boys,* Universal, 1915.) "Digby Bell, Actor, Dies in 69th Year; Comedian and Opera Singer Who Won First Successes in Gilbert and Sullivan's Works," *NYT,* 21 Jun 1917, 13:4 (age 68). "Digby Bell," *Variety,* 29 Jun 1917 (60). BHD, p. 103 (b. 1879). IFN, p. 23. SD. J. Van Cartmell, "Along the Pacific Coast," *NYDM,* 30 Oct 1915, 27:2 (filming *Father and the Boys,* 5 reels).

Bell, Emma *see* **Clifton, Emma Bell**

Bell, Frederick G[atenbury] [actor] (b. England, 1879?–10 Dec 1930 [51], Bronx NY [Death Certificate Index No. 9481]). m. Gladys Hopton. "Fred G. Bell," *Variety,* 24 Dec 1930. BHD, p. 103.

Bell, Gaston [actor] (b. Boston MA, 27 Sep 1877–11 Dec 1963 [86], Woodstock NY). "Gaston Bell," *Variety,* 18 Dec 1963. AMD, p. 36. BHD, p. 103. IFN, p. 23. Truitt, p. 23. "Gaston Bell Joins Lubin," *MPW,* 27 Dec 1913, 1545. "Gaston Bell," *MPW,* 15 Aug 1914, 946.

Bell, Genevieve [actress] (b. 1895?–3 Oct 1951 [56], Los Angeles CA). (Lasky; De Mille.) "Genevieve Bell," *Variety,* 10 Oct 1951 ("she was one of the early Hollywood film players"). BHD1, p. 42. IFN, p. 23.

Bell, Hank [actor] (*né* Henry Branch Bell, b. Los Angeles CA, 21 Jan 1892–4 Feb 1950 [58], Los Angeles CA; heart attack). "Henry Bell," *Variety,* 15 Feb 1950. BHD1, p. 42. IFN, p. 23. Truitt, p. 23. George Katchmer, "Remembering the Great Silents," *CI,* 183 (Sep 1990), 44. Mario DeMarco, "Hank Bell," *CI,* 201 (Mar 1992), 55.

Bell, Howard [head of advertising agency/radio announcer] (b. 1908?–9 Mar 1959 [51], Hollywood CA). "Howard Bell," *Variety,* 18 Mar 1959.

Bell, Karina [actress] (b. Copenhagen, Denmark, 26 Sep 1898–5 Jun 1979 [80], Helsinki, Finalnd). BHD1, p. 42.

Bell, Marie [actress] (b. Begles, France, 23 Dec 1900–15 Aug 1985 [84], Neuilly, France). BHD1, p. 42.

Bell, Mildred M. [script assistant]. No data found. LACD, r 6053 Selma Ave.

Bell, Monta [actor/director/producer/scenarist/editor] (*né* Louis Monta Bell, b. Washington DC, 5 Feb 1891–4 Feb 1958 [66], Woodland HIlls CA). m. Lucille, 1910; **Betty Lawford** (d. 1960). "Monta Bell Dies; Ex-Film Director; Maker of Silent and Early Sound Movies Was 66—Newsman and Actor," *NYT,* 5 Feb 1958, 28:1. "Monta Bell," *Variety,* 12 Feb 1958 (age 67). AMD, p. 36. AS, p. 114. BHD, p. 103; BHD2, p. 19. IFN, p. 23. Truitt, pp. 23–24. Jim Tully, "The Man Who Sold Himself," *MPC,* Nov 1924, 23, 85–86. "Bell to Direct 'Charm,'" *MPW,* 23 Jan 1926, 323. "Completing 'Boy Friend,'" *MPW,* 8 May 1926, 176. "Monta Bell to Supervise," *MPW,* 29 Nov 1926, 3. "Bell Gets New Contract," *MPW,* 19 Feb 1927, 545. "Bell Uses Large Party in His Current Production," *MPW,* 20 Aug 1927, 531. Homer Joseph Dodge, "Came the Dawn Like Thunder Across the Potomac and Brought Monta Bell Out of Darkness," *MPC,* Jan 1928, 25, 67. Robert S. Birchard, "Monta Bell; In the Shadow of the Stars," *Griffithiana,* Oct 1994, pp. 199–211.

Bell, Pearl Doles [novelist/scenarist] (*née?,* b. 1885?–11 Mar 1968 [83], New York NY). m. Gilbert E. Rubens. "Pearl Doles Bell, 83, Dead; A Novelist During Twenties," *NYT,* 13 Mar 1968, 53:5 (wrote *Sandra,* 1924). "Pearl D. Bell," *Variety,* 20 Mar 1968. AMD, p. 36. AS, p. 114 (d. 1966). "Fox Takes Option on Works of Mrs. Pearl Doles Bell," *MPW,* 17 Apr 1920, 443. "Pearl Doles Bell to Write Stories for Shirley Mason," *MPW,* 7 Aug 1920, 758. "Many Pictures Are Spoiled by Poor Subtitle, Says Mrs. Bell," *MPW,* 29 Jan 1921, 582.

Bell, Ralph W. [actor/director] (b. 1883?–14 Jul 1936 [53], San Francisco CA; pneumonia). m. (1) **Pert Kelton** (d. 1968); (2) Mary Bordon. (Columbia; Metro.) "Ralph W. Bell," *Variety,* 22 Jul 1936. AS, p. 115. BHD1, p. 43. IFN, p. 23. SD.

Bell, Rex [actor] (*né* George Francis Beldam, b. Chicago IL, 16 Oct 1903–4 Jul 1962 [58], Las Vegas NV; coronary occlusion). m. **Clara Bow** (d. 1965). "Lieut. Gov. Rex Bell of Nevada, ex-Cowboy Screen Star, Dies," *NYT,* 5 Jul 1962, 23:5; "Funeral Held for Rex Bell; Widow, Clara Bow, Attends," *NYT,* 10 Jul 1962, 33:1; "No Bequest to Clara Bow Made in Husband's Will," *NYT,* 12 Jul 1962, 18:3. "Rex Bell," *Variety,* 11 Jul 1962. AS, p. 115. BHD1, p. 43. IFN, p. 23. Truitt, p. 24 (b. 1905). Oscar Henning, "Thar's Gold in That Thar Boy; Mr. Fox Left No Doubt About It When He Signed Rex Bell to Whoop Up His W.-K. Westerns," *MPC,* Jul 1928, 63, 89 (replaced Rex King in Fox's cowboyland).

Bell, Spencer [actor] (b. Lexington KY, 25 Sep 1887–18 Aug 1935 [47]). AS, p. 115. BHD1, p. 43. IFN, p. 23.

Bell, William F. [actor] (b. New York NY, 1890). (Lubin; Reliance; Vitagraph.) 1918 Studio Directory, p. 65.

Bellamy, George [actor] (b. Bristol, England, 10 Jul 1866–26 Dec 1944 [78]). AS, p. 115. BHD1, p. 43. IFN, p. 23. SD.

Bellamy, Madge [stage/film actress] (*née* Margaret Philpott, b. Hillsboro TX, 30 Jun 1899–24 Jan 1990 [90], Upland CA; chronic heart ailment). m. Logan Metcalf, 1928, Tiajuana (lasted 4 days). *A Darling of the Twenties* (NY: The Vestal Press, Ltd., 1989). (Film debut: *The Riddle: Woman,* Pathé, 1920.) "Madge Bellamy, 90, 1920's Film Actress," *NYT,* 27 Jan 1990, 32:3. "Madge Bellamy," *Variety,* 31 Jan 1990, p. 94 (age 96?). Paul Feldman, "Silent Screen Actress Madge Bellamy, 89," *LA Times,* 26 Jan 1990, A22:4. AMD, p. 36. AS, p. 115. BHD1, p. 43. BR, pp. 101–05 (b. 1900). FFF, p. 120 (b. 1903). FSS, p. 28. HCH, p. 127. MH, p. 96 (b. 1903). "Madge Bellamy," SOS, pp. 6–35 (b. 1902). "Paramount Secures Miss Bellamy," *MPW,* 25 Sep 1920, 463. Joan Jordan, "Madge Make-Believe; A new little twinkler whose fairyland is a motion picture studio," *Photoplay,* Mar 1921, 54 (had a 3-year contract with Thomas H. Ince). "Madge Bellamy Makes Debut in Ince Picture," *MPW,* 30 Jul 1921, 533 (*Dear Brutus*). "Madge Bellamy," *MPW,* 25 Jul 1925, 445. Ramon Romeo, "Reeling Down Broadway; Fox Generous with Releases," *Paris and Hollywood Screen Secrets Magazine,* May 1927, 62–63 (Fox did not renew her contract after *Loose Ankles.* "The solution of this mystery might be that Fox believes that he has three big stars in George O'Brien, Olive Borden and Janet Gaynor, with Charles Farrel[l], Nancy Nash and Sally Phipps rapidly building. These youngsters are all under contract at small salaries, and the organization probably feels they will in the long run prove the most profitable bets."); "Madge May Join Players," 63 (Paramount offered her a five-year contract. "Now that spring is here it looks as if everything is going to be rosy for Madge!"). "Madge Bellamy," *MPW,* 13 Aug 1927, 456. Buck Rainey, "Madge Bellamy," *CI,* 99 (Sep 1983), 31–33; 100 (Oct 1983), 13. George Katchmer, "More Forgotten Cowboys and Cowgirls—Chapter 6," *CI,* 172 (Oct 1989), C12, C14. Michael G. Ankerich, "Madge Bellamy: Discovering the Stranger Within," *CI,* 174 (Dec 1989), 7–8, 16, 24. Chapter 4, "Madge Bellamy," *BS,* pp. 45–61 (includes filmography).

Bellamy, Ralph Rexford [actor] (b. Chicago IL, 17 Jun 1904–29 Nov 1991 [87], Santa Monica CA; respiratory failure). *When the Smoke Hit the Fan* (Garden City NY: Doubleday, 1979). m. Alice Delbridge; Catherine Willard; Ethel Smith; Alice Murphy, 1949. Peter B. Flint, "Ralph Bellamy, the Actor, Is Dead at 87," *NYT,* 30 Nov 1991, 9:1. Marianne Goldstein, "Ralph Bellamy Dead at 87," *New York Post,* 30 Nov 1991, p. 5:1. "Ralph Bellamy," *Variety,* 2 Dec 1991, p. 101. AS, p. 115. BHD1, p. 43. Eric Niderost, "'The Other Man': An Interview with Ralph Bellamy—Part I," *CI,* 198 (Dec 1991), 54–55; Part II, 199 (Jan 1992), 46–47.

Belle, Tula [actress] (b. Christina, Norway, 28 Jul 1906–13 Oct 1992 [86], Newport Beach CA). (Artcraft.) AMD, p. 36. AS, p. 115 (b. 1909). BHD, addendum. Spehr, p. 116. "Tula Belle," *MPW,* 21 Apr 1917, 403. "An Eight-Year-Old-Star of Big Picture," *MPW,* 12 Jan 1918, 214.

Bellew, Cosmo Kyrle (son of **Kyrle Bellew**) [stage/film actor] (b. London, England, 23 Nov 1885–25 Jan 1948 [62], Los Angeles CA). "Cosmo Kyrle Bellew," *Variety,* 4 Feb 1948, p. 63. AS, p. 115. BHD1, p. 43.

Bellew, Kyrle (father of **Cosmo Kyrle Bellew**) [actor] (*né* Harold Kyrle-Money Bellew, b. Calcutta, India, 28 Mar 1855–2 Nov 1911 [56], Salt Lake City UT; pneumonia). "Kyrle Bellew Is Dead; Actor Expires of Pneumonia in Salt Lake City—Funeral to Be Held Here," *NYT,* 3 Nov 1911, 11:4; "Kyrle Bellew's Funeral Tomorrow," *NYT,* 5 Nov 1911, 15:5. "Kyrle Bellew," *Variety,* 11 Nov 1911 (b. 1857; d. 3 Nov). AS, p. 115. BHD, p. 103 (b. Prescot, Lancastershire, England). IFN, p. 23 (b. Prescot, England). SD (b. Prescott).

Bellincioni, Gemma (mother of **Bianca Stagno-Bellincioni**) [soprano opera singer/actress/director] (aka Gemima Bellincioni Stagno, b. on a ship near Istanbul, Turkey, 17 Aug 1864–24 Apr 1950 [85], Roccabelvedere, Italy). JS, p. 35 (in Italian silents from 1916).

Bells, Running [actor] (b. 1919-Mar 1927 [8?], Glacier Park Reservation). BHD, p. 103.

Belmar, Henry [stage/film director/actor/producer/writer] (b. on a ship in the Atlantic Ocean, 1849–12 Jan 1931 [82], New Castle PA [Death Certificate No. 456–3035]). m. actress **Laurel Love.** (Powers Co.) "Henry Belmar," *Variety,* 21 Jan 1931. AMD, p. 36. AS, p. 116. BHD, p. 103; BHD2, p. 19. IFN, p. 23 (age 81). Truitt, p. 24. "Picture Personalities," *MPW,* 25 Feb 1911, 419:1. "Belmar Co.," *MPW,* 4 May 1912, 424. Eugene Michael Vazzana, "Henry Belmar (1849–1931) of Stage and Screen," *CI,* 191 (May 1991), 44–45, 48, 50.

Belmont, Joe A[rtessi] [actor] (b. 1860?–28 Mar 1930 [70], Toledo OH). m. Anna. "Old Circus Acrobat Dies," *Variety,* 2 Apr 1930 (at the time he had a serious accident, "he was doubling for Theda Bara in a picture in 1915"). AS, p. 116.

Belmont, Joseph T. "Baldy" [vaudeville: Belmont & Lewis/Belmont & Carleton; actor/director] (b. Port Huron MI, 18 Aug 1875–16 May 1939 [63], CA). (Victor; PDC.) AMD, p. 36. AS, p. 116. BHD1, p. 43 (b. 1874). IFN, p. 23. "Joseph T. 'Baldy' Belmont," *MPW,* 28 Apr 1917, 619.

Belmont, Mrs. Morgan [actress] (b. 1894–1 Nov 1945 [51?], New York NY). AMD, p. 36. BHD, p. 103. "Mrs. Morgan Belmont in Cast of Griffith's 'Way Down East,'" *MPW,* 14 Aug 1920, 853.

Belmont, Murray [actor] (b. 1889–15 Oct 1922 [33?], New York NY). "Murray Belmont," *Variety,* 20 Oct 1922, p. 9. BHD, p. 103.

Belmont, Ralf [actor/writer] (b. Italy, 9 Apr 1882–21 Sep 1964 [82], Los Angeles CA). AS, p. 116. BHD, p. 103. IFN, p. 23.

Belmore, Alice [actress] (b. London, England, 1870?–31 Jul 1943 [73]). "Alice Belmore," *Variety,* 4 Aug 1943, 46. BHD, p. 103. IFN, p. 23.

Belmore, Daisy [actress] (sister of Herbert and **Lionel Belmore**) (*née* Daisy Garstin, b. London, England, 30 Jun 1874–12 Dec 1954 [80], New York NY; heart attack). m. Samuel Waxman. "Daisy Belmore," *Variety,* 15 Dec 1954. AS, p. 116. BHD1, p. 43. IFN, p. 23. SD. Truitt 1983.

Belmore, Lionel [actor/director] (brother of **Daisy** and Herbert Belmore) (*né* Lionel Garstin, b. Wimbledon, Surrey, England, 12 May 1866–30 Jan 1953 [86], Woodland Hills CA). "Lionel Belmore, 86, Stage, Film Veteran," *NYT,* 3 Feb 1953, 25:4. "Lionel Belmore," *Variety,* 4 Feb 1953. AMD, p. 36. AS, p. 116. BHD1, p. 43; BHD2, p. 19 (b. 1868). Finch, p. 255 (b. London, England, 23 Mar 1878). IFN, p. 23 (b. 1868). Truitt, p. 24. "Belmore to Direct Pageant," *MPW,* 12 Jun 1915, 1791. Blackie Seymour, "'Vigilant Villagers'; Lionel Belmore," *CI,* 234 (Dec 1994), 35.

Belmour, Harry [actor] (b. San Francisco CA, 9 Jan 1882–8 Sep 1936 [54]). AS, p. 116. BHD1, p. 43 (b. 9 Feb). IFN, p. 23. George A. Katchmer, "Remembering the Great Silents," *CI,* 183 (Sep 1990), 44.

Belt, Glenn D. [assistant director] (b. Macy IN, 1890?–4 Sep 1940 [50], Hollywood CA; pneumonia). "Jackie Cooper's Tutor Dies," *NYT,* 6 Sep 1940, 21:5. "Glenn D. Belt," *Variety,* 11 Sep 1940.

Beltri, Ricardo [actor] (*né* Ricardo Beltri Llovera, b. Mexico, 1898?–17 May 1962 [63], Mexico City, Mexico). "Ricardo Beltri," *Variety,* 6 Jun 1962. AS, p. 116. BHD, p. 104. IFN, p. 23.

Belwin, Alma [actress] (b. San Francisco CA, 1894–8 May 1924 [29], Boston MA; following operation). (Film debut: *The Ivory Snuffbox,* World, 1915.) "Alma Belwin," *Variety,* 7 May 1924. AS, p. 116. BHD, p. 104 (b. 3 May). IFN, p. 23. "In the Picture Studios," *NYDM,* 4 Aug 1915, 27:1 (Alma Belvin).

Benassi, Memo [actor] (b. Sorbolo, Italy, 21 Jun 1886–24 Feb 1957 [70], Bologna, Italy). AS, p. 117 (b. Parma, Italy; d. 25 Feb). JS, pp. 35–36 (in Italian silents from 1916).

Benchley, Robert C[harles] [writer/film and radio actor/scenarist] (b. Worcester MA, 15 Sep 1889–21 Nov 1945 [56], New York NY [Death Certificate Index No. 24886]; cerebral hemorrhage). m. Gertrude Darling, 6 Jun 1914. (Stage acting, 1923; Fox; MGM; Paramount; WB.) "Bob Benchley Dies; Noted Humorist 56; Man Who Taught Americans How to Sleep [AA, 1935] Diffused Wit Throughout Varied Career; Actor, Author and Editor; Former Executive of Old Life [ca. 1922–29] and Vanity Fair [1919–20] Appears in Several Current Films," *NYT,* 22 Nov 1945, 35:1 (the current films were *Weekend at the Waldorf,* MGM; *Kiss and Tell,* Columbia; and *Duffy's Tavern,* Paramount. Six of his films were unreleased). "Robert Benchley," *Variety,* 28 Nov 1945 (AA for short, *How to Sleep,* 1936). AMD, p. 36. AS, p. 117. BHD1, p. 44; BHD2, p. 20.. IFN, p. 24. "To Write the Titles," *MPW,* 17 Nov 1923, 327.

Bencivenga, Edoardo [director] (b. Naples, Italy). JS, p. 36 (in Italian silents from1908).

Benda, Helena [actress] (b. 1903–24 Dec 1986 [83?], Woodland Hills CA). BHD1, p. 44.

Benda, W[ladyslaw] **T**[heodor] [artist/author/authority on masks] (b. Poznan, Poland, 1873?–30 Nov 1948 [75], Newark NJ). "Wladyslaw T. Benda," *NYT,* 1 Dec 1948, 29:2. "W.T. Benda," *Variety,* 8 Dec 1948.

Bender, Charles A[lbert] [baseball player/actor; full-blooded Chippewa Indian] (aka Chief Bender, b. Crow Wing Co. (Brainard) MN, 5 May 1883–22 May 1954 [71], Philadelphia PA; after cancer and heart attack). "Chief Bender Dies; A Famous Pitcher; He Led Philadelphia Athletics to 5 Pennants—Was Elected to Hall of Fame in 1953," *NYT,* 23 May 1954, 88:4. BHD, p. 104. "Who They Are; Some Handy Data on the Champion Ball Players Who Became Picture Players," *MPW,* 18 Nov 1911, 558 (full-blooded Chippewa Indian, b. OK). *The Baseball Bug* ("A Rattling Comedy"; Thanhouser ad), *MPW,* 11 Nov 1911, 514 (photo of Big Chief Bender).

Bender, Henry [actor] (b. Berlin, Germany, 1 Oct 1867–14 May 1933 [65]). BHD1, p. 44.

Bendix, William (descendant of Felix Mendelssohn) [film/TV actor] (b. New York NY, 14 Jan 1906 [Birth Certificate Index No. 4617, "Bendix, male"]–14 Dec 1964 [58], Los Angeles CA; lobar pneumonia and malnutrition). m. Therese Stefanotti, 27 Oct 1928. (Vitagraph, Brooklyn NY, 1911; Roach.) "Bendix Funeral on Coast Attended by 400 Persons," *NYT,* 17 Dec 1964, 33:4 (buried at San Fernando Mission Cemetery). "William Bendix," *Variety,* 16 Dec 1964. AS, p. 118 (b. 4 Jan). Katz, pp. 102–03.

Bendow, Wilhelm [actor] (*né* Emil Boden, b. Einbeck, Germany, 29 Sep 1884–29 May 1950 [65], Einbeck, Germany). BHD1, p. 44.

Bendsten, France [actor] (b. 1890). (Clara K. Young; Selig.) 1918 Studio Directory, p. 65.

Benedict, Brooks [actor] (b. New York NY, 6 Feb 1896–1 Jan 1968 [71], TX). BHD1, p. 44. IFN, p. 24.

Benedict, Kingsley [actor/scenarist] (b. Buffalo NY, 14 Nov 1878–27 Nov 1951 [73], Woodland Hills CA). (Vitagraph; Universal.) BHD1, p. 44; BHD2, p. 20. IFN, p. 24. George A. Katchmer, "Forgotten Cowboys and Cowgirls—Part XVI," *CI,* 193 (Aug 1991), 35.

Benelli, Sam [scenarist] (b. Filettole, Italy, 10 Aug 1877–18 Dec 1949 [72], Zoagli, Italy). "Sem [sic] Benelli," *Variety,* 21 Dec 1949, 55. JS, p. 36 (in Italian silents from 1914).

Benetti, Carlo [actor] (b. Florence, Italy, 4 Jul 1885–4 Jun 1949 [63], Rome, Italy). m. **Olga.** AS, p. 118. JS, p. 36 (in Italian silents from 1913).

Benetti, Olga [actress] (b. Ceprano, Italy). m. **Carlo Benetti** (d. 1949). JS, p. 36 (in Italian silents from 1913).

Benge, Wilson [actor] (*né* George F. Benge, b. Greenwich, London, England, 1 Mar 1875–1 Jul 1955 [80], Los Angeles CA). "Wilson Benge," *Variety,* 6 Jul 1955. AS, p. 118. BHD1, p. 44. IFN, p. 24. Truitt, p. 25.

Benham, Dorothy Lucile (daughter of **Harry Benham** and **Ethyl Cooke**; sister of **Leland Benham**) [actress] (b. Boston MA, 6 Sep 1910–19 Sep 1956 [46], Watertown WI; Hodgkin's disease). m. Jack Tutton. (Thanhouser; Universal.) AMD, p. 36. AS, p. 118. BHD, p. 104. IFN, p. 24.

"Notes of the Trade," *MPW,* 20 Dec 1913, 1428 (two years old). "Atlas to Begin Production December 1," *MPW,* 8 Dec 1917, 1503. Billy H. Doyle, "Lost Players," *CI,* 149 (Nov 1987), 17.

Benham, Elsa [actress] (*née* Elsa Hackmann, b. St. Louis MO, 20 Nov 1908). George Katchmer, "More Forgotten Cowboys and Cowgirls—Chapter 6," *CI,* 172 (Oct 1989), C12; "Update—Forgotten Cowboys/Girls," *CI,* 179 (May 1990), 43.

Benham, Ethyle *see* **Cooke, Ethyl**

Benham, Grace [actress] (b. KS, 25 Jun 1876–19 Nov 1968 [92], Pasadena CA). BHD, p. 104.

Benham, Harry (father of **Dorothy** and **Leland Benham**) [actor] (b. Valparaiso IN, 26 Feb 1884–17 Jul 1969 [85], Sarasota FL). m. **Ethyle Cooke** (d. 1949). (Thanhouser.) AMD, p. 36. BHD, p. 104 (b. 1883). IFN, p. 24 (b. 1886). MH, p. 97 (b. 1886). *Photoplay Arts Portfolio* (Thanhouser) (b. 1884). "Girls, Don't Write Benham!," *MPW,* 28 Dec 1912, 1282. "Eltinge of the Films," *MPW,* 28 Jun 1913, 1344. "Harry Benham; Youthful Lead with the Thanhouser Co.," *MPS,* 3 Oct 1913, 29 (began 1911). "Harry Benham No Villain," *MPW,* 7 Mar 1914, 1251. "How I Became a Photoplayer," *Motion Picture Magazine,* Feb 1915, 114. Billy H. Doyle, "Lost Players [the Benhams]," *CI,* 149 (Nov 1987), 17.

Benham, Leland (son of **Harry Benham** and **Ethyle Cooke**; brother of **Dorothy Benham**) [actor] (b. Boston MA, 10 Sep 1905–26 Sep 1976 [71], Boynton Beach FL). (Thanhouser; Reliance; Universal.) AMD, p. 36. BHD, p. 104. "Atlas to Begin Production December 1," *MPW,* 8 Dec 1917, 1503. Billy H. Doyle, "Lost Players," *CI,* 149 (Nov, 1987), 17.

Benkhoff, Fita [actress] (b. Dortmund, Germany, 1 Nov 1901–26 Oct 1967 [65], Munich, Germany). BHD1, p. 45.

Benner, William [scenic artist]. No data found. LACD, r 730 S. Figueroa.

Benner, Yale Delespine [actor] (b. New York NY, 17 Nov 1875–29 Sep 1952 [76], San Diego CA). (Edison; Thanhouser.) AMD, p. 36. BHD, p. 104. IFN, p. 24. "Yale Benner," *MPW,* 3 Jul 1915, 47.

Bennet, Buford [title writer]. No data found. FDY, p. 441.

Bennett, Alma [actress] (b. Seattle WA, 9 Apr 1904–16 Sep 1958 [54], Los Angeles CA). AMD, p. 36. AS, p. 119. BHD1, p. 45. FSS, p. 29. IFN, p. 24. Katz, p. 104 (b. 1889). MH, p. 97. "Joins Paramount Players," *MPW,* 12 May 1923, 174. "Alma Bennett Is Back to Sennett," *MPW,* 5 Mar 1927, 40. George A. Katchmer, "Forgotten Cowboys and Cowgirls—Part X," *CI,* 182 (Aug 1990), 37.

Bennett, Arnold [writer]. No data found. AMD, p. 37. "Pathé to Film Arnold Bennett's 'Hugo,'" *MPW,* 24 Jul 1915, 654.

Bennett, Barbara Jane [actress] (daughter of **Richard Bennett**; sister of **Constance** and **Joan Bennett**) (b. Palisades NJ, 13 Aug 1906–8 Aug 1958 [51], Montreal, Canada; heart attack). m. Morton Downey, 1929–40; Addison (Jack) Randall (d. 1945); Laurent Suprenant. "Barbara Bennett," *Variety,* 13 Aug 1958. AMD, p. 37. As, p. 119. BHD1, p. 45. IFN, p. 24. Truitt, p. 25 (b. 1911). "Buck Jones Picks Barbara Bennett," *MPW,* 11 Jun 1927, 420.

Bennett, Belle [stage/film actress] (b. Milaca MN, 6 Aug 1890?–4 Nov 1932 [42?], Hollywood CA). m. (1) William Macy; Jack Oaker; Fred Windsmire. ("Cub" Mutual farces; Triangle; Universal; Goldwyn.) "Belle Bennett Dies at 39 in Hollywood; Film Actress Was Noted for Her Portrayal of Mother Roles—Famous for 'Stella Dallas'; Once Trapeze Performer; Began Career with a Circus at Age of 13—Appeared Here in Belasco Productions," *NYT,* 6 Nov 1932, 38:1 (b. Milada MN). "Belle Bennett," *Variety,* 8 Nov 1932 (age 42). AMD, p. 37. AS, p. 119 (b. 22 Apr 1891). BHD1, p. 45 (b. Milcoon Rapids IA, 22 Apr 1891). FSS, p. 29. IFN, p. 24 (b. Milcoon Rapids IA, 22 Apr 1891). MSBB, p. 1032 (b. near Dublin, Ireland). SD. Truitt, p. 25. Belle Bennett, "Lives of the Players; My Experiences as a Child Actress," *MPS,* 14 Mar 1913, 30, 32. "Morosco Borrows Belle Bennett," *MPW,* 16 Feb 1918, 95. "Belle Bennett, Too, Adopts Some Boys," *MPW,* 16 Mar 1918, 1541. "Fell Down a Canyon," *MPW,* 17 Aug 1918, 969 (re Jack Oaker). "To Erect Studio in San Francisco," *MPW,* 22 Feb 1919, 1052. Sara Redway, "The Screen's Most Tragic Triumph," *MPC,* Feb 1926, 18–19, 83, 85–87. "Goldwyn and Belle Bennett Are Reconciled," *MPW,* 2 Jul 1927, 17.

Bennett, Billie [actress] (*née* Emily B. Mulhausen, b. Evansville IN, 23 Oct 1874–19 May 1951 [76], Los Angeles CA). AS, p. 119. BHD1, p. 45. IFN, p. 24. LACD, "photoplayer," r 210 S. Flower. George A. Katchmer, "Forgotten Cowboys and Cowgirls—Part X," *CI,* 182 (Aug 1990), 37.

Bennett, Billy [actor] (b. Glasgow, Scotland-d. 30 Jun 1942, Blackpool, England). "Billy Bennett," *Variety,* 8 Jul 1942, 54. BHD1, p. 45.

Bennett, Catherine (sister of **Enid** and **Marjorie Bennett**) [actress] (b. York, Australia, 17 Jan 1901–11 Oct 1978 [77], Westwood CA). AMD, p. 37. AS, p. 119. BHD, p. 104. "Catherine Bennett in Comedy," *MPW,* 13 Jan 1923, 161. "Katherine [sic] Bennett Signed," *MPW,* 20 Jun 1925, 895.

Bennett, Charles [actor] (d. Jul? 1925, New York NY; found dead in a livery stable where he worked). (Cosmopolitan.) "Charles Bennett," *Variety,* 8 Jul 1925. AMD, p. 37. BHD, p. 104. IFN, p. 24. "Charles Bennett," *MPW,* 3 Jul 1915, 54.

Bennett, Charles J. [actor] (b. Dunedin, New Zealand, 11 Mar 1889–15 Feb 1943 [53], Los Angeles CA). "Charles J. Bennett," *Variety,* 24 Feb 1943 (age 52). AS, p. 119. BHD1, p. 45. IFN, p. 24. Truitt, p. 25 (b. 1891).

Bennett, Chester M. [actor/director] (b. San Francisco CA-d. 29 Oct 1943, Hong Kong, China; died in a Japanese internment camp). (Vitagraph; Universal.) "Chester Bennett, Silent Director, Victim of Japs," *Variety,* 17 May 1944. AMD, p. 37. AS, p. 119. BHD, p. 104. LACD, h 6132 DeLongpre Ave. "Vitagraph Promotes Bennett," *MPW,* 13 Sep 1919, 1664. June Lee, "Dan Cupid's Bulletin Board," *Paris and Hollywood Screen Secrets,* Oct 1927, 37 ("Pauline Hampton, winner of several beauty contests, and film actress, has announced the breaking of her engagement to Chester Bennett, director. Disagreement over her entrance to the pictures is said to be the cause of the falling out.").

Bennett, Clarence [producer/writer] (b. 1860?–4 Jul 1930 [70], Springfield IL). "Clarence Bennett," *Variety,* 16 Jul 1930. AS, p. 119.

Bennett, Constance [actress]. No data found. "The First Woman to Do a 'Brodie,'" *MPW,* 21 Feb 1914, 966 (in *Fighting Death,* 1914, with Rodman Law).

Bennett, Constance Campbell (daughter of **Richard Bennett**; sister of **Barbara** and **Joan Bennett**) [actress/producer] (b. New York NY, 22 Oct 1905–24 Jul 1965 [59], Fort Dix NJ; cerebral hemorrhage). m. (1) Chester Moorhead; (2) Philip Morgan Plant, 3 Nov 1925, Greenwich CT (d. 18 Jun 1941); (3) Henri de la Falaise; (4) **Gilbert Roland**, 1941–44 (d. 1994); (5) John T. Coulter. (Film debut: *The Valley of Decision,* American/Mutual, 1916; WB.) "Constance Bennett Is Dead at 59; A Star Since the Silent Movies; Ghost in the 'Topper' Series Resumed Her Career Only Recently After 11 Years," *NYT,* 26 Jul 1965, 23:1; "200 Attend Rites for Miss Bennett; Simple, 12-Minute Ceremony Is Held for Film Star," *NYT,* 28 Jul 1965, 35:4. "Constance Bennett," *Variety,* 28 Jul 1965. AMD, p. 37. AS, p. 119 (b. 1904; d. Walston NJ). BHD1, p. 45 (b. 1904); BHD2, p. 20 (b. 1905). FFF, p. 147. FSFW, p. 4. FSS, p. 30. IFN, p. 24. Katz, p. 105 (b. 1904). MH, p. 97. Truitt, p. 25. "Miss Bennett Signed by Paramount," *MPW,* 22 Nov 1924, 343. Helen Cather, "Her Father's Daughter," *MW,* 13 Jun 1925, 26–27, 39. Sara Redway, "Maxims of the Super-Flapper of the Films; Constance Bennett Speaks Her Mind," *MPC,* Aug 1925, 36–37, 80. "Constance Bennett," *MPW,* 26 Sep 1925, 347. "Constance Bennett Signs Contract," *MPW,* 7 Nov 1925, 43. "'Why I've Come Back'; Three Years Ago, on the Threshold of Fame, She Retired to Marry a Millionaire. Now She Returns," *Screenland,* Aug 1929, 20–21, 105. Carol Benton, "Wedding Bells for Connie?; Constance Bennett and Marquis de la Falaise May Be Married When He Has Final Decree from Gloria Swanson in November," *Movie Classic,* Oct 1931, 37. Audrey Rivers, "Connie Bennett's Huge Salary Starts Trouble," *Movie Classic,* I, Dec 1931, 43. "Peter [Bennett] Plant [age 13] Barred as Heir to $550,000; Court Rules He Is Adopted and Not Son of Constance Bennett," *NYT,* 3 Sep 1942, 22:2 (in Jan 1930, Bennett informally adopted Dennis Arthur Armstrong in England. A month earlier, Bennett sued Philip Plant for divorce in Nice, which became final on 14 Feb. In Jan 1932, Bennett formally adopted Armstrong under California law and named him Peter Bennett Plant. Philip Plant died before his fortieth birthday, so his mother got his father's estate. The Court ruled that Plant died childless and that Peter Bennett Plant was not an heir.). Eve Golden, "The Public and Private Lives of Constance Bennett," *Films of the Golden Age,* 11 (Winter 1997–1998), 16–27 (with filmography by R.E. Braff).

Bennett, Enid (sister of **Catherine** and **Marjorie Bennett** and producer Alex [Anthony?] Bennett) [stage/film actress] (b. York, western Australia, 15 Jul 1893–14 May 1969 [75], Malibu CA; heart attack). m. **Fred Niblo**, Apr 1918, Los Angeles CA—div. 1920 (d. 1948); **Sidney Franklin** (d. 1972). (Ince; Paramount.) "Enid Bennett, 71, Actress, Appeared in Silent Films," *NYT,* 17 May 1969, 33:2 (age 71). "Enid Bennett," *Variety,* 28 May 1969 (age 71). AMD, p. 37. BHD1, p. 45. FFF, p. 118 (b. 22 Jan 1896). FSS, p. 31. IFN, p. 24 (b. 1893). Lowrey, p. 18. MH, p. 97 (b. 22 Jan 1896). MSBB, pp. 1030, 1032. Truitt, p. 25 (b. 2 Jan 1895). WWS, p. 31. "Enid Bennett Becomes Triangle-KayBee Star," *MPW,* 4 Nov 1916, 705. Cal York, "Plays and Players," *Photoplay Magazine,* Feb 1917, 89 ("Enid Bennett, a young Australian beauty discovered in New York by Tom Ince last summer," was to play opposite William Gargan at Universal). "Niblo-Bennett," *MPW,* 23 Mar 1918, 1645. "Little Miss Niblo," *MPW,* 27 Aug 1921,

888. "Miss Bennett Signed," *MPW,* 19 Jan 1924, 189. Michael Collins, "The Sunset Girls," *The Guardian Friday Review,* 4 Dec 1998, 2–5 (Frances Lee, Bennett's sister-in-law, was interviewed by twins Austin and Howard Mutti-Mewse for their documentary, *I Used to Be in Pictures.*)

Bennett, Frank Fisher [actor] (b. Bakersfield CA, 15 Sep 1890–29 Apr 1957 [66], Warren Township NJ). m. **Billie West** (d. 1967). AMD, p. 37. BHD, p. 104. IFN, p. 24. "Frank Bennett with Mutual," *MPW,* 27 Dec 1913, 1556. Billy H. Doyle, "Lost Players," *CI,* 142 (Apr 1987), C12-C13.

Bennett, Frederick [scenarist]. No data found. AMD, p. 37. "Frederick Bennett with Triangle-Keystone," *MPW,* 8 Dec 1917, 1475. "Bennett Writing for Hank Mann," *MPW,* 31 Jan 1920, 735.

Bennett, Hugh J. [actor/director/film editor] (b. New York NY, 22 Aug 1892–21 Mar 1950 [57], Malibu CA). (Edison; WB; Reliance; Goldwyn; Paramount.) "Hugh Bennett," *Variety,* 29 Mar 1950. AS, p. 120 (b. 1894). BHD, p. 104 (Hugh S.); BHD2, p. 20..

Bennett, Hunter W. [general manager]. No data found. (World.) AMD, p. 37. "H.W. Bennett Leaves; Goes to Mutual Film Corporation—Succeeded at Shuberts by A. Toxen Worm," *NYDM,* 11 Feb 1914. "Hunter Bennett Returns to New York," *MPW,* 3 Oct 1914, 72. "Hunter Bennett Leaves World Film," *MPW,* 24 Oct 1914, 512. "Hunter Bennett with Box Office," *MPW,* 21 Nov 1914, 1094. "Hunter Bennett Is 'Doing His Bit'; Motion Picture Man, Formerly Associated with Frank Hall, Mutual and World Film, Joins the Army," *MPW,* 31 Aug 1918, 1252:2.

Bennett, Joan Geraldine (daughter of **Richard Bennett**; sister of **Barbara** and **Constance Bennett**) [actress] (b. Palisades NJ, 27 Feb 1910–7 Dec 1990 [80], Scarsdale NY). m. (1) Jack Fox, NYC; (2) Gene Markey, 1932–37; (3) **Walter Wanger**, 1940–65 (d. 1968); (4) David Wilde, 1978. (UA.) Peter B. Flint, "Joan Bennett, 80, Dies; Actress Played Ingénues and Femme Fatale," *NYT,* 9 Dec 1990, 52. "Joan Bennett," *Variety,* 17 Dec 1990, p. 69. Dave Lesher, "Joan Bennett, Movie, Stage, TV Star, Dies," *LA Times,* 9 Dec 1990, A3:6. BHD1, p. 45. June Lee, "Dan Cupid's Bulletin Board," *Paris and Hollywood,* Oct 1926, 85 (wed Fox). Herbert Cruikshank, "In the Sub-Deb Manner; Joan, the Youngest of the Bennetts, Has Done Very Well by Herself," *MPC,* Mar 1930, 51, 100.

Bennett, John [foreman]. No data found. (Garson Studios.) LACD, "foreman."

Bennett, John Drew [actor] (b. Washington DC, 1884–18 Nov 1944 [60], New York NY [Death Certificate Index No. 24490]). BHD, p. 104. Slide, p. 157 (b. 1888). Billy H. Doyle, "Lost Players," *CI,* 137 (Nov 1986), C24.

Bennett, Joseph [actor] (b. Los Angeles CA, 28 Aug 1894–3 Dec 1931 [37], Los Angeles CA). (Ince.) "Joseph Bennett," *Variety,* 8 Dec 1931 (age 35). BHD1, p. 45. IFN, p. 24. Truitt, p. 25.

Bennett, Marjorie (sister of **Catherine** and **Enid Bennett**) [actress: Ince Bathing Beauty] (b. York, Australia, 15 Jan 1895–14 Jun 1982 [87], Los Angeles CA; cancer). (Began 1915.) BHD1, p. 45 (b. Perth).

Bennett, Mickey [actor] (b. Victoria, B.C., Canada, 28 Jan 1915–6 Sep 1950 [35], Los Angeles CA; heart attack). "Mickey Bennett," Variety, 13 Sep 1950. AMD, p. 37. BHD1, p. 45 (b. 1914). IFN, p. 25. Truitt, pp. 25–26. "New Faces in Comedies," *MPW,* 6 Jun 1925, 682.

Bennett, Monroe [lab head at WB] (b. 1894?–24 Apr 1949 [55], Hollywood CA). "Monroe Bennett," *Variety,* 4 May 1949.

Bennett, Red [actor] (*né* William Houghton, b. 1873?–10 May 1941 [68], Hollywood CA). "Red Bennett," *Variety,* 14 May 1941.

Bennett, Richard (father of **Barbara**, **Constance** and **Joan Bennett**) [stage/film actor] (b. Bennetts Switch IN, 21 May 1872–21 Oct 1944 [72], Los Angeles CA). m. (1) Grena Heller; (2) Angela Raisch; (3) **Adrienne Morrison**, 1903–25 (d. 1940). (American-Mutual.) "Richard Bennett's Death at 72 Ends Long Stage and Screen Career," *Variety,* 25 Oct 1944 (age 72). AMD, p. 37. BHD1, p. 46 (b. Deacon's Mills IN). FSS, p. 31. IFN, p. 25 (b. 1873). MH, p. 97 (b. 1873). MSBB, p. 1021 (b. 1873). SD. Truitt, p. 26 (b. Deacon's Mills [Cass County] IN, 21 May 1873). "Richard Bennett Trains to Be Picture Director," *MPW,* 19 Mar 1921, 289. B.F. Wilson, "It's All in the Family; After the Barrymores, the Bennetts are undoubtedly the best known and most talented family in this country…," *Classic,* Jul 1924, 36–38, 76. "Bennett Girls on Plane; Joan and Constance Flying Here to Be at Father's Bedside," *NYT,* 21 Jan 1936, 3:3 (Bennett was ill with pneumonia in New York City).

Bennett, Robert [sound engineer] (d. Oct 1929?, Toronto Canada?). "Cliff Bennett," *Variety,* 26 May 1965 (death reported in IATSE ranks [#173]).

Bennett, Spencer Gordon [actor/director] (b. Brooklyn NY, 5 Jan 1893–8 Oct 1987 [94], Santa Monica CA). (Edison.) "Spencer Gordon Bennett," *Variety,* 14 Oct 1987. AMD, p. 36. AS, p. 120. BHD, p. 104; BHD, p. 29 (Bennet). "Spencer Bennet [sic]," *MPW,* 5 Feb 1927, 419.

Bennett, Mrs. Spencer Gordon [actress] (d. 5 Dec 1983, Los Angeles CA). BHD, p. 104.

Bennett, Whitman [writer/producer/dealer in rare books] (b. Cambridge MA, 30 Dec 1883–17 Apr 1968 [84], New York NY). m. Lillias Livingston. "Whitman Bennett, a Book Dealer, 84," *NYT,* 19 Apr 1968, 47:4 (production manager for FP-L and Paramount). AMD, p. 37. BHD2, p. 20. "Circuit to Star Lionel Barrymore in Series to Be Made by Whitman Bennett," *MPW,* 27 Mar 1920, 2095. Edward Weitzel, "Enter Whitman Bennett as a Producing Manager, a New Force in Picture Making," *MPW,* 8 May 1920, 805. "Melodrama as Pure Entertainment Stands Highest of All, Says Whitman Bennett," *MPW,* 25 Feb 1922, 819. "Vitagraph to Release Six Big Productions by Whitman Bennett," *MPW,* 19 May 1923, 212. "Whitman Bennett Elected Vice-President of Arrow," *MPW,* 4 Jul 1925, 30.

Bennett, Wilda [actress] (b. Asbury Park NJ, 19 Dec 1894–20 Dec 1967 [73], Winnemucca NV). m. (1) **Robert Schable** (d. 1947); (2) Pepe d'Albrew; (3) Anthony J. Wettach; (4) Munro Whitmore. (Film debut: *Love, Honor and Obey,* Metro, 1920). "Wilda Bennett Dead at 73; Starred in Musicals Here," *NYT,* 23 Dec 1967, 23:2. "Wilda Bennett," *Variety,* 27 Dec 1967. AMD, p. 38. BHD1, p. 46. IFN, p. 25. SD. Truitt, p. 26. "Wilda Bennett Makes Screen Debut in 'S-L' Special Picture," *MPW,* 8 May 1920, 851. "Miss Wilda Bennett Appears at Equity Show in Smoked 'Specs,'" *MPW,* 29 May 1920, 1219 (had Klieg eyes).

Bennett, William H. [actor]. No data found. LACD, h 5419 Pasadena Ave.

Benninger, Otto [still photographer/scenarist/director] (b. 1893–3 Mar 1946 [52?], Los Angeles CA). "Otto Benninger," *Variety,* 6 Mar 1946, p. 62. BHD, p. 105; BHD2, p. 20.

Bennison, Andrew [actor/scenarist/director] (b. 1887?–7 Jan 1942 [55], Oxnard CA). "Andrew Bennison," *Variety,* 14 Jan 1942. AS, p. 120. BHD, p. 105; BHD2, p. 20. FDY, p. 417. IFN, p. 25.

Bennison, Louis [stage/film actor] (b. San Francisco CA, 1884?–9 Jun 1929 [45], New York NY [Death Certificate Index No. 16154; age 44]; suicide with a cowboy revolver; murdered **Margaret Lawrence**). (Betzwood Film Co., Philadelphia PA; Goldwyn.) "[Actress Margaret] Lawrence-Bennison Affair Ends in Killing and Suicide in New York," *Variety,* 12 Jun 1929. AMD, p. 38. AS, p. 120. BHD, p. 105. IFN, p. 25. MSBB, p. 1021. Truitt, p. 26. "Bennison's 'Oh, Johnny' to Be Issued by Goldwyn," *MPW,* 7 Dec 1918, 1096. "Louis Bennison's Second Goldwyn Is Now Ready," *MPW,* 19 Apr 1919, 423. "From Cow-puncher to Actor," *MPS,* 13 Jun 1919, 24 (b. Alturas CA; "The next time you happen to see one of my pictures, just pay a little attention to my horse, and you'll notice the brass setting in the harness that only cowboys use."). "United Cigarette Named After Louis Bennison," *MPW,* 13 Sep 1919, 1618 ("Bennison Smiles" brand). "Charles Stevenson and Louis Bennison Signed," *MPW,* 10 Dec 1921, 657. Joseph P. Eckhardt, "Louis Bennison Corrections [letter]," *CI,* 245 (Nov 1995), 6 (his suicide note read, "The sunset has a heart—look for us there.").

Bennoit, Joseph [actor] (b. 1875–23 Jun 1925 [50?], New York NY). BHD, p. 105. IFN, p. 25.

Benoit, Georges [cameraman] (b. Paris, France, 27 Nov 1883–1943 [60?]). (Gaumont, 1899; Eclair; American, 1912; Reliance-Majes-tic; Fox.) AMD, p. 38. BHD2, p. 21. FDY, p. 455. "G. Benoit, Cameraman," *MPN,* 21 Oct 1916, 182. "Benoit Comes East," *MPW,* 2 Dec 1916, 1330. "George Benoit Now Cameraman for Park-Whiteside Pictures," *MPW,* 10 Apr 1920, 243.

Benoit, Pierre [scenarist] (*né* Ferdinand Marie Pierre Benoit, b. Albi, France, 16 Jul 1886 [extrait de naissance no. 213/1886]-3 Mar 1962 [75], Ciboure, France). AS, p. 121. FDY, p. 417.

Benoit, Victor L[ucien] (b. Ottawa, Canada, 1876–16 Jan 1943 [66], Newburgh NY). "Victor L. Benoit," *Variety,* 20 Jan 1943. BHD, p. 105. IFN, p. 25.

Benson, Caroline [film cutter]. No data found. LACD, h 6276 Hollywood Blvd.

Benson, Clyde [actor] (b. Marshalltown IA). (NYMP Co.; Fox; Selig; Universal.)

Benson, Frank [actor] (b. Alresford, England, 4 Nov 1858–31 Dec 1939 [81], London, England). m. Constance Fetherstonhaugh, 1886. "Sir Frank Benson," *Variety,* 10 Jan 1940. BHD1, p. 46. IFN, p. 25.

Benson, Frank [actor] (b. Sydney, Australia, 6 Jan 1876–7 Apr 1950 [74]). BHD1, p. 46.

Benson, John William [actor] (b. Lowell MA, 1862?–2 Jul 1926 [64], New York NY [Death Certificate Index No. 18634]). "John William Benson," *Variety,* 7 Jul 1926. BHD, p. 105. IFN, p. 25. Truitt, p. 26.

Benson, Juliette V.P. [actress] (b. MA, 15 Aug 1875–22 Dec 1962 [87], Hollywood CA). "Juliette V.P. Benson," *Variety,* 2 Jan 1963 (in Hollywood 29 years). BHD1, p. 46. IFN, p. 25.

Benson, Mae or May *see* **Benson, Mary Elinor**

Benson, Mary Elinor "Mother" [actress] (d. 29 Sep 1916). AMD, p. 38. BHD, p. 105 (May Benson). IFN, p. 25. "'Mother' Benson of Universal," *MPW,* 26 Jun 1915, 2074. "Obituary," *MPW,* 4 Nov 1916, 708.

Benson, Patricia [actress]. No data found. AMD, p. 38. "Patricia Benson," *MPW,* 5 May 1917, 782.

Bent, Buena [actor] (b. London, England, 1890–15 Dec 1957 [67?], London, England). BHD, p. 105.

Bent, Marion S. [film/vaudeville dancer/actress: Rooney & Bent] (b. Tremont, Bronx NY, 23 Dec 1879–28 Jul 1940 [60], Bronx NY [Death Certificate Index No. 7286, "Marion S. Rooney"]; cancer). m. **Patrick James Rooney**, 10 Apr 1903, Boston (d. 1962) (d. 1962). "Mrs. Pat Rooney, Stage Dancer, 60; Member, with Husband, of Old Vaudeville Team of Rooney and Bent Dies Here; 'Straight-Line Actress' [fed lines to her husband]; Couple Toured for 27 Years Until Her Retirement in 1932—Appeared Again in 1935," *NYT,* 29 Jul 1940, 13:3. "Marion Bent, 37 Yrs. on Stage, Dies at 60," *Variety,* 31 Jul 1940 (interred at Evergreen Cemetery, Brooklyn). AS, p. 939 (Patricia Rooney). BHD, p. 105. "Rooney and Bent Comedy," *NYDM,* 28 Apr 1915, 28:3 (to make screen debut in *The Busy Bell Boy,* Lubin).

Benthall, Dwinelle [title writer]. No data found. FDY, p. 441.

Bentley, Alice [actress] (*née?,* b. Scranton PA, 1892–3 Sep 1956 [64], Beechurst, LI NY). m. (1) Wilton Bentley; (2) Mike P. Wear. (Equitable; Biograph; Kleine.) "Mrs. Mike Wear (Alice Bentley)," *Variety,* 5 Sep 1956 (age 58). BHD, p. 105. IFN, p. 25.

Bentley, Doria [actress] (d. 25 Feb 1944, England). BHD, p. 105.

Bentley, Grendon [actor] (b. Bromyard, England, 8 Apr 1877–27 Apr 1956 [79], London, England). BHD, p. 105.

Bentley, Robert [actor] (aka Bob Butt, b. 1895?–19 Apr 1958 [63], Benton Harbor MI). "Robert Bentley," *Variety,* 30 Apr 1958. BHD1, p. 46. IFN, p. 25. Truitt, p. 26.

Benton, Bessie [actress] (d. Jan 1917, Los Angeles CA). BHD, p. 105. IFN, p. 25.

Benton, Curtis [actor/scenarist] (*né* Horatio Curtis Benton, b. Toledo OH, 26 Aug 1885–14 Sep 1938 [53], Van Nuys CA). (Imp.) BHD1, p. 46 (d. LA CA). FDY, p. 417. IFN, p. 25. Truitt 1983 (b. 1880).

Benton, Marie Louise [actress] (b. Boston MA, 1884). BHD, p. 105.

Beradino, John [Our Gang] [film/TV actor/ball player] (b. 1917?–19 May 1996 [79], Los Angeles CA; cancer). m. Marjorie. William Grimes, "John Beradino, 79, an Enduring Soap Opera Star," *NYT,* 22 May 1996, D21:1. "John Beradino," *Variety,* 27 May 1996, 77:2 (he appeared in *General Hospital* and *The New Breed* on TV and "also appeared in a 1955 episode of 'Superman' and was in the silent 'Our Gang' comedies as a child.").

Beranger, Clara S. [scenarist] (b. Baltimore MD, 14 Jan 1886–10 Sep 1956 [70], Los Angeles CA; heart attack). m. **William C. DeMille** (d. 1955). "Mrs. William DeMille," *NYT,* 12 Sep 1956, 37:2. "Clara Beranger," *Variety,* 19 Sep 1956. AMD, p. 38. AS, p. 122. BHD2, p. 21. FDY, p. 417. IFN, p. 25. Lowrey, p. 20. Spehr, p. 116. "Clara Beranger with World Pictures," *MPW,* 30 Mar 1918, 1809. "Clara Beranger Writes Stage Play," *MPW,* 13 Mar 1920, 1773. "Beranger Leaves F.P.-L.," *MPW,* 23 Jan 1926, 316. "Returns to DeMille," *MPW,* 28 Aug 1926, 2. "Clara Beranger Busy," *MPW,* 10 Sep 1927, 93. Clara Beranger, "Good and Bad Authorship," *Classic,* Sep 1923, 11, 78.

Beranger, George Andre [actor/assistant director] (*né* George Auguste Alexandre Robert de L'Ile de Beranger, b. Sydney, New South Wales, Australia, 27 Mar 1895–8 Mar 1973 [77], Laguna Beach CA). (Griffith.) AMD, p. 38. AS, p. 122. BHD1, p. 46; BHD2, p. 21 (b. 1893). IFN, p. 25 (b. 1893). KOM, p. 128. LACD, "ass't director," r L.A.A.C. (Los Angeles Athletic Club). "Beranger Directing for Majestic," *MPW,* 12 Dec 1914, 1533. "The Roll of Honor," *MPW,* 7 Jul 1917, 64.

Berangere, Mme. [actress] (b. France-d. Nov 1928, Paris, France). BHD, p. 105. IFN, p. 25.

Berber, Anita [actress] (b. Dresden, Germany, 1899–3 Nov 1928 [29], Kreuzberg [near Berlin], Germany; tuberculosis). m. (1) Sebastian Droste; (2) Henri Chattin Hoffmann. (Film debut: *Das Dreimäderlhaus* [*The House of Three Girls,* 1918].) *Anita Berber: Dance Between Ecstasy and Death, 1918–1928 in Berlin* (1986, produced by Rosa von Praunheim). BHD, p. 105 (d. 14 Nov). Gene Vazzana, "Anita Berber—Nackt!," *The Silent Film Newsletter,* II (Jun 1994), 98–102.

Berchett, Ross [actor] (b. 1888). (Metro; Keystone; Universal.) 1918 Studio Directory, p. 65.

Bercovici, Konrad [writer] (b. Braila, Rumania, 22 Jun 1881–27 Dec 1961 [80], New York NY). m. Naomi Librescu (d. 1957). "Konrad Bercovici Is Dead at 80; Works Depicted Life of Gypsies; Romanticism of His Career Was Reflected in His Books—Journalist, Film Writer," *NYT,* 28 Dec 1961, 27:1 ("In 1947 his suit for $6,450,000 against Charlie Chaplin, charging that the motion picture actor had stolen ideas from Mr. Bercovici, for the film 'The Great Dictator,' was settled for payment of $95,000."). AMD, p. 38. *Twentieth Century Authors,* p. 128. WWWA (b. 1882). "Gypsy Writer Signed," *MPW,* 18 Apr 1925, 715.

Beregi, Oscar, Sr. (father of Oscar Beregi, Jr.) [actor] (b. Budapest, Hungary, 24 Jan 1876–18 Oct 1965 [89], Hollywood CA). "Oscar Beregi, Sr.," *Variety,* 27 Oct 1965 (age 90). AMD, p. 38. BHD1. p. 46. IFN, p. 25. Truitt, p. 26. "Oscar Beregi Signs Five-Year Contract with Universal," *MPW,* 8 May 1926, 142.

Beresford, Cynthia Vera (daughter of **Harry Beresford** and **Kitty Gordon**) [actress] (b. 1901). "Personal; Beresford," *NYDM,* 13 Nov 1915, 5:1 (14-year-old "is to make her debut as an actress on Dec. 1 by appearing in motion pictures with her mother.... It is said that Captain Beresford objects to a stage career for his daughter and will come to this country about Christmas time to oppose her [his wife's] action.").

Beresford, Frank S. [propman/technical director/scenarist]. No data found. FDY, p. 417. "Frank Beresford, Technical Director," *MPW,* 21 Apr 1917, 436. "Frank Beresford Triangle Script Editor," *MPW,* 3 Nov 1917, 683. "Universal Engages New Story Editor," *MPW,* 15 May 1926, 232.

Beresford, Harry (father of **Cynthia Vera Beresford**) [actor] (*né* Henry William Walter Horsley Beresford, b. London, England, 4 Nov 1863–4 Oct 1944 [80], Los Angeles CA). m. (1) **Kitty Gordon** (d. 1974); Edith Wyle. (Fox.) "Harry Beresford," *Variety,* 11 Oct 1944. BHD1, p. 47. IFN, p. 25. SD. Truitt, p. 26.

Berg, Stina [actress] (b. Sweden, 1869–1930 [60?], Sweden). BHD1, p. 47.

Bergdorf, Ferdinand [art titles]. No data found. AMD, p. 38. "Artist Painting DeMille Titles," *MPW,* 24 Jul 1920, 492.

Bergen, John [actor] (d. 25 Aug 1922, New York NY). BHD, p. 105.

Bergen, Thurlow [stage/film actor] (b. Washington DC). (Wharton.) AMD, p. 38. 1921 Directory, p. 157. Spehr, p. 116. "Thurlow Bergen with Pathé," *MPW,* 4 Apr 1914, 78. "To Feature Bergen; Wharton, Incorporated, Secures Stage Star for Coming Film Features," *NYDM,* 10 Jun 1914, 30:3 (on the cover). "Thurlow Bergen Again Appears in a Pathé Picture," *MPW,* 9 Sep 1916, 1690.

Berger, Leo Charles [actor]. No data found. m. Margaret McMahon, 20 Jan 1921. AMD, p. 38. "Picture Player Married," *MPW,* 27 Jan 1912, 298.

Berger, Ludwig [playwright/film/TV director] (*né* Ludwig Gottfried Heinrich Bamberger, b. Mainz, Germany, 6 Jan 1892–17 May 1969 [77], Schlagenbad, West Germany; heart failure). Autobiography: *We're Made of Such Stuff as Dreams.* (1st film, 1920; Paramount; Phoebus Films; last feature film: *Ballerina,* France, 1950.) "Ludwig Berger," *Variety,* 28 May 1969. AMD, p. 38. AS, p. 123. BHD2, p. 21. IFN, p. 26. Waldman, p. 24. "Berger to Make Fox's 'I Will Not Marry,'" *MPW,* 26 Nov 1927, 19. Gladys Hall, "Actors Should Not Act; Ludwig Berger, Doctor of Philosophy from Heidelberg and Now a Hollywood Director, Sets Forth Several New Ideas," *MPC,* Jan 1929, 26, 66.

Bergere, Dorothy [actress] (b. 1899–12 Jul 1979 [79?], Harrison NJ). BHD, p. 105.

Bergère, Ouida [stage/film actress/scenarist] (*née* Ida Berger, b. Spain, 1886?–29 Nov 1974 [88], New York NY [Death Certificate Index No. 21346]). m. (1) **Louis Weadock** (d. 1942); **Basil Rathbone** (d. 1967); (3) **George Fitzmaurice** (d. 1940). "Ouida Bergere Rathbone Dies; Dramatist Was Actor's Widow," *NYT,* 1 Dec 1974, 83:1 (brother's name was B.C. Branch). "Mrs. Basil Rathbone," *Variety,* 4 Dec 1974. AMD, p. 38. AS, p. 123. BHD2, p. 21. IFN, p. 26. Lowrey, p. 22. SD. WWS, p. 127. "Woman Heads Company; Ouida Bergere, Former Pathe Scenario Editor, to Manage Film Company," *NYDM,* 17 Feb 1915, 25:1. "Ouida Bergere Joins American Play Company," *MPW,* 15 Apr 1916, 417. "Ouida Bergere Prepares Scenario," *MPW,* 16 Aug 1919, 979. "Ouida Bergere to Direct," *MPW,* 19 Mar 1921, 266.

Bergere, Valerie [actress] (b. Metz, Alsace-Lorraine, France, 2 Feb 1867–16 Sep 1938 [71], Hollywood CA). m. Herbert Warren, Aug? 1917. (WB; RKO.) "Valerie Bergere," *Variety,* 21 Sep 1938. BHD, p. 105. IFN, p. 26. "Marriages," *Variety,* 31 Aug 1917, p. 15.

Bergman, Helmer Walton [scenarist] (b. Sundsvall, Sweden, 1883–1 Jan 1931 [47?]). AMD, p. 39. BHD2, p. 21 (Helmer Wilhelm Bergman). "Bergman Adapts Story for Bebe Daniels' Realart Debut," *MPW,* 19 Jun 1920, 1604.

Bergman, Henri [stage/film actor] (b. 1859–9 Jan 1917 [57?], New York NY). (Metro.) "Henry Bergman," *Variety*, 19 Jan 1917, p. 13. AMD, p. 39 (under Bergman, Henry). BHD, p. 105. "Henri Bergman," *MPW*, 5 Feb 1916, 787:2.

Bergman, Henry [actor/assistant director] (b. San Francisco CA, 23 Feb 1868–22 Oct 1946 [78], Hollywood CA; heart attack). "Henry Bergman; Old-Time Actor with Chaplin Had Operated a Cafe," *NYT*, 24 Oct 1946, 27:2. "Henry Bergman," *Variety*, 30 Oct 1946 (age 76). AMD, p. 39. AS, p. 124. BHD1, p. 47; BHD2, p. 21. IFN, p. 26 (age 76). Katz, p. 109 (b. Sweden). LACD, "actor," h 6511 1/2 Hollywood Blvd. Truitt, p. 26 (b. 1870). "The Cohns Sign Clark and Bergman for a New Series of Comedy Films," *MPW*, 17 Jan 1920, 429. "Henry Bergman Engaged by Lesser," *MPW*, 20 Nov 1920, 310.

Bergner, Elisabeth [actress] (*née* Elisabeth Ettel, b. Vienna, Austria, 22 Aug 1900–12 May 1986 [85], London, England). m. Dr. **Paul Czinner**, 1933 (d. 1972). (Ten German films, 1923–32; one American film: *Paris Calling*, 1942.) "Elisabeth Bergner, an Actress in Plays and Films, Dies at 85," *NYT*, 13 May 1986, 26:1. "Stage, Screen Great Elisabeth Bergner Dies at 85 in U.K.," *Variety*, 21 May 1986. BHD1, p. 47 (b. Drogobych, Ukraine). JS, p. 39 (appeared in *Michele Strogoff* in 1970). Waldman, p. 26 (b. Poland, 1897).

Bergquist, Rudolph J. [cameraman] (b. 1885?– Feb 1928 [42], Los Angeles CA). "Picture's [Madge Bellamy's *The Sport Girl*] 2d Death; Rudolph Berquist, Cameraman, Killed in Auto Smash," *Variety*, 29 Feb 1928. AMD, p. 39. FDY, p. 455. LACD, "cameraman," h 7292 Sunset Blvd. "Bergquist to Photograph Lockwood," *MPW*, 24 Aug 1918, 1103.

Bergstrom, Oscar [actor] (b. St. Paul MN, 18 Jul 1874–14 Nov 1931 [57], Stockholm, Sweden). BHD1, p. 604.

Bergvall, Sven [actor] (b. 1881–2 Nov 1960 [79?]). BHD1, p. 47.

Bériza, Marguerite [actress]. No data found. m. **Lucien Muratore** (d. 1954). (Selig). SD.

Berkeley, Claude [film editor] (b. Chicago IL-d. 6 Nov 1931, Los Angeles CA; taken ill while working on *Second Shot* for Pathé). "Claude Berkeley," *Variety*, 10 Nov 1931. BHD2, p. 21.

Berkeley, Gertrude (b. Plattsburg NY, 1864–15 Jun 1946 [81], Hollywood CA). m. Wilson Enos (d. 1904). (World.) BHD, p. 106. IFN, p. 26. SD.

Berkeley, Reginald Cheyne [writer] (b. London, England, 18 Aug 1881–30 Mar 1935 [54], Los Angeles CA; complications after surgery). m. (1) Gwendoline L.I. Cock; (2) Clara H.G. Digby. (Fox.) "Reginald Berkeley," *Variety*, 3 Apr 1935. AS, p. 124. BHD2, p. 21 (b. 19 Aug). IFN, p. 26. SD. Truitt 1983 (b. 1890).

Berle, Sandra [actress] (*née* Sandra Glanz, b. New York NY, 1877–31 May 1954 [77?], Los Angeles CA; cerebral hemorrhage). AS, p. 125. BHD1, p. 48.

Berley, André [actor] (*né* André Edmond Obrecht, b. Paris, France, 13 Jan 1880–27 Nov 1936 [56?], Paris, France [extrait de décès no. 7/1673/1936]). (MGM; Fox; TC-F.) AS, p. 125 (b. 1890). BHD1, p. 48. IFN, p. 26 (Berly). Waldman, p. 27.

Berlin, Irving [composer/producer] (*né* Israel Baline, b. Tyumen, Russia, 11 May 1888–22 Sep 1989 [101], New York NY; heart attack in his sleep). Marilyn Berger, "Irving Berlin, Nation's Songwriter, Dies," *NYT*, 23 Sep 1989, 1, 7. AMD, p. 39. As, p. 125. BHD2, p. 21. "Irving Berlin Goes Into Movie Business," *MPW*, 1 Oct 1921, 531.

Berlin, Minnie [actress] (b. Germany, 1864–13 Sep 1929 [65?], New York NY). BHD, p. 106.

Berliner, Rudolph [assistant director]. No data found. AMD, p. 39. "Made DeMille Assistant," *MPW*, 14 Jun 1924, 653.

Berlyn, Ivan [actor] (b. England, 1874–11 Dec 1934 [60?]). BHD1, p. 48.

Berman, Bobby Burns [actor] (b. London, England, 16 Sep 1896–15 Feb 1955 [58], San Francisco CA). BHD1, p. 48.

Berman, Pandro S[amuel] [producer] (b. Pittsburgh PA, 28 Mar 1905 [Birth Register, Vol. 82, p. 452; b. at 937 St. James St.]-13 Jul 1996 [91], Beverly Hills CA; congestive heart failure). m. (1) Viola Newman; (2) Kathryn Hereford, 1960. (Began 1923; RKO; MGM.) Eric Pace, "Pandro Berman, 91, a Producer of Classic Films,"*NYT*, 15 Jul 1996, B9:4. Fred Alvarez, "Pandro Berman; Produced Films for 4 Decades," *Los Angeles Times*, 14 Jul 1996, p. A-30. AS, p. 125. BHD2, p. 21.

Bern, Paul [scenarist/director] (*né* Paul Levy, b. Wannsbeck [Wandsbek], Germany, 3 Dec 1889–4 Sep 1932 [42], Beverly Hills CA; murder or suicide by shooting). m. (2) **Jean Harlow** (d. 1937). Samuel Marx and Joyce Vanderveen, *Deadly Illusions; Jean Harlow and the Murder of Paul Bern* (New York: Random House, 1990). (Conness-Till Film Co., Toronto; MGM.) "Paul Bern," *Variety*, 13 Sep 1932 (b. Wandabeck; body was cremated). AMD, p. 39. AS, p. 125. BHD2, p. 22. FDY, p. 417. IFN, p. 26. Truitt, p. 27. "Paul Bern a Director," *MPW*, 28 Aug 1920, 1210. "Bern with Universal," *MPW*, 13 Jan 1923, 123. "Paul Bern, Director, Signs with Metro-Goldwyn-Mayer," *MPW*, 29 Aug 1925, 944. "M-G-M Promotes Bern," *MPW*, 27 Nov 1926, 2. "Screen Stories Especially for a Personality," *MPW*, 29 Jan 1927, 354. Jim Tully, "'I'd Fight for Paul'; 'I Have Never Met a Man so Richly Endowed with that Strange Something Called "Soul" as Paul Bern...He Is One of the Greatest Men in Pictures...,'" *MPC*, May 1925, 23, 88 ("Paul will survive.").

Bernard, Adolph [stage/film actor] (aka Bernard A. Reinold, b. 1860–18 Mar 1940 [79?], Percy Williams Home, East Islip LI NY). "Major Bernard Reinold," *Variety*, 27 Mar 1940, p. 47. BHD, p. 106.

Bernard, Alex[ander] [actor] (b. Paris, France, 1882). JS, pp. 39–40 (in Italian silents from 1911).

Bernard, Armand [actor] (b. Paris, France, 21 May 1894–1968 [74?], Paris, France). BHD1, p. 48.

Bernard, Barney [actor] (b. Rochester NY, 17 Aug 1877– 21 Mar 1924 [46], New York NY [Death Certificate Index No. 8267, age 47]; bronchial pneumonia). "Barney Bernard," *Variety*, 26 Mar 1924. AMD, p. 39. BHD, p. 106. IFN, p. 26. Truitt, p. 27. "Barney Bernard in Yiddish Comedy," *MPW*, 10 Jun 1916, 1896. "Obituary," *MPW*, 5 Apr 1924, 444.

Bernard, Barry [actor] (b. England, 4 Oct 1899–24 Jun 1978 [78], Studio City CA). BHD1, p. 48.

Bernard, Dorothy [stage/film actress] (b. Port Elizabeth, South Africa, 25 Jul 1890–15 Dec 1955 [65], Los Angeles CA; heart attack). m. Arthur H. Van Buren (d. 1965). "Dorothy Bernard," *NYT*, 16 Dec 1955, 29:3 (age 61). "Dorothy Bernard," *Variety*, 21 Dec 1955. AMD, p. 39. AS, p. 126. BHD1, p. 48. IFN, p. 26. MSBB, p. 1032. SD. Truitt, p. 27. 1921 Directory, p. 211. "Dorothy Bernard," *MPW*, 2 Jan 1915, 59. "Dorothy Bernard," *MPW*, 27 Feb 1915, 1268. "Dorothy Bernard with Fox Forces Again," *MPW*, 13 Oct 1917, 217. Dunham Thorp, "Fade Out for Fort Lee; The Concrete Walls of Fort Lee's Studios Are Cracked and Crumbling. They Are Skeletons Now of a Dead Past. What Was Once the Movie Center Eighteen Years Ago Is But a Mass of Ruins, Débris and Decay," *MPC*, Feb 1927, 22–23, 72. George Katchmer, "Remembering the Great Silents," *CI*, 234 (Dec 1994), 43.

Bernard, Harry [actor] (b. San Francisco CA, 13 Jan 1878–4 Nov 1940 [62], Los Angeles CA; cancer). "Harry Bernard," *Variety*, 13 Nov 1940. AS, p. 126. BHD1, p. 48. IFN, p. 26. SD. Truitt, p. 27.

Bernard, Lester [actor]. No data found. AMD, p. 39. "Columbia Signs Bernard," *MPW*, 14 Aug 1926, 4.

Bernard, Nan [actress] (b. Peabody KS-d. 19 Jul 1938, Princess Bay NY). BHD, p. 106.

Bernard, Raymond (son of **Tristan Bernard**) [actor/composer/director] (b. Paris, France, 10 Oct 1891–10 Dec 1977 [86], Paris, France). "Raymond Bernard," *Variety*, 21 Dec 1977, p. 79. AS, p. 126. BHD, p. 106; BHD2, p. 22 (d. 12 Dec). IFN, p. 26 (d. Jan 1978).

Bernard, Richard [actor] (b. 1865–26 Dec 1925 [60?], New York NY). BHD, p. 106.

Bernard, Sam [stage/film actor] (aka Samuel Barnet, b. Birmingham, England, 3 Jun 1863–18 May 1927 [63]; apoplexy aboard the *Columbus*). m. (1) Lizzie Raymond (d. 1942); (2) Florence Deutsch. (FP-L.) "Sam Bernard Dies of Stroke on Liner; Comedian Stricken While on Vacation—News Shocks Theatrical World; On the Stage 50 Years; Actor, 64, Was Honored March 13 on Anniversary—Began Career in Oldtime Beer Gardens," *NYT*, 19 May 1927, 27:5. "Sam Bernard," *Variety*, 25 May 1927. AS, p. 126. BHD, p. 106 (b. 16 Jan). IFN, p. 26. Truitt, p. 27. "Famous Players Secures Sam Bernard," *MPW*, 5 Jun 1915, 1583:2 ("reputed to be the highest salaried comedy star on the stage to-day."). "Sam Bernard's Debut," *NYDM*, 7 Jul 1915, 37:3 (in *Poor Schmaltz*, 23 Aug 1915, FP-L). "Sam Bernard's Debut," *NYDM*, 11 Aug 1915, 21:3.

Bernard, Sam [actor] (b. New York NY, 23 Apr 1889–5 Jul 1950 [61], Los Angeles CA). m. Katherine. "Sam Bernard," *Variety*, 12 Jul 1950. AS, p. 126. BHD1, p. 49. IFN, p. 26. SD. Truitt, p. 27.

Bernard, Tristan (father of **Raymond Bernard**) [actor/scenarist] [*né* Paul Bernard, b. Besancon, France, 7 Sep 1886 [extrait de naissance no. 873]-7 Dec 1947 [61], Paris, France [extrait de décès no. 7/1512/1947]). "Tristan Bernard," *Variety*, 10 Dec 1947, 71. AS, p. 126. BHD, p. 22.

Bernardi, Nerio [actor] (*né* Nerino Bernardi, b. Bologna, Italy, 23 Jul 1899–12 Jan 1971 [71], Rome, Italy; uremic poisoning). AS, p. 126. BHD1, p. 49. IFN, p. 26. JS, p. 40 (in Italian silents from 1919).

Bernardo, Maurel [actor] (b. 1880?–16 May 1951 [71], New York NY [Death Certificate Index No. 10799]). "Manuel Bernardo," *Variety*, 23 May 1951. AS, p. 126.

Bernds, Edward L. [director] (b. Chicago IL, 12 Jul 1905–20 May 2000 [94], Van Nuys CA). AS, p. 127 (b. 1911). Harris Lentz, III, "Obituaries; Edward Bernds, 94," *CI,* 301 (Jul 2000), 46 ("He went to Hollywood in the late 1920's where he worked as a sound mixer on such early talking films as *Song of Love* [1929], *Dirigible* [1931], *Platinum Blonde* [1931]," and others).

Bernelli, Sem [librettist/poet/playwright] (b. Italy?, 1877?–18 Dec 1949 [72], Zoagli, Italy). AMD, p. 36. "Sem Bernelli," *Variety,* 21 Dec 1949, 55. "Sem Bernelli Who Wrote 'The Jester' Is Author of 'Tears of the Sea,'" *MPW,* 3 Dec 1921, 562.

Bernhard, Francis S. [actor]. No data found. LACD, h 1722 London.

Bernhard, Ilma Frances [actress] (b. Los Angeles CA, 23 Nov 1919–16 Aug 1997 [77], Los Angeles CA). BHD1, p. 604.

Bernhardt, Sarah [stage/film actress] (*née* Henriette Rosine Bernard, b. Paris, France, 23 Oct 1844–26 Mar 1923 [78], Paris, France). m. Jacques Damala, 1882. (Stage debut, 1862.) Joanna Richardson, *Sarah Bernhardt and Her World* (London: Weidenfeld & Nicolson, 1977). Arthur Gold and Robert Fizdale, *The Divine Sarah* (NY: Alfred A. Knopf, 1991). "Bernhardt Dies in Her Son's Arms in Paris, Aged 78; Throng Sorrows at Her Door as She Succumbs After Comment on Long Agony; Last Words for America; 'Greatest Actress' to Have a State Funeral—Flowers Cover Her Deathbed; Mourned in Many Lands; The Theatre Here Pays Tribute—Career Began Sixty Years Ago—Triumphs in Many Roles," *NYT,* 27 Mar 1923, 1:1, 8:1 (b. 22 Oct). "Sarah Bernhardt," *Variety,* 29 Mar 1923. AMD, p. 39. AS, p. 127 (b. 25 Oct). BHD1, p. 604 (b. 22 Oct). GSS, pp. 37–39 (age 79). IFN, p. 26. SD. Truitt, p. 27. WWVC, p. 23. "Bernhardt Coming Here, Signs a Contract with the Shuberts for a Tour Beginning Nov. 6," *NYT,* 29 Jun 1905, 9:4 (to play 30 weeks in *Angelo* and *Adrienne Le Couvreur*). "Eclair Presents Mme. Bernhardt in Pictures," *MPW,* 11 Nov 1911, 473. "Bernhardt and Réjane," *MPW,* 10 Feb 1912, 468. W. Stephen Bush, "Bernhardt and Réjane in Pictures," *MPW,* 2 Mar 1912, 760. "Bernhardt Conquers New World; Says Her Immortality Will Depend Upon the Record of the Films," *MPW,* 9 Mar 1912, 874–75. "Bernhardt Exclusively with Society Film D'Art," *MPW,* 23 Mar 1912, 1061. "Bernhardt in Motion Pictures," *The Literary Digest,* 3 Aug 1912, 190–91 ("Much has been heard of the moving-picture machine as the ignoble but dangerous rival of legitimate drama, crowding the players off the boards and debasing the public taste with its crude and tawdry substitute for dramatic art.... But to many it will doubtless be a surprize [sic] to learn that no less an artist than Sarah Bernhardt has entrusted her art to the films, and that she will be seen this season in the United States in a historical photo-play [21 scenes from Amiel Moreau's *Queen Elizabeth*). "Sarah Bernhardt Pleased with Pictures," *MPW,* 21 Sep 1912, 1174. M. Michelson, "Immortality in the Films," *Colliers, The National Weekly,* 12 Apr 1913, 11 (the best-known players in France are appearing in films; American players are doing the same, attracted only by extraordinary financial inducements "but also by the fascination of the idea so dramatically expressed by Mme. Sarah Bernhardt as the last clicks of a picture machine recorded the end of her performance of 'Queen Elizabeth.' 'I am immortal!' she exclaimed. 'I am a film!'" Less than eight months after the completion of the Bernhardt film, James K. Hackett made *The Prisoner of Zenda* and James O'Neil [sic] made *The Count of Monte Cristo.*" The argument that broke her down was that other great actress, such as Ristori and Rachel, "could only be remembered in memorials, while she had an opoortunity to be visualized to all nations for all time." Daniel Frohman said it took three months for Bernhardt to make the film. "Frequently she had to rest in the middle of a scene and the camera would be stopped. Thus she is seen at a better advantage in the pictures than she has been on the stage in several years." Americna and English players soon to make their movie debuts included Tree, Mrs. Fiske, Ethel Barrymore, Blanche Bates, Faversham, and Julie Opp in Shakespearean roles; and Sothern, Mrs. Langtry, and Mrs. Leslie Carter. Klaw & Erlanger recently "patched up their war with the Shuberts" and will produce films in America. "The managers express no fear that the appearance of their leading actors in films will injure the attraction of the legitimate." Frohman said films will help attendance at theaters, as proved in the case of Bernhardt. The living actor will never be supplanted—"The pictures are never the real thing, no matter how fine they may be. Rather, they make countless auditors for the actor; create an interest in him..."). "Films Immortalize Bernhardt," *NYDM,* 3 Mar 1915, 25:3 (had a "delicate operation" the week before). "No Operation for Bernhardt," *MPW,* 16 Nov 1918, 727. Gaston Glass, "Sarah Bernhardt: A Memory," *MM,* Apr 1926, 42–43, 94–96. Eve Golden, "From Stage to Screen: The Film Career of Sarah Bernhardt," *CI,* 264 (Jun 1997), C8-C9. D.J. Turner, "Sarah Bernhardt [letter]," *CI,* 268 (Oct 1997), 12 (mother's name was Judith Van Hard).

Bernie, Ben [actor] (b. Bayonne NJ, 30 May 1891–20 Oct 1943 [52], Beverly Hills CA). "Ben Bernie," *Variety,* 27 Oct 1943, 46. BHD1, p. 49.

Bernoudy, Jane [actress] (b. New Castle CO, 19 Aug 1893–28 Oct 1972 [79], Canoga Park CA). AMD, p. 39. AS, p. 127. BHD, p. 106. IFN, p. 27. "Jane Bernoudy at Home in the Saddle," *MPW,* 25 Dec 1915, 2394. George A. Katchmer, "Remembering the Great Silents," *CI,* 172 (Oct 1989), C14.

Bernstein, Isadore [publicist/actor/scenarist/title writer/producer/director] (b. New York NY, Nov 1876?–18 Oct 1944 [68], Los Angeles CA; heart attack). (Imp, 1910; Yankee Film Co., publicist and general manager.) "Isadore Bernstein," *Variety,* 25 Oct 1944 (persuaded Laemmle to buy Universal City). AMD, p. 39. AS, p. 127. BHD, p. 106 (b. 1877). FDY, pp. 417, 441. LACD, "manager, National Film Co.," h 5107 Harold Way. "Bernstein Resigns from Yankee," *MPW,* 11 Nov 1911, 480:1. "Isadore Bernstein to Manage Western Universal," *MPW,* 5 Jul 1913, 29. "Bernstein Resigns," *MPW,* 20 May 1916, 1322. "Bernstein to Produce Comedies," *MPW,* 7 Jul 1917, 73. "Bankruptcy Papers Filed by Isadore Bernstein," *MPW,* 3 Aug 1918, 687. "Bernstein Receives Flattering Offer," *MPW,* 31 Jan 1920, 759.

Bernstein, Jules [studio manager]. No data found. Jules Bernstein, "An Exchange-Man's Views; Pathe's New York Manager Decrys [sic] the Daily Change—He Favors Short Pictures and Has Faith in the Serial," *NYDM,* 27 Jan 1915, 43:1.

Bernstein, Leonard [general manager]. No data found. (Wizard Motion Pictures Corporation.) "'Pokes and Jabs,'" *MPW,* 11 Sep 1915, 1811:1.

Berquist, Rudolph J. [cinematographer] (b. Sweden, 1885–15 Feb 1928 [42?], Los Angeles CA; after a fall). AS, p. 128. BHD2, p. 22.

Berrell, George W. [stage/film actor] (aka George Burrell, b. Philadelphia PA, 16 Dec 1849–20 Apr 1933 [83], Los Angeles CA). m. actress Serena Tylor. (Climax; Lubin; Lasky; Bosworth; Metro; Universal; Imp.) BHD, p. 106. IFN, p. 27. LACD, Berrel, George B., "photoplayer," h 1465 N. Bronson Ave. MSBB, p. 1022. 1918 Studio Directory, p. 65. George A. Katchmer, "Forgotten Cowboys and Cowgirls—Part XVI," *CI,* 193 (Jul 1991), 35.

Berri, Maud Lillian [opera singer/producer]. No data found. AMD, p. 40. "Miss Berri to Make More Pictures," *MPW,* 17 Feb 1917, 1049.

Berry, Aline [actress] (b. 1904–3 Apr 1967 [62], Hollywood CA; heart attack). "Aline Berry," *Variety,* 12 Apr 1967. BHD, p. 106. IFN, p. 27. Truitt, p. 27.

Berry, Audrey C. [actress] (b. 23 Oct 1906). (Vitagraph juvenile.) AMD, p. 40. "Gossip of the Studios," *NYDM,* 13 Nov 1915, 33:1 (9 years old on 23 Oct. "She was given a birthday party at the studio.") "Little Audrey Berry Visits Old Friends," *MPW,* 17 Jun 1916, 2034.

Berry, James [actor] (b. Manchester, England, 11 May 1883–1 Aug 1915 [32]). AMD, p. 40. BHD, p. 106. "Sign Colored Comedian," *MPW,* 12 Apr 1924, 546.

Berry, Lillian [actress]. No data found. AMD, p. 40. "Biograph Player at Liberty," *MPW,* 9 Nov 1912, 539.

Berry, Mrs. Stella F. [actress]. No data found. LACD, "photoplayer," h 244 S. Figueroa.

Berry, William Henry [actor] (b. London, England, 23 Mar 1870–2 May 1951 [81], Herne Bay, Kent, England). BHD1, p. 49 (d. London). IFN, p. 27.

Berscia, Leandro [cinematographer]. No data found. JS, p. 40 (in Italian silents from 1914).

Berski, M. [cinematographer]. No data found. FDY, p. 455.

Berst, Jacques A. [vice-president of Selig]. No data found. AMD, p. 40. Louis Reeves Harrison, "Studio Saunterings," *MPW,* 16 Mar 1912, 944–45. "Berst Resigns Pathé Office," *MPW,* 13 Dec 1913, 1263. "Berst vs. Griffith," *MPW,* 17 Jul 1915, 465. "Cutting and Allied Arts," *NYDM,* 13 Nov 1915, 24:3, 30:3 ("An expert film technician should be able to quickly perceive the weaknesses in the completed film." As for tinting and toning, film shoiuld be toned then tinted, then given a coating of celluloid and retinted. For realism, a small portion of film could be colored, such as a flag. The expert is able to manufacture missing fades. Trimming scenes must be exact. "The Selig compamy pays careful attention to the sub-title.... A list of all sub-titles for every photoplay is made out, and these are carefully gone over and edited by three or four individuals, and the approved result appears on the screen. In comedy productions, the sub-title is of even more importance. I have known many a comedy film to be saved by original, cleverly written sub-titles."). "Berst Active for Hughes Bill," *MPW,* 29 Jul 1916, 778. "Berst Outlines Pathé Policy," *MPW,* 5 May 1917, 816. "Jacques A. Berst Resigns from Pathé," *MPW,* 23 Mar 1918, 1642.

Bert, Camille [actress] (b. Orleans, France, 27 Dec 1880-Jun 1970 [89], Paris, France). BHD1, p. 50.

Berte, Genevive [actress]. (Canyon Pictures Corp.) George A. Katchmer, "Forgotten Cowboys and Cowgirls—Part XIII," *CI*, 190 (Apr 1991), C6.

Bertel, Maurice [cinematographer] (d. Melbourne, Victoria, Australia, May 1930). BHD2, p. 22.

Berthelet, Arthur [actor/director] (b. Milwaukee WI, 12 Oct 1879–16 Sep 1949 [69], Vista CA). (Essanay.) "Arthur Berthelet," *Variety*, 28 Sep 1949 (d. 21 Sep). AMD, p. 40. AS, p. 128 (d. 21 Sep). BHD2, p. 22. IFN, p. 27. "Arthur Berthelet Goes West to Direct Miss Love in 'Penny of Tophill Trail,'" *MPW*, 11 Sep 1920, 236.

Bertini, Francesca [stage/film actress/singer] (*née* Elena Seracini Vitiello, b. Florence, Italy, 11 Apr 1888–13 Oct 1985 [97], Rome, Italy). *The Rest Doesn't Count. The Last Diva* (Italy, 1982; dir. Gianfranco Mingozzi; on tape). Costanzo Constantini, *La Diva Imperiale; Ritratto di Francesca Bertini* (Milano, Italia: Bompiani, 1982). (Cines; Kleine-Celio.) (Film debut: *La Dea del Mare*, 1904.) "Francesca Bertini," *Variety*, 23 Oct 1985. AMD, p. 40. AS, p. 129. BHD1, p. 50. JS, p. 41 (in Italian silents from1904. "Possibly Italy's first cinematic sex symbol."). Katz, p. 116. JS, p. 41 ("Possibly Italy's first cinematic sex symbol."). "Miss Francesca Bertini," *MPW*, 13 Dec 1913, 1269. "Cines-Kleine Players; Some of the Notable Ones Who Have Distinguished Themselves in a Number of Great Productions," *MPW*, 11 Jul 1914, 237–38 (26 years old…"a remarkably talented and graceful woman with a face and form of singular beauty."). "Kleine Subject Featuring Francesca Bertini," *MPW*, 31 Oct 1914, 652. "Metro Signs Popular Italian Actress," *MPW*, 20 Sep 1919, 1806.

Bertone, Alfredo [actor] (b. Naples, Italy-d. 15 Mar 1927, Liège, Belgium). AS, p. 129. BHD, p. 106. IFN, p. 27. JS, p. 42 (in Italian silents from 1913).

Bertoni, Alberto-Francis [director] (b. Rome, Italy). JS, p. 42 (in Italian silents 1917–20; "[w]orked mostly in Germany and France.").

Bertram, Vedah [actress] (*née* Adele Buck, b. Boston MA, 4 Dec 1891–26 Aug 1912 [20], Oakland CA; after surgery for appendicitis). (Essanay.) AMD, p. 40. AS, p. 129. BHD, pp. 7–8, 106. BR, p. 2. IFN, p. 27. "The 'Acting' Member of Essanay," *MPW*, 6 Jan 1912, 27–28. "Miss Bertram Ill," *MPW*, 20 Apr 1912, 234. James S. McQuade, "Miss 'Vedah Bertram' Very Ill," *MPW*, 10 Aug 1912, 531. "Greenroom Jottings," *MPSM*, Sep 1912, 110 ("As we go to press, the sad news comes from Niles, Cal., that Mr. Anderson's popular leading woman, Vedah Bertram, is hovering between life and death at the Samuel Merrit Hospital at Oakland."). "Death of Vedah Bertram," *MPW*, 7 Sep 1912, 966 (d. 27 Aug). Billy H. Doyle, "Lost Players," *CI*, 163 (Jan 1989), 30.

Bertram, William [actor/director] (*né* Benjamin Switzer, b. Walkerton, Ontario, Canada, 19 Jan 1880–1 May 1933 [53], Los Angeles CA). (Great Western Film Co.; Pathé; Imp; Bison.) "William Bertram," *Variety*, 9 May 1933. AMD, p. 40. AS, p. 129. BHD1, p. 50; BHD2, p. 23. FDY, p. 417 (Bartram). IFN, p. 27. Spehr, p. 116. Richard Willis, "Lives of the Players; William Bertram, 101 Bison 'Indian Chief,'" *MPS*, 18 Apr 1913, 30. "William Bertram," *MPW*, 25 Mar 1916, 1982. "Bertram Directs 'Hidden Dangers,'" *MPW*, 24 Apr 1920, 581.

Bertramo, Calisto (father of Letizia Bonini) [actor] (b. Turin, Italy, 28 Aug 1875–30 Sep 1941 [66], Viareggio, Italy). m. (daughter, Maria Letizia Bertrama, b. Florence, Italy, 13 May 1902). JS, p. 42 (in Italian silents from 1923).

Bertrand, Mary [actress] (b. 1881?–12 May 1955 [74], Woodland Hills CA). "Mrs. Mary Bertrand Rall," *Variety*, 25 May 1955. AS, p. 129. BHD1, p. 50. IFN, p. 27. Truitt, p. 28.

Bertsch, Marguerite [scenarist/director] (b. New York NY, 14 Dec 1889–1967 [77?]). AMD, p. 40. AS, p. 130. BHD2, p. 23. Slide, p. 135. "Vitagraph Employs Woman Director," *MPW*, 5 Aug 1916, 935.

Berwin, Isabel. No data found. (In *Prunella*, 1918.)

Beryl, Eddie [actress] (b. 1894–25 Nov 1922 [28?], Cincinnati OH). BHD, p. 107.

Besley, J.C. [cameraman]. No data found. AMD, p. 40. "Besley Expedition Successful," *MPW*, 7 Nov 1914, 763.

Bessent, Marie [actress] (b. 1898?–10 Oct 1947 [49], Los Angeles CA). "Marie Bessent," *Variety*, 15 Oct 1947. AS, p. 130. BHD, p. 107. IFN, p. 27.

Besserer, Eugenie [actress] (b. Watertown NY, 25 Dec 1868–28 May 1934 [65], Los Angeles CA; heart attack). "Eugenie Besserer," *Variety*, 5 Jun 1934 (age 64). AMD, p. 40. AS, p. 130 (b. Marseilles, France). BHD1, p. 50. FSS, p. 32. IFN, p. 27. Katz, p. 117 (b. Marseilles, France). LACD, "photoplayer," h 2215 Baxter. MH, p. 97. Truitt, p. 28 (b. 1870). "Selig Leading Woman Injured Second Time," *MPW*, 30 Mar 1912, 1152. "Eugenie Besserer," *MPW*, 10 Mar 1917, 1549. "Eugenie Besserer," *MPW*, 13 Aug 1927, 456.

Besserer, Loma [stock/film actress]. No data found. (Film debut: *The Heart of a Cowboy*, Essanay, 1909.) "The Essanay Company Out West," *MPW*, 4 Dec 1909, 801–02.

Best, Dolly [actress] (b. 1899?–6 Oct 1968 [69?], Los Angeles CA). BHD, p. 107. Truitt, p. 28.

Best, Edna (mother of actress Sarah Marshall) [stage/film actress] (b. Hove, Sussex, England, 3 Mar 1900–18 Sep 1974 [74], Gevena, Switzerland). m. (1) actor Seymour Beard—div.; (2) **Herbert Marshall**—div. (d. 1966); (3) Nat Wolff, 1940. "Edna Best," *Variety*, 25 Sep 1974, p. 62. BHD1, p. 50. IFN, p. 27.

Best, Martin (H.M. Best) [stage/film actor] (b. Chicago IL, 17 Sep 1880–2 Nov 1975 [95], Santa Monica CA). (Pathé; Unity; Vitagraph.) BHD, p. 107. LACD, "photoplayer," h 761 E. Kensington Rd. MSBB, p. 1022.

Bethew, Herbert [actor]. No data found. (Universal.) George A. Katchmer, "Forgotten Cowboys and Cowgirls—Part XVII," *CI*, 194 (Aug 1991),43.

Betrone, Annibale [actor] (b. Turin, Italy, 9 Dec 1883–11 Dec 1950 [67], Rome, Italy). AS, p. 131. JS, p. 42 (in Italian silents from 1916).

Betts, William E. [actor] (b. 1856?–4 Apr 1929 [73], New York NY [Death Certificate Index No. 10283, age 62]; pneumonia). "William E. Betts," *Variety*, 10 Apr 1929. BHD, p. 107 (d. 5 Apr). IFN, p. 27. Truitt, p. 28.

Betz, Matthew [actor] (*né* Matthew von Betz, b. St. Louis MO, 13 Sep 1881–26 Jan 1938 [56], Los Angeles CA). "Matthew Betz," *Variety*, 2 Feb 1938 (age 57). AS, p. 131. BHD1, p. 51. IFN, p. 27. Truitt, p. 28.

Bevan, Billy [stage/film actor] (*né* William Bevan Harris, b. Orange, Australia, 29 Sep 1887–26 Nov 1957 [70], Escondido CA). m. Leona Roberts (sister of Edith Roberts). AMD, p. 40. AS, p. 131. BHD1, p. 51. FSS, p. 32. IFN, p. 27. LACD, William Bevan, "photoplayer," h 6834 DeLongpre Ave. MSBB, p. 1022. "Romance Lends Interest to L-KO's," *MPW*, 27 Oct 1917, 511 (m. Roberts). "Bevan Is Back with Sennett," *MPW*, 28 May 1927, 276.

Bevani, Alexander [actor] (*né* Alexander Beaven, b. 1870?–24 Feb 1938 [67], Los Angeles CA). (Universal.) "Alexander Bevani," *Variety*, 2 Mar 1938 (age 75). AS, p. 131. BHD, p. 107. IFN, p. 27.

Bevans, Lionel [actor/director] (b. 1884?–17 Feb 1965 [81], Los Angeles CA). m. (1) Viola Roache (d. 1961); (2) Helen Lippe. "Lionel Bevans," *Variety*, 17 Mar 1965. SD.

Bevins, Mabel [actress] (d. 23 Dec 1916). BHD, p. 107. IFN, p. 27.

Bey, Ben Ali *see* **Auzinger, Max**

Beyer, Charles W. [actor/actors' agent since 1920] (b. Newark NJ, 28 Feb 1893–28 Nov 1953 [60], Los Angeles CA; cancer). (Vitagraph.) "Charles W. Beyer," *Variety*, 2 Dec 1953. AMD, p. 40. AS, p. 131. BHD1, p. 51; BHD2, p. 23. IFN, p. 27. Truitt, p. 21. "Beyer Engaged for Arliss Film," *MPW*, 29 Jul 1922, 352. George Katchmer, "Remembering the Great Silents," *CI* (Nov 1993), 51–52.

Beyers, Clara [actress]. No data found. (*Fl.* 1916–17.)

Beyfuss, Alexander E. [general manager] (d. 8 Jan 1925, New York NY). m. Wilhemina Speer-Hudson, 17 Feb 1916, SF CA. AMD, p. 41. BHD2, p. 23. "Western Picturemen in Town," *MPW*, 21 Nov 1914, 1093. "Alexander E. Beyfuss Marries," *MPW*, 18 Mar 1916, 1828. "Beyfuss Returns to Coast," *MPW*, 1 Apr 1916, 1828. "Beyfuss with Selznick," *MPW*, 9 Dec 1916, 1476.

Bianchetti, Suzanne [actress] (b. Paris, France, 24 Feb 1889–17 Oct 1936 [47], Paris, France [extrait de décès no. SN/1936]). m. journalist/scenariust René Jeanne (1887–1969). AS, p. 133. BHD1, p. 51 (b. 1894). IFN, p. 27 (age 42).

Bianchi, Giorgio [actor, 1925/dubbing director/director, 1942/producer] (b. Rome, Italy, 18 Feb 1904–9 Feb 1968 [63], Rome, Italy). (Last film: *The Two Motorcycle Cops*.) "Georgio Bianchi," *Variety*, 21 Feb 1968, p. 78 (age 64). AS, p. 132 (b. 1894). BHD1, p. 51; BHD2, p. 23. JS, pp. 43–44 (in Italian silents from 1928).

Bianchi, Vittorio [writer/actor] (b. Arezzano, Italy, 23 Dec 1865). AS, p. 132. JS, p. 44 (in Italian silents from 1916).

Biancini, Ferrucio Angelo Carlo [actor/producer/scenarist] (b. Pomponesco, Italy, 18 Aug 1890 [extrait de naissance no. 57]–19 Mar 1955 [64], Rome, Italy). AS, p. 132. BHD, p. 107. IFN, p. 28. JS, p. 44 (in Italian silents from 1925).

Bianco, Tranquillo [actor] (b. Turin-d. Jun 1926, Turin, Italy). JS, p. 44 (in Italian silents from 1913).

Bibo, Irving [composer] (b. San Francisco CA, 22 Aug 1889–2 May 1962 [72], Los Angeles CA; heart attack). m. Gertrude (; b. 10 Oct 1895-Nov 1983 [88], CA). "Irving Bibo, 72, Writer of Songs, Film Scores," *NYT*, 3 May 1962, 33:3 (composed scores for 300+ films; wrote *Huggable, Kissable You; Do You Believe in Dreams*). "Irving Bibo," *Variety*, 9 May 1962 (wrote *Cherie; Forever* *and a Day*). AS, p. 132. ASCAP, 1966, p. 55. BHD2, p. 23.

Biby, Edward [actor/scenarist] (b. Chicago IL, 8 Aug 1886–3 Oct 1952 [66], Los Angeles CA). (Chaplin.) AS, p. 132. LACD, "scenario writer," h 2174 Highland.

Bickel, George L. [actor/director] (b. Saginaw MI, 17 Feb 1863–5 Jun 1941 [78], Los Angeles CA). (Film debut: *The Fixer,* Kleine, 1915; Edison; Fox.) "George Bickel," *Variety,* 11 Jun 1941. AS, p. 133. BHD1, p. 51. IFN, p. 28. Truitt, p. 29. "Bickel and Watson Comedy," *NYDM,* 11 Aug 1915, 21:1 (to debut in *Hello, Bill,* Kleine, 15 Sep 1915).

Bickers, H. Sheridan [scenarist] (County Galway, Republic of Ireland, 1883). BHD2, p. 23. LACD, "scenario writer," h 7128 Hollywood Blvd.

Bickerton, Joseph P., Jr. [attorney/showman/producer]. (b. 1878?–20 Aug 1936 [58], Mt. Kisco NY). m. Lois Taber. "Joseph P. Bickerton, Jr.," *Variety,* 20 Aug 1936; "Joe Bickerton Dies at 58; Was Central Cog of All Legit Biz," 26 Aug 1936, p. 94. "Another Producer; Joseph P. Bickerton, Jr., Has Organized a Company to Produce Dramatic Novelties," *NYDM,* 22 Jan 1913, 13:3 (organized the Jungle Film Company, securing African hunt pictures from Paul J. Rainey).

Bidwell, Eli C. [business manager]. No data found. (Griffith.) LACD, "bus. mgr," h 1275 Lyman Pl.

Biensfeldt, Paul [actor] (b. Berlin, Germany, 4 Mar 1869–2 Apr 1933 [64]). AS, p. 133. BHD, p. 107. IFN, p. 28.

"Big Boy." *See* Sebastian, Malcolm.

Bigelow, Frank [actor] (b. 1870–10 Dec 1916 [46]). BHD, p. 107. IFN, p. 107.

Bigelow, Fred A. [actor] (b. Denver CO, 1877–8 Dec 1931 [54?], New York NY). BHD, p. 107.

Biggers, Earl Derr [creator of Charlie Chan/scenarist] (b. 24 Aug 1884–5 Apr 1933 [48], Pasadena CA; heart attack). "Earl Derr Biggers," *Variety,* 11 Apr 1933, 54. AS, p. 133. BHD2, p. 23.

Biggy, Frank [actor]. No data found. *MPW,* 11 Mar 1911, 520 (photograph of Pathé stock company).

Bilancia, Oreste [actor] (b. Catania, Italy, 24 Sep 1881–31 Oct 1945 [64], Rome, Italy). AS, p. 134. BHD1, p. 52. IFN, p. 107. JS, p. 45 (in Italian silents from 1914).

Bilbrooke, Lydia [actress] (b. Somerset, England, 6 May 1888–4 Jan 1990 [101], Suffolk, England). AS, p. 134 (d. 6 Dec 1989). BHD1, p. 52.

Bildt, Paul [actor] (b. Berlin, Germany, 19 May 1885–16 Mar 1957 [71], Berlin, Germany). BHD1, p. 52. IFN, p. 107.

Bilimoria, M[anchersha] **B**[urjorji] [pioneerof Indian cinema] (b. India, 1899–6 Jul 1959 [60>], Bombay, India). AS, p. 134.

Biliotti, Enzo [actor] (b. Livorno, Italy, 28 Jun 1887). JS, p. 45 (in Italian silents from 1923).

Billings, Benjamin [actor] (b. 1903–3 May 1923 [20], Los Angeles CA). AS, p. 134. IFN, p. 28.

Billlings, Billie [actress]. No data found. (*Fl.* 1916–17.)

Billings, Elmo G. [actor: Our Gang Comedies/film editor] (b. Los Angeles CA, 24 Jun 1912–6 Feb 1964 [51], Los Angeles CA; stroke). "Elmo Billings," *Variety,* 12 Feb 1964 (age 58). AS, p. 134. IFN, p. 28. Truitt, p. 29.

Billings, Florence B. [actress] (b. NY, 1896). (Vitagraph; Metro.) MSBB, p. 1032.

Billings, George A. [mailman/actor] (b. Preston MN, 22 Nov 1870–15 Apr 1934 [63], Sawtelle CA). "George A. Billings," *Variety,* 24 Apr 1934. AS, p. 134. BHD1, p. 52 (d. LA CA). IFN, p. 28. Truitt, p. 29. Dorothy Donnell, "Getting in by the Back Door," *MPS,* 26 Aug 1924, 20–21, 31 (he was a Hollywood letter carrier whose "picture career was based on an unusual physical resemblance to Lincoln...").

Billings, Richard E. [film editor] (b. 1908?–17 Aug 1965 [57], Los Angeles CA). "Richard E. Billings," *Variety,* 25 Aug 1965 (with TC-F for 30 years). BHD2, p. 23.

Billings, Ted [actor] (b. London, England, 7 Apr 1880–5 Jul 1947 [67], Los Angeles Co. CA). AS, p. 134. BHD1, p. 52. IFN, p. 28.

Billington, Francelia [actress] (b. Dallas TX, 1 Feb 1895–24 Nov 1934 [39], Glendale CA; tuberculosis). m. **Lester Cuneo**, 1920, Riverside CA—div. 1925 (d. 1925). (Kalem, 1912; Thanhouser [West Coast]; Reliance-Majestic [Apr 1913]; Universal; American). AMD, p. 41. AS, p. 134. BHD1, p. 52. FSS, p. 33. MH, p. 97 (b. 1897). "World Notice Brings Stardom," *MPW,* 31 May 1913, 926. "Miss Billington Does the 'Impossible,'" *MPW,* 21 Mar 1914, 1509. "Versatile Miss Billington," *Motography,* 11 Jul 1914, 58. "Francelia Billington," *MPW,* 18 Jul 1914, 410. "Francelia Billington Joins Universal," *MPW,* 4 Mar 1916, 1453. "Miss Billington Signed by Mutual," *MPW,* 30 Dec 1916, 1969. "Francelia Billington," *MPW,* 8 Sep 1917, 1529. "Wedding in Filmland," *MPW,* 6 Nov 1920, 55:1. Billy H. Doyle, "Lost Players," *CI,* 158 (Aug 1988), 26. George A. Katchmer, "Remembering the Great Silents," *CI,* 172 (Oct 1989), C14.

Binder, Ray Jerome [actor] (b. Chicago IL, 27 Jul 1884). (Fine Arts.) AS, p. 135. BHD, p. 107. 1918 Studio Directory, p. 65.

Bing, Herman [opera singer/actor/producer] (b. Frankfurt, Germany, 30 Mar 1888–9 Jan 1947 [58], Los Angeles CA; suicide). (Final film: *Where Do We Go From Here?,* 1944.) "Herman Bing," *Variety,* 15 Jan 1947 (production executive in Germany; notes to his daughter "complained of insomnia and added, 'I had to commit suicide.'"). AS, p. 135. BHD1, p. 52 (b. 1889). IFN, p. 28.

Binger, Maurits Herman [director] (b. Haarlem, Netherlands, 5 Apr 1868–9 Apr 1923 [55], Wiesbaden, Garmany). AS, p. 135. BHD2, p. 23.

Binger, Ray [cinematographer]. No data found. FDY, p. 455.

Bingham, Cecil [actor] (d. 6 May 1925, London, England). BHD, p. 107.

Bingham, Edfrid A. [scenarist] (b. 13 Jan 1906-Nov 1977 [71], CA). BHD2, p. 24 (b. Oak Hill OH-2 May 1930, New York NY). FDY, p. 417.

Bingham, J. Clarke [actor] (b. England, 1897?–4 Dec 1962 [65], New York NY [Death Certificate Index No. 25707; M.E. Case 9825]). "J. Clarke Bingham," *Variety,* 12 Dec 1962.

Bingham, Stanley J. [actor] (b. Cleveland OH, 28 Apr 1880–9 Jan 1962 [81], Riverside CA). AS, p. 135. BHD, p. 107. IFN, p. 28.

Binney, Constance (sister of **Faire Binney**) [actress] (b. New York NY, 28 Jun 1896–15 Nov 1989 [93], Whitestone NY). (Film Debut: *The Sporting Life,* 1918.) m. (1) Charles E. Cotting, 1926–1932; (2) Henry Wharton, Jr.; (3) Geoffrey Cheshire, 1947. AMD, p. 41. AS, p. 135. BHD, p. 107. Finch, p. 256 (b. 27 Jul 1899). MH, p. 97. WWS, p. 90. "Constance Binney Signed to Appear in Realart Films," *MPW,* 5 Jul 1919, 73. "Constance Binney to Begin Screen Work," *MPW,* 2 Aug 1919, 674. "Miss Binney's First Vehicle Will Be 'Erstwhile Susan,'" *MPW,* 13 Sep 1919, 1672. "Constance Binney to Go on Tour in Stage Play," *MPW,* 4 Oct 1919, 107. "Signs Constance Binney," *MPW,* 7 Jul 1923, 52. "Constance Binney on Stage and Screen," *MPW,* 24 Nov 1923, 409. Bown Adams, "Constance Binney Came to Our Christmas Party," *CFC,* 39 (Summer, 1973), 11. Billy H. Doyle, "Constance and Faire Binney," *CI,* 214 (Apr 1993), 16.

Binney, Faire (sister of **Constance Binney**) [actress] (*née* Frederica Gertrude Binney, b. New York NY [Morristown NJ?], 20 Aug 1898–28 Aug 1957 [59], Los Angeles CA; pneumonia). m. David C. Sloane, 1922–div.; Sering D. Wilson. AMPAS (b. PA or NY NY). (Film Debut: *The Sporting Life,* 1918.) AS, p. 135. BHD, p. 107 (b. PA, 24 Aug 1900). IFN, p. 28 (b. PA). MH, p. 98. 1921 Directory, p. 212. WWS, p. 206. Faith Service, "Starward Ho!; Airy Faire Binney Is on the Threshold of Fame," *MPC,* Feb 1919, 36–37, 70.

Binney, Harold J. (Josh) [actor/director/producer] (b. Kansas City MO, 3 Jun 1889–8 Nov 1956 [67], Los Angeles Co. CA). AMD, p. 41. BHD, p. 24. IFN, p. 28. "Harold J. Binney Comes to Town," *MPW,* 13 Oct 1917, 255. "Binney to Make Two-Reel Comedies," *MPW,* 4 May 1918, 680. "Funny Fatty Filbert Is Star in J. Binney Comedies," *MPW,* 18 May 1918, 1018. "New Haven to Be Home of Binney Productions," *MPW,* 7 Dec 1918, 1055.

Binns, George H. [actor] (b. England, 1886–27 Oct 1918 [32?], Glendale CA; double pneumonia). m. "Jerry" Melville. (Keystone; L-KO.) "George H. Binns," *Variety,* 15 Nov 1918. AS, p. 135. BHD, p. 107. IFN, p. 28.

Birch, Carolyn [actress]. No data found. AMD, p. 41. "Carolyn Birch," *MPW,* 25 Aug 1917, 1202.

Bird, Charles A. [General Manager of Fox Film Corp.] (b. Lockport NY, 1855?–11 Nov 1925 [ca. 70], Hornell NY; after two operations). "Charles A. Bird Dead; Veteran Theatrical Manager Was Long with the Shuberts," *NYT,* 12 Nov 1925, 25:5. "Charles A. Bird," *Variety,* 18 Nov 1925 (general manager for Fox studios).

Bird, Charlot [actress] (b. Philadelphia PA). (FP-L.) "Is She Richard Dix's Fiancée?," *MPC,* Dec 1925, 54.

Bird, Violet [actress]. No data found. (Christie.) "Beauties Who Make the Comedies Attractive," *Cinema Arts,* Aug 1926, 21 (photo).

Birell, Tala [stage/film/TV actress] (*née* Natalie Bierl, b. Bucharest, Rumania, 10 Sep 1907–17 Feb 1958 [50], U.S. military hospital at Landstuhl, Germany; cancer. Buried in the Bierl family plot in the cemetery at Marquartstein, Bavaria). (Film debut: bit in *Man Spielt nich mit der Liebe* [*Don't Play with Love*], 1926; Universal.) AS, p. 136 (b. Vienna, Austria, 1908–1959). Barrie Roberts, "Tala Birell: Second Garbo," *CI,* 287 (May 1999), 20–24 (includes filmography. Birell was publicized as another Garbo, which possibly ruined her subsequent career in films.).

Birkett, Viva [actress] (b. Exeter, Devon, England, 14 Feb 1887–26 Jun 1934 [47], London, England). AS, p. 136. BHD, p. 107. IFN, p. 29.

Biró, Lajos [playwright/scenarist] (*né* Lajos Blau, b. Nagyvarad, Hungary, 22 Aug 1880–9 Sep 1948 [68], London, England). "Lajos Biro," *Variety,* 15 Sep 1948. AMD, p. 41. AS, p. 136 (Lagos Biro). BHD2, p. 24 (b. 1883). FDY, p. 417. IFN, p. 29. Katz 1994. Waldman, p. 29. "Lajos Biro in Los Angeles," *MPW,* 14 Aug 1926, 400.

Biro, Ludwig [scenarist]. No data found. FDY, p. 417.

Biron, Lillian [actress]. No data found. AMD, p. 41. "Lillian Biron Is Comedy Lead," *MPW,* 20 Sep 1919, 1855.

Bischoff, Johann [actor]. No data found. LACD, "photoplayer," r 1137 Maple Ave.

Bischoff, Robert W. [film editor] (b. 1899?–12 May 1945 [46], Bethesda MD). (TC-F.) "Lt. Robert W. Bischoff," *Variety,* 9 May 1945 ("Bischoff has edited films at Fox since the days of 'The Covered Wagon.'"). BHD2, p. 24.

Bischoff, Samuel [producer/director] (b. Hartford CT, 11 Aug 1890–21 May 1975 [84], Los Angeles CA; general debilitation). (Columbia; RKO; MGM; Tiffany; WB.) "Sam Bischoff, 84, Succumbs; A Coast Producer Since 1923," *Variety,* 28 May 1975. AS, p. 136. BHD2, p. 24.

Bishop, Alfred (brother of actress Kate Bishop and uncle of Marie Lohr) [stage/film actor] (b. Liverpool, England, 7 Feb 1848–22 May 1928 [80], London, England). "Alfred Bishop," *Variety,* 6 Jun 1928, p. 58 (blind since 1922). BHD, p. 107.

Bishop, Andrew [actor] (b. 1893?–10 Sep 1959 [66], Cleveland OH). "Andrew Bishop," *Variety,* 23 Sep 1959. AS, p. 136.

Bishop, Chester [actor] (New Albany IN, 7 Feb 1871–23 May 1937 [66], El Nido CA). "Chester Bishop," *Variety,* 26 May 1937. AS, p. 136 (b. 1858). BHD, p. 108. IFN, p. 108. Truitt, p. 30.

Bishop, Fayette [actor] (d. 7 Mar 1927). BHD, p. 108. IFN, p. 108.

Bishop, Kenneth J. [producer/executive] (b. Sutton, England, 1893?–6 Sep 1941 [48], Vancouver, B.C., Canada). AMD, p. 41. BHD2, p. 24. "Kenneth J. Bishop," *Variety,* 144, 24 Sep 1941, 54:1 (launched Commonwealth Prods., Ltd., and Central Films, Ltd.). Kenneth D. Bishop, "Good Producers Laugh at Combines—B," *MPW,* 2 Jan 1926, 52.

Bispham, David [actor/opera singer/producer] (b. 1877?–2 Oct 1941 [64], New York NY; stomach ailment). m. Caroline Russel. *A Quaker Singer's Recollections.* (Professional stage debut, 1891; Gibraltar Films.) "David Bispham," *Variety,* 7 Oct 1941, 7:3 (had a repertoire of 2,000 songs). AMD, p. 41. "Bispham Heads Film Co.; Operatic Star Prominent in New Gibraltar Film Corporation," *NYDM,* 14 Oct 1914, 25:1 (1st release: *A Message to Garcia,* with Elbert Hubbard). "David Bispham Heads New Company," *MPW,* 24 Oct 1914, 476. "Bispham on Screen; Vitagraph Company Will Present Singer in First of Novel Series," *NYDM,* 16 Jun 1915, 22:3 (to appear as Beethoven in a screen version of the opera *Adelaide*).

Bistolfi, Gian [set designer/director/scenarist] (b. Turin, Italy, 16 Aug 1886). AS, p. 137. JS, p. 46 (in Italian silents from 1919).

Bittner, William [actor] (b. 1866?–5 Jul 1918 [52], Hotel St. Margaret, New York NY; hemorrhage). "William Bittner," *Variety,* 12 Jul 1918. AMD, p. 41. AS, p. 137. BHD, p. 108. IFN, p. 29. "Obituary," *MPW,* 20 Jul 1918, 384.

Bitzer, G.W. "Billy" [cinematographer] (*né* Johann Gottlob Wilhelm Bitzer, b. 15 Burton Street, Roxbury MA, 21 Apr 1872 [MVRB, Vol. 243, p. 72]–29 Apr 1944 [72], Woodland Hills CA; heart attack). m. Ethel. *Billy Bitzer: His Story* (NY: Farrar, Straus & Giroux, 1973). "G.W. Bitzer Dead; Noted Camera Man," *NYT,* 2 May 1944, 19:1 (age 73). "William G. Bitzer," *Variety,* 3 May 1944. *See* premature obituary, "John Carl Bitzer," *Variety,* 13 Sep 1923. AS, p. 24. BHD2, p. 24 (b. 1874). FDY, p. 455. IFN, p. 29 (b. 1870). LACD, Bitzer, George W., "cameraman," h 1834 Canyon Dr. SD. Spehr, p. 116 (b. Boston MA, 1870). WWVC, p. 24. "Billy Bitzer with C.C. Burr Forces," *MPW,* 12 Aug 1922, 512. "Billy Bitzer Back," *MPW,* 13 Nov 1926, 3. "D.W. Griffith Completes 'Drums of Love,' for U.A.," *MPW,* 5 Nov 1927, 42. "Billy Bitzer Re-elected," *MPW,* 17 Dec 1927, 6 (President, I.A.T.S.E., Local No. 644).

Bitzer, John Carl [cinematographer] (b. Boston MA, 1883–6 Sep 1923 [40?], Brooklyn NY; heart attack). AS, p. 137. BHD2, p. 24.

Bitzer, Louis C. [assistant cameraman]. No data found. LACD, "ass't cameraman," D.W. Griffith Studios.

Bixeley, Ethel [actress]. No data found. LACD, "photoplayer," r 240 S. Figueroa.

Bixeley, Mary [actress]. No data found. LACD, "photoplayer," r 240 S. Figueroa.

Bizeul, Jacques [cameraman] (d. Jul? 1925, Paris, France). "Jacques Bizeul," *Variety,* 15 Jul 1925. AMD, p. 41. BHD2, p. 24. "Voshell with Clara Kimball Young," *MPW,* 24 Nov 1917, 1157.

Björne, Hugo [actor] (b. 1886–14 Feb 1966 [79?], Stockholm, Sweden). "Hugo Bjorne," *Variety,* 23 Feb 1966, 71. AS, p. 137. BHD1, p. 53.

Blaché, Alice Guy- *see* **Guy-Blaché, Alice**

Blaché, Herbert [director/cinematographer] (*né* Herbert Reginald Hraton Blaché-Bolton, b. London, England, 5 Oct 1882–23 Oct 1953 [71], Santa Monica CA). m. **Alice Guy** (d. 1968). (Gaumont; Blaché; U.S. Amusement Co.; Pathé.) AMD, p. 42. AS, p. 137. BHD, p. 108; BHD2, p. 24. IFN, p. 29. LACD, "director," Metro Pictures Corp., Hotel Hollywood. Lowrey, p. 24. MSBB, p. 1044. Spehr, p. 116 (d. 1949). "Herbert Blaché Joins Solax," *MPW,* 14 Jun 1913, 1145. "Blaché American Features," *MPW,* 23 Aug 1913, 827. "Blaché Forms New Company," *MPW,* 2 May 1914, 653. Herbert Blaché, "The Life of a Photodrama," *MPW,* 11 Jul 1914, 196. "Will Pay $1,000 for Scenarios," *MPW,* 24 Jun 1916, 2250.

Black, Alexander [journalist/exhibitor/scenarist/producer/cinematographer/director] (b. Brooklyn NY, 7 Feb 1859–8 May 1940 [81], New York NY [Death Certificate Index No. 10434]). "Alex. Black Dies; Made Photoplays; Showed Still Pictures in '94 with Narrative—Cleveland and McKinley in Casts; A Journalist and Artist; Ex-World Sunday Editor and Kings Features ex-Art Head Published Paper When 11," *NYT,* 9 May 1940, 23:1. "Alexander Black," *Variety,* 15 May 1940. AS, p. 137. BHD2, p. 24. WWVC, p. 25. Burnes St. Patrick Hollyman, "Alexander Black's Picture Plays, 1893–1894," in *Film Before Griffith,* ed. John L. Fell (Berkeley CA: Univ. of CA Press, 1983), pp. 236–43.

Black, Buck [child actor]. No data found. Paul Paige, "Close-Ups and Fade-Outs," *Paris and Hollywood,* 2 (Oct 1926), 97 (played the Irish boy in *Senor Daredevil.* "When asked [by a casting director] what he could do, he replied that he could chew a dog's tail. He was taken at his word and given a chance—but he called their bluff, too—and did it. He's been working in the movies ever since."). George A. Katchmer, "Remembering the Great Silents," *CI,* 183 (Sep 1990), 45.

Black, Elinor (or Eleanor) [actress]. No data found. (Sennett.) "Six Reasons Why Mack Sennett Comedies Are Popular," *Cinema Arts,* Aug 1926, 23 (photo).

Black, G. Howe [actor]. No data found. (In *The Wizard of Oz,* 1925.)

Black, George [stage producer/director] (b. Birmingham, England, 20 Apr 1890–4 Mar 1945 [54], London, England). "George Black," *Variety,* 7 Mar 1945, p. 54 (Black and his father "established the first permanent motion picture theatre in Britain."). BHD2, p. 25.

Black, Harry [actor]. No data found. LACD, "photoplayer," r 120 W. 17th.

Black, Maurice [actor] (b. Warsaw, Poland, 14 Jan 1891–18 Jan 1938 [47], Los Angeles CA). "Maurice Black," *Variety,* 26 Jan 1938. AS, p. 137. BHD1, p. 53. IFN, p. 29. Truitt, p. 30.

Black, William W. (b. Irvington NY, 1871). (Fox; FP-L; Metro; Triangle; Frohman.) BHD, p. 108. 1918 Studio Directory, p. 65.

Blackburn, Bebe [actress]. No data found.

Blackhawk, Lawrence [actor] (d. 10 Aug 1978, Los Angeles Co. CA). BHD1, p. 54.

Blackmer, Sidney Alderman [actor] (b. Salisbury NC, 13 Jul 1895–5 Oct 1973 [78], New York NY [Death Certificate Index No. 18740]; cancer). m. Lenore Ulric, 1928–39 (d. 1970); (2) Suzanne Kaaren. "Sidney Blackmer," *Variety,* 10 Oct 1973. AS, p. 138 (b. 1896). BHD1, p. 54. IFN, p. 29. Katz, p. 124.

Blackmore, E. Willard [actor] (b. 1870?–20 Nov 1949 [79], East St. Louis MO). "E. Willard Blackmore," *Variety,* 23 Nov 1949. AS, p. 138. BHD, p. 108. Truitt, p. 30.

Blackston, Cliff [assistant cameraman]. No data found. FDY, p. 455. LACD, Blackstock, Clifford M., "ass't cameraman," Morosco Studio, r 1806 W. 50th.

Blackton, J[ames] Stuart, Jr. [actor] (son of J. Stuart Blackton, Sr.; brother of Marion C. Blackton) (b. England, 6 Nov 1907–16 Dec 1968 [61], England). AS, p. 138.

Blackton, J[ames] Stuart, Sr. (father of J. Stuart Blackton, Jr. and Marion C. Blackton; half-brother of Isabel S. Lyons) [actor/executive/ director/scenarist/producer] (b. Sheffield, Yorks, England, 5 Jan 1875–13 Aug 1941 [66], Los Angeles CA; about 5 days after being hit by a car). m. (1) Isabelle Mabel MacArthur; (2) Paula Hilburn (d. 1930); (3) Dr. Helen Stahle (d. 12 Dec 1933 [45]); (4) Evangeline Russell. Marion Blackton Trimble, *J. Stuart Blackton: A Personal Biography by His Daughter* (Metuchen NJ: Scarecrow Press, Inc., 1985). "Blackton, Pioneer in Movies, Dies, 66; ex-Commodore of Atlantic Yacht Club Here Is Victim of Auto Accident; A Founder of Vitagraph; Producer of 'Black Diamond Express' Thriller—Began as Marine Artist," *NYT,* 14 Aug 1941, 17:3. "Commodore Blackton, Who Went from Riches to Relief, Dies at 66," *Variety,* 20 Aug 1941. AMD,

p. 42. AS, p. 138. BHD, p. 108; BHD2, p. 25. IFN, p. 29. Lowrey, p. 26. WWVC, pp. 25–26. "Interviews with Manufacturers," *MPW,* 8 Feb 1908, 95. "Items of Interest," *MPW,* 24 Oct 1908, 317. "An Interview with J. Stuart Blackton," *MPW,* 19 Dec 1908, 497–98. "Blackton a Playwright; Vitagraph Official Writes Drama in Which Players Will Appear Saturday," *NYDM,* 4 Feb 1914, 31:2 (wrote The Honeymooners, to be played by Vitagraph players "as if they were producing a moving picture." At the Vitagraph Theater, ca. 7 Feb 1914, with John Bunny, Mary Charleson and James Morrison). "We've Made 3,000 Pictures," *NYDM,* 30 Jun 1915, 26:1 (including *The History of a Sardine Sandwich.* The films had an estimated value of $3-million, "a conservative estimate and does not include the cost of the production but is our valuation at market figures."). "Hot Shot from Blackton," *NYDM,* 21 Jul 1915, 19:2 ("...it has never been our object to secure any of the so-called stars of the theatrical firmament. Our policy has been to develop our own stars..." In his rebuttal to theatrical managers, Blackton stated that small towns do not know Broadway actors but they do recognize motion picture players.). J. Stuart Blackton, "A Glimpse Into the Past," *MPW,* 10 Mar 1917, 1527–28. "Blackton Begins Paramount Picture," *MPW,* 18 Aug 1917, 1055. "Blackton Resigns from Vitagraph," *MPW,* 15 Sep 1917, 1686. "Blackton, Jr., a Corporal 'Over There,'" *MPW,* 27 Jul 1918, 530 (son born). Robert Grau, "The Film Studio; A Gold Laden Haven for the Patriarchs of the Stage," *NYDM,* 8 Sep 1915, 3:1 (the weekly payrool for actors at Vitagraph was $20,000: 175 actors, $25 to $1,000 a week pay). "Blackton Organizes New Company," *MPW,* 21 Jun 1919, 1780. "Blackton Will Make Four a Year for Warner Bros.," *MPW,* 5 Dec 1925, 433. "On the Set and Off,"*MM,* May 1926, 84 (Lieut. Gerald de Merveux sued Blackton for $25,000 because Blackton horsewhipped him on 10 Apr 1925 for making an angry attack on Mrs. Blackton. Blackton "says that de Merveux is to be pitied, as he was shell-shocked during the war.").

Blackton, Marion Constance (daughter of J. Stuart Blackton, Sr.; brother of J. Stuart Blackton, Jr.) [actress/scennarist] (b. 18 Jan 1901–12 Dec 1993 [92], Los Angeles CA). m. (1) Gardner James, 26 Dec 1926 (d. 1953); (2) Gladden James (d. 1948). BHD2, p. 25. FDY, p. 417.

Blackton, Paula [actress] (*née* Pauline Dean, b. GA, 1 Aug 1881–27 Mar 1930 [48], Los Angeles CA). BHD, p. 108.

Blackton, Violet Virginia [actress] (b. New York NY, 22 Jun 1910–28 Mar 1973 [62], Pasadena CA). BHD1, p. 604.

Blackwell, Carlyle (father of Carlyle Blackwell, Jr.) [stage/film actor/scenarist/director/producer] (b. Troy PA, 20 Jan 1884–17 Jun 1955 [71], Miami FL). m. Ruth Hartman, 8 Jul 1909 (d. 1956); Leah P. Haxton, 1925, England; (3) Avonne Taylor; (4) Nancy Emmons; (5) Ann Enoch. (Vitagraph; Kalem; Lasky; International; World.) "Carlyle Blackwell, Idol of Silent Films Who Appeared in 300 Movies, Dies at 71," *NYT,* 18 Jun 1955, 17:3. "Carlyle Blackwell," *Variety,* 22 Jun 1955. AMD, p. 42. AS, p. 138. BHD, p. 1; BHD2, p. 25 (b. Troy NY). IFN, p. 29 (b. Troy PA). MH, p. 98 (b. 1888). MSSB, p. 1022. SD. Spehr, p. 118 (b. 1888). Truitt, p. 30. "Blackwell Remains with Kalem," *MPW,* 27 Sep 1913, 1396. "Carlyle Blackwell For Himself," *MPW,* 25 Jul 1914, 553. "Brief Biographies of Popular Players," *Motion Picture Magazine,* Feb 1915, 109 (b. Syracuse NY). "Blackwell and Actresses," *MPW,* 13 Mar 1915, 1618. "Engages Carlyle Blackwell," *MPW,* 22 May 1915, 1262. W.E. WIng, "Along the Pacific Coast," *NYDM,* 23 Jun 1915, 26:2 (filed for bankruptcy: assets of $11,800, liabilities of $8,080, of which $1,085 was due to William D. Taylor). "What One Player Does in a Few Short Years," *MPW,* 14 Dec 1918, 1219. "Now Vaudeville Favorite," *MPW,* 26 Nov 1921, 425. "Carlyle Blackwell to Return to Screen," *MPW,* 22 Oct 1927, 498. Billy H. Doyle, "Lost Players," *CI,* 155 (May 1988), 26, C28 (b. Syracuse NY, 12 May 1884 or b. Troy PA, 1885).

Blackwell, Carlyle, Jr. (son of Carlyle Blackwell) [actor] (b. Los Angeles CA, 22 May 1913–19 Sep 1974 [61], Los Angeles CA). AS, p. 138 (d. 20 Sep). BHD1, p. 54.

Blackwell, James [actor] (b. Richmond MO, 6 Jun 1876–27 Sep 1932 [56]). AS, p. 138. BHD, p. 108. IFN, p. 29.

Blackwood, John H. [producer/scenarist] (d. 10 Aug 1923, Los Angeles CA). (Universal.) "John H. Blackwood," *Variety,* 16 Aug 1923. AS, p. 138. AMD, p. 42. BHD2, p. 25. LACD, "scenario writer," r 941 Georgia. "Blackwood Heads Scenario Department," *MPW,* 28 Dec 1918, 1492. "Schulberg Engages Blackwood to Start Revolution in Publicity Copy Writing," *MPW,* 7 Jan 1922, 72.

Blackwood, Peggy [actress] (b. Portland OR, 15 Jun 1875–27 Feb 1956 [80], Los Angeles CA). BHD, p. 108.

Blade, Augusta [actress] (b. 1871–9 Nov 1953 [82], Copenhagen, Denmark). BHD, p. 108. IFN, p. 29.

Bladen, Ernest S. [cinematographer]. No data found. LACD, "ass't cameraman," h 5511 Bayer.

Blagoi, George [actor] (b. Russia, 26 Oct 1895–24 Jun 1971 [75], Los Angeles CA). "George Blagoi," *Variety,* 7 Jul 1971. AS, p. 138 (b. 1897; d. 23 Jun). BHD1, p. 54. IFN, p. 29. Truitt, p. 30.

Blaine, Joan [actress] (d. 18 Apr 1949, New York NY). BHD, p. 108. IFN, p. 108.

Blaine, Walker [cameraman]. No data found. LACD, "cameraman," h 1001 N. Figueroa, Van Nuys.

Blair, Betty [actress] (b. 1895–11 Jan 1981 [85?], Los Angeles CA). BHD, p. 108.

Blair, Ella S. [actress] (b. 1895–11 Dec 1917 [22], New York NY). AS, p. 139. BHD, p. 108. IFN, p. 108.

Blair, Lottie May [writer] (b. 1858?–5 Jan 1937 [78], Great Neck, LI NY). m. Harry Doel Parker. "Lottie Blair Parker," *Variety,* 13 Jan 1937 (wrote *Way Down East* and *Under Southern Skies*). AS, p. 139.

Blair, Nan [literary agent] (b. 1892?–15 Aug 1944 [52], Culver City CA). "Nan Blair," *Variety,* 23 Aug 1944.

Blair, Ruth [actress] (b. Williamsport PA, 1892?). (Smallwood Film Corp.; Fox.) AMD, p. 42. "Ruth Blair," *MPW,* 20 Mar 1915, 1769. "Ruth Blair," *MPW,* 22 May 1915, 1241. "Ruth Blair in Comedy," *MPW,* 2 Oct 1915, 85. "Ruth Blair," *MPW,* 20 Nov 1915, 1469. "Ruth Blair in Coveted Role," *MPW,* 27 Nov 1915, 1685. Al Ray, "Before the Stars Shone," *Picture-Play Magazine,* Sep 1917, 50.

Blair, Sidney [actor] (b. San Francisco CA, 1882). (Thanhouser.) BHD, p. 108.

Blaisdell, Charles "Big Bill" [actor] (b. 1874?–10 May 1930 [56], Los Angeles CA; heart attack). (Christie; WB.) "Charles Blaisdell," *Variety,* 14 May 1930. AS, p. 139. BHD, p. 108. IFN, p. 29. Truitt, p. 30.

Blaisdell, Evanne [scenarist]. No data found. FDY, p. 417.

Blaisdell, Roland E. (son of George Blaisdell, writer for the *MPW*) [part owner and treasurer of the Queen City Film Corp.]. No data found. m. Gertrude J. Stokes, Hamburg NY, 24 Nov 1915. "Roland E. Blaisdell Marries; Treasurer and Part Owner of the Queen City Film Corporation of Buffalo Takes a Wife, Gertrude J. Stokes, of Hamburg, N.Y.," *MPW,* 4 Dec 1915, 1835:2.

Blaisdell, William [actor] (b. 1865–1 Jan 1931 [65?], Brooklyn NY). "Mrs. William Blaisdell [stage actress Clara Lavine]," *Variety,* 5 Jan 1949 (b. New York NY, 1873?–30 Dec 1948 [75], NY NY). BHD, p. 108.

Blake, Al [actor/author] (*né* Alva D. Blake, b. Manitou CO, 31 Mar 1887–5 Nov 1966 [79], Los Angeles CA; heart attack). AS, p. 139. BHD, p. 108. IFN, p. 29.

Blake, Ben [director]. No data found. AMD, p. 43. "Ben Blake Joins Levey," *MPW,* 10 Jul 1920, 248.

Blake, Eubie [musician in early 20's talkies] (*né* James Hubert Hall, b. Baltimore MD, 7 Feb 1883–12 Feb 1983 [100], Brooklyn NY [Death Certificate Index No. 2593 (James H. Hall)]). m. (1) Avis Lee; (2) Marion Gant Tyler. Lawrence T. Carter, *Eubie Blake; Keys of Memory* (Detroit: Belamp Publishing, 1979). "Eubie Black, Ragtime Composer, Dies 5 Days After 100th Birthday," *NYT,* 13 Feb 1983, 36:1. "Blake Lasted a Century; Left Mark on Broadway," *Variety,* 16 Feb 1983. AS, p. 139. BHD1, p. 54. SD.

Blake, Lucy [actress] (b. Boston MA, 1888). (Balboa.) m. William Conklin (d. 1935). BHD, p. 108. J. Van Cartmell, "Along the Pacific Coast," *NYDM,* 6 Oct 1915, 31:2.

Blake, Marguerite [actress] (d. Toronto, Canada, 29 Apr 1927). BHD, p. 108.

Blake, Nina [actress] (*née* Nena Blake, b. 1887?–12 Oct 1924 [37], New York NY [Death Certificate Index No. 25044]; following operation for tumor of the intestines). "Nina Blake," *Variety,* 22 Oct 1924. AS, p. 139 (*née* Anita Blake). BHD, p. 108.

Blake, Tom [actor]. No data found. (In *Out of the Fog,* 1919, and other films.)

Blakeley, James [stage/film actor] (b. Hull, Yorks, England, 1873–19 Oct 1915 [42?], London, England). "James Blakeley," *Variety,* 22 Oct 1915, p. 4 (was appearing in *Tonight's the Night*). BHD, p. 108. IFN, p. 30.

Blakeley, Walter [cinematographer]. No data found. FDY, p. 455.

Blakemore, Harry D. [actor] (b. Gallatin TN, 1859–14 Feb 1936 [76], Bay Shore NY). BHD, p. 108.

Blakeslee, Louise [actress] (b. 1905–5 Aug 1920 [15], New York NY). BHD, p. 108. IFN, p. 30.

Blanchar, Pierre [actor] (*né* Gustave Pierre Blanchard, b. Phillippeville (Constantine), Algeria, 30 Jun 1892–21 Nov 1963 [71], Suresnes, France;

brain tumor [extrait de décès no. 824/1963]). m. Marthe d'Lagrange. "Pierre Blanchar," *Variety*, 27 Nov 1963 (age 67). AS, p. 140. BHD1, p. 55. IFN, p. 30. Truitt, p. 30.

Blanchard, Harry [actor] (b. 1876?–27 Apr 1944 [68], Los Angeles CA). AS, p. 140. BHD, p. 108. IFN, p. 30.

Blancke, Kate [actress] (b. Cheltenham, England, 14 Mar 1860–24 Jun 1942 [82], East Islip, LI NY). "Kate Blancke," *Variety*, 1 Jul 1942. AS, p. 140. BHD, p. 108. IFN, p. 30.

Bland, R. Henderson [actor] (b. England–d. 20 Aug 1941, London, England). AMD, p. 43. BHD, p. 109. IFN, p. 30. George Blaisdell, "R. Henderson Bland, Actor," *MPW*, 5 Sep 1914, 1355–56. "Actor Who Played Christ Now in Trenches," *MPW*, 10 Mar 1917, 1505. "Lieut. R. Henderson Bland in France," *MPW*, 19 Jan 1918, 345.

Blandick, Clara [stage/film actress] (b. on an American ship, Hong Kong, China, 4 Jun 1881–15 Apr 1962 [80], Los Angeles CA; suicide by pulling a plastic bag over her head). (Film debut: *The Maid's Double*, 1911; last film, *Key to the City*, 1950.) "Clara Blandick," *Variety*, 25 Apr 1962 (age 81; began 1929). AS, p. 140. BHD1, p. 55. IFN, p. 30. Katz, p. 128 (began 1908). "Personal; Miss Clara Blandick," *NYDM*, 5 May 1915, 5:1 (with photo; appearing in Owen Davis's *The 'Fraid Cat* in Wilmington DE). Charles Stumpf, "Clara Blandick: Auntie Em," *CI*, 296 (Feb 2000), 63 (b. 1880. Her suicide note read: "I am now about to make the great adventure. I cannot endure this agonizing pain any longer. It is all over my body [arthritis]. Neither can I face the impending blindness. I pray the Lord my soul to take. Amen.").

Blane, Sally (sister of Polly Ann and Loretta Young; half-sister of Gerogiana Young) [actress] (aka Betty Jane Young, *née* Elizabeth Jane Jung, b. Salida CO, 11 Jul 1910–27 Aug 1997 [87], Palm Springs CA). m. Norman Foster, ca. 1937 (d. 1976). (Film debut: *Sirens of the Sea*, 1917; last film: *A Bullet for Joey*, 1954.) AS, p. 140 (b. Salt Lake City UT). BHD1, p. 604. "Sally Blane, 87, Veteran Film Actress," *NYT*, 7 Sep 1997, 52. "Sally Blane," *Variety*, 27 Oct 1997, 59:1 (survived by Loretta Young, a daughter, another sister [Georgiana Montalban], and brother Jack Lindley). BR, pp. 105–08. FSS, p. 33. Katz, p. 128. Buck Rainey, "Sally Blane [filmography]," *CI*, 87 (Sep 1982), pp. 34–35 (last name Jung). "Beery's Leading Lady," *MPW*, 28 May 1927, 270. "Sally Blane Has Lead with Luden," *MPW*, 9 Jul 1927, 100. "Sally Blane," *MPW*, 30 Jul 1927, 318. "Sally Blane Injured," *MPW*, 19 Nov 1927, 25. George A. Katchmer, "Remembering the Great Silents," *CI*, 172 (Oct 1989), C14).

Blaney, Charles E[dward], "King of the Melodrama" (brother of Harry Clay Blaney) [actor/author/scenarist/producer] (b. Columbus OH, 1866?–21 Oct 1944 [78], New Canaan CT). m. (1) Lizzie Melrose (d. 1909); (2) Cecil Spooner, 1909 (d. 1953). "C.E. Blaney Dead; Old-Time Producer; Author of 'More to Be Pitied Than Scorned' and Others Once Ran Theatre Chain," *NYT*, 22 Oct 1944, 46:2 (d. Norwalk). "Charles E. Blaney," *Variety*, 25 Oct 1944 (wrote *King of the Opium Ring*). AMD, p. 43. AS, p. 140. BHD2, p. 25. SD. "Charles Blaney to Produce Independently," *MPW*, 2 Jun 1923, 403. "Blaney's 'Untamed Woman,' on Arrow List, Has Four Stars," *MPW*, 5 Sep 1925, 79.

Blaney, Harry Clay (brother of Charles E. Blaney) [actor/producer/scenarist] (b. Cincinnati OH, 14 Jul 1876?–22 Jan 1964 [87], New York NY). m. Kitty Woolfolk (actress Kitty Wolfe; d. 1944); Mae A. Planagan (d. 27 Apr 1966; her *NYT* obituary states that Blaney survived her). "Harry Clay Blaney," *Variety*, 12 Feb 1964. BHD1, p. 604; BHD2, p. 25. *Who's Who in Music and Drama*, p. 45.

Blaney, May [actress] (b. England, 6 Jul 1875–10 Feb 1953 [77], Wopener, So. Africa). BHD, p. 109.

Blanke, Henry [producer] (b. Berlin, Germany, 30 Dec 1901–28 May 1981 [79], Los Angeles CA; stroke). (Ufa; Efa; WB; Paramount.) "Henry Blanke," *Variety*, 3 Jun 1981 (began as film cutter, 1920). AS, p. 141. BHD2, p. 25.

Blankman, George [actor] (b. 1877?–13 Mar 1925 [48], Los Angeles CA; heart attack). "George Blankman," *Variety*, 18 Mar 1925. BHD, p. 109. IFN, p. 30. Truitt, p. 31.

Blasco-Ibanez, Vincente [novelist/scenarist] (b. Valencia, Spain, 29 Jan 1867–28 Jan 1928 [60], Menton, France). (Novels include *Mare Nostrum*, *The Torrent*, *Blood and Sand*, and *The Four Horsemen of the Apocalypse*.) AS, p. 141. BHD2, p. 25.

Blasetti, Alessandro [scenarist/producer/director] (b. Rome, Italy, 3 Jul 1900–2 Feb 1981 [80], Rome, Italy; heart attack). AS, p. 141. BHD2, p. 25. JS, pp. 47–48 (in Italian films from 1929).

Blauvelt, H.D. [cameraman]. No data found. AMD, p. 43. "Paramount Cameraman Returns," *MPW*, 18 Mar 1916, 1838.

Bleen, Harry [actor]. No data found. LACD, "photoplayer," r 2030 S. Normandie.

Bleibtreu, Hedwig [actress] (b. Linz, Austria, 23 Dec 1868–24 Jan 1958 [89], Vienna, Austria). AS, p. 141. BHD1, p. 56. IFN, p. 109.

Bleifer, John [actor] (b. Zawiercie, Poland, 26 Jul 1901–24 Jan 1992 [90], Los Angeles Co. CA). AS, p. 141. BHD1, p. 56.

Bletcher, Arline Roberts [actress: Sennett Bathing Beauty] (*née* Arline Roberts, b. 22 Mar 1893–3 Jul 1992 [99], Los Angeles CA; cardiac arrest). m. Billy Bletcher (d. 1979). (2 reelers; Sennett; Roach.) "Arline Bletcher," *Variety*, 20 Jul 1992, p. 76:5. AS, p. 142. BHD1, p. 56.

Bletcher, Billy [actor] (b. Lancaster PA, 24 Sep 1894–5 Jan 1979 [84], Los Angeles CA). m. Arline Roberts (d. 1992). (Sennett; Roach.) "William Bletcher," *Variety*, 17 Jan 1979. AS, p. 142. BHD1, p. 56. FSS, p. 33 (William Bletcher). IFN, p. 30. George A. Katchmer, "Forgotten Cowboys and Cowgirls—Part VIII," *CI*, 180 (Jun 1990), 51.

Blevins, Eleanor [actress] (b. Lincoln NB). (Lubin.) AMD, p. 43. "Eleanor Blevins, Screen Actress, an Aviator," *MPW*, 16 Dec 1916, 1647.

Blich, Mrs. Catto [actress] (*née* Helen Friedman, b. Germany, 1891–9 Jun 1926 [34?], Hollywood CA; suicide by veronal poisoning). "Miss Friedman, Film Extra, Kills Self in Despair," *Variety*, 16 Jun 1926. AS, p. 142. BHD, p. 109. IFN, p. 30 (age 33).

Blind, Eric [actor] (d. 31 Dec 1916, Reading PA; pneumonia). m. Frances Carson. "Eric Blind," *Variety*, 5 Jan 1917. BHD, p. 109.

Blinkhorn, Albert [producer/executive]. No data found. AMD, p. 43. "Albert Blinkhorn's Importations," *MPW*, 22 Nov 1913, 879. George Blaisdell, "Albert Blinkhorn in Educationals," *MPW*, 2 May 1914, 675. "Blinkhorn Photoplays Corporation," *MPW*, 14 Nov 1914, 950.

Blinn, Beatrice [actress] (b. WI, 7 Jul 1901–31 Mar 1979 [77], Oceanside CA). BHD, p. 109.

Blinn, Benjamin F. [actor] (b. Allentown PA, 3 Apr 1872–28 Apr 1941 [69], Los Angeles CA). (Goldwyn.) "Benjamin F. Blinn," *Variety*, 7 May 1941. AS, p. 142. BHD, p. 109. IFN, p. 30. Truitt, p. 31.

Blinn, Genevieve [actress] (*née* Genevieve Namary, b. St. John, New Brunswick, Canada, 1872–20 Jul 1956 [84?], Ross [San Francisco] CA). (Fox.) "Genevieve Blinn," *Variety*, 25 Jul 1956. AS, p. 142 (b. 1874). BHD1, p. 56. IFN, p. 30. Truitt, p. 31.

Blinn, Holbrook [actor] (b. San Francisco CA, 23 Jan 1872–24 Jun 1928 [56], Journey's End, Croton-on-Hudson NY; fall from a horse). m. Ruth Benson (d. 1948). (Film debut: *The Boss*, World, 1915.) "Holbrook Blinn Dies from Injury; Blood Transfusion Fails to Save Noted Actor Thrown from His Horse; Made Debut as a Child; A Native of San Francisco—His Last Appearance Here Was in 'The Play's the Thing,'" *NYT*, 25 Jun 1928, 21:3. "Holbrook Blinn," *Variety*, 27 Jun 1928. AMD, p. 43. AS, p. 142. BHD, p. 109. IFN, p. 30. MH, p. 98. Truitt, p. 31. "Holbrook Blinn," *MPW*, 10 Mar 1917, 1544. "Simple Services at Blinn Burial," *New York Evening World*, 28 Jun 1928.

Bliss, Edwin [magazine writer/scenarist] (b. 1879?–14 Apr 1915 [36], New York NY). AMD, p. 43. BHD2, p. 26 (d. St. Louis MO). "Edwin Bliss Drops Dead," *NYDM*, 21 Apr 1915, 24:1 (wrote *What Happened to Mary*). "Obituary," *MPW*, 24 Apr 1915, 535 (wrote *Who Pays?*).

Bliss, George [actor]. (Lubin.) No data found.

Bliss, James A. [actor]. No data found. AMD, p. 43. "Rex Invades Broadway," *MPW*, 3 Jun 1911, 1241.

Bliss, Lela [actress] (aka Lela Hayden, b. Los Angeles CA, 11 May 1896–15 May 1980 [84], Woodland Hills CA). AS, p. 511 (Lela Hayden). AS, p. 511 (Lela Hayden). BHD1, p. 56.

Block, Ralph [publicist/scenarist/producer] (b. 1889?–2 Jan 1974 [84], Wheaton MD. "Ralph Block Dies; Screen Producer," *NYT*, 3 Jan 1974 (founding member of the Screen Writers Guild). AMD, p. 43. "Kenneth Macgowan Is Made Goldwyn Advertising Head," *MPW*, 12 Apr 1919, 210. "Ralph Block Becomes Director of Goldwyn's Advertising and Publicity," *MPW*, 8 Nov 1919, 231. Ralph Block, "Says No More Favoritism Will Be Shown to Pictures," *MPW*, 31 Dec 1921, 1063. "Ralph Block Quits Paramount; Joins DeMille as a Producer," *MPW*, 17 Sep 1927, 162.

Block, Rudolph *see* **Lessing, Bruno**

Blood, Adele [stage/film actress] (b. San Francisco CA, 23 Apr 1886–13 Sep 1936 [50], Yonkers NY; suicide). (World.) m. Edward S. Davis. "Adele Blood Hope," *Variety*, 16 Sep 1936. AS, p. 143. BHD, p. 109 (d. Harrison NY). "Actress' Divorce Suit Is Enlivened by New Discovery," *The Pittsburgh Press*, 15 Jan 1915, p. 5:2 (Blood and Davis were divorced and it was discovered that Edward J. Mackay, vaudeville performer, deserted his wife Eloise for Miss Blood. Eloise was given substantial alimony.). "Actor Davis Will Fight Divorce Suit of Miss Adele Blood," *The Pittsburgh Press,* 16 Jan 1915, p. 1:5. "Miss Adele Blood Robbed of $3,200," *NYDM,* 23 Jun 1915, 7:1 (on 12 Jun in Buffalo NY).

Bloom, Phil [agent and booker] (b. 1903?–12 Nov 1956 [53], Hollywood CA; following surgery for brain tumor). "Phil Bloom," *Variety,* 14 Nov 1956. BHD2, p. 27.

Bloome, A.J. [director]. No data found. AMD, p. 43. "Count Tolstoi to Appear in Rivoli Productions," *MPW,* 1 Feb 1919, 631.

Bloomer, Raymond [actor]. No data found. (In *The Love Light,* 1921.)

Blore, Eric [actor] (b. London, England, 23 Dec 1887–1 Mar 1959 [71], Los Angeles CA; apparent heart attack). m. (1) Violet Winter; (2) Clara Macklin. (RKO; Paramount; MGM; WB.) "Eric Blore," *Variety,* 4 Mar 1959. BHD, p. 109. IFN, p. 30. SD. Truitt, p. 31. Dan Van Neste, "Eric Blore," *CI,* 236 (Feb 1995), 24 *et passim.*

Bloss, Johnny [actor/director] (b. MN, 4 Aug 1919–29 Oct 1988 [69], Los Angeles CA). BHD1, p. 604; BHD2, p. 26..

Blossom, Henry Martyn, Jr. [author/playwright] (b. St. Louis MO, 6 May 1866–23 Mar 1919 [52], New York NY [Death Certificate Index No. 11570, age 53]; pneumonia). m. Marjorie Seely. "Henry M. Blossom," *Variety,* 28 Mar 1919. AS, p. 143 (b. 1967). BHD, p. 109. SD. WWWA.

Blossom, Rose [actress] (b. St. Louis MO). (Universal.) Don Juan, "So This Is Hollywood," *Paris and Hollywood,* 2 (Oct 1926), 79. George A. Katchmer, "Forgotten Cowboys and Cowgirls—Part VIII," *CI,* 180 (Jun 1990), 51; 203 (May 1992), 41.

Blow, Leila [actress]. (Vitagraph.) No data found.

Blue, Ben [actor] (*né* Benjamin Bernstein, b. Montreal, Canada, 12 Sep 1901–7 Mar 1975 [73], Los Angeles CA). m. (1) Mary–div. 1937; (2) Axie Dunlap. (WB; Roach.) "Ben Blue," *Variety,* 12 Mar 1975. AS, p. 143. BHD, p. 109. IFN, p. 30. Katz, pp. 131–32. Percy Knighton, "Big Boy Blue Now Toots His Horn," *MPC,* Dec 1927, 55, 86.

Blue, Monte [actor/director/writer] (*né* George [or Gerard] Montgomery Blue, b. Indianapolis IN, 11 Jan 1887–18 Feb 1963 [76], Milwaukee WI; coronary attack and influenza). m. (1) Erma Gladys—div. 1923; (2) Tova Jansen [or Tove Danor], 11 Nov 1924 (d. 23 Mar 1956; daughter, Barbara Ann; son, Richard [d. 1962]); (3) Betty Jean Munson Mess, 1959. (Film debut: extra, *The Birth of a Nation,* 1915; Griffith; WB.) "Monte Blue Dies; Film Star Was 73; Turned to Western Roles After Advent of Talkies," *NYT,* 19 Feb 1963, 8:6. "Monte Blue," *Variety,* 20 Feb 1963. AMD, p. 43. AS, p. 143. BHD1, p. 57 (b. 1890). FFF, p. 18. FSS, p. 34. GK, pp. 67–86. HCH, p. 55. IFN, p. 30. KOM, pp. 128–29. MH, p. 98. Truitt, pp. 31–32. WWS, p. 249. "Monte Blue Seriously Ill," *MPW,* 26 Apr 1919, 521. "Famous Players-Lasky Signs Monte Blue for Five Years," *MPW,* 23 Aug 1919, 1114. "Monte Blue Ill," *MPW,* 30 Oct 1920, 1286 (appendicitis and Kleig eyes). "Monte Blue Injured," *MPW,* 28 Oct 1922, 765 (dragged by a runaway horse). Helen Carlisle, "Monte and Tove; A Love Story," *MW,* 24 Jan 1925, 17–18, 33. "Monte Blue," *MPW,* 7 May 1927, 24. "The Postal Pouch," *Paris and Hollywood Screen Secrets Magazine,* Aug 1927, 86 ("He has one small daughter, Barbara Ann, whose maternal grandmother is Bodil Rosing..."). Ruth Tildesley, "Hollywood Night's Entertainment," *Paris and Hollywood Screen Secrets Magazine,* Oct 1927, 92 (had his driver's license revoked for three convictions for speeding). "Monte Blue," *MPW,* 1 Oct 1927, 287. "Monte Blue," *MPW,* 22 Oct 1927, 486. Ruth Biery, "Live and Re-Live; Acting for Monte Blue Has Meant Merely Re-Enacting Real Experiences," *MPC,* May 1929, 37, 92. Michael R. Pitts, "The Career of Monte Blue," *CFC,* 30 (Spring, 1971), 22–25; Part II, 31, 43. Letter, *CFC,* 31 (Summer, 1971), 4 (more filmography). George A. Katchmer, "Monte Blue; From Shovel to Star," *CI,* 127 (Jan 1986), 17–20. David L. Smith, "Monte Blue: Rugged Romantic Star," *CI,* 302 (Aug 2000), 61–64 (b. 1887).

Blum, Sammy [actor] (b. New York NY, 25 May 1889–30 May 1945 [56], Los Angeles CA; heart attack). (Edison, Ft. Lee NJ; Imperial; RKO.) "Sammy Blum; Comedian, One of First to Play in Films, Dies in Hollywood," *NYT,* 2 Jun 1945, 15:1. "Sammy Blum," *Variety,* 6 Jun 1945 (d. 1 Jun). AS, p. 144 (d. 1 Jun). BHD1, p. 57. IFN, p. 31. Truitt, p. 32 (d. 1 Jun).

Blum, T. [carpenter]. No data found. (Vitagraph.) LACD, Vitagraph Co.

Blumenstock, Morton [publicist/scenarist/title writer] (b. New York NY, 26 Dec 1900–18 Jul 1956 [55], Beverly Hills CA; heart attack). m. Sandra. (1st National; Paramount.) "M. Blumenstock, Film Executive; Former Vice President for Publicity and Advertising at Warners Dies at 54," *NYT,* 19 Jul 1956, 27:5. "Mort Blumenstock," *Variety,* 25 Jul 1956 (film editor at First National). AMD, p. 43. BHD2, p. 26. FDY, pp. 417, 441. "In Titling Department," *MPW,* 16 Oct 1926, 4.

Blumenthal-Tamarina, Marie [actress] (b. 1859–4 Nov 1938 [79?]). BHD1, p. 57.

Blunt, Walter [cameraman]. No data found. LACD, "cameraman," h 835 W. 9th.

Blystone, Jasper [assistant director] (b. 30 Oct 1899–25 Sep 1965 [65], Los Angeles CA). (TC-F.) "Jasper Blystone," *Variety,* 6 Oct 1965. BHD2, p. 26.

Blystone, John G. [actor/director] (b. Rice Lake WI, 2 Dec 1892–6 Aug 1938 [45], Beverly Hills CA; heart attack). "[Warner] Oland's ex-Director Dies; John G. Blystone Started Chan Series—With Fox 17 Years," *NYT,* 7 Aug 1938, 32:6. "John G. Blystone," *Variety,* 10 Aug 1938. AMD, p. 43. AS, p. 144. BHD, p. 109; BHD2, p. 26.. IFN, p. 31. "Lehrman Engages Jack Blystone," *MPW,* 21 Dec 1918, 1324. "Signs Fox Contract," *MPW,* 21 Jul 1923, 243. "Blystone Signs," *MPW,* 16 Oct 1926, 1. "Blystone Starts 'Grand Flapper,'" *MPW,* 12 Mar 1927, 115 (41st Fox film). "Blystone Ends 41st Production," *MPW,* 2 May 1927, 834.

Blystone, Stanley [actor] (*né* William Stanley Blystone, b. Rice Lake WI, 1 Aug 1894–16 Jul 1956 [61], Los Angeles CA; heart attack). m. Alma Tell (d. 1937). AS, p. 144. BHD1, p. 57. IFN, p. 31. George Katchmer, "Remembering the Great Silents," *CI,* 197 (Nov 1991), 51–52.

Blythe, Betty [stage/film actress] (*née* Elizabeth Blythe Slaughter, b. Los Angeles CA, 18 May 1893–7 Apr 1972 [78], Woodland Hills CA). m. Paul Scardon (d. 1954). (Kalem; Selig; Vitagraph; Metro.) "Betty Blythe, Who Starred in Silent Films, Dead on Coast," *NYT,* 9 Apr 1972, 71:1 (age 72). "Betty Blythe," *Variety,* 12 Apr 1972 (age 72). AMD, p. 43. AS, p. 144. BHD1, p. 57 (b. 1 Sep). FFF, p. 116. FSS, p. 35. IFN, p. 31 (b. 1 Sep). MH, p. 98. MSBB, p. 1032. SD. WWS, p. 173. "Betty Blythe Has Been Signed by Thomas H. Ince," *MPW,* 1 Jan 1921, 55. Betty Blythe, "The True Story of My Life," *MW,* 12 Jul 1924, 8–9, 26–27, 29 (Part I); Part II, 19 Jul 1924, 3–4, 26–29; Part III, 26 Jul 1924, 7–8, 25–27; Part IV, 2 Aug 1924, 9–10, 26–27; Part V, 9 Aug 1924, 12–13, 25–26; Part VI, 16 Aug 1924, 9, 26–27; Part VII, 30 Aug 1924, 11, 27. "Betty Blythe Heads Cast," *MPW,* 9 Aug 1924, 435. "Miss Blythe in England," *MPW,* 9 Jan 1926, 154.

Blythe, Sidney [cinematographer]. No data found. FDY, p. 455.

Blythe, Violet [actress] (b. 1890–17 Mar 1983 [92?]). BHD, p. 109.

Boardman, Claude [actor] (b. 1871–10 Dec 1928 [57]). BHD, p. 109. IFN, p. 31.

Boardman, Eleanor, "The Eastman Kodak Girl" [actress] (Philadelphia PA, 19 Aug 1898–12 Dec 1991 [93], Santa Barbara CA). m. King Vidor, Sep 1926–31 (d. 1982); Harry D'Abbadie D'Arrast, 1940 (d. 1968). (MGM.) (Film debut: *The Stranger's Banquet,* Goldwyn, 1922; final film: *The Three-Cornered Hat,* 1934). "Eleanor Boardman; Actress, 93," *NYT,* 17 Dec 1991, D21:1. Myrna Oliver, "Eleanor Boardman; Was Actress in Silent Films," *LA Times,* 16 Dec 1991, A323:1. Joseph McBride, "Eleanor Boardman," *Variety,* 23 Dec 1991, p. 54. AMD, p. 44. AS, p. 144. BHD1, p. 57. FFF, p. 97. FSS, p. 35. MH, p. 98. "Eleanor Boardman," SOS, pp. 36–57. "Miss Boardman in a New Goldwyn Film," *MPW,* 19 May 1923, 250. Myrtle Gebhart, "From Beauty Contest to Cats' Claws," *Picture-Play Magazine,* Jun 1923, 82–84. Adele Whitely Fletcher, "It Isn't What She Wanted," *MW,* 2 May 1925, 10–11, 32. Tamar Lane, "The Puzzling Miss Boardman," *MPC,* Aug 1925, 64, 84. Helen Carlisle, "The Most Outspoken Girl in Hollywood," *MM,* Dec 1925, 37–38, 98–100 ("The interviewer has to protect Eleanor from herself."). "Vidor—Boardman," *MPW,* 25 Sep 1926, 1. "These Title Changes," *MPW,* 10 Dec 1927, 10 (birth of daughter, Antonia). "Eleanor Boardman Fails in Suit," *NYT,* 14 Dec 1935, 11:2 ("one-time screen star" lost plea for $943 a month from King Vidor for support of their 2 children. The amount stayed at $250 a month). DeWitt Bodeen, "Eleanor Boardman; On the Screen She Displayed Intelligence as Well as Beauty," *FIR* Dec 1973, 593–608 (includes filmography). William M. Drew, *Speaking of Silents* (Vestal NY: Vestal Press, Ltd., 1989), pp. 36–57. Michael G. Ankerich, "Eleanor Boardman's Glittering Role in Hollywood History," *CI,* 168 (Jun 1989), 7–8, 38. Chapter 5, "Eleanor Boardman," *BS,* pp. 62–74 (includes filmography).

Boardman, Nan [actress] (b. New York NY, 21 Mar 1903–9 Sep 1984 [81], Fallbrook CA). BHD1, p. 57.

Boardman, True, Sr. [actor] (*né* William True Boardman, b. Oakland CA, 21 Apr 1882–28 Sep 1918 [36], Los Angeles CA; nervous breakdown). m. Virginia Eames (d, 1971; son, True Boardman, Jr., b. Seattle WA, 25 Oct 1909). (Kalem.) "True Boardman Dies Suddenly," *Variety,* 4 Oct 1918. AMD, p. 44. AS, p. 144 (d. 30 Sep). BHD, p. 109 (b. 1881). IFN, p. 31. "True Boardman Again with Kalem," *MPW,* 10 Jun 1916, 1869. "Obituary," *MPW,* 26 Oct 1918, 497 (d. Norwalk CA). George A. Katchmer, "Remembering the Great Silents," *CI,* 172 (Oct 1989), C14 (d. 28 Sep 1918). Billy H. Doyle, "Lost Players," *CI,* 172 (Oct 1989), 36, 5.

Boardman, Virginia [actress] (*née* Virginia Eames, b. Ft. Davis TX, 23 May 1889–10 Jun 1971 [82], Los Angeles CA). m. True Boardman (d. 1918; son, True Boardman, Jr.). "Virginia Eames," *Variety,* 16 Jun 1971, p. 62. AS, p. 144; p. 351 (Virginia Eames). BHD1, p. 57. IFN, p. 31. Truitt, p. 32. George A. Katchmer, "Remembering the Great Silents," *CI,* 172 (Oct 1989), C14.

Boasberg, Al[bert] [publicist/gag writer /scenarist/title writer] (b. Buffalo NY, 5 Dec 1892–18 Jun 1937 [45], Beverly Hills CA; heart attack). m. (3) Roslyn Goldberg, 1927. (Metro; RKO.) "Al Boasberg, Writer of Jokes for Radio; Author of 'Gags' for Leading Comedians Dies While Telling One of His Own Stories," *NYT,* 19 Jun 1937, 17:1. Arthur Ungar, "Al Boasberg Does an 'Off to Buffalo'; Gagsters Will Miss His Ready Wit," *Variety,* 23 Jun 1937 (wrote titles for Buster Keaton films). AMD, p. 44. AS, p. 145 (d. 17 Jun). BHD2, p. 27 (d. 16 Jun). FDY, pp. 417, 441. "Boasberg Joins R-C Pictures," *MPW,* 6 May 1922, 56. "Albert Boasberg to Write Titles for Gotham Comedy," *MPW,* 12 Feb 1927, 501. "F.P. Signs Boasberg," *MPW,* 19 Feb 1927, 541. "Albert Writes a Nasty Title," *MPW,* 25 Jun 1927, 573. June Lee, "Dan Cupid's Bulletin Board," *Paris and Hollywood Screen Secrets Magazine,* Aug 1927, 37, 98 (after seven months of married life, Goldberg returned to live with her family. "Boasberg blames his profession for the failure of their marriage. He believes that the demands of motion picture work make a marriage impossible unless both parties are members of the profession."). "Boasberg Continues His Funny Stuff," *MPW,* 17 Sep 1927, 162 (m. Goldberg).

Bocci, Gildo [actor] (b. Rome, Italy, 1 Sep 1886–22 Jul 1964 [77], Rome, Italy). AMD, p. 44. BHD1, p. 57. "Metro Engages Gildo Bocci," *MPW,* 17 Jan 1925, 284.

Boccolino, Alfredo [actor] (b. La Spezia, Italy, 29 Dec 1885–6 Feb 1956 [70], Vladana, Italy). JS, p. 49 (in Italian silents from 1916).

Bock, Frederick [actor] (d. 13 Jan 1916, Flushing, LI NY). m. Jessaline Rogers. "Frederick Bock," *Variety,* 21 Jan 1916. AS, p. 144. BHD, p. 109.

Bodo, Eugene [actor/producer/director] (*né* Bogdan Eugeniusz Junod, b. Geneva, Poland, 29 Dec 1899–4 Jul 1941 [41], Russia; shot to death by Hitler's troops). AS, p. 145. BHD2, p. 27.

Boem, Carl [cinematographer]. No data found. FDY, p. 455.

Boesch, Zoe [child actress] (b. ca. 1910). S., "Packer Jim's Guardianship [review]," *NYDM,* 11 Dec 1915, 35:1 ("Although only five years of age she rides bareback on a galloping horse, and plays the part in style that would do credit to many of her elders in motion pictures.").

Boesnach, A. [producer] (d. Mar 1928, Schiedam, Netherlands). BHD2, p. 27.

Boggs, Francis W. [actor/cameraman/director] (b. Newman CA, 1870–27 Oct 1911 [41?], Los Angeles CA; shot to death). m. May Hosmer. (Alcazar Stock Co., San Francisco; May Hosmer Stock Co., Chicago; Selig.) AMD, p. 44. AS, p. 145. BHD, p. 110; BHD2, p. 27 (d. Edendale CA). "Pictures of Real Western Life Coming," *MPW,* 27 Jun 1908, 541. "Obituary," *MPW,* 11 Nov 1911, 455 (Japanese gardener was disturbed by the noise emanating from the Selig Studios; Col. Wm. Selig injured). "Japanese Murderer Gets Life Sentence," *MPW,* 30 Dec 1911, 1064. "Los Angeles," *MPW,* 13 Jan 1912, 114 (Boggs's murderer, Frank Minnematsu, was sent to San Quentin for life). Three of his almost 200 films are extant: *The Cattle Rustlers* (Selig, 1908); *Blackbeard* (Selig, 1910); and *The Little Widow* (Selig, 1911).

Bohnen, Michael [opera singer/actor] (b. Cologne, Germany, 2 May 1887–26 Apr 1965 [77], Berlin, Germany; heart ailment). m. (3) Ingeborg Behrend. "Michael Bohnen," *Variety,* 5 May 1965, p. 71 (b. Cologne). BHD1, p. 58. IFN, p. 31.

Boileau, Mrs. Philip [actress]. No data found. AMD, p. 44. "Mrs. Boileau Supporting Louise Huff," *MPW,* 29 Jun 1918, 1822.

Bois, Curt [stage/film actor] (b. Berlin, Germany, 5 Apr 1901–25 Dec 1991 [90], Berlin, Germany). (Began 1908; last film: *Adieu, Claire,* 1986–87.) AS, p. 147. BHD1, p. 58. Waldman, p. 31.

Boland, Eddie [stage/film actor] (b. San Francisco CA, 27 Dec 1883–3 Feb 1935 [51], Santa Monica CA; heart attack). m. Jean Hope, 28 May 1921. (Universal.) "Eddie Boland," *Variety,* 5 Feb 1935. AMD, p. 44. AS, p. 147. BHD1, p. 58 (b. 1885). IFN, p. 31 (b. 1885). MH, p. 98. MSBB, p. 1022. Truitt, p. 32. "Eddie Boland to Be Featured with the 'Vanity Fair Girls,'" *MPW,* 25 Sep 1920, 469. "Eddie Boland Married," *MPW,* 25 Jun 1921, 807. "Back from Honeymoon," *MPW,* 6 Aug 1921, 584. "Back with Jackie," *MPW,* 4 Aug 1923, 407. "All Roles in Lloyd Film Filled," *MPW,* 14 Aug 1926, 338.

Boland, Jack [assistant director]. No data found. AMD, p. 44. "Joins Paramount," *MPW,* 26 May 1923, 333.

Boland, John M. [salesman]. (Fox Film Corp.) LACD, r Glendale.

Boland, Mary [stage/film actress] (b. Philadelphia PA, 28 Jan 1880–23 Jun 1965 [85], New York NY [Death Certificate Index No. 13452; age 83]). (Ince.) (Film debut: *The Edge of the Abyss,* NYMP Co., 1915; World.) "Mary Boland, 83, Actress, Is Dead; Broadway and Film Veteran Played Comedy Roles," *NYT,* 24 Jun 1965, 35:1. "Mary Boland," *Variety,* 30 Jun 1965 (age 83). AMD, p. 44. AS, p. 147. BHD1, p. 57. FSS, p. 36. IFN, p. 31. MSBB, p. 1032. Truitt, p. 32 (b. 28 Jan 1880). "New York Signs Mary Boland," *MPW,* 24 Jul 1915, 631.

Bolder, Robert [actor] (b. London, England, 1859?–10 Dec 1937 [78], Beverly Hills CA). (Essanay.) "Bobbie Bolder," *Variety,* 15 Dec 1937. AS, p. 147. BHD1, p. 57. IFN, p. 31. Truitt, p. 32.

Boles, John [actor] (b. Greenville TX, 27 Oct 1895–27 Feb 1969 [73], San Angelo TX; heart attack). m. Marceline Dobbs. "John Boles," *Variety,* 5 Mar 1969. AS, p. 147. BHD1, p. 57. FSS, p. 36. IFN, p. 31. Truitt, p. 33. "John Boles," WBO2, pp. 172–73 (b. 1900).

Boleslawski, Richard (father of Jan Boleslawski, 1935–62) [stage/film actor/director] (*né* Ryszard Srzednicki Boleslawsky, b. Warsaw, Poland, 4 Feb 1889–17 Jan 1937 [47], Los Angeles CA; heart attack). m. (Began in Russia, 1915; Pathé; Columbia; RKO; MGM.) "Richard Boleslawski," *Variety,* 20 Jan 1937. AS, p. 147. BHD2, p. 27. IFN, p. 31. Katz, p. 137. Waldman, p. 31 (died from drinking contaminated river water during the making of *The Garden of Allah,* 1936).

Boley, Mary [actress] (b. Philadelphia PA, 28 Jan 1880–23 Jun 1965 [85], New York NY). BHD, p. 110.

Boley, May [actress] (b. Washington DC, 29 May 1881–7 Jan 1963 [81], Los Angeles CA; cancer). "May Boley," *Variety,* 16 Jan 1963. AS, p. 147. BHD1, p. 57.

Bolger, George [film editor]. No data found. LACD, r 1963 N. Bronson Ave.

Bolles, Florence C. [scenarist]. No data found. AMD, p. 44. "Florence Bolles Writes Goldwyn Script," *MPW,* 25 May 1918, 1124.

Bolson, Joan [private secretary]. No data found. LACD, Fairbanks Studio, r Hollywood Hotel.

Bolster, Harold [general manager]. No data found. AMD, p. 44. "Around the World for Goldwyn," *MPW,* 6 Oct 1917, 79.

Bolton, Guy [Reginald] [playwright/novelist/screenwriter] (b. Wilmington DE, 23 Nov 1883–5 Sep 1979 [95], London, England). m. (1) Julie A. Currie; (2) Marguerite Namara (d. 1974); (3) Mary Radford; (4) Virginia de Lanty. "Guy Bolton," *Variety,* 12 Sep 1979. AS, p. 148 (b. 1885). BHD2, p. 28 (b. 1885). Katz, p. 138 (b. 1885). SD, p. 138.

Bombard, Lottie Gertrude [child actress] (b. 1908–17 Nov 1913 [5?], Saranac Lake NY). (Pathé.) "Lottie Gertrude Bombard," *Variety,* 19 Dec 1913, p. 23. AS, p. 148. BHD, p. 110.

Bomear, Ona [actress]. No data found. LACD, "photoplayer," h 1401 W. 9th.

Bona, Alessandro [cinemtographer]. No data found. JS, pp. 50–51 (in Italian silents from 1911).

Bonanova, Fortunio [actor] (b. Palma de Mallorca, Spain, 13 Jan 1895–2 Apr 1969 [74], Woodland Hills CA; stroke). "Fortunio Bonanova," *Variety,* 9 Apr 1969 (age 73). AS, p. 148 (b. 1893). BHD1, p. 59. IFN, p. 31. Katz, pp. 138–39 (b. 1893). Truitt, p. 33.

Bonard, Henriette [actress] (*née* Enrica Bonardi, b. Cossila nel Biellese, Italy). JS, p. 51 (in Italian silents from 1916).

Bonavita, Capt. Jack [animal trainer/director] (b. Philadelphia PA, 1866?–19 Mar 1917 [51], Los Angeles CA; clawed to death by a bear at Bostock animal farm). "Polar Bear Kills Bonavita," *Variety,* 23 Mar 1917. AMD, p. 44. BHD, p. 110; BHD2, p. 28. IFN, p. 31. "Wants to Work in Pictures Again," *MPW,* 18 Apr 1914, 374. "Bonavita Was in 'Woman and Beast,'" *MPW,* 12 May 1917, 984.

Bond, Brenda [actress] (b. Winchester MA). AMD, p. 44. "Praise Brenda Bond," *MPW,* 13 Sep 1924, 146. "Brenda Bond Signed," *MPW,* 14 Nov 1925, 125. Nelle Dee, "The Story of Brenda Bond," *Cinema Art,* Jan 1926, p. 28. In *Rainbow Riley* (1st National, 1925) and *The Fool.*

Bond, Franklin G. [actor] (b. Salina KS, 1886–4 Oct 1929 [43], New York NY). AS, p. 148. BHD, p. 110. IFN, p. 31.

Bond, Frederick [actor] (*né* Frederick Drew, b. New York NY, 12 Sep 1861–9 Feb 1914 [52], Whitestone, LI NY). m. (1) Annie Rose (d. 1892); (2) Caroline Parker. "Frederick Bond," *Variety,* 13 Feb 1914 (age 53). AS, p. 148. SD, p. 138.

Bond, Lilian [actress] (b. London, England, 18 Jan 1907?–25 Jan 1991 [83], Reseda CA; heart attack). m. Lionel E. Lawrence (d. 1914). "Lillian Bond, 83, Dies; Film Actress in 30's," *NYT,* 29 Jan 1991, B5:2 (d. 25 Jan). "Lillian Bond," *Variety,* 4 Feb 1991, p. 104. AS, p. 148 (b. 1910). BHD1, p. 59 (b. 1908). Katz, p. 139. SD.

Bond, Raymond [actor] (b. IA, 21 Apr 1885–13 Feb 1972 [86], San Bernardino CA). (FP-L; All-Star.) AS, p. 148. BHD1, p. 59. IFN, p. 31. 1918 Studio Directory, p. 65.

Bondhill, Gertrude [actress] (*née* Gertrude Schafer, b. Cincinnati OH, 1880?–15 Sep 1960 [80], Chicago IL). (Essanay.) "Gertrude Bondhill," *Variety,* 28 Sep 1960. AMD, p. 44. AS, p. 149. BHD, p. 110. IFN, p. 32. Truitt, p. 33. "Gertrude Bondhill with United," *MPW,* 26 Jun 1915, 2103. "Pike's Peak Engages Miss Bondhill," *MPW,* 21 Aug 1915, 1297.

Bone, William N. [artist]. No data found. LACD, "motion picture artist," r 3851 University Ave., Belvedore.

Bonelli, Richard [actor] (b. Port Byron NY, 6 Feb 1889–7 Jun 1980 [91], Los Angeles CA). AS, p. 149. BHD1, p. 59.

Bonelli, Sam [writer]. No data found. AMD, p. 44. "Wounded Italian Poet Writes for Screen," *MPW,* 20 Oct 1917, 394.

Bonelli, William [actor]. No data found. AMD, p. 44. "William Bonelli," *MPW,* 18 Sep 1915, 2000.

Bonetti, Emiliano [writer] (b. Milan, Italy, 28 May 1874–14 Jan 1937 [62]). JS, p. 51 (in Italian silents from 1913).

Boni, Carmen [actress] (*née* Carmela Bonicatti, b. Rome, Italy, 17 Apr 1904–18 Nov 1963 [59], Paris, France). m. Augusto Genina (d. 1957). AS, p. 149. BHD1, p. 60. JS, p. 52 (in Italian silents from 1919).

Boniface, Symora [stage/film actress] (b. New York NY, 5 Mar 1894–2 Sep 1950 [56], Woodland Hills CA). m. Frank Pharr Sims. "Symora Boniface," *Variety,* 6 Sep 1950. AS, p. 149 (Symona Boniface, b. 1895). BHD1, p. 50. IFN, p. 32 (age 55).

Bonillas, Myrta [actress] (sister of Grace Morse) (*née* Myrtle Willis Morse, b. Boston MA, 3 Nov 1890 [MVRB, Vol. 405, p. 182]–13 Nov 1959 [69], Los Angeles CA; heart attack). (Fox.) "Myrna Bonillas," *Variety,* 25 Nov 1959. AS, p. 149. BHD1, p. 60. IFN, p. 32. Truitt, p. 33. John E. Thayer, "Stars in View—1922," *CI,* 61 (Winter, 1978), 36–38.

Bonn, Frank [actor] (*né* Ferdiand Franz Joseph Boon, b. 1872–4 Mar 1944 [71], Los Angeles CA). "Frank Bonn," *Variety,* 8 Mar 1944. AS, p. 149. BHD, p. 110. IFN, p. 32. Truitt, p. 33.

Bonns, Eddie [publicist]. No data found. AMD, p. 44. "Bonns Resigns from Metro," *MPW,* 20 Jun 1925, 850. "'Eddie' Bonns in Charge of Warner Bros. Exploitation," *MPW,* 11 Jul 1925, 144.

Bonnard, Mario (brother of composer Giulio Bonnard) [actor/director/producer/scenarist] (b. Rome, Italy, 21 Jun 1889–22 Mar 1965 [75], Rome, Italy; heart attack). "Mario Bonnard," *Variety,* 31 Mar 1965 (age 76). AS, p. 149. BHD1, p. 60; BHD2, p. 28. IFN, p. 32. JS, pp. 52–53 (b. 24 Dec; in Italian silents from 1909). Truitt, p. 34.

Bonnel, Cecile (actress]. No data found. (Film debut: *Hurricane Hutch,* ca. 1921.) (Pathé.) John E. Thayer, "Stars in View—1922," *CI,* 61 (Winter, 1978), 36–38.

Bonner, Ethel P. [actress] (*née* Ethel Penning, b. 1883–26 Dec 1928 [45], New York NY). "Ethel P. Bonner," *Variety,* 2 Jan 1929, p. 32. AS, p. 149.

Bonner, Joe [vaudevillian] (b. Pittsburgh PA, 1881–13 Apr 1959 [77], Burbank CA). (Vitagraph; Sennett; RKO; WB.) "Joe Bonner," *Variety,* 22 Apr 1959 ("silent comedy star"). BHD, p. 110 (b. England, 1992). IFN, p. 32.

Bonner, Marjorie (sister of Priscilla Bonner) [actress] (b.Washington DC, 17 Feb 1905–28 Sep 1988 [83], Los Angeles CA). m. Jerome Chaffee, Jr., Hollywood, 1924. (Progressive Motion Picture Co.; World.) AS, p. 150. BHD, p. 110. Dorothy Manners, "They're Doing Better by Little Nell," *MPC,* Aug 1927, 43. 91.

Bonner, Priscilla (sister of Marjorie Bonner) [actress] (b. Adrian MI, 18 Jul 1898–21 Feb 1996 [97], Los Angeles CA). m. Allen Wynes Alexander, 28 May 1922–26 (deserted her on 29 May 1922); Bertham Wollfan, 1928 (d. 1988). "Priscilla Bonner," *Variety,* 1 Apr 1996, 66:3 (born WA). "Priscilla Bonner," *Chicago Tribune,* 3 Mar 1996, IV, 4:3. MH, p. 98 (b. Washington DC). AMD, p. 44. AS, p. 150. BHD1, p. 604 (b. 17 Feb 1899). "To Play Opposite Barrymore," *MPW,* 18 Jul 1925, 359. "On the Set and Off," *MW,* 22 Aug 1925, 45 (Bonner intended to sue WB because Dolores Costello was used in *The Sea Beast,* a role for which Bonner had a contract. WB sent her a check for one week's salary and Barrymore gave her $1,000 "with a note of regret."). Helen Carlisle, "The Girl Who Lost and the Girl Who Won," *MW,* V, 19 Sep 1925, 30–31. Henriette, "From Hollywood to You," *MPS,* 1 Mar 1927, 7 (won her divorce decree from Alexander). George Katchmer, "Remembering the Great Silents," *CI,* 238 (Apr 1995), C9–10. Tony Villeco, "Priscilla Bonner; Innocence in Hollywood," *Films of the Golden Age,* No. 4, Spring 1996, pp. 44–49.

Bonomo, Joe [actor] (b. Brooklyn [Coney Island] NY, 24 Dec 1901–28 Mar 1978 [76], Los Angeles CA; pneumonia). m. Ethel Newman (d. 1995). *The Strongman; A True Life Pictorial Autobiography of the Hercules of the Screen, Joe Bonomo* (NY: J.W. Clement Co., 1968). George Katchmer, *Eighty Silent Film Stars* (Jefferson NC: McFarland & Co., 1993). "Joe Bonomo, Star of the Silent Films; Began as Stuntman," *NYT,* 1 Apr 1978, 24:2. "Joe Bonomo," *Variety,* 5 Apr 1978. "Ethel Ramona Bonomo, 92," *CI,* 245 (Nov 1995), 57. AMD, p. 45. AS, p. 150. BHD1, p. 60 (b. 1898). FSS, p. 38. GK, pp. 86–91. IFN, p. 32. "Joe Bonomo," *MPW,* 16 Jul 1927, 186. George A. Katchmer, "Joe Bonomo, All-American," *CI,* 68 (Mar 1980), 40–41, 43. R.E. Braff, "An Index to the Films of Joe Bonomo," *CI,* 20 (Jun 1992), 33, 59. George Katchmer, "Joe Bonomo," *CI,* 238 (Apr 1995), C10–11.

Bonzi, Camillo Bruto [scenarist/director] (b. Piedmont, Alessandria, Italy, 7 Mar ?). JS, p. 53 (in Italian silents from 1919).

Booker, Beula [actress] (b. Silverton CO, 27 Dec 1901–17 Sep 1973 [71], Oceanside CA). m. (1) Kenneth O'Hara, 1918; (2) Thomas O"Farrell, 1925.

Booker, Harry [actor/director] (b. KY, 1850?–28 Jun 1924 [74], San Diego CA). (Sennett; Fox.) "Harry Booker," *Variety,* 2 Jul 1924. AS, p. 150. BHD, p. 110; BHD2, p. 28. IFN, p. 32. Truitt, p. 34.

Booker, John I. [actor] (b. 22 Apr 1887–18 Jan 1982 [94], New Rochelle NY). BHD, p. 110.

Boone, Dell [actress] (b. Springfield MO, 28 Feb 1894–6 Sep 1960 [66], Burbank CA). BHD, p. 110.

Boone, J. Allen [publicity manager/writer] (b. Newport RI, 18 Feb 1882). (Lubin.) AMD, p. 45. BHD2, p. 28. "Boone a New York Visitor," *NYDM,* 14 Jul 1915, 24:2. "J. Allen Boone," *MPW,* 23 Oct 1915, 594.

Booth, Christopher B. [scenarist]. No data found. FDY, p. 419.

Booth, Christopher Henry Hudson [composer] (b. Accrington, Lancashire, England, 1866?–19 Apr 1939 [73], New York NY [Death Certificate Index No. 9251]; heart ailment). "Christopher Booth, Church Musician, 73; Organist and Composer Dies—Had Written Masses," *NYT,* 20 Apr 1939, 23:2 (wrote *Mass in E Flat* in Latin, 1892; *Divine Tragedy,* 1923). AS, p. 150.

Booth, Dolores [scenarist/actress]. No data found. m. Denver Dixon (d. 1972). Nick C. Nicholls, "Profiles; Denver Dixon," *Westerns and Serials* #43 (1997), p. 26.

Booth, Edwin [actor] (b. Provo UT, 13 Sep 1909–18 May 1991 [81], Long Beach CA). BHD1, p. 60.

Booth, Edwina [actress] (*née* Josephine Constance Woodruff, b. Provo UT, 13 Sep 1905?–18 May 1991 [86], Long Beach CA; heart attack). m. (1) Anthony E. Schuck; (2) Richard H. Cutting (d. 1972). "Edwina Booth, 86; Actress Who Won Fame Due to Illness," *NYT,* 24 May 1991, B8:2. "Edwina Booth," *Variety,* 3 Jun 1991. AS, p. 150. BHD, p. 110 (b. 1909). SD. Paul Paige, "Close-Ups and Fade-Outs," *Paris and Hollywood,* Oct 1926, 96–97 (she "happened to be an onlooker at one of the beaches where a film was in the process of making. The director saw her sceen possibilities, and asked her if she would like to be in the movies. Edwina thought that she might, and she was therefore engaged by Metropolitan and given a part in *For Wives Only.*").

Booth, Elmer (brother of Margaret Booth) [actor] (*né* William Elmer Booth, b. Los Angeles CA, 9 Dec 1882–16 Jun 1915 [32], Los Angeles CA; auto accident). (Famous Players.) "[Booth] Killed in Auto," *Variety,* 18 Jun 1915. AMD, p. 45. AS, p. 150. BHD, p. 110. IFN, p. 32. W.E. Wing, "Along the Pacific Coast," *NYDM,* 30 Jun 1915, 22:1 (killed almost instantly when the car he was in drove into a flat car loaded with steel rails. Also in the car were the driver, Tod Browning, and George Siegman). "Obituary," *MPW,* 3 Jul 1915, 75. "Funeral of Elmer Booth," *MPW,* 10 Jul 1915, 289.

Booth, Frank H. [cinematographer]. No data found.

Booth, George T. [director] (b. 1898–7 Aug 1957 [59?], Bracebridge, Ontario, Canada). AS, p. 150. BHD2, p. 28.

Booth, John Hunter [playwright/scenarist] (b. 27 Nov 1886–23 Nov 1971 [84], Norwood MA rest home; cancer). (Fox.) "John H. Booth," *Variety,* 1 Dec 1971. AS, p. 151 (b. 1884). BHD2, p. 28.

Booth, Margaret (sister of Elmer Booth) [film editor] (b. Los Angeles CA, 1898). (Griffith; Metro; MGM.) Katz, pp. 141–42. Brownlow, pp. 302–05.

Booth, Sidney Barton (nephew of Edwin Booth) [actor] (b. Boston MA, 29 Jan 1872–5 Feb 1937 [65], Stamford CT). "Sydney Barton Booth," *Variety,* 10 Feb 1937. AS, p. 151. BHD, p. 110 (b. 1873). IFN, p. 32 (age 64). Spehr, p. 118.

Booth, Sidney Scott [scenarist/radio script

writer/minister] (b. 50 Baker St., Aston, Birmingham, Warwickshire, England, 7 Mar 1880–5 Mar 1946 [65], Hamilton, Ontario, Canada. Buried in Woodlawn Cemetery near Burlington and Hamilton, Ontario). m. [Eliza] Margaret Nicholls, 20 Jul 1911, Toronto (d. 30 Jul 1967). (Edison, 1913; Bison.) John Nicholls Booth, *Booths in History: Their Roots and Lives, Encounters and Achievements* (Los Alamitos CA: Ridgeway Press, 1982).

Borboni, Paola [film/stage actress] (b. Golese, Italy, 10 Jan 1900–9 Apr 1995 [95], Bodio Lomnago, Varese, Italy; stroke). "El Primer Desnudo," *Clarin* [Buenos Aires], 11 Apr 1995 (Borboni provoked a scandal in 1925 when she appeared onstage with a breast exposed in Carlo Veneziani's *Alga marina.*) "Paola Borboni [obituary]," *CI,* 240 (Jun 1995), 57 (in *Jacopo Ortis,* 1917, and other silents). AS, p. 151 (b. 1 Jan). JS, p. 54 (in Italian silents from 1917).

Borcosque, Carlos F[rancisco] (father of director Carlos Borcosque, Jr.; cousin of actor-director Tito Davison) [director] (b. Valparaiso, Chile, 9 Sep 1894–5 Sep 1965 [70], Buenos Aires, Argentina). (Began in South America, 1923; MGM; Universal; Argentine Sono films.) AS, p. 151. BHD2, p. 28. Waldman, p. 32.

Bordeau, Joe [actor/assistant director] (b. CO, 9 Mar 1886–10 Sep 1950 [64], Los Angeles CA). (Sennett.) "Joe Bordeau," *Variety,* 13 Sep 1950. AS, p. 151 (b. 1894). BHD1, p. 61.

Borden, Eddie [actor] (b. Deer Lodge TN, 1 May 1888–30 Jun 1955 [67], Lows Angeles CA). "Eddie Borden," *Variety,* 6 Jul 1955. AS, p. 151. BHD1, p. 61. IFN, p. 32. Truitt, p. 34 (d. 1 Jul).

Borden, Ethel [playwright/scenarist] (*née* Ethel Harriman, b. NY-d. 4 Jul 1953, New York NY). "Ethel Borden," *Variety,* 8 Jul 1953 (Mrs. Ethel Harriman Russell). AS, p. 151. BHD2, p. 28.

Borden, Eugène [actor] (b. Paris, France, 22 Mar 1897–21 Jul 1971 [74], Woodland Hills CA). AS, p. 151 (b. 21 Mar). BHD1, p. 61. IFN, p. 32.

Borden, Olive M. [actress: Sennett Bathing Beauty/Wampas Star, 1925] (1st cousin of Natalie Joyce) (b. Richmond VA, 14 Jul 1906–1 Oct 1947 [45], Los Angeles CA; pneumonia). m. (1) Theodore Spector; (2) John Moeller. (Sennett.) "Olive Borden, Star of Silent Films, 40," *NYT,* 2 Oct 1947, 27:4. "Olive Borden," *Variety,* 8 Oct 1947 (b. Baltimore MD). AMD, p. 45. AS, p. 151 (b. Timpson TX, 20 Jul 1902). BHD1, p. 61. FSS, p. 38. HCH, p. 113. IFN, p. 32 (b. Richmond VA, 1906). Katz, p. 142 (b. Richmond, 14 Jul 1906). SD. Truitt, p. 34 (b. Richmond, 1907). "Olive Borden Signs Long Contract with Fox Films," *MPW,* 19 Dec 1925, 649. "Olive Borden," *MPW,* 23 Jan 1926, 323. "Olive Borden Operated on for Appendicitis," *MPW,* 11 Sep 1926, 96. "Miss Borden Ill," *MPW,* 6 Nov 1926, 1. "Olive Borden; The Girl on the Cover," *Cinema Arts,* Jan 1927, 33, 42. "Olive Borden," *MPW,* 24 Sep 1927, 228. Beth O'Shea, "Olive Borden, 'The Joy Girl,'" *Screenland,* Oct 1927, 52–53, 99–100. "Olive Borden to United Artists," *MPW,* 19 Nov 1927, 13. Hal K. Wells, "The Most Misunderstood Girl in Hollywood; Because She Wouldn't Cross Streets in a Nightie They Called Olive Borden High-Hat," *MPC,* Jul 1928, 25, 71. "Many Happy Returns," *The Film Daily,* 14 Jul 1931, p. 3 (birthday of 14 Jul). Michael G. Ankerich, "Olive Borden: The Joy Girl of the Silent Screen—Part I," *CI,* 185 (Nov 1990), 9–10; Part II, 187 (Jan 1991), 8–9. Henry R. Davis, "The Films of Olive Borden," *CI,* 188 (Feb 1991), 55. "Death Reveals Name," *Houston Press,* 23 Apr 1928 (clipping alleges that her brother was killed in an automobile accident, thus revealing her "real" name of "Sybil Tinkle." This report is an error. She was supposed to have been born in Timpson TX [20 Jul 1902] and to have lived in Lufkin).

Borders, Elizabeth [actress] (b. 1891?–1985 [93], San Antonio TX). "Elizabeth Borders Lee, 93," *CI,* 127 (Jan 1986), 60. Cited in the *AFI Catalog* as "Betty Borders" for one film. (Appeared in *When Knighthood Was in Flower.*)

Bordoni, Irene [vaudeville/film singer/actress] (b. Ajaccio, Corsica, Italy, 16 Jan 1895–19 Mar 1953 [58], New York NY [Death Certificate Index No. 6742, age 55]). m. (1) Edgar Becman; (2) E. Ray Goetz (annulled). "Irene Bordoni," *Variety,* 25 Mar 1953 (age 59). BHD1, p. 61 (b. Ajaccio, France). IFN, p. 32. "Personal; Bordoni," *NYDM,* 13 Nov 1915, 5:1 (to U.S. in 1912; decided to stay in this country permanently and is learning to speak English. "Frederic McKay has become her manager and is arranging to put her in motion pictures."). "...Bordoni for Vaudeville," *NYDM,* 13 Nov 1915, 20:2.

Borelli, Lyda [stage/film actress] (b. La Spezia, near Genoa, Italy, 22 Mar 1887–1 Jun 1959 [72], Rome, Italy). m. Vittorio Civi. "Lyda Borelli," *Variety,* 10 Jun 1959. AMD, p. 45. AS, p. 152. BHD, p. 110 (b. Rivarolo Ligure, Italy, 1884). IFN, p. 32 (age 71). JS, p. 54 (in Italian silents from 1913). Katz, p. 142 (b. Rivardo Ligure, Italy, 1884). Truitt, p. 34 (d. 2 Jun 1958). "Lyda Borelli Joins Kleine-Cines," *MPW,* 16 May 1914, 956. "Coming Kleine Films; Lyda Borelli to Be Seen in Unique Allegorical Photoplay," *NYDM,* 8 Jul 1914, 24:2 (*Satan's Rhapsody,* about a barter made with Satan to restore beauty and youth to an old woman."). "Cines-Kleine Players," *MPW,* 11 Jul 1914, 237–38 ("...unquestionably the most charming woman appearing in European films. Miss Borelli is not pretty; she is beautiful with a grace and refinement distinctly European.... Moreover, like most of the really great actresses of the present age, she is anxious to preserve her image for the future.").

Borello, Edith [actress] (b. Italy, 25 Nov 1890–6 Mar 1974 [83], Los Angeles CA). BHD, p. 110.

Borello, Marco [actor] (b. 1899–21 Jan 1966 [66?], Santa Cruz CA). AS, p. 152. BHD, p. 111.

Borg, Carl Oscar [art director] (b. Sweden, 1878?–9 May 1947 [69], Santa Barbara CA). "Carl Oscar Borg, Noted as Painter; Self-Taught Artist, a Specialist in Desert and Indian Scenics, Dies—Won Many Awards," *NYT,* 10 May 1947, 13:7. AS, p. 152.

Borg, Sven-Hugo [actor] (b. Winslow, Sweden, 26 Jul 1896–19 Feb 1981 [84], Los Angeles CA). AMD, p. 45. BHD1, p. 61. "Interpreter [for Greta Garbo] Is an Actor, Now," *MPW,* 5 Mar 1927, 35.

Borg, Washington [scenarist] (b. Alexandria, Egypt, 1866–26 Feb 1940 [74?], Rome, Italy). JS, p. 54 (in Italian silents from 1916).

Borgato, Agostino [actor] (b. Venice, Italy, 30 Jun 1871–14 Mar 1939 [67], Los Angeles CA; heart attack). "Agostino Borgato," *Variety,* 22 Mar 1939 (age 65). AMD, p. 45. AS, p. 152. BHD1, p. 61. IFN, p. 32. Truitt, p. 34. "Banks Retains I alian Actor," *MPW,* 16 Jul 1927, 184.

Borgelt, Edward S. [singer] (b. 1872?–15 Jul 1915 [43], St. Louis MO). "'Father of Illustrated Song' Dies," *NYDM,* 28 Jul 1915, 7:1 (at age 14 "he conceived the idea of illustrating songs with magic lantern slides, and is said to have sung the first illustrated song in the world in Pope's Theater.").

Borgström, Hilda [actress] (b. Stockholm, Sweden, 13 Oct 1871–2 Jan 1953 [82], Stockholm, Sweden). "Hilda Bergstrom," *Variety,* 14 Jan 1953. AS, p. 152. BHD, p. 111. IFN, p. 32. Truitt, p. 34.

Boring, Edward [actor] (d. 18 Jun 1923, New York NY). AS, p. 152. BHD, p. 111. IFN, p. 32.

Borio, Josephine [actress]. No data found. (In *Fazil,* 1928.)

Borland, Barlowe [actor] (b. Greenock, Scotland, 6 Aug 1877–31 Aug 1948 [71], Woodland Hills CA). AS, p. 152. BHD1, p. 61. IFN, p. 32.

Boros, Ferike [character actress] (*né* Ferike Weinstock, b. Nagyvarad, Hungary, 2 Aug 1880–16 Jan 1951 [70], Van Nuys CA). "Ferike Boros," *Variety,* 24 Jan 1951 (age 62). AS, p. 152. BHD1, p. 62 (b. Oradea, Romania). IFN, p. 33.

Borup, Dean [actor] (b. St. Louis MO, 27 Jun 1875–2 Oct 1944 [69], New York NY [Death Certificate Index No. 20960]). "Dean Borup," *Variety,* 11 Oct 1944, p. 46. AS, p. 153 (d. 3 Oct). BHD, p. 111 (Doan Borup).

Borzage, Frank (brother of Lew Borzage) [actor/director/producer] (b. Salt Lake City UT, 23 Apr 1893–19 Jun 1962 [69], Los Angeles CA; cancer). m. (1) Rena Rogers, ca. 1915 (d. 1966); (2) Edna Stillwell. (Ince.) (Directorial debut: *The Pitch o' Chance,* 1915.) Frederick Lamster, *Souls Made Great Through Love and Adversity; The Film Work of Frank Borzage* (Metuchen NJ: Scarecrow Press, 1981). "Frank Borzage, Director, 69, Dies; He Won Oscars for 'Seventh Heaven' and 'Bad Girl,'" *NYT,* 20 Jun 1962, 32:4 (d. Los Angeles CA). "Frank Borzage: Unique Career," *Variety,* 27 Jun 1962 (age 72). AMD, p. 45. AS, p. 153. BHD1, p. 62; BHD2, p. 28. IFN, p. 33. SD. Truitt, p. 34. "Newspaperman Writes Scenario," *MPW,* 25 Mar 1916, 2039. "Frank Borzage a Director," *MPW,* 8 Apr 1916, 275. "Borzage's Rise to Directorship Result of Experience and Work," *MPW,* 3 Apr 1920, 116. "Borzage Will Soon Start on Second Picture," *MPW,* 9 Jun 1923, 511. "Loew Engages Borzage," *MPW,* 19 Jan 1924, 185. "Frank Borzage Is Back from France," *MPW,* 18 Dec 1926, 502. George Katchmer, "Remembering the Great Silents," *CI,* 220 (Oct 1993), 40–41 (includes filmography).

Borzage, Lew (brother of Frank Borzage) [assistant director] (b. Salt Lake City UT, 1902–6 Dec 1974 [71], Santa Ana CA; found dead of apparent heart attack). m. Betty. "Lew Borzage," *Variety,* 11 Dec 1974, p. 63. AMD, p. 45. AS, p. 153. BHD2, p. 29. "Frank Borzage's Brother on Job," *MPW,* 12 Feb 1927, 497.

Bos, Annie [actress] (b. Amsterdam, Holland, 10 Dec 1886–3 Aug 1975 [88], Leiden, Holland). AS, p. 153. BHD, p. 111. IFN, p. 33.

Bosco, Wallace [actor] (b. London, England, 31 Jan 1880–1973 [93?]). BHD1, p. 62.

Boshell, Ada [actress] (b. 1854–31 Mar 1924 [71], Philadelphia PA). AS, p. 153 (d. Hollywood CA). BHD, p. 111. IFN, p. 33.

Boss, Yale F.F. [actor] (b. Utica NY, 18 Oct 1899–16 Nov 1977 [78], Augusta GA). (Edison.) AMD, p. 45. BHD, p. 111. W. Stephen Bush, "The

Screen Children's Gallery," *MPW,* 6 Jun 1914, 1413. Yale Boss, "The Disguise," *Motion Picture Magazine,* Feb 1915, 99–100. "Here and There," *NYDM,* 30 Jun 1915, 29:1 (at Edison six years). "Yale Boss Back in Pictures," *MPW,* 9 Dec 1916, 1470.

Bosse, Harriet [stage/film actress] (b. 1878-Nov 1961 [83?], Oslo, Norway). m. 3 times: August Stringberg (d. 1912). "Harriet Bosse," *Variety,* 15 Nov 1961, p. 71. BHD, p. 111.

Bosetti, Roméo [actor] (b. Paris, France, 1879–1946 [67?], France). AS, p. 153. BHD1, p. 604; BHD2, p. 29.

Bostick, Elwood F. [general manager]. No data found. AMD, p. 45. "New Producing Company," *MPW,* 4 Sep 1915, 1624.

Bostwick, Edith [actress] (b. Golden CO, 29 Jan 1882–3 Dec 1943 [51], Los Angeles CA). m. J. Farrell McDonald (d. 1952). BHD, p. 111. W.E. Wing, "On the Pacific Coast," *NYDM,* 9 Dec 1914, 26:2 (birth of son).

Boswell, Hugh [actor/assistant director] (b. Quebec, Canada, 30 Oct 1888–14 Jan 1964 [75], So. Pasadena CA). m. Maude Truax (d. 1939). (Metro.) BHD1, p. 62; BHD2, p. 29.

Bosworth, Hobart Van Zandt, "The Dean of Film Actors" [stage/film actor/scenarist/director/producer] (b. Marietta OH, 11 Aug 1867–30 Dec 1943 [76], Glendale CA; pneumonia). m. Adele Farrington—div. ca. 1919 (d. 1936); Cecile Kibre (Mrs. Percival), San Diego CA, 22 Dec 1920. (Selig, 1905?; Bosworth; Universal; FP-L; Fox.) "Hobart Bosworth, Film Pioneer, Dies; Played Lead in First Movie Made in Los Angeles—Star of Many Screen Epics," *NYT,* 31 Dec 1943, 15:1. "Hobart Bosworth," *Variety,* 5 Jan 1944, p. 242. AMD, p. 45. AS, p. 154. BHD1, p. 62; BHD2, p. 29. FFF, p. 16. FSS, p. 39. GK, pp. 91–109. IFN, p. 33. MH, p. 99. MSBB, p. 1022. Truitt, p. 35. "Mr. Robert Bosworth [sic]," *MPW,* 18 Mar 1911, 591. "Hobart Bosworth; Leading Man with Selig Polyscope," *MPS,* 15 Aug 1913, 30. "Brief Biographies of Popular Players," *Motion Picture Magazine,* Feb 1915, 107–08. Hobart Bosworth, "Entertaining the Indians; Hobart Bosworth's Company Gives a Unique Entertainment in the Mountains Which Attracts All People of Bear Valley," *MPC,* Oct 1916, 37–38, 70. "Hobart Bosworth Marries," *MPW,* 22 Jan 1921, 453 (m. Cecile Percival). Cal York, "Plays and Players," *Photoplay,* Mar 1921, 122 (married Mrs. Percival recently). "Hobart Bosworth Placed Under Five Year Contract by Goldwyn," *MPW,* 17 Feb 1923, 640. Frances Gilmore, "How Hollywood Happened; the First Movie that Started It All," *MPC,* Aug 1927, 49, 89–90 (claims the first film made in Hollywood was *The Roman;* the first western, *Told in the Golden West* [1909], both starring Bosworth. *The Power of the Sultan* [Selig] was made in Los Angeles). Richard E. Braff, "Index to the Films of Hobart Bosworth," *CI,* 121 (Jul 1985), 31; Part II, 122 (Aug 1985), 45–46; Part III, 123 (Sep 1985), C10–11, 44; "Additional Films," 228 (Jun 1994), 51. George A. Katchmer, "Hobart Bosworth; A Real Film Pioneer," *CI,* 120 (Jun 1985), 43–44, 51. George A. Katchmer, "Bosworth Update [letter]," *CI,* 124 (Oct 1985), 59, 63.

Boteler, Wade [actor/scenarist] (b. Santa Ana CA, 3 Oct 1888–7 May 1943 [54], Los Angeles CA; heart attack). "Wade Boteler," *Variety,* 12 May 1943 (age 52). AS, p. 154. BHD1, p. 62; BHD2, p. 29. FDY, p. 419. FSS, p. 39. IFN, p. 33. MH, p. 99. Truitt, p. 35. George A. Katchmer, "Remembering the Great Silents," *CI,* 184 (Oct 1990), 58. George Katchmer, "Remembering the Great Silents," *CI,* 250 (Apr 1996), 44.

Bothwell, John F. "Freckles" [actor] (b. 1920–7 Mar 1967 [46], Long Branch NJ). AS, p. 155 (d. 8 Mar). BHD1, p. 62. IFN, p. 33.

Botle, Charles [cinematographer]. No data found. FDY, p. 455.

Botsford, A.M. [advertising/producer/executive] (b. Rockford IL, 1884–15 May 1967 [83?], Encino CA). AMD, p. 45. BHD2, p. 29. "A.M. Botsford," *MPW,* 26 Mar 1927, 310.

Bottomley, Roland [stage/film actor] (b. Liverpool, England, 23 Sep 1879–5 Jan 1947 [67], New York NY). "Roland Bottomley, A Veteran of Stage," *NYT,* 6 Jan 1947, 23:4. AMD, p. 46. AS, p. 155 (b. 1880). BHD, p. 111 (b. 1880). IFN, p. 33. SD, p. 145 (b. 19 Oct). Truitt 1983 (b. 1880). "Roland Bottomley with Kalem," *MPW,* 23 Oct 1915, 590. "Roland Bottomley," *MPW,* 3 Mar 1917, 1355.

Boucher, Martha [stage/film actress]. No data found. (Selig.) AMD, p. 46. "Martha Boucher with Edendale Company," *MPW,* 29 May 1915, 1441. "Gossip of the Studios," *NYDM,* 2 Jun 1915, 30:4.

Boucher, Victor Louis Armand [actor/director] (b. Rouen, France, 24 Aug 1877–22 Feb 1942 [64], Ville-d'Avray, France; cerebral hemorrhage [extrait de décès no. 15]). AS, p. 154. BHD2, p. 29.

Bouchier, Chili "The Brunette Bombshell" [film/stage/TV actress] (*née* Dorothy Irene Boucher, b. London, England, 12 Sep 1909–9 Sep 1999 [89], London, England; after a fall). m. (1) Harry Milton, 28 Sep 1929, Paddington, England—div. 1936; (2) Peter de Greeff, 5 Apr 1946, Kensington, London—div. 1955; (3) Australian director Bluey Hill, 1 Apr 1977 (d. 1986). *For Dogs and Angels,* 1968; *Shooting Star; The Last of the Silent Film Stars; Chili Bouchier* (London: Atlantis, 1995). (Film debut: sound shorts for Phonofilms, Clapham Studios, 1927; feature, *Shooting Stars;* Stage debut: *Open Your Eyes,* Piccadilly Theatre, 1930.) "Chili Bouchier," *London Times,* 11 Sep 1999, p. 22 (changed her name from a popular song, *I Love My Chili Bom-Bom*). Tom Vallance, "Chili Bouchier," *Independent Review,* 13 Sep 1999, p. 6 ("With the British press comparing her to Clara Bow, she decided to change her surname to Bouchier because 'it sounded more French and glamorous,'"). "Chili Bouchier," *Daily Telegraph,* 13 Sep 1999, p. 23 ("Sex symbol of British silent films who never gave up her acting career despite a series of disastrous love affairs.... Towards the end of her life, Chili Bouchier lived in a council flat off the Edgeware Road in London, drinking quite a lot of whiskey."). Ronald Bergan, "Chili Bouchier; Britain's original 'It' girl, who rose from shop assistant to movie star," *The Guardian,* 13 Sep 1999, p. 18. Patrick Newley, "Chili Bouchier," *Stage,* 16 Sep 1999, p. 28. AS, p. 155 (b. Fulham, England, 17 Sep). Michael Grantside, "Chili Bouchier; Britain's 'It' Girl," *CI,* 276 (Jun 1998), 20–22. Jim Goodrich, "Chili Bouchier Fan [letter]," *CI,* 277 (Jul 1998), 14 (Teddy Joyce, b. Canada-d. 10 Feb 1941).

Boucicault, Dion G. (father of Nina Boucicault) [actor/director/producer] (b. New York NY, 23 May 1859–25 Jun 1929 [70], Hurley, Buckshire, England). m. Agnes Robertson (d. 1916). AS, p. 155. BHD, p. 111; BHD2, p. 29. "Mrs. Boucicault [his mother] Married; Widow of Actor Becomes Wife of William G. Cheney of Montreal," *NYT,* 10 Apr 1905, 2:5 (Mrs. Louise Thorndyke Boucicault m. Cheney at Marble Collegiate Church, 8 Apr 1905. She was an actress in Australia; married Boucicault in 1888; he died in 1890.).

Boucicault, Nina (daughter of Dion Boucicault) [stage/film actress] (b. Marylebone, London, England, 27 Feb 1867–2 Aug 1950 [83], Ealing, near London, England). m. Donald Innes-Smith. "Nina Boucicault," *Variety,* 9 Aug 1950, p. 63 ("first actress to play Peter Pan"). AS, p. 155 (d. 4 Aug). BHD1, p. 62. IFN, p. 33.

Boucicault, Renee [actress] (b. 1898–3 Jul 1935 [37?], New York NY). BHD, p. 111.

Boudrioz, Robert Pierre Frédéric [actor/director/scenarist] (b. Versailles, France, 12 Feb 1877–22 Jun 1949 [72], Paris, France). AS, p. 155. BHD2, p. 29.

Boulden, Edward [actor] (b. Roanoke VA). (Edison, 1909.) "Motography's Gallery of Picture Players," *Motography,* 4 Jul 1914, 17.

Boulton, Matthew [actor] (b. Lincoln, England, 20 Jan 1883–10 Feb 1962 [79], Los Angeles CA). AS, p. 155. BHD1, p. 63.

Bounds, Lillian Marie [animation inker] (b. Spalding ID, 1899–16 Dec 1997 [98], Los Angeles CA; following a stroke). m. Walt Disney (1 daughter, Diane; 10 grandchildren; 13 great-grandchildren), 13 Jul 1925, Lewiston ID (d. 1966). "Lillian Disney," *Variety,* 22 Dec 1997, 74:1 (went to Los Angeles in 1923 and got a job as a $15-a-week "inker" of film frames at the then-fledgling Disney Studio. She suggested Mickey, instead of Mortimer Mouse, as she thought the latter too formal.). AS, p. 326.

Bourber, Aaf [actor] (b. Amsterdam, Holland, 17 Oct 1885–23 May 1974 [88]). BHD1, p. 63.

Bourchier, Arthur [actor] (b. Speen, Berkshire, England, 22 Jun 1863–14 Sep 1927 [64], Johannesburg, South Africa). m. Violet Vanbrugh (d. 1942). AS, p. 156. BHD, p. 111. IFN, p. 33. SD, p. 146.

Bourgeois, Gérard [director] (b. Geneva, Switzerland, 18 Aug 1874–15 Dec 1944 [70], Paris, France). AS, p. 156. BHD2, p. 29.

Bourgeois, Paul [producer]. No data found. AMD, p. 46. "Paul Bourgeois Making Animal Pictures," *MPW,* 8 Aug 1914, 844. "Paul Bourgeois Joins Universal," *MPW,* 3 Jul 1915, 83.

Bourke, Fan [actress] (b. Brooklyn NY, 12 Jul 1886–9 Mar 1959 [73], Norwalk CT). "Fan Bourke," *Variety,* 18 Mar 1959. AMD, p. 46. AS, p. 157 (b. 1885). BHD1, p. 63. IFN, p. 33. SD. Truitt, p. 35. "Hite Engages Three," *MPW,* 14 Mar 1914, 1366. "Fan Bourke, Thanhouser Favorite," *MPW,* 6 Mar 1915, 1436.

Bourke, Peggy [actress]. No data found. AMD, p. 46. "Peggy Bourke, Girl-Reporter-Detective," *MPW,* 13 Feb 1915, 1002.

Bourne, Adeline [stage/film actress] (b. 1872–8 Feb 1965 [92?], England). "Adeline Bourne," *Variety,* 24 Feb 1965, p. 79. BHD, p. 111.

Bouton, Betty [actress]. No data found. m. Arthur Jackson, Apr? 1920. AMD, p. 46. "Marshall Neilan Engages Ingenue and Cameraman," *MPW,* 27 Dec 1919, 1131. "Betty Bouton Married," *MPW,* 24 Apr 1920, 565. "Betty Bouton in New York," *MPW,* 29 May 1920, 1212.

Boutsyma, Amroy Maximilianovich [actor/director] (b. Lemberg, Austria, 14 Mar 1891–6 Jan 1957 [65]). AS, p. 156.

Bouwmeester, Theo [director] (b. Rotterdam, Netherlands, 14 Jul 1871–20 Sep 1956 [85], Amsterdam, Netherlands). BHD2, p. 29.

Bow, Clara Gordon, "The 'It' Girl" [actress: Wampas Star, 1924] (b. Brooklyn NY, 29 Jul 1905–26 Sep 1965 [60], West Los Angeles CA; heart attack). m. Rex Bell (d. 1962). David Stenn, *Clara Bow; Runnin' Wild* (New York: Doubleday, 1988). "Clara Bow, the 'It' Girl, Dies at 60; Film Actress Set Vogue in 1920's," *NYT,* 28 Sep 1965, 1:6, 3:3. "Clara Bow," *Variety,* 29 Sep 1965 (d. 27 Sep). AMD, p. 46. AS, p. 157 (b. 25 Aug; d. 27 Sep). BHD1, p. 63 (d. 27 Sep). FFF, p. 121 (b. 8 Aug). FSS, p. 40. HCH, p. 9. IFN, p. 33 (b. 5 Aug 1906). Truitt, p. 35 (b. 25 Aug-d. 27 Sep). Martin Perry, "Seeing's Believing," *Classic,* Sep 1922, 66, 83. "Clara Bow Makes Personal Appearance," *MPW,* 7 Apr 1923, 665. "Schulberg Signs Clara Bow," *MPW,* 28 Jul 1923, 320. J.L. Johnston, "The Sort of Man I Could Love," *MW,* 5 Apr 1924, 8. Alma Talley, "What a Flapper Thinks About," *MW,* 15 Nov 1924, 13–14, 31. Harry Carr, "The Kid Who Sassed Lubitsch; Clara Bow's First Problem Was Making Her Eyes Behave...," *MPC,* Jun 1925, 21, 81. Alice L. Tildesley, "She Wants to Succeed; Clara Bow has one goal—Fame; Nothing else counts," *MPC,* Jun 1926, 36–37, 90. June Lee, "Clara Bow's Beau Ends Romance in Near Suicide," *Paris and Hollywood,* Sep 1926, 45–46, 76–77 (millionaire Robert S. Savage, former husband of Follies girl Geneva Mitchell, slashed his wrists after an unsuccessful courtship of Bow. Quotes a poem he wrote: "...Clara, you'd better beware,/Muster your wiles for protection,/This warns you, young lady—prepare!" Savage knew her a week, drove her to the license bureau [she never got out of the car], went to her home, where her father prevented his entry. Some time later, he was found "lying on a couch with his blood streaming out over a photograph of the girl of his dreams," and rushed to the hospital. Bow was quoted as saying that "when a man attempts suicide over a woman he doesn't but his wrists with a safety razor blade, then drape himself over a couch, with a cigarette between his lips.... That might work out fine in the pictures, but men don't think of dramatics when they kill themselves. They use pistols." Savage said that "it takes a lot of nerve to just sit there and calmly cut your wrists and then watch the blood flow." He still thought he could make her love him. Since it was against the law in California to attempt suicide, Savage was held in the psychopathic ward of the Los Angeles general hospital on suspicion of insanity. He was permitted to go to a sanitarium. Bow refused to appear before the Lunacy Board.). "A Real Star," *MPW,* 18 Sep 1926, 177. Don Juan, "So This Is Hollywood," *Paris and Hollywood,* Oct 1926, 19–20 (at his lunacy trial "he declared that Clara gave him a kiss so passionate that his lips were sore for three days. 'You're darned right!' testified Clara. 'The big boob grabbed me and started to kiss me. I jolly well bit him on the lip!"). "Clara Bow; The Girl on the Cover," *Cinema Arts,* Feb 1927, 33, 48–49. Helen Louise Walker, "The Glynization of Clara Bow; Famous Authoress Selects the Girl Sensation of the Screen to Carry a Message None Other Could Portray," *Paris and Hollywood Screen Secrets Magazine,* May 1927, 16–18, 81 ("'It,' says Madame Glyn, 'is a quality of personal magnetism which exerts an irresistible allure over members of the opposite sex, It is a spontaneous, ineffable something in here,' pointing to her forehead, 'which shines out through the eyes."). "Clara Bow Signed to New Long Term Contract," *MPW,* 30 Jul 1927, 329. Gordon R. Silver, "Real Sirens of Screenland; Would the Vamps Shatter Hearts Upon the Silversheet in Actual Life?," *Paris and Hollywood Screen Secrets Magazine,* Aug 1927, 72–74. June Lee, "Dan Cupid's Bulletin Board," *Paris and Hollywood Screen Secrets,* Oct 1927, 36–37 (her father, Robert W. Bow, filed suit for divorce against his young wife, whom he married 9 Jul 1924. "The couple separated the next day, and Bow declares that he spent the nuptial night sleeping on the hard floor. Mrs. Bow, who was Idella Elizabeth Mowery, on the other hand, alleges extreme cruelty on the part of Bow."). Walter Ramsey, "Imagine Their Embarrassment; Almost Married—Here's How," *MPC,* Apr 1928, 33, 73, 86 (re Mr. Bow). Cedric Belfrage, "Clara Bow Exposed; The 'It' Girl Is Discovered Flagrantly Living Like a Normal Human Being," *MPC,* Dec 1928, 22, 77, 79 (Belfrage discovered that she had a Cadillac—not a Rolls Royce. "It was at this juncture that I swooned."). Audrey Rivers, "Clara *Will* Come Back—A Bigger Star than Ever; So says Rex Bell, her fiancé, who believes she'll become one of the greatest actresses of her day when given the chance to make a *really big* picture," *Movie Classic,* Sep 1931, 22, 73. Raymond Lee, "The 'It' Girl," *CFC,* 27 (Spring/Summer, 1970), 36. John Korcz, "Clara Bow: The Irresistible 'It' Girl," *The Silent Film Newsletter,* Mar 1993, 1–12. Eve Golden, "Clara Bow: She Had It—But It Didn't Do Her No Good," *CI,* 225 (Mar 1994), 12, 16, 56. Walter Goodman, "In the Age of the Flapper There Was One Who Had It," *NYT,* 14 Jun 1999, E8 (review of *Clara Bow: Discovering the "It" Girl,* Turner Classic Movies documentary. "Although the writers of this affectionate documentary evidently read too many fan magazines at an impressionable age, and Courtney Love's narration is sloppily delivered, the story is worth telling, for what it reveals about the exploitation of performers by Hollywood studios and for the details of a sad life that belied a devil-may-care image.").

Bowen, J.E. [executive] (b. 1879–7 Apr 1930 [51?], Los Angeles CA). BHD2, p. 29.

Bower, Arthur [actor]. No data found. AMD, p. 46. "Hite Engages Three," *MPW,* 14 Mar 1914, 1366.

Bower, Bertha Muzzy [writer] (*née* Bertha Muzzy, b. Cleveland MN, 15 Nov 1871–23 Jul 1940 [68], Los Angeles CA). m. (1) Clayton J. Bower, ca. 1889–1906; (2) Bertrand W. Sinclair; (3) Robert Ellsworth Cowan. "Bertha Muzzy Bower; Author of Western Novels Dies in Los Angeles at 68," *NYT,* 24 Jul 1940, 21:5 (wrote *Chip of the Flying U,* magazine, 1904; book, 1906). AS, p. 157. Ralph Sutter, "Mrs. Chip of the Flying U; B.M. Bower Is a Name That Carries Magic to a Million Readers of Western Fiction. It Will Surprise Many to Know That This Author Is a Woman," *MPC,* Mar 1927, 54–55, 84, 86 (b. Lesueur County MN). *Newsweek,* 5 Aug 1940, p. 7. *Who Was Who in America,* Vol. 1, pp. 121–22. *Twentieth Century Authors,* pp. 169–70. Stanley R. Davidson, "The Author Was a Lady," *Montana: The Magazine of Western History,* 23, No. 2, 1973. Jon Tuska and Vicki Piekarski, edd., *Encyclopedia of Frontier and Western Fiction* (NY: McGraw Hill Book Co., 1983), pp. 28–32.

Bower, Lulu [actress]. No data found. m. Richard Johnson, Nov? 1915. (Balboa.) AMD, p. 46. J. Van Cartmell, "Studio News from the Coast," *NYDM,* 4 Dec 1915, 27:2 (married Johnson by announcing the marriage instead of eloping). "Another Balboa Bride," *MPW,* 11 Dec 1915, 2023.

Bowers, Charley [animator] (b. 1889). (Universal.) Lorenzo Codelli, "Forgotten Laughter; A Symposium on American Silent Comedy," *Griffithiana,* 53, May 1995, 44–75.

Bowers, John [actor] (b. Garrett IN, 27 Dec 1894–15 Nov 1936 [41], Malibu CA; suicide—possibly jumped from a boat into the ocean). m. Rita Heller, 1918; Marguerite de la Motte (d. 1950). (Film debut: *The Little Dutch Girl,* 1915.) "John Bowers Dies," *Variety,* 18 Nov 1936. AMD, p. 46. AS, p. 157 (b. 25 Dec 1899). BHD1, p. 63 (b. 25 Dec 1884-d. 17 Nov). FFF, p. 20. FSS, p. 41. IFN, p. 33. Truitt, p. 36 (b. 1899–17 Nov 1936). "John Bowers with World Film," *MPW,* 26 Jan 1918, 503. "John Bowers Takes to Himself a Bride," *MPW,* 4 May 1918, 671 (m. Heller). "John Bowers with Goldwyn," *MPW,* 2 Nov 1918, 596. "Bowers to Be Miss Minter's Leading Man," *MPW,* 3 Apr 1920, 143. "John Bowers," *MPW,* 20 Aug 1927, 517 (m. de la Motte). George Katchmer, "Remembering the Great Silents," *CI,* 220 (Oct 1993), 43.

Bowers, Lyle [actor] (b. IA, 22 May 1895–8 Mar 1943 [47], Los Angeles CA). "Lyle Bowers," *Variety,* 17 Mar 1943 (film cowboy for 20 years). AS, p. 157. BHD1, p. 63. IFN, p. 33. Truitt, p. 36.

Bowers, Robert Hood [composer] (b. Chambersburg PA, 24 May 1877–29 Dec 1941 [64], New York NY). "Robert Hood Bowers," *Variety,* 7 Jan 1942. AS, p. 157 (d. 1942). ASCAP 66, p. 72. WWWA.

Bowers, Sally [actress: Our Gang Comedies] (b. Los Angeles CA, 1924?–20 Aug 1987 [63], Beverly Hills CA). "Sally Bowers [obituary]," *CI,* 148 (Oct 1987), 60. AS, p. 157.

Bowers, William [story analyst/writer] (b. 1904?–30 Dec 1952 [48], Hollywood CA; cerebral hemorrhage). (Columbia; Paramount.) "William Bowers," *Variety,* 14 Jan 1953.

Bowes, Clifford W. [actor] (b. Pueblo CO, 14 Nov 1894–6 Jul 1929 [34]). AS, p. 158. BHD, p. 111. IFN, p. 33.

Bowes, Lawrence Alfred [actor] (b. Newark CA, 1 Jan 1885–5 Jun 1955 [70], Glendale CA). (Selig; Universal; Essanay-Chaplin.) BHD, p. 112. 1918 Studio Directory, p. 65.

Bowker, Virginia [actress]. No data found. (DeMille.)

Bowles, Donald [actor] (b. PA, 12 Feb 1879–3 Oct 1921 [42], Los Angeles CA). "Donald Bowles," *Variety,* 14 Oct 1921. AMD, p. 46. AS, p. 158. BHD, p. 112. "More Horsley Stars," *MPW,* 2 Oct 1915, 62. "Obituary," *MPW,* 22 Oct 1921, 920.

Bowman, Laura [actress] (b. Quincy IL, 3 Oct 1880?–29 Mar 1957 [76], Los Angeles CA; cerebral thrombosis). m. Le Roi Antoine, 1935. "Laura Bowman," *Variety,* 3 Apr 1957. AS, p. 158 (b. 1881). BHD1, p. 64 (b. 1881)). IFN, p. 33. SD.

Bowman, Lewis Edward [actor] (b. 1886–1961 [74?]). AS, p. 158. BHD, p. 112.

Bowman, Palmer [actor/producer/writer] (b. Chicago IL, 1883?–25 Sep 1933 [50], Chicago IL; heart attack). (Selig; Essanay.) "Palmer Bowman," *Variety,* 3 Oct 1933. AS, p. 158. BHD, p. 112 (b. Brazil IN, 1884). IFN, p. 33. Truitt, p. 36.

Bowman, William J. [actor/director] (b. Bakersville NC, 1876?–1 Jan 1960 [83], San Diego CA). (Vitagraph.) AMD, p. 46. AS, p. 158 (d. LA CA). BHD, p. 112; BHD2, p. 29. IFN, p. 33. "Bowman Joins David Horsley," *MPW,* 27 Nov 1915, 1666. "Bowman to Assist Director Balshofer," *MPW,* 8 Jun 1918, 1405. "William Bowman, Director, Ill," *MPW,* 14 Feb 1920, 1088.

Bowser, Charles [actor] (d. 17 Mar 1917). AS, p. 158. BHD, p. 112. IFN, p. 33.

Boyce, Jack [actor] (b. 1885–13 Dec 1923 [38?], New York NY). AS, p. 158. BHD, p. 112.

Boyce, St. Elmo [scenarist/cinematographer] (b. 1899?–30 Sep 1930 [31], Los Angeles CA; possible suicide with poison). "St. Elmo Boyce," *Variety,* 8 Oct 1930. AS, p. 158. BHD2, p. 30. FDY, p. 455.

Boyd, Ada [actress] (b. 1890–25 Mar 1978 [87], Barrington MA). BHD, p. 112. IFN, p. 34.

Boyd, Betty [actress: Wampas Star, 1929] (b. Kansas City MO, 11 May 1908–16 Sep 1971 [63], Los Angeles CA). (Christie.) "Mother of Betty Boyd," *Variety,* 4 Dec 1929 (d. 28 Nov 1929 [42]; auto accident). AS, p. 158. BHD1, p. 64. IFN, p. 34.

Boyd, Charles A. [actor] (b. Philadelphia PA, 1864?–25 Jul 1930 [66], Brooklyn NY). "Charles A. Boyd," *Variety,* 30 Jul 1930.

Boyd, Lois [actress]. No data found. AMD, p. 46. "Returns to Century," *MPW,* 18 Oct 1924, 611. "Lois Boyd in Fat Men Comedy," *MPW,* 31 Oct 1925, 724. "Lois Boyd Signed," *MPW,* 19 Jun 1926, 4.

Boyd, Storm V. [actor] (b. Watertown NY-d. 13 Oct 1919, Syracuse NY). BHD, p. 112.

Boyd, William Lawrence [film/TV actor/producer] (b. Cambridge OH, 5 Jun 1895–13 Sep 1972 [77], So. Laguna Beach CA; heart attack and Parkinson's disease). m. (1) Patsy Ruth Miller, 1921, LA CA (d. 1995); (2) Elinor Fair, Dec 1926–29 (d. 1957); (3) Dorothy Sebastian, 1930–36 (d. 1957); (5) Grace Bradley, 5 Jun 1937. (Film debut: extra work, 1918 or before; *Why Change Your Wife?,* FP-L, 1920; Fox; De Mille.) "William Boyd, 'Hopalong Cassidy,' Dies," *NYT,* 14 Sep 1972, 50:1 (b. Hendrysburg OH; age 74. Hopalong Cassidy created by Clarence E. Mulford [d. 1956]). "William Boyd," *Variety,* 20 Sep 1972. AMD, p. 46. AS, pp. 158–59 (b. Hedrysburg OH). BHD1, p. 64; BHD2, p. 30 (d. 12 Sep). FSS, p. 41. GK, pp. 109–22. HCH, p. 51. IFN, p. 18 (b. Hendrysburg). "William Boyd," WBO2, pp. 52–53. "Film Players Wed," *MPW,* 15 Oct 1921, 756. "Two Talented Players Signed for DeMille Stock Company," *MPW,* 18 Apr 1925, 698. "Boyd Assigned," *MPW,* 18 Jul 1925, 357. "DeMille Creates Another Star," *MPW,* 28 Nov 1925, 340. Alice L. Tildesley, "No Book Learnin'; Bill Boyd worked in a rolling-mill at twelve," *MPC,* Apr 1926, 19, 78. "William Boyd," *MPW,* 2 May 1927, 794. John Hanlon, "A Bill B(oy)d for Happiness; Everybody's For Him—'Cause He's Regular," *MPC,* Jan 1928, 23, 81. Dorothy Donnell, "A Tough Boyd; At One Time the Only Thing Hard-Boiled About Bill Was His Shirt," *MPC,* Apr 1929, 45, 87, 89 ("'I guess I've never got over being an extra,' says Bill."). George A. Katchmer, "William Boyd," *CI,* 115 (Jan 1985), 12–14, 59, 61. John Cocchi, "The 2nd Feature; A History of the B Movies—The Western, Part III," *CI,* 147 (Sep 1987), 18–19 (extra ca. 1918). Frank "Junior" Coghlan, "Hoppy and Me," *CI,* 202 (Apr 1992), 38–40. R.E. Braff, "An Index to the Films of William Boyd, Part I," *CI,* 213 (Mar 1993), C15; Part II, 214 (Apr 1993), 53–55. *Hoppy Talk* [newsletter], ed. Laura Bates, 6310 Friendship Drive, New Concord OH 43762–9708.

Boyd, William H. "Stage" [stage/film actor] (b. New York NY, 18 Dec 1889–20 Mar 1935 [45], Los Angeles CA; intestinal disorder). m. Clara Joel. (Film debut: *The Locked Door.*) "William Boyd," *Variety,* 27 Mar 1935. AS, p. 158. BHD1, p. 64. IFN, p. 34.

Boye, Billy [actor]. No data found. AMD, p. 46. "A Screen Find," *MPW,* 15 Nov 1924, 253.

Boyer, Charles [actor] (b. Figeac, France, 28 Aug 1899 [extrait de naissance no. 62]–26 Aug 1978 [78], Phoeniz AZ; suicide by an overdose of barbituates). m. actress Patricia Eliza Paterson (age 22), 14 Feb 1934, Yuma AZ. Larry Swindell, *Charles Boyer: The Reluctant Lover* (Garden City NY: Doubleday, 1983). (Began 1920; French-language films, MGM, 1931; Ufa; Fox.) "A Star for Four Decades," *NYT,* 6 Nov 1978, 56:2. "Charles Boyer, Despondent Over Wife's Death, Takes Life at 78," *Variety,* 30 Aug 1978. AS, p. 159. BHD1, p. 64. IFN, p. 34. Katz, pp. 150–51. SD. Waldman, p. 34. "Marriages," *Variety,* 113, 20 Feb 1934, 52:5 ("Bride is a native of England and has appeared in coast pix."). Robert A. Monsees, "Charles Boyer," *FIR,* May 1971, 258–74, 303 (b. 1897).

Boyer, Louise Rive-King Miller [scenarist]. No data found. AMD, p. 46. "Metro Engages Pageant Specialist," *MPW,* 25 May 1918, 1132.

Boylan, Malcolm Stuart (son of novelist Grace Duffle Boylan) [publicity director/title writer/scenarist] (b. Chicago IL, 13 Apr 1897–3 Apr 1967 [69], Los Angeles CA). m. Ladessa. (1st National.) "Malcolm (Mike) Boylan," *Variety,* 12 Apr 1967 (d. 2 Apr; as a title writer, he made $5,000 a week; supervising story editor of Fox Films, 1925–29). AMD, p. 46. AS, p. 159. BHD2, p. 30. FDY, p. 441. IFN, p. 34. "Boylan Signs with Fox," *MPW,* 21 Aug 1926, 4. "Malcolm Stuart Boylan, Title Expert, with Fox," *MPW,* 25 Dec 1926, 579. "Malcolm Stuart Boylan," *MPW,* 22 Oct 1927, 496.

Boyle, Charles P. [cinematographer] (b. IL, 26 Jul 1892–28 May 1968 [75], Los Angeles CA). (With Disney since the early 1920s.) "Charles P. Boyle," *Variety,* 251, 5 Jun 1968, 63:3. BHD2, p. 30. FDY, p. 455. IFN, p. 34.

Boyle, Edward G. [set decorator] (b. Cobden, Ontario, Canada-d. 17 Feb 1977, Los Angeles CA). "Edward G. Boyle," *Variety,* 9 Mar 1977 (AA for *The Apartment,* 1960). BHD2, p. 30. An Edward Boyle was born in the county of Wellington, Canada, on 8 April 1882; birth certificate #036083.

Boyle, John Francis [actor] (b. 1873?–8 Mar 1918 [45], New York NY). AS, p. 159. BHD1, p. 604. "John Francis Boyle," *Variety,* 15 Mar 1918. AS, p. 159. IFN, p. 34.

Boyle, John William [cinematographer] (b. Memphis TN, 1881?–28 Sep 1959 [78], Los Angeles CA). "John W. Boyle," *Variety,* 7 Oct 1959 (began 1915). AS, p. 159. BHD, p. 112; BHD2, p. 30. FDY, p. 455. IFN, p. 34.

Boyle, Joseph C[layton] [actor/director/production manager] (b. Philadelphia PA, 30 Sep 1888–24 Nov 1972 [84], Culver City CA). m. Maud Douglas, eloped 2 Jul 1915. (Lubin.) AMD, p. 47. BHD2, p. 30. "In the Picture Studios," *NYDM,* 21 Jul 1915, 19:2 (eloped with Douglas. "In company with Mr. [John] Ince and Crane Wilbur, they had motored to Elkton, the Maryland Gretna Green, and there entered on a life of connubial felicity."). "Just Mr. and Mrs. Boyle," *MPW,* 31 Jul 1915, 823.

Boyne, Clifton [actor] (b. 1874–16 Dec 1945 [71?]). BHD, p. 112. IFN, P. 112.

Boytler, Arcady [director] (b. Moscow, Russia, 31 Aug 1890–23 Nov 1965 [75], Mexico City, Mexico; heart ailment). "Arcady Boytler," *Variety,* 8 Dec 1965, p. 79. AS, p. 159. BHD2, p. 30.

Braban, Harvey [actor] (b. Brighton, England, 19 May 1883–1943 [60?]). BHD1, p. 65.

Brabin, Charles J. [actor/scenarist/director/producer] (b. Liverpool, England, 17 Apr 1883–3 Nov 1957 [74], Santa Monica CA; heart attack). m. (1) Susette Mosher, 14 Dec 1913, Bronx NY; (2) Theda Bara, 2 Jul 1921, Greenwich CT (d. 1955). (Edison, 1908; MGM.) "Charles J. Brabin," *NYT,* 6 Nov 1957, 35:4. "Charles J. Brabin," *Variety,* 13 Nov 1957. AS, p. 159. BHD, P. 112; BHD2, p. 30. FDY, p. 419. IFN, p. 34. "Credit Misplaced," *MPW,* 26 Apr 1913, 356. "Charles J. Brabin," *MPW,* 23 Aug 1913, 826. "Brabin-Mosher," *MPW,* 27 Dec 1913, 1528 (m. Mosher; Marc MacDermott, best man). "One Director's Hard Work," *MPW,* 19 Dec 1914, 1658. "Charles J. Brabin; Essanay Director," *NYDM,* 5 Feb 1916, 24:3 (began 1908: 1st stage-manager in the film business; director, 1910). "MacDermott and Brabin Again Together," *MPW,* 1 Jul 1916, 109. "Brabin Resigns from Metro," *MPW,* 23 Mar 1918, 1646. "Three Notable Directors Have Been Engaged by William Fox," *MPW,* 12 Oct 1918, 249. "Goldwyn Engages Brabin," *MPW,* 3 Mar 1923, 42. "Charles J. Brabin to Direct 'Ben Hur,'" *MPW,* 13 Oct 1923, 595. "Engages Brabin," *MPW,* 6 Jul 1924, 259. "Charles J. Brain," *MPW,* 20 Nov 1926, 143.

Bracco, Roberto [scenarist] (b. Naples, Italy, 10 Nov 1861–20 Apr 1943 [81], Sorrento, Italy). JS, p. 57 (in Italian silents from 1912).

Brace, Frederick S. [cameraman]. No data found.

Brace, Norman C. [actor/director] (b. 1892?–20 Jun 1954 [62], New York NY). "Norman C. Brace," *Variety,* 23 Jun 1954. AS, p. 160. BHD, p. 112; BHD2, p. 30. IFN, p. 34. Truitt, p. 36.

Bracey, Sidney [stage/film actor] (b. Melbourne, Australia, 18 Dec 1877–5 Aug 1942 [64], Los Angeles CA). (Kalem; Thanhouser.) "Sidney Bracey," *Variety,* 12 Aug 1942. AMD, p. 47. AS, p. 160. BHD1, p. 65. FSS, p. 42. IFN, p. 34. MSBB, p. 1022 (b. 1882). Truitt, p. 36. "Arrow Signs Sidney Bracy [sic]," *MPW,* 16 Sep 1916, 1849. "Bracy [sic] Joins Wanda Hawley Company," *MPW,* 26 Jun 1920, 1783.

Bracken, Bertram [actor/director/scenarist] (b. San Antonio TX, 1880–1 Nov 1952 [72?], Cathedral City CA). m. Margaret Landis, 6 Apr 1919—div. 1924 (d. 1981). (Stage debut: Hay Market Theatre, Chicago, 1898; Star Film, 1910; Western Lubin Co.; Fox.) AMD, p. 47. AS, p. 160. BHD, p. 112; BHD2, p. 30 (d. LA CA). IFN, p. 34. Spehr, p. 118. "Bracken Back with Balboa," *MPW,* 5 Dec 1914, 1386. "Bertram Bracken to Direct 'Jazz' Restaurant," *MPW,* 16 Mar 1918, 1497. "Bertram Bracken Engaged by Paralta," *MPW,* 6 Apr 1918, 69. "Bracken—Landis," *MPW,* 26 Apr 1919, 519. "Mistakes Will Happen," *MPW,* 20 Sep 1919, 1856. Billy H. Doyle, "Lost Players," *CI,* 153 (Mar 1988), 52. Jura, pp. 103–04.

Bracker, Leone [artist/publicist]. No data found. AMD, p. 47. "Leone Bracker, Famous Artist, to Design First National Posters; Begins with Holubar Production," *MPW*, 13 Nov 1920, 230. "M. Leone Bracker, of First National, Says the Cinema Is Attracting Renowned Artists," *MPW*, 20 Nov 1920, 375.

Bracy, Clara T. [actress] (*née* Clara Thompson, b. London, England, 1846–22 Feb 1941 [94], Los Angeles CA; cardiac arrest). (Kinemacolor; Biograph.) "Clara T. Bracy," *Variety*, 26 Feb 1941. AS, p. 160. BHD, p. 112. IFN, p. 34. Truitt, p. 36.

Bradbury, James H., Jr. [actor] (b. New York NY, 5 Oct 1894–21 Jun 1936 [41], Los Angeles CA; suicide). AS, p. 160. BHD1, p. 65. IFN, p. 34.

Bradbury, James H., Sr. [actor] (b. Old Towne ME, 12 Oct 1857–12 Oct 1940 [83], Clifton, Staten Island NY). (Selig.) "James Bradbury," *Variety*, 16 Oct 1940, p. 62. AMD, p. 47. AS, p. 160 (d. Clifton NY). 1918 Studio Directory, p. 65. BHD1, p. 65. IFN, p. 34. Truitt, p. 36. "James Bradbury with Selig," *MPW*, 4 Dec 1915, 1815.

Bradbury, Kitty [actress]. No data found. AMD, p. 47. "Miss Bradbury in 'The Turmoil,'" *MPW*, 15 Dec 1923, 636.

Bradbury, Robert North (father of Bob Steele) [actor/scenarist/director] (*né* Ronald Bradbury, b. Walla Walla WA, 23 Mar 1886–24 Nov 1949 [63], Glendale CA). (Universal; Lasky; Kalem.) AMD, p. 47. AS, p. 160. BHD, p. 112; BHD2, p. 30. FDY, p. 419. "To Direct Hoxie," *MPW*, 28 Jul 1923, 319. Billy H. Doyle, "Lost Players," *CI*, 197 (Nov 1991), 29–30.

Bradbury, William [actor] (b. Portland OR, 23 Jan 1907–15 Sep 1971 [64], Loma Linda CA). BHD, p. 112.

Braddon, John D. [art director]. No data found. AMD, p. 47. "Braddon Engaged by Capellani," *MPW*, 20 Dec 1919, 972.

Bradell, Maurice [actor] (b. Folkstone, England, 23 Nov 1901–28 Jul 1990 [89], England). AS, p. 160 (b. Brentford, England). BHD1, p. 65.

Bradford, Charles Avery [actor/director] (aka Charles Avery, b. Chicago IL, 28 May 1873–23 Jul 1926 [53], Los Angeles CA; suicide). "Charles Avery Bradford," *Variety*, 28 Jul 1926. AMD, p. 25. AS, p. 160. BHD, p. 96; BHD2, p. 11. IFN, p. 13 (Avery). 1921 Directory, p. 257. Truitt, p. 36. "Julius Stern Engages Avery to Direct L-KO's," *MPW*, 27 Jul 1918, 570.

Bradford, Gardner [title writer]. No data found. FDY, p. 441.

Bradford, James C. [actor] (b. Rochester NY, 1886?–11 May 1941 [55], Neponsit, LI NY). m. Edna. "James C. Bradford," *Variety*, 14 May 1941, p. 51. AS, p. 160. BHD2. p. 30.

Bradford, James M. [actor] (b. Cincinnati OH, 1844?–8 Jun 1933 [89], Akron OH). "J.M. Bradford Dead; Once a Noted Actor; Friend of Lincoln, Who Toured with Buffalo Bill, Wrote Poem, 'Somebody's Mother,'" *NYT*, 10 Jun 1933, 13:5 (does not mention film career). "James M. Bradford," *Variety*, 13 Jun 1933, p. 54 (d. 9 Jun). AS, p. 160.

Bradford, Virginia [actress]. No data found. m. Cedric Belfrage (writer for *MPC*), 12 Sep 1928, Tia Juana. (Pathé.)

Bradley, Amanda [actress] (d. 13 Dec 1916, New York NY; auto accident). AS, p. 160. BHD, p. 112. IFN, p. 35.

Bradley, Benjamin R. [actor] (b. 1898?–29 Sep 1950 [52], St. Louis MO; heart attack). "Benjamin R. Bradley," *Variety*, 18 Oct 1950 ("former magician and a film player in the silent picture days"). AS, p. 160. BHD, p. 112. IFN, p. 35. Truitt, p. 36.

Bradley, Curley [stuntman/actor] (*né* George Courtney, b. OK, 18 Sep 1910–3 Jun 1985 [74], Long Beach CA). AS, p. 160. BHD, p. 113.

Bradley, Estelle [actress] (b. Atlanta GA, 5 Apr 1908–28 Jun 1990 [82], Woodland Hills CA). BHD1, p. 65.

Bradley, George E. [publicist/writer]. No data found. AMD, p. 47. "Bradley Head of F.N. Publicity," *MPW*, 3 Jul 1926, 19. "To Adapt Universal Script," *MPW*, 11 Sep 1926, 97.

Bradley, Harry C. [actor] (b. San Francisco CA, 15 Apr 1869–18 Oct 1947 [78], Los Angeles CA). AS, p. 160. BHD, p. 113. IFN, p. 35.

Bradley, Mrs. Lillian Trimble [writer/director]. No data found. m. George H. Broadhurst (d. 1952). AMD, p. 47. "Mrs. L. Trimble Bradley Joins Paramount," *MPW*, 25 Feb 1922, 828.

Bradley, Russell F. [actor] (b. Palo Alto CA, 27 Mar 1894–17 Dec 1952 [58], Alameda CA). BHD, p. 113. IFN, p. 35.

Bradley, Willard King [writer]. No data found. AMD, p. 47. FDY, p. 419. "Universal Pays $1,200 for Synopsis," *MPW*, 19 Aug 1916, 1221.

Bradshaw, Eunice [actress] (b. 1893–1973 [80?]). AS, p. 161. BHD, p. 113.

Bradshaw, Lionel H. [actor] (b. Lima OH, 10 May 1892–17 Dec 1918 [26], Los Angeles CA; influenza). (Universal; Fine Arts; Fox.) "Lionel Bradshaw," *Variety*, 27 Dec 1918. AS, p. 161. BHD, p. 113. 1918 Studio Directory, p. 65. IFN, p. 35.

Brady, Alice (daughter of William A. Brady) [stage/film actress] (b. New York NY, 2 Nov 1892–28 Oct 1939 [46], New York NY; cancer). m. James L. Crane, 20 May 1919 (d. 1968). (World; Select.) "Alice Brady Dead; Stage, Film Star; Daughter of Producer, William A. Brady, Succumbs Here After Long Illness; Began Career in 'Mikado'; Last Work Was in Screen Play 'The Young Mr. Lincoln'—Won Academy Award in '38," *NYT*, 30 Oct 1939, 17:1. "Alice Brady Dies in N.Y.," *Variety*, 1 Nov 1939. AMD, p. 47. AS, p. 161. BHD1, p. 66. FSS, p. 43. IFN, p. 35. Lowrey, p. 28. MH, p. 99. MSBB, p. 1032. Spehr, p. 118. Truitt, p. 37. WWS, p. 42. "Alice Brady on Screen; Will Be Seen In Peerless Company Production of 'As Ye Sow,'" *NYDM*, 7 Oct 1914, 25:2 (to be made at Ft. Lee NJ). Cover (with Florence Nash), *NYDM*, 5 May 1915 (in play, *The Sinners*). "Alice Brady with Knickerbocker," *MPW*, 19 Jun 1915, 1922. "Alice Brady with World Film," *MPW*, 10 Jul 1915, 325. "Alice Brady Busy with Pictures," *MPW*, 5 Feb 1916, 785. "Alice Brady Multiple Star," *MPW*, 4 Nov 1916, 705. "Alice Brady Leaves World Film Corporation," *MPW*, 1 Sep 1917, 1362. "Select Pictures Signs Alice Brady," *MPW*, 6 Oct 1917, 61. "Alice Brady to Return to the Stage," *MPW*, 17 Aug 1918, 960. C. Blythe Sherwood, "Where There's an Alice Brady There's a Way," *MPC*, Jan 1919, 24–25, 70. "Alice Brady Completing Her Contract with Select," *MPW*, 1 Mar 1919, 1178. "Alice Brady Is Wedded to James Crane, Actor," *MPW*, 7 Jun 1919, 1462. "Alice Brady Signs with Realart," *MPW*, 12 Jul 1919, 209. "[The True Story of Alice] Brady and Jimmie Crane," *MW*, 7 Jan 1922, 19, 30. "Miss Brady Comes Back to Pictures," *MPW*, 17 Jun 1922, 623. Sonya Levien, "Diary of a Scenario Writer on Location with Alice Brady," *MW*, 12 May 1923, 13, 30; Part II, "On Location with Alice Brady in the Canada Wilds," 19 May 1923, 21, 30; Part III, "Breasting the Big Snows with Alice Brady," 26 May 1923, 21, 30. Alma Talley, "Will the Deserted Village of Moviedom Live Again?; Will Fort Lee, in New Jersey, which was once the eastern mecca of film production, find a new lease on life and become again the center of movie making?," *MW*, 17 May 1924, 12–13, 24 (Brady, June Elvidge, Ethel Clayton and others made films there).

Brady, Arthur [publicist]. No data found. AMD, p. 48. "Brady, the Post Man Moves," *MPW*, 13 Apr 1912, 117. "Brady, the Poster Man," *MPW*, 15 Mar 1913, 1111.

Brady, Cyrus Townsend (brother of Jasper Ewing Brady) [clergyman/author/historian/scenarist] (b. Allegheny PA, 20 Dec 1861–24 Jan 1920 [58], Yonkers NY; pneumonia). m. (1) Clarissa Sidney Guthrie, 1884 (d. 1890); (2) Mary Barrett, Nov 1891. AMD, p. 48. BHD2, p. 30. "Cyrus Townsend Brady's Works Secured," *MPW*, 4 Apr 1914, 41. "Cyrus Townsend Brady Sues Reliance," *MPW*, 25 Sep 1915, 2178. "Reliance Wins Against Dr. Brady," *MPW*, 18 Mar 1916, 1840. "Cyrus Townsend Brady Is Big Author for Vitagraph," *MPW*, 13 Sep 1919, 1636. "Obituary," *MPW*, 7 Feb 1920, 862 (age 59). "Brady, Cyrus Townsend," *National Cyclopedia of American Biography*, Vol. 10, p. 477 ("Townsend" was his mother's maiden name; ordained in 1888 to the Protestant Episcopal church; first novel, *For Love of Country*, 1898).

Brady, Edwin J. [actor] (b. New York NY, 6 Dec 1889–31 Mar 1942 [52], Los Angeles CA; heart attack). (Selig; Universal.) m. Lillian West. "Edward J. Brady," *Variety*, 8 Apr 1942 (age 54). AMD, p. 48. AS, p. 161. BHD1, p. 66. FSS, p. 43. IFN, p. 35. Truitt, p. 37 (Edward J. Brady). "Edwin J. Brady Married," *Motography*, 2 Oct 1915, 683. "Edward J. Brady," *MPW*, 12 Feb 1916, 963. Al Ray, "Before the Stars Shone," *Picture-Play Masgazine*, Sep 1917, 92.

Brady, Jasper Ewing (brother of Cyrus Townsend Brady) [scenarist]. No data found. AMD, p. 48. "A Script in Record Time," *MPW*, 23 Oct 1915, 594. "Colonel Brady Writes Novel," *MPW*, 19 Feb 1916, 1115. "Colonel Brady, Universal's Scenario Chief," *MPW*, 26 May 1917, 1284. "Metro Scenario Editor Is Author of a Novel," *MPW*, 3 Jan 1920, 144 (*The Case of Mary Sherman*).

Brady, William A[loysius] (father of Alice Brady) [actor/sports promoter/theatrical manager/producer/playwright/head of World Film Corp./President of the National Association of the Motion Picture Industry, 1915–22] (b. San Francisco CA, 19 Jun 1863–6 Jan 1950 [86], New York NY; heart ailment). m. French dancer Marie René, ca. 1885 (d. 1896; actress Alice Brady resulted from this marriage); Grace George, 8 Jan 1899 (d. 1961; William A. Brady, Jr., resulted from this marriage). *Showman*, 1937. "W.A. Brady, 86, Dies of Heart Ailment; Noted Showman's Wife, Grace George, Remains in Play [*The Velvet Glove*] Here After Being at Deathbed; Granddaughter [of WAB, Jr., Barbara Brady] in Cast; Theatrical Producer Managed Corbett and Jeffries—Was Father of Alice Brady," *NYT*, 8 Jan 1950, 76:1 ("Mr. Brady's biggest money maker in the theatre...was the old stand-by 'Way Down East,' which came to him in manuscript titled 'Annie Laurie.'" He earned over a million dollars on it.). "Vet Showman Wm. Brady Dies at 86; Produced 260 Shows, Handled Champs," *Variety,* 11 Jan 1950, p. 63. AS, p. 161. BHD2, p. 31. SD, p. 154. Spehr, p. 118. WWVC, p. 28. "William A. Brady in Pictures," *MPW,* 21 Feb 1914, 929. "Films Close 'Trilby'; Play Unable to Compete with Motion Picture Version—[producer Joseph] Brooks to Sue Brady," *NYDM,* 6 Nov 1915, 9:3 (the touring company was to close in Boston. Effective film ads proclaimed, "Why pay $2 when it can be seen for 25 cents?" Brooks to sue Brady because the film was not to be shown until the tour ended. Brady said his partners in the film venture would not agree to this. To sue for $50,000, "and may be more," said Brooks.). "Brady Assumes Active Control," *MPW,* 15 Apr 1916, 410. "William A. Brady Old Picture Man," *MPW,* 15 Jul 1916, 459. "Imprison Makers of Independent Pictures," *MPW,* 19 May 1917, 1094–95. "William A. Brady Quits Producing for World Film," *MPW,* 16 Feb 1918, 948. *Dictionary of American Biography,* Supp. 4 (1974), p. 103 (co-authored *Gentleman Jack,* 1892, for James J. Corbett; discovered David Warfield, 1891; managed Douglas Fairbanks in *All for a Girl,* 1908; produced *Street Scene,* 1929, with a cast of 50). Interred at Sleepy Hollow Cemetery, Tarrytown NY.

Brady, William J. [actor] (b. Putnam CT, 1870?–26 Dec 1936 [66], Queens, New York NY). m. Elizabeth Cunningham. "William J. Brady," *Variety,* 30 Dec 1936, p. 55. AS, p. 161. IFN, p. 35. SD.

Bragaglia, Carlo Ludovico (son of Francesco Bragaglia, managiong director of Cinès; uncle of producer Silvio Clementelli) [stills cameraman/director/scenarist] (b. Frosinone, Ciociaria province, so. of Rome, 8 Jul 1894 [extrait de naissance no. 224]-4 Jan 1998 [103], Rome, Italy; following operation for a broken hip). *Bragaglia racconta Bragaglia,* 1997. (First film as director: *O la borsa o la vita* (*Your Money or Your Life*), 1933; final film: *I 4 Moschettieri* [*The Four Musketeers,* 1963]; Cinès Studios.) David Rooney, "Carlo Ludovico Bragaglia," *Variety,* 19 Jan 1998, p. 100:1. John Francis Lane, "Carlo Bragaglia; A century of Italian cinema," *The Guardian,* 8 Jan 1998, p. 16. AS, p. 161. JS, p. 58.

Braham, Harry [actor] (b. London, England, 1850–21 Sep 1923 [73], Staten Island NY). m. Lillian Russell (d. 1922). "Harry Braham," *Variety,* 27 Sep 1923, p. 9. AS, p. 161. BHD, p. 113. IFN, p. 35. SD. Truitt, p. 37.

Braham, Horace [actor] (cousin of Lionel Braham) (b. London, England, 29 Jul 1892–7 Sep 1955 [63], New York NY). m. Gladys Feldman (d. 1974). "Horace Braham," *Variety,* 14 Sep 1955, p. 71 (age 62). AS, p. 161. BHD, p. 113. IFN, p. 35. Truitt, p. 37.

Braham, Lionel (cousin of Horace Braham) [actor] (b. Yorkshire, England, 1 Apr 1879–6 Oct 1947 [68], Los Angeles CA; heart attack). "Lionel Braham," *Variety,* 15 Oct 1947, p. 55. AS, p. 161. BHD1, p. 66. IFN, p. 35. Truitt, p. 37.

Brahms, Helene [actress] (b. 21 May 1872–22 Jul 1948 [76]). BHD1, p. 66.

Braidon, Thomas A. [actor] (b. London, England, 1 Mar 1870–22 Jun 1950 [80], Los Angeles Co. CA). AS, p. 161. BHD1, p. 66. IFN, p. 35.

Braidwood, Frank [actor]. No data found. (Universal.) George A. Katchmer, "More Forgotten Cowboys and Cowgirls—Chapter 6," *CI,* 172 (Oct 1989), C14.

Braithwaite, John [actor] (b. 1883-Oct 1963 [80?], Egremont, Cumberland, England). BHD, p. 113.

Braithwaite, Lilian [stage/film actress] (*née* Florence Lilian Braithwaite, b. Ramsgate, England, 9 Mar 1873–17 Sep 1948 [75], London, England; heart attack). "Dame Lillian Braithwaite," *Variety,* 22 Sep 1948, p. 55 (age 77). AS, p. 161. BHD1, p. 66. IFN, p. 35 (age 77).

Bramble, A[lbert] **V**[ictor] [actor/director/producer] (b. Portsmouth, England, 1880–17 May 1963 [83?], Fiern Barnett, England). AS, p. 162 (b. 1884). BHD1, p. 66; BHD2, p. 31.

Bramley, Flora [actress: Wampas Star, 1928] (b. London, England, 1909?–23 Jun 1993 [84], Moline IL). AS, p. 162. BHD1, p. 66. Roi Uselton, "The Wampas Baby Stars," *FIR,* Feb 1970, 73.

Bramley, Nellie [actress] (b. 1889–10 Jun 1982 [93?], Australia). BHD, p. 113.

Brammall, Jack (John) [actor]. George Katchmer, "Remembering the Great Silents," *CI,* 221 (Nov 1993), 31.

Branch, Houston [scenarist] (b. St. Paul MN, 5 Mar 1905–27 Jan 1958 [52]). WWWA.

Branch, William [scenarist]. No data found. FDY, p. 419.

Brand, Harry [publicist/scenarist] (b. New York NY, 16 Mar 1896–22 Feb 1989 [92], Beverly Hills CA). BHD2, p. 31. FDY, p. 419.

Brand, Mary Spoor [actress] (b. 1887–18 Oct 1985 [97?]). BHD, p. 113.

Brandeis, Madeline [actress/author/scenarist/producer] (*née* Madeleine Frank, b. San Francisco CA, 18 Dec 1897–27 Jun 1937 [39], Gallup NM; two weeks after auto accident). m. (1) E. John Brandeis, 28 Jan 1918—div. 25 Apr 1921, Omaha NE; (2) Dr. Joseph A. Sampson, 5 Oct 1933. "Mrs. Madeline Brandeis," *NYT,* 29 Jun 1937, 21 (d. 28 Jun). "Mrs. Brandeis Succumbs to Auto Accident," *Variety,* 30 Jun 1937. AS, p. 162. BHD2, p. 31 (b. 1898. IFN, p. 35. "Who's Who? On Stage and Screen," *MPC,* Nov 1924, 43. Ruth Tildesley, "Giving the Children a Chance; Madeline Brandeis has won Fame and Fortune Producing Pictures Starring—Just Kids!," *Screenland,* May 1929, 24–25, 98–99.

Brandes, Werner [cinematographer] (b. 10 Jul 1899-Sep 1968 [69], CA). FDY, p. 455.

Brandenberg, Chet [actor] (b. KY, 15 Oct 1897–17 Jul 1974 [76], Woodland Hills CA). BHD1, p. 67.

Brander, Ida [actress] (*née* Maria Charlotta Brander, b. Helsinki, Finland, 5 Oct 1857–15 May 1931 [73], Kauniainen, Finland). AS, p. 162.

Brandon, Mrs. F. Marlon [scenarist]. No data found. "Scenario Needs; Eclair Scenario Editor States Script Needs of That Company," *NYDM,* 11 Feb 1914, 28:2.

Brandon, Florence [actress] (b. 1879?–11 Oct 1961 [82], London, England). "Florence Brandon," *Variety,* 25 Oct 1961, p. 71. AS, p. 162. BHD, p. 113. IFN, p. 35. Truitt, p. 37.

Brandon, Francis [actor] (b. 1886–3 Oct 1924 [38], New York NY). AS, p. 162. BHD, p. 113. IFN, p. 35.

Brandon, Mary [actress]. No data found. m. Robert E. Sherwood, 1922. AMD, p. 49. "Film Critic Weds Leading Lady," *MPW,* 9 Dec 1922, 540.

Brandon-Thomas, Amy [actress] (b. London, England, 9 Mar 1890–9 May 1974 [84], London, England). BHD1, p. 67 (Bandon-Thomas). IFN, p. 35.

Brandt, Charles Christian [actor] (b. Philadelphia PA, 27 May 1862–9 Jun 1924 [62], Philadelphia PA). (Equitable; Lubin; World.) 1918 Studio Directory, p. 65 (b. 1864). AMD, p. 49. AS, p. 162. BHD, p. 113 (b. 1864). IFN, p. 35 (age 60). "Funny Things That Happen in the Studio," *MPW,* 15 Jun 1912, 1011 (cites birthday of 27 May). "Charles Christian Brandt; Lubin Character Actor," *MPS,* 13 Nov 1914, 25 (began at Lubin on 2 Jan 1911). Chas. C. Brandt, "The Joker," *Motion Picture Magazine,* Feb 1915, 100. "Charles Brandt," *MPW,* 23 Oct 1915, 596.

Brandt, Hohn [scenarist]. No data found. FDY, p. 419 (Hohn [sic]: may be a nickname for Johannes. *See* next entry.).

Brandt, Johannes [scenarist/producer/composer] (b. Austria-10 Mar 1955, Vienna, Austria). AS, p. 162.

Brandt, Joseph [actor] (d. ca. 1916). BHD, p. 113.

Brandt, Joseph [publicist] (*né* Joseph Brandenburg?, b. Troy NY, 20 Jul 1882–22 Feb 1939 [56], Beverly Hills CA). (Universal.) AMD, p. 49. "Joseph Brandt," *Variety,* 1 Mar 1939, p. 54 (organizer and first president of C.B.C. Sales Corp., later Columbia. Private secretary to Carl Laemmle in 1908). BHD2, p. 31. "Brandt Goes to Mirror," *MPW,* 15 Apr 1911, 818. "Brandt Joins Imp Company," *NYDM,* 3 Apr 1912, 25:2 (referred to as "Joe 'Brandt' Brandenburg"). "Flickers," *MPW,* 16 Aug 1913, 728. F.J. Beecroft, "Publicity Men I Have Met," *NYDM,* 14 Jan 1914, 48 (*see* Beecroft, Chester for full citation) "Universal Publicity Staff," *MPW,* 26 Sep 1914, 1756–57. "Some Job of Cutting," *MPW,* 4 Nov 1916, 714. "Joe Brandt Heads Film Adversiting Men," *MPW,* 8 Dec 1917, 1503. Joe Brandt, "How Independent Leaders See New Season," *MPW,* 8 Sep 1923, 158. "Joe Brandt Announces New Columbia Policy in Force," *MPW,* 11 Jul 1925, 182. "'Biggest Year,' Brandt Says," *MPW,* 18 Jul 1925, 310. "Prediction by Brandt Three Years Ago Now Fulfilled," *MPW,* 10 Oct 1925, 474. "Columbia Chief Back from Continent, Marks New Film Entente Against U.S.," *MPW,* 25 Dec 1926, 570. "Brandt Off to Feature 'Columbia' All Over Europe," *MPW,* 24 Sep 1927, 240.

Brandt, Louise [actress] (b. 1877–13 Jul 1959 [82], San Diego CA). AS, p. 162. BHD, p. 113. IFN, p. 35.

Branscombe, Lily [actress] (*née* Lily Rodman, b. New Zealand, 28 Feb 1876–26 Sep 1970 [94], San Francisco CA; pneumonia and heart attack). m. Herbert Ashton, New Zealand (d. 31 Jan 1930, NYC). (Essanay [Chicago], 1911.) Billy H. Doyle, "Lost Players," *CI,* 163 (Jan 1989), 30. AS, p. 163 (b. 1878). BHD, pp. 10–11 (widow of Ashton listed as "Lily Granstone"); 113.

Brantley, Nell [actress]. George A. Katchmer, "Forgotten Cowboys and Cowgirls—Part XIII," *CI,* 190 (Apr 1991), C4.

Brasseur, Pierre (father of actor Claude Brasseur, b. 15 Jun 1936) [actor/writer] (b. Paris, France, 22 Dec 1905–14 Aug 1972 [66], Brunice, Italy; during the filming of *La Panne* [*The Breakdown*]). m. actress Odette Joyeux (son, Claude);

Lina Magrini. *Ma Vie Envrac.* (Began 1925.) "Pierre Brasseur," *Variety,* 30 Aug 1972, p. 63. AS, p. 163. BHD1, p. 67 (d. Brunico, Italy). IFN, p. 35. Waldman, p. 36.

Braun, Curt J[ohannes] [scenarist] (b. 1903–18 Jun 1961 [58?], Munich, Germany). AS, p. 163 (b. Germany, 1898). BHD2, p. 31. FDY, p. 419.

Braun, Leo H. [composer] (b. Breslau, Germany, 1881?–12 Nov 1954 [73], Flushing NY). "Leo Braun," *Variety,* 17 Nov 1954.

Brausewetter, Hans [actor] (b. Malaga, Spain, 27 May 1896–29 Apr 1945 [48], Berlin, Germany). As, p. 164 (b. 1899). BHD1, p. 67. IFN, p. 36 (b. 1900).

Bravetta, Vittorio Emanuele [scenarist] (b. Livorno, Italy, 1 Dec 1889). JS, p. 59 (in Italian silents from 1912).

Brawn, John P. [stage/film actor] (b. New York NY, 1869–16 Jun 1943 [74], New York NY). m. Ethel Brooke Ferguson, 1904. (Vitagraph.) (Niblo's Gardens, 1888; Hoyt & McKee Co., 1894.) "John P. Brawn, Actor More than 50 Years; Began Career as Whistler at Niblo's Gardens in 1888," *NYT,* 17 Jun 1943, 21:4 (lead actor in *The Dream of a Rarebit Fiend,* Edison, 1906). "John P. Brawn," *Variety,* 23 Jun 1943, p. 63. AS, p. 164. BHD, p. 113. IFN, p. 36. Truitt, p. 37.

Braxton, Harry [title writer] (b. NY, 1893?–13 May 1952 [59], New York NY). m. Celia. "Harry Braxton," *NYT,* 14 May 1952, 27:2 (ran the Braxton Gallery in Hollywood). AS, p. 164. FDY, p. 441.

Bray, Helen [actress]. No data found. AMD, p. 49. "Miss Bray Visits Her Home," *MPW,* 1 Aug 1914, 714.

Bray, John Randolph [animator/producer] (b. Addison MI, 25 Aug 1879–10 Oct 1978 [99], Bridgeport CT). "Father of Animated Cartoons," *NYT,* 6 Nov 1978, 56. "John Bray," *Variety,* 18 Oct 1978 (age 81). AS, p. 164. BHD2, p. 31 (b. Detroit MI). "Bray Cartoons Score; Pathe News Now Contains Celebrated Series of Animated Cartoons," *NYDM,* 10 Mar 1915, 26:1. "Animated Cartoons in Motion Pictures," *MPW,* 3 Apr 1915, 54. "Cartoonists Go to Court," *MPW,* 24 Apr 1915, 532. "That Cartoon Suit; J.R. Bray Issues a Statement Concerning Criticism of the Suit to Protect His Patents on Animated Pictures," *NYDM,* 9 Jun 1915, 25:1. "Bray Withdraws Court Suit," *NYDM,* 20 Nov 1915, 26:3 (against Harry Palmer, "claiming infringement of the former's patents on the process of making animated cartoons." The defendant's attorneys protested and were to appeal. "The costs of the case were assessed against the plaintiff."). "Cartoonist Bray with Paramount," *MPW,* 11 Dec 1915, 1988. John R. Bray, "Development of Animated Cartoons," *MPW,* 21 Jul 1917, 395–97. "Bray Ready with Colored Cartoons," *MPW,* 13 Sep 1919, 1644. "Bray to Produce Comedies," *MPW,* 20 Mar 1926, 157. Mark Langer, "The Reflections of John Randolph Bray; An Interview with Annotations," *Griffithiana,* May 1995, pp. 94–131.

Brayfield, George W. [actor] (d. 17 Feb 1968, Denver CO). AS, p. 164 (d. LA CA). BHD, p. 113.

Brayton, Ethel [actress]. m. Carl Van Schiller, 1913 (d. 1962). "News Briefs," *MPW,* 24 May 1913, 798 (eloped with Van Schiller.)

Brayton, Lily [stage/film actress] (b. Hindley, Lancashire, England, 23 Jun 1876–30 Apr 1953 [76], Dawlish, Devonshire, England). m. (1) Oscar Asche (d. 1936). (Stage debut: *Richard II,* Manchester, 1896.) "Lily Brayton," *Variety,* 6 May 1953, p. 63. AS, p. 164. BHD, p. 113.

Brazier, Sara [actress]. No data found. AMD, p. 49. "Madame Sara Brazier to Make Debut in Pictures," *MPW,* 9 Oct 1920, 784.

Breamer, Sylvia [stage/film actress] (b. Sydney, Australia, 9 Jun 1897–7 Jun 1943 [45], New York NY). m. Harry W. Martin. (Ince; FP-L.) "Sylvia Breamer," *Variety,* 16 Jun 1943. AMD, p. 49. AS, p. 164. BHD1, p. 68 (b. 1903). FFF, p. 99. IFN, p. 36 (age 40). Lowrey, p. 30. MH, p. 99. MSBB, p. 1032. Truitt, p. 37 (b. 1903). "Sylvia Breamer," *MPW,* 30 Jun 1917, 2081. "Sylvia Breamer," *MPW,* 7 Apr 1917, 106. "Sylvia Breamer Leading Man for Hart," *MPW,* 15 Sep 1917, 1673. "Sylvia Breamer on Stage Early in Life," *MPW,* 26 Jul 1919, 584. "Sylvia Breamer in Coming Production," *MPW,* 19 May 1923, 249. Kenneth McGaffey, "The Story of Five Hundred Dollars," *MPC,* Dec 1921, 32–33, 79–80.

Bredel, Elwood [cinematographer]. No data found. FDY, p. 455.

Breen, Harry [actor] (d. 20 Jan 1918, Riverside CA; drowned in a lake). AS, p. 165 (d. 2 Mar 1918, Elsinore CA). BHD, p. 114.

Breen, Margaret [stage/film actress] (b. MO, 3 Feb 1907–5 Dec 1960 [53], Santa Monica CA). m. Arthur Hamburger. "Margaret Breen," *Variety,* 14 Dec 1960, p. 63. "Margaret Breen," *Variety,* 14 Dec 1960, p. 63. AS, p. 165. BHD1, p. 68. IFN, p. 36.

Breese, Edmund [stage/film actor] (b. Brooklyn NY, 18 Jun 1871–6 Apr 1936 [64], New York NY; peritonitis). m. (1) Genevieve Landry; (2) Harriet A. Beach. (Lasky; Fox; Metro.) "Edmund Breese Dies; Peritonitis Sets In," *Variety,* 8 Apr 1936, p. 62. AMD, p. 50. AS, p. 165. BHD1, p. 68. IFN, p. 36. SD. Truitt, p. 37. "Breese Joins Lasky; Broadway Star to Be Seen in Film Version of 'The Master Mind,'" *NYDM,* 4 Feb 1914, 39:1. "Edmund Breese for Metro," *MPW,* 16 Oct 1915, 454. "Edmund Breese Engaged by Raver," *MPW,* 10 Nov 1917, 894.

Breese, Vinton [actor]. No data found. m. actress Carlotta DeFelice, 11 Sep 1916, Newark NJ.

Breil, Joseph Carl [composer] (b. Pittsburgh PA, 29 Jun 1870–23 Jan 1926 [55], Los Angeles CA; heart disease after nervous breakdown). "Joseph Carl Breil," *Variety,* 27 Jan 1926, p. 48 (age 56). AS, p. 165. BHD2, p. 32. "Breil to Write Special Music," *NYDM,* 1 Sep 1915, 26:1 (hired by D.W. Griffith to contribute to Fine Arts films for Triangle).

Brendel, El, "The Synthetic Swede" [stage/film actor] (*né* Elmer Goodfellow Brendle, b. Philadelphia PA, 25 Mar 1891–9 Apr 1964 [73], Los Angeles CA; diabetes). m. Sophie Flo Bert. "El Brendel, 73, Dies on Coast; Film Comedian in 20's and 30's," *NYT,* 10 Apr 1964, 35:1. "El Brendel," *Variety,* 15 Apr 1964, p. 60. AMD, p. 50. AS, p. 165 (b. 1890). BHD1, p. 68. FSS, p. 43. IFN, p. 36. SD. Truitt, p. 38 (b. 1890). "Vaudeville Headliner Signs with Paramount," *MPW,* 15 May 1926, 238. "Brendel Pens His Own Gags," *MPW,* 11 Jun 1927, 409. Cedric Belfrage, "The Synthetic Swede," *Motion Picture Classics,* May 1930, pp. 52, 98.

Brennan, Edward [actor/director] (b. Rochester NY). AMD, p. 50. "New Rolfe-Metro Stars," *MPW,* 9 Oct 1915, 287. "Edward Brennan in Metro Subject," *MPW,* 17 Jun 1916, 2044. "Edward Brennan Now a Director," *MPW,* 15 Jul 1916, 433.

Brennan, F[rederick] H[azlitt] [novelist/scenarist/TV writer] (b. 1902?–1 Jul 1962 [60], Hidden Valley CA; suicide by shooting). "Frederick Hazlitt Brennan," *Variety,* 4 Jul 1962, p. 103 (survived by wife, 2 sons and a daughter). BHD2, p. 32 (d. 30 Jun). FDY, p. 419. IFN, p. 36 (d. 30 Jun).

Brennan, Jay [actor/scenarist] (b. Baltimore MD, 6 Dec 1882–14 Jan 1961 [77], Brooklyn NY). "Jay Brennan," *Variety,* 18 Jan 1961, p. 70. AS, p. 165. BHD2, p. 32.

Brennan, John E. [actor/producer] (b. Springfield MA, 17 Jul 1865–27 Dec 1940 [75], Los Angeles CA; heart attack). AS, p. 166. BHD, p. 114. IFN, p. 36. *Photoplay Arts Portfolio* [Kalem]. "Johnnie Brennan, Producer," *MPW,* 20 May 1916, 1340. "John Brennan 'Comes Back,'" *MPW,* 27 May 1916, 1516.

Brennan, Joe [actor] (b. 1883?–19 Jan 1931 [48], Cragmore CO, near Colorado Springs; tuberculosis). "Joe Brennan," *Variety,* 21 Jan 1931, p. 68.

Brennan, Joseph D. [actor] (b. 1859?–10 Dec 1940 [81]). AS, p. 166. IFN, p. 36.

Brennan, Joseph H. [actor] (d. 28 Feb 1949). IFN, p. 36.

Brennan, Robert [actor] (b. 1892?–17 Apr 1940 [48], Los Angeles CA). "Robert Brennan," *Variety,* 24 Apr 1940 (d. Sawtelle CA). AS, p. 166. BHD1, p. 69. IFN, p. 36. Truitt, p. 38.

Brennan, Walter Andrex [film/TV actor] (b. Swampscott MA, 25 Jul 1894–21 Sep 1974 [80], Oxnard CA; emphysema). m. Ruth C. Wells, 1920. (Film debut: *The Ridin' Rowdy,* 1927; AA in 1936, 1938, and 1940.) "Walter Brennan, Durable Character Actor, Dies at 80," *Variety,* 25 Sep 1974, p. 62. AS, p. 166. BHD1, p. 69. IFN, p. 36. SD. George A. Katchmer, "Remembering the Great Silents," *CI,* 183 (Sep 1990), 45. Eric Niderost, "Walter Brennan; Consummate Character Actor," *CI,* 217 (Jul 1993), 18, 20, 22, 24.

Brenner, Ida Netia [actress] (b. MO, 22 Sep 1888–21 Nov 1952 [64], Azusa CA). BHD1, p. 605.

Brenon, Herbert (brother of Roma Brenon) [stock player/vaudevillian/scenarist/director/producer] (*né* Alexander Herbert Reginald St. John Brenon, b. 25, Crosthwaite Park, Dun Laoghaire [formerly Kingston], near Dublin, Ireland, 13 Jan 1880–21 Jun 1958 [78], Los Angeles CA). (Directorial debut: *All for Her,* Imp, 1910; Champion; Fox; Universal; Paramount; UA.) m. Helen Oberg (stage name: Helen Dowling), 1904. "Herbert Brenon Dies; A 'Big 3' Movie Maker; In Silent Screen Days, He Was Ranked with DeMille, Griffith," *New York Herald Tribune,* 23 Jun 1958. "Herbert Brenon," *Variety,* 25 Jun 1958, p. 79. AMD, p. 50. AS, p. 166. BHD, p. 114; BHD2, p. 32. FDY, p. 419. IFN, p. 36. JS, p. 60 (worked in Italian films 1919–20. "Went to the U.S.A. in 1896, and to the U.K. in 1934.'). MSBB, p. 1044. SD (m. Oberg). Spehr, p. 118. Truitt, p. 38. "Herbert Brenon Returns from Europe," *MPW,* 8 Nov 1913, 615. "Herbert Brenon Resigns from Universal," *MPW,* 24 Oct 1914, 466. "A Director of Directors," *NYDM,* 12 May 1915, 22:4, 37:2 (when 1- and 2-relers were declared doomed, Brenon said, "At one time in vaudeville houses they were using single reels to fill in waits between acts and to end the performance. The future of the short reel is to be a similar relative position with the big features. They will fill in between and finish the performance.... And you can just say for me that I think the day of the 'good looking' actor who is not a finished artist is over."). "Newsy Notes," *NYDM,* 22 Sep 1915, 30:4 (on his way to Jamaica to film a Kellerman film, Brenon "received a wireless saythat that he inherited the whole estate of his uncle, Col. T. Lawrence Brenon, of Dublin. The bequest amounts to $20,000."). Herbert Brenon, "Directing Feature Productions," *Motography,* 2 Oct 1915, 681–83. "Court Denies Injunction to Brenon," *MPW,* 9 Sep 1916, 1671. "Brenon's Pretentious Plans," *MPW,* 28 Oct 1916, 527. "Death of Herbert Brenon's Father," *MPW,* 2 Jun 1917, 1455 (Edward St. John Brenon, d. 14 May 1917 [73], Clapham, London, England). "Chandos Brenon [brother] in New York," *MPW,* 23 Mar 1918, 1641. Charles Jameson, "The Stagnation of the Screen; Herbert Brenon, Fresh from Flanders Fields, Believes the American Photoplay Is at a Standstill," *MPC,* Mar 1919, 47, 84. "Brenon to Produce 'Peter Pan,'" *MPW,* 3 May 1924, 42. Alice L. Tildesley, "Filming *Beau Geste,*" *MPC,* Jun 1926, 26, 62, 73. DunhamThorp, "We Underrate Our Public, Says the Man Who Made 'Beau Geste,'" *MPC,* Jun 1927, 28, 90. Mary C. McCall, Jr., "The Box-Office Blasphemer; Herbert Brenon talks of his latest enthusiasm—the filming of 'Sorrell and Son,'" *Cinema Arts,* Jul 1927, 18, 46. Herbert Brenon, "Sorrell and Son—a Book for Fans," *Screenland,* Sep 1927, 12, 101. Burr C. Cook, "Herbert Brenon; A Portrait of the Producer of the Cinema Masterpieces: 'A Daughter of the Gods,' 'Peter Pan,' 'A Kiss for Cinderella,' 'Beau Gest' and His Latest, 'Sorrell and Son,'" *Cinema Arts,* Oct 1927, 22–23, 49 (arrived in America on 4 Jul 1896). "British Co. Sues Brenon," *MPW,* 15 Oct 1927, 411–12. "18th Anniversary for Herb Brenon," *MPW,* 17 Dec 1927, 6. Herbert Cruikshank, "From Fad to Worse; That's What Herbert Brenon Thinks of the Trend the Talkies Signify," *MPC,* Nov 1928, 33, 76 (succeeded William Collier, Sr., as a call-boy at Daly's theatre). Jack Lodge, "The Career of Herbert Brenon," *Griffithiana,* 57/58 (Oct 1996), 5–121; filmography, 122–133; Riccardo Redi, "Brenon in Italy," 135–143.

Brenon, Juliet [actress] (b. 1 Sep 1885–18 Nov 1979 [94], Bronx NY). BHD, p. 114.

Brenon, Roma (sister of Herbert Brenon) [actress] (b. Rome, Italy, 1870–9 Oct 1927 [57?], Brooklyn NY; interred in Woodlawn Cemetery). m. Oliver Gurney, 1892, London. "Mrs. Roma Brenon Gurney," *Variety,* 12 Oct 1927, p. 57. AS, p. 166 (d. 15 Oct). BHD, p. 114.

Brent, Evelyn [actress: Wampas Star, 1923] (*née* Mary Elizabeth Riggs, b. Tampa FL, 20 Oct 1899–4 Jun 1975 [75], Los Angeles CA; heart attack). m. (1) Bernard P. Fineman, 1 Nov 1922–27 (d. 1971); (2) Harry J. Edwards (d. 1952); (3) Harry Fox (d. 1959). (World, Ft. Lee NJ; film debut: *A Gentleman from Mississippi,* 1914; Metro.) "Evelyn Brent, 75, Film Star of 1920's; Made Transition to Talkies After Career in Silents," *NYT,* 8 Jun 1975, 55:3. "Evelyn Brent," *Variety,* 11 Jun 1975, p. 78 (age 74). AMD, p. 50. AS, p. 166 (b. 1894). BHD1, p. 69. BR, pp. 108–14. FSS, p. 44. IFN, p. 36. MH, p. 99. SD. Spehr, p. 120 (at World as Betty Riggs). "Betty Riggs Now Evelyn Brent," *MPW,* 5 Feb 1916, 782 (17 years old). "Evelyn Brent Plays with Metro," *MPW,* 4 Aug 1923, 419. "Gothic Signs Miss Brent," *MPW,* 13 Sep 1924, 114. "Evelyn Brent Gets Divorce from Fineman," *MPW,* 27 Aug 1927, 585 (separated Feb 1925). June Lee, "Dan Cupid's Bulletin Board," *Paris and Hollywood Screen Secrets,* Oct 1927, 37 ("Miss Brent accuses her husband [Fineman] of staying away days at a time without excuse and of mental cruelty, but this big part in the new Paramount picture [*Beau Sabreur*], the company in which Fineman is one of the chief executives, should be a very nice plum in the offing."). Gladys Hall, "Confessions of the Stars X; Evelyn Brent Tells Her Untold Tale," *MPC,* Jul 1929, 28–29, 66, 90 ("I was born when my mother was fourteen"; she died when Brent was fourteen). Buck Rainey, "Evelyn Brent; Innocence Was Hardly Her Forte," *CI,* 91 (Jan 1983), 6–7 (with filmography); Part II, 92 (Feb 1983), 48–50.

Brent, Romney [stage/film actor/playwright/scenarist/director] (*né* Romulo Larrade, b. Saltillo, Mexico, 26 Jan 1902–24 Sep 1976 [74], Mexico City, Mexico). m. actress Gina Malo (d. ca. 1966). "Romney Brent," *Variety,* 29 Sep 1976, p. 95. AS, p. 166. BHD, p. 114; BHD2, p. 32.

Brenton, Cranston [Chairman, National Board of Censorship of Motion Pictures]. No data found. AMD, p. 50. "New National Board Chairman," *MPW,* 17 Jul 1915, 498.

Breon, Edmund [acttor] (b. Hamilton, Scotland, 12 Dec 1882–1951 [68?]). AS, p. 166. BHD1, p. 69.

Brereton, Tyrone [actor] (b. Dublin, Ireland, 1894?–25 Apr 1939 [45], Los Angeles CA). "Tyrone Brerton," *Variety,* 3 May 1939. AS, p. 166. BHD1, p. 69 (b. 1893). IFN, p. 36. Truitt, p. 38.

Bresee, A.R. [actor] (b. 1851?–15 Feb 1918 [66], Brooklyn NY). "A.R. Bresee," *Variety,* 1 Mar 1918. AS, p. 166.

Breslow, Lew [cameraman/scenarist] (b. Boston MA, 18 Jul 1900–10 Nov 1987 [87], Woodland Hills CA). AS, p. 166. BHD2, p. 32. FDY, p. 419.

Bressart, Felix [stage/film actor] (b. Eydtkuhnen, Germany, 2 Mar 1895–17 Mar 1949 [54], Los Angeles CA; leukemia). "Felix Bressart," *Variety,* 30 Mar 1949, p. 55 (age 57). BHD1, p. 69 (Bressert; b. 1892). IFN, p. 36.

Bret, Tom [actor/editor/title writer for Vitagraph/scenarist] (b. Bolivar NY, 1883). m. AMD, p. 50. MSBB, p. 1022. "Tom Bret Joins Metro-Rolfe Scenario Staff," *MPW,* 21 Apr 1917, 434. Tom Bret, "Subtitles de Luxe," *MPW,* 19 May 1917, 1123. "Tom Bret Opens Script and Title Office," *MPW,* 25 Aug 1917, 1200. "Broadwell Engages Tom Bret," *MPW,* 28 Aug 1920, 1184.

Bretherton, Howard P. (father of film editor David Bretherton) [director] (b. Tacoma WA, 13 Feb 1896–12 Apr 1969 [73], San Diego CA). m. (son David). "Howard Bretherton," *Variety,* 16 Apr 1969, p. 79 ("pioneer film director" from 1914). Melissa Mielcarek, "David Bretherton," *Variety,* 29 May 2000, 70:2 (d. 11 May 2000 [76], John Douglas French Center, Los Angeles CA; pneumonia). AMD, p. 51. AS, p. 167. BHD2, p. 32 (b. 1890). IFN, p. 36. "Long Contract for Warner Director," *MPW,* 26 Feb 1927, 642. Tom Waller, "Howard Bretherton," *MPW,* 2 May 1927, 788–89.

Bretonne, May [actress] (b. 1860–28 Sep 1952 [92?], Englewood NJ). BHD, p. 114.

Bretty, Béatrice [actress] (*née* Béatrix Anne-Marie Bolchesi, b. La Fere, France, 26 Oct 1893 [extrait de naissance no. 175/1893]–4 Sep 1982 [88], Paris, France; heart attack). AS, p. 167. BHD, p. 114 (b. 1895).

Breuil, Mrs. Beta [*nom de plume*] [script editor/scenarist] (*née* Elizabeth Donner Van der Veer, b. New York NY, 1876). m. (1) Frank M. Willard, 1893 (d. 1903); (2) Hartmann Breuil, 1903 (d. 1908); (3) Gerrit Willem van Limburgh, Oct 1914). (Vitagraph, 1910.) AMD, p. 51. Slide, p. 36. *Woman's Who's Who of America* (NY: American Commonwealth Co., 1914) ("FIrst woman editor in this line of business to hold position."). "Misplaced Credit," *MPW,* 22 Jun 1912, 1113. Epes Winthrop Sargent, "Photoplaywright; Mrs. Breuil Retires," *MPW,* 9 Aug 1913, 630; "Mrs. Breuil's Plans," *MPW,* 16 Aug 1913, 738. "Photoplaywright; In Error," *MPW,* 18 Oct 1913, 257. "Among the Players," *NYDM,* 28 Oct 1914, 32:2 (married van Limburgh). "Beta Breuil with Mirror," *MPW,* 15 Jan 1916, 431.

Brewer, Jimmy [actor]. No data found. AMD, p. 51. "A New Fat Comedian," *MPW,* 19 Jan 1924, 226.

Brewster, Eugene V[alentine] [with *Motion Picture Magazine,* backed by Vitagraph/scenarist] (b. Bay Shore, LI NY, 7 Sep 1871–1 Jan 1939 [67], Brooklyn NY). m. Eleanor V.V. Cator, 1916; (3) Corliss Palmer, 1926 (d. 1952); (4) Liane Hill, 1935. "Eugene Brewster, Publisher, Was 67; Pioneer in the Film Magazine Field [*The Motion Picture Magazine*], Also Lawyer and Writer, Succumbs Here; Left Law for Pictures; Practiced 16 Years Before He Started Magazine in 1911—Made and Lost Millions," *NYT,* 2 Jan 1939, 23:3 ("...in 1911 he launched a pioneering motion-picture magazine that ultimately made him a millionaire." Also connected with *Motion Picture Classic; Movie Monthly; Beauty; Shadowland*). "Brewster Brothers' Deaths 3 Days Apart," *Variety,* 11 Jan 1939 (his brother Carleton E. d. 4 Jan 1939 [66], Smyrna FL; car accident). BHD2, p. 32. Eugene V. Brewster, "Trick Photography and Its Possibilities; How to Bring the Mammoth Monsters of Pre-Historic Times Before Your Eyes, as in *The Lost World,*" *MPC,* May 1925, 46, 84, 90–91, 94. "The Five Greatest Pictures of All Time; Opinions by the World's Greatest Reviewers, Expressed to Eugene V. Brewster," *MPC,* Jun 1925, 22–23, 83 (one reviewer listed *A Woman of Paris, Broken Blossoms, Tol'able David, The White Sister* and *The Birth of a Nation*).

Brewster, Percy D[ouglas] [producer] (b. 1866–7 Oct 1952 [86?], East Orange NJ). AS, p. 167.

Breyer, Mrs. Margarette [actress] (b. Fort Recovery OH, 1845?–11 Mar 1931 [86], Indianapolis IN). AS, p. 167. BHD, p. 114. IFN, p. 37.

Brian, Donald [stage/film actor] (b. St. John's, Newfoundland, Canada, 17 Feb 1875–22 Dec 1948 [73], Great Neck, LI NY). m. Virginia O'Brien. (Film debut: *The Voice in the Fog,* Lasky, 1915.) Joe Laurie, Jr., "Donald Brian (A Post-Mortem Salute)," *Variety,* 29 Dec 1948 (b. 1877). AMD, p. 51. AS, p. 167. BHD1, p. 69. IFN, p. 37. Truitt, p. 38 (b. 1871). "Donald Brian Signed; Will Make His Screen Debut with the Jesse Lasky Photoplay Company," *NYDM,* 10 Mar 1915, 25:1 (after his stint in the play, *The Girl from Utah*). "Donald Brian with Lasky," *MPW,* 20 Mar 1915, 1784. "Donald Brian's Screen Debut," *NYDM,* 7 Jul 1915, 36:2. "Donald Brian in 'The Voice in the Fog,'" *MPW,* 24 Jul 1915, 661. "Donald Brian at Lasky Studio," *MPW,* 21 Aug 1915, 1334. "Famous Players to Star Donald Brian," *MPW,* 17 Jun 1916, 2042.

Briant, Roy [Paramount title writer/actor/scenarist] (b. 1888?–16 Dec 1927 [39], Los Angeles CA; heart attack). m. Nila Mack (*née* Nila MacLaughlin, d. 1953). "Roy Briant," *Variety,* 21 Dec 1927, p. 57. AS, p. 167 (d. 18 Dec). BHD, p. 114; BHD2, p. 32. FDY, p. 419. IFN, p. 37. SD.

Brice, Fanny (sister of Lew Brice) [stage/film/radio actress] (*née* Fania Borach, b. New York NY, 29 Oct 1891–29 May 1951 [59], Beverly Hills CA; cerebral hemorrhage). m. (1) Frank White, 1909–11; (2) Jules Wilford "Nicky" Arnstein, 5 Apr 1919, NJ, and 18 Jun 1919, Brooklyn NY-Sep 1927; (3) Billy Rose, 9 Feb 1929–1938 (d. 1966). (Film debut: *My Man.*) Herbert G. Goldman, *Fanny Brice: The Original Funny Girl* (Oxford University Press, 1992). "Fanny Brice Stricken; The Baby Snooks of Radio Fame Suffers Brain Hemorrhage," *NYT,* 25 May 1951, 29:4; "Fanny Brice in Coma; Comedienne in Oxygen Tent at Cedars of Lebanon Hospital," 26 May 1951, 19:6; "Fanny Brice Still in Oxygen Tent," 27 May 1951, 58:4; "Fanny Brice Dies at the Age of 59; Comedienne, Famed in Role of Baby Snooks, First Scored with Song 'My Man'; "'Discovered' by Ziegfeld; She Got $75 a Week to Play in 'Follies' [from 1916]—Also Starred on Radio and in Movies," 30 May 1951, 21:1; "Fanny Brice's Will [29 Jul 1949] Filed; 2 Children and 3 Grandchildren Get Most of 2 Million Estate," 6 Jul 1951, 14:7. "Fanny Brice Dies on Coast at 59," *Variety,* 30 May 1951, p. 63. AMD, p. 51. AS, p. 167 (b. Delancey NY). BHD1, p. 70. Beatrice Wilson, "Fannie and Her English Rival [Beatrice Lillie]," *Classic,* Jun 1924, 34–35. "Films Get Fanny Brice," *MPW,* 11 Jun 1927, 400.

Brice, Lew (brother of Fanny Brice) [actor] (b. New York NY, 1894?–16 Jun 1966 [72], Los Angeles CA; heart attack). "Lew Brice," *Variety,* 22 Jun 1966. AS, p. 167. BHD1, p. 70. AMD, p. 51. "Lew Brice in Pictures," *MPW,* 12 Jun 1926, 540.

Brice, Marvelle Monte [actor/director/producer/scenarist/composer] (b. New York NY, 12 Jul 1891–8 Nov 1962 [71], London, England; following heart attack). "Monte Brice, Writer for Bob Hope, Dead," *NYT,* 9 Nov 1962, 35:1. "Monte Brice," *Variety,* 14 Nov 1962, p. 71 (wrote *Daughter of Rose O'Grady;* began in films in 1912 with Pearl White). AMD, p. 51. AS, p. 167. BHD2, p. 32. FDY, p. 419. IFN, p. 37. "Author Advanced to Director," *MPW,* 6 Nov 1926, 29.

Brice, Rosetta [stage/film actress] (aka Betty Brice, b. Washington DC [or Sunbury PA], 1890?–15 Feb 1935 [44?], Van Nuys CA). m. John La Gorce—div. (Lubin.) "Betty Brice," *Variety,* 6 Mar 1935 (Mrs. Betty Pratt). AMD, p. 51. BHD, p. 114 (b. Sunbury PA, 1892). IFN, p. 37. Truitt, p. 38. "Rosetta Brice," *MPW,* 27 Feb 1915, 1302. "Briefs of Biography; Rosetta Would See Herself," *NYDM,* 11 Aug 1915, 24:2 (one of the reasons she became a photoplayer is because she wanted to see herself act). "Near Death in Aeroplane," *NYDM,* 23 Oct 1915, 27:2 (filming *The Rights of Man; or, War's Red Blotch* at Mineola, LI NY, she flew in a plane piloted by George Grey 50 feet above ground when a puff of wind tilted the biplane and caused it to plunge headlong to earth. "The machine was badly damaged, but despite a severe scalding received by Mr. Grey and Miss Brice being rendered almost hysterical from shock, she insisted upon another flight being made in the afternoon."). "Rosetta Brice," *MPW,* 27 Nov 1915, 1646. "Film Actress Held in $800 Bail; Rosetta Brice of Lubin Forces Accused of the Larceny of Two Diamond Rings; Considers Charge [by Walter Lewis] a Joke," *The [NY] Morning Telegraph,* 11 Dec 1915, 10:2 ("Miss Brice's arrival in the courtroom created a sensation, as she drew up outside the building in a high-powered automobile. She was clad in a coat of tiger skin...the gruelling [sic] fire of questions to which she was subjected by the Congressman [J.R.K. Scott of Philadelphia] did not even bring a scowl of resentment to her pink and white face. She even smiled at a number of other motion picture actors and actresses in the courtroom." She made bail and "left the courtroom with an air that indicated she considered the proceedings to be a lark."). "Rosetta Brice [photo and quip]," *Photoplay Magazine,* April 1916, [p. 21].

Brick, Alfred D. [cameraman]. No data found. AMD, p. 51. "Fox Cameraman Slightly Hurt When Gasbag of Blimp Bursts," *MPW,* 22 May 1920, 1068.

Bricker, Betty [actress] (*née?,* b. 1890?–15 Feb 1954 [64], Los Angeles CA). m. Clarence Bricker. "Betty Bricker," *Variety,* 24 Feb 1954 ("...bit player in films for more than 40 years."). AS, p. 167. BHD1, p. 70 (b. 1889). IFN, p. 37.

Bricker, Clarence [assistant director/production manager]. No data found. m. Betty (d. 1954).

Brickert, Carlton [actor] (b. Martinsville IN, 14 May 1890–23 Dec 1943 [52], New York NY). (Metro.) "Carlton Brickert," *Variety,* 29 Dec 1943, p. 39. BHD, p. 114. IFN, p. 37. Truitt, p. 38. "Editor's Letter Box," *NYDM,* 19 Feb 1916, p. 6 (b. Indianapolis IN, 1886).

Brickley, Charles E. [actor] (b. 1891–28 Dec 1949 [58?], New York NY). AS, p. 167. BHD, p. 114.

Bridenbecker, Milton [2nd cameraman] (b. 1900?–17 Aug 1942 [42], Los Angeles CA; following operation). (Columbia.) "Milton Bridenbecker," *Variety,* 26 Aug 1942. FDY, p. 455.

Brierley, Thomas A. [actor/technical director] (b. 1880?–23 Jul 1928 [48], Los Angeles CA; following appendicitis operation). (Christie.) "Thomas Brierly," *Variety,* 1 Aug 1928, p. 50. AMD, p. 51. AS, p. 168. BHD2, p. 32. George Blaisdell, "New York Motion Picture Company," *MPW,* 10 Jul 1915, 233.

Briggs, Clare A. [cartoonist/scenarist] (b. Reedsburg WI, 5 Aug 1875–3 Jan 1930 [54], New York NY; complications of pneumonia). "Briggs Unafraid," *Variety,* 24 Jan 1919, p. 43 ("Clare Briggs, the cartoonist whose pictures 'make' the front pages of the Tribune every morning, has accepted an offer from an independent producer to go to L.A. to write one-reel comedies of his various kid characters..."). AMD, p. 51. "Work of Cartoonist Briggs to Be Put on the Screen," *MPW,* 8 Mar 1919, 1346. "Clare A. Briggs Heavily Insured," *MPW,* 5 Jul 1919, 45. "Briggs Supervises His Comedies," *MPW,* 2 Aug 1919, 672.

Briggs, Hal [actor/director] (b. Rockville Center NY, 1881–28 Apr 1925 [44?], Rockville Center NY). AS, p. 168. BHD, p. 114; BHD2, p. 32.

Briggs, Matt[ias] [Broadway/film character actor] (b. 18 Nov 1883–10 Jun 1962 [78], Seattle WA). "Matt Briggs," *Variety,* 20 Jun 1962, p. 71. AS, p. 168. IFN, p. 37.

Briggs, Oscar [actor] (b. WI, 1876?–17 Jan 1928 [51], Los Angeles CA; cerebral hemorrhage). "Oscar Briggs," *Variety,* 25 Jan 1928, p. 65. AS, p. 168. BHD, p. 114. IFN, p. 37.

Bright, Mildred [actress] (b. New York NY, 30 Apr 1892 [Birth Certificate Index No. 17452]–27 Sep 1967 [75], Woodland Hills CA). m. Robert W. Frazer, ca. 1913 (d. 1944). AMD, p. 51. AS, p. 168. BHD, p. 114. "Miss Millie Bright, Eclair," *MPW,* 30 Nov 1912, 886. Billy H. Doyle, "Lost Players," *CI,* 168 (Jun 1989), 26.

Brighton, Albert [stock/film actor] (b. 1876?–12 Jul 1911 [35], Brady's pond, Grassmere, Staten Island NY; drowned in a pond while filming). (Edison; Nestor; Henry Belmar M.P. Co.) "Albert Brighton," *Variety,* 22 Jul 1911, p. 28. AMD, p. 51. AS, p. 168. BHD, p. 114. "Moving Picture Actor Drowns," *MPW,* 22 Jul 1911, 112 (d. 11 Jul).

Brignon, Guy [scenarist]. No data found. FDY, p. 419.

Brignone, Guido (father of actress Lilla Brignone [1913–1984]; uncle of Mercedes Brignone) [director/ producer/scenarist] (b. Milan, Italy, 6 Dec 1887–6 Mar 1959 [71], Rome, Italy; during the shooting of his last film). m. Dolores Visconti (Lola Visconti-Brignone; d. 1924). AS, p. 168 (b. 1886; d. 6 May). BHD2, p. 33. JS, p. 61 (in Italian silents from 1916).

Brignone, Mercedes (daughter of actor Giuseppe Brignone; niece of Guido Brignone) [actress] (b. Madrid, Spain, 18 May 1885). m. Umberto Palmarini (d. 1934). AS, p. 168 (b. 1883). JS, p. 62 (in Italian silents from 1916).

Brilant, Arthur M. [publicist/scenarist]. No data found. AMD, p. 51. "Brilant Joins Universal Staff," *MPW,* 19 Dec 1914, 1657. "Brilant Now Scenario Editor," *MPW,* 31 Mar 1917, 2078. "Brilant Sells 'The Alibi' to Brady," *MPW,* 29 Sep 1917, 1973.

Brill, Patti [actress] (*née* Patricia Brilhante, b. San Francisco CA, 8 Mar 1923–18 Jan 1963 [39], No. Hollywood CA). AS, p. 168 (Patti Brill; d. 16 Jan, LA CA). BHD1, pp. 70; 615 (Patsy Paige).

Brimblecom, Stedman Buttrick [scenarist/composer] (b. 1871–26 Mar 1952 [81?], San Jose CA). AS, p. 169. BHD2, p. 33.

Brinckman, Elsie [actress] (b. 1893–22 Apr 1950 [57?], Los Angeles CA). BHD, p. 114.

Brink, Elga [actress] (b. Berlin, Germany, 1 Feb 1895-Dec 1986 [91]). AS, p. 169 (b. Weid-Mannslut, Germany, 2 Apr 1906). BHD1, p. 70.

Brinkley, Nell [artist] (b. 1888?–21 Oct 1944 [56], New Rochelle NY). m. Bruce MacRae, Jr. (son of actor Bruce MacRae). "Nell Brinkley, 56, Artist, Succumbs; Creator of Widely Syndicated Boy-and-Girl Drawings Leader in Her Field," *NYT,* 22 Oct 1944, 47:3. "Nell Brinkley," *Variety,* 25 Oct 1944 (created "The Brinkley Girl"). AS, p. 169.

Brinkman, Dolores [actress]. No data found. (MGM.) "Come Right In, Dolores," *MPC,* Jun 1928, 50.

Brinley, Charles E. [actor] (b. Yuma AZ, 15 Nov 1880–17 Feb 1946 [65], Los Angeles CA). (Universal.) AS, p. 169. BHD1, p. 70. IFN, p. 37.

Brisbane, Arthur [writer] (b. Buffalo NY, 12 Dec 1864–25 Dec 1936 [72], New York NY). m. Phoebe Cary. "Arthur Brisbane Dead," *Variety,* 30 Dec 1936. AS, p. 169. BHD, p. 115. *Century Cyclopedia of Names,* p. 652. WWWA.

Briscoe, Lottie [stage/film actress] (b. St. Louis MO, 19 Apr 1870?–21 Mar 1950 [79?], New

York NY). m. Harry McRae Webster—div. in Chicago; Harry Mountford (d. 1950). (Essanay, 1910; Majestic; Imp; Lubin.) "Lottie Briscoe Dies at 79; Former Star of Stage Played in Early Silent Films," *NYT,* 22 Mar 1950, 27:3. "Lottie Briscoe," *Variety,* 29 Mar 1950, p. 75 (age 69). AMD, p. 51. AS, p. 169 (1 Oct 1880; d. 19 Apr). BHD, p. 115. IFN, p. 37 (age 69; d. 19 Mar). SD. Truitt, p. 39 (b. 1881; d. 19 Mar). "Lottie Briscoe," *MPW,* 7 Sep 1912, 962. "Motion Pictures Ridiculed on Stage; Broadway Farce [*Kiss Me Quick* by Phillip Bartholomae] Seeks to Redeem the Waning Glory of the Stage by Affront—Miss Briscoe Serves Injunction," *MPW,* 6 Sep 1913, 1047. "Flickers," *MPW,* 22 Nov 1913, 871. "Lottie Briscoe a Girl of To-Day," *MPW,* 20 Dec 1913, 1419. "Artist Admires Lottie Briscoe," *NYDM,* 28 Jan 1914, 40:3 (Albert Shore of NY saw Briscoe in *The Parasite* [Lubin] and asked her to sit for him). "Lottie Briscoe, a Magnet for Artist," *MPW,* 14 Feb 1914, 825. "Lottie Briscoe: Leading Lady with the Lubin Company," *MPS,* 20 Feb 1914, 28. Mabel Condon, "Sans Grease Paint and Wig," *Motography,* 11 Jul 1914, 63–64. "Lottie Briscoe Leaves Lubin," *NYDM,* 19 May 1915, 25:1 (left on Saturday, 15 May, after 3 1/2 years with Lubin). "Lottie Briscoe Leaves Lubin," *MPW,* 5 Jun 1915, 1620. Sue Roberts, "Where Have They Gone?," *Motion Picture Magazine,* Feb 1918, 134 (Once part of a famous team with Arthur Johnson, "her cinematic shade flittered away into ethereal nothingness and no one knew the why nor wherefore of her disappearance." Of a sudden, Briscoe sent Roberts a photograph of herself and met her for an interview. She had had a "severe operation," but expected to be before the cameras soon.). "Lottie Briscoe Returns to Screen; Long Time Lubin Favorite Will Be Seen in Metro's 'The House of Mirth,'" *MPW,* 30 Mar 1918, 1820 (returned after operation). Billy H. Doyle, "Lost Players," *CI,* 151 (Jan 1988), C4-C5 (b. 1880).

Briskin, Irving (brother of Sam Briskin) [Columbia mogul] (b. New York NY, 28 Feb 1903–29 May 1981 [78], Los Angeles CA). (Banner Productions, 1923.) "Irving Briskin," *Variety,* 3 Jun 1981 (Banner Productions, 1923–25; Sterling Pictures, 1925–30). "Irving Briskin," *CI,* 76 (Jul 1981), 50. AS, p. 169. BHD2, p. 33.

Briskin, Samuel J[acob] (brother of Irving Briskin) [producer/executive] [Columbia V-P/director] (b. Russia, 8 Feb 1897–14 Nov 1968 [71], Los Angeles CA; following heart attack on 6 Nov). m. Sara Myers, 1918. (Columbia, 1920; RKO; Paramount.) "Samuel Briskin, Movie Aide, Dead; Columbia Executive Served Long as Production Chief," *NYT,* 15 Nov 1968, 47:1. "Samuel J. Briskin," *Variety,* 20 Nov 1968, p. 95 (motion picture accountant with C.B.C. Film Sales Corp. in 1920). AS, p. 169 (b. NYC, 9 Feb 1896). BHD2, p. 33 (b. NY NY). SD.

Brisson, Carl, "The Older Girls' Sinatra" (father of Frederick Brisson) [middleweight boxing champion, 1915; singer/stage and film actor] (*né* Carl Frederick Brisson Pederson, b. Copenhagen, Denmark, 24 Dec 1895–25 Sep 1958 [62], Copenhagen, Denmark; jaundice and cancer of the liver). m. Cleo Willard. (Stage debut, 1916, Denmark; Broadway debut, *Forbidden Melody,* Nov 1936; in *The Manxman,* 1929; Paramount.) "Carl Brisson, 62, Stage Star, Dead; Romantic Lead in Musicals Was Noted as Prince in 'The Merry Widow,'" *NYT,* 26 Sep 1958, 27:3 (his stage name of Brisson became his legal name). "Carl Brisson Buried; Requiem Mass Offered in Copenhagen for Singer," *NYT,* 30 Sep 1958, 31:5 (became a Roman Catholic the day before he died). "Carl Brisson," *Variety,* 1 Oct 1958, p. 70 (age 64). AS, p. 169. BHD1, p. 71 (b. 1893). Abel Green, "Remembrances of Carl Brisson," *Variety,* 8 Oct 1958.

Bristol, Cameron H. [publicist]. No data found. AMD, p. 51. "Cameron H. Bristol to Handle Advertising for Triangle," *MPW,* 7 Apr 1917, 105.

Bristol, Edith [title writer/scenarist] (*née* Edith McPhee, b. CA, 1886?–16 Feb 1946 [59], Oakland CA). "Mrs. Edith Bristol; Women's Editor of Call-Bulletin in San Francisco Dies at 59," *NYT,* 17 Feb 1946, 42:3 ("joined *The Call-Bulletin* in 1926 as a drama editor, leaving to write scenarios of a Hollywood studio"). FDY, p. 441.

Britt, Albert [film editor]. No data found. AMD, p. 51. "Outing Editor Discusses Value of Chester Pictures," *MPW,* 31 Aug 1918, 1288.

Britton, Edna [actress] (b. 28 Jun 1887–5 Aug 1960 [73], Mansfield MA). AS, p. 170. BHD, p. 115. IFN, p. 37. Truitt 1983.

Britton, Hutin [actor] (b. Reading, Berkshire, England, 24 Apr 1876–3 Sep 1965 [89], England). BHD, p. 115.

Britton, Leon [actor] (d. 8 Jan 1966, Tokyo, Japan). "Leon Britton," *Variety,* 19 Jan 1966 (foreign sales work for 45 years).

Brizzi, Anchise [cinematographer] (b. Poppi, Italy, 5 Oct 1887–1964 [77?], Rome, Italy). AS, p. 170. FDY, p. 455. JS, p. 62 (in Italian silents from 1914).

Broad, Kid [actor] (*né* William M. Thomas, b. Cornwall, England, 3 Mar 1878–11 Jun 1947 [69], New York NY). AS, p. 170. BHD, p. 115. Truitt 1983.

Broadhurst, George H[owells] [playwright/scenarist] (b. Walsall, Staffordshire, England, 3 Jun 1866–31 Jan 1952 [85], Santa Barbara CA). m. Lillian Trimble Bradley. "George H. Broadhurst," *Variety,* 6 Feb 1952, p. 63. AMD, p. 51. AS, p. 170. BHD2, p. 33. NNAT. SD, p. 165. "Oliver Morosco Signs Broadhurst," *MPW,* 22 Jan 1916, 575. "Famous Players Acquires Rights to All George Broadhurst's Plays," *MPW,* 20 Sep 1919, 1833.

Broadley, Edward [actor] (b. 1875?–24 Nov 1947 [72], New York NY). AS, p. 170. BHD1, p. 71. IFN, p. 37.

Broadwell, Robert B. [director]. No data found. m. Gladys Brockwell (d. 1929). AMD, p. 52. "Friday the 13th," *MPW,* 28 Aug 1920, 1186.

Brock, Baby Dorothy Marion [child actress] (b. Phoenix AZ?, 1920). (Film debut: *The Lullaby,* FBO.) AMD, p. 52. "A Three-Year-Old Doubles for Star," *MPW,* 3 Nov 1923, 98:1 ("Little Dorothy's mimetic abilities and her intelligent interpretation of Director Chester Bennett's instructions indicate a brilliant future for her.").

Brock, Henry J. [publicist/executive] (b. Buffalo NY?, 1869?–7 Sep 1917 [46], near Kingston NY; by the overturning of the car in which he was riding). "Henry J. Brock Killed," *Variety,* 14 Sep 1917, 27:4 (President of Kinemacolor Co. up to ca. 1913). Louis Reeves Harrison, "Sauntering with Kinemacolor," *MPW,* 15 Feb 1913, 661–62. "Obituary," *MPW,* 22 Sep 1917, 1833.

Brock, Tony [actor] (d. 26 Nov 1924, New York NY; auto accident during filming). AS, p. 170. BHD, p. 115.

Brockman, James [vaudevillian/actor/scenarist/composer] (b. NY, 8 Dec 1886–22 May 1967 [80], Santa Monica CA). "James Brockman, Composer-Lyricist of Hit Songs, Dies," *NYT,* 24 May 1967, 47:1 (wrote *Feather Your Nest,* 1920; *Golden Gate,* 1928; "Later in life Mr. Brockman went to Hollywood where he became a staff writer for motion-picture studios."). "James Brockman," *Variety,* 31 May 1967, p. 63 (wrote *I'm Forever Blowing Bubbles; I Faw Down and Go Boom; Down Among the Sheltering Palms;* and *Let's Grow Old Together.* ASCAP since 1921). ASCAP 66, p. 29. AS, p. 170. BHD2, p. 33 (b. 1878).

Brockwell, Gladys [stage/film actress] (*née* Gladys Lindeman, b. Brooklyn NY, 26 Sep 1894–2 Jul 1929 [34], Los Angeles CA; injuries sustained in auto accident). m. Robert B. Broadwell; Harry Edwards, 1918, Seattle WA. (Lubin; NYMP; Reliance; Ince; Fine Arts; Universal; Fox.) "Gladys Brockwell," *Variety,* 10 Jul 1929, p. 37. AMD, p. 52. AS, p. 171. BHD1, p. 71. FSS, p. 45. IFN, p. 37. MSBB, p. 1032. Truitt, p. 39. "'In Reply to Yours—,'" *Photoplay Magazine,* Jun 1917, 72–73. "Brockwell Divorce Suit Withdrawn," *Variety,* 21 Dec 1917, p. 50 (Brockwell withdrew the suit because her husband was then in the military). Dorothy Donnell, "Gladys Brockwell Does 'His' Bit," *Motion Picture Magazine,* Feb 1918, 36–41 (did research on women doing men's jobs during "the current crisis," with many photos of her in "male" professions. "When women begin to realize that they can perform almost any kind of manual labor, and in many instances do it more skillfully than the men, we will have made giant strides toward our political enfranchisement, as well as the right to expect higher wages. But first of all we will be one of the biggest factors in winning the war."). "Gladys Brockwell with Fox Three Years," *MPW,* 10 Aug 1918, 822–23. "Gladys Brockwell a Bride," *MPW,* 17 Aug 1918, 969. "Victory Pictures Feature Brockwell, Mix and Walsh," *MPW,* 19 Jul 1919, 355. "Gladys Brockwell," *MPW,* 19 Jul 1919, 359. "Gladys Brockwell Plays in Two Films During the Same Day," *MPW,* 17 Apr 1920, 388. Truman B. Handy, "Iconoclast," *MPC,* Sep 1922, 36–37, 90. George Katchmer, "Gladys Brockwell," *CI,* 148 (Oct 1987), 9, 11, 41. George Katchmer, "Remembering the Great Silents," *CI,* 250 (Apr 1996), 44–45.

Broderick, Helen (mother of Broderick Crawford, 1911–1986) [stage/film actress/scenarist] (b. Philadelphia PA, 11 Aug 1891–25 Sep 1959 [68], Beverly Hills CA). m. Lester Crawford. "Helen Broderick, Actress, 68, Dies; Comedienne Was the Mother of Broderick Crawford—Started in Vaudeville," *NYT,* 27 Sep 1959, 86:1; "Helen Broderick Rites Held [27 Sep]," *NYT,* 28 Sep 1959, 31:5 (funeral in Gloversville NY). "Helen Broderick," *Variety,* 30 Sep 1959, p. 63. AS, p. 171. BHD1, p. 71. FDY, p. 419. IFN, p. 38. Truitt, p. 39.

Broderick, Lillian [actress] (b. New York NY, 1895–28 Mar 1946 [50?], Long Island NY). "Lillian Broderick," *Variety,* 3 Apr 1946, p. 62. BHD, p. 115.

Broderick, Robert [actor]. No data found. AMD, p. 52. "Robert Broderick," *MPW,* 19 Dec 1914, 1663.

Brodie, Buster [actor] (b. Pittsburgh PA, 11 Oct 1885–9 Apr 1948 [62], Los Angeles CA; heart attack). "Buster Brodie," *Variety,* 14 Apr 1948, p. 55. AS, p. 171. BHD, p. 115. IFN, p. 38. Truitt, p. 39.

Brodine, Norbert F. [cinematographer] (b. Joseph MO, 16 Dec 1896–28 Feb 1970 [73], Los Angeles CA). m. Catherine Ferguson (sister of Helen Ferguson), Los Angeles CA, 1924. (TC-F.) AMD, p. 52. AS, p. 171. BHD2, p. 33. FDY, p. 455 (Brodin). Katz, pp. 166–67. "Norbert Brodin," *MPW,* 29 Jan 1927, 341. Dates supplied by ASC.

Brody, Anna G. [actress] (*née* Ann Brody Goldstein, b. Poland, 29 Aug 1884–16 Jul 1944 [59], New York NY). (Vitagraph.) "Ann Brody," *Variety,* 19 Jul 1944 (age 60). AMD, p. 52. AS, p. 171. BHD1, p. 72. IFN, p. 38. Truitt, p. 39. "Ann Brody Signed," *MPW,* 15 Sep 1923, 274.

Brody, Estelle [actress in British silents] (b. New York NY, 15 Aug 1900–3 Jun 1995 [94], La Vallette, Malta). "Estelle Brody; Silent-Film Actress, 90," *NYT,* 12 Jun 1995, B10:6 (b. in either NY or Montreal; age 90). "Deaths Last Week; Estelle Brody," *Chicago Tribune,* 18 Jun 1995, II, 6:3 (b. NY). *The Independent,* 6 Jun 1995. AS, p. 171 (b. Montreal, Canada, 5 Aug 1904). BHD1, p. 72. Ephraim Katz, *The International Film Encyclopedia,* p. 167.

Broedt, Edna Louise [stage (Frawley and Louise)/film actress (may have been billed under another name in films)]. No data found. m. William Frawley, 1914—separated 1921; div. 1927 (d. 1966). (Film debut: *Lord Loveland Discovers America,* American Film Manufacturing Co., 1916.) Michael Bernal, "William Frawley: Before and After Lucy," *CI,* 303 (Sep 2000), pp. 6–14, 67–69.

Broening, H[enry] Lyman [cameraman] (b. Baltimore MD, 30 Jun 1882-Jun 1983 [100], San Berbardino Co. CA). m. actress Amelia W. Daly, 23 Nov 1917, Greenwich CT. (FP-L.) "Marriages," *Variety,* 30 Nov 1917, p. 9. AMD, p. 52. BHD2, p. 33. FDY, p. 455. "Broening with Famous Players," *MPW,* 16 Aug 1913, 727. "Lyman H. Broening Marries Miss Daley," *MPW,* 8 Dec 1917, 1465. "Broening Leaves Famous Players," *MPW,* 16 Nov 1918, 747. "H. Lyman Broening to Photograph Neilan and Kaufman Subjects," *MPW,* 29 May 1920, 1219.

Brokaw, Charles [stage and film actor] (b. Columbus OH, 23 Sep 1898–23 Oct 1975 [77], New York NY). "Charles Brokaw Dies at 77; Acted on Stage and in Films," *NYT,* 24 Oct 1975, 40:4. "Charles Brokaw," *Variety,* 29 Oct 1975, p. 78. AS, p. 171. BHD1, p. 72. IFN, p. 38.

Bromhead, A[lfred] **C.** [executive] (b. 1877?–4 Mar 1963 [86], London, England; heart attack). "British Film Pioneer Dies," *NYT,* 7 Mar 1963, 7:4. "A.C. Bromhead," *Variety,* 13 Mar 1963, p. 70 (exhibited the Chronophone in 1909 with Gaumont; formed Gaumont-British Picture Corporation in 1927; "He was one of the pioneers of the British film..."). AMD, p. 52. AS, p. 171. BHD2, p. 33. "A.C. Bromhead," *MPW,* 11 Apr 1908, 318. "An Interview with A.C. Bromhead," *MPW,* 7 Feb 1914, 656.

Bromley-Davenport, Arthur [actor] (b. Baginton, England, 29 Oct 1867–15 Dec 1946 [79]). BHD1, p. 72.

Broneau, Helen [actress]. No data found. AMD, p. 52. "Helen Broneau a New Universal Beauty," *MPW,* 29 Nov 1919, 544.

Bronis, James [scenarist]. No data found. FDY, p. 419.

Bronson, Betty [actress] (*née* Elizabeth Ada Bronson, b. Trenton NJ, 17 Nov 1906–19 Oct 1971 [64], Pasadena CA; pneumonia). m. Ludwig Lauerhass. (Film debut: *Anna Ascends;* FP-L.) "Betty Bronson, '24 Peter Pan in Silent Film, Is Dead at 64; Actress Chosen by Barrie Became Star at 17—Won Over Stiff Competition," *NYT,* 22 Oct 1971, 42:1. "Betty Bronson," *Variety,* 27 Oct 1971, p. 79 (d. 21 Oct). AMD, p. 52. AS, p. 172. BHD1, p. 72. FFF, p. 107. FSS, p. 46. IFN, p. 38. MH, p. 99. SD. Truitt, p. 39. "Betty Bronson," *MPW,* 30 Aug 1924, 718. Helen Carlisle, "The Story of Betty Bronson; Chosen by Sir James Barrie as the Screen's Peter Pan," *MW,* 20 Sep 1924, 9, 27. Harry Carr, "'Out of the Nowhere,'" *MPC,* Nov 1924, 51. "Betty Bronson," *MPW,* 3 Jan 1925, 32. "Betty Bronson Welcomed by New Jersey Governor," *MPW,* 24 Jan 1925, 389. Charles Wyckoff, "Will Peter Pan Grow Up?," *MPC,* Dec 1925, 53, 83. "Betty Bronson to Warner Bros.," *MPW,* 24 Sep 1927, 232.

Bronston, Douglas [scenarist] (b. Richmond KY, 1887–9 Jul 1951 [64?], Santa Monica CA). AMD, p. 52. AS, p. 172 (Douglas Bronson). BHD2, p. 34. FDY, p. 419. "Pathé Scenario Man Writes a Song," *MPW,* 2 Oct 1915, 61. "Bronston Contracts to Write Scenarios for Famous Players," *MPW,* 3 Jul 1920, 109.

Brook, Clive [stage/film actor] (*né* Clifford Hardman Brook, b. London, England, 1 Jun 1887–17 Nov 1974 [87], London, England). m. Mildred Evelyn, 25 Sep 1921, London. (Ince.) Lawrence Van Gelder, "Clive Brook, 87, Suave Briton of Stage and Screen, Is Dead; Epitome of Stiff Upper Lip, He Chose Acting After an Unflappable Army Stint," *NYT,* 19 Nov 1974, 46:3. "Clive Brook," *Variety,* 20 Nov 1974, p. 63. AMD, p. 52. AS, p. 172. BHD1, p. 72; BHD2, p. 34. FSS, p. 47. IFN, p. 38. Waldman, p. 38. Norman Bruce, "A Gentleman from Piccadilly; Clive Brook Came to Hollywood via Flanders," *MPC,* Aug 1925, 32–33, 78–79. "Paramount Signs Brook to Contract," *MPW,* 21 Aug 1926, 466. "Clive Brook Signs New Paramount Contract," *MPW,* 30 Jul 1927, 333. Helen Bailey, "Everything's Quite Top Hole Y'-Know Except for the Bally Sex Appeal," *MPC,* Dec 1927, 33, 80.

Brook, Marion [actress] (b. Dallas TX, 1874–1914 [40?]). BHD1, p. 605.

Brooke, Claude [screen/stage actor] (b. Liverpool, Lancashire, England, 1853?–14 Dec 1933 [80], Leonia NJ). m. Cora Leslie. "Claude Brooke," *Variety,* 19 Dec 1933, p. 62. AS, p. 172. BHD, p. 115. IFN, p. 38. SD. Truitt, p. 39.

Brooke, E.H. [actor] (b. 1876–18 Jan 1929 [52?]). BHD, p. 115.

Brooke, Mrs. E.H. [actress] (b. 1835–19 Dec 1915 [80?], London, England). BHD, p. 115.

Brooke, Myra [actress] (*née?,* b. 1865–9 Feb 1944 [79], Amityville NY). "Mrs. Myra Brooke," *Variety,* 16 Feb 1944. AS, p. 172. BHD, p. 115. IFN, p. 38. Truitt, p. 40.

Brooke, Tyler [actor] (*né* Victor Huge de Biere, b. New York NY, 6 Jun 1885–2 Mar 1943 [57], Los Angeles CA; suicide by carbon monoxide poisoning in his car). "Tyler Brooke," *Variety,* 10 Mar 1943, p. 46 (age 52). AMD, p. 52. AS, p. 172 (d. No. Hollywood CA). BHD1, p. 72 (b. 1886). IFN, p. 38. Truitt, p. 40. "New Players Starting Work," *MPW,* 4 Jul 1925, 78. *Biographical Dictionary of Dance,* pp. 127–28.

Brooke, Van Dyke [actor/director] (*né* Stewart McKerrow, b. Detroit MI, 22 Jun 1859–17 Sep 1921 [62], Saratoga Springs NY; respiratory ailment). "Van Dyke Brooke Dead," *Variety,* 23 Sep 1921. (Last film: *The Son of Wallingford.*) AMD, p. 52. AS, p. 172. BHD, p. 115; BHD2, p. 34. IFN, p. 38. Robert Grau, "The Film Studio; A Gold Laden Haven for the Patriarchs of the Stage," *NYDM,* 8 Sep 1915, 3:1 ("Neither [he nor William Humphries] would leave his present environment and neither is expected to do so as long as life lasts."). "Two Famous Directors Join Thanhouser," *MPW,* 31 Mar 1917, 2084. "Obituary," *MPW,* 1 Oct 1921, 524.

Brooker, Tom [actor] (b. NY, 25 Jul 1886–29 Jan 1929 [42], New York NY). AS, p. 172. BHD, p. 115. IFN, p. 38.

Brooks, Alan [actor] (*né* Irving Hayward, b. Boston MA, 1888?–13 Sep 1936 [48], Saranac Lake NY). "Irving Hayward," *Variety,* 7 Oct 1936. AS, p. 172. BHD1, p. 72 (d. 28 Sep). Truitt, p. 40.

Brooks, Edgar O. [publicity]. No data found. AMD, p. 52. "Brooks Exploitation Manager for Pathé," *MPW,* 31 Aug 1918, 1236.

Brooks, Hank [actor] (d. 3 Dec 1925, Los Angeles CA). "Hank Brooks," *Variety,* 9 Dec 1925. AS, p. 173. BHD, p. 115. IFN, p. 38. Truitt, p. 40.

Brooks, Louise [dancer/stage/film actress/writer] (*née* Mary Louise Brooks, b. Cherryvale KS, 14 Nov 1906–8 Aug 1985 [78], Rochester NY; heart attack). m. (1) A. Edward Sutherland, New York NY, 1926–28 (d. 1973); (2) Dearing Davis. Barry Paris, *Louise Brooks* (NY: Alfred A. Knopf, 1989). (Film debut: *The Street of Forgotten Men,* FP-L, 1925.) Herbert Mitgang, "Louise Brooks, Proud Star of Silent Screen, Dead at 78," *NYT,* 10 Aug 1985, A29:4. Todd McCarthy, "Silents Legend Louise Brooks Succumbs After 30-Year Exile," *Variety,* 14 Aug 1985. AMD, p. 52. AS, p. 173. BHD1, p. 73. FSS, p. 48. SD. "In Lead Feminine Role," *MPW,* 30 Jan 1926, 443. "Louise Brooks," *MPW,* 12 Jun 1926, 550. "The Girl on the Cover," *Paris and Hollywood,* Sep 1926, 78 (she appeared in the Ziegfeld Follies and *Louie the Fourteenth,* "but it was her legs that got Louise Brooks off to a flying start in the films." A small part in *The Street of Forgotten Men,* Paramount, was followed by the lead in *The American Venus* and other films, which explains the "rocket-like rise of Louise Brooks from the extra-girl ranks to the featured player status during the space of considerably less than a year."). June Lee, "Dan Cupid's Bulletin Board," *Paris and Hollywood,* Oct 1926, 31 (married Sutherland). Ollie Woods, "Three Skips and a Jump!," *Paris and Hollywood Screen Secrets Magazine,* May 1927, 57. Carol Johnston, "Brooksy; A Credit to Kansas," *MPC,* Sep 1927, 53, 86. "New Contract," *MPW,* 24 Sep 1927, 232. Carol Stafford, "Paragraphs Pertaining to Players and Pictures; Louise Brooks," *Cinema Arts,* Dec 1927, 26. "Flat Broke," *Arizona Daily Star* [Tucson], 14 Mar 1931 (Brooks declared voluntary bankruptcy in New York City). Wayne Schutz, "Louise Brooks; A Magical Presence; Footnotes to a Career," *CI,* 94 (Apr 1983), 68–69; II, 95 (May 1993), 39–40. John Roberts, "Louise Brooks," *CI,* 92 (Feb 1983), 35. Wayne Schutz, "Louise Brooks: A Magical Presence [update]," *CI,* 100 (Oct 1983), 62. Jerry Vermile, "Louise Brooks (Part I); Attitude and rebellion would play a key role in the course of her career," *FIR,* Nov/Dec 1995, 24–35; Part II, Jan/Feb 1996, 44–53; Part III, *FIR,* Mar/Apr 1996, 43–51 (includes filmography).

Brooks, Ted [actor]. No data found. (In *Straight Shooting,* 1917.)

Brooks, Walter H. [publicist]. No data found. AMD, p. 52. "Educational Has New Publicity Man," *MPW,* 1 Mar 1919, 1204.

Brophy, Edward S. [actor] (b. New York NY, 27 Feb 1895–27 May 1960 [65], Los Angeles CA). m. Ann. "Edward Brophy," *Variety,* 8 Jun 1960, p. 71 (d. 30 May). AS, p. 173. BHD1, p. 73. IFN, p. 38. SD. Truitt, p. 40.

Broske, Octavia [actress] (b. Philadelphis PA, 4 Jun 1886–19 Mar 1967 [80], Los Angeles CA). m. George C. Burke—div. 12 Apr 1913 (interlocutory decree; infelidity). AS, p. 173 (d. NYC). BHD, p. 115. IFN, p. 38. "Divorce for Octavia Broske," *NYT,* 13 Apr 1913, p. 7.

Brotherhood, William E. [actor] (b. England). (International Feature Films; Vitagraph; Essanay.) 1918 Studio Directory, p. 65.

Brotherton, Joseph [cinematographer]. No data found. FDY, p. 456.

Brott, Robert [actor] (b. 1881–15 Aug 1933 [52], Welfare Island NY). BHD, p. 115. IFN, p. 38.

Brough, Antonia [actress] (b. London, England, 1900–1937 [37?]). BHD1, p. 73.

Brough, Mary [stage/film actress] (b. London, England, 16 Apr 1863–30 Sep 1934 [71], London, England; heart disease). "Mary Brough," *Variety,* 16 Oct 1934, p. 60. AS, p. 174. BHD1, p. 73. IFN, p. 38.

Brough, Widmer [actor] (b. WA, 6 May 1914–15 Apr 1958 [43], Los Angeles CA). BHD1, p. 605.

Broughton, Cliff [actor/director/producer] (*né* Clifton Broughton, b. Walnut IA, 20 Jul 1898–18 Apr 1979 [80], Woodland Hills CA). (b. 1898). m. Lena. "Cliff Broughton," *Variety,* 25 Apr 1979 (Ince, 1923). AS, p. 175 (b. 1897). BHD2, p. 34 (b. 1897; d. 17 Apr).

Brower, Otto [actor/director] (b. Grand Rapids MI, 2 Dec 1895–25 Jan 1946 [55], Los Angeles CA; heart attack). "Otto Brower," *Variety,* 30 Jan 1946, p. 50. AS, p. 174 (b. 1890). BHD1, p. 73; BHD2, p. 34. IFN, p. 38. Truitt, p. 40.

Brower, Robert [actor] (b. Point Pleasant NJ, 14 Jul 1850–8 Dec 1934 [84], West Hollywood CA; heart attack). (Edison.) AMD, p. 52. AS, p. 174. BHD1, p. 73. IFN, p. 38. "Robert Brower," *MPW,* 27 Dec 1913, 1524. "Robert Brower," *MPW,* 21 Nov 1914, 1094. "Robert Brower Says Farewell," *MPW,* 23 Sep 1916, 1957.

Brower, Thomas L. [actor] (b. Birmingham AL, 20 Feb 1878–19 Jul 1937 [59], Los Angeles CA). AS, p. 174 (b. 1875). BHD1, p. 73. IFN, p. 38.

Brown, Anita [stage/film actress] (b. New Haven CT, 1894). (Metro; Pathé; Fox; World; Wharton.) AMD, p. 53. MSBB, p. 1032. "Anita Brown, 280 Comedy Pounds," *MPW,* 11 May 1918, 872.

Brown, Beth [bit actress/author/scenarist]. No data found. "Miss Brown Appointed," *MPW,* 5 Jun 1926, 478. Beth Brown, "Making Movies for Women," *MPW,* 26 Mar 1927, 342. "Beth Brown Draws Big Fan Mail on 'Ballyhoo,' [WPCH Radio]" *MPW,* 26 Nov 1927, 12. "M-G-M Buys Beth Brown's 'Ballyhoo' for N. Shearer," *MPW,* 31 Dec 1927, 8. Sydney Valentine, "The Baby Author," *Screenland,* Aug 1929, 111 ("[I] went to Hollywood and worked in movie comedies"; wrote *Ballyhoo* and *Applause*).

Brown, Betty *see* **Browne, Betty Beckett**

Brown, Chamberlain [actor/agent] (b. Hartford CT, 1 Apr 1888–11 Nov 1955 [67], New York NY). BHD, p. 116; BHD2, p. 34.

Brown, Charles D. [actor] (b. Council Bluffs IA, 1 Jul 1887–25 Nov 1948 [61], Los Angeles CA; heart attack). m. Nellie Tallman. (Vitagraph.) "Charles D. Brown," *Variety,* 1 Dec 1948, p. 55 (age 60). AS, p. 174. BHD1, p. 74. IFN, p. 38. SD. Truitt, p. 40. Lester Sweyd, "What They Are Doing Now," *Motion Picture Magazine,* Feb 1918, 12 (appearing as "William Carlton in Geo. M. Cohan's stage production of 'Captain Kidd, Jr.'").

Brown, Clarence L[eon] [director] (b. Clinton MA, 10 May 1890 [MVRB, Vol. 405, p. 340]–17 Aug 1987 [97], Santa Monica CA). m. (1) **Alice Joyce** (d. 1955); (2) Marian R. Spies. "Clarence Brown, A Director and Six-Time Oscar Nominee," *NYT,* 20 Aug 1987, B15:6. Todd McCarthy, "Stylish Director Clarence Brown, Garbo's Favorite, Is Dead at 97," *Variety,* 26 Aug 1987. AMD, p. 53. AS, p. 174. BHD2, p. 34. SD. "Brown to Direct," *MPW,* 6 Dec 1924, 558. Peggy Snow, "Wife Made Him Good Director, Says Brown," *Paris and Hollywood,* Oct 1926, 65. "Director Brown May Double His Salary," *MPW,* 26 Mar 1927, 271. Dorothy Manners, "Without Benefit of Blow-Ups; Clarence Brown Never Displays His Temper," *MPC,* Apr 1928, 26, 78. William K. Everson, "Clarence Brown; A Survey of His Work," *FIR,* Dec 1973, 577–89.

Brown, Eleanor [actress]. No data found. (Thanhouser.) "In the Picture Studios," *NYDM,* 4 Aug 1915, 27:2 (a member of the female baseball team at Thanhouser).

Brown, Everett [actor] (b. TX, 1 Jan 1902–14 Oct 1953 [51]). AS, p. 174. BHD1, p. 74. IFN, p. 39.

Brown, Frank [actor] (b. England, 1854?–8 Apr 1943 [89], Buenos Aires, Argentina). m. Rosita de la Plata (d. 1941). "Frank Brown," *Variety,* 28 Apr 1943, p. 54. AS, p. 174.

Brown, Fred G. [stock/film actor/writer/painter] (b. London, England, 1878–Aug 1944 [66?],Toronto, Canada). "Fred G. Brown," *Variety,* 20 Sep 1944, p. 54. BHD, p. 116.

Brown, George E. [publicist] (d. 18 Nov 1946, Glens Falls NY). "George E. Brown," *Variety,* 27 Nov 1946 (with advertising department of Paramount-Publix in New York).

Brown, Halbert W. [actor] (b. 1865?–24 Oct 1942 [77], New York NY). AS, p. 175. BHD1, p. 74. IFN, p. 39.

Brown, Harold P. [cameraman]. No data found. (*Screen Telegram,* Mutual.) AMD, p. 23. "Brown Named Chief of Camera Staff," *MPW,* 23 Feb 1918, 1096:2.

Brown, Harry [actor] (b. 1844?–30 Jul 1916 [72], Patchogue, LI NY). m. Marie Stanley. "Harry Brown," *Variety,* 4 Aug 1916, p. 17. AS, p. 175.

Brown, Harry [actor] (b. NY, 22 Sep 1891–8 Jan 1966 [74], New York NY). AMD, p. 53. AS, p. 175. IFN, p. 39. "Harry Brown in Western Role," *MPW,* 27 May 1916, 1521.

Brown, Harry Joe [director/producer] (b. Pittsburgh PA, 22 Sep 1890–28 Apr 1972 [81], Palm Springs CA; heart attack). m. (1) **Sally Eilers,** 1933 (d. 1978); (2) Dorothy Gray. "Harry Joe Brown," *Variety,* 3 May 1972, p. 255 (age 78). AS, p. 175 (b. 1893). BHD2, p. 34. IFN, p. 39. Katz, p. 172.

Brown, Hiram S. (father of Hiram S. Brown, Jr.) [executive] (b. MD, 1883–4 May 1950 [67?], Chestertown MD). BHD2, p. 34.

Brown, Jack N. [casting director]. No data found. AMD, p. 53. "Brown Engaged as Casting Director," *MPW,* 31 May 1919, 1316.

Brown, J[ames] **Edwin** (twin of **Sedley Brown**) [actor] (b. Boston MA, 29 Feb 1856). (Universal.) AS, p. 175. 1918 Studio Directory, p. 65.

Brown, James [cinematographer]. No data found. FDY, p. 456.

Brown, James S. [military man/actor] (b. 1861?–7 Mar 1938 [77], Whitehall NY). "James S. Brown," *NYT,* 9 Mar 1938, 23:2 (in St. Louis, 1904, he staged a reproduction of the Boer War at the World's Fair. "Later he took the company on tour, which ended at Coney Island."). AS, p. 174.

Brown, Joe E[vans] [actor] (b. Holgate OH, 22 Sep 1890–6 Jul 1973 [82], Brentwood CA; cancer). *Laughter Is a Wonderful Thing* (1959). m. Kathryn McGraw, 24 Dec 1915, NYC. (Film debut: *Crooks Can't Win,* 1927.) (FBO; WB.) "Joe E. Brown, Comedian of Movies and Stage, Dies," *NYT,* 7 Jul 1973, 24:1 (age 80); Peter Millones, "A Favorite of the Young" (b. 28 Jul). "Joe E. Brown, 82, Dies in Hollywood," *Variety,* 11 Jul 1973, p. 63. AS, p. 175 (b. 1892). BHD1, p. 74 (b. 28 Jul 1892). IFN, p. 39 (b. Pittsburgh PA). Katz, p. 173. Joe Collura, "Joe E. Brown; 'The Mouth That Roared,'" Part I, *CI,* 118 (Apr 1985), 34–35 (b. 28 Jul); Part II, May 1985, 28–29, 31; Part III (Jun 1985), 34–35.

Brown, John J. [cinema pioneer] (b. Scotland, 1873–28 Jul 1955 [82?], Dundee, Scotland). AS, p. 175.

Brown, John "Jack" S[pencer] [cinematographer] (b. 1892?–1 Jun 1949 [56], Los Angeles CA). (Edison, 1912; FBO; Darmour; Universal; Columbia; Monogram.) "John S. Brown," *Variety,* 174, 8 Jun 1949, 63:2. BHD2, p. 35. FDY, p. 456.

Brown, John W[ebster] [cinematographer]. No data found.

Brown, Johnny Mack [actor] (b. Dothan AL, 1 Sep 1904–14 Nov 1974 [70], Woodland Hills CA; heart attack). (MGM; UA; Mascot; Paramount.) m. Connie Foster. Mario DeMarco, *All American Cowboy.* "Johnny Mack Brown, 70, Dies; Cowboy Star and Football Hero," *NYT,* 15 Nov 1974, 34:1. "Johnny Mack Brown," *Variety,* 20 Nov 1974, p. 63. AS, p. 175. BHD1, p. 74. FSS, p. 49. IFN, p. 39. Carolyn Dawson, "Bonenalabahmah and Johnny Mack Brown Forward-Passed from Stock-Shots to Stardom," *MPC,* Aug 1928, 42, 70. John Cocchi, "The 2nd Feature; A History of the B Movies," *CI,* 146 (Aug 1987), 28, C19. Frank Dolven, "Johnny Mack Brown; All American On and Off the Screen," *CI,* 218 (Aug 1993), 38–39.

Brown, Karl [cinematographer/director/scenarist] (b. McKeesport PA, 1897–25 Mar 1990 [93], Woodland Hills CA). m. **Edna Mae Cooper,** 1919 (d. 1986). *Adventures with D.W. Griffith* (NY: DeCapo Press, 1976). (Griffith.) "Karl Brown, 93, Hollywood Pioneer in Cinematography," *NYT,* 30 Mar 1990, D17:3. "Karl Brown," *Variety,* 4 Apr 1990, p. 70. AMD, p. 53. AS, p. 175 (b. 1896). BHD2, p. 35 (b. 1895). FDY, p. 419. KOM, pp. 129–30. "Weddings," *MPW,* 22 Nov 1919, 422. Bert A. Folkart, "Karl Brown; Pioneer in Cinematography," *LA Times,* 29 Mar 1990, 28:1. Sara Oyen, "High-High Up in the Hills; Real Life and

Rich Melodrama Are Captured in Stark Love,'" *MPC,* Jun 1927, 62–63, 77.

Brown, Katherine H[olland] [scenarist] (d. 2 Jun 1931, Orlando FL). "Katherine Holland Brown," *Variety,* 9 Jan 1931, p. 61. AS, p. 175. BHD2, p. 35.

Brown, Kirke [actor] (b. Braddock PA, 16 Jan 1879–11 Jan 1945 [65], Norwood NJ). BHD, p. 116.

Brown, Kirke [actor] (b. McKeesport PA, 1899–13 Jul 1953 [53?], Levittown NY; coronary thrombosis).

Brown, Kurt T. [scenarist]. No data found. FDY, p. 419.

Brown, Leete Rennick [scenarist]. No data found. FDY, p. 419.

Brown, Lena Viola [actress]. No data found. (Heine and Louie comedies, Pathé.) AMD, p. 53. "In the Picture Studios," *NYDM,* 18 Dec 1915, 34:3 (). "Lena Viola Brown," *MPW,* 25 Dec 1915, 2345.

Brown, Lew [composer] (*né* Louis Brownstein, b. Odessa, Russia, 10 Dec 1893–5 Feb 1958 [64], New York NY; heart attack). m. (1) Sylvia Fiske; (2) Catherine Junewich. "Lew Brown, 64, of Tin Pan 'Golden Era,' Personified Pro Tunesmith Tradition," *Variety,* 12 Feb 1958, p. 79 (first song: *Please Don't Take My Lovin' Man Away*). AS, p. 175 (b. 1894). BHD2, p. 35 (b. New Haven CT). CEPMJ, Vol. 2, pp. 629–30. NNAT. SD.

Brown, Louis Allen [scenarist] (b. 1876–24 May 1937 [61?]). BHD2, p. 35 (Lewis A. Brown). FDY, p. 419.

Brown, Lucille E. [Farina in Our Gang Comedies] (b. New York NY, 1918?–21 Aug 1992 [74], Buffalo NY). (Roach.) "Lucille E. Brown," *Variety,* 31 Aug 1992, p. 75. AS, p. 175.

Brown, Martin [actor/playwright] (b. Montreal, Quebec, Canada, 22 Jun 1884–13 Feb 1936 [51], New York NY). "Martin Brown," *Variety,* 19 Feb 1936, p. 79. AS, p. 175. BHD, p. 116; BHD2, p. 35 (b. 1895). NNAT (b. 1885). SD (b.1885).

Brown, Maxine V. [actress] (b. Denver CO, 1897–28 Dec 1956 [59], Alameda CA; result of burns received at Brass Rail Cafe). m. George H. Maines, 1921–35; Clarence Willard. (Griffith; Photo Film Corp.; Edison; Ivan Film Productions.) "Maxine V. Willard," *Variety,* 9 Jan 1957 (d. Oakland CA). "Maxine Brown," *Variety,* 20 and 27 Feb 1957. AS, p. 175. BHD, p. 116. Gene Vazzana, "Maxine Brown, a Griffith Discovery," *The Silent Film Newsletter,* II, Mar 1994, 39–41.

Brown, Melville W. [actor/director/scenarist] (b. Portland OR, 10 Mar 1887–31 Jan 1938 [50], Los Angeles CA; heart attack). "Melville Brown," *Variety,* 2 Feb 1938, p. 62. AMD, p. 53. AS, p. 175. BHD, p. 116; BHD2, p. 35.. FDY, p. 419. IFN, p. 39. Truitt, p. 41. "Engage Melville Brown," *MPW,* 5 Apr 1919, 58. "Vitagraph Engages Brown," *MPW,* 10 Jan 1920, 248. "Brown to Direct for 'U,'" *MPW,* 16 Jan 1926, 232. "Brown Recovering," *MPW,* 16 Oct 1926, 2 (auto accident). "Brown's Next a War Story," *MPW,* 2 May 1927, 795.

Brown, Milton [actor] (b. 1875–31 May 1935 [60?], Los Angeles CA). BHD, p. 116.

Brown, [L.] Milton [actor] (b. 1896?–29 Mar 1948 [52], Los Angeles CA). (Metro, 1920.) "Milton Brown," *Variety,* 31 Mar 1948. AS, p. 176. BHD1, p. 74; BHD2, p. 35..

Brown, Morgan [actor] (b. New York NY, 4 Dec 1884–4 Jan 1961 [76], Los Angeles CA). AS, p. 176 (d. NYC). BHD1, p. 74. IFN, p. 39.

Brown, N. Howland [executive] (d. 17 Nov 1910). AMD, p. 53. "Obituary," *MPW,* 3 Dec 1910, 1279.

Brown, Nacio Herb [composer/actor] (*né* Ignacio Herb Brown, b. Deming ND, 22 Feb 1896–28 Sep 1964 [68], San Francisco CA; cancer). m. Anita Page—div. "Nacio Herb Brown Dies at 68; Composer of Many Hit Songs," *NYT,* 30 Sep 1964, 43:4. "Nacio Herb Brown," *Variety,* 7 Oct 1964, p. 62. AS, p. 176 (b. Deming NM). BHD1, p. 74; BHD2, p. 35.

Brown, Raymond [film editor]. No data found. AMD, p. 53. "Raymond Brown Metro Film Editor," *MPW,* 5 May 1917, 778. (Not to be confused with stage/film actor Raymond Brown, d. 30 Jul 1939).

Brown, Royal [title writer]. No data found. FDY, p. 441 (*Across the Plains,* 1928).

Brown, Sally Joy [actress] (b. 1905–6 May 1986 [81?]). BHD, p. 116.

Brown, Samuel G. [scenarist/film editor] (b. 13 Apr 1904–10 Sep 1991 [87], Woodland Hills CA; pneumonia). "Samuel Brown," *CI,* 197 (Nov 1991), 61. AS, p. 176. BHD2, p. 35.

Brown, Sedley (twin brother of **J. Edwin Brown**) [actor] (b. Boston MA, 29 Feb 1856–19 Sep 1928 [72], Los Angeles CA). m. **Henrietta Crosman** (d. 1944). "Sedley Brown," *Variety,* 26 Sep 1928, p. 58. AS, p. 176. BHD, p. 116. IFN, p. 39. SD.

Brown, Southard [publicist]. No data found. AMD, p. 53. "Brown to Handle Publicity for Tiffany and Mae Murray," *MPW,* 10 Sep 1921, 188.

Brown, Tom [stage/film/TV actor] (*né* Thomas Edward Brown, b. New York NY, 6 Jan 1913–3 Jun 1990 [77], Woodland Hills CA; cancer). m. (2 sons, 1 daughter). (Universal.) "Tom Brown," *Variety,* 13 Jun 1990, 92:3. BHD1, p. 75. Katz, p. 174. "Ask the Answer Man," *Photoplay Magazine,* May 1932, 82. F. Harry Happeny, "Tom Brown," *CFC,* 59 (Summer, 1978), 39. SW.

Brown, Viola *see* **Brown, Lena Viola**

Brown, William H. [actor] (b. Northampton MA). (Yankee; Reliance-Majestic; Fine Arts.) 1918 Studio Directory, p. 65.

Brown, Judge Willis [educator/scenarist]. No data found. (Universal; General Film [Boy City Film Corp.]) AMD, p. 53. "Judge Brown to Write for Universal," *MPW,* 7 Jul 1917, 74:1. "Judge Willis Brown Writes for Universal," *MPW,* 15 Sep 1917, 1675:2. "Judge Brown as Producer; Children's Advocate to Release Characteristic 'Stories of Youth' Through General FIlm," *MPW,* 29 Dec 1917, 1938:1 (administrator of the Parental Court of Gary IN, and founder of the Boy City movement at Charlevoix MI). "Judge Says His Stories Are Designed for Adult Appeal," *MPW,* 1 Jun 1918, 1304:1.

Brown, Willis H. [stage/film actor] (d. Oct 1931, Columbus OH; shot to death by Mrs. Maude G. Malloy). "Willis Brown Killed by Jealous Widow," *Variety,* 27 Oct 1931 (Malloy "admitted having purchas[ed] the revolver the day before the slaying.").

Browne, Betty Beckett [stage/film actress] (b. 1902?–9 Mar 1923 [21], Toronto, Canada; pneumonia). (Essanay.) Lester Sweyd, "What They Are Doing Now," *Motion Picture Magazine,* Feb 1918, 13 ("...after closing with 'The Girl from Brazil,' joined one of the New England stock companies, where she is the leading ingénue."). "Betty Beckett Browne," *Variety,* 15 Mar 1923, p. 9.

Browne, Bothwell [actor/female impersonator] (*né* Walter Bothwell Bruhn, b. Copenhagen, Denmark, 7 Mar 1877–12 Dec 1947 [80], Los Angeles CA). AS, p. 176. BHD, p. 116. IFN, p. 39.

Browne, Earle [stage/film actor/scenarist] (b. Vallejo CA, 7 Sep 1872–26 Nov 1944 [72], Hollywood CA). (UA.) "Earle Brown," *NYT,* 29 Nov 1944, 23:5 (began acting in 1895). "Earle Browne," *Variety,* 6 Dec 1944 (d. 28 Nov; stage career began with the Henry Miller company in 1894). BHD1, p. 75. FDY, p. 419. IFN, p. 39. Truitt, p. 41.

Browne, Irene [actress] (b. London, England, 29 Jun 1896–24 Jul 1965 [69], London, England; cancer). "Irene Browne," *Variety,* 28 Jul 1965, p. 100. AS, p. 176 (b. 1891). BHD1, p. 75.

Browne, John Barton [writer] (b. 1887?–24 Jan 1942 [55], Los Angeles CA; suicide from self-inflicted gunshot wounds). "John Barton Browne," *Variety,* 28 Jan 1942, p. 54. AS, p. 176.

Browne, Lewis Allen [scenarist] (b. No. Sandwich NH, 18 Jan 1876–24 May 1937 [61], Englewood NJ). "Lewis A. Browne," *Variety,* 26 May 1937. AMD, p. 53. AS, p. 177. BHD2, p. 35. WWWA. "Makes Long Contract with Browne," *MPW,* 13 Mar 1920, 1821.

Browne, Lucile [actress] (b. Memphis TN, 18 Mar 1907–10 May 1976 [69], Los Angeles CA). m. James Flavin, ca. 1932 (d. 1976). "Lucile Browne Flavin," *Variety,* 16 Jun 1976. BHD1, p. 75 (d. Lexington VA). Buck Rainey, "Lucile Brown; Unobtrusively Alluring, She Exuded More Sex Appeal Accidentally than Most Other Actresses Did Purposefully," *CI,* 130 (Apr 1986), 31, C1, C23 (began 1929). The *AFI Catalog* lists a 1921 film for Lucille E. Browne.

Browne, Peggy [actress]. No data found. AMD, p. 53. "Peggy Browne in Warner Film," *MPW,* 11 Aug 1923, 500.

Browne, Porter E[merson] [playwright/scenarist] (b. Beverly MA, 22 Jun 1879 [MVRB, Vol. 304, p. 169, last name "Brown"]–20 Sep 1934 [55], Norwalk CT). m. Myrtle Suzanne May, Chicago IL, 10 Feb 1907. "Porter E. Browne, Playwright, Dead; Author of 'The Bad Man' and Other Successful Works on Stage and Screen Was 55; Bitter Foe of Pacifists; His Story 'Peace at Any Price' Won Him the Friendship of Late Theodore Roosevelt," *NYT,* 21 Dec 1934 ("He also wrote several film plays, the most prominent of which were 'Joan of Plattsburgh,' starring Mabel Normand; 'Too Many Millions,' starring Wallace Reid; and 'The Seventh Day,' with Richard Barthelmess."). AMD, p. 53. AS, p. 177. BHD2, p. 35. "Porter Emerson Browne with Goldwyn," *MPW,* 14 Apr 1917, 245.

Browne, W. Grahame [actor/director] (b. Ireland, 1 Jan 1870–11 Mar 1937 [67], Hampstead, England; double pneumonia). m. Madge McIntosh; **Marie Tempest**, 1921 (d. 1942). "W.G. Browne Dies; Actor-Producer, Husband of Marie Tempest Had Appeared in Many Plays Here with Her; Asked That 'Show Go On'; Wife Continues as Usual in Cast He Left Because of Illness Only a Week Ago," *NYT,* 12 Mar 1937, 23:3. "W. Grahame

Brown," *Variety*, 17 Mar 1937. AS, p. 177. BHD1, p. 75.

Browne-Decker, Kathryn [actress] (*née* Kathleen Brown, b. Richmond VA-d. 11 Feb 1919, Colombo, Ceylan, while on tour). (Pathé.) "Kathryn B. Decker," *Variety*, 21 Feb 1919. IFN, p. 39.

Brownell, Herbert H. [cinematographer]. No data found. FDY, p. 457.

Brownell, John C. [scenarist] (b. 5 Feb 1877–27 Aug 1961 [84], Starksboro VT). (RKO.) "John C. Brownell," *Variety*, 6 Sep 1961. AMD, p. 53. AS, p. 177. AS, p. 177. BHD1, p. 605; BHD2, p. 35. FDY, p. 419. "John C. Brownell," *MPW*, 18 Mar 1916, 1812. "Brownell, Universal Scenario Editor, Deplores Filming of Many Stage Plays," *MPW*, 3 Apr 1920, 105. Miss Vee Dee, "Ask Me!," *Screenland*, Aug 1929, 96 (photo).

Browning, Alice *see* **Houghton, Alice**

Browning, Ethel [stage/film actress]. No data found. m. **Ashley Miller** [d. 1949]. "In the Picture Studios," *NYDM*, 18 Dec 1915, 34:4 (worked in a film on child labor directed by her husband).

Browning, Irving [actor] (b. New York NY, 1893). (Began ca. 1907; Champion; Thanhouser; Ramo; Fox; World; Metro; Pickford; Vitagraph.) MSBB, p. 1022.

Browning, Tod [vaudeville and film actor/director/scenarist] (*né* Charles Albert Browning, b. Louisville KY, 12 Jul 1880–6 Oct 1962 [82], Santa Monica CA; following cancer surgery. Buried at Rosedale Cemetery, Los Angeles CA). m. (1) Amy Louise Stevens [aunt of Buster Collier], Louisville KY, 28 Mar 1906-div. 24 Dec 1910; (2) **Alice Lillian Houghton Wilson**, 9 Jun 1917, New Rochelle NY (d. 1944). Stuart Rosenthal and Judith M. Kass, *Tod Browning, Don Siegel* (1975). *Dark Carnival* (1995). (Film debut: *Scenting a Terrible Crime*, Biograph, Oct 1913, 1-reel; Mutual; Reliance-Majestic; Fine Arts/Triangle; Universal; Goldwyn; FBO; MGM.) "Tod Browning, 80, ex-Film Director; Maker of Chaney and Lugosi Films Dies—Former Actor," *NYT*, 10 Oct 1962, 47:4. "Tod Browning," *Variety*, 17 Oct 1962, p. 63. AMD, p. 53. AS, p. 177 (b. 1882). BHD, p. 116 (b. 1882); BHD2, p. 35.. IFN, p. 39 (age 80). KOM, p. 130 (b. 1882). *AFI Catalog*, p. 552, has m. Alice Rae (aka Alice Wilson), 1917. W.E. Wing, "Along the Pacific Coast," *NYDM*, 30 Jun 1915, 22:1 (in the car with George Siegman in which Elmer Booth was killed. Browning suffered internal injuries and a leg broken in three places). "Tod Browning Discusses Lighting," *MPW*, 23 Jun 1917, 1966. "Tod Browning with Universal," *MPW*, 25 May 1918, 1146. "Browning to Make Bluebirds," *MPW*, 1 Jun 1918, 1295. "Browning Leaves Universal," *MPW*, 10 Sep 1921, 169. "Tod Browning Has Again Signed with Universal," *MPW*, 19 Nov 1921, 298. "Goldwyn Signs Browning," *MPW*, 10 Mar 1923, 145. "Browning Signed to Long Term byMetro," *MPW*, 31 Dec 1927, 5. Joan Dickey, "A Maker of Mystery; Tod Browning Is a Specialist in Building Thrills and Chills," *MPC*, Mar 1928, 33, 80. Alan Buster, *DAB*, Supp. 7, 86–88 (played with Roy C. Jones as "Lizard and Coon," 1905).

Browning, William E. [actor] (b. 1871–21 Dec 1930 [59?], Middle Village, LI NY). m. Mae. "William E. Browning," *Variety*, 21 Jan 1931, p. 68. BHD1, p. 75. IFN, p. 39.

Brownlee, Frank [actor] (b. Dallas TX, 11 Oct 1874–10 Feb 1948 [73], Los Angeles Co. CA). BHD1, p. 75. IFN, p. 39. George Katchmer, "Remembering the Great Silents," *CI*, 245 (Nov 1995), 44.

Brox, Bobbe (sister of Lorayne [d. 1993] and Patricia [d. 1988]) [stage/film actress/singer] (b. 1901?–2 May 1999 [98], Glens Falls NY). "Bobbe Brox," *CI*, 288 (Jun 1999), 45.

Bruce, Becky [actress]. No data found. AMD, p. 53. "Becky Bruce with Raver," *NYDM*, 30 Oct 1915, 26:4 (to be in *The Other Girl*, with James J. Corbett). "Becky Bruce with Raver," *MPW*, 30 Oct 1915, 981. "Becky Bruce," *MPW*, 20 Nov 1915, 1489.

Bruce, Belle [actress] (b. Bridgeport CT-d. 15 Jun 1960, Winsted CT). m. Charles Pettijohn, 1917. (Vitagraph.) "Mrs. Helen L[ynch] Pettijohn," *Variety*, 29 Jun 1960. AMD, p. 53. BHD, p. 116. IFN, p. 39. "Charles Pettijohn Marries," *MPW*, 8 Dec 1917, 1503.

Bruce, Beverly [actress] (b. Montreal, Canada-d. Jul 1925, Bryn Mawr PA; cancer). (Vitagraph.) "Beverly Bruce," *Variety*, 29 Jul 1925, p. 45. BHD, p. 116. IFN, p. 39.

Bruce, Clifford [stage/film actor] (*né* Clifford Bruce Scott, b. Toronto, Canada, 1885–27 Aug 1919 [34], West Camp NY). (Selig; Pathé; Fox; Metro.) m. Marie Gaber. AMD, p. 53. BHD, p. 116. IFN, p. 40. MSBB, p. 1022. SD. "A New Leading Man for Selig," *MPW*, 26 Jul 1913, 416. "Motography's Gallery of Picture Players," *Motography*, 11 Jul 1914, 53. "Clifford Bruce Joins Metro," *MPW*, 25 Mar 1916, 2014. "Clifford Bruce Wants Salary," *MPW*, 6 Sep 1919, 1458.

Bruce, David [actor] (*né* Andrew McBroom, b. Kankakee IL, 6 Jan 1914–3 May 1976 [62], Los Angeles CA; heart attack). (Universal; WB.) "David Bruce," *Variety*, 12 May 1976 (age 60). AS, p. 177. BHD, p. 116. IFN, p. 40.

Bruce, Kate [actress] (b. 1858–2 Apr 1946 [88], New York NY). AS, p. 177. BHD, p. 116. IFN, p. 40. Spehr, p. 120. George A. Katcher, "More Forgotten Cowboys and Cowgirls," *CI*, 76 (Jul 1981), 17.

Bruce, Robert C[ameron] [cameraman/producer] (b. Stowe VT, 1885–6 Aug 1948 [63?], Los Angeles CA). AMD, p. 54. AS, p. 177 (b. 1875; "pioneer of Technicolor"). BHD2, p. 35. "Robert C. Bruce on Ten Months' Trip," *MPW*, 3 Feb 1917, 692. "Latest from Robert C. Bruce," *MPW*, 13 Jul 1918, 202. "Editing Film," *MPW*, 27 Jan 1923, 378. "Bruce Editing Eight Novel Films for Release Through Educational," *MPW*, 24 Nov 1923, 420.

Bruce, Tonie Edgar [stage/film actress] (b. London, England, 4 Jun 1892–28 Mar 1966 [73], Chertsey, Surrey, England). "Tonie Edgar Bruce," *Variety*, 6 Apr 1966, p. 71. BHD1, p. 76.

Bruce, Virginia [actress] (*née* Helen Virginia Briggs, b. Minneapolis MN, 29 Sep 1909–24 Feb 1982 [72], Woodland Hills CA; cancer). m. (1) **John Gilbert** (d. 1936); (2) **J. Walter Ruben** (d. 1942); (3) Ali Ipar. "Virginia Bruce, 72, Actress Portrayed Ziegfeld Showgirl," *NYT*, 26 Feb 1982, B5:3. "Virginia Bruce," *Variety*, 3 Mar 1982 (b. Fargo ND). AS, p. 177. BHD1, p. 76 (b. 1910). SD. "Virginia Bruce," WBO2, pp. 202–03 (b. 1910).

Bruch, Reinhard [director/scenarist] (b. Prague, Czechoslovakia, 1885–5 Jun 1929 [44?], Berlin, Germany). BHD2, p. 35.

Bruckman, Clyde [writer/cinematographer/director] (b. San Bernardino CA, 20 Sep 1894–4 Jan 1955 [60], Santa Monica CA; suicide by shooting). "Clyde Bruckman," *Variety*, 12 Jan 1955, p. 75. AMD, p. 54. AS, p. 178. BHD2, p. 35. FDY, p. 457. IFN, p. 40. O&W, pp. 202–04. Wheeler W. Dixon, *The "B" Director; A Biographical Directory* (Metuchen NJ: The Scarecrow Press, Inc., 1985), pp. 89–90 (b. 1894). "Lyons and Moran Increase Staff," *MPW*, 15 Feb 1919, 887. "Bruckman Again to Direct Banks," *MPW*, 29 Jan 1927, 355. "Roach Engages Clyde Bruckman," *MPW*, 28 May 1927, 277.

Bruggeman, George [actor] (b. Belgium, 1 Nov 1904–9 Jun 1967 [62], Los Angeles CA). AS, p. 178. IFN, p. 40.

Brulatour, Jules E. [producer] (b. New Orleans LA, 1870?–26 Oct 1946 [76], New York NY [Death Certificate Index No. 22703]). m. (2) **Dorothy Gibson**, 1917 (d. 1946); (3) **Hope Hampton** (d. 1982). "Jules E. Brulatour Dies in Hospital, 75; Motion-Picture Financier Was Well-Known 'First-Nighter'—Husband of Hope Hampton," *NYT*, 27 Oct 1946, 62:3; "Share Brulatour Estate; Widow and Three Children Are Named in Will of Financier," *NYT*, 27 Nov 1946, 46:2. "Jules Brulatour Dies at 76 in New York; Pioneer of Film Biz," *Variety*, 30 Oct 1946, p. 58. BHD2, p. 35. IFN, p. 40. Spehr, p. 120. "'Twelfth Night' and After," *MPW*, 7 Jan 1911, 35.

Brule, André [stage/film actor/producer/director] (*né* André Gresely, b. Bordeaux, France, 26 Sep 1879–14 Feb 1953 [73], Neuilly-sur-Seine, France). "Andre Brule," *Variety*, 18 Feb 1953, p. 63 ("created the role of Arsene Lupin on the French stage in 1908..."). AS, p. 178. BHD1, p. 76; BHD2, p. 35. IFN, p. 40.

Bruna, Ria [actress]. No data found. JS, p. 64 (in Italian silents from 1917).

Brundage, Mathilde [actress] (b. Louisville KY, 22 Sep 1859–6 May 1939 [79], Long Beach CA). (World.) "Bertha Brundage," *Variety*, 10 May 1939. AS, p. 178. BHD, p. 117. IFN, p. 40. George Katchmer, "Remembering the Great Silents," *CI*, 221 (Nov 1993), 51.

Brunel, Adrian [actor/director/scenarist] (b. Brighton, England, 4 Sep 1892–18 Feb 1958 [65], Gerrard's Cross, Buckshire, England). AS, p. 178. BHD, p. 117; BHD2, p. 35.

Brunel, Irene (Babs) [actress] (b. 1891–19 Mar 1987 [95?]). BHD, p. 117.

Bruner, Frank V. [publicist]. No data found. AMD, p. 54. "Frank Bruner with Rex Beach Pictures Co.," *MPW*, 5 May 1917, 780. "Bruner to Exploit Serial Stars," *MPW*, 21 Dec 1918, 1356. "Bruner Recovering from Operation," *MPW*, 13 Mar 1920, 1817.

Brunet, Paul [executive]. No data found. AMD, p. 54. "Pathé Executives Dine Paul Brunet," *MPW*, 30 Mar 1918, 1802. "Brunet Denies Statement of Universal," *MPW*, 6 Jul 1918, 42. "Brunet Discusses Open Booking," *MPW*, 19 Jul 1919, 369. "Paul Brunet Succeeds Charles Pathé as President of Great Film Organization," *MPW*, 25 Sep 1920, 457. "Brunet Resigns as Pathé Head," *MPW*, 23 Sep 1922, 259 (returned to France for personal reasons). "Brunet Resignation Accepted," *MPW*, 7 Oct 1922, 460.

Brunette, Fritzi [actress] (*née* Florence Brunet, b. Savannah GA, 27 May 1890–28 Sep 1943 [53], Los Angeles CA). m. **William Robert Daly**, 17 Jun 1914. (Yankee Film Co.) "Fritzi

Brunette," *NYT,* 30 Sep 1943, 21:2 (b. Boston MA). "Fritzi Brunette," *Variety,* 6 Oct 1943, p. 54. AMD, p. 55. AS, p. 178. BHD1, p. 76. FSS, p. 49. IFN, p. 40 (b. 1895). MH, p. 99 (b. 1894). Truitt, p. 41. "Two Powers Players," *MPW,* 13 Apr 1912, 126. "Fritzi Brunette with Universal," *MPW,* 16 Aug 1913, 749. "Fritzi Brunette," *MPW,* 30 May 1914, 1264. "Daly—Brunette," *MPW,* 27 Jun 1914, 1840. "Fritzi Brunette," *MPW,* 12 Dec 1914, 1545. "Fritzi Brunette," *MPW,* 24 Feb 1917, 1183. "Fritzi Brunette," *MPW,* 26 May 1917, 1291. "Selig Veterans Join Universal Forces," *MPW,* 6 Jul 1918, 51. "Fritzi Brunette Is Leading Woman for New Holt Production," *MPW,* 12 Nov 1921, 201.

Brunius, Jacques-Bernard [scenarist/director/actor] (*né* Jacques Henri Cottance, b. Paris, France, 16 Sep 1906–24 Apr 1967 [60], Exeter, England). AS, p. 178 (d. 23 May). BHD2, p. 36.

Brunius, John W. [actor/director] (b. Stockholm, Sweden, 26 Dec 1884–16 Feb 1937 [52], Stockholm, Sweden). (Skandia.) m. **Pauline** Brunius (d. 1954). AS, p. 179. BHD2, p. 36.

Brunius, Pauline [actress/director] (*née* Emma Maria Pauline Lindstedt, b. Stockholm, Sweden, 10 Feb 1881–31 Mar 1954 [73], Stockholm, Sweden). m. **John W. Brunius** (d. 1937). AS, p. 179 (d. 30 Mar). BHD1, p. 77. IFN, p. 40.

Bruns, Edna [actress] (b. 1880–23 Jul 1960 [80?], New York NY). BHD, p. 117. IFN, p. 40 (d. 25 Jul).

Bruns, Julia [actress] (b. St. Louis MO, 1895–24 Dec 1927 [32?], New York NY; acute alcoholism). "Julia Bruns," *Variety,* 28 Dec 1927, p. 49. AS, p. 179. BHD, p. 117.

Brunswick, Earl [actor] (aka Earl Brunswig). No data found. AMD, p. 55. "Earl Brunswick," *MPW,* 10 Jan 1914, 183. "Earl Brunswick," *MPW,* 29 Sep 1917, 1982. "Earl Brunswick," *MPW,* 3 Nov 1917, 684.

Brunton, Garland L[ewis] [actor/assistant director] (b. 24 Jul 1903–24 Jul 1975 [72], Los Angeles CA). "Garland Lewis Brunton," *Variety,* 6 Aug 1975, p. 62. BHD1, p. 77; BHD2, p. 36.

Brunton, Robert A. [stage/film scenic artist/film director] (b. Glasgow, Scotland-7 Mar 1923, London, England). (Ince-Triangle.) BHD2, p. 36. MSBB, p. 1044.

Brunton, William G. [stage/film actor] (b. Canada, 13 Mar 1883–19 Feb 1965 [81], Los Angeles CA). m. Louella Manan. AS, p. 179. BHD, p. 117. IFN, 40. MSBB, p. 1022.

Bruzovna, Halina [actress]. No data found. AMD, p. 55. "Popular Polish Actress Engaged by Selznick for Leading Role," *MPW,* 27 Dec 1919, 1184. "Polish Star Engaged by Selznick Marvels at America's Lavishness," *MPW,* 10 Jan 1920, 254.

Bruzzel, Maxwell S. [cameraman] (b. New York NY?, 1890?–Oct 1912 [22], AZ; accidentally shot). (Selig Polyscope Co.; Bison.) m. Miss Hunt, 1912. AMD, p. 55. "Doings at Los Angeles; Cameraman Loses Life," *MPW,* 12 Oct 1912, 129:2–30:1 (Bruzzel, his bride, and Robert Hunt, his father-in-law, went to Arizona to visit a mining project which Bruzzel owned. During one night, Hunter mistook him for a wild animal and shot him. Bruzzel died after a race to the nearest doctor.).

Bryan, Alfred [composer] (b. Brantford, Canada, 1870–1 Apr 1958 [88?], Morristown NJ). "Alfred Bryan," *Variety,* 9 Apr 1958, p. 119. AS, p. 179. BHD2, p. 36.

Bryan, Paul M. [scenarist/producer] (b. Sylvania GA, 1873?–4 Aug 1944 [71], Los Angeles CA). "Paul M. Bryan," *Variety,* 9 Aug 1944, p. 38. AMD, p. 55. AS, p. 179. BHD2, p. 36 (b. 1875). FDY, p. 419. "Gaumont Secures Editor for "Reel Life,'" *MPW,* 21 Oct 1916, 396.

Bryan, Vincent Patrick [director/scenarist] (b. St. John's, Newfoundland, Canada, 1877–27 Apr 1937 [60?], Los Angeles CA). AMD, p. 55. BHD2, p. 36. "Vincent Bryan to Write Stories for Billy West," *MPW,* 22 Feb 1919, 1077.

Bryan, William Jennings [writer]. No data found. AMD, p. 55. W.S. daPonte, "William Jennings Bryan Will Write Stories for Production on Screen," *MPW,* 8 Oct 1921, 641–42.

Bryant, Charles E. [actor/director] (b. Hartford, England, 8 Jan 1879–7 Aug 1948 [69], Mt. Kisco NY). m. (1) **Alla Nazimova** (d. 1945); (2) Marjorie Gilhooley. "Charles Bryant, Actor, Dies at 67; Former Husband and Leading Man of Nazimova Made London Debut in 1901," *NYT,* 8 Aug 1948, 57:1. "Charles Bryant," *Variety,* 11 Aug 1948 (age 67). AMD, p. 55. AS, p. 179. BHD, p. 117; BHD2, p. 36. IFN, p. 40 (age 67). MH, p. 99. SD. Truitt, p. 42. "G. Charles Bryant," *MPW,* 17 Jul 1915, 489. "Charles Bryant Returns to Support Mme. Nazimova," *MPW,* 8 Mar 1919, 1345. "Charles Bryant Conferring with Metro President," *MPW,* 12 Mar 1921, 189.

Bryant, Jack V. [actor] (b. Ayr, Scotland, 26 May 1889–2 Mar 1924 [34], London, England). "J.V. Bryant, 35, prominent English juvenile, is dead," *Variety,* 19 Mar 1924, p. 2. BHD, p. 117.

Bryant, Marguerite [actress] (d. Jan 1951, Brooklyn NY). BHD, p. 117. IFN, p. 40.

Bryant, Mayme [actress] (related to Frank Mayo) (b. 1874?–14 Oct 1930 [56], New York NY). "Mayme Bryant," *Variety,* 22 Oct 1930, p. 76.

Bryantsev, Alexandr A. [director/actor] (b. St. Petersburg, Russia, 15 Apr 1883–30 Sep 1961 [78]). BHD2, p. 36.

Bryde, Vilhelm [actor/director/producer] (b. Stockholm, Sweden, 28 Apr 1888—26 Apr 1974 [85], Stockholm, Sweden). AS, p. 180. BHD1, p. 605.

Brydone, Alfred [actor] (b. Edinburgh, Scotland, 9 Dec 1863–26 Nov 1920 [56], London, England). BHD, p. 117.

Bryson, James V[an Bibber] [actor] (d. 31 Dec 1935). (Universal.) AS, p. 180. IFN, p. 40. SD.

Bryson, Winifred [stage/film actress] (b. Columbus OH, 20 Dec 1892–20 Aug 1987 [94], Los Angeles CA). m. **Warner Baxter**, 1918 (d. 1951); (2) Ferdinand M. Menger. (Universal.) "Winifred Brison Manger," *Variety,* 328, 16 Sep 1987, 127:3. AS, p. 180. BHD, p. 117. SD. Maude Cheatham, "The Endless Honeymoon of the Warner Baxters," *Classic,* Jul 1923, 24–25, 78.

Bubb, Benjamin C. [advertising artist]. No data found. AMD, p. 55. "Bubb Joins American," *MPW,* 4 Feb 1922, 480.

Buchan [or Buchanan], Annabelle *see* **Annabelle**

Buchanan, Claud [actor]. No data found. AMD, p. 55. "Claud Buchanan," *MPW,* 26 Feb 1927, 644.

Buchanan, Jack [actor] (b. Helensburgh, Scotland, 2 Apr 1891–20 Oct 1957 [66], London, England; arthritis). m. Susan Bassett. (MGM.) "Jack Buchanan," *Variety,* 23 Oct 1957, p. 75 (age 64). AMD, p. 55. AS, p. 180 (b. 1890). BHD1, p. 78 (b. Glasgow). IFN, p. 40. Katz, p. 178 (b. Glasgow, Scotland). SD. Truitt, p. 42. "Buchanan Signed by DeMille," *MPW,* 31 Jul 1926, 278.

Buchanan, Thompson [scenarist/script editor] (b. New York NY, 21 Jun 1877–15 Oct 1937 [60], Louisville KY). m. (1) Katharine Winterbotham—div. 1927; (2) Joan Lowell, 16 Oct 1927–1929. (Wrote *Civilian Clothes;* Goldwyn; Lasky.) "Thompson Buchanan, Long a Playwright; Radio Sketch Writer and Former Newspaper Man Dies of Heart Stroke in Louisville," *NYT,* 16 Oct 1937, 19:5 (in 1919, he was editor of Goldwyn Pictures in Hollywood). AMD, p. 55. AS, p. 180. BHD2, p. 36. "Buchanan Joins Goldwyn," *MPW,* 29 Mar 1919, 1773. "Buchanan Made Supervising Director at Lasky's; Will Share Duties with Woods," *MPW,* 15 Jan 1921, 275. June Lee, "Dan Cupid's Bulletin Board," *Paris and Hollywood,* Oct 1926, 89 (sued for divorce by his wife. "...it is said that Buchanan's recent failures with plays and picture contracts disappointed his socially ambitious wife. There was also considerable comment in Hollywood as to the expensive mismanagement of the Writers Club while Buchanan was president and the necessity of the members making up a mysterious deficit of $17,000.... Mrs. Buchanan is often seen in Hollywood with a very young man of swarthy countenance.").

Buchman, Sidney R. [scenarist] (b. Duluth MN, 27 Mar 1902–23 Aug 1975 [73], Cannes, France). "Sidney Buchman," *Variety,* 27 Aug 1975, p. 63 (AA for *Here Comes Mr. Jordan*). BHD2, p. 36. IFN, p. 40.

Buchowetski, Dimitri [director/scenarist/producer] (b. Russia, 1885–1932 [46?], Los Angeles CA). AMD, p. 55. AS, p. 181. BHD2, p. 36. FDY, p. 419. Katz, p. 179. Waldman, p. 38 (fired from directing *Anna Karenina,* MGM, 1927, for standing up to his producers). "Buchowetzki to Direct" *MPW,* 5 Jan 1924, 24. "Laemmle Engages Buchowetzki," *MPW,* 21 Mar 1925, 279. "To Direct for M-G-M," *MPW,* 15 May 1926, 235. Alfred Dace, "Invited Invaders; The Foreign Legion Is Still Carrying On. Some Are Making Good, But...," *MPC,* Nov 1926, 18–19, 74 (also discusses von Stroheim, Christiansen, Lubitsch, Stiller).

Buchs, José [director] (father of Julio Buchs, 1926–1973) (*né* José Buchs Echeandia, b. Santander, Spain, 16 Jan 1893–30 Jan 1973 [80], Madrid, Spain). AS, p. 181. BHD2, p. 36.

Buck, Frank [actor/director/producer] (b. Gainesville TX, 17 Mar 1888–25 Mar 1950 [62], Houston TX; pulmonary embolism). AS, p. 181 (b. 1884). BHD2, p. 36.

Buck, Inez [stage/film actress] (b. Oelrichs SD, 1890?–6 Sep 1957 [67], Oakland CA). m. Arthur G. Robinson. (Lubin.) "Inez B. Robinson," *Variety,* 18 Sep 1957, p. 63. AS, p. 181. BHD, p. 117. IFN, p. 41. Truitt, p. 42.

Buck, Nell Roy [actress] (b. 1910?–28 Feb 1962 [51], Van Nuys CA). AS, p. 181. BHD, p. 117. IFN, p. 41.

Buckham, Hazel [actress]. No data found. (Universal.) J. Van Cartmell, "Along the Pacific Coast," *NYDM,* 4 Aug 1915, 26:1.

Buckingham, Thomas [actor/director/scenarist] (b. Chicago IL, 1895?–7 Sep 1934 [39], Los Angeles CA; complications after surgery). m. Jan Ridgeway. (WB; Fox; Pathé.) "Tom Buckingham," *Variety,* 11 Sep 1934, p. 62. AMD, p. 55. AS,

p. 181. BHD, p. 117; BHD2, p. 36. IFN, p. 41. "Buckingham with Fox," *MPW,* 10 Oct 1925, 493.

Buckland, Wilfred, Sr. [art director/producer/director] (b. 1866?–18 Jul 1946 [80], Los Angeles CA; suicide by shooting after killing his insane son). "Wilfred Buckland, Sr.," *Variety,* 24 Jul 1946, p. 62 ("first art director in Hollywood"). AMD, p. 55. AS, p. 181. BHD2, p. 36. IFN, p. 41. "Getting Belasco Atmosphere," *MPW,* 30 May 1914, 1271. "Buckland Switches," *MPW,* 7 May 1927, 36.

Buckler, Hugh C. [actor] (b. Southampton, England, 9 Sep 1881–30 Oct 1936 [55], Malibu Lake CA; drowned with his son John). m. AS, p. 181. BHD1, p. 78.

Buckley, Andrew M. [actor] (b. 1879?–15 Apr 1917 [38], Paterson NJ; following nervous breakdown). "Andrew M. Buckley," *NYDM,* 28 Apr 1917, 10:1. AS, p. 181.

Buckley, Floyd [actor] (b. Chatham NY, 1874?–14 Nov 1956 [82], New York NY; heart attack). m. Juliet. "Floyd Buckley," *Variety,* 21 Nov 1956, p. 63. AS, p. 181. BHD, p. 117; BHD2, p. 36. IFN, p. 41. SD. Truitt, p. 42.

Buckley, Harold R. [scenarist] (b. Westfield MA, 4 Apr 1896–13 Jun 1958 [62], Rigby ID; meningitis). "Harold Buckley Dies; Early Pilot and Film Writer Aided Hoover Relief Work," *NYT,* 17 Jun 1958, 29:5. "Harold R. Buckley," *Variety,* 25 Jun 1958 (d. 14 Jun). AS, p. 181 (d. 14 Jun). BHD2, p. 37.

Buckley, Joseph [actor] (b. 1875?–2 Dec 1930 [55], Van Nuys CA; struck by electric freight train). "Joseph Buckley," *Variety,* 10 Dec 1930. AS, p. 181. IFN, p. 41. Truitt, p. 42.

Buckley, May [actress] (b. San Francisco CA, 15 Dec 1875-ca. 1941 [45?]). AMD, p. 55. BHD, p. 117. "May Buckley," *MPW,* 27 Jan 1912, 291. "May Buckley," *MPW,* 8 Jun 1912, 919. "May Buckley with Selig," *MPW,* 5 Apr 1913, 60.

Buckley, William [actor]. No data found. (Paramount.) George A. Katchmer, "Forgotten Cowboys and Cowgirls—Part XVII," *CI,* 194 (Aug 1991), 43.

Bucko, Ralph [actor] (*né* Roy F. Bouckou, b. CA, 1891–6 Aug 1962 [70], Yakima WA). BHD1, p. 78. IFN, p. 41.

Bucko, Roy [actor] (b. CA, 22 Aug 1893–6 Aug 1954 [60], Los Angeles Co. CA). BHD1, p. 78.

Buckstone, John C[opeland] [actor] (b. Sydenham, England, 9 Dec 1858 [extrait de naissance no. 182/1859]–24 Sep 1924 [66?], London, England). AS, p. 182. BHD, p. 117.

Buckstone, Rowland [actor] (b. Syndeham, England, 29 Mar 1860–13 Sep 1922 [62], London, England). m. Cicely J. Wilson. (Vitagraph.) "Rowland Buckstone," *Variety,* 29 Sep 1922, p. 9 (age 60). BHD, p. 117. NNAT, p. 362. SD.

Buckwalter, H.H. [cameraman]. No data found. (Kleine.) AMD, p. 55. M.H. Walker, "How Buckwalter Saved the Show," *MPW,* 12 Aug 1911, 368. "Camera Difficulties in the Canal Zone," *MPW,* 20 Dec 1913, 1399. "Buckwalter Films Mitchel," *MPW,* 20 Dec 1913, 1426. "Buckwalter with Kleine," *NYDM,* 23 Oct 1915, 27:1 (now manager of the Denver office).

Bucquet, Harold Spencer [extra/set designer/producer/director] (b. London, England, 10 Apr 1891–13 Feb 1946 [54], Los Angeles CA). m. Louise Fremery (or de Fremory) Howard, 18 Sep 1920, Piedmont CA. "H.S. Bucquet Dead; Film Director, 54; M-G-M Guide, Best Known for 'Dr. Kildare' Series, Had Won an Academy Award," *NYT,* 15 Feb 1946, 26:2. "Harold S. Bucquet," *Variety,* 20 Feb 1946, p. 54 (directed *Dr. Kildaire* and *Dr. Gillespie* series and many shorts). AMD, p. 56. AS, p. 182. BHD, p. 117; BHD2, p. 37. IFN, p. 41. A.H. Giebler, "Los Angeles News Letter; Assistant Director Weds," *MPW,* 9 Oct 1920, 783 (married Fremery).

Buczkowski, Leonard Marian [director] (b. Warsaw, Poland, 5 Aug 1900–19 Feb 1966 [65], Warsaw, Poland). AS, p. 182 (d. 1967). BHD2, p. 37.

Budd, Leighton [cartoonist]. No data found. AMD, p. 56. "Budd Leighton," *MPW,* 21 Jul 1917, 397.

Buel, Keenan [actor/director] (*né* John William Adams, b. KY, 1873?–5 Nov 1948 [75], New York NY [Death Certificate Index No. 24348]). "Keenan Buel," *NYT,* 6 Nov 1948, 13:3. AMD, p. 56. AS, p. 182. BHD, p. 117; BHD2, p. 37. IFN, p. 41. 1921 Directory, p. 259. Spehr, p. 120. "New Kalem Company for Jacksonville," *MPW,* 16 Dec 1911, 880. "Keenan Buel," *MPW,* 1 Sep 1917, 1360. "Hall Signs Keenan Buel to Direct Series of Specials," *MPW,* 4 Oct 1919, 110.

Buffalo Bill, Jr *see* **Wilsey, Jay**

Buffington, Adele [western scenarist] (b. St. Louis MO, 12 Feb 1900–23 Nov 1973 [73], Woodland Hills CA; arteriosclerosis). (Ince.) "Adele Buffington," *Variety,* 5 Dec 1973, p. 62. AMD, p. 56. AS, p. 182. BHD2, p. 37. FDY, p. 419. IFN, p. 41. "Author Writes Scenario," *MPW,* 24 Jan 1925, 392.

Buffum, Jesse H. [cinematographer] (b. Boston MA, 1881–20 Feb 1956 [75?], North Adams MA). BHD2, p. 37.

Bughart, Charles [actor] (b. 1857–19 Feb 1927 [69], Los Angeles CA). BHD, p. 117.

Buhler, Richard [stage/film actor] (b. Washington DC, 21 Jun 1876–27 Mar 1925 [48], Washington DC). (Box Office Attraction Co.; Lubin.) "Richard Buhler," *Variety,* 1 Apr 1925, p. 51 (interred at Mt. Olivet Cemetery). AMD, p. 56. AS, p. 182. BHD, p. 117. IFN, p. 41. *MPN Studio Directory,* 21 Oct 1916 (b. Brooklyn). "Richard Buhler," *MPW,* 11 Sep 1915, 1840. Al Ray, "Before the Stars Shone," *Picture-Play Magazine,* Sep 1917, 93.

Buhr, Arturo Garcia [stage, film, radio actor/director] (b. Los Libres del Sur, Buenos Aires Argentina, 16 Dec 1905–4 Oct 1995 [89], Buenos Aires, Argentina). m. actress Aida Olivier. "García Buhr fue un señor de la escena," *La Nación* [Buenos Aires], 5 Oct 1995, p. 1:4 (appeared in the silent, *Manuelita Rosas*).

Bulgakov, Leo [actor/director/producer] (b. Tula, Russia, 22 Mar 1889–20 Jul 1948 [59], Binghamton NY). "Leo Bulgakov," *Variety,* 28 Jul 1948, p. 97 (age 60). AS, p. 183. BHD2, p. 37.

Bull, Charles Edward [actor] (b. TX, 26 Feb 1881–9 Sep 1971 [90], Los Angeles CA). (Fox.) AMD, p. 56. AS, p. 183. BHD1, p. 605 (d. Lynwood CA). IFN, p. 41. "Will Portray Lincoln Role," *MPW,* 14 May 1927, 111.

Bull, Clarence S. [photographer/cinematographer] (b. MT, 1896–8 Jun 1979 [83?], Brentwood CA). AS, p. 183. BHD2, p. 37.

Bullock, Boris *see* **Barrymore, William**

Bump, Edmond [actor] (b. 1877–6 Nov 1938 [61?], Los Angeles CA). AS, p. 183. BHD, p. 117. IFN, p. 41.

Bunker, Ralph [actor] (b. Boston MA, 1889?–28 Apr 1966 [77], New York NY; cerebral embolism [Death Certificate Index No. 9208; age 76]). "Ralph Bunker," *Variety,* 4 May 1966, p. 215. AS, p. 183. BHD1, p. 79. IFN, p. 41. Truitt, p. 42.

Bunny, George (father of **George Bunny, Jr.**; brother of **John Bunny**; uncle **of John Bunny, Jr.**) [actor] (b. New York NY, 13 Jul 1867–16 Apr 1952 [84], Los Angeles CA; heart attack). "George Bunny," *Variety,* 23 Apr 1952 (age 82). AMD, p. 56. AS, p. 183. BHD1, p. 79. IFN, p. 41. Truitt, p. 42. "George Bunny Resembles His Well-Known Brother," *MPW,* 10 Aug 1918, 867.

Bunny, George, Jr. (son of **George Bunny**; nephew of **John Bunny**; cousin of **John Bunny, Jr.**) [actor] (b. 1893–8 Dec 1958 [66?], Los Angeles CA). AMD, p. 56. BHD, p. 118. "George Bunny a National Star," *MPW,* 6 Nov 1920, 55:2 (states he is "son of the late John Bunny").

Bunny, John J. (father of **John Bunny, Jr.**; brother of **George Bunny**; uncle of **George Bunny, Jr.**) [stage/film actor] (b. at 115 Mott Street, New York NY, 21 Sep 1863 [Birth Certificate Index, Vol. II, p. 29]–26 Apr 1915 [51], Brooklyn NY [Death Certificate No. 8829]; Bright's disease). m. Clara Scanlan, 23 Jan 1890, Houston TX. (Vitagraph.) "John Bunny Dies; Movie Funmaker; Fat, Big, Round-Faced Actor Who Made Millions Laugh Succumbs at 52," *NYT,* 27 Apr 1915, 13:5. "John Bunny, probably one of the most well known actors known to fame through moving pictures, died Apr 26 of liver trouble, at his home in Brooklyn," *Variety,* 30 Apr 1915, p. 18. "John Bunny Left $6,536.89," *NYDM,* 15 Jan 1916, 33 (his widow, "of Valley Stream, LI," got the money). AMD, p. 56. AS, p. 183 (b. 1 Sep). BHD, p. 118. IFN, p. 41 (b. 1 Sep). "The Vitagraph Baseball Club," *MPW,* 20 May 1911, 1118. "John J. Bunny," *MPW,* 14 Oct 1911, 112. "John Bunny's Double," *MPW,* 10 Feb 1912, 466. "John Bunny in Vaudeville," *MPW,* 1 Feb 1913, 473. "John Bunny; Playing Character Leads with the Vitagraph Co.," *MPS,* 29 May 1914, 26 (b. New York NY, 21 Sep 1863). "Bunny to Tour World; Famous Comedian Will Head Company Organized by L.C. Wiswell and George Sidney," *NYDM,* 29 Jul 1914, 24:3 (to be advertised as Sunny Bunny, Funny Bunny, Honey Bunny, and Money Bunny. He was known on the stage as a Shakespearean actor of the old school). "Bunny 'Arrested' in Detroit," *MPW,* 5 Dec 1914, 1389. "John Bunny Ill; Famous Screen Comedian Confined to Home After Closing of His Road Show," *NYDM,* 21 Apr 1915, 24:4 (complication of diseases). "John Bunny Dead," *NYDM,* 28 Apr 1915, 22:2). "Bunny Seriously Ill," *MPW,* 1 May 1915, 704. "Mourn John Bunny; Screeners, Elks and Masons Pay Tribute to Memory of Bunny in New York," *NYDM,* 5 May 1915, 32:2. "Obituary," *MPW,* 8 May 1915, 876. H[ugh] A[ntoine] D'Arcy, "To the Memory of John Bunny [poem]," *NYDM,* 12 May 1915, 22:2 ("Good-bye, good clown/Indeed thou wert a merry fool…," by the poet/publicist). "Throng at Bunny's Funeral," *MPW,* 15 May 1915, 1048. "Observations by Our Man About Town," *MPW,* 15 May 1915, 1062. "Bunny Theatre Bills Vitagraph," *MPW,* 28 Jun 1919, 1998. James L. Neibaur, "John Bunny: The First Star of Comedy Movies," *CI,* 199 (Jan 1992), 33. Robert Klepper, "'Films of John Bunny, Volume One,' Vitagraph Company, A Bill Sprague

Video Release," *CI,* 263 (May 1997), 47 (three films with Flora Finch: *A Cure for Pokeritis,* 1912; *The Locket,* 1914; *Hearts and Diamonds,* 1914).

Bunny, John Francis, **Jr.** (son of **John Bunny**; nephew of **George Bunny**; cousin of **George Bunny, Jr.**) [actor/editor] (b. 1895–16 Apr 1971 [75?], Los Angeles CA; Bright's disease). AMD, p. 56. AS, p. 183. BHD, p. 118; BHD2, p. 37.

Bunton, Laura [actress] (b. 1895–6 Jun 1921 [26?], Los Angeles CA; suicide with chloroform). m. **Jack Mulhall** (d. 1979). "Laura Bunton, Suicide; Wife of Jack Mulhall Takes Chloroform at Home—No Message," *Variety,* 10 Jun 1921. BHD, p. 118 (Mulhall was playing opposite Mabel Normand in Sennett's *Molly O.* The Mulhalls had been married for seven years. "Mr. Mulhall says his wife had been despondent for some time."). AS, p. 183.

Burani, Michelette [actress] (b. Asnières [Paris] France, 1882?–27 Oct 1957 [75], Eastchester NY). m. Georges Barrere. "Michelette Burani," *Variety,* 30 Oct 1957, p. 87. AS, p. 183. BHD1, p. 79. IFN, p. 41.

Burbank, Goldie [actress] (*née* Ruth Caton, b. 1880?–1 Mar 1954 [74], Toledo OH). AS, p. 184. BHD, p. 118 (*née* Ruth Harris). IFN, p. 41. Truitt, p. 42.

Burbeck, Frank [actor] (b. Boston MA, 30 Dec 1855–20 Feb 1930 [74], New York NY). m. Nanette Comstock (d. 1942). "Frank Burbeck," *Variety,* 26 Feb 1930, p. 77. AS, p. 184. BHD, p. 118 (b. 1856). SD.

Burbridge, Ben [big game hunter/author] (b. 1876?–19 Jun 1936 [60], Jacksonville FL). "Ben Burbridge," *Variety,* 24 Jun 1936 (filmed *The Gorilla Hunt,* 1927; wrote *Gorilla,* 1928). AS, p. 184. Ben Burbridge, "Hunting Gorillas for the Screen; A Big Game Hunter Tells How He Made Pictures of Gigantic Ape-men in the Heart of an African Jungle," *Cinema Arts,* Oct 1926, 22–23, 43.

Burbridge, Charles J. [actor] (b. London, England, 1849–30 May 1922 [73], Amityville, LI NY). AS, p. 184. BHD1, p. 605. "Charles J. Burbridge," *Variety,* 2 Jun 1922, p. 21, and 9 Jun 1922, p. 7.

Burbridge, Elizabeth "Tommy" [actress/scenarist] (b. San Diego CA, 7 Dec 1895–19 Sep 1987 [91], Tarzana CA). (Ince.) AMD, p. 56. AS, p. 184. BHD, p. 118; BHD2, p. 37. FDY, p. 419 (Betty Burbridge). "Elizabeth Burbridge with Powell," *MPW,* 16 Sep 1916, 1806.

Burby, Gordon P. [actor] (b. NY, 1882–17 Oct 1951 [69?], Brightwaters NY). BHD, p. 118.

Burch, John E. [actor/assistant director] (b. Chicago IL, 17 Aug 1896–29 Jul 1969 [72], Honolulu HI). "John Burch," *Variety,* 6 Aug 1969, p. 63. AS, p. 184. BHD1, p. 79; BHD2, p. 37. IFN, p. 41. Truitt, p. 43.

Burchill, William [actor] (d. 1 Apr 1930). BHD, p. 118.

Burel, Lee [cinematographer/director] (*né* Léonce Henri Burel, b. Indre, France, 22 Nov 1892–21 Mar 1977 [84], Mougins, France [extrait de décès no. 28/1977]). AS, p. 184. BHD2, p. 37 (b. 23 Nov). FDY, p. 457.

Burford, Corinne (mother of Lana Morris) [actress]. No data found. "Lana Morris," *The London Times,* 2 Jun 1998, p. 23 (*née* Avril Maureen Anita Morris, b. The Hackney, London, England, 11 Mar 1930–27 May 1998 [68], Slough, England; of a drug overdose; "Her mother was the silent screen actress Corinne Burford, and her great-grandfather appeared with Sir Henry Irving at the Lyceum Theatre and Drury Lane."). "Lana Morris," *The Independent,* 30 May 1998, p. 24.

Burford, Ellen [actress]. No data found. AMD, p. 56. "Ellen Burford," *MPW,* 6 Oct 1917, 62.

Burg, Egen [actor/director] (b. Berlin, Germany, 6 Jan 1871–15 Nov 1944 [73], Camp de Theresienstadt, Germany). AS, p. 184. BHD1, p. 79. IFN, p. 42.

Burgarth, Theodore [actor]. No data found. (New York Film Co.) AMD, p. 56. "A New Star; Theodore Burgarth," *MPW,* 27 Sep 1913, 1383.

Burger, Paul F. [scenarist] (b. 1891–16 Jun 1937 [45?], Los Angeles CA). "Paul F. Burger," *Variety,* 29 Jun 1937, p. 70. AS, p. 184. BHD2, p. 37.

Burgermeister, Augusta *see* **Burmeister, Augusta**

Burgess, Earl [stuntman/actor] (b. Des Moines IA?, 1883?–5 Feb 1920 [36], Los Angeles CA). (Fox.) AS, p. 184. BHD, p. 118. IFN, p. 42. "Film Comedy's Grim Tragedy; Funny Man Plunges [500 feet] to Death from Fox Airplane; Heroic Effort at Rescue in Midair Fails Him; Camera's Remarkable Record of Fight for Life," *LA Times,* 6 Feb 1920, II, p. 1 ("When the film was developed in the Fox laboratories last night it revealed a gruesome picture of the unfortunate daredevil's fight for life up to the last minute." The photographer was P.H. Whitman.). "Movie Aviator Falls 500 Feet," *MPW,* 28 Feb 1920, 1480.

Burgess, William [actor] (b. 1867–30 Oct 1948 [81?], Los Angeles CA). AS, p. 185 (b. 1967).

Burghart, Charles [actor] (d. 19 Feb 1927, Los Angeles CA). BHD, p. 118.

Burkart, Theodore [actor] (b. Philadelphia PA, 1869). (Solax; Lubin; Eclair; World-Peerless.) 1918 Studio Directory, p. 65.

Burke, Billie [stage/film actress/singer] (*née* Mary William Ethelbert Appleton Burke, b. Washington DC, 7 Aug 1885–14 May 1970 [84], Los Angeles CA). m. **Florenz Ziegfeld, Jr.**, 11 Apr 1914, Hoboken NJ (d. 1932). With Cameron Shipp, *With a Feather on My Nose* (NY: Appleton-Century-Crofts, 1949); *With Powder on My Nose* (1959). (Film debut: *Peggy,* 1915; Triangle; Kleine; FP-L.) "Billie Burke, Film Comedienne and Once a Stage Beauty, Dead," *NYT,* 16 May 1970, 1:8, 25:1. "Billie Burke," *Variety,* 20 May 1970, p. 53 ("Ethelberg"). AMD, p. 56. AS, p. 184 (b. 1884). BHD1, p. 80. FSS, p. 50. IFN, p. 42. Katz, p. 183. MSBB, p. 1032 (b. 1886). Truitt, p. 43. William Hughes, *DAB,* Supp. 8 (1988), pp. 64–65 (b. 1886). "Burke—Ziegfeld; Marriage Takes Place in Hoboken Apr 11 After Saturday Matinee," *NYDM,* 15 Apr 1914, 19:1. "Stage Versus Screen; Merry War Between Theatrical Managers and Film Producers—Billie Burke Quits Frohman Company to Appear on Screen," *NYDM,* 21 Jul 1915, 9:1 (the NYMP Co. recruited Burke for 5 weeks at $8,000 a week. Theatrical manager A.H. Woods then announced that "henceforth no player in his empl[o]y would be allowed to act simultaneously for motion pictures, except in cases where previous contracts had to be fulfilled. ¶'The moving picture people derive all of the gain and we bear the loss,' said Mr. Woods. 'The reputations that the movies capitalize are made in the legitimate theater, and these same reputations come back to plague us from the screen with ten cent competitions.' ¶"Joseph Brooks has declared that any of his stars who enter the motion pictures can consider their contracts with him void, and Selwyn and Company have announced that they will hereafter carry a line in all their advertisements that 'this is not a motion picture.' This course has been made necessary...by the fact that by advertisements of motion pictures in which legitimate stars are featured, it is impossible to tell whether the offering has a company of living actors or screen presenttations." For more *see* Marc Klaw.). "Billie Burke Signed; New York Motion Picture Corporation Pays Record Figure to Former Frohman Star," *NYDM,* 21 Jul 1915, 25:1 ($40,000 for five weeks' work, plus an option of $50,000 for her continuous services for the next three years, which, if accepted, will give her $150,000 a year. "She in turn is to give twenty-six weeks of her time for motion picture work." All traveling expenses are to be paid, including a private car for the railroad journey and the exclusive use of a car while in CA. The NYMP Co. took out insurance of $50,000 with Lloyds of London in the event of rain (since she was to work for five continous weeks.). "Billie Burke Signs with New York," *MPW,* 31 Jul 1915, 825. J. Van Cartmell, "Along the Pacific Coast," *NYDM,* 22 Sep 1915, 29:2 ("Billie Burke's debut in the film world is evidently proving a great success.... A strange fact concerning Miss Burke's work—one that was immediately noted and commented upon—is that she exhibited not the slightest indication of camera fright. Usually, a stage star, making his or her initial appearance in front of the camera, gives way to a petty fear that something will go amiss and be observed which otherwise would escape detection on the stage."). J. Van Cartmell, "Along the Pacific Coast," *NYDM,* 29 Sep 1915, 33:1 (playing an American hoyden who visits Scotland, Burke was required to wear pink pajamas in 38 different scenes. She refused. Ince insisted. She was somewhat relieved when "energetic carpenters had overcome the difficulty by boxing in the scene, much to the sorrow of the many camera fiends and several bald headed visitors."). "Billie Burke Leaves Inceville," *MPW,* 30 Oct 1915, 776. "'My Lady o' the Roses,'" *MPC,* Aug 1916, 59–60, 70. "A New Gloria in the Field," *MPW,* 11 Nov 1916, 873 (Patricia Burke Ziegfeld b. 23 Oct 1916, NYC). "Billie Burke with Famous-Lasky," *MPW,* 21 Apr 1917, 405. C. Blythe Sherwood, "In Pursuit of Billie; Miss Burke Is Very, Very Busy," *MPC,* May 1919, 22–23, 76–77. "Bankrolls Win for Billie Burke as Movie Queen," *Daily News,* 11 May 1922 (eyebrows were lifted when Burke won the "Queen of the Movies" title. "She is 'Queen of the Movies' without being a movie queen. She has had her days in the pictures and has definitely abandoned the screen. Not since she completed *The Education of Elizabeth,* in the fall of 1920, has she been before the camera, and at that time she made public announcement of her retirement from filmland."). "Edward Earle and Billie Burke Are Crowned King and Queen of Movies," *MPW,* 20 May 1922, 261. Eve Golden, "Billie Burke: That Charming Mrs. Ziegfeld," *Films of the Golden Age,* No. 4, Spring 1996, pp. 66–70.

Burke, Edwin [director/scenarist] (b. Albany NY, 30 Aug 1889–26 Sep 1944 [55], New York NY). AS, p. 185. BHD2, p. 37.

Burke, Ethel [actress]. No data found. (World-Equitable). AMD, p. 57. "Ethel Burke with World Film," *MPW,* 13 May 1916, 1176.

Burke, James L. [actor] (b. New York NY, 24 Sep 1886–23 May 1968 [81], Los Angeles CA; heart attack). "James Burke," *Variety*, 5 Jun 1968, p. 63 (began 1933). AS, p. 185. BHD1, p. 80. IFN, p. 42.

Burke, J. Frank [vaudeville/film actor] (*né* John Franklin Burke, b. Hartland VT, Apr 1867–23 Jan 1918 [50?], Los Angeles CA; arteriosclerosis). (NYMPC; Ince; Triangle.) "J. Frank Burke," *Variety*, 8 Feb 1918. AS, p. 185. BHD, p. 118. IFN, p. 42. 1918 Studio Directory, p. 65. SD. George Katchmer, "Remembering the Great Silents," *CI*, 243 (Sep 1995), 42, 44.

Burke, Johnny [actor/composer] (b. Antioch CA, 3 Oct 1908–25 Feb 1964 [55], New York NY; heart attack in his sleep). "Johnny Burke," *Variety*, 3 Apr 1964, p. 79. AMD, p. 57. AS, p. 185. BHD2, p. 37. "Pathé Signs Up Johnny Burke," *MPW*, 10 Apr 1926, 454.

Burke, Joseph C. [actor] (b. New York NY, 1884?–17 Dec 1942 [58], New York NY). (Powers; Pathé; Reliance; FP-L; Triumph; Fox; Kleine; Ivan; Rolfe.) "Joseph C. Burke," *Variety*, 23 Dec 1942 (blind for 10 years up to his death). AS, p. 185. BHD1, p. 80. IFN, p. 42. 1918 Studio Directory, p. 65.

Burke, Marie (mother of actress Patricia Burke) [stage/film actress] (*née* Marie Rosa Holt, b. London, England, 18 Oct 1894–21 Mar 1988 [93], Menton, France). (Stage debut: *Afgar*, 1919, London Pavilion.) "Marie Burke," *The Times*, 23 Mar 1988, p. 12:7. m. (1) Tom Burke—div. (d. 1969; 1 daughter b. 1917); Guy Nelson King. AS, p. 185 (d. London, England). BHD1, p. 80. SD.

Burke, Melville [director] (b. St. Louis MO, 4 Nov 1884–22 Mar 1982 [97], Honolulu, Oahu HI). AS, p. 185. BHD2, p. 37.

Burke, Peggy [actress]. No data found. (Thanhouser.) "In the Picture Studios," *NYDM*, 4 Aug 1915, 27:2 (in the female baseball team at Thanhouser).

Burke, Thomas F. [actor] (d. 25 Mar 1941, Los Angeles CA). "Thomas Burke," *Variety*, 2 Apr 1941. AS, p. 185. BHD, p. 118. IFN, p. 42.

Burke, Tom [opera singer/actor] (*né* Thomas Aspinall Burke, b. Leigh, Lancashire, England, 2 Mar 1890–14 Sep 1969 [79], Carshalton, Surrey, England). "Tom Burke," *Variety*, 1 Oct 1969. AS, p. 185. IFN, p. 42. SD.

Burke, Virginia [extra actress] (b. ca. 1910). Paul Paige, "Close-Ups and Fade-Outs," *Paris and Hollywood Screen Secrets*, Oct 1927, 22 (attempting suicide, the seventeen-year-old took poison, but survived).

Burkett, Bartine [film/TV actress] (b. Robeline LA, 9 Feb 1898–20 May 1994 [96], Burbank CA; congestive heart failure). m. Ralph Zane (d. 1968). (FP-L; Universal, retired in 1928.) "Bartine Zane," *Variety*, 6 Jun 1994 (known as Bartine Burkette from 1916). AMD, p. 57. AS, p. 185; p. 1179 (Bartine Zane, b. 1897). BH p. 118. "Bartine Burkett Back," *MPW*, 1 Mar 1924, 72. "Bartine Burkett," *CI*, 229 (Jul 1994), 57.

Burkhardt, Addison [scenarist/title writer] (b. 1880–25 Jan 1937 [56?], Los Angeles CA). AS, p. 185. BHD2, p. 38. FDY, pp. 419, 441.

Burkhardt, Charles [actor] (d. 17 Feb 1925, Denver CO). m. **Mary Rothwell** (d. 1926). AS, p. 185.

Burkhardt, Harry [actor] (b. Boston MA, 27 Sep 1870–18 Sep 1943 [72], Los Angeles CA). (Fox; Pathé; Metro; Triumph.) BHD1, p. 80. IFN, p. 42.

Burleigh, Bertram [actor]. No data found. AMD, p. 57. "Engage Popular English Star for Lead in 'The Great Day,'" *MPW*, 31 Jul 1920, 613. "Paramount's English Studio Praised by Bertram Burleigh," *MPW*, 2 Oct 1920, 658.

Burlingham, Frederick [cinematographer]. No data found. AMD, p. 57. "Something New from Switzerland," *MPW*, 20 Apr 1918, 384–85. "Burlingham Film Full of Thrills," *MPW*, 14 Dec 1918, 1201. "Burlingham First to Film 'Suwanee Ribber,' Finds It Beauty-Festooned," *MPW*, 17 Jan 1920, 405.

Burmeister [or **Burmester**], **Augusta** [stage/film actress] (b. Hamburg, Germany, 1859–28 Mar 1934 [74], Los Angeles CA). (Kleine; Sun Photoplay Co.) "Augusta Burmeister," *Variety*, 3 Apr 1934. AMD, p. 57. AS, p. 185. BHD1, p. 80. IFN, p. 42. "Kleine Actress Has Played Lead with Edwin Booth," *MPW*, 27 Feb 1915, 1274.

Burnell, Gene [actress]. No data found. AMD, p. 57. "Showman Summer Adage on Personal Shows Again Substantiated by Miss Gene Burnell," *MPW*, 22 Jul 1922, 298.

Burnett, Coral [scenarist]. No data found. FDY, p. 419.

Burnett, James (Tex) [actor] (b. 1904–16 Sep 1984 [80?], Orange Co.,CA). BHD, p. 118.

Burnett, Jessie [actress] (b. France). No other data found. (Biograph; Balboa.) Al Ray, "Before the Stars Shone," *Picture-Play Magazine*, Sep 1917, 93 (b. in France, raised in Arizona).

Burnett, William Riley [scenarist/director] (b. Akron OH, 25 Nov 1899–25 Apr 1982 [82], Santa Monica CA). AS, p. 186. BHD2, p. 38.

Burnham, Beatrice [actress] (b. El Paso TX, 1897). AMD, p. 57. BR, pp. 118–19. MH, p. 100 (b. Galveston TX, 1902). "Beatrice Burnham Signs with Universal," *MPW*, 24 May 1919, 1179. "Beatrice Burnham to Lead," *MPW*, 31 Jul 1920, 568. "Beatrice Burnham with MacLean," *MPW*, 7 Aug 1920, 757. George A. Katchmer, "Remembering the Great Silents," *CI*, 175 (Jan 1990), C5.

Burnham, Clara L[ouise] (daughter of composer George Frederick Root) [writer] (*née* Clara Root, b. West Newton MA, 26 May 1854–20 Jun 1927 [73], Bailey Island, Casco Bay, near Portland ME; heart disease). m. Walter Burnham, 1873 (d. 1900). (First novel, *No Gentleman*, 1881.) "Clara L. Burnham, Novelist, Dead; Daughter of George F. Root, Composer, Stricken in Sleep at Maine Home; Had Written Many Books; Returned Recently from Hollywood, Where She Had Sold Movie Rights of Latest Work [*The Lavarons*]," *NYT*, 22 Jun 1927, 27:5. "Clara L. Burnham Dies," *Variety*, 29 Jun 1927 (wrote 26 novels between 1881 and 1925). AS, p. 186 (b. 1856). *NEAB*, Vol. 21 (1931), p. 151. *Twentieth Century Authors*, p. 226.

Burnham, Eunice [pianist/actress] (b. 1882?–13 Apr 1966 [84], Van Nuys CA). "Eunice Burnham," *Variety*, 27 Apr 1966 (was once partner of Charlotte Greenwood). AMD, p. 57. AS, p. 186. "Get Fat Female at Last for Paramount Film," *MPW*, 5 Feb 1921, 701.

Burnham, Frances [actress] (b. 1898?). (Fox; Fine Arts.) AMD, p. 57. "Frances Burnham," *MPW*, 16 Jun 1917, 1792. Al Ray, "Before the Stars Shone," *Picture-Play Magazine*, Sep 1917, 92 (19 years old). "Star to Organize Company," *MPW*, 26 Apr 1919, 520.

Burnham, Julia [scenarist]. No data found. AMD, p. 57. "Julia Burnham Joins Metro Scenario Staff," *MPW*, 22 May 1920, 1068.

Burnham, Nicholas [actor] (b. 1860–30 Jan 1925 [64?], Bernardsville NJ). AS, p. 186. BHD, p. 118.

Burns, Beulah [actress]. No data found. AMD, p. 57. "Beulah Burns, A Chip of the Old Block," *MPW*, 25 Nov 1916, 1190.

Burns, Bobby *see* **Burns, Robert P**

Burns, David [actor] (b. New York NY, 22 Jun 1901–12 Mar 1971 [69], Philadelphia PA). m. Mildred Todd. "David Burns," *Variety*, 17 Mar 1971, p. 79 (age 67). AS, p. 186 (b. 1903). NNAT, p. 363.

Burns, Edmund [or **Edward**] [actor] (*né* Edward J. Burns, b. Philadelphia PA, 27 Sep 1892–2 Apr 1980 [87], Los Angeles CA). (Fox; UA.) AMD, p. 57. AS, p. 186. BHD1, p. 81. FSS, p. 50. Katz, p. 185 (began 1918). Anthony Slide, *Silent Portraits* (Vestal NY: The Vestal Press, Ltd., 1989), p. 39 (d. 1980). "DeMille Renews with Three Featured Players," *MPW*, 22 May 1926, 4. George Katchmer, "Remembering the Great Silents," *CI*, 256 (Oct 1996), 41.

Burns, Edward W. [actor] (d. 1 Sep 1957). AMD, p. 57. BHD, p. 118. "Burns Goes to the Coast," *MPW*, 22 Feb 1919, 1057.

Burns, Fred [actor] (b. Ft. Keough MT, 24 Apr 1878–18 Jul 1955 [77], Los Angeles Co. CA). (Began 1914.) AS, p. 186. BHD1, p. 81. IFN, p. 43. Katz, p. 185 (began 1916).

Burns, George J. [actor] (b. Utica NY, 24 Nov 1889–15 Aug 1966 [76], Gloversville NY). BHD, p. 118.

Burns, Harry (step-father of **Bobby Vernon**) [director/actor] (b. 1883?–9 Jan 1939 [55], Los Angeles CA; heart attack at wheel of his car). m. **Dorothy Vernon** (d. 1970). "Harry Burns," *Variety*, 11 Jan 1939. AS, p. 186. IFN, p. 43.

Burns, Harry [actor] (b. Philadelphia PA, 1885–9 Jul 1948 [63?], Santa Monica CA). "Harry Burns," *Variety*, 14 Jul 1948, p. 55. AS, p. 186. BHD1, p. 81.

Burns, James W. [actor] (d. 16 Jul 1975, San Diego CA). AS, p. 186. BHD, p. 118.

Burns, Jesse [scenarist]. No data found. FDY, p. 419.

Burns, Neal [actor] (b. Bristol PA, 26 Jun 1890–3 Oct 1969 [79], Los Angeles CA). AMD, p. 57. AS, p. 186. BHD1, p. 81. FFF, p. 238. IFN, p. 43 (b. GA). MH, p. 100 (b. 4 Feb 1904). "Neil Burns," *MPN*, 21 Oct 1916, 166 (b. 1891). "Neal Burns," *MPW*, 24 Mar 1917, 1929. "Neal Burns," *MPW*, 23 Jun 1917, 1942. "Fire Singes Actors; Considerable Damage [$3,000] Done by the Flames on Movie Stage," *LA Times*, 7 Feb 1920, II, p. 9 (at National Film Corp. of America, Santa Monica, on 6 Feb. Also hurt was Lucille Rubey. "A flash pistol used in the picture sent sparks toward the cloth covering the set, which was quickly consumed by the flames...the studio fire department extinguished the flames. The loss is covered by insurance."). "Neal Burns Signs Long Contract," *MPW*, 12 Aug 1922, 500. "Who Challenges Burns?," *MPW*, 9 Jan 1926, 163.

Burns, Paul E. [actor] (b. Philadelphia PA, 26 Jan 1881–17 May 1967 [86], Los Angeles CA; heart attack). "Paul E. Burns," *Variety*, 24 May 1967, p. 63. AS, p. 186 (d. Van Nuys CA). BHD1, p. 81. IFN, p. 43.

Burns, Robert E. (Bob Burns) [stage/film acrobat/actor] (b. Glendive MT, 21 Nov 1884–14 Mar 1957 [72], Los Angeles Co. CA). AMD, p. 57. AS, p. 186. BHD1, p. 81. IFN, p. 43. "Pokes and Jabbs," *MPW,* 11 Sep 1915, 1811:2.

Burns, Robert P[aul] (Bobby Burns) [actor] (b. Philadelphia PA, 1 Sep 1878–16 Jan 1966 [87], Los Angeles Co. CA). AMD, p. 57. AS, p. 187. BHD1, p. 81. IFN, p. 43. "Robert Paul Burns," *MPW,* 6 Jan 1917, 78.

Burns, Sammy [actor] (b. England). "First Vogue Comedy Ready; New Brand of Slapstick Pictures Will Soon Be Released on the Mutual Program, with Sammy Burns in Leading Role," *Motography,* 1 Jan 1916, 24 (in *Sammy's Scandalous Scheme,* 27 Dec 1915).

Burns, Vinnie [actress] (aka June Daye, 1915–19). No data found. (Lubin.) AMD, p. 57. "Mexican War in Solax Features," *MPW,* 4 Jul 1914, 80. "What a Picture Has to Do," *MPW,* 5 Sep 1914, 1358. "Vinnie Burns Now June Daye," *NYDM,* 6 Nov 1915, 26:4 (300 admirers of hers in Philadelphia suggested the new name. "Impressed with the symphony of the two names, Miss Burns agreed."). "Actress Changes Name [to June Daye]," *MPW,* 27 Nov 1915, 1638. "Vinnie Burns with Doris Kenyon," *MPW,* 11 Jan 1919, 234 [changed name back to Vinnie Burns).

Burns, William John [detective/author/actor] (b. Baltimore MD, 19 Oct 1861–14 Apr 1932 [70], Sarasota FL; heart attack). m. Annie M. Ressler, 5 Jul 1880. "W.J. Burns Dead; Famous Detective; Former New Yorker Stricken at His Home in Sarasota, Fla., at the Age of 70; Once Secret Service Head; Career Began in 1885 with Unraveling of Tally-Sheet Forgeries in Ohio Election," *NYT,* 15 Apr 1932, 19:1. AMD, p. 57. AS, p. 187. BHD, p. 118. Alvin F. Harlow, *DAB,* Supp. 1 (1944), pp. 134–35 (appeared in *The $5,000,000 Counterfeiting Plot,* Dramascope, 1914, with Sir Arthur Conan Doyle). "Burns Acts in His Own Story," *MPW,* 8 Aug 1914, 843.

Burns, William "Willy" [actor] (b. 1902?–21 Jan 1966 [63], Los Angeles CA; pneumonia). "William Burns," *Variety,* 26 Jan 1966, p. 70. AS, p. 187.

Burnside, R[ichard] **H.** [director/producer/playwright/lyricist/librettist] (*né* Richard Hubber Thorne Burnside, b. Glasgow, Scotland, 13 Aug 1870–14 Sep 1952 [82], Metuchen NJ). "R.H. Burnside, 82, Producer, Is Dead; Former General Director of Old Hippodrome Staged 200 Shows During His Career," *NYT,* 15 Sep 1952, 25:1 (wrote *Ladder of Roses; Nice to Have a Sweetheart; Poor Butterfly* [with John Golden and Ray Hubbell]). "R.H. Burnside," *Variety,* 17 Sep 1952, p. 75. AS, p. 187. ASCAP 66, pp. 93–94. BHD2, p. 38. CEPMJ, Vol. 2, pp. 648–49. NNAT, p. 363. SD.

Burnstein, Norman [scenarist]. No data found. FDY, p. 419.

Burr, Charles C. [director/producer] (b. Brooklyn NY, 30 Jan 1891–4 Jun 1956 [65], Los Angeles CA). "C.C. Burr," *Variety,* 6 Jun 1956, p. 63. AMD, p. 57. AS, p. 187. BHD2, p. 38. "Charles C. Burr Is Promoted," *MPW,* 2 Mar 1918, 1208. "Burr Forms New Producing Company; Will Star Hines in Torchy Stories," *MPW,* 31 Jan 1920, 767. "48-Hour-a-Week Actors' Contract Would Prove a Menace—Charles C. Burr," *MPW,* 27 Jan 1923, 367. "Independent Is Exhibitor's Safeguard, States Charles C. Burr," *MPW,* 17 May 1924, 270.

Burr, Edmund [actor] (d. 16 Jul 1975). AS, p. 187. BHD1, p. 82.

Burr, Eugene [actor] (b. Leavenworth KS, 1884?–7 Jun 1940 [56], Los Angeles CA; pulmonary oedema). AS, p. 187. BHD1, p. 82. IFN, p. 43.

Burred, L.J. [cameraman]. No data found. AMD, p. 58. "Veteran Gaumont Cameraman on Duty," *MPW,* 8 Jul 1916, 271.

Burress, William [actor] (b. New Cornerstown OH, 19 Aug 1867–30 Oct 1948 [81], Los Angeles Co. CA). (Essanay; Fox; Universal.) AS, p. 187. BHD1, p. 82. IFN, p. 43. 1918 Studio Directory, p. 65.

Burris, James [actor/composer] (d. 2 Jun 1923, Washington DC). "James Burris," *Variety,* 21 Jun 1923. BHD, p. 119.

Burrough, Tom [actor] (b. Clinton County IL, 1869–8 Sep 1929 [60], Staten Island NY). AS, p. 187 (d. LA CA). BHD, p. 119. IFN, p. 43.

Burrows, James [actor] (b. 1842?–20 May 1926 [84], Lynn MA). "James Burrows," *Variety,* 26 May 1926, p. 56. BHD, p. 119.

Burston, Louis B. [producer] (*né* Louis Burstein, d. 4 Apr 1923, near Pomona CA; auto accident). (Metro.) "Auto Hit Train; Louis Burston and Others Fatally Injured in Crash Near Pomona," *Variety,* 5 Apr 1923. AMD, p. 58. AS, p. 187. BHD2, p. 38. "Louis Burstein with Equitable," *MPW,* 24 Jul 1915, 663. "Louis B. Burstein," *MPW,* 16 Jun 1917, 1769. "Louis B. Burstein, President of the King-Bee," *MPW,* 13 Oct 1917, 240. "Producer Sues Star," *MPW,* 13 Sep 1919, 1635–36. "Obituary," *MPW,* 7 Apr 1923, 618 (d. 25 Mar 1923, near Hollywood). Richard Alan Nelson, "Before Laurel: Oliver Hardy and the Vim Comedy Company, a Studio Biography," *Current Research in Film,* 2 (1986), 136–55.

Burt, Frederic [actor] (b. Onarga IL, 12 Feb 1876–2 Oct 1943 [67], Twenty-Nine Palms CA). m. Helen Ware. "Frederic Burt," *Variety,* 13 Oct 1943. AS, p. 187. BHD1, p. 82 (d. Los Angeles CA). IFN, p. 43. Truitt, p. 44.

Burt, Ida [stage/film actress] (b. New Orleans LA, 1852–26 Oct 1941 [89?], New York NY). "Ida Burt," *Variety,* 29 Oct 1941, p. 54 (interred in Evergreen Cemetery, Brooklyn). BHD, p. 119.

Burt, Katherine Newlin [writer]. No data found. AMD, p. 58. "Joins Author Colony," *MPW,* 29 Jan 1921, 579.

Burt, Laura [actress] (b. Ramsay, Isle of Man, 16 Sep 1872–16 Oct 1952 [80], Bronx NY). m. Henry Stanford. (World.) "Laura Burt," *Variety,* 22 Oct 1952, p. 63. AMD, p. 58. AS, p. 187. BHD1, p. 82. IFN, p. 43. "Famous Actress Seen in 'Love and the Woman,'" *MPW,* 31 May 1919, 1343.

Burt, Nellie (daughter of **William Presley Burt**) [actress] (b. 4 Jan 1900–3 Nov 1986 [86], East Rockaway NJ). AMD, p. 58. BHD, p. 119. "Director's Daughter in Pictures," *MPW,* 20 Dec 1924, 740:2.

Burt, William Presley (father of **Nellie Burt**) [actor] (b. St. Peter MN, 11 Feb 1867–23 Feb 1955 [88], Denver CO). "William P. Burt," *Variety,* 2 Mar 1955, p. 71. AS, p. 187. BHD1, p. 82; BHD2, p. 39. IFN, p. 43. Truitt, p. 44 (b. 1873).

Burton, Beatrice [scenarist]. No data found. AMD, p. 58. "Burton and W. Dugan Signed to Long Term," *MPW,* 10 Dec 1927, 24.

Burton, Blanche [actress] (b. Baltimore MD, 1879–24 Jul 1934 [55], New York NY). BHD, p. 119. IFN, p. 43.

Burton, C. Edgar [scenarist]. No data found. AMD, p. 58. "Premier Scenario Department," *MPW,* 11 Dec 1915, 1985.

Burton, Charlotte [actress] (b. San Francisco CA, 30 May 1881?–28 Mar 1942 [60], Los Angeles CA; heart attack). m. **William Russell**, 1917 (d. 1929). (American.) "Charlotte Burton," *NYT,* 31 Mar 1942, 21:2. "Charlotte Burton," *Variety,* 8 Apr 1942, p. 54 (d. 29 Mar). AMD, p. 58. AS, p. 188. BHD, p. 119 (b. 1882). IFN, p. 43. "Charlotte Burton," *MPW,* 15 Jun 1912, 667. "Charlotte Burton," *MPW,* 16 Nov 1912, 667. "Charlotte Burton Joins Essanay," *MPW,* 16 Dec 1916, 1629. "Russell—Burton," *MPW,* 9 Jun 1917, 1614. Cal York, "Plays and Players," *Photoplay,* Jul 1917, 110 (sued Essanay for $28,200. "Miss Burton alleges that the Chicago concern took her from her happy home in Santa Barbara, California, brought her to Chicago and then failed to live up to its contract."). "Don't Try to Make Your Tragedienne Do Comedy," *MPW,* 9 Oct 1920, 775. Billy H. Doyle, "Lost Players," *CI,* 152 (Feb 1988), C12 (b. 1891). Truitt, p. 44.

Burton, Clarence V. [actor] (b. Windsor MO, 10 May 1881–1 Dec 1933 [52], Los Angeles CA; heart attack). "Clarence Burton," *Variety,* 5 Dec 1933. AS, p. 188 (b. Ft. Lyons MO; d. 2 Dec). BHD1, p. 82 (b. Fort Lyons MO). IFN, p. 43. MH, p. 100. Truitt, p. 44.

Burton, David [actor/director] (b. Odessa, Ukraine, Russia, 22 May 1877–30 Dec 1963 [86], New York NY [Death Certificate Index No. 28155; M.E. Case No. 1140; age 77]). "David Burton," *Variety,* 8 Jan 1964, p. 274. AS, p. 186 (b. 1890). BHD1, p. 82; BHD2, p. 38 (b. 1890).

Burton, Ethel Marie [actress]. No data found. AMD, p. 58. "Ethel Marie Burton," *MPW,* 19 May 1917, 1119. "Ethel Burton Returns to 'King-Bee,'" *MPW,* 2 Feb 1918, 658. "Ethel Burton with King Bee," *MPW,* 23 Feb 1918, 1110.

Burton, Frederick [actor] (b. Indianapolis IN, 20 Oct 1871–23 Oct 1957 [86], Woodland Hills CA). "Frederick Burton," *Variety,* 30 Oct 1957. AMD, p. 58. AS, p. 188. BHD1, p. 82. IFN, p. 43. Truitt, p. 44. "Cosmopolitan Engages Burton," *MPW,* 10 Apr 1920, 225.

Burton, George H. [actor] (b. Butte MT, 17 Sep 1898–8 Dec 1955 [57], Los Angeles CA). "George H. Burton," *Variety,* 14 Dec 1955 (age 55). AS, p. 188. BHD1, p. 82. IFN, p. 43.

Burton, G. Marion [scenarist]. No data found. FDY, p. 419.

Burton, John W. [actor] (b. WI, 7 Jan 1853–25 Mar 1920 [67], Los Angeles CA; stroke). AMD, p. 58. AS, p. 188. BHD, p. 119. IFN, p. 43. "Obituary," *MPW,* 17 Apr 1920, 421 (b. 1857; d. 27 Mar).

Burton, Langhorne [actor] (b. Somersby, Lincolnshire, England, 25 Dec 1872–6 Dec 1949 [77], London, England). m. Marjorie Chard. AS, p. 188. BHD1, p. 82. IFN, p. 43. SD.

Burton, M.G. [actor]. No data found. AMD, p. 58. "Cited for Bravery," *MPW,* 1 Mar 1919, 1186.

Burton, Ned [actor] (b. 1850?–11 Dec 1922 [72], New York NY; heart attack). (Pathé Frères.) "Ned Burton," *Variety,* 15 Dec 1922, p. 9. AS, p. 188. BHD, p. 119. IFN, p. 43. Truitt, p. 45.

Burton, S.J. [actor] (b. 1860?–6 May 1920 [60+], Chicago IL; suicide by hanging). "S.J. Burton," *Variety,* 14 May 1920, p. 9.

Burton, William H. [actor] (b. 11 Apr 1844–15 Mar 1926 [81], New York NY). (Pilot Films Corp.) "William H. Burton," *Variety,* 17 Mar 1926, p. 47. AS, p. 188. BHD, p. 119. IFN, p. 44. Truitt, p. 45.

Busch, Mae [actress] (b. Melbourne, Australia, 19 Jan 1891?–19 Apr 1946 [55?], San Fernando CA). m. (1) **Francis J. McDonald**, 12 Dec 1915, Los Angeles CA—div. 1922 (d. 1968); (2) John Earl Cassell, Riverside CA, 30 Jun 1926; (3) Thomas C. Tate. (Sennett.) "Mae Busch, Known on Screen, Stage; Former Leading Actress, Who Began Career in Keystone Comedies, Is Dead at 44," *NYT,* 22 Apr 1946, 21:4. "Mae Busch," *Variety,* 24 Apr 1946, p. 62 (age 44). AMD, p. 58. AS, p. 188 (b. 20 Jan; d. Woodland Hills CA). BHD1, p. 83 (b. 1901-d. LA CA). FFF, p. 29. FSS, p. 51. IFN, p. 44 (age 44). Katz, p. 187 (b. 20 Jan 1897). Truitt, p. 45 (b. 20 Jan 1891). "Director Marries Comedy Star," *Motography,* 1 Jan 1916, 28. Elizabeth Petersen, "The Comedy Girl with the Serious Eyes," *MPC,* Sep 1916, 26. "Mae Busch in New Goldwyn Picture," *MPW,* 27 May 1922, 393 (*The Christian*). Helen Klumph, "The Minority Favorite," *Picture-Play Magazine,* Jun 1923, 26–27. "Put Under Contract," *MPW,* 3 Feb 1923, 434. "Mae Busch, Star in Movies, to Wed Director [Lewis King, brother of Henry King] in Fall," *Daily News,* 12 Jun 1925. "Busch—Cassell," *MPW,* 17 Jul 1926, 3. Don Juan, "So This Is Hollywood," *Paris and Hollywood,* 2 (Oct 1926), 18 (her new husband, Cassell, was an engineer of the General Petroleum Corp. States that he was 26; Busch, 29. June Lee, "Dan Cupid's Bulletin Board," *Paris and Hollywood,* Oct 1926, 86 (Mae, "29," wed Cassell, 26). "This marriage ought to wear well."). Larry Lee Holland, "Mae Busch," *FIR,* Sep 1986, 400–07 (1897–1946).

Bush, Anita [stage/film actress/secretary of the Negro Actors Guild] (b. Washington DC, 1883–16 Feb 1974 [91], New York NY). "Anita Bush," *Variety,* 20 Feb 1974, p. 55 (appeared in *The Bulldogger* and *The Crimson Skull*). AS, p. 188. BHD, p. 119. IFN, p. 44. SD, p. 193.

Bush, Pauline Elvira, "The Madonna of the Movies" [stock/film actress] (b. Wahoo [Lincoln] NB, 22 May 1886–1 Nov 1969 [83], San Diego CA; pneumonia). (American, 1911; Universal, 1911–15.) m. **Allan Dwan**, 24 Apr 1915, San Juan Capistrano—div. ca. 1919 (d. 1981). AMD, p. 58. AS, p. 188. BHD, pp. 11–12; 119. BR, pp. 2–6. IFN, p. 44. "Pauline Bush; The New Leading Lady in the 'Flying A' Western Company," *MPW,* 3 Jun 1911, 1249. "Pauline Bush; Leading Woman in Director Allan Dwan's Gold Seal Company," *MPS,* 20 Mar 1914, 26. "Brief Biographies of Popular Players," *Motion Picture Magazine,* Feb 1915, 109. William E. Wing, "Along the Pacific Coast," *NYDM,* 8 Apr 1915, 24:2 (imminent marriage to Dwan announced. They "met, sighed and palpitated" ["love at first sight"] four years earlier. "From that day until recent months Miss Bush played in Mr. Dwan's pictures while working havoc with his affections."). Billy H. Doyle, "Lost Players," *CI,* 151 (Jan 1988), C4-C5.

Bush, Robert Finlay [actor] (b. New Haven CT, 1888–2 Apr 1929 [41], Prescott AZ). BHD, p. 119. IFN, p. 44.

Bushman, Francis X[avier] [sculptor's model; stage/vaudeville/film/radio/TV actor] [father of **Virginia**, **Lenore** and **Francis X. Bushman, Jr.**; grandfather of actor Pat Conway) (aka Frank X. Bushman, and Cecil Stanhope in England, b. Baltimore MD, 10 Jan 1883–23 Aug 1966 [83], Pacific Palisades CA; heart attack after a fall). m. (1) Josephine Fladuenne, 1902 (mother of Ralph Everly [Francis X. Bushman, Jr.], b. 1902; Josephine, b. 1905; Virginia, b. 1906; Lenore Konti, b. 1909; and Bruce, b. 1911)—div. 5 Feb 1918; (2) **Beverly Bayne**, 31 Jul 1918, Baltimore MD—div. 1932 (d. 1982; son, Richard)—div. 15 Sep 1926; (3) Norma Atkins, 1932 (d. Feb 1956); (4) Iva Millicent Richardson, 15 Aug 1956, Las Vegas NV. Richard J. Maturi and Mary Buckingham Maturi, *Francis X. Bushman; A Biography and Filmography* (Jefferson NC: McFarland, 1998). (Stage debut, ca. 1907, Albaugh Lyceum Theater; film debut: *His Friend's Wife,* 6 Jun 1911; Essanay; Metro; Vitagraph.) "Francis X. Bushman of Silent Films Dies," *NYT,* 24 Aug 1966, 1:2, 45:1. "Francis X. Bushman, 83, Idol of Silent Screen Era, Dies in His H'wood Home," *Variety,* 24 Aug 1966, p. 71. AMD, p. 59. AS, p. 189. BHD1, p. 83. FSS, p. 51. IFN, p. 44. MH, p. 100 (b. Norfolk VA, 1885). MSBB, p. 1022 (b. 1885). SD. Truitt, p. 45. WWS, p. 263 (b. Norfolk). "Blank Cartridge Injures Player," *MPW,* 20 Apr 1912, 234. "Bushman a 'Champ' Wrestler," *MPW,* 3 Aug 1912, 452. "Bushman Returns to Essanay," *MPW,* 24 May 1913, 816. "Chats with the Players; Francis X. Bushman, of the Essanay Company," *Motion Picture Magazine,* Feb 1915, 89–91. "Bushman a Metro Player," *MPW,* 1 May 1915, 731. "Bushman with Metro; Screen Star Will Be Featured in Adaptations of Famous Books and Plays," *NYDM,* 21 Apr 1915, 21:1. "Editor's Letter Box," *NYDM,* 22 Jan 1916, p. 6 (Bushman was born in Norfolk VA and educated in Baltimore). "Bushman Buys Estate [Bushmanor, Riderwood MD]," *MPW,* 13 May 1916, 1155. "Who's Married to Who," *Photoplay,* Jul 1917, 79 ("This is possibly the only photograph of Mrs. Bushman [Josephine Fladune] with Mr. Bushman in existence."). Neil G. Caward, "Screen Gossip," *Picture-Play Magazine,* Sep 1917, 105 (Bushman and Bayne signed a new contract with Metro "calling for their joint appearance for a long term of years in Metro pictures."). "Francis X. Bushman Club," *Motion Picture Magazine,* Feb 1918, 18 (a fan club organized in the autumn of 1916, dedicated to improving the art of film by bringing pressure on the producers. Meetings were held at Bushmanor, Baltimore MD, in Feb and Jun of 1917. Membership fee, 25¢ a year.). "Francis X. Bushman Marries Beverly Bayne," *MPW,* 17 Aug 1918, 967. "Francis X. Bushman Signed by Morosco," *MPW,* 3 May 1919, 651. Susan Elizabeth Brady, "The Return of Francis X. Bushman," *Classic,* Jun 1923, 22–23, 83. Alma M. Talley, "Bushman to Play Villain in 'Ben Hur,'" *MW,* 8 Mar 1924, 8. "Bushman and Bayne—At Home," *MW,* 5 Apr 1924, 6 (photo layout of "The former screen stars..."). Dorothy Donnell, "From Hollywood to You," *MPS,* 24 Feb 1925, 8–9 (he and Bayne to separate. "...Bushman was married before and it is said that he had a large family of children, but for the sake of screen publicity, because the public was supposed to prefer its heroes unmarried and consequently marriageable, he would never admit his domesticity. When confronted with a picture of himself, his five or six little Bushmans sitting in a row on the steps of his house he said airily—so the story goes—that that was merely a picture of a 'house party' he had had."). "On the Set and Off," *MW,* 28 Feb 1925, 34 (separated from Bayne). Robert E. Sherwood, "The Changing Styles in Film Sex Appeal; Where Are the Vamps and He-Men of Yesteryear?," *MPC,* Aug 1925, 22–23, 82. "Conway—Bushman," *MPW,* 9 Oct 1926, 343 [daughter, Virginia Bushman, m. director Jack Conway, 22 Sep 1926). "Mrs. Bushman to Sue for Back Alimony," *MPW,* 1 Oct 1927, 291 (divorced 2 Jun 1925, desertion). James Bagley, "Are American Movies Corrupting Japan?; The Honorable August Nippon Stars Have Gone In for Sex Appeal," *MPC,* Dec 1927, 18–19, 74 (Bushman speaks on the Japanese film industry). "Back to Vaudeville," *MPW,* 3 Dec 1927, 21. "Bushman Goes Berserk," *MPW,* 10 Dec 1927, 5. Joe Hyams, "Ex-Star Pines for Lost Son," *New York Herald Tribune,* 10 Jun 1957. "Bushman Knew His Son [Richard S. Bayne; surname changed to Bayne in 1941] Was in Valley," *Phoenix Gazette,* 28 Jun 1957. Larry Lee Holland, "Francis X. Bushman, 1885–1966," *FIR,* Mar 1978, 157–73. William H. Mulligan, Jr., *DAB,* Supp. 8 (1988), pp. 65–67. Richard J. Maturi, "Francis X. Bushman: The Rest of the Story," *CI,* 206 (Aug 1992), 46–47.

Bushman, Francis X., Jr. (son of **Francis X. Bushman**; brother of **Virginia Bushman**) [actor] (*né* Ralph Everly Bushman, b. Baltimore MD, 1 May 1903–16 Apr 1978 [74], Los Angeles CA; respiratory failure). m. Beatrice Dante, 10 Jul 1924. (MGM.) AMD, p. 59. AS, p. 189. BHD1, p. 83. "Francis X. Bushman, Jr.," *MPW,* 7 Apr 1917, 485. "Al Christie Signs Ralph, Son of Francis X. Bushman," *MPW,* 6 Mar 1920, 1639."Young Bushman Married, *Variety,* 16 Jul 1924, p. 21 (Ralph E. Bushman m. Dante, both age 22). "Francis X. Bushman," *MPW,* 2 May 1927, 795.

Bushman, Lenore [actress] (daughter of **Francis X. Bushman**; sister of **Virginia**, and **Francis X. Bushman, Jr.**) (b. 1909). Appeared in *The Love Wager,* Platinum Pictures, 1927.

Bushman, Leonore [film critic] (b. 1918?–Nov 1950 [32], Philadelphia PA). "Leonore Bushman," *Variety,* 22 Nov 1950.

Bushman, Ralph *see* **Bushman, Francis X., Jr**

Bushman, Virginia (daughter of **Francis X. Bushman**; sister of **Lenore** and **Francis X. Bushman, Jr.**) [actress] (b. 1906). m. **Jack Conway**, 22 Sep 1926, LA CA (d. 1952). AMD, p. 59. "Metro-Goldwyn-Mayer Signs Virginia Bushman," *MPW,* 8 Aug 1925, 654. "Conway—Bushman," *MPW,* 9 Oct 1926, 343.

Buskirk, Bessie [actress] (b. IL, 21 Mar 1892–19 Nov 1952 [60], Los Angeles CA). BHD, p. 119.

Buskirk, Mrs. Hattie [actress] (b. Decatur IL, 7 Aug 1867–12 Jan 1942 [74], Los Angeles CA). BHD, p. 119.

Buster, Budd L. [actor] (b. Colorado Springs CO, 14 Jun 1891–22 Dec 1965 [74], Los Angeles CA). AS, p. 189. BHD, p. 119. IFN, p. 44.

Butcher, Edward W. [producer] (b. Troy NY, 15 May 1892–11 Dec 1960 [68], Los Angeles CA). "Edward W. Butcher," *Variety,* 21 Dec 1960, p. 63. AS, p. 189. BHD2, p. 39.

Butler, Barbara (Babs) [actress] (b. Ogdensburg NY, 1902–4 Jan 1975 [72?]). BHD, p. 119.

Butler, Charles [actor] (b. 1846?–17 Sep 1920 [74], New York NY). "Charles Butler, Actor," *NYT,* 18 Sep 1920, 9:2. "Charles Butler," *Variety,* 24 Sep 1920. AS, p. 189 (b. 1946). IFN, p. 44.

Butler, Cliff [sound engineer] (b. 1904?–10 May 1965 [61], Albuquerque NM). "Cliff Butler," *Variety,* 26 May 1965.

Butler, David W[ayne] (son of **Fred J. Butler**) [actor/director] (b. San Francisco CA, 17 Dec 1894–14 Jun 1979 [84], Arcadia CA; blood poisoning). (Griffith; Universal; Fox; Paramount; WB.) Irene Kahn, interviewer, *David Butler* (Directors Guild of America/Scarecrow Press, 1993). "David Butler Dies at 84; Actor-Turned-Director an 'Old Reliable' in Studio Days—Shirley Temple's Pics," *Variety,* 20 Jun 1979. AMD, p. 59. AS, p. 189. BHD1, p. 83; BHD2, p. 39 (b. 1895-d. LA CA). FFF, p. 254. IFN, p. 44 (b. 1895). Katz, p. 189. MH, p. 100 (b. 17 Dec 1894). "Butler to Head His Own Company; Young Film Star Receives Big Holiday Gift from His Dad," *LA Times,* 2 Jan 1920, III, 4 (stage director of the Morosco Stock Co.; received 51 shares of stock in David Butler Films, Inc.; to produce *Broadway or Bust* and 7 other films.). "David Butler Finishes His First Independent Picture," *MPW,* 3 Apr 1920, 115. "David Butler, Newest Star of Screen, Says: 'Watch Us Shoot,'" *MPW,* 10 Apr 1920, 293. "Irving Lesser Signs David Butler for Series of Five-Reel Pictures," *MPW,* 12 Mar 1921, 180. "Once with Griffith," *MPW,* 18 Nov 1922, 244. "David Butler," *MPW,* 20 Aug 1927, 516. George Katchmer, "Remembering the Great Silents," *CI,* 206 (Aug 1992), 40, 61.

Butler, Eddie [actor] (b. New York NY, 5 Jul 1888–21 May 1944 [55], Los Angeles CA). "Eddie Butler," *Variety,* 7 Jun 1944 (d. 31 May; age 56). AS, p. 190. IFN, p. 44.

Butler, Ellis Parker [writer] (b. Muscatine IA, 5 Dec 1869–13 Sep 1937 [67], Williamsville MA). m. Ida A. Zipser, 1899. "Film Famous Authors; Vitagraph Company Prepares Novel Series for Authors' League Benefit," *NYDM,* 28 Jan 1914, 30:4. "Contributors to Mirth," *LA Times,* 25 Jan 1920, 13:5. *Twentieth Century Authors,* pp. 230–31.

Butler, Emma Lathrop [actress] (b. 24 Mar 1845–8 Mar 1935 [89], Englewood NJ). BHD, p. 120.

Butler, Frank [actor/scenarist] (b. Oxford, England, 28 Dec 1890–10 Jun 1967 [76], Los Angeles CA). (Paramount; Roach.) "Frank Butler," *Variety,* 14 Jun 1967, p. 71 (age 77). AS, p. 190. BHD1, p. 84; BHD2, p. 39. FDY, p. 419. IFN, p. 44. Truitt, p. 45. George Katchmer, "Remembering the Great Silents," *CI,* 206 (Aug 1992), 61.

Butler, Fred J. (father of **David Butler**) [stage/film director] (*né* Alfred Joline Butler, b. ID, 22 Oct 1863?–22 Feb 1929 [65], Los Angeles CA). m. (1) Florence Rice (d. 1974); (2) Adele Belgarde (d. 1938). "Fred J. Butler," *Variety,* 6 Mar 1929, p. 59. AS, p. 190 (b. 1867). BHD, p. 120 (b. 1867). IFN, p. 44 (b. 1867). SD. "Butler to Head His Own Company; Young Film Star Receives Big Holiday Gift from His Dad," *LA Times,* 2 Jan 1920, III, 4 (stage director of the Morosco Stock Co.).

Butler, Irene [actress]. No data found. (Film debut: *The Fire Brigade,* MGM, 1926.) Paul Paige, "Close-Ups and Fade-Outs," *Paris and Hollywood,* Sep 1926, 92 (winner of MGM's Eastern "Million Dollar Baby Contest.").

Butler, John A. [actor] (b. Canada, 1 May 1884–9 Oct 1967 [83], Woodland Hills CA). AS, p. 190. BHD1, p. 84. IFN, p. 44.

Butler, Rachel Barton [playwright] (b. 1888?–24 Nov 1920 [ca. 32], New York NY). m. Boyd Agin, 1919. "Rachel Barton Butler, Playwright," *NYT,* 28 Nov 1920, 22:4. "Rachel Barton Butler," *Variety,* 3 Dec 1920, p. 19.

Butler, Royal (Roy) E. [actor] (*né* Edwin Richay, b. Atlanta GA, 4 May 1893–28 Jul 1973 [80], Desert Hot Springs CA). AS, p. 190 (b. 1895). BHD, p. 120. IFN, p. 44.

Butler, William J. [actor] (b. 1860?–27 Jan 1927 [67], Staten Island NY). (FP-L; Biograph; K&E; Metro.) "William J. Butler," *Variety,* 2 Feb 1927, p. 55. AMD, p. 59. AS, p. 190. BHD, p. 120. IFN, p. 44. Truitt, p. 46. "William J. Butler with Gaumont," *MPW,* 25 Dec 1915, 2343.

Butt, Johnny [actor] (d. 1930). AS, p. 190. BHD1, p. 84.

Butt, W[illiam] **Lawson "Billy"** [actor] (b. Isle of Jersey, Channel Islands, 1883–14 Jan 1956 [72]). AMD, p. 59. AS, p. 190. BHD1, p. 84. IFN, p. 44. "Forthcoming Kalem Feature," *NYDM,* 7 Jul 1915, 37:1 (in *Don Caesar de Bazan*). "W. Lawson Butt with Kleine," *MPW,* 7 Aug 1915, 982. "H.B. Warner a Selig Star," *MPW,* 21 Apr 1917, 428. "Wife a Hindrance," *Variety,* 6 Oct 1922, p. 47 "...William Butts brought an action for divorce against his French war bride. He was granted a decree late last week."). George A. Katchmer, "Remembering the Great Silents," *CI,* 183 (Sep 1990), 45.

Butterfield, Everett [stage/film actor] (b. Portland ME, 1885–6 Mar 1925 [40?], New York NY). m. Leah. "Everett Butterfield," *Variety,* 11 Mar 1925, p. 51. AMD, p. 59. AS, p. 190. BHD, p. 120. SD. "'The Magic Skin' Completed [to be released 13 Oct]," *NYDM,* 29 Sep 1915, 24:4 ("a newcomer in the ranks of picture-players"). "Everett Butterfield," *MPW,* 30 Oct 1915, 766.

Butterfield, Millie (granddaughter of a founder of the American Express Co.) [stage/film actress] (b. Utica NY-d. 19 Apr 1939, New York NY; found dead in her hotel apartment). "Millie Butterfield," *Variety,* 26 Apr 1939, p. 44. BHD, p. 120. "Gossip of the Studios," *NYDM,* 6 Nov 1915, 32:3 (returned to NYC after thirteen months' work in the picture ranks in Los Angeles.").

Butterworth, Ernest, Jr. [actor] (b. Lancashire, England, 8 May 1905–2 May 1986 [80], No Hollywood CA). (Began ca. 1915; Pickford; Universal; De Mille.) BHD, p. 120. MSBB, p. 1022 (b. 1907).

Butterworth, Ernest, Sr. [vaudeville/film actor/assistant director/scenarist] (b. Lancashire, England, 16 Dec 1876–22 Apr 1950 [73], rural Pearblossom CA). (American, 1911; Kriterion.) BHD, p. 120; BHD2, p. 39. MSBB, p. 1022.

Butterworth, Frank J. [actor] (b. Lancashire, England, 12 Dec 1903–6 Aug 1975 [71], Burbank CA). (Universal.) BHD, p. 120. MSBB, p. 1022 (b. 1906). J. Van Cartmell, "Along the Pacific Coast," *NYDM,* 4 Aug 1915, 26:2 (Butterworth, age 11, and Baby Early called by their director, H.C. Matthews, "the coming Mary Pickfords and Henry Walthalls.").

Butterworth, Joe [actor]. No data found. (1st National).

Butterworth, Walter T. [actor] (b. IN, 4 Apr 1892–10 Mar 1962 [69], Los Angeles CA). m. Mabel. "Walter T. Butterworth," *Variety,* 21 Mar 1962, p. 71. AS, p. 190. BHD1, p. 84 (d. Van Nuys CA). IFN, p. 44.

Buxbaum, Edward F. [actor] (b. 1892–21 Jan 1951 [58?], Punta Gorda FL). BHD1, p. 84.

Buxton, Henry James [journalist/writer] (b. Warren MA, 16 Oct 1881–30 Aug 1939 [58], Stockton Springs ME). m. Alice W. "Henry James Buxton, Newspaper Man, 58; Author of Three Books, Among Them 'Assignment Down East,'" *NYT,* 2 Sep 1939, 17:4. "Henry James Burton," *Variety,* 6 Sep 1939.

Buzzell, Edward (Eddie) [stage/film actor/director/scenarist] (b. Brooklyn NY, 13 Nov 1895?–11 Jan 1985 [89], Los Angeles CA). (Columbia; MGM.) m. **Ona Munson**, San Francisco CA, Jul 1927—div. (suicide, 1955); (2) Sarah Clarke. AS, p. 191. BHD1, p. 84; BHD2, p. 39 (b. 1897). SD, p. 96.

Buzzi, Pietro [actor] (b. Italy-d. 16 Feb 1921, Los Angeles CA). m. Helen Jackman, 1913. (Paramount.) "Pietro Buzzi," *Variety,* 25 Feb 1921. AMD, p. 59. AS, p. 191. BHD, p. 120. Truitt, p. 46. "Obituary," *MPW,* 5 Mar 1921, 38.

Byers, Nancy [actress] (b. 1900–14 Nov 1980 [80?]). BHD, p. 120.

Byford, Roy [actor] (b. London, England, 12 Jan 1873–31 Jan 1939 [66], London, England). "Roy Byford," *Variety,* 15 Feb 1939. AS, p. 191. BHD1, p. 84. IFN, p. 44. Truitt, p. 46.

Bylek, Rudolph [scenarist] (b. Vienna, Austria, 1 Mar 1885–3 Aug 1967 [82], Los Angeles CA). BHD2, p. 39.

Byram, Ronald [stage/film actor] (b. Brisbane, Australia-d. 17 Apr 1919, Calgary, Canada). AS, p. 191. BHD, p. 120. IFN, p. 44. MSBB, p. 1022.

Byrd, Anthony D. [actor] (b. 1865-Apr 1925 [59?], New York NY). "Anthony D. Byrd," *Variety,* 13 May 1925, p. 45. BHD, p. 120.

Byrd, Betty [actress]. No data found. (Christie.) "Beauties Who Make the Comedies Attractive," *Cinema Arts,* Aug 1926, 21 (photo).

Byrd, Violet *see* **Bird, Violet**

Byrens, Myer [actor] (b. 1839?–29 Jan 1933 [93], Los Angeles CA). "Myer Byrens," *Variety,* 11 Jul 1933. BHD, p. 120. IFN, p. 45. Truitt, p. 46.

Byrne, Donn [writer] (b. Brooklyn NY, 20 Nov 1889–18 Jun 1928 [38], Brandon, Cork, Ireland). m. Dorothea Cadogan, 1911. AMD, p. 59. BHD, p. 120. "Marshall Neilan Signs Donn Byrne," *MPW,* 4 Jun 1921, 522. *Twentieth Century Authors,* pp. 233–34.

Byrne, Francis M. [actor] (b. Newport RI, 3 Aug 1876–6 Feb 1923 [46], New York NY). m. actress Helen Vincent. "Francis M. Byrne," *Variety,* 15 Feb 1923, p. 9 (age 47). AS, p. 191. BHD, p. 120.

Byrne, James A. [actor] (b. Norwich CT, 1867–19 Mar 1927 [59?], Camden NJ). BHD, p. 120.

Byrne, John [actor] (b. Brooklyn NY, 1861?–14 Feb 1924 [62], Los Angeles CA). AS, p. 191 (d. NYC). BHD, p. 120. IFN, p. 45.

Byrne, John F. [actor] (b. 1859-19 Sep 1937 [78], Norwich CT). BHD, p. 120.

Byrne, John (Jack) [scenarist/film editor/director] (d. 4 Jul 1968, Greenwich CT). "John Byrne," *Variety,* 17 Jul 1968, p. 71. AMD, p. 59. BHD2, p. 39. "Jack Byrne, Kriterion Editor," *MPW,* 30 Jan 1915, 685.

Byron, Marion "Peanuts" [actress] (b. Dayton OH, 16 Jun 1910–5 Jul 1985 [75], Santa Monica CA). m. Mr. Breslow. (Film debut: *Steamboat Bill, Jr.,* 1928.) "Marion Byron [obituary],"

CI, 123 (Sep 1985), 9 (age 73). AS, p. 191. BHD1, p. 85 (b. 16 Mar 1911).

Byron, Nina (or **Nigne)** [actress] (b. Christchurch, New Zealand, 1900?). m. **Nicholas Dunaew.** (Pallas Pictures.) Eleanor Brewser, "That Hungry Look Brought Her a Chance; The Story of Nina Byron," *Motion Picture Magazine*, Jul 1917, pp. 63, 105.

Byron, Paul [actor] (b. New York NY, 1891?–12 May 1959 [68], San Diego CA; heart attack). (Metro.) "Paul Byron," *Variety*, 20 May 1959, p. 79. AS, p. 191. BHD, p. 120 (b. 1889). IFN, p. 45. Truitt, p. 46.

Byron, Royal James [actor] (b. 20 Feb 1887–4 Mar 1943 [56], Trenton NJ). (Vitagraph.) "Royal James Byron," *Variety*, 10 Mar 1943. AS, p. 191. BHD, p. 120. IFN, p. 45. Truitt, p. 46.

Byron, Walter [actor] (*né* Walter Clarence Butler, b. Leicester, England, 11 Jun 1899–2 Mar 1972 [72], Signal Hill CA). AS, p. 191 (d. LA CA). BHD1, p. 85. IFN, p. 45. Katz, p. 191 (b. 1901).

Bystrom, Walter E. [Keystone Cop] (b. 14 Oct 1893–13 Sep 1969 [75], San Diego CA). AS, p. 191. BHD, p. 120. Truitt, p. 46.

C

Cabanne, William Christy [stage actor/film director] (b. St. Louis MO, 16 Apr 1888–15 Oct 1950 [62], Philadelphia PA; heart attack). (Biograph, 1910; Reliance-Majestic; Fine Arts; Griffith; Metro.) "W.C. Cabanne Dies; Film Director, 62; Pioneer in the Movie Industry Started with D.W. Griffith in Old Biograph Films," *NYT*, 17 Oct 1950, 31:1. "William Christy Cabanne," *Variety*, 18 Oct 1950, p. 63. AMD, p. 60. AS, p. 193. BHD1, p. 85; BHD2, p. 39. IFN, p. 45. KOM, pp. 130–32. MSBB, p. 1044. 1921 Directory, p. 259. Truitt, p. 46. "Film Villa's Life; Mexican General Will Appear in Mutual Film Biography," *NYDM*, 18 Mar 1914, 30:2 (Cabanne directed). "Director Cabanne Leaves Fine Arts," *MPW*, 2 Sep 1916, 1526. "William Christy Cabanne Joins Metro," *MPW*, 2 Sep 1916, 1534. "To Direct in England," *MPW*, 7 May 1927, 11. John Roberts, "King of the B's—Christy Cabanne," *CI*, 183 (Sep 1990), C8-C9 (b. 1888).

Cabot, Elliot [actor] (b. Boston MA, 22 Jun 1899–17 Jun 1938 [39], New York NY; injuries after a fall). "Eliot Cabot Dies of Injuries After Fall; Was on Equity Council," *Variety*, 22 Jun 1938, p. 54. BHD, p. 121. IFN, p. 45.

Cade, James [actor] (d. 19 May 1985). BHD1, p. 85.

Cade, Sven [director] (b. 1877–25 Jun 1952 [75?], Aarhus, Denmark). BHD2, p. 39.

Cadell, Jean (mother of Simon John Cadell, 1950–1996) [actress] (b. Edinburgh, Scotland, 13 Sep 1884–24 Sep 1967 [83], London, England). m. actor P. Perceval-Clark. "Jean Cadell," *Variety*, 4 Oct 1967. p. 63 (d. 24 Sep); 18 Oct 1967 (d. 26 Sep). AS, p. 193. BHD1, p. 85. IFN, p. 45. Truitt, pp. 46–47.

Cadman, Charles Wakefield [composer] (b. Johnstown PA, 24 Dec 1881–30 Dec 1946 [65], Los Angeles CA; after heart attack). "Charles Cadman, Composer, Is Dead; Author of 'Land of Sky-Blue Water' Was First to Write Music on Indian Themes; Had Successful Opera; Called 'Shanewis,' It Was Initial American Work Presented Twice at Metropolitan," *NYT*, 31 Dec 1946, 17:1. "Charles Wakefield Cadman," *Variety*, 8 Jan 1947 (wrote *At Dawning*). AS, p. 193. ASCAP 66, p. 98. BHD2, p. 39. CEPMJ, Vol. 2, p. 660.

Cadwallader, Charles L. [art director] (b. 1883?–5 Apr 1935 [52], Los Angeles CA). "Charles L. Cadwallader," *Variety*, 17 Apr 1935. BHD2, p. 39.

Cadzaw, William [actor] (d. 28 Oct 1922). BHD, p. 121.

Caesar, Arthur (brother of **Irving Caesar**) [playwright/scenarist] (b. Bucharest, Romania, 9 Mar 1892–20 Jun 1953 [61], Beverly Hills CA; heart attack). m. Dora. "Arthur Caesar," *NYT*, 22 Jun 1953, 21:3 (d. 21 Jun). "Arthur Caesar," *Variety*, 24 Jun 1953, p. 71 (AA for script of *Manhattan Melodrama*, MGM, 1934). AS, p. 194. BHD2, p. 39. IFN, p. 45.

Caesar, Irving (brother of **Arthur Caesar**) [composer] (*né* Isaac Caesar, b. New York NY, 4 Jul 1895–17 Dec 1996 [101], New York NY). AS, p. 194. BHD2, p. 39.

Cahill, Lilly [actress] (b. San Antonio TX, 17 Jul 1886?–20 Jul 1955 [69], San Antonio TX). m. **Brandon Tynan** (d. 1967). "Lilly Cahill," *Variety*, 27 Jul 1955, p. 127. AS, p. 194 (b. 1889). BHD1, p. 85 (b. 1885). IFN, p. 45. Truitt, p. 47.

Cahill, Marie [actress] (b. Brooklyn NY, 7 Oct 1870–23 Aug 1933 [62], New York NY; heart attack). m. **Daniel V. Arthur**, 18 Jun 1903. "Marie Cahill Dies; Famed in Theatre; Her Singing of 'Nancy Brown' Won Wide Favor in Early Days of the Century; Created New Song Style; Pioneer in Stressing Story Rather Than Tune of a Ballad—Fought for Stage Censorship," *NYT*, 24 Aug 1933, 15:1 (age 59). "Marie Cahill," *Variety*, 29 Aug 1933 (age 59). AMD, p. 60. AS, p. 194 (b. 7 Feb). BHD, p. 121. IFN, p. 45. Truitt, p. 47 (b. 1874). "Miss Cahill Files Petition," *NYDM*, 17 Mar 1915, 7:3 (voluntary petition in bankruptcy; liabilities of $35,402, assets of $23,827. Due to "the suits filed against her husband, Daniel V. Arthur, as maker of notes which she indorsed."). "Marie Cahill on Universal Program," *MPW*, 15 May 1915, 1083. "Marie Cahill Comedies," *Variety*, 15 Dec 1916, 30:3 (to appear in 2-reel comedies directed by her husband, released through "the Mutual. They will start to grind about Jan. 1."). "Marie Cahill Mutual's Latest," *MPW*, 27 Jan 1917, 534. "Marie Cahill," *MPW*, 28 Apr 1917, 627.

Cahill, William (b. 1853–9 Feb 1926 [72?], Brooklyn NY). BHD, p. 121.

Cahn, Edward L. [cutter/director] (b. Brooklyn NY, 12 Feb 1899–25 Aug 1963 [64], Los Angeles CA). . (Began in 1917.) "Edward L. Cahn," *Variety*, 4 Sep 1963, p. 53. AS, p. 194 (d. NYC). BHD2, p. 40. IFN, p. 45.

Caillol, Pierrette Emmanuelle [actress] (b. Marseilles, France, 17 Jul 1898–8 Jun 1991 [92], Nice, France [extrait de décès no. AN71–701/2808]). m. **Yvon Noe** (d. 1963). AS, p. 194.

Cain, Robert [actor] (b. Chicago IL, 4 Jun 1886–27 Apr 1954 [67], New York NY [Death Certificate Index No. 9214]). "Robert Cain," *NYT*, 30 Apr 1954, 23:4. "Robert Cain," *Variety*, 5 May 1954 (age 67). AMD, p. 60. AS, p. 195 (d. 28 Apr). BHD, p. 121 (b. 1882). IFN, p. 45. MH, p. 100 (b. 1886). 1921 Directory, p. 161 (b. 1882). Truitt, p. 47. "Paramount Signs Robert Cain," *MPW*, 15 Nov 1924, 253. "Kane Signs Cain," *MPW*, 16 Jan 1926, 240.

Caine, Clarence J. [scenarist] (b. Milwaukee WI, 1895–21 Jun 1917 [22?], Sierra Madre CA). AMD, p. 60. BHD2, p. 40. "Obituary," *MPW*, 14 Jul 1917, 252.

Caine, Derwent Hall [scenarist] (b. Isle of Man, 14 May 1853–31 Aug 1931 [78], Greeba Castle, Isle of Man). m. Mary Chandler, 1882. "Sir Hall Caine Dies; Famous Novelist; Began Career as Journalist in Liverpool—Was Confidante of Dante Gabriel Rossetti; Made Isle of Man Noted—His Many Stories of His Birthplace Sold Widely and Were Adapted for the Stage and Screen," *NYT*, 1 Sep 1931, 23:1. "Hall Caine," *Variety*, 8 Sep 1931, p. 119. AMD, p. 60. BHD2, p. 40 (Hall Caine, b. Runcorn, England). "Derwent Hall Caine," *MPW*, 23 Sep 1916, 1975.

Caine, Derwent Hall [actor] (b. Keswick, England, 12 Sep 1892–2 Dec 1971 [79], Miami FL). BHD, p. 121.

Caine, Georgia [actress] (b. San Francisco CA, 30 Oct 1876–4 Apr 1964 [87], Los Angeles CA). "Georgia Caine," *Variety*, 15 Apr 1964, p. 60 (age 88). AS, p. 195. BHD1, p. 86. IFN, p. 45.

Caines, Eleanor [actress] (b. Philadelphia PA, 1880–2 Jun 1913 [33?], Philadelphia PA; after operation due to accident). m. **Jack Le Faint.** (Lubin; Scarlett M.P. Co.) BHD, p. 121. "Investigating Death [of Caines]," *Variety*, 6 Jun 1913. AS, p. 195. *MPW*, 12 Apr 1913, 148.

Cairns, Jay [publicist]. No data found. AMD, p. 60. "Jay Cairns Impersonal Booster," *MPW*, 25 Sep 1915, 2191.

Calabria, Rina [actress]. No data found. JS, p. 68 (In Italian silents from 1915).

Calapristi, Santo [actor] (*né* Samuel Calapristi, b. 1896–27 Apr 1987 [91?], Springfield PA). AS, p. 195. BHD1, p. 86.

Calcagni, David [producer]. No data found. AMD, p. 60. "Calcagni with Associated," *MPW*, 22 Aug 1925, 848.

Calcina, Vittorio [director/cinematographer] (b. Turin, Italy, 1847–1916 [69?]). JS, p. 68 ("Pioneer filmmaker, he was the Italian representative for Lumière Brothers, and made the first Italian film that people paid to see, a short documentary, *Umberto e Margherita di Savoia a passeggio per il parco* [1896].").

Caldara, Orme [actor] (b. Empire City OR, 9 Feb 1875–21 Oct 1925 [50], Saranac Lake NY). m. **Julia Dean** (d. 1952). "Orme Caldara," *Variety*, 20 Jan 1926, p. 49 (age 50). AS, p. 195 (Ormi Caldera, b. 1885). IFN, p. 45. SD.

Calderari, Antonietta [actress]. No data found. JS, pp. 68–69 (In Italian silents from 1911).

Caldwell, Anne [lyricist/composer/playwright] (*née* Annie Caldwell, b. Boston MA, 30 Jul 1876 [Massachusetts Vital Statistics, Births, Vol. 279, p. 149]–22 Oct 1936 [60], Beverly Hills CA). m. songwriter James O'Dea. (RKO.) "Anne Caldwell, 60, Librettist, Is Dead; Collaborator in 'Hitchy-Koo,' 'Chin-Chin,' 'Jack o' Lantern' and Many Other Shows; Joined Film Ranks in 1931; Successes in Hollywood Included 'Flying Down to Rio,' 'Babes in Toyland,' and 'Dixiana,'" *NYT,* 24 Oct 1936, 17:5 (wrote lyrics to *Kalua* and *Wait Till the Cows Come Home*). "Anne Caldwell," *Variety,* 28 Oct 1936, p. 63. AS, p. 195. BHD2, p. 40.

Caldwell, Betty [actress] (b. 14 Nov). George Katchmer, "Forgotten Cowboys and Cowgirls—Part X," *CI,* 182 (Aug 1990), 37.

Caldwell, Fred H. [vaudevillian: Caldwell & Wentworth] (d. 8 Feb 1928, Rochester NY; following operation). m. Miss Wentworth, 30 Sep 1901. "Fred H. Caldwell," *Variety,* 28 Mar 1928, p. 57. AS, p. 195.

Caldwell, H.H. [title writer/film editor]. No data found. m. **Katharine Hilliker**. AMD, p. 60. FDY, p. 441. "Caldwells to Assist June Mathis," *MPW,* 23 Dec 1922, 732.

Caldwell, Orville Robert [actor] (b. Oakland CA, 8 Feb 1896–24 Sep 1967 [71], Santa Rosa CA). m. Aubrey Anderson. "Orville Caldwell," *Variety,* 1 Nov 1967, p. 63. AMD, p. 60. AS, p. 195. BHD1, p. 86. IFN, p. 45. Truitt, p. 47. "Caldwell Signs New Contract," *MPW,* 7 Oct 1922, 473. David A. Balch, "The Man Elinor Glyn Called 'Perfect'; Meet Orville Caldwell, star of 'The Miracle,' and learn why the famous English novelist termed him without a peer," *MW,* 5 Jul 1924, 3, 27. Orville Caldwell, "The Romance of the Extra," *MPC,* Oct 1924, 35, 79. "Star Triumphs on Screen," *MPW,* 7 Feb 1925, 607.

Caldwell, Virginia [stage/film actress]. No data found. AMD, p. 60. "From Showgirl to Screen Player," *MPW,* 15 Nov 1919, 328.

Calhern, Louis Vogt [actor] (*né* Carl Henry Vogt, b. Brooklyn NY, 19 Feb 1895–12 May 1956 [61], Tokyo, Japan; heart attack). m. Ilka Chase, 1926 (d. 1978); Julia Hoyt (d. 1956); Natalie Schafer; Marianne Stewart. "Louis Calhern, Noted Actor, Dies; Star of Broadway and Films Succumbs in Japan on Location for 'Teahouse,'" *NYT,* 13 May 1956, 86:3; "Calhern's Body to Be Cremated," *NYT,* 14 May 1956, 25:3; "Calhern Will Names ex-Wife [Miriam Stewart Calhern]," *NYT,* 24 May 1956, 27:4. "Louis Calhern," *Variety,* 16 May 1956, p. 63. AS, p. 195 (d. Nara, Japan). BHD1, p. 86. FSS, p. 52. IFN, p. 43. Katz, p. 195 (b. New York NY, 16 Feb). MH, p. 100. Truitt, p. 47.

Calhoun, Alice Beatrice [actress] (b. Cleveland OH, 24 Nov 1900–3 Jun 1966 [65], Los Angeles CA; cancer). m. (1) Mendel B. Silberburg, 5 May 1926; (2) Max Chotiner. "Alice Calhoun Chotiner, 65, Started in Silent Movies," *NYT,* 6 Jun 1966, 41:2. "Alice Calhoun," *Variety,* 8 Jun 1966, p. 63. AMD, p. 60. AS, p. 195 (b. 21 Nov). BHD1, p. 86. FFF, p. 96. FSS, p. 52. IFN, p. 45. Katz, p. 195 (b. 1904). MH, p. 100. Slide, p. 137 (b. 1901). Truitt, p. 47. WWS, p. 231. "Vitagraph Engages Alice Calhoun," *MPW,* 3 Jan 1920, 74. "Vitagraph Raises Alice Calhoun to Stardom; Elevation Due to Request of the Public," *MPW,* 23 Oct 1920, 1136. Hazel Shelley, "Discoveries in Wonderland," *MPC,* Oct 1921, 18–19. "Alice Calhoun Signs as Featured Warner Player," *MPW,* 23 May 1925, 464. "On the Set and Off," *Pictures,* Aug 1926, 80 (her contract with WB expired 5 May 1926, and on that day she married Silberburg). "Sign Garon and Calhoun," *MPW,* 10 Sep 1927, 78. John E. Thayer, "Alice Calhoun; A Lovely Lady," *CFC,* 50 (Spring, 1976), X14 (Forest Lawn Cemetery). George A. Katchmer, "Remembering the Great Silents," *CI,* 184 (Oct 1990), 56–57.

Calhoun, Catherine [actress]. No data found. AMD, p. 60. "Catherine Calhoun with Metro," *MPW,* 4 Mar 1916, 1447. Paul Paige, "Close-Ups and Fade-Outs," *Paris and Hollywood,* Sep 1926, 92–93 (she had Frank C. Kingsley arrested for "striking her and blacking one eye.").

Calhoun, Cathleen or Kathleen [actress]. George A. Katchmer, "Remembering the Great Silents," *CI,* 184 (Oct 1990), 57.

Calhoun, Maude [actress]. No data found. AMD, p. 60. "Maude Calhoun," *MPW,* 22 Mar 1913, 1206 (played leads after the death of Vedah Bertram).

Calhoun, Patrick [actor] (b. Bray, Ireland, 1886). AMD, p. 60. BHD, p. 121. "She Saw Patrick Calhoun, Long Lost Brother, in film," *MPW,* 13 May 1916, 1145.

Calhoun, Richard A. (b. 1898–11 Apr 1977 [78?], Los Angeles CA). BHD, p. 121.

Call, Mildred [actress]. No data found. AMD, p. 60. "Mildred Call, Goldwynner," *MPW,* 30 Jun 1917, 2117.

Callaghan, Andrew J. [Vice-President of Technicolor] (b. 1 Aug 1889–4 Oct 1934 [46], Los Angeles CA). "Andrew J. Callaghan," *Variety,* 9 Oct 1934, p. 70. AMD, p. 60. BHD2, p. 40. "Callaghan Was a Lawyer Before Entering Industry," *MPW,* 4 Sep 1920, 87. "Callaghan of Monogram Warns Exhibitors Against Imposters," *MPW,* 1 Dec 1923, 460.

Callahan, Jerry [director]. No data found. AMD, p. 61. "Jimmy Callahan Will Produce Comedy Series in Atlantic City," *MPW,* 30 Apr 1921, 976. "Jimmy Callahan Meets Painful Injury in Hydroplane Accident," *MPW,* 9 Jul 1921, 215.

Calles, Guillermo "Indio" [actor] (*né* Guillermo Calles Guerrero, b. Chihuahua, Chihuahua, Mexico, ca. Mar 1891–28 Feb 1958 [67?], Mexico City, Mexico). AS, p. 196 (b. 1893).

Calley, Robert S. [extra film actor/stage/TV director] (b. Oakland CA, 1889–6 May 1977 [88], Kansas City MO). "Robert S. Calley," *Variety,* 8 Jun 1977, p. 79; 29 Jun 1977, p. 70. BHD, p. 121. IFN, p. 46.

Calliga, George [actor] (b. Rumania, 2 Jan 1897–18 Jan 1976 [79], Los Angeles Co. CA). AS, p. 196 (b. NYC). BHD1, p. 87. IFN, p. 46.

Callis, David M. [actor] (b. Baltimore MD, 4 Sep 1888–10 Sep 1934 [46], Los Angeles CA). "David M. Callis," *Variety,* 18 Sep 1934. AS, p. 196. BHD1, p. 87. IFN, p. 46.

Calmettes, André [actor] (b. Paris, France, 18 Apr 1861–1942 [81?], France). AS, p. 196. BHD, p. 121.

Caló, Romano [actor] (b. Rome, Italy, 6 May 1883–17 Aug 1952 [69], Lugano, Italy). JS, p. 70 (in Italian silents from 1917).

Calthrop, Donald Clayton (grandson of 19th-century dramatist and actor Dion Boucicault) [actor] (b. London, England, 11 Apr 1888–15 Jul 1940 [52], London, England; heart attack). m. Margaret Ledward. "Donald Calthrop," *Variety,* 7 Aug 1940, p. 46. AS, p. 196. BHD1, p. 87. IFN, p. 46. SD, p. 203. Truitt, p. 48 (d. Aug).

Calve, Olga [actress] (b. Russia, 1899?–12 May 1982 [82], Santa Paula CA; broncho-pneumonia). AMD, p. 61. AS, p. 197. BHD1, p. 87. (In *Ben Hur;* retired in 1930.) "Countess Goubarev Is Here," *MPW,* 5 Dec 1925, 442. "Olga Calve," *CI,* 85 (Jul 1982), 16.

Calvert, Alexander [actor] (b. England, 1861–31 Mar 1917 [55?], London, England). "Alexander Calvert; Two Deaths in London," *Variety,* 13 Apr 1917, p. 4 (and Charles Owen). AS, p. 197. *Green Room Book 1909,* pp. 80–81. SD, p. 204.

Calvert, Catherine [stage/film actress] (*née* Catherine ["Kittie"] Cassidy, b. Baltimore MD, 20 Jan 1890–18 Jan 1971 [80], Uniondale, LI NY). m. George A. Carrothers; **Paul Armstrong**, 10 Dec 1913 (d. 1915); **M. Paul Doucet** (d. 1928). (U.S. Amusement Co; Mutual; FP-L.) "Catherine Calvert," *Variety,* 27 Jan 1971, p. 63. AMD, p. 61. AS, p. 197 (b. 20 Mar). BHD, p. 121. IFN, p. 46. MH, p. 100. MSBB, p. 1032. SD. Truitt, p. 48. WWS, p. 272. "Catherine Calvert to Be Starred," *MPW,* 29 Dec 1917, 1928. "Catherine Calvert Joins Vitagraph, Signing Contract for Three Years; 'Dead Men Tell No Tales' Her First," *MPW,* 28 Aug 1920, 1203.

Calvert, Mrs. Charles [stage/film actress] (*née?,* b. 1835–20 Sep 1921 [86?], London, England). "Mrs. Charles Calvert," *Variety,* 30 Sep 1921, p. 7. BHD, p. 121.

Calvert, Elisha Helm [actor/director] (b. Alexandria VA, 27 Jun 1863–5 Oct 1941 [78], Los Angeles CA). m. **Lillian Drew** (d. 1924). "Elisha H. Calvert," *Variety,* 15 Oct 1941, p. 54. AMD, p. 61. AS, p. 197 (b. 1873). BHD1, p. 87. IFN, p. 46. Katz, p. 196 (b. 1873). Truitt, p. 48 (b. 1873). "Calvert Wants Wishbones," *MPW,* 21 Dec 1912, 1197. "Calvert Remains with Essanay," *MPW,* 9 Oct 1915, 267. "E.H. Calvert," *MPW,* 16 Oct 1915, 454. "Film Division Names Director Advisers," *MPW,* 20 Jul 1918, 363–64.

Calvert, Louis [actor] (b. Manchester, England, 25 Nov 1859–9 Jul 1923 [63], New York NY). AS, p. 197. BHD, p. 121.

Calvin, Lester [extra actor] (b. IA, 1890–30 May 1978 [88], Orlando FL). AS, p. 197. BHD, p. 121. IFN, p. 46.

Calvo, Rafael [actor] (b. 1886–1960 [74?]). (Began in Spain, 1924; Paramount; Fox.) Waldman, p. 42.

Calza-Bini, Piero [actor/cameraman/director] (*né* Luigi Calza Bini, b. Milan, Italy, 14 Dec 1883). AMD, p. 61. AS, p. 197. JS, p. 70 (in Italian silents from 1914). "Piero Calzabini," *MPW,* 18 Mar 1911, 591. "Arrest of Signor Calzabini," *MPW,* 22 Jul 1911, 129.

Camagni, Bianca Virginia [actress/director] (b. Milan, Italy). AS, p. 197. JS, p. 70 (1914).

Camasio, Sandro [playwright/scenarist/director] (*né* Alesjandro Pietor Paoli Eugénie Camasio, b. Isola della Scala, Italy, 5 Nov 1886 [extrait de naissance no. 195]–23 May 1913 [29?], Turin, Italy). AS, p. 197. JS, p. 71 (b. Turin, Italy, 1884).

Camelia, Muriel [actress] (b. 1913–15 Nov 1925 [12], Miami FL; bus accident). (Griffith.) "Muriel Camelia," *Variety,* 9 Dec 1925, p. 51. AS, p. 197. BHD, p. 121. Truitt, p. 48.

Camerini, Augusto (brother of **Mario**

Camerini; cousin of **Augusto Genina**) [director/scenarist] (b. Rome, Italy, 21 Jan 1894). AS, p. 197. JS, p. 71 (in Italian silents from 1920).

Camerini, Mario (brother of **Augusto Camerini**; cousin of **Augusto Genina**) [director/scenarist] (b. Rome, Italy, 6 Feb 1895–6 Feb 1981 [86], Gardone Riviera, Italy; pneumonia). m. Anastasia Noris von Gerzfeld (**Assia Noris** [d. 1998]). Sergio Gromek Germani, *Mario Camerini* (Florence, Italy: La Nuova Italia, 1980). AS, p. 197. JS, p. 71 (in Italian silents from 1920).

Cameron, Donald C. [actor] (b. St. Stephens, Canada, 1888–11 Jul 1955 [66], West Cornwall CT). "Donald Cameron, Actor, Dies at 66; Retired Leading Man of Stage and Silent Screen Made Debut on Coast in 1913," *NYT,* 13 Jul 1955, 25:1. "Donald Cameron," *Variety,* 20 Jul 1955, p. 63. AS, p. 197. BHD, p. 122. IFN, p. 46. SD, p. 205. Truitt, p. 48.

Cameron, Gene [actor] (b. 1901?–16 Nov 1927 [26], near Sentinel [Yuma] AZ; auto accident.) "Gene Cameron Killed, 2 Girls Hurt in Ariz.," *Variety,* 23 Nov 1927. AS, p. 197. BHD, p. 122. IFN, p. 46. Truitt, p. 48 (d. 1928).

Cameron, George *see* **Drew, Gladys S**

Cameron, Gladys [actress]. No data found. m. Robert Lackey. (Lubin.) "Greenroom Jottings," *MPSM,* Sep 1912, 108.

Cameron, Hugh V. [actor] (b. Duluth MN, 15 May 1879–9 Nov 1941 [62], New York NY). m. Louisa. "Hugh Cameron," *Variety,* 12 Nov 1941, p. 62. AMD, p. 61. AS, p. 198. BHD, p. 122. IFN, p. 46. SD. "Has Comedy Part," *MPW,* 2 Jul 1921, 60.

Cameron, Rudolph Willis B. [actor] (*né* Rudolph Brennan, b. Washington DC, 24 Oct 1892–17 Feb 1958 [65], Los Angeles CA; cerebral hemorrhage). m. **Anita Stewart** (d. 1961). AMD, p. 61. AS, p. 198 (b. 1894). BHD1, p. 87. IFN, p. 46 (age 63). 1921 Directory, p. 161 (b. 1892). "Anita Stewart's Husband in Cast," *MPW,* 14 Jan 1922, 170.

Cameron, Violet [stage/film actress] (b. 7 Dec 1839–25 Oct 1919 [79?], Worthing, England). "Violet Cameron," *Variety,* 31 Oct 1919, p. 4 (began on stage in 1849). BHD, p. 122.

Cammage, Maurice [director] (b. 1882–15 Apr 1946 [64?], Paris, France). AS, p. 198. BHD2, p. 40 (d. May 1946).

Camp, Sheppard [actor] (b. West Point GA, 16 Jul 1882–20 Nov 1929 [47], Los Angeles CA; from injuries sustained after falling off a horse while filming *Song of Flame* [WB] two days earlier.) "Sheppard Camp," *Variety,* 27 Nov 1929, p. 70. AS, p. 198. BHD1, p. 87. IFN, p. 46.

Campanile Mancini, Gaetano [scenarist/director] (b. Naples, Italy, 26 Jun 1868–1942 [74?], Naples, Italy). AS, p. 198. JS, p. 72 (in Italian silents from 1919).

Campbell, Alan [actor] (d. 30 Dec 1917). BHD, p. 122.

Campbell, Alan [stage actor/scenarist] (b. Homestead FL, 22 Apr 1905–14 Jun 1963 [58], Los Angeles CA). m. **Dorothy Parker** (d. 1967). "Alan Campbell," *Variety,* 231, 10 Jul 1963, 79:1. AS, p. 198. BHD2, p. 40. IFN, p. 46.

Campbell, Argyle [director] (b. 1887–4 Apr 1940 [53?], Shreveport LA). BHD2, p. 40.

Campbell, Colin [director] (aka J[ames] Colin Campbell, b. Scotland, 11 Oct 1859–26 Aug 1928 [68], Los Angeles CA; cerebral thrombosis). "Colin Campbell," *Variety,* 29 Aug 1928, p. 57 (age 62). AMD, p. 61. AS, p. 198. BHD, p. 122; BHD2, p. 41. IFN, p. 46. Katz, pp. 199–200. "James S. McQuade, "Director James Colin Campbell," *MPW,* 27 Mar 1915, 1916. "Selig to Produce "The Crisis,'" *MPW,* 15 Jan 1916, 400. "Selig Veteran Joins Universal Forces," *MPW,* 6 Jul 1918, 51. "To Direct Katherine MacDonald," *MPW,* 8 Mar 1919, 1329.

Campbell, Colin [actor] (b. Falkirk, Scotland, 20 Mar 1881–25 Mar 1966 [85], Woodland Hills CA; cerebral hemorrhage). . "Colin Campbell," *Variety,* 6 Apr 1966, p. 71 (began 1916). AS, p. 198 (b. 1883). BHD1, p. 88 (b. 1883). IFN, p. 46. Truitt, p. 48.

Campbell, Eric Alfred [actor] (b. Dunoon, Scotland, 26 Apr 1879–20 Dec 1917 [38], Los Angeles CA; auto accident). m. (1) d. Jul 1917; (2) Pearl Gilman, 1917. (Mutual.) "Eric Campbell," *Variety,* 28 Dec 1917, p. 48. BHD, p. 122. IFN, p. 46 (age 37). "Campbell's Tough Luck," *Variety,* 13 Jul 1917, p. 19 ("The wife of Eric Campbell…died suddenly the other evening, after dinner in a local café, from a heart attack…"). "Obituary," *MPW,* 5 Jan 1918, 53. "Additional Details of Campbell Tragedy," *MPW,* 12 Jan 1918, 220. AMD, p. 61. AS, p. 198 (b. 25 Apr). "Married After 4 Days," *Variety,* 10 Aug 1917, p. 1 ("Los Angeles, Aug. 8. Eric Campbell and Pearl Gilman, sister of Mabel Gilman Corey, were married here…. Campbell's wife died 14 days ago."). Gilman filed for divorce on 14 Nov 1917, *Variety,* 16 Nov 1917, p. 55. "Campbell Won't Be Seen in Pickford Picture," *MPW,* 19 Jan 1918, 355. "Actor's Widow Engaged," *MPW,* 28 Dec 1918, 1496.

Campbell, Evelyn [actress] (b. 4 Dec 1895–9 May 1992 [96], New York NY). . "Evelyn Campbell," *Variety,* 25 May 1992, p. 71 (Ziegfeld Follies girl). AMD, p. 61. AS, p. 199 (d. 1922). "'Yesterday's Wife' Pleases Author," *MPW,* 3 Nov 1923, 131.

Campbell, Frank G. [actor] (b. 1846–30 Apr 1934 [87], Los Angeles CA). AS, p. 199. BHD1, p. 88. IFN, p. 46.

Campbell, Frankie [actress] (b. 1882?–5 Oct 1933 [51], Los Angeles CA). m. Herbert Ingram. "Frankie Campbell," *Variety,* 17 Oct 1933, p. 62. AS, p. 199.

Campbell, James L. [scenarist]. No data found. FDY, p. 419.

Campbell, Lloyd [film editor]. No data found. AMD, p. 61. "Campbell Joins Bachmann," *MPW,* 11 Sep 1926, 119.

Campbell, Margaret [actress] (b. St. Louis MO, 24 Apr 1883–27 Jun 1939 [56], Los Angeles CA; murdered in a hammer attack by her son, Campbell McDonald). m. **Joseph Swickard** (d. 1940). "Margaret Campbell," *Variety,* 5 Jul 1939, p. 54. AS, p. 199. BHD1, p. 88. IFN, p. 46. Truitt, p. 48. Truitt 1983 (b. 1873).

Campbell, Maurice [scenarist/director]. No data found. AMD, p. 61. FDY, p. 419. "Major Campbell Is Directing Paramount's 'Burglar Proof,'" *MPW,* 22 May 1920, 1101. "To Direct May McAvoy," *MPW,* 3 Dec 1921, 549. "Campbell Signs Contract as Director for Arrow," *MPW,* 4 Jul 1925, 82.

Campbell, Mrs. Patrick (mother of **Alan Campbell**) [stage/film actress] (*née* Beatrice Stella Turner, b. Kensington, London, England, 9 Feb 1865–9 Apr 1940 [75], Pau, France [extrait de décès no. 408/1940]). m. Patrick Campbell; George Cornwallis-West, 1914. (Fox; MGM; Columbia.) "Mrs. Patrick Campbell," *Variety,* 17 Apr 1940, p. 55 (in *The Dancers,* Fox). AS, p. 199. BHD1, p. 88 (d. Pau, France). GSS, pp. 59–62. IFN, p. 46. Waldman, p. 42 (*née* Tanner; "The studios say I am too celebrated for small parts, and too English to star—that Kalamazoo and Butte, Montana, and Seattle would not understand my English style and speech."). "Mrs. Patrick Campbell Breaks a Kneecap [on 3 Jan]; Actress, Hampered by Dog [Pinky-Panky-Poo] Under Arm, Slips on Carriage Step; May Be Confined in a Philadelphia Hospital for Three Weeks—Engagements Canceled," *NYT,* 4 Jan 1905, 1:5 (was appearing in *The Sorceress,* Broad Street Theatre. She had a bundle of books and was tightly wrapped in a heavy cloak.). "Mrs. Campbell Out Again; Actress Leaves Hospital for First Time Since Her Accident," *NYT,* 1 Feb 1905, 9:4 (at University Hospital, Philadelphia PA; accident on 2 Jan). Alan Strachan, "Leslie French," *Independent Review,* 26 Jan 1999, p. 6 ("The production [*Strange Orchestra,* 1932] had not been helped by Mrs. Patrick Campbell, long considered unemployable, living up to her reputation as a sinking ship firing on its rescuers. [John] Gielgud risked casting her…but after rehearsing gloriously for for a fortnight and promising to deliver a magnificent comeback, she flounced out of the production, claiming to understand neither the play nor her characters.").

Campbell, Violet [actress] (*née* Violet Shelton, b. Hertfordshire, England, 24 Apr 1892–3 Jan 1970 [77], London, England). AS, p. 199. BHD1, p. 88.

Campbell, Webster [actor/scenarist/director] (*né* William Webster Campbell, b. Kansas City KS, 25 Jan 1893–28 Aug 1972 [79], Liberty KS; heart attack). . m. **Corinne Griffith**, 1916—div. 1923 (d. 1979); Beatrice, 1959. (Lubin; NYMP Co.; Ince; Vitagraph.) "Webster Campbell," *Variety,* 6 Sep 1972, p. 62. AS, p. 199. BHD1, p. 88; BHD2, p. 41. IFN, p. 46. "Webster Campbell," *NYDM,* 29 Jul 1914, 24:1 (graduate of the University of Michigan).

Campbell, W[illiam] **S.** [director] (b. Ashley PA). AMD, p. 61. AS, p. 199. "W.S. Campbell Plans to Make Greater Educational Comedies," *MPW,* 4 Jun 1921, 529.

Campeau, Frank [actor] (b. Detroit MI, 14 Dec 1864–5 Nov 1943 [78], Woodland Hills CA). "Frank Campeau, Stage, Film Actor; A Noted 'Villain' of the Silent Screen Dies—An Original Member of the Maskers," *NYT,* 9 Nov 1943, 21:5 (d. 6 Nov). "Frank Campeau," *Variety,* 10 Nov 1943, p. 70. AMD, p. 61. AS, p. 199 (d. 6 Nov). BHD1, p. 88. IFN, p. 46. MH, p. 100. Truitt, p. 48. "Frank Campeau Re-Engaged by Fairbanks," *MPW,* 20 Oct 1917, 394. "Campeau to Continue in Support of Fairbanks," *MPW,* 17 Jan 1920, 453.

Campogalliani, Carlo [stage/screen actor/director/scenarist] (b. Concordia, Italy, 10 Oct 1885–9 Aug 1974 [88], Rome, Italy). m. **Letizia Quaranta**, 1921 (d. 1977). AS, p. 199. BHD2, p. 41 (b. Modena, Italy). JS, p. 73 (in Italian silents from 1910; "In the 20s he went to Argentina for some years, working in the infant industry there.").

Canfield, Eugene [actor]. No data found. *MPN,* II, 2 May 1908, 390.

Canfield, William F. [actor] (b. 1860?–14 Feb 1925 [64], New York NY; fell down elevator shaft one month previously). "Wm. F. Canfield," *Variety*, 18 Feb 1925, p. 40. AS, p. 200. BHD, p. 122. IFN, p. 46.

Cann, Bert [cinematographer]. No data found. FDY, p. 457.

Cannon, Pomeroy [stage/opera singer/vaudeville/minstrels/circus actor/director] (b. New Albany IN, 1 Mar 1870–16 Sep 1928 [58], Los Angeles CA). (Began 1903; Triangle Paramount; Fox.) AMD, p. 61. BHD, p. 122; BHD2, p. 41. MSBB, p. 1922 (b. 1880). "Cannon with Metropolitan," *MPW*, 2 May 1927, 786.

Cannon, Raymond [actor/scenarist/director] (b. Long Hollow TN, 1 Sep 1892–7 Jun 1977 [84], Los Angeles CA; cancer). . "Raymond Cannon," *Variety*, 22 Jun 1977, p. 111. AS, p. 200. BHD1, p. 88; BHD2, p. 41. FDY, p. 419. FFF, p. 150. IFN, p. 46. MH, p. 101.

Cansino, Eduardo (father of Rita Hayworth and **Eduardo Cansino, Jr.**) [dancer/actor] (b. Madrid, Spain, 2 Mar 1895–23 Dec 1968 [73], Pompano Beach FL). m. Elisa. "Eduardo Cansino," *Variety*, 1 Jan 1969, p. 55. AS, p. 200. BHD1, p. 89. IFN, p. 46. "Vaudeville; The Cansinos Dance," *NYDM*, 7 Jul 1915, 17:2 (at the Palace). "Miss Elisa Cansino [photo]," *NYDM*, 14 Jul 1915, 16:1.

Cansino, Eduardo, Jr. (son of **Eduardo Cansino**; brother of Rita Hayworth) [actor] (b. New York NY, 13 Oct 1919–11 Mar 1974 [54], Los Angeles CA; cancer). AS, p. 200. BHD1, p. 89. IFN, p. 46.

Cantagrel, Marc [director] (b. Paris, France, 1 Dec 1879–6 Nov 1960 [80], Neuilly-sur-Seine, France). BHD, p. 200.

Canter, Nellie Bell [actress] (b. 1902–1 May 1981 [79?], Pittsburgh PA). AS, p. 201. BHD, p. 122.

Cantini, Guido [scenarist] (b. Livorno, Italy, 9 Apr 1889–1 Jan 1945 [55], Rome, Italy). JS, p. 74 (in Italian silents from 1920).

Cantor, Eddie [stage/film/TV actor/scenarist/producer] (*né* Edward Israel Iskowitz, b. New York NY, 31 Jan 1892–10 Oct 1964 [72], Beverly Hills CA; heart attack). m. Ida Tobias, 1914 (d. 1962). *My Life Is in Your Hands* (1928); *Take My Life* (1957); *The Way I See It* (1959); *As I Remember Them* (1963). "Eddie Cantor Dead; Comedy Star Was 72," *NYT*, 11 Oct 1964, 1:2; "Comedy Star of Vaudeville, Screen and Radio and TV Was a Discoverer of Talent," 85:3 (*né* Isidor Iskowitch). "Private Service Is Planned for Cantor," *NYT*, 12 Oct 1964, 29:2. "Cantor Estate to Daughters," *NYT*, 16 Oct 1964, 32:2. "Eddie Cantor Requested No Public Funeral; Star, Long Ailing, Was 72," *Variety*, 14 Oct 1964 (*né* Isidor Iskewitch). AMD, p. 61. AS, p. 201. BHD1, p. 89; BHD2, p. 41. IFN, p. 47. Truitt, p. 49. "Cantor Boosts 'Charley's Aunt,'" *MPW*, 7 Mar 1925, 74. "Cantor Returns to Stage Work," *MPW*, 4 Jun 1927, 344. "Cantor Packs F-P-L Suitcase Rumor Hath It," *MPW*, 18 Jun 1927, 479.

Cantzen, Conrad [stage/film actor] (b. New Orleans LA, 1867–28 Jun 1945 [78], New York NY). "Conrad Cantzen," *Variety*, 4 Jul 1945, p. 42. BHD, p. 122. IFN, p. 47.

Canudo, Ricciotto [scenarist] (b. Italy, 1878–10 Nov 1923 [45?], Paris, France). "Ricciotto Canudo," *Variety*, 15 Nov 1923, p. 19. BHD2, p. 41.

Canutt, Yakima (brother of Joe Canutt) [stuntman/actor/director] (*né* Enos Edward Canutt, b. Snake River Hills [Colfax] WA, 29 Nov 1895–24 May 1986 [90], No. Hollywood CA; cardiac arrest). . With Oliver Drake, *Stunt Man; The Autobiography of Yakima Canutt* (New York: Walker and Company, 1979). "Yakima Canutt Dies; Stunt Man in Movies," *NYT*, 27 May 1986, D18:6. Bill Edwards, "Pioneer Stuntman Yakima Canutt, 90, Dies in California," *Variety*, 28 May 1986 (b. 28 Nov). AMD, p. 62. AS, p. 201. BHD1, p. 89; BHD2, p. 41. FSS, p. 53. JS, p. 74 (Yakima Canutt appeared in Italian films from 1956 to 1965; Joe Canutt appeared in *Ben-Hur*, 1959, and *El Cid*, 1961). "Canutt Recovering," *MPW*, 29 Aug 1925, 947. George A. Katchmer, "Forgotten Cowboys and Cowgirls—Part X," *CI*, 182 (Aug 1990), 38.

Capellani, Albert [director] (brother of **Paul Capellani**) (b. Fumay, France, 1870–1931 [61?], Paris, France]. (Pathé Frères [Paris], 1905; World; Selznick; Mutual; Metro; directorial debut: *The Face in the Moonlight*, World, 1915.) AMD, p. 62. AS, p. 201. BHD2, p. 41. MSBB, p. 1044 (b. 1874). Spehr, p. 120. Waldman, p. 45. "Albert Capellani," *MPW*, 24 Apr 1915, 541. "Capellani a Metro Director," *MPW*, 20 Oct 1917, 393. "Cosmopolitan Signs Albert Capellani to Direct Five Special Productions," *MPW*, 24 Apr 1920, 590. "Albert Capellani Sues International Alleging $15,000 Due Him in Salary," *MPW*, 4 Sep 1920, 70. "Capellani Made Defendant," *MPW*, 4 Sep 1920, 94.

Capellani, Paul Henri [actor/director] (brother of **Albert Capellani**) (b. Paris, France, 9 Sep 1877–7 Nov 1960 [83], Cagnes-sur-mer, France [extrait de décès no. 96/1960]). m. Marie Léonie Bürckel. (Paramount, Joinville, France, 1930; World Pictures; Ivan; Metro.) AMD, p. 62. AS, p. 201. BHD2, p. 41. MSBB, p. 1044. Spehr, p. 120. Waldman, p. 45 (b. 1870).

Capellani, Paul [stage/film actor/sculptor] (d. 1914). IFN, p. 47 (d. 1914). "Another Pathe Hero; Paul Capellani, of French Pathe Stock Company, Killed in Battle," *NYDM*, 9 Dec 1914, 25:1 (the other player was Rene Alexander. "Word has also been received of the wounding of several players."). "Pathé Players Killed on the Firing Line," *MPW*, 12 Dec 1914, 1503.

Capellani, Paul [actor] (b. Paris, France, 1884–1944 [60?]). BHD, p. 122.

Capera, Mary [actress] (d. 21 May 1921, New York NY). BHD, p. 122.

Caples, Vivian [actress]. No data found. (Lubin). *MPN*, 9 Oct 1915, 73 (photo).

Capodaglio, Ruggero [actor] (b. Salerno, Italy, 1880–1946 [66?], Rome, Italy). m. Anna Gramatica (actress Anna Capodaglio). JS, p. 74 (in Italian silents from 1918).

Capodaglio, Wanda [actress] (b. Asti, Italy, 1 Jan 1890). JS, p. 74 (in Italian silents from 1914).

Capozzi, Alberto A. [actor] (b. Genoa, Italy, 8 Jul 1886–27 Jun 1945 [58], Rome, Italy). AS, p. 201 (b. 1884; d. 19 Mar). BHD1, p. 89. IFN, p. 47. JS, p. 75 ("One of the early silent stars," in Italian silents from 1909).

Cappelaro, Vittorio [actor/director] (b. Mongrande, Italy, 1877–1943 [66?], Rio de Janeiro, Brazil). AS, p. 201.

Cappellano, Francesca [actress] (b. 1896–13 Apr 1988 [91?], Los Angeles CA; pneumonia). AS, p. 201. BHD, p. 122.

Cappelli, Dante [actor] (b. Bologna, Italy). AS, p. 201. JS, p. 75 (in Italian silents from 1913).

Capra, Frank R. [director/scenarist] (*né* Francesco Capra, b. Bisaquino [Palermo], Sicily, Italy, 18 May 1897 [Register of Births, No. 171, Part I, 1897]–3 Sep 1991 [94], La Quinta [Palm Springs] CA; heart attack in his sleep). . Naturalized as a U.S. citizen on 4 Jul 1920. m. (1) Helen Howell, 29 Nov 1923, San Francisco CA—div. 19 Aug 1929; (2) Lucille Florence Warner, 1 Feb 1932, Brooklyn NY (d. 1 Jul 1984). *The Name Above the Title: An Autobiography* (NY: MacMillan, 1971). Joseph McBride, *The Catastrophe of Success* (NY: Simon & Schuster, 1992). (Christie, 1919; Columbia; AA in 1934, 1936, and 1938.) Peter B. Flint, "Frank Capra, Whose Films Helped America Keep Faith in Itself, Is Dead at 94," *NYT*, 4 Sep 1991, B10:1. "Frank Capra," *Variety*, 9 Sep 1991, p. 101. AMD, p. 62. AS, p. 201. BHD2, p. 41. FDY, p. 419. "Frank Capra," *MPW*, 22 Jan 1927, 265. Barry Gewen, "It Wasn't Such a Wonderful Life," *The NYT Book Review*, Sec. 7, 3 May 1992, 3, 37. (Memorabilia at Wesleyan University CT.) Robert Yates, "'A Wonderful Life' makes its way back to the big screen," *PP-G*, 15 Dec 1997, D-5:1 (Frank Capra, Jr., in London to promote a new print, big-screen reissue. In 1994, NBC bought the rights to show the film every Christmas on TV.).

Capri, Olga [actress] (b. Rome, Italy, 18 May 1893–ca. 1930 [37?]). AS, p. 202. JS, p. 75 (in Italian silents from 1919).

Caprice, June [actress] (*née* Betty Lawson, b. Arlington MA, 19 Nov 1898–9 Nov 1936 [37], Los Angeles CA). m. **Harry Millarde** (d. 1931). (Film debut: *Caprice of the Mountains*, Fox, 1916.) "June Caprice," *Variety*, 18 Nov 1936. AMD, p. 62. AS, p. 202 (b. 1899). BHD, pp. 12–14 (b. 1899); 122. IFN, p. 47. MSBB, p. 1032. Spehr, p. 120. Truitt, p. 49. "June Caprice," *MPW*, 17 Feb 1917, 1010. "June Caprice Signs Contract with Pathé; to Play in Serials," *MPW*, 10 Jul 1920, 238.

Capus, Alfred [scenarist]. No data found. AMD, p. 62. "Noted Dramatists to Write Moving Picture Plays," *MPW*, 28 Mar 1908, 263.

Caracciolo, Giuseppe [cinematographer] (*né* Luigi Sapelli, b. Naples, Italy, 17 Apr 1892). JS, pp. 76–77 (in Italian silents from 1918).

Caramba, Luigi [director/art director/costume designer] (*né* Luigi Sapelli, b. Pinerolo, Italy, 25 Feb 1865–10 Nov 1936 [71], Milan, Italy). AS, p. 202. JS, p. 77 (in Italian silents from 1913).

Carco, Francis [actor] (*né* Francis Carcopino-Tuscoli, b. Noumea, New Caledonia, 5 Jul 1886–25 May 1958 [71], Paris, France). "Francis Carco," *Variety*, 6 Apr 1958, p. 75. AS, p. 202.

Cardinal, Margaret [actress]. No data found. AMD, p. 62. "French Actress in American Films," *MPW*, 13 Dec 1919, 838.

Cardona, René [actor/director] (*né* René Cardona Andre, b. Havana, Cuba, 8 Sep 1905–25 Apr 1988 [82], Mexico City, Mexico; cancer). (Hollywood, 1926.) AS, p. 202. Waldman, p. 47.

Caress, William H. (Bill) [actor] (b. 1883–9 Aug 1938 [55?], French Lick IN). BHD1, p. 90.

Carew, James [stage/film/radio actor] (b. Goshen IN, 5 Feb 1876–4 Apr 1938 [62], London, England). m. **Ellen Terry**, Mar 1907, Pittsburgh PA (d. 1928). (Stage debut: *Damon and Pythias*, 1897, Irving Theatre, Chicago; Pathé, 1915; B&C, Ideal; London; Hepworth.) "James Carew,

62, Actor Since 1897; Third Husband of Ellen Terry Dies in London—Prominent on the British Stage; Was Native of Indiana—Began Career in Chicago—Also Had Been Successful in English Films and Radio," *NYT,* 5 Apr 1938, 21:3. "James Carew," *Variety,* 6 Apr 1938, p. 54 (age 67). AS, p. 203. BHD1, p. 90. IFN, p. 49. Truitt, p. 49. May Herschell Clarke, "James Carew on 'The Hero of To-Day,'" *Picture Show,* 5 Nov 1921, 17.

Carewe, Arthur Edmund [actor] (*né* Arthur Arman?, b. Trebizond, Armenia, 30 Dec 1884–21 Apr 1937 [52], Santa Monica CA; suicide). m. prima donna Irene Pavlowska, 1920. "Arthur Carewe," *Variety,* 28 Apr 1937, p. 70. AMD, p. 62. AS, p. 203. BHD1, p. 90 (b. Trabzon, Turkey). FSS, p. 53. IFN, p. 47. Katz, pp. 205–06 (*né* Jan Fox). MH, p. 101. 1921 Directory, p. 260 (b. Gainesville TX). Truitt, p. 49. "A Lead, Director, and Two Heavies Join Universal," *MPW,* 26 Jul 1919, 512. "Carew's Noted Wife," *LA Times,* 1 Feb 1920, III, p. 5.

Carewe, Ora (sister of **Grant Whytock**) [actress] (*née* Ora Whytock, b. Salt Lake City UT, 13 Apr 1893–26 Oct 1955 [62], Los Angeles CA). m. John C. Howard. (Triangle; Sennett; Universal; FP-L; Christie; Metro; Selznick.) "Ora Carewe," *Variety,* 2 Nov 1955. AMD, p. 62. AS, p. 203. BHD, p. 122. IFN, p. 47. MH, p. 101. Truitt, p. 49. WWS, p. 250. "Ora Carew Joins Universal," *MPW,* 4 Mar 1916, 1455. "Ora Carew," *MPW,* 31 Mar 1917, 2108. "Ora Carew," *MPW,* 7 Apr 1917, 103. "Ora Carew Engaged by Diando," *MPW,* 23 Mar 1918, 1645. "Ora Carew, Sennett Beauty, to Play Leads for DeMille," *MPW,* 3 Jul 1920, 50. Maude Cheatham, "Pink Roses Forever," *MPC,* Oct 1921, 50–51, 94 (Carew was her mother's maiden name). "On the Set and Off," *MW,* 13 Sep 1924, 30:1 (fled from the physical abuse of her husband). George A. Katchmer, "Forgotten Cowboys and Cowgirls—Part XVI," *CI,* 193 (Jul 1991), 35.

Carewe, Edwin (brother of **Finis** and **Wallace Fox**; father of **Yvonne Carewe**) [actor/scenarist/director] (*né* Jay J. Fox, b. Gainesville TX, 5 Mar 1881–22 Jan 1940 [58], Los Angeles CA; heart attack). m. Mary Akin, May 1925, Mexico. (1st National; Metro.) "Edwin Carewe, 56, Director of Films; Leader in Silent Era, Noted for Productions of 'Ramona' and 'Resurrection,' Dies," *NYT,* 23 Jan 1940, 21:6. "Edwin Carewe," *Variety,* 24 Jan 1940, 47 (age 56). AMD, p. 62. AS, p. 203. BHD, p. 123; BHD2, p. 41 (b. 1883). FDY, p. 419. IFN, p. 47. Lowrey, p. 32. Spehr, p. 122 (b. 1883). Truitt, p. 49. "Edwin Carewe," *MPW,* 22 Feb 1913, 782. "Edwin Carewe," *MPW,* 30 Oct 1915, 805. "Studio Gossip," *NYDM,* 20 Nov 1915, 24:2 (his assistant at Metro, Harry L. Franklin, acted in stock with him). "Carewe Returns to Metro," *MPW,* 16 Mar 1918, 1523. "Edwin Carewe Forms Own Company," *MPW,* 4 Oct 1919, 94. "Carewe Quits Mayer," *MPW,* 23 Jul 1921, 413. "Edwin Carewe, a Versatile First National Director," *MPW,* 9 Jun 1923, 509. Paul Paige, "Close-Ups and Fade-Outs," *Paris and Hollywood,* Sep 1926, 87 (granted a petition to change his surname of Fox to Carewe. This affected his three daughtrers, Sally Ann, 3 months; Mary, age 8; Violet; and his wife, Margaret.). "Edwin Carewe," *MPW,* 3 Sep 1927, 25. "Carewe and Inspiration Are Merged," *MPW,* 12 Nov 1927, 10.

Carewe, Rita (daughter of **Edwin Carewe**) (actress: Wampas Star, 1927] (*née* Violette Fox, b. New York NY, 9 Sep 1909–23 Oct 1955 [46], Torrance CA). m. **Leroy Mason** (d. 1947). "Rita Carewe," *Variety,* 21 Dec 1955 (aka Rita Mason; age 47). AS, p. 203 (d. 22 Oct). BHD1, p. 90. IFN, p. 47. SD. Truitt, p. 50 (b. 1908).

Carewe, Yvonne (daughter of **Edwin Carewe**; niece of **Finis** and **Wallace Fox**) [actress]. No data found. AMD, p. 62. "Carewe Signs Dolores Rel Rio and His Daughter Yvonne," *MPW,* 5 Dec 1925, 428.

Carey, Harold [writer]. No data found. AMD, p. 62. "Harold Carey with Paramount," *MPW,* 10 Jun 1916, 1858.

Carey, Harry, Sr. (father of Harry Carey, Jr.) [stage/film actor/playwright] (*né* Harry DeWitt Carey II, b. Bronx NY, 16 Jan 1878–21 Sep 1947 [69], Brentwood CA; coronary thrombosis). m. Alma Fern Foster (Fern Foster); **Olive Fuller Golden**, Jan 1920 (son, Harry Carey, Jr., b. 16 May 1921; d. 1988). (Biograph, 1909; Progressive; Universal.) "Harry Carey, Star of Stage, Screen; Veteran Actor Who Won Fame as Cowboy Hero Dies at 69—Scored in 'Trader Horn,'" *NYT,* 22 Sep 1947, 23:3. "Harry Carey," *Variety,* 24 Sep 1947, p. 55. AMD, p. 62. AS, p. 203. BHD1, p. 90 (d. LA CA). FFF, p. 248 (b. 1880). FSS, p. 54. GK, pp. 122–39. IFN, p. 47. MH, p. 101. MSBB, p. 1022 (b. 1880). Truitt, p. 50. WWS, p. 227 (b. NYC, 1880). "Harry Carey," *MPW,* 4 Dec 1915, 1806. "Harry Carey Returns to Universal," *MPW,* 11 Nov 1916, 829. "Secret Marriage Disclosed," *MPW,* 6 Nov 1920, 55 (m. Olive Golden). "Harry Carey Signs with R-C to Star in Special Productions," *MPW,* 25 Mar 1922, 359. "Pathé Has Harry Carey," *MPW,* 26 Sep 1925, 338. Geo. H. Ridley, "Harry Carey; A Cinema Cowboy Who Typifies the Old West," *Cinema Arts,* Aug 1926, 24–25. "Carey Brings Suit," *MPW,* 9 Oct 1926, 3. Charles H. Adair, "Harry Carey's Trading-Post," *MPC,* Nov 1926, 62–63, 70, 88. George A. Katchmer, "The Old, But Young Harry Carey," *CI,* 112 (Oct 1984), 16, 18–20. Roi Uselton, "Harry Carey's Marriage Status [letter]," *CI,* 115 (Jan 1985), C12. George Katchmer, "Remembering the Great Silents," *CI,* 256 (Oct 1996), 41–43.

Carey, Joyce Lillian Lawrence [actress] (b. London, England, 30 Mar 1898–28 Feb 1993 [94], Los Angeles CA; heart attack in her sleep). AS, p. 203. BHD1, p. 90.

Carey, Olive *see* **Golden, Olive Fuller**

Carini, Luigi [actor] (b. Cremona, Italy, 21 Dec 1869 [extrait de naissance no. 1089/1869]-28 Sep 1943 [73], Rome, Italy). AS, p. 204. JS, p. 78 (in Italian silents from 1914).

Carl, Renée [actress] (b. Paris, France, 1875–3 Aug 1954 [79?], Paris, France). AS, p. 204. AS, p. 204. BHD1, p. 605.

Carle, Philip [director]. No data found. AMD, p. 63. "Phillip Carle Resigns," *MPW,* 4 Jun 1921, 494. "Carle to Direct 'In a Moment of Temptation,'" *MPW,* 25 Jun 1927, 593. "Phillip Carle Gets Started on His First for FBO," *MPW,* 16 Jul 1927, 183.

Carle, Richard [stage/film actor] (*né* Charles Nicholas Carleton, b. Somerville MA, 7 Jul 1871–28 Jun 1941 [69], No. Hollywood CA; heart attack). "Richard Carle," *Variety,* 2 Jul 1941, p. 54. AMD, p. 63. AS, p. 204. BHD1, p. 90. IFN, p. 47. Truitt, p. 50. "Carle a Pathe Star," *NYDM,* 7 Jul 1915, 32:4 (to film his stage success, *Mary's Lamb*). "Richard Carle the New Pathé Star," *MPW,* 11 Sep 1915, 1808.

Carleton, George M. [actor] (b. NY, 28 Oct 1885–23 Sep 1950 [64], Los Angeles CA; heart attack). "George Carlton," *Variety,* 27 Sep 1950 (age 65). AS, p. 204. IFN, p. 47.

Carleton, Henry Guy [actor] (b. 1859?–31 Jan 1922 [62], Boston MA). AS, p. 204 (d. NYC). BHD, p. 123 (Harry G. Carleton). IFN, p. 47.

Carleton, John T. (brother of **Lloyd B. Carleton**) [executive]. No data found. "Flashes; New Film Company; Clermont Photoplays in Producing Field," *LA Times,* 30 Jan 1920, II, 9 (vice-president of Clermont Photoplays Corp.).

Carleton, Lloyd B. (brother of **John T. Carleton**) [actor/producer/stage and film director] (*né* Carleton B. Little, b. New York NY, 1872?–8 Aug 1933 [61], New York NY). (Lubin; Selig; Universal; Selznick.) "Lloyd B. Carleton," *Variety,* 15 Aug 1933, p. 55. AMD, p. 63. AS, p. 204. BHD, p. 123; BHD2, p. 42. Wray Bartlett Physioc, "Peptonized and Predigested Teachings," *MPW,* 1 Jun 1912, 806. "Carleton Goes to Fox," *MPW,* 31 Oct 1914, 660. "Box Office Producers," *MPW,* 7 Nov 1914, 791. "Carleton to Direct 'The Idler' and Capt. Jinks," *MPW,* 14 Nov 1914, 937. "Flashes; New Film Company; Clermont Photoplays in Producing Field," *LA Times,* 30 Jan 1920, II, 9.

Carleton, Thomas [producer] (d. Apr 1930). BHD2, p. 42.

Carleton, William C. [actor/scenario editor] (*né* Will C. Cummings, b. New York NY, 24 Sep 1872–21 Sep 1941 [68], Los Angeles CA). (Sennett.) "Will Carleton," *Variety,* 1 Oct 1941, p. 94 (age 70). AS, p. 204. BHD, p. 123; BHD2, p. 42.. IFN, p. 47. Truitt, p. 50.

Carleton, William P. (son of **William T. Carleton**) [stage/film actor] (b. London, England, 3 Oct 1872–5 Apr 1947 [74], Los Angeles CA; from injuries sustained in an auto accident). "William P. Carleton," *Variety,* 9 Apr 1947, p. 54 (d. 6 Apr; in films from 1937). AS, p. 204. AMD, p. 63. BHD1, p. 91. IFN, p. 47. Truitt, p. 50. "William P. Carleton," *NYDM,* 21 Oct 1914, 10:2. "William P. Carleton," *MPW,* 26 Aug 1916, 1416. "Carleton Returns to Famous," *MPW,* 7 Aug 1920, 756.

Carleton, William T. (father of **William P. Carleton**) [opera singer] (b. England, 1859–28 Sep 1930 [71?], St. John, New Brunswick, Canada). (Edison.) "William T. Carleton," *Variety,* 1 Oct 1930, p. 76 (stage director). AS, p. 204. BHD, p. 123. IFN, p. 47. SD, p. 212. "Carleton with Edison; Well-Known Baritone to Be Seen in the Multiple Reel Release, 'Fantasma,'" *NYDM,* 7 Oct 1914, 28:2.

Carlie, Edward [actor] (b. 1878?–25 Nov 1938 [59], Los Angeles CA; dropped dead while dancing in *I'm from Missouri* at Paramount). "Edward Carlie," *Variety,* 30 Nov 1938, p. 54 (age 60). AS, p. 204 (b. 1878). BHD1, p. 91. IFN, p. 47 (Edwin Carlie). Truitt, p. 50.

Carlin, George A. [publicist]. No data found. AMD, p. 63. "Carlin Joins Metro Publicity Staff," *MPW,* 28 Feb 1920, 1501.

Carlin, Tommy [stage/film actor] (b. Jersey City NJ, 20 Apr 1912–17 Jul 1990 [78], San Diego CA). BHD1, p. 605. MSBB, p. 1022.

Carlisle, Alexandra [actress] (*née* Alexandra Swift, b. London, England, 15 Jan 1886–21 Apr 1936 [50], New York NY; found dead of a heart attack). m. (1) Victor Herbert Miller; (2) Dr. Albert Pfeiffer; (3) Joseph Coyne (d. 1941); (4) John Elliott

Jenkins. (World Pictures.) "Alexandria Carlisle," *Variety,* 29 Apr 1936, p. 62. AMD, p. 63. AS, p. 204. BHD1, p. 91. IFN, p. 47. SD. "Alexandra Carlisle Signed," *NYDM,* 29 Sep 1915, 32:2 (to debut in *Creeping Tides* for Equitable). "Alexandra Carlisle with Equitable," *MPW,* 2 Oct 1915, 59. "Alexandra Carlisle," *MPW,* 1 Sep 1917, 1362. "English Beauty in 'Tides of Fate,'" *Motography,* 1 Sep 1917, 458.

Carlisle, Anne B *see* **Eline, Marie**

Carlisle, Lucille (sister of Helen Carlisle, writer for *Movie Weekly*) [actress]. No data found. m. **Larry Semon** (d. 1928). (Vitagraph.)

Carloni-Talli, Ida [actress] (b. Rome, Italy, 31 Jan 1860–23 Apr 1940 [79?], Milan, Italy). AS, p. 205 (b. 1869). JS, p. 79 (in Italian silents from 1912).

Carlsen, F. [scenarist]. No data found. FDY, p. 419.

Carlsen, Traute [actress] (*née* Gertrud Rosalie Kempner, b. Dresden, Germany, 16 Feb 1882–22 Nov 1968 [86], Kunsnacht, Switzerland). m. **Karl Forest** (d. 1944). AS, p. 205.

Carlson, Wallace [cartoonist/actor/director/scenarist] (b. St. Louis MO, 28 Mar 1894–9 May 1967 [73], Chicago IL). AMD, p. 63. BHD2, p. 42. "Wallace Carlson Joins Bray," *MPW,* 2 Jun 1917, 1444. "Wallace Carlson," *MPW,* 21 Jul 1917, 397.

Carlucci, Leopoldo [director]. No data found. JS, p. 79 (in Italian silents from 1915).

Carlyle, Aileen [actress] (b. San Francisco CA, 5 Mar 1906–3 May 1984 [78], Los Angeles CA). (Began 1926.) BHD1, p. 91. SD, p. 213.

Carlyle, Billie [actress] (b. Adelaide, Australia, 1901–23 Jul 1991 [90?], Staines, England). BHD1, p. 91.

Carlyle, Francis [actor] (b. England, 27 Aug 1868–15 Sep 1916 [48], Hartford CT). (Pathé.) "Francis Carlyle," *Variety,* 22 Sep 1916, p. 13. AMD, p. 63. AS, p. 205 (b. 1870). BHD, p. 123. IFN, p. 48. SD, p. 213. "Francis Carlyle," *MPW,* 31 Jan 1914, 524. "Francis Carlyle," *MPW,* 25 Apr 1914, 495. "Obituary," *MPW,* 14 Oct 1916, 238.

Carlyle, Grace [actress]. No data found. AMD, p. 63. "Miss Carlyle Returns to the Studio," *MPW,* 9 Oct 1926, 353.

Carlyle, Helen [actress] (b. Hollywood CA, 18 Oct 1892–30 Jun 1933 [40], Los Angeles CA; heart attack). m. **Hampton Del Ruth** (d. 1958). "Helen Carlyle," *Variety,* 11 Jul 1933. AS, p. 205. IFN, p. 48.

Carlyle, Jack [Montgomery] [actor]. No data found. George A. Katchmer, "Forgotten Cowboys and Cowgirls—Part XVI," *CI,* 193 (Jul 1991), 52.

Carlyle, Richard [actor] (b. Guelph, Ontario, Canada, 21 May 1876–12 Jun 1942 [66], San Fernando CA). m. Mirza Marston, 1909. "Richard Carlyle," *Variety,* 17 Jun 1942, p. 54 (in *The Copperhead* with Lionel Barrymore). AS, p. 205. BHD1, p. 91. IFN, p. 48. Truitt, p. 50 (b. 1879).

Carlyle, Sidney D. [actor] (b. Yarmouth, England, 29 Aug 1893–3 Nov 1962 [69], San Bernardino CA). BHD1, p. 91.

Carmen, Jewel [actress] (aka Evelyn Quick, *née* Florence Lavina Quick, b. Danville KY [or in Oregon], 13 Jul 1897–4 Mar 1984 [86], Helix View Nursing Home, El Cajon CA; lymphoma). m. **Roland West**, Dec 1918 (d. 1952). (Keystone, 1913; Pathé; Nestor; Triangle.) AMD, p. 63. AS, p. 205. BHD1, p. 605. KOM, pp. 132–33. Spehr, p. 122. "Doings at Los Angeles; Changes in Universal Staff," *MPW,* 10 May 1913, 582 (as Evelyn Quick, succeeded Louise Glaum as leading woman at Nestor). "Jewel Carmen Joins William Fox Forces," *MPW,* 25 Nov 1916, 1163. Cal York, "A Queen of Blondes; Jewel Carmen, the girl who 'photographs like a million dollars,'" *Photoplay,* Jul 1917, 108–09 (discovered by Douglas Fairbanks. "In that city [Los Angeles] she attended a convent and was studying there when induced to apply for a position in a moving picture studio about four years ago."). "Jewel Carmen Working as a Star," *MPW,* 22 Dec 1917, 1787. "Jewel Carmen, Under Keeney Contract, Will Be Directed by Sidney Olcott," *MPW,* 7 Sep 1918, 1403. "Jewel Carmen Enters Suit Against Fox Companies," *MPW,* 9 Nov 1918, 677. "Player Wins First Round in Fox Suit," *MPW,* 14 Dec 1918, 1188. "Jewel Carmen Again Wins Point in Contract Suit," *MPW,* 5 Apr 1919, 54. "Jewel Carmen Has Success in Court," *MPW,* 12 Jul 1919, 222. "Jewel Carmen Awarded $43,500 Damages from Fox," *MPW,* 26 Jul 1919, 483. "Burkan Takes Contract Dispute Between Jewel Carmen and Fox to Highest Court," *MPW,* 5 Feb 1921, 661. "Jewel Carmen Loses Law Suit Against Fox," *MPW,* 19 Mar 1921, 249. "Two Fox Companies Answer Damage Suit Brought Against Them by Jewel Carmen," *MPW,* 6 Aug 1921, 594. Capitola Williams Ashworth, "The Mermaid of Manhassett," *MPC,* Dec 1921, 16–17, 80. *See* Anita Loos, *The Talmadge Girls; A Memoir* (NY: The Viking Press, 1978), p. 123. Billy Doyle, "Jewel Carmen; Shaded for Scandal," *CI,* 287 (May 1999), C2-C3.

Carmen, Sybil [actress] (*née* Sybil Revnes, b. Parkersburg WV, 1891?–15 Apr 1929 [38?], Paris, France; pneumonia). m. Maurice Revnes. "Sybil Carmen Dies," *Variety,* 17 Apr 1929. AMD, p. 63. AS, p. 205. BHD, p. 123 (b. 1900). IFN, p. 48. "Keeney Engages Players," *MPW,* 16 Feb 1918, 954.

Carmi, Maria [actress] (*née* Norina Gilli, b. Florence, Italy, 3 Mar 1880–4 Aug 1957 [77], Myrtle Beach SC). AMD, p. 63. AS, p. 205. BHD, p. 123. IFN, p. 48. JS, p. 79 (in Italian silents from 1914). "Maria Carmi," *MPW,* 28 Mar 1914, 1693. Vittorio Martinelli, "Kino-Lieblinge," *Griffithiana,* 38/39 (Oct 1990), 11.

Carmichael, Myra [actress] (b. 22 Jan 1890–22 Oct 1974 [84], Port Washington NY). AS, p. 205 (d. 25 Oct, LA CA). BHD1, p. 605.

Carminati, Tullio [stage/film actor] (*né* Count Tullio Carminati de Brambilla, b. Zara [now in Yugoslavia], Dalmatia, Italy, 21 Sep 1894–26 Feb 1971 [76], Rome, Italy; stroke). (Began 1912; Ufa; UA.) "Tullio Carminati, Actor, Dies; Star in 'Strictly Dishonorable,'" *NYT,* 27 Feb 1971 (age 77). "Tullio Carminati," *Variety,* 3 Mar 1971, p. 71 (age 77). AMD, p. 64. AS, p. 206. BHD1, p. 92 (b. Zadar, Croatia). IFN, p. 48. JS, pp. 79–80 (b. 1895; "Star of early silent films," from 1912). Truitt, pp. 50–51. Waldman, p. 47 (b. 1895). "Schenck Signs Carminati," *MPW,* 7 Nov 1925, 40. "Italian Screen Actor Leading Man for Constance Talmadge," *MPW,* 24 Apr 1926, 599. Carolyn Darling, "Tullio Carminati; Constance Talmadge's New Leading Man [*The Duchess of Buffalo*] Tells Interesting Impressions of Stage and Screen," *Cinema Arts,* Aug 1926, 26, 47 (*né* Count Tullio Carminati di Branbills).

Carnahan, Thomas B., Jr. [actor] (b. Pittsburgh PA, 1904). AS, p. 206.

Carnegie, Andrew [industrialist] (b. Dunfermline, Scotland, 1835–1919 [84?]). m. Louise Whitfield (daughter Margaret, b. 1897). "Andrew Carnegie's Debut in Pictures [photo]," *NYDM,* 4 Feb 1914, 39:1.

Carney, Augustus [actor]. No data found. m. **Margaret Joslin** (d. 1956). (Essanay.) AMD, p. 64. "'Alkali Ike' on His Way to Paris," *MPW,* 8 Nov 1913, 598. "Augustus Carney Signs with Universal," *MPW,* 20 Dec 1913, 1417. "'Alkali Ike' Back from Abroad," *MPW,* 25 Jul 1914, 583.

Carney, [Uncle] Don [actor] (*né* Howard Rice, b. 1896?–14 Jan 1954 [57], Miami FL; heart attack). "Don (Uncle Don) Carney," *Variety,* 20 Jan 1954, p. 71. AS, p. 206. IFN, p. 48.

Carney, George [actor] (b. Bristol, England, 21 Nov 1887–9 Dec 1947 [60], London, England). AS, p. 206. BHD1, p. 92. IFN, p. 48.

Carney, Mary [actress] (b. 1904–21 Jul 1984 [80?]). BHD1, p. 92.

Carol, Sue (mother of David Ladd) [actress: Wampas Star, 1928/actors' agent] (*née* Evelyn Lederer, b. Chicago IL, 30 Oct 1903–4 Feb 1982 [78?], Los Angeles CA; heart attack). m. **Nick Stuart** (d. 1973); (4) Alan Ladd (son, David; d. 1964). "Sue Carol Ladd, ex-Actress and Widow of Alan Ladd, 72," *NYT,* 6 Feb 1982, 16:6. "Sue Carol Ladd," *Variety,* 10 Feb 1982. AMD, p. 64. AS, p. 206 (b. 1907); AS, p. 631 (Sue Carol Ladd, b. 1907; d. 1979). BHD1, p. 92. FSS, p. 55. "New Lead for MacLean," *MPW,* 7 May 1927, 23. "'U' Signs Sue Carol," *MPW,* 24 Sep 1927, 213. Helen Bailey, "Out of the Nowhere into the Here," *MPC,* Oct 1927, 63, 87 (discusses starlets Carol, Virginia Whiting, Patricia Caron, Anita Barnes, *et al.*). "Sue Carol," *MPW,* 10 Dec 1927, 48. Ann Cummings, "How to Tell Clara from Sue; Except to Themselves and Hollywood The Bow and the Carol Seem Indistinguishable," *MPC,* Aug 1928, 28–29, 73, 83.

Carotenuto, Nello (father of actor Mario Carotenuto [d. 1985]) [actor] (*né* Raffaele Carotenuto, b. Italy). AS, p. 206.

Carpenter, Charles [actor] (b. 1913–12 Nov 1990 [77], Oxnard CA; heart attack). "Charles Carpenter," *Variety,* 10 Dec 1990. AS, p. 207. BHD1, p. 92.

Carpenter, Edward Childs [actor/novelist/playwright] (b. Philadelphia PA, 13 Dec 1872–7 Oct 1950 [77], Torrington CT). m. Helen A. Knipe, 1907. "Edward Childs Carpenter," *Variety,* 11 Oct 1950, p. 63 (age 76). AS, p. 207 (b. 1874). BHD2, p. 42 (b. 1874). NNAT. SD. WWWA.

Carpenter, Francis [child actor] (b. 1906?). No other data found. AMD, p. 64. F.E. Hasty, "The Children Are Promoted," *NYDM,* 8 Sep 1915, 37:2 (Majestic Juvenile Co. members to appear in 2-reel features, Reliance brand, due to the popularity of child films for children acted by children. Mentioned were Carpenter, age 9, George Stone, age 6, Carmen de Rue, age 9, and Violet Radcliffe, age 6.). "Child Actor Gets Contract," *MPW,* 16 Oct 1920, 953.

Carpenter, Frederick L. [actor] (b. 1922–31 Mar 1984 [61?], Oxnard CA). AS, p. 207. BHD, p. 123.

Carpenter, George Melford [art director]. No data found. AMD, p. 64. "George Melford Carpenter Now Metro Art Director," *MPW,* 6 Dec 1919, 662.

Carpenter, Horace B. [actor/scenarist/

cinematographer] (b. Grand Rapids MI, 31 Jan 1875–21 May 1945 [70], Los Angeles CA; heart attack). "Horace B. Carpenter," *Variety*, 30 May 1945, p. 54. AS, p. 207. BHD1, p. 92; BHD2, p. 42. FDY, pp. 419, 457. IFN, p. 48. Truitt, p. 51. George A. Katchmer, "Remembering the Great Silents," *CI*, 172 (Oct 1989), C14.

Carpenter, Jeanne [actress] (b. 1916–5 Jan 1994 [77?], Oxnard CA). BHD, p. 123.

Carpenter, Roy [cinematographer]. No data found. FDY, p. 457.

Carpentier, Georges [actor] (b. Lens, France, 12 Jan 1876?–15 Aug 1929 [53], Paris, France; found dead, a probable victim of heart disease). "Carpentier, Comic, Dies," *Variety*, 11 Sep 1929. AS, p. 207.

Carpentier, Georges Jean-Baptiste Joseph [boxer/actor] (b. Lens, France, 10 May 1894 [extrait de naissance no. 229]–28 Oct 1975 [81], Paris, France). AMD, p. 64. AS, p. 207. BHD1, p. 93. IFN, p. 48. "Carpentier Here from France; to Start Work Soon on Robertson-Cole Special," *MPW*, 3 Apr 1920, 58. "Carpentier Has Qualities of an Actor, According to Tests," *MPW*, 24 Apr 1920, 590. "Carpentier Delights Notable Crowd at Solax Studio as Both Fighter and Actor," *MPW*, 8 May 1920, 856. "Georges Carpentier Is Signed to Three-Year Film Contract," *MPW*, 22 May 1920, 1058. "Carpentier's Smile Is Basis of Suit Against Distributors," *MPW*, 24 Jul 1920, 476. "Georges Carpentier to Return," *MPW*, 7 Aug 1920, 760. "Robertson-Cole Wins in Lumiere's Suit to Prevent Use of Carpentier Pictures," *MPW*, 4 Jun 1921, 492.

Carr, Alexander [actor] (b. Rumni, Russia, 7 Mar 1878–19 Sep 1946 [68], Los Angeles CA). m. (1) Mary; (2) Helen Cressman, 1924. "On the Set and Off," *MW*, 7 Mar 1925, 34 (reconciled with Cressman; first wife sued him for back alimony). "Alexander Carr, Comedian, 68, Dies; Stage, Screen Veteran Won Fame as Mawruss Perlmutter in Montague Glass Series," *NYT*, 20 Sep 1946, 31:1. "Alexander Carr," *Variety*, 25 Sep 1946, p. 62. AMD, p. 64. AS, p. 207. BHD1, p. 93 (b. Poltava, Ukraine). FSS, p. 56. IFN, p. 48. SD. "Gets Character Actor," *MPW*, 5 Dec 1925, 439.

Carr, Catherine [scenarist/film editor] (*née?*, b. Austin TX, 1880?–18 Jan 1941 [61], Los Angeles CA). (Lasky; Universal; Fox; Paramount.) "Mrs. Catherine Carr," *Variety*, 29 Jan 1941. AS, p. 207. BHD2, p. 42. "In the Picture Studios," *NYDM*, 7 Jul 1915, 9:2 (suffered a nervous breakdown).

Carr, Gladys M. [actress] (b. 1890?–26 Sep 1940 [50], Los Angeles CA). (Vitagraph.) m. Harold E. Roy. "Gladys M. Carr," *Variety*, 2 Oct 1940. BHD, p. 123. IFN, p. 48. SD.

Carr, Harry [title writer/scenarist] (b. 1877?–10 Jan 1936 [58], Los Angeles CA). (Griffith; Lasky; Paramount.) "Harry Carr Dead," *Variety*, 15 Jan 1936. AS, p. 207. BHD2, p. 42. FDY, pp. 419, 441. Harry, Carr, "Wild Extras I Have Known," *MPC*, Jul 1922, 46–47, 91–92, 94.

Carr, John [actor] (b. Philadelphia PA–d. 27 Nov 1956, Los Angeles CA). BHD, p. 124.

Carr, John J. [director of animated films] (b. 1901–3 Aug 1974 [73?], Los Angeles CA). AS, p. 207.

Carr, Luella [actress] (b. Philadelphia PA–d. 16 Jan 1937, Los Angeles CA). AS, p. 207. BHD, p. 124. IFN, p. 48.

Carr, Mary, "The Mother of the Movies" (mother of **Stephen** and **Thomas Carr**) [stage/film actress] (*née* Mary Kennivan, b. Germantown [Philadelphia] PA, 8 Jun 1874–24 Jun 1973 [99], Woodland Hills CA). m. **William C.D. Carr**, Philadelphia PA, ca. 1901 (d. 1937). (Lubin; Fox.) "Mary Carr," *Variety*, 1 Aug 1973, p. 55. AMD, p. 64. AS, p. 208 (b. 14 Mar). BHD1, p. 93 (b. 14 Mar). FFF, p. 208. FSS, p. 56. IFN, p. 48 (b. 14 Mar). SD. Sumner Smith, "The Mother Love of Mrs. Mary Carr, Who Preferred Babies to Stage Fame," *MPW*, 9 Oct 1920, 777. "Mary Carr to Be Seen in Person," *MPW*, 19 Nov 1921, 332. "Mary Carr in Schulberg Pictures," *MPW*, 3 Jan 1925, 75. "On the Set and Off; The Latest News of Plays and Players," *Movie Magazine*, Jan 1926, 76 ("Mary Carr, the famous 'screen mother[,]' has separated from her husband, W.C. Carr. She is living with her six children in a roomy house in Hollywood while Carr has taken an apartment. Mrs. Carr is quoted as saying that her children threatened to leave her if she did not part from their father, so she stuck to the youngsters. The Carrs were married in Philadelphia twenty-five years ago."). "Mary Carr," *MPW*, 2 Jan 1926, 68. "Mary Carr," *MPW*, 17 Sep 1927, 167. Richard Woods, "Mary Carr: Our Favorite Mom," *CI*, 260 (Feb 1997), C18.

Carr, Maybeth [actress] (b. Philadelphia PA, 1913–27 Dec 1996 [83?], Los Angeles CA). BHD1, p. 605.

Carr, Nat [actor] (*né* Nathan C. Carr, b. Poltava, Ukraine, Russia, 12 Aug 1886–6 Jul 1944 [57], Los Angeles CA). m. Madge. (WB.) "Nat Carr," *Variety*, 12 Jul 1944, p. 42. AMD, p. 64. AS, p. 208. BHD1, p. 93. IFN, p. 48. Truitt, p. 51. "Gets Character Actor," *MPW*, 5 Dec 1925, 439. "Sign Supporting Players for Universal Feature [*The Mystery Club*]," *MPW*, 30 Jan 1926, 448:3. "Carr Signs with Warner Bros.," *MPW*, 17 Jul 1926, 152.

Carr, Percy [actor] (b. England, 1875?–22 Nov 1926 [51], Saranac Lake NY). "Percy Carr," *Variety*, 1 Dec 1926. AS, p. 208 (b. 1865). BHD, p. 124. IFN, p. 48. Truitt, p. 51.

Carr, Rosemary [actress] (b. Philadelphia PA, 1911–24 Sep 1987 [76?], Ventura CA). BHD, p. 124.

Carr, Sade [actress] (*née* Sade Latham, b. London, England, 1889?–17 Nov 1940 [51], Carmel CA). (Essanay.) "Sade Carr," *Variety*, 20 Nov 1940. AS, p. 208. BHD, p. 124. IFN, p. 48. Truitt, p. 51.

Carr, Stephen (son of **Mary Carr**; brother of **Thomas Carr**) [actor] (b. Philadelphia PA, 23 Apr 1906–20 May 1986 [80], No. Hollywood CA). BHD1, p. 93.

Carr, Thomas (son of **Mary Carr**; brother of **Stephen Carr**) [actor/director] (b. Philadelphia PA, 4 Jul 1907–18 Aug 1946 [39], Los Angeles CA). AMD, p. 64. AS, p. 208. IFN, p. 48. Katz, p. 211. "Carr to Play in Coming Pathé Serial," *MPW*, 20 Mar 1920, 1989. "Tommy Carr," *MPW*, 17 Dec 1927, 27. Joe Collura, "Thomas Carr—Part I," *CI*, 178 (Apr 1990), 18, 24, 31; Part II, (May 1990), 30–32, 42.

Carr, Trem [director/producer/executive] (b. Trenton IL, 1892?–18 Aug 1946 [54], San Diego CA; heart attack). m. Margaret. (Rayart Pictures; Syndicate Pictures; Monogram; Republic; Universal.) "Trem Carr, Figure in Film Industry; Production Chief at Monogram Once Head of Independent Producers Group, Is Dead," *NYT*, 19 Aug 1946, 25:5. "Trem Carr," *Variety*, 21 Aug 1946, p. 42. AS, p. 208. BHD2, p. 42. IFN, p. 48.

Carr, William [actor] (b. NY, 6 May 1891–19 Mar 1945 [53]). IFN, p. 48.

Carr, William C.D. [director/actor] (b. Philadelphia PA, 6 Aug 1866–13 Feb 1937 [70], Los Angeles CA). (Lubin.) m. Mary Kennivan (**Mary Carr**). "William Carr," *Variety*, 17 Feb 1937, p. 62. AS, p. 208. BHD, p. 124; BHD2, p. 42. IFN, p. 48. SD. Truitt, p. 51.

Carre, Bartlett A. [stuntman/assistant director] (b. Melrose MA, 10 Jul 1897–26 Apr 1971 [73], Los Angeles CA; respiratory ailment). m. Isabel Ulric (Lenore's sister). "Bartlett A. Carre," *Variety*, 5 May 1971. AS, p. 208. BHD1, p. 93; BHD2, p. 42. IFN, p. 49. Truitt, p. 51.

Carré, Ben [art director] (*né* Benjamin S. Carré, b. Paris, France, 5 Dec 1883–28 May 1978 [94], Santa Monica CA). Wrote unpublished autobiography. "Ben Carre, an Art Director for the Early Movies, 94; Helped to Found Academy," *NYT*, 30 May 1978, 2:3. "Ben Carre," *Variety*, 31 May 1978, p. 105 (d. Hollywood CA, age 95). AMD, p. 64. AS, p. 208. BHD2, p. 42 (d. LA CA). IFN, p. 49. "New Eclair Artist," *MPW*, 30 Nov 1912, 883 (arrived in America with Maurice Tourneur on 9 Nov 1912). "Carre Going to France," *MPW*, 11 Oct 1924, 497.

Carrera, Liane (daughter of **Anna Held**) [actress]. No data found. AMD, p. 64. "Anna Held's Daughter in U. Picture," *MPW*, 16 Dec 1916, 1645. "Daughter of Anna Held in Fox Production," *MPW*, 6 Jul 1918, 40.

Carrico, Charles [actor] (b. 19 Feb 1887–18 Jan 1967 [79], Desert Hot Springs CA). . AS, p. 208. BHD1, p. 605. Truitt, p. 51.

Carrigan, Thomas Jay [actor] (b. Lapeer MI, 13 Apr 1886–2 Oct 1941 [55], Lapeer MI; cerebral hemorrhage). m. **Mabel Taliaferro** (d. 1979). "Thomas Jay Carrigan; Retired Actor, 55, ex-Husband of Mabel Taliaferro," *NYT*, 3 Oct 1941, 23:5. "Thomas J. Carrigan," *Variety*, 8 Oct 1941. p. 54. AMD, p. 64. AS, p. 209. BHD1, p. 93. IFN, p. 49. Truitt, pp. 51–52. "Tom Carrigan Again with Selig," *MPW*, 1 Mar 1913, 876. "Thomas J. Carrigan," *MPW*, 1 Jan 1916, 99.

Carrillo, Leo Antonio (cousin of **Eugene W. Castle**) [film/TV actor] (b. Los Angeles CA, 6 Aug 1881–10 Sep 1961 [80], Santa Monica CA; cancer). m. Edith. "Leo Carrillo," *Variety*, 13 Sep 1961, p. 79 (age 81). AS, p. 209 (b. 1880). BHD1, p. 93 (b. 1880). IFN, p. 49. SD.

Carrington, C.B. [scenarist]. No data found. FDY, p. 419.

Carrington, Elaine Stern, "Queen of the Soapers" [scenarist/producer/writer] (*née* Elaine Stern, b. New York NY, 14 Jun 1891–4 May 1958 [66], New York NY). m. George Dart Carrington, 23 Mar 1920 (d. 1945). "Elaine Carrington Is Dead at 66; Originator of Radio Soap Opera; Author of More Then 12,000 Daily Installments Wrote First Show in 1932," *NYT*, 5 May 1958. "Elaine Sterne Carrington," *Variety*, 7 May 1958, p. 79. *Dictionary of American Biography*, Suppl. Six, p. 103 (in 1911 "she won several short fiction and scenario-writing contests"; co-author of *Nightstick*, 1927).

Carrington, Evelyn Carter [actress] (b. 22 Sep 1876–21 Nov 1942 [66], Los Angeles CA). AS, p. 209. BHD1, p. 93. IFN, p. 48. Truitt, p. 52.

Carrington, Frank [actor] (b. Angel Island,

CA, 13 Sep 1901–3 Jul 1975 [73], Milburn NJ). AS, p. 209. BHD, p. 124. IFN, p. 49.

Carrington, Hereward [writer]. No data found. AMD, p. 64. "Hereward Carrington—Psychic Extraordinary," *MPW,* 1 Jul 1916, 83.

Carrington, Murray [stage/film actor] (b. Upper Norwood, England, 13 Mar 1885–2 Dec 1941 [56], Clivedon, Somerset, England). "Murray Carringtron," *Variety,* 7 Jan 1942, p. 210. BHD, p. 124.

Carroll, Earle [writer/producer] (b. Pittsburgh PA, 16 Sep 1893–17 Jun 1948 [54], Mount Carmel PA; airplane crash). "Earle Carroll," *Variety,* 23 Jun 1948, p. 40. AMD, p. 64. AS, p. 209. BHD2, p. 43. "Sues for One-Third of Money Paid to Film 'So Long Letty,'" *MPW,* 26 Jun 1920, 1771. "Carroll Testifies," *MPW,* 11 Feb 1922, 614.

Carroll, Francis (or Frank) J. [director/President of Stellar Photoplay Co.] (b. 1879?–5 Jun 1944 [65], Los Angeles CA). "Francis J. Carroll," *Variety,* 14 Jun 1944. AMD, p. 64. AS, p. 209. IFN, p. 49. "Frank J. Carroll Will Make Pictures," *MPW,* 3 Jan 1914, 54.

Carroll, Mabel Z. [scenarist]. No data found. FDY, p. 419.

Carroll, Madeleine [film/stage/radio actress] (*née* Marie-Madeleine Bernadette O'Carroll, b. West Bromwich, near Birmingham, England, 26 Feb 1906–2 Oct 1987 [81], Marbella, Spain; pancreatic cancer). m. (1) Captain Philip Astley, 25 Aug 1931, Varenna, Italy; (2) Sterling Hayden, 14 Feb 1942, MA—div. 1946 (d. 1986); (3) Henri Loverol, 13 Jul 1946—div.; (4) Andrew Heiskel, 1950—div. Jan 1965. (Film debut: *The Guns of Loos,* New Era, Feb 1928; Gaumont; Paramount). AS, p. 209. BHD1, p. 94. Barrie Roberts, "Madeleine Carroll; Courage, Brains, and Beauty," *CI,* 245 (Nov 1995), 14 *et passim.*

Carroll, Mae [actress]. No data found. AMD, p. 65. "Mae Carroll Signed," *MPW,* 3 Jan 1925, 67.

Carroll, Marcelle [actress] (b. Biarritz, France, 1897–18 Nov 1936 [39?], New York NY). BHD, p. 124.

Carroll, Nancy [stage/film actress] (*née* Ann Veronica Lahiff, b. New York NY, 19 Nov 1903 [Birth Certificate Index No. 50328]–6 Aug 1965 [61], New York NY; heart attack [Death Certificate No. 16580, M.E. Case No. 6698]). m. (1) **Jack Kirkland** (d. 1969); (2) Bolton Mallory; (3) C.H.J. Gaden. Paul Nemcek, *A Charmer's Almanac (1905–1965)* (1969). "Nancy Carroll, Actress, Is Dead; Is Found in Apartment After Failing to Appear for Play," *NYT,* 7 Aug 1965, 13:1. "Nancy Carroll," *Variety,* 11 Aug 1965, p. 55 (age 60). AMD, p. 65. AS, p. 209. BHD1, p. 94 (b. 1904). FSS, p. 56. HCH, p. 41. IFN, p. 49 (b. 1904). SD. Truitt, p. 52 (b. 1906). Quip, *Paris and Hollywood,* Oct 1926, 80 (in the cast of *Nancy* on Boradway, she made screen tests and was slated to appear in *Forever After* for First National). "Nancy Carroll," *MPW,* 17 Sep 1927, 166.

Carroll, Richard Field [actor/producer/scenarist] (b. Boston MA, 27 Oct 1865–26 Jun 1925 [59], New York NY). "Richard F. Carroll," *Variety,* 1 Jul 1925, p. 39. AS, p. 209. BHD2, p. 43. IFN, p. 49.

Carroll, William A[rthur] [actor/director] (b. NY, 1876–26 Dec 1927 [51], Glendale CA; cancer). (Bison.) "William A. Carroll," *Variety,* 11 Jan 1928, p. 57 (d. 6? Jan 1928 [sic]). AS, p. 210. BHD, p. 124. IFN, p. 49. Truitt, p. 52 (d. 26 Jan 1928). George A. Katchmer, "Forgotten Cowboys and Cowgirls—Part XVIII," *CI,* 195 (Sep 1991), C9-C10.

Carruth, Clyde [film editor]. No data found. AMD, p. 65. "Angry Bear Bites Fox Film Editor," *MPW,* 6 Aug 1927, 380.

Carson, J.W. [director] (b. 1872–27 Nov 1932 [60?], Des Moines IA). "J.W. Carson," *Variety,* 6 Dec 1932, p. 55. BHD2, p. 43.

Carson, James B. [actor] (b. MO, 22 Dec 1884–18 Nov 1958 [73], Los Angeles CA). "James B. Carson," *Variety,* 26 Nov 1958, p. 79. AS, p. 210 (b. 1886). IFN, p. 49 (b. 1886).

Carson, Kit [character comic] (*né* William A. Carson, b. 1854?–29 Nov 1930 [76], Wheeling WV). "William A. Carson," *Variety,* 3 Dec 1930, p. 68. AS, p. 210.

Carson, Madge [actress] (d. 16 Sep 1918, New York NY; "following the bursting of a blood vessel in her head shortly after going onto the street from her hotel for a walk to the stores."). "Madge Carson," *Variety,* 20 Sep 1918, p. 23. BHD, p. 124.

Carson, May [actress]. No data found. Edgar Wyatt, "Ranger Bill Miller," *CI,* 280 (Oct 1998), C-7 ("[Miller's] leading lady in both pictures, *The Fighting Ranger and Guilty(,)* was May Carson. They were the only two films that she appeared in."].

Carson, Robert L. [actor/cameraman]. No data found. AMD, p. 65. "Carson with Metro," *MPW,* 17 Feb 1917, 1015.

Carta, Alberto G. [cinematographer] (b. Sicily, Italy). JS, p. 83 (in Italian silents from 1914).

Carter, Ann [child actress]. No data found. "Nancy Ann Carter [mother of Ann Carter]," *Variety,* 9 Mar 1977 (d. 16 Feb 1977, Escondido CA).

Carter, Betty [actress] (b. England, 1906–22 Dec 1991 [85]). BHD1, p. 95. George A. Katchmer, "Forgotten Cowboys and Cowgirls—Part XVI," *CI,* 193 (Jul 1991), 35, 52.

Carter, Charles Calvert, "The Perfect Butler" (b. VA, 23 Oct 1858–26 Aug 1932 [73], Long Beach CA; heart attack). (Universal.) "Charles Calvert Carter," *Variety,* 6 Sep 1932 (in films 20 years). AS, p. 210 (d. 29 Aug). BHD1, p. 95. IFN, p. 49. Truitt, p. 52.

Carter, Dick [actor] (*né* Bill Mix). No data found. George Katchmer, "Remembering the Great Silents," *CI,* 208 (Oct 1992), 61.

Carter, Douglas [actor]. No data found. AMD, p. 65. "Negro Signed to Selznick Contract," *MPW,* 22 Jul 1922, 296.

Carter, Frank [actor] (b. Fairbbury NB, 22 Mar 1892–9 May 1920 [28], near Grantville MD; auto accident). m. **Marilyn Miller**, May 1919 (d. 1936). "Frank Carter Killed in an Auto Accident; Car Turns Over on Curve—Three Friends Slightly Injured," *Variety,* 14 May 1920, p. 12. AS, p. 211. Truitt, p. 52.

Carter, Harrison [film editor/scenarist] (b. 1893?–23 Oct 1943 [50], Los Angeles CA; heart attack). "Harrison Carter," *Variety,* 152, 27 Oct 1943, 46:2 ("...had been writing screenplays for past 20 years."). AS, p. 211.

Carter, Harry [actor] (b. Louisville KY, 1879). AMD, p. 65. BHD, p. 124. "How Harry Carter Doubled," *MPW,* 16 Oct 1915, 421. George Katchmer, "Remembering the Great Silents," *CI,* 243 (Sep 1995), 44.

Carter, Hubert [stage/film actor] (b. Great Horton, Yorkshire, England, 1869–26 Mar 1934 [65?], London, England). "Hubert Carter," *Variety,* 10 Apr 1934, p. 62 (d. 27 Mar; age 65). AS, p. 211. BHD1, p. 95 {b. 1868}. IFN, p. 49.

Carter, Katherine F. [producer]. No data found. AMD, p. 65. "The Picture in Education," *MPW,* 11 Apr 1914, 200. "Katherine F. Carter, Inc.," *MPW,* 2 May 1914, 657. "Mrs. Katherine Carter Embarks in New Enterprise," *MPW,* 13 May 1916, 1156.

Carter, Leslie [actor] (b. 1873–4 Oct 1921 [48?]). BHD, p. 124.

Carter, Mrs. Leslie [stage/film actress] (*née* Caroline Louise Dudley, b. Lexington KY, 10 Jun 1862–12 Nov 1937 [75], Brentwood Heights [Los Angeles] CA; endocarditis). m. (2) **William Louis Payne**, 1906 (d. 1953). "Mrs. Leslie Carter," *Variety,* 17 Nov 1937, p. 70 (d. 13 Nov). AMD, p. 65. AS, p. 211. BHD1, p. 95 (d. Santa Monica CA). IFN, p. 49. Truitt, p. 52. "Mrs. Leslie Carter Sails for Kleine," *MPW,* 13 Sep 1913, 1186. "Mrs. Leslie Carter in Film," *NYDM,* 3 Jun 1914, 25:2 (she and husband, Payne, filmed *Madame Pompadour* in Paris and Versailles). "Cannot Act in Pictures; United Booking Office After Actors Who Encroach on Other Fields," *NYDM,* 14 Jul 1915, 12:3 (her salary was reduced from $2,500 to $1,500 a week because her film *The Heart of Maryland* was shown in cities where she was billed as a vaudeville star. "Some managers have refused to let their stars act for pictures on the ground that it cheapened them and the action of the vaudeville managers is in keeping with this policy."). "Madame Critic," *NYDM,* 8 Apr 1916, 4 (Carter announced her alleged retirement from the stage).

Carter, Lincoln J. [playwright/scenarist] (b. Rochester NY, 15 Apr 1865–13 Jul 1926 [61], near Goshen IN; interred in Violet Cemetery, Goshen IN). m. (1) Mary L. Beane; (2) Mrs. Whitmer, 12 Feb 1916. (Fox.) "Lincoln J. Carter," *Variety,* 21 Jul 1926, p. 50 (born the day Lincoln was shot). AMD, p. 65. AS, p. 211. SD. "Lincoln J. Carter to Produce for Universal," *MPW,* 18 Jan 1913, 253. "Carter Stories for Fox," *MPW,* 5 Aug 1922, 414.

Carter, Louise [actress/writer] (*née* Louise Spligler Murray, b. Denison IA, 17 Mar 1875–10 Nov 1957 [82], Los Angeles CA). "Louise Carter," *Variety,* 20 Nov 1957, p. 79. AS, p. 211. BHD1, p. 95. IFN, p. 49. SD.

Carter, Monte [actor/director] (b. San Francisco CA, 1884?–14 Nov 1950 [66], San Francisco CA). "Monte Carter," *Variety,* 22 Nov 1950. AS, p. 211. BHD1, p. 95. IFN, p. 49.

Carter, Nellie Bell [actress] (b. 1902–1 May 1981 [79?]). BHD, p. 124.

Carter, Owen [assistant cameraman] (b. 1889–1 Jul 1914 [25?], near Canon City CO; drowned in the Arkansas River during filming). "Film Ends Fatally; Two Members [Carter and Grace McHugh] of Colorado M.P. Company Drowned While Producing Picture," *NYDM,* 8 Jul 1914, 32:1 (Carter tried to save McHugh). "Obituary," *MPW,* 18 Jul 1914, 439. AMD, p. 65. BHD2, p. 43.

Carton, Pauline [actress] (*née* Pauline Aimée Biarez, b. Geneva, Switzerland, 7 Apr 1884–17 Jun 1974 [90], Paris, France). AS, p. 211 (b. Biarritz, France, 4 Jul). BHD1, p. 95. IFN, p. 49 (age 89).

Caruso, Enrico (father of **Enrico Caruso, Jr.**) [opera singer/actor] (*né* Errico Caruso, b. Naples, Italy, 25 Feb 1873–2 Aug 1921 [48], Naples, Italy; peritonitis). m. Dorothy Benjamin, 1918, Marble Collegiate Church, NYC. (Operatic debut: *L'amico Francesco,* Teatro Nuovo, Naples, 1895; Artcraft.) "Enrico Caruso Dies in Native Naples; End Came Suddenly; Famous Tenor Succumbs When Taken from Sorrento for New Operation; National Mourning in Italy; Tenor, It Is Now Disclosed, Had Undergone Six Operations and Blood Transfusions; Colleagues Pay Tribute; Called 'Matchless Singer' by Those Who Sang with Him—Whole World Watched His Long Illness Here," *NYT,* 3 Aug 1921, 1:1, 12:4; 4 Aug 1921, 1:1, "King Victor Orders Special Obsequies in Caruso's Honor; Public Funeral in Structure Like Pantheon to Follow Day of Mourning in Naples; Throngs View Tenor's Body; Ambassador Child Sends Message to Mrs. Caruso on Behalf of America; No Trace of Will Found; Kept Affairs to Himself and None of Friends Can Estimate Value of Estate"; 3:5, "No Trace of Will, Estate a Secret; Caruso Kept Affairs to Himself and Made Careful Record of Even Small Matters [he did his own bookkeeping]; Never Told His Wealth; Had Prosperity in Italy, But It Is Doubtful If He Owned Any Elsewhere; 10 Aug 1921, 15:4, "Caruso's Will [of 1919] Is Read in Court at Naples; Omits Wife and Babe, Named in Copy Here" [but Italian law decreed that they must receive the greater part of the estate]. "Enrico Caruso," *Variety,* 5 Aug 1921. AMD, p. 65. AS, p. 211. BHD, p. 124. IFN, p. 49. MSBB, p. 1023. SD. Truitt, p. 53. "Caruso Turns Universal Cameraman," *MPW,* 13 Mar 1915, 1616. "Enrico Caruso Becomes a Screen Star," *MPW,* 13 Jul 1918, 185. "Caruso Will Debut in Special Play," *MPW,* 20 Jul 1918, 385. "Caruso's Screen Debut Will Be in 'My Cousin,'" *MPW,* 10 Aug 1918, 864. "[Oscar] Hammerstein Was Right—Caruso Did It," *MPW,* 24 Aug 1918, 1089–90. "Pathé Has Pictures of Caruso Made Four Days Before He Died," *MPW,* 3 Sep 1921, 74. Paul Fryer, "Enrico Caruso, the Reluctant Movie Star," *Griffithiana,* 64 (Oct 1998), 143–171.

Caruso, Enrico, Jr. (son of **Enrico Caruso**) [actor/singer] (b. 7 Sep 1904–9 Apr 1987 [82], Jacksonville FL; heart attack). AS, p. 211. BHD1, p. 95.

Caruso, Maria [actress] (b. 1922–13 Jun 1979 [57?], Las Vegas NV). BHD1, p. 95.

Carver, Kathryn [actress] (aka Kathryn Hill, b. New York NY, 24 Aug 1899–18 Jul 1947 [47], Elmhurst, LI NY). m. (1) Ira L. Hill, 1921–27; (2) **Adolphe Menjou**, 1928–34 (d. 1963); (3) Paul Vincent Hall. "Kathryn Carver Hall," *Variety,* 23 Jul 1947, p. 46. AS, p. 212. BHD1, p. 95. IFN, p. 49. Truitt, p. 53. June Lee, "Dan Cupid's Bulletin Board," *Paris and Hollywood Screen Secrets Magazine,* Aug 1927, 36 (obtained an interlocutory divorce decree from Hill. "Miss Carver charged a general 'hard-boiled' attitude on the part of Hill, often concluding in hair-pulling and cold showers.").

Carver, Louise [actress] (*née* Louise Spilger Murray, b. Davenport IA, 9 Jun 1868–19 Jan 1956 [87], Los Angeles CA). m. **Tom Murray** (d. 1935). "Louise Carver, Star of Films and Stage," *NYT,* 21 Jan 1956, 21:4. "Louise Carver," *Variety,* 25 Jan 1956, p. 63. AS, p. 212 (d. 18 Jan). BHD1, p. 95. IFN, p. 50. SD. Truitt, p. 53.

Carvill, Henry J. [actor] (b. St. Mary's, Nova Scotia, Canada, 11 May 1866–11 Mar 1941 [74]). AS, p. 212. BHD1, p. 95 (b. London, England). IFN, p. 50.

Carville, Virginia [actress/dancer] (b. 1894–18 Feb 1982 [87?], Los Angeles CA. AS, p. 212. BHD, p. 125.

Cary, Falkland L. [scenarist] (b. Kildare, Ireland, 2 Jan 1897–7 Apr 1989 [92], Fleet, England; cerebral hemorrhage). AS, p. 212 (b. 1886). BHD2, p. 43.

Casajuana, Maria [actress]. No data found. AMD, p. 65. "'Miss Spain [1927]' Here for Beauty Trials and Fox Contract," *MPW,* 2 May 1927, 785.

Casaleggio, Giovanni Domenico Celestino [actor/director] (b. Turin, Italy, 29 Jun 1876 [extrait de naissance no. 318]–11 Nov 1955 [79], Turin, Italy [extrait de décès no. 1963/1955]). AS, p. 212. BHD, p. 125 (b. 1880); BHD2, p. 43. IFN, p. 50 (age 75). JS, p. 83 (in Italian silents from 1911).

Casanave, Charles [actor/executive] (b. Chicago IL, 1895–7 May 1958 [62?], Rye NY). BHD, p. 125; BHD2, p. 43.

Casanova, Eve [actress]. No data found. AMD, p. 65. "New Face," *MPW,* 12 Jun 1926, 5.

Case, Anna [opera singer/actress] (b. Clinton NJ, 29 Oct 1889–7 Jan 1984 [94], New York NY). m. Clarence H. Mackay, 1931 (d. 1938). (Film debut: *The Hidden Truth,* Select, 1919.) "Anna Case," *Variety,* 8 Feb 1984. AMD, p. 65. AS, p. 212. BHD, p. 125. *Century Cyclopedia of Names,* p. 843. "Anna Case to Enter Pictures," *MPW,* 1 Sep 1917, 1357. "'Golden Hope' Selected for Anna Case's Debut," *MPW,* 13 Jul 1918, 233. "Will Soon Begin Work on First Anna Case Picture," *MPW,* 17 Aug 1918, 1005. A scathing review of *The Hidden Truth* in *Theatre Magazine,* Mar 1919, 29: "Anna Case should stick to concert work, for as a motion picutre actress she makes an excellent singer.... Anna Case's pantomimic ability is limited."

Case, Helen E. [actress] (b. Petersburgh IN, 8 May 1885-Mar 1977 [91], Tucson AZ). (Vitagraph.) BHD1, p. 605. "Doings in Los Angeles; Brevities," *MPW,* 6 Jul 1912, 35. "Helen Case," *MPW,* 5 Jun 1915, 1593.

Caserini, Maria [actress] (aka Maria Caserini Gasperini, b. Milan, Italy). m. **Mario Caserini** (d. 1920). JS, p. 84 (in Italian silents from1909).

Caserini, Mario [actor, 1905/director] (b. Rome, Italy, 1874–17 Nov 1920 [46], Rome, Italy). m. **Maria**. AS, p. 212. BHD1, p. 605; BHD2, p. 43. IFN, p. 50. JS, p. 84 (in Italian silents from 1905).

Casey, Jack [actor/stuntman/scenarist/makeup artist] (b. Ireland, 15 Aug 1888–30 Aug 1956 [68], Los Angeles CA; following heart attack). (MGM.) "Jack Casey," *Variety,* 5 Sep 1956 (age 71). AS, p. 213. BHD, p. 125; BHD2, p. 43. FDY, p. 419. IFN, p. 50.

Casey, Kenneth [child film actor/vaudeville] (b. New York NY, 10 Jan 1899–10 Aug 1965 [66], Newburgh NY; heart attack). (Vitagraph.) "Kenneth Casey, Song Writer, 66; One of 3 Collaborators on 'Sweet Georgia Brown' Dies," *NYT,* 11 Aug 1965, 35:3. "Kenneth Casey," *Variety,* 18 Aug 1965, p. 63. AMD, p. 65. AS, p. 213. ASCAP, p. 112. BHD1, p. 96 (b. Cornwall NY). IFN, p. 50. Slide, p. 137 (d. Cornwall NY). Truitt, p. 53. "The Moving Picture Boy Song," *MPW,* 2 Dec 1911, 740. "Kenneth Casey Bound for Africa," *MPW,* 18 Jul 1914, 447. "Kenneth Casey in South Africa," *MPW,* 29 Aug 1914, 1250. "Kenneth Casey Returns to Screen," *MPW,* 13 Jan 1917, 211. Lester Sweyd, "What They Are Doing Now," *Motion Picture Magazine,* Feb 1918, 13 ("...now grown to manhood, is appearing successfully as a vaudeville headliner."). Bert Ennis, "What Becomes of the Child Wonders?; A New Crop of Juveniles Is Coming Along. The Youngsters of Yesterday Have Grown Up or Have Stepped Completely Out of the Picture," *MPC,* Jan 1927, 48–49, 72, 77 (discusses Casey, Baby Peggy; Wesley Barry, Mary Miles Minter; Jackie Coogan; Baby Marie Osborne, *et al.*).

Casey, Leslie J. [actor] (b. Australia, 1891?–18 Feb 1942 [50], New York NY). AS, p. 213. BHD, p. 125. IFN, p. 50.

Casey, Pat [producer]. No data found. AMD, p. 65. "Theatrical Men in Pictures," *MPW,* 29 Mar 1913, 1314.

Cash, M. Lowell [publicist]. No data found. AMD, p. 65. "Lowell Cash Goes Over to Selznick from Universal," *MPW,* 27 Dec 1919, 1136.

Cashier, Izadore [actor] (b. Russia, 1887–15 Apr 1948 [61?], Savannah GA). "Izadore Cashier," *Variety,* 21 Apr 1948, p. 63. AS, p. 213. BHD1, p. 96.

Cashman, Harry [actor] (b. 20 Jun 1870–12 Dec 1912 [42], Chicago IL; pneumonia). AMD, p. 65. AS, p. 213 (d. 14 Dec). BHD, p. 125 (d. 14 Dec). IFN, p. 50 (d. 14 Apr). "Cashman's Perfect Impersonations," *MPW,* 8 Jun 1912, 910. "Obituary," *MPW,* 28 Dec 1912, 1301. James S. McQuade, "Chicago Letter; The Passing of Harry Cashman," *MPW,* 28 Dec 1912, 1301. "The Late Harry Cashman," *MPW,* 4 Jan 1913, 25.

Casilini, Umberto [actor] (b. Bologna, Italy, 4 Nov 1882). JS, p. 84 (in Italian silents from 1916).

Casler, Herman [inventor] (b. 1867–20 Jul 1939 [72?], Canastota NY; heart attack). "Herman Casler," *Variety,* 26 Jul 1939, p. 54. AS, p. 213. BHD2, p. 43.

Casperson, Karen [actress] (b. Copenhagen, Denmark, 20 Aug 1890–14 May 1941 [50], Copenhagen, Denmark). BHD1, p. 605.

Cass, Francis [actor] (d. May 1927, England). BHD, p. 125. IFN, p. 50 (d. Jun 1927).

Cass, Maurice [stage/film actor] (b. Vilna, Lithuania, 12 Oct 1884–8 Jun 1954 [69], Los Angeles CA; heart attack). "Maurice Cass," *Variety,* 16 Jun 1954 ("veteran stage and screen actor"). AS, p. 213 (d. 9 Jun). BHD1, p. 96 (b. Vilnius). IFN, p. 50. Truitt, p. 53.

Cassady, James H. [stage/film actor] (b. Philadelphia PA, 1869–23 Mar 1928 [58], Spokane WA; pneuomonia). (Lubin.) "James Cassady," *Variety,* 28 Mar 1928, p. 57. AS, p. 213. BHD, p. 125. IFN, p. 50.

Cassano, Riccardo [director/scenarist] (*né* Riccardo Cassano dei Maltagliati, b. Rome, Italy). AS, p. 213. JS, p. 84 (in Italian silents from 1916).

Cassidy, William E. [actor] (b. 1876?–6 Apr 1943 [67], Cincinnati OH). (Griffith.) "Bill Cassidy," *Variety,* 14 Apr 1943 ("He recently refused a Hollywood contract, offered through a silent screen star still in pictures, because he didn't want to return to Hollywood broke."). AS, p. 213. BHD, p. 125. IFN, p. 50. Truitt, p. 53.

Cassil, Dorothy [actress] (*née* Dorothy

Louise Cummins, b. 9 Sep 1902–19 Apr 1983 [80], Anderson CA). . (Sennett, 1918–23.) "Dorothy Cassil," *Variety*, 18 May 1983. AS, p. 214. BHD, p. 125.

Cassinelli, Dolores, "The Cameo Girl of the Movies" [actress] (*née* Elvere Dolores Cassinelli, b. Chicago IL, 4 Jul 1888–26 Apr 1984 [95], New Brunswick NJ). . Unmarried. (Essanay, 1911; Emerald.) AMD, p. 65. AS, p. 214 (b. 1893). BHD, pp. 14–15; 125. MH, p. 101. MSBB, p. 1032. Spehr, p. 122. WWS, p. 214. "Dolores Cassinelli in Dolly Sisters' Picture," *MPW*, 4 May 1918, 722. "Dolores Cassinelli Is Back on Screen," *MPW*, 17 Aug 1918, 975 (b. Genoa, Italy, 1894). "Dolores Cassinelli to Remain in Films," *MPW*, 12 Oct 1918, 262. "Organize Cameo Pictures to Star Miss Cassinelli," *MPW*, 12 Apr 1919, 225. "Casts Dolores Cassinelli," *MPW*, 5 Apr 1924, 446. Billy H. Doyle, "Lost Players," *CI*, 195 (Sep 1991), 18, 20.

Cassini, Alfonso [actor] (b. Bologna, Italy, 1858–6 Aug 1921 [63?], Rome, Italy). m. **Giulia Rizzotto**. JS, p. 85 (in Italian silents from 1912).

Cassity, Ellen [actress]. No data found. AMD, p. 66. "Ellen Cassity," *MPW*, 10 Aug 1918, 814. "Ellen Cassity Hurt in Making Scene," *MPW*, 5 Apr 1919, 76.

Casson, Lewis [actor/manager/director/producer] (*né* Louis Thomas Casson, b. Birkenhead, England, 26 Oct 1875–16 May 1969 [93], London, England). m. **Sybil Thorndike**, 25 Dec 1908 (4 children; d. 1976). "Sir Lewis Casson," *Variety*, 21 May 1969, p. 71. AS, p. 214. BHD1, p. 97. IFN, p. 50. SD.

Castellani, Bruto [actor] (d. 19 Jan 1933, Rome, Italy). AMD, p. 66. JS, p. 85 ("Muscleman of the silent screen, best remembered as Ursus, a character he played in *Quo Vadis?* [1912]..."). "Cines-Kleine Players," *MPW*, 11 Jul 1914, 237–38 (he "is a Herculean man physically and a splendid actor.").

Castle, Egerton [writer/producer/cinematographer] (b. 12 Mar 1858–17 Sep 1920 [62], London, England). "Egerton Castle," *Variety*, 24 Sep 1920, p. 6. BHD2, p. 44.

Castle, Eugene W. (cousin of **Leo Carrillo**) [cameraman/executive] (b. San Francisco CA, 1897?–6 Feb 1960 [62], New York NY; result of surgery of the esophagus the previous fall. Buried in SF CA). m. Mildred. (Castle Films.) AMD, p. 66. AS, p. 215 (d. 9 Feb). BHD2, p. 44. "Eugene W. Castle Dies at 62; Film Producer Fought U.S. 'Propaganda,'" *Variety*, 10 Feb 1960, 4:1. "Gaumont Enlarges Cameraman's Territory," *MPW*, 21 Oct 1916, 420.

Castle, Irene [stage/film dancer/actress] (*née* Irene Foote, b. New Rochelle NY, 7 Apr 1893–25 Jan 1969 [75], Eureka Springs AR; heart attack). m. 4 times: (1) **Vernon Castle**, 28 May 1911 (d. 1918); (2) Robert H. Treman, 21 May 1918 and 4 May 1919, NYC (public ceremony)—div. 1923; (3) Frederic McLaughlin, 26 Nov 1923 (d. 1944); (4) George Enzinger, 26 Nov 1946. *My Husband* (1919); with Bob and Wanda Duncan, *Castles in the Air* (1958). (Cort; Astra-Pathé.) "Irene Castle, Dancer, Dies at 75; Was Toast of World War I Era; She and Husband, Vernon, Started 'Castle Walk' Craze—Fought Vivisectionists," *NYT*, 26 Jan 1969, 72:7. "Irene Castle's Death Recalls Flapper Era," *Variety*, 29 Jan 1969, p. 79. AMD, p. 66. AS, p. 215. BHD, p. 125. IFN, p. 50 (b. 7 Apr). MH, p. 101. MSBB, p. 1032. SD. Truitt, p. 54. "Irene Castle," WBO1, pp. 128–29. "Castle's in Cort Pictures," *MPW*, 8 May 1915, 877. "Mrs. Castle Engaged for Gold Roosters," *MPW*, 28 Apr 1917, 629. "Irene Castle," *MPW*, 2 Jun 1917, 1420. "Irene Castle May Go Abroad," *MPW*, 20 Jul 1918, 386 (death of Vernon Castle). "Mrs. Castle, Famous Dancer, to Wed Ithaca Man," *MPW*, 10 May 1919, 823 (m. Treman). "Irene Castle Will Return to Pictures Through Medium of New Cawwood Company," *MPW*, 18 Dec 1920, 854. Chris Laube and Lewis G. Krohn, "The Film Career of Irene Castle," *CI*, 121 (Jul 1985), 23–24, C2 (includes filmography). Olive Hoogenboom, *DAB*, Supp. 8 (1988), pp. 76–78. Eve Golden, "Everybody Two-Step: The Story of Vernon and Irene Castle," *CI*, 249 (Mar 1996), C8-C9.

Castle, James W. [director]. No data found. AMD, p. 66. "James W. Castle," *MPW*, 19 Dec 1914, 1692. "Four Directors for Premier Program," *MPW*, 18 Dec 1915, 2160.

Castle, Lillian [actress] (b. 1865?–24 Apr 1959 [94], Los Angeles CA). "Lillian Castle," *Variety*, 6 May 1959, p. 63. AS, p. 215. IFN, p. 50.

Castle, Vernon [dancer/actor] (*né* Vernon Castle Blyth, b. Norwich, England, 2 May 1885?–15 Feb 1918 [32], Ft. Worth TX; airplane accident). m. **Irene** Foote, 28 May 1911 (d. 1969). "Capt. Vernon Castle," *Variety*, 22 Nov 1918 (no dates). AMD, p. 66. AS, p. 215 (b. 1887). BHD, p. 125 (b. 1887). IFN, p. 50. SD, p. 223. "Castle's in Cort Pictures," *MPW*, 8 May 1915, 877. "Vernon Castle to Enlist; Will Join Aviation Corps of British Army in December," *NYDM*, 4 Aug 1915, 8:3. "Captain Castle in Animated Weekly," *MPW*, 9 Mar 1918, 1344.

Castleton, Barbara [stage/film actress] (b. Little Rock AR, 14 Sep 1894–23 Dec 1978 [84], Boca Raton FL). . (Fox; Brenon-Selznick; Ivan.) AMD, p. 66. AS, p. 215 (b. 1895). BHD, p. 125 (b. 1895). Finch, p. 258. MH, p. 101. MSBB, p. 1032 (b. 1896). WWS, p. 221. "The Rise of Barbara Castleton," *MPW*, 17 Nov 1917, 1039. "Barbara Castleton with World Pictures," *MPW*, 2 Mar 1918, 1212. "Barbara Castleton to Lead for Warner," *MPW*, 22 Mar 1919, 1629. "Barbara Castleton Has Big Role in 'Peg o' My Heart,'" *MPW*, 31 May 1919, 1394.

Castro, Steven [actor] (b. 1864–19 Nov 1952 [88?], Los Angeles CA). AS, p. 215.

Catelain, Jaque [actor] (b. St. German-en-Laye, France, 9 Feb 1897–1965 [67?]). BHD1, p. 97.

Cathcart, Countess [scenarist]. No data found. FDY, p. 421.

Catlett, Walter (son of George C. Catlett) [stage/film actor] (b. San Francisco CA, 4 Feb 1889–14 Nov 1960 [71], Woodland Hills CA; apoplexy). m. (1) Zanetta Watrous; (2) Ruth Verney; Kathlene. (NY stage debut: *The Prince of Pilsen*, Lyric Theatre, 1911.) "Walter Catlett, Actor, 71, Is Dead; Comedian in Many Films Also Appeared on Stage During 50-Year Career," *NYT*, 15 Nov 1960, 39:1 ("He made his film debut in 1929 and since then had been characterized as a fidgety, goggle-eyed comic in scores of roles."). "Walter Catlett," *Variety*, 16 Nov 1960, p. 79. AS, p. 215 (d. Calabasas CA). BHD1, p. 98. FSS, p. 57. IFN, p. 51. Katz, p. 218. SD. Truitt, p. 54. "George C. Catlett," *Variety*, 23 Jan 1914, 23:3 (stage actor, d. 9 Jan 1914, Oakland CA; two sons).

Cattaneo, Carlo [actor/director]. No data found. JS, p. 87 (in Italian silents from 1912).

Caulfield, Ward [actor]. No data found. "Anna Driver [Mrs. Ward Caulfield of Caufield & Driver]," *Variety*, 7 May 1915 (d. 28 Apr 1915).

Cavagna, Cesare [cinematographer]. No data found. JS, p. 87 (in Italian silents from 1915).

Cavalcanti, Alberto [set designer/director] (*né* Alberto de Almeida-Cavalcanti, b. Rio de Janeiro, Brazil, 6 Feb 1897–23 Aug 1982 [85], Paris, France). AS, p. 216. BHD2, p. 44. Antonio Rodrigues and Alain Marchand, "Alberto Cavalcanti: An 'Extraordinary Ordinary Man,'" *Griffithiana*, 60/61 (Oct 1997), 191–99.

Cavaleri, Nita [actress]. No data found. m. (1) Prince Alexander Bariatinsky; (2) Winthrop Chanderl; (4) Paolo d'Arvanni. George A. Katchmer, "Remembering the Great Silents," *CI*, 183 (Sep 1990), 46.

Cavalieri, Lina [opera singer/actress] (*née* Natalina Cavalieri, b. Viterbo, Italy, 25 Dec 1874–8 Feb 1944 [69], Florence, Italy; during an air raid). m. **Lucien Muratore**, 1913 (d. 1954). (Paramount.) AMD, p. 66. AS, p. 216 (b. Onano, Italy; d. 7 Feb). BHD, p. 125 (b. Rome). IFN, p. 51. JS, p. 88 (in Italian silents from 1915; played by Gina Lollobrigida in *La donnappiú bella del mondo* [1955]). MSBB, p. 1032. SD. "Lina Cavalieri Paramount Star," *MPW*, 14 Jul 1917, 250.

Cavallius, R.H. [scenarist]. No data found. FDY, p. 421.

Cavan, Allan [actor] (b. Concord CA, 25 Mar 1880–20 Jan 1941 [60], Los Angeles CA). (Fox.) "Allan Cavan," *Variety*, 29 Jan 1941 (d. 19 Jan; bit player). AS, p. 216. BHD1, p. 98. IFN, p. 51. Truitt, p. 55.

Cavanagh, Paul [actor] (b. Chislehurst, Kent, England, 8 Dec 1888–15 Mar 1964 [75], Cockeysville MD). AS, p. 216 (d. 16 Mar). BHD1, p. 98.

Cavanagh, Raymond [publicist]. No data found. AMD, p. 66. "Cavanagh with Neilan," *MPW*, 16 May 1925, 347.

Cavanaugh, Hobart [actor] (b. Virginia City NV, 22 Sep 1886–25 Apr 1950 [63], Woodland Hills CA). m. Florence Heston. "Hobart Cavanaugh," *Variety*, 3 May 1950, p. 63 (b. SF CA). AS, p. 216. BHD1, p. 98. IFN, p. 51. SD.

Cavanaugh, Lucille (b. 1895–13 Jul 1983 [88?], Carmel CA). BHD, p. 125.

Cavanaugh, William H. [actor/director] (b. New York NY, 1876). (Imp.) BHD, p. 125; BHD2, p. 44.

Cavanna, Elise [actress] (b. PA, 30 Jun 1902–12 May 1963 [61], Los Angeles CA; cancer). m. James Welton. "Elsie Cananna," *Variety*, 22 May 1963, p. 79. AS, p. 216 (d. 25 Apr). BHD1, p. 98 (b. 30 Jan). IFN, p. 51. Truitt, p. 54.

Cave, George A. [cinematographer/V.P./Hollywood Sales Manager for Technicolor] (b. 1899?–30 Mar 1952 [53], Hollywood CA; heart attack). m. Louella. "George A. Cave," *NYT*, 1 Apr 1952, 29:2. "George A. Cave," *Variety*, 2 Apr 1952 (with Technicolor since 1921). FDY, p. 457.

Cave, Joseph A. [actor] (b. London, England, 21 Oct 1823–20 Nov 1912 [89], London, England). BHD, p. 125.

Cavender, Glenn W. [actor/Keystone Cop] (b. Tucson AZ, 19 Sep 1883–9 Feb 1962 [78], Los Angeles CA). "Glenn W. Cavender," *Variety*, 21 Feb 1962 (began in 1910). AS, p. 216. BHD1, p. 98; BHD2, p. 44. IFN, p. 51. Truitt, p. 55. "Glen Cavender, Director, Keystone," *MPN*, 21 Oct 1916, 206.

Cavendish, David [actor] (*né* Dennis D'Auburn, b. England, 29 Oct 1890?–9 Oct 1960 [69], Los Angeles CA; heart attack). "David Cavendish," *Variety,* 26 Oct 1960. AS, p. 216 (b. 1893). IFN, p. 51 (b. 1893).

Cavens, Fred [actor/fencing master] (*né* Frederic Adolphe Cavens, b. Belgium, 30 Aug 1882–30 Apr 1962 [79], Woodland Hills CA; uremic poisoning). "Fred Cavens," *Variety,* 9 May 1962, p. 87. AS, p. 216. BHD1, p. 98. IFN, p. 51. Fred Cavens, "Sword Play in the Movies," in Celebrity Articles from *The Screen Guild Magazine,* ed. Anna Kate Sterling (Metuchen NJ: The Scarecrow Press, Inc., 1987), pp. 54–58.

Caverly, Leon H. [cameraman]. No data found. AMD, p. 66. "Marine Have Official Cameraman," *MPW,* 7 Jul 1917, 64. "War Cameraman's Kit," *MPW,* 15 Sep 1917, 1673. "Difficulties of a War Cameraman," *MPW,* 22 Feb 1919, 1058.

Caviglia, Orestes [director] (b. Buenos Aires, Argentina, 9 Nov 1893–1 Apr 1971 [77], Tucuman, Argentina). AS, p. 216 (d. 2 Apr). BHD2, p. 44.

Cavin, Jess [actor] (b. IN, 5 May 1885–20 Jul 1967 [82], Los Angeles CA). BHD1, p. 98. IFN, p. 50.

Cawthorn, Joseph Bridges [actor] (b. New York NY, 29 Mar 1868–21 Jan 1949 [80], Beverly Hills CA; stroke). m. Queenie Vassar. "Joseph Cawthorn," *Variety,* 26 Jan 1949, p. 63 (age 81); began in 1926. AMD, p. 66. AS, p. 217. BHD1, p. 98. FSS, p. 58. IFN, p. 51. SD. Truitt, p. 55. "Joe Cawthorn Signed by Fox for a Comedy," *MPW,* 7 May 1927, 42. "Joe Cawthorn in Screen Debut," *MPW,* 18 Jun 1927, 509.

Cazenuve, Paul [actor/scenarist/director] (b. France, 11 May 1871–22 Jun 1925 [54], Los Angeles CA). m. Orpha. (Fox.) "Paul Cazenuve," *Variety,* 1 Jul 1925, p. 39. AMD, p. 66. AS, p. 217. BHD, p. 126; BHD2, p. 44. IFN, p. 51. SD. Truitt, p. 55. "Cazeneuve Succeeds Clift," *MPW,* 4 Sep 1920, 64.

Cecil, Edward [actor] (b. San Francisco CA, 13 Sep 1878–13 Dec 1940 [62], Los Angeles CA). "Edward Cecil," *Variety,* 18 Dec 1940. AMD, p. 66. AS, p. 217. BHD1, p. 99. IFN, p. 51. Truitt, p. 55 (b. 1888). "Edward Cecil to Be 'Heavy' in Bert Lytell's Next Film," *MPW,* 17 Apr 1920, 449. "Edward Cecil Joins Metro," *MPW,* 9 Oct 1920, 812.

Cecil, Mary [actress] (b. New York NY, 1885?–21 Dec 1940 [55], New York NY; pneumonia). m. Henry Parker. "Mary Cecil," *Variety,* 25 Dec 1940, p. 54. AS, p. 217. BHD, p. 126. IFN, p. 51.

Cecil[e], Nora [actress] (b. Ireland [or USA], 23 Oct 1879–1954 [74?], Los Angeles CA). (Began 1915.) AS, p. 217. BHD1, p. 99. George Katchmer, "Remembering the Great Silents," *CI,* 243 (Sep 1995), 44.

Ceder, Ralph [actor/director/scenarist] (b. Marinette WI, 2 Feb 1898–29 Nov 1951 [53], Los Angeles CA; pneumonia). (Sennett; FBO; Metro.) "Ralph Ceder," *Variety,* 5 Dec 1951, p. 75 (age 54). AS, p. 217. BHD2, p. 44. IFN, p. 51.

Cederlund, Gosta [actress] (b. Stockholm, Sweden, 6 Mar 1888–4 Dec 1980 [92], Stockholm, Sweden). AS, p. 217 (d. 1937). BHD1, p. 99.

Celeste, Olga [stuntwoman] (b. Sweden, 1887–31 Aug 1969 [82], Burbank CA). BHD1, p. 99. IFN, p. 51.

Cella, Marga [actress] (b. Milan, Italy, 1898). JS, p. 90 (in Italian silents from 1921).

Celli, Faith [actress] (b. London, England, 27 Nov 1888–16 Dec 1942 [54], Ascot, England). m. Arthur Murray. "Faith Celli," *Variety,* 23 Dec 1942, p. 54 (d. 17 Dec). BHD, p. 126.

Cellier, Frank [actor] (b. Surbiton, Surrey, England, 23 Feb 1884–27 Sep 1948 [64], London, England). m. Florence Glossop Harris (d. 1931). "Frank Cellier," *Variety,* 29 Sep 1948, p. 75. AS, p. 218. IFN, p. 51. SD.

Cennerazzo, Armando [actor] (b. 1886–10 Jan 1962 [75], New York NY). BHD, p. 126. IFN, p. 51.

Cerf, Georges [actor] (b. France, 10 Oct 1890). AS, p. 218.

Cesar, M. [actor] (d. 15 Sep 1921). AS, p. 218. BHD, p. 126.

Chadwick, Cyril [actor] (b. Kensington, London, England, 11 Jun 18—?). AMD, p. 66. AS, p. 219. MH, p. 101. "Cyril Chadwick for Film Comedies," *MPW,* 21 Feb 1914, 963.

Chadwick, Helene [actress] (*née?,* b. Chadwick [Utica] NY, 25 Nov 1897–5 Sep 1940 [42], New York NY; from injuries sustained in an accident in June 1940). m. **William Wellman** (d. 1975). (Film debut: *The Challenge,* Pathé, 1916.) "Helen Chadwick, 41, Once Star of Films; Actress Credited with Earning $2,000 a Week Is Dead," *NYT,* 6 Sep 1940, 21:4. "Helene Chadwick," *Variety,* 11 Sep 1940, p. 46. AMD, p. 66. AS, p. 219 (d. 4 Sep). BHD1, p. 99 (d. LA CA). FFF, p. 65 (b. 25 Nov 1897 and "is a direct descendant of Lord Chadwick"). FSS, p. 58. IFN, p. 51 (b. 1898). MH, p. 101 (b. 1897). Truitt, p. 55 (b. 1897). WWS, p. 217. "Helene Chadwick," *MPW,* 13 Jan 1917, 217. "Helen Chadwick Renews with Pathé," *MPW,* 20 Oct 1917, 391. Ethel Rosemon, "Fame Found Her in the Subway; Helene Chadwick Sought the Elusive God Success via Advertising Car Cards," *MPC,* Jan 1919, 41–42, 73. Ned Goldschmidt, "Lunchtime in the Biograph Studio; With star, director and cameraman during the midday lull in studio activities—Miss Chadwick prefers California to New York," *MW,* 28 Jun 1924, 8, 27. "Helene Chadwick," *MPW,* 12 Jul 1924.

Chadwick, I[saac] E. [executive: Merit Film Corp.; Ivan Film Productions] (b. London, England, 15 Feb 1884–19 Nov 1952 [68], Los Angeles CA; heart attack). m. Elizabeth. "Isaac E. Chadwick, A Film Leader, 68; Headed Independent Producers and Distributors Since '24—Succumbs to Heart Attack," *NYT,* 20 Nov 1952, 31:2. "I.E. Chadwick," *Variety,* 26 Nov 1952, p. 63 (began in 1910 at a film exchange [Exclusive Pictures, Inc.]; U.S. representative of Pathé Frérès of France; bought Ivan Film; organized Merit, 1914; made *The Bells*). AMD, p. 67. AS, p. 219. BHD2, p. 45. "Chadwick's Advertising Campaign to Benefit Showmen Everywhere," *MPW,* 16 Aug 1924, 576.

Chaffin, Ethel [costume designer] (*née?*). No data found. AMD, p. 67. "Mrs. Chaffin, Designer, Comes Back from Paris," *MPW,* 11 Dec 1920, 755.

Chagnon, Jack [stage/film actor] (b. 1880–21 Jul 1912 [32], Woonsocket RI; stroke of apoplexy). "Jack Chagnon Drops Dead," *Variety,* 26 Jul 1912, p. 17. BHD, p. 126.

Chaillie, Joseph S. [actor] (b. 1851?–17 Dec 1924 [73], Amityville NY). AS, p. 219 (d. 7 Dec, NYC). BHD, p. 126. IFN, p. 52.

Chaliapin, Feodor Ivanovich, **Jr.** (son of **Feodor Chaliapin**; twin of Tatiana Chaliapin Chernoff) [actor] (b. Moscow, Russia, 1905?–17 Sep 1992 [87], Rome, Italy). m. twice. "Feodor Chaliapin, Jr.," *Variety,* 5 Oct 1992, p. 95. AS, p. 219. BHD1, p. 99.

Chaliapin, Feodor Ivanovitch (father of **Feodor Chaliapin, Jr.**) [actor/opera singer] (b. Kazan-Kazan, a Tartar city, Russia, 13 Feb 1873–12 Apr 1938 [65], Paris, France; anemia from kidney ailment). m. (1) Julia Tornaghi (d. 1965); (2) Maria Petzhold. "Feodor Chaliapin," *Variety,* 13 Apr 1938. AMD, p. 67. AS, p. 219. IFN, p. 52. SD. "Feodor Chaliapin in Pictures," *MPW,* 20 Feb 1926, 720. "Won't Be Chaliapin," *MPW,* 10 Sep 1927, 80.

Challenger, Percy [actor] (b. England, 3 Sep 1858–23 Jul 1932 [73], Los Angeles CA). BHD1, p. 99. AS, p. 219. IFN, p. 52. George A. Katchmer, "Forgotten Cowboys and Cowgirls—Part XVII," *CI,* 194 (Aug 1991), 44.

Chalmers, James D.S. [scenarist] (b. 1855–8 Oct 1933 [78?]). BHD2, p. 45.

Chalmers, James Petrie [founder of *The Moving Picture World,* 1907] (b. Orkney Island, no. of Scotland, 8 Feb 1866–27 Mar 1912 [46], Dayton OH; fell down an elevator shaft of the National Cash Register Convention Hall building). AMD, p. 67. "Diplomacy on the Beach," *MPW,* V, 24 Jul 1909, 123. "Death of James P. Chalmers," *NYDM,* 2 Apr 1912, 25:1, 3 (an employee of the building "found Mr. Chalmers with his head horribly crushed from the eighteen-foot fall to the cement floor of the shaft." He died at the Miami Valley Hospital.). "A Martyr to Duty," *MPW,* 6 Apr 1912, 21. "Obituary," *MPW,* 6 Apr 1912, 21.

Chalmers, Steven [writer] (b. Dunoon, Scotland, 1880?–14 Dec 1935 [55], Laguna Beach CA). m. (2) Helen A. Brereton, 1924. "Stephen Chalmers Dead in California; Novelist and Writer of Short Stories Formerly Reporter on The Times; Author of Prize Essay; Predicted in 1910 the Election of Franklin Roosevelt to the Presidency 'Some Day,'" *NYT,* 15 Dec 1935, II, 10:8.

Chalmers, Thomas Hardie [actor/director/editor] (b. New York NY, 20 Oct 1884–11 Jun 1966 [81], Greenwich CT). m. Vilma Fiorelli. "Thomas Chalmers," *Variety,* 15 Jun 1966, p. 79 (age 82). AS, p. 219 (d. 12 Jun). BHD1, p. 99; BHD2, p. 45. IFN, p. 52. SD. Truitt, p. 55 (b. 1890).

Chamberlain, Riley C. [actor] (b. Byron MI, 7 Nov 1854–22 Jan 1917 [62], New Rochelle NY). AMD, p. 67. AS, p. 220 (b. Grand Rapids MI). BHD, p. 126. IFN, p. 52 (d. 16 Jan). *Photoplay Arts Portfolio* (Thanhouser). "Riley Chamberlain," *MPW,* 7 Aug 1915, 975. "Riley Chamberlain," *MPW,* 11 Nov 1916, 867. "Obituary," *MPW,* 10 Feb 1917, 819, 852.

Chamberlin, Belle [actress] (b. 1873–12 Oct 1930 [57?], Los Angeles CA). BHD, p. 126.

Chamberlin, Frank [cowboy/actor] (b. 1870?–29 Aug 1935 [65], Los Angeles CA). "Frank Chamberlin," *Variety,* 4 Sep 1935 (wrote *Strawberry Roan*). AS, p. 220. BHD1, p. 100. IFN, p. 52.

Chamberlin, J. Raymond [actor/director] (b. 1886?–2 Dec 1957 [71], Norristown PA). (Lubin.) "J. Raymond Chamberlin," *Variety,* 11 Dec 1957. AS, p. 220. BHD, p. 126; BHD2, p. 45. IFN, p. 52.

Chambers, C. Haddon [journalist/writer]

(b. Sydney, Australia, 22 Apr 1860–28 Mar 1921 [60], London, England). m. (2) Pepita Bobadilla (stage name). "C. Haddon Chambers," *Variety,* 1 Apr 1921, p. 17:4 (Chambers identified the body of his friend, Charles Frohman, after the sinking of the *Lusitania*). AMD, p. 67. "C. Haddon Chambers Sues Life Photo," *MPW,* 9 Oct 1915, 234.

Chambers, Lee [scenarist] (b. 1880–20 Apr 1935 [55?], Del Rio TX). BHD2, p. 45.

Chambers, Lyster [actor] (b. MI, 1876?–27 Jan 1947 [71], New York NY). m. Helen Ashmun. "Lyster Chambers," *Variety,* 29 Jan 1947. AS, p. 220. BHD1, p. 100. IFN, p. 52. SD.

Chambers, Margaret [actress] (b. KY, 16 Oct 1896–6 Oct 1965 [68], Los Angeles CA). "Margaret Chambers," *Variety,* 13 Oct 1965. BHD1, p. 100. IFN, p. 52. Truitt, p. 56.

Chambers, Marie [actress] (b. Philadelphia PA, 1889?–21 Mar 1933 [44], Paris, France). m. Otto Wagner. (World.) "Marie Chambers," *Variety,* 28 Mar 1933, p. 55 (brief screen appearances). AS, p. 220. BHD, p. 126. IFN, p. 52. Truitt, p. 56. *Photoplay Magazine,* Mar 1917, 18.

Chambers, Ralph [actor] (b. Uniontown PA, 1891–10 Mar 1968 [77?], New York NY). AS, p. 220 (d. 16 Mar). BHD1, p. 100.

Chambers, Robert W[illiam] [novelist] (b. Brooklyn NY, 26 May 1865–16 Dec 1933 [68], New York NY; after abdominal operation). m. Elsa V. Moller. "Robert Chambers, Novelist, Is Dead; Author of 72 Books Succumbs to Operation Here After 3 Months' Illness; Began Career as Painter; He Was a Prolific Writer and Had Three or Four Works Under Way at Same Time," *NYT,* 17 Dec 1933, 36:1 (descendant of Roger Williams). "Two Authors Die [Chambers & Louis Joseph Vance]," *Variety,* 19 Dec 1933. AMD, p. 67. BHD2, p. 45. SD. "All-Star Gets Chambers Stories," *MPW,* 23 May 1914, 1126.

Champagne, Pierre [scenarist] (d. May 1927, Fontainebleau, France). BHD2, p. 45.

Chance, Anna [actress] (b. Oxford MD, 25 Oct 1879–11 Sep 1943 [63], Los Angeles CA). m. Charley Grapewin (d. 1956). AS, p. 220. BHD1, p. 100 (b. 1884). IFN, p. 52. SD. Truitt, p. 56 (b. 1884).

Chance, Frank L[eroy] [baseball player/actor] (b. Fresno CA, 9 Sep 1877–15 Sep 1924 [47], Los Angeles CA; after long illness). (Appeared in *Baseball's Peerless Leader,* Pathé, 1913.) AS, p. 220 (b. 19 Sep 1879; d. 14 Sep 1974). BHD, p. 126 (b. 19 Sep 1879). "Frank Chance Dies in Coast Hospital; Suffers Sudden Relapse in Los Angeles Home and Succumbs Within Half an Hour," *NYT,* 16 Sep 1924, 18:3.

Chandlee, Harry [actor/title writer/scenarist] (aka Henry E. Chandler, b. Washington DC, 7 Dec 1882–3 Aug 1956 [73], Los Angeles CA). m. Edith Creel Spofford, 30 Jun 1918, Washington DC. (Lubin; Paralta.) "Harry Chandlee," *Variety,* 8 Aug 1956, p. 63 (began scripting in 1918, states *Variety,* but fails to note his scripts of 1914). AMD, p. 67. AS, p. 221. BHD2, p. 45. FDY, p. 421. IFN, p. 52. "Another Lubin Writer," *MPW,* 16 May 1914, 948. "Paralta's Eastern Scenario Department," *MPW,* 26 Jan 1918, 489. "Chandlee Heads Paralta Scenario Department," *MPW,* 30 Mar 1918, 1809. "Marriages," *Variety,* 15 Feb 1918, p. 9.

Chandler, Anna [actress] (b. 1887–10 Jul 1957 [70?], El Sereno CA). "Anna Chandler," *Variety,* 24 Jul 957, p. 79. AS, p. 221. BHD1, p. 100.

Chandler, Clement F. [advertising director/publicist] (b. China, 1880?–5 Sep 1936 [56], Los Angeles CA; coronary thrombosis). (Essanay, Chicago; WB.) "Clement F. Chandler," *Variety,* 9 Sep 1936, p. 62. AMD, p. 67. "Chandler Appointed Director of F.N. Advertising and Publicity," *MPW,* 19 Sep 1925, 237. "C.F. Chandler," *MPW,* 26 Mar 1927, 310.

Chandler, Chick [actor] (*né* Fehmer Chandler, b. Kingston NY, 18 Jan 1905–30 Sep 1988 [83], Laguna Beach CA). AS, p. 221. BHD1, p. 100. Katz, p. 222 (began 1925).

Chandler, Clarence (d. 26 Feb 1915, Los Angeles CA). BHD, p. 126.

Chandler, Edward [actor] (b. Wilton Junction IA, 12 Mar 1894–23 Mar 1948 [54], Los Angeles Co. CA). AS, p. 221. BHD1, p. 100. IFN, p. 52.

Chandler, George L. [actor] (b. Waukegan IL, 30 Jun 1898–10 Jun 1985 [86], Los Angeles CA; Alzheimer's disease). . "George L. Chandler, 86, Dies; Film Actor Who Headed Guild," *NYT,* 14 Jan 1985, D18. "George Chandler," *Variety,* 19 Jun 1985. AS, p. 221. BHD1, p. 100.

Chandler, Helen Frances [actress] (b. Charleston SC, 1 Feb 1906–30 Apr 1965 [59], Los Angeles CA). m. Cyril Hume; **Bramwell Fletcher** (d. 1988); Walter Piascik. "Helen Chandler," *Variety,* 5 May 1965. AS, p. 221. BHD1, p. 100 (b. NYC). IFN, p. 52 (b. 1909). Katz, p. 223.

Chandler, Howard [actor] (d. Jan 1933, San Antonio TX). BHD, p. 127.

Chandler, James Robert [actor] (b. 1860?–17 Mar 1950 [90], East Islip, LI NY). "James Robert Chandler," *Variety,* 22 Mar 1950 ("He also appeared in early silent films."). AS, p. 221. IFN, p. 52. Truitt, p. 56. George A. Katchmer, "Forgotten Cowboys and Cowgirls—Part XVII," *CI,* 194 (Aug 1991), 44, 46.

Chandler, Janet [actress] (*née* Lillian Guenther, b. Pine Bluff AR, 31 Dec 1916–16 Mar 1994 [77], Los Angeles CA; heart failure). m. (1) George E. Barrett, 1935–47; (2) Joseph A. Kramm. "Janet Chandler [obituary]," *CI,* 227 (May 1994), 58:1. (In *Inez of Hollywood,* with Anna Q. Nilsson.) AS, p. 221.

Chandler, Lane R. [actor] (*né* Robert Chandler Oakes, b. Culbertson MT, 4 Jun 1899–14 Sep 1972 [73], Los Angeles CA; cardio-vascular ailment). (Paramount.) AMD, p. 67. AS, p. 221. BHD1, p. 100. FSS, p. 59. IFN, p. 52. Katz, p. 223. "Lane Chandler," *MPW,* 28 May 1927, 271. "Contract Given Lane Chandler by Paramount," *MPW,* 9 Jul 1927, 95. "Lane Chandler," *MPW,* 15 Oct 1927, 431. Helen Carlisle, "He's No Drug-Store Cowboy; Lane Chandler Knows His Whoopees," *MPC,* Jun 1928, 55, 91 (b. MT; "You're to take Gary Cooper's place in Westerns, I hear.").

Chandler, Robert [actor] (b. 1860–16 Mar 1950 [89], East Islip NY). AS, p. 221 (d. 17 Mar, NYC). BHD, p. 127. IFN, p. 52 (d. 17 Mar).

Chaney, Lon, Sr. (father of Creighton Chaney; grandfather of Lon Ralph Chaney, 1929–1992) [stage/film actor/director] (*né* Leonidas Frank Chaney, b. Colorado Springs CO, 1 Apr 1883–26 Aug 1930 [47], Los Angeles CA; throat cancer). m. (1) Cleva Creighton (son Creighton, b. 10 Feb 1906-d. 12 Jul 1973); (2) Hazel Hastings, 26 Nov 1915, Santa Ana CA; Frances Cleveland Bush (d. 1967). Michael F. Blake, *Lon Chaney; The Man Behind the Thousand Faces* (Vestal NY: The Vestal Press, Ltd., 1993); *A Thousand Faces; Lon Chaney's Unique Artistry in Motion Pictures* (Vestal NY: The Vestal Press, Ltd., 1995). (Began 1912.) "Lon Chaney Dies After Brave Fight; On Road to Recovery, Screen Actor Is Stricken by Hemorrhage of the Throat; Was a Master of Make-Up; Son of Deaf and Dumb Parents, He Began Career as Property Boy—Excelled in Vivid Personations," *NYT,* 27 Aug 1930, 25:1. "Chaney Dies as Fan Thousands Swamp Phone; Scores Offer Blood," *Variety,* 27 Aug 1930. AMD, p. 67. AS, p. 221. BHD1, p. 101. FFF, p. 56. FSS, p. 59. HCH, p. 91. IFN, p. 52. SD. Truitt, p. 56. WWS, p. 216. "Lon Chaney and Leatrice Joy Signed for Leads in New Goldwyn Production," *MPW,* 19 Mar 1921, 289. "Lon Chaney Has Been Raised to Stardom; Will Play Chief Role in 'Wolf Breed,'" *MPW,* 17 Sep 1921, 279. Maude Cheatham, "The Darkest Hour, III," *Classic,* Sep 1922, 47, 97. "Lon Chaney Signs Contract with Metro-Goldwyn-Mayer," *MPW,* 7 Mar 1925, 73. Lon Chaney, "My Own Story [Part I]," *MM,* Oct 1925, 55–57, 86–89; Part II, Nov 1925, 55–56, 74–76. Isabel Darrow, "*The Tower of Lies* [novelization]," *MPC,* Nov 1925, 35–37, 68, 80, 89. "Chaney to Remain with M-G-M; Big Films Planned," *MPW,* 30 Jan 1926, 448:1. Milton Howe, "The Man Who Made Homeliness Pay; Lon Chaney draws more money per week than eighty per cent. of the stars," *MPC,* Mar 1926, 34–35, 80. "Chaney's Son Weds," *MPW,* 5 Jun 1926, 2 (Creighton Tull Chaney m. Dorothy Hinckley). Joseph Jackson, "Things I Have Seen," *Paris and Hollywood,* Sep 1926, 49 (he probably makes $2,500 a week, and "he has a clause in his contract which stipulates that no 'straight' photographs [pictures which show him as he actually looks in private life] shall be given out. He always wants to be pictured as the characters he plays. He says the straight pictures rob him of any mystery."). "Lon Chaney," *MPW,* 25 Sep 1926, 236. Paul Paige, "Close-Ups and Fade-Outs," *Paris and Hollywood,* Oct 1926, 95–96 ("Fourteen years ago Lon Chaney quit a musical comedy company because it was demanded that he direct, do a solo dance, and take the place of one of the scene shifters as well. He refused—and lost his job. Tht was how the famous star first entered the movies as an extra in a Western picture."). "Lon Chaney," *MPW,* 4 Dec 1926, 337. "They Are Real!," *MPW,* 23 Jul 1927, 252. "Chaney Pays," *MPW,* 31 Dec 1927, 25. Joseph Henry Steele, "It Might Be Pagliacci; The Man of a Thousand Moods and Faces," *MPC,* May 1928, 23, 92–93. Herbert Cruikshank, "There's Always Carpet-Laying; In Case the Powers Insist on Lon Chaney's Doing Talkies, Because He Won't," *MPC,* Mar 1929, 43, 70 ("...Lon did the megaphone yelping through a dozen J. Warren Kerrigan pictures.") Dan Thomas, "The Life Story of Lon Chaney," *CFC,* 49 (Winter, 1975), 24–26. Michael F. Blake, "Sincerely, Lon Chaney," *CI,* 214 (Apr 1993), C14, 16, 20. Michael F. Blake, "'Quincy Adams Sawyer'—Found!," *CI,* 224 (Feb 1994), 11:1. Gary Weinraub, "The Man of a Hundred Voices; Chaney's First Talkie [*The Unholy Three*]," *CI,* 225 (Mar 1994), 34–36. George Katchmer, "Remembering the Great Silents," *CI,* 243 (Sep 1995), 44–45. Rusk, Bob, "AFI finds silents are golden; Two films, one starring Lon Chaney, were thought to be lost," *The Hollywood Reporter,* 16 Sep 1996, 4, 42 (*When Bearcat Went*

Dry [Macauley Photoplays, 1919; dir: Ollie Sellers], with Chaney, Bernhard Durning, Vangie Valentine, and *The Life and Death of King Richard III* [M.B. Dudley Amusement Co., NYC, 1912], with British actor Frederick Warde, were donated to the AFI for preservation by Bill Buffum, 77, of Portland, Oregon). Michael F. Blake, "A Not-So-Distant Thunder; Long Considered Lost, Lon Chaney's Last Silent Film [*Thunder*, MGM, 1929] Has Been Partially Rediscovered," *CI*, 299 (May 2000), 75–77 (2 minutes of 16mm footage was discovered in 1996; 530 feet of 35mm footage was discovered later, to be restored).

Chaney, Norman "Chubby" Myers [actor: Our Gang Comedies] (b. Baltimore MD, 18 Jan 1918–29 May 1936 [18], Baltimore MD). "Norman Chaney," *Variety*, 3 Jun 1936 (age 17). BHD1, p. 101. IFN, p. 52. Truitt, p. 56. Leonard Maltin and Richard W. Bann, *The Little Rascals; The Life and Times of Our Gang* (NY: Crown Publishers, 1992), pp. 254–55. Photo of Chaney with Jackie Cooper and Fatty Joe Cobb, *MPC*, Mar 1930, 80.

Chanin, Irwin Salmon [architect] (b. Brooklyn NY, 29 Oct 1891–24 Feb 1988 [96], New York NY [Death Certificate Index No. 3397]). . David W. Dunlap, "Irwin Chanin, Builder of Theaters and Art Deco Towers, Dies at 96," *NYT*, 26 Feb 1988, D17:1. "Irwin Chanin," *Variety*, 2 Mar 1988.

Chapelle, Yvonne *see* **Gardelle, Yvonne**

Chapin, Alice [actress] (*née*?, b. Keene NH, 1858–6 Jul 1934 [76], Keene NH; of injuries suffered in a fall on 9 May). "Mrs. Alice Chapin," *Variety*, 10 Jul 1934. AS, p. 222. BHD, p. 127. *Green Room Book 1907*, p. 70. IFN, p. 52. SD.

Chapin, Benjamin C[hester] [actor] (b. Bristolville OH, 1875?–2 Jun 1918 [43], Loomis Sanitarium, Liberty NY; tuberculosis). "Benjamin C. Chapin Dies; Actor Noted for His Portrayals of Lincoln Expires in Liberty N.Y.," *NYT*, 4 Jun 1918, 13:4. "Benjamin Chester Chapin," *Variety*, 7 Jun 1918. AMD, p. 67. AS, p. 222. BHD, p. 127; BHD2, p. 45. IFN, p. 52 (d. NYC). Spehr, p. 122 (b. 1877). W. Stephen Bush, "Why Not a Biographic Masterpiece," *MPW*, 1 Feb 1913, 443. "Lincoln Impersonator in Films," *MPW*, 10 Jul 1915, 290. "Benjamin Chapin Sees Pictures as a Regular Job," *MPW*, 20 Oct 1917, 367. "Obituary," *MPW*, 22 Jun 1918, 1699.

Chapin, Frederick (father of **James Chapin**) [scenarist]. No data found. AMD, p. 68. FDY, p. 421. "Chapin Joins Pathé Scenario Staff," *MPW*, 28 Jun 1919, 1958.

Chapin, Harold [actor] (b. Brooklyn NY, 1886–26 Sep 1915 [29], France). BHD, p. 127. IFN, p. 52.

Chapin, Harry L. [scenarist] (d. Cleveland OH, 7 Nov 1917). BHD2, p. 45.

Chapin, James (son of scenarist **Frederick Chapin**; brother-in-law of **William Wellman**) [director/scenarist] (b. 1889?–5 Oct 1924 [35], Los Angeles CA; pneumonia). "James Chapin," *Variety*, 15 Oct 1924 (interred in Hollywood Cemetery). AMD, p. 68. AS, p. 222. BHD2, p. 45. "Jim Chapin Is Worsley's Assistant," *MPW*, 3 Jun 1922, 488.

Chapin, W. Francis [actor]. No data found. AMD, p. 68. "Brenon Finds Actor to Play Kerensky," *MPW*, 1 Sep 1917, 1401.

Chaplin, Charles Spencer (son of Lily [*née* Hannah] Chaplin, 1867–1928; half-brother of **Sydney Chaplin**) [stage/film actor/composer/title writer/scenarist/director] (b. Walworth, London, England, 16 Apr 1889–25 Dec 1977 [88], Corsier-sur-Vevey, Switzerland; bronchitis). m. (1) **Mildred Harris**, 23 Oct 1918, LA CA—div. 1920 (d. 1944); (2) **Lita Grey**, 25 Nov 1924, Guaymas, Mexico—div. 22 Aug 1927 (d. 1995); (3) **Paulette Goddard** (d. 1990); (4) Oona O'Neill (8 children; d. 1991). Gareth von Ulm, *King of Tragedy; My Autobiography* (NY: Simon & Schuster, 1964); Raoul Sobel and David Franncis, *Chaplin; Genesis of a Clown* (NY: Horizon Press, 1978); Wes D. Gehring, *Charlie Chaplin; A Bio-Bibliography* (Westport CT: Greenwood Press, 1983); Georgia Hale, *Charlie Chaplin; Intimate Close-Ups* (Metuchen NJ: Scarecrow Press, 1995); Joyce Milton, *Tramp; The Life of Charlie Chaplin* (NY: Harper Collins, 1996). "Charlie Chaplin Dead at 88; Made the Film an Art Form," *NYT*, 26 Dec 1977, 1:1; Alden Whitman, "Chaplin's Little Tramp, an Everyman Trying to Gild Cage of Life, Enthralled World," 28:1; "Private Funeral for Chaplin Today," 27 Dec 1977, 38:1; "Chaplin Is Interred in Brief, Private Rite; Family, Staff and a Few Friends at Cemetery Near Swiss Home," 28 Dec 1977, IV, 15:2. "Charles Chaplin, the Immortal Tramp of Int'l Cinema, Dies at 88," *Variety*, 28 Dec 1977. "Quiet Dignity Surrounds Chaplin's Final Exit; Simple Burial in Switzerland," *The Pittsburgh Press*, 27 Dec 1977, A-6:1 ("'There were floggings, deprivations and solitary confinement,' he recalled years later. 'But even when I was in the orphanage…I thought of myself as the greatest actor in the world.'") (Essanay; Mutual; UA.) AMD, p. 68. AS, p. 222. BHD1, p. 100; BHD2, p. 45. FDY, p. 421. FFF, p. 84. FSFM, p. 93. FSS, p. 60. HCH, p. 35. IFN, p. 52. MH, p. 102 (b. Paris). MSBB, p. 1023 (b. Paris). "Studio Gossip," *NYDM*, 28 Jan 1914, 40:1 ("Charles Chapmann [sic], formerly with Fred Karno's Company in the vaudeville hit, *A Night in an English Music Hall*, and one of the great English pantomime artists, has signed a long contract with the Keystone Company…"). "Essanay Signs Charles Chaplin," *MPW*, 26 Dec 1914, 1822. "Charles Chaplin," *MPW*, 9 Jan 1915, 197. "The Essanay Chaplin Comedies," *MPW*, 10 Jul 1915, 238. "Seize Chaplin Films; Essanay Company Plans Strong Campaign Against Spurious Chaplin Pictures," *NYDM*, 1 Sep 1915, 26:4 (spurious, i.e., copied, films were seized at Duluth MN and Chicago IL). "Chaplin Satisfied; Popular Comedian Denies Rumors That He Is Likely to Leave Essanay Company," *NYDM*, 22 Sep 1915, 36:1. "After the Pirates; Essanay Company Seeks to Punish Pirates 'Duping' Chaplin Subjects," *NYDM*, 6 Oct 1915, 24:3 (Abraham George Levi was arrested for infringing on the copyright of Essanay's *The Champion*. "It is declared that some one, realizing the great demand for Chaplin films, has gathered together scraps of some of his earlier plays, and assembled them, to foist them upon an unsuspecting public."). "Chaplin Will Stick," *MPW*, 9 Oct 1915, 279. "Chaplin Signs with Mutual," *MPW*, 11 Mar 1916, 1622. "Essanay vs. Chaplin," *MPW*, 3 Jun 1916, 1704. "No Injunction for Chaplin," *MPW*, 10 Jun 1916, 1897. "Chaplin Loses 'Carmen' Suit," *MPW*, 8 Jul 1916, 236. Stanley W. Todd, "The Real Charlie Chaplin; The Personal Side of the Famous Comedian as His Associates Know It," *MPC*, Sep 1916, 41–44. "Charles Chaplin," *MPW*, 14 Apr 1917, 279. John Ten Eyck, "When Charlie Chaplin Earned $25.00 a Week," *Photoplay Magazine*, Jun 1917, 19–22. Cal York, "Plays and Players," *Photoplay*, Jul 1917, 114 ("Charlie Chaplin is now a millionaire…Not that such an announcement will be received with bated breath, but he was only twenty-eight on his last birthday."). Warren Reed, "What Will Chaplin Do?," *Picture-Play Magazine*, Sep 1917, 100 (a British subject, he made no claim to exemption from military service, but instead of enlisting he bought thousands of dollars of war bonds). "Chaplin to Put Signature in Films," *MPW*, 27 Oct 1917, 512. "Charles Chaplin Organizes Company, *MPW*, 27 Oct 1917, 517. "Chaplin Files Many Suits," *MPW*, 10 Nov 1917, 864. "Chaplin Secures Injunction," *MPW*, 22 Dec 1917, 1762. H.H. Van Loan, "Our Picture Cruise Around the World; "Hook, Line and Sinker"—Our Round-the-World Reporter Meets Charlie Chaplin and Company in Hawaii," *Motion Picture Magazine*, Feb 1918, 107–114, 166 ("Somebody started the rumor that what he had hinted was a vacation was in reality his honeymoon and that Edna Purviance was the happiest woman in the world." Chaplin replied, "Well, dont treat that rumor the same way," he warned me; "dont be a heap of dirt on a windy corner."). "Chaplin and [Harry] Lauder Co-Star," *MPW*, 23 Feb 1918, 1103. "Mildred Harris Wife of Chas. Chaplin Since Oct. 23," *MPW*, 23 Nov 1918, 810. "Chaplin Sues to Protect His Inimitable Antics," *MPW*, 23 Nov 1918, 816. "Charlie Is Married," *MPW*, 30 Nov 1918, 937. Harry C. Carr, "A Dozen Chaplins, and They're All Charlie," *MPC*, Apr 1919, 18–19, 80. "Mr. and Mrs. Charles Chaplin Present Charles Chaplin, Jr.," *MPW*, 19 Jul 1919, 339 (b. 7 Jul 1919, 7 3/4 lbs.). "Death of Chaplin Baby Came Very Unexpectedly," *MPW*, 26 Jul 1919, 483. "Chaplin Greatest Artist the Screen Has Produced," *MPW*, 23 Aug 1919, 1146. "Charles Chaplin Takes Latest Film to Utah to Evade Wife's Process Servers," *MPW*, 28 Aug 1920, 1143. "Charles Chaplin Will Have New House Organ," *MPW*, 24 Feb 1923, 820. "Chaplin's First Serious Picture Is 'Public Opinion' in 10 Reels," *MPW*, 3 Mar 1923, 34. Grace Kingsley, "What Is Charlie Chaplin's Secret for Fascinating Women?; His Old Sweethearts Tell," *MW*, 9 Jun 1923, 9, 28. Ted Le Berthon, "Absolutely, Mr. Chaplin! Positively, Mr. Freud!; Psycho-analysis comes to the movies," *Classic*, Aug 1923, 37, 88. Lawrence Langdon, "Chaplin Defies Old Conventions in Movie-Making; World famous comedian completes his first picture and revolutionizes methods of film production—'A Woman of Paris' features Edna Purviance," *MW*, 22 Sep 1923, 18. Clemence Douglas, "'I Think Marriage Is Terrible!,' Says Charlie Chaplin," *MW*, 29 Mar 1924, 4–5, 41. Jim Tully, "The Loneliest Man in Hollywood," *Classic*, Mar 1924, 40–41, 79–81. "The Chaplin-Harris Divorce; A Hitherto Untold Tale of the Negotiations Preceding the Divorce," *Photoplay Magazine*, May 1924, 100. "Believes Chaplin Is Greatest Film Actor," *MPW*, 6 Dec 1924, 502. "Charles Chaplin Weds Lita Grey in Mexico," *MPW*, 6 Dec 1924, 510. "Charles Chaplin," *MPW*, 27 Jun 1925, 998. "Chaplin Enjoins Amador," *MPW*, 3 Oct 1925, 382. "Chaplin Turns Hostile; Fairbanks Says Film Comedian is Now Suspicious of Merger," *NYT*, 29 Nov 1925, 29:3 (UA was to merge releasing facilities with MGM—"…the merger contracts would have to be sent [to New York] for the approval of Gloria Swanson, one of the prominent recent additions to the United Artists group."). Harriette Underhill, "That Chaplin Complex," *MPC*, Apr 1926, 56, 90–91. Bert

Ennis, "Fame Came to Chaplin with Borrowed Clothes; The Inside Story of How the Comedian Borrowed Arbuckle's Pants and Ford Sterling's Shoes, Thereby Achieving Success," *MPC,* Jul 1926, 36–37, 76. As told by Myrna Kennedy to Frances Gilmore, Mordaunt Hall, "The Changeable Chaplin; Charlie Chaplin Is a Man of Moods...," *MPC,* Aug 1926, 16–17, 67, 83. June Lee, "Dan Cupid's Bulletin Board," *Paris and Hollywood,* Sep 1926, 21 (it was rumored that Negri and Chaplin were registered at the same hotel in Coranado CA while she was filming. "...have the shades of a romance of three years ago returned for a brief time?"). Paul Paige, "Close-Ups and Fade-Outs," *Paris and Hollywood,* Oct 1926, 67 (he "has signed her [Raquel Meller] to play Josephine to his Napoleon in a picture which he will direct. The gay little comedian must be the envy of many a married man. He has all of the joy of a home, a wife and babies and apparently all of the liberties of a gay and festive bachelor."). Paul Paige, "Close-Ups and Fade-Outs," *Paris and Hollywood,* Oct 1926, 93 ("The biggest gamble of all has recently been taken by Charlie Chaplin." Famous Players offered Raquel Meller $100,000 and Chaplin raised the ante, so that "the Spanish senorita of the meager voice, who has been so wondferfully exploited that she draws $20 per seat, is now under definite contract to Chaplin."). Paul Paige, "Charlie Awaits Another Smile from Cupid; And a champion rises to defend the kiddies' favorite," *Paris and Hollywood Screen Secrets Magazine,* May 1927, 26–27, 81. Paul Paige, "Close-Ups and Fade-Outs," *Paris and Hollywood Screen Secrets Magazine,* Aug 1927, 41–42 (seven prominent actresses were named as co-respondent in Grey's suit for divorce. The divorce will cost Chaplin between $650,000 and $1,250,000, plus 25% of the receipts of *The Circus.* Chaplin wanted sections deleted that attacked his moral character, the references to Mrs. Chaplin as "a virtuous and inexperienced girl of sixteen" at the time of the marriage, and charges that he sought to force his wife to undergo an illegal operation. She won temporary alimony of $1,500 a month. Leo Loeb'sd suit for $50,000 against Chaplin for plagiarizing his scenario, *The Rookie,* in *Shoulder Arms,* was dismissed.). "Chaplin's Studio Is Again Active; Divorce Settled," *MPW,* 27 Aug 1927, 581 (divorced Grey). Paul Thompson, "When *The Circus* Comes to Town," *MPC,* Oct 1927, 28–29, 80. James Bagley, "Movies You Will Never See; Some of Them Stay on the Shelf," *MPC,* Nov 1927, 18–19, 66 (re *The Woman from the Sea* and other unreleased films). "The Change in Chaplin," *MPC,* Jan 1928, 21, 77. Dorothy Manners, "What Love Has Cost Chaplin," *Movie Classic,* Nov 1931, 24–25, 79. "Mrs. Mai Belle Carr," *NYT,* 8 Apr 1944, 13:4 (b. 1871?–7 Apr 1944 [73], Memphis TN; 8 days after cerebral hemorrhage; m. Charles H. Carr. She was the mother of U.S. District Attorney Charles H. Carr, who prosecuted Charles Chaplin on charges of violating the Mann Act. Her husband [same name] flew in from Los Angeles "after a jury acquitted the film star of the Federal charges."). Newsletter: *Limelight;* Bonnie McCourt, Charlie Chaplin Film Company, 300 So. Topanga Canyon Blvd., Topanga CA 90290.

Chaplin, Sydney (son of [Lily] Hannah Chaplin; half-brother of **Charles Chaplin**) [actor/executive] (*né* Sidney Hawkes, b. Capetown, South Africa, 17 Mar 1885–16 Apr 1965 [80], Nice, France). "Sydney Chaplin," *Variety,* 21 Apr 1965. AMD, p. 69. AS, p. 222. BHD, p. 126; BHD2, p. 45. IFN, p. 53. MH, p. 102. Truitt, p. 56 (d. 1956). WWS, p. 23. John McCabe, *Charlie Chaplin* (Garden City NY: Doubleday & Company, Inc., 1978), p. 233 (d. 1956). "Sydney Chaplin," *MPW,* 7 Nov 1914, 767. "Syd and Charlie Still Chummy," *MPW,* 22 Jul 1916, 611. "Sydney Chaplin Returns to Screen," *MPW,* 31 May 1919, 1320. "Sydney Chaplin Going Abroad to Produce First of Four Pictures for Famous Players," *MPW,* 26 Jul 1919, 517. Harry Carr, "Charlie's Brother Sid; Tells Their Sad Story," *Classic,* Apr 1924, 20–21, 86–87. "Warners Sign Sydney Chaplin," *MPW,* 28 Mar 1925, 386. Don Ryan, "How Laughs Are Built; Syd Chaplin Explains the Gentle Art of Rough Humor," *MPC,* Jan 1926, 38–39, 64, 66. "Sydney Chaplin," *MPW,* 29 Jan 1927, 522. "Chaplin with M-G-M," *MPW,* 9 Jul 1927, 85. "Sydney Chaplin," *MPW,* 23 Jul 1927, 257.

Chapman, Blanche [actress] (*née* Ada Blanche Chapman, b. Covington KY, 1851?–7 Jun 1941 [90], Rutherford NJ). Widow of Henry Clay Ford, manager of Ford's Theatre, Washington DC. "Blanche Chapman," *Variety,* 11 Jun 1941. AMD, p. 69. AS, p. 222. BHD1, p. 101. IFN, p. 53. SD. Truitt, p. 56. "Blanche Chapman Joins California Corporation," *MPW,* 29 Aug 1914, 1224.

Chapman, C.C. [cameraman]. No data found. AMD, p. 69. "Pathé News Airplane Rushes Harding Death Films East," *MPW,* 18 Aug 1923, 550.

Chapman, Charley [art director] (b. 12 Aug). (Vitagraph.) "Charley Chapman's Birthday," *MPW,* 6 Sep 1913, 1047. "Chapman Is Art Director for First 'S-L' Picture," *MPW,* 21 Dec 1918, 1378.

Chapman, Edythe [actress] (b. Rochester NY, 8 Oct 1863–15 Oct 1948 [85], Glendale CA; heart attack). m. **James Neill** (d. 1931). (DeMille.) "Edythe Chapman," *Variety,* 20 Oct 1948. AMD, p. 69. AS, p. 222. BHD, p. 127. IFN, p. 53. MH, p. 102. Truitt, p. 56. "Edythe Chapman in Lytell Support," *MPW,* 14 Dec 1918, 1238. "Add Neil and Chapman to Goldwyn Repertory Players," *MPW,* 27 Sep 1919, 1974.

Chapman, Frank R. [actor] (b. 1844?–9 Jan 1940 [95], Philadelphia PA). "Frank R. Chapman," *Variety,* 17 Jan 1940. AS, p. 222.

Chapuis, Marius (brother of **Pierre Chapuis**) [cinematograher] (*né* Narcis Marius Chauis, b. Lyon, France, 30 May 1878–16 Nov 1961 [83], Champfromier, France). AS, p. 223.

Chapuis, Pierre (brother of **Marius Chapuis**) [cinematographer] (b. Lyon, France, 25 Jul 1879–23 Mar 1900 [20], Lyon, France). AS, p. 223.

Charbeneau, Oscar [actor] (d. 15 Sep 1915, Los Angeles CA; accident during filming). AS, p. 223. BHD, p. 127. IFN, p. 53.

Charles, Charles C. [actor] (d. 10 Mar 1957, Orlando FL). "Charles C. Charles," *Variety,* 20 Mar 1957. AS, p. 223.

Charles, John [actor] (b. 1835?–7 Nov 1921 [86], Whitestone NY). AMD, p. 69. AS, p. 223 (d. NYC). BHD, p. 127. IFN, p. 53. "John Charles—Villain of the Pictures," *MPW,* 19 Jun 1915, 1942.

Charleson, Mary (niece of **Kate Price**) [opera singer/actress] (b. Dunganon, Ireland, 18 May 1890–3 Dec 1961 [71], Los Angeles CA). m. **Henry B. Walthall**, 1917, IN (d. 1936). (Vitagraph; Equitable; Selig; Essanay; Paralta; National.) "Mary C. Walthall," *Variety,* 7 Feb 1962. AMD, p. 69 (Mary Charleston). AS, p. 223 (b. 1885; d. Woodland Hills CA). BHD, p. 127. IFN, p. 53. MSBB, p. 1032. 1921 Directory, p. 215 (b. 1893). "Vitagraph Notes," *MPW,* 2 Aug 1913, 515. "Mary Charleson," *MPW,* 27 Feb 1915, 1292. "Mary Charleson," *MPW,* 1 Apr 1916, 93. "Mary Charleson Joins Selig Forces," *MPW,* 1 Jul 1916, 85. "Mary Charleson," *MPW,* 31 Mar 1917, 2108.

Charlot, André Eugène Maurice [director/producer/scenarist] (b. Paris, France, 26 Jul 1882–20 May 1956 [73], Woodland Hills CA; cancer). AS, p. 224. BHD2, p. 45.

Charlton, Charles [cameraman]. No data found. AMD, p. 70. "Back from the Jungle," *MPW,* 5 Jul 1924, 49.

Charney, C. King [producer] (b. 1893–5 Jun 1958 [65?], Los Angeles CA; cerebral thrombosis). AS, p. 224 (b. 1883). BHD2, p. 45.

Charpentier, Gustave [producer/scenarist/composer] (b. Dieuze, France, 25 Jun 1860 [extrait de naissance no. 43/1860]–18 Feb 1956 [95], Paris, France). AS, p. 224. BHD2, p. 46.

Charrat, Jeanne [scenarist] (d. 9 Jan 1929). BHD2, p. 46.

Charsky, Boris [actor] (b. Petrograd, Russia, 28 May 1893–1 Jun 1956 [62], Inglewood CA). AS, p. 224 (d. Hollywood CA). BHD1, p. 102. IFN, p. 53 (age 63).

Charters, Spencer [actor] (b. Duncannon PA, 25 Mar 1875–25 Jan 1943 [67], Los Angeles CA; found dead in his garage of carbon monoxide poisoning and an overdose of sleeping pills). "Spencer Charters," *Variety,* 27 Jan 1943 (age 68). AS, p. 224. BHD1, p. 102. IFN, p. 53. Truitt, p. 57.

Chase, Arline [dancer/actress: Sennett Bathing Beauty] (b. 1900?–19 Apr 1926 [26], Sierra Madre CA; tuberculosis). m. Frank O'Leary. "Arline Chase," *Variety,* 28 Apr 1926. AS, p. 224. BHD, p. 127.

Chase, Charley (brother of **James Parrott**) [actor/director/scenarist] (*né* Charles Joseph Parrott, Jr., b. Baltimore MD, 20 Oct 1893–20 Jun 1940 [46], Los Angeles CA; heart attack). m. Bebe Eytinge, 25 Mar 1914. Brian Anthony and Andy Edmonds, *Smile When the Raindrops Fall; The Story of Charley Chase* (Lanham MD: Scarecrow Press, Inc., 1998). (Sennett; Roach.) "Charley Chase, 47, Comedian of Films; Started in Sennett's Keystone Kop Series—Dies in West," *NYT,* 21 Jun 1940, 21:4. "Charley Chase," *Variety,* 26 Jun 1940. AMD, p. 70 (Chase, Charley); p. 271 (Parrott, Charles). AS, p. 224 (b. 1892). BHD1, p. 102; BHD2, p. 46. FSS, p. 63. IFN, p. 53 (b. 1893). SD. Truitt, p. 57. "Parrott to Direct King-Bees," *MPW,* 6 Apr 1918, 103. "Mermaid Director Hurt," *MPW,* 30 Oct 1920, 1280. "New Pathé Series Stars Charley Chase," *MPW,* 22 Dec 1923, 723. "Charley Chase," *MPW,* 7 May 1927, 25. "Charley Chase," *MPW,* 24 Sep 1927, 221. "Chase Contract Renewed by Hal Roach for Five Years," *MPW,* 12 Nov 1927, 16. Sam Gill, "The Funnymen: Charlie Chase," *8mm Collector,* 11 (Spring, 1965), 12; Part II, 12 (Summer, 1965), 6. P.A. Carayannis, "Charley Chase; The Formative Years," *CI,* 128 (Feb 1986), 10–11, 46, 63; Part II, 129 (Mar 1986), C11-C12. Brian Anthony and Andy Edmonds, "Crazy Like a Fox; The Saga of Charley Chase," *Griffithiana,* 48/49 (Oct 1993), 21–33 (b. 1893); filmography, 34–53. Richard M. Roberts, "Charley Chase, Part I: The Life & Times of Charles Parrott," *CI,* 221 (Nov 1993), 42–44, 57; Part II, (Dec 1993), 36–38, 57; Park III (Feb 1994), 40–41, 47,

55; Part IV (Apr 1994), C18-C19; Part V (Aug 1994), C1 *et passim*. Richard M. Roberts, "The Motion Picture Career of Charles Parrott a/k/a Charley Chase; Part I," *CI,* 232 (Oct 1994), 45–47; Part II, 236 (Feb 1995), 41–46, 56; Part III, 237 (Mar 1995), 36, 38–40, 54.

Chase, Colin [stage/film actor] (*né* Colin Collings, b. Lewiston ID, 13 Apr 1886–24 Apr 1937 [51], Los Angeles CA; paralysis). "Colin Chase," *NYT,* 26 Apr 1937, 19:5 (d. 25 Apr). "Colin Chase," *Variety,* 28 Apr 1937. AMD, p. 70. AS, p. 224. BHD1, p. 102. IFN, p. 53. MH, p. 102 (b. 1888). Truitt, p. 57. "Colin Chase Escapes Death as Nick Carter Plane Falls," *MPW,* 28 Aug 1920, 1184. George Katchmer, "Remembering the Great Silents," *CI,* 243 (Sep 1995), 45–46.

Chase, Florence [actress] (b. 1854–12 May 1929 [74?], New York NY). AMD, p. 70. BHD, p. 127. "Florence Chase Is Star of Series of Features to Be Distributed by Aywon Film Corporation," *MPW,* 31 Jul 1920, 597.

Chase, George W. [actor] (b. Spokane WA, 1890–29 Jul 1918 [28?], Woodhaven NY). AMD, p. 70. AS, p. 225. BHD, p. 127. "George W. Chase Seriously Ill," *MPW,* 11 May 1918, 866.

Chase, Hal [actor] (*né* Harold W. Chase, b. Los Gatos CA, 13 Feb 1883–18 May 1947 [64], Colusas CA). AS, p. 225 (d. Colusa CA). BHD, p. 127.

Chase, Pauline [stage/film actress] (b. Washington DC, 20 May 1885–3 Mar 1962 [76], Tunbridge Wells, Kent, England). m. 1914. "Pauline Chase," *Variety,* 21 Mar 1962, p. 71. BHD, p. 127.

Chatelaine, Stella [actress] (b. 1886–7 Nov 1946 [60?], Los Angeles CA). m. **Leon Errol** (d. 1951). AS, p. 225.

Chatterdon, Arthur B. [actor] (b. 1885–9 Oct 1947 [62?], Absecon NJ). BHD, p. 127.

Chatterton, Ruth [stage/film actress] (b. New York NY, 24 Dec 1893–24 Nov 1961 [67], Norwalk CT). m. **Ralph Forbes**, 1924–32 (d. 1951); George Brent, 1932–34; Barry Thomson, 1942 (d. 1960). "Ruth Chatterton, Actress, 67, Dies; Stage and Screen Star Was Also a Successful Novelist," *NYT,* 25 Nov 1961, 23:1. "Ruth Chatterton," *Variety,* 29 Nov 1961. AMD, p. 70. AS, p. 225. BHD1, p. 102. IFN, p. 53. Katz, p. 230. Truitt, p. 57. "Ruth Chatterton Has Not Signed with Louis Mayer," *MPW,* 17 Jan 1920, 439. R.E. Braff, "An Index to the Films of Ruth Chatterton," *CI,* 269 (Nov 1997), 13.

Chatterton, Thomas [actor] (b. Geneva NY, 12 Feb 1881–17 Aug 1952 [71], Los Angeles CA). (American; Kay-Bee.) "Thomas Chatterton, 71, pioneer screen actor, died Aug. 17 at his Hollywood home," *Variety,* 27 Aug 1952. AMD, p. 70. AS, p. 225. BHD1, p. 102. IFN, p. 53. "Tom Chatterton Joins American," *MPW,* 22 Jan 1916, 574.

Chaudet, Louis William [director] (b. Manhattan KS, 1884?–10 May 1965 [81], Burbank CA). BHD2, p. 46. IFN, p. 53.

Chautard, Emile [actor/director] (b. Avignon, France, 1865?–24 Apr 1934 [69], Westwood CA). m. Alice Archainbaud (d. 12 Mar 1920, NYC). (Eclair [Paris]; World; Thanhouser; Lasky; CKY; Pathé; Paramount.) (1st U.S. film: *The Arrival of Perpetua,* World, 1915.) "Emile Chautard," *Variety,* 1 May 1934. AMD, p. 70. AS, p. 225 (b. Paris, France, 1881). BHD1, p. 102; BHD2, p. 46. IFN, p. 53. MSBB, p. 1044 (b. Paris). Spehr, p. 122 (b. 1881). Truitt, pp. 57–58 (b. 1881). "Emile Chautard," *MPW,* 6 Mar 1915, 1460. "Director Chautard Shaking Hands with Himself," *MPW,* 26 Jun 1915, 2080. "Emile Chautard," *MPW,* 27 May 1916, 1500. "Two Famous Directors Join Thanhouser," *MPW,* 31 Mar 1917, 2084. "Emile Chautard Renews Contract," *MPW,* 8 Jun 1918, 1440. "Alice Archainbaud Chautard Dies Suddenly of Paralysis," *MPW,* 27 Mar 1920, 2102. "Chautard Has Had Wide Experience," *MPW,* 3 Nov 1923, 70.

Chauvel, Charles Edward [actor] (b Warwick, Australia, 7 Oct 1897–11 Nov 1959 [62], Sydney, New South Wales, Australia). m. **Elsa** (d. 1983). (Roach.) "Charles Chauvel," *Variety,* 18 Nov 1959. AS, p. 225. BHD, p. 127; BHD2, p. 46. IFN, p. 53.

Chauvel, Elsa [actress/scenarist] (*née* Elsie Silvanez, b. Brisbane, Queensland, Australia, 10 Feb 1898–22 Aug 1983 [85], Toowoomba, Australia). m. **Charles Chauvel** (d. 1959). "Elsa Chauvel," *Variety,* 31 Aug 1983. AS, p. 226. BHD2, p. 46.

Chavanon, Antoine Michel [cinematographer] (b. Annonay, France, 23 Sep 1860–21 Oct 1927 [67], Sail-sous-Couzan, France). AS, p. 226.

Chavarous, Pierre [cameraman]. No data found. AMD, p. 70. "Pathé Cameraman Honored," *MPW,* 28 Nov 1914, 1250.

Chedister, America (b. IA, 21 Oct 1895–1 Nov 1975 [80], So. Laguna CA). BHD, p. 127.

Cheesman, Martin [actor] (b. 1859–9 Jun 1924 [65], New York NY). BHD, p. 127. IFN, p. 53.

Chefé, Jack (Jacques) [actor] (b. Kiev, Russia, 1 Apr 1894–1 Dec 1975 [81], Los Angeles CA). AMD, p. 70. AS, p. 226 (Jack Cheffe). BHD1, p. 102. IFN, p. 53. "French Lon Chaney Signed," *MPW,* 25 Apr 1925, 809.

Cheirel, Jeanne (brother of **Léon Leriche**) [actress] (*née* Jeanne Augustine Balthazar-le-Riche, b. Paris, France, 18 Mar 1869–2 Nov 1934 [65], Paris, France). AS, p. 226. BHD1, p. 103. IFN, p. 54.

Chellini, Amelia [actress] (b. Florence, Italy, ca. 1897-Apr/May 1943 [46?]). AS, p. 226. JS, p. 94 (in Italian silents from 1914).

Chene, Dixie [actress] (b. Detroit MI, 31 Jul 1894–30 Aug 1972 [78], Los Angeles CA). BHD, p. 128.

Chene, Hazel [actress] (b. MI, 22 Sep 1888–28 Apr 1976 [87], Glendale CA). BHD, p. 128.

Cherniavsky, Josef [music director] (b. Russia, 31 Mar 1891?–3 Nov 1959 [68], New York NY). m. Lara. (Universal.) "Josef Cherniavsky, 68; Cellist and Conductor Is Dead Led Saginaw Symphony," *NYT,* 4 Nov 1959, 35:2. "Josef Cherniavsky," *Variety,* 11 Nov 1959 (scored silent films). AS, p. 227. *ASCAP Biographical Dictionary*, p. 85 (b. 1895).

Cheron, André [actor] (*né* Andre Louis Duval, b. France, 24 Aug 1880–26 Jan 1952 [71], San Francisco CA). AS, p. 27 (d. Paris, France). BHD1, p. 103. IFN, p. 54.

Cherrill, Virginia [actress] (b. near Carthage IL, 12 Apr 1908–14 Nov 1996 [88], Santa Barbara CA). m. (1) Irving Adler; (2) Cary Grant, 1933–35; (3) 9th Earl of Jersey, 1937—div. 1946; (4) Florian Martini, 1948. Eric Pace, "Virginia Cherrill, 88, Actress in 30's Films, Including 'City Lights' [1931]," *NYT,* 18 Nov 1996, B10:4. "Virginia Cherrill Martini," *Variety,* 25 Nov 1996, 78:4. "Virginia Cherrill Martini; Actress in 'City Lights,' ex-wife of Cary Grant," *Pittsburgh Post-Gazette,* 22 Nov 1996, C-9:1 ("'I was no great shakes as an actress,' she once said.") AS, p. 227.

Cherry, Charles [actor] (b. Greenwich, England, 19 Nov 1872–2 Sep 1931 [59]). AMD, p. 70. AS, p. 227. BHD, p. 128. IFN, p. 54. "More Lasky Stars," *MPW,* 22 Aug 1914, 1107.

Cherry, Malcolm [stage/film actor/writer] (b. Liverpool, England, 17 May 1878–12 Apr 1925 [46], London, England). "Malcolm Cherry," *Variety,* 29 Apr 1925, p. 44 (d. 17 Apr; age 47). BHD, p. 128.

Cherry, William (Doc) [prop man] (b. 1878–9 Oct 1930 [52?], Palm City CA). BHD2, p. 46.

Cherryman, Rex [stage/film actor] (b. Grand Rapids MI, 30 Oct 1896–10 Aug 1928 [31], Le Havre, France; septic poisoning). m. and div. Esther Lamb. "Rex Cherryman," *Variety,* 15 Aug 1928. AS, p. 227. BHD, p. 128. IFN, p. 54. Truitt, p. 58. Axel Madsen, *Stanwyck* (NY: Harper Collins, 1994), pp. 24 *et passim* (Barbara Stanwyck was in *The Noose* with Cherryman in 1926).

Chesebro, George Newell [actor] (b. Minneapolis MN, 29 Jul 1888–28 May 1959 [70], Los Angeles CA; arteriosclerosis). AMD, p. 70. AS, p. 227 (d. Hermosa Beach CA). BHD1, p. 103. IFN, p. 54. Katz, p. 232. "Frohman Engages Three Stars to Appear with Texas Guinan," *MPW,* 29 Mar 1919, 1786. Ed Wyatt, "George Chesebro; Not Always the Bad Guy," *CI,* 234 (Dec 1994), 49–51 (b. 1889).

Chesney, Arthur (brother of **Edmund Gwenn**) [actor] (b. London, England, 1882?–27 Aug 1949 [67], London, England). m. Estelle Winwood (d. 1984). "Arthur Chesney," *Variety,* 31 Aug 1949. AS, p. 227. BHD1, p. 103. IFN, p. 54.

Chester, Alma [actress] (b. Canada, 30 Apr 1871–21 Jan 1953 [81], Woodland Hills CA). m. J. Irving White. "Alma Chester White," *Variety,* 28 Jan 1953. AS, p. 227 (d. Calabasas CA). BHD1, p. 103. IFN, p. 54.

Chester, George Randolph [actor/scenarist/producer] (b. OH, 1869–26 Feb 1924 [54?], New York NY; heart attack). m. (1) Elizabeth Bethermel; (2) **Lillian** Eleanor de Rimo. "George Randolph Chester," *Variety,* 28 Feb 1924. AMD, p. 70. AS, p. 227 (d. 15 Feb). BHD2, p. 46. SD. "Wallingford on Screen; George Randolph Chester Creation to Be Presented by Colonial M.P. Corp.," *NYDM,* 4 Nov 1914, 25:4. "Reliance Signs Up George Randolph Chester," *MPW,* 12 Dec 1914, 1507. "George Randolph Chester Is Vitagraph Script Chief," *MPW,* 8 Feb 1919, 757. "George Randolph Chester Forms Company; Plans to Make Two Big Films Yearly," *MPW,* 19 Nov 1921, 290. "Universal Signs George Randolph Chester," *MPW,* 8 Apr 1922, 614. "Author Praises Film," *MPW,* 9 Feb 1924, 457. "Obituary," *MPW,* 8 Mar 1924, 119.

Chester, Lillian [scenarist] (*née* Lillian Eleanor de Rimo). m. **George Randolph Chester** (d. 1924). SD.

Chester, Virginia Evelyn [actress] (b. San Francisco CA, 27 Aug 1896–28 Jul 1927 [30], Oakland CA). AMD, p. 70. AS, p. 227. BHD, p. 128. IFN, p. 54. Richard V. Spencer, "Los Angeles," *MPW,* 4 Mar 1911, 466; 29 Apr 1911, 944; 20 May 1911, 1125; 3 Jun 1911, 1244; 8 Jul 1911, 1576.

"Virginia Chester with Mena," *MPW,* 1 Dec 1917, 1311. "Virginia Chester," *MPW,* 29 Dec 1917, 1933.

Chevalier, Albert [stage/film actor/scenarist/composer] (b. London, England, 21 Mar 1861–11 Jul 1923 [62], London, England). (Legitimate stage debut: *To Parents and Guardians,* old Prince's, Sep 1877.) "Albert Chevalier Dies in London; Noted Comedian Had Been Ill Six Months—Made Six Tours of U.S.," *Variety,* 12 Jun 1923, p. 2; 26 Jul 1923, p. 10. AS, p. 227. BHD, p. 128. IDN, p. 54.

Chevalier, Maurice Auguste Saint-Léon [singer/actor] (b. Paris [Ménilmontant], France, 12 Sep 1888–1 Jan 1972 [83], Marnes-la-Coquette, France; cardiac arrest [extrait de décès no. 1/1972]). m. actress (Marguerite) **Yvonne Vallee**—div. (d. 1996). *Ma Route et Mes Chansons* (*My Road and My Songs*). (French film debut, 1901; French-language films in Hollywood, 1930–35; Paramount.) "Maurice Chevalier Dead; Singer and Actor Was 83," *NYT,* 2 Jan 1972, 1:4; "Chevalier's Rites Set for Wednesday," 3 Jan 1972, 30:2; "Maurice Chevalier Buried After a Quiet Ceremony," 6 Jan 1972, 40:1 (in suburban village of Marnes-la-Coquette next to his mother [d. 1929]). Abel Green, "Maurice Chevalier, 83, Was One of Few Authentic Superstars of This Century," *Variety,* 12 Jan 1972. AS, p. 227. BHD1, p. 103. IFN, p. 54. Katz, pp. 232–33 (began in France, 1908). Waldman, p. 53 (b. 1889). Ernest N. Corneau, "I Remember Maurice Chevalier," *CFC,* 28 (Fall, 1970), 16–64. Paris villa: La Louque.

Chevallier, Alyrie F. [scenarist] (b. 1851–23 Apr 1935 [84?], Los Angeles CA). BHD2, p. 46.

Cheyenne Bill [actor] (*né* Harold McKechnie, b. Sioux Ste. Marie, Ontario, Canada, 1900–1979 [79?]). m. Ruby. (Anchor Productions.) Ab Breeden, "Cheyenne Bill [letter], *CI,* 279 (Sep 1998), 17.

Chiantoni, Giannina [actress] (b. Macerata, Italy, 24 Jun 1884). JS, p. 94 (in Italian silents from 1910).

Chief Black Hawk [actor] (*né* Elmer Attear, d. 15 May 1975). AS, p. 228. BHD, p. 128.

Chief John Big Tree [actor] (*né* Isaac Johnny John, b. 1875?–6 Jul 1967 [92?], Onondaga Indian Reservation NY). (Posed for the 1912 Indian Head nickel.) "Chief Big Tree," *Variety,* 12 Jul 1967. AS, p. 228. BHD1, p. 103 (b. 1865). IFN, p. 28. Truitt, p. 58. George Katchmer, "Remembering the Great Silents," *CI,* 183 (Sep 1990), 44.

Chief Nipo Strongheart (grandson of Chief Standing Rock) [actor] (*né* Nee-hah-pow Tah-che-num, b. Wakima [Indian Reservation] WA, 15 May 1891–30 Dec 1966 [75], Woodland Hills CA). (Lubin, 1905.) "Chief Strongheart, 75, Dies; Actor Upheld Indian Rights," *NYT,* 6 Jan 1967, 35:3. "Nipo Strongheart," *Variety,* 11 Jan 1967 (Yakima Indian actor; age 82). AS, p. 228. IFN, p. 285. Truitt, p. 58.

Chief Standing Bear [stage/film actor] (*né* Chief Luther Standing Bear, b. Ft. Robinson NB, 1860–20 Feb 1939 [79], Huntington Park CA). (Ince.) "Chief Standing Bear; Author of 'My People, the Sioux,' Was Motion Picture Actor," *NYT,* 23 Feb 1939, 23:5 (b. Sioux Pine Ridge Reservation SD; age 74). AS, p. 228. BHD1, p. 103; p. 516 (Standing Bear, Chief Luther; b. SD, 1865). IFN, p. 280. MSBB, p. 1028 (age 53 in 1918). George Katchmer, "Remembering the Great Silents," *CI,* 222 (Dec 1993), C17.

Chief Thunderbird [actor] (b. Tongue River MT, 6 Aug 1866–6 Apr 1946 [79], CA). AS, p. 228. BHD1, p. 103. IFN, p. 293.

Chief Thunder Cloud [actor] (*né* Scott T. Williams, b. Cedar MI, 12 Apr 1898–31 Jan 1967 [68], Chicago IL). "Chief Thunder Cloud," *Variety,* 8 Feb 1967 (descended from Chief Pontiac). AS, p. 228. BHD1, p. 104.

Chief White Eagle [actor] (b. 1872?–18 Jan 1946 [73], Los Angeles CA). AS, p. 228. BHD, p. 128. IFN, p. 316.

Chief White Eagle [actor] (né Louis Scott, b. Poncia City OK, 5 May 1892–23 Feb 1926 [33], Clover Field CA). AS, p. 229. BHD, p. 336.

Chief Whitehorse [actor]. George A. Katchmer, "Forgotten Cowboys and Cowgirls—Part X," *CI,* 182 (Aug 1990), 41.

Chiesa, Luigi [actor] (b. Turin, Italy). JS, p. 95 (in Italian silents from 1913).

Childers, Naomi Weston [stage/film actress] (b. Pottstown PA, 15 Nov 1892–8 May 1964 [71], Woodland Hills CA). m. **Luther A. Reed** (d. 1961). (Kalem; Vitagraph; U.S. Amusement Co.; Metro.) "Naomi Childers," *Variety,* 20 May 1964. AMD, p. 70. AS, p. 229. BHD1, p. 104. IFN, p. .54 Katz, p. 233. MH, p. 102. MSBB, p. 1032 (b. St. Louis MO). Truitt, p. 58. "Naomi Weston Childrrs," *MPW,* 15 Aug 1914, 942. "Naomi Weston Childers," *MPW,* 20 Feb 1915, 1119. "Naomi Childers Joins Commonwealth," *MPW,* 8 Dec 1917, 1512. "Naomi Childers in Metro Play," *MPW,* 21 Sep 1918, 1715. "Naomi Childers in Lockwood Support," *MPW,* 26 Oct 1918, 529. "Naomi Childers Back to Screen," *MPW,* 10 Nov 1923, 248.

Childs, Mae (Mae Old Coyote) [actress] (b. 1891–22 Oct 1995 [104?], Billings MT). BHD1, p. 104.

Childs, Ray [actor]. No data found. George A. Katchmer, "Forgotten Cowboys and Cowgirls—Part XVI," *CI,* 193 (Jul 1991), 52.

Chippo, Josephine [scenarist]. No data found. FDY, p. 421.

Chirgwin, George H. [actor] (b. London, England, 13 Dec 1854–14 Nov 1922 [67], London, England). BHD, p. 128.

Chivvis, Chic [actor] (*né* Frederick W. Chivvis, b. White Plains NY, 2 Dec 1884–26 Oct 1963 [78], Reseda CA). "Chic Chivvis," *Variety,* 6 Nov 1963 (age 79; in silent westerns). AS, p. 229 (d. Hollywood CA). BHD1, p. 104. IFN, p. 54. Truitt, p. 58.

Chmara, Gregor [actor] (*né* Grigory Michaelovich Chmara, b. Poltava, Ukraine, 29 Jul 1886–3 Feb 1970 [77], Paris, France). AS, p. 229 (b. 1893). BHD1, p. 104. IFN, p. 54.

Chomette, Henri (brother of **René Clair**) [director] (b. Paris, France, 1896–15 Jun 1941 [45?], Rabat, Marocco). AS, p. 230. BHD2, p. 47 (d. Aug 1941).

Choux, Jean [actor/director/scenarist] (*né* Jean-Robert Choux, b. Geneva, Switzerland, 6 Mar 1887–6 Mar 1946 [59], Paris, France). AS, p. 230. BHD, p. 128.

Chrisander, Nils [actor/director] (*né* Waldemar Olaf Chrisander, b. Stockholm, Sweden, 14 Feb 1884–1947 [63?]). AMD, p. 70. AS, p. 230. BHD, p. 128; BHD2, p. 47. "DeMille Signs Chrisander," *MPW,* 17 Jul 1926, 3. Vittorio Martinelli, "Kino-Lieblinge," *Griffithiana,* 38/39 (Oct 1990), 45.

Chrisman, Ethylyn [actress] (b. MO, 7 Nov 1877–19 Apr 1943 [65], Burbank CA). (Selig.) BHD1, p. 605.

Chrisman, Pat [actor] (b. Meadville MO, 1882). (Lubin; Pathé; Reliance; Selig; Fox.) George Katchmer, "Forgotten Cowboys/Girls—Part VII," *CI,* 179 (May 1990), 44; 203 (May 1992), 42.

Christensen, Benjamin [actor/scenarist/director] (b. Viborg, Denmark, 28 Sep 1879–28 Sep 1959 [80], Copenhagen, Denmark). AMD, p. 71. AS, p. 230 (d. 1 Apr). BHD, p. 128; BHD2, p. 47. FDY, p. 421 (Christianson). Katz, p. 235 (began in Denmark, 1906). Waldman, p. 53. "Metro Signs European Director," *MPW,* 28 Mar 1925, 378.

Christensen, William O. [casting director] (b. 1877–2 Sep 1933 [56?]). BHD2, p. 47.

Christian, John [actor] (*né* Harry Albert Pihl, b. Lowell MA, 30 Oct 1883 [MVSB, Vol. 341, p. 130]–29 Aug 1950 [66], Los Angeles CA). m. **Dorothy Vernon** (d. 1970). "John Christian," *Variety,* 6 Sep 1950. AS, p. 231. IFN, p. 54.

Christians, Mady [stage/film actress] (*née* Marguerite Maria Christians, b. Vienna, Austria, 19 Jan 1900–28 Oct 1951 [51], So. Norwalk CT; cerebral hemorrhage). m. Dr. Sven von Mueller. "Mady Christians, Actress Is Dead; 'I Remember Mama' Star Had Roles in 'Watch on the Rhine,' 'Hamlet' and 'Henry IV,'" *NYT,* 29 Oct 1951, 23:1. "Mady Christians," *Variety,* 31 Oct 1951. AS, p. 231. BHD1, p. 104. IFN, p. 54. Katz, p. 236.

Christians, Rudolph [actor] (*né* Broekern Rudolph Christians, b. Middoge, Oldenburg, Germany, 15 Jan 1869–2 Feb 1921 [52], Pasadena CA; double pneumonia). "Rudolph Christians," *Variety,* 18 Feb 1921 (last film: *Foolish Wives*). AMD, p. 71. AS, p. 231. BHD, p. 128. IFN, p. 54. SD. "Obituary," *MPW,* 26 Feb 1921, 1067.

Christie, Al[bert] **E**[rnest] [actor/director/producer] (brother of **Charles H.V. Christie**) (b. London, Ontario, Canada, 23 Oct 1881 [birth certificate #019382, No. 393]–14 Apr 1951 [69], Los Angeles CA; heart attack). m. Shirley Collins. (Began at Nestor, 1909; Horsley; Universal.) "Al Christie," *NYT,* 15 Apr 1951, 93:2. "Al Christie," *Variety,* 18 Apr 1951 (d. Beverly Hills CA). AMD, p. 71. AS, p. 231 (b. 24 Nov). BHD2, p. 47 (b. 1886). IFN, p. 54. Katz, pp. 236–37. MH, p. 5 (arrived in Hollywood on 27 Oct 1911). MSBB, p. 1044. Spehr, p. 122. "Al E. Christie," *MPW,* 20 Feb 1915, 1148. J. Van Cartmell, "Along the Pacific Coast," *NYDM,* 23 Oct 1915, 30:4 (he had scratched his hand during production of *Sally's Blighted Career,* and thought nothing of it. "Blood poisoning set in, however, and it was regarded as so serious that an operation was considered imperative, if the director's arm was to be saved."). "Al Christie an Independent Producer," *MPW,* 9 Sep 1916, 1680. "The Christies Celebrate Third Comedy Anniversary," *MPW,* 20 Sep 1919, 1853. "Al Christie, the Comedy King," *MPW,* 12 Jul 1924, insert. "Hollywood's Fourteenth Anniversary," *MPW,* 14 Nov 1925, 113. "Mark Original Coast Studio," *MPW,* 13 Nov 1926, 83 (Nestor Studio, 27 Oct 1911, now Christie studio). Al Christie, "Building Christie Comedies," *MPW,* 17 Sep 1927, 176. Richard M. Roberts, "Al Christie," *CI,* 212 (Feb 1993), 42, 44–45, 56.

Christie, Charles H. V. (brother of **A.E. Christie**) [actor/director/producer] (b. London, Ontario, Canada, 13 Apr 1880–1 Oct 1955 [75], Los Angeles CA). m. 1902 (d. 16 Jul 1918, LA CA; stomach trouble). "Charles H. Christie," *Variety,* 5 Oct 1955. AMD, p. 71. AS, p. 231. BHD2, p. 47. IFN, p. 54. "The Christie Brothers Return from New York," *MPW,* 23 Sep 1916, 1982. "Mrs. Charles H. Christie Dies," *MPW,* 10 Aug 1918, 828–29. "Charles H. Christie Again Signs with Educational to Handle Product," *MPW,* 29 Mar 1924, 370.

Christie, Eileen [actress]. No data found. AMD, p. 71. "Makes Film Debut," *MPW,* 27 Jan 1923, 324.

Christie, George Stuart [actor] (b. Philadelphia PA, 27 Feb 1873–20 May 1949 [76], Tom's River NJ). "George Christie," *Variety,* 25 May 1949. AMD, p. 71. AS, p. 231. BHD, p. 128. IFN, p. 54. "George Stuart Christie," *MPW,* 3 Mar 1917, 1337.

Christie [or Christy], Ivan W. [actor] (b. Denmark, 23 Nov 1887–9 May 1949 [61], Burbank CA; heart attack in the Walt Disney studio). "Ivan Christy," *Variety,* 11 May 1949. BHD, p. 129. IFN, p. 54. Truitt, p. 59.

Christman, Pat [actor] (b. Meadville MO). BHD, p. 128. "Studio Gossip," *NYDM,* 11 Aug 1915, 26:2 (Pat Chriseman [sic] and Leo B. Maloney, Selig, were directed by Tom Mix at Las Vegas NV, and "carried realism a little too far in a fighting scene last week, with the result that they appeared on the main streets of the city, one with a black eye and the other a split lip.").

Christy, Ann [actress: Wampas Star, 1928] (*née* Gladys Cronin, b. Logansport IN, 31 May 1905–14 Nov 1987 [82], Vernon TX; heart attack). (Christie.) AMD, p. 71. AS, p. 231. BHD1, p. 105. FSS, p. 64. "Sign Ann Christy as Christie Player," *MPW,* 29 Jan 1927, 346. Henriette, "From Hollywood to You," *MPS,* 1 Mar 1927, 31 (to be leading lady to Jimmy Adams at Christie's. "Bobby Vernon deserves the credit for picking out Ann, for he noticed the little extra in "Wife Shy," and gave her a bit that was developed into a good part in that picture."). "Lloyd Acquires New Leading Lady," *MPW,* 16 Jul 1927, 155. "Ann Christy [obituary]," *CI,* 151 (Jan 1988), 60.

Christy, Ivan W. [actor] (b. Frederikshavn, Denmark, 23 Nov 1887–9 May 1949 [61], Burbank CA; heart attack at the Walt Disney studios). AS, p. 231 (b. 1890). BHD1, p. 105.

Christy, Lillian E. [actress]. No data found. (Kalem; Vitagraph; Frontier.) "Miss Lillian Christy," *MPW,* 21 Dec 1912, 1995 (at Vitagraph, Kalem, Bison, American). "Gossip of the Studios," *NYDM,* 7 Oct 1914, 27:2.

Church, Frederick Roosevelt [actor] (aka Montana Bill, b. IA, 19 Nov 1888–7 Jan 1983 [94], Blythe, Riverside County, CA). . (Film debut: *The Cowboy's Baby,* Selig, 1907; Essanay; Frontier Co. [Santa Paula Ca]; Universal; Fox; W.W. Hodkinson; Peninsula Studios; Mascot; Aywon Film Corp.) AMD, p. 71. AS, p. 232 (b. Grand Rapids MI, 1890; d. 1936, LA CA). BHD1, p. 105 (b. 17 Oct 1889). "Gossip of the Studios," *NYDM,* 5 Aug 1914, 23:2. "Frederick Church Now Plays Leads," *MPW,* 1 Jan 1916, 52. "Frederick Church, Leads, Universal," *MPN,* 21 Oct 1916, 231 (in films from 1907 with Francis Boggs). "Fred Church Undergoes Operation," *MPW,* 23 Dec 1916, 1794. George A. Katchmer, *CI,* 73; "Remembering the Great Silents," *CI,* 184 (Oct 1990), 56. Ed Wyatt, "Fred Church: From Broncho Billy to Montana Bill," *CI,* 252 (Jun 1996), C8-C9. Bill Cappello, "Fred Church Mystery Solved [letter]," *CI,* 257 (Nov 1996), 10, 12.

Churchill, Berton [film/stage actor] (b. Toronto, Canada, 9 Dec 1876–10 Oct 1940 [63], New York NY; uremic poisoning). m. Harriet. "Churchill's Death at 64 Delays 'Geo. Wash.' 2d Time; [Dudley] Digges Replaces," *Variety,* 16 Oct 1940. AS, p. 232. BHD1, p. 105. IFN, p. 55. Katz, p. 237. SD.

Cialente, Renato [actor] (b. Treviglio, Italy, 2 Feb 1897–25 Nov 1943 [46], Rome, Italy; run over by a car). IFN, p. 55. JS, p. 96 (in Italian silents from 1921).

Cianelli, Mrs. Alma [actress] (*née?,* b. 1892–23 Jun 1968 [76?], Villa San Pietro, Italy; pulmonary embolism). m. **Eduardo Cianelli** (d. 1969). AS, p. 232. BHD, p. 129.

Cianelli, Eduardo [opera singer/actor] (b. Ischia, Italy, 30 Aug 1889–8 Oct 1969 [80], Rome, Italy; cancer). m. **Alma** (d. 1968). "Eduardo Cianelli," *Variety,* 15 Oct 1969. AS, p. 232. BHD1, p. 106. IFN, p. 55. JS, p. 97 (in Italian films from 1949 to 1969). SD.

Cichy, Martin [actor] (b. New York NY, 9 Nov 1892–26 Apr 1962 [69], Los Angeles CA). BHD1, p. 106. IFN, p. 55. George Katchmer, "Martin Cichy," *CI,* 230 (Aug 1994), 39.

Cierkes, Vincent [extra] (b. 1906–14 Mar 1979 [73], Baltimore MD). AS, p. 232. BHD, p. 129.

Cinquevalli, Paul [actor] (b. Lissa, Poland, 1859–14 Jul 1918 [59?], London, England). BHD, p. 129. IFN, p. 55.

Clair, René (brother of **Henri Chomette**) [actor/director/producer/scenarist] (*né* René Lucien Chomette, b. Paris, France, 11 Nov 1898–15 Mar 1981 [82], Neuilly-sur-Seine, France; heart attack in his sleep [extrait de décès no. 174]). AS, p. 233. BHD2, p. 47.

Claire, Ethlyne [actress: Wampas Star, 1929] (*née* Ethlyne Williamson, b. Talladega AL, 23 Nov 1904–27 Feb 1996 [91], Los Angeles CA; respiratory failure after ulcer surgery). m. (1) Richard Lonsdale Hinshaw, 28 Jun 1928, Tijuana, Mexico—div. 14 Feb 1930; (2) Ernest Westmore, 22 Feb 1930, West Hollywood CA—div. 1937; (3) Merle Arthur Frost, Jr., Sep 1939 (d. 1968). (1st National, 1924; Universal; WB; last film: *God's Gift to Women,* 1931.) "Ethlyne Clair; Film Actress, 91," *NYT,* 4 Mar 1996, D10:5. Myrna Oliver, "Ethlyne Clair; Actress in silent movies," *Pittsburgh Post-Gazette,* 69, 2 Mar 1996, C-2:1. AMD, p. 71. AS, p. 233. BHD1, p. 106. BR, pp. 119–21. CNW, p. 144 (b. 1908). FSS, p. 64. "Ethlyne Claire," *MPW,* 24 Apr 1926, 602. George A. Katchmer, "More Forgotten Cowboys and Cowgirls—Chapter 6," *CI,* 172 (Oct 1989), C14, 52 (b. Atlanta GA). Billy H. Doyle, "Letter," *CI,* 178 (Apr 1990), 22 (b. Talladego AL, 23 Nov 1904). Chapter 6, "Ethlyne Clair," *BS,* pp. 75–85 (includes filmography).

Claire, Gertrude [actress] (b. Boston MA [IL?], 16 Jul 1852–28 Apr 1928 [75], Los Angeles CA). (Nestor; Rex; Pathé; Biograph; Paramount.) "Gertrude Claire," *Variety,* 2 May 1928 (age 76). AMD, p. 71. AS, p. 233. BHD, p. 129. BR, pp. 119–21. CNW, p. 144 (b. 1908). IFN, p. 55. "Doings in Los Angeles; Brevities," *MPW,* 6 Jul 1912, 35. "Lives of the Players; Gertrude Claire," *MPS,* 24 Jan 1913, 31. "Gertrude Claire Engaged by Universal," *MPW,* 31 May 1919, 1348. George Katchmer, "Gertrude Claire," *CI,* 230 (Aug 1994), 42.

Claire, Ina (sister of **Allen Fagan**) [stage/film actress] (*née* Ina Fagin, b. Washington DC, 15 Oct 1892–21 Feb 1985 [92], San Francisco CA; cerebral hemorrhage). m. (1) James Whittaker, Chicago IL, Jan? 1920—div. 1925 (d. 1964); (2) **John Gilbert**—div. 1932 (d. 1936); (2) William R. Wallace, Jr., 1939 (d. 1976). (Film debut: *The Wild Goose Chase,* Paramount, 1915.) Peter B. Flint, "Ina Claire, 92, Who Brought Comic Artistry to Stage Roles," *NYT,* 23 Feb 1985, 9:5. "Ina Claire," *Variety,* 27 Feb 1985. AMD, P. 71. AS, p. 233. BHD1, p. 106. SD. WWS, p. 138. "Ina Claire," WBO2, pp. 176–77 (b. 1895). "Ina Claire Added to Lasky Stars," *MPW,* 27 Feb 1915, 1291. "Signs for Long Term; Lasky Gets Ina Claire's Screen Services for Five-Year Period," *NYDM,* 14 Apr 1915, 22:1. Cover, *NYDM,* 28 Jul 1915 (as Marie-Odile in the Ziegfeld Follies). Cal York, "Plays and Players," *Photoplay,* Jul 1917, 114 (to marry Lieutenant Lawrence Townsend of the Navy). "Metro Signs Ina Clare and Secures Film Rights to Her Recent Successes," *MPW,* 3 Jan 1920, 106. "Ina Claire Marries Chicago Journalist; Star Kept Her Wedding a Secret; Expects Soon to Come West [to film *Polly with a Past* for Metro]," *LA Times,* 7 Feb 1920, II, p. 9 (m. Whittaker). "Ina Claire Starts Work for Metro on Her Stage Success 'Polly with a Past,'" *MPW,* 10 Jul 1920, 218. "Ina Claire in Picturees by Day, on Stage by Night—and Sleeps Whenever Possible," *MPW,* 14 Aug 1920, 924. Eve Golden, "Sophisticated Lady; The Long Happy Career of Ina Claire," *CI,* 245 (Nov 1995), 20, 22. Jim Watters, "Re: Ina Claire [letter]," *CI,* 246 (Dec 1995), 7, 13.

Clairval, M. [cinematographer] (d. May, 1925, Paris, France). BHD2, p. 47.

Clapham, Leonard *see* **London, Tom**

Clapp, Chester Blinn [scenarist]. No data found. (Biograph; Mutual; Universal.) AMD, p. 72. W.E. Wing, "Along the Pacific Coast," *NYDM,* 14 Apr 1915, 26:2. "Clapp Returns to Universal," *MPW,* 3 Feb 1917, 699.

Clare, Arthur [actor]. No data found. AMD, p. 72. "Clare Making 'Go' of Hippodrome," *MPW,* 23 Mar 1918, 1647 (owner of Hippodrome).

Clare, George, Jr. [actor]. No data found. AMD, p. 72. "Horsley Re-Engages Clare," *MPW,* 12 Feb 1916, 932.

Clare, Ida [actress]. No data found. AMD, p. 72. "Ida Clare," *MPW,* 16 Jun 1917, 1770.

Clare, Madelyn [actress] (b. Cleveland OH, 14 Nov 1894–20 Sep 1975 [81], Raleigh NC). (Madelyn Dixon). m. **Rev. Thomas Dixon** (d. 1946). "Madelyn Dixon," *Variety,* 1 Oct 1975. AMD, p. 72. AS, p. 233. BHD, p. 129. IFN, p. 55. "Madelyn Clare Is Leading Woman in 'Young America,'" *MPW,* 3 Aug 1918, 702. "Madelyn Clare Back in New York," *MPW,* 21 Sep 1918, 1747.

Clare, Mary [actress] (b. London, England, 17 Jul 1894–29 Aug 1970 [76], London, England). m. L. Mawhood. "Mary Clare," *Variety,* 2 Sep 1970. AS, p. 233. BHD1, p. 106. IFN, p. 55. SD. Truitt, p. 59.

Clarence, O[liver] **B.** [actor] (b. Hove, England, 25 Mar 1870–2 Oct 1955 [85], Hove, Sussex, England). m. Hilda Forseutt. BHD1, p. 106 (b. London). AS, p. 234. IFN, p. 55. SD. Truitt, p. 59.

Clarendon, Hal [actor/director]. No data found. AMD, p. 72. "Picture Shows Crowd Out Vaudeville," *MPW,* I, 9 Nov 1907, 577 (possibly the first actor written about in *MPW*). "'Alma, Where Do You Live?' directed by Hal Clarendon," *MPW,* 7 Feb 1920, 934.

Clarens, Elsie [actress] (b. 1881–20 Jun 1917 [36?], New York NY). BHD, p. 129. IFN, p. 55.

Clarens, Henry F. [actor] (b. 1860?–19 Dec 1928 [68], New York NY). "Henry F. Clarens," *Variety,* 26 Dec 1928. AS, p. 234. BHD, p. 129. IFN, p. 55. Truitt, p. 60.

Clarges, Verner or **Vernon** [actor] (b. Bath, Somersetshire, England, 1846?–11 Aug 1911 [65], New York NY). (Biograph.) "Verner Clarges," *Variety,* 19 Aug 1911 (age 63). AMD, p. 72. AS, p. 234. BHD, p. 129. IFN, p. 55. SD. "Death of Noted Film Actor," *MPW,* 26 Aug 1911, 530 (age 63).

Clark, Alexander [actor] (b. New York NY, 2 May 1900–30 Sep 1995 [95], New York NY). BHD1, p. 107.

Clark, Andrew J. [actor] (b. New York NY, 12 Mar 1903–16 Nov 1960 [57], New Rochelle NY). "Andrew J. Clark," *Variety,* 7 Dec 1960 (began with Edison, 1914; *Andy Clark* series). AMD, p. 72. AS, p. 234. BHD1, p. 107. IFN, p. 55. Truitt, p. 60. "Edison Touches Popular Chord," *MPW,* 3 Jan 1914, 28–29. W. Stephen Bush, "the Screen Children's Gallery," *MPW,* 28 Mar 1914, 1667. "Andy Clarke [sic]," *NYDM,* 22 Sep 1915, 26:4 (with photo; presently "at liberty").

Clark, Bert [stage/film actor] (*né* Albert Raymond Clark, b. San Francisco CA, 1885?–26 Jan 1920 [34], New York NY; interred at Calvary Cemetery). "Clark," *NYT,* 28 Jan 1920, 11:5. "Bert Clark," *Variety,* 6 Feb 1920, p. 16. AS, p. 234.

Clark, Bert [Clark & Arcaro] (*né* Herbert Knight Clark, b. London, England, 30 Jan 1873–9 May 1922 [48?], Brooklyn NY; following four major operations, including appendicitis, hernia and gaul [sic] stones). "Herbert Knight Clark," *NYT,* 11 May 1922, 17:4. "Bert Clark," *Variety,* 12 May 1922, p. 8 (age 45). AS, p. 234 (b. 1877). BHD, p. 129 (b. 1878).

Clark, Bobby [actor] (*né* Robert Edwin Clark, b. Springfield OH, 16 Jun 1888–12 Feb 1960 [71], New York NY). AS, p. 234. BHD1, p. 107.

Clark, Carroll [art director] (b. 1894?–17 May 1968 [74], Glendale CA; heart attack). (Disney; RKO.) "Carroll Clark," *Variety,* 29 May 1968. BHD2, p. 47.

Clark, Champ [actor] (b. Anderson County KY, 1850–1 Mar 1921 [70?], Washington DC). BHD, p. 129.

Clark, Charles [cinematographer]. No data found. FDY, p. 457.

Clark, Charles Dow [actor] (b. St. Albans VT, 1870?–26 Mar 1959 [89], New York NY [Death Certificate No. 6995]). m. Winifred. "Charles Dow Clark," *Variety,* 8 Apr 1959. AS, p. 234. BHD1, p. 107. IFN, p. 55.

Clark, Daniel B. [cinematographer] (b. Urbana MO, 28 Apr 1890–14 Dec 1961 [71], San Bernardino Co. CA). AMD, p. 72. BHD2, p. 47. FDY, p. 457. IFN, p. 55. "Clark Undergoes Operation," *MPW,* 9 Oct 1926, 342. "Explains Purpose of Cinematograph Unit," *MPW,* 13 Nov 1926, 85.

Clark, Davison [actor] (*né* George Davison Clark, b. CA, 15 Jan 1881–4 Nov 1972 [91], Ventura Co. CA). AS, p. 234. BHD1, p. 107. IFN, p. 55.

Clark, Don [director/TV producer] (b. 1897?–9 Jun 1963 [66?], Los Angeles CA). "Don Clark," *Variety,* 19 Jun 1963. AS, p. 234.

Clark, Dorothy Love [stage/film actress] (b. Mediterranean Sea, 1902). (Lasky; Universal.) MSBB, p. 1032.

Clark, E. Holman [actor] (b. East Hothley, Sussex, England, 22 Apr 1864–7 Sep 1925 [61], London, England). BHD, p. 129. IFN, p. 56.

Clark, Edward [scenarist/actor] (b. Russia, 6 May 1878–18 Nov 1954 [76], Los Angeles CA; heart attack). "Eddie Clark," *Variety,* 24 Nov 1954 (age 75). AMD, p. 72. AS, p. 234. BHD1, p. 107. FDY, p. 421. IFN, p. 56. Truitt, p. 60. "Clark Joins Scenario Staff," *MPW,* 27 Mar 1926, 258. "Warners Sign Edward Clark," *MPW,* 1 May 1926, 43. "Clark Remains with Warners," *MPW,* 25 Sep 1926, 215.

Clark, Estelle [actress] (*née* Stasia Zwolinska, b. Warsaw, Poland, 7 May 1898–3 Dec 1982 [84], Port Hueneme CA). (MGM.) BHD, p. 129. Katherine Albert, "A Comedienne from Poland; Estelle Clark Strives for Situations Which Will Appeal to All of Us," *Cinema Arts,* Nov 1926, 52, 58.

Clark, Frank [actor]. No data found. AMD, p. 72. "Fairbanks Discovers Boy Wonder," *MPW,* 13 Oct 1917, 239.

Clark, Frank Howard [scenarist]. No data found. FDY, p. 421.

Clark, Frank M. [actor] (b. Cincinnati OH, 22 Dec 1857–10 Apr 1945 [87], Woodland Hills CA). (Selig.) AS, p. 234. BHD1, p. 107. IFN, p. 56. George A. Katchmer, "Forgotten Cowboys and Cowgirls—Part XIII," *CI,* 190 (Apr 1991), C4.

Clark, Gladys [actress]. No data found. AMD, p. 72. "The Cohns Sign Clark and Bergman for a New Series of Comedy Films," *MPW,* 17 Jan 1920, 429.

Clark, Grant [songwriter] (*né* Grant Clarke, b. Akron OH, May 14, 1889–16 May 1931 [42], Los Angeles CA; heart failure induced by alcoholism). m. (2) Fay. (WB.) "Grant Clark Dies of Bad Heart and Bad Booze," *Variety,* 20 May 1931 (wrote *Mother o' Mine; I Still Love You; Weary River; Am I Blue?*). AS, p. 234. ASCAP 66, pp. 123–24. CEPMJ, Vol. 2, pp. 714–15 (b. 1891).

Clark, Harvey Thornton [actor] (b. Chelsea [Boston] MA, 4 Oct 1885–19 Jul 1938 [52], Los Angeles CA; heart attack). (NYMPC.) "Harvey Clark," *Variety,* 27 Jul 1938. AS, pp. 234–35. BHD1, p. 107. IFN, p. 56. Truitt, pp. 60–61. George A. Katchmer, "Forgotten Cowboys and Cowgirls—Part XVIII," *CI,* 195 (Sep 1991), C10, 44.

Clark, Herbert [actor]. No data found. AMD, p. 72. "Herbert Clark Back on the Screen," *MPW,* 4 Aug 1923, 412.

Clark, Herbert C. [scenarist/cinematographer]. No data found. FDY, pp. 421, 457.

Clark, J.A. [actor] (d. Seattle WA, 30 May 1921). BHD, p. 129.

Clark, James Bly [executive] (b. 1870–24 Jul 1951 [81?], Pittsburgh PA). BHD2, p. 47.

Clark, John (Jack) J. [actor/director] (b. 23 Sep 1876–12 Apr 1947 [70], Los Angeles CA). (Kalem, 1907.) m. **Gene Gautier**, 1912, Palestine—div. 1918 (d. 1966). "John J. Clark," *NYT,* 13 Apr 1947, 60:4 (in over 200 films). "John J. Clark," *Variety,* 16 Apr 1947. AMD, p. 72. AS, p. 235. BHD1, p. 107; BHD2, p. 47. IFN, p. 56. Truitt, p. 61. "Putting on a Picture in Egypt," *MPW,* 1 Jun 1912, 819–20. "Picture Players at a Turkish Wedding," *MPW,* 20 Jul 1912, 253–54 (m. Gautier). "Along the Pacific Coast," *NYDM,* 16 Jun 1915, 26:2 (following a nervous breakdown, he returned to directing chores at Universal). "Studio Gossip," *NYDM,* 7 Jul 1915, 41:1 (car collided into a fence; Gene Gauntier was injured). "Signs Contract," *MPW,* 6 Aug 1927, 382.

Clark, Lillian [actress] (b. 1909?–9 Nov 1931 [22], near Liberty NY; tuberculosis). "Lillian Clark Dies," *Variety,* 17 Nov 1931.

Clark, Marguerite [stage/film actress] (*née* Helen Marguerite Clark, b. Avondale [Cincinnati] OH, 22 Feb 1883–25 Sep 1940 [57], New York NY [Death Certificate Index No. 19970 (Marguerite C. Williams), age 53]; pneumonia after a heart attack and cerebral hemorrhage; cremated; ashes interred at Metaire [LA] cemetery). m. Harry Palmerston Williams, 16 Aug 1918, Greenwich CT (d. 19 May 1936, near Baton Rouge LA; airplane crash). Curtis Nunn, *Marguerite Clark; America's Darling of Broadway and the Silent Screen* (Ft. Worth TX: Texas Christian University Press, 1981). (FP-L.) "Marguerite Clark, ex-Actress, Dies; Star of Stage and Screen Twenty Years Ago Was the Widow of Harry Williams; Entered Theatre in 1899; First Snow White of Films in Many Plays, Including 'Babes in Toyland,'" *NYT,* 26 Sep 1940, 23:4 (b. 1887). "Marguerite Clark," *Variety,* 2 Oct 1940. AMD, p. 72. AS, p. 235. BHD, p. 129. IFN, p. 56 (b. 1887). MSBB, p. 1032 (b. 1887). Spehr, p. 122. Truitt, p. 61. "A Merry Monarch in a Merry Land; De Wolf Hopper Now Wanders in Elysian Fields; A Nearly Comic Opera; Or, Perhaps, Near Several Comic Operas, but it Pleases—Song Hits—Rich Pictures," *NYT,* 3 Oct 1905, 9:3 (Clark played Sylvia, last in the cast list of *Happyland*). "Marguerite Clark Renews Contract with Famous Players," *MPW,* 14 Oct 1916, 252. "Miss Clark in a Lasky Picture," *MPW,* 31 Oct 1914, 660. "Marguerite Clark," *MPW,* 7 Apr 1917, 100. "Miss Clark Not to Leave Paramount," *MPW,* 1 Dec 1917, 1314. "The Grand of Pittsburgh Opened," *MPW,* 23 Mar 1918, 1635. Marguerite Clark, "Filming Fairy Plays," *Motion Picture Magazine,* Feb 1918, 99–106, 162. "Marguerite Clark Has War Romance," *MPW,* 10 Aug 1918, 858. "Marguerite Clark Marries," *MPW,* 31 Aug 1918, 1254. "Marguerite Clark to Come East," *MPW,* 30 Aug 1919, 1300. Frederick James Smith, "The Lilliput Lady," *MPC,* Jul 1921, 44–45, 93. "Where Your Old Screen Favorite Is Now; Marguerite Clark, who used to be the idol of millions of fans, is now the demure little wife of a New Orleans millionaire [Harry Palmerston Williams]," *MW,* 3 May 1924, 8. Richard Alan Davis, "Marguerite Clark; Forgotten Silent Superstar," *Films of the Golden Age,* #1 (Summer 1995), pp. 62–66 (includes filmography). Karen Merritt, "Marguerite Clark as America's Snow White: The Resourceful Orphan Who Inspired Disney," *Griffithiana,* 69 (Oct 1998), 5–25.

Clark, R.M. [executive] (b. 1897–17 Nov 1934 [37?], Oklahoma City OK). BHD2, p. 48.

Clark, Roy [cinematographer]. No data found. FDY, p. 457.

Clark, T.C. [actor] (b. 1882–4 Oct 1954 [72?], Los Angeles CA). AS, p. 235. BHD, p. 129.

Clark, Trilby [actress]. No data found. AMD, p. 72. "Australian Beauty Engaged," *MPW,* 3 Jan 1925, 77. "Stromberg Signs Trilby Clark," *MPW,* 11 Apr 1925, 599. George A. Katchmer, "Forgotten Cowboys and Cowgirls—Part 2," *CI,* 173 (Nov 1989), C12.

Clark, Vera [scenarist]. No data found. FDY, p. 421.

Clark, Violet Taggart [scenarist]. No data found. AMD, p. 72. FDY, p. 421. "Violet Clark in New York," *MPW,* 27 Dec 1919, 1129. "Violet Clark Writing Continuity for Jans," *MPW,* 7 Feb 1920, 896.

Clark, Wallace C. [actor] (d. 30 Jan 1920, Philadelphia PA; Bright's disease). m. Blanche. "Wally Clark," *Variety,* 13 Feb 1920. BHD, p. 129. IFN, p. 56. SD.

Clark, Wallace V[incent] [actor: the voice of Popeye] (b. 1897?–24 Aug 1960 [63], Old Lyme CT). "Wallace V. Clark," *Variety,* 14 Sep 1960. AS, p. 235. IFN, p. 56.

Clark, Wallis H. [actor] (b. Essex, England, 2 Mar 1882–14 Feb 1961 [78], No. Hollywood CA). AS, p. 235. BHD, p. 129. IFN, p. 56.

Clark, William T. [actor] (b. Springfield OH, 1865?–14 Sep 1925 [60], Brooklyn NY). m. Mary Ellen Mullen. "William T. Clark," *Variety,* 23 Sep 1925. AS, p. 235 (b. 1845; d. 27 Feb, NYC). BHD, p. 129.

Clarke, Betty Ross [actress] (b. Langdon ND, 19 Apr 1896–31 Jan 1947 [50], Los Angeles CA; found dead). m. Lt. Arthur Collins, 1921, Riverside CA). "Betty C. Ross; Acrtress, Former Leading Lady for Tom Mix, Dies on Coast," *NYT,* 3 Feb 1947, 19:3. "Betty Ross," *Variety,* 5 Feb 1947 ("leads in Tom Mix westerns"). IFN, p. 55 (b. Pittsburgh PA, 1896). AMD, p. 73. AS, pp. 235 (b. Pittsburgh PA); 942 (Betty Ross, d. 1 Feb 1947). BHD1, p. 108 (b. Pittsburgh PA). Truitt, p. 291. WWS, p. 322. "Miss Clark Married," *MPW,* L, 18 Jun 1921, 703.

Clarke, Charles G[alloway] [cinematographer] (b. Potter Valley CA, 10 Mar 1899–1 Jul 1983 [84], Beverly Hills CA). *Early Film Making in Los Angeles.* (Universal; Griffith; Horsely; TC-F; FBO.) "Charles G. Clarke," *Variety,* 13 Jul 1983. AS, p. 235. BHD2, p. 48 (b. 19 Mar). Katz, p. 243.

Clarke, Edwin [actor]. No data found. AMD, p. 73. "Edwin Clarke Very Ill," *MPW,* 19 Dec 1914, 1694.

Clarke, Frank [actor/stuntman] (b. Paso Robles CA, 29 Dec 1898–12 Jun 1948 [49], Los Angeles CA). AS, p. 235. BHD1, p. 108. IFN, p. 56.

Clarke, George [actor] (*né* George Broome, b. Bromley, Kent, England, 11 Apr 1886–21 Dec 1946 [60], London, England). m. Isabelle Markey. (Lubin.) AS, p. 236 (b. 1888). BHD1, p. 108 (b. 1888). IFN, p. 56 (age 58). NNAT. SD, p. 250.

Clarke, George Downing [actor] (b. Birminham, England, 1859?–17 Aug 1930 [71], New Haven CT). (Vitagraph.) "George Downing Clarke," *Variety,* 27 Aug 1930. AS, p. 235 (Downing Clarke). BHD1, p. 108. IFN, p. 56 (Downing Clarke). Truitt, p. 61 (Downing George Clarke).

Clarke, Rev. George LeRoi [actor]. No data found. AMD, p. 73. "Year's Contract Signed by Preacher-Comedian," *MPW,* 5 Jun 1920, 1324.

Clarke, Gilbert [costume designer]. No data found. AMD, p. 73. "Gilbert Clarke, English Gown Designer, Is Now with M-G-M," *MPW,* 2 Jul 1927, 32.

Clarke, J[oseph] **I**[gnatius] **C**[onstantine] [actor/writer] (b. Kingstown, Ireland, 31 Jul 1845–27 Feb 1925 [79], New York NY). m. Mary A. Cahill. "J.I.C. Clarke," *Variety,* 4 Mar 1925. AS, p. 236. SD (b. 1846).

Clarke, Kenneth B. [scenarist]. No data found. FDY, p. 421.

Clarke, Kerry [scenarist]. No data found. FDY, p. 421.

Clarke, Redfield [actor] (b. Peru NY-d. 23 Oct 1928, Detroit MI). AS, p. 236. BHD, p. 130. IFN, p. 56.

Clarke, Robert "Buddy" [actor] (b. 1896?–20 May 1957 [61], Oakland CA). "Robert (Buddy) Clark," *Variety,* 5 Jun 1957.

Clarke, Wescott B. [actor] (b. Jersey City NJ, 27 Sep 1886–26 Jan 1959 [72], Los Angeles CA). AS, p. 236. BHD1, p. 108. IFN, p. 56.

Clarke, William [actor] (b. 1858?–13 Feb 1913 [55]). "William H. Clarke," *Variety,* 21 Feb 1913, p. 18.

Clarke-Warde, Carrie [actress] (b. Virginia City NV, 9 Jan 1862–6 Feb 1926 [64], Los Angeles CA). m. Mr. Brown. "Carrie Clarke-Warde," *Variety,* 10 Feb 1926. AS, p. 1129 (Carrie Ward). IFN, p. 309.

Clary, Charles [stage/film actor] (b. St. Charles IL, 24 Mar 1873–24 Mar 1931 [58], Los Angeles CA). m. Margaret Bechtel, Feb 1919, Santa Barbara CA. (Stage debut: 1897; *The Vampire,* Selig, May, 1910; Lasky; Fox.) AMD, p. 73. AS, p. 236 (b. 29 Mar). BHD1, p. 108 (b. Charleston IL). IFN, p. 56. MH, p. 102. "About Charles Clary," *MPW,* 12 Jun 1915, 1783. "Charles Clary," *MPW,* 21 Apr 1917, 427. "Charles Clary a Benedict," *MPW,* 7 Jun 1919, 1491–92. "Clary Quits Villain Roles for Lead in 'Sunset Jones,'" *MPW,* 29 Jan 1921, 549. "A Son," *MPW,* 20 Aug 1921, 793 (b. 30 Jul 1921). George Katchmer, "Remembering the Great Silents," *CI,* 196 (Oct 1991), 53. Clary appeared in *The Coming of Columbus* (Selig, 1910), one of the first 3-reel pictures.

Clausen, Claus [actor/director] (b. Eisenach, Germany, 15 Aug 1899–25 Nov 1989 [90], Essen, Germany). BHD1, p. 108; BHD2, p. 48.

Clawson, Dal [cinematographer] (*né* Lawrence Dallin [Dal] Clawson, b. Salt Lake City UT, 1886?–18 Jul 1937 [51], Englewood NJ). m. (d. in NY, 1920, of heart disease after acture indigestion). (Universal, 1914.) *Bangkok Daily Mail,* 25 Jun 1923 (worked on the first feature film produced in Siam [Thailand], *Miss Suwanna of Siam* [*Nangsao Suwan*], 1923). AMD, p. 73. BHD2, p. 48. FDY, p. 457. "Newsy Notes," *NYDM,* 1 Sep 1915, 29:1 (Clauson [sic] hired by Morosco as head cameraman. "It is said that his salary will surpass that of any other man in the business in like position."). "Morosco Signs Dal Clawson," *MPW,* 11 Sep 1915, 1809. "Clawson Heads Walsh Cameramen," *MPW,* 5 Jun 1920, 1342. "Mrs. Dal Clawson Dies," *MPW,* 31 Jul 1920, 615. "Lawrence Clawson, Movie Photographer; Pioneer in Field Dies Near Here Within Hour After Death of His Mother in Utah," *NYT,* 20 Jul 1937, 23:5.

Clawson, Elizabeth [scenarist]. No data found. FDY, p. 421.

Clawson, Elliott Jud [writer/scenarist] (b. Salt Lake City UT, 1891?–21 Jul 1942 [51], Vista CA). (Metro.) "Elliott Clawson," *Variety,* 29 Jul 1942. AMD, p. 73. AS, p. 236. FDY, p. 421. IFN, p. 56. "Masterpiece Film Men," *MPW,* 10 Oct 1914, 171. "Clawson Rejoins Universal," *MPW,* 25 Mar 1916, 1992.

Claxton, Kate [actress/playwright] (*née* Kate E. Wallace, b. Somerville NJ, 1850?–5 May 1924 [74], New York NY. Buried in Greenwood Cemetery, Brooklyn NY). m. **Charles A. Stevenson,** 1878 (d. 1929). (Began on stage, 1870; apex: 1873–1903 in *The Two Orphans,* as the blind girl). "Kate Claxton (Kate Cone)," *Variety,* 7 May 1924, 8:4. AMD, p. 73 (at the Brooklyn Theatre, 5 Dec 1876, a fire killed 289 people. She was dubbed "The Heroine of the Brooklyn Theatre Fire...through the presence of mind exhibited by her on that occasion." She also played at a St. Louis house and one in La Crosse WI which caught fire. Stevenson secretly divorced her in 1910, but she successfully contested this.). "Kate Claxton Sues William Fox," *MPW,* 9 Oct 1915, 259.

Clayton, Arthur [actor/assistant producer] (b. London, England, 29 Jan 1902–19 Feb 1955 [53], Liverpool, England). AMD, p. 73. AS, p. 237 (d. New Brighton, England). "Hampton Engages Arthur Clayton," *MPW,* 2 Aug 1919, 688.

Clayton, Donald [actor] (b. MO, 27 Oct 1889–18 Jan 1964 [74]). AS, p. 127. BHD1, p. 109. IFN, p. 56.

Clayton, Edward U[trecht] [actor/vaudevillian: Clayton & Lennie] (b. 1885?–25 Sep 1963 [78], Denville NJ). "Edward U. Clayton," *NYT,* 28 Sep 1963, 19:3. "Edward U. Clayton," *Variety,* 2 Oct 1963. AS, p. 237.

Clayton, Ethel [stage/film actress] (b. Champaign IL, 18 Nov 1883–11 Jun 1966 [82], Oxnard CA). m. (1) **Joseph Kaufman,** 1915 (d. 1918); (2) **Ian Keith,** ca. 1928 (d. 1960). (Began 1909; Essanay; Lubin; World; FP-L; Paramount.) "Ethel Clayton," *NYT,* 12 Jun 1966, 86:5. "Ethel Clayton," *Variety,* 15 Jun 1966 (brother's name was Donald Clayton Bloom). AMD, p. 73. AS, p. 237 (b. 8 Nov). BHD1, p. 109 (b. 8 Nov). FFF, p. 242 (b. 1890). FSS, p. 64. IFN, p. 56 (b. MO, 8 Nov). Lowrey, p. 34 (b. Champagne IL). MH, p. 102 (b. 1890). MSBB, p. 1032 (b. 1890). Spehr, p. 122 (b. 1884). Truitt, p. 61 (b. 1884). WWS, p. 15. "Ethel Clayton," *MPW,* 17 May 1913, 684. "Miss Ethel Clayton," *NYDM,* 4 Feb 1914, 29:3. "Ethel Clayton," *MPW,* 16 May 1914, 955. "Ethel Clayton; Leading Lady with the Lubin Company," *MPS,* 2 Oct 1914, 26. "Ethel Clayton," *MPW,* 13 Feb 1915, 997. "In the Picture Studios," *NYDM,* 14 Jul 1915, 27:1 (2nd annual contest of the Onyx Club [for motion picture enthusiasts] of Denver CO. Clayton, at Lubin, won with 378,235 votes. In 1914, Muriel Ostriche, now with Vitagraph, won and Clayton came in second.). "Ethel Clayton," *MPW,* 8 Apr 1916, 247. Howard Mann, "Shot Without Warning," *Picture-Play Magazine,* Sep 1917, 130. "Ethel Clayton Signs Paramount Contract," *MPW,* 11 May 1918, 867. "Who's Who in Starland," *Motion Picture Magazine,* Jun 1918, 108 (b. 8 Nov 1889). Elizabeth Peltret, "The Mysterious Miss Clayton," *MPC,* Mar 1919, 50–51, 62. "Famous Players Signs New Contract with Ethel Clayton," *MPW,* 10 Apr 1920, 295. Maude Cheathem, "Firelight Confessions," *MPC,* Oct 1921, 36–37, 78. "Ethel Clayton Returns," *MPW,* 24 Jan 1925, 380. Catti Merrick, "Ian Keith Says Goodby to Both Wife and Screen," *Movie Classic,* Oct 1931, 40.

Clayton, Frederic [actor] (b. 1874–2 Jan 1948 [73?], New York NY). BHD, p. 130.

Clayton, Gilbert [actor] (b. Polo IL, 18 Jan 1859–1 Mar 1950 [91], Los Angeles Co. CA). AS, p. 237. BHD1, p. 109. IFN, p. 56. George Katchmer, "Remembering the Great Silents," *CI,* 221 (Nov 1993), 52.

Clayton, Hadie [actress]. No data found. AMD, p. 73. "Hadie Clayton with Paralta," *MPW,* 15 Dec 1917, 1614.

Clayton, Hazel [actress] (b. 1885?–8 Mar

1963 [77], Forest Hills NY). (Fox, Ft. Lee NJ.) m. Hilliard Mack. "Hazel Clayton," *Variety,* 13 Mar 1963. AS, p. 237. BHD, pp. 130; 200. IFN, p. 56. Truitt, p. 154.

Clayton, Lou [actor] (*né* Louis Finkelstein, b. New York NY, 1887?–12 Sep 1950 [63], Santa Monica CA; cancer). m. Ida. "Lou Clayton's Death Recalls Close Kinship with Durante-Jackson," *Variety,* 13 Sep 1950 (teamed with Durante in 1924). AS, p. 237 (b. Brooklyn NY). BHD1, p. 109. IFN, p. 56. SD.

Clayton, Lucille [actress] (d. Birmingham AL, 26 Jun 1923). BHD, p. 130.

Clayton, Marguerite B. [actress] (b. Ogden UT, 12 Apr 1891–20 Dec 1968 [77], Los Angeles CA; from injuries after a car accident). (Essanay.) m. Mr. Bertrandias. AMD, p. 73. AS, p. 237 (b. Salt Lake City UT). BHD, p. 130. BR, pp. 8–12 (b. Salt Lake City UT). IFN, p. 56. Katz, p. 245. "Some Prominent Essanay Photoplayers," *MPW,* 11 Jul 1914, 234–35. "Marguerite Clayton," *MPW,* 20 Nov 1915, 1489. "Miss Clayton in Cohan Support," *MPW,* 8 Jun 1918, 1422. Billy H. Doyle, "Lost Players," *CI,* 155 (May 1988), 26 (Mrs. Marguerite Bertrandias). George A. Katchmer, "Forgotten Cowboys & Cowgirls—2," *CI,* 173 (Nov 1989), C12.

Cleary, Michael H. [composer] (b. Weymouth MA, 27 Apr 1902–15 Jun 1954 [52], New York NY). "Michael H. Cleary, Writer of Songs, 52," *NYT,* 16 Jun 1954, 31:4 (wrote *Is There Anything Wrong in That?; Hello Baby; When a Lady Meets a Gentleman Down South*). "Michael H. Cleary," *Variety,* 23 Jun 1954 (wrote *I'll Putcha Pitcha in the Papers; Here It Is Monday and I've Still Got a Dollar*). AS, p. 237. ASCAP 66, p. 125. BHD1, p. 109 (d. Westport CT). CEPMJ.

Cleary, Peggy [actress/scenarist] (b. Detroit MI, 29 Dec 1892–10 Jan 1972 [79], Los Angeles CA; cancer). "Peggy Cleary," *Variety,* 19 Jan 1972. AS, p. 237. BHD, p. 130; BHD2, p. 48. IFN, p. 57. MH, p. 102.

Clegg, Valce V. [actor] (b. MN, 27 Feb 1888–29 Jul 1947 [59], Los Angeles CA). "Valce V. Clegg," *Variety,* 6 Aug 1947. AS, p. 237. BHD, p. 130. IFN, p. 57. Truitt, p. 61.

Clemenceau, Georges [writer]. No data found. AMD, p. 73. "Fox Gets Screen Rights to Clemenceau's Novel," *MPW,* 3 Jan 1920, 130.

Clement, Clay [actor/founding member of Screen Actors Guild] (b. Greentree KY, 19 May 1888–20 Oct 1956 [68], Watertown NY). m. **Kathleen Kerrigan** (d. 1957); Mary Frey. "Clay Clement," *Variety,* 24 Oct 1956 (began 1914). AS, p. 237. BHD1, p. 109. IFN, p. 57. SD. Truitt, p. 61.

Clemento, Steve [actor] (aka Steve Clemente, *né* Steve Clemento Morro, b. Mexico, 22 Nov 1885–7 May 1950 [64], Los Angeles CA; cerebral hemorrhage). AS, p. 238. BHD1, p. 109. IFN, p. 157. George A. Katchmer, "Forgotten Cowboys and Cowgirls—Part VIII," *CI,* 180 (Jun 1990), 59, 61.

Clements, Colin Campbell [playwright/scenarist] (b. Omaha NB, 25 Feb 1894–29 Jan 1948 [53], Philadelphia PA; from heart attack on 26 Dec 1947). m. Florence Ryerson, 1927 (d. 1965). "Colin Clements, Playwright, 53, Husband of Florence Ryerson Dies—Wrote 'Harriet' and 'Bedfellows' with Wife," *NYT,* 30 Jan 1948, 23:4. "Colin Clements," *Variety,* 4 Feb 1948. AS, p. 238. BHD2, p. 48. FDY, p. 421. SD.

Clements, Dudley [actor] (b. New York NY, 31 Mar 1889–4 Nov 1947 [58], New York NY; heart attack). "Dudley Clements," *Variety,* 12 Nov 1947. AS, p. 238. BHD1, p. 109. IFN, p. 57. Truitt 1983.

Clements, Hal C. [director/actor]. No data found. m. **Olga Printzlau-Clark** (d. 1962). (Kalem.) AMD, p. 73. "Clements with Premier," *MPW,* 16 Jan 1915, 390. "Doings in Los Angeles," *MPW,* 23 Jan 1915 (mentions wife). Anthony Slide, *Silent Portraits* (Vestal NY: Vestal Press, 1989), p. 56.

Clements, Joseph I. [art/technical director] (b. 1889?–20 May 1929 [40], Camden NJ; pneumonia). (Columbia.) "Joseph Clements," *Variety,* 22 May 1929. AMD, p. 73. AS, p. 239 (d. 18 May). BHD2, p. 48 (d. 14 May). "Persons with DeLuxe Pictures," *MPW,* 5 Oct 1918, 73.

Clements, Roy S. [actor/director] (b. Sterling IL, 12 Jan 1877–15 Jul 1948 [71], Los Angeles CA). (Triangle.) AS, p. 238. BHD2, p. 48. IFN, p. 57.

Clemons, James K. [actor] (b. PA, 14 Jan 1883–5 Jun 1950 [67], Los Angeles CA). "James K. Clemons," *Variety,* 14 Jun 1950. AS, p. 238. BHD1, p. 109. IFN, p. 57.

Clerget, Paul Maurice [actor] (b. Paris, France, 31 Jul 1868–4 Dec 1935 [68], Paris, France [extrait de décès no. SN/1935]). "Paul Clerget," *Variety,* 18 Dec 1935. AS, p. 238. BHD, p. 130. IFN, p. 57. Truitt, p. 61.

Clermont, Harvey (Harry) [actor] (b. 1907–28 Jan 1978 [70?], Marina del Ray CA). BHD, p. 130.

Clermont, Rita [actress] (b. 4 Mar 1894-Dec 1969 [75]). BHD, p. 130.

Cleveland, Anna [stage/film actress] (b. New Orleans LA, 1880–7 Jan 1954 [73?], Manhasset NY). AS, p. 238. BHD1, p. 109. "Woman Forms Picture Company [at Waterville NY]," *NYDM,* 28 Jul 1915, 23:1.

Cleveland, Dorothy V. [publicist]. No data found. AMD, p. 73. "Dorothy Cleveland with Hodkinson," *MPW,* 18 Sep 1920, 381. "Writing for Rayart," *MPW,* 11 Oct 1924, 503.

Cleveland, Dwight [scenarist] (b. 1871?–5 Jan 1926 [54], Los Angeles CA). "Dwight Cleveland," *Variety,* 13 Jan 1926. AS, p. 238. BHD2, p. 48.

Cleveland, George (son of **Lavinia Cleveland**) [actor] (b. Sydney, Nova Scotia, Canada, 17 Sep 1885–15 Jul 1957 [71], Burbank CA; heart attack). "George Cleveland," *Variety,* 17 Jul 1957 (began 1936). AS, p. 238 (b. 1883). IFN, p. 57.

Cleveland, Lavinia (mother of **George Cleveland**) [actress] (b. 1857–10 May 1950 [93?], Stockton CA). AS, p. 238.

Cleveland, Val [title writer]. No data found. FDY, p. 441.

Clever, Willy [actor] (b. 11 Aug 1905-Dec 1969 [64]). BHD1, p. 605.

Clevinger, Beatrice [stage/film actress]. No data found. (All-Star.) "Beatrice Clevinger [photo only]," *NYDM,* 3 Jun 1914, 23:1.

Clewig, Carl [actor] (b. Schwerin, Germany, 22 Apr 1884–15 May 1954 [70], Badenweiler, Germany). BHD1, p. 605.

Cliff, Laddie [actor] (*né* Clifford Albyn Perry, b. Bristol, England, 3 Sep 1891–8 Dec 1937 [46], Montana, Valais, Switzerland). m. (1) Maybelle Parker; (2) Phyllis Monkman (d. 1976). "Laddie Cliff," *Variety,* 15 Dec 1937. AS, p. 238 (d. London, England). BHD1, p. 109 (d. London). IFN, p. 57. SD.

Cliffe, H. Cooper [actor] (b. Oxford, England, 19 Jul 1862–1 May 1939 [76], New York NY; pneumonia). m. Alice Belmore. "H. Cooper Cliffe," *Variety,* 10 May 1939. AMD, p. 73. AS, p. 238. BHD, p. 130. IFN, p. 57. Truitt, p. 62. "H. Cooper Cliffe," *MPW,* 30 Oct 1915, 803.

Clifford, Billy [actor/dancer] (*né* William Clifford Shyrigh, b. Urbana IL, 1869?–20 Nov 1930 [61], Urbana IL). m. (1) Maud Huth; (2) Mae. "Billy Clifford," *Variety,* 26 Nov 1930. AS, p. 238.

Clifford, Eugene [journalist/scenarist] (b. Elgin IL, 14 Jun 1886–2 Aug 1941 [55], Warwick NY). (1st National; Fox.) "Eugene Clifford, Publisher, Is Dead; Head of Orange County Leader Up-State, Former New York Journalist, Stricken at 55; Had Written for Films; Ex-Editor of The Bridge Forum Did Scripts in Hollywood and for Gaumont-British," *NYT,* 3 Aug 1941, 34:3 (d. 3 Aug). "Eugene Clifford," *Variety,* 6 Aug 1941 (…script writer for several Hollywood studios some 15 years ago…"). AS, p. 238. FDY, p. 421.

Clifford, Gordon [lyricist] (b. Providence RI, 28 Mar 1902–11 Jun 1968 [66], Las Vegas NV; traffic accident). "Gordon Clifford," *Variety,* 19 Jun 1968 (wrote *I Surrender Dear*). AS, p. 238. ASCAP 66, p. 126.

Clifford, Jack [actor] (*né* Virgil James Montani, b. Genoa, Italy, 1880?–10 Nov 1956 [76], New York NY). m. **Evelyn Nesbit Thaw**, 1916 (d. 1967). "Jack Clifford," *Variety,* 14 Nov 1956. AMD, p. 73. AS, p. 239 (b. San Francisco CA). BHD1, p. 110. IFN, p. 57. Truitt, p. 62. "Jack Clifford Signed," *MPW,* 18 Jul 1925, 313.

Clifford, Kathleen [actress] (b. Charlottesville VA, 16 Feb 1887–11 Jan 1963 [75], Los Angeles CA). m. LA banker Meo Illitch (from Belgrade, Serbia). "Kathleen Clifford," *Variety,* 16 Jan 1963. AMD, p. 73. AS, p. 239 (b. 1894). BHD, p. 130 (b. 1894). IFN, p. 57 (b. England, 14 Feb 1894). SD, p. 255. Truitt 1983. "Church Supports Kathleen Clifford," *MPW,* 31 Aug 1918, 1281. "Kathleen Clifford in Christie Comedy," *MPW,* 3 May 1924, 48. June Lee, "Dan Cupid's Bulletin Board," *Paris and Hollywood,* Sep 1926, 21–22 (she and Illitch had been secretly married for months).

Clifford, Molly Hamley [actress] (b. Exeter, England, 1 Aug 1885–7 Jun 1956 [70]). BHD, p. 130.

Clifford, Ruth [film/stage/TV actress] (b. Pawtucket RI, 17 Jul 1900–30 Nov 1998 [98], Woodland Hills CA; buried in Holy Cross Cemetery, Culver City CA). (Edison; Universal.) m. James A. Cornelius, 1924 (1 son, James). (Edison, 1914; Universal, 1916.) Myrna Oliver, "Ruth Clifford; Early Movie Star, Character Actress," *LA Times,* 31 Dec 1998, A22. Anthony Slide, "Ruth Clifford—A Tribute," *CI,* 283 (Jan 1999), 6. AS, p. 239. FFF, p. 244. FSS, p. 65. Katz, p. 246. MH, p. 103. WWS, p. 285. "Vitagraph Engages Ruth Clifford," *MPW,* 9 Aug 1919, 854. "Ruth Clifford Entertains Maeterlinck at Luncheon," *MPW,* 14 Feb 1920, 1052. "Ruth Clifford Is Signed for Frohman; Five Features Yearly," *MPW,* 7 Aug 1920, 776. John G. Holme, "Film-Flamming the Public; Exposing some further activities of those who prey on the public faith in the Motion Picture," *Photoplay,* Mar 1921, 60, 120–21 (sued William L. Sherrill of Frohman for breach of contract which was answered by a countersuit). Ed Wyatt, "The Talented Ruth Clifford," *CI,* 181 (Jul 1990), 37.

Clifford, William [actor] (b. Cincinnati OH, 27 Jun 1877–23 Dec 1941 [64], Los Angeles CA). (Bison; Fox.) "William Cliffom [sic]," *Variety,* 31 Dec 1941. AS, p. 239. BHD, p. 130. IFN, p. 57. Truitt, p. 62. "William Clifford, Leads,William Fox," *MPN,* 21 Oct 1916, 181 (b. New Orleans LA, 1882).

Clifford, William H. [playwright/actor/scenarist/producer] (*né* Clifford Williams, b. San Frtancisco CA, 1874?–9 Oct 1938 [64], Los Angeles CA). (Imp; Ince; FP-L.) "William H. Clifford," *Variety,* 12 Oct 1938. AMD, p. 74. AS, p. 239. BHD2, p. 49. FDY, p. 421. IFN, p. 57. "William H. Clifford," *MPW,* 23 May 1914, 1119. "Beat Stork by a Nose," *MPW,* 11 Jul 1914, 279 (birth of son). "Clifford Joins F.P.; Prominent Inceville Writer to Take Reins in Famous Players Script Department," *NYDM,* 29 Sep 1915, 31:2 (resigned from Ince to go to FP-L. "Ever since I have been in the motion picture business I seem to have been working under terrific pressure—always trying to meet some superhuman schedule apparently devised for the express purpose of wearing me to the proverbial frazzle. Can you imagine doing your best work at the rate of two scenarios a week for three years? But in my new work I shall be given a free rein with all the time I require for the completion of the minute details that constitute the deciding factor between real art and mere motion picture production…"). "Clifford Joins Famous Players," *MPW,* 9 Oct 1915, 266. "William H. Clifford Heads Own Company," *MPW,* 23 Jun 1917, 1942.

Clift, Denison H[aley] [writer/director] (b. San Francisco CA, 3 May 1885?–17 Dec 1961 [76], Beverly Hills CA; heart attack). m. Fay Holden. (FP-L.) "Denison Clift, 76, Dead; Film Director Was Also a Novelist and Playwright," *NYT,* 21 Dec 1961, 27:4. "Denison Clift," *Variety,* 27 Dec 1961. AMD, p. 74. AS, p. 239. BHD2, p. 49 (b. 2 May 1892). IFN, p. 57. Katz, p. 246 (b. 1892). "Denison Clift Writing for Fox Stars," *MPW,* 16 Nov 1918, 749. "Clift Made Head of Fox Coast Scenario Writers," *MPW,* 13 Sep 1919, 1648. "Denison Clift Is Directing Own Stories for Fox Film," *MPW,* 1 May 1920, 701. "Caseneuve Succeeds," *MPW,* 4 Sep 1920, 64. "Clift to Direct Big Film," *MPW,* 10 Oct 1925, 488.

Clifton, Elmer [actor/director/scenarist] (b. Chicago IL, 14 Mar 1890–15 Oct 1949 [59], Los Angeles CA; cerebral hemorrhage). (Griffith.) "Elmer Clifton, 59, Screen Director; Hollywood Veteran with 200 Picture Credits Dies—Discovered Clara Bow," *NYT,* 17 Oct 1949, 23:5. "Elmer Clifton," *Variety,* 19 Oct 1949. AMD, p. 74. AS, p. 239. BHD, p. 130; BHD2, p. 49. IFN, p. 57. Truitt, p. 62 (b. 1893). "Elmer Clifton Fine Arts Director," *MPW,* 3 Mar 1917, 1358. "Elmer Clifton May Leave Griffith to Organize His Own Producing Company," *MPW,* 16 Apr 1921, 720. "Elmer Clifton Will Direct Barthelmess Productions," *MPW,* 2 May 1925, 81. Faith Service, "Demi-Tasse Heroines; The screen is fostering a false ideal of American womanhood, says Elmer Clifton," *Pictures,* Jul 1926, 40, 81.

Clifton, Emma Bell [actress/scenarist] (*née* Emma MacGrew, b. Pittsburgh PA, 1 Nov 1874–3 Aug 1922 [47], Los Angeles CA). m. **Wallace C. Clifton**. AMD, p. 74. AS, p. 239. BHD, p. 130; BHD2, p. 49. IFN, p. 57. "Emma Clifton," *MPW,* 12 Dec 1914, 1532.

Clifton, Frank M. [scenarist]. No data found. FDY, p. 421.

Clifton, Ray D[elano] [scenarist/director] (b. 1878?–25 Apr 1940 [62], Los Angeles CA; "result of a rare tropical ailment contracted on location in India 18 years ago"). "Ray D. Clifton," *Variety,* 1 May 1940. AS, p. 239. BHD2, p. 49. IFN, p. 57.

Clifton, Wallace C. [scenarist]. No data found. m. **Emma Bell** (d. 1922). AMD, p. 74. William Lord Wright, "For Photoplay Authors Real and New," *NYDM,* 14 Jul 1915, p. 30. "Three Scenario Writers for World," *MPW,* 6 Apr 1918, 73.

Clifton, William F. [actor] (b. 1855–18 Sep 1931 [76?], Chicago IL). BHD, p. 130.

Cline, Edward "Eddie" F[rancis] [actor: Keystone Cop/director/cinematographer] (b. Kenosha WI, 7 Nov 1892–22 May 1961 [68], Los Angeles CA). m. (died 17 Sep 1918). (Sennett; Pathé.) "Edward F. Cline, 68, ex-Movie Director," *NYT,* 24 May 1961, 41:5. "Eddie Cline," *Variety,* 31 May 1961. AMD, p. 74. AS, p. 239. BHD, p. 131; BHD2, p. 49. FDY, p. 457. IFN, p. 57. Katz, p. 247. Truitt, p. 62. "Wife of Director Dies," *MPW,* 12 Oct 1918, 207. "Edward Cline with Principal," *MPW,* 17 Feb 1923, 693. "Brief Story on the Rise of Edward F. Cline," *MPW,* 6 Oct 1923, 505. "Edward F. Cline Signed," *MPW,* 12 Feb 1927, 501. "Edward Cline Returns to Mack Sennett," *MPW,* 23 Jul 1927, 259. "Edward F. Cline," *MPW,* 8 Oct 1927, 358.

Cline, Robert E. [cinematographer] (b. AZ, 12 Jul 1896?–30 Nov 1946 [50], Los Angeles CA). "Robert Cline," *Variety,* 4 Dec 1946 ("Cline started in films during early years of silents."). AS, p. 239. BHD2, p. 49 (b. 1898). FDY, p. 457. IFN, p. 57.

Cline, Wilfred [cinematographer]. No data found. FDY, p. 457.

Clisbee, Edward [actor] (b. Santa Rosa CA, 29 Dec 1878–24 Jul 1936 [57], Wentachee WA). AS, p. 239. BHD, p. 131. Billy H. Doyle, "Lost Players [Edward Clisbee]," *CI,* 156 (Jun 1988), C13.

Clive, Colin [actor] (*né* Colin Clive-Greig, b. St. Malo, north France, 9 Jan 1898–25 Jun 1937 [39], Los Angeles CA; pneumonia). m. Jeanne de Casalis. "Colin Clive, Actor, Dies in Hollywood; Star of Screen and Stage, 37, Scored First Hit as Stanhope in 'Journey's End'; Made Debut Here in 1930; Appeared in 'Clive of India,' a Picture Based on Life of His Ancestor," *NYT,* 26 Jun 1937, 17:3. "Colin Clive," *Variety,* 30 Jun 1937. AS, p. 239. BHD1, p. 110 (b. 20 Jan 1900). IFN, p. 57 (b. 20 Jun 1900). Katz, pp. 247–48 (b. 20 Jan). Truitt, p. 62. Gregory Mank, "Colin Clive; 1900–1937," *FIR,* May 1980, 257–68.

Clive, E[dward] E. [actor] (b. Monmouthshire, Wales, 28 Aug 1879–6 Jun 1940 [60], No. Hollywood CA; heart attack). "E.E. Clive," *Variety,* 12 Jun 1940. AS, p. 239 (b. Blenavon, Wales, 1880). IFN, p. 57 (age 56). Katz 1994.

Clive, Henry [actor/title writer] (*né* Henry Clive O'Hara, b. Melbourne, Australia, 3 Oct 1881–12 Dec 1960 [79], Los Angeles CA; lung cancer). Married 6 times. "Henry Clive, Illustrator, Dead; Known for Portraits of Women," *NYT,* 16 Dec 1960, 33:1 (in Chaplin's *City Lights*). "Henry Clive," *Variety,* 21 Dec 1960 (in silents on both coasts). AMD, p. 74. AS, p. 239. BHD1, p. 110. IFN, p. 57. Truitt, p. 63. "Henry Clive," *MPW,* 21 Apr 1917, 434. "Henry Clive Joins Walsh Staff," *MPW,* 25 Sep 1920, 509.

Clive, Vincent [actor] (b. Upper Norwood, England-d. 11 Apr 1943). BHD1, p. 110. IFN, p. 57.

Cloninger, Ralph [actor] (b. TX, 20 Apr 1888–17 Jun 1962 [74], Los Angeles Co., CA). AS, p. 239. BHD, p. 131. IFN, p. 57.

Close, Ivy [mother of Ronald Neame] [actress] (b. Stockton-on-Tees, England, 1890?–4 Dec 1968 [78], Goring, England). m. Elwin Neame (son, Ronald, b. 23 Apr 1911). (Hepworth; Kalem.) "Ivy Close," *Variety,* 18 Dec 1968. AMD, p. 74. AS, p. 239. BHD, p. 131. IFN, p. 57. "Beauty May Become Screen Star," *MPW,* 22 Apr 1916, 626. "Ivy Close Coming Here," *MPW,* 6 May 1916, 964. "Kalem Signs Ivy Close," *MPW,* 20 May 1916, 1338. "Ivy Close, Goes to Jacksonville; 'Most Beautiful Woman in the World,' Now Kalem Star, Takes Up New Duties in the Southern Studio," *MPW,* 28, 10 Jun 1916, 1869. "Ivy Close Returns to England," *MPW,* 7 Oct 1916, 86. Peter Wade, "The Eternal Quest for Beauty; How, in Spite of Herself, a Country Lass Became the Most Sought-After Maiden in England," *MPC,* Nov 1916, 39–40, 68.

Clothier, William J. [cinematographer] (b. Decatur IL, 1903?–14 Jan 1996 [92], Los Angeles CA). (WB; Paramount; RKO.) "William J. Clothier Dies," *CI,* 248 (Feb 1996), 52. AS, p. 240. BHD2, p. 49 (d. 7 Jan).

Cloud, Mabel [actress] (d. Newkirk OK, 17 Jun 1921). BHD, p. 131. IFN, p. 58.

Clovelly, Cecil [actor] (b. England, 25 May 1890–25 Apr 1965 [74], New York NY [Death Certificate Index No. 9051]). . "Cecil Clovelly," *Variety,* 5 May 1965. AS, p. 240. BHD1, p. 110. IFN, p. 58.

Cloy, May [stage/film actress] (b. Minneapolis MN, 7 May 1880–14 Feb 1977 [96], Los Angeles CA). m. Clarence Kolb, 1 Sep 1917, San Francisco CA. BHD1, p. 110. "Marriages," *Variety,* 7 Sep 1917, p. 8.

Clugston, H[oward] **N**[ewkirk] [actor] (b. Scotland, 18 Oct 1881–5 Apr 1944 [62], Los Angeles CA). BHD1, p. 110. IFN, p. 58.

Clune, W[illiam] **H.** [exhibitor/producer/executive] (b. 1860?–18 Oct 1927 [67], Los Angeles CA; apoplexy). "W.H. Clune," *Variety,* 26 Oct 1927. AMD, p. 74. AS, p. 240. BHD2, p. 49 (b. 1862). "Clune Buys Studio," *MPW,* 3 Jul 1915, 42. J. Van Cartmell, "Clune to Produce; Prominent Coast Exhibitor Enters Producing Field—News from the Pacific Colony," *NYDM,* 8 Sep 1915, 32:3 (to produce *Romona*).

Cluzetti, Jules [actor] (b. 1861–22 Apr 1927 [64?], New Orleans LA). BHD, p. 131.

Clyde, Andy (brother of **David** and **Jean Clyde**) [actor] (b. Blairgowrie, Scotland, 25 Mar 1892–18 May 1967 [75], Los Angeles CA; heart attack). m. **Elsie Maud Tarron** (d. 1990). (Sennett.) "Andy Clyde," *Variety,* 24 May 1967. AS, p. 240. BHD1, p. 110. IFN, p. 58. Katz, p. 249.

Clyde, David [actor/producer] (brother of **Andy** and **Jean Clyde**) (b. Blairgowrie, Scotland, 27 Mar 1885–16 May 1945 [60], Hollywood CA). m. Fay Holden, 24 Jun 1914. "David Clyde; Comedian of Screen, Producer, Theatre Owner Dies on Coast," *NYT,* 18 May 1945, 19:5. "David Clyde," *Variety,* 23 May 1945. AS, p. 240 (b. 1887; d. San Fernando Valley CA). IFN, p. 58 (age 57).

Clyde, Jean (sister of **Andy** and **David**

Clyde) [actress] (b. Blairgowrie, Scotland, 1889–13 Jul 1962 [73], Helensburgh, Scotland). "Jean Clyde," *Variety,* 11 Jul 1962. AS, p. 240.

Clyde, June [actress] (*née* June Tetrazini, b. St. Joseph MO, 2 Dec 1909–1 Oct 1987 [75], Fort Lauderdale FL). AS, p. 240. BHD1, p. 110.

Clymer, Beth [actress] (b. 1887?–14 Jan 1952 [65], Woodland Hills CA; heart attack). "Beth Clymer," *Variety,* 23 Jan 1952. AS, p. 240. IFN, p. 58.

Clymer, John B. [scenic artist] (b. 1881?–25 Mar 1936 [55], Los Angeles CA; "killed in fall from scaffolding on set at Metro"). "John Coakley," *Variety,* 1 Apr 1936.

Clymer, John B. [publicist/scenarist/title writer] (b. 1887?–24 May 1937 [50], Los Angeles CA). (Gaumont; Exclusive Supply Co.) "John Clymer," *Variety,* 26 May 1937. AMD, p. 74. AS, p. 240. BHD2, p. 49. FDY, p. 421. IFN, p. 58. "Tips on Titling," *MPW,* 9 Nov 1912, 532. "Posters, Pertinent and Impertinent," *MPW,* 23 Nov 1912, 778. J.B. Clymer, "Telling the Truth to the Exhibitor," *MPW,* 4 Jan 1913, 35. "Clymer Leaves Gaumont," *MPW,* 19 Apr 1913, 269. F.J. Beecroft, "Publicity Men I Have Met...," *NYDM,* 14 Jan 1914, 48 (*see* Beecroft, Chester for full citation). "John B. Clymer," *MPW,* 10 Oct 1914, 195. "John Clymer Now Pathé Scenario Editor," *MPW,* 18 Dec 1915, 2162. "Clymer Joins Yorke-Metro Scenario Staff," *MPW,* 2 Mar 1918, 1217. "Clymer Has a Play," *MPW,* 21 Mar 1925, 281.

Coad, Joyce [child actress] (b. WY, 14 Apr 1917–3 May 1987 [70], March Air Force Base CA). (Film debut: *The Scarlet Letter,* MGM.) AMD, p. 74. BHD1, p. 110. Paul Paige, "Close-Ups and Fade-Outs," *Paris and Hollywood,* 2 (Sep 1926), 92 (winner of the Southern California "Million Dollar Baby Contest"; photo, p. 70). "Joyce Coad," *MPW,* 25 Jun 1927, 572.

Coakley, John [actor] (b. 1881–25 Mar 1936 [55?], Los Angeles CA). AS, p. 240.

Coakley, Marion [actress]. No data found. AMD, p. 74. "Marion Coakley to Make Film Debut," *MPW,* 1 Dec 1923, 501.

Coates, Franklin B. [actor/writer/cameraman/director]. No data found. AMD, p. 75. George Blaisdell, "Franklin B. Coates, Explorer," *MPW,* 4 Apr 1914, 42–43. "Coates to Star in Jungle Picture," *MPW,* 30 Jan 1915, 683. "Coates Engaged by Raver," *MPW,* 13 Dec 1919, 781.

Cobb, Edmund Fessenden [film/TV actor] (b. Albuquerque NM, 23 Jun 1892–15 Aug 1974 [82], Woodland Hills CA; heart attack). (Extra, St. Louis Motion Picture Co., 1910; Lubin; Colorado Film Co.; Essanay; Art-O-Graf Film Co.; Universal, 1910; Arrow; final film: *Johnny Reno,* Paramount, 1966.) "Edmund Cobb," *Variety,* 28 Aug 1974. AMD, p. 75. AS, p. 240. BHD1, p. 111. FSS, p. 65. GK, pp. 139–63. IFN, p. 58. "A Handsome Boy," *The Daily Times* [Albuquerque NM], 3 Dec 1893. "Wrong Actor Given Credit," *MPW,* 4 Jul 1914, 87. Nick Williams, "A Tribute to Edmund Cobb," *Filmograph,* II, No. 2 (1971), 30–44 (includes filmography). Andrew C. McKay, "An Edmund Cobb Filmography, 1913–1966 (Addenda, Notes, and Corrections)," *Filmograph,* III, No. 1 (1972), 6–14. George A. Katchmer, "Cowboy Edmund Cobb," *CI,* 89 (Nov 1982), 20–22.

Cobb, F. Heath [publicist]. No data found. AMD, p. 75. "Cobb Joins C.B.C.," *MPW,* 3 May 1924, 70.

Cobb, Irvin S[hrewsbury] [journalist/novelist/humorist/scenarist/title writer/actor] (b. Paducah KY, 23 Jun 1876–11 Mar 1944 [67], New York NY). m. Laura Spencer Baker, 12 Jun 1900. *Exit Laughingly.* "Literati; Some Memories of Irv Cobb," *Variety,* 154, 15 Mar 1944, 58:4 (d. 10 Mar). AMD, p. 75. AS, p. 240. BHD1, p. 111; BHD2, p. 49. IFN, p. 58. Truitt, p. 63. "Irvin Cobb as a Picture Actor," *MPW,* 29 May 1915, 1447. "When Irvin Cobb Sold Cold Stuff," *MPW,* 26 Jan 1918, 490. Harold R. Hall, "Yessiree! They Could Be Better According to Irvin Cobb; Kentucky's Contribution to the Mirth of a Nation Is Terribly Frank About Films," *MPC,* May 1927, 16–17, 66. Irving Dilliard, *DAB,* Supp. 3 (1973), pp. 170–71 (includes bibliography).

Cobb, Ty [baseball player/actor] (*né* Tyrus Raymond Cobb, b. Narrows GA, 18 Dec 1886–17 Jul 1961 [74], Atlanta GA). AS, p. 240. BHD1, p. 111.

Cobe, Andrew J. [executive]. No data found. AMD, p. 75. "The Alliance Program," *MPW,* 10 Oct 1914, 166. "Alliance Has New Poster Policy," *MPW,* 8 May 1915, 925. "Head of Alliance Returns," *MPW,* 15 May 1915, 1079.

Coburn, Charles Douville [actor] (b. Macon GA, 19 Jun 1877–30 Aug 1961 [84], New York NY; cardiovascular ailment [Death Certificate Index #18903]). m. Ivah Wills; (2) Winifred J. Natzko. (AA, 1943). "Charles Coburn," *Variety,* 6 Sep 1961. AS, p. 241. IFN, p. 58. SD.

Coburn, Dorothy [actress] (b. Great Falls MT, 8 Jun 1905–15 May 1978 [72], Los Angeles CA). AS, p. 241. BHD, p. 131.

Coburn, Gladys [actress]. No data found. (Film debut: *The Battle of Life,* Fox, 1916.)

Coburn, Grace [actress]. No data found. AMD, p. 75. "Grace Coburn Makes Film Debut in Fox Film," *MPW,* 16 Dec 1916, 1661.

Coburn, Walter J. [scenarist]. No data found. FDY, p. 421.

Coccia, Aurelia [dance director] (b. Rome, Italy, 1868?–30 Sep 1938 [70], Englewood NJ). m. Minnie Amato (stage name; d. 1921). "Aurelia Coccia Dies; Ex-Ballet Master, 70; Formerly at Metropolitan and Dance Director of Films," *NYT,* 2 Oct 1938, 49:2 (danced with Swanson in *The Hummingbird* and with Gilda Gray in *Aloma of the South Seas*). SD.

Cochrane, Frank [actor] (b. Durham, England, 28 Oct 1882–21 May 1962 [79], London, England). AS, p. 241. BHD1, p. 111. IFN, p. 58.

Cochrane, George (brother of **Robert H. Cochrane**) [producer/director] (b. Wheeling WV, 1869). AMD, p. 75. BHD2, p. 49. "Cochrane to Direct Company," *MPW,* 5 Feb 1916, 781.

Cochrane, Robert H[enry] (brother of **George Cochrane**) [publicist/director/founding partner of Universal, 1906] (b. Wheeling WV, 27 Dec 1879–31 May 1973 [94], New Rochelle NY). "Robert H. Cochrane," *Variety,* 6 Jun 1973. AMD, p. 75. AS, p. 241. BHD2, p. 49. WWWA. "Universal Publicity Staff," *MPW,* 26 Sep 1914, 1756–57. "Robert H. Cochrane, Jr., Comes to Town," *MPW,* 14 Nov 1914, 945 (birth of son). Robert H. Cochrane, "Beginning of Motion Picture Press Agenting," *MPW,* 20 Jul 1918, 322–23. "Robert H. Cochrane Commissioned in the United States Army," *MPW,* 14 Nov 1925, 115.

Cochrane, Thomas D. [executive] (b. 1869–9 Nov 1937 [68?], New York NY). AMD, p. 75. BHD2, p. 49. "Another Independent Manufacturer," *MPW,* 30 Sep 1911, 983.

Cody, Albert R. [actor] (b. Portland OR, 6 June 1885–30 Mar 1966 [80], San Francisco CA). BHD, p. 131.

Cody, Bill (father of Bill Body, Jr.) [actor] (*né* William Frederick Cody, Sr., b. Winnipeg, Canada, 5 Jan 1891–24 Jan 1948 [57], Santa Monica CA; alkalosis). m. Virginia Kench (son, Bill, 1925–1989). (Biograph, 1912; Pathé; Universal.) "Bill Cody," *Variety,* 28 Jan 1948 ("silent film cowpoke star"). AMD, p. 75. AS, p. 241. BHD1, p. 111 (b. St. Paul MN). IFN, p. 58. Katz, p. 252 (*né* William Joseph Cody, Jr.). Truitt, p. 64. WWVC, p. 35. "Cody Starts Work on Next," *MPW,* 15 Nov 1924, 262. "Cody Signed for Five Years," *MPW,* 20 Dec 1924, 768. "Bill Cody's Lightnin'," *MPW,* 3 Jan 1925, 63. "Bill Cody," *MPW,* 9 Apr 1927, 550. Tom Waller, "Bill Cody," *MPW,* 7 May 1927, 20–21. "Bill Cody," *MPW,* 16 Jul 1927, 156. Jonathan Guyot Smith, "Bill Cody," *CI,* 133 (Jul 1986), 51–56, 63. George A. Katchmer, "Forgotten Cowboys and Cowgirls—Part XVIII," *CI,* 195 (Sep 1991), C9.

Cody, Gene [actor: Keystone Cop/stuntman/director/producer/writer] (*né* Gene Eubanks, b. Baltimore MD, 17 Mar 1894–10 Jul 1976 [82], Atlanta GA). (Last film: *Pay Day.*) "Gene (Cody) Eubanks," *Variety,* 4 Aug 1976, p. 63 (in *Birth of a Nation*). AS, p. 241. BHD1, p. 112.

Cody, Iron Eyes (son of **Thomas Longplume Cody**) [film/TV actor/technical advisor] (b. Oklahoma Territory OK, 5 Apr 1904?–1991 [87?]). m. Birdie Darkcloud, 1924 (d. ca. 1974). (Film debut: *The Massacre,* Griffith, 1912; final film: *Grayeagle,* American International, 1977.) AS, p. 241 (*né* Oakie Cody, b. 1907). Robert W. Phillips, "Iron Eyes Cody," *The Big Reel,* #304, Sep 1999, pp. 119–121 (includes filmography; may have been of Italian heritage, born in Brooklyn).

Cody, Lew, "The Butterfly Man" [actor] (*né* Louis Joseph Coté, b. Berlin NH, 22 Feb 1884–31 May 1934 [50], Beverly Hills CA; heart attack). m. **Dorothy Dalton** (d. 1972); **Mabel Normand**, 17 Sep 1926, Ventura CA (d. 1930). (Ince.) "Lew Cody, Actor, Dies in Sleep; Urbane 'Villain' of Silent Films Had Last Appearance on Screen Here in March; Married Mabel Normand; Creator of New Type in Pictures; Won Wide Following—Left Medical Studies for Stage," *NYT,* 1 Jun 1934, 23:1. "Lew Cody," *Variety,* 5 Jun 1934 (b. Waterville ME, 1887; age 47). AMD, p. 75. AS, p. 242. BHD1, p. 112 (b. Waterville ME, 1888). FFF, p. 58 (b. Waterville). FSS, p. 65. IFN, p. 58 (b. Waterville, 1888). MH, p. 103 (b. Waterville). Truitt, p. 64 (b. 1887). WWS, p. 78. Gladys Hall, "What Is a Playboy?," *MW,* 18 Oct 1924, 10, 28. Gladys Hall, "$ix Way$ to Attract a Woman; Famous male vampire of the screen reveals methods whereby weaker sex are certain to succumb to masculine charms," *MW,* 19 May 1925, 3. "King for a Day," *MPW,* 6 Jun 1925, 684. "Lew Cody, Screen Favorite, Signs M-G-M Contract," *MPW,* 29 Aug 1925, 938. "Mabel Normand and Lew Cody," *MPW,* 2 Oct 1926, 280. Florence Mae Jonstone, "A Villain Reforms," *Cinema Arts,* Feb 1927, 22–23, 42. "Lew Cody," *MPW,* 17 Dec 1927, 27. "Lew Cody Producer," *MPW,* 24 Dec 1927, 21. Gladys Hall, "The Code of Cody; Lew Chose to Face Starvation Rather Than Be the Butterfly Man," *MPC,* May 1929, 26, 84.

Cody, Thomas Longplume (father of **Iron Eyes Cody**) [technical advisor/assistant to Tim McCoy]. No data found. m. Robert W. Phillips, "Iron Eyes Cody," *The Big Reel,* #304, Sep 1999, pp. 119–121.

Cody, William [director] (b. 1889–24 Jun 1956 [67?], Los Angeles Co. CA). BHD2, p. 49.

Cody, Col. William F[rederick] "**Buffalo Bill**" (b. Scott County IA, 26 Feb 1846–10 Jan 1917 [71], Denver CO). m. Louisa Frederici, ca. 1865, St. Louis MO (22 years old). "Col. Wm. F. Cody, 'Buffalo Bill,' Dead; Body of Noted Plainsman and Scout to Lie in State in Colorado Capitol; End Came in 71st Year; One of Nation's Most Picturesque Characters Gained His First Fame as Indian Fighter," *NYT,* 11 Jan 1917, 15:3. "Col. William F. Cody," *Variety,* 12 Jan 1917. AMD, p. 75. AS, p. 242. BHD, p. 131. SD. "'Buffalo Bill's' Wife Denies His Charges; Never Tried to Poison Him, Says Mrs. Cody; Divorce Suit Testimony; Showman's Wife Tells How She and He Started Life Together—Says She Wants Reconciliation," *NYT,* 1 Mar 1905, 7:1 ("The Colonel went on the stage in 1874, and shortly after this [Ft. McPherson NB] he took us to Rochester, N.Y., where we lived for four years." Then they relocated to North Platte NB. Mrs. Cody denied she was ever intoxicated, as witnesses said. "She never drank liquor except for medicinal purposes, and never used profane language." She declared that she still loved Cody and desired a reconciliation, "but I think he ought to retract the poisoning accusation." Mrs. Cody read a letter from her deceased daughter Arta, written three years before she died, in which she wrote that her father's divorce suit had broken her heart.) "Col. Cody Will Not Relent; In Divorce Suit Trial He Rejects Reconciliation Offered," *NYT,* 8 Mar 1905, 9:3 ("...today [7 Mar] declared that he could not accept any reconciliation with Mrs. Cody. This declaration was made as the result...of Mrs. Cody having charged him with being the murderer of their daughter Arta, and announcing publicly that she would denounce him over her grave."). "No Divorce for Buffalo Bill; Court Calls Mrs. Cody Overindulgent Wife and Mother," *NYT,* 24 Mar 1905, 1:4 (Sheridan WY, 23 Mar. He lost his suit for divorce. The poisoning was supposed to have taken place on or about 26 Dec 1900; the evidence showed Mrs. Cody was trying to revive plaintiff from a state of intoxication, "and administered not poison but remedies which she deemed beneficial to him.... The poisoning of his pet dogs was accidental..." Cody's counsel successfully requested 60 days to file a petition for a rehearing.). "Buffalo Bill Loses Suit," *MPW,* 29 Jun 1912, 1238. "Buffalo Bill and Pawnee Bill Company to Sue Col. Cody and Maj. Lillie," *MPW,* 20 Jul 1912, 234. "Charlie Evans [obituary]," *Pittsburgh Post-Gazette,* 9 Aug 1997, A-10.1 (d. 5 Aug 1997 [89], North Platte NB. Evans was a Buffalo Bill look-alike who spent 35 years portraying Cody, including likenesses on the Nebraska highway map, the covers of telephone books, and in national commercials).

Coe, Arthur J. [producer]. No data found. AMD, p. 75. "Joins Sennett," *MPW,* 19 Nov 1921, 331.

Coe, Charles Francis [scenarist]. No data found. FDY, p. 421.

Coffee, Lenore J. [title and screenwriter/playwright/novelist] (b. San Francisco CA, 13 Jul 1896–2 Jul 1984 [87], Woodland Hills CA). m. **William J**[oyce] **Cowen**, ca. 1924. (d. ca. 1963) *Story-line: Recollections of a Hollywood Screenwriter.* (MGM; WB; Paramount.) "Lenore Coffee," *Variety,* 11 Jul 1984. AMD, p. 75. AS, p. 242. BHD2, p. 50. "Lenore Coffee Signed," *MPW,* 25 Jul 1925, 453. "Coffee Writes Story," *MPW,* 1 Jan 1927, 30. "Miss Coffee Signs," *MPW,* 7 May 1927, 39. "Lenore Coffee, Writer of Film Romances, Dies," *LA Times,* Sect. IV, 5 Jul 1984, p. 7 (wrote her first scenario for Clara Kimball Young in 1919; last script, *Cash McCall,* 1960). BHD, p. 131. FDY, p. 421. Katz, pp. 252–53.

Coffin, Charles Hayden [stage/film actor] (b. Manchester, England, 22 Apr 1862–8 Dec 1935 [73], Kensington, England [extrait de deecès no. 75/1935]). "Charles Hayden Coffin," *Variety,* 11 Dec 1935, p. 70. AS, p. 242 (Hayden Coffin). BHD1, p. 112.

Coffin, Ray [scenarist/actor] (b. Cherokee IA, 1890?–3 Mar 1942 [52], Dallas TX). (Kalem; Edison; Vitagraph; Fox.) "Ray Coffin," *Variety,* 11 Mar 1942 ("in the picture business since the early silents"). AMD, p. 75. AS, p. 242. "Ray Coffin Heads the Wampas with Reputation as Writer," *MPW,* 5 Mar 1927, 32.

Coffyn, Frank [cinematographer] (b. 1878?–10 Dec 1960 [82], Palo Alto CA). m. Mabel. "Frank Coffyn, 82, Early Flier, Dies; Original Member of Wright Brothers Exhibition Team Mapped Airmail Routes," *NYT,* 11 Dec 1960, 88:6 ("Mr. Coffyn took the first motion pictures from an aircraft. They were used as newsreels. Later he helped to develop an electric motion-picture camera for use in planes."). AS, p. 242 (Frank Coffy).

Cogan, Fanny Hay [actress] (*née* Hay?, b. Philadelphia PA, 1865–17 May 1929 [63], New York NY). "Fanny Hay Cogan," *Variety,* 22 May 1929 (d. 18 May). AS, p. 242 (d. 19 May). BHD, p. 131. IFN, p. 59. Truitt, p. 64.

Cogan, James P. [scenarist] (d. 21 Sep 1921; heart attack). AMD, p. 75. BHD, p. 132; BHD2, p. 50. "James P. Cogan with Famous Players," *MPW,* 8 Nov 1913, 598. "James P. Cogan, Premier Scenario Editor," *MPW,* 4 Dec 1915, 1838. "Obituary," *MPW,* 8 Oct 1921, 647.

Cogdell, Josephine [actress: Sennett Bathing Beauty] (b. 1901?–2 May 1969 [68], New York NY). AS, p. 242. BHD, p. 132. IFN, p. 59. Truitt, p. 65.

Coghlan, Charles F. (nephew and adopted son of **Rose Coghlan**) [actor/director/producer] (b. England–d. 16 Mar 1972, Hershey PA). "Charles F. Coghlan," *Variety,* 29 Mar 1972 (d. 18 Mar). AS, p. 242 (d. 18 Mar). BHD, p. 132. IFN, p. 59.

Coghlan, Gertrude Evelyn (niece of **Rose Coghlan**) [actress] (b. Hertfordshire, England, 1 Feb 1876–11 Sep 1952 [76], Bayside, LI NY). m. Augustus Pitou (d. 1915). "Gertrude Coghlan," *Variety,* 17 Sep 1952 (no age given). AMD, p. 76. AS, p. 242. BHD, p. 132. IFN, p. 59. SD. "Gertrude Coghlan Joins Selig," *MPW,* 9 Aug 1913, 641. "A New Leading Lady," *MPW,* 27 Sep 1913, 1371. "Gertrude Coghlan with Selig Co.," *MPW,* 11 Oct 1913, 135.

Coghlan, Katherine (mother of Junior Coghlan) (b. CT, 3 Sep 1889–20 Sep 1965 [76], Los Angeles CA; cancer). "Katherine Coghlan," *Variety,* 13 Oct 1965. AS, p. 242. BHD, p. 132. IFN, p. 59. Truitt, p. 65.

Coghlan, Rose (aunt of **Gertrude** and **Charles Coghlan**) [actress] [extra, 1919–20] (*née* Rosamond Marie Coghlan, b. Peterborough, England, 18 Mar 1851–2 Apr 1932 [81], Westchester [Harrison] NY; cerebral hemorrhage). m. (1) Clinton J. Edgerly; (2) John T. Sullivan (d. 1904). "Rose Coghlan Dies; Famous Actress; She Succumbs in Westchester Country Retreat After Long Illness at Age of 81; On Stage a Half Century; Later Appearance in 'Deburau' in 1921—Scored Success in All Departments Except Tragedy," *NYT,* 5 Apr 1932, 23:1 (b. 18 Mar 1851). "Rose Coghlan," *Variety,* 5 Apr 1932 (age 80). AMD, p. 76. AS, p. 242. BHD1, p. 112. IFN, p. 59. SD. Truitt, p. 65. "Rose Coghlan," *MPW,* 29 May 1915, 1413. "Rose Coghlan Free of Debt," *NYDM,* 21 Jul 1915, 7:1 (her petition of 4 Feb 1915 showed liabilities of $9,538 and assets of $100. Now discharged from bankruptcy.).

Cogley, Nick [actor/director] (*né* Nicholas P.J. Cogley, b. New York NY, 1869–20 May 1936 [67], Santa Monica CA). "Nicholas Cogley," *Variety,* 27 May 1936. AS, pp. 242–43. BHD1, p. 112; BHD2, p. 50. IFN, p. 59. Truitt, p. 65.

Cohan, George M[ichael] (father of **Georgette Cohan**) [actor/singer/dancer/composer/producer/writer] (b. Providence RI, 3 Jul 1878–5 Nov 1942 [64], New York NY; cancer [Death Certificate Index No. 21986]). Ward Morehouse, *George M. Cohan, Prince of the American Theater* (New York: J.B. Lippincott Co., 1943). m. Ethel Levey; Agnes Nolan. (Film debut: *Broadway Jones,* Artcraft, 1917.) "George M. Cohan, 64, Dies at Home Here; Veteran Actor, Producer and Playwright Called Himself 'a Song-and-Dance Man'; Trouper of Stage at 8; 'Original Yankee Doodle Boy' Composed 'Over There' and 'It's a Grand Old Flag,'" *NYT,* 6 Nov 1942, 20:1 (b. 4 Jul). AMD, p. 76. AS, p. 243. BHD1, p. 112; BHD2, p. 50. GSS, pp. 72–73. "George M. Cohan Is Laid to Rest Just 45 Minutes from Broadway," *Variety,* 11 Nov 1942. IFN, p. 59. Katz, p. 253. Spehr, p. 122. Truitt, p. 65. "George M. Cohan to Play for Artcraft," *MPW,* 18 Nov 1916, 990. "DeMille to Produce Cohan Subject," *MPW,* 23 Dec 1916, 1787. "Cohan to Produce 'Broadway Jones,'" *MPW,* 23 Dec 1916, 1809. "George M. Cohan," *MPW,* 24 Feb 1917, 1187.

Cohan, Georgette (daughter of **George M. Cohan**) [actress]. No data found. AMD, p. 76. "Georgette Cohan to Appear in Pictures," *MPW,* 4 Oct 1919, 68.

Cohen, Bennett R. [scenarist] (b. Trinidad CO, 28 Aug 1890–10 Jun 1964 [73], Los Angeles CA). . BHD2, p. 50. FDY, p. 421.

Cohen, Emmanuel [production manager] (b. Hartford CT, 5 Aug 1892–9 Sep 1977 [85], New York NY). m. Madeline Bender. (Newsreel editor, Pathé, 1914–26; Paramount, 1927, V-P, 1932–35.) "Emanuel Cohen, Officer of Paramount Pictures," *NYT,* 11 Sep 1977, 36:6. "Emanuel Cohen," *Variety,* 14 Sep 1977, p. 111. AMD, p. 76. BHD2, p. 50. "Cohen Now Head of Paramount's Short Features," *MPW,* 12 Feb 1927, 475. "The Story of the News Reel," *MPW,* 26 Mar 1927, 322.

Cohen, Harry J. [production manager/executive] (b. 1899–15 Dec 1952 [53?], Los Angeles CA). AMD, p. 76. BHD2, p. 50. "Harry J. Cohen," *MPW,* 23 May 1914, 1099.

Cohen, Max [title writer] (b. Pittsburgh PA, 20 Nov 1889–9 Dec 1935 [56], Los Angeles CA). BHD2, p. 50.

Cohen, Meyer [executive] (b. 1872–28 Dec 1937 [65], Dallas TX). BHD2, p. 50.

Cohen, Octavus Roy [scenarist] (b.

Charleston SC, 26 Jun 1891–6 Jan 1959 [67], Los Angeles CA). "Octavus Roy Cohen," *Variety,* 14 Jan 1959. AMD, p. 76. AS, p. 243 (d. 1958). BHD2, p. 50. IFN, p. 59. SD, p. 263/ "Octavius Roy Cohen Becomes Goldwyn Pictures Author," *MPW,* XLI, 26 Jul 1919, 496. "Cohen Completing First Photoplay for Goldwyn," *MPW,* 20 Sep 1919, 1831. "Colored Players in Films," *MPS,* 13 May 1921, 23 (tales similar to those by Cohen and Joel Chandler Harris were to be produced by the Mount Olympus Distributing Corp., chartered in Delaware, "and the cast to appear in each [26 productions] will be made up entirely of colored players." The MODC was housed in the *World* Tower Bldg., NYC).

Cohen, Sammy [actor] (b. Minneapolis MN, 8 Dec 1902–30 May 1981 [78], Santa Monica CA). (Fox.) AMD, p. 76. AS, p. 243 (d. 1979). BHD1, p. 112. "Sammy Cohen," *MPW,* 18 Jun 1927, 484.

Cohill, William Wright [actor/casting director] (b. PA, 6 Dec 1882–28 Apr 1931 [48], Garberville CA). m. Maybelle van Tassell, ca. 1907. "William S. Cohill," *Variety,* 6 May 1931. AMD, p. 76. AS, p. 243. BHD, p. 132. "New Casting Director," *MPW,* 25 Nov 1922, 330.

Cohl, Emile [animator] (*né* Emile Eugène Jean Louis Courtet, b. Paris, France, 4 Jan 1857–20 Jan 1938 [81], Villejuif, France; died in a fire). (Eclair, Ft. Lee NJ.) Donald Crafton, *Emil Cohl, Caricature, and Film* (Princeton NJ: Princeton University Press, 1990). "Emile Cohl; Frenchman Credited with First Animated Cartoon," *NYT,* 22 Jan 1938, 15:3. "Emile Cohl," *Variety,* 26 Jan 1938. AS, p. 243 (d. 27 Jan). BHD2, p. 50 (d. 21 Jan). Katz, p. 253. Waldman, p. 58.

Cohn, Alfred A. [title writer/scenarist] (b. Freeport IL, 1880?– 3 Feb 1951 [71], Los Angeles CA). "A.A. Cohn, Wrote 'The Jazz Singer'; Veteran Newsman and Screen Author Dies at 71—Headed Police in Los Angeles," *NYT,* 5 Feb 1951, 23:5. "Alfred A. Cohn," *Variety,* 7 Feb 1951 ("He began to write for the screen in 1918."). AS, p. 243. BHD2, p. 50. FDY, pp. 421, 441. IFN, p. 59.

Cohn, Ben [property man] (d. Apr 1926, Los Angeles CA; from burns "by an explosion of flaming torches, used during the filming of scenes with the Max Gold comedy company."). (Fox.) "Property Man Killed," *Variety,* 28 Apr 1926. BHD2, p. 50.

Cohn, Harry (brother of **Jack Cohn**) [executive/producer] (b. New York NY, 23 Jul 1891 [Birth Certificate Index No. 25447]–27 Feb 1958 [66], Phoenix AZ; heart attack). m. Joan Perry. Bob Thomas, *King Cohn: The Life and Times of Harry Cohn* (New York: G.P. Putnam's Sons, 1967). "Harry Cohn Dead; Movie Executive; Columbia President Since Its Founding Decorated Office with Studio's 45 'Oscars,'" *NYT,* 28 Feb 1958, 21:1; "Hollywood Pays Tribute to Cohn; Funeral for President of Columbia Held at Studio—1,500 Attend Rites," CVII, 3 Mar 1958, 27:2. "Death Strikes 'Last of Studio Czars'; Harry Cohn a Showman Who Knew Scripts, Stars, Editing and Everybody Else's Business," *Variety,* 5 Mar 1958. AMD, p. 76. AS, p. 243. BHD2 p. 50. IFN, p. 59. SD. "Harry Cohn—Author!," *MPW,* 18 Jul 1925, 310. "Harry Cohn Discusses Present Independent Situation Points," *MPW,* 10 Oct 1925, 476. "Harry Cohn in from Coast," *MPW,* 21 Nov 1925, 234.

Cohn, Jack (brother of **Harry Cohn**) [film editor/producer/executive] (b. New York NY, 27 Oct 1889–8 Dec 1956 [67], New York NY; pulmonary embolism). m. Jeanette Lesser. (Imp.) "Jack Cohn Dies; Once Film Editor at $7 a Week," *Variety,* 12 Dec 1956. AMD, p. 76. AS, p. 243. BHD2, p. 51. IFN, p. 59. SD. "Jack Cohn," *MPW,* 27 Feb 1915, 1298. "Jack Cohn Starts In as a Producer," *MPW,* 12 Apr 1919, 231. "Screen Supplement and Screen Snapshots Merge," *MPW,* 28 Aug 1920, 1167.

Cohn, Joseph Judson [scenarist/editor/founding member of AMPAS] (b. New York NY, 3 Dec 1895–12 Jan 1996 [100], Beverly Hills CA; heart attack in his sleep). (Fox Film Co., 1915; Goldwyn; MGM.) Chris Dray, "Joseph Judson Cohn," *Variety,* 22 Jan 1996, 111:3. AS, p. 243. BHD2, p. 50.

Cohn, Martin G. [editor] (b. New York NY, 5 May 1893–19 Nov 1953 [60], Los Angeles CA; heart attack). "Martin G. Cohn," *Variety,* 25 Nov 1953 (in film industry for 40 years). BHD2, p. 51.

Cohn, Morris [extra actor] (d. 1921, Redondo Beach CA; drowned during filming of *The Money Master*). No data found. AMD, p. 76. "Obituary," *MPW,* 19 Mar 1921, 258.

Coit, Sam [actor] (b. Bethlehem CT, 17 Nov 1871?–1 Jan 1933 [61], New York NY; pneumonia). "Sam Coit," *Variety,* 10 Jan 1933. AS, p. 243 (d. 2 Jan). BHD, p. 132. IFN, p. 59.

Colbert, Claudette [film/stage/TV actress] (*née* Lily Claudette Chauchoin, b. Saint-Mande, France, 13 Sep 1903 [extrait de naissance no. 171/1903]–30 Jul 1996 [92], Bridgetown, Barbados; heart attack). m. (1) Norman Foster, 1928–35; (2) Dr. Joel Pressman, 1935 (d. 1968). (Stage debut, 1923; film debut: *For the Love of Mike,* 1927; AA for *It Happened One Night,* Columbia, 1934; Paramount; last film: *Parrish,* 1961.) Eric Pace, "Claudette Colbert, Unflappable Heroine of Screwball Comedies, Is Dead at 92," *NYT,* 31 Jul 1996, D21:1. Richard Natale, "Claudette Colbert," *Variety,* 5 Aug 1996, 58:1 (in 64 films; married to Foster "although they never lived together"). "Actress Claudette Colbert Dies at 92," *The Washington Post,* 119, 31 Jul 1996, B4:1 (she refused to write her memoirs: "What am I going to say? I married a wonderful doctor, and I was very happy—period.") Stephen Hunter, "Claudette Colbert; Breezy, likable, sexy, a bit harebrained," *Pittsburgh Post-Gazette,* 31 Jul 1996, B-4:1. AMD, p. 76. AS, p. 244 (d. Speighstown, Barbados). BHD1, p. 112. "Kane Signs Miss Colbert," *MPW,* 18 Jun 1927, 474.

Colbourne, Maurice [actor] (b. Cuddington, Cheshire, England, 24 Sep 1894–22 Sep 1965 [70], Perelle, Isle of Guernsey Channel Islands). BHD1, p. 113 (b. Ouddington). IFN, p. 59.

Colburn, Carrie [actress] (b. 1858–23 May 1932 [73], New York NY). "Carrie Colburn," *Variety,* 21 May 1932 (silent character actress). AS, p. 244. BHD, p. 132. IFN, p. 59. Truitt, p. 65.

Colby, Charles [actor] (b. 1868?–31 Oct 1913 [45], San Francisco CA). AS, p. 244. BHD1, p. 605. "Charles Colby," *Variety,* 7 Nov 1913. George A. Katchmer, "Forgotten Cowboys and Cowgirls—Part XIII," *CI,* 190 (Apr 1991), C6.

Colby, Herbert [actor] (b. 1839–6 Feb 1912 [72?], Brooklyn NY; possible suicide by gas inhalation). "Herbert Colby," *Variety,* 10 Feb 1912, p. 16 (age 45–50). AS, p. 244 (b. 1868; d. 9 Feb). BHD, p. 132.

Colcord, Mabel [actress] (b. San Francisco CA, 13 Aug 1873–6 Jun 1952 [79?], Los Angeles CA). "Mabel Colcord," *Variety,* 11 Jun 1952. AS, p. 244. BHD1, p. 113. IFN, p. 59.

Coldewey, Anthony W. [scenarist] (b. Louisville KY, 1 Aug 1887–29 Jan 1963 [75], Los Angeles CA). . AMD, p. 76. BHD2, p. 51. FDY, p. 421. "L-KO Has New Scenario Editor," *MPW,* 12 Oct 1918, 206. "Coldewey Returns to Universal," *MPW,* 7 Jun 1919, 1486. "Anthony Coldewey Signs with Metropolitan," *MPW,* 22 May 1926, 320. "Coldeway Signed to Warner Contract," *MPW,* 22 Jan 1927, 272. "Anthony Coldeway," *MPW,* 3 Sep 1927, 24.

Cole, Alonzo Deen [scenarist/director/producer] (b. St. Paul MN, 22 Feb 1897–31 Mar 1971 [74], Glendale CA). BHD2, p. 51.

Cole, Charles "Slim" [actor]. No data found. (Vitagraph.) George A. Katchmer, "Forgotten Cowboys and Cowgirls—XVIII," *CI,* 195 (Sep 1991), 44.

Cole, Frederick [actor] (b. Los Angeles CA, 21 May 1901–19 Sep 1964 [63], Los Angeles CA). "Fred Cole," *Variety,* 23 Sep 1964. AS, p. 244. BHD, p. 132. IFN, p. 59. Truitt, p. 65.

Cole, Thornton [actor] (d. 1915; heart failure). (With Biograph five years; Klaw & Erlanger.) W.E. Wing, "Along the Pacific Coast," *NYDM,* 10 Mar 1915, 27:1.

Coleby, A.E. [actor/director/scenarist] (b. London, England–d. 15 Jul 1930). AS, p. 244. BHD2, p. 51.

Coleman, Brysis [scenarist]. No data found. FDY, p. 421.

Coleman, Charles C. "Buddy" [actor] (b. Sydney, Australia, 22 Dec 1885–7 Mar 1951 [65], Woodland Hills CA; pulmonary embolism). "Charles Coleman," *Variety,* 14 Mar 1951. AS, p. 244. BHD1, p. 113. IFN, p. 59. Katz, p. 255.

Coleman, Cherie [actress]. No data found. AMD, p. 76. "Cherie Coleman," *MPW,* 17 Mar 1917, 1785.

Coleman, Claudia [actress] (b. Hyram GA, 7 Jul 1886–17 Aug 1938 [52], Los Angeles CA). "Claudia Coleman," *Variety,* 24 Aug 1938 ("...she had been working in pictures for the past five years"; age 49). AS, p. 244 (d. 18 Aug). BHD1, p. 113. IFN, p. 59.

Coleman, Don [cowboy actor] (b. Sheridan WY, 15 Jan 1893–16 Dec 1985 [92], Willits CA). (Began 1924.) AS, p. 245 (b. 1898; d. LA CA). BHD1, p. 113.

Coleman, Harry [actor/vaudevillian] (b. 1883?–30 Jan 1928 [44], New York NY; pneumonia). m. Gladys Hart. "Harry Coleman," *Variety,* 1 Feb 1928. AMD, p. 76. "Coleman Signed for 'Sentimental Tommy,'" *MPW,* 2 Oct 1920, 637.

Coleman, John J. [writer/director]. No data found. AMD, p. 76. "Coleman Attends Masonic Council," *MPW,* 19 Sep 1914, 1650. John J. Coleman, "The Ultimate Triumph of the Single Reel Production," *MPW,* 17 Oct 1914, 325.

Coleman, Majel [actress] (b. OH, 22 Feb 1903–27 Jul 1980 [77], Paramount CA). (De Mille.) BHD1, p. 605. "Stars Who Will Shine," *MW,* 1 Aug 1925, 37 (others were Lawrence Gray, Evelyn Pierce, Hugh Allan, Estelle Clark, Richard Arlen, Sally Rand and William Boyd).

Coleman, Richard H. [actor/minstrel man: Primrose & West; Dockstader; *et al.*] (b. 1862?–4 Oct 1932 [70], Weehauken NJ). m. "Richard H. Coleman," *Variety,* 11 Oct 1932.

Coleman, Vincent (nephew of Shakespearean actor Richard Coleman) [stage/film actor] (aka Willie B. Coleman, b. LA, 16 Feb 1900–26 Oct 1971 [71], Los Angeles CA). AMD, p. 77. AS, p. 245 (b, NYC). MH, p. 103. MSBB, p. 1044 (b. NY, 1897). WWS, p. 142. "Vincent Coleman Joins Goldwyn," *MPW,* 29 Nov 1919, 543. Capitola Williams Ashworth, "The Distinguishing Mark," *MPC,* Oct 1921, 46–47, 88. Hariette Underhill, "He's an Actor, But—; Vincent Coleman doesn't look like one and that is part of the secret of his success," *Picture-Play Magazine,* Jun 1923, 85–86.

Coleman, William Robert [director]. No data found. AMD, p. 77. "Coleman to Direct First Meredith Picture," *MPW,* 30 Jun 1917, 2131.

Colenbrander, Col. Johann W.C.B. [actor] (d. Africa, 2 Mar 1918). BHD, p. 132.

Coles, Russell [actor] (b. TN, 14 May 1909–26 Sep 1960 [51], Los Angeles CA). AS, p. 245 (d. 23 Sep). BHD1, p. 114.

Colin, Jean [actress] (b. Brighton, England, 24 Mar 1905–7 Mar 1989 [83], London, England). AS, p. 245. BHD1, p. 114.

Coll, Owen G[riffith] [actor] (b. 1878?–7 Feb 1960 [81], Long Island City [Queens] NY [Death Certificate Index No. 1704; M.E. Case No. 470]). "Owen G. Coll," *Variety,* 10 Feb 1960. AS, p. 245. IFN, p. 59.

Collen, Henri [actor] (b. 1878–25 Jul 1924 [46?], Paris, France). "Henri Collen," *Variety,* 3 Sep 1924, p. 2. BHD, p. 132.

Collett, Lorraine Petersen (b. 9 Dec 1892–30 Mar 1983 [90], Fresno CA). BHD, p. 132.

Collette, John [scenic artist] (d. 19 Nov 1918, Los Angeles CA). BHD2, p. 51.

Collier, Constance [stage/film actress/scenarist] (*née* Laura Constance Hardie, b. Windsor Berks, England, 22 Jan 1878–25 Apr 1955 [77], New York NY [Death Certificate Index No. 9453]). m. **Julian L'Estrange** (d. 1918). *Harlequinade: The Story of My Life* (London: John Lane, 1929). (Griffith.) "Constance Collier, Actress, Dies; Leading Dramatic Coach Was 75; She Made Her Debut at Age of 4 in England—Cited by Shakespearean Theatre," *NYT,* 26 Apr 1955, 29:4 (b. 1880); "Rites for Constance Collier," *NYT,* 27 Apr 1955, 31:4. "Constance Collier," *Variety,* 27 Apr 1955 (b. 1880; age 75). AMD, p. 77. AS, p. 246. BHD1, p. 114; BHD2, p. 51. GSS, pp. 74–76. IFN, p. 59. Truitt, p. 66. "Constance Collier Signed; Oliver Morosco Will Present Star in Subject to Be Especially Written," *NYDM,* 23 Oct 1915, 25:4 (to debut in *Tongues of Men*). "Constance Collier in Second Morosco Subject," *MPW,* 12 Feb 1916, 940.

Collier, William "Buster," Jr. (son of **Paula Marr**; step son of **William Collier, Sr.**, adopted 12 Sep 1914) [stage/film actor] (*né* Charles F. Gall, Jr., b. New York NY, 12 Feb 1902–5 Feb 1987 [84], San Francisco CA; arteriosclerosis [Death Certificate No. 0166 3 87 380830]). . m. Marie "Stevie" Stevens, 31 Dec 1934 (1909–1981). (Ince; Paramount.) (Film debut: *The Bugle Call,* 1916). AMD, p. 77. AS, p. 246. BHD1, p. 114. FSS, p. 66. Katz, p. 256. "Buster Collier," *Variety,* 18 Feb 1987 ("at one time a leading romantic actor of silent films"). "Buster Collier in 'Tom Sawyer,'" *MPW,* 11 Aug 1917, 921. "William Collier, Jr., in Lasky Picture," *MPW,* 24 Apr 1920, 593. Cal York, "Plays and Players," *Photoplay,* Mar 1921, 80 ("Watch 'Buster' Collier. This only son [sic] of the celebrated comedian, William Collier, is, some day, going to be one of the great American actors or we don't know an embryo genius when we see one...Some producer ought to sign young Collier to a life contract right now, before all the other producers get wise to his talents." Collier had been filming *The Heart of Maryland,* Vitagraph, in Natchez MS.). "'Hottentot' Liked by Willie C.," *MPW,* 13 Jan 1923, 159. "William Collier, Jr., in 'Pleasure Mad,'" *MPW,* 1 Sep 1923, 159. Joan Cross, "The Heart of Young William Collier; Revealing a Bitter Struggle for Success," *MW,* 20 Jun 1925, 19–20, 45–46. June Lee, "Dan Cupid's Bulletin Board," *Paris and Hollywood,* Oct 1926, 31 ("escorting Mary Hay about New York these days. Buster was Mary's very first beau before Mary ever met Richard Barthelmess."). "William Collier, Jr.," *MPW,* 7 May 1927, 25. "Dolores Costello's New Leading Man," *MPW,* 20 Aug 1927, 534. "'Buster' Collier to Wed," *MPW,* 5 Nov 1927, 10 (Dorothy Vincentella McCarthy). "Girls, Pick Your Chiselers," *Picture Play,* Dec 1927, 51, 106. Roberta Ridgely, "Wm. (Buster) Collier Jr,; Reminiscences of 'old' Hollywood, its male idols and female sirens, from a retired star who knew them all," *Palm Springs Magazine,* Feb 1976. William J. Mann, *Wisecracker; The Life and Times of William Haines, Hollywood's First Openly Gay Star* (NY: Viking Penguin, 1998) (Haines, who died in 1973, mentioned Mrs. Collier in his will. "Stevie Collier, 'a warm and glorious friend besides being a refreshing and capable camp,' received a bronze spread-eagle clock on a marble base. Billy wrote the clock 'has always been in my bedroom where she would never come. Alas!'"). (Mrs. Chatty Eliason [daughter] of Newberg OR, verified data on the Colliers.)

Collier, William, Sr. (step-father of **William Collier, Jr.**) [stage/film actor] (*né* William Morenus, b. New York NY, 12 Nov 1864–13 Jan 1944 [79], Beverly Hills CA; pneumonia [Death Certificate No. 44-004143 cites birth year as 1864]). . (1920 census, b. 1867.) m. (1) Louise Allen (1875–1909); (2) **Paula Marr** (b.1885 [Death Certificate No. 7034 22285 cites 23 Sep 1883]-1960), 10 May 1910. "William Collier, Noted Actor, Dies; Stage and Screen Favorite More Than 60 Years Is Stricken on Coast, 77," *NYT,* 14 Jan 1944, 19:1. Jack Pulaski, "William Collier, Comedian-Author, 77, Dies on Coast After Long Illness," *Variety,* 19 Jan 1944. AMD, p. 77. AS, p. 246. BHD1, p. 114 (b. 1866). IFN, p. 59. Katz, pp. 255–56. MH, p. 103. Truitt, p. 66. "Flying Trip for Actors; Collier and Co. to Go to London for Four Weeks," *NYT,* 12 Apr 1905, 9:3 (Daniel Frohman sent him over in *The Dictator* for four weeks on the steamer *Majestic* on 19 Apr. He was to play at the Comedy Theatre from 3 May 31 May, and return 3 Jun on the *St. Louis* for New York, to open at the Hudson Theatre on 12 Jun. The trip "will consume, in all, fifty-three days."). "Collier with Triangle; Legitimate Star Closes Contract Calling for Two Years' Work Under Sennett," *NYDM,* 15 Sep 1915, 25:1 (to leave NY for LA on 1 Nov). J. Van Cartmell, "Along the Pacific Coast," *NYDM,* 13 Nov 1915, 31:1 (he was thoroughly fatigued from a long journey across the continent "but glad to be in the land of sunshine"; to debut at Triangle-Keystone. "By the way, this is Collier's first appearance before the camera. We expect great things, Willie."). J. Van Cartmell, "Film News from the Coast...," *NYDM,* 20 Nov 1915, 35:1 ("Collier succumbed to the persuasion of Producer Ince on condition that he receive a salary which according to all reports is to be a record breaker."). Alfred A. Cohn, "What They Really Get NOW!; A Story of Photoplay Salaries and the Conditions Governing Them," *Photoplay Magazine,* Mar 1916, 27–30. "William Collier, Popular Comedian, Presented by Selznick in a Feature, 'The New Butler,'" *MPW,* 17 Apr 1920, 394. Doris Curran, "The Modern Parable of the Prodigal Son; In the 1925 Version [*The Wanderer*], Willie Collier, Jr., Returns a Success," *MPC,* Oct 1925, 38–39, 83. Diana Barrymore and Gerold Frank, *Too Much, Too Soon* (NY: Henry Holt & Co., 1957) (in 1951 Diana Barrymore and her third husband, Robert Wilcox, toured Australia. The newspapers "recalled that Daddy [John Barrymore] had toured Australia forty-five years before with William Collier in *The Dictator.* They remembered him well, especially since he and Collier had been arrested one night for 'laughing too loudly in the street'" (p. 283). Roberta Ridgely, "Wm. (Buster) Collier, Jr.; Reminiscences of 'old' Hollywood, its male idols and female sirens, from a retired star who knew them all," *Palm Springs Magazine,* Feb 1976. Gene Vazzana, "William Collier, Sr.; Talented, Magnetic, and Amiable," *CI,* 221 (Nov 1993), 32 *et passim.*

Collings, Pierre [scenarist] (b. Nova Scotia, Canada, 1902?–21 Dec 1937 [35], No. Hollywood CA; pneumonia following nervous prostration). "Pierre Collings," *Variety,* 29 Dec 1937 (began at age 17 at Brunton Studios). AS, p. 246. BHD2, p. 51. FDY, p. 421. IFN, p. 60.

Collins, Arthur [director/producer] (b. 1866–13 Jan 1932 [65?], Surrey, England). BHD2, p. 51.

Collins, C[harles] **E.** [actor] (b. Anderson County, MO, 23 Jul 1873–15 Apr 1951 [77], Los Angeles CA). AS, p. 246. BHD, p. 132. IFN, p. 60.

Collins, Eddie [actor] (*né* Edward Bernard Collins, b. Jersey City NJ, 30 Jan 1883–1 Sep 1940 [57], Arcadia CA; heart attack). m. Florence Wilmot. "Eddie Collins," *Variety,* 4 Sep 1940 (age 56). AS, p. 246. IFN, p. 60. SD.

Collins, Eddy [actor] (*né* Edward Collins, b. 1866–17 Dec 1916 [50?], Los Angeles CA; suicide). AS, p. 246. BHD, p. 132.

Collins, Frederick L. [producer]. No data found. AMD, p. 77. "McClure Pictures Well Underway," *MPW,* 19 Aug 1916, 1221. "Collins on War and Pictures," *MPW,* 28 Apr 1917, 646. "Frederick L. Collins Sails for Europe," *MPW,* 5 Apr 1919, 47.

Collins, G. Pat [actor] (*né* George Percy Collins, b. Brooklyn NY, 16 Dec 1895–5 Aug 1959 [63], Los Angeles CA; cancer). m. **Billie Rhodes** (d. 1988). "G. Pat Collins," *Variety,* 12 Aug 1959 (age 64). AS, p. 246. BHD1, p. 114. IFN, p. 60. Truitt, p. 66.

Collins, Harry [publicist]. m. **Rita Hoyt**, 1927. No data found. (Fox.) AMD, p. 174. "Hoyt—Collins," *MPW,* 31 Dec 1927, 25.

Collins, Jack [scenarist/title writer] (d. 23 Aug 1926, Los Angeles CA). AS, p. 246. BHD2, p. 51.

Collins, John Hancock [director/scenarist] (b. New York NY, 31 Dec 1889–23 Oct 1918 [28], New York NY [Death Certificate No. 30772]; pneumonia and influenza). m. **Viola Dana**, 1915 (d. 1987). (Began with Edison as an errand boy, 1905.) "John Hancock Collins," *Variety,* 1 Nov 1918. AMD, p. 77. AS, p. 247. BHD2, p. 51. SD. "John Hancock Collins," *MPW,* 13 Dec 1913, 1263. "Collins New Edison Director," *MPW,* 8 Aug 1914,

840. "John Hancock Collins," *MPW,* 24 Jul 1915, 629. "Briefs of Biography; He's Only Twenty-three," *NYDM,* 4 Aug 1915, 25:1 (first film as director: *Jim's Vindication,* 1914). "Collins, Edison Director, Holds Unique Record," *MPN,* 28 Aug 1915, 64. "Collins to Direct Viola Dana," *MPW,* 27 May 1916, 1500. "John Hancock Collins Wins New Laurels," *MPW,* 18 Nov 1916, 1026. "John Collins, Director of Metro's 'Blue Jeans,' a Man with Wisdom," *MPW,* 15 Dec 1917, 1639. "Obituary," *MPW,* 9 Nov 1918, 651. Wheeler Winston Dixon, "The Curious Case of John Collins," *CI,* 261 (Mar 1997), C8-C11 (includes filmogtraphy).

Collins, Jose, "The Maid of the Mountains" (daughter of **Lottie Collins**) [Ziegfeld Follies/film actress] (*née* Josephine Collins, b. London, England, 23 May 1887–6 Dec 1958 [71], London, England). m. (1) Leslie Chatfield; (2) Sir Robert Innes-Ker; (3) G.B. Kirkland. *The Maid of the Mountains* (1932). (Film debut: *The Impostor,* World, 1915.) "Miss Jose Collins, British Stage Star," *NYT,* 7 Dec 1958, 88:8. "Jose Collins," *Variety,* 12 Dec 1958. AMD, p. 77. AS, p. 247. BHD1, p. 114. IFN, p. 60. SD. "Josie Collins on Screen," *NYDM,* 16 Jun 1915, 21:1 (to debut in *The Imposters*). "Jose Collins," *MPW,* 26 Jun 1915, 2075. "Equitable's Latest Star; Jose Collins Signs Contract to Appear in Equitable Release at Early Date," *NYDM,* 29 Sep 1915, 24:4 ("She will begin work within a fortnight.... No vehicle has yet been chosen for Miss Collins' initial Equitable appearance.").

Collins, Kathleen [actress] (b. San Antonio TX). BR, pp. 121–22. George A. Katchmer, "Forgotten Cowboys and Cowgirls—Part 2," *CI,* 173 (Nov 1989), C12; "Up-date," *CI,* 179 (May 1990), 43.

Collins, Lewis D. [director/scenarist] (b. Baltimore MD, 12 Jan 1899–24 Aug 1954 [55], Los Angeles CA, heart attack). (Began at Universal, 1926.) "Lewis D. Collins," *Variety,* 1 Sep 1954 (age 50). AS, p. 247. BHD2, p. 51 (b. 1895). IFN, p. 60.

Collins, Lottie (mother of **Jose Collins**) [stage/film actress] (b. London, England, ca. 1866–2 May 1910 [44?]). m. (1) Stephen Cooney (d. 1901); James W. Tate. "Lottie Collins," *Variety,* 14 May 1910,p. 12 (made *Ta-rara-boom-de-a* famous in England). AMD, p. 77. SD, p. 269. "Bits for Fans," *MPW,* 22 Mar 1913, 1206 (replaced Vedah Bertram).

Collins, May [actress] (b. New York NY, 1906–6 May 1955 [49?], Fairfield CT). m. (1) Carl H[enry] Leverage (d. 1931). Edmund E. Thomas. "May Collins," *Variety,* 11 May 1955. BHD, p. 132. IFN, p. 60. MH, p. 103. SD. Joyce Milton, *Tramp; The Life of Charlie Chaplin* (NY: Harper Collins, 1996), pp. 184–85.

Collins, Monte Francis, **Jr.** (son of **Monte Collins, Sr.**) [actor/director/scenarist/producer] (b. New York NY, 3 Dec 1898–1 Jun 1951 [52], No. Hollywood CA; heart attack). (Sennett; Educational.) "Monty F. Collins," *Variety,* 6 Jun 1951. AMD, p. 77. AS, p. 247. BHD1, p. 114; BHD2, p. 52 (b. 21 Dec 1897). IFN, p. 60. Truitt, p. 66. "Collins Scores," *MPW,* 22 Oct 1927, 498. George Katchmer, "Remembering the Great Silents; Monte Collins," *CI,* 205 (Jul 1992), 58.

Collins, Monte, Sr. (father of **Monte Collins, Jr.**) [actor] (b. 1856–4 Aug 1929 [73], Los Angeles CA; cancer). m. **Norma Wills**. AS, p. 247. BHD, p. 132. Ragan 2, p. 1828.

Collins, Richard (Dick) [actor] (b. 1861?–19 Jun 1939 [78]). AS, p. 247 (b. 1906). BHD, p. 133. IFN, p. 60.

Collins, Tom [director] (d. 17 Jun 1973, Los Angeles CA). AS, p. 247.

Collins, Treve, Jr. [writer]. No data found. AMD, p. 77. "Treve Collins Writing Two-Reelers for Legend," *MPW,* 14 Aug 1920, 899.

Collins, William E. [actor] (d. 15 Feb 1922, Chicago IL; found dead in bed, possibly from drugs). "Wm. E. Collins Dies in Bed," *Variety,* 3 Mar 1922. AS, p. 247.

Collo, Alberto [actor] (b. Piobesi, Italy, 6 Jul 1883–7 May 1955 [71]). AS, p. 247 (b. Turin, Italy; d. Turin, Italy). IFN, p. 60 (b. Torino, Italy). JS, p. 102 (in Italian silents from 1909).

Collyer, June (granddaughter of stage actor Dan Collyer; daughter of stage actress Carrie Collyer) [actress: Wampas Star, 1928] (*née* Dorothea Heermance, b. New York NY, 19 Aug 1906–16 Mar 1968 [61], Los Angeles CA; bronchial pneumonia). m. Stuart Erwin, 22 Jul 1931. (Fox, 1927; Paramount.) "June Collyer, 61, Actress, Is Dead; Widow of Stuart Erwin Was Star in Early Talkies," *NYT,* 19 Mar 1968, 47:1. "June Collyer," *Variety,* 20 Mar 1968. AMD, p. 77. AS, p. 247. BHD1, p. 115 (b. 1907). IFN, p. 60. Truitt, pp. 66–67 (b. 1907). "Fox Signs June Collyer," *MPW,* 9 Jul 1927, 77. Tollington Leigh, "June Collyer Makes Her Screen Début [*East Side, West Side*]," *Cinema Arts,* Nov 1927, 27, 49. "June Collyer," *MPW,* 10 Dec 1927, 48. Dorothy Manners, "Her Royal Shyness; June Collyer Doesn't Want to Capitalize Her Friendship with a Prince [George of England]," *MPC,* Dec 1928, 40, 86–87. Sydney Valentine, "The Rich Little Working Girl; June Collyer Only Works Because She Wants To," *Screenland,* May 1929, 40–41. Jean Dorman, "June Collyer Elopes with Stuart Erwin; Actress Becomes Bride of Comedian after All-Night Drive to Yuma, Arizona—Couple Surprise Everybody," *Movie Classic,* Oct 1931, 38.

Colman, Ben [actor] (b. 1906–22 Feb 1988 [81?], Tarzana CA; septicemia). AS, p. 247. BHD, p. 133.

Colman, Bruce [actor] (b. Cutler CA, 11 Nov 1910–16 Nov 1978 [68], San Mateo CA). BHD1, p. 115.

Colman, Ronald Charles [actor] (b. Richmond, Surrey, England, 9 Feb 1891–19 May 1958 [67], San Ysidro Ranch, Montecito CA; after surgery for a lung infection). m. Victoria Maud; Thelma Ray (1919–1934); Benita Hume (d. 1967).. (Film debut: *The Toilers,* 1916, British 2-reeler.) Juliet Benita Colman (daughter), *Ronald Colman—A Very Private Person* (NY: William Morrow & Co., 1975); R. Dixon Smith, *Ronald Colman, Gentleman of the Cinema; A Biography and Filmography* (Jefferson NC: McFarland & Company, Inc., 1991); Sam Frank, *Ronald Colman: A Bio-Bibliography* (Westport CT: Greenwood Pub. Group, 1997). "Ronald Colman, Actor, Is Dead; Won '48 Oscar for 'Double Life'; British-Born Star of Debonair Charm and Distinctive Voice Had 40-Year Career," *NYT,* 20 May 1958, 33:2. "Ronald Colman," *Variety,* 21 May 1958 (d. Santa Barbara CA). AMD, p. 77. AS, p. 247. BHD1, p. 115 (d. Santa Barbara CA). FFF, p. 209. FSFM, p. 133 (b. 1891). FSS, p. 67. IFN, p. 60. MH, p. 103 ("Coleman"). Truitt, p. 67. Ruth Mabrey, "What Every Actor Needs Most," *MW,* 14 Jun 1924, 11. "Goldwyn Signs Colman," *MPW,* 13 Sep 1924, 125. "Signs Ronald Colman," *MPW,* 11 Oct 1924, 507. "Ronald Colman Borrowed," *MPW,* 8 Nov 1924, 152. Dorothy Gish, "Ronald Colman *Minus* His Greasepaint," *MW,* 14 Mar 1925, 10–11, 28. "The Next Romeo," *MPC,* Jul 1925, 37. Isabel Darrow, "A Soldier and a Gentleman; Otherwise Ronald Colman, Silent and Reserved Briton," *MPC,* Dec 1925, 32–33, 77–78. Gladys Hall and Adele Whitely Fletcher, "We Interview Ronald Colman," *MM,* Jan 1926, 37–38, 98–99. Dorothy Donnell, "Not That They Mind, But—Being the Imaginary Thoughts of Ronald Colman and Vilma Banky on Seeing Each Other Make Love to a New Co-Star," *MPC,* Feb 1929, 58. Faith Service, "I Hope to Marry Again; Says Ronald Colman, who doesn't expect to find a wife in Hollywood—and who also claims he's no mystery man," *Movie Classic,* Oct 1931, 50, 70. George A. Schatz, "Tribute to a Gentleman; A Review of the Career of Ronald Colman," *CFC,* 29 (Winter, 1970), 18–23. George A. Katchmer, "The Professional Career of Ronald Colman in All Media," *CI,* 132 (Jun 1986), 58–61; 133 (Jul 1986), 22–25.

Colmann, M. [scenarist]. No data found. FDY, p. 421.

Colson, Kate [actress] (b. 1861–6 Sep 1944 [83], Los Angeles CA). BHD, p. 133. IFN, p. 60.

Colton, John B. [title writer] (b. near Minneapolis MN, 1886–26 Dec 1946 [60], Gainesville TX). "John Colton," *Variety,* 1 Jan 1947. AMD, p. 77. BHD2, p. 52. FDY, p. 441. IFN, p. 60. NNAT, p. 370. SD. "Colton to Do Stories for Kane," *MPW,* 28 Sep 1918, 1880. "Colton to Write for Universal," *MPW,* 29 May 1920, 1222. "To Write Scenario of 'Exciters,'" *MPW,* 3 Feb 1923, 493.

Colvig, Vance D. "Pinto" [actor/voice of Pluto and Goofy] (b. Jacksonville OR, 11 Sep 1892–3 Oct 1967 [75], Woodland Hills CA). m. (son, Vance, Jr., 1918–1991). (Sennett; Metro; Disney.) "Vance D. (Pinto) Colvig," *Variety,* 11 Oct 1967. AS, p. 248. BHD1, p. 115; BHD2, p. 52. IFN, p. 60. Truitt, p. 67.

Colvin, William G. [actor] (b. Sligo, No. Ireland, 20 Jul 1877–8 Aug 1930 [53], Los Angeles CA). (Keystone.) AS, p. 248. BHD1, p. 115. IFN, p. 60. Mabel Condon, "Keystone; The Home of Mack Sennett and the Film Comedy," *NYDM,* 9 Sep 1916, 36.

Colwell, Goldie [actress]. AMD, p. 77. BR, pp. 12–14. George A. Katchmer, "Remembering the Great Silents," *CI,* 231 (Sep 1994), 49. "New Players for MinA," *MPW,* 5 Jun 1915, 1614. "Miss Colwell in Centaur Features," *MPW,* 30 Oct 1915, 952.

Coman, Morgan [actor] (d. Mar 1947). BHD, p. 133. IFN, p. 60.

Comanche, Laurence [actor] (b. 1908–10 Oct 1932 [24?], Los Angeles CA; suicide or accident with a gun). AS, p. 248. BHD1, p. 115.

Comandini, Adele [scenarist] (b. 29 Apr 1898-Jul 1987 [89], CA). . FDY, p. 421.

Comerio, Luca [former photographer to the Royal Family; cinematographer] (b. Milan, Italy, 1878–6 Jul 1940 [62?], Milan, Italy; in poverty). AS, p. 249 (d. Monbello, Italy). JS, p. 104 (began filming news events in 1905).

Cominetti, Gian Maria [director/scenarist] (b. Salasco Vercellese, Italy, 14 Dec 1884). AS, p. 249. JS, p. 104 (in Italian silents from 1917).

Commerford, Thomas [actor] (b. New York NY, 1 Aug 1855–17 Feb 1920 [64], Chicago

IL). (Essanay.) AMD, p. 77. AS, p/ 249 (d. NYC). BHD, p. 133. IFN, p. 60. "Thomas Commerford Joins Essanay Company," *MPW,* 31 May 1913, 907. "Thomas Commerford," *MPW,* 15 Apr 1916, 450. "Obituary," *MPW,* 6 Mar 1920, 1648. "Request Brief History of 'Dad' Commerford's Career," *MPW,* 13 Mar 1920, 1788–89.

Comont, Mathilde [actress] (b. Bordeaux, France, 9 Sep 1886–21 Jun 1938 [51], Los Angeles CA; heart attack). "Mathilda Comant," *Variety,* 29 Jun 1938. AS, p. 249 (d. 1971). BHD1, p. 116. IFN, p. 60. Terese Rose Nagel, "Everybody Loves a Fat Woman in the Movies," *MW,* 5 Jan 1924, 9, 31 (name spelled Camont).

Compson, Betty, "The Prettiest Girl in Pictures" [actress] (*née* Eleanor Luicime Compson, b. Beaver City UT, 18 Mar 1897–18 Apr 1974 [77], Glendale CA). m. (1) **James Cruze**, 25 Oct 1924–div. 20 May 1930 (d. 1942); (2) **James Walker**, 18 Apr 1933, Cannes, France—div. 15 Mar 1941, Key West FL [d. 1946; Walker's obituary cites her death on 12 Jul 1944]; Irving Weinberg; Jack Gall (d. 1962); Theodore T. Knappen, 10 May 1942, Jersey City NJ. (Christie, 13 Oct 1915.) "Betty Compson, 77, Film Star, Is Dead; Played in 'Miracle Man' and Scores of Silent Movies," *NYT,* 24 Apr 1974, 47:3. "Betty Compson," *Variety,* 1 May 1974. AMD, p. 77. AS, p. 249. BHD1, p. 116. BR, pp. 122–29. FFF, p. 51 (b. Salt Lake City UT). FSS, p. 68. IFN, p. 60. MH, p. 103 (b. Salt Lake City, 18 Mar 1897). WWS, p. 170 (b. Salt Lake City). "Betty Compson," WBO2, pp. 84–85. "Betty Compson in Pathé Serial," *MPW,* 11 May 1918, 839. "Betty Compson with Desmond," *MPW,* 8 Feb 1919, 736. "Goldwyn to Release for Betty Compson; 'Prisoners of Love,' Her First Feature," *MPW,* 10 Jul 1920, 192. "Congratulate Betty Compson," *MPW,* 7 Aug 1920, 720. "Betty Compson Disguises Herself So as to Work in Office as Stenographer," *MPW,* 18 Sep 1920, 335. "Betty Compson Has Signed a Five Year Contract to Star in Paramount Pictures," *MPW,* 26 Feb 1921, 1084. "A Star in the Making," *MPC,* Sep 1922, 20–21 (photos from her films). Alma M. Talley, "Betty Compson Will Wed Movie Director [James Cruze] in Old Mining Camp," *MW,* 29 Mar 1924, 7, 43. "Lengthy Contract for Betty Compson," *MPW,* 17 May 1924, 303. "Betty Compson," *MPW,* 12 Jul 1924, insert. "Cruz[e] Weds Compson," *MPW,* 1 Nov 1924, 29 (home estate: Flintridge). "Betty Compson with Lon Chaney," *MPW,* 22 Oct 1927, 493. Nancy Pryor, "Betty Blooms Again; From the Limbo of Retirement and the Quickies, Miss Compson Emerges to Regain Her Stardom," *MPC,* Jul 1928, 23, 77 (returns to films after married life with James Cruze). Gladys Hall, "Confessions of the Stars; Betty Compson Tells Her Untold Tale," *MPC,* Dec 1928, 16–17, 72, 86 ("Live and let live—Make love and make money—that's my philosophy!"). DeWitt Bodeen, "Betty Compson," *FIR,* Aug/Sep 1966, 396–418. "Joyful, Silent Memories," *CFC,* 30 (Spring, 1971), X1. Jeannette Mazurki, "Glendale Star from Silent Film Era Feted," *CFC,* 33 (Winter, 1971), 13. William T. Leonard, "Fiddler on the Reel; The Story of Betty Compson," *CFC,* 36 (Fall, 1972), 9, 62; II, 37 (Winter, 1971), 42–44, 53; III, 38; Jeannette, Mazurski, "'Best Bad' Girl of the Silent Film Era Still Sparkles, Lives with Her Memories," *CFC,* 34 (Spring, 1972), X4. Buck Rainey, "Betty Compson," *CI,* 116 (Feb 1985), 21–22; 117 (Mar 1985), 18, C3; 118 (Apr 1985), C4-C6. George Katchmer, "Remembering the Great Silents," *CI,* 222 (Dec 1993), C18.

Compton, Charles [actor] (b. Mount Vernon NY, 14 Aug 1883–26 Apr 1964 [80], Laguna Beach CA). BHD1, p. 606.

Compton, Dixie [actress] (b. Louisville KY, 1886). BHD, p. 133.

Compton, Fay (sister of **Francis** and **Viola Compton**) [actress] (*née* Virginia Lilian Emeline MacKenzie, b. London, England, 18 Sep 1894–12 Dec 1978 [84], London, England). m. **H.G. Pelissier** (d. 1913); **Leon Quartermaine** (d. 1967). AS, p. 249. BHD1, p. 116. IFN, p. 60.

Compton, Francis (brother of **Fay** and **Viola Compton**) [actor] (*né* Francis Sidney MacKenzie, b. Malvern, England, 4 May 1885–17 Sep 1964 [79], Noroton CT). . m. Mary W. Wells. AS, p. 249 (Frank Compton). IFN, p. 60. SD. "Francis Compton," *Variety,* 23 Sep 1964.

Compton, Joyce [film/TV actress: Wampas Star, 1926] (*née* Eleanor Hunt, b. Lexington KY, 27 Jan 1907–13 Oct 1997 [90], Woodland Hills CA). m. 1956—annulled. (Film debut: *The Golden Bed,* FP-L, 1925; FBO; Paramount, 1st National; Fox.) "Joyce Compton [obituary]," *CI,* 270 (Dec 1997), 50. AS, p. 249. BHD1, p. 606. BR, pp. 279–85. FSS, p. 69. Katz, p. 262. Joe Collura, "Comedienne Joyce Compton," *CI,* 158 (Aug 1988), 32, 38; 159 (Sep 1988), 11, 20. Michael G. Ankerich, "Reel Stars; Hollywood's Favorite Dumb Blonde," *CI,* 167 (May 1989), 9–10. Buck Rainey, "Joyce Compton Filmography, Part I," *CI,* 84 (Jun 1982), pp. 52–53; Part II, 85 (Jul 1982), 24–25, 46. P.A. Carayannis, "Joyce Compton [letter]," *CI,* 87 (Sep 1982), 49 (lists Paramount shorts). Chapter 8, "Joyce Compton," *BS,* pp. 103–24 (includes filmography). Charles Stumpf, "Ageless Joyce Compton," *CI,* 271 (Dec 1997), 11.

Compton, Juliette [actress] (b. Columbus GA, 3 May 1899–19 Mar 1989 [89], Pasadena CA). BHD1, p. 116.

Compton, Viola (sister of **Fay** and **Francis Compton**) [actress] (*née* Viola MacKenzie, b. London, England, 1886–7 Apr 1971 [85], Birchington-on-Sea, England). m. Henry Crocker. "Viola Compton," *Variety,* 21 Apr 1971. AS, p. 249. BHD1, p. 116. IFN, p. 61.

Comstock, Clark [actor] (b. Yukatan MN, 7 Jan 1862–24 May 1934 [72], Los Angeles CA). (Universal.) AMD, p. 78. AS, p. 249. BHD1, p. 116. IFN, p. 61. "Lived with Ogalalla Sioux," *MPW,* 24 May 1919, 1228. George A. Katchmer, "Forgottten Cowboys and Cowgirls—Part 2," *CI,* 173 (Nov 1989), C12.

Comstock, Dr. Daniel Frost [inventor] (b. MA?, 14 Aug 1883–2 Mar 1970 [86], Lincoln MA). . (Technicolor.) "Dr. Daniel Comstock," *Variety,* 11 Mar 1970.

Concord, Lillian [actress] (b. Omaha NB, 18 Jul 1884–6 Aug 1973 [89], Highland Park CA). BHD, "Addendum."

Condon, Charles R. [publicist/title writer/scenarist] (b. Chicago IL, 10 Jul 1894–21 Sep 1960 [66], Los Angeles CA; heart attack). . (MGM; WB; Columbia.) "Charles R. Condon," *Variety,* 28 Sep 1960. AMD, p. 78. AS, p. 250. BHD2, p. 52. FDY, pp. 421, 441. "Charles Condon Joins Goldwyn's Press Staff," *MPW,* 27 Sep 1919, 1936. "Condon Enters Free Lance Field," *MPW,* 3 Jul 1926, 19.

Condon, Frank [writer] (b. Toledo OH, 1882?–19 Dec 1940 [58], Beverly Hills CA). m. Betty Esther. "Frank Condon," *Variety,* 25 Dec 1940. AMD, p. 78. AS, p. 250. BHD2, p. 52. "Condon to Write for Fairbanks," *MPW,* 18 Jan 1919, 313.

Condon, Jackie [actor: Our Gang] (*né* John Michael Condon, b. Los Angeles CA, 24 Mar 1918–13 Oct 1977 [59], Inglewood CA; cancer). m. Shirley, 1947, Washington D.C. Eric Grimm, "A Little Rascal Waves Goodbye," *The Evening Outlook,* 21 Oct 1977 (reprinted in *CFC,* 57 [Winter, 1977], 63). AS, p. 250. BHD, p. 133. IFN, p. 61.

Cone, Mrs. Nancy Stewart [actress] (d. Cincinnati OH, 23 Nov 1916). BHD, p. 133.

Conesa, Maria [actress] (b. 12 Dec 1892–4 Sep 1978 [85], Mexico City, Mexico). BHD1, p. 606.

Coniber, Elizabeth Jenkins [actress] (b. 1878–18 Jan 1965 [86?], Caldwell NJ). BHD, p. 133. IFN, p. 61.

Conklin, Charles (Heinie) [actor] (*né* Charles John Conklin, San Francisco CA, 16 Jul 1880–30 Jul 1959 [79], Los Angeles CA). (Sennett.) "Charles Conklin," *Variety,* 5 Aug 1959. AS, p. 250. BHD, p. 133. IFN, p. 61. Katz, pp. 262–63. Truitt, p. 67. George A. Katchmer, "Forgotten Cowboys and Cowgirls—Part XVII," *CI,* 194 (Aug 1991), 46.

Conklin, Chester [actor: Keystone Cop] (*né* Jules Cowles, b. Oskaloosa IA, 11 Jan 1886–11 Oct 1971 [85], Woodland Hills CA). m. (1) 1913–33; (2) Margherita Rouse, 5 May 1934 (d. 1937); (3) Valda C. Genessee, 1949, Las Vegas NV; (4) June Ayres Gunther, 23 Jun 1965, Las Vegas NV. (Sennett; Fox.) "Chester Conklin, Silent Film Star; Keystone Kop Is Dead at 83—Talkies Ended Career," *NYT,* 12 Oct 1971, 46:3 (b. 1888). "Chester Conklin," *Variety,* 13 Oct 1971 (age 83). AMD, p. 78. AS, p. 250. BHD1, p. 116. FSS, p. 70. IFN, p. 61. MH, p. 103. SD. Truitt, pp. 67–68. "Chester Conklin," WBO1, pp. 90–91. "Chester Conklin," *MPW,* 30 Jun 1917, 2081. "New Experiences for a Veteran," *MPW,* 31 May 1919, 1322. "Special Pictures Secures Chester Conklin, Comedian," *MPW,* 21 Aug 1920, 1059. Verne Kibbe, "Garnering the Guffaws; The Walrus-Faced Comic Talks of the Newer Taste in Silverscreen Humor," *MPC,* Feb 1926, 54–55, 88. "Chester Conklin Added to Paramount Company," *MPW,* 15 May 1926, 234. "Fields—Conklin a Comedy Team," *MPW,* 11 Jun 1927, 419. "Chester Conklin," *MPW,* 30 Jul 1927, 319. Dorothy Spensley, "Minus the Smootch [moustache]; The Bare-Faced Tale of Chester Conklin's Life," *MPC,* Mar 1929, 63, 96. Nick Lamberto, "A Lonely Boy Who Never Came Back to Iowa," *Des Moines Sunday Register,* 16 Feb 1969 (age given as 79 when he married his fourth wife on 23 Jun 1965 in Las Vegas). Nick Lamberto, "A Lonely Boy Who Never Came Back to Iowa," *CFC,* 24 (Summer, 1969), 15.

Conklin, Frank [actor] (b. Atchison KS, 15 Apr 1886–6 Jun 1945 [59]). AS, p. 250. BHD, p. 133. IFN, p. 61.

Conklin, Frank Roland [writer] (b. NJ, 1903?–8 Nov 1963 [60], Detroit MI; multiple sclerosis). m. Grace Haskins, 1925. "Frank R. Conklin," *Variety,* 20 Nov 1963 (Conklin [carnival] Shows). AMD, p. 78. AS, p. 250. "Conklin to Write for Christie," *MPW,* 9 Aug 1919, 793. "Conklin-Haskins," *MPW,* 5 Dec 1925, 459.

Conklin, Frederick Meade [actor] (b. 1873–22 Jan 1929 [55], Long Island NY). IFN, p. 61.

Conklin, Harold "Hal" [title writer/scenarist]. No data found. FDY, pp. 423, 441.

Conklin, William S. [actor] (b. Brooklyn NY, 25 Dec 1872–21 Mar 1935 [62], Los Angeles CA; cerebral hemorrhage). m. **Lucy Blake**. (Balboa.) "William Conklin," *Variety,* 27 Mar 1935 (b. NYC). AMD, p. 78. AS, p. 250. BHD1, p. 116. IFN, p. 61. Katz, p. 263. Truitt, p. 68. J. Van Cartmell, "Along the Pacific Coast," *NYDM,* 6 Oct 1915, 31:2. "William Conklin," *MPW,* 4 Dec 1915, 1812. "Conklin with Lasky," *MPW,* 16 Sep 1916, 1836. "Tom Ince Enlarges Staff at His Culver City Studio," *MPW,* 15 Mar 1919, 1481. George A. Katchmer, "Forgotten Cowboys and Cowgirls—Part XVII," *CI,* 194 (Aug 1991), 46–47.

Conkwright, Arthur Bliss [actor] (b. Siegel IL, 2 Mar 1882–3 Feb 1957 [74], Palm Springs CA). BHD, p. 133; BHD2, p. 52.

Conlan, Frank (or Francis) **X.** [actor] (*né* Peter Murphy, b. Belfast, Ireland, 22 Jul 1874–24 Aug 1955 [81], East Islip, LI NY). "Frank Conlan," *Variety,* 31 Aug 1955. BHD1, p. 116. IFN, p. 61.

Conley, Effie [actress] (b. Norwich CT, 1857). BHD, p. 133.

Conley, George [actor] (b. 1887-Nov 1929 [42?], Los Angeles CA). BHD, p. 133.

Conley, Harry J. [actor] (b. 1877–23 Jun 1975 [98?], Cleveland OH). AS, p. 250 (b. 1884). BHD1, p. 116 (b. 1884). IFN, p. 61.

Conley, Lige [actor] (*né* Elijah A. Crommie, b. St. Louis MO, 5 Dec 1897–11 Dec 1937 [40], Los Angeles CA; struck by car). "Lige Conley," *Variety,* 15 Dec 1937 (age 37). (Educational-Mermaid Comedies.) AMD, p. 78. AS, p.250 (b. LA CA, 5 Dec 1899). BHD, p. 133 (b. LA CA, 1899). FFF, p. 151. IFN, p. 61 (b. 1899). MH, p. 104. Truitt, p. 68. "Lige Has a Georgia Peach," *MPW,* 10 Jan 1925, 177:3 (chose Estelle Bradley, from Atlanta, Georgia, as his leading lady at Educational). "Hal Roach to Co-Feature Well-Known Fun Makers," *MPW,* 16 May 1925, 356.

Conley, Onest [actor] (b. Evanston IL, 25 Dec 1906–8 Oct 1989 [82], Los Angeles Co. CA). BHD1, p. 116.

Conlin, Jimmy [actor] (b. Camden NJ, 14 Oct 1884–7 May 1962 [77], Encino CA; cancer). m. (1) Myrtle Glass; (2) Dorothy Ryan. "Jimmy Conlin," *Variety,* 9 May 1962. AS, p. 250. BHD1, p. 117 (d. LA CA). IFN, p. 61.

Conlin, Tom [agent] (b. 1885–21 Aug 1953 [68?], Beverly Hills CA). BHD2, p. 52.

Conliss, Edward B., "Zam Zam the Clown" [actor] (b. 19 Sep 1900–3 Aug 1981 [80], Toledo OH). AS, p. 250. BHD1, p. 606.

Connelly, Bobby (brother of **Helen E. Connelly**) [child actor] (*né* Robert Joseph Connelly, b. Brooklyn NY, 4 Apr 1909 [Birth Certificate Index No. 11498]–5 Jul 1922 [13], Lynbrook, LI NY; acute bronchitis). (Kalem; Vitagraph.) "'Bobby' Connelly Dead; Child Screen Star Dies of Bronchitis at His Home, in Lynbrook," *NYT,* 7 Jul 1922, 17:6. "Bobby Connelly," *Variety,* 14 Jul 1922. AS, pp. 250–51. BHD, p. 134. IFN, p. 61. 1921 Directory, p. 246. Slide, p. 137. Truitt, p. 68. W. Stephen Bush, "The Screen Children's Gallery," *MPW,* 14 Mar 1914, 1371. "Bobby Connelly Very Busy," *MPW,* 14 Aug 1915, 1148. "Bobby's Bookstand Bookings," *MPW,* 30 Sep 1916, 2096. "Lost: One Small Star," *Photoplay,* Feb 1917, 71–72. "Bobby Connelly Plays with Drew," *MPW,* 16 Feb 1918, 979. "Bobby Connelly Joins Garson Forces," *MPW,* 5 Oct 1918, 91. "Bobby Connelly with Macdon Comedies," *MPW,* 29 Mar 1919, 1799. "Obituary," *MPW,* 15 Jul 1922, 204 (d. 6 Jul). Billy H. Doyle, "Lost Players," *CI,* 174 (Dec 1989), C13.

Connelly, Edward J. [actor] (b. New York NY, 30 Dec 1855–20 Nov 1928 [72], Hollywood CA; flu). "Edward Connolly," *Variety,* 28 Nov 1928 (age 73). AMD, p. 78. As, p. 251 (b. 1859). BHD, p. 134. IFN, p. 61. Truitt, p. 68. "Marse Connelly," *Photoplay Magazine,* Jun 1917, 71. "Connelly Engaged to Support Nazimova," *MPW,* 25 Jan 1919, 467. "Connelly's New Role," *MPW,* 3 Apr 1926, 345. "Metro Re-Signs Two," *MPW,* 4 Sep 1926, 4.

Connelly, Erwin [actor] (b. Chicago IL, 15 May 1872–12 Feb 1931 [58], Los Angeles CA; auto accident). m. **Jane** (d. 1925). (Metro; Universal.) "Erwin Connelly," *Variety,* 18 Feb 1931. AS, p. 251. BHD1, p. 117 (b. 1879). IFN, p. 61. Truitt, p. 68 (b. 1873).

Connelly, Helen E. (sister of **Bobby Connelly**) [actress]. No data found. AMD, p. 78. W. Stephen Bush, "The Screen Children's Gallery," *MPW,* 14 Mar 1914, 1371.

Connelly, Jane [actress] (*nee?*, b. Port Huron MI, 2 May 1883–25 Oct 1925 [42], Los Angeles CA; result of a nervous breakdown). m. **Erwin Connelly** (d. 1931). "Jane Connelly," *Variety,* 28 Oct 1925. AS, p. 251. BHD, p. 134. IFN, p. 61. Truitt, p. 68.

Connelly, Marc [actor/director/producer/scenarist] (*né* Marcus Cook Connelly, b. McKeesport PA, 13 Dec 1890–21 Dec 1980 [90], New York NY). AS, p. 251. BHD1, p. 117; BHD2, p. 52.

Conness, Robert [actor] (b. La Salle Co. IL, 24 Dec 1867–15 Jan 1941 [73], Portland ME). m. Helen Strickland. "Robert Conness; Veteran Actor Seen Here and in Europe for 46 Years," *NYT,* 17 Jan 1941, 17:4 (age 74). "Robert Conness," *Variety,* 22 Jan 1941. AMD, p. 78. AS, p. 251. BHD, p. 134. IFN, p. 61. "Robert Conness," *MPW,* 26 Sep 1914, 1766. Thornton Fisher, "Robert Conness," *MPW,* 24 Jul 1915, 633. "Robert Conness," *MPW,* 20 Jan 1917, 373.

Connolly, John S. (Jack) [actor/executive] (b. Wellesley MA, 1887?–22 Dec 1960 [73], New York NY; heart attack). m. Lucille. "Jack Connolly, 73, Trade-&-Capital Figure Succumbs," *Variety,* 28 Dec 1960.

Connolly, Mike [talent agent/casting director] (b. 1887?–19 Dec 1950 [63], Los Angeles CA). (Cosmopolitan Productions, 1917.) m. Marion. "Mike Connolly," *Variety,* 27 Dec 1950.

Connolly, Myles [scenarist/director/producer] (b. Boston MA, 7 Oct 1897–15 Jul 1964 [66], Santa Monica CA; open heart surgery). (FBO; RKO.) m. Agnes. "Myles Connolly, a Film Writer, 66; Author and Producer Dead—Edited K. of C. Magazine," *NYT,* 17 Jul 1964, 27:3. "Myles Connolly," *Variety,* 22 Jul 1964. AS, p. 251. BHD2, p. 52. IFN, p. 61.

Connolly, Regina [actress] (b. 1892–12 Mar 1926 [33?], New York NY). BHD, p. 134.

Connolly, Walter [actor] (b. Cincinnati OH, 8 Apr 1887–28 May 1940 [53], Los Angeles CA; cerebral thrombosis). m. Nedda Harrigan (d. 1989). "Walter Connolly," *Variety*, 29 May 1940. AS, p. 251. BHD1, p. 117. IFN, p. 61. SD.

Connor, Della [actress]. No data found. *Fl.* 1914–16. AMD, p. 78. "Della Connor in 'Stop Thief,'" *MPW,* 2 Jan 1915, 52. "Della Connor Signs Permanently with George Kleine," *MPW,* 16 Jan 1915, 378. "When Della Connor Smiles," *MPW,* 16 Sep 1916, 1814.

Connor, Edward [actor] (d. 14 May 1932, New York NY). (Edison, 1913.) "Edward Connor," *Variety,* 17 May 1932. AS, p. 251. BHD, p. 134. Ragan, p. 319. Truitt, p. 68.

Connor, Velma [actress] (b. 1 Dec 1904–19 Jul 1987 [82], Los Angeles CA). AS, p. 251. BHD1, p. 117.

Connor, Virginia M. [actress] (b. Los Angeles CA, 28 Jul 1920–27 Feb 1987 [66], Rancho Mirage CA). BHD, p. 134.

Connors, Barry [actor/scenarist] (b. Oil City PA, 31 May 1883–5 Jan 1933 [49]). BHD2, p. 52.

Connors, George "Buck" [actor] (b. San Sabag TX, 22 Nov 1880). BHD, p. 134. "Buck Connor's Stories for Ince; Ince May Release Two Five-Reel Subjects a Week—William S. Hart Renews His Contract," *MPW,* 21 Apr 1917, 430:1. "Cowboy Author to Write for Hart," *MPW,* 21 Apr 1917, 445:1 ("the literary Texas Ranger," published in *McClure's, The Saturday Evening Post,* and *The Popular Magazine*). George A. Katchmer, "Remembering the Great Silents," *CI,* 17 (Jan 1990), C5; "Update—Forgotten Cowboys/Girls," *CI,* 179 (May 1990), 43 (with Albuquerque Film Co.).

Conoly, Joseph [actor/general manager/producer] (b. 1871?–19 Apr 1926 [55], Saranac Lake NY). "Joseph Conoly," *Variety,* 28 Apr 1926, p. 83. AMD, p. 78. BHD2, p. 52. "Dobbs Will Make Pictures," *MPW,* 30 Aug 1913, 944. "Conoly with Helen Gardner Company," *MPW,* 7 Mar 1914, 1242.

Conover, Theresa Maxwell [actress] (b. Richmond IN, 26 Sep 1884-Sep 1968 [83?], Leavittown NY). AMD, p. 78. BHD1, p. 117. "Miss Conover Joins World Pictures," *MPW,* 1 Jun 1918, 1274.

Conquest, Arthur [actor] (b. London, England, 1875–6 Dec 1945 [70?], London, England). BHD, p. 134.

Conrad, Con [composer] (*né* Conrad K. Dober, b. New York NY, 18 Jun 1889–28 Sep 1938 [49], Van Nuys CA). AS, p. 251 (b. 1891). BHD2, p. 52.

Conrad, Edward [actor] (b. New York NY, 1890–27 Apr 1941 [51?], Los Angeles CA). AS, p. 251. BHD1, p. 117.

Conrad, Joseph [novelist/scenarist] (*né* Teodor Josef Konrad Korzenlowski, b. Ukraine, Russia, 6 Dec 1857–3 Aug 1924 [66], Bishopsbourne, near Canterbury, England). "Joseph Conrad Dies, Writer of the Sea; Author of 'Victory,' 'The Rover' and 'Youth' Succumbs in England at 67 Years; Began Sea Career at 17; Called 'Most Romantic Figure in English Literature'—Original Scripts Sold for $110,998," *NYT,* 4 Aug 1924, 1:7, 4:2. "Conrad Thoughtful of Others to the Last; In Dying Moments He Asked That Professional Nurse Relieve His Devoted Servant," *NYT,* 7 Aug 1924, 3:5. AMD, p. 78. "Joseph Conrad to Write for Paramount Pictures," *MPW,* 8 Jan 1921, 174. Cal York, "Plays and Players," *Photoplay,* Mar 1921, 122 ("engaged to write screen stories for Paramount.").

Conrad-Schlenther, Paula [actress] (b. Germany, 27 Feb 1860–9 Aug 1938 [78]). BHD, p. 134.

Conroy, Frank Parish [actor] (b. Derby, England, 14 Oct 1890–24 Feb 1964 [73], Paramus NJ; heart attack). . m. (1) Helen Robbins; (2) Ruth Mudie. "Frank Conroy," *Variety,* 26 Feb 1964. AS, p. 252. BHD1, p. 117. IFN, p. 61. SD, p. 278. Truitt, p. 69. James Robert Parish, *Hollywood Character Actors* (1978), pp. 137–38.

Conroy, Larry [actor] (b. NY, 1894–29 Jun 1922 [28?], New York NY). BHD, p. 134.

Consalvi, Achille [director]. No data found. JS, p. 105 (in Italian silents from 1914).

Conselman, William M[arien] [scenarist] (b. Brooklyn NY, 10 Jul 1896–25 May 1940 [43], Eagle Rock CA). "Wm. M. Conselman, Film Writer, Dies; Co-Creator of the Comic Strip 'Ella Cinders' Devised Many Plots—Also Producer; On Stage When a Child; Scenarist Since Silent Era Had Penned Roles for Will Rogers, Cantor, Temple and Crosby," *NYT,* 26 May 1940, 35:1. "William M. Conselman," *Variety,* 29 May 1940. AMD, p. 79. AS, p. 252. BHD2, p. 53. FDY, p. 423. IFN, p. 61. "M.-G.-M. New Title Writer," *MPW,* 22 Aug 1925, 804.

Considine, John William, Jr. [director/producer] (b. Spokane WA, 7 Oct 1898–22 Mar 1961 [63], Los Angeles Co. CA). m. Carmen Pantages. (MGM.) "John Considine, Jr., Movie Producer, 62," *NYT,* 23 Mar 1961, 33:3 (age 62; "Among the silent movies he made were 'Son of the Sheik,' 'Kiki' and 'The Tempest.'"). "John W. Considine," *Variety,* 29 Mar 1961. AS, p. 252. BHD2, p. 53. Harry D. Wilson, "Will Carmen Pantages Wed John Considine, Jr.?; All Hollywood Wonders Whether Carmen Pantages or Joan Bennett Will Be Film Executive's Bride," *Movie Classic,* Oct 1931, 42.

Considine, Mildred [scenarist]. No data found. AMD, p. 79. "Pickford Scenarist Arrives," *MPW,* 12 Apr 1919, 218. "Mildred Considine with Mary Pickford," *MPW,* 3 May 1919, 679.

Constance, Marion [scenarist]. No data found. AMD, p. 79. FDY, p. 423. "Bungalow for Marion Constance," *MPW,* 3 Jan 1925, 66.

Constant, Max [actor] (b. Bordeaux, France, 20 Oct 1889–d. May 1943 [53], Mojave Desert). "Max Constant," *Variety,* 26 May 1943. AS, p. 252 (d. 15 May). BHD, p. 134. IFN, p. 62. Truitt, p. 69.

Conti, Albert [actor] (*né* Alberto de Conti Cadassamare, b. Trieste, Italy, 29 Jan 1887–18 Jan 1967 [79], Los Angeles CA; pulmonary embolism during a flu attack). m. Miriam Wherry (*née* **Patricia Cross**), 1927. "Albert Conti," *Variety,* 25 Jan 1967 (b. Italy). AMD, p. 79. AS, p. 252. BHD1, p. 118. IFN, p. 62. Katz, p. 266. Truitt, p. 69. Tom Waller, "Albert Conti," *MPW,* 26 Mar 1927, 268–69. "Two Film Weddings," *MPW,* 16 Apr 1927, 632.

Contreras Torres, Miguel [actor/producer/director] (b. Sonoro, Mexico, 16 Sep 1899–1981 [82?], Culver City CA). m. actress Medea Novora. *El Libro Negro del Cine Mexicano,* 1960. AS, p. 252 (d. 30 Sep 1956). BHD2, p. 53 (b. 1904; d. Culver City CA, 30 Dec 1956). Waldman, p. 60.

Converse, Thelma Morgan [actress] (b. Lucerne, Switzerland, 1904–25 Jan 1970 [65?], New York NY). BHD, p. 134.

Conville, Robert [actor] (b. ME, 1881–28 Feb 1950 [68?], Los Angeles CA). (Westart Pictures.) BHD, p. 134. George Katchmer, "Remembering the Great Silents," *CI,* 196 (Oct 1991), 53.

Conway, H[ugh] **Ryan** [actor]. No data found. *Fl.* 1910–11 (Bison). AMD, p. 79. Richard V. Spencer, "Notes of the Los Angeles Studios," *MPW,* 14 Jan 1911, 93.

Conway, Jack [actor] (b. Ireland, 1886–3 May 1951 [65?], Forest Hills NY). AS, p. 253. BHD, p. 134.

Conway, Jack [title writer/actor/director/producer] (*né* Hugh Ryan Conway, b. Graceville MN, 17 Jul 1887–11 Oct 1952 [65], Pacific Palisades CA). m. (1) **Virginia Bushman**, 22 Sep 1926, LA CA; (2) **Viola Barry** (d. 1964); **We-Chock-Be** (d. 1937). (Nestor; Griffith; MGM.) "Jack Conway Dies; Film Director, 65; Star of Silent Screen Was Responsible for 'Hucksters' and 'Tale of Two Cities,'" *NYT,* 13 Oct 1952, 21:3. "Jack Conway," *Variety,* 15 Oct 1952. AMD, p. 79. AS, p. 253. BHD2, p. 53. FDY, p. 441. IFN, p. 62. SD. Truitt, p. 69. "Jack Conway," *MPW,* 27 Apr 1912, 334. "Jack Conway Directing Kerrigan," *MPW,* 13 May 1916, 1177. "Karger Engages Directors for Three Plays to Be Filmed by Screen Classics," *MPW,* 19 Jul 1919, 352. "Director Jack Conway Is Back with Metro Pictures," *MPW,* 26 Jul 1919, 527. "Conway a Metro Director," *MPW,* 2 May 1925, 82. "Conway Contract Renewed," *MPW,* 8 Aug 1925, 659. "Conway-Bushman," *MPW,* 9 Oct 1926, 343. "And These Titles Ought to Be Good!," *MPW,* 5 Mar 1927, 41.

Conway, Joseph [actor] (b. Philadelphia PA, 1889?–28 Feb 1959 [70?], near Philadelphia PA). (Lubin.) "Joseph Conway," *Variety,* 11 Mar 1959. AS, p. 253. BHD, p. 134. Truitt, p. 69.

Conway, Lizzie [stage/film actress] (*née?,* b. Philadelphia PA, 1845–4 May 1916 [70?], Milwaukee WI). m. George W. Conway (d. 1918). "Lizzie Conway," *Variety,* 12 May 1916. AS, p. 253. BHD, p. 134. IFN, p. 62. SD.

Conway, William [actor] (b. 1876–13 Oct 1924 [48?], New York NY). BHD, p. 134. IFN, p. 62.

Conwell, O'Kane [art supervisor]. No data found. AMD, p. 79. "Metro Engages Art Supervisor," *MPW,* 9 Feb 1918, 829.

Conyers, Joseph [actor] (b. County Mayo, Ireland, 1854–25 Jun 1920 [65?], New York NY). BHD, p. 134.

Coogan, Jack (John), Sr. (father of **Jackie Coogan**) [actor/director/producer] (*né* John Henry Coogan, b. Syracuse NY, 1880–4 May 1935 [55?], San Diego CA; auto accident). m. Lillian Dolliver. "2 Film Tragedies in 48 Hours; [John] Coogan—[Robert] Horner [aged 25]—[Junior] Durkin [aged 17] Auto Fatalities and Plane Crack-Up," *Variety,* 8 May 1935 (interred at Calvary Cemetery, LA CA). AMD, p. 79. BHD, p. 134; BHD2, p. 53. AS, p. 253. "Jack Coogan, Sr., Now Producing Independently," *MPW,* 17 Jun 1922, 619. "Son to Coogan's," *MPW,* 3 Jan 1925, 24 (b. Dec 1924).

Coogan, Jackie (son of **Jack Coogan, Sr.**) [film/TV actor] (*né* John Leslie Coogan, Jr., b. Los Angeles CA, 26 Oct 1914–1 Mar 1984 [69], Santa Monica CA; heart attack). m. (1) Betty Grable, 1937–39; (2) Flower Parry; (3) Ann McCormick; (4) Dodie. (MGM; Chaplin; 1st National.) (Film debut: *A Day's Pleasure,* 1st National, 1919.) James Barron, "Jackie Coogan, Child Star of Films, Dies at 69," *NYT,* 2 Mar 1984, B5:1. "Child Star Jackie Coogan, 69, Dies; Always Remembered for The Kid," *Variety,* 7 Mar 1984. AMD, p. 79. AS, p. 253. BHD1, p. 118. FFF, p. 53. FSS, p. 70. MH, p. 104. "Jack Coogan in 'Peck's Bad Boy,'" *MPW,* 23 Oct 1920, 1108. "I.M. Lesser Will Feature Jackie Coogan in Series of 'Peck's Bad Boy' Films," *MPW,* 13 Nov 1920, 218. "Jackie Coogan in Auto Smash," *MPW,* 4 Dec 1920, 586 (fractured skull). "Jackie Coogan Is Now Back at Work," *MPW,* 18 Dec 1920, 881. "Coogan, Jr., Writes Story of Life," *MPW,* 5 Aug 1922, 418. Faith Service, "Frank Lloyd's Jackie Coogan," *Classic,* Jun 1923, 42–43. Don Ryan, "Jackie and His Half Million; Never in all history has a child had so great an earning power as Jackie Coogan," *Picture-Play Magazine,* Jun 1923, 46–47. "Jackie Coogan 2-a-Year," *MPW,* 16 Feb 1924, 545. "Jackie Coogan," *MPW,* 30 Aug 1924, 721. "Jackie Coogan," *MPW,* 18 Oct 1924, 610. "Jackie Coogan Back with Lots of Toys; He Admired Athens and the Eiffel Tower in Paris"," *NYT,* 11 Nov 1924, 20:3 (aboard the *Leviathan* with Valentino and Nita Naldi aboard; 10 years old on 7 Oct 1924 [sic]; salary: $18 a week from his father, "with special tips of 50 cents when he accomplished anything really smart, like picking out a good actor or actress for some role in a picture that was difficult to fill."). "Jackie Coogan," *MPW,* 22 Nov 1924, 339. "Jackie Coogan Now Full-Fledged Star," *MPW,* 13 Nov 1926, 80. Jay Rubin, "Jackie Coogan," *CFC,* 52 (Fall, 1976), 6–9.

Coogan, Mrs. Lillian [actress] (b. 1892–23 Oct 1977 [85?], Los Angeles CA). BHD, p. 134.

Cook, C. Warren [stage/film actor] (b. Boston MA, 23 May 1878–2 May 1939 [60], East Islip NY). (Stage debut: *1492,* 1895; Vitagraph.) "Warren Cook," *Variety,* 10 May 1939, p. 52. AMD, p. 80. AS, p. 254 (d. NYC). BHD, p. 135. IFN, p. 62. Truitt, pp. 69–70. "Warren Cook Engaged for Selznick Stock Company," *MPW,* 12 Jun 1920, 1492.

Cook, Charles Emerson [publicist]. No data found. AMD, p. 79. "Charles Cook with Vitagraph," *MPW,* 25 Sep 1915, 2164.

Cook, Clyde Wilford [stage/film actor] (b. Port MacQuarie, NSW, Australia, 16 Dec 1891–13 Aug 1984 [92], Carpenteria CA; heart attack). m. (1) Alice Draper; (2) Constance. (Sennett; Fox; Roach.) "Clyde Cook," *Variety,* 3 Oct 1984. AMD, p. 79. AS, p. 253. BHD1, p. 118. FSS, p. 71. Katz, p. 268. SD, p. 280. "Clyde Cook Quits Hippodrome to Join Fox Sunshine Forces," *MPW,* 10 Apr 1920, 231. "New Sunshine Comedy Stars Clyde Cook, Stage Comedian," *MPW,* 21 Aug 1920, 1063. "Clyde Cook's India-Rubber Legs Wobble Wildly in Fox Comedy, 'Kiss Me Quick,'" *MPW,* 4 Sep 1920, 96. "Clyde Cook," *MPW,* 5 Mar 1927, 27. "Clyde Cook's Long Contract with Warners," *MPW,* 16 Apr 1927, 650. "Clyde Cook," *MPW,* 30 Jul 1927, 318.

Cook, Clyde R. [cameraman]. No data found.

Cook, Edward Bertram [director] (b. 1878–14 Mar 1930 [52?], Los Angeles CA). BHD2, p. 53.

Cook, James F. [actor] (b. 1868?–21 Jan 1931 [62], Brooklyn NY). "James F. Cook," *Variety,* 28 Jan 1931. AS, p. 253.

Cook, Joe [assistant director]. No data found. AMD, p. 80. "Bachmann Signs," *MPW,* 11 Sep 1926, 119.

Cook, Joe [stage/film actor/singer] (b. Evansville IN, 29 Mar 1890–15 May 1959 [69], Staatsburg NY; Parkinson's disease since 1942). m.

(1) Beatrice Helen; (2) Alice Boulders. "Joe Cook, 69, Dies; Famed Comedian; Vaudeville Star Appeared in 'Vanities'—Best Known for His 'Four Hawaiians' Act," *NYT*, 17 May 1959, 84:1. Glendon Allvine, "'Greatest Man in World': Atkinson on Joe Cook; Trouper-Wife's Loyalty," *Variety*, 20 May 1959. AS, p. 253 (d. 16 May, Clinton Hollows NY). BHD1, p. 118 (d. Poughkeepsie NY). IFN, p. 62.

Cook, Lillian [stage/film actress] (b. Hot Springs AR, 1898–14 Mar 1918 [19], New York NY). (World.) "Lillian Cook," *Variety*, 22 Mar 1918. AMD, p. 80. AS, p. 253. BHD, p. 135. IFN, p. 62. SD, p. 281. "Lillian Cook," *MPW*, 30 Oct 1915, 980. "Studio Gossip," *NYDM*, 20 Nov 1915, 34:4 ("Her success has been almost meteoric and she will be heard from in great things in the future.").

Cook, Madge Carr [actress] (b. Yorkshire, England, 28 Jun 1856–20 Sep 1933 [77], Syosset, LI NY). m. (1) Charles Robson; (2) Augustus Cook. "Madge Carr Cook," *Variety*, 26 Sep 1933 (age 71). AS, p. 253 (b. 1862; d. LA CA). SD, p. 283.

Cook, Will A. [actor] (b. 1873?–2 Feb 1924 [50], Cleveland OH; pneumonia). "Will A. Cook," *Variety*, 14 Feb 1924. AS, p. 254.

Cook, William Wallace [writer/scenarist] (b. Marshall MI, 11 Apr 1867–20 Jul 1933 [66], Marshall MI). m. (1) Anna Gertrude Slater, 28 Feb 1891 (d. 1913); (2) Mary Ackley, 1926 (widow). Stanley A. Pachon, "William Wallace Cook," *Dime Novel Round-Up*, 25, 15 Sep 1957, 67–75 (in 1910 Cook wrote scenarios for Buffalo Bill's Wild West Show and Pawnee Bill's Far East Show).

Cooke, Albert G[ardner] [actor] (b. Los Angeles CA, 1882–6 Jul 1935 [53], Santa Monica CA). (Film debut: *By Golly;* Sennett; Universal; FBO.) "Al Cook," *Variety*, 10 Jul 1935 ("veteran of silent motion pictures"). AMD, p. 79. BHD, p. 135. IFN, p. 62. Truitt, p. 69. "Cook Started as a 'Social Pest,'" *MPW*, 3 Nov 1923, 98:1 ("Cooke comes from one of the earliest of the pioneer families in Los Angeles." Photo with article.).

Cooke, Baldwin G. "Baldy" [actor] (b. New York NY, 10 Mar 1888–31 Dec 1953 [65], Los Angeles CA). AS, p. 254. BHD1, p. 119. IFN, p. 62.

Cooke, Ethyle (mother of **Dorothy** and **Leland Benham**) [actress] (aka Ethyle Benham, b. Lynn MA, 4 Aug 1880–20 Apr 1949 [68], Waukesha WI). m. **Harry Benham** (d. 1969). AMD, p. 80. BHD, p. 135. IFN, p. 24 (age 63). "In the Picture Studios," *NYDM*, 4 Aug 1915, 27:2 (on the female baseball team at Thanhouser). "Ethyle Cooke—Thanhouser Leading Woman," *MPW*, 14 Oct 1916, 247. "Ethyle Cooke," *MPW*, 7 Jul 1917, 90. Billy H. Doyle, "Lost Players," *CI*, 149 (Nov 1987), 17.

Cooke, John J. [actor] (b. NY, 1 Oct 1876–2 Oct 1921 [45]). AS, p. 254 (d. NYC). BHD, p. 135. IFN, p. 62.

Cooke, John M. [playwright/producer] (b. 1871?–Mar 1922 [51], Salt Lake City UT; Bright's disease). "John M. Cooke," *Variety*, 17 Mar 1922.

Cooke, Pearl [actress] (d. 15 Dec 1917, Portland OR). BHD, p. 135.

Cooke, Stephen Beach [actor] (b. 1898–16 Sep 1948 [50?], Cooperstown NY). AS, p. 254 (b. 1879). BHD, p. 135. IFN, p. 62.

Cooke, Thomas C[offin] [actor/director] (b. Montgomery AL, 1875–9 Jun 1939 [64?], Bayside NY). AMD, p. 80. BHD2, p. 53. "Thanhouser Again Raids 'Legit,'" *MPW*, 15 May 1915, 1084.

Cooksey, Curtis [actor] (b. IN, 9 Dec 1891–19 Apr 1962 [70], Los Angeles CA; suicide because of incurable cancer). "Curtis Cooksey," *Variety*, 25 Apr 1962 (age 71). AS, p. 254. BHD1, p. 119. IFN, p. 62. SD, p. 283. Truitt, p. 70.

Cookson, S.A. [actor] (b. 1869–27 Feb 1947 [77?]). BHD1, p. 119. IFN, p. 62.

Cooley, Frank L[ucius] [actor/director] (b. Natchez MS, 1870?–6 Jul 1941 [71], Los Angeles CA). m. Gladys Kingsbury. (Keystone; Chaplin; American.) "Frank Cooley," *Variety*, 16 Jul 1941. AS, p. 254. BHD, p. 135. IFN, p. 62. Truitt, p. 70. "Director Cooley Ill," *NYDM*, 14 Apr 1915, 34:2 (with a siege of the grippe).

Cooley, Hallam [actor] (aka Hallam Burr, b. Brooklyn NY, 8 Feb 1895–20 Mar 1971 [76], Tiburon CA). m. Elizabeth Bates, 24 Dec 1918. AMD, p. 80. AS, p. 254. BHD1, p. 119; BHD2, p. 53. IFN, p. 62. 1921 Directory, p. 164. "Some Facts About Hallam Cooley," *MPW*, 4 May 1918, 717. "Hallam Cooley Married," *MPW*, 18 Jan 1919, 330. "Hallam Cooley," *MPW*, 24 Sep 1927, 228.

Cooley, James R. [actor] (b. Nelsonville OH, 1880–5 Nov 1948 [68], Los Angeles CA). "James R. Cooley," *NYT*, 7 Nov 1948, 88:5. "James R. Cooley," *Variety*, 10 Nov 1948. AMD, p. 80. AS, p. 254. BHD1, p. 119. IFN, p. 62. Truitt, p. 70. "James Cooley Rejoins Reliance," *MPW*, 22 Jun 1912, 1118. "In the Catskills with Reliance," *MPW*, 24 Aug 1912, 748–51. "Moore and Cooley Join Reliance," *MPW*, 24 Jan 1914, 423. "James Cooley Joins Imp," *MPW*, 28 Nov 1914, 1219.

Coolidge, Cuba [actor] (aka Cuba Crutchfield). No data found. AMD, p. 80. "Seeling Offers Coolidge in Five-Reel Westerns," *MPW*, 16 Aug 1924, 559.

Coombs, Boyce Molyneaux (b. 1894?–11 Mar 1934 [40], Chicago IL; found dead in bed). "Find Boyce Coombs Dead in Bed in Chicago Hotel," *Variety*, 13 Mar 1934. AS, p. 254. BHD, p. 135 (b. 1890).

Coombs, Guy [stage/film actor] (b. Washington DC, 15 Jun 1882). m. Anna Nilsson. (Edison; Kalem, Sep 1911; Kleine; Metro.) AMD, p. 80. AS, p. 254. BHD, p. 135. Spehr, p. 124. "Essanay Company Plans Greatest Baseball Film," *MPW*, 14 Oct 1911, 114–15. "Who Are They?," *MPW*, 18 Nov 1911, 558. Thornton Fisher, "Guy Coombs, Silent Leading Man," *MPW*, 4 Jul 1914, 45. "Coombs Heads Own Co.; Kalem Star to Be Featured by New Organization with Strong Backing," *NYDM*, 29 Jul 1914, 24:1. "Gossip of the Studios," *NYDM*, 5 Aug 1914, 23:2 (Coombs "now states that he has no intentions of accepting the offer made to feature him in a company of his own and will continue with the Kalem Company, where he is entirely satisfied."). "Brief Biographies of Popular Players," *Motion Picture Magazine*, IX, Jun 1915, 108. "Guy Coombs," *MPW*, 16 Oct 1915, 426. Bert Ennis, "Them Were the Happy Days; The Custard Pie Era," *MPC*, Feb 1927, 30–31, 67, 85 ("He also gave up pictures to engage in real-estate operations in Florida," p. 67).

Coombs, Jack [baseball player/actor] (aka Colby Jack Coombs, b. Le Grand IA, 18 Nov 1882–15 Apr 1957 [74], Palestine TX; heart attack). "Jack Coombs, 74, Ballplayer, Dies; Pitcher in Both Leagues, 1906 to 1920, Won 5 Series Games—Coached at Duke U.," *NYT*, 16 Apr 1957, 33:1. AS, p. 254. BHD, p. 135.

Coombs, Wolcott [actor]. No data found. AMD, p. 80. "Wolcott Coombs, Deaf-Blind Marvel in Selig Film," *MPW*, 30 Mar 1912, 1181.

Cooper, Arthur Melbourne [director/producer] (b. St. Albans, England, 15 Apr 1874–24 Nov 1961 [87], Coton-on-Cambridge, England). AS, p. 254. BHD2, p. 53.

Cooper, Ashley [actor] (b. Sydney, Australia, 1881?–3 Jan 1952 [70], New York NY). "Ashley Cooper," *Variety*, 9 Jan 1952. AS, p. 255. BHD, p. 135. IFN, p. 62. Truitt, p. 70.

Cooper, Bigelow [actor]. No data found. m. Mabel. (Edison; Vitagraph.) AMD, p. 80. "Bigelow Cooper, Edison Players," *MPW*, 7 Aug 1915, 1010. "Newsy Notes," *NYDM*, 22 Sep 1915, 30:4 (recovering from a car accident while touring Pennsylvania recently. The car skidded and smashed another; he and his friend were thrown into a ditch "with the overturned car partly on top of them. Luckily, they were only slightly injured."). "Bigelow Cooper Joins Apollo," *MPW*, 6 Jan 1917, 64.

Cooper, Claude H. [actor/director] (b. London, England, 1881?–20 Jul 1932 [51], Laurelton NY; throat cancer). (Thanhouser.) "Claude Cooper," *Variety*, 26 Jul 1932. AS, p. 255. BHD1, p. 119. IFN, p. 62. Truitt, p. 70.

Cooper, Courtney Riley [writer/circus clown and publicist/director] (b. Kansas City MO, 31 Oct 1886–29 Sep 1940 [53], New York NY; suicide by hanging in a NY hotel room). m. Genevieve R. Furey, 1916. "Courtney Riley Cooper," *Variety*, 2 Oct 1940. AMD, p. 80. AS, p. 255. BHD2, p. 53. James Vinson, ed., *Twentieth Century Western Writers* (Detroit MI: Gale Research, 1982), p. 192. "Courtney Ryley Cooper, Editor for Wharton," *MPW*, 2 Jun 1917, 1453. "Courtney Ryley Cooper," *MPW*, 22 Dec 1917, 1788. "Cooper Made Marine Lieutenant," *MPW*, 15 Feb 1919, 886.

Cooper, D.P. [cinematographer]. No data found. FDY, p. 457.

Cooper, Dulcie [stage/film actress] (b. Sydney, Australia, 1904?–3 Sep 1981 [77], New York NY). m. Elmer Brown. AS, p. 255. BHD1, p. 119. SD.

Cooper, Earl P. [actor] (b. 1886–22 Oct 1965 [79?], Atwater CA). BHD, p. 135.

Cooper, Edna Mae [actress] (b. Baltimore MD, 19 Jul 1900–27 Jun 1986 [85], Woodland Hills CA). m. **Karl Brown**, 1919 (d. 1990). (Paramount.) "Edna Mae Cooper," *Variety*, 2 Jul 1986. AMD, p. 80. AS, p. 255. BHD1, p. 120. "Weddings," *MPW*, XLII, 22 Nov 1919, 422.

Cooper, Edward [actor] (b. 1883–15 Jul 1956 [73?], Surrey, England). AS, p. 155. BHD1, p. 120.

Cooper, Elizabeth [writer]. No data found. AMD, p. 80. "Author Attends Premiere," *MPW*, 6 Jun 1925, 672.

Cooper, Frederick [actor] (b. London, England, 1889–3 Jan 1945 [55?], London, England). BHD1, p. 120.

Cooper, Gary [actor/producer] (*né* Frank James Cooper, b. Helena MT, 7 May 1901–13 May 1961 [60], Los Angeles CA). m. (1) Sandra Shaw; Virginia Balfe. Hector Arce, *Gary Cooper; An Intimate Biography* (NY: William Morrow & Co., Inc., 1979). "Gary Cooper Dead of Cancer; Film

Star, 60, Won 2 Oscars; Honored for 'Sergeant York' [1941] and 'High Noon' [1952]—Played Movie Leads 35 Years," *NYT,* 14 May 1961, 1:4, 86:4. "Gary Cooper," *Variety,* 17 May 1961 (d. Hollywood CA, age 59). AMD, p. 80. AS, p. 255. BHD1, p. 120; BHD2, p. 53. FSFM, p. 155 (b. 1902). FSS, p. 72. HCH, p. 59. IFN, p. 63. Katz, pp. 269–70 (began 1925). Truitt, p. 70. "Paramount Creates a New Star," *MPW,* 20 Nov 1926, 146. "Gary Cooper Is Lead in 'Nevada,'" *MPW,* 28 May 1927, 255. Dorothy Manners, "The Cow-Punchin' Cinderella Man; Gary Cooper Drifted into Pictures *by Way of the* Plains—and Became a Star Overnight," *MPC,* Jun 1927, 54–55, 79. "New Role for Gary," *MPW,* 23 Jul 1927, 238. Elisabeth Goldbeck, "You Can't Trust Women; Gary Cooper Exhibits His Shattered Illusions," *MPC,* Feb 1929, 43, 80, 83 ("Ladies of every type have thrown all dignity to the winds and made it perfectly clear that they consider him the last word in sex appeal."). Julie Lang, "The Man of the Moment, Gary Cooper; A Big Boy from Montana Becomes the New Idol of Hollywood," *Screenland,* May 1929, 44–45, 100. Ruth Biery, "Don't You Dare Marry; Because Everyone's Said that to Gary Cooper and Lupe Velez, Is Why They Don't," *MPC,* Jul 1929, 22, 80–81.

Cooper, George A. [director/scenarist] (b. 29 Apr 1894-Aug 1947 [53]). BHD2, p. 53.

Cooper, George H. [actor] (*né* George Cooper Healy, b. Newark NJ, 18 Dec 1891–9 Dec 1943 [51], Sawtelle CA). (Vitagraph, 1908; Sennett.) "George Cooper," *Variety,* 15 Dec 1943. AMD, p. 80. AS, p. 255 (b. 1892). BHD1, p. 120; BHD2, p. 53. IFN, p. 63. "Cooper Signed by M-G-M," *MPW,* 26 Jun 1926, 683. George Katchmer, "Remembering the Great Silents," *CI,* 207 (Sep 1992), 42.

Cooper, Georgie (mother of George Stevens) [actress] (*née* Georgie Cooper Stevens, b. MI, 31 Jul 1882–3 Sep 1968 [86], Los Angeles CA). AS, p. 255. BHD1, p. 120 (Georgia Cooper). IFN, p. 63.

Cooper, Gladys Constance [actress] (b. Lewisham [London], England, 18 Dec 1888 [extrait de naissance no. 323/1889]–17 Nov 1971 [82], Remenham, England; cancer [extrait de décès no. 59/1971]). m. **Philip Merivale** (d. 1946); Capt. H.J. Buckmaster; Sir Neville Pearson. *Gladys Cooper* (1931); *Without Veils* (1953). "Gladys Cooper, British Actress, Dies," *NYT,* 18 Nov 1971, 50:3. "Gladys Cooper," *Variety,* 24 Nov 1971. AS, p. 255. BHD1, p. 120. IFN, p. 63. Katz, p. 270 (began in 1914). SD. Truitt, p. 70.

Cooper, Harry [cinematographer]. No data found. FDY, p. 457.

Cooper, Harry [stuntman/actor] (b. 1882? 28 Aug 1957 [75], Los Angeles CA). m. Mae Valli. (Vitagraph.) "Harry Cooper," *Variety,* 4 Sep 1957. AS, p. 255. BHD1, p. 120. IFN, p. 63. Truitt, p. 70.

Cooper, J. Gordon [director/producer] (b. Baltimore MD, 1895?–27 Jun 1939 [44], Beverly Hills CA; heart attack). (Paramount; Fox.) "J. Gordon Cooper," *Variety,* 28 Jun 1939 ("Was with Fox Film Corp. for 17 years directing silent pictures."). AMD, p. 80. AS, p. 255. BHD2, p. 53. "Cooper Directing," *MPW,* 17 Sep 1927, 155.

Cooper, Jack [actor/publicist] (b. England, 29 Oct 1903–9 Jun 1976 [72], Lake Tahoe CA). m. Marie. (WB.) "Jack Cooper," *Variety,* 16 Jun 1976. BHD2, p. 54.

Cooper, James [actor] (d. 26 Feb 1915, New York NY). "James Cooper, the actor, died in Bellevue Hospital, Feb. 26," *Variety,* 5 Mar 1915. AS, p. 255.

Cooper, Lillian Kemble [actress] (b. London, England, 21 Mar 1892–4 May 1977 [85], Los Angeles CA). AS, p. 255. BHD1, p. 120 (b. 1898). IFN, p. 63.

Cooper, Mabel (mother of Jackie Cooper) [actress] (*née?,* b. 1905?–27 Nov 1941 [36], Beverly Hills CA). m. (1) Johnny Cooper (son, Jackie, b. 15 Sep 1922). "Mabel Cooper Bigelow," *Variety,* 3 Dec 1941. AS p. 255.

Cooper, Merian C[aldwell] [director/producer] (b. Jacksonville FL, 24 Oct 1893–21 Apr 1973 [79], San Diego CA; cancer). m. **Dorothy Jordan**, 27 May 1933 (d. 1988). (RKO; Selznick International.) William M. Freeman, "Merian Cooper, Creator of 'King Kong,'" *NYT,* 22 Apr 1973, 55:1 (age 78). "Merian C. Cooper," *Variety,* 25 Apr 1973. AS, p. 255. BHD, p. 135; BHD2, p. 54 (d. Coronado CA). IFN, p. 63. Katz, p. 270. Dunham Thorp, "Fighting the Jungle; The Heroic Record of 'Chang,'" *MPC,* Jul 1927, 40–41, 68. Francis Jackson, "Two Men and a Camera Conquer the Jungle; How true is 'Chang,' that astonishing drama of the Siamese jungle?...," *Cinema Arts,* Jul 1927, 16–17, 46.

Cooper, Miriam [actress] (b. Baltimore MD, 7 Nov 1891–12 Apr 1976 [84?], Charlottesville VA; cerebral hemorrhage). With Bonnie Herndon, *Dark Lady of the Silents; My Life in Early Hollywood* (Indianapolis IN: The Bobbs-Merrill Co., Inc., 1973). (Kalem; Biograph.) m. **Raoul Walsh** [Albert Edward Walsh], Feb 1916, Hopi Indian Reservation near Albuquerque NM—div. 1926 (d. 1980). "Miriam Cooper Walsh, 84, Star in 'Birth of a Nation,'" *NYT,* 14 Apr 1976, 42:4; "Correction," *NYT,* 27 Apr 1976, 37:7. "Miriam C. Walsh," *Variety,* 5 May 1976. (Reliance-Majestic; Fine Arts; Fox.) AMD, p. 80. AS, p. 255. BHD, p. 136 (b. 1894). Katz, p. 271 (began 1910). MH, p. 104. MSBB, p. 1034. "Miriam Cooper with Fox," *MPW,* 20 Jan 1917, 350. "Miriam Cooper Returns to Screen," *MPW,* 2 Mar 1918, 1208 (from retirement in 1917). "Miriam Cooper Leads in First Independent Walsh Picture," *MPW,* 1 May 1920, 665. "Belasco Signs Miriam Cooper," *MPW,* 14 Oct 1922, 5765. "Sues Walsh for Divorce," *MPW,* 28 May 1927, 251 (decree final in 1927). June Lee, "Dan Cupid's Bulletin Board," *Paris and Hollywood Screen Secrets Magazine,* Aug 1927, 37 (Cooper, "once a favorite leading lady of the films, has filed suit for divorce, declaring that Walsh himself has often said that he is temperamentally unfit for matrimony...the director has evinced a decided disinclination to live at home, preferring the congenial atmosphere of a Hollywood hote. The couple were married in 1916, and separated last October. They have two adopted children."). Anthony Slide, *The Griffith Actresses* (NY: A.S. Barnes & Co., 1973), pp. 127–35. "Jay Rubin Interviews Miriam Cooper," *CFC,* 44 (Fall, 1974), 6–8.

Cooper, Olive (daughter of stage actress Georgie Woodthorpe and minstrel Fred A. Cooper) [actress/scenarist] (b. 31 Jul 1892–15 Jun 1950 [58], Los Angeles CA; pneumonia). AMD, p. 81. AS, p. 255 (d. 1987). BHD, p. 136 (d. 17 Jun 1987); BHD2, p. 54 (d. 12 Jun 1987). IFN, p. 63.

Cooper, Ollie [stage/film actress]. No data found. AMD, p. 81. "Ollie Cooper Making Screen Debut," *MPW,* 16 Feb 1918, 988:2 (in *The Brass Check,* Metro).

Cooper, Stephen [scenarist]. No data found. FDY, p. 423.

Cooper, Tex [actor] (*né* Judge Thomas Cooper, b. TX, 21 Apr 1876–29 Mar 1951 [74], Los Angeles CA). m. Nona, a former circus midget. (Bison, 1910.) "Tex Cooper," *Variety,* 4 Apr 1951 ("pioneer film cowboy"; began ca. 1916). AS, p. 255. BHD1, p. 120. IFN, p. 63. Truitt, p. 70.

Coote, Bert [actor] (*né* Albert Coote, b. London, England, 1868?–1 Sep 1938 [70], London, England). m. (1) Julie Kingsley; (2) Ada Russell. "Bert Coote," *Variety,* 7 Sep 1938. AS, p. 256. BHD1, p. 120. IFN, p. 63. SD.

Coover, L.G. [advertising] (b. 1882?–8 Jan 1913 [30]; appendicitis). AMD, p. 81. "Obituary," *MPW,* 18 Jan 1913, 275. "Burial of L.G. Coover," *MPW,* 25 Jan 1913, 349.

Copeau, Jacques [actor/director] (b. Paris, France, 4 Feb 1879–20 Oct 1949 [70], Beaune, France; cancer [extrait de décès no. 207/1949]). AS, p. 256.

Copeland, Nicholas W. [vaudevillian/actor/writer] (b. Omaha NB, 14 Oct 1894–17 Aug 1940 [45], Los Angeles CA). (Began 1921.) "Nick Copeland," *Variety,* 21 Aug 1940. AS, p. 256. IFN, p. 63.

Copper, R.C. [executive]. No data found. (Interstate Film Corp.; President of Reelcraft.) Grace Kingsley, "Flashes; New Film Concern; Reelcraft Latest to Enter Cinema Realm," *LA Times,* 11 Mar 1920, III, p. 4 (Reelcraft absorbed the Bullseye Comedy Company and the Interstate Film Corp., a distributing agency. Actors Conway Tearle and Ora Carew, and directors Jay Hunt and George Jeske joined the new comapny.).

Coquelin, Constant-Benoit [actor] (*né* Jules Constant Coquelin, b. Boulogne-sur-Mare, France, 11 Jan 1841 [extrait de naissance no. 29/1841]–27 Jan 1909 [68], Couilly-Pont-aux-Dames, France). AS, p. 256. BHD, p. 136.

Coquelin, Jean [actor/producer] (b. 1865–2 Oct 1944 [79?], France). AS, p. 256 (d. 3 Oct). BHD2, p. 54.

Corbaley, Kate [scenarist] (b. 1878?–23 Sep 1938 [60], Los Angeles CA). (Triangle; Palmer Photoplay; Metro.) "Kate Corbaley," *Variety,* 28 Sep 1938. AS, p. 256. IFN, p. 63.

Corbett, Ben[ny] [actor] (b. Hudson IL, 6 Feb 1892–19 May 1961 [69], Los Angeles CA). "Ben Corbett," *Variety,* 31 May 1961 (in films 46 years). AS, p. 256. BHD1, p. 121 (b. OH). IFN, p. 63 (b. OH). Truitt, p. 71.

Corbett, Bernard M. [general manager]. No data found. AMD, p. 81. "Corbett Resigns from Kriterion," *MPW,* 18 Dec 1915, 2155.

Corbett, James J[ohn], "Gentleman Jim" [prizefighter/actor/scenarist] (b. San Francisco CA, 1 Sep 1866–18 Feb 1933 [66], Bayside, LI NY [Death Certificate Index No. 1331]; liver cancer). m. (1) Olive Lake, 8 Jun 1886—div. 2 Aug 1895; (2) Jessie Taylor (Vera Stanwood), 15 Aug 1895. (Film debut: 1894 prizefight [against Peter Courtney] kinetograph documentary; *How Championships Are Won—And Lost,* Vitagraph, 1910 [also scenarist].) "James J. Corbett," *Variety,* 21 Feb 1933. AMD, p. 81. AS, p. 256. BHD1, p. 121. IFN, p. 63. SD. Spehr, p. 124. Truitt, p. 71. WWVC, pp. 35–36. "Corbett Smashes Things; Strenuous Doings in Harvard Playlet in Which ex-Pugilist

Shines," *NYT,* 28 Mar 1905, 9:1 (in *Pals* at the American Theatre, 27 Mar. "...when the climax came it was the hottest finish that the local stage has seen since the palmy days of the old Bowery. It was then that James J. Corbett of ex-championship fame, acting in concert with the villain of the play [J. Frank Burke], who had up to this time been his old college chum, smashed 150 incandescent electric lights, ten pieces of bric-à-brac, two mirrors, broke a balustrade, and tore up two carpets.... There is no gainsaying the argument that James J. Corbett takes to the stage as gracefully as he did to pugilism. He may not become a champion on the boards as he did in the roped arena, but there is no gainsaying the fact that he is easy, graceful, and natural, and that he played his part for all there was in it.... After the third act Corbett was called before the curtain to make a speech. He looked as much surprised as any veteran."). "Jim Corbett a Boniface; He and [Charles] Parson Davies to Take 'Tom' O'Rourke's Hotel Del[a]van," *NYT,* 13 Jun 1905, 5:2. "Notes of the Trade," *MPW,* 27 Sep 1913, 1399. "James Corbett to Appear in Blaché Features," *MPW,* 16 May 1914, 957. "James J. Corbett to Start Work for Universal Jan. 6," *MPW,* 11 Jan 1919, 240. "Corbett Itching to Stage a Real Screen Fist Fight," *MPW,* 18 Jan 1919, 313. "Corbett Now Film Star," *MPW,* 25 Jan 1919, 474. William J. Reilly, "Well, Goodbye, Jim—Take Keer Yourself," *MPW,* 2 Aug 1919, 661.

Corbin, Ruth (sister of **Virginia Lee Corbin**) [actress]. No data found. m. John Miehle—div. 1927. June Lee, "Dan Cupid's Bulletin Board," *Paris and Hollywood Screen Secrets,* Oct 1927, 37 (divorced her husband, "because, she says, she had to give up her own room to her mother-in-law and sleep in the kitchen.").

Corbin, Virginia Lee (sister of **Ruth Corbin**) [stage/film actress] (b. Prescott AZ, 5 Dec 1910–4 Jun 1942 [31], Winfield IL; heart attack). m. (1) Theodore Krol—div. 1937 (sons Harold and Robert); (2) Charles Jacobson. "Virginia Lee Corbin," *Variety,* 10 Jun 1942. (Fox; last film: *Knee High,* 1929.) AMD, p. 81. AS, p. 257. BHD1, p. 121. FSS, p. 74. IFN, p. 63. MSBB, p. 1034 (b. 1913). Truitt, p. 71. "Popular Picture Personalities," *MPW,* 14 Apr 1917, 279. "Miss Corbin in Cast," *MPW,* 20 Dec 1924, 279. "Virginia Lee Corbin," *MPW,* 13 Feb 1926, 631. "Miss Corbin Signs with I.E. Chadwick," *MPW,* 4 Dec 1926, 346. "Virginia Lee Corbin," *MPW,* 15 Jan 1927, 191. "Gotham Signs Miss Corbin," *MPW,* 22 Jan 1927, 274. "John McCormick Signs New Star," *MPW,* 16 Apr 1927, 645. "Virginia Lee Corbin," *MPW,* 4 Jun 1927, 332. "Virginia Lee Corbin," *MPW,* 13 Aug 1927, 925. Billy Doyle, "Lost Players," *CI,* 174 (Dec 1989), C12-C13.

Corby, Travers [scenarist]. No data found. FDY, p. 423.

Corcoran, Ethel M[argaret] *see* **Dayton, Ethel**

Corda, Maria [actress] (aka Maria Korda, *née* Maris Farkias, b. Deva, Hungary, 4 May 1902). m. director Alexander Korda. (Film in Germany, 1923–26; two U.S. silents: *The Private Life of Helen of Troy,* 1927, and *Love and the Devil,* 1929.) AMD, p. 81. AS, p. 257. BHD, p. 136. JS, p. 107 (in Italian silents from 1925). "Maria Corda," *MPW,* 18 Dec 1926, 496. Tom Waller, "Maria Corda," *MPW,* 2 Apr 1927, 478–79. "Maria Corda Here," *MPW,* 10 Dec 1927, 24. Carol Johnston, "So This Is—Helen; A Close-Up of Maria Corda," *MPC,* Mar 1928, 51, 86.

Corday, Marcelle [actress] (b. Brussels, Belgium, 8 Jan 1906). AS, p. 257. Ragan 2, p. 332.

Cording, Harry [actor] (b. England, 26 Apr 1891–1 Sep 1954 [63], Sun Valley CA). (Film debut: *Sins of the Father,* 1921.) AS, p. 257 (b. NYC). BHD1, p. 121. IFN, p. 63. Truitt, p. 71 (b. NYC, 29 Apr 1894). George A. Katchmer, "Forgotten Cowboys and Cowgirls—Part XVII," *CI,* 194 (Aug 1991), 47. Blackie Seymour, "The Many Faces of Harry Cording," *CI,* 209 (Nov 1992), 28, 30 (b. 1894).

Corelli, Marie [actress] (d. Detroit MI, 10 May 1954). BHD, p. 136.

Corey, Eugene *see* **Corrado, Gino**

Corey, James [actor] (*né* James Warren Corey, Sr., b. Tucson AZ, 1884–10 Jan 1956 [72], Los Angeles CA). m. Patrice. AS, p. 257 (Jim Corey, d. 12 Nov). BHD1, p. 122. GK, pp. 163–92. George Katchmer, "Remembering the Great Silents," *CI,* 203 (May 1992), 43; *CI,* 222 (Dec 1993), C18-C19.

Cormack, Bartlett [actor/director/scenarist] (b. Hammond IN, 12 Mar 1898–16 Sep 1942 [44], Phoenix AZ). "Bartlett Cormack; Playwright and Newspaperman Dies in Phoenix, Ariz., at 44," *NYT,* 18 Sep 1942, 21:5. "Bartlett Cormack," *Variety,* 23 Sep 1942. AS, p. 258. BHD2, p. 54. IFN, p. 64.

Cornwall, Anne [actress] (b. Brooklyn NY, 17 Jan 1897–2 Mar 1980 [82], Van Nuys CA). m. **Charles M. Maigne** (d. 1929). (Universal.) AMD, p. 81. AS, p. 258 (d. LA CA). BHD1, p. 122. FFF, p. 149. FSS, p. 74. WWS, p. 232. "Anne Cornwall Is Star of 'Virginia,'" *MPW,* 3 Apr 1920, 110. "Anne Cornwall Signed," *MPW,* 4 Apr 1925, 481. Alma Talley, "Life Is Full of Danger...for Anne Cornwall; When Studio Work Is One Thrill After Another," *MW,* 18 Jul 1925, 14–15, 44. "Christie Signs Anne Cornwall," *MPW,* 15 May 1926, 210. "Beauties Who Make the Comedies Attractive," *Cinema Arts,* Aug 1926, 21 (photo). "Anne Cornwall," *CI,* 69 (May 1980), 48.

Cornwall, Blanche [actress]. (Solax.) AMD, p. 81. Spehr, p. 124. "Solax Enlarging Studios," *MPW,* 4 Nov 1911, 386.

Corradini, Arnaldo Ginanni (brother of **Bruno Corradini**) [director] (b. Ravenna, Italy, 7 May 1890). AS, p. 258.

Corradini, Bruno (brother of **Arnaldo Corradini**) [director] (b. Ravenna, Italy, 9 Jun 1892–20 Nov 1974 [82], Varese, Italy). AS, p. 258.

Corrado, Gino [actor] (aka Eugene Corey, *né* Gino Liserani, b. Florence, Italy, 9 Feb 1893–23 Dec 1982 [89], Woodland Hills CA). "Gino Liserani (Corrado)," *Variety,* 5 Jan 1983 (age 87). (In *Her Bridal Night-Mare,* Christie, 1920). AS, p. 258. BHD1, p. 122. FSS, p. 74. "Coast Picture News," *Variety,* 19 Oct 1917, p. 28 ("Gino Liserini, the actor, has come to the conclusion that his name is too complicated for film publicity uses and has changed it to 'Eugene Corrie.'").

Corregan, Donald W. [scenic artist] (d. Syracuse NY, 2 May 1915). BHD, p. 136; BHD2, p. 54.

Corrigan, D'Arcy [actor] (b. County Cork, Ireland, 2 Jan 1870–25 Dec 1945 [75], Los Angeles CA). AS, p. 258. BHD1, p. 122. IFN, p. 64.

Corrigan, Emmett [vaudeville/film actor] (*né* Antoine Zilles, b. Amsterdam, Holland, 5 Jun 1868–29 Oct 1932 [64], Los Angeles CA; heart attack at Maskers Club). m. (1) Myra (d. 1896); (2) Molly I. Mack. (Metro.) "Emmett Corrigan, Actor, Dies Suddenly; Victim of Heart Attack at 65 While Watching Card Game—Made Stage Debut at 14," *NYT,* 30 Oct 1932, 37:2. "Emmett Corrigan," *Variety,* 1 Nov 1932 (age 65). AMD, p. 81. AS, p. 259. BHD1, p. 122 (b. 1871). IFN, p. 64. SD. Truitt, p. 71. "Emmet Corrigan on Screen," *NYDM,* 28 Apr 1915, 29:2. "Actor Withdraws from Success," *MPW,* 18 Dec 1915, 2194.

Corrigan, James [actor] (b. OH, 17 Oct 1867–28 Feb 1929 [61], Los Angeles CA). m. Lillian Elliot. "James Corrigan," *Variety,* 6 Mar 1929 (age 58). AMD, p. 81. AS, p. 259. BHD, p. 136. IFN, p. 64. Truitt, p. 71. "Has Stomach Trouble," *MPW,* 12 Feb 1921, 815.

Corrigan, Lloyd (son of **Lillian Elliott**; brother of **Jack Corrigan**) [actor/director/scenarist] (b. San Francisco CA, 16 Oct 1900–5 Nov 1969 [69], Woodland Hills CA). . "Lloyd Corrigan, a Movie Actor, 69; Gag Man, Also a Director and a Script Writer, Dies," *NYT,* 9 Nov 1969. "Lloyd Corrigan," *Variety,* 12 Nov 1969 (d. 7 Nov). AMD, p. 81. AS, p. 259 (d. 7 Nov). BHD1, p. 122; BHD2, p. 54. FDY, p. 423. IFN, p. 64. Katz, p. 275. Truitt, p. 72. "Corrigan Again Signs," *MPW,* 19 Feb 1927, 544.

Corsi, Antonio [model/actor] (b. 1868?–4 Dec 1924 [56], Los Angeles CA). "Famous Model Dead; Antonio Corsi, Who Posed for Great Painters, Dies at 56," *NYT,* 6 Dec 1924, 15:7. AS, p. 259 (d. 5 Dec). BHD, p. 136.

Corsi, Mario [scenarist/director] (b. Pistoia, Italy, 16 Jun 1882–3 Apr 1954 [71], Rome, Italy). AS, p. 259. JS, p. 109 (in Italian silents from 1917).

Cort, Harry L. [producer/director/scenarist] (b. Seattle WA, 1893–6 May 1937 [44?], New York NY). BHD2, p. 54.

Cort, John [stage/film producer] (b. Woodstock CT, 1859–17 Nov 1929 [70], Stamford CT, in a sanitarium). m. (1) **Maude Fealey**, 9 Jan 1920, Cincinnati OH (d. 1971). "John Cort," *Variety,* 20 Nov 1929, p. 68 (b. Newark NJ). AMD, p. 81. BHD, p. 136. "Cort Heads Talking Picture Company," *MPW,* 28 Sep 1912, 1285. "Cort with Morosco; Theatrical Manager Gives Exclusive Rights to His Plays and Stars to New Firm," *NYDM,* 18 Nov 1914, 24:4. "Farnums Sue Cort; Want Payment of $3,000 from Manager for Three Weeks' Work," *NYDM,* 18 Nov 1914, 9:2 (William Farnum). "Morosco and Cort Enter Picture Field," *MPW,* 21 Nov 1914, 1093. "Flashes; Maude Fealy Weds; Noted Actress is Now Mrs. John Cort, Jr.," *LA Times,* 17 Jan 1920, II, 7.

Cortes, Armand F. [actor] (*né* Armand Coetez, b. Nîmes, France, 16 Aug 1880–19 Nov 1948 [68], San Francisco CA). AMD, p. 81. AS, p. 259. BHD1, p. 123. IFN, p. 64. "Actor in 'Tarzan' Cast Narrowly Escapes Death," *MPW,* 31 Jan 1920, 713.

Cortez, Orlando [actor]. No data found. AMD, p. 81. "May Become Star," *MPW,* 30 Dec 1922, 884.

Cortez, Ricardo (brother of **Stanley Cortez**) [actor/director] (*né* Jake Krantz [or Krantzko], aka Jack Crane, b. Vienna, Austria [or Brooklyn NY], 19 Sep 1899–28 Apr 1977 [77], New York NY [Death Certificate Index No. 7346, age 76]). m. **Alma Rubens**, Apr 1926 (d. 1931); Christine Coniff Lee, 6 Jan 1934, Phoenix AZ—div. Jun 1940; Margaret Ball, 1950). (Paramount; MGM; Columbia; RKO.) "Ricardo Cortez, Actor in Movies, 77," *NYT*, 29 Apr 1977, B4:3. "Ricardo Cortez," *Variety*, 4 May 1977. AMD, p. 81. AS, p. 259. BHD1, p. 123; BHD2, p. 55 (b. Brooklyn NY). FFF, p. 89. FSS, p. 75. GK, pp. 192–203. IFN, p. 64. MH, p. 104 (b. Alsace-Lorraine, France). "Cortez Lead in 'Anna Karenina,'" *MPW*, 23 Apr 1927, 714. "Columbia Signs Three Stars of the First Magnitude," *MPW*, 30 Jul 1927, 331. De-Witt Bodeen, "Ricardo Cortez," *Films in Review*, Jun/Jul 1984, 322–35. "Ricardo Cortez," WBO2, pp. 138–39. George A. Katchmer, "Latin Lover? Ricardo Cortez," *CI*, 147 (Sep 1987), 25–28 (extra at Ft. Lee NJ). *CI*, 184; *CI*, 231, 44.

Cortez, Stanley (brother of **Ricardo Cortez**) [cinematographer] (*né* Stanislaus Krantzko, b. New York NY, 4 Nov 1905–23 Dec 1997 [92], Los Angeles CA; heart attack). "Stanley Cortez," *Variety*, 5 Jan 1998, 90:5. Katz, p. 276 (began 1926). AS, p. 259 (b. 1908).

Corthell, Herbert [actor] (*né* Joseph Bertram Corthel, b. Boston MA, 20 Jan 1878 [Massachusetts Vital Statistics, Births, Vol. 297, p. 192]–23 Jan 1947 [68], Los Angeles CA). "Herbert Corthell," *Variety*, 29 Jan 1917. AS, p. 259. BHD1, p. 123. IFN, p. 64. Truitt, p. 72 (b. 1875).

Corwin, Mary [actress] (*née* Maria Breninki, b. Warsaw, Poland, 1895). JS, p. 109 (in Italian silents from 1916).

Cory, Robert [actor] (b. 1883?–9 Nov 1955 [72], Los Angeles CA; cancer). m. Doreen Munroe. "Robert Cory," *Variety*, 23 Nov 1955. AS, p. 259. IFN, p. 64. Truitt, p. 72.

Cos, Joaquin [director] (*né* Joaquin Coss Malens, b. Barcelona, Spain, 6 Jan 1886–14 Jul 1949 [63], Mexico City, Mexico; cancer). AS, p. 259 (worked in Mexico).

Cosgrave, Jack [actor] (b. PA, 29 Sep 1875–27 Jan 1925 [49]). AS, p. 259 (d. NYC). BHD, p. 136. IFN, p. 64.

Cosgrave, Luke [actor] (*né* Sean Maccosggair, b. Ballaghderreen, County Mayo, Ireland, 6 Aug 1862–28 Jun 1949 [86], Woodland Hills CA). "Luke Cosgrave," *Variety*, 6 Jul 1949 (character actor). AS, p. 260. BHD1, p. 123 (d. Calabasas CA). IFN, p. 64. SD. Truitt, p. 72. George Katchmer, "Forgotten Cowboys and Cowgirls—Part XVII," *CI*, 194 (Aug 1991), 43–44.

Cosgrove, Charles [extra] (b. Delaware IA, 17 Nov 1865–12 Dec 1943 [78], Los Angeles CA). BHD, p. 136. IFN, p. 64.

Cosgrove, Larry Sheldon [actor] (b. Baltimore MD, 1882). BHD, p. 136.

Cosini, Nelo [director] (b. Macerata, Italy, 1894–5 Oct 1945 [51?], Buenos Aires, Argentina). BHD2, p. 55.

Coslow, Sam (father of actress Jacqueline Coslow) [composer/lyricist/publisher/producer] (*né* Samson Coslow, aka Leslie Barton, b. New York NY, 7 Sep 1902–2 Apr 1982 [79], Bronxville NY). . m. **Esther Muir** (d. 1995). "Sam Coslow Dies at 79, Songwriter, Finance Wiz, Former Variety Staffer," *Variety*, 7 Apr 1982 (wrote *My Old Flame; Mr. Paganini*). AS, p. 260 (b. 27 Dec). ASCAP 66, p. 140. BHD1, p. 123; BHD2, p. 55 (b. 1901). CEPMJ.

Cossar, John Hay [actor] (b. London, England, 2 Jan 1858–28 Apr 1935 [77], Los Angeles CA). (Essanay.) "John Hay Cossar," *Variety*, 8 May 1955. AS, p. 260. IFN, p. 64. Truitt, p. 72.

Cossart, Ernest (father of Valerie Cossart) [stage/film actor] (b. Cheltenham, England, 24 Sep 1876–21 Jan 1951 [74], Bronx NY). m. Maude Davis (daughter, Valerie, 1907–1949). "Ernest Cossart, 74, Veteran of Stage; Trouper for Half Century Who Appeared in Many Successes Dies—Acted in Films," *NYT*, 22 Jan 1951, 17:3. "Ernest Cossart," *Variety*, 24 Jan 1951. AS, p. 260. BHD1, p. 123. IFN, p. 64. Katz, p. 276. Truitt, p. 72.

Costa, Sebastiano [actor] (b. Italy, 1876–18 Jul 1935 [59], New Rochelle NY). AS, p. 260. BHD, p. 137. IFN, p. 64.

Costamagna, Adriana [actress] (*née* Maria Teresa Costamagna, b. Piedmonte, Italy, 1889). AMD, p. 81. JS, p. 110 (in Italian silents from 1911). "Photoplay Actress Disfigured by Leopard," *MPW*, 1 Nov 1913, 481.

Coste, Maurice R. [actor] (b. 1875–22 Mar 1963 [87?], Chatham, Canada). BHD, p. 137. IFN, p. 64.

Costello, Dolores (daughter of **Maurice Costello**; sister of **Helene Costello**) [actress: Wampas Star, 1926] (b. Pittsburgh PA, 17 Sep 1905–1 Mar 1979 [73], Fallbrook CA; emphysema). m. **John Barrymore**, 24 Nov 1928—div. 24 Aug 1934 (d. 1942); (4) John Vrywink. (Vitagraph; WB; RKO) Peter B. Flint, "Dolores Costello, 73, Film Star; Wife of Barrymore," *NYT*, 3 Mar 1979, 28:4. "Dolores Costello," *Variety*, 7 Mar 1979. AMD, p. 81. AS, p. 260. BHD1, p. 123. FSFW, p. 68 (b. 1906). FSS, p. 75. HCH, p. 53. IFN, p. 64. SD. "Dolores Costello," WBO2, pp. 106–107 (b. 1906). "Among the Players," *NYDM*, 22 Jul 1914, 28:3. "Barrymore Picks Dolores Costello," *MPW*, 25 Jul 1925, 445 (m. Barrymore). Hal K. Wells, "The House of Costello Carries On," *MPC*, Nov 1925, 34, 70. "Harry Warner Makes Dolores Costello a Star," *MPW*, 30 Jan 1926, 444. Elizabeth Greer, "Dolores...A Story About the Costello Girl," *MM*, Mar 1926, 69, 129–30. "Dolores Costello," *MPW*, 19 Jun 1926, 638. Paul Paige, "Close-Ups and Fade-Outs," *Paris and Hollywood*, Sep 1926, 90–91 (tried to give her sister Helene a boost by getting Raymond Griffith to give her the lead in *Wet Paint*. Warners did Dolores an injustice by giving her material like *The Bride of the Storm*, a poor film.). "Dolores Costello; The Girl on the Cover," *Cinema Arts*, Nov 1926, 35, 51. Dorothy H. Cartwright, "The Costello Constellation; Dolores and Helene in Starry Heights of Screen Heavens," *Paris and Hollywood Screen Secrets Magazine*, Aug 1927, 62–64, 93. Carol Johnston, "The Clinging Vine; A Close-Up of Dolores Costello," *MPC*, Oct 1927, 53, 84. "News From the Dailies," *Variety*, 4 Nov 1936, 62:1 ("Final divorce decree granted Dolores Costello Barrymore from John Barrymore in L.A. Actress was awarded custody of Dolores, five, and John, Jr., four.").

Costello, Helene (daughter of **Maurice Costello**; sister of **Dolores Costello**) [actress: Wampas Star, 1927] (*née* Helen Costello, b. New York NY, 18 Nov 1902 [Birth Certificate Index No. 13378D]–26 Jan 1957 [54], Los Angeles CA; pneumonia and overdose of TBC and narcotics). m. (1) John Regan, 29 Sep 1927; (2) **Lowell J. Sherman** (d. 1934); (3) Arturo del Barrio; (4) George L. LeBlanc. (Vitagraph.) "Helene Costello, Silent-Film Star, Dies; Had Brief Career in Nineteen Twenties," *NYT*, 29 Jan 1957, 31:3. "Helene Costello," *Variety*, 30 Jan 1957 (age 53). AMD, p. 82. AS, pp. 260–61 (d. Patton CA). BHD1, p. 122 (b. 21 Jun 1903). FSS, p. 76. IFN, p. 65 (b. 21 Jun 1903). Katz, p. 277 (b. 21 Jun 1903). SD. Truitt, p. 72. "Among the Players," *NYDM*, 22 Jul 1914, 28:3. "Helene Costello to Play Opposite Raymond Griffith," *MPW*, 6 Mar 1926, 29. "Helene Costello," *MPW*, 16 Apr 1927, 631. Dorothy H. Cartwright, "The Costello Constellation; Dolores and Helene in Starry Heights of Screen Heavens," *Paris and Hollywood Screen Secrets Magazine*, Aug 1927, 62–64, 93. "Helene Costello Engaged," *MPW*, 24 Sep 1927, 217. "Miss Costello Becomes Bride of Jack Regan," *MPW*, 8 Oct 1927, 339.

Costello, John L. [actor] (b. New York NY, 1878?–29 Jan 1946 [67], Los Angeles Co. CA). AS, p. 261. BHD, p. 137. IFN, p. 65.

Costello, Lou [stage/film/TV actor] (*né* Louis Francis Cristello, b. Paterson NJ, 6 Mar 1906–3 Mar 1959 [52], Los Angeles CA; heart attack). m. Anne, ca. 1934 (d. 1959). (WB; Metro.) "Lou Costello, 52, Dies on Coast; Comic Had Teamed with Abbott; 'Little Guy Trying to Be a Big Shot' in Films and on TV—Partners Broke Up in '57," *NYT*, 4 Mar 1959, 31:2 ("When I was a stunt man I was clawed on the top of the head by an eagle and bitten by a vulture. I wonder if anyone else in the world was ever bitten by a vulture. I was once supposed to lead a hundred Cossacks in a mob scene. I fell off my horse and all hundred rode over me."). "Lou Costello Rites Tomorrow," 6 Mar, 25:4; "Costello Rites Held; Comedian Mourned by 400 at Requiem Mass on Coast," 8 Mar, 86:7. "Mrs. Lou Costello, 47; Widow of Movie Comedian Is Dead in California," *NYT*, 6 Dec 1959, 86:2 (b. 1912?–5 Dec 1959 [47], Van Nuys CA; apparent heart attack). "Lou Costello," *Variety*, 11 Mar 1959 (age 53). AS, p. 261. IFN, p. 65. Truitt, pp. 72–73. Richard Bann, "Screening Notes on 'Battle of the Century,'" *CI*, 83 (May 1982), 51 (appeared as a ringside extra in *Battle of the Century* and as a double in MGM's *Rose Marie* and *Trail of '98*).

Costello, Mae A. [actress] (*née* Mae Altschul, b. Brooklyn NY, 1882–2 Aug 1929 [47?], Los Angeles CA). m. Maurice Costello. AS, p. 261. BHD, p. 137. IFN, p. 65. SD. Truitt 1983.

Costello, Maurice George Washington, "The Dimpled Darling" (father of **Dolores** and **Helene Costello**) [stage/film actor/director] (b. Pittsburgh PA, 22 Feb 1877–29 Oct 1950 [73], Los Angeles CA). m. Ruth Reeves, ca. 1902. (Edison; Vitagraph, 1907; Erbograph.) "Maurice Costello Dies in Hollywood; Stage, Film Star, 73, Matinee Idol Early in the Century, Is Victim of Heart Ailment," *NYT*, 30 Oct 1950, 27:1. "Maurice Costello," *Variety*, 1 Nov 1950. AMD, p. 82. AS, p. 261. BHD1, p. 124; BHD2, p. 55. FSS, p. 77. IFN, p. 65. Katz, pp. 277–78. MSBB, p. 1023. Slide, p. 138 (d. 28 Oct). Truitt, p. 73. "Picture Personalities," *MPW*, 17 Dec 1910, 1402. "Trading on Costello's Name," *MPW*, 7 Sep 1912, 977. "Maurice Costello; Vitagraph Moving Picture Star," *MPS*, 24 Apr 1914, 25 (b. 22 Feb 1877). "Costello Theater," *MPW*, 30 May 1914, 1269. "Costello Wins Contests Abroad," *MPW*, 27 Jun 1914, 1837. "Maurice Costello, Popular Player and Director of the Vitagraph Co.," *MPW*, 11 Jul 1914, 205. "Maurice Costello Out of Vitagraph," *MPW*, 25 Dec 1915, 2376. "Costello Came Back Strong," *MPW*, 18 Nov 1916, 1026. "Maurice Costello," *MPW*, 6 Jan 1917, 78. "Maurice Costello Signed for 'Determination' Film," *MPW*, 30 Oct 1920, 1277. "Costello as Villain," *MPW*, 14 Apr 1923, 773. Bert Ennis, "Them Were the Happy Days; The First of a Series of Articles About the Pioneer Days of the Motion Picture—Before It Became a Highly Specialized Industry," *MPC*, Oct 1926, 18–19, 65, 86 (discusses Vitagraph stars). Ann Cummings, "The Tragedy of Costello; The Past Creeps Up to Haunt the Favourite of Yesteryear, But He Still Carries On with a Smile," *MPC,* Jan 1928, 18–19, 78.

Costello, Tom [actor] (b. Birmingham, England, 30 Apr 1863–8 Nov 1943 [80], London, England). BHD1, p. 124.

Costello, William A. [actor/voice of Popeye] (b. 2 Feb 1898–9 Oct 1971 [73], San Jose CA). "William A. Costello," *Variety,* 20 Oct 1971. AS, p. 261. BHD1, p. 124. IFN, p. 65. Truitt, p. 73.

Costinha [actor] (*né* Ernestino Augusto da Costa, b. Santarem, Portugal, 24 Feb 1891–24 Jan 1976 [84], Lisbon, Portugal). AS, p. 261.

Coteret, Paul Ernest [cinematographer] (b. Aubervilliers, France, 2 Apr 1896 [extrait de naissance no. 256]). AS, p. 261.

Cotner, Frank [cinematographer]. No data found. FDY, p. 457.

Cotter, Harry A. [actor] (b. Philadelphia PA, 1880–10 Jun 1947 [67?], Chicago IL). BHD, p. 137.

Cotter, Louise [actress] (b. 1884–11 Jun 1930 [46?], Portland OR). BHD, p. 137. IFN, p. 65.

Cotterly, Mathilde [stage/film actress/singer] (b. Hamburg, Germany, 7 Feb 1851–15 Jun 1933 [82], Tuckerton NJ). m. (1) George Cottrell, ca. 1866–69; (2) Thomas J. Wilson (d. ca. 1923). "Mathilde Cotterly," *Variety,* 20 Jun 1933, p. 46 (d. 16 Jun). BHD, p. 137.

Cotton, Billy [composer] (*né* William Edward Cotton, b. Westminster, England, 6 May 1899–25 Mar 1969 [69], London, England; heart attack). "Billy Cotton," *Variety,* 2 Apr 1969 (wrote *Somebody Stole My Gal*). AS, p. 261. Truitt, p. 73.

Cotton, Lucy [stage/film actress] (*née* Lucy Cotton Magraw, b. Houston TX, 1891–12 Dec 1948 [57], Miami Beach FL; suicide with sleeping tablets). m. Edward L. Thomas; Lytton Ament; Charles Hann; Prince Vladimir Eristavi Tchitcherine. (Biograph.) "Lucy Cotton Magraw," *Variety,* 15 Dec 1948. AMD, p. 82. AS, p. 261. BHD, p. 137. IFN, p. 65. SD. WWS, p. 99. "Lucy Cotton, Broadway Star, Signed by Gerald Bacon," *MPW,* XL, 24 May 1919, 1148. "Lucy Cotton Signs with Inrternational," *MPW,* 29 Nov 1919, 555. "Lucy Cotton to Star in New Emile Chautard Production," *MPW,* 10 Apr 1920, 285.

Cotton, Richardson [actor] (b. Ephraim WI, 1868?–24 Sep 1916 [48], Ephraim WI; run down by car). (Essanay.) "Film Player Killed," *Variety,* 29 Sep 1916 (was to have filmed *The Chaperon*). AMD, p. 82. AS, p. 261 (d. 27 Sep). BHD, p. 137. IFN, p. 65. "Obituary," *MPW,* 14 Oct 1916, 245.

Cotton, William H. [artist]. No data found. AMD, p. 82. "Artist Cotton Joins Goldwyn," *MPW,* 30 Jun 1917, 2085.

Couderc, Pierre M. [actor/scenarist/director] (b. Paris, France, 18 Nov 1896–6 Oct 1966 [69], Santa Monica CA). (Fox.) BHD1, p. 124; BHD2, p. 55. FDY, p. 423. Waldman, p. 62.

Coudray, Peggy [actress] (b. New York NY, 17 Mar 1894). AS, p. 261.

Coulson, Roy [actor] (b. Streator IL, 13 Sep 1890–10 May 1944 [53], San Bernardino CA). AS, p. 262. BHD, p. 137. IFN, p. 65.

Coulter, Frazer [actor] (b. Smiths Falls, Ontario, Canada, 20 Aug 1848–26 Jan 1937 [88], East Islip, LI NY). m. Grace Thorne (d. 1916). "Frazer Coulter," *Variety,* 3 Feb 1937. AS, p. 262. IFN, p. 65. SD.

Coulter, Lucia [head of wardrobe department; known as "Mother"] (*née* Lucia Hays?, b. 1863?–24 Oct 1936 [73], Los Angeles CA). (MGM.) "Mrs. Lucia Hays Coulter," *Variety,* 28 Oct 1936.

Counihan, William J. [executive] (b. Ireland, 1872?–4 May 1923 [51], New York NY). "William J. Counihan," *Variety,* 10 May 1923. AS, p. 262.

Countiss, Cathrine [actress]. No data found. (Life Photo Film Corp.) "Cathrine Countiss on Screen," *NYDM,* 2 Dec 1914, 24:3. "Cathrine Countiss Signed," *NYDM,* 7 Apr 1915, 22:3 (signed by Dramatic Feature Film Co., to star in *The Gray Nun of Belgium,* her fourth film in five months).

Courant, Curtis [director of photography] (b. Berlin, Germany, 11 May 1899–20 Apr 1968 [68], Los Angeles CA). BHD2, p. 55. JS, p. 110 (b. ca. 1895; co-photographed *Quo vadis?,* 1924). Waldman, p. 63.

Court, Florence [actress] (*née* Lotta Miles, b. Buffalo NY, 18 Dec 1893–25 Jul 1937 [43], East Islip, LI NY). BHD1, p. 124.

Courteline, Georges [writer/scenarist] (*né* GeorgesVictor Marcel Moineau, b. Tours, France, 25 Jun 1858 [extrait de naissance no. 526/1858]–25 Jun 1929 [71], Paris, France; complications after an amputation). AS, p. 262.

Courtenay, William L[eonard] [stage/film actor] (*né* William Hancock Kelley, b. Worcester MA, 19 Jun 1875–20 Apr 1933 [57], Rye NY). m. Virginia Harned. "William Courtenay," *Variety,* 25 Apr 1933. AMD, p. 82. AS, p. 262. BHD1, p. 124. IFN, p. 65. Slide, p. 158 (b. 1894). Truitt, p. 73. Portrait, *Green Book Album,* 3, Feb 1910, 244. "Courtenay Legalizes Name; Well-Known Actor Prefers Stage Name to That of William Hancock Kelley," *NYDM,* 20 Nov 1912, 17:1 (Courtenay was the name of a relative. "William Hancock Kelley is about thirty-five years of age. He is one of the most competent leading men in the profession."). "Another 'Vita' Star; William Courtenay, Star of 'Under Cover," Signed for Screen Appearance," *NYDM,* 28 Apr 1915, 28:2 (to make screen debut). "Vitagraph Engages William Courtenay," *MPW,* 8 May 1915, 879. "Courtenay's First Vitagraph," *NYDM,* 30 Jun 1915, 20:2 (to debut in *The Island of Surprise*).

Courteney, Fay [stage/film actress] (b. San Francisco CA, 7 Oct 1895–18 Jul 1943 [48], New York NY; cerebral hemorrhage). "Fay Courteney," *Variety,* 28 Jul 1943, p. 46. BHD, p. 137.

Courtleigh, Edna (mother of **William Courtleigh, Jr.**) [actress] (*née?,* b. 1879–25 Jul 1962 [83?], Los Angeles CA). m. **William Courtleigh** (d. 1930). AS, p. 262.

Courtleigh, William (father of **William Courtleigh, Jr.**) [actor] (b. Guelph, Ontario, Canada, 28 Jun 1867–27 Dec 1930 [63], Rye NY; acute indigestion). m. **Edna** (d. 1962). "Wm. Courtleigh, Noted Actor, Dies; Portrayer of Important Roles for Last 40 Years a Victim of Indigestion; His First Success in 1891; Was 'Juvenile Lead' with Fanny Davenport—A Member of Augustin Daly's Famous Company," *NYT,* 28 Dec 1930, 26:8 (age 61). AMD, p. 82. AS, p. 262. IFN, p. 65. Truitt, p. 73. "Courtleigh Has Big Role in Young Film," *MPW,* XLI, 30 Aug 1919, 1324.

Courtleigh, William, Jr. (son of **Edna** and **William Courtleigh**) [stage/film actor] (b. Buffalo NY, 28 Jan 1892–13 Mar 1918 [26], Philadelphia PA; pleuro-pneumonia). m. **Ethel Fleming,** 1915. (Film debut: *The Nightingale,* 1914; FP-L; Fox.) "William Courtleigh, Jr.," *Variety,* 22 Mar 1918. AMD, p. 82. AS, p. 262. BHD, p. 137. IFN, p. 65. MSBB, p. 1023. "William Courtleigh, Jr., in New Serial," *MPW,* 26 Jun 1915, 2119. "William Courtleigh, Jr., Marries," *MPW,* 14 Aug 1915, 1138. "Obituary," *MPW,* 30 Mar 1918, 1828. Billy H. Doyle, "Lost Players," *CI,* 139 (Jan 1987), 55; *CI,* 143 (May 1987), C6-C7, 40.

Courtney, Dan [actor] (*né* David Bloomberg, b. 5 Aug 1896–30 Apr 1982 [85], Los Angeles CA). (Edison, 1912; in *The Perils of Pauline.*) BHD1, p. 125. "David Bloomberg," *CI,* 85 (Jul 1982), 16.

Courtney, Maude [actress] (b. 1880–26 Jul 1959 [79?], Gerrard's Cross, England). AS, p. 262.

Courtney, Oscar W[illis] [actor] (b. 18 Sep 1877–18 Jun 1962 [84], Chicago IL). (Essanay, 1912.) "Oscar W. Courtney," *Variety,* 4 Jul 1962. AS, p. 262. BHD, p. 137. IFN, p. 65. Truitt, p. 73.

Courtney, William Basil [scenarist] (b. Dover NH, 20 Dec 1894-Apr 1966 [71]).

Courtot, Marguerite Gabrielle [actress] (b. Summit NJ, 20 Aug 1897–28 May 1986 [88], Long Beach CA). m. **Raymond McKee,** 4 Aor 1923, NYC (d. 1984). (Kalem; Gaumont; FP-L; Arrow; France Film Co.) "Marguerite Courtot," *Variety,* 17 Dec 1986. AMD, p. 82. AS, p. 262 (b. 22 Apr). BHD, p. 137. FFF, p. 228. MH, p. 104. MSBB, p. 1034. Spehr, p. 124. *Photoplay Arts Portfolio* (Kalem) (b. Baltimore). "Marguerite Courtot," *MPW,* 21 Nov 1914, 1083. "How I Became a Photo-player; Marguerite Courtot," *Motion Picture Magazine,* Jan 1915, p. 75 (lived near the Kalem studio in Cliffside). "Kalem Player Wins; Marguerite Courtot's Beauty Gets Her a Hundred-Dollar Prize in Contest," *NYDM,* 3 Mar 1915, 25:4 (17 years old. Paintings for sale were made of her photograph.). "Kalem Star Wins Prize," *MPW,* 6 Mar 1915, 1465. "Marguerite Courtot Joins Gaumont," *MPW,* 25 Dec 1915, 2371. Grace Wynden-Vail, "A Play-Day with Marguerite Courtot," *MPC,* Jul 1916, 41–44. "Marguerite Courtot Joins Famous Players," *MPW,* 29 Jul 1916, 794. "Marguerite Courtot to Wed," *MPW,* 31 Mar 1923, 511. Alma M. Talley, "How I Intend to Make My Marriage a Success," *MW,* 12 May 1923, 9, 29.

Courtwright, William "Uncle Billy" [actor] (*né* Theodore Courtwright, b. New Milford IL, 10 Feb 1848–6 Mar 1933 [85], Ione CA). m. **Jennie Lee** (d. 1925). "William Courtwright," *Variety,* 21 Mar 1933. AS, p. 263. BHD, p. 137 (Courtright). IFN, p. 65. Truitt, p. 73 (b. 10 Mar). Edgar M. Wyatt, "'Parson Bill,' Venerable Actor of Silent Era," *CI,* 145 (Jul 1987), 11, C27-C28. "Forgotten Cowboys and Cowgirls—Part XIV," *CI,* 191 (May 1991), 22.

Coutable, Georges [producer/director] (b. Paris, France, 24 Nov 1893). AS, p. 263.

Coutant, André Clément [director] (b. Paris, France, 21 Oct 1906–25 May 1983 [76], Septeuil, France [extrait de décès no. 22/1983]). AS, p. 262.

Coutna, Leila [midget actress]. No data found. (Headline Amusement Co.) "First Headline Comedy [*Pee-Wee's Courtship*]," *NYDM,* 23 Jun 1915, 21:2.

Couzinet, Emile [director/producer] (*né* Robert Couzinet, b. Bourg-sur-Gironde, France, 12 Nov 1896–24 Oct 1964 [67], Bordeaux, France [extrait de décès no. 1188). AS, p. 263.

Coventry, Florence [actress] (b. New Brunswick, Canada, 1874?–22 Nov 1939 [65], New York NY). (World.) "Florence Coventry," *Variety,* 29 Nov 1939. AS, p. 263. BHD, p. 137. IFN, p. 65.

Coventry, Tom [actor]. (Kleine.) No data found.

Covington, Z. Wall [actor/scenarist] (b. Bonne Terre MO, 21 Jan 1876–25 Sep 1941 [65], Los Angeles Co. CA). AS, p. 263. BHD, p. 137; BHD2, p. 55. IFN, p. 65.

Cowan, James R. [executive] (b. Glasgow, Scotland, 25 Aug 1889–26 Mar 1940 [50], Beverly Hills CA). BHD2, p. 55.

Cowan, Lynn F. [composer] (b. Iowa Falls IA, 8 Jun 1888–29 Aug 1973 [85], Pensacola FL). . "Lynn F. Cowan," *Variety,* 12 Sep 1973. AS, p. 263 (b. 1894. ASCAP 66, p. 441. BHD, p. 137 (b. 1894). Truitt 1983.

Cowan, Sada [scenarist] (b. Boston MA, 1883?–31 Jul 1943 [60], Los Angeles CA). "Sada Cowan," *Variety,* 4 Aug 1943. AMD, p. 82. AS, p. 263/ BHD2, p. 55. FDY, p. 423. IFN, p. 65. "Garson Signs Sada Cowan," *MPW,* 26 Jun 1920, 1774. "On Paramount Staff," *MPW,* 3 Feb 1923, 437. "Higgin and Cowan Signed," *MPW,* 7 Feb 1925, 603.

Coward, Noël Peirce [actor/composer/scenarist/producer/playwright] (b. Teddington-on-Thames, Middlesex, England, 16 Dec 1899–26 Mar 1973 [73], Blue Harbor, Jamaica, British West Indies; heart attack). (Film debut: *Hearts of the World,* 1918.) Cole Lesley, *The Life of Noël Coward* (New York: Penguin Books, 1978). (Griffith.) "Coward Burial Tomorrow at His Estate in Jamaica," *NYT,* 28 Mar 1973, 50:1. "Noel Coward, 73, Playwright, Actor, Songwriter and Wit, Dies in Jamaica," *Variety,* 28 Mar 1973. AS, p. 263. BHD1, p. 125; BHD2, p. 55. GSS, pp. 88–91. IFN, p. 65. Waldman, p. 64.

Cowen, William J. [director[(b. New York NY, 1883-ca. 1963 [80?]). m. **Lenore J. Coffee**, ca. 1920 (d. 1984). BHD2, p. 55.

Cowie, Laura [actress] (b. Aberdeen, Scotland, 7 Apr 1892–11 Feb 1969 [76]). BHD1, p. 125.

Cowl, George [actor] (b. Blackpool, England, 24 Feb 1878–4 Apr 1942 [64], Los Angeles CA). AS, p. 263 (b. 1978). BHD1, p. 125 (d. West Hollywood CA). IFN, p. 65.

Cowl, Jane [stage/film actress/playwright/director] (*née* Grace Bailey, b. Boston MA, 14 Dec 1883 [IGI MA, Fiche #00519, p. 3411]–22 Jun 1950 [66], Santa Monica CA; cancer). m. Adolph E. Klauber, 18 Jun 1906 (d. 1935). "Jane Cowl Is Dead; Star of Stage, 65; Leading Actress for 38 Years Broke Records as Juliet—Recently Played in Films," *NYT,* 23 Jun 1950 (in *The Spreading Dawn,* Goldwyn, 1917; Ft. Lee NJ). "Jane Cowl," *Variety,* 28 Jun 1950 (age 64). AMD, p. 82. AS, p. 263 (b. 1884). BHD1, p. 125 (b. 1885). GSS, pp. 91–92. IFN, p. 65. Truitt, p. 73 (b. 1887). Clara M. Behringer, *DAB,* Suppl. 4 (1974), pp. 186–88. "Jane Cowl to Come to the Screen," *MPW,* 13 Jan 1917, 207. "Jane Cowl Active in War Charities," *MPW,* 26 May 1917, 1310. "Jane Cowl," *MPW,* 1 Dec 1917, 1303. "Picture Increases Vogue of Stage Star," *MPW,* 22 Dec 1917, 1819.

Cowles, Albert [scenarist]. No data found. AMD, p. 82. "Albert Cowles with Triangle," *MPW,* 4 Nov 1916, 713.

Cowles, Denis [actor] (b. London, England, 12 Sep 1889–31 Mar 1970 [80], London, England). BHD1, p. 125.

Cowles, Eugene C[hase] [actor/opera singer/composer] (b. Stanstead, Quebec, Canada, 1860?–22 Sep 1948 [88], Boston MA). m. Louise Cleary. "Eugene C. Cowles, a Noted Basso, 88; Singer on Concert and Opera Stages Here and Abroad for Many Years Dies," *NYT,* 24 Sep 1948, 25:3. "Eugene C. Cowles," *Variety,* 29 Sep 1948.

Cowles, Jules [actor] (*né* Julius D. Cowles, b. Farmington CT, 7 Oct 1877–22 May 1943 [65], Los Angeles CA). "Jules Cowles," *Variety,* 26 May 1943. AMD, p. 82. AS, p. 263. BHD1, p. 125. IFN, p. 65. Truitt, p. 73. "Julius D. Cowles," *MPW,* 4 Dec 1915, 1805. George Katchmer, "Remembering the Great Silents," *CI,* 196 (Oct 1991), 53–54.

Cowley, Eric [actor] (b. Southsea, England, 11 Jul 1886–8 Sep 1948 [62]). BHD1, p. 125.

Cowling, Herford Tynes [cameraman]. No data found. AMD, p. 82. "Photographer Cowling Working in Clouds," *MPW,* 2 Sep 1916, 1545. "Herford Tynes Cowling Joins Burton Holmes," *MPW,* 3 Mar 1917, 1358. "Cowling in Fiji Islands," *MPW,* 26 May 1917, 1291. "Cranking a Scenic Camera Far Away," *MPW,* 22 Mar 1919, 1642.

Cowper, William C. [actor] (b. Manchester, England, 1853?–13 Jun 1918 [65]). AS, p. 263. BHD, p. 138. IFN, p. 65.

Cox, David Wilson [poet/landscape artist/writer] (b. near Indianapolis IN, 1848?–29 Sep 1942 [94], St. Joseph MI). "David W. Cox; Michigan Landscape Artist and Poet Dies in St. Joseph at 93," *NYT,* 30 Sep 1942, 23:3 (d. 28 Sep; age 93). "David Wilson Cox," *Variety*, 7 Oct 1942.

Cox, Doran H. [assistant director] (b. Hinton WV, 1881–2 May 1957 [76?], Los Angeles Co. CA). AMD, p. 83. BHD2, p. 55. "Cox Assisting Forman," *MPW,* 26 Jul 1924, 256.

Cox, Edna Mae [scenarist] (d. 17 Apr 1934, Stuart FL). BHD2, p. 55.

Cox, George B. [President of World Film Co.] (d. 20 May 1916, Cincinnati OH; pneumonia). "New World Film Head; George B. Cox, of Cincinnati, Chosen President of Film Organization," *NYDM,* 5 May 1915, 24:1 (succeeded Van Horn Ely). "George B. Cox," *Variety,* 26 May 1916. BHD2, p. 55.

Cox, George L. [general manager/director]. No data found. (Advance Motion Picture Co., Chicago IL.) AMD, p. 83. "Cox Near Death; Chicago Film Man and Adrienne Kroell in Disastrous Railroad Wreck," *NYDM,* 27 Jan 1915, 60:3 (when train jumped tracks). "Director George Cox Has Been Ill," *MPW,* 31 Mar 1917, 2090.

Cox, Robert [actor: Keystone Cops] (b. 1895–8 Sep 1974 [79], Phoenix AZ). AS, p. 264. BHD1, p. 125.

Cox, Thomas F. (son of stage actor Thomas Wise) [actor] (b. 1892–6 Dec 1914 [22], La Crescenta CA). (Kalem.) "Tom Cox," *Variety,* 14 Dec 1914, p. 24. AMD, p. 83. AS, p. 264. BHD, p. 138. "Obituary," *MPW,* 30 Jan 1915, 686.

Coxen, Edward [actor] (*né* Albert Edward Coxen, b. London, England, 8 Aug 1884–21 Nov 1954 [70], Los Angeles CA). (American.) "Albert Edward Coxen," *Variety,* 1 Dec 1954. AMD, p. 83. AS, p. 264. BHD1, p. 125. IFN, p. 66. Truitt, p. 73. "Ed Coxen Again with Flying A," *MPW,* 12 Jul 1913, 189. "Edward Coxen," *MPW,* 6 Dec 1913, 1131. "Leading American Players," *MPW,* 11 Jul 1914, 240–42.

Coyan, Betty [actress] (b. 1901?–9 Feb 1935 [34], Council Bluffs IA). m. Dr. Harry C. Timberman. "Betty Coyan," *Variety,* 20 Feb 1935. AS, p. 264 (d. 10 Feb). BHD1, p. 125. IFN, p. 66. Truitt, p. 73.

Coygne, Frank [producer]. No data found. AMD, p. 83. "Frank Coygne Still with Ruby Company," *MPW,* 28 Mar 1914, 1659.

Coyle, Marion J. [actress] (b. 1897–23 May 1981 [83?], No. Hollywood CA). AS, p. 264. BHD, p. 138.

Coyle, Walter V. [actor/director] (b. 1888?–3 Aug 1948 [60], Freeport, LI NY). m. Alice Murrell (widow). (Universal; Biograph.) "Walter V. Coyle," *Variety,* 11 Aug 1948. AMD, p. 83. AS, p. 264. BHD, p. 138. IFN, p. 66. "Biograph Director," *MPW,* 10 Jul 1915, 243–44.

Coyote, Mae Old [actress] (*née* May Childs [Crow Indian], b. 1891?–22 Oct 1995 [104], Billings MT). Obituary, *CI,* 247 (Jan 1996), 58:2.

Cozine, Arthur [actor] (b. Brooklyn NY, 6 Apr 1894). (Vitagraph.) AMD, p. 83. AS, p. 264. "Arthur Cozine," *MPW,* 7 Aug 1915, 1135. "Arthur Cozine," *Motography,* 16 Oct 1915, 783.

Craddock, Claudia [actress] (b. Warsaw, Poland, 16 Feb 1889–15 Dec 1945 [56], Los Angeles CA). AS, p. 264.

Craft, Pliny P. [executive]. No data found. AMD, p. 83. Hugh Hoffman, "The Father of the Feature," *MPW,* 11 Jul 1914, 272–73.

Craft, William James [cinematographer/scenarist/director] (b. Toronto, Canada, 1887?–30 Jun 1931 [44], Los Angeles CA; auto accident). "William Craft," *Variety,* 7 Jul 1931. AMD, p. 83. AS, p. 264. BHD2, p. 56 (b. 1890). FDY, p. 423. IFN, p. 66 (age 41). "William James Craft," *MPW,* 29 Jan 1927, 341. "Craft Keeps Busy," *MPW,* 29 Jan 1927, 347. "Renew Craft's Contract," *MPW,* 28 May 1927, 251.

Craig, Alec [actor] (b. Dunfermline, Scotland, 30 Mar 1885–25 Jun 1945 [60], Glendale CA). AS, p. 264.

Craig, Blanche [actress] (*née* Blanche Sanderson, b. Cutler ME, 6 Jan 1866–23 Sep 1940 [74], Los Angeles CA). "Blanche Craig," *Variety,* 2 Oct 1940. AS, p. 264. BHD1, p. 126 (d. Culter ME). IFN, p. 66.

Craig, Charles G. [actor]. m. **Frances** (d. 1925). No data found.

Craig, Edith [actress] (b. Harpenden, England, 9 Dec 1869–27 Mar 1947 [77], Small Hythe, Kent, England). BHD1, p. 126.

Craig, Edith [actress] (b. 1908–2 Mar 1979 [71], Tenafly NJ). AS, p. 264. BHD, p. 138. IFN, p. 66.

Craig, Edward Anthony (son of **Edward Gordon Craig**; grandson of **Ellen Terry**) [writer/director/film and stage designer] (aka Edward Carrick, b. London, England, 3 Jan 1905–21 Jan 1998 [93], Thame, Oxfordshire, England). m. (1) Helen Godfrey, 1928 (1 son, 1 daughter; d. 1960); (2) Mary Timewell. (Art director, Welsh-Pearson Film Co., 1928–29; art director, Associated Talking Pictures, 1932–36; art director, Crown Film Unit, 1939–46, executive art director,

Independent Producers [Rank], 1947–49). Tom Craig, "Edward Craig," *The Independent*, 23 Jan 1998, 17.

Craig, Edward Gordon (son of **Ellen Terry**; father of **Edward Craig**; cousin of **John Gielgud**) [art director/producer/author/director] (*né* Edward Godwin, b. Stevenage, Hertfordshire, England, 16 Jan 1872–29 Jul 1966 [94], Vence, France). m. Elena Fortuna Meo. "Edward Gordon Craig," *Variety*, 3 Aug 1966, p. 71 (had a daughter with Isidora Duncan who drowned in 1913). BHD, p. 138; BHD2, p. 56.

Craig, Frances B. [actress] (*née?*, b. OR, 10 Oct 1866–21 Jul 1925 [58], Los Angeles CA). m. **Charles G. Craig**. "Frances B. Craig," *Variety*, 29 Jul 1925 (age 56). AS, p. 264. BHD, p. 138. IFN, p. 66. Truitt, p. 74 (b. ca. 1869).

Craig, Godfrey [actor] (b. Copper Cliff, Ontario, Canada, 20 Jan 1915–26 May 1941 [26], Los Angeles CA). BHD1, p. 126. IFN, p. 66.

Craig, Hal [actor] (b. CA, 8 Jan 1894–5 Oct 1964 [70], Camarillo CA). BHD1, p. 126.

Craig, Howard Charles [cinematographer] (b. 1887–9 May 1938 [51?], Youngstown OH). BHD2, p. 56.

Craig, Nell [actress] (b. Princeton, NJ, 13 Jun 1890–5 Jan 1965 [74], Los Angeles CA). (Lubin; Pathé; Essanay.) "Nell Craig," *Variety*, 13 Jan 1965 ("earlyday film actress"). AMD, p. 83. AS, p. 264 (b. 1891). BHD1, p. 126. IFN, p. 66. Truitt, p. 74. "Briefs of Biography," *NYDM*, 3 Jun 1914, 23:3 (Nelle Craig, with photo). "Nell Craig," *MPW*, 14 Aug 1915, 1135.

Cram, Mildred [scenarist] (b. 17 Oct 1889–Apr 1985 [95], CA). . FDY, p. 423.

Cramer, Richard [actor] (b. Bryan OH, 3 Jul 1890–9 Aug 1960 [70], Los Angeles CA). AS, p. 265 (b. 2 Jan 1899). BHD1, p. 126. IFN, p. 66.

Crampton, Howard [actor] (b. New York NY, 12 Dec 1865–15 Jun 1922 [56]). (Imp; Universal.) AMD, p. 83. AS, p. 265. BHD, p. 138. IFN, p. 66. "Howard Crampton," *MPW*, 9 May 1914, 811.

Crandall, James (Doc) [actor] (b. Wadena IN, 8 Oct 1887–17 Aug 1951 [63], Bell CA). BHD, p. 138.

Crandall, Milton [publicist]. No data found. AMD, p. 83. "Milton Crandall Joins Equity to Exploit Young Productions," *MPW*, 19 Feb 1921, 952. "Milton Crandall Joins Hodkinson," *MPW*, 23 Sep 1922, 282.

Crandall, Robert S. [cinematographer] (b. 1868–16 Aug 1949 [81?], Los Angeles CA). AS, p. 265. BHD2, p. 56.

Crane, Charles [actor]. No data found. "Sign Supporting Players for Universal Feature [*The Mystery Club*]," *MPW*, 30 Jan 1926, 448:3.

Crane, Dixie [actress] (b. 1888?–18 Nov 1936 [48], Los Angeles CA). m. Henry Johnson. "Dixie Crane," *Variety*, 25 Nov 1936. AS, p. 265. BHD, p. 138. IFN, p. 66. Truitt, p. 74.

Crane, Edith [actress] (b. New York NY, 1865–3 Jan 1912 [47?], New York NY). m. **Tyrone Power, Sr.** (d. 1931). "Edith Crane Is Dead; Well-Known Actress, Wife of Tyrone Power, Succumbs to Operation," *NYT*, 4 Jan 1912, 13:6. AS, p. 265.

Crane, Ethel G[ordon] [actress] (b. IL, 1877–13 Oct 1930 [53?], San Bernardino CA; suicide by poison). "Ethel G. Crane," *Variety*, 22 Oct 1930 (her only daughter committed suicide one week previously). AS, p. 265 (d. 12 Oct). BHD, p. 138. Truitt, p. 74.

Crane, Frank H[all] [actor/producer/director] (b. San Francisco CA, 1873–31 Aug 1948 [75], Woodland Hills CA). (Lubin; Thanhouser; Universal.) "Frank H. Crane," *NYT*, 4 Sep 1948, 15:2. AMD, p. 83. AS, p. 265 (d. 1 Sep). BHD1, p. 127; BHD2, p. 56 (d. LA CA). IFN, p. 66. Spehr, p. 126. "Crane Tells How Films Are Made," *MPW*, 8 Apr 1911, 763. "Frank Crane a Comet Director," *MPW*, 2 Dec 1911, 720. "Frank Crane a Canuck," *MPW*, 7 Dec 1912, 957. "Frank H. Crane," *NYDM*, 8 Apr 1914, 32:1. "Frank Crane a 'Soft Pedal' Director," *MPW*, XX, 11 Apr 1914, 217. "Frank H. Crane; Actor and Director with the Imp Company," *MPS*, 5 Jun 1914, 24. "Frank Crane Joins World Film," *MPW*, 17 Oct 1914, 359. "Frank Crane Directing 'As Ye Sow,'" *MPW*, 14 Nov 1914, 949. "Frank Crane Engaged to Direct Petrova," *MPW*, 22 Dec 1917, 1774. "Frank Crane Joins World Pictures," *MPW*, 20 Apr 1918, 396.

Crane, Gardner [actor] (b. Boston MA, 4 Jul 1867–8 Jun 1939 [71],Los Angeles CA). BHD, p. 138.

Crane, H[arry] **F.** [actor]. No data found. AMD, p. 83. "Harry F. Crane," *MPW*, 1 Aug 1914, 711.

Crane, Herbert [actor] (b. 1903?–1 Apr 1932 [29], Brooklyn NY; knee tumor). "Herbert Crane," *Variety*, 5 Apr 1932. AS, p. 265.

Crane, James L. [actor] (b. Rantoul IL, 9 Aug 1889–3 Jun 1968 [78], San Gabriel CA)). . m. **Alice Brady**, 20 May 1919 (d. 1939). AMD, p. 83. AS, p. 265 (d. NYC). BHD, p. 138; BHD1, p. 127. IFN, p. 66. "Alice Brady Is Wedded to James Crane, Actor," *MPW*, 7 Jun 1919, 1462.

Crane, Ogden [actor] (b. Brooklyn NY, 1 Sep 1873–14 May 1940 [66], West Hollywood CA). AMD, p. 83. AS, p. 265. BHD, p. 138. Truitt 1983. "Ogden Crane with Pallas Pictures," *MPW*, 22 Apr 1916, 631.

Crane, Ward [actor] (b. Albany NY, 18 May 1890–21 Jul 1928 [38], Saranac Lake NY; pneumonia after pleurisy). "Ward Crane," *Variety*, 25 Jul 1928. AMD, p. 83. AS, p. 265. BHD, p. 138. IFN, p. 67 (age 37). MH, p. 104. Truitt, p. 74. "Mayer Signs Ward Crane," *MPW*, 21 Feb 1920, 1258.

Crane, William H[enry] [actor] (b. Leicester MA, 30 Apr 1845–7 Mar 1928 [82], Los Angeles CA). m. Ella C. Myers, ca. 1870. (Paramount.) "William H. Crane, Noted Player, Dead; Comedian, Before American Public for 53 Years, Dies in Hollywood at 82; Long Associate of Robson; Best Known for His Roles in 'The Henrietta,' 'The Senator,' 'David Harum' and 'Comedy of Errors,'" *NYT*, 8 Mar 1928, 25:3 (age 82). "William H. Crane," *Variety*, 14 Mar 1928. AMD, p. 83. AS, p. 265. BHD, p. 138. IFN, p. 67. SD. Portrait (in group), *Green Book Album*, 3, Jan 1910, 21. "Crane with Famous Players," *MPW*, 24 Oct 1914, 476. June Lee, "Dan Cupid's Bulletin Board," *Paris and Hollywood*, Oct 1926, 88 (married for 56 years).

Crane, William H. [actor] (b. Brooklyn NY, 1886–22 Jan 1957 [70?], Scranton PA). AS, p. 265 (b. 1892). BHD, p. 138. IFN, p. 67 (age 65).

Craske, Leonard [actor] (b. England, 1877–29 Aug 1950 [73?], Boston MA). BHD, p. 138.

Craven, Frank [actor/playwright/scenarist/director] (*né* Francis Henry Craven, b. Malden [Boston] MA, 29 Apr 1876 [MVRB, Vol. 278, p. 137]–1 Sep 1945 [69], Beverly Hills CA; heart attack. Buried in Kensico Cemetery, Valhalla NY.). m. Mary Blyth (divorced wife of Arnold Daly), 8 May 1914, Stamford CT. (Last film: *Colonel Effingham*.) "Frank Craven," *Variety*, 5 Sep 1945 (age 70). *Dictionary of American Biography*, Supp. 3 (1973), pp. 197–99 (b. 24 Aug 1875?). AS, p. 266 (b. 24 Aug 1875). BHD1, p. 127; BHD2, p. 56 (b. 24 Aug 1875). IFN, p. 67. Katz, p. 283. Truitt, p. 74.

Craven, Helene [stage/film actress] (*née?*, b. London, England, 1860?–13 Dec 1943 [83], Yonkers NY). m. **Walter Scott Craven** (d. 1918). "Mrs. Walter Craven; Actress Is Dead in Yonkers at 83—Played with Sothern, Adams," *NYT*, 15 Dec 1943, 27:3. "Mrs. Helene Craven," *Variety*, 25 Nov 1936. AS, p. 266.

Craven, Walter Scott [actor/stage manager] (b. 1863?–25 Nov 1918 [55], Knoxville TN). m. **Helene** (d. 1943). "Walter Craven," *Variety*, 29 Nov 1918. AS, p. 266 (d. London, England). BHD, p. 138.

Cravens, Kathryn [actress] (b. 27 Oct 1898–29 Aug 1991 [92], Burkett TX; cancer). . (Fox.) "Kathryn Cravens," *Variety*, 9 Sep 1991, p. 103.

Craveri, Mario Emilio [film/TV cinematographer/director] (b. Turin, Italy, 2 May 1902 [extrait de naissance no. 1170/1.1/1892]–28 Feb 1990 [87], Bergame, Italy). AS, p. 266. JS, p. 111 (in Italian silents from 1923).

Crawford, Bessie [actress] (b. Chicago IL, 25 Jan 1883–11 Nov 1943 [60], Los Angeles CA; heart attack). m. T[homas] **Roy Barnes** (d. 1937). "Bessie Crawford," *Variety*, 17 Nov 1943. AS, p. 266. BHD1, p. 127. IFN, p. 67. SD. Truitt, p. 74.

Crawford, Clifton [music hall/vaudeville/film actor] (b. Edinburgh, Scotland, 1875?–3 Jun 1920 [45], London, England; fell from window). "Clifton Crawford," *Variety*, 11 Jun 1920. AMD, p. 83. AS, p. 266. BHD, p. 138. "Another Pathe Star; Clifton Crawford Signed by Pathe [in NJ] to Play in Production of 'The Galloper,'" *NYDM*, 30 Jun 1915, 20:1. "Clifton Crawford," *MPW*, 17 Jul 1915, 498.

Crawford, Florence [actress]. No data found. AMD, p. 83. "Florence Crawford," *MPW*, 23 Jan 1915, 525. "Florence Crawford," *MPW*, 24 Jul 1915, 632. "Florence Crawford," *MPW*, 2 Oct 1915, 85.

Crawford, Capt. Jack [actor] (b. County Donegal, Ireland, 4 Mar 1847–27 Feb 1917 [69]). AMD, p. 83. AS, p. 266. BHD, p. 138. "'Capt. Jack' for the Screen," *MPW*, 29 Aug 1914, 1219.

Crawford, Joan (brother of **Hal Le Sueur**) [stage/film/TV actress] (*née* Lucille Fay Le Sueur, aka Billie Cassin, b. San Antonio TX, 23 Mar 1904–10 May 1977 [73], New York NY [Death Certificate Index No. 8006; Medical Examiner No. 3357, age 69]; heart attack). m. **Douglas Fairbanks, Jr.**, 1929–33 (d. 2000); Franchot Tone, 1935–39; Philip Terry, 1942–46; Alfred N. Steele, 1955 (d. 1959). *A Portrait of Joan* (Doubleday & Co., 1962); *My Way of Life* (1971); Christina Crawford [adopted daughter], *Mommie Dearest* (1978); Bob Thomas, *Joan Crawford; A Biography* (NY: Simon and Schuster, 1978). (MGM; WB; Republic.) "Joan Crawford Dies at Home," *NYT*, 11 May 1977, A1:2, B8:2. "Joan Crawford Dies at 69; Metro and Warner Star Held Special Status Over Many Decades—A Pepsi Spokeswoman," *Variety*,

18 May 1977. (AA, *Mildred Pierce,* 1945.) AMD, p. 83. AS, p. 266. BHD1, p. 128. FSFW, p. 91 (b. 1908). FSS, p. 77. HCH, p. 25. IFN, p. 67. Joan Cross, "Introducing Lucille Le Sueur Who Needs Another Name for her Screen Career; Name Her and Win $1,000," *MW,* 28 Mar 1925, 5–31; Contest, pp. 6, 33; 11 Apr 1925, 17. "Lucille Le Sueur's Name Has Been Chosen," *MW,* 1 Aug 1925, 45 (to be announced shortly). "Joan Crawford Is the Winning Name," *MW,* 19 Sep 1925, 16–17, 47 (Mrs. J.B. Spradley of Dallas TX submitted the winning name and won $500. Other names suggested: June Carter, Betty Bowers, Margery Ames, Alma Dale, June Colby, etc.). "Constance Bennett Signed for 'Sally, Irene and Mary,'" *MPW,* 26 Sep 1925, 347. "Jackie Coogan's New M-G-M Film, 'Old Clothes,' Completed," *MPW,* 7 Nov 1925, 40. Charles J. Duranty, "A Chat with Joan Crawford; Who Thinks Her Career More Important Than a Husband," *Cinema Arts,* Oct 1926, 24–25. "Joan Jostles the Jinx!," *Paris and Hollywood Screen Secrets Magazine,* May 1927, 54–55 (appeared in one play in Chicago; in New York she was in *Innocent Eyes, The Passing Show,* and *The Winter Garden;* discovered by Harry Raft [Rapf]. "With only one picture released, Joan's fan mail began to pour in at a rate that was proof sufficient of her personality."). "Joan Crawford Assigned Role," *MPW,* 23 Jul 1927, 251. Ruth Tildesley, "Hollywood Nights' Entertainment," *Paris and Hollywood Screen Secrets Magazine,* Aug 1927, 29 ("Joan Crawford invited twenty-one girls to her twenty-first birthday party given at the popular Montmartre cafe. A catty soul at our table remarked that it might be a good idea for the twenty-one maidens to stick together so that they could celebrate all of Joan's twenty-first birthdays..."). "M-G-M Players Hurt," *MPW,* 3 Sep 1927, 10. "Joan Crawford," *MPW,* 29 Oct 1927, 555. "Joan Crawford, Star?," *MPW,* 24 Dec 1927, 23. Cedric Belfrage, "From Toast to Toast; Such Has Been Joan Crawford's Career. She Began by Eating It and Ended by Being It," *MPC,* Jul 1928, 37, 78 ("She recorded herself on celluloid...on the fateful morning of January 9, 1925...They made her play a little scene with Creighton Hale."). June Lee, "Dan Cupid's Bulletin Board," *Paris and Hollywood,* Sep 1926, 95 (seeing Michael Cudahy). Dorothy Spensley, "What Should a Poor Girl Do?; A Self-Confessed Beauty Asks Joan and Marian [Nixon] and Sue [Carol] About Short-Cuts to Stardom," *MPC,* Oct 1928, 30–31, 84. Ruth Biery, "O.K. with Oakie; Joan Crawford Is Still the World's Only Girl to Jack," *MPC,* Jan 1929, 40, 73, 79. Elisabeth Goldbeck, "Swopell; Dodo and Billy Play Just the Cutest Games Together," *MPC,* Jul 1929, 55, 79, 85. Jack Jamison, "Are Joan and Doug, Jr. Through Holding Hands?; The Younger Fairbankses Start Divorce Rumors by Declining to Pose Together and by Stepping Out with Others," *Movie Classic,* I, Nov 1931, 36. Noel Busch, "The Un-Real Joan Crawford; Closeup of a Onetime Waitress Named Billie Casson Who Became the Cinema's Most Consistently Successful Actress," *Cinema Arts,* Sep 1937, 48–50 (cover of Crawford by Jaro Fabry). Eve Golden, "Joan Crawford: A Reappraisal," *CI,* 221 (Nov 1993), 14 *et passim.* George Cukor, "She Was Consistently Joan Crawford, Star, " *NYT,* 22 May 1977 (Cukor's paean to Crawford). Aljean Harmetz, "For 50 Years, a Crawford Fan," *NYT,* 25 May 1977, C19 (an account of Dore Freeman's 40-year friendship with Crawford). Christopher Finch and Linda Rosenkrantz, *Gone Hollywood* (Garden City NY: Doubleday & Co., Inc., 1979), p. 41 ("Crawford had a dramatically harsh early life and achieved her position as a *grande dame* of the movies by sheer will power and discipline. [It is said that when she first went to M-G-M, she was so lax in her personal hygiene that wardrobe women were in the habit of picking up her discarded clothes with sticks.]"). Maurice Rapf, *Back Lot; Growing Up with the Movies* (Lanham MD: Scarecrow Press, 1999), pp. 8–9 ("I think I met Joan the first day she arrived at the studio. She was sixteen at the time and I was eleven, but that didn't stop me from fantasizing a relationship with her. She was a bit plump, with a face that was much rounder than the one we are familiar with, and the famous Crawford eyes had not yet exploded into those big saucers that we know so well. [Some people claimed it took an operation to accomplish that.] But she was a very attractive girl.").

Crawford, Kathryn [actress] (*née* Kathryn Moran, b. Wellsboro PA, 5 Oct 1908–7 Dec 1980 [72], Pasadena CA; cancer). m. Ralph M. Parson (d. 1974). "Kathryn Crawford," *Variety,* 28 Jan 1981. AS, p. 266. BHD1, p. 128. George A. Katchmer, 'Forgotten Cowboys and Cowgirls—Part V," *CI,* 177 (Mar 1990) (b. 1908–7 Dec 1980); "Update—Forgotten Cowboys/Girls," *CI,* 179 (May 1990), 43.

Crawford, Merritt [publicist/title writer/founded and co-edited *Motion Picture Today*] (b. New York NY, 1881?–11 Aug 1945 [64], Brooklyn NY). m. Ethel Donovan. (Began 1916; edited *Motion Pictures Today.*) "Merritt Crawford, Veteran Movie Publicist, Ex-Head of New Film Alliance," *NYT,* 13 Aug 1945, 19:5 (age 67). "Merritt Crawford," *Variety,* 15 Aug 1945. AMD, p. 84. FDY, p. 441. "Arthur James Goes to Metro," *MPW,* 21 Aug 1915, 1319. "Merritt Crawford Resigns from Fox to Form Own Publicity Organization," *MPW,* 3 Jul 1920, 64. "Crawford Leaves Bray," *MPW,* 5 Jul 1924, 21.

Crawford, Richard B. [actor] (b. 15 May 1915–21 Oct 1990 [85], Los Angeles CA). BHD1, p. 606.

Crawford, Roy [executive]. No data found. AMD, p. 84. "U.S. Film Favorite," *MPW,* 8 Sep 1923, 135. "Roy Crawford, After Survey, Predicts Big Year for Films," *MPW,* 3 Nov 1923, 45.

Crawford, Sam [actor] (b. Wahoo NB, 18 Apr 1880–15 Jun 1968 [88], Los Angeles CA). AS, p. 266. BHD, p. 139.

Crawford, Timothy [actor] (b. 24 Apr 1904–13 Jun 1978 [74], Reno NV). BHD, p. 606.

Crawley, Constance [stage/film actress/scenarist] (b. London, England, 30 Mar 1879–17 Mar 1919 [39], Los Angeles CA; heart failure). "Constance Crawley," *Variety,* 21 Mar 1919. AMD, p. 84. AS, p. 267. BHD, p. 139. IFN, p. 67. "Miss Crawley Writes Scenarios," *MPW,* 17 Jun 1916, 2043. "Obituary," *MPW,* 5 Apr 1919, 76 (daughter Vera d. Apr 1918). Billy H. Doyle, "Lost Players," *CI,* 171 (Sep 1989), C2.

Credi, Vasco [actor] (b. Florence, Italy, 1875–16 Oct 1945 [70?], Rome, Italy). AS, p. 267.

Creelman, James Ashmore [scenarist/director] (b. 1901?–9 Sep 1941 [40], New York NY; "suicided...by jumping from the roof of an apartment house on east 72nd street."). "James A. Creelman," and "James Creelman Dies in N.Y. Suicide Leap," *Variety,* 10 Sep 1941. AMD, p. 84. AS, p. 267. BHD2, p. 56. FDY, p. 423. "Addition to Paramount Staff," *MPW,* 6 Dec 1924, 559. "DeMille Engages Creelman," *MPW,* 9 May 1925, 213. "Creelman Will Direct 'The Duke of Ladies,'" *MPW,* 8 Jan 1927, 122.

Crehan, Joseph [actor] (b. Baltimore MD, 12 Jul 1884–15 Apr 1966 [81], No. Hollywood CA; cerebral hemorrhage). . "Joseph Crehan," *Variety,* 27 Apr 1966 (began 1934). AS, p. 267 (b. 1883). BHD1, p. 128. IFN, p. 67. *MPN Studio Directory,* 21 Oct 1916 (b. 18 Jul 1888).

Crespi, Daniele [set designer] (b. Ferrara, Italy, 1893-Jun 1954 [61?], Milan, Italy). JS, p. 112 (in Italian siletns from 1917).

Crespinel, William T. [inventor/cinematographer] (b. Weymouth, England, 9 Jul 1890–19 Jun 1987 [96], Laguna Beach CA). . "William Crespinel, 96, Pioneer in Color Films," *NYT,* 24 Jun 1987, B10:6. "William Crespinel," *Variety,* 1 Jul 1987. AS, p. 267. BHD2, p. 56.

Crespo, José [stage/film/TV actor/director] (*né* José Crespo Férez, b. Murcia, Spain, 7 Nov 1900–19 Mar 1997 [96], Murcia, Spain). "José Crespo, 96," *CI,* 264 (Jun 1997), 51:2. Waldman, p. 65.

Cressall, Maud (b. Demrera, British Guiana, 5 Dec 1886-May 1962 [75], Kingsdown, Kent, England). BHD, p. 139.

Cressy, Will M. [vaudevillian/film actor] (b. Bradford NH, 29 Oct 1864–7 May 1930 [65], St. Petersburg FL). m. Blanche Dayne. "William Cressy," *Variety,* 14 May 1930, p. 76 (ashes interred at Bradford NH). BHD, p. 139.

Creste, Rene Auguste [actor/director] (b. Paris, France, 5 Dec 1875–30 Nov 1922 [47], Paris, France). AS, p. 267 (b. 1881). BHD, p. 139. IFN, p. 67.

Crew, William [actor/producer]. No data found. m. **Gwendolyn Pates.** (Selig.) "Miss Pates with Selig," *NYDM,* 1 Apr 1914, 34:4. Lester Sweyd, "What They Are Doing Now," *Motion Picture Magazine,* Feb 1918, 12 ("Miss Pates is now delighting vaudeville audiences in her playlet, 'Solitaire,' in which she is supported by her husband, Wm. Grew [sic], who was formerly a Selig player.").

Crews, Kay C. [actress] (b. 1901?–29 Nov 1959 [58], San Antonio TX). "Kay C. Crews," *Variety,* 9 Dec 1959. AS, p. 267. BHD, p. 139. IFN, p. 67. Truitt, p. 75.

Crews, Laura Hope [actress] (b. San Francisco CA, 12 Dec 1879–13 Nov 1942 [62], New York NY). "Laura Hope Crews, Actress, 62, Is Dead; Stage and Screen Comedienne for 56 Years Appeared in Fluttery Roles Mostly; Made Debut at Age of 4; Played Shakespeare with John Drew—Last Seen Here in 'Arsenic and Old Lace,'" *NYT,* 14 Nov 1942, 15:1. "Laura Hope Crews," *Variety,* 18 Nov 1942. AS, p. 267. BHD1, p. 128. IFN, p. 67. Truitt, p. 75. "Lasky-Belasco Star; Laura Hope Crews to Be Presented in Screen Production of 'The Fighting Hope,'" *NYDM,* 21 Apr 1915, 21:1.

Crile, Jackie [extra actress]. No data found. Paul Paige, "Close-Ups and Fade-Outs," *Paris and Hollywood Screen Secrets,* Oct 1927, 22 ("Jackie Crile, another actress, took poison because her husband took other women driving. She also will survive.").

Crimmins, Daniel [actor] (*né* Alexander M. Lyon, b. Liverpool, England, 18 May 1863–12 Jul 1945 [82], Los Angeles CA). m. **Rosa Gore** (d. 1941). (Kleine.) "Dan Crimmins," *Variety,* 18 Jul 1945 (d. 11 Jul). AMD, p. 84. AS, p. 267. BHD1, p. 128. IFN, p. 67. "Crimmins and Gore Join

Vitagraph," *MPW,* 13 Jun 1914, 1523. "Crimmins and Gore in Kleine," *NYDM,* 21 Apr 1915, 21:3 (in Kleine's *The Commuters*). "Crimmins and Gore at Work," *NYDM,* 6 Nov 1915, 26:3 (at Kleine). "Crimmins and Gore," *MPW,* 22 Apr 1916, 628. George Katchmer, "Remembering the Great Silents," *CI,* 196 (Oct 1991), 54 (Don Crimmins).

Criner, J[ohn] **Lawrence** [actor] (b. TX, 19 Jul 1898–8 Mar 1965 [66], Los Angeles CA). . AS, p. 267. BHD, p. 139. IFN, 67.

Crinley, Adele [actress] (b. MO, 18 Jul 1879–29 Jan 1970 [90], Los Angeles CA). BHD1, p. 606.

Crinley, Myrtis [actress] (b. St. Louis MO, 8 Nov 1905–24 Jun 1996 [90], Los Angeles CA). BHD1, p. 128.

Crinley, William A. [actor/director] (b. 1882?–1 Jan 1927 [44], Los Angeles CA; stomach trouble). (Universal, 1914.) "William A. Crinley," *Variety,* 12 Jan 1927. AMD, p. 84. BHD, p. 139; BHD2, p. 56. IFN, p. 67. Ragan 2, p. 351. Truitt, p. 75. "New Universal Director," *MPW,* 6 Jun 1925, 674. "Obituary," *MPW,* 8 Jan 1927, 117.

Crisp, Donald [actor/director/producer] (b. Aberfeddy, Scotland, 27 Jul 1882–25 May 1974 [91], Van Nuys CA; after several cerebral hemorrhages). . m. **Marie Stark**, 1917 or 1918, San Juan Capistrano CA; **Jane Murfin**, 1932–44 (d. 1955). (Biograph; AA, 1941.) "Donald Crisp, 93, '41 Oscar Winner; Honored for Role in 'How Green Was My Valley,'" *NYT,* 27 May 1974, 20:5. "Donald Crisp, 93; Actor, Director, and Film Banker," *Variety,* 29 May 1974. AMD, p. 84. AS, p. 267 (b. 1880). BHD1, p. 128; BHD2, p. 56 (b. Aberfeldy, 1832; d. Woodland Hills CA). FSS, p. 79. GK, pp. 203–20. IFN, p. 67. Katz, pp. 285–86. Spehr, p. 126 (b. London). "Donald Crisp," *MPW,* 14 Feb 1914, 817. "Some 'Class' to This Mob," *MPW,* 12 Dec 1914, 1538. "Donald Crisp, Producer," *MPW,* 29 Apr 1916, 805. "Donald Crisp Leaves Lasky," *MPW,* 29 Dec 1917, 1947. "Crisp East with Bride [Marie Stark]," *Variety,* 11 Jan 1918, p. 45. "Donald Crisp Takes a Bride," *MPW,* 19 Jan 1918, 365. Sumner Smith, "Donald Crisp, Veteran Director, Actor, Will Pioneer in England and in India," *MPW,* 11 Sep 1920, 193. "Dr. James Crisp [father] Dies," *MPW,* 9 Jul 1921, 192 (age 90, Ilford, London, England). "Sam E. Rork Signs Crisp," *MPW,* 7 Jul 1923, 93. "Crisp Re-elected," *MPW,* 30 Oct 1926, 2. "Donald Crisp Is Signed to New Contract," *MPW,* 15 Jan 1927, 197. George A. Katchmer, "Donald Crisp," *CI,* 160 (Oct 1988), C9-C12.

Crist, Harry [scenarist]. No data found. FDY, p. 423.

Criswell, Floyd [actor] (b. TX, 17 Jun 1899–28 Dec 1974 [75], Los Angeles Co. CA). BHD, p. 139.

Crittenden, Trockwood Dwight [actor] (b. Oakland CA, 27 Sep 1878–17 Feb 1938 [59], Los Angeles CA). AS, p. 268. BHD, p. 139. IFN, p. 67.

Crizer, Thomas J. [scenarist]. No data found. AMD, p. 84. FDY, p. 423. "Crizer Assigned," *MPW,* 3 Sep 1927, 17.

Crocker, Harry [actor/assisant director] (b. San Francisco CA, 2 Jul 1893–23 May 1958 [64], Beverly Hills CA). (MGM.) "Harry Crocker," *Variety,* 28 May 1958. AS, p. 268. BHD1, p. 129; BHD2, p. 56 (d. LA CA). IFN, p. 67. Truitt 1983.

Crocker, May B. [actress] (d. 1 Nov 1930, New York NY). BHD, p. 139. IFN, p. 68.

Crockett, Charles B. [actor] (b. Baltimore MD, 29 Dec 1870–12 Jun 1934 [63], Los Angeles CA). "Charles B. Crockett," *Variety,* 19 Jun 1934 (age 62). AS, p. 268. BHD1, p. 129. IFN, p. 68. George Katchmer, "Remembering the Great Silents," *CI,* 196 (Oct 1991), 54.

Crockett, John [actor] (b. 1881?–21 Feb 1922 [40], Los Angeles CA). AS, p. 268. BHD, p. 139. IFN, p. 68.

Croker-King, Charles [actor] (b. Rook Holme, Yorkshire, England, 30 Apr 1873–25 Oct 1951 [78]). BHD1, p. 129. IFN, p. 68.

Crolius, Gladys [actress] (b. 6 Sep 1892–5 Apr 1972 [79], Los Angeles CA). AS, p. 268.

Crolius, Louise [actress] (d. 1 Jun 1931, Los Angeles CA). BHD, p. 139.

Crompton, Frank [technical director]. No data found. AMD, p. 84. "Two More Experts for Horsley," *MPW,* 20 Nov 1915, 1502.

Crone, George J. [director/film editor/scenarist]. No data found. AMD, p. 84. FDY, p. 423. "Crone Directing," *MPW,* 25 Oct 1924, 704.

Cronin, Timothy [actor] (b. 1860–6 Jan 1919 [59], Hawthorne NY). "Tim Cronin," *Variety,* 17 Jan 1919, p. 25. BHD, p. 139.

Cronjager, Edwin (nephew of **Jules Cronjager**) [cinematographer] (*né* Edward Cronjager, b. Los Angeles CA, 21 Mar 1904–15 Jun 1960 [56], Los Angeles CA; heart attack). . m. (5) Yvette. (RKO; Fox; Paramount.) "Film Man Found Dead; Cronjager, Cited for Camera Work on Coast, Was 56," *NYT,* 17 Jun 1960, 38:2. "Edwin Cronjager," *Variety,* 22 Jun 1960. AS, p. 269. BHD2, p. 57 (Edward Cronjager). FDY, p. 457 (Edward). IFN, p. 68 (Edward). Katz, p. 287 (Edward).

Cronjager, Henry [cinematographer] (b. Germany, 15 Feb 1877–1 Aug 1967 [90], Los Angeles CA). . (Edison; Biograph.) "Henry Cronjager," *Variety,* 9 Aug 1967. AMD, p. 84. AS, p. 269. BHD2, p. 57. FDY, p. 457. IFN, p. 68. Spehr, p. 126. "Henry Cronjager, Cameraman," *MPW,* 7 Oct 1916, 81.

Cronjager, Jules [cinematographer] (uncle of **Edward Cronjager**) (b. 1872?–28 Dec 1934 [62], Culver City CA). "Jules Cronjager," *Variety,* 1 Jan 1935 (d. 25 Dec). AS, p. 269. BHD2, p. 57 (d. LA CA). FDY, p. 457. IFN, p. 68.

Crosby, Gene [actor]. George A. Katchmer, "Forgotten Cowboys and Cowgirls—Part 2," *CI,* 173 (Nov 1989), C12. (There was a Jean Crosby in Eric Campbell's car in his final auto accident; see his obituary.)

Crosby, Walter Hull [actor] (d. 14 Apr 1921, New York NY). BHD, p. 139.

Crosby, Zelda [actress/scenarist] (d. 19 Jun 1921, New York NY). BHD, p. 139; BHD2, p. 57.

Crosland, Alan [actor/director/scenarist] (b. New York NY, 10 Aug 1894–16 Jul 1936 [42], Los Angeles CA; from injuries sustained in an auto accident). (Edison; WB.) "Alan Crosland," *Variety,* 22 Jul 1936. AMD, p. 84. AS, p. 269. BHD, p. 139; BHD2, p. 57. IFN, p. 68. Katz, p. 288. "Paramount Signs Crosland," *MPW,* 9 Feb 1924, 454. "Warners Sign Alan Crosland," *MPW,* 18 Dec 1926, 4. "Will Be First Vita[phone] Film Made on Coast," *MPW,* 23 Apr 1927, 707 (*The Jazz Singer*). "Alan Crosland Directs Jessel in 'Jazz' Film," *MPW,* 2 May 1927, 830 (filming to begin 16 May 1927). Dorothy Calhoun, "The Tamer of the Temperament; Handle-with-Care Stars, Says Alan Crosland, Are Bad-Actors in One Sense, But in the Other, and True, They're the Best," *MPC,* Jun 1928, 33, 80.

Crosman, Henrietta Foster [actress] (b. Wheeling WV, 2 Sep 1861–31 Oct 1944 [83], Pelham Manor NY). m. (1) **Sedley Brown** (d. 1928); (2) Maurice Campbell (d. 1942). (Film debut: *The Unwelcome Mrs. Hatch,* FP-L, 10 Sep 1914.) "Henrietta Crosman," *Variety,* 8 Nov 1944 (age 79). BHD1, p. 129. AS, p. 269. IFN, p. 68. SD. Truitt, p. 75. "Famous Players Presents Henrietta Crosman," *MPN,* 12 Sep 1914, 18. "Henriette Crosman," in *Celebrity Articles from The Screen Guild Magazine,* ed. Anna Kate Sterling (Metuchen NJ: Scarecrow Press, Inc., 1987), pp. 6–9.

Cross, Alfred Francis [actor] (b. 1891?–28 Jan 1938 [47], San Diego CA; heart attack). "Alfred Francis Cross," *Variety,* 2 Feb 1938. AS, p. 269. BHD1, p. 129. IFN, p. 68. Truitt, p. 75.

Cross, Barr [scenarist]. No data found. FDY, p. 423.

Cross, Leach [pugilist/actor] (b. New York NY, 12 Feb 1886–7 Sep 1957 [71], New York NY). BHD, p. 140. "Another Pug Joins U.," *LA Times,* 7 Mar 1920, III, p. 16 (to appear with Eddie Polo in *The Vanishing Dagger,* an 18-episode serial thriller. He is the third boxer to work at Universal, the other two being Corbett and Benny Leonard.).

Cross, Oliver [actor] (b. New York NY, 18 Jul 1894–19 Feb 1971 [76], Los Angeles Co. CA). AS, p. 270 (d. NYC). BHD1, p. 130. IFN, p. 68.

Cross, Patricia [actress] (*née* Miriam Wherry). m. **Albert Conti**, 1927. No data found. AMD, p. 84. "Two Film Weddings," *MPW,* 16 Apr 1927, 632.

Cross, Wellington [singer] (b. Boston IL, 3 Apr 1887–12 Oct 1975 [88], New York NY). . "Wellington Cross," *Variety,* 5 Nov 1975. AMD, p. 84. AS, p. 270 (d. Tudor City NY). BHD, p. 140. SD, p. 308. "Wellington Cross to Be Featured in Triangle Plays," *MPW,* 31 Aug 1918, 1279.

Crossley, Syd [actor] (b. London, England, 18 Nov 1885–18 Nov 1960 [75], Troon, England). "Sid Crossley, veteran film actor, died recently in Troon, England. He was a comedian of the silent days," *Variety,* 7 Dec 1960. AS, p. 269. BHD1, p. 130 (d. 15 Nov). IFN, p. 68. Truitt, p. 75.

Crothers, Rachel [playwright/scenarist] (b. Bloomington IL, 12 Dec 1870–6 Jul 1958 [87], Danbury CT). *NYT,* letter, 12 Jul 1958, 14:6. "Rachel Crothers," *Variety,* 9 Jul 1958 (age 75). BHD2, p. 57 (b. 1883; 5 Jul). SD, p. 309. WWWA.

Crothers, Wilson Gray [production manager for Blattnar Film Co.] (b. 1897?–21 Sep 1928 [31], Monte Carlo; suicide by overdose of veronal). "Wilson Gray Crothers," *Variety,* 31 Oct 1928.

Crothwaite, Ivy *see* **Barrett, Ivy Rice**

Crowell, Burt [actor] (*né* Walter J. Crowley, b. 1873–26 Mar 1946 [73?], Chicago IL). AS, p. 270.

Crowell, Josephine B[oneparte] [actress] (b. Halifax, Canada-d. 27 Jul 1932 [80s], Amityville, LI NY). [Griffith.] "Josephine C. Le Croix," *Variety,* 2 Aug 1932. AMD, p. 85. AS, p. 270. BHD, p. 140. IFN, p. 68. Ragan 2, p. 356. "Lloyd Picks Players," *MPW,* 3 May 1924, 44. "Josephine Crowell," *MPW,* 9 Apr 1927, 550.

Croy, Homer [humorist/novelist/scenarist] (b. Nodaway County MO, 11 Mar 1883–24 May 1965 [82], New York NY). m. Mae Bell Savell, 7

Feb 1915, NYC (2 sons who died in infancy, Creighton and Homer, and a daughter, Carol). *Country Cured* (1943). "Homer Croy Dies; Novelist Was 82; Also Did Biographies of Will Rogers [*Our Will Rogers*, 1953] and Jesse James," *NYT*, 25 May 1965, 41:3. "Homer Croy," *Variety*, 26 May 1965, p. 71 (born the year the Brooklyn Bridge was built). AMD, p. 85. AS, p. 270 (b. Marysville MO; d. Riverdale NY). BHD2, p. 57 (b. Maryville MO). George Blaisdell, "At the Sign of the Flaming Arcs," *MPW*, 4 Apr 1914, 67. "Homer Croy a Benedict," *NYDM*, 10 Feb 1915, 24:3. "Homer Croy Marries," *MPW*, 20 Feb 1915, 1126. Homer Croy, "Doughboy Wants Screen's Best," *MPW*, 14 Jun 1919, 1617. "Croy, Homer," *National Cyclopædia of American Biography*, XV (1969), pp. 663–64 (wrote *How Motion Pictures Are Made*, 1915; *Star Maker*, 1959).

Crozier, Emmet [scenarist] (b. 1893–5 Nov 1982 [89?]). BHD2, p. 57. FDY, p. 423.

Cruikshank, Herbert K. [author/scenarist] (b. 1890–27 Dec 1939 [49?], New York NY). AS, p. 270.

Crume, Camilla [actress] (b. 1874?–20 Mar 1952 [78], Norwalk CT). m. **Charles William Goodrich** (d. 1931). (Vitaphone Studios in Brooklyn.) "Camilla Crume," *Variety*, 26 Mar 1952. AS, p. 270. BHD, p. 140. IFN, p. 68. SD. Truitt, p. 76.

Cruster, Aud [actor] (*né* Cruster Aud Olsen, b. 1889?–18 May 1938 [49], Moline IL). "Aud Cruster," *Variety*, 25 May 1938. AS, p. 270. BHD, p. 140. IFN, p. 68. Truitt, p. 76.

Crute, Sally [actress] (*née* Sally C. Kirby, b. Chattanooga TN, 17 Jun 1886–12 Aug 1971 [85], Miami FL). (Edison, Bronx studio.) AMD, p. 85. AS, p. 271. BHD1, p. 606. IFN, p. 68 (b. 1893). MH, p. 105 (b. 1893). Truitt, p. 76. "Sally Crute Taken Ill," *NYDM*, 25 Feb 1914, 34:1. "Sally Crute," *MPW*, 25 Apr 1914, 496. "Sallie Crute," *MPW*, 13 Mar 1915, 1617 (b. near Huntsville AL). "Narrow Escape for Sally Crute," *NYDM*, 23 Oct 1915, 26:2 (driving from Yonkers to NYC, "the tires of her automobile caught in the trolley track and were instantly ripped to ribbons. Miss Crute was thrown bodily from the car and landed head first against a billboard. She was knocked unconscious and received several painful bruises."). "Sally Crute in Edison Feature," *MPW*, 9 Dec 1916, 1480. "Metro Engages Sally Crute," *MPW*, 1 Dec 1917, 1307. "Players Engaged for 'When Man Betrays,'" *MPW*, 18 May 1918, 1019. "Sally Crute Recovering," *MPW*, 17 May 1919, 1035. Billy H. Doyle, "Lost Players," *CI*, 150 (Dec 1987), 10–11.

Cruz, Charles [editor] (b. 1888?–31 Aug 1958 [70], New York NY; pneumonia). "Carlos Bareiro Cruz," *NYT*, 2 Sep 1958, 25:1 (translated South American motion pictures for Universal-International Films).

Cruze, James (brother of **Mae Cruze**) [actor/director/producer/scenarist] (*né* Jens Cruz Bosen, b. Five Points [Ogden] UT, 27 Mar 1884–3 Aug 1942 [58], Los Angeles CA; heart attack). m. **Marguerite Snow** (d. 1958); **Betty Compson**, 14 Oct 1924 (d. 1974); (3) Alberta B. McCoy. (Thanhouser, 1908; FP-L.) "James Cruze, 58, Screen Director; 'Covered Wagon' Among the Many Films He Made—Dies in California," *NYT*, 5 Aug 1942, 19:3. "James Cruze," *Variety*, 5 Aug 1942. AMD, p. 85. AS, p. 271. BHD, p. 140; BHD2, p. 57. IFN, p. 68 (b. 1894, but age 58). SD. Truitt, p. 76 (b. 1894). "Thanhouser Players Have Narrow Escape," *MPW*, 8 Jun 1912, 934. Thornton Fisher, "Off the Screen with James Cruze," *MPW*, 16 May 1914, 945. "James Cruze Engaged by Metro," *MPW*, 15 Apr 1916, 411. "James Cruze with Fox," *MPW*, 17 Mar 1917, 1786. "Paramount Won't Lose James Cruze," *MPW*, 31 Dec 1921, 1045. Jim Tully, "A Thousand Dollars a Day!," *MPC*, Oct 1924, 40, 77–78. "Cruze Weds Compson," *MPW*, 1 Nov 1924, 29. Dorothy Donnell, "Cruze, Trail-Breaker; The Runaway Utah Boy Who Became a Pioneer with Shadows," *MPC*, Sep 1925, 26–27, 78–79, 89. Don Juan, "So This Is Hollywood; Old Ironsides Takes Toll," *Paris and Hollywood*, Oct 1926, 22 (during the filming of *Old Ironsides* for Paramount, a cannon exploded, a mast fell, and two extra men who were in the rigging were killed.). "Cruze Will Not Renew Contract," *MPW*, 28 May 1927, 254. "James Cruze Joins P.D.C.-Pathé Unit; Walter Woods Also," *MPW*, 4 Jun 1927, 325. "Cruze Shoots Thirty Scenes in One Day," *MPW*, 8 Oct 1927, 348. Burr C. Cook, "The Uphill Climb of James Cruze; Tenacity Carried Him Along the Road from Tent Shows to Leadership as a Director," *Cinema Arts*, Nov 1927, 19, 47 (of Danish ancestry). Herbert Cruikshank, "The Rebel of the Megaphone; Jim Cruze's Shirts Have No Sleeves, He Likes Freedom of Movement, of Speech, of Everything," *MPC*, May 1928, 33, 70. George Geltzer, "James Cruze," *FIR*, Jun/Jul 1954, 283–91 (d. 4 Aug). Herb Gordon, "James Cruze and the Critics," *CI*, 76 (Jul 1981), 57, 59.

Cruze, Julie Jane [actress] (b. New York NY, 24 Oct 1913–27 Jul 1946 [32], San Diego CA). BHD, p. 140.

Cruze, Mae (sister of **James Cruze**) [actress] (*née* Mae Bosen, b. Five Points [?] UT, 24 May 1881–16 Aug 1965 [84], Los Angeles CA). Unpublished *My Big Brother*. "Mae Cruze," *Variety*, 25 Aug 1965 (age 74). AS, p. 271. BHD1, p. 130. IFN, p. 68. Truitt, p. 76 (b. 1891).

Csortos, Gyula [actor] (b. Munkacs, Hungary, 3 Mar 1883–1 Aug 1945 [62], Budapest, Hungary). AS, p. 271.

Cudahy, Michael (b. 1908–14 Feb 1947 [38?], Los Angeles CA). BHD, p. 140.

Cuenca, Carlos Fernandez [actor/director/writer] (b. Madrid, Spain, 8 May 1904–25 Nov 1977 [73], Madrid, Spain). AS, p. 386 (Fernandez Cuenca, Carlos).

Cuenca, Pedro Fernandez [actor] (b. Madrid, Spain, 5 Jun 1888–8 Dec 1940 [52], Madrid, Spain). AS, p. 386.

Cuerlis, Hans [director/producer] (b. Germany, 1889–6 Aug 1982 [93?], Berlin, Germany). AS, p. 271.

Cufaro, Antonio [cinematographer]. JS, p. 114 (in Italian silents from 1913).

Cukor, George [director] (*né* George I. Cukor, b. New York NY, 6 Jul 1899 [Birth Certificate Index No. 27202]–24 Jan 1983 [83], Los Angeles CA; heart attack). . m. Ruth Sinclair (d. 1984). Patrick McGilligan, *George Cukor: A Double Life* (New York: St. Martin's Press, 1991). Peter B. Flint, "George Cukor, 83, Film Director, Dies," *NYT*, 26 Jan 1983, 18:1. "Director George Cukor, 83, Dies in L.A., 50-Yr. Career, Many Hits," *Variety*, 26 Jan 1983. AS, p. 271. BHD2, p. 57 (b. 7 Jul).Katz, p. 290. SD.

Culhane, Shamus [animator] (b. Ware MA, 12 Nov 1908–2 Feb 1996 [87], New York NY). m. Maxine Marx; Juana Hegarty. (Disney.) *Talking Animals and Other People* (St. Martin's Press, 1986). Lawrence Van Gelder, "Shamus Culhane, a Pioneering Film Animator, Is Dead at 87," *NYT*, 4 Feb 1996, 43:1. AS, p. 271. BHD2, p. 57.

Cullen, Cleo [actress] (b. 1903–28 Oct 1993 [90?], Los Angeles CA). BHD1, p. 130.

Cullen, Edward L. [actor] (b. Buffalo NY, 10 Aug 1893–27 Jul 1964 [70], New York NY [Death Certificate Index No. 15752; M.E. Case No. 6217]). . "Edward L. Cullen," *Variety*, 12 Aug 1964. AS, p. 271 (b. 1895). BHD, p. 140 (b. 1895).

Cullen, Robert [scenarist]. No data found. FDY, p. 423.

Culley, Frederick [actor] (b. Plymouth, England, 9 Mar 1879–3 Nov 1942 [63], London, Rngland). AS, p. 271.

Cullington, Margaret [actress] (b. Philadelphia MA, 1886–18 Jul 1925 [39], Los Angeles CA; despondent over the death of her husband). m. William Fowler. (Christie.) "Margaret Cullington," *Variety*, 22 Jul 1925 (age 34). AS, p. 271. BHD, p. 140 (b. New Rochelle NY). IFN, p. 69.

Cullison, Webster [stage/film director] (b. Baltimore MD, 18 Feb 1880–7 Jul 1938 [58], Glendale CA sanitarium). "Webster Cullison," *Variety*, 13 Jul 1938 ("former stage and screen director"). AMD, p. 85. AS, p. 271. BHD, p. 140; BHD2, p. 57. Truitt 1983. "Eclair in Arizona; Webster Cullison Has Strong Company and Up-to-Date Studio at Tucson," *NYDM*, 11 Feb 1914, 34:1. "Eckels Signs Webster Cullison to Direct Neal Hart Features," *MPW*, 5 Feb 1921, 715.

Cumberland, John [actor]. No data found. AMD, p. 85. "John Cumberland Joins Goldwyn," *MPW*, 26 May 1917, 1289. "'Jimmie' Sticks to John Cumberland," *MPW*, 30 Aug 1919, 1306. "John Cumberland Makes His Debut for Pathé," *MPW*, 13 Dec 1919, 824.

Cumegys, Kathleen Foster [actress] (b. Shreveport LA, 25 Jul 1895). AS, p. 272.

Cumming, Dorothy [actress/script supervisor/title writer] (b. Burrows, Australia, 13 Nov 1900–22 Apr 1975 [74], Los Angeles CA). . (MGM.) "Dorothy Cumming," *Variety*, 7 May 1975. AMD, p. 85. AS, p. 272. BHD1, p. 131 (b. 12 Apr 1899–10 Dec 1983 [84], NYC). IFN, p. 69 (b. NC, 13 Nov 1913). MH, p. 105. WWS, p. 36. "Dorothy Cumming in Cast," *MPW*, 2 May 1925, 69. "Dorothy Cumming Returns East," *MPW*, 25 Jul 1925, 453. "Dorothy Cumming Is Queen," *MPW*, 26 Sep 1925, 339. "I'll Say It's Tough!," *MPW*, 16 Jan 1926, 238.

Cummings, Catherine [actress] (b. Grantsburg IL, 1871–8 Jul 1950 [79?], Los Angeles CA). AS, p. 272 (d. 10 Jul). BHD, p. 140. IFN, p. 69 (Katherine).

Cummings, Charles Eugene [actor] (b. IN-d. 4 Oct 1916, Los Angeles CA). BHD, p. 140.

Cummings, Dwight [scenarist]. No data found. FDY, p. 423.

Cummings, Forrest H. [stock director/film actor] (b. San Francisco CA, 1877–15 May 1929 [51?], Toronto, Canada; in a fire). m. Hazel Harrington. "Forrest H. Cummings," *Variety*, 15 May 1929, p. 67 (age 52). BHD, p. 140.

Cummings, Frances [actress] (d. 12 Aug 1923, New York NY; cancer). (Lubin; Famous Players.) "Frances Cummings," *Variety*, 23 Aug 1923. AS, p. 272. BHD, p. 140. Truitt, p. 76.

Cummings, George F. [actor] (b. Richmond VA, 4 Jul 1880–11 Mar 1946 [66], Los Angeles Co. CA). AS, p. 272. BHD, p. 140. IFN, p. 69.

Cummings, Harold [title writer]. No data found. FDY, p. 441.

Cummings, Irving (son of Irving Cummings, Jr.) [stage/film actor/scenarist/director/producer] (*né* Irving Caminsky, b. New York NY, 9 Oct 1888–18 Apr 1959 [70], Los Angeles CA; heart attack). m. **Ruth** Sinclair (d. 1984; son, Irving, Jr., 1918–1996). (Began 1910; American; Pathé; Horsley; FP-L; Fox; Metro.) "Irving Cummings, Director, Is Dead; Broadway Leading Man at Turn of Century Was with Fox—Won 1943 Medal," *NYT,* 19 Apr 1959, 86:1. "Irving Cummings," *Variety,* 22 Apr 1959. AMD, p. 85. AS, p. 272. BHD, p. 140; BHD2, p. 57. FDY, p. 423. IFN, p. 69. Katz, p. 291 (began 1909). MSBB, p. 1023. SD. Spehr, p. 126. Truitt, p. 76. "Irving Cummings," *MPW,* 1 Feb 1913, 446. "Lives of the Players; Irving Cummings; Leading Man with the Reliance Company," *MPS,* 30 May 1913, 30–31. "Irving Cummings Joins Universal," *MPW,* 13 Dec 1913, 1263. "Irving Cummings," *MPW,* 25 Apr 1914, 528. "Irving Cummings Joins Fox," *MPW,* 23 Dec 1916, 1810. "Cummings with Famous Players-Lasky," *MPW,* 10 May 1919, 810. "Cummings's 1st Independent Production," *MPW,* 6 Oct 1923, 505. "Cummings Is No Longer Fox Director," *MPW,* 8 Jan 1927, 111. "Irving Cummings with Warner Bros.," *MPW,* 22 Jan 1927, 267.

Cummings, Ralph E. [director] (b. 1867–20 Oct 1933 [66?], New York NY). BHD2, p. 58.

Cummings, Richard H[enry] [actor] (b. New Haven CT, 20 Aug 1858–25 Dec 1938 [80], Los Angeles CA). (Thanhouser, 1912; Griffith.) "Richard H. Cummings," *Variety,* 28 Dec 1928. AS, p. 272. BHD1, p. 131. IFN, p. 69. Truitt, p. 76. George Katchmer, "Remembering the Great Silents," *CI,* 222 (Dec 1993), C19.

Cummings, Robert W. [actor] (b. MA, 8 Feb 1865–22 Jul 1949 [84], Los Angeles Co. CA). (World; Metro.) AS, p. 272 (b. Richmond VA). BHD1, p. 131. IFN, p. 69. Spehr, p. 126 (b. Richmond VA, 1867).

Cummings, Ruth Sinclair (mother of Irving Cummins, Jr.) [actress/title writer/scenarist] (aka Ruth Cummings after 1924, *née* Ruth Sinclair, b. 4 Apr 1894–6 Dec 1984 [90], Woodland Hills CA). . m. **Irving Cummings** (d. 1959; son, Irving, Jr.). (MGM.) "Ruth Sinclair Cummings," *Variety,* 12 Dec 1984. AS, p. 272. BHD1, p. 131 (d. 11 Aug 1967, NY NY); BHD2, p. 245. FDY, pp. 423, 441.

Cummins, Dwight W. [writer] (b. San Francisco CA, 20 Feb 1902–31 May 1985 [83], Monrovia CA). m. **Dorothy Yost**, 1927 (d. 1967). . AMD, p. 85. BHD2, p. 58 (b. 1901). "Cummins, Yost Wed Soon," *MPW,* 1 Oct 1927, 284.

Cummins, Ralph [scenarist]. No data found. FDY, p. 423.

Cummins, Samuel [executive/producer] (b. New York NY, 5 Oct 1890–14 Dec 1967 [77], New York NY [Death Certificate Index No. 25391]). . m. Faith. "Samuel Cummins," *Variety,* 20 Dec 1967 (age 72). AS, p. 272 (b. 1895). BHD2, p. 58.

Cumpson, John R. [actor] (b. Buffalo NY, 1868?–15 Mar 1913 [45], New York NY [Death Certificate No. 8986]; pneumonia). (Biograph; Imp.) "John R. Cumpson," *Variety,* 21 Mar 1913. AMD, p. 85. AS, p. 272. BHD, p. 133. IFN, p. 60. SD. "Obituary," *MPW,* 29 Mar 1913, p. 1341 (played Bumptious and Mr. Jones).

Cunard, Grace (sister of **Myna Cunard**) [stage/vaudeville/film actress] (*née* Harriet Mildred Jeffries, b. Columbus OH, 8 Apr 1891–19 Jan 1967 [75], Woodland Hills CA; cancer). m. **Francis Ford** (d. 1953); **Joseph Moore**, 1917 (d. 1926); **Jack Shannon** (d. 1968). (Lubin; Bison; Biograph; Universal.) "Grace Cunard, 73, Silent-Film Star; Actress in Many Serials 50 Years Ago Is Dead," *NYT,* 24 Jan 1967, 37:2. "Grace Cunard," *Variety,* 25 Jan 1967 (b. France), but *see* Lahue, *CNW,* p. 20 (not born in Paris). AS, p. 272 (d. San Fernando Valley CA). BHD1, p. 131 (b. 1893). BR, pp. 14–17 (b. 1893). FSS, p. 80. IFN, p. 69 (b. 1893). LD, pp. 52–62. MH, p. 105 (b. Paris). MSBB, p. 1034 (b. Paris). Truitt, p. 76 (b. Paris, 1894). "Grace Cunard," *MPW,* 23 Dec 1911, 972. "Grace Cunard," *MPW,* 21 Feb 1914, 933. "Grace Cunard; Playing Leads in the Gold Seal Company," *MPS,* 27 Feb 1914, 27. "Grace Cunard," *NYDM,* 10 Jun 1914, 50:2. "Grace Cunard," *MPW,* 19 Feb 1916, 1115. "Grace Cunard," *MPW,* 27 Jan 1917, 522. "Grace Cunard Married to Joe Moore," *MPW,* 10 Feb 1917, 854. "Grace Cunard Has Much Experience," *MPW,* 1 Mar 1919, 1185. Eldon K. Everett, "The Great Grace Cunard-Francis Ford Mystery," *CFC,* 39 (Summer, 1973), 22–25.

Cunard, Myna (sister of **Grace Cunard**) [actress] (b. Columbus OH, 16 Dec 1894–9 Aug 1978 [83], Woodland Hills CA; cancer). . m. **Harry Seymour** (d. 1967). "Myra Cunard," *Variety,* 16 Aug 1978. AMD, p. 182 (Mina Jeffries). AS, p. 272. BHD1, p. 131 (Mina Cunard). IFN, p. 69. Truitt 1983. "Mina Jeffries," *MPW,* 25 Mar 1916, 1992.

Cuneo, Lester H. [actor/director] (b. Indian Territory, OK [or Chicago IL], 25 Oct 1888–1 Nov 1925 [37], Los Angeles CA; suicide by shooting). m. **Francelia Billington**, 1920, Riverside CA (d. 1934). "Film Actor Commits Suicide," *NYT,* 3 Nov 1925, 13:3. "Cuneo Kills Self," *Variety,* 4 Nov 1925. AMD, p. 85. AS, p. 272. BHD2, p. 58. IFN, p. 69. MH, p. 105. "Lester Cuneo Returns to Screen," *MPW,* 15 Apr 1916, 446. "Lester Cuneo," *MPW,* 1 Dec 1917, 1322. "Lester Cuneo in New Wanda Hawley Picture," *MPW,* 19 Jun 1920, 1628. "Cuneo's Car Runs Off Embankment," *MPW,* 10 Jul 1920, 213. "Capital Film Company Starts Work on Six Pictures Starring Lester Cuneo," *MPW,* 9 Oct 1920, 797. "Wedding in Filmland," *MPW,* 6 Nov 1920, 55. "Breaks Toe," *MPW,* 24 Sep 1921, 421. "Obituary," *MPW,* 14 Nov 1925, 118.

Cunning, Patrick Michael [actor] (b. Santa Clara CA, 23 May 1905–13 Mar 1973 [67], Fresno CA). AMD, p. 86. AS, p. 272. BHD1, p. 131. "Pat Cumming," *MPW,* 22 Oct 1927, 496.

Cunningham, Arthur [cinema pioneer] (b. 1868?–22 Mar 1953 [85], Morecambe, England). "Arthur Cunningham," *Variety,* 8 Apr 1953.

Cunningham, Arthur [dancer/singer/vaudevillian/actor] (b. San Francisco CA, 1888?–29 Nov 1955 [67], San Francisco CA; heart ailment). m. Edith (d. Nov 1955). "Arthur Cunningham," *Variety,* 7 Dec 1955. AS, p. 272. BHD, p. 141.

Cunningham, Cecil [actor] (b. St. Louis MO, 2 Aug 1888–17 Apr 1959 [70], Woodland Hills CA). AS, p. 272.

Cunningham, George R. [choreographer/stage director/actor] (b. New York NY, 11 Feb 1904–30 Apr 1962 [58], Los Angeles CA). AS, p. 272 (d. 1 May). BHD1, p. 131; BHD2, p. 58. IFN, p. 69.

Cunningham, Jack [scenarist] (b. Ionia IA, 1 Apr 1882–3 Oct 1941 [59], Santa Monica CA; cerebral hemorrhage). "Jack Cunningham," *Variety,* 8 Oct 1941. AMD, p. 86. AS, p. 272 (d. 4 Oct). BHD2, p. 58. FDY, p. 423. IFN, p. 69. "Cunningham Writes for Kerrigan," *MPW,* 5 Oct 1918, 58. "Jack Cunningham Writing 'Draws,'" *MPW,* 19 Mar 1927, 192.

Cunningham, Joseph A. [actor/scenarist] (b. Philadelphia PA, 22 Jun 1890–3 Apr 1943 [52], Los Angeles CA; coronary occlusion). AS, p. 272. BHD2, p. 58.

Cunningham, Zamah [actress] (b. 29 Nov 1892–2 Jun 1967 [74], New York NY [Death Certificate Index No. 11373]). . (Griffith.) "Zamah Cunningham," *Variety,* 7 Jun 1967. AS, p. 273. IFN, p. 69.

Curci, Gennaro [actor] (*né* Baron Gennaro Mario Curci, b. Italy, 9 Sep 1888–13 Apr 1955 [66], Los Angeles CA; cerebral thrombosis). AS, p. 272.

Curley, Leo [actor] (b. New York NY, 12 Apr 1878–11 Apr 1960 [81], Woodland Hills CA; complications from arteriosclerosis). AS, p. 273.

Curley, Robert D. [cameraman]. No data found. AMD, p. 86. "Robert D. Curley," *MPW,* 19 Mar 1927, 177.

Curran, Barry [publicist]. No data found. AMD, p. 86. "Curran Joins Columbia," *MPW,* 31 Oct 1925, 706.

Curran, J.P. [stage/film actor] (b. 1847?–11 Jan 1919 [71], Sawtelle CA). m. **Ruby LaFayette** (d. 1935). BHD, p. 141. IFN, p. 69. "Ruby LaFayette's Husband Dies," *MPW,* 1 Feb 1919, 616 (d. 12 Jan).

Curran, Thomas A. [actor] (b. Australia, 1879–24 Jan 1941 [61], Los Angeles CA; pneumonia). (Monogram.) "Thomas A. Curran," *Variety,* 29 Jan 1941. AMD, p. 86. AS, p. 273. BHD1, p. 132. IFN, p. 69. Truitt, p. 76. "Thomas A. Curran—Thanhouser Leading Man," *MPW,* 23 Dec 1916, 1778. "Thomas A. Curran," *MPW,* 14 Jul 1917, 229.

Currie, Clive [actor] (b. Birmingham, England, 26 Mar 1877–25 May 1935 [58], London, England). BHD1, p. 132. IFN, p. 69.

Currie, Finlay Jefferson [actor] (b. Edinburgh, Scotland, 20 Jan 1878–9 May 1968 [90], Gerrard's Cross, England). m. Maude Courtney (d. 1959). "Finlay Currie," *Variety,* 15 May 1968. AS, p. 273. BHD1, p. 132. IFN, p. 69.

Currier, Frank [stage/film actor] (b. Norwich CT, 4 Sep 1857–22 Apr 1928 [70], Los Angeles CA; blood poisoning). m. Mabel Olms, 1919, LA CA. (Began ca. 1914.) "Frank Currier," *Variety,* 25 Apr 1928 (age 71). AMD, p. 86. AS, p. 273. BHD, p. 141. IFN, 69. Truitt, p. 77. "Frank Currier Engaged by Metro," *MPW,* 14 Oct 1916, 237. "Frank Currier Married," *MPW,* 19 Apr 1919, 360. "Frank Currier Marries," *MPW,* 3 May 1919, 641. "Signs Long Term Contract," *MPW,* 29 Nov 1924, 429. "Currier Signs with M-G-M," *MPW,* 6 Feb 1926, 546. Ivan St. Johns, "The Daddy of Them All," *Photoplay,* Aug 1926, 32 *et passim.* Louise Helen Johnson, "Frank Currier—Veteran of Stage and Screen; An interesting chat with one who has grown up with the screen," *Cinema Arts,* Aug 1926, 22, 46–47. "Currier Recovers," *MPW,* 9 Oct 1926, 2 (from nervous breakdown). "Frank Currier

Celebrates 50 Years as Actor," *MPW,* 23 Apr 1927, 732. Percy Knighton, "The Famous Fore-4-Fathers of Filmdom," *MPC,* Jul 1927, 58, 81 (re Currier, Alec Francis, J. Farrell MacDonald and Clarence Burton).

Currier, Richard Carlton [film editor] (b. CO, 26 Aug 1892–14 Dec 1984 [92], El Toro CA). AMD, p. 86. BHD2, p. 58. "Hal Roach Signs Richard Currier as Chief Editor," *MPW,* 19 Mar 1927, 193.

Currier, Victor [title writer]. No data found. FDY, p. 441.

Curtis, Allen [director/actor] (b. NY, 1877?–24 Nov 1961 [84], Santa Anita CA). (Universal.) "Allen Curtis," *Variety,* 29 Nov 1961 (began 1912; "pioneer director"). AS, p. 273. BHD, p. 141 (b. 1879); BHD2, p. 58 (d. LA CA).

Curtis, Beatrice (sister of **Jack Curtis**) [actress] (b. New York NY, 23 Sep 1906–26 Mar 1963 [56], Los Angeles CA). m. Harry Fox; Sammy White. "Beatrice White," *Variety,* 3 Apr 1963 (age 62. AS, p. 273 (b. 1901). BHD1, p. 132. IFN, p. 70. Truitt, p. 77 (b. 1901).

Curtis, Catherine [actress/producer]. No data found. (Catherine Curtis Corporation.) AMD, p. 86. "George M. Taylor Dies," *MPW,* 4 Sep 1920, 48 (death of father). "Harry Collins, Modiste, Sues Catherine Curtis," *MPW,* 26 Nov 1921, 403.

Curtis, Dick [actor] (*né* Richard Curtis, b. Newport KY, 11 May 1902–3 Jan 1952 [49], Los Angeles CA). m. **Ruth Sullivan**. (Griffith.) "Dick Curtis," *Variety,* 9 Jan 1952. AS, p. 273. BHD1, p. 132. IFN, p. 70. Katz, p. 293 (began 1918). Truitt, p. 77.

Curtis, Graham [scenarist]. No data found. FDY, p. 423.

Curtis, Jack (brother of **Beatrice Curtis**) [actor] (b. San Francisco CA, 28 May 1880–16 Mar 1956 [75], Los Angeles CA). "Jack Curtis," *Variety,* 28 Mar 1956. AS, p. 273. BHD1, p. 132. IFN, p. 70. Truitt, p. 77. George A. Katchmer, "Forgotten Cowboys and Cowgirls—Part XIV," *CI,* 191 (May 1991), 20.

Curtis, John W. [actor] (b. 1846–21 Jul 1925 [79?], New York NY). BHD, p. 141. IFN, p. 70.

Curtis, Spencer M. [actor] (b. 1858?–13 Jul 1921 [63], Long Beach CA; dropped dead during filming at Long Beach High School). (Balboa.) "Spencer M. Curtis," *Variety,* 22 Jul 1921. AMD, p. 86. AS, p. 274. BHD, p. 141 (b. 1858). IFN, p. 70. Truitt, p. 77. "Obituary," *MPW,* 30 Jul 1921, 497.

Curtis, Willa Pearl [actress] (b. TX, 21 Mar 1886–19 Dec 1970 [84], Los Angeles CA; arteriosclerosis and diabetes). AS, p. 274.

Curtiz, David (brother of **Michael Curtiz**) [assistant director] (*né* Kertész, b. Budapest, Hungary, 24 May 1893–23 May 1962 [68], Los Angeles Co. CA). AS, p. 274 (b. 1894). BHD2, p. 58.

Curtiz, Michael (brother of **David Curtiz**) [actor/director/producer] (*né* Mihaly Kertész, b. Budapest, Hungary, 24 Dec 1888–10 Apr 1962 [73], No. Hollywood CA; cancer). m. (1) **Lucy Doraine**—div. 1923 (d. 1989); (2) Bess Meredyth. (Svenska Studios; Saccha Prods.; UFA; WB; AA, 1943.) James C. Robertson, *The Casablanca Man: The Cinema of Michael Curtiz* (Routledge, 1993). "Michael Curtiz, Director, 72, Dies; Oscar-Winner Made Many Films—'Discovered' Stars," *NYT,* 12 Apr 1962, 35:1 (age 72). "Michael Curtiz," *Variety,* 25 Apr 1962 (d. 11 Apr). AMD, p. 82 (Michael Courtice); p. 86. AS, p. 274. BHD2, p. 58. IFN, p. 70. JS, p. 114 (worked on *Miss Tutti Frutti,* Italy, 1921). Katz, pp. 293–94 (began in Hungary, 1912). "Sign Courtice," *MPW,* 24 Apr 1926, 2 (from Vienna; Warner Bros.). "Curtiz Will Direct 'Noah's Ark,'" *MPW,* 10 Jul 1926, 86. "Michael Curtiz," *MPW,* 2 May 1927, 787. "Curtiz Gets Meg for 'Noah's Ark,'" *MPW,* 2 May 1927, 795. Tom Waller, "Michael Curtiz," *MPW,* 9 Jul 1927, 82–83. "Director Michael Curtiz," *CI,* 91 (Jan 1983), 17–18, 38. Barry Paris, "The Little Tyrant Who Could," *American Film,* Jan 1991, 34–37, 44–45.

Curwood, Bob [stuntman/actor] (b. Romania, 17 Mar 1896-Nov 1980 [84], CA). (Began 1918.) AS, p. 274. BHD1, p. 132 (b. 1899).

Curwood, James Oliver [writer/scenarist] (b. Owosso MI, 12 Jun 1878–13 Aug 1927 [49], Owosso MI). m. (1) Cora Leon Johnson, 21 Jan 1900, Windsor, Ontario, Canada—div. Nov 1908, Detroit MI; (2) Ethel Greenwood, 27 Sep 1909, Owosso MI (d. 11 Apr 1965, CA). Judith A. Eldridge, *James Oliver Curwood; God's Country and the Man* (Bowling Green OH: Bowling Green State University, 1993). AMD, p. 86. AS, p. 274. BHD2, p. 58. *Twentieth Century Authors,* pp. 342–43. WWWA. James S. McQuade, "James Oliver Curwood," *MPW,* 5 Sep 1914, 1352–53. "Curwood to Write for Vitagraph Exclusively," *MPW,* 4 Sep 1915, 1630. "Curwood and Nell Shipman Form Producing Company," *MPW,* 9 Nov 1918, 678. "James Oliver Curwood Forms His Own Company to Picturize His Own Novels," *MPW,* 21 Feb 1920, 1243. "Court Fight Over 'I Am the Law' Prevents Showing of That Feature in Two Cities," *MPW,* 17 Jun 1922. "Curwood Wins in Court," *MPW,* 5 Aug 1922, 410.

Cusack, Cyril James (father of actresses Sinead, Sorcha, Niamh and Catherine Cusack) [stage/film actor] (b. Durban, South Africa, 26 Nov 1910–6 Oct 1993 [82], London, England; motor neuron disease). m. (1) Maureen Kiely; (2) Mary. (Early film: *Knockagow,* 1918.) Matt Wolf, "Cyril Cusack," *Variety,* 18 Oct 1993, 27:5, 65:5. AS, p. 274 (d. 7 Oct). BHD1, p. 132. JS, p. 115 (appeared in Italian films from 1967–77). Waldman, p. 69.

Cuscaden, Sarah D. [actress] (b. 1873?–18 Oct 1954 [81], Los Angeles CA). "Sarah D. Cuscaden," *Variety,* 27 Oct 1954. AS, p. 274. IFN, p. 70.

Cushing, Tom [scenarist] (*né* Charles Cyprian Strong Cushing, b. New Haven CT, 1880?–6 Mar 1941 [61], Boston MA). "Tom Cushing," *Variety,* 12 Mar 1941. AS, p. 274. BHD2, p. 58. SD.

Custer, Bob [actor] (*né* Raymond Anthony Glenn, b. Frankfort KY, 18 Oct 1898–27 Dec 1974 [76], Redondo Beach CA; heart attack). (FBO). m. Anne E. Cudahy; Mildred. "Raymond Glenn [Bob Custer]," *Variety,* 15 Jan 1975. "Silent Film Cowboy Star 'Bob Custer,'" *Washington Post,* 31 Dec 1974. AMD, p. 86. AS, p. 274; p. 451 (Raymond Glenn) (d. Torrance CA). BHD1, p. 133. IFN, p. 70. Katz, p. 295 (began 1924; in over 100 silents). "Custer to Marry Miss Cudahy," *MPW,* 29 Nov 1926, 3. "Bob Custer Out of 'Westerns' in Society Stuff,"' *MPW,* 21 May 1927, 196. George Katchmer, "Remembering the Great Silents," *CI,* 222 (Dec 1993), C17.

Cuttica, Primo [actor] (b. Genoa, Italy, 1876-Oct 1921 [45?], St. Bario Legure, Italy). "Primero Cuttica," *Variety,* 4 Nov 1921, p. 5. BHD, p. 141.

Cutts, Graham [director/producer] (*né* John Henry Graham Cutts, b. Brighton, England, 1885–7 Sep 1958 [73?], London, England). AS, p. 274. BHD2, p. 59.

Cwiklinska, Mieczylaslava [actress] (*née* Mieczyslava Trapszo, b. Posen, Germany, 1880). AS, p. 275 (worked in Poland).

Cytron, Maurice [assistant director]. No data found. AMD, p. 86. "Maurice Cytron Joins Horsley," *MPW,* 1 Jan 1916, 57.

Czepa, Friedl [actress] (née Friederike Pfaffeneder, b. Amstetten, Austria, 3 Sep 1898–22 Jun 1973 [74], Munich, Germany). AS, p. 75.

Czinner, Paul [scenarist/producer/director] (b. Hungary, 30 May 1890–22 Jun 1972 [82], London, England). m. **Elisabeth Bergner** (d. 1986). "Paul Czinner," *Variety,* 267, 9 Aug 1972, 63:4 (d. 23 Jun). AS, p. 275. BHD2, p. 59. FDY, p. 423. IFN, p. 70.

Czynxki, Kazimierz [director] (b. Przemysl, Poland, 6 Feb 1891–15 Nov 1956 [65], Sulechow, Germany). AS, p. 275.

D

Daab, Hyatt [publicist]. No data found. AMD, p. 87. "Hyatt Daab," *MPW,* 26 Mar 1927, 310.

D'Abbadie D'Arrast, Henri *see* **D'Arrast, Henri D'Abbadie**

Dac, Pierre [actor/singer/writer] (*né* André Isaac, b. Chalons-sur-Marne, France, 15 Aug 1893 [extrait de naissance no. 339]-9 Feb 1975 [81], Paris, France). AS, p. 279.

Dacia [dancer/actress] (*née* Minna Vandyck) (b. Jamaica, West Indies?, ca. 1902). W. Adolphe Roberts, "'American Movies Are Wild!' Declares Dacia, Fascinating Little English Vamp; Tiny star of *Weavers of Fortune* who formerly danced in Chu Chin Chow, announces to *Movie Weekly* representative that British films are as good as American," *MPW*, 2 Jun 1923, 4–5.

Da Cunha, José Maria Alves [actor] (*né* José Maria Alves da Cunha, b. Lisbon, Portugal, 19 Aug 1889–25 Sep 1956 [67], near Lisbon, Portugal). m. Berta de Bivar. "Jose Da Cunha," *Variety*, 10 Oct 1956. AS, p. 278. BHD1, p. 133.

Daghofer, Fritz [actor] (*né* Friedrich Gustav Josef Daghofer, b. Klosterneuberg, Austria, 5 Jul 1872–25 Nov 1936 [64], Vienna, Austria). m. **Lil Dagover**—div. 1919 (d. 1980). AS, p. 278.

Dagmar, Florence [actress]. No data found. m. Roy Somers, 1917. (Laksy.) AMD, p. 87. "Florence Dagmar in 'The Clown,'" *MPW*, 20 May 1916, 1346. Cal York, "Plays and Players," *Photoplay*, Jul 1917, 111 (married Somers. "It was a double wedding, the groom's brother marrying at the same time.").

Dagnall, Ells [actor] (b. 1860–26 Dec 1935 [75?], England). BHD, p. 141.

D'Agostino, Albert S. [art director] (b. New York NY, 27 Dec 1892–14 Mar 1970 [76], Los Angeles CA). . AS, p. 277 (b. 1893). BHD2, p. 59 (b. 1893). IFN, p. 70.

Dagover, Lil [actress] (*née* Antonia Maria Siegelinde Martha Seubert, b. Madiven, Java, Dutch East Indies, 30 Sep 1897–23 Jan 1980 [82], Munich, West Germany). m. **Fritz Daghofer**—div. 1919 (d. 1936). (Decla; Ufa; sole Hollywood film, *A Woman from Monte Carlo*, 1932; last film: *Tales from the Vienna Woods*, 1979.) "Lil Dagover," *Variety*, 30 Jan 1980. AMD, p. 87. AS, p. 279. BHD1, p. 133 (b. Pati, Java, Indonesia, 1894). IFN, p. 70. Truitt 1983 (*née* Marie Antonia Siegelinde Martha Seubert). "Idols of Berlin," *MPC*, Feb 1926, 41 (photo). "Lil Dagover," *MPW*, 1 Jan 1927, 29. Sue Dibble, "New Star Risks Life to Meet Fans; Lil Dagover, Famous German Actress, Makes Air Tour of United States on Way to Hollywood—in Three Airplane Accidents," *Movie Classic*, Dec 1931, 39.

Dague, Roswell [scenarist]. No data found. AMD, p. 87. "Roswell Dague in War Camp," *MPW*, 28 Sep 1918, 1868. "Dague Assumes New Editorial Duties at Famous Players," *MPW*, 3 Jul 1920, 96.

Daguerre, Mandé [inventor] (b. Cormeilles, France, 16 Nov 1789–10 Jul 1851 [70], Bry-sur-Marne, France). AS, p. 279.

Dahl, Andre [scenarist] (b. 1887–11 Sep 1932 [45?]). BHD2, p. 59.

Dahl, Helen [actress]. No data found. AMD, p. 87. "In Support of Billie Burke," *MPW*, 9 Oct 1920, 777.

Dahlberg, Camilla [actress] (b. Erfurt, Germany, 18 Jun 1870-Feb 1968 [97], Bronx NY). m. **Charles Kraus** (d. 1931). AMD, p. 87. BHD1, p. 606 (Camille Dalberg). "Camilla Dalberg," *MPW*, 3 Feb 1912, 399. "Camilla Dalberg," *MPW*, 15 Dec 1917, 1625. "Mme. Camilla Dalberg Ends Engagement with 'Buddies,'" *MPW*, 24 Sep 1921, 421.

Dailey, Joseph [singer/dancer/stage/film actor] (b. 1862–23 Sep 1940 [78], Englewood NJ, at the Actors' Fund Home). (Stage debut: 1883.) "Joseph Dailey," *Variety*, 25 Sep 1940, p. 62. AS, p. 280. BHD, p. 141.

D'Albert, Eugen [composer] (b. Glasgow, Scotland, 10 Apr 1864–3 Mar 1932 [67], Riga, Latvia). AS, p. 277.

D'Albrook, Sydney [stage/film actor] (b. Chicago IL, 3 May 1886–30 May 1948 [62], Los Angeles CA; heart attack). (Selig and Essanay [Chicago]; Biograph; World; Fox; Metro; FP-L.) AS, p. 277. BHD1, p. 134. IFN, p. 71. MSBB, p. 1023 (b. 1888). George A. Katchmer, "Forgotten Cowboys and Cowgirls—Part XVIII," *CI*, 195 (Sep 1991), C6.

D'Alcy, Jeanne [actress] (*née* Charlotte Lucie Marie Adèle Stephanie Adrienne Faës, b. Vaujours, France, 20 Mar 1865 [extrait de naissance no. 17]–14 Oct 1956 [91], Versailles, France). m. **Georges Méliès** (d. 1938). AS, p. 277. BHD, p. 141. Katz, p. 17 (began ca. 1898.)

Dale, Alan (father of **Margaret Dale**) [author/playwright/critic] (*né* Alfred J. Cohen, b. Birmingham, England, 14 May 1861–21 May 1928 [67], on train traveling from Plymouth to Birmingham, England). m. Carrie L. Frost. "Alan Dale Dies Suddenly Abroad; Dramatic Critic of New York American Stricken on a Railroad Train in England; On Way to Birthplace; Dean of Dramatic Reviewers Here Sailed Recently—Had Undergone Several Operations," *NYT*, 22 May 1928, 27:3. "Alan Dale," *Variety*, 30 May 1928. AS, p. 280. SD, p. 318.

Dale, Charles [actor] (*né* Charles Marks, b. New York NY, 6 Sep 1881–16 Nov 1971 [90], Teaneck NJ). m. Molly Cahill (d. 1968). "Chas. Dale (Smith &) Dies in Teaneck, N.J. Nursing Home at 90," *Variety*, 24 Nov 1971. AS, p. 280. BHD1, p. 134. IFN, p. 71.

Dale, Dorothy [actress] (b. 1882?–13 May 1957 [75?], Los Angeles CA; burned to death). "Dorothy Dale [Mrs. Alida Hyman], Silent Film Star, Dies in Coast Fire," *Variety*, 15 May 1957. AS, p. 280. BHD, p. 141. IFN, p. 71. SD, p. 318. Truitt, p. 78.

Dale, James [actor] (b. England, 1885–2 Mar 1985 [100?], London, England). AS, p. 280.

Dale, Margaret (daughter of **Alan Dale**) [actress] (*née* Margaret Rosendale Wallace, b. Philadelphia PA, 6 Mar 1876–23 Mar 1972 [96], New York NY [Death Certificate Index No. 6028]). m. Peter Goffin. "Margaret Dale," *Variety*, 29 Mar 1972. AMD, p. 87. AS, p. 280. BHD1, p. 134. IFN, p. 71. SD. "Alan Dale's Daughter in Metro Picture," *MPW*, 15 Apr 1916, 449.

Dale, Marjorie [actress] (b. 1897–21 Apr 1979 [81?], Boston MA). BHD, p. 141.

Dale, Olive [actress] (*née* Olive Simon). No data found. m. **Roy Del Ruth**, 14 Mar 1921—div. 1947 (d. 1961). AMD, p. 87. "Wedding in Hollywood," *MPW*, 2 Apr 1921, 477.

Dale, Virginia [novelist/critic on the *Chicago Journal*] (*née* Hermona Dale?, b. Chicago IL, 1897?–5 Sep 1957 [ca. 60], New York NY; found dead). m. Mr. Shirk-Johnstone. "Virginia Dale, Writer, Is Dead; Author of Three Novels [*Nan Thursday*, *They Waited for the Night* and *Honeyfogling* ("to coerce sweet words") *Time* (1946)] Had Been Movie and Drama Reviewer in Chicago," *NYT*, 6 Sep 1957, 21:1. "Virginia Dale [Mrs. Hermona Shirk-Johnstone]," *Variety*, 11 Sep 1957.

Dalgard, Olav [director/scenarist] (b. Folldal, Norway, 19 Jun 1898). AS, p. 281.

D'Algy, Antonio (brother of **Helena D'Algy**) [actor] (*né* Antonio Guedes Infante, b. Angola, Spain 1905?–29 Apr 1977 [72], Spain). AS, p. 277. BHD, p. 141. IFN, p. 71.

D'Algy, Helena (sister of **Antonio D'Algy**) [actress]. No data found. (Paramount; MGM; made French- and Spanish-language films at Joinville, France.) AMD, p. 87. Waldman, p. 71. "Singer Is 'Find' in His Latest, Says Blackton," *MPW*, 22 Dec 1923, 721. "Sign Helena D'Algy," *MPW*, 8 Oct 1924, 578.

Dali, Salvador [painter/director/scenarist] (b. Figueras, Spain, 11 May 1904–23 Jan 1989 [84], Figueras, Spain; heart ailment). m. Elena Diaranoff, 1935 (d. Jun 1982). John Russell, "Salvador Dali, Pioneer Surrealist, Dies at 84," *NYT*, 24 Jan 1989, 8:1 ("With Luis Buñuel, he produced two Surrealist films, 'Un Chien Andalou' [1929] and 'L'Age d'Or' [1931], which will live in the history of outrage."). AS, p. 281. BHD2, p. 59. Waldman, p. 72.

Dalla Porta, Azucena [actress]. No data found. JS, p. 115 (in Italian silents from 1912).

Dallas, Gertrude [actress]. No data found. AMD, p. 87. "Gertrude Dallas with Thanhouser," *MPW*, 10 Mar 1917, 1558.

Dallet, Henriette [gown designer]. No data found. AMD, p. 87. "DeMille Engages Fashion Creator," *MPW*, 7 Mar 1925, 90.

Dalleu, Gilbert [actor] (b. Saint-Pons, France, 5 Mar 1861–1 Mar 1931 [69], Paris, France; gangrene after an auto accident [extrait de décès no. SN/1931]). AS, p. 281.

Dalmores, Aimee [actress] (d. 22 Jan 1920). AMD, p. 87. BHD, p. 141. "Aimee Dalmores," *MPW*, 25 Aug 1917, 1204.

Dalroy, Harry "Rube," "The Mayor of Gower Gulch" [actor] (b. 1879?–8 Mar 1954 [75], Los Angeles CA). "Harry (Rube) Dalroy," *Variety*, 17 Mar 1954 ("pioneer western film actor"). AS, p. 281 (d. 3 Mar). BHD1, p. 134. IFN, p. 71. Truitt, p. 78.

Dalrymple, Frank [cameraman]. No data found. AMD, p. 87. "N.Y. Cameraman Saves Fiancee from Drowning," *MPW*, 13 Aug 1927, 445.

Dalsace, Lucien [actor] (*né* Gustave Louis Chalot, b. Chatou, France, 14 Jan 1893 [extrait de naissance no. 2]–30 Jul 1980 [87], L'Hay-les-Roses, France). AS, p. 281. BHD1, p. 135.

Dalsheim, Friderich [director] (b. Germany, 1895–1936 [41?], Germany). AS, p. 281.

Dalton, Charles [actor] (b. Rochester, Kent, England, 29 Aug 1864–11 Jun 1942 [77], Stamford CT). m. Rita Walton. "Charles Dalton," *Variety*, 17 Jun 1942. AS, p. 281. BHD, p. 142. IFN, p. 71. SD, p. 320.

Dalton, Dorothy [stage/film actress] (b. Chicago IL, 22 Sep 1893–13 Apr 1972 [78], Scarsdale NY). m. **Lew Cody** (d. 1934); Arthur Hammerstein. (Ince; Paramount; World; All-Star.) "Dorothy Dalton Is Dead at 78; Star of Stage and Silent Screen," *NYT*, 15 Apr 1972, 34:1. "Dorothy Dalton," *Variety*, 19 Apr 1972. AMD, p. 87. AS, p. 282 (b. 1894). BHD, p. 142. FFF, p. 232 (b. 1894). IFN, p. 71 (b. 1894). Lowrey, p. 36. MH, p. 105 (b. 1894). MSBB, p. 1034. Spehr, p. 126. Truitt, p. 78. WWS, p. 20. "Dorothy Dalton Becomes Paramount Star," *MPW*, 11 Aug 1917, 967. "Dorothy Dalton with Famous Players," *MPW*, 27 Dec 1919, 1037. Edward Weitzel, "Dorothy Dalton Trains for Stage While Rehearsing for the Screen," *MPW*, 21 Feb 1920, 1255. "Paramount Stars Lead in Rio de Janeiro Contest," *MPW*, 17 Apr 1920, 439 (Dalton won as "Most Beautiful Screen Actress"). Mary Kelly, "Dorothy Dalton Visualizes Time When Scenes Will Be Rehearsed in Sequence," *MPW*, 16

Oct 1920, 956. "Dorothy Dalton To Wed A. Hammerstein; Motion Picture Actress Will Be the Impresario's Fourth Wife; Chicago Ceremony Today; Film Star, Who Is 30, Is Former Wife of Lew Cody—New Husband Is 51," *NYT,* 22 Apr 1924, 1:2, 18:3. DeWitt Bodeen, "Dorothy Dalton; 1893–1972," *FIR,* Oct 1978, 449–63.

Dalton, Emmett [actor] [a member of the Dalton gang of outlaws who made 3 westerns] (b. Bellon MO, 3 May 1861–13 Jul 1937 [76], Los Angeles CA). AMD, p. 87. AS, p. 282 (b. 1872; d. 1927). BHD, p. 142. "Emmett Dalton," *MPW,* 14 Nov 1914, 940. "Ex-Bandit on Screen," *LA Times,* 11 Feb 1920, II, p. 7 (to appear in *Beyond the Law* at the Symphony Theater and will also make personal appearances).

Dalton, Irene [actress] (b. 1901?–15 Aug 1934 [33], Chicago IL). m. **Lloyd Hamilton,** 1927–28 (d. 1935). "Irene Dalton," *Variety,* 21 Aug 1934. AMD, p. 87. AS, p. 282. BHD, p. 142. IFN, p. 71. Truitt, p. 78. "Christie Engages Irene Dalton," *MPW,* 7 Aug 1920, 722.

D'Alvarez, Marguerite [actress] (b. Liverpool, England, 1884–18 Oct 1953 [69?], Alassio, Italy). BHD2, p. 277.

Daly, Arnold [stage/film actor] (*né* Peter Christopher Arnold, b. Brooklyn NY, 4 Oct 1874–13 Jan 1927 [52], New York NY [Death Certificate No. 1320; third degree burns of body conflagration at residence]). m. Mary Blythe, 1 Jul 1900—div. B[erthold] H[enry] Goldsmith, *Arnold Daly* (NY: James T. White & Co., 1927). (Pathé; Frohman.) "Arnold Daly," *Variety,* 19 Jan 1927. AMD, p. 87. AS, p. 282 (b. 1875). BHD, p. 142 (b. 1875). IFN, p. 71 (b. 1875). MSBB, p. 1023 (b. 1875). Spehr, p. 126. Truitt, p. 78. "Notes of the Foreign Stage; Arnold Daly on English and American Actors in the World of Art," *NYT,* 29 Jan 1905, IV, 2:1 ("There is the greatest difference in the world between the English and the American actor.... It is...the difference which exists in the temperament...due to environment. ¶The American actor is a man who is part of many nationalities.... ¶The English actor...is an Englishman. ¶The English actor...considers that...he is entitled to so much recognition upon his entrance into a scene, or at the finish of a scene. The American...is a conglomerate structure who may, and can, be molded into a stage picture which will suit what the tout ensemble should be."). "Arnold Daly Out of Cast; Absence from 'You Never Can Tell' Said to Be Due to Breakdown," *NYT,* 31 Mar 1905, 9:4 (Garrick Theatre, 30 Mar, "had broken down from nervous exhaustion." Winchell Smith substituted.). "Arnold Daly in Pictures; Famous Players to Present Prominent Star in 'Port of Missing Men,'" *NYDM,* 4 Feb 1914, 38:2. "Famous Players Secure Arnold Daly," *MPW,* 14 Feb 1914, 790. "Arnold Daly Breaks Leg," *NYDM,* 13 May 1914, 11:2 (slipped on pavement near Plaza Hotel, NYC. Frank Keenan replaced him in the play *She Lied to Her Husband*). "Arnold Daly on Shaw, Critics and—Arnold Daly; The Brilliant Young Actor Comments Upon the So-Called 'Intellectual Drama,'" *NYDM,* 2 Dec 1914, 17:1; photo, p. 16. (He was once Charles Frohman's office boy. "I was very well received in the Shaw playlet [*How He Lied to Her Husband*] in vaudeville—except in Cincinnati. But we will let that pass, as I hope to bring something to Cincinnati some day that they will understand."). "Vaudeville; Arnold Daly Makes His First Appearance as Anatol," *NYDM,* 9 Dec 1914, 17:1 (was in the episode *Ask No Questions.* "Mr. Daly's portrayal had shading and atmosphere where Mr. [Jack] Barrymore was just a smart, bored young American." He was forced to retuurn to *How He Lied to Her Husband* because of a legal controversy over the rights to *The Affairs of Anatol.*). "Arnold Daly a Pathé Player," *MPW,* 2 Jan 1915, 54. "Arnold Daly Injured; Star Has Bad Fall While Filming 'Exploits of Elaine,'" *NYDM,* 10 Feb 1915, 24:3 (fell from a studio-constructed steeple when he lost his balance and landed on his shoulder. "The cameraman succeeded in getting a portion of his fall."). "Daly a Film Man; Arnold Daly Now Making His Own Pictures for Release in the Pathe Programme," *NYDM,* 28 Jul 1915, 24:3 (Arnold Daly Series, directed by Ashley Miller, to be based on John C. McIntyre's "Ashton Kirk" novels.). "Arnold Daly Uses Gould Residence in a Motion Picture," *MPW,* 21 Aug 1915, 1334. "Pathé's 'Gold Rooster' Producers," *MPW,* 28 Aug 1915, 1485.

Daly, Hazel [actress] (b. IL, 8 Oct 1895–2 Jan 1987 [91], Santa Monica CA). AMD, p. 87. BHD, p. 606. "Hazel Daly," *MPW,* 30 Oct 1915, 763. "Hazel Daly," *MPW,* 6 Oct 1917, 63.

Daly, Herbert G. [actor] (b. 1902–12 May 1940 [38?], New York NY). AS, p. 282. BHD1, p. 135.

Daly, James L. [actor] (b. 1852?–9 Nov 1933 [80], Philadelphia PA; heart attack). m. **Clara Lambert** (d. 1921). (Lubin.) "James L. Daly," *Variety,* 14 Nov 1933 (age 81). AMD, p. 88. AS, p. 282. BHD, p. 142. IFN, p. 71. Truitt, p. 78. "James L. Daly," *MPW,* 30 Jan 1915, 684.

Daly, Jane *see* **Gadsden, Jacqueline**

Daly, Marcella [actress]. No data found. AMD, p. 88. "Strong Cast," *MPW,* 7 Nov 1925, 46. George Katchmer, "Remembering the Great Silents," *CI,* 221 (Nov 1993), 52–53.

Daly, Mark [actor] (b. Edinburg, Scotland, 23 Aug 1887–27 Sep 1957 [70], England). AS, p. 282.

Daly, Orlando [actor] (b. Leamington, England, 1872?–17 Jan 1929 [56], Boston MA). "Orlando Daly," *Variety,* 20 Feb 1929. AS, p. 282 (d. 15 Feb). BHD, p. 142.

Daly, William F. [actor] (b. Boston MA, 1872–11 May 1940 [68?]; under subway train). AS, p. 282. BHD1, p. 606 (d. Feb 1929). "*The Melody* [Imp, 1911; review]," *MPW,* 21 Jan 1911, 136–37 (praises Daly's acting). 1921 Directory.

Daly, William Robert [actor/director] (b. Boston MA, 1872). m. **Fritzi Brunette,** 17 Jun 1914 (d. 1943). AMD, p. 88. AS, p. 59. "Man Killed in Movie Riot," *MPW,* 29 Nov 1913, 994 (not Daly). "Daly—Brunette," *MPW,* 27 Jun 1914, 1840.

Dalzell, Lydia St. Clair [stage/film/TV actress] (d. 1 Jan 1970, New Milford CT). "Lydia St. Clair," *Variety,* 4 Feb 1970, p. 71. BHD, p. 142 (d. 28 Mar 1974).

D'Ambra, Lucio [scenarist/director/producer] (*né* Renato Eduardo Manganella, b. Rome, Italy, 1 Sep 1877–31 Dec 1939 [62], Rome, Italy). AS, p. 277. BHD2, p. 59 (b. 1 Nov 1880). JS, pp. 116–17 (in Italian silents from 1910).

D'Ambricourt, Adrienne [actress] (b. Paris, France, 2 Jun 1878–6 Dec 1957 [79], Los Angeles CA; auto accident). "Adrienne D'Ambricourt," *Variety,* 11 Dec 1957. AS, p. 277 (b. 1879). BHD1, p. 135. IFN, p. 71. Truitt, p. 78.

Dameral, Charles [actor]. No data found. AMD, p. 88. "Charles Dameral Joins MinA," *MPW,* 3 Jul 1915, 69.

Damia [singer/actress] (*née* Marie-Louise Damien, b. Bordeaux, France, 5 Dec 1889–30 Jan 1978 [88], La Celle-Saint- Cloud, France; accidental fall in a subway [extrait de décès no. 13/1978]). AS, p. 282. BHD1, p. 135 (d. Paris). IFN, p. 71.

Damita, Lili [actress] (aka Damita del Maillo Rojo, *née* Liliane Marie Madeleine Carré, b. Blaye, France, 10 Jul 1904 [extrait de naissance no. 39]–21 Mar 1994 [89; death certificate says 85], Palm Beach FL; Alzheimer's disease). m. (1) Errol Flynn, 1935–42 (d. 1959; son Sean, 1941–70); (2) Allen B. Loomis, 1962—div. mid-80's. (Film debut: *Rescue,* Goldwyn, 1928; quit films in 1935.) AS, p. 283. BHD1, p. 135. Wolfgang Saxon, "Lili Damita, Actress from France Who Starred in Hollywood, Dies," *NYT,* 25 Mar 1994, A22:1 ("Damita" means "little lady"). "Lili Damita," *Variety,* 28 Mar 1994, 72:5 (to be buried in Fort Dodge IA).

Damman, Gerhard [actor] (b. Cologne, Germany, 30 Mar 1883–21 Feb 1946 [62], Bad Ischl, Austria). BHD, p. 142.

D'Amore, Diana [actress] (*née* Floriana D'Amore Pasquali). No data found. JS, p. 118 (in Italian silents from 1915).

Dampier, Claude, "The Professional Idiot" [actor] (*né* Claude Cowan, b. Clapham, England, 1878–1 Jan 1955 [76], London, England; pneumonia). AS, p. 283. BHD1, p. 135. IFN, p. 71.

Damroth, George [actor/director] (b. 1894–10 Feb 1939 [45], New York NY). BHD, p. 142. IFN, p. 71.

Dan, Zhao [actress/director] (aka Chao Ming, *née* Zhao Fengao b. China, 1915–10 Oct 1980 [65?], Peking, China; cancer). AS, p. 283. BHD1, p. 135 (d. Beijing).

Dana, Clara L. [actress] (b. 1878–23 Jun 1956 [78], Los Angeles CA). AS, p. 283. BHD, p. 142. IFN, p. 72.

Dana, Frederick [actor]. George A. Katchmer, "Forgotten Cowboys and Cowgirls," *CI,* 195 (Sep 1991), C6.

Dana, Muriel Frances [actress] (b. Clinton IA, ca. 1919). MH, p. 105.

Dana, Viola (sister of **Edna Flugrath** and **Shirley Mason**) [stage/film actress] (*née* Virginia Flugrath, b. Brooklyn NY, 28 Jun 1897–3 Jul 1987 [90], Woodland Hills CA; heart attack). m. **John H. Collins** (d. 1918); **Maurice "Lefty" Flynn,** 20 Jun 1925—14 Feb 1929 (d. 1959); (3) **Omer L. Locklear** (d. 1920); (4) Jimmy Thomson. (Edison, 1910; Metro.) "Viola Dana," *Variety,* 8 Jul 1987. AMD, p. 88. AS, p. 283. BHD1, p. 135. FFF, p. 130. FSS, p. 80. Lowrey, p. 38. MH, p. 105 (b. 1900). MSBB, p. 1034 (b. 1898). WWS, p. 100. "Viola Dana," *MPW,* 13 Feb 1915, 990. "Viola Dana," *MPW,* 11 Sep 1915, 1808. "Viola Dana Joins Metro," *MPW,* 8 Apr 1916, 275. "A Double Twinkler; Viola Dana Shines Alike on Stage and Screen," *Photoplay,* Feb 1917, 74 (b. 1898; played in Thomas Jefferson's *Rip Van Winkle* company for three years from age 11. "She is 4 feet 11 inches in height, weighs 96 pounds and has light green—green, mind you—eyes and a wealth of beatiful brown hair. She is sensitive, emotional and has a wonderful sense of humor."). "Viola Dana an Apollo Star," *MPW,* 3 Feb 1917, 674. Faith Service, "The Poor Little Rich Star; Tragedy Has Come to Little Viola Dana," *MPC,* Jan 1919, 52–53, 67. "Viola Dana Makes New Contract with Metro," *MPW,* XL19 Feb 1921, 948. "Viola Dana to Make

2 for Paramount," *MPW,* 17 May 1924, 307. "The Kitten and the King," *MPW,* 7 Nov 1925, 43. Dorothy Spensley, "They Go Smiling On; A Story of Strange Destiny," *Photoplay Magazine,* Jun 1926, 38–39, 132–34. "Viola Dana Signed for F.B.O. specials," *MPW,* 31 Jul 1926, 2. "Columbia Signs Villa Dana," *MPW,* 1 Oct 1927, 285. Jeffrey M. Rollick, "Viola Dana: One of the Silent Screen's Shining Stars," *CI,* 236 (Feb 1995), 28–30.

D'Ancora, Maurizio [actor] (*né* Rodolfo Gucci, b. Florence Italy, 16 Jul 1912). m. actress Sandra Ravel, 1944 (1910–1954). AS, p. 277. JS, p. 118 (in Italian silents from 1929; part of the firm of Gucci).

D'Andrea, Goffredo [actor/director/producer] (b. Naples, Italy, 3 May 1889). AS, p. 277. BHD2, p. 277. JS, p. 118 (in Italian silents from 1916).

Dandy, Jess [actor] (*né* Jesse A. Danzig, b. Rochester NY, 9 Nov 1871–15 Apr 1923 [51], Brookline MA; septicemia). (Keystone.) "Jess Dandy," *Variety,* 19 Apr 1923. AS, p. 283. BHD, p. 142. SD, p. 322. Truitt, p. 79.

Dandy, Ned [scenarist] (b. 1888–8 Aug 1948 [60?], Los Angeles CA). AS, p. 283.

Dane, Clemence [actor] (*né* Winfred Ashton, b. Blackheath, England, 1887–28 Mar 1965 [78?], London, England). AS, p. 284.

Dane, Karl [actor] (*né* Rasmus Karl Thekelsen Gottlieb, b. Copenhagen, Denmark, 12 Oct 1886–14 Apr 1934 [47], Los Angeles CA; suicide by shooting). m. (2) Thais Valdemar, 4 May 1928. (Extra work at Fort Lee NJ.) "Karl Dane Ends Life; Actor in 'Big Parade' Film Had Been Idle Two Years," *NYT,* 15 Apr 1934, 30:6. "Karl Dane's Suicide," *Variety,* 17 Apr 1934. AMD, p. 88. AS, p. 284. BHD1, p. 136. FSS, p. 81. IFN, p. 72. Truitt, p. 79. Hal K. Wells, "Dane Goes Over the Top," *MPC,* Feb 1926, 56, 78. "Dane Signs New Contract," *MPW,* 5 Jun 1926, 468. Charles J. Duranty, "Karl Dane; A Serious Comedian; Read this, and learn of the fine art of manufacturing mirth," *Cinema Arts,* Aug 1926, pp. 16–17. "Dane Signed by Metro to Long Term Contract," *MPW,* 11 Jun 1927, 421. Dunham Thorp, "The Mutt and Jeff of the Movies," *MPC,* Sep 1927, 41, 85, 91. James Bagley, "The Perfect Crime as George Arthur and Karl Dane Would Do It," *MPC,* Apr 1928, 63, 72.

Danegger, Theodor [actor/singer] (b. Lienz, Austria, 31 Aug 1891–11 Oct 1959 [68], Vienna, Austria). AS, . 284.

Danforth, William [actor] (*né* William Daniels, b. Syracuse NY, 13 May 1867–16 Apr 1941 [73], Skaneateles NY [near Syracuse]). m. Norma Kopp, 1898. "William Danforth," *Variety,* 23 Apr 1941. BHD1, p. 136. IFN, p. 72. SD.

D'Angelo, Rodolfo [cinematographer]. No data found. JS, pp. 118–119 (in Italian silents from 1918).

Daniel, Maud [stage/film producer]. No data found. (Fred Made Feature Film Co.) m. A.L. Wilbur. "Shakeup at Universal...Notes of a Newsy Week on the Coast," *NYDM,* 13 May 1914, 39:1.

Daniel, Viora [actress]. No data found. AMD, p. 88. "Viora Daniel in 'Twas Ever Thus,'" *MPW,* 4 Feb 1922, 504.

Daniells, Kent [poster artist]. No data found. AMD, p. 88. "Kent Daniells Gets Lieutenantcy," *MPW,* 31 Aug 1918, 1258.

Daniels, Bebe [child actress on stage/film actress] (*née* Phyllis Daniels, b. Dallas TX, 14 Jan 1901–16 Mar 1971 [70], London, England; cerebral hemorrhage and cancer). m. **Ben Lyon**, 1930 (d. 1979). *Life with the Lyons; The Autobiography of Bebe Daniels and Ben Lyon* (London: Odhams Press, 1953). (Selig, 1910; 101-Bison; Vitagraph; Rollin Film Co.; Paramount; RKO; WB.) "Bebe Daniels, Screen Star, Dies in London," *NYT,* 16 Mar 1971, 40:1. "Bebe Daniels," *Variety,* 17 Mar 1971. AMD, p. 88. AS, p. 284. BHD1, p. 136. FFF, p. 42. FSFW, p. 113 (b. 14 Jan 1901). FSS, p. 82. HCH, p. 93. IFN, p. 72. MH, p. 105. MSBB, p. 1034. Truitt, p. 79 (*née* Virginia Daniels). "Bebe Daniels," WBO1, pp. 192–93. "Rollin Film Co. Plans Announced," *MPW,* 13 Nov 1915, 1290. "Bebe Daniels Recovers," *MPW,* 15 Sep 1917, 1699. "Bebe Daniels Signs Again with Rollin," *MPW,* 10 Aug 1918, 859. Fritzi Remont, "A Daniels Come to Judgment," *MPC,* May 1919, 42–43, 74. "Bebe Daniels, Ingenue, Engaged by Cecil DeMille," *MPW,* 21 Jul 1919, 205. "Realart Signs Its Fifth Star, A Woman; Will Disclose Her Identity Next Week," *MPW,* 29 May 1920, 1186. "Realart's New Star Is Bebe Daniels, Now Named 'The Good Little Bad Girl,'" *MPW,* 5 Jun 1920, 1316. "Bebe Daniels Begins Her Realart Career with 'You Never Can Tell' for Vehicle," *MPW,* 26 Jun 1920, 1762. "Sentenced for Speeding," *MPW,* 16 Apr 1921, 711. "Bebe Honored," *MPW,* 20 Aug 1921, 796 ("Most Beautiful Girl in California"). "Bebe Daniels Under Knife," *MPW,* 10 Feb 1923, 540. Maude Cheatham, "The Darkest Hour," *Classic,* Mar 1923, 66. "Bebe Daniels Forsakes Camera for Editorial Chair," *MW,* 23 Jun 1923, 3. David A. Balch, "Bebe Daniels First to Give Interview Over Radio," *MW,* 23 Jun 1923, 9, 30. Regina Cannon, "Bebe Daniels as Her Friends Know Her," *MW,* 23 Jun 1923, 10, 28. Regina Cannon, "Would I Marry a Poor Man? 'Yes!' Says Bebe Daniels," *MW,* 1 Mar 1924, 3, 27. John D. Mackie, "Minister Would Like to Marry Bebe Daniels," *MW,* 21 Jun 1924, 9, 31. Grace Kingsley, "The Home Life of Bebe Daniels," *MW,* 5 Jul 1924, 9, 29. Regina Cannon, "Bebe with Her Back to the Camera," *MW,* 4 Sep 1924, 9–10. Bebe Daniels, "The True Story of My Life," *MW,* 25 Jul 1925, 12–14, 43; 1 Aug 1925, 25–26, 41; 8 Aug 1925, 13–14, 42; 15 Aug 1925, 13–14, 46; 22 Aug 1925, 13–14, 46; 29 Aug 1925, 13–14, 46; 5 Sep 1925, 22–23, 43; 12 Sep 1925, 21–22, 40–42. Frederick Harris, "Shaking the Family Tree; Ancestor worship flourishes in the studios, and lucky is the star who can drag up an aristocratic ghost," *MPC,* Aug 1925, 42, 74. "Bebe Daniels to Head Own Unit for Production of Big Comedies," *MPW,* 2 Jan 1926, 74. "Bebe Crashes," *MPW,* 13 Mar 1926, 3. "Bebe Daniels Hurt; Thrown by Horse," *MPW,* 15 May 1926, 2. June Lee, "Dan Cupid's Bulletin Board," *Paris and Hollywood,* Oct 1926, 32 (announced her engagement to sprinting champion/actor Charles W. Paddock). "Famous Players Signs Bebe Daniels Until 1931," *MPW,* 23 Oct 1926, 482. "Bebe Daniels Better," *MPW,* 29 Oct 1927, 545. Grace Kingsley, "On Bebe's Beach," *Screenland,* Dec 1927, 46–47, 94, 96–97. Carol Johnston, "A Good Little Sport; A Close-Up of Bebe Daniels," *MPC,* Dec 1928, 51, 78 ("She is highly strung and nervous—temperamental in the best sense of the word."). Gladys Hall, "Confessions of the Stars IV; Bebe Daniels Tells Her Untold Tale," *MPC,* Jan 1929, 16–17, 82–83 ("Yes, I have known one great love... This man—he must be nameless—came into my life right after Harold and I had decided to take separate paths."). Eve Golden, "The Speed Girl: The Many Lives of Bebe Daniels," *CI,* 210 (Dec 1992), C12-C14. Robert N. Pinkerton, "Daniels in the Lyon's Den of Film Scholarship," *CI,* 210 (Dec 1992), C13-C14 (in *The Common Enemy,* Selig, 1910; her father's name was Melville Daniel MacNeal).

Daniels, Eleanor [actress] (b. 1887–18 Mar 1994 [106?]). BHD, addendum.

Daniels, Frank Albert [actor] (b. Dayton OH, 1860?–12 Jan 1935 [74], West Palm Beach FL). m. Bessie Samson. (Vitagraph.) "Frank Daniels," *Variety,* 15 Jan 1935. AMD, p. 88. AS, p. 284. BHD, p. 142. IFN, p. 72. SD. Truitt, p. 79. "Frank Daniels," *MPW,* 1 May 1915, 706. "Frank Daniels on the Screen," *MPW,* 12 Jun 1915, 1795. "Daniels Signs with Vitagraph Company," *MPW,* 25 Dec 1915, 2368. "Frank Daniels in Vitagraph Films," *MPW,* 26 Feb 1916, 1316.

Daniels, Josephus [journalist/actor/Secretary of the Navy under Wilson, 1913–21] (b. Washington NC, 18 May 1862–15 Jan 1948 [85], Raleigh NC). BHD, p. 142. *Century Cyclopedia of Names,* p. 1183.

Daniels, Mickey [actor: Our Gang comedies] (b. UT, 11 Oct 1914–20 Aug 1970 [55], San Ysidro CA). AMD, p. 89. AS, p. 285 (b. Rock Springs WY, 1916). BHD1, p. 136. "Mickey a Star," *MPW,* 7 Apr 1923, 675. "Daniels Leaves 'Our Gang,'" *MPW,* 22 May 1926, 301.

Daniels, Phyllis [actress] (b. 1886–20 Feb 1959 [72?], London, England). BHD, p. 142.

Daniels, Thelma [actress]. No data found. (Christie.) "Beauties Who Make the Comedies Attractive," *Cinema Arts,* Aug 1926, 21 (photo).

Daniels, Walter [actor] (b. 1875?–30 Mar 1928 [53], Los Angeles CA). m. Mina. "Walter Daniels," *Variety,* 11 Apr 1928. AS, p. 285. BHD, p. 142. IFN, p. 72. Truitt, p. 79.

Daniels, William H. [actor/cinematographer/producer] (b. Cleveland OH, 1895–14 Jun 1970 [75?], Los Angeles CA). (Triangle; MGM; Universal.) "William H. Daniels," *Variety,* 24 Jun 1970 (age 69). AS, p. 285. BHD2, p. 60. FDY, p. 457.

Danis, Ida [actress] (b. France-d. 9 Apr 1921, Nice, France). AS, p. 285. BHD, p. 142.

D'Annunzio, Gabriele (father of **Gabrielino D'Annunzio**) [writer/scenarist/title writer/director] (aka Duca Minimo, *né* Gabriele Rapagnetta, Principe di Monte Nevoso, b. Francavilla al Mare, Italy, 12 Mar 1863–1 Mar 1938 [74], Gardone Riviera, Italy). m. Maria di Gallese-Hardouin, 28 Jul 1883 (d. 18 Jan 1954, Gardone Riviera, Italy; sons, Mario, b. 1 Feb 1884; Gabriele Maria; and Hugo Veniero, d. 17 Jan 1945). "Maria D'Annunzio Dies in Italy at 94; Widow of Famed Poet-Soldier Figured in Stormy Romance—Princess and Duchess," *NYT,* 19 Jan 1954, 25:1. (Itala Film Co., Turin, Italy.) AMD, p. 89. BHD, p. 6 (Gabriel Annunzio). JS, p. 119 ("One of Italy's most famous Fascist poets and novelists."). "D'Annunzio Writing for Itala," *MPW,* 9 May 1914, 801. "D'Annunzio in the Movies," *The Literary Digest,* 48, 16 May 1914, 1183:1 (wrote the scenario for *Cabiria.* "D'Annunzio's 'notes of action,' as he calls the titles and subtitles of the pictures, did not allow for half-measures. This building showing the gate of the Temple of Moloch, for instance, was specially built of stone and plaster. It is nearly 100 feet high."). "D'Annunzio Has Another Sickness," *MPW,* 8 Aug 1914, 812. "D'Annunzio Signs with Ambrosio,"' *MPW,* 24 Jun 1916, 2217. Vittorio

Martinelli, "D'Annunziana," *Griffithiana*, 69 (Oct 1998), 27–49. Russell Merritt, "The Man Who Stole the Gioconda [i.e., the Mona Lisa]: Introduction," *Griffithiana*, 64 (Oct 1998), 51–59. Gabriele D'Annunzio, "The Man Who Stole the Gioconda [text of script]," *Griffithiana*, 64 (Oct 1998), 61–79.

D'Annunzio, Gabrielino (son of **Gabriele d'Annunzio**) [director] (b. 28 Jul 1885–8 Dec 1945 [60], Rome, Italy). "Gabrielino D'Annunzio; Son of Noted Poet and Soldier Was Film Director in Rome," *NYT*, 9 Dec 1945, 44:6. BHD2, p. 60.

Dansey, Herbert [actor] (*né* Conte Berte Danyell Tassinari, b. Rome, Italy, 6 Mar 1870–30 May 1917 [47], New York NY). "Herbert Dansey (Count Berto Danyell Tassinari)," *Variety*, 1 Jun 1917. AS, p. 285. BHD, p. 142. IFN, p. 72. Truitt 1983.

Dansford, Granville [actor] (d. Honolulu HI, 27 Jun 1924). BHD, p. 142.

Dantes, Suzanne [actress] (*née* Suzanne Havequez, b. Saint-Quentin, France, 29 Apr 1888–29 Jul 1958 [70], Saint-Leger-en-Yvelines, France; leukemia). AS, p. 286.

Danton, George [actor] (b. 1861–15 Mar 1918 [57?], New York NY; accidentally asphyxiated). AS, p. 286.

Danville, Charles [actor] (b. Savannah GA, 19 Jun 1877–15 Aug 1961 [84], Los Angeles CA). AS, p. 286.

Darby, John J. [actor] (b. Long Beach CA, 27 Aug 1893–13 Dec 1946 [53], Los Angeles Co. CA). BHD, p. 142. IFN, p. 72.

D'Arclay, Louis [actor]. No data found. "Belgian War Hero in Metro Film," *MPW*, 8 Mar 1919, 1326.

Darclea, Edi [actress]. No data found. JS, p. 120 (in Italian films from 1918).

D'Arcy, Alexander [actor] (aka Gheet Alex Gil, *né* Alexander Sarruf, b. Cairo, Eqypt, 10 Aug 1908–20 Apr 1996 [87], West Hollywood CA). (International film debut: *The Garden of Allah*, 1928; U.S. film debut: *Stolen Holiday*, 1937.) "Alexander D'Arcy; Film Actor, 87," *NYT*, 28 Apr 1996, 38:1. "Alexander D'Arcy," *Variety*, 13 May 1996, 70:2 ("worked in more than 15 countries as a film actor"; age 88). AS, p. 278. BHD1, p. 137.

D'Arcy, Camille [actress] (b. 1879?–27 Sep 1916 [37], Chicago IL; infected while bathing in Lake Michigan). m. Dr. Loren Wilder. (Essanay.) "Mrs. Loren Wilder," *Variety*, 6 Oct 1916. AMD, p. 89. AS, p. 278. BHD, p. 142. IFN, p. 72. "Obituary," *MPW*, 14 Oct 1916, 253.

D'Arcy, Hugh Antoine [writer/publicist] (b. Paris, France, 5 Mar 1843–11 Nov 1925 [82], New York NY). (Lubin.) "Hugh Antoine D'Arcy," *Variety*, 18 Nov 1925 (wrote *The Face on the Floor*, poem published in 1887). AMD, p. 89. BHD, p. 143. IFN, p. 72. "Letters and Questions," *NYDM*, 28 Feb 1912, 29:3 (D'Arcy explains that the title of his famous poem is not "The Face on the Barroom Floor." That was a title of an unauthorized song published about 10 years after the poem. The poem was published in the New York *Dispatch* in Aug 1888). "Hugh Antoine D'Arcy," *MPW*, Apr 1912, 53. H.A. D'Arcy, "To the Memory of John Bunny [poem]," *NYDM*, 12 May 1915, 22:2.

D'Arcy, Roy [stage/film singer/actor] (*né* Roy Francis Giusti, b. San Francisco CA, 10 Feb 1894–15 Nov 1969 [75], Redlands CA). m. Laura Rhinock Duffy, 31 Dec 1925—div.. (Film debut: *Oh, Boy*, 1919.) "Rites Set for Veteran Stage, Screen Actor," *LA Herald-Examiner*, 18 Nov 1970. "Roy D'Arcy," *Variety*, 26 Nov 1969. AS, p. 278. BHD1, p. 136. FSS, p. 83. IFN, p. 72. Truitt, p. 79. Helen Perrin, "The Gentleman Tramp," *MPC*, Nov 1925, 59, 82. Joan Cross, "The Man Who Laughed His Way Around the World," *MM*, May 1926, 53, 112–14. Katherine Albert, "A Cosmopolite of the Cinema; The Colorful Heritage of a Mixed Anmcestry Explains Roy D'Arcy's Versatility in Widely Different Roles," *Cinema Arts*, Sep 1926, 18–19. *Screenland*, May 1927, p.103 (re marriage). Don Juan, "So This Is Hollywood," *Paris and Hollywood Screen Secrets Magazine*, Aug 1927, 55 (*né* Roy Guasti. Re possible marriage rift.). Charles P. Mitchell, "Roy D'Arcy: Master of Melodrama," *CI*, 294 (Dec 1999), 12–15 (includes filmography).

Dare, Dorris [actress] (*née* Dorris Prince, b. 1899?–16 Aug 1927 [28], Los Angeles CA). "Dorris Prince," *Variety*, 24 Aug 1927. AMD, p. 89. AS, p. 287. BHD, p. 143. IFN, p. 72. Truitt, p. 79. "Obituary," *MPW*, 27 Aug 1927, 588.

Dare, Eva [actress] (d. 15 Oct 1931). BHD, p. 143.

Dare, Phyllis (sister of **Zena Dare**) [stage/film actress/singer] (b. London, England, 15 Aug 1890–27 Apr 1975 [84], Brighton, England). "Phyllis Dare," *Variety*, 7 May 1975, p. 351. AS, p. 287. BHD1, p. 137. IFN, p. 72.

Dare, Virginia [actress] (b. PA, 6 Aug 1882–8 Jul 1962 [79], Woodland Hills CA). m. **Sydney Jarvis** (d. 1939). (Vitagraph.) "Virginia Dare," *Variety*, 18 Jul 1962. AS, p. 287. BHD, p. 143. IFN, p. 72. Truitt, p. 79. "Birth Announcement," *MPW*, 1 Jan 1921, 78 (birth of a son).

Dare, Zena (sister of **Phyllis Dare**) [actress] (*née* Florence Henrietta Zena Dare, b. London, England, 4 Feb 1885–11 Mar 1975 [90], London, England). AS, p. 287 (b. 1887). BHD1, p. 137. IFN, p. 72 (b. 1887).

Darewski, Herman [director] (b. Minsk, Russia, 17 Apr 1883–21 Jun 1947 [64], London, England). BHD2, p. 60.

Dariel, Lyne [actreess] (*née* Jeanne Catherine Vercammen, b. Molenbeek Saint Jean, Belgium, 16 Apr 1898–15 Jan 1956 [57], Lille, France [extrait de décès no. 153/1956). AS, p. 287.

Darien, Frank, Jr. [stage/film actor] (b. New Orleans LA, 18 Mar 1876–20 Oct 1955 [79], Los Angeles CA). (Reliance-Majestic.) "Frank Darien, Jr.," *Variety*, 26 Oct 1955. AS, p. 287. BHD1, p. 137. IFN, p. 72. Truitt, pp. 79–80. W.E. Wing, "Along the Pacific Coast," *NYDM*, 23 Jun 1915, 26:2.

Dark, Stanley [*The Dial* editor/actor]. No data found. Dorothy Donnell, "A Little Light On Michael Dark," *MPC*, Dec 1924, 36, 80.

Darkcloud [actress] (*née* Elizah Tahamont, d. 1918). BHD, p. 143.

Dark Cloud [actress] (*née* Beulah Darkcloud, d. 2 Jan 1946, Thermolite CA). (Griffith.) "Mrs. Beulah T. Filson," *Variety*, 16 Jan 1946. AMD, p. 89. AS, p. 287 (b. India; d. 3 Jan). BHD, p. 143. IFN, p. 72. Slide, p. 159 (d. 1918). Spehr, p. 126. Truitt, p. 80. "Dark Cloud," *MPW*, 25 Apr 1914, 500. "Dark Cloud," *MPW*, 4 Dec 1915, 1812.

Darkfeather, Princess Mona [actress] (*née* Josephine M. Workman, b. Boyle Heights, Los Angeles CA, 13 Jan 1881–3 Sep 1977 [96], Los Angeles CA). m. Frank Akley; **Arthur Ortega** (d. 1960); Frank E. Montgomery (d. 18 Jul 1944)—div. 1928; re-wed, 1937. (Bison; Nestor; Kalem; Centaur.) AMD, p. 89. AS, p. 287 (b. 1882). BHD, p. 143. BR, pp. 17–19. "Princess Mona Darkfeather; Playing Leads with the Kalem Company," *MPS*, 19 Jun 1914, 25 (of Spanish heritage, not Indian). "Mona Darkfeather," *MPW*, 7 Nov 1914, 790. "Mona Darkfeather Returning to Star in Indian Features,"' *MPW*, 13 Sep 1919, 1676. "Film Pair Wed Second Time," Los Angeles Times, 24 Dec 1937 (re-wed Montgomery). Diana Serra Cary, *The Hollywood Possee* (Boston: Houghton Mifflin Co., 1975), pp. 208–209 (Cary [Baby Peggy] writes that Darkfeather was married to "Artie Ortega"). Eldon K. Everett, "Mona Darkfeather, the Indian Princess," *CFC*, 49 (Winter, 1975), 35. Billy H. Doyle, "Lost Players," *CI*, 156 (Jun 1988), C13; *CI*, 157 (Jul 1988), 23. "Princess Mona Darkfeather," *CI*, 219 (Sep 1993), 54–55.

Darley, Brian [actor] (b. England, 1857?–25 Feb 1924 [66], New York NY). AS, p. 287. BHD, p. 143. IFN, p. 72. Truitt 1983.

Darling, Anne [actress] (b. Lnsingburg NY, 16 Jul 1915–3 Aug 1991 [76], Los Angeles CA). BHD1, p. 138.

Darling, Gladys [actress] (*née* Gladys Stockham, b. Chicago IL, 18 Jul 1898–5 Jan 1983 [84], Garden Grove CA). m. Harry Moshier, Sr. "Gladys Darling," *Variety*, 19 Jan 1983. AS, p. 287. BHD1, p. 138 (d. Garden City CA).

Darling, Grace [actress] (b. New York NY, 7 Oct 1893-Oct 1971 [78?], New York NY; bronchial pneumonia). m. **Pat Rooney** (d. 1933). (Vitagraph; Sawyer-Lubin; Pathé; International.) AMD, p. 89. AS, p. 287. BHD1, p. 606. MSBB, p. 1034. 1921 Directory, p. 217. "Grace Darling Meets Colonel Selig," *MPW*, 27 Mar 1915, 1907. "Grace Darling to Appear in Canada," *MPW*, 9 Dec 1916, 1499. "Grace Darling," *MPW*, 14 Apr 1917, 279. "Popular Picture Personalities," *MPW*, 14 Apr 1917, 279. "Grace Darling to Support Lincoln in S-L Pictures," *MPW*, 14 Dec 1918, 1242. "Grace Darling, Traveler, Actress," *MPW*, 1 Feb 1919, 604. "Another Grace Darling Feature in J.W. Society Drama Series," *MPW*, 26 Nov 1921, 432.

Darling, Helen [dancer/actress]. No data found. AMD, p. 89. "Former Dancer Now Comedy Lead," *MPW*, 20 Sep 1919, 1855. "Helen Darling Playing in Universal Comedies," *MPW*, 12 Mar 1921, 168.

Darling, Ida [actress] (b. New York NY, 1875?–5 Jun 1936 [61], Los Angeles CA). "Ida Darling," *Variety*, 10 Jun 1936. AMD, p. 89. AS, p. 287. BHD1, p. 138. IFN, p. 72. Truitt, p. 80. "Ida Darling in Norma Talmadge Support," *MPW*, 8 Dec 1917, 1505. "Selznick Engages Ida Darling for Permanent Stock Company," *MPW*, 15 May 1920. "Ida Darling," *MPW*, 16 Apr 1927, 649.

Darling, Jean [child actress: Our Gang comedies] (*née* LaVerne P. Cumming, b. Santa Monica CA, 23 Aug 1922). AMD, p. 89. AS, p. 287 (*née* Dorothy Jean LeVake). "Jean Darling Is 'Our Gang' Lead," *MPW*, 19 Feb 1927, 563. Don Juan, "So This Is Hollywood," *Paris and Hollywood Screen Secrets Magazine*, May 1927, 32 (four years old; supplanted Mary Kornman in the *Our Gang* series).

Darling, Roy [actor/director] (b. England, 1884–1956 [72?], Sydney, Australia). AS, p. 287.

Darling, Ruth [actress] (b. 1896?–11 Sep 1918 [22], San Francisco CA; auto accident). m. **Chester M. Franklin** (d. 1954). "Killed by Auto,"

Variety, 20 Sep 1918. AMD, p. 89. AS, p. 287 (d. 15 Sep). BHD, p. 143. IFN, p. 72. "Obituary," *MPW,* 5 Oct 1918, 63.

Darling, W[illiam] **Scott** [scenarist/director] (b. Toronto, Ontario, Canada, 28 May 1898–29 Oct 1951 [53]; found floating in the Pacific about a mile from Santa Monica CA; missing since 29 Oct). "Wm. Scott Darling," *Variety,* 14 Nov 1951. AMD, p. 89. AS, p. 287. BHD2, p. 60 (b. 1891; d. 7 Nov). FDY, p. 423. IFN, p. 73. "Darling Now Scenario Editor," *MPW,* 31 Jan 1920, 709. "Darling Directs Universal Comedy with Salt Lake Beauty," *MPW,* 19 Dec 1925, 658. "Darling to Shift?," *MPW,* 23 Oct 1926, 494.

Darling, William S. [art director] (*né* Wilhelm Sandorhazi, b. Sandorhaz, Hungary, 14 Sep 1882–15 Dec 1963 [81], Laguna Beach CA). (TC-F.) "William S. Darling," *Variety,* 1 Jan 1964. AS, p. 287. BHD2, p. 60. Katz, p. 305 (began 1920).

D'Armelle, Suzanne [actress] (b. Paris, France). JS, p. 120 (in Italian silents from 1916).

Darmond, Grace [stage/film actress] (b. Toronto, Canada, 20 Nov 1898–7 Oct 1963 [65], Los Angeles CA). (Film debut: *Your Girl and Mine,* Selig, Chicago, 1914; Vitagraph; Astra; Sanger and Jordan; Technicolor.) "Grace Darmond," *Variety,* 16 Oct 1963. AMD, p. 89. AS, p. 287. BHD1, p. 138. IFN, p. 73. Katz, p. 305. MH, p. 105. MSBB, p. 1034. Truitt, p. 80. "Studio Gossip," *NYDM,* 3 Jun 1914, 26:2. "Grace Darmond," *MPW,* 6 Jun 1914, 1396. "Grace Darmond," *MPW,* Mar 1915, 1914f. Cover, *NYDM,* 28 Apr 1915. "Miss Darmond Writes as Well as Plays," *MPW,* 21 Aug 1915, 1331. "Grace Darmond," *MPW,* 1 Sep 1917, 1362. "Paramount Engages Grace Darmond," *MPW,* 8 Mar 1919, 1318. Elizabeth Peltret, "The Purple and Gold Darmond; An Interview in Sixteenth Century Negligée with a New Star," *MPC,* Apr 1919, 32–33, 68, 70. "Producer Sues Star," *MPW,* 13 Sep 1919, 1635. "Grace Darmond, 'Shadows of Jungle' Star, Seriously Hurt," *MPW,* 18 Feb 1922, 733 (fell from elephant). Buck Rainey, "Grace Darmond; A Model of Femininity for Her Time," *CI,* 134 (Aug 1986), C5–C7 (includes filmography).

Darmour, Lawrence J. [photographer/producer] (b. Flushing, LI NY, 8 Jan 1895–17 Mar 1942 [47], Los Angeles CA). "L.J. Darmour, 47, a Film Producer; Man Who Introduced Mickey Rooney to the Movie World Dies in Hollywood; Opened Own Studio in 1926; Was Camera Man for Gaumont on Ford Peace Ship—With Signal Corps in War," *NYT,* 18 Mar 1942, 23:5. "Lawrence J. Darmour," *Variety,* 25 Mar 1942. AMD, p. 89. AS, p. 287. BHD2, p. 60. IFN, p. 73. "Camera Man Under Fire," *MPW,* 6 Feb 1915, 807.

Darnell, Jean *see* **Matthews, June D**

Darnley, Herbert [actor] (b. Chatham, Kent, England, 1872–7 Feb 1947 [74?], London, England). BHD, p. 143.

Darnold, Blaine A. [actor] (b. 1886–11 Mar 1926 [39], Kansas City MO; pneumonia). AS, p. 288. BHD, p. 143. IFN, p. 73.

Darnton, Charles [scenarist] (b. Adrian MI, 1870?–18 May 1950 [80], Los Angeles CA). "Charles Darnton Dies; Drama Critic of Evening World Here, Later a Screen Writer," *NYT,* 21 May 1950, 104:4. "Darnton, Onetime Dean of N.Y. Drama Critics, Dies on Coast at 80," *Variety,* 24 May 1950. AS, p. 288. BHD2, p. 60 (d. 20 May). FDY, p. 423.

Daroy, Jacques [scenarist/director/producer] (*né* Jacques Schenck, b. Paris, France, 1896–1963 [67?], Paris, France). AS, p. 288.

Darr, Homa [actress] (b. AL, 31 Oct 1897–18 May 1980 [82], Encino CA). BHD1, p. 606.

Darr, [Baby] Vondell [child actress]. No data found.

D'Arrast, Harry D'Abbadie [scenarist-director] (*né* Henri Charles Armand D'Abbadie D'Arrast, b. Buenos Aires, Argentina, 6 May 1897–17 Mar 1968 [70], Monte Carlo, Monaco). m. **Eleanor Boardman** (d. 1991). (Paramount.) "Harry D'Arrast," *Variety,* 3 Apr 1968. AMD, p. 89. AS, p. 277 (d. 16 Mar). BHD2, p. 60. FDY, p. 423. IFN, p. 73. Katz, pp. 305–306 (began 1922). "Menjou Keeps His Director," *MPW,* 9 Jul 1927, 97.

Darrell, Steve [actor] (*né* J. Steven Darrell, b. Osage IA, 19 Nov 1904–14 Aug 1970 [65], Los Angeles CA; brain tumor). (Bison.) AS, p. 288. CP, p. 61. IFN, p. 73.

Darro, Frankie [actor] (*né* Frank Johnson, b. Chicago IL, 22 Dec 1917–25 Dec 1976 [59], Huntington Beach CA). (Monogram.) "Frankie Darro," *Variety,* 19 Jan 1977. AMD, p. 90. AS, p. 288. BHD1, p. 138 (b. 1918). FSS, p. 83. IFN, p. 73 (b. 1918). "Frankie Darro Created a Star on F.B.O. List," *MPW,* 28 May 1927, 268. "Frankie Darro," *MPW,* 12 Nov 1927, 22. Ken Law, "The Screen Life of Frankie Darro," *CI,* 105 (Mar 1984), 56–58 (b. 1918).

Darrow, Clarence S. [actor] (b. Kinsman OH, 18 Apr 1857–13 Mar 1938 [80], Chicago IL). AS, p. 288. BHD, p. 143.

Darrow, John [actor] (*né* Harry Simpson, b. New York NY, 17 Jul 1904–24 Feb 1980 [75], Malibu CA). . "Ask the Answer Man," *Photoplay,* Dec 1931, 113. AS, p. 288 (b. 1907). BHD1, p. 138 (b. Leonia NJ). IFN, p. 73.

Darteuil, Pierre [actor] (*né* Pierre Maisonnt, b. Paris, France, 12 Jul 1887 [extrait de naissance no. 1052/1887]–21 Mar 1955 [67], Paris, France). AS, p. 288.

Dartois, Robert [actor] (*né* Robert Edouard Marcel Delandres, b. Trouville-sur-mer, France, 11 Feb 1900 [extrait de naissance no. 20/1900]–13 Jan 1959 [58], Saint-Arnould, France). AS, p. 288.

Darvas, Charles [actor] (b. Budapest, Hungary, 2 Mar 1880–14 Apr 1930 [50]). BHD1, p. 138. IFN, p. 73.

Darwell, Jane [stage/film actress] (*née* Patti Woodard, b. Palmyra MO, 15 Oct 1879–13 Aug 1967 [87], Woodland Hills CA; heart attack). Unmarried. (Paramount; Fox.) "Jane Darwell, 87, Actress, Is Dead; Won Academy Award as Ma Joad in 'Grapes of Wrath,'" *NYT,* 15 Aug 1967, 39:1. "Jane Darwell," *Variety,* 16 Aug 1967. *St. Louis Post-Dispatch,* 15 Aug 1967. AS, p. 288. BHD1, p. 138. FSS, p. 84. IFN, p. 73. Katz, p. 307. Truitt, p. 80 (b. 1880). L. Moody Simms, Jr., DAB, Supp. 8 (1988), pp. 116–17 (b. 1880).

Dary, René [actor] (aka Kid René and René Duclos, *né* Anatole Antoine Clément Mary, b. Paris, France, 18 Jul 1905–7 Oct 1974 [69], Plan-de-Cuques, France [extrait de décès no. 42]). AS, p. 288.

Darzal, Noél [actor] (b. Paris, France, 11 Mar 1899). AS, p. 288.

Dashiell, Willard [actor] (b. Salisbury MD, 1867–19 Apr 1943 [76], Holyoke MA). m. Mabel Griffith. "Willard Dashiell," *Variety,* 21 Apr 1943. AS, p. 289. BHD1, p. 138. IFN, p. 73. Truitt, p. 80.

D'Asseau, Leon [art director/assistant director]. No data found. AMD, p. 90. "D'Asseau to Assist Holubar," *MPW,* 5 Apr 1919, 54.

Datig, Fred [casting director] (b. 1891–11 Dec 1951 [60?], Culver City CA). AMD, p. 90. BHD2, p. 61. "New Casting Director," *MPW,* 5 Sep 1925, 72. "Schuessler Succeeds," *MPW,* 3 Oct 1925, 415. "Datig Signs Again," *MPW,* 30 Jul 1927, 305.

Datlowe, Sam [title writer]. No data found. FDY, p. 443.

Daube, Belle [actress] (aka Harda Daube, b. Northampton, England, 1887–25 May 1959 [71], Los Angeles CA). m. Jacques Vinmont. "Belle Daube," *Variety,* 3 Jun 1959. AS, p. 289. BHD1, p. 139. IFN, p. 73.

D'Auburn, Dennis [actor] (b. England, 29 Oct 1893–9 Oct 1960 [66]). BHD1, p. 139.

Daugherty, Frank [title writer]. No data found. FDY, p. 443.

Daugherty, Terrence [title writer]. No data found. FDY, p. 443.

Daugherty, Virgil Jack [actor] (*né* Virgil A. Dougherty, b. Bowling Green MO, 16 Nov 1895–16 May 1938 [42], Los Angeles CA; carbon monoxide poisoning). m. **Barbara La Marr** (d. 1926); **Virginia Faire Browne**, 6 Feb 1927. "Virgil Jack Daugherty," *Variety,* 18 May 1938. AMD, p. 90. AS, p. 289. BHD1, p. 139 (Jack Daugherty). IFN, p. 73. Truitt, p. 92. "Miss MacDonald's Leading Man Husky," *MPW,* 29 Jul 1922, 350. *Screenland,* May 1927, p. 103 (married Browne).

Daumery, Carrie [actress] (b. Amsterdam, Holland, 25 Mar 1863–1 Jul 1938 [75], Los Angeles CA). (PDC.) AS, p. 289. BHD1, p. 139. IFN, p. 73.

Daumery, John [director] (b. Brussels, Belgium, 1898–May 1934 [36?], Lausanne, Switzerland). BHD2, p. 61.

Daussmond, Betty [actress] (*née* Marguerite Anne Bettina Doneau, b. Beaumont-sur-Sarthe, France, 29 Jul 1873–25 Sep 1957 [84], Paris, France [extrait de deecès no. 93]). AS, p. 290.

Daven, André [actor/producer] (b. Paris, France, 16 Mar 1900–17 Nov 1981 [81], Paris, France). m. Danièle Parola (b. 1903). "Andre Daven," *Variety,* 30 Dec 1981. AS, p. 290. BHD, p. 143; BHD2, p. 61 (b. 1990).

Davenport, A[rthur] **Bromnley** [actor] (b. Baginton, Warwickshire, England, 29 Oct 1867–15 Dec 1946 [79], London, England). BHD1, p. 139. IFN, p. 73.

Davenport, Alice (mother of **Dorothy** and **Harry Davenport**) [actress] (*née* Alice Shepard, b. New York NY, 29 Feb 1864–24 Jun 1936 [72], Los Angeles CA). m. **Harry Davenport** (d. 1949). AMD, p. 90. AS, p. 290. BHD1, p. 139. IFN, p. 73 (b. 1864). Katz, p. 308. 1921 Directory, p. 217 (b. 1864). Spehr, p. 126 (1853 or 1864). "Alice Davenport and Martha Trick, New Keystoners," *MPW,* 27 Oct 1917, 545.

Davenport, Blanche [actress] (b. London, England–d. 17 Oct 1921, New York NY). AS, p. 290. IFN, p. 73.

Davenport, C. Edward [producer]. No

data found. AMD, p. 90. "C. Edward Davenport Will Produce Feature Series," *MPW,* 8 Aug 1925, 652.

Davenport, Charles E. [director]. No data found. AMD, p. 90. "Charles E. Davenport 'Safety First' Director," *MPW,* 25 Aug 1917, 1203.

Davenport, Dorothy (daughter of **Harry** and **Alice Davenport**; niece of Fanny Davenport) [actress/scenarist/director] (b. Boston MA, 13 Mar 1895–12 Oct 1977 [82], Woodland Hills CA). m. **Wallace Reid**, 13 Oct 1913, Hollywood (d. 1923). (Biograph; Ince.) "Dorothy Davenport Reid," *Variety,* 19 Oct 1977. AMD, p. 90. AS, p. 290. BHD1, p. 139; BHD2, p. 221 (Dorothy Davenport Reid). FFF, p. 216. FSS, p. 84. IFN, p. 73 (age 81). Katz, p. 308 (began 1909). MH, p. 106. Spehr, p. 126 (d. 1937). "New Nestor Players," *MPW,* 14 Oct 1911, 136. "Dorothy Davenport," *MPW,* 4 Nov 1911, 372. "Dorothy Davenport Leaves Nestor," *MPW,* 16 Mar 1912, 972. "Universal Film Director Marries Leading Woman," *MPW,* 29 Nov 1913, 993. "Dorothy Davenport Member of Lasky Co., *MPW,* 6 Nov 1915, 1148. "Mrs. Wallace Reid Selected as Leading Woman for Lester Cuneo," *MPW,* 27 Aug 1921, 909. "Grauman Books 'Human Wreckage' for an Indefinite Run," *MPW,* 26 May 1923, 335. "Mrs. Reid Is Home; Finishes Crusade," *MPW,* 29 Dec 1923, 806. "Mrs. Reid's Plans," *MPW,* 2 Aug 1924, 353. Grace Kingsley, "Don't Worry About Your Children's Respect," *MW,* 8 Nov 1924, 8–9, 25. "Mrs. Wallace Reid to Produce Two Specials for Lumas Film," *MPW,* 12 Mar 1927, 112. "Mrs. Reid in 'Satin Woman,'" *MPW,* 23 Apr 1927, 715. "Mrs. Wallace Reid to Do Road 'Tour,'" *MPW,* 7 May 1927, 35. "Mrs. Wallace Reid's Tour Opens in San Francisco, *MPW,* 10 Sep 1927, 78. "Mrs. Wallace Reid's 'Stage and Screen' Tour Smashes Records," *MPW,* 22 Oct 1927, 489. "Mrs. Wallace Reid Has Busy Week in Buffalo," *MPW,* 5 Nov 1927, 13. "Mrs. Reid Completes Twenty Week Tour," *MPW,* 17 Dec 1927, 21.

Davenport, Edgar Loomis (son of Edward L. Davenport; brother of Fanny Davenport) [actor] (b. Roxbury MA, 7 Feb1862–25 Jul 1918 [56], Boston MA). (FP-L; Fox.) "Edgar Loomis Davenport," *Variety,* 2 Aug 1918. AMD, p. 90. AS, p.290. BHD, p. 144. IFN, p. 73. SD. Truitt 1983. "Davenport Leaves Fox," *NYDM,* 2 Jun 1915, 22:1 (in films three years). "Edgar L. Davenport Metro Actor," *MPW,* 6 May 1916, 996.

Davenport, Harry (brother of Fanny Davenport; father of **Dorothy**, **Kate** and Ann Davenport and **Arthur L. Rankin**; brother-in-law of **Sydney Drew**) [actor/scenarist/director] (*né* Harry George Bryant Davenport, b. New York NY, 19 Jan 1866–9 Aug 1949 [83], Los Angeles CA; heart attack). m. **Alice** Shepard (1936); (2) **Phyllis Rankin** (d. 1934). (Vitagraph, 1914.) "Harry Davenport, Veteran Actor, 83; Stage and Screen Star for 78 Years Dies—Had Appeared in 113 Films Since 1936," *NYT,* 10 Aug 1949, 22:4. "Harry Davenport," *Variety,* 17 Aug 1949. AMD, p. 90. AS, p. 290. BHD1, p. 139. IFN, p. 73. Truitt, p. 81. Robert Grau, "The Film Studio; A Gold Laden Haven for the Patriarchs of the Stage," *NYDM,* 8 Sep 1915, 3:1 (Grau mentions Charles Kent, Louise Beaudet, Cissy Fitzgerald, S. Rankin Drew, William Humphries [sic], Van Dyke Brooke, and Davenport, all from the stage. He and Sydney Drew married sisters.). "Harry Davenport Joins Metro Forces," *MPW,* 17 Feb 1917, 1028. "Harry Davenport to Direct Cummings," *MPW,* 30 Jun 1917, 2109.

Davenport, Harry J. [actor] (b. 7 May 1857–20 Feb 1929 [71], Glendale CA). AS, p. 290. BHD, p. 144. IFN, p. 73.

Davenport, Helene [actress] (*née* Helene Reynolds, b. 1865–31 May 1928 [63?], New York NY). "Helene Davenport," *Variety,* 6 Jun 1928, p. 58. BHD, p. 144.

Davenport, Kate (daughter of **Harry Davenport**) [actress] (b. New York NY, 7 Jun 1896–7 Dec 1954 [58], West Hollywood CA). "Kate Davenport," *Variety,* 15 Dec 1954. AMD, p. 90. AS, p. 290. IFN, p. 73. Truitt, p. 81. "Kate Davenport in 'Sentimental Tommy,'" *MPW,* 9 Oct 1920, 776.

Davenport, Kenneth [actor/scenarist] (b. Macon MO, 1879–10 Nov 1941 [62?], Los Angeles CA; heart attack). (K&E.) "Kenneth Davenport," *Variety,* 12 Nov 1941. AS, p. 290. BHD, p. 144; BHD2, p. 61. Truitt, p. 81.

Davenport, Milla [actress] (*née?*, b. Zurich, Switzerland, 14 Feb 1871–17 May 1936 [65], Los Angeles CA). m. Harry Davenport. In films from 1911. "Milla Davenport," *Variety,* 20 May 1936 (b. Sicily, Italy). AS, p. 290. BHD1, p. 139 (b. 4 Feb). IFN, p. 73. Truitt, p. 81 (b. Sicily, Italy). George A. Katchmer, "Remembering the Great Silents," *CI,* 184 (Oct 1990), 58.

Davenport, William [actor] (b. 1867–11 May 1941 [74], Philadelphia PA). AS, p. 290. BHD, p. 144. IFN, p. 74.

Davert, José [actor] (b. Marseilles, France, 6 Sep 1874-Apr/May 1934 [59]). AS, p. 291.

Davey, Allen M. (brother-in-law of **David Horsley**) [inventor/actor] (b. 1895?–5 Mar 1946 [51], Los Angeles CA). (Universal; TC-F.) m. Margaret M. Bronaugh, 30 Jun 1914. "Allen M. Davey," *Variety,* 13 Mar 1946 (pioneer in color photography). AS, p. 290. BHD2, p. 61. FDY, p. 457 (Allan Davey). "Gossip of the Studios," *NYDM,* 13 Aug 1914, p. 27 (re marriage).

Davey, Horace [director] (b. Bayonne NJ, 5 Nov 1889–22 Apr 1970 [80], Los Angeles CA). . (Universal; Christie.) BHD2, p. 61. *MPN Studio Directory,* 21 Oct 1916, 166.

David, Constantin J. [director/producer] (b. Constantinople, Turkey, 18 Feb 1886–19 Feb 1964 [78], Los Angeles CA). AS, p.290 (b. Hamburg, Germany). BHD2, p. 61.

David, Gertrude [director] (b. Leipzig, Germany, 25 Dec 1878). AS, p. 291.

David, William [actor] (b. Vicksburg MS, 5 Oct 1882–10 Apr 1965 [82], East Islip, LI NY; cancer). . "William David," *Variety,* 21 Apr 1965. AS, p. 291. BHD, p. 144 (b. 1881). IFN, p. 74. Truitt, p. 81.

Davids, Henriette "Heintje" [actress] (b. Rotterdam, Holland, 13 Feb 1888–14 Feb 1975 [87], Naarden, Holland). AS, p. 291.

Davidsen, Hjalmar [director/producer] (b. Copenhagen, Denmark, 2 Feb 1879–7 Feb 1958 [79], Copenhagen, Denmark). AS, p. 291.

Davidson, David [artist] (b. 1892?–7 Nov 1918 [26], France; war casualty). (Vitagraph publicity department.) AMD, p. 90. "Obituary," *MPW,* 14 Dec 1918, 1191.

Davidson, Dore [actor] (b. New York NY, 16 Oct 1848–7 Mar 1930 [81], Kings Park Hospital, New York NY; interred in Valhalla Cemetery NY). "Dore Davidson," *Variety,* 12 Mar 1930. AS, p. 291 (b. 1849). BHD, p. 144 (b. 1850). IFN, p. 74. MH, p. 106. SD, p. 332. Truitt, p. 81.

Davidson, E. Roy [cinematographer/director] (b. 1889–19 Aug 1962 [73?], Los Angeles CA). BHD2, p. 61.

Davidson, Elisabeth [actress] (b. Chicago IL-1 Jul 1914). AS, p. 291.

Davidson, John [actor] (b. New York NY, 25 Dec 1886–15 Jan 1968 [80], Los Angeles CA; heart attack). AS, p. 291. BHD1, p. 139. IFN, p. 74. Katz, p. 309.

Davidson, Lawford [actor] (b. London, England, 1 Jan 1890). AS, p. 291. George A. Katchmer, "Forgotten Cowboys and Cowgirls—Part XVII," *CI,* 194, Aug 1991, 47.

Davidson, Max [actor] (b. Berlin, Germany, 23 May 1875–4 Sep 1950 [75], Woodland Hills CA). m. Alice Marti, 1927, Honolulu HI. (Griffith; Roach.) "Max Davidson," *Variety,* 13 Sep 1950. AMD, p. 90. AS, p. 291. BHD1, p. 139. FSS, p. 84. IFN, p. 74. Truitt, p. 81. "Max Davidson Signed," *MPW,* 8 Aug 1925, 659. "Max Davidson, Roach Player, Achieves Wife," *MPW,* 12 Feb 1927, 501.

Davidson, William B. [actor] (b. Dobbs Ferry NY, 16 Jun 1888–28 Sep 1947 [59], Santa Monica CA; complications after surgery). m. Helen Bolton. (Vitagraph.) "William B. Davidson," *Variety,* 1 Oct 1947. AMD, p. 90. AS, p. 291. BHD1, p. 140. FSS, p. 85. IFN, p. 74. Katz, p. 309. Truitt, pp. 81–82. "William B. Davidson," *MPW,* 4 Mar 1916, 1447. "William B. Davidson Joins Officers' Training Camp," *MPW,* 21 Sep 1918, 1698. "Davidson Practised Law Prior to Entering Screendom," *MPW,* 26 Jul 1919, 578. "Davidson Engaged for Big Role in Hammerstein Film," *MPW,* 20 Nov 1920, 379. George A. Katchmer, "Forgotten Cowboys and Cowgirls—Part XVIII," *CI,* 195 (Sep 1991), C6.

Davidt, Michael [actor] (b. 1876–14 Mar 1944 [68?], Los Angeles CA). AS, p. 291.

Davies, Acton [drama critic] (b. St. Johns, Quebec, Canada, 1868?–12 Jun 1916 [48], Chicago IL; rheumatism of the heart). "Acton Davies," *Variety,* 16 Jun 1916. AMD, p. 90. SD. WWWA (b. 1870). "Action Davies Reviewing Edison Scenarios," *MPW,* 15 Nov 1913, 741. "Obituary," *MPW,* 24 Jun 1916, 2215.

Davies, David Thomas [actor] (d. 15 May 1920, Chicago IL). m. Margaret Kennedy. "David Davies," *Variety,* 28 May 1920. AS, p. 291. BHD, p. 144. SD.

Davies, Hamilton [actor] (d. 25 May 1922, Los Angeles CA). BHD, p. 144.

Davies, Howard O. [actor] (b. Liverpool, England, 18 May 1879–30 Dec 1947 [68], Los Angeles CA). (Majestic, 1912; Bison.) AMD, p. 90. AS, p. 292. BHD1, p. 140. IFN, p. 74. "Howard Davies in Accident," *MPW,* 21 Aug 1915, 1327. George Katchmer, "Remembering the Great Silents, CI, 222 (Dec 1993), C17-C18.

Davies, Hubert Henry [scenarist] (d. Robin Hood Bay, England, 17 Jan 1918). BHD2, p. 61.

Davies, Marion (sister of **Reine Davies**) [stage/film actress] [actress] (*née* Marion Cecilia Douras, b. Brooklyn NY, 3 Jan 1897–22 Sep 1961 [64], Los Angeles CA; cancer). Mistress of **William Randolph Hearst** (d. 1951); m. Horace G. Brown. Fred Laurence Guiles, *Marion Davies* (NY: McGraw Hill, 1972). *The Times We Had; Life with William Randolph Hearst* (NY: Bobbs-Merrill Co., Inc., 1975). (International; Select.) "Marion

Davies, Film Actress, Dead of Cancer; One of the Last Survivors of an Ultra-Lavish Period—Protégé of Hearst," *NYT,* 23 Sep 1961, 19:2. "Marion Davies [Mrs. Horace Brown] Dies at 64; Made Star by W.R. Hearst; Noted for Her Kindness," *Variety,* 27 Sep 1961. AMD, p. 90. AS, p. 292. BHD1, p. 140. FFF, p. 125 (b. 1900). FSS, p. 85. HCH, p. 33. IFN, p. 74. Katz, pp. 309–10 (began 1917). MH, p. 106. MSBB, p. 1034 (b. NYC). Truitt, p. 82 (b. 1898). WWS, p. 29. "Marion Davies," *MPW,* 8 Sep 1917, 1514. "Marion Davies a Hard Worker," *MPW,* 3 Nov 1917, 673. "Select to Release Marion Davies Films," *MPW,* 15 Jun 1918, 1580. "The Rapid Rise of Marion Davies," *MPW,* L, 14 May 1921, 141. "No Summer Letdown for Hearst; Miss Davies and Others Working," *MPW,* 16 Jul 1921, 324. Faith Service, "Medieval Marion," *Classic,* Sep 1922, 22–23, 89–90. "Variety of Roles for Marion Davies," *MPW,* 13 Jan 1923, 162. "Likes Her Work," *MPW,* 27 Jan 1923, 379. "Hello Fans!; Marion Davies, popular screen star, visits office of Movie Weekly and edits a special issue—Miss Davies' message to the fans," *MW,* 15 Mar 1924, 3. Alma M. Talley, "Just a Regular Girl!," *MW,* 15 Mar 1924, 9, 29. Ruth Mabrey, "The King and Queen of the Movies; Rudolph Valentino and Marion Davies are voted royal rulers of filmdom in the hearts of the fans," *MW,* 15 Mar 1924, 13, 27. "The Theater That Was Built for Marion Davies," *Classic,* Jun 1924, 18–19, 84 (the Cosmopolitan in Columbus Circle, NYC, formerly the Park Theater). Marion Davies, "The True Story of My Life," *MW,* 30 Aug 1924, 4–5, 25 (Part I); Part II, IV, 6 Sep 1924, 7–8, 26–27; Part III, 12–13, 27–28; Part IV, 20 Sep 1924, 13–14, 25, 27; Part V, 27 Sep 1924; Part VI, 4 Oct 1924, 12–13, 27; Part VII, 11 Oct 1924, 8–9, 30–31. "Marion Davies Again Signs with Metro-Godwyn-Mayer," *MPW,* 26 Sep 1925, 342. "Marion Davies," *MPW,* 10 Oct 1925, 467. Paul Paige, "Close-Ups and Fade-Outs," *Paris and Hollywood,* Sep 1926, 56–57 (at a convention is Los Angeles, theater owners complained that Eugene V. Brewster ordered a publicity blitz for his sweetheart, Corliss Palmer. "To be consistent they should discourage the featuring of Marion Davies. The radiant Marion is being starred at Metro-Goldwyn and is receiving more publicity through the Hearst papers than any magazine could ever hope to give his fair lady."). Paul Paige, "Close-Ups and Fade-Outs," *Paris and Hollywood,* Oct 1926, 67 (the news is that her last picture, *The Red Mill,* "when viewed in its entirety was a decided flop. Practically the entire picture is to be remade. King Vidor has been given the job of making it over."). "M-G-M Signs Davies," *MPW,* 6 Nov 1926, 4. Gladys Hall, "The Girl Friend; A Vignette of Marion Davies—Who Is the Toast of Hollywood and Everybody's Pal," *MPC,* Mar 1927, 53, 84. "Marion at Home Soon in 42 Rooms," *MPW,* 19 Mar 1927, 175. Katherine Albert, "Toiling With Tillie; Aided by Marion Davies, Another Comic Strip Steps Out of the Daily Papers and Comes to Life with the Familiar Characters of Office Life," *Cinema Arts,* Sep 1927, 24–25. Pauline Swanson, "Sunday Night at Marion Davies; An exclusive story of an intimate visit to Marion Davies' Beach House," *Cinema Arts,* Jun 1937, 34–35 ("Here was magnificence, and in the manner of the Europeans who know what magnificence is.... The great kitchens are stocked to the capacity of a 250 room hotel..."). Lewis G. Krohn and Chris Laube, "The Best of the Hearst: Marion Davies," *CI,* 89 (Nov 1982), 9–12, 22; Part II, 90 (Dec 1982), 55–56. Eve Golden, "Marion Davies: A Modern Du Barry," *CI,* 232 (Oct 1994), 14–15. Martha Sherrill, "San Simeon's Child," *Vanity Fair,* Apr 1995, 304–13, 319–21, 326–27. Robert Board, "Meeting Marion Davies," *CI,* 239 (May 1995), 26.

Davies, Reine (sister of **Marion Davies**; mother of Charles Lederer) [stage/film actress] (*née* Reine Douras, b. Montclair NJ, 6 Jun 1892–2 Apr 1938 [45], Beverly Hills CA; spinal meningitis). m. **George Regas** (d. 1940); **George W. Lederer** (d. 1938). "Reine Davies," *Variety,* 6 Apr 1938. AMD, p. 91. AS, p. 292. BHD, p. 144. IFN, p. 74. "Miss Davies Leaving Two-a-Day," *NYDM,* 25 Mar 1914, 23:4 (to support William Collier in *Forward March*). "Reine Davies," *MPW,* 12 Jun 1915, 1782. "Reine Davies in the World Film," *MPW,* 31 Jul 1915, 797.

Davies, Rosemary [actress] (*née* Rose Douras, b. Brooklyn NY, 15 Jun 1903–20 Sep 1963 [60], Bel Air CA). AMD, p. 91. BHD, p. 144. IFN, p. 74. "Rosemary Davies's First," *MPW,* 6 Sep 1924, 29.

Davis, Acton [senarist] (b. St. John, New Brunswick, Canada, 1870–12 Jun 1916 [46?], Chicago IL). BHD2, p. 61.

Davis, Alan [or **Allen**] [actor] (b. London, England, 30 Aug 1901?–11 Dec 1943 [42], West Los Angeles CA). m. **Peggy Shannon** ()d. 1941). "Alan Davis," *Variety,* 15 Dec 1943. IFN, p. 74.

Davis, Ann [actress] (b. 1893?–3 Sep 1961 [68], Bronx NY [Death Certificate Index No. 9493; M.E. Case No. 2623]). "Ann Davis," *Variety,* 6 Sep 1961. BHD, p. 144.

Davis, Anna [actress] (b. 1890–5 May 1945 [55?], Los Angeles CA). BHD1, p. 140.

Davis, Arthur [film/TV animator] (b. 1906?–9 May 2000 [94]). (WB.) Harris Lentz III, "Arthur Davis, 94," *CI,* 302 (Aug 2000), 50.

Davis, Ben [publicist]. No data found; may be next entry. AMD, p. 91. "Davis Joins Press Staff of Realart," *MPW,* 27 Sep 1919, 1960.

Davis, Benny [composer] (b. New York NY, 28 Aug 1893–20 Dec 1979 [86], No. Miami FL). . m. Gilda. "Benny Davis," *Variety,* 26 Dec 1979 (wrote *Margie; Baby Face; Carolina Moon*). ASCAP 1966, p. 157 (b. 21 Aug 1895). BHD2, p. 61 (b. 1895). CEPMJ, vol. 2, p. 782.

Davis, Boyd [actor] (b. Santa Rosa CA, 19 Jun 1885–25 Jan 1963 [77], Hollywood CA; heart attack). . "Boyd Davis," *Variety,* 6 Feb 1963. IFN, p. 74. Truitt, p. 82.

Davis, Charles Belmont [scenarist]. No data found. AMD, p. 91. "Charles Belmont Davis a Selznick Scenarist," *MPW,* 10 Jan 1920, 262.

Davis, Charles T. [cinematographer] (b. 1892–3 Oct 1936 [44?], Washington DC). BHD2, p. 61.

Davis, Conrad [actor] (b. 29 Feb 1915–22 Dec 1969 [54], Paramount CA). BHD, p. 144.

Davis, Donald [senarist]. No data found. FDY, p. 423.

Davis, Edwards [actor/writer/producer] (*né* Cader Edwards Davis, b. Santa Clara CA, 17 Jun 1867–17 May 1936 [68], Los Angeles CA). "Edwards Davis," *Variety,* 20 May 1936 (age 65). AMD, p. 91. BHD1, p. 140. IFN, p. 74. Truitt, p. 82 (b. 1871). "Edwards Davis," *MPW,* 27 Nov 1915, 1643. "Edwards Davis Was at One Time a Western Minister," *MPW,* 31 May 1919, 1328.

Davis, Emma [actress] (b. 1890?–14 Aug 1965 [75], Hollywood CA). "Emma Davis," *Variety,* 25 Aug 1965 (E.D. Edlund).

Davis, Fay [actress] (b. Houlton ME, 15 Dec 1872–26 Feb 1945 [72], London, England). BHD, p. 144.

Davis, Frank Foster [scenarist]. No data found. FDY, p. 423.

Davis, George Henry [producer] (b. 1861?–10 Aug 1932 [71], New York NY). m. Lillian. George Henry Davis," *Variety,* 16 Aug 1932. AMD, p. 91. BHD2, p. 61.

Davis, George T. [stage/film actor] (b. Amsterdam, Holland, 7 Nov 1889–19 Apr 1965 [75], Woodland Hills CA; cancer). (Began 1922; Educational; Universal.) BHD1, p. 140. IFN, p. 74. Truitt, p. 82. "George Davis," *MPW,* 9 Apr 1927, 549:2 (spoke seven languages).

Davis, Glenmore W. (Stuffy) [actor] (b. 1880–20 Aug 1958 [78?], Detroit MI). BHD, p. 144.

Davis, Hal [actor] (b. OH, 6 Oct 1909–4 Jan 1960 [50], Lancaster CA). BHD1, p. 141.

Davis, Hallie Flanagan [playwright/stage producer] (*née* Hallie Ferguson, b. Redfield SD, 27 Aug 1890–23 Jul 1969 [78], NY; Parkinson's disease). "Hallie Flanagan Davis," *Variety,* 30 Jul 1969.

Davis, Harry [pioneer entrepreneur] (b. Blackfriar's Row, London, England, 1861–2 Jan 1940 [78?], Pittsburgh PA). m. Queenie Ayres (d. 1976); Edith Pichel. "Harry Davis Dead; Pioneer in Movies; Opened the World's First Picture House 35 Years Ago in Pittsburgh; Called It 'Nickelodeon'; Made a Success in Legitimate Theatre—Sold Film Interests to the Stanleys," *NYT,* 3 Jan 1940, 21:1 (age 78). "Harry Davis Dies at 78 in Pittsburgh; Founder of the First Nickelodeon," *Variety,* 10 Jan 1940. AMD, p. 91. "A.M. Kennedy Combines with Harry Davis," *MPW,* 21 Oct 1911, 196. "Producers' Film Company," *MPW,* 28 Oct 1911, 282. Manley, "Pittsburgh, Pa., Has a Record Date for 'Store Shows'; Harry Davis Was a Real Pioneer and Set a Rapid Pace—Rowland and Clark Big Factors," *MPW,* 15 Jul 1916, pp. 405–06 (opened the Nickelodeon on Smithfield Street in Pittsburgh in 1903). Eugene L. Connelly, "The Life Story of Harry Davis; Showman Battled Way from Poor Boy to Millionaire; 'Nickelodeon' Founder Began Rise to Fame as Carnival Man," Pittsburgh Sun-Telegraph, 3 Jan 1940, pp. 15, 23 (Mr. Connelly claims to have coined the term "Nickelodeon.").

Davis, Harry [actor] (b. 1874?–4 Apr 1929 [55], New York NY). (Bison.) "Harry Davis," *Variety,* 10 Apr 1929. AS, p. 293. BHD, p. 144. IFN, p. 74. Truitt, p. 82.

Davis, Harry H. [cinematographer] (b. New York NY, 22 Oct 1896–9 Jun 1966 [69], Burbank CA). BHD2, p. 62. FDY, p. 457.

Davis, Howard O. [journalist/film executive] (b. 1877?–28 Aug 1964 [87], Palm Springs CA). (Universal; Triangle; Sennett.) "H.O. Davis," *Variety,* 2 Sep 1964. AMD, p. 91. BHD2, p. 61 (d. 23 Aug). "Universal City's New Head," *MPW,* 25 Dec 1915, 2345.

Davis, Hugh G. [executive]. No data found. "Davis Joins Rayart as an Executive; New Officer," *MPW,* 26 Dec 1925, 746.

Davis, J. Charles [theatrical manager/press agent] (b. 1850?–9 Apr 1919 [69], New York NY; complication of diseases). "J. Charles Davis,"

NYT, 10 Apr 1919, 11:2. "J. Charles Davis," *Variety,* 18 Apr 1919 (d. 10 Apr).

Davis, Jackie *see* **Davis, John H.**

Davis, James [actor] (d. Dec 1924, Chicago IL). BHD, p. 145.

Davis, James Gunnis [actor/assistant director] (b. Sunderland, England, 21 Dec 1873–22 Mar 1937 [63], Los Angeles CA). (Vitagraph.) "James G. Davis," *Variety,* 31 Mar 1937. AMD, p. 91. BHD1, p. 141; BHD2, p. 63. IFN, p. 74. Spehr, p. 126. Truitt, p. 82. "Davis Now an Assistant Director," *MPW,* 8 Jan 1916, 232. "Davis for Century," *MPW,* 27 Jan 1923, 385:4 (to direct Century Comedies for Julius Stern).

Davis, Jefferson [actor] (b. Cincinnati OH, 1884–5 Apr 1968 [83?], Cincinnati OH). AS, p. 293. BHD, p. 145.

Davis, John H[arold] (brother of **Mildred Davis**; brother-in-law of **Harold Lloyd**) (actor: "Jackie Davis" in Our Gang comedies] (b. Los Angeles CA, 5 Apr 1914–3 Nov 1992 [78], Santa Monica CA; respiratory ailment). m. Josephine. (Roach.) "John H. Davis," *Variety,* 16 Nov 1992, 78:5. AS, p. 293 (d. 15 Apr 1993); also listed under Jackie Davis. BHD, p. 145.

Davis, Mrs. Mary [actress] (b. 1846?–24 Jun 1918 [72], New York NY). "Mrs. Mary Davis," *Variety,* 28 Jun 1918. AS, p. 294. BHD, p. 145.

Davis, Mildred (sister of **John H. Davis**) [actress] (b. Philadelphia PA, 1 Jan 1900–18 Aug 1969 [69], Santa Monica CA; heart attack). m. **Harold Lloyd**, 10 Feb 1923, St. John's Episcopal Church, LA CA (d. 1971). "Mildred Davis, Wife of Harold Lloyd, 68," *NYT,* 20 Aug 1969, 47:3 (d. Beverly Hills CA). "Mildred Davis Lloyd," *Variety,* 27 Aug 1969. AMD, p. 91. AS, p. 294. BHD, p. 145 (b. 22 Feb 1901). IFN, p. 75 (b. PA, 22 Feb 1901). MH, p. 106. Truitt, p. 83 (b. Brooklyn NY, 1900). "Harold Lloyd Introduces New Fun in Third Comedy," *MPW,* 3 Jan 1920, 135. "Mildred Davis to Continue in Support of Harold Lloyd," *MPW,* 22 May 1920, 1098. "Lloyd Marries Mildred Davis," *MPW,* 3 Mar 1923, 35. "Back from Honeymoon," *MPW,* 17 Mar 1923, 310. "Lloyd and Bride Here," *MPW,* 7 Jul 1923, 54. "Mildred Davis Signed by Grand-Asher Co.," *MPW,* 20 Oct 1923, 673. "On the Set and Off," *MW,* 28 Aug 1925, 44 (was to return to the screen in John Golden's *The First Year* for Fox). "Mildred Davis Returns to Screen," *MPW,* 29 Aug 1925, 934. "On the Set and Off," *MM,* Jan 1926, 75 (Davis was to return to films in *Behind the Front* for FP-L but she contended the role was too small. "Mary Brian replaced Mildred."). Joan Cross, "The Girl Who Has Everything," *Pictures,* Sep 1926, 25–26, 78. "Miss Davis Returns; Signed by Paramount," *MPW,* 11 Dec 1926, 1.

Davis, Morgan [actor/cowboy] (b. Ethel MO, 2 May 1890–2 Sep 1941 [51], Riverside Co. CA). AS, p. 294. BHD, p. 145. IFN, p. 75.

Davis, Owen [playwright] (b. Portland ME, 29 Jan 1874–14 Oct 1956 [82], New York NY). m. Elizabeth Breyer. *My First Fifty Years in the Theatre* (1950). "Owen Davis Dies; A Playwright, 82; Prolific Author of Formula Melodramas Won Pulitzer Prize in '23 for 'Icebound,'" *NYT,* 15 Oct 1976, 25:3; George Middleton, "Some Reflections About a Stage-Struck Writer [letter]," 21 Oct 1956, II, 3:8. "Owen Davis," *Variety,* 17 Oct 1956. AMD, p. 91. BHD2, p. 62. "Owen Davis Originals for Famous Players," *MPW,* 23 Oct 1926, 484.

Davis, Phillip [social worker/actor/pioneer documentary film producer/President of National Motion Picture Bureau, Inc., from 1914–40] (b. Boston MA, 1876?–20 Nov 1951 [75], Boston MA). "Philip Davis," *NYT,* 21 Nov 1951, 25:3. "Phillip Davis," *Variety,* 28 Nov 1951. AS, p. 294.

Davis, Reed E. [actor] (b. 29 Aug 1893–12 Oct 1984 [91], Omaha NB). BHD1, p. 606.

Davis, Richard Harding [writer] (d. 11 Apr 1916, Mt. Kisco NY). "R. Harding Davis's Body Cremated," *NYT,* 15 Apr 1916, 13:7 (ashes to be interred in Leverington Cemetery). "Richard Harding Davis," *Variety,* 14 Apr 1916, p. 28. AMD, p. 91. "Fox Purchases Screen Rights for 67 Richard Harding Davis Stories," *MPW,* 21 Feb 1920, 1200.

Davis, Roger [stage/film actor] (b. 20 Jan 1884–3 Mar 1980 [96], Woodland Hills CA; cancer). "Roger Davis," *Variety,* 12 Mar 1980. AS, p. 294. BHD1, p. 141.

Davis, Ulysses [director] (b. South Amboy NJ 1872). AMD, p. 91. BHD2, p. 62. "Director Davis at Liberty," *MPW,* XI, 9 Mar 1912, 879. "Two More Experts for Horsley," *MPW,* 20 Nov 1915, 1502.

Davis, William S. [producer/director] (b. 1882?–16 Nov 1920 [38], Los Angeles CA; peritonitis). "William Davis Dies," *Variety,* 19 Nov 1920. AMD, p. 91. AS, p. 294. BHD2, p. 62 (d. 19 Nov). "Will S. Davis to Produce Art Dramas," *MPW,* 17 Feb 1917, 1028. "William S. Davis Metro Director," *MPW,* 13 Oct 1917, 240.

Davison, Grace [actress] (b. Oceanside, LI NY). AMD, p. 91. WWS, p. 146. "Grace Davison, Film Star, Entertains at Showing of 'Love, Hate and a Woman,'" *MPW,* 3 Dec 1921, 557.

D'Avril, Yola [stage/film actress] (b. Lille, France, 8 Apr 1907–2 Mar 1984 [76], Los Angeles CA). (First U.S. film: *The Dressmaker from Paris;* Christie; 1st National; Paramount.) AMD, p. 91. AS, p. 278. BHD1, p. 142 (b. Belgium; d. Port Hueneme CA). WFE, p. 69. "Yola D'Avril Signed by First National," *MPW,* 25 Sep 1926, 214. "Yola D'Avril," *MPW,* 9 Jul 1927, 87. Dorothy Cartwright, "Paris Comes to Hollywood; Charmingly Petite Yola D'Avril of France in Two Short Years Captures Our Film Mecca," *Paris and Hollywood Screen Secrets,* Oct 1927, 29–31 ("She has beautifully expressive grey eyes, reddish bobbed hair, and a delightful sprinkling of freckles.... ¶When Yola was fifteen her father died, leaving too little money for the family to live on comfortably. It was, therefore, necessary for Yola to work." Through M. Gaumont, she met Swanson during shooting of *Madame Sans Gene* in France. She came to the U.S. with a letter to Paramount. "...Yola d'Avril has one of filmdom's most interesting careers waiting for her just around the corner.").

Daw, Marjorie, "The Girl with the Nursery-Rhyme Name" (sister of Chandler House) [actress] (*née* Margaret House; aka Marguerita House, b. Colorado Springs CO, 19 Jan 1902–18 Mar 1979 [77], Huntington Beach CA). m. (1) **A[lbert] Edward Sutherland**—div. 1925 (d. 1973); (2) **Myron Selznick**, 1925–42 (d. 1944); (3) Mr. Myers. (Universal; FP-L, 1915; Paramount; 1st National; Selznick; Fox; FBO; Arrow; MGM; UA. Film debut: The Love Victorious, Universal.) AMD, p. 92. AS, p. 295. BHD, pp. 15–17; 145. BR, pp. 130–32. FFF, p. 93. MH, p. 106. WWS, p. 64. "Miss Farrar's Protége," *MPW,* XXV, 28 Aug 1915, 1460. "Marjorie Daw Has Her Chance at Last," *MPW,* 9 Oct 1915, 262. Elizabeth Peltret, "The Girl with the Nursery-Rhyme Name," *MPC,* Apr 1919, 48–49, 76. Grace Leslie, "Bubbles," *MPC,* Jul 1921, 16–17, 89. "Marjorie Daw," *MPW,* 29 Aug 1925, 933. "Marjorie Daw," *MPW,* 30 Oct 1926, 553. "Marjorie Daw," *MPW,* 3 Sep 1927, 24. Billy H. Doyle, "Lost Players," *CI,* 144 (Jun 1987), C58. George Katchmer, "Forgotten Cowboys and Cowgirls—Part XIII," *CI,* 190 (Apr 1991), C6.

Dawkins, Irma L. [actress] (b. Columbia SC, 25 Mar 1892–13 Oct 1972 [80], Raleigh NC). m. Roy R. English. (Biograph, 1912.) As, p. 294 (d. Knoxville TN). BHD, p. 145. IFN, p. 75. John E. Thayer, "A Diamond in the Sky," *CFC,* 39 (Summer, 1973), 51.

Dawley, Herbert M. [actor/director/] (b. 15 Mar 1880–15 Aug 1970 [90], New Providence NJ). . "Herbert M. Dawley," *Variety,* 19 Aug 1970. AS, p. 295. BHD2, p. 62 (d. 4 Aug 1976). IFN, p. 75.

Dawley, J. Searle [director/producer/scenarist] (b. Del Norte CO, 13 May 1877–29 Mar 1949 [71], Woodland Hills CA). (Edison; FP-L.) "J. Searle Dawley, Movie Pioneer, 71; Director for Edison at Studios Here in 1907 Dies—Later with Zukor, Frohman," *NYT,* 30 Mar 1949, 25:4. "J. Searle Dawley," *Variety,* 6 Apr 1949. AMD, p. 92. AS, p. 295. BHD2, p. 62. IFN, p. 75. Lowrey, p. 40. Spehr, p. 126. "Director Dawley Joins Famous Players," *MPW,* 24 May 1913, 822. "Famous Players Engage J. Searle Dawley," *MPW,* 21 Jun 1913, 1255. George Blaisdell, "J. Searle Dawley, Producer," *MPW,* 31 Jan 1914, 531. "Dawley's New Idea; Famous Players' Director Resigns to Become Free Lance Producer and Scenario Writer," *NYDM,* 13 May 1914, 36:4. "Films as Records," *NYDM,* 7 Oct 1914, 26:4. "Beck Signs J. Searle Dawley," *MPW,* 29 Nov 1919, 550. "Continuity Writers Are 'Curse' of the Director," *MPW,* 21 Feb 1920, 1213. "Fox Engages J. Searle Dawley to Direct Feature Productions," *MPW,* 9 Oct 1920, 830. "Achievement Films Has Signed Dawley as Director General," *MPW,* LV, 29 Apr 1922, 932.

Dawn, Hazel, "The Pink Lady" [actress] (*née* Hazel La Tout, b. Ogden UT, 23 Mar 1890–28 Aug 1988 [98], New York NY). m. Charles Gruelle (d. 1941). C. Gerald Fraser, "Hazel Dawn, Stage Actress, Is Dead at 98," *NYT,* 30 Aug 1988, D21:1 (d. 27 Aug). "Hazel Dawn," *Variety,* 7 Sep 1988. AMD, p. 92. AS, p. 295. BHD, p. 145. Alan Brock, "Younger than Springtime," *CFC,* 34 (Spring 1972), 30–31, 33. "Hazel Dawn," WBO2, pp. 100–101. "Hazel Dawn Returns to Famous Players," *MPW,* 13 Mar 1915, 1587. "Another Picture Recruit," *MPW,* 12 Jun 1915, 1757. "Hazel Dawn Will Return to Screen in Series of Modern Feature Dramas," *MPW,* 9 Oct 1920, 802. Billy H. Doyle, "Lost Players," *CI,* 161 (Nov 1988), C19.

Dawn, Jack (actor/makeup artist) (b. KY, 10 Feb 1892–20 Jun 1961 [69], Los Angeles CA). BHD1, p. 142; BHD2, p. 62.

Dawn, L.W. [makeup artist] (b. 1894–2 May 1944 [50?], Phoenix AZ). BHD2, p. 62.

Dawn, Norman O. [cinematographer/director] (b. Argentina, 25 May 1886–2 Feb 1975 [88], Santa Monica CA). . m. Katherine. "Norman O. Dawn," *Variety,* 12 Feb 1975 (age 88). AMD, p. 92. AS, p. 295 (b. 1994; d. 1 Feb, LA CA). BHD2, p. 62 (b. 1884; d. 1 Feb). IFN, p. 75. "Dawn with Universal," *MPW,* 29 Aug 1925, 949.

Dawson, Ben H. [scenarist] (b. 1874–4 Mar 1922 [48?], Los Angeles CA). BHD2, p. 62.

Dawson, Dorice [actress] (*née* Doris Dawson, b. 1894?–14 Nov 1950 [56], Riverside CA; heart attack). (Fox; 1st National.) "Dorice Dawson," *Variety,* 22 Nov 1950 (film actress for 28 years). AS, p. 295. BHD1, p. 142. IFN, p. 75.

Dawson, Doris [actress: Wampas Star, 1929] (b. Goldfield NV, 16 Apr 1909–20 Apr 1986 [77], Coral Gables FL). Truitt, p. 83. Dorothy Manners, "Reducing Herself to Riches; Doris Dawson's Soul-Struggle Is Caused by a Hunger for Both Cake and a Career," *MPC,* Jul 1928, 42, 82 ("When you're about eighteen, it's hard to give up whipped cream, but Doris put her mind to it.").

Dawson, Douglas [scenarist] (b. London, England, 25 Apr 1854–20 Jan 1933 [79], London, England). m. Mrs. Herbert Oakley, 1903. *A Soldier Diplomat* (1927). "Douglas Dawson Is Dead in London; State Chamberlain and Master of Ceremonies to King Edward Succumbs at 78; Won Fame as a Soldier; Served with Coldstream Guard in Egypt, Taking Part in Capture of Cairo—Won Many Medals," *NYT,* 21 Jan 1933, 15:3.

Dawson, Frank [actor] (b. England, 4 Jul 1870–11 Oct 1953 [83], Los Angeles CA). "Frank Dawson," *Variety,* 21 Oct 1953. AS, p. 295. BHD, p. 145. IFN, p. 75.

Dawson, Ivo [actor] (b. Rutlandshire, England, 13 Dec 1879–7 Mar 1934 [54], Los Angeles CA). AMD, p. 92. AS, p. 295. BHD1, p. 142. IFN, p. 75. "Ivo Dawson Engaged for 'Love Without Question,'" *MPW,* 10 Jan 1920, 259. "Ivo Dawson Becomes a Commuter," *MPW,* 15 May 1920, 965.

Dawson, Ralph (Pappy) [executive/film editor] (b. Waterloo MA, 18 Apr 1897–15 Nov 1962 [65], Woodland Hills CA). (Began as publicist in 1919 with Samuel Goldwyn Productions; WB; Batjac Productions.) "Ralph Dawson," *NYT,* 18 Nov 1962, 86:8 (AA for *A Midsummer Night's Dream* [1935]; Anthony Adverse [1936]; and *The Adventures of Robin Hood*). "Ralph Dawson," *Variety,* 21 Nov 1962. AS, p. 295. BHD2, p. 62.

Dax, Jean [actor] (*né* Gontran Théodore Louis Henri Willar, b. Paris, France, 17 Sep 1879–6 Jun 1962 [82], Paris, France [extrait de décès no. 18/1683]). AS, p. 295.

Day, Alice (sister of **Marceline Day**) [actress: Sennett Bathing Beauty/Wampas Star, 1928] (*née* Alice Newlin, b. Boulder [or Colorado Springs] CO, 7 Nov 1905–25 May 1995 [89], Integrated Health Service, Orange Hill, Orange CA [Certificate of Death No. 3-95-30-006460], respiratory failure due to cerebral hemorrhage infarction; cardiovascular disease due to hypertension. "Place of final dispostion: At sea off coast of Newport Beach California."). m. Mr. Hawkins—div. (1 son, Gary). (Sennett; Fox; MGM.) AMD, p. 92. AS, p. 295. FSS, p. 86. Katz, p. 313. Ragan 2, p. 392 (b. Pueblo CO, 1905). "Alice Day Signed," *MPW,* 23 Feb 1924, 674. "Mack Sennett Has New Star in Dainty Little Alice Day," *MPW,* 8 Aug 1925, 650 (19 years old). Mayadele Howard, "Enter—A New Comedienne; Alice Day Bids Fair to Make Her Mark in the Exclusive Field of Girl Comedy Stars," *Cinema Arts,* Sep 1926, 44, 57. "Alice Day Loaned by Mack Sennett," *MPW,* 6 Nov 1926, 32. "Alice Day," *MPW,* 10 Sep 1927, 89. Betty Standish, "Mother Knew Best; So the Day Sisters Went into the Movies," *MPC,* Dec 1927, 58, 87. Carol Johnston, "The Girl Who Wouldn't Undress; An Impression of Alice Day," *MPC,* Feb 1929, 51, 87 ("Her enthusiasm abated, however, when she was asked to don an abbreviated costume."). "Mrs. Day Bankrupt," *Variety,* 106, 26 Apr 1932, 3:4 (Irene Day, mother of Alice and Marceline, "former picture leads, has taken bankruptcy status for $1,026 liabilities. Assets zero. ¶Mrs. Day's debts are mostly bills at Hollywood shops, led by Magnin's with $397."). Data supplied by Frank Reichelt, Germany.

Day, Bingham [director] (b. Newark OH, 1883). BHD2, p. 62.

Day, Edith Marie [stage/film actress] (b. Minneapolis MN, 10 Apr 1896–1 May 1971 [75], London, England). m. (1) Carle E. Carlton; (2) **Pat Somerset**—div. 1927 (d. 1974). (Crest Pictures Corp.) "Edith Day, Starred in London Musicals," *NYT,* 3 May 1971, 40:1. "Edith Day," *Variety,* 5 May 1971. BHD, p. 145. AS, p. 296. IFN, p. 75. SD, p. 339. Lewis Richmond, "Crash! Another Romance on the Rocks!; Shaking the stage and screen world, Edith Day's second romance has smashed, and now everyone wonders who will be next to win the heart of the beautiful 'Rose Marie' Girl," *Paris and Hollywood Screen Secrets Magazine,* May 1927, 46–48 (Somerset was named as co-respondent in the divorce suit of Richard "Skeets" Gallagher against his wife, Irene Martin. In her deposition for her own divorce, Day asserted that Somerset "struck me and inflicted blows, treated me with no respect before his friends, brought low women of vile character into the home, expected me to support him and his valet, never contributed a cent to he home. He took all my earnings...").

Day, Frances [actress] (*née* Frances Victoria Schenck, b. New York NY, 16 Dec 1907-Apr 1984 [76?), Brighton, England. AS, p. 296. BHD1, p. 142.

Day, Harry Irving [publicist]. "Harry Day Joins Realart," *MPW,* XLII, 15 Nov 1919, 332. "Harry Irving Day, Ex-Buck Private, Now International Publicist," *MPW,* 13 Mar 1920, 1769. "Day Resigns as Publicity Head of Cosmopolitan Productions," *MPW,* 22 May 1920, 1101.

Day, Holman [scenairst] (b. ME, 1866–19 Feb 1935 [69?], Mill Valley CA). AMD, p. 92. AS, p. 296 (d. 27 Feb). BHD2, p. 62. "Increases Writing Staff," *MPW,* 8 Sep 1923, 130.

Day, Joel [actor]. No data found. CH, p. 37.

Day, Josette [actress] (*née* Josette Andrée Noëlle Claire Dagory, b. Paris, France, 31 Jul 1914–29 Jun 1978 [63], Paris, France). BHD, p. 145. AS, p. 296 (d. 27 Jun). IFN, p. 75.

Day, Julietta [actress] (b. Boston MA, 1894?–18 Sep 1957 [63], Huntington, LI NY). (American.) "Juliette Day [Mrs. Juliette Day Whitney]," *Variety,* 25 Sep 1957. AMD, p. 92. AS, p. 296 (d. 16 Sep). BHD, p. 145 (d. Northport NY). IFN, p. 75. "Juliette Day," *MPW,* 26 May 1917, 1294. "Dinner to Welcome Miss Day," *MPW,* 9 Jun 1917, 1609.

Day, Marceline (sister of **Alice Day**) [actress: Wampas Star, 1926] (*née* Marceline Newlin, b. Colorado Springs CO, 24 Apr 1907–16 Feb 2000 [92], Cathedral City CA). m. (1) Arthur J. Klein; (2) John Arthur, 1959. Bill Cappello, "Marceline Day: 1908–2000," *CI,* 300 (Jul 2000), p. 18 (b. 1908; "When she ended her film career [ca. 1937] she withdrew from the film world and would not talk or discuss her career with writers or fans."). Harris Lentz, III, "Obituaries; Marceline Day, 91," *CI,* 301 (Jul 2000), 47 (b. 1908). (Sennett; MGM.) AMD, p. 92. AS, p. 296. BR, pp. 132–35. FSS, p. 87. Katz, p. 314. "With Hoot Gibson," *MPW,* 13 Dec 1924, 654. "Marceline Day Signs New Contract," *MPW,* 6 Aug 1927, 399.

Day, Marie L. [actress] (*née?,* b. Troy NY, 1855?–7 Nov 1939 [84], Cleveland OH; pneumonia). m. Wilson Day (d. 1927). "Marie L. Day," *Variety,* 15 Nov 1939 (in the silent *Mother Carey's Chickens*). AS, p. 296. BHD1, p. 142. IFN, p. 75. Truitt, p. 83.

Day, Richard [art director] (b. Victoria, B.C., Canada, 9 May 1896–23 May 1972 [76], Los Angeles CA). . (MGM; TC-F; UA.) "Richard Day," *Variety,* 31 May 1972 (age 78). AMD, p. 92. AS, p. 296. BHD2, p. 62 (d. 19 May). Katz, p. 314 (began 1918). "Capt. Richard Day Signs with Associated Studios," *MPW,* 10 Apr 1926, 428.

Day, Shannon [actress] (*née* Sylvia Day, b. New York NY, 5 Aug 1896–24 Feb 1977 [80], New York NY [Death Certificate Index No. 3511; age 78]). AMD, p. 92. AS, p. 296. BHD1, p. 142 (b. Austria). FSS, p. 87. MH, p. 106. "DeMille Signs Shannon Day, Beauty of Midnight Frolics," *MPW,* 24 Jul 1920, 496. Alma M. Talley, "Why a 'Follies' Girl Can Get a Rich Husband," *MW,* 5 May 1923, 7, 29. George Katchmer, "Forgotten Cowboys and Cowgirls—Part XVIII," *CI,* 195 (Sep 1991), C6.

Day, Verne R. [executive] (b. 1870?–17 Aug 1945 [75], Los Angeles CA). (Essanay [Chicago and Los Angeles]). "Verne Day," *Variety,* 22 Aug 1945. BHD2, p. 62.

Day, Willperey [inventor/director] (b. Lutton, England, 1878–1950 [72?], England). AS, p.296.

Daye, June *see* **Burns, Vinnie**

Daykarhanova, Tamara [actress] (b. Moscow, Russia, 14 Jan 1889–2 Aug 1980 [91], Englewood NJ). AS, p. 296.

Dayne, Blanche [Cressy and Dane/stage/film actress] (b. Troy NY, 25 Dec 1871–27 Jun 1944 [72], Hackensack NJ). m. Will Cressy (d. 1930). "Blanche Dayne," *Variety,* 5 Jul 1944, p. 39 (age 73). BHD, p. 145.

Dayton, Ethel [actress] (*née* Ethel Margaret Corcoran) (b. New York NY, 28 Oct 1895). (Film debut: Disciplining Daisy; Vitagraph.) AMD, p. 92. "Ethel Corcoran," *MPW,* 18 Dec 1915, 2164. "Ethel Corcoran Becomes Ethel Dayton," *MPW,* 16 Dec 1916, 1650.

Dayton, Frank [stage/film actor] (b. Boston MA, 1865?–17 Oct 1924 [59], St. Vincent's Hospital, New York NY). (Essanay.) "Frank Dayton," *Variety,* 22 Oct 1924. AMD, p. 92. AS, p. 296 (d. LA CA). BHD, p. 145. IFN, p. 75. SD, p. 340. "Frank Dayton," *MPW,* 13 Dec 1913, 1270 (cites theater work).

Dayton, James [scenarist] (*né* Walker James Niceware, d. 18 Aug 1924, Los Angeles CA). "James Dayton," *Variety,* 20 Aug 1924. AMD, p. 92. AS, p. 296. BHD2, p. 62. "James Dayton," *MPW,* 28 Dec 1912, 1290.

Dayton, Lewis Seeley [writer] (b. Marlboro NJ, 1894?–24 Jun 1950 [56], Yonkers NY). m. Irene Rice. "Lewis Dayton Dies; Editor and Writer; Analyst in State Department Worked on Evening Journal Here and Yonkers Papers," *NYT,* 25 Jun 1950, 68:5.

Daze, Mercedes [actress] (b. 1892–18 Mar

1945 [52?], Los Angeles CA). AS, p. 296. BHD, p. 145. IFN, p. 75.

Dazey, Charles T[urner] (father of **Frank M. Dazey**) [playwright/scenarist] (b. Lima, Adams County, I, 12 Aug 1853–9 Feb 1938 [84], Quincy IL). m. Lucy Harding, Quincy IL. "C.T. Dazey, Wrote 'In Old Kentucky'; Will Rogers Was Featured in Movie of His Drama Written in 1891—Dies at 84," *NYT,* 10 Feb 1938, 21:2. "Charles T. Dazey," *Variety,* 16 Feb 1938. AMD, p. 93. BHD2, p. 62. Lowrey, p. 42. 1921 Directory, p. 286. NNAT. "Dazey Writes Script for Apollo," *MPW,* 30 Jun 1917, 2078. "Dazey Moves to Santa Barbara," *MPW,* 14 Jul 1917, 230. "Dazey on Scenario Staff of Beck," *MPW,* 23 Aug 1919, 1150.

Dazey, Frank M[itchell] (son of **Charles T. Dazey**) [scenarist] (b. 1892?–16 Jun 1970 [78], Los Angeles CA). m. **Agnes Christine Johnston**, Jul 1920, LI NY (d. 1978). "Francis M. Dazey," *Variety,* 24 Jun 1970. AMD, p. 93. AS, p. 296. BHD2, p. 62. "Frank Dazey Joins Mayer's Scenario Staff," *MPW,* 22 Nov 1919, 451. "Dazey a Rapid Worker," *MPW,* 3 Jan 1920, 131. "Agnes Johnston Will Wed," *LA Times,* 19 Feb 1920, III, p. 14. "Agnes Johnston to Return in September," *MPW,* 14 Aug 1920, 874. "Little Miss Dazey Arrives," *MPW,* L, 21 May 1921, 279 (daughter b. 1 May 1921). "Dazey Associate Editor of Selznick Scenarios," *MPW,* 22 Oct 1921, 920.

Dazie, Mlle. [dancer/actress] (b. 1885–12 Aug 1952 [67?], Miami Beach FL). BHD, p. 145. Frederick James Smith, "Vaudeville; Mlle. Dazie Triumphs in Sir James Barrie's Fantasy 'Pantaloon'...," *NYDM,* 25 Mar 1914, 21:1. "Dazie on the Art of the Toe Dancer; Charming Danseause Tells of Her Career and Her Plans for the Future," *NYDM,* 1 Apr 1914, 24:1.

De Acosta, Mercedes [composer/scenarist/novelist] (b. New York NY, 1893–9 May 1968 [75?], New York NY; cancer). m. portrait painter Abram Poole. (Composed *What Next.*) AS, p. 296. BHD2, p. 62.

Dean, Basil [stage/film producer/director] (b. Croydon, So, London, England, 27 Sep 1888–22 Apr 1978 [89], London, England). m. 3 times. "Basil Dean," *Variety,* 26 Apr 1978, p. 95. (Founded Associated Talking Pictures, 1928.) AS, p. 308. BHD, p. 145. IFN, p. 75. Waldman, p. 76.

Dean, Cecilia (actress]. No data found. "Cecilia Dean," *MPW,* 19 Apr 1913, 269 (plot synopsis of Dean vamping in *The Burden Bearer,* Lubin, 1913; 1 reel; with Arthur Johnson).

Dean, Dora *see* **Johnson, Dora Dean**

Dean, Faxon M. [cameraman] (b. Guyton GA, 26 May 1890-May 1965 [74?], CA).. BHD2, p. 63 (b. 1882). FDY, p. 457. Ruth Mabrey, "Only 1000 Film Faces in America, Says Movie Cameraman," *MW,* 31 May 1924, 14, 30.

Dean, Jack [actor] (*né* John Wooster Dean, b. Bridgeport CT, 1875?–23 Jun 1950 [75], New York NY). (Lasky.) m. **Fannie Ward**, 1916 (d. 1952). "Jack Dean," *Variety,* 28 Jun 1950. AMD, p. 93. AS, p. 308 (b. Washington DC). BHD1, p. 606. IFN, p. 75. "Fannie Ward and Jack Dean Married," *MPW,* 15 Jan 1916, 402. "Jack Dean," *MPW,* 17 Feb 1917, 1010.

Dean, Jerrie [vaudeville/film actress]. No data found. (Lasky.) m. Harry K. Evans, 19 Feb 1920. "The 1917-Model Bathing Girl," *Photoplay,* Jul 1917, 70–77 (called Jerrie Deen on p. 73). "Cupid Bulletin No. 9999," *LA Times,* 22 Feb 1920, III, p. 16.

Dean, Julia [stage/film actress] (b. St. Paul MN, 13 May 1878–18 Oct 1952 [74], Los Angeles CA). m. Ormi Caldara. (Ince.) "Miss Julia Dean, Stage Star, Dead; Actress Who Had Worked with Belasco and Brody Here Also Played in Movies," *NYT,* 19 Oct 1952, 89:1. "Julia Dean," *Variety,* 22 Oct 1952. AMD, p. 93. AS, p. 308. BHD1, p. 143. IFN, p. 75. Spehr, p. 126. Truitt, p. 83. "Julia Dean Featured in 'Ruling Passions,'" *MPW,* 28 Sep 1918, 1906 (b. Minneapolis).

Dean, Louis [actor/director] (b. Wilmington DE, 1875–8 Apr 1933 [57], Honolulu HI). m. Virginia Duncan (widow). "Louis Dean," *Variety,* 11 Apr 1933. AS, p. 308. BHD, p. 145. IFN, p. 75.

Dean, May (Mrs. Mary Bernard) [actress] (b. 1896–1 Sep 1937 [41?], New York NY). "May Dean," *Variety,* 8 Sep 1957 ("She was the original colored mammy of the Aunt Jamima pancake flour ads."). AS, p. 308. BHD, p. 145 (d. Jamaica NY, 28 Aug). IFN, p. 75. Truitt, p. 83. A Mae Dean appeared in *Riders of the Range* (1923).

Dean, Mildred [actress]. No data found. m. **Harry L. Franklin**, 27 Feb 1918 (d. 1927). AMD, p. 93. "Metro Director Marries Actress," *MPW,* 16 Mar 1918, 1515.

Dean, Nelson [actor] (*né* Nelson S. Whipple, b. 1882?–19 Dec 1923 [41], Detroit MI; apoplexy). "Nelson Dean," *Variety,* 27 Dec 1923. AS, p. 308. BHD, p. 145.

Dean, Pauline [actress] (*née* Pauline Hilburn, b. GA, 1 Aug 1881–27 Mar 1930 [48], Los Angeles CA). m. **J. Stuart Blackton** (d. 1941). AS, p. 308.

Dean, Priscilla [stage/film actress] (b. New York NY, 25 Nov 1896–27 Dec 1987 [91], Leonia NJ; result of a fall in Sept.). m. **Wheeler Oakman**, 10 Jan 1920, Reno NV (d. 1949); Gen. Leslie Arnold. (Biograph; Universal.) "Priscilla Dean," *Variety,* 2 Mar 1988 (d. Las Vegas). AMD, p. 93. AS, p. 308 (b. 16 Sep). BHD1, p. 143. FFF, p. 25. FSS, p. 87. Katz, p. 315. LD, pp. 74–82. MH, p. 106. MSBB, p. 1034. Spehr, p. 126. WWS, p. 246. "Priscilla Dean Wins Loving Cup," *MPW,* 4 Aug 1917, 771. "Miss Dean Renews Contract," *MPW,* 16 Nov 1918, 751. Fritzi Remont, "A Twentieth Century Priscilla; Most of All She Loves to Travel Fast—Be It in Auto or 'Plane," *MPC,* Feb 1919, 30–31, 71. "Priscilla Dean Renews Contract with Universal," *MPW,* 6 Sep 1919, 1477. "Oakman-Dean Marriage Announced," *MPW,* 17 Apr 1920, 421. Cover, *Photoplay,* Mar 1921. Truman B. Handy, "Differences and Priscilla," *Classic,* Oct 1922, 36–37, 79, 85. "Priscilla Dean," *MPW,* 27 Jun 1925, 977. "Star Praises Roach-Pathé Gown Creator," *MPW,* 18 Dec 1926, 508. Allan Brock, "Unforgettable—Priscilla Dean," *CFC,* 30 (Winter 1970), 6–7.

Dean, Ralph [actor/director] (b. 21 Mar 1868–15 Sep 1923 [55], New York NY). "Ralph Dean," *Variety,* 20 Sep 1923. AS, p. 308. BHD, p. 146; BHD2, p. 63.

Dean, Raye [actress]. No data found. AMD, p. 93. "Raye Dean Is Leading Woman for Bert Lytell," *MPW,* XL20 Nov 1920, 354.

Dean, Rosemary [actress] (b. Baltimore MD, 1898–12 Apr 1990 [91?]). BHD, p. 146.

Dean, Ruby [actress] (b. 1887–23 Feb 1935 [47?], Cleveland OH). AS, p. 308. BHD, p. 146. IFN, p. 75.

Dean, Wally [actor] (*né* Walter Perry Deal, b. PA, 26 Dec 1878–1 Oct 1955 [76]). BHD, p. 146. IFN, p. 75.

Deane, Doris [Ziegfeld Follies/actress] (b. La Crosse WI, 20 Jan 1900–24 Mar 1974 [74], Los Angeles CA; found dead of an apparent heart attack). m. **Roscoe (Fatty) Arbuckle** (d. 1933). "Doris Deane," *Variety,* 8 May 1974, p. 287 (age 73). AS, p. 308. BHD, p. 146. IFN, p. 76.

Deane, Ralph [actor/director] (b. 1875–4 Feb 1955 [79?], Los Angeles Co. CA). BHD, p. 146; BHD2, p. 63. IFN, p. 76.

Deane, Sydney [actor]. No data found. George Katchmer, "Remembering the Great Silents," *CI,* 243 (Sep 1995), 46.

De Angelis, Jefferson [actor] (b. San Francisco CA, 30 Nov 1859–20 Mar 1933 [73], Orange NJ). "Jefferson De Angelis," *Variety,* 21 Mar 1933 (age 74). AS, p. 297. BHD, p. 146. IFN, p. 76.

De Antoni, Alfredo [director/actor] (*né* Alfredo De Antonio, b. Alessandria in the Piedmonte, Italy, 14 Jul 1875–3 Dec 1953 [78], Rome, Italy). AS, p. 297. JS, p. 122 (in Italian silents from 1912).

Dearholt, Ashton [actor] (*né* Richard Holt, b. Milwaukee WI, 4 Apr 1894–27 Apr 1942 [48], Los Angeles CA). m. **Helene Rosson** (d. 1985). (Began 1915; American; Gerson Pictures Corp.) AMD, p. 93. AS, p. 308; p. 536 (Richard Holt). BHD1, p. 143. IFN, p. 76. MSBB, p. 1023 (b. 1895). "Carmel Myers Has New Leading Man," *MPW,* 22 Dec 1917, 1820. Gene Fernett, "Studios in Northern California," *CI,* 141 (Mar 1987), C9-C10.

Dearing, Edgar [actor] (b. Ceres CA, 4 May 1893–17 Aug 1974 [81], Woodland Hills CA; lung cancer). "Edgar Dearing," *Variety,* 2 Oct 1974. AS, p. 308. BHD1, p. 143. IFN, p. 76.

De Aubry, Diane, "The Girl with the Million Dollar Eyes" [actress] (*née* Diane Rubini, b. Sault St. Marie MI, 11 Nov 1889–23 May 1969 [79], Santa Monica CA). (Diane Rubini). m. Jan Rubini. (Biograph; World.) "Diane de Aubrey," *Variety,* 11 Jun 1969 (d. Santa Monica CA). AS, p. 297. BHD1, p. 144. IFN, p. 76. Truitt, p. 84.

Deaves, Ada (daughter of minstrel Edwin Deaves) [stage/film actress] (b. 1856–18 Sep 1920 [64?], New York NY; heart disease). "Ada Deaves," *Variety,* 1 Oct 1920, p. 9 (d. 16 Sep). BHD, p. 146.

Deavor, Nancy [actress] (b. Australia). (Film debut: *The Law of the Yukon;* Selznick.) AMD, p. 93. "June Elvidge Not Featured," *MPW,* 17 Jan 1920, 403. "Realart Signs Australian Girl for 'Law of the Yukon,'" *MPW,* 0 Mar 1920, 2000 (film debut). John E. Thayer, "Stars in View—1922," *CI,* 61 (Winter, 1978), 36–38. George A. Katchmer, "Forgotten Cowboys and Cowgirls—Part 2," *CI,* 173 (Nov 1989), C14.

Debain, Henry [actor/director] (b. Paris, France, 3 Aug 1886–15 Jan 1983 [96], Paris, France). AS, p. 308.

De Balzac, Jeanne (niece of Honoré Balzac) [actress] (b. France, 1891–8 Apr 1930 [39?], Paris, France). "Jeanne de Balzac," *Variety,* 21 May 1930, p. 60. AS, p. 297. BHD, p. 146.

De Banos, Richard [director/cinematograher] (*né* Ricardo de Banos Martinez, b. Barcelona, Spain, 27 Aug 1884–8 Aug 1939 [54?], Barcelona, Spain). AS, p. 297 (b. 1882). BHD2, p. 63.

De Baroncelli, Jacques [actor/director/scenarist] (*né* Marquis Marie Joseph Henri Jacques de Baroncelli de Javon, b. Bouillargues, France, 25 Jun 1881 [extrait de naissance no. 31]–12 Jan 1951 [69], Paris, France; heart attack). AS, p. 297. BHD2, p. 63.

De Barre, Vivian [actress] (d. 18 Jul 1985, Los Angeles CA). BHD1, p. 144.

De Barros, Leitão [director/scenarist] (*né* José Leitão de Barros, b. Lisbon, Portugal, 22 Oct 1896–29 Jun 1967 [70], Lisbon, Portugal; cancer). AS, p. 297 (Leitao De Barros); p. 658 (José Leitão de Barros).

De Barros, Luiz [director/producer] (b. Rio de Janeiro, Brazil, 1893–1981 [88?], Rio de Janeiro, Brazil). AS, p. 297.

De Bary, Jean Brice [actor] (b. 1906?–14 Mar 1959 [53], Washington DC; heart attack). AS, p. 297. "Brig. Gen. Jean de Bary," *NYT*, 15 Mar 1959, 88:4.

De Bear, Archie [director/producer] (b. 31 Mar 1888–15 Mar 1970 [81]). BHD2, p. 63.

De Beaumont, Etienne [producer] (*né* Bonnin de la Bonniere, Comte de Beaumont, b. Paris, France, 1883–1958 [75?], Paris, France). AS, p. 297.

De Beck, Billy [actor/animator] (b. 1890–11 Nov 1942 [52?], New York NY). BHD, p. 146; BHD2, p. 63.

De Becker, Harold [actor] (b. London, England, 8 Jun 1889–23 Jul 1947 [58], Los Angeles CA). "Harold De Becker," *Variety*, 30 Jul 1947. AS, p. 297. BHD, p. 146. IFN, p. 76.

De Becker, Marie [actress] (b. London, England, 13 Jun 1880–23 Mar 1946 [65], Los Angeles CA; heart attack). AS, p. 297.

De Belleville, Frederic [actor] (b. Liege, Belgium, 17 Feb 1855–25 Feb 1923 [68], New York NY). m. Emily; (2) Kate Massi (d. 1893). "Frederic de Belleville," *Variety*, 1 Mar 1923 (age 68). AMD, p. 93. AS, p. 297. BHD, p. 146 (b. 1857). IFN, p. 76 (age 66). SD. "Frederick DeBelleville with Dyreda," *MPW*, 19 Dec 1914, 1689. "Recover from Effects of Accident," *MPW*, 10 Jul 1915, 330.

De Benedetti, Aldo [scenarist/director] (b. Rome, Italy, 13 Aug 1892–19 Jan 1970 [77], Rome, Itlay). AS, p. 297. BHD2, p. 63. JS, p. 123 (in Italian silents from 1920).

De Beranger, Andre [actor] (*né* George André de Berenger, b. Sydney, Australia, 27 Mar 1893–8 Mar 1973 [79]). (Griffith; MGM.) IFN, p. 25 (Beranger). AS, p. 297. Katz, p. 107.

De Biccari, Violet [actress]. No data found. AMD, p. 93. "Violet deBiccari in 'The Battle of Life,'" *MPW*, 16 Dec 1916, 1648.

De Bles, Arthur [scenarist] (b. 1876–19 Jun 1935 [59?], Los Angeles CA). BHD2, p. 63.

De Bodamere, Madame [Mary Pickford's personal attendant/actress]. No data found. (MGM.) "Getting in by the Back Door," *MPS*, 26 Aug 1924, 20–21, 31 (played in *Tess of the d'Urbervilles*, and "every one around the lot is prophesying a brilliant future for her.").

De Bosset, Vera [actress] (b. St. Petersburg, Russia, 25 Dec 1888–17 Sep 1982 [93], New York NY). BHD, p. 146.

De Bray, Alexander [writer/producer]. No data found. AMD, p. 93. "Alexander DeBray," *MPW*, 23 Feb 1918, 1103. "Alexander DeBray," *MPW*, 16 Mar 1918, 1527.

De Bray, Harold [actor] (b. 1874?–31 Oct 1932 [58], Los Angeles CA). "Harold De Bray," *Variety*, 8 Nov 1932. AS, p. 298. BHD1, p. 144. IFN, p. 76.

De Bray, Yvonne Laurence Blanche [actress] (b. Paris, France, 12 May 1887–1 Feb 1954 [66], Paris, France; heart attack [extrait de décès no. 82/1954]). AS, p. 298.

De Briac, Charles (twin brother of **Raymond De Briac**). No data found.

De Briac, Jean [actor] (b. France, 15 Aug 1891–18 Oct 1970 [79], Los Angeles Co. CA). (Fox.) AS, p. 298. BHD1, p. 144 (d. Pasadena CA). IFN, p. 76.

De Briac, Raymond (twin brother of **Charles De Briac**) [actor] (b. France, 15 Aug 1891).

De Brier, Samson [actor] (b. NJ, 18 Mar 1909–1 Apr 1995 [86], Los Angeles CA). BHD1, p. 606 (Debrier). "Samson DeBrier," *CI*, 243 (Sep 1995), 56 (appeared in *Salome*, 1922).

De Brugh, Aimee [actress] (b. Aberdeen, Scotland-d. 2 Apr 1946). BHD, p. 146.

De Brulier, Nigel [actor] (b. Bristol, England, 8 Jul 1877–30 Jan 1948 [70], Los Angeles CA). AS, p. 298. BHD1, p. 144. FFF, p. 207. FSS, p. 88. IFN, p. 76. Truitt, p. 84. William K. Gibbs, "The Master of Make-Up; Nigel De Brulier Has Mastered All Kinds of Characterizations as Well as the Contents of the Make-Up Box. He Has Made Acting a Deep and Profound Study," *MPC*, Feb 1927, 48–49, 74.

Debucourt, Jean [stage/film actor] (*né* Jean Etienne Pelisse, b. Paris, France, 19 Jan 1894–22 Mar 1958 [64], Montgeron, France; leukemia [extrait de décès no. 43/1958]). "Jean Debucourt," *Variety*, 9 Apr 1958, p. 119. AS, p. 309. BHD1, p. 144. IFN, p. 76.

De Camp, Frank [actor] (b. London, England, 1865–18 Dec 1919 [54?], New York NY). BHD, p. 146.

De Canonge, Maurice [actor/director] (b. Toulon, France, 18 Mar 1894–29 Dec 1978 [85], Paris, France). AS, p. 298.

De Cardi, Laura [actress]. No data found. AMD, p. 93. "Josh Binney Makes a Find," *MPW*, 11 May 1918, 837.

De Carlton, George, "The Wonderful Boy Soprano" [stage/film actor/director/general supervisor of Ocean Film Corp.] (b. Boston MA, 30 Jun 1867–15 May 1935 [67], Saranac Lake NY). (The DeCarlton Players, Boston MA; Reliance, ca. 1911; Fox.) "George DeCarlton," *Variety*, 22 May 1935. AMD, p. 93. BHD, p. 146; BHD2, p. 63. "George DeCarlton," *MPW*, 5 Jun 1915, 1607. "Briefs of Biography; A Voice Wasted in Silent Drama," *NYDM*, 7 Jul 1915, 39:1. "DeCarlton Wins Suit," *NYDM*, 13 Nov 1915, 25:1 (won suit against Vaughn Glaser, actor-manager, for $1,287.32. He claimed he was on a 52-week contract to play in *The Grain of Dust;* Glaser denied this. He was with Glaser from 17 Sep 1912 to 1 Feb 1913, "when Glaser closed the show and disbanded the company.").

De Carlton, Grace [actress] (b. Boston MA, 1890-d. Portland ME). "Husband of silent screen actress Grace DeCarlton died March 9 in Portland, Me., after a long illness," *Variety*, 20 Mar 1963. BHD, p. 146.

De Casalis, Jeanne [actress/writer] (b. Basutoland, South Africa, 22 May 1892–19 Aug 1966 [74], London, England). BHD1, p. 144 (b. Lesotho, South Africa). AS, p. 298 (b. 1897). IFN, p. 76 (b. 1897).

De Casseres, Benjamin [author/title writer/scenarist] (descendant of Benedict de Spinoza; b. Philadelphia PA, 3 Apr 1873–6 Dec 1945 [72], New York NY). m. Bio Terrill, 12 Oct 1919. (FP-L, 1921–24; Universal, 1924–25.) "De Casseres Dies; Author, Columnist; Was Editorial Writer for The Mirror—Started Newspaper Career at the Age of 13," *NYT*, 7 Dec 1945, 22:3. AMD, p. 93. BHD2, p. 63 (b. 1883). "Benjamin DeCasseres Doing an Original," *MPW*, 13 Aug 1927, 468.

de Castrejon, Blanca [actress] (b. Mexico, 1916–26 Dec 1969 [53], Mexico City, Mexico). BHD1, p. 144.

Dechamp, Charles [actor] (*né* Emile CharlesFrançois Dechanmps, b. Paris, France, 13 Sep 1882 [extrait de naissance no. 981]–25 Sep 1959 [77], Paris, France [extrait de décès no. 2696/1959]). AS, p. 309.

De Chauveron, Andrée [actress] (b. Paris, France, 5 Sep 1890–9 Jun 1965 [74], Paris, France [extrait de décès no. 17/685]). AS, p. 299.

De Chomón, Segundo [cinematographer/animator/director/producer/special effects] (aka Sogon de Chomón and Segundo Chaumont, b. Teruel, Spain, 18 Oct 1871–2 May 1929 [57], Paris, France). AS, p. 299. JS, p. 124 (in Italian silents from 1912).

Decker, John [actor] (b. San Francisco CA, 8 Nov 1895–7 Jun 1947 [51], Los Angeles CA). AS, p. 309.

Decker, Kathryn Browne [actress] (b. Richmond VA-d. 12 Feb 1919, Colombo, Ceylon). "Kathryn Browne Decker," *Variety*, 21 Feb 1919. AS, p. 309. BHD, p. 146.

Decker, Phelps [film editor] (b. 1886?–5 Feb 1928 [41], New York NY; gas asphyxiation). m. Clarice. (Universal.) "Phelps Decker Dead; Killed by Gas in Apartment—Wife Denies Suicide," *Variety*, 8 Feb 1928. BHD2, p. 63.

Decoin, Henri (father of Didier Decoin) [director/producer/scenarist] (b. Paris, France, 18 Mar 1896–4 Jul 1969 [73], Paris, France). m. (son, Didier Françoise Decoin, b. 13 Mar 1945). AS, p. 309 (b. 1890). BHD2, p. 63.

De Coma, Eddie [actor/stuntman] (b. 1878–30 Jul 1938 [60?]). BHD, p. 146. IFN, p. 76.

De Conde, Syn M. [actor] (*né* Sinesio Mariano de Aguilar, b. Brazil, 14 Jun 1894–28 May 1990 [95], Rio de Janeiro, Brazil). BHD, p. 146. Ragan 2, p. 399.

De Cordoba, Pedro [stage/film actor] (b. New York NY, 28 Sep 1881–16 Sep 1950 [68], Sunland CA; found dead). m. (1) Antoinette Glover (d. 1921); (2) Eleanor M. Nolan, 1928. "Pedro de Cordoba, A Noted Actor, 68; Veteran of Stage and Screen, Star in Shakespearean Roles, Dies at Home on Coast," *NYT*, 18 Sep 1950, 23:3. "Pedro de Cordoba," *Variety*, 20 Sep 1950 (d. 17 Sep, Hollywood CA). AMD, p. 93. AS, p. 299. BHD1, p. 145 (d. LA CA). IFN, p. 76. Truitt, p. 84. "Personal," *NYDM*, 19 May 1915, 5:1 (cover portrait; to appear in *The White Violet*, Universal). "Pedro DeCordoba Joins the Lasky Company," *MPW*, 3 Jul 1915, 46. "DeCordoba in Cast of Second Faversham-Selznick Picture," *MPW*, 5 Jun 1920, 1356. Susan Elizabeth Brady, "The Aristocrat of the Screen, Thumbnail Sketches No. IV; Pedro De Cordoba," *MPC*, Mar 1925, 62, 80.

De Cordova, Leander (brother of **Rudolph De Cordova**) [actor/assistant director] (b. Kingston, Jamaica, West Indies, 5 Dec 1877–19 Sep 1969 [91], London, England). . AMD, p. 93 (b. 1878). AS, p. 299. BHD2, p. 63 (d. LA CA). IFN, p. 77. "DeCordova to Assist with Metro," *MPW,* 15 Apr 1916, 447.

De Cordova, Rienzi [actress]. No data found. AMD, p. 94. "Rienzi DeCordova in 'A Man's Shadow,'" *MPW,* 2 Jan 1915, 63.

De Cordova, Rudolph (brother of **Leander De Cordova**) [stage/film actor/scenarist] (b. Kingston, Jamaica, West Indies, b. 1860?–11 Jan 1941 [81], London, England). m. **Alicia Ramsey**, 14 Sep 1916, NY (d. 1933). (Metro.) "Rudolph DeCordova," *Variety,* 22 Jan 1941. AMD, p. 94. AS, p. 299. BHD, p. 147; BHD2, p. 63. IFN, p. 77. MSBB, p. 1023. SD. "Alicia Ramsey Weds Rudolph DeCordova," *MPW,* 30 Sep 1916, 2127.

De Cordova, Tessie [actress]. No data found. AMD, p. 94. "Picture Playhouse Gets Terriss," *MPW,* 17 Apr 1915, 377.

Decorps, Paul Auguste [cinematographer] (b. Saint-Etienne, France, 9 Dec 1876–29 Nov 1914 [37], France; in combat). AS, p. 309.

De Costa, Leon [scenarist] (b. 1882–10 May 1951 [68?], New York NY). AS, p. 299. BHD2, p. 63.

De Costa, Morris [actor] (*né* Morris Miller, b. 1890?–6 Oct 1957 [67], Phoenixville PA). "Morris Miller," *Variety,* 16 Oct 1957. AS, p. 299. BHD, p. 147. Truitt, p. 84.

De Courcy, Nenette [actress] (*née* Nan Boardman, b. New York NY, 21 Mar 1903–9 Sep 1984 [81], Fallbrook CA). BHD, p. 147.

De Courville, Albert P. [director/producer] (b. London, England, 26 Mar 1887–15 Mar 1960 [72], London, England). AS, p. 299. BHD2, p. 64.

De Croisset, Francis [actor/scenarist] (*né* Franz Wiener, b. Brussels, Belgium, 1877–8 Nov 1937 [60?], Neuilly, France). AS, p. 299 (d. Belgium). BHD2, p. 64.

Decserepy, Arzen [director]. No data found. AMD, p. 94. "To Make 'War of the Worlds,'" *MPW,* 10 Jul 1926, 87.

Deed, André [acrobat/stage/film actor/director] (*né* André Chapais, b. Le Havre, France, 24 Feb 1884–15 Apr 1938 [54], Paris, France). AS, p. 310 (b. 1879). BHD, p. 147 (b. 1879). JS, p. 125 (in Italian films from 1909; "Best known as an acrobat and comedian..."). *The Illustrated History of the Cinema,* consulting ed., David Robinson; ed., Ann Lloyd (NY: Macmillan, 1986), p. 25.

Deeley, Ben [actor] (*né* J. Bernard Deely, b. CA, 22 Jan 1878–23 Sep 1924 [46], Los Angeles CA; double pneumonia). m. Marie Wayne; **Barbara La Marr** (d. 1926). (FBO; Universal.) "Ben Deeley," *Variety,* 1 Oct 1924. AMD, p. 94. AS, p. 310 (d. 26 Sep). BHD, p. 147. IFN, p. 77. Truitt, p. 84. "Deely at Centaur Studios," *MPW,* 24 Jul 1915, 672.

Deen, Jerrie *see* **Dean, Jerrie**

Deer, Diane [actress] (*née* Diane Deering, b. 1894–30 May 1979 [84?], New York NY). AMD, p. 94. BHD, p. 147. "Diana Deer to Play in 'Hurricane Hutch,'" *MPW,* 14 May 1921, 157 (age 19).

Deer, James Young *see* **Young Deer, James**

Deer, John J. [actor] (b. 1861–31 Mar 1940 [79], St. Regis Reservation). BHD, p. 147. IFN, p. 77.

Deery, Jack [actor] (b. Australia, 31 Jul 1893–5 May 1965 [71], Los Angeles Co. CA). BHD1, p. 145.

Deesy, Alfred [actor/director] (b. Hungary, 1877). AS, p. 310. BHD2, p. 64.

De Felice, Carlotta [actress]. No data found. AMD, p. 94. "Carlotta DeFelice," *MPW,* 15 Aug 1914, 939. "Miss Felice Fears for Kinsmen," *MPW,* 22 Aug 1914, 1083.

De Feraudy, Jacques (son of **Maurice De Feraudy**) [actor] (*né* Marie Pierre Jacques de Feraudy, b. Paris, France, 1 Sep 1886 [extrait de naissance no. 993]–5 Feb 1971 [84], Draveil, France). AS, p. 299.

De Feraudy, Maurice "Crainquebille" [actor] (*né* Dominique Marie Maurice de Feraudy, b. Joinville-le-Pont, France, 3 Dec 1859–12 May 1932 [73], Paris, France). AS, p. 299. BHD, p. 147. IFN, p. 77.

Deffenbaugh, Elvo [actor]. No data found. (Southern Sun Corp.) "Spokane's First Picture," *NYDM,* 22 Jul 1914, 24:1 (*When Betty Marries* with Betty Thorpe).

De Ferrari, Gemma [actress] (b. Naples, Italy). JS, p. 126 (in Italian silents from 1912).

De Filippo, Eduardo (brother of **Peppino** and **Tina De Filippo**) [actor/director/scenarist] (*né* Eduardo Passarelli, b. Naples, Italy, 24 May 1900–31 Oct 1984 [84], Rome, Italy). AS, p. 299. BHD2, p. 64.

De Filippo, Peppino (brother of **Eduardo** and **Tina De Filippo**) [actor] (*né* Peppino Passarelli, b. Naples, Italy, 24 Aug 1903–12 Jan 1978 [74], Rome, Italy; heart and respiratory ailments). AS, p. 299.

De Filippo, Tina (sister of **Eduardo** and **Peppino De Filippo**) [actress/scenarist] (*née* Titina Passarelli, b. Naples, Italy, 23 Mar 1898–26 Dec 1963 [65], Rome, Italy). AS, p. 299. BHD2, p. 64.

De Fleuriel, Yvonne [actress/singer] (b. Frosinone, Italy). JS, p.127 (in Italian silents from 1915).

De Foe, Annette [actress] (b. 1889?–6 Aug 1960 [71], Los Angeles CA). AS, p. 299. BHD, p. 147. IFN, p. 77.

De Forest, Hal (father of **Buddy De Sylva**) [actor] (*né* Aloysius Joseph De Sylva, b. Portugal, 1862?–16 Feb 1938 [76], New York NY; heart attack). (Fox.) "Aloysius J. De Sylva (Hal De Forest)," *Variety,* 23 Feb 1938. AS, p. 299. BHD, p. 147. IFN, p. 77.

De Forest, Lee, "The Father of Radio" [inventor] (b. Council Bluffs IA, 26 Aug 1873–30 Jun 1961 [87], Los Angeles CA). m. (1) Lucille Sheardown, 1906—annulled 1907; (2) Nora Stanton Blatch, 14 Feb 1908—div. 1911; (3) Mary Mayo, 23 Dec 1912—div. ca. 1930; (4) **Marie Mosquini**, Oct 1930 (d. 1983). (De forest Phonofilm Co., 1923.) *Father of Radio,* 1950. I.E. Levine, Electronics Pioneer, Lee deForest (1964). (PhD., 1899; applied for patents on the triode [three-element vacuum tube] Audion, 1906.) "Lee De Forest, 87, Radio Pioneer, Dies," *NYT,* 2 Jul 1961, 1:2, 32:2. "Dr. Lee De Forest," *Variety,* 5 Jul 1961. AS, p. 299 (b. 25 Aug). BHD2, p. 64. Katz, p. 319. "Claims to Perfect Talking Pictures; De Forest Says Radio Process Synchroniously [sic] Records Voice With Action on Film; Uses Amplifier in Theatre; Gives Demonstration in Cleveland—Kentucky Man Charges Infringement of 1921 Patent [Lee. A. Collins, Patent 1,366,446, 25 Jan 1921]," *NYT,* 6 Jan 1924, II, 1. Donald DeB. Beaver, "De Forest, Lee," *DAB,* Suppl. 7 (1981), pp. 174–77 (presented the first commercial talking picture in NYC on 12 Apr 1923). His papers are at the DeForest Memorial Archives, Foothill College, Electronics Museum, 12345 El Monte Road, Los Altos CA 94022.

De Forest, Patsy [actress]. No data found. (Lubin.) AMD, p. 94. "Patsey DeForest," *MPW,* 10 Feb 1917, 847. "Patsey DeForest will Appear in Phillipp. Films," *MPW,* 2 Aug 1919, 688.

DeForrest, Charles [actor]. No data found. AMD, p. 94. "New Republic Player," *MPW,* 27 Jan 1912, 298. "Crystal Secures Two New Stars," *MPW,* 21 Mar 1914, 1537. "Charlie DeForrest Joins Crystal," *MPW,* 25 Apr 1914, 528.

De Francesco, Louis [composer] (b. Atessa, Italy, 26 Dec 1886–5 Oct 1974 [77], Northridge CA). AS, p. 300. BHD2, p. 64 (De Franesco).

De Frece, Lauri [actress] (b. Liverpool, England, 1880–25 Aug 1921 [41?], Deauville, France). BHD, p. 147.

De Frietas, Cecil [actor/cinematographer] (b. 1890–6 Dec 1925 [35?], Hawthorne CA). AS, p. 300 (d. 27 Dec). BHD, p. 147; BHD2, p. 64.

De Fuentes, Fernando [director/scenarist] (*né* Fernando de Fuentes Carrau, b. Vera Cruz, Mexico, 13 Dec 1894–4 Jul 1958 [65], Mexico City, Mexico; heart attack). (In Mexican silents from 1931; directed three classics of Mexican cinema: *El compadre Mendoza,* 1933; *Vámonos con Pancho Villa,* 1935; and *Allá en el Rancho Grande,* 1936.) AS, p. 300 (b. 1895). BHD2, p. 64 (b. 1895; d. 1952).

De Gaetano, Alfred [film editor] (b. 1894?–2 May 1958 [64], Los Angeles CA). "Al De Gaetano," *Variety,* 7 May 1958 ("He started in silent pictures."). BHD2, p. 64.

De Garde, Adele [actress]. No data found. (Biograph; Vitagraph; K&E). Hector Ames, "Child Player Becomes Leading Woman," *MPC,* May 1916, 13.

De Gastyne, Marc (brother of Guy de Gastyne) [director/art director] (*né* Marc Benoist, b. Paris, France, 15 Jul 1888–8 Nov 1982 [93], Paris France). "Silent Filmmaker De Gastyne Succumbs in Paris at Age 93," *Variety,* 1 Dec 1982. AS, p. 300. BHD2, p. 64 (b. 1889).

Degli Abbti, Alberto [actor, 1906/director, 1908] (b. Naples, Italy). JS, p. 127 (in Italian films from 1906).

De Grandcourt, G. [publicist]. No data found. AMD, p. 94. "Joins Preferred," *MPW,* 29 Sep 1923, 432.

Degrace, "Sylvette" [actress]. No data found. Rene de la Seine, "Moviettes from Gay Paree," *Paris and Hollywood Screen Secrets Magazine,* Aug 1927, 94.

De Grasse, Joseph (brother of **Sam de Grasse**; uncle of **Robert de Grasse**) [actor/director] (b. Bathurst, New Brunswick, Canada, 4 May 1873 –24 May 1940 [67], Los Angeles CA). m. **Ida May Park**, 1920 (d. 1954). "Joseph De Grasse," *NYT,* 26 May 1940, 35:2 (age 61). "Joseph De Grasse," *Variety,* 29 May 1940. AMD, p. 94. AS, p. 300 (d. Eagle Rock CA). BHD, p. 147; BHD2, p. 64. IFN, p. 77. Katz, p. 319. 1921 Directory, p. 261 (b. France). Truitt, p. 85. "Joseph and Sam DeGrasse at Last Get Together," *MPW,* 29 Sep

1917, 1979. "Tom Ince Engages DeGrasse," *MPW*, 5 Apr 1919, 74.

De Grasse, Robert (nephew of **Joseph** and **Sam de Grasse**) [cinematographer/director] (b. Maplewood NJ, 9 Feb 1900–28 Jan 1971 [70], Newport Beach CA). m. Eva. (RKO.) "Robert De Grasse," *Variety*, 3 Feb 1971. AS, p. 300. BHD2, p. 64. FDY, p. 457. IFN, p. 77. Katz, pp. 319–20.

De Grasse, Sam (brother of **Joseph De Grasse**; uncle of **Robert de Grasse**) [actor] (*né* Samuel Alfred de Grasse, b. Bathurst, New Brunswick, Canada, 20 Jun 1875–29 Nov 1953 [78], Los Angeles CA; heart attack). (Began 1911; Pathé; Ammex; Majestic; Reliance-Majestic; Fine Arts.) "Sam De Grasse," *Variety*, 9 Dec 1953. AMD, p. 94. AS, p. 300. BHD1, p. 146. FSS, p. 88. IFN, p. 77. Truitt, p. 85. "Joe and Sam DeGrasse at Last Get Together," *MPW*, 29 Sep 1917, 1979. George A. Katchmer, "Forgotten Cowboys and Cowgirls—Part XVIII," *CI*, 195 (Sep 1991), C6-C7.

De Gravone, Gabriel [actor] (b. France, 1885). AS, p. 64.

De Gresac, Frederique [scenarist] (b. 1867?–20 Feb 1943 [75], Los Angeles CA). m. Victor Maurel (d. 1923). "Frederique de Gresac," *Variety*, 3 Mar 1943. FDY, p. 423 (Madame De Gresac). AS, p. 300. BHD2, p. 64. SD.

De Grey, Sydney [actor] (b. Unn, England, 16 Jun 1866–30 Jun 1941 [75], Los Angeles Co. CA). AS, p. 300. BHD1, p. 146. IFN, p. 77.

De Guingand, Pierre [actor] (*né* Octave Pierre Deguingand, b. Paris, France, 6 Jun 1885–10 Jun 1964 [79], Versailles, France [extrait de décès no. 639/1964]). AS, p. 300. BHD1, p. 146.

De Haas, Max [director/producer] (b. Amsterdam, Holland, 12 Sep 1899–2 May 1983 [83], Gravenhage, Holland). AS, p. 300. BHD2, p. 64.

De Haven, Carter (father of Gloria and **Carter de Haven, Jr.**) [actor/director/producer] (b. Chicago IL, 5 Oct 1886–20 Jul 1977 [90], Woodland Hills CA). . m. Flora Parker (d. 1950). (Film debut: The College Orphan, Universal, 1915.) "Carter De Haven," *Variety*, 27 Jul 1977. AMD, p. 94. AS, p. 300. BHD1, p. 146; BHD2, p. 64. IFN, p. 77. WWS, p. 286. "DeHaven Directs Comedies," *MPW*, 7 Oct 1916, 86. "The DeHaven's with 'Smiling Bill' Parsons," *MPW*, 25 Jan 1919, 516. "DeHaven Writes for National Film," *MPW*, 15 Feb 1919, 897. "The Carter DeHaven's to Appear in Capitol Comedies," *MPW*, 19 Apr 1919, 375. "DeHaven's to Make for First National a New Series of High Class Comedies," *MPW*, 2 Oct 1920, 626. "DeHaven Is Host to N.Y. Showmen," *MPW*, 30 Sep 1922, 376.

De Haven, Carter, Jr. (son of **Carter De Haven**; brother of Gloria De Haven) [actor/assistant director] (b. New York NY, 23 Dec 1910–1 Mar 1979 [68], Encino CA). . (Chaplin; Columbia; Universal.) "Carter De Haven, Jr.," *Variety*, 7 Mar 1979. BHD2, p. 64.

De Haven, Evelyn [actress: Sennett Bathing Beauty] (*née* Evelyn Byrd, b. 1906?–10 Jan 1990 [83], Los Angeles CA; heart attack). m. **Carter de Haven** (d. 1977). "Evelyn de Haven," *Variety*, 17 Jan 1990. BHD, p. 147.

De Haven, Flora Parker *see* **Parker, Flora**

De Haven, Rose [actress] (b. 1881–23 Jul 1972 [91?], Los Angeles CA). AS, p. 301.

Dehelly, Jean [actor] (b. France, 1896–1964 [68?]). BHD1, p. 146. IFN, p. 77.

De Herain, Pierre [director/scenarist] (*né* Pierre Paul Henri Deherain, b. Avilly-Saint-Leonard, France, 24 Jul 1904–25 Sep 1972 [68], Paris, France). AS, p. 301. BHD2, p. 64 (d. Oct).

De Homs, Juan Canals (actor/director] (b. Spain). (Began in Mexico, 1917; Spanish-language films at MGM.) Waldman, p. 139.

Deibel, Ivy [actress]. No data found. AMD, p. 94. "Ivy Deibel Wins Fox Contest," *MPW*, 26 Jan 1918, 506. "Ivy Deibel Works with June Caprice," *MPW*, 2 Feb 1918, 700.

Deitrich, Theodore C. [publicist/producer]. No data found. AMD, p. 94. "Deitrich Forms New Company," *MPW*, 8 Dec 1917, 1506.

De Jonge, Harry [actor/director] (d. 13 Mar 1927, Chicago IL). AS, p. 301. BHD, p. 147; BHD2, p. 64.

De Kelety, Julia [actress]. No data found. AMD, p. 94. "Primagraf's New Leading Lady," *MPW*, 30 May 1914, 1271.

De Kobra, Maurice [actor/director] (b. France, 1884-Jun 1973 [89?], Paris, France). AS, p. 301. BHD2, p. 65.

De Kock, Hubert [actor] (b. 1863–25 Nov 1941 [78?], Montrose CA). AS, p. 301.

De Kowa, Viktor [actor/director of stage/TV/film/painter/sculptor] (*né* Viktor Paul Karl Kowarzik, b. Hochkirch-bel-Gorlitz, Germany, 8 Mar 1904–8 Apr 1973 [69], Berlin, Germany; cancer). m. **Michiko Tanaka** (d. 1968). "Victor de Kowa," *Variety*, 2 May 1973, p. 71 ("He had, at the time of his death, more than 100 films to his credit."). AS, p. 301. BHD, p. 147. IFN, p. 78.

Delac, Charles [director/producer] (*né* Ben Caled, b. Mascara, Algiers, 2 Jul 1885–14 Jan 1965 [80], Paris, France). AS, p. 312. BHD2, p. 65.

De Lacey, John [or **Jack**] [stage/film actor] (b. New York NY, 1872?–18 Dec 1924 [52], New York NY). (Metro; World; Fox; Artcraft; Universal; Pathé; FP-L.) AS, p. 302. BHD, p. 147. IFN, p. 78. MSBB, p. 1023.

De la Cruz, José [actor] (b. Mexico, 19 Mar 1892–14 Dec 1961 [69], Los Angeles CA). AS, p. 301. BHD1, p. 146 (Joseph De La Cruz). IFN, p. 78. George Katchmer, "Remembering the Great Silents," *CI*, 207 (Sep 1992), 42 (Juan De la Cruz).

De la Cruz, Juan [actor] (b. Copenhagen, Denmark, 4 Jun 1881–12 Nov 1953 [72], Orange Co. CA). AMD, p. 94. AS, p. 301 (José de la Cruz). BHD1, p. 147. IFN, p. 78. "Morosco Signs Juan de la Cruz," *MPW*, 24 Jul 1915, 640.

De Lacy, Philipe [child actor/director] (*né* Andreas? [adopted by Mrs. Edith De Lacy], b. Nancy, France, 25 Jul 1917–29 Jul 1995 [78], Carmel CA; cancer). (Began 1921.) "Philippe DeLacey [obituary]," *CI*, 261 (Mar 1997), 58. AS, p. 302. BHD1, p. 147; BHD2, p. 65. FSS, p. 89. MH, p. 106. Harry Carr, "Bombed into the Movies," *Classic*, Sep 1923, 26, 82.

De Lacy, Ralph [set designer] (d. 20 Jun 1978, Santa Cruz Co. CA). BHD2, p. 65.

De Lacy, Robert [film editor/director]. No data found. AMD, p. 94. "DeLacy Signed as Editor," *MPW*, 13 Sep 1924, 122. "To Direct Next Tyler Opus," *MPW*, 24 Oct 1925, 629. "Robert DeLacy," *MPW*, 17 Sep 1927, 166. "DeLacy Ready for 'Big Stuff,'" *MPW*, 24 Dec 1927, 25.

De Lacy, Van Epps John [actor/director] (b. 1879–15 Sep 1960 [81?], Teaneck NJ). AS, p. 302.

de la Falaise y de la Codraye, Henri [director/producer] (b. St. Cyr, France, 11 Feb 1898–10 Apr 1972 [74]). (Pathé; MGM; Paramount; Universal.) m. **Gloria Swanson** (d. 1983); **Constance Bennett** (d. 1965). BHD2, p. 65. Waldman, p. 102 (directed French-language films at RKO, 1931).

De la Maza, Armando Vargas [director/producer] (b. Mexico, 5 May 1890–16 Nov 1941 [51], Mexico City, Mexico). AS, p. 301.

De la Mothe, Leon [actor/director] (*né* Leon Kent, b. New Orleans LA, 26 Dec 1880–12 Jun 1943 [62], Woodland Hills CA). (Universal.) "Leon de la Mothe," *Variety*, 23 Jun 1943 (age 63). AMD, p. 192 (Leon Kent). AS, p. 301 (b. 28 Dec); p. 603 (Leon Kent). BHD1, p. 299; BHD2, p. 65. IFN, p. 163. Truitt, p. 85. "Kent Returns to the Universal," *MPW*, 5 Oct 1918, 124. George A. Katchmer, "Forgotten Cowboys and Cowgirls—XVII," *CI*, 194 (Aug 1991), 47.

De la Motte, Axel [actor] (b. Sweden, 1879–1937 [58?], Sweden). AS, p. 301.

De la Motte, Marguerite [actress] (b. Duluth MN, 22 Jun 1902–10 Mar 1950 [47], San Francisco CA; cerebral thrombosis). m. **John Bowers** (d. 1936). "Miss de la Motte, 47, Star of Silent Films," *NYT*, 11 Mar 1950, 15:2. "Marguerite de la Motte," *Variety*, 15 Mar 1950 (age 47). AMD, p. 94. AS, p. 301. BHD1, p. 147. FFF, p. 128. FSS, p. 89. IFN, p. 78. Katz, pp. 321–22. MH, p. 106 (b. 1903). Truitt, p. 85. WWS, p. 244. "Metro Star in Tragic Auto Accident," *MPW*, 10 Jan 1920, 233 (on 23 Dec 1919). "Marguerite de la Motte Signs with Frothingham for Long Term," *MPW*, 10 Sep 1921, 202. "An Ideal Flapper," *MPW*, 10 Mar 1923, 235. "Marguerite de la Motte Is Signed to Support LaRocque," *MPW*, 2 Jan 1926, 81. "Marguerite de la Motte," *MPW*, 20 Aug 1927, 516. Harry Carr, "Lady Luck and Marguerite de la Motte," *MPC*, Sep 1924, 38, 80.

De Landa, Juan [actor/singer] (*né* Juan Pison Pagoaga, b. Motrigo, Spain, 27 Jan 1894–17 Feb 1968 [74], Motrico, Spain). AS, p. 302.

De Lane, William [producer] (b. England, 1900–1964 [64?], England). AS, p. 302.

Delaney, Charles [actor] (b. New York NY, 9 Aug 1892–31 Aug 1959 [67], Los Angeles CA). "Charles Delaney," *Variety*, 2 Sep 1959. BHD1, p. 147. IFN, p. 78. Truitt, p. 85. Phil Lawlor, "It's the Old Blarney Game," *MPC*, Jan 1928, 58, 80.

Delaney, Jere A. [actor/film editor] (b. 1887?–2 Jan 1954 [66], Forest Hills NY). m. Mary O'Moore. "Jere A. Delaney," *Variety*, 13 Jan 1954. BHD1, p. 147. IFN, p. 78.

Delaney, Leo Patrick [stage/film actor] (b. Swanton VT, 15 Mar 1879–4 Feb 1920 [40], New York NY; pneumonia).AMD, p. 95. BHD, p. 148 (b. 1885). IFN, p. 78 (age 38). SD. "Leo Delaney Resigns from Vitagraph," *MPW*, 9 May 1914, 802. "Gossip of the Studios; Leo Delaney," *NYDM*, 15 Jul 1914, 23:1 (spent six years with the Kirk LaShelle stage company). "Leo Delaney Joins Raver's Apollo," *MPW*, 27 Jan 1917, 537. "Leo Delaney Dies After Illness of But Two Days," *MPW*, 21 Feb 1920, 1208 (age 38).

Delano, Edith Barnard [novelist/short story writer] (*née* Edith Barnard, b. WA, 1875?–7 Sep 1946 [71], Old Deerfield MA). "Edith Bernard Delano; Novelist and Short-Story Writer Dies in Old Deerfield, Mass.," *NYT*, 9 Sep 1946, 9:2 (She wrote *Rags*, "which provided a screen play for Mary Pickford. Hazel Dawn appeared in the film version of another of her works."). "Edith Barnard Delano," *Variety,* 164. 11 Sep 1946, 63:2. BHD2, p. 65. WWWA.

Delano, Gwen [actress] (b. 1882?–20 Nov 1954 [72], Los Angeles CA). "Gwen Delano," *Variety,* 24 Nov 1954. BHD1, p. 147. IFN, p. 78. Truitt, p. 66.

De Lanti [or Di Lanti], Stella [actress]. No data found.

De la Parelle, M. [director]. No data found. AMD, p. 95. "Masterpiece Film Men," *MPW,* 10 Oct 1914, 171.

De Lara, Antonio [director/scenarist] (*né* Antonio de Lara Gavilan, b. Jaen, Spain, 22 Sep 1896–4 Jan 1978 [81], Madrid, Spain). AS, p. 302.

De Lara, Mario [director] (*né* Mario de Lara Sainti-Banez, b. Mexico, 10 Jun 1896–5 Jul 1942 [46], Mexico City, Mexico). AS, p. 302. BHD2, p. 65.

Delargo, Celia [actress] (b. 1901–3 Oct 1927 [26], San Francisco CA). BHD, p. 148). IFN, p. 78.

Delaro, Hattie [stage/film actress] (b. Brooklyn NY, 1861?–18 Apr 1941 [80], New York NY). m. William S. Barnes. (Biograph; K&E; Vitagraph; Eclair; Reliance; Fox; FP-L.) "Hattie Delaro," *Variety,* 23 Apr 1941. AMD, p. 95. BHD, p. 148. IFN, p. 78. SD. MSBB, p. 1030. "Hattie Delaro in 'April Folly' Cast," *MPW,* 4 Jun 1919, 1675.

Delavan, Fred[erick] **M**[ontague], **Jr.** [cinematographer] (b. Chicago IL, 1886). AMD, p. 95. BHD2, p. 65. "Fox Cameraman Gets Pictures of Thrilling Alligator Hunt," *MPW,* 3 Jul 1920, 109.

De la Vega, Alfredo Gomez [actor] (b. Mexico, 24 Feb 1897–15 Jan 1958 [60], Mexico City, Mexico). AS, p. 302.

De la Vega, Alfredo Lasso [producer] (b. Mexico, 1882–7 Sep 1982 [100?], Mexico City, Mexico). AS, p. 302.

De Lay, Mel [actor/director/producer] (b. 1900–3 May 1947 [47?], near Saugus CA; heart attack). "Mel de Lay," *Variety,* 5 Mar 1947 (actor since 1923). AS, p. 302. BHD, p. 148; BHD2, p. 65. Truitt, p. 86.

Del Colle, Ubaldo Maria [director/actor] (b. Rome, Italy, 27 Jun 1883). JS, p. 129 (in Italian silents from 1905).

De Leon, Walter [actor/scenarist] (b. Oakland CA, 1884?–1 Aug 1947 [63], Los Angeles CA). "Walter De Leon," *Variety,* 6 Aug 1947. AS, p. 302. BHD2, p. 65. IFN, p. 78.

De Lespine, Edgena [actress] (b. Houston TX). (Reliance.) AMD, p. 95. "In the Catskills with Reliance," *MPW,* 24 Aug 1912, 748–51.

Del Giudice, Filippo [actor/producer] (b. Trani, Italy, 26 Mar 1892–31 Dec 1962 [70]). BHD2, p. 65.

Delight, June [actress] (*née* June Delight Canoles, b. Rochester NY, 16 Jun 1898–3 Oct 1975 [77], Carmel GA; cancer). AS, p. 313 (d. Carmel LA). BHD1, p. 606. IFN, p. 78.

De Liguoro, Giuseppe (father of **Wladimiro De Liguoro**) [actor/director] (*né* Giuseppe Dei Conti de Liguoro Presicce, b. Naples, Italy, 10 Jan 1869–19 Mar 1944 [75], Rome, Italy). AS, p. 302. BHD, p. 148. IFN, p. 78. JS, p. 131 (in Italian silents from 1909).

De Liguoro, Rina [actress] (*née* Elena Caterina Catardi na del Liguoro, b. De Liguero, b. Florence, Italy, 24 Jul 1892–7 Apr 1966 [73], Rome, Italy). m. Count **Wladimiro De Liguoro**. (Film debut: Messalina, 1923). "Rina de Liguoro," *Variety,* 4 May 1966. AS, p. 302. BHD1, p. 148. IFN, p. 78. JS, p. 130 (in Italian silents from 1920).

De Liguoro, Wladimiro (son of **Giuseppe De Liguoro**) [director/cinematographer/actor] (*né* Wladimiro dei Conti de Liguoro Presicce, b. Naples, Italy, 11 Oct 1893). m. Elena Caterina Catardi (**Rina De Liguoro**, d. 1966). AS, p. 303. JS, p. 130 (in Italian silents from 1912).

De Lima, Charles Abinon [actor/writer] (b. Brooklyn NY, 13 Jul 1872–7 Aug 1954 [82], Nice, France [Death Certificate No. 2183]). m. Florence Buchard. "Charles DeLima," *Variety,* 11 Aug 1954. AS, p. 303. BHD, p. 148 (d. 8 Aug).

De Limour, Jean [director/scenarist] (b. Vannes, France, 1887?–5 Jun 1976 [89], Paris, France). AS, p. 303 (b. 1896). BHD, p. 148; BHD2, p. 65. FDY, p. 423. IFN, p. 78. Truitt 1983.

De Linsky, Victor [actor: Adolphe Menjou's stand-in] (b. Moscow, Russia, 18 Mar 1883–9 May 1951 [68], Los Angeles CA; following auto accident). "Victor A. DeLinsky," *Variety,* 16 May 1951. AMD, p. 95. BHD1, p. 148. IFN, p. 78. "Russo-Japanese War Hero Now an Actor," *MPW,* 29 Apr 1916, 811.

De Lint, Fritz [actor]. No data found. AMD, p. 95. "Fritz deLint, New Metro Lead," *MPW,* 27 Nov 1915, 1634.

Dell, Dorothy [actress] (*née* Dorothy Goff, b. Hattiesburg MS, 30 Jan 1914–8 Jun 1934 [20], Pasadena CA; car accident). "Dorothy Dell," *Variety,* 12 Jun 1934. BHD1, p. 148. IFN, p. 79.

Dell, Rupert L. [actor] (b. Oxfordshire, England, 1881–25 Oct 1945 [64?], Los Angeles CA). BHD, p. 148. IFN, p. 79.

Della Garisenda, Gea [operette singer/actress] (*née* Alessandra Drudi, b. Carignola, Italy, 24 Sep 1878). JS, p. 130 (in Italian silents from 1916).

Della Valle, Umberto [cinematographer] (b. Florence, Italy, 15 Oct 1889). JS, p. 130 (in Italian silents from 1912; first film was in color).

Delluc, Louis [director/scenarist] (b. France, 14 Oct 1890–22 Mar 1924 [33], Paris, France). BHD2, p. 65.

Del Mar, Claire Eloise [actress] (b. 1901?–10 Jan 1959 [58], Carmel CA; murdered by stabbing). m. **Hal Mohr**, 1926–29 (d. 1974). "Clair del Mar," *Variety,* 21 Jan 1959. BHD, p. 148. IFN, p. 79. Truitt, p. 86.

Delmar, Eddie [actor] (b. Detroit MI, 17 Aug 1885–1 Mar 1944 [58], Los Angeles CA). BHD1, p. 148.

Delmar, Kenny (b. Boston MA, 1911–14 Jul 1984 [73?], Stamford CT). BHD, p. 148.

Delmar, Thomas [actor]. No data found. (Alliance Film Corp.) George Katchmer, "Forgotten Cowboys and Cowgirls—Part XVIII," *CI,* 195 (Sep 1991), C8.

Delmont, Gene [actor] (b. 28 Mar 1895–20 Sep 1987 [92], Memphis TN). BHD1, p. 606.

Delmont, Joseph [art director/actor/director] (*né* Charles Pyck, b. Loiwein, Austria, 8 May 1873–12 Mar 1935 [61], Bad Pystyan, Germany). AMD, p. 95. "An Interesting Character," *MPW,* 14 Mar 1914, 1393. Vittorio Martinelli, "Kino-Lieblinge," *Griffithiana,* 38/39 (Oct 1990), 46.

Delmore, Herbert [stage/film actor/artists' model] (b. NY). (World.) MSBB, p. 1023.

Delmore, Ralph [actor] (b. New York NY, 18 Dec 1853–21 Nov 1923 [69], New York NY). m. (1) Angy Griffith (d. 1888); (2) Gertrude Daws (d. 1916). (Selig.) AMD, p. 95. BHD, p. 148. IFN, p. 79. SD. Truitt 1983. "Ralph Delmore Joins the Selig Forces," *MPS,* 10 Oct 1913, 30.

De Lorenzo, Salvatore *see* **Higan, Kid (Society Kid Hogan)**

De Lorez, Claire [actress] (*née* Claire Schulz, b. France, 1900). Data from André Siscot.

Del Re, Fernando [actor] (b. Naples, Italy–d. Jan 1919). JS, p. 132 (in Italian silents from 1914).

Del Riccio, Lorenzo [inventer]. No data found. AMD, p. 95. "Magnascope for 'Wings' Effects," *MPW,* 9 Jul 1927, 97.

Del Rio, Dolores (second cousin of **Ramon Novarro**) [actress: Wampas Star, 1926] (*née* Lolita Dolores de Martinez Asunsolo Lopez Negrette, b. Durango, Mexico, 3 Aug 1905–11 Apr 1983 [77], Newport Beach CA; heart attack). m. (1) writer Jaime Del Rio—div. (d. Dec 1928, Berlin); (2) **Cedric Gibbons**, 1930–41 (d. 1960). Dorothy J. Gaiter, "Dolores Del Rio, 77, Is Dead; Film Star in U.S. and Mexico," *NYT,* 13 Apr 1983, D23:1. BHD1, p. 148 (b. 1904). FSS, p. 89. JS, p. 132. "Dolores Del Rio," *Variety,* 13 Apr 1983. AMD, p. 95. HCH, p. 65. "Carewe Signs Dolores Del Rio and His Daughter Yvonne," *MPW,* 5 Dec 1925, 428. Dwinelle Benthall, "Success with a Cup or Two of Tea; Dolores del Rio Played Hostess to Picture People and Became a Movie Heroine Overnight," *MPC,* Mar 1927, 48–49, 81. "Miss Del Rio Picked," *MPW,* 26 Mar 1927, 270. "Dolores Del Rio," *MPW,* 2 Apr 1927, 485. "Believe It or Not, But They Get That Way," *MPW,* 3 Sep 1927, 23. "Dolores Del Rio Plans Vacation in Mexico City," *MPW,* 5 Nov 1927, 42. Elisabeth Goldbeck, "The Lowdown on Divorce; Dolores del Rio Endorses an Old American Custom," *MPC,* Aug 1928, 23, 72–73 ("And my divorce has made me free to dedicate my life to my work."). Gladys Hall, "Dolores Del Rio Isn't Beaten Yet; Just as she found greater happiness in her second marriage, the Mexican beauty may find greater fame in her screen comeback. She looks too happy to fail," *Movie Classic,* Sep 1931, 24–25, 73. Allan R. Ellenberger, *Ramon Novarro; A Biography of the Silent Film Idol, 1899–1968; With a Filmography* (Jefferson NC: McFarland & Co. Inc., 1999) pp. 130–31 (When police raided Communist headquarters in Sacramento CA in Aug 1934, they found the names of Ramon Novarro and Del Rio among the effects of Caroline Decker, secretary of the Cannery and Agricultural Workers' Union. Cedric Gibbons vehemently denied that his wife was a Communist. "'It's too silly for words,' Del Rio added.").

Delroy, Irene [stage/film actress] (b. Bloomington IL, 1898). Ragan 2, p. 409. WWIT, p. 523.

Del Ruth, Hampton (brother of **Roy Del Ruth**) [scenarist/producer/director] (b. DE, 7 Sep 1879–15 May 1958 [78], Woodland Hills CA). m. Alta Crowin (**Alta Allen**), 1920; **Helen Carlyle** (d. 1933). "Hampton Del Ruth," *NYT,* 18 May 1958, 87:1. "Hampton Del Ruth," *Variety,* 21 May 1958 (d. Los Angeles CA, age 77). AMD, p. 95. BHD2, p. 65 (b. 1887). FDY, p. 423. IFN, p. 79. Lowrey, p. 44. 1921 Directory, p. 261 (b. Venice, Italy, 1888). Hampton Del Ruth, "Sympathetic Comedy to Rule Laughter's Realm," *MPW,* 9 Jun 1917, 1593. "Del Ruth Leaves Sennett Studio," *MPW,* 3 Aug 1918, 687. "Hampton Del Ruth with Lehrman," *MPW,* 2 Nov 1918, 607. "Hampton Del Ruth Weds," *MPW,* 18 Dec 1920, 889. "Hampton Del Ruth Now Independent Producer," *MPW,* 5 Aug 1922, 409. "Del Ruth with Chadwick," *MPW,* 29 Aug 1925, 930. "Hampton Del Ruth to Direct for Sax," *MPW,* 20 Aug 1927, 534.

Del Ruth, Roy (brother of **Hampton Del Ruth**) [scenarist/film/TV director/producer/scenarist] (b. Philadelphia PA, 18 Oct 1893–27 Apr 1961 [67], Sherman Oaks CA; heart attack). m. (1) Olive Simons (**Olive Dale**), 14 Mar 1921—div. 1947; (2) Winifred "**Winnie**" Reeves **Lightner**, 6 Aug 1947 (d. 1971). (Sennett; Fox; WB; MGM; TC-F; Paramount.) "Roy Del Ruth, 66, Directed Movies; Scenarist for Mack Sennett Dead—Wrote for Stars," *NYT,* 28 Apr 1961, 31:2. "Roy Del Ruth," *Variety,* 3 May 1961 (age 66). AMD, p. 95. BHD2, p. 65 (b. 1895; d. LA CA). IFN, p. 79 (b. 1893). Mario Salmi, "Roy Del Ruth," Film Dope, Sep 1976. G.F. Goodwin, "Del Ruth, Roy," DAB, Supp. 7 (1981), pp. 177–78 ("If not an artist, Del Ruth was a diligent and skilled craftsman created by the studio system of the 1930's."). "Wedding in Filmland," *MPW,* 2 Apr 1921, 477. "Roy DelRuth Joins Mermaid," *MPW,* 27 Jan 1923, 386. "DelRuth to Direct Features," *MPW,* 10 Jan 1925, 172. "DelRuth of the Fourth Estate, Now Star Director," *MPW,* 1 Jan 1927, 49. "DelRuth Given New Contract; with Warners," *MPW,* 2 May 1927, 834. "Roy DelRuth," *MPW,* 9 Jul 1927, 86.

Delschaft, Maly [actress] (b. Hamburg, Germany, 4 Dec 1898–20 Aug 1995 [96], Berlin, Germany). Obituary, *Der Katholische Filmdienst,* Sep 1995 (in *Variety,* 1925, and other films). BHD1, p. 148.

Delson, John J. [actor]. (Lubin.) No data found.

Deltry, William [actor] (*né* William Blackwell, d. 8 Oct 1924, London, England). BHD, p. 148. IFN, p. 79.

De Luca, Giuseppe [actor] (b. Rome, Italy, 25 Dec 1876–26 Aug 1950 [73], New York NY). BHD1, p. 148.

Delva, Yvonne [actress]. No data found. AMD, p. 95. "Yvonne Delva, from France, Is 'Thirteenth Chair' Star," *MPW,* 6 Sep 1919, 1485.

Delvair, Jeanne [actress] (b. Paris, France, 10 Oct 1877–13 Jan 1949 [71], France). BHD1, p. 606.

Del Val, Jean [actor] (b. Paris, France, 17 Nov 1891–13 Mar 1975 [83], Pacific Palisades CA; heart attack). "Jean Del Val," *Variety,* 9 Apr 1975. BHD1, p. 148. IFN, p. 79. Esther Steele, "Permittez Moi, Monsieur Jean Gauthier!," *MPC,* Jul 1921, 42, 77, 81.

Delys, Kay [stage/vaudeville/film actress] (b. London, England, 28 Sep 1899–15 Aug 1974 [74], West Covina CA).

Delysia, Alice [actress] (b. Paris, France, 3 Mar 1889–9 Feb 1979 [89], Brighton, England). BHD1, p. 148.

De Main, Gordon [actor] (*né* Gordon de Main Wood, b. IA, 28 Sep 1886–5 Mar 1954 [67]). AS, p. 303. BHD1, p. 149 (*né* De Woods). IFN, p. 79.

De Mar, Carrie [vaudevillian/actress/singer] (b. 1 Apr 1876–23 Feb 1963 [86], Cold Springs NY; stroke). m. songwriter/playwright Joe Hart (*né* Joseph Hart Boudrow). "Carrie De Mar," *Variety,* 20 Mar 1963, p. 87 (age 87; "...entered a Catholic order in 1950."). BHD, p. 148. "May Return to Stage; Carrie de Mar Offered $2,000 to Appear at Opening of Atlantic City Garden Theater," *NYDM,* 1 Apr 1914, 25:2.

De Mrguenat, Jean [actor/director] (b. Paris, France, 2 May 1893–1956 [63?]). AS, p. 303. BHD2, p. 65.

Demarest, William [actor] (b. St. Paul MN, 27 Feb 1892–27 Dec 1983 [91], Palm Springs CA). m. (1) Estelle Collette; Lucille Thayer. (Film debut: *Finger Prints,* 1927; Paramount.) Todd McCarthy, "William Demarest Dead at 91; 70 Years as Character Support," *Variety,* 4 Jan 1984 (b. 17 Feb; in Finger Prints, WB, 1927; discovered Jane Wyman and Ellen Drew). AMD, p. 95. AS, p. 315 (d. 28 Dec). BHD1, p. 149. FSS, p. 90. Katz, p. 325. "Demarest Signed," *MPW,* 1 Jan 1927, 36. "Warner's New Comedy Find," *MPW,* 28 May 1927, 256.

De Marguenat, Jean [actor] (b. Paris, France, 2 May 1893–1956 [63?], France). AS, p. 303.

De Mark, Bert [actor]. No data found. George Katchmer, "Forgotten Cowboys and Cowgirls—Part XVIII," *CI,* 195 (Sep 1991), C8.

De Marney, Derrick (brother of **Terrence De Marney**) [actor] (b. London, England, 21 Sep 1906–18 Feb 1978 [71], London, England). AS, p. 303. BHD1, p. 149; BHD2, p. 66.

De Marney, Terrence (brother of **Derrick De Marney**) [scenarist] (b. London, England, 1 Mar 1909–25 May 1971 [62], London, England; accident in the subway). AS, p. 303. BHD2, p. 66.

Demarsan, Maurice [scenarist] (b. 1863–Apr 1929 [66?]). BHD2, p. 66.

De Max, Edouard [stage/film actor] (b. Jassy, Romania, 14 Feb 1869–28 Oct 1924 [55], Paris, France). "M. De Max," *Variety,* 5 Nov 1924, p. 40. AS, p. 303. BHD, p. 148.

De Me, Shirley [actress] (b. 1898–27 Jul 1940 [42?], Petoskey MI). BHD, p. 148.

Demeny, Georges [inventor] (b. Douai, France, 12 Jun 1850–20 Dec 1917 [67], Paris, France). AS, p. 315 (b. 12 May; d. 26 Dec). BHD2, p. 66.

Demetrio, Anna [actress] (b. Rome, Italy, 8 Nov 1892- 8 Nov 1959 [67], San Mateo CA). BHD, p. 148.

De Mille, Beatrice M. (mother of **Cecil B.** and **William C. de Mille**; grandmother of **Cecilia De Mille**) (*née* Mathilda Beatrice Samuel, d. 8 Oct 1923, Hollywood CA). "Mrs. Beatrice M. DeMille," *Variety,* 11 Oct 1923. AS, p. 303.

De Mille, Cecil B[lount] (son of **Beatrice M. DeMille**; brother of **William C. de Mille**; father of **Cecilia De Mille**) [stage/film actor/director/producer] (b. Ashfield MA, 12 Aug 1881–21 Jan 1959 [77], Los Angeles CA; heart attack). m. **Constance Adams** (d. 1960). *Autobiography* (1959). Sumiko Higashi, *Cecil B. DeMille and American Culture: The Silent Era* (Univ. of California Press, 1997). (Lasky; Artcraft; Paramount.) "Cecil DeMille, 77, Pioneer of Movies, Dead in Hollywood," *NYT,* 22 Jan 1959, 1:4, 31:2; "DeMille Service Attended by 500; Short Religious Ceremony Held in Hollywood Church for Producer-Director," *NYT,* 24 Jan 1959, 19:5; "DeMille's Will Filed; Daughter Cecilia Gets Most of His Large Estate," *NYT,* 28 Jan 1959, 31:1. "DeMille: 'Founder' of Hollywood; Pioneered 'Rembrandt Lighting' When Sun Failed to Shine—Long, Unique, Creative Career," *Variety,* 28 Jan 1959. AMD, p. 95. AS, p. 303. BHD1, p. 149; BHD2, p. 66. IFN, p. 79. Lowrey, p. 46. MSBB, p. 1044. Truitt, p. 86. "DeMille 'Talks Shop,'" *MPW,* 29 Aug 1914, 1224. "Cecil B. De Mille," *NYDM,* 17 Mar 1915, 31:1. "Cecil B. DeMille," *MPW,* 27 Mar 1915, 1938. "Cecil B. DeMille at Work," *MPW,* 10 Jul 1915, 239–40. "Cecil DeMille Heads Morosco-Pallas," *MPW,* 11 Nov 1916, 875. "DeMille to Produce Cohan Subject," *MPW,* 23 Dec 1916, 1787. Cecil B. DeMille, "Photodrama a New Art," *MPW,* 21 Jul 1917, 374. Neil G. Caward, "Screen Gossip," *Picture-Play Magazine,* Feb 1917, 111 (he and his brother William became interested in "a new invention which they expect will make talking pictures practical." The record and the projector were to be operated by the man in the booth enabling him to synchronize the sound. They advised a Mr. Newman to invest in the new apparatus, which was brought to New York from California" and is being perfected at the present time. We sincerely hope that this project will prove successful, and solve the long-standing mystery of talking movies."). "Lasky Chiefs Working on Color Process," *MPW,* 9 Feb 1918, 832. Cecil B. DeMille, "DeMille Tells Why He Makes Stills," *MPW,* 19 Apr 1919, 370. "Cecil B. DeMille Renews Contract with Famous Players-Lasky; Rejects Big Offers," *MPW,* 22 May 1920, 1098. "Deny Absurd Story of DeMille-Glaum Marriage," *MPW,* 11 Dec 1920, 704. "Era of All-Star Picture Is Here to Stay, Believes Cecil DeMille," *MPW,* 14 May 1921, 197. "Made Vice-President," *MPW,* 11 Nov 1922, 141 (Federal Trust and Savings Bank, Hollywood). Grace Kingsley, "Cecil de Mille—Director and Daddy," *MW,* 12 May 1923, 18, 29. "Cecil DeMille Heads Bank," *MPW,* 4 Apr 1925, 439 (Culver City Commercial and Savings Bank). Barrett C. Kiesling, "The Boy Who Lived in the Haunted House," *MPC,* Nov 1925, 29, 68. "DeMille Sees New Screen Favorites," *MPW,* 19 Dec 1925, 656. C.K. Barrett, "'They Kick Themselves Out of the Movies...,' Says Cecil B. De Mille, and He Proceeds to Tell Tales Out of School About Several Prominent Movie Stars," *MM,* Dec 1925, 47, 120–21. Joseph Jackson, "Things I Have Seen," *Paris and Hollywood,* Oct 1926, 33 ("...Cecil has attained the dignity of a capital 'D' in his name."). "DeMille in Unique Deal with Players," *MPW,* 20 Nov 1926, 144. "DeMille Joins Hays Body," *MPW,* 18 Jun 1927, 475. "DeMille Is Spending $400,000 on Studio," *MPW,* 10 Sep 1927, 85. "Suratt Action Stirs DeMille; $1,000,000 Suit Names Many," *MPW,* 17 Sep 1927, 168. "Flashes from Filmland," *Paris and Hollywood Screen Secrets Magazine,* Oct 1927, 10 (to stand trial on 28 Nov "for alleged participation in the Julian Petroleum stock pool case. De Mille, charged with netting $12,800 usurious profit on a loan to the Julian corporation, has entered a plea of not guilty."). Burr C. Cook, "Cecil B. De Mille, A Super-Showman," *Cinema Arts,* Dec 1927, 19, 46. "DeMille to Defy to Hays Story Policy, Report," *MPW,* 31 Dec 1927, 5. Dunham Thorp, "Shouting from the Bathtubs; Cecil B. DeMille Thinks They Make Splendid Pulpits," *MPC,* Jun 1929, 23, 76 (he claimed to have an Unuttered Message for a future film).

De Mille, Cecilia (daughter of **Cecil B. De Mille**; grandaughter of **Beatrice M. De Mille**; niece of **William C. de Mille**) [actress] (b. Orange

NJ, 5 Oct 1908–23 Jun 1984 [75], Los Angeles CA). AMD, p. 97. AS, p. 303. BHD, p. 148. (In *The Squaw Man* and other films.) "Cecilia De Mille Harper," *NYT,* 25 Jun 1984, D13:6. "Cecil B. DeMille's Daughter Makes Hasty Screen Debut," *MPW,* 25 Jul 1925, 453.

De Mille, William C[hurchill] (son of **Beatrice M. De Mille**; brother of **Cecil B. De Mille**; uncle of **Cecilia De Mille**) [playwright/film director/producer] (b. Washington DC, 25 Jul 1878– 8 Mar 1955 [76], Playa del Rey CA). m. (1) Anna George, 30 Mar 1903 (2 children); (2) **Clara Beranger** (d. 1956). (Lasky.) "William C. De Mille," *Variety,* 9 Mar 1955. AMD, p. 97. AS, p. 303. BHD2, p. 66. IFN, p. 79. Katz, pp. 326–27. MSBB, p. 1044. SD. Truitt, p. 86. "The Outlook for a Native Drama as Reflected in the Works of One Week—What De Mille, [Clyde] Fitch and [John W.] Broadhurst Have Achieved—Criticising the Critics," *NYT,* 5 Feb 1905, IV, 2:1 ("William C. De Mille is to be congratulated upon achieving a hearing with a play that reveals him as something more than a promising young American dramatist, for 'Strongheart,' despite the fact that it is not without flaws, indicates the possession of an exceptional knowledge of dramatic values and uusual ability in craftsmanship on the part of its author." The play starred Edeson, Percita West, and Edmund Breeze.). "William C. DeMille," *MPW,* 3 Oct 1914, 48. "William C. DeMille Talks on the Drama," *MPW,* 9 Oct 1915, 258–59. "Scenario Department Again Expanded," *MPW,* 21 Oct 1916, 412. "William DeMille Adopts a Traveling Schedule," *MPW,* 4 Mar 1922, 43. Tom Doyle, "Whittling His Way In," *MPC,* Sep 1924, 66,82- 83. Herbert Cruikshank, "de Mille with a Small de; For Most People's Opinions, William C. Doesn't Give a Tinker's Damn," *MPC,* pr 1929, 35, 76–77. "William DeMille Cuts Titles," *MPW,* 7 Mar 1925, 79 (Men and Women: no titles after first thousand feet of film). "William DeMille Joins Cecil to Direct Leatrice Joy," *MPW,* 10 Apr 1926, 4. "Returns to DeMille," *MPW,* 28 Aug 1926, 2 (to brother's studio). June Lee, "Dan Cupid's Bulletin Board," *Paris and Hollywood Screen Secrets,* Oct 1927, 35 (to divorce George. "The couple have been living apart for over a year, and the customary charge of desertion has been made.").

De Miollis, François [scenarist] (aka Frédéric Mauzens, *né* Comte François de Miollis, b. Paris, France, 1873–26 Apr 1934 [61?], Los Angeles CA). AS, p. 303. BHD2, p. 66 (d. 25 Apr).

De Mond, Albert [title writer/scenarist/cinematographer] (b. 7 May 1901–20 Feb 1973 [71], Los Angeles CA). BHD2, p. 66. FDY, pp. 423, , 443, 457.

De Moos, Charles [inventor] (b. France, 1885–28 Oct 1959 [74?], Brunswick NJ). AS, p. 304. BHD2, p. 66.

De More, Harry C. [actor]. No data found. (Universal.)

De Morlhon, Camille de la Valette [director] (b. Paris, France, 1869–1952 [83?], France). AS, p. 304.

De Mott, John A. [actor: Our Gang comedies/producer] (b. 1912–19 Mar 1975 [62?], San Diego CA; heart failure). (Paramount.) "John A. De Mott," *Variety,* 26 Mar 1978, p. 79. AS, p. 304. BHD, p. 148.

Dempsey, Clifford [actor] (b. Winstead CT, 1865–4 Sep 1938 [73?], Highlands NJ). AS, p. 315.

Dempsey, Jack, "The Manassa Mauler" [boxer/actor] (*né* William Harrison Dempsey, b. Manassa CO, 24 Jun 1895–31 May 1983 [87], New York NY). m. (1) Maxine Gates; (2) **Estelle Taylor** (d. 1958); (3) Hannah Williams—div. 1943; (4) Deanna Piatelli, 1958. Nathaniel S. Fletcher, *Jack Dempsey* (New Rochelle NY: Arlington House, 1972); Jack Dempsey with Barbara Piattelli Dempsey, *Dempsey* (NY: Harper & Row, 1977); Randy Roberts, *Jack Dempsey, the Manassa Mauler* (Baton Rouge LA: LA State University Press, 1979). "Jack Dempsey Is Dead Here at 87; Heavyweight Champion in 1920's [4 Jul 1919 to 23 Sep 1926]," *NYT,* 1 Jun 1983, 1:1; Red Smith, "Jack Dempsey, 87, Is Dead; Boxing Champion of 1920's," B4; "Jack Dempsey Buried on Long Island," 5 Jun 1983, V, 3:6; "Dempsey Estate Under $250,000," 7 Jun 1983, II, 13:5 (painting by James Montgomery Flagg to Smithsonian Institution). AMD, p. 97. AS, p. 315. BHD1, p. 149. "Jack Dempsey Will Be Movie Star," *MPW,* 22 Nov 1919, 433. "Giebler Looks Over Jack Dempsey and Declares Him Regular Fellow," *MPW,* 10 Jan 1920, 227. "Jack Dempsey Did Not Evade Selective Draft, Jury Finds," *MPW,* 26 Jun 1920, 1714. "Jack Dempsey's Acquittal Is Signal for Serial Booking," *MPW,* 3 Jul 1920, 615. "Pathé Gets Exclusive Rights to Picture of Dempsey in Training," *MPW,* 14 May 1921, 180. "Winifred Westover Has Day Off to Visit Champion Jack Dempsey," *MPW,* 25 Jun 1921, 838. "Winik Insists He Has Foreign Rights to Quimby's Dempsey Figh Pictures," *MPW,* 20 Aug 1921, 784. Grace Kingsley, "Jack Dempsey, Heavyweight Champion, Doffs Ring Togs and Dons Movie Make-Up," *MW,* 24 May 1924, 8–9, 30. Gladys Hall and Adele Whitely Fletcher, "We Interview Jack Dempsey and Estelle Taylor," *MW,* 13 Jun 1925, 9–10, 43. James F. Taggart, "Rebuilding Noses for the Screen; Film Luminaries Face Knife in Plastic Surgery to Hide Blemishes and Obtain Larger Contracts," *Paris and Hollywood Screen Secrets,* Oct 1927, 41–43 (photos show his acquired "sheik" nose. The article lists many others who had their noses redone.). Eleanore Wilson, "I Owe It All to You, Babe," *MPC,* Oct 1927, 40, 79, 85. Carol Johnston, "Mister and Missus; Impressions of Mr. Ginsberg, the Manassa Mauler, and of His Wife, Estelle Dempsey," *MPC,* Sep 1928, 51, 87. Joan Standish, "Is Jack Dempsey Broke?; Manassa Mauler Is Said to Have Created Huge Trust Funds for Himself. But All Estelle Taylor Asks Is His Purchase of Their $100,000 Hollywood Home," *Movie Classic,* Nov 1931, 43. "News From the Dailies," *Variety,* 4 Nov 1936, 62:1 ("Indictments against restaurant racketeers reveal that Jack Dempsey paid $285, the Brass Rail was shaken down for $6,050, Hollywood Restaurant coughed up $750 and Steuben Taverns topped with $17,000. Total take is about $2,000,000 annually."). Alan Brock, "Jack Dempsey: Outside the Ring," *CI,* 214 (Apr 1993), 8.

Dempsey, Pauline [actress] (b. 1867–Sep 1923 [55], Harlem NY). AS, p. 315. BHD, p. 148. IFN, p. 79.

Dempsey, Thomas [actor] (b. Philadelphia PA, 20 Jan 1862–6 Oct 1947 [85], Los Angeles CA). (Sennett.) "Thomas Dempsey," *Variety,* 15 Oct 1947. AS, p. 315 (b. 1868). BHD1, p. 149 (b. 1868). IFN, p. 79 (b. 1868). Truitt, p. 86.

Dempster, Carol [actress] (b. Duluth MN, 8 Dec 1901–1 Feb 1991 [89], La Jolla CA). "Carol Dempster," *Variety,* 4 Mar 1991, p. 70 (b. Duluth). "Carol Dempster [obituary]," CI, 190 (Apr 1991), 60 (b. Duluth, 1902). AMD, p. 97. AS, p. 315. BHD, p. 149. FFF, p. 140 (b. Santa Maria CA, 16 Jan 1902). MH, p. 107 (b. Santa Marie, 16 Jan 1902). WWS, p. 228. "Carol Dempster," WBO2, pp. 192–93 (b. Duluth, 1902). "A New Griffith Star," *MPW,* 30 Nov 1918, 937. Ruth Mabrey, "'It Isn't the Cost of Clothes that Counts!' Says Carol Dempster," *MW,* 29 Mar 1924, 11. "The Case of Carol Dempster; Harry Carr Says She Will Never Achieve the Heights Until She Plays Sophisticated Rôles," *MPC,* Dec 1925, 38–39, 70. Faith Service, "The Girl Who Is Herself," *MM,* 38, 88–89. Gladys Hall, "The Gentle Gypsy; Carol Dempster Has the Soul of a Vagabond...," *MPC,* Oct 1926, 53, 86, 88. John McGee, "Carol Dempster's Gift to MoMA," *CFC,* 46 (Spring, 1975), 48–49 (rare photos).

Dempster, Hugh [actor] (b. London, England, 3 Aug 1900–30 Apr 1987 [86], Chicago IL). AS, p. 315. BHD1, p. 149.

De Napierkowska, Stacia [actress] (b. Paris, France, 19 Sep 1896–11 May 1945 [48], Paris, France). AS, p. 304.

De Navelle, Jean [actress]. No data found. AMD, p. 97. "New Famous Players Actress," *MPW,* 2 Oct 1926, 281.

De Nevers, Lucille [scenarist]. No data found. FDY, p. 423.

Denham, Reginald [stage/film director/scenarist] (b. London, England, 10 Jan 1894–4 Feb 1983 [89], Englewood NJ; apoplexy). m. Moyna McIldowie (**Moyna MacGill**; d. 1975). AS, p. 315. BHD2, p. 66.

Denege, Blanche [actress] (née Jeanne Céleste Antoinette Guy, b. 11 Aug 1876 [extrait de naissance no. 1115/1876]-13 Nov 1957 [81], Paris, France). AS, p. 315.

Denes, Oszkar [actor] (b. Magyarkeszi, Hungary, 8 May 1894–2 Jul 1950 [56], Italy). AS, p. 315.

Denham, Reginald [director/scenarist] (b. London, England, 10 Jan 1894–4 Feb 1983 [89], Englewood NJ; apoplexy). AS, p. 315. BHD2, p. 66.

Denig, Lynde [publicist] (d. 24 Sep 1938). "Lynde Denig," *Variety,* 28 Sep 1938, p. 62. AMD, p. 97. "Lynde Denig Leaves Wid's to Be a Goldwyn Publicist," *MPW,* 26 Jul 1919, 498. "Lynde Denig Resigns," *MPW,* 17 Feb 1923, 640. "Denig Addresses Collegians," *MPW,* 28 Feb 1925, 876 (Union College Syracuse NY, 18 Feb 1925; First National publicity manager).

Denis-D'Ines (father of Pierre Denis-D'Ines) [actor] (*né* Joseph Victor Octave Denis, b. Paris, France, 1 Sep 1885–25 Oct 1968 [83], Paris, France). m. (son, Pierre, b. 4 Jan 1927). AS, p. 316.

Denison, Edwin [actor] (b. 1862?–26 Jan 1928 [65]). AS, p. 316. BHD, p. 149. IFN, p. 79.

D'Ennery, Guy [actor] (b. CA, 4 Jun 1884–17 Oct 1978 [94], Alameda Co. CA). BHD1, p. 150 (d. Oakland CA).

Dennis, Amy Leah [stage/film actress] (b. Wyoming Valley PA, 1901?). (Selig.) AMD, p. 97. "Amy Leah Dennis," *MPW,* 9 Jun 1917, 1620 (age 16). "Amy Leah Dennis," *MPW,* 4 Aug 1917, 784. Al Ray, "Before the Stars Shone," *Picture-Play Masgazine,* Sep 1917, 92. "Amy Leah Dennis," *MPW,* 19 Jan 1918, 368.

Dennis, Crystal B. [actress] (b. KS, 15 May 1893–15 Dec 1973 [80], Los Angeles Co. CA). AS, p. 316. BHD, p. 149.

Dennis, Eddie [actor]. No data found. AMD, p. 97. "Eddie Dennis," *MPW,* 12 Mar 1927, 101.

Dennis, Nadine [actress] (b. 2 Dec 1896–11 Aug 1979 [82], Studio City CA). AS, p. 316 (d. Riverside CA). BHD1, p. 150.

Denniston, Reynolds [actor[(b. Dumedin, New Zealand, 1880–29 Jan 1943 [62?], New York NY). AS, p. 316.

Denny, Barbara [actress] (b. New York NY, 15 Aug 1916–5 Sep 1978 [62], Los Angeles CA). BHD1, p. 150.

Denny, Malcolm (brother of **Reginald Denny**) [actor]. No data found.

Denny, Orrin B. [studio man] (b. Louisville KY, 14 Mar 1882–6 Aug 1969 [87], Oakland CA). BHD2, p. 66.

Denny, Reginald (brother of **Malcolm Denny**) [actor] (*né* Reginald Leigh Daymore, b. Richmond, Surrey, England, 20 Nov 1891–16 Jun 1967 [75], Surrey, England; cerebral hemorrhage). m. (1) Irene "Renee" Haisman—div. 1928; Isobel (Bubbles) Steiffel, Nov? 1928; Betsy Lee. "Reginald Denny Is Dead at 75; Debonair Film and Stage Actor," *NYT,* 18 Jun 1967, 76:1; "Service for Denny Scheduled," *NYT,* 22 Jun 1967, 39:3. "Reginald Denny," *Variety,* 21 Jun 1967. AMD, p. 97. AS, p. 316. BHD1, p. 150 (b. 21 Nov). FFF, p. 103. FSS, p. 91. HCH, p. 23. GK, pp. 220–34. IFN, p. 80. Katz, p. 329. MH, p. 107. SD. Truitt, pp. 86–87. "Reginald Denny Has Had an Adventurous Career," *MPW,* 19 Jul 1919, 362. "Denny Wins Own Production Unit," *MPW,* 14 Jul 1923, 166. "Reginald Denny Hurt," *MPW,* 27 Oct 1923, 727. "Denny Recovering," *MPW,* 10 Nov 1923, p. 220. "Nails Denny Rumor," *MPW,* 2 May 1925, 32. "Reginald Denny," *MPW,* 15 Aug 1925, 753. Dorothy Spensley, "The Fall Guy; Is Reginald Denny going to win Wally Reid's place in the heart of the fans?," *Photoplay Magazine,* Jun 1926, 35, 132. Don Eddy, "Reg the Regular; It Speaks Volumes for a Man's Character When He Is Known by His Nickname...," *MPC,* Sep 1926, 48–49, 78, 83. Edwin Gallinagh, "Why Reginald Denny Prefers Brunettes," *Paris and Hollywood,* Oct 1926, 35–37 ("The principal reason why Denny prefers brunettes in his pictures is because he has learned, after careful observation, that dark-haried womenn are far more popular than their blonde sisters as film stars.... But the fact that Reginald Denny prefers brunettes as leading women should not be taken too seriously by his blonde haired admirers for Mr. Denny has a charming blonde haired wife in his Hollywood home."). "Reginald Denny Writes a Story for the Films," *MPW,* 6 Nov 1926, 29. Geo. H. Wilson, "A 'Typical American' Who Is British; Reginald Denny Believes in Living, Working, and Playing at Breakneck Speed," *Cinema Arts,* Nov 1926, 24–25, 47. "Reginald Denny," *MPW,* 27 Nov 1926, 209. "Denny Advanced to Super Picture Class by Laemmle," *MPW,* 14 May 1927, 115. "Reginald Denny," *MPW,* 4 Jun 1927, 333. "Denny's Separate?," *MPW,* 22 Oct 1927, 484 (from Haisman). "Denny—Seiter Reported Out," *MPW,* 31 Dec 1927, 25. Dorothy Manners, "Reggy Spank; Bubbles Leave Nasty Old Salad Alone and Drink Her Nice Milk," *MPC,* Oct 1928, 55, 73, 79 ("She's just surrounded by protection—and it's [sic] last name is Denny."). George A. Katchmer, "Reginald Denny; Subtle Comedian," *CI,* 131 (May 1986), 13–16. Richard E. Braff, "An Index to the Films of Reginald Denny," *CI,* 186 (Dec 1990), C8 *et passim.*

Dent, James [prop man] (b. 1888–28 Sep 1936 [48?], Savannah GA). BHD2, p. 66.

Dent, Josephine [actress] (b. England-d. 18 Aug 1978). BHD1, p. 150.

Dent, Maurice Arthur [producer] (b. 18 Dec 1887–25 Jun 1956 [68], London, England; coronary thrombosis). AS, p. 316. BHD2, p. 66.

Dent, Vernon [actor/scenarist] (b. San Jose CA, 16 Feb 1895–5 Nov 1963 [68], Los Angeles CA; coronary thrombosis). (Began 1919.) "Vernon Dent," *Variety,* 13 Nov 1963. AS, p. 316. BHD1, p. 150; BHD2, p. 66 (d. 4 Nov). FSS, p. 92. IFN, p. 80. O&W, pp. 208–212. Truitt, p. 87. Ted Okuda and Ed Watz, "Always in the Foreground—Vernon Dent," *CFC,* 52 (Fall, 1976), 52–53 (b. 1894; went blind in 1954).

Dentler, Marion [actress] (*née* Mary Ann Dentler, b. 24 Feb 1892–14 Dec 1988 [96], Kingston NY). AS, p. 316 (Mary Dentler). BHD, p. 149.

Denton, Frank [actor] (b. Louth, Lincolnshire, England, 1878–23 Feb 1945 [66?], Flauden, Hertfordshire, England). BHD, p. 149.

Denton, George [actor] (b. 1865–12 Mar 1918 [52?], New York NY; accidental asphyxiation). AS, p. 317. BHD, p. 149.

De Padua, Tramullas Antonio [producer] (b. Spain, 1879–15 Sep 1961 [82?], Stiges, Spain). AS, p. 304.

De Palma, Ralph [actor] (b. Italy, 1883–31 Mar 1956 [73?], So. Pasadena CA). BHD1, p. 607.

De Pesa, Joseph A. [publicist]. No data found. AMD, p. 98. "Joseph A. DePesa," *MPW,* XXIV, 24 Apr 1915, 544.

Depew, Ernest "Hap" [cameraman] (b. Brushton NY, 30 Mar 1887–11 Apr 1940 [53], Los Angeles CA; heart attack). "Ernest Depew," *Variety,* 17 Apr 1940. BHD2, p. 66. FDY, p. 457 (has an entry for both Ernest and Hap Depew).

De Pew, Joseph D. [actor] (b. Harrison NJ, 11 Jul 1912–30 Oct 1988 [76], Escondido CA). BHD1, p. 150.

De Pomes, Félix [actor/director] (b. Barcelona, Spain, 5 Feb 1889–17 Jul 1969 [80], Spain). AS, p. 304.

Depp, Harry [actor] (b. St. Louis MO, 22 Feb 1883–31 Mar 1957 [74], Los Angeles CA). "Harry Depp," *Variety,* 3 Apr 1957 (age 71). AMD, p. 98. AS, p. 317 (b. MS). BHD1, p. 150. IFN, p. 80. Truitt, p. 87 (b. 1886). "Harry Depp with Strand-Mutuals," *MPW,* 5 Oct 1918, 124.

Deppe, Hans Johannes Carl Otto [actor/director] (b. Berlin, Germany, 12 Nov 1897–23 Sep 1969, Berlin, Germany). AS, p. 317. BHD2, p. 67.

De Putti, Lya [film/stage actress] (*née* Amalya de Putti de Hoyos, b. Vesce, Hungary, 10 Jan 1899–27 Nov 1931 [32], New York NY [Death Certificate No. 27390]), from pneumonia and blood poisoning that resulted after a chicken bone lodged in her throat on 19 Nov was removed). Peter Hozog and Romano Tozzi, *Lya de Putti: "Loving Life and Not Fearing Death"* (NY: Corvin, 1993). "Chicken Bone Proves Fatal to Lya de Putti," *Variety,* 1 Dec 1931. "Cinema's Loss; Lya de Putti Is Dead," *Wisconsin News* [Milwaukee], 27 Nov 1931. AMD, p. 98. AS, p. 304. BHD, p. 149 (b. 1896). IFN, p. 80 (b. 1900). Katz, p. 330 (b. Vesce, Hungary). Truitt, p. 87 (b. 1901). "Idols of Berlin," *MPC,* Feb 1926, 40 (photos). "DePutti Here," *MPW,* 6 Mar 1926, 1. "DePutti Under Knife," *MPW,* 20 Mar 1926, 3. Heinrich Fraenkel, "The Toast of Berlin; Lya de Putti, the Famous Hungarian Screen Beauty, Is Now in America," *MPC,* May 1926, 18–19, 73. "Sign Lya DePutti," *MPW,* 17 Jul 1926, 3. "Lya Joins P.D.C.; Miss Murray and M-G-M in Break," *MPW,* 8 Jan 1927, 95. "With DeMille," *MPW,* 5 Mar 1927, 25. Faith Service, "Lya Goes Pollyanna; Why the De Putti Is Called a Vampire Is Nobody's Business. She Truly Believes in Healthy Slumber, Marriage and Picnics for Two," *MPC,* Mar 1927, 38–39, 84. "Lya DePutti," *MPW,* 28 May 1927, 256. George Marshall, "The Queen's English; An Interview with Lya de Putti," *Screenland,* Oct 1927, 20–21, 92, 94–95. "DePutti for 'U' Film," *MPW,* 24 Dec 1927, 12. Carol Johnston, "Domesticating De Putti; The Savage Siren of Variety Is More Tractable—and Attractive," *MPC,* Nov 1928, 51, 84.

Der Abrahamian, Arousiak Haskashian [actress] (b. Ankara, Turkey, 1890–2 Jul 1973 [83?], Philadelphia PA). AS, p. 317.

De Ravenne, Arthur [actor] (b. Nice, France, 13 May 1903–18 Sep 1962 [59], Los Angeles CA). BHD1, p. 150.

De Ravenne, Charles [actor] (b. Nice, France, 5 Apr 1917–5 Apr 1977 [60], Los Angeles CA). BHD1, p. 150.

De Ravenne, Charline Marie [actress] (b. Nice, France, 13 May 1882–8 May 1962 [79], Woodland Hills CA). AS, p. 304 (d. France). BHD1, p. 151.

De Ravenne, Raymond [actor] (b. 1904–14 Oct 1950 [46?], Los Angeles CA). AS, p. 305. BHD1, p. 151.

Derba, Mimi [actress] (*née* Maria Hermina Perez de Leon, b. Mexico, 8 May 1894–14 Jul 1953 [59], Mexico City, Mexico; pulmonary embolism). AS, p. 317. BHD1, p. 151.

De Recat, Emile [costumer]. No data found. AMD, p. 98. "Emile DeRecat, Authority on Costumes, Making Short Comedy-Drama in Chicago," *MPW,* 9 Oct 1920, 797.

De Remer, Rubye [stage/film actress] (*née* Ruby Burkhardt, b. Denver CO, 9 Jan 1892–18 Mar 1984 [92], Beverly Hills CA). m. Ben Throop. (Film debut: *The Auction Block,* 1917; Ivan; Rex; Edgar Lewis Prods.; Rex Beach.) "Rubye de Remer," *Variety,* 25 Apr 1984. AMD, p. 98. AS, p. 305 (b. 1895). BHD1, p. 151. FFF, p. 206. MH, p. 107. MSBB, p. 1034. SD. Slide, p. 159. "Two Noted Players for Metro's 'Pals First,'" *MPW,* 3 Aug 1918, 703. "Rubye DeRemer Re-Engaged," *MPW,* 7 Sep 1918, 1402. "Rubye DeRemer Signs Contract with World Film," *MPW,* 7 Jun 1919, 1462. "Niebuhr Signs Rubye DeRemer," *MPW,* 13 Sep 1919, 1678. "Paul Helleu [French artist] Calls Rubye DeRemer America's Most Beautiful Woman," *MPW,* 18 Dec 1920, 883. T. Howard Kelly, "How a Rich Young American Coal Baron [Ben Throop] Won the Heart of a Beautiful Screen Star," *MW,* 3 May 1924, 4–5. Regina Cannon, "Why I Married a Rich Man; Screen favorite who has just returned from abroad the wife of a miltimillionaire tells why she chose a wealthy husband," *MW,* 21 Jun 1924, 3, 30.

De Rieux, Max [actor/director] (b. Paris, France, 1898–12 Mar 1963 [65?], Nice, France). AS, p 305.

De Riso, Camillo [director/actor] (b. Naples, Italy, 20 Nov 1859–2 Apr 1924 [64], Rome, Italy). AS, p. 305. BHD, p. 149. JS, p. 136 (in Italian silents from 1913).

Dermoz, Germaine [actress] (*née* Germaine Deluermoz, b. Paris, France, 30 Jul 1888–6 Nov 1966 [78], Paris, France). AS, p. 318.

De Roberti, Lydia [actress] (*née* Lidi Bonelli, b. Turin, Italy). JS, p. 136 (in Italian films from 1908).

De Roche, Charles [actor/director] (*né* Charles d'Antier de Rochefort, b. Port Vendres, southern France, 7 Jul 1879–2 Feb 1952 [72], Paris, France). "Charles de Rochefort," *Variety,* 6 Feb 1952. AMD, p. 98. BHD, p. 149 (b. 1880). FFF, p. 246 (b. 1893). IFN, p. 80. MH, p. 107 (b. 1893). Truitt, p. 87. "Charles DeRoche in Paramount's 'Spanish Jade,'" *MPW,* LIV, 14 Jan 1922, 170. "Charles DeRoche, French Actor, to Star in Paramount Films," *MPW,* 18 Nov 1922, 246.

De Rochefort, Charles d'Authier [actor/scenarist/director] (b. Port-Vendres, France, 7 Jul 1887–1 Feb 1952 [64], Paris, France). AS, p. 305.

De Rosas, Enrique [actor] (b. Buenos Aires, Argentina, 14 Jul 1888–20 Jan 1948 [59], Ituzaingo, Argentina). AS, p. 305.

De Rosselli, Rex [actor/director] (b. KY, 1876–21 Jul 1941 [65?], East St. Louis IL). AMD, p. 98. BHD, p. 149; BHD2, p. 67. "Death Takes Rosselli's Sister," *MPW,* 26 Feb 1916, 1304. George Katchmer, "Remembering the Great Silents," *CI,* 207 (Sep 1992), 42. M.G. "Bud" Norris, *The Tom Mix Book.*

De Rossi, Camillo [director/writer/actor] (d. Jul 1953, Rome, Italy). JS, p. 137 (in Italian films from 1916).

D'Errico, Corrado [director] (b. Rome, Italy, 19 May 1902–3 Sep 1941 [39], Rome, Italy). AS, p. 278. JS, p. 137 (in Italian silents from 1927).

Derson, Ann [actress] (b. England). (Eaco Films.) "Gossip of the Studios," *NYDM,* 7 Oct 1914, 27:2.

De Rue, Carmen Fay [actress] (aka "Baby DeRue," b. Pueblo CO, 1908–28 Sep 1986 [78], No. Hollywood CA; heart attack). (Began 1913.) "Carmen DeRue," *NYT,* 3 Oct 1986, D18:6. "Carmen DeRue [Mrs. Carmen Schrott]," *Variety,* 8 Oct 1986. AS, p. 305. BHD, p. 149. 1921 Directory, p. 247 (b. 1908). F.E. Hasty, "The Children Are Promoted," *NYDM,* 8 Sep 1915, 37:2 (age 9). Luther Hancock, "Baby DeRue and Her Dad," *CI,* 134 (Aug 1986), 36–37.

De Rue, Eugene [actor/editor/director] (b. Pueblo CO, 21 Aug 1885–29 Sep 1985 [100], Woodland Hills CA). m. Grace. . Wrote unpublished "Silents Were Golden." "Eugene DeRue," *Variety,* 9 Oct 1985. AMD, p. 98. BHD, p. 149; BHD2, p. 67. "Engages DeRue," *MPW,* 3 Mar 1923, 89.

De Ruelle, Emile [film editor/actor/assistant director] (b. St. Louis MO, 24 Dec 1880–14 Sep 1948 [67], Woodland Hills CA). BHD2, p. 67.

De Ruiz, Nicholas [stage and film actor] (b. Santa Barbara CA, 1868–21 Jun 1959 [90?], Los Angeles CA). BHD1, p. 607. Hal K. Wells, "Quick-Lunch Route to Fame," *MPC,* Mar 1926, 55, 81. George Katchmer, "Remembering the Great Silents," *CI,* 207 (Sep 1992), 42.

Derwent, Clarence (brother of **Elfrida Derwent**) [actor] (b. London, England, 23 Mar 1884–6 Aug 1959 [75], New York NY [Death Certificate Index No. 17409; M.E. Case No. 6493; age 74]). "Clarence Derwent," *Variety,* 12 Aug 1959. AS, p. 318. BHD1, p. 151. IFN, p. 80.

Derwent, Elfrida (sister of **Clarence Derwent**) [actress] (b. London, England, 1886–5 Jul 1958 [72?], Islip, LI NY). AS, p. 318.

De Saint Girons, Henry [actor] (b. Paris, France, 15 Jul 1896). AS, p. 305.

De Sano, Marcel [director] (*né* Marcel Dragugeanu, b. Rumania, 10 May 1897–1939 [42?], France). m. **Arlette Marchal** (d. 1984). AMD, p. 98. AS, p. 305 (b. 18 May). BHD2, p. 67 (b. 18 May). "Schulberg Signs Marcel DeSano to Make Series of Special Films," *MPW,* 6 Jun 1925, 679. "Marcel DeSano Signs New Contract with B.P. Schulberg," *MPW,* 22 Aug 1925, 838. "Schulberg Releases DeSano," *MPW,* 26 Sep 1925, 344 (due to ill health). "DeSano Signed," *MPW,* 9 Oct 1926, 342. "Goldwyn Signs DeSano," *MPW,* 5 Mar 1927, 11.

De Sax, Guillaume [actor] (*né* Guillaume Henri Robert de Segur Lamoignon, b. Paris, France, 23 Dec 1889–6 Nov 1945 [55], Paris, France [extrait de naissance no. SN/16.1945]). AS, p. 306.

Descant, Cecilia [actress/scenarist] (b. 19 Dec 1885–3 Mar 1973 [87], Los Angeles CA). BHD2, p. 67.

Descours, Georges [producer] (b. Lyon, France, 26 Jul 1889). AS, p. 319.

De Segurola, Andréas [actor/vocal instructor] (*né* Count Andreas Perello de Segurola, b. Madrid, Spain, 27 Mar 1874–23 Jan 1953 [78], Barcelona, Spain). "Andreas de Segurola," *Variety,* 28 Jan 1953. AMD, p. 98. AS, p. 306 (b. Valencia, Spain). BHD1, p. 151 (b. Valencia, Spain). IFN, p. 80. Truitt, p. 87. "Andreas DeSegurola Cast for Role in M-G-M Film," *MPW,* 1 Oct 1927, 287.

Desfassiaux, Maurice [cinematographer] (*né* Henri Maurice desfassiaux, b. Paris, France, 1 Feb 1866–22 Dec 1956 [90], Deuil-la-Barre, France [extrait de décès no. 116/1956]). AS, p. 319.

Desfis, Angelo [actor] (b. Greece, 11 Dec 1888–27 Jul 1950 [61], Los Angeles CA). "Angelo Desfis," *Variety,* 2 Aug 1950 (He "appeared in 110 motion pictures, both silent and talkers"; age 62.) AS, p. 319. BHD1, p. 151. IFN, p. 80. Truitt, p. 87.

Desfontaines, Henri [actor] (b. 1878–7 Jan 1931 [52?], Paris, France). AS, p. 317 (b. 1885). BHD2, p. 67.

Deshon, Florence [actress] (*née* Florence Hanks, b. Tacoma WA, 1894?–4 Feb 1922 [27], New York NY [Death Certificate No. 3748; accidental illuminant gas poisoning]). "Actress Dies of Gas Poison; Found Unconscious in Her Apartment with Window Open," *NYT,* 5 Feb 1922, 3:5 (age 28). AMD, p. 98. AS, p. 319. BHD, p. 149. IFN, p. 80 (age 28). Joyce Milton, *Tramp; The Life of Charlie Chaplin* (NY: Harper Collins, 1996), pp. 156–57. "Florence Deshon Joins Goldwyn Repertory Company," *MPW,* 26 Jul 1919, 535. Deshon's affair with Charlie Chaplin (and simultaneously with Max Eastman) is recounted in Joyce Milton, *Tramp; The Life of Charlie Chaplin* (NY: Harper Collins, 1996); the author states that Deshon was 29 years old when she died, and that her death was a suicide (p. 204).

Deshon, Frank [actor] (b. 1858–28 Dec 1918 [60?], So. Pasadena CA). BHD, p. 149.

De Shon, Vila Sabra [actress] (b. 1850–20 Sep 1917 [67?], Brooklyn NY). (Eclair). AS, p. 306.

De Sica, Vittorio Dominico Stanislo Gaetano Sorano [film/TV actor/writer/director] (father of Christian and Manuel De Sica) (b. Sora, Italy, 7 Jul 1901–13 Nov 1974 [73], Neuilly-sur-Seine, France; after surgery for removal of cysts from his lungs [extrait de décès no. 667/1974]). m. (1) **Giuditta Rissoni,** 1937 (d. 1977; sons, actor Christian De Sica, and composer Manuel De Sica); (2) Maria Mercader, 1968. (First film, 1931; first direction, *Twenty-Four Roses;* AA for *Bicycle Thief,* 1949; 4 AAs, in 1946, 1947, 1949, and 1971). "Vittorio De Sica Dies; Actor Came to Renown as Director," *Variety,* 20 Nov 1974, p. 63. AS, p. 306. BHD1, p. 151; BHD2, p. 67 (b. Sera, Italy). JS, p. 138 (in Italian silents from 1918); Giuditta Rissone, p. 381 (b. Genoa, Italy, 28 Aug 1895; in Italian films from 1932 to 1963).

De Sicilia, Gustavo Sáenz [director/producer/scenarist] (b. Mexico). (In Mexican silents from 1923.)

De Silva, Fred [actor] (*né* Fred Lancaster, b. Lisbon, Portugal, 7 Feb 1885–16 Feb 1929 [44], Norwalk CT). "Fred De Silva (Fred Lancaster)," *Variety,* 6 Mar 1929 (d. 24 Feb, age 52). AS, p. 306 (d. LA CA). BHD, p. 149. IFN, p. 80. George A. Katchmer, "Forgotten Cowboys and Cowgirls—Part XVIII," *CI,* 195 (Sep 1991), C8-C9.

De Simone, Ugo [director/producer/actor]. No data found. JS, p. 140 (in Italian silents from 1915).

Desjardins, Maxime [actress] (b. Auxerre, France, 17 Sep 1861–1 Oct 1936 [75], Venice, Italy). AS, p. 317. BHD1, p. 152.

Deslys, Gaby [stage/film actress] (*née* Marie-Elsie-Gabrielle Caire, b. Marseilles, France, 4 Nov 1881–11 Feb 1920 [38], Paris, France; throat malady; interred at Marseilles). m. **Harry Pilcer** (d. 1961). James Gardiner, *Gaby Deslys; A Fatal Attraction* (London: Sidgwick & Jackson, 1986). (Film debut: *Her Triumph,* FP-L, 1915; Pathé.) "Gaby Deslys dies in Paris, February 11, of throat trouble which followed influenza," *Variety,* 20 Feb 1920 (age 36). AMD, p. 98. AS, p. 317. BHD, p. 149 (b. 4 Sep). IFN, p. 80. MSBB, p. 1034. Truitt, p. 87. "In Favor of Gaby; Cleveland Court Enjoins Gertrude Hoffman from Giving Imitation of Deslys," *NYDM,* 4 Feb 1914, 7:4 (imitations described as "improper, unbecoming burlesque"). "Famous Players Engage Gaby Deslys," *MPW,* 30 May 1914, 1239. "Gaby Deslys Nearly Drowned," *NYDM,* 22 Jul 1914, 7:4 (Deslys, Pilcer, Max Linder and four others were on a landing stage at Varenne-St. Hilaire [where Linder had a home] when it collapsed on 15 Jul. They were celebrating Bastille Day, 14 Jul. "All were quickly rescued."). "Gaby Deslys at Work for Famous Players," *MPW,* 15 Aug 1914, 975. "Funeral Service [13 Feb] for Gaby Held in Paris; Famous Pearls Left to Her Mother and Sister; All Were Remembered," *LA Times,* 14 Feb 1920, I, p. 4 (weighed 70 pounds when she died from the grippe and pneumonia. Hary Pilcer to receive a handsome set of diamonds. "Gaby's father, who was angry at his daughter for her stage career, and who never saw her perform, attended the funeral, having wired forgiveness just before she died.").

Deslys, Kay [actress] (b. London, England, 28 Sep 1899–15 Aug 1974 [74], West Covina CA). BHD1, p. 152.

d'Esme, Jean [director/scenarist] (*né* Jean d'Esmenard, b. Shanghai, China, 15 Sep 1883–1966 [83?], Paris, France). AS, p. 278.

Desmond, Ethel [actress] (b. 1873–5 Feb 1949 [76?], San Bernardino CA). AS, p. 317.

Desmond, Lucille (sister of **William Desmond**) [actress] (b. 1894?–20 Nov 1936 [42],

Los Angeles CA). "Lucille Desmond," *Variety,* 2 Dec 1936. AS, p. 317. BHD, p. 150. IFN, p. 80.

Desmond, Marcella [actress]. No data found. m. **Alf Goulding**, ca. Jul 1920 (d. 1972). A.H. Giebler, "Los Angeles News Letter," *MPW,* 17 Jul 1920, 327 (married Goulding).

Desmond, William, "King of the Silent Serials" (brother of **Lucille Desmond**) [stage/film actor] (*né* William Mannion, b. Dublin, Ireland, 23 Jan 1878–2 Nov 1949 [71], Los Angeles CA; heart attack). m. Lillian Lamson (d. 1917); (2) **Mary McIvor**, 22 Mar 1919, Pasadena CA (d. 1941). (Ince-Triangle; Mutual; Universal; FBO.) (Film debut: Peggy, 1915.) "William Desmond, Once Screen Star, Matinee Idol of Silent Films Dies at 71—Played for Many Years on Broadway Stage," *NYT,* 4 Nov 1949, 27:3. "William Desmond," *Variety,* 9 Nov 1949. AMD, p. 98. AS, p. 319. BHD1, p. 152. FFF, p. 52. FSS, p. 92. GK, pp. 234–66. IFN, p. 80 (b. NY NY). Katz, p. 333. MH, p. 107. MSBB, p. 1023. SD. Truitt, p. 87–88. "Two Morosco Stars; William Desmond and Lenore Ulrich to Be Seen in Feature Films," *NYDM,* 19 May 1915, 32:1 (to debut in their stage play, *The Bird of Paradise,* for the Oliver Morosco Photoplay Co.). "Morosco-Bosworth Secures William Desmond," *MPW,* 22 May 1915, 1279. Laurette Despard, "Desmond, the Distinctive," *Motion Picture Magazine,* Feb 1918, 93–95. Sue Roberts, "Desperate Raymond," *MPC,* Jan 1919, 18–19, 77. "William Desmond," *MPW,* 3 Feb 1917, 698. "Death of Mrs. Desmond," *MPW,* 24 Nov 1917, 1179 (Gertrude Lanson). "Bill Desmond Married," *MPW,* 12 Apr 1919, 218 (MacIvor). "Stahl Secures Desmond," *MPW,* 26 Feb 1921, 1060. "Desmond Badly Hurt," *MPW,* 29 Apr 1922, 916 (18 Apr 1922, fell into river at Truckee CA). "Desmond Recovering," *MPW,* 6 May 1922, 47. "Desmond Signed by 'U,'" *MPW,* 30 Aug 1924, 721. George Katchmer, "William Desmond; The Riddle Rider," *CI,* 93 (Mar 1983), 30–32. Mel Woods, "Favorite Hollywood Cowboy," *CI,* 162 (Dec 1988), 47–63 (includes filmography). George Katchmer, "Remembering the Great Silents," *CI,* 256 (Oct 1996), 43.

Desni, Xenia [actress] (b. Kiev, Ukraine, Russia, 19 Jan 1894). (Ufa.) AS, p. 319. "Idols of Berlin," *MPC,* Feb 1926, 41. (photo). Garth Pedler, "Ludwig Berger's 'The Waltz Dream' (1926)," *CI,* 131 (May 1986), C17–C19 (photo).

De Solla, Rachel [actress] (d. 24 Nov 1920). BHD, p. 150.

Despres, Suzanne [actress] (*née* Josephine Charlotte Bonvalet, b. Veddun, France, 18 Dec 1873 [extrait de naissance no. 2736]-29 Jun 1951 [77], Paris, France). AS, p. 319.

Dessauer, Siegfried [director] (b. Berlin, Germany, 20 Sep 1874). AS, p. 319.

Deste, Stephanie [actress] (b. Liege, Belgium, 22 Jan 1901-Apr 1996 [95]). BHD1, p. 607.

De Stefano, Vitale [actor/director]. No data found. JS, pp. 140–41 (in Italian silents from 1911).

De Stefani, Helen [actress] (*née?*, b. 1880–8 Jan 1938 [57?], Los Angeles CA). m. **Joseph DeStefani** (d. 1940). AS, p. 306.

De Stefani, Joseph [actor] (b. Venice, Italy, 3 Oct 1879–26 Oct 1940 [61], Los Angeles CA). m. **Helen** (d. 1938). AS, p. 306.

Destinn, Emmy [actress] (b. Prague, Czechoslovakia, 26 Feb 1878–28 Jan 1930 [51], Budweis, Czechoslovakia). AMD, p. 99. AS, p. 320. BHD, p. 150. Terese R. Nagel, "Operatic Star in Pictures," *MPW,* 11 Jul 1914, 281.

De Swirsky, Thamara [actress]. No data found. AMD, p. 99. "Classical Dancing on the Screen," *MPW,* 2 Mar 1912, 757.

De Sylva, Buddy (son of **Hal de Forest**) [songwriter/scenarist/producer] (*né* George Gard [Buddy] De Sylva, b. New York NY, 27 Jan 1895–11 Jul 1950 [55], Los Angeles CA; heart attack). m. Marie Wallace, New York NY, 1925. (Fox.) "Buddy De Sylva, 54, Film Leader, Dead; Producer of Hit Pictures and Plays Wrote Top Songs, Including 'Sonny Boy,'" *NYT,* 12 Jul 1950, 29:1. "B.G. DeSylva, 55, Dies in H'wood; Prolific in Music, Legit, Pix," *Variety,* 12 Jul 1950 (wrote *April Showers; Sonny Boy; You're the Cream in My Coffee;* "...he prepared a script for Betty Hutton, 'The Life of Theda Bara.'...she turned down the script."). AS, p. 306; p. 320 (B.G. Desylva). BHD2, p. 67. SD.

De Tellier, Mariette [actress] (b. France, 1891?–9 Dec 1957 [66], Cincinnati OH). BHD, p. 150. IFN, p. 81. Truitt, p. 88 (d. 11 Dec).

Detlefsen, Paul [actor] (*né* Otto Detlefsen, b. Copenhagen, Denmark, 3 Oct 1899–1 Aug 1986 [86], Los Angeles CA). . AS, p. 320 (b. 27 Nov 1866–15 Feb 1963).

Deutsch, Ernst [actor] (b. Prague, Czechoslovakia, 16 Sep 1890–22 Mar 1969 [78], Berlin, Germany). AS, p. 320. BHD1, p. 152.

Deval, Marguerite [actress] (*née* Marguerite Juliette Brulfer, b. Strasbourg, France, 19 Sep 1866–18 Dec 1955 [89], Paris, France). AS, p. 320.

Devalde, Jean [actor/producer] (*né* Jean Dewalde, b. Antwerp, Belgium, 8 Oct 1888-ca. 1933 [45?]). AS, p. 320.

De Valdez, Carlos J. [actor] (b. Arica, Peru, 19 Mar 1894–30 Oct 1939 [45], Encino CA). AS, p. 307.

Devant, David [actor] (b. London, England, 22 Feb 1868–13 Oct 1941 [73], London, England). BHD, p. 150.

Davarennes, Alex [actor/director/producer] (*né* Alexander Durand, b. Paris, France, 11 Jun 1887). AS, p. 320.

Devarney, Emile J. [actor/scenarist]. No data found.

Devaull, William P. [actor] (b. San Francisco CA, 12 Dec 1870–4 Jun 1945 [74], Los Angeles CA). (Griffith.) "William P. Devaull," *Variety,* 13 Jun 1945. BHD, p. 150. IFN, p. 81. Truitt, p. 88.

De Verdier, Anton [actor] (b. Skåne, Sweden, 14 Aug 1878–21 Apr 1954 [75]). BHD1, p. 607.

Devere, Arthur [vaudevillian, 1904/stage/film actor] (b. Brussels, Belgium, 24 Jan 1883–23 Sep 1961 [78], Brussels, Belgium). (Last film: *Midnight Circuit.*) "Arthur Devere," *Variety,* 11 Oct 1961, p. 79. BHD1, p. 152.

Devere, Francesca "Frisco" [actress] (b. 1891?–11 Sep 1952 [61], Port Townsend WA). (Keystone; Sennett.) "Francesca De Vere," *Variety,* 24 Sep 1952. BHD, p. 150. IFN, p. 81. Truitt, p. 88.

DeVere, Harry T. (b. New York NY, 1 Feb 1870–10 Oct 1923 [53]). (American; Santa Barbara M.P. Co.; Bosworth; Pallas; Fox.) BHD, p. 150. IFN, p. 81. George Katchmer, "Remembering the Great Silents," *CI,* 223 (Jan 1994), 47:1.

Devere, Lillian [actress]. No data found. (Edison.)

Devere, Margaret [actress] (b. 1889–24 Oct 1918 [29?], New York NY; pneumonia). "Margaret Devere," *Variety,* 1 Nov 1918 (age 22). BHD, p. 150 (Marjorie De Vere). Truitt 1983.

Devereaux, Jack (son-in-law of **John Drew**) [actor] (b. 22 Mar 1881–19 Jan 1958 [76], New York NY [Death Certificate Index No. 1513]). m. Louise Drew (d. 1954). "Jack Devereaux, Retired Actor, 76," *NYT,* 20 Jan 1958, 23:2. "Jack Devereaux," *Variety,* 22 Jan 1958. AMD, p. 99. AS, p. 320 (b. 12 Mar). BHD, p. 150. IFN, p. 81. SD. Truitt, p. 88. "Jack Devereaux," *MPW,* 21 Apr 1917, 440.

Devereaux, Jennings [cinematographer] (b. 1885–12 Mar 1952 [67?], Los Angeles CA). BHD2, p. 68.

Devereaux, Orra G. [actress] (aka Grace Gardner on stage, b. 1882?–11 Dec 1951 [69], Orange CA). "Orra G. Devereaux," *Variety,* 19 Dec 1951. AS, p. 320. BHD, p. 150.

Deverell, John W. [actor] (b. England, 30 May 1880–2 Mar 1965 [84], Haywards Heath, England). AS, p. 321. BHD1, p. 152.

Deverich, Nat [director/executive] (b. London, England, 20 Feb 1893–11 Apr 1963 [70], Los Angeles CA). . "Nat Deverich," *Variety,* 17 Apr 1963. AMD, p. 99. AS, p. 321. BHD2, p. 68. "Adds Director," *MPW,* 16 Apr 1921, 745.

De Vernon, Frank, "The Beau Brummel of Broadway" [actor] (b. New York NY, 1845?–19 Oct 1923 [78], New York NY; heart attack). "Frank de Vernon," *Variety,* 25 Oct 1923 (He received his epithet "due to his habit of changing his clothes as often as six times a day."). AS, p. 307. BHD, p. 150. IFN, p. 81. Truitt, p. 88.

Devienne, Maurice [actor] (*né* Maurice Helie, b. Paris, France, 20 Feb 1892-Apr/May 1953 [61]). AS, p. 321.

De Vilbiss, Robert [actor] (b. Richmond CA, 12 Mar 1915–4 Mar 1973 [57], Torrance CA). AS, p. 307 (b. 1918). BHD, p. 150. MH, p. 107.

De Villiers, Victor [scenarist]. No data found. AMD, p. 99. "Victor DeVilliers Scenario Editor for Ivan," *MPW,* 26 Aug 1916, 1414.

Devine, Andy [actor] (*né* Jeremiah Schwartz, b. Flagstaff AZ, 27 Oct 1905–18 Feb 1977 [71], Orange CA; leukemia). m. Dorothy Irene House, 1933. "Andy Devine, Squeaky-Voiced TV and Film Star, Dies"; Robert Hanley, "Football Saved His Career," *NYT,* 20 Feb 1977, 39:1. "Andy Devine," *Variety,* 23 Feb 1977. AS, p. 321. BHD1, p. 152 (b. 7 Oct). IFN, p. 81.

Devine, Jerry [actor: Our Gang comedies] (b. Boston MA, 11 Nov 1908–20 May 1994 [85], Santa Barbara CA). "Jerry Devine," CI, 230 (August, 1994), 54. AS, p. 321 (b. LA CA). BHD1, p. 153.

De Vinna, Clyde [cameraman] (b. Sedalia MO, 1892–26 Jul 1953 [60], Los Angeles CA). (MGM.) "Clyde De Vinna," *Variety,* 29 Jul 1953. AMD, p. 99. AS, p. 307. BHD2, p. 68. FDY, p. 457. IFN, p. 81. Katz, p. 334. "Cameraman DeVinna with Paralta," *MPW,* 16 Jun 1917, 1761. "DeVinna Continues with Barriscale," *MPW,* 25 Aug 1917, 1200. "Barriscale's Cameraman—Clyde DeVinna," *MPW,* 17 Nov 1917, 1028.

Devirys, Rachel [actress] (*née* Rachel Itzkovitz, b. Sympheropol, Ukraine, Russia, 28 Feb

1890–16 May 1983 [93], Nice, France [extrait de deecès no. 2396/1983]). AS, p. 321. BHD1, p. 153 (d. 1984).

DeVite, William [assistant director]. No data found. m. **Dorothy Gulliver**, May? 1926. AMD, p. 99. "DeVite—Gulliver," *MPW*, 29 Nov 1926, 3.

De Vito, Chester [assistant director] (b. 1892–1964 [72?]). BHD2, p. 68.

Devoe, Bert [actor] (b. 1884–17 Jan 1930 [45], Steelton PA). (Sennett.) "Bert Devoe," *Variety*, 29 Jan 1930. BHD, p. 150. IFN, p. 81. Truitt, p. 88.

De Vogt, Carl Bernhard [actor/singer] (b. Cologne, Germany, 14 Sep 1885–16 Feb 1970 [84], Berlin, Germany). AS, p. 307. BHD1, p. 153.

De Vol, Norman [cameraman] (b. Marietta OH, 7 Jun 1900–31 Jul 1933 [33], Hollywood CA). (Pathé.) "Cameraman Suicides," *Variety*, 1 Aug 1933 (d. 30 Jul; out of a job for two years). FDY, p. 457. IFN, p. 81.

Devore, Dorothy [actress: Wampas Star, 1923] (*née* Alma [or Ann] Inez Williams, b. Fort Worth TX, 22 Jun 1899–10 Sep 1976 [77], Woodland Hills CA). m. Albert Wylie Mather, 1926. (Christie.) "Dorothy Devore," *Variety*, 15 Sep 1976. AMD, p. 99. AS, p. 321. BHD1, p. 153. FFF, p. 69. FSS, p. 92. IFN, p. 81. "Christie Star Guest at Aerial Circus," *MPW*, 19 Apr 1919, 358. "Christie Loans Dorothy Devore," *MPW*, 17 Jul 1920, 357. "Miss Devore as Iron-Clad Knight," *MPW*, 24 Dec 1921, 937. "Dorothy Devore and St. Clair Sign Warner Bros. Contracts," *MPW*, 23 Aug 1924, 530. "Dorothy Devore in Many Pictures," *MPW*, 6 Dec 1924, 553. "Queen of Oakland Ball," *MPW*, 3 Jan 1925, 75. "Dorothy Devore," *MPW*, 16 Apr 1927, 652. "Dorothy Devore," *MPW*, 23 Apr 1927, 709. "Dot Starts Off with Own Unit," *MPW*, 11 Jun 1927, 408. June Lee, "Dan Cupid's Bulletin Board," *Paris and Hollywood*, Sep 1926, 22 (wed Mather, theater owner of San Francisco and Honolulu, "and she too will desert Hollywood."). June Lee, "Dan Cupid's Bulletin Board," *Paris and Hollywood Screen Secrets Magazine*, Aug 1927, 37 (returned to films but not because of marital unhappiness). "Miss Devore Studies Broadway Productions," *MPW*, 1 Oct 1927, 281. Roy A. Uselton, "Wampas Baby Stars [letter]," *FIR*, Nov 1977, 574.

De Vore, James [actor] (b. Kansas City MO, 15 Mar 1890). BHD, p. 150.

Devorska, Jess [actor]. No data found. AMD, p. 99. "He Made Firing Squads Laugh, So He Figures in the 'Movies,'" *MPW*, 5 Feb 1927, 422.

De Vries, Henri [actor] (b. 1863-May 1930 [67?]). BHD1, p. 153.

Devries, Paul [producer] (b. Paris, France, 20 Oct 1888-Apr/May 1953 [64]). AS, p. 321.

De Warfaz, George [actor/scenarist] (b. Belgium, 2 Dec 1884–14 Oct 1959 [74]). BHD2, p. 68.

Dewar, M.C. [title writer]. No data found. FDY, p. 443.

De Wavrin, Robert [director] (*né* Comte Robert Frédéric de Wavrin de Villers au Tertre, b. Bottelaere, Belgium, 29 Aug 1888–29 Jun 1971 [82], Uccle, Belgium). AS, p. 307. BHD2, p. 68.

De Weese, Frank [actor] (b. 1903–15 Apr 1928 [25?], Salina KS). BHD, p. 150.

DeWeil, Gus [actor]. No data found. AMD, p. 99. "Actor Elected," *MPW*, 22 Oct 1927, 492.

Dewey, Earl S. [actor] (b. Manhattan KS, 2 Jun 1881–5 Feb 1950 [68], Los Angeles CA). m. Billie Rogers. "Earl S. Dewey," *Variety*, 15 Feb 1950 (age 58). AS, p. 321. BHD1, p. 153. IFN, p. 82. Truitt, p. 88.

Dewey, Elmer [actor] (*né* Dan Danilo, b. 1884?–28 Oct 1954 [70?], Los Angeles CA). "Elmer Dewey," *Variety*, 3 Nov 1954. AS, p. 321. BHD1, p. 153. Truitt, p. 88.

Dewhurst, William [actor] (b. England, 1888–26 Oct 1937 [49?], London, England). AS, p. 321.

De Winton, Albert [actor] (d. May 1934, Brazil). BHD1, p. 153.

Dewitz, Baron [producer]. No data found. AMD, p. 99. "Here's the 'Regisseur,'" *MPW*, 22 Jan 1916, 583.

De Wolfe, Elsie [stage/film actress/interior decorator] (b. New York NY, 20 Dec 1865–12 Jul 1950 [84], Versailles, France). m. Sir Charles Mendl [British diplomat], 1926. *After All.* "Lady Mendl (Elsie De Wolfe)," *Variety*, 19 Jul 1950, p. 55. BHD, p. 150.

Dewsbury, Ralph [director] (b. England-d. 1921). BHD2, p. 68.

Dexter, Aubrey [actor] (b. London, England, 29 Mar 1896-May 1958 [62]). BHD1, p. 153 (b. 1898).

Dexter, Bob [publicist/writer]. No data found. AMD, p. 99. "Bob Dexter Resigns," *MPW*, XXVII, 22 Jan 1916, 583.

Dexter, Elliott [vaudevillian/actor] (b. Galveston TX, 21 Dec 1869– 23 Jun 1941 [71], Amityville, LI NY). m. **Marie Doro**, 1915 (d. 1956); Nina Untermeyer. "Elliott Dexter; Silent Screen, Vaudeville Actor Retired in 1930—Dies at 71," *NYT*, 24 Jun 1941, 19:2. "Elliott Dexter," *Variety*, 2 Jul 1941. AMD, p. 99. AS, p. 321. BHD, p. 150 (b. Houston TX, 29 Mar 1870). FFF, p. 40. IFN, p. 82. MH, p. 107. SD. Truitt, p. 88 (b. 1870). WWS, p. 35 (b. Houston TX). "Marie Doro Married," *MPW*, 25 Dec 1915, 2342. "Foote and Dexter with Morosco," *MPW*, 17 Jun 1916, 2050. "Elliott Dexter with Artcraft," *MPW*, 17 Nov 1917, 1026. "Elliott Dexter Renews Lasky Contract," *MPW*, 29 Jun 1918, 1855. "Dexter Too Ill to Work," *MPW*, 14 Jun 1919, 1632 (nervous breakdown). "Elliott Dexter Convalescing," *MPW*, 21 Jun 1919, 1767. "Elliott Dexter Is Reported Recovering from Breakdown," *MPW*, 23 Aug 1919, 1149. "Dexter Signed," *MPW*, 20 Aug 1921, 810. Lillian Montanye, "Dexter Philosophy," *MPC*, Oct 1921, 34–35, 81.

De Yong, Joseph [costumer/set designer/actor] (b. 12 Mar 1894–16 Apr 1975 [81], Los Angeles Co. CA). BHD2, p. 68.

D'Harcourt, Rita [actress/cinematographer]. No data found. JS, p. 142 (in Italian silents from 1919).

Dhelia, France [actress] (aka Mado Floreal, *née* Franceline Berthe Léontine Delia Benoit, b. Saint-Lubin-in-Vergonnois, France, 9 Nov 1894 [extrait de naissance no. 10]-3 May 1964 [66], Paris, France [extrait de décès no. 1311/1964]). AS, p. 322. BHD1, p. 154. IFN, p. 82.

Dhervilly, Marfa [actress] (*née* Marthe Dutreix, b. Paris, France, 9 Nov 1876–18 Nov 1963 [87], Lagny, France). AS, p. 322.

Dhirendranath, Ganguly [actor/director] (b. Calcutta, India, 26 Mar 1893–17 Dec 1978 [85], Bombay, India). AS, p. 322.

Dhurtal, Alain [actor] (né Henry Allain, b. France, 1887–6 Feb 1968 [80?], France). AS, p. 322.

Dial, Patterson [actress] (b. Madison FL, 19 May 1902–23 Mar 1945 [42], Los Angeles CA). m. **Rupert Hughes** (d. 1956). (Paramount.) BHD, p. 150. IFN, p. 82.

Diamant-Berger, Henri [director/producer/scenarist] (b. Paris, France, 9 Jun 1895–7 May 1972 [76], Paris, France). AS, p. 322. BHD2, p. 68.

Diamond, James R. [Diamond & Brennan/actor/singer/cinematographer] (b. 1881?–26 Jul 1930 [49], Freeport, LI NY; pneumonia). m. Sybil. "Jim Diamond," *Variety*, 30 Jul 1930. AS, p. 322. BHD2, p. 68 (b. 1894–17 Oct 1936, LA CA). FDY, p. 457.

Diamond, Lou S. [executive] (b. 1892–5 Apr 1940 [48?], New York NY). BHD2, p. 68.

Diana, Laure [actress] (*née* Lucienne Schwartz, b. Paris, France, 6 Feb 1897–1980 [83?], France). AS, p. 323.

Dianville, Max [producer/director/scenarist] (b. Vincelles, France, 18 Sep 1890–1954 [64?], France). AS, p. 323.

Díaz de Mendoza, Carlos (son of stage actors Fernando Díaz de Mendoza and María Guerrero) [actor] (b. 1898–1960 [62?]). (Spain, 1924; Paramount, Joinville, France; Fox.) Waldman, p. 87.

Dickens, Stafford [actor/director/scenarist] (b. Grays, England, 1896–12 Oct 1967 [71?], New York NY). AS, p. 323.

Dickerson, Homer [actor] (b. TX, 23 Mar 1890–6 Jun 1959 [69], Los Angeles CA). BHD1, p. 154.

Dickerson, Jennie [opera singer/actress] (b. Newburgh NY, 1855?–14 Aug 1943 [88], Philadelphia PA). "Jenny Dickerson," *Variety*, 25 Aug 1943. BHD, p. 150. IFN, p. 82.

Dickey, Basil [scenarist] (b. 1881?–17 Jun 1958 [77], Long Beach CA). "Basil Dickey," *Variety*, 25 Jun 1958. AS, p. 323. BHD2, p. 68. FDY, p. 423. IFN, p. 82.

Dickey, Paul [playwright/scenarist/actor/director] (b. Chicago IL, 12 May 1882–8 Jan 1933 [50], New York NY). m. Inez Plummer, 1915. "Paul Dickey," *Variety*, 10 Jan 1933. AMD, p. 99. AS, p. 323 (b. 1885). BHD, p. 150; BHD2, p. 68 (b. 1885). FDY, p. 423. IFN, p. 82. Truitt, p. 88 (b. 1885). "Paul Dickey a Lasky Director," *MPW*, 25 Dec 1915, 2336.

Dickinson, Arthur [executive] (b. Chattanooga TN, 21 Jan 1888–25 Oct 1947 [59], Santa Monica CA). BHD2, p. 68.

Dickinson, Weed [publicity]. No data found. AMD, p. 99. "Dickinson Is P.A. for Harry Langdon," *MPW*, 29 Oct 1927, 546.

Dickson, Charles [actor] (*né* Charles Doblin, b. New York NY, 1860?–11 Dec 1927 [67], New York NY). m. Lillian Burkhardt. "Charles Dickson," *Variety*, 14 Dec 1927. AMD, p. 99. AS, p. 323. BHD, p. 151. IFN, p. 82. "Charles Dickson with Reliance," *MPW*, 4 Oct 1913, 32.

Dickson, Dorothy (mother of **Dorothy Hyson**) [stage/film actress] (b. Chicago IL?, 20 Jul 1893–25 Sep 1995 [102], London, England). m.

Carl Hyson—div. 1935 (daughter Dorothy, 1914–1996). British biography by Michael Thornton. Robert McG. Thomas, Jr., "Dorothy Dickson, Musical Star of British Stage, Is Dead at 102," *NYT,* 27 Sep 1995, D23:1 (daughter married Anthony Quale). *The Guardian,* 27 Sep 1995. AS, p. 323 (b. Kansas City MO, 1900). BHD1, p. 154 (b. Kansas City MO, 6 Jul). Ragan, *Who's Who in Hollywood,* p. 426. "Dorothy Dickson, Famous Stage Dancer, Engaged for Fitzmaurice's 'Money Mad,'" *MPW,* 21 Aug 1920, 1004 (m. Carl Heisen).

Dickson, John V. [actor] (b. Bordentown NJ, 28 Mar 1875–1 May 1941 [66], Trenton NJ). BHD, p. 151. IFN, p. 82.

Dickson, Lydia [actress] (b. MO, 17 Apr 1887–26 Mar 1928 [40], Los Angeles CA). "Lydia Dickson," *Variety,* 4 Apr 1928 (age 50). AS, p. 323. BHD, p. 151. IFN, p. 82. Truitt, p. 89 (b. 1878; d. 2 Apr).

Dickson, William Kennedy Laurie [inventor/cinematographer] (b. Le Minihic-sur-Rance, France, 3 Aug 1860 [extrait de naissance no. SN/1860]–28 Sep 1935 [75], Twickenham, England). With Antonia Dickson, *History of the Kinetograph, Kinetoscope & Kinetophonograph* (NY: Arno Press and The New York Times, 1895; rpt. NY: Albert Bunn, 1970). "W.K. Laurie Dickson," *Variety,* 9 Oct 1935. AS, p. 323. BHD2, p. 69. Katz, p. 328. Spehr, pp. 126–27.

Dictor, David [actor] (b. 1896-Aug 1916 [20?], Baltimore MD). BHD, p. 151.

Didway, Ernest L. [actor] (b. 1871–3 Jan 1939 [66?], Los Angeles CA). AS, p. 324.

Diee, Ernest [cinematographer] (b. 1892–26 May 1916 [24?], Jacksonville FL). BHD2, p. 69.

Diege, Samuel [director/producer] (b. 1902–13 Oct 1939 [37?], Los Angeles CA). BHD2, p. 69.

Diegelmann, Wilhelm [actor] (b. Ellers bei Fulda, Germany, 28 Sep 1861–1 Mar 1934 [72], Berlin, Germany). BHD1, p. 154 (b. Worbeck, Germany). IFN, p. 82. Vittorio Martinelli, "Kino-Lieblinge," *Griffithiana,* 38/39 (Oct 1990), 44.

Diehl, Karl Ludwig [stage/film actor] (b. Halle, Germany, 14 Aug 1896–7 Mar 1958 [61], Oberbayern, Upper Bavaria, Germany). "Karl L. Diehl," *Variety,* 19 Mar 1958, p. 95 (d. 9 Mar; "Starting in silent films, he created more than 70 roles."). AS, p. 324 (d. Gut Berghofpenzberg, Germany). BHD1, p. 154. IFN, p. 82.

Dierker, Hugh [director]. No data found. (Pathé.) Mary McClintock, "The True Story Is the Thing; Thinks Hugh Dierker, the Director," *MW,* 19 Sep 1925, 21, 46.

Diessl, Gustav Karl Balthasar [actor] (b. Vienna, Austria, 30 Dec 1899–20 Mar 1948 [48], Vienna, Austria). m. **Camilla Horn** (d. 1996). (Made German- and French-language films for WB and Films Paramount.) AS, p. 325. BHD1, p. 154. IFN, p. 82. Waldman, p. 87.

Dieterle, Charlotte [actress] (*née* Charlotte Hagenbruch, b. Germany, 1897–12 May 1968 [71?], Vaduz, Lichtenstein). m. **William Dieterle** (d. 1972). AS, p . 324.

Dieterle, William [actor/director/producer] (*né* Wilhelm Doerr, b. Ludwigshafen, Rhenpflaz, Germany, 15 Jul 1893–8 Dec 1972 [79], Ottobrunn, Germany). m. **Charlotte** Haganbruch (d. 1968). (Debut as actor: *Fiesco,* Germany, 1911; as director: *Men at the Crossroads,* 1923.) "William Dieterle Dead at 79; A Director of Stage and Screen," *NYT,* 16 Dec 1972, 34:2 (d. near Munich). "William Dieterle," *Variety,* 20 Dec 1972, p. 63. AS, p. 324. BHD1, p. 154; BHD2, p. 69. IFN, p. 82. JS, p. 142 (d. 9 Dec; directed films in Italy in 1949 and 1959). SD. Harry Sanford, "The Screen Biography of William Dieterle," *CFC,* 50 (Spring, 1976), 39 *et passim.*

Dietl, Frank H. [actor] (b. Lakeville IN, 15 Nov 1875–24 Jan 1923 [47]). BHD, p. 151. IFN, p. 82.

Dietrich, Antonia [actress] (b. Vienna, Austria, 31 Jan 1900–1975 [74?]). BHD1, p. 607.

Dietrich, Marlene [stage/film/TV actress/singer] (*née* Maria Magdalena von Losch, b. Schoenberg, Germany, 27 Dec 1901–6 May 1992 [90], Paris, France; heart attack). m. Rudolf Sieber, 1924 (daughter, Maria Riva; d. 1976). *My Life Story* (Germany, 1979). Maria Riva, *Marlene Dietrich* (NY: Ballantine Books, 1992). (Film debut: *Der Kleine Napoleon,* 1923.) Peter B. Flint, "Marlene Dietrich, 90, Symbol of Glamour, Dies," *NYT,* 7 May 1992, A1, B16:1. Joseph McBride, "Marlene Dietrich," *Variety,* 11 May 1992, p. 135. AS, p. 324. BHD1, p. 154. JS, p. 142 (appeared in *Montecarlo,* Italy, 1956). Katz, pp. 338–39 (began in Germany, 1923). Stephen Kinzer, "Dietrich Buried in Berlin, and Sentiment Is Mixed," *NYT,* 17 May 1992, 8:13. Carol Benton, "Marlene Dietrich Denies Charge She Is 'Love Thief'; Accused by Wife of Josef von Sternberg of Alienating Director's Affections, Star Refuses to Settle Case Out of Court," *Movie Classic,* I, Nov 1931, 37. "Glamour Girl No. 1, Mary Magdalene 'Marlene' Dietrich," *Cinema Arts,* I, Jun 1937, 33 (painting by Jaro Fabry). "Dietrich by [Anton] Bruehl; A Color Portfolio," *Cinema Arts,* I, Sep 1937, 51–57. Caryn James, "The Dietrich Mystique," *NYT,* 29 Jan 1993, C1:3, C24:1. Rita Reif, "Dietrich: Picking Up the Pieces," *NYT,* Sec. 2, 26 Sep 1993, 35:1 ("Some 100,000 items from her collection that have been bought by the city of Berlin only prove that memorabilia help make the star."). "Briefs; World; Berlin honors Marlene Dietrich," *Pittsburgh Tribune-Review,* 109, 14 Aug 1997, 1:1 (stamp issued this date, and a Marlene Dietrich Square in central Berlin to be announced on 28 Aug). Miriam Hils, "Dietrich Devotions Cause Berlin Angst," *Variety,* 18 Aug 1997, 5:2 (efforts to name a street after her failed: "What did Dietrich ever do for us?" cried Berliners.)

Dietrich, Ralph [editor/producer/scenarist/director] (b. New York NY, 1902?–1 Dec 1961 [59], West Hollywood CA; heart attack). m. Katherine. (Universal; Pathé; TC-F; RKO.) "Ralph Dietrich," *NYT,* 4 Dec 1961, 37:1. AS, p. 324. BHD2, p. 69.

Dietz, Howard [scenarist/producer/composer] (b. New York NY, 9 Sep 1896–30 Jul 1983 [86], New York NY [Death Certificate Index No. 12254]). m. (1) Elizabeth Hall; (2) Tania G. Montagu; (3) Lucinda G. Ballard. *Dancing in the Dark; Words by Howard Dietz* (New York: Quadrangle/The New York Times Book Co., 1974). (Goldwyn; Metro; MGM.) Wolfgang Saxon, "Howard Dietz, 86; Pop-Song Lyricist; Worked with Arthur Schwartz on Musicals—Directed Publicity for M-G-M," *NYT,* 31 Jul 1983, 37:5. "Howard Dietz, Songwriter, Dies at 86," *NYT,* IV, 1 Aug 1983, 10:4. "Howard Dietz, 86, Renaissance Man for All Media, Dies in N.Y.," *Variety,* 3 Aug 1983. AMD, p. 99. AS, p. 324. BHD2, p. 69 (b. 8 Sep). SD. "Dietz Heads Metro's Advertising and Publicity," *MPW,* 11 Apr 1925, 541. "Howard Dietz," *MPW,* 26 Mar 1927, 310.

Dieudonne, Albert [actor] (b. Paris, France, 26 Nov 1889–19 Mar 1976 [86], Paris, France). AS, p. 324. BHD, p. 151 (b. 1892). IFN, p. 82.

Dieudonne, Hélène [actress] (*née* Hélène Jeanne Aimée Dieudonne, b. Paris, France, 24 Dec 1887–29 Sep 1980 [92], Chaumont-en-Vexin, France [extrait de décès no. 81]). AS, p. 324.

Digges, Dudley [actor] (b. Dublin, Ireland, 9 Jun 1879–24 Oct 1947 [68], New York NY; cerebral hemorrhage). m. Mary Quinn (d. 1946). "Dudley Digges," *Variety,* 29 Oct 1947. AS, p. 324. BHD1, p. 155. IFN, p. 82.

Digges, Mary R. [actress] (né Marie Quinn, b. Dublin, Ireland, 1885–21 Aug 1947 [62?], Bay Shore NY). AS, p. 324.

Digges, Richard H., Jr. [writer/film editor]. No data found.

Diggins, Eddie [boxer/actor] (*né* Edward Ayer Diggins, b. San Francisco CA, 8 Jan 1898–26 Mar 1927 [29], Los Angeles CA; stabbed to death). m. Marian. "Eddie Diggins Killed in Clubroom Brawl; Charles Meehan Held—Wives of Both Men in Hollywood Picture Colony," *Variety,* 30 Mar 1927 (d. 25 Mar; age 38; Meehan, alleged bootlegger, was husband of actress Irene Dalton; she was present with Lloyd Hamilton, Jack Wagner, *et al.*). AS, p. 324. BHD, p. 151 (b. 1903). IFN, p. 82. Truitt 1983 (b. 1903).

Di Giorgio, Ameriga [actor]. No data found. JS, p. 143 (in Italian silents from 1916).

Di Golconda, Ligia [actress] (b. 6 Apr 1883–10 Jan 1942 [58], Mexico City, Mexico; heart attack). AS, p. 322. BHD, p. 151. IFN, p. 83 (age 58).

Dikyi, Alexei Dimitrievich [actor/director] (b. Moscow, Russia, 24 Jan 1889–1 Nov 1955 [66], Moscow, Russia). AS, p. 325.

Dill, Jack *see* **Dillon, John**

Dill, Joseph L. [assistant director] (b. 1894–11 Dec 1959 [65?], Los Angeles CA). BHD2, p. 69.

Dill, Max M. [actor: Kolb & Dill/actor] (b. Cleveland OH, 1878–21 Nov 1949 [71], San Francisco CA). "Max M. Dill," *Variety,* 30 Nov 1949. AMD, p. 99. AS, p. 325. IFN, p. 83. Truitt 1983. "Max Dill," *MPW,* 17 Feb 1917, 1015.

Dillon, Dick [actor] (*né* Kenneth Bowstead, b. 1896?–17 Apr 1961 [65], Boston MA). m. Ann Darling. "Dick Dillon," *Variety,* 26 Apr 1961 (in *Perils of Pauline*). AS, p. 325. BHD1, p. 155. IFN, p. 83. Truitt, p. 89.

Dillon, Edward [actor/scenarist/director] (b. New York NY, 1 Jan 1879–11 Jul 1933 [54], Los Angeles CA; heart attack). (Biograph.) "Edw. Dillon, 60, Star of Early Films, Dies," *The Evening Herald-Express,* 11 Jul 1933, 1:1 (age 60). "Edward Dillon," *Variety,* 18 Jul 1933 (age 53). AMD, p. 100. AS, p. 325. BHD1, p. 155; BHD2, p. 69. IFN, p. 83. KOM, pp. 133–34 (b. 1873). Truitt, p. 89. "Director Edward Dillon Burned Out," *MPW,* 26 Jun 1915, 2108. "Director Dillon Has Had Much Experience," *MPW,* 22 Sep 1917, 1831. "Three Notable Directors Have Been Engaged by William Fox," *MPW,* 12 Oct 1918, 249. "Edward Dillon Will Direct Hammerstein Series," *MPW,* 15 Sep 1923, 267.

Dillon, Gregory T. [scenarist] (b. 1892–3 Jun 1957 [65?], Elmhurst IL). BHD2, p. 69.

Dillon, John Francis [actor/director] (brother of **Robert A. Dillon**) (aka Jack Dill, b. New York NY, 26 Nov 1883–4 Apr 1934 [50], Beverly Hills CA; heart attack). m. **Edith Hallor**, 1921 (d. 1971). (Kalem; Famous Players; Nestor; Universal; Keystone; Lubin; 1st National). "John F. Dillon," *Variety*, 10 Apr 1934. AMD, p. 100. AS, p. 325. BHD, p. 151; BHD2, p. 69. IFN, p. 83. Katz, p. 340 (b. 13 Jul 1887). Truitt, p. 89 (b. 1887). "John Dillon, Vogue Director," *MPW*, 1 Apr 1916, 70. "John Dillon Returns to Acting," *MPW*, 29 Mar 1919, 1779. "Edith Hallor Weds Director," *MPW*, 4 Jun 1921, 503. "Stork Visits Mr. and Mrs. John F. Dillon," *MPW*, 20 Dec 1924, 715 (son, John Francis, Jr., b. 29 Nov 1924). "Richard Rowland and Colleen Moore Are Godparents," *MPW*, 3 Jan 1925, 25. "Dillon Wields Mean Megaphone," *MPW*, 11 Jun 1927, 408. "F.N. Signs Dillon," *MPW*, 3 Sep 1927, 15.

Dillon, John T. [actor] (b. Deal Beach NJ, 19 Jun 1876–29 Dec 1937 [61], near Sawtelle CA; pneumonia). (Griffith; RKO.) "John Dillon," *Variety*, 5 Jan 1938. AS, p. 325 (b. 1866). BHD1, p. 155 (d. LA CA). IFN, p. 83. Truitt 1983 (b. 1866).

Dillon, John Webb [actor] (b. London, England, 6 Feb 1877–20 Dec 1949 [72], Los Angeles CA). m. **Catherine Earl** (d. 1946). "John W. Dillon," *Variety*, 28 Dec 1949. AMD, p. 99 (Dillion). AS, p. 325. BHD1, p. 155. FSS, p. 93. IFN, p. 83. Truitt, p. 89. "Make-Up Expert Signed by Fox," *MPW*, 11 Aug 1923, 497. George A. Katchmer, "Forgotten Cowboys and Cowgirls—Part XVIII," *CI*, 195 (Sep 1991), C7.

Dillon, Josephine [coach/actress] (b. CO, 26 Jan 1884–10 Nov 1971 [87], Verdugo CA). m. **Clark Gable**, 1924–30 (d. 1960). AS, p. 325. BHD2, p. 69.

Dillon, Robert A. (brother of **John F. Dillon**) [lyricist/scenarist] (b. New York NY, 1889–30 Nov 1944 [55], Los Angeles CA). "Robert A. Dillon," *Variety*, 6 Dec 1944. AMD, p. 100. AS, p. 325. BHD2. p. 69. FDY, p. 423. "Robert Dillon Under Contract with Warners," *MPW*, 19 Feb 1927, 571.

Dillon, Stella [actress] (b. 1877–28 Apr 1934 [57?], Los Angeles CA). AS, p. 325.

Dillon, Tom [actor] (b. 1888–22 Oct 1965 [77?], Burbank CA). BHD, p. 151.

Dills, William [actor] (b. Burlington IA, 1878–25 Mar 1932 [53?], Portland OR). BHD, p. 151. George Katchmer, "Remembering the Great Silents," *CI*, 197 (Nov 1991), 52.

Di Lorenzo, Tina [stage/film actress] (b. Turin, Italy, 4 Dec 1872–25 Mar 1930 [57], Milan, Italy). m. **Armando Falconi**, 1901 (d. 1954; son, Dino Falconi). AS, p. 322. JS, p. 144 (appeared in two Italian silents: *La mamma bella*, 1915, and *La scintilla*, 1915).

di Majo Durazzo, Duca Arturo [actor]. No data found. m. Elizabeth Hanan, 1913. "Duke as M.P. Actor," *NYDM*, 11 Dec 1915, 25:1 (already appeared in a film in Italy or France. "His work has been 'straight' parts and he has displayed, it is said, some ability for comedy.").

Di Marzio, Matilde [actress]. No data found. JS, p. 144 (in Italian silents from 1913).

Dime, James [actor] (b. Yugoslavia, 19 Dec 1897–11 May 1981 [83], Woodland Hills CA). (Pathé; last film: *Down to the Sea in Ships*, 1949) "James Dime," *Variety*, 27 May 1981 (in industry 29 years). AS, p. 325. BHD1, p. 155.

d'Indy, Vincent [composer] (*né* Paul Marie Théodore Vincent d'Indy, b. Paris, France, 27 Mar 1851–2 Dec 1931 [80], Paris, France). AS, p. 278.

Dinehart, Alan [director/producer/scenarist] (b. Missoula MT, 3 Oct 1886–17 Jul 1944 [57], Los Angeles CA). AS, p. 326.

Dinelli, Niní [actress] (*née* Alba Dinelli, b. Pisa, Italy). JS, p. 144 (in Italian silents from 1916).

Dinesen, Marie [actress] (b. Denmark, 3 Nov 1887–17 Aug 1935 [47], Denmark). AS, p. 326.

Dinesen, Robert [director/actor] (b. Copenhagen, Denmark, 23 Oct 1874–7 Mar 1930 [55], Berlin, Germany). AS, p. 326.

Dingle, Charles W. [actor] (b. Wabash IN, 28 Dec 1887–19 Jan 1956 [68], Worcester MA). AS, p. 326.

Dinis, Samwell [actor] (*né* Rodrigo Samwell Dinis, b. Lisbon, Portugal, 1888–29 Jul 1972 [84?], Lisbon, Portugal). AS, p. 326.

Dintenfass, Mark M. [producer/executive] (b. Austria, 1878?–23 Nov 1933 [55], Cliffside Park NJ). "Mark M. Dintenfass, Film Pioneer, Dies; Once Had Studio [Champion Film Company, 1908, later part of Universal] at Ft. Lee—Ran for Governor of New Jersey as Single-Taxer," *NYT*, 25 Nov 1933, 15:2. AMD, p. 100. AS, p. 326 (Dintenflas). Spehr, p. 128. "Wants $16,000 Divided; Mark Dintenfass Starts Suit to Have Independents Divide Earnings," *NYDM*, 11 Feb 1914, 32:1. "Ambassador Gerard's Story in Pictures," *MPW*, 22 Dec 1917, 1791. "Dintenfass Signs Noted Comedienne," *MPW*, 30 Aug 1919, 1327.

Dion, Hector [actor] (b. Boston MA, 1881). (Vitagraph; Reliance.) AMD, p. 100. BHD, p. 151. "Hector Dion Returns to Pictures," *MPW*, XII, 22 Jun 1912, 1139. Hugh Hoffman, "In the Catskills with Reliance," *MPW*, 24 Aug 1912, 748–51. "Hector Dion Leaves Reliance," *MPW*, 16 Nov 1912, 638 (claims that he was the first leading man at Vitagraph). "Hector Dion Goes to Biograph," *MPW*, 23 Nov 1912, 749. "Hector Dion with Florence Turner Co.," *MPW*, 18 Jul 1914, 447. "Hector Dion Returns from England," *MPW*, 27 Feb 1915, 1266.

Dione, Rose [actress] (b. Paris, France, 27 Oct 1875–29 Jan 1936 [60], Los Angeles CA). AMD, p. 100. AS, p. 326 (b. 1877). BHD1, p 156. IFN, p. 83 (age 58). Truitt 1983. "Parisian Star with Geraldine Farrer," *MPW*, 20 Sep 1919, 1790.

Dippel, Andreas [producer] (b. Kassel, Geramny, 30 Nov 1866–19 May 1932 [65], Los Angeles CA). BHD2, p. 69.

Di San Germano, Lucy (sister of **Linda Moglia**) [actress] (*née* Lucia Moglia, b. Turin, 1898). JS, p. 145 (in Italian silents from 1918).

Di Sangro, Elena [actress] (b. Vasto d'Aimone, Italy, 5 Sep 1901–26 Jan 1969 [67], Los Angeles CA). AS, p. 322. BHD, p. 151. IFN, p. 83.

Disney, Lillian *see* **Bounds, Lillian**

Disney, Walt (brother of Roy O. Disney, 1893–1971) [animator/producer/executive] (*né* Walter Elias Disney, b. Chicago IL, 5 Dec 1901–15 Dec 1966 [65], Burbank CA; complications after lung surgery). m. **Lillian Bounds**, 13 Jul 1925 (1 daughter, Diane; 10 grandchildren; 13 great-grandchildren), Lewiston ID (d. 1997). Bob Thomas, *Walt Disney; An American Original* (NY: Simon & Schuster, 1976). "Walt Disney, 65, Dies on Coast; Founded an Empire on a Mouse," *NYT*, 16 Dec 1966, 1:6, 40:1. "Lillian Disney; Widow of famed Hollywood producer," *PP-G*, 18 Dec 1997, B-7:1 (b. 1899?–16 Dec 1997 [98], Los Angeles CA; complications following a stroke). "After First Shock of Disney's Demise Spotlight Shifts to Brother & Staff," *Variety*, 21 Dec 1966. AS, p. 326 (b. 30 Dec 1890). BHD2, p. 69. IFN, p. 83. SD.

Ditcham, S. Frank [executive] (b. 1884–Oct 1953 [69?], London, England). BHD2, p. 69.

Ditmars, Raymond L. [producer] (d. New York NY, 12 May 1942). AMD, p. 100. BHD2, p. 69. W. Stephen Bush, "A New Star," *MPW*, 8 Feb 1914, 1095–96.

Ditrichstein, Leo [author/writer] (b. Temesbar, Hungary, 6 Jan 1865–28 Jun 1928 [63], Vienna, Austria). m. Josephine Wehrle. "Leo Ditrichstein," *Variety*, 4 Jul 1928. AS, p. 327. BHD, p. 151. Truitt 1983. Cover, *NYDM*, 27 Nov 1915 (onstage in *The Great Lover*).

Ditt, Josephine [actress] (b. Chicago IL, 7 Sep 1868–18 Oct 1939 [71], Los Angeles CA). m. **Thomas V. Ricketts** (d. 1939). (Nestor). AS, p. 327. BHD, p. 151. IFN, p. 83. Truitt 1983.

Dittenfass, Mark M. [producer] (b. Austria, 1872–23 Nov 1933 [61?], Cliffside Park NJ). BHD2, p. 69.

Dittenhoefer, Judge A.J. [actor] (b. Charleston SC, 17 Mar 1835–23 Feb 1919 [83], New York NY). BHD, p. 151.

Dittmars, Harry [scenarist]. No data found. FDY, p. 423.

Divad, David [director] (aka David Smith). No data found.

Dix, Beulah Marie [scenarist] (b. Kingston MA, 1876–25 Sep 1970 [93], Woodland Hills CA). m. George M. Flebbe. Evelyn F. Scott [daughter], *Hollywood When Silents Were Golden* (NY: McGraw-Hill Book Company, 1972). "Beulah M. Dix," *Variety*, 7 Oct 1970 (age 94). AS, p. 327. FDY, p. 423. IFN, p. 83 (age 94). 1921 Directory, p. 286.

Dix, Lillian [actress] (b. 1864–10 Oct 1922 [58?], New York NY). BHD, p. 151. IFN, p. 83.

Dix, Mae [actress] (b. Lake Ann MI, 1895?–21 Oct 1958 [63?], Los Angeles CA; from burns sustained in a fire). (Biograph.) "Mae Dix," *Variety*, 29 Oct 1958. AS, p. 327. BHD. p. 151. Truitt, p. 90.

Dix, Richard [actor] (*né* Ernest Carlton Brimmer, b. St. Paul MN, 10 Jul 1893–20 Sep 1949 [56], Los Angeles CA; heart attack). m. (1) Winifred Coe, 20 Oct 1931–33; Virginia Webster, 7 May 1935? (Paramount; RKO.) "Richard Dix Dead; Film Hero 25 Years; Noted for Virile Roles in 200 Movies, He Symbolized Law and Order on Screen," *NYT*, 21 Sep 1949, 31:1; "Richard Dix Will Filed; Widow and Four Children Share in Estate of Late Actor," *NYT*, 24 Sep 1949, 13:2 (b. 18 Jul 1895; age 54). "Richard Dix," *Variety*, 21 Sep 1949. AMD, p. 100. AS, p. 327 (b. 1894). BHD1, p. 156 (b. 18 Jul). FFF, p. 34. FSS, p. 93. GK, pp. 246–55. HCH, p. 15. IFN, p. 83. MH, p. 107. Truitt, p. 90 (b. 8 Aug 1894). "Richard Dix with Goldwyn Signs Two-Year Contract," *MPW*, 26 Mar 1921, 372. "Paramount Signs Dix," *MPW*, 10 Feb 1923, 546. Dana Rivers, "'It's the Women Who Are to Blame!', Says Richard Dix," *MW*, 5 Jan 1924, 13. Richard Dix, "A Message to the Fans," *MW*, 10 May 1924, 3 (Dix, on the cover, also edited this issue). David A. Balch, "The Most Popular Man in the Movies," *MW*, 10 May 1924, 8–9, 30. Lois Wilson,

"What I Think of Richard Dix," *MW,* 10 May 1924, 15, 30. Bland Johaneson, "That Saving Sense of Humor; The Face of a Hero and the Soul of a Comedian," *Photoplay Magazine,* May 1924, 67, 141. Adele Whitely Fletcher, "The Business of Being a Star," *MW,* 13 Sep 1924, 4–5, 29. "Dix Signed by DeMille," *MPW,* 17 Jan 1925, 280. Joan Cross, "Richard Seeks a Wife," *MM,* Nov 1925, 50–51, 111. Carol White, "He's Elected!; Richard Dix Wins Brewster Popularity Contest," *MPC,* Jul 1926, 16–17. "Richard Dix," *MPW,* 28 Aug 1926, 541. "Griffith Assigned to Direct Richard Dix in 'White Slave,'" *MPW,* 25 Sep 1926, 239. Harold R. Hall, "Here's a Star Who Doesn't Want to Twinkle; Richard Dix Says a Mouthful About This Starring Business," *MPC,* Jan 1927, 54–55, 89. Carol Johnston, "'Rich'—and Famous; A Regular—With Both Feet on the Ground," *MPC,* Aug 1927, 53, 86. "Paramount Stars Win in Popularity," *MPW,* 17 Dec 1927, 14. "Richard Himself Again; From His Illness the Rugged Mr. Dix Emerges as Sound in Health as in Popularity," *MPC,* Sep 1928, 38–39 (captioned photos). Helen Ludlam, "Heap Big Location; How They Made 'Redskin' with Richard Dix, and Real Indians and Everything," *Screenland,* Jan 1929, 48–50, 103–07. George A. Katchmer, "Richard Dix; Man of Diversified Talents," *CI,* 84 (Jun 1982), pp. 39–40. Richard E. Braff, "The Films of Richard Dix," *CI,* 166 (Apr 1989), 48, 50; #231, 43. Frank Dolven, "On the Surprising Longevity of Richard Dix's Star!," *CI,* 226 (Apr 1994), C10-C12.

Dixey, Henry E. [stage/film actor] (*né* Henry E. Dixon, b. Boston MA, 6 Jan 1859–25 Feb 1943 [84], Atlantic City NJ; from injuries sustained after having been struck by a bus on 21 Feb 1943). m. (2) Marie Nordstrom. (Universal.) "Henry Dixey Dies; An Actor 58 Years; Set Broadway Record Run as 'Adonis' in 1884—Succumbs to Accident Injuries at 84; An Idol of Gaslight Era; Was David Garrick in 'Oliver Goldsmith'—Also Seen in 'Erminie' and 'Pinafore,'" *NYT,* 26 Feb 1943, 19:1. "Henry E. Dixey," *Variety,* 3 Mar 1943. AMD, p. 100. AS, p. 327. BHD, p. 152. IFN, p. 83. Truitt, p. 90. "Henry E. Dixey Among Famous Players," *MPW,* 20 Sep 1913, 1262. "Dixey Wins Suit; Appellate Division Upholds $6,250 Judgment That Actor Obtained Against A.H. Woods," *NYDM,* 23 Jun 1915, 8:1. "In the Picture Studios," *NYDM,* 8 Sep 1915, 36:4 (one of the stage actors at Universal).

Dixon, Charlotte Louise [actress] (d. 4 Oct 1970, West Palm Beach FL). AS, p. 327. BHD, p. 152. IFN, p. 83. Truitt, p. 90.

Dixon, Conway [actor] (b. England, 1874–17 Jan 1943 [68?], London, England). AS, p. 327. BHD1, p. 156.

Dixon, Denver [stuntman/film and TV actor/director/producer] (*né* Victor Adamson; b. Kansas City MO, 4 Jan 1890–9 Nov 1972 [82], Los Angeles CA; heart attack). m. **Dolores Booth**. "Denver Dixon," *Variety,* 22 Nov 1972 (produced first western film in New Zealand; appeared in *Birth of a Nation* and *The Squaw Man.* "He built three indie studios in the 1917 period..."). AS, p. 327; p. 774 (Art Mix, b. IL, 12 Jun 1896). BHD1, p. 156; BHD2, p. 70. IFN, p. 84 (*né* Albert Adamson). Nick C. Nicholls, "Profiles; Denver Dixon," *Westerns and Serials,* #43 (1997), p. 26 (b. Auckland, New Zealand, 1890).

Dixon, Henry P. [actor] (b. New York NY, 21 Dec 1869–3 May 1943 [73], Los Angeles CA). "Henry Dixon," *Variety,* 12 May 1943 (age 72). AS, p. 327. BHD, p. 152. IFN, p. 84.

Dixon, Mrs. Madelyn *see* **Clare, Madelyn.**

Dixon, Ralph H. [pioneer motion picture executive/film editor] (b. 1897?–1 May 1948 [51], Los Angeles CA). (Selig, 1913; Fox; Universal.) "Ralph H. Dixon," *Variety,* 5 May 1948. AMD, p. 100. BHD2, p. 70. "Metropolitan Signs Dixon," *MPW,* 21 Nov 1925, 224.

Dixon, Rev. Thomas [Baptist minister/scenarist/author of *The Clansman*] (b. Shelby NC, 11 Jan 1864–3 Apr 1946 [82], Raleigh NC). m. (1) Harriet Bussey, 1896 (d. 1927); (2) **Madelyn** Donovan, 1939 (d. 1975). "Thomas Dixon Dies; Wrote 'Clansman' [1905]; Book Was Basis for 'Birth of a Nation,' Provocative Film—Supported Klu Klux Klan; He Had Held Pulpit Here; Also Was Lawyer, Lecturer—'White Supremacy' Was Subject of His Novels," *NYT,* 12 Jul 1950, 29:1 (wrote *The Flaming Sword,* 1939). "Thomas Dixon," *Variety,* 10 Apr 1946. CCN, p. 1294. WWWA. S.M. Wolfe, "'The Clansman'; Southerner's Plea That Memories of Civil War Be Allowed to Die [letter of 7 Apr 1905]," *NYT,* 9 Apr 1905, 8:5 [a]"It is hard to accuse Mr. Dixon of insincerity, in the face of his seeming earnestness, and yet it is diffucult to ascribe to one of his intuition, insight, and intelligence any motive in writing 'The Clansman' that would warrant his claim to sincerity."). Gene Vazzana, "Reading 'The Clansman' [letter]," *CI,* 248 (Feb 1996), C4, C9.

Dixon, Thomas, Jr. [scenarist]. No data found. FDY, p. 423.

Dmytryk, Edward [film editor/director] (b. Grand Forks, British Columbia, Canada, 4 Sep 1908–1 Jul 1999 [90], Encino CA; heart and kidney failure). m. (1) Madeleine Robinson, Mar 1932—div. 1948; (2) actress Jean Porter, 13 May 1948, Elliott City VA (2 sons, Richard and Michael; 2 daughters, Victoria and Rebecca). *It's a Hell of a Life but Not a Bad Living; Odd Man Out: A Memoir of the Hollywood Ten* (Time Books, 1978). "Edward Dmytryk, Film Director, Dies at 90," *NYT,* 3 Jul 1999, B6. Bob Thomas, "Edward Dmytryk; Director who went to prison during Red Scare," *PP-G,* 4 Jul 1999, p. B-5:1. (Began in 1923, FP-L; directorial debut: *The Hawk,* Monogram, 1935; RKO.) AS, p. 327. Michael Ankerich, "The Director & the Bobby-Soxer; The Story of Edward Dmytruk & Jean Porter," *CI,* 230 (August, 1994), 18 *et passim.*

Doane, Frank [actor] (b. England–d. 30 Apr 1943, Port Jefferson, LI NY). m. Bertha Blake (widow). "Frank Doane," *Variety,* 5 May 1943. AS, p. 327. BHD, p. 152.

Dobbs, Beverley B. [producer/cameraman]. No data found. m. May Kelly, 16 Mar 1924. AMD, p. 100. "Beverley B. Dobbs's Arctic Pictures," *MPW,* 12 Oct 1912, 128. "Dobbs's Alaska Pictures," *MPW,* 2 Nov 1912, 442. "No Injunction Against Dobbs," *MPW,* 30 Nov 1912, 866. "A Cinematograph Pioneer," *MPW,* 14 Dec 1912, 1071. "Dobbs Will Make Pictures," *MPW,* 30 Aug 1913, 944. "Dobbs a Benedict," *MPW,* 5 Apr 1924, 466.

Dobelin, Louis C. [actor] (b. 1880–13 Jun 1952 [72?], Los Angeles CA). AS, p. 328.

Doble, Budd [actor] (b. Philadelphia PA, 10 Oct 1841–29 Mar 1926 [84], Los Angeles CA). AS, p. 328 (d. Puente CA. AS, p. 328. BHD, p. 152.

Doble, Frances [stage/film actress] (b. Montreal, Canada, 10 Jun 1902–14 Dec 1969 [67], England). m. Lord Lindsay-Hogg. "Frances Doble," *Variety,* 31 Dec 1969, pp. 41, 47. AS, p. 328. BHD1, p. 157.

Doblin, Hugo [actor] (b. 1875-Nov 1960 [85?]). BHD, p. 152. IFN, p. 84.

Dobson, Fred [cameraman/scenarist/director]. No data found. (Lumiérè, Canada, 1897; Biograph, 1898; Morosco-Bosworthl; MGM.) AMD, p. 100. "Dobson with M-B Forces," *NYDM,* 16 Jun 1915, 21:3. "A Veteran Cameraman; The Unusual Record Made by Fred Dobson, Veteran Coast Photographer," *NYDM,* 20 Nov 1915, 33:2 (he had no retakes in 50,000 feet of film in five productions at Pallas Pictures. At Biograph he "was electrician and operator, carpenter, scenic artist, and photographer. It was the period when Biograph productions were dominant, and through his association with Griffith and the other graduates of this remarkable training school which has contributed so much to the present development of the business. Dobson now enjoys a unique prestige." He was descended from family members ["The Dobsons"] who "were the first professional performers upon the banjo in the history of the stage.... Pallas Pictures have a treasure in Fred Dobson."). "Fred Dobson Makes Record," *MPW,* 20 Nov 1915, 1464.

Dockson, Evelyn [actress] (b. MO, 8 Aug 1888–20 May 1952 [63], Burbank CA; cancer). AS, p. 328.

Dockstader, Lew [actor] (*né* George Alfred Clapp, b. Hartford CT, 7 Aug 1856–26 Oct 1924 [68], New York NY). "Lew Dockstader," *Variety,* 29 Oct 1924 (b. 1856). AMD, p. 100. AS, p. 328. BHD, p. 152. IFN, p. 84. "All-Star Gets Lew Dockstader," *MPW,* 2 May 1914, 650.

Dodd, Elizabeth [actress] (d. 19 Nov 1928, Los Angeles CA). BHD, p. 152. IFN, p. 84.

Dodd, Mrs. Ellen E. [actress] (*née?,* b. 1868–12 Mar 1935 [66], Brooklyn NY). (Vitagraph; WB.) "Mrs. Elan E. Dodd," *Variety,* 20 Mar 1935 (age 67). AS, p. 328. BHD1, p. 157. IFN, p. 84. Truitt, p. 90 (b. 1868).

Dodd, Rev. Neal [minister/actor] (b. Fort Madison IA, 6 Sep 1878–26 May 1966 [87], Los Angeles CA). "Rev. Neal Dodd," *Variety,* 1 Jun 1966 (age 88). AS, p. 328. BHD1, p. 157. IFN, p. 84 (b. 1879). Anthony Slide, "Letter," *FIR,* Apr 1977, 254. Helen Cotton, "Hollywood Parson; Rev. Neal Dodd Is Priest in Real and Reel Life," *NYT,* 3 Sep 1950, II, 4:1. Dunham Thorp, "The Marrying Parson of Hollywood," *MPC,* Oct 1927, 32, 77, 85.

Dodge, Anna [stage/film actress] (b. River Falls WI, 19 Oct 1867–4 May 1945 [77], Los Angeles CA; pneumonia). m. **George F. Hernandez**, ca. 1919 (d. 1922). (Began ca. 1911; Paramount.) AS, p. 328 (b. 18 Oct); p. 522 (Anna Hernandez). BHD1, p. 257 {Anna Hernandez). IFN, p. 84.

Dodge, Arthur B. [art director] (b. 1863–11 Jun 1952 [89?], Los Angeles CA). BHD2, p. 70.

Dodge, Louis [writer]. No data found. "Author of Love Picture Pleased with Choice of Star," *MPW,* 4 Sep 1920, 87.

Dodsworth, Betty [actress]. No data found. AMD, p. 100. "Betty Dodsworth," *MPW,* 7 Apr 1917, 69.

Doerry, Walter [actor] (b. Wilhelmshafen, Germany, 18 Jun 1880–24 Oct 1963 [83], Hildesheim, Germany). AS, p. 328.

Doherty, Ethel [scenarist]. No data found. (FP-L.) FDY, p. 423. Rob Wagner, "Times Do Not Change in Hollywood," *Screenland,* Dec 1927, 20–21, 101 (wrote the scripts for *The Vanishing*

American, Behind the Front, The Runaway and *Mantrap*).

Doherty, Mildred *see* **Frisby, Mildred**

Dol, Mona [actress] (*née* Amélie Alice Gabrielle Delbart, b. Lille, France, 28 May 1901–29 Dec 1990 [89], Paris, France [extrait de décès no. 18/2257]). AS, p. 328.

Dolenz, George [actor] (b. Trieste, Italy, 5 Jan 1908–8 Feb 1963 [55], Los Angeles CA). AS, p. 329. BHD1, p. 157.

Dolina, Pavel Trofimovich [director] (b. Ukraine, Russia, 12 Nov 1888–15 Nov 1955 [67], Ukraine, Russia). AS, p. 329.

Doller, Mikhail Ivanovich [director] (b. 1889–2 Mar 1952 [63?], Moscow, Russia). AS, p. 329. BHD2, p. 70.

Dolly, Roszika (twin sister of **Yansci Dolly**) [stage/film actress] (*née* Roszicka Deutsch, b. Budapest, Hungary, 25 Oct 1890–1 Feb 1970 [79], New York NY [Death Certificate Index No. 2586 (Rosie Netcher); age 75]; heart attack; buried at Forest Lawn Cemetery). m. (1) composer Jean A. Schwartz—div. 1921 (d. 1956); (2) tobacco multimillionaire Mortimer (Philip) Davis, Jr., 1927, NYC—div. ca. 1931; (3) Irving Netcher (brother of Townsend Netcher who married Constance Talmadge), 1932—sep 1940 (d. 1953). "Roszika Dolly," *Variety*, 4 Feb 1970 (Roszika [Rosie] Dolly Netcher; b. 1892). AMD, p. 100. AS, p. 329. BHD, p. 152. IFN, p. 84. SD. Truitt, p. 91 (*née* Roszicka Deutsch, b. 15 Oct 1892). J. Van Cartmell, "Along the Pacific Coast," *NYDM*, 29 Sep 1915, 33:1 (married Schwartz). "Dolly Sisters Dance for Metro Production," *MPW*, 27 Apr 1918, 574. June Lee, "Dan Cupid's Bulletin Board," *Paris and Hollywood Screen Secrets Magazine*, Aug 1927, 37 ("It is understood that Philip disobeyed all parental discretion in contracting the alliance with the famous music-hall star, and diplomatic relations have also been suspended with his family."). Max Pierce, "The Dolly Sisters: Glamour, Real to Reel," *CI*, 295 (Jan 2000), 14, 71–72 (b. 1892).

Dolly, Yansci [Jenny] (twin sister of **Roszika Dolly**) [stage/film actress] (*née* Janszieka Deutsch, b. Budapest, Hungary, 25 Oct 1890–1 Jun 1941 [50], Los Angeles CA; suicide by hanging with drapes; buried at Forest Lawn Cemetery). m. Jerome Schwartz; Harry Fox, 1914—div. 1920; Bernard W. Vinissky, 1935. (Film debut: *The Call of the Dance*, Kalem, 1915.) "Jenny Dolly, of Famed Sister Team, Suicides," *Variety*, 4 Jun 1941 (age 48). AMD, p. 101. AS, p. 329. BHD, p. 152. IFN, p. 84. Spehr, p. 188 (b. 1892). SD. Truitt, p. 91 (b. 1892). "Cupid Invades Jardin de Danse," *NYDM*, 15 Jul 1914, 19:2 (to marry Fox on 15 Aug at Long Beach, LI NY). "Kalem Procures Yancsi Dolly," *NYDM*, 1 Sep 1915, 26:4 (to debut in *The Call of the Dance*. "Until she received the flattering offer of the Kalem Company, Miss Dolly refused to turn her back on the vaudeville stage, and it was only when her present salary was doubled that she finally gave her consent. A fact not generally known is that this talented young denseuse [sic] has never received a dancing lesson in her life, having acquired all her ability, first, by watching others and then constantly practising what she had seen."). "Yancsi Dolly in Kalem Feature," *MPW*, XXV, 4 Sep 1915, 1658. "Dolly Sisters Dance for Metro Production," *MPW*, 27 Apr 1918, 574. Max Pierce, "The Dolly Sisters: Glamour, Real to Reel," *CI*, 295 (Jan 2000), 14, 71–72 (b. 1892).

Dolores, Miss [Ziegfeld Follies/actress] (*née* Kathleen Mary Rose, b. 1892–7 Nov 1975 [83], Paris, France). m. Tudor Wilkinson, 1923, France. "Dolores," *Variety*, 26 Nov 1975, p. 63. BHD, p. 152.

Doman, R.S. [publicist]. No data found. AMD, p. 101. "Doman Joins Universal Publicity Staff," *MPW*, XXII, 12 Dec 1914, 1531.

Domenighini, Anton Gino [director] (b. Darfo, Italy, 30 Apr 1897 [extrait de naissance no. 37/1897]-6 Nov 1966 [69], Milan, Italy). AS, p. 329.

Dominguez, Beatrice [actress/dancer] (b. San Bernardino CA, 6 Sep 1897–27 Feb 1921 [23], Los Angeles CA; after operation for appendicitis). (Vitagraph.) "Beatrice Dominguez," *Variety*, 4 Mar 1921. AMD, p. 101. AS, p. 329 (d. 12 Mar). BHD, p. 152. IFN, p. 84. Truitt, p. 91 (d. Mar 1921). "Obituary," *MPW*, 26 Mar 1921, 372.

Dominguez, Joe [actor] (b. Chihuahua, Mexico, 19 Mar 1894–12 Apr 1970 [76], Woodland Hills CA). AS, p. 329 (d. 11 Apr). BHD, p. 152.

Don, David L. [acrobat/minstrel/light opera comedian/stage and film actor] (aka Davy Don, b. Utica NY, 1867–27 Oct 1949 [82], New York NY). m. Mary Brady. (Eclair; Lubin; Davy Don Comedies.) "David L. Don," *NYT*, 28 Oct 1949, 23:3. AS, p. 330. BHD, p. 152. IFN, p. 84. "New Lubin Comedy Star," *NYDM*, 8 Sep 1915, 25:3 (to make his film debut). "Lubin Secures New Comedy Star," *Motography*, 2 Oct 1915, 680. "To Multiply D.L. Don," *NYDM*, 20 Nov 1915, 25:4 (Lubin to produce more Don pictures in response to public demand).

Donague, James T. [scenarist]. No data found. AMD, p. 101. "Select O," *MPW*, 26 Feb 1927, 638 (surname O'Dohoghoe in article). "Donague Will Prepare Script for 'Maryland,'" *MPW*, 26 Feb 1927, 644.

Donahue, Jack [actor/director/producer] (*né* John J. Donahue, b. New York NY, 29 Dec 1888–1 Oct 1930 [41], New York NY). AS, p. 330.

Donald, Dorothy [actress]. No data found. George A. Katchmer, "Forgotten Cowboys and Cowgirls—Part X," *CI*, 182 (Aug 1990), 38.

Donaldson, Arthur [stage/film actor/director] (*né* Arthur Danielson, b. Norsholm, Sweden, 5 Apr 1869–28 Sep 1955 [86], Long Island NY). (Vitagraph.) "Arthur Donaldson," *Variety*, 5 Oct 1955. AMD, p. 101. AS, p. 330. BHD1, p. 158; BHD2, p. 70.. IFN, p. 84. SD. "Kalem Sends Stock Company to Ireland," *MPW*, 3 Jun 1911, 1242. "A Royal Send Off," *MPW*, VIII, 24 Jun 1911, 1427. "Fine Engagement for Donaldson," *MPW*, 16 Sep 1911, 794. "Donaldson Leaves Screen for Stage," *MPW*, 26 Aug 1916, 1411. "Form Company to Star Arthur Donaldson Both on Stage and in Motion Pictures," *MPW*, 28 Aug 1920, 1187.

Donaldson, Lyn [actor] (b. Utica NY, 1867–27 Oct 1949 [82?], New York NY). BHD, p. 152.

Donaldson, Robert A. [scenarist] (b. 1888–11 Oct 1937 [49?], Los Angeles CA). AS, p. 330 (b. 1896). BHD2, p. 70.

Donaldson, Walter [actor/composer/lyricist] (b. Brooklyn NY, 15 Feb 1893–15 Jul 1947 [54], Santa Monica CA; liver ailment). m. Dorothy; m. stage actress Walda Mansfield—div. 1945. "W. Donaldson, 54, Song Writer, Dies; Composer of 'My Blue Heaven' [1927], 'Mammy,' Other Hits, Wrote Scores for Stage, Screen," *NYT*, 16 Jul 1947, 23:1 (wrote *Nobody Loves No Baby Like My Baby Loves Me; You're Driving Me Crazy; If I Can't Have You; After I Say I'm Sorry; Sam the Accordion Man; At Sundown; Back Home in Tennessee*). "Walter Donaldson Dies at 54; Turned Out String of Hits Spanning 30 Yrs.," *Variety*, 23 Jul 1947 (wrote *My Blue Heaven, My Buddy, et al.*). AS, p. 330. BHD1, p. 158; BHD2, p. 70. CEPMJ.

Donatien [actor] (*né* Charles Emile Bernard Wessbecher, b. Paris, France, 20 Jun 1887–8 Nov 1955 [68], Paris, France). AS, p. 330.

Dondi, Guglielmina [stage/film actress]. No data found. JS, p. 147 (appeared in Italian silents in 1919–20).

Dondini, Ada [actress] (*née* Itala Dondini, b. Cosenza, Italy, 18 Mar 1883–3 Jan 1958 [74], Chieti, Italy). AS, p. 330.

Donelli, Alfredo [cinematographer] (b. Udine, Italy). JS, pp. 147–48 (in Italian silents from 1915).

Doner, Hugh [scenic designer] (b. 1890–25 Oct 1918 [28?], Camp Fremont CA). AS, p. 330. BHD2, p. 70.

Doner, Martin J. [art director] (b. 1865?–15 Oct 1949 [84], Los Angeles CA). "Martin J. Doner," *Variety*, 26 Oct 1949. AMD, p. 101. AS, p. 330. BHD2, p. 70. "Famous Sculptor Gets Goldwyn Contract," *MPW*, 10 Mar 1923, 233.

Doner, Rose (daughter of vaudevillians Joe and Nellie Doner) [vaudevillian/film/stage actress] (b. 1905–15 Aug 1926 [21], New York NY; following appendicitis operation). "Rose Doner Dies; Sister of Ted and Kitty Succumbs to Appendicitis Operation," *Variety*, 18 Aug 1926, p. 90. AS, p. 330. BHD, p. 152. IFN, p. 85.

Donlan, James [actor] (father of Yolanda Donlan) (b. San Francisco CA, 23 Jul 1888–7 Jun 1938 [49], Los Angeles CA; heart attack). m. (daughter Yolanda b. 1920). "James Donlan," *Variety*, 15 Jun 1938 (last film: Lloyd's *Professor Beware*). AS, p. 331. BHD1, p. 158.

Donlevy, Brian [actor] (*né* Waldo Brian Donlevy, b. Portadown County, Armaugh, Ireland, 9 Feb 1899–5 Apr 1972 [73], Woodland Hills CA; throat cancer). m. (1) Lillian Arch; (2) Marjorie Lane. "Brian Donlevy, Film Tough Guy, Dies," *NYT*, 5 Apr 1972, 46:1 (age 69). "Brian Donlevy," *Variety*, 12 Apr 1972. AS, p. 331. BHD1, p. 158 (b. Ohio, 1901). IFN, p. 85 (b. 1901). John Roberts, "Brian Donlevy: Irish Tough Guy Becomes Hollywood Star," *CI*, 185 (Nov 1990), 18–19, 22, C2. Katz 1994. SD. Truitt 1983.

Donlin, Mike [actor] (b. Peoria IL, 30 May 1877–24 Sep 1933 [56], Los Angeles CA). m. Mabel Hite; (2) Rita Ros. "Mike Donlin," *Variety*, 26 Sep 1933 (age 55). AS, p. 331. BHD1, p. 159. IFN, p. 85. SD. Truitt, p. 91.

Donnelly, Dorothy Agnes [stage/film actress/writer] (b. New York NY, 28 Jan 1880–3 Jan 1928 [47], New York NY; nephritis and pneumonia). "Dorothy Donnelly," *Variety*, 11 Jan 1928 (age 48). AMD, p. 101. AS, p. 331. BHD, p. 152. IFN, p. 85. SD, p. 370. WWWA. "'The Thief' on Screen; With Dorothy Donnelly in Leading Role—Box Office Company to Film Stage Success," *NYDM*, 14 Oct 1914, 32:2 (debut film). "Dorothy Donnelly with Box Office," *MPW*, 17 Oct 1914, 348. "Another Metro Star; Dorothy Donnelly Engaged to Appear in Dyreda Productions Under J. Searle Dawley," *NYDM*, 19 May 1915, 22:4 (to debut in *The Iron Woman* for release on 1 Aug). "Dorothy Donnelly," *MPW,* 29 May 1915, 1435.

Donnelly, James A. [actor] (b. Boston MA, 1865?–13 Apr 1937 [72], Los Angeles CA). (Sennett.) "James Donnelly," *Variety,* 21 Apr 1937 (in films 22 years). AS, p. 331. BHD1, p. 159. IFN, p. 85. Truitt, p. 91.

Donnelly, Leo [actor] (b. Philadelphia PA, 1878?–20 Aug 1935 [57], Atlantic City NJ). "Leo Donnelly," *Variety,* 28 Aug 1935. AS, p. 331. BHD1, p. 159. IFN, p. 85. Truitt, p. 91.

Donnelly, Ruth [actress] (b. Trenton NJ, 17 May 1896–17 Nov 1982 [86], New York NY). AS, p. 331. BHD1, p. 159.

Donnelly, Thomas [minstrel/actor] (b. 1863–20 Jul 1923 [60?], Springfield MA). m. Emma Lipman. "Thomas Donnelly," *Variety,* 26 Jul 1923. BHD, p. 152. Ragan 2, p. 439.

Donoghue, Steve [actor] (d. London, England, 23 Aug 1945). BHD1, p. 159.

Donohue, Joseph [actor] (b. 1884?–24 Oct 1921 [37], Flatbush [Brooklyn] NY). "Joseph Donohue," *Variety,* 28 Oct 1921. AMD, p. 101. AS, p. 331. BHD, p. 152. IFN, p. 85. Truitt, p. 91. "Sign Little Joseph," *MPW,* 4 Aug 1923, 412.

Donovan, Frank P. [director] (b. New York NY, 10 Mar 1894). AMD, p. 101. AS, p. 331. "Innovations by Donovan," *MPW,* 16 May 1925, 347.

Donovan, Michael Patrick [actor] (b. MA, 29 Nov 1878–11 Nov 1960 [81], Los Angeles Co. CA). BHD1, p. 159. IFN, p. 85.

Dooley, Billy [brother-in-law of **Edward Dowling**] [actor] (b. Chicago IL, 8 Feb 1893–4 Aug 1938 [45], Los Angeles CA; heart attack). (Christie.) "Billy Dooley," *Variety,* 10 Aug 1938 (age 44). AMD, p. 101. AS, p. 332. BHD1, p. 159. IFN, p. 85. Truitt, p. 91. "A Misfit Sailor," *MPW,* 26 Sep 1925, 338. "Dooley Undergoes for Stomach Disorder," *MPW,* 26 Dec 1925, 776. "Dooley In and Out," *MPW,* 2 Jan 1926, 172.

Dooley, J. Gordon (brother of **Ray Dooley** [Mrs. Eddie Dowling]) [Dooley and Morton/stage/film actor] (b. 1899–24 Jan 1930 [31], Philadelphia PA; tuberculosis). m. Martha Morton, Jul 1922. "J. Gordon Dooley," *Variety,* 29 Jan 1930, p. 92 (age 31). AS, p. 332. BHD, p. 153. IFN, p. 85.

Dooley, Jed [actor] (b. 1884?–4 Sep 1973 [89]). "Jed Dooley," *Variety,* 12 Sep 1973, p. 87. AMD, p. 101. IFN, p. 85. "Jed Dooley," *MPW,* 3 Apr 1926, 351. "Jed Dolley," *MPW,* 24 Apr 1926, 602.

Dooley, Johnny [actor] (*né* John D. Dool, b. Glasgow, Scotland, 1887?–7 Jun 1928 [41], Yonkers NY; appendicitis). m. Florence Harris; Yvette Rugel; Maria Fruscella (aka Constance Madison), 1924. "Johnny Dooley," *Variety,* 13 Jun 1928. AMD, p. 101. AS, p. 332. BHD, p. 153. IFN, p. 85. Truitt, p. 91. "Johnny Dooley in Two Reelers," *MPW,* 10 May 1919, 802.

Dooley, Ray (sister of **J. Gordon Dooley**) [actress] (*née* Rachel Rice, b. Glasgow, Scotland, 30 Oct 1896–28 Jan 1984 [87], Los Angeles CA). m. **Eddie Dowling** (d. 1976). AS, p. 332 (b. 1890). BHD1, p. 159 (d. East Hampton NY).

Doolittle, W.C.J. [executive]. No data found. AMD, p. 101. "Producers' Trust Fund Plan Told of by W.C.J. Doolittle," *MPW,* 25 Aug 1923, 668.

Doone, Allen [actor] (d. Reno NV, 4 May 1948). BHD, p. 153.

Dor, Christiane [actress] (*née* Blanche Marguerite Sauty, b. Arras, France, 7 Mar 1892–14 May 1939 [47], Paris, France [extrait de décès no. SN/1939]). AS, p. 332.

Dora, Isa [actress in Italian silents]. No data found.

Dora, Josefine [actress] (b. Vienna, Ausria, 13 Nov 1867–28 May 1944 [76], Germany). BHD1, p. 159. IFN, p. 85.

Doraine, Lucy [actress] (*née* Ilonka Kovacks, b. Budapest, Hungary, 22 May 1898–14 Oct 1989 [91], Los Angeles CA). m. **Michael Curtiz** (d. 1962). (Ufa; Paramount.) AMD, p. 101. AS, p. 332. BHD1, p. 607. "Lucy Doraine, the Star of 'Good and Evil,' Preparing to Come to the United States," *MPW,* 7 Jan 1922, 77. "Lucy Doraine, Star of 'The Love Slave,' Will Tour United States," *MPW,* 4 Feb 1922, 514. Gladys Hall, "What Hollywood Did to Pola; Her Five American Years Find Her Still Imperial, Yet Not Unchanged," *MPC,* Aug 1928, 21, 68, 77 ("And the new importation, Lucy Doraine, was being rumored about as the Negri successor. They didn't even wait for the body to cool."). Gladys Hall, "A Pollyannic Pola; Lucy Doraine, Chosen to Succeed the Abdicant Miss Negri, Has Just the Gladdest Thoughts!," *MPC,* Sep 1928, 22, 70.

Doraldina [dancer/actress] (*née* Dora Saunders, b. San Francisco CA, 1887–13 Feb 1936 [48], Los Angeles CA). m. Frank Saunders. (Metro; Pathé.) "Doraldina," *Variety,* 19 Feb 1936. AMD, p. 101. AS, p. 332. BHD, p. 153. IFN, p. 85. Truitt, p. 91. WWS, p. 148. "New York Sensation in 'The Naulahka,'" *MPW,* 29 Dec 1917, 1975. "Doraldina, Actress and Dancer, Enters Independent Picture Producing Field," *MPW,* 9 Aug 1919, 852. "Los Angeles Studio Shots," *MPW,* 17 Jul 1920, 327 (arrived in Los Angeles with Saunders). "Doraldina Is to Begin Making Pictures on Her Own Account," *MPW,* 23 Apr 1921, 866.

Doran, Ann (daughter of **Carrie Barnett**) [film/TV actress] (b. Amarillo TX, 1911?–19 Sep 2000 [89], Carmichael CA). (Began ca. 1915; her sole lead role: *Rio Grande,* 1939.) "Ann Doran, 89, Character Actress," *NYT,* 3 Oct 2000, B10. Myrna Oliver, "Ann Doran; Appeared in 500 movies, 1,000 TV shows," *PP-G,* 3 Oct 2000, B:8.

Doran, Bob [cinematographer] (b. 1890?–30 Aug 1938 [48], Los Angeles CA). (Ince.) "Bob Doran," *Variety,* 7 Sep 1938. BHD2, p. 71.

Doran, Carrie A. [actress] (aka Rose Allen, b. 31 Mar 1885–3 May 1977 [92], Los Angeles CA). "Carrie A. Doran," *Variety,* 25 May 1977. AS, p. 332. BHD, p. 91 (Rose Allen). IFN, p. 7 (Rose Allen).

Doran, Dan [assistant director]. No data found. AMD, p. 101. "Made Assistant Director," *MPW,* 1 May 1926, 42.

Doran, Mary [actress] (*née* Florence Arnot, b. New York NY, 3 Sep 1907).

D'Orcy, Georgia [actress] (b. Bordeaux, France, 1878). BHD, p. 153.

Dore, Adrienne [actress] (b. Coeur d'Alene ID, 22 May 1907–26 Nov 1992 [85], Woodland Hills CA). AMD, p. 101. BHD1, p. 159. "Adrienne Dore Signed for Stern Bros. Comedies," *MPW,* 24 Apr 1926, 605.

Doree, Jean [actress]. No data found. AMD, p. 101. "Jean Doree Signed by Stern Bros. for Leads," *MPW,* 24 Sep 1927, 221.

Dorety, Charles R. [actor] (b. San Francisco CA, 20 May 1898–2 Apr 1957 [58], Los Angeles CA). "Charles R. Dorety," *Variety,* 10 Apr 1957. AS, p. 332. BHD1, p. 159. IFN, p. 85.

Dorfman, Nat N. [publicist] (b. 19 Nov 1894–3 Jul 1977 [82], New York NY [Death Certificate Index No. 11101; M.E. Case No. 4643]). . m. Belle (d. 1977). (Metro.) "Nat N. Dorfman," *Variety,* 13 Jul 1977. AS, p. 332. BHD2, p. 71.

Dorgan, T[homas] A[loysius] [animator] (b. San Francisco CA, 29 Apr 1877–2 May 1929 [52], Great Neck, LI NY). "'Tad' Drawing for International," *Variety,* 24 Jan 1919, p. 43 ("'Tad' [T.A. Dorgan], the cartoonist, will draw animated 'Indoor Sports' for the International Film Service weeklies."). AMD, p. 101. "Tad Will Draw for Universal," *MPW,* 1 Feb 1919, 662.

Dorgeles, Roland Maurice Lecavele [actor/scenarist] (b. Amiens, France, 15 Jun 1885 [extrait de naissance no. 1087]-18 Mar 1973 [87], Paris, France). AS, p. 332.

Doria, Luciano [director/writer]. No data found. JS, p. 148 (in Italian silents from 1918).

Doria, Max [actor] (*né* Marcel Georges Nicolas Dauphin, b. Amiens, France, 20 Nov 1896 [extrait de naissance no. 1992]-19 Dec 1989 [93], Noyers-sur-Serein, France). AS, p. 332.

Doria, Vera (sister of Charles Eyton) [opera/stage/film actress]. No data found. AMD, p. 101. "New Morosco Star; Morosco-Bosworth Combination Will Present Well-Known European Opera Star [lyric soprano] on Screen," *NYDM,* 23 Jun 1915, 25:1 (to debut in *The Majesty of the Law* and to appear in *As the Years Go By,* with Cyril Maude). "Vera Doria Latest Film Recruit," *MPW,* 17 Jul 1915, 489.

Dorian, Charles W. [assistant director/actor] (b. Santa Monica CA, 1893–21 Oct 1942 [49], on train near Albuquerque NM; heart attack). "Charles Dorian," *Variety,* 28 Oct 1942 (began 1917). AS, p. 332. BHD2, p. 71 (b. 1891). IFN, p. 85. Truitt, p. 92.

Dorin, René [actor/singer] (b. France, 13 Nov 1892–15 Aug 1969 [76], France). AS, p. 332.

Dorleac, Maurice (father of Catherine, Françoise and Sylvie Dorleac) [actor] (*né* Georges Maurice Edmond Dorleac, b. Paris, France, 26 Mar 1901 [extrait de naissance no. SN/6/1901]-4 Dec 1979 [78], Paris, France). m. (daughters Catherine; Françcoise, 1942–67; Sylvie, b. 14 Dec 1946). AS, p. 333.

Dorman, Shirley [actress]. No data found. Photograph and quip, *Picture Play,* Dec 1927, 91. ("A Second Gloria Swanson?" Appeared in *Honeyman Hate, The One Woman Idea, The City Gone Wild* and *One Woman to Another.*)

Dorny, Thérèse [actress] (*née* Thérèse Jeanne Longo-Dorni, b. Paris, France, 18 Sep 1891–14 Mar 1976 [84], Saint-Tropez, France [extrait de décès no. 22.1976]). AS, p. 333.

Doro, Marie [stage/film actress] (*née* Marie Kathryn Stewart, b. Duncannon PA, 25 May 1882–9 Oct 1956 [74], New York NY [Death Certificate Index No. 21152]). m. **Elliott Dexter,** 1915 (d. 1941). (British film debut: *Twelve-Ten.*) "Marie Doro, 74, Retired Actress; Star of Stage and Movies Dies—Appeared in Plays Produced by Frohman," *NYT,* 10 Oct 1956, 39:3. "Marie Doro," *Variety,* 17 Oct 1956 (b. Kansas City KS). AMD, p. 102. AS, p. 333. BHD, p. 153. IFN, p. 85. JS, p. 148 (made films in Italy in 1919 and

1920). Truitt, p. 92. "A Conventional Play of Life in the Circus; Marie Doro Knocks Out One Actor in 'Friquet'; Drama Lays Others Low," *NYT,* 1 Feb 1905, 9:4 ("In occasional passages where the demands are in harmony with her natural natural endowments she may be said to be succeessful."). "Now It's Marie Doro; Frohman Star the Latest 'Legitimate' Brilliant to Be Captured for the Screen," *NYDM,* 11 Nov 1914, 25:4 (to debut in *The Morals of Marcus,* FP-L). "Famous Players Engage Marie Doro," *MPW,* 21 Nov 1914, 1084. Cover, *NYDM,* 4 Aug 1915. "Marie Doro Married," *MPW,* 25 Dec 1915, 2342. "Marie Doro," *MPW,* 10 Feb 1917, 857. "Marie Doro Forms Her Own Company," *MPW,* 4 May 1918, 699. Hazel Simpson Naylor, "Sunlight on White Velvet," *MPC,* Mar 1919, 20–21, 62, 81 ("Marie Doro is to the American stage what the Renaissance was to Rome."). M.H.C., "The Girl from America; Marie Doro Chats on British Films and Film Studios," *The Picture Show,* No. 11, 12 Jul 1919, 12 (disliked the British artificial lighting). "Herbert Brenon Scores a Beat," *MPW,* 16 Aug 1919, 968. Billy H. Doyle, "Lost Players," *CI,* 161 (Nov 1988), C19.

Dorr, Lester [actor] (*né* Harry Lester Dorr, b. MA, 8 May 1893–25 Aug 1980 [87], Los Angeles CA). AS, p. 333.

Dorris, Albert B. [assistant director] (b. 1878?–5 Nov 1952 [74], No. Hollywood CA). (Vitagraph [NY]; Universal.) "Albert B. Dorris," *Variety,* 12 Nov 1952. AS, p. 333. BHD2, p. 71 (d. LA CA).

D'Orsa, Lonnie [director] (b. MO, 2 Nov 1897–24 Jul 1993 [95], Beverly Hills CA). . (Sennett.) m. Florence Green, early '30's, Egypt. "Lonnie D'Orsa," *Variety,* 11 Oct 1993, p. 201:5 ("director of silent-era films"). AS, p. 278. BHD2, p. 71.

Dorsay, Edmund [actor] (b. 1897?–12 Jun 1959 [62], New York NY [Death Certificate Index No. 13402]). "Edmund Dorsay," *Variety,* 17 Jun 1959. AS, p. 333. BHD, p. 153. IFN, p. 85.

D'Orsay, Lawrence [stage/film actor] (*né* William Lawrence Dorset, b. Peterborough, Northamptonshire, England, 19 Aug 1853–13 Sep 1931 [78], London, England). m. (1) Marie Dagmar; (2) Susan Rucholme. "Lawrence D'Orsay, British Actor, Dead; Made London Debut in 1877—First Major Success Here Was in 'The Earl of Pawtucket'; In John Drew's Last Play; His Final Role in London Was with Paul Robeson in 'Othello'—Injured in a Fall a Year Ago," *NYT,* 14 Sep 1931, 17:1 (age 71). "Lawrence D'Orsay," *Variety,* 22 Sep 1931. AS, p. 278. BHD, p. 153. IFN, p. 85. NNAT. SD. Truitt, p. 92 (b. 1860).

Dorsch, Kaethe [actress] (*née* Katharina Dorsch, b. Nuremberg, Germany, 29 Dec 1890–27 Dec 1957 [66], Vienna, Austria). AS, p. 333.

Dorsch, Kaethe [stage/film actress] (b. Nurenburg, Germany, 29 Dec 1889–25 Dec 1957 [67], Vienna, Austria; liver infection). "Kaethe Dorsch," *Variety,* 1 Jan 1958, p. 55; 15 Jan 1958, p. 70 (b. 1890; age 66). BHD1, p. 160. IFN, p. 85 (age 66).

Dorsey, Dee [actress]. No data found. AMD, p. 102. "Alaska Girl in Metro Play," *MPW,* 21 Jul 1917, 488.

D'Orvella, Mina [actress]. No data found. JS, p. 149 (in Italian silents from 1917).

Dorville [actor] (*né* Georges-Henri Dobane, b. Paris, France, 1 Mar 1883–10 Aug 1941 [58], Souillac, France). AS, p. 334.

Dorziat, Gabrielle [actress] (*née* Marie Odile Léonie Gabrielle Sigrist, b. Epernay, France, 25 Jan 1880–30 Nov 1979 [93], Biarritz, France [extrait de décès no. 396/1979]). AS, p. 334. BHD1, p. 160 (b. 1886).

Doscher, Doris [actress] (b. 24 Jun 1882–9 Mar 1970 [88], Farmingdale, LI NY). . m. Dr. H. William Baum. (Griffith.) "Mrs. H. William Baum," *Variety,* 18 Mar 1970 (played Eve in *The Birth of a Nation* and was the model for the U.S. Liberty 25¢ piece). AS, p. 334. BHD, p. 153. IFN, p. 86. Truitt, p. 20 (model for the U.S. Liberty 25-cent piece).

Dossett, Chappell [actor] (b. London, England, 1 Jan 1883–19 Dec 1961 [78], Los Angeles Co. CA). BHD1, p. 160.

Dostal, Karel [actor/director] (b. Nymburk, Germany, 14 Mar 1884). AS, p. 334 (in Czechoslovakian films).

Doty, Douglas Z[abriskie] [magazine editor/title writer/scenarist] (b. New York NY, 15 Oct 1874–20 Feb 1935 [60], Los Angeles CA; heart attack). (Metro; Paramount; WB.) "Douglas Z. Doty," *Variety,* 27 Feb 1935. AMD, p. 102. AS, p. 334. BHD2, p. 71. FDY, pp. 423, 443. IFN, p. 86. WWWA. "Doty a Scenario Writer," *MPW,* 1 Jan 1921, 87. "Joins DeMille Staff," *MPW,* 8 Aug 1925, 657. "Doty Writes Plot," *MPW,* 2 Apr 1927, 488.

Doty, Weston and Winston [actors] (twins, b. Malta OH, 18 Feb 1913–1 Jan 1934 [20], CA; drowned in flood). "Winston and Weston Doty," *Variety,* 9 Jan 1934 (age 19). AS, p. 334. BHD, p. 153. IFN, p. 86. Truitt, p. 92 (b. 1915).

Doublepatte [actor] (*né* Karl Schenstrom, b. Copenhagen, Denmark, 13 Nov 1881–10 Apr 1942 [60], Copenhagen, Denmark). AS, p. 334.

Doublier, François [boy on bicycle in *Workers Leaving the Lumière Factory,* 1895/actor/producer] (*né* Francisque Doublier, b. Lyons, France, 11 Apr 1878–3 Apr 1948 [69], Englewood NJ). "Francois Doublier, Film Pioneer, Dies; Producer at Fort Lee During Silent Movie Era Shot Photos of Czar's Coronation in '96," *NYT,* 4 Apr 1948, 60:6. "Francis Doublier," *Variety,* 7 Apr 1948. AS, p. 334. BHD2, p. 71.

Doucet, Catherine [actress] (*née* Catherina Green, b. Richmond VA, 20 Jun 1875–24 Jun 1958 [83], New York NY). AS, p. 334. BHD1, p. 160.

Doucet, M. Paul [actor] (b. France, 1886?–10 Oct 1928 [42?], New York NY; septic poisoning). m. **Catherine Calvert** (d. 1971). "M. Paul Doucet," *Variety,* 17 Oct 1928. AS, p. 334. BHD, p. 153. Truitt, p. 92.

Doud, Omar F. [publicist]. No data found. AMD, p. 102. "Omer F. Doud Goes West," *MPW,* XIV, 23 Nov 1912, 773. "O.F. Doud Joins George Kleine," *MPW,* 28 Jun 1913, 1366.

Dougherty, Daniel W. [songwriter] (b. Lansdowne PA, 17 Jul 1897–13 Jun 1955 [57], Hollywood CA). (Columbia.) "Daniel W. Dougherty," *NYT,* 15 Jun 1955, 31:4. "Dan Dougherty," *Variety,* 15 Jun 1955 (b. 1900). ASCAP 1966, p. 182.

Dougherty, Hughey [minstrel/vaudevillian/actor] (b. Philadelphia PA, 4 Jul 1844–20 Aug 1918 [75], Philadelphia PA; at Kirkbride's, hospital for the insane). "Hughie Dougherty Dies," *Variety,* 23 Aug 1918.

Dougherty, Lee E. [executive/film editor]. No data found. AMD, p. 102. Lee E. Dougherty, "Conditions and Features," *MPW,* 11 Jul 1914, 224–26 (installed an Eidoloscope in the Boston Museum in 1896, then became "stage director" for Biograph with their new machine. He didn't then nnd doesn't now think that films would supplant the legitimate drama. "My greatest objection to the feature film, I mean the program monopolizers, is that it is in opposition to the very motive that brought the moving picture to the front." One has to be present at the beginning of the first reel to understand the whole film, while shorter films can be caught on the fly.). J. Van Cartmell, "Film News from the Coast; Biograph Studio Comes to Live—Reincarnation of a Lot of Reliable Old Directors," *NYDM,* 20 Nov 1915, 32:3 (the returnees included Daugherty [sic] as manager of production, Travis Vale, Wray Physioc, Walter Coyle, J. Farrell McDonald, and Thomas Walsh). "Lee Doughertry Recalls Early Days," *MPW,* 23 Sep 1916, 1952. "Unhonored and Unsung Is Film Editor; That is, Usually, but Such Is Not the Situation with Lee Dougherty at World Pictures," *MPW,* 31 Aug 1918, 1252:2 ("If the story was honestly told of many of the great hits instead of directors and stars getting the credit the film editor would be entitled to all the praise and glory."). "Lee Dougherty Looks with Envy on a Coast Contract," *MPW,* 31 Jan 1920, 766:2 (with Biograph 19 years; with World 2 years; now at liberty and longing for California). "Mary O'Connor Will Now Give Scenarios Entire Attention," *MPW,* 25 Sep 1920, 514 (Daugherty [sic] was "...said to have been the first scenario editor in the motion picture business, having acted in that capacity with Biograph in 1906. He accepted the first story ever written for the screen by Frank E. Woods, now supervising director at the Lasky studio."). "Lee Dougherty, 26 Years in Industry, Recalls Incidents in Its Progress," *MPW,* 11 Mar 1922, 142:1 (he says that films were "dailies" and scenics until Gaston and George Méliès produced a fairyland story in 1903. Then *The Poacher* from England had "the first chase ever recorded that we awoke to the story possibilities. As far as I know, *Hiawatha* was the first American-made motion picture that claimed to have a story. Shortly after that we made *The Pioneers* in the Adirondacks. It had a thin Indian story—but a story nevertheless." The first comedy was *Personal,* at Biograph, which consisted almost entirely of chase scenes. In 1908 a one-reel picture without a chase was made—*After Many Years,* written by Frnnk Woods and directed by D.W. Griffith.).

Dougherty, Lew E. [director/publicist]. No data found. m. Mayme Elinore Butt, 26 Oct 1910. AMD, p. 102. "Nuptials," *MPW,* 5 Nov 1910, 1040. "Dougherty Leaves Biograph," *MPW,* 5 Apr 1913, 33. "Biograph Directors," *MPW,* 10 Jul 1915, 243–44. "Dougherty Out of Biograph," *MPW,* 16 Sep 1916, 1849 (Lee E. Dougherty in article).

Dougherty, Virgil Jack [actor] (b. 1895–16 May 1938 [43?], Los Angeles CA; suicide by carbon monoxide). m. **Barbara La Marr** (d. 1926). "Virgil Jack Dougherty," *Variety,* 18 May 1938 ("Dougherty was found dead in his car in the Hollywood Hills of carbon monoxide"). BHD2, p. 334. Truitt, p. 92.

Doughty, Francis W[orcester] (son of playwright Sara P. Doughty) [writer/scenarist] (b. Brooklyn NY, 5 Nov 1850–30 Oct 1917 [66], Cresskill NJ; after a fall). (Thanhouser, 1913.) "Francis W. Doughty Dead; Author of 1,200 Detective Stories and Creator of 'Nick Carter,'" *NYT,* 1 Nov 1917, 15:3 (Doughty Street in Brooklyn is named after his grandfather). "The Roundup," *The Dime Novel Roundup,* XXV, Feb 1957, 16–17 (reprint from *MPS,* 3 Sep 1915). "Francis W. Doughty," *Variety,* 9 Nov 1917. AMD, p. 102. BHD2, p. 71. "Doughty to Write for Horsley," *MPW,* 21 Aug 1915, 1293. "Francis Worcester Doughty," *MPW,* 18 Sep 1915, 2003. "Obituary," *MPW,* 17 Nov 1917, 1028 (d. 29 Oct).

Douglas, Byron [actor] (b. 1865–21 Apr 1935 [70], New York NY). m. Marie Booth (d. 1932). "Byron Douglas," *Variety,* 24 Apr 1935. AS, p. 334. BHD1, p. 160. IFN, p. 86. SD. Truitt, p. 92. George Katchmer, "Forgotten Cowboys and Cowgirls—Part XVIII," *CI,* 195 (Sep 1991), C7-C8.

Douglas, Frederic C. [stock/stage/manager/film actor] (b. Newark NJ, 1867–17 Jul 1929 [62], Los Angeles CA; cancer). "Frederic C. Douglas," *Variety,* 24 Jul 1929, p. 75. AS, p. 334. BHD, p. 153. IFN, p. 86.

Douglas, Gertrude [vaudevillian/actress] (d. 21 Apr 1929, Cambridge MA; pneumonia). m. H.J. Hollick. "Gertrude Douglas," *Variety,* 24 Apr 1929.

Douglas, Gilbert [stage/film actor] (b. Southampton, England, 1881?–11 Oct 1959 [78], Philadelphia PA). "Gilbert Douglas," *Variety,* 14 Oct 1959 ("veteran actor"). AMD, p. 102. AS, p. 334. BHD, p. 153. IFN, p. 86. "Belasco Player Makes His Screen Debut," *MPW,* 5 Oct 1918, 102.

Douglas, Gordon [actor] (b. New York NY, 15 Dec 1909–30 Sep 1993 [84], Los Angeles CA; cancer). m. Julia Mock. "Gordon Douglas," *Variety,* 25 Oct 1993, 68:3 (began on the East Coast in 1920's). AS, p. 335. BHD1, p. 160; BHD2, p. 71 (d. 29 Sep).

Douglas, Kenneth [stage/film actor] (b. London, England, 1873–17 Oct 1923 [50?], New York NY, of alcoholic poisoning at Mrs. Alston's sanitarium). "Kenneth Douglas," *Variety,* 25 Oct 1923, p. 6. BHD, p. 153.

Douglas, Lillian [actress]. No data found. AMD, p. 102. "Miss Walker Has Changed Her Name," *MPW,* 10 Dec 1921, 668 (to avoid confusion with Lillian Walker).

Douglas, Lloyd C. [actor] (b. 1877–13 Feb 1951 [72?], Los Angeles CA). AS, p. 335.

Douglas, Marian *see* **Gregory, Ena**

Douglas, Maud [actress]. No data found. m. John Boyle, 1915 (eloped). AMD, p. 102. "Just Mr. and Mrs. Boyle," *MPW,* 31 Jul 1915, 823.

Douglas, Royal [actor] (b. Canada, 17 Aug 1888–29 Jun 1924 [35], Cleveland OH). AS, p. 335 (b. 1884-d. 15 Jun). BHD, p. 153; BHD2, p. 71. IFN, p. 86.

Douglas, Tom [actor] (*né* Lee Doolan, b. Louisville KY, 4 Sep 1895–4 May 1978 [82], Cuernavaca, Mexico; heart attack). (Paramount.) "Tom Douglas," *Variety,* 12 Jul 1978. AS, p. 335. BHD1, p. 161. IFN, p. 86. SD.

Douglas, William A.S. [director] (b. Bushmills, Northern Ireland, 1886–21 Jul 1951 [65?], New York NY). BHD2, p. 71.

Douglass, Leon F. [executive/inventor/founded the Victor Talking Machine Co.] (b. Lincoln NB, 1869?–7 Sep 1940 [71], near San Francisco CA). "Leon F. Douglass," *Variety,* 11 Sep 1940. BHD2, p. 71.

Dounel [actor] (*né* Louis Alfred Doumet, b. Marseilles, France, 2 Dec 1889–23 May 1954 [64], Reillanne, France [extrait de décès no. 3/1954]). AS, p. 335.

Dove, Billie, "The American Beauty" [Ziegfeld Follies dancer/actress] (*née* Lillian Bohney, b. New York NY, 14 May 1900–31 Dec 1997 [97], Woodland Hills CA; pneumonia). m. (1) **Irvin V. Willat**, 27 Oct 1923, Santa Monica CA—div. Jul 1930 (d. 1976); (2) Robert Kenaston, May 1933 (d. 1973; 1 son, Robert, d. 1996); (3) John Miller, m. and div., 1973. (Began 1921; bit part in *Diamond Head,* 1962.) Mel Gussow, "Billie Dove, Damsel in Distress in Silent Films, Is Dead at 97," *NYT,* 6 Jan 1998, D21. "Billie Dove," *Variety,* 16 Feb 1998,71:3 ("Willat, who had appeared in several Mary Pickford films before turning to directing, was paid $350,000 by [Howard] Hughes to divorce Dove, according to [Gail] Adelson [adopted daughter]."). "Billie Dove; Silent film star who was celebrated for her beauty," *PP-G,* 9 Jan 1998, B-6:3 ("When a photographer told her she looked like a dove, she adopted it as her professional surname."). "Murió Billie Dove," *La Nación* [Buenos Aires, Argentina], 4 Jan 1998, IV, 9 ("Desde 1920 actuó en decenas de películas del cine mudo. En 1932, dejó la actividad para casarse."). AMD, p. 102. AS, p. 335. BHD1, p. 607. FFF, p. 138 (b. 1903). FSS, p. 94. HCH, p. 13. Katz, p. 356. MH, p. 108 (b. 1903). "Billie Dove," WBO2, pp. 168–69 (b. 1903). "Miss Billie Dove New Metro Star; Popularity Impressed Marcus Loew," *MPW,* 29 Apr 1922, 932. "Billie Dove," *MPW,* 5 Dec 1925, 441. "Billie Dove Signed," *MPW,* 5 Jun 1926, 4. "Billie Dove Signs with Lois Weber," *MPW,* 7 Aug 1926, 339. "Billie Dove Signed," *MPW,* 2 Oct 1926, 2. "Billie Dove, the "Rainbow Girl,'" *MPW,* 8 Jan 1927, 125. "Billie Dove," *MPW,* 19 Mar 1927, 177. Carol Johnston, "Even the Girls Are for Her; A Close-Up of Billie Dove," *MPC,* Dec 1927, 53, 83. Elisabeth Goldbeck, "Are You Up-to-Date About Billie Dove?," *Movie Classic,* Dec 1931, 50, 81. DeWitt Bodeen, "Billie Dove; An American Beauty," *FIR,* Apr 1979, 193–208. George A. Katchmer, "Forgotten Cowboys & Cowgirls—Part XIII," *CI,* 190 (Apr 1991), C8 (b. 4 May). Michael Ankerich, "The Flight of the Elusive Dove: Billie Dove Looks Back," *CI,* 228 (Jun 1994), 12 *et passim* (1920 U.S. census lists birth year of 1903; includes filmography).

Dove Eyes [actress] (d. 13 Jul 1969, Los Angeles Co. CA). BHD, p. 153.

Dovey, Alice [Broadway musical comedy/film actress] (b. Plattsmouth NB, 28 Aug 1884–12 Jan 1969 [84], Tarzana CA). (FP-L.) m. **John E. Hazzard**, 1916 (d. 1935). "Alice Dovey Hazzard," *Variety,* 22 Jan 1969. AMD, p. 102. AS, p. 335. BHD, p. 153 (b. 1885). IFN, p. 86. SD, p. 375 (b. 1885). Truitt, p. 92. "Alice Dovey with Gaumont," *NYDM,* 23 Oct 1915, 30:4 (to debut in *The Reformer,* 1 reel, with "Budd" Ross and James Levering). "Gaumont Gets Alice Dovey," *MPW,* 30 Oct 1915, 952. "Alive Dovey," *MPW,* 30 Dec 1916, 1936.

Dovjenko, Alexandre Petrovich [actor/director/scenarist] (b. Sosnitsa, Ukraine, Russia, 11 Sep 1894–25 Nov 1956 [62], Moscow, Russia; heart attack). AS, p. 335. BHD2, p. 72.

Dowerman, C.L. [cameraman]. No data found. AMD, p. 102. "Dowerman to Take Pictures in West," *MPW,* 14 Aug 1915, 1138.

Dowlan, William C. [actor/director] (b. St. Paul MN, 21 Sep 1882–6 Nov 1947 [65], Los Angeles CA). (American-Mutual; Universal.) AMD, p. 102. AS, p. 336. BHD, p. 154; BHD2, p. 72. IFN, p. 86. "Dowlan Secured by Universal," *MPW,* 14 Feb 1914, 825. Quip, *NYDM,* 19 May 1915, 32:1 (first directorial effort, *Out of the Night*). "William Dowlan in New York," *MPW,* 2 Jun 1917, 1449. "Dowlan, Metro Director," *Motography,* 11 Aug 1917, 312 (to work at 3 West 61st Street, NYC). "William C. Dowlan Director for Metro," *MPW,* 25 Aug 1917, 1202.

Dowling, Ambrose [executive] (b. 1877–19 Dec 1934 [57], London, England). BHD2, p. 72.

Dowling, Andrew [actor/assistant director] (b. 1878–6 Apr 1919 [41?], Brooklyn NY). (Vitagraph.) BHD2, p. 72.

Dowling, Edward [actor/scenarist] (*né* Joseph Nelson Goucher, b. Woonsocket RI, 9 Dec 1894–18 Feb 1976 [81], Smithfield RI). m. Rae (or **Ray) Dooley** (d. 1984). "Eddie Dowling," *Variety,* 25 Feb 1976 (Broadway debut, *The Velvet Lady,* 1919; "Dowling" was father's middle name). AS, p. 336. BHD1, p. 161 (b. 1895); BHD2, p. 72 (b. 1895). IFN, p. 86. Bert Ennis, "He's Gotta Hear 'Em Laugh; Eddie Dowling Won't Eat His Applause Unless It's Fresh," *MPC,* Aug 1929, 60, 88, 92 (b. Providence RI).

Dowling, Joseph J[ohnson] [actor] b. Pittsburgh PA, 4 Sep 1848–8 Jul 1928 [80], Los Angeles CA). m. Sadie Hesen. (Film debut: *The Trail of the Lonesome Star,* 19 Oct 1913, Flying A.) "Joseph J. Dowling," *Variety,* 11 Jul 1928. AMD, p. 103. AS, p. 336. BHD, p. 154. IFN, p. 86. MH, p. 108 (b. 1850). SD. Truitt, p. 93 (d. 10). "Joseph J. Dowling," *MPW,* 26 May 1917, 1296. "Joseph J. Dowling with Paralta," *MPW,* 4 Aug 1917, 781. "Casting Coincidence," *LA Times,* 7 Mar 1920, III, p. 16 (he and Roy Stewart made their film debuts in the same film, and also on 19 Oct 1919, both were cast in B.B. Hampton's *Desert Wheat*). George Katchmer, "Remembering the Great Silents," *CI,* 197 (Nov 1991), 52–53.

Dowling, Pat [publicist]. No data found. m. Ruth Mohrman, 25 Oct 1919. AMD, p. 103. "Weddings," *MPW,* 22 Nov 1919, 422. Charles Edward Hastings, "Pat Dowling, In His Little French Car, Sells Christie Comedies Enroute West," *MPW,* 11 Sep 1926, 121. "Dowling, on Auto Trip to Coast, Hits Chicago," *MPW,* 9 Oct 1926, 353. "Writes Christie History," *MPW,* 25 Dec 1926, 571.

Downes, Olin [actor] (*né* Edwin Olin Downes, b. 1886–22 Aug 1955 [69?], New York NY). AS, p. 336.

Downing, Harry [actor] (b. 1893–9 Jan 1972 [78], Boston MA). AS, p. 336. BHD, p. 154. IFN, p. 86.

Downing, Walter [actor] (b. Rochester NY, 28 Oct 1874–22 Dec 1937 [63], Los Angeles CA). "Walter Downing," *Variety,* 29 Dec 1937 ("...veteran western actor...had been in pictures since 1915."). AS, p. 336. BHD1, p. 161. IFN, p. 86. Truitt, p. 93.

Downs, Johnny [actor: Our Gang, 1922/vaudevillian/dancer/TV host] (b. Brooklyn NY, 10 Oct 1913–6 Jun 1994 [80], Coronado CA; cancer). m. June. (Roach; Paramount.) "Johnny Downs, 80, Star of 'Our Gang,'" *NYT,* CXLIII, 14 Jun 1994, D21:6. "Johnny Downs," *Variety,* 18 Jul 1994 (age 81). AMD, p. 103. BHD1, p. 161. Katz, p. 357. "'Our Gang' Has New Member in Their Newest Production," *MPW,* 7 Mar 1925, 83. "Downs in Vaudeville," *MPW,* 11 Dec 1926, 409.

Chris Farlekas, "The Reign of the 'King of Hollywood's B Movies,'" *CFC,* 41 (Winter, 1973), 51.

Downs, Rex E. [actor] (b. Waterville OH, 22 Aug 1885–3 Feb 1975 [89], Indio CA). (Kalem.) Appeared in *Gray Eagle's Revenge; At the End of the Rope;* and *Kidnapped by Indians.*

Doxat-Pratt, B[ernard] **E**[dwin] [director] (b. Upper Norwood, England, 26 Jul 1886). AS, p. 336.

Doxat-Pratt, Norman [actor] (b. England, 1 Jun 1916–1982 [66?]). BHD, p. 154.

Doyle, Arthur Conan [physician/writer] (b. Edinburgh, Scotland, 22 May 1859–7 Jul 1930 [71], at Windlesham in Crowborough, Sussex, England). m. (1) Louisa Hawkins, 1885, Minsterworth, England (d. 4 Jul 1906, London; 2 children); (2) Jean Leckie, 1907 (3 children). "Conan Doyle Dead from Heart Attack; Spiritist, Novelist and Creator of Famous Fiction Detective [Sherlock Holmes] Ill Two Months—Was 71; Family Awaits 'Message'; Son [Adrian Conan Doyle] Is Confident Father Will Confirm Existence, in Which He Believed," *NYT,* 8 Jul 1930, 1:4, 9:3 (Holmes first appeared in 1887, based on Dr. Joseph Bell, a Scotch surgeon; Holmes was "killed off" in 1904 and 1927). "Sir Conan Doyle Dead," *Variety,* 9 Jul 1930. "Sir Conan Doyle's Wife Dead," *NYT,* 6 Jul 1906, 7:6. "Who's Who? On Stage and Screen," *MPC,* Dec 1924, 43.

Doyle, Buddy (brother of actor Gene Doyle) [singer/actor] (*né* Benjamin Taubenhaus, b. 1901–9 Nov 1939 [38?], New York NY; after appendix operation). "Buddy Doyle," *Variety,* 15 Nov 1939, p. 62. AS, p. 336. BHD1, p. 162. IFN, p. 86.

Doyle, Charley J. [director] (b. 1880–31 Mar 1957 [77?], Liverpool, England). AS, p. 336. BHD2, p. 72.

Doyle, Jack [director/executive] (d. Oct 1914, NB). BHD2, p. 72.

Doyle, Johnny [actor] (b. England-d. 24 Mar 1919, Chattanooga TN; pneumonia). "Johnny Doyle," *Variety,* 18 Apr 1919. BHD, p. 154.

Doyle, John T. [actor/playwright] (b. St. Louis MO, 1873?–16 Oct 1935 [62], New York NY). m. Marion Willard. "John T. Doyle," *Variety,* 23 Oct 1935. AS, p. 336. BHD1, p. 162. IFN, p. 87. SD.

Doyle, Larry [actor] (b. Caseyville IL, 31 Jul 1886–1 Mar 1974 [87], Saranac Lake NY). BHD, p. 154.

Doyle, Ray[mond] [actor/vaudevillian/title writer/scenarist] (b. South Boston MA, 6 Oct 1898 [MVRB, Births, Vol. 477, p. 319]-15 Jun 1954 [55], New York NY; heart attack). m. Lillian Gormley. "Ray Doyle, Manager of Cavanagh's Here," *NYT,* 16 Jun 1954, 31:4 (in stock at age 7). "Ray Doyle," *Variety,* 23 Jun 1954. BHD2, p. 72. FDY, pp. 423, 443. IFN, p. 87 (age 56).

Doyle, Regina [actress] (b. 1904–30 Sep 1931 [27?], No. Hollywood CA; auto struck train). "Regina Doyle," *Variety,* 6 Oct 1931. AS, p. 337 (b. 1907). BHD, p. 154. BR, p. 135. IFN, p. 87. Truitt, p. 93. George A. Katchmer, "Forgotten Cowboys and Cowgirls—Part V," *CI,* 177 (Mar 1990), C2.

Drago, Harry Sinclair [writer] (b. Toledo OH, 20 Mar 1888–25 Oct 1979 [91], White Plains NY). AMD, p. 103. "Fox Signs Drago," *MPW,* 21 May 1927, 171.

Drain, Emile Pierre Charles [actor] (b. Paris, France, 1 Feb 1890–22 Nov 1966 [76], Paris, France [extrait de décès no. 12/3022/1966]). AS, p. 337.

Drake, Fabia [actress] (b. Herne Bay, England, 20 Jan 1904–28 Feb 1990 [86], London, England). AS, p. 337. BHD1, p. 162.

Drake, Josephine Smart [actress] (b. 1904–7 Jan 1929 [24?], New York NY; pneumonia). m. Sir **Ernest O.C. Lambert** (d. 1945). "Josephine S. Drake," *Variety,* 16 Jan 1929. AS, p. 337. BHD, p. 154. IFN, p. 87. Truitt, p. 93.

Drake, Margot [actress] (*née* Marjorie Alexa Thomson Drake, b. Deptford South, England, 11 Dec 1899 [extrait de naissance no. 499/1900]-15 May 1948 [48], Kensington, England; cancer). AS, p. 337.

Drake, Oliver [sceararist/director/producer of B westerns] (b. Boise ID, 1903?–5 Aug 1991 [88], Las Vegas NV). *Written, Produced and Directed by Oliver Drake.* m. June. "Oliver Drake," *Variety,* 19 Aug 1991, pp. 55–56. AS, p. 337. BHD2, p. 72. FDY, p. 423. George Katchmer, "Remembering the Great Silents," *CI,* 221 (Nov 1993), 53.

Drane, Sam Dade [actor/director] (b. 1869–15 Aug 1916 [47?], New York NY). "Sam Dade Drane," *Variety,* 25 Aug 1916. AMD, p. 103. AS, p. 337. BHD, p. 154. "'The Crisis' Player a Lincoln Student," *MPW,* 1 Jul 1916, 78. "Obituary," *MPW,* 16 Sep 1916, 1845.

Dranem [actor] (*né* Charles Armand Menard, b. Paris, France, 23 May 1869–13 Oct 1935 [66], Paris, France). AS, p. 337. BHD1, p. 162. IFN, p. 87.

Draper, Jack [cinematographer] (b. Spencer IN, 5 Mar 1892-Oct? 1962 [70], Mexico City, Mexico; heart attack). "Jack Draper," *Variety,* 24 Oct 1962. Draper also worked on Mexican films. BHD2, p. 72 (d. Sep 1962).

Draper, L.A. [cinematographer]. No data found. FDY, p. 457.

Draper, Col. T. Wain-Mogan [actor] (d. 8 Nov 1915). AMD, p. 103. AS, p. 338 (b. 1885). BHD, p. 154. "Obituary," *MPW,* 20 Nov 1915, 1511.

Draper, William H. [producer]. No data found. AMD, p. 103. "Draper Joins American," *MPW,* 18 Apr 1925, 715.

Drayton, Alfred [actor] (*né* Alfred Varick, b. Brighton, England, 1 Nov 1881–26 Apr 1949 [67], London, England). m. Enid Sass (d. 1959). "Alfred Drayton," *Variety,* 27 Apr 1949. AS, p. 338. BHD1, p. 163. IFN, p. 87. SD. Truitt, p. 93.

Drean [actor] (*né* Roch Alexandre Vincentelli, b. Marseilles, France, 12 Nov 1884 [extrait de naissance no. 968/1884]-8 Mar 1977 [92], Corbeilessones, France). AS, p. 338.

Dreier, Hans [art director] (b. Bremen, Germany, 21 Aug 1885–24 Oct 1966 [81], Bernardsville NJ; heart ailment). . (Began at Paramount, 1923.) "Hans Dreieer," *Variety,* 9 Nov 1966 (age 71). AS, p. 338. BHD2, p. 72.

Dresser, Louise [actress] (*née* Louise Josephine Kerlin, b. Evansville IN, 5 Oct 1878–24 Apr 1965 [86], Woodland Hills CA; intestinal obstruction). m. Jack Norworth (d. 1959); (2) **Jack Gardner** (d. 1950). "Louise Dresser, Actress, 84, Dies; Singer in Vaudeville Became Will Rogers Film Co-Star," *NYT,* 25 Apr 1965, 87:3. "Louise Dresser," *Variety,* 28 Apr 1965 (b. Indianapolis IN). AMD, p. 103. AS, p. 338 (b. 1880). BHD1, p. 163. FSS, p. 95. IFN, p. 87. Katz, p. 359. SD. Truitt, p. 93. "Louise Dresser in Comedy Series," *MPW,* 16 Apr 1921, 737. Dorothy Donnell, "Photo by Sarony; Louise Dresser Was Old Fashioned at Sixteen and Is Young at Forty-Six [she was 49]," *MPC,* Sep 1928, 25, 78, 90.

Dressler, Marie [stage/film actress] (*née* Leila Maria von Koerber, b. Cobourg, Ontario, Canada, 9 Nov 1869–28 Jul 1934 [64], Santa Barbara CA; cancer). m. James Hoeppert, 1900; (2) James H. Dalton, 1917. *The Life Story of an Ugly Duckling* (NY: Robert M. McBride & Co., 1924); *My Own Story* (Boston: Little, Brown, and Company, 1934); Betty Lee, *Marie Dressler: The Unlikeliest Star;* Matthew Kennedy, *Marie Dressler: A Biography; With a Listing of Major Stage Performances, a Filmography, and a Discography* (Jefferson NC; McFarland, 1998). (Lubin; MGM.) "Marie Dressler, Noted Actress, Dies; Succumbs at the Age of 64 to a Long Illness at Santa Barbara, Calif.; 'Best Film Actress' in '31; Became Motion Picture Star at Age of 61 After Waiting 14 Years for a Comeback," *NYT,* 29 Jul 1934, 1:6, 22:3. "Marie Dressler," *Variety,* 31 Jul 1934 (age 62). May Robson, "My Friend Marie," *The New Movie Magazine,* Oct 1934, 34–35, 100–01. AMD, p. 103. AS, p. 338. BHD1, p. 163. FSFW, p. 160). FSS, p. 96. IFN, p. 87. SD (m. George F. Hoppert). Spehr, p. 128 (b. 1871). Truitt, p. 93. "Miss Dressler's Troubles; 'Frisco Managers Prevent Her Performance of 'The Merry Gambols' by Force," *NYDM,* 4 Feb 1914, 7:4 (prevented from entering the Gaity Theater; management had advertised a moving picture show instead. "J.J. Rosenthal, the manager, has been angry because his wife, Katherine Osterman, was not permitted to have a part in the play," G.M. Anderson, associate manager, said that the show was not strong enough. Rosenthal continued: "...we have been dictated to by these high-priced stars befor, and nothing can be done under the circumstances."). "J.J. Rosenthal Out; George M. Anderson Transfers Manager of Gaiety to Morosco Theater in Los Angeles," *NYDM,* :25 Feb 1914, 14:2 (Rosenthal had arranged for Dressler to appear and yet "a contract had been signed for the showing of certain white-slave films at the house at the same time." Anderson had to forfeit a $1,500 cash bond that the films would be shown. Rosenthal was succeeded by Jack Dalton, Dressler's husband!). "Dressler Case in U.S. Court," *NYDM,* 1 Apr 1914, 9:2 (Gaiety Theater against Dressler. "Miss Dressler is going to cross complain for $50,000 for defamation of character, the Gaiety folks having accused her of not being married to Mr. Dalton."). "Keystone Wins Suit; Court Denies Marie Dressler Injunction Preventing Release of 'Tillie's Punctured Romance,'" *NYDM,* 17 Mar 1915, 21:4 ("The plaintiff claimed that her contract with the producing company prevented the release of the picture without her consent..."). "Lubin Signs Dressler; Comedienne Will Be Starred in Series of Specially Written Comedies," *NYDM,* 14 Apr 1915, 22:1 (to make three 5-reel comedies a year). "Marie Dressler with Lubin," *MPW,* 1 May 1915, 733. "McNaughton with Lubin; Eccentric Lubin Comedian to Be Seen with Marie Dressler on the Screen [in *Tillie's Tomato Surprise*]," *NYDM,* 16 Jun 1915, 21:4 (Dressler rode a horse for the camera, but audiences would not be told of the "half dozen cowpunchers who assisted Miss Dressler into the saddle, nor of the surprise of the horse who had long ago been pensioned off on the Betzwood ranch." Photo of Dressler and director Howell Hansel, p. 21:2; another photo on p. 32:1.). "Marie Dressler," *MPW,* 19 Jun 1915, 1944. Photo,

NYDM, 7 Jul 1915 (production still from *Tillie's Tomato Surprise,* Lubin, illustrating the Herculean task of getting Dressler over a fence). "Keystone Wins Suit," *NYDM,* 11 Aug 1915, 22:3 ("The court held that Miss Dressler had failed to prove her contentions of fraud or misconduct and was entitled only to the royalties agreed upon in the original contract. The film company has always been willing to pay the royalties, but Miss Dressler refused to accept them, alleging that they were insufficient."). "Marie Dressler Wins Against Keystone," *MPW,* 14 Aug 1915, 1141. Cover, "Marie Dressler, Lubin Comedy Star," *NYDM,* 15 Sep 1915. "Tillie's Tomato Surprise [review]," *NYDM,* 6 Oct 1915, 28:1 (released 27 Sep). "No Double for Marie," *NYDM,* 30 Oct 1915, 33>2 (an actress in Tillie's Tomato Surprise madfe statements that she doubled for Dressler in some of the hazardous scenes. "Both the Lubin Company and Miss Dressler strenuously and emphatically deny this and state that whenever Miss Dressler appears in the picture it is the redoubtable Marie in reality. The Lubin Company wishes to assure exhibitors and the public that Miss Dressler plays each and every scene of the photoplay without substitution of any kind or any doubles, and neither did her director, Mr. Hansel, find it necessary to resort to trick photography to secure effects."). "Marie Dressler to Play for Mutual," *MPW,* 30 Dec 1916, 1941. "Dressler Pictures for Goldwyn," *MPW,* 11 Aug 1917, 951. "Marie Dressler Goes to California," *MPW,* 29 Sep 1917, 1991. "Marie Dressler Strong for the Impromptu," *MPW,* 29 Dec 1917, 1974. "Marie's Beauty Not of Garden *Variety,*" *MPW,* 5 Jan 1918, 74. "Marie Dressler Signs Contract with World," *MPW,* 4 May 1918, 706. "Marie Dressler Pictures Occupy Court's Attention," *MPW,* 15 Mar 1919, 1471. "Dressler-World Suit Is Settled Outside Court," *MPW,* 6 Nov 1920, 97. "Marie Dressler Short Features," *MPW,* 11 Sep 1926, 120. DeWitt Bodeen, "The Four Dowagers of MGM," *Focus on Film,* No. 24, Spring 1976, 20–26 (includes filmography). Charles E. Carley, "Marie Dressler," *CFC,* 35 (Summer, 1972), 20–21. John Thayer, "The Most Beloved Crook," *CFC,* 59 (Summer, 1978), 16, 37. Anthony Slide, "The Slide Area: Film Book Notes," *CI,* 272 (Feb 1998), 46 (review of Lee's book which notes that Lee had access to Claire DuBrey's unpublished autobiography which describes her lesbian relationship with Dressler).

Dréville, Jean François Alexandre [director] (b. Vitry-sur-Seine, France, 20 Sep 1906 [extrait de naissance no. 173/1906]-5 Mar 1997 [90], Vallangouiard, France). m. (2) Veronique Descha*MPS,* 1960. James Kirkup, "Jean Dréville," *The Independent* [England], 12 Mar 1997, p. 14 (made a documentary, *Autour de l'argent,* 1928, which documents the production of Marcel L'Herbier's *L'Argent,* 1929.). *The Bavarian Videotext,* 5 Mar 1997. AS, p. 338. Katz, *The International Film Encyclopedia,* p. 359.

Drew, Ann[e] [actress] (b. New York NY, 13 Jul 1890–6 Feb 1974 [83], Miami FL). m. Hawley B. Turner; Harry Speicher. (Griffith.) "Ann Drew Speicher," *Variety,* 13 Feb 1974 (won *New York Herald* beauty contest in 1909). AMD, p. 103. AS, p. 338 (b. 1888). BHD, p. 154. IFN, p. 87. "Ann Drew Visits New York," *MPW,* 22 Nov 1913, 878. George A. Katchmer, "Forgotten Cowboys and Cowgirls—Part XVIII," *CI,* 195 (Sep 1991), C8.

Drew, Cora Rankin [stage/film actress/scenarist]. (Selig; Kalem; Lubin; Universal; Bosworth; Majestic; Fine Arts; Fox.) MSBB, p. 1034 (age 46). AMD, p. 103. "Cora Drew," *MPW,* 1 Dec 1917, 1322.

Drew, Dorothy [actress]. No data found. AMD, p. 103. "Baum Signs Dorothy Drew," *MPW,* 13 Jun 1925, 800.

Drew, Elizabeth [actress]. No data found. AMD, p. 103. "Elizabeth Drew," *MPW,* 6 Mar 1915, 1458.

Drew, Gladys S. [actress/scenarist] (*née?*; George Cameron [*nom de plume*], ca. 1874–9 Jan 1914 [39?], New York NY). m. **Sidney Drew** (d. 1919). "Mrs. Gladys Drew," *Variety,* 16 Jan 1914. AFI2, p. 612. AS, p. 338. BHD, p. 154; BHD2, p. 72 (Gladys Rankin Drew).

Drew, Jerry *see* **Beauchamp, Clement H.**

Drew, John [stage/film actor] (b. Philadelphia PA, 13 Nov 1853–9 Jul 1927 [73], San Francisco CA). m. Josephine Baker (d. 1918). "John Drew," *Variety,* 13 Jul 1927. AS, p. 338. SD, p. 380. "Players Elect John Drew; Succeeds Joseph Jefferson—Is Third President of Club," *NYT,* 9 May 1905, 1:6 (16 Gramercy Park, NYC. Edwin Booth was the first president for five years; Jefferson the second for twelve years. William Bispham was elected Vice-President.). "Drew as Head of Players; Jefferson Told Him He Would Be His Natural Successor," *NYT,* 10 May 1905, 9:4 (Kansas City MO, 9 May. Drew was playing at the Willis Wood Theatre. "Mr. Jefferson, you know, succeeded Mr. Booth as President, and it was one of the ideas of his generous mind that since the three families, Booth, Jefferson, and Drew, had been so long associated with the stage, it would be right and natural that I should continue the succession in The Players.").

Drew, Joseph Lee (nephew of **Sidney Drew**) [actor]. No data found.

Drew, Lillian, "The Lily of the Essanay" [actress] (b. Chicago IL, 1883–4 Feb 1924 [41], Chicago IL; veronal poisoning). m. **Elisha H. Calvert** (d. 1941). "Mysterious Death of Lillian Drew; Dies in Chicago Hospital—Estranged from Husband, E.H. Calvert," *Variety,* 7 Feb 1924. AMD, p. 103. AS, p. 338. BHD, p. 154. IFN, p. 87. "Some Prominent Essanay Photoplayers," *MPW,* 11 Jul 1914, 234–35. "Lillian Drew," *MPW,* 18 Dec 1915, 2179. Billy H. Doyle, "Lost Players," *CI,* 158 (Aug 1988), 26.

Drew, Morton [director] (d. 3 Sep 1916). BHD2, p. 72.

Drew, Philip Yale [actor] (b. 15 Mar 1880–2 Jul 1940 [60], Kensington, Surrey, England). AS, p. 338 (d. 9 Jul 1940, LA CA). BHD, p. 154. IFN, p. 87.

Drew, Roland [actor] (*né* Walter D. Goss, b. Elmhurst [New York] NY, 4 Aug 1900–17 Mar 1988 [87], Santa Monica CA). AS, p. 338 (d. 16 Mar). BHD1, p. 163. *Classic Images* obituary, May 1988.

Drew, Mrs. Sidney *see* **Drew, Gladys S. and McVey, Lucille**

Drew, Sidney (brother of **John Drew**; father of **Sidney Rankin Drew**; uncle of the **Barrymores** and **Joseph Lee Drew**; brother in-law of **Harry Davenport**) [stage/film actor/producer] (b. New York NY, 28 Aug 1864–9 Apr 1919 [54], New York NY [Death Certificate No. 13331; uraemia exhaustion from nervous breakdown]). m. **Lucille McVey**, 29 Jul 1914, Little Church Around the Corner, NYC (d. 1925). (Vitagraph; Paramount; Metro.) "Sidney Drew, Film and Stage Star, Dies; Comedian Succumbs to Uraemia, at His Park Avenue Home After Brief Illness; Gave Up Law for Theatre; Brother of John Drew Made His Debut in 'Our Boarding House' at $12 a Week," *NYT,* 10 Apr 1919, 11:1. "Sidney Drew," *Variety,* 11 Apr 1919. AMD, p. 103. AS, p. 339. BHD, p. 154. IFN, p. 87 (age 55). MSBB, p. 1023. Slide, p. 159. "When Two Hearts Are Won," *MPW,* 2 Sep 1911, 610. "Sidney Drew to Wed," *NYDM,* 22 Jul 1914, 22:1. "Sidney Drew," *MPW,* 15 May 1915, 1078. Robert Grau, "The Film Studio; A Gold Laden Haven for the Patriarchs of the Stage," *NYDM,* 8 Sep 1915, 3:1 (Grau mentions Charles Kent, Louise Beaudet, Cissy Fitzgerald, Sydney [sic] Drew, S. Rankin Drew, William Humphries [sic], Van Dyke Brooke, and Harry Davenport, all from the stage. He and Davenport married sisters.). "Sidney Drew with Metro," *MPW,* 8 Jan 1916, 218. "The Sidney Drew's Celebrate Second Wedding Anniversary," *MPW,* 12 Aug 1916, 1089. "Sidney Drew," *MPW,* 20 Jan 1917, 373. "R. Sidney Drew Falls in Battle," *MPW,* 8 Jun 1918, 1407 (son shot down in France, 23 May 1918). "Paramount to Release Drew Films," *MPW,* 30 Nov 1918, 936. "Obituary," *MPW,* 19 Apr 1919, 339. "The Passing of Sidney Drew," *MPW,* 26 Apr 1919, 511–12. "Sidney Drew Film Found," *CI,* 265 (Jul 1997), 5:3, 61:3 (*Mr. and Mrs. Sidney Drew and Gravy,* 1916. A Mr. Barry dug the film can out of the ground in Chicago. The film studios don't want it and UCLA wants Mr. Barry to donate the film, which he declined to do).

Drew, S[idney] **Rankin** (son of **Gladys** Rankin and **Sidney Drew**; nephew of **Harry Davenport**; cousin of the **Barrymores**) [stage/film actor/director/scenarist] (b. New York NY, 1892–19 May 1918 [26?], Ardillieries, France; shot down). (Vitagraph, 1913; Metro.) AMD, p. 104. AS, p. 338. BHD, pp. 17–19; 154; BHD2, p. 72. IFN, p. 87. Slide, p. 159 (b. 1891). Robert Grau, "The Film Studio; A Gold Laden Haven for the Patriarchs of the Stage," *NYDM,* 8 Sep 1915, 3:1 (Grau mentions Charles Kent, Louise Beaudet, Cissy Fitzgerald, Sydney Drew [sic], William Humphries [sic], Van Dyke Brooke, and Harry Davenport, all from the stage). "R. Sidney Drew Falls in Battle," *MPW,* 8 Jun 1918, 1407. "Sidney Drew Now Counted as Dead," *MPW,* 29 Jun 1918, 1854 (age 27). "The Late Sidney Rankin Drew," *MPW,* 6 Jul 1918, 88. Billy H. Doyle, "Lost Players," *CI,* 162 (Dec 1988), 44–45.

Drexel, Nancy [actress] (aka Dorothy Kitchen, b. New York NY, 6 Apr 1910–19 Nov 1989 [79], San Juan Capistrano CA). m. **Thomas H. Ince, Jr.**, 1932–47 (d. 1924). BHD1, p. 163. BR, pp. 168–69 (b. 1912). George Katchmer, "Remembering the Great Silents," *CI,* 178 (Apr 1990), 40.

Dreyer, Carl Th[eodor] [title writer/actor/director/producer/scenarist] (b. Copenhagen, Denmark, 3 Feb 1889–20 Mar 1968 [79], Copenhagen, Denmark). m. Ebba Frederike Larsen, 19 Nov 1911, Vor Frue Kirke, Copenhagen, Denmark (daughter Gunni, b. 24 Sep 1913; son Erik, b. 20 Feb 1923). (Det Skandinavisk-Russiske Handelshus [The Scandanavian-Russian Co., later Filmfabriken Danmark]; Nordisk, 1912.) Martin Drouzy, *Carl Th. Dreyser fodt Nilsson* (Copenhagen: Glydendals Ugleboger, 1964); Martin Drouzy, Kildemateriale til en biografi om Carl Th. Dreyer (Copenhagen, 1987); Jean Drum and Dale D. Drum, *My Only Great Passion; The Life and*

Films of Carl Th. Dreyer (Lanham MD: Scarecrow Press, 2000). AS, p. 339; p. 340 (Carl Th. Dryer). BHD2, p. 72.

Dreyer, Dave [composer/author] (b. Brooklyn NY, 22 Sep 1894–2 Mar 1967 [72], New York NY). . m. Anna. (RKO.) "Dave Dreyer, 72, Song Writer, Dies; Pianist Wrote 'Cecilia' and Other 20's and 30's Hits," *NYT*, 3 Mar 1967, 35:4. "Dave Dreyer," *Variety*, 8 Mar 1967 (wrote *Me and My Shadow; Back in Your Own Backyard; You Can't Be True, Dear*). AS, p. 339. ASCAP 66, p. 186. CEPMJ [1974], pp. 838–39. BHD2, p. 72.

Drigo, Riccardo [composer] (b. Padua, Italy, 30 Jun 1846–1 Oct 1930 [84], Padua, Italy). BHD2, p. 72.

Drinkwater, John [scenarist] (b. Leytonstone, England, 1 Jun 1882–25 Mar 1937 [54], London, England). BHD2, p. 73.

Driscoll, Frank Tex [actor] (aka Frank Driscoll, *né* John W. Morris, b. IN, 7 Sep 1889–1 Jun 1970 [80], Los Angeles Co. CA). IFN, p. 87.

Driscoll, G.C. (father of **Harold Driscoll**) [studio manager of Mina]. No data found.

Driscoll, Harold (son of **G.C. Driscoll**) [child actor] (b. 1905). "Coast Picture News," *Variety*, 19 Oct 1917, p. 28.

Driscoll, Sam Wallace [actor] (b. 1868–13 Dec 1956 [88], Los Angeles CA). AS, p. 339.

Driscoll, Tex [actor] (b. IN, 7 Sep 1889–1 Jun 1970 [80], Los Angeles Co. CA). AS, p. 339. BHD1, p. 163.

Driver, Adabelle [actress] (b. England, 6 Dec 1874–23 Oct 1952 [77], So. San Gabriel CA). BHD1, p. 163.

Droeshout, Adrian [actor/publicist] (b. NY, 1897–25 Dec 1965 [68], Los Angeles CA). AS, p. 339 (d. 26 Dec). BHD2, p. 73.

Drogmund, Freddie [actor] (b. MO, 5 Oct 1915–15 Apr 1995 [79], Burbank CA). BHD1, p. 607.

Dromgold, George C. [title writer/actor/director/scenarist] (b. Los Angeles CA, 1894–9 Apr 1948 [54], Ft. Lauderdale FL). AS, p. 339 (LA CA); p. 340 (George Drumgold). BHD, p. 154; BHD2, p. 73. FDY, pp. 423, 443 (George Drumgold). IFN, p. 87.

Droop, Marie Louise [director/producer] (b. Stettin, Germany, 15 Jan 1890–22 Aug 1959 [69], Gnegenbach, Germany). AS, p. 339. BHD2, p. 73.

Drouet, Robert [actor] (b. Clinton IA, 27 Mar 1870–17 Aug 1914 [44], New York NY). m. Mildred Loring. (K&E.) "Robert Drouet," *Variety*, 21 Aug 1914. AS, p. 339. BHD, p. 155. IFN, p. 87. SD. "Little Blaze in Theatre; Actor Smothers Burning Flowers of Herald Square Stage," *NYT*, 4 Mar 1905, 9:2 (while performing in *The Woman in the Case* with George Fawcett, he set a box of matches aflame and a vase of artificial flowers caught fire. He smothered the flames with his hands. "The audience calmed down and gave him a hearty round of appleause.").

Drought, Doris [film editor]. No data found.

Druce, Hubert [actor] (b. Twickenham, Middlesex, England, 20 May 1870–6 Apr 1931 [60], New York NY; pneumonia). m. Frances Dillon. "Hubert Druce," *Variety*, 8 Apr 1931. AS, p. 339. BHD1, p. 164. IFN, p. 87.

Druet, Robert [actor]. No data found. AMD, p. 104. "Robert Druet," *MPW*, 12 Jul 1913, 187.

Drumier, Jack [actor] (b. Philadelphia PA, 1869–2 Apr 1929 [60], Clearwater FL; pneumonia). "Jack Drumier," *Variety*, 24 Apr 1929. AMD, p. 104. AS, p. 340. BHD, p. 607. IFN, p. 87. 1921 Directory, p. 168 (b. 1864). Spehr, p. 128. Truitt, p. 94 (d. 22 Apr). "Drumier Has Strong Role in World Film's 'Heredity,'" *MPW*, 6 Jul 1918, 87.

Drury, Weston [actor/casting director] (b. London, England, 24 Dec 1892–15 Feb 1983 [90], Reading, England). BHD2, p. 73.

Dryden, Ernest [costumer] (b. 1887–17 Mar 1938 [51?], Los Angeles CA). BHD2, p. 73.

Dryden, Leo [actor] (b. London, England, 6 Jun 1863–21 Apr 1939 [75], London, England). BHD, p. 155. IFN, p. 87.

Dryden, Wheeler [actor/scenarist] (b. London, England, 31 Aug 1893–30 Sep 1957 [64], Los Angeles CA). AMD, p. 104. AS, p. 340. BHD1, p. 164. FDY, p. 423. IFN, p. 87. "Wheeler Dryden Signs with Fitzpatrick for 'Melodies,'" *MPW*, 6 Mar 1926, 34.

Dryhurst, Edward [gag writer] (*né* Edward Dryhurst Roberts, b. Kettering, Northamptshire, England, 28 Dec 1904–7 Mar 1989 [84], Islington, London, England). *Gilt Off the Gingerbread* (1988). (Roach.) "Edward Dryhurst," *Variety*, 15 Mar 1989 (began 1920). AS, p. 340 (b. Desborough, England). BHD2, p. 73 (b. Desborough, England).

Dubin, Al[exander] [actor/composer/lyricist] (b. Zurich, Switzerland, 10 Jan 1890–11 Feb 1945 [55], New York NY). "Al Dubin, Author of Song Hits, Dies; Lyricist of 'Broadway Lullaby' Credited with Turning Out 60 Numbers a Year," *NYT*, 12 Feb 1945, 19:1. "Al Dubin, ASCAP's Bob Murray Dead," *Variety*, 14 Feb 1945 (wrote *Just a Girl That Men Forget; A Cup of Coffee, a Sandwich and You*). AS, p. 340. CEPMJ (b. 1891). BHD2, p. 73. IFN, p. 88 (age 54). Truitt 1983.

Du Bois, Jean [cameraman/actor] (b. Sumatra, West Indonesia, 1888?–28 Oct 1957 [69?], Denver CO). "Jean Dubois," *Variety*, 30 Oct 1957 (began 1925). AS p. 340. BHD2, p. 73. Truitt, p. 94.

Dubosc, André [actor] (*né* Auguste César Dubosc, b. Paris, France, 30 Mar 1866–20 Dec 1935 [69], Paris, France). AS, p. 341.

Dubosc, Gaston Anatole [actor] (b. Paris, France, 9 Aug 1861–28 Jun 1941 [79], Paris, France [extrait de décès no. SN/1941]). AS, p. 341.

Dubray, Joseph A. [cinematographer]. No data found. AMD, p. 104. FDY, p. 457. "Dubray Wounded Five Times in Four Years Against Hun," *MPW*, XL, 19 Apr 1919, 374.

Du Brey, Claire [actress] (aka Clara Gates, b. Bonner's Ferry ID, 31 Aug 1892–1 Aug 1993 [100], Los Angeles CA). (Lubin; Ince, 1915.) Luther Hancock, "Claire Du Brey [obituary]," *CI*, 222 (Dec 1993), 59:1. AMD, p. 104. AS, p. 340 (b. NY NY). BHD1, p. 164. FSS, p. 97. MH, p. 108. 1921 Directory, p. 219. WWS, p. 248 (b. 1893). "Claire DuBrey," *MPW*, 24 Mar 1917, 1929. "Claire DuBrey in Bluebird Leads," *MPW*, 8 Dec 1917, 1508. "Ben Wilson in Another Accident," *MPW*, 22 Dec 1917, 1787. "Claire Du Brey: Film Pioneer," *Screen Actor*, Summer 1979, pp. 28–29. George Katchmer, "Remembering the Great Silents," *CI*, 223 (Jan 1994), 47:1.

Duc, Paul [actor] (b. France, 1906-Sep 1923 [17?]). BHD, p. 155.

Du Cello, Countess [actress] (*née* Mary du Cello, b. Buffalo NY, 1864–20 Nov 1921 [57], Los Angeles CA; possible suicide with lethal drugs). m. H.C. Bunting. "Countess Ducella," *Variety*, 2 Dec 1921. AS, p. 262 (Countess Ducella; d. 28 Nov); p. 340 (b. London, England). BHD, p. 155. IFN, p. 88.

Ducey, Lillian [scenarist]. No data found. FDY, p. 423.

Duchamp, Marcel Henri Robert [actor/director/scenarist] (b. Blainsville, Normandy, France, 28 Jul 1887–2 Oct 1968 [81], Neuilly-sur-Seine, France [extrait de décès no. 721/1968]). AS, p. 341. BHD1, p. 164; BHD2, p. 73.

Ducos, Yvonne [actress] (b. Marseilles, France, 1 Aug 1887). AS, p. 341.

Ducos du Hauron, Louis [producer] (b. Langon, France, 8 Dec 1837–31 Aug 1920 [82], Agen, France [extrait de décès no. 401/1920]). AS, p. 341.

Ducouret, Marguerite Victorine [actress] (b. Paris, France, 11 Dec 1893–12 Apr 1971 [77], Paris, France [extrait de décès no. SN/1971]). AS, p. 341.

Du Crow, Tote G. [circus clown/film actor] (b. Watsonville CA, 1858?–12 Dec 1927 [69]). AS, p. 340. BHD, p. 155. IFN, p. 88. "Clown of 50 Years Ago to Clown Again Now," *Camera*, Apr 1923, 13 (Du Crow had been a circus clown for almost 50 years, entering pictures "where he has been an interesting figure for fourteen years or more."). George A. Katchmer, "Forgotten Cowboys/Girls—Part VII," *CI*, 179 (May 1990), 44.

Dudgeon, Elspeth [actor] (b. England, 4 Dec 1871–11 Dec 1955 [84], England). AS, p. 341.

Dudley, Bernard [actor/singer] (b. Ireland, 1878-Oct 1964 [86], London, England). "Bernard Dudley," *Variety*, 21 Oct 1964, p. 79. BHD1, p. 164.

Dudley, Charles [actor] (*né* Charles Dudley Heaslip, b. Fort Grant AZ, 10 Oct 1883–9 Mar 1952 [68], Woodland Hills CA). (Universal; Monopol; Keystone; Balboa, 1913.) "Charles Dudley," *NYT*, 13 Mar 1952, 29:4. "Charles Dudley," *Variety*, 19 Mar 1952 (d. Hollywood CA). AS, p. 342. BHD, p. 155; BHD2, p. 73. Billy H. Doyle, "Lost Players," *CI*, 153 (Mar 1988), 52. Jura, p. 104.

Dudley, Florence [stage/film actress] (d. 2 Oct? 1912, London, England; "shot dead in a taxicab by a non-professional 'gentleman friend.'"). "Killed by Gentleman Friend," *Variety*, 4 Oct 1912, p. 4.

Dudley, John E. [actor] (b. 1861?–10 Mar 1932 [71], Englewood NJ; pneumonia). "John E. Dudley," *Variety*, 15 Mar 1932. AS, p. 342.

Dudley, John Stuart [actor] (b. 1894? 1 May 1966 [72], Wilmington NC). "John S. Dudley," *Variety*, 18 May 1966. IFN, p. 88.

Dudley, Robert Y. [actor] (b. Cincinnati OH, 13 Sep 1869–12 Nov 1955 [86], San Clemente CA). (Griffith; founded Troupers Club.) "Robert Y. Dudley," *Variety*, 23 Nov 1955. AS, p. 342 (b. 1875). BHD1, p. 165. IFN, p. 88. Truitt, p. 94 (b. 1875).

Dudley, Sherman H. [stage/film actor]. No data found. "Start Negro Film Co.; Smart Set Film Company, Inc., Organized for the Production of Negro Comedies," *NYDM*, 18 Aug 1915, 23:2 (studios at Washington DC; J. Martin McKee, general manager; George E. Power, technical director. Dudley was to appear in *The Porter,* 1 reel, with his trick mule.).

Dudow, Slatan Theodor [director/scenarist] (b. Zaribrod, Bulgaria, 30 Jan 1903–12 Jul 1963 [60], East Berlin, Germany; following auto accident). "Slatan Dudow," *Variety,* 24 Jul 1963. AS, p. 342. BHD2, p. 73. IFN, p. 88.

Duff, Sadie [actress] (b. 1870–10 Jun 1942 [72?], New York NY). BHD, p. 155.

Duffield, Harry S. [actor] (b. 1850–13 Oct 1921 [71?], Los Angeles CA). m. Phosa McAllister (d. 1909). AMD, p. 104. AS, p. 342. BHD, p. 155. IFN, p. 88. SD. Truitt 1983. "Duffield an Old Timer," *MPW,* 29 Jan 1921, 553. "Obituary," *MPW,* 5 Nov 1921, 51 (d. 31 Oct).

Duffy, Gerald C. [title writer/scenarist] (b. 1896?–25 Jun 1928 [32], CA; dropped dead while dictating a scenario to secretary at 1st National). "Gerald C. Duffy," *Variety,* 27 Jun 1928. AMD, p. 104. AS, p. 342. BHD2, p 73. FDY, pp. 423, 443. "Gerald C. Duffy Joins Goldwyn," *MPW,* 9 Aug 1919, 844.

Duffy, Jack [silent film comic/make-up artist] (brother of **Kate Price**) (b. Pawtucket RI, 4 Sep 1882–23 Jul 1939 [56], Los Angeles CA). (Vitagraph.) "Jack Duffy," *Variety,* 26 Jul 1939 (age 57). AMD, p. 104. AS, p. 342. BHD1, p. 165. IFN, p. 88. Truitt, p. 94. "Plays Grandpa Parts," *MPW,* 20 Sep 1924, 202. "Duffy Signs with Christie," *MPW,* 14 Aug 1926, 401.

Dufkin, Sam [actor] (b. 1890?–19 Feb 1952 [61], Los Angeles CA). (Sennett.) "Sam Dufkin," *Variety,* 27 Feb 1952 ("Starting in silent film days, he played for several years with Mack Sennett company."). AS, p. 343. BHD, p. 155.

Duflos, Hugette [actress] (*née* Hermance Joséphine Meurs, b. Limoges, France, 24 Aug 1887–12 Apr 1982 [95?], Paris, France [extrait de décès no. 8/109/1982]). AS, p. 343. BHD1, p. 165.

Dufraine, Rosa [actress] (b. 1901–29 Apr 1935 [34], Duarte CA). AS, p. 343. BHD, p. 155. IFN, p. 88.

Dugan, James E. [director] (b. 1898?–5 Aug 1937 [39], Los Angeles CA; heart ailment). "James Dugan," *Variety,* 11 Aug 1937 (interred in Calvary Cemetery). AMD, p. 104. AS, p. 343. BHD2, p. 73. "James Dugan," *MPW,* 15 Oct 1927, 431.

Dugan, Tom [actor] (*né* Thomas J. Dugan, b. Dublin, Ireland, 1 Jan 1889–6 Mar 1955 [66], Redlands CA; auto accident). m. Marie Engle; Marie Raymond. "Tom Dugan," *Variety,* 9 Mar 1955 (m. Marie Raymond). AS, p. 343. BHD1, p. 165. IFN, p. 88. Truitt, p. 94.

Dugan, William Francis [scenarist]. No data found. AMD, p. 104. "Burton and William Dugan Signed to Long Term," *MPW,* 10 Dec 1927, 24.

Duhen, V.L. No data found. *Fl.* 1911.

Dukas, Paul [composer] (b. Paris, France, 1 Oct 1865–17 May 1935 [69], Paris, France). AS, p. 343.

Duke, Ivy [actress] (b. England, 1895). AS, p. 343.

Dukes, Ashley [scenarist] (b. Bridgewater, England, 29 May 1885–4 May 1959 [73], London, England). BHD2, p. 74.

Dulac, Germaine [director/producer/scenarist] (*née* Germaine Charlotte Elisabeth Saisset-Schneider, b. Amiens, France, 18 Nov 1882–20 Jul 1942 [59], Paris, France; heart attack). AS, p. 344. BHD2, p. 74.

Dull, Orville O. [actor/assistant director/producer] (b. Lima OH, 25 Apr 1890–29 Dec 1978 [88], Los Angeles CA). (MGM.) AS, p. 344. BHD, p. 155; BHD2, p. 74. Truitt 1983.

Dullac, Paul [actor] (*né* Paul Aurel Gouteredonde, b. Begles, France, 9 Mar 1882 [extrait de naissance no. 43]-17 Aug 1941 [59], Vichy, France [extrait de décès no. 578/1941]). AS, p. 344.

Dullin, Charles [actor/writer/director] (aka Louis Adlon, b. Yenne, France, 8 May 1885–11 Dec 1949 [64], Paris, France; complications from an operation [extrait de décès no. 12/3465/1949]). AS, p. 344 (b. 12 May). BHD1, p. 165.

Dumar, Jean [actress]. No data found. AMD, p. 104. "Jean Dumar, a New Edison Star," *MPW,* 30 Jan 1915, 687.

Du Maurier, Sir Gerald (father of writer Daphne Du Maurier) [actor] (b. London, England, 26 Mar 1873–11 Apr 1934 [61], London, England). m. (daughter Daphne, 1907–1989). AS, p. 340 (b. Hampstead, England). BHD1, p. 166. IFN, p. 88 (b. Hampstead).

Dumbrille, Douglas Rupert [stage/film actor] (b. Hamilton, Ontario, Canada, 13 Oct 1889 [Birth certificate #040798, no. 376]-2 Apr 1974 [84], Woodland Hills CA; heart attack). m. (1) Jessie Lawson (d. 1957); (2) Patricia Mowbray (Alan Mowbray's daughter), May, 1960. "Douglass Dumbrille," *Variety,* 10 Apr 1974, p. 70. "Dumbrille Rites Slated Tomorrow," *Los Angeles Herald-Examiner,* 4 Apr 1974. AS, p. 344. IFN, p. 88. SD.

Dumeny [actor] (*né* Camille Georges Richomme, b. France, 1857–1920 [63?], France). AS, p. 344.

Dumont, Gordon [actor] (*né* Raymond R. Bourgeois, b. Milwaukee WI, 24 Apr 1894–7 Mar 1966 [71], Los Angeles Co. CA). AS, p. 344. BHD, p. 155. IFN, p. 89.

Dumont, J[ohn] **M**[onte] [actor] (aka George McNamara, b. Paris KY, 7 Feb 1879–19 Dec 1959 [80]; Los Angeles Co CA). AMD, p. 104. AS, p. 344. BHD, p. 155 (b. LA). IFN, p. 89. "Dumont Signs Contract with Famous Players," *MPW,* 4 Oct 1919, 59 (Jean Monte Dumont).

Dunaew [or **Dunaev**], **Nicholas A.** [actor/writer] (b. Moscow, Russia, 26 May 1884). (Vitagraph.) m. writer Edith Donnerberg, 20 Sep 1914, NYC; **Nina Byron**. AMD, p. 104. BHD, p. 155. "Nicholas Dunaew," *MPW,* 26 Sep 1914, 1785. "Notes Written on the Screen," *NYT,* 27 Sep 1914, p. 6:8 (re marriage). "Studio Gossip," *NYDM,* 30 Sep 1914, 28:2 (re marriage).

Dunbar, Blanche [actress] (b. 1894–7 Mar 1926 [31?], Los Angeles CA). BHD, p. 155. IFN, p. 89 (d. 1932).

Dunbar, David [actor] (brother of Charles Dunbar) (b. West Maitland, N.S.W., Australia, 14 Sep 1886–7 Nov 1953 [67], Woodland Hills CA). "David Dunbar," *Variety,* 18 Nov 1953 (in films for 31 years). AS, p. 344. BHD1, p. 165. IFN, p. 89. Truitt, p. 95.

Dunbar, Dorothy [actress] (b. Colorado Springs [or Cripple Creek] CO, 28 May 1902–23 Oct 1992 [90], Seattle WA). m. Max Baer; Thomas B. Wells, 6 Oct 1926; (7) Russell Lawson. AS, p. 345. BHD, p. 156. Paul Paige, "Close-Ups and Fade-Outs," *Paris and Hollywood,* Sep 1926, 91 (the screen "find" leased the former home of Tito Schipa of grand opera, recently vacated by Constance Bennett upon her marriage to Plant). George A. Katchmer, "Forgotten Cowboys and Cowgirls—Part XVIII," *CI,* 195 (Sep 1991), C8. "Dorothy Dunbar Lawson [obituary]," *CI,* 210 (Dec 1992), 59.

Dunbar, Helen [actrress] (*née* Katheryn Burke Lackey, b. Philadelphia PA, 10 Oct 1863–28 Aug 1933 [69], Los Angeles CA). (Essanay.) "Helen Dunbar," *NYT,* 30 Aug 1933, 19:2. "Helen Dunbar," *Variety,* 5 Sep 1933. AMD, p. 104. AS, p. 345. BHD, p. 156. IFN, p. 89. Truitt, p. 95. "Helen Dunbar," *MPW,* 4 Apr 1914, 41.

Dunbar, John Sutherland [actor/executive] (b. 1896–15 Oct 1961 [65], Edinburgh, Scotland). AS, p. 345 (Jack Dunbar). BHD, p. 156; BHD2, p. 74. IFN, p. 89.

Dunbar, Robert N. [actor] (b. Beaver PA, 1 Jul 1858–16 Jan 1943 [84], Los Angeles Co CA). AS, p. 345. BHD, p. 156. IFN, p. 89.

Duncan, Bud [actor] (*né* Albert Edward Duncan, b. Brooklyn, NY, 31 Oct 1883–26 Nov 1960 [77], Los Angeles CA). "Bud Duncan," *Variety,* 7 Dec 1960. AMD, p. 104. AS, p. 345. BHD1, p. 166. IFN, p. 89. "Bud Duncan," *MPW,* 19 Jun 1915, 1921. "Kalem Ham Comedy Company," *MPN,* 21 Oct 1916, 197. "Kalem Signs Ham and Bud," *MPW,* 10 Mar 1917, 1554. "Bud Duncan Signs with National," *MPW,* 18 May 1918, 1007. "Bud Duncan Re-enters Field and Will Appear in One Reel Comedies Which Reelcraft Will Handle," *MPW,* 21 Aug 1920, 1019.

Duncan, Charles [actor] (b. 1920–15 Oct 1942 [22?], Los Angeles CA). AS, p. 345. IFN, p. 89.

Duncan, Evelyn (sister of **Rosetta** and **Vivian Duncan**) [stage/film actress] (b. Bellflower CA, 21 Jan 1893–8 Jun 1972 [79], Los Angeles CA). AS, p. 345. BHD1, p. 166 (b. LA CA). IFN, p. 89 (b. LA CA).

Duncan, Isidora (mother of Anna Duncan) [dancer/actress] (b. San Francisco CA, 27 May 1877–14 Sep 1927 [60], Nice, France). m. (daughter Anna, 1894–1980). AS, p. 345.

Duncan, Malcolm [actor] (b. Brooklyn NY, 19 Sep 1872–2 May 1942 [70], Bay Shore, LI NY). m. Edith Barker. "Malcolm Duncan," *Variety,* 6 May 1942 (age 60). AMD, p. 104. BHD, p. 156 (b. 1881) SD, p. 388. Truitt 1983 (b. 1872). "Malcolm Duncan in 'The Money Master,'" *MPW,* 7 Aug 1915, 1007.

Duncan, Mary [stage/film actress] (b. Luttrellville VA, 13 Aug 1894–9 May 1993 [98], Palm Beach FL). m. Stephen "Laddie" Sanford. "Mary Duncan Sanford, 98, former actress, died May 9 in Palm Beach," *Variety,* 7 Jun 1993, p. 57:2. AMD, p. 104. BHD1, p. 166. Katz, p. 363 (b. 1903; began 1927).. "W.R. Sheehan Signs Mary Duncan; Talented Stage Star in Fox Films," *MPW,* 2 May 1927, 832.

Duncan, Rosetta (sister of **Evelyn** and **Vivian Duncan**) [stage/film actress] (b. Los Angeles CA, 23 Nov 1894–4 Dec 1959 [65], Acero IL; from injuries sustained in an auto accident). "Rosetta Duncan, Stage Star, Dies; Teamed with Sister Vivian in Vaudeville Comedy Act—Noted for Role of Topsy," *NYT,* 5 Dec 1959, 23:1. "Rosetta Duncan, 58; Made Topsy Household Word," *Variety,* 9 Dec 1959. AMD, p. 105. AS, p. 345 (b. 1896). BHD1, p. 166 (b. 1896; d. Berwyn IL). IFN, p. 89 (age 63). Truitt, p. 95 (b. 1900). "Duncan Sisters in Damage Suit," *MPW,* 14 May 1927, 93. "Says Films Are Harder Than Stage," *MPW,* 25 Jun 1927,

572. Don Eddy, "The Heavenly Twins Are Captured by the Movies," *MPC,* Sep 1927, 42, 77, 87 ("When we marry, we will even marry brothers!"). Peter Ryder, "'It All Comes Out in the Wash,' Say the Duncan Sisters," *Screenland,* Oct 1927, 34–35, 86, 88. Ruth Tildesley, "Hollywood Night's Entertainment," *Paris and Hollywood Screen Secrets,* Oct 1927, 21 (Rosetta and Vivian were lured to the stage on the opening night of *Topsy and Eva;* in "spite of the fact that the picture was an obvious 'flop,' the talented sisters were given a prolonged ovation on their personal appearance in the prologue and their many friends gathered around after the fall of the curtain at midnight."). Elisabeth Goldbeck, "It's All Jake with Hyme; Not Even the Siamese Twins Have Anything on the Duncan Sisters," *MPC,* Mar 1930, 58, 91, 93. Eve Golden, "The Real Broadway Melody: The Life and Career of The Duncan Sisters," *CI,* 261 (Mar 1997), 42–43 (includes filmography).

Duncan, Taylor E. [studio personnel/actor] b. Kansas City MO,4 Jul 1875?–23 Jul 1957 [82], Los AngelesCA). "Taylor E. Duncan," *Variety,* 31 Jul 1957 (on Columbia's police force). AMD, p. 105. BHD, p. 156 (b. 1877). "Duncan Returns to Lasky Fold," *MPW,* 10 May 1919, 837.

Duncan, Ted E. [music arranger] (b. 1902–9 Mar 1976 [74], Burbank CA; cancer). (MGM; Universal.) "Ted Duncan," *Variety,* 17 Mar 1976, p. 103 (age 74). AS, p. 345.

Duncan, Vivian (sister of **Evelyn** and **Rosetta Duncan**) [stage/film actress] (b. Los Angeles CA, 17 Jun 1897–19 Sep 1986 [89], Los Angeles CA; Alzheimer's disease). m. **Nils Asther,** 1930–32 (d. 1981); Frank Herman, 1957. BHD, p. 156 (b. 1902). "Vivian Duncan," *Variety,* 15 Oct 1986. AMD, p. 105. AS, p. 345 (b. 1899). BHD1, p. 166 (b. 1903). "Duncan Sisters Sued; G.C. Reed Asks $250,000, Charging Breach of Movie Contracts," *NYT,* 8 May 1927, 29:5 (a contract of July 1926 with Reed and S.S. McClelland was breached. They earned $83,000 from films and refused to pay 10% commission and "will not perform under the contract"). As Vivian Herman, Duncan was listed at the Social Security Office with a birthdate of 17 Jun 1902, but the 1900 Census lists her birth year as 1897. "Duncan Sisters in Damage Suit," *MPW,* 14 May 1927, 93. (*See* Duncan, Rosetta.)

Duncan, Walter [actor]. No data found. (Lubin.)

Duncan, William A[llan] [scenarist/director/stage/film actor] (b. Dundee, Scotland, 16 Dec 1879–7 Feb 1961 [81], Los Angeles CA). m. (2) **Edith Johnson,** 1921 (d. 1969). (Began 1910; Selig, 1912; Vitagraph, 1916; Universal.) George Katchmer, *Eighty Silent Film Stars* (Jefferson NC: McFarland, 1993; includes filmography). "William A. Duncan," *Variety,* 15 Feb 1961 (age 80). AMD, p. 105. AS, p. 345 (b. 18 May 1880). BHD, p. 156; BHD2, p. 74. GK, pp. 256–65. IFN, p. 89. Katz, pp. 363–64. MSBB, p. 1023, 1046. Truitt, p. 95. "Selig Actor Has Thrilling Experience," *MPW,* 17 Aug 1912, 656. "William Duncan," *MPW,* 24 Jul 1915, 652. "William Duncan Goes to Pathé," *MPW,* 9 Feb 1918, 838. "William Duncan Vitagraph's Popular Serial Director," *MPW,* 16 Nov 1918, 725. "Vitagraph Star in Vaudeville Show," *MPW,* 19 Jul 1919, 342. "Smith Signs Big Contract with Duncan, Serial Star," *MPW,* 20 Dec 1919, 947. "William Duncan, Vitagraph Serial Star, Is Making New Film with Edith Johnson," *MPW,* 25 Dec 1920, 1073. "Duncan Day Was a Great Success," *MPW,* 26 Feb 1921, 1073 (in Arizona). "Duncan May Resume Work in Serial Films," *MPW,* 6 Jan 1923, 68. "William Duncan Is Signed by Universal; To Make Big Serials," *MPW,* 3 Feb 1923, 432. Buck Rainey, "The Film Career of William Duncan," *CFC,* 55 (Summer, 1977), 24–26. George A. Katchmer, "The Athletic William Duncan," *CI,* 75 (May 1981), 24–25. Richard E. Braff, "An Index to the Silent Films of Wm. Duncan," *CI,* 177 (Mar 1990), 28 ff. George Katchmer, "William Duncan," *CI,* 238 (Apr 1995), C9 (Forepaugh Acting Stock Co., Philadelphia; Baker Stock Co., Rochester; Hopkins Repertoire, Memphis TN).

Duncan, William Cary [actor/scenarist] (b. North Brookfield MA, 6 Feb 1874–21 Nov 1945 [71], North Brookfield MA). AS, p. 345. BHD2, p. 74.

Dunham, John S. [publicist]. No data found. AMD, p. 105. "Dunham on Ince Press Staff," *MPW,* 7 Feb 1920, 935.

Dunham, Maudie (b. Essex, England, 1902–3 Oct 1982). BHD, p. 156.

Dunham, Phil [actor/director] (*né* Philip Gray Dunham, b. London, England, 23 Apr 1885–5 Sep 1972 [87], Los Angeles CA). AS, p. 345. BHD1, p. 167. IFN, p. 89.

Dunkinson, Harry L. [actor] (*né* Henry Leopold, b. New York NY, 16 Dec 1876–14 Mar 1936 [59], Los Angeles CA). (Essanay.) AMD, p. 105. AS, p. 345. BHD1, p. 167. IFN, p. 89. "Harry Dunkinson," *MPW,* 3 Jun 1916, 1700. George Katchmer, "Forgotten Cowboys and Cowgirls—Part X," *CI,* 182 (Aug 1990), 38.

Dunlap, Louise [actress] (b. 1865–31 Mar 1940 [74?], Los Angeles CA). BHD, p. 156.

Dunlap, Scott R. "Scotty" [director/producer/scenarist] (b. Chicago IL, 20 Jun 1892–30 Mar 1970 [77], Los Angeles CA). m. Alsie. (Fox; Monogram.) "Scott R. Dunlap," *Variety,* 1 Apr 1970 (began 1915; with Buck Jones at the Cocoanut Grove fire in 1942). AS, p. 345. BHD, p. 156; BHD2, p. 74. FDY, p. 423. IFN, p. 89.

Dunmyre, Louis H. [cinematographer]. No data found.

Dunn, Bobby [actor] (*né* Robert V. Dunn, b. Milwaukee WI, 28 Aug 1890–24 Mar 1937 [46], Los Angeles CA; possible suicide). "Robert V. Dunn," *Variety,* 31 Mar 1937. AS, p. 346. BHD1, p. 167. IFN, p. 89. Truitt, p. 96 (d. 1939). Tay Garnett and Fredda Dudley Balling, *Light Your Torches and Pull Up Your Tights* (New Rochelle NY: Arlington House, 1973), p. 72. George A. Katchmer, "Forgotten Cowboys and Cowgirls—Part V," *CI,* 177 (Mar 1990); "Update—Forgotten Cowboys/Girls," 179 (May 1990), 43–44.

Dunn, Dorothy [actress/writer/cinematographer]. No data found. AMD, p. 105. "Enter the Camerawoman," *MPW,* XXXII, 9 Jun 1917, 1609.

Dunn, Edward F[rank] [actor] (b. Brooklyn NY, 31 Mar 1896–5 May 1951 [55], Los Angeles CA). (Vitagraph.) "Edward F. Dunn," *Variety,* 9 May 1951. AMD, p. 105. AS, p. 346. BHD1, p. 167. IFN, p. 89. "Blackton Signs Dunn and Alexander," *MPW,* 14 Jun 1919, 1640.

Dunn, Eleanor [actress]. No data found. (Lubin.)

Dunn, Emma [actress] (b. Cheshire, England, 26 Feb 1875–14 Dec 1966 [91], Los Angeles CA). m. John Stokes. (MGM.) "Emma Dunn," *Variety,* 5 Apr 1967. AMD, p. 105. AS, p. 346. BHD1, p. 167 (d. Moorpark CA). IFN, p. 89. SD. Spehr, p. 128. Truitt, pp. 95–96. Cover, *NYDM,* 21 Apr 1915. "Emma Dunn Speaks of Her Work as a Screen Actress," *MPW,* 10 Apr 1920, 281.

Dunn, Herbert S[tanley] [actor: the Cisco Kid from 1913–15] (b. Brooklyn NY, 1892?–14 Apr 1979 [87], Costa Mesa CA; stroke). "Herbert S. Dunn," *CI,* 64 (Jul 1979), p. 68. AS, p. 346. BHD, p. 156. IFN, p. 89.

Dunn, J[ames] **Malcolm** [actor] (b. London, England, 25 May 1876–10 Oct 1946 [70], Beechurst, LI NY). m. Violette Kimball. "J. Malcolm Dunn," *Variety,* 16 Oct 1946. AS, p. 346. BHD1, p. 167. IFN, p. 89.

Dunn, Jack [title writer/editor] (*né* Jack Dunn Trop, b. New York NY, 17 May 1900–17 May 1992 [92], Miami FL). (Paramount.) "Jack Dunn [obituary]," *CI,* 205 (Jul 1992), 61. BHD2, p. 74.

Dunn, James Howard [actor] (b. New York NY, 2 Nov 1901–1 Sep 1967 [65], Santa Monica CA). m. (1) Frances Gifford—div. 1938; (2) Edna Rush. (Extra at Paramount [Astoria]; Fox.) "James Dunn," *Variety,* 6 Sep 1967 (age 61; began in *Bad Girl,* 1931). AS, p. 346. IFN, p. 90. Terry Costello, "Jimmy Dunn Is in the Money Now," *Movie Classic,* Nov 1931, 59, 72 (b. 1905).

Dunn, John J. [actor/assistant director] (b. New York NY, 1874-May 1928 [53?], Binghamton NY). BHD, p. 156; BHD2, p. 74.

Dunn, John J. (Johnny) [actor] (b. Binghamton NY, 1906?–2 Apr 1938 [32], Bluefield WV; pneumonia). "John J. Dunn," *Variety,* 20 Apr 1938. AS, p. 346. BHD, p. 156. IFN, p. 90. Truitt, p. 96.

Dunn, Josephine [actress: Wampas Star, 1929] (*née* Mary Josephine Dunn, b. New York NY, 1 May 1906–3 Feb 1983 [76], Thousand Oaks CA; cancer). m. **William P. Cameron,** 1925–28; Clyde Greathouse, 1931. "Josephine Dunn," *Variety,* 11 May 1983. (MGM; Paramount.) AS, p. 346. BHD1, p. 167. FSS, p. 97. Katz, pp. 365–66.

Dunn, Linwood Gale [cinematographer/special effects expert] (b. Brooklyn NY, 1904?–20 May 1998 [94], St. Joseph's Hospital, Glendale CA; cancer). m. Alice (4 daughters). (Pathé; RKO; AA for the Acme-Dunn special-effects optical printer, 1981.) Myrna Oliver, "Linwood Dunn; Legendary creator of special effects," *PP-G,* 23 May 1998, A-14:1. "Linwood Gale Dunn," *Variety,* 1 Jun 1998, 57:5 (age 93). AS, p. 346. Joe Collura, "Dialogue in Athens, Ohio with Linwood G. Dunn, A.S.C., Ph.d.," *CI,* 66 (Nov 1979), 26–27.

Dunn, William R[obert] [actor] (b. Astoria NY, 1884). AMD, p. 105. BHD, p. 156. "William Robert Dunn," *MPW,* XXVI, 16 Oct 1915, 449. "William Robert Dunn," *MPW,* 3 Feb 1917, 691. "After 20 Years, Actor Makes Debut in Print," *MPW,* 22 Nov 1924, 307.

Dunn, Winifred [scenarist] (b. 1899?). No data found. AMD, p. 105. FDY, p. 423. "Winifred Dunn a Star Writer," *MPW,* 10 Dec 1921, 686. "Miss Dunn Metro Editor," *MPW,* 17 Mar 1923, 308 (age 24).

Dunne, James J. [director]. No data found. AMD, p. 105. "Joins Production Forces," *MPW,* 4 Aug 1923, 415.

Dunning, Philip Hart [scenarist] (b. New York NY, 11 Dec 1890–20 Jul 1968 [77], Westport CT). AS, p. 346 (b. Meriden CT, 1891). BHD2, p. 74.

Dunrobin, Lionel Claude [actor] (b. 1875?–15 Aug 1950 [75], Hollywood CA; suicide). "Lionel Claude Dunrobin," *Variety*, 23 Aug 1950. AS, p. 347. IFN, p. 90.

Dunskus, Erich Adolf [actor] (b. Pillkallen, Germany, 27 Jul 1890–25 Nov 1967 [77], Hagenhelfe, Germany). AS, p. 347.

Dunsmuir, Alexander [actor] (b. Scotland, 1877–19 Jul 1938 [61?], Los Angeles CA; auto accident). AS, p. 347.

Dunton, Helen [actress] (d. 20 Nov 1920, San Francisco CA; suicide with poison). "Helen Dunton," *Variety*, 19 Nov 1920. AS, p. 347 (d. 15 Nov). BHD, p. 156. Truitt, p. 96.

Dupar, Edwin B. [cinematographer] (b. 1890?–4 Jun 1961 [71], Los Angeles CA). (Vitagraph; WB.) "Edwin Dupar," *Variety*, 223, 21 Jun 1961, 71:4 ("pioneer cameraman who started lensing with the old Vitagraph company in New York"). BHD2, p. 74.

Duplessy, Armand [director/scenarist] (*né* Armand de Prins, b. Ixelles, Belgium, 19 Jul 1883–2 Feb 1924 [40], Nice, France). AS, p. 340. BHD2, p. 74.

Dupon-Joyce, Mrs. [film/stage actress]. No data found. (Balboa.) J. Van Cartmell, "Along the Pacific Coast," *NYDM*, 30 Oct 1915, 27:2 (former understudy to Mrs. Pat Campbell. "She is appearing in vampire parts for the Balboa company.").

Dupont, E[wald] **A**[ndre] [director/scenarist] (b. Leitz, Germany, 25 Dec 1891–12 Dec 1956 [64], Los Angeles CA; cancer). (UFA; Universal; Paramount.) "E.A. Dupont," *Variety*, 19 Dec 1956. AMD, p. 105. AS, p. 347. BHD2, . 74. FDY, p. 423. IFN, p. 90. "Dupont to Direct for 'U,'" *MPW*, 26 Dec 1925, 761. Heinrich Fraenkel, "Presenting Dupont of Berlin; Another German Director, a Graduate Journalist, Comes to America," *MPC*, Apr 1926, 52–53 ("He was the first man who ever wrote a film review in Germany.").

Du Pont, Floyd [producer] (b. 1895–23 Oct 1937 [42?]). BHD2, p. 74.

Dupont, Gretl [actress] (*née* Gretl Scherk-Dupont, b. Germany, 1894–6 Feb 1973 [78?], Los Angeles CA). AS, p. 347.

Dupont, Jean [title writer/scenarist]. No data found. AMD, p. 105. FDY, pp. 423, 443. "Jean Dupont Now Scenarist," *MPW*, 5 Mar 1927, 10. "Jean Steps Up," *MPW*, 9 Apr 1927, 569. "Put Spice in Witwer Yarns," *MPW*, 16 Apr 1927, 633.

Dupont, Max [cinematographer]. No data found. FDY, p. 457.

Du Pont, Miss [actress] (aka Marguerite Armstrong; *née* Patricia Blanche Heiser, b. Frankfort KY, 28 Apr 1894–6 Feb 1973 [78], Palm Beach FL). m. Joseph Hannan; Sylvanus Stokes. AMD, p. 105. BHD, p. 156. Blum, p. 229 (*née* Marguerite Armstrong). IFN, p. 90. Katz, p. 366. MH, p. 108. "Carl Laemmle Announces the Engagement of New Film Star," *MPW*, 18 Jun 1921, 726. Kenneth McGaffey, "A Million Dollar Miss," *MPC*, Oct 1921, 63, 82. Harry Carr, "The Hollywood Boulevardier Chats," *MPC*, Sep 1924, 63 (maiden name given as Patricia Day). "Miss DuPont Signs with Warners," *MPW*, 25 Nov 1922, 336.

Dupray, Gaston [actor] (*né* Gaston Joseph Dopere, b. Schaerbeek, Belgium, 8 Jun 1886–12 Dec 1976 [90], Ixelles, Belgium). AS, p. 347.

Du Pre, Louise [actress]. No data found. (Charles K. Harris films.) AMD, p. 105. "Among the Players," *NYDM*, 6 Nov 1915, 23:2. "Louise DuPre," *MPW*, 17 Feb 1917, 987. "Louise DuPre Opposite Earl Williams," *MPW*, 8 Dec 1917, 1465. "Mary Pickford's Understudy to Be Starred in Pictures," *MPW*, 31 Jul 1920, 566. "Louise DuPre Is Signed by Casco," *MPW*, 11 Jun 1921, 620.

Dupree, George [actor] (b. Cincinnati OH, 1874–29 Jul 1951 [76?], New York NY). "George Dupree," *Variety*, 1 Aug 1951. AS, p. 347 (b. 1877). BHD, p. 156. IFN, p. 90 (age 74). Truitt 1983 (b. 1874).

Dupree, Minnie [actress] (b. La Crosse WI, 19 Jan 1873–23 May 1947 [74], New York NY). AS, p. 347. BHD1, p. 168.

Duprez, Charles J. [publicist/photographer]. No data found. AMD, p. 105. "Duprez Engaged by World," *MPW*, 7 Sep 1918, 1417.

Duprez, Fred [actor] (b. Detroit MI, 6 Sep 1884–27 Oct 1938 [54], aboard ship; heart attack). AS, p. 347.

Dupuy-Mazeul, Henri [scenarist] (b. Perpignan, France, 17 May 1885). AS, p. 347.

Dura, Ethel [actress]. No data found. AMD, p. 105. "Ethel Dura Is in 'Back Pay' Cast," *MPW*, 21 May 1921, 310.

Duran, Carlos [actor]. No data found. AMD, p. 105. Tom Waller, "Carlos Duran," *MPW*, 16 Apr 1927, 628–29.

Duran, Val [actor] (b. 1895–1 Feb 1937 [41?], Los Angeles CA). AS, p. 347.

Durand, David [child actor: Our Gang] (*né* David Parker Grey, b. Los Angeles CA, 29 Sep 1920–25 Jul 1998 [77], Bridgeview IL). (Film debut: two *Our Gang* comedies, 1925; last film: *Naval Academy*, 1941.) "Other Deaths; David Durand," *PP-G*, 5 Aug 1998, B-5:2. "David Durand [obituary]," *CI*, 279 (Sep 1998), 54–55 (includes filmography).

Durand, Edouard [actor] (b. France, 1871?–31 Jul 1926 [55], Port Chester NY; cerebral hemorrhage). m. Madeline Foster. "Edouard Durand," *Variety*, 4 Aug 1926. AS, p. 348 (b. 1861). BHD, p. 156. IFN, p. 90. Truitt, p. 96.

Durand, Jean [actor/director] (b. Paris, France, 15 Dec 1882–1946 [64?], Paris, France). AS, p. 348. BHD, p. 157; BHD2, p. 74.

Durant, Addie J. [actress] (d. 20 Aug 1914). m. **Charles E. Eldridge** (d. 1922). AMD, p. 106. "Obituary," *MPW*, 12 Sep 1914, 1495.

Durant, Harold Riggs [author/scenarist] (b. 1869?–22 Apr 1957 [88], Guilford CT). "Harry R. Durant, 88, Legislator, Author," *NYT*, 23 Apr 1957, 31:5 ("Mr. Durant was agent and adviser for many stage and screen stars, among them Mabel Normand, Gloria Swanson, Geraldine Farrar, Elsie Ferguson and Lucille Langhanke, whose name he changed to Mary Astor."). AMD, p. 106. "Famous Players Engage Harry Riggs Durant," *MPW*, 22 Apr 1916, 636. "Durant to Write for Kay-Bee," *MPW*, 18 Nov 1916, 994. "Durant in Receipt of Many Scripts," *MPW*, 7 Jul 1917, 100. "Durant Joins Goldwyn," *MPW*, 29 Dec 1917, 1931. "Durant Sells Four Plays for Broadway Production," *MPW*, 27 Mar 1920, 2171.

Durant, Thomas [actor] (b. 1899–7 Dec 1984 [85?], Santa Monica CA). BHD, p. 157.

Durell, Jean [actress]. No data found. AMD, p. 106. "Jean Durell Joins American," *MPW*, 29 Mar 1913, 1338.

Durfée, Dorothy [actress]. (Keystone). No data found.

Durfee, Minta E. [actress] (*née* Arminta E. Durfee, b. Los Angeles CA, 1 Oct 1889–9 Sep 1975 [85], Woodland Hills CA; heart attack). m. **Roscoe Arbuckle**, 5 Aug 1908, Long Beach CA, onstage at the Byde a Whyle Theatre—div. 25 (d. 1933). (Sennett.) "Minta Durfee, Actress, 85, Dies; Former Wife of Fatty Arbuckle," *NYT*, 12 Sep 1975, 31:5 (d. 9 Sep 1975). "Minta Durfee Arbuckle," *Variety*, 17 Sep 1975. Paul F. Kneeland, "Minta Durfee, at 85; Starred with Chaplin," *Boston Evening Globe*, 12 Sep 1975. AS, p. 348 (d. 10 Sep). BHD1, p. 169. FSS, p. 98. IFN, p. 90. Stuart Oderman, "Minta Durfee Arbuckle—A Friend Remembered," *CFC*, 49 (Winter 1975), 11 *et passim*. Stuart Oderman, "Fatty's First," *CI*, 64 (Jul 1979), 8–9, 14 (b. 1899); continued in every issue through No. 79 (Jan 1982).

Durham, Lewis (or **Louis**) [actor] (b. New Oxford PA, 19 Aug 1852–16 Oct 1937 [85]). AS, p. 348. BHD, p. 157. IFN, p. 90. George Katchmer, "Remembering the Great Silents," *CI*, 245 (Nov 1995), 42. *See* next entry.

Durham, Louis "Bull" Raphael [baseball player (1898–09)/actor] (*né* Louis Raphael Staub, b. New Oxford PA, 27 Jun 1877–28 Jun 1960 [83], Bentley KS). m. (1) ca. 1906–09; (2) Edith C. Smithman, 1914; (3) 1927. (Mutual; Ince.) "The World of the Movies," *NYT*, Sect. VIII, 24 May 1914, 6:1 ("Bull" Durham in Keystone comedies). "Gossip of the Studios," *NYDM*, 4 Nov 1914, 29:2 (married Smithman). "Durham Continues with Horsley," *MPW*, 8 Apr 1916, 267. Bill Haber, "In Pursuit of Bull Durham," *Society for American Baseball Research* (1983). Victor A. Berch, "Louis Durham Confusion [letter]," *CI*, 246 (Dec 1995), 14, 28.

Durieux, Tilla [actress/director] (*née* Ottilie Godeffroy, b. Vienna, Austria, 18 Aug 1880–21 Feb 1971 [90], Berlin, Germany). AS, p. 348. BHD1, p. 169. IFN, p. 90.

Durkin, James Peter [actor/director] (b. Quebec, Canada, 21 May 1879–12 Mar 1934 [64], Los Angeles CA). m. Alice. (Thanhouser; FP-L.) "James Peter Durkin," *Variety*, 20 Mar 1934 (age 55). AS, p. 348. BHD1, p. 169. IFN, p. 90. "Durkin with F.P.; Feature DIrector Latest Addition to the Famous Players Increasing Staff," *NYDM*, 23 Jun 1915, 21:4 (producing debut at FP-L with *The Incorrigible Dukane*).

Durlam, George Arthur [scenarist/producer]. No data found. FDY, p. 423.

Durling, E[dgar] **V**[incent] [writer/executive] (b. New York NY, 24 Jul 1893–13 Sep 1957 [64], New York NY; brain tumor). m. Joan Marie. "E.V. Durling Dies; Columnist Was 64; King Features Writer Did 'Life with Salt on Side' for Journal-American," *NYT*, 14 Sep 1957, 19:3. "E.V. Durling," *Variety*, 18 Sep 1957 ("In 1924, he returned to Hollywood to head a comedy film studio."). BHD2, p. 74 (b. 1892). WWWA.

Durning, Bernard J. [actor/director] (b. New York NY, 1893?–29 Aug 1923 [30], New York NY; typhoid). m. **Shirley Mason** (d. 1979). "Bernard J. Durning," *Variety*, 6 Sep 1923. AS, p. 348. BHD, p. 157; BHD2, p. 75. IFN, p. 90. Truitt, pp. 96–97.

Duryea, George *see* **Keene, Tom**

Duse, Carlo [actor] (b. Udine, Italy, 5 Jan 1899–9 Sep 1956 [57], Rome, Italy). AS, p. 348. BHD1, p. 169. IFN, p. 90.

Duse, Eleanora Giulia Amalia (daughter of

actor Alessandro Duse) [stage/film actress/director/writer] (b. Vigevano, Pavia [Venice], Italy, 3 Oct 1858–21 Apr 1924 [65], Pittsburgh PA; influenza and pneumonia). m. Tebaldo Checci. Jeanne Bordeux, *Eleonora Duse: The Story of Her Life* (London: Hutchinson & Co., 1924?). Arthur Symons, *Eleonora Duse* (London: Elkin Mathews, Ltd., 1926). Edoardo Schneider, *Gli Ultimi Anni di Eleonora Duse* (Milan: L'Eroica, 1928). Olga Resnevic Signorelli, *La Duse* (Rome, 1938). Leonardo Vergani, *Eleonora Duse* (Milan: Aldo Martello, 1958). Giovanni Pontiero, trans. and ed., *Duse on Tour; Guido Noccioli's Diaries, 1906–07* (Manchester, England: Manchester Univ., 1982). William Weaver, *Duse; A Biography* (London: Thames and Hudson, Ltd., 1984). Gerardo Guerrieri, *Eleonora Duse; Nove Saggi* (Rome: Bulzoni Editore, 1993). "Mme. Duse's Body to Be Sent Home; Famous Actress Who Died in Pittsburgh to Be Buried in Her Native Italy; Her Whole Life a Tragedy; Last Illness Ascribed to Drain Upon Her Strength in Making Farewell Tour," *NYT*, 22 Apr 1924, 6:2 (b. 1859). "Duse," *Variety*, 23 Apr 1924. AS, p. 348. BHD, p. 157 (b. 1859). GSS, pp. 114–15. IFN, p. 91. JS, p. 151 (appeared in *Cenere*, Italy, 1916). SD.

Dussane, Béatrix [actress] (*née* Béatrix Coulond-Dussan, b. France, 8 Mar 1888–3 Mar 1969 [80], France). AS, p. 348.

d'Usseau, Leon [director/scenarist] (b. Toledo OH, 1886?–6 Jun 1963 [77], en route to Europe). AS, p. 278. BHD2, p. 75. FDY, p. 423. IFN, p. 91.

Duval, Paulette [actress] (b. Buenos Aires, Argentina). (MGM). Hal K. Wells, "From Argentine to Films," *MPC*, Jan 1926, 41, 74.

Duvaleix [actor] (*né* Jean Albert Duvaleix, b. Bordeaux, France, 8 Jun 1893 [extrait de naissamce no. 835ED/1893]-21 Dec 1962 [69], Paris, France [extrait de décès no. 14/5200/1962]). AS, p. 349.

Duvalles [actor] (*né* Charles Frédéric Coffinieres, b. Paris, France, 26 Sep 1894–14 Feb 1971 [76], Paris, France). AS, p. 349.

Duvivier, Julien Henri Nicolas [actor/director/scenarist] (b. Lille, France, 8 Oct 1896 [extrait de naissance no. 4922/CD]-29 Oct 1967 [71], Paris, France). AS, p. 349.

Dvorak, Ann (daughter of **Sam McKim**) [actress] (*née* Anna McKim, aka Anna Lehr, b. New York NY, 2 Aug 1911 [Birth Certificate Index No. 40777]–10 Dec 1979 [68], Honolulu HI). m. **Leslie Fenton**, 17 Mar 1932 (d. 1978). "Ann Dvorak Dies; Screen Actress, 67; Made Debut as Paul Muni's Sister in 'Scarface' in 1932," *NYT*, 20 Dec 1977, D19:4. "Ann Dvorak," *Variety*, 19 Dec 1979. AS, p. 349. BHD1, p. 170 (b. 1912). IFN, p. 91 (b. 1912). "Ann Dvorak," WBO2, pp. 160–61 (b. 1912). John Roberts, "Ann Dvorak," *CI*, 154 (Apr 1988), C24-C25, 48. Dan Van Neste, "Ann Dvorak: Talent and Determination, *CI*, 247 (Jan 1996), 14 *et passim*.

Dvorska, Jesse [vaudeville/film actor] (b. Kovno, Lithuania, 1898–27 Dec 1999 [101], Westwood CA). (Appeared in the *Jake the Plumber* series.) "Jesse Dvorska [obituary]," *CI*, 296 (Feb 2000), 48 (to the U.S. in 1914).

Dwan, Allan [scenarist/director] (*né* Joseph Aloysius Dwan, b. Toronto, Canada, 3 Apr 1885–21 Dec 1981 [96], Woodland Hills CA; apoplexy). . Peter Bogdanovich, *Allan Dwan; The Last Pioneer* (New York: Praeger, 1971). m. **Pauline Bush**, 24 Apr 1915, San Jua Capistano (d. 1969); Marie Shelton (d. 1954). (Essanay; American; Universal; FP-L; Eastern Triangle.) Janet Maslin, "Allan Dwan, Director, Dead; Began Movie Career in 1909," *NYT*, 23 Dec 1981, B5:3. "Allan Dwan, 96, Most Prolific Hollywood Director, Dies in L.A.," *Variety*, 23 Dec 1981. AS, p. 349. BHD2, p. 75. FDY, p. 423. KOM, p. 134. Lowrey, p. 48. MSBB, p. 1044, 1046. Spehr, p. 128. "Allen [sic] Dwan's Play First Vehicle for Warren Kerrigan," *MPW*, 20 Sep 1913, 1292. William E. Wing, "Along the Pacific Coast," *NYDM*, 8 Apr 1915, 24:2 (to marry Bush). "More fr N.Y.M.P.; Helen Ware Added to List of Stars and Allan Dwan Signed to Produce," *NYDM*, 30 Jun 1915, 20:1. Doris Irving, "How the Director Knows," *Picture-Play Magazine*, Jun 1923, 59, 92. Beatrice Wilson, "The Great Firm of Dwan and Swanson," *MPC*, Dec 1924, 28–29. O.A.G., "Screen: Three Films Have Premieres [review of Escape to Burma, RKO, 1955]," *NYT*, 21 May 1955, 11:3 ("...one must pin down some of the responsibility, and we fear the choice must be Allan Dwan, the director. Mr. Dwan displays little or no talent in his chosen craft. His work is so inept that he even allows off-stage people to be seen.").

Dwan, Dorothy [actress] (aka Molly Mills, *née* Dorothy Illgenfritz, b. Sedalia MO, 26 Apr 1906–17 Mar 1981 [74], Ventura Community Hospital, Ventura CA; lung disease; cremated at the Grand View Crematory, Glendale CA on 20 Mar 1981. Certificate of Death: County of Ventura, 800 So. Victoria Ave., Ventura CA 93009, #5600-687). . m. **Larry Semon**, 22 Jan 1925; Little Church Around the Corner, NYC (d. 1928); (2) Paul Northcutt Boggs, Jr., 23 May 1930—div. 3 Dec 1935 (1 son, Paul Boggs Crikelair, b. 22 Nov 1931); (3) Fred Buckels—div. (Vitagraph; Educational.) AS, p. 349 (b. 1907). BR, pp. 135–37. FSS, p. 98. George A. Katchmer, "Famous Cowboys & Cowgirls—2," *CI*, 173 (Nov 1989), C14. Billy Doyle, "Dorothy Dwan: The Forgotten 'Dorothy,'" *CI*, 280 (Oct 1998), C-6. Richard M. Roberts, "Larry Semon Part Three: Trouble Brewing," *CI*, 301 (Jul 2000), p. 59 (Dwan is quoted as saying that her maiden name was Smith; states that Dwan died in 1980. "After Larry died—I really lost interest in my own film career, and I didn't like the thought of talking pictures. Ken [Maynard] called me and begged me to do one talking film with him [*The Fighting Legion*, 1930], and I did it, and hated it, and after that experience I called it quits.").

Dwiggins, Jay [actor] (d. 8 Sep 1919, Los Angeles CA; heart failure in a Hollywood theater). (Vitagraph.) AMD, p. 106. BHD, p. 157. IFN, p. 91. Truitt 1983. "Jay Dwiggins," *MPW*, 4 Mar 1916, 1447. "Obituary," *MPW*, 27 Sep 1919, 1959–60.

Dwire, Earl [actor] (b. Rockport MO, 3 Oct 1883–16 Jan 1940 [56], Carmichael CA). AS, p. 350. BHD, p. 157. IFN, p. 91.

Dwyer, Ethel [actress] (*née* Ethel Dwyer McCrady, b. Tarrytown NY, 1898–2 Sep 1985 [86], Pittsburgh PA). "Ethel Dwyer," *Variety*, 11 Sep 1985 ("She made a number of silent films..."). AS, p. 350. BHD, p. 157.

Dwyer, John T. [stage/film/radio actor] (b. 1877?–7 Dec 1936 [59], New York NY). (Stage debut: 1897, Boyd's Opera House, Omaha NB). "John T. Dwyer," *Variety*, 16 Dec 1936, p. 70 (interred in Calvary Cemetery). AS, p. 350. BHD, p. 157.

Dwyer, Leslie Gilbert [actor] (b. London, England, 28 Aug 1906–26 Dec 1986 [80], London, England; pulmonary embolism). AS, p. 350 (b. Catford, England). BHD1, p. 170.

Dwyer, Ruth [actress] (b. Brooklyn NY, 25 Jan 1898–2 Mar 1978 [80], Woodland Hills CA). m. William Jackie. "Ruth Dwyer," *Variety*, 8 Mar 1978. AMD, p. 106. AS, p. 350. BHD1, p. 170. IFN, p. 91. "Sign Miss Dwyer," *MPW*, 8 Sep 1923, 191. "Ruth Dwyer Is Horton's Lead," *MPW*, 21 May 1927, 181. George A. Katchmer, "Forgotten Cowboys and Cowgirls—Part XVII, *CI*, 194 (Aug 1991), 47.

Dwyer, William [vaudevillian: Clapham & Dwyer/actor] (b. 1890?–11 Jan 1943 [52], Rutland, England; heart attack). "William Dwyer," *Variety*, 3 Feb 1943.

Dyall, Franklin [actor/producer] (b. Liverpool, England, 3 Feb 1874–8 May 1950 [76], Worthing, England). (Stage debut: *The Masqueraders*, 1894, London.) "Franklin Dyall," *Variety*, 10 May 1950, p. 55 (age 80). AS, p. 350. BHD1, p. 170. IFN, p. 91.

Dyas, Dave [actor] (b. MO, 11 Apr 1895–5 Nov 1929 [34]). AS, p. 350. BHD, p. 157. IFN, p. 91.

d'Yd, Jean [actor] (*né* Paul Didier Perret, b. Paris, France, 17 Mar 1880–15 May 1964 [84], Paris, France). AS, p. 278. BHD, p. 157. IFN, p. 91.

Dye, Florence [actress]. BR, pp. 19–20.

Dyer, Anson [director/producer] (b. Brighton, England, 1876). AS, p. 350.

Dyer, Frank Lewis (brother of **Richard Nott Dyer**) [writer/inventor/executive] (b. NJ, 1871–4 Jun 1941 [70], Ventnor NJ). "Frank Lewis Dyer, Edison Biographer; Attorney and Inventor, Noted as Deviser of 'Talking Book' for Blind, Dies at 70; Holder of 100 Patents; Served as Counsel for Edison Interests—Head of the General Film Company," *NYT*, 5 Jun 1941, 23:5. AMD, p. 106. Spehr, p. 128 (b. 1871). Frank L. Dyer, "Edison's Place in the Moving Picture Art," *MPW*, 21 Dec 1907, 679–80. "Facts Concerning the New Arrangement of the Principal Factors of the Motion Picture Manufacturing Interests in America," *MPW*, 26 Dec 1908, 519. "Concerning Mr. Dyer," *MPW*, 30 Nov 1912, 864 (resignation as President of Editon). "Dyer President of General Film," *MPW*, 28 Dec 1912, 1276. George Blaisdell, "President Dyer Talks on General Film," *MPW*, 22 Mar 1913, 1197–98. "Dyreda—New Producing Company," *MPW*, 3 Oct 1914, 69.

Dyer, John E. [actor] (b. 1884?–11 Oct 1951 [67], Detroit MI). "John E. Dyer," *Variety*, 24 Oct 1951. AS, p. 350. IFN, p. 91.

Dyer, Richard Nott (brother of **Frank Lewis Dyer**) [Edison patent lawyer] (b. 1858?–13 Jan 1914 [56], E. Orange NJ). "Richard Nott Dyer [obituary]," *NYDM*, 21 Jan 1914, 30:3.

Dyer, William J. [actor] (b. Atlanta GA, 11 Mar 1881–22 Dec 1933 [52], Los Angeles CA). (Vitagraph.) "William Dyer," *Variety*, 2 Jan 1934 (d. 23 Dec). AS, p. 350. BHD1, p. 170. IFN, p. 91. George A. Katchmer, "Forgotten Cowboys and Cowgirls—Part XV," *CI*, 192 (Jun 1991), 42. George Katchmer, "Remembering the Great Silents; William J. Dyer," *CI*, 205 (Jul 1992), 58.

Dymo, Ossip [actor/scenarist] (b. Bialystok, Poland, 16 Feb 1878–9 Feb 1959 [80], New York NY). BHD2, p. 75.

Dynes, Odette [actress] (*née* Odette Marthe Dinet, b. Le Petit-Quevilly, France, 1 May 1903 [extrait de naissamce no. 136]-24 Oct 1963 [60], Asnieres-sur-Seine, France). AS, p. 350.

Dzigan, Yefim Lvovich [director] (b. Moscow, Russia, 2 Dec 1898–5 Jan 1982 [83], Moscow, Russia). AS, p. 350.

E

Eadia, Dennis [actor] (b. Glasgow, Scotland, 14 Jan 1875–10 Jun 1928 [53], London, England). BHD, p. 157.

Eagels, Jeanne [stage/film actress] (b. Kansas City MO, 26 Jun 1890–3 Oct 1929 [39], New York NY [Death Certificate No. 23947, age 36; general visceral congestion; autopsy]). m. (1) Morris Dubinsky; (2) Edward H. Coy. Edward Joseph Doherty, *The Rain Girl; The Tragic Story of Jeanne Eagels* (Philadelphia: Macrae Smith Co., 1930). (Pathé, 1915.) "Jeanne Eagels Collapses, Dies in Hospital on Visit to Be Treated for Nerve Ailment," *NYT,* 4 Oct 1929, 1:4 (b. 1894). "Jeanne Eagels," *Variety,* 16 Oct 1929 (age 35). AS, p. 351 (b. Kansas City KS). BHD1, p. 170. GSS, p. 116 (b. Kansas City MO, 26 Jun 1890). IFN, p. 91 (age 35). Katz, p. 371. SD. Spehr, p. 128. Truitt, p. 97 (b. 1894). AMD, p. 107. "Jeanne Eagels to Be in New Arnold Daly Picture for Pathé," *MPW,* 16 Oct 1915, 449. "Miss Jeanne Eagels Joins Thanhouser," *MPW,* 19 Aug 1916, 1224. "Jeanne Eagels—Thanhouser Star," *MPW,* 18 Nov 1916, 1027. Beatrice Wilson, "Should a Star Stick to Broadway?," *MPC,* XX, Jan 1925, 33, 77. Ann Cummings, "She's Come in Out of the Rain; Jeanne Eagels Leaves Pango Pango for Hollywood," *MPC,* Dec 1927, 21, 77. Eve Golden, "Jeanne Eagels: Sadie Thompson Is Going Straight to Hell," *CI,* 241 (Jul 1995), C10-C11.

Eagle Eye [actor] (aka William Eagle Eye and William Ens) (b. Globe AZ, 1876?–17 Jan 1927 [50], Los Angeles CA; result of skull fracture in a fight on 16 Jan 1927). "Indian Actor Dies," *Variety,* 19 Jan 1927 (age 32). AS, p. 351; p. 365 (William Ens); p. 371 (Eye, Eagle, d. 16 Jan). BHD, p. 162. IFN, p. 91. George Katchmer, "Remembering the Great Silents," *CI,* 196, Oct 1991, 54.

Eagle, James C[rump] [actor] (b. Norfolk VA, 10 Sep 1907–15 Dec 1959 [52], Los Angeles CA; cirrhosis of the liver). BHD1, p. 171. IFN, p. 91. Truitt 83, p. 212.

Eagle, Oscar [stage/film actor/director] (b. Gallipolis OH, 21 Jan 1861–14 Mar 1930 [69], New York NY). m. Esther Lyon (d. 1958). (Selig; Reliance-Mutual; FP-L.) AMD, p. 107. AS, p. 351. BHD2, p. 75. IFN, p. 91 (Eagles). "Mrs. Oscar Eagle," *NYT,* 16 Jul 1958, 29:1 (b. 30 Oct 1868–15 Jul 1958 [89], New York NY). "Oscar Eagle Directing 'Runaway June,'" *MPW,* 12 Dec 1914, 1539. "Oscar Eagle to F.P.; Director Sails for Cuba to Direct John Barrymore in 'The Dictator,'" *NYDM,* 12 May 1915, 21:2. "Famous Players Engage Oscar Eagle," *MPW,* 15 May 1915, 1076.

Eagler, Paul E. [cinematographer] (b. Newman IL, 24 Sep 1890–30 Sep 1961 [71], Sherman Oaks CA; cerebral hemorrhage). (Ince, 1918.) "Paul Eagler," *Variety,* 11 Oct 1961. AS, p. 351. BHD2, p. 75.

Eames, Clare [stage/film actress] (b. Hartford CT, 5 Aug 1896–8 Nov 1930 [34], Richmond, London, England). m. Sidney Coe Howard, 1922 (Cleveland OH). "Clare Eames Dead; Brilliant Actress; American Star Underwent Two Operations During Illness of Three Weeks; Won Success in London; Enthusiastically Received by Critics and Public—Had Made Reputation Before Going Abroad," *NYT,* 9 Nov 1930, 31:1. "Clare Eames," *Variety,* 12 Nov 1930. AS, p. 351. BHD, p. 157. IFN, p. 91. Truitt, p. 97.

Eames, Virginia *see* **Boardman, Virginia Eames**

Earl, Catherine V. [stage/film actress] (b. 1886–14 Aug 1946 [60], Los Angeles CA; heart attack). m. **John Webb Dillion** (d. 1949). (Biograph.) "Catherine Earl," *Variety,* 21 Aug 1946, p. 62 ("She retired from the screen in 1923."). AS, p. 351. BHD, p. 157. IFN, p. 91.

Earl, Edna *see* **Skirvan, Marguerite**

Earl, Edward [executive]. No data found. AMD, p. 107. "Edward Earl Now Vice-President," *MPW,* 5 Aug 1916, 925. "Mixed Identities," *MPW,* 23 Dec 1916, 1794. "Edward Earl Is Guest at Dinner," *MPW,* 6 Apr 1918, 67. "Edward Earl," *MPW,* 20 Jul 1918, 380.

Earlcott, Gladys [actress] (d. 18 May 1939, Los Angeles CA; cancer). "Gladys Earlcott," *Variety,* 24 May 1939. BHD, p. 157. IFN, p. 91. Truitt, p. 97.

Earle, Blanche "Bonnie" [actress] (*née?,* b. 1883?–22 Jan 1952 [69], Woodland Hills CA). (Vitagraph; retired 1920.) m. **William P.S. Earle** (d. 1972). "Blanche (Bonnie) Earle," *Variety,* 30 Jan 1952. AS, p. 351. BHD, p. 157. IFN, p. 91. Truitt, p. 97.

Earle, Dorothy [actress] (b. NJ, 4 Sep 1892–5 Jul 1957 [64], Burbank CA). m. Gabby Hayes. BHD, p. 157. Truitt, p. 97.

Earle, Edna [actress] (b. Kansas City KS). (Metro [under another name]; Pathé; FP-L; Universal.) *Fl.* 1918. *Theatre Magazine,* XXVII, Jun 1918, 403, 405.

Earle, Edward [cameraman]. No data found. AMD, p. 107. "Has Photographed 150 Featuers," *MPW,* Apr 1920, 394.

Earle, Edward C. [stage/film actor] (b. Toronto, Canada, 16 Jul 1882–15 Dec 1972 [90], Woodland Hills CA 92627). (Valentine Stock Co. [of which Mary Pickford was a member], Toronto; Edison, 1916; FP-L; General Film Co.; Pathé; Metro; Frohman; Vitagraph.) AMD, p. 107. AS, p. 351. BHD1, p. 171. FFF, p. 162. IFN, p. 91. Katz, p. 371. MH, p. 108. MSBB, p. 1023. "Edward Earle, the Edison Leading Man," *MPW,* 27 Feb 1915, 1294. "Mixed Identities," *MPW,* 23 Dec 1916, 1794. "Edward Earle," *MPW,* 24 Mar 1917, 1929. "Edward Earle," *MPW,* 21 Apr 1917, 434. "Edward Earle Goes to Vitagraph," *MPW,* 21 Jul 1917, 432. "Personal and Otherwise," *MPW,* 18 Jan 1919, 342 (left Vitagraph). Cyrene Howard, "Making Love at 32 Degrees Below Zero; Edward Earle Doesn't Find the Position of Lover in the Yukon as Attractive as You Might Imagine," *Photo-Play Journal,* Aug 1920, pp. 48–49, 52 ("I've made love to a number of women, in pictures, of course, and I always enjoyed it, too, but making the love 'shots' for *The Law of the Yukon* was no bed of roses. I think we took about five re-takes on them and then, you know, there are always a number of scenes taken that never appear in the picture.... Miss [Nancy] Deaver, who played opposite me, was just a little tiny girl and she kept crying that she knew the wind was going to blow her away or that she was going to be frozen to death.... The result was a couple of hundred feet of ruined film and a retake. And with the retake, just as we were about to reach the climax, Miss Deaver's foot slipped and she sank into the snow. Another retake! So you see things weren't quite so pleasant as one might imagine."). "Bijou; The Law of the Yukon," *Telegraph,* 30 Jan 1921 (Mayflower, 7 reels, directed by Charles Miller). W.R.W., "Ballin's 'East Lynne' Artistic Success," *Exhibitor's Herald,* 5 Mar 1921, p. 45 ("Edward Earle, as the husband, satisfies. He disposes of the comparatively slender 'part' capably, gaining by restraint the realism that his stage predecessors lost by lack of it."). Boyle, "A Bit Out of Date Is Dear Old 'East Lynne' in This Age," *News,* 24 Mar 1921 (Mabel Ballin is attractive as the hapless heroine, but she greatly overacts in certain scenes. I like Barbara, played by Gladys Coburn, not at all, but Doris Sheerin as the wicked gardener's daughter is attractively fierce. As for the men, they are so so."). "Constance Binney and Earle Lead; Movie Star Gains 5,000 Votes in a Day—Mrs. [Lydig] Hoyt [society screen star] Drops to Sixth Place," *N.Y. World,* 8 May 1922 (Billie Burke, Madge Kennedy, Mary Pickford and Marion Davies trailed Binney; Tom Mix, Larry Semon, Will Rogers and Charlie Chaplin trailed Earle). "Edward Earle and Billie Burke Are Crowned King and Queen of Movies," *MPW,* 0 May 1922, 261 (in NY). Milton Silver, "Real Movie Stars Not Made; They Make Themselves, Says Edward Earle," *MW,* 26 May 1923, 8, 29. Earle began in 1914 with Lester Lonergan as an extra at five whole dollars a week. Many stage engagements followed, such as *The Quaker Girl* with Ina Claire. He and Agnes Ayres were "married" 15 times in films made for the General Film Co., as in *The Sisters of the Golden Circle,* by O. Henry. "We have been honeymooning so many weeks in making pictures that if I were ever to get married I am afraid honeymooning would become rather a tiresome and monotonous business."

Earle, Ferdinand Pinney [art director/producer] (b. New York NY, 8 Jun 1878–13 Jul 1951 [73], Los Angeles CA). "Ferdinand P. Earle," *Variety,* 18 Jul 1951. AMD, p. 107. AS, p. 351. BHD2, p. 75. Slide, p. 159. WWS, p. 174. "Day of the Painter Coming, Says Earle," *MPW,* 27 Jul 1918, 533. "Earle to Title Cuneo Features," *MPW,* 26 Feb 1921, 1038.

Earle, Jack [actor] (b. Denver CO, 3 Jul 1906–18 Jul 1952 [46], El Paso TX). AS, p. 351. BHD, p. 158.

Earle, Josephine, "The Vitagraph Vamp" [actress] (*née* Josephine McEwan, b. Brooklyn NY, 23 Feb 1892–15 Aug 1929 [37], Brooklyn NY). m. Capt. James Glen, 1918. (Vitagraph.) AMD, p. 107. AS, p. 351. BHD1, p. 171. IFN, p. 91. Truitt 1983, p. 212. "Josephine Earle," *MPW,* 5 Jun 1915, 1612. "In the Picture Studios," *NYDM,* 22 Sep 1915, 32:3 (to debut in Vitagraph's *Gone to the Dogs,* directed by Harry handworth). "Josephine Earle," *MPW,* 5 Aug 1916, 928. "Josephine Earle," *MPW,* 19 May 1917, 1119. "Josephine Earle," *MPW,* 8 Dec 1917, 1470. "Keeping in Personal Touch," *MPW,* 31 Jul 1920, 578 ("...known in days gone by as the 'Vitagraph Vamp,' was married two years ago to Captain James Glen of the Royal Air Force.").

Earle, Ralph E. [cameraman]. No data found. m. Hazel Brown, ca. Jan 1914. AMD, p. 107. "Camera Man's Romance; Pathe Camera Man Weds Girl He Met While Taking Picture for

'Weekly,'" *NYDM,* 4 Mar 1914, 31:2. "Pathé Secures Cameraman Earle," *MPW,* 26 Aug 1916, 1415. "Ralph E. Earle Ends Trip," *MPW,* 19 Jan 1918, 355. "Hurricane Smashes Theatres; Pathé News Cameraman a Hero," *MPW,* 2 Oct 1926, 1–2. "Earle Discharged from Hospital," *MPW,* 16 Oct 1926, 422.

Earle, William P.S. [writer/playwright/photographer/director/producer] (b. New York NY, 28 Dec 1882–30 Nov 1972 [89], Los Angeles CA). m. **Blanche** (d. 1952). (Vitagraph.) AMD, p. 107. AS, p. 351. BHD1, p. 607; BHD2, p. 75.. IFN, p. 92. MSBB, p. 1046 (b. 1884). Slide, p. 139. Spehr, p. 128 (1884–1974). "William Earle Directs Earle Williams," *MPW,* 21 Jul 1917, 460. "William P.S. Earle Joins World Pictures," *MPW,* 25 May 1918, 1129. Grace Greenwood, "Tut! Tut! King Tut!; Popoular fad created by the opening of King Tutankhamen's Egyptian tomb is now responsible for a movie [released as *The Dancer of the Nile,* FBO, 23 Oct 1923] based upon the love of one of the Pharaohs," *MW,* 2 Jun 1923, 21, 31.

Earles, Harry [actor] (aka Harry Doll, *né* Kurt Schneider, b. Germany, 3 Apr 1902–4 May 1985 [83], Sarasota FL). "Harry Earles," *Variety,* 25 Dec 1985. AS, p. 351. BHD1, p. 171.

Early, Dudley [title writer]. No data found. FDY, p. 443.

Early, Pearl M[ay] [actress] (b. Wooster OH, 30 Dec 1878–17 Jun 1960 [81], Oceanside CA). AS, p. 351.

Eason, B. Reaves "Breezy" (father of **Reaves Barnes Eason, Jr.**) [director/scenarist] (*né* William Reaves Eason, b. Friars Point MS, 2 Oct 1886–9 Jun 1956 [69], Sherman Oaks CA; heart attack). m. 1914 (son, Breezy Eason, Jr., 1914–1921). "B. Reeves Eason," *NYT,* 13 Jun 1956, 37:1. "B. Reeves Eason," *Variety,* 13 Jun 1956. AMD, p. 107. AS, p. 351. BHD, p. 158; BHD2, p. 75. FDY, p. 423. IFN, p. 92. Katz, pp. 371–72 (b. Friar Point). 1921 Directory, p. 262 (b. Prize Point). "Reaves Eason, Benedict," *NYDM,* 8 Apr 1914, 41:3. "Breezy Directing Carey," *MPW,* 28 Jun 1924, 788. "'Breezy' Eason Directing," *MPW,* 18 Oct 1924, 605. "To Direct Fred Thomson," *MPW,* 12 Jun 1926, 548. Ezra Goodman, "Step Right Up and Call Him 'Breezy'; But It's Mr. B. Reeves Eason When He's Directing Inserts for Grade A Films," *NYT,* 19 Apr 1942, 3:4 (b. MA). George Katchmer, "Remembering the Great Silents," *CI,* 199 (Jan 1992), 12.

Eason, Lorraine [actress]. AMD, p. 107. "Lorraine Eason," *MPW,* 8 Oct 1927, 359. George A. Katchmer, "Remembering the Great Silents," *CI,* 184 (Oct 1990), 58.

Eason, Reaves Barnes, Jr. [actor] (son of **B. Reaves Eason**) (b. CA, 19 Nov 1914–25 Oct 1921 [6], Hollywood, Los Angeles CA; auto accident). (Jewel; final film: *The Fox,* with Harry Carey.) AMD, p. 107. BHD, p. 158. IFN, p. 92. "Obituary," *MPW,* 5 Nov 1921, 41. George Katchmer, "Remembering the Great Silents," *CI,* 199 (Jan 1992), 12.

East, Henry [casting director]. No data found. AMD, p. 108. "Henry East Directing," *MPW,* 31 Jan 1920, 710.

East, John M. [actor] (b. 1861–18 Aug 1924 [63?], London, England). BHD, p. 158. IFN, p. 92.

Eastman, George [inventor/manufacturer] (*né* Luigi Montefiore, b. Waterville ME, 12 Jul 1854–14 Mar 1932 [77], Rochester NY; suicide by shooting). "Eastman a Suicide; Note to His Friends Says 'Work Is Done'; Sends Doctor and Nurses from Room at Rochester Home and Then Fires Shot; Long Broken in Health; Only a Moment Before Fatal Act He Was Chatting with His Physician; Had Given Away $75,000,000, Manufacturer Blazed the Trail for Large-Scale Industry and World-Wide Marketing," *NYT,* 15 Mar 1932, 1:8, 14:4. "George Eastman," *Variety,* 15 Mar 1932. AMD, p. 108. IFN, p. 92. Katz, p. 372. WWVC, p. 47. Thomas Bedding, "The Largest Manufacturer of Films for Moving Pictures in the World," *MPW,* 7 Aug 1909, 186. "The Cradle of the Moving Picture," *MPW,* 7 Aug 1909, 190–91. "Handsome Theatre Is Eastman"s Gift," *MPW,* 29 Mar 1919, 1790. "George Eastman, the King of Film, Proves to Be a Right Royal Host," *MPW,* 16 Aug 1919, 937. "Rise of Eastman Kodak Company Constitutes Industrial Romance," *MPW,* 16 Aug 1919, 957. "Eastman Tells Why He Chose Name of Kodak," *MPW,* 16 Aug 1919, 962. "The 'Mysterious Mr. Smith' Who Gave 'Tech' $4,000,000 May Be Eastman," *MPW,* 3 Jan 1920, 60. "George Eastman Is Disclosed as Mysterious Donor of $11,000,000," *MPW,* 24 Jan 1920, 591. Mr. Eastman's Birthday," *MPW,* 16 Jul 1927, 147. Re André Siscot: *né* Luigi Montefiore.

Eastman, George [cinematographer] (b. 1900–2 Jan 1930 [29?], Santa Monica CA). BHD, p. 75.

Eastman, Janet [actress]. No data found. *Fl.* 1917–19. (Universal.) BR, p. 20. George Katchmer, "Remembering the Great Silents," *CI,* 245 (Nov 1995), 42–43.

Easton, Henry Clement [director] (b. Summit NJ, 1879). AMD, p. 108. BHD2, p. 75. "Clement Easton and Edgar Jones Join Thanhouser," *MPW,* 17 Jul 1915, 489. "Clement Easton," *MPW,* 13 May 1916, 1141. Clement Easton, "What to Photograph—A Prophecy," *MPW,* 13 May 1916, 1144.

Easton, W. Richard [production assistant/assistant director] (b. 1900?–19 Dec 1928 [28], Los Angeles CA; pneumonia). m. Marcella C. Fay, 1927. (Inspiration Pictures.) "Richard Waston," *Variety,* 26 Dec 1928 ("...for seven years assistant to [producer] Edwin Carewe.") BHD2, p. 75. June Lee, "Dan Cupid's Bulletin Board," *Paris and Hollywood Screen Secrets Magazine,* May 1927, 53 (wed Fay).

Eaton, Charles (brother of **Mary**, Joseph, and **Doris Eaton**) [actor] (b. Washington DC, 22 Jun 1910).

Eaton, Doris (sister of **Charles**, **Mary**, and Joseph Eaton) [actress] (b. Norfolk VA, 4 May 1891). (RKO.) AS, p. 352. MH, p. 108.

Eaton, Elwyn [actor] (b. England, 16 Oct 1864–30 Apr 1937 [72], Los Angeles CA). AS, p. 352. BHD, p. 158. IFN, p. 92.

Eaton, Jay K. [actor] (b. NJ, 17 Mar 1899–5 Feb 1970 [70], Los Angeles CA; heart attack). "Jay Eaton," *Variety,* 25 Feb 1970 (began 1919). AS, p. 352. BHD1, p. 171. IFN, p. 92. Truitt, p. 97.

Eaton, Mabel [actress] (d. 10 Jan 1916, Chicago IL). m. William Farnum; Leo Kamerman. "Mabel Eaton," *Variety,* 21 Jan 1916. AS, p. 352. BHD, p. 158.

Eaton, Mary (sister of **Charles**, **Doris**, and Joseph Eaton) [actress] (b. Norfolk VA, 29 Jan 1901–10 Oct 1948 [47], Los Angeles CA; heart attack). m. (1) **Millard Webb** (d. 1935); (2) Charles Emery; Edward Laughton (d. 21 May 1952). "Mary Eaton," *Variety,* 20 Oct 1948 (age 46). AMD, p. 108. AS, p. 352. BHD1, p. 171. IFN, p. 92. SD. Truitt, p. 97. "Mary Eaton Makes Film Debut," *MPW,* 4 Aug 1923, 412. Nanette Kutner, "'The Natural Girl Is Worst Kind of Vamp!,' Says Mary Eaton," *MW,* 15 Mar 1924, 7.

Ebbesen, Jenny [actress] (b. 1854–1934 [80?]). BHD1, p. 607.

Ebele, Ed[ward] (actor] (b. Turkheim, France, 22 May 1861–19 Feb 1936 [74], Los Angeles CA). AS, p. 352.

Eberle, Eugene A. [actor] (b. Bangor ME, 7 Apr 1840–23 Oct 1917 [77], Chatham NY; pneumonia). m. Mrs. G.F. Tyrell (d. 1919). "Eugene A. Eberle," *Variety,* 9 Nov 1917. AS, p. 352 (d. NY NY). SD.

Eberle, Mrs. Eugene A. (*née* G.F. Tyrell, b. Glasgow, Scotland, 1841-Jul 1919 [78?], Chatham NY). BHD, p. 158.

Eberson, John [architect] (b. Austria, 1875–5 Mar 1954 [79], Stamford CT). "John Eberson, 79, Architect, Is Dead; Designed 500 Theatres in U.S. and Abroad, Including the Paradise [Bronx], Valencia [Jamaica, Queens] Here," *NYT,* 7 Mar 1954, 90:4. "John Eberson," *Variety,* 10 Mar 1954. "Eberson: A Valentino of Theater Architecture," *NYT,* 13 Dec 1990, C3.

Ebert, Carl [actor] (b. 20 Feb 1887–14 May 1980 [93], Los Angeles CA). BHD1, p. 607.

Ebert, Paula [actress] (b. Berlin, Germany, 8 Sep 1869–5 Feb 1929 [59]). BHD, p. 158. IFN, p. 92.

Eburne, Maude [stage/film actress] (b. Bronte-on-the-Lake, near Toronto, Canada, 10 Nov 1875–8 Oct 1960 [84], Los Angeles CA). m. actor/director Eugene Hall. (Began on the stage in 1904; Broadway debut: *A Pair of Sixes,* 1914; film debut: *A Pair of Sixes,* 1916; last film: *Arson, Inc.,* 1949.) "Maude Eburne," *Variety,* 26 Oct 1960 (age 85). AS, p. 353. BHD1, p. 172. IFN, p. 92. Charles Stumpf, "Queen of the Zanies: Maude Eburne," *CI,* 292 (Oct 1999), 6–8.

Eckerlein, John Elwood [actor] (b. New York NY, 1884?–9 Sep 1926 [42], New York NY). (FP-L.) "John E. Eckerlein," *Variety,* 15 Sep 1926. AS, p. 353. BHD, p. 158; BHD2, p. 76.. IFN, p. 92. Truitt, p. 98.

Eckersberg, Elsie [actress] (b. 1895-Nov 1989 [94?], Bavaria). BHD, p. 158.

Eckhardt, Oliver J. [actor] (b. MO, 14 Sep 1873–15 Sep 1952 [79], Los Angeles CA). "Oliver J. Eckhardt," *Variety,* 24 Sep 1952. AS, p. 353. BHD1, p. 172. IFN, p. 92. Truitt, p. 98.

Eckles, Lew [actor] (*né* Lewis C. Eckles, b. 1888–26 Mar 1950 [62?], Kansas City KS). AS, p. 353.

Eckstein, William, "Mr. Fingers" [actor] (b. 1890–15 Sep 1963 [73?], Montreal, Canada). "Billy Eckstein," *Variety,* 2 Oct 1963 ("gained particular fame during the silent screen days..."). AS, p. 353.

Eddinger, Wallace [actor] (b. Albany NY, 14 Jul 1881–8 Jan 1929 [47], Pittsburgh PA; pneumonia). m. (1) Mrs. Ivy Lee Moore-La Grove; (2) Margaret Lawrence. (Film debut: *A Gentleman of Leisure,* Paramount, 1915.) "Wallace Eddinger," *Variety,* 16 Jan 1929. AS, p. 353. BHD, p. 158. IFN, p. 92. "Wallace Eddinger Signed," *NYDM,* 30 Dec 1914, 24:1 (to replace an ailing Harry Woodruff in *A Gentleman of Leisure*). "Wallace Eddinger," *NYDM,* 6 Jan 1915, 24:4 (photo).

Eddy, Mrs. Augusta F. [actress] (*née?*, b. 1860–21 Sep 1925 [65?], Staten Island NY). BHD, p. 158.

Eddy, Don [publicist] (b. Hannibal MO, 1 Jul 1896–1 Jan 1956 [59], Los Gatos CA; heart attack). m. Doris Denbo. (FP-L; FBO; RKO.) "Don Eddy," *Variety*, 201, 11 Jan 1956, 70:2. AMD, p. 108. BHD2, p. 76. "Eddy with Langdon," *MPW*, 9 Oct 1926, 343. "Audiences Expect More Than Comedy from Langdon—Eddy," *MPW*, 8 Oct 1927, 356.

Eddy, Helen Jerome [film/stage actress/real estate agent] (b. New York NY, 25 Feb 1897–27 Jan 1990 [92], Alhambra CA; heart attack). Unmarried. (Film debut: *Jealousy*, Lubin, 1 reel, 1915; Pallas; Paramount.) "Helen Jerome Eddy," *NYT*, 2 Feb 1990, D18:3. "Helen Jerome Eddy," *Variety*, 7 Feb 1990, p. 183. "Helen Jerome Eddy; Silent Screen Actress Played High-Class Heroines," *LA Times*, 31 Jan 1990, p. A16:1. "Helen Jerome Eddy; Played Heroines in Silent Movie Era," *Chicago Tribune*, 2 Feb 1990. AS, p. 353. BHD1, p. 172. FFF, p. 205. FSS, p. 98. MH, p. 108. WWS, p. 71. "In the Picture Studios," *NYDM*, 4 Aug 1915, 27:1 (debuted in *Jealousy*, Lubin, 1 reel, with L.C. Shumway). "Studio Gossip," *NYDM*, 16 Oct 1915, 32:3 ("Pallas Picture directors believe they have a 'find' in Helen Eddy, who plays a small role as a slavey in 'The Gentleman from Indiana.'"). "Helen Eddy Engaged by Universal," *MPW*, 15 Jun 1918, 1570. "Sidelights and Reflections," *MPW*, 5 Apr 1919, 121.Elizabeth Peltret, "An Untroubled Eddy in the Silverscreen Stream; Helen—Original Philosophess," *Motion Picture Magazine*, Sep 1919, 58–59–111. "In the Plays," *LA Times*, 8 Feb 1920, III, p. 1 (photo). "She Covets a Director's Job," *MPS*, 28 May 1920, 24–25 ("She is so genuine and unaffected, that a moment after meeting the feeling comes that you've known her a lifetime."; during WWI, Eddy entertained soldiers at Camp Fremont, near San Francisco; "My ambition is to become a director. I have had six years of valuable experience with the leading companies of the film world and some day I am going to burst forth as a director with an invaluable combination of ideas I have gathered from many angles and sources."). "Helen Jerome Eddy with the 'Flying A,'" *MPW*, 5 Jun 1920, 1358. "Will Star Helen Jerome Eddy," *MPW*, 26 Jun 1920, 1727. "Helen Eddy to Star," *MPW*, 24 Jul 1920, 447. Cal York, "Plays and Players," *Photoplay*, Mar 1921, 80 (apppered with Conrad Nagel in *Paolo and Francesca* at the Hollywood Community Theater). Barbara Beach, "The Saintly Eddy," *Motion Picture Magazine*, May 1921, 28–29. "Helen Jerome Eddy to Star for F.B.O.," *MPW*, 9 Dec 1922, 547. "Helen Eddy in 'Padlocked,'" *MPW*, 20 Mar 1926, 166. Merton, "He'll Help You Get in the Movies!," *Paris and Hollywood Screen Secrets Magazine*, May 1927, 22–25 (states that Beban discovered Eddy and put her in his play, *The Sign of the Rose*, at $35 per week, soon raised to $750 per week. "Sometime during her earlier association with Beban, she became the actor's wife." Eddy never married.).

Eddy, Robert [director/scenarist]. No data found. FDY, p. 423.

Edelman, Joseph S. [publicist]. No data found. AMD, p. 108. "Joseph S. Edelman," *MPW*, XXII, 17 Oct 1914, 358.

Edelstein, "Dad" [actor] (b. 1845-Jun 1927 [82], Sydney, Australia). BHD, p. 158. IFN, p. 92.

Ederle, Gertrude [champion swimmer/actress]. No data found. (Paramount.) Don Juan, "So This Is Hollywood; Graduated from Newsreel," *Paris and Hollywood Screen Secrets*, Oct 1927, 62 (filming *Swim, Girl, Swim* at Paramount).

Edeson, Arthur [cinematographer] (b. New York NY, 24 Oct 1891–14 Feb 1970 [78], Los Angeles CA). (Eclair, 1911.) "Arthur Edeson," *Variety*, 18 Feb 1970. AS, p. 354. BHD2, p. 76. FDY, p. 457. IFN, p. 92. Katz, p. 373.

Edeson, Robert [stage/film actor] (b. New Orleans LA, 3 Jun 1868–24 Mar 1931 [62], Los Angeles CA). m. (1) Ellen Berg (d. 1906); (2) Georgia E. Porter; **Mary Newcomb** (d. 1966); (4) Aida de Martinez (Banker?). "Robert Edeson Dies in Hollywood Home; Actor, Long Famous on Stage and in Films, Succumbs to Heart Disease; Was Star in 'Strongheart'; Last of Quartet of Theatre Favorites Who Pioneered in Movies—Before Public 45 Years," *NYT*, 25 Mar 1931, 25:1. "Robert Edeson," *Variety*, 1 Apr 1931 (age 63). "Robert Edeson, Last of Famed Pioneers of Movies, Is Dead; Follows Roberts, Farnum and Neill, Who Heard Call of Filmland 17 Years Ago and Helped Establish Hollywood; Best Known for 'Strongheart,'" *The Arizona Daily Star*, 24 Mar 1931. AMD, p. 108. BHD1, p. 172. FSS, p. 99. IFN, p. 92. Katz, pp. 373–74. SD. Spehr, p. 128. Truitt, p. 98. "Edeson wi Lasky," *MPW*, 4 Apr 1914, 78. "Edeson Signs a Contract," *MPW*, 23 May 1914, 1102. "Robert Edeson, Lasky Star," *MPW*, 8 Aug 1914, 839. "Edeson—Mitchell—Hart," *MPW*, 19 Dec 1914, 1682. "'Bob' Edeson's Home Troubles," *MPW*, 18 Dec 1915, 2158. "Robert Edeson Will Direct for Metro After Playing Lead with May Allison," *MPW*, 30 Oct 1920, 1274. "Robert Edeson Will Play in the Metro Production of 'Are Wives to Blame?,'" *MPW*, 6 Nov 1920, 75. "Robert Edeson Will direct Metro Films When 'Are Wives to Blame?' Is Finished," *MPW*, 4 Dec 1920, 637. "Rober Edeson in Metro Production," *MPW*, 12 Nov 1921, 209. "Edeson Is Engaged for Metro Picture," *MPW*, 17 Nov 1923, 322. George A. Katchmer, "Famous Cowboys & Cowgirls—2," *CI*, 173 (Nov 1989), C14.

Edgar, Marriott [actor/scenarist] (b. Colvend, England, 8 Oct 1880–4 May 1951 [70], London, England). AS, p. 354.

Edgar-Bruce, Tonie [actress] (*née* Sybil Etonia Bruce, b. London, England, 4 Jun 1892–29 Mar 1966 [73], Chertsey, England). AS, p. 354.

Edgard, Lewis [actor] (b. 1878–8 Dec 1917 [39?], New York NY). BHD, p. 158.

Edginton, May [scenarist]. No data found. FDY, p. 423.

Edgren, Gustaf [director/scenarist] (*né* Erik Gustaf Edgren, b. Ostra Fagelvik, Sweden, 1 Apr 1895–10 Jun 1954 [59], Stockholm, Sweden). AS, p. 354. BHD2, p. 76.

Edgren, Robert W. [actor] (b. 1874–9 Sep 1939 [65?], Del Monte CA). BHD, p. 158.

Edhofer, Anton [actor] (b. Vienna, Austria, 18 Sep 1883). AS, p. 354.

Edington, Harry E. [producer] (b. 1890?–10 Mar 1949 [59], Beverly Hills CA). (Goldwyn; Metro; Universal; RKO.) "Harry E. Edington," *NYT*, 12 Mar 1949, 17:5. "Harry Eddington," *Variety*, 16 Mar 1949 (age 62). AS, p. 354.

Edington, May [writer]. No data found. AMD, p. 108. "Write for Fox," *MPW*, 21 May 1921, 199.

Edison, Thomas Alva [inventor] (b. Milan OH, 11 Feb 1847–18 Oct 1931 [84], West Orange NJ). Wyn Wachhorst, *Thomas Alva Edison; An American Myth* (Cambridge MA: MIT Press, 1981). "Thomas Edison Dies in Coma at 84; Family with Him as the End Comes; Inventor Succumbs at 3:24 A.M. After Fight for Life Since He Was Stricken on Aug. 1—World-Wide Tribute Is Paid to Him as a Benefactor of Mankind," *NYT*, 18 Oct 1931, 1:4. AMD, p. 108. AS, p. 354. BHD2, p. 76. IFN, p. 93. Katz, p. 374. Spehr, p. 128. WWVC, pp. 47–49. "Dangerous Operation on Thomas A. Edison; Surgeons Remove Mastoid Abscess Near the Inventor's [left] Ear; Successful, Doctors Say; Action Hurried to Prevent Blood Poisoning—Patient Has Long Suffered from Trouble," *NYT*, 24 Jan 1905, 1:3 (at his home at Glenmont NJ; "very close to the brain"; 57 years old). "Thomas Edison Improving; Inventor Quickly Rallies After Delicate Surgical Operation," *NYT*, 25 Jan 1905, 2:5 ("He is cheerful, and his greatest worry seems to be that he is not permitted to read the newspapers about the situation in Russia."). "Edison vs. Biograph," *MPW*, 16 Mar 1907, 21–23. "Trade Notes," *MPW*, 24 Aug 1907, 390–91. Frank L. Dyer, "Edison's Place in the Moving Picture Art," *MPW*, 21 Dec 1907, 679–80. "Biograpih vs. Editon," *MPW*, 29 Feb 1908, 155–56. "Edison Compoany Brings Suits," *MPW*, 28 Mar 1908, 259–60. "Edison Manufacturing Company vs. Kleine Optical Company and George Kleine," *MPW*, 11 Apr 1908, 314–16. "A Word from Mr. Edison," *MPW*, 28 Aug 1909, 283. "Mr. Edison and the Color Problem," *MPW*, 12 Nov 1910, 1098. Thomas Bedding, "Edison: His Life and Inventions," *MPW*, 3 Dec 1910, 1280–81. "Edison Celebrates Silver Wedding," *MPW*, 4 Mar 1911, 487. Frank Parker Hulette, "An Interview with Thomas Alva Edison," *MPW*, 22 Jul 1911, 104–05. "Thomas Alva Edison, Inc., vs. Swanson," *MPW*, 14 Oct 1911, 117–18. "Edison Camera Patent Re-Issued," *MPW*, 16 Dec 1911, 876. "Monopoly in Moving Pictures," *The Literary Digest*, 45, 31 Aug 1912, 322:2 (a suit by the Federal government against the General Film Co. and the Motion Picture Patents Co. alleged "that an exhibitor must pay $2 a week to the Patents company on every exhibiting machine he owns.... It is alleged that the defendants overstept [sic] the bounds of lawful monopoly by interlocking their various patents and then refusing to grant a license to any exhibitor except a license obligating him to use exclusively the films of the 'combination.'" The defendants included Thomas A. Edison [Inc.], and other companies and individuals.). "Fire Sweeps Edison Studio [Bronx NY]; Loss Heavy, But Films, Scenarios, Etc., Are Saved. No Interruption in Release Schedule," *NYDM*, 1 Apr 1914, 32:1. "Sued for Filming Cat," *NYDM*, 8 Jul 1914, 32:2 (a woman sued the Edison Co. for $5,000 for filming her cat at a Madison Square Garden exhibition. "Her chief complaint is that the pictures hold her up to ridicule, since she was not 'dressed to pose.'"). "Edison Celebrates Birthday," *MPW*, 27 Feb 1915, 1266. James S. McQuade, "Kleine-Edison Merger Formed," *MPW*, 24 Jul 1915, 626–27. "Testimonial to Edison," *MPW*, 16 Feb 1924, 562 (on 15 Feb 1924, for 77th birthday). "Industry Pays Tribute to Edison; Always Serve the Public, He Urges," *MPW*, 1 Mar 1924, 27. "Thos. Edison Lauds Movietone Pictures," *MPW*, 24 Dec 1927, 12. Joseph C. Szymanski, "Thomas Edison on Long Island," *CI*, 150 (Dec 1987), C7. Gloria Hayes Kremer, "Discovering Edison's Winter Home," *New York Post*, 3 Nov

1992, 45:1. Scott Johnson, "The Sensation That Failed: The Story of Edison's Kinetophone," *CI,* 214 (Apr 1993), C22–C24, 33–34. Niel Baldwin, "The Lesser Known Edison; In addition to his famous inventions, Thomas Edison's fertile imagination gave the world a host of little known technologies, from talking dolls to poured-concrete houses," *Scientific American,* 276, Feb 1997, 62–67 (copiously illustrated with rare prints).

Edler, Charles [actor] (b. NJ, 13 Aug 1864–29 Mar 1942 [77], Santa Monica CA). (Sennett; Falcon Features.) "Charles Edler," *Variety,* 1 Apr 1942 (age 65). AS, p. 354. BHD1, p. 173. IFN, p. 93. Truitt, p. 98 (b. 1877).

Edlin, Theodore M. [actor] (b. CA, 3 Oct 1894–7 Jul 1974 [79], Woodland Hills CA 91311). BHD, p. 158. IFN, p. 93.

Edmonde, Frances [producer]. No data found. AMD, p. 109. "Frances Edmonde Now Heads Her Own Producing Company," *MPW,* 19 Jun 1920, 1582.

Edmondson, Albert [actor] (b. Pueblo CO, 1896–11 May 1954 [58?], Hollywood CA). (World; Universal; Kalem.) "Kalem Ham Comedy Company," *MPN,* 21 Oct 1916, 197. AS, p. 354 (Al Edmundsen). BHD, p. 158. Truitt 1983, p. 214.

Edmonson, Frank [cameraman]. No data found. No data found. "Frank Edmonson to Fly with Camera," *MPW,* 6 May 1916, 956.

Edmondson, Harry B. [actor] (b. Baltimore MD, 1873). BHD, p. 158.

Edmondson, William [stage/film/TV actor] (b. Spokane WA, 15 Oct 1902–28 May 1979 [76], Los Angeles CA; heart attack). "William Edmonson," *Variety,* 6 Jun 1979. BHD1, p. 173. IFN, p. 93. Truitt 1983, p. 214.

Edmunds, Charles [actor] (b. NY, 1877). BHD, p. 158.

Edney, Florence [actress] (b. London, England, 2 Jun 1879–24 Nov 1950 [71], New York NY). m. John H. Brewer. "Florence Edney," *Variety,* 29 Nov 1950. AS, p. 354. BHD, p. 158. IFN, p. 93. SD. Truitt 1983, p. 214.

Edouard, Farcilt [cinematographer] (b. CA, 1894–17 Mar 1980 [86?], Kenwood CA). BHD2, p. 76 (Fargiot Edouart). FDY, p. 457.

Edstrom, Katherine [actress] (b. 28 Jul 1901–2 Jun 1973 [72], Los Angeles CA; cancer). AS, p. 354. BHD1, p. 607. IFN, p. 93.

Edthofer, Anton [actor] (b. Vienna, Austria, 18 Sep 1883–21 Feb 1971 [77], Vienna, Austria). AS, p. 354. BHD1, p. 173.

Edwardes-Hall, George [actor] (b. Dublin, Ireland, 8 Oct 1852–10 Jul 1934 [81], London, England). m. Julia Gwynne. "Julia Gwynne," *Variety,* 17 Jul 1934. SD, p. 401.

Edwards, Aaron [actor]. No data found. *Fl.* 1917–20. George Katchmer, "Remembering the Great Silents," *CI,* 245 (Nov 1995), 43.

Edwards, Alan [actor] (b. New York NY, 3 Jun 1892–8 May 1954 [61], Los Angeles CA). (Edison, 1912; Vitagraph; Paramount; Metro; Fox; Republic; Universal.) "Alan Edwards," *Variety,* 12 May 1954. AMD, p. 109. AS, p. 354 (b. Chatham, England). BHD1, p. 173. IFN, p. 93. Truitt, p. 98 (b. 1900). "Alan Edwards, World Star, Has Had an Inusual Career," *MPW,* 0 May 1919, 835.

Edwards, Charles [actor] (b. 1869?–17 Mar 1922 [53], New York NY). "Charles Edwards," *Variety,* 24 Mar 1922. AS, p. 354.

Edwards, Charles E. [actor] (*né* Charles Edwards Virian, b. 1898–18 Aug 1978 [80?], Los Angeles CA). AS, p. 354. BHD, p. 159.

Edwards, Cliff (Ukelele Ike) [singer/stage/film/radio/TV actor/voice of Jiminy Cricket in *Pinocchio,* 1940] (b. Hannibal MO, 14 Jun 1895–17 Jul 1971 [76], Los Angeles CA). m. (1) Gertrude Benson, 1919–21 (son, Cliff, Jr.); (2) Irene Wiley; (3) actress Nancy Dover, 1932—div. 1936. (MGM.) "Cliff Edwards, 76, 'Ukelele Ike' of Stage and Film, Dies on Coast," *NYT,* 22 Jul 1971, 36:2. "Cliff Edwards," *Variety,* 28 Jul 1971. AS, p. 355. BHD1, p. 173. IFN, p. 93. Eve Golden, "The Ballad of Ukulele Ike," *CI,* 304 (Oct 2000), 74–75 (d. 21 Jul).

Edwards, David [executive] (d. 13 May 1923). BHD2, p. 76.

Edwards, Edna Park [actress] (b. Pittsburgh PA, 17 Feb 1895–5 Jun 1967 [72], Los Angeles CA). AS, p. 355. BHD, p. 159. IFN, p. 93.

Edwards, Edyth Paula [actress] (b. Breslau, Germany, 14 May 1899–6 Mar 1956 [56], Berlin, Germany). BHD1, p. 172 (b. Wroklaw, Poland).

Edwards, Eleanor [actress] (*née?,* b. New York NY, 13 Jan 1884–22 Oct 1968 [84], Los Angeles CA). m. **Snitz Edwards** (d. 1937). "Eleanor Edwards," *Variety,* 30 Oct 1968 (began 1922). AS, p. 355 (d. Burbank CA). BHD, p. 159 (b. 1882). IFN, p. 93. Truitt, p. 98.

Edwards, Gus (brother of **Leo Edwards**) [stage/film actor/lyricist/director/producer] (*né* Gus Simon, b. Hohensalza, Germany, 18 Aug 1878–7 Nov 1945 [67], Los Angeles CA; cancer). m. Lillian Boulanger, 1 Dec 1905. Film biography: *The Star Maker,* 1940. (Began 1928; MGM.) "Gus Edwards Dies; Song Writer 66; Actor, Director, Talent Scout 'Discovered' Cantor, Jessel, Groucho Marx, Winchell," *NYT,* 8 Nov 1945, 19:1 (wrote *By the Light of the Silvery Moon; Good-bye, Little Girl, Good-bye; Tammany; Schooldays; Wonderful; Every Day Is Mother's Day for Me; Orange Blossom Time; When the Roses Bloom Again; I'm Gonna Meet Minnie Tonight; I Just Can't Make My Eyes Behave*). "Gus Edwards," and "Star-Maker Gus Edwards Dies Broke; Kern was 'Songwriter's Songwriter,'" *Variety,* 14 Nov 1945 (interred at Woodlawn). AS, p. 355 (*né* Simon Edwards, b. 1879). BHD1, p. 173 (b. Inowroclaw, Poland, 1879); BHD2, p. 76 (b. 1879). SD, p. 401. Maurice Rapf, *Back Lot; Growing Up with the Movies* (Lanham MD: Scarecrow Press, 1999), pp. 5–6 (gave Harry Rapf a job as road manager of *Gus Edwards' School Boys and Girls*).

Edwards, Harry [actor] (b. New York NY, 1859?–27 Nov 1924 [65], New York NY). "Harry Edwards," *Variety,* 3 Dec 1924. AS, p. 355.

Edwards, Harry J. [actor/director] (b. London, Ontario, Canada, 11 Oct 1888–26 May 1952 [63], Los Angeles CA; carbon tetrachloride poisoning). m. **Louise Glaum,** 1915—div. 1919 (d. 1970); **Evelyn Brent** (d. 1975). (LK-O, Sennett.) "Harry J. Edwards," *Variety,* 4 Jun 1952. AMD, p. 109. AS, p. 355. BHD, p. 159; BHD2, p. 76. IFN, p. 93. Katz, p. 377. Lynde Denig, "Larry Trimble Brings Turner Films," *MPW,* 19 Aug 1916, 1223. "National Director Has New Method of Filming Scenes," *MPW,* 20 Mar 1920, 1951. "Edwards with Camero," *MPW,* 26 Jan 1924, 279. "Edwards Joins Warner Staff," *MPW,* 24 Jan 1925, 383. "Edwards to Direct," *MPW,* 21 May 1927, 195.

Edwards, Henry [actor/director] (*né* Arthur Harold Ethelbert Edwards, b. Weston-super-Mare, England, 18 Sep 1882–2 Nov 1952 [70], Chobham, England). m. **Chrissie White** (d. 1989). "British Actor Is Dead; Henry Edwards, 69, Remembered Here for His Stage Roles," *NYT,* 4 Nov 1952, 29:4. "Henry Edwards," *Variety,* 5 Nov 1952. AS, p. 355. BHD1, p. 173 (b. 1883); BHD, p. 76. IFN, p. 93 (b. 1883). Truitt, p. 99.

Edwards, J. Gordon [stage/film director] (b. Montreal, Quebec, Canada, 24 Jun 1867–31 Dec 1925 [58], Plaza Hotel, New York NY [Death Certificate No. 131]; pneumonia). (Fox.) "J. Gordon Edwards," *Variety,* 6 Jan 1926. AMD, p. 109. AS, p. 355. BHD2, p. 76. IFN, p. 93. Katz, p. 377. MSBB, p. 1046. Spehr, p. 128. "Box Office Producers," *MPW,* 7 Nov 1914, 791. "Too Much directing Will Spoil Stories, Says Edwards," *MPW,* 16 Aug 1919, 950. Grace Lamb, "A Cinema Crusade," *Classic,* XI, Mar 1923, 38–39, 75 (making *The Shepherd King* for Fox). "J. Gordon Edwards Tells of Picture Activities Abroad," *MPW,* 3 Nov 1923, 43. "Obituary," *MPW,* 16 Jan 1926, 217 (age 58; buried in Montreal, Canada). Ruth Waterbury, "The Final Fade-Outs; Even Death Is Not Simple in the Movie Colonies," *Photoplay,* Mar 1926, 34.

Edwards, John [actor] (*né* John Marnill, b. Natick [Boston] MA, 22 May 1868–16 Oct 1929 [60], New York NY [Massachusetts Vital Statistics, Births, Vol. 206, p. 209]). m. Daisy Sinclair. "John Edwards," *Variety,* 23 Oct 1929. AS, p. 355. BHD, p. 159 (b. 1869). IFN, p. 93.

Edwards, John [director] (b. 1889?–25 Aug 1934 [45], Yonkers NY; in a brawl). "John Edwards," *Variety,* 28 Aug 1934 ("said to have been a former director"; a vagrant for 4 years). AS, p. 355. BHD2, p. 76.

Edwards, Julia [actress] (b. 1883–16 Apr 1976 [92?], Stockton CA). BHD, p. 159. IFN, p. 93.

Edwards, Leo (brother of **Gus Edwards**) [actor/songwriter] (*né* Leo Simon, b. Germany, 21 Feb 1886–12 Jul 1978 [92], New York NY). "Leo Edwards," *Variety,* 18 Jul 1978 (first score: *The Merry Whirl,* 1911; wrote Fanny Brice's *I'm an Indian; Sweetheart, Let's Grow Old Together; My Fantasy; That's What the Rose Said to Me*). AS, p. 355. BHD1, p. 607.

Edwards, Mrs. Margaret *see* **Sinclair, Daisy**

Edwards, Mattie [actress] (*née* Martha Mattie Edwards, b. 1866?–26 Jun 1944 [78], Los Angeles CA). m. Edward Settle. (DeMille.) "Mattie Edwards," *Variety,* 28 Jun 1944. AS, p. 355. BHD1, p. 173. IFN, p. 93.

Edwards, Nate [extra/stuntman/actor/casting director/producer] (b. 18 Mar 1902–12 Sep 1972 [70], Van Nuys CA). (Republic.) "Nate Edwards," *Variety,* 20 Sep 1972, p. 63 (helped to organize SAG). AS, p. 355. BHD, p. 159; BHD2, p. 76.

Edwards, Neely [actor] (*né* Cornelius Limbach, b. Delphos OH, 16 Sep 1883–10 Jul 1965 [81], Woodland Hills CA). m. **Marguerite Snow** (d. 1958). ("The Hallroom Boys" series.) "Neely Edwards," *Variety,* 14 Jul 1965 (age 82). AMD, p. 109. AS, p. 355. BHD1, p. 173. FSS, p. 99 (d. 1957). IFN, p. 93. SD. Truitt, p. 99 (b. 1889). "Cohns to Feature Neely Edwards in Future Hall Room Boys Comedies," *MPW,* 28 Feb 1920, 1470. "Neely Edwards Signs Three-Year Contract rto Appear Under Management of the Cohns," *MPW,* 27 Mar 1920, 2141.

Edwards, Nelson E. [cameraman]. No data found. AMD, p. 109. "Nelson E. Edwards, War Photographer," *MPW*, 21 Oct 1916, 409.

Edwards, Rowland G. [actor/director/producer] (b. New York NY-10 Aug 1953, Glendale CA). m. Doris Paxgter (widow). "Rowland G. Edwards," *Variety*, 19 Aug 1953. BHD2, p. 76.

Edwards, Sam [actor] (b. San Francisco CA, 1851–2 May 1921 [69?], Chicago IL). BHD, p. 159.

Edwards, Snitz [stage/film actor] (b. Budapest, Hungary, 1 Jan 1862–1 May 1937 [75], Los Angeles CA; arthritis). m. **Eleanor** (d. 1968). "Snitz Edwards," *Variety*, 5 May 1937. AMD, p. 109. AS, p. 355. BHD1, p. 173. IFN, p. 93. Truitt, p. 99. "'Snitz' Edwards with Kleine," *NYDM*, 29 Sep 1915, 24:4 (on stage for 30 years; to debut for George Kleine.). "Snitz Edwards with Kleine," *MPW*, 9 Oct 1915, 259. "Cissie Fitzgerald with Kleine," *NYDM*, 30 Oct 1915, 25:4 (along with Edwards, the "one hundred-poound star of *The Queen of the Moulin Rouge* and *The Silver Slipper*, and others).

Edwards, Ted [Keystone Cop/actor] (*né* M.E. Burrell, b. Sheffield, England, 1883?–29 Sep 1945 [62], Los Angeles CA). (Sennett.) "Ted Edwards," *Variety*, 3 Oct 1945. AS, p. 355. BHD, p. 159. Truitt, p. 99.

Edwards, Walter [actor/director] (b. MI, 8 Jan 1870–12 Apr 1920 [50], Honolulu HI). "Obituary," *MPW*, 24 Apr 1920, 544. (Ince; Select). AMD, p. 109. AS, p. 356 (d. 15 Apr). BHD, p. 159; BHD2, p. 76. "Edwards Wouldn't Stay Dead," *MPW*, 23 Jan 1915, 518.

Edwin, Walter [actor/director/producer]. No data found. AMD, p. 109. "Edison Touches Popular Chrod," *MPW*, 3 Jan 1914, 28–29. "Walter Edwin," *MPW*, 26 Jun 1915, 2101. "Walter Edwin Signed by Van D[y]ke," *MPW*, 19 May 1917, 1108.

Egan, Betty [actress] (b. 5 Aug 1909). m. **John Harron** (d. 1939).

Egan, George [actor] (b. 1883–26 Sep 1943 [60], Cincinnati, OH). (Lubin.) BHD, p. 159. IFN, p. 93.

Egan, Gladys [actress]. (Biograph, 1908). No data found.

Egan, Jack [press agent for big bands] (*né* John Egan, b. 14 Oct 1911–21 May 1986 [74], Yonkers NY; cancer). "Jack Egan," *Variety*, 28 May 1986.

Egan, Mischa [actor] (b. Russia, 28 Nov 1888–15 Feb 1964 [75], Los Angeles CA). AS, p. 356.

Egbert, Albert [actor] (d. 18 Mar 1942). BHD, p. 159.

Egede-Nissen, Aud [actress] (b. Bergen, Norway, 30 May 1893–15 Nov 1974 [81], Oslo, Norway). m. **Paul Richter** (d. 1961). AS, p. 356. Vittorio Martinelli, "Kino-Lieblinge," *Griffithiana*, 38/39 (Oct 1990), 12.

Eggeling, Viktor [director] (b. Lund, Sweden, 21 Oct 1880–1925 [45?], Berlin, Germany). AS, p. 356 (Viking Eggeling). BHD2, p. 77.

Eggenton, Joseph [actor] (b. Ponfert CT, 29 Feb 1871–3 Jul 1946 [75], Los Angeles CA). AS, p. 356.

Egger, Josef [actor] (b. Waasen, Austria, 22 Feb 1899–29 Aug 1966 [67], Gablitz, Austria). AS, p. 356.

Eggert, Constantin Vladimirovich [actor/director] (b. Russia, 9 Oct 1883–24 Dec 1955 [72], Russia). AS, p. 356.

Eggleston, Mrs. Ann [actress] (*née?*, b. 1866?–19 May 1934 [68], New York NY). "Ann Eggleston," *Variety*, 22 May 1934. AS, p. 356. BHD, p. 159.

Eggleston, Katherine [writer/editor]. No data found. AMD, p. 109. "Katherine Eggleston," *MPW*, XVIII, 20 Dec 1913, 1415. "Katherine Eggleston," *MPW*, 11 Jul 1914, 259.

Ehfe, William C[arl] [actor] (b. Payette ID, 19 Jun 1887–1 Aug 1940 [53], Los Angeles CA; heart attack). AS, p. 356. BHD, p. 159. IFN, p. 93. Billy H. Doyle, "Lost Players," *CI*, 156 (Jun 1988), C13.

Ehmann, Karl [actor] (b. Vienna, Austria, 13 Aug 1882–1 Nov 1967 [85], Vienna, Austria). AS, p. 356.

Ehrenburg, Arthur Ilva [scenarist]. No data found. FDY, p. 423.

Ehrle, Curt [actor/director] (b. Reichenhofen, Germany, 26 May 1884–17 Apr 1967 [82], Saarbrucken, Germany). AS, p. 357.

Ehrlich, Max [actor] (b. Dresden, Germany, 25 Nov 1892–30 Oct 1944 [51], Auschwitz (Oswiecim), Germany, 1943). BHD1, p. 174.

Eibenschutz, Lia [actress] (b. 19 Mar 1899–Mar 1985 [86?]). AS, p. 357. BHD, p. 159.

Eichberg, Richard Albert [actor/scenarist/producer/director] (b. Berlin, Germany, 27 Oct 1888–8 May 1952 [63], Munich, Germany). AS, p. 357. BHD2, p. 77.

Eide, Egil Naess [actor/director] (b. Sweden, 1868–1946 [78?], Sweden). AS, p. 357.

Eiler, Ray [title writer]. No data found. FDY, p. 443.

Eilers, Sally [actress] (*née* Dorothea Eilers, b. New York NY, 11 Dec 1908 [Birth Certificate Index No. 64634]–5 Jan 1978 [69], Woodland Hills CA). m. 4 times: (1) **Hoot Gibson**, 1930–33 (d. 1962); (2) **Harry Joe Brown**, 1933–43 (d. 1972); (3) Howard Barney; (4) John H. Morse. (Fox; WB; Sennett; MGM.) "Sally Eilers, Actress, Is Dead; Appeared in More Than 40 Films," *NYT*, 7 Jan 1978, 42:4. "Sally Eilers," *Variety*, 11 Jan 1978. AMD, p. 109. AS, p. 357. BHD1, p. 174. BR, pp. 296–300. FSS, p. 100. IFN, p. 93. Katz, p. 379. SD. "Miss Eilers Ill," *MPW*, 22 Oct 1927, 498. Dorothy Manners, "Hotta Dogga!; Honest, It Sounds Funny When Sally Eilers Says It," *MPC*, Jul 1929, 58, 91. James M. Fidler, "Her Trial Career; Said Sally Eilers: 'If I don't make good in the movies within six months, I'll quit.' Read her story," *Screenland*, Aug 1929, 41, 109. "Classic Images Salutes...Sally Eilers," *CI*, 169 (Jul 1989), 7.

Einfeld, Charles [producer] (*né* Sigmund Charles Einfeld, b. New York NY, 25 Oct 1901–27 Dec 1971 [70], Ascona, Switzerland). AS, p. 357. BHD2, p. 77 (d. 1974).

Einhorn, Herman [executive] (b. 1870–23 Apr 1934 [64?], New York NY). AS, p. 77.

Einhorn, Lizzie [stage/film actress/singer] (aka Liza Einhorn, b. Rumania, 1856?–14 Jan 1945 [88], New York NY). m. (1) Mr. Gould; (2) **Ivan Abramson** (d. 1934). "Mrs. Ivan Abramson; Retired Actress and Singer, 88, Appeared with Jacob Adler," *NYT*, 16 Jan 1945, 19:5 (retired from films in 1924). AS, p. 357. BHD, p. 88. IFN, p. 1 (Mrs. Ivan Abramson; age 87).

Eis, Alice [stage dancer/film actress]. No data found. In *The Vampire* (Kalem, 15 Oct 1913); *MPW*, 4 Oct 1913, 51 (review). "Miss Alice Els; Dancing with Bert French at the Victoria in 'The Temptress,'" *NYDM*, 1 Jul 1914, 16 (photo).

Eis, Maria Theresia [actress] (b. Prague, Czechoslovakia, 22 Feb 1896–18 Dec 1954 [58], Vienna, Austria). AS, p. 357.

Eischbrich, Julius [assistant director] (d. 29 Mar 1921). BHD2, p. 77.

Eisenstein, Sergei Mikhailovich [director/producer/scenarist] (b. Riga, Russia [Latvia], 23 Jan 1898–10 Feb 1948 [50], Moscow, Russia; massive heart attack). m. **Pera Atasheva**, 1929 (d. 1965). (Paramount.) "Sergei Eisenstein," *Variety*, 18 Feb 1948 (wrote *Film Sense*, published in U.S. in 1942). AS, p. 357. BHD2, p. 77. FDY, p. 423. Waldman, p. 94.

Ekert, Alexander [actor] (b. 1875-Nov 1920 [45?]). BHD, p. 159.

Eklund, Alice [actress/director] (b. Stockholm, Sweden, 21 Jul 1896–6 Oct 1983 [87], Sweden). AS, p. 358.

Eklund, Ernst Olof [actor/director] (b. Ostervala, Sweden, 6 Aug 1882–3 Aug 1971 [88], Sweden). AS, p. 358.

Ekman, Gôsta (father of Hasse Ekman) [stage/film actor] (b. Stockholm, Sweden, 28 Dec 1887–12 Jan 1938 [50], Stockholm, Sweden). m. Pauline Brunius (d. 1954; son, Hasse, b. 10 Sep 1915). (UFA.) "Goesta Ekman, 48, Swedish Film Star; Actor Who Had Appeared with Greta Garbo Before She Came Here Is Dead; Was Also Stage Favorite; Noted for Work in Classics—Producer and Manager and Created Popular Roles," *NYT*, 13 Jan 1938, 21:5. "Goesta Ekman," *Variety*, 19 Jan 1938 (age 48). AS, p. 358 (b. 1888). BHD1, p. 174 (b. 1890). IFN, p. 94. Katz, p. 385 (began in Germany, 1912). SD. Truitt, p. 98 (Edman).

Ekman, John [actor] (b. Stockholm, Sweden, 15 Nov 1880–22 Nov 1949 [69], Karlstad, Sweden). AS, p. 358. BHD1, p. 174.

Ekstrom, Marta [actress] (b. Varmdo, Sweden, 28 Jan 1899–23 Jan 1952 [52], Stockholm, Sweden). AS, p. 358.

Elder, Ethel [actress]. No data found. AMD, p. 109. "Ethel Elder with Powers," *MPW*, 3 Feb 1912, 380.

Elder, Ruth [aviatrix/actress] (b. Anniston AL, 8 Sep 1905–9 Oct 1977 [73], San Francisco CA). (Thanhouser; Paramount.) "Ruth Elder," *Variety*, 19 Oct 1977. AS, p. 358. BHD, p. 159. IFN, p. 94. Truitt 1983, p. 217. "In the Picture Studios," *NYDM*, 4 Aug 1915, 27:2 (on the female baseball team at Thanhouser).

Eldredge, Ruth [actress] (b. 1879–3 Nov 1939 [60?], Los Angeles CA). AS, p. 358.

Eldridge, Anna Mae *see* **Walthall, Anna Mae**

Eldridge, Charles E. [stage/film actor] (b. Saratoga Springs NY, 1854–29 Oct 1922 [68], New York NY; cancer). m. Addie J. Dunant (d. 20 Aug 1914). (World; Viragraph; Goldwyn; Metro.) "Chas. Eldridge," *Variety*, 3 Nov 1922. AMD, p. 109. AS, p. 358. BHD, p. 159. IFN, p. 94. MSBB, p. 1023. SD. Truitt 1983, p. 217. George Blaisdell, "At the Sign of the Flaming Arcs," *MPW*, 24 Jan 1914, 415. "Charles E. Eldridge; Playing Character Leads with the Imp Co.," *MPS*, 1 May 1914, 27. "Charles Eldridge Returns to Vitagraph," *MPW*,

23 May 1914, 1097. "Death of Mrs. Charles Eldridge," *MPW,* 12 Sep 1914, 1495.

Eldridge, Florence [actress] (*née* Florence McKechnie, b. Brooklyn NY, 5 Sep 1900–1 Aug 1988 [87], Santa Barbara CA; heart attack). m. **Fredric March**, 1927, Mexico (d. 1975). "Florence Eldridge," *Variety,* 10 Aug 1988. AMD, p. 109. AS, p. 358 (b. 1901; d. 31 Jul). BHD1, p. 175 (b. 1901). Katz, p. 385. "Florence Eldridge Is Engaged," *MPW,* 30 Jun 1923, 764.

Eldridge, Frances [actress]. No data found. AMD, p. 109. "Frances Eldridge in 'The Foreigner,'" *MPW,* 9 Oct 1920, 797. "Frances Eldridge Signed with Superior Pictures," *MPW,* XLVII, 6 Nov 1920, 84. "Not to Return to Stage," *MPW,* 22 Jan 1921, 421. "Frances Eldridge Sues World Film Corporation," *MPW,* 12 Mar 1921, 141 (for $9,750).

Elffors, Nils [actor] (b. 1885–1925 [40?]). BHD1, p. 607.

Elias, Francisco [director/producer] (*né* Francisco Elias Riquelme, b. Huelva, Spain, 26 Jun 1890–8 Jun 1977 [86], Barcelona, Spain). AS, p. 359.

Eline, Mrs. Grace [costumer/actress] (b. 1874–24 Jul 1935 [61?], New York NY). BHD, p. 160; BHD2, p. 77.

Eline, Marie, "The Thanhouser Kid" (sister of Grace Eline) [child actress] (aka Anne B. Carlisle, b. Milwaukee WI, 27 Feb 1902–3 Jan 1981 [78?], Longview WA; heart attack). "Marie Eline," *Variety,* 28 Jan 1981 (no age). AMD, p. 110. AS, p. 359. BHD, p. 160 (b. 1905). "'The Thanhouser Kid' on the Stump," *MPW,* 15 Apr 1911, 825. "Who the 'Princess Man' Is," *MPW,* 15 Nov 1913, 745. "'Thanhouser Kid' No Longer," *MPW,* 6 Dec 1913, 1131 (age ten).

Elinor, Carli D. [composer] (b. Bucharest, Romania, 21 Sep 1890–20 Oct 1958 [68], Los Angeles CA; heart attack). "Carli Elinor," *Variety,* 29 Oct 1958 (age 66; "scored many early D.W. Griffith pix, and scored more than 1,000 films, being one of first to intro sound effects in films"). AS, p. 359. Truitt, p. 100.

Eliscu, Fernanda [actress] (b. Bucharest, Rumania, 24 Apr 1880–27 Sep 1968 [88], Los Angeles CA). AS, p. 359.

Elizondo, Fernando R. [actor]. No data found. AMD, p. 110. "Albert E. Fortoul Discovers New Screen Star by Chance," *MPW,* 1 May 1920, 667.

Elizondo, Joaquin [actor] (b. 1896–15 Jan 1952 [55], Los Angeles CA). AS, p. 359. BHD, p. 160. IFN, p. 94.

Elkas, Edward [stage manager/tenor/actor] (b. New York NY, 8 Feb 1862). m. Helen Solters, NYC. (Columbia Singing Society, 1882; Marie Geistinger Opera Co.; Germania and Thalia Theaters; Aaronson Opera Co.; Alice Nielsen Opera Co.; Vitagraph.) AMD, p. 110. BHD, p. 160. "Edward Elkas," *MPW,* 22 May 1915, 1238:2.

Ellery, Arthur [actor] (b. 1870–27 Aug 1945 [75], Elizabeth NJ). BHD, p. 160. IFN, p. 94.

Ellingford, William [stage/film actor] (b. Morgan UT, 1863?–20 May 1936 [73], Los Angeles CA). (Fox.) "William Ellingford," *Variety,* 27 May 1936 ("veteran of stage and screen"). AS, p. 359. BHD, p. 160. IFN, p. 94. Truitt, p. 100.

Elliott, Adelbert S. [actor/director]. No data found. AMD, p. 110. "Adelbert S. Elliott," *MPW,* 2 Jan 1915, 84.

Elliott, Alice Claire. No data found. AMD, p. 110. "Universal Engages Alice Elliott," *MPW,* 29 Mar 1919, 1786.

Elliott, Clyde E. [cinematographer/director/producer] (b. Concord NE, 23 Jul 1891–12 Jun 1959 [67], Los Angeles CA). AS, p. 359.

Elliott, Dick [actor] (*né* Richard Damon Elliott, b. MA, 30 Apr 1886–22 Dec 1961 [75], Burbank CA). AS, p. 360.

Elliott, Frank [actor] (b. Cheshire, England, 11 Feb 1880–Jul 1970 [90]). AMD, p. 110. AS, p. 360. BHD1, p. 175. "Frank Elliott Rejoins Universal," *MPW,* 26 Feb 1916, 1321. "Karger Signs Frank Elliott," *MPW,* 27 Dec 1919, 1179.

Elliott, Gertrude (sister of **Maxine Elliott**) [actress] (*née* Gertrude Dermott, b. Rockland ME, 14 Dec 1874–24 Dec 1950 [76], Kent, England). m. **Johnston Forbes-Robertson** (d. 1937). "Gertrude Elliott," *Variety,* 3 Jan 1951. AS, p. 360. BHD, p. 160. IFN, p. 94. Truitt, p. 100.

Elliott, Gordon *see* **Elliott, William "Wild Bill**

Elliott, John H. [actor] (b. Pella IA, 5 Jul 1876–12 Dec 1956 [80], Los Angeles CA; heart attack). AS, p. 360 (b. Keosauqua IA). BHD1, p. 176 (b. Keosaugua IA). IFN, p. 94.

Elliott, Lillian (mother of Jack and **Lloyd Corrigan**) [stage/film actress] (b. Canada, 24 Apr 1874–15 Jan 1959 [84], Los Angeles CA; heart attack). m. Corrigan. "Lillian Elliott," *Variety,* 21 Jan 1959. AS, p. 360. BHD1, p. 176. IFN, p. 94. SD. Truitt, p. 100. "Lillian Elliott in Morosco Film," *NYDM,* 10 Mar 1915, 26:1 (*Help Wanted,* Bosworth-Morosco).

Elliott, Madge [stage/film/TV actress/director/dancer] (b. London, England, 12 May 1898–8 Aug 1955 [57], New York NY). m. Cyril Ritchard. "Madge Elliott," *Variety,* 10 Aug 1955, p. 63 (age 59). AS, p. 360 (b. 1896). BHD, p. 160.

Elliott, Maxine (sister of **Gertrude Elliott**) [stage/film actress] (*née* Jessie C. Dermott, b. Rockland ME, 5 Feb 1868–5 Mar 1940 [72], Juan-le-Pins, France). m. (1) George A. McDermott; **Nat Goodwin** (d. 1919). (Film debut: *Fighting Odds,* Goldwyn, 1917.) "Maxine Elliott, 69, Stage Beauty, Dies; Noted American Actress Was Stricken at Her Chateau L'Horizon in France; Starred Here and Abroad; She Made Debut in 1890 and Retired in 1920—'Trimmed in Scarlet' Last Play," *NYT,* 7 May 1940, 23:1. "Maxine Elliott Dead at 69," *Variety,* 13 Mar 1940. AMD, p. 110. AS, p. 360. BHD, p. 160 (b. 1871; d. Cannes, France). GSS, pp. 117–18 (b. 5 Feb 1868). IFN, p. 94 (age 69). SD. Spehr, pp. 128, 130 (b. 1873). Truitt, p. 100 (b. 1873; d. Juan Les Pins, France). "Fitch Play in London; 'Her Own Way' Well Received—Hearty Welcome for Miss Elliott," *NYT,* 26 Apr 1905, 11:4 (Lyric Theatre, London, 26 Apr. *The Daily Telegraph* wrote of her: "She was always beautiful and is beautiful still, but she now possesses ease of manner, charm of action, and a direct, convincing power of making her effects."). "Maxine Elliott Joins Goldwyn," *MPW,* 20 Jan1917, 384. "Maxine Elliott," *MPW,* 3 Mar 1917, 1357.

Elliott, Milton "Skeets" [stuntman] (b. Gadsden AL, 1896–2 Aug 1920 [24?], Los Angeles CA; airplane crash during the filming of *The Skywayman*). AS, p. 360. BHD, p. 160. IFN, p. 94. Truitt 1983, p. 218.

Elliott, Robert [actor] (b. OH, 9 Oct 1879–15 Nov 1951 [72], Los Angeles CA). m. **Ruth** Thorp (d. 1971). (WB.) AMD, p. 110. AS, p. 360. BHD1, p. 176. IFN, p. 94. Truitt, p. 100 (b. Ireland). "Robert Elliott Appears in New Graphic Picture," *MPW,* 8 Jun 1918, 1455.

Elliott, Ruth [actress] (*née* Ruth Thorp, b. CT, 17 Apr 1889–15 Feb 1971 [81], Hollywood CA). m. **Robert Elliott**, 1920 (d. 1951). "Ruth Elliott," *Variety,* 24 Feb 1971. AS, p. 360. IFN, p. 94.

Elliott, William (son-in-law of David Belasco) [stage/film actor] (b. Boston MA, 4 Dec 1879–5 Feb 1932 [52], New York NY). m. Augusta Belasco; (2) Louise LaGrange. "William Elliott," *Variety,* 9 Feb 1932. AMD, p. 110. AS, p. 360. BHD, p. 160 (b. 1885). IFN, p. 94. SD. "Famous Players Secure William Elliott," *MPW,* 9 Jan 1915, 198. "Mrs. Thomas Not Married; Denies Report of Her Wedding to William Elliott, the Actor," *NYT,* 29 Jan 1915, 9:2 (in *Experience* at the Casino, Elliott "was very much perturbed over the report. ¶'I do not care so much for myself, but it was inexcusable to mention the name of Mrs. Thomas,' he said. ¶Mrs. [Helen Kelly Gould] Thomas followed her denial by placing the matter in the hands of her attorney..."). "William Elliott," *MPW,* 3 Apr 1915, 54.

Elliott, William "Wild Bill" [actor] (*né* Gordon Nance, b. near Pattonsburg MO, 16 Oct 1903–26 Nov 1965 [62], Las Vegas NV; cancer). m. (2) Dolly Moore. "'Wild Bill' Elliott," *Variety,* 1 Dec 1965 (age 61). AS, p. 360. BHD1, p. 176. FSS, p. 100. IFN, p. 94. Katz, p. 386 (*né* Gordon Elliott). Truitt, p. 100.

Ellis, Albert B. [executive] (b. 1901?–May 1969 [68], England). (Pathé, 1918.) "Bert Ellis," *Variety,* 21 May 1969. AS, p. 360.

Ellis, Carlyle [producer/director] (b. Toronto, Ontario, Canada, 1879–2 Apr 1942 [63?], Palmdale CA). BhD2, p. 77.

Ellis, Celie [stage/film actress/playwright] (aka Mrs. Celie G. Turner, *née?,* b. 1874?–2 Oct 1924 [50]). "Mrs. Cecilia Turner," *Variety,* 8 Oct 1924, 44 ("October 2 she proceeded to make the rounds of producers with her latest play. Late in the afternoon she reached the office of William H. Gilmore in the Empire Theatre, and while he read the manuscript she toppled off her chair. A doctor was summoned, who pronounced Mrs. Turner dead."). AMD, p. 110. "Damages for Moving Picture Accident," *MPW,* 1 Jan 1916, 86.

Ellis, Daniel [scenarist]. No data found. m. Anna C. Duffy, 1 Dec 1915, Baltimore MD. (Lubin.) "Editor Commits Matrimony," *NYDM,* 18 Dec 1915, 23:2 ("Daniel [of Lubin] has succumbed tot he charms of a fair one, and slying so, too, for on Wednesday, Dec. 1, taking with him a grim determination to end the lonesomeness of life, and, with the little shining band of gold safely tucked away in the lower left-hand corner of the right-side waistcoat pocket, he led pretty Anna C. Duffy, a charming daughter of 'William Penn,' to Baltimore, Md., where they pledged to one another to 'Love, honor, and obey.'").

Ellis, Diane [actress] (b. Los Angeles CA, 20 Dec 1909–15 Dec 1930 [20], Madras, India; heart attack). m. Stephen C. Millet. "Diane Ellis Dies in India on Honeymoon," *Variety,* 17 Dec 1930. AS, p. 360. BHD1, p. 176. IFN, p. 94. Truitt, p. 101.

Ellis, Earle [regional director of Coronet Instructional Films] (b. 1906?–8 Dec 1964 [58], near Maumee OH; plane crash). "Earl Ellis," *Variety,* 23 Dec 1964.

Ellis, Edith (sister of **Edward Ellis**) [actress/scenarist] (b. Coldwater MI, 1874?–27 Dec 1960 [86], New York NY). m. C. Becher Furness. (Goldwyn; MGM.) "Edith Ellis," *Variety,* 4 Jan 1961. AMD, p. 110. AS, p. 360. BHD2, p. 78. IFN, p. 95. SD. "Edith Ellis Joins Goldwyn," *MPW,* 6 Jan 1917, 92.

Ellis, Edna Small [actress] (b. 1898–14 Jul 1917 [19?], Cincinnati OH; convulsions). AS, p. 360.

Ellis, Edward (brother of **Edith Ellis**) [actor] (b. Coldwater MI, 12 Nov 1870–26 Jul 1952 [81], Beverly Hills CA). m. **Josephine Stevens**, 5 Apr 1917. "Edward Ellis," *Variety,* 30 Jul 1952. AMD, p. 110. AS, p. 360. BHD1, p. 176. IFN, p. 95. Truitt, p. 101. "Edward Ellis Succumbs to Pictures," *MPW,* 17 Feb 1917, 1014. "Edward Ellis and Josephine Stevens," *MPW,* 28 Apr 1917, 600.

Ellis, Edwin [actor] (b. London, England, 22 Nov 1895–21 Mar 1959 [63]). AS, p. 360 (b. 1890; d. 1958). BHD1, p. 176.

Ellis, Elis [actor/director] (b. Sweden, 1879–1956 [77?], Sweden). AS, p. 361.

Ellis, Frank B[irney] [actor] (b. OK, 26 Feb 1897–23 Feb 1969 [71], Los Angeles Co. CA). "Wife of Frank Ellis," *Variety,* 26 Feb 1964 (d. 11 Feb 1964 [55], Hollywood CA). AS, p. 361 (b. 1867; d. 11 Feb 1964). BHD1, p. 176. IFN, p. 95. George A. Katchmer, "Famous Cowboys & Cowgirls—2," *CI,* 173 (Nov 1989), C14. Mario DeMarco, "Frank Ellis," *CI,* 199 (Jan 1992), 48.

Ellis, George [actor] (b. 1891-Mar 1929 [37?], Bloomibngton IL). BHD, p. 160.

Ellis, Houston [actor] (b. 1893–13 Feb 1928 [34?], Delana CA). AS, p. 361 (d. 12 Feb). BHD, p. 160. IFN, p. 95.

Ellis, John [still photographer] (b. 1886?–11 Oct 1951 [65], Hollywood CA). (Ince; WB; U-I.) "John Ellis," *Variety,* 17 Oct 1951.

Ellis, Lillian [actress] (b. Denmark, 25 May 1909–21 Feb 1951 [41], Copenhagen, Denmark). BHD1, p. 176. IFN, p. 95.

Ellis, Melville [art director/costume designer/musician] (b. San Francisco CA, San Francisco CA, 1876?–4 Apr 1917 [41?], New York NY; typhoid fever). "Melville Ellis," *Variety,* 6 Apr 1917. AS, p. 361. BHD1, p. 607.

Ellis, Paul [actor] (b. Buenos Aires, Argentina, 4 Nov 1896). AS, p. 361.

Ellis, Robert du Reel [actor/writer] (*né* Robert Ellis Reel, b. Brooklyn NY, 27 Jun 1892–29 Dec 1974 [82], Los Angeles CA). AS, p. 361 (d. Santa Monica CA). BHD1, p. 176. IFN, p. 95.

Ellis, Robert J. [art director/actor/director] (b. Pasadena CA, 5 Sep 1888–20 May 1935 [46], Los Angeles CA). m. **May Allison** (d. 1989); **Vera Reynolds** (d. 1962). "Robert Ellis," *Variety,* 29 May 1935 (age 42). AMD, p. 110. AS, p. 361. BHD2, p. 78. FSS, p. 101. IFN, p. 95. Katz, pp. 386–87 (b. Brooklyn, 27 Jun 1892). MH, p. 108. Truitt, p. 101 (b. Brooklyn NY, 27 Jun 1892–19 May 1935). "Ellis Directs 'Ventures,'" *MPW,* 4 Dec 1915, 1812. "Ellis to Direct 'Sis Hopkins,'" *MPW,* 1 Jan 1916, 62. "Robert Ellis Signs with Selznick for Long Term," *MPW,* 21 Jun 1919, 1768. "Robert Ellis Loaned to Tucker," *MPW,* 9 Aug 1919, 843. "Selznick Pictures Begins Suit Against Ellis for Alleged Breach of Contract," *MPW,* 16 Oct 1920, 928. "Selznick Sues Director," *MPW,* 13 Nov 1920, 226. "Ellis Files Answer to Suit," *MPW,* 4 Dec 1920, 596. "Record Made in Filming Advertising Men's First Picture; Ellis Finishes in One Day," *MPW,* 1 Apr 1922, 458.

Ellis, Will E. [actor/writer] (d. 31 Mar 1915, Los Angeles CA). "William E. Ellis," *Variety,* 9 Apr 1915, p. 6. AMD, p. 110. BHD2, p. 78. "Wrong Actor Given Credit," *MPW,* XXI, 4 Jul 1914, 87.

Ellison, Marjorie [actress]. No data found. (Edison, 1913.) AMD, p. 110. "Gossip of the Studios," *NYDM,* 1 Sep 1915, 32:2 (after two years' constant work at Edison, she was to take a vacation on the Pacific coast). "Marjorie Ellison," *MPW,* 4 Sep 1915, 1655. "In the Picture Studios," *NYDM,* 29 Sep 1915, 26:3 (to leave NY to work at a film company in LA). "Marjorie Ellison Now with Universal," *MPW,* 22 Jan 1916, 630.

Elliston, Grace [actress] (*née* Grace Rutter, b. Memphis TN, 1878?–14 Dec 1950 [72], Lenox MA). (Film debut: *Black Fear,* Metro, 1915.) "Grace Elliston," *Variety,* 20 Dec 1950. AMD, p. 110. AS, p. 361. BHD, p. 160. SD, p. 409. "Grace Elliston," *MPW,* 6 Nov 1915, 1123.

Elliston, Mark [actor] (b. 1889–27 Feb 1925 [35?], Chicago IL). BHD, p. 160.

Ellsler, Effie [actress] (b. Cleveland OH, 17 Sep 1855–8 Oct 1942 [87], Los Angeles CA). m. Frank Weston (d. 1922). "Effie Ellsler," *Variety,* 14 Oct 1942. AS, p. 361. BHD1, p. 176. IFN, p. 95. SD. Truitt, p. 101 (b. Philadelphia PA).

Ellsworth, Elmer [costumer] (b. 4 Jan 1900–4 Apr 1969 [69], Los Angeles CA; heart attack). (Western Costume.) "Elmer Ellsworth," *Variety,* 16 Apr 1969 (for 40 years). AS, p. 361. BHD2, p. 78.

Elmendorf, Dwight L. [cameraman]. No data found. AMD, p. 110. "Elmendorf Travel Talks, Inc.," *MPW,* 7 Apr 1917, 74. "Elmendorf Signs with Educational," *MPW,* 13 Jul 1918, 191.

Elmer, Clarence Jay [actor] (b. San Francisco CA, 1886). (Lubin.) AMD, p. 110. BHD, p. 160. "Gossip of the Studios," *NYDM,* 20 Jan 1915, 33:1 (Elner [sic] to marry Lubin actress Edith Stout Anderton on 13 Feb). "Lubin Players to Wed Before Camera," *MPW,* 30 Jan 1915, 662.

Elmer, William "Billy" [actor] (*né* William E. Johns, b. Council Bluffs IA, 25 Apr 1869–24 Feb 1945 [75], Los Angeles CA). "Billy Elmer," *Variety,* 7 Mar 1945. AS, p. 361. BHD1, p. 176. IFN, p. 95. Truitt, p. 101. George Katchmer, "Remembering the Great Silents," *CI,* 196 (Oct 1991), 54.

Elmore, Bruce [actor] (*né* Alfred G. Kennedy, b. 1885–14 May 1940 [55?], New York NY). AS, p. 361.

Elmore, Pearl [actress] (b. Kansas City MO, 1879). (Griffith.) BHD, p. 160.

Elsie, Lily [vaudeville/stage/film actress] (b. Worsley, Lancashire, England, 8 Apr 1886–16 Dec 1962 [76], Pelehouse Common, Sussex, England). "Lily Elsie," *Variety,* 26 Dec 1962, p. 47. BHD, p. 160.

Elsom, Isobel [actress] (aka Isobel Harbord, *née* Isobel Jeannette Reed, b. Chesterton, Cambridge, England, 16 Mar 1893–12 Jan 1981 [87], Woodland Hills CA). m. **Maurice Elvey** (d. 1967); (2) Carl Harbord. "Isobel Elsom," *Variety,* 28 Jan 1981. AS, pp. 361–62. BHD1, p. 177. Katz, p. 387. SD.

Eltinge, Juilian [stage/film actor/female impersonator] (*né* William Dalton, b. Newtonville MA, 14 May 1881–7 Mar 1941 [59], New York NY; kidney ailment [Death Certificate Index No. 5664 (William Dalton)]). (Lasky-Paramount.) "Julian Eltinge, Impersonator, 57; Actor Famous for His Female Characterizations 2 Decades Ago Dies at Home Here; Theatre Named for Him; Scored Hits with 'Fascinating Widow' and 'Crinoline Girl'—Lost Three Fortunes," *NYT,* 8 Mar 1941, 19:3. "Julian Eltinge Dies at 57; B'way Recalls His Fisticuffs, Parties," *Variety,* 12 Mar 1941. AMD, p. 110. AS, p. 362. BHD1, p. 177 (b. 1882). IFN, p. 95 (b. 1883). MSBB, p. 1023. Truitt, p. 101 (b. 1893). Cover, *NYDM,* 6 Oct 1915 (in *Cousin Lucy*). "Julian Eltinge Comes to the Screen," *MPW,* 16 Jun 1917, 1791. "Eltinge Becomes Male Impersonator," *MPW,* 30 Nov 1918, 937. "Name of Eltinge Legalized," *MPW,* 21 Dec 1918, 1327. "Eltinge Better," *MPW,* 23 Jul 1921, 413 (appendicitis),. "Eltinge Ill," *MPW,* 27 Aug 1921, 888 (Clara Barton Hospital). "Eltinge Leaves Hospital," *MPW,* 17 Sep 1921, 293. "Al Christie Signs Julian Eltinge," *MPW,* 16 May 1925, 344. "Introducing a Beautiful New Movie Star, 'Madame Lucy,'" *MW,* 26 Sep 1925, 34 (photo spread). Michael Moore, "The Mr. Lillian Russell of the Silent Screen: Julian Eltinge," *CI,* 152 (Feb 1988), 58 (b. 1882). John Holusha, "A Theater's Muses, Rescued; Mural Figures Recall Celebrity of a (Well-Painted) Face," *NYT,* 24 Mar 2000, B1, B6 (restoration at the Empire Theater on 42nd Street—formerly the Eltinge Theater—uncovered murals of the impersonator. "With the restoration completed and the mural back in place, Julian Eltinge's image is once again where he surely would have wanted it to be, overlooking audiences coming to see a show.").

Elton, Edmund J. [actor] (b. England, 5 Feb 1871–4 Jan 1952 [80], Los Angeles Co. CA). AS, p. 362. BHD1, p. 177. IFN, p. 95.

Elton, Leslie [cartoonist]. No data found. AMD, p. 111. "Leslie Elton, Cartoonist, Joins Paramount-Bray Forces," *MPW,* 9 Sep 1916, 1709.

Elvey, Maurice [producer/director] (*né* William Seward Folkard, b. Darlington, Yorkshire, England, b. 11 Nov 1887–28 Aug 1967 [79], Brighton, England). m. (1) Philippa Preston; **Isobel Elsom** (d. 1981). (Fox.) "Maurice Elvey," *Variety,* 6 Sep 1967 (made 300+ films). AMD, p. 111. AS, p. 362. BHD, p. 161; BHD2, p. 78. IFN, p. 95. Katz, pp. 387–88. SD, p. 411. Waldman, p. 97. "Elvey's Second for Fox," *MPW,* 13 Sep 1924, 117. "The Early Memoirs of Maurice Elvey," recorded by Denis Gifford, *Griffithiana,* 60/61 (Oct 1997), 77–125 (includes filmography).

Elvidge, June C. [stage/film actress] (b. St. Paul MN, 30 Jun 1893–1 May 1965 [71], Eatontown NJ). m. (2) Lt. Frank C. Badgely, 19 Nov 1918, NY; (3) Briton N. Busch (d. 1950). (World Film Corp.; Metro; Cosmopolitan; FP-L; Universal; Fox; film debut: *The Lure of Woman,* 1915.) "June Elvidge," *NYT,* 3 May 1965, 33:3. "June Elvidge," *Variety,* 5 May 1965 (age 72). AMD, p. 111. AS, p. 362. BHD, p. 1616. IFN, p. 95 (age 72). MH, p. 108. MSBB, p. 1034. Spehr, p. 130. Truitt, p. 101. WWS, p. 254. "June Elvidge," *MPW,* 1 Jan 1916, 88. "Claims Exemption for Gown Taxation," *MPW,* 13 Jul 1918, 189. "June Elvidge Hangs Up a Record," *MPW,* 31 Aug 1918, 1245. Edward Weitzel, "Dual Personality of June Elvidge," *MPW,* 5 Oct 1918, 59–60. "June Elvidge Marries Canadian Soldier Hero," *MPW,* 7 Dec 1918, 1091. "June Elvidge to Be One of Stars in Metro Production," *MPW,* 28 Aug 1920, 1206. "C.B.C. Signs June Elvidge," *MPW,* 17 Feb 1923, 697. Billy Doyle, "June Elvidge," *CI,* 222 (Dec 1993), C8.

Elvin, Joe [music hall/film actor] (b. London, England, 29 Nov 1862–3 Mar 1935 [72], London, England). "Joe Elvin," *Variety*, 20 Mar 1935, p. 62 (d. 4 Mar). BHD, p. 161.

Elwell, George Edwin [actor] (b. Detroit MI, 21 Apr 1893–13 Nov 1916 [23], Los Angeles CA; heart attack). (Ince.) AMD, p. 111. AS, p. 362 (d. 3 Nov). BHD, p. 161. IFN, p. 95. *MPN Studio Directory*, XIV, 21 Oct 1916 (b. 1893). "Obituary," *MPW*, 9 Dec 1916, 1485. Cal York, "Plays and Players," *Photoplay Magazine*, Feb 1917, 88 ("George H. [sic] Elwell, a youthful protege of Thomas H. Ince who was fast approaching stardom, dropped dead several weeks ago while dancing at a beach resort near Los Angeles. Young Elwell enlisted in the California militia when President Wilson asked for volunteers last summer but was rejected because of a weak heart...He was just 21.").

Elwell, Harry [property head] (d. 9 Jun 1918, Hollywood CA). (FP-L.) "Harry Elwell," *Variety*, LI, 28 Jun 1918, 16:3. AMD, p. 111. "Obituary," *MPW*, 13 Jul 1918, 215.

Ely, Eleazer [actor] (b. 1839–9 Feb 1929 [90], Cooperstown NY). BHD, p. 161. IFN, p. 95.

Ely, Harry R. [actor] (b. 1883?–15 Jul 1951 [68], Los Angeles CA). "Harry R. Ely, 68, actor whose career dated back to silent films, died July 15 in Hollywood," *Variety*, 25 Jul 1951. AS, p. 362. BHD, p. 161. IFN, p. 95. Truitt, p. 101.

Ely, Nora [casting director]. No data found. AMD, p. 111. "Gaylord Lloyd to Resume Acting," *MPW*, 3 Oct 1925, 415 (succeeded him in Harold Lloyd Corporation).

Ely, S. Gilbert (father of Robert R. Ely) [actor/director] (b. 1858?–4 Apr 1920 [62], Osgood IN). m. (2) Marie Bailey. (Lubin.) "S. Gilbert Ely," *Variety*, 9 Apr 1920. AS, p. 362. BHD, p. 161; BHD2, p. 78. IFN, p. 95.

Elzer, Karl Conrad [actor] (b. Karlsrühe, Germany, 2 Aug 1881–30 Aug 1938 [57], Rottach-Egern, Bavaria). BHD1, p. 177 (d. Germany).

Emden, Margaret [actress] (b. 1890–13 Feb 1946 [55?], England). AS, p. 362. BHD, p. 161.

Emerick, Bessie or Besse [actress] (b. Rochester IN, 1875–13 Dec 1939 [64], Boston MA). m. Leopold D. Wharton. "Besse Emerick," *NYT*, 14 Dec 1939, 27:2. "Besse Emerick," *Variety*, 20 Dec 1939. AS, p. 362. BHD, p. 161. IFN, p. 95. Truitt, p. 101.

Emerson, John [stage actor/film director/scenarist] (b. Sandusky OH, 28 May 1871–7 Mar 1956 [84], Pasadena CA). m. Anita Loos, m. 15 Jun 1919, Bayside NY. (Triangle; Paramount.) "John Emerson of Theatre Dies; Playwright with Wife, Anita Loos, Directed Many Films and Led Actors Equity," *NYT*, 9 Mar 1956, 23:1 (age 81). "John Emerson," *Variety*, 14 Mar 1956. AMD, p. 111. AS, p. 362 (*né* Clifton Paden). BHD, p. 161; BHD2, p. 78. FDY, p. 423. IFN, p. 95. KOM, pp. 134–35 (b. 1874). MSBB, p. 1046 (b. NY). Spehr, p. 130 (b. 1874). Truitt, p. 101 (b. 1874). "John Emmerson [sic] in Another Film," *NYDM*, LXXIII, 24:1 (to debut in *The Conspiracy*, FP-L, and then to appear in *The Bachelor's Romance*). "Emerson to Direct Fairbanks," *MPW*, 16 Oct 1915, 449. "John Emerson," *MPW*, 8 Apr 1916, 251. "Emerson Goes to Famous Players," *MPW*, 29 Jul 1916, 773 (on loan). "Emerson Back with Triangle," *MPW*, 4 Nov 1916, 707. Ethel Rosemon, "The Extra Girl, Anita and John; An Emerson-Loos Comedy in the Making," *MPC*, Mar 1917, 52–53, 79, 85. "Emerson and Loos Leave Fairbanks," *MPW*, 29 Dec 1917, 1948. "Emerson and Loos Go to Paramount," *MPW*, 26 Jan 1918, 492. Edward Weitzel, "Corralling Practical Experience," *MPW*, 8 Feb 1919, 737–38. "Emerson and Anita Loos Make Permanent Alliance," *MPW*, 28 Jun 1919, 1955. "Emerson Nominated as Actors' President," *MPW*, 8 May 1920, 790. "Emerson and Loos Find Screen Material in Europe," *MPW*, 28 Aug 1920, 1205. "Emerson and Loos Tell How They Write Their Scenarios," *MPW*, 25 Sep 1920, 465 (published *How to Write Photoplays*, James A. McCann Co.). "Emerson-Loos to Retire?," *MPW*, 1 Oct 1927, 289.

Emerson, Ralph (Walter) [stage/film actor/scenarist] (b. Kalispell MT, 9 Aug 1898–22 Feb 1984 [85], West Lafayette IN). "Ralph Emerson," *Variety*, 314, 14 Mar 1984, 46:4. AS, p. 362. BHD1, p. 177 (b. 1899).

Emerton, Roy [actor] (*né* Hugh Fitzroy Emerton, b. Burford, England, 9 Oct 1892–30 Nov 1944 [52], England). AS, p. 362.

Emery, Gilbert [actor] (*né* Arthur MacArthur, b. Naples NY, 11 Jun 1875–28 Oct 1945 [70], Los Angeles CA). (Vitagraph.) AS, p. 362. BHD1, p. 177. IFN, p. 95. Truitt, p. 105.

Emery, Gilbert [actor] (b. Australia, 1882?–31 Dec 1934 [52], Los Angeles CA). "Gilbert Emery," *Variety*, 8 Jan 1935 (began 1924). AS, p. 362. BHD, p. 161. IFN, p. 95. Truitt, p. 102.

Emery, Pollie [actress] (b. Bolton, England, 10 May 1875–31 Oct 1958 [83], London, England). BHD1, p. 177. IFN, p. 95.

Emery, Winifred [actress] (b. Manchester, England, 1 Aug 1862–15 Jul 1924 [61], Bexhill, Sussex, England). BHD, p. 161.

Emmet, Katherine [actress] (b. San Francisco CA, 1882?–6 Jun 1960 [78], New York NY). m. painter Alon Bement (d. 1954). "Katherine Emmet, a Stage Actress," *NYT*, 7 Jun 1960, 35:5. "Katherine Emmet," *Variety*, 15 Jun 1960. AMD, p. 111. AS, p. 363. BHD1, p. 178. IFN, p. 95. Truitt, p. 102. "Katherine Emmet with Selig," *MPW*, 29 Nov 1913, 995.

Emmett, Fern [stage and screen actress] (b. Oakland CA, 22 Mar 1896–3 Sep 1946 [50], Los Angeles CA; cancer). m. Henry Roquemore. "Fern Emmett," *Variety*, 11 Sep 1946. AS, p. 363. BHD1, p. 178. IFN, p. 96. Truitt 1983, p. 221.

Emmons, Louise [actress] (b. 1852?–6 Mar 1935 [85], Los Angeles CA). "Louise Emmons," *Variety*, 13 Mar 1935 ("played character parts in pictures since 1909"). AS, p. 363. BHD, p. 161. IFN, p. 96. Truitt, p. 102.

Emney, Fred, Sr. (father of Fred Emney, Jr.) [stage/film actor] (b. London, England, 5 Mar 1865–7 Jan 1917 [51], New Malden, Surrey, England; result of a fall). m. (son, Fred, 1900–1980). "Fred Emney Dies," *Variety*, 12 Jan 1917, p. 4 ("...slipped during a performance recently [of *Cinderella*, at the London opera house] and, although seriously injured, pluckily continued the performance and also appeared the next day. He was then confined to his bed..."). AS, p. 363 (Fred Emsey, Sr., d. London, England). BHD, p. 161.

Emo, E[merich] **W**[alter] [actor] (*né* Emerich Walter Wojtek, b. Seebarn, Austria, 11 Jul 1898–1 Dec 1975 [77], Vienna, Austria). AS, p. 363. BHD1, p. 607; BHD2, p. 78.

Emory, Thomas V. [actor] (b. 1883?–18 Mar 1921 [38], New York NY; pneumonia). "Thomas V. Emory," *Variety*, 11 Mar 1921. AS, p. 363.

Empey, Arthur Guy [actor/scenarist/director/producer/President of Guy Empey Pictures, Inc.] (b. Ogden UT, 11 Dec 1883–22 Feb 1963 [79], Wadsworth KS). (Vitagraph.) "Arthur Guy Emtey [sic] Dead; He Wrote 'Over the Top,'" *NYT*, 27 Feb 1963, 16:1. "Guy Empey," *Variety*, 6 Mar 1963. AMD, p. 111. AS, p. 363. BHD1, p. 178; BHD2, p. 78.. FDY, p. 423. IFN, p. 95. Truitt, p. 102. "'Over the Top' 's Hero, Arthur Guy Empey, in Khaki," *MPW*, 14 Sep 1918, 1591. "Guy Empey in the South Hunts Locations for Comedy-Dramas," *MPW*, 14 Aug 1920, 866. "Watchword of Guy Empey Productions Is Quality, Not Quantity—'Oil' Completed," *MPW*, 14 Aug 1920, 867. "Arthur Guy Empey Plans to Picturize His First Novel," *MPW*, 28 Aug 1920, 1193.

Empress, Marie [actress] (b. England-d. 1919, Atlantic Ocean; fell overboard from ship to U.S.). AMD, p. 111. BHD, p. 161. IFN, p. 96. Truitt 1983, p. 222. "New Rolfe-Metro Players," *MPW*, Oct 1915, 287. "Marie Empress," *MPW*, 23 Dec 1916, 1808.

Encinas, Lalo [actor] (b. AZ, 27 Jun 1886–5 May 1959 [72], Los Angeles Co. CA). AS, p. 363. BHD1, p. 178. IFN, p. 96.

Endresse, Clara [actress] (b. MT, 20 Mar 1898–2 Dec 1979 [81], Los Angeles CA). AS, p. 363. BHD1, p. 178 (b. 1896). IFN, p. 96.

Enfield, S. Charles [publicist]. No data found. m. May Band, 15 Jun 1927. AMD, p. 111. "Enfield Marries," *MPW*, 18 Jun 1927, 475.

Engdahl, Catl [actor/director] (b. Sweden, 1864–1939 [65?], Sweden). AS, p. 363.

Engel, Alexander [stage/film actor] (b. Berlin, Germany, 4 Jun 1902–25 Aug 1968 [66], Saarbruecken, Germany). "Alexander Engel," *Variety*, 11 Sep 1968, p. 111 ("He had appeared in more than 100 films including many silents."). AS, p. 363. BHD, p. 161. IFN, p. 96 (d. Jul 1968).

Engel, Joseph W. [actor/director/producer] (b. 1883?–18 Apr 1943 [60], New York NY). (FP-L; Universal; MGM.) "Joseph W. Engel," *Variety*, 21 Apr 1943 ("film production pioneer"). AMD, p. 111. AS, p. 364. BHD, p. 161; BHD2, p. 78. IFN, p. 96. "Course of Film Empire Sways to South; So Declares Treasurer Joseph W. Engel of Metro Following Visit to Florida—Pictures Gaining in Havana," *MPW*, 22 Apr 1916, 624:1 ("...I am willing to hazard a good guess that the big features which cannot be made in the North during the winter months will, in a majority of cases, before very long be produced in Flordia, especially in Jacksonville..."). "'Joe' Engel, a Metro Founder, Joins Ranks of Producers," *MPW*, 6 Dec 1924, 509.

Engelmann, Andrews [actor] (b. St. Petersburg, Russia, 3 Mar 1901–25 Feb 1992 [90], Basel, Switzerland). Polizei-und Militärdepartement des Kantons, Basel-Stadt, 14 Jan 1999, Einwohnerdienste. AS, p. 364. (Data contributed by Frank Reichelt.)

Engels, Erich [director/scenarist] (b. Remscheid, Germany, 23 May 1889–25 Apr 1971 [81], Munich, Germany). AS, p. 364.

Engels, Vera [actress] (b. Kiel, Germany, 12 May 1909–16 Nov 1988 [79], Germany). m. **Ivan Lebedeff** (d. 1953). AS, p. 364 (b. 1904). BHD, p. 607.

Engl, Olga [actress] (b. Prague, Czechoslovakia, 30 May 1871–21 Sep 1946 [75], Berlin, Germany). BHD1, p. 178.

England, Daisy [actress] (b. 1862–7 Mar 1943 [80?]). BHD, p. 161.

England, Paul [scenarist] (b. London, England, 17 Jun 1893–21 Nov 1968 [75], Devonshire, England). AS, p. 364 (b. Streatham, England). BHD1, p. 178; BHD2, p. 79.

Engle, Billy [actor] (b. Austria, 28 May 1889–28 Nov 1966 [77], Woodland Hills CA; heart attack). (Christie.) "Billy Engle," *Variety*, 7 Dec 1966. AMD, p. 112. AS, p. 364. BHD1, p. 178. IFN, p. 96. Truitt, p. 102. "Signs Billy Engle," *MPW*, 24 Feb 1923, 801.

Engle, Marie [actress] (b. 1902?–23 Mar 1971 [69?], Los Angeles CA). m. Tom Dugan. "Marie Engle Dugan," *Variety*, 31 Mar 1971. AS, p. 364. Truitt, p. 102.

Engler, Gustav A. [executive]. No data found. AMD, p. 112. "Malitz and Engler Out of Piedmont," *MPW*, 26 Jan 1918, 480. "Malitz and Engler Sentenced to Prison," *MPW*, XXXVI, 25 May 1918, 1123 (got 1 1/2 yearw for smuggling rubber into Germany).

Englid, Arvid [actor/director] (b. Helskini, Finland, 18 Jun 1882–12 Sep 1972 [90], Helsinki, Finland). AS, p. 364.

Englisch, Lucie [actress] (*née* Paula Aloisia Englisch, b. Baden, Germany, 8 Feb 1897–12 Oct 1965 [68], Erlangen, Germany; cirrhosis of the liver). m. **Heinrich Fuchs**. AS, p. 364 (b. 1902). BHD1, p. 178 (b. Austria). IFN, p. 96 (age 63).

English, John W[ilkinson] [director] (b. Cumberland, England, 25 Jun 1903–11 Oct 1969 [66], Los Angeles CA). m. Nina. (Republic; Universal.) "John W. English," *Variety*, 22 Oct 1969. AS, p. 364. BHD2, p. 79. IFN, p. 96.

English, Harry [actor] (b. 1861–3 Apr 1939 [77?], Englewood NJ). BHD, p. 161.

English, Robert [actor] (b. Cheltenham, England, 2 Dec 1878). BHD, p. 161.

Enk, Florence [publicist]. No data found. AMD, p. 112. "Is with American," *MPW*, L, 28 May 1921, 417.

Ennis, Bert G. (grandson of Henry F. Hughes, pioneer piano manufacturer) [vaudevillian/publicist with Vitagraph and the New York Motion Picture Company/writer] (b. Brooklyn NY). m. Clara Muriel Pirung, Nov 1913, St. Rose of Lima Church, Washington Avenue, Flatbush NY (officiated by Rev. Father Leo Ennis, a cousin). (Vitagraph; NYMP Co.; Eclair.) Father's obituary (Richard J. Ennis, 31 Aug 1927) cites Brooklyn as the family hometown. (Sennett.) AMD, p. 112. "News Notes," *MPS*, 10 Oct 1913, 30 (worked with Eclair after leaving NYMPC). G.F. Blaisdell, "At the Sign of the Flaming Arcs," *MPW*, 23 Nov 1912, 775; *MPW*, 13 Dec 1913, 1264 (Ennis, then publicity manager of the Edison Company, m. Clara Muriel Pirung on Thanksgiving evening, 1913). "Bert Ennis and Miss Pirung Wed," *MPN*, 6 Dec 1913, p. 32 ("George Bunny, son of John Bunny, the Vitagraph star, took motion pictures of the bride and groom entering and leaving the church, and of the festivities following the ceremony."). F.J. Beecroft, "Publicity Men I Have Met...," *NYDM*, 14 Jan 1914, 48 (*see* Beecroft, Chester for full citation. "For several years Bert was 'on the big time' in vaudeville."). "Bert Ennis Off for Texas," *MPW*, 18 Apr 1914, 362. "Ennis Leaves Eclair," *NYDM*, 19 May 1915, 32:2 (scenario editor, publicity expert, and advance man for Eclair). "Eastern Co. Preparing," *Variety*, 27 Aug 1915, 6 (general press rep for the Eastern Co., he and wife moved to Providence RI). Bert Ennis, "How the Keystone Kops Happened," *MPC*, Jun 1926, 34–35, 74 (Ennis claims to have discovered the Cops' costumes.). Bert Ennis, "Them Were the Happy Days; Part I, "The Vitagraph Years," *MPC*, Oct 1926, 18–19, 65, 86; Part II, "The Keystone Comedies," *MPC*, Nov 1926, 20–21, 68, 79; Part III, "The Screen Club and Biograph-Reliance Era," *MPC*, Dec 1926, 26–27, 67, 77, 83; Part IV, "The Eclair-World-Metro Era," *MPC*, Jan 1927, 32–33, 67, 88; Part V, "The Custard Pie Era," *MPC*, Feb 1927, 30–31, 67, 85; Part VI, "L'Envoi," *MPC*, Mar 1927, 42–43, 68. Bert Ennis, "Up From the Two-a-Day; or, Vaudeville, We Owe a Lot to You," *MPC*, Mar 1927, 35, 70. Bert Ennis, "Whoopee—Horse Opera; They Have Hoofed Their Way to the Top," *MPC*, Jul 1927, 26–27, 66. "Bert G. Ennis," *MPW*, 26 Mar 1927, 311. Bert Ennis, "The Grind That Was Worth While," *MPC*, Aug 1927, 28–29, 80 (discusses directors Phil Rosen, Richard Walling, *et al.*). Bert Ennis, "Papa Whip!," *MPC*, Nov 1927, 27, 84 (re high salaries and Wall Street). Bert Ennis, "When It Comes to Stars' Children Does History Repeat?," *MPC*, Nov 1927, 48–49, 65.

Ennis, Harry [publicist] (b. 1880–12 Oct 1924 [44?], Brooklyn NY; appendicitis). AMD, p. 112. BHD, p. 161. "Obituary," *MPW*, LXXI, 1 Nov 1924, 30.

Enright, Florence [actress] (b. New York NY, 4 Dec 1883–3 Apr 1961 [77], Los Angeles CA). AS, p. 365.

Enright, Ray [director] (*né* Raymond E. Enright, b. Anderson IN, 25 Mar 1896–3 Apr 1965 [69], Los Angeles CA; heart attack). (Sennett; Ince; WB; 1st National; Universal; Columbia; RKO.) "Ray Enright," *Variety*, 7 Apr 1965 ("earlyday director"). AMD, p. 112. AS, p. 365. BHD2, p. 79. IFN, p. 96. Katz, 390. "Now He Directs," *MPW*, 22 Jan 1927, 266. "Ray Enright Is Back from Work on First Picture," *MPW*, 12 Mar 1927, 103. "Ray Enright to Direct Dog Star," *MPW*, 28 May 1927, 270. "Presenting the Director of Rinty," *MPW*, 2 Jul 1927, 19.

Ens, William *see* **Eagle Eye**

Enstedt, Howard [actor] (b. IL, 7 May 1906–13 Dec 1928 [22]). AS, p. 365 (d. NY NY). BHD, p. 162. IFN, p. 96.

Entwistle, Harold [actor] (*né* Charles H. Entwistle, b. London, England, 5 Sep 1865–1 Apr 1944 [78], Los Angeles CA). m. Jane Ross. (Famous Players, 1910.) "Harold Entwistle," *Variety*, 5 Apr 1944 (age 77). AMD, p. 112. AS, p. 365. BHD1, p. 179. IFN, p. 96. Truitt, p. 102. "Harold Entwistle," *MPW*, 26 Aug 1916, 1415. "Harold Entwistle," *MPW*, 24 Feb 1917, 1186. "Harry Entwistle," *MPW*, 31 Mar 1917, 2108.

Entwistle, Robert S. [actor/stage manager] (b. London, England, 1872–19 Dec 1922 [50?], Brooklyn NY; from injuries sustained in an auto accident). "Robert S. Entwistle," *Variety*, 22 Dec 1922. BHD, p. 162. SD.

Enuteseak, Columbia [actress]. No data found. AMD, p. 112. "American-Born Eskimo Girl Plays Leading Part in Selig Film," *MPW*, 5 Aug 1911, 291.

Epping, Florence Luella [actress] (b. 1888–1986 [97?]). BHD, p. 162.

Epstein, Jean (brother of **Marie Epstein**) [director/producer/scenarist] (b. Warsaw, Poland, 26 Mar 1897–2 Apr 1953 [56], Paris, France). AS, p. 365. BHD2, p. 79.

Epstein, Marie (sisten of **Jean Epstein**) [director/scenarist] (b. Warsaw, Poland, 14 Aug 1899–1995 [96?], Paris, France). AS, p. 366.

Erastoff, Edith [actress] (*née* Edith Alma Frederika Lundberg, b. Helsinki, Finland, 8 Apr 1887–28 Aug 1945 [58], Stockholm, Sweden). m. **Victor Seastrom** (d. 1960). (Began in Sweden, 1913). AS, p. 366. BHD1, p. 607. IFN, p. 96.

Erb, Ludwig G.B. [President of the Crystal Film Co.]. No data found. AMD, p. 112. "'Picture Plays' and Their Production," *MPW*, 23 Apr 1910, 636–37. "The Crystal Film Company, New York; The Superb Equipment of This New Studio and Factory, One of the Surprises of the Week," *MPW*, 16 Mar 1912, 946–47. "Ludwig Erb, Pioneer, Always Insists on Big, Clean Dramas," *MPW*, 24 Jan 1925, 388.

Ercole, George [cameraman]. No data found. AMD, p. 112. "Saw First Allies at Vladivostock," *MPW*, 14 Sep 1918, 1550. "Pathé News Has complete Record of Smyrna Fire," *MPW*, 14 Oct 1922, 567. "Ercole Is Lauded by Paramount," *MPW*, 22 Oct 1927, 478.

Eric, Fred [stage/film actor] (*né* Frederick Murphy, b. Peru IN, 1874–16 Apr 1935 [61], New York NY). (Pathé.) "Fred Eric," *Variety*, 24 Apr 1935, p. 62 (d. 17 Apr). AS, p. 366. BHD, p. 162. IFN, p. 96. SD.

Erickson, A.F. "Buddy" [producer] (b. Bloomington IL, 3 May 1879–15 Jan 1956 [76], Los Angeles CA). (Began with Inceville Studios; Paramount; Metro; Columbia; TC-F; Hal Roach.) "A.F. Erickson," *Variety*, 25 Jan 1956. AS, p. 366 (b. 1898). BHD2, p. 79.

Erickson, Bob [actor/horseman] (*né* Robert E. Erickson, b. Minneapolis MN, 10 Oct 1898–21 Jan 1941 [42], Los Angeles Co. CA). BHD1, p. 179. IFN, p. 96.

Erickson, Knute [actor] (b. Norrkoping, Sweden, 27 May 1870–31 Dec 1945 [75], Los Angeles CA). "Knute Erickson," *Variety*, 9 Jan 1946 (d. 1 Jan 1946). AMD, p. 112. BHD1, p. 179 (b. Ogden UT, 1872). IFN, p. 97. Truitt, p. 103 (d. 1 Jan 1946). "Knute Erickson in Cort Films," *MPW*, 1 May 1915, 747.

Eriksen, Erich [director/scenarist] (*né* Fritz Max Erich Joseph Eriksen, b. Berlin, Germany, 13 Sep 1882). AS, p. 366.

Eristoff, Nestor [actor] (b. Russia, 15 Nov 1875–24 Oct 1961 [85], Los Angeles CA). AS, p. 366.

Erlanger, Abraham Lincoln, "Little Napoleon" [theater owner/executive] (b. Buffalo NY, 4 May 1859–7 Mar 1930 [70], New York NY [Death Certificate No. 6032]). m. (1) Louise Balfe; (2) Charlotte Fiscal (common law); Adelaide Louise—div. 1911. "A.L. Erlanger Dies After Long Illness; Largest Individual Owner of Playhouses and Former 'Czar' of Stage Succumbs at 69; 'Widow' Retains Counsel; [Max D.] Steuer Asserts the Estate Is $75,000,000—Brother Insists Theatre Man Left No Wife," *NYT*, 8 Mar 1930, 1, 10. "A.L. Erlanger," *Variety*, 12 Mar 1930. SD. WWVC, pp. 49–50. "Divorce for Mrs. Erlanger," *NYDM*, 10 Jan 1912, 11. "Stage Versus Screen; Merry War Between Theatrical Managers and Film Producers...," *NYDM*, 21 Jul 1915, 9:1 (see more at Billie Burke, Marc Klaw, and Joseph Brooks).

Ermelli, Claudio [actor] (*né* Ettore Foa, b.

Turin, Italy, 24 Jun 1892–29 Oct 1964 [72], Rome, Italy; cancer). AS, p. 367.

Ermolieff, Joseph N. [director/producer] (b. 1890–20 Feb 1962 [72?], Los Angeles CA). AS, p. 367. BHD2, p. 79.

Ermolova, Maria Nikolaevna [actress] (b. Moscow, Russia, 17 Feb 1853–9 Oct 1926 [73], Moscow, Russia). BhD2, p. 367.

Ernemann, Dr. Alexander [inventor] (b. Dresden, Germany, 1878–14 Oct 1956 [78?], Stuttgart, Germany). AS, p. 367.

Errol, Leon [stage/film actor] (*né* Errol Simms, b. Sydney, Australia, 3 Jul 1881–12 Oct 1951 [70], Los Angeles CA; heart attack). m. **Stella Chatelaine** (d. 1946). "Leon Errol Dies; Film Comedian, 70; R.K.O. Star 20 Years Played in Ziegfeld 'Follies,' 'Sally'—Noted for Lord Epping Role," *NYT,* 13 Oct 1951, 17:3; "Errol's $100,000 to Relatives," *NYT,* 21 Oct 1951, 58:5. "Leon Errol," *Variety,* 17 Oct 1951. AMD, p. 112. AS, p. 367. BHD1, p. 179. IFN, p. 97. Katz, p. 392 (began 1924). SD. Truitt, p. 103. "New Series of Two Reel Comedies for Reelcraft; Leon Errol One of Stars," *MPW,* 3 Jul 1920, 89. "First National Signs Errol, Noted Comedian, for 8 Pictures," *MPW,* 13 Jun 1925, 798. Ramon Romeo, "Reeling Down Broadway; Leon Errol in 'Little Cafe,'" *Paris and Hollywood Screen Secrets Magazine,* May 1927, 63 (made a hit in *The Lunatic at Large;* to film *The Little Cafe* at First Natioal's Burbank studios).

Erskine, Chester [actor/scenarist/director/producer] (*né* Charles Erskine, b. Hudson NY, 29 Nov 1905–7 Apr 1986 [80], Beverly Hills CA; pneumonia). m. Sally. "Chester Erskine Dies; Director and Producer," *NYT,* 15 Apr 1986, B8:6 (b. 1905; age 83). "Chester Erskine," *Variety,* 16 Apr 1986. AS, p. 367. BHD2, p. 79 (b. NY NY, 1903). SD.

Erskine, Wallace [actor] (b. England, 8 Aug 1862–6 Jan 1943 [80], Massapequa, LI NY). m. Margaret Bonney. "Wallace Erskine," *Variety,* 13 Jan 1943. AS, p. 367 (b. 1861). BHD, p. 162. IFN, p. 97. SD. Truitt, p. 103.

Erskine, Mrs. Wallace [actress] (*née* Margaret Bonney). m. **Erskine Wallace** (d. 1943). No data found. SD, p. 417.

Erte [costume designer] (*né* Romain de Tirkoff, b. St. Petersburg, Russia, 23 Nov 1892–21 Apr 1990 [97], Paris, France). AMD, p. 112. AS, p. 367. BHD2, p. 79. "Sign Famous Costume Designer," *MPW,* 7 Mar 1925, 90. "Erte at Work," *MPW,* 22 Aug 1925, 840.

Ertugrul, Mushin [director/producer] (b. Istanbul, Turkey, 1888). AS, p. 367.

Erwin, June [actress] (b. 1918–27 Dec 1965 [47?], Carmichael CA). AS, p. 367. BHD, p. 162. IFN, p. 97.

Erwin, Madge [actress] (d. 30 Jun 1967, Alameda Co. CA). BHD1, p. 179.

Erwin, Stuart Philip [actor] (b. Squaw Valley CA, 14 Feb 1902–21 Dec 1967 [65], Beverly Hills CA; heart attack). m. June Collyer. (Fox.) "Stuart Erwin, the Lovable Yokel of 115 Films and TV; Dies at 64; Actor with Hound-Dog Look Typecast for 30 Years as Amiable 'Mr. Average,'" *NYT,* 22 Dec 1967, 31:2 (b. 1903). "Stuart Erwin," *Variety,* 27 Dec 1967 (began 1928). AS, p. 367. BHD1, p. 179 (b. 1903). IFN, p. 97 (b. 1903). Katz, p. 393. Truitt, p. 103.

Erwing, Jack [title writer]. No data found. FDY, p. 443.

Esary, Howard [actor] (b. 1906?–17 Nov 1950 [44], Burbank CA; after surgery). "Howard Esary," *Variety,* 22 Nov 1950.

Escande, Maurice René [actor] (b. Paris, France, 14 Nov 1892–10 Feb 1973 [80], Paris, France; cancer). AS, p. 367.

Eschbrich, Julius [assistant director] (b. 1895?–29 Mar 1921 [25], Los Angeles CA; acute appendicitis). (FP-L.) "Julius Eschbrich," *Variety,* 8 Apr 1921, p. 43. AMD, p. 112 (Eschrich). "Studio Man Dies," *Variety,* 8 Apr 1921. "Obituary," *MPW,* 16 Apr 1921, 711.

Eschert, Arthur L. [actor]. No data found. AMD, p. 112. "Paramount's Handsomest Man," *MPW,* 15 Apr 1916, 452.

Escoffier, Paul [actor] (*né* Adolphe Jean-Marie Escoffier, b. Cahors, France, 30 Jun 1875–30 Jul 1941 [66], Paris, France). AS, p. 367 (d. 19 Jul). BHD1, p. 179. IFN, p. 97.

Esdale, Charles [actor] (b. 1873?–10 Jul 1937 [64], New York NY; complications of diseases). "Charles Esdale; Actor Had Appeared with Jeanne Eagels and Jane Cowl," *NYT,* 12 Jul 1937, 17:2. "Charles Esdale," *Variety,* 14 Jul 1937 (interred at Kensico). AS, p. 368. BHD, p. 162. IFN, p. 97.

Eslick, Roy [cinematographer]. No data found. FDY, p. 457.

Esmelton, Frederick [actor] (b. Melbourne, Australia, 22 Jun 1872–23 Oct 1933 [61], Los Angeles CA). (Fox.) AS, p. 368. BHD1, p. 180. IFN, p. 97. Truitt 1983, p. 224.

Esmond, Annie [actress] (b. Surrey, England, 27 Sep 1873–4 Jan 1945 [81]). BHD1, p. 180.

Esmond, H[arry] **V**[ernon] [actor/playwright] (b. London, England, 30 Nov 1869–17 Apr 1922 [52], Paris, France; heart disease). m. actress Eva Moore, 1891. (1st play: *One Summer's Day,* 1897.) "Henry V. Esmond," *Variety,* 21 Apr 1922, p. 3; 5 May 1922, p. 2 (age 53). BHD, p. 162. IFN, p. 97.

Esmond, Merceita [actress] (b. Philadelphia PA, 1869–22 Nov 1929 [60?], Brooklyn NY). m. **Harry S. Northrup** (d. 1936); Dr. Frank Farra Lyne. "Mercita Esmond," *Variety,* 4 Dec 1929. AS, p. 368. BHD, p. 162.

Espinosa, Edouard [actor] (b. London, England, 2 Feb 1872–23 Mar 1950 [78], Worthing, Sussex, England). BHD, p. 162.

Esser, Peter [actor] (b. Germany, 4 Apr 1886–23 Jun 1970 [84], Dusseldorf, Germany). AS, p. 368. BHD, p. 162. IFN, p. 97.

Essler, Fred [actor] (b. Vienna, Austria, 13 Feb 1895–17 Jan 1973 [77], Woodland Hills CA). AS, p. 368.

Estabrook, Edward T. [cinematographer] (b. 1893–24 Oct 1979 [86?], Los Angeles CA). BHD2, p. 80. FDY, p. 457.

Estabrook, Howard [stage/film actor/director/scenarist] (*né* Howard Bolles, b. Detroit MI, 11 Jul 1884–16 Jul 1978 [94], Woodland Hills CA; cancer). m. Margaret (d. 1975). (Kleine; World; Pathé; Metro; International; Paramount; Selznick-Select.) Eric Pace, "Howard Estabrook, Won Oscar for 'Cimarron' Screenplay, at 94," *NYT,* 26 Jul 1978, B2:3. "Howard Estabrook," *Variety,* 26 Jul 1978. AMD, p. 112. AS, p. 368. BHD, p. 162; BHD2, p. 80. FDY, p. 423. IFN, p. 97. Katz, p. 394. MSBB, p. 1046. SD. "Howard Estabrook," *MPW,* 14 Nov 1914, 912. "Howard Estabrook; Star of Kleine's 'Officer 666,'" *NYDM,* 2 Dec 1914, 26:4. "Estabrook for World; Will Be Seen in Film Adaptation of the Novel 'The Butterfly,'" *NYDM,* 6 Jan 1915, 28:1. "Estabrook Honored," *MPW,* 15 May 1915, 1078. "Gossip of the Studios," *NYDM,* 16 Jun 1915, 25:2 (while filming *Four Feathers* for Metro, Estabrook was thrown into a cell by an actor playing a jailer with such force "that the star lost a large part of the epidermal covering of his shin bone and knee cap, but not enough, says our informant, to prevent his filling his vaudeville engagements."). "Personal; Estabrook," *NYDM,* 25 Aug 1915, 24:4. "Editor's Letter Box," *NYDM,* 15 Sep 1915, 6:4 (date of birth given). "Howard Estabrook Signs with Arrow," *MPW,* 30 Oct 1915, 977. "Howard Estabrook with International," *MPW,* 13 May 1916, 1173. "Estabrook Popular with College Boys," *MPW,* 24 Jun 1916, 2244. "To Speak at Columbia," *MPW,* 9 Jun 1923, 461 (on Tuesdayt, 29 May 1923).

Estee, Adelyn [actress/singer] (b. 1870–3 Jun 1941 [71?], Los Angeles CA). AS, p. 368.

Estepanian, Henry [director/scenarist] (b. Tabriz, Iran, 1891–1959 [68?], Teheran, Iran). AS, p. 368.

Esway, Alexandre [director/producer/scenarist] (*né* Alexander Ezryesway, b. Budapest, Hungary, 20 Jan 1895–23 Aug 1947 [52], Saint-Tropez, France [extrait de décès no. 42/1947]). AS, p. 369. BHD2, p. 80 (b. Debrecen, Hungary, 1898).

Etchepare, Pierre Paul Lucien Salvat [actor] (b. Paris, France, 2 Oct 1891–20 Apr 1943 [51], Paris, France [extrait de décès no. SN/1943]). AS, p. 369.

Ethier, Alphonse [actor] (b. Virginia City NV, 10 Dec 1874–5 Jan 1943 [68], Los Angeles CA). "Alphonse Ethier," *Variety,* 13 Jan 1943. AS, p. 369 (d. 4 Jan). BHD1, p. 180. IFN, p. 97. Truitt, p. 103.

Etievant, Henri [actor/director] (b. Paris, France, 1870). AS, p. 369.

Etlinger, Karl [actor] (b. Frankfort, Germany, 22 Jan 1882–8 Apr 1946 [64], Berlin, Germany). AS, p. 369.

Etris, Robert [cinematographer/executive] (b. 1874?–11 Apr 1956 [82], Philadelphia PA). (Lubin.) "Robert Etris," *Variety,* 11 Apr 1956 ("He helped film *The Birth of a Nation,* parts of which were shot in Fairmount Park, Philly.").

Etting, Ruth [singer/actress] (b. David City NB, 23 Nov 1896–24 Sep 1978 [81], Colorado Springs CO). m. Martin Snyder; Myrl Alderman, 1938. "A Ziegfeld Girl," *NYT,* 6 Nov 1978, 56:4 (age 80?). "Ruth Etting Dies at 81; Actress-Singer Had Stormy Career in '30s," *Variety,* 27 Sep 1978. AS, p. 369. BHD1, p. 180. IFN, p. 97. Katz, p. 394.

Ettinger, Karl [actor] (Frankfurt, Germany, 22 Jan 1882–8 May 1946 [64]). BHD1, p. 180. IFN, p. 97.

Eugster, Al [animator]. No data found. (Pat Sullivan; Fleischer.) Graham Webb and G. Michael Dobbs, "In Memory of Al Eugster," *Animato!,* Spring 1997, 66–67.

Europe, James Reese [composer/musician] (b. Mobile AL, 1878–9 May 1919 [41?], Boston MA). "James Reese Europe," *Variety,* 16 May 1919, p. 17. BHD, p. 162.

Evans, Arthur R. [stage manager] (b. 1872?–Oct? 1916 [44], Watkins Glen NY). m.

Bertie E. Britton. "Arthur R. Evans," *Variety,* 6 Oct 1916. AS, p. 369 (d. 5 Sep 1916, Wathing Falls NY). SD.

Evans, Cecilia, "The Girl with the $100,000 Legs" [Sennett Bathing Beauty/actress] (b. Oxford KS, 7 May 1902–11 Nov 1960 [58], San Rafael CA). "Cecilia Evans [Mrs. Cecilia Graham]," *Variety,* 23 Nov 1960. AMD, p. 112. AS, p. 369. BHD, p. 162. IFN, p. 97. Truitt, p. 103. "Cecile Evans in Lead Role," *MPW,* 12 Dec 1925, 546.

Evans, Charles Evan [actor] (b. Rochester NY, 6 Sep 1856–16 Apr 1945 [88], Santa Monica CA). m. Helena Phillips. "Charles Evan Evans," *Variety,* 18 Apr 1945. AS, p. 369. BHD1, p. 180. IFN, p. 98.

Evans, Daniel [scenarist] (b. 1898–4 Aug 1934 [36?], Los Angeles CA; auto accident). AS, p. 369.

Evans, Edith [actress] (*née* Edith W. Snowden, b. 1894?–12 Oct 1962 [68], Morristown NJ). "Mrs. Edith W. Snowden," *Variety,* 17 Oct 1962. AS, p. 369 (d. Madison NJ). BHD, p. 163. IFN, p. 98. Truitt, p. 104.

Evans, Dame Edith Mary [actress] (b. London, England, 8 Feb 1888–14 Oct 1976 [88], Cranbrook, Kent, England). m. George (Guy) Booth, 9 Sep 1925 (d. 1935). *NYT,* 15 Oct 1976, I, 29:2. Joseph Collins, "Dame Edith Evans Is Dead at 88; A Legend of the EnglishTheater," *NYT,* 15 Oct 1976, 29:2. "Edith Evans," *Variety,* 20 Oct 1976. Sheridan Morley, *The Great Stage Stars* (New York: Facts on File, 1986), pp. 118–22. AS, p. 369. BHD1, p. 181. IFN, p. 98. Patrick Brock, "Dame Edith Evans," *CI,* 215 (May 1993), 38–39 (was in *A Welsh Singer,* Walton-on-Thames Studios, 1915, and *East Is East,* 1916).

Evans, Estelle [actress] (b. FL, 1 Oct 1906–20 Jul 1985 [78], New York NY). BHD1, p. 181.

Evans, Esther [actress] (b. 1863–7 Nov 1943 [70?], Santa Monica CA). BHD, p. 163.

Evans, Frank [actor]. No data found. (Biograph, 1908; K&E).

Evans, Frank [cinematographer]. No data found. FDY, p. 457.

Evans, Fred [actor] (b. 1840–31 Oct 1909 [69?], Bristol, England). BHD, p. 163. IFN, p. 98.

Evans, Fred (Pimple) [actor] (b. England, 1889–1951 [60?], England). AS, p. 370. BHD, p. 163.

Evans, Helen St. Clair [actress] (b. 1905–6 Jun 1927 [22?], Los Angeles CA). AS, p. 370. BHD, p. 163. IFN, p. 98.

Evans, Helena Phillips *see* **Phillips, Helena**

Evans, Herbert D. [actor] (b. London, England, 16 Apr 1882–10 Feb 1952 [69], San Gabriel CA). "Herbert Evans," *Variety,* 20 Feb 1952 (in films 30 years). AS, p. 370. BHD1, p. 181. IFN, p. 98. Truitt, p. 104.

Evans, Jack [actor] (b. NC, 5 Mar 1893–7 Mar 1950 [57], Los Angeles CA; heart attack). "Jack Evans," *Variety,* 15 Mar 1950 (d. 14 Mar 1950; "western actor and honorary mayor of Gower Gulch"). AS, p. 370. BHD1, p. 181. IFN, p. 98. Truitt, p. 104 (d. 14 Mar).

Evans, Joe [actor] (b. 1891–1967 [75?]). AS, p. 370. BHD, p. 163.

Evans, Lawrence [playwright/author] (d. 26 Apr 1925, Tucson AZ; tuberculosis). "Lawrence Evans," *Variety,* 29 Apr, pp. 44:5, 54:5, and 6 May 1925 (wrote *Someone in the House,* produced by George Tyler ca. 1915). AMD, p. 112. AS, p. 370. "Fox Strengthens Scenario Staff," *MPW,* 12 May 1917, 958. "Schulberg Signs Larry Evans," *MPW,* 18 Nov 1922, 240.

Evans, Madge [child stage/film actress] (*née* Margherita Evans, b. New York NY, 1 Jul 1909 [Birth Certificate Index No. 31952]–26 Apr 1981 [71], Oakland NJ). m. playwright Sidney Kingsley, 1939 (d. 20 Mar 1995). (World; FP-L.) Herbert Mitgang, "Madge Evans, Stage-Film Actress," *NYT,* 28 Apr 1981, B18:4. "Madge Evans, All-American Girl of Stage & Screen, Dies at 71," *Variety,* 29 Apr 1981. AMD, p. 112. AS, p. 370. BHD1, p. 181. FSS, p. 101. Katz, p. 395. MSBB, p. 1034. "Little Madge Evans in 'Alias Jimmy Valentine,'" *MPW,* 20 Mar 1915, 1751. "Madge Evans, Stamp Booster," *MPW,* 20 Apr 1918, 378. "Madge Evans Wins Honors," *MPW,* 8 Jun 1918, 1453. "Film Star Selling Hats," *MPW,* 28 Sep 1918, 1904. "Madge Evans in Natural Color Film," *MPW,* 15 Mar 1919, 1456. "Prizma Secures Miss Madge Evans as a Star for Multiple Reel Pictures in Natural Colors," *MPW,* 22 Nov 1919, 447. "Presenting a Grown-Up Madge; Madge Evans Comes Back to the Screen with Her Curls Pinned Up and Her Skirts Lengthened," *MW,* 25 Oct 1924, 12. Ruth Biery, "How Madge Evans Grew to Stardom," *Photoplay,* Dec 1931, 40–41, 122–24. "Madge Evans—The Little Girl Who Grew Up and Became Famous Again," *Movie Classic,* Nov 1931, 30–31 (photo layout). Jay Rubin, "Madge Evans," *CFC,* 55 (Summer, 1977), 7–9, 60.

Evans, Millicent [actress]. No data found. m. T[homas] Hayes Hunter, 4 Apr 1919, LA CA. AMD, p. 113. "Hunter-Evans," *MPW,* 26 Apr 1919, 519. "Director Hunter Marries Millicent Evans," *MPW,* 3 May 1919, 660.

Evans, Nelson [still photographer]. No data found. *Fl.* 1910's and early 1920's. P.M. Powell, "Doings at Los Angeles; Brevities," *MPW,* 7 Dec 1912, 969 (mentions a "Nelson Evans" as "head of American Feature Film Company"); *MPW,* 12 Apr 1913, 150 ("N.F. Evans"): these may not be the photographer. John Kobal, *Hollywood; The Years of Innocence* (New York: Abbeville Press, 1985), pp. 19 ff.

Evans, Netta [actress]. No data found. AMD, p. 113. "Netta Evans in Paramount Pictures," *MPW,* 13 Oct 1917, 224.

Evans, Robert [minstrel/actor] (d. 15 May 1919, Revere MA). "Robert Evans," *Variety,* 23 May 1919. AS, p. 370 (d. 19 May).

Evans, Thomas [executive]. No data found. AMD, p. 113. "Thomas Evans an Early Bird," *MPW,* 10 Mar 1917, 1544.

Evans, Wainwright [scenarist]. No data found. FDY, p. 423.

Evans, Will [actor] (*né* William Edward Evans, b. London, England, 29 May 1873–11 Apr 1931 [57], London, England). m. Ada Luxmore; (2) Evelyn Poole. "Will Evans," *Variety,* 29 Apr 1931. AS, p. 370 (d. 1981). BHD, p. 163. IFN, p. 98 (age 55). SD.

Evans, Will [driector] (b. 1878–8 Mar 1941 [63?], Epsom, England). BHD2, p. 80.

Evans, William A. [actor] (b. 1876-Sep 1937 [63?], Los Angeles CA). BHD, p. 163.

Evans, William Arthur [cameraman/actor] (b. Kent, England, 1860?–2 Jan 1940 [79], Englewood NJ). "William Arthur Evans," *Variety,* 10 Jan 1940. AMD, p. 113. AS, p. 370. "Pictures from China and Japan," *MPW,* 14 Sep 1912, 1076.

Evarts, Hal G[eorge] [scenarist] (*né* Harry George Evarts, b. Topeka KS, 24 Aug 1887–18 Oct 1934 [47] aboard the *Malolo;* buried at sea near Brazil). m. Sylvia Abraham (1890–1977), 1911. "Hal G. Evarts Dies; Novelist of West; Succumbs on Liner near Rio de Janeiro—Seeking Health After Severe Heart Attacks; Long Rancher and Guide; Authority on Hunting and Trapping—Writer of Many Articles, Short Stories and Novels [e.g., *The Cross Pull* and *Tumbleweeds*]," *NYT,* 19 Oct 1934, 23:1. BHD2, p. 80 (d. 23 Oct, Boston MA). Hal Evarts, Jr., *Skunk Ranch to Hollywood; The West of Author Hal Evarts* (Santa Barbara CA: Capra Press, 1989).

Evarts, L.V. [scenarist]. No data found. FDY, p. 423.

Evelyn, Fay [actrerss] (b. 1895–22 Jun 1947 [52?], Washington DC). BHD, p. 163.

Evelyn, Mildred [actress] (b. York, England, 26 Sep 1898–1989 [90?], England). BHD1, p. 181.

Evelynne, May [actress] (*née* Mollie McCarthy Tinker, b. 1855–3 Apr 1943 [87], Los Angeles CA). AS, p. 371. BHD, p. 163. IFN, p. 98.

Evennett, Wallace [actor] (b. London, England, 17 Dec 1887-Oct 1973 [85]). BHD, p. 163. IFN, p. 98.

Everest, Barbara [actress] (b. London, England, 8 Jun 1890–9 Feb 1968 [77], London, England). "Barbara Everest," *Variety,* 21 Feb 1968, p. 78. AS, p. 371. BHD1, p. 182. IFN, p. 98.

Everett, Charles Frohman (nephew of **Charles, Daniel** and **Gustave Frohman**) [stage actor] (b. 1903?). No data found. (Edison; Thanhouser; Kalem; Vitagraph; Essanay, Chicago.) AMD, p. 113. MSBB, p. 1023. "Young America's Star a Long Time on Stage," *MPW,* 13 Jul 1918, 224 (15 years old).

Everett, George [director]. No data found. AMD, p. 113. "Director Everett a Sculptor," *MPW,* 30 Oct 1920, 1243.

Evers, Arthur [actor]. No data found. AMD, p. 113. "Arthur Evers," *MPW,* 26 Dec 1914, 1844.

Evers, Ernest P. [actor] (b. Villa Ridge IL, 12 Sep 1874–22 Jul 1945 [70], Los Angeles CA). "Ernest P. Evers," *Variety,* 25 Jul 1945 (age 71; began ca. 1915). AS, p. 371. BHD, p. 163. IFN, p. 98. Truitt, p. 104.

Everton, Paul [actor] (b. New York NY, 19 Sep 1868–26 Feb 1948 [79], Woodland Hills CA; heart attack). "Paul Everton," *Variety,* 3 Mar 1948. AMD, p. 113. AS, p. 371 (d. Calabasas CA). BHD1, p. 182. IFN, p. 98. Truitt, p. 104. "'Elaine' Actor Injured," *NYDM,* 4 Aug 1915, 21:3 (while filming *The Romance of Elaine* at the Triphammer Gorge, "[t]he Pathe-Wharton actor fell over a cliff and suffered a painful injury to one of his legs. It was intended that he should fall at a place where there was only a six foot drop, but he accidentally picked out the wrong spot and fell twenty-five feet instead.") "'Elaine' Actor Injured," *MPW,* 14 Aug 1915, 1170. "World Pictures Announces 'Ginger' as a May Release," *MPW,* 29 Mar 1919, 1829.

Evesson, Isabelle [actress] (d. Stamford CT, 9 Aug 1914). BHD, p. 163.

Evison, Millicent [scenarist] (b. 1876–29 Jan 1970 [93?], Morristown NJ). BHD2, p. 80.

Evreinoff, Nicolas [director/writer] (b. Moscow, Russia, 13 Feb 1879–1953 [74?], France). AS, p. 371.

Evremont, David J. [actor] (b. Le Havre, France, 1890). AS, p. 371.

Ewald, O. [cinematographer]. No data found. FDY, p. 457.

Ewers, Hans Heinz [scenarist] (b. Dusseldorf, Germany, 3 Nov 1871–12 Jun 1943 [71]). BHD2, p. 80. FDY, p. 423. IFN, p. 98.

Ewing, Elinor [scenarist]. No data found. FDY, p. 423.

Eycke, Leon [still photographer] (b. 1899?–6 Feb 1926 [26], Los Angeles CA; of injuries from auto accident). (Ince; FBO.) "Leon Eycke," *Variety,* 10 Feb 1926. BHD2, p. 80.

Eysoldt, Gertrud Franziska Gabriele [stage/film actress/director] (b. Pirna, Germany, 11 Nov 1870–6 Jan 1955 [84], Ohlstadt, Germany). "Gertrud Eysoldt," *Variety,* 26 Jan 1955, p. 63 ("She reportedly was the first actress to portray 'Salome' in Germany..."). AS, p. 372 (b. 30 Nov). BHD, p. 182. IFN, p. 98.

Eysoldt, Peter [actor] (b. Berlin, Germany, 1 Oct 1910–4 Nov 1985 [75], Munich, Germany). BHD1, p. 606.

Eytinge, Pearl [actress] (d. 8 Mar 1914, Atlantic City NJ). m. Robert W. Yard. "Pearl Eytinge," *Variety,* 13 Mar 1914. AS, p. 372. SD.

Eyton, Alice (sister of **Charles F. Eyton**) [actress/scenarist] (b. New Zealand, 1875?–3 Nov 1929 [54], Pasadena CA; from burns when clothing caught fire). m. Robert Von Saxmer. "Alice Eyton," *Variety,* 6 Nov 1929. AS, p. 372. BHD2, p. 80. IFN, p. 98.

Eyton, Bessie [actress] (*née* Bessie Harrison, b. Santa Barbara CA, 5 Jul 1890–22 Jan 1965 [74], Thousand Oaks CA). m. (1) **Charles F. Eyton**—div. 1915 (d. 1941); (2) Clarke Brewer Coffey, 29 Sep 1916, Santa Barbara CA—div. 3 Jul 1923. (Pathé; Selig.) AMD, p. 113. AS, p. 372. BHD1, p. 606. BR, pp. 20–24. FSS, p. 102. "Lives of the Players; Bessie Eyton; Selig's Popular 'Wild Animal' Actress," *MPS,* 8 Aug 1913, 31. "Bessie Eyton," *MPW,* 3 Apr 1915, 79. "Bessie Eyton Visits New York," *MPW,* 24 Jun 1916, 2217. "Bessie Eyton," *MPW,* 17 Feb 1917, 1010. Bessie Eyton, "A Few Ideas," *MPW,* 21 Jul 1917, 394. "Bessie Eyton to Support Lockwood," *MPW,* 15 Jun 1918, 1586. Billy H. Doyle, "Lost Players," *CI,* 166 (Apr 1989), 20.

Eyton, Charles F. (brother of **Vera Doria** and **Alice Eyton**) [producer/executive] (b. Auckland, New Zealand, 24 Jun 1871–2 Jul 1941 [70], Los Angeles CA; pneumonia). m. **Bessie** Harrison—div. 1915 (d. 1965); **Kathlyn Williams** (d. 1960). "Charles F. Eyton, 70; ex-Film Executive; He Was General Manager for Paramount in Silent Era," *NYT,* 3 Jul 1941, 19:6. "Charles F. Eyton," *Variety,* 9 Jul 1941. AS, p. 372. BHD2, p. 80. IFN, p. 98 (d. 1 Jul).

Eywo, Hugh [cinematographer]. No data found. FDY, p. 457.

F

Faasen, William [actor] (b. 1897–15 Apr 1978 [80?]). BHD, p. 163.

Faber, Leslie [actor] (b. Newcastle-on-Tyne, England, 30 Aug 1879–5 Aug 1929 [49], London, England). "Leslie Faber," *Variety,* 21 Aug 1929, p. 59. AS, p. 373. BHD1, p. 182. IFN, p. 98.

Fabian, Maximilian [cinematographer] (b. Austria, 1 May 1891–30 Jun 1969 [78], Los Angeles CA). AMD, p. 113. BHD2, p. 80. FDY, p. 457. "Max Fabian Renews M-G-M Contract," *MPW,* 26 Dec 1925, 763.

Fables, William "Billy" [actor]. No data found. AMD, p. 113. "Gossip of the Studios," *NYDM,* 15 Jul 1914, 23:2 (he was "to take the part of the goat in the forthcoming Edison split-reel Buster Brown comedies." He had twenty-two years' experience at playing animals.). "Billy Fables with Edison," *MPW,* 18 Jul 1914, 437. "William 'Billy' Fables," *MPW,* 16 Jun 1917, 1792.

Fabre, Marcel [director]. No data found. JS, pp. 154–55 (in Italian silents from 1914).

Fábregas, Virginia (cousin of **Manuel Arbó**) [stage/film actress] (b. Yautepec, Morelos State, Mexico, 1870–17 Nov 1950 [80], Mexico City, Mexico). m. (1) Francesco Dardona. (Stage debut: 1892; *La Fruz Amarga,* MGM, 1931.) "Virginia Fabregas," *Variety,* 22 Nov 1950 ("made Spanish-language pictures in Hollywood in 1919 and in 1937–38"). IFN, p. 98. Waldman, p. 101 (b. Oacalco, Morales, Mexico).

Fabrèges, Fabienne [actress] (b. Paris, France). JS, p. 155 (in Italian silents from 1916).

Factor, Max (father of Max Factor, Jr.) [makeup artist] (b. Lodz, Poland, 1872–30 Aug 1938 [66?], Beverly Hills CA). m. (son, Max, 1904–1996). BHD2, p. 81.

Fadman, Edwin Miles [producer]. No data found. AMD, p. 113. "Fadman's New Company," *MPW,* 13 Mar 1926, 103. "Edwin Miles Fadman Off to Europe to Buy and Sell," *MPW,* 22 May 1926, 324.

Fagan, Allen (brother of **Ina Claire**) [actor] (b. Washington DC, 1890–17 Sep 1937 [47?], New York NY; heart attack). AS, . 374.

Fagan, Allan H. [actor/dialogue director] (b. 1890–17 Sep 1937 [47?], New York NY). BHD2, p. 81.

Fagan, Myron C. [scenarist] (b. 31 Oct 1887–12 May 1972 [84], Los Angeles Co. CA). BHD2, p. 81.

Fager, Karl Georg [director] (b. Helsinki, Finland, 3 Jun 1883–30 Jun 1962 [79], Helsinki, Finland). AS, p. 374.

Fahrney, Milton H. [actor/scenarist/producer/director] (b. Dayton OH, 24 Jun 1872–26 Mar 1941 [68], Culver City CA). (Nestor.) m. **Alexandra Phillips**, 12 Jan 1911 (d. 1936). "Milton H. Fahrney," *NYT,* 27 Mar 1941, 23:4. "Milton H. Fahrney," *Variety,* 2 Apr 1941. AMD, p. 113. AS, p. 374. BHD1, p. 183; BHD2, p. 81. IFN, p. 98. SD. Spehr, p. 130 (b. 1871). Truitt, p. 105. "Milton H. Fahrney," *MPW,* 2 Mar 1912, 786. "Horsley Adds to His Forces," *MPW,* 8 Aug 1914, 821. "Milton H. Fahrney," *MPW,* 19 Sep 1914, 1618. "Horsley Renews Contract with Fahrney," *MPW,* 14 Apr 1917, 246.

Fair, Elinor [actress: Wampas Star, 1924] (b. Richmond VA, 21 Dec 1903–26 Apr 1957 [53], Seattle WA). m. **William Boyd**, Santa Ana CA (d. 1972). AMD, p. 113. AS, p. 374. BHD1, p. 183 (b. 1902). FFF, p. 201. IFN, p. 99. MH, p. 109. Truitt 1983, p. 228. "William Fox Engages Two Bright Youngsters," *MPW,* 15 Feb 1919, 887 (17 years old). "Ray and Fair," *MPW,* 19 Jul 1919, 360. "Elinor Fair," *MPW,* 21 Nov 1925, 234. "Elinor Fair Signed by DeMille Under Big Contract," *MPW,* 27 Mar 1926, 258. Mary B. Chapman, "All's Fair in Love; How Elinor Fair Met and Married Bill Boyd," *MPC,* Jun 1926, 56–57, 78 ("We've been married two months, and I still think of Bill as my 'boy friend.' Isn't that wonderful?"). Paul Paige, "Close-Ups and Fade-Outs," *Paris and Hollywood,* Oct 1926, 92 ("...a Filipino formerly in her employ attempted to stab her. William Boyd, her husband, and Jimmie Adams, another picture player, both nurse slight cuts which they received in overpowering the Filipino, who is charged with having signed Boyd's name to a number of checks.").

Fair, Joyce [actress/playwright/politician] (*née* Ann Clare Boothe, b. New York NY, 10 Apr 1903–9 Oct 1987 [84], Washington DC; cancer). m. (1) George Tuttle Brokaw, 1923–29; (2) Henry R. Luce, 1935. Stephen C. Shadegg, *Clare Boothe Luce: A Biography* (NY: Simon & Schuster, 1970). Wilfred Sheed, *Clare Boothe Luce* (NY: Dutton, 1982). "Clare Booth Luce, Playwright and Politician, Succumbs at 84," *Variety,* 14 Oct 1987 (elected to the House of Representatives, Republican-CT, 1943). AMD, p. 113. BHD1, p. 607. "Joyce Fair with Edison," *MPW,* 8 Aug 1914, 840. "Joyce Fair Joins Essanay," *MPW,* 25 Mar 1916, 2014. "Joyce Fair," *MPW,* 8 Jul 1916, 241. Do not confuse with actress Clair Luce (1903–1989). *See* Gay Pauley, "Actress, Writer—and Confusion; There's Luce and Luce, But Only One Is ClaIre!," *NY World-Telegram and The Sun,* 15 May 1959, p. 18:1.

Fair, Justin [publicist]. No data found. AMD, p. 113. "Justin Fair with Pathé," *MPW,* 18 May 1918, 973.

Fair, Virginia [actress] (b. Comstock TX, 23 Aug 1899–5 Sep 1948 [49], Los Angeles CA). AS, p. 374 (d. 8 Sep). BHD, p. 163. IFN, p. 99.

Fairbanks, Douglas Elton, **Jr.** (son of **Douglas Fairbanks** and actress Anna Beth Sully) [film/stage/TV actor/title writer/producer] (b. New York NY, 9 Dec 1909 [Birth Certificate Index No. 60746]–7 May 2000 [90], Mount Sinai Medical Center, New York NY). m. (1) **Joan Crawford**, 3 Jun 1929–33; (2) Mary Lee Epping (Mrs. Huntington Hartford), 22 Apr 1939 (d. 1988; 3 daughters, Daphne, Victoria and Melissa); (3) Vera Shelton, 1991. *The Salad Days* (NY: Doubleday, 1988) (includes filmography, 1923–41); *A Hell* *of a War* (St. Martin's Press, 1993). "Douglas Fairbanks Jr., Film Star, TV Producer and Good-Will Ambassador, Dies at 90," *NYT,* 8 May 2000, B7 ("He said his father had given his mother $500,000 in a divorce settlement, and she spent nearly all of it within five years."). Adam Bernstein, "Douglas Fairbanks Jr.; Hollywood leading man, producer, war hero, socialite," *PP-G,* 8 May 2000, C-4:1 ("In 1923, he made his movie debut in the comedy *Stephen Steps Out.* But Mr. Fairbanks, who once said his father 'had no more paternal feelings than a tiger in the jungle for his cub,' broke a $2,000 a week film contract that year after learning he got it because of his father's name."). "Douglas Fairbanks, Jr.," *Variety,* 15 May 2000, 77:3. (Film debut: *American Aristocracy,* 1916; major film debut: *Stephen Steps Out,* 1923; final film: *Ghost Story,* 1981; stage debut: *Young Woodley,* 1927, LA CA.) AMD, p. 113. AS, p. 374. EK, pp. 399–400. FFF, p. 243. "'Doug' Jr., to Be Starred," *MPW,* 2 Jun 1923, 376. "Young 'Doug' Given a Hearty Reception," *MPW,* 7 Jul 1923, 90. "Father Praises Doug, Jr.'s Work in First Picture," *MPW,* 24 Nov 1923, 414. "Doug, Jr., with Famous Players-Lasky," *MPW,* 11 Oct 1924, 499. Helen Carlisle, "Why Douglas Fairbanks Junior Wants to Change His Name," *MW,* V, 12 Sep 1925, 10–11. "Young Fairbanks in F.B.O. Film," *MPW,* 20 Aug 1927, 529. David A. Balch, "Just Like His Dad!; Douglas Fairbanks, Junior, who is a new addition to the ranks of screen stars, has same engaging charm that made his father popular," *MW,* 22 Dec 1927, 29. Ruth Biery, "For the Love of Joan; Douglas Fairbanks, Jr., Owes All His Success to the Girl He Calls Billie Crawford," *MPC,* Feb 1929, 37, 76 ("It is not easy to live up to anyone like Billie Joan Crawford. She is pretty big herself in this racket."). Elisabeth Goldbeck, "Swopell; Dodo and Billy Play Just the Cutest Games Together," *MPC,* Jul 1929, 55, 79. Jay Rubin, "Douglas Fairbanks, Jr.," *CFC,* 49 (Winter, 1975), 4 *et passim.* John Gruen, "Douglas Fairbanks Jr. Is Turning 80, Going Like 60," *NYT,* 12 Mar 1989, 19. Eric Niderost, "The Dashing Douglas Fairbanks, Jr.: An Interview," *CI,* 207 (Sep 1992), 10, 12, 14. Chapter 9, "Douglas Fairbanks, Jr.," *BS,* pp. 125–39 (includes filmography). Geraldine Hawkins, "Douglas Fairbanks, Jr. [an interview]," *CI,* 300 (Jun 2000), pp. 64–69. Cathie Christie, "Douglas Fairbanks, Jr.: A Fitting Farewell, December 9, 1909-May 7, 2000," *CI,* 301 (Jul 2000), 15–16 (a service was held at the Hollywood Forever Cemetery on 24 May 2000, attended by Mickey Rooney, Mary Brian [at age 91], Mary Carlisle, Ann Rutherford, Betty Lasky, Buddy Ebsen, *et al.*).

Fairbanks, Douglas, Sr. (father of **Douglas Fairbanks, Jr.**; brother of **John** and **Robert P. Fairbanks**; uncle of **Florence Faire**) [stage/film actor/producer/director/scenarist] (*né* Douglas Elton Thomas Ullman, b. Denver CO, 23 May 1883–12 Dec 1939 [56], Santa Monica CA). m. actress Anna Beth Sully, 1907; **Mary Pickford**, 28 Mar 1920, LA CA (d. 1979); Sylvia Ashley. (Triangle-Fine Arts; Artcraft.) "Douglas Fairbanks Dies in His Sleep; Stage and Screen Actor Is Victim of a Sudden Heart Attack at Santa Monica; Saw Football Saturday; Mary Pickford, Lasky, James Roosevelt and Goldwyn Pay Tribute to Famous Star," *NYT,* 13 Dec 1939, 29:8; "Fairbanks a Star of Silent Movies; Most Spectacular Actor of Era Before Talking Films Noted for Acrobatics; A Glittering Personality; Ranked with Mary Pickford, Former Wife, and Charlie Chaplin in Public Eye," 30:1. "Douglas Fairbanks Dies in His Sleep Suddenly on Coast at 55," *Variety,* 13 Dec 1939. AS, p. 374. BHD1, p. 183; BHD2, p. 81. FFF, p. 78 (b. 1894). FSFM, p. 177 (b. 1884). FSS, p. 102. HCH, p. 31. IFN, p. 99. Lowrey, p. 50 (b. 1884). MH, p. 109 (b. 1884). MSBB, p. 1024. Anthony Slide, ed., *Before, In and After Hollywood; The Autobiography of Joseph E. Henabery* (Lanham MD: Scarecrow Press, 1997), pp. xi (Henabery left Fairbanks "when the star conducted a secret liaison with Mary Pickford before his divorce."). Spehr, p. 130. Truitt, p. 105. WWS, p. 86. "Douglas Fairbanks in Fine Arts Pictures," *MPW,* 2 Oct 1915, 86. "Douglas Fairbanks in Comedy," *MPW,* 23 Oct 1915, 598. "Fairbanks Will Live in California," *MPW,* 22 Jan 1916, 571. "Douglas Fairbanks the Irrepressible," *MPW,* 22 Apr 1916, 624. "Douglas Fairbanks in New York," *MPW,* 24 Jun 1916, 2213. Hector Ames, "Always Up Against It; Douglas Fairbanks' Rapid Road to Fame Is Beset with Black Eyes and Mangled Wardrobe," *MPC,* Jul 1916, 18–19, 64. "Fairbanks and Chaplin Do a Turn Together," *MPW,* 9 Dec 1916, 1485–86. "Douglas Fairbanks Bids Goodbye to California," *MPW,* 6 Jan 1917, 85. "Fairbanks Retires from Triangle," *MPW,* 27 Jan 1917, 537. "Douglas Fairbanks, Sr.," *MPW,* 3 Feb 1917, 691. "Douglas Fairbanks Signs with Artcraft," *MPW,* 24 Feb 1917, 1166. "Majestic Sues Fairbanks," *MPW,* 3 Mar 1917, 1334. "Fairbanks Wins Injunction Suit," *MPW,* 10 Mar 1917, 1538. "Pickford and Fairbanks Most Popular," *MPW,* 10 Mar 1917, 1558. "Douglas Fairbanks, Sr.," *MPW,* 26 May 1917, 1268. "Fairbanks Using Stage Methods," *MPW,* 26 May 1917, 1284. "Douglas Fairbanks Celebrates Birthday," *MPW,* 9 Jun 1917, 1619. Douglas Fairbanks, "The Development of the Screen," *MPW,* 21 Jul 1917, 375–76. "Fairbanks Is Called into Court," *MPW,* 27 Apr 1918, 545. "Fire at Fairbanks Studio," *MPW,* 27 Jul 1918, 534 (on 4 Jul 1918). "Fairbanks Writes Another Book," *MPW,* 2 Nov 1918, 607 (*Making Life Worth While*). "United Artists Association Formed," *MPW,* 25 Jan 1919, 455. "Star Combination Was Unexpected," *MPW,* 1 Feb 1919, 619. "Douglas Fairbanks Opens New Studio at Hollywood," *MPW,* 21 Jun 1919, 1785. "Douglas Fairbanks; The Man Who Romps and Laughs Through Life," *The Picture Show,* No. 11, 12 Jul 1919, 14–15. "Pickford-Fairbanks Wedding Celebrated in Los Angeles," *MPW,* 10 Apr 1920, 214. "Thousands Greet Mary and Doug on Arrival in England," *MPW,* 3 Jul 1920, 72. "Fairbanks Injuries Will Not Delay His Next Production," *MPW,* 26 Feb 1921, 1085. "Novel Copyright Suit Involves Fairbanks," *MPW,* 10 Sep 1921, 156. "No Alliance Between United Artists and the First National," *MPW,* 8 Oct 1921, 654. "'No man knows the strain I was under in creating and acting *Robin Hood,*' Says Douglas Fairbanks," *MW,* 28 Oct 1922, 9. Willis Goldbeck, "Who Are the Movie Millionaires?," *Classic,* Sep 1922, 32–34, 76 (the rich include the Talmadge sisters, Doug and Mary, Chaplin, William Farnum, Alla Nazimova, Rex Ingram, Adolph Zukor, Jesse Lasky, DeMille, and Charles Ray). "Lips of Players Read from Screen," *MPW,* 13 Jan 1923, 166. "Fairbanks Wins Suit," *MPW,* 14 Jul 1923, 130. "Court Decides Against Re-Editing of Old Douglas Fairbanks Pictures," *MPW,* 17 Nov 1923, 295. "Mary and Doug, New York Visitors, Hope for End of Internal Discord," *MPW,* 1 Mar 1924, 31. Grace Kingsley, "How 'The Thief of Bagdad' Was Made," *MW,* 29 Mar 1924, 22–23, 40. "Fairbanks Honored," *MPW,* 12 Apr 1924, 539. "Douglas and Mary Unknown as They Try to See Danish King," *NYT,* 8 May 1924, 21:2 (Douglas's press agent called a Danish newspaper to arrange an audience; an editor called the King's Chamberlain, who asked who these people were. "Learning their vocations and nationality, the Chamberlain replied that 'American citizens must apply for an audience through the American Minister.'"). Hubert V. Coryell, "How Doug Gets Away with Murder," *MW,* 6 Jun 1925, 7–8, 45. Hubert V. Coryell, "Doug; The Only Man Who Can Do Doug's Stunts or Produce Doug's Pictures," *MW,* 13 Jun 1925, 22–23, 45. "Fairbanks Leads Taxpayers with a Check for $182,190," *MPW,* 12 Sep 1925, 142. Gladys Hall and Adele Whitely Fletcher, "We Interview Mary and Doug," *Pictures,* Jul 1926, 31–32, 76, 78–80. "(John) Fairbanks Passes On," *MPW,* 29 Nov 1926, 4. "Douglas Fairbanks, Sr.," *MPW,* 2 May 1927, 794. "Solona Beach 'Pickfair' Site," *MPW,* 24 Dec 1927, 23. Dorothy Manners, "He'd Like to Be a Bum; But Mr. Fairbanks the Elder Keeps on Working with *Dougged* Determination," *MPC,* Nov 1928, 21, 75. Ruth Biery, "Hollywood Sob-Stories; Douglas Fairbanks, Doug, Jr.'s Father," *MPC,* Mar 1930, 29, 96. George Katchmer, "Remembering the Great Silents," *CI,* 245 (Nov 1995), 43.

Fairbanks, Eleanor [actress]. No data found. AMD, p. 115. "Eleanor Fairbanks," *MPW,* 3 Jul 1915, 69. "Miss Eleanor Fairbanks Goes with Gaumont," *MPW,* 13 Nov 1915, 1330.

Fairbanks, Flobelle (daughter of **John Fairbanks**) [actress] (aka Florence Fair, b. Hollywood CA, 1908?–5 Jan 1969 [60], News York NY; heart attack). AS, p. 375. BHD, p. 164. IFN, p. 99.

Fairbanks, Fred T. [actor] (b. 1871–15 May 1927 [55?], Coney Island NY). BHD, p. 164. IFN, p. 99.

Fairbanks, Jerry [cinematographer/producer] (b. San Francisco CA, 1 Nov 1904–21 Jun 1995 [90], Santa Barbara CA). AS, p. 375. BHD2, p. 81. FDY, p. 457.

Fairbanks, John (brother of **Robert P.** and **Douglas Fairbanks, Sr.**; uncle of **Douglas Fairbanks, Jr.**, and **Florence Faire**) [executive] (b. 1874?–20 Nov 1926 [52], Beverly Hills CA; paralysis). "John Fairbanks," *Variety,* 24 Nov 1926, 56:4 (age 23; interred at Denver CO; father of Flobelle, 18, and Mary, 14. States that John was the brother of Doug and William.). AMD, p. 115. BHD2, p. 81 (b. 1903; d. 10 Nov). "Fairbanks to Make a 'Pep' Film," *MPW,* 27 Jul 1918, 561. "Obituary," *MPW,* 29 Nov 1926, 4.

Fairbanks, Madeleine (twin sister of **Marion Fairbanks**) [actress] (b. New York NY, 15 Nov 1900–26 Jan 1989 [88], New York NY). (Madeleine Sherman). "Madeleine Fairbanks Sherman," *Variety,* 12 Apr 1989 (age 82). AMD, p. 115. AS, p. 375. BHD1, p. 183 (b. 1906). "Madeline Fairbanks," *MPW,* 20 May 1916, 1338. "Twins Engaged," *MPW,* 20 Aug 1921, 814.

Fairbanks, Marion (twin sister of **Madeleine Fairbanks**) [actress] (b. New York NY, 15 Nov 1900–20 Sep 1973 [73], New York NY). AMD, p. 115. AS, p. 375. BHD1, p. 183 (b. 1906). "Marion Fairbanks," *MPW,* 20 May 1916, 1338. "Twins Engaged," *MPW,* 20 Aug 1921, 814.

Fairbanks, Robert P. (brother of **John** and **Douglas Fairbanks, Sr.**; uncle of **Douglas Fairbanks, Jr.**) [actor] (b. 1880?–22 Feb 1948 [67], Los Angeles CA). "Robert P. Fairbanks," *Variety,* 25 Feb 1948. AS, p. 375 (d. 23 Feb).

Fairbanks, William [actor] (aka Carl Ullman [from Douglas Fairbanks's real name], b. St.

Louis MO, 24 May 1889–1 Apr 1945 [55], Los Angeles CA; lobar pneumonia). (Triangle; MGM; Columbia.) AMD, p. 115. AS, p. 375 (b. 1894). BHD, p. 164. IFN, p. 99. "September Is Set as Arrow Month, Sign William Fairbanks and Lyons," *MPW,* 19 Aug 1922, 585. "Pauline Garon Signs," *MPW,* 9 May 1925, 190. "Sax Pictures to Feature William Fairbanks," *MPW,* 2 Jan 1926, 72. Edgar M. Wyatt, "The Naming of William Fairbanks," *CI,* 221 (Nov 1993), C18, C19 (includes filmography).

Fairbrother, Sydney [actress] (*née* Sydney Parselle Cowell [or Tapping], b. London, England, 31 Jul 1872–3 Jan 1941 [68], London, England). m. (1) Percy Sydney Buckler; (2) Trevor Lowe (d. 1910). "Sydney Fairbrother," *Variety,* 29 Jan 1941 ("She had also appeared in many films."). AS, p. 375. BHD1, p. 183. IFN, p. 99 (b. 1894). SD. Truitt, p. 105.

Fairchild, Dorothy [actress]. No data found. (World Pictures.) Spehr, p. 130.

Fairchild, Madeline [actress] (b. CA). AMD, p. 115. WWS, p. 319. "Declaring Intention to Specialize in Heavy Roles, Miss Fairchild Tells Why," *MPW,* 28 Aug 1920, 1197.

Fairchild, Roy [actor] (b. 1872?–20 Apr 1918 [46], OH; on train to Columbus). m. Dallas Tyler (d. 1953). "Roy Fairchild," *Variety,* 10 May 1918. AS, p. 375 (d. Columbus OH, 30 Apr). BHD, p. 164. SD.

Faire, Florence (niece of **Douglas** and **John Fairbanks**) [actress] (*née* Florence Belle Fairbanks). No data found. AMD, p. 115. "Doug's Niece Signed," *MPW,* 2 Oct 1926, 4.

Faire, Virginia Brown [actress: Wampas Star, 1923] (*née* Virginia La Buna, b. Brooklyn NY, 26 Jun 1904–30 Jun 1980 [76], Laguna Beach CA). m. **Howard B. Worne** (d. 1933); Dick Durham; Jack Daugherty; (3) William Bayer. "Virginia Brown Faire, 75, Actress Starred in 1922 'Monte Cristo,'" *NYT,* 11 Jul 1980, A15:6. "Virginia Brown Faire," *Variety,* 16 Jul 1980. AMD, p. 115. AS, p. 375. BHD1, p. 183 (d. 1 Jul). BR, pp. 137–41. FSS, p. 104. MH, p. 109. SD. Truitt, p. 105. WWS, p. 212. "Virginia Browne Faire Wins Heroine Role in Pathé's Kipling Picture After Tests," *MPW,* 26 Mar 1921, 366. "Two Columbia Stars Staged Surprise Weddings Last Week," *MPW,* 19 Feb 1927, 568. Buck Rainey, "Virginia Brown Faire; The Rolls Royce of Poverty Row," *CI,* 142 (Apr 1987), 13–16 (d. 1976). "Clippings," *CI,* 143 (May 1987), 4.

Fairfax, James [actor] (b. England, b. 10 Aug 1896–8 May 1961 [64], Papeete, Tahiti; heart attack). m. Jessie C. Adams (widow). "James Fairfax," *Variety,* 17 May 1961. AS, p. 375 (d. 7 May). IFN, p. 99 (age 63).

Fairfax, Lance [actor] (b. Wellington, New Zealand, Apr 1899–Jan 1974 [74?]). BHD1, p. 183.

Fairfax, Lettice [actress] (b. 26 Mar 1876–25 Dec 1948 [72]). BHD, p. 164.

Fairfax, Marion [playwright/scenarist/director] (*née* Marion Neiswanger, b. Richmond VA, 24 Oct 1875–2 Oct 1970 [94], Los Angeles CA). m. **Tully Marshall** (d. 1943). AMD, p. 115. AS, p. 375. BHD2, p. 81. FDY, p. 423. IFN, p. 99. Lowrey, p. 52. 1921 Directory, p. 286. Slide, *Early Women Directors,* p. 113. "Add to Lasky Staff; Marion Fairfax Latest Addition to Scenario Department at the Coast," *NYDM,* 2 Jun 1915, 21:3 (wrote *The Builders,* 1907; *The Chaperone; The Talker*). "Marshall Neilan Signs Marion Fairfax," *MPW,* 22 Nov 1919, 434. "Marion Fairfax Will Write Scripts of Next Four Neilan Pictures Under New Contract," *MPW,* 16 Oct 1920, 968. "Marion Fairfax Forms Production Unit; First Offering to Be 'The Lying Truth,'" *MPW,* 23 Apr 1921, 847. "Marion Fairfax Has Decided to Direct Personally Her Own Films," *MPW,* 30 Apr 1921, 982. "Metro Engages Marion Fairfax," *MPW,* 22 Jul 1922, 282. "Marion Fairfax Forms Own Producing Company [Marion Fairfax Productions]," *MPS,* 13 May 1921, 21 (first production was to be *The Lying Truth,* with Pat O'Malley, Marjoie Daw and Tully Marshall; co-directed by Fairfax and Hugh Mcclung; photography by Rene Guissart). "Increases Writing Staff," *MPW,* 8 Sep 1923, 130.

Fairman, Austin (father of Churton Fairman) [actor] (b. London, England, 4 Mar 1892–26 Mar 1964 [72], Dedham MA). m. **Hilda Moore** (d. 1929; son Austin Churton, 15 Nov 1924–24 Apr 1997). AS, p. 375.

Fais, Charles C. [director] (b. 1877–17 Aug 1945 [68?], Los Angeles CA). AS, p. 375.

Faivre, Paul [actor] (*né* Henri Paul Faivre, b. Belfort, France, 3 Mar 1886 [extrait de naissance no. 117]–5 Mar 1973 [87], Paris, France). AS, p. 375.

Falconetti, Renée Jeanne (mother of Gérard Falconetti) [stage/film actress] (b. Pantin, France, 21 Jul 1892–12 Dec 1946 [54], Buenos Aires, Argentina). m. (son, Gérard, 1949–1984). Hélène Falconetti, *Falconetti* (Paris: Les Editions du Cerf, 1987). "Renee Falconetti," *Variety,* 15 Jan 1947. AS, p. 376. BHD, p. 164 (b. Sermano, Corsica). IFN, p. 99 (1893–1944). Truitt 1983, p. 229. The NYPL holds a box of articles and correspondence from 1962 collected by William Boroson on Falconetti's career and identity (call #8-MWEZ); he attempts to prove that Renée and Marie Falconetti were the same person.

Falconi, Armando [actor] (b. Rome, Italy, 10 Jul 1871–4 Sep 1954 [83], Milan, Italy). m. **Tina Di Lorenzo**, 1901 (d. 1930; son, scenarist/director Dino Falconi, b. Livorno, Italy, 18 Sep 1902). AS, p. 376. JS, p. 156 (in Italian silents from 1915).

Falena, Ugo [director] (b. Rome, Italy, 25 Apr 1875–20 Sep 1931 [56], Rome, Italy). AS, p. 376. BHD2, p. 81. JS, p. 156 (in Italian silents from 1909).

Falk, Norbert [scenarist]. No data found. FDY, p. 423.

Falk, Norman [scenarist]. No data found. FDY, p. 423.

Falkenstein, Julius [actor] (b. Berlin, Germany, 25 Feb 1879–9 Dec 1933 [54], Berlin, Germany). AS, p. 376. BHD1, p. 183. IFN, p. 99.

Faller, Ray [cinematographer]. No data found. FDY, p. 457.

Fallon, Charles [actor/director/producer] (*né* Charles Ludovic van der Belen, b. Antwerp, Belgium, 6 Mar 1875–12 Mar 1936 [61], Los Angeles CA). AS, p. 376. BHD2, p. 81.

Fallon, Thomas F. [actor] (b. New York NY, 8 Sep 1855). (FP-L; Biograph; Edison; Universal; Crystal; Rex.) AS, p. 376.

Fanck, Arnold [scenarist/director] (Frankenthal, Germany, 6 Mar 1889–27 Sep 1974 [85]. Freiburg, Germany; cancer). AS, p. 376 (d. 28 Sep). BHD2, p. 81. FDY, p. 423. IFN, 99.

Fang, Charles A. [actor]. No data found. AMD, p. 116. "Chinese Actor in 'The Jury of Fate,'" *MPW,* 21 Jul 1917, 486. "Scrantonia Photoplay Corporation Making Comedies," *MPW,* 30 Mar 1918, 1840.

Fanning, Frank B. [actor] (b. Los Angeles CA, 25 Dec 1879–1 Mar 1934 [54], Los Angeles CA). "Frank B. Fanning," *Variety,* 5 Mar 1934 (d. 3 Mar; "He also played minor parts on the screen."). AS, p. 376 (d. 3 Mar). BHD1, p. 183. IFN, p. 99. Truitt, p. 105 (d. 3 Mar).

Fanning, George Francis [actor] (b. St. Joseph MO, 6 Sep 1885–8 Jan 1946 [60], Los Angeles CA). BHD1, p. 184.

Fanning, Katherine [scenarist]. No data found. FDY, p. 423.

Fantis, Enrica [actress] (b. Turin, Italy, 21 Sep 1906). JS, p. 157 (in Italian silents from 1926).

Faralla, Dario Lucien [producer] (b. Italy, 19 Jul 1886–10 Jun 1944 [57], Los Angeles CA). AS, p. 377 (d. 10 Jun). BHD2, p. 81.

Farebrother, Violet [actress] (b. Grimsby, Lincolnshire, England, 22 Aug 1888–27 Sep 1969 [81], Eastbourne, Sussex, England). AS, p. 376. BHD1, p. 184. IFN, p. 99.

Farfariello [actor] (*né* Eduardo Migliaccio, b. Salerno, Italy, 1881–28 Mar 1946 [65?], New York NY). AS, p. 377.

Farina [actor] (*né* Allen Clayton Hoskins, Jr., b. Chelsea [Boston] MA, 9 Aug 1920–26 Jul 1980 [59], Oakland CA). "Allen (Farina) Hoskins," *Variety,* 30 Jul 1980. AMD, p. 171. AS, p. 377. BHD1, p. 269 (Allen "Farina" Hoskins). "Long Term Contract for 'Farina,'" *MPW,* 6 Oct 1923, 515. "Song Dedicated to Farina," *MPW,* 3 Jul 1926, 42 (from Harold Lloyd). "Ask the Answer Man," *Photoplay,* Dec 1931, 112.

Farjeon, Herbert V. [actor/dialogue director] (b. San Francisco CA, 27 Oct 1879–3 Nov 1972 [93], San Diego Co. CA). AS, p. 377. BHD1, p. 184; BHD2, p. 81 (b. 1883). IFN, p. 99.

Farkas, Marae [actress] (b. Hungary). m. **Alexander Korda**, 1919–29.

Farley, Dorothea "Dot" [actress] (b. Chicago IL, 6 Feb 1881–21 May 1971 [90], Woodland Hills CA). (Essanay; American; St. Louis; Keystone; Fox; Sunshine; Century; Sennett; Pathé; Manhattan; RKO; Universal.) AMD, p. 116. AS, p. 378. BHD1, p. 184. IFN, p. 99. Billy H. Doyle, "Lost Players," *CI,* 152 (Feb 1988), C12. "News Notes," *MPW,* 29 Mar 1913, 1323 (Farley resigned from Keystone to join the St. Louis Motion Picture Co. at Albuquerque NM). "Big Picture from Albuquerque Company," *MPW,* 30 May 1914, 1275. "Dot Farley to Direct," *MPW,* 3 Sep 1921, 50. George Katchmer, "Remembering the Great Silents," *CI,* 223 (Jan 1994), 47:3 (d. Pasadena CA).

Farley, James Lee [actor] (b. Waldron AR, 8 Jan 1882–12 Oct 1947 [65], in a sanitarium in Pacoima CA; cancer). (De Mille.) "James Lee Farley," *Variety,* 22 Oct 1947. AS, p. 378. BHD1, p. 184. IFN, p. 99 (b. TX). Truitt, p. 105. George A. Katchmer, "Forgotten Cowboys and Cowgirls—Part X," *CI,* 182 (Aug 1990), 38–39.

Farley, [Francis] Morgan [actor] (*né* Francis Morgan, b. Mamaroneck NY, 3 Oct 1898–11 Oct 1988 [90], San Pedro CA). AS, p. 378. BHD1, p. 184. NNAT. SD, p. 428.

Farnam, Dorothy [scenarist]. No data found. FDY, p. 423.

Farnham, Joseph W[hite] [scenarist/publicist/title writer/producer] (aka Gordon Trent, b. New York NY, 1884?–2 Jun 1931 [47], Beverly Hills CA; heart attack). m. Rose Alma LeCourt, 1914 (d. 1922). (All-Star Picture Corp.; Metro.) "Joseph

W. Farnham," *Variety,* 9 Jun 1931. AMD, p. 116. AS, p. 378. BHD2, p. 81 (d. 3 Jun). FDY, p. 443. F.J. Beecroft, "Publicity Men I Have Met...," *NYDM,* 14 Jan 1914, 48 (*see* Beecroft, Chester for full citation). "On the Battlefields of France," *MPW,* 1 May 1915, 718. "Joseph White Farnham," *MPW,* 2 Oct 1915, 55. "Joe Farnham Marries," *MPW,* 15 Jul 1916, 442 (announced two years after marriage). "Joe Farnham with Sherrill," *MPW,* 17 Feb 1917, 1028. "Farnham President of Screen Club," *MPW,* 10 Nov 1917, 847. "G. Fred Farnham Dead," *MPW,* 15 Dec 1917, 1652 (father d. 26 Nov 1917, Greenwich CT). "Joe Farnham Is a Very Busy Man," *MPW,* 25 Feb 1922, 827. "Mrs. Joseph White Farnham Dies," *MPW,* 6 Jan 1923, 33 (Alma Cour, 26 Dec 1922, So. Orange NJ). "Engages Farnham," *MPW,* 9 Jun 1923, 524. "The Big Parade," *MPW,* 22 Aug 1925, 848. "Record for 'Joe' Farnham," *MPW,* 7 Nov 1925, 45.

Farnsworth, F. Eugene [executive]. No data found. AMD, p. 116. "Mastercraft Photoplay Corporation," *MPW,* 19 Jan 1918, 368. "Farnsworth Returns to California," *MPW,* 11 May 1918, 836.

Farnum, Dorothy [scenarist] (b. 10 Jun 1900). AMD, p. 116. "Dorothy Farnum," *MPW,* 26 Jun 1915, 2098. "Dorothy Farnum Signed by Schenck," *MPW,* 29 May 1920, 1227. "'Babbitt' Soon," *MPW,* 1 Mar 1924, 41. Alma Talley, "Have You a Little Scenario in Your Home?," *MW,* 31 May 1924, 15, 29.

Farnum, Dustin (son of stage actor Greenleaf Dustin Farnum and actress/opera singer Clara Adele Legros; brother of **Marshall** and **William Farnum**) [stage/film actor] (b. Hampton Beach NH, 27 May 1874–3 Jul 1929 [55], New York NY [Death Certificate No. 17769]). m. (1) actress Agnes Muir Johnston, 1898–1908 (d. 1927); (2) actress Mary Bessie (or Elizabeth) Cornwell, 1909-div. 1924, Reno NV; (3) actress Winifred Kingston, 1924. (Began on stage in 1897 with the Ethel Tucker Repertoire Co.; began in films in 1913; Triangle; FP-L; Pallas-Paramount; Fox; United.) "Dustin Farnum Dies After Long Illness; Stage and Screen Star, 55, Was Born in Hampton Beach, Me., of Theatrical Parents; Debut in Stock in 1897; He Scored First Big Success in 'The Virginian'—with Brother William in 'The Littlest Rebel,'" *NYT,* 5 Jul 1929, 17:3. "Dustin Farnum," *Variety,* 10 Jul 1929 (b. ME). AMD, p. 116. AS, p. 378. BHD, p. 164. GK, pp. 265–70. IFN, p. 99. Lowrey, p. 54. MH, p. 109. MSBB, p. 1023. SD. Truitt, p. 105. WWS, p. 81. "Dustin Farnum Visits Universal's Ranch," *MPW,* 11 Jan 1913, 140. "Farnum in 'Squaw Man,'" *MPW,* 24 Jan 1914, 421. George Blaisdell, "A Man with the Bark On," *MPW,* 7 Mar 1914, 1243. "Dustin Farnum Leaves for Coast," *MPW,* 11 Sep 1915, 1837. "Dustin Farnum Ill," *MPW,* 25 Dec 1915, 2339. "Hart and Farnum Most Popular Cowboys," *MPW,* 2 Jun 1917, 1471. "Dustin Farnum Starts Own Company," *MPW,* 23 Feb 1918, 1107. "Dustin Farnum Company Starts Production," *MPW,* 6 Apr 1918, 97. "Dustin Farnum Joins Robertson-Cole; Signs Three-Year Contract; Limit on Pictures," *MPW,* 20 Mar 1920, 1948. "Dustin Farnum Is Now Wm. Fox Star," *MPW,* 18 Jun 1921, 704. "Farnum Returns to Screen," *MPW,* 25 Jul 1925, 450. Peter Grid Schmid, "The Big Boy of the Open Country; How Dustin Farnum Amuses Himself When Away from the Grind of the Camera," *MPC,* Apr 1916, 16–17. George A. Katchmer, "Dustin Farnum: The Actor's Actor," *CI,* 82 (Apr 1982), 45–47. George Katchmer, "Remembering the Great Silents," *CI,* 239 (May 1995), C6. R. Philip Loy, "Dustan Farnum: The Forgotten Cowboy," *CI,* 260 (Feb 1997), 24–27 (western fiolmography included).

Farnum, Franklyn (father of actress Geraldine Farnum) [stage/film actor/singer] (no relation to William and Dustin Farnum) (*né* William Franklin Smith, b. Boston MA, 5 Jun 1878 [MVRB Vol. 297, p. 192]–4 Jul 1961 [83], Woodland Hills CA; cancer). m. **Alma Rubens**, 14 Jun 1918 (d. 1931); Edith (Walker?) Goodwin, 24 Feb 1921 (d. 1959). (Broadway debut: *The Dollar Princess,* 1909; Triangle; Bluebird; Metro; Universal; FP-L; Good Seal.) "Franklyn Farnum, Actor, Dies; Performer in 1,100 Films Was 83," *NYT,* 6 Jul 1961, 29:4. "Franklyn Farnum," *Variety,* 12 Jul 1961 (age 85). *The LA Times,* 5 Jul 1961. AMD, p. 116. AS, p. 378 (b. 1876). BHD1, p. 184. FSS, p. 105. GK, pp. 270–80. IFN, p. 99. MH, p. 109 (b. 1883). MSBB, p. 1023–24. Truitt, pp. 105–106. "Franklyn Farnum Joins Universal," *MPW,* 5 Aug 1916, 923. "Franklyn Farnum Joins Universal," *MPW,* 7 Oct 1916, 79. "Farnum Signs Universal Contract," *MPW,* 2 Dec 1916, 1309. "Identifying Franklyn Farnum," *MPW,* 19 May 1917, 1101. "Franklyn Farnum," *MPW,* 21 Jul 1917, 450. "Universal Players' Contracts Expire," *MPW,* 1 Jun 1918, 1267. "Franklyn Farnum in Court," *MPW,* 2 Nov 1918, 595 (re auto accident of 16 Aug 1917). "Franklyn Farnum Signed for Art-O-Graf Feature," *MPW,* 1 Mar 1919, 1237. Doris Delvigne, "From Plain Bill Smith to Franklyn Farnum," *MPM,* Apr 1919. "Franklyn Farnum Reappears in Films in 'The Gutter,'" *MPW,* 31 May 1919, 1344. "Franklyn Farnum in Short Westerns," *MPW,* 21 Jun 1919, 1754. "Franklyn Farnum Meets with Unusual Accident," *MPW,* 26 Jul 1919, 552. "W.N. Selig to Make Six Features Starring Franklyn Farnum; Cannon Will Distribute," *MPW,* 22 May 1920, 1079. "Franklyn Marries," *MPW,* 19 Mar 1921, 262. George A. Katchmer, "Franklyn Farnum; The Smiling Cowboy," *CI,* 97 (Jul 1983), 38–39 (b. 1883). Elizabeth R. Nelson, "Farnum, Franklyn," *DAB,* Supp. 7 (1981), pp. 229–30 (appeared in 1,100 films).

Farnum, Marshall (brother of **Dustin** and **William Farnum**) [actor/director/producer] (b. 1880?–19 Feb 1917 [36], Prescott AZ). "Marshall Farnum," *Variety,* 23 Feb 1917. AMD, p. 117. AS, p. 378. BHD2, p. 82 (d. 18 Feb). IFN, p. 99. Spehr, p. 130. "A New Producer," *MPW,* 27 Sep 1913, 1398. "Farnum Joins Miller Brothers," *MPW,* 9 May 1914, 798. "Obituary," *MPW,* 17 Mar 1917, 1782 (d. 18 Feb).

Farnum, William (brother of **Dustin** and **Marshall Farnum**) [stage/film actor] (b. Boston MA, 4 Jul 1876–5 Jun 1953 [76], Los Angeles CA; cancer). m. Olive White (daughter, Sara Adele). (Stage debut: *Julius Caesar,* Boston Academy, 1890; established the William Farnum Stock Co. in Buffalo NY and Cleveland OH; Selig; Fox.) "William Farnum, Actor, 76, Is Dead; Star of Silent Screen Earned $10,000 a Week in Heyday—Famed for 'Spoilers,'" *NYT,* 6 Jun 1953, 17:1. "William Farnum," *Variety,* 10 Jun 1953. AMD, p. 117. AS, p. 378. BHD1, p. 184. FFF, p. 113. FSS, p. 105. GK, pp. 280–88. IFN, p. 99. Lowrey, p. 56. MH, p. 109. MSBB, p. 1024. SD. Spehr, p. 130. Truitt, p. 106. WWS, p. 200. "Famous Players Engage William Farnum," *MPW,* 21 Mar 1914, 1529. "Two More Stars for Famous Players," *MPW,* 28 Mar 1914, 1692. "William Farnum Hurt," *NYDM,* 14 Oct 1914, 25:1 (in *The Battle Cry;* thrown from his horse and splintered a bone in his arm). "William Farnum Returns to Screen," *MPW,* 11 Nov 1916, 874. "Farnums Sue [John] Cort; Want Payment of $3,000 from Manager for Three Weeks' Work," *NYDM,* 18 Nov 1914, 9:2 (on 17 May 1913 Mr. and Mrs. Farnum were to appear in *VIiginius* for 18 weeks; the engagement lasted 15 weeks.). "William Farnum," *MPW,* 16 Jun 1917, 1793. William Farnum, "Greater Opportunities in Pictures," *MPW,* 21 Jul 1917, 425. William Farnum, "Booming the Cheer Market," *Picture-Play Magazine,* Sep 1917, 46–49 (includes photo of daughter Olive). "Illness of Mrs. Farnum Brings Fox Player East," *MPW,* 12 Oct 1918, 204. "William Farnum Hangs Up $33,000,000 in Bond Sale," *MPW,* 2 Nov 1918, 577. "William Farnum Signs Long Time Fox Contract," *MPW,* 28 Dec 1918, 1488. "Farnum's Tonsils Removed," *MPW,* 19 Apr 1919, 360. "Farnum Recovers from Operation," *MPW,* XL, 26 Apr 1919, 508. "William Farnum," *MPW,* 19 Jul 1919, 358. "Precious Old Clothes," *MPS,* 13 May 1921, 22–23 (Farnum "has twenty or thirty trunks full of costumes which he used in his many stage productions."). "Contest Won by William Farnum," *MPW,* 1 Oct 1921, 560 (star popularity contest in Japan). "William Farnum Returns from Europe; In Fine Condition and Ready to Work," *MPW,* 5 Nov 1921, 52. "Farnum About to Begin Work with Fox, Ending Seven Months' Rest in Europe," *MPW,* 19 Nov 1921, 290. "Famous Players-Lasky Gets Farnum," *MPW,* 8 Mar 1924, 111. June Lee, "Dan Cupid's Bulletin Board," *Paris and Hollywood Screen Secrets Magazine,* Aug 1927, 37 (Sara Adele Farnum, 18 years old, m. William Gerard Tuttle, an oil engineer). "William Farnum Returns," *MPW,* 29 Oct 1927, 541. George A. Katchmer, "William Farnum, the ACTOR!," *CI,* 69 (May 1980), 58. Filmography, *CI,* 193, 231 (Sep 1994). George Katchmer, "Remembering the Great Silents," *CI,* 256 (Oct 1996), 43–44.

Farquharson, Robert [actor] (b. London, England, 6 Nov 1877–11 Jan 1966 [88], Ticiono, Switzerland). BHD2, p. 378.

Farra, Abe [actor]. No data found. AMD, p. 117. "Triangle Puncher Has Serious Fall," *MPW,* 23 Mar 1918, 1688.

Farrar, Geraldine [opera singer/actress] (*née* Alice Geraldine Farrar, b. Melrose MA, 28 Feb 1882 [extrait de naissance no. 2348]–11 Mar 1967 [85], Ridgefield CT). m. **Lou-Tellegen**, 8 Feb 1916, NY NY (d. 1934). *Such Sweet Compulsions; The Autobiography of Geraldine Farrar* (New York: Greyston Press, 1938). (FP-L; Artcraft.) "Geraldine Farrar, Met Soprano Dies," *NYT,* 12 Mar 1967, 1:7; Harold C. Schonberg, "Link with Golden Age; Geraldine Farrar Was Blessed with Beauty, Intelligence, Spirit and Voice," 86:1. "Geraldine Farrar, 85; Her Pre-1922 Fans Put System Into Hysteria," *Variety,* 15 Mar 1967. AMD, p. 117. AS, p. 378. BHD, p. 164. IFN, p. 100. MSBB, p. 1934. Spehr, p. 130. Truitt, p. 106. "Vast Audience at 'Carmen'; Miss Farrar, Caruso, and Amato in the Leading Roles," *NYT,* 28 Jan 1915, 9:5 ("The most obvious reason for this fact is the participation of Miss Farrar and Mr. Caruso..."). "Will Farrar Stay in Opera?; Charles A. Ellis Has Disposed of Singer's Services for Next Season," *NYT,* 9 Feb 1915, 9:3 (with a salary of between $1,200 and $1,500 a performance, her contract with the Metropolitan Opera Co. was to expire. "The impression prevails in operatic circles that the singer is intrenching herself against a possible reduction in salary following cuts that have been made recently at the expiration of contracts."). "Lasky Signs Farrar; Famous Metropolitan Favorite Receives Record Salary to Appear on Screen," *NYDM,* 5 May 1915, 22:1. "Geraldine Farrar for the Screen," *MPW,* 8 May 1915, 879. "Geraldine Farrar on Her Way," *MPW,* 19 Jun 1915, 1944. "Dinner to Farrar," *MPW,* 26 Jun 1915, 2100. "Geraldine Farrar: Woman," *MPW,* 10 Jul 1915, 257–58. "Farrar Energetic," *MPW,* 24 Jul 1915, 660. "Miss Farrar's Protége," *MPW,* 28 Aug 1915, 1460 (Marjorie Daw). Geraldine Farrar, "Why I Went Into Motion Pictures," *MPW,* 9 Oct 1915, 266. Allan Douglas Brodie, "Geraldine Farrar; Famous Diva Will Place the Noted Heroines of Grand Opera in Motion Pictures, as a Record of Her Splendid Art for Future Generations to See," *MPC,* Dec 1915, 57–58. "Geraldine Farrar Weds," *NYDM,* 19 Feb 1916, 10:4. "Geraldine Farrar Leaves for California," *MPW,* 17 Jun 1916, 2042. "Geraldine Farrar Returns to Screen," *MPW,* 12 May 1917, 973. [Farrar Starts Work on First Artcraft," *MPW,* 28 Jul 1917, 667. "Farrar Again Faces the Camera," *MPW,* 6 Jul 1918, 80. "Farrar Sells $1,200,000 Bonds," *MPW,* 26 Oct 1918, 501. "Lou Tellegen to Star with Farrar," *MPW,* 17 May 1919, 1010. "Geraldine Farrar Signs with Associated Exhibitors; Production to Begin in New York," *MPW,* 24 Apr 1920, 586. "Farrar Not to Resume Film Work Until Spring of 1921," *MPW,* 30 Oct 1920, 1259.

Farrar, Margaret [actress] (b. Kansas City MO, 8 Apr 1901–9 Aug 1925 [24], Los Angeles CA; suicide with poison). "Margaret Farrar," *Variety,* 12 Aug 1925 ("Before her death she said that she was tired of living."). BHD, p. 164; BHD2, p. 378. Truitt, p. 106.

Farrell, Charles [actor] (b. Dublin, Ireland, 6 Aug 1900–27 Aug 1988 [88], London, England). AS, p. 379 (b. 1901). BHD1, p. 185.

Farrell, Charles [actor] (b. Onset Bay MA, 9 Aug 1901–6 May 1990 [88], Palm Springs CA; heart attack). m. **Virginia Valli** (d. 1968). Eric Pace, "Charles Farrell, Actor, Dies at 88; Made Debut in 'Seventh Heaven,'" *NYT,* 12 May 1990, 29:1. "Charles Farrell," *Variety,* 16 May 1990 (age 89). Burt A. Folkart, "Charles Farrell, 89; Film and TV Actor, Developer, Former Palm Springs Mayor," *LA Times,* 11 May 1990, A24:1. "Charlie Farrell [obituary]," *CI,* 180 (Jun 1990), 60 (b. Walpole MA). AMD, p. 117. AS, p. 379. BHD1, p. 185 (b. Walepole MA, 1900). FSS, p. 106. "Charles Farrell," WBO2, p. 68–69 (b. Cape Cod MA, 1902). "Warners Sign Charles Farrell," *MPW,* lxxiv, 6 Jun 1925, 679. Alma Whitaker, "'Old Ironsides' Sails the Seven Seas Again, How a Screen Spectacle Is Being Built About the Famous *Old Constitution* Off Catalina," *MPC,* XXIII, Jun 1926, 20–21, 85–87 (Ferrell [sic], star of *Old Ironsides,* had been an extra for two years, as in *The Ten Commandments*). Mary B. Chapman, "The Kid from Cape Cod," *MPC,* Jul 1926, 57, 74. Dorothy Manners, "'Atta Boy Charlie'; Just a Young Fellow Getting Along," *MPC,* Nov 1926, 54, 89. "Charles Farrell," *MPW,* 28 May 1927, 273. Marian Newcomb, "A Very Remarkable Fellow; Charlie Farrell Is Winning the Popularity Stakes," *MPC,* May 1928, 58, 77. Cover (with Janet Gaynor), *Screen Book,* Jul 1928; illustrated novelization of *Street Angel,* pp. 4–59.

Farrell, Glenda [stage/film/TV actress] (b. Enid OK, 30 Jun 1904–1 May 1971 [67], New York NY; lung cancer). m. [1] Thomas Richards, 1920–29 (1 son, Thomas, b. 7 Oct 1921); Dr. Henry Ross, 19 Jan 1941. (Tiffany; WB.) (Film debut: *Lucky Boy,* Tiffany, 1929). "Glenda Farrell," *Variety,* 5 May 1971 (debut: *Little Caesar,* 1931). AS, p. 379. BHD1, p. 185. IFN, p. 100. SD. Dan Van Neste, "Glenda Farrell: Diamond in the Rough," *CI,* 275 (May 1998), 20–31 (includes filmography).

Farrell, John W. [actor] (b. 1885?–8 Jul 1953 [68], Brooklyn NY). m. Josephine Saxton. "John W. Farrell," *Variety,* 15 Jul 1953 ("The couple also appeared in films"). AS, p. 379. IFN, p. 100.

Farrell, Marguerite [actress] (b. 1889?–26 Jan 1951 [62], Buffalo NY). "Marguerite Farrell," *Variety,* 7 Feb 1951 (Mrs. Marguerite Farrell Wheeler). AS, p. 379.

Farrell, Vessie [actress] (b. 1888–30 Sep 1935 [47?], Los Angeles CA). AS, p. 379.

Farren, Fred [actor] (b. London, England, 1874–7 May 1956 [81?], London, England). BHD, p. 164.

Farren, George F[rancis] (father of Mary Farren, 1907–1977) [actor] (b. Boston MA, 14 Sep 1858–21 Apr 1935 [76], New York NY). AS, p. 379 (b. 1860). BHD, p. 164. IFN, p. 100 (age 74).

Farren, William [actor] (b. 2 Aug 1853–7 Sep 1937 [84], London, England). BHD, p. 164.

Farrington, Adele [actress] (b. Brooklyn NY, 1867?–19 Dec 1936 [69], Los Angeles CA). m. **Hobart Bosworth**—div. ca. 1919 (d. 1936). (Film debut: *The Country Mouse,* Paramount, 1914.) "Adele Farrington," *Variety,* 23 Dec 1936. AMD, p. 117. AS, p. 379. BHD, p. 165. IFN, p. 100. Truitt, p. 108. "Miss Farrington's First Film," *NYDM,* 18 Nov 1914, 24:1. "Adele Farrington," *MPW,* 16 Oct 1915, 455. "Adele Farrington to Be Seen in Neilan Picture," *MPW,* 7 Feb 1920, 871.

Farrington, Frank [actor] (b. Bruxton, London, England, 8 Jul 1873–27 May 1924 [50], Los Angeles CA). "Frank Farrington," *Variety,* 4 Jun 1924. AMD, p. 117. AS, p. 379. BHD, p. 165. IFN, p. 100. Truitt, pp. 106–107. "Farrington in an Edison," *NYDM,* 2 Jun 1915, 21:3 (*Through Turbulent Waters,* with Edward Earle and Robert Brower). "Frank Farrington," *MPW,* 3 Mar 1917, 1355.

Farrington, Mrs. Frank [wardrobe]. No data found. AMD, p. 117. Mrs. Frank Farrington, "In the Costume Room," *MPW,* 21 Jul 1917, 389–90.

Farris, Evelyn [actress]. No data found. AMD, p. 117. "Evelyn Farris Joins International," *MPW,* 28 Oct 1916, 565.

Farrow, John Villiers (father of Mia Farrow) [director/title writer/scenarist/producer] (b. Sydney, NSW, Australia, 10 Feb 1904–27 Jan 1963 [58], Beverly Hills CA; apparent heart attack). m. (1) Felice Lewin; (2) Maureen O'Sullivan, 1936 (daughter Mia, b. 9 Feb 1945; Stephanie, b. 1949; Tisa, b. 1951). "John Farrow, 56, Movie Director; Hollywood Producer Also Wrote Some Scripts," *NYT,* 29 Jan 1963, 7:6. "John Farrow," *Variety,* 30 Jan 1963. AS, p. 379. BHD2, p. 82. FDY, pp. 423, 443. IFN, p. 100.

Farulli, Adele [actress] (*née* Adele Accansi; d. Sep 1929, Rome, Italy). JS, p. 158 (in Italian silents in 1928 and 1929).

Fassini, Baron [executive]. No data found. AMD, p. 118. "Baron Fassini—Head of Ambrosio," *MPW,* 22 Nov 1913, 882. "Baron Fassini Not Head of Ambrosio," *MPW,* 29 Nov 1913, 1021.

Fassy, Fernanda [actress] (*née* Fernanda Bucalossi, b. Rome, Italy, 1898). JS, p. 158 (in Italian silents from 1916).

Fatima, "La Belle" [actress] (b. Syria, 1880–14 Mar 1921 [40?], Venice CA). AS, p. 380. BHD, p. 165.

Fauchois, René Charles André [actor] (b. Rouen, France, 31 Aug 1882 [extrait de naissance no. 1615]–10 Feb 1962 [79], Paris, France). AS, p. 380.

Fauley, Wilbur Finley [writer]. No data found. AMD, p. 118. "New York Newspaperman [*NY Times*] an Author of 'Jenny Be Good,'" *MPW,* 3 Jul 1920, 114.

Faulkner, John [actor] (d. 1940). BHD, p. 165.

Faulkner, Ralph B. [actor] (b. Aberdeen WA, 1891–28 Jan 1987 [95?], Burbank CA). AS, p. 380. BHD1, p. 185.

Faulkner, Ralph C., Sr. [actor] (b. San Antonio TX, 1890?–21 Aug 1948 [58], Washington DC). "Ralph C. Faulkner, Sr.," *Variety,* 25 Aug 1948 (b. Washington DC). AS, p. 380. BHD1, p. 185 (b. San Antonio NY-d. 1984).

Faure, Elie [writer/historian] (b. Sainte-Foye-la-Grande, France, 4 Apr 1873–29 Oct 1937 [64], Paris, France). AS, p. 380.

Faussett, James, Jr. [actor] (b. 1878–13 Nov 1940 [62?], Los Angeles CA). BHD, p. 165. IFN, p. 100.

Faust, Edward A. [trainer] (b. 1897?–23 Nov 1958 [61], Las Vegas NV; run over by train). "Edward A. Faust," *Variety,* 3 Dec 1958 (trained Strongheart and Peter the Great).

Faust, Martin J. [actor] (b. Poughkeepsie NY, 16 Jan 1886–19 Jul 1943 [57], Los Angeles CA). "Martin J. Faust," *Variety,* 28 Jul 1943. AS, p. 380 (d. 20 Jul). BHD1, p. 185. IFN, p. 100 (b. Germany). Truitt, p. 107.

Favar, Margaret [actress] (b. Greenwood MS?–21 Sep 1915, Memphis TN; murdered.) (Bison.) "Margaret Favar Murdered," *Variety,* 24 Sep 1915. AS, p. 380. BHD1, p. 608.

Faversham, William [stage/film actor] (b. London, England, 12 Feb 1868–7 Apr 1940 [72], Bay Shore, LI NY; coronary embolism). m. **Julie Opp**, 1902 (d. 1921). (Paramount.) "Faver-sham Dies; Famous as Actor; Formerly Called the Greatest 'Matinee Idol' of His Day—Is Stricken at 72; Noted for 'Squaw Man'; Versatility Revealed in Varied List of His Successes—He Delighted in Shakespeare," *NYT,* 8 Apr 1940, 20:2. "Wm. Faversham Passes at 73," *Variety,* 4 Apr 1940 (age 73). AMD, p. 118. AS, p. 380. BHD1, p. 186. IFN, p. 100. MSBB, p. 1024. SD. Truitt, p. 107. WWS, p. 154. "Faversham in New Play; 'The Squawman' Mixes Up a Nobleman and Wyoming Cowboys," *NYT,* 25 Apr 1905, 7:2 (Buffalo NY, 24 Apr, at the Star Theatre. Four-act comedy written for him by Edwin Milton Royle.). "Faversham to Act for Playgoers," *MPW,* 21 Mar 1914, 1531. "Faversham for All-Star," *MPW,* 1 Aug 1914, 713. "William Faversham with Rolfe," *MPW,* 3 Apr 1915, 75. "Faversham to Be Starred in 'The Silver King,'" *MPW,* 21 Sep 1918, 1722. Edward Weitzel, "William Faversham Reaches High Rank as the Star of 'The Sin That Was His,'" *MPW,* 18 Dec 1920, 859. "William Faversham Replies to Chadbourne's $4,000 Suit," *MPW,* 23 Jul 1921, 398. David

Carroll, *The Matinee Idols* (New York: Galahad Books, 1972), pp. 80–82.

Favieres, Guy [actor] (*né* Guy Jean Marie Perret, b. Paris, France, 1 Jun 1876 [extrait de naissance no. 1027/1876]–30 Mar 1963 [86], Paris, France). AS, p. 381.

Favor, Edward M. [actor] (b. 1856–10 Jan 1936 [79?], Brooklyn NY). m. Edith Sinclair. "Ed M. Favor," *Variety,* 15 Jan 1936. AS, p. 381. BHD, p. 165. Truitt 1983, p. 232.

Fawcett, Charles S. [actor] (b. 1855–23 Nov 1922 [67?], London, England). "Charles Fawcett," *Variety,* 1 and 15 Dec 1922. BHD, p. 165.

Fawcett, George D[eneale] [actor/director] (b. Alexandria [Fairfax County] VA, 25 Aug 1860–6 Jun 1939 [78], Nantucket Island MA). m. **Percy Haswell** (d. 1945). (Began on stage, 1886; founded the Fawcett Stock company of Baltimore; film debut: *The Majesty of the Law,* Paramount, 1915; Universal.) (Ince.) "George D. Fawcett, Famous Actor, 77; Star of the Stage and Screen Dies of Heart Ailment on Nantucket Sound; Career Began in 1886—Had Filled Character Parts in Pictures with Garbo and John Barrymore," *NYT,* 7 Jun 1939, 23:5. "George D. Fawcett," *Variety,* 14 Jun 1939 (age 77). AMD, p. 118. AS, p. 381. BHD1, p. 186; BHD2, p. 82. FFF, p. 109 (b. 1863). FSS, p. 107. IFN, p. 100. MH, p. 109 (b. 1863). Truitt, p. 107. "Little Blaze in Theatre; Actor Smothers Burning Flowers of Herald Square Stage," *NYT,* 4 Mar 1905, 9:2 (while performing in *The Woman in the Case* with Robert Drouet, the latter set a box of matches aflame and a vase of artificial flowers caught fire. He smothered the flames with his hands. "The audience calmed down and gave him a hearty round of appleause."). "Fawcett with Bosworth; Another Stage Star to Make His First Appearance on the Motion Picture Screen," *NYDM,* 12 May 1915, 21:4 ("In the Picture Studios," *NYDM,* 8 Sep 1915, 36:4 (one of the stage stars at Universal). "Fawcett in 'The Frame Up' for Universal," *MPW,* 18 Sep 1915, 2000. "George D. Fawcett," *MPW,* 10 Feb 1917, 847. Fritzi Remont, "The Man Who Is Never Himself; George Fawcett Lives the Characters He Plays," *MPC,* Jan 1919, 39–40, 71, 80. "Fawcett Becomes Vitagraph Director," *MPW,* 13 Dec 1919, 851. "Fawcett Joins Lasky Stock," *MPW,* 29 Apr 1922, 932. "George D. Fawcett," *MPW,* 16 Jul 1927, 156. George A. Katchmer, "Forgotten Cowboys & Cowgirls—IV," *CI,* 175 (Jan 1990), C6.

Fay, Alleen [stage/film actress]. No data found. "Alleen Fay," *NYDM,* Nov 1915, 35:1 (with photo. Made films in England and New York City. "Her decided beauty is aided materially in screen work by a wealth of Titian red hair, but her chief charm consists in her vivacity and a smile that won't come off.").

Fay, Elfie [actress] (daughter of **Hugh Fay**) (b. 11 Jan 1872?–16 Sep 1927 [55?], Los Angeles CA; tuberculosis). m. (1) Eugene Elwood; (2) Samuel A. Brenner. "Elfie Fay," *Variety,* 21 Sep 1927. AS, p. 381 (b. 1881). BHD, p. 165 (b. 1881). IFN, p. 100 (age 46; d. 18 Sep). SD.

Fay, Essie [actress] (b. 1883–7 Apr 1949 [65?], St. Petersburg FL). BHD, p. 165.

Fay, Hugh [actor] (father of **Elfie Fay**) (b. NY, 1879–4 Dec 1926 [47], Los Angeles CA; "stomach trouble"). (Keystone.) "Hugh Fay," *Variety,* 8 Dec 1926. AS, p. 381. BHD, p. 165. 1921 Directory, p. 171. "What's Happening," *Picture-Play Masgazine,* VII (Sep 1917), 80 (photo of Fay giving his dog a drink from a hose).

Fay, Jack [actor] (b. 1903?–15 Nov 1928 [25], Los Angeles CA; from injuries sustained in an explosion at Fox Studios while filming *What Price Glory?,* 1926). "Jack Fay," *Variety,* 21 Nov 1928. AS, p. 381. BHD, p. 165. IFN, p. 100. Truitt, p. 107.

Fay, Olive [actress] (b. 1925–23 Nov 1977 [52?], Los Angeles CA). AS, p. 381. BHD, p. 165.

Fay, William George [actor/producer] (b. Dublin, Ireland, 12 Nov 1872–27 Oct 1947 [75], London, England). m. Bridget O'Dempsey (d. 1952). *The Fays of the Abbey Theatre.* "William George Fay," *Variety,* 5 Nov 1947. AS, p. 381. BHD1, p. 186; BHD2, p. 82. IFN, p. 100. SD.

Faye, Alice Louisa Ernestine [actress] (b. Lille, France, 8 Sep 1879–29 Sep 1962 [83], Paris, France). AS, p. 381.

Faye, Alleen [actress]. No data found. AMD, p. 118. "Alleen Faye," *MPW,* 8 Jan 1916, 225.

Faye, Julia [actress/Sennett Bathing Beauty] (*née* Julia Faye Conell, b. Richmond VA, 28 Sep 1893–6 Apr 1966 [72], Santa Monica CA; cancer). (Keystone.) "Julia Faye," *Variety,* 13 Apr 1966. AMD, p. 118. AS, p. 381. BHD1, p. 186. FFF, p. 224 (b. 1898). IFN, p. 100. Katz, p. 405. MH, p. 110 (b. 1898). Truitt, p. 107 (b. 1896). *Stars of the Photoplay* (Chicago: Photoplay Publishing Co., 1930). "New DeMille 'Discovery,'" *MPW,* 16 Jan 1926, 241. Ellen Willis, "The Fan Mail of a Bad Girl," *Pictures,* Jun 1926, 68, 126–28. "Has Been in All DeMille's Films," *MPW,* 23 Apr 1927, 715. Ramon Romeo, "Thru the Day with Julia Faye; A Keyhole Slant on a Movie Star's Morning, Noon and Night," *Paris and Hollywood Screen Secrets,* Oct 1927, 68–71. Joan Dickey, "A Private Life—That's Fairly Private; Julia Faye Minds Her Cues and Her Own Business as Well," *MPC,* Dec 1927, 40, 78.

Faye, Randall H. [director/producer/scenarist]. No data found. FDY, p. 423.

Faylauer, Adolph [actor] (b. OH, 16 Nov 1882–11 Jan 1961 [78], Los Angeles CA). AS, p. 381. BHD1, p. 186. IFN, p. 100.

Fazenda, Louise [actress] (b. Lafayette IN, 17 Jun 1889–17 Apr 1962 [72], Holmby Hills (Los Angeles] CA; cerebral hemorrhage). m. (1) **Noel Mason Smith**, 1917–26; **Hal Wallis**, Nov 1927. (Universal; Sennett.) "Louise Fazenda Is Dead at 67; Comedienne of the Silent Films; Wife of Hal Wallis Started in Mack Sennett Pictures in '15—Continued Acting Until '39," *NYT,* 18 Apr 1962, 39:3. "Louise Fazenda," *Variety,* 25 Apr 1962. AMD, p. 118. AS, p. 381. BHD1, p. 186 {b. 1895}. FFF, p. 202 (b. 1895). FSS, p. 107. IFN, p. 100 (b. 1895). Katz, pp. 406–406 (b. 1895; began 1913). MH, p. 110. Truitt, p. 107. WWS, p. 190. "Younger Keystoners," *MPW,* 5 Feb 1916, 783. "Discouragement of Vamping," *MPW,* 14 Sep 1918, 1573. Louise Fazenda, "Me by Myself; The Confessions of a Comedienne," *MPC,* May 1919, 34–35, 69. "Special Pictures Signs Louise Fazenda; Comedy Star to Come East for Vacation," *MPW,* 2 Oct 1920, 649. "Louise's 'Bank' Draws 'Interest,'" *MPW,* 18 Dec 1920, 909. Alma Talley, "Louise Fazenda Forsakes Laughter for Tears," *MW,* 21 Jun 1924, 8, 28. "Serious Role for Miss Fazenda," *MPW,* 2 Aug 1924, 383. Dorothy Donnell, "Who Is Nadine Mason?," *MPS,* 26 Aug 1924, 2–3, 28–29 (she assumed the name of Nadine Mason in order to mingle with the common folk in LA). "Playing Dramatic Lead," *MPW,* 27 Sep 1924, 321. "Fjazenda Signed by Paramount," *MPW,* 28 Feb 1925, 925. Harry Carr, "Louise Gives a Party," *MPC,* Apr 1925, 20–21, 83 (also on the cover). Catharine Brody, "A Star with Whom You Can Be Poor; Is Louise Fazenda—Who Loves to Hunt Bargains—Buy Her Own Vegetables and Is Willing to Marry a Newspaper Man and Live on Sixty Dollars a Week," *MW,* 25 Sep 1925, 26–27. "Louise Fazenda Made a Star by Warners," *MPW,* 13 Feb 1926, 635. "Louise Fazenda," *MPW,* 16 Apr 1927, 631. Tom Waller, "Louise Fazenda," *MPW,* 30 Jul 1927, 314–16. "Wedding March," *MPW,* 3 Dec 1927, 23.

Fealy, Margaret (mother of **Maude Fealey**) [actress] (b. Memphis TN, 18 Jul 1865–11 Feb 1955 [89], Woodland Hills CA). AS, p. 382 (b. 15 Jul). BHD1, p. 186. IFN, p. 100.

Fealy, Maude (daughter of **Margaret Fealey**) [stage/film actress/playwright] (b. Memphis TN, 4 Mar 1881–9 Nov 1971 [90], Woodland Hills CA). m. James Durkin (3) **John Cort, Jr.** (son of the theatrical producer), 9 Jan 1920, Cincinnati OH (d. 1929). "Maude Fealy," *Variety,* 17 Nov 1971. AMD, p. 118. AS, p. 382 (b. 1883). BHD1, p. 186 (b. 1883). IFN, p. 100 (b. 1883). SD, p. 434. Truitt, p. 108. "Miss Maude Fealy, In Pictures," *MPW,* 17 May 1913, 684. Arthur Edwin Krows, "Maude Fealy 45 Minutes from Broadway," *NYDM,* 24 Jun 1914, 14:3 (traces her entire theatrical career). "Maude Fealy Starring for Hub Company," *MPW,* 24 Oct 1914, 469. Albert L. Roat, "The Drama in Pictures; Reminiscences of the Dramatic Actress Maude Fealey," *Motion Picture Magazine,* Feb 1915, 115–16. "Personal; Fealy," *NYDM,* 29 Sep 1915, 5:1 (on the cover. The dramatic critic of the Denver *Post,* F.W. White, wrote of Fealy's recent stage work that "in her advancing maturity [she] shows the value of stock experience." To appear in *The Average Woman* for Kleine-Edison.). "Maude Fealy in Knickerbocker," *MPW,* 16 Oct 1915, 424. "Maude Fealy with Kleine," *MPW,* 23 Oct 1915, 597. "Maude Fealy Optimistic," *MPW,* 20 Nov 1915, 1465. "'Bondwomen' [Kleine-Edison, 15 Dec 1915] in the Bronx," *NYDM,* 11 Dec 1915, 24:4 (her film premiere completed). "Maude Fealy with Lasky," *MPW,* 13 Jan 1917, 209. "Flashes; Maude Fealy Weds; Noted Actress Is Now Mrs. John Cort, Jr.," *LA Times,* 17 Jan 1920, II, 7.

Fearnley, Jane [actress] (b. ca. 1885). (Imp.) m. (1) Louis F. Sherwin; (2) John E. Cort (d. 1929). (Reliance.) BHD, p. 165. "Lives of the Players; Jane Fearnley," *MPS,* I, 31 Jan 1913, 31.

Featherly, William [actor] (b. 1870–11 May 1925 [54?], Los Angeles CA). AS, p. 382 (d. 10 May). BHD, p. 165.

Featherston, Vane [actor] (b. London, England, 16 Dec 1864–6 Nov 1948 [83], Maidenhead, Berkshire, England). BHD, p. 165.

Featherstone, Eddie [actor] *see* **Fetherston, Edward A.**

Fegte, Ernst [art director] (b. Hamburg, Germany, 28 Sep 1900–15 Dec 1976 [76], Los Angeles CA). (Paramount; Republic.) "Ernst Fegte," *Variety,* 22 Dec 1976 (began in Germany, 1919). Katz, p. 406.

Feher, Friedrich [actor/director/scenarist] (*né* Friedrich Weiss, b. Vienna, Austria, 16 Mar 1889–30 Sep 1950 [61], Stuttgart, Germany). AS, p. 382. FDY, p. 423.

Fehim, Ahmet [director/scenarist] (b. Constantinople, Turkey, 1857–1930 [73?], Istanbul, Turkey). AS, p. 382.

Feinman, Al [publicist]. No datra found.

AMD, p. 118. "Warner Exploitation Man Takes Detroit by Storm," *MPW,* 17 Feb 1923, 695.

Feist, Felix F. [film salesman/cameraman/executive/director/producer/scenarist] (b. New York NY, 28 Feb 1906–2 Sep 1965 [59]; Encino CA; cancer). (RKO; Universal.) "Felix Feist," *Variety,* 240, 8 Sep 1965, 69:1 (age 55). AMD, p. 118. AS, p. 382. IFN, p. 101. "Feist Says: 'Get Busy,'" *MPW,* 30 Jan 1915, 658. "Felix F. Feist," *MPW,* 24 Apr 1915, 558. "The Men Back of Equitable," *MPW,* 18 Sep 1915, 1999. "Felix Feist Is Elected Goldwyn Vice-President," *MPW,* 4 Jan 1919, 54. Felix F. Feist, "Service Is First Plank in Platform of Goldwyn; More Prints on Each Film," *MPW,* 17 Jul 1920, 343.

Fejos, Paul [film director, 1926–30/scenarist] (*né* Pâl Fegos, b. Budapest, Hungary, 24 Jan 1897–23 Apr 1963 [66], New York NY; heart ailment). m. Lita Binns. (Universal; MGM.) "Dr. Paul Fejos, Anthropologist; President of Wenner-Gren Foundation Is Dead at 66," *NYT,* 24 Apr 1963, 35:4. AS, p. 382. FDY, p. 423. IFN, p. 101. Katz 1994.

Fekete, Fritz [scenarist] (b. Enghien-les-Bains, France, 1880–1954 [74?], France). AS, p. 382.

Feld, Fritz [actor] (b. Berlin, Germany, 15 Oct 1900–18 Nov 1993 [93], Santa Monica CA). (Film debut: *Der Golem und die Tanzerin,* 1917.) m. Virginia Christine (widow). "Fritz Feld; Actor, 93," *NYT,* 23 Nov 1993, B10:1. "Fritz Feld," *Variety,* 6 Dec 1993, p. 47:3. AS, p. 383. BHD1, p. 186. FSS, p. 108. Katz, pp. 406–07 (in 425 major film productions; about 30 silent movies).

Feld, Hans [film critic (*Film-Kurier*); editor] (b. Germany, 1902?–15 Jul 1992 [90], London, England). "Hans Feld," *Variety,* 3 Aug 1992, p. 52 ("authority on the silent cinema of his native Germany").

Feldman, Gladys [actress] (b. Chicago IL?, 28 Sep 1886–12 Feb 1974 [87], New York NY). m. Horace Braham (d. 1955). "Gladys Feldman," *Variety,* 20 Feb 1974. AS, p. 383 (b. 1891). BHD, p. 165 (b. 1891). IFN, p. 101. Paul Rochester, "Former Ziegfeld Beauty Becomes Movie Star—on Stage; Gladys Feldman, who once won honors as a star in a musical comedy, is now a movie star—but not on the screen," *MW,* 9 Jun 1923, 11, 29.

Feldman, Herbert [publicist]. No data found. AMD, p. 118. "Feldman Now Free-Lancing," *MPW,* 21 Aug 1920, 1050.

Felicia, Norma [actress]. No data found. m. **Billy Gilbert** (d. 1961). (Keystone). J. Van Cartmell, "Along the Pacific Coast," *NYDM,* 15 Sep 1915, 30:4.

Felix, George [actor] (b. Canada, 20 Jun 1866–12 May 1949 [83?], New York NY). m. Lydia Barry. "George Felix," *Variety,* 18 May 1949. AS, p. 383. BHD, p. 165. SD. Truitt, p. 108.

Felix, Hugo [composer] (b. 1872–25 Aug 1934 [62?], Los Angeles CA). AS, p. 383.

Fellner, Herman [producer] (b. Germany, 1877–22 Mar 1936 [59?], London, England; suicide by hanging). AS, p. 383.

Fellner, P.P. [producer] (b. Germany, 1884–Oct 1927 [43?]). BHD2, p. 82.

Fellowes, Rockliffe [stage/film actor] (b. Ottawa, Canada, 7 Mar 1883–28 Jan 1950 [66], Los Angeles CA; heart attack). m. **Lucile Watson**—div. (d. 1962). (Began 1912; film debut: *The Rejuvenation,* Fox.) "R. Fellowes, 65, Dies; Stage, Screen Actor," *NYT,* 29 Jan 1950, 68:4. "Rockliffe Fellowes," *Variety,* 1 Feb 1950. AS, p. 383. BHD1, p. 187 (b. 17 Mar). FFF, p. 203. FSS, p. 108. IFN, p. 101. MH, p. 110. Slide, p. 160. Truitt, p. 108. "Rockliffe Fellowes," *MPW,* 23 Jul 1927, 239:3 ("He has fought shy of long term contracts and has been a free lance player from the very first.").

Fellows, Doris [actress] (d. 19 Oct 1918, Camp Funston KS; influenza). "Doris Fellows," *Variety,* 25 Oct 1918.

Fellows, George G[regson] [actor] (b. London, England, 1903–26 Dec 1928 [25], Liverpool, England; pneumonia). AS, p. 383.

Fellows, Robert [actor/director/producer] (*né* Robert Followes, b. Los Angeles CA, 23 Aug 1903–11 May 1969 [66], Los Angeles CA; heart attack). m. Donna. "Robert Fellows," *Variety,* May 1969. AS, pp. 383–84. BHD, p. 165; BHD2, p. 82. Truitt 1983, p. 234.

Felner, Peter Paul [director] (b. Budapest, Hungary, 1884–1927 [43?], Germany). AS, p. 384 (worked in Germany).

Felsenstein, Walter Theodor [actor/director] (b. Vienna, Austria, 30 May 1901–8 Oct 1975 [74], Berlin, Germany). AS, p. 384.

Felt, Edward H. [actor] (b. 1857–7 Jul 1928 [71], New York NY). "Edward H. Felt," *Variety,* 11 Jul 1928. BHD, p. 166. IFN, p. 101.

Felton, Verna [actress] (b. Salinas CA, 20 Jul 1890–14 Dec 1966 [76], No. Hollywood CA; pulmonary embolism). m. Lee Millar. "Verna Felton, 76, TV Actress, Dead; Radio and Movie Performer Was in 'December Bride,'" *NYT,* 16 Dec 1966, 47:1. "Verna Felton," *Variety,* 21 Dec 1966. AS, p. 384. BHD1, p. 187. IFN, p. 101.

Fenimore, Ford [actor] (*né* Ford Fenimore Hoft, d. 20 Apr 1941, El Paso TX; tuberculosis). m. Dorothy Armstrong. (Griffith.) "Ford Fenimore," *Variety,* 30 Apr 1941. AS, p. 384. BHD, p. 166. IFN, p. 101. Truitt, p. 108.

Fenner, Walter S. [actor] (b. Akron OH, 1882?–7 Nov 1947 [65]; Los Angeles CA; diabetic coma). AS, p. 384. BHD, p. 166. IFN, p. 101.

Fenton, Francis (Frank) (brother of **Leslie Fenton**) [scenarist] (b. Liverpool, England, 13 Feb 1903–23 Aug 1971 [68], Los Angeles CA). BHD2, p. 83. FDY, p. 423.

Fenton, Leslie C[arter] (brother of **Francis Fenton**) [actor/director/producer] (b. Liverpool, England, 12 Mar 1902–25 Mar 1978 [76], Montecito CA). m. **Ann Dvorak**, 1932–45 (d. 1979); (2) Marcela Zabala Howard. "Leslie C. Fenton," *Variety,* 19 Apr 1978). AS, p. 384. BHD1, p. 187; BHD2, p. 83. IFN, p. 101. Katz, p. 409. SD. Truitt 1983, p. 235.

Fenton, Mabel [actress] (*née* Ada Towne, b. Van Buren Co. MI, 29 Mar 1868–19 Apr 1931 [63?], Los Angeles CA). m. **Charles J. Ross**, 1887 (d. 1918). "Mabel Fenton Ross," *Variety,* 22 Apr 1931. AS, p. 384 (b. 1867). BHD, p. 166. IFN, p. 104 (Mabel Fenton Ross). SD. Truitt, p. 108.

Fenton, Mark [actor] (b. Crestline OH, 11 Nov 1866–29 Jul 1925 [58], Los Angeles CA; after amputation of leg crushed in auto accident). "Three Masses for Mark Fenton," *NYT,* 4 Aug 1925, 19:4 (b. near Shelby OH; began 1910). "Mark Fenton," *Variety,* 5 Aug 1925 (age 55). AS, p. 384. BHD, p. 166. IFN, p. 101. Truitt, p. 108. George Katchmer, "Remembering the Great Silents," *CI,* 197 (Nov 1991), 51.

Fenwick, Harry [actor] (b. Cincinnati OH, 1 Aug 1880–24 Dec 1932 [52]). BHD, p. 166. IFN, p. 101.

Fenwick, Irene [stage/film actress] (*née* Irene Frizzel, b. Chicago IL, 5 Sep 1887–24 Dec 1936 [49], Beverly Hills CA). m. (1) Felix Isman, 1909; (2) **Lionel Barrymore**, 16 Jul 1923, Rome, Italy (d. 1954); J.F. O'Brien. (Film debut: *The Commuters,* Kleine, 1915.) "Irene Fenwick, Actress, Is Dead; Wife of Lionel Barrymore Was Married to Him After They Had Been in Same Play; Long His Leading Lady; They Had Appeared Together on Broadway Until He Left the Stage for the Movies," *NYT,* 25 Dec 1936, 23:4. "Irene Fenwick Barrymore," *Variety,* 30 Dec 1936. AMD, p. 118. AS, p. 384. BHD, p. 166. IFN, p. 101. SD. Truitt, p. 108. "Irene Fenwick's Plans; Stage Star Signs Contract Giving Kleine Exclusive Rights to Screen Appearances," *NYDM,* 3 Mar 19145, 25:1. "Irene Fenwick," *MPW,* 13 Mar 1915, 1621. "Irene Fenwick," *MPW,* 14 Aug 1915, 1171. "Irene Fenwick Metro Star," *MPW,* 29 Jul 1916, 781. "Irene Fenwick Joins Famous Players," *MPW,* 28 Oct 1916, 533.

Feodoroff, Leo [actor] (b. Odessa, Russia, 1867?–23 Nov 1949 [82], Long Beach NY; auto accident injuries). "Leo Feodoroff," *Variety,* 30 Nov 1949 (in silents in New York and Hollywood). AS, p. 385. BHD, p. 166. IFN, p. 101. Truitt, p. 108.

Fera, Gertrude M. [actress] (b. NY, 1893). MSBB, p. 1034.

Ferguson, Alfred [actor] (b. Rosslare, Ireland, 19 Apr 1888–4 Dec 1971 [83], Burbank CA). AS, p. 385. BHD1, p. 187. IFN, p. 101. SD, p. 437 (b. Baltimore MD).

Ferguson, Casson [actor] (b. Alexandria LA, 29 May 1891–12 Feb 1929 [37], Culver City [Los Angeles] CA; pneumonia). "Casson Ferguson," *Variety,* 20 Feb 1929 (age 35). AS, p. 385. BHD, p. 166. IFN, p. 101. MH, p. 110. Truitt, p. 108. Billy H. Doyle, "Lost Players," *CI,* 172 (Oct 1989), 36. George Katchmer, "Remembering the Great Silents," *CI,* 223 (Jan 1994), 48:2.

Ferguson, Elsie Louise [stage/film actress] (b. New York NY, 19 Aug 1883–15 Nov 1961 [78], New London CT). m. (1) Frederick C. Hoey, 1907–div. 1911; (2) Thomas B. Clarke, Jr.; (3) British stage actor Frederick Worlock—div. 1930 (d. 1973); (4) Victor Augustus Seymour Egan, London, England, 17 Mar 1934 (d. 1956). (Stage debut: *The Belle of New York* [chorus girl], NYC, 1900. Film debut: *Barbary Sheep,* Artcraft, 1917; FP-L; Paramount; final film: *Scarlet Pages,* 1st National, 1930.) "Elsie Ferguson Is Dead at 76; Former Stage and Screen Star; Actress Won Fame in 1909 for 'Such a Little Queen'—Last Seen Here in 1943," *NYT,* 16 Nov 1961, 39:4; "$500,000 Is Willed to Animal Center by Elsie Ferguson," *NYT,* 28 Aug 1962, 33:8. "Elsie Ferguson," *Variety,* 22 Nov 1961. AMD, p. 118. AS, p. 385 (b. 18 Aug). BHD1, p. 187. FFF, p. 114. FSS, p. 109. IFN, p. 101 (b. 1885). MH, p. 110 (b. 19 Aug 1893). MSBB, p. 1034. SD. Spehr, p. 130 (b. 1883). Truitt, p. 108. WWS, p. 17. "Elsie Ferguson to Wed; Actress Engaged to T.B. Clarke, Jr., Vice-President of the Harriman National Bank," *NYDM,* 4 Aug 1915, 7:3 (b. 1886). "Elsie Ferguson with Cardinal," *MPW,* 10 Feb 1917, 858. "Tourneur to Direct Elsie Ferguson," *MPW,* 2 Jun 1917, 1462. "Elsie Ferguson Starts Work for Artcraft," *MPW,* 21 Jul 1917, 470. Frederick James Smith, "The Patrician of the Photoplay," *MPC,* VIII, Jun 1919, 18–19, 87, 89. "Elsie Ferguson to Resume Work on Dramatic Stage," *MPW,* 20 Dec 1919, 974. "Returns to Screen," *MPW,* 23 Sep 1922,

279. Regina Cannon, "'All Women Are Actresses!' Says Elsie Ferguson," *MW,* 5 Apr 1924, 7 (was then appearing onstage, "between pictures," in *The Moon Flower*). "Elsie Ferguson Signed," *MPW,* 28 Mar 1925, 391. DeWitt Bodeen, "Elsie Ferguson Personified the Cultivated Graces of Half a Century Ago," *FIR,* Nov 1964, 551–63 (includes filmography). Robert K. Klepper, "Elsie Ferguson: Aristocrat of the Silent Screen," *CI,* 261 (Mar 1997), 26–28.

Ferguson, George S. [actor] (b. 1884?–24 Apr 1944 [60], Los Angeles CA). "George S. Ferguson," *Variety,* 26 Apr 1944 ("player in silent films"). AS, p. 385. BHD, p. 166. IFN, p. 101. Truitt, p. 109.

Ferguson, Helen [actress: Wampas Star, 1922/publicist] (b. Decatur IL, 23 Jul 1900–14 Mar 1977 [76], Clearwater FL). m. **William Russell,** 1925, LA CA (d. 1929); Richard L. Hargreaves, 1930 (d. 1941). (Essanay; Metro.) "Helen Ferguson," *Variety,* 23 Mar 1977. AMD, p. 119. AS, p. 385. BHD1, p. 187; BHD2, p. 83 (b. 1901. BR, pp. 141–42 (b. 1901). FFF, p. 142. FSS, p. 109. IFN, p. 101 (b. 1901). Katz, p. 410. MH, p. 110. MSBB, p. 1034 (b. 1901). "Helen Ferguson Has Role in Screen Classic Feature," *MPW,* 18 Jan 1919, 325. "Helen Ferguson Will Support Lewis [Mitchell] in Picturization of 'Burning Daylight,'" *MPW,* 28 Feb 1920, 1495. June Lee, "Dan Cupid's Bulletin Board," *Paris and Hollywood,* 2 (Oct 1926), 86 ("At the time of their marriage a written contract was drawn up...they agreed to deposit $5,000 each year from their combined earnings to the credit of one of their best friends, Norman Brodin. Should they ever agree to cut the marriage bonds, the one first making the overtures forfeits all right to this joint account."). Robert A. Evans, "Evans' 1977 Chronicle," *FIR,* Mar 1978, 148 (age 76).

Ferguson, Hilda [actress] (*née* Hildegarde Gibbons, b. Baltimore MD, 1903–3 Sep 1933 [30?], New York NY; heart attack). m. Robert B. Ugarte. (Sennett.) "Hilda Ferguson," *Variety,* 10 Oct 1933. AS, p. 385. BHD, p. 166. Truitt, p. 109.

Ferguson, Lee S. [publicist]. No data found. AMD, p. 119. "Selznick Makes Ferguson Publicity Department Head," *MPW,* 7 Aug 1920, 758.

Ferguson, Lile [stuntman] (d. Yuma AZ, 21 Nov 1921). BHD, p. 166. IFN, p. 101.

Ferguson, Mattie [actress] (b. Minneapolis MN, 1862–31 Mar 1929 [67], New York NY). m. Fred Reichelt. "Mattie Ferguson," *Variety,* 3 Apr 1929. AS, p. 385. BHD, p. 166.

Ferguson, Robert V. [actor] (b. Scotland, 1848?–21 Apr 1913 [65], New York NY [Death Certificate No. 12895]; asthma). (Imp.) AMD, p. 119. AS, p. 385. BHD1, p. 608. "Death of Robert Ferguson, Comedian," *MPW,* 3 May 1913, 467.

Ferguson, William J[ason] [actor] (b. Baltimore MD, 8 Jun 1844–4 May 1930 [85], Pikesville MD). m. Fannie Pierson (d. 1878). "William J. Ferguson," *Variety,* 14 May 1930 ("last surviving member of the 'Our American Cousin' cast that played at Ford's, Washington"). AMD, p. 119. AS, p. 385. BHD, p. 166 (b. 1845). IFN, p. 101. SD. Truitt, p. 109. "World Film Actor Witness of Lincoln's Assassination," *MPW,* 19 Jun 1915, 1951.

Ferguson, William R. [publicist] (b. Gloucester MA-6 Jul 1959, Welles ME). AMD, p. 119. BHD2, p. 83. "William R. Ferguson Heads Metro-Goldwyn Exploitation," *MPW,* 20 Jun 1925, 846.

Fern, Fritzie [actress] (b. Akron OH, 19 Sep 1901–20 Sep 1932 [31], Los Angeles CA). (Began 1922.) "Fritzie Fern," *Variety,* 27 Sep 1932, p. 63 (age 24). AS, p. 385. BHD1, p. 188. IFN, p. 101 (age 24).

Fernandes, Nascimento [circus clown/stage/film actor/producer] (*né* Manuel Fernandes do Nascimento, b. Faro, Portugal, 6 Nov 1886–15 Aug 1955 [68], Lisbon, Portugal; cancer). "Nascimento Fernandes," *Variety,* 11 Jan 1956, p. 70 (in films produced in Lisbon, Paris and Brazil). AS, p. 386. BHD1, p. 188; BHD2, p. 83. IFN, p. 101 (d. Jan 1956, age 76).

Fernandez, Bijou [Goldwyn talent scout/stage/film actress] (b. New York NY, 1877?–7 Nov 1961 [84], New York NY). m. **William L. Abingdon** (d. 1959). "Bijou Fernandez," *Variety,* 15 Nov 1961. AS, p. 386. BHD, p. 166. IFN, p. 101. SD. Truitt, p. 109.

Fernández, Emilio, "El Indio" [actor/director/scenarist] (b. El Seco Hondo, Mexico, 26 Mar 1904–6 Aug 1986 [82], Mexico City, Mexico; heart attack). AS, p. 386. BHD2, p. 83. Waldman, p. 103.

Fernandez, Escamillo [actor] (b. CT, 6 Sep 1879–31 Mar 1952 [72], Los Angeles CA). BHD, "Addendum."

Fernandez, Felix [actor] (*né* Felix Fernandez Garcia, b. Cangas de Onis, Spain, 21 Sep 1899–5 Jul 1966 [66], Madrid, Spain). AS, p. 386.

Fernandez, George M. [actor] (b. 1864–1923 [58?]). BHD, p. 166.

Fernandez, Roy [actor] (b. 1888–22 Jun 1927 [39], Los Angeles CA). AS, p. 386. BHD, p. 166. IFN, p. 102.

Fernau, Rudolf [actor] (*né* Andreas Rudolf Neuberger, b. Munich, Germany, 7 Jun 1898–4 Nov 1985 [87], Munich, Germany). AS, p. 386.

Ferrara, Luigi [director/producer] (b. Italy, 1882–13 Aug 1962 [80?], Naples, Italy). BHD2, p. 83.

Ferrari, Angelo [skating champion/actor] (b. Lombardy, Italy, 14 Aug 1897–1945 [48?], Berlin, Germany; after an apoleptic fit). AS, p. 386 (b. Rome, Italy). BHD1, p. 188 (b. Rome). JS, p. 161 (in Italian silents from 1916).

Ferrari, Mario [actor[(b. Rome, Italy, 3 Sep 1894–Apr/May 1975 [80]). AS, p. 386.

Ferrari, Martin [director] (b. Russia, 1879–18 May 1927 [47?]). BHD, p. 166. "Martin Ferrari," *Variety,* 5 May 1927.

Ferrell, Cullen H. [director] (d. 7 Feb 1930, New York NY). BHD2, p. 83.

Ferreira, José A[ugustin] [director] (b. Buenos Aires, Argentina, 28 Aug 1889-Feb 1943 [53], Buenos Aires, Argentina). AS, p. 387 (under Ferreira and Ferreyra). BHD2, p.83.

Ferrers, Helen [actress] (b. Cookham, England, 1865–1 Feb 1943 [77?], London, England). AS, p. 387.

Ferrez, Julio [director] (b. Rio de Janeiro, Brazil, 1881–1946 [65?], Rio de Janeiro, Brazil). AS, p. 387.

Ferriere, Yvonne [actress] (*née* Yvonne Ponsard, b. France, 1889–14 Jun 1929 [40?], Paris, France). AS, p. 387.

Ferrieres, Ann-Marie [actress] (*née* Jeanne Laure Alvina Hovine, b. Tournai, Belgium, 7 Feb 1888–30 Aug 1992 [104], Ixelles, Belgium). AS, p. 387.

Ferris, Audrey [actress: Wampas Star, 1928] (*née* Audrey Kellar, b. Detroit MI, 30 Aug 1909–3 May 1990 [81], Los Angeles CA). (WB.) AMD, p. 119. AS, p. 387 (b. 1908). "A New Comer Gets Contract," *MPW,* 16 Jul 1927, 186. "Audrey Ferris," *MPW,* 20 Aug 1927, 517. Ragan, *Who's Who in Hollywood,* p. 527.

Ferris, Walter [scenarist] (b. Green Bay wI, 23 Apr 1886). AS, p. 387.

Ferriz, Miguel Angel [actor] (*né* Miguel Angel Ferriz Mendoza, b. Mexico, 29 Nov 1899–1 Jan 1967 [67], Mexico City, Mexico; heart attack). AS, p. 387.

Ferry, Felix [actor/singer] (b. Bucharest, Romania, 1897–12 Nov 1953 [56?], Bad Bomburg, Germany). AS, p. 388.

Fertner, Antoni [actor] (b. Czenstochowa, Poland, 23 May 1874–16 Apr 1959 [84]). AS, p. 388.

Ferval, Pierre [actor] (*né* Pierre Fabregues, b. Asnieres-sur-Seine, France, 18 May 1899). AS, p. 388.

Fery, Claude [director] (b. Munich, Germany, 1890). AS, p. 388.

Fescourt, Henri [director/writer] (*né* Marcellin Henri Fescourt, b. Beziers, so. France, 22 Nov 1880–9 Aug 1966 [85?], Neuilly-sur-Seine, France). Garth Pedler, "Garth's Vintage Viewing," *CI,* 232 (Oct 1994), C6-C7. AS, p. 388 (b. 23 Nov). BHD2, p. 83 (b. 23 Nov).

Fetchit, Stepin [actor] (*né* Lincoln Theodore Monroe Andrew Perry, b. Key West FL, 30 May 1898 or 1902–19 Nov 1985 [83?], Woodland Hills CA). m. (3)Bernice Sims. Donald Bogle, *Toms, Coons, Mulattoes, Mammies and Bucks; An Interpretive History of Blacks in American Films* (New York: Continuum, 1989), pp. 38–44. "Stepin Fetchit, the First Black to Win Film Fame, Dies at 83," *NYT,* 20 Nov 1985, D31:1 (age 83). "Stepin Fetchit Dead at 83; Comic Actor in Over 40 Films," *Variety,* 27 Nov 1985 (age 83). AS, p. 388. BHD1, p. 188 (b. 1902). FSS, p. 109. SD. Jim Arpy, "Even as a Has-Been Stepin Was Special," *CI,* 127 (Jan 1985), 60 (reprinted from *Quad City Times,* Davenport IA). "Stepin Fetchit," WBO1, pp. 194–95 (b. 1902).

Fetherston, Edward A. [actor] (aka Eddie Featherstone, b. New York NY, 9 Sep 1896–12 Jun 1965 [68], Yucca Valley CA; heart attack). m. Roselle Novello. "Eddie Fetherston," *Variety,* 23 Jun 1965. AMD, p. 119. AS, p. 388. BHD1, p. 188. IFN, p. 102. Truitt, p. 109. "Eddie Fetherston," *MPW,* 15 May 1926, 239.

Fetner, Tanya [actress]. No data found. AMD, p. 119. "Tanya Fetner," *MPW,* 15 Sep 1917, 1672.

Feuhrer, Bobby [actor] (*né* Wilhelm Robert McBain Feuhrer). No data found. AMD, p. 119. "Universal Ike, Jr.," *MPW,* 25 Jul 1914, 558.

Feuillade, Louis Jean [actor/director/producer/scenarist] (b. Lunel, France, 20 Feb 1873–26 Feb 1925 [52], Nice, France [extrait de deecès no. 608/1925]). AS, p. 388. BHD2, p. 83 (b. 9 Feb).

Feusier, Norman [actor] (b. San Francisco CA, 24 Mar 1886–27 Dec 1945 [59], Los Angeles CA). AS, p. 388.

Feydeau, Georges Léon Jules Marie [actor/scenarist] (b. Paris, France, 8 Dec 1862–5 Jun 1921 [58], Rueil-Malmaison, France). AS, p. 388.

Feyder, Jacques (brother of actor/director Bernard Farrel, b. 22 Jun 1926; father of Paul Feyder, b. 18 Apr 1922) [director/scenarist/producer] (*né* Jacques Frederix, b. Ixelles, Belgium, 21 Jul 1885–24 May 1948 [62], Rives-de-Prangins, France). m. Francoise Bandy de Naleche (**Francoise Rosay**), 26 Jul 1917 (d. 1974). (MGM.) "Jacques Feyder," *Variety,* 2 Jun 1948 ("died in Switzerland recently"; age 54). AS, p. 388. BHD, p. 166; BHD2, p. 83 (d. Switzerland). FDY, p. 425. IFN, p. 102. Katz, p. 414. Waldman, p. 105. Garth Pedler, "Jacques Feyder, Before Hollywood," *CI,* 107 (May 1984), 34–36.

Feyer, Ernst B. [scenarist]. No data found. FDY, p. 425.

Ffolliott, Gladys [actress] (b. Ireland, 1879–1 Feb 1928 [48?], London, England). BHD, p. 166. "Gladys Ffolliott," *Variety,* 15 Feb 1928.

Ffrangcon-Davies, Gwen [actress] (b. London, England, 25 Jan 1891–27 Jan 1992 [101], Essex, England). AS, p. 388.

Fidler, Ben [actor] (b. 1867?–19 Oct 1932 [65], Los Angeles CA). "Ben Fidler," *Variety,* 25 Oct 1932. AS, p. 389. IFN, p. 102.

Field, Alexander [actor] (b. London, England 6 Jun 1892–17 Aug 1971 [79], London, England). AS, p. 389. BHD1, p. 188. IFN, p. 102.

Field, Ben [actor] (b. England, 1878–21 Oct 1939 [61], Los Angeles CA). AS, p. 389 (d. London, England). BHD1, p. 188. IFN, p. 102.

Field, Edward Salisbury [scenarist] (d. 20 Sep 1936, Zaca Lake CA). BHD2, p. 83.

Field, Elinor [actress] (b. Plymouth PA, 1902). (Universal.) AMD, p. 119. AS, p. 389. MH, p. 110. "Elinor Field to Star in One-Reel Strands," *MPW,* 27 Jul 1918, 572. George Katchmer, "Remembering the Great Silents," *CI,* 245 (Nov 1995), 43–44.

Field, George [actor] (b. San Francisco CA, 18 Mar 1877–9 Mar 1925 [47], CA; tuberculosis). m. (Mutual, 1912; American.) AS, p. 389. BHD, p. 167. IFN, p. 102. "Players in Accidents; Fields Hurt in Motorcycle Spill…," *NYDM,* 15 Jul 1914, 22:2. George Katchmer, "Remembering the Great Silents," *CI,* 223 (Jan 1994), 48:3.

Field, Gladys [actress] (*née* Gladys Wesley, b. San Francisco CA, 1895–2 Sep 1920 [25?], Mt. Vernon NY; in childbirth). m. John M. O'Brien. (Essanay.) "Mrs. John [M.] O'Brien," *Variety,* 10 Sep 1920. AMD, p. 119. AS, p. 389. BHD, p. 167. Truitt, p. 109 (d. Aug 1920). *MPW,* 26 Apr 1913, 490 (returned to films after a prolonged illness). "Gladys Field," *MPW,* 3 May 1913, 490.

Field, Madalynne [actress] (b. MI, 1 Apr 1907–1 Oct 1974 [67], Palm Springs CA). BHD, p. 167.

Field, Norman [actor] (b. Montreal, Canada, 4 Jan 1881–11 Sep 1956 [75], Los Angeles CA). AS, p. 389.

Field, Salisbury [writer]. No data found. AMD, p. 119. "Salisbury Field Joins DeMille," *MPW,* 21 Feb 1920, 1264.

Field, Walter [actor] (b. on a boart on the way to New York NY, 19 Aug 1874–5 Jun 1976 [101], Los Angeles CA). AS, p. 389.

Fielding, Edward [actor] (*né* Edward B. Elkins, b. Brooklyn NY, 19 Mar 1879–10 Jan 1945 [65], Los Angeles CA; heart attack after mowing lawn). "Edward Fielding," *Variety,* 17 Jan 1945. AS, p.389. BHD1, p. 189. IFN, p. 102. SD.

Fielding, Maggie [stage/film actress] (*née?,* d. 15 Jul 1913, NY). m. John Fielding. "Maggie Fielding," *Variety,* 25 Jul 1913. SD.

Fielding, Margaret [actress] (b. Jersey City NJ, 22 Jun 1895–25 Nov 1974 [79], Los Angeles CA). BHD1, p. 189.

Fielding, Minnie [actress] (*née* Minnie Flynn, b. 1871?–22 Jul 1936 [65] Los Angeles). (Biograph.) "Minnie Flynn," *Variety,* 29 Jul 1936. AS, p. 390. BHD, p. 167. IFN, p. 102. Truitt, p. 109.

Fielding, Romaine [actor/director/producer/scenarist] (b. Bowling Green KY, 26 May 1879–15 Dec 1927 [48], Los Angeles CA; blood clot from infected tooth). m. Mabel Vann (*née* Mabel Van Valkenburg)—div. Sep? 1917, Minneapolis MN. (Lubin.) "Romaine Fielding," *Variety,* 21 Dec 1927 (age 45). AMD, p. 119. AS, p. 390 (d. 16 Sep). BHD, p. 167; BHD2, p. 84. IFN, p. 102. Spehr, p. 130 (b. Corsica, Italy, 1882). Truitt, p. 109. "A Crack Shot," *MPW,* IX, 12 Aug 1911, 379. "Romaine Fielding, Lubin Director—An Expert Shot," *MPW,* 21 Dec 1912, 1197. "Romaine Fielding Stages Spectacle," *MPW,* 13 Dec 1913, 1266. "Romaine Fielding," *NYDM,* 15 Jul 1914, 22:1. "The Moving Picture of the Future," *MPW,* 15 Aug 1914, 941. "Produces Five Features at Same Time," *MPW,* 12 Dec 1914, 1541. "Fielding to Head Round-the-World Co.," *MPW,* 9 Jan 1915, 223. Romaine Fielding, "Who Gets the Credit?; A Surprisingly Frank Article on the Relative Importance of Author, Director, Player—and Press Agent—By 'One Who Knows' and Who Is Not Afraid to Speak," *NYDM,* 27 Jan 1915, 41:1, 46:1. "Fielding's Collapsible Studio," *MPW,* 6 Feb 1915, 840. "Romaine Fielding Jons Universal," *MPW,* 11 Dec 1915, 2020. "Romaine Fielding with World Film," *MPW,* 31 Mar 1917, 2090. "Romaine Fielding Divorced," *Variety,* 7 Sep 1917, p. 26. "Obituary," *MPW,* 24 Dec 1927, 23 (d. 16 Dec). Eldon K. Everett, "The Search for Romaine Fielding," *CFC,* 44 (Fall, 1974), 28, 32, 35. P. St. George Cooke, "Romaine Fielding and the Lubin Motion Picture Co., Silver City, New Mexico, 1913," *CI,* 85 (Jul 1982), 37; Part II, 86 (Aug 1982), 38–39; Part III, 87 (Sep 1982), 24–25, 45. "Romaine Fielding and the Luibin Moving Picture Company," *CI,* 97 (Jul 1983), 9–11, 25; Part II, 98 (Aug 1983), 29–31, 69, 71; Part III, 99 (Sep 1983), 40–42. Anthony Slide, *Silent Portraits* (Vestal NY: The Vestal Press, Ltd., 1989). Linda Kowall Woal, "Romaine Fielding: The West's touring auteur," *Film History,* Winter 1995, 401–25. Joseph P. Eckhardt, *The King of the Movies; Film Pioneer Siegmund Lubin* (Madison WI: Farleigh Dickinson University Press, 1998), p. 129 ("Though he had been born William Grant Blandin in Iowa, he claimed to be the son of wealthy Spanish and Italian-French parents living on the island of Corsica.").

Fields, Benny [singer/actor] (*né* Benjamin Geisenfeld, b. Milwaukee WI, 14 Jun 1894–16 Aug 1959 [65], New York NY; heart attack). m. Blossom Seeley. "Benny Fields, 65; Created 'Croon' Style of Singing," *Variety,* 19 Aug 1959. AS, p. 390. IFN, p. 102.

Fields, Dorothy (daughter of **Lew Fields**; sister of **Herbert** and **Joseph Fields**) [composer/scenarist] (b. Allenhurst NJ, 15 Jul 1905–28 Mar 1974 [68], New York NY). AS, p. 390. BHD2, p. 84.

Fields, Herbert [scenarist/librettist] (son of **Lew Fields**; brother of **Dorothy Fields** and **Joseph**) (b. New York NY, 26 Jul 1897–24 Mar 1958 [60], New York NY; heart attack). (Paramount.) AS, p. 390 (b. 1898). BHD, p. 167; BHD2, p. 84. "Herbert Fields," *Variety,* 26 Mar 1958, 79:1.

Fields, John F. [actor] (b. 1855?–30 May 1921 [66], Belleville NJ). m. Emma. "John F. Fields," *Variety,* 20 May 1921. AS, p. 390.

Fields, Joseph A[lbert] (son of **Lew Fields**; brother of **Dorothy** and **Herbert Fields**) [scenarist] (b. New York NY, 21 Feb 1895–3 Mar 1966 [], Beverly Hills CA). AS, p. 390.

Fields, Lew (father of **Herbert**, **Joseph** and **Dorothy Fields**) [actor] (*né* Lewis Maurice Schanfield, b. New York NY, 1 Jan 1867–21 Jul 1941 [74], Beverly Hills CA; pneumonia). m. Rose Harris. "Lew Fields Dies; Noted Comedian, 74; Joe Weber, Vaudeville Partner for 60 Years, and Family Only Ones at Secret Burial; Began Career on Bowery; Team at 30 Years' Jubilee Scored Broadway Record—Noted Players in Company," *NYT,* 22 Jul 1941, 19:1. "Lew Fields Dies in Cal. at 73, Joe Weber at His Bedside," *Variety,* 23 Jul 1941. AMD, p. 119. AS, p. 390. BHD1, p. 189 (d. 20 Jul). IFN, p. 102. SD. Spehr, p. 130. Truitt, p. 110. "Weber & Fields in Pictures," *MPW,* 6 Sep 1913, 1051. "A Famous Team," *MPW,* 22 May 1915, 1239. "Lew Fields Sued for Breach of Contract," *MPW,* 4 Sep 1915, 1625. "Fields Makes Counterclaim," *MPW,* 25 Sep 1915, 2178. "Weber & Fields Have Narrow Escape," *MPW,* 9 Oct 1915, 273. "Now Weber and Fields," *MPW,* 10 Jan 1925, 169.

Fields, Nat [actor] (b. 1880–3 Feb 1934 [53?], Detroit MI). BHD1, p. 608.

Fields, Stanley [stage/film actor] (*né* Walter L. Agnew, b. Allegheny [Pittsburgh] PA, 20 May 1884–23 Apr 1941 [56], Los Angeles CA; heart attack). "Stanley Fields, 57, Character Actor; Noted for His Gangster Roles in 'Little Caesar' and Similar Films—Dies in West; Appeared in Vaudeville [with Frank Fay]; Began Stage Career in Chorus with George M. Cohan—In Films 15 Years," *NYT,* 24 Apr 1941, 21:6 (fighter Bennie Leonard broke his nose. "The injury is said to have left a disfigurement which appealed to casting directors looking for ferocious villains."). "Stanley Fields," *Variety,* 30 Apr 1941 (age 57). AS, p. 391 (b. 1880). BHD1, p. 189. IFN, p. 102. Truitt 1983 (b. 1880).

Fields, W.C. [stage/film actor/scenarist] (*né* William Claude Dukenfield, b. Philadelphia PA, 29 Jan 1879–25 Dec 1946 [67], Pasadena CA). m. Harriet (Hattie) Hughes, 8 Apr 1900, San Francisco CA. Ronald J. Fields, commentator, *W.C. Fields by Himself; His Intended Autobiography* (Englewood Cliffs NJ: Prentice-Hall, 1973) (b. 1980). David T. Rocks, *W.C. Fields—An Annotated Guide: Chronology, Bibliographies, Discography, Filmographies, Press Books, Cigarette Cards, Film Clips, and Impersonators* (Jefferson NC: McFarland, 1993). "W.C. Fields, 66, Dies; Famed as Comedian; Mimicry Star of the Films Since 1924 Got Start as a $5-a-Week Juggler; Rarely Followed Script; Raspy Remarks and 'Know-It-All' Perspective Made Him Nation-Wide Character," *NYT,* 26 Dec 1946, 25:1 (b. 1880). Jack Pulaski, "Show Biz in Tribute to W.C. Fields; Cantor Recalls Terrif Sense of Humor," *Variety,* 1 Jan 1947. AMD, p. 119. AS, p. 390 (b. 10 Feb). BHD1, p. 189; BHD2, p. 84 (b. 1880). FSS, p. 110. IFN, p. 102. Katz, p. 416 (b. 10 Feb). SD. "W.C. Fields," *MPW,* 25 Sep 1915, 2162. "Engage Popular Pla¥ers," *MPW,* 26 Apr 1924, 735. "Fields in New Production," *MPW,* 5 Sep 1925, 88. Sara Redway, "W.C. Fields Pleads for Rough Humor," *MPC*, Sep 1925, 32–33, 73. Nanette Kutner, "Introducing Bill Fields; 'Famous Ziegfeld Follies' Comedian Who Has Just Made His Motion Picture Debut [in *Sally of the Sawdust*]," *MW*, 26 Sep 1925, 17, 46 (*Sally* was *not* his film debut). Dunham Thorp, "The Up-to-Date Timer; W.C. Fields Is an Old Hand at the Comedy Game...," *MPC*, Sep 1926, 38–39, 88–89. "Fields Signs Contractg to Star for Paramount," *MPW*, 21 Nov 1925, 229. "Sue Over W.C. Fields," *MPW*, 5 Mar 1927, 9. "Fields—Conklin a Comedy Team," *MPW*, 11 Jun 1927, 419. "Fields Due to Stay in Hospital 6 Weeks," *MPW*, 8 Oct 1927, 343.

Fieling, Edward [actor] (b. Brooklyn NY, 1879–10 Jan 1945 [65?], Beverly Hills CA). BHD2, p. 390.

Fierce, Louis [actor] (b. 1852?–11 Mar 1926 [74], Bernardsville NJ). "Louis Fierce," *Variety*, 17 Mar 1926. AS, p. 390. BHD, p. 167.

Fife, Shannon [scenarist] (b. TX, 16 Dec 1888–7 May 1972 [83], Dallas TX). "Obituaries; Shannon Fife," *Lake Placid News*, 25 May 1972 (he is buried in Old Cavalry Cemetery TX on 9 May). (Lubin.) AMD, p. 120. FDY, p. 425. "Briefs of Biography," *NYDM*, 13 May 1914, 34:3. "Gossip of the Studios," *NYDM*, 7 Oct 1914, 27:1 (visiting family in Dallas TX). "Shannon Fife Is Prolific," *MPW*, 20 Mar 1915, 1782. "Former Screen Writer Once Again at Work," *MPW*, 8 Mar 1919, 1342.

Figman, Max [actor] (b. Vienna, Austria, 1866?–13 Feb 1952 [85], Bayside [New York] NY). m. (1) Sadie Martinot (*née* Sarah Frances Marie Martinot, d. 1923); (2) **Lolita Robertson**. "Max Figman," *Variety*, 20 Feb 1952. AMD, p. 120. AS, p. 390. BHD, p. 167 (b. 1868); BHD2, p. 84. IFN, p. 102. SD. "New Lasky Picture Starts," *MPW*, 16 May 1914, 953. "Rolfe Gets Stars; Lois Meredith and Max Figman Among Latest Signed by Metro Ally," *NYDM*, 21 Apr 1915, 22:1. "Max Figman Plays the Hero in Real Life," *MPW*, 4 Sep 1915, 1662. "Figman—Robertson Comedies for Metro," *MPW*, 8 Jul 1916, 241.

Figman, Oscar Brimberton [actor] (b. 1882–18 Jul 1930 [48?], Neponsit NY). "Oscar Figman," *Variety*, 23 Jul 1930. AS, p. 390. BHD, p. 167.

Fijewski, Tadzio [actor] (b. Poland, 14 Aug 1911–1977 [65?]). BHD, p. 167.

Filauri, Antonio [actor] (b. Italy, 9 Mar 1889–18 Jan 1964 [74], San Gabriel CA). BHD2, p. 391.

Filbert, Fatty [actor]. No data found. AMD, p. 120. "Funny Fatty Filbert Is Star in Josh Binney Comedies," *MPW*, 18 May 1918, 1018.

Fildes, Glenn [actor] (b. MN, 13 Nov 1914–21 Sep 1968 [53], Alhambra CA). BHD1, p. 608.

Fildes, Roy [actor] (b. MO, 29 Jul 1910–22 Jan 1990 [79], San Diego CA). BHD1, p. 608.

Fildew, William E. [cameraman] (b. 1890?–17 Jul 1943 [53], Los Angeles CA). (Biograph; Reliance; Griffith; Goldwyn.) "William E. Fildew," *Variety*, 28 Jul 1943. AMD, p. 120. AS, p. 391. BHD2, p. 84. FDY, p. 457. William E. Fildew, "Trials of the Cameraman," *MPW*, 21 Jul 1917, 391–92. "Fildew Becomes Member of Allison Staff," *MPW*, 20 Jul 1918, 388. "Cameraman, Looking for Snow, Travels Across the Continent," *MPW*, 19 Mar 1921, 307.

Fillmore, Clyde [actor] (*né* Clyde Fogle, b. McConnelsville OH, 25 Sep 1875–19 Dec 1946 [71], Santa Monica CA). AS, p. 391. BHD1, p. 189. IFN, p. 103. Billy H. Doyle, "Lost Players," *CI*, 16 (Oct 1988), 30.

Fillmore, Nellie [actress] (b. 1864?–20 Jun 1942 [78], Winthrop MA). "Nellie Fillmore," *Variety*, 8 Jul 1942 (Mrs. Nellie Dorsey Brown). AS, p. 391. BHD, p. 167.

Fillmore, Russell [actor/director] (b. TN, 7 Sep 1888–18 Aug 1950 [62], Los Angeles CA). AS, p. 391.

Filson, Al W. [actor] (b. Blufton IN, 27 Jan 1857–14 Nov 1925 [68], Elsinore CA). m. Lea Errol. AS, p. 391. BHD, p. 167. IFN, p. 103.

Filson, Mrs. Beulah T *see* **Darkcloud**

Finaly, Pierre Auguste [actor] (b. Paris, France, 7 Aug 1889–4 Apr 1937 [47], Paris, France [extrait de décès no. 293/1937]). AS, p. 391.

Finch, Flora [actress] (b. Sussex, England, 17 Jun 1869–4 Jan 1940 [71], Los Angeles CA; streptococcus infection). m. Harold March. (Biograph, 1908; MGM.) "Flora Finch, Star of Film Comedies; Original 'Ugly Duckling' of the Screen Dies in Hollywood—Appeared with John Bunny; Began Her Career in 1910; Played in 'Those Awful Hats' and 'A Night Out'—On Stage with Sir Phillip Ben Greet," *NYT*, 5 Jan 1940, 19:3. "Flora Finch," *Variety*, 10 Jan 1940. AMD, p. 120. AS, p. 391. BHD1, p. 189. FSS, p. 110. IFN, p. 103. MH, p. 110. Slide, pp. 139–40. Truitt, p. 110. "Flora Finch, of the Vitagraph Company," *Motion Picture Story Magazine* (Nov 1913), 109. "Flora Finch; Comedienne of the Vitagraph Company," *MPS*, 8 Jan 1915, 26. "Flora Finch," *MPS* (Apr 1915), p. 112. "In the Picture Studios," *NYDM*, 21 Jul 1915, 19:2 (as a member of "Vitagraph's Big Comedy Four [filming *A Night Out* with Hughie Mack, Kate Price, and WIlliam Shea]," she was "the lightweight of the quartette who refuses to weight more than 110 pounds."). "Flora Finch Has Own Company," *MPW*, 23 Dec 1916, 1792. "Flora Finch's First Fun Film," *MPW*, 28 Apr 1917, 629. "Film Frolics Pictures to Produce Six Two-Reel Comedies Yearly Starring Flora Finch," *MPW*, 7 Aug 1920, 719. Flora Finch, "Old Days in the Movies," *Movie Weekly*, 7 May 1921, 10–11; Part II, *Movie Weekly*, 14 May 1921, 22–23. "Flora Finch 'No Extra,'" *MPW*, 23 Feb 1924, 632. "Flora Finch with Chadwick," *MPW*, 21 Feb 1925, 811. "Flora Finch," *MPW*, 26 Jun 1926, 706.

Finch, Veronica Cavendish [actress] (b. 1900–16 Jul 1924 [24?], New York NY). BHD, p. 167.

Findlay, John [actor] (b. England, 1858–10 Apr 1918 [59?], New York NY). m. (1) Patricia Cutts (*née* Patricia Graham, d. 1974); (2) Agnes. "John Findlay," *Variety*, 19 Apr 1918. AS, p. 391 (d. 9 Apr). BHD, p. 167. SD.

Findlay, Ruth [actress] (b. New York NY, b. 1904?–13 Jul 1949 [45], New York NY). m. Donald W. Lamb, 1927. "Ruth Findlay," *Variety*, 20 Jul 1949. AMD, p. 120. AS, p. 391. BHD, p. 167. IFN, p. 103. "Ruth Findlay Star of 'The Salamander,'" *MPW*, 15 Jan 1916, 392.

Findlay, Thomas B[ruce] [actor] (b. Guelph, Ontario, Canada, 28 Dec 1873–29 May 1941 [67], Aylmer, Quebec, Canada). "Thomas Bruce Findlay; Character Actor Was Seen Here in 'Mice and Men,' 'First Lady,'" *NYT*, 30 May 1941, 15:2. "Thomas B. Findley," *Variety*, 4 Jun 1941. AS, p. 391. BHD, p. 167. IFN, p. 103. Truitt, p. 110.

Fine, Budd [actor] (b. CT, 9 Sep 1894–9 Feb 1966 [71], West Los Angeles CA). BHD1, p. 190.

Fineman, Bernard P. [producer] (b. NY, 23 Feb 1895–28 Sep 1971 [76], Culver City CA; cancer). m. (1) **Evelyn Brent**, 1 Nov 1922–27 (d. 1975); (2) Margaret de Mille; (3) Miriam Hayman. (Began 1918; Paramount; RKO; MGM.) "Bernard P. Fineman," *Variety*, 6 Oct 1971. AMD, p. 120. AS, p. 391. BHD2, p. 84 (b. 22 Feb). IFN, p. 103. "Fineman Gets Ready to 'Treat 'em Rough,'" *MPW*, 29 Jun 1918, 1857. "Fineman Rejoins Schulberg," *MPW*, 18 Sep 1926, 156. "Evelyn Brent Gets Divorce from Fineman," *MPW*, 27 Aug 1927, 585 (separated Feb 1925; $52,000 settlement). June Lee, "Dan Cupid's Bulletin Board," *Paris and Hollywood Screen Secrets*, Oct 1927, 37 (accused of staying away from Brent for days at a time and mental cruelty).

Finkel, Abem [scenarist] (b. New York NY, 6 Dec 1889–10 Mar 1948 [58], San Diego CA). AS, p. 392. BHD2, p. 84.

Finlay, Currie [actress] (b. Edinburg, Scotland, 20 Jan 1878–9 May 1968 [90], England). AS, p. 392.

Finlay, Robert [actor] (*né* Robert Finlay Bush, b. New Haven CT, 1888?–2 Apr 1929 [41], Prescott AZ). "Robert Finlay," *Variety*, 17 Apr 1929. AS, p. 392. BHD, p. 167. Truitt, p. 110.

Finlayson, Alex [actor/assistant director] (b. Los Angeles CA, 13 Nov 1912–7 Feb 1954 [41], Culver City CA; internal hemorrhages). m. Patricia. (Panoramic Prods.; RKO Pathé.) "Alex Finlayson," *NYT*, 9 Feb 1954, 27:4. "Alex Finlayson," *Variety*, 17 Feb 1954. BHD2, p. 84 (b. Scotland). IFN, p. 103 (b. Scotland).

Finlayson, James H[enderson] [actor/Keystone Cop] (b. Falkirk, Scotland, 27 Aug 1887–9 Oct 1953 [66], Los Angeles CA; heart attack). m. Emily Gilbert, Jul 1919. (Sennett; Ince; L-KO; Roach.) "James H. Finlayson, of 'Keystone Kops'; 'Villain' of Mack Sennett and Hal Roach Comedies Dies—Seen with Laurel and Hardy," *NYT*, 10 Oct 1953, 17:5. "James H. Finlayson," *Variety*, 14 Oct 1953 (d. Hollywood). AMD, p. 120. AS, p. 392. BHD1, p. 190. FSS, p. 112. IFN, p. 103. Katz, p. 420. Truitt, p. 110. "Finlayson Just Finishing Third Year of Film Work," *MPW*, 13 Dec 1919, 831.

Finley, Ned [stage/film actor/director/producer] (b. 10 Jul 1870–27 Sep 1920 [50], New York NY [Death Certificate No. 26491; strychnine poisoning (suicide) and chronic morphinism]). (Vitagraph.) "Ned Finley a Suicide; Actor-Producer Pens Death Note—Takes Strychnine," *Variety*, 1 Oct 1920. AMD, p. 120. AS, p. 392. BHD, p. 167. IFN, p. 103. Slide, p. 140. "Ned Finley Joins Vitagraph," *MPW*, 5 Apr 1913, 30. "Vitagrpah Director Ned Finley and His Company Starting for North Carolina," *NYDM*, 15 Jul 1914, 24:2 (photo of company with names). "Editorials in Films; 'Semi-Educationals' as Seen by David W. Griffith and Ned Finley," *NYDM*, 1 Jul 1914, 21:3. "Finley Off for Carolina," *NYDM*, 1 Jul 1914, 24:3 (to produce "a number of mountain pictures" at Hendersonville NC). "Ned Finley's Vitagraphers Flit South," *MPW*, 11 Jul 1914, 269. "Finley Lost and Found; Director Disappears from Carolina, Turns Up in New York, a Victim of Aphasia," *NYDM*, 5 Aug 1914, 25:1 (a blow on the head received when he fell from a boat. On a park bench in NYC he kept saying, "Finley, Screen Club," which was contacted. He was taken to a hospital.). "Where Is Ned Finley?," *MPW,* 15 Aug 1914, 966. "Ned Finley Has Own Company," *MPW,* 16 Feb 1918, 972. "Personally and Otherwise," *MPW,* 8 Feb 1919, 742 (in hospital). "Obituary," *MPW,* 16 Oct 1920, 961.

Finn, Adelaide [stage/film actress] (*nee?,* b. 4 Jan 1894–20 Jan 1978 [84], Addingham PA). m. Albert Hugh Finn. "Adelaide Finn," *Variety,* 8 Feb 1978, 74:3 (d. Drexel Hill PA). BHD, p. 167. IFN, p. 103.

Finn, James H. [director/scenarist: Our Gang comedies] (b. 1887–12 Oct 1952 [65?], Los Angeles CA). AS, p. 392.

Finn, Jonathan [scenarist] (b. 1884–4 Jun 1971 [87?], New York NY). AS, p. 392.

Finnegan, Frank X. [scenarist/title writer]. No data found. AMD, p. 120. "Finnegan Joins Goldwyn's Scenario Staff," *MPW,* 19 Apr 1919, 350. "Finnegan Joins Famous Players," *MPW,* 17 May 1919, 1018. "Universal Signs New Title Writer," *MPW,* 22 May 1926, 317.

Finnegan, Walter [actor] (b. 1872–30 May 1943 [71?], Los Angeles CA). AS, p. 392.

Finnerty, Louis [actor] (b. 1883–4 Aug 1937 [54?], Los Angeles CA). AS, p. 392.

Finston, Joseph [producer] (b. 1899–1 Mar 1936 [37?], Monrovia CA). BHD2, p. 85.

Fiorenza, Alfredo [actor] (b. Italy, 1868?–24 Feb 1931 [63], Los Angeles CA). "Alfredo Fiorenza," *Variety,* 4 Mar 1931. AS, p. 392. BHD1, p. 190. IFN, p. 103. Truitt, p. 111.

Fiorini, Guido [art decorator] (b. Bologna, Italy, 1 Jul 1891 [extrait de naissance no. 2018]–28 Dec 1965 [74], Parigi, Italy). AS, p. 392.

Fiorio, Luigi [cinematographer/director]. No data found. JS, pp. 167–68 (in Italian silents from 1915).

Firestone, Rose [actress]. No data found. AMD, p. 120. "Rose Firestone," *MPW,* 27 Jul 1912, 337.

Firth, Thomas Preston [actor] (b. 1883–9 Jan 1945 [61?], Los Angeles CA). AS, p. 392 (d. No. Hollywood CA. BHD1, p. 608.

Fischbeck, Harry A. [cinematographer] (b. Hanover, Germany, 3 Jun 1879–May 1968 [88]). BHD2, p. 85. FDY, p. 457.

Fischer, Adelbert [executive] (b. Germany, 1865–31 Mar 1922 [57?], New Rochelle NY). BHD2, p. 85.

Fischer, Alice [actress] (b. Terre Haute IN, 16 Jan 1869–23 Jul 1947 [78], New York NY). m. William King Harcourt (widow). "Alice Fischer," *Variety,* 2 Jul 1947. AS, p. 393. SD, p. 445.

Fischer, David G. [playwright/stage/film director/actor] (b. 1891–21 Apr 1939 [48], Hartford CT). (American; Essanay; American Commercial; Premier.) AMD, p. 120. AS, p. 393. BHD, p. 167; BHD2, p. 85. IFN, p. 103. MSBB, p. 1046. "David Fischer Will Direct 'Dad's Girl' for World," *MPW,* 23 Aug 1919, 1148.

Fischer, Josef [actor] (b. 1874–1926 [52?]). BHD1, p. 608.

Fischer, Kathie [actress]. No data found. AMD, p. 120. "Kathie Fischer with Beauty Films," *MPW,* 21 Feb 1914, 975.

Fischer (or **Fisher**), **Margarita** [stage/film actress] (*née* Margarita Ficher, b. Missouri Valley IA, 12 Feb 1886–11 Mar 1975 [89], Encinatas CA; cerebral thrombosis). m. **Harry A. Pollard** (d. 1934). (Selig [Chicago], 1910; Imp; Nestor; Bison; Rex; Mutual; American; Pathé; Universal; Paramount.) AMD, p. 120. AS, p. 393. BHD, pp. 20–22; 167. IFN, p. 103. MSBB, p. 1034. WWS, p. 226. "Margaret Fisher," *MPW,* 23 Dec 1911, 983. "It's 'Margarita' Fischer," *MPW,* 6 Jan 1912, 39. "Margarita Fischer," *MPW,* 1 Nov 1913, 473. "Margarita Fischer," *MPW,* 24 Jan 1914, 396. "Leading American Players," *MPW,* 11 Jul 1914, 240–42. "Margarita Fischer," *MPW,* 31 Oct 1914, 649. "In the Picture Studios," *NYDM,* 4 Aug 1915, 27:1 (in *The Girl from His Town,* American, 5 Aug 1915, "a unique effect in double exposure...in which pretty Margareta Fischer is seen dancing on the polished side of a speeding automobile."). "New Equitable Stars," *MPW,* 11 Sep 1915, 1813. "Margarita's Menage," *Photoplay Magazine,* Feb 1917, 97 (played with a menagerie in *The Pearl of Paradise* for Mutual). "Margarita Fischer Recovers," *MPW,* 12 May 1917, 989. "Miss Fischer Has a Birthday," *MPW,* 16 Mar 1918, 1496. Edward Weitzel, "Margarita Fisher, Moving Picture Star, Learns a Most Important Screen Secret," *MPW,* 25 Dec 1920, 1065. Grace Kingsley, "Eliza Crosses the Jinx; Margarita Fischer and Harry Pollard Can't Click Without Each Other," *MPC,* Mar 1928, 42, 65. Billy H. Doyle, "Lost Players; Margarita Fisher and Harry Pollard," *CI,* 185 (Nov 1990), C4-C5.

Fischer, Robert A. [stage/film actor] (b. Louisville KY, 1853?–29 Apr 1919 [65], Amityville, LI NY). m. Margaret Casse. "Robert A. Fischer, Actor," *NYT,* 30 Apr 1919, 11:4. AMD, p. 120. AS, p. 393. SD. "Robert A. Fischer," *MPW,* XVII, 30 Aug 1913, 943.

Fischer, Robert C[arl] [actor] (b. Danzig, Germany, 28 May 1881–11 Mar 1973 [91], San Diego CA). AS, p. 393. BHD1, p. 190 (b. Gdansk, Poland). IFN, p. 103.

Fischer-Koeppe, Hugh [actor] (b. 13 Feb 1890–31 Dec 1937 [47]). BHD, p. 168. IFN, p. 103.

Fischinger, Oskar [animator] (*né* Wilhelm Oskar Fischinger, b. Gelnhausen, Germany, 22 Jun 1900–1 Feb 1967 [66], Los Angeles CA). (Ufa; Paramount; Metro; Disney.) "Oskar Fischinger," *Variety,* 245, 8 Feb 1967, 63:4. AS, p. 393 (d. 31 Jan). BHD2, p. 85. Waldman, p. 109.

Fishbeck, Fred [director] (b. New York NY, 1894?–6 Jan 1925 [30], Los Angeles CA; lung cancer). m. **Ethel Lynn**, 1919. (Sennett.) "Fred Fishbeck," *Variety,* 14 Jan 1925 (had a "suite adjoining that of Arbuckle in a San Francisco hotel at the time of the death of Virginia Rappe"). AMD, p. 121. AS, p. 393 (d. 17 Jan). BHD2, p. 85 (Fred Fishback, b. Bucharest, Romania). "Fishbeck Making Comedies for Lehrman Sunshiners," *MPW,* 14 Dec 1918, 1184. "Fred Fishbeck Joins Universal," *MPW,* XL, 3 May 1919, 669. "Comedienne Weds Director," *MPW,* 26 Jul 1919, 505–06. "Fishbeck Goes to Special," *MPW,* 30 Oct 1920, 1243. "Century Comedies Signs Director and Dog-Star," *MPW,* 19 Mar 1921, 291. "Obituary," *MPW,* 31 Jan 1925, 436.

Fisher, Alfred C. [actor] (b. Bristol, England, 14 Jan 1849–26 Aug 1933 [84], Glendale CA). "Alfred C. Fisher," *Variety,* 29 Aug 1933 (began 1918). AMD, p. 121. AS, p. 393. BHD, p. 168. IFN, p. 103. Truitt, p. 111. "Alfred Fisher," *MPW,* 15 Jan 1927, 191.

Fisher, Bud [cartoonist, creator of Mutt and Jeff]. No data found. m. **Pauline Welch**. (Fox.) AMD, p. 121. "Bud Fisher Likes Pictures," *MPW,* 19 May 1917, 1136. "Bud Fisher Is 'On the Job,'" *MPW,* 2 Jun 1917, 1464. "Bud Fisher Invites Suggestions," *MPW,* 2 Jun 1917, 1468. "How Mutt and Jeff Happened," *MPW,* 11 Aug 1917, 965. "The Roll of Honor," *MPW,* 1 Sep 1917, 1350. "Bud Fisher an Executive," *MPW,* 1 Sep 1917, 1393. "Mutt and Jeff to Continue Mad Career on Screen in Fisher's Comic Cartoons," *MPW,* 19 Jul 1919, 360:2 (comic strip in newspapers since 1909. "The biggest and most expensive advertising campaign in the history of merchandising cannot measure the public attention and interest that has been won for the 'Mutt and Jeff' cartoons.").

Fisher, Chad [cameraman] (d. 11 Aug 1914, near Grassy Springs Reservoir, Yonkers NY; struck by lightning while filming). (Imp; Vitagraph.) AMD, p. 121. BHD2, p. 85. "Camera Man Killed; Chad Fisher, of the Vitagraph Company, Struck by Lightning—Others Injured," *NYDM,* 19 Aug 1914, 24:4 ("Chad Fisher's parents are completely prostrated by the blow, as he was an only child."). "Lightning Kills Cameraman," *MPW,* 29 Aug 1914, 1253.

Fisher, Charles [actor] (d. 1 Jul 1916). BHD, p. 168.

Fisher, Edna [actress] (*née* Edna Levi, b. NB, 14 Aug 1879–23 Apr 1978 [98]. Los Angeles CA). m. **Rollin Sturgeon**, 26 Sep 1912, LA CA (d. 1961). (Vitagraph.) AMD, p. 121. BHD1, p. 608. "Serious Mishap of Picture Actress," *MPW,* 9 Dec 1911, 823. "Essanay Leading Woman a Real Heroine," *MPW,* 16 Dec 1911, 984. "Doings at Los Angeles," *MPW,* XIV, 12 Oct 1912, 129:1 ("Sturgeon kept his approaching marriage a profound secret from his friends and associates and the first information they received reached them after the ceremony had been performed.").

Fisher, Fred [orchestra leader] (b. 1904?–28 Mar 1967 [63]). AS, p. 393. IFN, p. 103.

Fisher, George B. [stage/film actor] (b. Republic MI, 10 Aug 1891–13 Aug 1960 [69], Sawtelle CA). (NYMP Co.; Ince.) "George B. Fisher," *NYT,* 15 Aug 1960, 23:1 (age 66). "George B. Fisher," *Variety,* 17 Aug 1960 (age 66; "one-time leading man of the silent films and the Broadway stage"). AMD, p. 121. AS, p. 393. BHD, p. 168. IFN, p. 103. Truitt, p. 111. "George Fisher to Appear with Miss Minter," *MPW,* 20 Jan 1917, 347. George Katchmer, "Remembering the Great Silents," *CI,* 199 (Jan 1992), 14–15.

Fisher, Grace Dorothea [stage/film actress] (b. Oakland CA, 1870?–4 Apr 1954 [84], Rye NY). "Grace Dothea Fisher," *Variety,* 7 Apr 1954. AS, p. 393. SD.

Fisher, Harry A. [actor] (b. New York NY, 13 Sep 1886–21 May 1917 [34], Los Angeles CA; auto accident). AS, p. 393 (b. 1885). BHD, p. 168 (b. 1885). IFN, p. 103. "Picture Actor Killed," *Variety,* 25 May 1917, p. 17 ("Harry Fisper [sic], a picture actor, was killed here in an automobile accident.").

Fisher, Harry E. [actor] (b. Bristol, England, 1868?–28 May 1923 [55], New York NY). "Harry Fisher," *Variety,* 30 May 1923. AS, p. 393 (d. Brooklyn NY). BHD, p. 168. IFN, p. 103. SD, p. 446.

Fisher, Lawrence (Larry) [actor] (b. New York NY, 19 Apr 1891–6 Dec 1937 [46]). AS, p. 393. BHD1, p. 191. IFN, p. 103.

Fisher, Lola [actress] (b. Chicago IL, 17 Mar 1892–15 Oct 1926 [34], Fleetwood [Yonkers] NY). m. actor Kenneth Thompson. "Lola Fisher," *Variety,* 10 Oct 1926. AS, p. 393. NNAT (b. 3 Feb 1896).

Fisher, Maggie [Margarita?] Halloway [actress] (b. Manchester, England, 10 Jun 1854–3 Nov 1938 [84], Glendale CA). "Maggie Fisher," *Variety,* 9 Nov 1938 ("had roles in several early films"). AS, p. 393. BHD, p. 168. IFN, p. 130 (Maggie Halloway).

Fisher, Millicent [actress] (b. Ashville NC, 4 Feb 1896–1 Jan 1979 [82], Ventura CA). AMD, p. 121. BHD, p. 168. "Millicent Fisher," *MPW,* 5 May 1917, 788.

Fisher, Paula R. [scenarist] (b. 1886–7 May 1921 [35?], Los Angeles CA). BHD2, p. 85.

Fisher, Ross [cinematographer]. No data found. AMD, p. 121. FDY, p. 459. "Lloyd Inhraham to Direct DeHavens in 'Twin Beds,'" *MPW,* 10 Jul 1920, 212.

Fisher, Sallie [actress] (b. WY, 10 Aug 1880–8 Jun 1950 [69], Twenty-Nine Palms CA; heart attack). m. Arthur Houghton, 1913. "Sallie Fisher Married," *NYDM,* 9 Apr 1913, 17. "Sallie Fisher," *NYT,* 11 Jun 1950, 92:1. "Sally Fisher," *Variety,* 14 Jun 1950. AMD, p. 121. AS, p. 394. BHD, p. 168. IFN, p. 104. SD, p. 447. Truitt, p. 111. "Sallie Fisher with Essanay," *MPW,* 22 Apr 1916, 627.

Fisher, Ursa [actress]. No data found. Photo, *Cinema Arts,* Feb 1927, 46.

Fisher, William [double up to 1926] (b. 1868?–4 Jul 1933 [65], Los Angeles CA; heart attack). "William Fisher," *Variety,* 11 Jul 1933. AS, p. 394. BHD, p. 168. Truitt, p. 111.

Fisher, William G. [actor] (b. 1883–4 Oct 1949 [66?], Los Angeles CA). AS, p. 394.

Fishter, Walter [actor]. No data found. AMD, p. 121. "Walter Fishter Joins United," *MPW,* 12 Jun 1915, 1790.

Fiske, Minnie Maddern (aunt of **Emily** and **Robert Stevens**) [stage/film actress] (*née* Mary Augusta Davey, b. New Orleans LA, 19 Dec 1865–15 Feb 1932 [66], Hollis [Queens], LI NY [Death Certificate Index No. 1098]). m. Harrison Grey Fiske. "Mrs. Fiske Dies Here as Role Awaits Her; Among Greatest of Actresses, She Succumbs at 67 to a Heart Attack; Began Career at Age of 3; Was Prominent on Stage More Than Half a Century and Had Come Home Only to Rest; Asked Private Funeral; Public Ceremony to Be Omitted in Deference to Her Wish—Lived Virtually as a Recluse," *NYT,* 17 Feb 1932, 23:1. "Minnie Maddern Fiske," *Variety,* 23 Feb 1932 (age 67). AMD, p. 121. AS, p. 394. BHD, p. 168. IFN, p. 104. "Mrs. Fiske in 'Tess of the d'Ubervilles,'" *MPW,* 6 Sep 1913, 1074. "Mrs. Fiske Enjoyed 'Vanity Fair,'" *MPW,* 16 Oct 1915, 449.

Fiske, Robert L. [actor] (b. Griggsville MO, 20 Oct 1889–12 Sep 1944 [54], Sunland CA; pulmonary congestion). AS, p. 394.

Fisper, Harry [actor] (b. New York NY, 13 Sep 1885–21 May 1917 [31], Los Angeles CA; auto accident). AS, p. 394.

Fitz, Hans [actor] (*né* James Theodor August Fitz, b. Neustadt, Germany, 21 Dec 1891–28 Oct 1972 [80], Krailing, Germany). AS, p. 394.

Fitz-Allen, Adelaide [actress] (b. 1855?–26 Feb 1935 [79], New York NY; bronchial pneumonia). "Adelaide Fitz-Allen," *Variety,* 6 Mar 1935. AS, p. 394. BHD, p. 168. IFN, p. 104.

Fitzgerald, Cissy, "The Girl With the Wink" (mother of **Osmund Mark Fitzgerald**) [stage/film actress] (b. England, 1873?–5 May 1941 [68], Ovingdean [Brighton], England). m. (1 son, Osmund Mark Fitzgerald; 1 daughter). (Kleine.) "Cissy Fitzgerald, Actress, Is Dead; Original 'Gayety Girl,' Star of Musicals Here in Nineties, Stricken in England; Was Pioneer in Movies [Edison, 1896]; Claimed to Have Been First Woman in Films—Known as 'Girl with the Wink,'" *NYT,* 11 May 1941, 44:5 (d. 10 May). "Cissy Fitzgerald," *Variety,* 14 May 1941. AMD, p. 121. BHD1, p. 191. IFN, p. 104. "Gossip of the Studios," *NYDM,* 9 Dec 1914, 27:2 (had her famous wink insured for $25,000, according to Sam Spedon). Robert Grau, "The Film Studio; A Gold Laden Haven for the Patriarchs of the Stage," *NYDM,* 8 Sep 1915, 3:1 (Grau mentions Charles Kent, Louise Beaudet, Fitzgerald, Sydney Drew, S. Rankin Drew, William Humphries, Van Dyke Brooke, and Harry Davenport, all from the stage). "Cissy Fitzgerald," *MPW,* 16 Oct 1915, 423. "Cissie Fitzgerald with Kleine," *NYDM,* 30 Oct 1915, 25:4 (along with Bickel & Watson, Crimmons & Gore, Snitz Edwards, Maxfield Moree, and Florence Morrison). "Cissy Fitzgerald Signs Contract with World Film," *MPW,* 13 Sep 1919, 1646. June Lee, "Dan Cupid's Bulletin Board," *Paris and Hollywood Screen Secrets Magazine,* May 1927, 53 (son married Walker). June Lee, "Dan Cupid's Bulletin Board," *Paris and Hollywood Screen Secrets Magazine,* Aug 1927, 98 (her daughter-in-law, Vera, who married her son, Osmund Mark Fitzgerald, filed suit against her for $50,000 heart balm. "...the mother-in-law took a violent dislike to the bride soon after their marriage last January, and began conversations with the son that soon cooled his love for his new wife. Cissie characterizes the charges as ridiculous.").

Fitzgerald, Dallas M. [director] (b. La Grange KY, 13 Aug 1876–9 May 1940 [63], Los Angeles CA). (Quality Distrib. Corp.) "Dallas M. Fitzgerald," *Variety,* 15 May 1940. AMD, p. 121. AS, p. 394. BHD2, p. 85. IFN, p. 104. "Fitzgerald on Metro Staff," *MPW,* 7 Feb 1920, 915. "Fitzgerald Believes Public Likes Pictures Made Outdoors," *MPW,* 4 Jun 1921, 522. "Director Caught Groom Napping," *MPW,* 2 Jul 1927, 29.

Fitzgerald, Edward P. [actor] (b. 1883–1 May 1942 [59], Buffalo NY). (Sennett.) "Edward P. Fitzgerald," *Variety,* 6 May 1942. AS, p. 394. BHD, p. 168. IFN, p. 104. Truitt, p. 111.

Fitzgerald, Florence Dimock [actress] (b. 1889–31 Jan 1962 [72?], Hartford CT). AS, p. 394. BHD, p. 168.

Fitzgerald, James M. "Big Slim" [actor] (b. MS, 19 Apr 1896–21 Jan 1919 [22], Los Angeles CA; double pneumonia following influenza). (Rolin.) AMD, p. 121. AS, p. 394. BHD, p. 168. IFN, p. 104. ""Obituary," *MPW,* 8 Feb 1919, 754 (6 ft. 6 in. tall).

Fitzgerald, Osmund Mark (son of **Cissie Fitzgerald**) [actor]. No data found. m. Florence Vera Walker, 1927. June Lee, "Dan Cupid's Bulletin Board," *Paris and Hollywood Screen Secrets Magazine,* May 1927, 52–53 (m. Walker).

Fitzgerald, Walter [actor] (*né* Walter Bond, b. Keyhm, England, 18 May 1896–20 Dec 1976 [80], London, England). AS, p. 394.

Fitzhamon, Lewin [director] (b. Aldingham, England, 5 Jun 1869–10 Oct 1961 [92], London, England). "Lewin Fitzhamon," *Variety,* 18 Oct 1961, 71:1 (first film: *Briton vs. Boer,* turn of the century; made *Rescued by Rover* and over 600 other silents). AS, p. 394. BHD, p. 168; BHD2, p. 85. IFN, p. 104.

Fitzharris, Edward (grandfather of actors Stuart Edward and Richard Brent) [actor/costumer] (b. England, 5 Feb 1890–12 Oct 1974 [84], Woodland Hills CA; pneumonia). (Paramount.) "Edward Fitzharris," *Variety,* 16 Oct 1974, p. 78. AS, p. 394. BHD, p. 168; BHD2, p. 85. IFN, p. 104.

Fitzhugh, Venita (daughter of Burt Shepherd) [actress] (b. 1895?–1 Jan 1920 [24], Philadelphia PA; auto accident). "Venita Fitzhugh," *Variety,* 9 Jan 1920. AS, p. 394. BHD, p. 168.

Fitzmaurice, George [director/scenarist] (*né* Georges Fitzmaurice, b. Paris, France, 13 Feb 1885–13 Jun 1940 [55], Los Angeles CA; streptococcus infection). m. **Ouida Bergere** (d. 1974); **Diana Kane** (sister of Lois Wilson), 1927, Santa Barbara CA (d. 1977). (Kleine; Pathé.) "George Fitzmaurice, Screen Director, 55; Producer of 'Perils of Pauline' Long a Film Executive," *NYT,* 14 Jun 1940, 21:2. "George Fitzmaurice," *Variety,* 19 Jun 1940 (d. Hollywood). AMD, p. 121. AS, p. 394. BHD, p. 168; BHD2, p. 85 (b. 1895). IFN, p. 104 (b. 1895). Katz, pp. 422–23. MSBB, p. 1046. Spehr, p. 130. Truitt, p. 111 (b. 1895). "Fizmaurice Back with Pathé," *MPW,* 19 Jun 1915, 1922. "Pathé's 'Gold Rooster' Producers," *MPW,* 28 Aug 1915, 1485. "Started Something," *MPW,* 15 Apr 1916, 467. "Lasky Engages Three More Directors," *MPW,* 25 Jan 1919, 454. Edward Weitzel, "Watching Fitzmaurice in Action," *MPW,* 2 Aug 1919, 683. "George Gitzmaurice-Ouida Bergere Join in New Deal with Famous Players-Lasky," *MPW,* 28 Feb 1920, 1490. "Fitzmaurice Has New Way of Introducing Past Action," *MPW,* 17 Jul 1920, 332. "George Fitzmaurice, Paramount Director, Has Left for London to Film Pictures," *MPW,* 4 Dec 1920, 636. "Mussolini Sends Wire," *MPW,* 9 Feb 1924, 471 (re *The Eternal City*). "Novel Under-Sea Dance in 'A Thief in Paradise [1st National],'" *MPW,* 10 Jan 1925, 177:1 (direction by Fitzmaurice; photographic effects by Arthur Miller; sets by Anton Grot). "Fitzmaurice Signed by First National," *MPW,* 17 Jul 1926, 3. "George Fitzmaurice," *MPW,* 19 Mar 1927, 177. "Fitzmaurice-Kane Wedding, Quiet," *MPW,* 12 Nov 1927, 19. Herbert Cruikshank, "Fitz and Starts; George Had to Make Several Before They'd Let Him Make Pictures," *MPC,* Feb 1929, 33, 73, 77 ("During his sixteen years behind a megaphone Fitz has been weighed in many balances, and the scales have always shown a comfortable margin in his favor.").

Fitz-Patrick, James A[lbert] [actor/director/producer/scenarist] (b. Shelton CT, 26 Feb 1895–12 Jun 1980 [85], Palm Springs CA). AMD, p. 121. AS, p. 395 (b. 1892). BHD2, p. 85. "Fitz-Patrick with Juvenile Film Co.," *MPW,* 4 Mar 1916, 1454.

Fitzroy, Emily [actress] (b. London, England, 24 May 1860–3 Mar 1954 [93], Gardena CA; cerebral hemorrhage). (MGM.) AS, p. 395. BHD1, p. 191. IFN, p. 104. MH, p. 110. Truitt, p. 111.

Fitzroy, Louis [actor] (b. Saulte Sainte Marie MI, 24 Nov 1870–26 Jan 1947 [76], Los Angeles CA). AMD, p. 122. AS, p. 395. BHD, p. 168. IFN, p. 104. "New Players for MinA," *MPW,* 5 Jun 1915, 1614. "Louis Fitzroy of MinA Films," *MPW,* 17 Jul 1915, 499. "Cub Player's Bereavement," *MPW,* 25 Mar 1916, 1992.

Fix, Paul [actor] (*né* Paul Fix Morrison, b. Dobbs Ferry NY, 9 Mar 1901–14 Oct 1983 [81], Santa Monica CA). AS, p. 395 (b. 13 Mar). BHD1, p. 191; BHD2, p. 85 (b. 13 Mar). Katz, p. 423. SD. *Screen World 1984,* p. 235.

Fix, Ress [actress] (*née* Ressie Mae Fix, b. IN, 9 Jun 1893–5 Jan 1975 [81], Los Angeles CA). AS, p. 395.

Fizzarotti, Armando [director] (b. Naples, Italy, 16 Feb 1892). AS, p. 395. JS, p. 168 (in Italian silents from 1923).

Fjord, Olav [actor] (b. Christiana, Norway, 12 Aug 1897). AS, p. 395.

Flagg, James Montgomery [actist/actor/scenarist] (b. Pelham Manor NY, 18 Jun 1877–27 May 1960 [82], New York NY). AMD, p. 122. AS, p. 395. BHD, p. 168; BHD2, p. 85. "James Montgomery Flagg on the Screen," *MPW,* 1 Dec 1917, 1351. "Edison Will Release Flagg Stories," *MPW,* 5 Jan 1918, 105. "Flagg to Make Series for Famous Players," *MPW,* 22 Jun 1918, 1695. "James Montgomery Flagg Talks on Art in Advertising Before A.M.P.A.," *MPW,* LX , 20 Jan 1923, 220. "Movie History in the Making Ten Years Ago," *Paris and Hollywood Screen Secrets,* Oct 1927, 93 (Flagg "was preparing a series of comedies for Paramount under the title of *Sweethearts and Wives.* Martin Justice...was selected as the director.").

Flagstad, Kirsten [actress/singer] (b. Hamar, Norway, 12 Jul 1895–7 Dec 1962 [67], Oslo, Norway). AS, p. 395.

Flaherty, Robert J[oseph] [scenarist/cinematographer/producer] (b. Iron Mountain MI, 16 Feb 1884–23 Jul 1951 [67], Dummerston VT; heart attack). m. Frances Hubbard. (Pathé; Paramount; MGM.) "Robert Flaherty, Film Producer, 67; 'Father' of Documentary Dies—Made 'Louisiana Story,' 'Man of Aran' and 'Elephant Boy,'" *NYT,* 24 Jul 1951, 25:3. "Robert J. Flaherty," *Variety,* 25 Jul 1951 (d. Brattleboro VT). AMD, p. 122. AS, p. 395. BHD2, p. 86 (d. Brattleboro VT). FDY, pp. 425, 459. IFN, p. 104. Katz, pp. 423–24. SD. "Flaherty Honored," *MPW,* 7 Apr 1923, 614. "Flaherty Leaves for Samoa to Make South Sea Islanders Film," *MPW,* 21 Apr 1923, 814. Matthew Josephson, "*Moana:* A Poem of the Cinema," *MPC,* May 1926, 37, 84–85, 91. "Metro Signs Robert J. Flaherty to Make South Sea Island Film," *MPW,* 18 Jun 1927, 505. "Flaherty N.Y. Film Done; To Direct M-G-M Feature," *MPW,* 25 Jun 1927, 563. S.M. Weller, "Mr. Flaherty Sees It Through; The Creator of *Nanook* Is a Motion Picture Idealist," *MPC,* Oct 1927, 25, 72.

Flamant, Georges François Louis [actor] (b. Tunis, Tunisia, 3 Sep 1903–20 Jul 1990 [86], Villiers-le-Bel, France [extrait de décès no. 227/1990). AS, p. 395.

Flament, Edouard [actor] (b. Douai, France, 27 Aug 1880–27 Dec 1958 [78], Bois-Colombes, France). AS, p. 395.

Flanagan, Ed *see* **O'Keefe, Dennis**

Flanagan, Edward J. [actor] (b. St. Louis MO, 1880?–18 Aug 1925 [45], Los Angeles CA; peritonitis). m. Charlotte Ravenscroft. "Edward J. Flanagan," *Variety,* 26 Aug 1925 (began 1921). AS, p. 395. BHD, p. 168. IFN, p. 104. Truitt, p. 112.

Flanagan, Hugh [actor] (d. 26 Dec 1925, New York NY). BHD, p. 168. IFN, p. 104.

Flanagan, Rebecca [actress] (*née?,* b. Philadelphia PA, 10 Feb 1875?–30 Jan 1938 [62], Los Angeles CA). m. D.J. Flanagan. "Rebecca Flanagan," *Variety,* 2 Feb 1938. AS, p. 395 (b. 1878). BHD, p. 168 (b. 1878). IFN, p. 104 (b. 1878).

Flander, Rolland Wilcox [actor] (b. 12 Nov 1893-Oct 1972 [78], FL). (Biograph; Thanhouser.) AMD, p. 122. "Rolland Flander Signed," *MPW,* 22 Aug 1925, 840. "Rolland Flander in Three Big Pictures Simultaneously," *MPW,* 5 Dec 1925, 438. Regina B. Crewe, "Rolland Flander Shatters a Tradition," *Cinema Art,* Mar 1926, 31, 51. "Rolland Flander Signed," *MPW,* 16 Jan 1926, 238. "Rolland Flander Injured by Taxi," *MPW,* 8 May 1926, 3.

Flandre, Géo [actor] (*né* Georges Louis Flandre, b. Paris, France, 31 May 1876). AS, p. 395.

Flanette, Jean [scenarist]. No data found. FDY, p. 425.

Flateau, Georges [actor] (b. France, 1881?–13 Feb 1953 [71], Paris, France). "Georges Flateau," *Variety,* 18 Feb 1953. AS, p. 396. BHD, p. 168. IFN, p. 104.

Flather, Charlotte Carter [scenarist] (d. 13 Mar 1925, New York NY). BHD2, p. 86.

Flatow, John L. [actor] (d. 3 Oct 1922, Washington DC). "John L. Flatow," *Variety,* 13 Oct 1922. BHD, p. 168.

Flaum, Mayer (father of Marshall Flaum) [actor] (b. 9 Feb 1901–26 Apr 1990 [89], Los Angeles CA). m. (1 son, Marshall, b. NYC, 13 Sep 1930). AS, p. 396. BHD1, p. 608.

Flavin, Harold [publicist]. No data found. AMD, p. 122. "Joins Paramount," *MPW,* 16 Jul 1927, 148.

Flavin, Martin [scenarist] (b. San Francisco CA, 2 Nov 1883–27 Dec 1967 [84], Carmel CA). AS, p. 396. BHD2, p. 86.

Fleck, Fred F. [stage/film actor/company manager] (d. 29 Jul 1925, NY). m. Grace Fielding. "Fred Fleck," *Variety,* 5 Aug 1925, p. 38.

Fleck, Frederick A. [producer] (b. New York NY, 4 Jun 1892–9 Nov 1961 [69], Los Angeles CA). (Paramount [NY]). "Frederick A. Fleck," *Variety,* 15 Nov 1961. BHD, p. 169; BHD2, p. 86 (d. No. Hollywood CA).

Fleck, Jacob Julius [director] (b. Vienna, Austria, 8 Nov 1881–19 Sep 1953 [71], Vienna, Austria). AS, p. 396.

Fleck, Luise [director] (b. Vienna, Austria, 1 Aug 1873–15 Mar 1950 [76], Vienna, Austria). AS, p. 396.

Fleckels, Maurice [actor] (b. Chicago IL, 1872?–5 Jun 1946 [74], Los Angeles CA). (Universal.) m. Anna Laemmle (sister of Carl Laemmle), 1906. "Maurice Fleckles," *Variety,* 12 Jun 1946. AMD, p. 122. AS, p. 396. "Maurice Fleckles," *MPW,* 11 Sep 1909, 343. "Fleckles Gets Back Into the Game," *MPW,* 31 Aug 1918, 1251.

Fleischer, Dave (brother of **Max Fleischer**; uncle of **Ruth Fleischer**) [animator/producer/director] (b. New York NY, 14 Jul 1894–25 Jun 1979 [84], Woodland Hills CA). Leslie Cabarga, *The Fleischer Story* (New York: DaCapo Press, 1988). (Bray; Paramount.) "Dave Fleischer," *Variety,* 4 Jul 1979. AS, p. 396. BHD2, p. 86. IFN, p. 105. Katz, p. 425.

Fleischer, Louis [animator] (b. 1891–16 Nov 1985 [94?], Woodland Hills CA). AS, p. 396. BHD2, p. 86.

Fleischer, Max[imilian] (brother of **Dave Fleischer**; father of director Richard and **Ruth Fleischer**) [animator] (b. Vienna, Austria, 19 Jul 1883–11 Sep 1972 [89], Woodland Hills CA). (Bray; Paramount.) m. Essie (son Richard, b. 1916; daughter Ruth). "Max Fleischer," *Variety,* 13 Sep 1972. AMD, p. 122. AS, p. 396 (b. 1889). BHD2, p. 86. IFN, p. 105. Katz, p. 425. "Progress in Animated Drawing," *MPW,* 22 Jun 1918, 1707. "Fleischer Advances Technical Art," *MPW,* 7 Jun 1919, 1497. "Fleischer Signs New Contract," *MPW,* 10 Oct 1925, 492. "Max Fleischer Will Be Editor of Two New Urban-Kineto Series," *MPW,* 7 Nov 1925, 67. "Max Fleischer, Creator of 'Ko-Ko,' Elected Head of Red Seal Pictures," *MPW,* 30 Jan 1926, 432. "Ko-Ko and His Boss, Max Fleischer, in chicago," *MPW,* 27 Mar 1926, 277. "Fleischer on the Air," *MPW,* 3 Apr 1926, 350. "Max Fleischer Goes to Brooklyn—Again!," *MPW,* 15 May 1926, 247. "Blind Man Gets Kick Out of Pictures," *MPW,* 22 May 1926, 323. Leonard Maltin, *Of Mice and Magic; A History of American Animated Cartoons* (NY: New American Library, 1980), pp. 79–120.

Fleischer, Ruth (daughter of **Max Fleischer**; niece of **Dave Fleischer**) [actress]. No data found. AMD, p. 122. "Max Fleischer's Daughter Makes Her Film Debut," *MPW,* 21 Nov 1925, 252.

Fleischmann, Harry [actor] (b. Segerstown PA, 7 Jan 1899–28 Nov 1943 [44], Bakersfield CA). AS, p. 396.

Fleming, Alice [actress] (b. Brooklyn NY, 9 Aug 1882–6 Dec 1952 [70], New York NY). m. William Day. 'Alice Fleming," *Variety,* 10 Dec 1952. AS, p. 396. BHD1, p. 192. BR, pp. 309–10. IFN, p. 105. Truitt, p. 112.

Fleming, Bob *see* **Fleming, Robert**

Fleming, Carroll [actor/director/producer] (b. Lexington KY, 1865-May 1930 [64?], Bronx NY). BHD, p. 169; BHD2, p. 86. "Fleming with Jose," *NYDM,* 20 Nov 1915, 31:1 (to direct for Feature Film Corp./Pathé). "Fleming Directing First Episode of 'The Iron Claw,'" *MPW,* 18 Mar 1916, 1842. "Caryl Fleming to Direct Serial," *MPW,* 7 Jul 1917, 113 (Flemming).

Fleming, Caryl S[tacey] [stage/film actor/director] (b. Cedar Rapids IA, 1894?–2 Sep 1940 [46], Beverly Hills CA). (Began 1909; Powers; Universal; Kalem; Kleine; Royal Comedies; Mutual.) "Caryl S. Fleming," *Variety,* 11 Sep 1940. AMD, p. 122. AS, p. 396. BHD, p. 169; BHD2, p. 86. MSBB, p. 1024 (aged 28 in 1918). "Caryl Fleming Injured," *MPW,* 7 Nov 1914, 767.

Fleming, Claude [actor] (b. Camden, New South Wales, Australia, 22 Feb 1884–23 Mar 1952 [68], Sydney, Australia). "Claude Fleming," *Variety,* 26 Mar and 2 Apr 1952. AS, p. 396. BHD1, p. 192. IFN, p. 105.

Fleming, Ethel [actress]. No data found. m. **William Courtleigh, Jr.**, 1915 (d. 1918). AMD, p. 122. "William Courtleigh, Jr., Marries," *MPW,* 14 Aug 1915, 1138.

Fleming, Ian [actor] (*né* Ian MacFarlane, b. Melbourne, Australia, 10 Sep 1888–1 Jan 1969 [80], London, England). "Ian Fleming," *Variety,* 19 Aug 1964, p. 71. AS, p. 396. BHD1, p. 192. IFN, p. 105.

Fleming, John [actor] (b. 1875?–Jun 1945 [70], Chicago IL). m. Emma Boulton. "John Fleming," *Variety,* 20 Jun 1945. IFN, p. 105.

Fleming, Robert [actor] (b. Ontario, Canada, 19 Feb 1878 or 1888–4 Oct 1933 [55?]). AS, p. 396. BHD1, p. 192. IFN, p. 105. George A. Katchmer, "Forgotten Cowboys and Cowgirls—Part XIV," *CI,* 191 (May 1991), 24–25.

Fleming, Victor L. [cameraman/director] (b. Pasadena CA, 23 Feb 1883–6 Jan 1949 [65], Cottonwood AZ; heart attack). m. Lucille Rosson.

"Victor Fleming, 60, Film Leader, Dies; Director Won Academy Award for 'Gone with the Wind' [1939]—Worked on 'Joan of Arc,'" *NYT,* 7 Jan 1949, 21:1. "Victor Fleming," *Variety,* 12 Jan 1949 (age 64). AMD, p. 122. AS, p. 397. BHD2, p. 86. IFN, p. 105. SD. Spehr, p. 130. "'Vic' Fleming Will Film Presidential Peace Party," *MPW,* 21 Dec 1918, 1324. "Fleming Back with Fairbanks," *MPW,* 12 Apr 1919, 233. "Victor Fleming to Direct," *MPW,* 3 Sep 1921, 69. "Paramount Signs Fleming," *MPW,* 7 Jun 1924, 534. "Victor Fleming Remains," *MPW,* 29 Aug 1925, 934. "Victor Fleming to Direct 'The Blind Goddess,'" *MPW,* 12 Dec 1925, 548. 'To Direct 'Rough Riders,'" *MPW,* 17 Apr 1926, 504. "Fleming Buys Ranch," *MPW,* 12 Feb 1927, 491.

Fletcher, Adele Whitely [scenarist] (b. 1898–24 Jun 1979 [81?], Huntington NY). BHD2, p. 86.

Fletcher, Art [actor] (b. Collinsville IL, 5 Jan 1885–6 Feb 1950 [64], Los Angeles CA). BHD, p. 169.

Fletcher, Bramwell [actor] (b. Bradford, Yorkshire, England, 20 Feb 1904–22 Jun 1988 [84], Westmoreland NH). m. (1) **Helen Chandler** (d. 1965); (2) Diana Barrymore, 30 Jul 1942 (d. 1960); (3) Susan Robinson; (4) Lael Wertenbaker. Unpublished "The Thistleball." Leslie Bennetts, "Bramwell Fletcher, 84, Actor in Many Shaw Plays," *NYT,* 24 Jun 1988, D17:2. "Bramwell Fletcher," *Variety,* 29 Jun 1988. AS, p. 397. BHD1, p. 192. Katz, p. 426. SD. Randolph Man, "Letter," *FIR,* Oct 1990, 510.

Fletcher, Cecil B. [actor] (b. Northampton, England-d. Nov 1918, Romford, Essex, England). BHD, p. 169.

Fletcher, Ora [actress] (d. Feb 1920). "Ora Fletcher," *Variety,* 13 Feb 1920. BHD, p. 169.

Fletcher, William [actor] (b. San Francisco CA, 1861?–11 Dec 1933 [72], Los Angeles CA). "William Fletcher," *Variety,* 12 Dec 1933. AS, p. 397.

Flick, John Michael [title writer]. No data found. FDY, p. 443.

Fliesler, Joseph R. [title writer]. No data found. FDY, p. 443.

Flin, Ray [cinematographer] (b. 1905?–29 Jul 1969 [64], CA; heart attack). (Paramount, MGM, Universal.) m. June McNulty (sister of Penny Singleton; : b. 20 Apr 1912-Jan 1984 [71], CA). "Ray Flin," *Variety,* 6 Aug 1969. "Ray Flin, 64; Cameraman," *The Evening Star* [Washington DC], 23 Aug 1969. AS, p. 397 (d. 19 Aug).

Flinn, John C[unningham] [journalist/executive] (b. Evanston IL, 6 May 1887–2 Mar 1946 [58], New York NY; after earlier operation). (Began 1915; FP-L; W.W. Hodkinson; PDC; Metropolitan Pictures Corp. of CA; Cinema Corp. of America; Cecil B. De Mille Pictures Corp.) m. Courtney Luella Ames, 1911. "John C. Flinn Dead; Film Executive, 58; Secretary of the Independent Producers Group Since 1942—With Lasky Firm in 1915," *NYT,* 3 Mar 1946, 44:6. "J.C. Flinn, Vet Pic Exec, Dies at 58," *Variety,* 6 Mar 1946 (interred in Evanston IL). AMD, p. 122. BHD2, p. 86. "John C. Flinn Joins the Lasky Staff," *MPW,* 10 Jul 1915, 330. "John C. Flinn, Jr., Arrives," *MPW,* 26 May 1917, 1291 (b. 4 May 1917, 10 1/2 lbs.). John C. Flinn, "Money Wasted in Picture Publicity," *MPW,* 20 Jul 1918, 329. "John Flinn Talks on Film Advertising," *MPW,* 8 Nov 1919, 232. "John C. Flinn Moves Higher Up with FP-L as Jerome Beatty Succeeds Him," *MPW,* 21 Feb 1920, 1204. "Flinn Says Advertising Must Be Kept Clean," *MPW,* 21 May 1921, 272. "John Flinn Returns Gratified at Producers' Studio Progress," *MPW,* 23 Aug 1924, 629. "John C. Flinn Discusse Advantages of Cecil B. DeMille's Stock Company Plan," *MPW,* 9 May 1925, 211. "Flinn Made General Manager of Producers Distributing Corp.," *MPW,* 16 May 1925, 289. John C. Flinn, "Psychological Magnetism of Program Diversity," *MPW,* 3 Jul 1926, 36–37. "John C. Flinn," *MPW,* 26 Mar 1927, 311. "Did Flinn Kidnap Doctor When Ill on Fast Flyer?," *MPW,* 18 Jun 1927, 476.

Flint, Hazel E. [actress] (b. 1893?–18 Aug 1959 [66], Los Angeles CA). "Hazel Flint," *Variety,* 2 Sep 1959 (extra since 1926). AS, p. 397. BHD, p. 169. IFN, p. 105. Truitt, p. 112.

Flint, Helen [actress] (b. Chicago IL, 14 Jun 1898–9 Sep 1967 [69], Washington DC; from injuries sustained in an auto accident). "Helen Flint," *Variety,* 13 Sep 1967 ("stage and film actress in the 1920s and 1930s"). AS, p. 397. BHD1, p. 193. IFN, p. 105. Truitt, p. 112.

Flint, Homer Eon [author/scenarist] (*né* Homer Eon Flindt, b. Albany OR, 9 Sep 1888–26 Mar 1924 [35], near San Jose CA; auto crash). m. Mabel Williams, 1912. (Kalem.) AS, p. 397 (b. San Jose CA). BHD2, p. 86. Eldon K. Everett, "The Strange Death of Homer Eon Flint," *CI,* 63 (May 1979), 49. Mike Ashley, "The Galactic Emancipator: Remembering Homer Eon Flint," *Fantasy Commentator,* VIII (Fall, 1995), 258–66.

Flint, Joseph W. [actor] (b. 1893?–5 May 1933 [40], Los Angeles CA; suicide with a gun). "Joseph W. Flint," *Variety,* 9 May 1933. AS, p. 397. IFN, p. 105.

Flood, James [director] (b. New York NY, 31 Jul 1895–4 Feb 1953 [57], Los Angeles CA; complications after surgery). (Biograph, 1912; Fox; WB; Tiffany.) "James Flood," *NYT,* 6 Feb 1953, 20:7 (age 63; "veteran film director"). "James Flood," *Variety,* 11 Feb 1953. AS, p. 398. BHD2, p. 86. IFN, p. 105 (age 57). Katz, p. 427.

Flor, Jean [actor/singer] (*né* Jean Florens, b. France, 1876–1946 [70?], France). AS, p. 398.

Florath, Albert Peter Adam [stage/film actor/producer] (b. Bielefeld, Germany, 14 Dec 1888–10 Mar 1957 [68], Gailsdorf-Nordwuertemberg, W. Germany). (Began on stage, 1908.) "Albert Florath," *Variety,* 3 Apr 1957, 95:3 (age 63). AS, p. 398. BHD1, p. 193; BHD2, p. 86. IFN, p. 105.

Florelle [actress/singer] (*née* Odette Elisa Joséphine Marguerite Rousseau, b. Les Sables d'Olonne, France, 9 Aug 1898 [extrait de naissance no. 49/1898]-28 Sep 1974 [76], La-Roche-sur-Yon, France). AS, p. 398.

Florencie, Louis Jean Baptiste [actor] (b. Paris, France, 4 Dec 1896 [extrait de naissance no. 5762]-4 Dec 1951 [55], Madrid, Spain). AS, p. 398.

Floresco, Michel [actor] (b. Husci, Rumania, 1831–14 Sep 1925 [94?], Venice, Italy). "Michel Floresco," *Variety,* 11 Nov 1925. AS, p. 398. BHD, p. 169. IFN, p. 105.

Florey, Robert [director/producer] (b. Paris, France, 14 Sep 1900–16 May 1979 [78], Santa Monica CA; cancer). "Robert Florey," *Variety,* 23 May 1979 (b. 1900). AS, p. 398. BHD, p. 169; BHD2, p. 86. IFN, p. 105. Katz, pp. 427–28. Edith Tarrent, "The $97 Masterpiece; Its Producer, Robert Florey, Says That with Another $500 He Could Make Norma Talmadge Famous," *MPC,* Aug 1928, 40, 86 (discusses the one-reel, avant-garde *The Blues—A Rhapsody of Hollywood,* with Jules Raucourt). Brian Taves, "Robert Florey," *CI,* 154 (Apr 1988), 57–59.

Flowers, Bess, "Queen of the Hollywood Extras" [actress] (b. Sherman TX, 23 Nov 1898–28 Jul 1984 [86], Woodland Hills CA). m. Cullen B. Tate. "Bess Flowers," *Variety,* 8 Aug 1984. AS, p. 398. BHD1, p. 193 (b. 23 Mar). FSS, p. 113. Katz, p. 428. O&W, pp. 214–15. George A. Katchmer, "Remembering the Great Silents," *CI,* 183 (Sep 1990), 46.

Flowerton, Consuelo (mother of actress Nina Foch) [actress/singer] (b. 9 Aug 1900–21 Dec 1965 [65], New York NY). m. Dick Foch; Robert E. Cushman. "Consuelo Flowerton," *Variety,* 29 Dec 1965 (appeared with Valentino, Nazimova and Neil Hamilton). AS, p. 398. BHD, p. 169. IFN, p. 105. Truitt, p. 112.

Floyd, Ethel [actress]. (Frontier Films.) m. Lloyd Hamilton, 1914—div. 8 Aug 1925.

Flugrath, Edna (sister of **Viola Dana** and **Shirley Mason**) [child actress on stage/dancer/film actress] (b. Brooklyn NY, 29 Dec 1893–6 Apr 1966 [72], San Diego CA). m. (1) **Harold Shaw,** Johannesburg, South Africa, Jan 1917 (killed in auto accident on 30 Jan 1926; (2) Halliburton Houghton, Reno NV, 21 Jul 1928 [d. 1977]). (Edison; London Film Co., Ltd.) AMD, p. 123. AS, p. 398. BHD, p. 169. Rachel Low, *The History of the British Film, 1914–1918* (Surrey, England: R.R. Bowker Co., 1973), p. 76. "Miss Edna Flugrath," *MPW,* 12 Sep 1914, 1519:2 (played in *Newport News* with Peter Daly and appeared with Joseph Jefferson. "Miss Flugrath thinks England a beautiful country and has been happy there."). "Edna Flugrath," *MPW,* 27 Feb 1915, 1304. "Edna Flugrath Weds Harold Shaw," *MPW,* 31 Mar 1917, 2113. Billy H. Doyle, "Edna Flugrath," *CI,* 215 (May 1993), C14. Billy Doyle, "Edna Flugrath," *CI,* 227 (May 1994), 42–43.

Flugrath, Leonie [actress]. No data found. (Edison.) AMD, p. 123. "Briefs of Biography...One of the 'Poor Little Rich Girls,'...," *NYDM,* 16 Jun 1915, 32:1. "Leonie Flugrath, Edison's Child Star," *MPW,* 26 Jun 1915, 2078. "Is the Venus di Milo Out of Date? Anyway, Leonie Flugrath Thinks So," *MPC,* Sep 1916, 45–47.

Fluker, Mack A. [actor] (b. Los Angeles CA, 22 Apr 1903–28 Apr 1929 [26], Los Angeles CA). AS, p. 398 (Flucker). BHD, p. 169. IFN, p. 105.

Flynn, Elinor [actress] (b. Chicago IL, 17 Mar 1910–4 Jul 1938 [28], Glens Falls NY). BHD1, p. 193.

Flynn, Emmett J. (brother of **Raymond A. Flynn**) [stage/film actor/director] (b. Denver CO, 9 Nov 1892–4 Jun 1937 [44], Los Angeles CA). m. (1) **Margaret Shelby** (d. 1939); Nita. "Emmett J. Flynn," *Variety,* 9 Jun 1937 (age 55). AMD, p. 123. AS, p. 398. BHD2, p. 86. IFN, p. 105. SD. "Emmett J. Flynn, Young But Efficient," *MPW,* 24 Nov 1917, 1196. "Emmett J. Flynn Will Direct William Russell for Fox," *MPW,* 30 Aug 1919, 1337. "Flynn Joins Goldwyn," *MPW,* 17 Mar 1923, 308. "Flynn to Pick Stars for Foreign Film," *MPW,* 18 Sep 1926, 156.

Flynn, Hazel E. [actress] (b. Chicago IL, 31 Mar 1899–15 May 1964 [65], Santa Monica CA; heart attack). (Essanay [Chicago IL]). "Hazel

Flynn," *Variety,* 20 May 1964. AS, p. 399. BHD, p. 169; BHD2, p. 87. Truitt, p. 113.

Flynn, Maurice Bennett "Lefty" [actor] (b. Greenwich CT, 26 May 1892–4 Mar 1959 [66], Camden SC). m. (1) Irene Claire, ca. 1913; (2) Nora Langhorne Phipps; (3) Blanche Shove Palmer, 1916; (4) **Viola Dana**, 20 Jun 1925–14 Feb 1929 (d. 1987); (5) Nora Langhorne, 1930; (6) Lesley Bogert. "Maurice B. Flynn, Rancher, Was 66; Former Yale Fullback Dies—Actor in Silent Films Wed Norah Langhorne," *NYT,* 6 Mar 1959, 25:3. AMD, p. 123. AS, p. 399 (b. 24 May 1893). BHD, p. 169. GK, pp. 289–93. IFN, p. 105. MH, p. 111. "Goldwyn Signs Football Star," *MPW,* 13 Mar 1920, 1778. "Maurice Flynn, Former Gridiron Star, Now Film Star," *MPW,* 10 Sep 1921, 184. "The Kitten and the King," *MPW,* 7 Nov 1925, 43 (m. Dana). Ramon Romeo, "Reeling Down Broadway," *Paris and Hollywood,* Sep 1926, 83 (to get out of his contract with Harry Garson, Flynn agreed to make *The Wild Bull of the Pampas* for nothing. He was then to sign with F.B.O.). George A. Katchmer, "Lefty Flynn; Rarely Remembered," *CI,* 90 (Dec 1982), 36–37. George Katchmer, "Remembering the Great Silents," *CI,* 239 (May 1995), C6.

Flynn, Raymond A. (brother of **Emmett J. Flynn**) [assistant director/producer] (b. 1890?–16 Apr 1937 [47], Los Angeles CA). "Raymond A. Flynn," *Variety,* 21 Apr 1937. AS, p. 399. BHD2, p. 87 (b. 1893).

Flynn, Thomas [actor] (b. 1852?–23 Feb 1926 [73], New York NY). m. Alice Sharpley. "Thomas Flynn," *Variety,* 3 Mar 1926. AS, p. 399.

Flynn, William J. [director] (d. 27 Apr 1931). BHD2, p. 87.

Fogel, Vladimir Petrovich [actor] (b. Moscow, Russia, 1902–8 Jun 1929 [27?], Moscow, Russia). AS, p. 399. BHD, p. 169. IFN, p. 105.

Fogg, Orian [actor] (b. 1849–24 May 1923 [74], New York NY). "Orian Fogg," *Variety,* 30 May 1923. AS, p. 399. BHD, p. 169. IFN, p. 105.

Fogwell, Reginald G. [scenarist/director] (b. Dartmouth, England, 23 Nov-ca. 1932). AS, p. 399. BHD2, p. 87. FDY, p. 425.

Foireri, Adoni [stage/film actress] (b. France). No further data found. (Reliance-Majestic.) W.E. Wing, "Along the Pacific Coast," *NYDM,* 30 Jun 1915, 22:2.

Follansbee, Oliver [actor] (b. IL, 18 Sep 1890–4 Apr 1969 [78], Los Angeles CA). BHD, p. 169.

Follett, F.M. [cartoonist]. No data found. AMD, p. 123. "F.M. Follett," *MPW,* 21 Jul 1917, 397.

Folsey, George J. (father of George Folsey, Jr.) [cinematographer] (b. New York NY, 1898–1 Nov 1988 [90], Santa Monica CA; cerebral hemorrhage). m. (son George, b. 17 Jan 1939). "George Folsey Dies; Film Maker Was 90," *NYT,* 4 Nov 1988, B4:5. "Esteemed Lenser George Folsey Dead at 90; Shot Over 150 Pics," *Variety,* 9 Nov 1988. AS, p. 399. BHD2, p. 87. FDY, p. 459. Katz, p. 430.

Foltz, Virginia [actress] (b. CA). m. 1913. AMD, p. 123. (Universal.) "Virginia Foltz Returns to Film Through Pallas Pictures," *MPN,* 16 Oct 1915, 54. "Virginia Foltz Joins Universal," *MPW,* 7 Oct 1916, 91. "Virginia Foltz a New Triangle Recruit," *MPW,* 17 Nov 1917, 1026.

Fonda, Gloria [actress] (b. St. Paul MN, 1896–20 Jan 1978 [81?], Alamos, Sonora, Mexico). AMD, p. 123. BHD, p. 169. "Gloria Fonda," *MPW,* 6 Nov 1915, 1122.

Fones, Gilbert A. [actor] (b. AR, 13 Sep 1887–5 Oct 1965 [78], Los Angeles CA). BHD, p. 169.

Fönss, Olaf [actor] (b. Aarhüs, Denmark, 17 Oct 1882–3 Nov 1949 [67], Copenhagen, Denmark). BHD, p. 169 (d. 4 Nov). IFN, p. 106 (d. 4 Nov). "Olaf Fonss," *Variety,* 16 Nov 1969. AS, p. 400. Vittorio Martinelli, "Kino-Lieblinge," *Griffithiana,* 38/39 (Oct 1990), 48.

Fontaine, Lillian (mother of Olivia de Havilland and Joan Fontaine) [actress] (b. Reading, England, 11 Jun 1886–20 Feb 1975 [88], Santa Barbara CA). AS, p. 400.

Fontan, Gabrielle [actrice] (*née* Gabrielle Marie Joséphine Penecastel, b. Bordeaux, France, 16 Apr 1873–9 Sep 1959 [86], Juvisy-sur-Orge, France [extrait de décès no. 116/1959]). AS, p. 400.

Fontana, Eugenio [director/producer] (b. Rome, Italy, 12 Dec 1889). AS, p. 400. JS, pp. 169–70 (in Italian silents from 1918; long in Argentina).

Fontanne, Lynn [stage/film actress] (*née* Lillie Louise Fontanne, b. Woodford, Essex, England, 5 Dec 1887–30 Jul 1983 [95?], Genesee Depot, near Milwaukee WI; pneumonia). m. **Alfred Lunt**, 22 May 1922, NY (d. 1977). (Broadway debut: *Mr. Preedy and the Countess,* 39th Street Theater, 7 Nov 1910.) "Lynne Fontanne Is Dead at 95; A Star with Lunt for 37 Years," *NYT,* 31 Jul 1983, 1:1, 36:1. Hobe Morrison, "Lynn Fontanne, 95, Dies in Sleep; Starred with Lunt for 37 Years," *Variety,* 3 Aug 1983. AMD, p. 123. AS, p. 400. BHD1, p. 194 (b. 6 Dec). GSS, pp. 241–47. "Lynne Fontanne in Distinctive Film," *MPW,* 28 Jul 1923, 318. Nanette Kutner, "When a Stage Star Turns to the Screen," *MW,* 8 Aug 1925, 21–22. Home: Ten Chimneys.

Fonteney, Catherine [actress] (*née* Marie Alexandrine Catherine Fontaine, b. Paris, France, 23 Jun 1879–5 May 1966 [86], Duon, France). AS, p.400.

Foo, Lee Tung [actor] (b. CA, 23 Apr 1875–1 May 1966 [91], Los Angeles CA). AS, p. 400.

Foote, Courtenay [actor] (b. Harrowgate, Yorkshire, England–d. 4 May 1925, Italy). (Griffith; Vitagraph; Bosworth; Fine Arts; Morosco; Mutual; Paramount; 1st National; UA.) AMD, p. 123. AS, p. 400 (d. 4 Mar). BHD, p. 169. IFN, p. 106. MH, p. 111. WWS, p. 204. "Courtenay Foote Taking a Rest," *MPW,* 4 Oct 1913, 137 (with Vitagraph). "Courtenay Foote Filling Dates," *MPW,* 18 Oct 1913, 246 (appearances at motion picture theaters). "Foote and Dexter with Morosco," *MPW,* 17 Jun 1916, 2050. "Courtenay Foote," *MPW,* 29 Jun 1918, 1859. "Courtenay Foote Leaves for California to Play Leading Role in 'Star Rover,'" *MPW,* 26 Jun 1920, 1780 (b. Yorkshire, England). Billy H. Doyle, "Lost Players," *CI,* 145 (Jul 1987), 47.

Foote, John Traintor [scenarist/producer] (b. 1880–30 Jan 1950 [69?], Los Angeles CA). BHD2, p. 87.

Footner, Hulbert [novelist/playwright] (b. Hamilton, Ontario, Canada, 2 Apr 1879–25 Nov 1944 [65], Lusby MD; heart attack). m. Gladys Marsh. "Hulbert Footner; Novelist and Playwright Dies in Maryland at Age of 65," *NYT,* 26 Nov 1944, 56:4 (d. Baltimore MD). "Hulbert Footner," *Variety,* 29 Nov 1944. AS, p. 400. "Footner at West Coast," *MPW,* 17 Jul 1920, 303. Source: *Twentieth-Century Crime and Mystery Writers,* 3rd 3d., p. 384.

Forbes, Harris L. [actor/assistant director] (b. Annapolis MD, 5 Feb 1877–26 Oct 1956 [79], Glendale CA). AMD, p. 123. BHD, p. 169; BHD2, p. 87. "H.L. Forbes Joins American Forces," *MPW,* 24 Jan 1914, 417.

Forbes, Harry W. [cinematographer] (b. Cincinnati OH, 1887?–17 Aug 1939 [52], Los Angeles CA). "Harry Forbes," *Variety,* 23 Aug 1939. AS, p. 400. BHD2, p. 87. FDY, p. 459. IFN, p. 106.

Forbes, Henry [producer] (b. 1888?–15 Nov 1958 [70], New York NY). "Henry Forbes," *Variety,* 19 Nov 1958. AS, p. 401.

Forbes, James [critic/writer] (*né* James Grant Forbes, b. Salem, Ontario, Canada, 6 Mar 1871 [Birth certificate #021088, p. 319]–26 May 1938 [67], Frankfort, Germany). m. Ada E. Fischer. "James Forbes Dies at 66 in Germany; Wrote 'Chorus Lady'; Critic," *Variety,* 1 Jun 1938. NNAT, p. 390. SD.

Forbes, Mary (mother of **Ralph Forbes**) [stage/film actress] (b. Hornsey, England, 30 Dec 1883–22 Jul 1974 [90], Beaumont CA). m. (1) E.J. Taylor; Wesley Wall; (2) Charles Quartermaine (d. 1958). "Mary Forbes," *Variety,* 31 Jul 1974 (d. 23 Jul, age 91). AMD, p. 123. AS, p. 401. BHD1, p. 194 (b. London, 1 Jan 1883). IFN, p. 106. SD, p. 457. Truitt 1983, p. 247 (b. 1 Jan 1880). "Famed Actress to Appear with Marion Davies," *MPW,* 19 Feb 1927, 566.

Forbes, Mary Elizabeth [actress] (b. Rochester NY, 8 Nov 1879–20 Aug 1964 [84], Los Angeles CA; heart attack). AS, p. 401. BHD1, p. 194. IFN, p. 106. Truitt, p. 113.

Forbes, Norman (b. Scotland, 24 Sep 1858–28 Sep 1932 [74], London, England). BHD, p. 170.

Forbes, Ralph (son of **Mary Forbes**) [stage/film actor] (*né* Ralph Taylor, b. London, England, 30 Sep 1896–31 Mar 1951 [54], Bronx NY [Death Certificate Index No. 3409, age 45]). m. **Ruth Chatterton** (d. 1961); Heather Angel; (3) Dora Sayers. (MGM.) "Ralph Forbes Dies; Stage, Film Actor; London-Born Player Got His First Role in U.S. in 1924—Was in 50 Pictures," *NYT,* 1 Apr 1951, 94:1. "Ralph Forbes," *Variety,* 4 Apr 1951 ("Forbes" was mother's surname). AMD, p. 123. AS, p. 401. BHD1, p. 194 (b. 1905). FSS, p. 113. IFN, p. 106 (b. 1905). SD. Truitt, p. 113. "On Long Contract," *MPW,* 2 Oct 1926, 281. Katherine Albert, "Has Frankness Destroyed the Stage?; Ralph Forbes, a well-known legitimate actor, believes that the stage is decadent, resembling 'a woman who has undressed herself.' Consequently he has returned to the cinema," *Cinema Arts,* Jul 1927, 20, 47. "Sign M-G-M Contract," *MPW,* 3 Sep 1927, 9. Elisabeth Goldbeck, "Ralph Forbes's London; There, Stable Boys Are Proud and Burglars Respect a Pocket," *MPC,* Mar 1930, 30, 78, 85, 94–95.

Forbes-Robertson, Eric [actor] (b. 1865–9 Mar 1935 [69?], London, England). BHD, p. 170.

Forbes-Robertson, Johnston (great-uncle of Meriel Forbes, 1913–2000) [stage/film actor] (b. London, England, 16 Jan 1853–6 Nov 1937 [84], St. Margaret's Bay, Dover, England). m. **Gertrude Elliott** (*née* May Gertrude Dermot, d.

1950). *A Player Under Three Reigns* (London: T. Fisher Unwin, Ltd., 1925). "Forbes-Robertson, 84, Dies in England; Sir Johnston Last and One of Greatest of the Victorian Actor-Managers; His Hamlet Still Famous; Supported Irving and Ellen Terry—Painter Before Going on the Stage," *NYT,* 7 Nov 1937, B8:1. "Forbes-Robertson, 84, Great British Actor, Succumbs in England," *Variety,* 10 Nov 1927. AMD, p. 123, 295 (Robertson, Sir. J. Forbes). AS, p. 401. BHD, p. 170. GSS, pp. 131–34. IFN, p. 106. SD. Truitt, p. 113. "Johnstone Forbes-Robertson,' *NYT,* 13 Mar 1905, 8:3 (editorial which bewailed the small audiences attending Forbes-Robertson's *Hamlet.* "For Shakespeare now has no other single interpreter in the theatre who surpasses Mr. Forbes-Robertson in maturity of intellect, in poetic sympathy, in lucidity and elegance of diction, or in personal grace. In other subtler attributes he has no livingt equal."). "Decries 'Stage Business'; Forbes-Robertson Advises Dramatic Graduates to Be Natural," *NYT,* 15 Mar 1905, 6:4 (14 Mar, American Academy of Dramatic Arts [AADA]; "The English actor tried to impress upon the graduates that while it is easy to make a sensation on the stage by kicking over all truth and time-honored conventions, no one can ever be a great actor or actress who strays too far from the advice of Hamlet to the players."). "The Hamlet of Johnstone Forbes-Robertson; Its Greatest Glory Found in Comparison with Edwin Booth—Critical Appreciation of a Great Achievement—A Perspective on Public Insincerity," *NYT,* 19 Mar 1905, 4 (poor attendance by the public). "Sir J. Forbes Robertson in Knickerbocker Production," *MPW,* 10 Jul 1915, 312. "Forbes-Robertson in Brenon Subject," *MPW,* 17 Nov 1917, 997. "Forbes-Robertson Bids Farewell to America," *MPW,* 29 Dec 1917, 1975.

Force, Floyd Charles [actor: Keystone Cop] (b. South Line MI, 22 Mar 1876–9 Jun 1947 [71], Los Angeles CA). "Floyd C. Force," *Variety,* 18 Jun 1947. AS, p. 401. BHD, p. 170. IFN, p. 106. Truitt, p. 113.

Ford, Eugene F[rancis] **(Gene)** [director] (b. Providence RI, 8 Nov 1898–5 Dec 1948 [53], Washington DC). m. Katherine. (Fox.) "Eugene F. (Gene) Ford," *Variety,* 15 Dec 1948. Katz, pp. 436–37. Wheeler W. Dixon, *The "B" Director; A Biographical Directory* (Metuchen NJ: Scarecrow Press, Inc., 1985), pp. 179–81.

Ford, Fenton [actor/playwright] (*né* Belford Forrest, b. 1878?–1 May 1938 [60], Los Angeles CA). (Roach.) "Belford Forrest," *Variety,* 4 May 1938. AS p. 401. BHD, p. 170. IFN, p. 106.

Ford, Francis (brother of **John Ford**; father of **Philip Ford**) [stage/film actor/scenarist/director] (*né* Francis O'Fienne or O'Fearna, b. Portland ME, 15 Aug 1882–5 Sep 1953 [71], Los Angeles CA). m. Mary Armstrong; **Grace Cunard** (d. 1967). (Edison, 1907; Centaur, 1908; Méliès; NYMP; Universal; Metro.) "Francis Ford," *NYT,* 7 Sep 1953, 19:2. "Francis Ford," *Variety,* 9 Sep 1953. AS, p. 401. BHD1, p. 195; BHD2, p. 87. FSS, p. 114. GK, pp. 293–315. IFN, p. 106. Katz, pp. 433–34. MSBB, p. 1046. SD. Truitt, p. 113. "Star and Producer of 'The Broken Coin,'" *MPW,* 19 Jun 1915, 1920. "How I Became a Photoplayer," *Motion Picture Magazine,* Feb 1915, 112–13. "Francis Ford to Return West," *MPW,* 13 Apr 1918, 255. "Francis Ford an Inventor as Well as Egyptologist," *MPW,* 18 Jan 1919, 370. "Francis Ford Explains Origin of 'Phil Kelly,'" *MPW,* 8 Feb 1919, 802. "Francis Ford Building a Studio," *MPW,* 3 May 1919, 661. "Francis Ford Expresses His Ideas on Serials Based on Long Experience as Actor and Director," *MPW,* 16 Aug 1919, 998. "Francis Ford Will Appear in and Aldo Direct Texas Guinan Films," *MPW,* 29 Jan 1921, 572. "Francis Ford," *MPW,* 27 Aug 1927, 588. George A. Katchmer, "Francis Ford; A Prolific Man," *CI,* 109 (Jul 1984), 33–36, 59. R.E. Braff, "An Index to the Films of Francis Ford," *CI,* 224 (Feb 1994), 42–44; Part II, 225 (Mar 1994), C8, 42; Part III, 226 (Apr 1994), 52–55, 61.

Ford, Harrison [stage/film actor] (b. Kansas City MO, 16 Mar 1884–2 Dec 1957 [73], Woodland Hills CA). m. Beatrice Prentice. (Film debut: *Excuse Me,* Pathé, 1915.) "Harrison Ford," *Variety,* 11 Dec 1957. AMD, p. 124. AS, p. 401 (d. Calabasas CA). BHD1, p. 195. FFF, p. 204 (b. 1892). FSS, p. 114. IFN, p. 106. MH, p. 111. Truitt, p. 114. WWS, p. 24. "New Actors in Harlem Stock," *NYDM,* 7 Jan 1914, 13:2 (engaged as leading man of the Harlem Opera House Stock Co. He had played stock at Richmond VA, "and is said to be the youngest leading man in stock in the United States."). Cal York, "Plays and Players," *Photoplay Magazine,* Feb 1917, 89 (Ford "is a recent acquisition by Universal to take the place of J. Warren Kerrigan. He has been playing in stock in Los Angeles."). Sara Redway, "A Jazz Interview with Harrison Ford," *MPC,* Oct 1925, 60–61, 71. "Harrison Ford Is Signed by Metropolitan Pictures," *MPW,* 15 May 1926, 213. Tom Waller, "Harrison Ford," *MPW,* 29 Jan 1927, 342–43. George A. Katchmer, "Harrison Ford," *CI,* 157 (Jul 1988), C4-C6, C8. Eve Golden, "A Harrison Ford by Any Other Name," *CI,* 267 (Sep 1997), C7-C11 (includes filmography by R.E. Braff).

Ford, Hugh [director/[roducer/scenarist]. No data found. AMD, p. 124. "Hugh Ford at Work; Prominent Producer Leaves for Coast to Begin First Screen Play," *NYDM,* 11 Feb 1914, 32:1. "Hugh Ford Joins Famous Players," *MPW,* 14 Feb 1914, 823. "Two Producers Go Abroad," *MPW,* 16 May 1914, 975. "Send-Off [Edwin S.] Porter and Ford," *MPW,* 23 May 1914, 1096. "Porter and Ford Return Home," *MPW,* 1 Aug 1914, 681. "Hugh Ford Signs for Long Term with Famous Players," *MPW,* 2 Aug 1919, 643. "Hugh Ford of Famous Players Predicts a Rise in the Status of Photoplay Authors," *MPW,* 30 Aug 1919, 1294. "Hugh Ford Sails for London to Produce Marie Corelli's 'The Sorrows of Satan,'" *MPW,* 8 May 1920, 843. "Motion Pictures Have Elevating Effect on Drama and Literature, Says Hugh Ford," *MPW,* 25 Dec 1920, 1067.

Ford, Jack [actor] (b. England, 1883?–15 Feb 1962 [79], Consett, England). "Jack Ford," *Variety,* 21 Mar 1962. AS, p. 401.

Ford, James [actor] (b. Lawrence MA, 21 Mar 1903–13 Feb 1977 [73], San Diego CA). (First National.) BHD1, p. 195.

Ford, John (brother of **Francis Ford**; uncle of **Philip Ford**) [director] (*né* Sean Aloysius O'Fearna, b. Cape Elizabeth ME, 1 Feb 1894–31 Aug 1973 [79], Palm Desert CA; cancer). m. Mary Smith, 4 Jul 1920, San Juan Capistrano Mission CA. (Universal; Ford's 1st film: *Cactus My Pal* [*see* obituary of Duke R. Lee].) "John Ford, the Movie Director Who Won 5 Oscars, Dies at 78," *NYT,* 1 Sep 1973, 1:2, 24:1 (b. 1895). "Legenday John Ford, 78, Dies; Personally Honored by U.S.," *Variety,* 5 Sep 1973 (b. 1895, Portland ME; age 78). AMD, p. 124. AS, p. 401. BHD1, p. 195. IFN, p. 106. A.H. Giebler, "Los Angeles Studio Shots; Jack Ford Marries," *MPW,* 24 Jul 1920, 447 (married Smith). "John Ford Engaged by Fox to Direct Buck Jones Film," *MPW,* 25 Sep 1920, 465. "Ford Directs Mix," *MPW,* 27 Jan 1923, 377. "Production Costs Climbing, John Ford Informs English," *MPW,* 20 Jun 1925, 901. "John Ford Back from Europe," *MPW,* 7 May 1927, 37. "John Ford," *MPW,* 12 Nov 1927, 23. Eldon K. Everett, "John Ford...Movie Actor," *CFC,* 58 (Spring, 1978), 15, 51. Brian Miller, "Portland Celebrates Its Native Son: John Ford," *CI,* 279 (Sep 1998), 8 (Portland erected a monument to Ford, a bronze statue of him sitting with a pipe directing a scene, and placed it overlooking the site of Feeny's, the pub owned by Ford's father).

Ford, Lettie [actress] (*née?,* b. 1847?–26 Sep 1936 [89], New York NY). "Lettie Ford," *Variety,* 30 Sep 1936. AS, p. 402. BHD, p. 170. IFN, p. 106.

Ford, Marty [actor] (b. 1900–12 Nov 1954 [54], Los Angeles CA). AS, p. 402. BHD, p. 170. IFN, p. 106.

Ford, Philip [actor/director] (son of **Francis Ford**; nephew of **John Ford**) (b. Portland ME, 16 Oct 1900–12 Jan 1976 [75], Woodland Hills CA; cancer). (Universal; Republic.) "Philip Ford," *Variety,* 28 Jan 1976 (acted at age 5). AS, p. 402. BHD1, p. 195; BHD2, p. 87. IFN, p. 106.

Ford, Reginald [producer]. No data found. AMD, p. 124. "Reginald Ford to Produce in France for American Market," *MPW,* 15 Sep 1923, 234.

Ford, Wallace [actor] (*né* Samuel Jones Grundy, b. Batton, England, 13 Feb 1898–11 Jun 1966 [68], Woodland Hills CA). AS, p. 402.

Forde, Arthur [actor/casting director] (*né* Arthur Hanna-Forde, b. Plymouth, England, 29 Jul 1871–30 Dec 1952 [81], Culver City CA). m. **Maude George**—div. 1918 (d. 1963). AS, p. 402 (b. 1876). BHD, p. 170; BHD2, p. 87.

Forde, Eugene [ctor/director] (b. Providence RI, 8 Nov 1896–27 Feb 1986 [89], Port Hueneme CA). BHD, p. 170; BHD2, p. 87 (b. 1898).

Forde, Eugenie (mother of **Victoria Forde**) [actress] (b. New York NY, 22 Jun 1879–5 Sep 1940 [61], Van Nuys CA). m. Guy H. Fetters, 1920, Mission Inn, Riverside CA. (Nestor.) AMD, p. 124. AS, p. 402 (d. 6 Sep). BHD, p. 170. IFN, p. 106. "New Nestor Players," *MPW,* 14 Oct 1911, 136. "Eugenie Forde," *MPW,* 5 Jun 1915, 1619. "Eugenie Forde in Strand Comedies," *MPW,* 14 Sep 1918, 1586. "Flashes; Eugenie Forde Marries," *LA Times,* 24 Jan 1920, 7. "Eugenie Forde Marries," *MPW,* 14 Feb 1920, 1059.

Forde, Hal C. [stage/film actor] (b. Ireland, 1877?–4 Dec 1955 [78], Philadelphia PA). (Pathé.) "Hal Forde," *NYT,* 6 Dec 1955, 37:2. "Hal Forde," *Variety,* 7 Dec 1955. AS, p. 402. BHD, p. 170. IFN, p. 106. Spehr, p. 130. "Another Kalem Star; Hal Forde Engaged to Appear in a 'Broadway Favorite' Production [*The Maker of Dreams*]," *NYDM,* 21 Jul 1915, 28:2 (on stage at age 8.).

Forde, Stanley H. [actor] (b. Buffalo NY, 9 Feb 1878–28 Jan 1929 [50], New York NY; cancer). "Stanley H. Forde," *Variety,* 6 Feb 1929. AS, p. 402 (b. 1881). BHD, p. 170.

Forde, Victoria (daughter of **Eugenie Forde**) [stage/film actress/producer] (*née* Victoria Hannaford, b. New York NY, 21 Apr 1896–24 Jul 1964 [68], Beverly Hills CA). m. **Tom Mix**, May 1918, Mission Inn, Riverside CA—div. 24 Dec

1930 (d. 1940). (Centaur; Biograph; Nestor; Bison; Selig.) AS, p. 402. BHD, p. 170. BR, pp. 24–27 (d. 29 Jul). IFN, p. 106. "Victoria Forde," *MPW,* 10 Feb 1912, 488. "Victoria Forde," *MPW,* 9 May 1914, 807. "Gossip of the Studios," *NYDM,* 19 May 1915, 26:1 (with Nestor; celebrated her 19th birthday "last week"). Richard Wallace, "'Vicky' Forde; The Girl Who Is Always Willing to Take a Chance," *MPC,* Nov 1916, 22–23. "Victoria Forde Produces Selig Comedy," *MPW,* 11 Nov 1916, 844. "Tom Mix Married," *Variety,* 10 May 1918, p. 44. Buck Rainey, "Victoria Forde; Venturesome in an Era When There Was No Alternative," *CI,* 141 (Mar 1987), 20–21. Nick Nicholls, "Additional Victoria Forde Movies," *CI,* 143 (May 19878), 13. Billy H. Doyle, "Lost Players," *CI,* 170 (Aug 1989), 51.

Forde, Walter [actor] (*né* Thomas Seymour, b. Bradford, Yorkshire, England, 21 Apr 1896–7 Jan 1984 [87], Santa Monica CA). AS, p. 402 (b. 6 Aug; d. London, England). BHD1, p. 195 (b. LA CA); BHD2, p. 88 (d. LA CA).

Fordred, Dorice [actress] (b. Port Elizabeth, So. Africa, 25 Nov 1902–4 Aug 1980 [77], London, England). BHD1, p. 195.

Forest, Frank [actor] (b. St. Paul MN, 17 Oct 1896–23 Dec 1976 [80], Santa Monica CA). AS, p. 402 (b. 1899). BHD1, p. 195. IFN, p. 106.

Forest, Jean [actor] (b. Paris, France, 27 Sep 1912–27 Mar 1980 [66]). BHD, p. 170.

Forest, Karl [actor] (*né* Karl Obertimpfler, b. Vienna, Austria, 12 Nov 1874–3 Jun 1944 [69], Vienna, Austria). m. **Trute Carlsen** (d. 1968). AS, p. 402. BHD, p. 170. IFN, p. 106.

Foresti, L. [cinematographer]. No data found. FDY, p. 459.

Forman, Ethel [actress] (b. Englnnd, 1877–8 Sep 1976 [99?], London, England). m. **Basil Rathbone**—div. (d. 1967). AS, p. 403.

Forman, Tom (1st cousin of Maude Bellamy) [actor/director] (b. Mitchell Co. TX, 22 Feb 1892–7 Nov 1926 [34], Venice CA; suicide by shooting). "Tom Forman Kills Himself at Home; Picture Director, 34, Had Just Started Making New Picture—War Veteran," *Variety,* 10 Nov 1926. AMD, p. 124. AS, p. 403 (b. 1893). BHD, p. 170; BHD2, p. 88 (b. 1893). IFN, p. 106. Truitt, p. 250 (b. 1893). "Tom Forman," *MPW,* 12 Jun 1915, 1782. "Briefs of Biography...One of the 'Comers,'" *NYDM,* 16 Jun 1915, 32:1. "Forman Renews Lasky Contract," *MPW,* 27 Jan 1917, 537. "The Roll of Honor," *MPW,* 25 Aug 1917, 1224. "We Congratulate Lieutenant Tom Forman," *MPW,* 20 Jul 1918, 373. "Forman Re-Engaged by Famous Players," *MPW,* 15 Feb 1919, 893. "Preferred Signs Director Forman," *MPW,* 12 Aug 1922, 504. "Gasnier and Forman Sign with Preferred Pictures," *MPW,* 19 Aug 1922, 583. "Forman Is Screen's Man of the Hour," *MPW,* 27 Jan 1923, 363. "Forman to Direct Carey," *MPW,* 12 Jul 1924, 100. "Stromberg Signs Forman," *MPW,* 8 Nov 1924, 159.

Forman, Tom B. [actor] (*né* Thomas S. Farmer, b. MN, 29 Oct 1891–16 Nov 1951 [60], Los Angeles CA). BHD, p. 170. IFN, p. 106. George A. Katchmer, "Forgotten Cowboys/Girls—Part VII," *CI,* 179 (May 1990), 44.

Formby, George, Jr. [stage/film/TV actor/composer] (aka George Hoy, b. Wigan, Lancashire, England, 26 May 1904–6 Mar 1961 [56], Preston, Lancashire, England). "George Formby," *Variety,* 8 Mar 1961, 79:1. AS, p. 403. BHD1, p. 196; BHD2, p. 88. IFN, p. 107.

Formes, Carl, Jr. [opera singer/actor] (b. London, England, 3 Jul 1841–18 Nov 1939 [98], Los Angeles CA). AMD, p. 124. AS, p. 403. BHD, p. 170. IFN, p. 107. "Karl Formes Joins Vitagrpah," *MPW,* 17 May 1919, 1040.

Formia, Lia [actress] (b. Naples, Italy). JS, p. 170 (in Italian silents from 1919).

Fornaroli, Cia [ballerina/actress] (*née* Lucia Fornaroli, b. Milan, Italy, 16 Oct 1887–17 Aug 1954 [66], Riverdale NY). JS, p. 170 (in Italian silents from 1916).

Forney, Pauline [scenarist]. No data found. FDY, p. 425.

Forns, José [composer/scenarist] (b. Spain, 1897–7 Sep 1953 [56?], Geneva, Switzerland). AS, p. 403.

Forrest, Allan [actor] (*né* Emil or Allan Forrest Fisher, b. Brooklyn NY, 1 Sep 1884 or 1885–25 Jul 1941 [56], Detroit MI). m. **Anna Little**—19 Aug 1916, Santa Barbara CA—div. 1918 (d. 1984); **Lottie Pickford**, 8 Jan 1922–28 (d. 1936). "Allan Forrest, 56, ex-Film Star, Dead; He Was Leading Man for Mary Pickford and Talmadges in Era of Silent Pictures; Left Hollywood in 1929; Appeared in Productions with Jackie Coogan—In Detroit Studio for Eight Years," *NYT,* 27 Jul 1941, 30:4 (b. New York NY; age 55). "Allan Forrest," *Variety,* 30 Jul 1941. AMD, p. 124. AS, p. 403. BHD1, p. 196 (b. 1889). IFN, p. 107 (age 55). MH, p. 111. Truitt, p. 114 (b. 1889). "Mary Brooks [Anna Little] and Allan Fisher Marry," *MPW,* 16 Sep 1916, 1807. "Majtrimony Claims Anna Little," *MPW,* 30 Sep 1916, 2115.

Forrest, Ann, "The Little Weeper" [stage/film actress] (*née* Anna Kroman, b. Sønderho, Denmark, 14 Apr 1895–25 Oct 1985 [90], San Diego CA). m. (1) ?, 1916; (2) F. Steel Bain, 1 Feb 1933; (3) Mr. D'Lisle. (Began 1915; American Film Manufacturing Co.; Universal; Triangle; Fox; Lasky; UA.) AMD, p. 124. BHD1, p. 608. MH, p. 111. Hans J. Wollstein, *Strangers in Hollywood: The History of Scandinavian Actors in American Films.* "Ann Forrest Will Have Feminine Role in 'Other Wife,'" *MPW,* 10 JUL 1920, 247. "Ann Forrest Is Shifted," *MPW,* 28 Aug 1920, 1146. "Ann Forrest in Hospital," *MPW,* 9 Apr 1921, 590 (appendicitis). "Foreign Actors Barred [in England]," *MPW,* 5 Aug 1922, 412. Billy Doyle, "Ann For[r]est; The Melancholy Dane," *CI,* 245 (Nov 1995), 33.

Forrest, Arthur [stage/film actor] (b. Bayreuth, Germany, 1859–14 May 1933 [74], New York NY). "Arthur Forrest," *Variety,* 23 May 1933, p. 54 (age 76). BHD, p. 170; BHD2, p. 88. IFN, p. 107.

Forrest, Belford *see* **Ford, Fenton**

Forrest, Mabel [actress] (*née* Mabel Chidester?, b. Kinsman OH, 5 Nov 1894–5 Jul 1967 [72], Woodland Hills CA). m. Bryant Washburn, 1914. (Essanay.) AS, p. 403. BHD1, p. 196 (b. IL). IFN, p. 107 (b. IL). Roberta Courtlandt, "Bryant Washburn's Family," *MPC,* Sep 1916, 31–32. Billy H. Doyle, "Lost Players," *CI,* 150 (Dec 1987), 24, 29.

Forrest, William H. [stage/film actor] (b. Princeton CA, 1902?–29 Jan 1989 [86], Santa Monica CA; heart attack). m. Wilhelmina. "William Forrest, Actor, 86," *NYT,* 7 Feb 1989, 8:3. "William H. Forrest," *Variety,* 8 Feb 1989 (d. 26 Jan). AS, p. 403. SD.

Forrester, Frederick C. [actor] (b. 1872?–14 Oct 1952 [80], New York NY). "Frederick Forrester," *Variety,* 22 Oct 1952. AS, p. 403. BHD1, p. 196. IFN, p. 107.

Forrester, Izola [scenarist]. No data found. FDY, p. 425.

Forrester, Melville S. [director] (b. 1881–15 Nov 1949 [68?], Los Angeles CA). AS, p. 403 (b. 1885). BHD2, p. 88.

Forsberg, Edwin Forrest [actor] (b. Cleveland OH, 1873?–11 May 1947 [74], New York NY). m. Helen Courtney (d. 1939). "Edwin Forrest Forsberg," *Variety,* 14 May 1947. AMD, p. 124. BHD, p. 171. "Edwin Forsberg," *MPW,* 20 Jun 1914, 1677. "Kenney Engages Play'rs," *MPW,* 16 Feb 1918, 954.

Forshay, Harold [actor] (b. 1883?–23 Feb 1953 [69]). AMD, p. 124. IFN, p. 107. "Harold Forshay to Appear in Person," *MPW,* 20 Aug 1921, 817.

Forst, Emil [scenarist]. No data found. FDY, p. 425.

Forst, Willi [actor/scenarist/director/producer] (*né* Wilhelm Anton Frohs, b. Vienna, Austria, 7 Apr 1903–12 Aug 1980 [77], Vienna, Austria; complications after an operation). AS, p. 403. BHD1, p. 196; BHD2, p. 88.

Forstberg, Edwin Forrest [actor] (b. Cleveland OH, 1873–11 May 1947 [74?], New York NY). AS, p. 403.

Forster, Froedrich [actor/scenarist] (*né* August Theodor Waldfried Burggraf, b. Bremen, Germany, 11 Aug 1895–1 Mar 1958 [62], Bremen, Germany). AS, p. 403.

Forster, Hedda [actress] (b. Frankfort-on-the-Main, Germany, 27 Jun 1895–2 Jan 1933 [37], Berlin, Germany). BHD, p. 171.

Forster, Oscar W. [actor] (b. New York NY, 17 Feb 1885–12 Jun 1951 [66], Santa Barbara CA). BHD, p. 171; BHD2, p. 88.

Forster, Rudolf Herbert Anton [actor] (b. Groebming, Germany, 30 Oct 1884–25 Oct 1968 [83], Vienna, Austria). "Rudolf Forster," *Variety,* 30 Oct 1968. AS, p. 403. BHD1, p. 196. IFN, p. 107 (b. Grobming, Austria).

Forsyne, Ida [actress/daner] (b. Chicago IL, 1883-Apr/May 1936 [53?]). AS, p. 403.

Forsyth, James [publicist] (b. 31 May 1888–18 Feb 1963 [74], St. Leonard's-on-Sea, England). BHD2, p. 88.

Forsythe, Robert [actor] (b. Belfast, Ireland, 1876–9 Feb 1922 [47?], New York NY). BHD, p. 171.

Forsythe, Robert [stage/film actor] (*né* Kyle S. Crichton, b. Peale PA, 6 Nov 1896–24 Nov 1960 [64], New York NY). m. Mary Collier. "Kyle Crichton," *Variety,* 30 Nov 1960. SD.

Forsythe, Victor Clyde [actor/artist] (b. 1886–24 May 1962 [75?], Pasadena CA). AMD, p. 124. BHD, p. 171. Thornton Fisher, "Vic Forsythe," *MPW,* 19 Sep 1914, 1658.

Fort, Garrett Elsden [actor/scenarist] (b. New York NY, 5 Jun 1898–26 Oct 1945 [47], Beverly Hills CA; overdose of sleeping tablets). Garrett Fort," *Variety,* 31 Oct 1945. AMD, p. 125. AS, p. 404 (b. 1900). BHD2, p. 88. FDY, p. 425. IFN, p. 107. "Script Being Prepared," *MPW,* 8 Nov 1924, 168. "Scenarist Leaves Warners," *MPW,* 9 Jul 1927, 87.

Forte, Joe [film/radio/TV actor] (*né* Josef Forte, b. England, 14 Jun 1893–11 Mar 1967 [73], Los Angeles CA; heart attack). "Joe Forte," *Variety,*

22 Mar 1967 (age 71). AS, p. 404 (d. 22 Feb). IFN, p. 107.

Fortescue, Viola A. [stage/film actress] (b. Columbus GA, 1875?–16 Sep 1953 [78], New York NY). "Viola Fortescue," *Variety,* 23 Sep 1953. AS, p. 404. BHD, p. 171. SD.

Forth, George J. [actor]. No data found. AMD, p. 125. "George J. Forth," *MPW,* 29 Sep 1917, 1994.

Fortier, Herbert [stage/film actor] (b. Toronto, Canada, 1867?–16 Feb 1949 [82], Philadelphia PA). (Lubin.) "Herbert Fortier," *Variety,* 23 Feb 1949 ("in legit and films for 50 years before he retired in 1938"). AS, p. 404. BHD1, p. 196. IFN, p. 107. Truitt, p 114.

Fortune, Aimé [actor] (b. France, 20 Sep 1872–1962 [90?], France). AS, p. 404.

Fortune, Edmund [actor] (b. Geneva NY, 27 Mar 1851–21 Sep 1939 [88], CA). AS, p. 404. BHD1, p. 196. IFN, p. 107.

Fortune, Thomas George [actor] (b. Toronto, Canada, 1877?–16 Mar 1943 [65], Los Angeles CA). (Vitagraph; purchasing agent for Paramount.) "Thomas George Fortune," *Variety,* 24 Mar 1943. AS, p. 404 (d. 16 Feb 1949).

Fortune, Wallace [director/stage manager] (b. 1884?–12 Jan 1926 [42], New York NY; typhoid pneumonia). "Wallace Fortune," *Variety,* 20 Jan 1926. BHD, p. 171.

Forzano, Giovacchino [scenarist/director] (b. Borgo San Lorenzo, Italy, 13 Nov 1884–28 Oct 1970 [85], Rome, Italy). AS, p. 404. BHD2, p. 88.

Fosberg, Harold [actor]. No data found. AMD, p. 125. BHD1, p. 196. "Harold Fosberg Joins Selig Stock," *MPW,* 15 Nov 1913, 718.

Fosco, Piero [actor] (*né* Giovanni Pastrone, b. Montechiaro d'Asti, Italy, 13 Sep 1882–27 Jun 1959 [76], Turin, Italy). AS, p. 404.

Foshay, Harold A[dams] [stage/film actor/director/producer] (b. Charleston SC, 1884?–23 Feb 1953 [69], Charleston SC). "Harold A. Foshay," *Variety,* 4 Mar 1953 ("career spanned practically all aspects of film work during the era of silent pix"). AS, p. 404. BHD, p. 171; BHD2, p. 88 (b. Brooklyn NY). IFN, p. 107. SD. Truitt, p. 114.

Foss, Darrell Burton [actor] (b. Oconomowoc WI, 28 Mar 1893–15 Sep 1962 [69], Los Angeles CA). (In films from 1917 to 1922; Metro.) AMD, p. 125. AS, p. 404. (b. 1892) BHD, p. 171 (b. 1892). MSBB, p. 1024 (b. 1893). "Darrell Foss Again with May Allison," *MPW,* 17 Aug 1918, 998.

Foss, Kenelm [actor/director] (b. England, 13 Dec 1885–28 Nov 1963 [77], London, England). AS, p. 404. BHD, p. 171; BHD2, p. 88.

Foster, Art [actor] (*né* Arthur Turner Foster, b. Brooklyn NY, 21 Oct 1867–4 Jul 1947 [79], Los Angeles CA). AS, p. 405.

Foster, Basil [actor/director] (b. Malvern, England, 12 Feb 1882–30 Sep 1959 [77], Uxbridge, England). BHD2, p. 88.

Foster, Edna (sister of **Flora Foster**; aka "Billy," one of the Biograph Kids) [actress] (b. Chicago IL, 1899?). (Biograph, 1909.) "Biograph Kids Are Wonderful Girls; Chicago Exhibitor's Daughters," *Motography,* 4 Jul 1914, 3–4.

Foster, Fern [actress] (b. Somerville MA, 2 Oct 1885–10 Jun 1949 [63], Somerville MA). BHD, p. 171.

Foster, Flora (sister of **Edna Foster**; one of the Biograph Kids) [actress] (b. Boston MA, 1898–16 Sep 1914 [16?], Chicago IL). (Biograph, 1909.) AMD, p. 125. BHD, p. 171. ""Death of a Biograph Favorite," *MPW,* 10 Oct 1914, 197.

Foster, Helen [actress: Wampas Star, 1929] (b. Independence KS, 23 May 1906–25 Dec 1982 [76], Los Angeles CA). AS p. 405 (d. 22 Dec). BHD1, p. 197. BR, pp. 142–44 (b. 1907). George A. Katchmer, "Forgotten Cowboys and Cowgirls—Part III," *CI,* 174 (Dec 1989), 38.

Foster, J. Morris [stage/film actor] (b. Foxberg PA, 9 Sep 1881–24 Apr 1966 [84], Los Angeles CA). m. **Mignon Anderson**, 13 Apr 1915 (d. 1983). (Central Theater, San Francisco CA; Thanhouser; FP-L; Cort Stock at Wheeling WV.) AMD, p. 125. AS, p. 405. BHD, p. 171. IFN, p. 107. Truitt 1983, p. 251 (b. 1882). "Hite Engages Three," *MPW,* 14 Mar 1914, 1366. "Marriages," *NYDM,* 19 May 1915, 9:2. "Foster in Big U Pictures," *MPW,* 13 Jan 1917, 209. "Morris Foster [photo]," *Photoplay,* Jul 1917, Popular Photoplayers section. George Katchmer, "Remembering the Great Silents," *CI,* 242 (Aug 1995), 35.

Foster, John [prop man] (b. 1854–23 Nov 1916 [62?], New Orleans LA). BHD2, p. 88.

Foster, Maximillian [scenrist] (b. 1872–21 Sep 1943 [71?]). BHD2, p. 88.

Foster, May [actress] (aka May Campbell, b. IL, 27 Mar 1873–6 Jan 1951 [76], Los Angeles CA; heart disease). AS, p. 405. BHD1, p. 197. Truitt 1983, p. 251.

Foster, Norman [actor/scenarist/director] (*né* Norman Hoeffer, b. Richmond IN, 13 Dec 1900–7 Jul 1976 [75], Santa Monica CA; cancer). AS, p. 405. BHD1, p. 197; BHD2, p. 88.

Foster, Phoebe [actress] (b. Center Harbor NH, 1896–1975 [79?]). BHD1, p. 197.

Foster, Pop [actor] (*né* George Murphy Foster, b. McCall LA, 18 May 1892–7 Dec 1928 [36], Cleveland OH). AS, p. 405.

Foster, William [Manager, Foster Photoplay Company] (b. 1884). (Pathé.) *MPW,* 25 Oct 1913, 363. Donald Bogle, *Tom, Coons, Mulattoes, Mammies, & Bucks* (NY: Continuum, 1989), p. 102.

Foster, William C. [cinematographer]. No data found.

Fouce, Frank [actor/writer/executive] (b. HI, 26 Oct 1899–11 Jan 1962 [62], Los Angeles CA). AS, p. 405. BHD, p. 171. IFN, p. 107.

Fouche, Miriam [actress]. No data found. AMD, p. 125. "Miriam Fouche with Fox," *MPW,* 10 Mar 1917, 1542.

Fougere, Pierre [actor] (b. France-d. 28 Nov 1921, Paris, France). AS, p. 405. BHD, p. 171 (Pierre Fougers).

Fougez, Anna [actress/singer] (*née* Anna-Maria Appacena Laganà, b. Taranto, Italy, 9 Jul 1894–11 Sep 1966 [72], Santa Marinella, near Rome, Italy). "Anna Fougez," *Variety,* 21 Sep 1966. AS, p. 405. BHD, p. 171. IFN, p. 107. JS, p. 171 (in Italian silents from 1916).

Foulston, George [actor] (b. England, 1883–9 Sep 1960 [77?], St. Albans, England). AS, p. 405.

Fowler, Albert Bela [director] (b. 1887–6 Feb 1922 [34?]). BHD2, p. 88.

Fowler, Brenda [actress] (b. Jamestown ND, 16 Feb 1883–27 Oct 1942 [59], Los Angeles CA). m. John W. Sherman. (Kalem; Rex; Para.) "Brenda Fowler," *Variety,* 4 Nov 1942. AS, p. 406. BHD1, p. 197. IFN, p. 107. Truitt, p. 115 (b. Los Angeles CA).

Fowler, Harry M. [cinematogrpher] (b. Alliance OH, 1884?–17 Sep 1954 [70], Los Angeles CA). "Harry M. Fowler," *Variety,* 29 Sep 1954 ("motion picture technician"). BHD2, p. 89.

Fowler, John C[rawford] [actor] (b. New York NY, 25 Jul 1869–27 Jun 1952 [82], Los Angeles CA; arteriosclerosis). AS, p. 406. BHD1, p. 197. IFN, p. 107. George Katchmer, "Remembering the Great Silents," *CI,* 223 (Jan 1994), 49:1.

Fowler, Robert G. [aviator] (b. CA, 10 Aug 1883–15 Jun 1966 [82], San Jose CA). "Robert G. Fowler, Aviator, 81, Dead; Pilot Flew Biplane From West to East Coast in 1911," *NYT,* 16 Jun 1966 [in 1913 Fowler took pictures of the Panama Canal, then under construction, which activity was later banned). AS, p. 406 (b. KY). BHD, p. 171. "Champion Enterprise,"*MPW,* 11 Dec 1916, 907 (pilot for Champion cameraman).

Fox, Arthur P. [scenarist] (b. 1875–1 Nov 1928 [53?], Los Angeles CA). BHD2, p. 89.

Fox, DeWitt [executive]. No data found. AMD, p. 125. "Renfax Musical Pictures a Year Old," *MPW,* 6 Feb 1915, 833.

Fox, Finis (brother of **Wallace W. Fox** and **Edwin Carewe;** uncle of **Yvonne Carewe**) [title writer/scenarist] (b. Caddo OK, 8 Oct 1884–7 Nov 1949 [65], San Antonio TX). m. Conchita. "Finis Fox," *Variety,* 16 Nov 1949. AMD, p. 125. BHD2, p. 89 (b. 1881). FDY, pp. 425, 443. IFN, p. 107. "Finis Fox Joins Brother in Picture Field," *MPW,* 8 Sep 1917, 1543. "Fox Injured in Train Collision," *MPW,* 14 Feb 1920, 1060. "Finis Fox Recovering from Accident," *MPW,* 21 Feb 1920, 1230. "About: Finis Fox," *MPW,* 22 Sep 1923, 344. David A. Balch, "The Apostle of Heart Throb; Meet Finis Fox, author, director and producer of 'A Woman Who Sinned,' and learn how he made good against supendous obstacles," *MW,* 17 May 1924, 7, 25. "Sign Finis Fox," *MPW,* 7 Nov 1925, 41. "Fox Is Finis in Name Only," *MPW,* 4 Jun 1927, 332.

Fox, Franklyn [actor] (b. England, 1894–2 Nov 1967 [73?], Wantagh NY). AS, p. 406.

Fox, Fred [title writer/actor/assistant director] (*né* Frederick Strachan Fox, b. London, England, 22 Jan 1884–1 Dec 1949 [65], Los Angeles CA; heart attack). AS, p. 406. BHD2, p. 89. FDY, p. 443. IFN, p. 107.

Fox, Harry [stage/film actor/singer] (*né* Arthur Carringford) (b. NY, 25 May 1882–20 Jul 1959 [77], Woodland Hills CA). m. Evelyn Brent; Beatrice Curtis; Yancsi Dolly; Florrie Millership. (WB; TC-F.) "Harry Fox Is Dead at 76; Stage and Movie Comedian Acted with Dolly Sisters," *NYT,* 21 Jul 1959, 29:5. "Harry Fox," *Variety,* 22 Jul 1959. AMD, p. 125. AS, p. 406 (b. Pomona CA). BHD1, p. 197. IFN, p. 107. SD, p. 466 (b. Pomona CA). Truitt, p. 115 (b. Pomona CA). "Harry Fox," *MPW,* 13 Jan 1917, 234.

Fox, John, Jr. [actor] (b. Chicago IL-d. 6 Jul 1919, Big Stone Gap VA). AMD, p. 125. BHD, p. 171. "John Fox's First," *MPW,* LXVI, 19 Jan 1924, 226. "John Fox Signed," *MPW,* 26 Dec 1925, 798. George Katchmer, "Remembering the Great Silents," *CI,* 218 (Aug 1993), 42.

Fox, Josephine (sister of actress Elizabeth Malone) [stage/film/radio actress] (b. 1869–2 Aug 1953 [84], Englewood NJ). m. actor William

Marble. "Josephine Fox," *Variety,* 5 Aug 1953, p. 63. AS, p. 406. BHD, p. 171. IFN, p. 107.

Fox, Lucy [actress]. No data found. AMD, p. 125. "Lucy Fox Signs with Pathé to Play Leading Parts in Serials," *MPW,* 28 May 1921, 423. Alma M. Talley, "'No Girl Is Safe in Naples Without an Escort,' Says Lucy Fox," *MW,* 16 Jun 1923, 11, 31. "Lucy Fox and Alan Hale Added to Cast," *MPW,* 4 Aug 1923, 414. "Lucy Fox Is with Gallagher and Shean," *MPW,* 11 Aug 1923, 500.

Fox, Sidney [actress] (*né* Sidney Liefer, b. New York NY, 10 Dec 1910–14 Nov 1942 [31], Hollywood CA; found dead in bed from an overdose of sleeping pills). m. Charles Beahan. "Sidney Fox," *Variety,* 18 Nov 1942. BHD1, p. 198 (15 Nov). IFN, p. 108 (b. 1911; d. 15 Nov). Truitt 1983, p. 253.

Fox, Virginia [actress: Sennett Bathing Beauty] (b. Wheeling WV, 19 Apr 1902–14 Oct 1982 [80], Palm Springs CA; emphysema and cerebral thrombosis). (Virginia Zanuck; b. 1903). m. **Darryl F. Zanuck**, 24 Jan 1924 (d. 1979). Marlys J. Harris, *The Zanucks of Hollywood; The Dark Legacy of an American Dynasty* (NY: Crown Publishers, Inc., 1989). Mel Gussow, "Virginia F. Zanuck, Silent Movie Star; A Buster Keaton Leading Lady—Widow of Tycoon Was Prominent Hostess," *NYT,* 15 Oct 1982, D18:4. "Virginia Fox Zanuck," *Variety,* 20 Oct 1982 (b. Charleston WV; d. Santa Monica CA, age ca. 79). AMD, p. 125. AS, p. 407. BHD, p. 171 (b. Charleston; d. Santa Monica). MH, p. 111 (b. Charleston). "Virginia Fox Now Leading Woman for Buster Keaton," *MPW,* 9 Oct 1920, 829.

Fox, Wallace W. (brother of **Finis Fox** and **Edwin Carewe**; uncle of **Yvonne Carewe**) [director] (b. Purcell OK, 9 Mar 1895–30 Jun 1958 [63], Los Angeles CA). "Wallace Fox," *Variety,* 9 Jul 1958. AS, p. 407. BHD2, p. 89. IFN, p. 108. Katz, p. 441.

Fox, William [founder of Fox Films/executive] (*né* William Fuchs, b. Tulcheva, Hungary, 1 Jan 1879–8 May 1952 [73], New York NY [Death Certificate Index No. 10480]). m. Eve Leo. Glendon Allvine, *The Greatest Fox of Them All* (NY: Lyle Stewart, Inc., 1969). "William Fox Dies; Pioneer in Movies; Former Head of $300,000,000 Motion-Picture Empire Lost Hold in Market Crash; Started Film Firm in 1915," *NYT,* 9 May 1952, 23:1. "Wm. Fox Dies in N.Y. After Long Illness," *Variety,* 14 May 1952. AMD, p. 125. AS, p. 407. BHD2, p. 89. IFN, p. 108 (b. Tulchva, Hungary). SD. Spehr, p. 132. "Advent of the 'Talking' Picture...," *MPW,* 28 Jan 1911, 177–78 (opened the first "store" theater in Brooklyn). "United States vs. Motion Picture Patents Co.," *MPW,* 15 Mar 1913, 1082–83. "A Disclaimer from Wiliam Fox," *MPW,* 3 Oct 1914, 44. "Fox to Sell State Rights," *MPW,* 16 May 1914, 977. "Independents Propose Organization," *MPW,* 12 Sep 1914, 1521–22. "Fox Agrees with Bush," *MPW,* 21 Nov 1914, 1097. "Kate Claxton Sues William Fox," *MPW,* 9 Oct 1915, 259. "S.P.C.A. on the Job; Society Makes Five Arrests as Result of Scene in Fox's 'Carmen,'" *NYDM,* 6 Nov 1915, 26:4 (Art Jarvis and horse had to leap 80 feet into a lake at Ausable Chasm in the Adirondacks. The horse was uninjured, but Jarvis broke a leg. Warrants for 3 of the alleged misdemeanants brought about an arraignment; they were released on $100 bond. Thomas F. Freel contended that the horse was not a trained diving animal; that he balked at the jump; that he was blindfolded and plunged through a trap door, and that witnesses could be produced, which was denied by the Fox Film Corp.). "William Fox to Produce Comedies," *MPW,* 11 Nov 1916, 874. "Fox Talks 'Sunshine Comedies,'" *MPW,* 3 Nov 1917, 683. "Lehrman Pleases Fox," *MPW,* 10 Nov 1917, 894. "Fox Invests $400,000 in Bonds," *MPW,* 17 Nov 1917, 1025. "William Fox Takes Over Victor Studio," *MPW,* 5 Jan 1918, 57. "William Fox Will Dismiss Pro-Germans," *MPW,* 29 Jun 1918, 1859. "Fox Has Large Plans for 1918–19," *MPW,* 10 Aug 1918, 820–21. "Fox to Increase Admissions This Fall," *MPW,* 10 Aug 1918, 847. "Do Repeat Engagements Pay? Yes, Says William Fox," *MPW,* 18 Jan 1919, 369. "William Fox Gives Prizes to Employees for Captions," *MPW,* 19 Apr 1919, 375. "Penn¥ Arcade to Theatre Chain," *MPW,* 12 Jul 1919, 233–34. "Official Statement by William Fox," *MPW,* 19 Jul 1919, 354. "William Fox Will Open Cafeteria in New Building," *MPW,* 13 Sep 1919, 1630. "William Fox Reviews Company's Work for Past Year; Sees 1920 Bigger," *MPW,* 3 Jan 1920, 94. William Fox, "On Eve of New Season, William Fox Extends Greetings to All Exhibitors," *MPW,* 14 Aug 1920, 889. William Fox, "Fox Film Corporation Ends Its Most Successful Year with Close of 1920," *MPW,* 25 Dec 1920, 1012. "William Fox to Produce Abroad," *MPW,* 2 Apr 1921, 481. "William Fox Denies Rumor," *MPW,* 16 Jun 1923, 560. "Fox Corporation to Spend $27,000,000 on Production and Development," *MPW,* 17 Nov 1923, 329. "Author's Rights Upheld," *MPW,* 5 Jan 1924, 32. "Fox's Daughter Marries," *MPW,* 19 Apr 1924, 624 (Belle Fox m. Milton S. Schwartz, 2 Apr 1924, LA CA, her 20th birthday). "Fox Is Gold Wizard," *MPW,* 1 Nov 1924, 27. "Fox Is Grandfather," *MPW,* 11 Apr 1925, 550. "Fox Again a Grandfather," *MPW,* 2 May 1925, 33 (William Fox Jerome Schwartz, b. 8 Apr 1925). "William Fox Forging Ahead Faster During 22nd Year Than Ever Before," *MPW,* 16 May 1925, 327. "William Fox to Build New Academy of Music," *MPW,* 5 Sep 1925, 35. "They Control Your Films!," *MPC,* Jan 1926, 26. R.M. Hyams, "Fox Started with a Penny Arcade,' *Cinema Arts,* Nov 1926, 17, 46–47 ("A little more than two decades ago Mr. Fox was in a cloth-sponging business on the lower East Side of New York City.").

Foxe, Earle Aldrich (cousin of **Robert T. Haines**) [stock/film actor] (b. Oxford OH, 25 Dec 1887–10 Dec 1973 [85], Los Angeles CA). (b. 1891). (Kalem; Victor, 1909; Reliance; Universal.) AMD, p. 126. AS, p. 407. BHD1, p. 198 (b. 1891). FSS, p. 115. IFN, p. 108 (b. 1891). MH, p. 111 (b. 1888). "Earle Foxe Joins Metro Forces," *MPW,* 4 Nov 1916, 676. "Earle Aldrich Foxe," *MPW,* 28 Apr 1917, 619. "Earle Foxe Engaged by Triangle," *MPW,* 29 Sep 1917, 1978. "Earle Foxe, Constance Talmadge's Leading Man," *MPW,* 3 Nov 1917, 685. "Earle Foxe Signed by Ziegfeld Film to Star in Nine Pictures After 'The Black Panther's Club,'" *MPW,* XLVI, 30 Oct 1920, 1248. "Earle Foxe Now a Star," *MPW,* 14 Feb 1925, 714. "Earle Foxe in 'Van Bibbers,'" *MPW,* 20 Feb 1926, 707. "Sheehan Signs Earle Foxe to Long Contract," *MPW,* 7 May 1927, 43. Herbert Cruikshank, "The Menacin' Man; The Villainy of Earle Foxe Includes Stealing His Son's Toys," *MPC,* Oct 1928, 63, 85, 88 (his grandfather's buggy works evolved into Buick).

Foy, Bryan, "The Keeper of the B's" (son of **Eddie Foy, Sr.**; brother of **Eddie, Jr.**, **Madeline**, **Mary**, and **Richard Foy**) [actor/scenarist/producer/director] (*né* Bryan Fitzgerald, b. Chicago IL, 8 Dec 1894–20 Apr 1977 [82], Los Angeles CA; after heart attack). (b. 1896). m. Vivian (d. 4 Dec 1949 [53], Encino CA). (Began in 1920; Fox; WB.) "Bryan Foy, Vaudevillian and Film Producer, 80, Dies," *NYT,* 22 Apr 1977, IV, 19:2 (made 2-reelers for Fox). "Bryan Foy," and Joseph McBride, "Bryan Foy, 82, Rajah of 'B' Pics; Eldest of Eddie Foy's Brood Was Strictly for Fast Bucks—Resented 'Dialog,'" *Variety,* 27 Apr 1977. "Mrs. Bryan Foy," *NYT,* 6 Dec 1949, 31:2. AMD, p. 126. AS, p. 407. BHD1, p. 198; BHD2, p. 89 (b. 1896). FDY, p. 425. IFN, p. 108. Truitt 1983, p. 253 (b. 1896). "Bryan Foy Promoted to Be Director," *MPW,* 15 Sep 1923, 280. "Bryan for Directing," *MPW,* 20 Mar 1926, 173. "Bryan Foy," *MPW,* 20 Aug 1927, 517.

Foy, Charles [actor] (*né* Charles Fitzgerald, b. IL, 12 Jun 1898–22 Aug 1984 [86], Los Angeles CA). AS, p. 407. BHD1, p. 198.

Foy, Eddie, Jr. (son of **Eddie Foy Sr.**, and Madeline Morando; brother of **Madeline**, **Mary** and **Richard Foy**) [stage/film actor] (b. New Rochelle NY, 4 Feb 1905–15 Jul 1983 [78], Woodland Hills CA; pancreatic cancer). m. (d. 1952). (Film debut: *Queen of the Night Clubs,* 1929; Universal.) "Eddie Foy Jr., 78, Show Business Vet, Dies in California," *Variety,* 20 Jul 1983. AS, p. 407. BHD1, p. 198.

Foy, Eddie, Sr. (father of **Bryan**, **Madeline**, **Mary** and **Richard Foy**) [Eddie and the Seven Little Foys/stage/film actor] (*né* Edward Fitzgerald, b. Greenwich Village, New York NY, 9 Mar 1856–16 Feb 1928 [71], Kansas City MO; heart attack). m. (1) Rose Howland; (2) Lola Sefton; (3) ballerina Madeline Morando, 1896 (d. 14 Jun 1918); (4) Mrs. Marie Coombs. "Eddie Foy Dies Suddenly on Tour; Musical Comedy Star and the Father of the 'Seven Little Foys' Stricken in Kansas City; On Stage for 57 Years; Was Making Farewell Round in 'The Fallen Star'—Hero of the Iroquois [Theatre] Fire," *NYT,* 17 Feb 1928, 21:3. "Eddie Foy," *Variety,* 22 Feb 1928. AMD, p. 126. AS, p. 407. IFN, p. 108. Truitt, p. 115. "Foy Arrives at Keystone Studio," *MPW,* 7 Aug 1915, 975. "Nine Foys Keystoning with Sennett," *MPW,* 28 Aug 1915, 1488. "Eddie Foy vs. Keystone," *MPW,* 23 Oct 1915, 602. "Eddie Foy to Make Comedies," *MPW,* 14 Jun 1919, 1650.

Foy, Freddie [scenarist]. No data found. FDY, p. 425.

Foy, Harry (father of actress Gloria Foy) [actor/vaudeville: Foy & Clark] (b. 1868?–4 Mar 1931 [63], New York NY; pneumonia). "Harry Foy," *Variety,* 11 Mar 1931. BHD, p. 172.

Foy, Madeline (daughter of **Eddie Foy, Sr.**; sister of **Bryan**, **Eddie, Jr.**, **Mary**, and **Richard Foy**) [actress] (b. 21 Sep 1903–5 Jul 1988 [84], Los Angeles CA). AS, p. 407. BHD1, p. 198.

Foy, Magda, "The Solax Kid" [stage/film child actress] (b. 1905). "Magda Foy; Nine Years Old, First Juvenile Life Member of the Actors' Fund," *NYDM,* 20 May 1914, 11:1 ("If she lives, she will be able to say that she is the oldest member of the Fund."). Anthony Slide, *Early Women Directors* (New York: A.S. Barnes and Co., 1977), p. 20.

Foy, Mary (daughter of **Eddie Foy, Sr.**; sister of **Bryan**, **Eddie Foy, Jr.**, **Madeline**, and **Richard Foy**) [actress] (*née* Mary Fitzgerald, b. New York NY, 15 Aug 1902–13 Dec 1987 [85], Los Angeles CA; complications after surgery). m. Lyle Latell (d. 1967). AS, p. 407. BHD1, p. 198. SD.

Foy, Patrick C. [actor] (d. 4 Sep 1920). BHD, p. 172.

Foy, Richard (son of **Eddie Foy, Sr.**; brother of **Bryan, Eddie, Jr., Madeline** and **Mary Foy**) [vaudeville/ stage/film actor] (b. 1905–4 Apr 1947 [42], Dallas TX; heart attack). "Richard Foy," *Variety,* 9 Apr 1947, p. 54. AS, p. 407. BHD, p. 172. IFN, p. 108.

Foyer, Eddie [actor] (b. 1882–15 Jun 1934 [52?], Los Angeles CA). AS, p. 407.

Fracchia, Umberto [director/scenarist] (b. Lucca, Italy, 5 Apr 1889–5 Dec 1930 [41], Rome, Italy). AS, p. 407. JS, p. 171 (in Italian silents from 1919).

Fraiz, Birtine F. [actress] (*née?*, b. 1889–15 Feb 1949 [59?], New York NY). m. AS, p. 407.

Fralick, Allen (Freddie) [actor/casting director/agent] (b. Detroit MI, 4 Jun 1888–13 May 1958 [69], Los Angeles CA). (Biograph, 1912; Ince.) "Freddie Fralick," *Variety,* 21 May 1958. AS, p. 407. BHD, p. 172; BHD2, p. 89. IFN, p. 108. Truitt, p. 115.

Frambers, Clarence A. [playwright/scenarist]. No data found. AMD, p. 126. "Clarence A. Frambers," *MPW,* 3 Jul 1915, 70.

Frame, Park B. [actor/director] (b. Seattle WA, 1888?–2 Jun 1943 [55], on train near San Bernardino CA). (WB.) "Park Frame," *Variety,* 9 Jun 1943. AS, p. 407. BHD, p. 172; BHD2, p. 89.

France, Charles H. [director] (b. Decatur IN, 1870?–15 Jun 1940 [70], Onarga IL). (Sennett; Roach.) "Charles H. France," *Variety,* 26 Jun 1940. AS, p. 407. BHD2, p. 89. IFN, p. 108.

France, Charles V[ernon] [actor] (b. Bradford, England, 30 Jun 1868–13 Apr 1949 [80], Gerrard's Cross, England). AS, p. 407. BHD1, p. 198. IFN, p. 108.

France, Claude [actress] (*née* Jane Joséphine Anna Françoise Wittig, b. Emden, Germany, 9 Mar 1893–3 Jan 1928 [34), Paris, France; suicide by gas inhalation [extrait de décès no. 90/1928]). AS, p. 408. BHD, p. 172. IFN, p. 108.

France, R.W. [general manager] (b. Lowville NY, 27 Jul 1883). AMD, p. 126. "France Is Triangle's General Manager," *MPW,* 10 Mar 1917, 1552.

Francell, Fernand [actor] (*né* Fernand Clauge Eugène Francois, b. Gevrey-Chambertin, France, 9 Nov 1879–18 Feb 1966 [86], Paris, France). AS, p. 408.

Francen, Victor [stage/film actor] (*né* Victor Charles Sidonie Franssen, b. Tienen, Belgium, 5 Aug 1888–17 Nov 1977 [89], Aix-en-Provence, France [extrait de décès no. 959/1977]). m. **Mary Marquet** (d. 1979). (French film debut: *Twilight of Horror.*) Obituary in *CFC,* 58 (Spring, 1978), X4. "Victor Francen," *Variety,* 14 Dec 1977, p. 94 (age 88). AS, p. 408 (b. 1889). BHD1, p. 198. IFN, 108. SD. Parish, *Hollywood Character Actors.*

Frances, Alma [stage/film actress]. No data found. m. **Robert Gordon**, 25 Mar 1919, Hollywood CA (d. 1971). AMD, p. 126. "Gordon—Francis," *MPW,* 3 May 1919, 661.

Frances, Owen [scenarist]. No data found. FDY, p. 425.

Frances, Rose [actress] (b. Milwaukee WI, 1881–27 Jan 1962 [80?], Los Angeles CA). AS, p. 408. BHD, p. 172.

Franchini, Fabio [director/producer/scenarist] (b. Verona, Italy, 11 Aug 1891). AS, p. 408.

Francis, Alec B[udd] [actor] (b. Suffolk, England, 2 Dec 1867–6 Jul 1934 [66], Los Angeles CA; following surgery). m. Lucy Smith. (Vitagraph, 1910; World; Goldwyn.) "Alec B. Francis," *Variety,* 10 Jul 1934 (age 65). AMD, p. 126. AS, p. 408. BHD1, p. 198 (b. London)). FFF, p. 108. FSS, p. 115. IFN, p. 108. MH, p. 111. Spehr, p. 132. Truitt, p. 116. "Alex B. Francis," *MPW,* 3 Jan 1914, 57. "A Chat with Alec B. Francis," *MPW,* 7 Aug 1915, 1010. "Alec Francis with World Film," *MPW,* 24 Jun 1916, 2246. "Alec B. Francis," *MPW,* 6 Apr 1918, 77. "Francis Renews Goldwyn Contract," *MPW,* 10 Jan 1920, 294. Maude Cheatham, "Turning the Pages with Alec B. Francis," *MPC,* Jul 1922, 20–21, 83. "Warners Signs Francis," *MPW,* 15 Sep 1923, 233. Doris Denbo, "It's the Spirit That Counts; There's a Spiritual Quality About Alec Francis Which Is Always Manifested in His Personality and Work. No Wonder He Appears in Character in the Rôle of Peter Grimm," *MPC,* Dec 1926, 62–63, 87. "Alec Francis Busy," *MPW,* 10 Dec 1927, 46. George Katchmer, "Remembering the Great Silents," *CI,* 221 (Nov 1993), 52. Katz, pp. 446–47.

Francis, Charles [director]. No data found. AMD, p. 126. "Edison Touches Popular Chord," *MPW,* 3 Jan 1914, 28–29.

Francis, Eve [actress] (*née* Eve Louise Francois, b. Saint-Josse-Tennoode, Belgium, 24 Aug 1886–6 Dec 1980 [94], Neuilly-sur-Seine, France). AS, p. 409. BHD1, p. 198 (b. 1896).

Francis, Evelyn [actress]. No data found. AMD, p. 126. "Evelyn Francis," *MPW,* 27 Jan 1912, 296.

Francis, Jack [actor]. No data found. AMD, p. 126. "Jack Francis," *MPW,* 27 Nov 1926, 209.

Francis, Kay [actress] (*née* Katherine Edwina Gibas, b. Oklahoma City OK, 13 Jan 1905–26 Aug 1968 [63], New York NY; cancer). m. (1) James Dwight Francis; (2) William Gaston; (3) John Meehan; (4) **Kenneth McKenna**, Jan 1931–34 (d. 1962). (Film debut: *The Marriage Playground,* Paramount, 1929.) "Kay Francis, Actress, Dies at 63; Epitome of Glamour in the '30s; Her 50 Films Included 'Give Me Your Heart,' 'Raffles,' and 'I Found Stella Parish,'" *NYT,* 27 Aug 1968, 41:2 ("Miss Francis had lived a rather secluded life here [in NYC] lately and expressed some bitterness at how her Hollywood fortunes had risen so high and sunk so low."). "Kay Francis Left $1 Million to Train Dogs for Blind," *NYT,* 17 Dec 1968, 54:1 (will was drawn in March, 1967. She donated her press notice books and film stills to the theater and music collection of the Museum of the City of NewYork). "Kay Francis," *Variety,* 28 Aug 1968. AS, p. 409 (b. 1899). BHD1, p. 198; BHD2, p. 89 (b. 1899). IFN, p. 108. Truitt 1983, p. 254 (b. 1903). Sara Hamilton, "The Most Baffling Brunette; Who Is She?," *Movie Classic,* Dec 1930, 19, 68. Gene Fernett, "Kay Francis, Popular Star," *CI,* 61 (Winter, 1978), 22. Leon V. Calanquin, "The Saga of Kay Francis," *CI,* 111 (Sep 1984), 58–59 ("she only did it for the money").

Francis, Martha [actress]. No data found. AMD, p. 126. "New Screen Personality," *MPW,* 8 Aug 1925, 664.

Francis, Noel [actress] (*né* Noel Francis Sweeney, b. Temple TX, 31 Aug 1906–30 Oct 1959 [53], Los Angeles CA). (Fox.) AS, p. 409 (b. 1 Nov 1910). BHD1, p. 198 (b. 21 Nov 1910). IFN, p. 108 (b. 21 Nov 1910).

Francis, Olin [stage/film actor] (b. Mooreville MS, 13 Sep 1891–30 Jun 1952 [60], Los Angeles CA). "Olin Francis," *Variety,* 9 Jul 1952 ("legit and screen actor for 40 years"). AMD, p. 126. AS, p. 409. BHD1, p. 198 (b. 1892). IFN, p. 108. Truitt, p. 116 (b. 1892). "Olin Francis," *MPW,* 24 Sep 1927, 229. George Katchmer, "Remembering the Great Silents," *CI,* 221 (Nov 1993), 52.

Francis, Rae [actress]. (*Fl.* 1912.) No data found.

Francis, Thelma [actress]. No data found. AMD, p. 126. "Laemmle Picks Prize Beauty," *MPW,* 22 Jan 1916, 603.

Francisa, Fanny [actress] (*née* Fanny Michelsen, b. San Francisco CA, 31 Aug 1869). AS, p. 409.

Francisco, Betty (sister of **Evelyn Francisco**) [actress: Wampas Star, 1923] (*née* Elizabeth Bartman, b. Little Rock AR, 26 Sep 1900–25 Nov 1950 [50], El Cerito CA; heart attack). "Betty Francisco," *NYT,* 27 Nov 1950, 25:3 (d. Corona Ranch CA; age 50). "Betty Francisco," *Variety,* 29 Nov 1950 (d. Corona CA). AMD, p. 127. AS, p. 409. BHD1, p. 199 (d. Corona CA). IFN, p. 108. Truitt, p. 116. Willis Goldbeck, "Betty, in Profile," *MPC,* Dec 1921, 44–45, 92 ("I cultivated [my profile]. That is what got me into the movies..."). "Betty Francisco," *MPW,* 22 Jan 1927, 265. George Katchmer, "Remembering the Great Silents," *CI,* 246 (Dec 1995), 46.

Francisco, Evelyn (sister of **Betty Francisco**) [extra actress]. No data found. Robert Donaldson, "Famous Extras," *MPC,* Feb 1927, 32 [photo]-33, 68, 80.

Franck, John L. [actor] (b. Louisville KY, 31 Jul 1852–22 Oct 1920 [68], Los Angeles CA; "result of burns sustained in an explosion during the making of scenes in *The Bronze Bell*). AMD, p. 127. AS, p. 409. BHD, p. 172. IFN, p. 108. Truitt 1983, p. 254 (b. 1850). ""Obituary," *MPW,* 13 Nov 1920, 212.

Franck, Walter [actor] (b. Huttenstenach, Germany, 16 Apr 1884–10 Aug 1961 [77], Garmisch-Partenkirchen, Germany). AS, p. 409.

Franco, Francisco [director] (*né* Francisco Franco y Bahamonte, b. El Ferreol, Spain, 4 Dec 1892–20 Nov 1975 [82], Madrid, Spain). AS, p. 409.

Francoeur, Richard [actor] (b. France, 1894-Apr 1961 [67?], Paris, France). AS, p. 409.

Franconi-Nief, Leon E. [film editor of newsreels/producer/writer] (b. San Francisco CA, 1867?–20 Feb 1951 [83]; White Plains NY). (Pathé Frérès; Castle Films.) "Leon E. Franconi-Nief," *Variety,* 181, 28 Feb 1951, 63:2. AMD, p. 127. AS, p. 410. "Zecca and Franconi Return," *MPW,* 10 Aug 1918, 849.

Franek, Katherine [actress]. No data found. AMD, p. 127. "Katherine Franek," *MPW,* 27 Nov 1915, 1652.

Franey, William "Billy" [actor] (b. Chicago IL, 23 Jun 1889–6 Dec 1940 [51], Los Angeles CA; influenza). (Keystone; RKO.) "Billy Franey," *Variety,* 11 Dec 1940 (age 55). AMD, p. 127. AS, p. 410 (d. 9 Dec). BHD1, p. 199. IFN, p. 108. Truitt, p. 116 (b. 1885). Billy Franey, "I Am the Screen Comedy," *MPW,* 15 Jul 1922, 228. "Franey Story Is Syndicated," *MPW,* 15 Jul 1922, 228. George A. Katchmer, "Forgotten Cowboys/Girls—Part VII," *CI,* 179 (May 1990), 45, 53.

Frank, Alexander F. [actor] (b. England, 1866?–14 Dec 1939 [73], Long Island City NY). "Alexander Frank," *Variety,* 20 Dec 1939. AS, p. 410. BHD, p. 172.

Frank, Amy [actress] (*née* Emilie Rosenthal, b. Susice, Germany, 15 Dec 1896–6 May 1980 [83], Berlin, Germany). AS, p. 410.

Frank, Bruno [scenarist] (b. 1886–20 Jun 1945 [59?], Los Angeles CA). BHD2, p. 89.

Frank, Christian Julius [actor] (b. New York NY, 13 Mar 1890–10 Dec 1967 [77], Los Angeles CA; cancer). AS, p. 410. BHD1, p. 199. IFN, p. 108. George A. Katchmer, "Forgotten Cowboys and Cowgirls—Part XIII," *CI*, 190 (Apr 1991), C8.

Frank, Harry [actor] (b. Berlin, Germany, 15 Oct 1896–1948 [52?], Berlin, Germany). BHD1, p. 199.

Frank, J. Herbert [actor] (b. New York NY, 12 May 1885–9 Mar 1926 [40], Los Angeles CA; suicide by gas inhalation). (Fox.) "J. Herbert Frank Is Suicide in Coast Home," *Variety*, 17 Mar 1926 (arrests for dope peddling and bootlegging; d. 11 Mar). AMD, p. 127. AS, p. 410 (b. Chicago IL; d. 7 Mar). BHD, p. 172. IFN, p. 108 (d. 11 Mar). Truitt 1983, p. 255. "J. Herbert Frank to Support Marion Davies," *MPW*, 7 Jun 1919, p. 1538.

Frank, W[illiam] **B.** [executive]. No data found. AMD, p. 127. "Frank in New York," *MPW*, 30 Aug 1924, 716.

Frank, William [actor] (b. Chicago IL, 1880?–23 Dec 1925 [45], Los Angeles CA; Bright's disease). (Hal Roach.) "William Frank," *Variety*, 30 Dec 1925. BHD, p. 172. IFN, p. 108. Truitt, p. 116.

Frankau, Ronald [actor/scenarist] (b. London, England, 22 Feb 1894–11 Sep 1951 [57], Eastbourne, England). AS, p. 410.

Franke, Constant Louis [actor/director] (b. Brussels, Belgium, 5 May 1893–31 Oct 1943 [50], Los Angeles CA). AS, p. 410 (d. Brussels, Belgium). BHD, p. 172; BHD2, p. 90. IFN, p. 108.

Frankel, Ben [cinematograher] (b. New York NY, 1903–2 Jan 1930 [26?], Santa Monica CA). BHD2, p.90.

Frankel, Franchon [actress] (b. St. Louis MO, 28 Apr 1874–12 Aug 1937 [63], Los Angeles CA). "Fanchon [sic] Frankel," *Variety*, 18 Aug 1937 ("stage and screen actress"). AS, p. 411. BHD1, p. 199. IFN, p. 108. Truitt, p. 116.

Frankel, Harry [actor] (b. 27 Jan 1888–12 Jun 1948 [60]). AS, p. 411.

Frankel, Serge [director/producer] (b. Russia-d. 10 Sep 1927, Juan-les-Pins, France; accidental gas explosion). AS, p. 411. BHD2, p. 90.

Frankel, Theo [director] (b. 14 Jul 1871–20 Sep 1956 [85]). BHD2, p. 90.

Franken, Mannus [director] (*né* Marinus Herman Karel Franken, b. Deventer, Netherlands, 6 Feb 1899–1 Aug 1953 [54], Lochem, Netherlands). AS, p. 411. BHD2, p. 90.

Franken, Rose [scenarist] (b. Gainesville TX, 28 Dec 1896–22 Jun 1988 [91], Tucson AZ). BHD2, p. 90.

Frankiel, Mieszyslaw [actor] (*né* Adam Bonaventura Papr¥zyca Niwenski, b. Buszow, Poland, 15 Jul 1858–19 Apr 1935 [76], Warsaw, Poland). AS, p. 411.

Franklin, Alberta [actress] (*née* Alberta Levy, b. San Francisco CA, 1897?–14 Mar 1976 [79], Mountain View CA). m. "Alberta Franklin," *Variety*, 7 Apr 1976. AS, p. 411. BHD, p. 172. IFN, p. 108.

Franklin, Chester M. (brother of **Martha** and **Sidney A. Franklin**) [director/scenarist] (b. San Francisco CA, 1 Sep 1890–12 Mar 1954 [64], Los Angeles CA). m. **Ruth Darling** (d. 1918); Mildred Nadel, 9 Oct 1926, Hollywood CA. (Triangle, 1915.) AMD, p. 127. AS, p. 411. BHD2, p. 90 (d. Bel Air CA). FDY, p. 425. IFN, p. 108. KOM, pp. 135–36. "Chester Franklin to Direct Annette Kellerman Film," *MPW*, 31 Jan 1920, 711. "Franklin Becomes a Realart Director," *MPW*, 19 Jun 1920, 1625. "Chester Franklin Weds," *MPW*, 23 Oct 1926, 494.

Franklin, Harold B. [producer] (b. New York NY, 4 Apr 1894–21 Apr 1941 [47], Mexico City, Mexico). AS, p. 411.

Franklin, Harry L. [actor/director] (b. St. Louis MO, 5 Sep 1880–3 Jul 1927 [47], Los Angeles CA; found dead). m. **Mildred Dean**, 27 Feb 1918. (Universal; Metro.) "Harry Franklin Dead," *Variety*, 6 Jul 1927. AMD, p. 127. AS, p. 411 (d. 2 Jul). BHD2, p. 90. IFN, p. 109. "Studio Gossip," *NYDM*, 20 Nov 1915, 24:3 (acted in stock with Edwin Carewe for 13 years). "Metro Director Marries Actress," *MPW*, 16 Mar 1918, 1515. "Obituary," *MPW*, 16 Jul 1927, 151 ("autopsy shows natural death").

Franklin, Irene Lucille Marguerite [stage/film actress] (b. New York NY, 13 Jun 1876–16 Jun 1941 [65], Englewood NJ; cerebral hemorrhage). m. Burton Green (d. 1922); Jeremiah (Jerry) Jarnagin, 1925–34 (suicide). "Irene Franklin, 57, Dies in N.J.," *Variety*, 18 Jun 1941 (age 57). AS, p. 411. BHD1, p. 200 (b. St. Louis MO). IFN, p. 109. SD. Cover, *NYDM*, 18 Aug 1915 (in *Hands Up*).

Franklin, Martha [actress] (sister of **Chester M.** and **Sidney Franklin**) (*née* Martha Cohn, b. Germany, 13 Nov 1868–19 Apr 1929 [60], Los Angeles CA; heart attack). "Martha Franklin Dies," *Variety*, 1 May 1929. AS, p. 411. BHD1, p. 200. IFN, p. 109.

Franklin, Rupert [actor] (b. 1862?–14 Jan 1939 [77], Los Angeles CA). "Rupert Franklin," *Variety*, 18 Jan 1939 ("veteran character actor in pictures"). AS, p. 411. BHD, p. 173. IFN, p. 109. Truitt, p. 117.

Franklin, Sidney [stage/film actor] (b. Germany, 1870–18 Mar 1931 [61], Los Angeles CA). m. Ruth Helms (d. 1960). "Sidney Franklin," *Variety*, 25 Mar 1931. AS, p. 411. BHD1, p. 200. IFN, p. 109. SD. Truitt, p. 117.

Franklin, Sidney A[rnold] [stage/film director/producer] (brother of **Chester M.** and **Martha Franklin**) (b. San Francisco CA, 21 Mar 1893–18 May 1972 [79], Santa Monica CA; heart attack). m. (1) Ann Denitz; (2) **Enid Bennett** (d. 1969). (1st National; WB; MGM.) "Sidney Franklin, Producer, Dies; His 'Mrs. Miniver' Won Oscar," *NYT*, 20 May 1972, 36:5. "Sydney A. Franklin," *Variety*, 24 May 1972. AMD, p. 127. AS, p. 411. BHD2, p. 90. IFN, p. 109. KOM, p. 136. SD. "New Film Manufacturer [Arrow Co.]," *MPW*, 28 Sep 1912, 1282. "Franklin Signs to Direct Norman Talmadge," *MPW*, 12 Oct 1918, 243. "Long Term Contract Calls for Franklin to Make Four Films Yearly for Kaufman," *MPW*, 12 Jun 1920, 1493. "Franklin to Remain with the Talmadges," *MPW*, LIII, 19 Nov 1921, 290. "Sid Franklin Will Direct Warner Film," *MPW*, 2 Sep 1922, 44. "Sidney Franklin Signs with Warners," *MPW*, 3 Feb 1923, 482. Alma M. Talley, "'Directors Are Eager to Give Unknown Girls a Chance,' Says Sidney Franklin,' *MW*, 22 Dec 1923, 13. "Sidney Franklin Signs," *MPW*, 19 Apr 1924, 650. "Franklin Signs," *MPW*, 6 Nov 1926, 2.

Franklyn, Beth [actress] (b. 1873?–5 Mar 1956 [83], Baltimore MD). "Beth Franklyn," *Variety*, 14 Mar 1956. BHD, p. 173.

Franklyn, Irwin [stage/film actor/publicist/novelist] (b. New York NY, 8 Jan 1904–7 Sep 1966 [62], Los Angeles CA; heart attack). m. actress Katherine Green. (NY stage 1912–18; Ince; 1st National; Columbia; Goldwyn.) "Irwin Franklyn," *Variety*, 14 Sep 1966, p. 79. AS, p. 411. BHD, p. 173; BHD2, p. 90.

Franklyn, Leo [actor] (b. London, England, 7 Apr 1897–17 Sep 1975 [78], London, England; heart attack). AS, p. 411.

Frankman, Charles U. [actor] (b. New York NY, 23 Sep 1883). BHD, p. 173.

Franz, Joseph J. [actor/director] (b. Utica NY, 12 Oct 1883–9 Sep 1970 [86], Los Angeles Co. CA). AS, p. 412 (b. 1884). BHD1, p. 200; BHD2, p. 90. IFN, p. 109 (b. 1884). Truitt 1983, p. 255.

Franzen, Nell [actress]. (Mustang.) No data found.

Frascaroli, Valentina [actress] (b. Turin, Italy-d. Turin, Italy, 18 Jan 1955, Paris, France). AS, p. 412. JS, p. 174 (in Italian silents from 1912).

Fraser, Alec [stage/film actor/singer] (b. Fife, Scotland, 16 Feb 1884–20 Jun 1956 [72], London, England). "Alec Fraser," *Variety*, 27 Jun 1956, p. 63 (d. 21 Jun). BHD, p. 173.

Fraser, Harry C. [actor] (b. SD, 15 Mar 1894–2 Aug 1949 [55]). AS, p. 412. IFN, p. 109.

Fraser, Harry L. [director] (b. San Francisco CA, 31 Mar 1889–8 Apr 1974 [85], Pomona Valley CA). "Harry Fraser, 85; Directed Westerns," *Des Moines Register* (n.d.). AS, p. 412. BHD, p. 173; BHD2, p. 90. IFN, p. 109.

Fraser, James S. [actor] (b. Dundee, Scotland, 31 Jul 1873–19 Oct 1943 [70], Los Angeles CA). AS, p. 412.

Fraser, Jean [actress]. No data found. AMD, p. 127. "Baby Jean Fraser," *MPW*, 25 Dec 1915, 2351.

Fraser, Margaret E. [film editor] (b. 1900–2 Oct 1929 [29?], Los Angeles CA). BHD2, p. 90.

Fraser, William R. (uncle of **Gaylord** and **Harold Lloyd**) [general manager/executive] (b. Central City CO, 13 Dec 1879–5 Nov 1952 [72], Encino CA). AMD, p. 127. BHD2, p. 90. "Says Report Is Untrue," *MPW*, 11 Aug 1923, 464. "Lloyd Executive Senses Big Production Boom on West Coast," *MPW*, 21 Nov 1925, 225. "Comedies Scored During 1926, Declares Fraser," *MPW*, 25 Dec 1926, 586. "Fraser of Lloyd Corporation Eastward to Confer wi Kent," *MPW*, 16 Apr 1927, 627. William R. Fraser, "Fraser, of Lloyd Corp., Discusses Production," *MPW*, 3 Sep 1927, 34. "Fraser Finds American Films Still continue to Amuse World," *MPW*, 3 Dec 1927, 20. "Oh! Woodman, Spare That Tree!," *MPW*, 17 Dec 1927, 22.

Frateili, Arnaldo [director/scenarist] (b. Piediluco, Italy, 23 Aug 1888 [extrait de naissance no. 33/1/1888]-30 Dec 1965 [77], Rome, Italy). AS, p. 412.

Frawley, T. Daniel [stage/film/radio actor/director] (b. Washington DC, 8 Nov 1864?–26 Apr 1936 [72], Staten Island NY; complication of diseases). "T. Daniel Frawley," *Variety,* 122, 29 Apr 1936, 62:1 (interred in Washington DC). AMD, p. 127. BHD2, p. 90 (b. 1876; d. Richmond VA). "Becomes Metro Director," *MPW,* 19 Feb 1921, 943.

Frawley, William Clement [stage (Frawley and Louise)/film/radio/TV actor] (b. Burlington IA, 26 Feb 1887–3 Mar 1966 [79], Los Angeles CA; heart attack. Interred in the Fernando Mission Cemetery, San Fernando Valley CA). m. Edna Louise Broedt, 1914—div. 1927. (Film debut: *Lord Loveland Discovers America,* American Film Manufacturing Co., 1916; Paramount; Universal; Mascot; Grand National; MGM; TC-F; Columbia; Republic; UA.) "William Frawley, Actor, Dead; Played Lucy's Landlord on TV; Co-Star of 'My Three Sons,' 72, Was Also Familiar for His Roles in Many Films," *NYT,* 4 Mar 1966, 33:1 (age 72). "William Frawley," *Variety,* 9 Mar 1966. AS, p. 412. BHD1, p. 200. IFN, p. 109. Katz, pp. 450–51. Truitt, p. 117. Michael Bernal, "William Frawley: Before and After Lucy," *CI,* 303 (Sep 2000), pp. 6–14, 67–69 (Desi Arnaz planned to produce a spin-off series with the Mertzes of *I Love Lucy.* Vivian Vance refused. "I loathed Bill Frawley, and the feeling was mutual.").

Frayne, Frank I. [stage/film actor] (Kingston MD, b. 1863?–20 Sep 1938 [75], Valley Stream, LI NY). m. Adelaide Goundre. "Frank I. Frayne," *Variety,* 12 Oct 1938. AS, p. 413. SD.

Frazer, Alex [actor] (b. Cupar, Scotland, 27 May 1900–30 Jul 1958 [58], Los Angeles CA). AS, p. 413. BHD1, p. 200.

Frazer, Nitra [actress] (*née* Anitra Frazer MacTavish, b. Brooklyn NY, 21 Apr 1888–2 May 1979 [91], Englewood NJ). m. **Wally Van** (d. 1974). (Vitagraph.) AMD, p. 127. AS, p. 413 (d. 17 Aug 1944). BHD, p. 173. "Nitra Frazer," *MPW,* 31 Jul 1915, 804.

Frazer, Robert W. [actor] (b. Worcester MA, 29 Jun 1889–17 Aug 1944 [55], Los Angeles CA; leukemia). m. **Mildred Bright**, ca. 1913 (d. 1967). (Film debut: *Robin Hood,* Eclair, 1912.) "Robert W. Frazer," *Variety,* 23 Aug 1944. AMD, p. 127. AS, p. 413. BHD1, p. 200 (b. Farmington MA). FSS, p. 115. GK, pp. 315–26. IFN, p. 109. Katz, p. 451. MH, p. 111. Spehr, p. 132 (b. 1891). Truitt, p. 117. "Robert Frazer in Eclair Subject," *MPW,* 5 Oct 1912, 56. "Robert Frazer," *MPW,* 25 Jul 1914, 587. "Lubin Engages Robert Frazer," *MPW,* 3 Jun 1916, 1697. "Frazer in Negri Film," *MPW,* 1 Mar 1924, 30. Jim Tully, "An Edison Enters," *MPC,* Apr 1925, 36, 90. "First National Adds Several to List of Contract Players," *MPW,* 18 Apr 1925, 713. "Robert Frazer," *MPW,* 28 May 1927, 257. George A. Katchmer, "Who Was Robert Frazer?," *CI,* 132 (Jun 1986), 14–16, 51. Henry R. Davis, "Robert Frazer Filmography," *CI,* 133 (Jul 1986), 40–41.

Frazin, Gladys [actress] (b. 1901?–9 Mar 1939 [38], New York NY; suicide by jumping out of a window). m. Monte Banks. "Gladys Frazin Banks," *Variety,* 15 Mar 1939. AS, p. 413. BHD1, p. 200. IFN, p. 109. Truitt, p. 117.

Frederici, Blanche [actress] (b. Brooklyn NY, 21 Jan 1878–23 Dec 1933 [55], Visalia CA; heart attack). m. Donald Campbell. "Blanche F. Campbell," *Variety,* 2 Jan 1934 ("Had been in pix since 1920."). AS, p. 413. BHD1, p. 200.

Frederick, Freddie Burke [actor] (b. San Francisco CA, 13 Jan 1921–31 Jan 1986 [65], Glendale CA). BHD1, p. 201.

Frederick, Joseph [scenarist]. "Joseph Frederick with Premier," *MPW,* 4 Dec 1915, 1804.

Frederick, Pauline [stage/film actress] (*née* Pauline Beatrice Libbey, b. Boston MA, 12 Aug 1883 [MVRB, vol. 342, p. 94]–19 Sep 1938 [55], Beverly Hills CA; asthma). m. (1) Frank Mills Andrews, 8 Sep 1909, NY NY; (2) Willard Mack, 24 Sep 1917, Washington DC; (3) Dr. C.A. Rutherford (her 2nd cousin), 4 Feb 1922; (4) Hugh C. Leighton, 19 Apr 1930, NYC; (5) Col. Joseph A. Marmon, 21 Jan 1934, Scarsdale NY (d. 4 Dec 1934). Muriel Elwood, *Pauline Frederick; On and Off the Stage* (Chicago: A. Kroch, 1940). (Stage debut: *The Rogers Brothers at Harvard,* 1 Sep 1902; chorus; film debut: *The Eternal City,* FP-L, 1915; Paramount.) "Pauline Frederick Dies on the Coast; Stage and Film Actress, Who Made Theatrical Debut Here in 1902, Succumbs at 53; A Success in 'Madame X'; Last New York Appearance in 'Masque of Kings,' 1937—Known for Her Beauty," *NYT,* 20 Sep 1938, 23:1. "Pauline Frederick," *Variety,* 21 Sep 1938. AMD, p. 128. AS, p. 413. BHD1, p. 201 (b. 26 Aug). FFF, p. 222 (b. 1885). FSS, p. 116. IFN, p. 109 (b. 1885). Katz, p. 451. MH, p. 112 (b. 1885). Truitt, p. 117 (b. 1884). WWS, p. 84. "Famous Players Engage Pauline Frederick," *MPW,* 13 Jun 1914, 1521. "The Progress of Pauline; A Pictorial History of the Girl Who Graces The Cover," *Photoplay Magazine,* Jun 1917, 67–70. "Pauline Frederick with Famous Players," *MPW,* 7 Nov 1914, 767. "Famous Players Secure Pauline Frederick," *MPW,* 5 Jun 1915, 1612. "Pauline Frederick Quits Legitimate Stage," *MPW,* 18 Sep 1915, 2002. "Work Resumed on 'Bella Donna'; Pauline Frederick Being Starred by Famous Players Under Direction of Edwin S. Porter and Hugh Ford," *MPW,* 30 Oct 1915, 989:2 (work resumed after a fire at the 26th Street studio on 11 Sep destrooyed negatives of unreleased work. Frederick had returned from Florida where scenes had been shot; these scenes were found intact in a vault after the fire.). "Pauline Frederick Signs with Famous," *MPW,* 19 Aug 1916, 1258. "Pauline Frederick Nearly Asphyxiated," *MPW,* 23 Jun 1917, 1919. "Marriages," *Variety,* 28 Sep 1917, p. 9 (m. Mack). "Two Screen Players Hear Themselves Talk," *MPW,* 22 Dec 1917, 1818. "Frederick to Release Through Goldwyn," *MPW,* 25 May 1918, 1153. "Pauline Frederick Soon Makes Her Goldwyn Debut," *MPW,* 15 Feb 1919, 902. "Robertson-Cole Signs Pauline Frederick for a Series of Special Productions," *MPW,* 1 May 1920, 700. "Pauline Frederick Is Released from Her Goldwyn Contract," *MPW,* 8 May 1920, 816. "Tribute to Miss Frederick," *MPW,* 21 Aug 1920, 1060. "Pauline Frederick Asks for Divorce from Willard Mack," *MPW,* 28 Aug 1920, 1148. "Pauline Frederick Announces Plans of Returning to Stage," *MPW,* 8 Apr 1922, 623. "Miss Frederick's Last Screen Appearance Is in R-C Picture," *MPW,* 3 Jun 1922, 470 (*The Glory of Clementina*). Regina Cannon, "Is Style a Greater Asset Than Beauty?," *MW,* 8 Dec 1923, 3, 29. "Pauline Frederick Returning," *MPW,* 5 Dec 1925, 442. "Pauline Frederick to Star in an F.B.O. Gold Bond Film," *MPW,* 3 Apr 1926, 343. "Star and Director Pay Tribute to Each Other," *MPW,* 8 May 1926, 128. "Pauline Frederick Couples Theatre and Screen Work," *MPW,* 16 Oct 1926, 420. Ramon Romeo, "Reeling Down Broadway," *Paris and Hollywood Screen Secrets Magazine,* May 1927, 63 (recently closed in *Lady Frederick* in New York, then was on her way to London to film *Mumsy.* "If Pauline only realized how badly the screen needed her art she would not stay away so long."). Paul Paige, "Close-Ups and Fade-Outs," *Paris and Hollywood Screen Secrets Magazine,* May 1927, 82 (claimed she lost 26 pounds. "But kind critics contend that she is only counting her calories in a new way."). Beatrice Wilson, "She Hates the Screen; And as for the Talkies: Pauline Frederick Thinks They're Odorous," *MPC,* Mar 1929, 40, 74 ("For the past eight years I have been making pictures—almost all of them terrible."). Neville James, "Pauline Frederick, Star from the Past," *CI,* 63 (May 1979), 47 (b. 1881).

Frederick, William [actor] (b. 1861?–2 Mar 1931 [70], Astoria, LI NY). "William Frederic," *Variety,* 11 Mar 1931. AMD, p. 128. AS, p.413. BHD, p. 173. IFN, p. 109. "Metro Actor Works 385 Days," *MPW,* 24 Aug 1918, 1141.

Fredricksen, Lilly [actress]. No data found. AMD, p. 128. "Lilly Fredricksen," *MPW,* 18 Jan 1913, 266.

Freear, Louie [actor] (b. 26 Nov 1871–23 Mar 1939 [67], London, England). BHD, p. 173. IFN, p. 109 (age 62).

Freed, Arthur [composer/producer/scenarist] (*né* Arthur Grossman, b. Charleston SC, 9 Sep 1894–12 Apr 1973 [78], Bel Air CA; heart attack). m. Renée Klein, 14 Mar 1923, San Francisco CA. Hugh Fordin, *Hollywood's Royal Family: The Freed Unit* (Doubleday, 1973). (MGM.) "Arthur Freed, Screen Producer Who Won 2 Oscars, Dead at 78," *NYT,* 13 Apr 1973, 42:5 (AA for *An American in Paris,* 1951, and *Gigi,* 1958). Whitney Williams, "Arthur Freed, Producer, Songsmith, Film Musical Pioneer, Dies at 78," *Variety,* 18 Apr 1973. AS, p. 413. BHD2, p. 90. IFN, p. 109. SD. Dennis Lee Galling, "Arthur Freed Proved that a Lyricist Can Become Part of Hollywood's Establishment," *FIR,* Nov 1964, 521–44 (includes filmography).

Freed, Lazar [actor] (b. 30 May 1889–11 Mar 1944 [54], Monrovia CA). BHD1, p. 201.

Freeland, Thornton [director] (b. Hope ND, 10 Feb 1898–22 May 1987 [89], Fort Lauderdale FL). AS, p. 414 (d. 1938). BHD2, p. 91. Katz, 1979.

Freeman, Al [actor] (b. 1884?–22 Mar 1956 [72], Los Angeles CA). "Al Freeman," *Variety,* 28 Mar 1956. AS, p. 414. IFN, p. 109.

Freeman, Helen [actress] (b. St. Louis MO, 3 Aug 1886–25 Dec 1960 [74], Los Angeles CA). BHD1, p. 201.

Freeman, Jennie [actress] (b. 1817?–1925 [108], New York NY). AS, p. 414. "Jennie Freeman," *CI,* 100 (Oct 1983), 61. Appeared in *Salome of the Tenements* (Paramount, 1925), at age 108.

Freeman, Maurice [actor] (b. 1872?–26 Mar 1953 [81], Bayshore, LI NY). m. Nadine Winston. "Maurice Freeman," *Variety,* 1 Apr 1953 (in films 1915–18). AS, p. 414. BHD1, p. 201. IFN, p. 109. Truitt, p. 118.

Freeman, Otto C. [cinematographer] (b. 1899–13 Feb 1934 [34?], Los Angeles CA). BHD2, p. 91.

Freeman, William B. [actor] (b. 1870–7 Jun 1932 [62?], Brockton MA). "William B. Freeman," *Variety,* 21 Jun 1932. BHD, p. 173.

Freeman, William F. [sentry in *The Birth of a Nation,* Griffith, 1915]. No data found. *Photoplay,* X, Oct 1916, 94 (photograph). Bert Ennis, "I Wonder What Became of Him?; There Are Many Extras Who Have Made Good [e.g., Constance Talmadge and Barbara LaMarr], But Most of Them Continue to Furnish Atmosphere...," *MPC,* Aug 1926, 26–27, 84 ("...he apparently sank back into the ranks of obscurity after his few brilliant moments with Miss Gish.").

Freeman-Mitford, Rupert [actor] (b. England, 1895–7 Aug 1939 [44?], London, England). AS, p. 414.

Fregoli, Leopoldo [stage/film actor/director] (b. Rome, Italy, 2 Jul 1867–26 Nov 1936 [69], Viareggio, Italy; heart attack). "Leopoldo Fregoli," *Variety,* 2 Dec 1936, p. 70 (age 68). BHD, p. 173. IFN, p. 110. JS, p. 176 (in Italian silents from 1897).

Frehel [actress/singer] (*née* Marguerite Boulc'h, b. Paris, France, 13 Jul 1891–3 Feb 1951 [59], Paris, France). AS, p. 414.

Freil, Edward [actor] (b. 1878–30 Jul 1938 [60?], Los Angeles CA). AS, p. 414.

Freil, Raymond A. (Dick) [actor/director/writer] (b. 1894?–24 May 1939 [45], Yonkers NY; heart ailment). (Disney; Sennett; Fox; Paramount.) "Raymond A. Freil," *Variety,* 31 May 1939, p. 46. AS, p. 414 (d. LA CA). BHD, p. 173; BHD2, p. 91. IFN, p. 110.

Freis, John [cinematographer]. No data found. FDY, p. 459.

Friesler, Fritz [director] (b. Trubau, Germany, 21 Jan 1881–1955 [74?], Vienna, Austria). AS, p. 414.

Freleng, Isadore "Friz" [animator] (b. Kansas City KS, 20 Aug 1905–26 May 1995 [89], Los Angeles CA). (Disney, 1922; WB, 1930; Depatie-Freleng Enterprises; MGM.) m. Lily. "Isadore (Friz) Freleng Dies; Creator of Cartoons Was 89," *NYT,* 28 May 1995, 38:1 (won four Academy Awards). AS, p. 414 (b. Kansas City MO, 21 Aug 1906). BHD2, p. 91. *The World of Animation* (Rochester NY: Eastman Kodak Co., 1979), pp. 13 *et passim.* Leonard Maltin, *Of Mice and Magic; A History of American Animated Cartoons* (NY: New American Library, 1980), pp. 223 *et passim. The American Animated Cartoon; A Critical Anthology,* Danny Peary and Gerald Peary, edd. (NY: E.P. Dutton, 1980), pp. 105 *et passim.* Jeff Lenburg, *The Encyclopedia of Animated Cartoon Series* (NY: Da Capo, 1981), pp. 22 *et passim.*

Frelich, Oleg Nikolaievich [actor/director] (b. Russia, 1887–1953 [66?], Russia). AS, p. 414.

Fremont, Alfred W. [actor] (b. Cohoes NY, 23 Feb 1860–16 Jun 1930 [70], Los Angeles CA). (Fox.) AS, p. 414. BHD1, p. 608. IFN, p. 110. George Katchmer, "Remembering the Great Silents," *CI,* 199 (Jan 1992), 14.

French, Charles K. [actor/director] (*né* Charles E. Krauss, b. Columbus OH, 17 Jan 1860–2 Aug 1952 [92], Los Angeles CA; heart attack). "Charles K. French," *Variety,* 6 Aug 1952. AS, p. 415. BHD1, p. 201; BHD2, p. 91. IFN, p. 110. Nick Nicholls, "Charles K. French," *CI,* 138 (Dec 1986), 55. Ed Wyatt, "Charles French," *CI,* 158 (Aug 1988), C8.

French, George B. [actor] (b. Storm Lake IA, 14 Apr 1883–9 Jun 1961 [78], Los Angeles CA; heart attack). (Universal, 1912; Christie Comedies.) "George B. French," *Variety,* 21 Jun 1961. AS, p. 415. BHD1, p. 201. IFN, p. 110. Truitt, p. 118.

French, Harold [actor] (b. London, England, 23 Apr 1897–19 Oct 1997 [100]). AS, p. 415. BHD1, p. 201.

French, Helen K. [actress] (b. OH, 13 Feb 1863–12 Mar 1917 [54], Los Angeles CA). AS, p. 415. BHD, p. 173. IFN, p. 110.

French, Henry Leon [executive] (b. Portsmouth, England, 30 Dec 1883–3 Apr 1966 [82], London, England). BHD2, p. 91.

French, Herbert C. (Bert) [actor] (b. 1891–27 Jan 1924 [33], New London CT). IFN, p. 101.

French, Lloyd A. [director/scenarist] (b. San Francisco CA, 11 Jan 1900–24 May 1950 [50], Beverly Hills CA). AS, p. 415. BHD2, p. 91.

French, Park M. [stage/film art director] (b. Denver CO, 13 Dec 1881–18 Mar 1974 [92], Los Angeles CA). "Park M. French," *Variety,* 27 Mar 1974. AS, p. 415. BHD2, p. 91.

Frenkel, Theo[dore], **Jr.** (son of **Theo Frenkel, Sr.**) [actor] (b. Chicago IL, 1 Mar 1893–1 Jun 1955 [62], Gravenhage, Holland). AS, p. 415.

Frenkel, Theo, Sr. (father of **Theo Frenekl, Jr.**) [actor/director] (*né* theodorus Maurits Frenkel, b. Rotterdam, Holland, 14 Jul 1871–20 Sep 1956 [85], Amsterdam, Holland). AS, p. 415.

Fresnay, Pierre [actor] (*né* Pierre Jules Louis Laudenbach, b. Paris, France, 4 Apr 1897–9 Jan 1975 [77], Neuilly-sur-Seine, France [extrait de décès no. 25]). "Pierre Fresnay," *Variety,* 15 Jan 1975, p. 94. AS, p. 415. BHD1, p. 202. IFN, p. 110.

Fresno, Fernando (father of Maruchi Fresno) [actor] (*né* Fernando Lourdes Gomez Pamo del Fresno, b. Madrid, Spain, 31 May 1881–28 Apr 1949 [67], Madrid, Spain). m. (son, Maruchi, b. 14 Feb 1916). AS, p. 415.

Freuchen, Peter [actor] (b. Nykobing Falster, Denmark, 1886–3 Sep 1967 [81?], Denmark; heart attack). AS, p. 415.

Freuler, Jack [still photographer] (b. 1880–17 Oct 1936 [56?], Los Angeles CA). BHD2, p. 91.

Freuler, John Rudolph [President of Mutual Film Corp.] (b. Monroe WI, 17 Nov 1872–19 Dec 1958 [86]). m. Augusta Jess (d. 15 Nov 1917, Milwaukee WI). "Mrs. Augusta Freuler," *Variety,* 23 Nov 1917 (d. 8 Nov 1917, Milwaukee WI). AMD, p. 128. WWWA. "American Film Company Banquet," *MPW,* 13 Jan 1912, 121. "Freuler Heads Mutual; Aitken, Out of Mutual, Will Devote Time to Four-Million-Dollar Combination," *NYDM,* 30 Jun 1915, 21:4. "Freuler President of Mutual," *MPW,* 3 Jul 1915, 40–41. "President Freuler Says," *MPW,* 24 Jul 1915, 631. "Important Moves by Mutual," *MPW,* 31 Jul 1915, 797. "Freuler Buys Aitken Stock," *NYDM,* 13 Nov 1915, 27:2 ($720,000 worth of stock from H.E. Aitken). John R. Freuler, "Freuler Reviews the Year," *MPW,* 1 Jan 1916, 51. "Freuler Favors Film Organization," *MPW,* 1 Jul 1916, 67. "Freuler Strong for 'Stars,'" *MPW,* 5 Aug 1916, 929. "Freuler and Chaplin Confer," *MPW,* 24 Feb 1917, 1165. "Freuler Gives 'Em the 'Once Over,'" *MPW,* 7 Apr 1917, 104. "Admission Prices Should Be Raised," *MPW,* 9 Jun 1917, 1620. "Mrs. John R. Freuler Dies," *MPW,* 24 Nov 1917, 1148. "Death of Mrs. John R. Freuler," *MPW,* 1 Dec 1917, 1303. "Freuler Announces 'Screen Telegram,'" *MPW,* 26 Jan 1918, 490. John R. Freuler, "Industry Still Has Large Task Before It," *MPW,* 27 Apr 1918, 548. "Freuler Resigns as Mutual's President," *MPW,* 18 May 1918, 971. "American Extremely Active on Coast," *MPW,* 8 Mar 1919, 1333.

Freund, Karl [projectionist/technical director/film/TV cinematographer/scenarist/director/producer] (b. Koeniginhof, Czechoslovakia [later in Soviet Russia], 16 Jan 1890–3 May 1969 [79], Santa Monica CA). (Began 1908; Ufa; Fox-Europa; MGM; Universal.) "Karl Freund," *Variety,* 254, 7 May 1969, 263:1 (AA for *The Good Earth,* MGM, 1937; developed the Norwich lightmeter). AMD, p. 128. AS, p. 415. BHD2, p. 91. FDY, p. 425. IFN, p. 110. "Made Technical Head," *MPW,* 14 Aug 1926, 3.

Frey, Callie [actress] (b. 1875–29 Apr 1948 [72], Los Angeles CA). BHD, p. 173. IFN, p. 110.

Frey, Fernand [actor] (b. Asnieres, France, 15 Jun 1877–19 Mar 1959 [81], Escaudoeuvres, France). AS, p. 415.

Fric, Martin [actor/director/scenarist] (b. Prague, Czechoslovakia, 2 Mar 1902–26 Jul 1968 [66], Prague, Czechoslovakia). AS, p. 416. BHD, p. 173; BHD2, p. 91.

Friebus, Theodore [stage/film actor] (b. Washington DC, 1879?–26 Dec 1917 [38], New York NY; heart attack). m. (1) Georgine Flagg; (2) Beatrice Mosier. (Film debut: *Pearl of the Army;* Astra-Pathé; Warren Company.) "Theodore Friebus," *Variety,* 4 Jan 1918. AMD, p. 128. AS, p. 416. BHD, p. 173. IFN, p. 110. SD. "Theodore Friebus Dies on Stage," *MPW,* 19 Jan 1918, 355. Lester Sweyd, "What They Are Doing Now," *Motion Picture Magazine,* Feb 1918, 11 (playing Dr. Gustavus Sonntag in "A Tailor-Made Man" at the Cohan & Harris Theater, New York.").

Fried, Abe [cinematographer/film editor] (*né* Conrad Wells, b. New York NY, 1897?–2 Jan 1930 [32], Santa Monica CA). m. Gypsy, 1926. (Fox; Universal.) "Conrad Wells [Abe Fried]," *Variety,* 15 Jan 1930. AS, p. 416. BHD2, p. 279 (Conrad Wells). FDY, pp. 459, 471.

Fried, Alfred [producer] (b. England, 1885–15 Jan 1964 [78?], London, England). AS, p. 416.

Fried, Eleanor [film editor]. No data found. AMD, p. 128. "Miss Fried Goes to Universal City," *MPW,* 19 Oct 1918, 368.

Friedberger, Louis [actor] (b. Germany-d. 16 Feb 1924, Los Angeles CA). BHD, p. 173. IFN, p. 110.

Friedgen, Raymond [actor/director/producer] (*né* John Raymond Friedgen, b. New York NY, 1893–1 Mar 1966 [82?], Los Angeles CA). AS, p. 416. BHD, p. 174; BHD2, p. 91.

Friedkin, Joel [actor] (b. Russia, 15 Mar 1885–19 Sep 1954 [69], Burbank CA). AS, p. 416.

Friedlander, Al [executive/producer] (b. 7 Jul 1891–12 May 1937 [45], New York NY). BHD2, p. 91.

Friedman, Helen [film extra] (b. 1893?–8 Jun 1926 [33], Los Angeles CA; suicide by overdose of veronal). m. Catto Blich. "Miss Friedman, Film Extra, Kills Self in Despair," *Variety,* 16 Jun 1926 ("Despondency because she could not get roles in pictures was given as the reason for the suicide"). AS, p. 416 (d. 13 Jun).

Friedman, Henry [actor] (b. 1897–18 Aug 1983 [86?], Bryn Mawr PA). AS, p. 416. BHD, p. 174.

Friedman, Leopold [executive] (b. Saalfeld, Germany, 10 Jun 1887–18 Dec 1978 [91], New York NY). BHD2, p. 92.

Friedmann-Frederick, Fritz [director] (b. Berlin, Germany, 13 Mar 1883–16 Mar 1934 [51], Prague, Czechoslovakia). BHD2, p. 92.

Friel, Dick [scenarist]. No data found. FDY, p. 425.

Friend, Arthur S. [executive]. No data found. AMD, p. 128. "Brady Praises Friend," *MPW,* 1 Sep 1917, 1349. "Distinctive Plans Busy Year; Arthur S. Friend Issues Statement," *MPW,* 13 Jan 1923, 123. Arthur S. Friend, "Distinctive's

Schedule," *MPW,* 4 Aug 1923, 407. "The Industry Must Cure Own Ills, Says Arthur S. Friend," *MPW,* 8 Dec 1923, 540. "Friend Resigns as Head of Distinctive," *MPW,* 12 Jan 1924, 110.

Friend, Cliff [composer] (b. 1 Oct 1893–27 Jun 1974 [80], Las Vegas NV). "Cliff Friend Dead at 80; Composer and Song Writer," *NYT,* 29 Jun 1974, 32:6. "Cliff Friend," *Variety,* 3 Jul 1974 (wrote *You Tell Her, I Stutter; The Merry-Go-Round Broke Down; When My Dream Boat Comes Home*). AS, p. 416. CEPMJ.

Friend, Nathan H. [publicist]. No data found. AMD, p. 129. "Nathan H. Friend," *MPW,* 6 Jan 1917, 94.

Fries, Otto H. [actor] (b. St. Louis MO, 28 Oct 1887–15 Sep 1938 [50], Los Angeles CA). AS, p. 416. BHD1, p. 202. IFN, p. 110.

Friese-Greene, William (grandfather of Richard Greene) [inventor] (*né* William Edward Green, b. Bristol, England, 7 Sep 1855–5 May 1921 [65], London, England). AS, p. 417. Katz, p. 456. WWVC, pp. 53–54. Claude Friese-Greene, "How Films Began [reprint]," *CI,* 173 (Nov 1989), C4. "The New Colour Processes; Important Developments Outlined," *Kinematograph Weekly,* 91, 25 Sep 1924, 54 (formation of the Friese-Greene Colour Film Co.).

Friganza, Trixie (sister of Therese Thompson) [actress] (*née* Brigid O'Callaghan, b. Grenola KS, 29 Nov 1870–27 Feb 1955 [84], Flintridge CA; arthritis). m. (1) William J.M. Barry; (2) Charles A. Goetler. "Trixie Friganza Is Dead at 84; Starred in Musical Comedies; 'Champagne Girl' of Earlier Generation Succumbs in California—Appeared in Vaudeville and in the Movies," *NYT,* 28 Feb 1955, 19:2; "700 at Trixie Friganza Mass," *NYT,* 3 Mar 1955, 27:1 (age 83). "Trixie Friganza," *Variety,* 2 Mar 1955. AMD, p. 129. AS, p. 417. BHD1, p. 202. FSS, p. 116. IFN, p. 110. SD. Truitt, p. 118 (*née* Delia O'Callahan). On cover of *NYDM,* 23 Dec 1914. Walter J. Kingsley, "Trixie Friganza Finishes Record Vaudeville Engagement; Plays Seventy-five Weeks, Never Misses a Performance, Was Never Late, and Never Held the Curtain," *NYDM,* 21 Jul 1915, 15:1 ("...and never had words with the stage-manager or house manager.... Her record went to show what a pleasant life is possible to the vaudeville star who knows when they are well treated and highly paid and appreciate that fact."). Cover, *NYDM,* 25 Dec 1915. "Trixie Friganza Back on Screen," *MPW,* 6 Jan 1923, 68. "The Life of the Party," *Picture-Play Magazine,* Jun 1925, 50 (mother's name was Friganza). "Trixie Ends 'Blondes' Role," *MPW,* 22 Oct 1927, 486.

Frigerio, Jone [actress] (*née* Jone Frigerio Cristina, b. Rome, Italy, 1877). AS, p. 417.

Frink, Lola B. [actress] (b. 1900–15 Nov 1952 [52?], Chicago IL). BHD, p. 174.

Frisby, Mildred [actress/writer] (b. 1898–15 Mar 1939 [41], West Los Angeles CA; fell down a mountainside). m. Edward Doherty (2 sons, Edward, Jr., and Jack). BHD, p. 174. "Writer's Wife Found Dead on Mountain; Mrs. Edward Doherty Fell While Hiking in California," *NYT,* 16 Mar 1939, p. 48 ("She apparently had fallen about ten feet down the mountainside from a lonely trail along which she had been hiking. Her throat was lodged in the crotch of a mesquite bush." She was motion-picture editor of *The Chicago Tribune* and writer of a column under the name of Mildred Spain. "She had been an actress in silent pictures under the name of Mildred Frisby."). "Mrs. Doherty Strangled; Throat Caught in Branches of Tree in a Fall, Doctor Thinks," *NYT,* 17 Mar 1939, p. 44 (the coroner "ordered a chemical analysis to determine whether an overdose of sleeping powders might have caused her to lose her footing. ¶Detectives discovered sleeping powders in her room at the home of Richard Carroll, a writer, where she and her husband...had been guests for several weeks.").

Frisco, Joe [actor] (*né* Lewis W. Joseph, b. Milan IL, 1889–16 Feb 1958 [68?], Calabasas CA). AS, p. 417.

Fritch, Hanson (Pete) [film editor] (b. 1888–6 Aug 1954 [66?], Los Angeles CA). BHD2, p. 92.

Frith, John Leslie [scenarist] (b. London, England, 28 Sep 1884–2 Feb 1961 [76], London, England). AS, p. 417.

Frith, Thomas Preston [actor] (b. 1883?–7 Jan 1945 [62], Los Angeles CA). "Thomas Preston Frith," *Variety,* 17 Jan 1945 ("a picture actor for 27 years"). AS, p. 417 (d. 9 Jan). BHD1, p. 202. IFN, p. 110. Truitt, p. 118.

Fritsch, Willy [stage/film actor] (*né* Wilhelm Egon Fritz Fritsch, b. Kattowitz, Germany, 27 Jan 1901–12 Jul 1973 [72], Hamburg, Germany; heart attack). m. Dinah Grace; (2) Lilian Harvey (*née* Lilian Muriel Helen Harvey, d. 1968). "Willy Fritsch," *Variety,* 25 Jul 1973. AS, p. 417. BHD1, p. 203. IFN, p. 110. SD.

Fritz (horse) (d. 6 Feb 1938). IFN, p. 110. "Hart's Artcraft Debut Is Fritz's Finale," *MPW,* 20 Oct 1917, 411.

Fritz, Bruno [actor] (b. Berlin, Germany, 4 Mar 1900–12 Jun 1984 [84], Berlin, Germany). AS, p. 417.

Fritzsche, K.J. [producer] (b. Germany, 1883–12 Oct 1954 [71?], Munich, Germany). AS, p. 417.

Froelich, Carl August Hugo [director/producer/scenarist] (b. Berlin, Germany, 5 Sep 1875–13 Feb 1953 [77], Berlin, Germany). AS, P. 417. BHD2, p. 92.

Froeschel, George [scenarist] (b. Vienna, Austria, 8 Mar 1891–22 Nov 1979 [88], Los Angeles CA). AS, p. 417. BHD2, p. 92.

Frogerais, Jacques Pierre René [producer] (b. Bordeaux, France, 6 Jun 1893 [extrait de naissance no. 1E358/767]-19 Jan 1980 [86], Paris, France). AS, p. 417.

Frohlich, Gustav [actor/director] (*né* Gustav Froehlich, b. Hanover, Germany, 21 Mar 1902–22 Dec 1987 [85], Lugano, Switzerland; complications after an operation). AS, p. 417 (d. 26 Dec). BHD1, p. 123; BHD2, p. 92. Waldman, p. 111.

Frohman, Charles (brother of **Daniel** and **Gustave Frohman**; uncle of **Charles Frohman Everett**) (b. Lawrence Street, Sandusky OH, 17 Jun 1860–7 May 1915 [54], drowned on the *Lusitania*). AMD, p. 129. BHD2, p. 92. "Charles Frohman," *MPW,* 28 Mar 1914, 1659. "Tribute to 'C.F.'; Augustus Thomas's Eulogy Over the Remains of Charles Frohman," *NYDM,* 2 Jun 1915, 5:2). "Frohman Estate $350,000; Total Does Not Include Real Estate, the Value of Which Is Unknown," *NYDM,* 14 Jul 1915, 7:3 (heirs: brothers Daniel and Gustave; sisters Caryl, Emma, Ella, and Mrs. Rachael Davidson, all of NYC). "Approves Final Accounting of Charles Frohman Estate," *MPW,* 28 Aug 1920, 1143 (estate valued at $919,282).

Frohman, Daniel (brother of **Charles** and **Gustave Frohman**; uncle of **Charles Frohman Everett**) [stage manager/film executive] (b. Sandusky OH, 22 Aug 1851–26 Dec 1940 [89], New York NY). m. Margaret Illington, 1903–09. *Memories of a Manager; Daniel Frohman Presents* (1935). "Daniel Frohman, 'Grand Old Man' of the Theatre, Dies in N.Y. at 89," *Variety,* 1 Jan 1941 (possibly born in 1849). AMD, p. 129. AS, p. 417. BHD2, p. 92. Daniel Frohman, "Future of Motion Pictures," *MPW,* 18 Jun 1910, 1044–45. Hugh Hoffman, "Daniel Frohman and the Photoplay," *MPW,* 26 Oct 1912, 335. Louis Reeves Harrison, "Studio Saunterings," *MPW,* 4 Jan 1913, 26–28. "Daniel Frohman Visits World Staff," *MPW,* 22 Feb 1913, 771. "Daniel Frohman Talks Pictures," *MPW,* 11 Apr 1914, 194–95. "[Third] Anniversary for F.P. ...," *NYDM,* 14 Apr 1915, 24:2 (one of the trio that formed FP-L, along with Zukor and Edwin Porter). "Daniel Frohman Still with Famous Players," *MPW,* 16 Mar 1918, 1516.

Frohman, Gustave (brother of **Charles** and **Daniel Frohman**; uncle of **Charles Frohman Everett**) [manager/producer] (b. Sandusky OH, 1854?–16 Aug 1930 [76], New York NY). m. Marie Hubert. "Gustave Frohman," *Variety,* 20 Aug 1930. AMD, p. 129. AS, p. 417. BHD2, p. 92. "Gustave Frohman in Picture Field," *MPW,* 12 Dec 1914, 1528.

Frolik, Anneska [actress] (d. 1 Sep 1917, Los Angeles CA; shot to death by **Harry Leonard**). AS, p. 417. "Harry Leonard Dead," *Variety,* 7 Sep 1917, p. 26 ("Los Angeles, Sept. 5. Harry Leonard, picture actor, who tried to kill Anneska Frolik, actress, by shooting and throwing vitriol at her, died from self-inflicted wounds.").

Frondaie, Pierre [actor] (b. France-d. 25 Sep 1984, France). AS, p. 418.

Frontec, Georges-François [actor] (b. Saint-Malo, France, 13 Aug 1899). AS, p. 418.

Frost, Lorraine [actress]. No data found. AMD, p. 129. "Lorraine Frost, New Metro Ingenue," *MPW,* 26 Aug 1916, 1412.

Frothingham, J.L. [producer]. No data found. AMD, p. 129. "Frothingham Defies 'Dead Season' by Releasing Spectable, 'Bride of Gods,'" *MPW,* 31 Dec 1921, 1060.

Frouhins, Eugène [actor] (*né* Eugène Frouin, b. Estang, France, 9 May 1888–29 May 1966 [78], Paris, France). AS, p. 418.

Frowein, Eberhard [director/scenarist] (b. Elberfeld, Germany, 24 May 1881–15 Jan 1944 [62], Alt Aussee, Austria). AS, p. 418.

Frusta, Arrigo [scenarist] (*né* Augusto Ferraris, b. Turin, Italy, 26 Nov 1875–1965 [89?], Turin, Italy). AS, p. 418. JS, p. 176 (in Italian silents from 1908).

Frye, Dwight [stage/film actor] (b. Salina KS, 22 Feb 1899–9 Nov 1943 [44], Los Angeles CA; heart attack on a bus). m. Laura Lee. Gregory William Mank, James T. Coughlin, and Dwight D. Frye, *Dwight Frye's Last Laugh: An Authorized Biography* (Midnight Marquee Press, 1997). (Film debut?: *The Night Bird,* 1928). "Dwight Frye," *Variety,* 17 Nov 1943. AS, p. 418. BHD1, p. 123 (d. 7 Nov). IFN, p. 111. Gregory W. Mank, "Dwight Frye [letter]," *Films in Review,* Dec 1973, 638–39 (includes partial filmography). Blackie Seymour, "Dwight Frye: 'The Ultimate Villager,'" *CI,* 252 (ZJun 1996), 18–19.

Fryer, Richard [cameraman] (b. England, 1894?–9 Feb 1953 [58], Washington DC). m. actress Joyce Carroll. (Mutual; Biograph; Thanhouser; Pathé News; Universal [14 years]; Paramount; WB; UA). "Richard Fryer," *Variety,* 11 Feb 1953. AS, p. 418. BHD2, p. 92.

Fryland, Alphons Friedrich [actor] (b. Vienna, Austria, 1 May 1890). AS, p. 418.

Fuchs, Heinrich [actor] (b. Vienna, Austria, 6 Jul 1896). m. **Lucie Englisch** (d. 1965). AS, p. 418.

Fuchs, Oskar [actor] (b. Germany, 9 Jan 1866–19 Oct 1927 [61]). BHD, p. 174.

Fuglsang, Frederick [cinematographer]. No data found. FDY, p. 459.

Fujino, Hideo [actor] (*né* Uhei Shimada, b. Tokyo, Japan, 16 May 1878–11 Feb 1956 [77], Japan). AS, p. 419.

Fuller, Dale [stage/film actress] (b. Santa Ana CA, 17 Jun 1897). (Keystone.) AS, p. 419. MH, p. 112. MSBB, p. 1034.

Fuller, Elsie [actress]. No data found. AMD, p. 129. "Elsie Fuller Engaged by Vitagraph," *MPW,* 27 Dec 1919, 1146.

Fuller, Everett A. [cinematographer] (b. 1892–24 Nov 1963 [71?], Schenectady NY). BHD2, p. 92.

Fuller, Irene [actress] (b. 1898?–20 Mar 1945 [47], Los Angeles CA). "Irene Fuller," *Variety,* 28 Mar 1945 ("actress in silent days"). AS, p. 419. BHD, p. 174. IFN, p. 111. Truitt, p. 118.

Fuller, Jesse "Lone Cat" [actor/jazz musician] (b. Jonesboro GA, 12 Mar 1896–29 Jan 1976 [79], Oakland CA). BHD1, p. 203. IFN, p. 111.

Fuller, Leslie [actor/scenarist] (b. Hackney, England, 16 May 1890–24 Apr 1948 [57], Margate, England). AS, p. 419.

Fuller, Lew H. [actor] (b. 1887–13 Nov 1939 [52?], Chicago IL). BHD, p. 174.

Fuller, Loïe [actress] (*née* Marie-Louise Fuller, b. Fullesburg, Germany, 1862–1928 [66?], Berlin, Germany). AS, p. 419.

Fuller, Mary [actress] (*née* Mary Claire Fuller, b. Washington DC, 5 Oct 1888–9 Dec 1973 [85], Washington DC; at St. Elizabeth Hospital from 1 Jul 1947). (Vitagraph, 1906; Edison, 1909; Universal; Lasky.) AMD, p. 129. AS, p. 419. BHD, pp. 23–26; 174. MSBB, p. 1034 (b. 1893). Spehr, p. 132 (b. 1893). "Edison-McClure," *MPW,* 29 Jun 1912, 1212. "Edison Players Return," *MPW,* 16 Nov 1912, 647. Louis Reeves Harrison, "What Happened to Mary [review]," *MPW,* 5 Jul 1913, 26. Cover painting, *NYDM,* 25 Mar 1914. "Winsome Mary Fuller Wins," *MPW,* 2 May 1914, 648. "Gossip of the Studios," *NYDM,* 6 May 1914, 42:3 (at the Edison studio, "Dick Neil was carrying Mary downstairs, while rehearsing, when he tripped over a loose end of carpet. Both rolled down the flight of stairs. Neil, a trained athlete, arrived at the bottom unhurt, and Miss Fuller, by dint of much experience gained in previous tumbles, bobbed up, smiling, and equally undamaged."). "Mary Fuller Signs with Universal," *MPW,* 4 Jul 1914, 49. Mary Fuller, "Photoplay Acting Is Mental Radiation," *MPW,* 11 Jul 1914, 227. "Mary Fuller Does Battle with Snake," *MPW,* 22 Aug 1914, 1076. "Mary Fuller Returns from Shohola," *MPW,* 26 Sep 1914, 1753. "Mary Fuller a Prolific Writer," *MPW,* 10 Oct 1914, 195. Mary Fuller, "Morals Behind the Screen and Curtain," *Motion Picture Magazine,* Feb 1915, 85–88. "Mary Fuller," *MPW,* 14 Aug 1915, 1146. "Mary Fuller to Support Lou Tellegen," *MPW,* 27 Jan 1917, 534. Billy H. Doyle, "Lost Players," *CI,* 164 (Feb 1989), 40–41 (*née* Mary Pearl Fuller, b. 1890 or 1893). Billy H. Doyle, "Lost Players [Mary Fuller]," *CI,* 191 (May 1991), 7, 17 (*née* Mary Claire Fuller). George Katchmer, "Remembering the Great Silents," *CI,* 241 (Jul 1995), 37.

Fuller, P[aul] **Fairfax** [scenarist] (b. 1897–6 Oct 1927 [30?], New York NY; from fall out of 9th floor window of Park Central Hotel). BHD2, p. 93. FDY, p. 425. "Obituary," *MPW,* 8 Oct 1927, 337.

Fuller, Rene *see* **Lygo, Mary**

Fuller, "Ving" [cartoonist]. No data found. AMD, p. 129. "Fuller on Bray Staff," *MPW,* LXXV, 15 Aug 1925, 751.

Fulton, Helen [stage/film actress]. No data found. (Thanhouser; Edison.) "Helen Fulton," *NYDM,* LXXIV, 16 Oct 1915, 32:4.

Fulton, Maude [actress/playwright/title writer/scenarist] (b. Eldorado KS, 14 May 1881–9 Nov 1950 [69], San Fernando CA). m. **Robert H**[oward] **Ober** (d. 1950). (Wrote *The Brat* and *The Hummingbird.*) "Maude Fulton," *Variety,* 15 Nov 1950. AMD, p. 129. AS, p. 419 (d. San Fernando CA). BHD1, p. 204; BHD2, p. 93. FDY, p. 443. IFN, p. 111. SD. Truitt, p. 119. "Titling 'His Hour,'" *MPW,* 6 Sep 1924, 25. "To Write Titles for Metropolitan," *MPW,* 5 Jun 1926, 459. June Lee, "Dan Cupid's Bulletin Board," *Paris and Hollywood,* Oct 1926, 89 (she and Ober "are not residing together in their Laurel Canyon home. Whether this well known couple will make up their differences or go into court is a matter of conjecture."). "Maude Fulton," *MPW,* 7 May 1927, 39.

Fumet, Stanislas Marie Raphaël Louis Paul [actor/scenarist] (b. Lescar, France, 10 May 1896 [extrait de naissance no. 13]-1 Sep 1983 [87], Rozes, France). AS, p. 419.

Funes, Roque [director] (b. Buenos Aires, Argentina, 1 Dec 1897–15 Jun 1981 [83], Buenos Aires, Argentina). AS, p. 419.

Fung, Willie [actor] (b. Canton, China, 3 Mar 1896–16 Apr 1945 [49], Los Angeles CA; coronary occlusion). AS, p. 419. BHD1, p. 204 (b. Guangzhou, China). IFN, p. 111.

Funquist, Georg [actor] (b. Uppsala, Sweden, 13 Mar 1900). AS, p. 420.

Fuqua, Jack [cinematographer]. No data found. FDY, p. 459.

Fuqua, Wilbur [cinematographer] (b. 1882–31 Jan 1953 [70?], No. Hollywood CA). AS, p. 420 (b. 1878; d. 1952). BHD2, p. 93.

Furber, Douglas [stage/film actor, 1917–26/composer/scenarist] (b. London, England, 13 May 1885–20 Feb 1961 [75], London, England). m. (1) Elsa Cutler (d. 1945); (2) Diana Christiansen. "Douglas Furber, Song Writer, 75; Author of 'Limehouse Blues,' 'Bells of St. Mary's' Dies—Producer Did Musicals," *NYT,* 21 Feb 1961, 35:4. "Douglas Furber," *Variety,* 22 Feb 1961 (wrote *Lambeth Walk*). AS, p. 420. BHD2, p. 93 (d. 19 Feb). FDY, p. 425. NNAT. SD, p. 480.

Furbringer, E[rnst] **F**[ritz] [actor] (b. Braunschweig, Germany, 27 Jul 1900–30 Oct 1988 [88], Munich, Germany). AS, p. 420.

Furey, Barney [actor] (b. Boise ID, 7 Sep 1886–18 Jan 1938 [51], Los Angeles CA; cirrhosis of the liver). m. Florence. (Selig, 1911; Biograph; Kalem; Universal; Fox.) AMD, p. 129. AS, p. 420. BHD1, p. 204 (b. 1888). IFN, p. 111. "Barney Furey," *MPW,* 10 Sep 1927, 92. Billy H. Doyle, "Lost Players," *CI,* 148 (Oct 1987), 52. George A. Katchmer, "Forgotten Cowboys and Cowgirls—Part V," *CI,* 177 (Mar 1990), C2.

Furey, James A. [stage manager/singer/actor] (b. New York NY, 1845?–18 Apr 1922 [77], Brooklyn NY). "James A. Furey," *Variety,* 28 Apr 1922. AS, p. 420. SD.

Furey, James A. [actor] (b. Ogdenburg NY, 10 May 1865–7 Jul 1930 [65], New York NY). AS, p. 420 (d. LA CA). BHD, p. 174. IFN, p. 111.

Furniss, Harry [actor/cartoonist](b. Wexford, Ireland, 1854–15 Jan 1925 [70?], Hastings, England). AMD, p. 129. AS, p. 420. BHD, p. 174. "Harry Furniss in Edison Pictures," *MPW,* 30 Mar 1912, 1145. "Harry Furniss Sails," *MPW,* 18 May 1912, 617. Louis Reeves Harrison, "The Harry Furniss Photoplays," *MPW,* 25 May 1912, 719–23.

Furry, Elda *see* **Hopper, Hedda**

Fursman, Georgia May [actress] (b. 1860–10 Feb 1926 [65?]). BHD, p. 174.

Furst, Sigge [actor] (b. Stockholm, Sweden, 3 Nov 1901–11 Jun 1984 [82], Stockholm, Sweden). AS, p. 420. BHD1, p. 204.

Furst, William Wallace [stage/film actor] (b. Baltimore MD, 25 Mar 1852–11 Jul 1917 [65?], Freeport, LI NY). "William Furst," *Variety,* 13 Jul 1917. AS, p. 420. SD.

Furth, Jaro [actor/director] (*né* Edwin Furth-Jaro, b. Germany, 21 Apr 1877). AS, p. 420.

Furthman, Charles (brother of **Jules Furthman**) [scenarist] (b. Chicago IL, 3 Oct 1880?–7 Nov 1936 [56], Los Angeles CA; pneumonia following operation). "Charles Furthman," *Variety,* 11 Nov 1936. AMD, p. 129. AS, p. 420. BHD2, p. 93 (b. 1884). IFN, p. 111. "Furthman Is Scenario Editor-in-Chief at Lasky Studios," *MPW,* 6 Feb 1926, 554.

Furthman, Jules Grinnell (brother of **Charles Furthman**) [scenarist/director/producer] (b. Chicago IL, 5 Mar 1888–22 Sep 1966 [78], Oxford, England; cerebral hemorrhage). m. **Sybil Sealey**, ca. Jun 1920. "Jules Furthman," *Variety,* 5 Oct 1966. AMD, p. 129. AS, p. 420 (d. 1960). BHD2, p. 93. FDY, p. 425. IFN, p. 111. A.H. Giebler, "Los Angeles News Letter; Furthman—Sealey," *MPW,* 26 Jun 1920, 1753. "Jules Furthman Signed," *MPW,* 21 Aug 1926, 481. "Furthman Remains Another Year," *MPW,* 30 Jul 1927, 310.

Fusier-Gir, Jeanne (son of François Gir) [actress] (*née* Jeanne Fusier, b. Paris, France, 22 Apr 1885–24 Apr 1973 [88], Maisons-Laffitte, France [extrait de décès no. 132]). m. (son, director François Pierre Girard, b. 13 Mar 1920). AS, p. 420.

Fuss, Kurt [actor] (b. Leipzig, Germany, 11 Jan 1892–22 Mar 1976 [93]). BHD1, p. 608.

Fuster, Louis R. [cameraman]. No data found. AMD, p. 129. "Louis R. Fuster Missing," *MPW,* 3 Mar 1917, 1334.

Futter, Walter A. [producer/founded Vidoscope Corp. of America] (b. Omaha NB, 2 Jan 1900–3 Mar 1958 [58], New York NY; heart attack). m. (1) **Adele Lacey**, 1937 (d. 1953); (2) Betty Bartley. "Walter A. Futter, Movie Producer, 58," *NYT,* 5 Mar 1958, 31:4. "Walter A. Futter," *Variety,* 12 Mar 1958 (began as a film cutter in Hollywood, "and then became editor of Cosmopolitan Productions."). AMD, p. 129. AS, p. 420. BHD2, p. 93. "Walter Futter Tackles 'Mike' Next Thursday," *MPW,* 26 Nov 1927, 12 (WPCH Radio). "Airaids," *MPW,* 3 Dec 1927, 16.

G

Gaal, Bela [director] (b. Dombrad (Dombovar), Hungary, 2 Jan 1894–1945 [51?], Budapest, Hungary). AS, p. 423 (Géla Gaal). BHD2, p. 93.

Gaal, Franciska [actress] (*née* Franziska Zilverich, b. Budapest, Hungary, 1 Feb 1901–13 Aug 1972 [71], New York NY). AS, p. 423. BHD1, p. 204.

Gabaroche [actor] (*né* Gaston Gabaroche, b. Bordeaux, France, 29 Sep 1884–28 Aug 1961 [76], Marseilles, France). AS, p. 423.

Gabert [actor] (b. Marseilles, France, 24 Mar 1892). AS, p. 423.

Gabillat, Henri Eugène Marius [cinematographer] (b. Lyon, France, 9 Aug 1869–9 Jul 1934 [64], Saint-Bernard, France; accidental drowning). AS, p. 423.

Gable, Clark, "The King" (father of actor John Clark Gable) [stage/film actor] (b. Cadiz OH, 1 Feb 1901–16 Nov 1960 [59], Los Angeles CA; heart attack). Lyn Tornabene, *Long Live the King; A Biography of Clark Gable* (New York: Putnam, 1976). m. (1) **Josephine Dillon**, 1924–30 (d. 1971); (2) Rhea Langham, 1931; (3) **Carole Lombard**, 1939 (d. 1942); (4) Sylvia Ashley, 1949; (5) Kay Spreckels, 1955 (1 son, John Clark, b. 20 Mar 1961). (AA, *It Happened One Night*, 1934.) "Clark Gable Dies in Hollywood of Heart Ailment at Age of 59; 'King' of Film Capital Was One of Ten Top Box-office Attractions for Years," *NYT*, 17 Nov 1960, 1:4, 37:4. "Clark Gable" and "Gable's Last Pic Paid Him $800,000," *Variety*, 23 Nov 1960 (d. 17 Nov 1960). AS, p. 423. BHD1, p. 204. IFN, p. 112. Katz, pp. 460–61. Truitt, p. 119. Dorothy Calhoun, "How Many Marriages for Clark Gable?; Popular Actor Says He Has Been Wed Twice, But Friends Claim Four Marriages for Him," *Movie Classic*, Sep 1931, 42. Gladys Hall, "Will Gable Take the Place of Valentino?," *Movie Classic*, Oct 1931, 15, 73–74. Dorothy Calhoun, "Clark Gable's Fight for Fame," *Movie Classic*, Dec 1931, 20–21 (as told by Josephine Dillon. "Though he is now married again, I'm still Mrs. Gable and I shall keep the name always. You see—I'm terribly in love with him—"). Jim Tully, "Clark Gable Without Women' The Story of a Onetime Medical Student Who Was Bashful in the Presence of High School Girls," *Cinema Arts*, Sep 1937, 28–29, 100. T. Ross Milton, "Clark Gable Flew a Tough Mission [letter]," *The Wall Street Journal*, 24 Dec 1996, A9:2 (Milton writes that Gable was not, as Walter Cronkite recollects, "a celebrity manipulated by the PR machines" during WWII. He went through a formal gunnery program and flew on dangerous missions.). Dan Van Neste, "The Clark Gable Reconstructed Birthhome: 'Fit for a King,'" *CI*, 286 (Apr 1999), 20–22. Clark Gable Foundation, 140 Charleston Street, Cadiz OH 43907; (614) 942-GWTW; $12 annual membership.

Gable, Gilbert E. [producer]. No data found. AMD, p. 130. "Signs New Producer," *MPW*, 3 Mar 1923, 37.

Gabourie, Fred [techinical director] (b. Ontario, Canada, 19 Sep 1881–1 Mar 1951 [69], Los Angeles CA). "Fred Gabourie," *Variety*, 7 Mar 1951 (at MGM since 1921). AS, p. 423. BHD2, p. 93.

Gabriel, Carl [actor] (d. Feb 1931). BHD, p. 174.

Gabriel, Gilbert W. [scenarist] (b. 1890–3 Sep 1952 [62?], Mount Kisco NY). (Paramount.) AS, p. 423. BHD2, p. 93.

Gabriel, Jean [director/actor] (*né* Jean Gabriel Citarella, b. 1898–9 Oct 1977 [79], Newark NJ). AS, p. 423. BHD, p. 174; BHD2, p. 93. IFN, p. 111.

Gabriello [actor/singer] (*né* André Adrien Marie Galopet, b. Paris, France, 15 Oct 1896–19 Mar 1975 [78], Paris, France). AS, p. 423.

Gabrielsen, Holger [actor/director] (b. Copenhagen, Denmark, 27 Nov 1896–7 May 1956 [59], Copenhagen, Denmark). AS, p. 424. BHD2, p. 93.

Gabrio, Gabriel [actor] (*né* Edouard Gabriel Lelievre, b. Rheims, France, 13 Jan 1887–31 Oct 1946 [58], Bercheres-sur-Vesgre, France). AS, p. 424. BHD, p. 174. IFN, p. 111.

Gaby, Frank [actor] (b. 1895?–12 Feb 1945 [49], St. Louis MO; suicide by hanging himself in a clothes rack in a hotel). "Frank Gaby," *Variety*, 14 Feb 1945 (age 49). AS, p. 424. BHD1, p. 204. IFN, p. 111.

Gad, Henri [director] (b. 1884–8 Apr 1930 [46?], Paris, France). AS, p. 424. BHD2, p. 93.

Gad, Urban [director] (*né* Peter Urban Gad, b. Skaelsor, Denmark, 12 Feb 1879–26 Dec 1947 [68], Copenhagen, Denmark). AS, p. 424. BHD2, p. 93 (b. Copenhagen, Denmark).

Gaddis, Peggy [novelist; editor for *MPM* and *MPC*] (aka Roberta Courtland, Georgia Craig, Gail Jordan, Carolina Lee, Perry Lindsay and Joan Sherman, *née* Erolie Pearl Gaddis, b. Gaddistown GA, 5 Mar 1895–14 Jun 1966 [71], Tucker GA). m. John Sherman Dern, 13 Mar 1931 (d. 29 Nov 1950). "Peggy Dern," *Variety*, 29 Jun 1966.

Gade, Sven[d] [stage/film art director/director] (b. Copenhagen, Denmark, 9 Feb 1877–25 Jun 1952 [75], Aarhus, Denmark). (Last film: *Ballet Dancer*, 1938.) AMD, p. 130. AS, p. 424. BHD2, p. 93. IFN, p. 111. Katz, p. 461 (began in Denmark). Waldman, p. 115. "Svend Gade Engaged as Art Director," *MPW*, 24 Mar 1923, 458. "Carl Laemmle Signs Gade, Noted European Director," *MPW*, 21 Jun 1924, 704. "Svend Gade Starts Work," *MPW*, 17 Jan 1925, 276. "Gade Loaned to First National," *MPW*, 31 Jul 1926, 279. "Gade Free-Lancing," *MPW*, 16 Oct 1926, 440.

Gaden, Alexander [actor] (b. Montreal, Canada, 20 Feb 1880). (FP-L; Universal; Vitagraph; Gaumont.) AMD, p. 130. AS, p. 424. BHD, p. 174. 1921 Directory, p. 173. "Lives of the Players; Alexander Gaden," *MPS*, 31 Jan 1913, 31. "Alexander Gaden," *MPS*, 12 Jun 1914, 26 (b. 1881). "Alexander Gaden," *MPW*, 1 May 1915, 731. "Alexander Gaden to Be Gaumont Lead," *MPW*, 3 Jun 1916, 1678. "Alexander Gaden Returns to the Screen," *MPW*, 2 Aug 1919, 697. "Gaden Returning to Pictures," *MPW*, 30 Aug 1919, 1303.

Gadsby, C. Rivers [actor/singer] (b. England, 1887–24 Mar 1961 [74?], London, England). AS, p. 424.

Gadsden, Jacqueline [actress] (aka Jane Daly, b. Lompoc CA, 3 Aug 1900–10 Aug 1986 [86], Lake San Marcos CA). (MGM). AMD, p. 130. BHD1, p. 608 (Gadsdon). "Plays Opposite Jones," *MPW*, 30 Jun 1923, 754. "Extra Wins Contract," *MPW*, 30 Oct 1926, 4. George Katchmer, "Remembering the Great Silents," *CI*, 241 (Jul 1995), 37.

Gaffney, Arch [scenarist] (b. 1903–26 Feb 1935 [32?], Los Angeles CA; meningitis). AS, p. 424. BHD2, p. 93.

Gaidarov, Vladimir [actor] (*né* Wladimir Gaidarow, b. Poltava, Ukraine, 25 Jul 1893–17 Dec 1976 [83], Siberia, Russia). AS, p. 424 (b. 27 Jul 1895; d. 27 Dec); p. 425 (Vladimir Gajdarov). BHD1, p. 205.

Gaido, Domenico [director/costumer] (b. Turin, Italy). JS, p. 179 (in Italian silents from 1915).

Gail, Jane [stage/film actress] (*née* Ethel S. Magee, b. Salem NY, 16 Aug 1880–30 Jan 1963 [82], St. Petersburg FL; buried at Ferncliff Mausoleum, NYC). B. m. Edwin C. Hill (d. 13 Feb 1957, St. Petersburg FL). (Lubin.) AMD, p. 130. AS, p. 424 (b. 1890). BHD1, p. 608. George Blaisdell, "At the Sign of the Flaming Arcs," *MPW*, 20 Dec 1913, 1420 (cites theater work). "Jane Gail; Leading Woman of the Imp Company," *MPS*, 2 Jan 1914, 28. "In and Out of the Studio; Jane Gail's New Home," *Pictures and the Picturegoer*, 3 Apr 1915, 30. "Jane Gail Leaving California," *MPW*, 9 Sep 1916, 1715. James Trottier, "Just Jane: or Jane Gail's Story," *CI*, 267 (Sep 1997), 44. (Death certificate data supplied by James Trottier, Biddeford Pool ME).

Gaillard, Robert [actor/co-director] (b. Adrian MI, 14 Nov 1868–24 Sep 1941 [73], Glendale CA). BHD, p. 174.

Gaillard, Roger Louis Auguste [actor] (b. Salon-de-Provence, France, 17 Apr 1893–22 Feb 1970 [76], Bourg-la-Reine, France). AS, p. 425.

Gain, John J. [executive] (b. Philadelphia PA, 28 May 1888–15 Sep 1955 [67], Escondido CA). BHD2, p. 93.

Galal, Ahmad [actor/director/producer] (b. Cairo, Egypt, 1897–1947 [50?], Alexandria, Egypt). AS, p. 425.

Galbraith, Joseph [actor] (d. 4 Mar 1918, Los Angeles CA). BHD, p. 174. "Galbraith's Screen Debut," *NYDM*, 12 May 1915, 24:2 (to debut in *In the Purple Hills*, American).

Gale, Alice [actress] (b. Philadelphia PA, 5 Dec 1858–27 Mar 1941 [82], Harrisburg PA). "Alice Gale," *Variety*, 16 Apr 1941 (starred in Harry Davis and Avenue Theatre stock companies in Pittsburgh at turn of century). BHD, p. 174. IFN, p. 111.

Gale, Franklyn [stage/film actress/writer] (*née* Frances Cecilia Gale, d. 31 Dec 1922, St. Paul MN). "Miss Franklyn Gale," *Variety*, LXIX, 12 Jan 1923, 8:5. "Franklyn Gale," *MPW*, 6 Mar 1915, 1452.

Gale, Lillian [actress] (b. 8 Jun 1885–2 Apr 1972 [86], Englewood NJ). BHD, p. 175. IFN, p. 112.

Gale, Mrs. Marguerite H. [actress] (*née?*, b. 1885?–20 Aug 1948 [63], Amsterdam NY). (Film debut: *How Molly Malone Made Good*, Photo Drama Co., 1915.) "Mrs. Marguerite Gale," *Variety*, 1 Sep 1948 (in films 1914–18). AMD, p. 130. AS,

p. 425. BHD, p. 175. IFN, p. 112. Truitt, p. 119. "'How Molly Made Good' in Washington," *MPW,* 11 Dec 1915, 1986.

Gale, Mildred [actress] (d. 1915, San Francisco CA). "Mildred Gale," *Variety,* 2 Apr 1915.

Gale, Minna [actress] (aka Minna Gale Haines). No data found.

Galeen, Henrik [actor/director/scenarist] (b. Berlin, Germany, 1882–30 Jul 1949 [67?], Rochester NY). AS, p. 425. BHD, p. 175; BHD2, p. 94. IFN, p. 112 (age 57). Waldman, p. 116 (b. 1881; d. Randolph VT).

Gallagher, Donald [child actor/director] (b. IL, 25 Jun 1895–14 Aug 1961 [66], Los Angeles CA). (Film debut: *Zudora,* 11 Jan 1915; Chapter 8, "The Failed Elopement"). AMD, p. 130. BHD, p. 1765 ("Gallaher"). "Donald Gallagher in Zudora," *MPW,* 2 Jan 1915, 81. "Donald Gallagher a Goldwyn Player," *MPW,* 21 Apr 1917, 439.

Gallagher, Eward F. [actor] (b. San Francisco CA, 1876?–28 May 1929 [53], Astoria, Queens NY). m. (3) Helen Gallagher; (4) Anne Luther. "Edward Gallagher," *Variety,* 5 Jun 1929 (age 56; of Gallagher & Shean on stage). AMD, p. 130. IFN, p. 112. "William Fox Signs Gallagher and Shean as Stars in Big Special Picture," *MPW,* 30 Jun 1923, 759. "Mr. Gallagher and Mr. Shean at Work," *MPW,* 21 Jul 1923, 246. "Fox Suing Comedians," *MPW,* 4 Dec 1926, 4.

Gallagher, Frank [actor/director] (b. 1901–16 Feb 1929 [28?], Burbank CA). AS, p. 426 (d. 17 Feb). BHD2, p. 94.

Gallagher, Raymond [actor] (b. San Francisco CA, 17 Apr 1885–6 Mar 1953 [67], Camarillo CA). (Méliès; Lubin; Universal; Paramount; MGM; Columbia; WB.) AS, p. 426. BHD1, p. 205. IFN, p. 112. Billy H. Doyle, "Lost Players," *CI,* 148 (Oct 1987), 52.

Gallagher, Richard "Skeets" [actor] (b. Terre Haute IN, 28 Jul 1886–22 May 1955 [68], Santa Monica CA; heart attack). m. Pauline Mason. "Skeets Gallagher," *Variety,* 25 May 1955. AS, p. 426 (b. 1890). BHD1, p. 205 (b. 1890). FSS, p. 117. IFN, p. 12 (b. 1890). Truitt, p. 119.

Gallagher, Toy. No data found. AMD, p. 130. "'Toy' Gallagher," *MPW,* 22 Jan 1927, 277.

Gallaher, Donald [actor/producer] (b. IL, 25 Jun 1895–14 Aug 1961 [66], Los Angeles CA). BHD1, p. 205; BHD2, p. 94.

Galland, Jean Charles Pierre [actor] (aka Jean Gallot, b. Laval, France, 28 Mai 1897–18 Jul 1967 [70], Evian, France). AS, p. 426.

Gallatin, Alberta [actress] (*née* Alberta Jenkins, b. Campbell Co. WV, 5 Apr 1861–25 Aug 1948 [87], New York NY). m. (1) Percy S. Richardson; (2) Edwin O. Childe. "Alberta Gallatin," *Variety,* 1 Sep 1948. AS, p. 426. BHD, p. 175. IFN, p. 112. SD, p. 485 (b. 1870).

Gallea, Arturo [cinematographer/director] (b. Turin, Italy, 18 Sep 1895). JS, p. 180 (in Italian silents from 1915).

Gallery, Tom [journalist/actor] (*né* Thomas Patrick Scarsfield Gallery, b. Chicago IL, 27 Nov 1897–25 Aug 1993 [95], Encino CA). m. **ZaSu Pitts** (d. 1963); Lillian Fette. (Extra, 1919.) AMD, p. 130. AS, p. 426 (d. Chicago IL). BHD, p. 175 (b. 1898). "Parks His Pencil," *LA Times,* 22 Jan 1920, II, 9 (a writer for a Chicago newspaper, Gallery persuaded director Henry Kolker on the set of ZaSu Pitts's *Seeing It Through* that he could "be a tear-teaser on the screen"; Kolker gave him the lead opposite Pitts in *Bright Skies*). "Tom Galleryu Heading Toward Stardom, Visits Chicago Home," *MPW,* 3 Jul 1920, 74. "Zasu Pitts a Bride," *MPW,* 14 Aug 1920, 903. "Tom Gallery," *MPW,* 13 Aug 1927, 455. Billy H. Doyle, "Tom Gallery," *The S2lent Film Newsletter,* II, Mar 1994, 35:1. Mike Parker, *The Silent Film Monthly,* Mar 1995, 8–9.

Gallet, Gustave [actor] (b. Nantes, France, 1882). AS, p. 426.

Galli, Georges Henri Nicolas [actor] (b. Aix-en-Provence, France, 22 Nov 1902–3 Jul 1982 [79], Marseilles, France). AS, p. 426. BHD, p. 175.

Gallico, Paul [scenarist] (b. NY, 26 Jul 1897–15 Jul 1976 [78], Monte Carlo, Monaco). AS, p. 426 (d. 16 Jul). BHD2, p. 94.

Galli-Curci, Amelita [actress] (b. Milan, Italy, 18 Nov 1882–26 Nov 1963 [81], La Jolla CA). BHD, p. 175.

Galligan, Tom [cinematographer] (b. 24 Sep 1891–10 May 1965 [73], Los Angeles CA). BHD2, p. 94.

Gallina, Angelo [actor]. No data found. JS, p. 181 (in Italian silents from 1912).

Gallina, Pina [actress] (b. Ferrara, Italy, 19 Mar 1888–31 Jan 1974 [85], Ferrara, Italy). AS, p. 426.

Gallo, Mario [actor/director] (b. Barletta, Italy, 31 Jul 1878–1945 [67?], Buenos Aires, Argentina). AS, p. 426 (b. 31 Jan; d. 30 Oct 1984, Ontario CA). BHD2, p. 94.

Gallone, Carmine [actor/scenarist/director/producer] (b. Taggia, Italy, 18 Sep 1886–4 Apr 1973 [87], Frascati, Italy; bronchial pneumonia). m. Stanislava Winawerovna (**Soava Gallone**, 1912 (d. 1957). AS, p. 427 (d. 11 Mar). BHD2, p. 94 (d. 11 Mar). JS, p. 181 (in Italian silents from 1913).

Gallone, Soava [actress] (*née* Stanislava Winawerovna, b. Warsaw, Poland, 1880–30 May 1957 [76?], Rome, Italy). m. **Carmine Gallone**, 1912 (d. 1973). AS, p. 427. BHD1, p. 608. JS, p. 182 (in Italian silents from 1914).

Gallup, George B., Jr. [publicist]. No data found. AMD, p. 130. "Harvey Succeeds Gallup," *MPW,* 22 Sep 1923, 326. "George B. Gallup, Jr.," *MPW,* 26 Mar 1927, 311.

Galsworth, John [scenarist] (b. England, 14 Aug 1867–1933 [66?], London, England). AS, p. 427.

Galton, Blanche *see* **Whiffen, Mrs. Thomas**

Galvani, Ciro [actor] (*né* Giuseppe Chiamato Ciro Galvani, b. Castel San Pietro, Italy, 10 Apr 1867 [extrait de naissance no. 155]–29 Jan 1956 [88], Castel San Pietro, Italy [extrait de décès no 15/1956]). AS, p. 427. BHD, p. 175. IFN, p. 112. JS, p. 182 (in Italian silents from 1916).

Galvani, Dino [actor] (b. Milan, Italy, 27 Oct 1890–14 Sep 1960 [69], London, England). AS, p. 427. BHD1, p. 206. IFN, p. 112. JS, p. 182 (in Italian silents from 1915; long in the U.K.).

Gambardella, Giuseppe [actor] (aka Checcho, b. Naples, Italy). JS, pp. 182–83 (in Italian silents from 1912).

Gambarelli, Maria [actress/dancer] (b. La Spezia, Italy, 1900–4 Feb 1990 [89?], Huntington NY; cerebral hemorrhage). AS, p. 427. BHD1, p. 206.

Gambino, Domenico M. [actor/scenarist/director] (b. Turin, Italy, 17 May 1896–17 Apr 1968 [71], Rome, Italy). AS, p. 427 (b. 1890). JS, p. 183 (in Italian silents from 1915).

Gamble, Elias [actor] (*né* Elias Gamboa Robles, b. Mexico, 29 Jul 1895–9 Dec 1939 [44], Mecixo; auto accident). AS, p. 427.

Gamble, Fred A. [actor] (*né* Frederick Alvin Gambold, b. Indianapolis IN, 26 Oct 1868–17 Feb 1939 [70], Los Angeles CA). (Universal; Keystone; American; Nestor.) "Fred Gamble," *Variety,* 22 Feb 1939. AS, p. 427. BHD, p. 175. IFN, p. 112. Truitt, p. 119. Billy H. Doyle, "Lost Players [Fred A. Gamble]," *CI,* 152 (Feb 1988), C12–C13. George A. Katchmer, "Forgotten Cowboys/Girls—Part VII," *CI,* 179 (May 1990), 53.

Gamble, Warburton [actor] (b. England, 1883?–27 Aug 1945 [62]). m. Gillian Amy Scaife (d. 1976). AS, p. 427 (d. 25 Aug, LA CA). BHD1, p. 206. IFN, p. 112. SD.

Gamboa, Elias [actor] (b. Mexico, 20 Jul 1895–9 Dec 1959 [64], Los Angeles CA). BHD, p. 175.

Gance, Abel [scenarist/actor/director/producer] (*né* Eugène Alexandre Perethon, b. Paris, France, 25 Oct 1889–10 Nov 1981 [92], Paris, France; pulmonary edema). Lenny Borger, "Abel Gance, 92, Dies in Paris; Reputation Recently Restored," *Variety,* 18 Nov 1981. AMD, p. 130. AS, pp. 427–28. BHD, p. 175; BHD2, p. 94. FDY, p. 425. "Abel Gance Goes Back to France," *MPW,* 22 Oct 1921, 932. "Gance Announces Future Plans in Cable Dispatch," *MPW,* 19 Nov 1921, 322. Carl Bennett, "New Restoration of *Napoleon* Premieres," *CI,* 301 (Jul 2000), 17 (35 minutes have been added to the 1980 restortion; "An estimated 50 minutes of footage remains lost.").

Gandera, Félix [scenarist/director/producer] (b. Paris, France, 17 Feb 1885–15 Dec 1957 [72], Bougival, France). AS, p. 428. BHD2, p. 94.

Gandillot, Léon [actor/scenarist] (b. France, 1862–22 Sep 1912 [50?], Paris, France). AS, p. 428.

Gandolfi, Alfredo E. [singer/cameraman/executive] (b. Italy, 1885?–9 Jun 1963 [78], New York NY; anemia). m. Alice Kurkjian, 1934. (Cines [Rome]; Itila [Torino]; Pathè; American; Lasky; Morosco; Fox.) "Alfredo Gandolfi, 78, Dies; Former Baritone at Met [1929–36]," *NYT,* 10 Jun 1963, 31:2. AMD, p. 130 (Gandolfi); p. 141 (Gondolfi). "Ambrosio in America," *MPW,* 28 Sep 1912, 1260–61. "Gondolfi with Lasky," *MPW,* 27 Dec 1913, 1551. "Alfredo Gandolfi, Cameraman, Fox," *MPN,* 21 Oct 1916, 182.

Gandusio, Antonio [actor] (b. Rovigno d'Astria, Italy, 29 Jul 1875–23 May 1951 [75], Milan, Italy). AS, p. 428.

Gane, Nolan [actor/director/writer] (*né* Nolan Gagne, b. Houma LA–d. Sep 1914; pneumonia). AMD, p. 130. AS, p. 428 (d. 12 Feb 1915). BHD, p. 175 (d 12 Feb 1915). Truitt 1983, p. 263 (d. 12 Feb 1915). "Nolan Gane," *MPW,* 25 Apr 1914, 523. "Nolan Gane," *MPW,* 23 Jan 1915, 518. Q. David Bowers, *Muriel Ostriche; Princess of Silent Films* (NY: The Vestal Press, Ltd., 1987), p. 98.

Gangelin, Paul [scenarist] (b. Milwaukee WI, 1897?–25 Sep 1961 [64], Los Angeles CA; heart attack). (Began 1922.) "Paul Gangelin," *Variety,* 4 Oct 1961. AS, p. 428. BHD2, p. 94. FDY, p. 425. IFN, p. 112.

Ganguly, Dhiren [director/producer] (*né* Dhirenda Nath Gangopadhaya, b. Calcutta, India,

26 Mar 1893–18 Nov 1978 [85], Calcutta, India). AS, p. 428.

Gano, Glen [cinematographer, 1921–71]. No other data found.

Gant, Harry [actor/director/cinematographer] (b. Des Moines IA, 11 Feb 1881–26 Jul 1967 [86], Sunland CA). AS, p. 428 (d. LA CA). BHD, p. 175; BHD2, p. 94 (d. LA CA). IFN, p. 112.

Gantillon, Simon [writer/scenarist] (b. Lyon, France, 7 Jan 1891–9 Sep 1961 [70], France). AS, p. 428.

Gantvoort, Carl [actor/opera singer] (b. Bowling Green KY, 1883?–28 Sep 1935 [52], Los Angeles CA; from injuries received in a fall). "Carl Gantvoort," *Variety,* 9 Oct 1935 (d. 30 Sep; "He also did some picture work in the silent days."). AS, p. 428. IFN, p. 112.

Gantvoort, Herman L. [scenarist/producer] (aka William "Bill" Holland, b. Oxford OH, 1887?–17 Sep 1937 [50], New York NY). "Herman L. Gantvoort," *Variety,* 22 Sep 1937 ("active in pictures in the pre-sound era"). AMD, p. 130. AS, p. 428. BHD2, p. 94. "Gantvoort a Producer," *MPW,* 3 Jan 1925, 72 (produced *Fool's Gold* w8ith Shirley Booth and Humphrey Bogart). "This Producer is Producing," *MPW,* 6 Jun 1925, 626.

Ganzhorn, John W. [actor] (aka Jack Ganshorn, b. Ft. Thomas AR, 21 Mar 1881–19 Sep 1956 [75], Los Angeles CA). "John W. Ganzhorn," *Variety,* 26 Sep 1956 ("retired screen actor"). AS, p. 428. BHD, p. 175. IFN, p. 112. Truitt, p. 120.

Garat, Edouard [actor] (*né* Edouard Garasse, b. France, 1865–6 Jun 1909 [44?], Paris, France; suicide by shooting). AS, p. 428.

Garat, Henri [actor] (*né* Emile Henri Camille Garassu, b. Paris, France, 3 Apr 1902–13 Aug 1959 [57], Hyeres, France [extrait de décès no. 209/1959]). AS, p. 428.

Garavaglia, Ferruccio Giovita [stage/film actor] (b. San Zenone, Po, Italy, 1 May 1868–29 Apr 1912 [43], Naples, Italy). AS, p. 428. BHD, p. 175 (b. Poland). IFN, p. 112. JS, p. 183 (in Italian silents from 1909).

Garaveo, Onorato [actor] (b. Genoa, Italy, 2 Dec 1888–31 Mar 1926 [37], Genoa, Italy). JS, p. 183 (in Italian silents from 1919).

Garber, David S. [art director] (b. Floyd Knobbs IN, 9 Oct 1900–30 Mar 1984 [83], Beverly Hills CA). BHD2, p. 94. MPG.

Garbo, Greta (sister of **Alva Gustafsson**; brother of **Sven Garbo**) [actress] (*née* Greta Lovisa [her mother's name] Gustafsson, b. Stockholm, Sweden, 18 Sep 1905–15 Apr 1990 [84], New York NY [Death Certificate Index No. 36064]). Mercedes de Acosta, *Here Lies the Heart.* Barry Paris, *Garbo; A Biography* (NY: Alfred A. Knopf, 1995. In her eighth decade, Garbo had no great 'last' project to complete, no discernible personal dilemma to be resolved."). Karen Swenson, *Greta Garbo: A Life Apart* (NY: Scribner, 1997). (Film debut: *How Not to Dress,* 1921; short for Paul U. Bergström [PUB] department store emporium; MGM). "Greta Garbo, 84, Screen Icon Who Fled Her Stardom, Dies," 1;5; "Greta Garbo Dies at 84; Traded Stardom for Silence," *NYT,* 16 Apr 1990, D11:1; "Garbo Funeral Service Is Conducted in Private," *NYT,* 18 Apr 1990, B6. Lawrence Cohn, "Garbo, Screen's Classiest Siren, Dies at 84," *Variety,* 18 Apr 1990. AMD, p. 131. AS, p. 429. BHD1, p. 206. FSFW, p. 203 (b. 1906). FSS, p. 117. HCH, p. 37. "Greta Garbo's First Film," *MPW,* 28 Nov 1925, 337. Alice L. Tildesley, "The Northern Star; The Screen's Newest Meteor Is a Moody Daughter of Sweden," *MPC,* May 1926, 52–53, 71, 77. Don Juan, "So This Is Hollywood," *Paris and Hollywood,* Oct 1926, 80 (*The Temptress,* filming at MGM, contains some vivid love scenes, such as "the one in which Greta Garbo confesses her love for Antonio Moreno after flouting the hero through seveal reels."). "Greta Garbo Is Triumphant Now," *MPW,* 12 Feb 1927, 490. "Greta Garbo Idle, as Fight Is Waged Over Her Contract," *MPW,* 19 Feb 1927, 557. "John Gilbert and Greta Garbo Not Married, They Tell the World," *MPW,* 5 Mar 1927, 32. "Temperament Proves Costly to Greta Garbo, Now Only Featured," *MPW,* 26 Mar 1927, 274. "Greta Garbo Signs Contract with Metro," *MPW,* 2 Apr 1927, 462. "Greta Is Really Ill This Time," *MPW,* 14 May 1927, 96. Dorothy Calhoun, "They Learned About Women from Her," *MPC,* Aug 1927, 36, 80. Katherin Albert, "Greta Garbo—Mysterious Star of the North," *Cinema Arts,* Oct 1927, 20–21, 45 ("At first I was not happy in my work. I could not understand the language and everyone talked too fast. Now I enjoy it. Now I am glad when the day begins and I can be at the studio to work."). Mary Sharon, "The Loneliest Girl in Pictures; Why Greta Garbo Contents Herself by Remaining in Seclusion," *Paris and Hollywood Screen Secrets,* Oct 1927, 64–66, 95 ("When questioned about her reported romance with John Gilbert, she denies that there has ever been a love affair...Greta Garbo has built a wall of reserve about herself and it is in her aloofness that lies the secret of much of her charm."). "Greta Garbo; The Girl on the Cover," *Cinema Arts,* Dec 1927, 29. Gilbert Adrian, "The Garbo Girl Sways the Mode," *Screenland,* Jan 1929, 26–27, 90, 101. Rilla Page Palmborg, "Greta Garbo Goes Home; For the Holidays Ostensibly. Will She Ever Retuirn?," *MPC,* Feb 1929, 21, 74 ("I have been yust dying to go home..."). Faith Service, "Garbo Never Sleeps; Insomnia Has Robbed Her of Romance and Happiness," *Movie Classic,* Sep 1931, 41. Toni Gallant, "Science Reveals Garbo's Character; Careful Study of Her Features Brings to Light the Real Reasons for Her Silence and Aloofness," *Movie Classic,* Oct 1931, 23, 75. "Garbo Won't Bite," *Variety,* 26 Apr 1932, 3:3 (contract negotiations with Metro "are definitely cold, star refusing to consider all stories held out thus far as bait. ¶Foreign girl evidently intends to go through with her plan to return to Sweden next month."). Cover, *Cinema Arts,* Jun 1937 (by Jaro Fabry). Janet Graves, "Hollywood Trademarks," *Cinema Arts,* Sep 1937, 38–39, 102 (a painting of Garbo, *Economy,* by Martin Kosleck, a satire of her "well-known habit of thrift"). Patti Goldstein, "Garbo Walks; ...The 72-year-old legend prowls the East Side of Manhattan causing waves of ditherish pleasure whenever she's recognized...," *New York,* 12 Dec 1977, 83–84 ("Some knowledgeable observers say she covers as much as four miles a day."). Jerome E. Shipman, "Cole Porter's Waspish Words [letter]," *NYTBR,* 15 Aug 1993, 27:1 (*Let's Not Talk About Love,* 1941: "If you know Garbo, then tell me this news/Is it a fact the Navy's launched all her old shoes?"). Eve Golden, "Garbo: The Mysterious Lady," *CI,* 228 (Jun 1994), C6, C8, C10. Patrick McGilligan, "Less Than Met the Eye," *NYTBR,* Sec. 7, 2 Apr 1995, p. 3 (review of Barry Paris, *Garbo* [NY: Alfred A. Knopf, 1995]; "According to this biography, the private Garbo was not nearly as fascinating as the one on screen."). Gray Horan, "Lost and Found: 10 Rich Minutes of Early Garbo," *NYT,* 11 Jun 1995, II, 15:1. "Sweden Lays Garbo, Native Daughter, to Rest," *NYT,* 17 Jun 1999, C23 ("Nine years after her death at 84 in New York, Greta Garbo's ashes were buried at her birtthplace outside Stockholm yesterday. Caroline Krook, Bishop of Stockholm, led Garbo's relatives through the cemetary."). Barry Paris, "Letter Bombs?; [Rosenbach] Museum [Philadelphia] will open [on April 15, the 10th anniversary of her death] Garbo correspondence to alleged socialite lover [Mercedes de Acosta, 1893–1968]," *Pittsburgh Post-Gazette,* 13 Apr 2000, D1, D2 ["Mercedes was in love with Garbo and felt linked to her by destiny. In 1931, she moved to Hollywood to work on the script of a Pola Negri film and met Garbo. Mercedes was swept away. Garbo was reciprocally delighted with her new playmate, and 48 hours later they spent an intimate day alone together."]. Dinitia Smith, "Letters Push Garbo Slightly into View; Unsealing clues to a long, ambiguous relationship with another woman," *NYT,* 18 Apr 2000, E-3 ("The nature of Garbo's sexuality has always been debated because for more than 20 years she communicated an electreic and ambiguous sexuality that riveted moviegoers and a larger public.... In 1960 Acosta published her autobiography, and Garbo never spoke to her again."). Barry Paris, "Letters opened [written from 1931 to 1959], but mystery around Garbo lives on; 'There is no concrete evidence that any sexual relationship between these two women ever existed,'" *PP-G,* 18 Apr 2000, D-7 (Garbo's great niece, Gray Horan, said of the letters: "The letters indicate that they had a long-lasting friendship, one that had its ups and downs, but one that could not be characterized as tumultuous or amorous."). Barry Paris, "Garbo and Mercedes: Read between the lines [to solve the mystery]," *PP-G,* 24 Apr 2000, D1, D5 {"The new cache of Garbo letters does not confirm their 'lover' status in overt Harlequin romance or American sexual terms—hence the general conclusion of a mystery unsolved. ¶But the answer is wonderfully simple and obvious in the newly revealed letters to anyone who stops to think about the objective reality and DUALITY of the relationship..."}.

Garbo, Sven (brother of **Greta Garbo**) [actor] (*né* Sven Gustafsson, b. Stockholm, Sweden, 1898–1967 [69?], Santa Fe NM). AS, p. 429.

Garbutt, Frank A. [cinematographer/producer/executive] (b. 1869?–19 Nov 1947 [78], Los Angeles CA). "Frank A. Garbutt," *Variety,* 26 Nov 1947 (helped to organize Paramount in 1912). AMD, p. 131. AS, p. 428. BHD, p. 175. IFN, p. 113. "Another Combination of Picture Companies," *MPW,* 21 Oct 1916, 376.

Garbutt, Frank E. [actor] (b. 1895?–14 Nov 1938 [43], Los Angeles CA). (Paramount.) "Frank E. Garbutt," *Variety,* 23 Nov 1938. AS, p. 429.

Garchery, Gaston [actor] (b. Paris, France, 23 Feb 1896). AS, p. 429.

Garcia, Allan Ernest [actor] (b. San Francisco CA, 11 Mar 1887–4 Sep 1938 [51], Los Angeles CA). (Selig; Vitagraph; Chaplin.) "Allen Garcia," *Variety,* 7 Sep 1938. AS, p. 429. BHD1, p. 207. IFN, p. 113. George Katchmer, "Remembering the Great Silents," *CI,* 223 (Jan 1994), 49:1.

Garcia, Luce [actress] (*née* Lucienne Garcia-Ville, b. France, 1905–13 May 1965 [60?], Paris, France). AS, p. 429.

Garcia, May [actress/costume designer] (b. 1868?–17 Aug 1950 [82], New York NY). "Mrs. May Garcia Storey," *Variety,* 23 Aug 1950. AS, p. 429. BHD, p. 175.

Garcia, Roberto Seanu]producer/director] (b. Mexico, 6 Jun 1901–17 Jul 1951 [50], Mexico City, Mexico; suicide after the muder of Su Muy Key). AS, p. 429.

Garcia, Rosita [actress] (*née* Olga Garcia-Iniguez Ramirez, b. Montevideo, Uruguary, 11 Aug 1906–23 May 1997 [90], Culver City CA). "Rosita Garcia [obituary]," *CI,* 267 (Sep 1997), 54:3. AS, p. 429 (*née* Rosita Garcia Iniguez Enamorado). BHD1, p. 608.

Garcia, Sara [actress] (b. Orizaba, Mexico, 8 Sep 1895–21 Nov 1980 [85], Mexico City, Mexico). AS, p. 429. BHD, p. 175.

Garcon, Maurice [actor/scenarist] (b. Lille, France, 25 Nov 1889-Apr/May 1961 [71]). AS, p. 429.

Gardan, Julius [director] (*né* Juliusz Gardan, b. Warsaw, Poland, 1902–1945 [43?], Alma-Ata, Kazakistan). AS, p. 430. BHD2, p. 94.

Gardel, Carlos [singer/actor] (*né* Charles Romuald Gardes, b. Toulouse, France, 11 Dec 1890–24 Jun 1935 [44], Medellin, Columbia; plane crash). AS, p. 430 (b. 1887). BHD, p. 175. IFN, p. 113 (age 46). Waldman, p. 117 (b. 1891).

Gardelle, Yvonne (daughter of sculptor Carlton Gardelle) [actress] (aka Yvonne Chappelle, b. Chicago IL, 7 Oct 1897–21 Jul 1979 [81], Oceanside CA). BHD, p. 175. "Fooling Them in the Films; Noted Sculptor Bats for Thomas Meighan, Ladies' Man," *LA Times,* 2 Feb 1920, II, p. 12 (re sculptures in *The Prince Chap.* "Speaking of realism in motion pictures, Mr. [William] DeMille asserted that the public has begun to demand the real instead of camourflage in films, and that the producer who has the educational interest of the public at heart is dong his best to answer the demand.").

Garden, Mary [opera singer/actress] (b. Aberdeen, Scotland, 20 Feb 1874–3 Jan 1967 [92], Aberdeen, Scotland). "Mary Garden, 92, Opera Star, Dead; Soprano Won Distinction in Wide Variety of Roles," *NYT,* 5 Jan 1967, 1:5; "Mary Garden to Be Cremated," *NYT,* 6 Jan 1967, 35:3. "Mary Garden," *Variety,* 11 Jan 1967. AMD, p. 131. AS, p. 430. BHD, p. 175. IFN, p. 113. Spehr, p. 132. Truitt, p. 120. "Mary Garden Does Not Sail; Cancels Her Trip on the Lusitania, as Her Father Is Ill [with pneumonia]," *NYT,* 30 Jan 1915, 9:5 (transferred her reservation to the *Adriatic,* Feb,. 10). "Mary Garden Signs with Goldwyn," *MPW,* 17 Feb 1917, 1016. "Mary Garden," *MPW,* 24 Mar 1917, 1943. "Mary Garden Will Sing in Pictures," *MPW,* 23 Jun 1917, 1965. "Mary Garden to Arrive September 1," *MPW,* 25 Aug 1917, 1239. "Miss Farrar Calls on Miss Garden," *MPW,* 10 Nov 1917, 893. "Mary Garden," *MPW,* 24 Nov 1917, 1183. "Vampire Is Eternal, Says Mary Garden," *MPW,* 12 Jan 1918, 230. "Mary Garden in Paris Sees Herself on Screen," *MPW,* 8 Jun 1918, 1450. Paul Paige, "Close-Ups and Fade-Outs," *Paris and Hollywood,* Sep 1926, 90 (DeMille may film *Thais* again. Filmed about eight years previously by Goldwyn, the latter admitted that "his picture was far from being a masterpiece, and Mary Garden as a film actress was distinctly disappointing.").

Gardes, Renée [actress] (*née* Marie Noémie Gardes, b. Paris, France, 11 Jan 1887 [extrait de naissance no. 147]-6 Jan 1972 [], Paris, France [84]). AS, p. 430.

Gardin, Vladimir R. [actor/director/scenarist] (*né* Vladimir Rostislavovich, b. Moscow, Russia, 18 Jan 1877–28 May 1965 [88], Moscow, Russia). AS, p. 430 (Vladimir Gardine, b. 12 Jan; d. St. Petersburg, Russia). BHD, p. 175; BHD2, p. 94. IFN, p. 113.

Gardiner, Becky [scenarist]. No data found. FDY, p. 425.

Gardiner, Don [actor] (b. Peoria IL, 1902–5 Jun 1926 [24?], Los Angeles CA; suicide by gas inhalation). AS, p. 430. BHD, p. 176.

Gardiner, Reginald [actor] (*né* William Reginald Gardiner, b. Wimbledon, Surrey, England, 27 Feb 1903–7 Jul 1980 [77], Westwood CA; pneumonia and heart attack). AS, p. 430. BHD, p. 176.

Gardner, Amelia [actress] (b. Pittsburgh PA, 4 Sep 1866–11 Jan 1947 [80], Baltimore MD). BHD, p. 176.

Gardner, Buster [actor]. No data found. George A. Katchmer, "Forgotten Cowboys and Cowgirls—Part XIII," *CI,* 190 (Apr 1991), C6.

Gardner, Charles A. Karl, "The Sweet Singer of the Fatherland" [stage/film actor/composer/lyricist/singer] (b. 1847?–15 Feb 1924 [76]). (Began with Hooley Minstrels, Brooklyn NY, 1865.) "Charles A. Gardner," *Variety,* 21 Feb 1924, 6:5 ("He has been in poor financial circumstances for a number of years and, it is said, that the privations he suffered undermined his health.". AMD, p. 131. "Charles A. Gardner in Selig Specials," *MPW,* 3 Apr 1915, 83.

Gardner, Cyril [actor/director/producer/scenarist] (b. Paris, France, 30 May 1898–30 Dec 1942 [44], Los Angeles CA). (Ince; Universal; UA; Paramount.) "Cyril Gardner," *Variety,* 6 Jan 1943. AS, p. 430. BHD, p. 176; BHD2, p. 94. IFN, p. 113. Truitt, p. 120.

Gardner, George [actor] (b. 1868?–12 May 1929 [61], East Islip NY). m. Amelia Phillips. "George Gardner," *Variety,* 15 May 1929 ("He had appeared in a number of pictures"). AS, p. 430. BHD, p. 176. IFN, p. 113.

Gardner, Helen Louise [actress/producer] (b. Binghamton NY, 2 Sep 1884–20 Nov 1968 [84], Orlando FL). m. **Charles L. Gaskill** (d. 1943). (Vitagraph, 1911.) "Helen Louise Gardner," *Variety,* 4 Dec 1968. AMD, p. 131. AS, p. 430. BHD, p. 176. IFN, p. 113. Katz, p. 466 (b. 1885?). Slide, p. 140. "Helen Gardner to Have a Company of Her Own," *MPW,* 8 Jun 1912, 917. "Flickers," *MPW,* 19 Apr 1913, 289 (Helen Gardner Picture Players studio built in Tappan NY, 1912). "To Enlarge Helen Gardner Studio," *MPW,* 27 Sep 1913, 1378. "Address of Helen Gardner Features," *MPW,* 11 Oct 1913, 161. "Some Gardner Pictures for Warner," *MPW,* 22 Nov 1913, 873. "Helen Gardner," *MPW,* 19 Dec 1914, 1694. "Gaskill Leaves Vitagraph," *NYDM,* 14 Apr 1915, 34:2 (Gardner left with him). "Helen Gardner," *MPW,* 9 Oct 1915, 262. "Helen Gardner to Have Own Company," *MPW,* 5 Jan 1918, 56.

Gardner, Hunter [actor] (b. 1898?–16 Jan 1952 [53], Los Angeles CA; suicide by slashing wrists with a razor). "Hunter Gardner," *Variety,* 23 Jan 1952. AS, p. 430. IFN, p. 113.

Gardner, Jack [stage/film actor/casting director at Fox] (*né* John Edward Gardner, b. 1873–30 Sep 1950 [77], Encino CA). m. **Louise Dresser** (d.). "Jack Gardner," *Variety,* 4 Oct 1950, 63:4. AMD, p. 131. AS, p. 430. BHD, p. 176. IFN, p. 113. "Louise Dresser in Comedy Series," *MPW,* 16 Apr 1921, 737.

Gardner, Jack (brother of Horace Gardner) [vaudeville/film actor] (*né* John H. Gardner, b. 1876?–29 Dec 1929 [53], Glendale CA; heart attack). (Essanay; 1st National.) "Jack Gardner," *Variety,* XCVII, 1 Jan 1930, 59:4. AMD, p. 131. AS, p. 430. BHD, 176. IFN, p. 113. Truitt, p. 120. "Jack Gardner," *MPW,* 23 Jun 1917, 1969. "Richards and Flynn to Make Westerns Featuring Jack Gardner, Vaudevillian," *MPW,* 19 Jun 1920, 1616.

Gardner, Karl *see* **Gardner, Charles A.**

Gardner, Peter [stage/film actor] (b. 1898?–13 Nov 1953 [55], Studio City CA). "Peter Gardner," *Variety,* 25 Nov 1953 ("stage and screen actor for 35 years"). AS, p. 430. BHD, p. 176. IFN, p. 113. Truitt, p. 120.

Gardner, Shayle [actor] (b. Auckland, New Zealand, 22 Aug 1890–17 May 1945 [54]). BHD1, p. 208. IFN, p. 113.

Gargan, William Dennis (brother of Edward Gargan) (b. Brooklyn NY, 17 Jul 1905–17 Feb 1979 [73], on plane from NY to San Diego; heart attack). m. Mary Elizabeth Patrick Kenney, 19 Jan 1928, Baltimore MD. *Why Me?; An Autobiography* (Garden City NY: Doubleday & Co., Inc., 1969 (made film debut at Vitagraph with John Bunny and Lillian Walker; pp. 50–51). (Stage debut: Lyric Theatre, *Aloma of the South Seas,* 20 Apr 1925; adult film debut: *Misleading Lady,* Paramount, 1932.) Donald G. McNeil, Jr., "William Gargan, 73, Stage and TV Actor; Musical Star Taught Speech After Losing His Larnyx to Cancer [in 1960]," *NYT,* 18 Feb 1979, 40:1. AS, p. 431. BHD1, p. 208 (William Gargon, d. 16 Feb).

Gargiulo, Mario [director] (b. Naples, Italy). AS, p. 431. JS, p. 184 (in Italian silents from 1916).

Gariazzo, Pier Antonio [producer/director] (*né* Pietro Antonio Paolo Gariazzo, b. Turin, Italy, 7 Jun 1879 [extrait de naissance no. 102/1]-10 Jan 1964 [84], Turin, Italy). AMD, p. 131. AS, p. 431. JS, p. 184 (in Italian silents from 1912). "Famous Italian Director Made Weiss Brothers' Bible Films," *MPW,* 3 Dec 1921, 564.

Garland, Frank [actor] (d. 17 Nov 1935, Los Angeles CA; spinal meningitis). "Frank Garland," *Variety,* 20 Nov 1935.

Garland, Franklin [actor] (b. 1864?–5 May 1945 [81], Los Angeles CA). AS, p. 431. BHD, p. 176. IFN, p. 113.

Garland, Robert [scenarist] (b. Baltimore MD, 29 Apr 1895–27 Dec 1955 [60], New York NY). BHD2, p. 95.

Garmes, Lee [cinematographer/director/producer] (b. Peoria IL, 27 May 1898–31 Aug 1978 [80], Los Angeles CA). m. Ruth Hall. "Lee Garmes," *Variety,* 6 Sep 1978. AMD, p. 131. AS, p. 431. BHD2, p. 95. FDY, p. 459. IFN, p. 113. Katz, p. 468 (began 1916). "Ingram's Cameraman Arrives in France," *MPW,* 5 Feb 1927, 429. Joe Collura, "Artist with the Lens, Lee Garmes," *CI,* 99 (Sep 1983), 22 *et passim.*

Garnett, Tay [scenarist/director/producer] (*né* William Taylor Garnett, b. Santa Ana CA, 13 Jun 1894–3 Oct 1977 [83], Sawtelle CA; leukemia). m. (1) Helga Moray; **Patsy Ruth Miller** (d. 1995); (3) Mari Aldon. With Fredda Dudley Balling, *Light Your Torches, Pull Up Your Tights* (Arlington House, 1973). (Sennett; Roach; Pathé; Fox;

MGM.) Richard F. Shepard, "Tay Garnett, Film Director for Half Century, Dies," *NYT,* 19 Oct 1977, B2:2. "Tay Garnett," *Variety,* 12 Oct 1977. AS, p. 431. BHD, p. 176; BHD2, p. 95 (b. LA CA). FDY, pp. 425, 443 (dialogue for *The Spieler,* 1928). IFN, p. 113 (b. LA CA, 13 Jun). SD. Truitt 1983, p. 265 (b. 13 Jun 1893). John Roberts, "Films of Tay Garnett," *CI,* 173 (Nov 1989), 26, 43. John Wakeman, ed., *World Film Directors, Vol. I, 1890–1945* (NY: The H.W. Wilson Co., 1987), p. 385.

Garnier, Robert-Jules [set decorator] (*né* Jules Robert Garnier, b. Sevres, France, 29 Apr 1883–15 Apr 1958 [74], Condeau, France). AS, p.4 31.

Garon, Pauline [actress: Wampas Star, 1923] (*née* Marie Pauline Garon, b. Montreal, Canada, 9 Sep 1901–27 Aug 1965 [63], Patton CA). m. **Lowell J. Sherman** (d. 1934). AMD, p. 131. AS, p. 432 (d. Canada). BHD1, p. 208 (b. 1904). FFF, p. 231. FSS, p. 120. IFN, p. 113 (b. 1904). Katz, p. 469. MH, p. 112 (b. 1904). Truitt, p. 121. "With Paramount," *MPW,* 23 Sep 1922, 277. Faith Service, "The Eleventh Child," *Classic,* May 1923, 32–33, 75. "Two New Stars Signed by C.B.C.," *MPW,* 11 Aug 1923, 494. "Hodkinson Star Wins Popularity Contest," *MPW,* 29 Sep 1923, 434. Carolyn Carter, "Flap! Flap! Falp!; Here's Pauline Garon, the screen's flappiest flapper—Learn what Pauline has to say about 'em," *MW,* 22 Dec 1923, 3. "Pauline Garon Signed," *MPW,* 29 Mar 1924, 358. "Pauline Garon Signs," *MPW,* 9 May 1925, 190. "Sign Garon and Calhoun," *MPW,* 10 Sep 1927, 78. Elisabeth Greer, "Pauline Garon Advises Everyone to Keep on Dreaming," *Pictures,* Jun 1926, 57, 114–15.

Garrett, Oliver H.P. [journalist/scenarist/playwright/director] (b. New Bedford MA, 23 Jun 1897 [MVRB, Vol. 466, p. 291]–22 Feb 1952 [54], New York NY; heart attack). m. Charlcie Hedge, 1939. "O.H.P. Garrett, 54, Film Writer, Dies; Former Newspaper Man Here Was Co-Winner in 1934 of 'Oscar' for Screen Play," *NYT,* 4 Feb 1952, 84:3 (age 54). "Oliver H.P. Garrett," *Variety,* 27 Feb 1952 (age 58). AS, p. 432 (b. 1893). BHD2, p. 95 (b. 6 May 1894). FDY, p. 425. IFN, p. 114 (age 58). SD, p. 489.

Garrett, Otis [director/editor/scenarist] (b. 1893–24 May 1941 [48?], Glendale CA; complications from a stomach operation). AS, p. 432 (b. 1895). BHD2, p. 95.

Garrett, Pat [actor] (b. 1850–1908 [58?]). AS, p. 432.

Garrett, Pauline (mother of **Clara Kimball Young**) [actress] (aka Pauline Kimball, b. Chicago IL, 15 Mar 1860–11 Dec 1919 [59], Los Angeles CA). m. **Edward M. Kimball** (d. 1938). AMD, p. 373 (under Young, Clara Kimball). AS, p. 609 (Puline Kimball). BHD, p. 218 (Pauline Garrett Kimball). IFN, p. 165 (Pauline Garrett Kimball). "Clara Kimball Young's Mother Dead in Los Angeles," *MPW,* 27 Dec 1919, 1108 (*née* Pauline Maddern, d. 12 Dec).

Garrick, Alice [scenarist]. No data found. FDY, p. 425.

Garrick, John [actor] (*né* Reginald Dandy, b. Brighton, England, 31 Aug 1902–22 Oct 1966 [64], San Francisco CA). AS, p. 432. BHD1, p. 208. MPG.

Garrick, Richard T. [actor/director/producer] (b. Ireland, 27 Dec 1878–21 Aug 1962 [83], Los Angeles CA). "Richard T. Garrick," *Variety,* 5 Sep 1962 ("longtime actor"). AMD, p. 131. AS, p. 432 (b. 28 Dec). BHD, p. 176; BHD2, p. 95. IFN, p. 114. "Richard Garrick Joins the Gaumont Co.," *MPW,* 11 Sep 1915, 1835. "Garrick Makes Flying Trip to New York," *MPW,* 1 Jan 1916, 85. "RIichard Garrick's Company in Everglades," *MPW,* 4 Mar 1916, 1457.

Garrison, Lindley Miller [actor] (b. Camden NJ, 28 Nov 1864–18 Oct 1932 [67], Sea Bright NJ). BHD, p. 176.

Garrison, Lurleen [actress]. No data found. AMD, p. 131. "New Talent," *MPW,* 12 Jun 1926, 7.

Garrity, Harry [actor] (b. NJ, 15 Nov 1872–13 Dec 1928 [56], Los Angeles CA). AS, p. 432. BHD, p. 176. IFN, p. 114. Truitt 1983, p. 266.

Garrity, Marie "Baby Marie" [actress]. No data found. AMD, p. 131. "Marie Garrity," *MPW,* 22 Aug 1914, 1098.

Garry, Claude [actor] (b. 1877-Aug 1918 [41?], Paris, France). BHD, p. 176.

Garry, Joseph R. [actor] (b. Marietta OH, 14 Aug 1877–7 Jun 1954 [76], Marietta OH). AS, p. 432 (b. 1876). BHD1, p. 209. IFN, p. 114 (age 77).

Garson, Harry I. [director] (b. Rochester NY, 1882?–21 Sep 1938 [56], Los Angeles CA). m. **Clara Kimball Young** (d. 1960). "Harry Garson," *Variety,* 28 Sep 1938. AMD, p. 131. AS, p. 432. BHD, p. 176; BHD2, p. 95. IFN, p. 114. "Harry Garson Gets Ready to Expand,m" *MPW,* 4 Jan 1919, 62. "Harry Garson to Make Katterjohn Specials," *MPW,* 31 May 1919, 1388. "Mrs. Garson Dies," *MPW,* 25 Dec 1920, 1057 (mother, Mrs. I. Harry Garson, d. 13 Dec 1920 [55]; heart trouble).

Garson, Isaac [producer] (b. 1857–10 Sep 1939 [82?], Los Angeles CA). AS, p. 432. BHD2, p. 95.

Garsson, Murray W. [entrepreneur] (b. London, England, 14 May 1891–26 Mar 1957 [65], New York NY; brain hemorrhage after fall down stairs). m. (1) Rose (d. 1942); (2) Ruth Levy—div. 1952. "Murray Garsson Dies in Poverty; War Profiteer Imprisoned in 1949 for Bribery, Was a Homeless Man at 65," *NYT,* 28 Mar 1957, 32:1 ("active in various motion picture and real estate ventures").

Gartner, Adolph [actor/director/producer] (b. Berlin, Germany, 24 Jul 1880–9 Jan 1958 [77], Los Angeles CA). AS, p. 432. BHD, p. 176; BHD2, p. 95.

Gartner, Heinrich [cinematographer]. No data found. FDY, p. 459.

Garver, Oliver B. [publicist] (b. Peoria IL, 11 Mar 1900–13 Mar 1952 [52], Sawtelle CA). AMD, p. 131. BHD2, p. 95. "Garver Joins DeMille," *MPW,* 28 Nov 1925, 336.

Garvey, Louis [publicist]. No data found. AMD, p. 131. "Garvey on Job," *MPW,* 5 Feb 1927, 423.

Garvie, Edward E. [actor] (b. Meriden CT, 30 Oct 1864–17 Feb 1939 [74], New York NY). "Edward E. Garvie," *Variety,* 22 Feb 1939, p. 71 (age 73). AS, p. 432. BHD1, p. 209. IFN, p. 114 (age 73).

Garvin, Anita [descendant of Stonewall Jackson] [actress] (b. New York NY, 11 Feb 1906–7 Jul 1994 [88], Woodland Hills CA). (Sennett; Christie; Roach; Columbia; RKO.) m. Clifford "Red" Stanley, 1930 (d. 1980). AMD, p. 132. AS, p. 433 (b. 1907). BHD1, p. 209. FSS, p. 120. "Anita Garvin Off 'Vamp' Characters," *MPW,* 5 Feb 1927, 432. "Anita Garvin," *MPW,* 26 Mar 1927, 386. Steve Randisi, "The Gal Who Knew the Boys; An Interview with Anita Garvin," *Filmfax,* Aug/Sep 1993, 42–49 (retired in 1942). William T. Sherman, "Remembering Anita Garvin," *CI,* 240 (Jun 1995), 38, 40.

Garwood, William Davis, Jr. [stage/film actor/director] (b. Springfield MO, 28 Apr 1884–28 Dec 1950 [66], Los Angeles CA; cirrhosis of the liver from chronic alcoholism and coronary occlusion). (Thanhouser, 1909; Majestic; American; Imp; Victor; Bluebird; Universal; Ince; FP-L; Rolfe.) AMD, p. 132. AS, p. 433. BHD, pp. 26–28; 176; BHD2, p. 95. IFN, p. 114. "Garwood Rejoins Thanhouser," *MPW,* 13 Jul 1912, 135. "'Billy' Garwood, Motor Maniac," *MPW,* 5 Oct 1912, 56. "Billy Garwood Joins 'Flying A,'" *MPW,* 11 Apr 1914, 196. "Leading American Players," *MPW,* 11 Jul 1914, 240–42. "Garwood Playing Characters," *MPW,* 5 Sep 1914, 1384. "William Garwood with Universal," *MPW,* 28 Nov 1914, 1238. "William Garwood; Star of the Imp Company," *MPS,* 1 Jan 1915, 25. "Garwood Now Directs," *MPW,* 30 Jan 1915, 654. "William Garwood to Support Enid Bennett," *MPW,* 30 Dec 1916, 1936. Billy H. Doyle, "Lost Players," *CI,* 143 (May 1987), C6-C7, 40.

Gascon, Edward E. [vaudevillian/actor/director] (b. 1873?–10 Jan 1965 [93], Conesus NY). m. (1) Lillian (d. 1950); (2) d. 1962. "Edward E. Gascon," *Variety,* 20 Jan 1965, p. 71 (blind during his last five years).

Gaskill, Charles L[enoir] [actor/director/producer] (b. New Bern NC, 29 Jan 1869–9 Dec 1943 [74], Los Angeles CA; heart attack). m. **Helen Gardner** (d. 1968). (Vitagraph.) "Charles Gaskell," *Variety,* 15 Dec 1943. AMD, p. 132. AS, p. 433 (Gaskell, b. 19 Jan 1870). BHD, p. 176; BHD2, p. 95 (b. 1870). IFN, p. 114. Truitt 1983, p. 266 (b. 1870). "Gossip of the Studios; Charles L. Gaskill," *NYDM,* 1 Apr 1914, 39:2 (produced the first 6,000-foot film in the U.S.). "New Vitagraph Play by Gaskill," *MPW,* 5 Dec 1914, 1398. "Gaskill Leaves Vitagraph," *NYDM,* 14 Apr 1915, 34:2.

Gasnier, Louis J. [actor/stage/film director/producer] (b. Paris, France, 15 Sep 1875–15 Feb 1963 [87], Los Angeles CA). (Began 1906; French and American Pathé; MGM; Paramount; Astra Film Co.) "Louis Gasnier," *Variety,* 27 Feb 1963. AMD, p. 132. AS, p. 433 (b. 26 Sep). BHD2, p. 95. Katz, p. 470 (b. 1878). Waldman, p. 118 (b. 1878). Louis Reeves Harrison, "Studio Saunterings," *MPW,* 16 Mar 1912, 944–45. "He Makes the Rooster Crow," *NYDM,* 28 Jul 1915, 21:3 (stage actor at age 16, Paris; estabished the Film D'Art in Italy, 1910.). "Gasnier Forms Producing Company," *MPW,* 18 Mar 1916, 1834. "Asta in the Front Ranks of Producers," *MPW,* 2 Sep 1916, 1519. "Louis Gasnier Returns to Direct Mae Marsh in Special Productions," *MPW,* 24 Jan 1920, 603. "Robertson-Cole Signs Louis J. Gasnier to Make Four Great Productions Yearly," *MPW,* 23 Oct 1920, 1122. "Gasnier and Forman Sign with Preferred Pictures," *MPW,* 19 Aug 1922, 583. "Gasneir Is Doing His Supreme Work," *MPW,* 27 Jan 1923, 365. "Gasneir to Continue to Direct for Schulberg," *MPW,* 30 Aug 1924, 723. "Roach Signs Up Henry Lehrman and Louis J. Gasnier," *MPW,* 7 May 1927, 41.

Gaston, George [actor] (b. 1844–14 Jan 1937 [92?], Englewood NJ). BHD, p. 176.

Gaston, Mae [actress] (b. Boston MA, 1894). (Majestic; Fine Arts; Horsley; Universal; Selig; Paul Smith Picture Co.; Francis Ford Prods.) AMD, p. 132. BHD, p. 176 (b. ca. 1890). MSBB, p. 1034. "Mae Gaston with Horsley," *MPW,* 25 Mar 1916, 2017.

Gastrock, Philip [actor] (b. Los Angeles CA, 26 Oct 1876–10 Apr 1956 [79], Woodland Hills CA). (Paramount.) AS, p. 433. BHD, p. 176. IFN, p. 114.

Gates, Bert [actor] (b. 1883?–18 Dec 1952 [69?], Aberdeen, Scotland). "Bert Gates," *Variety,* 31 Dec 1952 ("early film pioneer"). AS, p. 433 (b. England). Truitt, p. 121.

Gates, Eleanor [writer] (b. Shakopee MN, 26 Sep 1875–7 Mar 1951 [75], Los Angeles CA; blood clot in the lungs after being struck by an autonmobile). m. (1) Richard Walton Tully, 1901–14 (d. 1945); (2) Frederick E. Moore—div. (d. 1924). "Eleanor Gates, 75, Wrote Many Plays; Author of 'Poor Little Rich Girl' and Other Productions Dies on Coast After Accident," *NYT,* 8 Mar 1951, 29. "Eleanor Gates," *Variety,* 14 Mar 1951. AMD, p. 132. "Eleanor Gates in Photoplay Field," *MPW,* 30 May 1914, 1269. "First Eleanor Gates Film," *NYDM,* 1 Jul 1914, p. 24 (*Doc,* run serially in *The Saturday Evening Post,* was to be the first 3-reel film released by the Eleanor Gates Photo Play Company, Mt. Kisco NY, directed by Richard Garrick). "Reorganize Gates Company," *NYDM,* 8 Jul 1914, p. 32 (moved from Mt. Kisco).

Gates, Harvey H. [publicist/scenarist] (b. HI, 19 Jan 1894–4 Nov 1948 [54], Los Angeles CA). m. Eleanor Brown. (Began 1912; last film, *Flashing Guns,* Monogram, 1947.) AMD, p. 132. FDY, pp. 425, 443 (dialogue for *The Terror,* 1928). "Universal Publicity Staff," *MPW,* XXI, 26 Sep 1914, 1756–57. "Harvey Gates a Free Lance Writer," *MPW,* 20 Feb 1915, 1144. "Harvey Gates Added to Goldwyn's Scenario Staff," *MPW,* 24 May 1919, 1142. "Gates Returns to Universal," *MPW,* XL, 28 Jun 1919, 1909. "Metro Adds Harvey H. Gates and Percy Heath as Writers," *MPW,* 3 Apr 1920, 126. "Signs Harvey Gates," *MPW,* 21 Jun 1924, 702. "Warners Sign Harvety Gates," *MPW,* 29 Jan 1927, 351. Ravished Armenia *and the Story of Aurora Mardiganian,* comp. Anthony Slide (Scarecrow: Lanham MD, 1997), p. 6.

Gates, Ruth [actress] (*née* Pearson Gates, b. Denton TX, 26 Oct 1884–23 May 1964 [79], New York NY). AS, p. 433.

Gatzert, Nate [art director/scenarist] (b. IL, 15 Dec 1890–1 Sep 1959 [68], Los Angeles Co. CA). BHD2, p. 95.

Gaudio, Eugene (brother of **Antonio Gaudio**) [cinematographer] (b. Italy, 1886–1 Aug 1920 [34?], Los Angeles CA; after appendicitis operation). A.H. Giebler, "Los Angeles News Letter; Noted Cinematographer Dies," *MPW,* 21 Aug 1920, 1009 (buried in Hollywood Cemetery). AMD, p. 132. BHD2, p. 95. "Jean Gaudio Was Submarine Comeraman," *MPW,* 7 Oct 1916, 78 (pohotographed *20,000 Leagues Under the Sea,* Universal, 1916). "Cameraman Gaudio Battles with Old Altnatic's Waves," *MPW,* 19 Oct 1918, 389. "High Grade Double-Exposure Work Seen in 'Life's Twist,'" *MPW,* 24 Jul 1920, 483.

Gaudio, Tony [Antonio] (brother of **Eugene Gaudio**) [cinematographer/director] (*né* Gaetano Antonio Gaudio, b. Cosenza, Italy, 2 Apr 1885 [extrait de naissance no. 174]–9 Aug 1951 [66], Burlingame CA). (Vitagraph.) "Tony Gaudio, 66, Film Cameraman, 1937 Academy Award Winner for 'Anthony Adverse' Dies—First to Use Montage," *NYT,* 11 Aug 1951, 11:6. "Gaetano (Tony) Gaudio," *Variety,* 15 Aug 1951. AMD, p. 132. AS, p. 434. BHD2, p. 95 (d. 8 Aug). FDY, p. 459. IFN, p. 114. Katz, pp. 471–72. *The International Dictionary of Films and Filmmakers,* Vol. IV (London: St. James Press, 1987) (b. Cosenza, Italy). "Cameraman Gaudio Joins Mutual," *MPW,* 1 Jul 1916, 78. Antonio Gaudio, "Difficulties of Screen Photography," *MPW,* 21 Jul 1917, 392–93. "Gaudio Joins Mayer's Staff," *MPW,* 13 Sep 1919, 1630. "Gaudio to Photograph 'Kismet,'" *MPW,* 17 Jul 1920, 354.

Gaultier, Henry [actor] (b. France, 1888–29 Apr 1972 [84?], Paris, France). AS, p. 434.

Gaumont, Léon Ernest (father of **Louis** and **Raymond Gaumont**) [inventor/producer] (b. Paris, France, 10 May 1864–11 Aug 1946 [82], Sainte-Maxime-sur-Mer, the Riviera, France). m. (sons Louis and Raymond). "Leon Gaumont, 82, Film Pioneer, Dies; Early French Producer Made Synchronized Talkies in 1910—Began Color Pictures," *NYT,* 12 Aug 1946, 21:3. "Leon Gaumont, Pioneer in Film Production, Dies in France at 82," *Variety,* 14 Aug 1946. AMD, p. 132. AS, p. 434 (d. 9 Aug). BHD2, p. 95. IFN, p. 114. WWVC, pp. 55–56. "Leon Gaumont Coming to New York," *MPW,* 10 May 1913, 574. "Leon Gaumont in New York," *MPW,* 7 Jun 1913, 1033. Hugh Hoffman, "The Gaumont Chronochrome," *MPW,* 28 Jun 1913, 1346. "Leon Gaumont Visits America," *MPW,* 1 Apr 1916, 95. W. Stephen Bush, "Leon Gaumont on a Visit," *MPW,* 8 Apr 1916, 233. "Gaumont Finds Conditions Good," *MPW,* 22 Apr 1916, 597. "Gaumont Returning to France, Says He Will Organize American Company in Fall," *MPW,* 31 Jul 1920, 582.

Gaumont, Louis (son of **Léon Gaumont**; brother of **Raymond Gaumont**) [producer] (b. Paris, France, 7 May 1899). AS, p. 434.

Gaumont, Raymond (son of **Léon Gaumont**; brother of **Louis Gaumont**) [cameraman]. No data found. AMD, p. 132. "Gaumont, Jr., in America," *MPW,* 1 Jun 1912, 813.

Gauntier, Gene, "The Kalem Girl" [actress/scenarist] (*née* Genevieve Liggett, b. Kansas City MO, 17 May 1885–18 Dec 1966 [81], Cuernavaca, Mexico). m. **Jack J. Clark**, 1912, Palestine (d. 1947). "Genevieve G. Liggett (Gene Gauntier)," *Variety,* 28 Dec 1966. AMD, p. 132. AS, p. 434. BHD, p. 176 (b. ca. 1880); BHD2, p. 95 (b. 1891). IFN, p. 114. Truitt, p. 121 (b. 1880). "Taking Pictures Under Difficulties," *MPW,* 16 Sep 1911, 784. "O'Kalems Return," *MPW,* 14 Oct 1911, 136. "Kalem Players Go South," *MPW,* 18 Nov 1911, 560. "A Voice from the Desert," *MPW,* 2 Mar 1912, 771. "Miss Gene Gauntier Returns," *MPW,* 13 Jul 1912, 153 (parents lived in Beaumont TX). "Picture Players at a Turkish Wedding," *MPW,* 20 Jul 1912, 253–54 (married Clark). "Gauntier Feature Players," *MPW,* 21 Dec 1912, 1169. "Miss Gauntier Wants," *MPW,* 18 Jan 1913, 258. "Gene Gauntier Players at Work," *MPW,* 18 Jan 1913, 274. "Gene Gauntier Players Return," *MPW,* 31 May 1913, 926. "Gauntier Players in Ireland," *MPW,* 4 Oct 1913, 39. George Blaisdell, "At the Sign of the Flaming Arcs," *MPW,* 27 Dec 1913, 1548 ("22 years old"). "Gene Gauntier Players' New Studio," *MPW,* 21 Feb 1914, 964. "Gene Gauntier Entertains Brooklyn Fans," *MPW,* 28 Mar 1914, 1662. Hanford C. Judson, "Gene Gauntier and Players in New Studio," *MPW,* 4 Jul 1914, 73. "Gene Gauntier Takes European Vacation," *MPW,* 18 Jul 1914, 439. "Miss Gauntier Returns from Europe," *MPW,* 12 Sep 1914, 1524. "Gene Gauntier with Universal," *MPW,* 27 Mar 1915, 1942. "Studio Gossip," *NYDM,* 7 Jul 1915, 41:1 (director Jack Clark and Gauntier crashed their car into a fence. Gauntier was thrown against an iron rail "sustaining very bad bruises over the entire head and cuts and abrasions on the face and neck. Mr. Clark was fortunately uninjured."). "Gene Gauntier Has Narrow Escape," *MPW,* 17 Jul 1915, 501. "Gene Gauntier Is Photoplay Editor," *MPW,* 22 Feb 1919, 1021 (*Daily Post,* Kansas City MO).

Gauthier, Georges [actor/director] (b. France, 1894). AS, p. 434.

Gauthier, Suzanne [actress] (b. 1926–26 Jan 1988 [61?], Los Angeles CA). AS, p. 434. BHD, p. 176.

Gavette, Marie [actress]. (Centaur.) No data found.

Gavin, John F. [actor/director/producer] (d. Bronte, New South Wales, Australia, Feb 1938). BHD, p. 176; BHD2, p. 96.

Gawlikowski, Wieslaw [actress] (*née* Ludwik Pacholski, b. Poland, 1890–19 Mar 1933 [43?], Warsaw, Poland). AS, p. 434.

Gawne, John N. [production manager] (b. 1888–30 Dec 1930 [42?], Los Angeles CA). BHD2, p. 96.

Gawood, Al [cameraman]. No data found. AMD, p. 133. "Lyons and Moran Complete Their 250th Production," *MPW,* 17 May 1919, 1064 ("...has been photographing the two comedians ever since they entered Universal's service").

Gawthorne, Peter [actor/writer] (b. Queen's County, Ireland, 1 Sep 1884–17 Mar 1962 [77], London, England). AS, p. 434.

Gaxton, William [actor] (*né* Arturo Gaxiola, b. San Francisco CA, 2 Dec 1893–2 Feb 1963 [69], New York NY). m. Madeline Cameron. "William Gaxton," *Variety,* 6 Feb 1963 (began 1926). AS, p. 435. BHD1, p. 210. IFN, p. 114. Truitt, p. 121.

Gay, Charles [actor/lion tamer] (b. France, 1887–23 Feb 1950 [62?], Nrwport Beach CA). BHD, p. 176. IFN, p. 114.

Gay, Dixie [actress] (b. 4 Oct 1911). MPG.

Gay, Fred [actor] (b. 1882?–11 Jun 1955 [73], Long Beach CA). "Fred Gay," *Variety,* 15 Jun 1955. AS, p. 435. BHD1, p. 210. IFN, p. 114.

Gay, Maisie [actress] (*née* Maisie Munro-Noble, b. London, England, 7 Jan 1878–13 Sep 1945 [67], London, England). "Maisie Gay," *Variety,* 19 Sep 1945 (age 62). AS, p. 435. BHD1, p. 210. IFN, p. 114. SD, p. 493 (b. 1883).

Gay, Walter [actor] (d. 8 Jan 1936). BHD, p. 176.

Gaye, Howard [actor] (b. Hitchin, Hertfordshire, England, 23 May 1878–26 Dec 1955 [77], London, England). (Kalem, 1912.) Unpublished "So This Was Hollywood" [at MoMA]. AS, p. 435. BHD, p. 177. IFN, p. 114.

Gayer, Echlin Philip [actor] (b. 1877?–14 Feb 1926 [48], New York NY; pneumonia). "Echlin Gayer," *Variety,* 17 Feb 1926. AS, p. 435. BHD, p. 177. IFN, p. 114.

Gaynor, Janet [actress: Wampas Star, 1926] (*née* Laura Augusta Gainer, b. Germantown, Philadelphia PA, 6 Oct 1906–14 Sep 1984 [77],

Palm Springs CA; pneumonia and complications from auto accident). m. **Gilbert A. Adrian**, 1939, Yuma AZ (d. 1959). Connie Billips, *Janet Gaynor; A Bio-Bibliography* (Westport CT: Greenwood Press, 1992). m. Jesse Lydell Peck, 11 Sep 1929–34; Gilbert Adrian, 14 Aug 1939 (d. 1957); Paul Gregory, 1964. (Film debut: *All Wet,* Roach 2-reeler, 1925; Universal; Fox; AA, 1927–28.) David Bird, "Janet Gaynor Is Dead at 77; First 'Best Actress' Winner," *NYT,* 15 Sep 1984, 30:1 (b. Philadelphia PA, 1906). "Janet Gaynor, 77, First Actress to Win Oscar, Dies in California," *Variety,* 19 Sep 1984. AMD, p. 133. AS, p. 435. BHD1, p. 210. FSFW, p. 222 (b. 1907). FSS, p. 120. Katz, pp. 472–73. "Janet Gaynor," WBO2, pp. 178–79. "Janet Gaynor," *MPW,* 26 Dec 1925, 768. "Janet Gaynor Signed by Fox to Long Term Contract," *MPW,* 30 Jan 1926, 442. Dorothy Cartwright, "Janet Gaynor, the Waltz Girl in a Jazz-Mad Age," *Parris and Hollywood,* Sep 1926, 9–10, 77 (the little Quaker maid from PA did extra work in six comedies at Universal, then appeared in *The Johnstown Flood* for Fox. First lead in *The Shamrock Handicap,* Fox. "One learns so much more by being versatile. I just won't get into a rut if I can help it!"). "Janet Gaynor," *MPW,* 30 Oct 1926, 549. "Janet Gaynor Elevated to Stardom," *MPW,* 2 Jul 1927, 36. Dorothy Calhoun, "Paging Cinderella; Janet's Life Is Just Like a Dream," *MPC,* Sep 1927, 37, 68. "Janet Gaynor," *MPW,* 29 Oct 1927, 550. Cover (with Charles Farrell), *Screen Book,* Jul 1928; illustrated novelization of *Street Angel,* pp. 4–59. "Janet Gaynor," *Cinema Arts,* Sep 1937, 13 (drawing by Theresa Schroder). David Ragan, *Movie Stars of the '30s* (Englewood Cliffs NJ: Prentice-Hall, Inc., 1985), p. 76.

Gaynor, Ruth [actress] (b. 1902–28 May 1919 [17?], Seattle WA). BHD, p. 177. IFN, p. 114.

Gaynor, Mayor William J. [actor] (b. Oneida NY, 1851–10 Sep 1913 [62?], aboard ship). BHD, p. 177.

Gear, Burton E[ugene] [actor] (b. 1865–23 Mar 1949 [84?], Los Angeles CA). AS, p. 435.

Gear, Luella Gardner van Nort [actress] (b. New York NY, 5 Sep 1897–3 Apr 1980 [82], New York NY). AS, p. 435. BHD1, p. 210.

Geary, [Maine] Bud [actor] (b. Salt Lake City UT, 15 Feb 1898–22 Feb 1946 [48], Los Angeles CA; result of injuries sustained in an auto crash). (Republic.) "Bud Geary," *Variety,* 27 Feb 1946 (age 47). AS, pp. 435–36. BHD1, p. 210. IFN, p. 114.

Gebhardt, Frank [actor] (d. 23 May 1951). BHD, p. 177. IFN, p. 114.

Gebhardt, George M. [actor] (b. Basle, Switzerland, 1879–2 May 1919 [40], Edensdale CA; tuberculosis). m. **Madeline West**. (Biograph, 1908; Bison.) AMD, p. 133. AS, p. 436. BHD, p. 177. IFN, p. 114. "The Most Perfect Indian Type," *MPW,* 22 Feb 1913, 766. "Gebhardt Joins Ramo," *MPW,* 16 May 1914, 942. "Praise for George Gebhardt," *MPW,* 13 Feb 1915, 995. "Obituary," *MPW,* 24 May 1919, 1161.

Gebhart, Albert [actor] (b. 1887–4 Jan 1950 [62?], East Orange NJ). BHD, p. 177. IFN, p. 114.

Gebuehr, Otto [stage/film actor] (b. Kettwig, Germany, 19 May 1877–13 Mar 1954 [76], Wiesbaden, West Germany; during production of *Rosen-Reslie*). m. (d. 1951). (Began in early 1920s.) "Otto Gebuehr," *Variety,* 31 Mar 1954, p. 71 (age 77). AS, p. 436. BHD1, p. 210. IFN, p. 115 (b. 29 May).

Gee, George D. [musicomedy/film actor] (b. Yorkshire, England, 1895–17 Oct 1959 [64?], Coventry, Warwick, England; during a performance of *The Merry Widow*). "George Gee," *Variety,* 28 Oct 1959, p. 71. AS, p. 436. BHD1, p. 210. IFN, p. 115.

Gee, George D. [actor/government informant] (d. 13 Dec 1917, 511 Rogers Avenue, Brooklyn NY; murdered). AMD, p. 133. AS, p. 436. BHD, p. 177. "Film Actor Murdered," *MPW,* 5 Jan 1918, 57 ("For many years, Gee had been an informant of the Government and aided the revenue agents trailing the scores of traffickers in drugs with the result that a price of $500 is said to have been placed on his head by tongs interested in the opium traffic.... Assistant United States District Attorney Edwin A. Stanton, who has successfully prosecuted many offtenders during the past few years, attributes the success of the Government to the information supplied by Gee." He was featured with Edna Goodrich in *Queen X,* "a sensational but realistic expose of the opium traffic.").

Geen, Frederick L[awrence] [actor/scenarist] (b. England, 1901–14 Apr 1953 [52?], Bristol, England). AS, p. 436.

Gehret, Jean [actor/director/scenarist] (b. Geneva, Switzerland, 10 Jan 1900–25 May 1956 [56], Paris, France). AS, p. 436.

Gehri, Alfred [director/scenarist] (b. Morges, Switzerland, 28 Mar 1895–8 Jan 1972 [76], Morges, Switzerland). AS, p. 436.

Gehrig, "Baby" Early *see* **Baby Early**

Gehring, Viktor [actor] (b. 10 Jan 1889–24 Apr 1978 [89]). BHD1, p. 210.

Gehrue, Mayme [actress]. No data found. "Grace Heather," *Variety,* 27 Jun 1913 (mother of Mayme d. 6 Jun 1913, New York NY).

Gehrung, Gene [actor] (b. 1882–19 Oct 1938 [55], Jacksonville FL). BHD, p. 177. IFN, p. 115 (Jean Gehrung).

Geisha, G. [actor/bull fighter] (d. 1913; killed by a bull). AMD, p. 133. "Cines Actor Is Killed by Maddened Bull," *MPW,* 6 Sep 1913, 1048.

Gelabert, Fructuoso [director/producer] (*né* Fructuoso Gelabert Badiella, b. Gracia, Spain, 15 Jan 1874–27 Feb 1955 [81], Barcelona, Spain). AS, p. 437.

Geldert, Clarence H. [stage/film actor] (b. St. John, N.B., Canada, 9 Jun 1867–13 May 1935 [67], Calabassas CA; heart attack). (Griffith; De Mille.) "Clarence Geldert," *Variety,* 15 May 1935 (age 68). AS, p. 437. BHD1, p. 210 (d. LA CA). IFN, p. 115. MSBB, p. 1024. Truitt, p. 122. George Katchmer, "Remembering the Great Silents," *CI,* 207 (Sep 1992), 42.

Geleng, Louis A.J. [cinematographer] (b. London, England, 24 Jul 1880-Dec 1962 [82]). BHD2, p. 96.

Gelman, Aleksandar Isaakovich [scenarist] (b. Russia, 25 Oct 1933). AS, p. 437.

Gelsey, Erwin S. [scenarist] (b. Poland, 1 Jan 1900–12 Dec 1988 [88], Beverly Hills CA). "Erwin S. Gelsey Dead; Screenwriter Was 88," *NYT,* 13 Dec 1988, B17:5. "Erwin Gelsey," *Variety,* 28 Dec 1988 (d. Los Angeles CA). AS, p. 437. BHD2, p. 96.

Gemelli, Enrico [actor] (b. Sant'Agata, Italy, 1841–7 May 1926 [85], Turin, Italy). BHD, p. 177 (Gamelli). JS, p. 188 (in Italian silents from 1914).

Gemier, Firmin [stage/film actor/director/scenarist/producer] (*né* Firmin Tonnerre, b. Aubervilliers, France, 13 Feb 1865–26 Nov 1933 [68], Paris, France; heart failure). "Firmin Gemier," *Variety,* 28 Nov 1933, p. 63. AMD, p. 133. AS, . 437. BHD1, p. 210. IFN, p. 115. "Firmin Gemier," *MPW,* 3 Apr 1926, 344.

Gemini, Italo [producer] (b. Italy, 1902–11 Sep 1984 [82?], Rome, Italy). AS, p. 437.

Gemora, Charles [actor] (b. Philippines, 15 Jun 1903–19 Aug 1961 [58], Los Angeles CA; heart attack). "Charlie Gemora," *Variety,* 30 Aug 1961. AS, p. 437 (b. 15 Aug). BHD1, p. 210 (b. 15 Aug). IFN, p. 115.

Gemp, Robert [actor] (d. Oct 1911). BHD1, p. 609.

Genaro, Frankie [actor] (b. 26 Aug 1901–12 Dec 1966 [65], Staten Island NY). BHD1, p. 609.

Gendron, Leon Pierre [actor/dialogue writer] (b. Toledo OH, 4 Mar 1896–27 Nov 1956 [60], Los Angeles CA). "Pierre Gendron," *Variety,* 5 Dec 1956. AMD, p. 133. AS, p. 437. BHD, p. 177; BHD2, p. 96. FDY, p. 443 (dialogue for *Sal of Singapore,* 1928) IFN, p. 115. Truitt, p. 122. "Leon Gendron Signed for Madge Kennedy," *MPW,* 15 May 1920, 969.

Genevois, Simone Roland Marthe [actress] (b. Paris, France, 13 Feb 1912 [extrait de naissance no. 489]-16 Dec 1995 [83], Ascona, Switzerland). m. (1) Jacques Pathé; (2) André Conti. (Eclipse; Eclair; early film: *Protéa ou les Mystères de Malmort,* 1917; last film: *Quand les feuilles tombent,* 1935.) Kevin Brownlow, "Simone Genevois," *The Independent,* 22 Dec 1995, p. 12. AS, p. 438. BHD1, p. 609.

Genevoix, Maurice [actor/scenarist] (*né* Charles Louis Maurice Genevoix, b. Decize, France, 29 Nov 1890–8 Sep 1980 [89], Alcante, Spain). AS, p. 438.

Geniat, Marcelle (mother of Gilberte Geniat) [actress] (*née* Eugénie Pauline Martin, b. St. Petersburg, Russia, 10 Jul 1881–27 Sep 1959 [78], L'Hay-les-Roses, France; cancer [extrait de décès no. 15/195]). AS, p. 438.

Genin, René [actor] (*né* Prosper René Genin, b. Aix-en-Provence, France, 25 Jan 1890–24 Oct 1967 [77], Paris, France). AS, p. 438.

Genina, Augusto (cousin of **Augusto** and **Mario Camerini**) [scenarist/director] (b. Rome, Italy, 28 Jan 1892–28 Sep 1957 [65], Rome, Italy; bronchial pneumonia). m. Carmela Bonicatti (**Carmen Boni**). (Scenarist, 1913; last film: *Frou-Frou,* France, 1955). "Augusto Genina," *Variety,* 9 Oct 1957, p. 71 (d. 29 Sep). AS, p. 438. BHD2, p. 96. IFN, p. 115. JS, pp. 189–90 (in Italian silents from 1913).

Gent, W.T. [director] (b. 1884–27 Aug 1952 [68?], Buxton, England). BHD2, p. 96.

Genthe, Arnold [photographer] (b. Berlin, Germany, 8 Jan 1869–9 Aug 1942 [73], Lake Candlewood CT). *As I Remember* (NY: Reynal & Hitchcock, 1936). "Dr. Genthe Is Dead; Photographer, 73; His Portraits of Presidents and Leading Figures of Stage Brought World Fame; Started in San Francisco; Took Notable Pictures of Fire and Earthquake in 1906—Art Patron and Writer," *NYT,* 11 Aug 1942, 19:1. WWWA (d. 8 Aug).

Gentry, Caroline [writer]. No data found.

AMD, p. 133. "Miss Gentry Meets Coal Operators," *MPW,* 25 May 1918, 1150.

Gentry, Gladys [actress]. No data found. AMD, p. 133. "Kentucky Society Girl Is to Be Screen Star," *MPW,* 9 Apr 1921, 624. "Gladys Gentry Productions, Inc., to Make Series of Productions," *MPW,* 21 May 1921, 310.

George, A.E. [actor] (b. Lincoln, England, 22 Jul 1889–28 Nov 1960 [71], Los Angeles Co. CA). BHD, p. 177.

George, Burton [actor/director/scenarist]. No data found. (Edison.) AMD, p. 133. "Another Edison Director," *NYDM,* LXXIV, 20 Nov 1915, 25:4 ("Mr. George is known as one of the most energetic directors in the business, the speed with which he turns out footage in no wise affecting the quality of the production."). "Burton George," *MPW,* 20 Nov 1915, 1481. "George Now a Fox Director," *MPW,* 25 May 1918, 1160. "Burton George Goes to New Hampshire for Scenes," *MPW,* 21 Feb 1920, 1239. "Burton George Signed by Selznick to Long Contract," *MPW,* 29 May 1920, 1220.

George, Ella Mae [actress] (b. 1883–27 May 1984 [101?], Los Angeles CA). AS, p. 438.

George, Franklin [actor] (b. Oil City PA, 1881?–16 Feb 1951 [69], Aberdeen WA). "Franklin George," *Variety,* 21 Feb 1951. AS, p. 438. BHD, p. 177.

George, George M. [actor] (b. St. Louis MO, 1888?–28 Nov 1960 [72], Los Angeles Co. CA). BHD, p. 177. IFN, p. 115.

George, Gladys [actress] (*née* Gladys Anna Clare, b. Patton ME, 13 Sep 1900–8 Dec 1954 [54], Los Angeles CA; cerebral hemorrhage). m. (1) Arthur Erway; (2) Leonard Penn (d. 1975); (3) Edward Fowler; (4) Kenneth Bradley. "Gladys George," *Variety,* 15 Dec 1954 (age 50; 1st film: *Straight Is the Way,* 1934 [in films from 1920]). AMD, p. 133. AS, p. 438. BHD1, p. 210 (b. 1904). FSS, p. 121. IFN, p. 115 (b. 1904). Katz, p. 475. SD. Truitt, p. 122. "Paramount Signs Gladys George," *MPW,* 25 Sep 1920, 466. "Lasky Signs Gladys George for Paramount Productions," *MPW,* 30 Oct 1920, 1271.

George, Grace (step-mother of **Alice Brady**) [actress] (*née* Grace Dougherty, b. New York NY, 25 Dec 1879–19 May 1961 [81], New York NY). m. **William A. Brady**, 8 Jan 1899 (1 son; d. 1950). "Grace George," *Variety,* 24 May 1961. AS, p. 439. IFN, p. 115. SD. "'Abigail' as Pretty as a Picture Book; Grace George in a Play of Syrupy Sentiment at the Savoy; Progress of a Country Girl; Begins Her Life in Poverty, Falls Heir to Millions, and Does Not Marry a Duke," *NYT,* 22 Feb 1905, 7:3 (with Louise Closser, Viva Ogden, Conway Tearle, and others. "Grace George has a natural and pleasing comedy method, which she employs agreeably at times. In the part of Abigail, however, she is most frequently called upon to lend sincerity to passages of sugary sentiment, a task beyond her powers.").

George, Heinrich [stage/film actor/director] (*né* George August Friedrich Schultz, b. Stettin, Germany, 9 Oct 1883–27 Sep 1946 [52], Sachsenhausen, Germany, Soviet internment camp). m. Bertha Drews. (MGM German-language films, 1931.) "Heinrich George," *Variety,* 20 Nov 1946, p. 70 (age 53). AS, p. 439 (b. 1893; d. 26 Sep). BHD1, p. 210 (b. Szczecin, Poland; d. 26 Sep). IFN, p. 115 (b. 1893). Waldman, p. 118 (b. 1893).

George, John [actor] (b. Iraq, 21 Jan 1898–25 Aug 1968 [70], Los Angeles CA; emphysema). (Began ca. 1916.) AS, p. 439 (b. Syria). BHD1, p. 210. IFN, p. 115. Kip-Xool, "John George: Just Another Face in the Crowd?," *CI,* 257 (Nov 1996), C18 (b. Syria; includes incomplete filmography).

George, Maude [actress/scenarist] (b. Riverside CA, 15 Aug 1888–10 Oct 1963 [75], Sepulveda CA). m. (1) **Arthur Forde**—div. 1918 (d. 1952); (2) Frank Passmore, 10 Jun 1927. (Universal, 1915; Weber; Ince; Goldwyn.) AMD, p. 133. AS, p. 439. BHD, pp. 28–30; 177. "Maude George," *MPW,* 13 Nov 1915, 1280. "Maude George," *MPW,* 12 Feb 1916, 968. Billy H. Doyle, "Lost Players," *CI,* 159 (Sep 1988), 22.

George, Muriel [actress] (b. London, England, 29 Aug 1883–22 Oct 1965 [82], London, England). AS, p. 439.

George, Voya [actor] (*né* Voya George Djordjevich, b. 1895?–8 May 1951 [56], New York NY). "Voya George," *Variety,* 16 May 1951. AS, p. 439. BHD, p. 177. IFN, p. 115. Truitt, p. 122.

George-Blankensee, Walter [director/scenarist] (b. Warren, Germany, 7 Jul 1896). AS, p. 439.

Georgey, Géo [actor] (*né* Georges Fernand Gasquy, b. Marseilles, France, 3 Dec 1890–29 Mar 1975 [84], Marseilles, France [extrait de décès no. 591/1975]). AS, p. 439.

Georgius [actor/composer/singer] (*né* Georges Auguste Charles Guibourg, b. Mantes-la-Jolie, France, 3 Jun 1891–8 Jan 1970 [78], Paris, France). AS, p. 439.

Geraghty, Carmelita (daughter of **Tom J. Geraghty**; sister of Maurice Geraghty) [actress: Wampas Star, 1924] (b. Rushville IN, 21 Mar 1901–7 Jul 1966 [65], New York NY [Death Certificate Index No. 14298]). m. **Carey Wilson** (d. 1962). "Carmelita Geraghty Dies at 65; Painter Played in Silent Films," *NYT,* Jul 1966, 35:4. "Carmelita Geraghty [Wilson]," *Variety,* 13 Jul 1966. AMD, p. 133. AS, p. 439. BHD1, p. 210. BR, pp. 144–46 (b. 22 Mar). FSS, p. 122. IFN, p. 115. MH, p. 112. Truitt, pp. 122–23 (d. 7 Jun). "Carmelita Geraghty," *MPW,* 22 Oct 1927, 490. George A. Katchmer, "Forgotten Cowboys and Cowgirls—Part XIV," *CI,* 191 (May 1991), 20.

Geraghty, Tom J. (father of **Carmelita** and Maurice **Geraghty**) [actor/title writer/scenarist/producer] (b. Rushville IN, 10 Apr 1883–5 Jun 1945 [62], Los Angeles CA). m. (daughter, Carmelita; son, Maurice, 1908–87). "T.C. Geraghty Dies; Pioneer Scenarist; Screen Writer and Producer, Associate of Fairbanks Sr., Swanson and Pickford," *NYT,* 6 Jun 1945, 21:1. "Tom Geraghty," *Variety,* 13 Jun 1945 (d. Culver City CA). AMD, p. 133. AS, p. 439 (d. 21 Jun). BHD2, p. 96. FDY, pp. 425, 443. IFN, p. 115. Lowrey, p. 58. 1921 Directory, p. 287. "Geraghty at Western Metro," *MPW,* 7 Sep 1918, 1389. "Geraghty Writing Western Series for Clifford Bruce," *MPW,* 3 May 1919, 664. "Roswell Dague on Vacation; Tom Geraghty in His Place," *MPW,* 21 Aug 1920, 996. "New Production Editor Comes to Paramount's Eastern Office," *MPW,* 18 Sep 1920, 382. "Enters Producing Field," *MPW,* 29 Mar 1924, 372. "Geraghty a Busy Invalid," *MPW,* 10 Jan 1925, 126. Peter Milne, "Join the Movies and See the World; That's How Tom Geraghty Does It," *MPC,* May 1927, 42, 85, 87. "Geraghty with Kane," *MPW,* 12 Nov 1927, 19.

Gerald, Jim [actor] (*né* Gérald Ernest Cuenod, b. Paris, France, 4 Jul 1889–2 Jul 1958 [68], Paris, France [extrait de décès no. 8/445]; heart attack). AS, p. 439. BHD1, p. 212. IFN, p. 115 (d. 1962). Truitt, p. 123. AS, p. 439.

Gerald, Pete [actor] (Piacenza, Italy, 1864). BHD, p. 177.

Geraldy, Paul Lefevre [actor/scenarist] (b. Paris, France, 6 Mar 1885–ca. Apr 1961 [76?]). AS, p. 439.

Gerard, Barney [scenarist/producer] (b. New York NY, 12 Jun 1870–30 Jun 1962 [92], Los Angeles CA). AS, p. 439 (b. 1882). BHD2, p. 96.

Gerard, Carl [actor] (b. Copenhagen, Denmark, 28 Sep 1885–6 Jan 1966 [80], Los Angeles CA). (Fox.) BHD1, p. 212.

Gerard, Charles K. [actor] (b. Carlow, ireland, 25 Dec 1887). AMD, p. 134. "Gerard's Work Gets Him a Contract," *MPW,* 18 Aug 1917, 1052. "Versatile Charles Gerard Popular Character Actor," *MPW,* 20 Sep 1919, 1836. Ragan, p. 604.

Gerard, Claire Elisa Julienne [actress] (b. Saint-Gilles, Belgium, 12 Mar 1889–24 Mar 1971 [82], Paris, France [extrait de décès no. 18/741]). AS, p. 439.

Gerard, Joseph Smith [actor] (b. 1871–20 Aug 1949 [78?], Woodland Hills CA). BHD, p. 178.

Gerard, Teddie [actress/dancer/singer] (*née* Teresa Gabre, b. Buenos Aires, Argentina, 2 May 1892–31 Aug 1942 [50], London, England). "Teddie Gerard," *Variety,* 9 Sep 1942, p. 46. AS, p. 440 (b. 1890). BHD, p. 178. IFN, p. 115 (age 52).

Gerasch, Alfred [actor] (b. Berlin, Germany, 17 Aug 1877–Aug 1955 [78]). BHD, p. 178. IFN, p. 116.

Gerasimov, Sergei Apollinarevic [actor/director/scenarist] (b. Zlatoust, Russia, 21 May 1906–28 Nov 1985 [79], Moscow, Russia). AS, p. 440 (b. Cheliabinsk, Russia). BHD1, p. 212.

Geray, Steven [actor] (*né* Stefan Gyergyay, b. Uzhord, Czechoslovakia, 10 Nov 1898–26 Dec 1973 [75], Los Angeles CA). AS, p. 440.

Gerber, Neva Delorez [actress] (aka Jean Dolores, b. Chicago IL, b. Chicago IL, 3 Apr 1894–2 Jan 1974 [79], Palm Springs CA). (Kalem; Balboa; Universal; Edwin August Feature Films; Metro; Favorite Players.) AMD, p. 134. BHD, p. 178. BR, pp. 146–50. *See* CNW, p. 53. MH, p. 112. MSBB, p. 1036. "Items of Interest," *MPS,* 28 Aug 1914, 31 (to start filming with William Desmond Taylor). "Neva Gerber," *MPW,* 20 Mar 1915, 1781. "New 'Beauty Star,'" *NYDM,* 14 Apr 1915, 24:1 (first film for American Beauty, *Life's Staircase,* directed by Frank Cooley. "The story will be partly allegorical and contain many effects in double and triple exposures.").

Gerdes, Emily [actress] (b. Jefferson KS, 29 Dec 1890–17 Sep 1974 [83], Los Angeles CA). BHD1, p. 212.

Gereghty, Frank L. [assistant director/production manager] (b. New York NY, 2 Aug 1888–1 Jan 1934 [45], No. Hollywood CA). "Frank Gereghty," *Variety,* 9 Jan 1934. AS, p. 440. BHD2, p. 96 (d. LA CA).

Gerety, Thomas W. [publicist]. No data found. AMD, p. 134. "Gerety Joins Hodkinson," *MPW,* 1 Jan 1921, 59. "Gerety with Universal," *MPW,* 25 Nov 1922, 324.

Gerlatta [actress] (*née* Germaine Louise Latappy, b. Bordeaux, France, 15 Sep 1899 [extrait de naissance no. 1899.2.1271. AC]-26 Nov 1967 [68], Marseilles, France). AS, p. 440.

German, Edward [composer] (b. 1862–11 Nov 1936 [74?], London, England). BHD2, p. 97.

German, William J. [executive] (b. Port Hope, Ontario, Canada, 1887–17 Feb 1963 [75?], Los Angeles CA). BHD2, p. 97.

Germonprez, Louis [art director] (b. MI, 14 May 1892–7 Jul 1963 [71], Woodland Hills CA). BHD2, p. 97.

Germonprez, Valerie Marguerite (mother of **Erich von Stroheim, Jr.**) [actress] (b. 14 Apr 1897–22 Oct 1988 [91], Sherman Oaks CA; cardiac arrest). m. **Erich von Stroheim**, ca. 1920 (d. 1957). AS, p. 440. BHD, p. 178.

Gerold, Hermann [actor] (b. Austria, 1862?–19 Nov 1920 [58], New York NY). AS, p. 440. BHD, p. 178. IFN, p. 116.

Gerrard, Charles (brother of **Douglas Gerrard**) (*né* Charles Kavanagh, b. Carlow, Ireland, 25 Dec 1883-Jan 1969 [85], New York NY). AMD, p. 134. AS, p. 440 (b. 1886; d. Apr 1933). BHD1, p. 212. "Charles Gerrard," *MPW,* 3 Sep 1927, 24.

Gerrard, Douglas (brother of **Charles Gerrard**) [actor/director] (*né* Douglas Gerrard McMurrough Kavanagh, b. Dublin, Ireland, 12 Aug 1891–5 Jun 1950 [58], Los Angeles CA; found unconscious on street). (Universal; 1st National; WB; TC-F.) "Injuries Fatal to Actor; Douglas Gerrard Was Found Unconscious in Los Angeles," *NYT,* 7 Jun 1950, 33:1 (age 62; began 1913). "Douglas Gerrard," *Variety,* 7 Jun 1950 (age 62). AMD, p. 134. AS, p. 440 (b. 1888). BHD1, p. 212; BHD2, p. 97. IFN, p. 116. Truitt 1983, p. 270 (b. 1888). "Douglas Gerrard," *MPW,* 6 Mar 1915, 1459. "Gerrard Again with Universal Company," *MPW,* 3 Nov 1917, 704.

Gerrard, Gene [actor/director] (*né* Eugene O'Sullivan, b. Clapham, England, 31 Aug 1889–1 Jun 1971 [81], Sidmouth, Devon, England). "Gene Gerrard," *Variety,* 16 Jun 1971. AS, p. 440. BHD, p. 178 (b. 1892). IFN, p. 116. SD.

Gerrard, Henry [cinematographer] (b, 1894–19 Nov 1934 [40?]). BHD2, p. 97. FDY, p. 459.

Gerron, Kurt [actor/director] (*né* Kurt Gerson, b. Berlin, Germany, 11 May 1897–28 Oct 1944 [47], Auschwitz, Poland; executed). AS, p. 441. BHD1, p. 212; BHD2, p. 97.

Gerson, Dora [actress] (*née* Dorothea Gerson, b. Berlin, Germany, 23 Mar 1899–14 Feb 1943 [43], Auschwitz, Poland). AS, . 441.

Gerson, Paul [actor/director] (b. Bradford, England, 25 Jan 1871–6 Jun 1957 [86], Los Angeles CA). "Paul Gerson," *Variety,* 12 Jun 1957. AS, p. 441 (d. 6 Jun). BHD, p. 178; BHD2, p. 97. IFN, p. 116. Truitt, p. 123.

Gerstad, Harry W. [film editor/cinematographer] (b. Chicago IL, 11 Aug 1886–26 Sep 1966 [80], So. Pasadena CA). BHD2, p. 97.

Gerstad, Merritt B. [cameraman] (b. Chicago IL, 5 Jul 1900–1 Mar 1974 [73], Laguna Beach CA). BHD2, p. 97. FDY, p. 459.

Gert, Valeska [actress] (*née* Gertrud Samosch, b. Berlin, Germany, 11 Jan 1891–18 Mar 1978 [87], Kampen, Germany). AS, p. 441 (b. 1892; d. 15 Mar). BHD1, p. 213 (b. 1896).

Gerwing, George [actor] (b. CO, 25 Nov 1902–9 Jan 1979 [76], Riverside CA). BHD, p. 178.

Gessner, Adrienne [actress] (b. Mariaschutz-am-Semmering, Austria, 23 Jul 1896–23 Jun 1987 [90], Vienna, Austria). AS, p. 441.

Gest, Morris (b. Vilna, Russia, 17 Jan 1881–16 May 1942 [61], New York NY). m. Reine Belasco. "Morris Gest, Colorful Showman, Dies Suddenly in N.Y. Hospital at 61," *Variety,* 20 May 1942. AMD, p. 134. AS, p. 441 (b. 1861). SD, p. 498. "Morris Gest Joins United Artists," *MPW,* 8 May 1926, 3. "Gest to Divide Time Between Stage and Film," *MPW,* 9 Apr 1927, 536.

Getchell, Sumner [actor/photographer] (b. Oakland CA, 20 Oct 1906–21 Sep 1990 [83], Sebastopol CA). (Universal.) BHD1, p. 213; BHD2, p. 79.

Gettinger, William *see* **Steele, Bill**

Getwell, Anetha [actress]. No data found. AMD, p. 134. "Amateur Contest Winner in American Legion Film," *MPW,* 13 Nov 1920, 236. "Anetha Getwell Signed for Pantheon Pictures," *MPW,* 12 Mar 1921, 141.

Gevaert, Liévin [producer] (b. Antwerp, Belgium, 28 May 1868–2 Feb 1935 [66], 's-Gravenhage, Netherlands). AS, p. 441.

Geymonat, Ermanno [director/writer] (b. Torre Pellice, Italy, 1893–7 Jul 1925 [32?], Torre Pellice, Italy [extrait de décès no. 45/1/1925]). AS, p. 441 [b. Turin, Italy]. JS, p. 192 (in Italian silents from 1913).

Geymond, Vital Bernard [actor] (b. Le Pont-de-Claix, France, 24 Jan 1897–6 Dec 1987 [90], Paris, France [extrait de décès no. 16/2195/1987]). AS, p. 442.

Gheller, Edward [cinematographer]. No data found. FDY, p. 459.

Gherardi, Gherardo [scenarist/director] (b. 1891–10 Mar 1949 [58?], Rome, Italy). AS, p. 442. BHD2, p. 97.

Ghio, Nino [actor/singer] (*né* Antonio Ghio, b. 1886–15 Jan 1956 [69?], Culver City CA). AS, . 442.

Ghione, Emilio Luigi Carlo Giuseppe Maria (father of actor Emilio Ghione, Jr.) [actor/director/scenarist] (b. Turin, Italy, 30 Jul 1879 [extrait de naissance no. 2031]-7 Jan 1930 [50], Rome, Italy; tuberculosis). (Cines-Kleine.) AMD, p. 134. AS, p. 442. BHD, p. 178; BHD2, p. 97 (d. Turin, Italy). JS, p. 193 (extra, 1909). "Cines-Kleine Players," *MPW,* 11 Jul 1914, 237–38 ("Ghione is tall and extremely slender. His lean, cadaverous face marks him a splendid type for character work of all kinds.... His peculiar power lies in his remarkable personality as well as in his odd physical characteristics.").

Ghosh, Sarath [writer]. No data found. AMD, p. 134. "Prince Ghosh After Pathé, By Gosh!," *MPW,* 22 Dec 1917, 1790.

Giachetti, Enrico (brother of **Fosco** and **Gianfranco Giachetti**) [composer] (b. Florence, Italy, 1890–1954 [64?], Italy). AS, p. 442.

Giachetti, Fosco [actor] (brother of **Enrico** and **Gianfranco Giachetti**) (b. Livorno, Italy, 28 Mar 1904–22 Dec 1974 [70], Rome, Italy). AS, p. 442.

Giachetti, Gianfranco (brother of **Enrico** and **Fosco Giachetti**) [actor] (b. Florence, Italy, 17 Sep 1888–29 Nov 1936 [48], Rome, Italy). AS, p. 442.

Giacomino [actor] (*né* Giuseppe Cirenia, b. 1884-Aug 1956 [72?], Milan, Italy). AS, p. 442 (*né* Cireni). BHD, p. 178.

Giannini, Guglielmo [director/scenarist] (aka Albert Vario, b. Pozzuoli, Italy, 14 Oct 1891–13 Oct 1960 [68], Rome, Italy). AS, p. 442.

Giannini, Nino [director/scenarist] (*né* Virgilio Pietro Giannini, b. San Remo, Italy, 10 Jul 1894 [extrait de naissance no. 243]-17 Jan 1978 [83], Rome, Italy [extrait de décès no. 441/1978]). AS, p. 442.

Giatintova, Sofia Vladimirovna [actress] (b. Moscow, Russia, 4 Aug 1895–12 Apr 1958 [62], Moscow, Russia). AS, p. 442.

Gibbons, Cedric [art director/director] (*né* Arthur Cedric Gibbons, b. Dublin, Ireland, 23 Mar 1893–26 Jul 1960 [67], Los Angeles CA). m. **Dolores Del Rio**, 1930–41 (d. 1983); Hazel Brooks. (Edison [Bedford] Park NY, 1915: art director; Goldwyn; MGM, 1924.) "Cedric Gibbons, M-G-M Artist, 65; Retired Head of Department Dead—Designer of Oscar Won 11 Academy Awards," *NYT,* 27 Jul 1960, 29:4 (b. NYC; age 65). "Cedric Gibbons," *Variety,* 3 Aug 1960 (age 65). AMD, p. 134. AS, p. 443 (d. Westwood CA). BHD2, p. 97 (b. Brooklyn NY). Katz, p. 480 (b. 1893). "Gibbons Renews Contract," *MPW,* 7 Jan 1922, 45.

Gibbons, Rose [actress] (b. 1886–13 Aug 1964 [78], Oakland CA). "Rose Gibbons," *Variety,* 26 Aug 1964 (acted with J.W. Kerrigan, 1913–15). BHD, p. 178. IFN, p. 116. In *The Conflict* (1899; dir. C.B. DeMille) at Eltich's Gardens, Denver CO. Truit 1983, p. 271.

Gibbs, Irving [actor] (b. 1875–5 Apr 1955 [80?], Los Angeles CA). AS, p. 443.

Gibbs, Joseph F. [actor] (b. England-d. 14 Apr 1921, New York NY). BHD, p. 178.

Gibbs, Robert P[atton] [actor] (b. Scranton PA, 1859?–22 Feb 1941 [81], Clifton, Staten Island NY). "Robert P. Gibbs," *Variety,* 26 Feb 1941. AS, p. 443. BHD, p. 178 (b. 1860). IFN, p. 116.

Gibbs, William K. [publicist] (b. 1886–23 Aug 1956 [70?], Los Angeles CA). BHD2, p. 98.

Gibler, R.A. [assistant director] (b. 1869–27 Jan 1925 [55?], Los Angeles CA). BHD2, p. 98.

Giblyn, Charles [actor/scenarist/director] (b. Watertown NY, 6 Sep 1871–14 Mar 1934 [62], Los Angeles CA). (Ince.) "Charles Giblyn," *Variety,* 20 Mar 1934 (age 63; began 1908). AMD, p. 134. AS, p. 443. BHD1, p. 213; BHD2, p. 98. IFN, 116. "Giblyn Writes New Story," *MPW,* 17 Oct 1914, 351. "Charles Giblyn Now with Selznick," *MPW,* 11 Nov 1916, 870. "Director Giblyn Honored by Furnishers," *MPW,* 21 Jul 1917, 449. "Goldwyn Engages Two Directors," *MPW,* 8 Jun 1918, 1418. "Film Division Names Director Advisors," *MPW,* 20 Jul 1918, 363–64. "Goldwyn Proud of Its Quintet of Directors," *MPW,* 27 Jul 1918, 547.

Gibney, Louise [actress] (*née* Lillian Harrington, b. Boston MA, 1896–22 Sep 1986 [90?], Santa Maria CA). AS, p. 443. BHD, p. 178.

Gibson, Charles Dana [artist/actor] (b. Roxbury MA, 14 Sep 1867–23 Dec 1944 [77], New York NY). AS, p. 443. BHD, p. 178.

Gibson, Dorothy [actress] (b. Hoboken NJ-d. 20 Feb 1946, Paris, France). m. **Jules Brulatour**, 1917 (d. 1946). (Eclair.) AMD, p. 134. BHD, p. 178. "A New Star in the Picture Firmament," *MPW,* 2 Dec 1911, 720. "Dorothy Gibson," *MPW,* 27 Apr 1912, 344. "Dorothy Gibson Tells Her Story of the Titanic Wreck to Our 'Roving Commissioner,'" *MPN,* 27 Apr 1912, p. 7 ("Miss

Gibson, although she assured me that it would take more than a shipwreck to knock her out, at the same time has the appearance of one whose nerves had been greatly shocked. She will, however, start work again with the Eclair Company almost immediately.").Chauncey L. Parsons, "Dorothy Gibson from the Titanic; An Account of the Shipwreck According to an Actress Who Was In It," *NYDM*, 1 May 1912, p. 13 ("A panic broke out on the *Titanic* after the first boats had left, and men had been shot to keep them from filling the remaining boats.... A pause of silence held everything and everybody spellbound, until the stern shot back into sight and immediately sank again. Then, there burst out the most ghastly cries, shrieks, yells, and moans that a mortal could ever imagine. No one can describe the frightful sounds that gradually died away to nothing.... But I've had quite enough ocean travel for some time."). "Saved from the Titanic [review of Eclair film]," *MPN*, 4 May 1912, p. 27 (written by Gibson; to be released on 14 May 1912, one month from the date of the disaster. Starred Gibson, Alec Francis, Miss Stuart, Jack Adolfi, William Dunn and Guy Oliver, "in strong characterizations." Ad for the film on p. 30.). Hans J. Wollstein, "Dorothy Gibson: 'Saved from the Titanic,'" *CI*, 268 (Oct 1997), 35–36 (d. NYC).

Gibson, Ella Margaret [stage/film actress] (b. Colorado Springs CO, 1896?). (Vitagraph.) AMD, p. 134. "Briefs of Biography," *NYDM*, 6 May 1914, 27:3 (age 18). "Ella Margaret Gibson," *MPW*, 16 May 1914, 982.

Gibson, Ethelyn [actress]. No data found. AMD, p. 134. "Ethelyn Gibson," *MPW*, 1 Dec 1917, 1322.

Gibson, Frances [actress]. No data found. AMD, p. 134. "Frances Gibson," *MPW*, 21 Nov 1914, 1085.

Gibson, Grace [actress]. No data found. AMD, p. 134. "More Horsley Stars," *MPW*, XXVI, 2 Oct 1915, 62.

Gibson, Helen Rose [actress] (*née* Rose Helen Wenger, b. Cleveland OH, 27 Aug 1892–10 Oct 1977 [85], Roseburg OR; hepatitis and heart attack). m. **Hoot Gibson**, 1918 (d. 1962). (Kalem; Universal.) AMD, p. 134. AS, p. 443. BHD1, p. 213. BR, pp. 27–31. FSS, p. 122. IFN, p. 116 (b. 1894). CNW, p. 25. MSBB, p. 1034 (b. 1894). "Kalem Has a New 'H,'" *MPW*, 28 Aug 1915, 1494. "Briefs of Biography; Filmdom's New Helen," *NYDM*, 6 Oct 1915, 33:1. "Kalem's New 'H,'" *MPW*, 9 Oct 1915, 260. "'Helen' Has a Birthday; Kalem's Hazardous Heroine Starts Second Year of Her Charmed Life This Month," *NYDM*, 4 Dec 1915, 34:3 (the series was one year old in November. E.W. Matlack, the Pittsburgh railroad official, was responsible for most of the Helen stories. New episodes: *The Tramp Telegrapher*, rel. 4 Dec 1915; *Crossed Wires*, to be rel. 11 Dec; *The Wrong Train Order*, rel. 18 Dec; *A Boy at the Thottle*, 25 Dec.). "Refuse Insurances to Kalem's 'H,'" *MPW*, 25 Dec 1915, 2344. "Helen Receives a Present," *MPW*, 26 Feb 1916, 1288. "Helen Gets Grim Warning," *MPW*, 25 Mar 1916, 2035. "Helen Gibson in Rodeo," *MPW*, 16 Sep 1916, 1841. "Helen Gibson," *MPW*, 29 Sep 1917, 1994. "Helen Gibson," *MPW*, 12 Oct 1918, 238. Nick C. Nicholls, "Helen, Mrs. Hoot, Gibson," *CI*, 168 (Jun 1989), C11.

Gibson, Hoot [actor/director] (*né* Edmund Richard Gibson, b. Tekamah NB, 6 Aug 1892–23 Aug 1962 [70], Woodland Hills CA; cancer). m. (1) **Helen** Johnson, 1918 (d. 1977); **Sally Eilers**, 1930–33 (d. 1978); Dorothy Dunstan, 3 Jul 1942. (American Biograph, 1910; Universal; Monogram.) "Hoot Gibson," *Variety*, 29 Aug 1962. AMD, p. 135. AS, p. 443. BHD1, p. 213 (Hoot Edward Gibson); BHD2, p. 98 (Edward [Hoot] Gibson). FFF, p. 126. FSS, p. 122. GK, pp. 327–40. HCH, 119. IFN, p. 116. Katz, p. 480. MH, p. 112. SD. Truitt, p. 123. "Hoot Gibson," *MPW*, 12 Oct 1918, 238. "Marie Prevost and Hoot Gibson Are to Star in Universal Attractions," *MPW*, 4 Jun 1921, 521. "Gibson Will Make Universal Specials," *MPW*, 16 Jun 1923, 594. "Gibson Film Goes Big on Broadway," *MPW*, 22 Sep 1923, 360. "Hoot Gibson to Be a Jewel Star," *MPW*, 2 May 1925, 65. "Gibson Will Direct Westerns for Universal," *MPW*, 10 Apr 1926, 418. "A Cowboy Who Became an Actor; Hoot Gibson Started His Career by Becoming Champion of a Roundup," *Cinema Arts*, Oct 1926, 41, 47. "'Hoot' Signs New Contract," *MPW*, 29 Nov 1926, 4. "Universal Is Losing Gibvson; Western Star," *MPW*, 9 Jul 1927, 85. "'Hoot' Names Personnel of His Company," *MPW*, 12 Nov 1927, 10. Lynn Fairfield, "The Ornery West; Hoot Gibson Argues for Old Time Law and Order," *MPC*, Apr 1928, 58, 90. Cedric Belfrage, "Wings Over the West; The Airplane, Reckons Hoot Gibson, Is Changing Things in the Cowboy Country," *MPC*, Mar 1930, 63, 97. George A. Katchmer, "The Lucky Man Hoot Gibson," *CI*, 72 (Nov 1980), 70–72. Richard E. Braff, "An Index to the Films of Hoot Gibson," *CI*, 190 (Apr 1991), 16 *et passim*; 231, 43. George Katchmer, "Remembering the Great Silents," *CI*, 257 (Nov 1996), 48–49. Bobby J. Copeland, "Hoot Gibson; The Smiling Whirlwind," *CI*, 259 (Jan 1997), C6-C-7.

Gibson, Jack [actor] (*née* John T. Tumulty, d. 23 Nov 1930, Chester PA). m. Isabelle Dean. "Jack Gibson," *Variety*, 3 Dec 1930. AS, p. 443.

Gibson, James Edwin [actor] (b. Jefferson IN, 24 Oct 1865–13 Oct 1938 [72], Redondo Beach CA). "James Gibson," *Variety*, 19 Oct 1938. AS, p. 443. BHD1, p. 214. IFN, p. 116. Truitt, p. 123.

Gibson, Kenneth [actor] (b. Sandusky OH, 17 Jan 1898–26 Nov 1972 [74], Los Angeles CA). m. **Paulette Paquet**, 1926. AS, p. 443. BHD1, p. 214. IFN, p. 116. June Lee, "Dan Cupid's Bulletin Board," *Paris and Hollywood*, Sep 1926, 96 (recently married Paquet. "Gibson is the son of Idah McGlone Gibson, a well-known newspaper woman.").

Gibson, Margaret [actress] (*née* Patricia Palmer, b. Colorado Springs CO, 14 Sep 1894–21 Oct 1964 [70], Los Angeles CA). (Vitagraph; NYMP Co.) AMD, pp. 135, 270. AS, p. 444. BHD1, p. 214. IFN, p. 116. Truitt 1983, p. 263. "Margaret Gibson," *MPW*, 3 Oct 1914, 42. "Margaret Gibson Signs with N.Y.M.P. Corp.," *MPW*, 22 May 1915, p. 1238. "Stars Added to Horsley's Array," *MPW*, 25 Sep 1915, 2187. "Margaret Gibson on Long Contract," *MPW*, 25 Dec 1915, 2354. "Patricia Palmer Back in Comedies," *MPW*, 20 Nov 1920, 375. George Katchmer, "Forgotten Cowboys and Cowgirls—Part IX," *CI*, 181 (Jul 1990), 56 (b. 1895).

Gibson, Ralph [actor]. No data found. June Lee, "Dan Cupid's Bulletin Board," *Paris and Hollywood*, Oct 1926, 89 (Gibson, "Hollywood actor," was named as co-respondent" in the divorce suit of Alfred D. Elsworth against his movie actress wife, Kathryn, whom he married in 1924. "He testified that his wife deserted him a few hours after their marriage.").

Gibson, Thomas V. [director/scenarist] (b. Boston MA, 1887–6 Dec 1950 [63?], Burbank CA) . m. Anna M. Gaylean, 2 Sep 1915, Santa Ana CA. (Lubin.) AMD, p. 135. FDY, p. 425. "In the Picture Studios," *NYDM*, 29 Sep 1915, 26:4 (married Gaylean. "The action was short and snappy and was directed by Justice Cox who put the stamp of approval on the scenario of what promises to be the biggest never finished serial ever begun."). "Tom Gibson Now with Universal," *MPW*, 10 Feb 1917, 827. "Tom Gibson Will direct Series of Hank Mann Comedies Which Are to Be Distributed by Arrow," *MPW*, 30 Aug 1919, 1350. "Gibson Writing a Book," *MPW*, 31 Jan 1920, 700. "Scott Engages Gibson," *MPW*, 7 Mar 1925, 77.

Gibson, Vivian [actress] (b. Liverpool, England, 14 May 18—?). (In Mexican and U.S. silents, e.g., *Why Men Forget*, 1921.) AS, p. 444.

Gibson, William H. "Willie" [actor]. No data found. AMD, p. 135. "Gibson, Wooden Footed Dancer, in thomas Film," *MPW*, 10 May 1919, 926. "One-Legged Actor Dacnes in Thomas' 'The Volcano,'" *MPW*, 12 Jul 1919, 290.

Gibson, William L. [actor] (b. 1888?–4 Aug 1926 [38], Huntington, LI NY). "William L. Gibson," *Variety*, 15 Sep 1926. AS, p. 444 (b. 1968).

Gibson, Wynne [stage/film actress] (*née* Winifred Gibson, b. New York NY, 3 Jul 1905–15 May 1987 [82], Laguna Niguel CA; cerebral thrombosis). "Wynne Gibson Is Dead; Stage and Film Actress," *NYT*, 21 May 1987, B14:4 (d. 14 May, age 81). "Wynne Gibson," *Variety*, 27 May 1987 (age 82). AS, p. 444. BHD1, p. 214. Katz, pp. 480–81.

Gide, André (actor/scenarist/director/producer] (b. Paris, France, 22 Nov 1869–19 Feb 1951 [81], Paris, France). AS, p. 444. BHD2, p. 98.

Giebler, Alfred R. [title writer/scenarist] (b. 1872–12 Dec 1950 [78?], Los Angeles CA). AMD, p. 135. BHD2, p. 98. FDY, p. 443. "Giebler to Write Scenarios," *MPW*, XXXIV, 22 Dec 1917, 1790. "To Write Comedies," *MPW*, 6 Oct 1923, 478.

Giegerich, Charles J. [publicist]. No data found. (VLSE.) AMD, p. 135. F.J.B., "With the Film Men," *NYDM*, 28 Apr 1915, 22:4. "Giegerich with Pathé," *MPW*, 5 Jan 1918, 61. "Giegerich at Work in Hollywood," *MPW*, 16 Nov 1918, 736. "Giegerich Leaves Vitagraph," *MPW*, 17 Jan 1920, 438.

Giehse, Therese [actress] (*née* Therese Gift, b. Munich, Germany, 6 Mar 1898–3 Mar 1975 [76], Munich, Germany). AS, p. 444.

Gielgud, John (brother of **Val Gielgud**; grandson of Kate Terry; great-nephew of **Ellen Terry**; cousin of **Dennis** and **Phyllis Neilson-Terry** and **Edward Gordon Craig**) [stage/radio/film/TV actor/director/producer] (*né* Arthur John Gielgud, b. London, England, 14 Apr 1904–21 May 2000 [96], near Aylesbury, west of London, England). *Early Stages; An Actor and His Time*, 1979; *Prospero's Books*, 1991. (Stage debut: *Henry V*, Old Vic, London, 1921; Broadway debut: *The Patriot*, 1928; film debut: *Who Is the Man?*, 1924; AA for *Arthur*, 1981; final film, *Catastrophe*, 2000.) Mel Gussow, "Sir John Gielgud, 96, Dies; Beacon of Classical Stage," *NYT*, 23 May 2000, A1, B10. Mel Gussow, "Sir John Gielgud; Eloquent English actor thrived on Shakespeare," *PP-G*, 23 May 2000, C-8. Matt Wolf, "John Gielgud," *Variety*, 29 May 2000, 70:3 ("Gielgud's longtime companion, Martin Heusler, died last year. He leaves no survivors.").

AS, p. 444. Waldman, p. 119 (b. 1903). Garth Pedler, "The Silent Films of Sir John Gielgud," *CI,* 106 (Apr 1984), 50–52 (two silents: *Who Is the Man?* [1924] and *The Clue of the New Pin* [1929]).

Gielgud, Val (brother of **John Gielgud**) [actor/scenarist/playwright/novelist/director] (b. London, England, 28 Apr 1900–20 Nov 1981 [81], London, England). AS, p. 444. BHD1, p. 214; BHD2, p. 98.

Gierasienski, Romuald [actor] (b. Lublin, Poland, 6 Feb 1885–21 May 1956 [71], Kasimierz, Poland). AS, p. 444.

Gierum, Ellen [actress]. No data found. AMD, p. 135. "Christie Gets Leading Lady," *MPW,* 20 Jan 1917, 351.

Gifford, Ada [actress] (b. Rahway NJ, 22 May ca. 1885). (Vitagraph.) BHD, p. 178. *MPW,* 2 Aug 1913, 515.

Gigli, Beniamino [actor/composer] (b. Recanati, Italy, 20 Mar 1890–30 Nov 1957 [67], London, England). AS, p. 444 (d. Rome, Italy). BHD1, p. 214; BHD2, p. 98.

Gignoret, Gabriel [actor] (b. France, 1879–16 Mar 1937 [58?], Paris, France). BHD, p. 179.

Gilbert, Bessie [actress] (b. 1876?–1 Oct 1944 [68], New York NY). m. Louis Wells. "Bessie Gilbert," *Variety,* 4 Oct 1944. AS, p. 444.

Gilbert, Billy [actor] (*né* William V. Campbell, b. Hollywood CA, 15 Sep 1891–29 Apr 1961 [69], Los Angeles CA). m. **Norma Felicia.** (Keystone.) AS, p. 444. BHD, p. 179. J. Van Cartmell, "Along the Pacific Coast," *NYDM,* 15 Sep 1915, 30:4.

Gilbert, Billy [actor] (*né* William J. Barron, b. Louisville KY, 12 Jan 1894–23 Sep 1971 [77], Los Angeles CA; cerebral hemorrhage). m. **Ella McKenzie** (d. 1987). "Billy Gilbert, Actor, 77, Dead; Noted as Man with the Sneeze," *NYT,* 24 Sep 1971, 44:4. "Billy Gilbert," *Variety,* 29 Sep 1971 (age 78). AS, p. 444 (d. No. Hollywood CA). BHD1, p. 214. IFN, p. 117 (b. 12 Sep). SD. Truitt, pp. 123–24. "Billy Gilbert," WBO2, pp. 76–77).

Gilbert, C. Allen [artist]. No data found. AMD, p. 135. "Drawing Art Titles for Metro," *MPW,* 19 Jun 1920, 1582.

Gilbert, Dick [actor/composer]. m. Ruth Wimp (vaudeville: Gilbert & Wimp). No data found. "Ruth (Mrs. Dick) Gilbert Killed in Auto Crash," *Variety,* 25 Jun 1952 (d. 20 Jun 1952, near Whittman AZ).

Gilbert, Eugenia [actress] (b. East Orange NJ). AMD, p. 135. BR, pp. 150–52. "Eugenia Gilbert," *MPW,* 16 Apr 1927, 631.

Gilbert, Florence A.P. [actress] (b. London, England, 1862?–2 May 1940 [78], Medford MA). m. James Gilbert (d. 1918). "Florence A.P. Gilbert," *Variety,* 8 May 1940. AMD, p. 135. AS, p. 445. "Florence Gilbert Signs with Fox," *MPW,* 13 Dec 1924, 650.

Gilbert, Florence L. [painted art titles] (b. Chicago IL, 20 Feb 1904–27 Feb 1991 [87], Sylmar CA). m. Edward Le Veque. BHD1, p. 609.

Gilbert, Joe [actor] (b. 1902–26 May 1959 [56], Los Angeles CA). "Joe Gilbert," *Variety,* 3 Jun 1959 (began 1923). AS, p. 445. BHD, p. 179. IFN, p. 117. Truitt, p. 124.

Gilbert, John, "The Great Lover" (son of **John Pringle**) [actor/scenarist] (*né* John Cecil Pringle, b. Logan UT, 10 Jul 1899–9 Jan 1936 [36], Los Angeles CA; heart attack). Leatrice Gilbert Fountain, *Dark Star* (New York: St. Martin's Press, 1985), p. 6 (b. 1899). m. (1) **Olivia Burwell,** 1918; (2) **Leatrice Joy,** Jan 1921, Tia Juana, Mexico, and remarriage on 3 Mar 1923—div. 29 May 1925 (d. 1985; 1 daughter); (3) **Ina Claire,** 9 May 1929, Las Vegas NV—div. 5 Aug 1931 (d. 1985); (4) **Virginia Bruce** (d. 1982). (Ince; Fox; MGM, 1 May 1923; Columbia.) "John Gilbert, 38, Movie Star, Dies; Romantic Silent Screen Star Lost Public When Voice Was Found Unsuitable to Talkies; He Married Four Times; Ina Claire and Virginia Bruce Among Brides—Leading Man for Greta Garbo," *NYT,* 10 Jan 1936, 19:1. "John Gilbert," *Variety,* 15 Jan 1936 (d. 9 Jul 1936, age 38, Hollywood CA). AMD, p. 135. AS, p. 445. BHD1, p. 214; BHD2, p. 98. FFF, p. 91. FSS, p. 123. HCH, p. 11. IFN, p. 117 (b. 1897). Katz, p. 481 (b. 1895). MH, p. 112 (b. 1895). Truitt 1983, p. 273 (b. 1897). "Jack Gilbert Returns to Triangle Fold," *MPW,* 2 Feb 1918, 646. "Actor Marries Mississippi Girl," *MPW,* 12 Oct 1918, 207. "Jack Gilbert with Universal," *MPW,* 24 May 1919, 1180. "Jack Gilbert Engaged by Metro," *MPW,* 22 Nov 1919, 431. Cal York, "Plays and Players," *Photoplay,* Mar 1921, 91 (the rumor was that Joy would marry John Gilbert. "At any rate, Miss Joy is wearing a diamond on the correct finger and neither of the parties has denied the engagement." [They were already married.]). "Jack Gilbert Is Made a Fox Star," *MPW,* 11 Jun 1921, 634. Maude Cheatham, "Ten Per Cent Romance," *MPC,* Dec 1921, 49, 86–87. "Gilbert to Star for Fox," *MPW,* 4 Nov 1922, 52. "Supporting Gilbert," *MPW,* 16 Jun 1923, 595. "Gilbert to Play in 'Cameo Kirby,'" *MPW,* 30 Jun 1923, 754. Gladys Hall and Adele Whitely Fletcher, "We Interview John Gilbert," *MW,* 9 May 1925, 10–12, 32–33. Dorothy Donnell, "Sequel; How John Gilbert Is Building a New Life Out of the Wreckage of the Old," *MPC,* Nov 1925, 33, 87–88. Eugene V. Brewster, "The Battle of the Romeos; Who Will Be the Great Lover of 1926?," *MPC,* Dec 1925, 16–17, 64, 79–80. "The Screen's Man of the Moment," *MPC,* Jan 1926, 52, 88. Gladys Hall, "Are Men Capable of Platonic Friendship?," *MM,* May 1926, 34–35, 116–17. Louise Helen Johnson, "When Realist and Idealist Meet; A Captivating Study at Close Range of Two Opposite Types—John Gilbert and Ramon Navarro," *Cinema Arts,* Sep 1926, 22, 55. Ramon Romeo, "Reeling Down Broadway," *Paris and Hollywood,* Sep 1926, 82 (recently divorced Joy. "John may be a great lover on the screen but he didn't do any of his rehearsing at home. They do say that no man is a hero to his valet."). "Gilbert Keeps Busy," *MPW,* 29 Nov 1926, 278. Hugh Miller [English actor], "An Actor's Tribute to an Actor; An Appreciation of an Actor's Art by a Member of the Acting Profession," *MPC,* Dec 1926, 20–21, 79, 85. "Deny Famous Is Angling to Sign Gilbert," *MPW,* 15 Jan 1927, 189. "John Gilbert and Greta Garbo Not Married, They Tell the World," *MPW,* LXXXV, 5 Mar 1927, 32. "Gilbert's Arrest Publicity Stunt? No! No! They Say," *MPW,* 23 Apr 1927, 704. "Gilbert and Mayer Clash Over Story," *MPW,* 23 Jul 1927, 238. "Gilbert Uses No 'Make-Up,'" *MPW,* 23 Jul 1927, 255. Paul Paige, "Close-Ups and Fade-Outs," *Paris and Hollywood Screen Secrets,* Oct 1927, 23 (not on speaking terms with L.B. Mayer. Hated his latest, *Twelve Miles Out,* and complained that his current Russian picture is under-budgeted. His MGM contract had 18 months to go, "but already he is threatening to take an extended vacation of several years from picture-making, or else form his own company and make pictures to suit himself."). Carolyn Dawson, "Ask Dad—He Knows; John Gilbert's Father Stalks Out of the Past to Release a Flood of Memories," *MPC,* Jan 1928, 23, 82. Helen Ludlam, "On Location with John Gilbert," *Screenland,* Aug 1929, 30–31, 102–05 (on location during the filming of *Redemption*). "And So They Were Married!," *Screenland,* Aug 1929, 65 (Gilbert and Ina Claire). Dorothy Donnell, "The Gilbert-Bennett Romance Fades Out; The Lonely John and the Wistful Joan Are Not That Way About Each Other at All," *Movie Classic,* Sep 1931, 44. Dorothy Calhoun, "Ina and John Reach Parting of the Ways; After Two Years of Trying to Make a Go of Marriage Ina Claire Divorces John Gilbert," *Movie Classic,* Oct 1931, 36. Muriel Babcock, "The Headline Career of John Gilbert 1922–1931," *Movie Classic,* Dec 1931, 24–25, 80.

Gilbert, John E. [actor] (b. ca. 1867–15 Feb 1916 [48?], New York NY; gas poisoning from leaky gas jet). m. Ruth Hayes. "John E. Gilbert," *Variety,* 3 Mar 1916. AS, p. 445 (d. 1915). SD.

Gilbert, L[azarius] **Wolfe** [composer] (b. Odessa, Ukraine, Russia, 31 Aug 1886–12 Jul 1970 [83], Los Angeles CA; stroke). m. (1) Kate; (2) Rose. *Without Rhyme or Reason* (1956). "J. Wolfe Gilbert, Composer, Dead; Wrote 'Ramona' and Many Other Successful Songs," *NYT,* 13 Jul 1970, 31:4 (wrote *Waitin' for the Robert E. Lee* [1912]; *Green Eyes; Peanut Vendor; Down Yonder; Hopalong Cassidy March; Lucky Lindy*). "L. Wolfe Gilbert, 83, Chas. Tobias, 72; Both ASCAPERs with Top Catalogue," *Variety,* 15 Jul 1970 (wrote*Jeannine, I Dream of Lilac Time*). AS, p. 445. ASCAP 66, p. 260. BHD2, p. 98.

Gilbert, Mae Edwards [actress] (*née* Mae Burke Edwards, b. 1871–18 Aug 1947 [76?], Los Angeles CA). AS, p. 445. BHD, p. 179.

Gilbert, Maude [actress] (b. 24 May 1883–7 Jul 1953 [70], Laguna Beach CA). m. Hayward J. Ginn. "Maude Gilbert," *Variety,* 15 Jul 1953. AS, p. 445. BHD, p. 179. IFN, p. 117.

Gilbert, Mercedes [stage/radio/TV actress] (b. Jacksonville FL, 1894–1 Mar 1952 [58?], New York NY). "Mercedes Gilbert," *Variety,* 12 Mar 1952, p. 63 ("Negro actress"). BHD, p. 179.

Gilbert, O[scar] **P**[aul] [actor/director] (b. Wanfercee-Baulet, Belgium, 21 Sep 1898–1973 [75?], Brussels, Belgium). AS, p. 445.

Gilbert, Richard [actor]. No data found. AMD, p. 135. "Richard Gilbert," *MPW,* 5 Feb 1927, 419.

Gilbert, Walter [actor] (b. Brooklyn NY, 1887–12 Jan 1947 [59?], Brooklyn NY). AS, p. 445. BHD1, p. 215.

Gilchrist, Charles A. [cinematographer] (d. May 1920). BHD2, p. 98.

Gildemeyer, Johan Hendrik [director/scenarist] (b. Alkmaar, Netherlands, 27 Mar 1871–31 Jan 1945 [83], Amsterdam, Netherlands). AS, p. 445.

Gilder, Jeannette [writer/critic/playwright] (b. 1849?–17 Jan 1916 [66], New York NY; stroke caused by a blood clot on the brain). "Jeannette Leonard Gilder," *Variety,* 21 Jan 1916, 28:1 (for the stage wrote *Quits, Seven Oaks, and A Wonderful Woman*). AMD, p. 135. "Jeannette Gilder Writes for Joan Sawyer," *MPW,* 9 May 1914, 797.

Gildes, Anthony [actor] (*né* Anatole Gleizes, b. Metz, France, 13 Aug 1856–6 Oct 1941 [85], Paris, France [extrait de décès no. 1434]). AS, p. 445.

Giles, Anna [actress] (b. IL, 23 Nov 1873–2 Feb 1973 [99], Los Angeles CA). AS, p. 445. BHD, p. 179.

Giles, Corliss [actress]. No data found. AMD, p. 135. "Clara Kimball Young Engages Corliss Giles for Leads," *MPW,* 8 Dec 1917, 1470.

Giles, Cyprian [actress]. No data found. AMD, p. 135. "Truex Announces Cast," *MPW,* 31 Jan 1920, 764.

Gilfether, Daniel [stage/film actor] (b. Boston MA, 17 Jan 1849–2 May 1919 [70], Long Beach CA; kidney illness). (Balboa.) "Daniel Gilfether," *Variety,* 9 and 16 May 1919 (interred in Boston MA). AMD, p. 136. AS, p. 445 (d. 3 May). BHD1, p. 609 (Daniel Gilfeather, b. 1854). IFN, p. 117. Jura, pp. 124–28. "Daniel Gilfether," *MPW,* 12 May 1917, 971. "Obituary," *MPW,* 24 May 1919, 1161 (d. 3 May). "Bulk of Estate to Charity," *MPW,* 31 May 1919, 1333 ($10,000).

Gilks, Alfred L. [cameraman] (b. CA, 29 Dec 1891–7 Sep 1970 [78], Los Angeles CA). "Al Gilks," *Variety,* 16 Sep 1970. BHD2, p. 98. FDY, p. 459.

Gill, Basil [actor] (b. Birkenhead, Cheshire, England, 10 Mar 1877–23 Apr 1955 [78], Hove, England). m. Margaret von Cavania. "Basil Gill," *Variety,* 27 Apr 1955. AS, p. 445. BHD1, p. 215. IFN, p. 117. SD. Truitt, p. 124. Davis Beams, "Letter," *Films in Review,* Mar 1977, 189–90.

Gill, Florence [actress] (b. London, England, 27 Jul 1877–19 Feb 1965 [87], Woodland Hills CA). AS, p. 446.

Gill, Robert Stowe [actor] (d. Sep 1918, France). BHD, p. 179.

Gillain, Maurice [actor] (*né* Maurice Auguste Alfred Gilain, b. Belgium, 25 Jan 1891–13 Dec 1971 [80], Etterbeek, Belgium). AS, p. 446.

Gillen, Ernest *see* **Reed, Donald**

Gilles, Pierre [actor/scenarist/composer] (*né* Jean Villard, b. Montreux, Switzerland, 2 Jun 1895–26 Mar 1982 [86], Vevey, Switzerland). AS, p. 446.

Gillespie, A. Arnold "Buddy" [special effects/art director] (b. El Paso TX, 14 Oct 1898–3 May 1978 [79], Los Angeles CA). (Goldwyn; MGM; Paramount.) "A. Arnold Gillespie," *Variety,* 10 May 1978. AS, p. 446 (Buddy Gillespie). BHD2, p. 987 (b. 1899). Katz, p. 483 (b. 1899).

Gillespie, Albert T. (Bert) [actor] (b. Hancock MI, 1888-May 1922 [34?]). BHD, p. 179.

Gillespie, Edward Charles [actor] (b. 1874?–23 Jul 1918 [44], New York NY). AS, p. 446. BHD, p. 179. IFN, p. 117

Gillespie, William [actor] (b. Aberdeen, Scotland, 24 Jan 1894). AMD, p. 136. BHD, p. 179. "Bill Gillespie Joins Rolin," *MPW,* 8 Sep 1917, 1521 (daughter, Margaret Ann, b. Aug 1917).

Gillette, Burton F. [animator/director] (b. Elmira NY, 15 Oct 1891–28 Dec 1971 [79], Glendale CA). (Charles Bowers, 1915; Disney, 1929; Walter Lantz.) "Burton Gillette," *Variety,* 12 Jan 1972. BHD2, p. 98 (d. LA CA).

Gillette, Elma [stage/film actress] (b. 3 Jul 1874–9 Jul 1941 [67], Los Angeles CA). AS, p. 446 (d. 23 Jul). BHD, p. 179. "Elma Gillette," *NYDM,* 3 Feb 1915, 23:1.

Gillette, Ethel [scenarist]. No data found. AMD, p. 136. "Mayer Adds to Scenario Staff," *MPW,* 27 Mar 1920, 2155. "Governor's [ex-Governor James N. Gillette of CA] Daughter Joins Mayer," *MPW,* 29 May 1920, 1217.

Gillette, William [actor] (b. Hartford CT, 24 Jul 1853–29 Apr 1937 [83], Hartford CT; pulmonary hemorrhage). "William Gillette, Actor, Dead at 81; Director and Playwright Had Gained Chief Fame in Role of Sherlock Holmes; Was Still on Tour at 80; Made First Stage Appearance in 1875 and His Last in 1936 in New York," *NYT,* 30 Apr 1937, 21:1. "Wm. Gillette, Author-Star, Dies at 81; One of Wealthiest Actors," *Variety,* 5 May 1937. AMD, p. 136. AS, p. 446. BHD, p. 179. GSS, pp. 141–43. IFN, p. 117. Truitt, p. 124. "Gillette in Essanay Production," *MPW,* 11 Mar 1916, 1656. *MPN Studio Directory,* 21 Oct 1916 (b. 1853).

Gilliat, Sidney [scenarist/director] (b. Edgeley, England, 15 Feb 1908–31 May 1994 [86], Pewsey Vale, England; leukemia). m. Beryl (d. 1981). "Sidney Gilliat, 86, British Screenwriter and Movie Director," *The New York Times,* 2 Jun 1994, D23:2 ("began his career writing lines [and titles] for silent movies"). "Sidney Gilliat," *Variety,* 6 Jun 1994, 45:2. AS, p. 446 (d. Pensey Vale, England). BHD2, p. 98.

Gillingwater, Claude [actor] (*né* Claude Gillenwater, b. Louisiana MO, 2 Aug 1870–1 Nov 1939 [69], Beverly Hills CA; suicide by shooting). m. Carlyn Stelleth. "Claude Gillingwater," *Variety,* 8 Nov 1939. AS, p. 447. BHD1, p. 215. FSS, p. 124. IFN, p. 117. MH, p. 112. Truitt, p. 124 (b. 1870). Lewis G. Krohn, "Who in the Heck Was Claude Gilling-water?," *CFC,* 57 (Winter, 1977), 32.

Gillis, Bill [actor] (*né* William S. Gillis, b. TX, 17 Nov 1867–24 Apr 1946 [78], Los Angeles CA). *Cf.* Diana Serra Cary, *The Hollywood Posse* (Boston MA: Houghton Mifflin Co., 1975). "William S. Gillis," *Variety,* 1 May 1946 ("he had appeared in films for over 40 years"). AS, p. 447. BHD1, p. 215. IFN, p. 117. Truitt, p. 124. George A. Katchmer, "Remembering the Great Silents," *CI,* 1 (Sep 1990), 44–45.

Gillman, Mary Arriea [actress]. No data found. AMD, p. 136. "Wallace Beery to Wed," *MPW,* 9 Aug 1924, 436 (did not marry her).

Gillman, Rita [actress] (b. Roanoke VA, 1898–14 Nov 1986 [88?], Canoga Park CA). BHD1, p. 215.

Gillmore, Frank (father of **Margalo Gillmore**) [actor/Equity President] (b. New York NY, 14 May 1867–29 Mar 1943 [75], New York NY). Jack Pulaski, "Frank Gillmore Dies in New York at 76; Was Equity Prez 8 Years," *Variety,* 150, 31 Mar 1943, 41:1, 44:3 (age 76; helped to form Equity in 1913; held #1 Equity membership card). BHD, p. 179.

Gillmore, Margalo (daughter of **Frank Gillmore**) (b. London, England, 21 May 1897–30 Jun 1986 [89], New York NY). AS, p. 447. BHD1, p. 216.

Gills, Norbert M. [actor] (d. 21 Feb 1920, San Francisco CA). BHD, p. 179.

Gillstrom, Arvid E. [director] (b. Götenberg, Sweden, 13 Aug 1890?–21 May 1935 [44?], Los Angeles CA). (Began with Christie, 1911; Educational; Universal; Paramount.) "Arvid Gillstrom," *Variety,* 29 May 1935. AMD, p. 136. AS, p. 447. BHD2, p. 99. "Arvid E. Gillstrom," *MPW,* 23 Mar 1918, 1680. "Gillstrom on from the Coast," *MPW,* 29 Jun 1918, 1828. "Gillstrom to Direct the Lees," *MPW,* 24 Aug 1918, 1123. "Gillstrom Goes to Coast to Make Fox Comedies," *MPW,* 12 Oct 1918, 236. William J. Reilly, "Gillstrom Mixes Sublime, Ridiculous and Ring Lardner in Scenic Cocktail," *MPW,* 10 Jan 1920, 287. "Christie Signs Arvid Gillstrom," *MPW,* 12 Feb 1927, 500.

Gilman, Ada [actress] (b. 6 Oct 1854–18 Dec 1921 [67], Holmesburg PA). "Ada Gilman," *Variety,* 23 Dec 1921. AS, p. 447. BHD, p. 179. IFN, p. 117.

Gilman, Fred [actor] (b. 24 Nov 1902–30 Mar 1988 [85], Capistrano Beach CA). BHD1, p. 216.

Gilmer, Reuben [scenarist/producer] (d. 4 Jan 1920, London, England; after an accident). AS, p. 447. BHD2, p. 99.

Gilmore, Barney (father of **Lillian Gilmore**) [stage/film actor] (b. Philadelphia PA, 1869?–19 Apr 1949 [80], Los Angeles CA). AMD, p. 136. AS, p. 447. BHD, p. 179. IFN, p. 117. Spehr, p. 134 (b. 1867). "Barney Gilmore with Solax," *MPW,* XV, 8 Mar 1913, 1002. "Barney Gilmore," *MPW,* 2 Oct 1915, 57. "Barney Gilmore in F.B.O. Feature with Daughter," *MPW,* 25 Jun 1927, 592. "Barney Gilmore Names Warner Bros. in Damage Suit," *MPW,* 27 Aug 1927, 585.

Gilmore, Billie [director] (*née* Ada Marie Maloney, b. New haven CT-d. 27 Jun 1931, Los Angeles CA). "Billie Gilmore," *Variety,* 28 Jul 1931. BHD2, p. 99. IFN, p. 117. SD.

Gilmore, Douglas [actor] (*né* Harris Augustin Gilmore, b. Boston MA, 25 Jun 1903–26 Jul 1950 [47], New York NY; buried in Woodlawn Cemetery NY). m. (1) Gladys Frazin, Chicago IL, 1924; Ruth Mix, Yuma AZ, Jun 1930—annulled; (2) Kay Kenny. (Film debut: *His Buddy's Wife,* Assoc. Distr., 4 Oct 1925.) AMD, p. 136. AS, p. 447. BHD1, p. 216. FSS, p. 125 (b. Marion IA). IFN, p. 117. "Douglas Gilmore Signed by Mayer," *MPW,* 4 Jul 1925, 85. "Gilmore Signs Famous Players Contract," *MPW,* 29 Nov 1926, 3. Bill Wilson, "Douglas Wilson," *CI,* 102 (Dec 1983), 72–73, 79 (b. Marion IA, 21 Jun; includes filmography).

Gilmore, Elinor [actress]. No data found. AMD, p. 136. "Rogers Has New Star," *MPW,* 5 Nov 1927, 10.

Gilmore, Faye [actress] (b. 1900–12 Aug 1984 [84?]). BHD, p. 179.

Gilmore, H.G. [scenarist] (b. 1886–4 Jul 1921 [35?], Chicago IL). BHD2, p. 99.

Gilmore, Helen [actress] (b. Washington DC, 4 Jan 1862–16 Nov 1936 [74], Los Angeles CA). AMD, p. 136. BHD, p. 179. "Vim Secures Helen Gilmore," *MPW,* 13 Nov 1915, 1327.

Gilmore, Helen [actress] (b. Chicago IL, 1900?–8 Oct 1947 [47], New York NY; leukemia). "Helen Gilmore," *Variety,* 15 Oct 1947. AS, p. 447.

Gilmore, Lillian (daughter of **Barney Gilmore**) [actress]. AMD, p. 136. BR, pp. 152–53. "'U' signs Stage Star's Daughter," *MPW,* 21 May 1927, 190. "Barney Gilmore in F.B.O. Feature with Daughter," *MPW,* 25 Jun 1927, 592. "'U' Signs Miss Gilmore," *MPW,* 10 Sep 1927, 78. George A. Katchmer, "Forgotten Cowboys and Cowgirls—Part V," *CI,* 177 (Mar 1990), C2.

Gilmore, Paul [stage/film actor/producer] (b. Rochester NY). (Metro; Raver, Staten Island NY; Kalem.) AMD, p. 136. J. Van Cartmell, "...News from the Pacific Colony," *NYDM,* 8 Sep 1915, 32:3 (to appear in *Penitents*). "Paul Gilmore at Liberty," *MPW,* 18 Sep 1915, 2011. "Another Raver Star; Paul Gilmore Engaged to Appear in

'Other Girl,' Initial Raver Feature," *NYDM*, 6 Nov 1915, 25:1 (had appeared in Grittith's *The Penitents*). "Paul Gilmore with Raver," *MPW*, 6 Nov 1915, 1109. "Gilmore Reaches Raver Studio," *NYDM*, 20 Nov 1915, 31:2 (to film *The Other Girl*, with James J. Corbett). "Character Signs Paul Gilmore for a Series of Productions," *MPW*, 13 Mar 1920, 1785.

Gilmore, William [executive] (d. 7 Jun 1919). BHD2, p. 99.

Gilmore, William E[dward] [general manager] (b. New York NY, 1863–1928 [65?]). AMD, p. 136. Spehr, p. 134. William E. Gilmore, "Edison Company's Stawtement," *MPW*, 29 Feb 1908, 158–59.

Gilmour, Boyd J. (actor/producer] (b. Kilmarnock, Scotland, 1873–13 Jul 1934 [61?], Gaffney SC). BHD2, p. 99.

Gilmour, John H. [actor] (b. Ottawa, Canada, 1857?–24 Nov 1922 [65], Yonkers NY). "John H. Gilmour," *Variety*, 1 Dec 1922. AS, p. 447. BHD, p. 179. IFN, p. 118. SD. WWVC, pp. 57–58.

Gilmour, Wesley [executive] (b. 1870–6 Jul 1935 [65?], Los Angeles CA). BHD2, p. 99.

Gilpin, Charles S[idney] [actor/playwright] (b. Richmond VA, 20 Nov 1878–6 May 1930 [51], Eldredge Park NJ). m. Alice Bynum. "Charles S. Gilpin," *Variety*, 14 May 1930 ("starred in a number of colored cast pictures [silents]"). AMD, p. 136. AS, p. 447. BHD, p. 179. SD, p. 506. Truitt, p. 124. WWWA. "Gilpin will Play 'Uncle Tom,'" *MPW*, 12 Jun 1926, 7.

Gilroy, Barbara [actress]. No data found. (Universal.)

Gilson, Charles E. [cinematographer]. No data found. AMD, p. 136. FDY, p. 459. "New Cameraman Shooting Hines' 'The Brown Derby,'" *MPW*, 1 May 1926, 41.

Gil-Spear, Adrian [scenarist]. No data found. AMD, p. 136. "Gil-Spear Made Goldwyn Scenario Chief," *MPW*, 14 Apr 1917, 292.

Ginet, René [director/scenarist] (*né* Joseph René Ginet, b. Vienne, France, 12 Jul 1896 [extrait de naissance no. 317/1896]-30 Sep 1971 [75], Neuilly-sur-Seine, France). AS, p. 448.

Gingold, Baroness Helene [actress] (d. 10 Dec 1926). BHD, p. 179.

Giniva, John "Alaska Jack" [actor] (b. 1867–22 Feb 1936 [], Los Angeles CA). AS, p. 448.

Ginn, Hayward J. [actor] (b. Virginia City NV, 8 Sep 1877–14 Feb 1926 [48], Sawtell CA; suicide by gas inhalation). m. Maude Gilbert. "2 Gas Suicides," *Variety*, 24 Feb 1926. AS, p. 448 (b. 1878). BHD, p. 179 (b. 1878). IFN, p. 118. Truitt 1983, p. 274 (b. 1878).

Ginn, Wells Watson [actor/director] (b. Bellefontaine OH, 1891?–15 Apr 1959 [68], Cincinnati OH). m. Nancy (d. 1957). "Wells W. Ginn," *Variety*, 22 Apr 1959. AS, p. 448. BHD, p. 179; BHD2, p. 99. IFN, p. 118. Truitt, p. 124.

Ginna, Arnaldo [director/cinematographer]. No data found. JS, p. 195 (one film, Vita futurista, Italy, 1916).

Ginoris, Marie [head film cutter] (*nee?*). No data found. AMD, p. 136. "Mrs. Ginoris Now with Paramount," *MPW*, 7 Jan 1922, 79.

Giono, Jean Fernand [director/producer/scenarist] (b. Manosque, France, 30 Mar 1895 [extrait de naissance no. 35/1895]-8 Oct 1970 [75], Manosque, France [extrait de décès no. 144/1970]). AS, p. 448.

Giordani, Arturo [cinematographer] (b. Rome, Italy, 9 Jan—?). JS, p. 196 (in Italian silents from 1919).

Gipsy, Maude [actress] (*née* Germaine Garnon, b. France, 1892–6 Dec 1969 [77?], France). AS, p. 448.

Giraci (or Geraci), May [actress]. No data found. (Universal.) MPG.

Girard, Joseph W. [actor] (b. Williamsport PA, 2 Apr 1871–21 Aug 1949 [78], Woodland Hills CA). (Universal.) AMD, p. 136. AS, p. 449. BHD1, p. 216. IFN, p. 118. "Joseph Girard," *MPW*, 1 Sep 1917, 1356. "Girard Added to Cast," *MPW*, 15 Nov 1924, 253.

Girardot, Etienne [stage/film actor] (b. London, England, 22 Feb 1856–10 Nov 1939 [83], Los Angeles CA). "Etienne Girardot, Character Actor; Veteran of Stage and Screen, Once with Old Vitagraph Co., Dies in Hollywood at 83; A Shakespearean Player; Appeared with Ellen Terry—Originated Title Role Here in 'Charley's Aunt,'" *NYT*, 11 Nov 1939, 15:3. "Etienne Girardot," *Variety*, 15 Nov 1939. AS, p. 449. BHD1, p. 216. IFN, p. 118. Truitt, p. 125.

Giraud, Octavio [actor] (b. Havana, Cuba, 1 Apr 1890–3 Jun 1958 [68], Los Angeles CA). AS, p. 449.

Giraudoux, Jean [scenarist/producer] (*né* Hippol¥te Jean Giraudoux, b. Bellac, France, 29 Oct 1882–31 Jan 1944 [61], Paris, France). AS, p. 449. BHD2, p. 99.

Girel, Constant Marie [director] (b. Seyssel, France, 28 Dec 1873–14 Feb 1952 [78], Arinthod, France). AS, p. 449.

Girod, Norman [producer] (b. Manchester, England, 19 Jan 1894). AS, p. 449 (worked in France).

Gish, Dorothy Elizabeth (daughter of **Mrs. Mary Gish**; sister of **Dorothy Gish**) [stage/film actress] (*née* Dorothy Elizabeth de Guiche, b. Dayton OH, 11 Mar 1898–4 Jun 1968 [70], Rapallo, Italy; bronchial pneumonia [extrait de décès no. 103/1968]). m. **James Rennie**, 26 Dec 1920, Greenwich CT—div. 1935 (d. 1965). (Biograph, 1912; Paramount; Reliance-Majestic; Fine Arts.) (Official film debut: *An Unseen Enemy*, 1912.) "Dorothy Gish, Actress, Is Dead; In Theater and Films 50 Years; Starred with Sister, Lillian, in Griffith Silent Classics—Many Broadway Roles," *NYT*, 6 Jun 1968, 47:1. "Dorothy Gish," *Variety*, 12 Jun 1968. AMD, p. 136. AS, p. 449. BHD1, p. 216. FFF, p. 123. FSS, p. 125. IFN, p. 118 (b. Massilon OH). KOM, pp. 136–38. MH, p. 112. MSBB, p. 1034, 1036 (b. Springfield OH, 1896). Truitt, p. 125. WWS, p. 62. "Dorothy Gish," *MPW*, 18 Apr 1914, 337. W.E. Wing, "Film Stars Near Death," *NYDM*, 2 Dec 1914, 24:2 (Gish was struck by a car and dragged forty feet; her left side was torn and a toe cut off. J.P. McGowan [Kalem] fell from a telegraph pole; three months to recover. Ford Sterling [Universal] had typhoid pneumonia. Helen Holmes [Kalem] was a victim of double pneumonia). W.E. Wing, "On the Pacific Coast," *NYDM*, 9 Dec 1914, 26:2 (Gish, Mae Marsh, and Miriam Cooper "had just left the Mutual studio and were crossing the Hollywood boulevard when a machine swept down upon them." Only Gish was hurt. "'Don't tell Lillian! Don't let mother know!' cried the crushed victim when friendly hands carried her from the scene.... 'I am so glad it wasn't Lillian. She is so small it would have hurt her much worse...'" McGowan injured the pelvis bone.) W.E. Wing, "Along the Pacific Coast," *NYDM*, 13 Jan 1915, 26:3 (Gish "is prancing about the Mutual studio once more, only a little worse for wear..." after her recent accident.). "The Coast in Review," *NYDM*, 27 Jan 1915, 50:3 ("After tripping a few measures with Dorothy Gish at the big hop [exhibitors' ball], we have decided to lose a toe also...."). "Dorothy Gish—Triangle Star," *MPW*, 30 Oct 1915, 764. "One on Dorothy," *MPW*, 8 Apr 1916, 243. "Dorothy Gish Saves Natalie Talmadge from Drowning," *MPW*, 9 Jul 1916, 775. "Dorothy Gish," *MPW*, 20 Jan 1917, 373. "Dorothy Gish Engaged by Selznick," *MPW*, 14 Apr 1917, 257. "Dorothy Gish Visits Chicago," *MPW*, 29 Jun 1918, 1845. "Dorothy Gish Is to Be Starred by Paramount," *MPW*, 29 Jun 1918. 1864. "Seven Players New to Artcraf -Paramount," *MPW*, 6 Jul 1918, 57. Edward Weitzel, "Novel Interview with Dorothy Gish," *MPW*, 13 Jul 1918, 215. "Gish Sisters Contract Flu," *MPW*, 30 Nov 1918, 937. E.M. Robbins, "Before and After Taking," *MPC*, Jan 1919, 52–53, 67. "Lillian Gish Directed Dorothy," *MPW*, 26 Jun 1920, 1777. E. Weitzel, "Talking It Over with Miss Dorothy Gish After she Took That Trip to Greenwich," *MPW*, 15 Jan 1921, 293 (married Rennie). "They're Married!; The double romance and marriage of Constance Talmadge and Dorothy Gish," *Photoplay*, Mar 1921, 59, 113 (honeymooned in NY since Rennie was appearing at the Rialto in *.Spanish Love*). "Signs Players," *MPW*, 7 Oct 1922, 469. "Dorothy Gish in New Feature," *MPW*, 16 Dec 1922, 647. "Dorothy Gish's Inspiration Films for Release byu Metro," *MPW*, 31 May 1924, 456. Kenneth Alexander, "An Unretouched Portrait of Dorothy Gish," *MW*, 6 Dec 1924, 12–13, 23. "Inspiration Signs Dorothy Gish," *MPW*, 23 May 1925, 468. Sara Redway, "Normalcy and Miss Gish," *MPC*, Sep 1925, 62, 86. "'Jaydee' Signs Dorothy Gish," *MPW*, 6 Feb 1926, 3. Mabel Livingstone, "Dorothy Gish Prefers London to Paris; For the Past Year This Beloved American Cinema Actress Has Been Working in British Studios—And She Has Enjoyed It," *Cinema Arts*, Dec 1926, 24–25. Eve Golden, "Dorothy—'The Other Side of the Story,'" *CI*, 206 (Aug 1992), C8-C10.

Gish, Lillian, "The Duse of the Silver Screen" (daughter of **Mrs. Mary Gish**; sister of **Dorothy Gish**) [stage/film actress/director] (*née* Lillian Diana de Guiche, b. Springfield OH, 14 Oct 1893–27 Feb 1993 [99], New York NY; heart failure). Unmarried. With Ann Pinchot, *The Movies, Mr. Griffith and Me* (Englewood Cliffs NJ: Prentice-Hall, Inc., 1969); Stuart Oderman, Lillian Gish; *A Life on Stage and Screen* (Jefferson NC: McFarland, 2000). (Biograph; Artcraft.) Albin Krebs, "Lillian Gish, 99, a Movie Star Since Movies Began, Is Dead," *NYT*, 1 Mar 1993, A1:5, B10:1. Glenn Collins, "Hundreds [nearly 700] Gather to Mourn a Friend, Lillian Gish," *NYT*, 12 Mar 1993, A19:4. Leonard Klady, "Lillian Gish," *Variety*, 8 Mar 1993, p. 75:1 ("the china doll icon of seven decades of cinema"). AMD, p. 137. AS, p. 449. BHD, p. 180; BHD2, p. 99. FFF, p. 112. FSS, p. 126. Katz, pp. 485–86. KOM, p. 138 (b. 1896). MSBB, p. 1036 (b. 1896). "Lillian Gish," *MPW*, 20 Jun 1914, 1702. "Gish Sisters Contract Flu," *MPW*, 30 Nov 1918, 937. "Award for Lilian Gish Photograph," *MPW*, 19 Apr 1919, 362. Edward Weitzel, "Lillian Gish Takes a Look Ahead," *MPW*, 12 Jul 1919, 221. "Lillian Gish Leaves David W. Griffith to Star for Frohman Amusement Company,"

MPW, 5 Jun 1920, 1308. "Lillian Gish Directed Dorothy," *MPW,* 26 Jun 1920, 1777. E. Weitzel, "When Lillian Gish Goes on Location on an Ice Cake in the Arctic Sea," *MPW,* 30 Oct 1920, 1231. John G. Holme, "Film-Flamming the Public; Exposing some further activities of those who prey on the public faith in the Motion Picture," *Photoplay,* Mar 1921, 60, 120–21 (under her contract with William L. Sherrill of Frohman, Gish was to receive $3,500 per week for the first year; $4,500 per week the second year, and $7,000 per week the third year; and was to be on the payroll 52 weeks a year. She also was to receive a percentage of the profits of the 15 pictures she was to make over a three-year period. But by Sep 1920, Sherrill failed to sell enough stock to float himself. Ruth Clifford sued him for breach of contract and the Gish production was halted. The Frohman Amusement Co.'s "bill of complaint asserts that the company has already spent $54,000 on the unfinished Gish masterpiece which it is unable to complete for lack of funds."). "At the Woods," *MPW,* 2 Apr 1921, 483. "Miss Lillian Gish Says," *MPW,* 4 Mar 1922, 38. "Signs Players," *MPW,* 7 Oct 1922, 469. "Lillian Gish Is Exclusive Metro-Goldwyn Star," *MPW,* 8 Nov 1924, 122. "Lillian Gish to Appear for Metro in Specials," *MPW,* 15 Nov 1924, 265. "Ask for Injunction to Keep Lillian Gish with Duell Co.," *MPW,* 14 Feb 1925, 653. "Lillian Gish Wins; Duell Charged with Perjury," *MPW,* 18 Apr 1925, 654. "Schenck Signs Lillian Gish," *MPW,* 25 Apr 1925, 763. "Lillian Gish," *MPW,* 2 May 1925, 82. "Lillian Gish Named Defendant in Five Million Dollar Suit," *MPW,* 2 Jul 1927, 17. Lillian Gish, "Go West, Young Woman!—If You've the Stuff; Hollywood Offers Great Opportunities...," *Cinema Art,* Sep 1927, 16–17, 49. "Lillian Gish Answers Charles Duell's Action," *MPW,* 8 Oct 1927, 357. "Lillian Gish to Testify," *MPW,* 31 Dec 1927, 25. Richard A. Blake, "Lillian Gish: A Passing," *America,* 168, March 20–27, 1993, 14 ("Lillian Gish invented much more than the close-up. She invented film acting, and with Griffith, she invented the movies.") Maude Cheatham, "The Darkest Hour, VI," *Classic,* Dec 1922, 43. Gladys Hall and Adele Whitely Fletcher, "We Interview the Gish Girls," *MW,* 26 Jul 1924, 4–5, 28–29. "She Says She Won't [get married]," *MPC,* Jul 1925, 64, 87. Gladys Hall, "The Grave and Guileless Gish; She Sees No Evil, Hears No Evil, Speaks No Evil," *MPC,* Jul 1927, 53, 85. Frank Cullen, "Off-Screen Moments: Lillian Gish," *CI,* 262 (Apr 1997), C8-C9.

Gish, Mrs. Mary (mother of **Lillian** and **Dorothy Gish**) [actress] (aka Mary Bernard, *née* Mary Robinson McConnell, b. Urbana IL, 1860–16 Sep 1948 [88?], New York NY). AS, p. 449. BHD, p. 180.

Gittens, Wyndham [director/scenarist] (b. Barbados, West Indies, 7 Feb 1885–18 Jun 1967 [82], Dunedin FL). BHD2, p. 99. FDY, p. 425.

Giunchi, Lea (sister-in-law of Polidor) [actress] (b. 1888?). (Cines-Kleine, 1911.) AMD, p. 137. JS, p. 199 (in Italian silents from 1910). "Cines-Kleine Players," *MPW,* 11 Jul 1914, 237–38 ("She is twenty-six years old, rides like a centaur, is a splendid swimmer, and a master with the foils.").

Giustini, Carlo [actor] (b. Rome, Italy, 16 Aug 1889). AS, p. 450.

Glackens, Louis M. [animator] (b. 1866–10 Sep 1933 [67?], New York NY). AS, p. 450. BHD2, p. 99.

Glagolin, Boris S. [director/producer] (b. Russia, 1878–12 Dec 1948 [70?], Los Angeles CA). AS, p. 450.

Glaser, Ben [director/producer/scenarist] (b. Belfast, Ireland, 7 May 1892–18 Mar 1956 [63], Los Angeles CA). AS, p. 450.

Glaser, Lulu [actress] (b. Allegheny [North Side, Pittsburgh] PA, 2 Jun 1874–5 Sep 1958 [84], Weston CT). m. **Ralph Herz** (d. 1921); (2) Thomas D. Richards. (Christie.) "Lulu Glaser at Work," *Variety,* 27 Aug 1915, 16. AS, p. 450. BHD, p. 180 (d. Norwalk CT). IFN, p. 118.

Glaser, Vaughan [actor] (b. OH, 17 Nov 1872–23 Nov 1958 [86], Van Nuys CA). AS, p. 450.

Glasmon, Kubec [scenarist] (b. Racioz, Poland, 1889–13 Mar 1938 [49?], Los Angeles CA). AS, p. 450 (b. 1897). BHD2, p. 99.

Glass, Gaston J. [stage/film actor] (b. Paris, France, 31 Dec 1895–11 Nov 1965 [69], Santa Monica CA). m. **Bo-Peep Karlin** (d. 1969). (Fox.) "Gaston J. Glass Dies at 66; TV Official Began as Actor," *NYT,* 13 Nov 1965, 29:6. "Gaston J. Glass," *Variety,* 17 Nov 1965. AMD, p. 137. AS, p. 450 (b. 1898). BHD1, p. 217. IFN, p. 118 (b. 1899). MH, p. 113. Truitt, p. 125. Waldman, p. 120 (b. 1899). WWS, p. 59. "Glass in Title Role," *MPW,* 7 Aug 1920, 722. "Gaston Glass Engaged," *MPW,* 31 May 1924, 457.

Glass, James Douglas [actor]. No data found. AMD, p. 137. "Who Has Seen This Boy?," *MPW,* 8 Apr 1916, 236.

Glass, Max [producer] (b. Vienna, Austria, 1884–18 Jul 1964 [80?], Paris, France). AS, p. 450. BHD2, p. 99.

Glass, Montague Marsden [author/title writer] (b. Manchester, England, 23 Jul 1877–3 Feb 1934 [56], Westport CT; cerebral hemorrhage). m. Caroline Patterson, 14 Feb 1907, Port Jervis NY (d. 1948). "Montague Glass, Writer, Dies at 56; Cerebral Hemorrhage Fatal to the Creator of 'Potash and Perlmutter' Stories; Began Career as Lawyer; Author and Playwright Was Active Until Recently on Radio Continuity," *NYT,* 4 Feb 1934, 30:1. "Mrs. Glass, Widow of the Author, 71," *NYT,* 26 Jan 1948, 19:2. "Montagu Glass Passes," *Variety,* 6 Feb 1934. AMD, p. 137. "Montague Glass to Write Titles," *MPW,* 3 Jun 1922, 471. "Glass Joins Fox Authors," *MPW,* 18 Jul 1925, 356.

Glassmire, Albert [actor/scenarist/director] (b. Philadelphia PA, 1881?–2 Dec 1926 [45], Los Angeles CA). (Biograph; Triangle; Keystone.) "Albert Glassmire," *Variety,* 15 Dec 1926. AS, p. 450. BHD2, p. 99.

Glassmire, Gus [actor] (*né* Augustin J. Glassmire, b. Philadelphia PA, 29 Aug 1879–23 Jul 1946 [66], Los Angeles CA). AS, p. 450.

Glässner, Erika [actress] (b. Germany, 28 Feb 1896–1951 [55?]). BHD, p. 180. Vittorio Martinelli, "Kino-Lieblinge," *Griffithiana,* 38/39 (Oct 1990), 13 (in silent and sound films).

Glauber, Jack [scenarist/cameraman]. No data found. FDY, pp. 425, 459.

Glaum, Louise [stage/film actress] (b. Baltimore MD, 10 Sep 1895?–25 Nov 1970 [75?], Los Angeles CA; pneumonia). m. (1) **Harry J. Edwards,** 1915—div. 1919 (d. 1952); (2) Zachary M. Harris, Kansas City MO, Jan 1926. (Pathé; Nestor; Ince; Paralta.) "Louise Glaum," *Variety,* 2 Dec 1970 (age 70). AMD, p. 137. AS, p. 450 (b. 1900; d. 26 Nov). BHD, p. 180 (b. 4 Sep 1900). IFN, p. 118 (b. 1900). Lowrey, p. 62. MH, p. 113. MSBB, p. 1036. Truitt, p. 125. "Notes from Nestor," *MPW,* 27 Jul 1912, 331. "Louise Glaum Starts the Baboon Kiss," *MPW,* 11 Apr 1914, 222. W.E. Wing, "Along the Pacific Coast," *NYDM,* 19 May 1915, 24:2 (m. Edwards, LK-O director). "Louise Glaum to Be Starred by Triangle," *MPW,* 17 Feb 1917, 1015. "Louise Glaum Visits New York," *MPW,* 29 Sep 1917, 1981. "Louise Glaum Returns to Coast," *MPW,* 6 Oct 1917, 77. "Paramount Getting Ready for Miss Glaum," *MPW,* 9 Feb 1918, 846. "In Photodrama of France Louise Glaum Finds Ideal," *MPW,* 3 Aug 1918, 701. "Louise Glaum to Marry Again," *Variety,* 28 Mar 1919, 96:3 (recently divorced from Harry Edwards, who married Gladys Brockwell, Glaum was "to marry J. Parker Reid, confidential man for Thomas H. Ince."). "Louise Glaum Files Judgment," *MPW,* 26 Apr 1919, 539. "Louise Glaum in New York; Star Acclaimed Enroute," *MPW,* 28 Feb 1920, 1506. Edward Weitzel, "Louise Glaum's Human Document Story Is Interrupted by the Nameless One," *MPW,* 27 Mar 1920, 2149. ⅔Louise Glaum to Write on Screen Life," *MPW,* 15 May 1920, 936. "Fred Warren Pays Tribute to Louise Glaum's Rapid Rise in Popular Esteem" *MPW,* 2 Oct 1920, 662. "Deny Absurd Story of DeMille-Glaum Marriage," *MPW,* 11 Dec 1920, 704. "Louise Glaum Is Signed," *MPW,* 28 Jan 1922, 400.

Glavey, John J. [director] (b. Philadelphia PA, 1884?–2 Jan 1925 [40], Los Angeles CA; effects of gas fumes). (Keystone; Normand.) "John J. Glavey," *Variety,* 14 Jan 1925. AS, p. 450. BHD2, p. 99 (b. 1886).

Glazer, Benjamin F. (Barney) [scenarist/producer/director] (b. Belfast, No. Ireland, 7 May 1887–18 Mar 1956 [68], Los Angeles CA). m. **Sharon Lynn** (d. 1963). (Pathé; WB; Paramount; UA.) "B.F. Glazer Dies, Movie Writer, 68; Won Academy Award for Scripts of 'Arise My Love' and 'Seventh Heaven,'" *NYT,* 19 Mar 1956, 31:3. "Benjamin F. Glazer," *Variety,* 21 Mar 1956. AMD, p. 137. AS, p. 450. BHD2, p. 100. FDY, p. 425. Katz, p. 486 (d. 1958). "Benjamin Glazer Signed by M-G-M," *MPW,* 20 Feb 1926, 714.

Glazer, Eve F. [actress] (b. PA, 4 Jun 1903–29 Jun 1960 [57], Los Angeles CA). AS, p. 450. BHD, p. 180.

Gleason, Adda [actress] (b. Chicago IL, 19 Dec 1888–6 Feb 1971 [82], Woodland Hills CA). BHD1, p. 217. IFN, p. 118. NNAT 3, p. 276. Truitt 1983, p. 276.

Gleason, Fred [actor] (b. 1854?–9 Jun 1933 [79], New York NY). "Fred Gleason," *Variety,* 13 Jun 1933 ("had done considerable screen work"). BHD, p. 180. IFN, p. 118.

Glazer, Herbert [director/scenarist] (b. Philadelphia PA, 4 Dec 1895). AS, p. 450.

Gleason, Adda [actress] (b. Chicago IL, 19 Dec 1888–6 Feb 1971 [82], Woodland Hills CA). AS, p. 450.

Gleason, Fred [actor] (b. 1853–9 Jun 1933 [80?], New York NY). AS, p. 450.

Gleason, James Austin (father of **Russell Gleason**) [actor/scenarist] (b. New York NY, 23 May 1882–12 Apr 1959 [76], Woodland Hills CA; asthma). m. Lucille Webster (1888–1947). (Began 1922.) "James Gleason," *Variety,* 15 Apr 1959 (age 72). AS, p. 451 (b. 1886). BHD1, p. 217; BHD2, p. 100. IFN, p. 118. Truitt, p. 125 (b. 1886). Herbert Cruikshank, "Troupers Three; Jimmy and Lucille and Russell, the Last Names Being Gleason," *MPC,* Feb 1929, 40, 78.

Gleason, John J. [actor] (b. San Francisco CA, 1872?–12 Mar 1923 [51], New York NY). "John J. Gleason," *Variety,* 15 Mar 1923. AS, p. 451. SD, p. 509.

Gleason, Mina [actress] (*née* Mina Crolius, b. Boston MA, 1858–27 Jun 1931 [73?], Beverly Hills CA). AS, p. 451. BHD, p. 180.

Gleason, Russell (son of **James Gleason** and Lucille Webster) [actor] (b. Portland OR, 6 Feb 1908–26 Dec 1945 [39], New York NY; fell from window of Hotel Sutton). m. Cynthia. "Russell Gleason's Death by a Fall Accidental," *Variety,* 2 Jan 1946. AS, p. 451. BHD1, p. 217 (b. 1907). IFN, p. 118.

Gleckler, Robert P. [actor] (b. Pierre SD, 11 Jan 1887–25 Feb 1939 [52], No. Hollywood CA; uremic poisoning). m. **Norma S. Phillips** (d. 1931); Adelaide Kendall, 1930. "Robert Gleckler," *Variety,* 1 Mar 1939 (was to have been in *Gone with the Wind*). AS, p. 451. BHD1, p. 217. IFN, p. 118. Truitt, p. 126 (b. 1890).

Gleichman, Phil [executive/manufacturer]. No data found. AMD, p. 137. "Gleichman Heads New Company," *MPW,* XXIII, 6 Feb 1915, 806. "Gleichman's New Enterprise," *MPW,* 10 Apr 1915, 224.

Gleize, Maurice [director] (b. Enghien-les-Bains, France, 4 Apr 1898–1974 [76?], France). AS, p. 451.

Glendinning, Ernest [actor] (b. Ulverston, England, 19 Feb 1884–17 May 1936 [52], So. Coventry CT). m. Marie J. Horne. "Ernest Glendenning," *Variety,* 20 May 1936 (age 42). AS, p. 451. BHD, p. 180. IFN, p. 118. SD. Truitt, p. 126.

Glendinning, John [actor] (b. Whitehaven, Cumberland, England, 30 Nov 1856?–15 Jul 1916 [60], Cheltenham, England). m. (1) Clara Louise Braithwaite (d. 1904); Jessie Millward. "John Glendinning," *Variety,* 21 Jul 1916. AS, p. 451. SD, p. 510 (b. 1857).

Glendon, J[onathan] **Frank** [actor] (b. Chateau MT, 25 Oct 1884–17 Mar 1937 [52], Los Angeles CA). (Lubin; Kalem; B.S. Moss; Metro; Rialto; Gaumont.) "Jonathan Glendon," *Variety,* 24 Mar 1937. AMD, p. 137. AS, p. 451. BHD1, p. 217. IFN, p. 118. Truitt, p. 126. "J. Frank Glendon," *MPW,* 16 Oct 1915, 455. *MPN Studio Directory,* 21 Oct 1916, 25.

Glenn, Forrest [actor] (b. Marissa IL, 1900–24 Aug 1954 [54?], Saranac Lake NY). BHD, p. 180.

Glenn, Raymond *see* **Custer, Bob**

Glennon, Bert L[awrence] [actor/cinematographer/scenarist/director] (*né* Herbert Glennon, b. Anaconda MT, 19 Nov 1893–29 Jun 1967 [73], Sherman Oaks CA). "Bert Glennon, Cameraman on Coast Since 1918, Dies," *NYT,* 1 Jul 1967, 23:6. "Bert Glennon," *Variety,* 5 Jul 1967. AMD, p. 138. AS, p. 451. BHD2, p. 100 (d. LA CA). FDY, p. 459. IFN, p. 119. "He's a Veteran," *MPW,* 19 Mar 1927, 182.

Glett, Charles Lester [actor]. No data found. AMD, p. 138. "He'a a Veteran," *MPW,* 19 Mar 1927, 182.

Glickman, Ellis P. [Yiddish showman/actor] (b. Kiev, Russia, 1869?–3 Oct 1931 [62], Chicago IL). "Ellis P. Glickman," *Variety,* 6 Oct 1931. AMD, p. 138. AS, p. 451. BHD, p. 180. "Glickman to Appear in 'The Last Concert,'" *MPW,* 6 Jun 1914, 1396.

Gliddon, John [actor/director/producer] (b. 24 Aug 1897–18 Jul 1990 [92], Worthing, England). BHD, p. 180; BHD2, p. 100.

Gliese, Rochus [scenarist/director] (b. Berlin, Germany, 6 Jan 1891–22 Dec 1978 [87], Berlin, Germany). AS, p. 451. BHD2, p. 100. FDY, p. 425.

Gloeckner-Kramer, Pepi [actress] (b. Austria, 17 Jan 1874–2 Mar 1954 [80], Vienna, Austria). AS, p. 452.

Gloria, Leda [actress] (*née* Leda Nicoletti, b. Rome, Italy, 30 Aug 1912). JS, p. 200 ("She started in silent movies.")

Glouner, Charles [cinematographer] (b. 1886–11 Apr 1967 [81?], Los Angeles CA). BHD2, p. 100.

Glover, Emlye [actress] (d. Sep 1923, Los Angeles CA). BHD, p. 180.

Glover, Gertrude [actress] (b. Chicago IL, 24 Sep 1895–1 Mar 1977 [81], Boulder CO). m. Robert Jeffress Watt, 1917 (d. 1939). (Essanay [Chicago]; retired 1917.) AMD, p. 138. BHD, p. 180. "Gertrude Glover," *MPW,* 30 Dec 1916, 1945. "Essanay Leading Lady [age 78] Now Lives in Boulder Colo.," *CFC,* 44 (Fall, 1974), X4 (reprint from *Billboard*).

Glowner, M. Lee [actor] (b. CA, 21 Oct 1866–9 Jul 1923 [56], CA). AS, p. 452. BHD, p. 180.

Glyn, Elinor [novelist/actress/scenarist/director] (*née* Elinor Sutherland, b. Isle of Jersey, Channel Islands, 17 Oct 1864–23 Sep 1943 [78], London, England). m. Clayton Glyn, 1892 (d. 1915). *Romantic Adventure.* Anthony Glyn (pseudonym of Sir Geoffrey Davson, Glyn's grandson), *Elinor Glyn* (NY: Doubleday, 1955). (Paramount; Goldwyn.) "Elinor Glyn Dies; Novelist, Age 78; Self-Styled 'High Priestess of God of Love' Shocked Many Readers of 2 Continents; Gave 'It' New Meaning; Author of 'Three Weeks' [1907] Had Vogue in the Pre-First World War and 'Flapper-Age' Days," *NYT,* 24 Sep 1943, 23:1. "Elinor Glyn," *Variety,* 29 Sep 1943. AMD, p. 138. AS, p. 452. BHD, p. 180; BHD2, p. 100. FDY, p. 425. IFN, p. 119. Waldman, p. 121. "Elinor Glyn Here to Write Scenarios for Paramount," *MPW,* 30 Oct 1920, 1222. Mary Kelly, "Elinor Glyn Discusses Scenario Writing; Picks American Business Man for Hero," *MPW,* 13 Nov 1920, 235. Edward Weitzel, "Elinor Glyn Throned on Her Tiger Skin Sets a New Pace for Speedy Interviews," *MPW,* 11 Dec 1920, 721. Elinor Glyn, "In Filmdom's Boudoir," *Photoplay,* Mar 1921, 28–30 ("Marriage is good, and art is good—but they do not appear to assimilate to perfection!"). "To Film Marriage of Elinor Glyn's Daughter," *MPW,* 12 Mar 1921, 186 (Juliet to Sir Rhys Williams in St. Margaret's, Westminster, England). "New Alliance," *MPW,* 13 Aug 1921, 700. "Elinor Glyn Goes Back to Hollywood," *MPW,* 24 Dec 1921, 938. "Elinor Glyn Made Supervisor of Paramount Film," *MPW,* 11 Feb 1922, 617. M. Kelly, "Elinor Glyn Says Hollywood Needs Personal Self-Respect, Not Reformers," *MPW,* 29 Apr 1922, 928. "Goldwyn Buys Screen Rights to Elinor Glyn's 'Six Days,'" *MPW,* 6 May 1922, 54. "Elinor Glyn Is Directing," *MPW,* 23 Sep 1922, 281. "Elinor Glyn"s Name Aids Attendance," *MPW,* 18 Nov 1922, 247. T. Howard Kelly, "Will the Screen Version of 'Three Weeks' Be a Challenge to the Censors?; How will the National Board Of Censorship receive Elinor Glyn's daring novel of unfettered love? Will they order it cut or will they ban itcompletely?," *MW,* 12 May 1923, 4–5. "Elinor Glyn Here to Supervise," *MPW,* 23 Jun 1923, 678. "Mayer Signs Miss Glyn," *MPW,* 15 Mar 1924, 183. "Goes to Coast for Mayer," *MPW,* 22 Mar 1924, 268. Ivan St. Johns, "Glyn & Glynne; How Madame Elinor's candidate for *Paul* in 'Three Weeks' got only a bleached head, while Conrad Nagel got the role," *Photoplay Magazine,* May 1924, 53, 129. "Elinor Glyun Tells How She Came to Write 'His Hour,'" *MPW,* 26 Jul 1924, 292. Dorothy Donnell, "Elinor Glyn on Summer Flirtations," *MW,* 9 Aug 1924, 4–5, 30. "Elinor Glyn signed by M-G-M," *MPW,* 5 Sep 1925, 90. "Elinor Glyn to Scenarize and Supervise 'Love's Blindness,'" *MPW,* 2 Jan 1926, 68. Don Ryan, "They Took the Megaphone Away from Mme. Glyn," *MPC,* Jan 1926, 27, 73–74 ("But I do think I know better than any director what my own characters should express."). "Elinor Glyn's 'It' for Paramount," *MPW,* 21 Aug 1926, 466. "Elinor Glyn Rejoins F.P.-L.," *MPW,* 28 Aug 1926, 541. "Elinor Glyn Will Be Seen in 'It,'" *MPW,* 23 Oct 1926, 479. Milton Howe, "Who's IT Defines What's 'It'?; Elinor Glyn Tells You the Meaning and Clara Bow Gives You the Answer," *MPC,* Feb 1927, 59, 88, 91. Orville Prescott, "Books of the Times," *NYT,* 6 Jul 1955, 25:4 (review of Glyn's book. "Such nonsense [praise of *Three Weeks*], makes one question all Mr. Glyn's opinions. Nevertheless, he has a bizarre woman to write about, and he might have produced an amusing book about her if he had taken her work less seriously and emphasized her follies more. Even so, Elinor Glyn probably does not deserve a biography.").

Glynne, Mary [stage/film actress] (*née* Mary Aitken, b. Penarth, Glamorganshire, Wales, 25 Jan 1898–19 Sep 1954 [56], London, England). m. (1) **Dennis Neilson-Terry** (d. 1932); (2) John Mannell. (In films from 1919; Paramount.) "Mary Glynne," *Variety,* 29 Sep 1954. AS, p. 452. BHD1, p. 218 (b. 1895). IFN, p. 119. SD, p. 512. Truitt, p. 126.

Gmur, Walburga [actress] (b. Weimar, Germany, 1901–9 Dec 1974 [73], Dortmund, Germany). m. actor/director Max Haufleur (1910–1965). AS, p. 452.

Gnass, Friedrich [actor] (*né* Fritz Gnass, b. Bochum, Germany, 13 Nov 1892–8 May 1958 [63], Berlin, Germany). AS, p. 452.

Goan, O.S. [producer]. No data found. AMD, p. 138. "Warners Celebrates Anniversary," *MPW,* 3 Oct 1914, 70.

Gobbett, David W. [cinematographer]. No data found. FDY, p. 459.

Gobet, Jean [actor] (*né* Joseph Paul Louis Gobet, b. Mornant, France, 20 Jul 1888 [extrait de naissance no. 21/1888]–29 Apr 1980 [91], Creteil, France). AS, p. 452.

Godard, Jean [director] (b. France, 1894). AS, p. 453.

Goddard, Alf [actor/boxer] (b. London, England, 28 Nov 1897–25 Feb 1981 [83], England). AS, p. 453. BHD1, p. 218.

Goddard, Charles W[illiam] [scenarist] (b. Portland ME, 1880–11 Jan 1951 [70?], Miami FL). AS, p. 453. BHD2, p. 100.

Goddard, Paulette [stage/film actress] (*née* Pauline Marian Levy, b. Whitestone Landing, Great Neck, LI NY, 3 Jun 1905–23 Apr 1990 [84], Porto Ronco, Lake Maggiore, Switzerland; heart attack [extrait de décès no. 7/3/1990]). m. (1) Edgar W. James–div. 1931; (2) **Charles Chaplin**—

div. 1942 (d. 1977); (3) Burgess Meredith, 1944–50; (4) Erich Maria Remarque, 1958 (d. 1970). (Film debut:*Berth Marks*, Roach, 1929.) Joe Morella and Edward Z. Epstein, *Paulette* (NY: St. Martin's Press, 1985). Joyce Milton, *Tramp; The Life of Charlie Chaplin* (NY: Harper Collins, 1996), pp. 330 ff. Peter B. Flint, "Paulette Goddard, 78, Is Dead; Film Star of 1930's Through 50's," *NYT*, 24 Apr 1990, D22:5 ("Goddard" was mother's maiden name). AS, p. 453. BHD1, p. 218. Katz, p. 469.

Godden, Jimmy [actor] (b. Maidstone, England, 11 Aug 1879–5 Mar 1955 [75], England). AS, p. 453.

Godderis, Albert [actor] (b. Belgium, 4 Nov 1880–2 Feb 1971 [90], Los Angeles CA). AS, p. 453 (b. 1889). BHD1, p. 218.

Godfrey, George [vaudevillian/talent scout/casting director] (b. 1888?–15 Apr 1974 [86], Miami Beach FL). (Columbia.) "George Godfrey," *Variety*, 8 May 1974. AS, p. 453.

Godfrey, George [boxer/actor] (b. Mobile AL, 25 Jan 1897–13 Aug 1947 [50], Los Angeles CA). Bachelor. "George Godfrey, 50, Noted Negro Boxer," *NYT*, 14 Aug 1947, 23:6 ("Godfrey had played movie roles at one time, but of late had been working as a cafe bouncer."). AS, p. 453. BHD1, p. 218.

Godfrey, Peter [actor/director] (b. London, England, 16 Oct 1899–4 Mar 1970 [70], Los Angeles CA). AS, p. 453. BHD2, p. 100.

Godfrey, Samuel T. [actor] (b. Brooklyn NY, 5 Oct 1891–18 Apr 1935 [43], Los Angeles CA). AS, p. 453.

Godik, Wladislaw [actor] (b. Warsaw, Poland, 1 Apr 1892–18 Dec 1952 [60], Warsaw, Poland). AS, p. 453.

Godowsky, Dagmar [actress] (b. Vilna, Lithuania, 24 Nov 1897–13 Feb 1975 [77], New York NY [Death Certificate Index No. 2927]). m. **Frank L. Mayo**, 1921–annulled 1928 (d. 1963). *First Person Plural; The Lives of Dagmar Godowsky* (New York: Viking Press, 1958). "Dagmar Godowsky, 78, 'Vamp' of the Silent Screen, Is Dead," *NYT*, 14 Feb 1975, 35:4. "Dagmar Godowsky," *Variety*, 19 Feb 1975. AMD, p. 138. AS, p. 453. BHD, p. 180 (b. Petrograd, Russia, 1896). FFF, p. 198 (b. Petrograd). IFN, p. 119, age 78. Katz, p. 489. MH, p. 113 (b. Petrograd). "Dagmar Godowsky," WBO1, pp. 182–83. "Mayo Answers Wife; Says Charge of Friendship for Film Actress Caused Him Anguish," *LA Times*, 20 Feb 1920, III, p. 4 ("He says his wife has no cause for suspicion in his associations with Miss Dagmar Godowsky. The latter has pending a $16,000 suit for libel against Mrs. Mayo [Joyce Eleanor Mayo]."). "Godowsky Recovering," *MPW*, 11 Dec 1920, 716 (from appendicitis). "Mayo-Godowsky," *MPW*, 22 Oct 1921, 920 (married Mayo a week after his divorce). Dagmar Godowsky, "She Wants to Be the Wickedest Woman on the Screen," *Photoplay Magazine*, May 1924, 86.

Godsay, Ellen [actress]. (Kalem.) No data found.

Godsol, Frank J. [executive]. No data found. AMD, p. 138. "Samuel Goldwyn Is Returned as President and Frank J. Godsol as Executive Head of Corporation," *MPW*, 6 Nov 1920, 25. "Godsol Succeeds Goldwyn as President," *MPW*, 25 Mar 1922, 347. "Godsol Announces Goldw¥n Will Release 49 Pictures Next Year," *MPW*, 12 May 1923, 125. "Godsol Off to Europe," *MPW*, 2 Jun 1923, 376. Frank J. Godsol, "Goldwyn's Production Policy," *MPW*, 4 Aug 1923, 407. Frank J. Godsol, "Godsol Calls Exhibitor Control Industry's Real Menace," *MPW*, 24 Nov 1923, 373.

Goebel, Otto E. [scenarist/executive]. No data found. "Gossip of the Studios," *NYDM*, 7 Oct 1914, 27:1 (President of the St. Louis Motion Picture Co.).

Goergens, George H. [inventor] (b. 1877–4 Jun 1952 [75?], St. Petersburg FL). AS, p. 453.

Goethals, Stanley [actor] (b. Culver City CA, 1 Dec 1916–8 Mar 2000 [83], Redding CA). m. (sons Stephen and Michael). (Began ca. 1920; Universal.)

Goetz, Ben [manager of Crystal Co./director] (b. New York NY, 2 Jun 1891–22 Aug 1979 [87], Los Angeles CA). m. Goldie Feldstone, Mar 1914. BHD2, p. 100. "Goetz a Benedict," *NYDM*, 1 Apr 1914, 32:3.

Goetz, Curt [actor] (*né* Kurt Walter Gotz, b. Mainz, Germany, 17 Nov 1888–12 Sep 1960 [71], Grabs, Switzerland). AS, p. 454. BHD, p. 180.

Goetz, E. Ray [composer/lyricist/producer] (b. Buffalo NY, 12 Jun 1886–12 Jun 1954 [68], Greenwich CT). m. (1) Elizabeth Leyland; (2) Ethel Johnson; (3) Irene Bordoni. "E. Ray Goetz," *Variety*, 16 Jun 1954, p. 63. BHD, p. 180; BHD2, p. 100.

Goetz, Fred [cinematographer] (b. 1888–18 Nov 1977 [89?]). BHD2, p. 100.

Goetz, Harry M. [executive] (b. New York NY, 9 Jan 1888–19 Dec 1978 [90], Los Angeles CA). BHD2, p. 100.

Goetz, Jack [executive] (b. New York NY, 17 Jan 1893–14 Dec 1962 [69], Beverly Hills CA). BHD2, p. 100.

Goetz, Paul P. (Pop) [actor] (b. 1865–26 Sep 1929 [64?], Los Angeles CA). AS, p. 454. BHD, p. 180.

Goetzke, Bernhard [actor] (b. Danzig, Germany, 5 Jun 1884–7 Oct 1964 [80], Berlin, Germany). AS, p. 454. BHD1, p. 219.

Gofton, E. Story [actor] (b. England, 1847–1 May 1939 [92?]). BHD, p. 181.

Goines, Betty [actress] (b. 1904-Jan 1929 [25?]). BHD, p. 181.

Going, Frederica [actress] (b. New York NY, 13 Aug 1895–11 Apr 1959 [63], New York NY). AS, p. 454 (b. 1894). BHD1, p. 219.

Gokhle, Kamalbai (mother of actor Chandrakant Gokhle; grandmother of stage/film/TV actor Vikram Gokhle) [film/stage actress] (b. 1900–1 May 1997 [97], Pune City, India). m. actor Raghumath Gokhle. Uma de Cunha, "Kamalbai Gokhle," *Variety*, 26 May 1996, 89:4 ("...the first Indian woman to act in an Indian movie, died in Pune City May 17 in the centenary year of Indian cinema." In 1913, aged 13, she was in *Bhasmasur Mohini* [1913], her only film, directed by Dadasaheb Phalke, thereby breaking the taboo of women parading themselves for public display in front of men, as on the stage. In film, men had played women's parts.). AS, p. 454.

Gold, Harry L. [executive] (b. 1894–11 Feb 1971 [75?], New York NY). BHD2, p. 101.

Gold, Jimmy [actor] (*né* James McConigal, b. Gasgow, Scotland, 1886–7 Oct 1967 [81?], London, England). AS, p. 454.

Gold, Max [assistant director] (b. New York NY, 1897?–2 Jan 1930 [32], near Santa Monica CA; airplane crash). "Max Gold," *Variety*, 15 Jan 1930. AS, p. 454 (d. 10 Jan). BHD2, p. 101.

Goldbeck, Willis [scenarist/director/producer] (b. New York NY, 1899?–17 Sep 1979 [80], Sag Harbor, LI NY). (Metro.) "Willis Goldbeck," *Variety*, 26 Sep 1979. AMD, p. 138. AS, p. 454. BHD2, p. 101 (d. Southampton NY). FDY, p. 425. IFN, p. 119. "Goldbeck Writes for Pola Negri," *MPW*, 27 Jun 1925, 977. "Goldbeck Made Director," *MPW*, 21 Nov 1925, 228 (27 years old). "Willis Goldbeck Return to U.S." *MPW*, 2 Apr 1927, 488.

Goldberg, Harry [general manager]. No data found. AMD, p. 138. "Harry Goldberg," *MPW*, 17 Oct 1914, 324.

Goldberg, Heinz [scenarist] (b. Konigsberg, Germany, 30 May 1891–2 Jul 1969 [78], Berlin, Germany). AS, p. 454. BHD2, p. 101.

Goldberg, Jack [executive] (b. 1889–4 Dec 1959 [70?], New York NY). BHD2, p. 101.

Goldberg, Maurice [photographer] (b. 1893–23 Nov 1949 [56?], Beverly Hills CA). BHD2, p. 101.

Goldberg, Rube L. [cartoonist/title writer/sculptor] (*né* Reuben Lucius Goldberg, b. San Francisco CA, 4 Jul 1883–7 Dec 1970 [87], New York NY; cancer). m. Irma Seeman, 1916. "Rube L. Goldberg," *Variety*, 9 Dec 1970 (Pulitzer Prize, 1948). AMD, p. 138. AS, p. 454. BHD1, p. 219. "Goldberg Joins Vitagraph," *MPW*, 30 May 1914, 1270. "Pathé Signs Rube L. Goldberg," *MPW*, 25 Mar 1916, 2021. "Plan Boob McNutt Two Reel Comedies," *MPW*, 21 Aug 1926, 467.

Goldberg, Sammy [actor]. No data found. AMD, p. 138. "The Associated Signs Up Another Star," *MPW*, 20 Nov 1915, 1457.

Goldburg, Jesse J[ames] [producer] (b. New York NY, 21 Oct 1881–27 Aug 1959 [77], Los Angeles CA). (Chadwick; FBO.) "Jesse J. Goldburg," *Variety*, 2 Sep 1959 ("He was identified with a number of early-day indie companies, including Independent Picture Corp., Ocean Film Corp. and Rialto Film Corp."). AMD, p. 138. AS, p. 454. BHD2, p. 101. "Jesse Goldburg Announces Big Production and Campaign Plans," *MPW*, 5 Apr 1924, 472. "Jesse Goldburg Outlines His Policy as an Independent Producer," *MPW*, 19 Apr 1924, 651. "Goldburg Believes in Advertising Co-operation," *MPW*, 19 Apr 1924, 651. "Wave of Optimism Sweeps Independent Market," *MPW*, 19 Apr 1924, 651. "Jesse J. Goldburg Makes Study of Needs in Independent Field," *MPW*, 10 May 1924, 172. "Independent Corporation Dividend of 15 Per Cent," *MPW*, 29 Nov 1924, 434. "Chadwick Productions at High Peak as Jesse Goldburg Directs," *MPW*, 15 Jan 1927, 189. "Jesse J. Goldburg Goes to London; To Make 'Comrades,' a War Film," *MPW*, 20 Aug 1927, 532.

Golden, Mrs. Bella [actress] (*née* Emma I. Llewellyn, b. London, England, 1842–10 Apr 1919 [77?], Evansville IN). m. Martin Golden (d. 1915). "Mrs. Bella Golden," *Variety*, 18 Apr 1919. AS, p. 455.

Golden, Edward A. [producer] (b. New York NY, 17 Mar 1887–26 Sep 1972 [85], Los Angeles CA). BHD2, p. 101.

Golden, John [stage producer/actor/director/composer/lyricist] (b. 27 Jun 1874–17 Jun 1955 [80], Bayside, Queens, LI NY; heart attack). m. Margaret, 1909. "John Golden Is Dead; Was

Colorful Showman, Songwriter, Benefactor," *Variety,* 22 Jun 1955, 62:4 ("...worked as a bricklayer on the construction of the old Garrick Theatre, N.Y., and later was employed as an actor."). AMD, p. 139. "John Golden Is at Fox Coast Studio," *MPW,* 28 Feb 1925, 912.

Golden, Joseph A. [director] (b. 1897–8 Jul 1942 [45?], Los Angeles CA). AMD, p. 139. AS, p. 455. "'Picture Plays' and Their Production," *MPW,* 23 Apr 1910, 636–37. "The Crystal Film Company, New York," *MPW,* 16 Mar 1912, 946–47. "Joseph A. Golden," *MPW,* 29 Aug 1914, 1226. "Thirteen Years in the film Field Is the Record of Joseph A. Golden," *MPW,* 21 Feb 1920, 1252.

Golden, Marta [actress]. No data found. (Keystone.) J. Van Cartmell, "Along the Pacific Coast," *NYDM,* 6 Nov 1915, 3:1 (in *A Janitor's Wife's Temptation,* with Fred Mace).

Golden, Mignonne [actress] (b. London, England, 29 Feb 1903–27 Sep 1997 [94], New York NY). BHD1, p. 609.

Golden, Olive Fuller (sister of **Ruth Fuller Golden**) [actress] (b. New York NY, 31 Jan 1896–13 Mar 1988 [92], Carpenteria CA). m. **Harry Carey**, Jan 1920 (d. 1947). "Olive Carey Dies at 92; Longtime Film Actress," *NYT,* 17 Mar 1988, B10:5. "Olive Carey," *Variety,* 23 Mar 1988. AS, p. 203 (Olive Carey). BHD1, p. 90 (Olive Carey). BR, pp. 6–8. FSS, p. 55 (Olive Carey). "Olive Fuller Gordon [sic]," *MPW,* 15 Jan 1916, 394. George A. Katchmer, "Forgotten Cowboys and Cowgirls—Part V," *CI,* 177 (Mar 1990), C2; "Update—Forgotten Cowboys/Girls," *CI,* 179 (May 1990), 44.

Golden, Robert A. [assistant director] (b. 1897?–8 Jul 1942 [45], Los Angeles CA; choked to death on a steak in a cafe). (MGM.) "Robert Golden," *Variety,* 15 Jul 1942. BHD2, p. 101 (b. 1894).

Golden, Ruth Fuller (sister of **Olive Fuller Golden**) [actress] (b. New York NY, 19 May 1901–15 Aug 1931 [30], Los Angeles CA). AS, p. 455. BHD, p. 181. IFN, p. 119.

Goldenberg, Carl Theodore [executive] (b. 22 Feb 1877–1 Aug 1929 [52]). BHD2, p. 101.

Goldenberg, Samuel (b. 1886–31 Oct 1945 [59?], Brooklyn NY). AS, p. 455.

Golder, Lew [producer] (b. 1884–7 Dec 1962 [78?], Philadelphia PA). AS, p. 455. BHD2, p. 101.

Goldfrap, John Henry [publicist] (b. England, 1877?–2 Nov 1917 [40], Staten Island NY; tuberculosis). AMD, p. 139. "Goldfrap with World Film," *MPW,* 11 Dec 1915, 2016. "Obituary," *MPW,* 8 Dec 1917, 1467.

Goldin, Sidney M. [actor/director] (b. Odessa, Ukraine, 1880?–19 Sep 1937 [57], Los Angeles CA). AMD, p. 139. AS, p. 455. BHD, p. 181; BHD2, p. 101 (d. NY NY). IFN, p. 120. "Sidney Golden Joins Cosmopolitan," *MPW,* 5 Sep 1914, 1387.

Goldina, Marian [actress] (b. Volgograd, Russia, 28 Mar 1898–14 Jan 1979 [80], New York NY). AS, p. 455.

Golding, Louis [scenarist] (b. 1897–9 Aug 1958 [61?], Manchester, England). BHD2, p. 101.

Golding, Samuel R. [scenarist] (b. 1889–14 Nov 1957 [68?], Los Angeles CA). AS, p. 455. BHD2, p. 101.

Goldman, Harold [scenarist] (b. New York NY, 1890–18 Jan 1956 [65?], Los Angeles CA). BHD2, p. 101.

Goldner, Charles [actor] (b. Vienna, Austria, 7 Dec 1900–15 Apr 1955 [54], London, England). AS, p. 455.

Goldsmith, I.G. [producer] (b. Australia, 1894–8 Oct 1964 [70?], Vermont IL). AS, p. 455.

Goldstein, Abe [actor] (b. 1895–9 Feb 1990 [94?], Los Angeles CA). AS, p. 455. BHD, p. 181.

Goldstein, Becky [actress] (b. England, 1887–12 May 1971 [84?], London, England). AS, p. 455.

Goldstein, Irving E. [producer]. No data found. AMD, p. 139. "Goldstein Organizes Gwendolyn Films," *MPW,* 23 Feb 1918, 1096.

Goldstein, Robert [costumer] (b. London, England, 1904?–6 Apr 1974 [70], London, England; cerebral hemorrhage). "Robert Goldstein," *Variety,* 10 Apr 1974. AMD, p. 139. AS, p. 456. "Goldstein Is Found Guilty," *MPW,* 11 May 1918 (of espionage). "Goldstein Is Sentenced to Ten Years," *MPW,* 25 May 1918, 1145 (29 Apr 1918, McNeil Island, $5,000 fine). "Sentence Cut to Three Years," *MPW,* 22 Mar 1919, 1628.

Goldstone, Phil [producer] (b. 1893?–19 Jun 1963 [70], W. Los Angeles CA; lung cancer). "Phil Goldstone," *Variety,* 26 Jun 1963. AS, p. 456. BHD2, p. 102.

Goldsworthy, John H[eath] [actor] (b. England, 28 Apr 1884–10 Jul 1958 [74], Los Angeles Co. CA). AS, p. 456. BHD1, p. 219. IFN, p. 120.

Goldwyn, Samuel (father of Samuel Goldwyn, Jr.) [producer/executive] (*né* Schmuel Gelbfisz, aka Samuel Goldfish, b. Warsaw, Poland, Jul 1879?–31 Jan 1974 [94?], Beverly Hills CA). m. (1) Blanche Lasky (son, Samuel, Jr., b. 7 Sep 1926); (2) **Frances Howard**, 1930, Jersey City NJ (d. 1976). A. Scott Berg, *Goldwyn; A Biography* (NY: Alfred A. Knopf, 1989). Albin Krebs, "Samuel Goldwyn Dies at 91," *NYT,* 1 Feb 1974, 1:1; "Samuel Goldwyn, Pioneer Film Producer, Noted for 'Goldwynisms,' Dies on Coast," 34:1. "Goldwyn, One of the Greats, Dies at 91; Respected, Feared," *Variety,* 6 Feb 1974 (age 91). AMD, p. 139. AS, p. 456 (b. 27 Aug 1882). BHD2, p. 102 (b. 27 Aug 1882). IFN, p. 120 (b. 27 Aug 1882). Spehr, p. 134 (b. 1884). "Goldfish on Western Trip," *MPW,* 9 May 1914, 795. "Goldfish on His Way to Europe," *MPW,* 13 Jun 1914, 1517. "Samuel Goldfish," *MPW,* 11 Jul 1914, 223. W. Stephen Bush, "Europe Hungry for Quality," *MPW,* 25 Jul 1914, 583. "Production Versus Menufacture," *MPW,* 6 Mar 1915, 1454. "Another Quality Triumph," *MPW,* 24 Apr 1915, 536. "Applaud Freedom of Screen," *MPW,* 8 May 1915, 872–73. "Lasky Will Build Studio," *MPW,* 3 Jul 1915, 43. "Lasky Chief Defends Photoplay," *MPW,* 14 Aug 1915, 1137. "Convention of Paramount Pictures Corporation," *MPW,* 18 Sep 1915, 1970–71. "Aid Actor's Fund; Cooperation of Picture Men Secured to Aid Million Dollar Campaign," *NYDM,* 13 Nov 1915, 30:4 (with FP-L at the time; made chairman of a committee to seek funds for the Million Dollar Campaign for the Actor' Fund. "The work of Mr. Goldfish and Mr. Lasky will be the easier for the fact that so many of the legitimate actors and actresses have gone into the films this season. Motion pictures have often been accused of having done more to make the actors' home a necessity than any other factor, but they appear to have evened the score by their present voluntary offer to help."). "Film Men Will Aid Actors' Fund," *MPW,* 13 Nov 1915, 1284. "Goldfish Now a Golder," *MPW,* 4 Dec 1915, 1809. "Samuel Goldfish Is Sued by Wife [Blanche]; She Gets an Interlocutory Decree of Divorce and Heavy Alimony, Too; Names 'Actress' ['Kathleen'] in Papers," *The [NY] Morning Telegraph,* 12 Dec 1915, 1:3 ("He put in an answer and contested the allegations of infidelity."). "Working for Actors' Fund," *MPW,* 26 Feb 1916, 1416. "Goldfish Resigns from Famous Players-Lasky," *MPW,* 30 Sep 1916, 2089. "Goldfish in New Company," *MPW,* 9 Dec 1916, 1482. "Goldwyn Pictures Enter the Field," *MPW,* 16 Dec 1916, 1627. "Goldfish Recovers from Accident," *MPW,* 24 Mar 1917, 1935. "Goldfish Recovers from Injury," *MPW,* 14 Apr 1917, 269. "Goldfish Talks About Goldwyn," *MPW,* 23 Jun 1917, 1914. "Goldfish Denounces Extravagance in Industry," *MPW,* 15 Dec 1917, 1613. "Goldwyn to Double Its Output," *MPW,* 1 Jun 1918, 1266. Samuel Goldfish, "Goldfish Praises Review Board's Work," *MPW,* 15 Jun 1918, 1578. "Goldwyn on Threshold of Second Year," *MPW,* 20 Jul 1918, 374–78. "Goldfish Describes Evils of 20 Per Cent Theatre Tax," *MPW,* 19 Oct 1918, 354. "Goldwyn Leases Triangle's Plant," *MPW,* 19 Oct 1918, 368. William E. Mulligan, "Goldfish Predicts New Screen Era," *MPW,* 21 Dec 1918, 1319–20. "Samuel Goldwyn Now Heads Goldwyn," *MPW,* 4 Jan 1919, 59 ("Samuel Goldfish Is Dead. Long Live Samuel Goldwyn."). "Goldwyn Purchases Triangle Studios," *MPW,* 7 Jun 1919, 1470. "Goldwyn Talks of Writers' Plans," *MPW,* 14 Jun 1919, 1639. "Goldwyn Capital Now $20,000,000," *MPW,* 9 Aug 1919, 785. "Samuel Goldwyn Points Out the Great Improvements Made in His Organization," *MPW,* XLI, 16 Aug 1919, 993. Samuel Goldwyn, "'Factory Production' Fails; Time Must Be Given to Artistic Harmony," *MPW,* 27 Dec 1919, 1121. Samuel Goldwyn, "Motion Picture Abroad Is Salesman for America's Expanding Commerce," *MPW,* 28 Feb 1920, 1387, 1391, 1393. "Samuel Goldwyn Warns Industry Against Causing Inflation of Production Costs," *MPW,* 3 Apr 1920, 53. "Samuel Goldwyn and F.J. Godsol Resign; Both to Remain on Board of Directors; Kendall Temporarily Head of Concern," *MPW,* 11 Sep 1920, 179. "Rex Beach to Samuel Goldwyn," *MPW,* 9 Oct 1920, 758. "Samuel Goldwyn Is Returned as President and F.J. Godsol as Executive Head of Corporation," *MPW,* 6 Nov 1920, 25. "Studio Wage Reduction Is Due, Says Goldwyn," *MPW,* 30 Jul 1921, 494. Samuel Goldwyn, "Sees No Permanent Setback of Industry in Spite of Patronage Fluctuations," *MPW,* 7 Jan 1922, 62. "'World' Honest, Fearless and Just, Says Goldwyn," *MPW,* 11 Mar 1922, 137. "Godsol Succeeds Goldwyn as President," *MPW,* 25 Mar 1922, 347. "First National and Samuel Goldwyn Make Important Arrangement," *MPW,* 28 Apr 1923, 909. Samuel Goldwyn, "Will Concentrate on a Few Big Pictures," *MPW,* 9 Jun 1923, 522. Thomas Tarrington, "Why New York's Opinion of Pictures Is Now Worthless," *MW,* III, 9 Jun 1923, 8, 28. "Goldwyn Restricted in Use of His Name According to Court Ruling," *MPW,* 3 Nov 1923, 44. "Sam Goldwyn Says West Better for Production; to Quit East," *MPW,* 16 Feb 1924, 557. "Warns 'Wampas' Against Evils of Thoughtless Publicity," *MPW,* 15 Mar 1924, 184. "Original Story for Screen Is Thing of Past, Says Goldwyn," *MPW,* 22 Mar 1924, 287. Tom Waller, "Censors Cannot Cut One Inch of 'Cytherea,' Says Goldwyn," *MPW,* 19 Apr 1924, 653. "Gets Use of

Name; Samuel Goldwyn by Amicable Arrangement Again Has Right to 'Be Himself,'" *MPW,* 26 Jul 1924, 258. "Goldwyn Coming East," *MPW,* 27 Sep 1924, 316. "'Life Blood of Industry,' Says Goldwyn of Independent Films," *MPW,* 25 Oct 1924, 676. "U.F.A. Representatives Dined by Samuel Goldwyn on Coast," *MPW,* 6 Dec 1924, 816. "German Competition Impending Factor in England, Says Goldwyn," *MPW,* 7 Mar 1925, 38. "Samuel Goldwyn Finds American Productions Dominating Europe," *MPW,* 21 Mar 1925, 244. "Samuel Goldwyn on Bank Board," *MPW,* 23 May 1925, 408 (Commercial National Bank, Hollywood). Faith Service, "That Whirlwind Romance of Frances Howard and Sam Goldwyn," *MW,* 23 May 1925, 4–5, 31. "Goldwyn Joins United Artists; No Change in Programs Planned," *MPW,* 18 Jul 1925, 358. Covarrubias, "Distinguished Picture People," *MPW,* 6 Feb 1926, 520. "Makes His Bow," *MPW,* 25 Sep 1926, 1 (son, Samuel, Jr., b. 7 Sep 1926, LA CA; mother, Frances Howard). R.M. Hyams, "Goldwyn Faces Life With a Loaf of Bread," *Cinema Arts,* Dec 1926, 21–22. "Replies to Charges," *MPW,* 26 Feb 1927, 619. "Goldwyn Cleans Slate," *MPW,* 7 May 1927, 17. "Goldwyn Joins U.A.," *MPW,* 22 Oct 1927, 476. "'Fight Censorship,' Goldwyn Urges Catholic M.P. Guild," *MPW,* 29 Oct 1927, 551. Noel F. Busch, "Maker of Stars; A Closeup of Samuel Goldwyn," *Cinema Arts,* Jun 1937, 66–67, 84 (emphasizes the recent discovery of Robert Taylor).

Goling, Louis [scenarist] (b. 1897–9 Aug 1958 [61?]). BHD2, p. 102.

Gollan, Campbell [actor/director] (*né* David Gollan, b. Cults, Scotland, 1866–13 Dec 1916 [50?], New York NY). AMD, p. 140. BHD, p. 181; BHD2, p. 102. "Gollan Campbell," *MPW,* 20 Feb 1915, 1143. "Obituary," *MPW,* Jan 1917, 91.

Gollomb, Joseph [scenarist] (b. St. Petersburg, Russia, 15 Nov 1881–23 May 1950 [68], New York NY). AMD, p. 140. AS, p. 456 (d. 24 May). BHD2, p. 102. "Universal Has New Scenario Man," *MPW,* 21 Nov 1914, 1089. "A New Vitagrapher," *MPW,* 3 Apr 1915, 71.

Golm, Ernest [actor] (b. Germany, 21 Dec 1885–29 May 1962 [76], Los Angeles CA). AS, p. 456.

Golovnya, Anatoli Dimitryevich [cinematographer/director] (b. Simferinol, Russia, 1900–1982 [82?], Moscow, Russia). AS, p. 456. FDY, p. 459.

Golubeff, Gregory [actor] (b. New York NY, 22 Feb 1891–11 Feb 1958 [66], Los Angeles CA). AS, p. 456.

Golz, Rosemay [actress/singer] (b. 1880–14 Apr 1963 [83?], Rome, Italy). AS, p. 456.

Gombell, Minna [stage/film actress] (b. Baltimore MD, 28 May 1893–14 Apr 1973 [79], Santa Monica CA). m. Joseph Sefton. (Broadway debut, 1919.) (Fox, 1930.) "Minna Gombell," *Variety,* 16 May 1973, p. 126 (age 91). AS, p. 456 (b. 1892). BHD1, p. 220 (Gombill).

Gomez, Leopold [director/producer/scenarist] (b. Sidi-bel-Abbes, Algeria, 2 Nov 1896). AS, p. 456.

Gomez, Ralph [actor] (b. 1897?–18 Apr 1954 [57], Los Angeles CA; cancer). "Ralph Gomez," *Variety,* 28 Apr 1954 ("screen actor and stuntman for 30 years"). AS, p. 457. BHD1, p. 220. IFN, p. 120. Truitt, p. 127.

Gomez Carillo, Enrique [director] (b. Guatemala, 1873–1927 [54?], Paris, France). AS, p. 457.

Gondi, Harry [actor] (b. Germany, 16 Jul 1900–20 Oct 1968 [68], Hamburg, Germany). AS, p. 457. BHD1, p. 220.

Gontcharoff, Vasily [director/scenarist] (*né* Vasily Michaelovich Goncharoff, b. St. Petersburg, Russia, 30 Aug 1861–2 Jan 1915 [53], St. Petersburg, Russia). AS, p. 457.

Gonzalez, Myrtle, "The Virgin Lily of the Screen" [actress] (b. Los Angeles CA, 28 Sep 1891–22 Oct 1918 [27], Los Angeles CA; influenza and heart trouble). m. (1) James P. Jones; (2) **Allen M. Watt**, 1 Dec 1917 (d. 1944). (Vitagraph, 1912; Universal.) AMD, p. 141. AS, p. 457. BHD, pp. 30–31; 181. BR, pp. 31–33. IFN, p. 120. Slide, p. 140. "Myrtle Gonzalez," *MPW,* 12 May 1917, 953. "Myrtle Gonzalez Weds," *MPW,* 29 Dec 1917, 1948. "Obituary," *MPW,* 16 Nov 1918, 727. "Requiem Mass for Actress," *MPW,* 15 Feb 1919, 882 (29 Jan 1919, St. Vincent's Church, Grand and Washington Sts., LA CA). Billy H. Doyle, "Lost Players," *CI,* 139 (Jan 1987), 55. George Katchmer, "Remembering the Great Silents," *CI,* 223 (Jan 1994), 49:3.

Good, Frank B. [actor/cameraman] (b. Columbus OH, 3 Oct 1884–1 Jun 1939 [55], Los Angeles CA). "Frank Good," *Variety,* 7 Jun 1939 ("Veteran of the silent days, Good was chief cameraman for Norma Talmadge, Tom Mix, Jackie Coogan and George O'Brien."). AS, p. 457. BHD, p. 181; BHD2, p. 102 (d. 31 May). FDY, p. 459. KOM, pp. 138–40 (d. 31 May). Truitt 1983, p. 280.

Goodall, Edyth [actress] (b. Dundee, Scotland, 20 Feb 1886–22 Jul 1929 [43], London, England). m. Leonard Francis Schuster. "Edyth Goodall," *Variety,* 7 Aug 1929.

Goodall, Grace [actress] (b. San Francisco CA, 12 Jun 1889–27 Sep 1940 [51], Los Angeles CA). AS, p. 457. BHD1, p. 220. IFN, p. 120.

Goode, Lizzie [actress] (b. ca. 1871–27 Jan 1921 [49?], New York NY). m. George Bothner. "Lizzie Goode," *Variety,* 4 Feb 1921. AS, p. 458. BHD, p. 181.

Goodfellow, Philo [prop man] (b. 1890–27 Aug 1937 [47?], Los Angeles CA). BHD2, p. 102.

Goodfriend, Pliny [cinematographer/actor] (b. Drayton ND, 5 Sep 1891–20 Jan 1981 [89], Santa Monica CA). m. Mary Barbara McEvoy [**Mary Anderson**?]—div. 1937. AMD, p. 141. BHD, p. 181; BHD2, p. 102. "Goodfriend on Mayer's Camera," *MPW,* 27 Mar 1920, 2096. Diane Goodfriend Walker was the daughter of Pliny Goodfriend. Her step-daughter thinks that Mary Barbara McEvoy and actress Mary Anderson are the same person. Philo Goodfriend, Pliny's brother, was a prop man who was killed on the set of 20th Century Fox's *Ali Baba Goes to Town* on 28 Aug 1937. The prop was a magic carpet that Eddie Cantor was to ride in the film. Data from Carol Walker Scherer of Orange CA.

Goodman, Dr. Daniel Carson [novelist/playwright/director/executive, International Films Corp. and Cosmopolitan] (b. Chicago IL, 24 Aug 1883–16 May 1957 [73], Wilmington NJ). m. **Alma Rubens** (d. 1931); Winifred Spear, 19 Oct 1935. "Daniel Goodman, Author, 73, Dead; Former Medical Specialist Wrote Novels, Plays and Motion Picture Scripts," *NYT,* 17 May 1957, 25:1. AMD, p. 141. AS, p. 458. BHD2, p. 102 (b. 1881; d. Flemington NJ). WWWA. "$60,000 for Writer; Dr. Goodman to Receive That Amount for Writing Twelve Features for Lubin," *NYDM,* 21 Jul 1915, 28:2. "Daniel Carson Goodman," *MPW,* 31 Jul 1915, 796. "More Lubin Enterprise," *MPW,* 9 Oct 1915, 236. "New Editorial Head for Triangle," *MPW,* 10 Aug 1918, 829. "Scenario Editor Retires," *MPW,* 2 Nov 1918, 595. "Pathé Contracts for Rubens-Goodman Plays," *MPW,* 10 May 1919, 794. "Dr. Goodman Is Author of Georges Carpentier Story," *MPW,* 17 Apr 1920, 452. Daniel Carson Goodman, "A Pledge to My Conscience," *MPW,* 4 Dec 1920, 579. "Daniel Carson Goodman Will Make Four Equitys," *MPW,* 11 Nov 1922, 161. "Daniel Carson Goodman Has Another Box Office Title Film," *MPW,* 20 Jan 1923, 255. Stanton Leeds, "Put Your Message Across," *Classic,* Jul 1923, 38, 77–78.

Goodman, Edward [director] (b. New York NY, 1888–2 Oct 1962 [74?], New York NY). AS, p. 458. BHD2, p. 102.

Goodman, Jack [actor] (aka Jack Powell, b. Brooklyn NY, 1901?–6 Apr 1976 [75], White Plains NY). "Jack Powell," *Variety,* 14 Apr 1976. AS, p. 458.

Goodman, Jules Eckert [scenarist] (b. Gervais OR, 2 Nov 1876–10 Jul 1962 [85], Peekskill NY). m. Mai Pfouts. "Jules Eckert Goodman," *Variety,* 18 Jul 1962. AMD, p. 141. AS, p. 458. SD, p. 578. WWWA. "Jules Eckert Goodman to Write for Lasky Company," *MPW,* 18 Mar 1916, 1835.

Goodman, Kenneth Sawyer [playwright] (b. Chicago IL, 19 Sep 1883–30 Nov 1918 [35], at Great Lakes Naval Training Station IL; influenza). m. Marjorie Robbins. "Lieut. Kenneth Sawyer Goodman," *Variety,* 6 Dec 1918. BHD2, p. 102. SD.

Goodrich, Amy Florench [actress] (b. 1889–20 Jul 1939 [50?], Los Angeles CA). AS, p. 458.

Goodrich, Charles W[illiam] [actor] (b. Philadelphia PA, 1861?–20 Mar 1931 [70], Norwalk CT). m. **Camilla Crume** (d. 1952). "Charles W. Goodrich," *Variety,* 25 Mar 1931 (stage debut, 1874). BHD, p. 181. IFN, p. 120. SD.

Goodrich, Edna [actress] (*née* Bessie Edna Stephens, b. Logansport IN, 22 Dec 1883–26 May 1971 [87], New York NY). m. (1) Nat C. Goodwin; (2) Baron Keane. (Film debut: *Armstrong's Wife,* Paramount, 1915.) AMD, p. 141. AS, p. 458. BHD, p. 181. IFN, p. 120. SD, p. 518. "Actresses Upset in Auto; Sixth Avenue Car Crashed Into Machine—Women and Chauffer Hurt," *NYT,* 17 Jan 1905, 1:6 (Nellie Stevens and Goodrich were thrown out of a car; Goodrich was cut about the arms and body). "Edna Goodrich," *MPW,* 1 Aug 1914, 712. "Edna Goodrich in War's Toils," *MPW,* 5 Sep 1914, 1354. "Edna Goodrich in Lasky Photoplays," *MPW,* 28 Aug 1915, 1456. "Edna Goodrich's Debut," *NYDM,* 30 Oct 1915, 26:3 (in *Armstrong's Wife,* FP-L, 18 Nov). "New Stars for Morosco," *MPW,* 6 May 1916, 960. "Mutual Gets Edna Goodrich," *MPW,* 20 Jan 1917, 350. "Edna Goodrich Designs Military Gown," *MPW,* 2 Feb 1918, 699. "Edna Goodrich to Make Series of Mutual Productions," *MPW,* 8 Jun 1918, 1452.

Goodrich, John Fish [writer/scenarist] (b. Delavan WI, 18 Feb 1887–11 Mar 1937 [50]. Los Angeles CA; after abdominal operation). m. Frances Munnally. "John Fish Goodrich; Early

Writer for Motion Pictures Collaborated in 'The Deluge [1933],'" *NYT,* 13 Mar 1937, 19:3. "John Fish Goodrich," *Variety,* 17 Mar 1937. AMD, p. 141. AS, p. 458. BHD2, p. 102 (d. 12 Mar). FDY, p. 425. "Goodrich Is Eager to Get Novel Ideas," *MPW,* 1 Jan 1927, 51.

Goodrich, Joseph [cinematographer] (d. Nov 1925, Los Angeles CA). BHD2, p. 102.

Goodrich, Katherine [actress] (b. Austin TX, 1880). m. **Thomas G. Lingham** (d. 1950). AMD, p. 141. BHD, p. 181. "Katherine Goodrich," *MPW,* 17 Mar 1917, 1778.

Goodrich, Louis [actor] (*né* Louis Goodrich Abbott Anderson, b. Sandhurst, England, 1865–31 Jan 1945 [79?], London, England). AS, p. 458.

Goodrich, William *see* **Arbuckle, Roscoe "Fatty**

Goodstadt, Louis M. [casting director] (b. 1877–24 May 1928 [51?], Los Angeles CA). BHD2, p. 103.

Goodwin, Aline [actress]. No data found. George A. Katchmer, "Remembering the Great Silents," *CI,* 183 (Sep 1990), 46.

Goodwin, Betty [actress] George A. Katchmer, "Forgotten Cowboys and Cowgirls—Part X," *CI,* 182 (Aug 1990), 39.

Goodwin, George [actor] (b. 1864–12 Jul 1926 [62?], England). BHD, p. 181.

Goodwin, Gloria [actress]. m. Foye Fossett Staniford, 24 Jul 1917, New London CT. "Marriages," *Variety,* 26 Oct 1917, p. 9.

Goodwin, Rev. Hannibal Williston [inventor] (b. Taughannock NY, 30 Apr 1822–31 Dec 1900 [78], Newark NJ). m. Rebecca Allen, 1852. *NYT,* 1 Jan 1901, 9:6 (missing on microfilm). "Mrs. Hannibal Goodwin Dies at 81," *NYT,* 23 Sep 1914, 9:4 (d. 22 Sep 1914 [81], Newark NJ). Spehr, p. 134 (1824–1901). "Eastman Company Loses Patent Suit; Buffalo Court Decides That Kodak Concern Has Infringed on Rights of Hannibal Goodwin, Deceased," *MPW,* 30 Aug 1913, 939. "The Tragedy of Rev. H. Goodwin; Some Interesting Data of His Life and Work," *MPW,* 13 Sep 1913, 1165. *The National Cyclopedia of American Biography,* vol. 23, pp. 377–78.

Goodwin, (Harold) Harry [vaudevillian/actor] (b. 1880?–24 Oct 1942 [62], New York NY). (Began ca. 1910.) "Harry Goodwin," *Variety,* 28 Oct 1942. AMD, p. 141. "Harold Goodwin Becomes Fox Film Star; Began Screen Experience Ten Years Ago," *MPW,* 5 Feb 1921, 679. "Fox Issues Folder for a New Star," *MPW,* 5 Mar 1921, 76.

Goodwin, Harold [actor] (b. Peoria IL, 1 Dec 1902–12 Jul 1987 [84], Woodland Hills CA). AS, p. 458. BHD1, p. 220.

Goodwin, Murray (nephew of **Nat Goodwin**) [actor]. No data found. "Nat Goodwin's Nephew's Suit," *Variety,* 21 Feb 1924, 3:3 ("...picture actor, a nephew of the late Nat Goodwin, is suing Joseph Guarino, owner of the make of films known as Audax, for breach of contract.").

Goodwin, Nat C[arl], Jr. (uncle of **Murray Goodwin**) [actor] (*né* Nathaniel Carll Goodwin, b. Boston MA, 25 Jul 1859 [Intl. Genealogical Index, MA, Fiche 00584, p. 33495]–31 Jan 1919 [59], New York NY [Death Certificate No. 4691; cerebral thrombosis]). m. 5 times; **Maxine Elliott** (d. 1940). "Nat C. Goodwin Dies of Apoplexy; Famous Comedian, Briefly Ill, Never Recovered from Operation for Removal of Eye; Actress at His Bedside; Georgia Gardner, It Was Said, Was to Be His Sixth Wife—61, He Began His Notable Career at 17," *NYT,* 1 Feb 1919, 13:3 (age 61). "Nat C. Goodwin," *Variety,* 7 Feb 1919 (age 59). AMD, p. 141. AS, p. 458. BHD, p. 181 (b. 1857). IFN, p. 120 (b. 1857). SD. Truitt, p. 127 (1857–1920). "Nathaniel Goodwin in Pictures," *MPW,* 12 Aug 1911, 367. "Nat Goodwin in Moving Pictures," *MPW,* XII, 18 May 1912, 616. "Nat Goodwin's Book," *NYDM,* 9 Dec 1914, 6:2 (re autobiography). "Nat Goodwin in 'The Master Hand,'" *MPW,* 26 Jun 1915, 2109. "Sues Because of Wet Feet," *NYDM,* 4 Aug 1915, 9:4 (sued a railroad in Milwaukee because a train wreck forced him and his company to wade through two feet of snow to another train. He missed an engagement at Dubuque IA and could not appear in Milwaukee because of a cold he caught.). "Goodwin}s Imitation of Robson," *NYDM,* 11 Aug 1915, 5:3 (Goodwin "is—the attested birthday register as guide—fifty-eight years and one week old..."). "Nat Goodwin Starts Work for Universal," *MPW,* 14 Aug 1915, 1137. "Nat Goodwin Joins Mirror," *MPW,* 4 Dec 1915, 1824. "'Fagin' Fessed Up, Nat C. Goodwin Was the First 'Star' to Fall for the Films," *NYDM,* 19 Feb 1916, 23:4 (made *Oliver Twist* in 1912?). "Nat Goodwin Sues Mirror," *MPW,* 24 Jun 1916, 2243. Gladys Hall, "Nat Goodwin, Bachelor; An Interview Without a Word About His Former Wives—Is That Not Remarkable? At Least He Thinks So," *MPC,* Jul 1916, 20–21. Joseph Jackson, "Things I Have Seen," *Paris and Hollywood,* Oct 1926, 34 (a marriage epidemic has hit Hollywood. When someone criticizes Goodwin for his many affairs of the heart, he shot back 'What's wrong about it?...I married them all, didn't I?")).

Goodwins, Fred [director] (b. London, England, 1891-Aug 1923 [32?], London, England). AMD, p. 141. AS, p. 459. BHD1, p. 609. "New Comedy Man with Christie," *MPW,* 1 Dec 1917, 1295. "Fred Goodwins Off to War," *MPW,* 5 Oct 1918, 66.

Goodwins, Leslie [writer/director] (b. London, England, 17 Sep 1899–8 Jan 1969 [69], Los Angeles CA; pneumonia). (Christie.) "Leslie Goodwins," *Variety,* 15 Jan 1969. AS, p. 459. BHD, p. 181; BHD2, p. 103. IFN, p. 120. Truitt, p. 127.

Goosson, Stephen [art director] (b. Grand Rapids MI, 24 Mar 1889–25 Mar 1973 [84], Woodland Hills CA; stroke). (Began 1919; Columbia; Univ.) "Stephen Goosson," *Variety,* 4 Apr 1973. AMD, p. 141. AS, p. 459. BHD2, p. 103. "Goossen Becomes Art Director," *MPW,* 28 Feb 1920, 1443.

Gopal, Govind Pathak [actor] (b. India, 24 Jun 1899–8 Apr 1974 [74], India). AS, p. 459.

Gorcey, Bernard (father of Leo and David Gorcey) [actor] (b. Russia, 9 Jan 1886–11 Sep 1955 [69], Los Angeles CA; injuries sustained from auto accident on 31 Aug). m. (sons, David [1921–1984]; Leo [1915–1969]. (Allied Artists.) "Bernard Gorcey, Long an Actor, 67; Creator of Isaac Cohen Role in 'Abie's Irish Rose' Dies—Also Appeared in Movies," *NYT,* 13 Sep 1955, 31:3 (b. Switzerland; age 67). "Bernard Gorcey," *Variety,* 14 Sep 1955 (age 67). AS, p. 459 (b. Switzerland, 1888). BHD1, p. 221. IFN, p. 120. Truitt, p. 127 (b. Switzerland, 1888). Ann Cummings, "A Kosher View of Movink Pichers," *MPC,* Mar 1928, 21, 78 (interview with Gorcey and Ida Kramer).

Gorczynska, Maria [actress] (b. Lublin, Poland, 27 Jan 1899–23 May 1959 [60], Warsaw, Poland). AS, p. 459.

Gordon, A. George [actor] (b. 1882?–27 Dec 1953 [71], Chicago IL; heart attack). (Selig Polyscope.) "A. George Gordon," *Variety,* 13 Jan 1954. AS, p. 459. BHD, p. 181. IFN, p. 120. Truitt, p. 128.

Gordon, Alice [actress] (b. St. Andrews, Scotland, 1879). BHD, p. 181.

Gordon, Anna R. [actress] (*née* Anna Rothwell, d. 4 Oct 1920, Cleveland OH; suicide). AS, p. 459.

Gordon, Bobby [actor/director] (b. Pittsburgh PA, 21 Aug 1913–1 Dec 1990 [87], Los Angeles CA). AS, p. 459 (d. 17 Feb 1973, NYC). BHD1, p. 221; BHD2, p. 103.

Gordon, Bruce [actor] (b. Fichburg MA, 1916). (1st U.S. film: *Forbidden Valley,* Pathé, 1920; 1st National.) AMD, p. 141. "English Actor-Athlete to 'Invade' American Field," *MPW,* 28 Feb 1920, 1517.

Gordon, C. Henry [actor] (*né* Charles Henry Racke, b. New York NY, 17 Jun 1884–3 Dec 1940 [56], Los Angeles CA; complications after a leg amputation). (Fox, 1930; Metro; TC-F.) "C. Henry Gordon," *Variety,* 11 Dec 1940. AS, p. 459 (b. 1883). BHD1, p. 221. IFN, p. 120. SD. Truitt 1983, p. 281 (b. 1883).

Gordon, Cole [actor] (b. 1889–25 May 1929 [40?], Baltimore MD; airplane crash). AS, p. 459.

Gordon, Constance "Kitty" [actress] (b. England, 1888–26 May 1974 [86?], Brentwood NY). AS, p. 459.

Gordon, Douglas [actor/producer] (b. London, England, 12 Mar 1871–26 Oct 1935 [64]). BHD2, p. 103.

Gordon, Dorothy [moderator of radio and TV programs] (*née* Dorothy Lerner, b. Odessa, Russia, 4 Apr 1889–11 May 1970 [81], New York NY). m. Mr. Gordon (d. 1944). Alden Whitman, "Dorothy Gordon, 81, Moderator of Times Youth Forums, Is Dead; Started Radio and TV Series in '43—Earlier, Had Career as Folk Song Singer," *NYT,* 12 May 1970, 39:1. "Dorothy Gordon," *Variety,* 13 May 1970.

Gordon, Edward R. [actor] (b. 1886?–10 Nov 1938 [52], Los Angeles CA). "Edward Gordon," *Variety,* 16 Nov 1938 ("a veteran of the silent pictures"). AMD, p. 141. AS, p. 460. BHD, p. 182. IFN, p. 120. Truitt, p. 128. "Julius and Abe Stern Pick Four Century Comedy Stars," *MPW,* 13 Dec 1924, 652.

Gordon, Eva [actress]. No data found. AMD, p. 141. "Eva Gordon," *MPW,* 26 Jan 1918, 521. "Eva Gordon Signed by Universal," *MPW,* 17 Feb 1923, 704.

Gordon, G. Swayne [actor] (b. Baltimore MD, 15 Mar 1879–23 Jun 1949 [70], New York NY). AS, p. 460.

Gordon, Gilbert (*né* Henry Moore, b. 1889?–20 Mar 1967 [78], London, England). m. Cissie Cane. "Gilbert Gordon," *Variety,* 5 Apr 1967. AS, p. 460.

Gordon, Gladys [scenarist]. No data found. FDY, p. 427.

Gordon, Glen Charles [actor] (b. New York NY, 13 Mar 1914–16 Sep 1977 [63], Los Angeles CA). AS, p. 460. BHD1, p. 221.

Gordon, Gloria (mother of actor Gale Gordon) [actress] (b. 1881–23 Nov 1962 [81?], Los Angeles CA). "Gloria Gordon," *Variety,* 5 Dec 1962. AMD, p. 141. AS, p. 460. BHD1, p. 221. IFN, p. 121. Truitt, p. 128. "From Extra to Lead in Four Days," *MPW,* 12 Jun 1926, 546. In *Dancing Days* (1926) and *Exclusive Rights* (1926).

Gordon, Grace [actress]. No data found. AMD, p. 142. Photo, *Paris and Hollywood,* Sep 1926, 68 (in *Butterflies in the Rain,* Universal). "Grace Gordon," *MPW,* 28 May 1927, 268.

Gordon, Hal [actor] (b. London, England, 18 Apr 1894–1946 [62?], England). AS, p. 460. BHD1, p. 221.

Gordon, Harris [stage/film actor] (b. Glenside PA, 4 Jul 1884–31 Mar 1947 [62], Burbank CA; heart attack). m. Babette; Kathryn Clark. (Reliance, 1911–14; FP-L; Universal; Solax; Thanhouse; Mutual; FP-Lr.) "Harris Gordon," *Variety,* 9 Apr 1947. AMD, p. 142. AS, p. 460. BHD1, p. 221. IFN, p. 121. MSBB, p. 1024 (b. 1886). Truitt, p. 128 (b. 1887; d. 2 Apr). "Harris Gordon," *MPW,* 5 Jun 1915, 1617. "Harris Gordon Engaged by Metro," *MPW,* 5 Aug 1916, 961. "Gordon Back on Screen Following Auto Smash," *MPW,* 29 Jun 1918, 1873 (after almost 2 years). "Gordon with Screencraft," *MPW,* 9 Nov 1918, 676.

Gordon, Harry G. [actor] (b. Buffalo NY, 1884–20 Nov 1948 [64?]). BHD, p. 182.

Gordon, Henry C. [actor] (b. New York NY, 12 Jun 1883–3 Dec 1940 [57], Los Angeles CA). AS, p. 460.

Gordon, Huntley [actor] (b. Montreal, Canada, 8 Oct 1887–8 Dec 1956 [69], Van Nuys CA). "Huntley Gordon, 69, Silent Screen Star," *NYT,* 10 Dec 1956, 31:2. "Huntley Gordon," *Variety,* 12 Dec 1956. AMD, p. 142. AS, p. 460 (d. 7 Dec). BHD1, p. 221 (d. LA CA). FFF, p. 199. IFN, p. 121. MH, p. 113. Truitt, p. 128 (b. 1897). "Huntley Gordon," *MPW,* 29 Apr 1916, 810. "Gordon Is Leading Man for Ethel Barrymore," *MPW,* 20 Jul 1918, 407. "Take Your Choice," *Classic,* Mar 1924, 35 (name given as Spurr Huntley Gordon). Jim Tully, "Married to Thirteen Women; The Arch-Bigamist of the Screen Discusses Them All…," *MPC,* Feb 1925, 24–25, 78, 94. Helen Carlisle, "The Truth About Huntley Gordon," *MW,* 2 May 1925, 4–5, 33.

Gordon, James (actor/director/a founder of The Troupers) (b. Pittsburgh PA, 23 Apr 1871–12 May 1941 [70], Los Angeles CA; complications after surgery). m. **Mabel Van Buren** (d. 1947). "James Gordon," *Variety,* 21 May 1941 (age 60). AMD, p. 142. AS, p. 460. BHD1, p. 221; BHD2, p. 103. IFN, p. 121. Truitt, p. 128 (b. 1881). "James Gordon Back from Bermuda," *MPW,* 10 Oct 1914, 168.

Gordon, Josie [actress] (b. Scotland, 1896–6 Mar 1959 [63?], Hove, England). AS, p. 460.

Gordon, Julia Swayne [actress] (*née* Sarah Victoria Swayne, b. Columbus OH, 29 Oct 1878–28 May 1933 [54], Los Angeles CA). (Edison; Vitagraph.) "Julia Swayne Gordon," *Variety,* 13 Jun 1933. AMD, p. 142. AS, p. 460. BHD1, p. 222. FSS, p. 128. IFN, p. 121. Katz, p. 493. Lowrey, p. 64. Slide, p. 141. Truitt, p. 129. "Julia Swayne Gordon, Vitagraph Woman of Moods," *MPW,* 11 Jul 1914, 236. "Julia Swayne Gordon," *MPW,* Jul 1915, 500. "Miss Gordon Comes to Paramount," *MPW,* 25 Sep 1920, 505.

Gordon, Kilbourn [publicist]. No data found. AMD, p. 142. "Gordon Handles Powell Publicity," *MPW,* 9 Sep 1916, 1706. Kilbourn Gordon, "Publicizing Pictures," *MPW,* 20 Jul 1918, 342.

Gordon, Kitty (mother of **Cynthia Vera Beresford**) [actress] (*née* Constance Blades, b. Folkstone, England, 27 Apr 1878–29 May 1974 [96], Brentwood, LI NY). m. (1) Michael Levenson; (2); **Capt. Henry William Walter Horsley Beresford** (d. 1944); (3) Ralph Ranlet; (4) **Jack Wilson** (d. 1931). (Film debut: *As in a Looking Glass,* World, 1916; Selznick.) "Kitty Gordon, Star of 1911 'Enchantress,' Is Dead; Actress for Whom Herbert Composed the Musical Also Played in Early Films," *NYT,* 29 May, 44:2. "Kitty Gordon [Mrs. Ralph Ranlet]," *Variety,* 29 May 1974 (age 96). "Kitty Gordon, Star of 1911 Herbert Production, 'The Enchantress,'" *Washington Post,* 31 May 1974 (age 96). AMD, p. 142. AS, p. 460 (b. 22 Apr; d. 26 May). BHD, p. 182 (b. 1878). IFN, p. 121 (b. 1878). MSBB, p. 1036. SD. Spehr, p. 134 (b. Folkstone, England, 1870). Truitt, p. 129. "Kitty Gordon on Screen; World Films Signs Famous Beauty for Appearance in Feature," *NYDM,* 20 Nov 1915, 25:4 (to debut in *As in a Looking-Glass* at World). "Kitty Gordon," *MPW,* 27 Nov 1915, 1648. "Kitty Gordon Working on New Feature," *MPW,* 23 Sep 1916, 1956. "Kitty Gordon's New Picture Nearly Ready," *MPW,* 14 Oct 1916, 261. "Brady Engages Kitty Gordon," *MPW,* 30 Dec 1916, 1969. "Kitty Gordon Renews World Contract," *MPW,* 28 Jul 1917, 658. "Kitty Gordon Forms Picture Company," *MPW,* 24 Aug 1918, 1131. "Kitty Gordon Leases a Home," *MPW,* 12 Oct 1918, 207. "World Film Appeals Kitty Gordon Case; Actress Was Injured in Battle Scenes," *MPW,* 30 Oct 1920, 1252. "Kitty Gordon Wins Suit," *MPW,* 13 Nov 1920, 229. "Supreme Court Awards Kitty Gordon $20,000," *MPW,* 14 May 1921, 162.

Gordon, Leon [actor/producer/playwright/scenarist] (b. Brighton, England, 12 Jan 1884–4 Jan 1960 [75], Los Angeles CA). (MGM, 1930.) "Leon Gordon," *Variety,* 13 Jan 1960, p. 63 (age 66). AS, p. 460. BHD, p. 182; BHD2, p. 103 (b. 1894). FDY, p. 427 (L.H. Gordon).

Gordon, Marian [actress] (b. 1897–8 Jan 1927 [29?], Los Angeles CA; suicide with poison). AS, p. 460. BHD, p. 182.

Gordon, Mary [actress] (*née* Mary Gilmour, b. Glasgow, Scotland, 16 May 1882–23 Aug 1963 [81], Pasadena CA). "Mary Gordon," *Variety,* 4 Sep 1963 (began 1920). AS, p. 460. BHD1, p. 222. IFN, p. 121. Katz, pp. 493–94. Truitt, p. 129.

Gordon, Maude Turner [actress] (b. Franklin IN, 10 Nov 1868–12 Jan 1940 [71], Los Angeles CA; pneumonia). (1st National.) AS, p. 460 (b. 10 May). BHD1, p. 222. IFN, p. 121.

Gordon, Nora [actress] (b. Westhardlepool, England, 1894–11 May 1970 [76?], London, England). AS, p. 461.

Gordon, Olive Fuller *see* Golden, Olive Fuller

Gordon, Paul [actor] (*né* Thomas Achelis, b. Brooklyn NY, 1886?–3 May 1929 [43], Florence, Italy). m. Ann Mason. "Thomas Achelis," *Variety,* 8 May 1929. AS, p. 461. BHD, p. 182 (b. 1883). IFN, p. 121.

Gordon, Peter [actor] (b. Naples, Italy, 1888?–25 May 1943 [55], near Los Angeles CA). (Vitagraph.) "Peter Gordon," *Variety,* 9 Jun 1943. AS, p. 461. BHD, p. 182. IFN, p. 121. Truitt, p. 129.

Gordon, Phyllis [actress] (b. Suffolk VA, ca 1889). m. **Eugene Pallette** (d. 1954). *Fl.* 1912.

Gordon, Richard H. [actor] (*né* Richard Henry Towey, b. Philadelphia PA, 21 Jun 1893–20 Sep 1956 [63], Los Angeles CA). m. Emily Ann Wellman (d. 1946). "Richard H. Gordon," *Variety,* 26 Sep 1956 (began 1918). AS, p. 461. BHD1, p. 222. IFN, p. 121. SD. Truitt, p. 129.

Gordon, Robert [actor] (*né* Robert Gordon Duncan, b. KS, 3 Mar 1895–26 Oct 1971 [76], Victorville CA). m. **Alma Francis**, 25 Mar 1919, Hollywood CA). "Robert Gordon," *Variety,* 3 Nov 1971. AMD, p. 142. AS, p. 461. BHD, p. 182. IFN, p. 121. Katz, p. 494. Truitt, p. 129. WWS, p. 74. "Bessie Love Introduces New Leading Man," *MPW,* 15 Mar 1919, 1518. "Gordon—Francis," *MPW,* 3 May 1919, 661. "Robert Gordon Starred," *LA Times,* 22 Jan 1920, II, 9 (signed with Vitagraph). "Robert Gordon Photoplays in Preparation with Star Who Has Worked Way to Fame," *MPW,* 1 May 1920, 698. "Gordon Finishes Second Vitagraph," *MPW,* 3 Jul 1920, 56.

Gordon, Roy Wells [actor] (b. OH, 18 Oct 1884–23 Jul 1972 [87], Sherman Oaks CA). AS, p. 461. BHD1, p. 222.

Gordon, Ruth [actress/scenarist] (*née* Ruth Gordon Jones, b. Wollaston MA, 30 Oct 1896–28 Aug 1985 [88], Edgartown MA; cerebral hemorrhage). m. (1) Gregory Kelly, 1921 (d. 1927); (2) Garson Kanin, 1942 (widower). *Myself Among Others* (1971); *My Side* (1976). (AA, 1968.) Todd McCarthy, "Ruth Gordon Dies at 88; Feisty Actress-Writer Found 2nd Wind," *Variety,* 4 Sep 1985 (extra at Ft. Lee NJ). AS, p. 461. BHD1, p. 222; BHD2, p. 103. Katz, p. 494.

Gordon, Vera [stage/film actress] (*née* Vera Nemirou, b. Edkerternoslav, Russia, 11 Jun 1886–8 May 1948 [61], Beverly Hills CA). "Vera Gordon, 61, Screen Actress; Former Vaudeville Player, Known in Films for Mother Roles, Dies on Coast," *NYT,* 10 May 1948, 21:4. "Vera Gordon," *Variety,* 12 May 1948. AMD, p. 142. AS, p. 461. BHD1, p. 222 (b. Edketernoslav). FFF, p. 197. FSS, p. 128. IFN, p. 121. Katz, p. 494. Truitt, p. 129. "Vera Gordon Portrays Mother Role in 'North Wind's Malice,'" *MPW,* 9 Oct 1920, 767. "Vera Gordon in Vaudeville," *MPW,* 6 Nov 1920, 86. "Vera Gordon at Sing Sing," *MPW,* 1 Jan 1921, 87.

Gordon, W. Lindsay [general manager/executive]. No data found. AMD, p. 142. "Gordon Heads Company; Maker of Illustrated Lectures Enters the Film Producing Field," *NYDM,* 24 Feb 1915, 25:2 (to erect a studio at Dongan Hills, Staten Island NY). "W. Lindsay Gordon Heads Beaver Film Corporation," *MPW,* 6 Mar 1915, 1467.

Gordoni, Arthur [actor] (b. NY, 17 Mar 1893–10 Aug 1966 [83], Los Angeles CA). AS, p. 461 (*né* Arthur Gordon). BHD, p. 182.

Gore, Rosa [Crimmins and Gore/film actress] (b. New York NY, 15 Sep 1866–4 Feb 1941 [74], Los Angeles CA). m. Alexander M. Lyon (**Daniel Crimmins**) (d. 1945). (Pathé [NJ], 1912.) "Rosa Gore [Mrs. Minnie Lyon]," *Variety,* 12 Feb 1941. AMD, p. 142. AS, p. 461. BHD1, p. 222. IFN, p. 121. Truitt, p. 129. "Crimmins and Gore Join Vitagraph," *MPW,* 13 Jun 1914, 1523. "Crimmins and Gore at Work," *NYDM,* 6 Nov 1915, 26:3 (with Kleine). "Crimmins and Gore," *MPW,*

22 Apr 1916, 628. George Katchmer, "Remembering the Great Silents," *CI*, 246 (Dec 1995), 46, 48.

Gorezov, Boris [director] (b. Plovdiv, Bulgaria, 4 Apr 1899). AS, p. 461.

Goring, Frederica [stage/film actress] (b. New York NY, 13 Aug 1895–11 Apr 1959 [63], New York NY). "Frederica Goring," *Variety*, 22 Apr 1959, p. 87. BHD, p. 181.

Gorki, Alexis Maximovich [actor/scenarist] (b. Nizny Novgorod, Russia, 14 Mar 1868–5 Dec 1936 [68], Moscow, Russia). AS, p. 461.

Gorlett [actor] (*né* Joseph Auguste Fabre, b. Pelissanne, France, 13 Jun 1898–27 Jan 1963 [64], Salon-de-Proence, France [extrait de décès no. 4/1963]). AS, p. 461.

Gorman, Baby Early *see* **Baby Early**

Gorman, Charles [actor] (b. 1864?–25 Jan 1928 [63, New York NY]). AS, p. 461 (d. LA CA). BHD, p. 182. IFN, p. 121.

Gorman, Eddie [actor] (b. Jersey City NJ, 1872–28 Jun 1919 [47?], New York NY). BHD, p. 182.

Gorman, Eric [actor] (*né* Frederick Eric Gorman, b. England, 1886–24 Nov 1971 [85?], Dublin, Ireland). AS, p. 461.

Gorman, James J. [minstrel/stage manager] (b. 1860–14 Aug 1921 [61?], Boston MA; dropsy). "James Gorman," *Variety*, 19 Aug 1921. AS, p. 461. BHD, p. 182.

Gorman, John P. [treasurer of B.F. Keith Circuit] (b. Boston MA, 1858?–12 Feb 1927 [68], West Medford MA). m. Agnes C. Maguire. "John P. Gorman," *Variety*, 16 Feb 1927 (interred at Holyhood Cemetery, Brookline MA).

Gorman, John W. [director] (b. Boston MA, 4 Sep 1884–2 Apr 1936 [51]). m. (2) **Clara Hamon**, 22 Aug 1921, Hollywood CA; (3) Vola Smith (**Vola Vale**), Dec 1926, Santa Ana CA. AMD, p. 142. BHD2, p. 103. "Clara Hamon Weds Director," *MPW*, 10 Sep 1921, 169. "Gorman Joins Chadwick," *MPW*, 9 Feb 1924, 460. "'Home, Sweet Home' to Be Gorman's first for A.E.," *MPW*, 1 May 1926, 23. "Gorman's Six Go to Independent Buyers," *MPW*, 3 Jul 1926, 1. "John Gorman Produces and Builds His Own Pictures," *MPW*, 1 Jan 1927, 52. "Now We Know It," *MPW*, 12 Feb 1927, 492. June Lee, "Dan Cupid's Bulletin Board," *Paris and Hollywood Screen Secrets Magazine*, May 1927, 53 (m. Vale).

Gos, Emile [director of documentaries] (b. Geneva, Switzerland, 8 Aug 1888–8 Jul 1969 [80], Lausanne, Switzerland). AS, p. 462.

Gosden, Alfred G. [pioneer in color films/cinematographer] (b. London, England, 1873?–15 Sep 1941 [68], Los Angeles CA). (Biograph; Lubin; Universal; RKO.) "Al Gosden," *Variety*, 1 Oct 1941 (Kinema Colour, 1911). AS, p. 462. BHD2, p. 103. FDY, p. 459.

Gosford, Alice Peckham [stage/film actress] (b. RI, 1886–23 Jan 1919 [32?], New York NY). "Alice Peckham Gosford," *Variety*, 31 Jan 1919, 15:3 (age 31). AS, p. 462. BHD, p. 182.

Gosho, Heinosuké [actor/director/producer] (*né* Heiuemon Gosho, b. Tokyo, Japan, 2 Feb 1902–1 May 1981 [79], Mishima, Japan). AS, p. 462.

Gosnell, Evelyn F. [actress] (b. IL, 1895?–11 Nov 1946 [51], New York NY; from injuries suffered from a fall). (Paramount-Flagg comedies.) "Evelyn F. Gosnell," *Variety*, 20 Nov 1946. AS, p. 462. BHD, p. 182. IFN, p. 121.

Goss, Walter *see* **Drew, Roland**

Gotho, Heinrich [actor] (*né* Heinrich Gottesmann, b. Dolina, Austria, 3 May 1872). AS, p. 462.

Gothson, Manne [actor/director] (b. Sweden, 1879–1933 [54?], Sweden). AS, p. 462.

Gott, Barbara [actress] (b. Stirling, Scotland-d. 18 Nov 1944, London, England). AS, p. 462. BHD1, p. 223.

Gottler, Archie [actor/composer/director] (b. New York NY, 14 May 1896–24 Jun 1959 [63], Los Angeles CA). AS, p. 463. BHD1, p. 223; BHD2, p. 104.

Gottout, John [actor] (d. 1934). BHD, p. 182.

Gottschalk, Ferdinand [actor] (b. London, England, 28 Feb 1858–10 Nov 1944 [86], London, England). (Empire All-Star Corp.) "Ferdinand Gottschalk," *Variety*, 29 Nov 1944 (d. 17 Nov). AMD, p. 142. AS, p. 463 (b. 1859; d. 17 Nov). BHD1, p. 223. IFN, p. 121. Truitt, pp. 129–30. "Ferdinand Gottschalk," *MPW*, 27 Oct 1917, 543.

Gottschalk, Louis F[erdinand] [conductor/composer] (b. St. Louis MO, 7 Oct 1864–15 Jul 1934 [70], Los Angeles CA; cerebral hemorrhage). m. Marie Millard. (Griffith.) "Louis F. Gottschalk," *Variety*, 17 Jul 1934. AMD, p. 142. AS, p. 463 (b. 1863). BHD2, p. 104. WWWA (b. 1868). "Dwan Engages Gottschalk," *MPW*, 3 Jul 1920, 62.

Goudal, Jetta [stage/film actress] (*née* Julie Henriette Goudeket, b. Amsterdam, Holland, 12 Jul 1891–14 Jan 1985 [93], Los Angeles CA). m. Harold Grieve, 11 Oct 1930, Yuma AZ. (Film debut: *Timothy's Quest*; Paramount; UA; last film, *Business and Pleasure*, Fox, 1932.) "Jetta Goudal," *NYT*, 16 Jan 1985, B5:4 (b. France). "Jetta Goudal," *Variety*, 23 Jan 1985 (b. Versailles, France). AMD, p. 142. AS, p. 463 (b. Versailles, France, 18 Jul 1878). BHD1, p. 223. FFF, p. 239 (b. Versailles, 1901). FSS, p. 129. Katz 1994 (b. Versailles, 18 Jul). MH, p. 113 (b. Versailles, 1901). Ragan, 2, p. 637 (b. 1891). Harry Carr, "Jetta and Her Temperament; Elle Est Française, Mais Oui! Et Ce N'Est Pas Tout!," *MPC*, Oct 1924, 20–21, 78. "DeMille Signs Jetta Goudal; 'Coming of Amos,' Her 1st Film," *MPW*, 18 Apr 1925, 706. "On the Set and Off," *MW*, V, 18 Jul 1925, 29 (sued FP-L for $23,250 for being fired; FP-L said she displayed too much temperament and suffered no financial loss as she immediately signed with De Mille). Dorothy Donnell, "From Hollywood to You," *MPS*, 28 Jul 1925, 15–16, 35 ("Jetta Goudal has brought suit against Lasky for breaking his contract with her, which she claims was to have run until October, 1926." Lasky replies that it was her uncontrollable temper that was the cause, "that she refused to portray her roles according to the instructions of her directors and that her temperamental flares cost the company at least twenty-five thousand dollars—and so they are suing Jetta for that sum in a cross-complaint!"). Dorothy Donnell, "You May Say of the Goudal; Is Jetta Goudal's Exotic Pose Real or a Sham? Here Is an Attempt to Penetrate the Mask," *MPC*, Feb 1926, 36–37, 81–83 ("I asked Jetta where she was born...[s]he bit her lip...admitted that Versailles, France, was her birthplace.... I had been sent to find out about Jetta Goudal and I had failed."). "Jetta Goudal Elevated to Stardom by DeMille," *MPW*, 20 Mar 1926, 166. Charles J. Durantz, "Jetta Goudal—Aloof and Mysterious; Of an Intensely Emotional Temperament, This French Actress Avoids Both Society and Publicity," *Cinema Arts*, Nov 1926, 18–19, 47 (b. Versailles). "Jetta Goudal," *MPW*, 5 Mar 1927, 27. "DeMille O.K.'s, Goudal Scoffs at Story of a Split," *MPW*, 17 Sep 1927, 153. Grace Simpson, "Hollywood's Lady of Mystery; Jetta Goudal, the enigmatic star who came to America to forget her tragic romance with a soldier boy [killed in WWI]," *Paris and Hollywood Screen Secrets Magazine*, Aug 1927, 44–45, 96 (b. Versailles, France.). "Jetta Goudal O)ut of Pathé," *MPW*, 24 Dec 1927, 21. Margaret Reid, "Goudal and Velez Fight to Draw; All of Jedda's Generalship Needed to Withstand Lupe's Tearing Attack," *MPC*, Dec 1928, 58, 78 (they fought on the set of *The Love Song*). Dorothy Donnell, "The Mistress of Mystery; Does the Career of Mata Hari, the Spy, Bear Upon the Riddle of Jetta Goudal's Past?," *MPC*, Feb 1929, 22, 84. Helen Louise Walker, "They Had to Pay Jetta Goudal Plenty to Come Back," *Movie Classic*, Nov 1931, 64, 78, 81 (sued Paramount and was out of films for 3 years). DeWitt Bodeen, "Jetta Goudal; Brought Mystery and Exoticism as Well as Beauty to Her Acting," *FIR*, Oct 1974, 449–66. Anthony Slide, *Silent Portraits* (Vestal NY: Vestal Press, 1989), p. 114 (b. 1891). Charles C. Benham, "Jetta Goudal: The Exotic," *CI*, 291 (Sep 1999), 6–13. Frank "Junior" Coughlan, "Jetta Goudal and Me," *CI*, 292 (Oct 1999), 11–12 (Coughlan remembers her as temperamental on the set; Anthony Slide notes her place of birth as in Amsterdam in 1891; includes filmography).

Gough, John [son of actor William Gough) [actor] (b. Boston MA, 22 Sep 1894 [MVRB, Vol. 441, p. 183; unnamed at birth]–29 Jun 1968 [73], Los Angeles CA; cancer). (American; FBO.) "John Gough," *Variety*, 10 Jul 1968 (age 74; "in silent pix played opposite such stars as Mary Miles Minter and the late Lottie Pickford"). AS, p. 463. BHD1, p. 223. IFN, p. Truitt, p. 130 (b. 1897). George Katchmer, "Remembering the Great Silents," *CI*, 242 (Aug 1995), 35.

Gould, Billy [actor] (b. New York NY, 1869–1 Feb 1950 [80?], New York NY; cancer). AS, p. 463. BHD, p. 183.

Gould, Gypsy *see* **Vaughn, Vivian**

Gould, Myrtle [actress] (b. 1880?–25 Feb 1941 [61], Los Angeles CA). m. William Jacobs Gould. "Myrtle Gould [Myrtle L. Jacobs]," *Variety*, 5 Mar 1941 ("She also played in silent pictures up to 1918."). AS, p. 463. BHD, p. 183. IFN, p. 122. Truitt, p. 130.

Gould, Violet [actress] (b. England, 1883–29 Mar 1962 [79?], London, England). AS, p. 463.

Gould, William A. [actor] (b. 1914–29 Mar 1960 [45?], Long Beach CA; in a fire). AS, p. 463. IFN, p. 122. Truitt 1983, p. 285.

Goulden, Louis B. [producer]. No data found. AMD, p. 143. "Goulden to Produce in Milwaukee," *MPW*, 18 Sep 1915, 1971.

Goulding, Alf [actor/director] (*né* Alfred John Goulding, b. Melbourne, Victoria, Australia, 26 Jan 1896–25 Apr 1972 [76], Los Angeles CA; pneumonia). (Rolin; Sennett; MGM.) m. (1) **Marcella Desmond**, ca. Jul 1920; (2) Suzanne Raphael. "Alfred Goulding," *Variety*, 3 May 1972. AMD, p. 143. AS, p. 463 (b. Katoomba, Australia, 29 Jan).

BHD, p. 183; BHD2, p. 104. IFN, p. 122. A.H. Giebler, "Los Angeles News Letter," *MPW*, 17 Jul 1920, 327 (married Desmond). "Alf Goulding Is to Direct Harry Sweet," *MPW*, LII, 15 Oct 1921, 795. "Alf Goulding Signed by Mack Sennett for Comedies," *MPW*, 1 Aug 1925, 575. "Goulding Signed by Metro," *MPW*, 21 Feb 1925, 811. "Births," *MPW*, 4 Sep 1926, 3 (daughter, Aldra, b. Hollywood CA). "Alf Goulding with Roach Now," *MPW*, 13 Nov 1926, 87. "Warners Sign Goulding," *MPW*, 29 Nov 1926, 3. "Mack Sennett at Megaphone; Goulding Ill," *MPW*, 3 Sep 1927, 231.

Goulding, Christopher [scenarist] (b. London, England, 1892–3 Nov 1928 [36?], Los Angeles CA). AS, p. 464. BHD2, p. 104.

Goulding, Edmund [actor/director/producer/scenarist/composer] (b. London, England, 20 Mar 1891–24 Dec 1959 [68], Los Angeles CA). "Edmund Goulding Dies on Coast; Film Director and Composer, 68," *NYT*, 25 Dec 1959, 24:2. "Edmund Goulding," *Variety*, 30 Dec 1959. AMD, p. 143. AS, p. 464. BHD, p. 183; BHD2, p. 104. IFN, p. 122. Katz, p. 496. "Thalberg Returns to West Coast; Has New Scripts; Signs Goulding," *MPW*, 14 Feb 1925, 716. "Goulding Adapts 'La Boheme,'" *MPW*, 4 Jul 1925, 65. "Goulding to Direct 'Paris,' Original Story by Himself," *MPW*, 27 Mar 1926, 266. "Ed. Goulding in New Áork on His Vacation," *MPW*, 12 Feb 1927, 494. "Goulding Shows Columbia How Pictures Are Made," *MPW*, 19 Feb 1927, 546.

Goulven, Jerome [actor] (*né* Henry Felix Marie Joseph Lasnet, b. Riom, France, 15 Aug 1901). AS, p. 464.

Goupillieres, Roger [director] (b. France, 1896). AS, p. 464.

Gove, Otis M. [actor/cinematographer] (b. 1852–23 Jan 1931 [78?], Los Angeles CA). (Biograph; Edison.) "Otis M. Gove," *Variety*, 28 Jan 1931, 86:3 (age 81; to Hollywood ca. 1904). AS, p. 464. BHD, p. 183; BHD2, p. 104.

Govi, Gilberto [actor] (*né* Amerigo Armando Govi, b. Genoa, Italy, 22 Oct 1885–27 Apr 1966 [80], Genoa, Italy). AS, p. 464.

Gowan, George [publicist] (b. 1893–12 Oct 1952 [59?], Woodland Hills CA). BHD2, p. 104.

Gowland, Gibson [actor] (*né* T.H. Gibson-Gowland, b. Spennymoor, England, 4 Jan 1872–9 Sep 1951 [79], London, England). AMD, p. 143. AS, p. 464. BHD, p. 183 (b. Carlisle, England, 1877). FSS, p. 129. IFN, p. 122 (b. 1877). MH, p. 113. Truitt, p. 130 (b. 4 Jan 1872). "Gowland to Star in 'McTeague,'" *MPW*, 3 Jan 1920, 107. George Katchmer, "Remembering the Great Silents," *CI*, 198 (Dec 1991), 11, C11.

Gowman, Clarence H. [producer] (b. 1871–2 Jan 1954 [82?], Los Angeles CA). AS, p. 464. BHD2, p. 104.

Goya, Mona [stage/film actress] (*née* Simone Isabelle Marchand, b. Mexico City, Mexico, 25 Nov 1912–8 Oct 1961 [48], Clichy-la-Garenne, France; cancer [extrait de décès no. 1585/1961]). (Film debut: Paris, ca. 1928; French-language films for MGM.) AS, p. 464 (b. 1909). BHD1, p. 224. IFN, p. 122. Waldman, p. 121.

Grabowski, Wladyslaw [actor] (b. Warsaw, Poland, 10 Jun 1883–6 Jul 1961 [78], Warsaw, Poland). AS, p. 465.

Grabowski-Magister, Hans [actor/director] (b. Germany, 21 Jul 1898). AS, p. 465.

Gracci, Ugo [actor/director] (b. Florence, Italy-d. 1937). JS, p. 203 (in Italian silents from 1916).

Grace, Charity [actress] (b. 1879–28 Nov 1965 [86?], St. Louis MO). AS, p. 465.

Grace, Dick [stunt flyer and actor] (b. MN, 10 Jan 1898–25 Jun 1965 [67]; Los Angeles Co. CA; cancer). AS, p. 465. BHD1, p. 224. IFN, p. 122. Dorothy Lubou, "His Crack-Ups and Downs; Dick Grace's One Fear Is of Killing Someone Else," *MPC*, Jan 1929, 58, 88 (did flying stunts for *Lilac Time, The Big Hop, Wings*, etc.).

Gradwell, Richard [executive] (b. 1875–25 Jul 1926 [51?]). AMD, p. 143. BHD2, p. 104. "Gradwell President of World Pictures," *MPW*, 25 May 1918, 1125.

Grady, Billy, Sr. [casting director/executive] (b. Lynn MA, 15 Sep 1885–5 Mar 1973 [87], Los Angeles CA). AS, p. 465. BHD2, p. 104.

Grady, James H. [vaudeville/musical comedy/film actor] (b. Boston MA, 1869–17 Feb 1941 [71?], Lynn MA). "James H. Grady," *Variety*, 141, 26 Feb 1941, 54:3 (age 70). BHD, p. 183.

Grady, Lottie [actress]. No data found. (Foster Photoplay Company.) *MPW*, 25 Oct 1913, 363.

Graetz, Paul [actor/director/producer] (b. Glogau, Germany, 4 Aug 1889–16 Feb 1937 [47], Los Angeles CA; cerebral hemorrhage). m. Bella. (British-International; Gaumont; WB.) "Paul Graetz Dies; German Actor, 47; In Hollywood After Success in Europe, He Is the Victim of a Stroke; Was to Be in Garbo Film; Had Been Assigned Part in Her Next Picture—Was Associated with Ernst Lubitsch," *NYT*, 18 Feb 1937, 21:1. AS, p. 465 (b. 1890). BHD1, p. 224. IFN, p. 122. Truitt, p. 130 (in films from 1923).

Graetz, Paul [producer] (b. Leipzig, Germany, 3 Apr 1899–5 Feb 1966 [66], Neuilly-sur-Seine, France [extrait de décès no. 117/1966]). AS, p. 465 (producer in France). BHD2, p. 104 (b. 4 Apr). "Paul Graetz," *Variety*, 2 Mar 1966, p. 63.

Graf, Louis C. (brother of **Max Graf**) [producer/director] (b. 1890?–21 Jul 1967 [77], Los Angeles CA; heart attack). AS, p. 465 (d. 1966). BHD2, p. 104.

Graf, Max (brother of **Louis Graf**) [scenarist/producer] (b. San Francisco CA, 29 Dec 1893–2 Jun 1940 [46], San Francisco CA). (F.B. Warren Corp.) AMD, p. 143. BHD2, p. 104. FDY, p. 427. "Max Graf to Produce," *MPW*, 30 Jul 1921, 513. "Max Graf Arrives in New York from Coast," *MPW*, 26 Nov 1921, 398.

Graf, Otto Ludwig Fritz [actor] (b. Haina, Germany, 28 Nov 1896–22 Feb 1977 [80], Berlin, Germany). AS, p. 465.

Graf, Peter [actor/singer] (b. 1872–20 Oct 1951 [79?], New York NY). AS, p. 465.

Graf, Wilhelm [director] (b. Vienna, Austria, 26 Dec 1866). AS, p. 465.

Graham, Ben R. [actor] (b. 1851–25 Mar 1924 [72?], New Brighton NY). BHD, p. 183.

Graham, Charles E. [actor] (b. Carthage MS, 16 Feb 1895–9 Oct 1943 [48], Los Angeles CA). "Charlie Graham," *Variety*, 13 Oct 1943 (age 46; "cowboy actor in films since silent days"). AS, p. 466. BHD1, p. 224. IFN, p. 122. Truitt, p. 130 (b. 1897).

Graham, Frederick [actor] (b. London, England, 18 Jun 1866–26 Sep 1947 [81], Sharon CT). AS, p. 466 (d. LA CA). BHD1, p. 224. IFN, p. 122.

Graham, Garrett [producer/title writer/scenarist] (b. 1895?–25 Sep 1964 [69], Los Angeles CA; following a stroke). "Garrett Graham," *Variety*, 30 Sep 1964 (began as title writer; wrote novel, *Queen People*, with his brother, Carroll: a satire on Hollywood). AS, p. 466. BHD2, p. 104. FDY, pp. 427, 443.

Graham, Harry [playwright/composer] (b. London, England, 1874–30 Oct 1936 [61], London, England). "Harry Graham," *Variety*, 124, 4 Nov 1936, 62:5. BHD, p. 183.

Graham, John C[ecil] [executive] (b. 1873–23 Nov 1949 [76?]). AMD, p. 143. BHD2, p. 104. "Reliance Under New Management," *MPW*, 14 Oct 1911, 135. Lynde Denig, "John C. Graham," *MPW*, 20 Mar 1915, 1740. "Important Moves by Mutual," *MPW*, 31 Jul 1915, 797. "Freuler Working Out Plans," *MPW*, 2 Oct 1915, 57.

Graham, Joseph H. [director/scenarist] (b. Portsmouth OH, 1893–29 Apr 1976 [83?], Woodland Hills CA). BHD2, p. 104.

Graham, Morland [actress] (*née* Moreland Graham, b. Glasgow, Scotland, 8 Aug 1891–9 Apr 1949 [57], London, England). AS, p. 466.

Graham, Robert Ernest [stage/film actor] (*né* Robert McGee, b. Baltimore MD, 17 Dec 1858–17 Jul 1916 [57], New York NY). "Robert Graham," *Variety*, 21 Jul 1916. BHD, p. 183. SD.

Graham, Shad E. [actor/director/producer] (b. 1896–28 Jan 1969 [72?], Houston TX). AS, p. 466 (b. 1898). BHD1, p. 609; BHD2, p. 104.

Graham, Violet [actress] (b. England, 9 Nov 1890–1967 [76?]). BHD, p. 183.

Grahame, Bert [actor] (*né* Robert A.S. Stanford, b. 1892?–23 Mar 1971 [79], England). "Bert Grahame," *Variety*, 21 Apr 1971 ("Featured in many early silent pix."). AS, p. 466. BHD, p. 183. IFN, p. 122. Truitt, p. 130.

Grahame, Margot [stage/film/TV actress] (*née* Margaret Clark, b. Canterbury, England, 20 Feb 1911–1 Jan 1982 [70], London, England; respiratory ailments). m. (1) Francis Lister, Mar 1934—div. 1936, Reno NV (d. 28 Oct 1951); (2) Allan McMartin, 28 Sep 1938, Montreal, Canada—div. 10 Apr 1946; (3) Augustus Dudley Peters. (Extra work, 1928–29; RKO; Columbia; Gainsborough; last film: *St. Joan*, 1957.) Barrie Roberts, "Margot Grahame: The Aluminum Blonde," *CI*, 281 (Nov 1998), C6-C10 (includes filmography).

Grainger, James R. [executive] (b. 1890–14 Aug 1968 [78?], Santa Monica CA). BHD2 p. 105.

Gralla, Dinna [Polish film actress]. No data found. m. newspaper correspondent Lincoln Eyre, 1926, aboard the *President Roosevelt* in the North Sea. June Lee, "Dan Cupid's Bulletin Board," *Paris and Hollywood*, Sep 1926, 96 ().

Gramatica, Emma (sister of **Irma** and Anna Gramatica [actress Anna Capodaglio] and **Irma Gramatica**) [actress] (b. Fidenza, Italy, 22 Mar 1875–8 Nov 1965 [90], Rome, Italy). AS, p. 466 (d. Ostia, Italy). BHD1, p. 225. JS, p. 203 (in films from 1916).

Gramatica, Irma (sister of Anna and **Emma Gramatica**) [actress] (b. Rijeka, Croatia, 24 Nov 1873–14 Oct 1962 [88], Florence, Italy). AS, p. 466 (b. Fiume, Italy, 25 Nov). BHD1, p. 225.

Gran, Albert [actor] (b. Bergen, Norway, 4 Aug 1862–16 Dec 1932 [70], Los Angeles CA; from injuries sustained in an auto accident). "Albert Gran," *Variety,* 20 Dec 1932. AS, p. 466. BHD1, p. 225. IFN, p. 122. Truitt, p. 131.

Granach, Alexander [stage/film actor] (*né* Jessaja Granach, b. Werbowitz, Poland, 18 Apr 1890–14 Mar 1945 [54], New York NY). "Alexander Granach," *Variety,* 158, 21 Mar 1945, 49:1. AS, p. 466 (b. Werbowitz, Germany). BHD1, p. 225.

Granby, Joseph [actor] (b. Boston MA, 24 Mar 1885–22 Sep 1965 [80], Los Angeles CA; cerebral hemorrhage). "Joseph Granby," *Variety,* 29 Sep 1965. AS, p. 466. BHD1, p. 225. IFN, p. 123. Spehr, p. 134 (b. Boston MA). Truitt, p. 131.

Grancher, Marcel E[tienne] [actor/scenarist] (b. Lons-le-Saulnier, France, 12 Aug 1897 [extrait de naissance no. 132]-7 Jan 1976 [78], Nice, France). AS, p. 466.

Grandais, Suzanne [actress] (*née* Suzanne Gueudret, b. Paris, France, 14 Jul 1893–28 Aug 1920 [27], Vadoy-en-Brie, France; auto accident [extrait de décès no. 27/1920]). "Susanne Grandais," *Variety,* 3 Sep 1920, 21:5 ("She was young and beautiful and had done much for France in picture propaganda. Long the idol of the French fans, she was called the 'Mary Pickford of France.'"). AMD, p. 143. AS, p. 467 (b. 14 Jun). BHD, p. 183. "Obituary," *MPW,* 11 Sep 1920, 201.

Grandee, George [actor] (b. Bridgeport CT, 22 May 1903–1 Aug 1985 [82], Long Beach CA). "George Grandee," *Variety,* 14 Aug 1985. AS, p. 467. BHD1, p. 225.

Grandi, Oreste [actor]. JS, p. 204 (in Italian silents from 1913).

Grandin, Elmer [actor] (b. 1861?–19 May 1933 [72], Patchogue, LI NY). (Stage debut, 1879.) "Elmer Grandin," *Variety,* 23 May 1933. AS, p. 467. BHD1, p. 225. IFN, p. 123.

Grandin, Ethel [stock/vaudeville/film actress] (b. New York NY, 3 Mar 1894–28 Sep 1988 [94], Woodland Hills CA). m. **Ray C. Smallwood**, 1912 (d. 1964). (Stage debut: *Rip Van Winkle,* with Joseph Jefferson; Laemmle, 1910; Imp, 1911; Pathé; Smallwood Film Corp., 1914.) "Ethel Grandin," *Variety,* 12 Oct 1988. AMD, p. 143. AS, p. 467. BHD, p. 183. Slide, *Aspects,* p. 27. Spehr, p. 136 (b. 1896). Spehr, p. 136 (b. 1896). Richard Willis, "Lives of the Players; Ethel Grandon, Playing Leads in Rex Pictures," *MPS,* 21 Mar 1913, 31. "The Smallwoods in New York," *MPW,* 21 Jun 1913, 1237. "Ethel Grandin," *MPW,* 6 Dec 1913, 1127. "Miss Ethel Grandin; Interesting Career of Photoplay Star Whose Portrait Appears on This Week's Cover," *NYDM,* 28 Jan 1914, 27:1 (age 19; in Joseph Jefferson's stock company in vaudeville). "Smallwood and Grandin Leave Universal," *MPW,* 20 Jun 1914, 1706. "Ethel Grandin," *MPW,* 12 Dec 1914, 1538. "Ethel Grandin Returns to Films," *MPW,* 11 Jun 1921, 629. "Ethel Grandin Smallwood," *CI,* 161 (Nov 1988) 60. James Trottier, "Ethel Grandin: The IMP Girl," *CI,* 275 (May 1998), 34–35.

Grandon, Francis J. [actor/director/producer] (*né* Frank Grandin, b. Chicago IL, 1879?–11 Jul 1929 [50], Los Angeles CA). (Biograph, 1910 Imp; Lubin; Griffith-Triangle; Majestic; Reliance.) "Frances [sic] J. Grandon," *Variety,* 17 Jul 1929. AMD, p. 143. AS, p. 467. BHD, p. 183; BHD2, p. 105. IFN, p. 123. KOM, p. 140. 1921 Directory, p. 264. Spehr, p. 136. "Grandon with Reliance and Majestic," *MPW,* 27 Mar 1915, 1918. "Director Francis J. Grandon Goes to Metro," *MPW,* 22 Jan 1916, 612.

Grandville [inventor] (*né* Jean Gerard, b. Nancy, France, 15 Sep 1903–1947 [44?], France). AS, p. 467.

Grange, Harold "Red" (*né* Harold E. Grange, b. Forksville PA, 13 Jun 1903–28 Jan 1991 [87], Lake Wales FL). BHD1, p. 225. June Lee, "Dan Cupid's Bulletin Board," *Paris and Hollywood,* Sep 1926, 94 (reportedly engaged to light opera star Vivienne Segal).

Granger, Dorothy [actress] (b. New London OH, 21 Nov 1911–4 Jan 1995 [83], San Bernardino CA). AS, p. 467 (d. 1994, LA CA). BHD1, p. 225.

Granger, Elsa G. [actress] (b. Australia, 1904–8 Feb 1955 [50?], New York NY). AS, p. 467. BHD, p. 183.

Granger, Maude [actress] (*née* Anna E. Brainard, b. Middletown CT, 1851?–17 Aug 1928 [77], New York NY). m. (1) Alfred Cecil (d. 1912); (2) W.R. Baxter. AS, p. 467 (b. 1831). BHD, p. 183. IFN, p. 123. SD.

Granger, William F. [actor] (b. Philadelphia PA, 24 May 1854–21 Dec 1938 [84], Los Angeles CA). AS, p. 467.

Granichstaedten, Bruno [composer] (b. Vienna, Austria, 1 Sep 1879–30 May 1944 [64], New York NY). AS, p. 467.

Granier, Jeanne [actress] (b. Paris, France, 1882–1939 [57?], Paris, France). AS, p. 467.

Granowsky, Alexis [director/scenarist] (*né* Alexander Abraham Azarch Granowsky, b. Moscow, Russia, 1890–11 Mar 1937 [47?], Paris, France). AS, p. 467.

Granstedt, Greta [actress] (*née* Irene Granstedt, b. Malmö, Sweden, 13 Jul 1907–7 Oct 1987 [80], Los Angeles CA). AS, p. 467. BHD1, p. 225. BR, p. 313. Ragan 2, p. 643. WFE, p. 89.

Grant, Billy [director] (b. 1892–29 Jan 1927 [34?], Los Angeles CA). AS, p. 467 (d. 1937). BHD2, p. 105.

Grant, Corinne [actress] (b. New Orleans LA, 1888). BHD, p. 184.

Grant, Henry Clay [actor/director/scenarist] (b. NY, 1885–30 Nov 1953 [68?], New York NY). BHD, p. 184; BHD2, p. 105.

Grant, John [scenarist] (b. 27 Dec 1891–19 Nov 1955 [63], Palm Desert CA). AS, p. 468. BHD2, p. 105.

Grant, Katherine [actress]. No data found. AMD, p. 143. "Katherine Grant Is Awarded 5-Year Contract by Roach," *MPW,* 4 Jul 1925, 80. Paul Paige, "Close-Ups and Fade-Outs," *Paris and Hollywood Screen Secrets,* Oct 1927, 23 ("Catherine Grant, who suffered a nervous breakdown more than a year ago, after, what was reported to be an attack made on the yacht of a certain movie millionaire [Hal Roach] is slowly recovering and it is said will be able to return to the pictures within a few months.").

Grant, Lawrence [actor] (*né* Percy Reginald Lawrence-Grant, b. Bournemouth, England, 30 Oct 1869–19 Feb 1952 [82], Santa Barbara CA). m. Iphigenia Hay. "Lawrence Grant," *Variety,* 27 Feb 1952. AMD, p. 143. AS, p. 468. BHD1, p. 226. IFN, p. 123. Truitt, p. 131. "Lawrence Grant Bears Likeness to Kaiser," *MPW,* 22 Jun 1918, 1704. "Lawrence Grant Under Metro Banner," *MPW,* 1 May 1920, 718.

Grant, Nellie [actress]. No data found. AMD, p. 143. "Nellie Grant," *MPW,* 29 Oct 1910, 983.

Grant, Sydney [actor/singer] (b. Boston MA, 20 Feb 1873–12 Jul 1953 [80], Santa Monica CA). m. Harriet. (Morosco.) "Sydney Grant," *Variety,* 15 Jul 1953. AS, p. 468 (d. 11 Jul). BHD, p. 184. IFN, p. 123. Truitt, p. 131.

Grant, Valentine [concert singer/actress] (b. IN, 14 Feb 1881–12 Mar 1949 [68], Dana Point CA). (Film debut: *A Mother of Men;* Lubin.) AMD, p. 143. AS, p. 468. BHD, p. 184. IFN, p. 123. "Valentine Grant with Cort," *MPW,* 1 May 1915, 714. "Valentine Grant," *NYDM,* 14 Jul 1915, 24:1 (b. Seattle WA?). "Miss Grant with Famous Players," *MPW,* 8 Apr 1916, 233. "Valentine Grant at Heroland," *MPW,* 29 Dec 1917, 1965. "Screen Star in Unique Role," *MPW,* 16 Mar 1918, 1515.

Granval, Charles [actor] (*né* Charles-Louis Gribouval, b. Rouen, France, 21 Dec 1882 [extrait de naissance no. 2421]–28 Jul 1943 [60], Honfleur, France). AS, p. 468.

Granville, Audrey [child actress/film editor] (b. 1910?–20 Oct 1972 [62], Encino CA; cancer). m. Roy. (Began ca. 1924; Selznick.) "Audrey Granville," *Variety,* 8 Nov 1972, p. 63:1. BHD, p. 184.

Granville, Bunny (father of Bonita Granville) [actor] (*né* Bernard Granville, b. Chicago IL, 4 Jul 1886–5 Oct 1936 [50], New York NY). m. (daughter Bonita, 1923–1988). AS, p. 468.

Granville, Charlotte [actress] (b. London, England, 9 May 1860–8 Jul 1942 [82], Los Angeles CA). AMD, p. 143. AS p. 468 (d. London, England). BHD1, p. 226. "Charlotte Granville," *MPW,* 19 Jan 1918, 369.

Granville, Dorothy [actress]. No data found. AMD, p. 143. "Dorothy Granville," *MPW,* 12 Dec 1914, 1533.

Granville, Fred[erick] **Le Roy** [cameraman/director] (b. Warnamabool, Victoria, Australia, 1886–14 Nov 1932 [45?], London, England; Bright's disease). m. (1) **Peggy Hyland**, Mar 1923?–div. "Fred Granville," *Variety,* 22 Nov 1932. AMD, p. 143. AS, p. 468. BHD2, p. 105. "Granville Leaves for Villa Camp," *MPW,* 18 Mar 1916, 1836.

Granville, Louise [actress] (b. Sydney, Australia, 29 Sep 1895–22 Dec 1968 [73], Woodland Hills CA; influenza). m. Joe Rock ca. 1923. (Vitagraph.) "Louise Granville," *Variety,* 1 Jan 1969. AS, p. 468. BHD, p. 184. IFN, p. 123. Truitt, p. 131 (d. 1969).

Granville, Taylor [actor/director] (b. 1873?–14 Apr 1923 [50], Los Angeles CA). m. Laura Pierpoint. "Taylor Granville," *Variety,* 19 Apr 1923 (ca. 45). AS, p. 468. BHD, p. 184; BHD2, p. 105 (b. 1877). IFN, p. 123 (age 50).

Granville-Dansford, Robert [actor] (b. Honolulu HI, 1888–27 Jun 1924 [36?], Los Angeles CA; blood poisoning). AS, p. 468.

Grassby, Bertram [actor] (b. Lincolnshire, England, 23 Dec 1880–7 Dec 1953 [72], Scottsdale AZ). m. **Gerard Alexander**, 1916 (d. 1962). (Selig, 1915; Universal.) AMD, p. 143. AS, p. 469. BHD, p. 184. IFN, p. 123 (1880–1953). MH, p. 113. "Universal Players Marry," *MPW,* 12 Feb 1916, 936. "Bertram Grassby," *MPW,* 17 Mar 1917, 1784. "Bertram Grassby Is Injured," *MPW,* 27 Apr 1918, 549.

Grassby, Mrs. Bertram (Gertrude) *see* **Alexander, Gerard**

Grasso, Giovanni (cousin of actor **Giovanni Grasso** [same name]) [actor] (b. Aci-Catania, Italy, 1875–13 Oct 1930 [55?], Catania, Italy). AS, p. 469 (b. 19 Dec 1873). BHD, p. 184. JS, p. 204 (in Italian silents from 1910).

Grasso, Giovanni (cousin of **Giovanni Grasso** [same name]) (b. Catania, Italy, 11 Nov 1888–3 May 1963 [74], Catania, Italy). AS, p. 469.

Grattan, Lawrence [stage/film actor/writer] (b. Concord NH, 1870?–9 Dec 1941 [71], New York NY). m. Eva Taylor. "Lawrence Grattan," *Variety,* 17 Dec 1941. BHD, p. 184 (Gratton). NNAT, p. 397. SD.

Grau, Robert [scenarist] (b. 1854–9 Aug 1916 [62?], Mount Vernon NY). BHD2, p. 105.

Grauer, Ben [actor/announcer] (b. Staten Island NY, 2 Jan 1908–31 May 1977 [69], New York NY). "NBC's Ben Grauer, Pioneer Announcer, Is Dead at Age 68," *Variety,* 1 Jun 1977. BHD1, p. 226 (b. Staten Island NY).

Grauman, Sid [executive] (b. Indianapolis IN, 17 Mar 1879–4 Mar 1950 [70], Los Angeles CA; heart ailment). "Sid Grauman, Famed Showman and Prankster, Dies in L.A. at 71," *Variety,* 8 Mar 1950, p. 26:1 (d. 5 Mar. "In the early 1900s the Graumans opened the first picture theatre in Frisco, a store large enough for 800 kitchen chairs, screen, scenery and piano. Called the Unique, the house was transformed by Sid Grauman from a crude establishment into a colorful entertainment spot. Out in front a big banner was planted, reading 'One Hundred Feet of New Film Being Shown.' The house also featured vaudeville and one of the acts that played there was the Musical Laskys [Jesse Lasky and his sister]." He built the Million Dollar theatre in LA, "then considered the finest film house in the country." In 1927 he built the Chinese theatre). AS, p. 459 (d. 5 Mar). BHD1, p. 226.

Graves, George [stage/film actor] (b. London, England, 1 Jan 1876–2 Apr 1949 [73], London, England). (Sole U.S. stage appearance: *The Little Michus,* 1907.) "George Graves," *Variety,* 6 Apr 1949, p. 63:1 ("His perfect diction, rich voice, and comedies delighted playgoers for nearly 50 years."). AS, p. 469. BHD, p. 184.

Graves, Jesse [actor] (b. IA, 11 Mar 1879–4 Mar 1949 [70], Los Angeles CA). AS, p. 469.

Graves, Kathryn [actress] (b. MN, 1 Dec 1898–26 Feb 1977 [78], San Diego CA). "Kathryn Graves, 78, silent screen actress from 1925 to 1930, died Feb. 26 in a hospital in San Diego, Calif. She was noted for wearing exotic apparel and jewelry," *Variety,* 9 Mar 1977. AS, p. 469 (b. 1899). BHD1, p. 226 (b. 1899). IFN, p. 123 (b. 1899).

Graves, Ralph [actor/director/scenarist] (*né* Ralph Hosburgh, b. Cleveland OH, 23 Jul 1900–18 Feb 1977 [76], Santa Barbara CA; heart attack). m. (1) Marjorie Seaman; (2) Virginia Goodwin; (3) Betty Flournoy. (Griffith; Columbia; WB.) "Ralph Graves," *Variety,* 2 Mar 1977). AMD, p. 144. AS, p. 469 (b. 23 Jan). BHD1, p. 226. FFF, p. 235 (b. 3 Jan). FSS, p. 129. IFN, p. 123. MH, p. 114. SD. WFE, p. 89. "Ralph Graves Rejoins Universal," *MPW,* 13 Apr 1918, 263. "Laemmle Loans Graves to Tourneur," *MPW,* 27 Apr 1918, 518. "Ralph Graves Joins Goldwyn," *MPW,* 5 Nov 1921, 80. Helen Greenwood, "The Young American; ...[Mack Sennett] declares that Graves is a comedian of the first water...and typical of young American manhood," *MW,* 16 Aug 1924, 11, 31. "Ralph Graves," *MPW,* 24 Sep 1927, 229. "Flashes from Filmland," *Paris and Hollywood Screen Secrets Magazine,* Oct 1927, 10 (to direct *Roulette* at Warners). "Ask the Answer Man," *Photoplay,* Jan 1932, 82 (b. 1 Jun). George A. Katchmer, "Ralph Graves," *CI,* 159 (Sep 1988), C6-C9, C17.

Graves, Robert, Jr. [actor] (b. New York NY, 22 Oct 1888–19 Aug 1954 [65], Los Angeles CA). AS, p. 469 (d. NYC). BHD1, p. 226. IFN, p. 123. George Katchmer, "Remembering the Great Silents," *CI,* 218 (Aug 1993), 41.

Gravet, Fernand [stage/film actor] (aka Fernand Gravey, *né* Fernand Maurice Noël Mertens, b. Brussels, Belgium, 25 Dec 1904–2 Nov 1970 [65], Paris, France [extrait de décès no. 445]). m. Jane Renouardt—div. 1966. (MGM; WB.) "Fernand, Gravet," *Variety,* 11 Nov 1970, p. 54:4 (WB changed his name to Gravet; it "feared, perhaps rightly, that the original Gravey spelling could conjure up an unromantic English pronunciation [like in the sauce]."). AS, p. 469 (Fernand Gravey; b. 1905). BHD1, p. 226. Waldman, p. 123.

Graveure, Louis [actor/singer] (*né* Wilfred Douthitt, b. London, England, 18 Mar 1888–27 Apr 1965 [77], San Francisco CA). m. **Camilla Horn** (d. 1996). AS, p. 469.

Gravina, Cesare [stage/film actor] (b. Naples, Italy, 23 Jan 1858–1954 [96], Italy). AMD, p. 144. AS, p. 469. BHD1, p. 226. Truitt 1983, p. 289. "Gravina Plays Comedy Role," *MPW,* 11 May 1918, 868. George Katchmer, "Remembering the Great Silents," *CI,* 246 (Dec 1995), 48.

Gray, Arnold *see* **Gregg, Arnold**

Gray, Beata Lily "Betty" [actress] (*née* Lily Pederson, b. Passaic NJ, 1895–15 Jun 1919 [24?], New York NY; influenza). (K&E.) AMD, p. 144. AS, pp. 469–70. BHD, p. 184. IFN, p. 123. "Beata Lily Gray," *MPW,* 20 Feb 1915, 1146. "Beata Lily Gray," *MPW,* 20 Nov 1915, 1475.

Gray, Daniel J. [film editor] (b. 1890?–17 May 1955 [65], Hollywood CA). (Metro; MGM.) "Danny Gray," *Variety,* 25 May 1955.

Gray, Dorothy [actress] (b. Los Angeles CA, 23 Oct 1922–9 May 1976 [53], Los Angeles CA). AS, p. 470. BHD1, p. 227.

Gray, Gene [actor] (b. 1881–10 Feb 1950 [68?], Los Angeles CA). AS, p. 470.

Gray, George G. [actor: Keystone Cop/director/stuntman/writer] (b. 1894?–8 Sep 1967 [73], Asheville NC; stroke). m. Elsie Clyde, Aug 1967. (Sennett.) "George G. Gray," *Variety,* 20 Sep 1967 (age 78). AMD, p. 144. AS, p. 470. BHD1, p. 227. IFN, p. 124. Truitt, p. 132. "George Gray Goes West to Build Up His Serial," *MPW,* 12 Mar 1927, 117.

Gray, Gilda [stage/film actress] (aka May Gray, *née* Maryana Michalska, b. Kraków, Poland, 24 Oct 1899–22 Dec 1959 [60?], Los Angeles CA; heart attack). m. (1) John Gorecki; (2) Gaillard "Gill" T. Boag, Apr 1923—div. 1929 (d. 1959); (3) Hector de Briceno. (Film debut: *Aloma of the South Seas;* Paramount.) "Gilda Gray Dead on Coast at 58; Creator of Shimmy Was Singer," *NYT,* 23 Dec 1959, 27:4 (age 58); "Gilda Gray Rites Tomorrow," *NYT,* 25 Dec 1959, 21:3. "Shimmy Exponent Gilda Gray Dies in H'wood at 60," *Variety,* 30 Dec 1959. AMD, p. 144. AS, p. 470 (b. 1898). BHD1, p. 227. FSS, p. 130. IFN, p. 124. Katz, p. 502. SD. Truitt, p. 132 (b. 1901). Regina Cannon, "Shimmying into the Camera—with Gilda Gray," *MW,* 26 May 1923, 7, 29. "Lasky Signs Gilda Gray; New Paramount Film Star," *MPW,* 20 Jun 1925, 900. "Gilda Gray in Paramount Picture," *MPW,* 18 Jul 1925, 352. Alma Talley, "Gilda—Without Any Gilding; The Story of a Star Who Can See Herself as Others Cannot See Her," *MW,* 26 Sep 1925, 20–42. Cover, *Paris and Hollywood Screen Secrets Magazine,* May 1927. "Gilda Gray; The Girl on the Cover," *Cinema Arts,* Jun 1927, 33, 47. "Gilda to Goldwyn," *MPW,* 4 Jun 1927, 325. Coral Clyce, "Bend Way Down and Shuffle Aroun'; The Girl Who Made the Shimmy Famous," *MPC,* Jul 1927, 54–55, 87. "Prologue Co. for Gilda Gray," *MPW,* 17 Sep 1927, 146. Beau Broadway, "Reeling Down Broadway," *Paris and Hollywood Screen Secrets Magazine,* Aug 1927, 77 (Gray, "the whilom torso tosser of the Chicago shoot-to-kill caves...hit out for Yurop with her husband, Gil Boag"). Herbert Cruikshank, "The Girl Who Closed Broadway; The Story of Gil and Gilda, of Gilda and Gil: Their Rise, Their Romance and Their Ruin," *MPC,* Jun 1928, 37, 86. Richard Woods, "Gilda Gray: Shimmy Queen," *CI,* 263 (May 1997), 16–18 (*née* Marianna Winchalska, b. 1901).

Gray, Gloria [actress] (*née* Lillian Halpren, b. 1900–4 Apr 1918 [18?], Walla Walla WA). BHD, p. 184.

Gray, Gordon [actor]. No data found. AMD, p. 144. "Gordon Gray, Vitagrpah Player," *MPW,* 16 Sep 1916, 1843.

Gray, Jack [actor] (b. 1880–13 Apr 1956 [76?], Woodland Hills CA). AS, p. 470. BHD1, p. 227.

Gray, Jeanne [actress] (d. 30 Jan 1996, Bel Air CA). BHD1, p. 227.

Gray, Johnny [scenarist]. No data found. FDY, p. 427.

Gray, Katherine [actress]. No data found. AMD, p. 144. "Katherine Gray," *MPW,* 15 Jan 1916, 398.

Gray, King D. [cinematographer] (b. Danville VA, 9 Mar 1886–30 Jun 1938 [52], Los Angeles CA; found dead in his car with a bullet wound in his chest). (At Universal for 22 years.) "King D. Gray," *Variety,* 6 Jul 1938. AS, p. 470. BHD2, p. 105. FDY, p. 459.

Gray, Laurence [actor] (b. 1894–5 May 1951 [57?], Oakland CA). AS, p. 470.

Gray, Lawrence [actor] (b. San Francisco CA, 28 Jul 1898–2 Feb 1970 [71], Mexico City, Mexico). "Lawrence Gray," *Variety,* 11 Feb 1970. AS, p. 470. BHD1, p. 227. FSS, p. 130. IFN, p. 124. Truitt, p. 132. Sarah Edmonton, "He Looked Like a Gentleman," *MPC,* Sep 1925, 64, 83. Grace Mack, "Sheiks Have Gone Out," *MM,* II, Apr 1926, 49, 98–99. "Questions and Answers," *Photoplay,* Aug 1926, 94. Charleson Gray, "The Sports of the Stars; III—Play Tennis, Lawrence Gray Urges, and Meet Nice People," *MPC,* Mar 1930, 33, 84.

Gray, Phyllis [actress] (b. 1887?–21 Jan 1922 [35], Los Angeles CA; suicide from poison taken 5 days previously). "Sudden Death in L.A.," *Variety,* 27 Jan 1922. AS, p. 470. BHD, p. 184.

Gray, Ray [actor/director] (b. 1899–18 Apr 1925 [26?], Glendale CA). AS, p. 470. BHD2, p. 105.

Gray, Robert [actor] (b. Houlton ME). AMD, p. 144. "Robert Gray and 'Billy' West New Leads for American," *MPW,* 24 May 1913, 799.

Gray, Schuyler [technical director] (b. 1895–2 Jul 1933 [38?], Stamford CT). BHD2, p. 105.

Gray, Stella *see* **La Rue, Grace**

Gray, Thomas J. [playwright/composer/scenarist/producer] (b. New York NY, 22 Mar 1888–30 Nov 1924 [36], New York NY; bronchial ailment). (Universal.) "Thomas J. Gray Dead; Playwright, Song Writer and Humorist Dies of a Bronchial Ailment," *NYT,* 1 Dec 1924, 17:4 ("He helped devise funny scenes for 'Fatty' Arbuckle and wrote the titles for the pictures, later performing somewhat similar services for 'Buster' Keaton, Chaplin and Harold Lloyd."). "Tommy Gray," *Variety,* 3 Dec 1924 (worked on Lloyd's *Girl Shy* and *Hot Water*). AS, p. 470. BHD2, p. 105. SD, p. 533. "Tommie Gray Joins Keaton," *MPW,* 14 Jan 1922, 170. "Thomas Gray Finds Topical Comedies Most Successful," *MPW,* 29 Sep 1923, 439. *ASCAP Biographical Dictionary,* p. 198.

Gray, William *see* **John W. Kolb**

Gray, William L. [executive] (b. 1881–24 Jan 1919 [37?], New York NY). BHD2, p. 105.

Gray, William Stanley [film editor] (b. 1896–16 Dec 1946 [50?], Los Angeles CA). BHD2, p. 105.

Graybill, Joseph [actor] (b. Kansas MO, 1882?–3 Aug 1913 [31], New York NY [Death Certificate Index No. 26426; acute spinal meningitis]). (Biograph, 1910.) "Joseph Graybill," *Variety,* 8 Aug 1913. "Death of Joseph Graybill," *MPW,* 23 Aug 1913, 846 (b. 1887). AMD, p. 144. AS, p. 470. BHD, p. 184 (b. Milwaukee WI, 1877).

Grazi, René [director/producer] (b. Paris, France, 6 Jun 1895). AS, p. 471.

Grazioso, Guido [actor]. No data found. JS, p. 205 (in Italian silents from 1912).

Grebner, G. [scenarist]. No data found. FDY, p. 427.

Greeley, Evelyn [actress] (*née* Evelyn Huber, b. Lexington KY, 3 Nov 1888–25 Mar 1975 [86], West Palm Beach FL). m. (1) actor John Smiley; (2) James H. Rand—div. 1960; (3) Morgan Laity. (Essanay [Chicago], 1914; Dixie Film Co.; World; Fox.) AMD, p. 144. AS, p. 471. BHD, pp. 31–32; 184 (b. Austria). Spehr, p. 136 (b. Lexington KY). "Evelyn Greeley," *MPW,* 23 Dec 1916, 1809. "Evelyn Greeley in World Film," *MPW,* 6 Jan 1917, 64. "Evelyn Greeley Renews World Contract," *MPW,* 23 Mar 1918, 1667. "Evelyn Greeley Presented with Genuine Dog of War," *MPW,* 30 Nov 1918, 971. "Evelyn Greeley Now Shines as Star in Her Own Right," *MPW,* 12 Apr 1919, 232. "Evelyn Greeley Recovers from Influenza," *MPW,* 10 May 1919, 795. Billy H Doyle, "Lost Players [Evelyn Greeley]," *CI,* 150 (Dec 1987), 10–11. 1921 Directory, p. 222 (b. Lexington KY).

Green, Alfred E. [actor/director] (b. Perris CA, 11 Jul 1889–4 Sep 1960 [71], Los Angeles CA). (Selig, 1912.) m. **Vivian Reed** (d. 1989). "Alfred E. Green, Director, 71, Dies; Guided Filming of 'Disraeli,' 'Dangerous,' 'The Jolson Story,' in 48-Year Career," *NYT,* 6 Sep 1960, 33:4. "Alfred E. Green," *Variety,* 7 Sep 1960. "Vivian Reid," *Variety,* 2 Aug 1989 (d. 20 Jul 1989 [95], Woodland Hills CA). AMD, p. 144. AS, p. 471. BHD, p. 184; BHD2, p. 106. IFN, p. 124. 1921 Directory, p. 264. "Alfred Green, Director," *MPW,* 21 Apr 1917, 441. "Alfred Green Joins Goldwyn to Be a Culver City Director," *MPW,* 3 Apr 1920, 115. "Green Back After 'Flu,'" *MPW,* 6 Jan 1923, 32. "Al Green to Direct It," *MPW,* 29 Mar 1924, 354. "Director Green Signed," *MPW,* 5 Sep 1925, 87.

Green, Anna Katherine [scenarist] (b. 1946–11 Apr 1935 [89?], Buffalo NY). BHD2, p. 106.

Green, Bert [scenarist] (b. 1885–5 Oct 1948 [63?], New York NY). AS, p. 471 (b. 1875). BHD2, p. 106.

Green, Burton [actor] (*né* James Burton Green, b. 1874?–17 Nov 1922 [48], Mt. Vernon NY). m. (1) Helen Green-Van Campen; (2) Irene Franklin. "Burton Green," *Variety,* 24 Nov 1922. AS, p. 471. BHD, p. 184.

Green, Denis [actor/scenarist] (b. London, England, 11 Apr 1903–6 Nov 1954 [51], New York NY). AS, p. 471. BHD2, p. 106.

Green, Dorothy [actress] (b. Petrograd, Russia, 1892–16 Nov 1963 [71], New York NY [Death Certificate Index No.24573]). m. Sam Pomerance; Norman November. "Dorothy Green, 71, Star of Silent Movies, Is Dead," *NYT,* 18 Nov 1963, 33:5. "Dorothy Green [Mrs. Dorothy Green November]," *Variety*, 20 Nov 1963. AMD, p. 144. AS, p. 471. BHD, p. 184. IFN, p. 124. 1921 Directory, p. 222. SD. Truitt, p. 132. "Manny Chappelle Divorced," *Variety,* 22 Feb 1918, p.47 ("...Dorothy Green, picture actress and wife of Sam Pomerance, was named as co-respondendent."). "Dorothy Green Leading woman for Montagu Love," *MPW,* 20 Jul 1918, 373. "Dorothy Green to Star in Series of World Pictures," *MPW,* 31 May 1919, 1330.

Green, Duke [actor] (d. 22 Nov 1984, Woodland Hills CA). BHD1, p. 228.

Green, Emily [actress] (b. Philadelphia PA, 1888–26 Mar 1980 [92?], Willow Grove PA). AS, p. 471. BHD, p. 185.

Green, Fred E. [actor] (b. 1890?–5 Aug 1940 [50?], near San Mateo CA; auto accident injuries). "Fred E. Green," *Variety,* 14 Aug 1940. AS, p. 471 (d. 15 Aug). BHD, p. 185. Truitt, p. 132. In *Topsy and Eva* (1927).

Green, George [actor/scenarist] (b. Dublin, Ireland, 1910?–24 May 1985 [75], Dublin, Ireland). "George Green," *Variety,* 19 Jun 1985. AS, p. 471. FDY, p. 427.

Green, Harry [actor] (*né* Henry Blitzer, b. New York NY, 1 Apr 1892–31 May 1958 [66], London, England; heart attack). m. Alva Larsen. "Harry Green," *Variety,* 4 Jun 1958 (age 60). AS, pp. 471–72. BHD1, p. 228. IFN, p. 124. SD.

Green, Howard J. [scenarist] (b. San Francisco CA, 20 Mar 1893–2 Sep 1965 [72], New York NY; heart attack). m. "Howard J. Green," *Variety,* 8 Sep 1965. AMD, p. 144. AS, p. 472. BHD2, p. 106 (d. LA CA). FDY, p. 427. MPG. "Howard Green," *MPW,* 3 Sep 1927, 24.

Green, James [scenarist] (b. 1893–19 Mar 1967 [74?], Woodland Hills CA). BHD2, p. 106.

Green, John W. [journalist] (b. 1848?–26 Jan 1926 [77], Los Angeles CA; following a stroke of paralysis). "John W. Green," *Variety,* 3 Feb 1926.

Green, Joseph [actor/producer/director] (b. Lódz, Poland, 23 Apr 1900–20 Jun 1996 [96], Great Neck, LI NY; emphysema). (Film debut: *Yiddle with a Fiddle,* 1925.) "Johnny Green," *Variety,* 1 Jul 1996, 41:3 (in *The Jazz Singer,* WB, 1927). AS, p. 472. BHD1, p. 228; BHD2, p. 106.

Green, Judd [actor] (b. Portsmouth, England, 1866–1932 [66?]). BHD1, p. 228.

Green[e], Kempton [actor] (b. Shreveport LA, 28 Jun 1887?). (Lubin; Joseph W. Farnham; Paramount.) AMD, p. 144. AS, p. 472. BHD, p. 185 (b. 1890). "Kempton Green," *MPW,* 22 Mar 1913, 1208. "Kempton Green," *MPW,* 21 Feb 1914, 958 (26 years old). Kempton Green, "Kempton Green," *MPW,* 7 Nov 1914, 770. "Kempton Green, "Kempton Green," *MPW,* 31 Jul 1915, 823. "How I Became a Photo Player," *MPC,* I, Feb 1916, 40. *MPN Studio Directory,* 21 Oct 1916, 26 (b. 1890). 1921 Directory, p. 175 (b. 1890).

Green, Kenneth [actor] (b. London, England, 1908?–24 Feb 1969 [61], Los Angeles CA; heart attack). (Hal Roach.) "Kenneth Green," *Variety,* 5 Mar 1969. AS, p. 472. BHD, p. 185. IFN, p. 124. Truitt, p. 132.

Green, L. Worthington [scenarist] (b. 1858–19 Dec 1932 [74?], Los Angeles CA). BHD2, p. 106.

Green, Mabel B. [actress] (b. 1886–19 Feb 1916 [29?], New York NY; pneumonia). AS, p. 472.

Green, Margaret [actress] (b. NY, 1890–30 Jan 1967 [76?], New York NY). BHD, p. 185.

Green, Marshall [actor/executive] (b. Los Angeles CA, 19 Apr 1919–18 Oct 1997 [78], Los Angeles CA). BHD1, p. 609; BHD2, p. 106.

Green, Martyn [actor] (*né* William Martyn Green, b. London, England, 22 Apr 1899–8 Feb 1975 [75], Los Angeles CA; blood poisoning). AS, p. 472.

Green, Paul [scenarist] (b. Illington NC, 17 Mar 1894–4 May 1981 [87], Chapel Hill NC). AS, p. 472. BHD2, p. 106.

Green, Thomas [actor?]. No data found. "Sentenced to Be Hanged," *NYDM,* 4 Feb 1914, 13:3 ("Thomas Green, who was a member of one of the film companies located at Los Angeles, has been sentenced to be hanged on April 3...." He robbed the Palo Verde CA bank and killed the cashier. He and his alleged confederate "have been in the amusement field for a number of years.").

Green, Vivian [actress] (*née* Vivian Reid, b. CA, 1894–20 Jul 1989 [95?], Woodland Hills CA). AS, p. 472.

Green, W. Freeze [inventor of the Kinematograph] (b. England-d. 5 May 1921, London, England). AS, p. 472.

Green, William Burnham [judge/actor] (b. 1852?–10 Apr 1926 [74], Utica NY). (Film debut: *When Samuel Skidded,* with Kate Price, Vitagraph, in which he played a judge.) AS, p. 472. BHD, p. 185. IFN, p. 124. Hazel Simpson Naylor, "How a Real Judge Became a Movie Judge," *Motion Picture Magazine,* Feb 1918, 91–92 ("...I was Justice of the Peace in Flatbush, and after that Associate Justice of the County Court of King's County. Then one day I was taken severely ill, and when I recovered I found that it had affected my memory.").

Greene, Clay M[eredith] (father of **Helen Greene**) [playwright/scenarist/director] (b. San Francisco CA, 12 Mar 1850–5 Sep 1933 [83], San Francisco CA). m. (1) writer Mrs. Laura H. Robinson; (2) Alice Wheeler (*née* Alice Randolph Wheeler, d. 1910). (Lubin, 1913–16.) "Clay M. Greene," *Variety,* 12 Sep 1933 (first American born in SF CA; wrote memoirs; member of Lambs, NYC). AMD, p. 144. BHD, p. 185. SD. WWWA. "Clay Greene to Direct," *NYDM,* 8 Sep 1915, 28:3 (to direct Kempton Greene). "Clay M. Greene," *MPW,* 22 Jul 1916, 615. "How to Get in the Pictures; Clay M. Greene, Lubin's Distinguished

Author-Director, Gives Some Succinct 'Donts,'" *MPC,* Dec 1916, 40. "Clay M. Greene Stricken Blind; Author of Many Plays and Scenarios and Former Lubin Director Victim of Vitreous Hemorrhage," *MPW,* 30 Mar 1918, p. 1820 (stricken in left eye [vitreous hemorrhage] on 16 Mar; author of *M'liss, Struck Oil* and *Blue Beard*). "Mrs. Clay M. Greene," *NYT,* 28 Jun 1949, 27:2.

Greene, Harrison [actor] (b. Portland OR, 18 Jan 1884–28 Sep 1945 [61], Los Angeles CA). AS, p. 473.

Greene, Helen (daughter of **Clay M. Greene**) [actress] (b. New York NY, 1896–10 Oct 1947 [51?], Oakland CA). (Lubin.) AMD, p. 144. BHD, p. 185. IFN, p. 124. "Helen Greene," *MPW,* 19 Feb 1916, 1117. "Helen Greene Featured in Serial by Prominent Newspaper," *MPN,* 11 Mar 1916, 1464:3. "Helen Greene," *MPW,* 5 Aug 1916, 940.

Greene, Howard [animator]. No data found. AMD, p. 145. "Howard Greene Joins Levey," *MPW,* 17 Jul 1920, 347.

Greene, J. Irving [publicist]. No data found. AMD, p. 145. "J. Irving Greene," *MPW,* 26 Mar 1927, 311.

Greene, Mabel B. [actress] (b. 1886?–19 Feb 1916 [29] New York NY; pneumonia). (Lubin; Historical Feature Co.). "Mabel Green," *Variety,* 25 Feb 1916.

Greene, Margaret [stage/film actress] (b. 1892?). No other data found. AMD, p. 145. "Pathe's New Star," *NYDM,* 6 Oct 1915, 30:3 (23 years old). "Margaret Greene, the New Pathé Star," *MPW,* 16 Oct 1915, 427. "Margaret Greene Believes in Dramatic Schools," *MPW,* 23 Jul 1916, 613.

Greene, Walter D. [actor] (b. Baltimore MD, 1872?–20 Feb 1941 [68], Great Neck, LI NY). "Walter D. Greene," *Variety,* 26 Feb 1941. AS, p. 473. BHD, p. 185.

Greene, Walter E. [executive]. No data found. AMD, p. 145. "Greene Outlines Artcraft"s Scope," *MPW,* 4 Nov 1916, 679. "Walter E. Greene Back from Vacation," *MPW,* 6 Oct 1917, 67. "Walter Greene Directs Paramount," *MPW,* 19 Jan 1918, 352. "Greene Says Business Clouds Are Passing," *MPW,* 16 Mar 1918, 1487. "Greene Talks of Reissues and of the Reasons Why," *MPW,* 14 Sep 1918, 1590. "Greene Puts Up 161-Reel Show for Seagoing Gobs," *MPW,* 11 Jan 1919, 202. "Famous Players Defines Advertising," *MPW,* 12 Apr 1919, 204. Walter E. Greene, "The Selective Booking of Motion Pictures," *MPW,* 28 Jun 1919, 1921–22. "Greene Resigns from Famous Players; to Reveal Plans on return from Trip," *MPW,* 22 Nov 1919, 417. "Greene Warns Against Domination," *MPW,* 20 Dec 1919, 978. "New Distributing Company Organized for Individual Producers by Walter E. Greene," *MPW,* 13 Nov 1920, 232. "Walter E. Greene Has Been Named President of Pyramid Pictures," *MPW,* 2 Jul 1921, 94. Walter E. Greene, "Why American Releasing Has Been Built; Free from Partiality in Distribution," *MPW,* 5 Aug 1922, 429. "Letters to Santa Claus," *MPW,* 30 Dec 1922, 835.

Greene, William H. (Duke) [cinematographer] (b. CT, 16 Aug 1895–28 Feb 1956 [60], Los Angeles CA). (Three-time AA winner.) AS, p. 473. BHD2, p. 106.

Greenidge, Terence [actor] (b. London, England, 14 Jan 1902). AS, p. 473.

Greenleaf, Mace [stage/film actor] (b. ME–d. 24 Mar 1912, Philadelphia PA; typhoid pneumonia. Interred in Dixfield ME). (Reliance, 1911; Solax; Lubin.) AMD, p. 145. BHD, p. 185. IFN, p. 125. "To Find Burke; A Puzzle with a Little of Everything by Chauncey Olcott," *NYT,* 3 Oct 1905, 9:3 (Greenleaf played Frederick, Prince of Wales, third in cast list). "Handsome Mace Greenleaf with Solax," *MPW,* 10 Feb 1912, 486. "Death of Mace Greenleaf," *NYDM,* 3 Apr 1912, 25:1 (caught a fatal cold one week after joining Lubin; d. Sunday, 23 Mar). "Mace Greenleaf Dead," *MPW,* 6 Apr 1912, 22. "In Memoriam—Mace Greenleaf," *MPW,* 6 Apr 1912, 22.

Greenleaf, Raymond [actor] (b. MA, 27 Nov 1892–29 Oct 1963 [70], Woodland Hills CA). AS, p. 473.

Greenwald, Morris J. [assistant director] (b. 1891–6 Feb 1981 [89?], Los Angeles CA). BHD2, p. 106.

Greenwald, S[anford] **E.** [cameraman]. No data found. AMD, p. 145. "Fox News Photographer Secures First Aeroplane Views of Yosemite Valley," *MPW,* 10 Jul 1920, 248. "Fox Cameraman Does Big Job," *MPW,* 3 Dec 1921, 543.

Greenway, Ann [actress/singer] (b. Alexandria, Egypt, 15 Aug 1898–26 Jun 1977 [78], Van Nuys CA). AS, p. 473.

Greenwood, Charlotte [stage/film actress] (*née* Frances Charlotte Greenwood, b. Philadelphia PA, 25 Jun 1890–18 Jan 1978 [87], Beverly Hills CA). m. (1) **Cyril Ring**, 24 Jul 1915, LA CA (d. 1967); (2) Martin Broones (d. 1971). (TC-F.) "Charlotte Greenwood, 87, Stage and Film Comedian [sic] Known for Her High Kick," *NYT,* 14 Feb 1978, 38:1. "Charlotte Greenwood," *Variety,* 8 Feb 1978 ("she began her film career in the silent era"). AMD, p. 145. AS, p. 473. BHD1, p. 229. Katz, p. 505 (b. 1893). "Weds Charlotte Greenwood," *NYDM,* 28 Jul 1915, 7:3 ("Miss Greenwood established a new matrimonial record by being proposed to and married within thirty minutes."). "Three New Stars; Morosco Captures Blanche Ring, Cyril Maude and Charlotte Greenwood," *NYDM,* 11 Aug 1915, 22:4. "Everybody Wish!," *MPW,* 22 Oct 1927, 492.

Greenwood, Ethel [actress] (b. MO, 10 Jun 1888–8 Dec 1970 [82], Los Angeles CA). AS, p. 473.

Greenwood, Hubert F. [actor] (b. England, 1 Apr 1884–7 Apr 1950 [66], Los Angeles Co. CA). BHD, p. 185.

Greenwood, Milton E. [executive] (b. La Place AL, 15 Oct 1883–5 Jan 1937 [53], Beverly Hills CA). BHD2, p. 106.

Greenwood, Reeva [actress]. No data found. AMD, p. 145. "It Was Reeva, Not Winnifred," *MPW,* 19 Jun 1915, 1922. "Reeva Green wood Joins 'Lariat,'" *MPW,* 19 Jun 1915, 1929.

Greenwood, Winnifred [stage/film actress] (b. Geneseo NY, 1 Jan 1885–23 Nov 1961 [76], Woodland Hills CA). m. (1) George Field, 1913–18. (Selig, 1910; American; Balboa; Marine; Bluebird; FP-L.) AMD, p. 145. AS, p. 473. BHD, pp. 33–34; 185. BR, pp. 33–36. IFN, p. 125. "Picture Personalitites," *MPW,* 1 Feb 1913, 471. "Winnifred Greenwood Gets Stage Fright," *MPW,* 10 May 1913, 577. "Winnifred Greenwood Joins American," *MPW,* 30 Aug 1913, 942. "Leading American Players," *MPW,* 11 Jul 1914, 240–42. "It Was Reeva, Not Winnifred," *MPW,* 19 Jun 1915, 1922. Roberta Courtlandt, "Winifred Greenwood, of the American Company," *MPC,* I, Dec 1915, 55–56. "Greenwood Returns," *MPW,* 22 May 1926, 317. Billy H Doyle, "Lost Players," *CI,* 181 (Jul 1990), 42.

Greer, Bernice [actress] (b. 1893–16 Apr 1983 [90?], Pasadena CA). AS, p. 473.

Greer, Howard [costume designer] (b. Rushville IL, 1896?–17 Apr 1974 [78], Culver City CA). (FP-L, 1923; Paramount.) *Designing Male* (1951). "Howard Greer, Designer, Dies; Couturier for Hollywood Stars," *NYT,* 21 Apr 1974, 53:1. "Howard Greer," *Variety,* 1 May 1974. AMD, p. 145. BHD2, p. 106. SD. "Greer Joins," *MPW,* 13 Jan 1923, 165 (joined Paramount). "The Evolution of a Gown for the Decoration of a Star," *MW,* 1 Aug 1925, 25.

Greer, Jesse [composer] (b. New York NY, 26 Aug 1896–3 Oct 1970 [74], Columbia CT). m. Josephine Lauter (d. 9 Dec 1969). "Jesse Greer, 74, Composer for Broadway Shows, Dies," *NYT,* 4 Oct 1970, 93:1 (wrote *Just You, Just Me; Kitty from Kansas City; Gonna Meet My Sweetie Now; Baby Blue Eyes*). "Jesse Greer," *Variety,* 7 Oct 1970 (wrote *Sleepy Head; Flapperette*). AS, p. 474. CEPMJ.

Greer, Julian [actor] (b. London, England, 1871?–15 Apr 1928 [56], New York NY). "Julian Greer," *Variety,* 25 Apr 1928. AS, p. 474. BHD, p. 185. IFN, p. 125. Truitt, p. 133.

Greet, Ben [actor] (b. London, England, 24 Sep 1857–17 May 1936 [78], London, England). BHD, p. 185.

Greet, Clare [actress] (b. England, 14 Jun 1871–14 Feb 1939 [67], London, England). (Paramount.) "Clare Greet," *Variety,* 22 Feb 1939. AS, p. 474. BHD1, p. 229. IFN, p. 125.

Gregers, Emmanuel [actor/director] (b. Horsens, Denmark, 28 Dec 1881–21 Mar 1957 [75], Copenhagen, Denmark). AS, p. 474.

Gregg, Arnold [actor] (aka Arnold Gray, *né* Arnold R. Samberg, b. Toledo OH, 20 Apr 1899–3 May 1936 [37], Alpine CA). "Arnold Samberg," *Variety,* 6 May 1936. AMD, p. 144 (Arnold Gray). AS, p. 474 (Arnold Gregg); p. 961 (Arnold R. Samberg). BHD1, p. 226 (Arnold Gray). IFN, p. 125 (Arnold Gregg). Truitt, p. 295. "Arnold Gray," *MPW,* 13 Aug 1927, 456. George Katchmer, "Remembering the Great Silents," *CI,* 207 (Sep 1992), 42–43.

Gregg, Everley [actress] (b. Bishop Stoke, England, 26 Oct 1898–9 Jun 1959 [60], Beaconsfield, England). AS, p. 474.

Gregg, Helen [title writer]. No data found. FDY, p. 443.

Gregor, Arthur [actor/director/scenarist] (b. Vienna, Austria, 9 Apr 1890–2 Feb 1948 [57], Los Angeles CA). (Metro; Universal.) "Arthur Gregor," *Variety,* 4 Feb 1948 (production veepee of United International, 16mm outfit). AS, p. 474. BHD2, p. 107. FDY, p. 427.

Gregor, Nora [stage/film actress] (b. Gorizia, Italy, 3 Feb 1900–20 Jan 1949 [48], Viña del Mar, Chile; heart attack during a vacation). m. Prince Ernst von Starhemberg. (MGM German-language films.) AS, p. 474 (b. 1901; d. Santiago, Chile). BHD1, p. 229. Waldman, p. 124 (b. Austria).

Gregori, Ferdinand [actor] (b. Germany, 13 Apr 1870–12 Dec 1928 [58]). BHD, p. 185.

Gregory, Carl Louis [cameraman/director] (b. KS, 9 Sep 1882–11 Mar 1951 [68], Ventura Co. CA). AMD, p. 145. BHD2, p. 107. "Rejoins Thanhouser After Record Trip," *MPW,* 31 May

1913, 905. "Gregory Made Aide to Fleming," *MPW,* 14 Feb 1914, 825. John William Kellette, "Under Water Photography," *MPW,* 25 Apr 1914, 497–98. "Gregory Joins Metro," *MPW,* 17 Jul 1915, 469.

Gregory, Dora [actress] (b. Dulwich, England, 2 Sep 1872–5 Mar 1954 [81], London, England). AS, p. 474. BHD1, p. 229.

Gregory, Edna [actress] (*née* Edna Steinberg, b. Winnipeg, Canada, 25 Jan 1905–3 Jul 1965 [56], Los Angeles CA; complications after surgery). m. Abe Steinberg. (Educational; Christie; Fox; WB.) "Edna Gregory," *Variety,* 14 Jul 1965. AS, p. 474. BHD1, p. 229 (b. Antelope OR). IFN, p. 125. Truitt, p. 133.

Gregory, Ena [actress: Wampas Star, 1925] (aka Marian Douglas, b. Melbourne, Australia, 18 Apr 1905–13 Jun 1993 [88], Los Angeles CA). (Universal.) m. (1) Theodore W. Flannery, 1927; (2) Dr. Frank G. Nolan, 5 Nov 1937, LA CA. Premature obituary: *Variety,* 17 Nov 1937. AMD, p. 102 (Marion Douglas). AS, p. 335 (Marian Douglas). BHD1, p. 229 (b. 1907; d. Laguna Beach CA). BR, pp. 153–54 (d. 3 Jul 1965). "Marion Douglas in F.B.O. Lead," *MPW,* 10 Dec 1927, 45. Billy H. Doyle, "Obituaries," *FIR,* Mar/Apr 1994, 35. June Lee, "Dan Cupid's Bulletin Board," *Paris and Hollywood Screen Secrets,* Oct 1927, 36 (married Flannery). "Ena Gregory Wins Divorce," *NY Herald Tribune,* 25 Jul 1939 (her husband would go out on a professional call, and she wouldn't see him for days). "Doctor Needn't Take Trek to South Seas; Actress-Wife Gets Divorce on Grounds of Long Absences from Home," *NY Journal-American,* 26 Jul 1939. "Hubby Out Late—So She Sues," *Daily Mirror,* 14 Jun 1939.

Gregory, Fan [actress]. No data found. (Thanhouser.) "In the Picture Studios," *NYDM,* 4 Aug 1915, 27:2 (on the female baseball team at Thanhouser).

Gregory, Gilbert [actor] (d. 9 Dec 1919). BHD, p. 185.

Gregory, Jackson [writer]. No data found. AMD, p. 145. "Jackson Gregory Pleased with American's Film Version of His Novel, 'Six Feet Four,'" *MPW,* 27 Sep 1919, 1968.

Gregory, Mildred [actress]. No data found. (Lubin). AMD, p. 145. "Mildred Gregory with Gaumont," *MPW,* 12 Feb 1916, 968.

Gregory, William H. [actor] (d. 24 Dec 1926, Los Angeles CA). "William H. Gregory," *Variety,* 5 Jan 1927. AS, p. 474. BHD, p. 185. Truitt, p. 133.

Greig, Robert [actor] (b. Melbourne, Australia, 27 Dec 1879–27 Jun 1958 [78], Los Angeles CA). AS, p. 474.

Gresham, Edith F. [actress] (b. 1897?–31 Dec 1976 [79], Riverdale NY). "Edith F. Gresham," *Variety,* 19 Jan 1977. AS, p. 475. BHD, p. 185.

Grethe, Hildegard [actress] (b. Germany, 1899–26 Dec 1961 [62?], Berlin, Germany). AS, p. 475.

Gretillat, Jacques Marie Gaëtan [actor/director/scenarist/singer] (b. Vitry-sur-Seine, France, 26 Aug 1885 [extrait de naissance no. 112]–19 Dec 1950 [65], Paris, France). AS, p. 475.

Gretler, Heinrich [stage/film actor] (b. Zurich, Switzerland, 1 Oct 1897–30 Sep 1977 [79], Zurich, Switzerland). m. actress Marion Wuensche. "Heinrich Gretler," *Variety,* 12 Oct 1977, p. 95 (age 80; in about 24 Swiss and 60 German films). AS, p. 475. BHD1, p. 230.

Grey, Clifford [actor/lyricist/scenarist] (*né* Clifford Davis, b. Birmingham, England, 5 Jan 1887–26 Sep 1941 [54], Ipswich, England). m. Dorothy Gould. (Stage, 1907; lyrics, 1913.) "Clifford Grey, 54, English Lyricist; Wrote Words for 'Hit the Deck' and 'The Three Musketeers' Tunes—Dies in Ipswich; He Went on Stage in 1907; 'If You Were the Only Girl in the World' One of His Songs—Also Worked for Films," *NYT,* 27 Sep 1941, 17:6. "Clifford Grey," *Variety,* 1 Oct 1941. AS, p. 475. BHD2, p. 107. CEPMJ, II, p. 1011. SD.

Grey, Denise (mother of Suzanne Grey) [actress] (*née* Jeanne Marie Laurentine Edouardine Verthuy, b. Chatillon, Italy, 17 Sep 1896–13 Jan 1996 [99], Paris, France [extrait de décès no. 4/1996]). m. (daughter Suzanne, b. 28 Jun 1917.). AS, p. 475.

Grey, Dolly [actress] (*née* Clara Galassi, b. 27 Mar 1904). AS, p. 475. JS, p. 206 (in Italian silents from 1924).

Grey, E. Henry [actor]. No data found. AMD, p. 145. "E. Henry Grey," *MPW,* 2 Dec 1916, 1337.

Grey, Gloria (actress: Wampas Star, 1924) (*née* Marie Draga, b. Portland OR, 23 Oct 1909–22 Nov 1947 [38], Los Anbgeles CA). m. **Ramon Romero** (d. 1981). (MGM; American Releasing Co.; FBO; Universal.) "Gloria Grey," *Variety,* 26 Nov 1947. AS, p. 475. BHD1, p. 230. BR, pp. 154–56 (b. Stockton CA). IFN, p. 125. Truitt, p. 133. Grace Kingsley, "'Girls Who Play Grown-Up Roles Seldom Marry Young,' Says Gloria Grey," *MW,* 22 Sep 1923, 19, 31 (17 years old). George A. Katchmer, "Forgotten Cowboys and Cowgirls—V," *CI,* 177 (Mar 1990), C2, C4; "Update—Forgotten Cowboys/Girls," *CI,* 179 (May 1990), 45.

Grey, Jane [stage/film actress] (aka Mamie Larock and Gladys Grey, *née* Mary Edith———, b. Middlebury VT, 22 May 1883–9 Nov 1944 [61], New York NY). m. (1) Riccardo Martin (*né* Hugh Whitfield Martin, d. 1952); (2) William E. Tyrrel. (Ince.) "Jane Grey [Mary E. Tyrrell]," *Variety,* 15 Nov 1944 (age 56). AMD, p. 145. AS, p. 475. BHD, p. 185. IFN, p. 125. KOM, pp. 140–41. SD. Truitt, p. 133. "World-Equitable Engagements," *MPW,* 4 Mar 1916, 1483. "Jane Grey on Screen and Stage," *MPW,* 9 Jun 1917, 1630.

Grey, John Wesley [director/scenarist/publicist] (b. San Jose CA, 1873?–27 Jun 1933 [60], Los Angeles CA). (Ince; Vitagraph, 1913; Sennett; Lloyd.) "John Grey," *Variety,* 4 Jul 1933. AMD, p. 146. AS, p. 475. BHD2, p. 107 (1887–1964). FDY, p. 427. IFN, p. 125. "John Wesley Grey," *MPW,* 18 Jul 1914, 418. "Now Father Jack, If You Please," *MPW,* 4 Sep 1915, 1645.

Grey, Katherine [actress] (b. San Francisco CA, 27 Dec 1873–21 Mar 1950 [76], Orleans MA). "Katharine Grey," *Variety,* 29 Mar 1950, p. 75 (age 77). AS, p. 475. BHD, p. 185.

Grey, King [cinematographer] (b. 1886–30 Jun 1938 [52?], Los Angeles CA; auto accident). AS, p. 475.

Grey, Leonard [actor] (b. England-d. 3 Aug 1918, New York NY). AS, p. 475. BHD, p. 185.

Grey, Lillian [actress] (d. 22 Apr 1985, Los Angeles CA). BHD, p. 186.

Grey, Lita [actress] (*née* Lillita Louise MacMurray, b. Cincinnati OH, 15 Apr 1907–29 Dec 1995 [88], Woodland Hills CA). *My Life with Chaplin; An Intimate Memoir* (1966). m. (1) **Charles Chaplin**, 25 Nov 1924, Guaymas, Mexico—div. 22 Aug 1927 (d. 1977); (2) Henry Aguirre; (3) Arthur Day; (4) Pat Longo. "Lita Grey Chaplin," *CI,* 248 (Feb 1996), 55:1 (obituary). AMD, p. 146. AS, p. 475 (b. 1908). BHD1, p. 230 (b. LA CA); p. 609. FFF, p. 83. MH, p. 114 (b. Hollywood CA). "Picks Lita Grey," *MPW,* 29 Mar 1924, 351. Grace Kingsley, "Charlie Chaplin's New Leading Lady—Lita Grey!," *MW,* 19 Apr 1924, 7, 26. Jim Tully, "The Picture Plum of 1924," *Classic,* Jul 1924, 62, 78. "Charlie Chaplin Weds Lita Grey in Mexico," *MPW,* 6 Dec 1924, 510 (m. 26 Nov). "Mrs, Chaplin May Return to Films," *MPW,* 26 Mar 1927, 267. Steve Randisi, "The Flirting Angel and the Tramp; An Exclusive Interview with Charlie Chaplin's Second Wife, Lita Grey Chaplin," *Filmfax,* 38 (Jun/Jul 1993), pp. 50–57 (b. 1908; met Chaplin on 15 Apr 1914). Jeff Vance, "In Memoriam: Lita Grey Chaplin," *CI,* 248 (Feb 1996), 8 (b. Hollywood CA).

Grey, Madeline [actress] (b. CA, 18 Jul 1887–16 Aug 1950 [63], Los Angeles CA). AS, p. 475.

Grey, Olga [stage/film actress] (*née* Anushka Zacsek, b. Budapest, Hungary, 1897–25 Apr 1973 [75?], Los Angeles CA). AMD, p. 146. AS, p. 475. BHD, p. 186. IFN, p. 125. KOM, p. 141. "A Vamp with a Goulash Name; So you see that she was quite justified in changing it," *Photoplay,* Feb 1917, 73 (extra work with Griffith). "Olga Grey Returns to Triangle," *MPW,* 20 Oct 1917, 367.

Grey, Paola (sister of **Umberto Paradisi**) [actress] (*née* Clelia Paradisi, b. Turin, Italy, 24 Mar 1886–27 Nov 1951 [65], Genoa, Italy). AS, p. 475. JS, p. 206 (in Italian silents from 1919).

Grey, Ray [director] (father of Virginia Grey) (b. 1899?–18 Apr 1925 [26], Glendale CA; pneumonia). (Universal.) "Ray Gray," *Variety,* 22 Apr 1925. AS, p. 475. BHD, p. 186.

Grey, R[obert] **Henry** [stage/film actor] (*né* Henry Virtue Goerner, b. Oakland CA, 17 Jul 1891–26 Apr 1934 [42], Los Angeles CA). (Began 1911; Essanay; American; Kalem; Balboa.) AS, p. 475. BHD1, p. 230. IFN, p. 125 (age 40). MSBB, p. 1024 (b. 1890). Truitt 1983, p. 293.

Grey, Schuyler E. [scenarist] (b. 1895?–2 Jul 1933 [38], Stamford CA; after an operation). "Schuyler Gray," *Variety,* 4 Jul 1933. AS, p. 475.

Grey, Zane [writer/scenarist] (b. Zanesville OH, 31 Jan 1875–23 Oct 1939 [64], Altadena CA; heart attack). m. Lina Elise Roth, 21 Nov 1905 (d. 26 Jul 1957 [74], LA CA; after a stroke and unconsciousness). Carlton Jackson, *Zane Grey* (NY: Twayne Publishers, 1973). Ann Ronald, *Zane Grey* (Boise ID: Boise State Univ., 1975). "Zane Grey, 64, Dies Suddenly on Coast; Wrote More Than 50 Novels [all of them in longhand], Most of Them Dealing with Western Adventure; 17,000,000 Copies Sold; Noted for His Catches of Game Fish—Once a Dentist [31st St. in NYC], Won Fame After Hardships," *NYT,* 24 Oct 1939, 23:1 (wrote *Betty Zane,* 1904; *Riders of the Purple Sage,* 1912. "Like most authors, Mr. Grey began writing because of an irresistable urge for self-expression." Published 5r books with 3 mss. unpublished. Descendant of Col. Ebenezer Zane, a Dane who came to America with William Penn.). "Mrs. Zane Grey Dies; Widow of Novelist, 74, Edited His Tales of the Old West," *NYT,* 27 Jul 1957, 17:5

(a graduate of Hunter College, 1905; moved to CA, 1920; 2 sons, 1 daughter). "Grey's Widow Left $500,000," *NYT*, 21 Aug 1957, 55:5 (Mrs. Lina Elise Grey's will filed for probate on 19 Aug 1957, Superior Court, LA CA). AMD, p. 146. AS, p. 476. BHD2, p. 107 (b. 1872). FDY, p. 427. "Zane Grey, Noted Author, Signs New Contract with Paramount," *MPW*, 24 May 1924, 397.

Gribbon, Eddie [Keystone Cop] (brother of **Harry Gribbon**) (*né* Edward T. Gribbon, b. New York NY, 3 Jan 1890–28 Sep 1965 [75], No. Hollywood CA; cancer). (Sennett; Metro; Paramount; Universal; TC-F; WB.) "Eddie T. Gribbon," *Variety*, 6 Oct 1965. AMD, p. 146. AS, p. 476. BHD1, p. 230. IFN, p. 126. Truitt, pp. 133–34. "Fine in Comedy Roles," *MPW*, 10 Jan 1925, 163. "Edward 'Eddie' Gribbon," *MPW*, 4 Jun 1927, 333. George Katchmer, "Remembering the Great Silents," *CI*, 246 (Dec 1995), 48–49.

Gribbon, Harry, "Silk Hat Harry" (brother of **Eddie Gribbon**) [actor] (b. New York NY, 9 Jun 1885–28 Jul 1961 [76], Los Angeles CA). m. Mae Emory. (Sennett.) "Harry Gribbon," *Variety*, 2 Aug 1961 (age 75). AMD, p. 146. AS, p. 476. BHD1, p. 230. IFN, p. 126. SD. Truitt, p. 134. "Younger Keystoners," *MPW*, 5 Feb 1916, 783.

Gridoux, Lucas [actor] (*né* Lucas Grimberg, b. Hertza, Romania, 16 Apr 1896–19 Apr 1952 [56], Paris, France [extrait de décès no. 13/1384]). AS, p. 476.

Griener, A. Leroy [cinematographer] (b. 1894-Oct 1929 [35?]). BHD2, p. 107.

Grieve, Adelaide [actress] (b. 10 Feb 1902–17 May 1993 [91], San Francisco CA). Billy H. Doyle, "Obituaries," *FIR*, Nov/Dec 1993, 429:1. AS, p. 476 (d. LA CA, 1992). BHD1, p. 609.

Grieve, Harold W. [art director] (b. Los Angeles CA, 1 Feb 1901–3 Nov 1993 [92], Los Angeles CA). BHD2, p. 107.

Griffell, Jose Martinez (son of **Paco Martinez** and **Prudencia Griffell**) [actor] (*né* José Luis Martinez Griffell, b. Mexico, 3 May 1905–15 Nov 1955 [50], Mexico City, Mexico). AS, p. 476.

Griffell, Prudencia (mother of **Jose Martinez Griffell**) [actress] (b. Lugo, Spain, 1881–7 Jun 1970 [89?], Mexico). m. **Paco Martinez** (d. 1956). AS, p. 476.

Griffen, Nannie [actress] (d. 17 Jul 1925, New York NY). BHD, p. 186.

Griffies, Ethel (daughter of actors Samuel Rupert Woods and Lillie Roberts) [stage/film actress] (*née* Ethel Woods, b. Sheffield, England, 26 Apr 1878–9 Sep 1975 [97], London, England; stroke). "Ethel Griffies," *Variety*, 17 Sep 1975, p. 86:1 (onstage as a baby in 1881). AS, p. 476. BHD1, p. 230 (b. Halifax).

Griffin, Al [technical director]. NO data found. AMD, p. 146. "Al Griffin with Rolin," *MPW*, Sep 1917, 1517.

Griffin, Alexander R.M. [executive] (b. 1903?–27 Jun 1959 [56], Philadelphia PA). "Alexander R.M. Griffin," *Variety*, 1 Jul 1959. AS, p. 476.

Griffin, Carlton E[lliot] [actor] (b. New York NY, 23 May 1893–24 Jul 1940 [47], Los Angeles CA; heart attack. Buried 25 Jul, Forrest Lawn Cemetery, Hollywood). m. (1) Pauline Saxon; (2) Verna. (Lubin; last film: *Before I Die*, Columbia.) "Carlton E. Griffin; Stage and Screen Actor Served in France During World War," *NYT*, 25 Jul 1940, 17:2 (worked with Griffith, Lloyd, Langdon, and Chase). "Carlton E. Griffin," *Variety*, 139, 31 Jul 1940, 142:4 ("Magic Glasses" vaudeville act with Grace Gordon). AS, p. 476. BHD1, p. 230. IFN, p. 126. Truitt, p. 134. "New American Feature Players," *NYDM*, 28 Apr 1915, 24:1 (with Beatrice Van).

Griffin, Charles [actor] (b. PA, 2 Sep 1888–17 Aug 1956 [67], Los Angeles CA). AS, p. 476.

Griffin, Frank C. [director/scenarist]. No data found. AMD, p. 146. FDY, p. 427. "Griffin to Sterling," *MPW*, 29 Aug 1914, 1219. "Frank Griffin Now Directing L-KO's," *MPW*, 5 Oct 1918, 105.

Griffin, Frank L. [actor/director] (b. 1889?–17 Mar 1953 [64?], Los Angeles CA; heart attack). (Lubin, 1906; Sennett; Fox; 1st National.) "Frank L. Griffin," *Variety*, 25 Mar 1953. AS, p. 476. BHD, p. 186; BHD2, p. 107. Truitt, p. 134.

Griffin, Gerald [stage/film actor/producer/director] (b. Hanley, Staffordshire, England, 1854?–16 Mar 1919 [65], Venice CA). (Gaumont; Serial Film Co.; Metro-Rolfe) "Gerald Griffin," *Variety*, 11 Apr 1919. AMD, p. 146. AS, p. 476 (b. Pittsburgh PA). BHD, p. 186. IFN, p. 126. "Gerald Griffin Engaged by Metro," *MPW*, 28 Oct 1916, 551 (family settled in Pittsburgh). "Gerald Griffin," *MPW*, 21 Jul 1917, 446. "Gerald Griffin," *MPW*, 4 Aug 1917, 786. "Gerald Griffin Out of Hospital," *MPW*, 22 Jun 1918, 1690.

Griffin, Gerald [actor] (b. Chicago IL, 1891–11 Jan 1962 [70?], Rhinebeck NY). AS, p. 476.

Griffin, Phyllis (mother of **Bebe Daniels**) [actress] (d. 20 Feb 1959, London, England). *Fl.* 1911. AS, p. 477. BHD, p. 186. In a group picture of the Bison Stock Co., *MPW*, 23 Dec 1911, 987.

Griffin, Walter L. [cinematographer]. No data found. FDY, p. 459.

Griffith, Albert L. (brother of **D.W. Griffith**) [producer] (b. La Grange KY, 1879–3 Apr 1963 [84?], Medina NY). AS, p. 477.

Griffith, Aileen [actress]. No data found. AMD, p. 146. "Aileen Griffith Deserting Comedy for Serious Roles," *MPW*, 21 Feb 1920, 1264.

Griffith, Beverly [stuntman/cinematographer/actor/director] (b. Butler GA, 27 Sep 1887–16 Apr 1970 [82], New York NY). (Sennett; Universal.) m. Edna Maison, Dec? 1917, Los Angeles CA (d. 1946). "Beverly Griffith," *Variety*, 6 May 1970. "Marriages," *Variety*, 14 Dec 1917, p. 9. AS, p. 477. BHD2, p. 107.

Griffith, Corinne, "The Orchid Lady of the Screen" [actress/author] (*née* Corinne Scott, b. Texarkana TX, 24 Nov 1894–13 Jul 1979 [84], Santa Monica CA; heart attack). m. (1) **Webster Campbell**, 1916–23 (d. 1972); (2) **Walter Morosco**, 1933–34 (d. 1948); (3) Preston Marshall, 1936–58; (4) Danny Scholl. *Papa's Delicate Condition. Hollywood Stories* (NY: Frederick Fell, [1962]). *My Life with the Redskins. I Can't Boil Water* (cookbook). *This You Won't Believe* (NY: Frederick Fell, 1972). (Vitagraph, $15 a week; Goldwyn; Selznick, 1st National, $10,000 a week.) George Goodman, Jr., "Corinne Griffith, Silent Movie Star; Beauty Brought Nickname, 'Orchid of the Screen.'—Was Also Real Estate Investor," *NYT*, 22 Jul 1979, 34:1 (b. Waco TX, 1906; d. Beverly Hills CA, age 73. "'I got my money without the help of any man,' she once told an interviewer. 'Women wise enough to earn their own money will get a broader understanding of life, a new respect from their husbands and a bank account which they can use without resorting to the old tricks that sicken every wife at heart.'). "Corinne Griffith Dies at 81; Early Star, Wily Business Woman," *Variety*, 25 Jul 1979 (b. Waco TX?, 24 Nov 1898; age ca. 81). AMD, p. 146. AS, p. 477. BHD1, p. 231 (b. 21 Nov). FFF, p. 31 (b. 1898). FSS, p. 131. HCH, p. 97. IFN, p. 126 (1894–1979). Katz, p. 509. MH, p. 114 (b. 1890). MSBB, p. 1036. SD. Slide, p. 141 (b. 1899). WWS, p. 58 (b. 1898). "Corinne Griffith," WBO2, pp. 198–99 (b. 1896). Frederick James Smith, "Corinne, Chocolate Cake and a Deep, Dark Secret," *MPC*, Apr 1919, 20–21, 80 (Irish/Italian extraction; won a beauty contest prize at a ball in New Orleans and was noticed by Rolin Sturgeon of Vitagraph). *Corinne Griffith, as She Is to Those Who Know Her* (NY: Ross Publishing Co., Inc., 1920 (claims that Rollin S. Sturgeon, a Vitagraph director, discovered her at the New Orleans Mardi Gras, p. 9). Edward Weitzel, "Corinne Griffith on Police Beat Meets a Courteous Taxicab Driver," *MPW*, 28 Feb 1920, 1491. "Corinne Griffith Renews Vitagraph Contract," *MPW*, 13 Mar 1920, 1782. "Silent Drama to Entertain the Spoken, with Corinne Griffith as the Hostess," *MPW*, 28 Aug 1920, 1150. "Corinne Griffith Starts Work Under G.L. Sargent," *MPW*, 27 Nov 1920, 506. "Corinne Griffith Wins First Place," *MPW*, 24 Dec 1921, 943 (popularity contest in Brooklyn). "Corinne Griffith Productions Will Be Released Through W.W. Hodkinson," *MPW*, 23 Dec 1922, 737. "Miss Sweet Named for Lead in Film," *MPW*, 3 Feb 1923, 491. Herbert Gleason, "Why I Am Quitting the Films to Rear a Family," *MW*, 22 Mar 1924, 3. Alma Talley, "Why All Women Love to Cry; Charming film star, who is shortly to leave screen, tells why members of her own sex delight in lachrymose tendency," *MW*, 26 Apr 1924, 8. "Corinne Griffith Finishes One, Prepares for Another," *MPW*, 5 Jul 1924, 22. Adele Whitely Fletcher, "Corinne Griffith as Mrs. Walter Morosco," *MW*, 19 Jul 1924, 8–9. "Corinne Griffith feted at Dansant," *MPW*, 6 Jun 1925, 618. Alice L. Tildesley, "Her Royal Highness," *MPC*, Jun 1926, 30–31, 88. Paul Paige, "Close-Ups and Fade-Outs," *Paris and Hollywood*, Oct 1926, 93 (purchased the *Edris*, formerly Thomas Ince's yacht built in New York in 1909. To be rechristened The Wanderlust. It was 80 feet long with a 19-foot beam, carried a crew of 4, and could accommodate 10 passengers.). Paul Blaine, "Corinne Griffith Predicts—That Einar Hansen Will Prove One of Our Great Romantic Actors," *MPC*, Nov 1926, 22–23, 83 (an idol in Europe, he was down to his last can of food before Griffith chose him as her leading man). "Miss Griffith wi United," *MPW*, 5 Mar 1927, 12. "Corinne Griffith Signed by United Artists Corporation," *MPW*, 5 Mar 1927, 35. Adele Whitely Fletcher, "A Portrait of Corinne Griffith; Thoroughly Modern in All Her Views and Reactions, Corinne Is, However, Always Feminine and Always Interested in Feminine Things and in Matters of Taste and Beauty," *Cinema Arts*, VI (Sep 1927), 21, 46. "Who's Who in Hollywood; Corinne Griffith," *Paris and Hollywood Screen Secrets*, Oct 1927, 45, 94. Frances Carpen, "The Divine Lady Herself; Corinne Griffith Is an Orchid that Flowered Only When Hardship Came," *MPC*, Aug 1928, 37, 89. Gladys Hall, "Confessions of the Stars VII; Corinne Griffith Tells Her Untold Tale," *MPC*, May 1929, 18–19, 72, 86 ("I have had a poison in my life...It is called an inferiority complex.").

Griffith, David Llewelyn **Wark** (brother of **Albert L. Griffith**) [stage/film actor/composer/scenarist/director/producer] (aka Lawrence Griffith, b. Crestwood KY, 22 Jan 1875–23 Jul 1948 [73], Los Angeles CA; stroke). m. (1) **Linda Arvidson**, 14 May 1906, Boston MA (d. 1949); (2) Evelyn E. Baldwin. (Edison; Biograph, 1908; Reliance-Majestic, 1915; Triangle; UA.) Richard Schickel, *D.W. Griffith; An American Life* (NY: Simon & Schuster, 1984). "David W. Griffith, Film Pioneer, Dies; Producer of 'Birth of Nation,' 'Intolerance' and 'America'; Made Nearly 500 Pictures; Set Screen Standards; Co-Founder of United Artists Gave Mary Pickford and Fairbanks Their Starts," *NYT*, 24 Jul 1948, 15:1. "D.W. Griffith, Film Pioneer, Dead at 73," *Variety*, 28 Jul 1948. AMD, p. 146. AS, p. 477. BHD, p. 186; BHD2, p. 107. IFN, p. 126 (b. La Grange KY). Katz, pp. 509–14. KOM, pp. 141–42. Lowrey, p. 60 (b. 1880). MSBB, p. 1046 (b. LaGrange KY, 1880). SD. Anthony Slide, ed., *The Autobiography of Joseph E. Henabery* (Lanham MD: Scarecrow Press, 1997), p. 67 ("He [Griffith] was patient with many rather stupid people."). Spehr, p. 136 (1875). Truitt, p. 134. Louis Reeves Harrison, "Studio Saunterings," *MPW*, 24 Feb 1912, 657. "Lawrence Griffith Out of Biograph; Famous Director Severed Connection with That Company on October 1—Has Been Making Pictures Five Years," *MPW*, 4 Oct 1913, 159. "Lawrence Griffith Out of Biograph," *MPW*, 11 Oct 1913, 159. "D.W. (Lawrence) Griffith withy Mutual," *MPW*, 8 Nov 1913, 591. L.R. Harrison, "D.W. Griffith," *MPW*, 22 Nov 1913, 847–48. "Actresses Must Be Young," *MPW*, 27 Dec 1913, 1556. Robert E. Welsh, "David W. Griffith Speaks; Among Other Things He Discusses the Director's Lot, the Development of Picture Players and Throws New Light on the Question of the Stage Versus the Drama," *NYDM*, 14 Jan 1914, 49, 54 ("You say that some stage players look down on the motion picture. I say that I woud not have the average stage player in a picture of mine..."). "Griffith on the Job," *MPW*, 28 Feb 1914, 1096. W.E. Wing, "Out on the Coast," *NYDM*, 8 Apr 1914, 36:2 (the Advertising Club of LA held a "Movie Festival" at the Auditorium Theater and "[t]he most unique event was the appearance upon the stage of D.W. Griffith, who had kept so far in the background druing his film career that the public almost came to regard him as a mighty fine myth."). "Talk Along the Coast...Griffith Production of 'The Clansman,'" *NYDM*, 17 Jun 1914, 31:1. "Editorials in Films; 'Semi-Educationals' as Seen by David W. Griffith and Ned Finley," *NYDM*, 1 Jul 1914, 21:3. "D.W. Griffith, Motion Picture Director," *MPW*, 11 Jul 1914, 184. Edward Mott Woolley, "The $100,000 Salary Man of the Movies; The Story of D.W. Griffith," *McClure's* (Sep 1914), 109–16 ("Six years ago Griffith escaped a fruitless tramping of the streets by securing a job as a 'super' in a struggling film company. To-day he ranks with the highest paid men in America and presides over a gigantic film-producing plant in Los Angeles—and he is only thirty-five years of age. *A Motion Picture Reformer:* Griffith reached New York in 1908, penniless, having acted in Louisville (and more lately in California), once a leading man for Nance O'Neil. His play, *A Fool and a Girl* failed in Washington DC. He applied for a job at Kalem with Frank Marion, who told him to try the Biograph in the Bronx, where he got a $5-a-day job and studied movie-making. This article includes sub-headings under *Griffith Produces the First Modern Photo-Play; The French Influence in Motion Pictures; Getting Realistic Emotional Effects; The Camera Man's Presence of Mind;* and *Robert Browning as a Scenario-Writer.* Illustrated, with one photo on p. 111 captioned, "Appraising a Candidate for a job. Mr. Griffith is discussing with this young girl the photographic value of her beauty." The "young girl" in the photo is Lillian Gish.). "Griffith Engages Theater," *MPW*, 20 Feb 1915, 1121. W., "'The Birth of a Nation' Summit of Picture Art; Griffith Blends Spectacle, History and Drama with Hand of a Master in His Latest Screen Production," *NYDM*, 10 Mar 1915, 28:1. "Griffith Film Scores," *MPW*, 13 Mar 1915, 1587. W.E. Wing, "Along the Pacific Coast," *NYDM*, 19 May 1915, 24:1 (to film *The Holy Grail* after *The Clansman*). Frank E. Woods, "D.W. Griffith," *MPW*, 10 Jul 1915, 256. "Berst vs. Griffith," *MPW*, 17 Jul 1915, 465. "San Francisco Convention," *MPW*, 31 Jul 1915, 790–94, 819–20. "Triangle Debut Brilliant Success; Trio of Strong Offerings from Griffith, Ince and Sennett Studios Receive Enthusiastic Reception—Many Notables at Initial Performance," *NYDM*, 29 Sep 1915, 30:1 (with photo, "The Men Who Made the 'Triangle'": Charles Kessel, Harry E. Aitken, Adam Kessel, Mack Sennett, Griffith, Thomas Ince, and Charles O. Bauman. *The Iron Strain, The Lamb,* and *My Valet* were shown at the reception. Reviews of these films on the same page.). W. Stephen Bush, "Schools of Motion Picture Art," *MPW*, 2 Oct 1915, 54–55. "Griffith First Producer in Trade Board," *MPW*, 9 Oct 1915, 260. "Mother of D.W. Griffith Is Dead," *MPW*, 18 Dec 1915, 2184 (b. 12 Dec 1828–6 Dec 1915 [86], Lagrange KY; penumonia). C.W. Curtis, "Death of Mother Griffith," *NYDM*, 18 Dec 1915, 23:3 (aged 85; survived by D.W. Griffith; Albert Griffith, NYC; William Griffith, Lagrange KY; Mrs. Ruth Houghton, Lagrange KY. "D.W. Griffith was daily notified by wire of his mother's condition, but owing to her sudden relapse was not able to arrive in time for her funeral. The other children were at her bedside."). "D.W. Griffith's Flying Trip," *MPW*, 25 Dec 1915, 2344. Epes Winthrop Sargent, "Griffith, His Book," *MPW*, 20 May 1916, 1320 (*The Rise and Fall of Free Speech in America*). Edward Weitzel, "The Making of a Masterpiece," *MPW*, 30 Sep 1916, 2084. "Griffith Bids Mae Marsh Godspeed," *MPW*, 23 Dec 1916, 1787. Cal York, "Plays and Players," *Photoplay Magazine*, Feb 1917, 86 (re the disintegration of the Griffith combination of players.). "Griffith a Busy Man," *MPW*, 17 Feb 1917, 1018. "Griffith to Contribute to Artcraft," *MPW*, 31 Mar 1917, 2074. "Griffith Leaves Fine Arts," *MPW*, 31 Mar 1917, 2087. "Griffith to Start Production in May," *MPW*, 21 Apr 1917, 433. "Griffith in London," *MPW*, 26 May 1917, 1270. "D.W. Griffith Champions England's Natural Light," *MPW*, 15 Sep 1917, 1678. "Griffith Arrives in Los Angeles," *MPW*, 24 Nov 1917, 1179. E. Weitzel, "The Showmanship of D.W. Griffith," *MPW*, 9 Mar 1918, 1342–43. L.R. Harrison, "Comedies of Married Life," *MPW*, 17 Aug 1918, 977. "United Artists Association Formed," *MPW*, 25 Jan 1919, 455. "Griffith Has Not Signed with Circuit, Says Tally," *MPW*, 8 Feb 1919, 731. "Griffith to Make First Nationals," *MPW*, 15 Feb 1919, 881. E. Weitzel, "Griffith Converts the Critics," *MPW*, 21 Jun 1919, 1757–58. "Griffith Forces Purchase New York Studio Site," *MPW*, 20 Sep 1919, 1771. "Griffith Warns of Films Issued as Made by Him," *MPW*, 24 Jan 1920, 602. "Griffith Pays Brady $175,000 for Picture Rights to 'Way Down East,'" *MPW*, 7 Feb 1920, 935. "Griffith's Speech Deals Death Blow to Censorship Movement in Virginia," *MPW*, 21 Feb 1920, 1198. "D.W. Griffith Patents Apparatus for Picture Projection with Color Effects," *MPW*, 17 Apr 1920, 388. "How D.W. Griffith's New Invention for Color Effects in Projection Operates," *MPW*, 17 Apr 1920, 474. "Insuring of Griffith's Life Set a Precedent, Says Paper," *MPW*, 24 Jul 1920, 428 (insured for $500,000). "Griffith to Omit Scenes of Inhumanity in Next," *MPW*, 8 Jan 1921, 168. "Receiver Appointed for Work Company on Application of the D.W. Griffith Corporation," *MPW*, 15 Jan 1921, 289. "Griffith Changes Name of 'The Two Orphans,'" *MPW*, 31 Dec 1921, 1069 (to *Orphans of the Storm*). "An Intimate Closeup of D.W. Griffith; 'The Shakespeare of the Motion Pictures,'" *MW*, 7 Jan 1922, 11. "Mr. Griffith Rises to a Dizzy Heigfht," *MPW*, 14 Jan 1922, 168. "Griffith Goes on Tour," *MPW*, 17 Feb 1923, 653. Stanton Leeds, "We Call Your Attention to—David Wark Griffith," *Classic*, Mar 1923, 23, 83. "May Lease His Studio," *MPW*, 17 Mar 1923, 311. W.S. Bush, "Griffith Reported Planning to Make Film in Italy," *MPW*, 21 Apr 1923, 809. "Griffith Meets the President," *MPW*, 24 Nov 1923, 412. "D.W. Griffith to Italy," *MPW*, 5 Apr 1924, 470. "Griffith with F.P.-L.," *MPW*, 26 Jul 1924, 254. "Griffith Makes Denial," *MPW*, 11 Oct 1924, 494. "Griffith Explains," *MPW*, 1 Nov 1924, 63. "American Movies Depend Less of Plot, More on Life," *NYT*, 16 Nov 1924, VIII, 4:1 (European critics told Griffith to eschew melodrama; he said he abandoned theatrical plot in *Isn't Life Wonderful?*, and "has thrown his artistic and financial fortunes into picturing life. He believes that this is an abrupt and active departure from all precedent in films"). Tamar Lane, "The Famous Film Plays and What They Earned; Inside Facts on the Millions Paid for the Screen Hits," *MPC*, Sep 1925, 18–19, 80, 82 ("D.W. Griffith leads all the directors in producing pictures of high earning capacity."). Tamar Lane, "Famous Failures; The Great Screen Flops," *MPC*, Oct 1925, 24–25, 66, 68 (discusses the financial failure of *Intolerance* and other films). Sara Redway, "The Man Who Kept Nothing for Himself; Why D.W. Griffith Is Struggling to Pay His Debts," *MPC*, Oct 1925, 30–31, 70, 77. Harry Carr, "The Status of the Directors; The Men with the Megaphone," *MPC*, Nov 1925, 20–21, 80 (discusses Griffith and others). "'Untrue and Absurd,' Is Griffith's Denial of Rumors," *MPW*, 3 Apr 1926, 344. "D.W. Griffith Reported to Have British Offer," *MPW*, 13 Nov 1926, 1. "Griffith with 'U'?," *MPW*, 20 Nov 1926, 2. Tom Waller, "Griffith May Sign with United Artists; Also Considers Pathé-lKeith-Albee Offer," *MPW*, 18 Dec 1926, 1, 2. Charles Hastings, "Griffith Returning to United Artists, to Attempt Stock," *MPW*, 25 Dec 1926, 562. D.W. Griffith, "The Greatest Theatrical Force," *MPW*, 26 Mar 1927, 408. "D.W. Griffith Returns to U.A.; No M-G-M Merger, Says Schenck," *MPW*, 23 Apr 1927, 703. "Rumor Griffith to Work Abroad Another Bubble," *MPW*, 7 May 1927, 17. "Griffith on Coast," *MPW*, 28 May 1927, 254. Harold R. Hall, "Biograph, The Magic Name of the Movies," *MPC*, Jun 1927, 59, 85. "Harvard Asks Griffith Film," *MPW*, 10 Sep 1927, 81. "His Best Pictures Were the Least Expensive, Says 'D.W.,'" *MPW*, 24 Sep 1927, 232. B.F. Wilson, "He Made 'Em What They Are Today and They're Not Satisfied," *MPC*, Nov 1927, 21, 72. Russell Merritt, "Griffith Biographs for the

1990s," *Griffithiana*, 60/61 (Oct 1997), 5–15. Yuri Tsivian, "Homeless Images: D.W. Griffith in the Eye of Soviet Filmmakers," *Griffithiana*, 60/61 (Oct 1997), 51–75.

Griffith, Edward H[ilaire] [director/producer/scenarist] (b. IL, 23 Aug 1888–3 Mar 1975 [86], South Laguna CA). (Edison, 1915.) AMD, p. 148. AS, p. 477 (b. Lynchburg VA; d. LA CA). BHD, p. 186; BHD2, p. 107. FDY, pp. 427, 443 (dialogue for *Shady Lady*, 1928). IFN, p. 126. Katz, p. 514. 1921 Directory, p. 265. Edward H. Griffith, "Hopping to a Close-Up," *MPW*, 21 Jul 1917, 415–16. "The Roll of Honor," *MPW*, 10 Nov 1917, 845. "Another Director for Vitagraph," *MPW*, 13 Dec 1919, 792. "Take 90 Interiors in a Day," *MPW*, 27 Mar 1920, 2135. "Griffith Leaves Vitagraph to Direct for Cayuga Pictures," *MPW*, 10 Jul 1920, 188. "Edward H. Griffith Signed," *MPW*, 1 Nov 1924, 54. "Banks Signs Griffith," *MPW*, 22 May 1926, 311. "Edward H. Griffith with Columbia," *MPW*, 2 May 1927, 833.

Griffith, Gordon (son of **Harry S.** and **Katherine Griffith**) [actor/assistant director] (b. Chicago IL, 4 Jul 1907–12 Oct 1958 [51], Los Angeles CA; heart attack). (Vitagraph; Keystone; Metro; Monogram.) "Gordon Griffith," *Variety*, 22 Oct 1958. AMD, p. 148. AS, p. 477. BHD1, p. 231; BHD2, p. 107. IFN, p. 126. MSBB, p. 1024. Truitt, p. 134. "Metro Has Youthful Actor," *MPW*, 28 Sep 1918, 1866. "'Katherine Griffith Dies Suddenly in Los Angeles," *MPW*, 5 Nov 1921, 40 (mother, d. 17 Oct 1921; stroke).

Griffith, Harry S[utherland] (father of **Gordon Griffith**) [actor] (b. IN, 19 Jul 1866–4 May 1926 [59], Pasadena CA). m. **Katherine** (d. 1921). AS, p. 477. BHD, p. 186. Truitt 1983, p. 295.

Griffith, Katherine (mother of **Gordon Griffith**) [actress] (*née* Katherine Kierman, b. San Francisco CA, 30 Sep 1876–17 Oct 1921 [45], Los Angeles CA). m. **Harry S. Griffith** (d. 1926; son, Gordon). (Universal; National; Fox; Pickford; Lasky.) AS, p. 477. BHD, p. 186. IFN, p. 126. MSBB, p. 1034. SD.

Griffith, Kate [actress] (b. Dublin, Ireland, 1859?–13 Mar 1934 [75], East Islip NY). m. Harry S. Austin (d. 1931). "Kate Griffith," *Variety*, 20 Mar 1934.

Griffith, Lawrence *see* **Griffith, David Llewelyn Wark**

Griffith, Linda A *see* **Arvidson, Linda**

Griffith, Raymond [actor/scenarist/producer] (b. Boston MA, 23 Jan 1887?–25 Nov 1957 [70], Los Angeles CA; heart attack). "Raymond Griffith, Screen Comedian," *NYT*, 27 Nov 1957, 31:4 (age 70). "Raymond Griffith," *Variety*, 4 Dec 1957. AMD, p. 148. AS, p. 477 (b. 1890). BHD1, p. 231; BHD2, p. 107 (b. 1890). FFF, p. 60 (b. 1890). FSS, p. 132. IFN, p. 126. Katz, p. 515. MH, p. 114 (b. 1890). Truitt, p. 134 (b. 1890). "Neilan Signs Raymond Griffith," *MPW*, 22 Apr 1922, 840. "Raymond Griffith Signed," *MPW*, 7 Feb 1923, 645. "Griffith with Goldburg," *MPW*, 11 Oct 1924, 476. "Famous Bows to Demands; Will Star Raymond Griffith," *MPW*, 14 Mar 1925, 180. Elisabeth Greer, "This Serious Business of Being Funny," *MW*, 22 Aug 1925, 24–25. "Griffith Severs Relations with Paramount for Free Lance Career," *MPW*, 14 May 1927, 97. Lance Gary Lester, "Forgotten King?," *CFC*, 46 (Spring, 1975), 46–47.

Griffith, Robert E. [stage actor/TV producer] (b. Methuen MA, 1907–7 Jun 1961 [54], Port Chester NY; heart attack). "Robert E. Griffith," *Variety*, 14 Jun 1961, p. 63:1. AS, p. 477. BHD, p. 186.

Griffith, Sunderland [actress]. No data found. AMD, p. 148. "Sunderland Griffith Goes from Movies to Y.W.C.A.," *MPW*, 15 Mar 1919, 1490.

Griffith, Walter L. [publicist]. No data found. AMD, op. 148. "Selznick Hires Explotationist Griffith," *MPW*, 22 Nov 1919, 433.

Griffiths, Charles [actor]. (Lubin.) No data found.

Grimaldi, Giovanni (father of cinematographer Domenico Grimaldi) [cinematographer] (b. Naples, Italy, 1872). JS, p. 207 (in Italian silents from 1919).

Grimault, Paul [director/producer/scenarist] (b. Neuilly-sur-Seine, France, 23 Mar 1905 [extrait de naissance no. 122]–29 Mar 1994 [89], Mesnil-Saint-Denis, France [extrait de décès no. 12/1994]). AS, pp. 477–78.

Grimes, Marcella [actress] (b. Dublin, Ireland, 1900–4 Aug 1983 [83?], Dublin, Ireland). AS, p. 478.

Grimes, Tommy [stunt rider] (b. Marysville KS, 4 Nov 1887–19 Aug 1934 [46], Tujunga CA). "Tommy Grimes," *Variety*, 28 Aug 1934 (age 47). AS, p. 478. BHD, p. 186. IFN, p. 126.

Grimm, Ben [publicist]. No data found. AMD, op. 148. "Ben Grimm Joins Selznick as Team-Mate for Bartlett," *MPW*, 4 Oct 1919, 86. "Ben Grimm," *MPW*, 26 Mar 1927, 311.

Grimmer, Frank [director] (b. New York NY, 8 Aug 1886–13 Oct 1942 [56], New Rochelle NY). BHD2, p. 108.

Grimoin-Samson, Raoul [inventor/producer] (*né* Raoul Adrien Grimoin, b. Elbeuf, France, 7 May 1860 [extrait de naissance no. 134/1860]–3 Nov 1941 [81], Oissel-sur-Seine, France). AS, p. 478.

Grimwood, Herbert [stage/film actor] (b. Walthamstow, England, 7 Mar 1875–1 Dec 1929 [54], England). BHD, p. 186. AS, p. 478. IFN, p. 126. "English Actor's Film Debut," *LA Times*, 8 Jan 1920, III, 4 (to appear in Fairbanks's *When the Clouds Roll By*.).

Grinda, Bernard [actor] (b. Nice, France, 17 Jul 1866–27 Jul 1934 [68], Nice, France). AS, p. 478.

Grinde, Harry A. "Nick" [director] (b. Madison WI, 12 Jan 1894–19 Jun 1979 [85], Los Angeles CA). (MGM.) "Harry A. Grinde," *Variety*, 27 Jun 1979 ("career went from silent to sound motion pictures and television"). AS, p. 478 (b. 1891). BHD2, p. 108. IFN, p. 126.

Gripenberg, Maggie [actress/dancer] (b. Helsinki, Finland, 11 Jun 1881–28 Jul 1976 [95], Mariehamn, Finland). AS, p. 478.

Gripp[e], Harry [actor] (b. Tyrone PA, 20 Nov 1885). BHD, p. 186. George Katchmer, "Remembering the Great Silents," *CI*, 207 (Sep 1992), 43. MPG.

Grisel, Louis R[acine] [stage/film actor] (b. New Castle DE, 26 Nov 1849–19 Nov 1928 [78], Fort Lee NJ). m. Mary Johnstone. "Louis R. Grisel," *Variety*, 21 Nov 1928 ("In later years when engagements were not so easy to obtain Mr. Grisel went into pictures."). AS, p. 478. BHD, p. 186. IFN, p. 126. SD, p. 593. Truitt, p. 134.

Grismer, Joseph R[hode] [playwright/scenarist/actor/manager] (b. Albany NY, 4 Nov 1849–5 Mar 1922 [72], New York NY; from a fractured skull sustained in a streetcar accident while on his way to the movies). m. Phoebe Davis; Olive Chamberlain, ca. 1917. (Stage debut: ca. 1870.) "J.R. Grismer Killed by a Broadway Car; Veteran Theatrical Manager Struck at 106th Street, Near His Home; Twice Lambs' Shepherd [1910 and 1917]; His Wife Hurries to Hospital, Where Victim of Accident Dies Under Operation," *NYT*, 4 Mar 1922, 1:5 (rewrote *Way Down East* in a partnership with Wiliam A. Brady; wife's name given as Allen Chamberlain). "Joseph R. Grismer," *Variety*, 10 Mar 1922. AS, p. 478. SD, p. 295 (b. 1848).

Griswold, Grace [actress/author] (*née* Grace Griswold Hall, b. Ashtabula OH, 1871–13 Jun 1927 [55], New York NY). AS, p. 478 (d. 14 Jun). BHD, p. 186. IFN, p. 126. SD.

Griswold, James [actor] (b. New Britain CT, 30 Apr 1882–4 Oct 1935 [53], Glendale CA). AS, p. 478. BHD, p. 186. IFN, p. 126.

Griswold, Nathaniel [actor] (d. Nov 1918, Albany NY). BHD, p. 186.

Grock [actor/clown] (*né* Carlo Adriano Wettach, b. Moulin-de-Loveresse, Switzerland, 10 Jan 1880–14 Jul 1959 [79], Imperia, Italy). AS, p. 478. BHD, p. 186.

Groeneeld, Ben [actor] (*né* Gijsberius Pieter Marius Groeneveld, b. Breda, Netherlands, 5 May 1898–14 Feb 1962 [63], Amsterdam, Netherlands). AS, p. 478.

Gronau, Ernst Alfred [actor] b. Memel, Germany, 21 Aug 1887–11 Aug 1938 [50]). BHD, p. 196.

Gronroos, Georg [actor] (b. Helsinki, Finland, 17 Sep 1885–8 May 1927 [41], Helsinki, Finland). AS, p. 479.

Groom, Victoria [actress]. No data found. AMD, op. 148. "Miss Groom Makes Her Bow," *MPW*, 10 Jan 1920, 273.

Grooney, Ernest G. [actor/musical director] (b. London, England, 1 Nov 1880–20 Jan 1946 [65], Los Angeles CA). AS, p. 479.

Gropper, Milton H. [scenarist] (b. 25 Dec 1896–27 Oct 1955 [58], New York NY). AS, p. 479. BHD2, p. 108.

Gropper, William [artist]. No data found. AMD, op. 148. "Goldwyn Engages Artist to Push Fan Publicity," *MPW*, 30 Aug 1919, 1295.

Gross, Milton [sports columnist/gag man] (b. 1912?–9 May 1973 [61], Rockeville Center, LI NY; cardiac arrest). "Milton Gross of 'The Post' Dies; A Sports Columnist Since 1949"; Sam Goldaper, "Dignified the Athlete, *NYT*, 10 May 1973, 48:3. Dorothy Donnell, "Nize Baby End de Baby Stozz; Witt Blonde Hair de Mettresses Are Stuffed in Hollywood, end de Vemps Get Ahead by Decrees," *MPC*, Aug 1928, 25, 90.

Gross, William J. [actor] (b. 1837?–11 Apr 1924 [87?], Brooklyn NY). m. Julia Parker (d. 16 Nov 1922). "William J. Gross," *Variety*, 16 Apr 1924. AS, p. 479. BHD, p. 186. Truitt, p. 134.

Grossman, Bernard "Bernie" L. [writer of songs and special material for motion pictures] (b. Baltimore MD, 21 Aug 1885?–2 Oct 1951 [66], Los Angeles CA). "Bernard L. Grossman," *NYT*, 4 Oct 1951, 33:4 (composed *When the Parson Hands the Wedding Band for Me to Mandy Lee; There's Something About You Makes Me Love You*).

"Bernard L. Grossman," *Variety*, 10 Oct 1951 (wrote *Linger Longer Letty; That Barcarolle Tune*). AS, p. 479. ASCAP 66, p. 294. BHD2, p. 108.

Grossmith, Ena (daughter of **George Grossmith, Jr.**) [stage/film actress] (b. London, England, 14 Aug 1896–20 Mar 1944 [47], London, England). BHD1, p. 231.

Grossmith, George, Jr. (son of stage actor George Grossmith [1847–1912]; father of **Ena Grossmith**; brother of **Lawrence Grossmith**) [stage/film actor and director/founder of English Film Co.] (b. London, England, 11 May 1874–6 Jun 1935 [61], London, England). m. Adelaide Astor (*née* Gertrude Rudge, d. 1951). (English stage debut: Criterion, 1892; American stage debut: *The Shop Girl*, 1895.) "George Grossmith," *Variety*, 118, 12 Jun 1935, 70:4. AS, p. 479. BHD1, p. 231. IFN, p. 127. SD, p. 545.

Grossmith, Lawrence R. (son of stage actor George Grossmith [1847–1912]; brother of **George Grossmith, Jr.**; brother-in-law of Vernon and Irene Castle) [stage/film actor] (b. London, England, 29 Mar 1877–21 Feb 1944 [66], Woodland Hills CA). m. Coralie Blyth. (Stage debut: Court Theatre, London, 1896; Vitagraph.) "Lawrence Grossmith," *Variety*, 1 Mar 1944 (age 67). AS, p. 479. BHD1, p. 231. MSBB, p. 1024. SD. Cover, *NYDM*, 6 Jun 1915 (with Adele Rowland onstage in *Nobody Home*). *Oxford Companion to the Theatre*, 3rd ed., ed. Phyllis Harnoll (London: Oxford University Press, 1967), p. 418 (his son and daughter were both on the stage).

Grossmith, Weedon (brother of stage actor George Grossmith, 1847–1912) [portrait painter/stage and film actor/author] (*né* Walter Weedon Grossmith, b. London, England, 9 Jun 1852–14 Jun 1919 [67], London, England). (Began on stage, Liverpool, 1885.) "Weedon Grossmith," *Variety*, 20 Jun 1919, 15:2 (b. 1892). BHD, p. 187.

Grosso, Paul [actor] (b. 26 Sep 1897–5 Jul 1979 [81], Fort Bragg SC). AS, p. 479. BHD1, p. 231.

Grossowna, Helena [actress] (*née* Helena Grossowna Cieslinska, b. Torun, Poland, 24 Nov 1904). AS, p. 479.

Grot, Anton [set designer/painter] (*né* Antoncz Franztiszek Groszewski, b. Kelbasin, Poland, 18 Jan 1884–21 Mar 1974 [90], Stanton CA). (Lubin, 1917–18; Blaché; Pathé, 1918–21; Fairbanks/Pickford, 1922; De Mille, 1922–27; WB, 1927–48). AMD, op. 148. AS, p. 480 (b. 1894; d. LA CA). "Long Contract for Anton Grot," *MPW*, 12 Mar 1927, 115.

Grothers, William [casting director]. No data found. m. **Molly Malone**—div. 1927 (d. 1952). AMD, op. 148. "Divorce Follows Trial Separation," *MPW*, 3 Sep 1927, 21.

Grouer, Jones [director/producer/scenarist] (b. 1888–24 Sep 1940 [52?], Los Angeles CA). AS, p. 480.

Grovas, Jesus [actor/producer] (*né* Jesus Grovas Pontones, b. Mexico, 4 Apr 1899–10 Sep 1967 [68], Mexico City, Mexico). AS, p. 480.

Grove, Sybil [actress] (*née* Sybil Westmacott, b. Teddington-on-Thames, England, 4 Oct 1891). AS, p. 480. MPG. WFE, p. 91.

Grover, Leonard, Jr. [actor] (b. Baltimore MD, 1859?–24 Mar 1947 [88], Brooklyn NY). m. Kitty O'Neill. "Leonard Grover," *Variety*, 2 Apr 1947. AS, p. 480. BHD, p. 187.

Grover, Leonard, Sr. [playwright/manager/operatic impressario/writer] (b. Springwater NY, 9 Dec 1835–7 Mar 1926 [90], New York NY). "Leonard Grover," *Variety*, 10 Mar 1926, 45:2 (age 92; d. Brooklyn NY. Wrote *Our Boarding House*, produced 31 Jan 1877, Park Theatre, NYC, with William H. Crane and Stuart Robson). BHD, p. 187.

Groves, Charles [actor] b. Manchester, England, 22 Nov 1875–3 May 1955 [79], London, England). AS, p. 480.

Groves, Frederick [actor] (b. London, England, 8 Aug 1880–4 Jun 1955 [74], London, England). AS, p. 480. BHD1, p. 232.

Groves, George R. [editor/sound engineer] (b. England, 1902?–4 Sep 1976 [74], No. Hollywood CA). m. Jane. (WB, 1925.) "George Groves," *Variety*, 15 Sep 1976. BHD2, p. 108.

Gruell, Johnny B. [cartoonist]. No data found. AMD, op. 148. "Quacky Doodles Hooks Up with Paramount," *MPW*, 17 Feb 1917, 1050.

Gruen, James [scenarist] (b. 1894?–19 Mar 1967 [73], Woodland Hills CA). (Sennett.) "James Gruen," *Variety*, 29 Mar 1967. AS, p. 480. BHD2, p. 108. FDY, p. 427.

Gruenberg, Louis [composer] (b. Brest Litovsk, Russia, 3 Aug 1884–9 Jun 1964 [79], Los Angeles CA). AS, p. 480.

Gruendgens, Gustaf Heinrich Arnold [stage/film actor/director/producer] (b. Dusseldorf, Germany, 22 Dec 1899–7 Oct 1963 [63], Manila, Philippines; internal hemorrhages). "Gustaf Gruendgens," *Variety*, 232, 23 Oct 1963, 71:2. AS, p. 480. BHD, p. 187; BHD2, p. 109.

Grune, Karl [scenarist/director] (b. Vienna, Austria, 22 Jun 1890–2 Oct 1962 [72], Bournemouth, Germany). AS, p. 480 (b. 22 Jan). BHD2, p. 109. FDY, p. 427. IFN, p. 127.

Gruning, Ilka [actress] (b. Vienna, Austria, 4 Sep 1876–14 Nov 1964 [88], Los Angeles CA). AS, p. 480 (b. 1868). BHD1, p. 232.

Gsell, Henry [actor] (b. 1899). AMD, p. 148. BHD, p. 187. "Lily Langtry's Leading Man with Crystal," *MPW*, 6 Sep 1913, 1074.

Guaita, Mario [actor] (b. Modena, Italy, 1882–1957 [74?], Marseille, France). JS, p. 207 (in Italian silents from 1913).

Gualandri, Carlo [actor]. No data found. JS, p. 207 (in Italian silents from 1919).

Gualino, Riccardo [producer] (b. Italy, 1879–7 Jun 1964 [85?], Florence, Italy). AS, p. 481.

Guard, A. Sully [actor] (d. 21 Mar 1916, Jacksonville FL; auto accident). "Sully Guard," *Variety*, 24 Mar 1916. "Movie Actor Killed; A. Sully Guard of Thanhouser Co. Dies in Auto Collision," *MPW*, 22 Mar 1916, 11:4. "Actor Killed by Auto; A. Sully Guard of Thanhouser Co. Dies in Collision with Telephone Pole," *NYDM*, 1 Apr 1916, 23.4. AS, p. 481. BHD, p. 187. IFN, p. 127.

Guard, Kit [actor] (*né* Christen Klitgaard, b. Hals, Denmark, 5 May 1894–18 Jul 1961 [67], Los Angeles CA; cancer). (FBO.) "Kit Guard," *Variety*, 26 Jul 1961 ("vet silent pix comic and heavy"). AMD, p. 149. AS, p. 481. BHD1, p. 232. IFN, p. 127. Truitt, p. 135. "Kit Guard Has Had Varied Career," *MPW*, 3 Nov 1923, 100. "Kit Guard," *MPW*, 13 Aug 1927, 455.

Guarino, Giuseppe [director] (b. Alexandria, Italy, 27 Jan 1885–12 Feb 1963 [78], Rome, Italy). AS, p. 481. JS, pp. 207–08 (in Italian silents from 1919).

Guarracino, Umberto [actor]. No data found. JS, p. 208 (in Italian silents from 1920).

Guattari, Emilio [cinematographer]. No data found. JS, pp. 208–09 (in Italian silents from 1914).

Guazzoni, Enrico [director/producer/scenarist/set designer/costume designer] (b. Rome, Italy, 18 Sep 1876–23 Sep 1949 [73], Rome, Italy). "Enrico Guazzoni," *NYT*, 25 Sep 1949, 92:7. AMD, p. 149. AS, p. 481. BHD2, p. 109. JS, p. 208. Katz, p. 517. "Enrico Guazzoni Arrives with Print of Big Film 'Messalina,'" *MPW*, 1 Dec 1923, 496.

Gudgeon, Bertrand C. (b. OK, 1899–22 Oct 1948 [49?], No. Bergen NJ). "Bertrand C. Gudgeon," *Variety*, 27 Oct 1948 (began 1908). AS, p. 481. BHD, p. 187 (Bernard Gudgeon). IFN, p. 127. Truitt, p. 135.

Guelstorff, Max [actor] (b. Germany, 22 Mar 1882–6 Feb 1947 [64], Berlin, Germany). AS, p. 481.

Guensteq, F[erdinand] **F**[rançois] (b. Pittsburgh PA, 16 Feb 1862–28 Mar 1936 [74], Glendale CA). "F.F. Guensteq," *Variety*, 1 Apr 1936 ("in pictures for past 20 years...he became prominent for butler roles."). AS, p. 481. BHD1, p. 232. IFN, p. 127. Truitt, p. 135.

Guerin, Bruce [actor] (b. 1919?). No data found. (Metro.) AMD, p. 149. "Clever Child Actor," *MPW*, 1 Jul 1922, 27 (3 years old).

Guerini, Camille [actor] (*né* Camille Adolphe Georges Le Pape, b. Lorient, France, 29 Jun 1900–15 Apr 1963 [62], Clichy-la-Garenne, France [extrait de décès no. 882/1963]). AS, p. 482.

Guest, Edgar A. [writer/poet] (b. Birmingham, England, 20 Aug 1881–5 Aug 1959 [77], Detroit MI). AS, p. 482. IFN, p. 127. WWWA.

Guest, Frederick [actor] (d. 20 Jan 1922, New York NY). (Bio-graph; Reliance.) "Frederick Guest," *Variety*, 27 Jan 1922. AMD, p. 149. BHD, p. 187. "Mr. Frederick Guest," *MPW*, 23 Mar 1912, 1071; *MPW*, 20 Apr 1912, 215 (resigned from Champion).

Guest, Harry R. [scenarist]. No data found. AMD, p. 149. "Guest to Write Stories for Nelson Productions, Inc.," *MPW*, 17 May 1919, 1031.

Guhl, George [actor] (b. St. Louis MO, 27 Sep 1875–27 Jun 1943 [67], Los Angeles CA). AS, p. 482.

Guide, Paul [actor/writer] (b. Paris, France, 1890). AS, p. 482.

Guihan, Frances E. [title writer/scenarist]. No data found. m. Ivan Behrendt Kahn, 1919. AMD, p. 149. FDY, pp. 427, 443. "Scenarist Weds," *MPW*, 5 Jul 1919, 76.

Guilbert, Yvette [actress/singer] (*née* Emma Laure Esther Guilbert, b. Paris, France, 20 Jan 1865–3 Feb 1944 [79], Aix-en-Provence, France [extrait de décès no. 123]). m. Max Schiller. "Yvette Guilbert," *Variety*, 9 Feb 1944 (age 76). AS, p. 483. BHD1, p. 232. IFN, p. 127. SD, p. 547.

Guilfoyle, James Ancel [actor] (b. MI, 18 Apr 1892–13 Nov 1964 [72], Woodland Hills CA). AS, p. 483.

Guilfoyle, Paul [actor] (b. Jersey City NJ, 14 Jul 1902–27 Jun 1961 [58], Los Angeles CA). AS, p.483.

Guillot de Saix [scenarist/author] (*né* Léon

Marie Guillot, b. Paris, France, 25 May 1885–4 Sep 1964 [79], Paris, France [extrait de décès no. 3/224]). AS, p. 482.

Guillou, Ernest Marie Clément [composer] (b. Rennes, France, 4 Oct 1894 [extrait de naissance no. 1060). AS, p. 483.

Guimond, Lou F. [publicist] (b. New York NY, 1886–23 May 1950 [64?], New York NY). BHD2, p. 109.

Guinan, Texas [actress] (*née* Mary Louise Cecilia Guinan, b. Waco TX, 12 Jan 1884–5 Nov 1933 [49], Vancouver, British Columbia, Canada; intestinal infection). m. (1) Jack Moynahan; (2) **Julian Johnson** (d. 1965); (3) George E. Townley. Glenn Shirley, *Hello, Sucker!; The Story of Texas Guinan* (Stillwater OK: Western Publications, 1992). "Texas Guinan Dies After Operation; Succumbs in a Hospital to Which She Was Taken from Theatre in Vancouver; Coined Broadway Slang; After a Girlhood on Ranch, She Became Colorful Figure in Night Club Life Here," *NYT,* 6 Nov 1933, 19:1. "Texas Guinan," *Variety,* 7 Nov 1933. AMD, p. 149. AS, p. 483. BHD1, p. 233. BR, pp. 36–38. FSS, p. 132. IFN, p. 127 (age 48). MH, p. 114. 1921 Directory, p. 223 (b. 1891). SD. Truitt, p. 135. "World Engages Texas Guinan," *MPW,* 19 Oct 1918, 365. "Miss Texas Guinan Is a Native Daughter of Texas," *MPW,* 22 Mar 1919, 1694 (b. 15 miles from Waco). "Texas Guinan Signs with Bull's Eye to Make Series of Twenty-Six Two-Reel Western Films," *MPW,* 13 Dec 1919, 797. "Texas Guinan to Appear in a Feature," *MPW,* 6 Mar 1920, 1677. "Texas Guinan Signed by Kremer to Star in the Making of Eight Five Reel Westerns Annually," *MPW,* 30 Oct 1920, 1247. "Texas Guinan Sues Reelcraft Pictures for $50,000 Over Bull's eye Contract," *MPW,* 24 Sep 1921, 402. Texas Guinan, "Pictures of New York's Night Club Life," *Pictures,* Jun 1926, 26–27, 69, 82–87; Part II, Jul 1926, 28–29, 67, 112–20; Part III, Aug 1926, 34–35, 69, 87–94; Part IV, Sep 1926, 38–39, 69, 85–90, 92–93. Cedric Belfrage, "Hollywood Gives Texas Guinan a Great Big Foot; A Surging Crowd of Six People Welcomes Her Back to the Coast," *MPC,* Nov 1928, 22, 68 ("This dump has changed some. When I was here making westerns ten years ago, we used to go down in a mob to meet returning friends at the station.").

Guiol, Fred L. [writer/director/producer/composer] (b. San Francisco CA, 1898?–23 May 1964 [66], Bishop CA). (Griffith; Roach, 1921.) "Fred Guiol," *Variety,* 27 May 1964. AS, p. 483. BHD2, p. 109.

Guise, Thomas S. [actor] (b. Detroit MI–d. 1930). AMD, p. 149. BHD, p. 187. IFN, p. 127. "Tom Guise Has Big Part," *MPW,* 24 Apr 1920, 589. George Katchmer, "Remembering the Great Silents," *CI,* 242 (Aug 1995), 35–36.

Guisol, Henri [actor] (*né* Henry Paul Julien Bonhomme, b. Aix-en-Provence, France, 12 Oct 1904 [extrait de naissance no. 350/1904]–11 May 1994 [89], Saint-Raphael, France). AS, p. 483.

Guissart, René [cinematographer/director] (b. Paris, France, 24 Oct 1888–19 May 1960 [71], Monaco [extrait de décès no. 171]). AMD, p. 149. AS, p. 483. FDY, p. 459. "Mayer Engages Rene Guissart," *MPW,* 28 Feb 1920, 1499. "Cameraman Declines to Photograph Hamon Film," *MPW,* 14 May 1921, 164. Photocopy of death certificate supplied by André Siscot, Brussels.

Guisti, Roy *see* **D'Arcy, Roy**

Guitry, Lucien Germain (father of **Sacha Guitry**) [actor] (b. Paris, France, 13 Dec 1860–1 Jun 1925 [64], Paris, France). AS, p. 483.

Guitry, Sacha (son of **Lucien Guitry**) [actor/producer/scenarist/director/humorist] (*né* Alexandre Georges Pierre Guitry, b. St. Petersburg, Russia, 21 Feb 1885–24 Jul 1957 [72], Paris, France). m. (1) **Charlotte Lyses** (d. 1956); Yvonne Printemps; (5) Lana Marconi (widow). "Sacha Guitry," *Variety,* 207, 31 Jul 1957, 119:1. BHD1, p. 233; BHD2, p. 109.

Guitton, Jean [actor/scenarist] (b. France, 29 Mar 1889–15 Apr 1973 [84], Juan-les-Pins, France). AS, p. 484 (Jean Guittoni). BHD2, p. 109.

Guitty, Madeline [actress] (*née* Marguerite Madeleine Guichard, b. Corbeilessonnes, France, 5 Jul 1870 [extrait de naissance no. 87/1870]–12 Apr 1936 [65], Paris, France; septicemia). AS, p. 484. BHD1, p. 233.

Gulick, Paul [publicist/title writer]. No data found. AMD, p. 149. FDY, p. 443. "Universal Publicity Staff," *MPW,* 26 Sep 1914, 1756–57. "Paul Gulick," *MPW,* 20 Nov 1915, 1471. "Rev. Gulick Dies," *MPW,* 10 May 1924, 123 (father, Rev. Hervey Gulick, d. 24 Apr 1924 [78], Salisbury CT). "Gulick Wins at Golf," *MPW,* 9 Jul 1927, 79.

Gullan, Campbell [actor/director] (b. Glasgow, Scotland–d. 1 Dec 1939, Glasgow, Scotland). BHD1, p. 233; BHD2, p. 109 (d. NY NY). SD, p. 547. Truitt 1983, p. 298.

Gulliver, Dorothy [actress: Wampas Star, 1928] (b. Salt Lake City UT, 6 Sep 1908–23 May 1997 [88], Escondido CA). m. (1) Chester William DeVito (**William DeVite**), May? 1926—div. 1932; (2) Jack Proctor, Mar 1947 (d. 1976). (Universal; WB.) AMD, p. 149. Ankerich, *Broken Silence,* pp. 140–50. BR, pp. 156–58. FSS, p. 133. Katz, pp. 518–19. Roy Liebman, *From Silents to Sound,* p. 133. Ragan, *Who's Who in Hollywood,* p. 669. Chapter 10, "Dorothy Gulliver," *BS,* pp. 140–50 (includes filmography). "DeVite—Gulliver," *MPW,* 29 Nov 1926, 3. "Her First Lead," *MPW,* 16 Jul 1927, 157. "Dorothy Gulliver Signed," *MPW,* 10 Sep 1927, 79. Joe Collura, "Dorothy Gulliver; Western Heroine Corrals Fans in Raleigh," *CI,* 113 (Nov 1984), 23–24.

Gulsdorff, Max [actor] (b. Sovetsk, Russia, 23 Mar 1882–6 Feb 1947 [64], Berlin, Germany). BHD1, p. 609.

Gunn, Charles [actor] (b. WI, 31 Jul 1883–6 Dec 1918 [35], Los Angeles CA; influenza). "Charles Gunn," *Variety,* 13 Dec 1918. AMD, p. 149. AS, p. 484. BHD, p. 187. IFN, p. 128. "Charles Gunn, New Leading Man for Triangle," *MPW,* 13 Jan 1917, 215. "Gunn in Barriscale Company," *MPW,* 23 Mar 1918, 1646. "Gunn to Support Bessie Barriscale," *MPW,* 30 Mar 1918, 1829. "Obituary," *MPW,* 28 Dec 1918, 1496 (age 36).

Gunn, Earl [actor] (b. MI, 8 May 1901–14 Apr 1963 [61], San Francisco CA). AS, p. 484. BHD1, p. 233.

Gunn, Thomas Patrick [vaudeville/stage/film/radio actor] (b. Cleveland OH, 1872?–11 Dec 1943 [71], Brooklyn NY; bronchial pneumonia). m. Rose Hazlin. (Stage debut: *San Toy.*) "Thomas Patrick Gunn; Character Actor, 71, Sheriff in Original 'Show Boat,' Dies," *NYT,* 12 Dec 1943, 69:5.

Gunnarsson, Algot [actor] (b. 1883–1937 [54?]). BHD1, p. 609.

Gunning, F.C. [publicist/general manager]. No data found. AMD, p. 149. "Gunning Joins Olcott," *MPW,* 6 Jun 1914, 1410. "Who Wants Gunning?," *MPW,* 17 Oct 1914, 359.

Gunning, Wid [executive/producer/writer/founder of *Wid's Daily*] (b. OH, 30 Jan 1886–5 Apr 1963 [77], Los Angeles CA). AMD, p. 149. BHD2, p. 109. MPG. "Future of the Industry Lies in the Hands of the Directors, Wid Gunning Declares," *MPW,* 31 Dec 1921, 1067. "Wid Gunning," *MPW,* 7 May 1927, 19.

Gurgo-Salice, Pierre [producer] (b. Casale Monferrato, Italy, 12 Aug 1894–1 Jan 1974 [79], Rome, Italy). AS, p. 484 (produced films in France).

Gurney, Edmund [actor] (b. Ireland, 1851?–14 Jan 1925 [73], New York NY). m. Olive Ripman; (2) Beatrice May Cooper (d. 1948). "Edmund Gurney," *Variety,* 28 Jan 1925. AS, p. 484. BHD, p. 187. IFN, p. 128. SD. Truitt, p. 135. In *Tol'able David.*

Gustafsson, Alva (sister of **Greta Garbo**) [actress] (b. Stockholm, Sweden, 1902–24 Jun 1926 [23], Stockholm, Sweden; cancer). AS, p. 484 (b. 1904). BHD, p. 187 (b. 1904). In *Tva Konungår* (*Two Kings*), Sweden, 1925.

Guter, Johannes [director] (b. Riga, Latvia, 25 Apr 1881–1967 [86?]). BHD2, p. 109.

Guterson, Mischa [composer] (b. 1879–27 Sep 1951 [72?], Los Angeles CA). BHD2, p. 109.

Guthrie, Charles W. [actor] (b. 1871?–30 Jun 1939 [68], Washington DC). "Charles W. Guthrie," *Variety,* 5 Jul 1939. AS, p. 485. BHD, p. 187. IFN, p. 128.

Guthrie, Jane [scenarist]. No data found. AMD, p. 149. "Jane Guthrie a Goldwyn Scenario Reader," *MPW,* 28 Apr 1917, 607.

Guthrie, Thomas Anstey [actor/director/producer] (b. England, 1856–11 Mar 1934 [78?], London, England). AS, p. 485.

Guthrie, Tyrone [actor/director/producer] (b. Tunbridge Wells, England, 2 Jul 1900–15 May 1971 [70], Dublin, Ireland). AS, p. 485. BHD2, p. 109.

Guthrie, William L. [executive] (b. 1882–9 Nov 1959 [77?], Burbank CA). BHD2, p. 109.

Guttman, Arthur [composer] (b. Vienna, Austria, 1 Jul 1877–3 Jun 1956 [78], Vienna, Austria). BHD2, p. 110.

Gutmann, Arthur [composer] (b. Vienna, Austria, 21 Aug 1891–4 Sep 1945 [54], Los Angeles CA). AS, p. 485.

Guy-Blaché, Alice [director/producer] (*née* Alice Ida Antoinette Guy, b. Sainte-Mandé, France, 1 Jul 1873 [extrait de naissance no. 66]–24 Mar 1968 [92], Mahwah NJ). m. **Herbert Blaché** (d. 1953). (Gaumont, 1897; Solax, 1910; Pathé.) AS, p. 485 (d. Wayne NJ). BHD2, p. 24 (b. 1875). IFN, p. 128 (b. 1875). Katz, p. 519 (b. 1873). MSBB, p. 1044 (b. 1878). Spehr, p. 116 (1873–1968). WWVC, pp. 61–62. "The Solax Company," *MPW,* 8 Oct 1910, 812. "Solax Enlarging Studios," *MPW,* 4 Nov 1911, 386. "Solax Engages Prominent Comedian," *MPW,* 2 Dec 1911, 732. ""Feature Production," *MPW,* 17 May 1913, 711. "The Director—Present and Future," *MPW,* 4 Apr 1914, 49. "Alice Blaché, "Woman's Place in Photoplay Production," *MPW,* 11 Jul 1914, 195. "Mme. Blache Endangered; Narrowly Escapes Injury When Tank Bursts at Fort Lee Studio," *NYDM,* 5 Jul 1914, 28:1 (while filming *The Mysterious Bride* with Kenneth D. Harlan). "Perret Engages Mme. Blaché," *MPW,* 2 Nov 1918, 602. "Madame Alice Blaché to Make 'Peace' Film" *MPW,* 7 Dec 1918, 1106. Anthony Slide, ed., *The Memoirs of Alice Guy Blaché,* trans. Roberta and Simone Blaché (Metuchen NJ: Scarecrow Press, Inc., 1986). Mrs. Blaché states that she was born "on the first of July, 1873," but this is corrected in Slide's *Early Women Directors* (NY: A.S. Barnes and Co., 1977), p. 15.

Gwenn, Edmund (brother of **Arthur Chesney**) [actor] (*né* Edmund Kellaway, b. Glamorgan, Wales, 26 Sep 1874–6 Sep 1959 [84], Woodland Hills CA). m. Minnie Terry (d. 1964). (AA, 1947.) "Edmund Gwenn Is Dead at 84; Famed for His Character Roles," *NYT,* 7 Sep 1959, 15:2. "Edmund Gwenn," *Variety,* 23 Sep 1959. AS, p. 485. BHD1, p. 233 (b. 1875). IFN, p. 128 (b. London, England, 1875). SD. Truitt, p. 135 (b. 1875). John Roberts, "Forever Santa—Edmund Gwenn," *CI,* 160 (Oct 1988), 20 (b. 1877). Eric Niderost, "Edmund Gwenn, Everybody's St. Nick," *CI,* 196 (Oct 1991), C2, C4, C6.

Gwynne, Dorothy [actress]. No data found. (Metro.) (In the 4-reel *The Yellow Streak.*)

Gwynne, Harold William [actor] (d. Aug 1927, Kew Gardens NY). BHD, p. 187. IFN, p. 128.

Gwyther, Geoffrey [actor] (b. 1890–27 Jul 1944 [54?]). BHD, p. 187.

Gynt, Arne [actor]. No data found. AMD, p. 149. "Kaj and Arne Gynt," *MPW,* 6 Nov 1915, 1151.

Gynt, Kaj [actor]. No data found. AMD, p. 149. "Kaj and Arne Gynt," *MPW,* 6 Nov 1915, 1151.

Gyorgy, Istvan [director] (b. Budapest, Hungary, 29 Nov 1899–14 Apr 1958 [58], Budapest, Hungary). AS, p. 486.

Gys, Leda [actress] (*née* Giselda Lombardi, b. Rome, Italy, 10 Mar 1892–2 Oct 1957 [65], Rome, Italy). m. **Gustavo Lombardo** (son, producer Goffredo Lombardo; d. 1951). AS, p. 486. BHD, p. 187. JS, p. 211 (in Italian silents from 1913).

H

Haack, Käthe [actress] (*née* Lisbeth Minna Sophie Isolde Haack, b. Berlin, Germany, 8 Aug 1896–5 May 1986 [89], Berlin, Germany). m. Heinrich Schroth (d. 1945). AS, p. 487 (b. 11 Aug 1897). BHD1, p. 234 (b. 11 Aug 1892). Vittorio Martinelli, "Kino-Lieblinge," *Griffithiana,* 38/39 (Oct 1990), 14.

Haagen, Al H. [actor] (b. 1871–8 Mar 1953 [82?], Los Angeles CA). AS, p. 487.

Haagen, Margarete [actress] (b. Nuremberg, Germany, 29 Nov 1889–14 Dec 1966 [77], Los Angeles Co. CA). AS, p. 487. BHD1, p. 234.

Haas, Dolly [actress] (*née* Dorothy Clara Louise Haas, b. Hamburg, Germany, 29 Apr 1910–16 Sep 1994 [84], New York NY). AS, p. 487. BHD1, p. 234.

Haas, Hugo [actor/director/producer/scenarist] (b. Brno, Czechoslovakia, 19 Feb 1901–1 Dec 1968 [67], Vienna, Austria; asthma). "Hugo Haas," *Variety,* 18 Dec 1968. AS, p. 487. BHD1, p. 234; BHD2, p. 110. IFN, p. 128 (age 66).

Haas, Robert M. [art director] (b. Newark NJ, 1889?–17 Dec 1962 [73], Costa Mesa CA). (Fox; WB.) "Robert M. Haas," *Variety,* 26 Dec 1962. AMD, p. 150. AS, p. 487. BHD2, p. 110 (b. 1887). "Robert M. Haas Renews Contract as Art Director with Famous Players," *MPW,* 9 Oct 1920, 780. "Haas to Plan Sets in Hollywood Plant," *MPW,* 9 Jul 1921, 226.

Haas, Walter [cameraman]. No data found. FDY, p. 459.

Haas, Willy [scenarist]. No data found. FDY, p. 427.

Habay, André [actor/director] (b. France, 1883–1941 [58?], Rome, Italy). AS, p. 487. JS, pp. 211–12 (in Italian silents from 1914).

Hackathorne, George [actor] (*né* George Hackthorne, b. Pendleton OR, 13 Feb 1896–25 Jun 1940 [44], Los Angeles CA). "George Hackathorne; Silent Films Actor Had Title Role in 'Little Minister,'" *NYT,* 27 Jun 1940, 23:4. "George Hackathorne," *Variety,* 3 Jul 1940. AS, p. 487. BHD1, p. 234. FFF, p. 119. IFN, p. 128. MH, p. 114 (b. 1898). Truitt, p. 136. Richard Wickstead, "If It's in You—You'll Get There, Says George Hackathorne; Close-up of noted young character actor who left his small town home in Oregon and went to Hollywood to become a screen star," *MW,* III, 22 Sep 1923, 7, 31. Alma Talley, "He Wants to Kiss the Heroine; So George Hackathorne Casts Aside His Character Make-Up Box," *MW,* IV, 1024, 17, 34.

Hackel, A.W. [producer] (b. 1883–21 Oct 1959 [76?], Los Angeles CA). AS, p. 487.

Hackenschmidt, George [actor] (b. Estonia, 1877–19 Feb 1968 [90?], London, England). BHD, p. 188.

Hacker, Maria [actress] (b. Germany, 1903?–20 Feb 1963 [59], Sherman Oaks CA; heart attack). m. (1) Inger Nathensen (d. 1925); (2) Lauritz Melchior. "Maria Hacker," *Variety,* 27 Feb 1963. IFN, p. 128.

Hackett, Albert M. [actor/playwright/scenarist] (son of **Florence Hackett**; brother of **Raymond Hackett**) [playwright/scenarist/actor] (b. New York NY, 16 Feb 1900–16 Mar 1995 [95], New York NY; pneumonia). m. (1) Frances Goodrich, 1931—div. (d. 1984); (2) Gisele Svetlik, 1985. (Lubin.) Mel Gussow, "Albert Hackett, 95, Half of Prolific Drama Team," *NYT,* 18 Mar 1995, 10:4 (Pulitzer Prize with Goodrich for *The Diary of Anne Frank*). Susan Shields, "Albert Hackett," *Variety,* 3 Apr 1995, p. 140 (actor in silents). AS, p. 487. BHD1, p. 234; BHD2, p. 110.

Hackett, Arline or **Arleen** [stage/film actress]. No data found. AMD, p. 150. "Three New Stars for Essanay," *NYDM,* 1 Sep 1915, 28:1 (to appear in *In the Palace of the King,* to be released Oct 1915, with E.J. Radcliffe and Edgar Lewis. "Five thousand extra people will be used, including over a hundred professional dancing girls."). "Personal; Hackett," *NYDM,* 15 Sep 1915, 5:2 (Arleen Hackett; with photo). "Arline Hackett," *MPW,* 9 Oct 1915, 265.

Hackett, Charles [actor] (b. Worcester MA, 21 Nov 1888–1 Jan 1942 [53], Jamaica NY). BHD1, p. 234.

Hackett, Flora Mae [actress]. No data found. AMD, p. 150. "Famous Beauty Is Aid to Archer Bros." Business," *MPW,* 23 Jul 1921, 397.

Hackett, Florence (mother of **Albert** and **Raymond Hackett**) [stage/film actress] (b. Buffalo NY, 1882?–21 Aug 1954 [72], New York NY). (Lubin.) "Florence Hackett," *Variety,* 25 Aug 1954. AMD, p. 150. AS, p. 487. BHD, p. 188. IFN, p. 128. SD, p. 551. Truitt, p. 131. Hector Ames, "Chats with the Players; Florence Hackett, of the Lubin Company," *MPSM,* Sep 1912, 132. "Florence Hackett," *MPW,* 4 Apr 1914, 39. "Florence Hackett," *MPW,* 21 Nov 1914, 1064. "Florence Hackett with United," *MPW,* 12 Jun 1915, 1757.

Hackett, James K[eteltas] [stage/film actor] (b. Wolfe Island, Ontario, Canada, 8 Sep 1869–8 Nov 1926 [57], Paris, France; cirrhosis of the liver). m. (1) actress Mary Mannering (d. 1953); (2) Beatrice Mary Beckley. "James K. Hackett, Actor, Dies in Paris; American Star Planned to Appear Before British King and Queen Today; Had Inherited $1,200,000; Death Due to Liver Malady—Ashes to Be Brought Here—Loss Shocks the Stage," *NYT,* 9 Nov 1926, 27:1. "James K. Hackett," *Variety,* 10 Nov 1926. AMD, p. 150. AS, p. 487. BHD, p. 188. IFN, p. 128. SD. Truitt, p. 136. "Hackett Gets a Theatre; To Control the Savoy for His Own Productions After Oct 1," *NYT,* 31 Mar 1905, 9:4 (with Frank McKee). "James K. Hackett Again Faces the Camera," *MPW,* 12 Jul 1913, 192. "$1,171,847 for Hackett; Actor Must Wait at Least a Year Before Receiving Share of Estate," *NYDM,* 24 Jun 1914, 10:1 (from Mrs. Minnie Hackett Trowbridge, his aunt. "Other relatives theeatened contests, but these were all dropped when it was made clear that no contest would stand in the courts."). "Hackett Gets Another Fortune," *NYDM,* 9 Dec 1914, 9:2 (to get $197,858 from the estate of his uncle, Francis Emory Trowbridge. As Mrs. Trowbridge was his sole beneficiary, "his estate reverts to Mr. Hackett, the next of kin."). "James K. Hackett Returns to Screen," *MPW,* 20 Jul 1918, 367.

Hackett, Jeanette [actress] (b. 1898–16 Aug 1979 [81?], New York NY). BHD, p. 188.

Hackett, Karl [actor] (b. Carthage MO, 5 Sep 1893–24 Oct 1948 [55], Sawtelle CA). AS, p. 488.

Hackett, Lillian [actress] (b. Chicago IL, 11 Oct 1896–28 Feb 1973 [76], Los Angeles CA; cerebral hemorrhage). m. William Schary. "Lillian Hackett," *Variety,* 7 Mar 1973. AS, p. 488. BHD, p. 188. IFN, p. 128.

Hackett, Raymond (son of **Florence Hackett**; brother of **Albert Hackett**) [actor] (b.

New York NY, 15 Jul 1902–7 Jul 1958 [55], Los Angeles CA). m. Myra Hampton, 1927; **Blanche Sweet** (d. 1986). "Raymond Hackett," *Variety,* 9 Jul 1958. AS, p. 488. BHD1, p. 234. FSS, p. 133. IFN, p. 128. Truitt, p. 136.

Hackett, Walter [scenarist] (b. 1876–20 Jan 1944 [67?], New York NY). BHD2, p. 110.

Hadank, Gunther Eugen Reinhold [actor] (b. Berlin, Germany, 20 Oct 1892). AS, p. 488.

Haddock, William Frederick, "Silent Bill" [director of Edison's "Casey" series/producer] (b. Portsmouth NH, 27 Nov 1877–30 Jun 1969 [91], New York NY). m. Rosa Koch, Nov 1913. (Edison; Méliès; Eclair; All Star Co.; Life Photo Film Corp.; Kalem; Gotham Film Co.) AMD, p. 150. AS, p. 488 (d. LA CA). BHD, p. 188; BHD2, p. 110.. IFN, p. 129. 1921 Directory, p. 265. Spehr, p. 138. George D. Proctor, "Oh, It's an Interesting Life!" *MPN,* 29 Nov 1913 (m. Koch that Wednesday). "William Haddock with the Holland Film Company," *MPW,* 19 Sep 1914, 1654. "William F. Haddock; Well-Known Moving Picture Director," *MPS,* 26 Feb 1915, 27. "William Frederick Haddock," *MPW,* 27 Feb 1915, 1297. "William Frederick Haddock," *MPW,* 12 Jun 1915, 1753. "Briefs of Biography: Famed for His Silence...," *NYDM,* 16 Jun 1915, 32:1. *Motography,* 26 Jun 1915, 1063. "'Silent Bill's' First Baby," *MPW,* XXV, 7 Aug 1915, 975 (b. 20 Jul 1915). "Film Fun in Florida; Sunday Shows with Invited Audiences, Balls and Banquets Galore," *NYDM,* 11 Dec 1915, 25:1 ("On the second anniversary of 'Silent Bill' Haddock's [so named because his voice cannot be heard above the roar of cannons] wedding," the Gaumont players presented him with an elaborate desk set. They, in turn, threw a dance for them the next night at the Burbridge Hotel). William F. Haddock, "Directing in Other Days Was no Snap," *MPW,* 10 Mar 1917, 1522. "'Silent Bill' Haddock Is Assistant to Miller," *MPW,* 15 Oct 1927, 419.

Haddon, Peter [stage/film actor] (*né* Peter Tildsley, b. Rawtenstall, England, 31 Mar 1898–7 Sep 1962 [64], London, England). m. Rosalie Courtneidge (d. 1926), sister of Cicely Courtneidge. "Peter Haddon," *Variety,* 228, 19 Sep 1962, 71:2. AS, p. 488. BHD1, p. 234. IFN, p. 129.

Hadfield, Harry [director]. No data found. AMD, p. 150. "Harry Hadfield with Lasky," *MPW,* 30 Oct 1915, 808.

Hading, Janie [actress] (*née* Jane Trefrouret, b. France, 1859–1934 [75?], France). AS, p. 488.

Hadley, Alberta Elizabeth [actress] (b. 1863?–8 Jan 1931 [67], Chicago IL). m. "Alberta Hadley," *Variety,* 14 Jan 1931. AS, p. 488.

Hadley, Bert [actor/makeup artist] (b. Walla Walla WA, 12 Apr 1882–30 Dec 1968 [86], Woodland Hills CA). (Began 1915.) BHD1, p. 610; BHD2, p. 110. George Katchmer, "Remembering the Great Silents," *CI,* 246 (Dec 1995), 44.

Hadley, Hap [actor] (*né* Alvan C. Hadley, b. Findlay IL, 16 Mar 1895–4 Aug 1976 [81], New York NY). BHD, p. 188.

Hadley, S[amuel] **H**[opkins] **"Hopp"** [scenarist/publicist] (b. New York NY, 1878–11 Oct 1943 [65?], Winter Park FL). m. Catherine McDonnell, 3 Aug 1912. (Reliance; Mutual.) AMD, p. 150. "Hopp Hadley Walks the Plank," *MPW,* XIII, 10 Aug 1912, 554. "Here's Hopp Hadley," *MPW,* 26 Oct 1912, 340–41. F.J. Beecroft, "Publicity Men I Have Met...," *NYDM,* 14 Jan 1914, 48 (*see* Beecroft, Chester for full citation). "Hopp Hadley with United," *MPW,* 27 Mar 1915, 1945. "Hopp Hadley to Open Airdome," *MPW,* 1 May 1915, 734. Hopp Hadley, "Our 'Hopp' Some Pioneer Picture Man," *MPW,* 15 Jul 1916, 421. "Hopp Hadley Resigns from Mutual," *MPW,* 7 Apr 1917, 105. "Hopp Completing a Cinema-Symphony," *MPW,* 4 May 1918, 699. "Hopp Picks Subject for Cinema-Symphony," *MPW,* 11 May 1918, 835. Hopp Hadley, "Press Agent's Debt to His Profession," *MPW,* 20 Jul 1918, 344. "Anderson Signs Hadley," *MPW,* 5 Jan 1924, 30. "S.H. Hadley," *MPW,* 26 Mar 1927, 311.

Haefeli, Charles "Jockey" [stuntman/assistant director] (b. New York NY, 16 Jul 1887–12 Feb 1955 [67], Los Angeles CA). "Charles (Jockey) Haefeli," *Variety,* 23 Feb 1955 (age 66). AS, p. 488. BHD1, p. 235; BHD2, p. 110.. IFN, p. 129. Truitt, p. 136 (b. 1889).

Haenel, Gunther Hans Ludwig [actor/director] (b. Dresden, Germany, 1898–1973 [75?], Germany). AS, p. 488.

Haesaerts, Luc (brother of **Paul Haesaerts**) [director/scenarist/composer] (b. Boom, Belgium, 15 Feb 1901–1 Feb 1974 [72], Brussels, Belgium). AS, p. 488.

Haesaerts, Paul (brother of **Luc Haesaerts**) [director/scenarist] (b. Boom, Belgium, 21 Sep 1899–1974 [75?], Brussels, Belgium). AS, p. 488.

Hafter, Robert M[ark] [actor] (b. London, England, 7 Jan 1897–9 Aug 1955 [58], Los Angeles CA). m. Kitty O'Neill. "Robert M. Hafter," *Variety,* 17 Aug 1955 (age 50). AS, p. 488. IFN, p. 129.

Hagan, James P. [scenarist] (b. Lowell MA, 1888–1 Sep 1947 [59?], Cincinnati OH). AS, p. 488 (b. 1872). BHD2, p. 110.

Hageman, Richard [composer] (b. Leeuwarden, Netherlands, 9 Jul 1882–6 Mar 1966 [83], Beverly Hills CA). AS, p. 488.

Hagen, Charles F. [actor] (b. MI, 19 Dec 1871–13 Jun 1958 [86], Los Angeles CA). (Griffith.) "Charles F. Hagen," *Variety,* 25 Jun 1958. AS, p. 488 (b. 1862). BHD1, p. 235. IFN, p. 129. Truitt, p. 136.

Hagen, Margarethe [actress] (b. Germany, 1890–14 Dec 1966 [76?], Gruenwald, Germany). AS, p. 488.

Hagen, Walter [actor] (b. Rochester NY, 21 Dec 1892–5 Oct 1969 [76], Traverse City MI). BHD1, p. 235.

Hagenah, Harry [writer/director]. No data found. AMD, p. 150. "Hagenah Joins Mayer Staff," *MPW,* 6 Mar 1920, 1655.

Hagenbruch, Charlotte [actress] (b. Austria, 1895–19 May 1968 [72], Lichtenstein). BHD, p. 188. IFN, p. 129.

Hager, Clyde [actor] (b. Mitcehll SD, 2 Dec 1887–21 May 1944 [56], Harrisburg PA; heart attack). "Clyde Hager," *Variety,* 24 May 1944. AS, p. 489. BHD1, p. 235. IFN, p. 129.

Hagerman, Arthur Q. [publicist/title writer]. No data found. AMD, p. 150. FDY, p. 443. "From Office Boy to Boss," *MPW,* 3 Jan 1925, 74.

Haggar, William [director/producer] (b. Dedham, England, 23 Mar 1851–1924 [73?], Wales). AS, p. 489. BHD2, p. 110.

Haggard, H[enry] **Rider** [writer/scenarist] (b. Bradenham Hall, Ipswich, Norfolk, England, 22 Jun 1856–14 May 1925 [68], London, England). m. Mariana Margitson, 1879. Philip Leibfried, *Rudyard Kipling and Sir Henry Rider Haggard on Screen, Stage, Radio and Television* (Jefferson NC: McFarland, 2000). "Rider Haggard Dies in London Hospital; Author of 'She,' 'King Solomon's Mines' and Many Other Novels Was Nearly 69; He Was Knighted in 1912; An Authority on Agriculture and Sociology—Served on Government Missions," *NYT,* 15 May 1925, 19:4 (Danish ancestors from the family of Aagard). AS, p. 489 (b. 28 Jun). "H. Rider Haggard's Mission; Coming to America to Study Salvation Army Land Settlements," *NYT,* 24 Jan 1905, 5:2. "Rider Haggard Here; To Get Suggestions for Rhodes South African Colony Scheme," *NYT,* 3 Mar 1905, 2:6 (came with daughter to inspect Salvation Army Industrial and Agricultural colonies in the U.S.). "Slum Talk by Haggard; Life of Family Only Three Generations, Says Novelist—Lauds Japan," *NYT,* 12 Mar 1905, 9:3 ("As a commissioner of the British government at a luncheon in Washington DC on 11 Mar, Haggard was "to investigate city garden work, colonization schemes, and the general problem of how 'to bring the landless man to the manless land.'" It had been almost proved, Haggard said, that three generations in the London slums "would wipe out a family absolutely." Japan's success, he said, was due to its affinity with the land.). "Rider Haggard's Prediction; Conquering Eastern People May Sweep Away Western Civilization," *NYT,* 2 Apr 1905, 1:6 (he gave an address at the University of CA at Berkeley on 1 Apr. "He drew a vivid picture of the wretchedness of life in London, and said: ¶'Unless the evils brought about by this congestion of the masses in cities is stopped, Western civilization is in danger of being swept away by a conquering Eastern people, who have the virtues of their country and are not afflicted with Western evils.'"). "Haggard Off for England; Talks on Pier of Economic Problems That He Has Met," *NYT,* 20 Apr 1905, 6:2 ("He was much interested in the municipal ownership agitation."). Philip Leibfried, "H. Rider Haggard on the Silent Screen," *The Silent Film Newsletter,* II (Nov 1993), 141–43. Philip Leibfr[i]ed, "H. Rider Haggard on the Screen," *FIR,* Sep/Oct 1995, 20–29.

Hagney, Frank S. [actor] (b. Sydney, Australia, 20 Mar 1884–25 Jun 1973 [89], Los Angeles CA). AS, p. 489. BHD1, p. 235. IFN, p. 129. George A. Katchmer, "Forgotten Cowboys and Cowgirls—Part III," *CI,* 174 (Dec 1989), 38, 48.

Hague, Clair [executive] (b. Brantford, Ontario, Canada, 18 Jul 1885–9 Feb 1945 [59], Toronto, Ontario, Canada). BHD2, p. 110.

Haguet, André Eugène Henri [director/producer/scenarist] (b. Suresnes, France, 9 Nov 1900 [extrait de naissance no. 198/1900]-20 Aug 1973 [72], Cannes, France). AS, p. 489.

Hahn, Philip [actor/director] (b. Amsterdam, Holland, 1884–4 Aug 1976 [92?], NY). (FP-L; All Star; Fox; Equitable; Metro; International.) AMD, p. 150. BHD, p. 188. "Philip Hahn," *MPW,* 26 Jun 1915, 2101.

Haid, Grit [actress] (*née* Grete Haid, b. Vienna, Austria, 14 Mar-d. 13 Aug 1938, Schwarzwald, Germany). AS, p. 489.

Haid, Liane [actress/dancer] (*née* Juliane Haid, b. Vienna, Austria, 16 Aug 1895). m. Baron von Haymerle. (Possible film debut: *Mitt Herz Und Hand Fur Vaterland,* 1915; Art Film Co.) AS, p. 489. Ragan 2, pp. 676–77. Garth Pedler, "The Silent Films of Liane Haid," *CI,* 124 (Oct 1985), 51–52, 54. "Idols of Berlin," *MPC,* Feb 1926, 41 (photo and quip).

Haik, Jacques (brother of **Maurice Haik**) [producer] (b. Tunisia, 1893–30 Aug 1950 [57?], Paris, France; cerebral hemorrhage on a train). AS, p. 490.

Haik, Maurice (brother of **Jacques Haik**) [producer] (b. Bone, Algeria, 17 Jul 1888-ca. Apr 1956 [67]). AS, p. 490.

Haine, Horace J. [actor] (b. Detroit MI, 1868?–26 Sep 1940 [72], New York NY). m. Maude LeRoy. "Horace J. Haine," *Variety*, 2 Oct 1940 (acted at Ft. Lee NJ). AS, p. 490. BHD, p. 188. IFN, p. 129. Truitt, p. 136.

Haines, Bert [cameraman]. No data found. FDY, p. 459.

Haines, Louis [actor] (b. 1877–25 Jul 1929 [52?], New York NY). BHD, p. 188.

Haines, Rhea [actress] (b. IN, 2 Oct 1894–12 Mar 1964 [69], Los Angeles CA). "Rhea Haines [Mrs. Rhea Haines Case]," *Variety*, 25 Mar 1964. AS, p. 490. BHD, p. 188. IFN, p. 129. Truitt, pp. 129–30. George Katchmer, "Remembering the Great Silents," *CI*, 242 (Aug 1995), 36.

Haines, Robert T[errell] (cousin of **Earle Foxe**) [stage/film actor/director/producer] (b. Muncie IN, 3 Feb 1868–6 May 1943 [75], New York NY [Death Certificate Index No. 10896]). m. (1) Genevieve Greville; (2) Mrs. William McDowell. (Equitable; Gaumont.) "Robert T. Haines, on Stage 40 Years; Actor, Director, Producer Dies in His Hotel Apartment," *NYT*, 7 May 1943, 19:2. "Robert T. Haines," *Variety*, 12 May 1943. AS, p. 490. BHD1, p. 235 (b. 1870). IFN, p. 129. MH, p. 114. SD. Truitt, p. 137 (b. 1870). "Haines with Gaumont," *NYDM*, 20 Nov 1915, 31:2 (to be in *The Secret Agent*, 3 reels, at Jacksonville FL).

Haines, Mrs. Robert T. [advisor]. No data found. AMD, p. 150. "Enter 'Social Mentor,'" *MPW*, 21 Aug 1915, 1303.

Haines, William [actor/interior decorator] (b. Staunton [Shenandoah Valley] VA, 1 Jan 1900–26 Dec 1973 [73], Santa Monica CA; cancer). Companion, James Shields (d. 5 Mar 1974 [68] of acute barbituate intoxication; "Goodbye to all of you who have tried so hard to comfort me in my loss of William Haines, whom I have been with since 1926. I now find it impossible to go it alone—I am much too lonely."). William J. Mann, *Wisecracker; The Life and Times of William Haines, Hollywood's First Openly Gay Star* (NY: Viking Penguin, 1998). (MGM.) "William Haines, 73, Film Comedian, Dies," *NYT*, 28 Dec 1973, 32:3. "William Haines," *Variety*, 16 Jan 1974. AMD, p. 150. AS, p. 490. BHD1, p. 235 (d. LA CA). FSS, p. 134. HCH, p. 83. IFN, p. 129. "New Juvenile Actor," *MPW*, 31 Mar 1923, 572. "Haines Re-Signed," *MPW*, 3 Apr 1926, 344. Dorothy Spensley, "The Kidding Kid," *Photoplay* (Oct 1926), 81–82, 117. Charles Paton, "One in a Million; Just the Story of a Level-Headed Young Fellow Trying to Get Along in the World," *MPC*, Jan 1927, 59, 86, 88. "William Haines Wins Starring Contract from Metro-Goldwyn," *MPW*, 5 Feb 1927, 426. "William Haines," *MPW*, 2 Apr 1927, 477. "M-G-M Players Hurt," *MPW*, 3 Sep 1927, 10. Malcolm H. Oettinger, "The Young Man of the Hour," *Picture Play* (Aug 1928), 34, 92. Ralph Wheeler, "The Bad Boy of Hollywood," *Screenland*, Aug 1929, 46–47, 112. Marquis Busby, "The Wisecracker Reveals Himself," *Photoplay* (Sep 1929), 68–69, 122–124; (Oct 1929), 56–57, 127–28. Madeline Glass, "He's Cut Out the Cut-Ups," *Picture Play* (Sep 1929), 74, 110, 114. Robert Fender, "Ballyhoodooed Bill," *Motion Picture* (Aug 1930), 66. 96. Helen Louise Walker, "Who's Popular in Hollywood?," *Motion Picture Classic* (Mar 1931), 68–69, 95. Charles Grayson, "The Life and Times of a Wisecracker," *Motion Picture Classic* (Apr 1931), 48, 91, 95. Constance Blake, "Why Billy Haines Stayed at Metro," *Movie Mirror* (Jan 1932), 23–24, 130. Ruth Biery, "The Assassins of Hollywood," *Silver Screen* (Mar 1934), 24–25. Gloria Emerson, "Million-Dollar Sparkle Added to Envoy's Residence," *NYT*, 22 Nov 1969. Murray Summers, "The Film Career of William Haines (Part One)," *Filmograph*, III, No. 3 (1973), 2–19, 49 ("During a jobless stretch, he earned money posing for advertising photos. One day [ca. 1922], walking down Broadway, he was approached by a woman talent scout for Samuel Goldwyn; she asked him whether he would like to go into the movies and mentioned a 'New Faces' contest. Borrowing clothes from his friend again, he had some portraits made and entered the contest. Without ever having entertained the notion of getting into either theater or film, within three months he would leave for Hollywood, his prize having been a contract with the Goldwyn studio." Includes filmography.); Part II, No. 4 (1973), 21–41, 49 (concludes filmography). Larry Lee Holland, "William Haines," *FIR*, Mar 1984, 165–72. Eve Golden, "William Haines; Fresh as Paint," *CI*, 246 (Dec 1995), 26, 28.

Hainia, Marcelle [actress] (b. Paris, France, 13 Nov 1896–15 Aug 1968 [71], Paris, France). AS, p. 490.

Haisman, Irene [actress] (b. Rochester, England, 7 Mar 1897–19 Aug 1950 [53], Los Angeles CA). BHD1, p. 235.

Hajos, Karl [composer] (b. Budapest, Hungary, 1889–1 Feb 1950 [60?], Los Angeles CA). AS, p. 490.

Halati, Rafi [actor] (b. Teheran, Iran, 1899–1981 [82?], Teheran, Iran). AS, p. 490.

Hale, Alan, Sr. (father of Alan Hale, Jr.) [actordirector] (*né* Rufus Edward MacKahan, b. Washington DC, 10 Feb 1892–22 Jan 1950 [57], Los Angeles CA; pneumonia). m. **Gretchen Hartman**, 1914 (d. 1979; daughter, Jean, b. 27 Dec 1916; daughter, Karen, b. 1917; son, Alan Hale, Jr., 1918–1990). (Champion Motion Picture Co., 1911; Lubin.) "Alan Hale, Actor in Popular Films; Player 40 Years Last Seen in 'Inspector General'—'Covered Wagon' Villain," *NYT*, 23 Jan 1950, 23:3. "Alan Hale," *Variety*, 25 Jan 1950. AMD, p. 150. AS, p. 490. BHD1, p. 235; BHD2, p. 110. FSS, p. 135. GK, pp. 340–57. IFN, p. 129. Truitt, p. 137. Slide, p. 160. "Alan Hale, Biograph," *MPW*, 5 Dec 1914, 1391. Thornton Fisher, "Alan Hale, Biograph," *MPW*, 6 Nov 1915, 1124. "Alan Hale," *MPW*, 7 Apr 1917, 75. "Lucy Fox and Alan Hale Added to Cast," *MPW*, 4 Aug 1923, 414. "Alan Hale, Director," *MPW*, 6 Dec 1924, 553. "Hale to Direct Valentino," *MPW*, 14 Mar 1925, 172. "Hale Will direct 'Rubber Tires,'" *MPW*, 18 Sep 1926, 175. "Alan Hale, an Actor Again, in One Photoplay," *MPW*, 19 Feb 1927, 569. "Hale Goes Back to His Megaphone," *MPW*, 26 Feb 1927, 649. "Alan Hale Acting Again," *MPW*, 30 Jul 1927, 332. "Alan Hale," *MPW*, 17 Sep 1927, 155. Gladys Hall, "The Osteopath to Success; This Is the One That Alan Hale Chose—and Traveled Without Even So Much as Stubbing a Thumb," *MPC*, Jun 1928, 25, 90. George A. Katchmer, "The Jovial Actor Alan Hale," *CI*, 122 (Aug 1985), 20–22, 63. Richard E. Braff, "An Index to the Films of Alan Hale," *CI*, 194 (Aug 1991), 16–18, 22–23; Part II, *CI*, 195, (Sep 1991), 26, 28, 30, 32. Eric Niderost, "Alan Hale: The Indispensable Sidekick," *CI*, 227 (May 1994), 12 *et passim*. George Katchmer, "Remembering the Great Silents," *CI*, 239 (May 1995), 38.

Hale, Albert W. [producer/director] (b. Bordeaux, France, 1 Jan 1882–27 Feb 1947 [65], Los Angeles CA). m. Julia F. Johnson, 31 Jan 1918. AMD, p. 151. AS, p. 490. BHD2, p. 110. "New Majestic Director," *MPW*, XIV, 19 Oct 1912, 231. "Albert W. Hale Joins Majestic," *MPW*, 26 Jul 1913, 434. "Director Albert Hale a Benedict," *MPW*, 16 Feb 1918, 9769.

Hale, Binnie (sister of **Sonnie Hale**) [actress/singer] (b. *née* Bernice Hale Monro, b. Liverpool, England, 22 May 1899–10 Jan 1984 [84], Hastings, England). AS, p. 490.

Hale, Bobbie [actor] (b. London, England, 27 May 1886–27 Sep 1977 [91], Woodland Hills CA). AS, p. 490. BHD1, p. 236 (Bobby). IFN, p. 129.

Hale, Creighton [stage/film actor] (*né* Patrick Fitzgerald, b. County Cork, Ireland, 24 May 1882–9 Aug 1965 [83], So. Pasadena CA). (b. 1888). m. Victoire Lowe, NYC, 1912–26 (children: Robert Lowe Hale and Creighton Hale, Jr.); (2) Kathleen Bering. (Pathé; Metro.) "Creighton Hale, Actor, Is Dead; Star of the Silent Screen Was 83," *NYT*, 12 Aug 1965, 27:3. AMD, p. 151. AS, p. 491 (b. 14 May). BHD1, p. 236. FSS, p. 135. IFN, p. 129. Katz, p. 524 (b. 14 May). MH, p. 114. MSBB, p. 1024. SD. Truitt, p. 137. "Creighton Hale Back with Pathé," *MPW*, 16 Jan 1915, 371. "Gossipy Items," *MPS*, 12 Feb 1915, 32 (Hale claimed to be 25 years old). "Creighton Hale, the Pathé Actor," *MPW*, 10 Jul 1915, 289. "Briefs of Biography; He Aids the Exploiting Elaine," *NYDM*, 4 Aug 1915, 25:1 (Hale got into pictures when a Pathé director noticed him on Broadway in *Indian Summer*). "Hale an Aviator," *MPW*, 29 Jul 1916, 772. "Creighton Hale Signed for Pathé Pictures," *MPW*, 17 Mar 1917, 1786. "Creighton Hale," *MPW*, 5 May 1917, 782. "The Hero with the Irish Smile; Creighton Hale, the Popular Pathe Hero, Who Possesses Cleverness, Youth, and Personal Charm," *The Picture Show*, No. 11, 12 Jul 1919, 8–9 (b. 1892; the son of an actor, Hale began on the stage at age 5). "Creighton Hale, Serial Actor, Joins with World," *MPW*, 30 Aug 1919, 1334. "On the Set and Off," *MW*, 4 Oct 1924, 19, 29 (Hale fired a gun at his wife and she sued for divorce). Dorothy Donnell, "From Hollywood to You," *MPS*, 28 Jul 1925), 15–16, 35 (in court, Mrs. Hale claimed "that her husband earns eight hundred a week and should give her half." She admitted to the court that she did leave him, but that "he was right back of me with a shotgun at the time!" Hale's accountants and auditors tried to prove that he lived on a net of $35 a week. "The rest goes, so he says pathetically, to business managers, press agents, clothiers, haberdashers and photographers."). "Creighton Hale Signed to Long Contract by Associated," *MPW*, 20 Feb 1926, 718. June Lee, "Dan Cupid's Bulletin Board," *Paris and Hollywood Screen Secrets Magazine*, Aug 1927, 36 (Victoria Lowe announced her engagement to John Miljan. She was given custody of her and Hale's children.).

Hale, George C. [showman: Hale's Tours] (b. Colton [St. Lawrence County] NY, 28 Oct 1849–14 Jul 1923 [73], Kansas City MO). AS, p.

491. Raymond Fielding, "Hale's Tours: Ultrarealism in the Pre-1910 Motion Picture," *Film Before Griffith*, John L. Fell, ed. (Berkeley CA: Univ. of CA Press, 1983), pp. 116–30.

Hale, Georgia [actress] (*née* Georgia Theorora Hale, b. St. Joseph MO, 25 Jun 1905–7 Jun 1985 [79], Los Angeles CA). *Charlie Chaplin; Intimate Close-Ups* (Metuchen NJ: Scarecrow Press, 1995). (Chaplin.) AS, p. 491. BHD, p. 188. FSS, p. 136. Katz, p. 524 (began 1924). Sarah Edmonton, "The Girl with the Hungry Eyes; The Extra Girl Who Leaped to Fame," *MPC*, Jul 1925, 60–61, 85–86. Dunham Thorp, "Hale-Fellow-Well-Met; Georgia Hale Lives the Moment by Being Natural and Accepting Gracefully What Life Has to Offer," *MPC*, Sep 1926, 58–59, 82. George Katchmer, "Forgotten Cowboys and Cowgirls—Part XIII," *CI*, 190 (Apr 1991), C6.

Hale, John F. [stage/film actor] (b. Baltimore MD, 1859?–4 May 1947 [88], Englewood NJ). m. Margot Merriam (*née* Case; d. 1942). "John Hale," *Variety*, 7 May 1947. AS, p. 491. BHD1, p. 236. IFN, p. 129. SD.

Hale, Jonathan [actor] (*né* Jonathan Hatley, b. Ontario, Canada, 29 Mar 1891–28 Feb 1966 [74], Woodland Hills CA; suicide by shooting). "Jonathan Hale," *Variety*, 9 Mar 1966. AS, p. 491 (b. 21 Mar). BHD1, p. 236 (b. 21 Mar). IFN, p. 129 (b. 21 Mar).

Hale, Louise Closser [stage/film actress] (*née* Louise Closser, b. Chicago IL, 13 Oct 1872–26 Jul 1933 [60], Los Angeles CA; cerebral hemorrhage). m. Walter Hale (d. 1917). (Film debut: *The Hole in the Wall*, Paramount.) "Louise Closser Hale," *Variety*, 1 Aug 1933. AS, p. 491. BHD, p. 126 (b. 1870). IFN, p. 129. SD, p. 555.

Hale, Richard [actor] (*né* Richard S. Bagg, b. Springfield MA-d. 15 Nov 1916, New York NY; apoplexy). "Richard S. Bagg," *Variety*, 20 Oct 1916. AS, p. 491.

Hale, Richard [actor] (b. Rogersville TN, 16 Nov 1892–18 May 1981 [88], Los Angeles CA). BHD1, p. 236.

Hale, Robert [stage/film actor/singer] (*né* J. Robert Hale-Munro, b. Newton Abbot, Devonshire, England, 25 Mar 1874–18 Apr 1940 [66], Maidenhead, Berkshire, England; from injuries in a car crash.) m. Belle Reynolds. "Robert Hale," *Variety*, 24 Apr 1940 ("he never came to America"). AS, p. 491. BHD1, p. 236. IFN, p. 129. SD, p. 555. Truitt 1983.

Hale, Robertson [actor] (b. England, 1891–1967 [76?], England). AS, p. 491.

Hale, Sonnie (brother of **Binnie Hale**) [actor/director/scenarist] (*né* John Robert Hale-Munro, b. London, England, 1 May 1902–9 Jun 1959 [57], London, England). m. **Evelyn Laye** (d. 1996). AS, p. 491. BHD1, p. 236; BHD2, p. 111.

Hales, Ethelbert D[unlop] [stage/film actor] (b. New Zealand, 1882?–26 Jan 1933 [50], Riverdale NY). m. Molly Pearson (d. 1959). "Ethelbert D. Hales," *Variety*, 31 Jan 1933. AS, p. 491. BHD, p. 189. SD.

Hales, Norman St. Clair [actor] (b. New Zealand, 1887–1 Jan 1929 [41?], New York NY). AS, p. 491.

Haley, Jack [actor] (father of Jack Haley, Jr.) (*né* John Joseph Haley, b. Boston MA, 10 Aug 1898–6 Jun 1979 [80], Los Angeles CA; after heart attack on 1 Jun). m. actress Florence McFadden (d. 1996; son, Jack, Jr., b. 25 Oct 1933). Eric Pace, "Jack Haley, Actor, 79, Dead; Was Tin Woodman in 'Oz,' [1939]" *NYT*, 7 Jun 1979, IV, 23:2. "Jack Haley," *Variety*, 13 Jun 1979. AS, p. 491 (b. 1899). BHD1, p. 236 (b. 1900). IFN, p. 129 (age 79).

Hall, Alexander C. [stage/film actor/director] (b. Boston MA, 11 Jan 1894–30 Jul 1968 [74], San Francisco CA; stroke). m. Lola Lane; (2) Marjorie M. Hunter. (Paramount; 1st National.) "Alexander Hall," *Variety*, 7 Aug 1968. AS, p. 491. AMD, p. 151. BHD, p. 189; BHD2, p. 111 (b. 1895). IFN, p. 129. Katz, pp. 524–25 (began 1914). SD. Truitt, p. 138. "Assistant Director Al Hall Signed by Robert Broadwell," *MPW*, 28 Aug 1920, 1185.

Hall, Alfred Henry [actor] (b. Brockton MA, 2 Dec 1879–21 Apr 1943 [63], Los Angeles CA; heart attack on the set of *McLeod's Folly*, Goldwyn). "Alfred Henry Hall," *Variety*, 28 Apr 1943. AS, p. 491 (b. Boston MA). IFN, p. 129 (age 61).

Hall, Ben[jamin J.] [actor/assistant director] (b. Brooklyn NY, 18 Mar 1899–20 May 1985 [86], No. Hollywood CA). BHD1, p. 236; BHD2, p. 111. Maltin, *Our Gang*, p. 74.

Hall, Bert [actor]. No data found. AMD, p. 151. "Lieutenant Hall Talks to Ohio Business Men," *MPW*, 29 Mar 1919, 1834.

Hall, Cameron [actor] (b. Hull, England, 6 Jan 1897-ca. Apr 1965 [68?]). AS, p. 492.

Hall, Charles "Cliff" [actor] (*né* Robert Clifford Hall, b. Birmingham, England, 4 Oct 1894–6 Oct 1972 [78], Englewood NJ; throat cancer). "Cliff Hall," *Variety*, 6 Oct 1972 (age 76). AS, p. 492 (b. Brooklyn NY). IFN, p. 129. Katz, p. 525.

Hall, Charles D. [stage/film actor/art director] (b. Birmingham, England, 19 Aug 1899–7 Dec 1959 [60], No. Hollywood CA). m. Dolly Gray (d. 1937). (Chaplin; Roach.) "Charles Hall," *Variety*, 16 Dec 1959. AS, p. 492 (under Charles R. Hall and Charlie Hall). BHD1, p. 237; BHD2, p. 111 (d. 13 Apr). IFN, p. 129. Katz, p. 525. SD. Truitt, p. 138.

Hall, Donald [actor] (b. Murree, North West Province, East India, 14 Aug 1867?–18 Jul 1948 [80], Woodland Hills CA). m. Frankie Mann. (Vitagraph; Ivan.) AMD, p. 151. AS, p. 492 (b. 1878; d. 25 Jul). BHD1, p. 237 (b. 1868). IFN, p. 129. L.C.R., "Chats with the Players; Donald Hall, of the Vitagraph Company," *Motion Picture Magazine*, Jan 1915, 108–11. "Donald Hall," *MPW*, 23 Jun 1917, 1945. *Motion Picture Magazine*, Jul 1918, 98 (b. East India, 1888).

Hall, Dorothy [actress] (b. Bradford PA, 1906?–3 Feb 1953 [47], New York NY). m. (1) Ned Andrews; (2) Albert D. Heath. "Dorothy Hall," *Variety*, 11 Feb 1953. AS, p. 492. BHD1, p. 237. IFN, p. 129. SD, p. 557. Truitt, p. 138.

Hall, Edna [stage/film actress] (b. 1886?–17 Jul 1945 [59], Culver City CA). "Edna Hall," *Variety*, 25 Jul 1945 ("In silent picture days, she appeared in *Lights of Paris, Shadows of Paris*, and other films after an earlier career in legit productions and stock companies."). AS, p. 492. BHD1, p. 237. IFN, p. 129.

Hall, Ella Augusta (mother of Richard Emory [d. 1994] and Ellen Hall) [actress] (b. New York NY, 17 Mar 1896–3 Sep 1981 [85], Canoga Park CA). m. **Emory Johnson**, 6 Sep 1917, Santa Barbara CA. (Biograph; Reliance; Universal.) "Ella Hall," *Variety*, 27 Jan 1982. AMD, p. 151. AS, p. 492. BHD1, p. 237 (b. NJ, 1897). MSBB, p. 1034 (b. NY, 1897). 1921 Directory, p. 222. "Ella Hall," *MPW*, 9 May 1914, 797. "Ella Hall a Bluebird," *MPW*, 17 Jun 1916, 2018. "Ella Hall," *MPW*, 14 Apr 1917, 279. "Ella Hall to Marry Emory Johnson," *MPW*, 28 Jul 1917, 628. "Universal Players' Contracts Expire," *MPW*, 1 Jun 1918, 1267. "Ella Hall to Support Stone in Screen Debut," *MPW*, 13 Jul 1918, 228. "Ella Hall Mother of Boy," *MPW*, 15 Mar 1919, 1473 (b. 29 Jan 1919). Ruth Mabrey, "Are Society Pictures More Popular Than Homespun Variety? 'No!,' Says Emory Johnson," *MW*, 8 Dec 1923, 23, 27. Thomas Fullbright, "Ella Hall," *CFC*, 21 (Summer, 1968), 12–13.

Hall, Emmett Campbnell [scenarist] (b. Tolbottom GA, 18 Nov 1882). (First scenario, *Indian Blood*, Lubin, 1910.) AMD, p. 151. BHD2, p. 111. Epes Winthrop Sargent, "The Photoplaywright," *MPW*, 14 Feb 1914, 802. "Gave Hall a Dinner," *MPW*, XXIV, 8 May 1915, 919. "Hall Leaves Lubin," *NYDM*, 14 Jul 1915, 24:1 (after 2 1/2 years; wrote *The Beloved Vagabond* and *Road o' Strife* series). "Hall Wins Universal Scenario Contest," *MPW*, 21 Oct 1916, 415. "Emmett Campbell Hall Joins Goldwyn," *MPW*, 24 Mar 1917, 1935. "Emmett Hall with Goldwyn," *MPW*, 31 Mar 1917, 2116. Emmett Campbell Hall, "The Trouble Is," *MPW*, 21 Jul 1917, 399–400. "Hall Leaves Goldwyn," *MPW*, 25 Aug 1917, 1212. Edward Azlant, "Screenwriting for the early silent film: forgotten pioneers, 1897–1911," *Film History*, 9 (1997), 243.

Hall, Ethel [actress/stunt woman] (b. 1905–28 Jun 1927 [22?], Merced CA; doing a dangerous stunt). AS, p. 492. BHD, p. 189. IFN, p. 129 (d. 30 Jun).

Hall, Evelyn [actress] (b. Harrogate, Yorkshire, England, 24 Dec ?). AMD, p. 151. AS, p. 492 (b. 1958). "Evelyn Hall," *MPW*, 23 Jul 1927, 257.

Hall, Frank [stage manager] (b. Trenton NJ–d. 25 Nov 1959, Trenton NJ). m. "Frank Hall," *Variety*, 9 Dec 1959. AS, p. 492.

Hall, Gabrielle [actress] (b. MO, 18 Apr 1898–1 Jan 1967 [68], El Cajon CA). AS, p. 492. BHD1, p. 237. IFN, p. 130. Truitt, p. 138.

Hall, Mrs. George [title writer/scenarist]. No data found. FDY, pp. 427, 443.

Hall, George Edwardes [actor/durector/scenarist] (b. Brooklyn NY, 1872–1 Jul 1922 [50?], Los Angeles CA). BHD, p. 189; BHD2, p. 111.

Hall, George Edwardes, Jr. [actor] (b. Brooklyn NY, 1901-Dec 1991 [90?]). BHD, p. 189.

Hall, George F. [actor] (b. 1867?–15 Oct 1934 [67], NY). "George F. Hall," *Variety*, 6 Nov 1934. AS, p. 492.

Hall, George M. [actor] (b. Sweden, 1890?–24 Apr 1930 [40?], Saranac Lake NY). "George M. Hall," *Variety*, 30 Apr 1930. AS, p. 492. BHD, p. 189. Truitt, p. 138.

Hall, Geraldine [actress] (b. IL, 31 Jan 1905–18 Sep 1970 [65], Woodland Hills CA; heart attack). m. **Porter Hall** (d. 1953). AS, p. 492.

Hall, Hal [publicist/director]. No data found. AMD, p. 151. "Hal Hall's New Color Classics," *MPW*, 15 Oct 1927, 433.

Hall, Henry Leonard [actor] (b. MO, 5 Nov 1876–11 Dec 1954 [78], Calabasas CA). AS, p. 492.

Hall, Howard [actor] (b. MI, 30 May 1867–25 Jul 1921 [54], Long Beach CA). "Howard Hall," *Variety*, 29 Jul 1921. AMD, p. 151. AS, p. 492 (b. Michigantown IN). BHD, p. 189. IFN, p. 130.

"Howard Hall Now a Gaumont Star," *MPW,* 19 Feb 1916, 1137. "Howard Hall, Leading Man for Emily Stevens," *MPW,* 3 Nov 1917, 683.

Hall, J. Albert [stage/film actor] (b. Calcutta, India, 1884–18 Apr 1920 [36?], Cumberland MD). m. Betty. "J. Albert Hall Dies," *Variety,* 23 Apr 1920. AMD, p. 151. AS, p. 492. BHD, p. 189. IFN, p. 130. "J. Albert Hall Has Great Record," *MPW,* 22 Jul 1916, 647. "J. Albert Hall Back to Stage," *MPW,* 23 Sep 1916, 1974.

Hall, James [actor] (*né* James E. Brown, aka James Hamilton, b. Dallas TX, 22 Oct 1900–7 Jun 1940 [39], Jersey City NJ; cirrhosis). m. Irene Gardner. (Film debut: *The Man Alone,* 1923.) "James Hall, Star of Silent Movies; Famous Leading Man, 1926 to 1930, in 'Hell's Angels'; Had Role with Jean Harlow—Went from $2,500 a Week to Small Night Club Jobs," *NYT,* 8 Jun 1940, 15:3. "James Hall, Once Film Star, Dies Broke at 39," *Variety,* 12 Jun 1940. AMD, p. 151. AS, p. 492. BHD1, p. 237. FSS, p. 136. IFN, p. 130. Katz, p. 325. Truitt, p. 138. "Hall Signed by Paramount," *MPW,* 24 Apr 1926, 581. George Mitchell, "One of the Boys That Ran Away—James Hall," *Screenland,* Sep 1927, 18–19, 103–04. Dorothy Spensley, "Knight Life in Hollywood; If You Think It Is the Woman Who Pays, Ask James Hall," *MPC,* Sep 1928, 42, 77 ("It's tough to be a knight in errant Hollywood."). George A. Katchmer, "The Short-Lived Career of James Hall," *CI,* 158 (Aug 1988), 7, 9–10. Arnold Berson, "James Hall," *FIR,* Jan/Feb 1992, 16–22.

Hall, James Norman [actor] (*né* James Norman Weight, b. IA, 22 Apr 1887–6 Jul 1951 [64], Vaipoopoo, Tahiti [extrait de décès no. 8/1951]). AS, p. 492.

Hall, Jane [actress] (b. Winona MN, 15 Feb 1880–13 Oct 1975 [95], St. Paul MN). AS, p. 492. BHD, p. 189. IFN, p. 130 (b. 1800).

Hall, Jefferson [actor] (b. AL, 1875?–26 May 1945 [70], New York NY). m. **Gertrude Maitland** (d. 1938). "Jefferson Hall," *Variety,* 30 May 1945. AS, p. 492. IFN, p. 130.

Hall, John [actor] (*né* Michael Braughal, b. 1878?–25 Apr 1936 [58], Los Angeles CA). "Michael Braughal," *Variety,* 29 Apr 1936. AS, p. 492. BHD, p. 189. IFN, p. 130.

Hall, John [actor] (b. Dallas TX, 22 Oct 1900–7 Jun 1940 [39], Jersey City NJ). AS, p. 492. Truitt, p. 138.

Hall, Jule [actress]. No data found. AMD, p. 151. "Jule Hall," *MPW,* 29 Jul 1922, 342.

Hall, Ken[neth] George [actor/director/producer/scenarist] (b. Sydney, New South Wales, Australia, 22 Feb 1901–8 Feb 1994 [92], Sydney, New South Wales, Australia). Mike Harris, "Ken Hall," *Variety,* 14 Feb 1994, 56A:2 (first Australian to win an Academy Award—as producer of *Kokoda Front Line,* 1942). AS, p. 493. BHD2, p. 111.

Hall, Laura Nelson [actress] (b. Philadelphia PA, 11 Jul 1876). BHD, p. 189.

Hall, Lillian [stage/film actress] (b. Brooklyn NY, 15 Mar 1896–18 Mar 1959 [63], Los Angeles CA; overdose from barbituate intoxication). m. **Glenn Tryon,** 19 Oct 1924. (Talmadge; World; Fox; Triangle; Brady Radin Co.; Eminent Authors Pictures; Haworth; D.N. Schwab Prods.) AMD, p. 151. AS, p. 493. BHD, pp. 35–36; 189. MSBB, p. 1034 (b. 1897). "Ingenue of Rapf Picture Greeted by Harlem Crowd," *MPW,* 8 Feb 1919, 802. "World Signs Lillian Hall," *MPW,* 21 Jun 1919, 1790. Billy H. Doyle, "Lost Players," *CI,* 159 (Sep 1988), 22.

Hall, Lou [actor] (*né* Louis F. Balzer, b. 1871?–18 Jun 1921 [50], Chicago IL; blood poisoning after tonsilectomy). "Lou Hall," *Variety,* 24 Jun 1921. AS, p. 493.

Hall, Louis Leon [actor] (b. Oneida NY, 1879–17 Apr 1930 [50?], Houghton ME). m. Ethel Robertson. "Louis Leon Hall," *Variety,* 21 May 1930. AS, p. 493. BHD, p. 189. Truitt 1983.

Hall, Mary [stage/film actress] (b. 1876?–8 Dec 1960 [84], New York NY). m. Urbain J. Ledoux. "Mary Hall," *Variety,* 14 Dec 1960 (Mrs. Mary Hall Ledoux). AMD, p. 151. AS, p. 493. SD. "Mary V. Hall," *MPW,* 9 Mar 1912, 853. "Mary Hall to Play Opposite George Walsh," *MPW,* 22 Nov 1919, 429.

Hall, Maud [actress[(b. New Orleans LA, 1881–1 May 1938 [57?], Liberty NY). AS, p. 493. BHD, p. 189.

Hall, May [actress] (b. 11 Sep 1877–21 Dec 1962 [85]). BHD, p. 189.

Hall, Mayre [actress]. No data found. AMD, p. 151. "Mayre Hall," *MPW,* 14 Nov 1914, 913.

Hall, Nelson L. [stuntman/actor] (b. Philadelphia PA, 1881?–28 Jul 1944 [63], Philadelphia PA). "Nelson L. Hall," *Variety,* 2 Aug 1944. AS, p. 493. BHD, p. 189. IFN, p. 130.

Hall, Oliver M. [executive] (d. Oct 1915). BHD2, p. 111.

Hall, Pauline [stage/film actress] (*née* Pauline Fredericka Schmidgall, b. Cincinnati OH, 1859?–29 Dec 1919 [60], Yonkers NY). m. (1) Edward R. White; (2) George B[rinton] MacLellan (d. 1932). "Pauline Hall," *Variety,* 2 Jan 1920. AS, p. 493. IFN, p. 129. SD.

Hall, Pauline [actress] (b. 1891–6 Oct 1974 [83?], Los Angeles CA; leukemia). AS, p. 493 (d. Reseda CA). BHD1, p. 610.

Hall, Philip [actor] (b. 1900–2 Jul 1983 [83?]). BHD1, p. 237.

Hall, Porter [actor] (*né* Clifford Porter Hall, b. Cincinnati OH, 19 Sep 1888–6 Oct 1953 [65], Los Angeles CA). m. **Geraldine** (d. 1970). AS, p. 493.

Hall, Ray [news editor]. No data found. AMD, p. 151. "Hearst-Vitagraph News Editor," *MPW,* 25 Dec 1915, 2352. "Hall Returns to Edit Screen Telegram," *MPW,* 19 Oct 1918, 363. "To Direct 'Fox Varieties,'" *MPW,* 14 Feb 1925, 710. "Ray Hall Will Give Pathé News 'Inside,'" *MPW,* 24 Dec 1927 (WPCH Radio). "Ray Hall, on Pathé News," *MPW,* 31 Dec 1927, 14.

Hall, Sheridan [director]. No data found. AMD, p. 152. "Hall Making Debut as Director," *MPW,* 7 Apr 1923, 663.

Hall, Thurston [stage/film actor] (b. Boston MA, 10 May 1882–20 Feb 1958 [75], Beverly Hills CA; heart attack). (Lubin, 1915; Fox; Ince; Universal.) "Thurston Hall," *Variety,* 26 Feb 1958. AMD, p. 152. AS, p. 493. BHD1, p. 237. FSS, p. 137. IFN, p. 130. Katz, p. 526. MSBB, p. 1024. Truitt, p. 139. "In the Picture Studios," *NYDM,* 7 Jul 1915, 9:2 (to debut in *The Earl's Adventure*). "Thurston Hall Returns to Universal," *MPW,* 22 Mar 1919, 1621. "Thurston Hall Leaves Screen," *MPW,* 26 Jul 1919, 512.

Hall, Walter Richard [director/producer/scenarist] (d. 30 Mar 1950, Caldwell NJ). AMD, p. 152. BHD2, p. 111. "Hall Back with Feature," *MPW,* 3 May 1924, 45.

Hall, Weston B[irch] **(Bert)** [aviator/actor] (b. near Higginsville MO, 7 Nov 1885–6 Dec 1948 [63], Fremont OH; auto accident). m. (1) Della Byers, 12 Apr 1918, Paris—div. 1921; (2) Helen; (3) Genevieve; (4) Elizabeth Chapline, 25 Jun 1937, Las Vegas NV. (TC-F, 1921–29.) "Weston Hall, 62, Flier of Fortune; One of Founders of Lafayette Escadrille Dies—Had Fought for Many Nations in Wars," *NYT,* 8 Dec 1948, 31 (age 62; made *A Romance of the Air,* 1918). Dennis Gordon, *Lafayette Escadrille Pilot Biographies* (Missoula MT: The Doughboy Historical Society, 1991), pp. 69–80.

Hall, Willard Lee [actor] (b. Altoona PA, 1863–30 Oct 1936 [73], San Francisco CA). (Metro.) AS, p. 493 (d. Hollywood CA). BHD, p. 189. IFN, p. 130. "Mother of Willard Lee Hall," *Variety,* 16 Mar 1912.

Hall, William H. ("Swede") [actor] (b. 1874?–24 Oct 1944 [70], Chicago IL). m. "Jolly Jennie" Colborn (d. 1942). "William H. ('Swede') Hall," *Variety,* 1 Nov 1944. AS, p. 493. IFN, p. 130.

Hall, Winter [actor] (b. Christchurch, New Zealand, 21 Jun 1872–10 Feb 1947 [74], Los Angeles CA). (Lasky/ Paramount.) AMD, p. 152. AS, p. 493 (d. London, England). BHD1, p. 237. IFN, p. 130. "Universal Engages Winter Hall," *MPW,* 3 May 1919, 642.

Hall-Davis, Lilian [actress] (b. Hampstead, London, England, 23 Jun 1898–25 Oct 1933 [35], London, England; gas poisoning). "Lilian Hall-Davis," *Variety,* 112, 7 Nov 1933, 62:3 ("Depression caused through her inability to continue film work owing to illness is believed to have been the cause of her death. Survived by husband and 14-year-old son."). AS, p. 493. BHD1, p. 237.

Hallam, Basil [stage/film actor] (*né* Basil Hallam Radford, b. London, England, 3 Apr 1889–17 Aug 1916 [27]; killed at the front). "Basil Hallam Killed," *Variety,* 1 Sep 1916. AS, p. 493. SD.

Hallam, Henry [actor] (b. London, England, 1867–9 Nov 1921 [54]). AS, p. 493 (d. NY NY). BHD, p. 189. IFN, p. 130.

Hallard, C[harles] **M**[aitland] [stage/film actor] (b. Edinburgh, Scotland, 26 Oct 1865–21 Apr 1942 [76], Surrey, England). "C.M. Hallard," *Variety,* 29 Apr 1942 (in films from 1917). AS, p. 493. BHD1, p. 237 (d. 21 Mar). IFN, p. 130. SD. Truitt, p. 139 (b. England).

Hallatt, Henry [actor] (b. Whitehaven, England, 1 Feb 1888–24 Jul 1952 [64], Cambridge, England). AS, p. 493 (b. Whitchaven, England). BHD1, p. 238. IFN, p. 130.

Hallatt, May [actress] (b. England, 1882–20 May 1969 [87?], London, England). AS, p. 493.

Halleck, Selah [actress] (d. 13 May 1919, Perth Amboy NJ; auto accident). m. Roland Carr. "Selah Halleck," *Variety,* 23 May 1919. AS, p. 493.

Hallenberger, Henry [cinematographer]. No data found. FDY, p. 459.

Haller, Carl [actor] (b. Strassbourg, France, 1883–9 Nov 1955 [72], Baden-Baden, Germany; heart attack). (Began 1910 in Strassbourg.) "Carl Haller," *Variety,* 23 Nov 1955. AS, p. 493 (b. 1873).

Haller, Ernest [cinematographer] (b. Los Angeles CA, 31 May 1896–21 Oct 1970 [74], Marina del Rey CA; auto accident). (Biograph.)

"Ernest Haller," *Variety*, 28 Oct 1970. AS, p. 494. BHD, p. 190; BHD2, p. 111. FDY, p. 459. IFN, p. 130. Katz, p. 526.

Halleran, Edith Kingdon [actress]. No data found. (Vitagraph.) AMD, p. 152. Slide, p. 141 (no dates). "Edith Kingdon Halleran," *MPW*, 19 Sep 1914, 1647 (Haller in article).

Hallett, Agnes [actress] (*née* Agnes Johns, b. 1880–19 Nov 1954 [74?], Los Angeles CA). m. **Albert Hallett** (d. 1935). AS, p. 494.

Hallett, Albert [actor] (b. 1870?–3 Apr 1935 [65], Los Angeles CA). m. **Agnes** Johns (d. 1954). "Albert Hallett," *Variety*, 10 Apr 1935. AS, p. 494. BHD1, p. 238. IFN, p. 130. Truitt, p. 139.

Halliburton, Jeanne [actress/agent] (b. Lonoke AR, 5 May 1894–23 Jan 1986 [91], Falls Church VA). BHD, p. 190; BHD2, p. 111.

Halliday, John [stage/film actor] (b. Brooklyn NY, 14 Sep 1880–17 Oct 1947 [67], Honolulu HI; heart attack). m. (1) Camille Personi; (2) Eva Lang; (3) Eleanor Griffith. "John Halliday," *Variety*, 22 Oct 1947 (began in 1930). AMD, p. 152. AS, p. 494. BHD1, p. 238 (b. 1886). IFN, p. 130. Katz, pp. 526–27 (began in 1920). SD. Truitt, p. 139. "Schenck Engages Halliday," *MPW*, 7 Feb 1920, 911.

Halliday, Lena [actress] (b. London, England-d. 19 Dec 1937). BHD1, p. 238.

Halligan, William [actor/writer] (b. IL, 29 Mar 1883–28 Jan 1957 [73], Woodland Hills CA). "William Halligan," *Variety*, 6 Feb 1957 (age 63; began in *The Wonder Man*, 1919). AS, p. 494. BHD1, p. 238; BHD2, p. 111. IFN, p. 130. Truitt, p. 139 (b. 1884).

Hallings, Carl [director] (b. Sweden, 1895–1938 [43?], Sweden). AS, p. 494.

Hallor, Edith Kingdon (sister of **Ray Hallor**) [stage/film actress] (b. Washington DC, 26 Mar 1896–21 May 1971 [75], Newport Beach CA; cancer). m. **L Laurence Weber**—div. 1920 (d. 1940); **John Francis Dillon**, Hollywood CA (d. 1934). (Stage: Columbia and Poll Players; Ramo; TC-F.) "Edith Hallor," *Variety*, 2 Jun 1971. AMD, p. 152. AS, p. 494. BHD1, p. 238. IFN, p. 130. Truitt, p. 139. "Gossip of the Studios," *NYDM*, 16 Sep 1914, 27:1. "Scjreening 'The Blue Pearl,'" *MPW*, 13 Sep 1919, 1627. "Miss Hallor Becomes Star of Lawrence Weber Series," *MPW*, 17 Jan 1920, 435. "Cosmopolitan Signs Edith Hallor," *MPW*, 15 May 1920, 966. "Edith Hallor Weds Director," *MPW*, 4 Jun 1921, 503.

Hallor, Ethel [actress] (b. 1882–1967 [85?]). BHD, p. 190.

Hallor, Ray (brother of **Edith Hallor**) [actor] (b. Washington DC, 11 Jan 1900–16 Apr 1944 [44], near Palm Springs CA; auto accident). "Ray Hallor," *Variety*, 19 Apr 1944 (played juvenile roles in early silents). AMD, p. 152. AS, p. 494. BHD1, p. 238. IFN, p. 130. Truitt, p. 139. "Ray Hallor Signed," *MPW*, 16 Jan 1926, 241.

Halloway, Maggie. *See* Fisher, Maggie Halloway.

Halls, Ethyl May [actress] (b. 20 Nov 1882–16 Sep 1967 [84], Woodland Hills CA). (Biograph.) "Ethel May Halls," *Variety*, 27 Sep 1967. AS, p. 494. BHD, p. 190. IFN, p. 130. Truitt, p. 139.

Halm, ALfred [scenarist] (b. Vienna, Austria, 9 Dec 1861–5 Feb 1951 [89], Berlin, Germany). BHD2, p. 112. FDY, p. 427.

Halm, Harry [actor/scenarist] (b. Berlin, Germany, 17 Jan 1901-Nov 1980 [79], Munich, Germany). AS, p. 494. BHD1, p. 238; BHD2, p. 112.

Halperin, Edward (brother of **Victor Hugo Halperin**) [producer] (b. Chicago IL, 12 May 1898–2 Mar 1981 [82], Rancho Mirage CA). AMD, p. 152. "Edward and Victor Halperin to Be Producers on Unique Lines," *MPW*, 7 May 1927, 40.

Halperin, Sol [cinematographer] (b. Newark NJ, 16 Feb 1902–4 May 1977 [75], Los Angeles CA). BHD2, p. 112 (Sol Halprin). FDY, p. 459.

Halperin, Victor Hugo (brother of **Edward Halperin**) [producer/director/scenarist] (b. Chicago IL, 24 Aug 1894–17 May 1983 [88], Woodland Manor, Benton County, Siloam Springs AR [Certificate of Death, Arkansas Dept. of Health, #09083009181. Buried in Eastlawn Cemetery, Marshall AK]). m. Venita Sergeant. AMD, p. 152. AS, p. 494. BHD2, p. 112. Katz, p. 527. "Edward and Victor Halperin to Be Producers on Unique Lines," *MPW*, 7 May 1927, 40.

Halsey, Forrest [title writer/scenarist]. No data found. AMD, p. 152. FDY, pp. 427, 443. "Halsey with F.P.-L.," *MPW*, 28 Jun 1924, 816.

Halston, Margaret E. [actress] (b. London, England, 25 Dec 1879–8 Jan 1967 [87], Hornchurch, Essex, England). BHD1, p. 238. IFN, p. 131.

Halton, Charles [stage/film actor] (b. Washington DC, 16 Mar 1876–16 Apr 1959 [83], Los Angeles CA). m. Lelah. "Charles Halton," *Variety*, 22 Apr 1959. AS, p. 495. BHD1, p. 238. IFN, p. 131. SD.

Ham, Harry Breden [actor/director] (b. Napanee, Ontario, Canada, 25 May 1886–27 Jul 1943 [57], Beverly Hills CA; heart attack). (Christie; Paramount; 1st National.) "Harry Ham," *Variety*, 4 Aug 1943. AMD, p. 152. AS, p. 495 (b. 1891). BHD1, p. 610. IFN, p. 131. "Ham Again in Christie Comedies," *MPW*, 5 Apr 1919, 74. "Harry Ham Back with Christie," *MPW*, 12 Apr 1919, 231.

Hamberg, Alfred P. [director] (d. 1 Nov 1922, Los Angeles CA). BHD2, p. 112.

Hambling, Arthur [actor] (b. Reading, England, 1888). AS, p. 495.

Hamburg, Alfred T. [director] (d. 1 Nov 1922, Los Angeles CA). AS, p. 495.

Hamby, William H. [scenarist] (b. 1875–26 Jan 1928 [52?], San Diego CA). AMD, p. 152. BHD2, p. 112. "Author Sues Willard Film Owners," *MPW*, 12 Jul 1919, 205.

Hamel, Edna [actress]. No data found. AMD, p. 15? W. Stephen Bush, "The Screen Children's Gallery," *MPW*, 28 Mar 1914, 166/.

Hamer, Fred B[ooth] [actor] (b. Lancashire, England, 1873?–30 Dec 1953 [80?], Los Angeles CA). (Griffith.) "Fred B. Hamer," *Variety*, 6 Jan 1954. AS, p. 495. BHD, p. 190; BHD2, p. 112. Truitt, p. 140.

Hamer, Gerald [actor] (*né* Geoffrey Earl Watton, b. Ireland, 16 Nov 1886–6 Jul 1972 [85], Los Angeles CA). AS, p. 495.

Hamil, Lucille Budd [actress] (b. Carthage NY, 1902–17 Jun 1939 [37], New York NY). AS, p. 495. BHD, p. 190. IFN, p. 131.

Hamilton, Christine [publicist]. No data found. AMD, p. 152. "Joins Bray," *MPW*, 16 Oct 1926, 2.

Hamilton, Clayton [playwright/scenarist] (b. Brooklyn NY, 1881?–17 Sep 1946 [65], New York NY). "Clayton Hamilton," *Variety*, 164, 18 Sep 1946, 54:1. AMD, p. 152. "Clayton Hamilton Is Signed to Write Goldwyn Scenarios," *MPW*, 19 Jun 1920, 1624.

Hamilton, George Gordon [actor] (b. Coytesville NJ, 1883?–16 Jan 1939 [55], Fort Lee NJ; heart attack). "George Gordon Hamilton," *Variety*, 25 Jan 1939 (in *Perils of Pauline*). AS, p. 495. BHD, p. 190 (Gordon Hamilton, b. 1884). IFN, p. 131.

Hamilton, G.P., Jr. [actor/director/producer]. No data found. AMD, p. 152. "G.P. Hamilton, Jr.," *MPW*, 7 Jul 1917, 89. "G.P. Hamilton a New Triangle Director," *MPW*, 20 Oct 1917, 393.

Hamilton, Gilbert P. [executive]. No data found. AMD, p. 152. "The Albuquerque Company," *MPW*, 10 Jul 1915, 226.

Hamilton, Hale Rice [stage/film actor] (b. Topeka KS, 28 Feb 1880–19 May 1942 [62], Los Angeles CA; cerebral hemorrhage). m. (1) Jane Oaker (*née* Minnie Dorothy Peper; d. 1960); (2) Maude M. Tannehill (**Myrtle Tannahill**) (d. 1977); **Grace La Rue** (d. 1956). (Metro.) "Hale Hamilton, 62, Noted Actor, Dies; Creator of Wallingford Role in Cohan Play Began Career on the Stage in 1899; Appeared at Drury Lane; Toured with James K. Hackett and Wilton Lackaye—In the Films in Recent Years," *NYT*, 20 May 1942, 19:1. "Hale Hamilton," *Variety*, 20 May 1942 (b. Ft. Madison IA, 1883; age 59). AMD, p. 152. AS, p. 495 (b. Fort Madison IA, 1881). BHD1, p. 239 (b. Fort Madison IA). FSS, p. 137. IFN, p. 131 (b. Ft. Madison IA, 1881). SD. Truitt, p. 140 (b. 1880). "Hale Hamilton Plays for Metro," *MPW*, 13 Apr 1918, 254. "Metro Engages Two Stars; Each Will Head Company," *MPW*, 20 Jul 1918, 408. "Grace La Rue Sued," *LA Times*, 11 Feb 1920, II, p. 7 (sued by Myrtle Tannehill Hamilton in New York for alienation of the affections of Hamilton. La Rue "denied that she lured Mr. Hamilton away from his wife.").

Hamilton, Jack (Shorty). *See* Hamilton, "Shorty."

Hamilton, James Shelley [stage/film composer/scenarist] (b. Orange MA, 17 Jan 1884–5 Jun 1953 [69], Rutland VT). (Paramount; Fox.) "James S. Hamilton, Wrote College Hit; Author and Composer of 'Lord Jeffrey Arnherst' Was 69—Headed Film Review Board," *NYT*, 6 Jun 1953, 17:3 ("Mr. Hamilton went to Hollywood in the early years of the moving picture industry and wrote many of the scripts for the famous movie serial 'The Perils of Pauline,' starring Pearl White. His first Hollywood post was with G.B. Seitz, Inc. Later he wrote several original scripts for Paramount including 'North of Thirty Six.' He was the author of a number of films in which Allan Dwan and Billie Dove starred for Fox."). "James S. Hamilton," *Variety*, 10 Jun 1953. AS, p. 495. FDY, p. 427. SD.

Hamilton, John [actor] (*né* Gianni Medici, b. Philadelphia PA, 16 Jan 1887–15 Oct 1958 [71], Los Angeles CA; heart attack). "John Hamilton," *Variety*, 22 Oct 1958 (began 1937). AS, p. 496. BHD1, p. 239. IFN, p. 131. Truitt, p. 140.

Hamilton, John Frank [actor] (b. New York NY, 7 Nov 1893–11 Jul 1967 [73], Paramus NJ). "John F. Hamilton," *Variety*, 19 Jul 1967. AS, p. 496. BHD, p. 190. IFN, p. 131. Truitt, p. 140.

Hamilton, Laurel Lee [actress] (d. 15 Dec 1955, Los Angeles CA). (Sennett.) "Laurel L. Hamilton," *Variety,* 21 Dec 1955. AS, p. 496. BHD, p. 190. IFN, p. 131. Truitt, p. 140.

Hamilton, Lillian [actress]. No data found. AMD, p. 152. "Lillian Hamilton," *MPW,* 12 Jun 1915, 1764. "Lillian Hamilton in Strand Comedies," *MPW,* 13 Apr 1918, 226.

Hamilton, Lloyd V[ernon] [actor] (b. Oakland CA, 19 Aug 1887–18 Jan 1935 [47], Los Angeles CA). m. Ethel Floyd, 1914; **Irene Dalton**, Santa Ana CA, Sep 1927—div. 1928 (d. 1934). (Began 1912; St. Louis Film Co.; Ham and Bud comedies for Kalem [Mar 1915-Aug 1917]; Fox [11 Nov 1917]; Educational [Mermaid Comedies, 7 Aug 1920].) "Lloyd Hamilton," *Variety,* 22 Jan 1935 (age 43). AMD, p. 152. AS, p. 496. BHD1, p. 239; BHD2, p. 112 (b. 1891). FFF, p. 143. FSS, p. 137. IFN, p. 131 (b. 1891). Katz, p. 528. MH, p. 114. Truitt, p. 140. "Lloyd V. Hamilton," *MPW,* 24 Jul 1915, 652. "Ham in the Hospital," *MPW,* 30 Oct 1915, 944. "Extry! 'Ham' Is Back," *MPW,* 18 Dec 1915, 2194. "'Ham' on Long-Term Contract," *MPW,* 22 Jan 1916, 623. Hector Ames, "'Ham' and 'Bud,'" *MPC,* Mar 1916, 41–42. "Kalem Ham Comedy Company," *MPN,* 21 Oct 1916, 197. "Kalem Signs Ham and Bud," *MPW,* 10 Mar 1917, 1554. "Educational Makes Big Comedy Contjract; White,. Hamilton, and Adams Are Signed," *MPW,* 2 Apr 1921, 474. "Lloyd Hamilton Making 307th Comedy in Ten Years in Films," *MPW,* 20 Aug 1921, 814. "Griffith Engages Lloyd Hamilton," *MPW,* 18 Aug 1923, 581. "Six Lloyd Hamilton Comedies to Be Supplied Educational in Year," *MPW,* 1 Sep 1923, 62. "'Be Yourself' the Title," *MPW,* 22 Sep 1923, 324. "Lloyd Hamilton's Injury," *MPW,* 5 Jun 1926, 467. Frank Capron, "He Who Gets 'Soaked'; Lloyd Hamilton Is Still Taking Falls and Ducking Custard Pies, But Has Hopes of Tossing His Checkered Cap at Bigger Targets," *MPC,* Feb 1927, 62, 82. Margaret G. Monks, "Lloyd Hamilton; When he was twelve years old, this comedian appeared as 'Dr. Jekyll and Mr. Hyde' in a stock company recruited in his back yard," *Cinema Arts,* Feb 1927, 26–27, 47. "Lloyd V. Hamilton," *MPW,* 23 Apr 1927, 709. Sam Gill, "Lloyd Hamilton," *8mm Collector,* 14 (Spring, 1966), 8, 26–27. Richard M. Roberts, with Robert Farr and Joe Moore, "Lloyd Hamilton: Silent Comedy's Poor Soul; Part I," *CI,* 216 (Jun 1993), C20 *et passim* (b. 1891); Part II, 217 (Jul 1993), 12, 14, 57; filmography, 218 (Aug 1993), 44–46.

Hamilton, Mahlon [actor] (b. Baltimore MD, 15 Jun 1880–20 Jun 1960 [80], Woodland Hills CA; cancer). m. Aleta Farnum, Jersey City NJ, 26 Aug 1918—div. 1925. (Began at Kinemacolor, LI NY, 1913.) AMD, p. 153. AS, p. 496. BHD1, p. 239. FFF, p. 193 (b. 1885). FSS, p. 138. IFN, p. 131. MH, p. 115. "Mahlon Hamilton," *MPW,* 20 Oct 1917, 369. Mary Winship, "An Involuntary Idol; Mahlon Hamilton refuses to be worshipped—except by his wife," *Photoplay,* Mar 1921, 55. "Hamilton to Play Opposite Ayres," *MPW,* 24 Mar 1923, 456.

Hamilton, Mark [actor]. No data found. George Katchmer, "Remembering the Great Silents," *CI,* 198 (Dec 1991), 11.

Hamilton, Neil [actor] (*né* James Neil Hamilton, b. Lynn MA, 9 Sep 1899–24 Sep 1984 [85], Escondido CA). (Griffith; Paramount.) m. Elsa Whitner. "Neil Hamilton, 85, Veteran Film Lead and TV Actor, Dies," *Variety,* 3 Oct 1984. AMD, p. 153. AS, p. 496. BHD1, p. 239. FSS, p. 138. Katz, p. 528. SD. "New Griffith Player," *MPW,* 21 Apr 1923, 814. Regina Cannon, "Woman"s Greatest Possession; Neil Hamilton Tells What It Is," *MW,* 19 Apr 1924, 16 (it's graciousness). "Hamilton Signed by Paramount," *MPW,* 6 Jun 1925, 679. Leatrice Hagen, "Just a New England Boy Who Made Good," *MPC,* Nov 1925, 60–61, 74. Walter Ramsey, "Houdini Hamilton; Neil's Parlor Tricks Would Be Worth the Price of Admission If There Was Any," *MPC,* May 1929, 58, 96. John McGee, "Reel Reviewer," *CI,* 115 (Jan 1985), 43.

Hamilton, "Shorty" [actor] (*né* John F. Hamilton, b. Chicago IL, 9 Nov 1879 or 1888–7 Mar 1925 [45?], Los Angeles CA). (NYMP Co.; Bison; Mutual; Monogram; Merit.) "Film Cowboy Killed," *Variety,* 11 Mar 1925. AMD, p. 153. AS, p. 495 (Jack Hamilton). BHD, p. 190. IFN, p. 131 (Jack [Shorty] Hamilton. "'Shorty' Hamilton," *MPW,* 17 Oct 1914, 354. "'Shorty' Finds His Mate," *MPW,* 14 Nov 1914, 920. Eldon K. Everett, "'Shorty' Hamilton, the Funny Little Cowboy," *CI,* 61 (Winter, 1978), 44. Edgar M. Wyatt, "Was Shorty Hamilton Another Broncho Billy?," *CI,* 233 (Nov 1994), C11-C14 (d. 1925? Appeared in *The Masked Menace,* 1927, perhaps released posthumously).

Hamilton, William E. [actor/film editor/director of shorts/scenarist] (b. NY, 1894–2 Aug 1942 [48], No. Hollywood CA; heart attack). (RKO.) m. Gloria. "William Hamilton," *NYT,* 4 Aug 1942, 20:2 (He "was a veteran of the film industry, having entered the technical end of the motion picture business as a young man."). AMD, p. 153. AS, p. 496. BHD2, p. 112. "William E. Hamilton," *MPW,* 15 Jul 1916, 435.

Hamlin, William H[ugh] [actor] (b. 1885?–27 Sep 1951 [66], Los Angeles CA). (Vitagraph.) "William H. Hamlin," *Variety,* 3 Oct 1951. AS, p. 496. BHD, p. 190. IFN, p. 131. Truitt, p. 140.

Hamlisch, Leopold [actor/director/producer] (b. Vienna, Austria, 2 Nov 1891–21 Feb 1979 [87], Hamburg, Germany). AS, p. 496.

Hamman, Joe [actor/director] (*né* Jean Hamman, b. Paris, France, 26 Oct 1885–30 Jun 1974 [88], Paris, France). AS, p. 496. BHD1, p. 239; BHD2, p. 112.

Hammer, Ever [boxer/actor]. No data found. AMD, p. 153. "Pugilist Joins Sennett Forces," *MPW,* 27 Dec 1919, 1129.

Hammer, Fred[erick] William [actor/director] (b. New York NY, 26 Jan 1889–8 Mar 1939 [49], Los Angeles CA). AS, p. 496.

Hammer, Ina [actress] (d. Brattleboro VT, 9 Aug 1953). BHD, p. 190.

Hammeras, Ralph [cinematographer] (b. Minneapolis MN, 24 Mar 1894–3 Feb 1970 [75], Los Angeles CA). BHD2, p. 112. FDY, p. 459.

Hammerstein, Elaine [granddaughter of **Oscar Hammerstein I**] [actress] (b. Philadelphia PA, 16 Jun 1897–13 Aug 1948 [51], near Tiajuana, Mexico; car accident with husband). m. James Walter Hays, 1926. (World, 1915; Selznick; Jewell.) "Elaine Hammerstein," *Variety,* 18 Aug 1948. AMD, p. 153. AS, p. 496. BHD, p. 190. IFN, p. 131. Katz, p. 529 (began 1915). MH, p. 115 (b. 1898). MSBB, p. 1034 (b. NY). Spehr, p. 138. WWS, p. 141. Truitt, p. 140. "Elaine Hammerstein," *MPW,* 10 Feb 1917, 850. "Large Crowds Greet Star of 'Wanted for Murder,'" *MPW,* 25 Jan 1919, 524. "Star to Appear in Person in Several Large Cities," *MPW,* 15 Feb 1919, 939. "Elaine Hammerstein Is Selznick's Third Star," *MPW,* 3 May 1919, 645. "To Elaine Hammerstein, Selznick Stawr," *MPW,* 6 Mar 1920, 1659 (poem by Herbert J. Hoose). "Elaine Hammerstein Renews Her Contract with Selznick," *MPW,* 24 Apr 1920, 588. "Miss Hammerstein Recovers Health," *MPW,* 2 Apr 1921, 501. "Elaine Hammerstein to Be Starred in Six Big Productions," *MPW,* 6 Aug 1921, 615. "Elaine Hammerstein Signed," *MPW,* 28 Feb 1925, 919. June Lee, "Dan Cupid's Bulletin Board," *Paris and Hollywood,* Sep 1926, 94 (wed to Hays, a Los Angeles business man). Billy H. Doyle, "Elaine Hammerstein," *CI,* 216 (Jun 1993), C10.

Hammerstein I, Oscar (grandfather of **Elaine Hammerstein**) (composer/lyricist/executive) (b. Berlin, Germany, 1852–1 Aug 1919 [67], Lenox Hill Hospital, New York NY; diabetes and other illnesses; nterment at Woodlawn Cemetery.). m. (3) Mrs. Mary Emma Swift (son Arthur; 2 daughters, Stella and Rose. Three sons, William, Abraham, and Harry, by his first wife, died within the past 5 years.). "Oscar Hammerstein," *Variety,* LV, 8 Aug 1919, 20:2. "Oscar Loses Film Suit," *Variety,* 23 Jan 1914, 14:4 (had brought suit "against David Belasco to throuw the movies out of the Republic, the managers denying the Hammrstein claim that a theatre's association with movies is degrading.").

Hammerstein, Reggie [director/producer] (*né* Reginald Hammerstein, b. 1897?–9 Aug 1958 [61], New York NY). "Reggie Hammerstein," *Variety,* 13 Aug 1958. AS, p. 496. BHD2, p. 112.

Hammerstein, Stella [actress] (b. New York NY, 2 Jan 1880–7 Jun 1975 [95], Englewood NJ). AMD, p. 153. BHD, p. 191. "Stella Hammerstein in Rialto Star Feature," *MPW,* 11 Dec 1915, 2014.

Hammett, Melville [scenarist]. No data found. AMD, p. 153. "Newspaper Man Selznick Scenarist," *MPW,* 10 Jan 1920, 226.

Hammil, Edna May [child actress]. No data found. (Edison.) Lester Sweyd, "What They Are Doing Now," *Motion Picture Magazine,* Feb 1918, 13 ("...one of the Edison children, but now grown to be quite a smart young lade, was one of the ponies in the musical-comedy, 'The Love Mill.'").

Hammond, Charles Norman [actor] (b. San Jose CA, 1878?–5 Jun 1941 [63], New York NY). "Charles N. Hammond," *Variety,* 11 Jun 1941. AS, p. 497. BHD, p. 191. IFN, p. 131.

Hammond, Dorothy [actress] (b. London, England, 1874–23 Nov 1950 [76?], London, England). AS, p. 497.

Hammond, Harriet [actress: Sennett Bathing Beauty] (b. Bay City NY, or KS, 1898). (MGM.) AMD, p. 153. WWS, p. 191. "To Play Features," *MPW,* 28 May 1921, 423. "Bathing Beauty in Neilan Film," *MPW,* 30 Jul 1921, 533. "Harriet Hammond Signed," *MPW,* 15 Aug 1925, 749.

Hammond, Kay [actress] (b. Kansas City MO, 14 Oct 1901–7 Jan 1982 [80], Los Angeles CA). (Griffith.) "Kay Hammond," *Variety,* 20 Jan 1980. AS, p. 497. BHD1, p. 240.

Hammond, Virginia [film/stage actress] (b. Staunton VA, 20 Aug 1893–6 Apr 1972 [78], Washington DC). "Virginia Hammond," *Variety,* 10 May 1972. AMD, p. 153. AS, p. 497. BHD1, p. 240. IFN, p. 131. "Virginia Hammond," *MPW,* 19

Feb 1916, 1138. "Virginia Hammond to Support Louise Huff," *MPW,* 28 Sep 1918, 1900. "Virginia Hammond Signs Contract with World Film," *MPW,* 5 Jul 1919, 63. "Virginia Hammond Is Made a Star in Her Own Right," *MPW,* 23 Aug 1919, 1151.

Hammond, W[illiam] **C**[harles] [director] (b. London, England, 28 Jan 1890). AS, p. 497.

Hammons, Earle W[ooldridge] [executive] (b. Winona MS, 1887?–31 Jul 1962 [75], New Rochelle NY). "Earle W. Hammons," *Variety,* 8 Aug 1962 (established Educational Pictures, 1915). AMD, p. 153. BHD2, p. 112 (b. 2 Dec 1882). "E.W. Hammons Drives More Nails," *MPW,* 22 Sep 1917, 1845. "Hammons Does Not Believe Radio Will Hurt Pictures," *MPW,* 29 Sep 1923, 439. E.W. Hammons, "Padding of Feature Another Cause of Enormous Waste," *MPW,* 8 Dec 1923, 539. E.W. Hammons, "The Public's Voice Demands Diversified Entertainment," *MPW,* 29 Dec 1923, 792. "Showmen 'Playing Up' Shorts, Says Head of Educational," *MPW,* Dec 1924, 862. "'Big Names—Little Comedies,' Discussed by E.W. Hammons," *MPW,* 28 Feb 1925, 921. E.W. Hammons, "1926–1927," *MPW,* 5 Jun 1926, 476. "Hammons Sails; Chats About Europe," *MPW,* 3 Jul 1926, 41. "E.W. Hammons Sends the World English Poster via Wireless," *MPW,* 10 Jul 1926, 1 (illustration of poster on p. 83). "Shrot Feature Studios Reflect Public's Enthusiasm—Hammons," *MPW,* 25 Sep 1926, 240. R.M. Hyams, "E.W. Hammons; Films for 'Entertainment Only'; The Man Who First Thought of Takng Trouble With the Despised 'One Reelers,'" *Cinema Arts,* V (Oct 1926), 15, 42. E.W. Hammons, "Business Can Be Built by Giving Full Exploitation to Your Short Feturs," *MPW,* 27 Aug 1927, 615–16, 618, 629.

Hamon, Clara Smith [actress]. No data found. m. **John W. Gorman**, 22 Aug 1921, Hollywood CA. AMD, p. 153. "Bumpy Road Awaiting Clara Hamon in Movies," *MPW,* 9 Apr 1921, 573. "Clara Hamon Weds Director," *MPW,* 10 Sep 1921, 169.

Hamon, Count Louis [scenarist] (b. 1867–8 Oct 1936 [69?], Los Angeles CA). BHD2, p. 112.

Hampden, Walter [actor] (*né* Walter Hempden Daughterty, b. Brooklyn NY, 30 Jun 1879–11 Jun 1955 [75], Los Angeles CA; cerebral hemorrhage). m. Mabel Moore. "Walter Hampden," *Variety,* 15 Jun 1955. AMD, p. 154. AS, p. 497. BHD1, p. 240. IFN, p. 131. Katz, pp. 529–30. Truitt, p. 141. "Walt4er Hampden, Knickerbocker Star," *MPW,* 2 Oct 1915, 61.

Hamper, Genevieve [stage/film actress] (b. Detroit MI, 8 Sep 1888–13 Feb 1971 [82], New York NY). m. **Robert B. Mantell**, 1916 (d. 1928); John Alexander (d. 1982). (Film debut: *The Blindness of Devotion,* Fox, 1915.) "Genevieve Hamper," *Variety,* 24 Feb 1971. AS, p. 497. BHD, p. 191 (b. Greenville MI, 1889). IFN, p. 131. SD. Truitt, p. 141.

Hampton, Benjamin B. [actor/director/producer/executive] (b. Macomb IL, 1875?–31 Jan 1932 [56], New York NY). m. (1) Martha Bartleson; (2) **Claire Adams** (d. 1978). *A History of the Movies.* (Vitagraph.) "B.B. Hampton, Promoter, Died in N.Y. Hospital," *Variety,* 2 Feb 1932. AMD, p. 154. AS, p. 497. BHD2, p. 112. "Ben B. Hampton Heads General Film Company," *MPW,* 2 Dec 1916, 1303. "Hampton Continues General Film Head," *MPW,* 13 Jan 1917, 201. "Hampton Resigns G.F. Presidency," *MPW,* 28 Apr 1917, 601. "Benjamin B. Hampton raises Work of Strong Cast of 'The Sagebrusher,'" *MPW,* 27 Dec 1919, 1176. "Benjamin B. Hampton Tells Why the Industry Needs and Must Have Support of Public Opinion," *MPW,* 5 Feb 1921, 669. Benjamin B. Hampton, "United Industry Is Hampton's Aim," *MPW,* 12 Feb 1921, 779. "To Benjamin B. Hampton," *MPW,* 12 Mar 1921, 127.

Hampton, Crystal [actress/director/producer] (d. 17 Jun 1922, New York NY). AS, p. 497. BHD, p. 191; BHD2, p. 113. IFN, p. 131.

Hampton, Faith [actress] (b. 1909?–31 Mar 1949 [40], Los Angeles CA; suffocated with husband in fire). m. **Don Short** (d. 1949). (Sennett.) "Faith Hampton," *Variety,* 6 Apr 1949. AS, p. 497 (d. 1 Apr). BHD, p. 191. IFN, p. 141 (d. 1 Apr). Truitt, p. 131. Photo, *Paris and Hollywood,* 2 (Oct 1926), 15.

Hampton, Grayce [actress] (b. Devonshire, England, 28 Mar 1876–20 Dec 1963 [87], Woodland Hills CA). AS, p. 497. BHD1, p. 240. IFN, p. 131.

Hampton, Hope [actress] (*née* Mae Elizabeth Hampton, b. Houston TX, 19 Feb 1897–23 Jan 1982 [84], New York NY; heart attack [Death Certificate Index No. 1363]). m. **Jules Brulatour** (d. 1946). Joyce Purnick, "Hope Hampton, Opera Singer and First-Nighter, Dies at 84," *NYT,* 25 Jan 1982, 28:1 (b. Philadelphia PA). "Hope Hampton," *Variety,* 27 Jan 1982 (b. Philadelphia). AMD, p. 154. AS, p. 497. BHD1, p. 240. FFF, p. 88. FSS, p. 139. MH, p. 115 (b. 1902). Spehr, p. 138 (b. 1902). WWS, p. 158 (b. Dallas TX). "Hope Hampton Back from Trip to Europe; Closes Contracts," *MPW,* 20 Mar 1920, 1982. "Hope Hampton a Deputy Sheriff," *MPW,* 26 Jun 1920, 1753. "Hope Hampton's Screen Gowns Cost Her $50,000 This Year," *MPW,* 30 Oct 1920, 1279. "Hope Hampton Travelled Abroad and Studied to Fit Herself for Her Work," *MPW,* 25 Dec 1920, 1024. Gladys Hall, "The Little Girl and the Stern Grandmother," *MPC,* Jul 1921, 54–55, 94. "Hope Hampton Begins Work, Ending Her Tour," *MPW,* 3 Dec 1921, 557. "Paramount and Fox Sign Hope Hampton," *MPW,* 23 Dec 1922, 734. "Hope Hampton Goes West," *MPW,* 28 Apr 1923, 905. "Uxtry Uxtry! Conducted by Ima Gossip," *MPS,* 12 Aug 1924, 25–26 ("Not content with being a picture star and having a husband whose aim in life seems to be to grant her every wish, she has set out to master some of the arts that will advance her career."). "Hope Hampton to Sue; Replaced in 'Madame Pompadour,' She Will Seek Damages," *NYT,* 11 Nov 1924, 20:2 (replaced by Wilda Bennett; attorney was Max D. Steuer; not to close the show but to sue Martin Beck and Charles B. Dillingham for payment of damages "for an alleged breaking of their contract with Miss Hampton," who played in the on the road try-out, although Bennett was advertised in the role: "[T]here was no possibility of a last-minute readjustment restoring Miss Hampton to her original role."). "Hope Hampton," *MPW,* 8 Aug 1925, 659. "Hope Hampton Sails," *MPW,* 29 May 1926, 2. Victoria Willis, "Shopping in Paris with Hope Hampton," *MW,* 1924, IV, 8, 29.

Hampton, Jesse D. [director/producer]. No data found. AMD, p. 154. "Industry Needs Ideals, Says Hodkinson Producers," *MPW,* 14 Sep 1918, 1572. "Jesse D. Hampton to Produce Three Films Based on Bret Harte's Western Narratives," *MPW,* 28 Jun 1919, 1949. "Hampton Likes His Special Featuring Blanche Sweet," *MPW,* 20 Sep 1919, 1813. "Capitalists May Back Jesse D. Hampton to Produce for Stage as Well as Films," *MPW,* 18 Sep 1920, 341. "Jesse D. Hampton Sues Variety for $150,000 on a Charge of Libel," *MPW,* 30 Oct 1920, 1273.

Hampton, Louise [stage/film actress] (b. Stockport, England, 1880–10 Feb 1954 [73], London, England; bronchial ailment). m. actor Edward Thane (d. three weeks previously). "Louise Hampton," *Variety,* 193, 17 Feb 1954, 63:1 (d. 11 Feb). AS, p. 497. BHD1, p. 240. IFN, p. 131.

Hampton, Pauline [actress]. No data found. June Lee, "Dan Cupid's Bulletin Board," *Paris and Hollywood Screen Secrets,* III (Oct 1927), 37 (broke off her engagement to director Chester Bennett).

Hampton, Raye. No data found. George Katchmer, "Remembering the Great Silents," *CI,* 197 (Nov 1991), 50–51.

Hamrick, Burwell Filson [actor/set designer] (b. 24 Nov 1905–21 Sep 1970 [64], Los Angeles CA). (Universal.) "Burwell Ham-rick," *Variety,* 30 Sep 1970. AMD, p. 154. AS, p. 497. BHD1, p. 610; BHD2, p. 112. IFN, p. 131. "Burwell Filson Hamrick," *MPW,* 3 Nov 1917, 684.

Hanbury, Ralph [executive] (b. Ballarat, Victoria, Australia, 2 May 1891–26 Sep 1940 [49], England). BHD2, p. 113.

Hanbury, Victor W. [director/producer/scenarist] (b. London, England, 1897–14 Dec 1954 [57], London, England). AS, p. 497. BHD2, p. 112.

Hancock, Don [director/producer/scenarist] (b. London, England, 21 Oct 1888–5 Jan 1951 [62], No. Hollywood CA). AS, p. 497. BHD2, p. 112.

Hancock, Elinor or **Eleanor** [actress]. No data found. (Universal.)

Hancock, Herbert E. [managing director] (b. London, England, 31 Aug 1879–7 Jan 1943 [63]). AMD, p. 154. BHD2, p. 113. "Hancock to Be Made Manager of Producing Company," *MPW,* 18 Jan 1919, 333. "Herbert E. Hancock Made Fox News Head," *MPW,* 9 Aug 1919, 817.

Hand, Horace E. [casting director] (b. 1863–13 Apr 1930 [67?], Los Angeles CA). BHD2, p. 113.

Handforth, Ruth [actress] (b. Springfield MA, 11 Jul 1882–10 Sep 1965 [83], Los Angeles Co. CA). AS, p. 498. BHD, p. 191. IFN, p. 132.

Handley, Tommy [actor] (b. Liverpool, England, 1894–9 Jan 1949 [54?], London, England; cerebral hemorrhage). AS, p. 498.

Handworth, Elsie [actress] (d. Hemet CA, 20 Sep 1994). BHD1, p. 610.

Handworth, Harry [actor/director] (*né* Henry Handworth, b. 1882?–22 Mar 1916 [34], Brooklyn NY [Death Certificate No. 6579]; pneumonia). AMD, p. 154. AS, p. 498 (b. 1892). BHD, p. 191; BHD2, p. 113. "Harry Handworth," *MPW,* 2 May 1914, 677. "Handworth Out of Excelsior," *MPW,* 16 Jan 1915, 381. Handworth was the head of the Excelsior Feature Film Co., Inc., Lake Placid NY, incorporated 3 Feb 1914 (released four features, from 19 Jun 1914 to 4 Jan 1915. (Another Excelsior company produced films in Florida from 10 Mar 1913 to 5 May 1913.)

Handworth, Octavia [actress] (*née* Octavia Boas, b. New York NY, 24 Dec 1887–3 Oct 1978 [90], Hemet CA). (Octavia Wood). AMD, p.

154. AS, p. 498. BHD, p. 191. "Octavia Handworth at Home," *MPW,* 2 Jan 1915, 55. "Octavia Handworth with Lubin," *MPW,* 8 May 1915, 880. "Octavia Handworth Returns," *MPW,* 17 Jun 1916, 2053. Billy H. Doyle, "Lost Players," *CI,* 182 (Aug 1990), 23.

Handy, Will C[hristopher] [composer] (b. Muscle Shoals AL, 16 Nov 1873–29 Mar 1958 [84], New York NY). AS, p. 498.

Handysides, J. Clarence [actor] (b. Montreal, Canada, 1854?–20 Dec 1931 [77], Philadelphia PA). m. Blanche Sharp (d. 1937). (Paramount.) *Variety,* 29 Dec 1931. AS, p. 498. BHD, p. 191 (Handyside). IFN, p. 132.

Hanford, Charles B. [stage/film actor] (b. Sutter Creek CA, 5 May 1859–16 Oct 1926 [67], Washington DC). "Charles B. Hanford," *Variety,* 20 Oct 1926, 105:1 ("During the war the late actor gained considerable fame with his recitation of the 'Star Spangled Banner,' which became identified with him to a great degree. Also during the world strife he co-operated with Thomas A. Edison in developing the American system of camouflage to protect troops."). AMD, p. 154. AS, p. 498. BHD, p. 191. "Charles Hanford in Pictures," *MPW,* 27 Jul 1912, 354.

Hanford, Raymond [actor]. No data found. AMD, p. 154. "Cleo Madison and Ray Hanford Stricken with Pneumonia," *MPW,* 3 Jul 1915, 67.

Hanft, Jules [actor] (*né* Julian O. Hanft, b. Jersey City NJ, 16 Sep 1859–6 Aug 1936 [76]). AS, p. 498. BHD, p. 191. IFN, p. 132.

Hanley, James F. [composer/scenarist] (b. Rensselaer IN, 17 Feb 1892–8 Feb 1942 [49], Douglaston NY; heart atttack). BHD2, p. 113. CEPMJ (wrote *Second Hand Rose* and *Rose of Washington Square*); Kinkle.

Hanley, Michael E. [actor/director/producer] (b. 1858?–18 Jun 1942 [84], Ft. Wayne IN; suicide by shooting). "Michael E. Hanley," *Variety,* 24 Jun 1942. BHD2, p. 113.

Hanley, William B., Jr. [actor] (b. 1900?–2 Oct 1959 [59?], Hollywood CA; heart attack). m. **Madge Kennedy** (d. 1987). "William B. Hanley," *Variety,* 7 Oct 1959. AS, p. 498. BHD1, p. 240. Truitt, p. 141.

Hanlon, Alma (mother of Dorothy Kingsley) [stage/film actress] (b. NJ, 30 Apr 1890–26 Oct 1977 [87], Monterey CA). m. Walter J. Kingsley. AMD, p. 154. BHD, p. 191. MSBB, p. 1034. SD. "Alma Hanlon," *MPW,* 5 Jun 1915, 1615. "Alma Hanlon in Special Kleine Drama," *MPW,* 20 Nov 1915, 1480. "Other Deaths; Dorothy Kingsley," *Pittsburgh Post-Gazette,* 3 Oct 1997, B-5:3 (scenarist, MGM, b. 1910?–26 Sep 1997 [87], Carmel CA).

Hanlon, Daniel E. [actor]. No data found. AMD, p. 154. "Daniel E. Hanlon," *MPW,* 10 Feb 1917, 847.

Hanlon, Edward [actor] (b. Manchester, England, 1854–15 Mar 1931 [77?], St. Petersburg FL). BHD, p. 191.

Hanna, Edward J. [actor] (b. 1872–16 Jun 1963 [91?], Brattleboro VT). AS, p. 499.

Hanna, Franklyn [actor] (b. MO, 1875–19 Jan 1931 [55]). (World.) AMD, p. 154. AS, p. 499. BHD, p. 191. IFN, p. 132. "Franklyn Hanna," *MPW,* 7 Apr 1917, 82.

Hanna, Wylie J. [actor] (b. 1887–7 Aug 1947 [60?], San Jose CA). AS, p. 499.

Hannah, James [actor] (b. 19 Sep 1905–11 Sep 1978 [72], Fresno CA). BHD, p. 191. IFN, p. 132.

Hannan, Roy Irving [cinematographer/director/scenarist] (b. 1882–22 Oct 1926 [44?], Green Bay WI). BHD2, p. 113.

Hanneford, Edwin Poodles [actor] (b. Barnsley, Yorkshire, England, 14 Jun 1891–9 Dec 1967 [75], Kattskill Bay NY). m. Grace Norma. "Edwin Poodles Hanneford," *Variety,* 13 Dec 1967. AS, p. 499. BHD1, p. 241. IFN, p. 132. Truitt, p. 141.

Hannelore [dancer/actress]. No data found. AMD, p. 154. "Noted Dancer to Be in New Picture," *MPW,* Dec 1922, 538.

Hannerman, Frederick G. [actor: Our Gang comedies] (b. 1914–3 Oct 1980 [66?], Santa Barbara CA). AS, p. 499 (Hanneman). BHD1, p. 241.

Hannen, Nicholas 9actor/director] (b. London, England, 1 May 1881–25 Jun 1972 [91], London, England). AS, p. 499.

Hannon, William Morgan [scenarist]. No data found. AMD, p. 154. "William Morgan Hannon," *MPW,* 18 Dec 1915, 2163.

Hanofer, Frank [actor/stuntman] (b. Hungary, 1897–16 Dec 1955 [58?], Newhall CA). AS, p. 499.

Hanray, Lawrence [actor] (b. London, England, 16 May 1874–28 Nov 1947 [73], England). AS, p. 499. BHD1, p. 241. IFN, p. 132.

Hansell, Howell [actor/director] (b. IN, 1852–5 Nov 1917 [65?], New York NY; pneumonia). (Thanhouser; World; FP-L.) "Howell Hansel," *Variety,* 9 Nov 1917 (age 57). AMD, p. 154. BHD, p. 191; BHD2, p. 113. "Howel Hansel [sic]," *NYDM,* 5 Aug 1914, 25:1. "Howell Hansel," *MPW,* 28 Aug 1915, 1488. "Obituary," *MPW,* 24 Nov 1917, 1154 (age 56).

Hansen, A. [cinematographer]. No data found. FDY, p. 459.

Hansen, Hans [actor] (b. Germany, 1885–18 Jun 1962 [77?], New York NY). AS, p. 499.

Hansen, Juanita, "Queen of Thrills" [actress: Sennett Bathing Beauty] (aka Wahneta Hanson, b. Des Moines IA, 31 Mar 1895–26 Sep 1961 [66], West Hollywood CA; found dead, apparently from natural causes). "Juanita Hansen, 66, Film-Serials Star," *NYT,* 28 Sep 1961, 41:4. "Juanita Hansen," *Variety,* 4 Oct 1961. AMD, p. 154. AS, p. 499. BHD, p. 191. FSS, p. 139. IFN, p. 132. MH, p. 115 (b. 1897). WWS, p. 143. Truitt, p. 141. "Juanita Hansen Joins Triangle," *MPW,* 4 Nov 1916, 680. "Juanita Hansen Becomes Triangle Star," *MPW,* 18 Nov 1916, 987. "Juanita Hansen—The Star in 'Glory,'" *MPW,* 13 Jan 1917, 215. "Juanita Hansen Leading Woman for Mix," *MPW,* 29 Mar 1919, 1830. "Juanita Hansen Signs to Appear in Pathé Serials," *MPW,* 20 Dec 1919, 952. Edward Weitzel, "When Juanita Hensen, New Pathé Star[,] First Met a Quintette of Lions," *MPW,* 24 Jan 1920, 579. "Will Probably Start Company," *MPW,* 2 Oct 1920, 636. "Juanita Hansen to Continue Making Serials; Decision Based on Opinions from Exhibitors," *MPW,* 6 Nov 1920, 90. "Juanita Hansen Ill," *MPW,* 7 May 1921, 55 (nervous breakdown). "Juanita Hansen on Tour," *MPW,* 28 Apr 1923, 911. George Katchmer, "Remembering the Great Silents," *CI,* 223 (Jan 1994), 56:1.

Hansen, Max [actor] (b. Mannheim, Germany, 22 Dec 1887–12 Nov 1961 [73], Copenhagen, Denmark). BHD1, p. 241. IFN, p. 132.

Hanshaw, Dale [assistant director] (b. Grafton WV, 1892). BHD2, p. 113.

Hanshew, Thomas W. [writer/scenarist] (b. Brooklyn NY, 1857–3 Mar 1914 [56?], Annesley, London, England). (Edison.)

Hanson, Einar [actor] (b. Stockholm, Sweden, 15 Jun 1899–3 Jun 1927 [27], Santa Monica CA; auto accident). "Einar Hanson Killed in Unsolved Accident; Found Crushed Under Auto with His Dog Impeding Rescue Work," *Variety,* 8 Jun 1927 (age 29). AMD, p. 155. AS, p. 499. BHD, p. 191 (Hansen). IFN, p. 132. Truitt, p. 141. WWS, p. 141. Paul Blaine, "Corinne Griffith Predicts—That Einar Hansen [sic] Will Prove One of Our Great Romantic Actors," *MPC,* Nov 1926, 22–23, 83 (tested and let go by Universal and MGM, 1st National signed him). "Obituary," *MPW,* 25 Jun 1927, 574.

Hanson, Frank (Spook) [actor] (b. Brooklyn NY, 1874–16 Jun 1924 [50?], New York NY). BHD, p. 191.

Hanson, Gladys [stage/film actress] (*née* Gladys Snook, b. Atlanta GA, 5 Sep 1883–23 Feb 1973 [89], Atlanta GA). m. Charles Emerson Cook, 12 Apr 1916 (d. 1941). (Essanay; Lubin.) "Gladys Hanson," *NYT,* 26 Feb 1973, 34:4. "Gladys Hanson, 89," *New York Post,* 26 Feb 1973, p. 17. "Gladys Hanson," *Variety,* 7 Mar 1973. AMD, p. 155. AS, p. 499. BHD, p. 192. IFN, p. 132. "New Lubin Star; Gladys Hanson Joins Company to Appear in Adaptation of 'The Evangelist,'" *NYDM,* 13 Jan 1915, 24:1. "Gladys Hanson," *MPW,* 16 Jan 1915, 372. "Personal; Hanson," *NYDM,* 9 Jun 1915, 5:1 (on cover). "Gladys Hanson Marries," *MPW,* 6 May 1916, 943. Gene Vazzana, "Gladys Hanson: Southern Belle, Stage Actress, Movie Actress," *CI,* 204 (Jun 1992), C10–11, C16–17. Roi Uselton, "Remembering Gladys Hanson [letter]," *CI,* 205 (Jul 1992), 4.

Hanson, Lars [stage/film actor] (b. Göteberg, Sweden, 26 Jul 1886–8 Apr 1965 [78], Stockholm, Sweden). m. actress Karin Nolander. (MGM.) (Film debut: *Dolken,* Swedish, 1914.) Margít Síwertz, *Lars Hanson* (Stockholm: P.A. Norstedt and Söners Förlag, 1947) (in Swedish). "Lars Hanson Dead; Swedish Stage Star," *NYT,* 9 Apr 1965, 33:2. "Lars Hanson," *Variety,* 14 Apr 1965. AMD, p. 155. AS, p. 499. BHD1, p. 241. IFN, p. 132. Katz, p. 531. Truitt, p. 141. Waldman, p. 128 (b. 1887). "Lars Hanson Signs with M-G-M," *MPW,* Oct 1925, 415. "Hanson Discovers America," *MPC,* Jan 1926, 40. Katherine Albert, "Sweden Sends Us Her Leading Actor; An Interview With Lars Hanson Showing That He Can Be Cool Under Any Conditions," *Cinema Arts,* V (Oct 1926), 33, 45. "Divorce Floors Lars," *MPW,* 6 Aug 1927, 398.

Hanson, "Spook." *See* Hanson, Frank (Spook).

Hanus, Emmerich [actor/director] (b. Vienna, Austria, 24 Aug 1884–1956 [72], Vienna, Austria). AS, p. 499.

Harbach, Otto [composer] (b. Salt Lake City UT, 18 Aug 1873–24 Jan 1963 [89], New York NY). BHD2, p. 113.

Harbacher, Karl [actor] (b. Klagenfurt, Austria, 2 Nov 1879–8 Mar 1943 [63], Berlin, Germany). BHD1, p. 241.

Harbaugh, Carl [actor/title writer/scenarist/director] (b. Washington DC, 10 Nov 1886–26 Feb 1960 [73], Woodland Hills CA). (Fox.) "Carl Harbaugh," *Variety,* 9 Mar 1960. AMD, p. 155. AS, p. 500. BHD1, p. 241; BHD2, p. 113. FDY, pp. 427, 443. IFN, p. 132. Truitt, p. 141. "Director Harbaugh Has New Actress," *MPW,* 16 Dec 1916, 1621 (his 1-year-old daughter). "Virginia Pearson Has New Director," *MPW,* 21 Jul 1917, 490. "George Now a Fox Firector," *MPW,* 25 May 1918, 1160.

Harbaugh, William [stuntman] (b. 1899?–19 Oct 1924 [25], Yuma AZ; drowned during filming of Charles Ray's *Desert Fiddler*). "Wm. Harbaugh Drowned," *Variety,* 22 Oct 1924. AS, p. 500 (d. 15 Oct). BHD, p. 192. IFN, p. 132. Truitt, p. 141 (Harborough).

Harbeck, William H. [cameraman/producer] (b. 1867?–15 Apr 1912 [45], *Titanic* disaster). AMD, p. 155. "Remarkable Demonstration of the Educational Picture," *MPW,* 17 Feb 1912, 561. Hugh H. Hoffman, "Harbeck Lost on the Titanic," *MPW,* 11 May 1912, 506. "Harbeck Pictures ijn Litigation," *MPW,* 1 Jun 1912, 805. "Unexhibited Films Sink with Titanic," *MPW,* 29 Jun 1912, 1231. "Wynward Represents Harbeck Estate Pictures," *MPW,* 3 Aug 1912, 455. "Does Not Represent the Harbeck Estate," *MPW,* 17 Aug 1912, 659.

Harben, Hubert [actor] (b. London, England, 12 Jul 1878–24 Aug 1941 [63], London, England). AS, p. 500. BHD1, p. 241. IFN, p. 132.

Harbord, Carl [actor] (b. Salcombe, England, 26 Jan 1908–18 Oct 1958 [50], Los Angeles CA). BHD1, p. 241.

Harburg, Edelaine [actress] (b. 1900–26 Apr 1989 [89?], Los Angeles CA; coronary occlusion and pneumonia). AS, p. 500.

Harcourt, George [stage/film actor]. No data found. m. **Peggy** (d. 1916). AMD, p. 155. "Pathé Player on Stage," *MPW,* 22 Oct 1927, 492.

Harcourt, Gerald [actor] (b. 1886–1 Jun 1924 [38?], Sydney, Australia). BHD, p. 192.

Harcourt, James [actor] (b. Leeds, England, 20 Apr 1873–18 Feb 1951 [77], London, England). AS, p. 500.

Harcourt, Mrs. Peggy [actress] (*née?,* d. 31 Jul 1916, Hewletts, LI NY; auto accident). m. **George Harcourt**. "Mrs. Peggie Harcourt," *Variety,* 4 Aug 1916. AS, p. 500. BHD, p. 192. IFN, p. 132.

Harcourt, William K. [actor] (b. Gallatin TX, 1866?–27 Nov 1923 [57], New York NY; apoplexy). m. Alice Fisher. "William K. Harcourt," *Variety,* 6 Dec 1923. AS, p. 500. BHD, p. 192.

Harde, Harry [cameraman]. No data found. AMD, p. 155. "Pathé Camera Photographs Bottling Up of Rum Fleet," *MPW,* 23 May 1925, 438.

Hardee, Kvikland [actor] (b. 1864–20 Feb 1929 [65?], Los Angeles CA). AS, p. 500.

Harden, Viola [actress] (b. 1897?–15 Aug 1988 [91?], Miami Beach FL).AS, p. 500. BHD, p. 192.

Harder, Emil [actor] (b. Saint Gall, Switzerland, 1885). AS, p. 500.

Hardin, Edward [publicist]. No data found. AMD, p. 155. "'Eddie' Hardin Joins Cusack," *MPW,* 6 Apr 1918, 67.

Hardin, Neil Cameron, Jr. [actor] (b. Louisiana MO, 20 Sep 1880–22 Nov 1969 [89], Louisiana MO). m. Gloria Payton. (Universal; Balboa.) AMD, p. 155. BHD, p. 192. MSBB, p. 1024. "Neil Cameron Hardin," *MPW,* 10 Mar 1917, 1571.

Harding, Alma [actress] (d. Woodstock NY, 17 Oct 1961). BHD, p. 192.

Harding, Ann [stage/film actress] (*née* Dorothy Walton [or Anna] Gately, b. Fort Sam Houston, San Antonio TX, 17 Aug 1902–1 Sep 1981 [79], Sherman Oaks CA). m. (1) **Harry Bannister**, Oct 1926–32 (d. 1961); (2) Werner Janssen, 1937–62. (Broadway debut: *Like a King,* 1921; RKO Pathé; reader for FP-L.) Carol Lawson, "Ann Harding, Actress Hailed for Roles as Elegant Women," *NYT,* 4 Sep 1981, 12:4 ("...she was much in demand in the early days of talking pictures when there was a scarcity of beautiful actresses in Hollywood who knew how to deliver a line."). "Ann Harding," *Variety,* 9 Sep 1981. AS, p. 500. BHD1, p. 242 (b. 7 Aug 1901; d. LA CA). "On the Set and Off," *MM,* Mar 1926, 83 (to appear in MGM films after her play, *Stolen Fruit,* closes). Ruth Biery, "Sisters Under Their Biographies; Are the Stage and the Screen Stars—If Ann Harding's Story Is a Fair Example," *MPC,* Aug 1929, 25, 78. Jack Grant, "Ann Harding's Double Caused Divorce Rumor; Diane Ballard Was Innocent Cause of Reports About Happily-Married Star—Is Mistaken for Ann Wherever She Goes," *Movie Classic,* Nov 1931, 42.

Harding, J. Rudge [actor] (b. Elvethan, England, 1862–24 Apr 1932 [70?]). BHD, p. 192.

Harding, Lorraine [actress]. No data found. AMD, p. 155. "Edward Keppler, Lorraine Harding and Greta Hartman Are Added to 'Bandbox' Cast," *MPW,* 9 Aug 1919, 853.

Harding, Lyn [actor] (*né* David Llewellyn Harding, b. Newport, Wales, 12 Oct 1867–26 Dec 1952 [85], Southend, Sussex, England). "Lyn Harding," *Variety,* 31 Dec 1952. AS, p. 500 (d. London, England). BHD1, p. 242. IFN, p. 132. Truitt, pp. 141–42.

Hards, Ira M. [actor] (b. Geneva IL, 24 Jun 1872–2 May 1938 [65?], West Norwalk CT). AS, p. 500. BHD, p. 192; BHD2, p. 113.

Hardt, Harry [actor] (*né* Hermann Karl Viktor Klimbacher Edler von Rechtswahl, b. Pola, Austria, 4 Aug 1889–1980 [91?], Germany). AS, p. 500.

Hardtmuth, Paul [actor] (b. Germany, 1889–5 Feb 1962 [72?], London, England; possible suicide). AS, p. 500.

Hardwicke, Cedric (father of Edward Hardwicke, b. 7 Aug 1932) [actor/director/producer] (*né* Cecil Webster Hardwicke, b. Stourbridge [Birmingham], England, 13 Feb 1893–6 Aug 1964 [71], New York NY; stomach cancer). m. (1) **Helena Pickard** (d. 1959); (2) Mary Scott. AS, p. 500. BHD1, p. 242 (b. Lye, England); BHD2, p. 113 (b. 19 Feb). AS, p. 500. IFN, p. 133. SD. "Sir Cedric Hardwicke," *CI,* 204 (Jun 1992), 9, 62.

Hardy, Loo [actor] (b. Berlin, Germany, 1898–1934 [36?], London, England). BHD, p. 192.

Hardy, Oliver "Babe" [actor] (*né* Norvell Hardy, b. Harlem GA, 18 Jan 1892–7 Aug 1957 [65], No. Hollywood CA). m. (1) **Myrtle Reeves**, 24 Nov 1917, Thankgiving Day (d. 1983); (2) Lucille. (Lubin [Jacksonville FL]; Roach). John McCabe and Al Kilgore, *Laurel & Hardy* (NY: Bonanza Books, 1975). "Oliver Hardy of Film Team Dies; Co-Star of 200 Slapstick Movies; Portly Master of the Withering Look and 'Slow Burn'—Features Popular on TV," *NYT,* 8 Aug 1957 (b. Atlanta); "Oliver Hardy Service; Final Tribute Is Paid to Film Comedian in Los Angeles," 10 Aug 1957, 15:5 (among those attending were Adolphe Menjou, Wallace Ford, Andy Clyde, Clyde Cook, Hal Roach, "and a few members of the original Keystone Kops"). "Oliver Hardy," *Variety,* 14 Aug 1957. AMD, p. 155. AS, p. 501. BHD1, p. 242. FSS, p. 175. IFN, p. 133. JS, p. 236 (made *Atollo K* in Italy in 1951). Katz, p. 533. Truitt, p. 142. "'Babe' Hardy, Vim Fat Man," *MPW,* 4 Dec 1915, 1862. "He Wants His Pound of Flesh," *MPW,* 20 Oct 1917, 405. "Hardy Married," *MPW,* 17 Dec 1921, 829 (to Reeves on Thanksgiving Day). Bo Berglund, "Addition to the Oliver Hardy Filmography," *CI,* 174 (Dec 1989), C22-C23.

Hardy, Sam B. [stage/film actor] (b. New Haven CT, 21 Mar 1883–16 Oct 1935 [52], Los Angeles CA; complications from surgery). m. Betty Scott. (World.) "Sam Hardy," *Variety,* 23 Oct 1935. AMD, p. 155. AS, p. 501. BHD1, p. 242. IFN, p. 133. MH, p. 115. SD. Truitt, p. 142. Cover, *NYDM,* 30 Oct 1915 (in *The Princess Pat* with Eleanor Painter). "Sam Hardy Engaged by World Pictures," *MPW,* 2 Aug 1919, 696.

Hare, F. Lumsden [stage/film actor] (*né* Francis Lumsden Hare, b. Tipperary, Ireland, 17 Oct 1874–28 Aug 1964 [89], Beverly Hills CA). m. (1) Frances Ruttledge; (2) Selene Johnson. "Lumsden Hare Dies; Long an Actor, 90," *NYT,* 1 Sep 1964, 36:2. "Lumsden Hare," *Variety,* 2 Sep 1964. AMD, p. 155. AS, p. 501. BHD1, p. 242 (b. Cashel, Ireland, 27 Apr 1875). FSS, p. 139. IFN, p. 133 (b. 27 Apr 1875). MSBB, p. 1024 (b. 1885). SD. Spehr, p. 138 (b. 1875). Truitt, p. 142. "F. Lumsden Hare," *MPW,* 12 Feb 1916, 940. "Lumsden Hare Engaged by Madame Petrova," *MPW,* 1 Dec 1917, 1301.

Hare, John [stage/film actor] (*né* John Fairs, b. Giggleswick, England, 16 May 1844–28 Dec 1921 [77], London, England). "Sir John Hare," *Variety,* 6 Jan 1922, 7:4. AS, p. 501. BHD, p. 192.

Hare, Rene Vivian [actress] (*née* Rene Vivian, b. England, 1897–4 Aug 1969 [72?], London, England). AS, p. 501.

Hare, Robertson [actor] (*né* John Robertson Hare, b. London, England, 17 Dec 1891–25 Jan 1979 [87], London, England). AS, p. 501.

Harford, Harry [actor] (b. Boston MA, 1851?–20 Sep 1925 [74], Bernardsville NJ). "Harry Harford," *Variety,* 7 Oct 1925. AS, p. 501. IFN, p. 133. Truitt, 1983 (b. 1841).

Hari, Mata [actress/dancer] (*née* Margaretha Geertruida Zelba, b. Leewaarden, Holland, 7 Aug 1876–15 Oct 1917 [41], Vincennes, France; executed by the French). AS, p. 728 ("actrice et danseuse hollandaise du cinéma muet").

Harispuru, Edouard (father of François Harispuru) [producer] (b. Paris, France, 15 Jan 1890). AS, p. 501.

Harker, Gordon [actor] (b. London, England, 7 Aug 1885–2 Mar 1967 [81], London, England). m. Christine Barrie (d. 1964). (Film debut: *The Ring,* 1927.) "Gordon Harker," *Variety,* 8 Mar 1967. AS, p. 501. BHD1, p. 243. IFN, p. 133. Truitt, p. 142.

Harkins, Dixie (Ruth?) [actress] (b. 1906?–1 Sep 1963 [57], Jacksonville FL). (MGM.) "Dixie Harkins," *Variety,* 4 Sep 1963 (acted with Valentino). AS, p. 501. BHD, p. 192. IFN, p. 133. Truitt, p. 142.

Harkins, Jim [actor] (b. 1888–25 Oct 1970 [82?], Media PA). AS, p. 501.

Harkins, William S. [actor] (b. NY, 1856?–1 Jul 1945 [89], Patchogue, LI NY). "William S. Harkins," *Variety,* 4 Jul 1945. AS, p. 501.

Harkrider, John W. [actor] (b. Abilene TX, 16 Nov 1899–7 Jul 1982 [82], Santa Monica CA). BHD1, p. 243.

Harlam, Macey [actor] (b. New York NY–d. 17 Jun 1923, Saranac Lake NY). (Goldwyn; Para.) "Macey Harlam," *Variety,* 21 Jun 1923. AMD, p. 155. IFN, p. 133 (d. 9 Apr 1924). Truitt, p. 143 (Harlan). "Harlam to Play in Support of Negri," *MPW,* 25 Nov 1922, 331.

Harlan, Kenneth D. (nephew of **Otis Harlan**) [actor] (b. Boston MA, 26 Jul 1895–6 Mar 1967 [71], Sacramento CA; aneurysm). m. 7 times: (1) **Florence Hart**, 26 Jun 1920 (d. 1960); (2) **Marie Prevost**, 24 Oct 1924, Hollywood—div. 21 Nov 1927 (d. 1937); Doris Booth; Phyllis McClure; Rhea Walker. (Griffith.) (Film debut: *Betsy's Burglar,* Triangle-Fine Arts, 4 Mar 1917.) "Kenneth Harlan of Silent Screen; Actor, 71, Who Ran Agency After Talkies Began, Dies," *NYT,* 8 Mar 1967, 45:3. "Kenneth Harlan," *Variety,* 8 Mar 1967. AMD, p. 155. AS, p. 501. BHD1, p. 243. FFF, p. 73 (b. NYC). FSS, p. 140. GK, pp. 357–69. IFN, p. 133. Katz, p. 533. MH, p. 115 (b. NYC). SD. Truitt, pp. 142–43. WWS, p. 184. "Kenneth D. Harlan Joins Fine Arts," *MPW,* 10 Mar 1917, 1554. "Kenneth D. Harlan," *MPW,* 7 Jul 1917, 90. "Kenneth Harlan at Camp Kearny," *MPW,* 20 Jul 1918, 391. "Kenneth Harlan Mustered Out," *MPW,* 15 Feb 1919, 892. "Schenck Signs Kenneth Harlan," *MPW,* 4 Dec 1920, 628. "Kenneth Harlan Is Sued for Separation by Wife," *MPW,* 29 Oct 1921, 1018 (from Hart). "Preferred Pictures to Form Stock company; Sign Harlan," *MPW,* 7 Oct 1922, 477. "Harlan Is Wounded Working on Picture," *MPW,* 25 Aug 1923, 667. "Harlan to Be Starred," *MPW,* 22 Sep 1923, 327. "To Appear in Person," *MPW,* 10 Nov 1923, 243. "Harlan Will Star in 'Poisoned Paradise,'" *MPW,* 1 Dec 1923, 495. "Kenneth Harlan at Home," *MW,* IV, 26 Apr 1924, 15 (photo layout). "Harlan Finishes Role," *MPW,* LXX, 25 Oct 1924, 685. "Stars in Wreck," *MPW,* 9 May 1925, 144. "Presenting Mr. and Mrs. Harlan," *MPC,* Jan 1926, 41. "Harlan Is Acquitted," *MPW,* 2 May 1927, 793. "Rift in Harlan—Prevost Family," *MPW,* 4 Jun 1927, 330. "Prevost Sues Harlan," *MPW,* 22 Oct 1927, 484. George A. Katchmer, "Kenneth Harlan, The Virginian," *CI,* 103 (Jan 1984), 33–35. Gerald Hamm, "Kenneth Harlan Info [letter]," *CI,* 105 (Mar 1984), C3. Richard E. Braff, "An Index to the Films of Kenneth Harlan," *CI,* 182 (Aug 1990), C10, C12; 183 (Sep 1990), 40–43, 54.

Harlan, Marion (daughter of **Otis Harlan**, cousin of **Kenneth Harlan**) [actress]. No data found. m. Walter Kennedy, 1926, Los Angeles CA. (Selig; Fox; Universal.) AMD, p. 156. "Studio Gossip," *NYDM,* 20 Nov 1915, 27:1 (to debut in *A Temperance Town* at Selig). "Adds New Leading Lady," *MPW,* 27 Sep 1924, 286. "Marion Harlan Selected," *MPW,* 11 Jul 1925, 193.

Harlan, Nellie [actress] (d. 27 Jun 1919, New York NY). "Nellie Harlan," *Variety,* 4 Jul 1919. AS, p. 501.

Harlan, Otis [stage/film actor] (father of **Marion Harlan**, uncle of **Kennth Harlan**) (b. Zanesville OH, 29 Dec 1864–20 Jan 1940 [75], Martinsville IN; cerebral hemorrhage). m. Nellie Harvey (d. 1919). (Film debut: *A Black Sheep,* Selig, 1915.) "Otis Harlan Dies; Noted Comedian, 75; Spent 33 Years on the Stage and 19 Years on Screen—Succumbs in Indiana; Made Debut Here in 1887; Appeared with Weber & Fields, Anna Held and Elsie Janis—Was Star in 'Broken Idol,'" *NYT,* 21 Jan 1940, 35:1. "Otis Harlan," *Variety,* 24 Jan 1940. AMD, p. 156. AS, p. 501. BHD1, p. 243 (b. 1865). FSS, p. 140. IFN, p. 133. MH, p. 115. SD. Truitt, p. 143. "Otis Harlan on Screen," *NYDM,* 19 May 1915, 25:2 (to join Selig Polyscope). "Otis Harlan Goes to Selig," *MPW,* 5 Jun 1915, 1585. "Otis Harlan with Selig," *MPW,* 3 Jul 1915, 70. "The Screen for Harlan; Comedian Gives Up Stage and Hopes to Become a Picture Director in Time," *NYDM,* 22 Sep 1915, 25:4. "Otis Harlan in 'A Black Sheep,'" *MPW,* 9 Oct 1915, 261. "English Actress" Debut Here in 'Redeeming Sin,'" *MPW,* 6 Dec 1924, 555. "Otis Harlan with Chadwick," *MPW,* 13 Mar 1926, 100. George Katchmer, "Remembering the Great Silents," *CI,* 218 (Aug 1993), 42.

Harlan, Richard [director] (*né* Ricardo Garlan, b. Lima, Peru, 19 Apr 1900–20 Oct 1968 [68], San Clemente CA). (Famous Players; UA; Fox; made Spanigh-language films in Hollywood). AS, p. 501. BHD, p. 192; BHD2, p. 114 (d. So. Laguna CA). Waldman, p. 128 (d. 1941).

Harlan, Veit [director/producer/actor/scenarist] (*né* Veit Stoss, b. Berlin, Germany, 22 Sep 1899–13 Apr 1964 [64], Capri, Italy; cancer). m. actress Christina Soderbaum. "Veit Harlan," *Variety,* 234, 15 Apr 1964, 60:4 (directed *Jew Suss* for the Nazi regime). AS, p. 502. BHD1, p. 243; BHD2, p. 114. IFN, p. 133.

Harland, Russell [cinematographer]. No data found. FDY, p. 459.

Harley, Edwin [actor] (b. Philadelphia PA, 1848?–29 Oct 1933 [85], Milwaukee WI). AS, p. 502. BHD, p. 192. IFN, p. 133. Truitt, 1983.

Harling, W. Franke [composer] (b. London, England, 18 Jan 1887–22 Nov 1958 [71], Sierra Madre CA). "Franke Harling, Composer, Dead; Writer of Hit Tunes and Serious Music Shared an Oscar for 'Stagecoach,'" *NYT,* 23 Nov 1958, 88:3 (wrote *Sing You Sinners*). "W. Franke Harling," *Variety,* 26 Nov 1958. AS, p. 502. ASCAP, p. 311. BHD2, p. 114.

Harlow, Jean [actress] (*née* Harlean Carpenter, b. Kansas City MO, 3 Mar 1911–7 Jun 1937 [26], Los Angeles CA; uremic poisoning). m. (1) Charles McGraw (*né* Charles Bulters, d. 1980); (2) **Paul Bern**, 1932 (d. 1932); (3) **Harold G. Rosson**, 1933–34 (d. 1988). (Chaplin; Roach; Paramount; Christie; MGM.) Eve Golden, *Platinum Girl; The Life and Legends of Jean Harlow* (New York: Abbeville Press, 1992). David Stenn, *Bombshell; The Life and Death of Jean Harlow* (NY: Doubleday, 1993). "Jean Harlow, Film Star, Dies in Hollywood at 26 After an Illness of Only a Few Days," *NYT,* 8 Jun 1937, 1:4, 30:4. "Private Services for Jean Harlow; Reputedly Insured for $1,000,000," *Variety,* 9 Jun 1937. AS, p. 502. BHD1, p. 243. IFN, p. 133. Katz, p. 534. SD. Truitt, p. 143. *Variety,* 113, 20 Feb 1934, 52:4 (Harlow filed a demurrer in LA, "to a suit attempting to claim a part of the estate of Paul Bern for his asserted former common-law wife, charging it is ambiguous."). Jean Harlow (as told to Eleanor Packer), "The Authentic Story of My Life," *The New Movie Magazine,* X, Oct 1934, 32–33, 91–93. Eve Golden, "Jean Harlow; A New and True Look at Hollywood's Blonde Bombshell," *CI,* 199 (Jan 1992), 16–18. Caryn James, "A No-Apologies Woman for the 90's: Harlow," *NYT,* 1 Oct 1993, C1:1, C24:1. Jeanine Basinger, "Lived Fast, Died Young," *NYT Book Review,* Sect. 7, 13:1 (review of Stenn's book).

Harlow, John R. [director/scenarist] (b. Ross-on-Wye, England, 19 Aug 1896–15 May 1946 [49], England). AS, p. 502.

Harman, Fred (brother of **Hugh** and **Walker Harman**) [animator] (b. CO, 1902–2 Jan 1982 [79?], Phoenix AZ). AS, p. 502.

Harman, Hugh (brother of **Fred** and **Walker Harman**) [animator] (b. Pagosa Springs CO, 31 Aug 1903–25 Nov 1982 [79], Chatsworth CA). "Hugh Harman, 79, Creator of 'Looney Tunes,' Cartoons," *NYT,* 30 Nov 1982, B12:5 (began 1922). "Harman, 79, Dies in California; Pioneer Animator with Rudy Ising," *Variety,* 1 Dec 1982. AS, p. 502. BHD2, p. 114. Katz, p. 534. Allan Greenfield, "Frame by Frame," *CFC,* 60 (Fall, 1978), 16 (began 1920 with Disney in Kansas City); Part II, 61 (Winter, 1978), 16. Allan Greenfield, "Frame by Frame," *CI,* 71 (Sep 1980), 14–15. Will Friedwald, "Hugh Harman," *CI,* 94 (Apr 1983), 51–52, 69.

Harman, Walker (brother of **Fred** and **Hugh Harman**) [animator] (b. Pagosa Springs CO, 1904–11 Mar 1938 [34?], Glendale CA). AS, p. 502.

Harmer, David [executive] (d. 16 Nov 1923). BHD2, p. 114.

Harmer, Frances [scenarist]. No data found. AMD, p. 156. "Miss Harmer Promoted to DeMille Scenario Staff," *MPW,* 15 Jan 1921, 319.

Harmer, Lillian [actress] (b. 1885–15 May 1946 [61?], Los Angeles CA). AS, p. 502. BHD1, p. 243.

Harmon, Pat [actor] (b. Lewiston IL, 3 Feb 1886–26 Nov 1958 [72], Riverside CA). "Pat Harmon," *Variety,* 3 Dec 1958. AS, p. 502 (b. 1888). BHD1, p. 243. IFN, p. 133. Truitt, p. 143. George Katchmer, "Forgotten Cowboys and Cowgirls—Part V," *CI,* 177 (Mar 1990), C4; "Update," 179 (May 1990), 44.

Harolde, Ralf [actor] (*né* Ralf Harold Wigger, b. Pittsburgh PA, 17 May 1899–1 Nov 1974 [75], Santa Monica CA; pneumonia). "Ralf Harold," *Variety,* 11 Dec 1974. AS, p. 502. BHD1, p. 243. IFN, p. 133.

Harout, Yeghishe Nerses [actor] (b. Armenia, 1 Oct 1898–7 Jun 1974 [75], Los Angeles CA; cancer). AS, p. 502.

Harr, Silver [actor] (*né* Arlie Silver Harr, b. ID, 21 Sep 1892–19 Sep 1968 [75], Los Angeles Co. CA). BHD1, p. 243. IFN, p. 133.

Harrigan, William [stage/film actor] (b. New York NY, 27 Mar 1886–1 Feb 1966 [79], New York NY [Death Certificate Index No. 2396]). m. (1) Dorothy Langdon; (2) Louise Groody (d. 1961); (3) Grace Culbert. "William Harrigan, Stage and Screen Veteran, Dies," *NYT,* 2 Feb 1966, 32:1. "William Harrigan," *Variety,* 9 Feb 1966 (age 72). AS, pp. 502–03. BHD1, p. 243 (b. 1894). IFN, p. 133. SD.

Harriman, Moses H. [stage/film actor] (b. 1861–16 Sep 1928 [67?], Percy Williams Home, East Islip, LI NY). "Moses H. Harriman," *Variety,* 19 Sep 1928, 58:4 (age 73; "...interment in Actors' Fund Plot in Kensico Cemetery."). BHD, p. 193.

Harrington, Alice [actress] (*née* Alice Augusta Harrington, b. Southboro MA, 4 Mar 1873

[MVRB, Vol. 252, p. 326]–6 Jun 1954 [81], Greenwich CT). m. William Parke. "Mrs. Parke, Coach of Stage Stars, 81; Actress Under Name of Alice Harrington Is Dead—Taught Jennifer Jones, Grace Kelly," *NYT,* 7 Jun 1954, 23:5. "Alice Harrington," *Variety,* 9 Jun 1954. AS, p. 503 (b. Marlboro MA).

Harrington, Buck [actor] (*né* Cyril J. Harrington, b. IA, 18 Mar 1897–2 Feb 1971 [73], Los Angeles CA). AS, p. 503.

Harrington, George [actor] (d. 14 Jun 1922, England). BHD, p. 193.

Harrington, John Daniel [actor] (b. Riverside Co. CA, 23 Jul 1882–9 Sep 1945 [63], San Francisco Co. CA). BHD1, p. 243. IFN, p. 133.

Harris, Averell (son of **William Harris**; brother of **Mitchell Harris**) [actor] (b. 19 Jun 1881–25 Sep 1966 [85], New York NY). AS, p. 503. BHD1, p. 244. IFN, p. 133.

Harris, Bernard [actor] (b. 1892–12 Jul 1981 [89?], Encino CA). BHD, p. 193.

Harris, Buddy [cameraman] (*né* Emil Harris Birnkrant, b. 28 Mar 1891–5 Sep 1971 [80]). AMD, p. 156. AS, p. 503. BHD2, p. 114. IFN, p. 134. "Busy Little 'Buddy,'" *MPW,* 28 Feb 1925, 916. "Three-Year-Old Boy 'Find,'" *MPW,* 28 Feb 1925, 919.

Harris, Caroline E. (mother of **Richard Barthelmess**) (b. 1867?–23 Apr 1937 [70], New York NY). "Caroline H. Barthelmess," *Variety,* 28 Apr 1937. AS, p. 503. BHD, p. 193. IFN, p. 19.

Harris, Charles K[assell] [stage/film composer] (b. Poughkeepsie NY, 1 May 1865–22 Dec 1930 [65], New York NY). m. Cora Lehrberg. "Charles K. Harris," *Variety,* 24 Dec 1930 (wrote *After the Ball*). AMD, p. 156. AS, p. 503. BHD1, p. 244. SD. "More Harris Pictures Coming," *MPW,* 30 Dec 1916, 1941. Charles K. Harris, "Song Slide the Little Father of Photodrama," *MPW,* 10 Mar 1917, 1520–21.

Harris, Rev. Clarence J[osiah] [scenarist] (b. Northbridge MA, 12 Mar 1873 [MVRB, Vol. 252, p. 309]–27 Nov 1941 [68], Bronx? NY). m. Muriel Seibel. "The Rev. C.J. Harris; Pastor of Washington Heights Universalist Church, 1918–38," *NYT,* 29 Nov 1941, 17:4. BHD2, p. 114. "Pastor Writes a Film Play," *NYT,* 7 Jun 1915, 11:4 (wrote *The Spender,* 2 reels).

Harris, Delmore [pioneer film sound technician] (b. CT, 27 Mar 1903–10 Jul 1991 [88], Los Angeles CA; leukemia). "Delmore Harris," *Variety,* 29 Jul 1991, p. 45. AS, p. 503. BHD2, p. 114 (d. 8 Jul).

Harris, Eddie [actor]. No data found. George Katchmer, "Remembering the Great Silents," *CI,* 207 (Apr 1992), 43.

Harris, Elmer B[laney] [actor/scenarist] (b. Chicago IL, 11 Jan 1878–6 Sep 1966 [88], Washington DC). m. Wilhelmina B. Henderson. (Realart; Columbia; MGM.) "Elmer B. Harris," *Variety,* 14 Sep 1966. AMD, p. 156. AS, p. 503. BHD, p. 193; BHD2, p. 114. FDY, p. 427. SD, p. 575. "Elmer Harris Renews Contract," *MPW,* 7 Feb 1920, 933. Elmer Harris, "European Writers Will Reap Rewards Unless Our American Authors Awaken," *MPW,* 7 Aug 1920, 715. "Elmer Harris Made Supervising Director of Realart's Studios on the West Coast," *MPW,* 27 Nov 1920, 485. "Elmer Harris to Supervise Mary Pickford Pictures," *MPW,* 13 May 1922, 155. "Harris to Make Series of Big Films for Hodkinson Release," *MPW,* 5 Apr 1924, 444. "Elmer Harris's Life One of Versatility," *MPW,* 12 Jul 1924, insert. "Harris Enlists Aid of Noted Psychiatrists for New Picture," *MPW,* 13 Sep 1924, 145. "Harris Joins DeMille," *MPW,* 9 May 1925, 221.

Harris, Elsie Lowe [actress] (b. 1891–17 May 1953 [62?], Los Angeles CA). AS, p. 503.

Harris, George [vaudevillian/film actor] (b. 1891?–16 Apr 1954 [63], Youngstown OH). "George Harris," *NYT,* 18 Apr 1954, 89:2 (age 60). "George Harris," *Variety,* 21 Apr 1954. AS, p. 503.

Harris, Georgie [actor] (b. Liverpool, England, 19 Jun 1898–14 Mar 1986 [87], England). BHD1, p. 244.

Harris, Harry B. [cinematographer/director]. No data found. FDY, p. 459.

Harris, Jack [actor]. No data found. AMD, p. 156. "Clown Leaves Circus to Join Keystone Forces," *MPW,* 5 Nov 1916, 1147.

Harris, James [actor]. No data found. AMD, p. 156. "James Harris," *MPW,* 16 Jun 1917, 1792.

Harris, Jed [director/producer] (b. Vienna, Austria, 25 Feb 1900–15 Nov 1979 [79], New York NY). AS, p. 503.

Harris, John P[aul] [theater entrepreneur] (b. Pittsburgh PA, 1872?–26 Jan 1926 [53?], Harrisburg PA). "John P. Harris [state senator]," *Variety,* 3 Feb 1926 (age 54). AS, p. 503.

Harris, Joseph [executive] (b. 1853?–10 Aug 1926 [73], near NY). m. Lena. "Joseph Harris," *Variety,* 18 Aug 1926 (former president of Esskay-Harris Feature Film Co.).

Harris, Joseph [actor] (b. ME, 11 Jan 1870–11 Jun 1953 [83], Los Angeles CA). (Universal; American.) "Joseph Harris," *Variety,* 17 Jun 1953 (d. at the home of Harry Carey, Jr.). AS, p. 503. BHD, p. 193. IFN, p. 134. Truitt, p. 143. Billy H. Doyle, "Lost Players," *CI,* 152 (Feb 1988), C13. George Katchmer, "Remembering the Great Silents," *CI,* 206 (Aug 1992), 39.

Harris, Katherine Corri [actress] (b. New York NY, 1893–2 May 1927 [34?], New York NY). m. **John Barrymore**—div. 1927. AS, p. 503. BHD, p. 193. IFN, p. 134. Truitt, 1983.

Harris, Kathryn [actress]. No data found. m. photographer Melbourne Spurr, May 1925. June Lee, "Dan Cupid's Bulletin Board," *Paris and Hollywood,* Oct 1926, 87–88 (charged desertion in her suit for divorce against Spurr. At the time of her marriage, she had her back "insured with Lloyds against injury for $50,000.").

Harris, Lawson (father of John Derek, 1926–98) [director]. No data found. m. **Dorothy Johnson**.

Harris, Lenore [actress] (b. New York NY, 1879?–27 Sep 1953 [74], New York NY). AS, p. 503. BHD, p. 193 (Leonore). IFN, p. 134.

Harris, Marcia [actress] (b. Providence RI, 14 Feb 1880). *Fl.* 1918–32. BHD, p. 193.

Harris, Margie [actress] (d. 17 Feb 1931, Houston TX). "Margie Harris," *Variety,* 18 Feb 1931.

Harris, Mildred [actress] (b. Cheyenne WY, 18 Apr 1901–20 Jul 1944 [43], Los Angeles CA; pneumonia). m. (1) **Charles Chaplin**, 23 Oct 1918, LA CA—div. 1920 (d. 1977); (2) Everett Terrance McGovern, 29 Nov 1924, Mexico and again in Greenwich CT; (3) William P. Fleckenstein. (Vitagraph; NYMP Co.; Reliance-Majestic; Fine Arts; Universal.) "Mildred Harris, in Silent Movies; Film and Stage Actress, Secret Bride of Chaplin When 15, Dies in Los Angeles at 41," *NYT,* 21 Jul 1944, 19:2. "Mildred Harris," *Variety,* 26 Jul 1944 (age 41). AMD, p. 156. AS, p. 504. BHD1, p. 244 (b. 29 Nov 1902). FSS, p. 141. IFN, p. 134 (b. 1902). Katz, p. 535 (b. 29 Nov). MH, p. 115. MSBB, p. 1030. SD. Truitt, p. 144 (b. 29 Nov). WWS, p. 93. "Mildred Harris," *MPW,* Nov 1914, 768. "Mildred Harris with Griffith-Mutual," *MPW,* 20 Feb 1915, 1127. "Mildred Harris," *MPW,* 26 May 1917, 1296. "Mildred Harris with Lois Weber," *MPW,* 27 Oct 1917, 511. "Mildred Harris Wife of Chas. Chaplin Since Oct. 23," *MPW,* 23 Nov 1918, 810. "Chaplin and His Bride Appear on Same Screen," *MPW,* 30 Nov 1918, 970. "Exhibitors Quick to Seek Film of Chaplin's Bride," *MPW,* 7 Dec 1918, 1104. "Mildred Harris Close-Up Makes a Hit in Animated," *MPW,* 14 Dec 1918, 1232. "Louis B. Mayer Signs Mildred Harris," *MPW,* 28 Jun 1919, 1948. "Mr. and Mrs. C.C. P:resent C.C., Jr.," *MPW,* 19 Jul 1919, 339 (b. 7 Jul 1919). "Death of Chaplin Baby Came Very Unexpectantly," *MPW,* 26 Jul 1919, 483 (d. 10 Jul 1919, intestinal trouble). "Mildred Harris Chaplin Recovered," *MPW,* 23 Aug 1919, 1151. "Wyoming Home Folks Plan to Honor Mrs. C.C.," *MPW,* 6 Mar 1920, 1674. "Mildred Harris in New York," *MPW,* 14 Aug 1920, 898. "Charlie Chaplin Takes Latest Film to Utah to Evade Wife's Process Servers," *MPW,* 28 Aug 1920, 1143. "Two Stars Ill," *MPW,* 6 Aug 1921, 591. "Mildred Harris Signed," *MPW,* 10 Jan 1925, 168. "Camera Scoops," *MW,* 16 May 1925, 19 (photo of Harris and Terrance McGovern). George Katchmer, "Remembering the Great Silents," *CI,* 224 (Feb 1994), 53:1.

Harris, Mitchell (son of **William Harris**; brother of **Averell Harris**) [actor] (b. New York NY, 1883?–16 Nov 1948 [65], New York NY). "Mitchell Harris," *Variety,* 24 Nov 1948. AS, p. 504. BHD1, p. 244. IFN, p. 134.

Harris, Raymond S. [scenarist] (b. 1885?–10 Apr 1971 [86], New York NY). "Raymond S. Harris, a Screenwriter, 86," *NYT,* 11 Apr 1971, 59:2 ("Mr. Harris's name appeared in comedies starring Harold Lloyd and W.C. Fields.... He began writing for the silent films in the Vitagraph Studios on Long Island, then spent 20 years in Hollywood..."). "Raymond S. Harris," *Variety,* 14 Apr 1971 ("He...spent 20 years in Hollywood for Paramount, 20th, Universal and other studios."). AS, p. 504. BHD2, p. 114. FDY, p. 427.

Harris, Robert [actor] (b. England, 28 Mar 1900–18 May 1995 [95], Denville Hall, England). AS, p. 504.

Harris, Sadie [actress] (b. 1892–15 May 1933 [41?], New York NY). BHD, p. 193.

Harris, Sam [actor/producer] (b. 1872? 2 Jul 1941 [69], New York NY; cancer). m. (3) Kathleen Nolan, 1939 (sister of George Brent). Jack Pulaski, "Sam Harris' Rise, a Chronicle of Success, Recalled by His Death," *Variety,* 143, 9 Jul 1941, 49:1, 50:3 ("...the passing of Harris was spoken of as a calamity to show business." He, George M. Cohan, and Joseph Schenck built the Music Box Theatre on Broadway. He and Cohan married the Nolan sisters of Boston. Cohan and Harris "lasted 15 years, team splitting after the actors strike of 1919.").

Harris, Mrs. Sam H. *See* Nolan, Alice.

Harris, Theodora [writer]. No data found. AMD, p. 156. "Joins Horsley Writers," *MPW,* 23 Oct 1915, 595.

Harris, Val [actor: Harris and Griffin] (*né* Valle E. Harris, b. IL, 14 Feb 1882–17 Mar 1961 [79], Van Nuys CA). AS, p. 504. BHD1, p. 245.

Harris, Wadsworth [actor] (*né* Lewis Wadsworth Harris, b. Boston MA, 9 Oct 1864–1 Nov 1942 [78], Los Angeles CA). (Red Feather Productions; Fox; Universal.) "Wadsworth Harris," *Variety*, 16 Dec 1942 (b. Calais ME). AS, p. 504. BHD1, p. 245. IFN, p. 134. Truitt, p. 144 (b. Calais; d. Dec 1942).

Harris, William (father of **Averell** and **Mitchell Harris**) [stage/film actor] (b. 1836?–4 Apr 1924 [88], 539 Bramhall Avenue, Jersey City NJ). m. Emma Mitchell (d. 1917). (Began on the stage in the late 1850s). "William Harris," *Variety*, 9 Apr 1924, 21:4. AS, p. 504.

Harris, Winifred [actress] (b. England, 17 Mar 1879–18 Apr 1972 [93], Evanston IL). BHD1, p. 245. Ragan 2.

Harrison, Arthur [assistant director] (b. Lakeside OH, 1888). BHD2, p. 115.

Harrison, Carey [actor] (*né* Carey Harrison Reppeteau, b. 1889–25 Mar 1957 [68?], Los Angeles CA). AS, p. 504.

Harrison, Doane [film editor] (b. 1894?–11 Nov 1968 [74], Riverside CA). "Doane Harrison," *Variety*, 20 Nov 1968. BHD2, p. 115.

Harrison, Edith Ogden [writer]. No data found. AMD, p. 156. "Mrs. Carter H. Harrison's Novel to Be Picturized," *MPW*, 6 Feb 1915, 818. "Filming 'The Lady of the Snows,'" *MPW*, 27 Feb 1915, p. 1274.

Harrison, Hoy [actor] (b. 1868–29 Dec 1928 [60], Concord NH). AS, p. 504.

Harrison, Irma [actress] (b. New Orleans LA, 24 Feb 1903–22 Jan 1975 [71], Los Angeles CA). AMD, p. 157. "Irma Harrison Back from Georgia," *MPW*, 27 Mar 1920, 2161.

Harrison, James A. [actor] (b. TX, 26 May 1908–9 Nov 1977 [69], Woodland Hills CA). (American.) "James Harrison," *Variety*, 16 Nov 1977. AMD, p. 157. AS, p. 504 (b. Milwaukee WI). BHD1, p. 245 (b. Milwaukee). IFN, p. 134. Truitt, 1983 (b. Milwaukee). "Jimmie Proved He Was an Actor," *MPW*, 19 Apr 1919, 362. "Harrison ill Be a Free Lance," *MPW*, 17 Jul 1920, 351.

Harrison, Kathleen [film/TV actress] (b. Blackburn, Lancashire, England, 23 Feb 1892–7 Dec 1995 [103], London, England). (Film debut: *Our Boys*, 1915; last film: *The London Connection*, Disney, 1979.) Anthony Hayward, "Kathleen Harrison," *The Independent*, 8 Dec 1995, p. 19. AS, p. 504. BHD1, p. 245 (d. 1 Dec).

Harrison, Louis Reeves [editor of *Moving Picture World*/scenarist] (b. 1858?–8 May 1921 [63], Hempstead NY). "Louis Reeves Harrison Dies," *Variety*, 13 May 1921. AMD, p. 157. BHD2, p. 115 (d. 7 May). "Harrison Writing for Apollo," *MPW*, 27 Jan 1917, 532.

Harrison, Mark [actor] (b. 1864?–1 Jun 1952 [88]). AS, p. 505. BHD, p. 193. IFN, p. 134.

Harrison, Mona K. [actress] (b. Edinburgh, Scotland-d. 2 Jan 1957). BHD, p. 193.

Harrison, Richard Berry [actor/scenarist] (b. London, Canada, 28 Sep 1864–14 Mar 1935 [70], New York NY). AS, p. 505.

Harrison, Saul E. [actor/director] (b. Brenham TX, 1888?–13 Oct 1944 [56], New York NY). (Kalem; Edison; Universal; Metro; Town and Country Films.) "Saul E. Harrison," *Variety*, 18 Oct 1944. AS, p. 505. BHD, p. 193; BHD2, p. 115. MSBB, p. 1046 (b. 1890).

Harrison, Stanley [stage/film actor] (b. Glasgow, Scotland, 1877–16 Feb 1950 [72], New York NY). "Stanley Harrison," *Variety*, 177, 22 Feb 1950, 63:1. BHD, p. 193.

Harron, Anna (sister of **Charles**, **John**, **Robert** and **Tessie Harron**) [actress] (b. 1899?–8 Nov 1918 [19], Hollywood CA; influenza). AMD, p. 157. "Obituary," *MPW*, 30 Nov 1918, 938.

Harron, Charles (brother of **Anna**, **John**, **Robert** and **Tessie Harron**) [actor] (d. 24 Dec 1915, Los Angeles CA; auto accident). "Film Actor Killed," *Variety*, 31 Dec 1915. AMD, p. 157. BHD, p. 193. "Obituary," *MPW*, Jan 1916, 228.

Harron, John (brother of **Anna**, **Charles**, **Robert** and **Tessie Harron**) [actor] (b. New York NY, 31 Mar 1903–24 Nov 1939 [36], Seattle WA; heart attack). m. **Betty Egan**. (MGM.) AMD, p. 157. AS, p. 505. BHD1, p. 245. FSS, p. 141. IFN, p. 134. Katz, 536. Truitt, p. 144. "Woods Signs Harron," *MPW*, 1 Mar 1924, 35. "Johnny Carries On," *MPC*, XXII, Jan 1926, 40. "John Harron," *MPW*, 4 Jun 1927, 333. Eve Golden, "Robert Harron: America's Kid Brother," *CI*, 235 (Jan 1995), C4-C5.

Harron, Robert Emmett (brother of **Anna**, **Charles**, **John** and **Tessie Harron**) [actor] (b. New York NY, 24 Apr 1893–5 Sep 1920 [27], New York NY [Death Certificate No. 24963; bullet wound of left lung]). (Biograph, ca. 1907; Griffith; Reliance-Majestic; Fine Arts; Goldwyn.) "Robert Harron Dies, Actor Succumbs to Wound Received in Pistol Accident," *NYT*, 6 Sep 1920, 7:5. "Robert Harron," *Variety*, 10 Sep 1920 (d. 6 Sep). AMD, p. 157. AS, p. 505 (d. 6 Sep). BHD, p. 193. IFN, p. 134. Katz, p. 536. KOM, p. 142 (b. 1896). Lowrey, p. 66. MSBB, p. 1024. Spehr, pp. 138–39 (b. 1894). Truitt, p. 144. WWS, p. 63. *See* Celia McGerr, "Griffith's Boy: An Introduction to the Career of Robert Harron," Dissertation, Sarah Lawrence College, 1978 (b. 1896, citing 1894 in other sources). "Film Actor Killed," *MPW*, 8 Jan 1916, 228 (Charles Harron, in car accident). "Robert Harron in the East," *MPW*, 15 Jan 1916, 405. "Riobert Harron to Be Starred," *MPW*, 13 Jan 1917, 210. "Harron to Star," *MPW*, 3 Feb 1917, 666. "Robet Harron Joins Goldwyn," *MPW*, 31 Mar 1917, 2113. "Sister of Robert Harron Dies," *MPW*, 30 Nov 1918, 938 (Anna Harron). "Robert Harron Badly Hurt When Pistol Is Discharged," *MPW*, 1 Sep 1920, 201 (on 1 Sep 1920, at Hotel Seymour, NYC; taken to Bellevue Hospital). "Obituary," *MPW*, 25 Sep 1920, 471–72. George Katchmer, "Remembering the Great Silents," *CI*, 241 (Jul 1995), 36.

Harron, Tessie (sister of **Anna**, **Charles**, **John** and **Robert Harron**) [actress] (*née* Therese Harron, b. New York NY, 16 Feb 1896–8 Nov 1918 [22], Los Angeles CA; influenza epidemic casualty). "Tessie Harron," *Variety*, 15 Nov 1918 (age 19). AS, p. 505. BHD, p. 193. IFN, p. 135 (Theresa Harron). Truitt, p. 144 (d. 1920).

Harry-Krimer [actor] (*né* Félix Désiré Rosenthal, b. Paris, France, 10 Mar 1896–4 Jan 1991 [94], Saint-Josse-sur-Mer, France [extrait de décès no. 1/1991]). AS, p. 505.

Harry-Max [actor] (*né* Maxime Louis Charles Dihamp, b. Paris, France, 23 Nov 1901–13 Mar 1979 [77], Ivry-sur-Seine, France [extrait de décès no. 238]). AS, p. 505.

Harsanyi, Tibor [composer/musician] (b. Magyarkamzsa, Hungary, 27 Jun 1898–19 Sep 1954 [56], Paris, France). AS, p. 505.

Hart, Albert S. [actor] (b. Liverpool, England, 6 Dec 1875–10 Jan 1940 [64], Los Angeles CA). (World [Ft. Lee NJ]; Universal; Paramount.) "Albert Hart," *Variety*, 17 Jan 1940 (age 63). AS, p. 505. BHD1, p. 245. IFN, p. 134. Truitt, p. 144.

Hart, Billy [actor] (*né* William Lenhart, b. 1863–18 Jun 1942 [79?], Los Angeles CA). AS, p. 505.

Hart, Charles [actor] (b. San Jose CA, 1873–15 Nov 1917 [44?], London, England; pneumonia). "Charles Hart Dies," *Variety*, 14 Dec 1917. AS, p. 505.

Hart, Florence [stage/film actress] (d. 30 Mar 1960, Germantown PA). m. **Kenneth Harlan**, 26 Jun 1920 (d. 1967). "Florence Hart," *Variety*, 6 Apr 1960. AS, p. 505. BHD, p.193. IFN, p. 134. SD.

Hart, Fred C. [stage/film actor] (d. 9 Nov 1927, Apollo Theatre, Chicago IL; heart disease). "Fred C. Hart," *Variety*, 23 Nov 1927, 58:4 ("Hart for the past 15 years had played with different colored troupes, among them Sandy Burns', Sam Russell's and his own, the Fred Hart Co., playing the Standard, Philadelphia, for two consecutive years."). BHD, p. 193.

Hart, "Indian" Jack [actor] (b. 1872–23 Sep 1974 [102?], Las Vegas NV). AS, p. 505. BHD1, p. 245.

Hart, James T. [actor] (b. 1868?–12 Aug 1926 [58], Los Angeles CA; apoplexy). m. Blance Trojan. "James T. Hart," *Variety*, 18 Aug 1926. AS, p. 505. BHD, p. 193. IFN, p. 134. Truitt, p. 144.

Hart, Joseph [actor: minstrel/Hallen & Hart/stage producer/writer] (*né* Joseph Hart Boudrow, b. Boston MA, 8 Jun 1864–3 Oct 1921 [57], New York NY; apoplexy after paralysis). m. Carrie De Mar, 1899. "Joseph Hart," *Variety*, Oct 1921, 7:2 (interred in Calvary Cemetery). BHD, p. 193.

Hart, Lewis O. [stage/film actor] (b. 1846?–9 Jan 1920 [73], Staten Island NY). m. Louise Plunkett. "Lewis O. Hart," *Variety*, 16 Jan 1920. AS, p. 505. BHD, p. 193. IFN, p. 134. SD.

Hart, Louis [actor] (b. TX, 27 Jan 1917–25 Apr 1972 [55]). AS, p. 505. IFN, p. 134.

Hart, Lucia (Sunshine) [actress] (b. Indianapolis IN, 6 Jul 1886–3 Jan 1930 [43], Los Angeles CA). AS, p. 506 (Sunshine Hart). BHD1, p. 245.

Hart, Mabel [actress] (b. IL, 29 Apr 1886–9 Jun 1960 [74], Los Angeles CA). AS, p. 505.

Hart, Neal, "America's Pal" [actor/director] (*né* Cornelius Augustus Neal Hart, Jr., b. Richmond NY, 7 Apr 1870?–2 Apr 1949 [78], Woodland Hills CA). (Began ca. 1914; Blue Streak serials, Universal.) "Neal Hart," *NYT*, 4 Apr 1949, 23:1 (d. 3 Apr). "Neal Hart," *Variety*, 6 Apr 1949 (age 70; "film cowboy in the days of the silent screen"). AS, p. 505 (b. 1879). BHD1, p. 246; BHD2, p. 115 (b. 1879). GK, pp. 369–75. IFN, p. 134 (b. 1879). Truitt, p. 144 (b. 1879). Eldon K. Everett, "Neal Hart; The Educated Cowboy," *CFC*, 40 (Fall, 1973), 36–37. Diana Serra Cary, *The Hollywood Possee* (Boston: Houghton Mifflin Co., 1975), pp. 47 *et passim*. George A. Katchmer, "Neal Hart; America's Cowboy Pal," *CI*, 91 (Jan 1983), 20–21. George Katchmer, "Remembering the Great Silents," *CI*, 241 (Jul 1995), 33.

Hart, Ruth [actress] (b. 1893?–2 May 1952

[59], New York NY [Death Certificate Index No. 9947]). m. Walter J. Moore. (Griffith.) "Ruth Hart Moore," *Variety*, 7 May 1952. AS, p. 506. BHD1, p. 610. IFN, p. 134. Truitt, p. 237.

Hart, Sunshine [actress] (*née* Lucia Hart, b. Indianapolis IN, 6 Jul 1886–3 Jan 1930 [43], Los Angeles CA). IFN, p. 134.

Hart, Thomas A. [actor] (b. 1894?–19 Apr 1929 [35], NY). m. Hazel Hurd. "Thomas A. Hart," *Variety*, 24 Apr 1929. AS, p. 506.

Hart, Virgil [assistant director] (b. Pontiac MI, 9 Feb 1894–22 Aug 1969 [75], Los Angeles CA; following recent surgery). "Virgil Hart," *Variety*, 27 Aug 1969. AS, p. 506. BHD2, p. 115.

Hart, William S[urrey] [stage/film actor/ director] (b. Newburgh NY, 6 Dec 1864–23 Jun 1946 [81], Saugus CA; apoplexy). m. **Winifred Westover**, 7 Dec 1921, LA CA; separated May 1922—div. Feb 1927, Reno NV (d. 1978). *My Life East and West* (Boston: Houghton Mifflin Co., 1929). (Ince; Artcraft.) "William S. Hart, 75, Film Veteran, Dies; 'Wild West' Idol During Era of Silent Screen Was Figure on Stage for Many Years; An Eastern-Born Cowboy; Considered Good Horseman—Contributed Old Pictures to Museum, Estate to Public," *NYT*, 25 Jun 1946, 21:1. "Wm. S. Hart Dies After Long Illness," *Variety*, 26 Jun 1946 (d. 24 Jun, LA CA). AMD, p. 157. AS, p. 506. BHD, p. 194; BHD2, p. 115. FFF, p. 101. FSS, p. 141. IFN, p. 134. MH, p. 115. MSBB, p. 1024. WWS, p. 22. Truitt, p. 144 (b. 1862). "William S. Hart," *MPW*, 14 Nov 1914, 920. "Edeson-Mitchell-Hart," *MPW*, 19 Dec 1914, 1682. "William S. Hart," *MPW*, 0 Jul 1915, 259. "William S. Hart in the Wilds," *MPW*, 5 Feb 1916, 782. "The Man Who Knows His West," *MPC*, Mar 1916, 48 ("Raised among the Sioux Indians on the plains of North Dakota..."). "William S. Hart," *MPW*, 20 Jan 1917, 373. "Hart to Stay with Triangle," *MPW*, 31 Mar 1917, 2126. "Hart and [Dustin] Farnum Most Popular Cowboys," *MPW*, 2 Jun 1917, 1471. "William S. Hart," *MPW*, 16 Jun 1917, 1783. "Hart to Make Pictures for Artcraft," *MPW*, 28 Jul 1917, 620. "Hart Controversy Reaches Court," *MPW*, 11 Aug 1917, 918. "Initial Hart Picture Nearing Completion," *MPW*, 15 Sep 1917, 1717. "Hart Picture Held Up," *MPW*, 27 Oct 1917, 513. "Hart Has New Horse in 'Silent Man,'" *MPW*, 24 Nov 1917, 1192. "Bill Hart Breaks a Finger," *MPW*, 1 Dec 1917, 1311. "Artcraft Wins William S. Hart Case," *MPW*, 22 Dec 1917, 1790. "Hart Takes on More Studio Space," *MPW*, 23 Feb 1918, 1118. "Artcraft Wins in Hart Suit," *MPW*, 6 Apr 1918, 71. "Hart Ends First Year of Artcraft Contract," *MPW*, 13 Jul 1918, 197 98. "Hart Completes Loan Film," *MPW*, 14 Sep 1918, 1570. Faith Service, "Have a Hart!; Might as Well—He Has—And Plenty of It," *MPC*, Jan 1919, 31–32, 80. "United Artists Association Formed," *MPW*, 25 Jan 1919, 455. "Hart Declares Himself Out of United Artists' Combine," *MPW*, 1 Mar 1919, 1166. "Hart to Make Nine Pictures for Famous Players-Lasky," *MPW*, 2 Aug 1919, 644. 'Famous Players Signs Hart to Make Nine Productions," *MPW*, 9 Aug 1919, 807. "Hart Refuses Generous Offer to Give Part Time to Stage," *MPW*, 29 May 1920, 1190. "William S. Hart for Sheriff," *MPW*, 12 Jun 1920, 1424 (Hood River County OR). "William S. Hart Files Two Suits to Prevent Exhibitions of His Old Films for New Under False Titles," *MPW*, 6 Nov 1920, 34. "Hart Wins Judgment for $87,000 from Tom Ince," *MPW*, 11 Dec 1920, 724. "Paramount Exchanges to Distribute Book by William S. Hart for Benefit of Hoover Fund," *MPW*, 5 Feb 1921, 685 (*Pinto Ben*). "William S. Hart Marries Winifred Westover," *MPW*, 17 Dec 1921, 786. "'No Truth in Rumors That I Am to Retire,' Says William S. Hart," *MPW*, 15 Apr 1922, 719. "The William S. Hart Company," *MPW*, 6 May 1922, 35. Maude Cheatham, "The Darkest Hour," *MPC*, Jul 1922, 51 (a series on the unhappiest period in the lives of well-known stars). "William S. Hart Signs New Paramount Contract," *MPW*, 7 Jul 1923, 53. "Hart to Work at the Paramount Studios," *MPW*, 14 Jul 1923, 162. Dorothy Donnell, "From Hollywood to You," *MPS*, 24 Feb 1925, 8 (news of the Hart trial—his divorce against Westover). Sumner Smith, "Bill Hart Finally Corralled to Talk About New Westerns," *MPW*, 9 May 1925, 144. Alma Talley, "Two-Gun Baby Bill," *MW*, 6 Jun 1925, 28–29 (Hart's son was born 6 Sep 1922). "On the Set and Off," *MW*, 1 Aug 1925, 43 (his wife was to get a $103,000 trust fund, his son one for $100,000. She wanted her trust fund set aside so that she could appear on the screen again; Hart said he would fight her court victory to do so). "'Bill' Hart 'Set' to Start for United Artists Corporation," *MPW*, 15 Aug 1925, 763. "Hart with Hays," *MPW*, 19 Sep 1925, 236. "Hart Ridicules Ideas That 'Westerns' Have Lost Appeal," *MPW*, 2 Jan 1926, 80. "Hart and Son Ill," *MPW*, 26 Feb 1927, 620. June Lee, "Dan Cupid's Bulletin Board," *Paris and Hollywood Screen Secrets Magazine*, May 1927, 51 (the public was excluded from the courtroom during the granting of Hart's divorce decree. In May 1922, "it was rumored that the separation was caused by the presence of Hart's sister, Mary Hart, in their home."). "Noted Gun Fighter of Old West Dea End Comes to Wyatt Earp at Los Angeles After Life of Battling 'Bad Men'; Defeated Clinton Gang; As Referee with a Pistol at Sharky-Fitzsimmons Fight, His Decision Stood," *NYT*, 14 Jan 1929, 23:3 (d. 13 Jan 1929 [78], LA CA; "In Alaska, during the gold rush, Earp met Bill Hart, the motion-picture actor; Wilson Mizner, playwright, and the late Tex Rickard, all of whom were close friends."). Mario de Marco, "William S. Hart; Pioneer of the Western," *CI*, 63 (May 1979), 48. Gene Fernett, "When William S. Hart Had His Own Studio," *CI*, 117 (Mar 1985), 21–22. Robert K. Klepper, "William S. Hart: The Man Behind the Legend," *CI*, 254 (Aug 1996), 34–37. George Katchmer, "Remembering the Great Silents," *CI* (Nov 1996). 49–50.

Hart, William Valentine (Pop) [actor] (b. 1865?–14 Oct 1925 [60], New York NY). AS, p. 506. BHD, p. 194. IFN, p. 134.

Harte, Betty [actress] (*née* Daisy Mae Light, b. Philadelphia PA, 13 May 1882–3 Jan 1965 [83], Sunland CA). (Selig, 1909.) AMD, p. 158. AS, p. 506. BHD, p. 194 (b. Lebanon PA). BR, pp. 38–40. IFN, p. 134 (age 82). Truitt, p. 145. "With the Western Producers," *MPW*, 8 Jul 1911, 1576. "Betty Harte at Grand Canyon," *MPW*, 10 Aug 1912, 530. "Betty Harte," *MPW*, 30 May 1914, 1237. "Betty Harte," *MPW*, 31 Oct 1914, 651. George Katchmer, "Remembering the Great Silents," *CI*, 246 (Dec 1995), 44–45.

Harte, Bret (grmndfather of **Richard Bret Harte**) [playwright]. No data found. "Another Harte Play; 'A Phyllis of the Sierras' to Be Released by the California Corporation," *NYDM*, 12 May 1915, 21:4.

Harte, Richard Bret (grandson of **Bret Harte**) [scenarist] (b. Philadelphia PA, 1890–18 Nov 1925 [35?], Paris France). AMD, p. 158. BHD2, p. 115. "Richard Bret Harte," *MPW*, 8 Sep 1917, 1518.

Hartford, David M. [actor/producer/director] (b. Ontonian MI, 11 Jan 1873–29 Oct 1932 [59], Los Angeles CA; heart attack). (Ince; Universal; Fox.) "David Hartford," *Variety*, 1 Nov 1932 (age 56). AMD, p. 158. AS, p. 506 (b. 16 Jan). BHD1, p. 246 (b. Rockland MI)' BHD2, p. 115 (d. 30 Oct). IFN, p. 135. Truitt, p. 145 (b. 1876). "May Direct Again," *MPW*, 21 May 1927, 179.

Hartford, Harry [actor] (b. 1851–20 Sep 1925 [74?], Bernardsville NJ). BHD, p. 194.

Hartigan, Patrick C. [actor/director] (b. New York NY, 21 Dec 1881–8 May 1951 [69], Los Angeles CA; coronary occlusion). AMD, p. 158. AS, p. 506. BHD1, p. 246; BHD2, p. 115. IFN, p. 135. 1921 Directory, p. 265 (b. Cork, Ireland). Slide, p. 161 (1881–1954). "Hartigan in Town," *MPW*, 28 Feb 1914, 1071 (C.P. Hartigan). George A. Katchmer, "Forgotten Cowboys & Cowgirls—IV," *CI*, 175 (Jan 1990), C6.

Hartigan, William [actor] (b. 1866?–3 Jul 1920 [54], Johannesburg, South Africa). "William Hartigan," *Variety*, 13 Aug 1920. AS, p. 506. BHD, p. 194.

Hartl, Karl Anton [actor/director/producer/scenarist] (b. Vienna, Austria, 10 May 1899–29 Aug 1978 [79], Vienna, Austria). AS, p. 506. BHD2, p. 115.

Hartley, Charles T. [actor] (b. 1852?–13 Oct 1930 [78], Fort Lee NJ; pneumonia). "Charles T. Hartley," *Variety*, 22 Oct 1930. AS, p. 506. BHD, p. 194. IFN, p. 135. Truitt, p. 145.

Hartley, Helen [actress/circus performer] (b. 1892–30 Oct 1954 [62?], Denison TX). BHD, p. 194. IFN, p. 135.

Hartley, K. Baron [director] (b. Enfield, England, 1886). AS, p. 506.

Hartley, Mary [stage/film actress] (b. 1879?–4 Aug 1919 [40], New York NY; suicide: "A gas tube connected with a nearby jet was in her mouth"). m. N.K. Lewis. "Mary Hartley," *Variety*, 8 Aug 1919. AS, p. 506. SD.

Hartman, Agnes A. (mother of **Gretchen Hartman**) [actress] (b. Sweden, 1860?–22 Dec 1932 [72?], Los Angeles CA). "Agnes A. Hartman," *Variety*, 3 Jan 1933. AS, p. 506. BHD1, p. 610. Truitt, p. 145.

Hartman, Ferris [stage/film actor/director] (b. 1861?–1 Sep 1931 [70], San Francisco CA; starvation). m. Josie Davis. "Ferris Hartman," *Variety*, 8 Sep 1931. AS, p. 506. BHD, p. 194; BHD2, p. 115. IFN, p. 135. SD.

Hartman, Gretchen (daughter of **Agnes A. Hartman**) [actress] (aka Sonia Markova, *née* Gretchin Arbin, b. Chicago IL, 28 Aug 1897–27 Jan 1979 [81], Los Angeles CA). m. **Alan Hale**. "Gretchen Hartman Hale," *Variety*, 7 Feb 1979. AMD, p. 158. AS, p. 506. BHD1, p. 246. IFN, p. 135. MH, p. 116 ("Greta"). "Gretchen Hartman," *MPW*, 28 Jul 1917, 625. "Edward Keppler, Lorraine Harding and Gretchen Hartman Are Added to 'Bandbox' Cast," *MPW*, 9 Aug 1919, 853.

Hartman, Jonathan William "Pop" [actor] (b. Louisville KY, 1872?–19 Oct 1965 [93], Tampa FL). "Jonathan William (Pop) Hartman," *Variety*, 27 Oct 1965. AS, p. 506. BHD, p. 194. IFN, p. 135.

Hartman, Ruth [actress] (b. IL, 3 Apr 1893–9 Jul 1956 [63], Los Angeles CA). m. **Carlyle Blackwell**, 8 Jul 1909 (d. 1955). AS, p. 506. BHD, p. 194. IFN, p. 135.

Hartmann, Paul Wilhelm Constantin [actor] (b. Fürth, Germany, 8 Jan 1889–30 Jun

1977 [88], Munich, Germany). AS, p. 507. BHD1, p. 246. IFN, p. 135 (d. Furth, Bayern, Germany). Vittorio Martinelli, "Kino-Lieblinge," *Griffithiana,* 38/39 (Oct 1990), 49.

Hartmann, Sadakichi [actor/dancer] (b. Japan, 1866–21 Nov 1944 [78?], St. Petersburg FL). AS, p. 507 (b. 1864). BHD, p. 194.

Hartsell, Harold [actor] (b. 1874–1 Oct 1930 [56?], Beechurst NY). BHD, p. 194.

Hartsook, Fred [photographer] (b. 1875–30 Sep 1930 [55?], Burbank CA). BHD2, p. 115.

Hartt, Heinz S. [director] (*né* Paul Erich Ernst Scheffer, b. Berlin, Germany, 17 Oct 1895). AS, p. 507.

Hartwig, Walter [director] (b. Milwaukee WI, 1880–17 Jan 1941 [60?], New York NY). BHD2, p. 115.

Harty, Veola [actress] (b. 1896–13 Jul 1936 [40?], New York NY). BHD, p. 194.

Harvey, Clarence [actor] (b. New York NY, 1865?–3 May 1945 [80], New York NY). AS, p. 507. BHD1, p. 246. IFN, p. 135.

Harvey, Donald [actor] (*né* James H. Brundage, b. 1863–1 Feb 1931 [67?], Los Angeles CA). BHD, p. 194. IFN, p. 135.

Harvey, Edward [actor] (b. England, 1893–5 Nov 1975 [82?], Ventor, England). AS, p. 507.

Harvey, Edwin L. [film editor] (b. 1884–18 Aug 1953 [69?], New York NY). BHD2, p. 115.

Harvey, Fletcher [actor] (b. 1865?–8 Sep 1931 [66], Bayshore LI NY). "Fletcher Harvey," *Variety,* 15 Sep 1931. AS, p. 507. BHD, p. 194. IFN, p. 135.

Harvey, Forrester [actor] (b. County Cork, Ireland, 27 Jun 1884–14 Dec 1945 [61], Laguna Beach CA). "Forrester Harvey," *Variety,* 19 Dec 1945. AS, p. 507. BHD1, p. 246. IFN, p. 135. Truitt, 1983 (b. 1880).

Harvey, George W. [publicist]. No data found. AMD, p. 158. "Harvey Succeeds Gallup," *MPW,* 22 Sep 1923, 326. "George W. Harvey," *MPW,* 26 Mar 1927, 311.

Harvey, Georgette [singer/actress] (b. St. Louis MO, 1882?–17 Feb 1952 [69], New York NY). "Georgette Harvey," *Variety,* 20 Feb 1952. AS, p. 507. IFN, p. 135.

Harvey, Georgia [actress] (b. Nova Scotia, Canada, 1875–17 May 1960 [85?], New York NY). BHD1, p. 246.

Harvey, Harry, Jr. (son of **Harry Harvey, Sr.**) [actor/director/writer] (d. 8 Dec 1978). AMD, p. 158. AS, p. 507. IFN, p. 135. "Harvey Writes for Gilda," *MPW,* 21 May 1927, 172.

Harvey, Harry, Sr. (father of **Harry Harvey, Jr.**) [actor/producer/director] (b. Indian Territory OK, 10 Jan 1901–27 Nov 1985 [84], Sylmar CA). (Monogram; RKO.) "Harry Harvey, Sr.," *Variety,* 4 Dec 1985. AMD, p. 158. AS, p. 507. "Some Horsemanship," *MPW,* 10 Feb 1912, 490. "Harry Harvey, Sr.," *MPW,* 26 Dec 1914, 1849. "Harry Harvey, Sr.," *MPW,* 18 Sep 1915, 1974.

Harvey, Herman (Hank) (father of **Billie McCormack**) [actor] (*né* Herman Heacker, b. 1849–4 Dec 1929 [80], Los Angeles CA). (Universal.) "Hank Harvey," *Variety,* 11 Dec 1929, 78:4 (interred in Culver City CA. "Harvey was of the old school of film actors and for many years appeared for Universal."). AS, p. 507. BHD, p. 194. IFN, p. 135.

Harvey, John Joseph [director]. No data found. AMD, p. 159. "Night Photography," *MPW,* 29 May 1915, 1410–11. "Harvey Joins Universal," *MPW,* 26 Jun 1915, 2076. "Jack Harvey Joins Universal," *MPW,* 17 Jul 1915, 501. "Taking Pictures in the Rain," *MPW,* 7 Aug 1915, 977. "John Harvey, Director, Joins Universal," *MPW,* 7 Aug 1915, 986. "John Joseph Harvcey," *MPW,* 9 Nov 1918, 674. "Harvey to Direct Ernest Truex," *MPW,* 19 Jul 1919, 372.

Harvey, John M. "Jack" [actor/director] (b. Cleveland OH, 1881?–10 Nov 1954 [73], Los Angeles CA; found dead). "John M. 'Jack' Harvey," *Variety,* 17 Nov 1954 ("pioneer cowboy actor"). AS, p. 507. BHD, p. 194; BHD2, p. 116. IFN, p. 135. Truitt, p. 145.

Harvey, Lee F. [actor] (b. 1895–19 Apr 1950 [55?], Philadelphia PA). BHD, p. 194. IFN, p. 135.

Harvey, Lew P. [actor] (b. WI, 6 Oct 1887–19 Dec 1953 [66], Los Angeles Co. CA). AS, p. 507. BHD1, p. 247. IFN, p. 135. George Katchmer, "Remembering the Great Silents," *CI,* 196 (Oct 1991), 55.

Harvey, Lilian [stage/film dancer/actress] (b. Edmonton, England, 19 Jan 1906–27 Jul 1968 [62], Cap d'Antibes, France [extrait de décès no. 391/1968]). (Began 1925, film debut: *The Crowd Entertains Itself;* Ufa; Fox; Columbia.) "Lilian Harvey," *Variety,* 251, 31 Jul 1968, 63:1 ("She had been operating a souvenir shop and raising edible snails."; "At the height of her career she was offered a Hungarian castle and the village that surrounded it by a Hungarian nobleman."). AS, p. 507 (b. Hornsey, England). BHD1, p. 247. IFN, p. 135 (b. 1907). Waldman, p. 130 (b. 1907; Fox canceled her contract after a dispute over *Serenade,* which she didn't like).

Harvey, Lottie [actress] (*née* Charlotte Action, b. 1890–2 Aug 1948 [58?], Los Angeles CA). AS, p. 507.

Harvey, Paul [stage/film actor] (b. Sandwich IL, 10 Sep 1882–15 Dec 1955 [73], Los Angeles CA; coronary thrombosis). m. Ottye. (Essanay.) "Paul Harvey, Acted in Films 40 Years," *NYT,* 16 Dec 1955, 30:1 (age 71). "Paul Harvey," *Variety,* 21 Dec 1955. AS, p. 507. BHD1, p. 247. IFN, p. 135. SD. Truitt, pp. 145–46 (b. 1884).

Harvey, Rupert [actor] (b. Ironbridge, England, 1 Jan 1887–7 Jul 1954 [67], London, England). AS, p. 507. BHD, p. 194.

Harvey, William Leo [actor]. No data found. AMD, p. 159. "William Leo Harvey," *MPW,* 7 Apr 1917, 100. "William Harvey Wearing Sergeant's Stripes," *MPW,* 22 Dec 1917, 1769.

Harwood, H.M. [scenarist] (b. 1873–20 Apr 1959 [86?], London, England). BHD2, p. 116.

Harwood, John Gomar [actor] (b. London, England, 29 Feb 1876–26 Dec 1944 [68], London, England). "John Gomar Harwood," *Variety,* 7 Feb 1945. AS, p. 507. BHD1, p. 247. IFN, p. 135.

Hasbrouck, Olive [actress] (b. Lewiston ID, 1 Jan 1905). (Universal.) AMD, p. 159. BR, pp. 159–61. "Real Western Girl," *MPW,* 9 Jul 1927, 103.

Hasegawa, Kazuo [actor] (b. Kyoto, Japan, 29 Feb 1908–6 Apr 1984 [76], Tokyo, Japan). AS, p. 507 (b. 27 Feb). BHD1, p. 247.

Haskel, Leonhard [actor] (b. Seelow, Germany, 7 Apr 1872–30 Dec 1923 [51]). BHD, p. 195. IFN, p. 135.

Haskell, Al[bert] B. [actor] (b. CA, 4 Dec 1886–6 Jan 1969 [82], Los Angeles CA). AS, p. 508.

Haskell, Jean [actress]. No data found. AMD, p. 159. "Jean Haskell Wins," *MPW,* LXI, 3 Mar 1923, 33.

Haskin, Byron [cinematographer/diretor] (*né* Byron Haskin Amor, b. Portland OR, 22 Apr 1899–16 Apr 1984 [84], Montecito CA). *Byron Haskin; Interviewed by Joe Adamson* (Metuchen NJ: Directors Guild of America and Scarecrow Press, Inc., 1984). "Byron Haskin Is Dead at 84; Directed 'War of the Worlds,'" *NYT,* 19 Apr 1984, B15:3. "Byron Haskin Succumbs at 84; Diverse Career Began in Silents," *Variety,* 25 Apr 1984 (d. Santa Barbara CA). AMD, p. 159. AS, p. 508 (d. Santa Barbara CA). BHD2, p. 116 (d. Santa Barbara). FDY, p. 459. Katz, p. 539 (began 1918). Tom Waller, "Byron Haskin," *MPW,* 9 Apr 1927, 542–43. "Byron Haskin," *MPW,* 27 Aug 1927, 589.

Haskin, Charles W[ilson] [stage manager/film actor] (b. 1868?–10 Jun 1927 [59], New York NY). "Charles W. Haskin," *Variety,* 15 Jun 1927. AS, p. 508. BHD, p. 195. IFN, p. 135.

Haskin, Harry R. [actor] (b. 1870–7 Feb 1953 [82?]). BHD, p. 195.

Haslup, Marion [actor]. NO data found. AMD, p. 159. "Selects Actor from Moving Pictures," *MPW,* 11 Aug 1923, 505. "Marion Haslup Signed," *MPW,* 21 Mar 1925, 282.

Hass, Willy [scenarist] (b. Prague, Czechoslovakia, 1891–4 Sep 1973 [82?], Hamburg, Germany). AS, p. 508. BHD2, p. 116.

Hassan, Princess Ibrahim *see* Humphrey, Ola.

Hassell, George (father of Virginia Hassell) [stage/film actor] (b. Birmingham, England, 4 May 1881–17 Feb 1937 [55], Chatsworth CA; heart attack). (Film debut: *Old Dutch,* 1915.) "George Hassell, 56, Dies in Hollywood; Former Broadway Comedian Is Stricken in Auto on His Way to Play in Film [*Wee Willie Winkle*]; Had a Colorful Career; Native of England, He Sold Real Estate, Farmed and Served Three Years in Boer War," *NYT,* 18 Feb 1937, 21:3 (age 56). "George Hassell," *Variety,* 24 Feb 1937. AS, p. 508. BHD1, p. 247. IFN, p. 136. Truitt, p. 146.

Hasselmann, Karl [cinematographer]. No data found. FDY, p. 459.

Hasselquist, Jenny [actress] (b. Stockholm, Sweden, 31 Jul 1894–1978 [84?], Stockholm, Sweden). AS, p. 508. BHD1, p. 610.

Hasti, Robert [actor] (b. Paris, France, 6 Mar 1880–ca. Apr 1956 [76?]). AS, p. 508.

Hastings, Adelaide [actress] (d. 22 May 1921, Toledo OH). BHD, p. 195.

Hastings, Ann [actress]. No data found. AMD, p. 159. "Ann Hastings Has Painful Accident," *MPW,* 18 Jun 1921, 718.

Hastings, Carey L. [actress] (b. New Orleans LA–ca. 1929, New York NY). AMD, p. 159. BHD, p. 195. 1921 Directory, p. 224. "Film Favorite Stock Star, 'By Permission,'" *MPW,* 5 Oct 1912, 34. "Carey L. Hastings," *MPW,* 2 Jun 1917, 1439.

Hastings, Victoria [actress] (d. 24 May 1934, Los Angeles CA; heart attack). AS, p. 508.

Hastings, Wells [scenarist] (d. 8 May 1923, Los Angeles CA). (Griffith; FP-L.) "Wells Hastings,"

Variety, 10 May 1923. AS, p. 508 (d. 15 Apr). BHD2, p. 116.

Haswell, Percy [stage/film actress] (b. Austin TX, 30 Apr 1871–14 Jun 1945 [74], Nantucket MA). m. **George Fawcett** (d. 1939). "Percy Haswell Fawcett," *Variety*, 20 Jun 1945. AS, p. 508. BHD1, p. 248 (d. 13 Jun). IFN, p. 136. SD, p. 585. Truitt, p. 146.

Hatch, Frank [stage/film actor] (b. Marysville CA, 1864?–25 Oct 1938 [74], Richmond Hill, Queens, LI NY). "Frank Hatch," *Variety*, 2 Nov 1938. AS, p. 508. SD.

Hatch, Harry E. [actor] (b. 1882–22 Oct 1926 [44?], New York NY). BHD, p. 195.

Hatch, Ike [actor] (*né* Isaac Flower Hatch, b. England, 1892–26 Dec 1961 [69?], London, England). AS, p. 508.

Hatch, William Riley [stage/film actor] (b. Cleveland OH, 2 Sep 1861–6 Sep 1925 [64], Bayshore, LI NY). (Began 1914; Wharton, Ithaca NY; Pathé; Paramount.) AMD, p. 159. AS, p. 508 (d. 6 Jun). BHD, p. 195 (b. 1862). IFN, p. 136. "William Riley Hatch with Pathé," *MPW*, 20 Jun 1914, 1700. "Riley Hatch with Whartons," *NYDM*, 20 Nov 1915, 31:2 (on stage for 30 years). "Riley Hatch with Wharton, Inc.," *MPW*, 25 Dec 1915, 2357. George A. Katchmer, "Remembering the Great Silents," *CI*, 241 (Jul 1995), 36–37 (b. 1865).

Hathaway, Henry (son of **Jean** and **Rhody Hathaway**) [director/producer] (*né* Henri Leopold de Fiennes, b. Sacramento CA, 13 Mar 1898–11 Feb 1985 [86], Los Angeles CA). m. Blanche. (American; Universal; Paramount; Fox.) Albin Krebs, "Henry Hathaway Dies at 86; Directed More than 60 Films," *NYT*, 13 Feb 1985, D27:1 (b. 1896). Todd McCarthy, "Veteran Helmer Henry Hathaway, 'Studio Workhorse,' Dead at 86," *Variety*, 20 Feb 1985. AS, p. 508. BHD, p. 195; BHD2, p. 116. SD.

Hathaway, Jean (mother of **Henry Hathaway**) [actress] (*née* Lillie de Fiennes, b. Hungary, 15 Jun 1876–23 Aug 1938 [62], Los Angeles CA). m. **Rhody Hathaway**. (American.) "Jean Hathaway," *Variety*, 31 Aug 1938. AS, p. 508. BHD, p. 195 (*née* Jane). IFN, p. 136. Truitt, p. 146.

Hathaway, Joan [actress] (d. 6 Feb 1981, Los Angeles CA). BHD1, p. 248.

Hathaway, Lillian [actress] (b. Liverpool, England, 1875?–12 Jan 1954 [78], Englewood Cliffs NJ). "Lillian Hathaway," *Variety*, 20 Jan 1954. AS, p. 508. BHD, p. 195 (b. 1876). IFN, p. 136.

Hathaway, Rhody (father of **Henry Hathaway**) [actor] (b. San Francisco CA, 5 Oct 1868–18 Feb 1944 [75], Los Angeles CA). m. **Jean** de Fiennes. (American.) "Rhody Hathaway," *Variety*, 23 Feb 1944 (began 1908). AS, p. 509. BHD1, p. 248. IFN, p. 136. Truitt, p. 146.

Hatot, Georges [director/producer] (b. Paris, France, 22 Dec 1876–14 Aug 1959 [82], Paris, France). AS, p. 509.

Hatrick, Edgar B. [cameraman/general manager/executive] (b. PA, 1885–15 Sep 1949 [64?], Colorado Springs CO). AMD, p. 159. AS, p. 509. BHD2, p. 116. "Hatrick to Photograph World-War Fighters," *MPW*, 16 Mar 1918, 1491. "Hatrick of International Sees News Reel Demand," *MPW*, 10 Jan 1925, 176.

Hatswell, Donald R.O. [actor] (b. England, 3 Jul 1898–29 Jun 1976 [77], Encino CA). BHD1, p. 248.

Hatton, Charles Edward [actor]. No data found. AMD, p. 159. "Hatton Injured," *MPW*, LI, 27 Aug 1921, 917.

Hatton, Clare L. [actress] (b. 1869?–5 Jul 1943 [74], Denver CO). "Clare L. Hatton," *Variety*, 7 Jul 1943. AS, p. 509. BHD, p. 195 (d. 26 Jun).

Hatton, Fanny [playwright/title writer/scenarist] (*née* Fanny Cottinet Locke, b. Chicago IL, 1870?–27 Nov 1939 [69], New York NY). m. (1) John Kenneth MacKenzie; (2) **Frederick H. Hatton** (d. 1946). "Fanny Hatton, 69, Noted Playwright; Writer of Series of Successes in Collaboration with Her Husband, Frederic, Dies," *NYT*, 28 Nov 1939, 25:5. "Fanny Hatton," *Variety*, 29 Nov 1939 (she and Hatton "did several adaptations and also film writing for almost all the major filmers."). AMD, p. 159. AS, p. 509. BHD2, p. 116. FDY, pp. 427, 443. IFN, p. 136. SD. "Banner Engages [Frederick] Hatton's," *MPW*, 20 Jun 1925, 898.

Hatton, Frances. *See* Roberts, Frances.

Hatton, Frederick H. [playwright/title writer/scenarist] (b. Peru IL, 7 Jul 1879–13 Apr 1946 [66], Rutland IL). m. **Fanny** Cottinet Locke (d. 1939). "Frederick H. Hatton," *Variety*, 17 Apr 1946. AMD, p. 159. BHD2, p. 116. FDY, pp. 427, 443. SD. "Banner Engages Hatton's," *MPW*, 20 Jun 1925, 898.

Hatton, Raymond Wallace [stage/film/radio/TV actor] (b. Red Oak IA, 7 Jul 1887–21 Oct 1971 [84], Palmdale CA; found dead of heart attack). m. **Frances Roberts**, 17 Apr 1909, Vancouver WA [Marriage Certificate, Clarke County WA, 1 May 1909, Book 1, page 150 of Marriage Records] (age 21; d. 1971. They resided in Portland OR at the time.). (Biograph; Kalem, 1911; Paramount.) "Raymond Hatton, Actor, Dead; In First Hollywood Feature Film; 'Squaw Man' of '12 Followed by Wallace Beery Movies—Also in Vaudeville," *NYT*, 23 Oct 1971, 36:1. "Raymond Hatton," *Variety*, 27 Oct 1971. AMD, p. 159. AS, p. 509. BHD1, p. 248. FFF, p. 233. FSS, p. 142. GK, pp. 375–97. IFN, p. 136. Katz, p. 540. MH, p. 116. Truitt, p. 146. "Goldwyn Engages Hatton," *MPW*, 10 Jan 1920, 227. Joan Tully, "Wagons and Windmills," *MPC*, Jul 1921, 34–35, 83. "F.P.L. Signs Hatton," *MPW*, 8 Nov 1924, 154. Glenn Chaffin, "The Off-Stage Laugh; The Part Played by Mrs. Raymond Hatton in Her Husband's Career," *MPC*, Jun 1926, 55, 81. Nick Williams, "A Tribute to Raymond Hatton," *Filmograph*, I, No. 3 (1970), 2–15 (b. 1892; includes filmography). George A. Katchmer, "Character Actor Raymond Hatton," *CI*, 143 (May 1987), 42 *et passim*. "Buck Rainey's Filmographies; The Sidekick Portrayals of Raymond Hatton," *CI*, 163 (Jan 1989), 46–47, 49. Buck Rainey, "The Films of Raymond Hatton," *CI*, 164 (Feb 1988), 47–48, 55; 165 (Mar 1988), 42, 44, 46–47. Photocopy of Marriage Certificate supplied by Charles R. Roberts, Steilacoom WA.

Hatton, Richard [cowboy actor/director] (*né* Clarence Hatton, b. KY, 1886–9 Jul 1931 [45?], Los Angeles CA; crushed to death in an auto accident). "Richard Hatton," *Variety*, 14 Jul 1931 (cowboy actor and film director). AS, p. 509 (Dick Hatton, b. 1891). BHD1, p. 248; BHD2, p. 117 (b. 1888). IFN, p. 136 (age 40). Truitt, p. 147.

Hatton, Rondo [actor] (b. Hagerstown MD, 29 Apr 1894–2 Feb 1946 [51], Beverly Hills CA). AS, p. 509.

Hatvany, Lili [scenarist] (b. Hatvan, Hungary, 8 Jun 1890–12 Nov 1967 [77], New York NY). AS, p. 509 (d. 7 Oct 1968). BHD2, p. 116.

Hauber, William C. [actor] (b. WI, 1891?–17 Jul 1929 [38], near Reseda CA; plane crash). "Camera and Stunt Men Killed in Plane Crash," *Variety*, 24 Jul 1929. AS, p. 509. BHD, p. 195 (b. Brownsville MN). IFN, p. 136. *Los Angeles Times*, 18 Jul 1929 (b. Brownsville MN). Bo Berglund, "The Elusive Protean, William C. Hauber," *CI*, 156 (Jun 1988), C19-C20.

Hauck, Roy [actor]. No data found. AMD, p. 159. "Roy Hauck," *MPW*, 17 Jun 1916, 2043.

Haught, Albert B. [actor] (b. Dallas TX, 30 Apr 1899–29 Oct 1936 [37], Los Angeles CA). AS, p. 509 (d. 1 Nov). BHD1, p. 248. IFN, p. 136 (d. 1 Nov 1936).

Haupt, Ullrich [actor] (b. Prussia, 8 Aug 1887–5 Aug 1931 [43], near Santa Maria CA; hunting accident). "Ullrich Haupt," *Variety*, 11 Aug 1931 (began 1928). AS, p. 509 (d. 5 Jul). BHD1, p. 248 (d. Santa Barbara CA). IFN, p. 136. Truitt, p. 147.

Hauptmann, Gerhart [writer]. No data found. AMD, p. 159. "Hauptmann's Atlantis," *MPW*, 6 Sep 1913, 1074.

Hauser, William [actor]. No data found. "Suicide Follows Quarrel," *Variety*, 19 Aug 1925 ("Following a quarrel with her husband, Imogene Hauser, wife of William Hauser, screen actor, attempted to commit suicide. She was taken to the Angelus Hospital and died shortly after her arrival." She died in Aug 1925).

Haussermann, Reinhold (father of Ernst Haussermann, 1916–1984) [actor] (b. Stuttgart, Germany, 10 Feb 1884–1947 [63], Germany). AS, p. 509.

Havel, Joseph [actor] (b. 1869?–24 Jan 1932 [63?], Los Angeles CA). "Joe Havel," *Variety*, 2 Feb 1932 (began ca. 1920). AS, p. 509 (d. 27 Jan). BHD1, p. 248. Truitt, p. 147.

Havens, Beckwith [actor] (b. 1890–7 May 1969 [79?], New York NY). BHD, p. 195.

Havens, Harry "Hank" [publicist]. No data found. AMD, p. 159. "Hank Havens Hooked Up with Ultra," *MPW*, 13 Jan 1917, 208.

Haver, Phyllis [actress: Sennett Bathing Beauty] (*née* Phyllis O'Haver, b. Douglas KS, 6 Jan 1899–19 Nov 1960 [61], Falls Village CT; suicide with barbituates). m. William Seeman, Apr 1929, NYC. (Sennett; Griffith.) "Phyllis Haver," *Variety*, 30 Nov 1960 (age 60). AMD, p. 159. AS, p. 510. BHD1, p. 248. FFF, p. 223. FSS, p. 142. HCH, p. 45. IFN, p. 136. Katz, p. 541. MH, p. 116. Truitt, p. 147 (b. 16 Jan). WWS, p. 188. "Phyllis Haver Signs Contract," *MPW*, Aug 1921, 626 (with Sennett). "Phyllis Haver Awaits Turpin," *MPW*, 19 Nov 1921, 332. "Actresses Ill," *MPW*, 10 Dec 1921, 685 (appendicitis). "Phyllis Haver Signed," *MPW*, 15 Aug 1925, 764. "Phyllis Haver Signs Long Term Contract with Metropolitan," *MPW*, 8 May 1926, 140. "Phyllis Haver's New Contract," *MPW*, 19 Mar 1927, 190. "Phyllis Haver," *MPW*, 9 Apr 1927, 550. Frederick Packard, "Tantalizing Phyllis; Once a bathing girl, little Phyllis Haver is now one of our most able comediennes, and will soon be seen opposite Emil Jannings in a serious rôle," *Cinema Arts*, VI (Jul 1927), 26–27, 48. Carol Johnston, "The Home-Loving Home-Wrecker; Phyllis Haver Vamps for Professional Purposes Only," *MPC*, Oct 1928, 51, 83 (in *The Christian*, she "bridged the gap from beauty to actress in one graceful leap."). "Phyllis Haver and Bill Seeman"s Great Wedding Act Ran 8 Hrs. in N.Y.," *Variety*, 1 May 1929, 4:1.

Havez, Jean C. [songwriter/scenarist] (b. Baltimore MD, 24 Dec 1869–11 Feb 1925 [55], Beverly Hills CA; heart attack). m. (1) Cecil Cunningham. "Jean Havez, Song Writer," *NYT,* 13 Feb 1925, 17:4 (age 52; wrote *Everybody Works But Father* and 100 other songs. "Recently he had been preparing a motion picture scenario for Harold Lloyd, tentatively entitled 'East Side, West Side.'"). "Jean Havez," *Variety,* 18 Feb 1925 ("At the time of his death Havez was working for Harold Lloyd on a scenario which was temporarily titled 'Eastside, Westside.'"; in LA since 1915; worked for Chaplin, Arbuckle, Keaton and Lloyd). AMD, p. 159. AS, p. 510. BHD, p. 195; BHD2, p. 116 (b. 1870). SD, p. 587 (b. 1874). "Havez Writes Scripts for Keaton," *MPW,* 15 May 1920, 938. "Jean havez Has Been Added to Lloyd Staff," *MPW,* 25 Jun 1921, 796. "Jean Havez En Route for Europe," *MPW,* 12 Aug 1922, 499.

Haviland, Auguste [actor] (d. 25 Oct 1925, New York NY). BHD, p. 195.

Haviland, Rena [actress] (b. 1878?–20 Feb 1954 [76], Woodland Hills CA). "Rena Haviland," *Variety,* 24 Feb 1954 (began 1911). AS, p. 510. BHD, p. 195. IFN, p. 136. Truitt, p. 147.

Haviland-Taylor, Katherine [scenarist] (d. 28 Nov 1941, Saint Cloud FL). AS, p. 510. BHD2, p. 116.

Havlick, Gene [film editor] (b. 1894?–11 May 1959 [65], Los Angeles CA). (Columbia.) "Gene Havlick," *Variety,* 20 May 1959 (AA for *The Lost Horizon*). BHD2, p. 116.

Hawker, Albert [actor]. No data found. AMD, p. 159. "Wide Newspaper Publicity Gets Sunshine Film a New Comedian," *MPW,* 23 Apr 1921, 869.

Hawkins, "Puny" [actor] (d. 30 Mar 1947, Wichita KS; heart attack). (Universal.) "'Puny' Hawkins," *Variety,* 2 Apr 1947. AS, p. 510. BHD, p. 195. Truitt, p. 147.

Hawkins, Ralph S. [cinematographer]. No data found. (Selig; American; Bosworth; Lasky.)

Hawks, Charles Monroe [actor] (b. 1874?–15 Dec 1951 [77], Los Angeles CA). "Charles Monroe Hawks," *Variety,* 26 Dec 1951 ("screen actor in the silent days"). AS, p. 510. BHD, p. 195. IFN, p. 136. Truitt, p. 147.

Hawks, Howard Winchester (brother of William Hawks; 2nd cousin of **Carole Lombard**) [scenarist/director] (b. Goshen IN, 30 May 1896–26 Dec 1977 [81], Palm Springs CA; complications from a concussion). m. (1) **Athole Shearer** (d. 1985); (2) Nancy Gross; (3) Dee Hartford; (4) Virginia Walker. Gerald Mast, *Howard Hawks, Storyteller* (NY: Oxford University Press, 1982). (Began in 1917 as a prop boy at Famous Players-Lasky; Fox.) Jennifer Dunning, "Howard Hawks, Director of Films and Developer of Stars, Dies at 81," *NYT,* 28 Dec 1977, IV, 14:1. "Howard Hawks, 81, Story Teller Who Became a Pantheon Figure," *Variety,* 28 Dec 1977. Gary Arnold, "Hollywood Director Howard Hawks Dies," *The Washington Post,* 28 Dec 1977. AMD, p. 160. AS, p. 510. BHD2, p. 116 (d. LA CA). IFN, p. 136. Katz, p. 542. SD. "Howard Hawks Joins Metro," *MPW,* 18 Apr 1925, 714. "Howard Hawks to Direct 'Gaby' for Fox," *MPW,* 28 Aug 1926, 543.

Hawks, J[ohn] **G.** [scenarist/editor] (b. San Francisco CA, 1875?–11 Apr 1940 [65], Los Angeles CA). (Ince, 1914.) "John G. Hawks," *Variety,* 17 Apr 1940. AMD, p. 160. AS, p. 510. BHD2, p. 117. FDY, p. 427. "Hawks's Sixty-Second Script Accepted," *MPW,* 24 Nov 1917, 1154. J.G. Hawks, "The Day of the Story Is Here!," *MPW,* 12 Jul 1919, 212. "J.G. Hawks Signs Contract to Continue as Head of goldwyn Editorial Forces," *MPW,* 6 Nov 1920, 92. "Hawks to Prepare Sea Story Continuity," *MPW,* 17 Nov 1923, 327.

Hawks, Kenneth (brother of **Howard** and William Hawks [1901–1969]; brother-in-law of **Bessie Love**) [cinematographer/ director/scenarist] (b. Goshen IN, 12 Aug 1896?–2 Jan 1930 [33], Santa Monica CA; plane crash). m. **Mary Astor**, 24 Feb 1928 (d. 1987). (Paramount; Fox.) "Hawks' Unit on Retakes When Air Crash Kills 10—'Overloading' Probe; Total Film Aviation Fatalities Now 24," *Variety,* 8 Jan 1930. Others who died in the crash during the filming of *Such Men Are Dangerous* (Fox): Max Gold, 32, assistant director; George Eastman, 29, cameraman; Conrad Wells, 32, cameraman; Thomas Harris, 30, property man; Henry Johaneesm, 28, grip; Otto Jordan, 26 (assistant cameraman). AS, p. 510 (b. 1898). BHD2, p. 117. FDY, p. 459. IFN, p. 136.

Hawks, Wells [publicist]. No data found. AMD, p. 160. "Wells Hawks on Road," *MPW,* Oct 1916, 93. "Mary Engages Hawks," *MPW,* 5 Apr 1924, 476. "Wells Hawks 'There,'" *MPW,* 19 Jul 1924, 204. "Wells Hawks with 'What Price Glory,'" *MPW,* 11 Dec 1926, 412. "Hawks Seriously Ill," *MPW,* 4 Jun 1927, 324 (apoplexy). "Wells Hawks Improves," *MPW,* 11 Jun 1927, 404.

Hawley, Allen Burton [actor] (b. Albany NY, 1895?–12 Sep 1925 [30?], near Troy NY). m. Wanda. "Allen Burton Hawley," *Variety,* 16 Sep 1925 (began 1915). AS, p. 510 (d. 8 Sep). BHD1, p. 610. Truitt, p. 147.

Hawley, H. Dudley [stage/film actor] (b. Styal, Cheshire, England, 1879?–29 Mar 1941 [62], New York NY; coronary thrombosis). m. Dolly Belden. "Dudley Hawley," *Variety,* 2 Apr 1941. AS, p. 510. BHD1, p. 249. IFN, p. 136. SD, p. 588. Truitt, p. 147.

Hawley, Ormi [actress/scenarist] (*née* Ormetta Grace Hawley, b. Holyoke MA, 21 Feb 1889 [MVRB, Vol. 394, p. 465]–3 Jun 1942 [53], Rome NY). (Lubin; World; Popular Players; Mutual; Fox; Ardsley; FP-L.) "Ormi Hawley Dies; Ex-Star of Screen; Was Seen in 370 Pictures—Dies in Rome, N.Y., Hospital at 52," *NYT,* 5 Jun 1942, 17:5. AMD, p. 160. AS, p. 510 (b. 1890). BHD, p. 195. IFN, p. 136. MSBB, p. 1034 (b. 1890). "Ormi Hawley," *MPW,* XI, 23 Mar 1912, 1059. "Ormi Hawley, of the Lubin Company," *Motion Picture Story Magazine,* Nov 1913, p. 109. "Brief Biographies of Popular Players," *Motion Picture Magazine,* IX, Jun 1915, 107. "Ormi Hawley Engaged as Caruso's Leading Woman," *MPW,* 21 Sep 1918, 1734.

Hawley, Wanda [actress] (aka Wanda Petit, *née* Selma Pittack, b. Scranton PA, 30 Jul 1895–18 Mar 1963 [67], Los Angeles CA). m. Allen Burton Hawley–div. 1922; Jay Stuart Wilkinson, Hollywood CA, 1925. (Began 1917; Paramount.) AMD, p. 160; (Wanda Petit), p. 275. AS, p. 510. BHD1, p. 249 (BHD, p. 196, *née* Wanda Petit). BR, pp. 161–63. FFF, p. 241 (b. 1897). FSS, p. 143. IFN, p. 136. Katz, p. 542. MH, p. 116 (b. 1897). Slide, p. 161. WWS, p. 68. "Wanda Petit One Year in Films," *MPW,* 26 Jan 1918, 485. "Famous Players Signs Wanda Hawley," *MPW,* 6 Jul 1918, 58. "Wanda Hawley Signs with Famous Players-Lasky," *MPW,* 17 May 1919, 1033. "Work the Psychic Hunch and Guess Who Is This Golden Girl with Azure Eyes," *MPW,* 13 Mar 1920, 1819. "Who's the Golden Girl wi the Azure Eyes? Why, Wanda Hawley, the New Realartist," *MPW,* 20 Mar 1920, 1928. "Wanda Hawley Makes Her Realart Debut in 'Miss Hobbes,' by Jerome K. Jerome," *MPW,* 10 Apr 1920, 280. Wanda Hawley, "Discussing Her Work, Realart Star Says 'Never So Happy,'" *MPW,* 10 Jul 1920, 236–37. "'Her Beloved Villain' Has Wanda Hawley for the Star," *MPW,* 25 Sep 1920, 508. "Wanda Hawley's Mother Is Dead," *MPW,* 24 Sep 1921, 404 (Mrs. Martha S. Hittack, d. at 51, Bremerton WA). "Wanda Hawley in Sea Story," *MPW,* 13 Jan 1923, 166. "On the Set and Off," *MW,* 29 Aug 1925, 44 (married J. Stuart Wilkinson, racing-driver). Anthony Slide, *Silent Portraits* (Vestal NY: The Vestal Press, Ltd., 1989), p. 127 (became a San Francisco call girl in the early 1930's).

Hawley-Clifford, Molly [actress] (b. Exeter, England, 1 Aug 1885–7 Jun 1956 [70]). BHD1, p. 249.

Hawn, John Allen [actor/stuntman] (b. CA, 4 May 1882–12 Feb 1964 [81], Fresno CA). AS, p. 510.

Hawthorne, David [actor] (b. Kettering, England, 22 May 1888–18 Jun 1942 [53], London, England). AS, p. 510. BHD1, p. 249. IFN, p. 137.

Hawtrey, Charles [actor] (b. Hounslow, England, 30 Nov 1914–27 Oct 1988 [73], Walmer, England). AS, p. 511. BHD1, p. 249.

Hawtrey, Charles Henry [stage/film actor] (b. Slough, Buckinghamshire, England, 21 Sep 1858–30 Jul 1923 [64], London, England; pneumonia). m. (1) Madeline Harriet Sheriffe; (2) Helen M. Durand; (3) Elsie Clark (née Katherine Elsie Clark, d. 1930). "Charles Hawtrey, Noted Actor, Dies; Long an English Favorite, He Won Fame in America in 'A Message from Mars'; Created a Knight in 1922; 'Where the Rainbow Ends' and 'The Private Secretary' Among His Greatest Successes," *NYT,* 31 Jul 1923, 17:1 (b. 21 Sep 1858). "Sir Charles Hawtrey," *Variety,* 2 Aug 1923 (age 66). AS, p. 511 (b. Eton, England). BHD, p. 196. IFN, p. 137. SD.

Hay, Fanny [actress/singer] (b. Philadelphia PA, 1866–18 May 1929 [83?], New York NY). AS, p. 511.

Hay, Ian [playwright/novelist/scenarist] (*né* John Hay Beith, b. Manchester, England, 1876?–22 Sep 1952 [76], near Peterfield, Hampshire, England; lung ailment). (First novel, *Pip,* 1907.) "Ian Hay, Novelist, a British General; World War I Favorite for His Humorous Sketches of Army Life, Also Playwright, Dies," *NYT,* 23 Sep 1962, 33:3 (age 79). "Ian Hay," *Variety,* 188, 24 Sep 1952, 63:3. BHD2, p. 117. FDY, p. 427.

Hay, Mary [stage/film actress] (*née* Mary Hay Caldwell, b. Ft. Bliss TX, 22 Aug 1901–4 Jun 1957 [55], Inverness CA). m. **Richard Barthelmess**, 18 Jun 1920, NYC (d. 1963); (2) David Bath; (3) Richard Hastings. "Mary Hay, Star of Stage, Was 56; Musical Comedy Performer, Former 'Ziegfeld Follies' Girl, Dies on Coast," *NYT,* 5 Jun 1957, 35:3. "Mary Hay [Mrs. Mary Hay Hastings]," *Variety,* 12 Jun 1957. AMD, p. 160. AS, p. 511. BHD, p. 196. IFN, p. 137. MH, p. 116. SD. Truitt, p. 147. WWS, p. 180. "Cupid Clinched Job in 'Way Down East' and Now 'Dick' Barthelmess Is Married," *MPW,* 26 Jun 1920, 1758. "Mary Hay," *MPW,* 4 Oct 1924, 378. Gladys Hall, "An Interview with Richard Barthelmess' Leading Lady," *MW,* 1 Nov 1924, 12–13, 25. Paul Paige, "Close-Ups and Fade-Outs," *Paris and Hollywood,*

Oct 1926, 96 (the meanest woman in the world stole her Scotch terrier, Snifter, at her Santa Monica beach house).

Hay, Will [stage/film actor] (*né* William Thompson Hay, b. Stockton-on-Tees, England, 6 Dec 1888–18 Apr 1949 [60], London, England). m. Gladys Perkins. "Will Hay," *Variety*, 20 Apr 1949. AS, p. 511. IFN, p. 137. SD, p. 590.

Hayakawa, Sessue [stage/film actor] (*né* Kintaro Hayakawa, b. Nanaura, Honshu, Japan, 10 Jun 1889–23 Nov 1973 [84], Tokyo, Japan). m. **Tsuru Aoki**, 1 May 1914 (d. 1961). (Began 1914; Ince; Paramount.) *Zen Showed Me the Way* (Indianapolis: Bobbs-Merrill, 1960). (NYMP Co.; FP-L) "Sessue Hayakawa Is Dead at 83; Silent Star Was in 'River Kwai'; Japanese Aristocrat Acted in More Than 120 Movies—Nominated for '57 Oscar," *NYT*, 25 Nov 1973, 85:1; Paul L. Montgomery, "Silent Lover and Villain" (b. 1890). "Sessue Hayakawa," *Variety*, 28 Nov 1973. AMD, p. 160. AS, p. 511 (b. Naaurachiba, Japan). BHD1, p. 249. FSS, p. 143. IFN, p. 137. Katz, 543. Lowrey, p. 68. MH, p. 116 (b. Tokio, Japan). MSBB, p. 1024 (b. Tokio; "foremost Japanese actor on screen."). Waldman, p. 132 (b. 1886). WWS, p. 116 (b. Tokyo). "Sessue Hayakawa," *MPW*, 4 Dec 1915, 1810. Pearl Gaddis, "A Romance of Nippon-Land," *MPC*, Dec 1916, 18–20. "Hayakawa an Ideal Hashimura Togo," *MPW*, 18 Aug 1917, 1087. "Hayakawa Talks of His Art," *MPW*, 27 Oct 1917, 550. "Haworth Pictures Signs Hayakawa," *MPW*, 16 Mar 1918, 1497. "Hayakawa to Release Through Mutual," *MPW*, 1 Jun 1918, 1292. "Hayakawa Names First Two Productions," *MPW*, 6 Jul 1918, 76. "Hayakawa's Both Ill of Flu," *MPW*, 28 Dec 1918, 1495. Harry C. Carr, "Sessue the Samurai; Hayakawa is the Proud Old Japanese Cast with the Manners of Modern America," *MPC*, Jan 1919, 24–25, 70. "Sessue Hayakawa Signs Four Year Contract Renewal with Robertson-Cole," *MPW*, 27 Mar 1920, 2170. "Hayakawa to Leave Haworth," *MPW*, 10 Apr 1920, 247. "Sessue Hayakawa Talks of His Future Productions While Visiting New York," *MPW*, 29 May 1920, 1184. "Sessue Hayakawa Leaves for Coast with His New Contract," *MPW*, 12 Jun 1920, 1442. "Sessue Hayakawa's 'Recuperative Trip' Develops Into a Mighty Busy Vacation," *MPW*, 9 Jul 1921, 212. "Hayakawa Has Great Time on His Visit in the East," *MPW*, 16 Jul 1921, 296. "Hayakawa Denies," *MPW*, 3 Sep 1921, 73. Harry Carr, "Son of the Manurai," *MPC*, Jul 1922, 31–33, 81. Sara Redway, "Old Pictures in New Frames; Screen Dramas Are Bigger and More Expensive, Says Sessue Hayakawa, But They Are Not Different," *MPC*, May 1926, 54–55, 78, 86. Alan Brock, "Sessue Hayakawa; American Style," *CFC*, 27 (Spring/Summer, 1970), 12–13. Hayakawa is mentioned in the 1925 opera, *L'Enfant et les Sortileges* (*The Child and the Sorcerers*) by Maurice Ravel. Art Stephan, "Hayakawa in Opera [letter]," *CI*, 75 (May 1981), 61. Michelle Locke, "Hayakawa Broke Barriers But Never Got the Girl," *CI*, 239 (1995), 20.

Hayden, Harry [actor] (b. Indian Territory OK, 8 Nov 1882–24 Jul 1955 [72], Los Angeles CA). AS, p. 511.

Hayden, J. Charles [actor/director/producer] (b. Frederick MD, 1876?–15 Oct 1943 [67], Baltimore MD). (Pioneer.) AS, p. 511. BHD, p. 196; BHD2, p. 117. IFN, p. 137.

Hayden, Joseph [film editor]. No data found. AMD, p. 160. "Hayden Joins a Selznick Editor," *MPW*, 16 Aug 1919, 992.

Hayden, Lela. *See* Bliss, Lela.

Haydock, John [actor] (b. New York NY, 1845–19 Jan 1918 [72?], New York NY). AS, p. 511. BHD, p. 196. IFN, p. 137.

Haye, Helen Mary [stage/film actress] (b. Assam, India, 28 Aug 1874–1 Sep 1957 [83], London, England). m. Ernest Attenborough. "Helen Haye," *Variety*, 4 Sep 1957. AS, p. 511. BHD1, p. 250. IFN, p. 137. SD.

Hayer, Nicolas [cinematographer] (*né* Lucien Nicolas Hayer, b. Paris, France, 1 May 1898–29 Oct 1978 [80], Saint-Laurent-du-Var, France [extrait de décès no. 156]). AS, p. 511.

Hayes, Ada [actress] (b. 1875?–8 Jun 1962 [87], Brooklyn NY). "Ada Hayes," *Variety*, 20 Jun 1962. AS, p. 511.

Hayes, Carrie [actress] (b. 1878?–22 Dec 1954 [76], Philadelphia PA). "Mrs. Carrie Miller," *Variety*, 29 Dec 1954 ("appeared in several silent films"). AS, p. 511. BHD, p. 196. IFN, p. 137. Truitt, p. 148.

Hayes, Catherine [actress] (b. 1885–4 Jan 1941 [56?], Los Angeles CA). AS, p. 511. BHD1, p. 250.

Hayes, Donn [film editor]. No data found. AMD, p. 160. "Donn Hayes," *MPW*, 16 Jul 1927, 156.

Hayes, Edmund J. [burlesque/vaudeville/film actor/director] (b. 1866–12 Jun 1921 [55?], Los Angeles CA; dropsy). "Edmund J. Hayes," *Variety*, LXIII, 17 Jun 1921, 9:3 ("At one time of his career Mr. Hayes essayed a serious role and was universally praised for his work in it."; interred in Calvary Cemetery). AMD, p. 160. BHD, p. 196. "Edmund Hayes to Head Own Feature Co.," *MPW*, 3 Mar 1915, 1588.

Hayes, Frank [actor] (b. San Francisco CA, 17 May 1871–28 Dec 1923 [52], Los Angeles CA; pneumonia). "Frank Hayes," *Variety*, 3 Jan 1924 (age 48). AS, p. 512 (b. 1878). BHD, p. 196. IFN, p. 137. Slide, p. 161. Truitt, p. 148 (b. 1879).

Hayes, George [actor] (b. London, England, 13 Nov 1888–13 Jul 1967 [78], London, England). m. Margaret Scobie. "George Hayes," *Variety*, 26 Jul 1967. AS, p. 512. IFN, p. 137. Truitt, 1983.

Hayes, George "Gabby" [stage/film actor] (*né* George Francis Hayes, b. Wellesville NY, 7 May 1885–9 Feb 1969 [83], Burbank CA; heart attack). m. Dorothy Earle (d. 1958). "Gabby Hayes, Actor, Dies at 83; Comic in 200 Western Pictures; Hopalong Cassidy's Pardner Was Best-Known Role—His First Career on Stage," *NYT*, 10 Feb 1969, 39:4. "George Gabby Hayes," *Variety*, 12 Feb 1969. AS, p. 512. BHD1, p. 250. IFN, p. 137. Katz, pp. 544–45. Truitt, p. 148.

Hayes, Helen (adoptive mother of James MacArthur) [stage/film/TV actress] (*née* Helen Hayes Brown, b. Washington DC, 10 Oct 1900–17 Mar 1993 [92], Nyack NY; pulmonary embolism). (Vitagraph, 1910; *The Weavers of Life*, 1920; *Babs*, 1920; AA, 1931–32 and 1970). m. Charles MacArthur, 1929–d. 1956. *On Reflection* (1968); with Katherine Hatch, *My Life in Three Acts* (New York: Harcourt Brace Jovanovich, 1990). Eric Pace, "Helen Hayes, Flower of the Stage, Dies at 92," *NYT*, 18 Mar 1993, A1:3, B9:1. Dennis Hevesi, "Helen Hayes, 92, Is Recalled in Church She Loved," *NYT*, 21 Mar 1993, 45:1. Jeremy Gerard, "Helen Hayes," *Variety*, 22 Mar 1993, p. 63:1. AMD, p. 160. AS, p. 512. BHD1, p. 250. "Warren Makes a Discovery," *MPW*, 21 Jul 1917, 476 (Helen Hayes Brown). Muriel Babcock, "Star Annoyed by Wisecrack; Helen Hayes Will Not Raise Her Daughter to Be an Actress," *Movie Classic*, I, Sep 1931, 40.

Hayes, Helen M. [actress] (b. Chattanooga TN-d. Jul 1974). BHD, p. 196.

Hayes, Jack [actor] (b. Malden MA, 1870–26 Dec 1928 [58?], Newark NJ). "Jack Hayes," *Variety*, 9 Jan 1929 (interred at Malden MA). AS, p. 512.

Hayes, Max E. [director/producer] (b. Minsk, Belarus, 25 Feb 1883–9 Apr 1950 [67], Los Angeles Co. CA). AS, p. 512. BHD2, p. 117.

Hayes, Sidney [actor] (b. 1865?–2 May 1940 [75], Beverly Hills CA). "Sidney Hayes," *Variety*, 8 May 1940. AS, p. 512. BHD1, p. 250. IFN, p. 137.

Hayes, Walter A. [actor/assistant director] (b. Los Angeles CA, 1880). BHD2, p. 117.

Hayes, Ward [director] (b. 1894?–28 Jan 1925 [30], Los Angeles CA; peritonitis after appendicitis operation). (Ben Wilson comedy studio.) "Ward Hayes," *Variety*, 4 Feb 1925. AMD, p. 160. AS, p. 512. BHD2, p. 117. "Ward Hayes Continues to Direct Bill Franey Films," *MPW*, 15 Jul 1922, 231.

Hayes, William T. [actor] (b. 1887?–13 Jul 1937 [50], Los Angeles CA; heart attack at Paramount Studio). "William Hayes," *Variety*, 21 Jul 1937 ("veteran cowboy actor"). AS, p. 512. BHD1, p. 250. IFN, p. 137. Truitt, p. 148.

Hayle, Grace [actress] (b. 1888–20 Mar 1963 [75?], Los Angeles CA). AS, p. 512.

Hayman, Adam Charles [actor/director] (b. New York NY, 1880–11 Jul 1945 [65?], Niagara Falls NY). AS, p. 512 (b. 1884; d. 10 Jul). BHD, p. 196; BHD2, p. 117.

Haynes, Daniel L. [actor] (b. Atlanta GA, 1894–28 Jul 1954 [60?], Kingston NY). AS, p. 512. BHD1, p. 251.

Haynes, L.C. [executive]. No data found. AMD, p. 161. "Intrigue Not Romance, Says Haynes," *MPW*, 7 Jun 1919, 1497. "L.C. Haynes of Robertson-Cole Praises Film Showing Results of War on Young Men," *MPW*, 30 Aug 1919, 1298.

Haynes, Mannig [actor] (b. Lyminster, England-d. 1957). BHD, p. 196.

Haynes, Marie [stage/film actress] (b. South Sutton NH, 10 May 1856–3 Apr 1934 [77], Amityville, LI NY). m. Ralph Howard. "Marie Haynes," *Variety*, 10 Apr 1934 (stage debut: *Uncle Tom's Cabin*, 1881). AS, p. 512. BHD, p. 196.

Haynes, Minna Gale [actress] (*née* Minna Gale, b. NJ, 26 Sep 1869–4 Mar 1944 [74], Riverside CT). BHD, p. 196.

Hays, Will [actor] (b. 1887–1937 [50?]). BHD1, p. 251.

Hays, Will H. [censor/executive] (*né* William Harrison Hays, b. Sullivan IN, 5 Nov 1879–7 Mar 1954 [74], Sullivan IN). Will H. Hays, Jr., *Come Home with Me Now... The Untold Story of Movie Czar Will Hays* (Indianapolis IN: Guild Press of Indiana, Inc., 1993). "Will Hays, First Film Czar, Dies; Former G.O.P. Leader was 74; Arbiter of Hollywood's Morals 23 Years Was Postmaster General Under Harding," *NYT*, 8 Mar 1954, 1:4, 27:4; "Funeral for Will Hays," 11 Mar, 31:5; "Will H. Hays Left $1,770,000," 21 Mar, 50:4. Gene Arneel, "Will Hays Came Into the

Picture Biz Under Conditions Similar to Today," *Variety,* 10 Mar 1954. AMD, p. 161. AS, p. 513. BHD2, p. 117. Katz, pp. 545–46. "Hays Will Head Picture Organization; Contract Signed Wednesday in New York," *MPW,* 8 Jan 1922, 369–70. "M.P.T.O.A. Disclaims Any Hand in Appointment of Will Hays as Head of Industry at Salary of $150,000," *MPW,* 28 Jan 1922, 377. "M.P.D.A. Dinner Dance in Hays's Honor Will Be Attended by Many Celebrities," *MPW,* 4 Mar 1922, 47. "Will Hays Expected at Naked Truth Dinner of A.M.P.A. on March 25," *MPW,* 11 Mar 1922, 154. "Motion Pictures Will Become National Stabilizer in This Country, Says Hays, at National Press Club Dinner," *MPW,* 11 Mar 1922, 155. Arthur James, "A Word to Will H. Hays," *MPW,* 11 Mar 1922, 156. "Will Hays Interviews Trade Paper Men; Begins Work by Studying the Industry," *MPW,* 18 Mar 1922, 255. William J. Reilly, "Will Hays Makes His Debut as Guardian of the 'Infant' That Is to Be Colossus," *MPW,* 1 Apr 1922, 453–54. "Hays Says Censorship Brought on America's Revolt Against Tyranny," *MPW,* LVII, 15 Jul 1922, 207–08. "Hays Answers Ministers," *MPW,* 6 Jan 1923, 34. "Hays Says Public Shall Decide Whether Arbuckle Is Wanted on Screen," *MPW,* 20 Jan 1923, 219. "The Best and the Worst," *MPW,* 22 Sep 1923, 326. "Will Hayus's Contract Extended," *MPW,* 12 Apr 1924, 538. "Hays Announces 'Open Door' Policy for Film Industry," *MPW,* 4 Apr 1925, 440. "President Coolidge Writes Hays Endorsement of Movie Season," *MPW,* 8 Aug 1925, 616. "Hays Commended for Care of Children in the Studio," *MPW,* 14 Nov 1925, 109. Marie Chomel, "An Interesting Account of How Will Hays Earns His Salary," *MM,* Jan 1926, 68–69, 94. "Best Acting Is Found in Films, Says Will Hays," *MPW,* 13 Feb 1926, 2. "Will H. Hays Delivers an Epochal Address on Advertising Problems," *MPW,* 10 Apr 1926, 410–13. "Will Hays Continues to 1936," *MPW,* 3 Jul 1926, 1. "Trade Notes," *Paris and Hollywood,* Oct 1926, 62 ("The motion picture industry…must have respect for the enforcement of the law. With this idea in mind, I shall insist that no ridicule of this or any other law be allowed to creep into our films, either through a subtitle or in a descriptive scene." Books and plays barred from the screen included *The Green Hat, Rain, The Constant Nymph, The Shanghai Gesture, Miss Lulu Belle, Ladies of the Evening, Desire Under the Elms,* and others.). "Hays Silent on Hollywood Winter Visit," *MPW,* 29 Jan 1927, 344. "The 'Czar,'" *MPW,* 26 Mar 1927, 314, 315. "From Will H. Hays," *MPW,* 26 Mar 1927, 359. "Hays Urges a 'Sympathetic, Constructive Study,'" *MPW,* 15 Oct 1927, 415–16. "Hays Working with Authors' Guilds on Scjreen Material," *MPW,* 24 Dec 1927, 10.

Hayward, Leland [theatrical producer/scenarist/agent] (b. Nebraska City NB, 13 Sep 1902–18 Mar 1971 [68], Yorktown Heights NY). m. (1) Lola Gibbs, 1921–22, 1930–34; (2) actress Margaret Sullavan, 1935–49; (3) Mrs. Nancy (Slim) Hawks; (4) Mrs. Pamela Digby Churchill, 1960. "Leland Hayward, Producer, Is Dead," *NYT,* 19 Mar 1971, 1:7, 42:1; Albin Krebs, "A Flamboyant Figure," 42:1 ("…Mr. Hayward wound up in Hollywood, working first as a press agent for United Artists and then as a producer of a dozen silent movies for First National Pictures. 'They stunk,' he was to say of the movies years later."). "Hayward Memorial April 2," *NYT,* 23 Mar 1971, 40:4 (at St. James' Episcopal Church, Madison Avenue at 71st Street). "Leland Hayward, Famed Producer, Former Agent, 68," *Variety,* 24 Mar 1971. AS, p. 513. BHD2, p. 117. FDY, p. 429 (Heyward).

Hayward, Lillian C. [actress/scenarist] (b. St. Paul MN, 12 Sep 1891–29 Jun 1977 [85], Los Angeles CA). m. Jerry Sockheim. (Selig; Cosmopolitan; Disney.) "Lillie Hayward," *Variety,* 6 Jul 1977. AS, p. 513 (b. 1892). BHD2, p. 117. FDY, p. 427 (Lillie Hawyard). IFN, p. 137.

Hayward, Lydia [scenarist]. No data found. FDY, p. 427.

Hayward, Richard [actor/producer] (b. Ireland, 1892–13 Oct 1964 [72?], Belfast, No. Ireland; auto accident). AS, p. 513. BHD2, p. 117.

Hazen, Joseph H. [lawyer/film producer] (b. Kingston NY, 1898?–13 Nov 1994 [96], Boca Raton FL). m. Lita Annenberg. "Joseph H. Hazen, 96, Is Dead; Lawyer [17 years for WB] and Movie Producer," *NYT,* 16 Nov 1994, 25:1 (wrote the contract between Warner Bros. and Edison Vitaphone that resulted in *The Jazz Singer*). AS, p. 513. BHD2, p. 117.

Hazleton, George C. [actor] (b. Boscobel WI, 1868?–23 Jun 1921 [53], New York NY). "George C. Hazleton," *Variety,* 1 Jul 1921. AS, p. 513. BHD2, p. 117 (Hazelton). NNAT, p. 404.

Hazleton, Joseph M. [actor] (b. 1853?–8 Oct 1936 [83], Los Angeles CA). "Joseph Hazleton," *Variety,* 14 Oct 1936 (program boy at Ford's theatre who saw Lincoln assassinated). AS, p. 513. BHD1, p. 251. IFN, p. 137. Truitt, pp. 148–49.

Hazzard, John E. (Jack) [stage/film actor/writer] (b. New York NY, 22 Feb 1881–2 Dec 1935 [54], Great Neck, LI NY). m. **Alice Dovey,** 1916 (d. 1969). "John E. Hazzard," *Variety,* 4 Dec 1935 (wrote poem, *Ain't It Awful, Mabel*). AS, p. 513. SD.

Headrick, Richard [actor] (b. 1918?). No data found. AMD, p. 161. "3-Year Old Player in 'Retribution' Wins Big Applause," *MPW,* L, 18 Jun 1921, 731.

Healy, Ted (son of **Eugenia Nash**) [vaudevillian/actor] (b. Houston TX, 1 Oct 1892–21 Dec 1937 [45], Los Angeles CA; heart attack). (1) Betty Braun—div. 1932; (2) Betty Hickman, 14 May 1936, Yuma AZ. (MGM; Roach.) "Ted Healy Dies; Autopsy Ordered; Rumors of Cafe Fight Add Some Mystery to Passing of Actor in California Home; Built Act on 'Stooges'; Former Vaudeville Headliner Leaves Wife and Son, Born in Culver City Friday," *NYT,* 22 Dec 1937, 3:4. "Ted Healy Dies of a Heart Attack on Coast; Was Suddenly Stricken," *Variety,* 22 Dec 1937 (son born 4 days before he died). AS, p. 514 (b. 1896; d. 19 Dec). BHD1, p. 252 (b. 1896). IFN, p. 137 (age 41).

Hearn, Edward [actor] (*né* Guy Edward Hearn, b. Dayton WA, 6 Sep 1888–15 Apr 1963 [74], Los Angeles CA). AMD, p. 162. AS, p. 514. BHD1, p. 252. IFN, p. 138. MH, p. 116). WWS, p. 334. "Actor Hearn Is Proud Father," *MPW,* 20 Jan 1917, 382. "Printer's Devil to Matinee Idol," *MPW,* 3 Nov 1923, 100. "Edward Hearn Featured," *MPW,* 15 Aug 1925, 760.

Hearn, Fred G. [actor/assistant director] (b. Louisville KY, 20 Dec 1871–20 Jan 1923 [51], Woodland Hills CA). AS, p. 514. BHD, p. 196; BHD2, p. 117 (d. Pasadena CA). IFN, p. 138.

Hearst, William Randolph [newspaper tycoon/film executive] (b. San Francisco CA, 29 Apr 1863–14 Aug 1951 [88], Beverly Hills CA). m. Millicent Willson, 28 Apr 1903 (sons John, twins Randolph and David, George, and William, Jr.). William Randolph Hearst, Jr., with Jack Casserly, *The Hearsts; Father and Son* (NY: Roberts Rinehart, 1991). Gladwin Hill, "William Randolph Hearst Dies at 88 in California; Builder of Vast Newspaper Empire Was Controversial Figure in Press, Politics," *NYT,* 15 Aug 1951, 1:2, 20:3. "William Randolph Hearst," *Variety,* 15 Aug 1951. AMD, p. 162. AS, p. 514. BHD2, p. 117. "Hearst Opens Exchanges," *MPW,* 8 Apr 1916, 230. "Hearst Has No Interest in Wharton's," *MPW,* 22 Apr 1916, 653. "'Visiting Star' System Introduced by Hearst," *MPW,* 16 Sep 1916, 1834. W.R. Hearst, "Cosmopolitan Productions," *MPW,* 4 Aug 1923, 407. "Loew and Hearst Honored at Striking Los Angeles Dinner," *MPW,* 9 Jan 1926, 131. Gene Fernett, "Citizen Hearst Creates a Studio," *CI,* 128 (Feb 1986), 12–13, 18.

Heath, Arch B. [director] (b. Brooklyn NY, 1890–6 Jan 1945 [54?]). AMD, p. 162. AS, p. 514. BHD2, p. 118. "Heath Co-Directing on Tunne¥ Film," *MPW,* 19 Jun 1926, 617.

Heath, Frank [actor/assistant director] (b. 1892–31 Oct 1952 [60?], Los Angeles CA). BHD, p. 196; BHD2, p. 118.

Heath, Percy [actor/scenarist] (b. Perry MO, 1884?–9 Feb 1933 [48], Los Angeles CA). (Universal, 1918; Metro; Realart; FBO; Metropolitan; Paramount.) "Percy Heath's Death," *Variety,* 14 Feb 1933. AMD, p. 162. AS, p. 514 (b. Perth Amboy NJ). BHD2, p. 118. FDY, p. 427. IFN, p. 138. "Percy Heath Hopes to Move Away from the Conventional Happy Ending in 'Laska' Film," *MPW,* 27 Sep 1919, 1986. "Metro Adds Harvey H. Gates and Percy Heath as Writers," *MPW,* 3 Apr 1920, 126. "Joins Realart Staff," *MPW,* 26 Feb 1921, 1071. "Heath with Realart," *MPW,* 12 Mar 1921, 168. "Heath and Katterjohn Signed by Metropolitan," *MPW,* 21 Nov 1925, 227.

Heatherley, Clifford [actor] (b. Preston, Lancashire, England, 8 Oct 1888–15 Sep 1937 [48], London, England). AS, p. 514. BHD1, p. 252. IFN, p. 138.

Heazlett, Eva [actress] (*née* Eva B. McKenzie, b. Toledo OH, 5 Nov 1889–15 Sep 1967 [77], Los Angeles CA). BHD, p. 196. IFN, p. 138.

Hebert, Henry J. [actor] (b. Providence RI, 12 Nov 1879–18 Jan 1956 [76], Los Angeles CA). AS, p. 514. BHD1, p. 252. IFN, p. 138.

Hecht, Ben [author/scenarist/producer/stage and film actor] (b. New York NY, 28 Feb 1893–18 Apr 1964 [71], New York NY; cerebral thrombosis). m. (1) Maria Armstrong; (2) Rose Caylor. *A Child of the Century* (1954); Florice Whyte Kovan, *Rediscovering Ben Hecht: Selling the Celluloid Serpent,* Vol. I (Washington DC: Snickersnee Press, 1999). "Ben Hecht, 70, Dies at His Home Here," *NYT,* 19 Apr 1964, 1:3, 84:1. "Ben Hecht," *Variety,* 22 Apr 1964. AS, p. 514 (b. 1894). BHD1, p. 252; BHD2, p. 1181. IFN, p. 138. SD.

Hechy, Alice [actress] (b. Berlin, Germany, 21 Jul 1895–26 May 1935 [39], Berlin, Germany). BHD1, p. 252 (b. Anklam, Germany 1898-d. 1973). Vittorio Martinelli, "Kino-Lieblinge," *Griffithiana,* 38/39 (Oct 1990), 15.

Heck, Stanton P. [actor] (b. Wilmington DE, 8 Jan 1877–16 Dec 1929 [52], Los Angeles CA). (MGM.) AS, p. 515. BHD, p. 197. IFN, p. 138. Truitt, 1983. George A. Katchmer, "Forgotten Cowboys and Cowgirls—Part XIV," *CI,* 191 (May 1991), 22–23.

Hedin, Sven [director] (b. Sweden, 1865–1952 [87?], Sweden). AS, p. 515.

Hedlund, Greg [actor] (d. Culver City CA). (Eclair.) Spehr, p. 140.

Hedlund, Guy [actor/director/producer/scenarist] (b. CT, 21 Aug 1884–29 Dec 1964 [80], Culver City CA; from injuries after a car accident). (Biograph, 1910.) AMD, p. 162. AS, p. 515. BHD1, p. 252; BHD2, p. 118. IFN, 138. "Guy Hedlund Now Universal Director," *MPW,* 8 Apr 1916, 248.

Hedman, Martha [stage/film actress] (b. Östersund, N. Sweden, 12 Aug 1883–20 Jun 1974 [90], Deland FL). (World.) AMD, p. 162. BHD1, p. 610. Spehr, p. 140. "Personal," *NYDM,* 13 Jan 1915, 5:1 (one of her dramatic teachers was Siri von Essen, the first wife of Strindberg. "Though Miss Hedman's beauty has won for her an international reputation, she is above all an actress."). "Martha Hedman in 'The Cub,'" *MPW,* 15 May 1915, 1085. "Metro Signs Three New Stars," *NYDM,* 22 Sep 1915, 35:1 (Hedman, Lionel Barrymore, and Hamilton Revelle).

Hedqvist, Ivan [actor/director] (b . Stockholm, Sweden, 8 Jun 1880–23 Aug 1935 [55], Stockholm, Sweden). AS, p. 515 (b. Gottroro, Sweden). BHD1, p. 252; BHD2, p. 118.

Heerman, Victor [director/screenwriter] (b. London, England, 27 Aug 1893–3 Nov 1977 [84], Los Angeles CA). m. **Sarah Y. Mason**, 1921, Hollywood CA (d. 1980). (Sennett; Paramount.) AMD, p. 162. AS, p. 515 (d. London, England). BHD2, p. 118 (b. Barnes, England). Katz, pp. 549–50. 1921 Directory, p. 265. "Victor Heerman to Direct Marshall Neilan Pictures," *MPW,* 6 Dec 1919, 661. "Weds Scenario Writer," *MPW,* 7 May 1921, 55. "Selznick Signs Victor Heerman," *MPW,* 12 Nov 1921, 213. "Schenck Signs Heernam," *MPW,* 17 Feb 1923, 643. "Heerman Will Direct [Ed] Wynn in Fun Film," *MPW,* 11 Dec 1926, 411. "Victor Heerman," *MPW,* 17 Sep 1927, 166.

Heffron, Thomas N. [stage/stock/film director/producer/scenarist]. No data found. (Began 1912; FP-L; Selig [Chicago]; Thanhouser; Biograph-Klaw & Erlanger; FP-L.) AMD, p. 162. "Heffron Join Selig," *NYDM,* 14 Apr 1915, 22:4. "T.N. Heffron," *NYDM,* 14 Jul 1915, 27:1. "Thomas N. Heffron with Selig," *MPW,* 17 Jul 1915, 474. "A Director's Answer," *NYDM,* 1 Sep 1915, 25:3, 29:2 (answers Harry Riechenbach's article on wastage in the studios which he attributes to the indifference of directors. "If an efficient director is given a good scenario, he evolves an excellent film from it, and if given a bad story he occasionally makes a good film of it, but I do not know of a single instance where an efficient director has made a bad film out of a good scenario. That prerogative belongs to the cutter."). "Efficiency in Directors," *MPW,* 11 Sep 1915, 1810. "Tom Heffron Believes in Giving Actor Long Leash," *MPW,* 10 Jan 1920, 274. "Thomas Heffron Signed by Fox to Direct Buck Jones," *MPW,* 1 May 1920, 674.

Hegetschweiler, Emile Johannes [actor] (b. Zurich, Switzerland, 15 Oct 1887–1 Oct 1959 [71], Zurich, Switzerland). AS, p. 515.

Heggie, O[tto] **P**[eters] [stage/film actor] (b. Angaston, So. Australia, 16 Sep 1876–7 Feb 1936 [59], Los Angeles CA; pneumonia). m. Nancy. "O.P. Heggie," *Variety,* 12 Feb 1936 (appeared in talkies and one silent, *The Actress*). AS, p. 515 (b. 17 Sep). BHD1, p. 253 (b. 1879). IFN, p. 138. SD. Truitt, p. 149.

Heidemann, Paul [actor] (b. Cologne, France, 26 Oct 1884–20 Jun 1968 [83], Berlin, Germany). AS, p. 515. BHD1, p. 253. IFN, p. 138. Vittorio Martinelli, "Kino-Lieblinge," *Griffithiana,* 38/39 (Oct 1990), 44.

Heilbron, Adelaide [scenarist]. No data found. FDY, p. 427.

Heilman, Vada Lee [actress] (b. IL, 25 Dec 1907–13 Oct 1953 [45], Inglewood CA). BHD addendum.

Heim, Edward [actor]. No data found. George Katchmer, "Edward Heim," *CI,* 230 (Aug 1994), 39. (In *The Lone Rider,* 1922.)

Heims, Else [actress] (b. Berlin, Germany, 3 Oct 1878–20 Feb 1958 [79], Santa Monica CA). AS, p. 515

Heisey, Mart E. [actor] (b. 1865?–21 Apr 1925 [60], Chicago IL). "Mart E. Heisey," *Variety,* 29 Apr 1925. BHD, p. 197.

Heisler, Elfriede [actress] (b. 31 Mar 1885–21 Feb 1919 [33]). BHD, p. 197.

Heisler, Frank [cinematographer]. No data found. FDY, p. 459.

Heisler, Stuart R. [film editor/director] (b. Los Angeles CA, 5 Dec 1896–21 Aug 1979 [82], Carlsbad, San Diego CA 92008). (b. 5 Dec 1896). AMD, p. 162. BHD2, p. 118 (d. Oceanside CA). IFN, p. 138. "Editor Advanced," *MPW,* 14 May 1927, 112. "The Past Put on Tape," *Tucson Daily Citizen,* 16 Apr 1971, p. 40 (Heisler recorded his memories of early filmmaking for Kenneth Hufford, Arizona Pioneers' Historical Society).

Helbling, Jeanne [actress] (*née* Johanna Marie Helbling, b. Thann, France, 28 Jul 1903 [extrait de naissance no. 149]-6 Aug 1985 [82], New York NY). (1st National; Columbia; made French-language films at MGM.) AS, p. 516. Waldman, p. 133.

Held, Anna [stage/film actress] (b. Paris, France, 18 Mar 1873–13 Aug 1918 [45], New York NY; pernicious anemia and bronchial pneumonia; multiple myeloma [bone cancer]). m. **Florenz Ziegfeld** (d. 1932). Eve Golden, *Anna Held and the Birth of Ziegfeld's Broadway* (2000). "Anna Held," *Variety,* 16 Aug 1918. AMD, p. 162. AS, p. 516 (1865). BHD, p. 197. IFN, p. 138. "Vaudeville," *NYDM,* 7 Jan 1914, 21:3 (appeared in a two-scene musical comedy, *Mlle. Baby.* "Too much dependence was placed on Miss Held's inability to make her eyes behave. Anything can be overdone," said critic Frederick James Smith). "Anna Held Wants Damages," *MPW,* 14 Mar 1914, 1389. "Anna Held Comes to the Screen," *MPW,* 30 Oct 1915, 948. "The Fair Anna Starts; Anna Held Departs Amid Throng of Admirers and Newspaper Men for Coast," *NYDM,* 13 Nov 1915, 30:4 (to debut at Morosco-Paralta. "I can hardly wait until I get to the studios. I have heard so much about these wonderful motion pictures and have seen such marvelous things on the screen that now it really surprises me when I think that I have kept away from this new field so long."). Hector Ames, "A 'Close Up' of Anna Held; Another Light Opera Star Has Fled to the Camera Stage. This Time It Is Anna Held, the Girl Who 'Just Couldn't Make Her Eyes Behave,'" *MPC,* Apr 1916, 57–58. "Anna Held Sees 'Joan of Plattsburg,'" *MPW,* 15 Jun 1918, 1577. "Screen Play as Monument to Memory of Anna Held," *MPW,* 14 Nov 1925, 123.

Held, George C. [cinematographer[(d. May 1919, Portland OR). BHD2, p. 118.

Held, John, Jr. [stage costumer/artist] (b. Salt Lake City UT, 10 Jan 1889–2 Mar 1958 [69], Belmar NJ). With Frank B. Gilbre, Jr., *Held's Angels* (NY: Thomas Y. Crowell Co., 1952?). Shelley Armitage, *John Held, Jr.* (Syracuse: Syracuse University Press, 1987) (designed film posters for MGM). "John Held Jr., Cartoonist, Dies; Satirist of the Twenties Was 69; Creator of Flapper Drawings Portrayed Flaming Youth—Had Revival in 1949," *NYT,* 3 Mar 1958, 27:4. "John Held Jr.," *Variety,* 5 Mar 1958. John Held, Jr., "Beginning the Adventures of Miss Cella Lloyd," *MPC,* Dec 1925, 28–29 (#1 in a monthly series of caricatures). WWWA.

Held, Max [cameraman]. No data found. m. Nellie McCoy, 2 Jun 1911. (Vitagraph.) "Vitagraph Notes," *NY Clipper,* 10 Jun 1911, p. 15 (re marriage).

Held, Thomas [film editor/assistant director] (b. 1890?–13 Mar 1962 [72], Los Angeles CA; pneumonia). (Neilan; Metro, 1924.) "Tom Held," *Variety,* 21 Mar 1962 (assistant to Marshall Neilan). BHD2, p. 118.

Helen, Marie [actress]. No data found. AMD, p. 162. "No!—Not 'Helen Maria'! Call Her Helen Marie!," *MPW,* 8 May 1926, 142.

Hell, René [actor] (*né* René Jules Legendre, b. Orbec, France, 1 May 1891 [extrait de naissance no. 21/1891]-11 Oct 1965 [74], Paris, France). AS, p. 516.

Helland, Heinz-Karl [director] (b. Germany, 10 Feb 1876). AS, p. 516.

Heller, Gloria. *See* Sheridan, Ann.

Heller, Herman [executive]. (Vitagraph.) Armand Falnieres, "Enter—The Silent Director; A personal narrative of a day spentin the Vitagraph studio—where the director must give all his directions in pantomime," *Cinema Arts,* June 1927, 26–27.

Heller, Otto [cinematographer] (b. Prague, Czechoslovakia, 8 Mar 1896–19 Feb 1970 [73], London, England). AS, p. 516. BHD2, p. 118.

Heller, William [stage/film actor] (*né* Owen Dale, b. 1851–21 Feb 1919 [67], San Francisco CA). "Dale Owen," *Variety,* LIV, 21 Mar 1919, 22:3. BHD, p. 197.

Hellman, Ella Paulina [actress] (b. Vipura, Finland, 13 Jul 1896–6 May 1981 [84], Tampere, Finland). AS, p. 517.

Hellman, Nancy [actress]. No data found. (Sennett.) "Six Reasons Why Mack Sennett Comedies Are Popular," *Cinema Arts,* V (Aug 1926), 23 (photo).

Hellman, Sam [writer/scenarist//title writer] (b. San Francisco CA, 4 Jul 1885–11 Aug 1950 [65], Beverly Hills CA; heart attack). m. Selma. (The *Leather Pushers* series, Paramount, 1927; TC-F; MGM; WB.) "Sam Hellman," *Variety,* 179, 16 Aug 1950, 55:1 (journalist, 1916). AMD, p. 162. AS, p. 517. BHD2, p. 119. IFN, p. 138. "Writer Praises Series," *MPW,* 6 Sep 1924, 33. "Titles Three Leonard Pictures," *MPW,* 22 Nov 1924, 348.

Hellmer, Karl [actor] (b. Vienna, Austria, 11 Mar 1896–18 May 1974 [78], Berlin, Germany). AS, p. 517.

Hellum, Barney [actor] (b. Seavyanv, Norway, 1 Jan 1895–22 Dec 1935 [40]). BHD, p. 197. IFN, p. 138.

Helm, Brigitte [actress] (*née* Eva Gisela Schittenhelm, b. Berlin, Germany, 17 Mar 1908–11 Jun 1996 [88], Ascona, Switzerland; heart failure). m. (1) Rudolf Weissbach; (2) Dr. Hugo von

Künheim, 1935. (Extra; feature film debut: *Metropolis,* 1926; Ufa.) Peter Herzog and Gene Vazzana, *Brigitte Helm; From Metropolis to Gold; Portrait of a Goddess* (NY: Corvin, 1994). Robert McG. Thomas, Jr., "Brigitte Helm, 88, Cool Star of Fritz Lang's 'Metropolis,'" *NYT,* 14 Jun 1996, B7:5 ("She was the most sought-after actress of the glory days of the German film industry, a tall blond beauty who starred in more than 35 movies, set directors against one another in the competition for her services, and was regarded as such a perfect embodiment of the era's ideal of cool sophistication that when she turned him down for the starring role in 'Blue Angel,' Josef von Sternberg had to settle for Marlene Dietrich."). "Brigitte Helm," *Variety,* 19 Aug 1996, p. 59:5 ("Helm quit the business after a series of harsh reviews, a two-month jail term because of a car accident she caused, and her trouble with the Nazis."). "Murió la mujer-robot de 'Metropolis,'" *La Voz del Interior,* 13 Jun 1996, 4C:1. "Brigitte Helm, Star of Silent Movies, Talkies," *Chicago Tribune,* 14 Jun 1996, II, 11 (age 90). "Brigette [sic] Helm; Actress Starred in 'Metropolis,'" *Los Angeles Times,* 17 Jun 1996, p. A-16 (age 90). *The Guardian,* 15 Jun 1996. AS, p. 517. BHD1, p. 253 (b. 1906) Ragan, *Who's Who in Hollywood,* p. 730. Katz, p. 557.

Helm, William P., Jr. [editor]. No data found. AMD, p. 162. "Newspaper Man for Pathé's Weekly," *MPW,* 0 Jan 1914, 182.

Helmers, Peter O[to] [actor] (b. Vienna, Austria, 16 Feb 1901–2 Jan 1976 [74], Los Angeles CA). AS, p. 517.

Helmore, Arthur [actor] (b. 1858–14 Jun 1941 [83?]). BHD, p. 197.

Helmore, Tom [stage/film/TV actor/novelist] (b. London, England, 4 Jan 1904–12 Sep 1995 [91], Longboat Key FL). m. Mary Drayton (d. 1994). (Broadway debut: *No Time for Comedy,* 1939.) "Tom Helmore, 91, Actor Known Best for Comedy," *NYT,* 15 Sep 1995, D17:4 (extra in English films in the 1920s). AS, p. 517. BHD1, p. 253.

Helms, Ruth [actress] (b. 1897?–27 Oct 1960 [63?], Los Angeles CA). AS, p. 517. BHD, p. 197. IFN, p. 138.

Helston, Wally [actor/director] (*né* Walter Ellis, b. England, 1873–1 Sep 1933 [60], Wildwood NJ; heart attack). m. Lottie. "Wally Helston," *Variety,* 112, 19 Sep 1933, 54:2 (with sister Kitty, "The Helstons, english Top Boot Dancers," with sisters Gussie and Dolly, "The Helston Trio," with wife, "Wally and Lottie Helston." Interred in Greenwood Cemetery, Philadelphia PA). BHD, p. 197.

Helton, Percy [stage/film actor] (b. New York NY, 31 Jan 1894–11 Sep 1971 [77], Los Angeles CA). m. Edna Eustace. "Percy Helton," *Variety,* 15 Sep 1971 (in 200 feature films). AS, p. 517. BHD1, p. 254. IFN, p. 138. Cover, *NYDM,* 22 Sep 1915 (Benny Sweeney, Helton and Jasper [dog] in *Young America*).

Helwig, Paul Julius Adolf [actor/scenarist] (b. Lubeck, Germany, 27 May 1893–7 Aug 1963 [70], Munich, Germany). AS, p. 517.

Heming, Violet (daughter of Mabel Allen and **Alfred Hemming**) [stage/film actress] (*née* Violet Hemming, b. Leeds, Yorkshire, England, 27 Jan 1895–4 Jul 1981 [86], New York NY). m. (1) Grant Mills (d. 1973); (2) Bennett C. Clark. "Violet Heming," *Variety,* 8 Jul 1981. AMD, p. 162. AS, p. 517. BHD1, p. 254 (b. 1893). MH, p. 116. SD. Truitt, 1983. WWS, p. 12. "Star Miss Heming; Pre-Eminent Film Company to Produce Under Direction of James Durkin," *NYDM,* 14 Apr 1915, 22:3. "H.B. Warner a Selig Star," *MPW,* 21 Apr 1917, 428. "Violet Heming in Blackton Picture," *MPW,* 29 Sep 1917, 1993. Charles Jameson, "She Doesn't Talk of Her Art; Violet Heming Looks Upon Acting as a Business," *MPC,* VIII, Apr 1919, 46–47, 74. "Violet Heming Has Title Role in 'Everywoman,'" *MPW,* 5 Jul 1919, 52.

Hemingway, Marie [actress] (b. Yorkshire, England, 1893–11 Jun 1996 [103?], England). BHD1, p. 254.

Hemment, J.C. [writer/cameraman]. No data found. AMD, p. 162. "Arrives in Africa," *MPW,* 6 May 1911, 1007. F.H. Richardson, "Hemment Making good," *MPW,* 1 Aug 1914, 694. "Hemment Brings African Scenes," *MPW,* 26 Sep 1914, 1762.

Hemmer, Esward [executive]. No data found. AMD, p. 163. "Edward Hemmer Describes Novel Plan for Determining Wants of Film Fans," *MPW,* 28 Aug 1920, 1194. "Cameraman Just as Important as Star, Says Edward Hemmer, Lauding Bill Tuers," *MPW,* 4 Sep 1920, 99. "Hemmer Production Asks Public's Ideas About Plays," *MPW,* 18 Sep 1920, 343.

Hemming, Alfred (father of **Violet Heming**) [stage/film actor] (b. London, England, 1851?–17 Dec 1942 [91], New York NY). m. Mabel Allen. "Alfred Hemming," *Variety,* 23 Dec 1942. AS, p. 517. BHD, p. 197. SD.

Hemp, Pierre [title writer]. No data found. FDY, p. 445.

Hempel, Frieda [actress]. No data found. AMD, p. 163. "Frieda Hempel in Pictures," *MPW,* 17 Nov 1917, 1029. "Frieda Hempel in Pictures," *MPW,* 29 Dec 1917, 1950.

Hemphill, Frank L. [actor] (b. Mobile AL, 6 Oct 1870–12 Dec 1966 [96], Oakland CA). BHD1, p. 254.

Hemsley, Estelle E. [actress] (b. Boston MA, 5 May 1887–4 Nov 1968 [81], Los Angeles CA). AS, p. 517.

Henabery, Joseph E. [actor/director] (b. Omaha NB, 15 Jan 1888–18 Feb 1976 [88], Woodland Hills CA). m. (1) Maeceal Nolan, 1918 (d. ca. 1922, flu); (2) Lil Nolan (1st wife's sister). Anthony Slide, ed., *Before, In and After Hollywood; The Autobiography of Joseph E. Henabery* (Lanham MD: Scarecrow Press, 1997). "Joseph Henabery, Film Director, Dies," *NYT,* 20 Feb 1976, 30:6. "Joseph Henabery," *Variety,* 25 Feb 1976. AMD, p. 163. AS, p. 517. BHD, p. 197; BHD2, p. 119 (b. 1887). IFN, p. 139. Katz, p. 552. Lowrey, p. 70. "Joseph Henabery Engaged by Fairbanks," *MPW,* 19 May 1917, 1099. "Henabery Returns to Fairbanks," *MPW,* 25 Jan 1919, 474. "Henabery Is Directing at Douglas Fairbanks Studios," *MPW,* 28 Jun 1919, 1962. "Joseph Henabery Will Direct Mildred Chaplin," *MPW,* 13 Sep 1919, 1651. "Henabery to Direct Mrs. Chaplin," *MPW,* 20 Sep 1919, 1799. "Joseph Henabery Is Now a Daddy," *MPW,* 10 Apr 1920, 232 (daughter b. at Clara Barton Hospital, LA CA).

Henckles, Paul [actor] (b. Hurth, Germany, 9 Sep 1885–27 May 1967 [81], Kettwich-Dusseldorf, Germany). AS, p. 517. BHD1, p. 254. IFN, p. 139.

Hendee, Harold F. [actor] (b. 4 Dec 1879–24 Jun 1966 [86], New York NY). "Harold F. Hendee," *Variety,* 29 Jun 1966 ("He also played bit parts in some early films"). AS, p. 517. BHD, p. 197. IFN, p. 139.

Henderson, Alice Palmer [scenarist] (b. 1861-Oct 1935 [74?], Los Angeles CA). BHD2, p. 119.

Henderson, Daniel M. [publicist]. No data found. AMD, p. 163. "Henderson Writes War Song," *MPW,* 24 Nov 1917, 1183 (The Road to France). "Henderson Returns to Petrova," *MPW,* 17 Aug 1918, 961.

Henderson, Dell [actor/scenarist/director] (*né* George Delbert Henderson, b. St. Thomas, Ontario, Canada, 5 Jul 1877–2 Dec 1956 [79], Woodland Hills CA). m. **Florence D. Lee** (d. 1962). (Biograph, 1909; K&E; NYMPC.) "Del Henderson, 79, Former Film Actor," *NYT,* 5 Dec 1956, 39:2. "Del Henderson," *Variety,* 5 Dec 1956. AMD, p. 163. AS, p. 518. BHD1, p. 254; BHD2, p. 119. FSS, p. 144. IFN, p. 139. Katz, pp. 552–53 (b. 1883). Spehr, p. 140 (b. 1883). Truitt, pp. 149–50. "Dell Henderson Doubles," *MPW,* 12 Jun 1915, 1781. "Dell Henderson," *MPW,* 27 Oct 1917, 516. "Henderson Writes Comedy," *MPW,* 21 Sep 1918, 1725. "Henderson Signed to Direct Fox Features," *MPW,* 15 Nov 1919, 332. "Henderson Enthuses Over Johnny Hines," *MPW,* 26 Aug 1922, 687. "Henderson to Discuss New Series of Pictures with Arrow Officials," *MPW,* 17 May 1924, 307. "Henderson Productions Will Make New Serial for Rayart," *MPW,* 18 Oct 1924, 602. "Finishing Rayart Serial," *MPW,* 29 Nov 1924, 433. "Henderson in 'Clinging Vine,'" *MPW,* 5 Jun 1926, 458.

Henderson, George A. [actor] (b. New York NY, 1851?–28 Nov 1923 [72?], San Francisco CA; stroke). AS, p. 518. BHD, p. 197. Truitt, p. 150.

Henderson, Grace [stage/film actress] (*née?,* b. Ann Arbor MI, 1860?–30 Oct 1944 [84], New York NY). m. David Henderson (d. 1908). (Biograph, 1909.) AMD, p. 163. AS, p. 518. BHD, p. 197. IFN, p. 139. SD. Truitt, 1983. "Grace Henderson in World Pictures," *MPW,* 27 Jul 1918, 536.

Henderson, J. Ernest [executive]. No data found. AMD, p. 163. John William Kellette, "Under Water Photography," *MPW,* 25 Apr 1914, 497–98.

Henderson, Jack [actor] (b. Syracuse NY, 1877–1 Jan 1957 [79], New York NY). AS, p. 518. BHD1, p. 254. IFN, p. 139. Truitt, 1983. George Katchmer, "Remembering the Great Silents," *CI,* 246 (Dec 1995), 45.

Henderson, Jack E. [actor] (b. 1895–31 Aug 1983 [88?], Woodland Hills CA). AS, p. 518. BHD1, p. 254.

Henderson, James [director] (b. England, 1876–7 Oct 1952 [76?], Stockton-on-Tees, England). AS, p. 518.

Henderson, Jessie [publicist] (b. 1889–27 Mar 1945 [56?], Los Angeles Co. CA). BHD2, p. 119.

Henderson, Lucius J. [stage/film actor/director/producer] (b. Chicago IL, 1860?–18 Feb 1947 [86], New York NY). (Thanhouser; Majestic.) "Lucius Henderson," *Variety,* 19 Feb 1947 (age 99). AMD, p. 163. AS, p. 518. BHD1, p. 254; BHD2, p. 119 (b. Aledo IL). IFN, p. 139. SD. Truitt, p. 150. "Lucius Henderson; Managing Director of New Majestic to Retire from That Company," *NYDM,* 4 Feb 1914, 33:2 (an ad announcing his being "at liberty after Feb. 7th, 1914" appears on p. 37). "Henderson's New Post; Producer Will Handle Feature Productions of California Motion Picture Company," *NYDM,* 25 Mar 1914, 30:1.

"Lucius J. Henderson," *MPW,* 11 Apr 1914, 189. "New Imp Director, Comes from Thanhouser," *MPW,* 28 Nov 1914, 1220.

Henderson, Ray [stage/film composer] (*né* Raymond Brost, b. Buffalo NY, 1 Dec 1896–31 Dec 1970 [74], Greenwich CT; heart attack). m. (1) Marie Armstrong—div. 1925; Florence Hoffman. Autobiographical film: *The Best Things in Life Are Free* (1966). "Ray Henderson, the Songwriter, Is Dead at 74; Partner in Trio with [Lew] Brown and [Buddy] DeSylva Provided Hit Scores for Many Years," *NYT,* 2 Jan 1971, 20:3; "Ben Hecht Is Buried in Nyack Near Charles MacArthur Grave," 22 Apr 1964, 47:4. "Ray Henderson," *Variety,* 13 Jan 1971. AS, p. 518. BHD2, p. 119. SD.

Henderson, Talbot V. [character actor] (b. Phelps Mills NY, 9 Feb 1879–24 May 1946 [67], Los Angeles CA). "Talbot V. Henderson," *Variety,* 5 Jun 1946. AS, p. 518. BHD, p. 197 (V. Talbot Henderson). IFN, p. 139.

Henderson, Ted [actor] (*né* Haines Theodore Henderson, b. CA, 6 Jul 1888–19 Jul 1962 [74], Santa Paula CA). AS, p. 518. BHD1, p. 254. IFN, p. 139.

Henderson-Bland, Robert [actor] (b. England–d. 18 Aug 1941, London, England). (Kalem.) "Robert Henderson-Bland," *Variety,* 24 Sep 1941. AS, p. 518. Truitt, p. 150.

Hendricks, Benjamin, Jr. (son of **Ben Hendricks, Sr.**) [actor] (b. New York NY, 2 Nov 1893–15 Aug 1938 [44], Los Angeles CA). "Ben Hendricks, Jr.," *Variety,* 17 Aug 1938. AS, p. 518. BHD1, p. 255. IFN, p. 139. George Katchmer, "Remembering the Great Silents," *CI,* 199 (Jan 1992), 14.

Hendricks, Ben, Sr. [stage/film actor] (b. Buffalo NY, 5 Jul 1865?–30 Apr 1930 [65], Los Angeles CA). m. Isabella (son **Benjamin, Jr.**). "Ben Hendricks," *Variety,* 7 May 1930. AS, p. 518 (b. 1862). BHD1, p. 255 (b. 1868). IFN, p. 139. SD. Truitt, p. 150.

Hendricks, Dudley C. [actor] (b. LaGrange KY, 3 Aug 1870–3 Feb 1942 [71], Pasadena CA). AS, p. 518. BHD, p. 198. IFN, p. 139. George Katchmer, "Remembering the Great Silents," *CI,* 199 (Jan 1992), 14.

Hendricks, John B. [actor/singer] (b. 1872?–26 Feb 1949 [76], Elizabeth NJ). m. Mary Fanning (d. 1947). "John B. Hendricks," *Variety,* 2 Mar 1949. AS, p. 518. BHD, p. 198. IFN, p. 139.

Hendricks, Louis [actor] (b. Buffalo NY, 1860–18 Dec 1923 [63?], New York NY). m. Geraldine De Rohan. "Louis Hendricks," *Variety,* 20 Dec 1923. AS, p. 518. BHD, p. 198. Truitt, p. 150.

Hendrie, Ernest [actor] (b. England, 10 Jun 1859–11 Mar 1929 [69], Windsor, England). BHD, p. 198.

Hendrix, Noah E. "Shorty" [actor] (b. MO, 20 Dec 1889–4 Mar 1973 [83], Los Angeles CA). AS, p. 518. BHD1, p. 255. IFN, p. 139.

Hendry, Anita [actress] (b. 1868–15 Apr 1940 [72?], Brooklyn NY). m. **David Miles** (d. 1915). (Biograph, 1909.) BHD, p. 198 (Hendrie); BHD2, p. 119. IFN, p. 139. Truitt, 1983.

Henley, David [actor/casting director] (b. London, England, 1893–30 Jul 1986 [93?], London, England). AS, p. 519. BHD2, p. 119.

Henley, Hobart [actor/producer/director] (b. Louisville KY, 23 Nov 1886–22 May 1964 [77], Beverly Hills CA). m. **Corinne Barker**, Jul 1920 (d. 1928). (Universal.) "Hobart Henley," *Variety,* 3 Jun 1964 (age 68). AMD, p. 163. AS, p. 519 (b. 1887). BHD, p. 198; BHD2, p. 119 (b. 1886). IFN, p. 139. Lowrey, p. 72. Spehr, p. 140. Truitt, p. 150 (b. 1891). "Hobart Henley," *MPW,* 5 Sep 1914, 1388. "Mysterious Feature, Mysterious Part," *MPW,* 10 Apr 1915, 220. "Henley Improves Rapidly," *MPW,* 22 Jan 1916, 573. "Hobart Henley," *MPW,* 20 Jan 1917, 349. "Hobart Henley," *MPW,* 26 May 1917, 1271. "Hobart Henley Joins Pathé," *MPW,* 10 Nov 1917, 892. "Henley to Direct Mae Marsh," *MPW,* 9 Feb 1918, 807. "Hobart Henley, Director," *MPW,* 8 Jun 1918, 1409. "Hobart Henley Starts Own Company," *MPW,* 10 May 1919, 824. "Pathé Signs Hobart Henley and Mrs. Sidney Drew; Paul Brunt Predicts Brilliant Future of Both," *MPW,* 27 Sep 1919, 1963. "Hobart Henley Joins Directorial Staff of the Selznick Pictures Corporation," *MPW,* 10 Apr 1920, 282. "Hobart Henley Weds Suddenly Before Sailing for Europe," *MPW,* 7 Aug 1920, 706. "Henley Goes to Universal City," *MPW,* 27 Aug 1921, 924. "Hobart Henley Signed," *MPW,* 2 Feb 1924, 373. "Hobart Henley Signs New Contract," *MPW,* 12 Sep 1925, 184. "Mayer Signs New Contract; Henley Remains with Metro," *MPW,* 19 Dec 1925, 661. "Henley to Direct 'Tillie,'" *MPW,* 11 Sep 1926, 97. "Henley and His Mother Celebrate," *MPW,* 11 Dec 1926, 408.

Henley, Jack [scenarist] (b. London, England, 1894–2 Nov 1958 [64?], Los Angeles CA). AS, p. 519.

Henley, Rosina [actress/scenarist] (*née?,* b. 18 Nov 1890–Jul 1978 [87], New York NY). m. director **Harley Knoles** (d. 1936). BHD, p. 198. Lynn Munroe, "William Henley Knoles," in *Books Are Everything,* No. 26 (Winter 1993), pp. 71ff.

Hennecke, Clarence R. [actor: Keystone Cop] (b. Omaha NB, 16 Sep 1894–28 Aug 1969 [74], Santa Monica CA). (Vitagraph; Sennett; Roach.) "Clarence R. Hennecke," *Variety,* 10 Sep 1969. AS, p. 519. BHD1, p. 255; BHD2, p. 119. IFN, p. 139. Truitt, p. 150.

Hennery [actor] (*né* Henri Hennery, b. Paris, France, 18 Oct 1898). AS, p. 519.

Hennessey, David [stage/film actor] (b. 1852?–24 Mar 1926 [74], Chicago IL). "David Hennessey," *Variety,* 31 Mar 1926 ("He had appeared in many photoplays when not on the legitimate stage"). AS, p. 519. BHD, p. 198. IFN, p. 139.

Hennessey, John A. [actor] (b. Boston MA, 1853?–15 May 1920 [67], New York NY). AS, p. 519 (d. 16 May). BHD, p. 198. IFN, p. 139.

Hennesy, Hugh Patridge [actor] (b. 1890–14 Mar 1954 [64?], Death Valley CA). AS, p. 519.

Henning, Hanna [director/producer] (b. Cannstadt, Germany, 16 Aug 1884–9 Jan 1925 [40], Berlin, Germany). AS, p. 519.

Henning, Uno [actor] (b. Stockholm, Sweden, 11 May 1895–16 May 1970 [75]). AS, p. 519 (Udo Henning). BHD1, p. 255.

Hennings, John [actor] (d. 8 Nov 1933, St. Joseph MO; suicide by shooting). AS, p. 519.

Hennion, Robert Alexandre Célestin [director] (b. Colombes, France, 17 Feb 1898 [extrait de naissance no. 61/1898]–18 Jan 1984 [85], Paris, France). AS, p. 519.

Henri, Louis (Lady Lytton) [actress] (b. 1863?–2 May 1947 [84?], Surbiton, England). BHD, p. 198.

Henrikson, Anders [actor/director/scenarist] (b. Stockholm, Sweden, 3 Jun 1896–17 Oct 1965 [69], Stockholm, Sweden). AS, p. 519 (also listed under Hendrikson). BHD, p. 198; BHD1, p. 255; BHD2, p. 119 (Hendrikson); BHD2, p. 120.

Henry, Charlotte [actress] (b. Brooklyn NY, 3 Mar 1913–11 Apr 1980 [67], San Diego CA). BHD1, p. 255.

Henry, Dorothy [actress]. No data found. AMD, p. 163. "Dorothy Henry Signed," *MPW,* 22 Aug 1925, 840.

Henry, Frank [actor] (b. England, 1884–30 Nov 1963 [79?], Los Angeles CA). AS, p. 519.

Henry, Frank Thomas Patrick [actor] (b. 1894–3 Oct 1963 [69?], Los Angeles CA). AS, p. 519.

Henry, Gale [actress] (*née* Gale Trowbridge, b. Bear Valley CA, 15 Apr 1893–17 Jun 1972 [79], Palmdale CA). m. **Bruno C. Becker**, LA CA (d. 1926). (Universal.) AMD, p. 163. AS, p. 520. BHD1, p. 255. IFN, p. 139. MH, p. 117. Cal York, "Plays and Players," *Photoplay Magazine,* Feb 1917, 86 (married Becker). "Gale Henry Transfers to L-KO Comedies," *MPW,* 1 Dec 1917, 1354. "Gale Henry to Start Work on Five-Reel Comedy Soon," *MPW,* 3 Jan 1920, 142. "Comedienne Gale Henry Is No Longer with Bull's Eye," *MPW,* 14 Feb 1920, 1055. "Gale Henry to Make Twelve Two-Reel Films for Special," *MPW,* 31 Jul 1920, 582. Billy H. Doyle, "Gale Henry," *FIR,* Feb 1978, 122.

Henry, Janet [actress]. No data found. (Thanhouser.) "In the Picture Studios," *NYDM,* 4 Aug 1915, 27:2 (on the female baseball team at Thanhouser).

Henry, John [actor] (b. 1882?–12 Aug 1958 [76], Winthrop MA). "John Henry," *Variety,* 20 Aug 1958 ("silent film actor"). AS, p. 520. BHD, p. 198 (b. 1880). IFN, p. 139. Truitt, p. 150.

Henry, S. Creagh [actor] (b. Isle of Guernsey, 1 Jul 1863–26 Feb 1946 [82]). BHD, p. 198.

Henry, William [actor] (b. Los Angeles CA, 10 Nov 1918–10 Aug 1982 [63], Canoga Park CA). AS, p. 520. BHD1, p. 256 (b. 1914; d. LA CA). Katz, p. 554. Ragan 2, p. 735.

Henshaw, Roger [director/scenarist] (b. 1896–3 Apr 1938 [42?], Los Angeles CA). BHD2, p. 120.

Henson, Gladys [actress] (*née* Gladys Gunn, b. Dublin, Ireland, 27 Sep 1897–15 Dec 1982 [85], London, England). AS, p. 520.

Henson, Leslie [actor] (b. London, England, 3 Aug 1891–2 Dec 1957 [66], Harrow Weald, England). AS, p. 520 (d. London, England). BHD1, p. 256. IFN, p. 139.

Hepburn, Barton [actor] (b. Minneapolis MN, 28 Feb 1906–9 Oct 1955 [49], Los Angeles CA). "Barton Hepburn," *Variety,* 19 Oct 1955. AS, p. 520. BHD1, p. 256. IFN, p. 139. Truitt, p. 150.

Hepp, Joseph [director/producer] (b. Budapest, Hungary, 1897–1968 [71?], Athens, Greece). AS, p. 520.

Hepworth, Cecil M[ilton] [actor/director/producer/executive] (b. Lewisham, England [at 17 Somerset Gardens, off Loampit Hill], 19 Mar 1873–9 Feb 1953 [79], Greenford, Middlesex, England). *Came the Dawn; Memories of a Film Pioneer* (London: Phoenix House, Ltd., 1952). "Cecil Hepworth, 79, British Film Pioneer," *NYT,* 11 Feb 1953, 29:2. "Cecil Hepworth," *Variety,* 18 Feb 1953. AS, p. 520 (b. Lambeth, England, 1874). BHD, p. 198; BHD2, p. 120. Katz, 1994. WWVC, pp. 64–65. "Silent Star; As the cinema celebrates its centenary Nellie Redmond pays tribute to Lewisham-borm film-maker Cecil Hepworth," *Lewisham Mercury,* 13 Mar 1997, p. 9.

Herald, Heinz [scenarist] (b. Germany, 1887–22 Jul 1964 [77?], Kreuth, Germany). AS, p. 521. BHD2, p. 120.

Herbert, Alexander J. [actor]. No data found. AMD, p. 163. "Acted in First Australian Motion Picture," *MPW,* 15 Jul 1916, 478.

Herbert, F. Hugh [title writer/scenarist] (b. Binghamton NY, 10 Aug 1885–12 Mar 1952 [66], San Fernando CA; heart attack). m. Aileen Lavern [his secretary], Sep 1927, Hollywood Ca; Anita Pam. (WB; Columbia; U-I.) "Hugh Herbert," *Variety,* 19 Mar 1952 (wrote first WB talkie, *Lights of New York*). AMD, p. 164. AS, p. 521 (Hugh Herbert, b. 1887). BHD, p. 198. FDY, p. 445. IFN, p. 140. Katz, p. 557 (b. 1887). SD. "Added to Scenario Staff," *MPW,* 3 Jan 1926, 308.

Herbert, Frances [actress]. No data found. AMD, p. 164. "Frances Herbert," *MPW,* 21 Jul 1917, 450.

Herbert, Frederick Hugh [director/scenarist] (b. Vienna, Austria, 28 May 1897–17 May 1958 [60], Los Angeles CA). AS, p. 521 (b. 29 May). BHD2, p. 120.

Herbert, F[rederick] **Hugh** [writer/playwright/radio writer/scenarist/director/President of Screen Actors' Guild, 1953–54] (b. Vienna, 1898?–17 May 1958 [60], Hollywood CA). m. Mary. (Began as scenarist in 1921; Paramount.) "F. Hugh Herbert Is Dead at 60; Playwright Had Wide Success; Vienna-Born Author of Stage and Film Comedies Also Was Poet and Novelist," *NYT,* 18 May 1958, 86:4. "F. Hugh Herbert," *Variety,* 210, 21 May 1958,. 79:2 (wrote *The Moon Is Blue*). FDY, p. 427.

Herbert, Hans [actor] (*né* Hans Hausknect, b. Poland, 11 Jun 1882–21 Jun 1957 [75], Los Angeles CA). AS, p. 521.

Herbert, Helen (aunt of Dan Duryea) [actress] (*née?,* b. Brooklyn NY, 6 Apr 1873–27 Oct 1946 [73], Los Angeles CA). m. **Henry J. Herbert** (d. 1947). "Mrs. Helen Herbert," *Variety,* 30 Oct 1946. AS, p. 521. BHD, p. 196. IFN, p. 138. Truitt, p. 150.

Herbert, Henry J. [actor] (b. England, 1878?–20 Feb 1947 [68], Flushing NY). m. **Helen** (d. 1946). "Henry Herbert," *Variety,* 26 Feb 1947 (in *So Big*). AS, p. 521. BHD, p. 198. IFN, p. 140. Truitt, p. 150. George Katchmer, "Remembering the Great Silents," *CI,* 242 (Aug 1995), 36–37.

Herbert, Holmes E. [stage/film actor] (*né* Edward Sanger, b. Dublin, Ireland, 30 Jul 1878–26 Dec 1956 [78], Los Angeles CA). m. Beryl Mercier (d. 1939). "Holmes Herbert," *Variety,* 2 Jan 1957 (b. England). AMD, p. 164. AS, p. 521 (b. Mansfield Notts, England, 3 Jul 1882). BHD1, p. 256 (b. Mansfield, England). FSS, p. 144. IFN, p. 140 (b. Mansfield, England, 1882). Katz, pp. 556–57 (b. Mansfield, 1883). MH, p. 117 (b. 1882). FFF, p. 195. SD, p. 603 (b. Mansfield, Nottinghamshire, England). Slide, p. 161. Truitt, p. 151 (b. 1882). "Herbert, Metro Player, Has Been Long on Stage," *MPW,* 21 Sep 1918, 1716 (b. 1882). Susan Elizabeth Brady, "A Man of Parts," *Classic,* Oct 1922, 59, 86–87. "Holmes Herbert Signed," *MPW,* 29 Mar 1924, 367. David A. Balch, "'Being Sure of Yourself Is Movie Actor's Greatest Asset,' Says Screen Leading Man," *MW,* 31 May 1924, 7, 27. Donald Calhoun, "Our Very British Holmes Herbert; He Calls His Early Barnstorming Days, 'Bottling and Busking,' and Sips Tea Among the Ice-Cream Sodas of Hollywood," *MPC,* Jun 1925, 50, 95–96.

Herbert, Hugh (brother of **Thomas F. Herbert**) [actor] (b. Binghamton NY, 10 Aug 1885–12 Mar 1952 [66], No. Hollywood CA). AS, p. 521 (b. 1887). BHD1, p. 256.

Herbert, Jack [actor] (*né* Herbert N. Songcrant, b. 1891?–10 Jun 1957 [66], North Reading PA). m. Barbara Neely (d. 1955). "Jack Herbert," *Variety,* 19 Jun 1957. AS, p. 521.

Herbert, Joseph [actor/writer] (b. Liverpool, England, 1866?–18 Feb 1923 [56], New York NY). m. Marie Maynard. "Joseph Herbert," *Variety,* 22 Feb 1923. AS, p. 521. BHD, p. 198.

Herbert, Lillian [actress] (b. 1887?–27 Dec 1923 [36], Sommerville MA; died backstage at the Olympia theatre from brain hemorrhage followed by a stroke of apoplexy). (Edison.) m. George Herbert. "Lillian Herbert Mullen," *Variety,* 10 Jan 1924. AS, p. 521.

Herbert, Sydney [actor] (b. England–d. 24 Dec 1927, London, England). AS, p. 521 (d. LA CA). BHD, p. 198. IFN, p. 140.

Herbert, Thomas F. (brother of **Hugh Herbert**) [actor] (b. New York NY, 25 Nov 1888–3 Apr 1946 [57], Los Angeles CA). AS, p. 521.

Herbert, Victor [composer] (b. Dublin, Ireland, 1 Feb 1859–26 May 1924 [65], New York NY). BHD2, p. 120.

Herczeg, Ceza [scenarist] (b. Nagykanizsa, Hungary, 1 Mar 1888–19 Feb 1954 [65], Rome, Italy). AS, p. 521 (Geza Herczeg). BHD2, p. 120.

Herford, William B. [actor] (b. Yorkshire, England, 5 May 1853–27 Dec 1934 [81]). AS, p. 521. BHD, p. 198. IFN, p. 140.

Heriat, Philippe [actor/scenarist] (*né* Raymond Gérard Payelle, b. Paris, France, 15 Sep 1898–10 Oct 1971 [73], Paris, France). AS, p. 521. BHD1, p. 257. IFN, p. 140.

Heribel, Renée Eugénie Aimée [actress] (b. Caen, France, 9 Feb 1903 [extrait de naissance no. SN/1995]–25 Jul 1952 [49], Neuilly-sur-Seine, France). AS, p. 521.

Heritage, Clarence [actor] (*né* Clarence Gibson, b. 1854?–27 Oct 1940 [86?], New York NY). "Clarence Heritage," *Variety,* 30 Oct 1940. AS, p. 521 (d. 27 Dec 1934). BHD, p. 198.

Herlein, Lillian [actress] (b. 11 Mar 1895–13 Apr 1971 [76], New York NY). m. Charles G. Straikosh. "Lillian Herlein," *Variety,* 21 Apr 1971. AS, p. 521. BHD1, p. 257. IFN, p. 140. Truitt, p. 151 (b. ca. 1895).

Herlinger, Karl [actor/makeup artist] (b. Vienna, Austria, 1880?–8 Feb 1949 [69], Los Angeles CA). BHD, p. 199; BHD2, p. 120.

Herlth, Robert Paul Fritz [director] (b. Wriezen, Germany, 2 May 1893–6 Jan 1962 [68], Munich, Germany). AS, p. 521.

Herman, Al [actor] (b. Scotland, 25 Feb 1887–2 Jul 1967 [80], Los Angeles CA). AS, p. 521. BHD1, p. 257. IFN, p. 140.

Herman, Charles D. [actor]. No data found. AMD, p. 164. Hugh Hoffman, "In the Catskills with Reliance," *MPW,* 24 Aug 1912, 751.

Herman, Jay [singer/actor] (d. 20 Feb 1928, Bridgeport CT; pneumonia). m. Thelma Pritchard. "Jay Herman," *Variety,* 29 Feb 1928. AS, p. 522. BHD, p. 199.

Herman, Milton C. [film/radio/TV actor] (b. 1895?–21 Jan 1951 [55], Astoria, LI NY; coronary thrombosis). (Bejgan 1912.) "Milton C. Herman," *Variety,* 181, 24 Jan 1951, 55:2. AS, p. 522. BHD, p. 199. IFN, p. 140.

Hermann, Fernand [actor] (b. Paris, France, 1886–ca. Apr 1925 [39?]). AS, p. 523.

Hermann, Jacques [actor]. No data found. AMD, p. 164. "Jacques Hermann," *MPW,* 30 Dec 1916, 1940.

Hernandez, Albert [actor] (*né* Luis Albereto Hernandez Gatell, b. Mexico, Apr 1898?–2 Jan 1948 [49], Los Angeles CA). "Albert Hernandez," *Variety,* 14 Jan 1948. AS, p. 522. BHD, p. 199. IFN, p. 140. Truitt, p. 151.

Hernandez, Anna. *See* Dodge, Anna.

Hernandez, George F. [actor] (b. Placerville CA, 6 Jun 1863–31 Dec 1922 [59], Los Angeles CA). m. **Anna Dodge** (d. 1945). (Selig.) AMD, p. 164. AS, p. 522. BHD, p. 199. IFN, p. 140. "George F. Hernandez," *MPW,* Mar 1918, 1217. George Katchmer, "Remembering the Great Silents," *CI,* 224 (Feb 1994), 53:3.

Herne, Chrystal Katherine (daughter of actor/playwright James A. Herne; sister of actress **Julie Herne**) [stage/film actress] (b. Beale Street, Ashmont, Dorchester MA, 17 Jun 1882 [MVRB, Vol. 333, p.190]–19 Sep 1950 [68], Boston MA; cancer). m. Harold Stanley Pollard, 31 Aug 1914, Los Angeles CA. (Stage debut: *Griffith Davenport,* 1899.) "Chrystal Herne, Stage Star, Dies; Retired Actress Appeared in 'Craig's Wife,' 'Melting Pot,' 'Candida,' 'Squaw Man,'" *NYT,* 20 Sep 1950, 31:1. "Chrystal Herne," *Variety,* 27 Sep 1950. AS, p. 522 (b. 1883). IFN, p. 140 (age 67). DAB, Supp. 4, p. 368.

Herne, Julie (sister of **Chrystal Herne**) [playwright] (b. Boston MA, 31 Oct 1880?–24 Feb 1955 [74], New York NY; found dead). (Metro.) "Julie A. Herne," *Variety,* 2 Mar 1955. SD (b. 1881).

Hernfeld, Anton [actor] (b. Germany, 1865–20 Oct 1929 [64?], Berlin, Germany). AS, p. 523.

Herrand, Marcel [actor] (b. Paris, France, 8 Oct 1897–11 Jun 1953 [55], Montfort-L'Amaury, France [extrait de décès no. 23/1953]). AS, p. 522.

Herrick, F. Herrick [producer/director]. No data found. AMD, p. 164. Charles Edward Hastings, "Herrick," *MPW,* 29 May 1926, 416.

Herrick, Jack [actor] (b. Hungary, 4 Feb 1891–18 Jun 1952 [61], Los Angeles Co. CA). AS, p. 522. BHD1, p. 257. IFN, p. 140. George Katchmer, "Remembering the Great Silents," *CI,* 199 (Jan 1992), 12.

Herriman, George [director] (b. 1880–1944 [64?]), Los Angeles CA). AS, p. 522.

Herring, Aggie [actress] (b. San Francisco CA, 4 Feb 1876–28 Oct 1939 [63], Santa Monica CA). AS, p. 523. BHD1, p. 257. IFN, p. 140. MH, p. 117.

Herring, Jess [actor] (b. MO, 29 Oct 1895–5 Mar 1953 [57], Los Angeles Co. CA). (Vitagraph.) AS, p. 523. BHD, p. 199. IFN, p. 140.

Herrmann, Julius E. [actor] (b. Germany, 13 Jun 1883–1977 [94?]). BHD, p. 199.

Herschell, Charles [director] (b. Australia, 1878–30 May 1962 [84?], Melbourne, Australia). AS, p. 523.

Herschfield, Harry [actor] (*né* Abe

Kabible, b. Cedar Rapids IA, 13 Oct 1885–15 Dec 1974 [89], New York NY). AS, p. 523. BHD, p. 199.

Hershey, Burnet [scenarist] (b. 1896–13 Dec 1971 [75?], Miami FL). BHD2, p. 120. FDY, p. 429.

Hersholt, Allan [actor/publicist] (b. Copenhagen, Denmark, 4 Dec 1914–19 Feb 1990 [75], Los Angeles CA). BHD, p. 199; BHD2, p. 120.

Hersholt, Jean [stage/film actor] (b. Copenhagen, Denmark, 12 Jul 1886–2 Jun 1956 [69], Los Angeles CA; cancer). m. Via Anderson, 11 Apr 1914, San Francisco CA. (Great Northern Film Co. [Denmark]; Ince, *Bullets and Brown Eyes,* 1914; NYMP Co.; Universal; Goldwyn; MGM; Danish film debut: *Professor Morgenavis,* Nordisk Films Kompangni, 24 Mar 1906; American film debut: *The Deserter.*) "Jean Hersholt, 69, Is Dead on Coast; Screen Actor for 50 Years Was Former President of Motion Picture Academy; Known as Dr. Christian; Civic Leader in Hollywood Created Role on Radio—Knighted by Denmark," *NYT,* 3 Jun 1956, 86:1; "Hundreds at Hersholt Rites," *NYT,* 5 Jun 1956, 35:2. "Jean Hersholt," *Variety,* 6 Jun 1956. AMD, p. 164. AS, p. 523. BHD1, p. 257. FSS, p. 145. GK, pp. 398–411. HCH, p. 47. IFN, p. 140. Katz, p. 558 (began 1915). MSBB, p. 1024. 1921 Directory, p. 266. Truitt, p. 151. "Jean Hersholt," *MPW,* 24 Mar 1917, 1929. Peter Milne, "Just a Natural Actor—and BOY How He Can Act; Jean Hersholt Came Over from Denmark a Few Years Ago With a Family, a few Dollars and Some Press Notices. After Various Ups and Downs He Showed Them He Could Do His Stuff—And Do It Remarkably Well," *MPC,* Feb 1927, 26–27, 84, 86. Hal Hall, "Don't Be Yourself; Jean Hersholt Believes Lasting Favor Goes Only to Those Who Keep Being Somebody Else," *MPC,* Aug 1928, 55, 84 ("None of us has a personality strong enough to keep the public wanting us as ourselves forever."). Gladys Hall, "How to Be Happy Though in Hollywood; One Man—Jean Hersholt Has Found Out," *MPC,* Apr 1929, 44, 88. Ed Finney, "The Jean Hersholt Story," *CFC,* 25 (Fall, 1969), 18–20. George A. Katchmer, "Jean Hersholt; From Villain to Kind Doctor," *CI,* 141 (Mar 1987), C18 *et passim.* Richard E. Braff, "An Index to the Films of Jean Hersholt," *CI,* 190 (Apr 1991), 16 *et passim.* George Katchmer, "Remembering the Great Silents," *CI,* 242 (Aug 1995), 37.

Hertel, Adolph R. [actor/director] (b. 1877?–14 Mar 1958 [80], Los Angeles CA). "Adolph R. Hertel," *Variety,* 2 Apr 1958. AS, p. 523. BHD2, p. 120 IFN, p. 140.

Herts, Edwin Jay [actor/decorator] (b. NY, 27 May 1883–26 Dec 1951 [68]). AMD, p. 164. IFN, 140. Edwin Jay Herts, "The Importance to the Films of Interior Details," *MPW,* 30 Oct 1915, 781.

Hertz, Aleksander [director] (b. Warsaw, Poland, 1879–1928 [49?]. Warsaw, Poland). AS, p. 523. BHD2, p. 120.

Hertzig, Sig [scenarist]. No data found. (Christie.) June Lee, "Dan Cupid's Bulletin Board," *Paris and Hollywood,* Oct 1926, 89 (to marry Betty Reinhold of the Christie publicity department).

Hertzinger, Charles W. [actor] (b. San Francisco CA, 10 Aug 1864–18 Feb 1953 [88], Los Angeles CA). (Universal.) AS, p. 523 (b. Nevada City CA, 12 Aug); also listed under Charles W. Herzinger. BHD1, p. 258 (b. NV). IFN, p. 141.

Herve, Jean Louis Emile [actor] (b. Paris, France, 30 Mar 1884 [extrait de naissance no. 619]–27 Nov 1966 [84], Paris, France [extrait de décès no. 4948]). AS, p. 523.

Hervey, Grizelda [actress] (b. Plomesgate, England, 1901–17 Dec 1980 [79?]). BHD1, p. 258.

Hervil, René [director/producer] (b. France, 1883–1960 [77?], France). AS, p. 523.

Herz, Ralph [vaudeville/stage/film actor] (b. Paris, France, 25 Mar 1878–12 Jul 1921 [43], Atlantic City NJ; diabetes). m. (1) **Lulu Glaser,** 1916 (d. 1958); (2) Frances Logan. "Ralph Herz, Actor, Dies in Atlantic City; He Was Soon to Appear Here in 'Blossom Time'—Famed in Musical Plays," *NYT,* 13 Jul 1921, 9:4 (debut, London, 1900). "Ralph Herz," *Variety,* 15 Jul 1921 (b. England; ca. 50). AMD, p. 164. AS, p. 523. BHD, p. 199. IFN, p. 140. "Metro's Activities; Two More Stars Added to Roster of Metro Pictures Corporation Last Week," *NYDM,* 23 Jun 1915, 25:1. "And Still They Come; Metro Secures Services of More Stage Luminaries and Adds to Plays," *NYDM,* 30 Jun 1915, 24:1. "Ralph Herz wi Metro," *MPW,* 3 Jul 1915, 69. "Ralph Herz Marries," *MPW,* 24 Jun 1916, 2211. "Ralph Herz Playing with Selig," *MPW,* 26 May 1917, 1295.

Herzfield, Guido [actor] (b. Berlin, Germany, 1865–16 Nov 1923 [58?]). BHD, p. 199. IFN, p. 140.

Herzig, Siegfried M. (Sid) [scenarist] (b. New York NY, 1897–12 Mar 1985 [88?], Thousand Oaks CA). AS, p. 523. BHD2, p. 121. FDY, p. 429.

Herzog, Charles L. (Buck) [actor] (b. Baltimore MD, 9 Jul 1885–5 Feb 1970 [84], Baltimore MD). BHD, p. 199.

Herzog, Dorothy [title writer]. No data found. FDY, p. 445.

Herzog, Frederic [actor] (b. 1868–2 Mar 1928 [59], Glendale CA). BHD, p. 199. IFN, p. 141.

Heslewood, Tom [actor] (b. Hessle, York, England, 8 Apr 1868–28 Apr 1959 [91]). BHD, p. 199. IFN, p. 141.

Heslop, Charles [vaudeville/film actor] (b. Thames, Ditton, England, 8 Jun 1883–13 Apr 1966 [82], London, England). m. actress Madie Field (d. Mar 1966, age 81). "Charles Heslop," *Variety,* 242, 20 Apr 1966, 71:1 (d. 3 weeks after wife). AS, p. 524. BHD1, p. 258. IFN, p. 141.

Hesperia [variety/film actress] (aka Alda Hesperia and Olga Negroni, *née* Olga Mombelli, b. Bertinoro, Forlì, Italy, 9 Jul 1885–30 May 1959 [73], Rome, Italy). m. Count **Baldassare Negroni,** 1923 [d. 1948]. AS, p. 524. JS, p. 213 ("A diva of more personality than beauty, she came out of variety theater."). "Coming Kleine Releases," *NYDM,* 3 Mar 1915, 25:4 (Marie Hesperia, "the most popular photoplayer in Europe," appeared in *Bartered Lives,* playing herself and her wayward sister in a "double exposure negative.").

Hesse, Baron William [actor] (b. Moscow, Russia, 22 Jul 1885–4 Apr 1936 [50], Los Angeles CA). AS, p. 524. BHD1, p. 258 IFN, p. 141.

Hesser, Edwin Bower [playwright/executive] (b. Jersey City NJ, 23 Apr 1893–7 Aug 1962 [69], Los Angeles CA). AMD, p. 164. BHD2, p. 121. "Hesser Film Company; Edwin Bower Hesser Heads New Film Feature Producing Organization," *NYDM,* 3 Feb 1915, 24:2 (capitalized at $50,000; first production: *The Royal Pretender*). "Hesser Organizes Producing Company," *MPW,* 13 Feb 1915, 959.

Hesslewood, Tom [actor] (b. Hessle, England, 8 Apr 1868–28 Apr 1959 [91]). BHD1, p. 258.

Hessling, Catherine [actor] (*née* Andrée Madeleine Heuschling, b. Moronvilliers, Alsace, France, 22 Jun 1900–28 Sep 1979 [79], La-Celle-Saint-Cloud, France [extrait de décès no. 140/76/CC66781]). AS, p. 524. BHD1, p. 258.

Hester, James [actor] (b. 1867–16 Feb 1924 [56?], Brooklyn NY). BHD, p. 199.

Hesterberg, Trude [actress] (*née* Gertrude Johanna Dorothea Helene Hesterberg, b. Berlin, Germany, 2 May 1892–31 Aug 1967 [75], Munich, Germany). AS, p. 524. BHD1, p. 258. IFN, p. 141.

Hetrick, Don [assistant director]. No data found. AMD, p. 164. "Don Hetrick Promoted to Assistant Director," *MPW,* 7 Nov 1925, 49.

Heuberger, Carl Edmund [director] (b. Aarau, Switzerland, 28 Apr 1883–9 Apr 1962 [78], Zurich, Switzerland). AS, p. 524. BHD2, p. 121.

Heurtzur, Fernand [director] (d. Dec 1930, Paris, France). BHD2, p. 121.

Heustis, Reed [scenarist/title writer]. No data found. AMD, p. 164. "Another Reporter!," *MPW,* 2 Apr 1927, 481.

Heuze, André Léon Louis [director] (b. Saint-Arnoult, France, 5 Dec 1880–16 Aug 1942 [61], Paris, France). AS, p. 524.

Hevener, Gerald "Little Jerry" [actor] (b. Philadelphia PA, 30 Apr 1873). AMD, p. 164. BHD, p. 199. "Jerold 'Little Jerry' Hevener," *MPW,* 4 Sep 1915, 1659.

Hewitt, Douglas D. [title writer]. No data found. AMD, p. 164. "Hewitt Now with Selznick," *MPW,* 27 Dec 1919, 1125.

Hewitt, Henry [actor] (b. London, England, 28 Dec 1885–23 Aug 1968 [82], Newbury, England). AS, p. 524.

Hewitt, Sanford [scenarist]. No data found. FDY, p. 429.

Hewlett, Ben [actor] (b. Oakland CA, 27 Feb 1892–16 Aug 1948 [56], Santa Monica CA). BHD1, p. 258.

Hewston, Alfred H. [actor] (b. San Francisco CA, 12 Sep 1880–6 Sep 1947 [66], Los Angeles CA). AS, p. 524 (b. 1882). BHD1, p. 258. IFN, p. 141 (b. 1882). Truitt, 1983. George Katchmer, "Remembering the Great Silents," *CI,* 198 (Dec 1991), 11.

Heyburn, Weldon [actor] (b. Selma AL, 19 Sep 1904–18 May 1951 [46], Los Angeles CA). m. (1) **Greta Nisson**; (2) Jane Eichelberger; (3) Virginia Haggard, Sep 1939, Tijuana, Mexico. "Weldon Heyburn," *Variety,* 23 May 1951. AS, p. 524. BHD1, p. 258. IFN, p. 141. Truitt, 1983. "Heyburn, Film Actor, Weds," *NYT,* 10 Sep 1939, 48:7.

Heyes, Herbert H. [actor] (b. Vader [Little Falls?] WA, 3 Aug 1889–31 May 1958 [68], No. Hollywood CA). (Essanay; Kleine; Fox.) "Herbert Heyes," *Variety,* 11 Jun 1958 ("leading man in silent pictures"). AMD, p. 164. AS, p. 524. BHD1, p. 258 (d. LA CA). FSS, p. 145. IFN, p. 141. Truitt, p. 152. "Hayes Returns to Fox Forces," *MPW,* 1 Jun 1918, 1276. "Hayes Plays Opposite to May Allison," *MPW,* 14 Sep 1918, 1596. "Herbert H. Heyes in Roland Serial," *MPW,* 27 Sep 1919, 1956. "Herbert Heyes Has Had a Long Dramatic Career," *MPW,*

20 Dec 1919, 995. George Katchmer, "Remembering the Great Silents," *CI,* 241 (Jul 1995), 35.

Heyward, Du Bose [scenarist] (b. Charleston SC, 1885–16 Jun 1940 [55?], Tryon NC). BHD2, p. 121.

Heywood, Herbert [actor] (b. IL, 1 Feb 1881–15 Sep 1964 [83], Van Nuys CA). AS, p. 525.

Hiatt, Ruth [actress: Wampas Star, 1924] (b. Cripple Creek CO, 6 Jan 1906–21 Apr 1994 [88], Montrose CA; congestive heart failure). (Sennett, ca. 1917; late film: *Double Trouble,* 1941.) AMD, p. 164. AS, p. 525 (b. 1908). BHD1, p. 259. "Engage Ruth Hiatt as Lead," *MPW,* 26 Aug 1922, 668. "Ruth Hiatt Wins Beauty Contest," *MPW,* 15 Sep 1923, 280. "Alfred Goulding Signed by Mack Sennett for Comedies," *MPW,* 1 Aug 1925, 575. "Ruth Hiatt," *CI,* 230 (August, 1994), 55.

Hibbard, Edna [actress] (b. Detroit MI, 12 May 1895–26 Dec 1942 [47], New York NY). m. (1) actor Stuart Gage; (2) John C. Seager, Jr.; (3) Lester Bryant. "Edna Hibbard," *Variety,* 30 Dec 1942. AS, p. 525. BHD1, p. 259.

Hibbard, Enid [title writer/scenarist]. No data found. FDY, pp. 429, 445.

Hibben, Edwin H. [director] (b. Omaha NB, 1883–18 May 1921 [38?], Phoenix AZ). BHD2, p. 121.

Hiby, Charles [actor] (b. Hamilton, Canada, 27 Dec 1880–15 Feb 1947 [66], Los Angeles CA). AS, p. 525.

Hichens, Robert [writer] (b. 14 Nov 1864–20 Jul 1950 [85], Zurich, Switzerland). AMD, p. 164. BHD2, p. 121. "Lasky Signs Contract with Prominent London Author to Write Scropts," *MPW,* 19 Feb 1921, 945.

Hickey, Howard L. [actor] (b. 1896–25 Mar 1942 [46?], San Fernando CA). AS, p. 525.

Hickman, Alfred D. [actor] (b. London, England, 25 Feb 1872–9 Apr 1931 [59], Los Angeles CA; cerebral hemorrhage). m. **Blanche Walsh**, 1896 (d. 1915); **Nance O'Neil**, 11 Aug 1916 (d. 1965). "Alfred D. Hickman," *Variety,* 15 Apr 1931 (age 57). AMD, p. 164. AS, p. 525. BHD1, p. 259. IFN, p. 141. Truitt, p. 152 (b. 1873). "Nance O'Neill Acting for McClure Pictures," *MPW,* 21 Oct 1916, 413. "Alfred Hickman in New Brenon Picture," *MPW,* 22 Dec 1917, 1793.

Hickman, Bill [actor] (b. Los Angeles CA, 25 Jan 1921–24 Feb 1986 [65], Indio CA). BHD1, p. 259.

Hickman, Charles H. [director] (b. 1876?–19 Sep 1938 [62], Sawtrelle CA). "Charles H. Hickman," *Variety,* 28 Sep 1938 ("He retired in 1932 after 24 years in the picture business"). AS, p. 525. BHD, p. 200; BHD2, p. 121. IFN, p. 141.

Hickman, Howard C. [stage/film actor/director] (b. Columbia MO, 9 Feb 1880–30 Dec 1949 [69], San Anselmo CA). m. **Bessie Bariscale** (d. 1965). (Universal; FP-L; Triangle-Ince; Paralta.) "Howard C. Hickman," *NYT,* 1 Jan 1950, 42:5. "Howard C. Hickman," *Variety,* 11 Jan 1950 (d. LA CA). AMD, p. 164. AS, p. 525 (d. 31 Dec). BHD1, p. 259; BHD2, p. 121 (d. LA CA). IFN, p. 141. Lowrey, p. 74. MSBB, p. 1024. 1921 Directory, p. 266. SD. Truitt, 1983. "Howard C. Hickman," *MPW,* 10 Mar 1917, 1571. "The Man Who Always Makes Good," *Motion Picture Magazine,* Feb 1918, 53 (photo of him as Lafe Grandoken in *Rose o' Paradise*). "Howard Hickman to Become Director," *MPW,* 11 May 1918, 862. "Hickman Ill with Pneumonia," *MPW,* 21 Jun 1919, 1776.

Hickman, Roberta [actress]. No data found. AMD, p. 164. "Roberta Hickman," *MPW,* 3 Jul 1915, 71.

Hickok, Lida [actress] (b. 1863–23 Aug 1928 [65?], Los Angeles CA). BHD, p. 200.

Hickok, Rodney [actor] (b. 1892?–9 Mar 1942 [50], Los Angeles CA). "Rodney Hickok," *Variety,* 11 Mar 1942. AS, p. 525. BHD, p. 200. IFN, p. 141. Truitt, p. 153.

Hickox, Sidney B. [cinematographer] (b. New York NY, 15 Jul 1889–16 May 1982 [92], La Canada CA). (Biograph.) AS, p. 525 (d. ca. Apr 1955). BHD2, p. 121. Katz, p. 560 (began 1915). FDY, p. 459. *Halliwell Filmgoers Companion,* 12th ed., p. 200.

Hicks, Don. *See* Hix, Don.

Hicks, Eleanor [actress] (b. 1886–11 Jul 1936 [50?], Aurora IL). BHD, p. 200.

Hicks, E[dward] **Seymour** [stage/film actor/director/scenarist] (b. St. Heliers, Jersey, England, 30 Jan 1871–6 Apr 1949 [78], Hampshire, England). m. **Ellaline Terriss**, 1893 (d. 1971). *The Stage as I Know It.* "Sir Seymour Hicks," *Variety,* 13 Apr 1949. AS, pp. 525–26. BHD1, p. 259; BHD2, p. 121. IFN, p. 141. Truitt, p. 153.

Hicks, John W., Jr. [actor] (b. Sedalia MO, 1887?–1 Jun 1945 [58], New York NY). m. Arline Phipps. (General Film Co., 1914; Paramount, 1919.) "John W. Hicks, Jr., Film Executive, 58; Paramount International Head Dies—Entered Industry as Theatre Operator in 1912," *NYT,* 2 Jun 1945, 15:3. AS, p. 525.

Hicks, Maxine Elliott [stage/film/TV actress] (b. Denver CO, 5 Oct 1904–10 Jan 2000 [95], San Clemente CA). m. Frank Dodge, 1938. (Edison; film debut: *The Borrowed Finery,* 1914; final film, *The Linguini Incident,* 1991.) Harris Lentz, III, "Marine Elliott, 95," *CI,* 297 (Mar 2000), 57. Chapter 11, "Maxine Elliott Hicks," *BS,* pp. 151–63 (includes filmography).

Hicks, Orton Havergal [executive] (b. Minneapolis MN, 1901?–10 May 1997 [96], Hanover NH). (Eastman Kodak Co. as film salesman; founded Films, Inc., 1928, and Seven Seas Film Corp.; Loew's International Corp.) "Orton Havergal Hicks," *Variety,* 2 Jun 1997, 69:4. BHD2, p. 121.

Hicks, Russell [actor] (*né* Edward Russell Hicks, b. Baltimore MD, 4 Jun 1895–1 Jun 1957 [61], Los Angeles CA; heart attack after traffic accident). "Russell Hicks," *Variety,* 5 Jun 1957 (film debut: *Happiness Ahead,* 1928). AS, p. 525. BHD1, p. 259. IFN, p. 141. Katz, pp. 560–61. Truitt, p. 153.

Hidari, Bokuzen [actor] (*né* Ichiro Mikajima, b. Saitama, Japan, 20 Feb 1894–26 May 1971 [77], Tokyo, Japan). As, p. 526.

Hieronimus, René [actor] (*né* René Marie Hieronimus, b. Sasint-Servan, France, 22 Jul 1893 [extrait de naissance no. SN/1894]-11 Aug 1971 [78], Vernon, France). AS, p. 526.

Hiers, Walter [stage/film actor] (b. Cordele GA, 18 Jul 1893–27 Feb 1933 [39], Los Angeles CA; pneumonia). m. Adah McWilliams. (Biograph.) "Walter Hiers," *Variety,* 28 Feb 1933. AMD, p. 164. AS, p. 526. BHD1, p. 259. FFF, p. 76. IFN, p. 141. MH, p. 116 ("Heirs"). SD. Truitt, p. 153. WWS, p. 238. "Walter Hiers Engaged by Ince," *MPW,* 2 Nov 1918, 600. "Famous Players to Star Walter Hiers," *MPW,* 9 Dec 1922, 543. "Walter Hiers to Marry," *MPW,* 13 Jan 1923, 123. "Walter Hiers to Star in Educational Two-Reelers," *MPW,* 14 Jun 1924, 651. "Walter Hiers," *MPW,* 20 Sep 1924, insert. "Walter Hiers Injured," *MPW,* 26 Sep 1925, 338. "Hiers Back at Studio," *MPW,* 31 Oct 1925, 722. "Walter Hiers Is Recovering," *MPW,* 21 Nov 1925, 150. "Hiers's 'Laughometer,'" *MPW,* 2 Jan 1926, 43.

Higashiyama, Chieko [actress] (*née* Sen Kono, b. Chiba, Japan, 30 Sep 1890–8 May 1980 [89], Gotenba, Japan). AS, p. 526.

Higby, Wilbur [stage/film actor] (*né* Wilbur Higby Jones, b. Meridian MS, 21 Aug 1867–1 Dec 1934 [67], Los Angeles CA; heart attack). m. Carolyn. (Began ca. 1913; Griffith; Fine Arts.) "Wilbur Higby," *Variety,* 11 Dec 1934 (began ca. 1913). AS, p. 526. BHD1, p. 259 (b. Churchill MS). IFN, p. 141. MSBB, p. 1024–25. Truitt, p. 153. George Katchmer, "Remembering the Great Silents," *CI,* 241 (Jul 1995), 31.

Higgin, Howard [art director/title writer/scenarist/director] (b. Denver CO, 15 Feb 1891?–16 Dec 1938 [47], Los Angeles CA; pneumonia). "Howard Higgin," *Variety,* 21 Dec 1938 (began in 1917). AMD, p. 165. AS, p. 526. BHD2, p. 121. FDY, p. 445. IFN, p. 141. Katz, p. 561 (b. 1893). "Howard and Cowan Signed," *MPW,* 7 Feb 1925, 603. "Robert Kane Picks Howard to Direct 'Invisible Wounds,'" *MPW,* 8 Aug 1925, 651.

Higgins, David H. [stage/film actor/writer] (b. Chicago IL, 21 Jun 1858–29 Jun 1936 [78], Brooklyn NY). (FP-L.) "David Higgins," *Variety,* 8 Jul 1936 (lived with the Carleton Macys). AS, p. 526 (d. 30 Jun). BHD, p. 200. IFN, p. 141. SD, p. 610.

Higgins, Ruth. *See* Hutton, Lucille.

Hignett, H.R. [actor] (b. Ringway, Cheshire, England, 29 Jan 1870–17 Dec 1959 [89]). BHD1, p. 259. IFN, p. 141.

Hilburn, Percy [cinematographer]. No data found. FDY, p. 459.

Hildebrand, Hilde [actress] (*née* Emma Minna Hildebrand, b. Hanover, Germany, 10 Sep 1897–28 Apr 1976 [78], Berlin, Germany). AS, p. 526. BHD1, p. 260.

Hildebrand, Lo [actor] (b. 1894?–11 Sep 1936 [42], Los Angeles CA; heart attack). "Lo Hildebrand," *Variety,* 16 Sep 1936. AS, p. 526. BHD1, p. 260. IFN, p. 142.

Hildebrand, Rodney W. [actor] (b. IL, 22 Mar 1892–22 Feb 1962 [69], Los Angeles CA). AS, p. 526. BHD1, p. 260. IFN, p. 142.

Hildebrand, Weyler [actor/director] (b. Vastervik, Sweden, 4 Jan 1890–17 Nov 1944 [54]). AS, p. 526. BHD2, p. 121.

Hilforde, Mary [actress] (*née* Mary Griggs, b. Carbondale PA, 1853?–12 Dec 1927 [74], Amityville, LI NY). "Mary Hilforde," *Variety,* 14 Dec 1927. AS, p. 526. BHD, p. 200. IFN, p. 142. Truitt, p. 153. WWS, p. 153.

Hilger, Winifred S. *See* Stockwell, Winifred.

Hill, Al [actor] (b. New York NY, 14 Jul 1892–14 Jul 1954 [62], Los Angeles Co. CA). AS, p. 526. BHD1, p. 260. IFN, p. 142.

Hill, Arthur [actor] (b. 1875?–9 Apr 1932 [57], Los Angeles CA; heart attack). (Gaumont American Productions.) "Arthur Hill," *Variety,* 12 Apr 1932. AS, p. 526. BHD, p. 200. IFN, p. 142.

Hill, Arthur R. [actor] (b. 1890–17 Apr 1941 [51?], Los Angeles CA). BHD1, p. 260.

Hill, Ben A. [actor/publicist] (b. 19 Oct 1894–30 Nov 1969 [75], Dallas TX). "Ben A. Hill," *Variety*, 17 Dec 1969. AS, p. 526. BHD, p. 200; BHD2, p. 121. Truitt, p. 153.

Hill, Bonnie [actress]. No data found. (Universal.)

Hill, Dale P. [actor] (d. 1918; Spanish flu). AS, p. 526.

Hill, Doris [actress: Wampas Star, 1929] (b. Columbus NE, 31 Mar 1911–3 Mar 1976 [64], Kingman AZ). AS, p. 527 (b. 1905; d. LA CA). BHD1, p. 260 (b. Roswell NM, 21 Mar 1905). BR, pp. 330–31. Katz, pp. 560–61. Ragan 2, p. 748 (age 109). George Katchmer, "Remembering the Great Silents," *CI*, 218 (Aug 1993), 42–43.

Hill, Dudley Sloan [actor] (b. 1881?–7 Jan 1960 [79], Wilkesboro NC). "Dudley S. Hill," *Variety*, 20 Jan 1960 (began in NY, 1913). AS, p. 527. BHD, p. 200. IFN, p. 142. Truitt, p. 153.

Hill, Edwin C. [scenarist] (b. Aurora IN, 23 Apr 1884–12 Feb 1957 [72], St. Petersburg FL). AS, p. 527.

Hill, Ethel [actress/scenarist] (b. Sacramento CA, 1898?–17 May 1954 [56], Los Angeles CA). (Metro; TC-F; Columbia.) "Ethel Hill," *Variety*, 26 May 1954. AS, p. 527. BHD2, p. 122. FDY, p. 429. IFN, p. 142.

Hill, George [actor] (b. 1871–2 Mar 1945 [74?], Los Angeles CA). AS, p. 527.

Hill, George F. [actor] (b. 1879–1 Dec 1956 [77], Tynemouth, England). "George F. Hill," *Variety*, 12 Dec 1956.

Hill, George William [cameraman/director] (b. Douglas KS, 25 Apr 1894–10 Aug 1934 [40], Venice CA; suicide by shooting). m. **Frances Marion** (d. 1973). (Griffith; MGM.) "George William Hill," *Variety*, 14 Aug 1934. AMD, p. 165. AS, p. 527. BHD2, p. 122 (b. 1895; d. 9 Aug). IFN, p. 142. Katz, p. 562 (b. 1895). "The Roll of Honor," *MPW*, 1 Jul 1917, 433. "Lieutenant George Hill, U.S.S.C.," *MPW*, 19 Jan 1918, 390. "Canmera to Directorship," *MPW*, 18 Dec 1920, 889. "Hill to Direct 'Limited Mail,'" *MPW*, 18 Apr 1925, 714. "George W. Hill," *MPW*, 4 Dec 1926, 339. "Was Almost a Bridge Builder," *MPW*, 14 May 1927, 99.

Hill, Gus [actor/producer] (*né* Gustave Metz, b. 1859?–20 Apr 1937 [78], New York NY). Epes W. Sargent, "Gus Hill, Dead at 78, a Pioneer Showman with His Cartoon Revues," *Variety*, 28 Apr 1937. IFN, p. 142.

Hill, Hallene Christian [actress] (b. MO, 12 Sep 1876–6 Jan 1966 [89], Los Angeles CA; arteriosclerosis and cerebral thrombosis). AS, p. 527.

Hill, Jack. *See* Keefe, Cornelius.

Hill, John Durbin [scenarist] (b. 1868–13 Mar 1952 [84?], Los Angeles CA). AS, p. 527. BHD2, p. 122.

Hill, Josephine [actress] (b. San Francisco CA, 3 Oct 1899–17 Dec 1989 [90], Palm Springs CA). m. **Jack Perrin**, 17 Sep 1920—div. 1937 (d. 1967); Jack Brown. (Universal, 1919; Metro.) AMD, p. 165. AS, p. 527. BHD1, p. 260. BR, pp. 163–67 (b. 1902). "Universal Introduces Two New Western Actors," *MPW*, 2 Aug 1919, 694. "Two Weddings in Filmland," *MPW*, 8 May 1920, 833. Marion Lake, "Cuddles Grows Up," *MPC*, Dec 1921, 38, 73–74. Buck Rainey, "Josephine Hill; The Real Queen of B Westerns," *CI*, 135 (Sep 1986), 35–38 (b. 1902; includes filmography). Luther Hathcock, "Josephine Hill," *CI*, 198 (Dec 1991), 41.

Hill, Kenneth [actor] (b. Boston MA–d. 15 Jan 1929, St. Moritz, Switzerland). AS, p. 527 (b. England; d. 16 Jan). BHD, p. 200.

Hill, Lee [actor] (b. Minneapolis MN). (Majestic; Selig Crown City Co.; Univ.) *MPN Studio Directory*, 21 Oct 1916.

Hill, Maude [actress] (b. St. Louis MO, 1885). (Universal; Equitable; World; Metro.) AMD, p. 165. BHD, p. 200. MSBB, p. 1034. "Maud Hill," *MPW*, 29 Apr 1916, 813.

Hill, Ralph [art titles]. No data found. AMD, p. 165. "Ralph Hill with Rolfe," *MPW*, 3 Jan 1920, 99.

Hill, Raymond C. [actor] (b. 1891?–16 Apr 1941 [50], Los Angeles CA). "Raymond Hill," *Variety*, 23 Apr 1941. AS, p. 527 (*né* Arthur Raymond Hill). IFN, p. 142.

Hill, Robert F. [actor/scenarist/director] (b. Port Rohen, Ontario, Canada, 14 Apr 1886 [Birth certificate #023409, no. 48, division of Walsingham]–18 Mar 1966 [79], Los Angeles CA). (Triangle; Universal, 1923; RKO.) "Robert F. Hill," *Variety*, 30 Mar 1966. AMD, p. 165. AS, p. 527. BHD, p. 200; BHD2, p. 122 (b. Ft. Rohen, Canada). IFN, p. 142. Katz, p. 562. "Robert Hill, Universal Director," *MPW*, 8 Jan 1916, 248. "Robert Hill on Triangle Staff," *MPW*, 5 Oct 1918, 73.

Hill, Sinclair [director/scenarist] (b. Kingston-upon-Thames, England, 10 Jun 1896–15 Mar 1945 [48], England). AS, p. 527 (b. Surbiton, England, 1894). BHD2, p. 122.

Hill, "Smiling" Roland [actor]. No data found. AMD, p. 165. "Stahl to Exploit New Comedian," *MPW*, 11 Aug 1917, 969.

Hill, Thelma [actress: Sennett Bathing Beauty] (*né* Thelma Hillerman, b. Emporia KS, 12 Dec 1906–11 May 1938 [32], Culver City CA). m. **John Sinclair** (d. 1945). "Thelma Hill," *Variety*, 18 May 1938. AS, p. 528. BHD1, p. 260. IFN, p. 142. Truitt, p. 153.

Hill, Walter L. [publicist]. No data found. AMD, p. 165. "Hill Leaves Famous Players," *MPW*, 3 Jan 1920, 134.

Hill, Walter O[sborne] [actor] (b. 1876–24 Aug 1963 [87?], Albany NY). AS, p. 528.

Hill, Walton [scenarist/publicist] (d. Apr 1924, Santa Monica CA). BHD2, p. 122.

Hill, Wesley [actor] (b. Baltimore MD, 1875–10 Dec 1930 [55], New York NY; struck by a taxi). (Began ca. 1890 as a barker with a medicine show; Gabriel in *Green Pastures;* member of Negro Masons and Elks.) "Wesley Hill," *Variety*, 101, 17 Dec 1930, 60:4. BHD, p. 200.

Hille, Heinz [director/scenarist] (b. Germany, 1891–15 May 1954 [63?], Dusseldorf, Germany). AS, p. 528. BHD2, p. 122.

Hilliard, Ernest [actor] (b. New York NY, 31 Jan 1890–3 Sep 1947 [57], Santa Monica CA; heart attack). AS, p. 528. BHD1, p. 260. IFN, p. 142. Truitt, pp. 153–54.

Hilliard, Harry S. [actor] (b. Cincinnati OH, 24 Oct 1886–21 Apr 1966 [79], St. Petersburg FL; from injuries sustained in a fall). (Fox.) "Harry S. Hilliard," *Variety*, 18 May 1966. AMD, p. 165. AS, p. 528. BHD1, p. 261. IFN, p. 142. Spehr, p. 140. Truitt, p. 154. "Harry Hilliard Leaves Fox," *MPW*, 9 Sep 1917, 1978.

Hilliard, Houston [actor] (d. 12 Feb 1928, Bakersfield CA). BHD, p. 201.

Hilliard, John (father of Frank Hilliard) [actor] (b. 1871?–31 Oct 1939 [68], Los Angeles CA). "Frank Hilliard's Father Dies," *NYT*, 2 Nov 1939, 23:3.

Hilliard, Mrs. Mack. *See* Clayton, Hazel.

Hilliker, Katherine [scenarist/title writer]. No data found. m. H.H. Caldwell. AMD, p. 165. FDY, p. 445. "Caldwells to Assist June Mathis," *MPW*, 23 Dec 1922, 732. "Katharine Hilliker Signs New Contract," *MPW*, 25 Jul 1925, 451.

Hillyer, Lambert H. [scenarist/director] (b. South Bend IN, 8 Jul 1889–5 Jul 1969 [79], Los Angeles CA). m. Lucille Stein, 26 Mar 1921. (Monogram.) AMD, p. 165. AS, p. 528. BHD2, p. 122 (b. 1893). FDY, p. 429. IFN, p. 142 (b. 1893). Katz, pp. 563–64. "Lambert Hillyer, Director," *MPW*, 9 Jun 1917, 1640. "Lambert Hillyer Now a Director," *MPW*, 16 Jun 1917, 1761. "Lambert Hillyer Marries," *MPW*, 16 Apr 1921, 711. "Hillyer with Ince," *MPW*, 28 May 1921, 422. Catharine Brody, "Funny Things That Happen During Love Scenes," *MW*, 3 Jan 1925, 4–6 (Hillyer and some actors comment on the subject).

Hilpert, Heinz [actor/director/scenarist] (b. Berlin, Germany, 1 Mar 1890–26 Nov 1967 [77], Goettingen, Germany). AS, p. 528. BHD2, p. 122.

Hilton, Frank [actor] (b. 1871?–16 Feb 1932 [61], New York NY). AS, p. 528. BHD, p. 201. IFN, p. 142.

Hilton, Haran [actor] (b. 1900–Aug 1930 [30], Los Angeles CA). BHD, p. 201. IFN, p. 142.

Hilton, James [scenarist] (b. Leigh, England, 9 Sep 1900–20 Sep 1954 [54], Long Beach CA). AS, p. 528.

Himm, Carl W. [film editor/title writer] (b. 1894?–12 Mar 1948 [54], Chicago IL). "Carl W. Himm," *Variety*, 17 Mar 1948. BHD2, p. 122. FDY, p. 445.

Himm, Otto [cinematographer] (b. 1893?–2 Apr 1940 [47], No. Hollywood CA; heart attack). m. Anna. (Selig, 1912; Essanay; Hearst Newsreel.) "Otto Himm," *Variety*, 10 Apr 1940. BHD2, p. 122 (b. 1890).

Hin, Jan [director] (b. Haarlem, Netherlands, 1899–1957 [58?], Haarlem, Netherlands). AS, p. 528.

Hinckley, William L. [actor] (b. 11 Sep 1894–14 May 1918 [23], New York NY). AS, p. 529. BHD, p. 201 (d. 4 May). IFN, p. 142. Truitt, 1983.

Hinding, Alma [actress]. No data found. AMD, p. 165. T.S. daPonte, "Norwegian Film Actress Visiting Here Expects to Sign an American Contract," *MPW*, 10 Jun 1922, 545.

Hinds, Errol R. [cinematographer] (b. 1888–5 May 1942 [54?], Los Angeles CA). BHD2, p. 122.

Hinds, Nina [singer/stage/film actress] (b. Eureka CA, 1904–24 May 1961 [57], Reno NV; cancer). "Nina Hinds Reed," *Variety*, 223, 31 May 1961, 63 (Keith and Franchon & Marco circuits; recorded for Victor Records). BHD, p. 201.

Hinds, Samuel S. [actor] (b. Brooklyn NY, 4 Apr 1875–13 Oct 1948 [73], Pasadena CA). AS, p. 529. BHD1, p. 261.

Hines, Charles J. (brother of **Johnny** and **Samuel E. Hines**) [actor/director] (b. Pittsburgh PA, 1891–16 Jul 1936 [45?], Los Angeles CA). AMD, p. 165. BHD, p. 201; BHD2, p. 122.

"Charles Hines," *MPW,* 12 Mar 1927, 101. "Charles Hines," *MPW,* 9 Jul 1927, 87.

Hines, George Henry "Daddy" (b. Panola IL, 1856?–17 Dec 1946 [90], Los Angeles CA). "George H. Hines; Retired Circus Figure, 90, Once Operator of Movie Theatres," *NYT,* 18 Dec 1946, 29:6. "George H. Hines," *Variety,* 25 Dec 1946.

Hines, Johnny [actor] (brother of **Samuel E.** and **Charles Hines**) (b. Golden CO, 25 Jul 1895–24 Oct 1970 [75], Los Angeles CA; heart attack). m. Irma Warner. (2-reel silents; Paramount; MGM.) "J. Hines, 72; Ex-Actor," *Los Angeles Times,* II, 8:5, 26 Oct 1970. "Johnny Hines Death Report," *The Hollywood Reporter,* 27 Oct 1970 (age 72). AMD, p. 165. AS, p. 529. BHD1, p. 261 (b, 1897). FSS, p. 146. GK, pp. 412–19. IFN, p. 142 (b. 1898). MH, p. 117. Spehr, p. 140 (b. 1897). Truitt, p. 54. "Johnny Hines," *MPW,* 19 Jun 1915, 1943. "Johnny Hines Signs with World," *MPW,* 3 Mar 1918, 1668. "Burr Forms New Producing Company; Will Star Hines in Torchy Stories," *MPW,* 31 Jan 1920, 767. "Henderson Enthuses Over Johnny Hines," *MPW,* 26 Aug 1922, 687. "Warner Brothers Signs Johnny Hines for Indefinite Period," *MPW,* 14 Jul 1923, 160. Grace Greenwood, "Some Hidden Engagement Rings," *MW,* 22 Sep 1923, 11, 30 (rumored to be engaged to Bessie Love). "Johnny Hines Again with C.C. Burr," *MPW,* 10 May 1924, 163. "Johnny Hines," *MPW,* 2 May 1925, 82. "Johnn¥ Hines," *MPW,* 23 May 1925, 471. Nanette Kutner, "Will Radio Keep the Stars at Home?," *MW,* 9 Aug 1925, 17–18. Paul Paige, "Funny Questions Film Fans Ask Johnny Hines," *Paris and Hollywood,* Sep 1926, 65, 79. "Hines Denies," *MPW,* 27 Feb 1926, 3. David E. Weshner, "Crowning a King of Comedy," *Cinema Art,* Mar 1926, 12–13. Paul Paige, "Close-Ups and Fade-Outs," *Paris and Hollywood,* Sep 1926, 87–88 (Adolphe Menjou had been invited to appear on the radio with Johnny¥ Hines, but didn't show up. Hines proceeded to impersonate Menjou, his mimicking said to have been "quite undignifed," and with a strong foreign accent. They almost came to blows at the Gotham night club, but "[c]ooler friends interceded, apologies were forthcoming, and all is serene again."). Geo. Q. Hamilton, "How Happy Is 'One, Big, Happy Family?'; Johnny Hines Makes Play of Work and Work of Play in the Studio," *Cinema Arts,* Jan 1927, 26–27. "Johnny Hines," *MPW,* 12 Mar 1927, 101. "Johnny and Charlie Expect a Prosperous Three Years," *MPW,* 16 Apr 1927, 632. "First Fitzer Star Talk Is Presented," *MPW,* 12 Nov 1927, 8. Carol Johnston, "The Life of the Party; Johnny Hines Serves Rubber Rolls at Dinner, Likes His Cars Fast and His Women Sober," *MPC,* Jul 1928, 51, 85 ("Probably Billy Haines is Johnny Hines' only rival as a wow with the girls."). Ed Finney, "Anecdotes About Stars I Have Known," *CFC,* 44 (Fall, 1974), 53. George Katchmer, "Happy-Go-Lucky, Forgotten Johnny Hines," *CI,* 142 (Apr 1987), 44–48, 61. Richard E. Braff, "The Films of Johnny Hines," *CI,* 145 (Jul 1987), 56. Richard M. Roberts, "Past Humor, Present Laughter; The Comedy Film Industry 1914–1945; Odds and Ends," *CI,* 238 (Apr 1995), C4 (cites films of Hines available on tape).

Hines, Samuel E. (brother of **Charles** and **Johnny Hines**) [actor] (b. 1881?–16 Nov 1939 [58], Los Angeles CA; in a sanatorium). (Roach.) "Samuel E. Hines," *Variety,* 22 Nov 1939. AS, p. 529 (d. 17 Nov). BHD1, p. 261. IFN, p. 142.

Hinsdale, Harriet [scenarist]. No data found. FDY, p. 429.

Hinz, Werner Heinz Alfons [actor] (b. Berlin-Lankwicz, Germany, 18 Jan 1903–10 Feb 1985 [82], Hamburg, Germany). AS, p. 529. BHD1, p. 261.

Hippard, George R. [journalist] (b. Dayton OH, 1868?–7 Feb 1939 [70], Los Angeles CA; heart attack). "George R. Hippard; Editor on California Papers for Last Two Decades," *NYT,* 9 Feb 1939, 21:4.

Hippe, Lew[is] [actor] (b. 1880?–19 Jul 1952 [72], Los Angeles CA). (Sennett.) "Lew Hippe," *Variety,* 23 Jul 1952. BHD1, p. 261. IFN, p. 142.

Hirsch, Hugo [composer] (b. Bimbaum, Germany, 12 Mar 1884–16 Aug 1961 [77], Berlin, Germany). AS, p. 529.

Hirsh, Nathan [executive]. No data found. AMD, p. 165. "Pioneer's First Production Ready," *MPW,* 19 Aug 1916, 1220. Nathan Hirsh, "How Independent Leaders See New Season," *MPW,* 8 Sep 1923, 158. "Hirsh Optimistic Regarding Outlook," *MPW,* 10 May 1924, 162.

Hirshbein, Peretz [scenarist] (b. 1883–16 Jul 1948 [65?], Los Angeles CA). AS, p. 529 (b. 1871). BHD2, p. 122.

Hiscott, Leslie Stephenson [assistant director/director/producer/novelist] (b. London, England, 25 Jul 1894–2 May 1968 [74), London, England]. (Began 1919.) "Leslie Hiscott," *Variety,* 250, 15 May 1968, 79:3. AMD, p. 166. AS, p. 530. BHD2, p. 123. IFN, p. 142. "Hiscott Now Assistant Director to Fitzmaurice," *MPW,* 22 Oct 1921, 921.

Hitchcock, Alfred Joseph (father of Patricia Hitchcock) [film/TV director/producer/scenarist] (b. London, England, 13 Aug 1899–29 Apr 1980 [80], Beverly Hills CA). m. **Alma Reville,** 1926 (d. 1982; daughter Patricia, b. 1930). (Paramount [London], 1920). William Rothman, *Hitchcock–The Murderous Gaze* (Cambridge MA: Harvard Univ. Press, 1982). Peter B. Flint, "Alfred Hitchcock Dies; A Master of Suspense," *NYT,* 30 Apr 1980, 1:1; "Hundreds at Funeral for Hitchcock Include Set Workers and Stars," 3 May 1980, 28:3. Todd McCarthy, "Alfred Hitchcock, 80, Dies in Hollywood; Master of Suspense," *Variety,* 7 May 1980. AS, p. 520 (b. Leytonstone, England). BHD1, p. 262; BHD2, p. 123. Katz, pp. 564–66.

Hitchcock, Keith Kenneth [actor] (b. London, England, 29 May 1887–11 Apr 1966 [78], Los Angeles CA). AS, p. 530.

Hitchcock, Raymond [stage/film actor] (b. near Auburn NY, 22 Oct 1865–24 Nov 1929 [64], Beverly Hills CA; in his car). m. **Flora Zabelle,** 1905 (d. 1968). "Raymond Hitchcock Dies in California; Musical Comedy Star, Long Ill, Collapses at His Wife's Side in Automobile; on Stage Nearly 40 Years; 'The Yankee Consul' [Boston, 21 Sep 1903] and 'Hitchy Koo' [Jun 1918] Outstanding Successes in Long List of Plays," *NYT,* 26 Nov 1929, 31:1. "Raymond Hitchcock Dies; Sudden Heart Attack," *Variety,* 27 Nov 1929 (age 53). AS, p. 530. BHD, p. 201. IFN, p. 143. Truitt, p. 154 (b. 1870). Cover, *NYDM,* 6 Nov 1915 (with Roscoe Arbuckle and Flora Zabelle).

Hitchcock, Walter Edwin [stage/film actor] (b. New Castle ME, 1872?–23 Jun 1917 [45], New York NY). m. Terasa Michelene. "Walter Hitchcock," *Variety,* 29 Jun 1917. AMD, p. 166. AS, p. 530. BHD, p. 201 (b. Walden MA). IFN, p. 143. SD. "Walter Hitchcock in New Rolfe Feature," *MPW,* 30 Oct 1915, 795. "Walter Hitchcock Engaged by Erbograph," *MPW,* 24 Feb 1917, 1192.

Hite, Charles J. [director/executive/bought Thanhouser, 1912] (b. Pleasantville OH, 1875?–22 Aug 1914 [39], New York NY; automobile accident). (Began in Chicago, Hite & Hutchinson [exchange business], 1905; C.J. Hite Moving Picture Co., Chicago, 1906; American; Film Supply Co.; Mutual.) AMD, p. 166. BHD2, p. 123. "The Charles J. Hite Film Company," *MPW,* 13 Mar 1909, 299. "An Important Change in the Motion Picture Map," *MPW,* 24 Jul 1909, 126. "Busy Days for Hite & Hite," *MPW,* 18 Nov 1911, 558. "Thanhouser Sells Plant," *MPW,* 20 Apr 1912, 207. "Messrs. Hite and Thanhouser 'Together,'" *MPW,* 11 May 1912, 522. "Peaceful Days with Hite," *MPW,* 29 Mar 1913, 1326. "A Bit of the 'Yellow,'" *MPW,* 24 May 1913, 814. "Has Yacht and Steward," *MPW,* 26 Jul 1913, 407. "Hite Plans Surprises," *MPW,* 15 Nov 1913, 721. "Bigger Majestic Company," *MPW,* 15 Nov 1913, 721. "C.J. Hite and His Career; Eventful Career of Head of Thanhouser and Majestic Companies," *NYDM,* 31 Dec 1913. George Blaisdell, "Thanhouser in New Studio," *MPW,* 17 Jan 1914, 268–69. Charles J. Hite, "Advertising for the Exhibitor," *MPW,* 11 Jul 1914, 187. "Mr. Hite Shows Underwater Pictures," *MPW,* 8 Aug 1914, 816. "Charles J. Hite Dead; Fatally Injured when Auto Plunges from [Central] Bridge [in Harlem NY]—Universally Liked, His Rise in Film World Rapid," *NYDM,* 26 Aug 1914, 24:2 (age 38). "Memoriam," *Reel Life* [house organ of the Mutual Film Co.], 29 Aug 1914, pp. 6–7. "Obituary," *MPW,* 5 Sep 1914, 1375–76. Bert Adler, "Charles J. Hite, the Man," *MPW,* 5 Sep 1914, 1376. "In Memory of Charles J. Hite," *MPW,* 26 Dec 1914, 1761. "Death's Toll for the Decade," *MPW,* 10 Mar 1917, p. 1528.

Hite, Violet [actress]. No data found. (Thanhouser.) "In the Picture Studios," *NYDM,* 4 Aug 1915, 27:2 (on the female baseball team at Thanhouser).

Hitt, Laurence W. [art director]. No data found. AMD, p. 166. "Art Director Goes to Coast," *MPW,* 16 Apr 1927, 627.

Hively, George O. [film editor/scenarist/director] (father of Jack Hively) (b. Springfield MO, 1887?–2 Mar 1950 [63], Los Angeles Co. CA). m. (son Jack, 1910–1995). (Universal; Metro; RKO.) "George O. Hively," *Variety,* 8 Mar 1950. AS, p. 530. BHD2j, p. 123. FDY, p. 429.

Hively, Georgenia [stuntwoman/actress] (b. 1890?–21 May 1977 [86], No. Hollywood CA). "Georgenia Hively," *Variety,* 1 Jun 1977. AS, p. 530. BHD, p. 201. IFN, p. 143. Robert A. Evans, "Evans' 1977 Chronicle," *FIR,* Mar 1978, 150.

Hix, Don [actor] (*né* Don T. Hicks, b. OH, 2 Mar 1891–31 Dec 1964 [73], Los Angeles CA). (Universal, 1914.) "Don Hix," *Variety,* 13 Jan 1965. AS, p. 530. BHD1, p. 262 (d. Santa Monica CA). IFN, p. 141 (Don Hicks). Truitt, p. 155.

Hoadley, C[harles] **B**[yron] **"Pop"** (father of **Harold Hoadley**) [scenarist] (b. Elyria OH-d. 18 Feb 1922, Los Angeles CA). "C.B. Hoadley," *Variety,* 3 Mar 1922. "Obituary," *MPW,* 4 Mar 1922, 44 (d. Sherman CA). AMD, p. 166. AS, p. 530 (d. 26 Feb). BHD2, p. 123.

Hoadley, Hal (son of **Charles Byron Hoadley**) [scenarist] (*né* Harold William Hoadley, b. Defiance OH, 7 Sep 1893–31 Jan 1974 [80], Santa Monica CA). m. stage actress Violet Shannon, Feb?

1920. (Universal.) AMD, p. 166. BHD2, p. 123. "Hoadley Finishes Scenario," *MPW,* 27 May 1916, 1531. "Cupid Bulletin No. 9999," *LA Times,* 20 Feb 1920, III, p. 4.

Hoagland, Harland [actor] (b. 28 Mar 1895–9 Jan 1971 [75], Los Angeles CA). m. Maude. "Harland Hoagland," *Variety,* 20 Jan 1971 (began 1921). AS, p. 530. BHD1, p. 262. IFN, p. 143. Truitt, p. 155.

Hoagland, Herbert C. [director/executive] (b. 1879–19 Apr 1946 [67?], Chicago IL). BHD2, p. 123.

Hoare, Frank Alan [diretor/producer] (b. Cobham, England, 4 Oct 1894). AS, p. 530.

Hoban, Stella [actress] (b. 1890–24 Jan 1962 [71?], Muskegon MI). BHD, p. 201.

Hobart, C. Doty [scenarist] (b. Brattleboro VT, 1886?–16 Nov 1958 [72], New York NY). "Doty Hobart, 72, Dies; Playwright, Movie Scenarist, Wrote 3 Broadway Shows," *NYT,* 17 Nov 1958, 31:3. "Doty Hobart," *Variety,* 19 Nov 1958 (wrote for Pickford and the Gish sisters). AMD, p. 166. AS, p. 530. BHD2, p. 123. "H.I. Young and C. Doty Hobart Join Fox Scenario Staff," *MPW,* 23 Aug 1919, 1153. "Hobart Will Write Briggs' Scenarios," *MPW,* 6 Sep 1919, 1502.

Hobart, George V[ero] [scenarist] (b. Cape Breton, Nova Scotia, Canada, 16 Jan 1867–31 Jan 1926 [59], Cumberland MD). "George V. Hobart," *Variety,* 3 Feb 1926. AMD, p. 166. AS, p. 530. "Hobart to Write for Paramount," *MPW,* 8 Sep 1917, 1543.

Hobart, Henry Morgan [producer/President of Distinctive Pictures Corp.] (b. 1884?–12 Feb 1954 [69], New York NY). m. **Olive Tell** (d. 1951). "Henry M. Hobart," *NYT,* 13 Feb 1954, 13:4. AMD, p. 166. "Distinctive Plays Busy Year; A.S. Friend Issues Statement," *MPW,* 13 Jan 1923, 123. "Distinctive Election," *MPW,* 3 May 1924, 43.

Hobbes, Halliwell [actor] (*né* Herbert Halliwell Hobbes, b. Stratford-upon-Avon, England, 16 Nov 1877–20 Feb 1962 [84], Santa Monica CA). AS, p. 530.

Hobble, John L. [scenarist] (b. 1886–15 Aug 1942 [56?], Los Angeles CA). BHD2, p. 123.

Hobbs, Hayford [actor]. No data found. (Universal.)

Hobbs, Jack [stage/film actor] (b. London, England, 28 Sep 1893–4 Jun 1968 [74], Brighton, England). (Stage debut: 1906.) "Jack Hobbs," *Variety,* 251, 19 Jun 1968, 79:3 (toured America and Canada with Cyril Maude's company in 1913). AS, p. 530. BHD1, p. 262.

Hobbs, Stephen [scenarist] (b. 1889–23 Aug 1951 [62?], Scarsdale NY). BHD2, p. 123.

Hobson, Violet [actress] (b. San Francisco CA, 16 Dec 1891). AMD, p. 166. AS, p. 539 (Violet Hopson). "Kremer Signs Violet Hobson for His First International Film," *MPW,* 18 Dec 1920, 884.

Hoch, Emil H. [actor] (b. Pforzheim, Germany, 27 Oct 1866–13 Oct 1944 [79], Los Angeles CA; heart attack). (Paramount.) AS, p. 530. BHD1, p. 262. IFN, p. 143.

Hoch, Rudolf [director] (b. Friburg, Germany, 19 Sep 1880–17 Jul 1936 [55], Fischen, Germany). AS, p. 530.

Hochbaum, Werner Paul Adolf [actor/director/scenarist] (b. Kiel, Germany, 7 Mar 1889–15 Apr 1946 [57], Potsdam, Germany). AS, p. 530.

Hochreich, David R. [producer] (b. 1895–31 Mar 1956 [61?], Forrest Hills NY). AS, p. 530.

Hockey, Harry G. [actor] (b. London, England, 1864–3 Feb 1936 [71?], New York NY). BHD, p. 201.

Hodd, Joseph B., Sr. [actor] (b. 1896?–26 Jun 1965 [69?], Philadelphia PA). BHD, p. 201. Truitt, p. 155.

Hodes, Hal [editor/executive] (b. New York NY, 8 Mar 1889–7 Apr 1949 [60], Forest Hills NY). AMD, p. 166. BHD2, p. 123 (Hal Hode). "Hodes Succeeds Cohn as Screen Magazine Editor," *MPW,* 12 Apr 1919, 216. "Hodes Resigns from Universal," *MPW,* 29 May 1920, 1183.

Hodgeman, Thomas [actor] (b. 1875?–24 Apr 1931 [56], Los Angeles CA). "Thomas Hodgeman," *Variety,* 29 Apr 1931. AS, p. 531. BHD1, p. 262.

Hodges, Eddie [actress]. No data found. AMD, p. 166. "Eddie Hodges, Younger Salvation Army Lassie, Has Returned to the Screen in 'If I Were King,'" *MPW,* 27 Sep 1919, 1971.

Hodges, Horace [actor/scenarist] (b. England, 19 Dec 1865–6 Jul 1951 [85]). BHD2, p. 123.

Hodges, Leslie [actor] (b. 1885?–30 Aug 1927 [42]; carbuncle). AMD, p. 166. "Obituary," *MPW,* 10 Sep 1927, 81.

Hodges, Maxine [actress]. No data found. m. Tex Rickard, 1926. June Lee, "Dan Cupid's Bulletin Board," *Paris and Hollywood,* Oct 1926, 86 (her friends said she was 18; Rickard said she was 24).

Hodges, Runa [child actress]. No data found. AMD, p. 166. "Little Runa Hodges on the Road," *MPW,* 6 Jul 1913, 419.

Hodges, William Cullen [actor] (b. Newbury Township OH, 6 Feb 1876–26 Jul 1961 [85], near Claridon OH). "William Cullen Hodges," *Variety,* 16 Aug 1961. AS, p. 531. BHD1, p. 610. IFN, p. 143.

Hodgins, Leslie [actor] (b. 1885?–15 Sep 1927 [42], St. Louis MO). "Leslie Hodgins," *Variety,* 14 Sep 1927 (film comic). AS, p. 531. BHD, p. 201. IFN, p. 143.

Hodgkins, Gene [stage/film actor] (*né* Eugene Knott Hodgkins, d. 31 Jul 1916, Louisville KY). m. Irene Hammond, 25 Dec 1914. "Gene Hodgkins Is Dead," *Variety,* 4 Aug 1916. AS, p. 531. SD.

Hodgson, Leland [actor] (*né* John Leyland Hodgson, b. London, England, 5 Oct 1892–16 Mar 1949 [56], Los Angeles CA). AS, p. 531.

Hodkinson, W.W. [executive] (b. Pueblo CO, 16 Aug 1881–2 Jun 1971 [89], Los Angeles CA). (Paramount.) "W.W. Hodkinson, 90, Zukor Contemporary; Pioneered Quality," *Variety,* 9 Jun 1971 (b. UT). AMD, p. 166. AS, p. 531. BHD2, p. 123. Katz, pp. 567–68 (designed Paramount logo). W. Stephen Bush, "Hodkinson—Conservative Iconoclast," *MPW,* 14 Feb 1914, 816–17. "Feature Producers Affiliate," *MPW,* 30 May 1914, 1268–69. W.S. Bush, "New Blood in New Programs," *MPW,* 6 Jun 1914, 1394. "Williams No Longer with Hodkinson," *MPW,* 4 Jul 1914, 84. "Paramount Celebrates," *MPW,* 27 Mar 1915, 1910. W.S. Bush, "Hodkinson Loquitur," *MPW,* 14 Aug 1915, 1139. W.W. Hodkinson, "What Is a Clean Picture?," *MPW,* 10 Jun 1916, 1858. "Hodkinson to Head Superpictures," *MPW,* 25 Nov 1916, 1140. W.W. Hodkinson, "Basic Business Principles Should Govern," *MPW,* 10 Mar 1917, 1499–1500. "Hodkinson Comes Back," *MPW,* 10 Nov 1917, 843. "Hodkinson Discusses Film Advertising," *MPW,* 1 Dec 1917, 1300. "Hodkinson's Prophetic Vision," *MPW,* 15 Dec 1917, 1619. "Hodkinson and General Film in Combination," *MPW,* 22 Dec 1917, 1764. "Hodkinson Will Explain," *MPW,* 29 Dec 1917, 1918. "W.W. Hodkinson Not in New Concern," *MPW,* 22 Jun 1918, 1702. "Hodkinson to Release Walker Pictures," *MPW,* 24 Aug 1918, 1092. "Hodkinson Explains the Selected Program," *MPW,* 7 Sep 1918, 1394. "Hodkinson Offers Remedy," *MPW,* 16 Nov 1918, 733–34. "Warren Joins Hodkinson Corporation," *MPW,* 5 Apr 1919, 48. "Hodkinson Secures Fourth Big Line," *MPW,* 12 Apr 1919, 229. "Hodkinson Cuts Out the Program," *MPW,* 19 Apr 1919, 351. "Hodkinson Primes Soem Dynamite," *MPW,* 24 May 1919, 1151. W.W. Hodkinson, "'Big Money' in Industry Means 'Big Price' for Use; Exhibitor Must 'Watch His Step,'" *MPW,* 27 Dec 1919, 1124. "Hodkinson Says Increased Bookings Indicate Endorsement of His Policies," *MPW,* 3 Jul 1920, 101. W.W. Hodkinson, "Dean of Independents Warns Producers to 'Spurn Twin Evils—Rut and Routine,'" *MPW,* 7 Aug 1920, 711. "Hodkinson Explains Why His Business Methods Are Best," *MPW,* 2 Oct 1920, 666. W.W. Hodkinson, "General Outlook Is Not Encouraging but There Are Many Rays of Sunshine," *MPW,* 25 Dec 1920, 1009. "W.W. Hodkinson Gives Details of New 'Backbone Service Contract,'" *MPW,* 20 Aug 1921, 814. "Hodkinson to Have Own Exchange System After November 1; Pathé Contract Ended," *MPW,* 10 Sep 1921, 159. W.W. Hodkinson, "Closer Co-operation with Exhibitor to Add Strength," *MPW,* 31 Dec 1921, 1052. "Marion Sues Hodkinson, Collins, Duell and Pawley for $500,000 Over Disposal of Stock Holdings," *MPW,* 21 Jan 1922, 260. "'World' Has Record to Be Proud Of, Says Hodkinson," *MPW,* 11 Mar 1922, 138–39. "Letters to Santa Claus," *MPW,* 30 Dec 1922, 833.

Hodson, J.L. [scenarist] (b. Hazelhurst, England, 1891–28 Aug 1956 [65?], London, England). BHD2, p. 123.

Hoeflich, Lucie [stage/film actress] (b. Hanover, Germany, 20 Feb 1883–9 Oct 1956 [73], Berlin, Germany; heart attack). "Lucie Hoeflich," *Variety,* 204, 24 Oct 1956, 79:1. BHD, p. 201. IFN, p. 143.

Hoerbiger, Paul [actor] (b. Budapest, Hungary, 29 Apr 1893–18 Mar 1981 [87], Vienna, Austria). BHD1, p. 262.

Hoeree, Arthur [composer/scenarist] (*né* Charles Ernest Hoeree, b. Brussels, Belgium, 16 Apr 1897–2 Jun 1986 [89], Paris, France). AS, p. 531.

Hoerl, Arthur [title writer/scenarist/director] (b. New York NY, 17 Dec 1892–6 Feb 1968 [75], Los Angeles CA). "Arthur Hoerl," *Variety,* 14 Feb 1968 ("He started as an exhibitor in 1912 and later wrote screenplays for many silent[s] before talkies." Wrote for Barbara LaMarr). AS, p. 531. BHD2, p. 123. FDY, pp. 429, 445. IFN, p. 143.

Hoesch, Eduard [director/producer] (b. Vienna, Austria, 15 Mar 1890–6 Nov 1983 [93], Vienna, Austria). AS, p. 531.

Hoey, Charles M. [actor/writer] (b. New York NY, 1872?–7 Mar 1922 [50?], New York NY). "Chas. M. Hoey," *Variety,* 10 Mar 1922. AS, p. 531.

Hoey, Dennis [actor] (b. London, England, 30 Mar 1893–25 Jul 1960 [67], Palm Beach FL).

"Dennis Hoey," *Variety,* 3 Aug 1960, p. 54 (age 65). AS, p. 530 (Dennis Hoby); p. 531. BHD1, p. 262. IFN, p. 143.

Hoey, George J. [actor] (b. 1884–17 Feb 1955 [70?], Los Angeles CA). AS, p. 531.

Hoey, Herbert [actor] (b. Atlanta GA, 24 Sep 1894–7 Dec 1970 [76], Miami Shores FL). BHD, p. 201.

Hoey, Iris [actress] (b. London, England, 17 Jul 1885–13 May 1979 [93], London, England). AS, p. 531. BHD1, p. 263. IFN, p. 143.

Hofer, Franz [director/scenarist] (b. Saarbrucken, Germany, 31 Aug 1883). AS, p. 531.

Hofer, Karl [producer] (b. Austria, 1894–1 Dec 1954 [60?], Vienna, Austria; suicide during a nervous depression). AS, p. 531.

Hoffe, Monckton [scenarist] (b. Connemara, Ireland, 26 Dec 1880–4 Nov 1951 [70], London, England). AS, p. 531. BHD2, p. 123.

Hoffenstein, Samuel [scenarist] (b. Lithuania, 1890–6 Oct 1947 [57?], Los Angeles CA). AS, p. 531. BHD2, p. 123.

Hoffman, Aaron [stage/film actor] (b. St. Louis MO, 31 Oct 1880–27 May 1924 [43], New York NY). m. Minnie. "Aaron Hoffman," *Variety,* 28 May 1924. AS, p. 531. BHD2, p. 123. SD.

Hoffman, Carl [cinematographer]. No data found. FDY, p. 459.

Hoffman, Charles W. [cinematographer]. No data found.

Hoffman, Eberhard [actor] (b. Germany, 1883?–16 Jun 1957 [74], Denville NJ). "Eberhard Hoffman," *Variety,* 26 Jun 1957 ("former silent film actor"). AS, p. 532. BHD, p. 201. IFN, p. 143. Truitt, p. 156.

Hoffman, Gertrude *see* Anderson, Gertrude.

Hoffman, Gladys [actress] (d. 5 Feb 1962, San Francisco CA). m. **Joseph M. Attie**, Aug 1923 (d. 1971). BHD, p. 201. "Gladys Hoffman Weds," *Variety,* 23 Aug 1923, p. 18.

Hoffman, Harry [actor?/real estate operator] (b. 1866?–17 Aug 1947 [81], Milford CT). m. Hannah. "Harry Hoffman," *NYT,* 19 Aug 1947, 23:5 (his three sons were "all executives of the Warner Brothers Theatre Corporation").

Hoffman, Hugh [publicist/scenarist] (b. Madison WI, 1877?–5 Dec 1942 [65], Los Angeles CA). (Universal.) "Hugh Hoffman," *Variety,* 9 Dec 1942. AMD, p. 167. AS, p. 532. BHD2, p. 124. "Hugh Hoffman Brances Out," *MPW,* 13 Feb 1915, 1002.

Hoffman, M[aurice] **H**[enry] [producer/general manager] (b. Chicago IL, 21 Mar 1881–6 Mar 1944 [62], Los Angeles CA). m. 25 Feb [1906?]. (Universal, 1912.) "M.H. Hoffman," *Variety,* 8 Mar 1944 (age 63). AMD, p. 167. AS, p. 532. BHD2, p. 124. IFN, p. 143. "M.H. Hoffman Talks on Bluebird," *MPW,* 15 Jan 1916, 402. "M.H. Hoffman Takes a Vacation 'Trip,'" *MPW,* 5 Aug 1916, 963. "M.H. Hoffman Explains," *MPW,* 21 Apr 1917, 410. "M.H. Hoffman Announces Policy," *MPW,* 12 May 1917, 994. "Picture Business Healthy, Says Hoffman," *MPW,* 9 Jun 1917, 1604. M.H. Hoffman, "How Independent Leaders See New Season," *MPW,* 8 Sep 1923, 158. "M.H. Hoffman Goes West to Supervise Productions," *MPW,* 18 Jul 1925, 295. Merritt Crawford, "M.H. Hoffman...The Tiffany Man," *MPW,* 4 Dec 1926, 333, 336. "Celebrate Silver Wedding," *MPW,* 5 Mar 1927, 12.

Hoffman, Michael H. [a founder of Tiffany-Stahl Co.] (b. Chicago IL, 1884?–6 Mar 1944 [62], Los Angeles CA). m. Mary. "Michael H. Hoffman; Motion Picture Producer; Active in Industry Since 1912, Dies," *NYT,* 8 Mar 1944, 19:2 (Owned Liberty Picture Corp. "which in 1937 was merged with two other companies to form Republic Pictures.").

Hoffman, Milton E[ly] [publicist/general manager/executive] (b. 1880–21 Jul 1952 [72?], Woodland Hills CA). m. Lydia Koch, 14 Oct 1914, NYC. (World.) AMD, p. 167. BHD2, p. 124. "Milton E. Hoffman," *MPW,* 6 Dec 1913, 1156. "With the Film Men," *NYDM,* 30 Dec 1914, 24:4 (m. Koch). "Milton E. Hoffman Joins Lasky," *MPW,* 13 May 1916, 1155. "Hoffman with DeMille," *MPW,* 11 Jul 1925, 193.

Hoffman, Otto Franklin [actor/director] (b. New York NY, 2 May 1879–23 Jun 1944 [65], Woodland Hills CA; cancer). AMD, p. 167. AS, p. 532. BHD1, p. 263; BHD2, p. 124. IFN, p. 143. "Otto Hoffman a Finished Actor of Character Parts," *MPW,* 27 Sep 1919, 1967. George Katchmer, "Otto Hoffman," *CI,* 230 (Aug 1994), 42.

Hoffman, Renaud [producer/director/scenarist] (b. Germany, 1900–19 Nov 1952 [52?], near Palm Springs CA). (First Hollywood film: *Not One to Spare.*) "Renaud Hoffman," *Variety,* 26 Nov 1952 ("early-day film producer-director"). AS, p. 532. BHD2, p. 124.

Hoffman, Ruby [vaudeville/stage/.film actress]. No data found. (Kleine.) AMD, p. 167. "Ruby Hoffman," *MPW,* XXI, 25 Jul 1914, 574. "Ruby Hoffman with Kleine," *MPW,* 20 Nov 1915, 1483:1.

Hoffman, William D. [scenarist] (b. 1884–10 Mar 1952 [68?], Glendale CA). AS, p. 532. BHD2, p. 124.

Hofman-Uddgren, Anna [actress/director] (b. Sweden, 1868–1947 [80?], Sweden). AS, p. 532.

Hoffmann, Carl [cinematographer] (b. Neisse an der Wobert, Silesia, Germany, 9 Jun 1881–13 Jul 1947 [66], Minden, Germany). AS, p. 532 (d. 5 Aug). BHD2, p. 124.

Hoffman, Gertrude W. [actress/dancer] (b. Heidelberg, Germany, 17 May 1874–13 Feb 1968 [93], Los Angeles CA). AS, p. 532.

Hoffmann-Harnisch, Wolfgang [actor/director] (*né* Friedrich Wolfgang Hoffmann, b. Frankfort, Germany, 13 May 1893–3 Jan 1965 [71], Boon, Germany). AS, p. 532.

Hoffmeir, Harry J. [art director] (b. 1873–18 Jul 1933 [60?], Ocean Grove NJ). BHD2, p. 124.

Hoflich, Lucie [actress] (*née* Helene Lucie von Holwede, b. Hanover, Germany, 20 Feb 1882–9 Oct 1956 [74], Berlin, Germany). AS, p. 532. BHD1, p. 263.

Hofmann, Ernst [actor] (*né* Ernst Carl Heinrich Hofmann von Schönholtz, b. Wroclaw [Breslau], Poland, 7 Dec 1890–27 Apr 1944 [53], Potsdam, Germany). BHD, p. 201 (b. Berlin, Germany; d. 1945). Vittorio Martinelli, "Kino-Lieblinge," *Griffithiana,* 38/39 (Oct 1990), 51.

Hogan, Charles E. [producer] (b. Cleveland OH, 1890–9 Jun 1927 [37?], Los Angeles CA; peritonitis). AS, p. 533 (also listed under Chas. E. Hohan).

Hogan, Dan [actor] (b. Stigler OK, 1923–22 Jun 1978 [54], New York NY). IFN, p. 144.

Hogan, Earl (Hap) [actor] (*né* Earl Richard Traynor, d. 14 Oct 1944, Los Angeles CA). AS, p. 533. BHD1, p. 263.

Hogan, James P[atrick] [scenarist/director/producer] (b. Lowell MA, 1891–4 Nov 1943 [52], No. Hollywood CA; heart attack). (Pickford, 1918; FBO, 1923; Universal; Paramount; Columbia.) "James Hogan," *Variety,* 10 Nov 1943. AMD, p. 168. AS, p. 533. BHD, p. 201; BHD2, p. 124. IFN, p. 144. "Director Hogan Seriously Ill," *MPW,* 19 Apr 1919, 351. "Schulberg Signs Director Hogan," *MPW,* 13 Dec 1924, 658. "James Patrick Hogan Is Directing 'Mansion of Aching Hearts,'" *MPW,* 24 Jan 1925, 382. "James Patrick Hogan to Direct 'S.O.S. Perils of the Sea,'" *MPW,* 18 Jul 1925, 307. "Hogan and Withey Added to F.B.O. Directorial Staff," *MPW,* 19 Dec 1925, 656. 'James Patrick Hogan Recovered," *MPW,* 24 Jul 1926, 217 (appendicitis). Tom Waller, "James Patrick Hogan," *MPW,* 19 Feb 1927, 558–59.

Hogan, Kid (Society Kid Hogan) [pugilist/property man/actor] (*né* Salvatore de Lorenzo, b. 1899?–10 Apr 1962 [63], Chicago IL). AS, p. 533. IFN, p. 144. "In the Picture Studios," *NYDM,* 11 Dec 1915, 34:3 (when a pugilist was needed for Metro's *Rose of the Alley,* Hogan was signed to make his film debut)..

Hohenvest, John [director]. No data found. AMD, p. 168. "Swiss Director Signed by Laemmle to Make Comedies," *MPW,* 29 May 1920, 1222.

Hohl, Arthur [actor] (b. Pittsburgh PA, 21 May 1889–10 Mar 1964 [74], Santa Monica CA). AS, p. 533. BHD1, p. 263. IFN, p. 144.

Holbrook, John K[night] [actor/director/cinematographer/scenarist] (b. Ripley TN-d. 17 Nov 1934, Los Angeles CA). BHD1, p. 263; BHD2, p. 124.

Holcomb, Willard [writer/publicist]. No data found. (Kinemacolor.) AMD, p. 168. F.J. Beecroft, "Publicity Men I Have Met...," *NYDM,* 14 Jan 1914, 48 (*see* Beecroft, Chester for full citation). "Holcomb Lands with Hatch," *MPW,* 12 Aug 1916, 1089. "Willard Holcomb," *MPW,* 22 Jun 1918, 1720.

Holcomb, Wynn [artist]. No data found. AMD, p. 168. "Drawing Posters," *MPW,* 25 Aug 1923, 669.

Holden, Fay [actress] (*née* Dorothy Fay Hammerton, b. Birmingham, England, 26 Sep 1893–23 Jun 1973 [79], Woodland Hills CA; cancer). AS, p. 533.

Holden, Harry Moore [stage/film actor] (b. Franklin OH, 15 May 1867–4 Feb 1944 [76], Woodland Hills CA). (Pioneer.) "Harry Moore Holden," *Variety,* 9 Feb 1944 ("veteran legit and film actor"). AS, p. 533. BHD1, p. 264. IFN, p. 144. Truitt, p. 156.

Holden, John K. [director] (b. Toronto, Canada–d. 11 Jul 1967, Toronto, Canada). "John Holden," *Variety,* 19 Jul 1967 (stage director).

Holden, William [actor] (b. Rochester NY, 22 May 1872–2 Mar 1932 [59], Los Angeles CA; heart attack). (Film debut: *Roadhouse,* 1928; Pathé; Vitagraph; Fox.) "William Holden," *Variety,* 8 Mar 1932 (age 57; began 1928). AS, p. 533. BHD1, p. 264. IFN, p. 144 (age 57).

Holderness, Fay [actress] (b. Oconto WI, 16 Apr 1888 [or 1890]–13 May 1963 [75?], Santa Monica CA).

Holding, Thomas J. [stage/film actor] (b.

Blackheath, Kent, England, 25 Jan 1880–4 May 1929 [49], New York NY; heart attack). (FP-L; Pallas.) "Thomas J. Holding Dies in Dressing Room," *Variety*, 8 May 1929. AMD, p. 168. AS, p. 533. BHD, p. 202. IFN, p. 144. Truitt, 1983. "Thomas Holding to Co-Star with Kathlyn Williams," *MPW*, 9 Sep 1916, 1712. "Thomas Holding Leading Man for Petrova," *MPW*, 13 Oct 1917, 240. "Gun Flash Injures Thomas Holding," *MPW*, 31 May 1919, 1346. "Many Prominent Picture Players in the Cast of 'The Honey Bee,'" *MPW*, 28 Feb 1920, 1492. Hazel Shelley, "The Costume Man," *MPC*, Dec 1921, 26, 82.

Holger-Madsen, Forest [director] (b. Copenhagen, Denmark, 11 Apr 1878–30 Nov 1943 [65]). AS, p. 534 (*né* Holger Madsen, d. 1 Dec, Copenhagen, Denmark). BHD2, p. 124.

Holl, Fritz [director] (b. Worms, Germany, 14 Oct 1883–3 Apr 1942 [58], Vienna, Austria). AS, p. 534.

Holland, Cecil [actor] (b. Gravesend, Kent, England, 29 May 1887–29 Jun 1973 [86], Los Angeles CA). AS, p. 534. BHD1, p. 264. IFN, p. 144.

Holland, Clifford E. [actor] (b. Kenosha WI, 1919–26 Sep 1990 [71?], Los Angeles Co. CA). (Fox.) AMD, p. 168. BHD1, p. 264. "Cliff Holland," *MPW*, 12 Nov 1927, 23.

Holland, Edna M. [actress] (b. New York NY, 20 Sep 1895–4 May 1982 [86], Los Angeles CA; ruptured aorta). AS, p. 534. BHD1, p. 264.

Holland, Edward [title writer/scenarist]. No data found. AMD, p. 168. FDY, p. 445. "Fleischer Engages Scenario Writer," *MPW*, 10 Jul 1926, 117.

Holland, Frank [actor] (b. Hope RI, 1862–6 Nov 1924 [62?], New York NY). BHD1, p. 611.

Holland, Frank J. [actor] (b. 1883?–8 Jul 1950 [67], Ft. Wayne IN). *Trials and Smiles of Show Business*. "Frank J. Holland," *Variety*, 12 Jul 1950. AS, p. 534.

Holland, John [cinematographer]. No data found. FDY, p. 459.

Holland, Joseph Jefferson (son of actor George Holland; brother of actor E.M. Holland) [stage/film actor] (b. 1859–25 Sep 1926 [67], Murray Hill Sanitarium, New York NY; bronchial pneumonia and paralysis). Unmarried. (Frohman comedies, 1890–1902.) "Joseph Jefferson Holland," *Variety*, 29 Sep 1926, 54:4 (had been an invalid for 20 years; affiliated with the Lambs since 1883. Pallbearers at his funeral included John Drew, Otis Skinner, Jules Huran, Russ Whytal, Daniel Frohman, Sam A. Scribner, Cyril Scott, Fritz Williams, Tom Wise and Henry E. Dixey). BHD, p. 202.

Holland, Mildred [actress] (b. Chicago IL, 9 Apr 1869–27 Jan 1944 [74], New York NY). m. Edward C. White. (Powers.) "Mildred Holland," *Variety*, 2 Feb 1944 (age 67). AMD, p. 168. AS, p. 534. BHD, p. 202. IFN, p. 144. "Mildred Holland in Pictures," *MPW*, 16 Dec 1911, 881. "Mildred Holland," *MPW*, 3 Feb 1912, 399. "That Mildred Holland Picture," *MPW*, 17 Feb 1912, 593.

Holland, Ralph [actor] (b. 1888?–7 Dec 1939 [51], Los Angeles CA). "Ralph Holland," *Variety*, 13 Dec 1939 (began ca. 1927). AS, p. 534. BHD1, p. 264. IFN, p. 144. Truitt, p. 156.

Holland, W. Bob [publicist]. "New Mutual Publicity Man," *MPW*, 30 May 1914, 1246.

Holles, Anthony [actor] (b. London, England, 17 Jan 1901–4 Mar 1950 [49]). AS, p. 534. BHD1, p. 264. IFN, p. 144.

Hollingshead, Ebba Mona [actress] (b. Oslo, Norway, 7 Jan 1904–15 Jun 1985 [81], Santa Ana CA). BHD1, p. 611.

Hollingshead, Gordon [actor/stage/film director/producer] (b. Garfield NJ, 8 Jan 1892–8 Jul 1952 [60], Balboa CA). m. Axeliana. (Thanhouser, 1914; WB.) "Gordon Hollingshead," *Variety*, 16 Jul 1952. AS, p. 534 (b. 6 Jan). BHD, p. 202; BHD2, p. 124 (b. 1891). IFN, p. 144. SD.

Hollingsworth, Alfred F. [actor] (b. NB, Apr 1869–20 Jun 1926 [57], Glendale CA). "Alfred Hollingsworth," *Variety*, 23 Jun 1926 (b. Lewiston ID). AS, p. 534. BHD, p. 202 (b. NY state). IFN, p. 144 (age 52). Truitt, p. 156. George Katchmer, "Remembering the Great Silents," *CI*, 241 (Jul 1995), 35–36.

Hollingsworth, Harry [actor] (b. Los Angeles CA, 3 Sep 1888–4 Nov 1947 [59], Inglewood CA). m. Nan Crawford. AS, p. 534. BHD1, p. 265. IFN, p. 144. Truitt, p. 156.

Hollis, Hylda [actress] (b. Philadelphia PA, 10 Jul 1891–9 Dec 1961 [70], Woodland Hills CA). BHD, p. 202.

Hollis, T. Beresford (Jack) [actor] (b. London, England, 1859?–15 Dec 1940 [81], Amityville NY). "Wife of Jack Hollis," *Variety*, 24 Jan 1919 (d. 18 Jan 1919, New York NY; pneumonia). BHD, p. 202. IFN, p. 144.

Hollister, Alice [actress] (*nee?*, b. Worcester MA, 28 Sep 1886–24 Feb 1973 [86], Costa Mesa CA). (b. 1885) m. **George K. Hollister, Jr.** (d. 1976). AMD, p. 168. AS, p. 534. BHD, p. 202. IFN, p. 144. Spehr, p. 140 (b. 1890). "Alice Hollister, Kalem Leading Woman," *MPW*, 7 May 1913, 707. Roberta Courtlandt, "Alice Hollister, of the Kalem Company," *Motion Picture Magazine*, Feb 1915, 94–96. "Alice Hollister, First Vampire," *MPW*, 24 Jun 1916, 2246. "Alice Hollister Resigns from Kalem," *MPW*, 15 Jul 1916, 468. "Alice Hollister Is Leading Woman in 'The Money Master,'" *MPW*, 5 Feb 1921, 714. Hazel Shelley, "The Original Vampire," *MPC*, Jul 1921, 62–63, 89. Billy H. Doyle, "Lost Players," *CI*, 182 (Aug 1990), 22–23.

Hollister, Doris [actress] (b. NY, 2 Dec 1906–26 Jul 1990 [83], Tustin CA). BHD, p. 202.

Hollister, George K. (father of **George K. Hollister, Jr.**) [cinematographer] (b. New York NY, 7 Mar 1873–28 Mar 1952 [79], Los Angeles CA). BHD2, p. 124.

Hollister, George K., Jr. (son of **George K. Hollister**) [cinematographer] (b. 6 Jun 1908–22 Jan 1976 [67], Vista CA). m. **Alice** (d. 1973). BHD, p. 202; BHD2, p. 124.

Holloway, Carol [stage/film actress] (b. Williamstown MA, 30 Apr 1890–18 Dec 1974 [84], Van Nuys CA). (Thanhouser, 1913; Pilot; Lubin; Eclair; Lasky; NYMP; American; Fine Arts; Vitagraph.) AMD, p. 168. AS, P. 534 (b. 1892). BHD1, p. 611. BR, pp. 40–43. MSBB, p. 1036. "Gossip of the Studios; Carol Holloway," *NYDM*, 7 Oct 1914, 27:1. "Carol Holloway," *MPW*, 26 May 1917, 1309. "Carol Holloway Returns," *MPW*, 6 Aug 1927, 402. Billy H. Doyle, "Letter," *CI*, 178 (Apr 1990), 22 (b. Lochee, Scotland); "Letter," *CI*, 179 (May 1990), 50. George A. Katchmer, "Forgotten Cowboys and Cowgirls—Part III," *CI*, 174 (Dec 1989), 48. Buck Rainey, *Sweethearts of the Sage* and *Those Fabulous Serial Queens*.

Holloway, Stanley Augustus (father of Julian Holloway, b. 24 Oct 1944) [stage/film actor] (b. East London, England, 1 Oct 1890–30 Jan 1982 [91], Littlehampton, England). m. (1) Alice Foran, 1913 (d. 1937); (2) Violet Lane, 1939. (Film debut: *The Rotters*, 1921.) AS, p. 535. BHD1, p. 265. SD, p. 622. John Roberts, "Stanley Holloway; His Music Was Laughter," *CI*, 211 (Jan 1992), 36–37.

Holloway, Sterling [actor] (b. Cedartown GA, 4 Jan 1905–22 Nov 1992 [87], Los Angeles CA.) m. AMD, p. 168. AS, p. 535 (b. 14 Jan). BHD1, p. 265. Katz, p. 571 (began 1927). "Sterling Holloway Signs Sennett Contract," *MPW*, 6 Aug 1927, 397. "Sterling Holloway, Actor, 87, Is Dead; Voice of Pooh Bear," *NYT*, 24 Nov 1992, D19:6. "Sterling Holloway," *Variety*, 30 Nov 1992, 103:2. Joe Collura, "Sterling Holloway," *FIR*, May/Jun 1991, 172–81.

Holloway, W[illiam] **E**[dwyn] [actor] (b. Adelaide, Australia, 18 Sep 1885–30 Jun 1952 [66], London, England). AS, p. 535.

Holly, Mary [actress] (b. 1887–17 May 1976 [89], Palm Springs CA). AS, p. 535. BHD, p. 202. IFN, p. 144.

Hollys, Hylda [actress] (b. Philadelphia PA, 10 Jul 1889–9 Dec 1961 [72], Woodland Hills CA). AS, p. 535.

Hollywood, Edwin L[arry] [director] (b. New York NY, 9 Oct 1892–15 May 1958 [65], Glendale CA). "Edwin L. Hollywood," *NYT*, 17 May 1958, 19:5. "Edwin L. Hollywood," *Variety*, 21 May 1958. AMD, p. 168. AS, p. 535. BHD2, p. 125 (LA CA). 1921 Directory, p. 266. "Hollywood Directs Arden Subject," *MPW*, 28 Dec 1918, 1488. "Hollywood to Direct Morey," *MPW*, 13 Sep 1919, 1662. "Hollywood Resigns," *MPW*, 1 Apr 1922, 465. "Hollywood Signs with Associated," *MPW*, 30 May 1925, 554.

Holm, Dary [actor] (b. Hamburg, Germany, 16 Apr 1897-Aug 1960 [63]). BHD1, p. 265.

Holm, Magda [actress] (b. Sweden, 1899–10 Oct 1982 [83?]). BHD, p. 202.

Holman, Harry [actor] (b. Lebanon MO, 15 Mar 1862–3 May 1947 [85], Los Angeles CA). AS, p. 535 (d. 2 May). BHD1, p. 265.

Holman, Richard [actor] (b. 1900–12 Aug 1955 [55], San Francisco CA). BHD, p. 202. IFN, p. 144.

Holman, Russell [writer/publicist/production manager] (b. 29 Oct 1893–1 May 1979 [85], Old Greenwich CT). AMD, p. 168. BHD2, p. 125. "Russell Holman," *MPW*, 6 Mar 1927, 311.

Holme, Randle [director] (b. England, 1864–23 Dec 1957 [93?], London, England). AS, p. 535.

Holmes, Ben [actor/director/writer] (b. Richmond VA, 1890?–2 Dec 1943 [53], Los Angeles CA; bronchial pneumonia). (Fox; Universal; RKO.) "Ben Holmes," *Variety*, 8 Dec 1943 (began 1927). AS, p. 535. BHD2, p. 125. IFN, p. 145.

Holmes, Elias Burton, "Dean of Travelog Producers" [travelog producer/cameraman] (b. Chicago IL, 8 Jan 1870–22 Jul 1958 [88], Los Angeles CA). m. Margaret Elise Oliver, 21 Mar 1914, NYC (Holmes "immediately took her to the top of the Woolworth Building and explained the view to her. She accompanied him on many of his travels."). *The World Is Mine*, 1953. (*Burton Holmes Travelogs*, FP-L; Paramount; Metro.) "Burton Holmes, Lecturer, 88, Dies; Originator of the Travelogue Used Slides, Later Films, to Illustrate His Talks; Took First Trip in 1886 [to Europe];

Retired in '50 but Company Continued to Put Out Five Productions a Year," *NYT,* 23 Jul 1958, 27:1 (to earn funds for the Chicago Camera Club he showed some of his travel pictures, "and that is how the travelogue was born.... The first use of motion pictures was in a primitive sort of way in 1897, with a twenty-second sequence of the Omaha Fire Department and one of equal length showing 'Neopolitans eating spaghetti.' The term travelogue was coined in 1904."). "Burton Holmes," *Variety,* 211, 30 Jul 1958, 127:1. AMD, p. 168. AS, p. 535. BHD1, p. 265; BHD2, p. 125. IFN, p. 145. Truitt, p. 157. WWVC, pp. 67–68. "Theatrical Notes," *NYT,* 19 Mar 1905, IV, 5:6 ("Burton Holmes delivers the first of his Lenten travelogues in Carnegie Hall tonight, his subject being 'In London.' In this lecture he uses nineteen moving picture films and 154 colored lantern slides..."). "In London with Holmes; Lecturer Entertains a Large Audience at Carnegie Hall," *NYT,* 27 Mar 1905, 9:1 (two hours of '*Round About London* at Carnegie Hall, using more than twenty moving picture films in illustrating his "travelogue," telling the audience "how the Englishman enjoys himself..."). "Trade Notes," *MPW,* 25 Jan 1908, 58. "A Novelty from Kalem," *MPW,* 20 Mar 1909, 326. "E. Burton Holmes Married," *NYT,* 22 Mar 1914, III, 4:5. "Burton Holmes Marries," *MPW,* 4 Apr 1914, 38. "Burton Holmes Travelettes," *MPW,* 13 Jun 1914, 1552. "Burton Holmes with Paramount," *MPW,* 25 Dec 1915, 2374. "A Year's Program," *MPW,* 14 Apr 1917, 269 (1917 releases by week). "Burton Holmes Brings Harvest of Films," *MPW,* 20 Oct 1917, 371. "Burton Holmes Will Film Reconstruction in Europe; Leaves on Four-Month Trip," *MPW,* 5 Jul 1919, 68. "Holmes Leaves for three Months' Tour of Near East, Turkey, Spain and Bohemia," *MPW,* 22 May 1920, 1097. Paul S. Boyer, "Holmes, Elias Burton," *Dictionary of American Biography,* Supp. Vol. 6, p. 302 ("In 1897 Holmes introduced motion-picture segments into his program [*Neapolitans Eating Spaghetti*], and eventually he abandoned slides altogether in favor of beautifully photographed color films complete with sound effects and musical backgrounds." Prior to that he had presented Burton Holmes Travelogues).

Holmes, Gerda [actress] (b. Chicago IL). (Essanay.) AMD, p. 169. "Gerda Holmes," *MPW,* 30 Oct 1915, 981. "Allan Douglas Brodie, "Photoplayer Whose Power of Song Is a Great Social Asset," *MPC,* Feb 1916, 37.

Holmes, Gilbert "Pee Wee" [actor] (b. Miles City MT, 15 Jun 1895–17 Aug 1936 [41], Los Angeles CA). "Gilbert Holmes," *Variety,* 26 Aug 1936 (b. Great Falls MT; age 42; "...for 20 years a cowboy-comedian in pictures."). AS, p. 535 (b. Great Falls MT). BHD1, p. 266. IFN, p. 145. Truitt, 1983 (b. 1894).

Holmes, Helen [actress] (b. Chicago IL, 19 Jun 1892–8 Jul 1950 [58], Los Angeles CA; buried in Forest Lawn Cemetery). m. **J.P. McGowan** (d. 1952); H.H. Saunders. (Sennett, 1911; Kalem; Universal; Signal [Mutual].) "Helen Holmes [Mrs. H.H. Saunders]," *Variety,* 12 Jul 1950. AMD, p. 169. AS, p. 535 (d. 9 Jul). BHD1, p. 266 (b. 1893). BR, pp. 43–45 (b. Louisville KY). FSS, p. 146. IFN, p. 145. Katz, p. 572. MH, p. 117. Truitt, p. 157. Clarke Irvine, "Helen Holmes," *MPW,* 16 Jan 1915, 382. "Helen Holmes to Be Featured by Universal," *MPW,* 9 Oct 1915, 241. "Helen Holmes Buys Pullman," *MPW,* 25 Nov 1916, 1167. "Helen Holmes," *MPW,* 24 Feb 1917, 1183. Helen Holmes, "Variety the Spice of Picture Life," *MPW,* 21 Jul 1917, 410–11. "Helen Holmes Has Narrow Escape," *MPW,* 24 Nov 1917, 1179. "Helen Holmes to Star in New Serial," *MPW,* 21 Jun 1919, 1785. "Production Work Started on Helen Holmes Serial," *MPW,* 5 Jul 1919, 100. "Helen Holmes to Perform a Daring Aviation Stunt," *MPW,* 9 Aug 1919, 871. "S.L.K. Announces Song Featuring Helen Holmes," *MPW,* 30 Aug 1919, 1355. Eldon K. Everett, "Helen Holmes—The Railroad Girl," *CFC,* 41 (Winter, 1973), 37–39 (b. South Bend IN). Billy H. Doyle, "Lost Players," *CI,* 156 (Jun 1988), C13 (b. 1893).

Holmes, J[ack] **Merrill** [actor] (b. PA, 21 Jul 1889–27 Feb 1950 [60], Los Angeles CA). AS, p. 535.

Holmes, Lois [actress] (b. Galion OH, 1899–12 Mar 1986 [86?], New York NY). AS, p. 535. BHD1, p. 266.

Holmes, Madeleine Taylor (daughter of **Taylor Holmes**) [actress] (d. 18 Dec 1987).

Holmes, Milton [actor/scenarist/producer] (b. Syracuse NY, 30 Jul 1907–19 Sep 1987 [80], Los Angeles CA). BHD1, p. 266; BHD2, p. 125.

Holmes, Peewee. *See* Holmes, Gilbert.

Holmes, Phillips R. (son of **Taylor Holmes**; brother of **Ralph Holmes**) [actor] (b. Grand Rapids MI, 22 Jul 1907–12 Aug 1942 [35], near Armstrong, Ontario, Canada; plane crash). (Paramount.) (Film debut: *Varsity,* 1928.) "Phillips Holmes," *Variety,* 19 Aug 1942 (began 1928). AS, p. 536 (b. 1909). BHD1, p. 266. IFN, p. 145. JS, p. 217 (appeared in *Casta Diva,* 1935, English version shot in Italy). Katz, pp. 572–73. Eve Golden, "Phillips Holmes; When Bad Things Happen to Blonde People," *CI,* 217 (Jul 1993), 44–45.

Holmes, Ralph (son of **Taylor Holmes**; brother of **Phillips R. Holmes**) [actor] (b. New York NY, 20 May 1915–15 Nov 1945 [30], New York NY). AS, p. 536 (b. Detroit MI). BHD1, p. 266.

Holmes, Rapley [stage/film actor] (b. Canada, 1 Jun 1867–11 Jan 1928 [60], Strathroy, Ontario, Canada). (Essanay.) AMD, p. 169. AS, p. 536. BHD, p. 203. IFN, p. 145. Truitt, 1983. "Holmes Joins Essanay; Rapley Holmes, Well-Known Dramatic Star, to Make His Motion Picture Debut," *NYDM,* 4 Feb 1914, 31:2 it was his desire "to remain in Chicago permanently, and so it was that he entered the ranks of motion-picture players."). "Some Prominent Essanay Photoplayers," *MPW,* 11 Jul 1914, 234–35. Lester Sweyd, "What They Are Doing Now," *Motion Picture Magazine,* Feb 1918, 12 (appeared 250 times "as E.M. Ralston with William Collier in his laugh-provoker, 'Nothing But the Truth.'").

Holmes, Robert [actor] (b. Newport, England, 7 Jan 1899–10 Jul 1945 [46]). BHD1, p. 266.

Holmes, Stuart [stage/film/TV actor] (*né* Joseph Liebchen, b. Chicago IL, 10 Mar 1884–29 Dec 1971 [87], Los Angeles CA; aneurism). (Ramo; Biograph; Fox; Selznick.) "Stuart Holmes," *Variety,* 12 Jan 1972. AMD, p. 169. AS, p. 536 (b. 20 Mar). BHD1, p. 266. FFF, p. 194 (b. 1887). FSS, p. 147. IFN, p. 145. Katz, p. 573 (b. 1887). MH, p. 117 (b. 1887). MSBB, p. 1025 (b. 1887). Spehr, p. 140 (b. 1887). Truitt, p. 157. "Prominent Players to Be Featured in Pathé Serials for the Next Two Years," *MPW,* 19 Jul 1919, 377. "Beck Signs Stuart Holmes," *MPW,* 2 Aug 1919, 679. Raymond Lee, "Villainy with a Velvet Touch," *CFC,* 28 (Fall, 1970), 47.

Holmes, Taylor [stage/film actor] (father of **Phillips** and **Ralph Holmes**) (b. Newark NJ, 16 May 1878–30 Sep 1959 [81], Los Angeles CA). m. **Edna Phillips** (d. 1952). (Essanay; Triangle.) "Taylor Holmes, Actor, Dies at 80; Stage, Screen and TV Player for 66 Years—A Matinee Idol of Early 1900's," *NYT,* 2 Oct 1959, 29:1. "Taylor Holmes," *Variety,* 7 Oct 1959. AMD, p. 169. AS, p. 536. BHD1, p. 266. FSS, p. 147. IFN, p. 145. MH, p. 117. MSBB, p. 1025. SD. Truitt, p. 157 (b. 1872). WWS, p. 91. "Taylor Holmes with Essanay," *MPW,* 2 Jun 1917, 1445. "Holmes Well Into First Essanay," *MPW,* 21 Jul 1917, 490. Neil G. Caward, "Screen Gossip," *Picture-Play Magazine,* VII (Sep 1917), 103 (Holmes signed a contract with Essanay the same week that Henry B. Walthall resigned). "Holmes Agrees to Appear for Red Cross," *MPW,* 23 Feb 1918, 1085. "Taylor Holmes Signs Triangle Contract," *MPW,* 13 Jul 1918, 189. "Taylor Holmes Comes to See Himself and Stops to Talk," *MPW,* 22 Mar 1919, 1610. William H. Reilly, "I'll Take My Comedy Straight," *MPW,* 28 Jun 1919, 1964. "Taylor Holmes Productions to Be Distributed by Metro," *MPW,* 29 Nov 1919, 526. "Taylor Holmes Built Up Own Strength Like Character He Plays in New Film," *MPW,* 20 Mar 1920, 1990. "Taylor Holmes's Next Vehicle to Be Melodrama, Not Comedy," *MPW,* 17 Jul 1920, 329. "Gaiety Signs Taylor Holmes to Star in Short Comedy Series," *MPW,* 19 Feb 1927, 572. "Holmes Ideal Domestic Type," *MPW,* 16 Apr 1927, 632.

Holmes, William J. [actor] (b. Watertown NY, 17 Mar 1877–1 Dec 1946 [69], Los Angeles CA). "William J. Holmes," *Variety,* 4 Dec 1946. AS, p. 536. IFN, p. 145.

Holmes-Gore, Arthur [actor] (b. England, 1871–12 Aug 1915 [44], Dardanelles). BHD, p. 203. IFN, p. 145.

Holmes-Gore, Dorothy [actress] (b. London, England, 26 May 1896–14 Oct 1977 [81], London, England). BHD1, p. 266.

Holmquist, Sigrid [actress] (b. Baros, Sweden, 1 Feb 1894–12 Jan 1970 [75], Sacramento CA). AMD, p. 169. AS, p. 536. BHD, p. 203. MH, p. 117. "Swedish Star Is Feminine Lead in Film, 'Prophet's Paradise,'" *MPW,* 10 Sep 1921, 192. "Sigrid Holmquist Chosen for Patricia Role," *MPW,* 16 Dec 1922, 647. "Sigrid Holmquist Engaged as Lead to Hines in Next Film," *MPW,* 27 Sep 1924, 311. "Sigrid Holmquist Signed," *MPW,* 10 Jan 1925, 176. "Sigrid Holmquist Is Seen in Remarkable Fashion Color Film," *MPW,* 29 Jan 1927, 351.

Holt, Edwin [actor] (b. ME, 12 Apr ?–d. 5 Jul 1920, New York NY). AS, p. 536. BHD, p. 203. IFN, p. 145.

Holt, George [actor/director]. No data found. AMD, p. 169. "George Holt," *MPW,* 16 Oct 1915, 429.

Holt, Helen [actress] (b. 1890?–17 Jan 1927 [37], Vancouver, British Columbia, Canada; pneumonia). AS, p. 536. BHD, p. 203. IFN, p. 145.

Holt, Helen Maude (Lady Tree) (b. London, England, 5 Oct 1858–7 Aug 1937 [78], London, England). m. **Sir Herbert Beerbohm Tree** (d. 1917). "Lady Tree," *Variety,* 11 Aug 1937 (age 72). AS, p. 536. BHD1, p. 546 (Helen Maude Holt Tree). IFN, p. 296.

Holt, Jack (father of Jennifer [d. 21 Sep 1997] and **Tim Holt**) [actor] (*né* Charles John Holt, b. Winchester VA, 31 May 1888–18 Jan 1951 [62], West Los Angeles CA). m. Margaret Stanley.

(Debut: *Salomy Jane,* ca. 1914.) Bill Wilson, *The Fabulous Holts* (1976). "Jack Holt, 62, Dies; Veteran Film Star; Western Hero in Movies for Many Years Succumbs on Coast of Heart Ailment," *NYT,* 19 Jan 1951, 25:1. "Jack Holt," *Variety,* 24 Jan 1951 (d. Sawtelle CA). AMD, p. 169. AS, p. 536 (b. 1881). BHD1, p. 266 (b. NYC; d. Sawtelle CA). FFF, p. 122. FSS, p. 147. IFN, p. 145. Katz, p. 573. MH, p. 117. Truitt, p. 157. WWS, p. 33. Mary Keane Taylor, "Holt—Who Goes There?; In This Case It's Jack, the Fascinating Scoundrel of the Silversheet," *MPC,* Jan 1919, 28–29, 66–67. "Holt Does Thrilling Stunt in Robertson-Cole Film," *MPW,* 2 Aug 1919, 671. "Jack Holt Signs to Play Leads for Famous Players," *MPW,* 17 Jan 1920, 424. "Holt Is Loaned," *MPW,* 16 Apr 1921, 706. "Jack Holt to Star in a Series of Productions for Paramount," *MPW,* 25 Jun 1921, 836. Jim Tully, "The Toss of a Coin; How Jack Holt Came to Hollywood, Footsore and Hungry," *MPC,* Jul 1925, 31, 76. Dorothy Manners, "A Screen Cowboy *Really* Goes in for Cows," *MPC,* Mar 1927, 58, 75, 87. "Holt May Return to Paramount," *MPW,* 28 May 1927, 257. "Jack Holt Undergoes Operation on Throat," *MPW,* 22 Oct 1927, 493. Helen Carlisle, "He Plays Polo and Between Chukkers, Jack Holt Does a Little Motion Picture Starring," *MPC,* Jul 1928, 26, 75. Bill Wilson, "Jack Holt Filmography," *CI,* 74 (Mar 1981), 29–31, 49. Bill Wilson, "About Jack Holt [letter]," *CI,* 75 (May 1981), 56–57 (b. in NY). Mike Newton, "The Holts—The First Family of Westerns," *CI,* 215 (May 1993), 28 *et passim.* George Katchmer, "Remembering the Great Silents," *CI,* 239 (May 1995), 36–38.

Holt, Richard. *See* Dearholt, Ashton.

Holt, Skip [actor] (b. 1921–2 Feb 1986 [64?]). BHD, p. 203.

Holt, Tim (son of **Jack Holt**; brother of Jennifer Holt) [actor] (*né* Charles John Holt, Jr., b. Beverly Hills CA, 5 Feb 1919–15 Feb 1973 [54], Shawnee OK; brain cancer). (Debut: *The Vanishing Pioneer,* 1928.) m. (1) Virginia Asheroff; (2) Alice Harrison; (3) Birdie Stephens. "Tim Holt, Western Film Star Who Made 149 Pictures, Dead," *NYT,* 16 Feb 1973, 42:1. "Tim Holt," *Variety,* 21 Feb 1973. AS, p. 536. BHD1, p. 266 (b. 1918). IFN, p. 145. Katz, p. 574 (b. 1918). SD. Buck Rainey, "Tim Holt," *CFC,* 54 (Spring, 1977), X19 *et passim.*

Holton, Joseph J. [assistant director/casting director] (b. Newburgh NY, 16 Dec 1895–18 Feb 1958 [62], Los Angeles CA). BHD2, p. 125.

Holtz, Lou [actor] (b. San Francisco CA, 11 Apr 1893–22 Sep 1980 [87], Beverly Hills CA). AS, p. 536. BHD1, p. 266.

Holtz, Tenen [actor] (*né* Elihu Tenenholtz, b. Russia, 17 Feb 1887–1 Jul 1971 [84], Los Angeles CA). (MGM.) AS, p. 536. BHD1, p. 266. IFN, p. 145.

Holubar, Allen J[oseph] [stage/film actor/director/writer] (b. San Francisco CA, 3 Aug 1888–20 Nov 1923 [35], Los Angeles CA; pneumonia). m. **Dorothy Phillips**, Wildwood NJ, 1912—div. 1923 (d. 1980). (Universal, 1914; Bluerbird.) "Alan Holubar Dies; Director Passes Away After Operation—Was Ill for Three Months," *Variety,* 22 Nov 1923. AMD, p. 169. AS, p. 537. BHD, p. 203; BHD2, p. 125 (b. 1890). IFN, p. 145. Lowrey, p. 76. MSBB, p. 1046 (b. 1889). "Allen Holubar," *MPW,* 13 Jan 1917, 222. "Allen Holubar Ill," *MPW,* 18 Jan 1919, 344. "Another Super-Drama for Dorothy Phillips," *MPW,* 22 Mar 1919, 1685. Fritzi Remont, "Dorothy, Alan and Gwen [their 4-year-old daughter]," *MPC,* Apr 1919, 34–35, 70. "Holubar Signs with Kaufman," *MPW,* 13 Mar 1920, 1781. "Holubar Starts Producing," *MPW,* 5 Jun 1920, 1321. "Holubar Recovering," *MPW,* 1 Jan 1921, 80 (appendicitis). "First National Retains Allen Holubar; Has Ambitious Plans for Future Films," *MPW,* 30 Apr 1921, 950. "Obituary," *MPW,* 1 Dec 1923, 456 (age 34). Billy H. Doyle, "Lost Players; Dorothy Phillips and Allen J. Holubar," *CI,* 186 (Dec 1990), 36–37.

Homan, Gertrude [actor] (b. 1880–29 May 1951 [71?], Glen Grove NY). BHD, p. 203.

Homans, Robert E[dward] [actor] (b. Malden MA, 8 Nov 1877 [MVRB, Vol. 287, p. 152]–27 Jul 1947 [69], Los Angeles CA; heart attack). "Robert Homans," *Variety,* 30 Jul 1947 (age 72). AS, p. 537. BHD1, p. 266. IFN, p. 145. Truitt, p. 158 (b. 1875). George A. Katchmer, "Forgotten Cowboys and Cowgirls—Part III," *CI,* 174 (Dec 1989), 48 (b. 1875).

Homolka, Oscar [stage/film actor] (b. Vienna, Austria, 12 Aug 1898–27 Jan 1978 [79], Sussex, England). m. 5 times: Grete Mosheim; Baroness Vally Hatvany; (4) Florence Meyer; (5) Joan Tetzel. "Oscar Homolka, Actor, Dies at 79; The Uncle in 'I Remember Mama,'" *NYT,* 29 Jan 1978, 42:1. "Oscar Homolka," *Variety,* 1 Feb 1978. AS, p. 537. BHD1, p. 267 (d. London). IFN, p. 145. Katz, p. 574 (began in Germany). SD.

Honda, Frank K. [actor] (b. Japan, 1884?–3 Feb 1924 [40], New York NY). "Frank Honda," *Variety,* 14 Feb 1924 ("Japanese picture actor"). AS, p. 537. BHD, p. 203. IFN, p. 145. Truitt, p. 158.

Hong, Shen [director/scenarist] (b. Jiangsu, China, 1894–1955 [61?], Peking, China). AS, p. 537.

Honn, Eldon [actor] (b. 1890–11 Aug 1927 [37?], San Diego CA). AS, p. 537. BHD, p. 203.

Hood, Darla Jean [actress: Our Gang Comedies] (b. Leedey OK, 4 Nov 1931?–13 Jun 1979 [48], Canoga Park CA). "Darla Hood," *Variety,* 20 Jun 1979. AS, p. 537. BHD1, p. 267. IFN, p. 145. Appeared in *His Wooden Wedding* (1925), so her birth year is incorrect.

Hood, Joseph B., Sr. [actor/stuntman] (b. 5 Jan 1893–26 Jun 1965 [72], Philadelphia PA). (Began 1927.) "Joseph B. Hood, Sr.," *Variety,* 239, 7 Jul 1965, 52:1. AS, p. 537 (b. 1896). BHD1, p. 267. IFN, p. 145.

Hood, Wally [actor] (b. Whittier CA, 9 Feb 1895–2 May 1965 [70], Los Angeles CA). AS, p. 537. BHD, p. 203.

Hooper, Louis [casting director]. No data found. AMD, p. 169. "The Roll of Honor," *MPW,* 16 Jun 1917, 1784.

Hoopes, Isabella [actress] (b. 21 Apr 1893–7 Aug 1987 [94], Far Rockaway NY). BHD1, p. 267.

Hoopii, Sol [actor] (*né* Sol Hoopii Kaaiai, b. Honolulu HI, 1902–16 Nov 1953 [51?], Seattle WA). AS, p. 538 (b. 1905). BHD1, p. 267.

Hoops, Arthur [stasge/film actor] (b. Middleton CT, 1870?–17 Sep 1916 [46], Los Angeles CA; heart attack). (FP-L; Metro.) "Arthur Hoops," *Variety,* 22 Sep 1916. AMD, p. 169. AS, p. 538. BHD, p. 203 (d. 16 Sep, LI NY). IFN, p. 145. SD. "Arthur Hoops Joins George Kleine," *MPW,* XXVI, 30 Oct 1915, 767. "Arthur Hoops," *MPW,* 19 Feb 1916, 1138. "Obituary," *MPW,* 7 Oct 1916, 60.

Hoover, Frank S. [cinematographer] (b. Lancaster PA, 1875?–11 Dec 1946 [71], WY; on a train). "F.S. Hoover, Gave Hollywood Start; Pioneer Camera Man Induced Acting Troupe to Make Films There—Dies on Train at 71," *NYT,* 12 Dec 1946, 29:6. "Frank S. Hoover," *Variety,* 18 Dec 1946. AS, p. 538 (b. 1865). BHD2, p. 125 (d. LA CA).

Hope, Diana [actress] (b. London, England, 1872–20 Nov 1942 [70?], Los Angeles CA). AS, p. 538.

Hope, Edward [scenarist] (b. 1896–24 Feb 1958 [61?], Los Angeles CA). BHD2, p. 125.

Hope, Evelyn [actress] (b. London, England-d. 23 Dec 1966). BHD, p. 203.

Hope, Faith [actress]. No data found. AMD, p. 170. "Faith Hope, Serial Player[,] Starts for the West Coast," *MPW,* 19 Mar 1921, 262.

Hope, Frederic [associate art director] (b. New Brighton PA, 22 Jan 1900–20 Apr 1937 [37], Los Angeles CA; after appendectomy). (Metro, 1924; UA.) "Frederic Hope," *NYT,* 22 Apr 1937, 23:1. "Frederic Hope," *Variety,* 28 Apr 1937. BHD2, p. 125.

Hope, Gloria [actress] (*née* Olive Francis, b. Pittsburgh PA, 9 Nov 1899–29 Oct 1976 [76], Pasadena CA; cardiac arrest). m. **Lloyd Hughes**, 30 Jun 1921. Methodist Church, Hollywood CA (d. 1958). (Film debut: *Free and Equal,* 1917. Ince; Griffith; Goldwyn; Garson; Universal; Selznick; Fox; Robertson-Cole; FP-L; Select.) AMD, p. 170. AS, p. 538. BHD1, p. 267. MH, p. 118. WWS, p. 281 (b. 1901). "Gloria Hope with Griffith," *MPW,* 25 May 1918, 1146. "Hughes-Hope," *MPW,* 23 Jul 1921, 413. Maude Stacey, "Red-Head," *MPC,* Dec 1921, 65, 84. Billy H. Doyle, "Lost Players," *CI,* 15 (Sep 1988), 22.

Hope, Jean [actress]. No data found. m. **Eddie Boland**, 28 May 1921 (d. 1935). AMD, p. 170. "Eddie Boland Married," *MPW,* 25 Jun 1921, 807.

Hope, Lelia [actress]. No data found. AMD, p. 170. "Strauss to Produce Series of Comedies," *MPW,* 22 Mar 1919, 1695.

Hope, Maidie [actress] (b. London, England, 15 Feb 1881–18 Apr 1937 [56], London, England). AS, p. 538 (d. 20 Apr). BHD1, p. 267.

Hope, Thelma P. [portrait and landscape artist/art director] (*née?,* b. 6 Nov 1898–13 Dec 1991 [93], Newport Beach CA). m. Fredric Hope. "Thelma P. Hope," *Variety,* 23 Dec 1991, p. 55. BHD2, p. 125.

Hopkins, Arthur Melancthon [tiutle writer/director/producer/writer] (b. Cleveland OH, 4 Oct 1878–22 Mar 1950 [71], New York NY [Death Certificate Index No. 6863]). m. (1) Eve O'Brien; (2) **Doris Kenyon** (d. 1979). "Arthur Hopkins, 71, Producer, Is Dead; Theatrical Leader Here More Than 30 Years Had Directed and Sponsored Many Hits; Introduced Great Actors; Among Stage Successes Were 'Magnificent Yankee,' 'Hairy Ape,' 'What Price Glory?,'" *NYT,* 23 Mar 1950, 29:1. "Arthur Hopkins Directed His Plays 'On Honor System' in Bow to the Actor," *Variety,* 29 Mar 1950. AMD, p. 170 (Arthur G. Hopkins). AS, p. 538. BHD2, p. 125. IFN, p. 146. SD. Spehr, p. 142. "Arthur Hopkins to Direct Maxine Elliott," *MPW,* 14 Apr 1917, 259. "Hopkins Signed by Special," *MPW,* 25 Sep 1920, 466.

Hopkins, Ben [bit actor] (b. Buffalo NY, 9 May 1870–8 Feb 1941 [70], Los Angeles CA). "Ben Hopkins," *Variety*, 19 Feb 1941. AS, p. 538. BHD1, p. 267. IFN, p. 146.

Hopkins, Charles R. [stage/film actor/producer] (b. Philadelphia PA, 1 Jan 1884–1 Jan 1953 [69], New York NY). m. Violet V. Clarke. "Charles Hopkins," *Variety*, 7 Jan 1953. AS, p. 538 (d. LA CA). IFN, p. 146. SD, p. 627.

Hopkins, Clyde E. [actor] (b. Garnett KS, 25 Jun 1893–19 Nov 1958 [65], Los Angeles CA). BHD, p. 203.

Hopkins, George James [scenarist/art director] (b. Pasadena CA, 23 Mar 1896–11 Feb 1985 [88], Los Angeles CA). AMD, p. 170. AS, p. 538. BHD2, p. 125. "Hopkins Goes to Mayer as Art Director," *MPW*, 15 Nov 1919, 345.

Hopkins, Jack (or John) [actor]. No data found. AMD, p. 170. "Jack Hopkins," *MPW*, 6 Jan 1912, 39. "Jack Hopkins," *MPW*, 14 Mar 1914, 1370. "Jack Hopkins," *MPW*, 27 Feb 1915, 1295.

Hopkins, Robert Evans "Hoppy" (step-father of Peter Lind Hayes) [title writer/scenarist] (b. Ottawa KS, 21 Sep 1886–22 Dec 1966 [80], Los Angeles CA; heart ailment). m. (2) Grace Hayes. "Robert Evans Hopkins," *Variety*, 28 Dec 1966 ("one of the early film writers and at Metro for 30 years"). AS, p. 538. BHD2, p. 125 (d. 21 Dec). FDY, p. 445.

Hopkins, Thomas J. [scenarist]. No data found. FDY, p. 429.

Hopkins, Una Nixon [writer/art director]. No data found. AMD, p. 170. "Morosco's New Art Director," *NYDM*, 8 Sep 1915, 25:3. "Morosco Engages Una Nixon Hopkins as Art Director," *MPW*, 18 Sep 1915, 2002.

Hopley, George. *See* Woolrich, Cornell.

Hopper, DeWolf (father of **William DeWolf Hopper, Jr.**) [stage/film actor] (*né* William DeWolf Hopper, b. New York NY, 30 Mar 1858–23 Sep 1935 [77], Kansas City MO). m. (1) Helen Gardner; (2) Ida Mosher; (3) **Edna Wallace** (d. 1959); (4) Nella Bergen; (5) Elda Furry [**Hedda Hopper**], 8 May 1913—div. 1922 (d. 1966); (6) Lillan Glaser. (Fine Arts.) "DeWolf Hopper," *Variety*, 25 Sep 1935. AMD, p. 170. AS, p. 538 (d. Kansas City KS). BHD1, p. 268. IFN, p. 146. MSBB, p. 1025. Truitt, p. 158. "Personal," *NYDM*, 3 Feb 1915, 5:1 (son born 26 Jan 1915). "Hopper in Modern Comedy," *MPW*, 18 Dec 1915, 2182.

Hopper, E. Mason [cartoonist/producer/director] (b. Enosberg VT, 6 Dec 1885–3 Jan 1967 [81], Woodland Hills CA). (Essanay, 1911; Pathé; 1st National; Goldwyn.) "E. Mason Hopper," *Variety*, 11 Jan 1967 (age 82). AMD, p. 170. AS, p. 538. BHD2, p. 126 (b. 1881). IFN, p. 146. Katz, p. 576 (d. 1966). "Hopper Takes to Vaudeville," *MPW*, 3 May 1913, 490. "Hopper Joins Metro's Western Forces," *MPW*, 25 May 1918, 1155. "Goldwyn Engages E. Mason Hopper," *MPW*, 29 Nov 1919, 553. E. Mason Hopper, "Events Move Rapidly," *MPW*, 31 Dec 1921, 1065. "Hopper to Direct," *MPW*, 2 Feb 1924, 391. "Hopper to Direct Big Christie Special," *MPW*, 27 Mar 1926, 270. "Hopper Is to Continue with Marie Prevost," *MPW*, 15 Jan 1927, 195. "E. Mason Hopper," *MPW*, 24 Sep 1927, 228. "Hopper to Europe," *MPW*, 10 Dec 1927, 21.

Hopper, Edna Wallace. *See* Wallace, Edna.

Hopper, Hedda (mother of **William DeWolf Hopper, Jr.**) [film/radio actress/gossip columnist] (*née* Elda Furry, b. Hollidaysburg [Altoona] PA, 2 May 1885–1 Feb 1966 [80], Los Angeles CA; pneumonia). m. **DeWolf Hopper**, 8 May 1913–22 (d. 1935). (MGM.) *From Under My Hat* (Garden City NY: Doubleday & Co., 1953); with James Brough, *The Whole Truth and Nothing But* (NY: Pyramid Books, 1963). George Eells, *Hedda and Louella* (1972). (Film debut: *Battle of Hearts*, 1916.) "Hedda Hopper, Columnist, Dies; Chronicled Gossip of Hollywood; Confidante of Leading Stars Noted for Flamboyant Hats and Caustic Comments," *NYT*, 2 Feb 1966, 32:1 (b. 2 Jun 1890). "Hedda Hopper, 75, Pneumonia Victim," *Variety*, 2 Feb 1966. AMD, p. 170. AS, p. 539 (b. 1890). BHD1, p. 268; BHD2, p. 126 (b. 2 Jun 1890). FFF, p. 192. FSS, p. 148. IFN, p. 146 (b. 2 Jun 1890). Katz, pp. 576–77 (b. 2 Jun 1890). MH, p. 118 (b. Hollydaysburg PA). Truitt, pp. 158–59. Olive Hoogenboom, *DAB*, Supp. 8 (1988), pp. 281–83 (her husband was about four years older than her father; her first gossip column appeared on 15 Feb 1938 in five newspapers). "Elda Furry," *MPW*, 28 Apr 1917, 607. "Hedda Hopper in 'The Cruel Truth,'" *MPW*, 25 Jun 1927, 597.

Hopper, William DeWolfe, Jr. (son of **DeWolfe** and **Hedda Hopper**) [film/TV actor] (b. New York NY, 26 Jan 1915–6 Mar 1970 [55], Palm Springs CA; pneumonia). m. Jan. "William Hopper," *Variety*, 11 Mar 1970. AS, p. 539. BHD1, p. 268. IFN, p. 146. "Personal," *NYDM*, 3 Feb 1915, 5:1 (birth of son to Hopper and Elda Curry [sic]).

Hopton, Russell [actor] (*né* Harry Russel Hopton, b. New York NY, 18 Feb 1900–7 Apr 1945 [45], No. Hollywood CA; suicide with sleeping tablets). "Harry Russell Hopton," *Variety*, 11 Apr 1945 (began 1930). AS, p. 539. BHD1, p. 268. IFN, p. 146. Truitt, p. 159.

Hopwood, Avery [playwright/scenarist] (b. Cleveland OH, 28 May 1882–1 Jul 1928 [46], Nice, France; drowned during a swim after dinner). Unmarried. "Avery Hopwood," *Variety*, 4 Jul 1928, 67:5 (first play: *Clothes*, produced in 1906; wrote *Fair and Warmer; The Gold Diggers; Naughty Cinderella; Little Miss Bluebeard*). AMD, p. 170. BHD2, p. 126 (d. 2 Jul 1928, Juan-les-Pins, France). "Avery Hopwood Has Signed a Three Year Contract to Write Plays for Paramount," *MPW*, 27 Nov 1920, 466. "Will Write Titles," *MPW*, 18 Nov 1922, 245.

Horan, Charles T[homas] [actor/director/scenarist] (b. New York NY, 6 Apr 1881?–11 Jan 1928 [46], Los Angeles CA; heart attack). "Charles T. Horan," *Variety*, 18 Jan 1928. AS, p. 539. BHD, p. 204; BHD2, p. 126 (b. 1886). FDY, p. 429.

Horbiger, Attila (brother of **Paul Horbiger**; father of Christiane Horbiger-Wessely) [actor] (b. Budapest, Hungary, 21 Apr 1896–27 Apr 1987 [91], Vienna, Austria). m. (son, Christiane, b. 13 Oct 1938). AS, p. 539. BHD1, p. 268.

Horbiger, Paul (brother of **Attila Horbiger**) [actor] (*né* Pat Janos Horbiger, b. Budapest, Hungary, 29 Apr 1894–5 Mar 1981 [86], Vienna, Austria). AS, p. 539.

Horkheimer, Elwood D[avid] (brother of **Herbert M. Horkheimer**) [secretary/treasurer of Balboa/director] (b. Wheeling WV, 8 Feb 1881–14 Aug 1966 [85], Los Angeles Co. CA). m. **Jackie Saunders** (d. 1954). Jean-Jacques Jura and Rodney Norman Bardin, II, *Balboa Films; A History and Filmography of the Silent Film Studio* (Jefferson NC: McFarland & Co., 1999). "Motion Pictures; On the Subject of Waste," *NYDM*, 6 Oct 1915, 23:3. BHD2, p. 126. *See* next entry, article from *NYDM*, 13 Nov 1915.

Horkheimer, Herbert M[orris] (brother of **Elwood D. Horkheimer**) [actor/theatrical producer/executive] (b. Wheeling WV, 9 Jul 1882–25 Apr 1962 [80], Cedars of Lebanon Hospital, Los Angeles CA; acute pulmonary edema). m. (1); (2) Agnes. Jean-Jacques Jura and Rodney Norman Bardin, II, *Balboa Films; A History and Filmography of the Silent Film Studio* (Jefferson NC: McFarland & Co., 1999). (President and General Manager of Balboa Studios, Long Beach CA, 1913–18, the largest indepdendent studio at the time. Originally the California Motion Picture Manufacturing Co., it was acquired by Thomas Edison, who sold the small lot to Horkheimer in 1913. He named the studio after the Spanish explore and he and his brother Elwood enlarged the facility and turned out more than 50 silent films the first year alone. The Horkheimers declared bankruptcy in 1918. The studio folded in 1924 and was demolished in 1925.). "Herbert M. Horkheimer," *Variety*, 2 May 1962. AMD, p. 170. AS, p. 539 (d. 27 Apr). BHD2, p. 126. IFN, p. 146 (d. 25 Apr). "Horkheimer Believes in Stars," *MPW*, 23 Jan 1915, 524. "Veterans of Balboa," *MPW*, 9 Oct 1915, 267. "A Word on Behalf of the West; H.M. Horkheimer Doesn't Agree with Writer [Donald A. Meaney] Who Advised Picture Men to Produce in the East—'There's No Comparison,' He Says," *NYDM*, 13 Nov 1915, 27:2 (E.D. Horkheimer [and not H.M.] rebuts Meaney: The climate in the West can't be excelled. Artificially lighted films are never as good as those using natural light. "Furthermore, working under artificial lights is extremely hard on the eyes. It is well known that many persons are laid up from the strain. It takes most players a long while to get used to the brilliant arcs; while some of the bes ones never do." A lack of props and costumes in the West is the fault of the studio involved. Producers are interferred with in the East, too—"...the law there requires all film to be carried in double lined galvanized iron cases; and it may not be taken in subways, streetcars or elevated railroads." Permission to work in public places is granted unless the privilege is abused. There may be better actors in the East, but there are better *film* actors out West. "As for the charge that California climate is enervating, well all I can say is that the steady growth of the picture industry in this vicinity doesn't indicate it."). "Horkheimer on the Job," *MPW*, 15 Jan 1916, 399. "Horkheimer Wrote It," *MPW*, 4 Mar 1916, 1485. "Horkheimer Nearly Beheaded," *MPW*, 25 Mar 1916, 1989. Herbert M. Horkheimer, "A View of Trade Conditions," *MPW*, 27 Jan 1917, 535. Herbert M. Horkheimer, "Independent Production Made Balboa," *MPW*, 10 Mar 1917, 1526. "Horkheimer to Make Mutual Series," *MPW*, 17 Mar 1917, 1786. Billy H. Doyle, "Lost Players [Balboa Feature Film Company]," *CI*, 153 (Mar 1988), 52–54 (d. 25 Apr).

Horn, Camilla Martha [dancer/film/stage/TV actress] (b. Frankfurt-am-Main, Germany, 25 Apr 1903–14 Aug 1996 [93], Gilchung, Germany; of natural causes in a nursing home). m. (1) **Gustav Diessl** (d. 1948); (2) **Louis Graveure** (d. 1965); (3) Klaus Geerz; (4) Kurt Kurfis; (5) Robert Schnyder; (6) Rudolf Mühlfenzl. *Verliebt in Die Leben* (*In Love with Life*), 1985. (Film debut: extra in *Madame Wunscht Keine Kinder?* [*Madame Doesn't*

Want Any Children], Ufa, Ufa, 1926; UA; Universal; 7 silents in U.S.) "Camilla Horn," *Variety,* 2 Sep 1996, p. 76:1. "Camilla Horn," *Pittsburgh Post-Gazette,* 19 Aug 1996, C-4:1. Tom Vallance, "Camilla Horn," *The Independent,* 22 Aug 1996, p. 14. *The Bavarian Videotext,* 16 Aug 1996. AMD, p. 170. AS, p. 539. BHD1, p. 268 (d. Gilching, Germany). JS, p. 218 (b. 1906, daughter of a German father and an Italian mother; appeared in Italian films in 1941, 1942, and 1968). Katz, *The International Film Encyclopedia,* p. 577. Ragan, *Who's Who in Hollywood,* p. 771. "Camilla Horn to Be John Barrymore's Leading Lady," *MPW,* 8 Oct 1927, 346. "Camilla Horn in Barrymore Film," *MPW,* 17 Dec 1927, 33. Tony Villecco, "Camilla Horn: The Girl from 'Faust,'" *CI,* 292 (Oct 1999), 9–10 (includes filmography).

Horn, Edward J. [cinematographer] (b. 1881–6 Mar 1937 [56?], Miami FL). BHD2, p. 126.

Hornbeck, William [film editor] (b. Los Angeles CA, 23 Aug 1901–11 Oct 1983 [82], Ventura CA; pancreatic cancer). m. Rosemary (Sennett actress; d. 1979). (Sennett; Korda; Universal; AA, 1951.) "William Hornbeck, 82, Vet Film Editor, Dies of Cancer in Calif.," *Variety,* 19 Oct 1983 (memorabilia at Wesleyan University CT). AS, p. 539. BHD2, p. 126. Katz, p. 577.

Hornblow, Arthur, Jr. [production assistant/stage and film producer] (b. New York NY, 15 Mar 1893–17 Jul 1976 [83], New York NY). m. (1) Juliette Crosby; (2) **Myrna Loy**, 1936–42 (d. 1993); (3) writer Leonora Schinasi. (Goldwyn, 1927; Paramount, 1933; MGM, 1949.) "Arthur Hornblow, Jr.," *Variety,* 283, 21 Jul 1976, 71:1. AMD, p. 170. AS, p. 539. BHD2, p. 126. IFN, p. 146. "Assists Goldwyn," *MPW,* 12 Mar 1927, 85.

Hornbrook, Charles (Gus) [actor] (b. 1874?–8 May 1937 [63], Los Angeles CA; pneumonia). (Metro.) "Charles Hornbrook," *Variety,* 12 May 1937. AS, p. 539. BHD1, p. 268. IFN, p. 146.

Horne, David [actor] (b. Balcombe, England, 14 Jul 1898–15 Mar 1970 [71], London, England). AS, p. 539.

Horne, Edna [actress] (*née* Frankie Ashley, b. 1886–17 Jul 1945 [59?], Culver City CA). AS, p. 539. BHD, p. 204. IFN, p. 146.

Horne, Harold (Hal) [actor] (b. Boston MA, 12 Aug 1896–8 Jun 1955 [58], New York NY). BHD, p. 204; BHD2, p. 126.

Horne, James W. [stage actor/scenarist/director] (nephew of **Georgia Woodthorpe**) (b. San Francisco CA, 14 Dec 1881–29 Jun 1942 [60], Los Angeles CA; cerebral hemorrhage). (Kalem, 1912.) m. **Cleo Ridgely** (d. 1962). (Kalem; Biograph.) "James W. Horne," *NYT,* 30 Jun 1942, 21:2. "James W. Horne," *Variety,* 1 Jul 1942. AMD, p. 170. AS, p. 539 (d. 28 Jun). BHD1, p. 268; BHD2, p. 126. IFN, p. 146. Katz, p. 578 (b. 1880). "New Producing Company," *MPW,* 22 Mar 1913, 1208. "Horne a Product of Stage; Kalem Director Brought Into Limelight by Success of 'Girl from Frisco,'" *MPW,* 7 Oct 1916, 88. "105 Pounds of Director Land 125 Pounds of Tuna," *MPW,* 16 Aug 1919, 978. "James Horne Finishes Another Picture," *MPW,* 17 Nov 1923, 319. Billy H. Doyle, "Lost Players," *CI,* 157 (Jul 1988), 25.

Horne, Pliny W. [cinematographer] (b. CT, 23 May 1891–17 Oct 1966 [75], Los Angeles CA). BHD2, p. 126.

Horne, William T. [actor] (b. Batavia IL, 4 Jun 1869–15 Dec 1942 [73], Los Angeles Co. CA). (Biograph.) AS, p. 540. BHD, p. 204. IFN, p. 146. P.M. Powell, "Doings at Los Angeles," *MPW,* 24 May 1913, 798.

Horner, Louise [actress] (b. 6 Jun 1877–6 Feb 1962 [84], Los Angeles CA). AMD, p. 171. BHD, p. 204. "Louise Horner, New Horsley Player," *MPW,* 9 Jan 1916, 237. "Louise Horner with Horsley," *MPW,* 5 Feb 1916, 781.

Horner, Robert J. [title writer/scenarist] (b. 1910?–4 May 1935 [25], near San Diego CA). (Paramount.) "2 Film Tragedies in 48 Hours; Coogan-Horner-Duncan Auto Fatalities and Plane Crack-Up," *Variety,* 8 May 1935. AMD, p. 171. FDY, pp. 429, 445. "Scenario Writer Elected President," *MPW,* 15 Apr 1916, 412. "Bob Horner to Write for Ebony," *MPW,* 13 Apr 1918, 227.

Hornick, Harry [actor] (b. Charleston SC–d. 7 Feb 1975). BHD, p. 204.

Horniman, Annie Elizabeth Fredericka [actress] (b. London, England, 3 Oct 1860–6 Aug 1937 [76], Surrey, England). "Annie Horniman," *Variety,* 18 Aug 1937. AS, p. 540. SD, p. 629.

Horning, Benjamin [actor] (b. 1853–18 Jan 1936 [82?], Los Angeles CA). AS, p. 540. BHD, p. 204.

Hornung, E[rnest] **W**[illiam] [writer] (b. London, England). AMD, p. 171. "The Author of 'Stingaree,'" *MPW,* 20 Nov 1915, 1471. "The Creator of 'Stingaree,'" *NYDM,* 20 Nov 1915, 34:3 (the first episode of twelve of *Stingaree,* called *An Enemy of Mankind,* to be released on 24 Nov by Kalem, with True Boardman and Paul Hurst). "Studio Gossip," *NYDM,* 20 Nov 1915, 34:4 (Kalem filming *To the Vile Dust,* episode four of *Stingaree,* in the Mojave Desert).

Horsley, David [founder of Centaur, Bayonne NJ, 1907–08; Nestor; Universal, 1912; MinA, 1914/director] (b. West Stanley, England, 11 Mar 1873–23 Feb 1933 [59], Sunland CA). "Pioneer Trust Buster Dies," *Variety,* 28 Feb 1933. AMD, p. 171. AS, p. 540. BHD, p. 204 (b. 1874; d. Los Angeles CA; BHD2, p. 126). IFN, p. 146. Spehr, p. 142. "Manufacturers Balk at Sales Company," *MPW,* 28 May 1910, 893. "Picture Personalities," *MPW,* 2 Jul 1910, 17. "A Chat with David Horsley," *MPW,* 11 May 1912, 511. "Nestor Not Bought by Mutual," *MPW,* 11 May 1912, 534. "David Horsley Back in Universal," *MPW,* 11 Oct 1913, 138. "David Horsley Opens Lumiere Agency," *MPW,* 22 Nov 1913, 878. "Horsley Arrives at Coast Studios," *MPW,* 7 Mar 1914, 1214. "David Horsley to Do One-Reel Comedies," *MPW,* 18 Jul 1914, 417. "Horsley at the Front; Harry Palmer, Cartoonist, Will Picture Events in Europe for Centaur Films," *NYDM,* 2 Sep 1914, 28:3. "David Horsley Announces a New Boy," *MPW,* 3 Oct 1914, 70 (birth of son). "Horsley in Licensed Group," *MPW,* 3 Oct 1914, 71. "Centaur Activities," *MPW,* 10 Oct 1914, 175. "Horsley Wants a Name," *MPW,* 17 Oct 1914, 311. "New Horsley Studio in Los Angeles," *MPW,* 31 Oct 1914, 656. "Horsley Opens Café de Centaur," *MPW,* 21 Nov 1914, 1096. "A Double Exposure Camera," *MPW,* 23 Jan 1915, 493. "Horsley's Animal Arena Formally Opened," *MPW,* 6 Feb 1915, 841. "David Horsley's Big Plans," *MPW,* 13 Mar 1915, 1584. "New Horsley Printer Successful," *MPW,* 20 Mar 1915, 1914d. "Horsley Entertains Picture Men," *MPW,* 17 Apr 1915, 380. George Blaisdell, "Mecca of the Motion Picture," *MPW,* 10 Jul 1915, 215–20. "Important Moves by Mutual," *MPW,* 31 Jul 1915, 797. "Horsley Off of General Program," *MPW,* 4 Aug 1915, 1169. "To Record Photographic Conditions," *MPW,* 6 Nov 1915, 1111. W. Stephen Bush, "Horsley's Animal Features," *MPW,* 11 Dec 1915, 1982–83. "Horsley Talks for Picturemen's Rights," *MPW,* 22 Jan 1916, 613. "Horsley for Congress," *MPW,* 26 Feb 1916, 1279 (from LA). "Horsley Drops in on New York," *MPW,* 1 Apr 1916, 60. "Horsley Roasts Promoters," *MPW,* 15 Apr 1916, 450. "Commuter Horsley in Again, Out Again," *MPW,* 6 Jan 1917, 89. "David Horsley Returns to the Coast," *MPW,* 17 Feb 1917, 1029. "Newcomer in Horsley Family," *MPW,* 24 Feb 1917, 1166 (birth of daughter). David Horsley, "How the First 'Independent' Started," *MPW,* 10 Mar 1917, 1518–19.

Horsley, Wallace [director]. No data found. AMD, p. 171. Wallace Horsley, "Look for Industry to Make Steady Advancement," *MPW,* 31 Dec 1921, 1064.

Horsley, William [producer] (b. Durham, England, 21 Nov 1870–2 Oct 1958 [87], Los Angeles CA). AS, p. 540. BHD2, p. 126.

Horton, Benjamin [actor] (b. 1872–6 Aug 1952 [80?], Los Angeles CA). AS, p. 540.

Horton, Clara, "The Eclair Kid" [actress] (*née* Clara Marie Horton, b. Brooklyn NY, 29 Jul 1904 [Birth Certificate Index No. 25919]–4 Dec 1976 [72], Whittier CA). m. (1) Hyman Brand, 1925; (2) Edwin H. Laufer. (Eclair, 1912; Ideal; Powers; Universal; Bison; Eminent Authors Pictures Corp.; Radio.) AMD, p. 171. AS, p. 540. BHD1, p. 268. IFN, p. 146. MH, p. 118 (b. Jun 1904). Spehr, p. 142. "Clara Horton," *MPW,* 28 Sep 1912, 1268. "Clara Horton," *MPW,* 21 Nov 1914, 1080. "Clara Horton," *MPW,* 5 Jun 1915, 1616. "Suit for Breach of Contract," *MPW,* 23 Nov 1918, 819. "Clara Horton Falls Off Boat," *MPW,* 31 May 1919, 1333. Billy H. Doyle, "Lost Players," *CI,* 168 (Jun 1989), 26, 38.

Horton, Edward Everett, Jr. [stage/film actor/singer) (b. Brooklyn NY, 18 Mar 1886–29 Sep 1970 [84], Encino CA; cancer). (Broadway debut: *The Cheater,* 1910; film debut: *Leave It to Me,* 1920.) "Edward Everett Horton Is Dead; Comic Character Actor Was 83; Star of Stage, Film and TV Played 'Befuddled' Role in a 60-Year Career," *NYT,* 1 Oct 1970, 44:1 (b. 1887). "E.E. Horton Dies in L.A. at 83; Veteran Character Comedian Had Notable Career in Legit, Films, Radio, TV," *Variety,* 7 Oct 1970. AMD, p. 171. AS, p. 540. BHD1, p. 268 (b. 1887). FSS, p. 149. IFN, p. 146. Katz, pp. 578–79. Truitt, p. 159. "Horton to Play on Orpheum," *MPW,* 6 Oct 1923, 504. Thomas Tarrington, "What Will the Screen Stars in Hollywood Do Now?; Recent shut-down of Famous Players' studio forces many actors out of work—Query is raised concerning their future source of livelihood," *MW,* 8 Dec 1923, 8–9, 28. "Edward Everett Horton," *MPW,* 2 Apr 1927, 486. "Clever Female Impersonator," *MPW,* 9 Apr 1927, 549:3 (making two-reelers produced by Harold Lloyd. "While he does not make the striking figure of a Julian Eltinge, he does succeed in getting plenty of laughs even from the electricians and other case-hardened individuals that [sic] have become blase through constant association with picture making."). Dorothy Spensley, "Horton Is Horton; He's the Stage Actor Who Throws Film Stars Completely Off Their Orbits," *MPC,* May 1929, 22, 80–81. Kyle Crichton, "Comedy—Six Days a Week," *Collier's,* 18 Jul 1936. Bernard Rosenberg and Harry Silverstein, eds., *The Real Tinsel* (1970). G.F. Goodwin, *DAB,* Supp. 8 (1988), pp. 283–84 (named after Edward Everett, orator and politician, who spoke at Gettysburg with Lincoln; estate: Belleigh Acres in the San Fernando Valley).

Horton, Marvin Perry [assistant director] (b. Peekskill NY, 13 Oct 1889). BHD2, p. 126.

Horwitz, Joseph [actor] (b. 1858?–25 Oct 1922 [64], Mt. Clemens MI; uremia). "Joseph Horwitz," *Variety,* 27 Oct 1922. AS, p. 540. BHD, p. 204.

Horwood, Robert [scenarist]. No data found. FDY, p. 429.

Hosch, Eduard [director] (b. Vienna, Austria, 1890–1983 [93?], Vienna, Austria). AS, p. 540.

Hosford, Maude [actress] (b. 1864–14 Oct 1935 [71?], Corinth VT). BHD, p. 204.

Hoskins, Alan Clay, Jr. *See* Farina.

Hosmer, May [actress]. No data found. m. **Francis Boggs** (d. 1911). AMD, p. 171. "Pictures of Real Western Life Coming," *MPW,* 27 Jun 1908, 541.

Hostetter, Roy [actor] (b. 1885?–22 Sep 1951 [66], near Carlsbad CA; auto accident). "Roy Hostetter," *Variety,* 3 Oct 1951. AS, p. 540. IFN, p. 146.

Hotaling, Arthur Douglas [(Fred) Mace & Douglas; actor/director/producer] (b. Albany NY, 3 Feb 1873–13 Jul 1938 [65], enroute to San Pedro CA). m. **Mae Hotely** (d. 1954; daughter, Leola May). (Lubin.) "Arthur D. Hotaling," *Variety,* 20 Jul 1938. AMD, p. 171. AS, pp. 540–41. BHD1, p. 269; BHD2, p. 127 (d. Palm Springs CA). IFN, p. 146. Truitt, p. 160. "Ziz—It's Hotaling!," *MPW,* 16 Sep 1911, 780. "Rip Van Hotaling," *MPW,* 23 Dec 1911, 978. "A Lubin Foreign Section," *MPW,* 1 Jun 1912, 808. "In the Field with Hotaling," *MPW,* 11 Jan 1913, 139–40. "Holtaling's New Company," *MPW,* 19 Jul 1913, 308. "Lubin Forms a New Company," *MPW,* 18 Apr 1914, 372. "Arthur D. Hotaling," *MPW,* 12 Dec 1914, 1541. "Arthur Hotaling Recalls the 'Good Old Days,'" *MPW,* 15 Jul 1916, 380–81. "Hotaling's 700th Comedy," *MPW,* 2 Feb 1918, 700. "Hotaling Director in L-KO Comedy," *MPW,* 8 Jun 1918, 1411.

Hotaling, Frank [actor/art director] (b. 4 Jul 1900–13 Apr 1977 [76], Woodland Hills CA). (Draftsman, 1923; art director, 1944; Republic.) "Frank Hotaling," *Variety,* 286, 20 Apr 1977, 126:3. AS, p. 541. BHD1, p. 269; BHD2, p. 127. IFN, p. 146.

Hotely, Mae [actress] (b. MD, 7 Oct 1872–6 Apr 1954 [81], Coronado CA). (Began 1900 or earlier; Lubin.) m. **Arthur Hotaling** (daughter, Leola May, d. 1938). (Lubin, 1909.) AMD, p. 172. AS, p. 541. BHD, pp. 39–40; 204. IFN, p. 146. "Mae Hotely," *MPW,* 13 Jan 1912, 111. "Going in for Racing," *MPW,* 14 Dec 1912, 1062. "Mae Hotely's New Boots," *MPW,* 31 Jul 1915, 815. "Mae Hotely; Lubin Comedienne Takes a Vacation for the First Time in Four Years," *MPW,* 20 Nov 1915, 1483:1. Billy H. Doyle, "Lost Players," *CI,* 141 (Mar 1987), 31, C10, 45.

Houdini, Harry [magician/actor] (*né* Ehrich Weiss, b. Budapest, Hungary, 6 Apr 1872?–31 Oct 1926 [54?], Detroit MI; peritonitis). m. Wilhelmina Beatrice Rahner. "Harry Houdini Dies After Operations; Magician, Conscious to Last, Loses Fight for Life in Detroit Hospital; Death Due to Poisoning; Playful Blow Given by Montreal Student as Test Caused Appendix to Break," *NYT,* 1 Nov 1926, 1:2, 6:2. "Harry Houdini," *Variety,* 3 Nov 1926 (age 54). AMD, p. 172. AS, p. 541 (b. 24 Mar 1874). BHD, p. 204 (b. 24 Mar 1874); BHD2, p. 127 (b. 24 Mar 1974). IFN, p. 146 (b. 24 Mar 1874). Katz, p. 579. SD. "Houdini for Pictures," *MPW,* 28 Apr 1917, 622. "Unprecedented Opening for Houdini Serial in New York," *MPW,* 25 Jan 1919, 520. "Arrange for Houdini to Make Own-Story Features," *MPW,* 8 Mar 1919, 1311. "Harry Houdini Signed by Famous Players-Lasky," *MPW,* 22 Mar 1919, 1606. "Houdini Will Start Work on Paramount Film May 1," *MPW,* 19 Apr 1919, 366. "Houdini Signs New Contract with Famous Players-Lasky," *MPW,* 13 Sep 1919, 1667. "Houdini Forms Own Company, Will Make Four Features a Year," *MPW,* 12 Mar 1921, 181. "Houdini-Octagon Suit Postponed to June 1," *MPW,* 13 May 1922, 158. "Houdini Wins Suit," *MPW,* 27 May 1922, 376 ($32,795.18 profit from *Master Mystery,* 1919). Eugene Pinetti, "Houdini Denounces Spirit Motion Pictures," *MM,* May 1926, 25–26, 114–16. "Houdini Alleges Money Is Due; Brings Suit," *MPW,* 9 Oct 1926, 4. "Obituary," *MPW,* 13 Nov 1926, 71 (b. 1874). Epes Winthrip Sargent, "Houdini—The Great Mystifier, Most Picturesque Figure of the Show World," *MPW,* 13 Nov 1926, 71, 105. Truitt, p. 160. Jack R. White, "Houdini and His Movies," *CFC,* 29 (Winter, 1970), 46–47. William J. Burgess, "The Films of Harry Houdini," *CI,* 104 (Feb 1984), 61.

Hough, Emerson [writer] (b. Newton IA, 1856–30 Apr 1923 [67?], Evanston IL). AMD, p. 172. BHD2, p. 127. "Author of 'The Broken Coin,'" *MPW,* 12 Jun 1915, 1753. "Obituary," *MPW,* 12 May 1923, 116.

Hough, Horace S. [assistant director/production manager] (b. 1891?–19 Aug 1965 [74], Los Angeles CA; heart ailment). m. Loretta Rush. (Universal, 1913; Metro; Fox; Paramount.) "Horace S. Hough," *Variety,* 25 Aug 1965. AS, p. 541. BHD2, p. 127.

Houghton, Alice [actress] (b. Offalan MO, 14 Jun 1887–12 May 1944 [56], Los Angeles CA). m. **Tod Browning**. "Mrs. Tod Browning," *NYT,* 14 May 1944, 46:1. "Mrs. Tod Browning," *Variety,* 17 May 1944. AS, p. 541. IFN, p. 147.

Houghton, Edward [actor/producer] (b. Quebec City, Quebec, Canada, 1867–20 May 1956 [89?], Niagara Falls NY). BHD2, p. 127.

Houry, Henri [director]. No data found. AMD, p. 172. "Henry Houry Finishes Bushman-Bayne Picture," *MPW,* 1 Feb 1919, 613.

House, Billy [actor] (b. MN, 7 May 1890–23 Sep 1961 [71], Los Angeles CA). AS, p. 541.

House, Chandler [actor/film editor/cinematographer] (b. CO, 26 Jan 1904–17 Mar 1982 [78], Westminster CA). BHD, p. 204; BHD2, p. 127. FDY, p. 459.

House, Jack [stuntman/actor] (b. TX, 18 Feb 1887–20 Nov 1963 [76], Los Angeles CA). AS, p. 541. BHD, p. 204. IFN, p. 147.

House, Newton [actor] (b. TX, 10 Jan 1865–16 Dec 1948 [83]). AS, p. 541. IFN, p. 147.

House, Newton [actor] (*né* Charles Newton House, b. Holly CO, 1 Nov 1911–23 Jul 1987 [75], Colton CA). AS, p. 541. BHD1, p. 269. Luther Hancock, "Newton House [obituary]," *CI,* 149 (Nov 1987), 60–61.

Housman, Arthur [actor] (b. New York NY, 10 Oct 1889–8 Apr 1942 [52], Los Angeles CA; pneumonia). (Edison.) "Arthur Houseman," *Variety,* 15 Apr 1942. AMD, p. 172. AS, p. 541. BHD1, p. 269. IFN, p. 147. Truitt, p. 160. "Arthur Housman, Gloom Dispeller," *MPW,* 13 Feb 1915, 988. "Housman with Lubin," *MPW,* 27 Nov 1915, 1637.

Houston, Billie (b. Scotland, 1906–30 Sep 1972 [66?], Walton-on-Thames, England). BHD1, p. 269.

Houston, George F. [actor] (b. Hampton NJ, 11 Jan 1896–12 Nov 1944 [48], Los Angeles CA). AS, p. 541.

Houston, Norman Francis [scenarist] (b. Denison TX, 1900). AS, p. 541.

Houston, Renee [actress] (*née* Katherina Houston Gribbin, b. Johnstone, Scotland, 24 Jul 1902–9 Feb 1980 [77], London, England). AS, p. 541. BHD1, p. 269. IFN, p. 147.

Hovenden, Valery [actress] (b. Barnes, England, 7 Apr 1902–1 Dec 1992 [90], London, England). BHD1, p. 269.

Hovey, Carl [scenarist/film editor] (b. 1876–25 Jun 1956 [80?], Los Angeles CA). BHD2, p. 127.

Hovey, Sonya [scenarist]. No data found. FDY, p. 429.

Howard, Arthur [actor] (b. MA, 1 Jan 1887–28 May 1963 [76], Los Angeles CA; coronary thrombosis). m. Naomi. "Art Howard," *Variety,* 5 Jun 1963 (age 71). AS, p. 542. IFN, p. 147.

Howard, Arthur B. [actor] (b. 1857-May 1928 [71?], Ware MA). BHD, p. 204.

Howard, Bert [actor] (b. Salmon Falls NH, 7 Aug 1873?–27 Oct 1958 [85], Los Angeles CA). "Bert Howard," *Variety,* 5 Nov 1958. AS, p. 542. BHD, p. 204 (b. 1878). IFN, p. 147 (age 80).

Howard, Blanche [actress] (d. 8 Jun 1932, Astoria, LI NY). m. John Seymour. "Blanche Howard," *Variety,* 14 Jun 1932.

Howard, Booth [actor] (b. Hammond WI, 2 Oct 1889–4 Oct 1936 [47], Los Angeles CA; run down by auto). "Booth Howard," *Variety,* 7 Oct 1936. AS, p. 542. BHD1, p. 269. IFN, p. 147.

Howard, Charles Ray [vaudeville/burlesque/stage/film actor] (b. San Diego CA, 1882–28 Jun 1947 [65], New York NY; heart attack in drawing room of Shubert Theatre). "Charles Ray Howard," *Variety,* 167, 2 Jul 1947, 55:2. AS, p. 542. BHD1, p. 270. IFN, p. 147.

Howard, Clifford [author/scenarist] (b. Bethlehem PA, 12 Oct 1868–19 May 1942 [73], Los Angeles CA). (First scenario: *The Woman in the Case,* 500 feet [split reel], Vitagraph, 1908, receiving $10 for it; Balboa; American.) "Clifford Howard," *Variety,* 27 May 1942. BHD2, p. 127. WWWA. Edward Azlant, "Screenwriting for the early silent film: forgotten pioneers, 1897–1911," *Film History,* 9 (1997), 239.

Howard, Constance (sister of **Frances Howard**) [actress] (b. Chicago IL, 4 Oct 1906–5 Dec 1980 [74], Los Angeles CA). AMD, p. 172. AS, p. 542 (d. 7 Dec). BHD1, p. 270 (b. Omaha NE; d. San Diego CA). Ragan 2, p. 777. "Constance Howard Gets Featured Role," *MPW,* 30 Oct 1926, 547.

Howard, David [actor/director] (*né* David Paget Davis III, b. Philadelphia PA, 6 Oct 1896–21 Dec 1941 [45], Los Angeles CA; heart attack). "David Howard," *Variety,* 24 Dec 1941. AS, p. 542 (d. 22 Dec). BHD, p. 204; BHD2, p. 127. IFN, p. 147.

Howard, David H. [actor] (b. New York NY, 1860?–9 Dec 1944 [84], Woodland Hills CA). "David H. Howard," *Variety*, 20 Dec 1944. AS, p. 542. BHD1, p. 270 (d. 20 Dec).

Howard, Ernest [actor] (*né* Ernest Ladd, b. Falls Village CT, 1875?–8 Nov 1940 [65?], Brooklyn NY). "Ernest Howard," *Variety*, 13 Nov 1940 ("film player during the early silent days"). AS, p. 542. BHD, p. 205. Truitt, p. 160.

Howard, Eugene (brother of **Willie Howard**) [actor] (*né* Isidore Levkowitz, b. Prudnik, Poland, 7 Jul 1881–1 Aug 1965 [84], New York NY). AS, p. 542 (b. Neustadt, Germany). BHD1, p. 270.

Howard, Florence [actress] (b. 1888?–11 Aug 1954 [66], Beverly Hills CA). m. Finis W. Henderson. "Florence Howard," *Variety*, 18 Aug 1954. AS, p. 542. IFN, p. 147.

Howard, Frances (sister of **Constance Howard**) [actress] (*né* Frances McLaughlin, b. Kansas City KS, 4 Jun 1903–2 Jul 1976 [73], Beverly Hills CA). m. **Samuel Goldwyn** (d. 1974). "Frances Howard Goldwyn," *Variety*, 7 Jul 1976. AMD, p. 172. AS, p. 542. BHD, p. 205 (b. Omaha NE); BHD2, p. 542. IFN, p. 147. SD. Alma Talley, "She Became a Princess Overnight," *MW*, 22 Nov 1924, 15–16. "Frances Howard Opposite Dix," *MPW*, 13 Dec 1924, 648. Faith Service, "That Whirlwind Romance of Frances Howard and SAM Goldwyn," *MW*, 23 May 1925, 4–5, 31. "Frances Howard," *MPW*, 30 May 1925, 579. "Makes His Bow," *MPW*, 25 Sep 1926, 1 (Samuel Goldwyn, Jr., b. 7 Sep 1926, LA CA).

Howard, George [actor] (b. 1866?–17 Mar 1921 [55], Vancouver, Canada). "George Howard," *Variety*, 25 Mar 1921. AS, p. 542.

Howard, George Bronson [playwright/scenarist/director] (b. "The Relay," Howard County MD, 7 Jan 1884–20 Nov 1922 [38], Los Angeles CA; suicide by inhaling gas through a tube). m. (1) Doss Skinner; (2) Margaret Sackville; (3) Jean. "George Bronson Howard," *Variety*, 24 Nov 1922. AMD, p. 172. BHD2, p. 127. SD, p. 633. WWWA. "New Kalem Series," *MPW*, 1 Jan 1916, 53. "George Bronson Howard Joins Lasky Company," *MPW*, 8 Jan 1916, 248. "The Screen and the Novelist," *MPW*, 26 Feb 1916, 1277. "Bronson Howard an Actor," *MPW*, 22 Apr 1916, 629. "Universal to Produce Howard's Works," *MPW*, 2 Dec 1916, 1308. "Fox Engages George Bronson Howard," *MPW*, 28 Apr 1917, 600. "New Scenarist," *MPW*, 26 Aug 1922, 668. "Obituary," *MPW*, 2 Dec 1922, 408. "Mrs. George Bronson Howard to Sell Playwright's Stories," *MPW*, 29 Aug 1925, 945.

Howard, George W. [actor] (b. Philadelphia PA, 1873?–25 Aug 1928 [55], New York NY; septic poisoning following leg amputation). "George W. Howard," *Variety*, 5 Sep 1928. AMD, p. 172. AS, p. 542 (d. LA CA). BHD, p. 205. IFN, p. 147. "George W. Howard," *MPW*, 22 May 1915, 1270.

Howard, Gertrude [actress] (b. Hot Springs AR, 13 Oct 1892–30 Sep 1934 [41], Los Angeles CA). "Gertrude Howard," *Variety*, 9 Oct 1934. AS, p. 542 (b. 2 Oct). BHD1, p. 270 (b. 2 Oct 1893). IFN, p. 147 (b. 2 Oct 1893). Truitt, p. 160.

Howard, Harold [stage/film actor] (*né* David Harold Howard, b. Rutland NY, 22 Aug 1870–9 Dec 1944 [74], Woodland Hills CA). (Kleine; Selig; Lasky.) AS, p. 542. BHD1, p. 270. IFN, p. 147. SD.

Howard, Helen [actress] (b. Colorado Springs CO, 2 May 1903–14 Mar 1927 [24], Los Angeles CA; accidental fall). (American.) AMD, p. 172. AS, p. 542 (d. 13 Mar). BHD, p. 205. IFN, p. 147. Truitt, 1983. "National Engages Helen Howard," *MPW*, 27 Mar 1920, 2142.

Howard, Joe E[dgar] [stage/film actor/composer] (*né* Joseph E. Dooley, b. New York NY, 12 Feb 1878–19 May 1961 [83], Chicago IL). m. Ida Emerson. m. (1) Margaret Clark; (2) Mabel Barrison (*née* Eva Farrance, d. 1912); (3) Irma Kilgallen. "Joe E. Howard, 83, Dies on Chi Stage," *Variety*, 24 May 1961 (wrote *Hello, My Baby*). AS, p. 542. ASCAP 66, p. 348. CEPMJ; Kindle (b. 1878). SD, p. 634 (b. Bellivere IL, 1867/68).

Howard, Leslie (brother of Arthur Howard, 1910–1995, and Ronald Howard, 1918–1996) [stage/film actor/director/producer] (*né* Leslie H. Stainer, b. Sydeham, England, 3 Apr 1893 [extrait de naissance no. 310/1893]–1 Jun 1943 [50], plane disappeared over Bay of Biscay?). m. Ruth Evelyn Martin. "Howard Won Fame in Romantic Roles; Peak of His Art Achieved in 'Petrified Forest' and 'Of Human Bondage'; His Manager Also Lost," *NYT*, 3 Jun 1943, 4:1 (b. 3 Apr); "No Trace Is Found of Howard's Plane; Spanish Destroyer Searches Bay of Biscay for Airliner Shot Down by Germans," 4 Jun, 4:3. "Priestley in BBC Howard Tribute"; "Little Hope Left; Hope Wanes for Howard; 12 Others in Lost Plane," *Variety*, 9 Jun 1943. AS, p. 543. BHD1, p. 270; BHD2, p. 127 (b. 3 Apr). IFN, p. 147. Katz, pp. 580–81 (began in England, 1917). SD. Waldman, p. 139. Whitney Williams, "Pals; Though their tastes are widely different, there is a strong tie that binds Leslie Howard and William Gargan to one of the finest friendships in Hollywood," *The New Movie Magazine*, Oct 1934, 43, 89–90.

Howard, May [actress] (b. 1870?–1 Feb 1935 [65], Los Angeles CA; heart attack). m. Henry Morris. "May Howard," *Variety*, 5 Feb 1935. AS, p. 543. BHD, p. 205. IFN, p. 147.

Howard, Moe [stage/film actor: The Three Stooges] (*né* Moses Harry Horowitz, b. Brooklyn NY, 19 Jun 1893–4 May 1975 [81], Hollywood CA; lung cancer). m. Helen. (Vitagraph.) AS, p. 543. BHD1, p. 270 (b. 1897). IFN, p. 147. SD. Truitt, 1983.

Howard, Norah [actress] (b. London, England, 12 Dec 1901–2 May 1968 [66], New York NY). BHD1, p. 271. IFN, p. 147.

Howard, Paula [actress]. No data found. AMD, p. 172. "Once an Extra, Paula Howard Now Featured," *MPW*, 29 Jan 1927, 345. "Paula Howard," *MPW*, 19 Mar 1927, 177. "Champion 'Extra' Publicity Gleaner," *MPW*, 14 May 1927, 98.

Howard, Peter [actor] (b. Knocklong, Ireland, 26 Jun 1878–14 Mar 1969 [91], Los Angeles CA). AS, p. 543. BHD, p. 205. IFN, p. 147. Truitt, p. 161.

Howard, Richard [vaudevillian/songwriter] (b. 1890?–Dec? 1981 [91], Brentwood NH). "Richard Howard," *Variety*, 30 Dec 1981 (wrote *Somebody Else Is Taking My Place*).

Howard, Ruth [actress] (b. 1894–28 Dec 1944 [50?], Los Angeles CA). AS, p. 543.

Howard, Sam [actor] (b. 1903?–20 Apr 1964 [61], Los Angeles CA; heart attack). "Sam Howard," *Variety*, 29 Apr 1964. AS, p. 543.

Howard, Sidney [scenarist] (b. Oakland CA, 26 Jun 1891–23 Aug 1939 [48], Tyringham MA). AS, p. 543. BHD2, p.1 27.

Howard, Sydney [actor] (b. Yeadon, England, 7 Aug 1885–12 Jun 1946 [60], London, England). AS, p. 543. BHD1, p. 271.

Howard, Tom [actor] (County Tyrone, Ireland, 16 Jun 1885–27 Feb 1955 [69], Long Branch NJ). AS, p. 543.

Howard, Vincent[e] [actor] (b. Los Angeles CA, 19 Jul 1869–2 Nov 1946 [77], Los Angeles Co. CA). (Began ca. 1913.) AMD, p. 172. AS, p. 543. BHD, p. 205. IFN, p. 148. "Vitagraph President Aids in Rescuing Daredevil Actor Torn by Savage Bear," *MPW*, 10 Apr 1920, 297. "Vincent Howard, Vitagraph Daredevil, Is Recovering," *MPW*, 17 Apr 1920, 441. George Katchmer, "Remembering the Great Silents," *CI*, 241 (Jul 1995), 36.

Howard, Violet [midget actress]. No data found. m. (1) Tom Thumb; (2) **Count Primo Magri** (d. 1920). (Headline Amusement Co.) "First Headline Comedy [*Pee-Wee's Courtship*]," *NYDM*, 23 Jun 1915, 21:2.

Howard, Walter [dramatist/actor-manager] (b. Leamington Spa, England, 7 Mar 1866–6 Oct 1922 [56], London, England; after a severe operation). "Walter Howard," *Variety*, LXVIII, 3 Nov 1922, 40:3 ("During his lifetime he has served 10 years as a soldier, been a sailor, a lighterman and a cowboy."). BHD, p. 205.

Howard, Warda [stage/film actress] (b. San Francisco CA, 1880?–17 Mar 1943 [63], New York NY). m. Leo Kennedy (d. 1939). "Warda Howard Kennedy," *Variety*, 24 Mar 1943. AMD, p. 173. AS, p. 543. BHD, p. 205. IFN, p. 148. "Miss Warda Howard," *NYDM*, 13 May 1914, 12:2. "Warda Howard," *MPW*, 28 Aug 1915, 1486. "Warda Howard," *MPW*, 25 Dec 1915, 2333.

Howard, William [actor] (b. Germany, 1883?–23 Jan 1944 [60], Los Angeles CA). "William Howard," *Variety*, 2 Feb 1944. AS, p. 543. BHD, p. 205. IFN, p. 148.

Howard, William K[errigan] [director/film editor/scenarist/actor] (b. St. Mary's OH, 16 Jun 1899–21 Feb 1954 [54], Los Angeles CA; throat cancer). m. (1) Nan—div. (Vitagraph; Fox; Metro; TC-F; WB; Para.; UA; Republic.) "William K. Howard," *Variety*, 24 Feb 1954 (began 1924). AMD, p. 173. AS, p. 543. BHD2, p. 128. IFN, p. 148. Katz, p. 582. "F.P.L. Signs Howard," *MPW*, 19 Jul 1924, 205. "Signs Five-Year Contract," *MPW*, 30 May 1925, 566. "Howard Signs to Direct for Cecil BN. DeMille," *MPW*, 19 Dec 1925, 660. "William K. Howard Edits 'White Gold,'" *MPW*, 29 Jan 1927, 357. "DeMille's 'White Gold' Is Hailed as Picture That 'Made' Director," *MPW*, 5 Mar 1927, 25, 30. "William K. Howard," *MPW*, 5 Mar 1927, 27. "A Director's Tribute to an Actor," *MPW*, 5 Mar 1927, 29. "Resignation Denied," *MPW*, 15 Oct 1927, 432. Herbert J. Cruikshank, "Conscience Doth Make Howards; At Last It Has Converted One—William K.—from High-Pressure Salesman into White-Haired Boy," *MPC*, Jul 1928, 21, 72.

Howard, Willie (brother of **Eugene Howard**) (*né* William Levkowitz, b. Prudnik, Poland, 13 Apr 1886–12 Jan 1949 [62], New York NY). AS, p. 543 (b. Neustadt, Germany; d. 14 Jan). BHD1, p. 271.

Howarth, Jack [actor] (b. Rochdale, England, 19 Feb 1896–31 Mar 1984 [88], Llandudno, Netherlands). AS, p. 543.

Howe, Ann [actress]. No data found. AMD, p. 173. "Ann Howe, New Screen Personality," *MPW,* 28 Aug 1926, 547.

Howe, Betty [actress] (b. New York NY, 23 May 1895–21 Jun 1969 [74], New York NY). AMD, p. 173. BHD, p. 205. "Vitagraph Adds Betty Howe to Roster of Stock Players," *MPN,* 11 Mar 1916, 1464:1. "Betty Howe, Latest Vitagrapher," *MPW,* 18 Mar 1916, 1834. "Betty Howe Recovering from Appendicitis," *MPW,* 17 Feb 1917, 1018. "Betty Howe Under Knife," *MPW,* 14 Sep 1918, 1561.

Howe, Edward J. [actor] (b. 1874?–23 Aug 1927 [53], New York NY; appendicitis). m. Diana Lee. "Edward J. Howe," *Variety,* 31 Aug 1927. AS, p. 544.

Howe, Eilot C. [director] (b. Boston MA, 23 Dec 1886–18 Dec 1921 [34], Los Angeles CA). AS, p. 544 (d. NY NY). BHD2, p. 128. IFN, p. 148.

Howe, Florence [actress]. No data found. m. **Fred Jackson**, 6 Jun 1915, Bayside, LI NY (d. 1953). (Vitagraph.) "Fred Jackson Marries; Author of 'A Full House' Weds Florence Howe, Motion Picture Actress," *NYDM,* 9 Jun 1915, 7:2.

Howe, Jay A. [director]. No data found. AMD, p. 173. "Big V Comedies to Star Aubrey," *MPW,* 11 Jan 1919, 240.

Howe, James Wong [cinematographer] (*né* Wong Tung Jim, b. Kwangtung [Canton], China, 28 Aug 1899–12 Jul 1976 [76], West Hollywood CA). m. Samora Babb. Robert Hanley, "James Wong Howe Dies; Noted Cinematographer," *NYT,* 16 Jul 1976, IV, 17:1. "James Wong Howe, Camera Wiz, Dies," *Variety,* 21 Jul 1976. AS, p. 544. BHD2, p. 128 (b. LA CA). FDY, p. 459. IFN, p. 148. Katz, p. 582. SD.

Howe, Lyman H[akes] [producer/exhibitor] (b. Wilkes-Barre PA, 9 Jun 1856–30 Jan 1923 [66], Brookline MA). *Lyman H. Howe's High Class Moving Pictures* [documentary], 1983. Charles Musser, *High-Class Moving Pictures: Lyman H. Howe and the Forgotten Era of Traveling Exhibition, 1880–1920* (Princeton Univ. Press, 1991). "Lyman H. Howe Dead," *Variety,* 1 Feb 1923. AS, p. 544 (d. 1926). BHD2, p. 128. WWVC, pp. 68–69. Joe Collura, "Howe Film Fascinating," *CI,* 102 (Dec 1983), 26.

Howe, Walter J[oseph] [actor] (b. London, England, 1856–9 Jan 1929 [72?], East Moriches NY). AS, p. 544.

Howe, Walter L. [actor/publicist/executive] (b. London, England, 12 Apr 1879–31 Jul 1957 [78], Toronto, Canada). m. actress Muriel Dean. "Walter L. Howe," *Variety,* 207, 7 Aug 1957, 63:1. BHD1, p. 271.

Howell, Albert S. [inventor] (b. 1879–3 Jan 1951 [71?], Chicago IL). AS, p. 544.

Howell, Alice [actress] (*née* Alice Clark, b. New York NY, 5 May 1888–12 Apr 1961 [72], Los Angeles CA). m. Richard Smith (d. 1937). (Sennett; L-KO.) AMD, p. 173. AS, p. 544. BHD, p. 205. IFN, p. 148. MH, p. 118. Slide, *Aspects,* p. 13. "Alice Howell in New Comedies," *MPW,* 19 May 1917, 1135. "Alice Howell Ascending Comedy Star," *MPW,* 23 Jun 1917, 1960. "Alice Howell," *MPW,* 29 Sep 1917, 1994. "Alice Howell Without Make-Up," *MPW,* 15 Dec 1917, 1625. "Alice Howell," *MPW,* 2 Mar 1918, 1215.

Howell, Dorothy [scenarist/assistant production manager]. No data found. AMD, p. 173. FDY, p. 429. "Miss Dorothy Howell Assistant Prod. Manager," *MPW,* 3 Apr 1926, 326.

Howell, Helen Edith [actress] (b. IL-d. ca. 1960). m. (1) **George Barnes**; (2) Ben Reynolds; (3) **Frank Capra**, 29 Nov 1923, San Francisco CA. Joseph McBride, *Frank Capra; The Catastrophe of Success* (NY: Simon & Schuster, 1992), pp. 134 *et passim.*

Howell, Lottice [actress] (b. Bowling Green KY, 14 Nov 1897–24 Oct 1982 [84], Greensboro AL). "Lottice Howell," *Variety,* 10 Nov 1982 ("silent film leading lady"). AS, p. 544. BHD1, p. 271.

Howell, Maude [scenarist/director] (b. 1887–24 Oct 1964 [77?], New Orleans LA). BHD2, p. 128.

Howell, William A. [actor/producer]. No data found. Related to Helen Edith Howell.

Howes, Bobby [actor] (b. London, England, 4 Aug 1895–27 Apr 1972 [76], London, England). AS, p. 544. BHD1, p. 271.

Howes, Reed, "Arrow Collar Man" [model/actor] (*né* Herman Reed Howe, b. Washington DC, 5 Jul 1900–6 Aug 1964 [64], Woodland Hills CA). AS, p. 544. BHD1, p. 271. FSS, p. 149. IFN, p. 148. Katz, pp. 582–83. Truitt, 1983. George Katchmer, "Remembering the Great Silents," *CI,* 246 (Dec 1995), 45–46.

Howey, Walter C. [scenarist] (b. 1881–21 Mar 1954 [73?], Boston MA). BHD2, p. 128.

Howland, Eugene [assistant director]. No data found. AMD, p. 173. "Eugene Howland Joins Metro," *MPW,* 27 May 1916, 1498.

Howland, Harry [scenarist] (b. 15 Nov 1933). BHD2, p. 128.

Howland, Jobyna (sister of **Olin Howlin**) [stage/film actress] (b. Indianapolis IN, 31 Mar 1880–7 Jun 1936 [56], Los Angeles CA; heart attack). m. **Arthur Stringer, 1900**—div. "Jobyna Howland," *Variety,* 10 Jun 1936. AMD, p. 173. AS, p. 544. BHD1, p. 271. IFN, p. 148. Truitt, p. 162. "Jobyna Howland Plays with Norma Talmadge," *MPW,* 20 Jul 1918, 411. "It's Miss Howland," *MPW,* 30 Jun 1923, 775.

Howland, Louis A. [actor/assistant director] (b. Chicago IL, 1889?–9 Aug 1931 [42], Los Angeles CA). "Louis A. Howland," *Variety,* 11 Aug 1931. AS, p. 544. BHD2, p. 128 (b. 1886).

Howland, Phillip [actor]. No data found. AMD, p. 173. "Phillip Howland Now Film Actor," *MPW,* 16 Jul 1921, 332.

Howley, Irene [actress]. No data found. AMD, p. 173. "Irene Howley in 'The Purple Lady,'" *MPW,* 10 Jun 1916, 1858. "Irene Howley," *MPW,* 20 Jan 1917, 377.

Howlin, Olin [actor] (*né* Olin Howland; brother of **Jobyna Howland**) (b. Denver CO, 10 Feb 1886–19 Sep 1959 [73], Los Angeles CA). "Olin Howlin," *Variety,* 23 Sep 1959 (age 63; began 1934). AS, p. 544 (b. 1896). BHD1, p. 272. IFN, p. 148. Truitt, p. 162 (b. 1896).

Howson, Albert Sydney [actor] (b. Brooklyn NY, 3 Feb 1881–2 Aug 1960 [79], Forest Hills NY). (WB.) "Albert Sydney Howson," *Variety,* 10 Aug 1960. AS, p. 544. BHD, p. 205; BHD2, p. 128. Truitt, 1983.

Hoxie, Al[ton] (brother of **Jack Hoxie**) [actor] (b. Nez Perce ID, 7 Oct 1901–6 Apr 1982 [80], Fontana [Redlands] CA). m. (1) Marie Nutsch; (2) Merlene Hull; (3) Marie Goss Wyman. Edgar Wyatt, *The Hoxie Boys.* "Al Hoxie," *Variety,* 26 May 1982. (Film debut: bit part in *Kentucky Colonel,* ca. 1919.) AS, p. 544. BHD1, p. 272 (b. Lewis County ID). Buck Rainey, "Al Hoxie and His Cow-Dung Westerns," *Filmograph,* IV, No. 1 (1973), 22–23, 26–323 (includes filmography). George Katchmer, "Remembering the Great Silents," *CI,* 224 (Feb 1994), 54:1 (b. Lewis County OK).

Hoxie, Edna Pearl (daughter of **Jack Hoxie**) [child actress] (b. 8 Nov 1910–1996 [85], Phoenix AZ; massive stroke). m. Zachary Taylor Maloby, 1931 (2 daughters)—div. 1951. Harris Lentz, III, and Ed Wyatt, "Edna Pearl Hoxie [obituary]," *CI,* 268 (Oct 1997), 56–57 (her grandson, John A. Green of Littlerock CA, said that his grandmother went out in style: "unconscious from a massive stroke, the ambulance gets knocked on its side on the way to the hospital.").

Hoxie, Jack (brother of **Al Hoxie**; father of **Edna Pearl Hoxie**) [stuntman/actor/director] (aka Hart Hoxie, *né* John F. [or Jack] Stone, b. Kingfisher [Guthrie] OK, 11 Jan 1885–28 Mar 1965 [80], Elkhart KS). m. Hazel Panky; **Marin Sais**, 1921 (d. 1971). Tom Trusky, *Retold in the Hills* (Boise ID: Boise State University, 1990). (Began 1912; Pathé.) Edgar M. Wyatt, *The Hoxie Boys; The Lives and Films of Jack and Al Hoxie* (Raleigh NC: Wyatt Classics, Inc., 1992). AMD, p. 173. AS, p. 544 (b. 24 Jan; d. Keyes OK). BHD1, p. 272 (b. Kingfish Creek OK). FSS, p. 150. GK, pp. 419–30. IFN, p. 148. Katz, 583. MH, p. 118. Truitt, p. 162 (b. 1890; d. Keyes OK). "Hoxie and O'Dell with Universal," *MPW,* 13 Oct 1917, 217. "Hoxie to Be a Director," *MPW,* 31 Jan 1920, 735. "Hoxie to Remain with National," *MPW,* 6 Mar 1920, 1640. "National Film Corporation Will Star Jack Hoxie in Five Reel Western Films," *MPW,* 22 May 1920, 1079. "Arrow Announces New Series of Eight Films Starring Jack Hoxie," *MPW,* 18 Jun 1921, 724. "Hoxie Continues Triumphal Tour," *MPW,* 23 Jul 1921, 419. "Jack Hoxie Is Guest of Honor at Dinner," *MPW,* 20 Aug 1921, 790. "Surprise Weddings," *MPW,* 3 Dec 1921, 566. George A. Katchmer, "In Complete and Utter Admiration of Jack Hoxie," *CI,* 85 (Jul 1982), 31–33; Part II, 86 (Aug 1982), 30–32, 46 (includes filmography). Billy H. Doyle, "Lost Players," *CI,* 157 (Jul 1988), 24. Richard E. Braff, "An Index to the Films of Jack Hoxie," *CI,* 170 (Aug 1989), 16 ff. Mike Newton, "Jack and Al Hoxie—Brothers of the Saddle," *CI,* 213 (Mar 1993), 28, 36.

Hoy, Danny. *See* Formby, George, Jr.

Hoyos, Rudolfo, Sr. (father of Rodolfo Hoyos, Jr.) [actor] (*né* Rodolfo Hoyos Mendiolea, b. Mexico City, Mexico, Jul 1896–24 May 1980 [83], Los Angeles CA). m. (son Rodolfo, Jr., 1914–1983). AS, p. 544.

Hoyt, Arthur [stage/film actor/director] (b. Georgetown CO, 19 Mar 1874–4 Jan 1953 [78], Woodland Hills CA). (Stage director for Henry W. Savage, 6 years, and for George Tyler, 5 years; began in films in 1916, Universal; Metropolitan Picture Co.) "Arthur Hoyt," *Variety,* 14 Jan 1953 (age 79). AMD, p. 173. AS, p. 544. BHD1, p. 272. IFN, p. 148. Truitt, p. 162. "Hoyt Kept Busy in Comedy Roles," *MPW,* 9 Apr 1927, 549:4. George Katchmer, "Remembering the Great Silents," *CI,* 250 (Apr 1996), 46; *CI,* 253 (Jul 1996), 47.

Hoyt, Artthur G. [casting director]. No data found. AMD, p. 173. "Arthur Hoyt Engaged by Triangle," *MPW,* 27 Oct 1917, 511. "Perhaps He Walked in His Sleep," *MPW,* 22 Dec 1917, 1787.

Hoyt, Charles B[amberger] [playwright] (b. Topeka KS?, 1896?–2 Feb 1929 [32], New York NY; pneumonia). m. painter and etcher Mary Parsons. "Charles B. Hoyt," *Variety,* 27 Feb 1929, 122:1. AMD, p. 173 (Charles H. Hoyt). "Charles Ray Productions, Inc., Buys Fourteen of Charles Hoyt's Comedies," *MPW,* 17 Apr 1920, 446.

Hoyt, Harry O. [director/scenarist] (b. Minneapolis MN, 6 Aug 1891–29 Jul 1961 [70?], Woodland Hills CA). AMD, p. 173. AS, p. 544. BHD2, p. 128 (b. 1895). FDY, p. 429. "Harry O. Hoyt with Metro," *MPW,* 18 Dec 1915, 2182. "Harry Hoyt, of Metro, 'Expert,'" *MPW,* 15 Jan 1916, 415. "Harry O. Hoyt as Sing Sing Warden," *MPW,* 3 Jun 1916, 1703. "Director Hoyut Gives View on Film Continuity Writing," *MPW,* 28 Jun 1919, 1943. "Harry O. Hoyt Is to Direct Warner Film," *MPW,* 29 Nov 1926, 279.

Hoyt, Helen [actress] (b. 1904–9 Apr 1979 [75?], Orange Co. CA). BHD, p. 205.

Hoyt, Julia [actress] (*née* Julia Robbins, b. New York NY, 15 Sep 1897–31 Oct 1955 [58], New York NY). m. (1) Lydig Hoyt; (2) **Louis Calhern** (d. 1956); (3) Aquila C. Giles. "Julia Hoyt," *Variety,* 2 Nov 1955 (began 1921). AS, p. 545. BHD, p. 205. IFN, p. 148. SD. Truitt, p. 163.

Hoyt, Rheata [actress]. No data found. m. **Harry Collins**, 1927. AMD, p. 174. June Lee, "Dan Cupid's Bulletin Board," *Paris and Hollywood Screen Secrets Magazine,* Aug 1927, 36 (received a tiny silver anklet for her birthday, but refused to divulge the name on it). "Hoyt—Collins," *MPW,* 31 Dec 1927, p. 25 (Rita Hoyt).

Hoyt, Ruth [actress]. No data found. AMD, p. 174. "Ruth Hoyt Burned in Studio Explosion," *MPW,* 6 Nov 1915, 1156.

Huban, Eileen [actress] (b. 1897–23 Oct 1935 [38?], New York NY). "Eileen Huban," *Variety,* 120, 30 Oct 1935, 70:1 (survived by five sisters). BHD1, p. 611.

Hubbard, H.L. "Bud" [actor/stuntman/special effects] (d. 10 Feb 1973, Burbank CA). (In *The Birth of a Nation;* WB, 1941.) "H.L. Hubbard," *Variety,* 270, 21 Feb 1973, 63:1.

Hubbard, Kin [writer/artist]. No data found. AMD, p. 174. "Hubbard to Draw for Universal," *MPW,* 22 Mar 1919, 1639.

Hubbard, Lucien [director/producer/scenarist] (b. Ft. Thomas KY, 22 Dec 1888–31 Dec 1971 [83], Beverly Hills CA; heart attack). "Lucien Hubbard, Film Director, Producer and Author, Is Dead," *NYT,* 1 Jan 1972, 22:1. "Lucien Hubbard," *Variety,* 12 Jan 1972. AMD, p. 174. AS, p. 545 (b. 1889). BHD2, p. 128 (b. 25 Dec 1889). FDY, p. 429 IFN, p. 148. Spehr, p. 142. "Three Scenario Writers for World," *MPW,* 6 Apr 1918, 73. "Lucien Hubbard Joins Universal," *MPW,* 20 Mar 1920, 2008. "With paramount," *MPW,* 11 Nov 1922, 154.

Hubbell, C.J. [cameraman]. No data found. AMD, p. 174. "Hubbell Returns from Three-Year Trip," *MPW,* 18 Aug 1917, 1066.

Hubbell, Edwin [actor]. No data found. AMD, p. 174. "Hubbell with Dempsey," *MPW,* 21 Jun 1924, 730.

Huber, Charles C. [actor] (b. IL, 11 Jul 1885–19 May 1960 [74], Altadena CA). BHD, p. 205.

Huber, Walter [actor] (b. 1887–1945 [58?]). BHD1, p. 611.

Huberdeau, Gustave [actor] (b. Paris, France, 1874–1945 [71?], Paris, France). AS, p. 545.

Hubert, Ali [set designer] (b. 1878?–1 Jun 1940 [62], Hollywood CA). "Ali Hubert," *Variety,* 5 Jun 1940.

Hubert, George [actor] (b. 1881?–8 May 1963 [82], Los Angeles CA). (Metro, 1917.) "George Hubert," *Variety,* 15 May 1963. AS, p. 545. BHD1, p. 272.

Hubert, Harold [actor] (*né* Harold Bourke, b. 1858–31 Mar 1916 [57], New York NY; struck by car). "Harold Bourke," *Variety,* 7 Apr 1916. AS, p. 545. BHD, p. 205. IFN, p. 148. Truitt, 1983.

Hubert, Marie [actress] (aka Louis de Coucy, d. 4 Jul 1939, Bronxville NY). m. **Gustave Frohman**. "Marie Hubert Frohman," *Variety,* 12 Jul 1939.

Hubert, Paul [actor] (b. Brussels, Belgium, 28 Dec 1879–1926 [46?], France; after an accident). AS, p. 545.

Hubner, Herbert Richard Eberhard Hermann [actor] (b. Breslau, Poland, 6 Feb 1889–27 Jan 1972 [82], Munich, Germany). AS, p. 546.

Hudd, Walter [actor] (b. London, England, 20 Feb 1898–20 Jan 1963 [64], London, England). AS, p. 546.

Hudson, Earl[e] J. [publicist/scenarist/producer/director] (b. Elgin IL, 1892?–20 Aug 1959 [67], Los Angeles CA; aplastic anemia). (Universal; 1st National; Metro.) "Earl Hudson," *Variety,* 26 Aug 1959. AMD, p. 174. AS, p. 546. BHD2, p. 128. FDY, p. 429. "Earl J. Hudson Goes to Centaur," *MPW,* 21 Jun 1913, 1261. "Hudson at the Megaphone," *MPW,* 21 Mar 1925, 282. Gladys Hall and Adele Whitely Fletcher, "We Interview the Stars' Boss," *MW,* 18 Apr 1925, 8–9, 27, 31. "Earl Hudson Addresses A.M.P.A.," *MPW,* 2 May 1925, 32. "Earl Hudson Busy," *MPW,* 13 Jun 1925, 801. "Earl Hudson Given Farewell Dinner," *MPW,* 17 Jul 1926, 4. "Earl Hudson Arrives," *MPW,* 31 Jul 1926, 278. "Hudson with M-G-M," *MPW,* 25 Dec 1926, 556.

Hudson, Eric [actor] (b. Notingham, England, 23 Nov 1862–4 Oct 1918 [55], New York NY). BHD, p. 205.

Hudson, Hazel [actress]. No data found. AMD, p. 174. "Hazel Hudson Is Signed by Character Pictures," *MPW,* 24 Apr 1920, 596.

Hudson, Virginia Tyler [scenarist]. No data found. AMD, p. 174. "New Thanhouser Writers," *MPW,* 25 Sep 1915, 2185. "Scenarist Gains Salary Verdict in Appeals Court," *MPW,* 3 May 1919, 677.

Hudson, Wilbur Collier [actor/assistant director]. No data found. AMD, p. 174. "Wilbur Collier Hudson," *MPW,* 23 Jan 1915, 524.

Huebler-Kahla, J.A. [actor] (b. Germany, 1900–2 Apr 1965 [65?], Berlin, Germany). AS, p. 546.

Huebnerova, Marie [actress] (b. Czechoslovakia, 1865–14 Aug 1931 [66?], Prague, Czechoslovakia). AS, p. 546.

Huff, Forrest [stage/film actor] (b. 22 Aug 1876–21 Aug 1947 [70], New York NY). m. Fritzi Von Busing (d. 1948). "Forrest Huff," *Variety,* 27 Aug 1947. AS, p. 546. BHD, p. 206. SD. Truitt, p. 163.

Huff, Jack. *See* Kirk, Jack.

Huff, Justina [actress] (b. Columbua GA, 8 Sep 1893–29 Jun 1977 [83], Philadelphia PA). m. **Edgar Jones**, 27 Jan 1914. AMD, p. 174. BHD, p. 206. "Justina Huff," *MPW,* 7 Feb 1914, 658. "A True Lubin Romance," *MPW,* 14 Feb 1914, 799. "This Is One of the Cameraman Lost," *MPW,* 11 Apr 1914, 198. "Justina Huff Ill," *NYDM,* 23 Jun 1915, 21:3 (recovering from an operation for appendicitis in Philadelphia PA).

Huff, Louise, "The Kate Greenaway Girl of the Screen" [stage/film actress] (descendant of President James K. Polk, b. Columbus GA, 14 Nov 1895–22 Aug 1973 [77], New York NY [Death Certificate Index No. 15744]). m. (1) (daughter, Mary Louise, b. ca. 1917); (2) Edwin A. Stillman, 16 Feb 1920, Marble Collegiate Church (1 son). (Lubin; Metro; Fox; Paramount.) "Mrs. E[dwin] A. Stillman, Movie Actress, 77," *NYT,* 23 Aug 1973, 40:3. "Louise Huff [Mrs. E.A. Stillman]," *Variety,* 10 Oct 1973. AMD, p. 174. AS, p. 546. BHD, p. 206. IFN, p. 149. Lowrey, p. 78. MH, p. 118. MSBB, p. 1034. WWS, p. 155. "Louise Huff—Lubin Ingeune [sic]," *MPW,* 8 Nov 1913, 726. "Louise Huff," *MPW,* 15 Nov 1913, 726. "Louise Huff," *MPW,* 19 Dec 1914, 1668. "Louise Huff Departs for Lasky Studio," *MPW,* 13 Jan 1917, 215. "Louise Huff to Star in World Picture," *MPW,* 15 Jun 1918, 1578. "West Is Not in It with East, Says Louise Huff," *MPW,* 6 Jul 1918, 87. "Migratory Star a Diminishing Light," *MPW,* 31 Aug 1918, 1248. "Miss Louise Huff Weds Wealthy Manufacturer," *MPW,* 28 Feb 1920, 1506. "Louise Huff Is Engaged to Star in Selznick Pictures," *MPW,* 24 Apr 1920, 589. Edward Weitzel, "Louise Huff Answers That Important Question, Why Are Southern Girls Flirts?," *MPW,* 5 Jun 1920, 1311. Cal York, "Plays and Players," *Photoplay,* Mar 1921, 89 (birth of son). "American Cinema Denies Actress Is Owed Salary," *MPW,* 9 Jul 1921, 186. Charles E. Dexter, "Why a Girl Can't Do as She Likes; Charming young screen star and mother discusses [sic] present day flapper and tells why a young girl is not free to do as her fancy prompts her," *MW,* 19 May 1923, 11, 27.

Huff, Theodore [historian] (*né* Edmund N. Huff, b. 1905–15 Mar 1953 [48?], Farmingdale NY). AS, p. 546.

Huffsmith, Art [title writer]. No data found. FDY, p. 445.

Hughes, C. Anthony [actor] (b. Augusta GA, 21 Mar 1890–1968 [78?]). BHD1, p. 273.

Hughes, Dorothy [actress]. No data found. (Paramount.) AMD, p. 174. "Dorothy Hughes Chosen for 'Flapper' Role by Griffith," *MPW,* 3 Apr 1926, 344. Renee Van Dyke, "Paragraphs Pertaining to Players and Pictures," *Cinema Arts,* Sep 1926, 53.

Hughes, Gareth [actor] (b. Llanelly, Wales, 23 Aug 1894–1 Oct 1965 [71], Woodland Hills CA). "Gareth Hughes," *Variety,* 13 Oct 1965. AMD, p. 174. AS, p. 547. BHD1, p. 273. FSS, p. 150. IFN, p. 149. Katz, p. 584 Truitt, p. 163. "World Pictures Announces 'Ginger' as a May Release," *MPW,* 29 Mar 1919, 1829. "Hughes Engaged for Talmadge Picture," *MPW,* 31 May 1919, 1330. "Gareth Hughes Plays as 'Eyes of Youth' Male Lead," *MPW,* 30 Aug 1919, 1286. "Hughes to Lead in Barrie Film," *MPW,* 2 Oct 1920, 665. "Metro Signs Gareth Hughes as One of Featured Play'rs," *MPW,* 2 Oct 1920, 673. "Gareth Hughes Cast for Title Role in Paramount Feature 'Sentimental Tommy,'" *MPW,* 2 Oct 1920, 681. "Gareth Hughes, of Metro, Named One of Filmdom's Best Dressers," *MPW,* 5 Feb 1921, 710.

Hughes, Howard R[obard] (nephew of **Rupert Hughes**) [director/producer/executive] (b.

Houston TX, 24 Dec 1905–5 Apr 1976 [70], over south Texas, en route by plane from Alcapulco, Mexico to Houston TX). m. (1) Ella Rice, 1925–29; [(2) Terry Moore?]; (2) Jean Peters, 1957–71. Albert B. Gerber, *Bashful Billionaire; The Story of Howard Hughes* (NY: Lyle Stuart, 1967); Noah Dietrich and Bob Thomas, *Howard; The Amazing Mr. Hughes* (Greenwich CT: Fawcett Pubs., 1972). (RKO.) James P. Sterba, "Howard Hughes Dies at 70 on Flight to Texas Hospital; Stroke Given as Cause of Billionaire's Death—Security Is Tight"; "Life of Howard Hughes Was Marked by a Series of Bizarre and Dramatic Events," *NYT*, 6 Apr 1976, 1:1, 58:1; Wallace Turner, "Secrecy Shrouds Hughes Empire's Fate," 59:1. "Howard Hughes, 70, Whilom Film Showman, Dies on Medico Flight," *Variety*, 7 Apr 1976. AS, p. 547. BHD2, p. 128 (b. 1901). Katz, pp. 584–85. SD. Helen Louise Walker, "Rich Producer Can't Marry Them All; Because of His Youth, Wealth, and Good Looks, Howard Hughes Is Considered Most Eligible Bachelor in Hollywood. Has Been Rumored Engaged to Five Different Stars," *Movie Classic*, I, Nov 1931, 41. Arthur c. Peterson, "The Films of Howard Hughes," *Filmograph*, II, No. 4 (1972), 14–19.

Hughes, John J. [actor/art director/cinematographer/director] (d. 22 Sep 1927, Flushing, LI NY; pneumonia). m. Adelaide, 1913. "John J. Hughes," *Variety*, 5 Oct 1927 (Adelaide & Hughes of vaudeville). AMD, p. 174. FDY, p. 459. "Hughes, Art Director," *MPW*, 2 Jun 1923, 415.

Hughes, Laurence A. [actor/director/scenarist] (b. Melbourne, Victoria, Australia, 1 Aug 1891–29 Sep 1952 [61], Los Angeles CA). BHD1, p. 611; BHD2, p. 128.

Hughes, Lloyd [actor] (b. Bisbee AZ, 21 Oct 1897–6 Jun 1958 [60], San Gabriel CA). m. **Gloria Hope**, 30 Jun 1921, Methodist Church, Hollywood CA (d. 1976). (Film debut: *Turn of the Road*, 1915.) "Lloyd Hughes Is Dead; Screen Actor Had Appeared with Many Noted Stars," *NYT*, 9 Jun 1958, 23:3. "Lloyd Hughes," *Variety*, 11 Jun 1958. AMD, p. 174. AS, p. 547. BHD1, p. 273. FFF, p. 219. FSS, p. 151. IFN, p. 149. MH, p. 118. Truitt, p. 163. "Tom Ince Enlarges Staff at His Culver City Studio," *MPW*, 15 Mar 1919, 1481 (age 21). "Lloyd Hughes Signed as New thomas H. Ince Stjar," *MPW*, 20 Dec 1919, 965. "Hughes—Hope," *MPW*, 23 Jul 1921, 413. Gladys Hall and Adele Whitely Fletcher, "We See New York with Lloyd Hughes," *MW*, 25 Jul 1925, 9–10, 42–43. "Just Like Papa," *MPW*, 13 Nov 1926, 3 (son b. 21 Oct 1926, Hughes's birthday). "Lloyd Hughes," *MPW*, 18 Jun 1927, 483. George Katchmer, "Remembering the Great Silents; Lloyd Hughes," *CI*, 162 (Dec 1988), C15-C16, 42. Henry R. Davis. "The Films of Lloyd Hughes," *CI*, 164 (Feb 1988), 53, 59. George Katchmer, "Remembering the Great Silents," *CI*, 250 (Apr 1996), 46, 48; *CI*, 253 (Jul 1996), 47–48.

Hughes, Roy [actor] (b. Kinmundy IL, 11 Jan 1894–12 Jan 1928 [34]). BHD, p. 206. IFN, p. 149.

Hughes, Rupert (uncle of **Howard Hughes**) [producer/title writer] (b. Lancaster MO, 31 Jan 1872–9 Sep 1956 [84], Los Angeles CA). m. **Paterson Dial** (d. 1945); (2) Adelaide Manola (d. 1923); (3) Elizabeth P. Dial. "Rupert Hughes," *Variety*, 12 Sep 1956. AMD, p. 175. AS, p. 547. BHD, p. 206; BHD2, p. 128. FDY, p. 445. IFN, p. 149. SD. Rupert Hughes, "What We Are Trying to Do," *MPW*, 29 Apr 1916, 781. "Rupert Hughes Leaves for Work in Goldwyn Studio," *MPW*, 26 Jul 1919, 488. Edward Weitzel, "Why Rupert Hughes Only Chuckled While Gazing at 'The Cup of Fury,'" *MPW*, 6 Dec 1919, 677. "Rupert Hughes Sits Up with the Critics and Tells Our Case Better Than Before," *MPW*, 14 Jan 1922, 154–55. "Why Don't 'Depravities' of the Films Affect Morals of Censors, Asks Hughes," *MPW*, 4 Feb 1922, 487. "Rupert Hughes Renews Goldwyn Contract," *MPW*, 13 May 1922, 168. Jim Tully, "The Wittiest Man in America; Rupert Hughes is one of the most remarkable men in the Cinema story. He has been called the 'social historian of these times.' He is the most brilliant defender of the profession he has elected to follow, the movies," *MPC*, Sep 1924, 34–35, 81. "Hughes Remains as Head of Writers," *MPW*, 15 Oct 1927, 432 (President of Writers Club).

Hughes, Rush [actor] (*né* Russell Sheldon Hughes, b. OH, 15 Jan 1910–16 Apr 1958 [48], Studio City CA). AS, p. 547. BHD1, p. 273.

Hughes, T[homas] **Arthur** [actor] (b. 1887–25 Nov 1953 [66], Los Angeles CA). AS, p. 547. BHD1, p. 273. IFN, p. 149.

Hughes, Yvonne Evelyn [actress] (b. 1900?–26 Dec 1950 [50], New York NY; strangled to death). m. Gordon Godowsky; John McDonald. (Paramount.) "Yvonne Evelyn Hughes," *Variety*, 3 Jan 1951. AS, p. 547. BHD, p. 206. IFN, p. 149.

Hughston, Regan [actor] (b. Chicago IL, 3 Sep 1875–2 Oct 1951 [76], Siasconset MA). BHD, p. 206.

Hugon, Andre [director/producer/scenarist] (*né* Jean Victor Félicien André Hugon, b. Algiers, Algeria, 13 Dec 1886–22 Aug 1960 [73], Cannes, France [extrait de décès no. 586]). AS, p. 547 (b. 17 Dec). BHD2, p. 129.

Huhn, Austin Oscar [actor/stage manager/director] (b. Hanover KS, 1884?–23 Jan 1933 [48], New York NY; heart attack). m. **Charlotte Wilkens**. (Excelsior Feature Film Co.) Photo of Excelsior personnel, *MPW*, 30 May 1914, 1251. A.O. Huhn, "Huhn Was in 'The Path Forbidden,'" *MPW*, 14 Nov 1914, 920. "Austin Oscar Huhn," *NYT*, 24 Jan 1933, 19:1. BHD2, p. 129.

Hulbert, Claude Noel (brother of **Jack Hulbert**) [actor] (b. London, England, 24 Dec 1900–22 Jan 1964 [63], Sydney, New South Wales, Australia). AS, p. 548 (b. 25 Dec). BHD1, p. 274; BHD2, p. 129 (b. 25 Dec).

Hulbert, Jack (brother of **Claude Hulbert**) [stage/film actor] (b. Ely, Cambridge, England, 24 Apr 1892–25 Mar 1978 [85], London, England). m. Cicely Courtneidge. *The Little Woman's Always Right*, 1976. "Jack Hulbert," *Variety*, 290, 29 Mar 1978, 94:2. AS, p. 548. BHD1, p. 274; BHD2, p. 129. IFN, p. 149.

Hulburd, H.L. (Bud) [special effects] (d. 10 Feb 1973, Burbank CA). "H.L. 'Bud' Hulburd," *Variety*, 21 Feb 1973, p. 62. AS, p. 548. BHD, p. 206.

Hulette, Gladys [stage/film actress] (b. Arcade NY, 21 Jul 1896–8 Aug 1991 [95], Montebello CA). (Vitagraph; Imp; Biograph; Edison; Thanhouser; Astra; First National; Universal; PDC.) (Film debut: *Princess Nicotine*, Vitagraph, 1909.) m. William Parke, Jr.—div. 1924. AMD, p. 175. AS, p. 548. BHD1, p. 274. FSS, p. 151. MH, p. 118. Slide, p. 142. "Gladys Hulette," *MPW*, 22 Oct 1910, 923. "Gladys Hulette in Legitimate," *MPW*, 12 Oct 1912, 131. "Gladys Hulette Again with Edison," *MPW*, 30 Aug 1913, 965. "Gladys Hulette," *MPW*, 25 Apr 1914, 521. "In the Picture Studios," *NYDM*, 11 Aug 1915, 27:1 (to leave pictures at Edison for the stage, reversing the exodus of stage stars to films). "Gladys Hulette Joins Thanhouser," *MPW*, 9 Oct 1915, 237. "Hoffman Signs Gladys Hulette," *MPW*, 13 Dec 1924, 660. "Gladys Hulette Signed," *MPW*, 31 Jan 1925, 489. Billy H. Doyle, "Gladys Hulette," *CI*, 218 (Aug 1993), C28 (died as "Gladys Parke"). George Katchmer, "Remembering the Great Silents," *CI*, 248 (Feb 1996), 45.

Huley, Pete [actor] (*né* Pete Klondike, b. Austria, 1892–6 Feb 1973 [80], Vancouver, Canada). AS, p. 548. BHD, p. 206. IFN, p. 149.

Huling, Lorraine [actress]. No data found. AMD, p. 175. "Thanhouser's Triple Coup," *MPW*, 17 Apr 1915, 374.

Hull, Arthur Stewart [actor] (b. PA, 8 May 1878–28 Feb 1951 [72], Los Angeles CA). AS, p. 548. BHD1, p. 274. IFN, p. 149.

Hull, George C. [scenarist]. No data found. FDY, p. 429.

Hull, Henry Watterson (brother of **Shelley Hull**) [stage/film actor] (aka Wallace Morgan, *né* Henry Vaughan, b. Louisville KY, 3 Oct 1890–8 Mar 1977 [86], Cornwall, England). "Henry Hull, 87, Star of Stage and Screen; Actor Who Created Jeeter Lester in 'Tobacco Road' on Broadway Also Appeared in 46 Movies," *NYT*, 9 Mar 1977, B4:2. "Henry Hull," *Variety*, 16 Mar 1977. AMD, p. 175. AS, p. 548. BHD1, p. 274 (b. 1888). FSS, p. 152. IFN, p. 149. Katz, p. 586 (began 1916). SD. Spehr, p. 144. "Brady Finds a 'Kerensky' Too," *MPW*, 22 Sep 1917, 1828. Leon V. Calanquin, "The Saga of Henry Hull," *CI*, 108 (Jun 1984), 9. Leon Calanquin, "Henry Hull: A Dedicated Actor," *CI*, 181 (Jul 1990), 12, 61 (includes filmography; d. 9 Mar).

Hull, Shelley (brother of **Henry Hull**) [actor] (*né* Shelley Vaughan, b. Louisville KY, 17 Jun 1884–14 Jan 1919 [34], New York NY; influenza). m. Josephine Sherwood [Josephine Hull], 1910. "Shelley Hull," *Variety*, 17 Jan 1919. AS, p. 548. BHD, p. 206 (b. 1885). IFN, p. 149.

Human, Bob [actor] (b. 1922?–5 Apr 1979 [57], Los Angeles CA). (Metro.) "Bob Human," *Variety*, 6 Jun 1979. IFN, p. 149.

Humberstone, H. Bruce "Lucky" [director] (b. Buffalo NY, 18 Nov 1903–11 Oct 1984 [80], Woodland Hills CA; pneumonia and stomah cancer). "H. Bruce Humberstone, 82; A Film Director for 30 Years," *NYT*, 18 Oct 1984, D25:6 (d. 16 Oct; age 82). "Lucky Humberstone," *Variety*, 17 Oct 1984 (age 81). AS, p. 548. BHD, p. 206; BHD2, p. 129. Katz, pp. 586–87.

Humbert, George [actor] (b. Florence, Italy, 29 Jul 1880–8 May 1963 [82], Los Angeles CA). AS, p. 548. BHD1, p. 274. IFN, p. 149.

Hume, Benita [stage/film/radio actress] (*née* Benita Humm, b. Beckenham, England, 14 Oct 1906–1 Nov 1967 [61], Egerton, England). m. (1) Eric Otto Siepman, Jun 1926–31; **Ronald Colman**, 30 Dep 1938, San Ysidro CA (d. 1958; 1 daughter, Juliet, b. 24 Jul 1944); George Sanders, 10 Feb 1959, Madrid, Spain. (Stage debut: *Kismet*, New Oxford Theater, 1925; film debut: *The Happy Ending*, 1925; Gainsborough; MGM; Paramount; final film: *Peck's Bad Boy with the Circus*, 1938.) "Benita Hume," *Variety*, 8 Nov 1967 (age 60). AS, p. 548. BHD1, p. 274 (b. London). IFN, p. 149. Katz, p. 587. Truitt, p. 164. Barrie Roberts, "Benita

Hume: Incontrovertibly English," *CI,* 279 (Sep 1998), 20–24 (includes filmography).

Hume, Ilean [vaudeville/film actress] (b. Toronto, Canada, 26 Feb 1896–20 Nov 1978 [82], Culver City CA). (Champion, Coytesville NJ; Eclair; Kalem.) AMD, p. 175. AS, p. 548 (Eileen Hume). BHD, p. 206 (d. Studio City). IFN, p. 149. "Ilean Hume," *MPW,* 25 Jul 1914, 586. "Gossip of the Studios," *NYDM,* 23 Sep 1914, 27:1 (Ilene Hume, 18 years old). "Ilean Hume," *MPW,* 20 Jan 1917, 350.

Hume, Marjorie [actress]. No data found. AMD, p. 175. "Marjorie Hume Has Heroine Part in First Famous Players Picture Made in Europe," *MPW,* 7 Aug 1920, 774 (*The Great Day*).

Humes, Fred [actor] (b. Dent's Run [Elks County, near DuBois] PA, 9 Jun 1900-disappeared after 1935). (Universal; American; MGM; Reliable; Columbia.) AMD, p. 175. AS, p. 548. "Humes Starts First Picture," *MPW,* 18 Jul 1925, 344. Ed Wyatt, "Fred Humes: The Other Cowboy from DuBois," *CI,* 240 (Jun 1995), 18, 20 (partial filmography).

Hummel, Mary Rockwell [actress] (b. 1889?–16 Feb 1946 [57], Los Angeles CA). "Mary R. Hummel," *Variety,* 27 Feb 1946 ("she had been in pictures for 30 years"). AS, p. 548. BHD1, p. 274. IFN, p. 149. Truitt, p. 164.

Hummel, Wilson [actor] (b. Cincinnati OH, 17 Nov 1876–5 Oct 1941 [64], Los Angeles CA). BHD1, p. 274.

Humphrey, Bessie [actress] (*née?,* b. Boston MA–d. 8 Mar 1933, Los Angeles CA). m. **William Humphrey** (d. 1942). (Vitagraph.) "Bessie Humphrey," *Variety,* 28 Mar 1933. AS, p. 548. BHD, p. 206. IFN, p. 149.

Humphrey, Floyd [cameraman]. NO data found. AMD, p. 175. "Humphrey Taking Aeroplane Pictures," *MPW,* 8 Jun 1912, 914.

Humphrey, Harry [actor] (b. San Francisco CA, 15 Dec 1873–1 Apr 1947 [73], Los Angeles CA). AS, p. 548.

Humphrey, Ola [actress] (aka Princess Ibrahim Hassan) (b. CA). No other data found. Related by marriage to the Khedive of Egypt. "Universal Feature; Princess Hassan to Be Presented in a Novel Dramatic Feature," *NYDM,* 20 Jan 1915, 32:2. Grace Kingsley, "Flashes; Star Gets Fortune; Princess Hassan's Husband Leaves Big Estate," *LA Times,* 8 Mar 1920, II, p. 9 (inherited $4,000,000 from her husband (one half of his estate], who died in the winter of 1919. Ironically, "Miss Humphrey was on her way to Paris to prosecute divorce proceedings...when she received news of his death...the action was at once annulled, and [she] has received notification that she is now the owner of a mansion situated in Versailles, used as a hospital during the war." In 1915, Universal sent her to Egypt to make a picture; there, she met Prince Hassan and they wed. "The marriage proved an unhappy one, however, and the pair soon separated, but the Princess continued the use of her title in connection with her pictures.").

Humphrey, Orral [actor/director] (*né* Thomas Orral Humphrey, b. Louisville KY, 3 Apr 1880–12 Aug 1929 [49], Los Angeles CA). AMD, p. 175. AS, p. 548. BHD, p. 206. IFN, p. 149. "Orral Humphrey Retires; Plans to Take Up Ranching," *MPW,* XL, 10 May 1919, 829. "Orral Humphrey to Retire," *MPW,* 17 May 1919, 1025.

Humphrey, Paul [director] (b. 1903–4 Apr 1926 [23?], San Diego CA; in an explosion). AS, p. 548.

Humphrey, William J[onathan] [actor/director] (b. Chicopee Falls MA, 2 Jan 1875–4 Oct 1942 [67], Woodland Hills CA; coronary thrombosis). m. **Bessie** (d. 1933). (Vitagraph, 1909–17.) AMD, p. 175. AS, p. 549 (b. 1874). BHD1, p. 274; BHD2, p. 129 (b. 1874). IFN, p. 149. Katz, p. 587 (b. 1874). Slide, p. 142. Truitt, 1983 (b. 1874). "Humphrey Joins Ivan," *MPW,* 27 Jan 1917, 536. "William Humphrey with Ivan," *MPW,* 21 Apr 1917, 409. "Humphrey to Direct Gladys Leslie," *MPW,* 4 Oct 1919, 97.

Humphreys, Cecil [actor] (b. Cheltenham, Gloucestershire, England, 21 Jul 1883–6 Nov 1947 [64], New York NY). (Universal.) "Cecil Humphreys," *Variety,* 12 Nov 1947. AS, p. 549. BHD1, p. 274. IFN, p. 149. Truitt, p. 164.

Humphreys, William [actor] (b. 1874?–24 Mar 1953 [79], Haddon Heights NJ). "William Humphreys," *NYT,* 25 Mar 1953, 31:5. AS, p. 549. Robert Grau, "The Film Studio; A Gold Laden Haven for the Patriarchs of the Stage," *NYDM,* 8 Sep 1915, 3:1 (Grau mentions Charles Kent, Louise Beaudet, Cissy Fitzgerald, Sydney Drew, S. Rankin Drew, Humphries [sic], Van Dyke Brooke, and Harry Davenport, all from the stage. "Neither [Humphries nor Van Dyke Brooke] would leave his present environment and neither is expected to do so as long as life lasts.").

Humphries, John [stage/film actor] (b. 1867?–27 Sep 1927 [60], Birmingham, England). m. Isabel Innes. "John Humphries," *Variety,* 12 Oct 1927. AS, p. 549. SD.

Hunebelle, André Henri [director/producer] (b. Meudon, France, 1 Sep 1896–26 Nov 1985 [89]. Nice, France [extrait de décès no. 5638/1985]). AS, p. 549.

Hung, Shen [actor/director/scenarist] (b. Changchow, China, 31 Dec 1894–29 Aug 1955 [60], China). AS, p. 549.

Hungerford, J[ames] **Edward** [scenarist]. No data found. AMD, p. 175. "Three Authors Added to Universal Forces," *MPW,* 20 Octr 1917, 364.

Hungerford, Mona [actress] (b. England, 1900–17 Jul 1942 [42?], New York NY). BHD, p. 206.

Hunlington, Wright [actor] (b. 1864–21 Sep 1916 [52?], New York NY). AS, p. 549.

Hunt, Charles J. [title writer/film editor]. No data found. FDY, p. 445.

Hunt, Frances [actress] (b. 1880–1963 [83?], Los Angeles CA). AS, p. 549.

Hunt, Governor George W[ylie] **P**[aul] (b. Huntsville MO, 1 Nov 1856–24 Dec 1934 [78], Phoenix AZ). AS, p. 549 (b. 1859). BHD, p. 206.

Hunt, Irene "Pat" [actress] (b. New York NY, 22 Feb.) m. Lester Scott, Santa Ana CA. (Reliance; Lubin.) AMD, p. 175. "Miss Hunt Breaks as Arm," *MPW,* 15 Mar 1913, 1090. "Irene Hunt; Clever Young Actress with the Reliance Co.," *MPS,* 19 Sep 1913, 30. "Irene Hunt Tries Scenario Reading," *MPW,* 30 Mar 1918, 1845. George Katchmer, "Irene Hunt," *CI,* 235 (Jan 1995), 37.

Hunt, J. Roy [cinematographer]. No data found. FDY, p. 459.

Hunt, Jay [stage/film actor/director] (b. Philadelphia PA, 4 Aug 1855–18 Nov 1932 [77], Los Angeles CA). m. Florence Hale. (Kay-Bee.) "Jay Hunt," *Variety,* 22 Nov 1932 (age 75). AMD, p. 175. AS, p. 549. BHD1, p. 275; BHD2, p. 129. IFN, p. 150. SD. Truitt, p. 164 (b. 1857). "Jay Hunt with Eclair," *MPW,* 11 Nov 1911, 455. "Jay Hunt, Burlesque Magnate," *MPW,* 10 Aug 1912, 552. "Jay Hunt Loses Father," *MPW,* 14 Sep 1912, 1082 (Henry J. Hunt, d. 21 Aug 1912, NYC, age 79). "Jay Hunt in Kay-Bee Drama," *MPW,* 13 Mar 1915, 1621. "Horsley Signs New People," *MPW,* 11 Sep 1915, 1809. Jay Hunt on Flying visit," *MPW,* 2 Oct 1915, 88. "Hunt Directing Two Reelers," *MPW,* 23 Oct 1915, 595. "Jay Hunt with Universal," *MPW,* 26 Feb 1916, 1288. George Katchmer, "Remembering the Great Silents," *CI,* 208 (Oct 1992), 48.

Hunt, Jewel [society dancer/actress]. No data found. (Vitagraph.) AMD, p. 175. "Jewel Hunt," *MPW,* 6 Nov 1915, 1147. "Studio Gossip," *NYDM,* 20 Nov 1915, 34:3 (joined Vitagraph). "Jewel Hunt Joins Vitagraph," *MPW,* 27 Nov 1915, p. 1679.

Hunt, Leslie M. [stage/film actor] (b. 1885). (Selig; Thanhouser; Fox; Goldwyn.) MBB, p. 1025.

Hunt, Madge [actress] (b. New York NY, 27 Nov 1875–2 Aug 1935 [59], Los Angeles CA). AS, p. 549. BHD1, p. 275. IFN, p. 150.

Hunt, Martita [stage/film actress] (b. Buenos Aires, Argentina, 30 Jan 1900–13 Jun 1969 [69], London, England). (Legit debut: Liverpool, England, 1921.) "Majrtita Hunt, Who Played Lead in 'Madwoman of Chaillot,' Dies; Performance Won a Tony—Was Miss Havisham in Film of 'Great Expectations,'" *NYT,* 14 Jun 1969, 33:1 (1949 interview: "Between my first play and my success with the Old Vic [1929], I did exactly 51 opening nights in some frightful plays. I vowed not to do an awful play again. So I carefully chose my stage parts and did dozens of stinking movies to pay the rent." First film cited as *I Was a Spy.*). "Martita Hunt," *Variety,* 255, 18 Jun 1969, 71:1. AS, p. 549. BHD1, p. 275. IFN, p. 150.

Hunt, Phoebe [actress]. No data found. AMD, p. 175. "Phoebe Hunt to Appear in Her First Picture," *MPW,* 9 Apr 1921, 590 (*The Grim Comedian*).

Hunt, Rea M. [actor/director] (b. NM, 5 Nov 1892–21 Jun 1961 [68], Los Angeles CA). AS, p. 549. BHD, p. 207. IFN, p. 150.

Hunte, Otto [art director] (b. Hamburg, Germany, 1881–1947 [66?]). AS, p. 549. BHD2, p. 129.

Hunter, C. Roy [cameraman] (b. 1891?–1 Jul 1954 [63], Pittsburgh PA; heart attack). (Began 1916; Paramount.) "C. Roy Hunter," *Variety,* 14 Jul 1954. AS, p. 549.

Hunter, Edna [stage/film actress] (*née* Edna Hunt, b. Toledo OH, 1876–5 Feb 1920 [43?], New York NY; pneumonia). m. Mr. Woods. (Fox; Red Feather-Universal; CKY-Selznick; Vitagraph; Monmouth.) "Edna Hunter," *Variety,* 13 Feb 1920. AMD, p. 176. AS, p. 549. BHD, p. 207. IFN, p. 150. MSBB, p. 1034. SD. "Edna Hunter," *MPW,* 18 Mar 1916, 1817. Billy H. Doyle, "Lost Players," *CI,* 163 (Jan 1989), 30.

Hunter, Glenn [stage/film actor] (b. Highland Mills NY, 26 Sep 1894–30 Dec 1945 [51], Bronx NY [Death Certificate Index No. 32]). m. May Eagan. "Glenn Hunter Dies; Stage, Film Actor; Won First Success in 'Merton of the Movies'—Early Career Paralleled That of Hero,"

NYT, 31 Dec 1945, 17:1. "Glenn Hunter," *Variety,* 2 Jan 1946. AMD, p. 176. AS, p. 549. BHD, p. 207. FFF, p. 200 (b. 1897). IFN, p. 150. MH, p. 118. SD. Truitt, p. 164. "Glenn Hunter Is a Hard Worker," *MPW,* 27 Jan 1923, 384. "Sign with Paramount," *MPW,* 24 Mar 1923, 403. Susan Elizabeth Brady, "Oh, Youth!," *Classic,* XI, May 1923, 20–21, 75. Barbara Litte, "Our Boy Atlas," *Picture-Play Magazine,* Jun 1923, 74–75, 95. Rgina Cannon, "Is Screen Success Harder to Win Than Stage Fame? 'Yes!', Says Glenn Hunter," *MW,* 22 Dec 1923, 20.

Hunter, Florence. *See* Baby Twinkles.

Hunter, Harrison [stage/film actor] (b. England, 1869?–2 Jan 1923 [53], Boston MA; following operation). m. Sidney Crowe. "Harrison Hunter," *Variety,* 5 Jan 1923. "Harrison Hunter Dies," *NYT,* 3 Jan 1923. "Recent Deaths," *The Boston Evening Transcript,* 3 Jan 1923, p. 4. BHD, p. 207. SD, p. 645.

Hunter, Ian [stage/film actor] (b. Kenilworth, South Africa, 13 Jun 1900–23 Sep 1975 [75], London, England). m. Catherine Pringle. AS, p. 549 (d. 24 Sep). BHD1, p. 275 (b. Capetown). IFN, p. 150. Katz, pp. 588–89 (began in England, 1924). SD, p. 646. Truitt, 1983.

Hunter, Kenneth [actor] (b. Capetown, South Africa, 19 Feb 1882–21 Dec 1961 [79], Los Angeles Co. CA). AS, p. 549 (d. London, England). BHD1, p. 275. IFN, p. 150.

Hunter, Richard [actor] (b. CA, 21 Apr 1875–22 Dec 1962 [87], Santa Monica CA). "Richard Hunter," *Variety,* 16 Jan 1963 (early film cowboy). AS, p. 550. BHD1, p. 275. IFN, p. 150.

Hunter, T[homas] **Hayes** [director] (b. Philadelphia PA, 1 Dec 1882–14 Apr 1944 [61], London, England). m. Millicent Evans, 4 Apr 1919, LA CA. (Goldwyn.) "T. Hayes Hunter; Motion Picture Director, Agent Is Dead in London at 62," *NYT,* 18 Apr 1944, 21:3 (age 62). "T. Hayes Hunter," *Variety,* 19 Apr 1944 (age 62; "he was one of the pioneers in motion pictures"). AMD, p. 176. AS, p. 550 (b. 1884; d. Hollywood CA). BHD2, p. 129. IFN, p. 150. Katz, p. 590. "Hunter—Evans," *MPW,* 26 Apr 1919, 519. "Director Hunter Marries Millicent Evans," *MPW,* 3 May 1919, 660. "T. Hayes Hunter Signs to Direct for Goldwyn," *MPW,* 19 Jul 1919, 386. "Three New Directors Are Signed by Goldwyn," *MPW,* 16 Aug 1919, 942. "Good Stories Are Needed as Well as Good Acting," *MPW,* 24 Jan 1920, 590. "T. Hayes Hunter Directing 'Wildfire' at Vitagraph," *MPW,* 14 Feb 1925, 707.

Hunting, Gardner [actor/scenarist] (b. 1872?–21 Nov 1958 [86], Burbank CA). (FP-L, 1912–18.) "Gardner Hunting," *Variety,* 26 Nov 1958. AMD, p. 176. AS, p. 550. BHD2, p. 129 (b. 1875). "Gardner Hunting with Wharton," *MPW,* 1 Jan 1916, 56.

Huntington, Wright [stage/film actor] (*né* John L. Sillimann, b. 1864–21 Sep 1916 [52], New York NY?). "Wright Huntington," *Variety,* 29 Sep 1916. BHD, p. 207 (b. 1866). SD. In *The Spatulate Thumb* (Gaumont, 22 Jun 1916, 3 reels, with Lionel Barrymore.)

Huntley, Ben [producer] (b. 1876–17 May 1961 [85?], Black River Falls WI). AS, p. 550. BHD2, p. 129.

Huntley, Hugh [stage/film actor] (b. London, England, 14 Dec 1889–9 Feb 1977 [87], Capistrano Beach CA). (Vitagraph.) BHD1, p. 275. Lillian May, "The Moss of a Rolling Stone," *MPC,* XII, Jul 1921, 65, 82.

Huntley, Luray. *See* Long, Luray.

Huntly, Fred [stage/film actor] (*né* Frederick William Huntly, b. London, England, 29 Aug 1862?–1 Nov 1931 [69?], Los Angeles CA). "Fred Huntly," *Variety,* 10 Nov 1931 ("Huntly came to Hollywood from the New York stage six years ago, but never worked in pictures"). AS, p. 550 (b. 1864). BHD, p. 207 (b. 1864). IFN, p. 150 (b. 1864). Truitt, p. 164. George Katchmer, "Remembering the Great Silents," *CI,* 218 (Aug 1993), 43 (b. 1864).

Huntress, Mary [actress] (b. Richmond VA–d. 11 Dec 1933, Manila, Philippines). BHD, p. 207. IFN, p. 150. Truitt, 1983.

Hurd, Earl [cartoonist/animator/inventor] (b. Kansas City MO, 1880?–28 Sep 1940 [60], Burbank CA). (1915: Bobby Bumps film cartoons.) "Earl Hurd," *Variety,* 140, 2 Oct 1940, 62:3 ("inventor of the first camera used in cartoon animation...devised the Bray-Hurd process for animated cartooning, now in use in all studios. For past six years he's been with Walt Disney, with whom he started drawing on Kansas City newspapers."). AMD, p. 176. AS, p. 550. BHD2, p. 129. "Comedies of a Cartoonist," *MPW,* 6 May 1916, 995. "Earl Hurd," *MPW,* 21 Jul 1917, 398. "Hurd with Bray Studios," *MPW,* 24 Oct 1925, 641.

Hurel, Robert [producer] (b. Bologne-sur-Mer, France, 1895–13 Jan 1938 [42], Paris, France). AS, p. 550.

Hurlbert, Mary [actress]. No data found. AMD, p. 176. "Southern Society Girl Dares Rigors of North to Play in Pictures," *MPW,* 3 Dec 1921, 551.

Hurlbut, Gladys [actress/scenarist] (b. 9 Dec 1898–25 Jan 1988 [89], Woodstock NY). BHD2, p. 129.

Hurlbut, William J[ames] [playwright/screenwriter] (b. Belvidere IL, 13 Jul 1882?–4 May 1957 [74], Los Angeles CA). "William Hurlbut," *Variety,* 8 May 1957. AS, p. 550. BHD2, p. 129 (b. 1883). SD, p. 647 (b. 1883).

Hurley, Arthur [stage/film director] (b. Boston MA, 1876?–2 Nov 1941 [65], Los Angeles CA). m. stage actress Irene Shirley. (WB; Fox.) "Arthur Hurley," *Variety,* 144, 5 Nov 1941, 62:1. AS, p. 550. AMD, p. 176. "Arthur Hurley to Direct Callaghan Productions," *MPW,* 27 Nov 1920, 491.

Hurley, Julia R. [actress] (*nee?,* b. Greenwich Village [New York] NY, 1847?–4 Jun 1927 [80], New York NY [Death Certificate No. 14148; chronic myocarditis and nephritis]). "[Mrs.] Julia Hurley," *Variety,* 8 Jun 1927. AMD, p. 176. AS, p. 550. BHD, p. 207. IFN, p. 150. 1921 Directory, p. 226. "Julia R. Hurley—45 Years an Actress," *MPW,* 30 Mar 1912, 1180. "Mrs. Hurley to Solax," *MPW,* 8? Mar 1913, 1001. "Horsley Adds to His Forces," *MPW,* 8 Aug 1914, 821. "Julia R. Hurley," *MPW,* 2 Jan 1915, 80. "Julia R. Hurley," *MPW,* 13 Nov 1915, 1277. "Julia Hurley Signed," *MPW,* 10 Jan 1925, 165.

Hurlock, Madeline [actress: Sennett Bathing Beatuy/Wampas Star, 1925] (b. Federalsburg MD, 17 Dec 1899–4 Apr 1989 [89], New York NY). m. (1) Marc Connelly, 1930–35; Robert E. Sherwood, 1935 (d. 1955). (Sennett.) "Madeline H. Sherwood," *Variety,* 12 Apr 1989. AMD, p. 176. AS, p. 550 (d. LA CA). BHD, p. 207. FFF, p. 158. Katz, p. 590. MH, p. 118. "Madeline Hurlock Renews Contract," *MPW,* 17 Jul 1926, 167. "Six Reasons Why Mack Sennett Comedies Are Popular," *Cinema Arts,* V (Aug 1926), 23 (photo).

Hurn, Philip J. [scenarist]. No data found. AMD, p. 176. "Jokes About Marriage," *MPW,* 16 Mar 1918, 1541.

Hurrell, George [photographer] (b. Cincinnati OH, 1 Jun 1904–17 May 1992 [87], Van Nuys CA). *The Hurrell Style; 50 Years of Photographing Hollywood,* text by Whitney Stine (NY: The John Day Co., 1976). "George Hurrell," *Variety,* 25 May 1992, p. 70. BHD2, p. 129.

Hurst, Brandon [actor] (b. London, England, 30 Nov 1866–15 Jul 1947 [80], Los Angeles CA). (MGM.) "Brandon Hurst," *Variety,* 23 Jul 1947 (age 81). AS, p. 551. BHD1, p. 275. FSS, p. 152. IFN, p. 150. Truitt, p. 164.

Hurst, Fannie, "The 'Sob Sister' of American Letters" [novelist/scenarist] (b. Hamilton OH, 18 Oct 1889–23 Feb 1968 [78], New York NY). m. pianist Jacques S. Danielson, 1915 (d. 1952). *Anatomy of Me: A Wonderer in Search of Herself* (NY: Doubleday, 1958. Grant Overton, *The Women Who Make Our Novels* (NY: Dodd, Mead & Co., 1928. "Fannie Hurst, Popular Author of Romantic Stories, Dies at 78," *NYT,* 24 Feb 1968, 37:4, 29:1 ("Young Fannie suffered embarrassment that her Jewish background seemed to set her off from schoolmates." After dieting, Hurst went to President Franklin D. Roosevelt to show him her new figure. His comment: "The Hurst may have changed, but it's the same old fanny." Hurst "was always mortified at this slang word and she spoke bitterly about her mother for the choice she made of a name for her daughter, between Beulah and Fannie. Miss Hurst observed, "No one ever sat on her beulah." She was "a gifted salonnière who enjoyed the company of celebrities" and was also "at ease with the unsophisticated."). Alden Whitman, "Hurst Bequests Aid Universities; Brandeis and Washington May Get $1-Million Each," *NYT,* 29 Feb 1968, 37:4 (will signed 8 Feb 1968, filed for probate in Surrogate Court on 28 Feb. "Miss Hurst's other bequests were $200 each to two household employees."). "200 at Private Rite Mourn Fannie Hurst," *NYT,* 1 Mar 1968, 37:1 (held at Frank B. Campbell's, 81st and Madison, NYC. The room was filled with calla lillies, her favorite flower. "Some 50 fans stood outside in the rain." She was to be cremated in Ferncliff Crematory, Hartsdale NY; ashes to St. Louis MO, her childhood home). AMD, p. 176. AS, p. 551. BHD2, p. 130. "Laemmle Buys a Fannie Hurst Story," *MPW,* 10 May 1919, 804 (*The Petal on the Current*). "Miss Hurst Lands Picturized Story," *MPW,* 4 Mar 1922, 51. "Fannie Hurst Sees Films as Potential Aid to Mentality," *MPW,* 1 Mar 1924, 45. "Fannie Hurst Wins Prize," *MPW,* 29 Aug 1925, 896 (*Liberty* magazine prize of $50,000 for *The Moving Finger*).

Hurst, Paul Causkey [actor/director] (b. Traver CA, 15 Oct 1888–27 Feb 1953 [64], Los Angeles CA; of self-inflicted gunshot wound]). m. **Hedda Nova**, 4 Nov 1919, Santa Ana CA. (Kalem, 1912; Vitagraph.) "Paul Hurst," *Variety,* 11 Mar 1953. AMD, p. 176. AS, p. 551. BHD1, p. 276; BHD2, p. 130. FSS, p. 153. IFN, p. 150. Truitt, p. 165. "Paul Hurst Joins Universal," *MPW,* 3 Nov 1917, 683. "Paul Hurst Joins Vitagraph," *MPW,* 2 Mar 1918, 1251. "Weddings," *MPW,* 22 Nov 1919, 422. "Hurst Signed by F.N.," *MPW,* 1 Jan 1927, 14. June Lee, "Dan Cupid's Bulletin Board," *Paris and Hollywood Screen Secrets Magazine,* Aug 1927, 37 (Nova filed a divorce complaint against him). Billy H. Doyle, "Lost Players," *CI,* 156 (Jun 1988), C13, 56.

Hurst, Vida [scenarist] (b. 1890–8 Jan 1958 [67?]). BHD2, p. 130.

Hurst, W.O. [production manager]. No data found. AMD, p. 176. "W.O. Hurst Invents New Type of Animated Cartoon," *MPW,* 30 Aug 1919, 1289.

Hurt, Mary [actress] (b. 7 May 1889–6 Oct 1976 [87], Los Angeles CA). AS, p. 551. BHD1, p. 276. IFN, p. 150.

Hussey, James J. [property man] (b. 1894?–Mar? 1917 [23], Lakewood NJ; heart failure). AMD, p. 176. "Obituary," *MPW,* 7 Apr 1917, 107.

Hussy, Jimmy [actor] (b. Chicago IL, 19 Jan 1891–20 Nov 1930 [39], Woodcliff NY; tuberculosis). AS, p. 551.

Huston, Walter (father of John Huston [1906–1987]; grandfather of Angelica Huston, b. 8 Jul 1951) [stage/film actor] (*né* Walter Houghton, b. Toronto, Ontario, Canada, 6 Apr 1884–7 Apr 1950 [66], Beverly Hills CA; aneurism). m. (1) Rhea Gore, 1905–13; (2) Bayonne Whipple; (3) Nan Sutherland, Nov 1931. "Walter Huston, 66, Noted Actor, Dead; Leading Stage and Screen Star for Generation First Played on Broadway in 1924; Won 'Oscar' in Son's Film; Both Honored for 'Treasure of the Sierra Madre' [1948]—Here He Scored in 'Dodsworth,'" *NYT,* 8 Apr 1950, 13:1. "Walter Huston," *Variety,* 12 Apr 1950. AS, p. 551. BHD1, p. 276. FSFM, p. 221. IFN, p. 150. Katz, p. 592. SD. Truitt, p. 165. Ernest Corneau, "The Walter Huston Story," *CFC,* 54 (Summer, 1977), 51–52. A Walter George Houghton was born in Toronto on 8 Feb 1888; birth certificate #039833, no. 15, division of Beverly (RL).

Hustwick, Alfred [title writer]. No data found. FDY, p. 445.

Huszar-Puffy, Karl [actor] (b. Budapest, Hungary, 3 Nov 1884–1940 [55?], Tokyo, Japan). BHD1, p. 276.

Hutchins, Bobby "Wheezer" [actor: Our Gang comedies] (*né* Bobby Hutcheons, b. Tacoma WA, 29 Mar 1925–17 May 1945 [20], Merced CA). AS, p. 551. BHD1, p. 276. IFN, p. 150.

Hutchins, George C. [actor] (b. 1869–10 Oct 1952 [83?]). BHD, p. 207. IFN, p. 150.

Hutchinson, Betty [actress]. No data found. AMD, p. 176. "English Beauty Appears in 'Man Who Stayed at Home,'" *MPW,* XLI, 26 Jul 1919, 520.

Hutchinson, Canon Charles [actor] (b. England, 1887–22 Apr 1969 [82?], Brighton, England). AS, p. 551.

Hutchinson, Craig [director]. No data found. AMD, p. 176. "Cut by Broken Glass," *MPW,* 28 Sep 1918, 1862.

Hutchinson, Harry [actor] (b. Dublin, Ireland, 1893–16 Mar 1980 [87?], Milan, Italy). AS, p. 551.

Hutchinson, Josephine [stock/stage/film actress] (b. Seattle WA, 12 Oct 1898/1903–4 Jun 1998 [99?], Florence Nightingale Nursing Home, New York NY). m. (1) Robert Bell—div. 1930; (2) Robert Townsend, 1935; (3) Staats Cotsworth. (Film debut: *The Little Princess,* 1917; WB; MGM.) "Josephine Hutchinson, 94, Movie Actress," *NYT,* 10 Jun 1998, B10. Markland Taylor, "Josephine Hutchinson," *Variety,* 15 Jun 1998, 109:4. AS, p. 551. Katz, p. 592 (child actress). John Roberts, "Reels from Hollywood," *CI,* 129 (Mar 1986), 45. *The Independent,* 13 Jun 1998. Katz, *The International Film Encyclopedia,* p. 592. Ragan, *Who's Who in Hollywood,* p. 797.

Hutchinson, Mildred [child actress]. No data found. (Pathé Frérès.) AMD, p. 176. "Picture Personalities," *MPW,* VII, 10 Dec 1910, 1341. Photo, *MPSM,* Sep 1912, 11.

Hutchinson, Samuel S. [producer/executive]. No data found. AMD, p. 176. "An Important Change in the Motion Picture Map," *MPW,* V, 24 Jul 1909, 126. "Samuel S. Hutchinson," *MPW,* VII, 29 Oct 1910, 988. "The American Film Manufacturing Co.," *MPW,* 19 Nov 1910, 1162. "Samuel S. Hutchinson to Erect Mansion," *MPW,* 25 Nov 1911, 644. "American Backgrounds Attract Attention," *MPW,* 17 Feb 1912, 580. "Samuel S. Hutchinson Buys Winter Home," *MPW,* 9 Mar 1912, 875. James S. McQuare, "Chicago Letter," *MPW,* 14 Sep 1912, 1065. "Samuel S. Hutchinson Has Narrow Escape," *MPW,* 26 Apr 1913, 366. "Samuel S. Hutchinson and Family in California," *MPW,* 1 Nov 1913, 473. Samuel S. Hutchinson, "Idealistic Motography," *MPW,* 11 Jul 1914, 183–84. "Hutchison [sic] Now Safe; American Company President Escapes from War-Swept Europe to London," *NYDM,* 16 Sep 1914, 24:4. George Blaisdell, "Mecca of the Motion Picture," *MPW,* 10 Jul 1915, 215–20. Samuel S. Hutchinson, "Hutchinson Says 'It Happened,'" *MPW,* 25 Sep 1915, 2199. "New Idea in Comedy Production," *MPW,* 2 Oct 1915, 101–02. Samuel S. Huitchinson, "The Railroad Screen Novel," *MPW,* 18 Dec 1915, 2188. Samuel S. Hutchinson, "America's President Talks of Ten Years," *MPW,* 10 Mar 1917, 1502–03. "An Optimistic Outlook," *MPW,* 2 Jun 1917, 1440. "New Plans for American," *MPW,* 13 Oct 1917, 220. "Hutchinson to Spend More Money," *MPW,* 13 Oct 1917, 230. "Samuel S. Hutchinson Talks About Margarita Fischer's Work and of Other American Stars," *MPW,* 20 Oct 1917, 387. "Samuel S. Hutchinson's Son Enlists as Private," *MPW,* 12 Jan 1918, 213. "Freuler Resigns as Mutual's President," *MPW,* 18 May 1918, 971. "Hutchinson Offers Big Money for Scripts," *MPW,* 22 Jun 1918, 1725. "American Film Company Outlines Plans,m" *MPW,* 13 Jul 1918, 195. "American Plans Fully Outlined," *MPW,* 27 Jul 1918, 537. "Hutchinson Enthusiastic Over Success of Stars," *MPW,* 5 Oct 1918, 100. J.S. McQuade, "American Evolves New Sales Plan," *MPW,* 26 Oct 1918, 494. "Samuel S. Hutchinson Off to Europe," *MPW,* 28 Dec 1918, 1501. "Samuel S. Hutchinson Talks of America's Productions," *MPW,* 10 May 1919, 820. "American Head Makes Announcement," *MPW,* 6 Sep 1919, 1457. "Mrs. Hutchinson Honored," *MPW,* 4 Sep 1920, 94. Samuel S. Hutchinson, "Hutchinson, of American, Sees Greater Prosperity with Coming of New Year," *MPW,* 25 Dec 1920, 1021. "Hutchinson Tells Difference Between Re-Constructed Picture and Re-Issue," *MPW,* 2 Apr 1921, 479.

Hutchinson, William [actor] (b. Edinburgh, Scotland, 16 May 1869–7 Sep 1918 [49], Los Angeles CA). (Selig.) AMD, p. 176 (Hutchison). AS, p. 551. BHD, p. 207. "Obituary," *MPW,* 5 Oct 1918, 63 (Hutchinson).

Hutchison, Charles A. [actor/director] (b. Pittsburgh [Allegheny Co.] PA, 3 Dec 1879–30 May 1949 [69], Los Angeles CA). m. **Edith Thornton**, 1918 (d. 1984). AMD, p. 176. AS, p. 551 (Hutchinson). BHD1, p. 276; BHD2, p. 130. IFN, p. 150. Lowrey, p. 80 (b. Allegheny PA). MH, p. 119 ("Hutchinson"). WWS, p. 107. "Hutchison Seriously Injured," *MPW,* 6 Jul 1918, 96. "Charles Hutchison Recovers," *MPW,* 3 Aug 1918, 700. "Charles Hutchison Injured," *MPW,* 29 Mar 1919, 1801. "Charles Hutchison Recovered," *MPW,* 12 Apr 1919, 239. "Prominent Players to Be Featured in Pathé Serials for e Next Two Years," *MPW,* 19 Jul 1919, 377–78. "Charles Hutchison Refused to Have Double Take Dangerous Parts in 'Great Gamble,'" *MPW,* 9 Aug 1919, 845. "Hutchison Resigns from Western," *MPW,* 20 Sep 1919, 1809. "Hutchison Goes North to Make Serial for Allgood," *MPW,* 20 Sep 1919, 1832. "Allgood's 'Daredevil' Star Enacts Unusually Thrilling Awroplane Stunt," *MPW,* 14 Feb 1920, 1058. "Charles Hutchison, Serial Daredevil, to Appear in Four Serials for Pathé," *MPW,* 10 Apr 1920, 292. "Charles Hutchison Seriously Injured; Has Both Wrists Broekn Doing 'Stunt,'" *MPW,* 9 Oct 1920, 770. "Charles Hutchison, Who Was Injured Making a Pathte Serial, Is Recovering," *MPW,* 23 Oct 1920, 1124. Sumner Smith, "If Daredevil Hutchison Is Ever Sick, Think of the Nightmares He Will Have," *MPW,* 15 Jan 1921, 295. "Pathé Stunt Star Progressing Well," *MPW,* 5 Feb 1921, 708. Edward Weitzel, "Star-Author-Stuntster Hutchison Is Hanged to Everyone's Satisfaction But His Own," *MPW,* 22 Oct 1921, 921. "Charles Hutchison Signed by Steiner for Features," *MPW,* 5 Apr 1924, 478. Billy H. Doyle, "Lost Players," *CI,* 142 (Apr 1987), C12–C13. Ed Finney, "Anecdotes About Stars I Have Known," *CFC,* 44 (Fall, 1974), 53. George Katchmer, "Remembering the Great Silents," *CI,* 248 (Feb 1996), 45. Joe Moore, "Rare Find of Many 35mm Nitrate Silent Films in Boston Basement," *CI,* 263 (May 1997), 8 (including *Lightning Hutch,* Hurricane Films, 1920, with Hutchison).

Huth, Harold [actor/director/producer/scenarist] (b. Huddersfield, Yorkshire, England, 20 Jan 1892–26 Oct 1967 [75], London, England). "Harold Huth," *Variety,* 248, 8 Nov 1967, 71:2. AS, pp. 551–52. BHD1, p. 276; BHD2, p. 130. IFN, p. 151.

Hutton, Edward [cameraman] (b. MO, 1895?–31 Aug 1989 [94], Woodland Hills CA). (Paramount.) "Edward Hutton," *Variety,* 20 Sep 1989 (in silents in Colorado Springs CO). AS, p. 552.

Hutton, Leona (aunt of June Clyde) [actress] (b. 1892?–1 Apr 1949 [57], Toledo OH; overdose of sleeping pills). (American.) "Leona Hutton," *Variety,* 6 Apr 1949 (Mrs. Mary Epstein; in films 1913–24). AMD, p. 176. AS, p. 552. BHD, p. 207. IFN, p. 151. Truitt, p. 165. "Leona Hutton," *MPW,* 30 Jan 1915, 680. "Stars Added to Horsley's Array," *MPW,* 25 Sep 1915, 2187.

Hutton, Lucille [actress] (aka Ruth Higgins). No data found. AMD, p. 176. "Hutton with Century," *MPW,* 4 Oct 1924, 416. George Katchmer, "Remembering the Great Silents," *CI,* 199 (Jan 1992), 12.

Huxham, Kendrick [actor] (*né* Frank Kendrick Huxham, b. England, 22 Feb 1898–24 Jul 1967 [69], Los Angeles CA). AS, p. 552.

Hyams, John (father of **Leila Hyams**) [actor] (b. Syracuse NY, 6 Jul 1869–9 Dec 1940 [71], Los Angeles CA). m. Leila McIntyre. "John Hyams," *Variety,* 11 Dec 1940. AS, p. 552. BHD1, p. 277. IFN, p. 151. Truitt, p. 165 (b. 1877).

Hyams, Leila (daughter of vaudevillians **John Hyams** and **Leila McIntyre**) [Listerine model/actress] (b. New York NY, 1 May 1905

[Birth Certificate Index No. 21138]–4 Dec 1977 [72], Bel Air CA). m. Phil Berg, 6 Oct 1927, New York NY. (Last film: *Yellow Dust,* 1936; WB; MGM.) C. Gerald Fraser, "Leila Hyams, 72, 'Golden Girl' of the Movies in 20's and 30's, Dies," *NYT,* 9 Dec 1977, B2:1. "Leila Hyams," *Variety,* 14 Dec 1977. AMD, p. 176. AS, p. 552. BHD1, p. 277. FSS, p. 153. IFN, p. 151. Katz, pp. 593–94. "Miss Hyams Signed," *MPW,* 23 Apr 1927, 736. "Leila Hyams," *MPW,* 21 May 1927, 180. Milton Howe, "A Neat Lil' Package—That's Leila Hyams," *MPC,* Aug 1927, 63, 88. "Marriages," *Variety,* 9 Nov 1927, 36:3. "Berg—Hyams," *MPW,* 12 Nov 1927, 8. "Long Terms for McAvoy, Hyams," *MPW,* 24 Dec 1927, 10. Helen Varden, "Born to the Spotlight; Leila Hyams was bound to make good in the movies because she was reared in the theater. The daughter of well-known vaudeville parents brought her poise and talent to the screen—and uses them to fine advantage," *Movie Classic,* Sep 1931, 60, 79.

Hyams, Phil (brother of Sid Hyams) [cinema owner/impresario] (b. 26 Mar 1894–8 Jan 1997 [102], London, England). m. Yetta Kramer, 1919. (Began 1912; founded Eros, production and distribution company.) "Phil Hyams," *The London Times,* 8 Feb 1997, p. 25.

Hyatt, Clayton [actor] (d. Jun 1932, Windsor, Ontario, Canada; suicide by hanging). "Clayton Hyatt," *Variety,* 5 Jul 1932 (dieting led to nervous breakdown). AS, p. 552. BHD, p. 207. IFN, p. 151.

Hyatt, John W[esley] [inventor of celluloid film] (b. Starkey NY, 1837–1920 [83?], Millburn NJ). AS, p. 552.

Hyde, Harry [actor]. (Biograph, 1911.) No data found.

Hyde, Raymond Newton [art director]. No data found. "Consulting Art Director," *NYDM,* 11 Dec 1915, 24:3 (to producers and directors. Trained at the Boston Academy of Fine Arts, Hyde pursued art studies in Paris and Bruessels [sic], embracing landscape painting and magazine illustration. He was art director on the *Herald* and *World.* Knowledgeable about costuming and accessories, historical and modern, "incident to the practice of the art of motion photography.").

Hyer, William C. [cinematographer] (b. Ravenna NB, 20 Dec 1896–7 Feb 1947 [50], Los Angeles CA). BHD2, p. 130. FDY, p. 459.

Hylan, Donald [actor] (b. 29 May 1899–20 Jun 1968 [69], New York NY; heart attack). "Donald Hylan," *Variety,* 26 Jun 1968 (in silents at Astoria, Queens NY). AS, p. 552. BHD1, p. 611. IFN, p. 151. Truitt, p. 165.

Hyland, Frances [scenarist]. No data found. FDY, p. 429.

Hyland, Peggy [stage/film actress] (*née* Gladys Hutchinson, b. Harborne, Staffordshire, England, 11 Jun 1884). m. (2) Owen Grant Evan-Thomas, 1914; (3) **Fred Leroy Granville**, 1923–div. (d. 1932). (Vitagraph; Fox; Windsor, Bromley Road, Catford, S.E. London; Pathé; Mayfair.) (Film debut: *The Love of an Actress,* British, 1914.) AMD, p. 178. AS, p. 552. Lowrey, p. 82. MSBB, p. 1034 (b. 1897). 1921 Directory, p. 226. "Peggy Hyland Joins Famous Players," *MPW,* 15 Apr 1916. Peggy Hyland, "Artistry and Motion Pictures," *MPW,* 21 Jul 1917, 382. "Peggy Hyland—Mayfair," *MPW,* 1 Dec 1917, 1345. "Peggy Hyland Begins Work for Fox," *MPW,* 9 Feb 1918, 831. "Father of Peggy Hyland Dead," *MPW,* 26 Oct 1918, 524 (Dr. Cyril George Hutchinson, buried at sea). Gladys Hall, "Alias Peggy Hyland," *Motion Picture Magazine,* Jan 1919, 69–70, 110. "Peggy Hyland Near Death as Auto Plunges Into Sea," *MPW,* 5 Apr 1919, 64. "Peggy Hyland," *MPW,* 19 Jul 1919, 360:1. Gene Vazzana, "Peggy Hyland; A Horse of a Different Color, Part I," *CI,* 207 (Sep 1992), 22, 24; Part II, 208 (Oct 1992), C20, 33–34; Part III, 209 (Nov 1992), 46–48. Mr. Wilf Stevenson, Director, "Letter," British Film Institute, 21 Stephen Street, London W1P 1PL, 15 Dec 1992 ("She married Fred Leroy Granville, a Universal producer, in September 1921 and there are no career details beyond that date, neither is there a record of her death."). Birth date from Mrs. Janice Healey, London, Great Britain.

Hylten-Cavallius, Ragnar [producer/scenarist] (b. Stockholm, Sweden, 27 Nov 1885–15 Nov 1970 [84]). AS, p. 552. BHD2, p. 130.

Hyman, Bernard H. [producer] (b. Grafton WV, 20 Aug 1895–7 Sep 1942 [47], Los Angeles Co. CA). (Triangle, 1919; Metro, 1924.) "Bernard H. Hyman; MGM Executive, 45; Produced 'The Great Waltz' and 'Saratoga,' Jean Harlow's Last Film—Dies on Coast; In Industry 23 Years; Ex-Scenarist [*The Black Bag,* 1921] Became Aide of Thalberg at Universal Studio—Went to Metro with Him," *NYT,* 9 Sep 1942, 23:3. AS, p. 552 (b. 1897; d. 15 Sep). BHD2, p. 130. IFN, p. 151.

Hyman, Louis [actor] (b. 1875–3 Aug 1929 [54?]). BHD, p. 207.

Hymer, John B. (father of **Warren Hymer**) [actor/scenarist/playwright] (b. 1876?–16 Jun 1953 [77], Los Angeles CA). m. **Elinor Kent** (d. 1957) (Metro.) "John B. Hymer," *Variety,* 24 Jun 1953. AS, p. 553. BHD, p. 207; BHD2, p. 130.

Hymer, Warren (son of **John B. Hymer** and **Elsie Kent**) [actor] (b. New York NY, 25 Feb 1906–26 Mar 1948 [42], Los Angeles CA; stomach ailment). m. (1) Beau Williams—div. 1931; (2) actress Virginia Meyer. (Fox.) "Warren Hymer, 42, in Films 2 Decades; Actor Who Played Soft-Hearted Tough Guy in Movies Dies—Began in Father's Play [*Crime*]," *NYT,* 27 Mar 1948, 13:5 ("When Mr. Hymer was making $1,000 a week in Hollywood in 1935 he was the principal in a test case over a contract in which a ruling of the California Appellate Court decided that he was a 'white-collar worker' rather than a 'laborer.'"). "Warren Hymer," *Variety,* 31 Mar 1948. AS, p. 553. BHD1, p. 277. IFN, p. 151. Truitt, 1983.

Hynes, John E. [stage/film actor] (b. Clinton MA, 1853?–12 Apr 1931 [78], Long Island NY). "John E. Hynes," *Variety,* 15 Apr 1931. AS, p. 553. BHD, p. 207 (d. LA CA). IFN, p. 151. SD.

Hyson, Dorothy (daughter of **Dorothy Dickson**, d. 1995) [stage/film actress] (*née* Dorothy Wardell Heisen, b. Chicago IL, 24 Dec 1914–23 May 1996 [81], London, England; complications from a stroke). m. (1) Robert Douglas, 1935–45; (2) Anthony Quayle, 1947. (Film debut: *Money Mad,* 1917.) Adam Benedick, "Dorothy Hyson," *The Independent,* 25 May 1996, p. 14. AS, p. 553.

Hyspa, Vincent Ernest [actor/singer] (b. Narbonne, France, 7 Nov 1865 [extrait de naissance no. 358/1865]–12 Oct 1938 [72], Villiers-sous-Gretz, France). AS, p. 553.

Hytten, Olaf [actor] (b. Glasgow, Scotland, 3 Mar 1888–11 Mar 1955 [67], Los Angeles CA; heart attack on the set of TC-F's *Sir Walter Raleigh*). "Olaf Hytten," *Variety,* 16 Mar 1955. AS, p. 553. BHD1, p. 277. IFN, p. 151. Truitt, p. 166.

I

Ibañez, Bonaventura W. [actor] (b. Spain). JS, p. 219 (in Italian silents from 1910).

Ibanez, Vicente Blasco [poet/journalist/novelist/scenarist/translator/editor] (b. 1 Jan 1867, Valencia, Spain–28 Jan 1928 [61], Mentone, France; pneumonia). m. (1) d. Jun 1925, Valencia (sons Sigfrido Blasco and Mario); (2) Dona Elena Ortuzr Bulnes, Jul 1925. "Blasco Ibanez Dies, Spanish Novelist; Worry Over Plot Charges Said to Have Hastened Disease Causing His End at Mentone; Writing 'Peace' Horseman; It Would Centre About the Leauge—Wide Fame Won by Author in His 60 Years of Life," *NYT,* 29 Jan 1928, 23:1. AMD, p. 178. "Metro Buys Ibanez Novel," *MPW,* 29 Nov 1919, 555 (*The Four Horsemen of the Apocalypse*). "June Mathis Confers with Ibanez on 'Four Horsemen of Apocalypse,'" *MPW,* 17 Jan 1920, 431. Tom Waller, "Ibanez to Pen for Films; Says Movies Excel Books as Outlet," *MPW,* 24 Nov 1923, 376.

Ibsen, Tancred [director] (b. Gausdal, Norway, 11 Jul 1893). AS, p. 555.

Iida, Chouko [actress] (*née* Cho Mobara, b. Tokyo, Japan, 15 Apr 1897–26 Dec 1992 [95], Tokyo, Japan). AS, p. 555.

Ikeda, Yoshinobu [director] (b. Nagano, Japan, 10 Mar 1892–1 Sep 1973 [81], Tokyo, Japan). AS, p. 555.

Ikonnikoff, Alexander [actor] (b. Kiev, Russia, 1884–17 Nov 1936 [52], Los Angeles CA). BHD, p. 208. IFN, p. 151.

Illes, Eugen [director/scenarist] (*né* Jenô Illes, b. Debreczen, Hungary, 28 Jan 1877–17 Oct 1951 [74], Budapest, Hungary). AS, p. 556.

Illian, Isolde [actress] (b. Milwaukee WI, 28 May 1898–5 Nov 1963 [65], Beverly Hills CA). BHD, p. 208.

Illing, Peter [actor] (b. Vienna, Austria, 4 Mar 1899–29 Oct 1966 [67], London, England). AS, p. 556.

Illington, Margaret [stage/film actress] (*née* Maude Light, b. Bloomington IL, 23 Jul

1881–11 Mar 1934 [52], Miami Beach FL). m. Daniel Frohman, 1903; Major E.J. Bowes. (Film debut: *The Inner Shrine,* 1917.) "Margaret Illington," *Variety,* 13 Mar 1934. AMD, p. 178. AS, p. 556. BHD, p. 208. IFN, p. 151. Truitt, p. 166. "Margaret Illington a Lasky Star," *MPW,* 13 Jan 1917, 203. "Margaret Illington Departs for Lasky Studio," *MPW,* 17 Feb 1917, 1028.

Illington, Marie [actress] (b. London, England, 1856–3 Feb 1927 [70?], London, England). BHD, p. 208.

Illuminati, Ivo [director] (b. Ripatranzone, Italy, 11 Jun 1892–6 Sep 1963 [71], Rome, Italy). AS, p. 556. JS, p. 219 (in Italian silents from 1914).

Ilmari, Wilho [actor/director] (b. Hymi, Finland, 24 Apr 1888–18 Aug 1983 [95], Turku, Finland). AS, p. 556. BHD2, p. 131.

Imboden, David C. [actor] (b. Kansas City MO, 6 Mar 1887–18 Mar 1974 [87], Kansas City MO). m. **Hazel** Bourne (d. 1956). "David Imboden," *Variety,* 27 Mar 1974 (in over 100 silents). AS, p. 556 (d. 19 Mar). BHD, p. 208. IFN, p. 151. Truitt, 1983.

Imboden, Hazel [actress] (*née* Hazel Bourne, b. Washburn IL–d. 8 Oct 1956, Kansas City MO). m. **David C. Imboden** (d. 1974). AS, p. 556. IFN, p. 151. Truitt, p. 166.

Imhof, Marcelle [actress] (*née* Marcelle Coreen, b. 1888–15 Jan 1977 [88?], Los Angeles CA). m. **Roger Imhof** (d. 1958). AS, p. 556.

Imhof, Roger [actor] (*né* Fred Roger Imhof, b. Rock Island IL, 15 Apr 1875–15 Apr 1958 [83], Los Angeles CA). m. **Marcelle** (d. 1977). AS, p. 556.

Impekoven, Sabine [actress] (b. 1889–5 May 1970 [81?]). BHD, p. 208.

Imperio, Pastora [actress] (b. Seville, Spain, 1889–14 Sep 1979 [90], Madrid, Spain). BHD1, p. 278. IFN, p. 152.

Impolito, John [actor] (b. Italy, 1 Sep 1886–1 May 1962 [75], Los Angeles CA). AS, p. 556.

Inagaki, Hiroshi [actor] (b. Japan, 1905–21 May 1980 [75?], Tokyo, Japan). BHD, p. 208.

Ince, John Edward [stage actor/director] (brother of **Thomas H.** and **Ralph Ince**) (b. New York NY, 29 Aug 1878–10 Apr 1947 [68], Los Angeles CA; pneumonia). m. Emma G., 10 Jul 1899—sep. 14 Nov 1923; **Ethel Kent** (d. 1952). (Lubin; World; Equitable.) "John Ince; Old-Time Actor on Stage and Screen Is Dead at 60," *NYT,* 11 Apr 1947, 25:5. "John E. Ince," *Variety,* 16 Apr 1947. AMD, p. 178. AS, p. 556. BHD1, p. 278; BHD2, p. 131. IFN, p. 152. Katz, p. 597. MSBB, p. 1046 (b. 1879). Truitt, p. 166. "John Ince," *MPW,* 14 Feb 1914, 817. "John Ince," *MPW,* 18 Jul 1914, 443. "John Ince," *MPW,* 12 Sep 1914, 1488. "John Ince Joins Equitable," *NYDM,* 11 Aug 1915, 21:4 (left Lubin to direct *The Cowardly Way* for World). "John Ince, Equitable Director," *MPW,* 21 Aug 1915, 1304. "Ralph and John Ince Join," *MPW,* 21 Apr 1917, 408. "Karger Engages Directors for Three Plays to Be Filmed by Screen Classics," *MPW,* 19 Jul 1919, 352. "John Edward Ince to Continue as Metro Director; Denies Plan to Leave," *MPW,* 20 Mar 1920, 1984. "Ince to Direct 'Girl of Gold,'" *MPW,* 6 Dec 1924, 553. June Lee, "Dan Cupid's Bulletin Board," *Paris and Hollywood Screen Secrets,* Oct 1927, 36 (to divorce Emma. "Mrs. Ince complains of cruelty and desertion, and Ince makes substantially the same charges.").

Ince, Ralph Waldo [stage/film actor/director] (brother of **Thomas H.** and **John Ince**) (b. 36 Dennis Street, Boston MA, 15 Jan 1887 [MVRB, Vol. 378, p. 225]–11 Apr 1937 [50], Kensington, London, England; car crash). m. **Lucille Lee Stewart**, 1907, Sheepshead Bay, LI NY—div. 1 Jul 1926; (2) Lucilla Mendez, 1926; (3) Helen Tigges. (Vitagraph.) "Ralph W. Ince," *Variety,* 14 Apr 1927. AMD, p. 178. AS, p. 556 (b. 16 Jan; d. 10 Apr). BHD1, p. 278; BHD2, p. 131 (b. 16 Jan 1882). IFN, p. 152. Katz, p. 597. MSBB, p. 1046. SD. Slide, p. 142 (b. 1882). Spehr, p. 144 (b. 1887). Truitt, p. 166 (b. 1887). "Ralph Ince as Lincoln Agjain," *MPW,* 3 Jan 1914, 56. "Ralph Ince as Lincoln," *MPW,* 28 Feb 1914, 1102. "Learned Business from Bottom Up," *MPW,* 11 Jul 1914, 285. "Ralph W. Ince; Director and Actor in the Vitagraph Company," *MPS,* 9 Oct 1914, 27 (b. 1887). "Ralph Ince—Actor, Cartoonist, Etc.," *MPW,* 26 Dec 1914, 1828. "Ralph Ince to Remain with Vitagrpah," *MPW,* 23 Jan 1915, 492. "Ralph Ince Leaves Vitagraph," *MPW,* 11 Nov 1916, 876. "Ralph Waldo Ince Engaged by Goldwyn," *MPW,* 13 Jan 1917, 211. "Ralph and John Ince Join," *MPW,* 21 Apr 1917, 408. "Ralph Waldo Ince," *MPW,* 23 Mar 1918, 1678. "Ralph Ince at Head of New Company," *MPW,* 8 Jun 1918 (*Ralph Ince Film Attractions*). "Ralpoh Ince to Direct Ethel Barrymore," *MPW,* 29 Jun 1918, 1857. "Ralph Ince Gets Praise from E.K. Lincoln," *MPW,* 28 Dec 1918, 1547. "Vitagraph Engages Ince to Make Leslie Subject," *MPW,* 22 Feb 1919, 1058. "Ralph Ince Will Make But One Vitagraph Film," *MPW,* 1 Mar 1919, 1197. "Ralph Ince to Produce for Selznick Pictures," *MPW,* 24 May 1919, 1139. "Ralph Ince Will Direct Myron Selznick Features," *MPW,* 10 Jan 1920, 260. "Myron Selznick Assigns Ralph Ince to Direct Faversham in 'Justice,'" *MPW,* 9 Jul 1921, 227. "'A Man's Home' Crowns Career of Actor-Director Ralph Ince," *MPW,* 29 Oct 1921, 1064. "Ralph Waldo Ince Enters Production Field as an Independent, with David M. Thomas," *MPW,* 23 May 1925, 406. "On the Set and Off," *MW,* 1 Aug 1925, 43 (divorced Stewart because of her unreasonable jealousy). June Lee, "Dan Cupid's Bulletin Board," *Paris and Hollywood,* Oct 1926, 85–86 (married Mendez, a former chorus girl and "now under contract in motion pictures."). "F.B.O. Signs Director Ralph Ince," *MPW,* 16 Oct 1926, 440. "Ralph Ince on F.B.O. Contract," *MPW,* 2 Apr 1927, 489. "Ince at Work on Script for F.B.O.'s 'Coney Island,'" *MPW,* 30 Jul 1927, 331. "Ralph Ince Judges Coney Beauty Contest," *MPW,* 20 Aug 1927, 532. "Ralph Waldo Ince," *MPW,* 10 Sep 1927, 93.

Ince, Richard W. (son of **Thomas H. Ince**) [actor] (b. Beverly Hills CA, 1915–27 Nov 1938 [23?], Oakland CA; racing accident). AS, p. 556.

Ince, Thomas Harper [stage actor/director/producer] (brother of **John** and **Ralph Ince**; father of **Richard W. Ince**) (b. Newport RI, 6 Nov 1881–20 Nov 1924 [43], Beverly Hills CA; acute indigestion, but under mysterious circumstances; had been guest at Hearst ranch). m. **Eleanor Kahn**; **Alice Kershaw** (d. 1971). (Biograph; Imp; NYMPC; Triangle.) "Ince Left $4,000,000; Widow and Three Children Inherit Film Producer's Estate," *NYT,* 12 Dec 1924, 21:3. "Thomas H. Ince," *Variety,* 26 Nov 1924. AMD, p. 179. AS, p. 556. BHD, p. 208 (b. 1882; d. 19 Nov); BHD2, p. 131 (d. 19 Nov). IFN, p. 152 (b. 16 Nov 1882). Katz, pp. 597–98. Lowrey, p. 84. MSBB, p. 1046. Slide, p. 161. Truitt, p. 152. "Thomas H. Ince," *MPW,* 20 May 1911, 1123. "Thomas H. Ince," *MPW,* 3 Aug 1912, 447. "Handed It to Ince," *MPW,* 7 Dec 1912, 969 (b. 15 Nov). "Lives of the Players; Thomas H. Ince; Director of Kay-Bee and Broncho Companies," *MPS,* 23 May 1913, 29. "Ince to Make Japanese Picture," *MPW,* 31 Jan 1914, 554. "The Making of Ince; How Thomas H., of Inceville, Came to Enter Pictures and His Rapid Rise," *NYDM,* 10 Jun 1914, 32:1. "Tom Ince and 'Inceville,'" *MPW,* 11 Jul 1914, 182. "Ince Has His Own Indians and Cowboys," *MPW,* 14 Nov 1914, 949. "Thomas H. Ince," *MPW,* 2 Jan 1915, 79. "Emotional Mr. Ince," *MPW,* 13 Feb 1915, 1000. W.E. Wing, "Ince Seriously Injured; Doctors Fear for Life of Thomas Ince, New York Motion Picture Producer and Official, Injured When Automobile Skids and Overturns," *NYDM,* 28 Apr 1915, 22.2 ("...his machine struck a wet spot and turned over twice." He received a broken collar bone and possible internal injuries. "The doctors state that the film man was near a nervous breakdown anyway as a result of the long hours and constant hard work while producing 'The Sign of the Rose'..."). "Thomas Ince Recovering; Producer Injured in Auto Accident Thought on Way to Recovery," *NYDM,* 5 May 1915, 22:4. "Picking the Screen 'Type,'" *NYDM,* 14 Jul 1915, 12:2 (interview re "What are the requirements for a GIRL who wishes to go into pictures?"). "Ince Directs Four Features at Once," *MPW,* 31 Jul 1915, 839. "The Feature Has a Future," *MPW,* 14 Aug 1915, 1166. 'Ince to Move to Culver City," *MPW,* 9 Oct 1915, 272. 'Ince to Start School," *MPW,* 19 Feb 1916, 111–12. "Ince Talks of Culver City," *MPW,* 3 Jun 1916, 1697. "Tom Ince Offers $1,000 for an Idea," *MPW,* 22 Jul 1916, 615. "Ince Discovers New Musical Instrument," *MPW,* 7 Oct 1916, 83. "Thomas H. Ince Back at Culver City," *MPW,* 28 Oct 1916, 557–58. "Ince and Sennett Continue in Triangle," *MPW,* 10 Feb 1917, 827. Thomas H. Ince, 'Looking Back," *MPW,* 10 Mar 1917, 1506. "Ince Definitely Out of Triangle," *MPW,* 30 Jun 1917, 2071. "Ince to Build Los Angeles Studio," *MPW,* 7 Jul 1917, 73. "Ince Goes to Art-Craft-Paramount," *MPW,* 14 Jul 1917, 216. "Ince Arrives in Los Angeles," *MPW,* 28 Jul 1917, 628. Neil G. Caward, "Screen Gossip," *Picture-Play Magazine,* Sep 1917, 101 (Ince and Sennett resigned from Triangle). "Ince to Build Studio in Culver City," *MPW,* 8 Dec 1917, 1474. "Tom Ince Lays Out Work for His Chief Players," *MPW,* 1 Jun 1918, 1334. "Ince Culver City Studios Rapidly Near Completion," *MPW,* XXXVIII, 7 Dec 1918, 1073. "Ince Re-Signs with Famous Players," *MPW,* 15 Feb 1919, 895. "Ince Chosen Producers' President; Tucker Is Latest Member of Group," *MPW,* 13 Dec 1919, 777. Thomas H. Ince, "Past Year Was One of Enexampled Prosperity for Picture Industry," *MPW,* 3 Jan 1920, 97. Hunt Stromberg, "East Cannot Hope to Desplace West as Picutre Centre, Says Thomas H. Ince," *MPW,* 21 Feb 1920, 1205. "Thomas Ince Offers Columbis Students $2,000 for Photoplays Suited to Needs," *MPW,* 20 Mar 1920, 1976. "Ince Thanks Press for Co-operation and Says Industry Is Booming Rapidly," *MPW,* 10 Apr 1920, 289. "Reputable Schools for Budding Genius Can Advance Screen Art, Says Director," *MPW,* 15 May 1920, 966. 'Thomas H. Ince completing Newspaper and Exhibitor Exploitation Photoplay," *MPW,* 14 Aug 1920, 879 (*A Trip Through the World's Greatest Motion Picture Studio*). "Ince Buys Home Site," *MPW,* 9 Jul 1921, 211. "Too Much Tinsel, Not Enough Truth Is Trouble with Pictures, Says Ince," *MPW,* 3 Sep 1921, 91. "Ince Declares the Industry Must Satisfy the Public's

Appetite for Human Drama," *MPW,* 17 Dec 1921, 820. Thomas H. Ince, "The Outlook for 1922," *MPW,* 31 Dec 1921, 1050. Thomas H. Ince, "Must Cater to Demand for Bigger and Better Pictures," *MPW,* 31 Dec 1921, 1052. "Public Unutterably Opposes Censorship, Star System Passing, Ince Survey Shows," *MPW,* 4 Mar 1922, 37. "Thomas H. Ince Called Back to Los Angeles," *MPW,* 8 Apr 1922, 606. "'Leech Pictures' Endanger Confidence of Public in Screen, Says Tom Ince," *MPW,* LV, 8 Apr 1922, 611. "Thomas Ince to Produce for Warners," *MPW,* 20 May 1922, 253. "Mr. Ince to Produce for Mr. Ince," *MPW,* 27 May 1922, 376 (not with Warners). "First National Sues Thomas H. Ince Over Alleged Violation of Contract," *MPW,* 24 Jun 1922, 698. "Ince Denies Rumore Regarding His Plans," *MPW,* 15 Jul 1922, 208. "Thomas Ince Predicts Big Boom for Picture Industry," *MPW,* 30 Dec 1922, 838. "Amplifies Statement," *MPW,* 27 Jan 1923, 319. "First National Renews Contract with Ince for Series of Specials," *MPW,* 24 Mar 1923, 407. "Ince Makes Special Print of 'Civilization' for U.S. Archives," *MPW,* 7 Apr 1923, 611. "Ince to Direct Personally One Special a Year for First National," *MPW,* 14 Apr 1923, 718. "Elaborate Specials Planned by Thomas H. Ince for Coming Year," *MPW,* 9 Jun 1923, 506. Thomas H. Ince, "Originality the Ince Keynote," *MPW,* 9 Jun 1923, 522. "Ince Denies Rumor," *MPW,* 3 Nov 1923, 38. "Ince Forecast Optimistic," *MPW,* 29 Dec 1923, 802. "Ince Production Plans Involve Reorganization of Studio Force," *MPW,* 23 Feb 1924, 629. "Ince Acquires Hollywood Laboratory and Equipment," *MPW,* 29 Mar 1924, 361. "Charles Ray Signs for Series Under Old Director, Tom Ince," *MPW,* 29 Mar 1924, 368. "Thomas Ince Renews Contract; To Make Six First Nationals," *MPW,* 14 Jun 1924, 652. "Ince to Stay West," *MPW,* 2 Aug 1924, 346. "Ince Finishes Cutting," *MPW,* 11 Oct 1924, 507 (*Christine of the Hungry Heart*). "Obituary," *MPW,* 29 Nov 1924, 403–04 (d. 19 Nov, age 44). "Ince to Star Jacqueline Logan," *MPW,* 29 Nov 1924, 428 (to be under his personal direction for more than five years). "Ince to Make 'Enchanted Hill,'" *MPW,* 29 Nov 1924, 432. "Philadelphia Critics Acclaim Ince's 'Barbara Frietchie,'" *MPW,* 29 Nov 1924, 433. "Ince's Widow Takes Helm; Corporation Will Continue; Tributes to Decedent," *MPW,* 6 Dec 1924, 513. "Ince's Death Natural, Prosecutor Asserts; District Attorney Announces That No Investigation Will Be Made by County Authorities," *NYT,* 11 Dec 1924, 6:2 ("heart failure as the result of acute indigestion." Ince's doctor and nurse said that Ince said he had had too much bad liquor on the yacht. "If there is any liquor investigation made it will have to be made in Los Angeles, where, presumably, the liquor was secured," said D.A. Chester C. Kempley."). Dorothy Donnell, "From Hollywood to You," *MPS,* 30 Dec 1924, 10 ("The Ince studios are shutting down. Eighty-five employees were given their notice..." Mrs. Ince said this was normal to shut down and release completed films. She planned to run the studio herself.). "Last Minute Flashes," *MPW,* 13 Nov 1926, 4. Fred S. Walburn and Will Wayne, "Inceville—The Ghost City of the Movies; Inceville-on-the-Pacific Is Now a Stretch of California Landscape. A Few Years Ago It Was the Capital of Movieland Where Stars Were Made Overnight," *MPC,* Jul 1927, 18–19, 70; Part II, *MPC,* Aug 1927, 41. 68, 88 (mentions Frank Borzage, Jerome Storm and N. Dick Stanton).

Inclan, Miguel [actor] (*né* Miguel Inclan Camacho, b. Mexico, Jun 1900–25 Jul 1956 [56], Tijuana, Mexico; cirrhosis of the liver). AS, p. 556.

Inescort, Elaine (mother of Frieda Inescort [1901–1976]) [stage/film actress] (*née* Charlotte Elizabeth Ihle, b. London, England, 1877?–7 Jul 1964 [87], Brighton, England). m. (1) John Wightman; (2) Harry de Lindt. "Elaine Inescort," *Variety,* 15 Jul 1964. AS, p. 557. BHD, p. 208. SD, p. 654.

Ingalls, Bernice [actress] (b. 1895–25 Feb 1987 [91?], Jacksonville FL). AS, p. 557. BHD, p. 208.

Ingersoll, George [publicist]. No data found. AMD, p. 180. "Ingersoll Joins Goldwyn's Press Staff," *MPW,* XL, 21 Jun 1919, 1780.

Ingersoll, Helene Marjorie [actress]. No data found. m. **Joe Ryan**, Oct? 1918, Merced CA. AMD, p. 180. "Joe Ryan Married," *MPW,* 2 Nov 1918, 595.

Ingersoll, William [stage/film actor] (b. New York NY, 9 Oct 1860–7 May 1936 [75], Los Angeles CA; acute indigestion). "William Ingersoll," *Variety,* 13 May 1936. AS, p. 557. BHD1, p. 278 (b. Lafayette IN, 1862). IFN, p. 152. SD. Truitt, p. 167.

Ingles, W.A. [actor/director/scenarist] (b. 1882–4 Aug 1952 [70?], Burbank CA). BHD2, p. 131.

Ingleton, E[ugenie] **Magnus** [scenarist] (b. London, England, 1886-Jul 1936 [50?]). BHD2, p. 131.

Ingleton, George [actor/scenarist/historian] (b. 1861?–19 May 1926 [65], Dark Canyon CA; auto accident). m. Midge. "George Ingleton," *Variety,* 26 May 1926. Edwin Gallinagh, quip, *Paris and Hollywood,* Oct 1926, 37 (he recently "sold a library to which he has been adding and collecting for over forty years, to the Fox company for $100,000 cash. His widow, 'Midge' Ingleton, is also widely known in the theatrical world, and is the author of the musical comedy, *Patsy.*"). BHD2, p. 131.

Inglis, W.A. "Gus" [actor] (b. 1882–4 Aug 1952 [70?], Burbank CA). AS, p. 557. BHD, p. 208.

Ingraham, Frank L. [scenarist]. No data found. FDY, p. 429.

Ingraham, Harrish [actor/scenarist/director] (b. London, England, 1881). (Pathé Frérès; Whitman's Features; Centaur.) BHD, p. 208. "Among the Players," *NYDM,* 29 Jul 1914, 25:3. "Harrish Ingraham with Horsley," *MPW,* 10 Jun 1916, 1872.

Ingraham, Lloyd [actor/scenarist/director] (b. Rochelle IL, 30 Nov 1874–4 Apr 1956 [81], Woodland Hills CA). "Lloyd Ingraham," *Variety,* 11 Apr 1956 (began 1912). AMD, p. 180. AS, p. 557. BHD1, p. 278; BHD2, p. 131 (d. Calabasas CA). FDY, p. 429. IFN, p. 152. Katz, p. 600 (began 1912). KOM, p. 144. Truitt, p. 167. "Lloyd Ingraham to Direct DeHavens in 'Twin Beds,'" *MPW,* 10 Jul 1920, 212. "Lloyd Ingraham Will Direct New DeHaven Comedy Feature," *MPW,* 16 Oct 1920, 976. "Associated Authors Sign Ingraham," *MPW,* 4 Aug 1923, 419. "Lloyd Ingraham," *MPW,* 27 Aug 1927, 588.

Ingram, Carl [actor] (b. Atchison KS, 1878). BHD, p. 208.

Ingram, Rex [actor/director] (*né* Reginald Ingram Montgomery Hitchcock, b. Rathmines, Dublin, Ireland, 15 Jan 1893–21 Jul 1950 [57], Los Angeles CA). m. **Doris Pawn** (d. 1988); **Alice Terry**, Nov 1921, Pasadena CA. (d. 1987). (Edison; Vitagraph; Fox; Universal; MGM.) Liam O'Leary, *Rex Ingram: Master of the Silent Cinema* (Le Giornate del Cinema Muto/British Film Institute, 1993). "Rex Ingram Dead; Film Director, 58; Screen Leader of Silent Era Credited with Discovery of Rudolph Valentino," *NYT,* 23 Jul 1950, 57:1 (age 58). "Rex Ingram," *Variety,* 26 Jul 1950 (*né* "Fitchcock," d. No. Hollywood CA, age 58). AS, p. 557. BHD, p. 208; BHD2, p. 131. IFN, p. 152. Katz, p. 600 (b. 1892). Lowrey, p. 86. 1921 Directory, p. 267 (b. 1892). Slide, p. 143. Truitt, p. 167. "Rex Ingram Joins Paralta Forces," *MPW,* 20 Oct 1917, 388. "Ingram Joins Metro Directorial Staff," *MPW,* 6 Dec 1919, 658. Edward Weitzel, "Director Rex Ingram of Metro Appraises 'The Four Horsemen of the Apocalypse,'" *MPW,* 19 Feb 1921, 923. "Rex Ingram Has Returned to Hollywood to Begin Work on Series of Productions," *MPW,* 23 Apr 1921, 852. Lillian Montanye, "The Master Hand," *MPC,* Jul 1921, 58, 84. "Rex Ingram Says Direjctor and Photographer Must Cooperate," *MPW,* 22 Oct 1921, 937. "Surprise Weddings," *MPW,* 3 Dec 1921, 566. "Rex Ingram at Work Instead of Resting," *MPW,* 2 Sep 1922, 35. "Ingram and Company in New York," *MPW,* 13 Jan 1923, 166. "Ince Has Arrived in Egypt," *MPW,* 10 Nov 1923, 244. "Rex Ingram in Tunis," *MPW,* 2 Feb 1924, 379. "Metro Studio Preparing for Ingram's Return Here," *MPW,* 8 Mar 1924, 120. 'Ingram Sails This Week," *MPW,* 15 Mar 1924, 197 (left 15 Mar 1924). "Rex Ingram Returns," *MPW,* 22 Mar 1924, 286. Ralph Willoughby, "Why I Am Leaving the Movies at the Height of My Career," *MW,* 19 Apr 1924, 13, 26. "Ingram to Start Work on 'The Magician' February 15," *MPW,* 20 Feb 1926, 714. Henry Albert Phillips, "The Hollywood of France; Rex Ingram Has Found a Paradise—a Perfect Arcadia by the Sea...," *MPC,* Sep 1926, 32–33, 66, 87.

Ingram, Rex [stage/film actor] (b. near Cairo IL, 20 Oct 1895–19 Sep 1969 [73], Los Angeles CA). m. (1) Lauwaune Kennard; (2) Dena Guillroy; (3) Francine Everett (d. 1999). "Rex Ingram, the Actor, Dies in Hollywood at 73; His Portrayal of De Lawd in 'Green Pastures' Hailed—Medical School Graduate," *NYT,* 20 Sep 1969, 29:2. "Rex Ingram," *Variety,* 23 Sep 1969. AS, p. 557. BHD1, p. 278. IFN, p. 152. Katz, pp. 600–601. SD. Truitt, p. 167.

Ingram, William D. [actor] (b. 1852?–2 Feb 1926 [73], New York NY [Death Certificate Index No. 3507 (Will D. Ingram)]). "William D. Ingram," *Variety,* 10 Feb 1926 (age 69). AS, p. 557 (b. 1856). BHD, p. 208 (b. 1857). IFN, p. 152. WWS, p. 167.

Inkijinoff, Valery Invanovich [actor] (b. Irkoutsk, Russia, 26 Mar 1895–27 Sep 1973 [78], Brunoy, France [extrait de décès no. 167/1973]). AS, p. 557.

Innes, T.A. [scenarist]. No data found. FDY, p. 429.

Inokuchi, Makoto [stage/film actor] (b. Japan). (Balboa; Selig.) AMD, p. 180. "Makoto Inokuchi in Selig Character Parts," *MPW,* 27 Feb 1915, 1295. "A Japanese Photoplayer," *MPW,* 29 May 1915, 1421. J. Van Cartmell, "...News from the Pacific Colony," *NYDM,* 8 Sep 1915, 33:2. Cal York, "Plays and Players," *Photoplay Magazine,* Feb 1917, 88 (Makato Inokuchi returned to Japan. "The former Balboa players believes that there is a great future for a film-wise Jap boy in his native land and he will endeavor to rake in the yens and sens with a company of Nipponese actors.").

Inouye, Masao [actor]. No data found. AMD, p. 180. "Inouye, Japanese Artist, May Play in This Country," *MPW,* 14 Aug 1920, 882.

Inslee, Charles E. [actor] (Biograph, 1908; Bison; Kalem.) AMD, p. 181. Spehr, p. 144. "The Universal in the Hawaiian Islands," *MPW,* 28 Dec 1912, 1302. "Film Comedian Victim of Thugs," *MPW,* 28 Sep 1918, 1902. Quip, *NYDM,* 23 Oct 1915, 26:3 (added to the Kalem staff of comedians. "He will appear under the euphonious title of Spike.").

Intropidi, Ethel [stage/film actress] (b. New York NY, 1896–18 Dec 1946 [50?], New York NY). (Last Broadway appearance: *Doctors Disagree,* 1943.) "Ethel Intropodi [sic]," *Variety,* 165, 25 Dec 1946, 44:4. BHD, p. 208.

Inwood, Alice [actress/writer]. No data found. AMD, p. 181. "From the War Zone to the Cycle," *MPW,* 28 Aug 1915, 1501.

Iny, Flore [actress] (b. Liege, Belgium, 1 Jul 1899). AS, p. 558.

Ipsen, Bodil [actress/director] (b. Copenhagen, Denmark, 30 Aug 1889–26 Nov 1964 [75], Copenhagen, Denmark). AS, p. 558. BHD2, p. 131.

Irani, Ardeshir M. [director/producer] (b. Poona, India, 5 Dec 1880–24 Oct 1969 [88], Bombay, India). AS, p. 558. BHD2. p. 131.

Ireland, Frederick J. [actor] (d. 22 Jun 1939, Detroit MI). m. Nema Catto. "Fred Ireland," *Variety,* 28 Jun 1939.

Irene [actress: Sennett Bathing Beauty/costume designer] (*né* Irene Lentz, b. Baker MT, 8 Dec 1900–15 Nov 1962 [61], Los Angeles CA; suicide by jumping from a window at the Knickerbocker Hotel). m. F. Richard Jones; Elliott Gibbons. (Sennett; MGM.) "Irene," *Variety,* 21 Nov 1962. AS, p. 558. BHD, p. 228 (Lentz, b. 1907); BHD2, p. 131. Katz, p. 602 (*née* Irene Gibbons). SD. Truitt, 1983 (b. 1907).

Iribe, Marie-Louise [actress/director] (*née* Pauline Marie Louise Lavoisot, b. Paris, France, 29 Nov 1894 [extrait de naissance no. 5563]-1930 [36?], France). AS, p. 558.

Iribe, Paul Joseph [setting and costume designer/director/art director] (b. Angouleme, France, 8 Jun 1885–21 Sep 1935 [50], Roquebrune-cap-Martin, France [extrait de décès no. 6/1935]). AMD, p. 181. AS, p. 558. "Paul Iribe, French Designer of Gowns and Decorations, Joins Famous Players," *MPW,* 14 Aug 1920, 886. "Paul Iribe Goes to Coast to Aid in Making 'Anatol,'" *MPW,* 20 Nov 1920, 375. "Art Director Hurt," *MPW,* 29 Oct 1921, 1026. "Iribe to Go with Cecil B. DeMille," *MPW,* 19 Nov 1921, 332. "C. DeMille and Paul Iribe Introduced to the Pope," *MPW,* LIV, 14 Jan 1922, 167. "C.B. DeMille and Paul Iribe Are Coming from Europe," *MPW,* 11 Feb 1922, 609.

Irish, William [title writer] (*né* Cornell George Hopley-Woolrich, b. New York NY, 4 Dec 1903–25 Sep 1968 [64], New York NY). Frank M. Nevins, Jr., *Cornell Woolrich: First You Dream, Then You Die* (NY: Mysterious Press, 1988). "Cornell Woolrich, Author, Dies; Mysteries Adapted for Movies," *NYT,* 26 Sep 1968, 47:2; "Writer Leaves $825,000 to Aid Columbia Students," 12 Dec 1968, 29:3. "Cornel Woolrich," *Variety,* 2 Oct 1968 (age 64). FDY, p. 445.

Irvin, Victor [scenarist]. No data found. FDY, p. 429.

Irvine, Clarke [publicist]. No data found. AMD, p. 181. "Irvine Resigns from Goldwyn," *MPW,* 12 Jun 1920, 1448. "Irvine Joins 'Big Six'; To Exploit Tourneur Productions," *MPW,* 26 Jun 1920, 1776. "Wild Waves Call Irvine, Who Quits Exploitation," *MPW,* 1 Jan 1921, 91.

Irvine, Robin [actor] (b. London, England, 21 Dec 1901–28 Apr 1933 [31], London, England). BHD1, p. 279 (b. Irvinestown, No. Ireland, 1899). IFN, p. 152.

Irvine, William H. [actor/director] (b. 1867–18 Feb 1934 [66?], Miami FL). BHD2, p. 131.

Irving, Ethel[yn] [stage/film actress] (aka Birdie Irving, b. England, 5 Sep 1869–3 May 1963 [93], Bexhill-on-Sea, England). m. Gilbert Porteous (d. 1928). "Ethel Irving," *Variety,* 15 May 1963. AS, p. 558. BHD, p. 208. IFN, p. 153. SD.

Irving, George [Henry] [actor/director] (b. New York NY, 5 Oct 1874–11 Sep 1961 [86], Los Angeles CA). "George Irving," *Variety,* 13 Sep 1961 (age 87). AMD, p. 181. AS, p. 558. BHD1, p. 279; BHD2, p. 131. IFN, p. 152. Katz, pp. 602–603 (began 1913). Truitt, pp. 167–68. "Director Irving Takes Vacation," *MPW,* 21 Apr 1917, 410. "George Irving with Popular Plays," *MPW,* 23 Jun 1917, 1945. "George Irving to Direct for Metro," *MPW,* 26 Jan 1918, 492. "George Irving Joins Goldwyn," *MPW,* 22 Jun 1918, 1700. "Film Division Names Director Advisors," *MPW,* 20 Jul 1918, 363–64. "Goldwyn Proud of Its Quintet of Directors," *MPW,* 27 Jul 1918, 547. Edward Weitzel, "As Director George Irving Thinks," *MPW,* 1 Mar 1919, 1177. "Irving Will Direct Edith Hallor," *MPW,* 31 Jan 1920, 737. "Terwilliger Ill, Irving Is Directing 'Misleading Lady,'" *MPW,* 4 Sep 1920, 66. "George Irving Signed to Direct Mollie King," *MPW,* 6 Nov 1920, 64. George Katchmer, "Remembering the Great Silents," *CI,* 206 (Aug 1992), 38–39.

Irving, H[enry] **B**[roadrib] [actor] (b. London, England, 5 Aug 1870–17 Oct 1919 [49], London, England). AS, p. 558. BHD, p. 208.

Irving, Harry R. [actor/scenarist] (b. 1895–24 May 1960 [65?], New York NY). AS, p. 558. BHD2, p. 132.

Irving, Kelville E. [composer] (b. England, 1878–24 Oct 1953 [75?], London, England). AS, p. 558.

Irving, Margaret [actress] (b. Pittsburgh PA, 18 Jan 1898–5 Mar 1988 [90], Stanton CA). BHD1, p. 279.

Irving, Mary Jane [actress] (*née?,* b. Columbis SC, 20 Oct 1913–17 Jul 1983 [69], Bel Air CA; suicide by shooting). m. Robert Carson. BHD1, p. 279. Billy H. Doyle, "Lost Players," *CI,* 174 (Dec 1989), C12.

Irving, Paul [actor] (b. Boston MA, 24 Aug 1877–8 May 1959 [81], Los Angeles CA). AS, p. 558.

Irving, Wallace [actor/scenarist] (b. Oneida NY, 15 Mar 1875–14 Feb 1959 [83], Southern Pines NC). BHD2, p. 132.

Irving, William J. [actor] (*né* Gustav Ludderman, b. Hamburg, Germany, 17 May 1893–25 Dec 1943 [50], Los Angeles CA). "William J. Irving," *Variety,* 5 Jan 1944. AMD, p. 181. AS, p. 559. BHD1, p. 279. IFN, p. 152. Truitt, p. 168. "William 'Bill' Iiving," *MPW,* 12 Nov 1927, 23.

Irwin, Boyd [actor] (b. Brighton, England, 12 Mar 1880–22 Jan 1957 [76], Woodland Hills CA). "Boyd Irwin," *Variety,* 30 Jan 1957. AS, p. 559. BHD1, p. 279. IFN, p. 152. Truitt, p. 168.

Irwin, Charles W[esley] [actor] (b. Curragh, Ireland, 31 Jan 1887–12 Jan 1969 [81], Woodland Hills CA; cancer). "Charles W. Irwin," *Variety,* 15 Jan 1969. AS, p. 559. BHD1, p. 279. IFN, p. 152.

Irwin, May [vaudeville/stage/film actress] (*née* May Campbell, b. Whitby, Ontario, Canada, 27 Jun 1862–22 Oct 1938 [76], Part Crescent Hotel, New York NY; bronchial pneumonia). m. (1) Frederick W. Keller (d. 1886; 2 sons, Harry and Walter); (2) Kurt Eisfeldt, 1907. (Film debut: *The Kiss,* Edison, Apr 1896; second and final film, *Mrs. Black Is Back,* Paramount, 30 Nov 1914.) "May Irwin Dead; Comedienne, 76; Stage Favorite of 90s and Early Part of This Century Was 50 Years in Theatre; Introduced Noted Songs; Began Career with Sister at 12—Named 'Secretary of Laughter' by Wilson," *NYT,* 23 Oct 1938, 41:1; May Irwin's Will Filed; Estate of More Than $100,000 Is Divided Between Husband and Son," 5 Nov 1938, 17:6. AMD, p. 181. AS, p. 559. BHD, p. 209. IFN, p. 152. Katz, p. 603. SD. Spehr, p. 144 (d. 1958). Truitt, p. 168. WWVC, p. 70. "Fire in May Irwin's House; Cracker Thrown from Street Starts Blaze in Basement," *NYT,* 17 Jun 1905, 16:4 (at 255 W. 52nd St. A giant firecracker was thrown into a basement window igniting a rug). "May Irwin Ill in Portland; Caught Cold on Train and Is Attacked by Acute Neuritis—Engagement Cancelled [*The Widow by Proxy*]," *NYDM,* 4 Feb 1914, 18:1. "May Irwin Sues Road; Actress Asks $50,000 from Southern Pacific for Illness Caused by Exposure to Cold," *NYDM,* 11 Feb 1914, 16:1. "May Irwin in Her Greatest Comedy Triumph," *MPW,* XXII, 21 Nov 1914, 1087. Epes W. Sargent, "Memories of May Irwin, Dead at 76," *Variety,* 26 Oct 1938. Eve Golden, "Masy Irwin: 'The First Movie Star,'" *CI,* 278 (Aug 1998), C14-C15 (she made a fortune in New York real estate).

Irwin, Wallace [actor] (b. Oneida NY, 15 Mar 1875–14 Feb 1959 [83], Southern Pines NC). AS, p. 559. BHD, p. 209.

Irwin, Will [actor] (b. Oneida NY, 14 Sep 1873–24 Feb 1948 [74], New York NY). AS, p. 559. BHD, p. 209.

Isaacs, John Dove [cinematographer] (b. Richmond VA, 1848–26 Apr 1929 [81?], Palo Alta CA). AS, p. 559 (b. 1898). BHD2, p. 132.

Isbert, José (Pepe) [actor] (*né* José Isbert Alvarruiz, b. Madrid, Spain, 3 Mar 1886–29 Nov 1966 [80], Madrid, Spain). "Jose Isbert," *Variety,* 7 Dec 1966, p. 71. AS, p. 559. BHD, p. 209. IFN, p. 152.

Isham, Frederic S[tewart] [actor] (b. Detroit MI, 29 Mar 1865?–6 Sep 1922 [57], New York NY). m. Helen Frue. "Frederic S. Isham," *Variety,* 15 Sep 1922. AS, p. 559. BHD2, p. 132. SD, p. 659 (b. 1866).

Ishert, Jose [actor] (b. 1884?–28 Nov 1966 [82], Madrid, Spain; heart ailment). (Stage, 1902; films, 1912.) "Jose Ishert," *Variety,* 245, 7 Dec 1966, 71:2 (in 120 films).

Ishii, Kan [film/TV/stage actor] (*né* Seichi Ishii, b. 27 Feb 1901–29 Apr 1972 [71], Tokyo, Japan; liver cancer). (Shochiku Motion Picture Co., 1922; stage debut, 1928.) "Kan Ishii," *Variety,* 267, 17 May 1972, 71:3. AS, p. 559. BHD, p. 209. IFN, p. 152.

Ising, Rudolf C. [animator] (b. Kansas

City KS, 7 Sep 1903–18 Jul 1992 [88], Newport Beach CA; cancer). m. Cynthia Westlake. (Disney, 1922; MGM.) Bruce Lambert, "Rudolf C. Ising, 80, a Cartoonist and Creator of 'Looney Toons,'" *NYT,* 23 Jul 1992, B9:4. "Rudolf Ising," *Variety,* 27 Jul 1992, p. 72. AS, p. 559. BHD2, p. 132 (b. Kansas City MO, 7 Aug).

Ito, Michio [choreographer/dancer] (b. Tokyo, Japan, 13 Apr 1892–6 Nov 1961 [69], Tokyo, Japan). "Machio Ito," *Variety,* 15 Nov 1961. AS, p. 560 (b. 1893). BHD, p. 209.

Ivan, Rosalind [actress] (b. London, England, 27 Nov 1880–6 Apr 1959 [78], New York NY). "Rosalind Ivan," *Variety,* 8 Apr 1959. AS, p. 560. BHD1, p. 279. IFN, p. 153 (age 75).

Ivano, Paul [cinematographer] (*né* Paul Ivano-Ivanichevitch, b. Nice, France, 13 May 1900 [extrait de naissance no. 1170]–9 Apr 1984 [83], Woodland Hills CA). m. Greta. "Paul Ivano, Cinematographer from Silent Era to Television," *NYT,* 21 Apr 1984, 24:6. "Cinematographer Paul Ivano Dies on Coast; Career Spanned 50 Yrs.," *Variety,* 18 Apr 1984 (co-directed *Seven Years' Bad Luck,* 1920). Brian Taves, "Paul Ivano [obituary]," *CI,* 109 (Jul 1984), 12. AS, p. 560. BHD2, p. 132. FDY, p. 459. Brian Taves, "Paul Ivano; Cameraman for Hollywood's Greats," *CI,* 111 (Sep 1984), 30–32.

Ivanoff, Alexander N. [film editor] (b. 19 Aug 1886–Mar 1942 [55], Cassville NJ). BHD2, p. 132.

Ivanov-Barkov, Evgueni Alexandrovich [director] (b. Kostroma, Russia, 4 Mar 1892–20 May 1965 [73], Moscow, Russia). AS, p. 560.

Ivnovsky, Alexander Victorovich [director] (b. Moscow, Russia, 29 Nov 1881–12 Jan 1968 [86], Moscow, Russia). AS, p. 560.

Ivans, Elaine [actress] (b. New York NY, 1900–5 Apr 1975 [75?], New York NY). AMD, p. 181. AS, p. 560. BHD, p. 209. "Elaine Ivans at Liberty," *MPW,* 13 Mar 1915, 1619. "Elaine Ivans," *MPW,* 3 Jul 1915, 298. "Elaine Ivans in Kleine-Edison Feature," *MPW,* 6 Jan 1917, 107.

Ive, Bert [actor/cinematographer] (b. Queensland, Australia, 1875–1939 [64?]). BHD2, p. 132.

Ivens, Joris [actor/director] (*né* George Henry Anton Ivens, b. Nijmegan, Netherlands, 18 Nov 1898–28 Jun 1989 [90], Paris, France; heart attack). AS, p. 560. BHD1, p. 611; BHD2, p. 132.

Ivers, Jeanne [actress]. No data found. AMD, p. 181. "Jeanne Ivers," *MPW,* 18 Mar 1916, 1842.

Iversen, Jon [actor/director] (b. Sakskobing, Denmark, 1 Dec 1889–17 Aug 1964 [74], Denmark). AS, p. 560.

Ives, Ann Florinda [actress] (b. Providence RI, 1887–15 May 1979 [92], Dakota NY; heart attack in her sleep). AS, p. 560. IFN, p. 153.

Ives, Charlotte [actress] (b. 27 Nov 1891–Sep 1976 [84]). BHD, p. 209.

Ives, Herbert E. [inventor] (b. 1882–13 Nov 1953 [71?], Upper Montclair NJ). AS, p. 560.

Ivins, Perry [actor/director] (*né* Carrell Perry Ivins, b. Trenton NJ, 19 Nov 1894–22 Aug 1963 [68], Los Angeles CA; arteriosclerosis). AS, p. 560. BHD1, p. 280; BHD2, p. 132. IFN, p. 153.

Ivors, Julia Crawford [director/scenarist] (mother of **James C. Van Trees**) (b. Los Angeles CA, 3 Oct 1869–8 May 1930 [60], Los Angeles CA). m. twice. AMD, p. 181. AS, p. 560 (Ivers). BHD2, p. 132 (Ivers). IFN, p. 153. Anthony Slide, *Early Women Directors* (New York: A.S. Barnes and Co., 1977), p. 111. "Returns to Direct," *MPW,* 14 Oct 1922, 557. Douglas J. Whitton, "Mystery Woman Director," *CI,* 121 (Jul 1985), 27. Bruce Long, "Julia Crawford Ives Circa: The Taylor Murder," *CI,* 126 (Dec 1985), C10–C12.

Iwerks, Ub [animator] (*né* Ubbe Ert Iwwerks, b. Kansas City MO, 24 Mar 1901–7 Jul 1971 [70], Burbank CA). m. Mildred Sarah Henderson, 1926. (Laugh-O-Grams [4 Nov 1922–5 May 1923]; Disney.) "Ub Iwerks, Artist with Disney, Dead," *NYT,* 10 Jul 1971, 26:6. "Ub Iwerks," *Variety,* 14 Jul 1971 (age 71). AS, p. 561. Katz, p. 609. David R. Smith, "Ub Iwerks, 1901–1971; A Quiet Man Who Left a Deep Mark on Animation," *CFC,* 38 (Spring, 1973), 20–23. "Ub Iwerks," in Leonard Maltin, *Of Mice and Magic; A History of American Animated Cartoons* (New York: New American Library, 1980), pp. 185–94.

J

Jaccard, Jacques [actor/director] (b. New York NY, 11 Sep 1886–24 Jul 1960 [73], Los Angeles CA). m. **Helen Leslie**. (Universal.) AMD, p. 181. AS, p. 563. BHD, p. 209; BHD2, p. 132. IFN, p. 153. "Jacques Jaccard Recovering," *MPW,* 13 Mar 1915, 1613. J. Van Cartmell, "Along the Pacific Coast," *NYDM,* 15 Sep 1915, 30:4 (Leslie mentioned). "Jaccard to Direct Sydney Ayres," *MPW,* 22 Jan 1916, 627. "Jaccard to Film Series," *MPW,* 17 Jun 1916, 2034. "Jacques Jaccard Commissioned to Direct a Five-Reel Picture," *MPW,* 12 Jun 1920, 1484. June Lee, "Dan Cupid's Bulletin Board," *Paris and Hollywood,* Oct 1926, 88 (wed recently. "Some two weeks after the ceremony, the bride exhibited a ukulele which had been shattered over her head. Other musical instruments and bric a brac also appeared as evidence, and the bride's mama called the Hollywood police. Jaccard and some of his pet liquor were jailed.").

Jack, T.C. [actor] (b. 1882?–4 Oct 1954 [72], Los Angeles CA; heart attack). (Sennett.) "T.C. Jack," *Variety,* 13 Oct 1954. AS, p. 563. BHD, p. 209. IFN, p. 153. Truitt, p. 168.

Jackie, William [actor] (b. 1890?–19 Sep 1954 [64], San Francisco CA). m. Ruth Dwyer. "William Jackie," *Variety,* 22 Sep 1954 ("silent screen actor and talent agent"). AS, p. 563 (d. 1960). BHD, p. 209. IFN, p. 153. Truitt, p. 168.

Jackman, Fred W. (brother of **G. Floyd Jackman**) [cinematographer] (b. Toledo IA, 1881?–27 Aug 1959 [78], Los Angeles CA). (Sennett; Roach; Lloyd.) "Fred W. Jackman," *Variety,* 2 Sep 1959 (began 1913). AS, p. 563. BHD2, p. 132. IFN, p. 153.

Jackman, Dr. G. Floyd [cameraman] (brother of **Fred Jackman**) (b. IA, 27 Mar 1885–27 Nov 1962 [76], West Hollywood CA; heart attack). (Sennett.) "Dr. G. Floyd Jackman," *Variety,* 5 Dec 1962. AS, p. 563. BHD2, p. 132. FDY, p. 459.

Jackson, Andrew [actor] (b. 1886–23 May 1953 [67?], Los Angeles CA). AS, p. 563.

Jackson, Arthur [playwright/actor/scenarist]. No data found. m. **Betty Bouton**, Apr? 1920. AMD, p. 181. "Arthur Jackson Is Pleased wi His First Production," *MPW,* 3 Apr 1920, 119. "Betty Bouton Married," *MPW,* 24 Apr 1920, 565.

Jackson, Charles [scenarist] (b. 1902?–21 Sep 1968 [66], New York NY; suicidal ingestion of sleeping pills). m. "Charles Jackson," *Variety,* 25 Sep 1968 (wrote *Lost Weekend*). AS, p. 563. BHD2, p. 132.

Jackson, Ethel [actress] (*née* Ethel Kent, b. New York NY, 31 Jul 1883–27 Jul 1952 [68], Los Angeles CA). AS, p. 563 (wife of John Ince). BHD, p. 209.

Jackson, Frederick J. [scenarist] (aka Victor Thorne, b. Pittsburgh PA, 21 Sep 1886–22 May 1953 [66], Los Angeles CA). m. **Florence Howe**, 6 Jun 1915, Bayside, LI NY. "Frederick Jackson," *Variety,* 27 May 1953 (age 67; began screenwriting in 1912; Pearl White serials). AMD, p. 181. AS, p. 563. BHD2, p. 133. IFN, p. 153. SD. "Fred Jackson Marries; Author of 'A Full House' Weds Florence Howe, Motion Picture Actress," *NYDM,* 9 Jun 1915, 7:2. "Frederick Jackson to Write for Pathé," *MPW,* 24 Jul 1915, 633.

Jackson, Geraldine [child actress] (b. 1914?). AMD, p. 181. "Good Fairy Sees That Little Geraldine Has Her Chance as Motion Picture Star," *MPW,* 31 Jul 1920, 618 (6 years old).

Jackson, Harry [stage/film actor/director] (b. 1863?–15 May 1923 [60], New York NY; suicide with poison). m. Kate Sefton (d. 2 Apr 1923, Poughkeepsie NY). "Harry Jackson," *Variety,* 30 May 1923 (despondent over death of wife). AS, p. 564. SD.

Jackson, Harry [cinematographer] (b. 1896?–3 Aug 1953 [57], Los Angeles CA). (Warners, 1927; MGM; TC-F.) "Harry Jackson," *Variety,* 5 Aug 1953. AS, p. 564. FDY, p. 459.

Jackson, Horace A. [scenarist/playwright] (b. 1899?–26 Jan 1952 [53], Los Angeles CA; from injuries received in an auto accident on 24 Jan). "Horace A. Jackson," *NYT,* 29 Jan 1952, 25:1. "Horace A. Jackson," *Variety,* 30 Jan 1952 (wrote play, *Bedside Manner*). AS, p. 564. BHD2, p. 133. IFN, p. 153.

Jackson, Joe [stage/film actor] (*né* Joseph Francis Jiranek, b. Vienna, Austria, 1875?–14 May 1942 [67], New York NY). m. Marie Rialto. "Joe Jackson, Noted Tramp Cyclist, Dies at Roxy After 5 Curtain Calls; Final Words of the Comedian, 'They're Still Applauding,' an Epitaph to 50-Year Career—Act Seen Throughout World," *NYT,* 15 May 1942, 21:6, 24:2. AS, p. 564. BHD, p. 209. IFN, p. 153.

Jackson, Joseph [title writer/scenarist] (b. Winchester KY, 8 Jun 1894–26 May 1932 [37], Laguna Beach CA; drowned after collapsing in the water from heart failure). m. **Ethel Shannon** (d. 1951). (Began 1918 as press agent for Sam Goldwyn; President of Wampas; early Vitagraph talkers; WB.) "Joseph Jackson," *Variety,* 106, 31 May 1932, 63:4 (the speakers at his service were Rupert Hughes, Father Dodd and Ted Cook, "with most of writing fraternity present."). AMD, p. 181. AS, p. 564 (d. 24 Jun). BHD2, p. 133. FDY, pp. 429, 445. Joseph Jackson, "Things I Have Seen," *Paris and Hollywood,* Sep 1926, 49–50 (this was a monthly column he wrote in which such observations as the following would appear: "Every once in a while I have a stomach ache, and it brings me nothing but pain and misery. But Percy Marmont and Conway Tearle earn thousands of dollars a week with theirs. At least, I suppose it's a stomach-ache that makes them look that way."). "Joseph Jackson Signed for Warner Scenarios," *MPW,* 22 Oct 1927, 489.

Jackson, Lois [scenarist]. No data found. FDY, p. 429.

Jackson, Marion [scenarist]. No data found. FDY, p. 429.

Jackson, Marjorie Manning [actress] (b. 1898?–3 Jun 1922 [24], Los Angeles CA). m. Joseph A. Jackson. "Screen Favorite Dies," *Variety,* 9 Jun 1922. AS, p. 564.

Jackson, Mary Ann (sister of **Peaches Jackson**) [child actress] (b. Los Angeles CA, 14 Jan 1923–1991 [68?], Los Angeles CA). (Sennett.) AMD, p. 182. AS, p. 564. "Alfred Goulding Signed by Mack Sennett for Comedies," *MPW,* 1 Aug 1925, 575. Maude Robinson Toombs, "She Walked Through Custard to Fame; Being the complete life-history of Mary Ann Jackson, the pug-nosed little four-year-old star of the 'Jimmy Smiths' comedy series," *Cinema Art,* VI (Jun 1927), 25, 48.

Jackson, Orin [cameraman] (b. Terre Haute IN, 1874–14 May 1942 [68?], New York NY). BHD, p. 209.

Jackson, Peaches (sister of **Mary Ann Jackson**) [child actress] (b. ca. 1915). Ragan 2, p. 810.

Jackson, Selmer [stage/film actor] (*né* Salmer Adolph Jackson, b. Lake Mills IA, 7 May 1888–30 Mar 1971 [82], Burbank CA; heart attack). AS, p. 564. BHD1, p. 280. IFN, p. 153. SD. Truitt, 1983.

Jackson, Thomas E. [actor] (b. New York NY, 4 Jul 1886–7 Sep 1967 [81], Tarzana CA; heart attack). "Thomas Jackson," *Variety,* 13 Sep 1967. AS, p. 564 (d. 8 Sep). BHD1, p. 280. IFN, p. 153 (d. 8 Sep).

Jackson, Thomas F. [cinematographer] (b. 1893–1 Feb 1970 [76?], Los Angeles CA). BHD2, p. 133.

Jackson, Warren [actor] (b. Paris TX, 12 Feb 1892–10 May 1950 [58], Los Angeles CA; auto accident). AS, p. 564.

Jacobini, Diomira (sister of **Maria** and actress Bianca Jacobini [b. 1888]; niece of Cardinal Jacobini, Minister of State to Pope Leo XIII) [actress] (b. Rome, Italy, 1896–1959 [63?], Rome, Italy). AS, p. 564. JS, p. 223 ("Not very beautiful, she always lived in Maria's shadow."; in Italian silents from 1915).

Jacobini, Maria (sister of **Diomira** and Bianca Jacobini; niece of Cardinal Jcobini, Minister of State to Pope Leo XIII) [actress] (b. Rome, Italy, 17 Feb 1890–20 Nov 1944 [54], Rome, Italy). AS, p. 565. IFN, p. 153. JS, pp. 223–24 (in films from 1910).

Jacobs, Arthur H. [producer]. No data found. AMD, p. 182. "Arthur Jacobs to Manage Talmadge Film Corporation," *MPW,* 28 Sep 1918, 1881. "Arthur Jacobs Points Out Contrasting Requirements," *MPW,* 21 Aug 1920, 1045.

Jacobs, Billy [cameraman/assistant director] (b. 1888?–30 Sep 1953 [65]). (WB.) "William Jacobs," *Variety,* 7 Oct 1953. AS, p. 565.

Jacobs, Harrison W. [film scenarist/TV writer] (b. PA, 5 Oct 1893–9 Apr 1968 [75], Woodland Hills CA). "Harrison Jacobs," *Variety,* 17 Apr 1968 (wrote scripts for TV's "Hopalong Cassidy"). AS, p. 565. BHD2, p. 133. FDY, p. 429. IFN, p. 153.

Jacobs, Leigh [scenarist]. No data found. FDY, p. 429.

Jacobs, W.W. [scenarist] (b. 8 Sep 1863–1 Sep 1943 [79]). BHD2, p. 133.

Jacobs, William [scenarist/producer] (b. Chicago IL, 31 Oct 1887–30 Sep 1953 [65], Beverly Hills CA). BHD2, p. 133.

Jacobson, Arthur Aaron [cameraman/assistant director] (b. New York NY, 23 Oct 1901–6 Oct 1993 [92], Woodland Hills CA). "Arthur Jacobson," *Variety,* 25 Oct 1993, 68:5. AS, p. 565. BHD2, p. 133.

Jacoby, Georg Gustav Franz [director] (b. Mainz, Germany, 23 Jul 1882–21 Feb 1964 [81], Munich, Germany). AS, p. 565. BHD2, p. 133.

Jacquemar, Charles Hanns Wilhelm Eugène [actor/director] (b. Belfort, France, 2 Aug 1887). AS, p. 565.

Jacquemin, André [actor/director] (b. Leuven, Belgium, 20 Feb 1891-ca. Apr 1956 [65?]). AS, p. 565.

Jacquet, Gaston [actor] (b. Marseilles, France, 14 Aug 1883). AS, p. 565.

Jacquin, Abel Louis [actor/director] (b. Colombes, France, 14 Jul 1893–12 May 1968 [74], Colombes, France [extrait de décès no. 117/1968]). AS, p. 565.

Jaenzon, Julius [cameraman/director] (b. Goteberg, Sweden, 8 Jul 1885–1961 [76?]. Stockholm, Sweden). AS, p. 566. BHD2, p. 133.

Jaffe, Sam [actor] (b. New York NY, 10 Mar 1891–24 Mar 1984 [93], Beverly Hills CA; cancer and a heart attack). AS, p. 566 (b. 8 Mar). BHD1, p. 281.

Jaggers, Dean [actor] (*né* Dean Jeffries, b. Lima OH, 7 Nov 1903–5 Feb 1991 [87], Santa Monica CA). AS, p. 566 (b. Columbus Groves OH; d. LA CA). BHD1, p. 281.

Jahnke, Marion Diggs [actress] (b. 1890–6 May 1986 [96?]). BHD, p. 209.

Jahns, Robert [film editor] (d. 23 Feb 1974, Burbank CA; heart failure). (TC-F; Columbia; MGM.) "Robert Jahns," *Variety,* 6 Mar 1974.

Jahr, Adolf, "The Swedish Douglas Fairbanks" [stage/film actor/director/operetta singer] (b. Sundsvall, Sweden, 23 Jun 1893–19 Apr 1964 [70], Stockholm, Sweden). (Film debut: *Den Gamla Harrgarden* [*The Old Mansion*], 1924.) "Adolf Jahr," *Variety,* 234, 29 Apr 1964, 191:1. AS, p. 566. BHD1, p. 281. IFN, p. 153.

Jalovec, Aloïs [director/producer] (b. Prague, Czechoslovkia, 28 Feb 1867–16 Dec 1932 [65], Prague, Czechoslovakia). AS, p. 567.

Jambon, Marcel [decorator] (b. Barbezieux-Saint-Hilaire, France, 19 Oct 1848–30 Sep 1908 [59], Paris, France). AS, p. 567.

James, Alan [title writer/scenarist/director] (*né* Alvin James Neitz, b. WA, 23 Mar 1890–30 Dec 1952 [62], Los Angeles CA). "Alan James," *Variety,* 14 Jan 1953 (pioneer western producer; organized the American Film Co. in Santa Barbara CA). AMD, p. 260. AS, p. 567. BHD2, p. 133. FDY, pp. 435 (Alvin J. Neitz), 447. IFN, p. 153. "Horsley Engages Neitz, Author," *MPW,* 23 Dec 1916, 1792. "New Writer Added to Triangfle Staff," *MPW,* 13 Oct 1917, 218.

James, Alf[red] **P.** [actor] (b. Australia, 12 Oct 1865–9 Oct 1946 [80], Los Angeles CA). AS, p. 567. BHD1, p. 281. IFN, p. 153.

James, Arthur [publicist]. No data found. AMD, p. 182. "New Mutual Publicity Man," *MPW,* 30 May 1914, 1246. "Arthur James Goes to Metro," *MPW,* Aug 1915, 1319. Arthur James, "How Shall I advertise Pictures," *MPW,* 20 Jul 1918, 326. Epes Winthrop Sargent, "Arthur James Talks Salesmanship," *MPW,* 14 Dec 1918, 1231–32. "James to Direct Fox Advertising," *MPW,* 21 Jun 1919, 1751. "Arthur James Resigns from Fox Film to Form His Own Publicity Organization," *MPW,* 17 Apr 1920, 391. "Arthur James," *MPW,* 26 Mar 1927, 311.

James, Clifton [actor/scenarist] (*né* M.E. Clifton-Jones, b. England, 1897–8 Mar 1963 [66?], Worthing, England). AS, p. 567.

James, David [chief of Amalgamated Pictures] (b. 1888?–7 Mar 1967 [79], Barcombe, England). (Began 1920.) "Sir David James," *Variety,* 15 Mar 1967.

James, Eddie [actor/director] (b. 1880?–22 Dec 1944 [64], New York NY). (Griffith.) "Eddie James," *Variety,* 31 Jan 1945. AS, p. 567. BHD, p. 209; BHD2, p. 133. IFN, p. 153. Truitt, p. 169.

James, Gardner [actor] (b. New York NY, 16 Mar 1903–23 Jun 1953 [50], West Los Angeles CA). m. **Marion Constance Blackton**, 26 Dec 1926 (d. 1993). (MGM.) AMD, p. 182. AS, p. 567. BHD1, p. 281. IFN, p. 153. "Gardner James Signed on 5-Year Contract," *MPW,* 3 Jul 1926, 4. "M-G-M Borrows Gardner James," *MPW,* 7 Aug 1926, 338. "James Not to Succeed Barthelmess," *MPW,* 18 Dec 1926, 489. "Gardner James's Future Hangs in the Balance," *MPW,* 14 May 1927, 96. "James Is Signed by Chadwick," *MPW,* 2 Jul 1927, 13. George Katchmer, "Remembering the Great Silents," *CI,* 199 (Jan 1992), 15. Truitt, 1983 (b. 1901).

James, Gladden [actor] (b. Zanesville OH, 26 Feb 1888–28 Aug 1948 [60], Los Angeles CA; leukemia). m. **Marian Constance Blackton** (d. 1993). (Vitagraph, 1912.) AMD, p. 182. AS, p. 567 (b. 1892). BHD1, p. 281. IFN, p. 153 [age 56]. Truitt, p. 169. "Lucky Escape From Drowning," *MPW,* 5 Aug 1911, 291. "Solax Enlarging Studios," *MPW,* 4 Nov 1911, 386. George Katchmer, "Remembering the Great Silents," *CI,* 250 (Apr 1996), 48; *CI,* 253 (Jul 1996), 48.

James, H.T. [executive] (b. 1851–12 Feb 1952 [100?], Los Angeles CA). BHD2, p. 133.

James, Henry [publicist/scenarist] (b. 15 Apr 1843–1916 [73?]). AMD, p. 182. AS, p. 567. "Henry James with Metro," *MPW,* 4 Sep 1915, 1627.

James, Horace D. [actor] (b. Baltimore MD, 17 Jan 1853–16 Oct 1925 [72], Orange NJ). (Paramount.) "Horace D. James," *Variety*, 21 Oct 1925. AS, p. 567. BHD, p. 210. IFN, p. 153. Truitt, p. 169.

James, Jesse, Jr. [actor] (*né* Jesse E. James, b. MO, 1876–26 Mar 1951 [75], Los Angeles CA). AS, p. 567. BHD, p. 210. IFN, p. 154. Warren Nolan, "The Real Jesse James; The Outlaw Hero Gallops on the Screen; A Robin Hood from Missouri," *MPC*, Dec 1927, 28–29, 68, 84 (photo of Jesse James, Jr.). "Court Approves Exhumation of Remains of Jesse James [Sr.]," *NYT*, 9 Jul 1995, 21:1 (Jesse James, Sr., [aka Tom Howard] was killed on 3 Apr 1882, St. Joseph MO. In 1902 his remains were removed from his mother's backyard outside Kearney MO, near Kansas City, to Mount Olivet Cemetery, northwest of Kansas City). George Katchmer, "Jesse James, Jr.," *CI*, 230 (Aug 1994), 39.

James, Vera [actress] (b. New Zealand, 1892–1980 [88?]). AS, p. 568. Neville James, "Vera James, Girl of the Bush," *CFC*, 60 (Fall, 1978), 6 (began in Australia; Universal).

James, Walter [stage/film actor] (b. Gardena CA, 3 Jun 1882–27 Jun 1946 [64], Gardena CA; heart attack). m. Ida. "Walter James," *Variety*, 3 Jul 1946 (age 60). AS, p. 568 (b. Chattanooga TN). BHD1, p. 281 (b.Chattanooga). IFN, p. 154 (b. Chattanooga). SD. Truitt, p. 169 (b. 1886).

James, Will [actor/scenarist] (b. Pryor MT, 1892–3 Sep 1942 [50?], Los Angeles CA). AS, p. 568.

Jami[e]son, William "Bud" [vaudeville/stock/film actor] (b. Vallejo CA, 15 Feb 1894–30 Sep 1944 [50], Los Angeles CA; heart attack). (Chaplin; Sennett.) "William (Bud) Jamison," *Variety*, 4 Oct 1944. AS, p. 568 (d. 28 Sep). BHD1, p. 281. IFN, p. 154. Truitt, p. 169.

Jamison, Frank W. [art titles]. No data found.

Jamois, Marguerite [actress] (b. Paris, France, 8 Mar 1901–20 Nov 1964 [63], Paris, France; cancer). AS, p. 568.

Jandolo, Augusto [actor/poet] (b. Italy, 1873–12 Jan 1952 [78?], Rome, Italy). AS, p. 568.

Janis, Elsie [stage/film actress/writer/scenarist/composer] (*née* Elsie Bierbauer, b. Columbus OH, 16 Mar 1889–26 Feb 1956 [66], Beverly Hills CA; complications from an operation for ulcers). m. Gilbert Wilson. *So Far, So Good!; An Autobiography* (New York: E.P. Dutton & Co., 1932). (Film debut: *The Caprices of Kitty*, Paramount, 1915.) "Elsie Janis Is Dead in California; 'Sweetheart of A.E.F.' Was 66; Entertainer, Famed as Mimic, Made Stage Debut at 8—Author and Song Writer," *NYT*, 28 Feb 1956, 1:2; "Elsie Janis' Will Probated," *NYT*, 11 Mar 1956, 75:1. "Elsie Janis Dies at 67; A Giant Show Biz Figure," *Variety*, 29 Feb 1956 (b. 6 Mar; d. 27 Feb). AMD, p. 182. AS, p. 568. BHD1, p. 282 (b. 15 Mar); BHD2, p. 134. FSS, p. 153. IFN, p. 154. SD. Spehr, p. 144. Truitt, pp. 169–70. "Elsie Janis with Bosworth," *MPW*, 14 Nov 1914, 940. "Elsie Janis," *MPW*, 16 Jan 1915, 388. "Four Janis Films; Stage Star Completed That Number of Features in Six Weeks," *NYDM*, 27 Jan 1915, 48:4 (at Bosworth LA studio, then off to London to comply with a stage contract with Alfred Butt). "Elsie Janis Becomes Selznick Star," *MPW*, 28 Jun 1919, 1913. "Elsie Janis Collaborates on Script," *MPW*, 9 Aug 1919, 843.

Janney, Leon [actor] (*né* Leon Ramon, b. Ogden UT, 1 Apr 1917–28 Oct 1980 [63], Chapala, Jalisco, Guadalajara, Mexico; cancer). AS, p. 569. BHD1, p. 282. Truitt, 1983. "Ask the Answer Man," *Photoplay*, May 1932, 82 (began 1925).

Janney, Russell [publicist] (b. Wilmington OH, 1884–14 Jul 1943 [59?], New York NY). BHD2, p. 134.

Janney, Samuel [playwright/scenarist] (b. 1893?–Jun? 1929 [36], Victorville CA; auto accident). m. Carlotta Dietz, Mar 1929. (1st National.) "Samuel Janney," *Variety*, XCV, 12 Jun 1929, 68:2. AMD, p. 182. "M-G-M Signs a Dramatist," *MPW*, 12 Mar 1927, 110.

Janney, William [actor] (*né* Russell Dixon Janney, b. New York NY, 15 Feb 1908–22 Dec 1992 [84], Fayette ID). m. (1) Madlyn Hobbs, 1940 (d. 1968); (2) Venice Daniels, 1970 (d. 1989). BHD1, p. 282. Michael Ankerich, "William Janney: His Life and Career," *CI*, 212 (Feb 1993), 32, C2, C4, C9 (includes filmography).

Jannings, Emil [stage/film actor/producer] (*né* Theodor Friedrich Emil Janenz [American father and German mother], b. Rorschach, Switzerland, 23 Jul 1884–2 Jan 1950 [65], Lake Wolfgang, Stroblhof, Austria; cancer). m. (1) **Lucie Hoeflich**; (3) Gussie Holl. (Began 1914; AA, 1927–28.) "Emil Jannings, 63, Veteran of Films; German Actor Who Achieved Success Here in 'Way of All Flesh' Is Dead in Austria," *NYT*, 3 Jan 1950, 25:3. AMD, p. 182. AS, p. 569. BHD1, p. 282; BHD2, p. 134 (b. 1886). FSFM, p. 243 (b. 29 Jul 1886). HCH, p. 87. IFN, p. 154 (b. Brooklyn NY, 26 Jul 1886). JS, p. 224 (in the Italian *Quo vadis?*, 1924). Katz, pp. 612–13 (b. Rorschach, Switzerland; began 1914 in Germany). SD. Truitt, p. 170 (b. 1886). Waldman, p. 145. Charles Edward Hastings, "Emil Jannings," *MPW*, 6 May 1925, 345–46. Emil Jannings, "Janning's Own Story of His Film Career; The Famous Actor Tells His Life Story for the First Time; Born in New York, He Speaks but Six Words of English," *MPC*, Dec 1925, 20–21, 77. Hal K. Wells, "The Real Jannings; The German Star Has Become the One Big Topic in Which All Hollywood Is Genuinely Interested. Classic Presents the Real Jannings and His Impressions Since He Settled Down in California," *MPC*, Mar 1927, 16–17, 80, 87. Alexander Johns, "The True Story of the Emil Jannings Triangle," *Paris and Hollywood Screen Secrets Magazine*, May 1927, 34–37 (b. Brooklyn NY. States that Jannings married Holl after Conrad Veidt divorced her.). "Emil Jannings," *MPW*, 30 Jul 1927, 319. "Re-Sign Jannings," *MPW*, 20 Aug 1927, 533. Hugh Miller [stage actor], "The Flame and the Lamp [Jannings and Barrymore]," *MPC*, Sep 1927, 33, 81, 88. Emil Jannings, "Why I Left the Films," *Living Age*, 338: 554–7, 1 Jul 1930.

Janowitz, Hans [scenarist] (b. Czechoslovaki, 1891–25 May 1954 [63?], New York NY). BHD2, p. 134.

Jans, Herman F. [producer]. No data found. AMD, p. 182. "Jans Pleased with Outlook on His Initial Sales Tour," *MPW*, 20 Mar 1920, 1950. "Jans to Produce," *MPW*, 16 Aug 1924, 580. "Herman Jans Promises Eight Big Independent Productions," *MPW*, 2 May 1925, 65. "Mrs. Herman F. Jans Dies," *MPW*, 22 Jan 1927, 246 (d. Maplewood NJ).

Jans, Van A. [scenarist]. No data found. FDY, p. 429.

Jansen, Marie [actress/comic opera soubret] (b. Boston MA, 1849–20 Mar 1914 [64?], Milford MA). "Marie Jansen," *Variety*, 27 Mar 1914, 21:2 (ca. age 65). BHD, p. 210.

Janson, Victor [actor/director] (b. Riga, Latvia, 25 Sep 1884–29 Jun 1960 [75], Berlin, Germany). "Victor Janson," *Variety*, 219, 20 Jul 1960, 63:2. AS, p. 569. BHD1, p. 282; BHD2, p. 134. IFN, p. 154.

Janssen, Walter [actor/director] (*né* Walther Philipp Janssen, b. Krefeld, Germany, 7 Feb 1887–1 Jan 1976 [88], Munich, Germany). AS, p. 569. BHD1, p. 282; BHD2, p. 134. IFN, p. 154.

Janvier, Jean-Louis [actor] (b. Paris, France, 15 Jan 1871). AS, p. 569.

Janvier, Philippe [actor] (b. Paris, France, 17 Sep 1903). AS, p. 569.

Jaque-Catelain [actor/director] (*né* Jacques Maxime Guerin, b. Saint-Germain-en-Laye, France, 9 Feb 1897–5 Mar 1965 [68], Paris, France). AS, p. 569.

Jaquet, Frank Garnier [actor] (b. WI, 16 Mar 1885–11 May 1958 [73], Los Angeles CA). AS, p. 569.

Jaray, Hans [actor] (b. Vienna, Austria, 24 Jun 1906–6 Jan 1990 [83], Vienna, Austria). AS, p. 569. BHD1, p. 282.

Jardon, Dorothy [vaudeville/film actress/opera singer] (b. 1883?–30 Sep 1966 [83], Hollywood CA). (Headliner on Keith Circuit, 1915–21.) "Dorothy Jardon [Oelrichs]," *Variety*, 244, 5 Oct 1966, 71:3. AMD, p. 182. "Dorothy Jardon," *MPW*, 6 Apr 1918, 74.

Jarmuth, Jack [title writer/scenarist]. No data found. FDY, p. 445.

Jarnegan, Jerry [actor] (b. 1893–19 Aug 1934 [41?], Toluca Lake CA). AS, p. 569.

Jarrett, Arthur L. (brother of **Daniel Jarrett**) [actor] (b. Marysville CA, 5 Feb 1884–12 Jun 1960 [76], New York NY). m. Mary Powers. (Ince.) "Arthur L. Jarrett," *Variety*, 15 Jun 1960. AS, p. 570. BHD, p. 210. IFN, p. 154. Truitt, p. 170 (b. 1888).

Jarrett, Daniel [actor] (b. Wales, 1854–23 Sep 1917 [63?], Brooklyn NY). BHD, p. 210.

Jarrett, Daniel [actor/scenarist] (brother of **Arthur Jarrett**) (b. Marysville CA, 4 Apr 1894–13 Mar 1938 [43], Los Angeles CA; heart attack). "Dan Jarrett," *Variety*, 16 Mar 1938. AS, p. 570. BHD1, p. 282; BHD2, p. 134. IFN, p. 154. Truitt, p. 170.

Jarrott, Jack (John) [dancer/actor/producer] (b. 1883?–14 Jun 1938 [55], New York NY; malnutrition). (Kleine.) "Jack Jarrott," *Variety*, 22 Jun 1938 (arrested in 1923 on a narcotics charge). AMD, p. 182. AS, p. 570. BHD, p. 210. "John Jarrott with Kleine," *MPW*, 20 Nov 1915, 1463. "In the Picture Studios," *NYDM*, 31:1 (gained fame dancing with Joan Sawyer; joined Kleine in the Bronx).

Jarvis, Jean [actress] (b. Denver CO, 23 May 1903–16 Mar 1933 [29], Los Angeles CA; in a sanitarium). "Jean Jarvis," *Variety*, 21 Mar 1933 (age 30; began ca. 1927). AS, p. 570. BHD, p. 210. IFN, p. 154. Truitt, p. 170.

Jarvis, Laura E. [actress] (b. 1866?–9 Mar 1933 [67], near Downey CA; injuries sustained from hit and run driver). "Laura E. Jarvis," *Variety*, 14 Mar 1933. AS, p. 570. IFN, p. 154. Truitt, p. 170.

Jarvis, Sydney [baritone/actor/film representative] (b. Toronto, Canada, 11 Jan 1878–6 Jun

1939 [61], Los Angeles CA). m. **Virginia Dare** (d. 1962). "Sydney Jarvis," *Variety*, 14 Jun 1939 (age 58). AS, p. 570. BHD1, p. 283. IFN, p. 154. Truitt, p. 170 (b. New York NY, 1881). "Birth Announcement," *MPW*, 1 Jan 1921, 78 (birth of a son).

Jason, Leigh [director/scenarist] (*né* Leigh Jacobson, b. New York NY, 26 Jul 1904–19 Feb 1979 [74], Woodland Hills CA). m. Ruth Harriet Louise (d. 1944). (Universal; RKO; Columbia.) "Leigh Jason," *Variety*, 7 Mar 1979. AS, p. 570. BHD2, p. 134. IFN, p. 154.

Jasper, John [general manager] (b. 1877–29 Aug 1935 [58?], Beverly Hills CA). AMD, p. 182. BHD2, p. 134. "Jasper Recovers from Illness," *MPW*, 15 Dec 1917, 1625.

Jasset, Victorin [director] (*né* Hippolyte Victoria Jasset, b. Fumay, France, 30 Mar 1862 [extrait de naissance no. 76]–22 Jun 1913 [51], Paris, France; complications from an operation). AS, p. 570. BHD2, p. 134.

Jaubert, Maurice Jacques Joseph Eugène [composer] (b. Nice, France, 3 Jan 1900 [extrait de naissance no. 41]–19 Jun 1940 [40], Azerailles, France; in combat). AS, pp. 570–71. BHD2, p. 134.

Jaudenes, Jose Alvares "Lepe" [actor] (b. Spain, 1891–14 Jul 1967 [76?], Madrid, Spain). AS, p. 571.

Jaux, Lise [actress]. No data found. Rene de la Seine, "Latest Gossip from Paris; Foreign Stars Look to Hollywood," *Paris and Hollywood*, Oct 1926, 43–44 ("...a charming little brunette *without* bobbed hair (that alone ought to send her far) who has starred in a number of routine French films, among them *Bibi-La Puree, Parisette, Une Fille Bien Gardee*, and *Vindicta*. She is essentially a comedienne and is a natural actress with eyes so brimful of humor that you can't help laughing with, not at, her." She has been approached by Paramount.).

Javor, Pal [actor] (*né* Paul Javor, b. Arad, Rumania, 31 Jan 1902–14 Aug 1959 [57], Budapest, Hungary). AS, p. 571.

Jay, Dorothy [actress] (b. 1908–28 Jul 1936 [28?], Los Angeles CA). AS, p. 571. BHD, p. 210.

Jay, Ernest [actor] (b. London, England, 18 Sep 1893–8 Feb 1957 [63], London, England). AS, p. 571. BHD1, p. 283. IFN, p. 154.

Jay, Jean [actress]. No data found. AMD, p. 182. "Norma's Protége," *MPW*, 16 Feb 1924, 583.

Jean [dog]. No data found. AMD, p. 182. "Jean Comes Back," *MPW*, 1 Dec 1917, 1301.

Jeanne, René Victor Paul [journalist/title writer/scenarist] (b. Paris, France, 6 Jan 1887–1 Feb 1969 [81], Paris, France). AS, p. 571. FDY, pp. 429, 445.

Jeanning, Irène [actress] (*née* Irène Andrée Jeanningros, b. Asnieres-sur-Seine, France, 10 Jun 1903 [extrait de naissance no. 277]–22 Nov 1991 [88], Saint-Nazaire, France [extrait de décès no. 962]). AS, p. 571.

Jeans, Isabel [stage/film actress] (b. London, England, 16 Sep 1891–4 Sep 1985 [93], London, England). m. (1) Claude Rains (d. 1967); (2) Gilbert Wakefield (d. 1963). AS, p. 571. BHD1, p. 283. Katz, 1994. SD, p. 668.

Jeans, Ursula [stage/film actress] (*née* Ursula McMinn, b. Simla, India, 5 May 1906–21 Apr 1973 [66], near London, England). m. (1) Robin Irvine (d. 1933); (2) Roger Livesey. "Ursula Jeans," *Variety*, 270, 2 May 1973, 71:2. AS, p. 571. BHD1, p. 283. IFN, p. 155.

Jeayes, Allan [stage/film actor] (b. London, England, 19 Jan 1885–20 Sep 1963 [78], London, England; heart attack). m. Frances Hamerton. "Allan Jeayes," *Variety*, 25 Sep 1963 (in British films since 1932). AS, p. 571. BHD1, p. 283. IFN, p. 155. SD.

Jeffers, John S. [actor] (b. 1874?–3 Jan 1939 [65], Long Beach, LI NY). (Bison.) "John S. Jeffers," *Variety*, 11 Jan 1939. AS, p. 571. BHD, p. 210. IFN, p. 155. Truitt, p. 170.

Jeffers, William L. [actor] (b. 1898?–18 Apr 1959 [61], Los Angeles CA). (Universal.) "William L. Jeffers," *Variety*, 29 Apr 1959. AS, p. 571. BHD, p. 210. IFN, p. 155. Truitt, p. 170.

Jefferson, Catherine [actress]. No data found. *MPN*, 2 May 1908, 390.

Jefferson, Daisy [actress] (b. 1889–3 Jun 1967 [78?], Los Angeles CA). AS, p. 571. BHD, p. 210.

Jefferson, Joseph, Sr. (father of **Thomas, Joseph, William**, and Josephine **Jefferson**) [stage/film actor] (b. Philadelphia PA, 20 Feb 1829–23 Apr 1905 [76], The Reefs, Palm Beach FL; pneumonia). "The Autobiography of Joseph Jefferson," *Century Magazine*, Nov 1889, 3–25 to XL, Jul 1890, 406–18. "Joseph Jefferson Dies at His Florida Home; End Comes After Day of Anxious Watching by Family; Ill on Visit to Cleveland; Caught Pneumonia While on Trip to Meet ex-President—To Be Buried at Buzzards Bay," *NYT*, 24 Apr 1905, 1:1, 2:3. AS, p. 571. BHD, p. 210. GSS, pp. 190–92. WWVC, p. 72. "Joseph Jefferson Very Ill; Aged Actor Suffering from Pneumonia After a Fishing Trip," *NYT*, 14 Apr 1905, 1:6 ("Tonight the patient is resting easily."). "Joseph Jefferson Very Low; Veteran Actor Has Relapse and the Worst Is Feared," *NYT*, 15 Apr 1905, 1:4 (14 Apr. "Mr. Jefferson has a highly nervous temperament, and this, Dr. Potter argues, is much against him."). "Joseph Jefferson Better; Still Very Weak; but Is Not at Present in Danger," *NYT*, 16 Apr 1905, 1:6. "Joseph Jefferson Sinking; Aged Actor's Condition Takes a Serious Turn for the Worse," *NYT*, 18 Apr 1905, 1:6 (17 Apr. "...the members of his family who are not already with him have been telegraphed to come."). "Joseph Jefferson Weaker; His Family at His Bedside Awaiting the End," *NYT*, 19 Apr 1905, 1:6 ("There seems to be no particular ailment and only his advanced age is against him."). "Jefferson Much Better; Some of His Relatives Now Think Actor May Recover," *NYT*, 20 Apr 1905, 1:6 (19 Apr. "...Mr. Jefferson has a room on the second floor of his cottage, The Reef, where he can see the ocean."). "Jefferson Getting Better; Every Indication That the Veteran Actor Will Recover," *NYT*, 21 Apr 1905, 9:5 (his illness was actually caused "by overexertion while on a visit to Hobe Sound. Added to this was a general weakness due to indigestion, from which he suffered last Spring, and which returned.... To-Day he has been talking cheerfully and asking that arrangements be made for his return to his Northern home."). "Mr. Jefferson Not So Well; Patient's Appetite Fails and Physicians Are Worried," *NYT*, 22 Apr 1905, 1:2 (21 Apr. "The patient refuses to take food..."). "Jefferson About the Same," *NYT*, 23 Apr 1905, 3:4 (as of 10pm, 22 Apr). "Son Cancels Boston Dates; Was Booked for This Week to Play 'Rip Van Winkle,'" *NYT*, 24 Apr 1905, 2:4 (Boston Theatre, 23 Apr). "Sorrow at Buzzard's Bay; Jefferson's Summer Home 15 Years—Was Old Colony Club President," *NYT*, 24 Apr 1905, 2:4 (Charles Jefferson was at Sandwich; Thomas, Joseph, and Josephine Jefferson were at Buzzard's Bay). "Jefferson About the Same; Improved Yesterday Afternoon, but Was Not So Well at Night," *NYT*, 24 Apr 1905,—? (22 Apr. "His fever was lower and he appeared to be a little stronger."). 'Jefferson Burial Plans; Actor Expressed Wish for Private Interment at Buzzard's Bay [MA]," *NYT*, 26 Apr 1905, 11:3 (The Players' Club wanted himn buried at The Little Church Around the Corner. His body arrived at Jacksonville on 25 Apr.). "Body of Jefferson Passes Through City; Taken Away on Midnight Train for Boston; Station Crowds Bare Heads; Family in H.M. Flagler's Private Car Accompanies Body on Journey from [Palm Beach] Florida," *NYT*, 27 Apr 1905, 11:6 (26 Apr. Arived at Jersey City NJ at 5pm, accompanied by Mrs. Jefferson, his four sons [Frank, Charles, James, and William], a granddaughter, and Carl Kettler, "Mr. Jefferson's faithful valet, and several servants of the family... Before being placed in the hearse the casket was taken out of the white pine box. It was covered with roses and floral pieces." Joseph Jefferson, Jr., said: "Through my father's death...I become Joseph Jefferson, but I hesitate in assuming that name. I think that I will be 'Jr.' for the rest of my life. It is hard to realize that my father is dead."). "Jefferson Buried Sunday; Funeral Services to Be Held at His Old Home, Near Buzzard's Bay," *NYT*, 28 Apr 1905, 9:2 (funeral to be held on 30 Apr at 11 o'clock at Crow's Nest. Burial in Bay View Cemetery.). "Players to Hold Service; Club Adopts Resolutions in Honor of Joseph Jefferson," *NYT*, 29 Apr 1905, 11:3 (ushers at their service for him were to include David Warfield, Vincent Serrano, and Joseph Kilgour). "Joseph Jefferson as Lawrence Hulton Knew Him," *NYT*, 30 Apr 1905, III, 1. "Jefferson Family's Thanks; Son of Dead Actor Issues a General Acknowledgement of Condolences," *NYT*, 2 May 1905, 11:5 (his son, C.B. Jefferson, through the press, thanked the public for its many letters, telegrams, and other messages of condolence). "Players Elect John Drew; Succeeds Joseph Jefferson—Is Third President of Club," *NYT*, 9 May 1905, 1:6 (16 Gramercy Park, NYC. Edwin Booth was the first president for five years; Jefferson the second for twelve years. William Bispham was elected Vice-President.). "Drew as Head of Players; Jefferson Told Him He Would Be His Natural Successor," *NYT*, 10 May 1905, 9:4 (Kansas City MO, 9 May. Drew was playing at the Willis Wood Theatre. "Mr. Jefferson, you know, succeeded Mr. Booth as President, and it was one of the ideas of his generous mind that since the three families, Booth, Jefferson, and Drew, had been so long associated with the stage, it would be right and natural that I should continue the succession in The Players."). "Jefferson Birthplace Sold; Philadelphia Speculator Buys Actor's Old Home for $8,125." *NYT*, 18 May 1905, 9:5 (at Sixth and Spruce Streets. Attorney William H. Ramsey bought it. Used as a store and dwelling, it had this plaque above the store: Joseph Jefferson, the Actor/Was Born Here/Feb. 20, 1829./Here's Your Good Health and/Your Family's—May they/Live Long and Prosper."). "Jefferson Plunder Found; Actor's Son Recovers Goods Stolen from Buzzard's Bay Home," *NYT*, 19 May 1905, 1:3 (in Providence RI, Thomas Jefferson identified property stolen while the family was in Florida that Spring).

Jefferson, Joseph W[arren], **Jr.** (son of **Joseph Jefferson, Sr.**, and brother of **Thomas** and

William Jefferson) [actor] (b. New York NY, 6 Jul 1869–1 May 1919 [49], New York NY). (Film debut: *The Hoosier Romance,* Selig). "Joseph W. Jefferson," *Variety,* 9 May 1919. AS, p. 572. SD, p. 670.

Jefferson, L[ouis] **V.** [story editor/scenarist] (b. Carthage MO, 14 May 1873–30 Nov 1959 [86], Los Angeles CA). (Universal; 1st National.) "L.V. Jefferson," *Variety,* 9 Dec 1959. AMD, p. 182. BHD2, p. 134. FDY, p. 429. "Jefferson Joins Horsley," *MPW,* 6 Nov 1915, 1141.

Jefferson, Thomas (son of **Joseph Jefferson, Sr.**; brother of **Joseph Jefferson, Jr.**, and **William Winter Jefferson**) [actor] (b. New York NY, 10 Sep 1856–2 Apr 1932 [75], Los Angeles CA). (Biograph, 1913; K&E.) "Thomas Jefferson," *Variety,* 12 Apr 1932 (age 76). AMD, p. 182. AS, p. 572. BHD1, p. 283 (b. 1857). IFN, p. 155. Katz, p. 617 (b. 1859). Truitt, p. 171 (b. 1859). "Thomas Jefferson Returns to Fine Arts," *MPW,* 10 Feb 1917, 844. "Jefferson in Lytell Support," *MPW,* 12 Oct 1918, 253. "Thomas Jefferson in Character Role," *MPW,* 13 Sep 1919, 1627.

Jefferson, William Winter (son of **Joseph Jefferson, Sr.**; brother of **Thomas Jefferson**) [stage/film actor] (b. London, England, 1875?–10 Feb 1946 [70], Honolulu HI). m. (1) Christie MacDonald (d. 1962); (2) **Vivian Martin** (d. 1987); (3) Mary Schwartz. (K&E.) "William Winter Jefferson," *Variety,* 20 Feb 1946. "Christie MacDonald Dies at 87; Musical Comedy Star, 1910–20," *NYT,* 27 Jul 1962, 25:4 (d. 26 Jul 1962 [87], Fairfield CT). AMD, p. 182. AS, p. 572. BHD, p. 210. SD. Truitt, 1983. "William Jefferson Injured," *MPW,* 1 Jul 1916, 73.

Jeffrey, Hugh S. [actor/casting director] (b. Belfast, Ireland, 1880?–18 Jan 1927 [46], Los Angeles CA; from carbon monoxide poisoning in his home). "Hugh S. Jeffrey," *Variety,* 26 Jan 1927. AS, p. 572. BHD, p. 210; BHD2, p. 134 (b. 1873). Truitt, 1983.

Jeffries, Ellis [actress] (b. Sri Lanka, 17 May 1872–21 Jan 1943 [70], Surrey, England). AS, p. 572.

Jeffries, Herbert E. [actor] (b. Pittsburgh PA, 1886). AS, p. 572.

Jeffries, James J. [actor] (b. Carroll OH, 15 Apr 1875–3 Mar 1953 [77], Burbank CA). AS, p. 572. BHD1, p. 283. IFN, p. 155. Truitt, 1983. WWVC, p. 72.

Jeffries, Mina *see* **Cunard, Myna**

Jeffries, Norman [actor] (b. 1866?–25 May 1933 [67], Philadelphia PA). "Norman Jeffries," *Variety,* 30 May 1933. AS, p. 572.

Jeffries, Wes [costume designer] (b. Provo UT, 1907–12 Jul 2000 [93], Palm Desert CA). Harris Lentz, III, "Wes Jeffries, 93," *CI,* 303 (Sep 2000), pp. 57–58.

Jeliabujski, Yuri [director] (b. Tbilissi, Georgia, 1888–1955 [67?], Moscow, Russia). AS, p. 572.

Jellett, Jack [cinematographer]. No data found. FDY, p. 459.

Jelley, Herbert E[ugene] [actor] (b. Pittsburgh PA, 18 Mar 1882 [Birth Register Index, Vol. 21, p. 265, dtd. 6 Apr 1882; born on Willow Street, 17th Ward]). (Universal; Champion; FP-L; Metro.) BHD, p. 210 (b. 1886).

Jenkins, Dr. C[harles] **Francis** [inventor] (b. Dayton OH, 22 Aug 1867–6 Jun 1934 [66], Washington DC). "C.F. Jenkins Dead; Television Expert; Inventor Was Active in Field of Motion Picture as Well as Wireless Devices; Showed Movies in 1892; Cut Photographic Film into Strips for Experiment—Sent Weather Maps to Ships," *NYT,* 7 Jun 1934, 23:4. "C. Francis Jenkins," *Variety,* 12 Jun 1934 (age 67). AS, p. 572. BHD2, p. 135. Katz, p. 618. Spehr, p. 144. WWVC, p. 72. WWWA. Frederick James Smith, "Are Radio Movies Coming? Will the Radio and the Motion Picture Combine?," *MPC,* Jul 1925, 18–20, 83.

Jenkins, Elizabeth [actress] (b. 1879?–18 Jan 1965 [86?], Caldwell NY). AS, p. 572. BHD, p. 211. Truitt, p. 171.

Jenkins, Felix A. [executive] (b. Pelham Manor NY, 22 Nov 1889–4 Mar 1947 [57], Los Angeles CA). BHD2, p. 135.

Jenkins, J[ohn] **W**[esley] [actor/singer] (b. Winchester, England, 1859-d. 1930 [71?], Brooklyn NY).

Jenks, George Elwood [writer/scenarist]. No data found. AMD, p. 182. "Jenks Joins Metro Writers," *MPW,* XLVII, 25 Dec 1920, 1070.

Jenks, Lulu Burns [actress] (b. 1870?–15 Apr 1939 [69], Los Angeles CA). (Universal.) "Lulu Burns Jenks, 69, former character actress, died April 15 in Los Angeles," *Variety,* 19 Apr 1939. AS, p. 573 (Lou Burns Jenks). BHD, p. 211 (Lula). IFN, p. 155.

Jenks, Si [actor] (*né* Howard H. Jenkins, b. Norristown PA, 23 Sep 1876–6 Jan 1970 [93], Woodland Hills CA). m. Lillian. (Fox, 1922.) "Si Jenks," *Variety,* 4 Feb 1970. AS, p. 573. BHD, p. 211. IFN, p. 155.

Jenner, George [actor] (b. Kent, England, 19 Dec 1875–16 Dec 1946 [70], Los Angeles CA). AS, p. 573.

Jennings, Al J. [outlaw/actor] (b. VA, 26 Dec 1863–26 Dec 1961 [98], Tarzana CA). "Al Jennings, ex-Outlaw, Dies at 98," *NYT,* 27 Dec 1961, 10:5. "Al Jennings," *Variety,* 3 Jan 1962. AMD, p. 183. AS, p. 573. BHD1, p. 283 (b. 25 Nov). IFN, p. 155 (b. 25 Nov). Katz, p. 618. Truitt, p. 171. "Film 'Beating Back'; Life Story of Al Jennings to Be Produced by Thanhouser Company," *NYDM,* 15 Apr 1914, 31:4 (from a story published in *The Saturday Evening Post*). "Al Jennings," *MPW,* 23 May 1914, 1123. "Al Jennings in New Film Seeks to Show Real Bandit," *MPW,* 1 Sep 1918, 1724.

Jennings, DeWitt C. [actor] (b. Cameron MO, 21 Jun 1872–28 Feb 1937 [64], Los Angeles CA). m. Ethel Conroy. (MGM.) "DeWitt Jennings," *Variety,* 3 Mar 1937 (age 65; began 1920). AS, p. 573. BHD1, p. 284. IFN, p. 155. SD. Truitt, p. 171 (b. 1879–1 Mar). George Katchmer, "Remembering the Great Silents," *CI,* 196 (Oct 1991), 55–56.

Jennings, Jane, "The Cameo Mother of the Screen" [actress]. (Vitagraph, 1916.) AMD, p. 183. "Jane Jennings Signed," *MPW,* 28 Feb 1925, 925. "Jane Jennings in Cast," *MPW,* 15 Aug 1925, 760. "Jane Jennings Busy," *MPW,* 14 Nov 1925, 126. "Jane Jennings Signed," *MPW,* 26 Jun 1926, 703. Nina Newman, "Speaking of Mothers," *Cinema Art,* Feb 1926, 31.

Jennings, J. Devereaux [cinematographer] (b. UT, 22 Sep 1884–12 Mar 1952 [67], Los Angeles CA). (Griffith; Neilan; Paramount.) "Devereaux Jennings," *Variety,* 19 Mar 1952. AS, p. 573. BHD2, p. 135. FDY, p. 459 (under Dev Jennings and J.D. Jennings).

Jennnings, Louis [cinematographer] (b. 1901–3 Jul 1982 [81?], Roseville CA). BHD2, p. 135. FDY, p. 459.

Jennings, S[ylvester] **E**[nnis] [actor/makeup artist] (b. Chicago IL, 8 Apr 1880–3 Feb 1932 [51], Los Angeles CA). AS, p. 573. BHD1, p. 284; BHD2, p. 135. IFN, p. 155. George A. Katchmer, "Forgotten Cowboys and Cowgirls—Part VIII," *CI,* 180 (Jun 1990), 53.

Jennings, Talbot L. [scenarist] (b. Shoshone ID, 25 Aug 1894–30 May 1985 [90], Cut Bank MT). BHD2, p. 135.

Jensen, Emil C. [executive] (b. 23 Feb 1892–15 Nov 1954 [62], New York NY). BHD2, p. 135.

Jensen, Eulalie [actress] (b. St. Louis MO, 24 Dec 1884–7 Oct 1952 [67], Los Angeles CA). AMD, p. 183. AS, p. 573. BHD1, p. 284. IFN, p. 155. MH, p. 119. "Eulalie Jensen to Play in 'the Passion Flower,'" *MPW,* 5 Feb 1921, 678. "Noted Additions to Cast of 'The Happy Warrior,'" *MPW,* 25 Apr 1925, 808.

Jensen, Franz E. [cameraman] (b. San Francisco CA, 1886-Mar 1918 [32?], Los Angeles CA; found dead). "Franz Jensen Found Dead," *Variety,* 22 Mar 1918. BHD2, p. 135.

Jensen, Frederick [actor[(b. Nyborg, Sweden, 25 Jun 1863–14 Feb 1934 [70], Copenhagen, Denmark). BHD1, p. 611.

Jepp, Mary [actress] (b. West Point MS, 1 Oct 1898–28 Apr 1980 [81], Monterey CA). BHD, p. 211. WWS, p. 124.

Jepson, Kate [actress] (b. Clinton NJ, 1868–27 Sep 1923 [55?], Philadelphia PA). BHD, p. 211.

Jerge, Eugene [actor] (b. 1873?–26 Feb 1926 [53], Buffalo NY; cirrhosis of the liver). "Eugene Jerge," *Variety,* 3 Mar 1926. AS, p. 573.

Jerome, Edwin [actor] (b. New York NY, 30 Dec 1885–10 Sep 1959 [73], Pasadena CA). AS, p. 573.

Jerome, Elmer [actor] (b. IL, 30 Jan 1872–10 Aug 1947 [75], Los Angeles Co. CA). BHD1, p. 284. IFN, p. 155.

Jerome, William [composer/scenarist] (b. 1865–25 Jun 1932 [67?], New York NY). BHD2, p. 135.

Jerrold, Mary [stage/film/radio actress] (*née* Mary Allen, b. London, England, 4 Dec 1877–3 Mar 1955 [77], London, England). (Stage debut: *Mary Pennington,* St. James Theatre, Lond, 1896). "Mary Jerrold," *Variety,* 9 Mar 1955, 79:2 ("She first entered films in 1931…'). AS, p. 573. BHD1, p. 284. IFN, p. 155.

Jeske, George [actor: Keystone Cop/director] (b. 1891–28 Oct 1951 [60], Los Angeles CA). "George Jeske," *Variety,* 31 Oct 1951. AS, p. 573. BHD, p. 211; BHD2, p. 135. IFN, p. 155. Truitt, p. 171.

Jessel, George Albert [actor] (b. New York [Harlem] NY, 3 Apr 1898–23 May 1981 [83], Los Angeles CA; heart attack). m. (1 & 2) Florence Courtney, 1919; (3) **Norma Talmadge**, 1932–34 (d. 1957); (4) Lois Andrews (16 yrs. old), 1942. William E. Geist, "George Jessel, Comedian, Dead; Known as 'Toastmaster General,'" *NYT,* 26 May 1981, IV, 12:1. "Jessel Service on Coast Today," *NYT,* 27 May 1981, 22:3 (Milton Berle delivered the eulogy). "George Jessel Dies in L.A. at 83; Of Many Talents and Romances," *Variety,* 27 May 1981. AMD, p. 183. AS, p. 573. BHD1, p. 284. FSS, p. 154. Katz, p. 619. "First Jessel Picture,"

MPW, 8 May 1926, 126. "Vitaphone Signs Jolson, Jessel, and Warrenrath," *MPW,* 11 Sep 1926, 3. Joseph Jackson, "Things I Have Seen," *Paris and Hollywood,* Oct 1926, 33 (to play in *Private Izzy Murphy* for WB. Of the Warner brothers, he said, "I can remember when they didn't have a dime apiece...[n]ow look at them—they've all got umbrellas."). "Jessel Wins Postponement," *MPW,* 29 Nov 1926, 3. "Jolson to Get Title Role in 'Jazz Singer,'" *MPW,* 4 Jun 1927, 330. "George Jessel," *MPW,* 6 Aug 1927, 384.

Jessner, Leopold [director] (b. Koningsberg, Germany, 3 Mar 1878–13 Dec 1945 [67], Los Angeles CA). AS, p. 574. BHD2, p. 135.

Jessup, Stanley [actor] (b. Chester NY, 1878–26 Oct 1945 [67?], Bronx NY). AS, p. 574.

Jett, Sheldon [film/TV actor] (b. 1901–1 Feb 1960 [59], New York NY). "Sheldon Jett," *Variety,* 217, 24 Feb 1960, 111:2. AS, p. 574. BHD, p. 211. IFN, p. 155.

Jevne, Jack A. [of H. Jevne & Co., a pioneer grocery and bakery enterprise/scenarist] (b. 1875?–6 Sep 1941 [66], Los Angeles CA; heart attack). "Jack A. Jevne," *NYT,* 7 Sep 1941, 50:1. AMD, p. 183. FDY, p. 429. "Jevne Signed by Considine for United Artists," *MPW,* 19 Feb 1927, 570.

Jewel, Betty [actress] (b. Omaha NB). AMD, p. 183. "Betty Jewel Signed," *MPW,* 15 Aug 1925, 753. "Betty Jewel Signs with Paramount," *MPW,* 17 Jul 1926, 153. George A. Katchmer, "Forgotten Cowboys and Cowgirls—Part III," *CI,* 174 (Dec 1989), 48; "Update—Forgotten Cowboys/Girls," *CI,* 179 (May 1990), 43.

Jewell, Edward C. [art director] (b. 1894?–25 Sep 1963 [69], Los Angeles CA; cancer). (Columbia; Paramount; Eagle Lion.) "Edward C. Jewell," *Variety,* 2 Oct 1963. BHD2, p. 135.

Jewett, Ethel [actress] (b. Portland OR, 8 Sep 1877–8 Dec 1944 [67], Los Angeles CA). (Edison.) BHD1, p. 611. Kay Sloan, *The Loud Silents; Origins of the Social Problem Film* (Chicago: University of Illinois Press, 1988; photo of Jewett in *Eighty Million Women Want?*).

Jimenez, Carmen [actress] (b. Spain). No other data found. (Paramount, Joinville, Paris; Fox; last film: *La Bien Pagada,* Spain, 1935.) Waldman, p. 149.

Jiminez, Soledad [actress] (b. Santander, Spain, 10 Mar 1874–17 Oct 1966 [92], Woodland Hills CA; following a stroke). "Soledad Jiminez," *Variety,* 26 Oct 1966 ("She was in many silents and played Warner Baxter's mother in the first talking western, 'In Old Arizona.'"). AS, p. 574 (b. 28 Feb). BHD1, p. 284 (b. Cantabria, Spain, 28 Feb). IFN, p. 155.

Jingu, Miyoshi [actress] (b. Japan, 1894–19 Jan 1969 [74?], Los Angeles CA). AS, p. 574.

Job, Herbert K. [cinematographer] (b. Boston MA, 1865–17 Jun 1933 [68?], Delmar NY). BHD2, p. 135.

Jobson, Edward [actor] (*né* Edwin C. Jobson, b. Philadelphia PA, 29 Feb 1861–7 Feb 1925 [63], San Jose CA). "Edward Johnson [sic]," *Variety,* 18 Feb 1925 ("veteran movie actor"). AMD, p. 183. AS, p. 574. BHD, p. 211. IFN, p. 156. Truitt, p. 172. "Triangle Adds Two New Players," *MPW,* 17 Nov 1917, 1028. "Jobson Joins Metro Stock Forces," *MPW,* 24 Jul 1920, 500.

Joby, Hans [actor] (b. Kronstadt, Hungary, 3 Aug 1884–1 May 1943 [58], Los Angeles CA). (Imperial.) "Hans Joby," *Variety,* 28 Apr 1943 (d. 30 Apr; age 59). AS, p. 574 (d. 30 Apr). BHD1, p. 284 (b. Brasov, Romania); BHD2, p. 135 (b. Kronstadt, Kotlin Island, Russia). IFN, p. 156.

Joffre, Jean François Omer [actor] (b. Rivesltes, France, 12 Nov 1872–21 Feb 1944 [71], Paris, France [extrait de décès no. SN/1944]). AS, p. 575.

Johansson, Ivar [actor/director] (b. Sweden, 1889–1963 [74?], Sweden). AS, p. 575.

John, Edmund [cinematographer]. No data found. FDY, p. 459.

John, Georg [actor] (d. 1934). BHD, p. 211.

Johns, Bertram "Bertie" [actor/technical director] (b. Plymouth, England, 1873–9 May 1934 [60], Los Angeles CA; heart attack). (Fox.) AMD, p. 183. AS, p. 575. BHD1, p. 285. IFN, p. 156. "Technical Director," *MPW,* 2 Jul 1927, 34.

Johns, Mervyn (father of Glynis Johns) [actor] (b. Pembroke, Wales, 18 Feb 1899–1992 [93?], England). AS, p. 575.

Johns, Phil [actor] (b. 1900–28 Mar 1929 [29?], Pacoima CA; airplane crash). AS, p. 575.

Johnson, A.L. [actor]. No data found. Paul J. Eisloeffel and Andrea I. Paul, "Hollywood on the Plains; Nebraska's Contribution to Early American Cinema," *Journal of the West,* Apr 1994, 13–19.

Johnson, Al [actor/stuntman] (b. 1896–19 Jan 1927 [30?], Glendale CA; airplane crash). AS, p. 575.

Johnson, Adrian [scenarist]. No data found. FDY, p. 429.

Johnson, Arthur Vaughan [actor] (b. Davenport IA, 1 Jun 1876–17 Jan 1916 [39], Philadelphia PA; alcoholism). m. **Florence Hackett**; Evelyn Graham. (Biograph, 1908; Reliance; Lubin.) "Arthur V. Johnson," *NYT,* 18 Jan 1916, 11:4. AMD, p. 183. AS, p. 575 (b. Cincinnati OH, 2 Feb). BHD, p. 211 (b. Cincinnati OH); BHD2, p. 135. IFN, p. 156 (age 39). Katz, p. 621. Spehr, p. 144. Truitt, 1983 (b. Cincinnati OH, 2 Feb). "Picture Personalities," *MPW,* 18 Feb 1911, 351. "Concerning Arthur Johnson," *NYDM,* 12 Mar 1913, p. 30 (b. Cincinnati OH). "Arthur Johnson Makes a Speech," *MPW,* 24 Jan 1914, 393. "Arthur Johnson, Leading Man," *MPW,* 24 Apr 1915, 545. 'Only Nervous Breakdown,' Says Johnson," *MPW,* 22 May 1915, 1269. "Arthur Johnson Recovering," *NYDM,* 9 Jun 1915, 25:2 (39 years old on 1 Jun). "Obituary," *MPW,* 22 Jan 1916, 574. "Arthur V. Johnson Dead; Famous Lubin Actor Who Was Known to Millions Passes Away," *NYDM,* 29 Jan 1916, 46:1. Eve Golden, "Arthur Johnson: Griffith's Matchless Star," *CI,* 208 (Oct 1992), 42–43 (b. Cincinnati).

Johnson, Benjamin [actor] (b. 1866–23 Jun 1928 [62?], New York NY). BHD, p. 211.

Johnson, Burges [actor] (b. 1873–23 Feb 1963 [89?], Schenectady NY). AS, p. 576 (b. 1878). BHD, p. 211.

Johnson, Carmencita [child actress] (b. Los Angeles CA, 31 Mar 1923–26 Sep 2000 [77], Ventura CA; result of a car accident). m. Jack Robertson, ca. 1950 (5 children). Harris Lentz, III, "Carmencita Johnson, 71," *CI,* 305 (Nov 2000), p. 55.

Johnson, Chic [actor] (*né* Harold Ogden Johnson, b. Chicago IL, 5 Mar 1891–25 Feb 1962 [70], Las Vegas NV). AS, p. 576.

Johnson, Dolores (mother of John Derek, 1926–98) [actress]. No data found. m. director **Lawson Harris**. No data found.

Johnson, Dora Dean [stage/film actress/dancer/vaudevillian] (*née* Dora Babbige, b. Covington KY, 1872?–Jan 1950 [78], Minneapolis MN). m. Charles Johnson. "Dora Dean Johnson," *Variety,* 11 Jan 1950 (Johnson & Dean, originators of the cakewalk). SD.

Johnson, Duke [actor] (b. 1871–12 Apr 1929 [58?], Los Angeles CA). AS, p. 576.

Johnson, Earle W. [scenarist]. No data found. FDY, p. 429.

Johnson, Edith [actress] (b. Rochester NY, 10 Aug 1893–5 Sep 1969 [76], Los Angeles CA; of injuries from a fall). (Edith Duncan). m. (1) Albert S. Dampman—div. Feb? 1920; (2) William Duncan, 1921. (Selig, 1914; Vitagraph.) AMD, p. 183. AS, p. 576 (b. 1894; d. 6 Sep). BHD, p. 211 (b. 1894). BR, pp. 45–48. IFN, p. 156. MH, p. 1119 (b. 1895). Slide, p. 162 (b. 1894). Truitt, p. 172. WWS, p. 245 (b. 1895). "Pretty Edith Johnson Writes of Art," *MPW,* 6 Nov 1915, 1123. "Looking for Edith Johnson," *MPW,* 15 Jan 1916, 388. "Studio Shots," *MPW,* 3 Apr 1920, 70 (cites divorce from Dampman). George Katchmer, "Remembering the Great Silents," *CI,* 224 (Feb 1994), 54:3.

Johnson, Edward [actor] (b. 1861–7 Feb 1925 [63?], San Jose CA). AS, p. 576.

Johnson, Emilie (mother of **Emory Johnson**) [scenarist] (b. Gothenberg, Sweden, 3 Jun 1867–23 Sep 1941 [74], Los Angeles CA). "Mrs. Emilie Johnson," *Variety,* 1 Oct 1941. AS, p. 576. BHD2, p. 136. FDY, p. 429. IFN, p. 156.

Johnson, [A.] Emory (son of **Emilie Johnson**) [actor/director/scenarist] (b. San Francisco CA, 16 Mar 1894–18 Apr 1960 [66], San Mateo CA; a result of burns suffered when his bed caught fire). m. **Ella Hall**, 6 Sep 1917, Santa Barbara CA (d. 1981). (Universal.) "Emory Johnson," *Variety,* 27 Apr 1960. AMD, p. 183. AS, p. 576. BHD1, p. 285; BHD2, p. 136 (b. 1895). IFN, p. 156. "Emory Johnson," *MPW,* 30 Jun 1917, 2081. "Ella Hall to Marry Emory Johnson," *MPW,* 28 Jul 1917, 628. "Universal Players' Contracts Expire," *MPW,* 1 Jun 1918, 1267. "Ella Hall Mother of Boy," *MPW,* 15 Mar 1919, 1473 (b. 29 Jan 1919, Santa Barbara CA). Ruth Mabrey, "Are Society Pictures More Popular Than Homespun Variety? 'No!,' Says Emory Johnson, *MW,* 8 Dec 1923, 23, 27. "Producing in Secret," *MPW,* 16 Aug 1924, 527. "Behind Locked Doors," *MPW,* 16 Aug 1924, 557. George Katchmer, "Remembering the Great Silents," *CI,* 250 (Apr 1996), 48.

Johnson, Frances [actress] (b. 1911?–1 Jan 1933 [21], Paris, France). *See NYT* obituary of Jack Pickford. IFN, p. 156.

Johnson, George Lorimer [actor/director] (b. 1859–20 Feb 1941 [81?], Los Angeles CA). AS, p. 576.

Johnson, George M. [scenarist]. No data found. FDY, p. 429.

Johnson, George Perry [producer] (b. Feb 1887–3 Apr 1939 [52], Los Angeles CA). BHD2, p. 136.

Johnson, J. Rosamond [actor/composer] (b. Jacksonville FL, 11 Aug 1873–11 Nov 1954 [81], New York NY). BHD2, p. 136.

Johnson, Jack [actor] (b. Galveston TX, 21 Mar 1878–10 Jun 1946 [68], Raleigh NC). AS, p. 576 (b. 31 Mar). BHD1, p. 285.

Johnson, John Lester [actor] (b. SC, 13 Aug 1893–27 Mar 1968 [74], Los Angeles CA). BHD, p. 211.

Johnson, Julian [scenario editor/title writer] (b. Chicago IL, 26 Nov 1885–12 Nov 1965 [79], Los Angeles CA). m. **Texas Guinan** (d. 1933). FP-L. "Julian Johnson," *Variety*, 17 Nov 1965. AMD, p. 183. AS, p. 576. BHD2, p. 136. FDY, p. 445. "Julian Johnson Joins Selznick," *MPW*, 14 Jul 1917, 251. "Julian Johnson Appointed to High Place in Paramount Company by Jesse L. Lasky," *MPW*, 25 Feb 1922, 818. Charles E. Dexter, "Pity the Poor Scenario Editor!; He gets more than his share when it comes to wading through daily stacks of unsolicited manuscripts—Ask Julian Johnston [sic]—He knows," *MW*, 22 Sep 1923, 10, 28. "Julian Johnson to West Coast as Title Editor," *MPW*, 23 Apr 1927, 734.

Johnson, Katie [actress] (*née* Katherine Johnson, b. England, 1878–4 Mar 1957 [78?], Elham, England). AS, p. 576.

Johnson, Kay [actress] (*née* Catherine Townsend, b. Mt. Vernon NY, 29 Nov 1904–17 Nov 1975 [70], Waterford CT). m. director/producer John Cromwell (d. 26 Sep 1979). AS, p. 576. BHD1, p. 286. IFN, p. 156. SD. Truitt, 1983.

Johnson, Keith [actor] (*né* Colin Keith Johnson, b. Lee, England, 8 Oct 1896 [extrait de naissance no. 144/1896]). AS, p. 576.

Johnson, Krag [writer]. No data found. AMD, p. 183. "Adds to Writing Staff," *MPW*, 26 Dec 1925, 776.

Johnson, Lawrence E. [scenarist] (b. Cobourg, Ontario, Canada, 1869–13 Oct 1933 [64?], Los Angeles CA). BHD2, p. 136.

Johnson, Martin E. [cameraman/producer] (b. Rockford IL, 9 Oct 1884–13 Jan 1937 [52], Newhall CA; result of plane crash injuries). m. **Osa** Leighty (d. 1953). "Martin Johnson," *Variety*, 20 Jan 1937 (age 53). AMD, p. 183. AS, p. 577. BHD1, p. 286; BHD2, p. 136. IFN, p. 156. "Johnson Brings Pictures of Cannibals," *MPW*, 3 Aug 1918, 671. S.M. Weller, "Martin Johnson tells readers of 'The Picture Show' his own story of how he nearly lost his wife and his life," *The Picture Show*, No. 11, 12 Jul 1919, 10–12. "Shooting Big Game with the Martin Johnsons in Africa," *MPC*, Aug 1927, 18–19, 67.

Johnson, Mary [actress] (*née* Astrid Maria Carlsson, b. Eskilstuna, Sweden, 11 May 1895–1975 [80?], Sweden). AMD, p. 183. AS, p. 577. "Sweden, Too, Has a Mary Who Is a 'Movie Queen,'" *MPW*, 10 Jan 1920, 258.

Johnson, Noble Mark [actor] (b. Marshall MO, 18 Apr 1881–9 Jan 1978 [96], Yucaipa, near San Bernardino CA). m. Ruth Thornton, 19 Oct 1912, Denver CO; Gladys Blackwell. (Film debut: *The Eagle's Nest*, Lubin, 1909; Griffith; Universal; RKO.) Henry T. Sampson, *Black in Black and White: A Source Book on Black Films* (Metuchen NJ: The Scarecrow Press, 1977). AS, p. 577. BHD1, p. 286. FSS, p. 155. MSBB, p. 1025. 1921 Directory, p. 181 (b. Colorado Springs CO, 1897). Luther Hancock, "Whatever Happened to Noble Johnson?," *CI*, 129 (Mar 1986), 48–49, 51 (b. Colorado Springs CO). Bill Cappello, "Noble Johnson—Part I," *CI*, 199 (Jan 1992), 42 *et passim;* Part II, *CI*, 200 (Feb 1992), 50–51. George Katchmer, "Remembering the Great Silents," *CI*, 224 (Feb 1994), 55:1.

Johnson, Nunally [journalist/writer/director/producer] (b. Columbus GA, 5 Dec 1897–25 Mar 1977 [79], Los Angeles CA; pneumonia). m. (1) Alice Mason, ca. 1919, NJ; (2) Marion Byrnes, ca. 1926, Portchester NY and in 1927, Hackensack NJ—div. 1938; (3) Dorris Bowdon, Feb 1940, Nyack NY. Nora Johnson [daughter], *Flashback: Nora Johnson on Nunnally Johnson* (Garden City NY: Doubleday & Co., Inc., 1979) (wrote *Rough House Rosie*, Paramount, 1927). Peter B. Flint, "Nunnally Johnson, Screenwriter, Producer and Director, Is Dead," *NYT*, 26 Mar 1977, 22:3. AS, p. 577.

Johnson, Olive [actress]. No data found. AMD, p. 183. "Olive Johnson," *MPW*, 29 May 1915, 1408.

Johnson, Ormi Hawley (sister of **Roswell "Buster" Johnson**) [actress]. No data found. AMD, p. 183. "Buster's Sister," *MPW*, 5 Apr 1913, 56.

Johnson, Orrin [stage/film actor] (b. Louisville KY, 1 Dec 1864?–24 Nov 1943 [78], Neenah WI). m. (1) Katherine Grey (*née* Katherine Best, d. 1950); (2) Isabel E. Smith. "Orrin Johnson, 78, Stage Star, Dead; A Player in Many Successes Around Turn of Century Stricken in Wisconsin," *NYT*, 25 Nov 1943, 25:1. *See* "Mrs. Orrin Johnson," *Variety*, 6 Sep 1950. AMD, p. 183. AS, p. 577. BHD, p. 211 (b. 1865). IFN, p. 156. SD. "Orrin Johnson," *MPW*, 19 Dec 1914, 1693. "More N.Y.M.P. Stars; Katherine Kaelred and Orrin Johnson Signed to Appear in Ince Screen Productions," *NYDM*, LXXIII, 9 Jun 1915, 25:1.

Johnson, Osa [producer/author] (*né* Osa Leighty, b. Chanute KS, 14 Mar 1894–7 Jan 1953 [58], New York NY; heart attack). m. **Martin Johnson** (d. 1937). "Osa (Mrs. Martin) Johnson," *Variety*, 14 Jan 1953. AS, p. 577. BHD1, p. 286; BHD2, p. 136. IFN, p. 156. Truitt, 1983.

Johnson, Pauline [actress] (b. England, 1902–1947 [45?], England). BHD1, p. 286.

Johnson, Richard [actor] (b. Denver CO, 1891). m. **Lulu Bower**, Nov? 1915. (Balboa.) AMD, p. 183. BHD, p. 212. J. Van Cartmell, "Studio News from the Coast," *NYUDM*, 4 Dec 1915, 27:2 (married Bower by announcing the marriage instead of eloping). "Another Balboa Bride," *MPW*, 11 Dec 1915, 2023.

Johnson, Roswell "Buster" (brother of Ormi Hawley Johnson) [actor] (b. New York NY, 1908?). AMD, p. 183. "The Lubin Child Wonder," *MPW*, 6 Apr 1912, 39. "One of the Lubin Troupes," *MPN*, 13 Jul 1912, 21 (Johnson was 3 1/2 years old).

Johnson, S. Kenneth [actor: Our Gang] (b. 1912–1 Nov 1974 [62], Los Angeles CA). "S. Kenneth Johnson," *Variety*, 277, 13 Nov 1974, 63:3 (...moppet star during the silent pix era..."). BHD, p. 211. IFN, p. 156.

Johnson, Tefft [stage/film actor/scenarist/director] (b. Washington DC, 23 Sep 1887–15 Oct 1956 [69]). (Edison; Vitagraph; Tefft Johnson Films; Fox.) AMD, p. 184. AS, p. 577. BHD, p. 212; BHD2, p. 136. IFN, p. 156. MSBB, p. 1046. 1921 Directory, pp. 267–68. Slide, p. 143. Spehr, p. 144. "An Edison Baseball Team of Other Days," *MPW*, 27 Jul 1912, 423 (photograph of 1905 Edison baseball team). "Tefft Johnson a Manufacturer," *MPW*, 17 Jun 1916, 2046. "Tefft Johnson to Direct Madge Evans for World," *MPW*, 10 Aug 1918, 860. "Johnson Has Studied Children's Ways," *MPW*, 24 Aug 1918, 1130. "Tefft Johnson Believes in Trade Paper Reviews," *MPW*, 5 Oct 1918, 91. "Tefft Johnson Outlines Defects in Picturemaking," *MPW*, 30 Nov 1918, 936.

Johnson, Victor B. [publicist]. No data found. (Warner's Features.) AMD, p. 184. F.J. Beecroft, "Publicity Men I Have Met...," *NYDM*, 14 Jan 1914, 48 (*see* Beecroft, Chester for full citation). "Vic Johnson with Williamson Brothers," *MPW*, 14 Apr 1917, 260.

Johnson, Victor L. [actor] (b. New York NY, 1907–16 May 1988 [81?], Honolulu HI). AS, p. 577. BHD, p. 212.

Johnson, Walter [actor] (b. 6 Nov 1887–1964 [76?]). AS, p. 577.

Johnson, Walter [actor/director] (b. Chicago IL, 25 Feb 1906–28 Jun 1946 [40], Pacific Palisades CA). m. Virginia. "Walter Johnson," *Variety*, 3 Jul 1946 (age 38). AS, p. 577. BHD2, p. 136. IFN, p. 156.

Johnson, William S[idney] [stage/film actor] (b. 1887?–31 May 1953 [66], Los Angeles CA). "William Sidney (Billy) Johnson," *Variety*, 10 Jun 1953 (in vaudeville as Vardon & Johnson). AS, p. 577.

Johnston, Agnes Christine [scenarist] (b. Swissvale PA, 11 Jan 1897–19 Jul 1978 [81], San Diego CA). m. **Frank M. Dazey**, Jul 1920, LI NY (d. 1970). (Vitagraph, 1912.) "Agnes Christine Johnston," *Variety*, 9 Aug 1978. AMD, p. 184. AS, p. 577. BHD2, p. 136. FDY, p. 429. IFN, p. 156. Agnes Christine Johnston, "The Comedy Scenario," *MPW*, 21 Jul 1917, 413–14. "Agnes Christine Johnston," *MPW*, 8 Feb 1919, 744. "Agnes Johnston Will Wed," *LA Times*, 19 Feb 1920, III, p. 14. "Agnes Johnston to Return in September," *MPW*, 14 Aug 1920, 874. "Little Miss Dazey Arrives," *MPW*, 21 May 1921, 279 (b. 1 May 1921, Good Samaritan Hospital). "Signed by Paramount," *MPW*, 30 Aug 1924, 701. "Signs with M-G-M," *MPW*, 24 Oct 1925, 629. Paul Paige, "Close-Ups and Fade-Outs," *Paris and Hollywood*, Oct 1926, 96. "Miss Johnston Asserts women 'Will Make Good,'" *MPW*, 29 Jan 1927, 350. "Gets New M-G-M Contract," *MPW*, 12 Mar 1927, 86. Arthur Cates, "Author, Author; The Real Stars of the Films," *MPC*, Sep 1927, 20–21, 72 (discusses Johnston, Glazer, Younger, Kate Corbaley, Mathis, Glyn, Dorothy Farnum, Byron Morgan, McPherson).

Johnston, Caroline K. [actress] (*née* Caroline Cook, b. IL, 29 Dec 1875–8 Jul 1962 [86], Los Angeles CA). AS, p. 577.

Johnston, John W[illiam] [actor] (b. Kilkee Co. Clain, Ireland, 2 Oct 1876–29 Jul 1946 [69], Los Angeles CA). (Reliance; Lasky; Pathé; Eclair; Hanover; FP-L; Metro.) "John W. Johnston," *Variety*, 7 Aug 1946 (began 1912). AS, p. 578. BHD1, p. 286. IFN, p. 157. Truitt, p. 172 (d. 1 Aug). George Katchmer, "Remembering the Great Silents," *CI*, 208 (Oct 1992), 48.

Johnston, Johnny [actor] (b. St. Louis MO, 1869–4 Jan 1931 [61?], Los Angeles CA). AS, p. 578.

Johnston, Julanne [actress: Wampas Star, 1924] (b. Indianapolis IN, 1 May 1900–26 Dec 1988 [88], Grosse Pointe MI). m. David W. Rust, 1933. AMD, p. 184. AS, p. 578 (b. 1906; d. LA CA). BHD1, p. 286. FFF, p. 191. FSS, p. 155. Katz, 1994. MH, p. 119. 1921 Directory, p. 226. Ragan 2, p. 835. "To Support Lew Brice," *MPW*, 30 Jun 1923, 763. "Miss Johnston Honored," *MPW*, 31 Jan 1925, 489. Eleanor Breitmeyer, "Surprise! For a Silent Star," *The Sunday News* [Detroit MI], 2 Jul 1972.

Johnston, Katherine [actress]. No data found. m. **George Archainbaud**, 18 May 1921, Mamaroneck NY (d. 1959). AMD, p. 184. "G.

Archainbaud, Director, Weds Katherine Johnston," *MPW,* 4 Jun 1921, 503.

Johnston, Lorimer George [actor/director/producer] (b. Maysville KY, 2 Nov 1858–20 Feb 1941 [82], Los Angeles CA). m. Caroline Frances Cooke. AMD, p. 184. AS, p. 578. BHD1, p. 286; BHD2, p. 136. IFN, p. 157. Truitt, p. 172 (Johnson). "Lorimer Johnston Is Now Selig Producer," *MPW,* 4 Jan 1913, 32. "Lorimer Johnston Joins American," *MPW,* 28 Jun 1913, 1364. "Lorimer Johnston," *MPW,* 30 Aug 1913, 964. "Lorimer Johnston Joins South African Company," *MPW,* 4 Sep 1915, 1651. "Lorimer Johnston Sails for Africa," *MPW,* 6 Nov 1915, 1147. "Lorimer Johnston Heard From," *MPW,* 18 Mar 1916, 1839. "Lorimer Johnston Returns to America," *MPW,* 19 May 1917, 1136.

Johnston, Mac (father of actor/director Jerry-Mac Johnston) [vaudeville/film actor/dancer] (b. Doniphan MO, 1906–22 Mar 1977 [71], Mt. Vernon MO). "Mac Johnston," *Variety,* 286, 13 Apr 1977, 86:4 (Hamel and Johnston; had "a brief fling at motion pictures (one film)..."). BHD, p. 212. IFN, p. 157.

Johnston, Moffat [actor] (b. Edinburgh, Scotland, 18 Aug 1886–3 Nov 1935 [49], Norwalk CT; complications after an operation for appendicitis). AS, p. 577 (Moffat Johnson). BHD1, p. 286.

Johnston, Oliver [actor] (b. England, 1888–22 Dec 1966 [78?], London, England). AS, p. 578.

Johnston, W. Ray [producer/executive] (b. Bristow IA, 2 Jan 1892–14 Oct 1966 [74], Los Angeles CA). AMD, p. 184. BHD, p. 212; BHD2, p. 136. "Independent Back to Normal—Johnston," *MPW,* 20 Jan 1923, 260. "W. Ray Johnston Leaves Arrow to Form Distributing Company," *MPW,* 2 Aug 1924, 346.

Johnston, Will B. [scenarist/lyricist] (b. 1881–6 Feb 1944 [62?], West Palm Beach FL). BHD2, p. 136.

Johnston, William [cinematographer]. No data found. FDY, p. 459.

Johnstone, Calder [scenarist]. No data found. AMD, p. 184. "Calder Johnstone Arrives at Coast," *MPW,* 1 Mar 1914, 1526.

Johnstone, Justine [stage/film actress] (b. Englewood NJ, 31 Jan 1895–3 Sep 1982 [87], Santa Monica CA; congestive heart failure). m. **Walter Wanger**, 1919–38 (d. 1968). (FP-L; Realart; Metro.) AMD, p. 184. AS, p. 578 (b. Hoboken NJ). BHD, pp. 40–42; 212. MH, p. 119. WWS, p. 115. "Justine Johnstone Is Realart's Sixth Star; Picked by Jury Composed of Professionals," *MPW,* 10 Jul 1920, 232. Justine Johnstone, "Says She Will Make Pictures of Redblooded American Women," *MPW,* 10 Jul 1920, 235. "Johnstone Company Returns," *MPW,* Aug 1920, 703. Edward Weitzel, "As Lola the Dancer, Justine Johnstone Attends the Banquet of the Thirty Club," *MPW,* 20 Nov 1920, 319. Billy H. Doyle, "Lost Players," *CI,* 173 (Nov 1989), 28, 56.

Johnstone, Lamar [actor] (b. Fairfax VA, 1885–21 May 1919 [34], Palm Springs CA). (Kalem, 1911; Eclair; Majestic, 1913; Selig, 1914; Lubin; American; Pallas; Morosco; Bluebird; Fox; Ince; Selznick.) AMD, p. 184. AS, p. 578. BHD, pp. 42–43 (b. 1886); p. 212. IFN, p. 157. "Johnstone Still a New Majestic," *MPW,* 12 Jul 1913, 209. "Obituary," *MPW,* 14 Jun 1919, 1631. Billy H. Doyle, "Lost Players," *CI,* 148 (Oct 1987), 52 (b. 1886). George Katchmer, "Lamar Johnstone," *CI,* 225 (Mar 1994), 43:1.

Jolivet, René Joseph [director/producer/scenarist] (b. Albertville, France, 28 Dec 1898–27 Feb 1975 [76], Bandol, France). AS, p. 578.

Jolivet, Rita [stage/film actress] (b. New York NY, 1894–26 Jul 1972 [78?], Barcelona, Spain). (Morosco; Lasky; Ivan; Selznick.) AMD, p. 184. AS, p. 578. BHD, p. 212 (b. Paris, France, ca. 1890; d. 1962). JS, p. 225 (in Italian silents, 1914–23). MSBB, p. 1034. Ragan 2, p. 836. "Rita Jolivet Engaged by Lasky," *MPW,* 23 Jan 1915, 523. "'The Unafraid' on Film; Ingram Novel Chosen as Vehicle for Rita Jolivet's Debut on Screen," *NYDM,* 27 Jan 1915, 65:1 (b. Paris. Review of film, 7 Apr 1915, 28:1). "Madame Critic," *NYDM,* 2 Jun 1915, 4:1 (photo; survivor of the *Lusitania*). "New Stars for Morosco," *MPW,* 6 May 1916, 960. "Rita Jolivet in Lusitania Story," *MPW,* 11 Aug 1917, 923. "Jolivet Sells Liberty Bonds," *MPW,* 4 May 1918, 678.

Jolson, Al [stage/film singer/actor] (*né* Asa Yoelson, b. Srednike, St. Petersburg, Russia, 26 May 1885–23 Oct 1950 [65?], San Francisco CA). m. (1) Henrietta Keller (d. 1967); (2) Ethel Delmar (*née* Alma Osborne, d. 1976); (3) Ruby Keeler, 1928–39; (4) Erle C. Galbraith. Herbert G. Goldman, *Jolson; The Legend Comes to Life* (NY: Oxford University Press, 1988). James Fisher, *Al Jolson: A Bio-Bibliography* (Greenwood Press, 1994). "Al Jolson Dead After Korea Tour; Noted Singer of Stage, Screen Has Heart Attack as He Plays Cards—Was 64," *NYT,* 24 Oct 1950, 1:7, 26:3 (b. Washington DC, 1886). "'Jolson Story' Finales with World's No. 1 Single Entertainer Dead at 64," *Variety,* 25 Oct 1950 (b. 1886, age 64). AMD, p. 184. AS, p. 578 (b. 1886). BHD1, p. 287; BHD2, p. 136 (b. 1886). HCH, p. 71. IFN, p. 157 (b. 1886). Katz, p. 623. SD. Truitt, p. 172 (b. 1886). "Al Jolson Praises 'Grandma's Boy,'" *MPW,* 26 Aug 1922, 670. "Vitaphone Signs Jolson, Jessel and Warrenrath," *MPW,* 11 Sep 1926, 3. "Jolson in 'Jazz Singer,'" *MPW,* 28 May 1927, 252. "Jolson to Get Title Role in 'Jazz Singer,'" *MPW,* 4 Jun 1927, 330. "Flashes from Filmland," *Paris and Hollywood Screen Secrets Magazine,* Aug 1927, 10 (Jolson added to the cast of *The Jazz Singer*). "Warners Insure Jolson," *MPW,* 6 Aug 1927, 376. "Al Jolson Begins Vitaphone Sequences for 'Jazz Singer,'" *MPW,* 20 Aug 1927, 530. "Jolson Reported Investing $50,000 in Stock of Warner Brothers Company," *MPW,* 10 Sep 1927, 94. "Personal Appearances of Barrymore Denied," *MPW,* 17 Sep 1927, 153. Francis Gilmore, "Oh Mammy; Al Jolson Sings the Celluloid Blues," *MPC,* Nov 1927, 25, 67. Donald Trowbridge, "Al Jolson Relives and Relates," *Cinema Arts,* Dec 1927, 14, 42. Carol Johnston, "The Mammy Man, An Impression of Al Jolson," *MPC,* Jan 1929, 51, 84 (b. Washington DC; "He didn't think much of 'The Jazz Singer,' although he is proud of the fact that it was a picture of his that started the talking craze."). Dave Greim, "Jolson's 'Back in His Own Backyard' Festival in Washington, D.C.," *CI,* 269 (Nov 1997), C29. The International Al Jolson Society (IAJS), Mr. Jim Brockson, 933 Fifth Avenue, Prospect Park PA 19076.

Joly, Henri [inventor] (*né* Marie Joseph Henri Joly, b. Viomenil, France, 2 Apr 1866–27 Dec 1945 [79], Paris, France). AS, p. 578.

Jonasson, Frank [actor] (b. UT, 1881). m. Jessie Alice Nash, 9 Dec 1916. (Kalem.) AMD, p. 185. BHD, p. 212. "Frank Jonasson Marries a Portland, Oregon Beauty," *MPN,* 6 Jan 1917, 95. "Kalem Player a Benedict," *MPW,* 6 Jan 1917, 61. "Frank Jonasson," *MPW,* 28 Apr 1917, 619. "Frank Jonasson," *MPW,* 6 Oct 1917, 93.

Jones, A[lexander] **L.** [producer/President of Broadway Theatre Ticket Corp.] (b. KS, 1880?–29 Oct 1943 [63], Desert Grove [Phoenix] AZ; tuberculosis). m. Della Vanna. "A.L. Jones, Head of Ticket Agency; President of Broadway Firm, a Theatrical Producer for 35 Years, Dies in Phoenix," *NYT,* 30 Oct 1943, 15:6 (produced *Rain or Shine,* with Joe Cook; *The Squaw* [with Clark Gable in a minor part]; *Brief Moment*). "Al Jones," *Variety,* 3 Nov 1943. AS, p. 578.

Jones, Al [cinematographer]. No data found. FDY, p. 459.

Jones, Alida V. [actress] (b. Philadelphia PA, Oct 1868–31 Jul 1945 [76], Los Angeles CA). BHD1, p. 611.

Jones, Barry [actor] (b. Guernsey, England, 6 Mar 1893–1981 [88?], England). AS, p. 578.

Jones, "Billy" Red [actor] (b. Wheeling WV, 9 Feb 1913). (Film debut: *Two Wagons Both Covered.*) Luther Hachcock, "The Billy 'Red' Jones Story," *CI,* 99 (Sep 1983), 26.

Jones, Beulah Hall [actress] (b. Goliad TX, 28 Jun 1900–8 Oct 1952 [52], Los Angeles CA). BHD, p. 212.

Jones, Charles **"Buck"** [actor] (*né* Charles Frederick Gebhart, b. Vincennes IN, 4 Dec 1889–30 Nov 1942 [52], Boston MA; in a nightclub fire). m. Odelle Osborne, 11 Aug 1915, Lima OH. (Fox.) "Cocoanut Grove, Boston, Fire [on 28 Nov 1942] Stuns Show Biz; Buck Jones, Pix Sales Execs and Cafe Artists Among Fatalities," *Variety,* 2 Dec 1942; "Buck Jones Was Long-Time Fave of Cowboy Fans," (age 53). AMD, p. 185. AS, p. 579. BHD1, p. 287. FFF, p. 41. FSS, p. 156. IFN, p. 157. Katz, p. 624 (began 1917). MH, p. 119. Truitt, p. 173. WWS, p. 222. "Buck Jones' Bad Luck," *LA Times,* 23 Jan 1920, 11, 9 (broke a toe when his horse fell on his foot). "Jones Recovers from Wound," *MPW,* 25 Sep 1920, 522. "Now It's Charles Jones, Fox Film Star; 'B.' Discarded at Church Christening," *MPW,* 12 Nov 1921, 190. "More Opportunity for Charles Jones," *MPW,* 30 Jun 1923, 765. "Charles 'Buck' Jones," *MPW,* 15 Aug 1925, 754. Helen Starr, "Buck Jones—Actor," *MW,* 19 Sep 1925, 10–11, 47. "Charles 'Buck' Jones," *MPW,* 24 Sep 1927, 215. Ernest N. Corneau, "I Remember Buck Jones," *CFC* , 27 (Spring/Summer, 1970), 28–29.

Jones, Curt [actor/stuntman] (*né* Curtis Ashy Jones, b. 1873–17 Dec 1956 [83?], Winchester IL). AS, p. 579.

Jones, Edgar [actor/director]. No data found. m. **Louise Vale** (d. 1918); **Justina Huff**, 27 Jan 1914 (d. 1977). (Lubin.) AMD, p. 185. "Edgar Jones," *MPW,* 26 Oct 1912, 329. "Edgar Jones; Accomplished Actor-Director of the Lubin Company Who Excels in Western Character Portrayal," *MPW,* 3 Jan 1914, 57. *MPS,* 30 Jan 1914, 21 (m. Louise Vale). "A True Lubin Romance," *MPW,* 14 Feb 1914, 799. "Clement Easton and Edgar Jones Join Thanhouser," *MPW,* 17 Jul 1915, 489. "Edgar Jones Produces Metro Subject," *MPW,* 11 Sep 1915, 1851.

Jones, Elizabeth "Tiny" [extra] (b. Cardiff, Wales, 25 Nov 1875–21 Mar 1952 [76], Los Angeles CA). "Elizabeth 'Tiny' Jones," *Variety,* 2 Apr 1952. AS, p. 579. BHD1, p. 287. IFN, p. 157. Truitt, p. 173.

Jones, Freda M. (mother of actors Marvin Jones and Marcia Mae Jones) [actress] (b. 9 Jun 1897–24 Oct 1976 [79], Los Angeles CA; bone cancer). "Freda M. Jones," *Variety,* 286, 3 Nov 1976, 79:2. BHD1, p. 287. IFN, p. 157.

Jones, F. Richard [actor] (b. St. Louis MO, 7 Sep 1893–14 Dec 1930 [37], Los Angeles CA; bronchial pneumonia). m. (2) **Irene Lentz** (Hollywood fashion designer). (Sennett; Roach; UA; Paramount.) "F. Richard Jones," *Variety,* 17 Dec 1930. AMD, p. 185. AS, p. 579. BHD2, p. 137. Katz, p. 625. "Pie-Throwing Is Passing Out," *MPW,* 14 Aug 1926, 423. "Jones to Direct Fairbanks Films," *MPW,* 12 Mar 1927, 102.

Jones, Grover [director/title writer/scenarist/producer] (b. Terre Haute IN, 1888?–24 Sep 1940 [52], Los Angeles CA; following a kidney operation). (At Vitagraph wrote 100 shorts; Universal; Paramount.) m. Susan. "Grover Jones, 47, Noted Film Writer; Author or Collaborator of 400 Feature Pictures, Coal Miner in Youth, Dies on Coast; First Sale to Laemmle; Former Gag Man for the Old Vitagrph Comedies Wrote Fiction for Magazines," *NYT,* 25 Sep 1940, 27:6 (began as a sign painter at Universal; last scenario, *Three Girls and a Gob,* for Harold Lloyd). "Grover Jones Dies in Hollywood at 52," *Variety,* 25 Sep 1940 (d. 23 Sep; had just completed the first draft of Harold Lloyd's "Three Girls and a Gob"). AMD, p. 185. AS, p. 579 (d. 23 Sep). BHD2, p. 137. FDY, p. 429. IFN, p. 157. "Adds to Writing Staff," *MPW,* 26 Dec 1925, 776.

Jones, Hazel [actress] (b. Swarraton, England, 17 Oct 1896–13 Nov 1974 [78], New York NY). "Hazel Jones," *Variety,* 27 Nov 1974, p. 87 (age 79). AS, p. 579. BHD1, p. 287. IFN, p. 157 (age 79).

Jones, Henry Arthur [playwright] (b. 1851?–7 Jan 1929 [77], London, England; following 3rd operation for kidney trouble). "Henry Arthur Jones," *Variety,* 9 Jan 1929, 67:2. "Suit Over Film Rights; Isaac S. Plaut Asks Danages from Henry Arthur Jones, the Famous Playwright," *NYDM,* 7 Oct 1914, 29:2 (Plaut sued Jones for $15,000 for failing "to deliver the motion picture rights to his play, 'Hoodman Blind.'").

Jones, Herbert [director/scenarist] (b. 1886–31 Aug 1923 [37?], Santa Monica CA). BHD2, p. 137.

Jones, James Parks [actor] (b. Cincinnati OH, 22 Aug 1890–11 Jan 1950 [59], Los Angeles CA). AS, p. 579. BHD, p. 212. IFN, p. 157. Truitt, 1983.

Jones, Jessie [actor] (b. Garden City KS, 1892). BHD, p. 212.

Jones, John W. (Johnny Jones) [actor] (d. 15 Feb 1926, Towson MD). "John W. Jones," *Variety,* 10 Mar 1926. AS, p. 579.

Jones, Johnny (son of **Edward J. Peil, Sr.**) [actor] (*né* Charles Edward Peil, Jr., b. Beloit, WI, 18 Nov 1907–7 Nov 1962 [54], San Andreas CA). AMD, p. 185. AS, pp. 579–80 (Johnny Jones); p. 857 (Edward Peil, Jr.). BHD1, p. 430 (Peil, Edward, Jr.). IFN, p. 233. "Johnny Jones to Be Edgar in Booth Tarkington Film," *MPW,* 3 Jan 1920, 108. "What Kind of an Edgar Is Little Johnny Jones?," *MPW,* 10 Jan 1920, 226. "Johnny Jones to Appear in New York Theatres," *MPW,* 16 Apr 1921, 709 (age 12). Arthur James, "Johnn¥ Jones—His Comedies," *MPW,* 24 Jun 1922, 703. George A. Katchmer, "Remembering the Great Silents," *CI,* 178 (Apr 1990), 42.

Jones, Marc Edmund [actor/scenarist] (b. CA, 9 Dec 1889–14 Apr 1965 [75], Los Angeles CA). m. **Lela Owens Leibrand**, Nov 1917. (Pathé.) AMD, p. 185. AS, p. 580. BHD, p. 212. IFN, p. 157. "Scenario 'Valueless'; Decision of Los Angeles Court—Full Account of Case from Marc Edmund Jones, Who Suffered Loss," *NYDM,* 18 Feb 1914, 34:2, 38:2 (Jones wrote *Hatred's Endless Chain* on 6 Sep 1913 and submitted it to Kalem and other companies. On 24 Sep, he submitted it to Universal. On 18 Oct, Phil Lang at Kalem received it from a "G.G. Paul" [Hampton del Ruth]. A manuscript was not adjudged a proper subject of larceny). "Jones to Do Free Lance Work," *MPW,* 15 Apr 1916, 410. "Marriages," *Variety,* 30 Nov 1917, p. 9. "Scenario Writers Get Married," *MPW,* 15 Dec 1917, 1621.

Jones, Morgan [actor] (b. Denver CO, 1879?–21 Sep 1951 [72], New York NY). (Metro.) "Morgan Jones," *Variety,* 26 Sep 1951 ("pioneer silent film actor"; in *The Great Train Robbery,* Edison, 1903). AS, p. 580. BHD, p. 212. IFN, p. 157. Truitt, p. 173.

Jones, Paul Meredith [actor/producer] (b. Bristol TN, 14 Mar 1897–30 Dec 1966 [69], No. Hollywood CA). (Realart; Griffith; Paramount.) "Paul Jones," *Variety,* 11 Jan 1967. AS, p. 580. BHD1, p. 288; BHD2, p. 137. Truitt, p. 173.

Jones, Paul R. [actor] (*né* John Byrd, b. 1910–24 Feb 1987 [76?], New Milford CT). BHD, p. 212.

Jones, R.D. [actor/stuntman] (d. 12 Jun 1925, Marsfield OR; during filming). AS, p. 580. BHD, p. 212. IFN, p. 157.

Jones, Robert Edmond [art director] (b. NH, 1887–26 Nov 1954 [67?], Milton NH). BHD2, p. 137.

Jones, S. Parke [extra]. No data found. Robert Donaldson, "Famous Extras," *MPC,* Feb 1927, 32–33 [photo], 68, 80.

Jones, Sam [actor] (b. Birkenhead, England, 1863–25 Aug 1952 [89?], Bournemouth, England). BHD, p. 212.

Jones, Thomas [actor] (b. 1884–8 Oct 1952 [68?], Los Angeles CA). AS, p. 580.

Jones, Wallace [stage/film actor] (b. London, England, 1883?–7 Oct 1936 [53], Los Angeles CA). "Wallace Jones," *Variety,* 14 Oct 1936 (actor for 27 years). AS, p. 580. BHD1, p. 288. IFN, p. 158. Truitt, p. 173.

Jones, Walter [actor] (b. Springfield OH, 2 Oct 1874–26 May 1922 [47], Bensonhurst NY). m. Blanche Deys. "Walter Jones," *Variety,* 2 Jun 1922. AS, p. 580. SD, p. 683.

Jordan, Dorothy [stage/film dancer/actress] (b. Clarkesville TN, 9 Aug 1906–7 Dec 1988 [82], Los Angeles CA). m. **Merrian C. Cooper**, 27 May 1933 (d. 1973); (2) Paul J. Barnes. "Dorothy Jordan, 82; Entered Movies in '29," *NYT,* 13 Dec 1988, B17:5. "Dorothy J. Cooper," *Variety,* 21 Dec 1988. BHD1, p. 288 (b. 1908). SD. "Dorothy Jordan, Dancer and Film Actress in '30s," *LA Times,* 14 Dec 1988, I, 32:1.

Jordan, Egon [actor] (b. 19 Mar 1902–27 Dec 1978 [76], Vienna, Austria). BHD1, p. 288. IFN, p. 158.

Jordan, Gladys [scenarist]. No data found. FDY, p. 429.

Jordan, Leslie [press agent]. No data found. AMD, p. 185. Leslie Jordan, "Troubles of a Press Agent," *MPW,* 20 Jul 1918, 347.

Jordan, Marion [actress] (*née* Marian Driscoll, b. Peoria IL, 15 Apr 1897–7 Apr 1961 [63], Encino CA). AS, p. 581. BHD1, p. 288.

Jordan, Sid [actor] (b. Muskogee OK, 12 Aug 1889–30 Sep 1970 [81], Hemet CA). (Selig, 1913; Fox.) AS, p. 581. BHD1, p. 288. IFN, p. 158.

Jordon, Harry J. [actor] (b. 1902–7 Jun 1945 [43], Los Angeles CA). BHD1, p. 288 (b. 1901). IFN, p. 158.

Jordon, Jules [actor] (b. Birmingham, England, 1871–22 Jul 1925 [54?], Toledo OH). BHD, p. 213.

Jorge, Paul [actor] (b. Belgium, 1848?–31 Dec 1928 [80], Paris, France). "Deaths Abroad; Paul Jorge," *Variety,* XCIV, 23 Jan 1929, 59:5 (in *La Passion de Jeanne d'Arc*). AS, p. 581. BHD, p. 213 (b. 1849). IFN, p. 158.

Jorge, Ricardo [director/founder of Tobis Films] (b. Portugal, 1887–10 Apr 1971 [84?], Lisbon, Portugal). AS, p. 581. BHD2, p. 137.

Jorgensen, Emilius A. [actor] (b. Denmark, 15 Mar 1888–5 Dec 1963 [75]). AS, p. 581 (b. 1883). BHD, p. 213. IFN, p. 158.

José, Edward [stage/film actor/scenarist/director/producer] (b. Rotterdam, Holland, 1880–18 Dec 1930 [50?], Nice, France [extrait de décès no. 3401/1930]). (Pathé; Selznick.) AMD, p. 185. AS, p. 581. BHD, p. 213; BHD2, p. 137. FDY, p. 429. IFN, p. 158. Katz, p. 627. Lowrey, p. 88. 1921 Directory, p. 268. Spehr, p. 144. Truitt, 1983. "Edward Jose," *MPW,* 15 May 1915, 1080. "Edwin Arden," *MPW,* 5 Jun 1915, 1586. "Pathé's 'Gold Rooster' Producers," *MPW,* 28 Aug 1915, 1485. "Edward Jose, Producer of 'The Iron Claw,'" *MPW,* 8 Apr 1916, 270. "Edward Jose Makes Remarkable Record," *MPW,* 6 May 1916, 960. "Edward Jose Now with Astra," *MPW,* 12 Aug 1916, 1079. "Stork Visits the Home of Edward Jose," *MPW,* 28 Oct 1916, 567 (daughter Helene b. 6 Oct 1916). "Jose Out of Astra," *MPW,* 17 Feb 1917, 1009. "Edward Jose, Producer of 'The Moth,'" *MPW,* 7 Jul 1917, 101. "Jose Has Miniature Studio," *MPW,* 11 Aug 1917, 921. "Edward Jose Making 'Gismonda,'" *MPW,* 27 Apr 1918, 547. "Jose to Direct Geraldine Farrar's First Picture for Associated Exhibitors," *MPW,* 1 May 1920, 701. "Edward Jose to Make Special Production for Associated to Be Released by Pathé," *MPW,* 14 Aug 1920, 878. "Vitagrpah Has Engaged Edward Jose as Director," *MPW,* 27 Nov 1920, 468. Alma Talley, "The Pearl [White] Her Director Knows," *MW,* 9 Aug 1924, 10–11, 26.

José, Richard J. [stage/film actor] (b. Lanner, Cornwall, England, 5 Jun 1870–20 Oct 1941 [71], San Francisco CA). m. Therese Shrieve. AMD, p. 185. AS, p. 581. BHD, p. 213. IFN, p. 158. SD. "Richard J. Jose," *MPW,* 17 Jul 1915, 512.

Josephson, Julien [scenarist] (b. Roseburg OR, 1884?–13 Apr 1959 [75], Los Angeles CA). "Julien Josephson," *Variety,* 22 Apr 1959. AMD, p. 185. AS, p. 582. BHD2, p. 137. FDY, p. 429. IFN, p. 158. "Signs Josephson on Long Contract," *MPW,* 5 Jun 1920, 1344. "Julien Josephson Joins Goldwyn Scenario Staff," *MPW,* 8 Jan 1921, 180. "Julien Josephson Joins Paramount," *MPW,* 11 Mar 1922, 162.

Joslin, Margaret [actress] (*née* Margaret Lucy Gosling, b. Cleveland OH, 6 Aug 1881–14 Oct 1956 [75], Glendale CA; cancer). m. **Augustus Carney**; Harry Todd (d. 15 Feb 1935). (Essanay.) AMD, p. 185. AS, p. 582 (b. 1883). BHD, p. 213. IFN, p. 158. Truitt, 1983. "Bits for Fans,"

MPW, XV, 22 Mar 1913, 1206. "Some Prominent Essanay Photoplayers," *MPW,* 11 Jul 1914, 234–35. "Back from Visit to Honolulu," *MPW,* 12 Sep 1914, 1515. "Margaret Joslin an Expert Cook," *MPW,* 26 Sep 1914, 1789. "Laughmakers Join Universal Company," *MPW,* 18 Mar 1916, 1833.

Jossenberger, Phil [actor] (*né* Phil Rich, b. 1896–22 Feb 1956 [59?], Woodland Hills CA). BHD, p. 213.

Jossey, William J. [actor/scenarist] (b. Macon GA, 1867–25 Jun 1937 [70?], Macon GA). BHD, p. 213; BHD2, p. 137.

Josz, Marcel [actor] (b. Molenbeek-Saint-Jean, Belgium, 9 May 1899–23 Sep 1984 [85], Brussels, Belgium). AS, p. 582.

Jouassain, Clémentine [actress] (*née* Catherine Julie Clémentine Jouassain, b. Saint-Leonard-de-Noblat, France, 3 Dec 1829–7 May 1902 [72], Paris, France; fall from a bicycle). AS, p. 582.

Joubé, Romuald Charles Eugène Goudins Jean Sylve [actor] (b. Mazeres, France, 20 Jun 1876 [extrait de naissance no. 82]–14 Sep 1949 [73], Givors, France). (Kleine-Eclipse.) AS, p. 582. BHD, p. 213. IFN, p. 158. JS, p. 226 (b. Saint-Gaufdens, France; d. Gisors, France; in Italian silents from 1924).

Jourdain, Jules [executive] (b. Charleroi, Belgium, 1854–19 Mar 1936 [82?], Schaerbeek, Belgium). AS, p. 582.

Jourjon, Charles [executive] (b. Chavanges, France, 1877–19 Sep 1934 [57?], Paris, France). AMD, p. 185. AS, p. 582. BHD2, p. 137. "Eclair's President in New York," *MPW,* 23 Sep 1911, 882. "Mr. Charles Jourjon Returns from Paris," *MPW,* 24 Aug 1912, 758. "Jourjon in New York," *MPW,* 10 Jan 1914, 176. George Blaisdell, "Jourjon Outlines Plans," *MPW,* 11 Apr 1914, 216–17. Charles Jourjon, "Concerning Eclair Enterprises," *MPW,* 11 Jul 1914, 207. "Jourjon Expected in New York," *MPW,* 3 Jun 1916, 1702. "Lieutenant Jourjon in Good Health," *MPW,* 21 Oct 1916, 370. "American Eclair to Resume Business," *MPW,* 21 Apr 1917, 405.

Journet, Marcel [actor] (b. Lyon, France, 8 Aug 1897). AS, p. 582.

Jouvet, Louis [film actor/stage director/producer] (*né* Jules Eugène Louis Jouvet, b. Crozon, France, 24 Dec 1887–16 Aug 1951 [63], Paris, France; heart attack). "Louis Jouvet," *Variety,* 183, 22 Aug 1951, 71:1. AS, p. 582 (d. 17 Aug). BHD1, p. 289; BHD2, p. 137. IFN, p. 158.

Jowitt, Anthony [actor] (b. Leeds, England, 14 Sep 1900–21 Nov 1977 [77], Great Barrington MA). AMD, p. 186. BHD1, p. 289. "Paramount Makes New Find," *MPW,* 7 Feb 1925, 589.

Joy, Ernest C. [actor] (b. IA, 20 Jan 1878–12 Feb 1924 [46], Los Angeles CA; peritonitis). m. **Mabel Van Buren** (d. 1947). "Ernest Joy Dies," *Variety,* 14 Feb 1924. AS, p. 582 (b. Minneapolis MN). BHD, p. 213. IFN, p. 158. Truitt, 1983 (b. Minneapolis MN).

Joy, Baby Gloria [stage/film child actress] (b. Los Angeles CA, 7 Oct 1910–25 Jan 1970 [59], Woodland Hills CA). (Universal; Balboa.) AMD, p. 186. BHD1, pp. 289; 611. MSBB, p. 1034. "Joy Among the Oakdales," *MPW,* 17 Aug 1918, 997.

Joy, Leatrice [actress] (*née* Leatrice Joy Zeidler, b. New Orleans LA, 7 Nov 1893–13 May 1985 [91], Bronx NY; pernicious anemia). m. (1) **John Gilbert**, Jan 1921, Tia Juana, Mexico, and remarriage on 3 Mar 1923—div. 29 May 1925 (d. 1936; daughter, Leatrice); (2) W.S. Hook. "Leatrice Joy, 91, Dies; Actress in Silent Films," *NYT,* 18 May 1985, 33:4. "Leatrice Joy," *Variety,* 22 May 1985 (d. Riverdale NY). AMD, pp. 186, 375 (under Zeidler, Leatrice Joy). AS, pp. 582–83. BHD1, p. 289 (d. Riverdale NY). FFF, p. 86. FSS, p. 157. HCH, p. 81. Katz, p. 628 (b. 1896). MH, p. 119. SD. "Leatrice Joy," SOS, pp. 58–87. "Miss Zeidler in Big 'A' Features," *MPW,* 18 Dec 1915, 2206. "Leatrice Joy," *MPW,* 30 Jun 1917, 2084. Cal York, "Plays and Players," *Photoplay,* Mar 1921, 91 (the rumor was that Joy would marry John Gilbert. "At any rate, Miss Joy is wearing a diamond on the correct finger and neither of the parties has denied the engagement." [They were already married.]). "Lon Chaney and Leatrice Joy Signed for Leads in New Goldwyn Production," *MPW,* 19 Mar 1921, 289. "Wave Sweeps Miss Joy into the Sea," *MPW,* 26 Aug 1922, 673. "First Starring Play Is Named for Leatrice Joy," *MPW,* 9 Feb 1924, 462. "Leatrice Joy Released," *MPW,* 11 Apr 1925, 596. Helen Carlisle, "Why Leatrice Joy Came Back to the Screen," *MW,* 25 Apr 1925, 9–10, 29. "Leatrice Joy in Culver City," *MPW,* 30 May 1925, 579. "On the Set and Off," *MW,* 27 Jun 1925, 33 (her divorce from Gilbert gave her $15,000, payable at $300 a week and $150 a week for the baby until age eighteen). "Leatrice Joy's Next," *MPW,* 12 Sep 1925, 182. "DeMille Exercises Option oon Leatrice Joy's Contract," *MPW,* 3 Apr 1926, 343. "Playing with Leatrice Joy," *MPW,* 16 Jul 1927, 188:1 (Elsie Bartlett and Clarence Burton added to the cast of *The Angel of Broadway*). Tom Waller, "Leatrice Joy," *MPW,* 5 Nov 1927, 38–39. Alan Brock, "Remembering Leatrice," *CI,* 133 (Jul 1986), 10. "Leatrice Joy," WBO1, pp. 148–49 (claims "Joy" is real surname). William M. Drew, *Speaking of Silents* (Vestal NY: Vestal Press, Ltd., 1989), pp. 58–87. Jimmy Bangley, "Leatrice Gilbert Fountain: Superstars' Daughter," *CI,* 257 (Nov 1996), 28–32, C1-C3.

Joy, Moses [cinematographer] (b. 1855–30 Apr 1937 [82?], New York NY). BHD2, p. 137.

Joy, Nicholas [actor] (b. Paris, France, 31 Jan 1884–16 Mar 1964 [80], Philadelphia PA). AS, p. 583.

Joyce, Alice, "The Madonna of the Screen" [actress] (b. Kansas City MO, 1 Oct 1890–9 Oct 1955 [65], Los Angeles CA; heart attack). m. (1) **Tom Moore**, 11 May 1914, Jacksonville FL (d. 1955); (2) James B. Regan, Jr.—div. 1932; (3) **Clarence Brown**, 1933–45 (d. 1987). (Kalem, 1910; Vitagraph; Paramount; Universal-Jewel; 1st National; WB; Fox; RKO.) "Alice Joyce Dies; Silent Film Star," *NYT,* 10 Oct 1955, 27:3. "Alice Joyce," *Variety,* 12 Oct 1955 (age 65). AMD, p. 186. AS, p. 583. BHD1, p. 289. FSS, p. 157. IFN, p. 158. Katz, p. 628. Lowrey, p. 90. MH, p. 119. MSBB, p. 1038. SD. Spehr, p. 144 (b. 1889). Truitt, p. 174. WWS, p. 52 (b. 1890). "Views of the Movies," *Cosmopolitan,* LV, Nov 1913, 839–40. "Alice Joyce Dances; Kalem Star in Forthcoming Release [*The Cabaret Dancer,* 6 Apr 1914] Shows Skill as Danseuse," *NYDM,* 25 Mar 1914, 28:2. "Alice Joyce Running," *MPW,* 28 Mar 1914, 1693. "Alice Joyce in Serial," *MPW,* 16 May 1914, 973. "Alice Joyce Weds; Kalem Star the Bride of Tom Moore in Jacksonville, Fla.," *NYDM,* 20 May 1914, 29:1. "Alice Joyce Marries Tom Moore," *MPW,* 30 May 1914, 1238. "A Million in Jewels; Alice Joyce Wears That Amount in a Forthcoming Kalem Picture [*Lucille*]," *NYDM,* 30 Sep 1914, 29:2. "New Alice Joyce Picture," *MPW,* 3 Oct 1914, 75. "Alice Joyce Contributes to Actors' Fund," *MPW,* 2 Jan 1915, 78. "Alice Joyce's Picture Blocks Street," *MPW,* 9 Jan 1915, 228. "Alice Joyce Looking Around," *MPW,* 25 Mar 1916, 2020. "Alice Joyce Joins Vitagraph," *MPW,* 3 Jun 1916. 1670. Roberta Courtland, "Mr. and Mrs. Tom Moore at Home," *MPC,* II, Aug 1916, 35–36, 70. "Alice Joyce," *MPW,* 3 Mar 1917, 1355. "Distinctive Engages Alice Joyce for 'The Green Goddess,'" *MPW,* 5 May 1923, 25. E.V. Durling, "Alice Where Have You Been?; 'I've been getting married...,'" *Photoplay Magazine,* May 1924, 72–73, 119. Regina Cannon, "Must an Actress Know Life to Portray It?; Alice Joyce Tells," *MW,* 12 Apr 1924, 3, 27. Regina Cannon, "The Madonna of the Movies," *MW,* 28 Jun 1924, 9. "Alice Joyce Returning to the Screen," *MPW,* 27 Sep 1924, 325. "Laemmle Signs Alice Joyce," *MPW,* 4 Apr 1925, 492. "Alice Joyce in Hollywood," *MPW,* 25 Jul 1925, 443. Faith Service, "'They Say...' a Number of Things of Alice Joyce," *MW,* 25 Jul 1925, 16–17, 44. "Paramount Signs Alice Joyce," *MPW,* 3 Oct 1925, 419. Sara Redway, "This Business of Being a Screen Lady; Alice Joyce was the first film actress to dress with distinction and taste...," *MPC,* Mar 1926, 32–33, 77. Gladys Hall, "Let Your Children Educate You," *Pictures,* II, Sep 1926, 65, 84–85. Gladys Hall, "Alice the Enigma; A Miniature of Alice Joyce—the Inscrutable Personality of the Screen," *MPC,* Jan 1927, 53, 84. DeWitt Bodeen, "Alice Joyce; 1890–1955," *FIR,* Dec 1976, 599–618. Eve Golden, "Alice Joyce: The Dark Madonna of the Silent Screen," *CI,* 248 (Feb 1996), 28, 30.

Joyce, Anna [actress] (b. 1912–23 Nov 1986 [74?], Hialeah FL). BHD, p. 213.

Joyce, James [author/movie entrepreneur] (b. 1883?–13 Jan 1941 [58], Zurich, Switzerland; after operation for an intestinal ailment). "James Joyce," *Variety,* 15 Jan 1941. John Rocco, "Silents, Exile, Cunning," *NYT Book Review,* 7 Jul 1996, 4:3 ("Joyce actually opened the first movie house in Dublin in 1909 (up until then movies were shown on portable screens at traveling shows and exhibitions. ¶When he noticed that his home city had no cinemas, Joyce got a consortium of businessmen from Trieste—the city in which he and Nora had settled after leaving Dublin—to back him, and he helped them open the Volta cinema on Mary Street. Joyce had a hand in almost every aspect of the opening, from hiring the staff to designing the movie posters. The Volta showed silent Italian films until a British company bought Joyce's partners out of the project. Movies were shown at the Volta until 1948.")

Joyce, Mike [cinematographer]. No data found. FDY, p. 461.

Joyce, Natalie [actress: Wampas Star, 1925] (b. Norfolk VA, 1902? 9 Nov 1992 [90], Poway CA). BHD1, p. 289.

Joyce, Peggy Hopkins (sister of **Lucille Upton**) [actress] (*née* Margaret Upton, b. Norfolk VA, 26 May 1893–12 Jun 1957 [63], New York NY). m. (1) Everett A. Archibald; (2) Shelburne G. Hopkins—div. ca. 1915; (3) J. Stanley Joyce; (4) Count Costa Morner de Moreland, Jun 1924, Atlantic City NJ; (5) Anthony Easton; (6) Andrew C. Mayer. "Peggy Hopkins Joyce," *Variety,* 19 Jun 1957. AMD, p. 186. AS, p. 583. BHD1, p. 289 (b. Farmville VA). IFN, p. 158. SD. Truitt, p. 174. "Vaudeville Gossip," *NYDM,* 4 Aug 1915, 18:1 (to divorce Hopkins, a lawyer from Washington DC). "Also Against Peggy Joyce," *MPW,* 27 May 1922,

376. "J.M. Mullin signs Peggy Hopkins Joyce," *MPW,* 27 Sep 1924, 318. "Adele Whitely Fletcher Tells of Peggy Hopkins Joyce," *MW,* 18 Oct 1924, 4–5, 28. "Peggy Hopkins Joyce Signed to Appear in Series of Pictures," *MPW,* 14 Mar 1925, 179. Nanette Kutner, "'Every Woman Has Seven Loves' According to Peggy Hopkins Joyce Who Ought to Know," *MM,* Oct 1925, 63, 92. "Peggy Hopkins Joyce," *MPW,* 7 Nov 1925, 48. "Peggy Hopkins Joyce," *MPW,* 28 Nov 1925, 339. "Peggy Hopkins Joyce," *MPW,* 5 Dec 1925, 441. "As We Go to Press," *Movie Magazine,* Jan 1926, 12 ("Strike four for Peggy, and four husbands out! Peggy Hopkins Joyce has filed suit for divorce in Paris. This time, her fourth husband, Count Costa Morner de Moreland[,] is being charged with desertion and non-support.... It will be remembered that shortly after the wedding, her husband filed suit for annulment and Peggy filed a counter suit. Both suits were dropped."). Elizabeth Forman, "Why Men Marry Peggy Hopkins Joyce," *MM,* May 1926, 42–43, 96. Sara Redway, "Men; In a recent *Classic,* Adolphe Menjou talked about Women—Here Miss Joyce answers him," *MPC,* May 1926, 22–23, 72, 83. "Peggy Hopkins Joyce to Appear at the Capitol, Detroit," *MPW,* 15 May 1926, 237. "Peggy Hopkins Joyce Reported Returning," *MPW,* 24 Sep 1927, 232.

Joyner, Francis [actor] (b. New Orleans LA, 1887). (Lubin.) AMD, p. 186. BHD, p. 213. "Francis Joyner," *MPW,* 5 Jun 1915, 1586.

Joyzelle, Rosamonde [actress] (sometimes billed as Joyzelle, b. England, 10 Jun 1883–12 Jul 1964 [81], Richmond CA). BHD, p. 213.

Judd, John [actor] (b. 1893?–7 Oct 1950 [57], Los Angeles Co. CA). (Universal.) AS, p. 583. BHD, p. 213. IFN, p. 158. George Katchmer, "John Judd," *CI,* 230 (Aug 1994), 41.

Judels, Charles [actor] (b. Amsterdam, Holland, 17 Aug 1881–14 Feb 1969 [87], San Francisco CA). AS, p. 583. BHD1, p. 289 (b. 1882). IFN, p. 158.

Judic, Anna [singer/actress] (*née* Anne Marie Louise Damiens, b. Semur-en-Auxois, France, 18 Jul 1850–15 Apr 1911 [60], Golfejuan, France). AS, p. 583.

Judic, Simone [actress] (*née* Simone Loisel, b. Paris, France, 1895). AS, p. 583.

Judson, Sheldon [actor] (b. 1896–5 Feb 1923 [26?], Los Angeles CA). BHD, p. 213.

Jul, Christen [director/scenarist] (*né* Christen Jul Viggo Pedersen, b. Copenhagen, Denmark, 25 Dec 1887–6 Feb 1955 [67], Denmark). AS, p. 583.

Julian, Alexander [actor] (b. Constantinople, Turkey, 27 May 1893?–18 May 1945 [52], Los Angeles CA). "Alexander Julian," *Variety,* 23 May 1945 ("film character actor"). AS, p. 583 (b. 1897).

Julian, Rupert [actor/director] (*né* Percival T. Hayes, b. Auckland, New Zealand, 25 Jan 1879–27 Dec 1943 [64], Los Angeles CA; cerebral thrombosis). m. **Elsie Jane Wilson** (d. 1965). "Rupert Julian," *NYT,* 31 Dec 1943, 16:6. "Rupert Julian," *Variety,* 5 Jan 1944. AMD, p. 186. AS, p. 583. BHD, p. 213; BHD2, p. 137 (b. 26 Jan). IFN, p. 158. Katz, p. 629. Truitt, p. 174 (b. 1889). "Rupert Julian," *MPW,* 21 Mar 1914, 1515. "Elsie Wilson and Rupert Julian wi Rex," *MPW,* 4 Jul 1914, 79. "Julian to Direct Exclusively," *MPW,* 8 Jul 1916, 269. "How to Get in the Pictures; Rupert Julian, Whose 'Heavy Leads' Have Made Him Famous, Says One Must Fight Upward from the Ranks," *MPC,* Dec 1916, 39–40. "Julian Combines Acting and Directing," *MPW,* 16 Jun 1917, 1769. "Three New Directors Are Signed by Goldwyn," *MPW,* 16 Aug 1919, 942. "Rupert Julian Completes 'The Phantom of the Opera,'" *MPW,* 7 Feb 1925, 605. "Rupert Julian Signed by Cecil DeMille," *MPW,* 2 May 1925, 78. "To Direct 'Silence,'" *MPW,* 6 Feb 1926, 541. "Two for Julian," *MPW,* 12 Jun 1926, 7. "Rupert Julian Started Young," *MPW,* 16 Apr 1927, 633.

Julias, J. [cinematographer]. No data found. FDY, p. 461.

Jullien, Henri Christian [actor] (b. Aix-en-Provence, France, 31 Jul 1879 [extrait de naissance no. 338]–23 May 1961 [81], Aix-en-Provence, France). AS, p. 584.

June [actress] (*née* June Tripp, b. Blackpool, England, 11 Jun 1901–14 Jan 1985 [83], New York NY). BHD1, p. 290.

June, Mildred [actress] (b. St. Louis MO, 1906?–19 Jun 1940 [34], Los Angeles CA). m. Edward H. Capps. (Sennett.) "Mildred June," *Variety,* 26 Jun 1940. AS, p. 584. BHD, p. 213. IFN, p. 158. Truitt, p. 174.

June, Ray [cinematographer] (b. Ithaca NY, 1898–27 May 1958 [60], Los Angeles CA). (MGM.) "Ray June," *Variety,* 4 Jun 1958. AS, p. 584. BHD2, p. 138. FDY, p. 461. Katz, p. 629.

Junge, Alfred [director] (b. Gorlitz, Germany, 29 Jan 1886–1964 [78?], England). AS, p. 584. BHD2, p. 138.

Jungmeyer, Jack [scenarist] (b. IA, 1883?–27 Jun 1961 [78], Encino CA). (Fox.) "Jack Jungmeyer," *NYT,* 29 Jun 1961, 33:4 ("story editor for the old Fox Film Corp."; d. LA CA). "Jack Jungmeyer," *Variety,* 5 Jul 1961. AS, p. 584. BHD2, p. 138. FDY, p. 429.

Junior, John [actor] (b. Minneapolis MN, 17 Dec 1890). (Essanay.) AMD, p. 186. AS, p. 584. BHD, p. 213. "John Junior Essanay Star," *MPW,* 18 Mar 1916, 1829. JCL.

Junkermann, Hans Ferdinand [actor] (b. Stuttgart, Germany, 24 Feb 1872–12 Jun 1943 [71], Berlin, Germany). (MGM; German-language films in Hollywood.) AS, p. 584. BHD1, p. 290. IFN, p. 158. Waldman, p. 150.

Jury, William [executive] (b. 1870–2 Aug 1944 [74?], London, England). BHD2, p. 138.

Justice, Ewan [publicist]. No data found. AMD, p. 186. "Ewan Justice Seriously Ill," *MPW,* 9 Jun 1917, 1579. "Ewan Justice on the Job," *MPW,* 18 Aug 1917, 1058. "Justice Joins Kellerman Company," *MPW,* 25 Aug 1917, 1192.

Justice, Maibelle Heikes Monroe [scenarist] (b. Logansport IN, 1871–11 Mar 1926 [55], New York NY; interred in Kensico Cemetery). "Maibelle Heikes Justice," *NYT,* 13 Mar 1926, 17:5. AMD, p. 186. BHD2, p. 138 (Maybelle Justice). "Miss Maibelle Heikes Justice Wrote 'The Final Judgment,'" *MPW,* 28 Jun 1913, 1361. "Maibelle Heikes Justice," *MPW,* 6 Mar 1915, 1456. "Authoress of 'Bloom Center' Series Back," *MPW,* 18 Dec 1915, 2190. "Miss Justice in Wider Field," *MPW,* 24 Jun 1916, 2226. "Maibelle Heikes Justice Recovering," *MPW,* 15 Feb 1919, 887:3 (critically ill for five weeks; escaped influenza then "underwent a complete nervous breakdown, caused by her incessant war work" as hostess of the Comrade Club and Canteen for enlisted men.). "$10,000,000 Company Features Works of Maibelle Heikes Justice, Screen Writer," *MPW,* 24 Jul 1920, 489. "Spoke at Convention," *MPW,* 26 May 1923, 300. "Miss Justice Better," *MPW,* 22 Sep 1923, 324 (fell on 29 May 1923).

Justice, Martin [director] (b. IA, 4 Apr 1869–3 Oct 1961 [92], Los Angeles CA). BHD2, p. 138.

Justitz, Emil [actor/director] (b. Vienna, Austria, 3 May 1878–1920 [42?], Germany). AS, p. 584.

Jutzi, Phil[ipp] [director/scenarist] (b. Alteiningen, Germany, 22 Jul 1896–1 May 1946 [49], Neustadt, Germany). AS, p. 584. BHD2, p. 138.

Juul, Ralph [actor] (b. 1888–5 Nov 1955 [67?], Chicago IL). AS, p. 584.

Juvenet, Pierre [actor] (*né* Ednie André Juvenet, b. Lyon, France, 9 May 1883 [extrait de naissance no. 770]–13 Oct 1951 [68], Neuilly-sur-Seine, France). AS, pp. 584–85.

K

Kabierske, Henry [director] (d. 18 Jun 1918, Los Angeles CA). "Henry Kabiersky," *Variety,* 28 Jun 1918. AS, p. 587. BHD2, p. 138 (Kabiersky).

Kachalov, Vassili I. [actor] (b. Vilnius, Lithuania, 11 Feb 1875–30 Sep 1948 [73], Moscow, Russia). BHD1, p. 290. IFN, p. 159.

Kademova, Litka (b. Bulgaria, 1908–15 Oct 1979 [71?], Marina CA). BHD, p. 213.

Kaelred, Katherine [actress] (b. England, 9 May 1882–26 Mar 1942 [59], New York NY). (World Pictures; Triangle-Kaybee.) m. J[oseph] Harry Benrimo. AS, p. 587 (b. 1874; d. 26 Mar 1942). BHD, p. 213. SD. Spehr, p. 144. "J. Harry Benrimo," *Variety,* 1 Apr 1942 (b. San Francisco CA, 1874?–26 Mar 1942 [67], New York NY). AMD, p. 187. "More N.Y.M.P. Stars; Katherine Kaelred and Orrin Johnson Signed to Appear in Ince Screen Productions," *NYDM,* 9 Jun 1915, 24:4. "New Star for Ivan," *MPW,* 9 Dec 1916, 1479.

Kaffenburg, Abe [executive] (b. Germany, 1875–5 Jun 1979 [104?], Paris, France). AS, p. 587.

Kahal, Irving [composer] (b. Houtzdale PA, 5 Mar 1901?–7 Feb 1942 [40], New York NY;

uremic poisoning). m. Alice. "Irving Kahal Is Dead; Writer of Songs, 40; Author of 'Moonlight Saving Time' and Other Tunes," *NYT,* 8 Feb 1942, 49:2. "Irving Kahal Dies at 40," *Variety,* 11 Feb 1942 (wrote *By a Waterfall; The Night Is Young and You're So Beautiful; Let a Smile Be Your Umbrella; I Can Dream, Can't I?; Nobody Knows What a Red-headed Momma Can Do*). AS, p. 587. ASCAP 1966, pp. 366–67 (b. 1903). BHD2, p. 138. CEPMJ; Kinkle (b. 1903).

Kahanamoku, Duke P. [actor/swimmer] (b. Honolulu HI, 24 Aug 1890–22 Jan 1968 [77], Honolulu HI). "Duke Kahanamoku," *Variety,* 31 Jan 1968 (began 1925). AS, p. 587. BHD1, p. 290. IFN, p. 159. Truitt, p. 174. Renee Van Dyke, "Paragraphs Pertaining to Plays and Players," *Cinema Arts,* V (Oct 1926), 49 (quip).

Kahane, Benjamin B. [executive] (b. Chicago IL, 30 Nov 1891–18 Sep 1960 [68], Las Vegas NV). AS, p. 587. BHD2, p. 138.

Kahn, Don [writer]. No data found. AMD, p. 187. "Kahn to Write for Universal," *MPW,* 12 Jun 1920, 1493.

Kahn, Eleanor [actress]. No data found. m. **Thomas H. Ince** (d. 1924). (Essanay.)

Kahn, Florence [actress] (b. Memphis TN, 3 Mar 1878–13 Mar 1951 [73], Rapallo, Italy). AS, p. 587.

Kahn, Gus [songwriter] (*né* Gustav Gerson Kahn, b. Coblenz, Germany, 6 Nov 1886–8 Oct 1941 [54], Beverly Hills CA; heart attack). m. Grace Leroy. "Gus Kahn, Writer of Popular Songs; Lyricist Who Created 'Mammy' and 'Carolina in the Morning' Dies in Beverly Hills," *NYT,* 9 Oct 1941, 23:4. "Gus Kahn Dies in L.A. at 54; Prolific Songwriter Was Highly Regarded in Publishing Trade as a Craftsman," *Variety,* 15 Oct 1941 (interred at Forest Lawn, L.A.). AS, p. 587. ASCAP 1966, p. 377. BHD2, p. 138. CEPMJ; Kinkle. SD.

Kahn, Lester [actor] (b. 1889–13 May 1913 [24?], Los Angeles CA). AS, p. 587.

Kahn, Otto (b. Mannheinm, Germany, 21 Feb 1867–29 Mar 1934 [67], New York NY). BHD, p. 214. "[Otto H.] Kahn Country Home Burned; Servants Have Narrow Escape from Cedar Court, Morristown [NJ]," *NYT,* 4 Feb 1905, 1:5 (residence on Normandie Heights, $200,000 damage. "An effort to save the household furnishings was futile." Is this Otto H. Kahn the actor?)

Kahn, Richard C. [actor/director] (b. 1896?–28 Jan 1960 [63?], Los Angeles CA). "Richard C. Kahn," *Variety,* 3 Feb 1960. AS, p. 588. BHD, p. 214; BHD2, p. 138. Truitt, p. 174.

Kains, Maurice [actor]. No data found. AMD, p. 187. "Maurice Kains," *MPW,* 4 Dec 1926, 339.

Kaipainen, Eino [actor] (*né* Enno Hermani Kaipainen, b. Pieksamaki, Finland, 2 Dec 1899–31 Jan 1955 [55], Helsinki, Filnand). AS, p. 588.

Kaiser-Titz, Erich [actor] (né Heinrich Felix Erich Kaiser-Titz, b. 7 Oct 1875–22 Nov 1928 [53], Berlin, Germany). AS, p. 588 (b. 1878; d. 22 Nov). BHD, p. 214 (b. 1878). Vittorio Martinelli, "Kino-Lieblinge," *Griffithiana,* 38/39 (Oct 1990), 53 (appeared in 275 films).

Kalatozov, Mikhail [actor/cinematographer/director] (b. Tbilisi, Soviet Georgia, 28 Dec 1903–27 Mar 1973 [69], Moscow, Russia). (Began 1923.) "Mikhail Kalatozov," *Variety,* 270, 4 Apr 1973, 127:2. BHD2, p. 138. Waldman, p. 151.

Kalb, Mary Caroline [actress] (b. La Chapelle, France, 5 Nov 1854–7 Jan 1930 [75], Ville D'Avray, France). AS, p. 588.

Kalich, Bertha [stage/film actress] (b. Lemberg, Galicia, Poland, 17 May 1874–18 Apr 1939 [64], New York NY [Death Certificate Index No. 9246 (Bertha Kalish)]). m. (1) Leopold Spachner; (2) K. Hunter. (Film debut: *Marta of the Lowlands,* Paramount, 1914.) "Mme. Kalich Dies; Famous Actress; Last on the Stage Feb. 23 at Testimonial to Her When She Acted Heine's Death; First Triumphs in Europe; Had Brilliant Career on Both Yiddish and English Stages in This Country," *NYT,* 19 Apr 1939, 23:1. "Bertha Kalich, Top Yiddish Star, Dies," *Variety,* 26 Apr 1939. AMD, p. 187. AS, p. 588. BHD, p. 214. IFN, p. 159. SD. Spehr, p. 144. Truitt, p. 174. "'Acting Is All Impulse,' Says Bertha Kalisch; Yiddish Duse About to Make Her Debut on the English Stage in 'Fedora,' Discusses Her Art and Her Ambitions," *NYT,* 14 May 1905, III, 5. "Famous Players Secure Madame Kalich," *MPW,* 24 Jan 1914, 417. "Mme. Kalich's Screen Debut," *NYDM,* 30 Sep 1914, 28:1 (*Marta of the Lowlands,* Paramount).

Kalich, Jacob [Yiddish theater director/producer/actor/writer] (b. Rymanov, Poland, 18 Nov 1891–16 Mar 1975 [83], Lake Mahopac NY; cancer). m. **Molly Picon**, 1919 (d. 1992). "Jacob Kalich," *Variety,* 278, 19 Mar 1975, 87:3 (past President of Hebrew Actors Union). AS, p. 588. BHD1, p. 291. IFN, p. 159.

Kaliz, Armand [actor/scenarist] (b. Paris, France, 23 Oct 1887–1 Feb 1941 [53], Beverly Hills CA). (MGM.) AMD, p. 187. AS, p. 588. BHD1, p. 291. FDY, p. 429. IFN, p. 159. Truitt, p. 174 (b. 1892). "Armand Kalicz Engaged by World Pictures," *MPW,* 13 Jul 1918, 216.

Kalkhurst, Eric [actor] (b. 1902?–13 Oct 1957 [55], Washington DC). "Eric Kalkhurst," *Variety,* 16 Oct 1957 (began ca. 1922). AS, p. 588. BHD1, p. 291. IFN, p. 159. Truitt, p. 174.

Kalmar, Bert [actor/scenarist/composer] (b. New York NY, 16 Feb 1884–17 Sep 1947 [63], Los Angeles CA). AS, p. 588.

Kalmus, Herbert T[homas] [founder of Technicolor Corp., 1912] (b. Chelsea MA, 9 Nov 1881–11 Jul 1963 [81], Los Angeles CA; heart attack). m. (1) Natalie [1892–1965]; (2) Eleanor. "Kalmus, Dead at 81, Founder of and 48 Years with, Technicolor Corp.," *Variety,* 17 Jul 1963. AS, p. 588. BHD2, p. 138.

Kalser, Erwin [actor] (*né* Erwin Kalischer, b. Berlin, Germany, 22 Feb 1883–26 Mar 1958 [75], Berlin, Germany). AS, p. 589.

Kalser, Georg [actor/director] (*né* Georg Karl Lorenz Kaiser, b. Germany, 31 Dec 1870). AS, p. 589.

Kalthoum, Um [actress] (b. Tamay-al-Zahirah, Egypt, 1898–3 Feb 1975 [76?], Cairo, Egypt). AS, p. 589.

Kamban, Gudmundur [director] (b. Reykjavik, Iceland, 8 Jun 1888–1945 [57?], Denmark). AS, p. 589.

Kamenka, Alexandre (father of Sacha Kamenka, 1910–1970) [director/producer] (*né* Aleksandr Petrovich Kamenka, b. Odessa, Ukraine, 18 May 1888–3 Dec 1969 [81], Paris, France). AS, p. 589.

Kamensky, Elizer [actor] (b. Russia, 1888–26 Feb 1957 68?], Lisbon, Portugal). AS, p. 589.

Kaminska, Ida [actress] (*née* Ida Kaminski, b. Odessa, Ukraine, Russia, 4 Sep 1899–21 May 1980 [80], New York NY). AS, p. 589. BHD1, p. 291.

Kamiyama, Sojin *see* **Sojin**

Kampers, Fritz [actor/director] (*né* Friedrich Kampers, b. Garmisch-Partenkirchen, Germany, 14 Jul 1891–1 Sep 1950 [59], Gamisch-Partenkirchen, Germany). AS, p. 589 (b. Munich, Germany). BHD1, p. 291; BHD2, p. 139. IFN, p. 159.

Kane, Arthur S. (father of **Arthur S. Kane, Jr.**) [general manager/executive] (b. 1874?–2 Aug 1945 [71], Woodland Hills CA). (General Film Co.; Eclectic; World.) "Arthur S. Kane," *Variety,* 8 Aug 1945. AMD, p. 187. AS, p. 590. BHD2, p. 139. "Eclectic Shows 'Em," *MPW,* 31 Oct 1914, 644. "Kane Joins World Co.; Former Eclectic Manager to Become Assistant Manager of World Film," *NYDM,* 18 Nov 1914, 25:1 (as assistant to Lewis J. Selznick). "Arthur S. Kane with World Film Corporation," *MPW,* 28 Nov 1914, 1218. "Kane Back from Trip," *MPW,* 2 Jan 1915, 46. F.J.B., "With the Film Men," *NYDM,* 27 Jan 1915, 52:2. "Kane Resigns from World Film," *MPW,* 27 Feb 1915, 1310. "How Arthur Kane Got His Start," *MPW,* 18 Mar 1916, 1837. "Kane Goes to Coast for Artcraft," *MPW,* 9 Sep 1916, 1670. "Kane with Selznick," *MPW,* 25 Aug 1917, 1192. "Kane to Make Extended Trip for Select," *MPW,* 8 Dec 1917, 1508. "Arthur S. Kane Resigns as President of Realart Films," *MPW,* 6 Dec 1919, 641. "Kane Visits Chicago, But Says He Has Made No Future Plans Yet," *MPW,* 27 Dec 1919, 1145. "Mystery Ends as Arthur S. Kane Forms Corporation Under Own Name," *MPW,* 31 Jan 1920, 755. Arthur S. Kane, "Impossible Scripts Responsible for Amazing Waste, Says Film Executive," *MPW,* 21 Aug 1920, 1001. "Real Stars Have Survived Popularity of Special Production, Says Arthur S. Kane," *MPW,* 18 Dec 1920, 849. "Arthur S. Kane, Back from Coast, Says Charles Ray Will Be Revelation in 1921," *MPW,* 25 Dec 1920, 1003. "Arthur S. Kane Company Expects Great Invention in 1921 to Help Movie Art," *MPW,* 25 Dec 1920, 1007. "Quality Led Rothafel to 'Star' Harold Lloyd, Says Arthur Kane," *MPW,* 23 Jul 1921, 426. "Kane Heads Associated Exhibitors; Continues Arrangement with Ray," *MPW,* 18 Mar 1922, 253–54. "Kane Sees Big Advance in Industry During Year 1923," *MPW,* 30 Dec 1922, 845. "Kane's Son Honored," *MPW,* 21 Apr 1923, 809 (Lawrence J. Kane elected to editorial staff of *Yale Daily News*). "Kane Resigns as Manager [of Charles Ray]," *MPW,* 21 Jul 1923, 210. Arthur S. Kane, "Associated Exhibitors Announces Great Lineup of Productions," *MPW,* 10 Nov 1923, 250. "Arthur S. Kane Goes to Los Angeles to Negotiate for New Product," *MPW,* 10 Nov 1923, 253. "Wants More Pictures," *MPW,* 24 Nov 1923, 375. "Arthur S. Kane Says Day of the Independent Producer Is Here," *MPW,* 26 Apr 1924, 735. "Arthur S. Kane with Universal; Resigned Associated Presidency," *MPW,* 28 Mar 1925, 343. "Kane Addresses A.M.P.A.," *MPW,* 16 May 1925, 287.

Kane, Arthur S., Jr. (son of Arthur S. Kane) [publicist]. No data found. m. Flavia A. Cavanaugh, 1923, New Haven CT. AMD, p. 187. "Arthur S. Kane, Jr., Doing Publicity," *MPW,* 1 Sep 1923, 34. "Kane, Jr., Marries," *MPW,* 3 Nov 1923, 44.

Kane, Blanche [actress] (b. 1889–24 Aug 1937 [48?], Los Angeles CA). AS, p. 590.

Kane, Diana (sister of **Lois** and **Constance Wilson**) [actress] (*née* Roberta Wilson, b. Birmingham AL, 10 Jan 1901–20 Apr 1977 [76], Beverly Hills CA). m. **George Fitzmaurice** (d. 1940). AS, p. 590. BHD, p. 214. IFN, p. 159. SD. "That Protegée of Bebe's; Presenting Diana Kane," *MW,* 30 Aug 1924, 3. "Diana Kane Off to Hollywood," *MPW,* 29 Jan 1927, 349:1 (screen name supplied by Bebe Daniels after a character in Arthur Train's *His Children's Children.*).

Kane, Eddie [vaudevillian: Kane & Herman/actor] (b. St. Louis MO, 12 Aug 1888–30 Apr 1969 [80], Los Angeles CA; heart attack). m. Madeleine. "Eddie Kane," *Variety,* 7 May 1969. AS, p. 590. BHD1, p. 291 (b. 1889). IFN, p. 159 (age 79).

Kane, Edward Vincent [scenarist] (b. 1889–26 Mar 1936 [47?], Beverly Hills CA). BHD2, p. 139.

Kane, Gail [stage/film actress] (*née* Abigail Kane, b. Philadelphia PA, 10 Jul 1885–17 Feb 1966 [80], Augusta ME). m. Iden Ottman. (American; Pathé; World; Mutual.) "Gail Kane [Mrs. Abigail Kane Ottman]," *Variety,* 23 Feb 1966. AMD, p. 187. AS, p. 590 (b. 1884). BHD, p. 214 (b. 1887). IFN, p. 159. MH, p. 120. SD. Spehr, p. 144. Truitt, p. 175. "Gail Kane," *MPW,* 25 Apr 1914, 493. "Metro's Activities; Two More Stars Added to Roster of Metro Pictures Corporation Last Week," *NYDM,* 23 Jun 1915, 25:1 (Kane, to debut in *Her Great Match,* with Ralph Herz). "Ralph Herz with Metro," *MPW,* 3 Jul 1915, 69. Cover, *NYDM,* 1 Sep 1915 (in Pathé's *Via Wireless*). "American Signs Gail Kane," *MPW,* 20 Jan 1917, 385. Gail Kane, "The Director's Importance," *MPW,* 21 Jul 1917, 381. "Gail Kane," *MPW,* 15 Sep 1917, 1690. "Graphic Engages Gail Kane," *MPW,* 27 Apr 1918, 557. "Gail Kane Sues," *MPW,* 26 Mar 1921, 364 (P&W Pictures, Inc., for $2,500 from Feb 1920 contract). "Judgment for $2,719 Is Awarded Gail Kane," *MPW,* 2 Jul 1921, 94.

Kane, Helen [singer/actress] (*née* Helen Schroeder, b. New York NY, 4 Aug 1904–26 Sep 1966 [62], Jackson Heights, LI NY; cancer). m. (1) Joseph Kane; (2) actor Max Hoffman, Jr.; (3) Daniel Joseph Healy, 1939. AS, p. 590. BHD1, p. 291. IFN, p. 159. "Helen Kane Dead; Boop-a-Doop Girl; Singer Known for 'Button Up Your Overcoat,'" *NYT,* 27 Sep 1966, 47:3. "Helen Kane," *Variety,* 28 Sep 1966 (famous for singing *That's My Weakness Now* [1928] and *I Wanna Be Loved by You* [1933]; "She lost a $250,000 suit against Paramount on the claim that Betty Boop was based upon her character and creation.").

Kane, Jay Inman [scenarist]. No data found. FDY, p. 429.

Kane, John P. [actor] (b. 1885?–1 Dec 1945 [60]). AS, p. 590. IFN, p. 159.

Kane, Joseph Forman [director] (b. San Diego CA, 19 May 1894–25 Aug 1975 [81], Santa Monica CA; heart attack). m. Helen Schroeder. (Pathé; RKO; Republic.) "Joseph Kane," *Variety,* 3 Sep 1975. AS, p. 590. BHD2, p. 139. IFN, p. 159. SD.

Kane, Lida [stage/film/rjadio/TV actress] (b. 1885?–7 Oct 1955 [70?], New York NY). (Began 1895.) "Lida Kane," *Variety,* 200, 2 Nov 1955, 79 ("She appeared in silent films with Mary Pickford, Theda Bara and Alice Joyce…"). AS, p. 590. BHD1, p. 291. IFN, p. 159.

Kane, Robert T. [executive/director/producer] (b. Jamestown NY, 1890?–5 Jan 1957 [67], Honolulu HI; cerebral hemorrhage). "Robert T. Kane," *Variety,* 16 Jan 1957. AMD, p. 188. AS, p. 590. BHD2, p. 139. "Kane Off to Close Contracts," *MPW,* 29 May 1915, 1436. "Bid Farewell to Robert Kane," *MPW,* 27 Oct 1917, 517. "Robert T. Kane, Producer, Back from France a Hero," *MPW,* XL, 10 May 1919, 823. "Sympathy for 'Bob' Kane," *MPW,* 15 Jan 1927, 176 (death of father). "Deny Kane Rumor," *MPW,* 2 Jul 1927, 9.

Kane, Whitford [actor] (b. Larne, Ireland, 30 Jan 1881–17 Dec 1956 [75], New York NY). AS, p. 590.

Kann, Maurice [publicist]. No data found. AMD, p. 188. "Joins Lichtman," *MPW,* 23 Sep 1922, 256.

Kanski, Tadeusz [actor/director/scenarist] (b. Rajbrzezany, Poland, 19 Aug 1902–5 Aug 1950 [47], Warsaw, Poland). AS, p. 590.

Kanturek, Otto [cinematographer/editor/director] (d. England, Jun 1941). (Directed silents in Mexico.) BHD2, p. 139.

Kaplan, Virginia [actress] (b. 1914–5 Jan 1993 [79?], Chicago IL). BHD1, p. 292.

Kapleau, R. Carol [scenarist]. No data found. AMD, p. 188. "Ince Adds to Scenario Staff," *MPW,* 21 Feb 1920, 1243.

Kapoor, Prithvi Raj [actor] (b. India, 1906–29 May 1972 [66], Bombay, India). BHD, p. 214. IFN, p. 159.

Kappeler, Alfred [actor] (b. Zurich, Switzerland, 1876?–29 Oct 1945 [69], New York NY). (Paramount; TC-F; Robert T. Kane Productions.) "Alfred Kappeler," *Variety,* 31 Oct 1945. AS, p. 591. BHD, p. 214. IFN, p. 159.

Karels, Harvey [actor] (b. IL, 4 Mar 1905–17 Nov 1975 [70], Los Angeles Co. CA). AS, p. 591. BHD1, p. 292. IFN, p. 160.

Karenne, Diana [actress/director] (*née* Leucadia Konstantia, b. Dantzig, Germany, 1888–14 Oct 1940 [52?], Aix-la-Chapelle, Germany). AS, p. 591. BHD1, p. 292 (b. Gdansk, Poland). JS, pp. 226–27 (in Italian silents from 1916; "One of the stars of her time" in Italian films).

Karger, Maxwell [director/producer] (b. Cincinnati, OH, 1879–5 May 1922 [43], Ft. Wayne IN; found dead on train of heart attack). (Metro.) "Maxwell Karger," *Variety,* 12 May 1922. AMD, p. 188. AS, p. 592. BHD2, p. 139 (d. Chicago IL). Lowrey, p. 92. "To Mr. and Mrs. Karger—a Son," *MPW,* 4 Mar 1916, 1456 (Frederick M. Karger, b. 13 Feb 1916). "Karger Arrives," *MPW,* 21 Dec 1918, 1327. Charles Jameson, "Temperance Drove Him to the Movies," *MPC,* VII, Feb 1919, 24, 79–80. "Not a Single Interior View Seen in 'Fair and Warmer,'" *MPW,* 16 Aug 1919, 974. "Karger Recovering from Blood Poisoning," *MPW,* 22 Nov 1919, 429. "Maxwell Karger, Metro Director General, Sees Dawning of New Era for Pictures," *MPW,* 24 Apr 1920, 555. "Karger, Introducing Innovations, Sets Metro's Eastern Studios Humming Again," *MPW,* 10 Jul 1920, 216. "Karger Makes Record for Metro in East; Films Three and Starts on Second Trio Within Threee Months," *MPW,* 21 Aug 1920, 1061. "Obituary," *MPW,* 20 May 1922, 308.

Karin, Vladimir Nicolaievich [director] (b. Russia, 1881–1951 [70?], Russia). AS, p. 592.

Karjnov, Vladimir Pavlovich [director] (b. Russia, 12 Jul 1893–24 Nov 1960 [67], Russia). AS, p. 592.

Karl, Roger [actor/director] (*né* Roger Trouve, b. Bourges, France, 29 Apr 1882–4 May 1984 [102], Paris, France [extrait de décès no. 768/1984]). AS, p. 592. BHD1, p. 292.

Karlin, Bo-Beep [actress] (d. 25 Feb 1969, Los Angeles CA). m. **Gaston Glass** (d. 1965). AS, p. 592. BHD1, p. 292. Truitt, p. 175.

Karloff, Boris [actor] (aka Boris Korlin, *né* William Henry Pratt, b. Dulwich, England, 23 Nov 1887 [extrait de naissance no. 28/1887]–2 Feb 1969 [81], Cambeswell [London suburb], England; respiratory ailment). (Film debut: *The Dumb Girl of Portici,* Universal, 1916; extra.) m. (1) Olive de Wilton, ca. 1912—div.; (2) Montana Laurena Williams, Jul 1920—div.; (3) Helene Vivian Soule, 3 Feb 1924—div. ca. 1928; (4) Dorothy Stine, ca. 1930 (daughter, Sara Jane, b. 23 Nov 1938)—div. 10 Apr 1946; (5) Evelyn Hope Helmore (former wife of actor Tom Helmore), 11 Apr 1946, Las Vegas NV. Forrest J. Ackerman, ed., *Boris Karloff: The Frankenstein Monster* (NY: Ace Publishing Corp., 1969). Richard Bojarski and Kenneth Beale, *The Films of Boris Karloff* (Secaucus NJ: Citadel Press, 1974). Denis Gifford, Karloff: *The Man, the Monster, the Movies* (NY: Curtis Books, 1973). Paul M. Jensen, *Boris Karloff and His Films* (NY: A.S. Barnes & Co., 1974). Cynthia Lindsay, *Dear Boris: The Life of William Henry Pratt a.k.a. Boris Karloff* (NY: Alfred A. Knopf, 1975). Peter Underwood, *Karloff* (NY: Drake Publishers, 1972). Scott Allen Nollen, *Boris Karloff; A Critical Account of His Screen, Stage, Radio, Television, and Recording Work* (Jefferson NC: McFarland & Co., 1991). "Boris Karloff Dead; Horror-Movie Star"; Alden Whitman, "Role [Frankenstein] Changed His Life," *NYT,* 4 Feb 1969, 1:8. "Boris Karloff," *Variety,* 5 Feb 1969 (d. London). "Evelyn Karloff," *CI,* 220 (Oct 1993), 58:2 (d. 1 Jun 1993, England; cancer). AS, p. 592 (b. Cambeswell, England). BHD1, p. 292. FSS, p. 158. IFN, p. 160. JS, p. 227 (made films in Italy in 1953, 1963, and 1964). Katz, pp. 635–36 (began 1916). SD. Truitt, p. 175. Sara Karloff, "Help Sought for Stamps," *CI,* 248 (Feb 1996), 6 (proposed stamps for Lugosi, Chaney and Karloff). George Katchmer, "Remembering the Great Silents," *CI,* 250 (Apr 1996), 48, 50. Ron Weiskind, "Cover Story; Daughter of Frankenstein; Sara Karloff [born on her father's 51st birthday] says her dad wasn't the monster we see on the screen," "Weekend," *Pittsburgh-Post Gazette,* 70, 18 Jul 1997, 2 (at the Monster Bash Convention in Ligonier PA, 18–20- Jul 1997, Sara Karloff, Bela Lugosi, Jr., and Ron Chaney, the grandson of Lon Chaney, Jr., were scheduled to appear).

Karlov, Sonia [actress] (*née* Alma Jean Williams, b. Syracuse NY?). (Sennett.) Ann Cummings, "The Girl Who Fooled Hollywood," *MPC,* Apr 1928, 37, 80, 89.

Karlstadt, Liesl [actress] (*née* Elisabeth Wellano, b. Munich, Germany, 12 Dec 1892–27 Jul 1960 [67], Garmisch-Partenkirchen, Germany). AS, p. 592.

Karlweiss, Oscar [actor] (*né* Oscar Weiss, b. Hinterbruhl, Austria, 10 Jun 1894–22 Jan 1956 [61], New York NY). AS, p. 592.

Karma, Geraldine [actress]. No data found. AMD, p. 188. "Geraldine Karma, Exotic Dancer, Seen in Federated Film," *MPW,* 16 Oct 1920, 985.

Karno, Fred [actor/stage producer] (*né* John Westcott, b. Exeter, England, 26 May 1866–17 Sep 1941 [75], Parkstone, Dorsetshire, England). "Fred

Karno," *Variety,* 144, 24 Sep 1941, 54:2; "Fred Karno Dies at 75 in England; Discovered Chaplin and Stan Laurel," 45:2 ("By 1910, IKarno's production setup was so prosperous, he virtually retired, though he was still comparatively a young man,"). BHD, p. 214.

Karns, Roscoe [film/TV actor] (b. San Bernardino CA, 7 Sep 1891–6 Feb 1970 [78], Los Angeles CA). m. Mary Matilda Frass, 1920. "Roscoe Karns," *Variety,* 11 Feb 1970. AMD, p. 188. AS, p. 592. BHD1, p. 292. FSS, p. 160. IFN, p. 160. Katz, p. 636 (began 1920). Truitt, p. 176 (b. 1893). A.H. Giebler, "Los Angeles News Letter," *MPW,* 26 Jun 1920, 1753 (married Frass).

Karpen, Clarence Alfred [publicist/title writer]. No data found. m. Jessie, 11 Mar 1916. AMD, p. 188. "Clarence Alfred Karpen, Universal Title Editor," *MPW,* 1 Jan 1916, 87. "Karpen—Christie," *MPW,* 25 Mar 1916, 2015. "Karpen a Universal Film Editor," *MPW,* 5 Aug 1916, 920. "Karpen Now on Realart's Press Staff," *MPW,* 27 Sep 1919, 1973.

Karr, Darwin [actor] (b. Almond NY, 25 Jul 1875–31 Dec 1945 [70], Los Angeles CA). AMD, p. 188. AS, p. 592. BHD, p. 214. IFN, p. 160. Spehr, p. 146 (b. 1885). "Solax Engages Prominent Comedian," *MPW,* 2 Dec 1911, 732. "Darwin Karr," *MPW,* 19 Dec 1914, 1687. "Darwin Karr," *MPW,* 12 Jun 1915, 1762. "Darwin Karr Joins Essanay," *MPW,* 21 Aug 1915, 1323. "Karr Says 'Home' Is Fiction," *MPW,* 4 Dec 1915, 1856. "Personal and Otherwise," *MPW,* 18 Jan 1919, 342 (in hospital). Billy H. Doyle, "Lost Players," *CI,* 169 (Jul 1989), 7.

Karr, "Fatty" [actor]. Nio data found. AMD, p. 188. "'Fatty' Karr Signs with T.R. Coffin," *MPW,* 9 Sep 1922, 126.

Karrington, Frank [actor] (b. 9 Mar 1858–5 Mar 1936 [77], Cornwall NY). "Frank Karrington," *Variety,* 11 Mar 1936 (age 78). AS, p. 592. Truitt, p. 176.

Kartoschinsky, Oscar K. [scenarist]. No data found. "Russian Writer and Translater," *MPW,* 4 Sep 1915, 1630. Oscar K. Kartoschinsky, "The Motion Picture in Russia," *MPW,* 4 Sep 1915, 1660.

Karu, Erkki [director] (b. Helsinki, Finland, 10 Apr 1887–8 Dec 1935 [48], Helsinki, Finland). AS, p. 592.

Kassay, Tilde [actress] (*née* Matilde Cassai, b. Naples, Italy). SJ, p. 227 (in Italian silents from 1915–20).

Kastner, Bruno [actor] (b. Soest, Prussia, 3 Jan 1880–30 Jun 1932 [52], Bad Kreuznach, Germany; suicide). BHD, p. 214 (b. 1890; d. 10 Jun). IFN, p. 160 (b. 1890; d. 10 Jun). Vittorio Martinelli, "Kino-Lieblinge," *Griffithiana,* 38/39 (Oct 1990), 54.

Kastner, Bruno Richard Otto [actor] (b. Forst-Lausitz, Germany, 3 Jan 1890–9 Jul 1932 [42], Bad Kreuznach, Germany). AS, p. 593.

Kasznar, Kurt [stage/film actor] (*né* Kurt Serwicher, b. Vienna, Austria, 13 Aug 1913–6 Aug 1979 [65], Santa Monica CA; cancer). m. (1) Cornelia Whooly (d. 1948); (2) Leora Dana—div. C. Gerald Fraser, "Kurt Kasznar Dies; Broadway Actor; Appeared in 'Barefoot in the Park,' 'Sound of Music' and 'Godot' and in Films and on TV," *NYT,* 8 Aug 1979, II, 6:3. "Kurt Kasznar," *Variety,* 15 Aug 1979. "Kurt Kaszner," *CI,* 65 (Sep 1979), 66 (in silents at age 7 in *Max, King of the Circus*). AS, p. 593 (b. 1914; d. 15 Jul). BHD, p. 214 (b. 12 Aug). IFN, p. 160. JS, p. 227.

Katch, Kurt [actor] (*né* Kurt Serwischer, b. Vienna, Austria, 12 Aug 1913–6 Aug 1979 [65], Santa Monica CA). AS, p. 593.

Katterjohn, Monte M[elchior] [scenarist/producer] (b. Warrick Co., Boonville IN, 20 Oct 1891–8 Sep 1949 [57], Evansville IN). (Universal, 1914; Vitagraph, Fox; Ince; Essanay.) "Monte Katterjohn," *NYT,* 11 Sep 1949, 94:5. "Monte Katterjohn," *Variety,* 14 Sep 1949 (adjudged insane in 1933; recovered. Wrote scenario for *The Shiek* and published *Motion Picture Topics*). AMD, p. 188. AS, p. 594. BHD2, p. 140. IFN, p. 160. "Monte Katterjohn Leaves Triangle for Essanay; Well-Known Writer to Take Complete Charge of Essanay Scenario Department and Prepare Scenarios for Henry Walthall—Change to Take Effect at Once," *MPN,* 21 Oct 1916, 2511. "Katterjohn Resigns from Paralta," *MPW,* 8 Jun 1918, 1417. "Monte Katterjohn with Famous Players," *MPW,* 13 Jul 1918, 189. "Katterjohn Plans Big Production," *MPW,* 21 Dec 1918, 1327. "Monte M. Katterjohn Adapted Harold McGrath Story," *MPW,* 21 Feb 1920, 1238. "Heath and Katterjohn Signed by Metropolitan," *MPW,* 21 Nov 1925, 227. "Katterjohn Leaving Paramount Production," *MPW,* 8 Oct 1927, 339.

Katz, Sam [producer] (*né* Samuel Katzman, b. Yampola, Poland, 3 Apr 1892–11 Jan 1961 [69], Beverly Hills CA). "Sam Katz, Film Executive, Dies; Leader in Exhibition, Production," *NYT,* 13 Jan 1961, 29:1. Robert J. Landry, "When Sam Katz Was in Flower; Obits Called Him a Film Producer—But His Heyday Was as a Theatre Emperor," *Variety,* 18 Jan 1961 (d. 12 Jan). AS, p. 594. BHD2, p. 140. "They Control Your Films!," *MPC,* Jan 1926, 26.

Kauffman, Charles [cameraman]. No data found. AMD, p. 188. "Kauffman Is Kerrigan's Photographic Chief," *MPW,* 23 Jun 1917, 1944.

Kauffman, Reginald Wright [writer/scenarist]. No data found. m. Ruth. (Humanology Film Producing Co., Medford MA, Jack Rose, president.) "Author Kauffman Signed; 'House of Bondage' Writer Will Supply Scenarios to Humanology Film Company," *NYDM,* 27 Jan 1915, 48:3.

Kauffmann, Eddie [scenarist/gag man]. No data found. AMD, p. 188. "Eddie Kauffmann to Educational," *MPW,* 3 Jul 1926, 42.

Kaufman, Albert A. [actor/producer/scenarist] (b. Devils Lake ND, 25 Sep 1888–7 Apr 1957 [68], Los Angeles CA). m. Rita Krone, 18 Jul 1918, Washington DC. (Paramount.) "Albert A. Kaufman," *Variety,* 10 Apr 1957. AMD, p. 188. AS, p. 594. BHD2, p. 140. "Lieutenant Kaufman Is Married," *MPW,* 10 Aug 1918, 818. "Kaufman Resigns to Be Independent Producer," *MPW,* 24 Jan 1920, 583. "Kaufman Given Desk Set on Leaving Famous Players," *MPW,* 7 Feb 1920, 931. "Albert Kaufman Buys Twenty Actres on Sunset Boulevard for Big Studio," *MPW,* 28 Feb 1920, 1479. "Marshall Neilan and Albert Kaufman Form Co-operative Producing Alliacne," *MPW,* 10 Apr 1920, 223.

Kaufman, Boris [cinematographer] (b. Bialystock, Russia [Poland], 24 Aug 1897–24 Jun 1980 [82], New York NY). AS, p. 594 (b. 1906). BHD2, p. 140.

Kaufman, Charles W. [actor] (d. Oct 1915, New York NY). "Chas. W. Kaufman," *Variety,* 15 Oct 1915. AS, p. 594.

Kaufman, Edward [scenarist] (b. Chicago IL, 20 Aug 1893–9 Jan 1955 [61], Los Angeles CA). BHD2, p. 140. FDY, p. 429.

Kaufman, Joseph [actor/director] (b. Washington DC, 1882–1 Feb 1918 [35?], New York NY; influenza). m. **Ethel Clayton** (d. 1966). (Lubin.) "Kaufman's Parents Die," *Variety,* 26 Apr 1918 (his mother died on 9 Apr; his father, on 18 Apr). AMD, p. 189. AS, p. 594. BHD, p. 214; BHD2, p. 140 (b. Russia). IFN, p. 160. "Joseph Kaufman," *MPW,* 4 Jul 1914, 67. "A Popular Lubinite," *Motography,* 11 Jul 1914, 54. "In the Studios," *NYDM,* 5 May 1915, 21:2 (had three teeth knocked out in a screen fight with Earl Metcalfe while filming *Darkness Before Dawn,* Lubin). "Joseph Kaufman, a Famous Players Director," *MPW,* 29 Apr 1916, 807. "Joseph Kaufman Directing M'Intyre," *MPW,* 2 Dec 1916, 1337. "Joe Kaufman to Direct George M. Cohan," *MPW,* 20 Jan 1917, 385. "Picture Folk in Auto Crash," *MPW,* 14 Apr 1917, 246. "Obituary," *MPW,* 16 Feb 1918, 974. Billy H. Doyle, "Lost Players," *CI,* 139 (Jan 1987), 55.

Kaufman, S. Jay [writer]. No data found. AMD, p. 189. "S. Jay Kaufman Author of 'Wanted for Murder,'" *MPW,* 14 Dec 1918, 1241. "Kaufman to Write for Selznick," *MPW,* 24 May 1919, 1172.

Kaufman, Sam [actor/producer] (b. New York NY, 14 Jul 1901–4 Aug 1973 [72]). AMD, p. 189. IFN, p. 160. "Sam Kaufman Joins Universal," *MPW,* 24 May 1919, 1150.

Kaufman, William [actor] (b. Germany, 10 Oct 1891–21 Dec 1966 [75], Los Angeles CA). AS, p. 594.

Kaus, Gina [scenarist] (b. Vienna, Austria, 21 Oct 1894–23 Dec 1985 [91]). BHD2, p. 140.

Kavannaugh, Katherine [scenarist]. No data found. AMD, p. 189. "Added to Staff," *MPW,* 3 Feb 1923, 486.

Kawakita, Magamasa [producer] (b. Tokyo, Japan, 30 Jan 1903–24 May 1981 [78], Tokyo, Japan). AS, p. 595..

Kay, Arthur [composer/musical director/conductor for Fox Movietone] (b. Germany, 16 Jan 1881–19 Dec 1969 [88], Los Angeles CA). "Arthur Kay," *Variety,* 24 Dec 1969. AMD, p. 189. BHD2, p. 141. "Tourneur Signs Music Writer," *MPW,* 27 Nov 1920, 491 (for *The Last of the Mohicans*).

Kay, Honey Beatrice [actress] (*née* Hannah Beatrice Kuper, b. New York NY, 11 Apr 1907–8 Nov 1986 [79], No. Hollywood CA). AS, p. 595 (b. 21 Apr). BHD1, p. 293.

Kay, Marjorie [actress] (d. 25 Jun 1949, Hartford CT). AS, p. 595. BHD, p. 214. IFN, p. 160. Truitt, 1983.

Kaye, A[lbert] **P**[atrick] [stage/film actor] (b. Ringwood, England, 1878?–7 Sep 1946 [68], Washingtonville NY). (Stage debut: London, 1906.) "A.P. Kaye," *Variety,* 164, 16 Oct 1946, 62:1. AS, p. 595. BHD, p. 214. IFN, p. 160.

Kaye, Frances [actress] (b. 1919?–3 Nov 1981 [62], Culver City CA). m. Gig Henry. "Frances Kaye," *Variety,* 18 Nov 1981.

Kayser, Charles Willy [actor] (b. Metz, Germany, 28 Jan 1881–10 Jul 1942 [61]). BHD, p. 214. IFN, p. 160.

Kayssler, Christian Friedrich [actor] (b. Breslau, Poland, 14 Jan 1898–10 Mar 1944 [45], Blankenfelde, Germany). AS, p. 596.

Kayssler, Friedrich Martin Adalbert

[actor] (b. Neurode/Grafschaft, Glatz, Germany, 7 Apr 1874–24 Apr 1945 [71], Kleinmachnow, Germany). AS, p. 596 (d. Berlin, Germany, during a bombardment). BHD1, p. 293. IFN, p. 160.

Kealey, Ed F. [actor] (d. 5 Jul 1933, Rockaway Beach NY; peritonitis). "Ed. F. Kealey," *Variety,* 11 Jul 1933. AS, p. 596.

Kean, Richard [actor] (b. England, 1 Jan 1881–29 Dec 1959 [78], Laguna Beach CA). AS, p. 596.

Keane, Doris [stage/film actress] (*née* Dora Keane, b. St. Joseph MI, 12 Dec 1881–25 Nov 1945 [63], New York NY). (Griffith.) m. Basil Sydney, 3 Jan 1918–25. "Doris Keane," *Variety,* 28 Nov 1945. AMD, p. 189. AS, p. 596. BHD, p. 214. IFN, p. 160. SD. Truitt, p. 176 (b. 1885). "Doris Keane, Stage Star, Joins Griffith Forces," *MPW,* 13 Dec 1919, 828. "Doris Keane Soon to Make Screen Debut in 'Romance,'" *MPW,* 13 Mar 1920, 1782. Edward Weitzel, "Doris Keane Has Received Many Tributes to the Great Popularity of 'Romance,'" *MPW,* 10 Apr 1920, 233.

Keane, Edward [actor] (b. New York NY, 28 May 1884–12 Oct 1959 [75], Los Angeles Co. CA). AS, p. 596. BHD1, p. 293. IFN, p. 160.

Keane, James [director]. No data found. AMD, p. 189. "James Keane and 'Money,'" *MPW,* 26 Sep 1914, 1780.

Keane, Raymond [actor] (*né* Raymond Kortz, b. Denver CO, 6 Sep 1906–24 Aug 1973 [66], Los Angeles CA). AS, p. 596. BHD1, p. 294. IFN, p. 160. Truitt, 1983 (b. 1900).

Keane, Robert Emmett [actor] (b. New York NY, 8 Mar 1885–2 Jul 1981 [96], Los Angeles CA). m. **Claire Whitney** (d. 1969). AS, p. 596 (b. 4 Mar 1883). BHD1, p. 294.

Kearney, John L. [actor] (b. New York NY 1871?–3 Aug 1945 [74?], New York NY). AS, p. 596. BHD1, p. 294.

Kearney, Patrick [publicist/scenarist] (b. Delaware OH, 1893–28 Mar 1933 [40?], New York NY; gas poisoning). "Patrick Kearney," *Variety,* 110, 4 Apr 1933, 47:1 ("Despondency was believed to have been the cause, the recent bank holiday having prevented the production of his most recent play, 'Veiled Eyes.'" Wrote *A Man's Man.*). AMD, p. 189. BHD2, p. 141. "Goes to Preferred," *MPW,* 25 Aug 1923, 632.

Kearns, Allen B. [stage/film/TV actor] (*né* Allan Bishop Kearns, b. Brockville, Ontario, Canada, 14 Aug 1893 [Birth certificate #016413, no. 43, division of Brockery, Canada]-20 Apr 1956 [62], Albany NY). "Allen B. Kearns Dead; Sang in Musicals; Featured Player in Three of Gershwin Shows Appeared in London and on TV," *NYT,* 22 Apr 1956, 85:3 (age 61). "Allen B. Kearns," *Variety,* 25 Apr 1956 (age 61). AS, p. 596 (b. 1894). BHD1, p. 294 (b. 1894). IFN, p. 160.

Kearton, Cherry [cameraman] (d. 15 Jun 1915, East Africa). AS, p. 596. AMD, p. 189. "Cherry Kearton and His Work," *MPW,* VII, 10 Sep 1910, 567–68. "Cherry Kearton," *MPW,* 1 Oct 1910, 739.

Kearton, Cherry [producer] (b. England, 1871–1940 [69?], England). AS, p. 596.

Keatan, A. Harry [actor/producer/writer/director] (b. Russia, 26 May 1896–18 Jun 1966 [70], Los Angeles CA). "A. Harry Keatan," *Variety,* 29 Jun 1966. AS, p. 596. BHD, p. 215; BHD2, p. 141. IFN, p. 160. Truitt, p. 176.

Keating, Fred [magician/writer/stage and film actor] (b. New York NY, 27 Mar 1897?–29 Jun 1961 [64], New York NY; apparent heart attack). "Fred Keating, 64, Magician, Is Dead; Stage and Screen Actor Had Been Vaudeville Headliner," *NYT,* 1 Jul 1961, 17:1. AS, p. 596. BHD1, p. 294 (b. 1902). Truitt, 1983 (b. 1902).

Keaton, Buster (son of **Myra** and **Joseph Keaton, Sr.**; brother of **Louise Keaton**; cousin of **Winona Shirley**) [stage/film/TV actor/scenarist/director/producer] (*né* Joseph Francis Keaton, b. Piqua KS, 4 Oct 1895–1 Feb 1966 [70], Woodland Hills CA; lung cancer). m. (1) **Natalie Talmadge**, 31 May 1921, Bayside, LI NY—div. 1932 (d. 1969); (2) Mae Scribbins—div. 1935; (3) Eleanor Norris (d. 1998). *My Wonderful World of Slapstick;* Tom Dardis, *Keaton; The Man Who Wouldn't Lie Down* (Charles Scribner's Sons, 1979); Joanna E. Rapf and Gary L. Green, *Buster Keaton; A Bio-Bibliography* (Westport CT: Greenwood Press, 1995); Larry Edwards, *Buster: A Legend in Laughter* (Bradenton FL: McGuinn & McGuire Publishing, 1995) (in 1898, Keaton's right index finger was crushed in the wringer of a washer and amputated above the first joint). "Buster Keaton, 70, Dies on Coast; Poker-Faced Comedian of Films," *NYT,* 2 Feb 1966, 1:3, 32:3. "Buster Keaton, 70, Victim of Cancer," *Variety,* 2 Feb 1966. AMD, p. 189. AS, p. 597. BHD1, p. 294; BHD2, p. 141. FFF, p. 71 (b. Pickway KS, 1896). FSS, p. 160. HCH, p. 111. IFN, p. 160. JS, p. 227 (made films in Italy in 1953 and 1965). Katz, pp. 641–42. MH, p. 120 (b. Pickway KS, 1896). SD. Truitt, pp. 176–77. WWS, p. 171. "Why Not Try a Number on the Screen?," *MPW,* 9 Mar 1918, 1361. "Uncle Sam Puts Buster Keaton in Class 1-A," *MPW,* 13 Apr 1918, 254. "'Buster' Keaton on His Way," *MPW,* 31 Aug 1918, 1255. "Buster Keaton in Arbuckle Cast," *MPW,* 12 Jul 1919, 273. "Buster Keaton Drafted form Comedy for 'New Henrietta,'" *MPW,* 10 Apr 1920, 280. "Under New Contract," *MPW,* 17 Apr 1920, 421. "Metro to Annually Release Eight Buster Keaton Films," *MPW,* 17 Apr 1920, 440. "'The New Henrietta' is Retitled," *MPW,* 24 Apr 1920, 583 (to *The Saphead*). "'One Week' Shows Buster Keaton in First Appearance as Individual Star," *MPW,* 2 Oct 1920, 671. "'Fatty' Arbuckle Lauds Keaton Comedy, Boosting 'Buster' as His Successor," *MPW,* 2 Oct 1920, 671. "Buster Keaton Disregards Birthday to Finish Film," *MPW,* 27 Nov 1920, 498. "Rowland Considers Buster Keaton a Real Screen Comedy Sensation; Metro Fins Films Book Rapidly," *MPW,* 11 Dec 1920, 751. "Buster Keaton Begins Work on Second Series of Two Reelers," *MPW,* 26 Mar 1921, 394. "Buster Keaton Says Five-Reel 'Funny' Is Making Rapid Gains in Popularity," *MPW,* 30 Apr 1921, 974. "Keaton and Bride Arrive," *MPW,* 25 Jun 1921, 807 (m. Talmadge). "Keaton Family All in One Film," *MPW,* 19 Aug 1922, 570 (parents in *The Electric House*). "Coogan, Keaton and Novarro Are New Metro Stars," *MPW,* 27 Jan 1923, 317. "Metro and Schenck Sign for Release of New Keaton Films," *MPW,* 16 Jun 1923, 558. "Buster Keaton Making Five-Reel Comedies," *MPW,* 11 Aug 1923, 498. "Keaton Picks New Lead," *MPW,* 29 Dec 1923, 794. Harry Brand, "They Told Buster to Stick to It," *MPC,* Jun 1926, 32, 80, 89. "Keaton to Change?," *MPW,* 22 Oct 1927, 475. "Keaton Signs a New Contract with M-G-M," *MPW,* 3 Dec 1927, 10. "News From the Dailies," *Variety,* 4 Nov 1936, 62:1 ("Mae [Scribbins] Keaton, former wife of Buster Keaton, won suit in L.A. from secretary, who was withholding $500 check, alleging Mrs. Keaton owed her back salary. Mrs. Keaton also granted final divorce decree from comedian."). P.A. Carayannis, "Keaton at Columbia," *CI,* 114 (Dec 1984), 42–44. John C. Tibbetts, "Railroad Man; The Last Ride of Buster Keaton," *FIR,* XLVI, Jul/Aug 1995, 2–11. Shirley Christian, "In a Little Kansas Town [Iola KS, 7 miles west of Piqua], a Feast for Buster Keaton Fans; Every year [since 1993] the faithful gather to celebrate a silent-era comic hero who still has the power to keep them laughing," *NYT,* 9 Oct 2000, E3. Patricia Eliot Tobias, "The Buster Keaton Myths," *CI,* 281 (Nov 1998), 24–28. Newsletter: *The Keaton Chronicle,* Patricia Eliot Tobias, *Editor,* 1117 Washington Street, Hoboken NJ 07030. John Bengtson, "Discovering Keaton's *Cops* Locations," *CI,* 305 (Nov 2000), 6–12.

Keaton, Harry S. [actor] (b. NY, 25 Aug 1904–20 May 1983 [78], San Diego CA). BHD1, p. 294.

Keaton, Joseph Holley, **Sr.** (father of **Buster Keaton**) [actor] (b. Dogwatch [Terre Haute] IN, 1867–13 Jan 1946 [79], Los Angeles CA). m. **Myra** Cutler, 1894 (d. 1955). AS, p. 597. BHD1, p. 294. IFN, p. 161. Truitt, p. 177. *Cf.* Dardis, *op. cit.,* p. 6.

Keaton, Louise (sister of **Buster Keaton**; cousin of **Winona Shirley**) [actress] (b. 30 Oct 1901–18 Feb 1981 [80?], Van Nuys CA). AS, p. 597. BHD1, p. 294 (b. 1906).

Keaton, Myra (mother of **Buster Keaton**) [actress] (*née* Myra Edith Cutler, b. Modale IA, 1882?–21 Jul 1955 [73], Los Angeles CA). m. **Joseph H. Keaton, Sr.**, 1894 (d. 1946). AS, p. 597 (b. 1870). BHD1, p. 294 (b. 1877). SD. Truitt, p. 177. *Cf.* Dardis, *op. cit.,* p. 264.

Keckley, Jane [actress] (b. Charleston SC, 10 Sep 1876–14 Aug 1963 [86], So. Pasadena CA). AMD, p. 189. AS, p. 597. BHD1, p. 294. IFN, p. 161. "Jane Keckley with Pallas Pictures," *MPW,* 19 Aug 1916, 1225. George Katchmer, "Jane Keckley," *CI,* 225 (Mar 1994), 43:1 (began ca. 1911).

Kedrov, Mikhail N[icolaievich] [actor/director] (b. Russia, 1894–22 Mar 1972 [78?], Moscow, Russia). AS, p. 597. BHD2, p. 141.

Keefe, Cornelius [actor] (*né* Jack Hill, b. Boston MA, 13 Jul 1900–11 Dec 1972 [72], Los Angeles CA). (Paramount.) AS, p. 527 (Jack Hill). AS, p. 597. BHD1, p. 294. IFN, p. 161. Truitt, 1983.

Keefe, Daniel [production manager/director] (d. 12 Oct 1971, Hollywood CA; after heart attack on 9 Oct). (Paramount.) "Daniel Keefe," *Variety,* 15 Dec 1971. AMD, p. 189. "To Direct O'Henry Series," *MPW,* 18 Jul 1925, 356.

Keefe, William E. [publicist]. No data found. AMD, p. 189. "Keefe Resigns from Griffith Forces," *MPW,* 22 Mar 1919, 1606.

Keefe, Zena [actress] (*née* Zena Virginia Keefe, b. Kansas City MO, 26 Jun 1895–16 Nov 1977 [82], Danvers MA). m. William M. Brownell. (Vitagraph, 1909.) AMD, p. 190. AS, p. 597. BHD, p. 215 (b. 1896). IFN, p. 161 (b. 1895). MH, p. 120 (b. San Francisco CA, 1896). Slide, p. 143, Spehr, p. 146, and WWS, p. 151 (b. San Francisco). "Zena Keefe," *MPW,* 11 Sep 1915, 1835. "Zena Keefe," *MPW,* 24 Feb 1917, 1166. "Zena Keefe as a Girl Reporter," *MPW,* 10 Mar 1917, 1553. "Zena Keefe," *MPW,* 22 Sep 1917, 1865 (b.1896). "World to Star Zena Keefe in 'The Amateur Widow,'" *MPW,* 26 Apr 1919, 540. "To Make Fair Women Fairer Scientists Would Solve Mystery of Actinic Ray," *MPW,* 20 Mar 1920, 1945. "Zena Keefe Does

Some Quick Thinking and Makes Rapid Trip to Fill Vaudeville Date," *MPW,* 2 Apr 1921, 478. Tom Fullbright, "Zeena Keefe; The Baby of Old Vitagraph," *CFC,* 35 (Summer, 1972), 16.

Keegan, Jack [publicist]. No data found. AMD, p. 190. "Keegan Joins Franklin," *MPW,* 26 Jul 1924, 262.

Keeler, H. P[ixley] [scenarist/director] (b. Danbury CT, 1887). AMD, p. 190. BHD2, p. 141. "Director H. Pixley Keeler Is Strong for West Coast Colony," *MPW,* 27 Mar 1920, 2102.

Keen, Malcolm (father of Geoffrey Keen, b. 21 Aug 1918) [actor] (b. Bristol, England, 8 Aug 1887–30 Jan 1970 [82], London, England). AS, p. 597. BHD1, p. 295. IFN, p. 161.

Keenan, Frances (daughter of **Frank Keenan**) [actress] (b. Boston MA, 1886–28 Feb 1950 [63?], Los Angeles CA). AS, p. 597. AS, p. 597.

Keenan, Frank (father of **Frances Keenan**) [stage/film actor/producer] (*né* James Francis Keenan, b. Dubuque IA, 8 Apr 1858–24 Feb 1929 [70], Los Angeles CA; pneumonia). m. (1) Katherine A. Long; (2) Margaret White; (3) Hilda Sloan. (Pathé; Universal; Ince.) "Frank Keenan Dies in Hollywood at 70; Noted Character Actor of the Stage and Screen Succumbs to Pneumonia; Made His Debut in 1880; He Won His Greatest Success as the Sheriff in 'The Girl of the Golden West,'" *NYT,* 25 Feb 1929, 23:3. "Frank Keenan," *Variety,* 27 Feb 1929. AMD, p. 190. AS, p. 597. BHD, p. 215. FFF, p. 68. IFN, p. 161. MH, p. 120. MSBB, p. 1025. SD. Slide, p. 162. Truitt, p. 177. "Keenan in a New Play [*A Passion in a Suburb,* by Algernon Boyesen]; One-Act Horror is a Study of Madness, but is Cleverly Acted," *NYT,* 17 Mar 1905, 6:3 (a man murders his wife whom he wrongly suspected of infidelity. "Taken with the rest of the bill it carries the actor through a whole gamut of emotions."). "Frank Keenan on Screen," *NYDM,* 18 Nov 1914, 24:1. "Frank Keenan Makes Promisejs," *MPW,* 7 Dec 1918, 1067. "Frank Keenan Addresses Northwest," *MPW,* 9 Aug 1919, 846. "Frank Keenan in New York; To Stay to See Premier[e] of 'Smoldering Embers,'" *MPW,* 14 Feb 1920, 1106.

Keenan, Harry G. [actor] (b. Richmond IN, 15 Jun 1867–18 Apr 1944 [76], Santa Ana CA). (Essanay [Niles CA], 14 Apr 1913; NYMP Co.; Ince.) BHD, p. 215. *Motography,* 17 Oct 1914, 535.

Keenan, Hilda [actress] (b. 1890–20 Aug 1940 [50?], New York NY). AS, p. 597.

Keene, Mattie [actress] (b. 1862?–1 Sep 1944 [82], New York NY). m. Joseph Phillips. "Mattie Keene," *Variety,* 6 Sep 1944. AS, p. 597. BHD, p. 215. IFN, p. 161. SD.

Keene, Tom [stage/film actor] (*né* George Duryea, aka Richard Powers, b. Rochester NY, 30 Dec 1896–4 Aug 1963 [66], Woodland Hills CA). m. Grace Stafford (*née* Boyle), Del Mar CA; Florence. (De Mille; MGM; RKO-Pathé; Monogram; Paramount; Crescent.) (Film debut: *Marked Money,* Pathé, 1928.) Don Miller, *Hollywood Corral* (Popular Library, 1976.) "Tom Keene, Actor, of Films and Stage," *NYT,* 7 Aug 1963, 33:2 (age 65). "Tom Keene," *Variety,* 7 Aug 1963 (age 67). AS, pp. 597–98. BHD1, p. 295. IFN, p. 161 (b. 1896). Truitt, p. 177 (b. 1898). Michael R. Pitts, "Tom Keene; Man of Many Names," *CI,* 87 (Sep 1982), 39–42 (includes filmography). John Cocchi, "The 2nd Feature; A History of the B Movies—The Western, Part III," *CI,* 147 (Sep 1987), 19–20 (b. 1898; began 1928). Frank Dolven, "Tom Keene; The On and Off Again Cowboy Star," *CI,* 224 (Feb 1994), C14, C16, 34 (b. Smokey Hollow NY, 1904).

Keener, Hazel [actress: Wampas Star, 1924] (b. Fairbury IL, 22 Oct 1904–7 Aug 1979 [74], Ventura CA). AS, p. 598 (b. 10 Oct). BHD1, p. 295 (d. Pacific Grove CA). BR, pp. 167–68. George A. Katchmer, "Forgotten Cowboys and Cowgirls—Part III," *CI,* 174 (Dec 1989), 48; "Update—Forgotten Cowboys/Girls," *CI,* 179 (May 1990), 43. Truitt, 1983.

Keeney, Frank A. [producer]. No data found. AMD, p. 190. "Frank A. Keeney," *MPW,* 12 Jan 1918, 247. "Keeney Will Continue Making Pictures," *MPW,* 8 Jun 1918, 1411. "New Keeney Studios to Be Brought Up to the Minute," *MPW,* 21 Sep 1918, 1716–17.

Keepers, Harry L. [cinematographer] (b. Newark NJ, 6 Apr 1883–17 Sep 1963 [80], San Diego CA). BHD2, p. 141.

Keh, Lu [actor] (d. May 1922). BHD, p. 215.

Keighley, William Jackson [stage/film actor/director] (b. Philadelphia PA, 4 Aug 1889–24 Jun 1984 [94], New York NY; pulmonary embolism [Death Certificate Index No. 10520]). m. **Genevieve Tobin** (d. 1995). (WB.) Jon Pereles, "William Keighley Dies at 94; Theater and Movie Director," *NYT,* 26 Jun 1984, B8:3. "William Keighley, Vet Film Director, Was a WB Reliable," *Variety,* 4 Jul 1984. AS, p. 598. BHD1, p. 295; BHD2, p. 141. Katz, pp. 643–44. SD.

Keightly, Cyril [actor] (b. Wellington, New South Wales, Australia, 10 Nov 1875–14 Aug 1929 [53], Wellington, New Zealand). m. (1) Ethel Dane—div. 1925; (2) Isabel Wright, 19 Jan 1929. "Cyril Keightly," *Variety,* 21 Aug 1929. AMD, p. 190. AS, p. 598 (d. NY NY). BHD, p. 215. IFN, p. 161. "Kleine Actor Has Varied Career," *MPW,* 26 Jun 1915, 2113.

Keil-Moller, Carlo [actor/director] (b. Sweden, 1890–20 Dec 1958 [68?], Sweden). AS, p. 598.

Keinz, Barbara Leone [actress] (b. 1888–4 Nov 1939 [51?], Oklahoma City OK). BHD, p. 215.

Keith, Brian (son of **Robert Keith**) [stage/radio/film/TV actor] (*né* Robert Brian Keith, Jr., b. Bayonne NJ, 14 Nov 1921–24 Jun 1997 [75], Malibu CA; suffered from cancer and committed suicide by shooting). m. actress Victoria Young. (Film debut: *Pied Piper Malone,* 1924; adult film debut: *Arrowhead,* 1953.) Lawrence Van Gelder, "Brian Keith, Hardy Actor, 75; Played Dads and Desperadoes," *NYT,* 25 Jun 1997, D20. Ray Richmond, "Brian Keith," *Variety,* 30 Jun 1997, 73:1 (his daughrter Daisy committed suicide six weeks earlier). Lawrence van Gelder, "Brian Keith; Gruff actor best known for 'Family Affair,'" *Pittsburgh Post-Gazette,* 70, 25 Jun 1997, B-5:1. Katz, p. 644 (began in *Pied Piper Malone,* 1924). Robert Bianco, "Farewell, Uncle Bill; Looking back on the career of Brian Keith," *Pittsburgh Post-Gazette,* 70, 28 Jun 1997, D18. AS, p. 598. BHD1, p. 611.

Keith, Donald [actor] (*né* Francis Feeney, b. Boston MA, 6 Sep 1903–1 Aug 1969 [65], Los Angeles CA). m. Kathryn Spicuzza, 1927, "who had never seen his films."). AMD, p. 190. AS, p. 598 (b. 5 Sep 1905; d. Apr 1968). BHD1, p. 295. FSS, p. 163. "Schulberg Signs Youth," *MPW,* 31 Jan 1925, 483. "Donald Keith Marries," *MPW,* 5 Mar 1927, 10.

Keith, Eugene [actor] (b. 1878?–6 Feb 1955 [76], New York NY). (Paramount.) "Eugene Keith," *Variety,* 9 Feb 1955. BHD, p. 215. IFN, p. 161.

Keith, Ian [stage/film actor] (*né* Ian Sylvester Ross, b. Boston MA, 9 Feb 1898 [extrait de naissance no. 6267]–26 Mar 1960 [62], New York NY [Death Certificate Index No. 6947]). m. (1) **Blanche Yurka** (d. 1974); (2) **Ethel Clayton** (d. 1966); (3) **Fern Andra**, 1932 and 15 Feb 1934, Tia Juana, Mexico (d. 1974); (4) Hildegarde Pabst. "Ian Keith, 61, Dies; Stage, Film Actor; Appeared in More Than 350 Roles—Had Part of Doctor in 'Andersonville Trial,'" *NYT,* 27 May 1960, 86:6. "Ian Keith," *Variety,* 6 Apr 1960. AS, p. 598. BHD1, p. 295 (b. 27 Feb 1899). FFF, p. 190. FSS, p. 163. IFN, p. 161. Katz, p. 644. MH, p. 120. SD. Truitt, p. 177. June Lee, "Dan Cupid's Bulletin Board," *Paris and Hollywood,* Oct 1926, 87 (owed Yurka back alimony of $6.050. She was awarded $125 a week from their separation last year. "Last December he was declared in arrears, and paid $4,800 on account. Now unless Keith ponys up again the court declares that he must go to jawil."). Catti Merrick, "Ian Keith Says Goodby to Both Wife and Screen; Handsome 'Heavy' Takes Full Blame for Marital Troubles, Returns to Stage," *Movie Classic,* Oct 1931, 40. "Marriages," *Variety,* 113, 20 Feb 1934, 52:5 (m. Keith "to insure the legeality of their first ceremony in 1932.").

Keith, Isabelle [actress] (aka Claudel Kay and Isabel Fowler, b. Omaha NB or New York NY, 1898–20 Jul 1979 [81?], Mill Valley CA). AS, p. 598. BHD1, p. 295. Truitt, 1983.

Keith, June [actress]. No data found. AMD, p. 190. m. Edwin C. Slater, Jun 1917, Hubbard Woods IL. "June Keith," *MPW,* 11 Sep 1915, 1806. "Marriages," *Variety,* 22 Jun 1917, p. 7. "June Keith's Exciting Experience," *NYDM,* 1 Sep 1915, 27:1 (a man stepped in front of Keith's car while she was filming *The Man Trail* for Essanay in Chicago, and the chauffeur, thinking him a robber, sped away. A bullet was fired, missing "Miss Keith's head by about six inches, passing through the windowshield...The man proved to be a policeman, who arrested the chauffeur for speeding.").

Keith, Robert (father of **Brian Keith**) [stage/film actor/scenarist/playwright] (*né* Robert Richey, b. Fowler IN, 10 Feb 1898–23 Dec 1966 [68], Los Angeles CA). m. Dorothy Tierney. AS, p. 598. BHD1, p. 295. IFN, p. 161. Katz, p. 644. SD. Truitt, p. 177.

Keith-Johnston, Colin [actor] (b. London, England, 8 Oct 1896–3 Jan 1980 [83]). BHD1, p. 295.

Kelcey, Herbert [stage/film actor] (*né* Herbert Henry Lamb, b. London, England, 10 Oct 1855–10 Jul 1917 [61], Bayport, LI NY). m. Effie Shannon. (Film debut: *After the Ball,* Photo Drama Co., 1914.) "Herbert Kelcey," *Variety,* 13 Jul 1917 (b. 1856). AMD, p. 190. AS, p. 598. BHD, p. 215 (b. 1856). IFN, p. 161. SD. "Kelcey and Shannon Sign for Pictures," *MPW,* 20 Jun 1914, 1671.

Keleher, Daniel F. [actor] (b. 1869-Jun 1917 [48?], Rochelle NY). BHD, p. 215; BHD2, p. 141.

Kellar, Julie [actress/harpist] (b. 1882–7 Oct 1976 [94?], Los Angeles CA). AS, p. 598.

Kellard, John E. [actor] (b. London, England, 14 May 1862–8 Jun 1929 [67], Yonkers NY; apoplexy). "John E. Kellerd," *Variety,* 12 Jun 1929 (age 67). AS, p. 598. BHD, p. 215 (Kellerd; b. 1863; d. 6 Jun). IFN, p. 161 (age 66).

Kellard, Ralph [stage/film actor] (*né* Thomas J.J. Kelly, b. New York NY, 16 Jun 1871?–5 Feb 1955 [83], New York NY). (Fox; Pathé.) AMD, p. 190. AS, p. 598 (b. 1882; d. NY NY). BHD1, p. 295 (b. 1882). IFN, p. 161. MSBB, p. 1025 (b. 1887). SD. "Ralph Kellard with Pathé," *MPW,* 11 Dec 1915, 1988. "Ralph Kellard," *MPW,* 31 Mar 1917, 2108. "Kellard Returns to the Stage," *MPW,* 14 Jul 1917, 250. "Kellard Comes Back to Screen," *MPW,* 29 Mar 1919, 1801.

Keller, Alfred S. [child actor/cameraman] (b. PA, 1911?–6 Sep 1989 [78], Santa Monica CA). "Alfred S. Keller," *Variety,* 13 Sep 1989. BHD, p. 215 (d. Palisades CA).

Keller, Brooklyn [actor] (b. Lakeland FL, 20 Mar 1890). AS, p. 598. BHD, p. 215.

Keller, Edgar M. [actor]. *Fl.* 1912 (Bison). No data found.

Keller, Edward [executive] (b. 1869?–4 Apr 1924 [55], New York NY; pneumonia). "Edward Keller," *Variety,* 9 Apr 1924. AS, p. 599.

Keller, Gertrude [actress] (b. Denver CO, 1881?–12 Jul 1951 [70], Los Angeles CA). "Mrs. Gertrude K. Bagley," *Variety,* 25 Jul 1951 ("Mrs. Bagley was in silent pictures for a brief period"). AS, p. 599. BHD1, p. 296. IFN, p. 161. Truitt, p. 177.

Keller, Gottfried [scenarist]. No data found. FDY, p. 429.

Keller, Helen Adams [deaf/blind/mute stage/film actress] (b. near Tuscumbia AL, 27 Jun 1880–1 Jun 1968 [87], Westport CT). "The Story of My Life," *Ladies Home Journal,* 1902. "Helen Keller, 87, Dies; Blind and Deaf Since Infancy, She Became Symbol of Courage," *NYT,* 2 Jun 1968, 1:2; "Helen Keller's Rites for Wednesday in Capital," *NYT,* 3 Jun 1968, 45:1; Alden Whitman, "Triumph Out of Tragedy," 1:2, 76:1. "Helen Keller Rites Held in Cathedral," *NYT,* 6 Jun 1968, 48:6 (her ashes were interred in a cathedral crypt next to those of Anne Sullivan Macy at Washington National Cathedral). "Helen Keller," *Variety,* 5 Jun 1968. AMD, p. 190. AS, p. 599 (b. 1881). BHD, p. 215 (b. 1881). Truitt, 1983. "Helen Keller to Make a Novel Picture," *MPW,* 17 Aug 1918, 968. "Visitors for Blind Film Star," *MPW,* 14 Sep 1918, 1549. "Helen Keller at Victory Tank," *MPW,* 2 Nov 1918, 595. "Keller Film to Be Surprise," *MPW,* 16 Nov 1918, 727. "Helen Keller Sightless, Laughs at 'Shoulder Arms,'" *MPW,* 21 Dec 1918, 1328. Maude S. Cheatham, "The Silent Star of the Silent Drama," *MPC,* Mar 1919, 38, 69–70. "Helen Keller Picture Is Booked in New York City," *MPW,* 23 Aug 1919, 1122 (*Deliverance*). "George Kleine Acquires 'Deliverance,'" *MPW,* 8 Nov 1919, 232. "Helen Keller in Vaudeville Duplicates Screen Success," *MPW,* 20 Mar 1920, 1950. "'Deliverance' Grips Chicago Society; Helen Keller Film Deeply Impressive," *MPW,* 13 Nov 1920, 211.

Keller, Nell Clark [actress] (b. 1876?–2 Sep 1965 [89], Tacoma WA). (Biograph.) "Nell Clark Keller," *Variety,* 15 Sep 1965. AS, p. 599. BHD, p. 215. IFN, p. 161. Truitt, p. 177.

Keller, Walter E. [art director] (b. 1893?–20 Mar 1962 [69], Los Angeles CA; hardening of the arteries). (RKO; WB; Paramount.) "Walter Keller," *Variety,* 28 Mar 1962. BHD2, p. 141.

Kellerman, Annette (sister of **Maurice Kellerman**) [swimmer/actress] (b. Sydney, New South Wales, Australia, 6 Jul 1888–5 Nov 1975 [87], Southport, Australia). m. James R. Sullivan. (Vitagraph, 1909; Universal; Fox) "Annette Kellerman," *Variety,* 12 Nov 1975. AMD, p. 190. AS, p. 599. BHD, p. 216 (b. 1887). IFN, p. 161. Katz, p. 645. MSBB, p. 1038. Spehr, p. 146. Truitt, 1983 (b. 1887). "Annette Kellerman," WBO2, pp. 108–109. "Miss Kellerman Injured; Glass Tank Bursts While Performing with Herbert Brenon," *NYDM,* 11 Feb 1914 (in Hamilton, Burmuda, 3 Feb). "Herbert Brenon Injured," *MPW,* 14 Feb 1914, 820 (accident during filming of *Neptune's Daughter* when glass tank filled with 8,000 gallons of water broke). "Miss Kellerman at the Globe," *MPW,* 25 Apr 1914, 531. "Annette Kellerman Loses Paris House," *MPW,* 19 Sep 1914, 1653. Cover, *NYDM,* 30 Jun 1915. "Kellerman Looking for 'Sea Stuff,'" *MPW,* 27 Oct 1917, 553. "Kellerman Films Ready in Fall," *MPW,* 6 Jul 1918, 91. "Kellerman in Another Spectacle," *MPW,* 27 Dec 1919, 1147. "Kellerman Saves Drowning Woman," *MPW,* 19 Jun 1920, 1607. "New Kellerman Company," *MPW,* 21 Aug 1920, 1009. "Annette in Two Slow-Speed Films," *MPW,* 22 Oct 1921, 941. "Kellerman Starred," *MPW,* 8 Jan 1927, 127.

Kellerman, Bernard [scenarist]. No data found. FDY, p. 429.

Kellerman, Maurice (brother of **Annette Kellerman**) [producer] (b. Sydney, Australia, 1883?–9 Nov 1943 [60], Long Island NY). "Maurice Kellerman," *Variety,* 17 Nov 1943. AS, p. 599. BHD2, p. 141.

Kellette, John William [director/composer/scenarist] (b. Lowell MA, Jun 1873–7 Aug 1922 [49], Worcester MA; cancer). (Fox.) "John William Kellette," *Variety,* 11 Aug 1922 (wrote *I'm Forever Blowing Bubbles*). AMD, p. 190. AS, p. 599 (b. 1885). BHD2, p. 141. "John William Kellette," *MPW,* 12 Feb 1916, 969. "John William Kellette Ill," *MPW,* 10 Mar 1917, 1549 (with grippe). "Kellette Writes Loan Song," *MPW,* 2 Nov 1918, 605. "Engage Kellette to Direct Paramount-Briggs Comedies," *MPW,* 14 Jun 1919, 1641. "Kellette Recovered, Is Back on Job," *MPW,* 9 Aug 1919 (quinsy sore throat).

Kelley, Albert J. [director]. No data found. AMD, p. 191. "Kelley Made a Director," *MPW,* 8 Jan 1921, 185. "Kelley on Second Preferred," *MPW,* 11 Sep 1926, 118.

Kelley, Daniel V. [casting director] (b. 1874?–9 Jun 1929 [55], Vallejo CA). "Daniel Kelley," *Variety,* 12 Jun 1929. AS, p. 599.

Kelley, George F. [cinematographer] (b. Wallingford CT, 11 Oct 1892–4 Oct 1947 [54], Los Angeles CA). BHD2, p. 141.

Kelley, Harry A. [cinematographer/producer] (b. 1873–4 Aug 1925 [52?], Tampa FL). BHD2, p. 141.

Kelley, Joseph L. [publicist/scenarist] (b. Hudson Falls NY, 1890). AMD, p. 191. BHD2, p. 141. "Kelley Joins Bacon as Publicity Director," *MPW,* 6 Mar 1920, 1620.

Kellino, Roy [actor/scenarist/TV director] (b. London, England, 22 Apr 1912–17 Nov 1956 [44], Los Angeles CA). m. (1) Pamela (d. 1996; she later married James Mason); (2) Barbara Billingsley. "Roy Kellino," *Variety,* 204, 21 Nov 1956, 63:3. AS, p. 599. BHD, p. 216; BHD2, p. 141.

Kellino, Will P. [actor/director] (b. London, England, 1873–1958 [85?]). AS, p. 599. BHD, p. 216; BHD2, p. 141.

Kellog, Mark [publicist]. No data found. AMD, p. 191. "Kellog in Charge," *MPW,* 12 Jan 1924, 108.

Kellogg, Charles [stage/film actor] (b. Plumas Co., CA, 1869?–3 Sep 1949 [80], Morgan Hill CA). "Charles Kellogg," *Variety,* 7 Sep 1949 (He did birdcalls in vaudeville. "Examination of his throat by scientists revealed that he was born with a normal larnyx plus that of a bird.") SD.

Kellogg, Cornelia [actress] (b. 1877–21 Feb 1934 [57], Los Angeles CA). AS, p. 599. BHD, p. 216. IFN, p. 161.

Kelly, Al V. [actor] (*né* Abraham Kalish, b. 1899?–6 Sep 1966 [67], New York NY). "Al Kelly, Double-Talking Comic Dies in N.Y. at 67; Overflow Crowd at Rites," *Variety,* 14 Sep 1966. BHD1, p. 296.

Kelly, Anthony Paul [scenarist] (b. Chicago IL, 1897?–26 Sep 1932 [35], New York NY; suicide by inhaling illuminating gas). (Vitagraph.) "Anthony Paul Kelly," *Variety,* 27 Sep 1932 (ca. 45; "windows and doors had been sealed before he turned on the gas"). AMD, p. 191. AS, p. 599. BHD2, p. 142 (b. 1892). IFN, p. 161 (age 35). "Anthony Kelly on Lubin Staff," *MPW,* 18 Sep 1915, 2002. "More Lubin Enterprise," *MPW,* 9 Oct 1915, 236. "Anthony Kelly's Star in the Ascendant," *MPW,* 16 Dec 1916, 1620. "Anthony Paul Kelly Not with Empire," *MPW,* 14 Apr 1917, 246. Edward Weitzel, "Talking It Over with Anthony Paul Kelly," *MPW,* 25 Jan 1919, 459–60. Barbara Beach, "A Fool of Fortune; Thus Anthony Paul Kelly Characterizes Himself," *MPC,* Feb 1919, 18–19, 77. "Anthony Kelly Has Been Ill," *MPW,* 15 Feb 1919, 892. "Anthony Paul Kelly Recovers," *MPW,* 22 Feb 1919, 1029. "Anthony Paul Kelly Writes First Vehicle for Lillian Gish as New Frohman Star," *MPW,* 31 Jul 1920, 584. "Anthony Paul Kelly Doing Adaptation of 'Tornado,'" *MPW,* 27 Nov 1920, 501. "An Anthony Paul Kelly Picture to Be Ready Within Threee Months," *MPW,* 10 Sep 1921, 199. "Anthony Paul Kelly to Write Scenario," *MPW,* 27 Jan 1923, 376.

Kelly, Dorothy Dupree "Dot" [actress] (b. Philadelphia PA, 12 Feb 1894–31 May 1966 [72], Minneapolis MN; cerebral hemorrhage). m. Harvey Hevenor [Havenot?], 28 Aug 1916, Jersey City NJ. (Vitagraph, 1911.) AMD, p. 191. AS, p. 600. BHD, p. 216. IFN, p. 161. Slide, p. 144. "Dorothy Dupree Kelly," *MPW,* 31 Oct 1914, 650. "'Dot' Kelly Marries Real Estate Man," *MPW,* 16 Sep 1916, 1812. "Dorothy Dupree Kelly," *MPW,* 10 Feb 1917, 847. "Newsy Bits from Filmdom," *MPS,* 19 Mar 1915, 26 (21st birthday on Friday, 12 Feb 1915). Allan Douglas Brodie, "'Dot' Kelly, Landscape Painter," *MPC,* Apr 1916, 43–44. "'Dot' Kelly Married," *NYDM,* 9 Sep 1916, 25 (age 22). Billy H. Doyle, "Lost Players," *CI,* 150 (Dec 1987), 10–11.

Kelly, Ed [actor] (*né* Arthur T. Higgins, 1853?–19 Sep 1926 [73], Kansas City KS). m. Ida Bertha. "Arthur T. Higgins (Ed. Kelly)," *Variety,* 29 Sep 1926. AS, p. 600.

Kelly, Eddie Thanks [actor] (b. 1887?–12 Apr 1924 [37], Staten Island NY). m. Marge. "Eddie Thanks Kelly," *Variety,* 16 Apr 1924. AS, p. 600.

Kelly, Mrs. Fannie [actress] (*née* Fannie McGrame, b. New York NY, 1875?–27 Jan 1925 [49], Los Angeles CA). m. Pat Kelly. (Sennett.) "Mrs. Fannie Kelly," *Variety,* 4 Feb 1925. AS, p. 600. BHD, p. 216. IFN, p. 162. Truitt, p. 178.

Kelly, George E. [actor/scenarist] (b. Philadelphia PA, 1887–18 Jun 1974 [87?], Bryn Mawr PA). BHD2, p. 142.

Kelly, Gregory [actor] (b. New York NY, 16 Mar 1891–9 Jul 1927 [36], New York NY; heart attack). m. Ruth Gordon. "Gregory Kelly," *Variety*, 13 Jul 1927. AMD, p. 191. AS, p. 600. BHD, p. 216. IFN, p. 162. Truitt, p. 178. "Gregory Kelly," *MPW*, 22 May 1926, 317.

Kelly, Harry [actor] (b. NY, 1873–19 Mar 1936 [62?], New York NY). BHD, p. 216.

Kelly, Jack [vaudevillian/actor/title writer/scenarist] (b. 1898?–21 Feb 1945 [46], Winchester NH; burned to death in conflagration of Strand Hotel). m. Sonia Petrocoff. "Jack Kelly," *Variety*, 7 Mar 1945. FDY, pp. 429, 445.

Kelly, James T. [actor] (b. Castlebar, County Mayo, Ireland, 10 Jul 1854–12 Nov 1933 [79], New York NY). (Essanay.) AS, p. 600. BHD, p. 216. IFN, p. 162. Truitt, 1983.

Kelly, John F. [actor] (b. Boston MA, 29 Jun 1901–9 Dec 1947 [46], Los Angeles Co. CA). AS, p. 600. BHD1, p. 296. IFN, p. 162.

Kelly, John T. [actor] (b. So. Boston MA, 26 Aug 1852–16 Jan 1922 [69], New York NY; Bright's disease). m. Florence Moore Eques, Aug 1915, Bayonne NJ. "John T. Kelly," *Variety*, 20 Jan 1922. AS, p. 600. BHD, p. 216. Truitt, p. 178. "In the Picture Studios," *NYDM*, 23 Oct 1915, 31:1 ("John T. Kelly has decided that the screen shall have his permanent allegiance, and he will continue a Vitagraph star.").

Kelly, Kitty [actress] (*née* Sue O'Neil, b. New York NY, 27 Apr 1902–29 Jun 1968 [66], Los Angeles CA). (Paramount; RKO.) "Kitty Kelly," *Variety*, 17 Jul 1968. AMD, p. 191. AS, p. 600. BHD1, p. 296. IFN, p. 162. Truitt, p. 178. "Kitty Kelly," *MPW*, 5 Feb 1927, 423.

Kelly, Lew [actor] (b. St. Louis MO, 24 Aug 1879–10 Jun 1944 [64], Los Angeles CA). AS, p. 600.

Kelly, Mabel [actress] (b. 1900?–25 Aug 1954 [54], So. Salem NY). m. Jack A. Pegler, 1917, Baltimore MD. "Mrs. Mabel Pegler," *Variety*, 1 Sep 1954. AS, p. 600.

Kelly, Margot [actress] (b. 1893–10 Mar 1976 [82?], New York NY). BHD, p. 216.

Kelly, Nan (mother of **Nancy Kelly**) [actress] (*née* Nan Kelly Yorke, b. 1895–26 Oct 1978 [83?], Camarillo CA). AS, p. 600. BHD, p. 216. IFN, p. 162.

Kelly, Nancy (daughter of **Nan Kelly Yorke**; sister of Jack Kelly) [stage/film actress] (b. Lowell MA, 25 Mar 1921–2 Jan 1995 [73], Bel Air CA; diabetes-related illness). m. 3 times: Edmund O'Brien. (Tony Award for *The Bad Seed*, 1954). Wolfgang Saxon, "Nancy Kelly, 73, Actress Noted in Hollywood and on Broadway," *NYT*, 14 Jan 1995, 30:4 ("As a child she appeared in some 50 Hollywood movies..."). Mentioned in Jack Kelly's *NYT* obituary as having been in films in the '20s. AS, p. 600. BHD1, p. 297. Ragan 2, pp. 870–71 (b. May 25). Doug McClelland, "Remembering Nancy Kelly; The Woman Who Came Back, Part II," *Films of the Golden Age*, Winter, 1997–1998, 52–62 (filmography from 1938 on).

Kelly, Nell [actress] (b. Memphis TN, 1910–16 Dec 1939 [29?], New York NY). AS, p. 600. BHD1, p. 297.

Kelly, Patrick J. [actor] (b. Philadelphia PA, 18 Jul 1891–19 Mar 1938 [46], Los Angeles CA). AS, p. 600. BHD1, p. 297. IFN, p. 162.

Kelly, Paul Michael [actor] (b. Brooklyn NY, 9 Aug 1899–6 Nov 1956 [57], Beverly Hills CA). m. Claire Owen; Dorothy MacKaye, 1931 (former wife of Ray Raymond). (Vitagraph, 1907.) "Paul Kelly, Actor on Stage, Screen; Performer, 57, Dies on Coast—Played in 400 Movies and in 'Command Decision' Here," *NYT*, 7 Nov 1956, 31:5. "Paul Kelly," *Variety*, 14 Nov 1956 (age 53). AMD, p. 191. AS, p. 600. BHD1, p. 297 (d. LA CA). FSS, p. 164. IFN, p. 162. Katz, p. 647. Truitt, p. 178. "Sign Paul Kelly to Play Leading Part for Warners," *MPW*, 12 Mar 1927, 103. "Actor's Death Sends Kelly to Jail," *MPW*, 23 Apr 1927, 703 (beating death of stage actor Ray Raymond on 15 Apr 1927). *See* "Dorothy Mackaye Indicted; Raymond's Wife, Florence Bain; Miss Bain Withdrew Contemplated Divorce Action in 1924, Naming Miss Mackaye as Correspondent—Paul Kelly Held Without Bail [for the murder of **Ray Raymond**] on Coast," *Variety*, 27 Apr 1927. Paul Paige, "Close-Ups and Fade-Outs," *Paris and Hollywood Screen Secrets Magazine*, Aug 1927, 42, 98 (Kelly was found guilty of manslaughter. Raymond's former wife, actress Florence Bain, claimed that she and Raymond were never divorced. MacKaye said that she and Kelly were married in Gretna Green MD; there is no such city, but Elkton MD is known as the Gretna Green of the State because of its lax marriage laws. "...there is no record there of the marriage of Raymond and Miss Mackaye."). Merton, "Reeling Down Broadway," *Paris and Hollywood Screen Secrets*, III (Oct 1927), 78 ("...the part of Sergeant O'Hara in *Sadie Thompson*...was to have been assigned to Paul Kelly, now in San Quentin prison for the murder of Ray Raymond.").

Kelly, Peggy [actress]. No data found. AMD, p. 191. "Peggy Kelly Is Voted Most Popular Fox Girl," *MPW*, 8 Oct 1927, 338.

Kelly, R. Guthrie [scenario editor] (b. 1888–24 Jan 1912 [23?], CA; auto accident "last Wednesday during the heavy fog in Los Angeles, near the Country Club House, on the road to Santa Monica."). (Nestor.) "R. Guthrie Kelly," *Variety*, 3 Feb 1912, 12:4. BHD2, p. 142. "R. Guthrie Kelly Killed," *MPN*, 27 Jan 1912, p. 6.

Kelly, Renee [actress] (b. London, England, 4 Jun 1888–28 Aug 1965 [77], London, England). BHD1, p. 297.

Kelly, Robert [stage/film actor] (b. Chicago IL, 1875?–19 Jun 1949 [74], Lewiston ME). m. Annie Mamlin. "Robert Kelly," *Variety*, 22 Jun 1949. AS, p. 600. BHD, p. 216. SD.

Kelly, Robert Henry [director] (b. 1884–19 Aug 1968 [84?], Los Angeles CA). BHD2, p. 142.

Kelly, Scotch [vaudeville/film actor] (*né* James Steele, b. 1889–19 Feb 1967 [77?], Laxey, Isle of Man, England). m. Edith Kebble. "Scotch Kelly," *Variety*, 246, 5 Apr 1967, 87:4. BHD1, p. 297.

Kelly, W.V.D. [inventor] (b. Trenton NJ, 1877–30 Sep 1934 [57?], Los Angeles CA). AS, p. 601.

Kelly, Walter C. [actor] (b. Mineville NY, 29 Oct 1873–6 Jan 1939 [65], Philadelphia PA). AS, p. 601.

Kelly, William [scenarist] (b. 1882–11 Apr 1978 [96?]). BHD2, p. 142.

Kelly, William J. [actor] (b. Newburyport MA, 16 Jun 1875–17 May 1949 [73], New York NY; heart attack). (Film debut: *A Woman's Resurrection*, Fox, 1915.) "William J. Kelly," *Variety*, 18 May 1949 (b. Boston MA). AS, p. 601. BHD1, p. 297. IFN, p. 162. Truitt, p. 178.

Kelsey, Fred A. [actor/director] (b. Sandusky OH, 20 Aug 1884–2 Sep 1961 [77], Woodland Hills CA). (Griffith; FBO.) "Fred Kelsey, 77, Dies; Was Among First Character Actors in Talking Pictures," *NYT*, 5 Sep 1961, 35:3. "Fred Kelsey," *Variety*, 6 Sep 1961. AS, p. 601. BHD1, p. 297; BHD2, p. 142. IFN, p. 162. 1921 Directory, p. 268. O&W, p. 218. Truitt, p. 178. "Kelsey Shines in 'Lights Out,'" *MPW*, 3 Nov 1923, 98:2.

Kelso, Mayme [actress] (b. Columbus OH, 28 Feb 1867–5 Jun 1946 [79], So. Pasadena CA; heart attack). AMD, p. 191. AS, p. 601 (b. Dayton OH). BHD, p. 216. IFN, p. 162. Truitt, 1983 (b. Dayton OH). "Mayme Kelso Buys a Bale," *MPW*, 24 Oct 1914, 473.

Kelson, George [director]. No data found.

Kelson, Stuart [cinematographer]. No data found.

Kelton, Pert Lizette [stage/film actress] (b. Great Falls MT, 14 Oct 1907–30 Oct 1968 [61], Ridgewood NJ). m. **Ralph W. Bell** (d. 1936). "Pert Kelton," *Variety*, 6 Nov 1968 (began in *Sally*, 1929). BHD1, p. 297. IFN, p. 162. Katz, p. 647. SD.

Kemble, William H. [producer]. No data found. AMD, p. 191. "Kemble Says He Will Produce," *MPW*, 29 Jul 1916, 813.

Kemble-Cooper, Violet [actress] (b. London, England, 1886–17 Aug 1961 [75?], Los Angeles CA; Parkinson's disease and cerebral thrombosis). AS, p. 601.

Kemm, Jean [actor/director] (b. France, 1874–1939 [65?], France). AS, p. 601.

Kemp, Everett [actor] (*né* Charles Everett Kemp, b. Shelbyville IL, 1874?–1 Oct 1958 [84?], Kansas City MO). "Everett Kemp," *Variety*, 8 Oct 1958 (made "some short films with Mr. and Mrs. Sidney Drew"). AS, p. 601 (d. Kansas City KS). BHD, p. 216. Truitt, p. 179.

Kemp, Mae [vaudeville/film actress] (*née* Mary Lange, b. 1877–6 Feb 1926 [49], New York NY; cancer). m. Bob Kemp. "Mae Kemp," *Variety*, 17 Feb 1926, 51:4 ("...one of the best known of colored theatrical women..." Interred in Woodlawn Cemetery NY). BHD, p. 216.

Kemp, Paul [actor] (b. Bad Godesburg, Germany, 20 May 1899–13 Aug 1953 [54], Bad Godesburg, Germany). AS, p. 601.

Kemp, Sam [scenarist] (b. 1869–20 Jun 1933 [64?], Redlands CA). BHD2, p. 142.

Kemp, Sylvia M. [actress]. No data found. (Horsely.)

Kemper, Joe [actor] (b. 1883–3 Aug 1948 [65?], Long Beach CA). AS, p. 601.

Kendall, Harry [actor] (b. Australia, 1872–27 Jul 1936 [64?], Brooklyn NY). BHD, p. 216.

Kendall, Henry [actor/scenarist] (b. London, England, 28 May 1897–9 Jun 1962 [65], London, England). "Henry Kendall," *Variety*, 4 Jul 1962. AS, p. 601. BHD1, p. 298. IFN, p. 162.

Kendall, Messmore [producer] (b. Grand Rapids MI, 9 Dec 1872–1 May 1959 [86], Palm Beach FL). BHD2, p. 142.

Kendig, Walter [actor]. No data found. AMD, p. 191. "'Heine and Louie' Comedies Going Well," *MPW*, 11 Sep 1915, 1840.

Kendis, J.D. [producer] (b. 1886–2 Aug 1957 [71?], Los Angeles CA). BHD2, p. 142.

Kennard, Victor [actor] (b. Hackensack NJ, 1887–14 Aug 1953 [66?], Bridgeport CT). BHD, p. 216.

Kennard, William C. [assistant director] (b. Batesville AR, 1876). BHD2, p. 142.

Kennedy, Aubrey M[ark] [director/producer/scenarist] (b. Winnipeg, Manitoba, Canada, 21 Jun 1887). AMD, p. 191. BHD2, p. 142. "Mr. Aubrey M. Kennedy in New Venture," *MPW,* 7 Oct 1911, 47. "Aubrey M. Kennedy Combines with Harry Davis," *MPW,* 21 Oct 1911, 196. "Producers' Film Company," *MPW,* 28 Oct 1911, 282. "An Animated Daily," *MPW,* 28 Sep 1912, 1261. "A Chance for Someone," *MPW,* 11 Jan 1913, 143. "United States vs. Motion Picture Patents Co.," *MPW,* 15 Mar 1913, 1082–83. "New Picture Concern," *MPW,* 17 Jan 1914, 300. "Aubrey M. Kennedy Leaves for the Coast," *MPW,* 4 Apr 1914, 79. "Aubrey M. Kennedy," *MPW,* 23 Jan 1915, 492. "Kennedy Returns to Coast," *MPW,* 6 Feb 1915, 808. "A New Producing Company for Kriterion," *MPW,* 6 Mar 1915, 1465. "Aubrey M. Kennedy, Manager of Production," *MPW,* 29 Sep 1917, 1975. "Aubrey M. Kennedy Resigns," *MPW,* 2 Feb 1918, 665 (from Goldwyn).

Kennedy, Charles Rann [actor/playwright] (b. Derby, England, 14 Feb 1871–16 Feb 1950 [79], Westwood CA). m. Edith Mathison. "Charles Rann Kennedy," *Variety,* 22 Feb 1950. AS, p. 602. BHD1, p. 298. IFN, p. 162. Truitt, p. 179.

Kennedy, Edgar Livingstone (brother of **Tom Kennedy**) [actor: Keystone Cop/director] (b. Monterey CA, 26 Apr 1890–9 Nov 1948 [58], Woodland Hills CA; throat cancer). m. Patricia Allwyn, 1924. (Last film: *My Dream Is Yours,* WB, 1947; Sennett; Roach; RKO; MGM; Goldwyn.) "Edgar Kennedy, 58, Comedian in Films; 37-Year Veteran of Industry Dies—An Original Keystone Cop, He Made 500 Movies," *NYT,* 10 Nov 1948, 29:3. "Edgar Kennedy," *Variety,* 10 Nov 1948. AMD, p. 191. AS, p. 602. BHD1, p. 298. FSS, p. 165. IFN, p. 163. Katz, pp. 648–49. Truitt, p. 179. "Kennedy to Direct 'U' Comedies," *MPW,* 17 Oct 1925, 570. "Edgar Kennedy," *MPW,* 27 Aug 1927, 588. Bill Cassara, "Edgar Kennedy: "Master of the Slow Burn,'" *CI,* 263 (May 1997), 34–36.

Kennedy, Elizabeth [actress] (b. 1908?). AMD, p. 191. "Elizabeth Has a Large Memory," *MPW,* 21 Sep 1918, 1718 (ten years old).

Kennedy, Harold [minstrel/vaudevillian/actor] (b. 1888?–1 Jun 1946 [58], NY). "Harold Kennedy," *Variety,* 5 Jun 1946. AS, p. 602.

Kennedy, Jack [actor] (b. 1902–27 Jan. 1961 [58?], Los Angeles, CA). BHD1, p. 299.

Kennedy, Jeremiah J. [executive]. No data found. AMD, p. 191. "Facts Concerning the New Arrangement of the Principal Factors of the Motion Picture Manufacturing Interests in America," *MPW,* 26 Dec 1908, 519.

Kennedy, John F. [actor: Keystone Cop] (d. 6 Nov 1960, Los Angeles CA). (Sennett.) "John F. Kennedy," *Variety,* 16 Nov 1960 (died 1 day after Sennett). AS, p. 602. BHD, p. 216. IFN, p. 163.

Kennedy, Joseph C. [actor] (b. Canada, 1890–4 May 1949 [59?], Halifax, Canada). AS, p. 602.

Kennedy, Joseph P[atrick] [executive/President of FBO] (b. Boston MA, 6 Sep 1888–18 Nov 1969 [81], Hyannis Port MA; after heart attacks). m. Rose Fitzgerald, 7 Oct 1914 (d. 22 Jan 1995 [104]). Charles Higham, *Rose; The Life and Times of Rose Fitzgerald Kennedy* (NY: Pocket Books, 1995). "Joseph P. Kennedy Dead; Forged a Political Dynasty; Family Tragedies Marred Success in Business and Government," *NYT,* 19 Nov 1969, 1:2, 51:1. "Jos. P. Kennedy, Once Film Prez [of RKO], Dead at 81," *Variety,* 19 Nov 1969, 2:1. AMD, p. 191. AS, p. 602. BHD2, p. 142. "Boston Financier Purchases Control of F.B.O.," *MPW,* 20 Feb 1926, 2. "A New Personality in Motion Pictures," *MPW,* 20 Feb 1926, 702. "Kennedy elected F.B.O. Chairman; Derr Treasurer," *MPW,* 20 Mar 1926, 1, 2. "F.B.O. Prides Itself on Its Standing with Exhibitors, Says Kennedy," *MPW,* 29 May 1926, 398. "Industry on Sane Basis, Says Kennedy," *MPW,* 29 May 1926, 2. "Broadway and F.B.O.," *MPW,* 24 Jul 1926, 215. "English Conditions Improved, Says Kennedy, Back in U.S.," *MPW,* 9 Oct 1926, 1–2. C.E. Hastings, "Will Hays Lauds Thomson and Kennedy at F.B.O. Luncheon; Tunney Greets 'Pal,'" *MPW,* 16 Oct 1926, 417. "Pictures' Greatest Development Now at Hand, Says 'Joe' Kennedy," *MPW,* 13 Nov 1926, 1, 2. Merritt Crawford, "Joseph P. Kennedy…A New, Big Figure," *MPW,* 11 Dec 1926, 396. "Kennedy Directs Course on Pictures at Harvard," *MPW,* 29 Jan 1927, 322 (Kennedy Class of 1912). "England Likes F.B.O. Pictures, Says Kennedy," *MPW,* 29 Jan 1927, 351. M. Crawford, "Harvard and the Newest Art," *MPW,* 9 Apr 1927, 556, 599. "F.B.O. Is Now FBO," *MPW,* 11 Jun 1927, 403. "Kennedy and F.P.," *MPW,* 9 Jul 1927, 75. "FBO Closes Saturdays," *MPW,* 16 Jul 1927, 145. Rosa Reilly, "Now He's in a Position to Help You," *Screenland,* Sep 1927, 38–39, 75, 102 (contest). "Deny FBO Rumor," *MPW,* 1 Oct 1927, 280. "Kennedy Heads Leaders Compiling Film History," *MPW,* 19 Nov 1927, 11 (book, *The Story of the Films* [Chicago: A.W. Shaw & Co.). "FBO Grand February Jubilee in Honor of Joseph P. Kennedy," *MPW,* 19 Nov 1927, 16. "Joseph P. Kennedy Will Broadcast Next Thursday," *MPW,* 26 Nov 1927 (WPCH Radio). Rosa Reilly, "Joseph P. Kennedy and His Christmas Guest," *Screenland,* Dec 1927, 36–37, 80, 82 (winner of the contest). Michael L. Simmons, "Impressions of Joseph P. Kennedy," *MPW,* 10 Dec 1927, 12. Abel Green, "Recall Joe Kennedy's Film Career; Review of Unreleased 800G Pic [*Queen Kelly*]," *Variety,* 26 Nov 1969.

Kennedy, Joyce [actress] (b. London, England, 1 Jul 1898–12 Mar 1943 [44], London, England). AS, p. 602.

Kennedy, Keith [actor] (b. England, 1887–11 Apr 1966 [79?], Los Angeles, CA). AS, p. 603.

Kennedy, Lem F. [director] (b. Jasper TN, 4 Feb 1885). AMD, p. 192. BHD2, p. 142. "Kennedy Rounding Up Cast," *MPW,* 31 Oct 1925, 707.

Kennedy, Leo A. [actor] (b. Wilmington DE, 1883–11 Dec 1939 [56?], New York NY). AS, p. 602 (d. LA CA). BHD, p. 216.

Kennedy, Madge [stage/film actress] (b. Chicago IL, 19 Apr 1891–9 Jun 1987 [96], Woodland Hills CA; respiratory ailment). m. (1) Harold Bolster; (2) **William B. Hanley, Jr.** (d. 1959). (Film debut: *Baby Mine,* Goldwyn, 1917.) "Madge Kennedy Dies; A Film and Stage Star," *NYT,* 13 Jun 1987, 44:6 (d. 8 Jun). "Madge Kennedy," *Variety,* 17 Jun 1987. AMD, p. 192. AS, p. 603. BHD1, p. 298. FSS, p. 165. Katz, p. 649. Lowrey, p. 94. MSBB, p. 1038 (b. CA). SD. Spehr, p. 146 (b. LA CA, 1892). WWS, p. 178 (b. CA). "Madge Kennedy Signs with Goldwyn," *MPW,* 10 Feb 1917, 830. "Madge Kennedy," *MPW,* 29 Dec 1917, 1936. "Madge Kennedy Gets Big Reception at Detroit Theater," *MPW,* 27 Apr 1918, 567. "Madge Kennedy Gets Longer Contraact," *MPW,* 1 Jun 1918, 1269. "Goldwyn Star Breaks Her Rule Against Face Powders," *MPW,* 19 Oct 1918, 401. Edward Weitzel, "Madge Kennedy: Her Day Dreams," *MPW,* 28 Dec 1918, 1510–11. "Flashes; Madge Kennedy to Flit," *LA Times,* 3 Jan 1`920, II, 9 (met Bolster on a train in San Bernardino CA at 2 a.m.). "Star Visited by Husband [Bolster]," *MPW,* 24 Jan 1920, 575. "Illness of Madge Kennedy Causes Delay to Her Picture," *MPW,* 12 Jun 1920, 1494. "Popularity Contest Enters Final Week; Madge Kennedy and Will Rogers Lead," *MPW,* 13 May 1922, 155. Gladys Hall, "Harmonies," *MPC,* Jul 1922, 44–45, 90. "Signed by St. Regis," *MPW,* 8 Nov 1924, 1453.

Kennedy, Merna [actress] (*née* Maude Kahler, b. Kankakee IL, 7 Sep 1908–20 Dec 1944 [36], Los Angeles CA; heart attack). m. (1) Busby Berkeley, 1934–35 (d. 1976); (2) Forrest Brayton. "Merna Kennedy, 35, Star of Silent Films," *NYT,* 21 Dec 1944, 21:2. "Merna Kennedy," *Variety,* 27 Dec 1944. AMD, p. 192. AS, p. 603. BHD1, p. 298. IFN, p. 163. Katz, pp. 649–50. SD. Truitt, p. 180. "Charlie Chaplin Has Completed 'The Circus,'" *MPW,* 29 Oct 1927, 556. Helen Louise Walker, "Honest, I Am Democratic; So Merna Kennedy, Lately Cart-Wheeled into the Limelight, Assures Us," *MPC,* Aug 1929, 65, 94. "News From the Dailies," *Variety,* 124, 4 Nov 1936, 62:2 ("Merna Kennedy granted divorce from Busby Berkeley in L.A.").

Kennedy, Tom (brother of **Edgar Kennedy**) [actor: Keystone Cop] (b. New York NY, 15 Jul 1885–6 Oct 1965 [80], Woodland Hills CA; bone cancer). (Sennett.) "Tom Kennedy," *Variety,* 13 Oct 1965. AMD, p. 192. AS, p. 603. BHD1, p. 298. FSS, p. 166. IFN, p. 163. Truitt, 1983 (b. 1884). "Paramount Signs Kennedy," *MPW,* 5 Jun 1926, 459.

Kennerly, Lew [artist]. No data found. AMD, p. 192. "Lew Kennerly to Design Buffalo Bill, Jr., Lithos," *MPW,* 24 Jan 1925, 346. "Lew Kennerly Engaged," *MPW,* 4 Apr 1925, 491.

Kenneth, Harry D. [actor] (b. 1854?–18 Jan 1929 [75], Newark NJ; cerebral hemorrhage). (Essanay [Chicago].) "Harry D. Kenneth," *Variety,* 30 Jan 1929. AS, p. 603. BHD, p. 217. IFN, p. 163. Truitt, p. 180.

Kenney, Jack [actor] (b. IL, 16 Nov 1886–26 May 1964 [77], Los Angeles CA). BHD1, p. 299. IFN, p. 163.

Kenny, Colin [actor] (*né* Oswald Joseph Collins, b. Dublin, Ireland, 4 Dec 1888–2 Dec 1968 [79], Los Angeles CA). AS, p. 603 (d. Dublin, Ireland). BHD1, p. 299. IFN, p. 163 (b. England).

Kent, Arnold *see* **Manetti, Lido**

Kent, Charles [actor/director] (b. London, England, 18 Jun 1852–21 May 1923 [70], Brooklyn NY [Death Certificate No. 10932]). (Vitagraph, 1906; Biograph, 1910.) "Charles Kent, Actor," *NYT,* 23 May 1923, 21:6. "Charles Kent," *Variety,* 24 May 1923 (age 69). AS, p. 603 (b. 1853). BHD, p. 217; BHD2, p. 143. IFN, p. 163 (age 69). Katz, p. 650. Slide, p. 144. Robert Grau, "The Film Studio; A Gold Laden Haven for the Patriarchs of the

Stage," *NYDM,* 8 Sep 1915, 3:1 (Grau mentions Kent, Louise Beaudet, Cissy Fitzgerald, Sydney Drew, S. Rankin Drew, William Humphries, Van Dyke Brooke, and Harry Davenport, all from the stage).

Kent, Crauford [stage/film actor] (b. London, England, 12 Oct 1881–14 May 1953 [71], Los Angeles CA). (Lubin; MGM.) "Crauford Kent," *NYT,* 15 May 1953, 23:1. "Crauford Kent," *Variety,* 20 May 1953. AMD, p. 192. AS, p. 603. BHD1, p. 299. FFF, p. 256. IFN, p. 163. Truitt, p. 181 (d. Los Angeles CA). "Crauford Kent," *MPW,* 2 Jan 1915, 83. "Briefs of Biography; Handicapped with a Yankee Accent," *NYDM,* 29 Sep 1915, 36:3 ("It is interesting to note that dramatic criticism in London was to the effect that 'Mr. [Craufurd (sic)] Kent's pronounced American accent hampered him in playing English parts.' The mother did not recognize her own child, in other words."). "Crauford Kent in Pathé Gold Rooster Plays," *MPW,* XXVI, 2 Oct 1915, 57. "Crauford Kent," *MPW,* 20 Nov 1915, 1463. Name variously spelled Craufurd, Crawford.

Kent, Cromwell [scenarist]. No data found. FDY, p. 429.

Kent, Elinor (mother of **Warren Hymer**) [actress] (d. 15 Sep 1957, Los Angeles CA). m. **John B. Hymer** (d. 1953). AS, p. 603. Truitt, p. 181.

Kent, Ethel [actress] (*née* Ethel Jackson, b. New York NY, 31 Jul 1883–27 Jul 1952 [68], West Hollywood CA). m. **John Ince** (d. 1947). AS, p. 603. IFN, p. 152 (Ethel Jackson Ince). Truitt, p. 181.

Kent, Herbert [actor] (b. England, 1877–13 Mar 1973 [95?], New York NY). AS, p. 603.

Kent, Kate [actress] (b. 1864–11 Dec 1934 [70], Van Nuys CA). AS, p. 603. BHD1, p. 299. IFN, p. 163.

Kent, Kenneth [actor/singer] (b. Liverpool, England, 20 Apr 1882–17 Nov 1963 [81], London, England). AS, p. 603.

Kent, Larry [actor] (*né* Henri W. Trumbull, b. Liverpool, England, 15 Sep 1900–7 Nov 1967 [67], Los Angeles CA). (2-reelers, FBO; 1st National.) AMD, p. 192. AS, p. 603. BHD1, p. 299. IFN, p. 163. "Colleen's New Lead," *MPW,* 17 Sep 1927, 158. Betty Standish, "Taking the Bumps; Larry Kent Bummed His Way to Stardom," *MPC,* Jun 1928, 40, 84.

Kent, Leon D *see* **de la Mothe, Leon**

Kent, Raymond [actor] (b. 1886–1 Nov 1948 [62], Amityville NY). AS, p. 603. BHD, p. 217. IFN, p. 163.

Kent, S[idney] **Miller** [stage/film actor] (b. 1862?–12 Nov 1948 [86], Amityville NY). m. Dorothy Dixon (d. 1946). "S. Miller Kent," *Variety,* 17 Nov 1948. AS, p. 603. BHD, p. 217; BHD2, p. 143 (b. 1882). SD, p. 706. "Rolfe Signs Kent; Well-Known Player to Be Seen in 'The Cowboy and the Lady,'" *NYDM,* 10 Mar 1915, 24:4.

Kent, Sidney R. [general manager] (b. Lincoln NB, 1885–19 Mar 1942 [57?], New York NY). AMD, p. 192. BHD2, p. 143. "Kent Made General Manager," *MPW,* 20 Sep 1924, 210. "Surprise Dinner to Kent," *MPW,* 11 Oct 1924, 476. "Tribute to Sidney R. Kent Closes Paramount Sales Convention," *MPW,* 8 Nov 1924, 119. "Kent Recovering," *MPW,* 20 Nov 1926, 1 (appendicitis). "Sidney R. Kent Goes Home," *MPW,* 29 Nov 1926, 1. Sidney R. Kent, "Pictures Aren't Bought—They're Sold," *MPW,* 26 Mar 1927, 342. "Kent Issues Denial," *MPW,* 2 Apr 1927, 463.

Kent, Stapleton [actor] (b. England, 15 May 1883–3 Apr 1962 [78], Los Angeles Co. CA). AS, p. 603. BHD, p. 217. IFN, p. 163. Ragan 2, p. 878. Truitt, 1983.

Kent, Willard [actor/director] (b. PA, 17 Mar 1882–5 Sep 1968 [86], Woodland Hills CA). AS, p. 603.

Kent, William T. [actor] (b. St. Paul MN, 1886?–5 Oct 1945 [59], New York NY). "William T. Kent," *Variety,* 10 Oct 1945. AS, p. 604. BHD1, p. 299 (d. 4 Oct). IFN, p. 163. Truitt, p. 181.

Kenton, Erle C[awthorn] [actor/director] (b. Norbonne MT, 1 Aug 1896–28 Jan 1980 [83], Glendale CA; Parkinson's disease and emphysema). (Sennett; Columbia.) "Erle C. Kenton," *Variety,* 6 Feb 1980. AMD, p. 193. AS, p. 604 (b. Norborne MO). BHD1, p. 299; BHD2, p. 143 (b. Norboro MO). IFN, p. 163. Katz, pp. 650–51. Truitt, 1983. "Erle Kenton Signed," *MPW,* 4 Oct 1924, 374. "C.B.C. Signs Erle Kenton," *MPW,* 11 Oct 1924, 474. "Erle C. Kenton Signed as New Warner Bros. Director," *MPW,* 30 May 1925, 554. "Erle C. Kenton," *MPW,* 9 Jul 1927, 87. Wheeler W. Dixon, *The "B" Director; A Biographical Directory* (Metuchen NJ: The Scarecrow Press, Inc., 1985), pp. 284–87.

Kentuck, Joe [actor] (d. 7 Feb 1923, Lapwai ID). BHD, p. 217. IFN, p. 163.

Kenyon, Albert G. [scenarist]. No data found. AMD, p. 193. "Kenyon Joins Metro," *MPW,* 21 Sep 1918, 1715. "Kenyon Joins Big 'U' Scenario Staff," *MPW,* 31 May 1919, 1318. "Kenyon Ill with Typhoid Fever," *MPW,* 21 Jun 1919, 1767. "Kenyon Joins Mayer Scenario Staff," *MPW,* 15 Nov 1919, 349. "Kenyon Joins Big 'U,'" *MPW,* 18 Nov 1922, 244.

Kenyon, Charles Arthur [playwright/scenarist] (b. San Francisco CA, 2 Nov 1880–27 Jun 1961 [80], Los Angeles CA; cerebral hemorrhage). (Universal.) m. (1) **Jane Winton**, 1927 (d. 1959). (Wrote the play, *Kindling,* and the script for *The Iron Horse.*) "Charles Kenyon," *Variety,* 5 Jul 1961 (age 79). AMD, p. 193. AS, p. 604. BHD2, p. 143. FDY, p. 429. IFN, p. 163. Martin Martin, "Chatter from Hollywood," *Screenland,* Oct 1927, 71. "Three Authors Added to Universal Forces," *MPW,* 20 Oct 1917, 364. "Kenyon at Work at Fox Studio," *MPW,* 22 Dec 1917, 1787. June Lee, "Dan Cupid's Bulletin Board," *Paris and Hollywood Screen Secrets,* Oct 1927, 35–36 (wed Winton).

Kenyon, Doris [stage/film actress] (*née* Margaret Doris Kenyon, b. Syracuse NY, 5 Sep 1897–1 Sep 1979 [81], Beverly Hills CA; cardiac failure). m. (1) **Milton Sills**, 12 Oct 1926, Adirondacks (d. 1930; 1 son b. 1927); (2) Arthur E. Hopkins, 1933—annulled 1934; (3) Albert D. Lesker, 1938—div. Jun 1939; (4) Bronislaw Mlynarski (d. 1971). (Film debut: *The Pawn of Fate,* World, 1916 [made in 1915]; FP-L; Pathé; Essanay; Wharton.) "Doris Kenyon Sills," *Variety,* 19 Sep 1979. AMD, p. 193. AS, p. 604. BHD1, p. 299. FFF, p. 225. FSS, p. 166. IFN, p. 163. Katz, p. 651. MH, p. 120. MSBB, p. 1038. Spehr, p. 146. WWS, p. 291. "Doris Kenyon," *MPW,* 19 Aug 1916, 1265. "Doris Kenyon," *MPW,* 10 Mar 1917, 1544. "Doris Kenyon with DeLux," *MPW,* 26 Jan 1918, 532. Edward Weitzel, "A Few Remarks De Luxe by Doris Kenyon," *MPW,* 10 Aug 1918, 849. "Doris Kenyon Returns from Trip," *MPW,* 31 Aug 1918, 1279. "Doris Kenyon to Increase Yearly Number of Pictures," *MPW,* 14 Sep 1918, 1568. "Doris Kenyon Offered $1,000 for Two War Zone Coins," *MPW,* 22 Mar 1919, 1692. "Doris Kenyon to Appear on Stage and on Screen," *MPW,* 14 Jun 1919, 1642. "Doris Kenyon Writes Book," *MPW,* 27 Sep 1919, 1974 (*Humorous Monologues* [NY: James T. White & Co.]). Mary Kelly, "Slim, Svelte, Smiling Doris Kenyon Talks About Art and Avoirdupois," *MPW,* 15 May 1920, 967. "Doris Kenyon Heads Stellar Cast Supporting Johnny Hines in Burr's 'Sure-Fire Flint,'" *MPW,* 29 Jul 1922, 367. "Burr Signs Doris Kenyon," *MPW,* 28 Apr 1923, 948. "Doris Kenyon Signs Long Term Burr Contract," *MPW,* 9 Jun 1923, 497. "Says New England Likes Burr Star," *MPW,* 22 Sep 1923, 345. "Silent and Spoken," *MPW,* 20 Oct 1923, 680. Faith Service, "'There Are No Mothers Any More,'" *Classic,* Mar 1924, 25, 86. "Doris Kenyon," *MPW,* 10 Jan 1925, 163. "Sills—Kenyon," *MPW,* 25 Sep 1926, 2. "Niagara Falls," *MPW,* 30 Oct 1926, 2. June Lee, "Dan Cupid's Bulletin Board," *Paris and Hollywood Screen Secrets Magazine,* Aug 1927, 36 (birth of son). DeWitt Bodeen, "Doris Kenyon," *FIR,* Apr 1980, 203–17 (includes filmography).

Kenyon, Robert [actor] (b. 1889?–19 Dec 1928 [39], Chicago IL). AS, p. 604 (d. LA CA). BHD, p. 217. IFN, p. 163.

Keough, Austin C[ampbell] [Vice President of Paramount] (b. New York NY, 11 Jun 1888–20 Apr 1955 [66], New York NY). m. Katherine Upton. (Began 1919.) "Austin C. Keough, 67, A Movie Executive," *NYT,* 21 Apr 1955, 29:4. WWWA (buried in Williamstown MA).

Keough, Edwin V. [vaudeville/film actor] (b. Cohoes NY, 1874?–17 Aug 1920 [46], Manhattan Hospital for the Insane, Ward's Island, New York NY; paresis). m. vaudeville actress Dorothy Ballard. (In vaudeville: Keough & Ballard; Keough & Nelson; Member of the White Rats.) "Edwin Keough," *Variety,* 27 Aug 1920, 4:5 ("Mr. Keough was the first to introduce a motion picture film as part of a vaudeville act…" He was first stricken in Jul 1919, "while engaged in motion picture work for Edgar Jones Productions at Atlanta, Ga."). BHD, p. 217 (Keogh).

Keppler, Edward [actor]. No data found. AMD, p. 193. "Edward Keppler, Lorraine Harding and Greta Hartman Added to 'Bandbox' Cast," *MPW,* 9 Aug 1919, 853.

Keppins, Emile [actor] (b. France-d. Oct 1926, France). BHD, p. 217.

Ker, Paul [stage/film actor] (b. 1875–31 Mar 1929 [54?], New York NY). BHD, p. 217. "From the Legitimate," *NYDM,* 2 Dec 1914, 26:3 (Ker, "eccentric German comedian," to debut in *The Million* for FP-L. He was in he play).

Kerby, Frederick [stage/film actor] (b. Hamilton, Canada, 1877–4 Apr 1927 [50], Saginaw MI). (Vaughan Glaser stock; Jeffres Strand stock.) "Fred Kerby," *Variety,* 13 Apr 1927, 58:4 (interred in the Catholic Actor's Guild Plot, Calvary Cemetery, Brooklyn NY). BHD, p. 217.

Kerby, Marion [actress] (b. 1877?–16 Dec 1956 [79], Los Angeles CA). (Biograph, 1912.) "Marion Kerby," *Variety,* 26 Dec 1956 (d. 18 Dec). AS, p. 604. BHD1, p. 300. IFN, p. 163.

Kerjean, Germaine [actress] (*née* Germaine Charlotte Rose Chapelle, b. Le Havre, France, 22 Jul 1893–6 May 1975 [81], Viry-Chatillon, France). AS, p. 604.

Kerker, Gustave Adolph [stage/film actor] (b. Herford, Westphalia, Germany, 28 Feb 1857–29 Jun 1923 [66], New York NY; apoplexy). m. (1) Rose Leighton, 1884; (2) Mattie Rivenberg, 1908. "Gustave Adolph Kerker," *Variety,* 4 Jul 1923. AS, p. 604. SD, p. 707.

Kern, [Miss] Cecil [actress] (b. Portland OR, 1892–4 Jun 1928 [35], New York NY). "Cecil Kern," *Variety,* 6 Jun 1928. AS, p. 604. BHD, p. 217. Truitt, 1983.

Kern, Hal C. [actor/film editor] (b. Anaconda MT, 14 Jul 1894–24 Feb 1985 [90], Los Angeles CA). BHD, p. 217; BHD2, p. 143.

Kernell, William [scenarist/title writer/composer] (b. 21 Feb 1891–12 Jul 1963 [72], Los Angeles CA; heart attack). AS, p. 604. BHD2, p. 143. FDY, pp. 429, 445.

Kerner, Gus [extra, most often a headwaiter] (b. 1869?). Robert Donaldson, "Famous Extras," *MPC,* Feb 1927, 32–33 [photo], 68, 80.

Kerr, Charles M. [assistant director/producer/title writer/scenarist] (b. 1892?–14 Feb 1954 [61], Los Angeles CA; muscular distrophy). "Charles Kerr," *Variety,* 17 Feb 1954 ("He started in films in 1918 as assistant director and was second unit director, writer, production manager with such companies as FBO, Famous Players, Goldwyn and various indies."). AS, p. 605. BHD2, p. 143. FDY, pp. 429, 445.

Kerr, Donald [actor] (b. Eagle Grove IA, 5 Aug 1891–25 Jan 1977 [85], Los Angeles CA). AMD, p. 193. AS, p. 605. "Donald Kerr," *MPW,* 27 Mar 1926, 277.

Kerr, Frederick Grinham [stage/film actor] (b. London, England, 11 Oct 1858–2 May 1933 [74], London, England). "Frederick Kerr," *Variety,* 110, 9 May 1933, 62:4. AS, p. 605. BHD1, p. 300.

Kerr, Geoffrey (father of John Kerr) [stage/film actor/scenarist] (*né* Geoffrey Keen, b. London, England, 28 Jan 1895). m. Jane Walker. AS, p. 605. Ragan 2, pp. 823–24. SD.

Kerr, Harry D. [composer] (b. Santa Rosa CA, 8 Oct 1886–20 May 1957 [71], Los Angeles CA). m. Ruth. "Harry D. Kerr Dies at 76; Lawyer and Song Writer Aided in Founding of ASCAP," *NYT,* 22 May 1957, 33:2 (age 76). "Harry D. Kerr," *Variety,* 22 May 1957 (composed *Do You Ever Think of Me?; Venetia; Rag Doll; Broken Dreams; Don't Be Too Sure*). AS, p. 605.

Kerr, James F. [composer] (b. Hamilton, Ontario, Canada, 1878?–14 Jun 1925 [47], New York NY). m. Edith Williams. "James F. Kerr," *Variety,* 17 Jun 1925 (wrote *Do You Ever Think of Me?; Neapolitan Night; Paradise; Me-Ow; Give Me Today*). SD.

Kerr, Jane [actress] (b. 1871–19 Nov 1954 [83?], Compton CA). AS, p. 605.

Kerr, Robert Perry [actor/director] (b. Burlington CT, 1895–5 Sep 1960 [65], Porterville CA; heart attack). m. Edna Barnes. (Sennett; Christie.) "Robert Kerr [sic]," *Variety,* 14 Sep 1960 ("silent comedy director"). AMD, p. 193. AS, p. 604 (Robert J. Kern; also listed under Bob Kerr). BHD1, p. 300; BHD2, p. 143. IFN, p. 163. "Kerr Signed by Fox," *MPW,* 6 Feb 1926, 553.

Kerr, Sophie [scenarist] (b. Denton MD, 1880–6 Feb 1965 [84?], New York NY). BHD2, p. 143.

Kerrick, Thomas [actor] (b. 1895–27 Apr 1927 [32], Los Angeles CA). AS, p. 605. BHD, p. 217. IFN, p. 164. Truitt, p. 181. Truitt, 1983.

Kerrigan, J[ack] **Warren** (twin of **William W. Kerrigan**; brother of **Kathleen Kerrigan**) [stage/film actor] (*né* George Warren Kerrigan, b. Louisville KY, 25 Jul 1879–9 Jun 1947 [67], Balboa Beach CA; pneumonia). *How I Became a Successful Motion Picture Star* (Los Angeles: self-published, 1914.) (Essanay; American; Universal; Paralta.) "J. Warren Kerrigan," *NYT,* 10 Jun 1947, 27:2. "J. Warren Kerrigan," *Variety,* 11 Jun 1947 (*né* George Warren Kerrigan). AMD, p. 193. AS, p. 605. BHD, p. 217. FFF, p. 124 (b. 1883). GK, pp. 430–41. IFN, p. 164. Katz, p. 652. MH, p. 120 (b. 1882). MSBB, p. 1025 (b. 1889). Truitt, p. 181 (b. 1889). "Warren Kerrigan Is Matinee Idol Hero," *MPW,* 3 Feb 1912, 382. "Kerrigan Has Bad Fall," *MPW,* 30 Mar 1912, 1179. "Dastardly Murder in American's Western Studio," *MPW,* 18 May 1912, 1179 (his dog). "American Film Company at Santa Barbara, Cal.," *MPW,* 7 Dec 1912, 984. "One on Kerrigan," *MPW,* 14 Jun 1913, 1116. "All to the Mustard," *MPW,* 27 Dec 1913, 1535. "Kerrigan's Father Dies," *MPW,* 15 Aug 1914, 970 (John Kerrigan, d. 29 Jul 1914, age 77). "Plucky Fight Saves Kerrigan from Shark," *MPW,* 29 Aug 1914, 1252. "J. Warren Kerrigan; The Universal Star," *MPS,* 11 Sep 1914, 25 (states his age as 25). "Kerrigan Renews Contract," *MPW,* 21 Nov 1914, 1097. "Mack Sennett's Forces," *NYDM,* 3 Feb 1915, 27:1 (Kerrigan "approached the window of the Universal studio post office and inquired, 'Any mail for me?' Looking him squarely in the face, the intelligent and gifted 'postmaster' asked, 'What name, please?' Needless to add there is a new face at that post office window."). W.E. Wing, "Along the Pacific Coast," *NYDM,* 19 May 1915, 24:1 ("It is said that J. Warren Kerrigan will recover nicely from his operation at the hospital for internal disarrangement. He delayed the ordeal so long that his case presented a serious problem to surgeons. However, he is gaining in strength and all seems well."). "Kerrigan is Improving Very Slowly," *MPW,* 12 Jun 1915, 1783. "Along the Pacific Coast," *NYDM,* 16 Jun 1915, 26:2 ("has recovered sufficiently to leave his bed."). William M. Henry, "The Great God Kerrigan," *Photoplay Magazine,* IX (Feb 1916), 32–36. "U. Suing Kerrigan," *Variety,* XLV, 8 Dec 1916, 23:1 (Kerrigna sued for $8,000 for breach of contract for walking out on *Mrs. Musselwhite* ("now being refilmed.... Universal contends there existed a verbal agreement with Kerrigan to complete the picture, but that he refused to continue after scenes had been taken for two weeks, saying that his contract had expired."). "Kerrigan Has Own Company," *MPW,* 13 Jan 1917, 210. Cal York, "Plays and Players," *Photoplay Magazine,* Feb 1917, 89 (stock actor Harrison Ford was hired by Universal "to take the place of J. Warren Kerrigan."). "J. Warren Kerrigan," *MPW,* 24 Mar 1917, 1935. "Kerrigan Production Begins June 5," *MPW,* 2 Jun 1917, 1454. "J. Warren Kerrigan," *MPW,* 30 Jun 1917, 2107. "J. Warren Kerrigan Breaks Leg," *MPW,* 25 Aug 1917, 1225–26. Neil G. Caward, "Screen Gossip," *Picture-Play Magazine,* Sep 1917, 110 (recently toured the country; now at Paralta). "J. Warren Kerrigan's Condition," *MPW,* 1 Sep 1917, 1361. "Kerrigan Out of Hospital," *MPW,* 29 Sep 1917, 1976. "Kerrigan Back at the Studio," *MPW,* 13 Oct 1917, 239. "J. Warren Kerrigan,"' *MPW,* 1 Dec 1917, 1322. "Kerrigan Back at Work," *MPW,* 1 Jun 1918, 1308. "Kerrigan making Own Films," *MPW,* 10 Aug 1918, 828. "Kerrigan Moves to Hollywood," *MPW,* 31 Aug 1918, 1238. "J. Warren Kerrigan Organizes Own Producing Company," *MPW,* 24 May 1919, 1161. "J. Warren Kerrigan Invited to Be Hero of a Novel," *MPW,* 26 Jul 1919, 532. "Kerrigan Adopts War Orphan," *MPW,* 6 Dec 1919, 659 (Stephen Myronoff, 6, Poland). Kenneth MacGowan, "The Play of the Month [*Outward Bound* by Sutton Vane]," *Classic,* May 1924, 46, 97 (J.M. Kerrigan is cited in the play on p. 42). "On the Set and Off," *MW,* 19 Jul 1924, 17 (was chosen for the lead in *Captain Blood* because of a poll and his work in *The Covered Wagon*). "Kerrigan Renews Contract," *NYDM,* 18 Nov 1924, 26:2 (at Universal for 2 years). "On the Set and Off," *MW,* 29 Aug 1925, 44 (to make 6 westerns after his personal appearance tour with *Captain Blood*). Dorothy Spensley, "The Living Ghosts of the Screen; Yesterday's Stars Wait Hopefully for the One Great Rôle That Will Renew Their Glory," *MPC,* Jul 1928, 18–19, 84 ("I don't miss it, really. I've had my day."). George A. Katchmer, "J. Warren Kerrigan: Impressive Star," *CI,* 87 (Sep 1982), 7–9. Richard E. Braff, "An Index to the Films of J. Warren Kerrigan," *CI,* 171 (Sep 1989), 54; 172 (Oct 1989), 33–34, 58.

Kerrigan, J[oseph] **M.** [actor] (b. Dublin, Ireland, 16 Dec 1884–29 Apr 1964 [79], Los Angeles CA). "Joseph M. Kerrigan," *Variety,* 13 May 1964 (age 76). AS, p. 605 (b. 1887). BHD1, p. 300. IFN, p. 164. Katz, p. 652. Truitt, p. 181 (b. 1887).

Kerrigan, Kathleen (sister of **J. Warren** and **William W. Kerrigan**) [actress] (b. New Albany IN, 11 Apr 1868–27 Jan 1957 [88], San Fernando CA). m. **Clay Clement** (d. 1956). AMD, p. 194. AS, p. 605. BHD1, p. 300 (b. Louisville KY). IFN, p. 164. Truitt, 1983. "New Universal Star; Kathleen Kerrigan to Join Brother Jack in Great Production of 'Samson and Delilah,'" *MPW,* 8 Nov 1913, 741. "Kathleen Kerrigan," *MPW,* 29 Nov 1913, 1015. "Kathleen's Father Dies," *MPW,* 15 Aug 1914, 970. Billy H. Doyle, "1957 Film Necrology [letter]," *FIR,* March 1958, 156.

Kerrigan, William Wallace (twin of **J.W. Kerrigan**; brother of **Kathleen Kerrigan**) [manager] (b. Louisville KY, 25 Jul 1879–20 Feb 1953 [73], Los Angeles CA). m. "William W. Kerrigan," *NYT,* 21 Feb 1953, 13:2. "William W. Kerrigan," *Variety,* 25 Feb 1953. AS, p. 605. "Important Changes at American's Santa Barbara Studio," *MPW,* 10 May 1913, 604. "Gossip of the Studios," *NYDM,* 20 May 1914, 33:2 (engaged to Nina May Richdale). J. Van Cartmell, "Film News from the Coast...," *NYDM,* 20 Nov 1915, 32:4 (child born recently). "On the Set and Off," *MW,* 31 Jan 1925, 23 (Kerrigan's eleven-year-old daughter Violet died "as a result of burns received when her dress caught fire at a Christmas party.").

Kerry, Norman [actor] (*né* Arnold Kaiser, b. Rochester NY, 16 Jun 1889–12 Jan 1956 [66?], Los Angeles CA). m. (1) Rosina Tripp, 1917–29; (2) Helen Mary Wells, 1932; (3) Kay English, 2 Nov 1946. "Norman Kerry, an ex-Film Star; Romantic Hero of the Silent Screen Dies—Figured in Real-Life Escapades," *NYT,* 13 Jan 1956, 23:5 (age 63). "Norman Kerry," *Variety,* 18 Jan 1956. AMD, p. 194. AS, p. 605. BHD1, p. 300. FFF, p. 66 (b. 1897). FSS, p. 167. GK, pp. 441–48. IFN, p. 164 (age 61). Katz, p. 652. MH, p. 120 (b. 1897). Truitt, p. 181 (*né* Arnold Kaiser). WWS, p. 120. "Report Kerry Injured," *MPW,* XXV, 28 Aug 1915, 896. Don Juan, "So This Is Hollywood; Black Eyes for Kerry," *Paris and Hollywood Screen Secrets,* Oct 1927, 60 (Kerry was having words with wife Rosine when someone misinterpreted and socked him). Walter Ramsey, "Eat, Drink and Be Kerry; Norman Goes in for the Squire Life," *MPC,* Mar

1929, 55, 92. George A. Katchmer, "Still Remembered Norman Kerry," *CI,* 128 (Feb 1986), 15–18. Richard E. Braff, "The Films of Norman Kerry," *CI,* 147 (Sep 1987), C17-C19.

Kershaw, Elinor [actress] (b. MO, 19 Nov 1884–13 Sep 1971 [86], Palos Verdes CA). m. **Thomas H. Ince** (d. 1924). "Mrs. Thomas H. Ince," *Variety,* 22 Sep 1971. AS, p. 605. BHD, p. 218. IFN, p. 164. Truitt, 1983.

Kershaw, Willette [stage/film actress[(*née* Willette Mansfield, b. Clifton Heights MO, 17 Jun 1881–4 May 1960 [78], Honolulu HI). m. (1) Albert Morrison-1909; (2) David Sturgis, 1923; (3) W.K. Lamar; (4) Richard Schuster. "Wilette Kershaw, Stage Actress, 78," *NYT,* 6 May 1960, 31:4. "Wilette Kershaw," *Variety,* 18 May 1960 (Mrs. Wilette Kershaw Lamar). AS, p. 605 (b. St. Louis LA, 1882). BHD, p. 218 (b. 1882). IFN, p. 164. SD.

Kershner, Glenn R. [cinematographer] (b. Findlay OH, 20 Jul 1884–9 May 1985 [100], Honolulu HI). (Helped to develop panchromatic color film.) AS, p. 605. BHD2, p. 143. FDY, p. 461.

Kerwood, Dick [actor/stuntman] (b. VA, 8 Oct 1892–15 Oct 1924 [32], Pico Canyon CA; accident during filming). AS, p. 605. BHD, p. 218. IFN, p. 164.

Keshavaro, Date [actor/director] (b. Adivare-Ratnagiri, India, 1889). AS, p. 606.

Kessel, Adam (brother of **Charles** and **William Kessel**) [executive/producer] (b. 1865?–21 Sep 1946 [80], Keeseville NY). "Adam Kessel, Got Chaplin into Films; Ex-Motion Picture Producer, Who Induced Comedian to Quit Stage, Is Dead," *NYT,* 23 Sep 1946, 23:2. "Adam Kessel," *Variety,* 25 Sep 1946. AMD, p. 194. AS, p. 606. BHD, p. 218; BHD2, p. 143. "Bison Company Gets 101 Ranch," *MPW,* 9 Dec 1911, 810. "Kessel Gets Loving Cup," *MPW,* 13 Dec 1913, 1288. "Kessel-Baumann-Aitken," *MPW,* 3 Jul 1915, 42. George Blaisdell, "Mecca of the Motion Picture," *MPW,* 10 Jul 1915, 215–20. "Ad. Kessel Convalescent," *MPW,* 30 Dec 1916, 1970. Adam Kessel, "When the Field Was Fresh," *MPW,* 10 Mar 1917, 1523–24. "Kessel's Lose Point in Triangle Suit; Superpictures History Heard in Court," *MPW,* 8 Jul 1922, 92. Douglas Gilbert, "Came the Dawn," *New York World-Telegram,* II, 22–27 Jun 1936, 1:1.

Kessel, Charles W. (brother of **Adam** and **William Kessel**) [secretary]. No data found. AMD, p. 194. "Charles Kessel Talks," *MPW,* 26 Sep 1914, 1786. "Kessel's Lose Point in Triangle Suit; Superpictures History Heard in Court," *MPW,* 8 Jul 1922, 92.

Kessel, Joseph [actor] (b. Clara, Argentina, 10 Feb 1898–24 Jul 1979 [81], Avesnes-sur-Meuse, France). AS, p. 606.

Kessel, William [director/manufacturer] (d 30 Oct 1914, Brooklyn NY). AMD, p. 194. BHD2, p. 143. "William Kessel Dies; Film Pioneer and Brother of Adam and Charles Kessel Passes Away Suddenly," *NYDM,* 4 Nov 1914, 28:4 ("This is the second of the Kessel brothers to die in the past six months."). "Obituary," *MPW,* 21 Nov 1914, 1089.

Kessler, David [actor] (b. Kishniev, Russia, 1859?–14 May 1920 [61], New York NY). m. twice. "David Kessler," *Variety,* 21 May 1920. SD.

Kesson, David [cinematographer]. No data found. FDY, p. 461.

Kesson, Frank [cinematographer]. No data found. AMD, p. 194. FDY, p. 461. "Warner Cameraman Burned on Location," *MPW,* 7 May 1927, 22 (*Simple Sis*).

Kester, Paul [scenarist] (b. 1871–21 Jun 1933 [62?], Lake Mohegan NY). BHD2, p. 143.

Kesterson, George *see* **Mix, Art**

Keszthelyi, A.S. [portrait painter] (b. Hungary). No other data found. (James D. Hampton Prods.) "Portrait Painter in Films," *LA Times,* 22 Feb 1920, III, p. 16 ("He will create decorative paintings for the elaborate interior sets of future Hampton productions, and will also illumine subtitles.").

Ketelbey, Albert W[illiam] [composer] (b. Birmingham, England, 4 Aug 1875–26 Nov 1959 [84], Cowes, England). AS, p. 606 (d. Cowes, England). Scott Johnson, "Ketelbey—A Notable Composer for Silent Film," *CI,* 127 (Jan 1986), C8.

Key, Kathleen [actress: Wampas Star, 1923] (*née* Kitty Lanahan, b. Buffalo NY, 1 Apr 1903–22 Dec 1954 [51?], Woodland Hills CA). "Kathleen Key," *Variety,* 29 Dec 1954 (age 48). AMD, p. 194. AS, p. 606 (b. 1907). BHD1, p. 300 (b. 1907). FFF, p. 189. IFN, p. 164 (b. 1907). MH, p. 120. Truitt, p. 182 (b. 1906). "Kathleen Key Signed for Goldwyn Stock," *MPW,* 31 Mar 1923, 570. "Kathleen Key Recovers," *MPW,* 18 Oct 1924, 603. George A. Katchmer, "Forgotten Cowboys/Cowgirls—Part VIII," *CI,* 180 (Jun 1990), 51, 53 (b. 1907).

Key, Pierre V.R. [publicist/scenarist] (b. Grand Haven MI, 1872–28 Nov 1945 [73?], New York NY). AMD, p. 194. BHD2, p. 143. Pierre V.R. Key, "Publicity Should Inform," *MPW,* 20 Jul 1918, 337–38.

Keyes, Donald Biddle [cinematographer]. No data found. FDY, p. 461.

Keyes, John [actor] (b. 1892–26 Aug 1966 [74?], Los Angeles CA). AS, p. 606.

Keys, Nelson (father of Anthony Nelson Keys) [actor] (b. London, England, 7 Aug 1886–26 Apr 1939 [52], London, England). AS, p. 606 (b. 1896). BHD1, p. 300. IFN, p. 164.

Khan, Mazhar [actor/director/producer] (b. India-d. 24 Sep 1950). AS, p. 606. BHD2, p. 144.

Khane, Eddie [actor] (b. MO, 12 Aug 1889–30 Apr 1968 [78], Los Angeles CA). AS, p. 606.

Kheifits, Iosif [director] (*né* Iosif Efimovic Hejfic, b. Minsk, Russia, 176 Dec 1905–24 Apr 1995 [89], St. Petersburg, Russia). (LenFilm Studios, 1928.) Tom Birchenough, "Iosif Kheifits," *Variety,* 29 May 1995, 72:2. AS, p. 607. BHD2, p. 144.

Khmara Ilia [actor] (b. Russia, 1896–5 Aug 1989 [93?], Reseda CA). AS, p. 607.

Khmelyov, Nikolai [actor/director] (b. Russia, 1901–15 Nov 1945 [44?], Russia). AS, p. 607. BHD2, p. 144.

Khokhlova, Aleksandra Sergeevna [actress] (b. Berlin, Germany, 1897–1985 [88?], Moscow, Russia). AS, p. 607.

Kholodnaia, Vera [actress] (b. Poltava, Ukraine, 1893–1919 [26?], Odessa, Ukraine; murdered). AS, p. 607.

Kidd, Jim [actor] (b. TX, 1846?–9 Dec 1916 [70], Los Angeles CA). "'Jim' Kidd," *Variety,* 29 Dec 1916 ("the most famous and likewise the oldest cowboy appearing in pictures"). AS, p. 607. BHD, p. 218. Truitt, 1983.

Kidd, Kathleen Maud [actress] (b. England, 1899?–23 Feb 1961 [62], Toronto, Canada). "Kathleen M[aud] Kidd," *Variety,* 1 Mar 1961. AS, p. 607. BHD, p. 218. IFN, p. 164. Truitt, p. 182.

Kidder, Edward E. [writer]. No data found. AMD, p. 194. "[Charles] Ray Praised by Author of 'Peaceful Valley,'" *MPW,* XLVII, 6 Nov 1920, 78.

Kidder, Hugh [actor] (b. 1879–3 Jun 1952 [73?], Los Angeles CA). AS, p. 607.

Kiesow, Doris [actress] (*née* Dorothea Charlotte Gertrud Kiesow, b. Cologne, Germany, 11 Dec 1902). AS, p. 608.

Kilgour, Joseph Turnbull [stage/film actor] (b. Ayr, Ontario, Canada, 11 Jul 1863–20 Apr 1933 [69], Bay Shore, LI NY). "Joseph Kilgour," *Variety,* 25 Apr 1933. AMD, p. 194. AS, p. 608 (d. 21 Apr). BHD, p. 218. FFF, p. 187. IFN, p. 164. MH, p. 121. SD. Slide, p. 162. "Joseph Turnbull Kilgour," *MPW,* 23 Oct 1915, 596. "Kilgour Joins Cast," *MPW,* 30 Jun 1923, 769. "Kilgour Signed by Bryant Washburn," *MPW,* 22 Sep 1923, 345.

Killifer, Jack [film editor] (b. CA, 19 Nov 1898–6 Aug 1956 [57], Los Angeles CA). "Jack Killifer," *Variety,* 15 Aug 1956. BHD2, p. 144.

Killiker, Katherine [title writer]. No data found. Paul Paige, "Close-Ups and Fade-Outs," *Paris and Hollywood,* Oct 1926, 96.

Kilpack, Bennett [actor] (b. London, England, 6 Feb 1883–17 Aug 1962 [79], Santa Monica CA). AS, p. 608. BHD, p. 218. IFN, p. 164.

Kilyenyi, Edward, Sr. [music director] (b. Bekes, Hungary, 25 Jan 1884–15 Aug 1968 [84], Tallahassee FL). "Edward Kilenyi [sic], Sr.," *Variety,* 21 Aug 1968 ("Kilyenyi began his association with films before sound. He wrote music and cue sheets that went out to exhibs with each picture."). AS, p. 628 (Edward Kylyenyi). BHD2, p. 144 (Kilenyi).

Kimball, Edward M[arshall] (father of **Clara Kimball Young**) [stage/film actor] (b. Keokuk IA, 26 Jun 1859–4 Jan 1938 [78], Los Angeles CA). m. **Pauline Garrett** (d. 1919). "Edward M. Kimball; Father of Clara Kimball Young Was Stage and Film Veteran," *NYT,* 5 Jan 1938, 21:4. "Edward M. Kimball," *Variety,* 12 Jan 1938. AS, p. 609. BHD1, p. 301. IFN, p. 165. Spehr, p. 146. Truitt, p. 182. AMD, p. 373 (under Young, Clara Kimball). "Clara Kimball Young's Mother Dead in Los Angeles," *MPW,* 27 Dec 1919, 1108 (*née* Pauline Maddern, d. 12 Dec 1919).

Kimball, Louis [actor] (b. Marshalltown IA, 19 May 1889–29 Jan 1936 [47], Orlando FL; pneumonia). "Louis Kimball," *Variety,* 5 Feb 1936. AS, p. 609. BHD, p. 218.

Kimball, Pauline Garrett *see* **Garrett, Pauline**

Kimball, Winifred [sxenarist]. No data found. AMD, p. 194. "Florida Woman Wins Scenario Contest Conducted b Goldwyn and Newspaper," *MPW,* 15 Apr 1922, 721.

Kimberley, Paul [executive] (b. 1882–5 Nov 1964 [82?], Chichester, England). BHD2, p. 144.

Kimmich, Max W[ilhelm] [scenarist/director] (b. Ulm, Germany, 4 Nov 1893–16 Jan 1980 [86], Icking, Germany). AMD, p. 194. AS, p. 609. "Will Direct," *MPW,* 14 May 1927, 120.

Kimura, Massa Kichi [actor] (b. Japan, 1890–3 Nov 1918 [28], New York NY; flu). "Massa

K. Kimura," *Variety,* 8 Nov 1918. AS, p. 609 (d. 2 Nov). BHD, p. 218. SD. Truitt, 1983. Billy H. Doyle, "Lost Players," *CI,* 139 (Jan 1987), 55.

Kindahl, Julian [actor] (b. Stockholm, Sweden, 12 Apr 1885-ca. Apr 1955 [70?]). AS, p. 609.

King, Ada [actress] (b. London, England, 1862–8 Jun 1940 [78?]). BHD, p. 218.

King, Alexander Boyne (b. Glasgow, Scotland, 1889–12 Feb 1973 [83?], Glasgow, Scotland). AS, p. 609.

King, Allyn [stage/film actress] (b. 1899?–30 Mar 1930 [31], New York NY; jumped from 5th floor of aunt's apartment on 29 Mar; arms and legs were broken). (Ziegfeld Follies, 1916–20.) "Allyn King," *Variety,* 2 Apr 1930, 76:4 (age 29; "Miss King recently attempted to stage a come-back on Broadway but failed, due to excess weight."). AS, p. 609 (b. 1901). BHD, p. 218 (b. 1901). IFN, p. 165.

King, Anita, "The Paramount Girl" [stage/film actress] (b. IN, 14 Nov 1889–10 Jun 1963 [74], Los Angeles CA; heart attack). m. Timothy KcKenna. "Anita King," *Variety,* 12 Jun 1963. AMD, p. 194. AS, p. 609. BHD, p. 218 (b. Chicago IL). IFN, p. 165. SD. Truitt, p. 182. "Lone Girl to Cross Continent," *NYDM,* 1 Sep 1915, 29:2 (King left the Lasky studio on Wednesday, 25 Aug, to make a trip across the continent [to NYC], accompanied by her English bulldog. She broke the record between LA and SF by ten minutes—"This is a remarkable performance, especially for a woman, for it is a rough mountain road, with few opportunities for real speed. ¶The trip is extremely dangerous. While crossing the desert she will be out of touch with civilization for two days at a time."). "Transcontinental Auto Trip," *MPW,* 4 Sep 1915, 1666. "Anita King Arrives; Paramount Girl Completes Daring Cross Country Trip in Auto," *NYDM,* 30 Oct 1915, 25:2 (arrived in NYC; escorted to City Hall; lunched at the Knickerbocker Hotel. Drove a 6-cylinder Kissel Kar.). "Anita King Reaches New York," *MPW,* 30 Oct 1915, 769. "Paramount Girl Entertained in Fresno," *MPW,* 4 Dec 1915, 1839. "Anita King Will Lecture," *MPW,* 14 Oct 1916, 256. "To Motor Across Continent," *MPW,* 28 Sep 1918, 1862 (cited as Anita King McKnight).

King, Basil [writer]. No data found. AMD, p. 194. "Basil King Starts for West Coast to Acquire First-Hand Information," *MPW,* 30 Aug 1919, 1299. "Goldwyn Studios Made Convert of Basil King," *MPW,* 20 Dec 1919, 994.

King, Boyd [actor] (b. 1906–19 Feb 1940 [34], Los Angeles CA). AS, p. 609. BHD1, p. 302. IFN, p. 165.

King, Bradley [title writer/scenarist] (b. New York NY, 8 Jul 1894–15 Jul 1929 [35]). m. **John Griffith Wray**, 7 Oct 1928, Riverside CA (d. 1929). AMD, p. 194. BHD2, p. 144. FDY, pp. 429, 445. "Bradley King Signs to Write Stories for Thomas H. Ince," *MPW,* 4 Sep 1920, 96. "T.H. Ince Praises Miss King," *MPW,* 25 Aug 1923, 665.

King, Burton L. [director/producer] (b. Cincinnati OH, 25 Aug 1877–4 May 1944 [66], Los Angeles CA). m. **Adele Lane** (d. 1957). (Solax; Lubin; NYMP Co.; Western Vitagraph; Bison; Universal; Selig; Kolb and Dill; Metro; Pathé.) "Burton King," *Variety,* 10 May 1944. AMD, p. 194. AS, p. 610. BHD, p. 218; BHD2, p. 144. IFN, p. 165. "Burton King; Metro Director," *NYDM,* 15 Aug 1916, 34 (b. 1887). "Rolfe Signs Director and Prominent Players," *MPW,* 10 Aug 1918, 868. "King to Produce Independently," *MPW,* 6 Mar 1920, 1659. "Burton King Now Directing Eddie Polo; MacGowan Forced to Go West," *MPW,* 22 Apr 1922, 858. "To Direct Banner Films," *MPW,* 6 Sep 1924, 50. "Burton King Signed," *MPW,* 25 Jul 1925, 442. "Burton King," *MPW,* 10 Sep 1927, 92.

King, Carlton S. [actor/director] (b. St. Louis MO, 15 Dec 1881–6 Jul 1932 [50], Glendale CA). (Edison.) "Carlton King," *Variety,* 12 Jul 1932 (radio announcer). AMD, p. 194. AS, p. 610. BHD1, p. 302; BHD2, p. 144. IFN, p. 165. "Carlton King," *MPW,* 1 Aug 1914, 711. "Three New Edison Directors," *MPW,* 24 Jul 1915, 632. "Carlton King," *MPW,* 27 Mar 1915, 1914g. "Studio Gossip," *NYDM,* 6 Nov 1915, 37:2 (though recently made a director at Edison, he was forced to act before the cameras again, "owing to the persistent demand of exhibitors and patrons. Popularity too has its drawbacks.").

King, Charles E. [stage/film actor] (b. New York NY, 31 Oct 1889–11 Jan 1944 [54], London, England; pneumonia). m. Lila Rhodes. "Charles E. King," *Variety,* 12 Jan 1944 (age 52). AS, p. 610 (b. 1891). BHD1, p. 302. SD, p. 712. Truitt, 1983. "Charles King a Versatile Actor," *MPW,* 3 Nov 1923, 98:2.

King, Charles L[afayette] **"Blackie," Sr.** [actor] (b. Hillsboro TX, 21 Feb 1895–7 May 1957 [62], Los Angeles CA; hepatic coma, cirrhosis, chronic alcoholism). (Film debut as extra: *Birth of a Nation.*) "Charles King, 58, western actor, died May 7 in Hollywood. Two sons survive," *Variety,* 15 May 1957. AS, p. 610. BHD1, p. 302 (b. Dallas TX). FSS, p. 167. IFN, p. 165. Katz, p. 655. Truitt, p. 182 (b. 1899). Kermit Slobb, "Resident Badman," *CI,* 133 (Jul 1986), 15. George A. Katchmer, "Forgotten Cowboys and Cowgirls—Part III," *CI,* 174 (Dec 1989), 48. Frank Dolven, "Three Bad Men I Would Have Liked to Know," *CI,* 221 (Nov 1993), C24-C25.

King, Charles W. [actor] (b. 1852?–12 Mar 1928 [76], Staten Island NY). "Charles W. King," *Variety,* 14 Mar 1928. AS, p. 610.

King, Claude Ewart [actor/founder of SAG] (b. Northampton, England, 15 Jan 1875–18 Sep 1941 [66], Los Angeles CA). m. (1) Violet Luddington; (2) Evelyn Hall. "Claude E. King," *Variety,* 24 Sep 1941 (began 1920). AS, p. 610 (b. 1879). BHD1, p. 302 (b. 1876). IFN, p. 165. SD. Truitt, p. 183 (b. 1879).

King, Cliff [cinematographer]. No data found. FDY, p. 461.

King, Cyrus W. [executive] (b. 1886–20 Sep 1951 [65?]). BHD2, p. 144.

King, Della M. [film cutter/scenarist] (b. 1886?–16 Oct 1935 [49], Los Angeles CA). "Della King," *Variety,* 23 Oct 1935. FDY, p. 429.

King, Dennis [actor/singer] (*né* Dennis Pratt, b. Warwickshire, Coventry, England, 2 Nov 1897–21 May 1971 [73], New York NY). m. Edith Wright. Hobe Morrison, "Dennis King, 73, Actor & Singer, Players' ex-Prez," *Variety,* 26 May 1971. AS, p. 610 (b. Hornchurch, England). BHD1, p. 302. IFN, p. 165. Truitt, p. 183.

King, Elinor [actress] (*née* Goldie Flynn). No data found. AMD, p. 195. "Elinor King Has F.B.O. Contract," *MPW,* 19 Mar 1927, 191.

King, Emmett Carleton [actor] (b. Griffin GA, 31 May 1865–21 Apr 1953 [87], Woodland Hills CA). "Emmett C. King," *Variety,* 29 Apr 1953. AS, p. 610. BHD1, p. 302. IFN, p. 165. Truitt, p. 183. George Katchmer, "Remembering the Great Silents; Emmett Carleton King," *CI,* 205 (Jul 1992), 58; "Emmett King," *CI,* 206 (Aug 1992), 38.

King, Eugene W. [actor] (b. 1884–26 Nov 1950 [66?], Los Angeles CA). AS, p. 610.

King, George [assistant director] (b. London, England, 1899–26 Jun 1966 [66?], London, England; bronchial pneumonia). "George King," *Variety,* 29 Jun 1966 (assistant director, 1922). AS, p. 610. BHD2, p. 144. *Winchester's Screen Encyclopedia,* p. 114.

King, Henry, "The Champion of Champion Directors" (brother of **Louis King**) [actor/director] (b. Christianburg VA, 24 Jan 1886–25 Jun 1982 [96], Toluca Lake CA; heart attack in his sleep). m. (2) **Gypsy Abbott**, ca. 1914 (d. 1952). (Balboa; Ince; Fox.) Janet Maslin, "Henry King, Movie Director Known for Book Adaptations," *NYT,* 1 Jul 1982, B8:1 (age 91). Todd McCarthy, "Henry King, 96, Film Director, Dies in Sleep; Fox Workhorse," *Variety,* 7 Jul 1982 (d. 29 Jun). AMD, p. 195. AS, p. 610. BHD1, p. 611; BHD2, p. 144 (b. 1888). Jura, 105–12. Katz, p. 656. SD. Spehr, p. 146 (b. 1892). Henry King, "Make Pictures Just 'Heart High,'" *MPW,* 21 Jul 1917, 376–77. "Henry King," *MPW,* 15 Sep 1917, 1690. "Henry King Productions," *MPW,* 21 Feb 1920, 1249 (first film, *Big Dick*). "Henry King," *MPW,* 19 Jul 1924, 199. "King Seeking Locations," *MPW,* 3 Apr 1926, 338. "United Artists Signs King," *MPW,* 20 Aug 1927, 510. "King to Go West," *MPW,* 24 Sep 1927, 211. Herbert Cruikshank, "A Miracle Is Foreseen; The Screen World Has Been Told to Watch Henry King," *MPC,* May 1929, 33, 88. Billy H. Doyle, "Lost Players," *CI,* 153 (Mar 1988), 52–53.

King, Irma Marion Helena "Bebe" [actress] (b. London, England). WWS, p. 135.

King, Jay A., Jr. [producer] (b. 1880–14 Apr 1950 [70?], Philadelphia PA). AS, p. 610.

King, James Wallace [actor]. No data found. AMD, p. 195. "James Wallace King," *MPW,* 8 Sep 1917, 1529.

King, Joseph [actor] (b. Austin TX, 9 Feb 1883–11 Apr 1951 [68], Woodland Hills CA). m. Hazel Buckham. (Selig.) AMD, p. 195. AS, p. 610. BHD1, p. 302. IFN, p. 165. Truitt, 1983. W.E. Wing, "On the Pacific Coast," *NYDM,* 9 Dec 1914, 26:2 (birth of daughter). "Joe King Is Engaged for Triangle Play," *MPW,* 10 Nov 1917, 893. "Selznick Engages Joe King," *MPW,* 15 Nov 1919, 327.

King, Judy [vaudeville/stage/film actress] (b. Montreal CN). (Film debut: *Safety Last;* Roach; Sennett.) AMD, p. 195. "Judy King Signs with Fox," *MPW,* 4 Apr 1925, 492. "Judy King Elevated to Stardom in New Contract," *Paris and Hollywood,* Oct 1926, 72 (photo with Jack Munhall. Signed by Associated Exhibitors to co-star in comedies directed by Thomas L. Griffith.). George Katchmer, "Remembering the Great Silents," *CI,* 209 (Nov 1992), 54.

King, Kewpie [actress]. No data found. *Fl.* 1924–25. George Katchmer, "Remembering the Great Silents," *CI,* 209 (Nov 1992), 54.

King, Leslie [actor] (b. Baltimore MD, 1876?–10 Oct 1947 [71], Amityville, LI NY). "Leslie King," *Variety,* 15 Oct 1947. AS, p. 610. BHD1, p. 302. IFN, p. 165. Truitt, 1983.

King, Louis (brother of **Henry King**) [director] (aka Luigi Capuano, b. Christiansburg VA, 28 Jun 1898–7 Sep 1962 [64], Los Angeles CA). (FBO; Fox; Columbia; WB; Paramount.) "Lewis King," *Variety,* 19 Sep 1962 (age 62). AS, p. 610. BHD1, p. 302; BHD2, p. 144. Katz, pp. 656–57.

King, Lucille [actress] (b. 1886?–15 Aug 1977 [91]). AS, p. 610. BHD, p. 218. IFN, p. 165.

King, Mollie (sister of Charles King) [stage/film actress] (b. New York NY, 16 Apr 1895?–28 Dec 1981 [86], Ft. Lauderdale FL; stroke). m. (1) Kenneth Dade Alexander, 26 May 1919; (2) Thomas Claffey. (Film debut: *A Woman's Power,* World, 1916; Astra-Pathé Co.; Ivan.) "Mollie King," *Variety,* 1 Sep 1982 (age 86). AMD, p. 195. AS, p. 610 (b. 1898). BHD, pp. 43–45 (b. 1898); 218 (b. 1896). MSBB, p. 1038 (b. 1898). Spehr, p. 146 (b. 1898). "World-Equitable Engagements," *MPW,* 4 Mar 1916, 1483. "Mollie King with Pathé," *MPW,* 4 Nov 1916, 712. "Led Neward Operators' Ball," *MPW,* 2 Dec 1916, 1338. "Mollie King with Ivan," *MPW,* 23 Feb 1918, 1111. "Mollie King, Serial Star, Again to Be Seen on Screen," *MPW,* 18 Jan 1919, 342. Sue Roberts, "Sugar and Spice and Everything Nice,"*MPC,* May 1919, 50–51, 89. "American Cinema to Star Mollie King in Six Films," *MPW,* 10 May 1919, 884. Billy H. Doyle, "Lost Players," *CI,* 179 (May 1990), 18, 30 (b. 1896).

King, Nellie [actress] (b. 1895–1 Jul 1935 [40?], West Palm Beach FL). BHD, p. 218.

King, R. Henry [actor]. No data found. AMD, p. 195. "Henry King with Knickerbocker," *MPW,* 19 Feb 1916, 1115. "R. Henry King," *MPW,* 21 Apr 1917, 440.

King, Rex [actor] (*né* Jim Doss). No data found. (Fox.) Oscar Henning, "How Not to Become a Movie Star In Six Easy Lessons; Rex King Hog-Tied Himself in World's Record Time," *MPC,* Jun 1928, 44, 82, 91 ("...the here-today-and-gone-tomorrow star.").

King, Ruth [actress]. No data found. George Katchmer, "Ruth King," *CI,* 225 (Mar 1994), 43–44 (began ca. 1917).

King, Stanley E. [actor] (b. London, England, 6 Feb 1904–3 Dec 1975 [71], Los Angeles Co. CA). AMD, p. 195. BHD1, p. 303. IFN, p. 165. Truitt, 1983. "Stanley King in New Play," *MPW,* 6 Oct 1917, 94.

King, W. George [cinematographer] (b. 1891–19 Nov 1928 [37?], Detroit MI). BHD2, p. 145.

King, Will [actor/producer/writer] (b. Brooklyn NY, 1886–22 Jan 1958 [71?], Oakland CA). m. Claire Starr, 1912. "Will King," *Variety,* 209, 29 Jan 1958, 71:1 (d. SF CA, age 72; "In 1925 he had a brief whirl at silent films in Hollywood..."). AS, p. 611. BHD, p. 218.

Kingdon, Dorothy [actress] (b. Auburn NY, 1894?–31 Mar 1939 [45], Los Angeles CA). m. Baron Van Raven. "Dorothy Kingdon [Mrs. Roche]," *Variety,* 5 Apr 1939. AMD, p. 195. AS, p. 611. BHD, p. 218. IFN, p. 165. Truitt, p. 183. Firoze Rangoonwalla, *75 Years of Indian Cinema* (New Delhi: Indian Book Company, 1975), pp. 46 ff. (Dorothy "Kimgdom" appeared in the Indian *Shakuntala* [*Fateful Ring,* 1920], providing "the unique interpretation of an Oriental character by an Occidental star"). "Dorothy Kingdon," *MPW,* 15 Jul 1916, 444. "Real Baroness a Metro Actress," *MPW,* 26 Aug 1916, 1382.

Kingdon, Frank [actor] (b. Providence RI, 1855?–9 Apr 1937 [82], Englewood NJ; bronchial pneumonia). "Frank Kingdon," *Variety,* 14 Apr 1937. AS, p. 611. BHD, p. 219 (b. 1865). IFN, p. 165.

Kingsford, Alison [actress] (*née?,* b. England, 1898–10 Jun 1950 [52?], No. Hollywood CA). m. **Walter Kingsford** (d. 1958). AS, p. 611.

Kingsford, Walter [actor] (b. Redhill, England, 20 Sep 1882–7 Feb 1958 [75], No. Hollywood CA). m. **Alison** (d. 1950). AS, p. 611.

Kingsley, Florida [actress] (b. Jacksonville FL, 1867?–19 Mar 1937 [70], Bay Shore, LI NY). m. Wright Huntingdon. (Goldwyn.) "Florida Kingsley," *Variety,* 24 Mar 1937. AS, p. 611. BHD, p. 219 (b. 1879). IFN, p. 165.

Kingsley, Pierce [producer/director/scenarist] (b. 1886?–30 Jun 1936 [50], near East Alton IL; auto accident.) "Killed in Crash," *Variety,* 8 Jul 1936. AMD, p. 195. AS, p. 611. BHD2, p. 145 (b. 1879–21 Feb 1935, Bayshore NY). "A Heavyweight Cast," *MPW,* 6 Apr 1912, 32.

Kingston, Natalie [actress: Wampas Star, 1927] (b. Sonoma CA, 19 May 1905–2 Feb 1991 [85?], West Hills CA). (Sennett; Paramount.) AMD, p. 195. AS, p. 611. BHD1, p. 303. FSS, p. 168. Katz, p. 657 (began 1924). Ragan 2, p. 891. Verne Kibbe, "The Smiling Venus; Like Other Famous Ex-Mack Sennetters, Natalie Kingston Longs for the Drama," *MPC,* Nov 1925, 50–51, 78–79. "Natalie Kingston," *MPW,* 28 May 1927, 268. "Very Natalie Attired; Miss Kingston's Costume Is Brief and Always to the Point," *MPC,* Nov 1928, 38–39.

Kingston, Samuel F. [casting/general manager for Fox] (b. Ireland, 1866?–17 Jun 1929 [63?]; meningitis). "Samuel F. Kingston," *Variety,* XCV, 19 Jun 1929, 68:4. AMD, p. 195. AS, p. 611. Samuel F. Kingston, "Casting for Pictures," *MPW,* 1 Jul 1917, 427.

Kingston, Winifred [stage/film actress] (b. London, England, 11 Nov 1894–3 Feb 1967 [72], La Jolla CA). m. **Dustin Farnum.** (Lasky; All-Star; Morosco; Fox.) "Winifred Kingston," *Variety,* 8 Feb 1967. AMD, p. 195. AS, p. 611. BHD, p. 219. BR, pp. 48–49. IFN, p. 165. Katz, p. 657. MSBB, p. 1038. Truitt, p. 183. "Special Engagement of Winifred Kingston," *MPW,* 25 Oct 1913, 387. "Winifred Kingston Joins Thanhouser," *MPW,* XXV, 21 Aug 1915, 1323. "Winifred Kingston," *MPW,* 18 Mar 1916, 1834. "Winifred Kingston to Play Opposite Dustin Farnum," *MPW,* 13 Jan 1917, 236. "Winifred Kingston," *MPW,* 10 Mar 1917, 1571.

Kinnel, Murray [actor] (b. London, England, 24 Jul 1889–11 Aug 1954 [65], Santa Barbara CA). AS, p. 611.

Kino, Goro [actor]. No data found. (Universal.)

Kinsella, Kathleen [actress] (*née* Kathleen Freeland, b. Liverpool, England, 1878?–25 Mar 1961 [83], Washington DC). (Biograph.) "Mrs. Kathleen Longheed Freeland," *Variety,* 29 Mar 1961. AS, pp. 611–12. BHD, p. 219. IFN, p. 165. Truitt, p. 184.

Kinsey, Arlene [actress] (b. 1891–30 Jan 1984 [92?]). BHD, p. 219.

Kinugasa, Teinosuke Kukame [actor/director/senarist] (b. Mie, Japan, 1 Jan 1896–26 Feb 1982 [86], Kyoto, Japan). AS, p. 612. BHD2, p. 145.

Kinz, Franziska Amalia [actress] (b. Kufstein, Austria, 21 Feb 1897–29 Apr 1980 [83], Merano, Italy). AS, p. 612.

Kionka, Helmuth [actor] (b. Germany-d. 4 Oct 1936, Berlin, Germany; condemned to death and executed). AS, p. 612.

Kipling, Richard [actor] (b. NY, 21 Aug 1879–11 Mar 1965 [85], Los Angeles Co. CA). AS, p. 612 (d. NY NY). BHD, p. 219. IFN, p. 165.

Kipling, Rudyard [writer/scenarist] (b. Bombay, India, 30 Dec 1865–18 Jan 1936 [70], London, England; five days after operation for a perforated stomach ulcer). m. Caroline Starr Balestier, 1892, NY. Philip Leibfried, *Rudyard Kipling and Sir Henry Rider Haggard on Screen, Stage, Radio and Television* (Jefferson NC: McFarland, 2000). (Nobel Prize, 1907.) "Rudyard Kipling Dies at Age of 70; Conscious at End; Wife and Daughter Are With Him at Death Resulting from Peritonitis After Operation; Rulers Showed Concern; Author's Works a Saga of the Glory of the Empire—Stirred Many Controversies," *NYT,* 18 Jan 1936, 1:4, 7:8; "Kipling a Champion of Imperial Glory; His Fame Is Expected to Rest on Vivid Tales of Britain in a Vast, Mysterious India; Stirred Many Disputes; 'Slight' to Victoria Closed the Laureateship to Him—Was 'Dated' in Recent Years," 18 Jan 1936, 7:1; "Mansfield Voices Praise of Kipling; He Was 'Best of the English Imperial Poets,' the British Laureate Says in the West; Walpole Adds Tribute; Novelist Extols Fellow-Author's Artistry, But Holds His Ideas Are 'Old-Fashioned' Now," 18 Jan 1936, 8:1. "Rudyard Kipling," *Variety,* 22 Jan 1936. AMD, p. 195. AS, p. 612. "Pathé Will Produce Kipling's Works; Author to Make His Own Adaptations," *MPW,* 16 Oct 1920, 915. "Kipling Enthuses Over Work for Pathé, Randolph Lewis Reports to Paul Bruner," *MPW,* 6 Nov 1920, 80. "Pathé Gets Kipling's First Scenario; Production Preliminaries All Prepared," *MPW,* 19 Feb 1921, 943. "Brunet Confers with Kipling, Who Will Continue to Write for Pathé," *MPW,* 30 Jul 1921, 488.

Kippen, Manart [actor] (b. 1894–12 Oct 1947 [53?], Claremore OK; auto accident). AS, p. 612.

Kirby, Audrew [actor]. No data found. (K&E.)

Kirby, David D. "Red" [actor] (b. St. Louis MO, 16 Jul 1880–4 Apr 1954 [73], Los Angeles CA). "David D. Kirby," *Variety,* 14 Apr 1954 (age 74; "pioneer screen actor"). AS, p. 612. BHD, p. 219 (b. 1883). IFN, p. 166 (b. 1883). Truitt, p. 184. George Katchmer, "Remembering the Great Silents," *CI,* 199 (Jan 1992), 12.

Kirby, Frank G[ordon] [actor] (aka Frank Kugler, b. Bremen, Germany, 1869?–22 Oct 1950 [81], Poughkeepsie NY). (Edison.) "Frank G. Kirby," *Variety,* 25 Oct 1950. AS, p. 612. BHD2, p. 145.

Kirby, George T. [actor] (b. London, England, 18 Feb 1879–2 Dec 1953 [74], Van Nuys CA). AS, p. 612.

Kirby, Madge [actress] (b. England). AMD, p. 195. WWS, p. 321. "Madge Kirby Engaged by Schlank," *MPW,* 24 Jan 1920, 616.

Kirby, Mae Elaine (b. Hillsdale County MI, 1881?–Oct? 1968 [87], Hillsdale MI). m. D.P. Dickinson (d. 1937). "Mae E. Kirby," *Variety,* 16 Oct 1968. AS, p. 612 (b. 1879).

Kirby, William W[arner] [lion tamer/

actor] (b. Germany, 4 Apr 1876–17 Apr 1914 [40], Los Angeles CA; clawed to death by a lioness from behind). "Killed in Picture Making," *Variety,* 24 Apr 1914, 20:2 ("William Warner Kirby has sacrificed his life for realism in photoplay activity. He died from blood poisoning due to wounds through being attacked by a maddened lion in a picture. The other players are in a panic." He was engaged to Lorena Lorenz, "The Girl in Red," who did a specialtiy of diving with a horse into a water tank.). "Lioness Kills Actor; Player at Universal Company's West Studio Fatally Hurt While Taking Picture," *NYDM,* 22 Apr 1914, 29:1. AS, p. 612. BHD, p. 219 (the lioness was shot).

Kirchhoff, Fritz [actor/director/scenarist] (b. Hanover, Germany, 10 Dec 1901–25 Jun 1953 [51], Hamburg, Germany). AS, p. 612.

Kirillov, Pjotr Klavdyevich [actor/director] (b. Russia, 17 May 1895–14 Jan 1942 [46], Russia). AS, p. 612.

Kirk, Ann [actress] (b. New York NY, 1894). (Essanay, Jul 1915). "Ann Kirk, Leads, Essanay," *MPN,* 21 Oct 1916, 168.

Kirk, Bertha W. [actress] (*nee?,* b. 1878?–9 Sep 1928 [50], Los Angeles CA; shot to death). "Murder and Suicide of Mrs. Kirk and Pepper," *Variety,* 12 Sep 1928 (age 45; Capt. Helsey James Pepper, age 54, shot himself to death). AS, p. 612. BHD, p. 219 (b. 1883). IFN, p. 166.

Kirk, Charles M. [art and set decorator] (b. PA, 16 May 1895–10 Dec 1969 [74], Los Angeles CA). BHD2, p. 145.

Kirk, Jack [actor] (*né* Jack Huff, b. 1895–3 Sep 1948 [53], Ketchican AK). AS, p. 612 (*né* Jack Kirkhuff). BHD1, p. 304. IFN, p. 166.

Kirk, James B. [publicist]. No data found. AMD, p. 195. "New Publicity Man at Warners," *MPW,* 11 Jul 1914, 279.

Kirkby, Ollie [actress] (b. Philadelphia PA, 26 Sep 1886–7 Oct 1964 [78], Glendale CA; pneumonia). m. **George Larkin**, 1918 (d. 1946). (Kalem, 1913.) AMD, p. 195. AS, p. 612 (Ollie Kirby). BHD, p. 219. IFN, p. 166. 1921 Directory, p. 227. "Ollie Kirby to Star with Larkin," *MPW,* 23 Sep 1916, 1985. Neil G. Caward, "Screen Gossip," *Picture-Play Magazine,* Sep 1917, 109 (after four years on the stage, she was to make films for George Backer films). "George Larkin Elopes with Ollie Kirby," *MPW,* 27 Apr 1918, 556.

Kirkham, Kathleen [stage/film actress] (b. Menominee MI, 15 Apr 1895–7 Nov 1961 [66], Santa Barbara CA; interred in Hollywood Cemetery). m. Harry N. Woodruff [LA insurance broker], ca. 1917. (Fine Arts; General; Morosco; Cline; American.) AMD, p. 195. AS, p. 613. BHD, pp. 45–46; 219. MH, p. 121. MSBB, p. 1038. WWS, p. 183. "Kathleen Kirkham," *MPW,* 12 May 1917, 971. "Kathleen Kirkham Engaged by American," *MPW,* 2 Jun 1917, 1475. "New Mutual Player," *MPW,* 23 Jun 1917, 1921. Neil G. Caward, "Screen Gossip," *Picture-Play Magazine,* Sep 1917, 110 (announced her recent marriage to Woodruff). Billy H. Doyle, "Lost Players," *CI,* 163 (Jan 1989), 30–31. George Katchmer, "Kathleen Kirkham," *CI,* 225 (Mar 1994), 44:1.

Kirkland, David S. [title writer/actor/director/producer] (*né* David Henry Swim, b. San Francisco CA, 26 Nov 1878–27 Oct 1964 [85], Los Angeles CA). m. Ann Page. AMD, p. 196. AS, p. 613. BHD, p. 219; BHD2, p. 145. FDY, p. 445. IFN, p. 166. "David Kirkland with Sterling," *MPW,* 20 Jun 1914, 1673. "Kirkland to Direct 'The Bachelor,'" *MPW,* 2 Aug 1919, 697. "David Kirkland Directed Holmes in New Metro Film," *MPW,* 3 Jan 1920, 130. "David Kirkland," *MPW,* 3 Sep 1927, 25.

Kirkland, Hardee [actor] (*né* Noble Rarda Kirkland, b. Savannah GA, 23 May 1866?–18 Feb 1929 [63], CA). "Hardee Kirkland," *Variety,* 6 Mar 1929 (b. England; d. 20 Feb; age 65). AMD, p. 196. AS, p. 613. BHD, p. 219 (b. 1868). IFN, p. 166. SD, p. 716 (b. 1868). Truitt, p. 18 (b. England). "Hardee Kirkland Joins Selig Staff," *MPW,* 21 Sep 1912, 1169.

Kirkland, Jack [playwright/scenarist/producer] (b. St. Louis MO, 1902?–22 Feb 1969 [66], New York NY; heart ailment). m. **Nancy Carroll** (d. 1965); Jayne Shadduck; Julia Laird; Haila Stoddard; Nancy Headley. "Jack Kirkland," *Variety,* 254, 26 Feb 1969, 79:1. AMD, p. 196. BHD2, p. 145. IFN, p. 166. "Personal Column," *Paris and Hollywood Screen Secrets Magazine,* May 1927, 8 (adapting the newspaper comic strip *Harold Teen* for the films). "Jack Kirkland," *MPW,* 22 Oct 1927, 496.

Kirkpatrick, Arthur S. [executive] (b. 14 Jan 1881–1934 [53]). BHD2, p. 145.

Kirkpatrick, Herbert [cinematographer]. No data found. FDY, p. 461.

Kirkwood, Jack [actor] (b. 6 Aug 1894–2 Aug 1964 [69], Las Vegas NV). AS, p. 613.

Kirkwood, James, Sr. [stage/film actor/director] (b. Grand Rapids MI, 22 Feb 1875–24 Aug 1963 [88], Woodland Hills CA). m. (1) **Gertrude Robinson**, 30 Sep 1916, Santa Barbara CA (d. 1962); (2) **Lila Lee** (d. 1973); Beatrice Power. (Biograph, 1909; Reliance; K&E; FP-L.) "James Kirkwood, Actor, Dead at 80; Hero of Silent Films Also Starred on the Stage," *NYT,* 25 Aug 1963, 82:7 (age 80). "James Kirkwood," *Variety,* 28 Aug 1963 (d. 21 Aug, age 80). AMD, p. 196. AS, p. 613. BHD1, p. 304; BHD2, p. 145. FFF, p. 188. FSS, p. 168. IFN, p. 166. Katz, pp. 658–59. MH, p. 121. Spehr, p. 146 (b. 1883). Truitt, p. 184 (b. 1883; d. 21 Aug). "Kirkwood Is Chosen; Heads Screen Club with Ben Wilson as VIce-President—Other Officers," *NYDM,* 7 Oct 1914, 25:4. "Kirkwood Screeners' President," *MPW,* 17 Oct 1914, 314 (The Screen Club, NY). "James Kirkwood," *Motion Picture Magazine,* Apr 1915, p. 112. "Briefs of Biography," *NYDM,* 7 Jul 1915, 39:1 (instrumental in getting Henry B. Walthall into films). "Kirkwood Joins American," *MPW,* 17 Jun 1916, 2047. "Kirkwood—Robinson," *MPW,* 21 Oct 1916, 412. "Kirkwood Writes on Scenarios," *MPW,* 11 Nov 1916, 876 (in 200 newspapers, 6-part series). "Kirkwood Comes Back to Famous Players," *MPW,* 22 Dec 1917, 1813. "Keeney Engages Kirkwood," *MPW,* 19 Jan 1918, 360. "Three Notable Directors Have Been Engaged by William Fox," *MPW,* 31 Mar 1923, 511. "Lee—Kirkwood," *MPW,* 18 Aug 1923, 548. "Kirkwood Badly Hurt," *MPW,* 8 Sep 1923, 131. "Kirkwood Improves," *MPW,* 15 Sep 1923, 233. "Hodkinson to Distribute Four Kirkwood-Lila Lee Features," *MPW,* 8 Dec 1923, 574. "F.P.L. Signs Kirkwood," *MPW,* 18 Oct 1924, 594.

Kirkwood, Ray [actor] (b. Dotter PA, 16 Jun 1893-Feb 1973 [79], Levittown NY). BHD, p. 219; BHD2, p. 145.

Kirkwood-Hackett, Eva [actress/singer] (b. England, 1877–9 Feb 1968 [90?], Dublin, Ireland). AS, p. 613.

Kirsanoff, Anatole Vladimirovich [director] (b. Moscow, Russia, 14 Jul 1902–2 May 1973 [70], Burbank CA). AS, p. 613.

Kirsanoff, Dimitri [director/scenarist] (*né* Mark David Kaplan, b. Dorpat, Estonia, 6 Mar 1899–11 Feb 1957 [57], Paris, France). AS, p. 613 (b. Russia). BHD2, p. 145.

Kirtley, Virginia [stage/film actress/scenarist] (*née* Virginia Saffell, b. Bowling Green MO, 11 Nov 1883–19 Aug 1956 [72], Sherman Oaks CA). m. **Eddie Lyons**, Aug 1917 (d. 1926). (Imp; Keystone; American, 1915; Selig; Centaur.) AMD, p. 196. AS, p. 613. BHD, p. 219; BHD2, p. 145. "Virginia Kirkley with Horsley," *MPW,* 11 Mar 1916, 1675. Billy H. Doyle, "Lost Players," *CI,* 173 (Nov 1989), 28.

Kisson, Dave [cameraman]. No data found. AMD, p. 196. "Marshall Neilan Engages Ingenue and Cameraman," *MPW,* 27 Dec 1919, 1131.

Kitchen, Dorothy *see* **Drexel, Nancy**

Kitchen, Fred [actor] (b. London, England, 15 Jun 1872–1 Apr 1951 [78], Hampton Hill, England). BHD1, p. 304.

Kitchen, H. Wilmer [scenarist]. No data found. FDY, p. 429.

Kithnou, Mlle. [actress]. No data found. AMD, p. 196. "Hindu Girl in Role," *MPW,* 6 Jun 1925, 672.

Klaffki, Roy H. [cinematographer] No data found. FDY, p. 461.

Klages, Raymond W. [songwriter] (b. Baltimore MD, 10 Jun 1888–20 Mar 1947 [58], sanitarium in Glendale CA; heart attack). m. May. "Raymond Klages," *NYT,* 22 Mar 1947, 13:6 (wrote lyrics for *Sally, Irene and Mary; Say When*). "Ray Klages," *Variety,* 26 Mar 1977 (wrote *Once in a Lifetime; Just You, Just Me; What Do I Care?*). ASCAP 66, p. 398. CEPMJ; Kinkle.

Klaren, Georg C. [director/scenarist] (*né* Georg Eugen Moritz Alexander Klaric, b. Vienna, Austria, 10 Sep 1900–18 Nov 1962 [62], Sawbridgeworth, England). AS, p. 614. BHD2, p. 146.

Klarke, Kerry [humorist/musical revue writer/gagman]. No data found. "Personal Column," *Paris and Hollywood Screen Secrets Magazine,* May 1927, 8.

Klaw, Marc [stage/film executive] (b. Paducah KY, 29 May 1858–14 Jun 1936 [78], Bracken Fell, Hassocks, Sussex, England). m. (1) Antoinette M. Morris; (2) Blanche V.D. Harris. Kemp R. Niver, *Klaw & Erlanger Present Famous Plays in Pictures,* ed. Bebe Bergsten (Los Angeles: John D. Roche, Inc., 1976). "Marc Klaw Dies in England at 78; Member of Noted Theatrical Firm of Klaw & Erlanger—Began Career as Lawyer; Retired Ten Years Ago; With Late A.L. Erlanger, Put Booking on Business Basis—Partnership Ended in 1919," *NYT,* 15 Jun 1936, 21:1. "Marc Klaw Dies in England at 78; Formerly Big Power in Show Biz," *Variety,* 17 Jun 1936. AS, p. 614. SD. T.B., "Marc Klaw; The 'K.' of K. & E.," *MPN,* 15 Nov 1913. "Stage Versus Screen; Merry War Between Theatrical Managers and Film Producers—Billie Burke Quits Frohman Company to Appear on Screen," *NYDM,* 21 Jul 1915, 9:1 ("...Klaw and Erlanger have adopted a plan whereby their players must obtain their permission if they wish to act on the screen. In cases where the permission is granted, Klaw and Erlanger may demand and receive half the money paid the actors by the film people. These conditions are said to be specified in all K.

and E. contracts." See Billie Burke and Joseph Brooks for more.). "Ask for Profits of Picture Play," *NYT,* 10 Feb 1915, 11:2 (Klaw & Erlanger and Robert Hilliard sued the General Film Co. for "an accounting of all the moneys made from a picture play entitled "A Fool There Was.' The plaintiffs had claimed the title of the photoplay, and a preliminary injunction restraining the defendants from using it had been issued. Decision was reserved.").

Klein, Al [actor] (b. New York NY, 1885–5 Sep 1951 [66?], Los Angeles CA). AS, p. 614.

Klein, Charles Jules Michel Alphonse [cinematographer] (b. Avignon, France, 13 Jan 1869–13 Feb 1904 [35], Marseilles, France). AS, p. 614.

Klein, Charles (brother of **Mnuel Klein**; father of **Philip Klein**) [director/scenarist] (*né* Friedrich Carl Klein, b. Namedy, Germany, 29 Jan 1878–1912 [34?], on the *Lusitania*). AS, p. 614.

Klein, Estelle ("Ma" Green) [vaudevillian/actress] (*née?,* b. 1874?–15 Jul 1946 [72], New York NY). m. Ed Klein (d. 1921). "Estelle Klein," *Variety,* 10 Jul 1946. AS, p. 614.

Klein, Harry [cinematographer]. No data found. FDY, p. 461.

Klein, Julius [actor] (b. Hungary, 20 Nov 1885–16 Jul 1966 [80], Los Angeles CA). AS, p. 614. BHD1, p. 305.

Klein, Manuel (brother of drammatist **Charles Klein**) [composer] (b. Namedy, Germany, 6 Dec 1876–1 Jun 1919 [42], Yonkers NY; result of being struck by a bomb in London in 1918). "Manuel Klein," *Variety,* 6 Jun 1919. "Death of Manuel Klein; Brother of Lusitania Victim Suffered in London Zeppelin Raids," *NYT,* 2 Jun 1919, 15:6. "Manuel Klein Writes Music for All-Star," *MPW,* 31 Jan 1914, 556. AS, p. 614 (b. Germany). ASCAP 66, pp. 399–400. Kurt Gänzl, *The Encyclopedia of the Musical Theatre,* Vol. I (NY: Schirmer Books, 1994).

Klein, Philip (son of drammatist **Charles Klein**) [actor/scenarist] (b. New York NY, 24 Apr 1889–8 Jun 1935 [46], Los Angeles CA; pneumonia). "Philip Klein," *Variety,* 12 Jun 1935 ("...he went to Hollywood in 1924 and turned his attention to scenario work."). AMD, p. 196. AS, p. 614 (b. Germany). BHD2, p. 146. FDY, p. 429. "Fox Signs Philip Klein," *MPW,* 26 Mar 1927, 266. "Klein Signed," *MPW,* 2 Apr 1927, 487.

Klein, Robert [actor] (b. Paris, France, 16 May 1880–21 Dec 1960 [80], Los Angeles Co. CA). AS, p. 614. BHD1, p. 305. IFN, p. 166. George Katchmer, "Remembering the Great Silents," *CI,* 196 (Oct 1991), 56.

Kleindenst, Harry [executive] (b. 1892–20 Nov 1959 [67?], New York NY). BHD2, p. 146.

Kleine, Charles [writer]. No data found. AMD, p. 196. "Lubin Gets Klein Plays," *MPW,* 8 Feb 1913, 552.

Kleine, George [Vice-President of General Film Co., Apr 1910-May 1913/producer/manufacturer] (b, 1864–8 Jun 1931 [67?], Los Angeles CA). (Kleine Opitcal Co., Chicago IL.) "George Kleine," *Variety,* 16 Jun 1931. AMD, p. 196. BHD2, p. 146 (d. NY NY). "Copy of Mr. Klein's Letter to the Chicago Tribune," *MPW,* 20 Apr 1907, 101–02. "Trade Notes," *MPW,* 4 May 1907, 136. "Kalem Company (Inc.)," *MPW,* 8 Jun 1907, 223. George Kleine, "Position of the Kleine Optical Co.," *MPW,* 7 Mar 1908, 182. "Statement by Mr. George Kleine," *MPW,* 14 Mar 1908, 205–06. "George Kleine Replies to Critics," *MPW,* 4 Apr 1908, 288–89. "Edison Manufacturing Company vs. Kleine Optical Company and George Kleine," *MPW,* 11 Apr 1908, 314–16. "Letter from George Kleine," *MPW,* 13 Feb 1909, 170–71. "Photoplay," *MPW,* 15 Oct 1910, 858. "Kleine to Release Cines Pictures," *MPW,* 6 Jan 1912, 26. James S. McQuade, "Pursuing the Pirates," *MPW,* 26 Oct 1912, 332–33 (re copyrighting). "How Big Companies Fight Illegitimate Competition," *MPW,* 23 Aug 1913, 825. "Kleine After Pirates," *MPW,* 11 Oct 1913, 163. "Kleine Builds Studio in Italy," *MPW,* 27 Dec 1913, 1532. "George Kleine Wants American Artists," *MPW,* 27 Dec 1913, 1558. "George Kleine Returns," *MPW,* 21 Feb 1914, 929. J.S. McQuade, "Chicago Letter," *MPW,* 28 Feb 1914, 1092. "George Kleine," *NYDM,* 15 Jul 1914, 28:1 (imported *Quo Vadis?* from Italy in 1913). "The Making of 'Julius Caesar,'" *MPW,* 26 Dec 1914, 1827. "Kleine Italian Studio; New Studio Near Turin Said to Be a Model of Construction and Beauty," *NYDM,* 12 May 1915, 24:3 (about five miles from Turin, covering ten acres). J.S. McQuade, "Kleine—Edison Merger Formed," *MPW,* 24 Jul 1915, 626–27. W. Stephen Bush, "George Kleine Talks," *MPW,* 20 Nov 1915, 1456–57. "Kleine, General Film President," *MPW,* 5 Feb 1916, 752. W.S. Bush, "Kleine Exalts Quality," *MPW,* 25 Mar 1916, 1984–85. "Kleine Enthusiastic Over 1917 Outlook," *MPW,* 30 Dec 1916, 1940. J.S. McQuade, "George Kleine Talks on the Trade Outlook," *MPW,* 13 Jan 1917, 214. George Kleine, "Advance Deposits to Guarantee Film Contracts," *MPW,* 3 Feb 1917, 671–72. George Kleine, "Big Profits Ten Years Ago," *MPW,* 10 Mar 1917, 1511. "Congratulations Coming to Kleine," *MPW,* 14 Jul 1917, 243. "Perfection Pictures Announces Plans," *MPW,* 29 Sep 1917, 1977–78. "Discussing the Situation," *MPW,* 16 Nov 1918, 733. "George Kleine to Produce," *MPW,* 19 Jul 1919, 349. J.S. McQuade, "Kleine Names Business Associates," *MPW,* 15 Nov 1919, 341. "George Kleine Becomes Treasurer of Ritz Pictures," *MPW,* 25 Aug 1923, 633.

Klein-Rogge, Rudolf [actor] (*né* Friedrich Rudolf Klein-Rogge, b. Cologne, Germany, 24 Nov 1888–30 Apr 1955 [66], Graz, Styria, Austria). m. Thea von Harbou; Mary Johnson. (Decla-Bioscop.) (Film debut: *The Cabinet of Dr. Caligari,* 1919.) AS, p. 614 (b. 1889). BHD1, p. 305. IFN, p. 166. Oscar G. Estes, Jr., "Rudolf Klein-Rogge; The German Chaney," *CFC,* 32 (Fall, 1971), 22–23, 42 (includes filmography).

Kleinschmidt, Captain Frank E. [producer]. No data found. AMD, p. 197. W. Stephen Bush, "The Camera in the Arctics," *MPW,* XIX, 14 Mar 1914, 1387. "Captain Kleinschmidt Off to Mexico," *MPW,* 16 May 1914, 970. "Captian Frank E. Kleinschmidt," *MPW,* 24 Apr 1915, 561. W.S. Bush, "Genuine War Films," *MPW,* 14 Aug 1915, 1134–35. "Capt. Kleinschmidt Now at Italian Front," *MPW,* 1 Jan 1916, 54. "Capt. Kleinschmidt Back from Europe," *MPW,* 11 Mar 1916, 1658. W.S. Bush, "War Pictures on Three Fronts," *MPW,* 1 Apr 1916, 65–65. "Captain Kleinschmidt Under Surveillance," *MPW,* 8 Dec 1917, 1503. "Capt. Kleinschmidt Now Returning from Alaska," *MPW,* 27 Nov 1920, 498.

Klempner, John [scenarist] (b. New York NY, 1898–30 Jul 1972 [74?], Redondo Beach CA). AS, p. 615.

Klendon, Jack [actor] (*né* Courtland J. Townsend, b. 1887–11 Apr 1952 [74?], Beacon NY). AS, p. 615.

Klercker, Georg Af [actor/scenarist/director] (b. Kristianstad, Sweden, 1877–1951 [74?]). AS, p. 615 (d. 1954). BHD2, p. 146.

Kley, Fred [executive] (b. Baltimore MD, 14 Aug 1885–14 Mar 1944 [58], Los Angeles CA). BHD, p. 219; BHD2, p. 146.

Kliegl, Anton (brother of **John H. Kliegl**) [inventor] (d. May 1927, Bad Kissingen, Bavaria, Germany). "Anton Kliegl Left Estate of $305,756; Widow of Stage Light Expert Sole Beneficiary—Stocks Form Bulk of Holdings; Huber Property Valued; Wife of Brewer's Son Left $506,343, Including $250,000 Necklace—Husband Gets Residue," *NYT,* 1 Dec 1928, 9:4 (d. May 1927).

Kliegl, John H. (brother of **Anton Kliegl**) [inventor] (b. Bad Kissingen, Bavaria, 1870?–30 Sep 1959 [89], New York NY [Death Certificate Index No. 21319]). "John H. Kliegl, 89, Made Klieg Lights [1911]; Co-Developer of Indoor Movie Unit Dead—Built War Projector System," *NYT,* 1 Oct 1959, 35:5 (states that Anton Kliegl died in 1928). "John H. Kliegl," *Variety,* 7 Oct 1959. AS, p. 615. "Kliegle [sic] Studio Lights; Company Equips Thanhouser and Eclair Plants [at Ft. Lee NJ] with New Arc Lamps," *NYDM,* 18 Mar 1914, 30:2. "Kleigl [sic] on European Trip," *NYDM,* 3 Jun 1914, 32:2 (on yearly trip to investigate "progress in stage and studio lighting" in Europe). Dorothy Donnell, "'Out, Damned Spot!'; Discusses the Scourge of the Movies, Kleig [sic] Eyes," *Classic,* May 1924, 14–16, 85.

Kline, Benjamin H. [cinematographer] (b. Birmingham AL, 11 Jul 1894–7 Jan 1974 [79], Los Angeles CA). (Fox [NY], 1914; Universal; Columbia.) "Ben Kline," *Variety,* 16 Jan 1974. AS, p. 615. BHD, p. 219; BHD2, p. 146. FDY, p. 461. IFN, p. 166.

Kline, Virginia [actress/scenarist] (b. 1881–16 Mar 1951 [70?], Commack IL). AS, p. 615.

Kline, Wilbur [cinematographer]. No data found. FDY, p. 461.

Kling, Saxon [actor] (b. 1892–29 Jul 1940 [48?], Marion OH). BHD, p. 219.

Klinger, Werner [actor/scenarist/director] (b. Stuttgart, Germany, 23 Oct 1903–23 Jun 1972 [68], Berlin, Germany). AS, p. 615 (b. 1900). BHD1, p. 305; BHD2, p. 146.

Klintberg, Gunnar [actor/director] (b. Sweden, 1870–1936 [66?], Sweden). AS, p. 615.

Klitzsch, Edgar [actor] (b. 11 Jul 1887–15 Sep 1955 [68]). BHD, p. 219; BHD2, p. 146.

Klopfer, Eugen Gottlob [actor] (b. Rauhenstichtalheim, Germany, 10 Mar 1886–3 Mar 1950 [63], Wiesbaden, Germany). AS, p. 615. BHD1, p. 305. IFN, p. 166.

Klotz, Florence [actress/costume designer] (*née* Kathrina E. Klotz, b. Brooklyn NY, 3 Dec 1901 [Birth Certificate Index No. 3906]). AMD, p. 197. AS, p. 615. WWIT 17, p. 397. "A Talented Child Artiste," *MPS,* 22 Feb 1913, 786.

Kluppell, Kitty [actress] (b. Holland, 1897–13 Oct 1982 [85?]). BHD, p. 219.

Knabb, Harry G. [actor] (b. 1891?–17 Dec 1955 [64], Cincinnati OH; heart attack). m. Margaret Bagnell. "Harry G. Knabb," *Variety,* 21 Dec 1955 (with a company in Wilkes-Barre PA). AS, p. 615 (b. 1901). BHD, p. 219. IFN, p. 166. Truitt, p. 184.

Knabenshue, Roy [actor] (b. 1876–6 Mar 1960 [83?], Los Angeles CA). BHD, p. 219.

Kneblova, Emma [actress] (d. Aug 1931, Prague, Czechoslovakia). BHD1, p. 305.

Knechtel, Alvin [cinematographer] (b. Ontario, Canada, 1901?–17 Jul 1929 [28], Los Angeles CA). (Pathé; First National.) m. Lillian Jane. "Alvin Knechtel," *Variety,* 24 Jul 1929. AS, p. 616. BHD2, p. 146. FDY, p. 461.

Knechtel, Lloyd [cinematographer] (b. Southampton, Ontario, Canada, 1 Jul 1907–22 Jun 1971 [63], Long Beach CA). BHD2, p. 146.

Knight, Charlott [actress/scenarist] (b. 1894–16 May 1977 [83?], Los Angeles CA). AS, p. 616. BHD2, p. 146.

Knight, Eric [scenarist] (b. Ilkley Moor, England, 10 Apr 1897-Jan 1943 [45], at sea). BHD2, p. 146.

Knight, Esmond [actor] (b. East Sheen, England, 4 May 1906–23 Feb 1987 [80], Egypt). BHD1, p. 305.

Knight, Harry [director] (b. 1895–30 Jan 1945 [49?], Los Angeles CA). BHD2, p. 146.

Knight, Henry K. "Hank" [extra actor] (b. 1847?–21 Apr 1930 [83], Los Angeles CA). AS, p. 616. BHD, p. 220. IFN, p. 166. Francis Gilmore, "He Knew the West When It Was Wild; Hank Knight Is Hollywood's Oldest Extra," *MPC,* Jun 1928, 63, 89 ("'Oh, *moving pictures,'* Hank Knight says, 'they're well enough when a man's eighty-two and can't do anything else.'").

Knight, James [stage/film actor] (b. Canterbury, England, 4 May 1891-ca. Apr 1947 [55?]). (Harma Co.) AS, p. 616. BHD1, p. 305. "A Hero's Many Expressions; James Knight; A British Actor who is endowed by nature with the Face and Figure of a Hero," *The Picture Show,* No. 11, 12 Jul 1919, 17 (...he does more than play his parts [on the screen]—he lives them—and, although still young, he has earned the right to be called 'A Father of the British Cinema.'").

Knight, Joe [actor]. No data found. (Ince.) "Joe Knight Trains a Substitute," *Photoplay,* Jul 1917, 98 (photo of Knight showing little Thelma Salter how to shoot a gun).

Knight, Lillian [actress] (b. 1881?–16 May 1946 [65], Pomona CA. BHD, p. 220. IFN, p. 166.

Knight, Percival [actor] (b. England, 1873?–27 Nov 1923 [50], Montreux, Switzerland; tuberculosis). "Percival Knight," *Variety,* 6 Dec 1923. AS, p. 616. BHD, p. 220 (b. Scotland). IFN, p. 166. Truitt, p. 185.

Knighton, Percy [actor] (b. Cismont VA, 14 May 1898–1 Jun 1971 [73], Little Rock AR). BHD, p. 220; BHD2, p. 147.

Knipper-Tschechowa, Olga [actress] (b. Glazov, Russia, 1870–22 Mar 1959 [89?], Moscow, Russia). BHD1, p. 305.

Knoblock, Edward [actor/playwright/scenarist] (*né* Edward Knoblauch, b. New York NY, 7 Apr 1874–19 Jul 1945 [71], London, England). *Round the Room* (1939). "E. Knoblock Dead; 'Kismet' [1911] Author, 71; One of Leading Playwrights in Britain Was Born Here—Scenarist of Fairbanks Films," *NYT,* 20 Jul 1945, 19:4. "Edward Knoblock," *Variety,* 25 Jul 1945 ("He...went to Hollywood, where he adapted for the screen 'Thief of Bagdad' for the late Douglas Fairbanks and 'Three Musketeers.'"; second most prolific playwright, after Owen Davis). AMD, p. 197. AS, p. 616. BHD2, p. 147. SD, p. 721.. Waldman, p. 153. William J. Reilly, "Edward Knoblock Starts form Scratch," *MPW,* 23 Oct 1920, 1079. "Edward Knoblock Named by Fairbanks to Write Screen Version of Dumas' Great Novel, 'The Three Musketeers,'" *MPW,* 26 Feb 1921, 1082.

Knoles, Harley [scenarist/director/producer] (b. Rotherham, England, 1880–6 Jun 1936 [56?], London, England). m. Rosina Henley. AMD, p. 197. AS, p. 616. BHD1, p. 612; BHD2, p. 147. IFN, p. 167. "Harley Knoles Walks into Acid," *MPW,* 2 Mar 1918, 1213 (accident on 17 Feb 1918). "Harley Knoles Renews World Contract," *MPW,* 30 Mar 1918, 1807. "Knoles to Direct Dorothy Dalton," *MPW,* 10 Jan 1920, 277. "Knoles Signs with Famous Players," *MPW,* 17 Jan 1920, 403. "Harley Knoles Honor Guest at Dinner Given to Speed Him Along to Big Job," *MPW,* 3 Jul 1920, 66. "A Little Girl Knoles," *MPW,* 27 Jan 1923, 320 (daughter b. 9 Jan 1923).

Knott, Clara [actress] (b. IN, 19 Jan 1871–11 Nov 1926 [55], Los Angeles CA). "Clara Knott," *Variety,* 17 Nov 1926 (age 44). AS, p. 616. BHD, p. 220. IFN, p. 167. Truitt, p. 185.

Knott, Ethelbert [actor] (*né* Adelbert Del Knott, 1858–3 May 1933 [75?], Los Angeles CA; from injuries after a fall). AS, p. 616. BHD, p. 220. Ragan 2, p. 701.

Knott, Else [actress] (b. Germany, 1872–10 Aug 1975 [103?], Frankfort, Germany; cancer). AS, p. 616.

Knott, Lydia [actress] (b. Tyner IN, 1 Oct 1866–30 Mar 1955 [88], Woodland Hills CA). AS, p. 617. BHD1, p. 306. IFN, p. 167.

Knowland, Alice [stage/film actress] (b. Ft. Fairfield ME, 6 Oct 1879–27 May 1930 [51], Los Angeles CA). (Eclair, Tucson AZ company.) AS, p. 617. BHD, p. 220. IFN, p. 167. Truitt, 1983. "Gossip of the Studios," *NYDM,* 9 Sep 1914, 27:1.

Knowles, Harry [actor] (b. 1878?–29 Feb 1936 [58], Kansas City KS). "Harry Knowles," *Variety,* 4 Mar 1936. AS, p. 617.

Knowles, J. Harry [actor] (b. England-d. Sep 1923, Orange FL). BHD, p. 220.

Knowles, Priscilla [actress] (b. 1886–15 Jul 1936 [50?], New York NY). AS, p. 617.

Knowles, R[ichard] **G**[eorge] [actor] (b. Hamilton, Canada, 7 Oct 1858–1 Jan 1919 [60], London, England). BHD, p. 220.

Knox, Hugh B. [stage/film actor/director] (*né* Hugo B. Koch, b. Chicago IL, 1881–9 Sep 1926 [45?], Seattle WA). m. stock actress Marie Dunkel. (Matinée idol in Chicago stock; assistant to Cecil B. DeMille.) "Hugh Knox," *Variety,* 15 Sep 1926, 57:2 (age 43: illegible on microfilm); 22 Sep 1926, 48:3. AS, p. 617. BHD, p. 220; BHD2, p. 147.

Knox, Teddy [actor] (b. Gateshead-on-Tyne, England,12 Jul 1894–1 Dec 1974 [80], Devon, England). AS, p. 617. BHD1, p. 306. IFN, p. 167 (age 78).

Kobayashi, Ichizo [executive] (b. Kofu, Japan, 3 Jan 1873–25 Jan 1960 [87], Osaka, Japan). AS, p. 617 (d. 1957). BHD2, p. 147.

Kobliansky, Nicholas V. [actor/technical director] (b. Russia, 15 Dec 1888–6 Nov 1976 [87], Monrovia CA). BHD2, p. 147.

Kobs, Alfred [actor] (b. Germany, 1881–20 Oct 1929 [48?], Los Angeles CA; tuberculosis). AS, p. 617. BHD, p. 220.

Koch, Carl [actor] (b. Numbrecht, Germany, 1892–1962 [70?], Germany). AS, p. 617.

Koch, Franz "Frany" [cinematographer] (b. 1898–28 Apr 1959 [61?], Munich, Germany; stomach infection). AS, p. 617. BHD2, p. 147.

Koenekamp, Hans F. [cinematographer] (father of Fred Koenekamp) (b. Denison IA, 3 Dec 1891–12 Sep 1992 [100], Northridge CA). (Sennett, 1913; Fox; Vitagraph; WB.) Joseph McBride, "Hans F. Koenekamp," *Variety,* 21 Sep 1992, p. 99. AS, p. 617. BHD2, p. 147. FDY, p. 461.

Koerner, Hermine [stage/film actress/musician] (b. 1882–14 Dec 1960 [78], Vienna, Austria; pneumonia with heart complications). "Hermine Koerner," *Variety,* 221, 28 Dec 1960, 55:1. BHD1, p. 306. IFN, p. 167.

Kohler, Fred, Sr. (father of Fred Kohler, Jr.) [actor] (b. Dubuque IA, 21 Apr 1888–28 Oct 1938 [50], Los Angeles CA). m. actress Marjorie Prole. "Fred Kohler, Actor, Dies in His Sleep; Veteran 'Bad Man' of Films Had Played in Many Pictures," *NYT,* 29 Oct 1938, 19:3. "Fred Kohler, Sr.," *Variety,* 2 Nov 1938. AMD, p. 197. AS, p. 618. BHD1, p. 305 (b. 1889). FSS, p. 169. GK, pp. 163–92. IFN, p. 167. Katz, p. 664 (b. Kansas City MO, 20 Apr 1889). "Fred Kohler," *MPW,* 6 Aug 1927, 383. Walter Ramsey, "The Worser the Better; Fred Kohler Enjoys Knocking the Hero Cold. And His Fans Enjoy Seeing Him," *MPX,* Apr 1929, 57, 83. George Katchmer, "Remembering the Great Silents," *CI,* 239 (May 1995), 53–54.

Kohler, Henry Noel [cinematographer] (b. 1890?–6 Aug 1936 [46], Santa Monica CA). "Henry Kohler," *Variety,* 12 Aug 1936 (cameraman for Harold Lloyd for 15 years). AS, p. 618. BHD2, p. 147.

Kohlmar, Lee [actor/director] (b. Nuremberg, Germany, 27 Feb 1873–14 May 1946 [73], No. Hollywood CA; heart attack). (Universal.) "Lee Kohlmar," *Variety,* 22 May 1946 (age 74). AMD, p. 197. AS, p. 618. BHD1, p. 306 (b. Fürth, Germany). IFN, p. 167 (b. Forth, Germany). Truitt, p. 185 (b. 1878). "Universal Signs Character Comedian for Comedy Series," *MPW,* 15 May 1920, 961. "Gladys Walton Working Under Kohmar Direction," *MPW,* L, 4 Jun 1921, 522.

Kohn, Ben G[rauman] [title writer/scenarist]. No data found. FDY, pp. 445, 491.

Kohn, Marion H. [executive]. No data found. Grace Kingsley, "Flashes; New Film Concern," *LA Times,* 12 Mar 1920, III, p. 4 (set up Marion H. Kohn Prods. at the National studio, using actors Grace Cunard, Polly Moran, and "Smiling" Bill Jones. To produce "dramas, comedies and two-reel featurettes.").

Kohn, Morris [executive] (b. 1864–20 Feb 1935 [70?], Nanuet NY). AMD, p. 197. BHD2, p. 147. "Morris Kohn Succeeds Arthur Kane as President of Realart Pictures," *MPW,* 10 Jan 1920, 262. Morris Kohn, "Confidence of Showmen Makes Possible Star Franchise and Increased Production—Kohn," *MPW,* 10 Jul 1920, 231. Morris Kohn, "Morris Kohn, of Realart, Says 1921 Is to Be a Banner Year for His Company," *MPW,* 25 Dec 1920, 1015.

Kohner, Paul (father of Susan Kohner) [scenarist/producer/talent agent] (b. Toplice-Sanov, now Czechoslovakia, 29 May 1902–16 Mar 1988 [85], Los Angeles CA; heart failure). AMD, p. 197. BHD2, p. 147. FDY, p. 491. "Kohner to Direct," *MPW,* 26 May 1923, 333.

Kokeny, Ilona [actress] (b. Bulgaria, 1891–17 Dec 1947 [56?], Bulgaria). AS, p. 618.

Kolb, Clarence William [actor] (b. Cleveland, OH, 31 Jul 1874–25 Nov 1964 [90], Los Angeles CA; pulmonary embolism). m. May Cloy, 1 Sep 1917, San Francisco CA; Mabel Sarah Larsen. (Film debut: *Glory,* 1917.) "Clarence Kolb," *Variety,* 2 Dec 1964. AS, p. 618. BHD1, p. 306. IFN, p. 167. Katz, p. 664. Truitt, p. 185. "Marriages," *Variety,* 7 Sep 1917, p. 8.

Kolb, Jean [actor] (*né* Sylvain Kolb, b. Lyon, France, 27 Nov 1880 [extrait de naissance no. 2448]-20 Jul 1959 [78], Letrait, France). AS, p. 618.

Kolb, John Philip [actor]. No data found. AMD, p. 197. "Richard A. Rowland Gives Two 'Unknowns' a Chance," *MPW,* 18 Jul 1925, 344. (Note: may be the same as the next entry.)

Kolb, John W. [stage/film actor] (b. Baltimore MD, 1860?–16 Feb 1943 [83], New York NY). "John W. Kolb, 83, Old-Time Minstrel; Known on Stage as Wm. Gray—With Primrose and West," *NYT,* 18 Feb 1943, 23:4. AS, p. 618.

Kolb, Marie Thérèse [actress] (b. Altkirch, France, 19 Jan 1856–19 Aug 1935 [79], Levallois-Perret, France). AS, p. 618. BHD1, p. 306 (d. Paris). IFN, p. 167.

Kolima, William [director]. No data found. AMD, p. 197. "Kolima to England," *MPW,* 23 Apr 1927, 702.

Kolin, Nicholas [actor] (b. Russia, 1878-d. ca. 1954 [66?]). BHD1, p. 306.

Kolker, Henry [stage/film actor/director] (b. Quincy IL, 13 Nov 1870–15 Jul 1947 [76], Los Angeles CA; from injuries sustained in a fall). m. Margaret Bruenn. "Henry Kolker, Star of Stage and Screen," *NYT,* 18 Jul 1947, 17:3. "Henry Kolker," *Variety,* 23 Jul 1947. AMD, p. 197. AS, p. 618. BHD1, p. 306; BHD2, p. 147. IFN, p. 167. 1921 Directory, p. 268. SD. Truitt, pp. 185–86 (b. Germany, 1874). "And Still They Come; Metro Secures Services of More Stage Luminaries and Adds to Plays," *NYDM,* 30 Jun 1915, 24:1. "Henry Kolker," *MPW,* 5 Aug 1916, 930. "Kolker Becomes Pupil of Capellani," *MPW,* 29 Jun 1918, 1859. "Hickman Ill with Pneumonia," *MPW,* 21 Jun 1919, 1776. "Henry Kolker to Direct for Selznick in Eastern Studios," *MPW,* 10 Jul 1920, 194. "Henry Kolker Directing Arliss in film Version of 'Disraeli,'" *MPW,* 2 Jul 1921, 66. "Kolker Leaves to Produce in Italy; F. Marion Crawford Stories Bought," *MPW,* 12 Nov 1921, 168.

Koller, Hermine [actress] (b. Germany-d. Mar 1920, Geneva, Switzerland). BHD, p. 220.

Kolster, Clarence [film editor] (b. 6 Sep 1900–6 May 1972 [71], Santa Monica CA; after abdominal surgery). "Clarence Kolster," *Variety,* 14 Jun 1972 (cutter in 1921). BHD2, p. 147.

Komai, Tetsu [actor] (*né* Tetsuo Komai, b. Kumamoto, Japan, 23 Apr 1894–10 Aug 1970 [76], Gardena CA; congestive heart failure). AS, p. 619. BHD1, p. 307. IFN, p. 167. Truitt, 1983.

Komarov, Sergei Petrovich [actor/director] (b. Moscow, Russia, 17 Apr 1891–23 Dec 1957 [66], St. Petersburg, Russia). AS, p. 619.

Konstam, Phyllis [stage/film actress/director/scenarist] (*née* Phyllis Kohnstamm, b. London, England, 14 Apr 1907–20 Aug 1976 [69], Stoke, St. Gregory, Somerset County, England). (Broadway debut: *Murder on the Second Floor,* 1928: also debut of Laurence Olivier.) "Phyllis Konstam," *Variety,* 284, 1 Sep 1976, 78:5. AS, p. 619. BHD1, p. 307 (d. Stoke St. Gregory, England). IFN, p. 167.

Konstantin, Leopoldine Eugenie Amelie [stage/film/TV actress] (b. Brno, Czechoslovakia, 12 Mar 1886–14 Dec 1965 [79], Vienna, Austria). AS, p. 619 (b. Moravia; d. Hitzing, Austria). BHD1, p. 307. Waldman, p. 155. Vittorio Martinelli, "Kino-Lieblinge," *Griffithiana,* 38/39 (Oct 1990), 17 (played the wicked poisoner in *Notorius*).

Koonen, Alisa Georgievna [actress] (b. St. Petersburg, Russia, 14 Sep 1889–3 May 1974 [84], Moscow, Russia). AS, p. 619.

Kopfstein, Jacques [writer/publicist/general manager] (b. Elmira NY, 25 Jul 1891–11 Jun 1957 [65], New York NY). AMD, p. 197. BHD2, p. 148. "Scenario for 'Anyman''s Wife' Almost Completed," *MPW,* 8 Apr 1916, 235. "Kopfstein Denies Pacemaker Is a Subsidiary," *MPW,* 29 Apr 1916, 809. "Kopfstein Joins B.S. Moss," *MPW,* 21 Oct 1916, 374.

Kopp, Erwin [actor] (b. Berlin, Germany, 3 Jul 1877–24 Apr 1928 [50]). BHD, p. 220. IFN, p. 167.

Korayim, Mohamed [director/actor/film editor/producer] (aka Mohamed Karim, b. Egypt, 1898–27 May 1972 [74], Cairo, Egypt). (First silent as producer: *Zinab.*) "Mohamed Korayim," *Variety,* 267, 14 Jun 1972, 70:5; 267, 21 Jun 1972, 71:3 ("He was the first Egyptian to direct a musical, *The White Rose*). BHD, p. 220; BHD2, p. 148. IFN, p. 167.

Korda, Alexander (brother of Vincent and Zoltan Korda) [director/producer] (*né* Sandor Laszlo Kordor, b. Pusztaturpaszlo, near Turkeve, Hungary, 16 Sep 1893–23 Jan 1956 [62], Kensington Gardens, London, England; heart attack). m. (1) **Marae Farkas** (Maria Corda), Hungarian film actress, 1919–29; (2) Merle Oberon, 1939–45; (3) Alexandra Irene Boycun, 1953. (Began 1915; Ufa; Paramount at Joinville.) "Korda Dies at 62; Movie Producer; Made 112 Pictures Including 'Henry VIII,' 'That Hamilton Woman' and 'Third Man'; 'Richard III' Due Here; Sir Alexander Raised British Standards, Brought Actors to Stardom, Aided in War," *NYT,* 24 Jan 1956, 31:1. "Sir Alexander Korda," *Variety,* 25 Jan 1956. AMD, p. 197. AS, p. 620. BHD2, p. 148. FDY, p. 491. IFN, p. 167. Waldman, p. 155. "Prominent German Director Signed by First National," *MPW,* 17 Apr 1926, 507. "Rowland Returns with Noted European Stars," *MPW,* 20 Nov 1926, 150. "Korda Will Direct," *MPW,* 16 Jul 1927, 156. "Alexander Korda," *MPW,* 8 Oct 1927, 358.

Korda, Vincent (brother of **Alexander** and **Zoltan Korda**) [art director] (b. [Pusztaturpaszlo?] Turkeve, Hungary, 1897–4 Jan 1979 [81], London, England). BHD2, p. 148. IFN, p. 167. Waldman, p. 155.

Korda, Zoltan (brother of **Alexander** and **Vincent Korda**) [producer/director] (b. [Pusztaturpaszlo?] Turkeve, Hungary, 3 May 1895–14 Oct 1961 [66], Beverly Hills CA). m. actress Joan Gardner (b. 26 Oct 1914). (London Films, Ltd.; Ufa; Fox.) "Zoltan Korda," *Variety,* 234, 18 Oct 1961, 71:1. AS, p. 620 (d. 13 Oct). BHD2, p. 148. IFN, p. 167 (d. 14 Oct). Waldman, p. 155.

Kordyoun, Arnold [director] (b. Ukeaine, 13 Jul 1890–26 Aug 1969 [79], Russia). AS, p. 620.

Korff, Arnold [stage/film/radio actor] (b. Vienna, Austria, 2 Aug 1870–2 Jun 1944 [73], New York NY; heart ailment). m. Amy Bauer, 1915. (Stage debut, Imperial Theatre Co., Vienna, 1897.) "Arnold Korff," *Variety,* 154, 7 Jun 1944, 46:1. BHD1, p. 307. IFN, p. 167.

Korhonen, Aku [actor] (*né* August Aleksander Korhonen, b. Kalisalmi, Finland, 29 Dec 1892–5 Sep 1960 [67], Helsinki, Finland). AS, p. 620.

Korlin, Boris [pseudonym of **Boris Karloff**).

Kornai, Richard [actor] (b. Budapest, Hungary, 1870–1931 [61?]). BHD1, p. 612.

Korner, Hermine [actress] (b. Berlin, Germany, 30 May 1878–14 Dec 1960 [82], Berlin, Germany). BHD1, p. 612.

Korner, Theo [scenarist] (b. 1882–10 May 1954 [72?], Los Angeles CA). AS, p. 620. BHD2, p. 148.

Kornman, Mary (daughter of **Verna K. Traver**; sister of **Mildred Kornman**) [actress] (b. Idaho Falls ID, 27 Dec 1915–1 Jun 1973 [57], Glendale CA; cancer). m. (1) Leo Tovar; (2) Ralph McCutcheon. (Film debut: *The Iron Heart,* 1920; Hal Roach; Paramount; Republic.) "Mary Kornman," *Variety,* 13 Jun 1973 (age 56). AS, p. 620. BHD1, p. 307. FSS, p. 169. IFN, p. 167. Buck Rainey, "Mary Kornman; A Spirited Ingenue Who Appeared Too Briefly on the Rugged Hinges of the Cinema," *CI,* 133 (Jul 1986), 58–61 (age 56; includes filmography).

Kornman, Mildred (daughter of **Verna K. Traver**; sister of **Mary Kornman**) [actress]. No data found. AMD, p. 198. "Mildred Kornman Returns to Work," *MPW,* 2 Apr 1927, 493.

Kornman, Tony [cinematographer] (b. 1887–17 Dec 1942 [55?], Los Angeles CA). BHD2, p. 148. FDY, p. 461.

Kortman, Bob [actor] (*né* Robert F. Kortman, b. Philadelphia PA, 24 Dec 1887–13 Mar 1967 [79], Long Beach CA; cancer). AS, p. 621. BHD1, p. 307 (b. NY NY). FSS, p. 170. GK, pp. 163–92. IFN, p. 167 (b. NY). Mario DeMarco, "Quickies," *CI,* 198 (Dec 1991), 50 (early cowboy character actor). Frank Dolven, "Three Bad Men I Would Have Liked to Know," *CI,* 221 (Nov 1993), 33–34.

Kortner, Fritz [stage/film actor/director] (*né* Fritz Nathan Kohn, b. Vienna, Austria, 12 May 1892–22 Jul 1970 [78], Munich, Germany; leukemia). m. Johanna Hofer. (Began 1915.) "Fritz Kortner," *Variety,* 29 Jul 1970. AS, p. 621. BHD1, p. 307; BHD2, p. 148. IFN, p. 167. SD. Truitt, p. 186. Waldman, p. 158.

Koser, Henry Francis [actor]. No data found. AMD, p. 198. "His Beard Was Long and His Hair Hung Down, and the Girl of His Heart Was Coming to Town," *MPW,* 4 Oct 1919, 66.

Koshetz, Nina [actress] (*né* Nina Koshetz Leonoff, b. Kiev, Ukraine, 30 Dec 1891–14 May 1965 [73], Santa Ana CA; cerebral thrombosis). AS, p. 621.

Kosic, Vaso [actor] (b. Cetinje, Monenegro, 2 Apr 1899–20 Dec 1957 [58], Sarajevo, Croatia). AS, p. 621.

Kosloff, Theodore [actor] (*né* Fijodor Mikailovitch Koslov, b. Moscow, Russia, 22 Jan 1882–22 Nov 1956 [74], Los Angeles CA). m. Maria "Alexandra" Baldina. (Film debut: *The Woman God Forgot,* DeMille, 1917.) "Theodore Kosloff," *Variety,* 28 Nov 1956 (age 74). AMD, p. 198. AS, p. 621. BHD1, p. 307. FFF, p. 70. FSS, p. 170. IFN, p. 167. Katz, p. 667. Lowrey, p. 96. MH, p. 121. Truitt, p. 186. Cover, *NYDM,* 7 Jul

1915 (with Mme. Baldina in *The Passing Show of 1915*). "Kosloff Joins Famous Players-Lasky," *MPW,* 23 Aug 1919, 1119. "Theodore Kosloff, Russian Dancer, with Famous Players," *MPW,* 13 Sep 1919, 1649. "Theodore Kosloff Becomes Member of DeMille's Staff," *MPW,* 3 Jan 1920, 64. "DeMille Engages Theodore Kosloff," *MPW,* 31 Jul 1920, 577. Theodore Kosloff, "Before Kings Fell," *Classic,* Sep 1922, 22–23, 81–82. Nellie B. Parker, "Dancing for the Screen," *MPC,* Sep 1927, 39, 84, 87 (discusses Kosloff and Ernest Belcher). "Kosloff's Application for Citizenship," *MPW,* 8 Oct 1927, 354.

Koster, Henry [director] (*né* Hermann Kosterlitz, b. Berlin, Germany, 1 May 1905–21 Sep 1988 [83], Camarillo CA). (Universal.) Andrew L. Yarrow, "Henry Koster, 83, Director of 'Harvey' and 'Bishop's Wife,'" *NYT,* 27 Sep 1988, B12:4. "Henry Koster," *Variety,* 28 Sep 1988. AS, p. 621. BHD2, p. 148.

Kotlowsky, Benjamin S *see* **Kutler, Benjamin S.**

Kotsonaros, George [actor] (b. Nauplie, Greece-d. 13 Jul 1933, Eutaw AL). AS, p. 622 (d. LA CA). BHD1, p. 308. IFN, p. 168.

Kottka, Otta [actress] (b. Germany, 5 May 1888–4 Apr 1952 [63], Los Angeles CA). BHD1, p. 308.

Koudelejev, Ian Nikolaievich [director/scenarist] (b. Russia, 1869–1932 [63?], Russia). AS, p. 622.

Koupal, T. Morse [actor] (b. New York NY, 24 Mar 1890–29 Mar 1970 [80], Toledo OH). BHD, p. 221.

Koval, René [actor] (*né* René Renouard, b. Paris, France, 1885–17 Aug 1936 [51?], Paris, France). AS, p. 622.

Koval-Samborsky, Ivan I[vanovich] [actor] (b. Russia, 16 Sep 1893–10 Jan 1962 [68]). AS, p. 622 (b. and d. in Moscow, Russia). BHD, p. 221. IFN, p. 168.

Kovanko, Nathalie [actress] (*née* Natalia Efimovna Kovanko, b. Yalta, Ukraine, 13 Sep 1899–23 May 1967 [67], Kiev, Ukraine). AS, p. 622.

Koverman, Ida R. [publicist] (b. 1876–24 Nov 1954 [80?], Los Angeles CA). BHD2, p. 148.

Ko Vert, Frederick [female impersonator/actor]. No data found. Dorothy Donnell, "From Hollywood to You," *MPS,* 30 Dec 1924, 11 (in *The Reel Virginian,* Sennett. He was "some six feet tall, weighs several stones and dazzlingly beautiful.").

Kozintsev, Grigory M[ikhailovich] [scenarist/actor/director] (b. Kiev, Ukraine, Russia, 9 Mar 1905–11 May 1973 [68], Leningrad, Russia). "Grigory Kozintsev," 271, *Variety,* 16 May 1973, 126:4. AS, p. 622 (d. St. Petersburg, Russia). BHD2, p. 148. FDY, p. 491 (G.M. Kozintosov).

Krafft, John W. [title writer]. No data found. FDY, p. 445.

Krafft, John [title writer/scenarist] (b. Indianapolis IN, 13 Jul 1888–23 Apr 1958 [69], Los Angeles CA). AMD, p. 198. BHD2, p. 148. "Titling Irvin Cobb Original," *MPW,* 16 Apr 1927, 631. "Krafft Keeps Busy," *MPW,* LXXXVI, 14 May 1927, 112.

Krafthefer, Hillis [actor]. No data found. AMD, p. 198. "Child Actor wi Essanay," *MPW,* 23 Mar 1912, 1069.

Kraly, Hans [scenarist] (b. Hamburg, Germany, 1885?–11 Nov 1950 [65], Los Angeles CA). "Hans Kraly," *NYT,* 13 Nov 1950, 27:4 (age 66). "Hans Kraly," *Variety,* 15 Nov 1950 (AA for script of *The Patriot,* 1929). AMD, p. 198. AS, p. 622. BHD, p. 221; BHD2, p. 148 (Hanns Krahly). FDY, p. 491. IFN, p. 168. "Will Write Talmadge Stories," *MPW,* 13 Jun 1925, 798 (Hans Kraely). "He Startled Even Hollywood," *MPC,* Dec 1925, 34, 71.

Kramer, Ida [stage/film actress] (b. 1878–14 Oct 1930 [52], Brooklyn NY; heart trouble). "Ida Kramer," *Variety,* 100, 22 Oct 1930, 76:1 (Mrs. Ida Schneider; d. 15 Oct; member of Hebrew Actors' Union, Equity, and the Jewish Theatrical Guild). AS, p. 623 (d. 15 Oct). BHD, p. 221. IFN, p. 168.

Kramer, Leopold [actor] (b. Prague, Czechoslovakia, 29 Sep 1869–29 Oct 1942 [73]). BHD1, p. 308. IFN, p. 168.

Kramer, Louie P. [publicist]. No data found. AMD, p. 198. "Louie Kramer Now In Hollywood; Associated with Grant E. Dodge," *MPW,* 26 Mar 1927, 270.

Kramer, Wright [actor] (b. Somerville MA, 19 May 1870–14 Nov 1941 [71], Los Angeles CA). "Wright Kramer," *Variety,* 26 Nov 1941. AS, p. 623. BHD, p. 221 (b. 1875). IFN, p. 168 (b. 1875).

Krampf, Gunther [cinematographer] (b. Vienna, Austria, 8 Feb 1899–1955 [56?], London, England). AS, p. 623.

Kranz, Alfred [actor] (b. Brooklyn NY, 1869–2 Dec 1937 [68?], Providence RI). BHD, p. 221.

Krasne, Mayme [actress]. No data found. AMD, p. 198. "Business Woman Makes Film Debut," *MPW,* 18 Jun 1921, 702.

Kraus, Charles [actor] (b. Budapest, Hungary, 1865?–12 Jul 1931 [66], New York NY). m. **Camille Dalberg**. "Charles Kraus," *Variety,* 21 Jul 1931. AS, p. 623 (d. 14 Nov 1941). BHD, p. 221. IFN, p. 168.

Kraus, Irni [actress] (*née* Helene Kraus, b. Germany, 1900–1960 [60?]). m. **Ernst Lubitsch** (d. 1947). AS, p. 623.

Krause, Charles [actor/producer] (b. France-d. 22 Oct 1926, Paris, France). AS, p. 623. BHD, p. 221; BHD2, p. 149.

Krauss, Henry (father of **Jacques Krauss**) [actor] (*né* Henri Kraus, b. Paris, France, 26 Apr 1866 [extrait de naissance no. 727]-15 Dec 1935 [69], Paris, France). AS, p. 623. BHD1, p. 308.

Krauss, Jacques (son of **Henry Krauss**) [art decorator] (*né* Jacques Kraus, b. Paris, France, 1900–1957 [57?], Paris, France). AS, p. 623.

Krauss, Werner [director/producer] (b. Vienna, Austria-d. 6 Nov 1936, Vienna, Austria; suicide). AS, p. 623. BHD2, p. 149.

Krauss, Werner Johnnes [actor] (b. Gestungshausen, Germany, 23 Jun 1884–20 Oct 1959 [75], Vienna, Austria). m. **Maria Bard** (d. 1944). AS, p. 623. BHD1, p. 308 (b. Coburg, Germany). IFN, p. 168. Katz, p. 670 (b. 23 Jul). SD. Truitt, p. 186.

Kraussneck, Arthur [actor] (b. Ostpreussen, Germany, 9 Apr 1856–21 Apr 1941 [85]). BHD, p. 221. IFN, p. 168.

Krawicz, Mieczyslaw [director] (d. Warsaw, Poland, 1944). BHD2, p. 149.

Kremer, Curt (son of **Victor Kremer**) [publicist]. No data found. AMD, p. 198. "Victor Kremer's Son, Curt, Joins Parent in Business," *MPW,* 21 Aug 1920, 1038.

Kremer, Victor (father of Curt Kremer) [producer]. No data found. AMD, p. 198. "Victor Kremer to Enter Production Field," *MPW,* 19 Jun 1920, 1611. Victor Kremer, "Following Progressive Expansion Plan, Victor Kremer Anticipates Bigger Year," *MPW,* 25 Dec 1920, 1026.

Krieg, Hans [director/scenarist] (b. Vaihingen, Germany, 18 Jun 1888–1970 [82?], Germany). AS, p. 624.

Krieg, Ursula Frida Erna Auguste [actress] (b. Berlin, Germany, 10 Oct 1900–11 Oct 1984 [84], Berlin, Germany). AS, p. 624.

Krimer, Harry [actor] (b. 10 Mar 1896–4 Jan 1991 [94]). BHD1, p. 308.

Krizenecky, Jan [director] (b. Czechoslovakia, 20 Mar 1868–9 Feb 1921 [52], Prague, Czechoslovakia). AS, p. 624.

Kroell, Adrienne [actress] (b. Chicago IL, 1892?–2 Oct 1949 [57], Evanston IL; complications from arthritis). (Selig; American; FP-L.) "Miss Adrienne Kroell," *NYT,* 3 Oct 1949, 17:6. "Adrienne Kroell," *Variety,* 5 Oct 1949. AMD, p. 198. AS, p. 624. BHD, p. 221. IFN, p. 168. "Adrienne Kroell," *MPW,* 22 Oct 1910, 923. "Adrienne Kroell," *MPW,* 21 Feb 1914, 931. "[George L.] Cox Near Death; Chicago Film Man and Adrienne Kroell in Disastrous Railroad Wreck," *NYDM,* 27 Jan 1915, 60:3 (sustained slight injuries when Illinois Central train jumped the tracks).

Krohner, Sarah [actress] (b. 1883–9 Jun 1959 [76?], Brooklyn NY). AS, p. 625.

Kromann, Ann *see* **Forrest, Ann**

Kromann, Mabel [actress] (b. Sønderho, Denmark, 15 Sep 1900–24 May 1964 [63]). BHD1, p. 612.

Krone, Rita A. [actress]. No data found. m. Albert A. Kaufman, 18 Jul 1918, Washington DC. AMD, p. 198. "Lieutenant Kaufman Is Married," *MPW,* 10 Aug 1918, 818.

Kronert, Max [actor] (d. 22 Jul 1925). BHD, p. 221. IFN, p. 168.

Krows, Arthur Edwin [title writer]. No data found. AMD, p. 198. FDY, p. 445. "Krows Joins Vitagraph," *MPW,* 2 Aug 1919, 670.

Krows, Arthur Henry [publicist]. No data found. AMD, p. 198. "Krows Goes to Goldwyn," *MPW,* 13 Oct 1917, 218.

Kruger, Alma [actress] (b. Pittsburgh PA, 13 Dec 1868–5 Apr 1960 [91], Seattle WA). AS, p. 625.

Kruger, Harold "Stubby" [swimmer/stuntman] (b. Honolulu HI, 16 Mar 1893–7 Oct 1965 [72], Los Angeles CA; heart attack). "Stubby Kruger," *Variety,* 240, 13 Oct 1965, 86:5 (doubled for Spencer Tracy in *The Old Man and the Sea*). AS, p. 625 (b. 23 Sep 1897). BHD1, p. 612. IFN, p. 168.

Kruger, Jules [cinematographer] (*né* Gustave Jules Kruger, b. Strasburg, France, 12 Jul 1891–13 Dec 1959 [68], Clichy-la-Garenne, France [extrait de décès no. 2024/1959]). AS, p. 625.

Kruger, Otto (grandnephew of Oom Paul Kruger, South Africa's President during the Boer War) [stage/film actor] (b. Toledo OH, 6 Sep 1885–6 Sep 1974 [89], Woodland Hills CA; stroke). m. Sue MacManamy, 30 Sep 1919. (Cosmopolitan, 1920; MGM.) "Otto Kruger, Suave Star of Stage and Screen, Dead," *NYT,* 7 Sep 1974, 30:1. "Otto Kruger," *Variety,* 11 Sep 1974 (1st film: *Under the Red Robe,* Cosmopolitan, 1920). AS, p.

625. BHD1, p. 309. Katz, pp. 671–72 (began 1923). IFN, p. 168.

Kruger, Paul [actor] (*né* Henry Paul Kreuger, b. Eau Claire WI, 24 Jul 1895–6 Nov 1960 [65], Los Angeles CA). AS, p. 625. BHD1, p. 309. IFN, p. 168.

Kruger, Stubby [actor] (b. Honolulu HI, 23 Sep 1897–7 Oct 1965 [68], Los Angeles CA). BHD1, p. 309.

Krusada, Carl [scenarist] (aka Val Cleveland). No data found. FDY, p. 491.

Kruse, George C. [actor] (b. Quincy IL–d. 2 Mar 1930, New Orleans LA). AS, p. 625.

Kubin, Josef Stefan [director/scenarist] (b. Czechoslovakia, 1864–1965 [101?], Czechoslovakia). AS, p. 625.

Kuehne, Edna [actress] (b. 1897–21 Jul 1922 [25?], Los Angeles CA; auto accident). AS, p. 626 (d. 31 Jul). BHD, p. 221.

Kugler, Frank *see* **Kirby, Frank**

Kuh, Anton [scenarist] (b. Vienna, Austria, 12 Jul 1891–18 Jan 1941 [49], New York NY). BHD2, p. 149.

Kuhn, Evelyn [actress] (b. 1893–29 Jun 1976 [83?]). BHD, p. 221.

Kuhn, Paul R. [vaudeville [Three White Kuhns] actor/advertising] (b. 1882?–17 Oct 1925 [43], Redwood City CA). "Paul Kuhn," *Variety,* 21 Oct 1925, 43. AMD, p. 198. "Kuhn Joins Mahin Agency," *MPW,* 5 Feb 1916, 757 (this *MPW* citation is for Paul Kuhn).

Kuhne, Friedrich [actor] (*né* Franz Michna, b. 1869-Oct 1958 [89]). BHD, p. 221. IFN, p. 168.

Kuleshov, Lev Vladimovich [actor/director] (b. Tambov, Ukraine, Russia, 14 Jan 1899–29 Mar 1970 [71]). AS, p. 626. BHD2, p. 149.

Kull, Edward A. [cameraman] (b. 1886?–22 Dec 1946 [60], Los Angeles CA). (Selig, 1907; Universal, 1915; De Mille.) "Edward Kull," *Variety,* 1 Jan 1947. AS, p. 626. BHD2, p. 149. FDY, p. 461.

Kummer, Clare B. [scenarist] (b. 1872–22 Apr 1958 [86?], Carmel CA). BHD2, p. 149.

Kummer, Frederick Arnold [writer/scenarist] (b. Catonsville MD, 5 Aug 1873–22 Nov 1943 [70], Baltimore MD). m. Marion McLean, 1907. "Frederick Arnold Kummer," *Variety,* 23 Nov 1943. AMD, p. 198. AS, p. 627. BHD2, p. 149. SD, p. 726. "Frederick Arnold Kummer," *MPW,* 31 Jul 1915, 823. "Frederick Arnold Kummer," *MPW,* 13 Nov 1915, 1281. "Frederick Arnold Kummer Author of 'Slave Market,'" *MPW,* 20 Jan 1917, 385. "Hyatt Daab Hits the Nail," *MPW,* 9 Mar 1918, 1378.

Kummer, Marion [actress]. No data found. AMD, p. 198. "Film Debut," *MPW,* 11 Dec 1926, 419.

Kunde, Al [actor] (*né* Emil Joseph Kunde, b. 19 Nov 1887–10 Aug 1952 [64], Los Angeles CA). AS, p. 627.

Kunkel, George (son of George Kunkel, Sr., who originated the role of Uncle Tom in *Uncle Tom's Cabin*) [stage/film actor] (b. 1867?–8 Nov 1937 [70], Los Angeles CA; heart attack). (Vitagraph.) "George Kunkel," *Variety,* 10 Nov 1937. AS, p. 627. BHD, p. 221. IFN, p. 169. Truitt, p. 187. "Gossip of the Studios; George Kunkel," *NYDM,* 4 Nov 1914, 29:1. George Katchmer, "George Kunkel," *CI,* 225 (Mar 1994), 44:2 (began ca. 1914).

Kunnecke, Eduard [actor/composer] (b. Emmerich, Germany, 27 Jan 1885–27 Oct 1953 [68], Berlin, Germany). AS, p. 627.

Kuntz, Reimar [cameramann] (b. Berlin, Germany, 27 Jan 1902–1949 [47?]). BHD2, p. 149. FDY, p. 461.

Kupfer, Margarethe [actress] (b. Freystadt, Germany, 10 Apr 1881–11 May 1953 [72]). BHD1, p. 309 (b. 1891). IFN, p. 169.

Kurihara, Thomas [director] (*né* Kisburo Kurihara, b. Kanagawa, Japan, 24 Jan 1885–8 Sep 1926 [41], Tokyo, Japan). AS, p. 627.

Kurrle, Robert B. [cameraman] (b. 1890?–27 Oct 1932 [42], Los Angeles CA). (WB.) "Rare Brain Germ Kills Cameraman After Week," *Variety,* 1 Nov 1932. AMD, p. 198. AS, p. 627. BHD2, p. 149 (b. 1880). FDY, p. 461. "Kurrle Returns as Metro Cameraman," *MPW,* 4 Sep 1920, 88.

Kurske, Erich [actor/director] (b. Schlichtingsheim, Germany, 2 Dec 1892). AS, p. 627.

Kusell, Maurice L. [actor/choreographer] (b. Champaign IL, 1902?–2 Feb 1992 [89], Los Angeles CA; pneumonia). m. Linda. "Maurice L. Kusell," *Variety,* 17 Feb 1992, p. 86 (1st film: *Love Never Dies,* 1916). AS, p. 628. BHD1, p. 310.

Kusell, Milton [executive] (b. Aurora IL, 27 Oct 1892–20 Jul 1971 [78], Port Chester NY). BHD2, p. 149.

Kuter, Leo E. [art director] (b. Shannon IL, 21 Jan 1897–10 Aug 1970 [73], Laguna Beach CA; cancer). m. Evelyn. (Metro; Fox; RKO [designed RKO's symbol]; WB.) "Leo E. Kuter," *Variety,* 19 Aug 1970. AS, p. 628. BHD2, p. 150.

Kutler, Benjamin S. [stage/film actor/scenarist] (aka Benjamin S. Kotlowsky). No data found. (Pathé; Universal; Biograph.) AMD, p. 198. "Kotlowsky Joins All-Star," *NYDM,* 11 Feb 1914, 35:1. "Kutler to Edit Apollo Scenarios," *MPW,* 24 Mar 1917, 1934. "Kutler Returns to Metro," *MPW,* 16 Jun 1917, 1793.

Kutschera, Viktor [actor] (b. Austria, 2 May 1863–20 Jan 1933 [69]). BHD, p. 221.

Kuwa, George K. [actor] (*né* Keiichi Kuwahara, b. Japan, 7 Apr 1885–13 Oct 1931 [46], Japan). AS, p. 628. BHD, p. 221. IFN, p. 169. George Katchmer, *CI,* 225 (Mar 1994), 44:3 (began ca. 1916).

Kuznetzoff, Adia [actor] (b. Russia, 1890–10 Aug 1954 [64?], Port Washington NY). AS, p. 628.

Kvapil, Jaroslav [actor/director/scenarist] (b. Czechoslovakia, 25 Sep 1868–10 Jan 1950 [81], Prague, Czechoslovakia). AS, p. 628.

Kyle, Austin C. [actor] (b. 1893–10 Nov 1916 [23], France; in combat). AS, p. 628. BHD, p. 221. IFN, p. 169.

Kyle, Bessie [actress] (b. 1889?–28 Nov 1926 [37], New York NY). m. Harry Richards. "Bessie Kyle," *Variety,* 8 Dec 1926. AS, p. 628 (d.1 Dec 1950).

Kyle, Howard [stage/film actor] (*né* Howard Anderson Vandergrift, b. Shullsburg WI, 22 Apr 1861–1 Dec 1950 [89], New York NY). m. Amy Urcilla Hodges. "Howard Kyle," *Variety,* 6 Dec 1950. BHD, p. 221. SD, p. 726.

Kyne, Peter Bernard [novelist/scenarist] (b. San Francisco CA, 12 Oct 1880–25 Nov 1957 [77], San Francisco CA). m. Helene C. (d. 26 Aug 1955). "Peter B. Kyne, 77, Novelist, Is Dead; Creator of Cappy Ricks Had Written 25 Books and 1,000 Stories and Articles," *NYT,* 26 Nov 1957, 30:3 (wrote *Valley of the Giants*). "Peter B. Kyne," *Variety,* 4 Dec 1957. AMD, p. 198. AS, p. 628. BHD2, p. 150. "Captain Kyne's Story for Films," *MPW,* 1 Mar 1919, 1191. "Shurtleff Signs Peter B. Kyne," *MPW,* 13 Mar 1920, 1781. "Fox Signs Peter B. Kyne," *MPW,* 14 Mar 1925, 171. "Fox Film Corporation to Screen the Kyne Stories," *MPW,* 21 Mar 1925, 285. "Kyne in Hollywood," *MPW,* 26 Dec 1925, 766.

Kyser, Hans [director] (b. 23 Jul 1882–24 Oct 1940 [58], Berlin, Germany). BHD2, p. 150.

Kyson, Charles H. [director/scenarist]. No data found.

L

Laakso, Uuno [actor] (*né* Uno Alarik Adamsson, b. Hollola, Finland, 1 Oct 1896–6 Dec 1956 [60], Helsinki, Finland). AS, p. 630.

La Badie, Florence [actress] (*née* Florence Russ, b. [Montreal, Canada?] New York NY, 27 Apr 1888–13 Oct 1917 [29], Ossining NY; from injuries sustained in an auto accident on 28 Aug 1917. Buried at Greenwood Cemetery, Brooklyn NY). (Biograph, 1909; Thanhouser; Pathé.) "Florence La Badie Dead; Motion-Picture Star Dies of Injuries in Motor Accident Two Months Ago," *NYT,* 14 Oct 1917, 23:3 (age 24 in Death Notice). "Florence La Badie," *Variety,* 19 Oct 1917 (age 24). AMD, p. 199. AS, p. 629. BHD, p. 222. IFN, p. 169. Katz, p. 675. *Photoplay Arts Portfolio* (Kalem) (b. NY NY, Apr 1893). "The Ever-in-Danger Actress," *MPW,* 26 Jul 1913, 408. "Miss LaBadie Jumps from Ship's Deck," *MPW,* 25 Jul 1914, 594. "Miss LaBadie Makes Some Jump," *MPW,* 15 Aug 1914, 975. "Florence LaBadie," *MPW,* 26 Jun 1915, 2075. "Florence LaBadie Does a 'Creatore,'" *MPW,* 25 Mar 1916, 2021. "Florence La Badie Dead; Well-Known Moving Picture Actress Succumbs to Injuries Sustained in Automobile Accident of Two Months Ago," *MPW,* 7 Oct 1917, 544 (age 23). "Florence LaBadie; From Out of the Past," *CFC,* 59 (Summer, 1978), 48. Eve Golden and Q. David Bowers, "Florence LaBadie: The Thanhouser Girl," *CI,* 213 (Mar 1993), C6, C8,

C16 (b. NYC, 27 Apr 1888). Eve Golden, "Florence LaBadie Update [letter]," *CI*, 215 (May 1993), 6:3 (adopted by Joseph E. and Amanda J. LaBadie).

La Badie, Hubert [producer] (b. 1866–15 Sep 1942 [76?], Brighton MI). BHD, p. 222; BHD2, p. 150.

Laban, Maurice [actor] (b. France, 20 May 1873). AS, p. 630.

La Barnette, Marguerita [actress]. No data found. AMD, p. 199. "Aviatrix Joins Fox News Staff," *MPW*, 31 Jan 1920, 758

La Bey, Louis [actor] (b. Lafontaine, Canada, 1870). BHD, p. 222.

La Bissoniere, Erin [actress] (b. Red Lake Falls MN, 5 Aug 1901–22 Sep 1976 [75], Los Angeles CA). (Universal.) AS, p. 629. BHD1, p. 310. IFN, p. 169.

La Brake, Harrison [actor] (b. 1888–2 Dec 1933 [45], Malone NY). AS, p. 629; p. 630 (LaBrake). BHD, p. 222. IFN, p. 169.

Labry, Pierre Honoré [actor] (b. Paris, France, 14 Dec 1885 [extrait de naissance no. 1681/1885]-23 Jun 1948 [62], Paris, France). AS, pp. 630–31.

Lacau-Pansini, Rose [director] (*née* Marie-Rose Lacau, b. Orthez, France, 7 Jun 1890–23 Mar 1985 [94], Paris, France). AS, p. 631.

La Cava, Gregory [scenarist/director] (*né* George Gregory La Cava, b. Towanda PA, 10 Mar 1892–1 Mar 1952 [59], Malibu CA; heart attack). m. (1) Beryl; (2) Grace O. Gerland. (FP-L.) "Gregory La Cava, Director, 59, Dead; Known for Movies 'Gabriel Over White House,' 'My Man Godfrey,' and 'Stage Door,'" *NYT*, 2 Mar 1952, 92:1. "Gregory La Cava," *Variety*, 5 Mar 1952. AMD, p. 199. AS, p. 629. BHD2, p. 150. FDY, p. 491. IFN, p. 169. Katz, pp. 675–76. SD. "Concerning...Gregory LaCava,, *MPW*, 29 Sep 1923, 418. "Gregory LaCava Signed to 2-Year Contract by Paramount," *MPW*, 17 Apr 1926, 497. Dunham Thorp, "Meet LaCava; With Two Richard Dix Comedies This Young Director Has Established Himself," *MPC*, May 1926, 62, 66. "LaCava Signs New Paramount Contract," *MPW*, 18 Jun 1927, 505.

Lacey, Adele [actress] (b. Mexico City, Mexico, 1914–3 Jul 1953 [39], Mexico City, Mexico). m. **Walter A. Futter**, 1937 (d. 1958). AS, p. 631. BHD1, p. 310. IFN, p. 169. Truitt, 1983.

Lachenbruch, Simon Herold [actor]. No data found. "Goldwyn's Latest Addition Has Youth—Just Youth," *MPW*, 9 Aug 1919, 854.

Lachman, Harry [director/painter] (b. La Salle IL, 29 Jun 1886–19 Mar 1975 [88], Beverly Hills CA; heart attack). m. Quon Tai. "Harry Lachman, A Film Director; Former Painter Dead at 88—Decorated by French," *NYT*, 21 Mar 1975, 40:3 (assistant to Rex Ingram on *Mare Nostrum*). "Harry Lachman," *Variety*, 26 Mar 1975. AS, p. 631. BHD2, p. 150. IFN, p. 169. Katz, p. 676.

Lachmann, Marc [publicist]. No data found. AMD, p. 199. "Lachmann with Metro," *MPW*, 23 Feb 1924, 638.

Lackaye, Helen (sister of **James M.** and **Wilton L. Lackaye**) [actress] (*née* Agnes Helen Lackaye, b. Loudon County VA, 10 Jan 1865–19 Oct 1940 [75?], Jersey City NJ; on train). m. H.J. Ridings. "Helen Lackaye [Mrs. Agnes Helene Ridings]; Actress, Sister of Late Wilton Lackaye, Dies on Train," *NYT*, 21 Oct 1940, 17:6. AS, p. 631. BHD, p. 222 (b. 1883). IFN, p. 169. SD.

Lackaye, James M. (brother of **Wilton** and **Helen Lackaye**) [actor] (b. Washington DC, 5 Dec 1866–8 Jun 1919 [52], New York NY; pneumonia). "Wilton Lackaye's Brother Dead," *NYT*, 10 Jun 1919, 13:4. "James M. Lackaye," *Variety*, 13 Jun 1919. AMD, p. 199. AS, p. 631. BHD, p. 222 (b. 1867). IFN, p. 169. "Two Noted Players for Metro's 'Pals First,'" *MPW*, 3 Aug 1918, 703. "Obituary," *MPW*, 21 Jun 1919, 1752 (b. 1867). Lester Sweyd, "What They Are Doing Now," *Motion Picture Magazine*, Feb 1918, 13 ("...is to head his own company in a rural comedy called 'Uncle Bill.'").

Lackaye, Richard [actor] (b. MI, 9 May 1873–5 Mar 1951 [77], Los Angeles CA). AS, p. 631.

Lackaye, Ruth [actress] (b. Oregon City OR, 1869). BHD, p. 222.

Lackaye, Wilton L. (brother of **James M.** and **Helen Lackaye**; father of Wilton Lackaye, Jr. [1902–1977]) [stage/film actor] (*né* Wilton A. Lackey, b. Loudon County VA, 30 Sep 1862–21 Aug 1932 [69], New York NY [Death Certificate Index No. 18747]). m. (1) Alice Evans (d. 1919); (2) Katherine Alberta Riley (d. 1945). "Wilton Lackaye, Noted Actor, Dies; Succumbs to Heart Attack at His Home Here at Age of 69—Made Stage Debut in 1883; Praised in Svengali Role; Active in Founding of Actors Equity—Prominent in Theatre for Forty Years," *NYT*, 22 Aug 1932, 15:1; "Mrs. Wilton Lackaye [Alice Evans]," 6 Aug 1919, 9:1; "Mrs. Wilton Lackaye [Katherine Alberta Riley]," 11 Mar 1945, 40:1. "Wilton Lackaye," *Variety*, 23 Aug 1932. AMD, p. 199. AS, p. 631. BHD, p. 222. IFN, p. 169. Spehr, p. 148. Truitt, p. 187 (b. London County VA). "Wilton L. Lackaye," *MPW*, 25 Sep 1915, 2184.

Lackteen, Frank [actor] (b. Kubber-Ilias, Lebanon, 29 Aug 1895–8 Jul 1968 [72], Woodland Hills CA). AS, p. 631. BHD1, p. 310 (b. 29 Aug 1927). FSS, p. 170. IFN, p. 169. Truitt, 1983 (b. 1894).

Lacroix, Georges-André [director] (d. 1920, France). AS, p. 631.

Lacroix, Julien [actor] (b. Paris, France, 15 Dec 1881-ca. 1960 [78?]). AS, p. 631.

Ladd, Schuyler [actor] (b. 1877–14 Apr 1961 [83?], Alhambra CA). BHD, p. 222. IFN, p. 169 (age 75).

La Deaux, Evelyn [actress] (b. 1905-Mar 1944 [39?], Philadelphia PA). BHD, p. 222.

Ladengast, Walter [actor] (b. Vienna, Austria, 4 Jul 1899–3 Jul 1980 [80], Munich, Germany). AS, p. 631.

Laemmle, Beth (niece of **Carl Laemmle**) [actress]. No data found. "Uncle Carl's Beth Girl," *MPC*, Jul 1928, 64 (photos).

Laemmle, Carl, Jr. (son of **Carl Laemmle, Sr.**; cousin of **Edward** and **Ernest Laemmle**) [head of production at Universal, 1929–36] (b. Chicago IL, 28 Apr 1908–24 Sep 1979 [71], Beverly Hills CA; stroke). Bachelor. "Carl (Jr.) Laemmle, 71, Dies in H'wood; Son of U Founder," *Variety*, 3 Oct 1979 (worked on Universal's Junior Jewell series, "The Collegians"). AMD, p. 199. AS, p. 632. BHD2, p. 150. "Young Laemmle Appointed Head of Production," *MPW*, 18 Jun 1927, 479. Herbert Cruikshank, "The Crown Prince of Hollywood; Junior, Heir to the Kingdom of Laemmle, Is as Open-Hearted as He Dares Be," *MPC*, Dec 1928, 33, 80 ("He says he won't marry for ten years because women interfere with a man's work."). Herbert Cruikshank, "Shooting His Million; Uncle Carl Gave Junior Laemmle That Much to Lavish on 'Broadway,'" *MPC*, Aug 1929, 23, 70.

Laemmle, Carl, Sr. (father of **Carl Laemmle, Jr.**; uncle of **Carla**, **Edward** and **Ernest Laemmle**) [President of Universal] (b. Laupheim, Württemberg, Germany, 17 Jan 1867–24 Sep 1939 [72], Beverly Hills CA; heart attack). m. Recha Stern (d. 13 Jan 1919 [43], NYC). Richard E. Braff, *The Universal Silents; A Filmography of the Universal Motion Picture Manufacturing Company, 1912–1929* (Jefferson NC: McFarland, 1998). "Carl Laemmle Sr., Film Pioneer, Dies; Man Who Ran $3,600 Invested in Nickelodeon into Millions Stricken in Hollywood; Formed First Exchange; Organized Independent Movie Companies into Universal, with Its Vast Studio," *NYT*, 25 Sep 1939, 19:1. "Carl Laemmle, Sr., Film Pioneer, Founder of Universal, Dies at 72," *Variety*, 27 Sep 1939. AMD, p. 199. AS, p. 632. BHD, p. 222; BHD2, p. 150. IFN, p. 169. Truitt, p. 187. "Carl Laemmle, Sr.," *MPW*, 9 Jan 1909, 35. "Carl Laemmle Interviewed," *MPW*, 17 Apr 1909, 472. "Laemmle Enters the Song Slide Field," *MPW*, 15 May 1909, 632–33. "Carl Laemmle Talks to Us," *MPW*, 22 May 1909, 673. "Laemmle Becomes a Manufacturer," *MPW*, 5 Jun 1909, 750. "Carl Laemmle," *MPW*, 3 Jul 1909, 11. "Laemmle Comes to New York," *MPW*, 10 Jul 1909, 48. "Laemmle Slow But Sure," *MPW*, 21 Aug 1909, 252. "Carl Laemmle Returns from Europe and Enthuses Over 'Imp' Filnms," *MPW*, 30 Oct 1909, 605. "Laemmle Case Postponed," *MPW*, 12 Feb 1910, 217. "The Motion Picture Distributing and Sales Company," *MPW*, 16 Apr 1910, 595. "The Imp Has a Birthday Party," *MPW*, 5 Nov 1910, 1048. "Three Reels a Week," *MPW*, 28 Oct 1911, 282. "Future Imp Releases," *MPW*, 6 Jan 1912, 30. Louis Reeves Harrison, "Studio Saunterings," *MPW*, 27 Apr 1912, 307–10. "Carl Laemmle Interviewed," *MPW*, 19 Oct 1912, 232. "Laemmle Controls Universal," *MPW*, 21 Jun 1913, 1237. "President Laemmle at the Coast," *MPW*, 28 Feb 1914, 1097. "Patents Company vs. Laemmle Argued," *MPW*, 28 Mar 1914, 1657. "Decision in Power—Laemmle Suit," *MPW*, 27 Jun 1914, 1834. Carl Laemmle, "Doom of Long Features Predicted," *MPW*, 11 Jul 1914, 185. "Laemmle Wins St. Louis Suit," *MPW*, 1 Aug 1914, 712. "Laemmle Replies to Fox," *MPW*, 19 Sep 1914, 1650. "Mrs. Laemmle Released by Germans," *MPW*, 31 Oct 1914, 646. George Blaisdell, "Universal Growing," *MPW*, 21 Nov 1914, 1050–51. Lynde Denig, "When Laemmle Forgets Business," *MPW*, 22 May 1915, 1237. George Blaisdell, "Mecca of the Motion Picture," *MPW*, 10 Jul 1915, 215–20. "Universal Not in Merger," *MPW*, 22 Apr 1916, 653 (Letter to the Editor, 7 Apr 1916). "Universal City Closed to Public," *MPW*, 10 Jun 1916, 1890 (tours of Universal City "interferred with studio efficiency, and anything that...interferes with efficiency must go."). Paul Gulick, "Carl Laemmle Made Start in Chicago 'Store Show,'" *MPW*, 15 Jul 1916, 420–21. "Laemmle Continues Salaries of Soldier Employees," *MPW*, 29 Jul 1916, 772. "President Laemmle Entertains Brothers," *MPW*, 12 Aug 1916, 1120 (Joseph and Louis). "Not Interested in New Company," *MPW*, 4 Nov 1916, 717. "Rumored Sale of Universal," *MPW*, 20 Jan 1917, 353. "Carl Laemmle Given Birthday Surprise," *MPW*, 3 Feb 1917, 673. Carl Laemmle, "Couldn't Get Film, Opened Exchange," *MPW*, 10 Mar 1917, 1501. "Arthur Leslie's Book," *MPW*, 15 Sep 1917, 1686 (*Who's Who and Why: The 100 Leading Lights* *of the Screen,* dedicated to Laemmle). "Universal's New Cartoon Plan," *MPW,* 6 Oct 1917, 63. "Laemmle Tells of Improvements," *MPW,* 13 Oct 1917, 218. "Carl Laemmle Takes Control of Bluebird," *MPW,* 20 Oct 1917, 414. "Laemmle Celebrates Twelfth Anniversary," *MPW,* 16 Mar 1918, 1526. "Exhibitor at Fault for Ruinous Overhead," *MPW,* 23 Mar 1918, 1668. "Laemmle to Push Short Subject," *MPW,* 11 May 1918, 838. "Laemmle Recognizes 'Vacuum Pan,'" *MPW,* 29 Jun 1918, 1856. "Laemmle Hammering on the Summer Stuff," *MPW,* 3 Aug 1918, 669. "Laemmle Shows Exhibitor How It's Done," *MPW,* 10 Aug 1918, 818. "Universal's President Bans Dreary Drama and Orders That Happiness Predominate," *MPW,* 7 Sep 1918, 1394. "Carl Laemmle Announces Finish of Eight-Reeler," *MPW,* 9 Nov 1918, 674. "Mr. Laemmle Explains Brandt's New Duties," *MPW,* 4 Jan 1919, 48. "Death of Mrs. Carl Laemmle Following Pneumonia Attack," *MPW,* 25 Jan 1919, 453 (leaving Rosabelle, 17, and Julius, 11). Carl Laemmle, "Read This and Pity the Scenarioist," *MPW,* 1 Feb 1919, 608. "Laemmle Predicts Year of Tremendous Development," *MPW,* 1 Mar 1919, 1165. "Laemmle Sees a Bright Path Ahead," *MPW,* 3 May 1919, 672, 675. "Universal Observes Anniversary," *MPW,* 17 May 1919, 1011–12. "New Universal Policy Announced," *MPW,* 31 May 1919, 1323. "Laemmle Visits Old Home Town," *MPW,* 14 Jun 1919, 1633 (Oshkosh WI). "Star Scarcity Plus Star Stealing Causing Big Rentals, Says Laemmle," *MPW,* 4 Oct 1919, 81. "Laemmle Believes Quality of Production Will Go Up," *MPW,* 27 Dec 1919, 1121–22. "Carl Laemmle Threatens to Sue Dorothy Phillips," *MPW,* 24 Jan 1920, 548. "Universal City Has Most People on Its Payroll, Declares Laemmle," *MPW,* 24 Jan 1920, 588. "Laemmle Explains 'Diploma System' for His Directors and Cameraman," *MPW,* 14 Feb 1920, 1104. "Use Crisp, Attractive Lobby Displays, Carl Laemmle Tells Small Exhibitors," *MPW,* 6 Mar 1920, 1672. "'Looks Like Fair Weather from Now On,' Says Carl Laemmle, Discussing Universal," *MPW,* 8 May 1920, 832. "Producers Polish Their Golden Harps and Haloes, Opinon of Carl Laemmle," *MPW,* 19 Jun 1920, 1589. "Laemmle Summons All Censors to Confer at Universal City, and to Pass on 'Folish Wives,'" *MPW,* 30 Jul 1921, 512. "Laemmle, Film Man, Gets Death Threat in Germany," *MPW,* 10 Sep 1921, 756. "Laemmle Denies 'Folish Wives' Is for Sale; Says Such Report Is Ridiculous," *MPW,* 26 Nov 1921, 426. Carl Laemmle, "The Outlook for 1922," *MPW,* 31 Dec 1921, 1053. "Laemmle Says 'Foolish Wives' Will Go Direct to Exhibitors; Production Will Be 14 Reels Long; Released January 15," *MPW,* 31 Dec 1921, 1077. "Laemmle Asks Bids on 'Folish Wives'; Salesmen to Cover Only the Big Cities," *MPW,* 7 Jan 1922, 67. "Carl Laemmle's Offer Brings Many Letters," *MPW,* 21 Jan 1922, 261. "Eddie Laemmle Ill," *MPW,* 2 Sep 1922, 31 (nephew; blood infection). "Laemmle Tells Why Universal Will Not Make Films in Europe," *MPW,* 14 Oct 1922, 555. "Laemmle Flays First Run System as Industry's Greatest Menace," *MPW,* 23 Dec 1922, 728. "Laemmle Says Plot Changing Necessary for Screen Needs," *MPW,* 27 Jan 1923, 325. "Motion Picture Renaissance Is at Hand, Says Laemmle," *MPW,* 3 Feb 1923, 434. "Laemmle Says Lower Admission Will Bring Bigger Patronage," *MPW,* 3 Feb 1923, 436. "Carl Laemmle Says Serials Are Good Medicine for the Summer," *MPW,* 16 Jun 1923, 596. "Put Personality in Advertising, Says Laemmle to Exhibitors," *MPW,* 14 Jul 1923, 133. Carl Laemmle, "Far-Reaching Results of the Scenario Scholarship Contest," *MPW,* 27 Oct 1923, 753. "Laemmle Optimistic," *MPW,* 17 Nov 1923, 290. Carl Laemmle, "Throw Out Your Chest," *MPW,* 24 Nov 1923, 374. "Lichtman with Universal," *MPW,* 8 Dec 1923, 544. Robert E. Welsh, "Carl Laemmle," *MPW,* 5 Jan 1924, 19. "Will Celebrate 40th Anniversary of Laemmle's Arrival in America," *MPW,* 12 Jan 1924, 97. "Carl Laemmle Moonth February 1924," *MPW,* 2 Feb 1924, 355–63, 372. "Laemmle Opens Virile Campaign for Clean, Wholesome Motion Pictures," *MPW,* 31 May 1924, 453. "Laemmle Talks for Radio (WGBS, NYC)," *MPW,* 17 Jan 1925, 223. "Old Timers' Tender Carl Laemmle Surprise," *MPW,* 28 Mar 1925, 340. "Laemmle Jubilee Celebrates Universal's 13th Birthday," *MPW,* 11 Apr 1925, 598. "Universal Confirms $4,000,000 Deal with Ufa; Laemmle Off for Berlin," *MPW,* 5 Dec 1925, 415–16. "Laemmle Off to Sign with Ufa; Names Stars to Be 'Swapped,'" *MPW,* 19 Dec 1925, 644. "They Control Your Films!," *MPC,* Jan 1926, 26 (photo and quip). "Laemmle Photoplay University Established at Universal City," *MPW,* 16 Jan 1926, 220. "Laemmle's Twentieth Anniversary Will Be Celebrated by Industry," *MPW,* 30 Jan 1926, 430–31. "Carl Laemmle's Brother Arrives," *MPW,* 20 Mar 1926, 3 (Siegfried). Carl Laemmle, "Laemmle Predicts Big 'Laugh Year,'" *MPW,* 3 Apr 1926, 336. "Laemmle as Correspondent for Moving Picture World," *MPW,* 3 Jul 1926, 1. "Laemmle Rallies After Operation," *MPW,* 10 Jul 1926, 1 (appendicitis). "Laemmle's Bed Side Message," *MPW,* 10 Jul 1926, 1. "Blood Transfusion for Laemmle," *MPW,* 17 Jul 1926, 1. "Laemmle Much Better; Offers Tip to Exhibitors," *MPW,* 24 Jul 1926, 1. Carl Laemmle, "Jay Dee Laughed When I Walked," *MPW,* 31 Jul 1926, 1. Carl Laemmle, "You Have to Hand It to UFA for Exploitation," *MPW,* 4 Sep 1926, 2. Carl Laemmle, "'Strogoff' Sells Out at UFA's Palast in Berlin," *MPW,* 11 Sep 1926, 1. "Miss [Rosabelle] Laemmle Ill," *MPW,* 18 Sep 1926, 3 (appendicitis). "Laemmle Smashes Rumor of Any Universal Merger," *MPW,* 11 Dec 1926, 409. "Plan Fete for Carl Laemmle, 60 Years Young," *MPW,* 1 Jan 1927, 30. "Film Folk Pay Tribute to Laemmle on 60th Birthday," *MPW,* 22 Jan 1927, 245–46. "Hollywood Pays Its Respects to Carl Laemmle," *MPW,* 29 Jan 1927, 345. "Laemmle Denies All Rumors of Universal Merjger," *MPW,* 2 Apr 1927, 461. "Laemmle Defies Balckmail by 'Old Uncle Tom' Film," *MPW,* 9 Apr 1927, 537. "Carl Laemmle's Twenty-First Year," *MPW,* 2 May 1927, 806. "Laemmle Makes $700,000 Bid for Lingburdh," *MPW,* 4 Jun 1927, 331. Paul Thompson, "Uncle Carl Sells Uncle Tom Down the Movie River," *MPC,* Sep 1927, 34–35, 87, 88 (Little Eva played by 9-year-old Virginia Grey). "Universal Buys 'Broadway' Laemmle Signs Via Radio," *MPW,* 8 Oct 1927, 370–71. "Laemmle Scans Universal Shorts, Demanding Nothing But the Best," *MPW,* 22 Oct 1927, 505, 507. "Universal Sound, Says Carl Laemmle," *MPW,* 19 Nov 1927, 26. Maurice Rapf, *Back Lot; Growing Up with the Movies* (Lanham MD: Scarecrow Press, 1999), p. 11 ("My father [Harry Rapf] was not alone in practising nepotism. It was said that Carl Laemmle, founder and head of Universal Pictures, made many trips to Europe, usually to take the baths at Bad Nauheim, and he always came back with relatives who became known as 'Laemmle's foreign legion.' When he died, more than seventy relatives or close friends were found on the Universal payroll, including two men who were dead.").

Laemmle, Edward [scenarist/director/cinematographer] (brother of **Ernest Laemmle**; nephew of **Carl Laemmle**; cousin of **Carl Laemmle, Jr.**) (b. Chicago IL, 25 Oct 1887–2 Apr 1937 [49], Beverly Hills CA). m. Peppi Heller. (Universal.) FDY, p. 491. "Edward Laemmle; Film Director, 49, Nephew of Carl Laemmle, Dies in Hollywood," *NYT,* 4 Apr 1937, II, 11:1; "$100,000 to Laemmle Widow," *NYT,* 2 May 1937, II, 10:6. "Edward Laemmle," *Variety,* 7 Apr 1937 (began 1916). AMD, p. 202. AS, p. 632. IFN, p. 169. "Eddie Laemmle Ill," *MPW,* 2 Sep 1922, 31 (blood infection). "Laemmle Promoted," *MPW,* 12 May 1923, 121. "Laemmle, Jr., Casting About," *MPW,* 2 Apr 1927, 480. "Edward Laemmle's Next Picture to Be 'Counsel for the Defense,'" *MPW,* 2 Apr 1927, 487. "Edward Laemmle Recovers," *MPW,* 28 May 1927, 252 (influenza).

Laemmle, Ernest [director] (brother of **Edward Laemmle**; nephew of **Carl Laemmle, Sr.**; cousin of **Carl Laemmle, Jr.**) (b. Munchen, Germany, 25 Sep 1900–1 May 1950 [49], Los Angeles CA). "Ernest Laemmle," *Variety,* 3 May 1950. AMD, p. 203. AS, p. 632. BHD2, p. 150. "Director Ernest Laemmle," *MPW,* 8 Mar 1924, 120. "New Director's First," *MPW,* 15 Mar 1924, 225. "Laemmle Promoted," *MPW,* 27 Nov 1926, 212.

Laemmle, Joseph [executive] (b. 1852–22 Mar 1929 [77?], Universal City CA). AS, p. 632. BHD2, p. 150.

Lafayette, Andrée [actress] (*née* Andrée Rose Godard de la Bigne, b. France, 1903). m. actor Arthur May Constant, 1923. (French films; First National). AS, p. 632. Barbara Little, "Introducing Trilby," *Picture-Play Magazine,* Jun 1923, 45–46, 92. Harry Carr, "The Hollywood Boulevardier Chats," *Classic,* Jul 1923, 72. Harry Carr, "The Girl Who Is Trilby," *Classic,* Aug 1923, 34–36, 89.

Lafayette, Ruby [actress] (b. Augusta KY, 22 Jul 1844–3 Apr 1935 [90], Bell CA). m. **John T. Curran** (d. 1919). (Film debut: *Mother O'Mine,* 1917.) "Ruby Lafayette," *Variety,* 10 Apr 1935. AMD, p. 203. AS, p. 632. BHD1, p. 310 (d. LA CA). IFN, p. 170. Truitt, 1983. "Julian Combines Acting and Directing," *MPW,* 16 Jun 1917, 1769. "Ruby LaFayette's Husband Dies," *MPW,* 1 Feb 1919, 616.

Laffon, Yolande [actress] (*née* Yolande Chamoux, b. Paris, France, 24 Aug 1895–15 Dec 1992 [97], Lou-Veciennes, France [extrait de décès no. 16/1626/1992]). AS, p. 632.

Lafon, Max Georges [actor] (b. Sete, France, 23 Jan 1888–14 Dec 1951 [63], Valence-en-Brie, France [extrait de décès no. 15/1951]). AS, p. 632.

Lafontaine, Victoria [actress] (*née* Victoria Valous, b. Lyons, France, 1841–4 Jan 1918 [76?], Versailles, France [extrait de décès no. 18/1918]). AS, p. 632.

Lafourcade, René [actor] (b. Libourne, France, 1892–1977 [85?], France). AS, p. 632.

Lagerlof, Selma [scenarist]. No data found. FDY, p. 491.

Lagrange, Louise [actress] (*née* Louise Vinot, b. Oran, Algeria, 18 Aug 1898–15 Feb 1979 [80], Paris, France). m. **Maurice Tournear** (d. 1961). AS, p. 632. BHD, p. 222.

Lagrenee, Maurice [actor] (*né* Maurice Jules Guichard, b. Sivry-Courtry, France, 1 Jul 1893 [extrait de naissance no. 18]–23 May 1955 [61], Paris, France). AS, p. 632.

La Groix, Josephine [actress]. No data found. (Quiloa Film Corp.) "Gossip of the Studios," *NYDM,* 13 Nov 1915, 33:1 (engaged by Robert Jewett to play ingenue parts).

La Houppa (Madame) [actress] (*née* Marcelle Capronnier, b. Vitry-sur-Seine, 29 May 1900–18 Jul 1987 [87], Paris, France). AS, p. 629.

Laidlaw, Ethan [actor] (b. Butte MT, 25 Nov 1899–25 May 1963 [63], Los Angeles CA). AS, p. 633. BHD1, p. 311. IFN, p. 170. Truitt, p. 188. George Katchmer, "Up-date—Forgotten Cowboys/Girls," *CI,* 179 (May 1990), 43.

Laidlaw, Roy [actor/makeup artist] (b. Comber, Ontario, Canada, 25 Mar 1883 [Birth certificate #007475, no. 112]–2 Feb 1936 [52], Los Angeles CA; heart attack). AS, p. 633. BHD2, p. 150. IFN, p. 170. George A. Katchmer, "Up-date—Forgotten Cowboys/Girls," *CI,* 179 (May 1990), 43.

Laidley, Alice [actress] (b. 1903–25 Jun 1926 [23?], Paris, France). BHD, p. 222.

Laing, Alfred Benson [actor] (b. 1890–3 Aug 1976 [86], Los Angeles CA; enphysema). AS, p. 633. BHD, p. 222. IFN, p. 170.

Lair, Grace [actress/singer] (*née* Grace Gaylor, d. 5 Jan 1955, Cleveland OH). AS, p. 633. BHD, p. 222. IFN, p. 170.

Laird, Margaret [actress]. No data found. AMD, p. 203. "Fox Gets Another Child Actress," *MPW,* 28 Apr 1917, 602.

Lait, Jack [scenarist] (*né* Joaquin Leonard Lait, b. New York NY, 13 Mar 1883–1 Apr 1954 [71], Beverly Hills CA). AMD, p. 203. AS, p. 633. BHD2, p. 150. IFN, p. 170. "Jack Lait Will Write for Selznick," *MPW,* 13 Sep 1919, 1649.

Laite, Charles [stage/film actor] (b. Warwick, England, 15 Jun 1883–17 Feb 1937 [53], Cleveland OH). (In films from 1915.) "Charles Laite, Actor, Dies at Stage Door [of Hanna Theatre]; Understudy for Roles in 'In a Nutshell' Is Victim of Heart Attack at Cleveland House," *NYT,* 18 Feb 1937, 21:5. AS, p. 633. BHD, p. 222.

La Jana [actress] (*née* Henriette Margarethe Hiebel, b. Berlin, Germany, 24 Feb 1905–13 Mar 1940 [35], Berlin, Germany). AS, p. 629 (b. Vienna, Austria, 28 Feb). BHD1, p. 311.

Lajthay, Karoly [actor/director] (*né* Karoly Le Derle, b. Hungary, 1885–1945 [60?], Hungary). AS, p. 633.

Lake, Alice [actress] (b. Brooklyn NY, 12 Sep 1889–15 Nov 1967 [78?], Los Angeles CA). m. Robert B. Williams, Hollywood, 22 Mar 1924. (Sennett; Metro.) "Alice Lake," *Variety,* 22 Nov 1967 (age 71). AMD, p. 203. AS, p. 633. BHD1, p. 311 (b. 1895). FFF, p. 229. FSS, p. 171. IFN, p. 170 (b. 1895). Katz, p. 678. MH, p. 121 (b. 1896). Slide, p. 162. Spehr, p. 148 (b. 1897). Truitt, p. 188 (d. Paradise CA). WWS, p. 96. "Alice Lake," *MPW,* 3 Nov 1917, 684. "Christie Signs Alice Lake," *MPW,* 14 Jun 1919, 1636. "Alice Lake Signs with Metro," *MPW,* 29 Nov 1919, 531. "Metro Makes Alice Lake Star in Her Own Right," *MPW,* 7 Feb 1920, 935. "Alice Lake Leads March at San Francisco Ball," *MPW,* 30 Oct 1920, 1260. "Metro Elevates Alice Lake to Stardom as Reward for Work in 'Body and Soul,'" *MPW,* 6 Nov 1920, 71. "Alice Lake Now with Big 'U,'" *MPW,* 6 Jan 1923, 33. "Thumbnail Sketches, No. V—Alice Lake," *MPC,* XXI, Apr 1925, 68, 90. "Alice Lake Is Cast with leatrice Joy," *MPW,* 23 Jul 1927, 252. "Alice Lake," *MPW,* 6 Aug 1927, 383.

Lake, Arthur (brother of **Florence Lake**) [actor] (*né* Arthur Silverlake, b. Corbin KY, 17 Apr 1905–9 Jan 1987 [81], Indian Wells CA; heart attack). m. Patricia Van Cleve (niece? daughter? of Marion Davies; d. 3 Oct 1993). "'Dagwood' of Movies, Arthur Lake, Is Dead," *NYT,* 11 Jan 1987, 22:5. AMD, p. 203. AS, p. 633. BHD1, p. 310 (b. 1906). FSS, p. 171. Katz, pp. 678–79 (began 1917). "Arthur Lake," WBO2, pp. 112–13 (b. Corbin KY). "Arthur Lake Is 'U' Choice for 'Betty's a Lady,'" *MPW,* 14 May 1927, 115.

Lake, Florence (sister of **Arthur Lake**) [actress] (b. Charleston SC, 27 Nov 1904–11 Apr 1980 [75], Woodland Hills CA). (RKO.) "Florence Lake," *Variety,* 23 Apr 1980 (Florence Lake Owens). AS, p. 633. BHD1, p. 311. Truitt, 1983.

Lake, Frank [actor] (b. 1848–19 Apr 1936 [88?], Los Angeles CA). AS, p. 633. BHD1, p. 311.

Lake, Harry [actor] (b. 1884–4 Mar 1947 [63?], Chicago IL). AS, p. 633. BHD1, p. 311.

Lake, Lew [actor] (b. England, 1874–5 Nov 1939 [65?], London, England). BHD1, p. 311.

Lake, Marjorie, "The Little Girl with the Big Voice" [actress]. (Universal.) No data found. J. Van Cartmell, "Along the Pacific Coast," *NYDM,* 30 Oct 1915, 27:1.

Lake, Stuart N. [publicist/scenarist] (b. Rome NY, 23 Sep 1889–27 Jan 1964 [74], San Diego CA). AMD, p. 203. BHD2, p. 150. "Stuart N. Lake with Aurora Film," *MPW,* 1 Jan 1916, 67.

Lakenan, Robert F., Jr. [scenarist]. No data found. m. **Leota Lorraine** (d. 1974). June Lee, "Dan Cupid's Bulletin Board," *Paris and Hollywood,* Sep 1926, 96 (he filed suit to divorce Lorraine). June Lee, "Dan Cupid's Bulletin Board," *Paris and Hollywood,* Oct 1926, 89 (in court over custody of his daughter, Nancy).

Lallement, François [actor] (b. France, 4 Feb 1877–ca. 1954 [77?]). AS, p. 634.

Lally, William [actor] (b. NY, 12 Mar 1908–20 Aug 1956 [48], Los Angeles CA). BHD1, p. 312.

Lalor, Fred [director] (d. 24 Jun 1924, Bayonne NJ). BHD2, p. 151.

Lamac, Karl [actor/director/producer/scenarist] (b. Prague, Czechoslovakia, 27 Jan 1897–2 Aug 1952 [55], Hamburg, Germany; apoplexy). AS, p. 634. BHD, p. 222; BHD2, p. 151.

La Manna, Marie [actress]. No data found. m. **Horace G. Plimpton, Jr.**, 11 Sep 1915, Church of the Ascension, 117th St. & Amsterdam, NYC. (Edison.) AMD, p. 203. "Edison Actress Marries; Marie La Manna Becomes Mrs. Horace Plimpton Jr., as Culmination of Romance," *NYDM,* 15 Sep 1915, 33:2. "Plimpton—LaManna," *MPW,* 25 Sep 1915, 2186.

La Marr, Barbara, "The Girl Who Was Too Beautiful" [actress] (*née* Rheatha Dale Watson, b. No. Yakima WA, 28 Jul 1896–30 Jan 1926 [29], Altadena CA; drug addiction). m. (1) Jack Lytell; (2) Lawrence Converse; (3) **Phil Ainsworth**—separated 1923; (4) N. **Bernard (Ben) Deeley**—div. (d. 1924); (5) **Virgil Jack Daugherty** (d. 1938). "Barbara La Marr," *Variety,* 3 Feb 1926 (age ca. 30). AMD, p. 203. AS, p. 629. BHD, p. 222. FFF, p. 39 (b. Richmond VA). IFN, p. 170. Katz, p. 679. LD, p. 156 ("Raetha"). MH, p. 121 (b. Richmond VA). Truitt, p. 188 (d. 1925). WWS, p. 188. "Again Signs," *MPW,* 15 Jul 1922, 214. "LaMarr Is Lead in 'Eternal City,'" *MPW,* 12 May 1923, 173. Alma M. Talley, "'I Never Knew What Love Was Before,' Says Barbara La Marr," *MW,* 23 Jun 1923, 11, 29–30. "Builds a Home," *MPW,* 30 Jun 1923, 755. "Five Year Contract," *MPW,* 8 Sep 1923, 170. "Barbara LaMarr to Be a Star," *MPW,* 22 Dec 1923, 718. John England, "Would You Forfeit Your Personal Liberty to Be a...Movie Star?," *MW,* 22 Mar 1924, 4–5 (La Marr's contract stated that she was to keep free of scandal. Attorney Herman L. Roth was charged with trying to extort [blackmail] $25,000 from La Marr's lawyer or Roth was going to implicate her involvement with 37 different men. The jury took eight minutes to convict Roth). Grace Kingsley, "The Home Life of the Hollywood Screen Stars," *MW,* IV, 5 Apr 1924, 14–15, 29. "Barbara's Married Troubles Again," *MW,* 5 Apr 1924, 21 (La Marr had to live apart from Jack Dougherty pending an action by Ben Deely, La Marr's former husband). Helen Ferguson, "'Unquenchable Ardor, Pitying, Wise'; Being an appreciation of one film player by another," *Classic,* May 1924, 34–36, 76. Regina Cannon, "'My Private Life's My Own Affiar!,' Declares Barbara La Marr," *MW,* 31 May 1924, 3, 29. "Lubin Announces LaMarr Unit Will Work in New York City," *MPW,* 21 Jun 1924, 709. "On the Set and Off; Barbara La Marr Said to Be Innocent Cause of Murder," *MW,* 12 Jul 1924, 29. "On the Set and Off," *MW,* 6 Dec 1924, 19 (La Marr took an overdose of *nux vomica*). Barbara La Marr, "The True Story of My Life," *MW,* 13 Dec 1924, 4–6, 27; Part II, 20 Dec 1924, 14–15, 29; Part III, 27 Dec 1924, 11–12, 29; Part IV, 3 Jan 1925, 11–12, 31; Part V, 10 Jan 1925, 14–15, 29–30; Part VI, 11–12, 30; Part VII, 24 Jan 1925, 19–20, 31; Part VIII, 31 Jan 1925, 18–19, 32; Part IX, 7 Feb 1925, 17–18, 27. "On the Set and Off," *MM,* Dec 1925, 74 ("returned to the studios too soon after her breakdown."). "Barbara LaMarr's Life Story," *MPW,* 3 Jan 1925, 71. "Barbara LaMarr Studying Role," *MPW,* 7 Mar 1925, 86. "Miss LaMarr Slightly Ill," *MPW,* 31 Oct 1925, 694. "Barbara LaMarr Recovering," *MPW,* 7 Nov 1925, 40. "Obituary," *MPW,* 20 Feb 1926, 3. "On the Set and Off," *MM,* May 1926, 84–85 (description of the morbid curiosity at La Marr's funeral). Bert Ennis, "The Truth About Barbara's Baby," *Pictures,* Jun 1926, 49, 97–98 (her son was legally adopted on 22 Feb 1923). Raymond Lee, "The Magic that Was Hollywood," *CFC,* 35 (Summer, 1972), 35–36. Jimmy Bangley, "The Legendary Barbara La Marr," *CI,* 251 (May 1996), pp. 14–21.

La Marr, Richard [actor] (b. Italy, 6 Nov 1895–24 Apr 1975 [79]). AS, p. 629. BHD1, p. 312. IFN, p. 170.

Lamb, Eugene [cameraman]. No data found. AMD, p. 203. "Expert News Cameraman in Far East for Kinograms," *MPW,* 14 Nov 1925, 146.

Lamb, Florence [actress] (b. 1884–9 May 1966 [84?], Los Angeles CA). AS, p. 634.

Lamb, Harold Albert [scenarist] (b. Alpine NJ, 1893–9 Apr 1962 [69?], Rochester NY). BHD2, p. 151.

Lambart, Ernest O[liver] **C**[avan] [actor] (b. Ireland, 1874?–27 Jun 1945 [71], New York NY). m. Josephine Teller (aka **Josephine Drake**, d. 1929). "Ernest O.C. Lambart, an Actor 30 Years," *NYT,* 28 Jun 1945, 19:5. "Ernest Lambart," *Variety,* 4 Jul 1945. AS, p. 634. BHD, p. 223 (Lambert; d. 27 Jan). IFN, p. 170.

Lambart, Capt. Harry [actor/director] (b. Dublin, Ireland, 9 Jul 1876–11 Jun 1949 [72], London, England). BHD, p. 223; BHD2, p. 151.

Lambart, Harry [actor] (d. Jul 1916). "Actor Killed in Action," *Variety*, 18 Aug 1916 (obituary of Charles Lambart, Harry's brother).

Lambert, Albert [actor] (b. France-d. 15 Aug 1918, Paris, France). AS, p. 634. BHD, p. 223.

Lambert, Charlotte [actress] (b. 1857–8 Sep 1935 [78?], Central Islip NY). BHD, p. 223.

Lambert, Clara [actress] (d. 1921). m. **James L. Daly** (d. 1933). (Lubin.) AMD, p. 203. BHD, p. 223. IFN, p. 170. Truitt, p. 188. "Clara Lambert," *MPW*, 20 Dec 1913, 1421.

Lambert, Eddie [actor/cinematographer]. No data found. FDY, p. 461.

Lambert, Glen [actor/director/scenarist] (*né* Lucian Glen Lambert, b. Richmond VA, 28 Jan 1896–9 Dec 1973 [77], Jacksonville Beach FL). AMD, p. 203. AS, p. 634 (b. 1894). BHD, p. 223; BHD2, p. 151. "Snooky Gets New Writer," *MPW*, 3 Sep 1921, 50.

Lambert, Harry [director]. No data found. AMD, p. 203. "Lambert Forms New Company," *MPW*, 9 Oct 1915, 276.

Lambert, Jack [actor] (b. Ardossan, Scotland, 20 Dec 1899–1976 [76?], Scotland). AS, p. 634.

Lambert, Madeleine Marie Joséphine [actress] (b. Saint-Pierre-Benouville, France, 7 May 1892 [extrait de naissance no. SN/1892]-24 Jul 1977 [85], Peymeinade, France). AS, p. 635.

Lambert, Paul [cinematographer]. No data found. FDY, p. 461.

Lambert, Theophile (Toby) J. (Skinny) [actor] (b. Edmonton, Alberta, Canada, 17 Sep 1916–14 Jun 1972 [55]). BHD, p. 223. IFN, p. 170.

Lambert, Will [costume designer]. No data found. AMD, p. 203. "Star Praises Roach-Pathé's Gown Creator," *MPW*, 18 Dec 1926, 508.

Lamberti, Edoardo [cinematographer] (b. Turin, Italy, 31 Mar 1897). JS, p. 232 (in Italian silents from 1921).

Lamberti, Michael [actor] (b. 1891–13 Mar 1950 [59?], Los Angeles CA). AS, p. 635.

La Meri [actress] (b. Louisville KY, 1898–7 Jan 1988 [89?], San Antonio TX). BHD, p. 223.

Lamon, Isabel (daughter of **Mrs. Mathilde Baring**) [actress]. No data found. (Eclair, 1912; Lubin, 1912; World.) "Two of 'Eclair's Stellar Beauties,'" *MPW*, 8 Jun 1912, 912. "Doings at Los Angeles," *MPW*, 12 Oct 1912, 130:2.

La Mont, Alice [actress]. No data found. AMD, p. 203. "Alice LaMont," *MPW*, 14 Jul 1917, 229. "Alice LaMont," *MPW*, 28 Jul 1917, 627.

Lamont, Bernard [actor]. No data found. AMD, p. 203. "Bernard Lamont, Daredevil," *MPW*, XXIII, 9 Jan 1915, 195.

Lamont, Charles W. [actor/director/producer] (b. San Francisco CA, 5 May 1895–11 Sep 1993 [98], Woodland Hills CA; pneumonia). m. **Estelle** Bradley (d. 1990). (Film debut: 1919; Sennett; Christie; Universal.) "Charles Lamont," *Variety*, 11 Oct 1993, p. 201:1. AMD, p. 203. AS, p. 635 (d. 12 Sep). BHD, p. 223; BHD2, p. 151 (b. 1898). Katz, p. 680 (began 1919). *The White Brothers: Jack, Jules, & Sam White* (Metuchen NJ: The Scarecrow Press, Inc., 1990), pp. 87–88. "Lamont Directs Juveniles," *MPW*, 5 Sep 1925, 66. "Charles Lamont," *MPW*, 26 Feb 1927, 635. "The Lamont's Take Off on a Vacation," *MPW*, 23 Apr 1927 (15 months). "Lamont Born in Show Business," *MPW*, 18 Jun 1927, 483. "Lamont En Route to Grand Canyon," *MPW*, 10 Dec 1927, 46.

Lamont, Estelle [actress] (*née* Estelle Bradley, b. 1908–28 Jun 1990 [82?], Woodland Hills CA; respiratory complications). m. **Charles Lamont** (d. 1993). "Estelle Lamont," *Variety*, 3 Sep 1990, p. 94. AS, p. 635 (Estelle Lamont).

La Mont, Harry [actor] (*né* Alfred Guibert, b. New York NY, 17 Jun 1882–8 May 1957 [74], Venice CA). m. Carmen. (Film debut: *A Tale of Two Cities*, 1915.) "Harry Lamont," *NYT*, 10 May 1957, 27:5. AS, p. 635. BHD1, p. 312. IFN, p. 170. Truitt, p. 188.

Lamont, Jack [actor: Keystone Cop] (*né* Jack Capitola, b. 1893?–28 Feb 1956 [63], Cleveland OH; heart attack). (Sennett.) "Jack Lamont," *Variety*, 7 Mar 1956. AS, p. 635. BHD, p. 223. IFN, p. 170. Truitt, 1983.

Lamothe, Julian Louis [scenarist] (b. New Orleans LA, 6 Oct 1893–20 Sep 1972 [78], Los Angeles CA). AMD, p. 203. BHD2, p. 151 (Lamonthe). "Julian LaMothe to Write for American," *MPW*, 17 Mar 1917, 1749. "Julian LaMothe at Camp Dix," *MPW*, 27 Jul 1918, 528.

Lampe, William [stage/film actor]. No data found. (Balboa.) J. Van Cartmell, "Along the Pacific Coast," *NYDM*, 4 Aug 1915, 26:1 ("succumbed to the lure of motion pictures").

Lampin, Georges [actor/director/producer/scenarist] (b. Ekaterinburg, Russia, 14 Oct 1901–6 May 1979 [78], Pau, France [extrait de décès no. 542/1979]). BHD, p. 223; BHD2, p. 151 (b. St. Petersburg, Russia; d. 11 May). IFN, p. 170.

Lampton, Dee "Fatty" [actor] (b. Ft. Worth TX, 1898?–2 Sep 1919 [21], New York NY; appendicitis). (Essanay; Rolin.) AMD, p. 204. AS, p. 636. BHD, p. 223. IFN, p. 170. "Obituary," *MPW*, 20 Sep 1919, 1799 (d. 1 Sep, Clara Barton Hospital, LA CA; 285 lbs.).

Lamy, Charles (brother of **Maurice Lamy**) [actor] (*né* Charles Désiré Casterede, b. Lyons, France, 28 Aug 1857–15 Jun 1940 [82], Orleans, France; from a war-time explosion). AS, p. 636.

Lamy, Henriette [actress] (*née* Henriette Adeline Genty, b. Paris, France, 28 Nov 1884–28 Aug 1978 [93], Paris, France). AS, p. 636.

Lamy, Maurice (brother of **Charles Lamy**) [actor] (*né* Maurice Henri Antoine Castarede, b. Lyons, France, 9 Sep 1863 [extrait de naissance no. 2301]). AS, p. 636.

Lancaster, Charles D. [scenarist] (b. Shelbyville IN, 1877–17 Oct 1928 [51?], Monrovia CA). BHD2, p. 151.

Lancaster, George [cinematographer] (b. 1893–10 Jun 1946 [53?], Los Angeles CA). BHD2, p. 151.

Lancaster, John [actor] (b. Richmond VA, 1857?–11 Oct 1935 [78], Washington DC). (Selig, 1911.) AS, p. 636. BHD, p. 223. IFN, p. 170.

Lancaster, John [production manager/agent] (b. 1876–14 Jul 1944 [70?], Los Angeles CA). BHD2, p. 151.

Lancaster, Leland L. [cinematographer] (b. Lafayette IN, 25 Sep 1888–6 Jan 1977 [88], Pasadena CA). BHD2, p. 151.

Lance, Chief Buffalo Child Long [actor] (d. 20 Mar 1932, Los Angeles CA). BHD, p. 223.

Lanchester, Elsa [stage/film/TV actress] (*née* Elizabeth Sullivan, b. Lewisham, England, 28 Oct 1902 [extrait de naissance no. 165/1903]-26 Dec 1986 [84], Woodland Hills CA; bronchiopneumonia). m. **Charles Laughton**, 1929 (d. 1962). *Charles and I* (1939); *Elsa Lanchester Herself* (1983). "Elsa Lanchester Dies on Coast; Screen, Stage Actress Was 84," *Variety*, pp. 4:4, 22:4 (AA nominations for *Come to the Stable*, 1949, and *Witness for the Prosecution*, 1958). AS, p. 636. BHD1, p. 313.

Land, Mary [actress]. No data found. m. **Howard M. Mitchell**, 22 Apr 1911, Jersey City NJ (d. 1958). (Lubin). AMD, p. 204. "Photoplayers Marry," *MPW*, 2 Dec 1911, 734.

Landa, Max [actor] (*né* Max Landau, b. Vienna, Austria (or Odessa), 24 Apr 1880–9 Nov 1933 [53], Bled, Yugoslavia). BHD, p. 223. Vittorio Martinelli, "Kino-Lieblinge," *Griffithiana*, 38/39 (Oct 1990), 56.

Landau, David [actor] (b. Philadelphia PA, 9 Mar 1879–20 Sep 1935 [56], Los Angeles CA). AS, p. 636 (Davis Landau, b. 1878). BHD1, p. 313. IFN, p. 170.

Landeau, Cecil [assistant director] (b. 1894–11 Apr 1982 [88?], London, England). BHD2, p. 151.

Landers, Lew [director] (*né* Louis Friedlander, b. New York NY, 2 Jan 1901–15 Dec 1962 [61], Palm Desert CA; heart attack). (Universal, 1922.) "Lew Landers," *Variety*, 19 Dec 1962. AS, p. 637. BHD2, p. 152. IFN, p. 170. SD.

Landers, Sam [cinematographer] (b. 1887?–5 Aug 1948 [61], Los Angeles CA). (Griffith.) "Sam Landers," *Variety*, 11 Aug 1948. AS, p. 637. BHD2, p. 152.

Landi, Elissa [stage/film/radio actress/novelist] (*née* Elizabeth Marie Christine Küehnelt, b. Venice, Italy, 6 Dec 1904–21 Oct 1948 [43], Kingston NY; melanoma). m. (1) John Cecil Lawrence, 1928-May 1937; (2) Curtiss Kinsey Thomas, 28 Aug 1943, Christ Presbyterian Church, NY NY (daughter, Caroline Maude Thomas, b. 11 Sep 1944). (Film debut: *London*, 1927; American debut: *Body and Soul*, 1931.) "Elissa Landi, 43, Actress, Writer; Stage, Screen and Radio Star in the 1930's Dies of Cancer—In 'Farewell to Arms,'" *NYT*, 22 Oct 1948, 245:3 ("Landi" was stepfather's surname). "Elissa Landi," *Variety*, 27 Oct 1948 (American film debut: *Body and Soul*, 1930.) AS, p. 637 (*née* Comtesse Elisabeth Maria-Christina Kuhnelt Zanardi-Landi). BHD1, p. 311. IFN, p. 170. SD. Truitt, pp. 188–89 (d. 31 Oct). John Roberts, "Elissa Landi," *CI*, 104 (Jan 1984), 10, 47. Martin A. Kelly, "Elissa Landi: Deposed Queen of the Movies," *CI*, 292 (Oct 1999), 20–27 (b. Vienna, Austria; last name from stepfather).

Landis, [J.] Cullen (brother of **Margaret Landis**) [actor/assistant director] (b. Nashville TN, 9 Jul 1895–26 Aug 1975 [80], Bloomfield Hills MI). m. (1) **Mignon Le Brun**—div. 1925 (d. 1941); (2) Jane Grenier, Detroit MI. (Christie.) William M. Freeman, "Cullen Landis, 79, Film Actor, Dead; Star of 'Lights of New York,' First Hollywood Talkie," *NYT*, 28 Aug 1975, 36:4 (age 79). "Cullen Landis," *Variety*, 3 Sep 1975 (age 79). AMD, p. 204. AS, p. 637. BHD1, p. 313. FFF, p. 79. FSS, p. 172. IFN, p. 171. Katz, pp. 683–84 (began 1917). MH, p. 121. WWS, p. 208. "Cullen landis, Assistant Director," *MPW*, 25 Nov 1916, 1176. "Wife of Landis Burned," *MPW*, 5 Mar 1921, 38 (LeBrun's dress caught fire from a gas stove). "Another Film Baby," *MPW*, 10 Dec 1921, 685 (daughter, joins sister, June). "Cullen landis Reaches Stardom, via F.B.O.," *MPW*, 26 Aug 1922,

668. "Cullen Landis Now with Vitagraph," *MPW,* 30 Dec 1922, 886. "Has Juvenile Lead Role," *MPW,* 17 May 1924, 271. "Joins 'Born Rich' Cast," *MPW,* 7 Jun 1924, 562. Dorothy Donnell, "From Hollywood to You," *MPS,* 28 Jul 1925, 15–16, 35 ("Mignon Le Brun Landis portrays Cullen as a jagging husband, and he retaliates by calling her publicly a nagging wife. Mrs. Landis says that one morning Cullen left the house for work and didn't return for six weeks..."). "Dan Cupid Chalks Up Two Weddings," *MPW,* 3 Sep 1927, 23. "Hoosegow Looms for Cullen Landis," *MPW,* 17 Sep 1927, 163. "Landis Agrees to Pay," *MPW,* 24 Sep 1927, 227 ($100-a-month child support). June Lee, "Dan Cupid's Bulletin Board," *Paris and Hollywood Screen Secrets,* Oct 1927, 36 (earned over $17,000 during the year but was $1,000 short in his alimony payments. Spent five days in the county jail. "Landis claims that his wife is trying to break his spirit. The couple was divorced two years ago, after a spirited legal battle."). James Goldsworthy, "The Cullen Landis Story," *CFC,* 27 (Spring/Summer, 1970), 6–8. George Katchmer, "Remembering the Great Silents," *CI,* 240 (Jun 1995), 43–44.

Landis, Margaret (sister of **Cullen Landis**) [actress] (aka Margaret Cullen, b. Nashville TN, 31 Aug 1890–8 Apr 1981 [90], Oakland CA). m. (1) **Bertram Bracken**, 6 Apr 1919–24 (d. 1952); (2) J. Hamilton Cooper, 1930-d. 1953. AMD, p. 204. AS, p. 637 (b. 1891; d. 1982). "Margaret Landis," *MPW,* 8 Apr 1916, 270. "Bracken—Landis," *MPW,* 26 Apr 1919, 519. "Miss Landis Signed," *MPW,* 19 Nov 1927, 11. John E. Thayer, "Remembering Margaret Landis," *CFC,* 51 (Summer 1976), X15. Billy H. Doyle, "Lost Players," *CI,* 168 (Jun 1989), 26; 171 (Sep 1989). Roi A. Uselton, "In Reference to Margaret Landis [letter]," *CI,* 221 (Nov 1993), 8.

Landis, Winifred [actress]. No data found. George Katchmer, "Remembering the Great Silents," *CI,* 199 (Jan 1992), 15.

Landon, George W. [advertising]. No data found. AMD, p. 204. George W. Landon, "I, Me, Myself," *MPW,* 20 Jul 1918, 328.

Landowska, Yona [actress]. No data found. AMD, p. 204. 'Yona Landowska," *MPW,* 29 Apr 1916, 778.

Landoy, Georges [producer] (b. France-d. 1929, accidentally during the eruption of a geyser). AS, p. 637.

Landray, Sabine [actress] (b. Blois, France, 1900). AS, p. 637.

Landregan, Jack [cinematographer] (b. 1898–17 Mar 1939 [40?], Barstow CA). BHD2, p. 152.

Landreth, Gertrude Griffith [actress] (b. New York NY, 26 Feb 1897–25 Nov 1969 [72], Palo Alto CA). (Sennett.) "Gertrude Griffith Landreth," *Variety,* 3 Dec 1969 (founded the Hollywood Studio Club). AS, p. 637. BHD, p. 223. IFN, p. 171. Truitt, p. 189.

Landy, Ludwig [producer] (b. Vienna, Austria, 1887–14 Apr 1953 [66?], New York NY). AS, p. 638.

Lane, Adele [stage/film actress] (b. Jersey City, NJ, 17 Jul 1877–24 Oct 1957 [80], Los Angeles CA). m. **Burton King** (d. 1944). (Lubin; Selig; Universal.) AMD, p. 204. AS, p. 638 (d. 1937). BHD, p. 223. IFN, p. 171. "Personal," *NYDM,* 26 May 1915, 5:2 (on cover). "Adele Lane," *MPW,* 5 Jun 1915, 1611. J. Van Cartmell, "Along the Pacific Coast," *NYDM,* 4 Aug 1915, 26:1 ("suffering from a nervous breakdown due to hard work, and may not be on the screen for some time.").

Lane, Allan "Rocky" [actor] (*né* Harry Albershart, b. Mishawaka IN, 22 Sep 1909–27 Oct 1973 [64], Woodland Hills CA). (Republic.) "Allan (Rocky) Lane," *Variety,* 7 Nov 1973. AS, p. 638. BHD1, p. 313. IFN, p. 171. Katz, 1994 (b. 1904).

Lane, Brenda H. [actress/writer] (b. 1910?–30 Nov 1942 [32], New York NY. "Brenda H. Lane," *Variety,* 2 Dec 1942. AS, p. 638.

Lane, Carol [actress]. No data found. George Katchmer, "Remembering the Great Silents," *CI,* 196 (Oct 1991), 54.

Lane, Charles Willis [actor] (b. Madison IL, 25 Jan 1869–17 Oct 1945 [76], Van Nuys CA; cancer). AMD, p. 204. AS, p. 638. BHD, p. 223. IFN, p. 171. "Charles Lane to Remain in Pictures," *MPW,* 10 Apr 1920, 250.

Lane, Chris [scenarist]. No data found. AMD, p. 204. "Chris Lane, Scenarioist," *MPW,* 20 Sep 1913, 1286.

Lane, Dorothy [actress] (b. 1905–7 Oct 1923 [18?], New York NY). AS, p. 638. BHD, p. 223.

Lane, Ed [cinematographer]. No data found. FDY, p. 461.

Lane, George W. [actor] (b. 1877?–15 Jun 1935 [58], New York NY). "George Lane," *Variety,* 5 Jun 1935. AS, p. 638.

Lane, Grace [actress] (b. England, 13 Jan 1876–14 Jan 1956 [80], Hove, England). BHD1, p. 313.

Lane, Harry J. [stage/film actor] (b. 1876–27 Oct 1943 [67], New York NY). "Harry J. Lane," *Variety,* 27 Oct 1943, p. 46:1 (won a membership drive contest prize of a life membership in Equity, when it cost $5 to join [in 1914]. "That is the only payment Lane ever made to Equity, his being the only instance of the kind in the association's records."). BHD, p. 223. IFN, p. 171.

Lane, Lupino (brother of **Wallace Lupino**; cousin of Ida and **Mark Lupino**) [stage/film actor/director/producer/ scenarist] (*né* Henry George Lupino, b. London, England, 16 Jun 1892–10 Nov 1959 [67], London, England). m. Violet Blythe, 1917. (Began 1915; Davison Film Sales, London; Fox; Educational; Paramount; WB; British International Pictures; St. George's Pictures.) "Lupino Lane, 67, Actor in Britain; Director, Producer and Star of 'Me and My Girl' Dead—Introduced Lambeth Walk," *NYT,* 11 Nov 1959, 35:3. "Lupino Lane," *Variety,* 18 Nov 1959. AMD, p. 204. AS, p. 638. BHD1, p. 313; BHD2, p. 152. FSS, p. 172. IFN, p. 171. Katz, pp. 684–85 (*né* Henry Lane; began in England, 1915). SD. Truitt, p. 189. "Lupino Lane Made One of William Fox Stars," *MPW,* 31 Dec 1921, 1041. "Lupino Lane Nears Completion of First Fox Special Comedy," *MPW,* 8 Apr 1922, 622. "Lupino Lane Makes Bow on August 20," *MPW,* 19 Aug 1922, 580. "Fox Presents Lupino Lane in Comedy Special," *MPW,* 13 Jan 1923, 168. "Lupino Lane to Star in New Fox Two-Reel Comedy Series," *MPW,* 24 Nov 1923, 419. "Lupino Lane Makes Debut with Educational in 2-Reel Comedy," *MPW,* 11 Oct 1924, 488. "Lupino Lane on Way to America," *MPW,* 7 Aug 1926, 363. "Insure Comedians," *MPW,* 13 Nov 1926, 4 (insured for $500,000). "Lupino Lane," *MPW,* 11 Dec 1926, 410. "Lupino Lane Asserts England Cannot Compete with America," *MPW,* 26 Feb 1927, 635. "Lupino Lane," *MPW,* 23 Apr 1927, 709. "Lane to Direct His Next Picture," *MPW,* 10 Sep 1927, 96. "Lupino Lane," *MPW,* 8 Oct 1927, 347. Lupino Lane, "The Ancient Art of Pantomime Revealed by a Scion of Clowns," *Cinema Arts,* Dec 1927, 10–11, 46–47 ("His Ancestors Since the Fifteenth Century Have Used the Legitimate Stage to Express the Art of Miming."). Richard M. Roberts, "Lupino Lane; Music Hall Comedian," *CI,* 256 (Oct 1996), 22–25. Robert Farr and Joe Moore with Richard M. Roberts, "The Filmography of Lupino Lane," *CI,* 257 (Nov 1996), C7-C9.

Lane, Magda [actress]. No data found. BR, pp. 49–50. George A. Katchmer, "Forgotten Cowboys and Cowgirls—Part III," *CI,* 174 (Dec 1989), 48, 49.

Lane, Nellie [actress]. No data found. Terese Rose Nagel, "Everybody Loves a Fat Woman in the Movies," *MW,* 5 Jan 1924, 9, 31 (photo from *Circus Days* with Jackie Coogan).

Lane, Nora [actress] (b. Chester IL, 12 Sep 1905–16 Oct 1948 [43], Glendale CA; suicide). AMD, p. 204. AS, p. 638. BHD1, p. 313. BR, pp. 169–72. Ragan 2, p. 927. "Nora Lane," *MPW,* 20 Aug 1927, 516. George A. Katchmer, "Forgotten Cowboys and Cowgirls—Part III," *CI,* 174 (Dec 1989), 49; "Update—Forgotten Cowboys/Girls," *CI,* 179 (May 1990), 43 (suicide).

Lane, Travers [scenarist]. No data found. FDY, p. 491.

Lane, Winifred [actress]. No data found. (Thanhouser.) "In the Picture Studios," *NYDM,* 4 Aug 1915, 27:1 (on the female baseball team at Thanhouser).

Lanfang, Mei [actreess] (b. 1894–8 Aug 1961 [67?]). BHD1, p. 612.

Lanfield, Sidney [scenarist/director] (b. Chicago IL, 20 Apr 1898–30 Jun 1972 [74], Marina del Rey CA; heart attack). m. **Shirley Mason**, Feb 1927 (d. 1979). "Sidney Lanfield," *Variety,* 12 Jul 1972. AS, p. 638. BHD2, p. 152. FDY, p. 491. Katz, 1994.

Lang, André [journalist/scenarist] (b. Paris, France, 12 Jan 1893–4 Oct 1986 [93], Paris, France). AS, p. 638.

Lang, Charles B[ryant] [cinematographer] (b. Bluff UT, 27 Mar 1902–16 Mar 1956 [53], Hollywood CA). "Charles B. Lang," *Variety,* 28 Mar 1956 (age 48). AS, p. 638 (d. 3 Apr 1998). FDY, p. 461. Katz, pp. 685–86.

Lang, Eva Clara [actress] (b. Columbus OH, 1884–6 Apr 1933 [49?], Los Angeles CA). AS, p. 638.

Lang, Fritz [actor/director/producer/scenarist] (*né* Friedrich Christian Anton Lang, b. Vienna, Austria, 5 Dec 1890–2 Aug 1976 [85], Beverly Hills CA). m. (1) **Thea Gabriele von Harbou**, 1920–div. (d. 1954); (2) **Lily Latte** (d. 1984). Albin Krebs, "Fritz Lang, Film Director Noted for 'M,' Dead at 85," *NYT,* 3 Aug 1976, 32:1. "Fritz Lang, 85; An Early Great; Film Fest Fave," *Variety,* 4 Aug 1976. AMD, p. 204. AS, p. 639. BHD, p. 223; BHD2, p. 152. IFN, p. 171. Katz, pp. 686–88. SD. Sumner Smith, "Ufa Heads Visit the U.S.; Expect Much of 'Siegfried,"' *MPW,* 1 Nov 1924, 29. Nora Sayre, "Fritz Lang's Dr. Mabuse Stalks the Screen Again," *NYT,* Sec. II, 3 Jan 1993, 9:1, 16:1. Heinrich Fraenkel, "The Story of Fritz Lang, Maker of 'Siegfried,'" *MPC,* Mar 1926, 38–39.

Lang, Harry [actor] (b. New York NY, 29

Dec 1894–3 Aug 1953 [58], Los Angeles CA). AS, p. 639.

Lang, Howard [film/stage actor] (*né* Frederick Lange, b. New Orleans LA, 12 May 1874–26 Jan 1941 [66], Los Angeles CA). m. Gwen Heller. "Howard Lang," *Variety,* 29 Jan 1941. AS, p. 639. BHD1, p. 314. IFN, p. 171. SD, p. 736. Truitt, p. 189 (b. 1876).

Lang, Louise [scenarist] (b. 1907–2 Feb 1977 [69], Los Angeles CA). AS, p. 639. BHD, p. 224. FDY, p. 491. Truitt, 1983. "Evans' 1977 Chronicle," *FIR,* Mar 1978.

Lang, Matheson [stage/film actor] (*né* Alexander Matheson Lang, b. Montreal, Canada, 15 May 1879–11 Apr 1948 [68], Bridgeton, Barbados, West Indies). m. Hutin Britton (*née* Nellie Hutin, d. 1965). "Matheson Lang, British Actor, 68; Shakespearean Performer Is Dead in Barbados—Seen with Ellen Terry, Mrs. Langtry," *NYT,* 13 Apr 1948, 27:3. "Matheson Lang," *Variety,* 11 Apr 1948. AS, p. 639 (b. 13 May). BHD1, p. 314. IFN, p. 171. SD. Truitt, p. 189.

Lang, Melvin [actor] (b. New York NY, 29 Dec 1894–14 Nov 1940 [45], Los Angeles CA). AS, p. 639.

Lang, Peter B. [actor] (b. 29 May 1859–20 Aug 1932 [73], New York NY [Death Certificate Index No. 18679]). (Lubin.) "Peter Lang," *Variety,* 23 Aug 1932. AMD, p. 204. AS, p. 639. BHD, p. 224. IFN, p. 171 (age 65). Truitt, p. 189. "Funny Things That Happen in the Studio," *MPW,* 15 Jun 1912, 1011. "Peter Lang," *MPW,* 29 Mar 1913, 1317.

Lang, Philip [actor/scenarist/editor/executive] (b. Xenia OH, 1887–24 Jan 1919 [31], New York NY; influenza). AMD, p. 204. AS, p. 639. BHD2, p. 152 (b. 1885). Epes Winthrop Sargent, "The Photoplaywright," *MPW,* 7 Feb 1914, 670. "Editor Becomes Vice-President," *MPW,* 21 Aug 1915, 1302. "Philip Lang Goes to Coast," *MPW,* 9 Dec 1916, 1477. "Philip Lang Shows Back to Camera," *MPW,* 7 Jul 1917, 73. Philip Lang, "The Scenario of Today," *MPW,* 21 Jul 1917, 406–07. "Philip Lang and Kalem Part at Last," *MPW,* 6 Apr 1918, 99 (began 1911). "Philip Lang Editing Films for Ordinance Department," *MPW,* 9 Nov 1918, 653. "Personal and Otherwise," *MPW,* 1 Feb 1919, 600 (joined Vitagraph). "Obituary," *MPW,* 8 Feb 1919, 732. "And Now It Is Philip Lang," *MPW,* 8 Feb 1919, 763 (interred at Xenia OH). Billy H. Doyle, "Lost Players," *CI,* 139 (Jan 1987), 55.

Lang, Walter [actor/scvenarist/director] (b. Memphis TN, 10 Aug 1896–7 Feb 1972 [75], Palm Springs CA; kidney ailment). m. Madelaine Fields. (TC-F.) "Walter Lang, 73, Director, Is Dead; Filmed 'King and I,' 'Call Me Madam' and 'Can Can,'" *NYT,* 8 Feb 1972, 37:1. "Walter Lang," *Variety,* 9 Feb 1972. AMD, p. 205. AS, p. 639 (b. 1898). BHD, p. 224; BHD2, p. 152. FDY, p. 491. IFN, p. 171. Katz, pp. 688–89. "Cohn Signs Lang for Columbia," *MPW,* 28 May 1927, 267.

Langdon, Harry, the "Little Elf" [stage/film actor/scenarist] (b. Council Bluffs IA, 15 Jun 1884–22 Dec 1944 [60], Los Angeles CA). m. (1) Rose Frances Mensolf, 1903; (2) Helen Walton, 1929; (3) Mabel Georgena Sheldon (native of Portsmouth, England), 12 Feb 1934, Tucson AZ. William Schelly, *Harry Langdon* (Metuchen NJ: The Scarecrow Press, Inc., 1982). "Harry Langdon, 60, Screen Comedian; Film 'Dead-Pan,' Who Began with Mack Sennett, Dies—Once Paid $7,500 a Week," *NYT,* 23 Dec 1944, 13:3. "Harry Langdon," *Variety,* 27 Dec 1944. AMD, p. 205. AS, p. 639. BHD1, p. 314; BHD2, p. 152. FDY, p. 491. FFF, p. 255. FSS, p. 173. IFN, p. 171. Katz, p. 689. MH, p. 121. Truitt, p. 189. "Title Changed," *MPW,* 24 Nov 1923, 409. "Sennett to Feature Harry Langdon," *MPW,* 1 Dec 1923, 504. "Harry Langdon," *MPW,* 10 Jan 1925, 160. "Langdon's Popularity Increasing," *MPW,* 14 Feb 1925, 706. "Harry Langdon," *MPW,* 16 May 1925, 348. LeRoy Green, "A Modest Clown," *MW,* 27 Jun 1925, 15–16, 45. Doris Curran, "The Sad-Faced Mr. Langdon," *MPC,* Jul 1925, 62, 87. Edward Watz, Laurence Reid, "The Celluloid Critic," *MPC,* Aug 1926, 50–51 (review of *Tramp, Tramp, Tramp*). "Harry Langdon, comedian, Signs wi First National," *MPW,* 26 Sep 1925, 312. "Harry Langdon to Join First National Soon," *MPW,* 5 Dec 1925, 442. Margaret G. Monks, "'Harry, Harry, Quite Contrary'; Being the Life History of the Little Man in 'Tramp, Tramp, Tramp,' and 'The Strong Man,'" *Cinema Arts,* Oct 1926, 18–19. "Langdon Figures on Hundred Laughs," *MPW,* 1 Jan 1927, 31. "Harry Langdon," *MPW,* 22 Jan 1927, 265. Tom Waller, "Harry Langdon: A Serious Man Who Makes the Whole World Laugh," *MPW,* 19 Mar 1927, 178–79. "Harry Langdon," *MPW,* 21 May 1927, 181. "Dictograph Used on Langdon Film," *MPW,* 24 Dec 1927, 21. "Harry Langdon Burned," *MPW,* 24 Dec 1927, 23. "Marriages," *Variety,* 113, 20 Feb 1934, 52:5 (reported twice in the same column, marriage to Sheldon on 12 Feb and 14 Feb). "Langdon, Silent and Sound (Part 1)," *CFC,* 45 (Winter, 1974), X9, X12, 55; Part II, 47 (Summer, 1975), 50–52. Newsletter: Mr. Floyd Bennett, ed., The Harry Langdon Society, PO Box 388, Downers Grove IL 60515.

Langdon, James [scenarist]. No data found. FDY, p. 491.

Langdon, Lillian [actress] (b. NJ, 1861?–8 Feb 1943 [81], Santa Monica CA). m. Mr. Bolles. "Lillian Langdon," *Variety,* 10 Feb 1943 ("one of the first stars of the silent screen"). AS, p. 639. BHD, p. 224. IFN, p. 171. Truitt, p. 189.

Lange, Willibald [actor/director] (*né* Georg Karl Willibald Lange, b. Bromberg, Germany, 15 Jan 1895). AS, p. 639.

Langer, Gilda [actress] (b. 1896–23 Jan 1920 [23?]). BHD, p. 224.

Langford, Edward J. [actor] (d. 10 Dec 1926, Indianapolis IN; pneumonia). m. Gonzell White. "Ed. Langford," *Variety,* 5 Jan 1927. AMD, p. 205. "Edward Langford Enlists," *MPW,* 9 Jun 1917, 1609. "Edward Langford," *MPW,* 16 Feb 1918, 951. "Edward Langford Returns," *MPW,* 5 Jul 1919, 73.

Langford, Howard [actor] (b. 1888?–20 Jan 1930 [41], Long Island NY). m. Myra. "Howard Langford," *Variety,* 22 Jan 1930. AS, p. 640.

Langford, John [title writer]. No data found. FDY, p. 445.

Langford, Martha [actress] (d. 21 Apr 1935, Syracuse NY). AS, p. 640. BHD, p. 224. IFN, p. 171.

Langhanke, Otto L. [actor] (b. 1871–3 Feb 1943 [71?], Los Angeles CA). BHD, p. 224.

Langley, Herbert [screen actor/opera baritone] (b. 1888?–13 Sep 1967 [79], London, England). "Herbert Langley," *Variety,* 18 Oct 1967. AS, p. 640 (d. 15 Oct). BHD1, pp. 314, 612. IFN, p. 171. Truitt, p. 190.

Langly, Dorothy [actress]. No data found. AMD, p. 205. "Dorothy Langly Makes Her Screen Debut in Fox Film," *MPW,* 27 Spe 1919, 1963.

Langston, Ruth [actress]. No data found. AMD, p. 205. "Ruth langston Has Big Role in Dempsey Serial," *MPW,* 7 Feb 1920, 917.

Langtry, Lily, "The Jersey Lily" [stage/film actress] (*née* Emilie Charlotte Le Breton, b. Isle of Jersey, England, 13 Oct 1852–12 Feb 1929 [76], Monte Carlo, Monaco). m. (1) Edward Langtry; (2) Sir Hugo de Bathe; (3) Frederick Gebhardt. (FP-L.) "Lily Langtry [Lady de Bathe] Dead," *Variety,* 13 Feb 1929 (age 77). AS, p. 640. BHD, p. 224 (b. 1851). GSS, pp. 210–14. IFN, p. 171. SD. Truitt, p. 190. "Lily Langtry's Leading Man [Henry Gsell] with Crystal," *MPW,* 6 Sep 1913, 1074.

Lani, Maria [actress] (b. Warsaw, Poland, 1906–11 Mar 1954 [48], Paris, France). AS, p. 640. BHD, p. 224. IFN, p. 171.

La Niece, Ed [actor]. George A. Katchmer, "Forgotten Cowboys and Cowgirls—Part V," *CI,* 177 (Mar 1990), C4.

Lannes, Georges [actor] (*né* Georges Henri Chrles Abraham, b. Paris, France, 27 Oct 1895–8 Jul 1983 [87], Paris, France [extrait de décès no. 17/791]). AS, p. 640.

Lanning, Edward (brother of **Frank Lanning**) [actor] (b. Marion IA, 21 Sep 1870–19 Sep 1918 [47], Los Angeles CA). (Universal.) AMD, p. 205. AS, p. 640 (d. 20 Sep). BHD, p. 224. IFN, p. 172 (d. 20 Sep). "Obituary," *MPW,* 12 Oct 1918, 207.

Lanning, Frank L. (brother of **Edward Lanning**) [actor] (b. Marion IA, 14 Aug 1872–17 Jun 1945 [72], Los Angeles Co. CA). m. Merva Eaton, Aug 1920. (Kalem.) AMD, p. 205. AS, p. 640. BHD1, p. 314. IFN, p. 172. "Frank Lanning," *MPW,* 4 Feb 1911, 245. "Fox Gets Frank Lanning," *MPW,* 17 Feb 1917, 1021. "Los Angeles Studio Shots," *MPW,* 28 Aug 1920, 1155 (married Eaton). "Lloyd's New Paramount Comedy, 'The Kid Brother,'" *MPW,* 11 Dec 1926, 417. George A. Katchmer, "Remembering the Great Silents," *CI,* 183 (Sep 1990), 46.

Lanning, George [actor] (b. Marion IA, 20 Feb 1877–5 Jun 1941 [64], Los Angeles Co. CA). BHD, p. 224. IFN, p. 172.

Lanning, Reggie [cinematographer] (b. AZ, 6 Oct 1893–6 Dec 1965 [72], Woodland Hills CA). BHD2, p. 152.

Lanphier, Faye [actress] (b. 1906?–21 Jun 1959 [53], Oakland CA; virus pneumonia). "Faye Lanphier," *Variety,* 1 Jul 1959 ("She was a screen actress for a brief period after winning the Atlantic City title."). AMD, p. 204. BHD, p. 224. "Beauty Pageant Winner Has Paramount Contract," *MPW,* 3 Oct 1925, 413 (Lamphier). Horace J. Gardner, "America's Beauty Pageant; This year's National Beauty Contest will select a winner from both the professional and amateur ranks," *Cinema Arts,* V (Aug 1926), 20, 45. "Fay Lanphier Shy," *Variety,* 9 Nov 1927, 29:1 (Electrical Products Corp. sued her for $842 for an electric sign in front of her beauty parlor in Oakland CA. "The sign has been up a year, and the company alleges the beaut has forgotten payments.").

Lansing, Alice [actress]. No data found. AMD, p. 205. "Alice Lansing," *MPW,* 31 Dec 1927, 26.

Lansing, Ruth Douglas [actress] (b. 1881?–19 Aug 1931 [50], Los Angeles CA; toxic poisoning from infected tooth.) "Ruth Douglas Lansing," *Variety*, 25 Aug 1931. AS, p. 641. BHD1, p. 315. IFN, p. 172.

Lantz, Adolf [scenarist]. No data found. FDY, p. 491.

Lantz, Walter [animator/scenarist] (*né* Walter Lanza, b. New Rochelle NY, 27 Apr 1900–22 Mar 1994 [93], Burbank CA; heart disease). m. Doris Hollister (daughter of George and Alice Hollister); Grace Stafford (the voice of Woody Woodpecker), 1941 (1903–1992). (AA, 1979.) Glenn Collins, "Walter Lantz, 93, the Creator of Woody Woodpecker, Is Dead," *NYT*, 23 Mar 1994, B20:1. Joe Adamson, *The Walter Lantz Story* (NY: G.P. Putnam's Sons, 1985). (Bray; Sennett.) AMD, p. 205. AS, p. 641. BHD2, p. 152 (b. 1899). Katz, pp. 690–91. Chapter 5, "Walter Lantz," in Leonard Maltin, *Of Mice and Magic; A History of Animated Cartoons* (NY: New American Library, 1980), pp. 155–184. "Fuller on Bray Staff," *MPW*, 15 Aug 1925, 751. "Lantz Completes Scenario," *MPW*, 22 Aug 1925, 848.

Lapaire, Leo [director/scenarist] (b. Fontenais, Switzerland, 26 Nov 1893–5 Feb 1963 [69], Berne, Switzerland). AS, p. 641.

Laparcerie, Cora [actress] (*née* Marie Caroline Laparcerie, b. Morcenx, France, 9 Nov 1875–20 Aug 1951 [75], Paris, France). AS, p. 641.

La Pearl, Harry [circus clown/film actor] (b. Danville IL, 1885?–13 Jan 1946 [61], Los Angeles CA). m. Loretta. "Harry La Pearl; Circus Clown Covered Sawdust Trail Since His Childhood," *NYT*, 15 Jan 1946, 23:2. "Harry La Pearl," *Variety*, 16 Jan 1946. AMD, p. 205. AS, p. 629. BHD, p. 224. IFN, p. 172. "Harry LaPearl," *MPW*, 16 Jan 1915, 349. "From Sawdust to Screen; Harry La Pearl, Chief MinA Fun-Maker, Gained His Fun-Makig Ability in Circus Arenas," *NYDM*, 27 Jan 1915, 60:3.

Lapkina, Maria Alexandrovna [actress] (b. Moscow, Russia, 17 Sep 1898–1 Jan 1936 [37], St. Petersburg, Russia). AS, p. 641.

La Plante, Beatrice [actress] (b. Paris, France, 1900). (Film debut: *Dangerous Water*, Robertson-Cole, 1919.) AMD, p. 205. BHD, p. 224. "Beatrice LaPlante in Rolin Comedy," *MPW*, 15 May 1920, 960.

La Plante, Laura (sister of **Violet La Plante**) [film/stage/TV actress: Wampas Star, 1923] (*née* Laura Isabelle La Plant, b. St. Louis MO, 1 Nov 1903–14 Oct 1996 [92], Woodland Hills CA). m. **William A. Seiter**, 14 Nov 1926, Wilshire Church, Hollywood CA—div. 1932 (d. 1964); **Irving Asher**, 19 Jun 1934, Paris, with James J. Walker and Betty Compson as witnesses (d. 1985). (Christie, 1919; Universal.) Robert McG. Thomas, Jr., "Laura La Plante Dies at 92; Archetypal Damsel in Distress," *NYT*, 17 Oct 1996, B14:1. AMD, p. 205. AS, p. 629. BHD1, p. 315 (b. 1904). BR, pp. 172–75. FFF, p. 102. FSS, p. 174. HCH, p. 21. MH, p. 121. Katz, p. 691. Ragan 2, pp. 933–34. "Laura La Plante," SOS, pp. 88–109. "Laura La Plante," WBO2, pp. 166–67. "Laura LaPlante in Leading Role," *MPW*, 22 Sep 1923, 355. "New Universal Star," *MPW*, 17 Nov 1923, 321. "Laura LaPlante," *MPW*, 10 Apr 1926, 418. Verne Kibbe, "The Candid Kid; I've No Particular Ambitions, Says Laura La Plante," *MPC*, Apr 1926, 34–35, 80. "LaPlante Renews," *MPW*, 7 May 1927, 13. "Laura La Plante; The Girl on the Cover," *Cinema Arts*, Jul 1927, 33. Tom Waller, "Bill and Laura," *MPW*, 10 Sep 1927, 86–87. "Laura Gets Her Haircut; The Story of a Star Who Sacrificed Beauty for Beauty; Movie Fans Ask What Will She Come to if She Has it Cut Again?," *Paris and Hollywood Screen Secrets Magazine*, Aug 1927, 26–27, 97. Cedric Belfrage, "Uncle Carl's Gabbin'; After Three Months' Talking and Testing, He Gives 'Show Boat' to Laura La Plante," *MPC*, Oct 1928, 40, 86–87 (Mary Philbin, Alice White and Zita Johan were in the running. "...kind Uncle Carl selected Laura La Plante, an absolute unknown who is most respectably married to an equally obscure gentleman by the name of Bill Seiter."). "It's a Great Life," *NYT*, 27 Sep 1955 (appeared with Michael O'Shea, 7 p.m., 20 Nov 1955, NBC-TV). Murray Summers, "Laura La Plante in 'Her Reel Life; With Reminiscences by Laura La Plante,'" Part I, *Filmograph*, II, No. 3 (1971), 22–25, 28–43, 51 (her mother was one of 19 children, including two sets of twins; La Plante's cousin, Mary Lee Burns, got her extra work in LA. "In 1921, she was earning about $20 a week; in 1922, $50; in 1923, $150. In 1925, she would be earning about $750 a week; in 1926, $1,500. In 1927, it was to be $2,000. Come the year 1929, she was to earn about $3,500 a week."; Part II, No. 4, 1972, 20–41). Buck Rainey, "Laura La Plante [filmography]," *CI*, 88 (Oct 1982), 53–55. William M. Drew, *Speaking of Silents* (Vestal NY: Vestal Press, Ltd., 1989), pp. 88–109. George A. Katchmer, "Forgotten Cowboys and Cowgirls—Part III," *CI*, 174 (Dec 1989), 49.

La Plante, Violet [actress: Wampas Star, 1925 (as Violet Avon)] (sister of **Laura La Plante**) (*née* Violet La Plant, b. St. Louis MO, 17 Jan 1907–1 Jun 1984 [77], La Jolla CA). AMD, p. 205. AS, p. 629. BHD, p. 224 (*née* Violet Avon; b. 1908). Ragan 2, p. 64. "To Be Featured," *MPW*, 16 Aug 1924, 561. Helen Carlisle, "The [WAMPAS] Baby Stars of 1925," *MW*, 7 Mar 1925, 4–5, 31 (the other 12 were Madeline Hurlock, Evelyn Pierce, Olive Borden, Joan Meredith, Duane Thompson, June Marlowe, Betty Arlen, Lola Todd, Dorothy Revier, Natalie Joyce, Ena Gregory and Ann Cornwall). George A. Katchmer, "Forgotten Cowboys and Cowgirls—Part V," *CI*, 177 (Mar 1990), C4.

Laporte, Léonie [actress] (b. France-d. 15 May 1924, Pont Canavese (Aosta), Italy). AS, p. 641. JS, p. 234 (in Italian silents from 1915–24).

Laporte, Marcel [actor] (b. Paris, France, 1895). AS, p. 641.

Lara, Augustin [actor/composer] (b. Veracruz, Mexico, 30 Oct 1897–5 Nov 1970 [73], Mexico City, Mexico). AS, p. 641 (b. and d., Tlacotalpan, Mexico). BHD2, p. 153.

Lara-Autant, Louise [actress] (*née* Louise Victorine Charlotte Larapidie Delisle, b. Chateau-Thierry, France, 22 Jul 1876 [extrait de naissance no. 108]-9 May 1952 [75], Paris, France). AS, p. 642.

Laraby, Nelson [cinematographer] (b. 1887–7 Nov 1937 [50?], Burbank CA). BHD2, p. 153.

Lardner, Ring W[ilmer] (son of Ring Lardner, Jr.) [writer/scenarist] (*né* Ringold Wilmer Lardner, b. Niles MI, 6 Mar 1885–25 Sep 1933 [48], Easthampton, LI NY). m. Ellis Abbott, 1911 (son, Ring Lardner, Jr., b. 19 Aug 1915). "Ring Lardner Dies; Noted as Writer; Won Early Laurels with Brilliant Sports Stories on Chicago Tribune; Author and Playwright; Wrote Baseball Scene for 'Follies,' with Will Rogers as Veteran Pitcher," *NYT*, 26 Sep 1933, 21:1. "Ring Lardner Gone," *Variety*, 3 Oct 1933. AMD, p. 205. AS, p. 642 (d. 27 Sep). BHD, p. 224. *Century Cyclopedia of Names*, p. 2584. "Rise of Ring W. Lardner in Literary Field Was Rapid," *MPW*, 6 Sep 1919, 1450. "Stern Bros. Sign Ring Lardner for 'You Know Me Al' Series," *MPW*, 6 Mar 1926, 34. B.F. Wilson, "Ring Lardner Hands Brickbats to the Movies; All Kidding to One Side, America's Greatest Humorist Becomes Deadly Serious for Once in Scoffing at the Screen," *MPC*, Jan 1927, 16–17, 84. WWWA.

La Reno, Richard [actor] (b. New York NY, 31 Oct 1863–26 Jul 1945 [81], Los Angeles CA). "Richard La Reno," *Variety*, 1 Aug 1945 (age 77). AS, p. 629. BHD1, p. 315 (b. County Limerick, Ireland). IFN, p. 172. Truitt, 1983 (b. County Limerick). George A. Katchmer, "Forgotten Cowboys and Cowgirls—Part V," *CI*, 177 (Mar 1990), C6 (b. 1873).

Largay, Ray[mond J.] [actor] (b. WI, 7 Mar 1876–28 Sep 1974 [98], Woodland Hills CA). AS, p. 642.

Larimore, Earle [actor] (*né* Earle Elton, b. Portland OR, 2 Aug 1899–22 Oct 1947 [48], New York NY; heart attack). m. **Selena Royle** (d. 1983). "Earle Larrimore, Actor, Dies at 48; Star of Many Theatre Guild Productions Played Leads in Broadway Successes," *NYT*, 24 Oct 1947, 23:1 ("Larimore" was mother's maiden name). "Earle Larimore," *Variety*, 29 Oct 1947. AS, p. 642. BHD, p. 224. IFN, p. 172. SD, p. 739. Truitt, p. 190.

Larive, Léon François [actor] (b. Paris, France, 28 Jun 1886–20 Jul 1961 [75], Paris, France [extrait de décès no. 12/1809]). AS, p. 642.

Larkin, Dolly [actress] (b. New York NY, 19 Apr 1891). AMD, p. 205. BHD, p. 224. "Dolly Larkin," *MPW*, 22 May 1915, 1243. "Dolly Larkin with MinA," *MPW*, XXIV, 5 Jun 1915, 1628.

Larkin, George Alan "Daredevil" [stage/film actor] (b. New York NY, 11 Nov 1887–27 Mar 1946 [59], New York NY [Death Certificate Index No. 7693]). m. **Ollie Kirkby**, 1918 (d. 1964). (On stage from 1900; Edison, 1907–10 [alleged film debut: *The Animated Snowball*, 1908]; Pathé. 1910–12; Eclair, 1912–13; FP-L; Kalem, 1913; Universal; Selig; Equitable; France Film; Newfield Prods; Fox.) AMD, p. 205. AS, p. 642 (b. 1886). BHD1, p. 315. GK, pp. 459–67. IFN, p. 172. MSBB, p. 1025 (b. 1892). "George Larkin Engaged by Eclair," *MPW*, 24 Feb 1912, 698. "George Larkin," *MPW*, 19 Sep 1914, 1627. "George Larkin," *MPW*, 25 Mar 1916, 1985:2. "Kalem Gets George Larkin," *MPW*, 9 Sep 1916, 1666. "Little Stories That Are True; One Perfect Day," *Motion Picture Magazine*, Feb 1918, 78 (cracked a rib one day; the next day he went to do exteriors for Grant, Police Reporter. He was to carry Ollie Kirkby down a trestle. She lost her grip but he got her down safely; his ribs were fine. Just then he sneezed and had to be taken to the doctor. Returning to the studio, he stepped on a tack and needed an "operation" to get it out. Later, heading for his hotel, his driver hit a milk wagon. Rushed to his hotel, he refused to take the elevator and walked up nine flights of stairs.). "George Larkin," *MPW*, 23 Feb 1918, 1096. "George Larkin Elopes with Olive Kirby," 27 Apr 1918, 556. "George Larkin, Hurt, Is Recovering," *MPW*, 29 Jun 1918, 1858. "George Larkin to Star," *MPW*, 24 May 1919, 1161. "Larkin in Auto Smash," *MPW*, 14 Feb 1925, 706. George Katchmer, "Daredevil George Larkin," *CI*, 104 (Feb 1984), 45–47. Billy H. Doyle, "Lost Players," *CI*, 162 (Dec 1988), 44.

Larkin, John [actor] (b. 1874–19 Mar 1936 [63], Los Angeles CA). AS, p. 642 (b. 1872). BHD, p. 224. IFN, p. 172.

Larkin, John A[ugustin] [actor] (b. 1874–7 Jan 1929 [54], New York NY). AS, p. 642.

Larkins, Carolyn [stage/film actress]. No data found. AMD, p. 206. "Forsakes Stage for the Screen," *MPW,* 12 Feb 1921, 847.

Larquey, Pierre Raphaël [actor] (b. Cenac, France, 10 Jul 1884–17 Apr 1962 [77], Maisons-Laffitte, France [extrait de décès no. 66/1962]). AS, p. 642.

La Roche, Edward [vaudeville/stage/film actor] (b. France, 1879–26 Dec 1935 [56], New York NY). "Edward La Roche," *Variety,* 121, 1 Jan 1936, 226 ("Recently he had been forced to appeal to Equity for assistance and was an applicant for home relief."). BHD, p. 224.

Laroche, Jules Félix Armand Laroche [actor] (b. Paris, France, 29 Jan 1841–14 Nov 1925 [84], Redene, France). AS, p. 642.

La Rocque, Rod [stage/film actor] (aka Rodney La Rock, *né* Roderick la Rocque de la Tour, b. Chicago IL, 29 Nov 1896–15 Oct 1969 [72], Beverly Hills CA). m. **Vilma Banky**, 26 Jun 1927, Beverly Hills CA (d. 1991). (Essanay; Goldwyn; Black Cat features.) "Rod La Rocque, a Leading Man of Silent Screen, Is Dead at 70; Matinee Idol of the 1920's Appeared as Villain in 'Ten Commandments,'" *NYT,* 17 Oct 1969, 47:1 (b. 1898). "Rod La Rocque," *Variety,* 22 Oct 1969 (age 70). AMD, p. 206. AS, p. 630. BHD1, p. 315. FFF, p. 49 ("La Roque," b. 1898). FSS, p. 174. GK, pp. 448–59. IFN, p. 172 (b. 1898). Katz, p. 691. MH, p. 122 ("La Roque," b. 1893). MSBB, p. 1025. SD. Truitt, p. 190 (b. 1898). WWS, p. 139. "Rod LaRocque with Brady," *MPW,* 17 Jul 1920, 325. "Rod Larocque Signs with Paramount," *MPW,* 21 Jul 1923, 239. "Rod LaRocque Off to Paris; Supporting Gloria Swanson," *MPW,* 27 Dec 1924, 857. Rod La Rocque, "The True Story of My Life," *MW,* 8–9. 30–31 (b. 1898); 14 Feb 1925, 14–15, 30; 21 Feb 1925, 12–13, 29; 28 Feb 1925, 13–14, 33; 7 Mar 1925, 13–14, 32–33; 14 Mar 1925, 22, 28. "Rod LaRocque, DeMille Star, Is Proud of Famous Players," *MPW,* 7 Mar 1925, 82. Gladys Hall and Adele Whitely Fletcher, "We Interview Rod La Rocque," *MW,* 28 Mar 1925, 8–10, 33. "Cecil B. DeMille Signs Tutor for Rod LaRocque," *MPW,* 6 Jun 1925, 688. Paul Paige, "Close-Ups and Fade-Outs," *Paris and Hollywood,* Sep 1926, 88 (voted the most popular star in Mexico, followed by Ramon Novarro, John Gilbert, Richard Dix, and Ronald Colman). "LaRocque Hols Ace Against His Chief, Is Belief," *MPW,* 19 Feb 1927, 560. "Record Broadcast," *MPW,* 16 Apr 1927, 622 (announcement of marriage to Vilma Banky). Paul Paige, "Close-Ups and Fade-Outs," *Paris and Hollywood Screen Secrets Magazine,* May 1927, 82 (his contract with DeMille, "dated 13 May 1925, calls for a sliding-scale salary, ranging from $2,500 to $6,000 a week." He sued to get out of it because his name did not appear in type as large as the name of the production he was in, as with the advertising for *Red Dice, Bachelor Brides, Gigolo,* and *Resurrection.* Loaned out to Inspiration Pictures for the latter film, he had $5,500 withheld by DeMille, which was returned to him, but at the time "it constituted a breach of contract and 'hurst his feelings.'"). "'No Foolin'; One marriage ceremony in Hollywood that was 'For Keeps'; The love match of Vilma Banky and Rod La Roque," *Screenland,* XV, Oct 1927, 22–23, 90, 92, 94–95. Ann Cummings, "I'll Bring Back My Bonnie with Me; Rod Set Sail for Budapest—He Couldn't Live Without Her," *MPC,* May 1928, 26, 72, 91. Dorothy Spensley, "Big Lens and Focus Men; Celebrities Who Are Always Behind a Camera When They're Not Before One," *MPC,* Jan 1929, 30–31, 87 (photographers include La Rocque, Ford Sterling, George Hackathorne, Edwin Carewe, Farrell MacDonald and Emory Johnson). George A. Katchmer, "Rod La Rocque; Matinee Idol," *CI,* 130 (Apr 1986), 19–22. Richard E. Braff, "The Films of Rod La Rocque," *CI,* 144 (Jun 1987), C55, C57, C43. R.E. Braff, "Additional Film Credits for Rod La Rocque," *CI,* 238 (Apr 1995), 44.

La Roux, Carmen [actress] (b. Durango, Mexico, 4 Sep 1909–24 Aug 1942 [32]). BHD1, p. 315.

Larrabeiti, Carmen [stage/film actress] (b. Bilboa, Spain, 1904–1968 [64?]). (Began 1925; Paramount, Joinville; Fox.) Waldman, p. 160.

Larrimore, Francine [actress] (*née* Francine La Remeé, b. Verdun, France, 22 Aug 1897–7 Mar 1975 [77], New York NY). m. (1) Conrad Conrad; (2) Alfred T. Mannon. "Francine Larrimore," *Variety,* 12 Mar 1975 (age 77). AMD, p. 206. AS, p. 642 (b. 1898). BHD1, p. 315. IFN, p. 172. SD. "Francine Larrimore," *MPW,* 30 Oct 1915, 803. "Francine Larrimore with Edison," *MPW,* 6 May 1916, 978.

Larry, Gaston [technical director] (d. 13 Sep 1911, NY; following an operation for mastoiditis). (Pathé; French Eclair; American Eclair.) AMD, p. 206. "Eclair Director Dies Suddenly," *MPW,* 30 Sep 1911, 983 (buried in Calvary Cemetery, Brooklyn NY).

Larry, Mike [actor] (b. 1882–22 Dec 1967 [85], Los Angeles CA). AS, p. 642.

Larsen, Viggo [actor/director] (b. Copenhagen, Denmark, 14 Aug 1880–6 Jan 1957 [76], Copenhagen, Denmark). (Messter Film Co.) AS, p. 642. BHD1, p. 315; BHD2, p. 153. IFN, p. 172. JS, p. 234 (in Italian silents from 1923). J.A. Fleitzer, "German Trade Notes," *MPW,* 15 Apr 1916, 431:2 (half of a popular team with Wanda Treumann, he signed to make 8 films a year with her with Messter Film Co.). Vittorio Martinelli, "Kino-Lieblinge," *Griffithiana,* 38/39 (Oct 1990), 57.

La Rue, Fontaine [actress]. No data found. (Universal.) AMD, p. 206. "Metro Signs Fontaine LaRue," *MPW,* 7 Aug 1920, 776 (actor).

La Rue, Frank H[erman] [actor] (b. OH, 5 Dec 1878–26 Sep 1960 [81], Woodland Hills CA). AS, p. 630.

La Rue, Grace [stage/film actress] (aka Stella Gray, b. Kansas City MO, b. 23 Apr 1880–12 Mar 1956 [75], Burlingame CA). m. (1) Byron D. Chandler; (2) **Hale Hamilton** (d. 1942). "Grace La Rue," *Variety,* 21 Mar 1956. AS, p. 630. BHD, p. 224. IFN, p. 172. SD. Truitt, p. 190. "Grace La Rue Sued," *LA Times,* 11 Feb 1920, II, p. 7 (sued by Myrtle Tannehill Hamilton in New York for alienation of the affections of Hale Hamilton. La Rue "denied that she lured Mr. Hamilton away from his wife.").

La Rue, Jean [actor] (*né* Eugene Marcus Bailey, b. 1901?–2 Jun 1956 [55], San Antonio TX). "Eugene Marcus Bailey," *Variety,* 13 Jun 1956. AS, p. 630. BHD, p. 224. IFN, p. 172. Truitt, p. 190.

La Salle, Katherine [stage/film actress]. No data found. AMD, p. 206. "Katherine LaSalle," *NYDM,* 1 Apr 1914, 34:1. "The Banker's Daughter," *MPW,* 4 Apr 1914, 75. "Katherine LaSalle," *MPW,* 3 Apr 1915, 54. "On Stage and Screen; Katherine La Salle Starts Tour in 'Kick In' [with John Barrymore] as Kalem Feature [*An Innocent Sinner,* released 15 May] Is Released," NYDM, 28 Apr 1915, 29:1.

Lascelle, Ward [actor/director/producer] (b. SD, 14 Dec 1882–19 Jan 1941 [58], Los Angeles CA; heart disease). m. Margaret. "Ward Lascelle," *NYT,* 20 Jan 1941, 12:1 ("early day motion picture director" who directed "some twenty-five pictures up to 1923. Later he produced independently. He had not been active in the industry since 1929."). "Ward Lascelle," *Variety,* 22 Jan 1941 ("directed more than a score of pictures in the early days of the industry"). AMD, p. 206. AS, p. 643. BHD2, p. 153. "Lascalle Makes Comedy Not Using Faces of Actors and Without the Use of Subtitles," *MPW,* 13 Mar 1920, 1829.

La Shelle, Joseph W. [cinematographer] (b. Los Angeles CA, 9 Jul 1900–20 Aug 1989 [89], La Jolla CA). "Joseph La Shelle, 89, Cameraman of 'Laura,'" *NYT,* 23 Aug 1989, B6:4. "Joseph LaShelle," *Variety,* 30 Aug 1989, p. 97 (age 80). AMD, p. 206. AS, p. 630. BHD2, p. 153. Katz, p. 692. "An Artist in Camera Angles," *MPW,* 23 Apr 1927, 714. "Cinematographer Joseph La Shelle," *LA Times,* 22 Aug 1989, 18:1.

Lasker, Dr. Emmanual [actor] (b. Berlin, Germany, 24 Dec 1868–11 Jan 1941 [72], New York NY). BHD, p. 224.

Lasker, Myles F. [publicist] (b. 1893–7 Dec 1940 [47], New York NY). BHD, p. 225; BHD2, p. 153.

Lasky, Jesse L[ouis] (father of Jesse Lasky, Jr.) [Jesse L. Lasky Feature Play Company; Famous Players-Lasky] (cousin of **Mervyn LeRoy**) (b. San Francisco CA, 13 Sep 1880–13 Jan 1958 [77], Beverly Hills CA). m. Bessie Gainnes (son, Jesse, Jr., 1908–1988). *I Blow My Own Horn* (1957). "Jesse L. Lasky, 77, Moviemaker, Dies; Associate of C.B. De Mille and Samuel Goldwyn in Infancy of Industry; Produced 1,000 Films; Made the First Full-Length Feature in Hollywood in '13 after Vaudeville Career," *NYT,* 14 Jan 1958, 33:1 (b. San Jose CA). "Jessie L. Lasky," *Variety,* 15 Jan 1958. AMD, p. 206. AS, p. 643. BHD2, p. 153. IFN, p. 172. Katz, p. 692. SD. "New Feature Company," *MPW,* 20 Dec 1913, 1417. George Blaisdell, "Jesse L. Lasky in Pictures," *MPW,* 3 Jan 1914, 35–36. "Name of Lasky Strong," *MPW,* 21 Feb 1914, 965. "Feature Producers Affiliate," *MPW,* 30 May 1914, 1268–69. W. Stephen Bush, "New Blood in New Programs," *MPW,* 6 Jun 1914, 1394. Jesse L. Lasky, "Accomplishments of the Feature," *MPW,* 11 Jul 1914, 214. "Lasky's First Year; In One Year of Existence Feature Company Has Reached Front Rank of Film Producwers—The Year's Record," *NYDM,* 30 Dec 1914, 24:2. "Lasky's First Year," *MPW,* 9 Jan 1915, 204. "Lasky Views the Future," *MPW,* 27 Mar 1915, 1911. J. Van Cartmell, "Along the Pacific Coast," *NYDM,* 13 Nov 1915, 31:1 (a printing press was installed at FP-L to produce a weekly *Lasky Leader,* confined to studio distribution). "Western Producers to Co-operate," *MPW,* 5 Feb 1916, 757. "Producing Plans Announced by Jesse L. Lasky," *MPW,* 19 May 1917, 1100. Jesse L. Lasky, "Famous Players to Make Cheerful Pictures," *MPW,* 15 Jun 1918, 1577. Jesse L. Lasky, "A Large Motion Picture Undertaking," *MPW,* 6 Jul 1918, 53–55. "Famous Players to Refilm Former Screen Successes,"

MPW, 12 Oct 1918, 243. "Lasky Talks of Company's Activities on West Coast," *MPW,* 12 Oct 1918, 248. "Lasky Wants San Francisco Studio," *MPW,* 29 Mar 1919, 1792. Jesse L. Lasky, "Specialized Production for the New Year," *MPW,* 28 Jun 1919, 1920–21. "Lasky Sees Prosperity Everywhere," *MPW,* 30 Aug 1919, 1293. "Lasky Defends Entry of Famous Players Into the Theatrical Producing Field," *MPW,* 8 May 1920, 806. Jesse L. Lasky, "Future Productions of Famous Players to Prove Value of Sound Organization," *MPW,* 12 Jun 1920, 1469. "Lasky Denies Paramount Will Hire Only Members of Actors Equity Association," *MPW,* 6 Nov 1920, 86. "Lasky Says Day of Extravagance and waste in Producing Films Is Ended," *MPW,* 15 Jan 1921, 281. "Jesse L. Lasky Says Thorough Organization Lessens Inefficiency in Studio Management," *MPW,* 26 Feb 1921, 1064. "Lasky Reveals Stupidity of Censorship in Strong Article in Pictorial Review," *MPW,* 23 Apr 1921, 831 (15 Apr 1921 issue). "Day for 'Show Down' Has Arrived, Says Lasky, in Detailing Paramount's Economy Program; To Cut Production Cost 25%," *MPW,* 9 Jul 1921, 177. Jesse L. Lasky, "Idle Promises Mean Failure, Says Lasky; Industry's Ideals Must Be Ever Higher," *MPW,* 10 Dec 1921, 704. Jesse L. Lasky, "Big Productions Have Made Good and Are Here to Stay," *MPW,* 31 Dec 1921, 1053. "Lasky Sues First National and Strand, Alleging Infringement on 'Sumurun,'" *MPW,* 7 Jan 1922, 62. "Buys Home Site," *MPW,* 4 Nov 1922, 42 (12 acres on Franklin Avenue, Hollywood; "Chief Cahuenga" tribal site). Jesse L. Lasky, "Challenge for Making of Better Pictures," *MPW,* 8 Sep 1923, 132. "Waste Eliminated, Says Lasky; New Production Plans Forming," *MPW,* 24 Nov 1923, 375. "Lasky Infuses New Blood in Paramount Directorial Staff," *MPW,* 12 Apr 1924, 569. "42,000 Scenarios Sent to Hollywood Studios; Few Taken," *MPW,* 24 May 1924, 366. "Writers Instructed," *MPW,* 25 Oct 1924, 675. "Lasky Tells Changes in the Producing Schedule," *MPW,* 20 Dec 1924, 759. "They're Off!," *MPW,* 1 Aug 1925, 569, 572 (formal opening of Paramount Picture School, Inc., 21 Jul 1925, LI City NY). "'Malicious Falsehood,' Comments Zukor on Lasky Rumor," *MPW,* 7 Nov 1925, 27. "Filmdom Pays Tribute to Lasky," *MPW,* 26 Dec 1925, 753. "They Control Your Films!," *MPC,* Jan 1926, 26. "Lasky Defines Function of 'Comedy Constructor,'" *MPW,* 2 Jan 1926, 73. "Studio Reorganization Pleases Lasky," *MPW,* 9 Jan 1926, 156. "'Famous' Buys United Studio in Hollywood, Lasky Reports," *MPW,* 16 Jan 1926, 225. "'Baby' Stars Graduated; Contracts Are Diplomas," *MPW,* 13 Mar 1926, pp. 1, 4. "Most Remarkable Production Era Here, Says Lasky," *MPW,* 15 May 1926, 236. Laurence Urbach, "Schulberg Responsible for F.P. Production," *MPW,* 31 Jul 1926, 1. "Lasky Writes," *MPW,* 28 Aug 1926, 4 (Edward L. Bernays' book on motion picture careers; Geo. H. Doran Co.). "Medal, Money for Directors of Best Films," *MPW,* 15 Jan 1927, 175. "Lasky Lauds Short Runs as Better Policy," *MPW,* 29 Jan 1927, 345. "Lasky Points the Way of All Art," *MPW,* 19 Feb 1927, 557. "Jesse L. Lasky Says," *MPW,* 26 Mar 1927, 326. "Nation-Wide Search for a Blonde," *MPW,* 14 May 1927, 112. Tom Waller, "Lasky Asks 10 Per Cent. Reductions in All Paramount Salaries Over $50," *MPW,* 25 Jun 1927, pp. 559, 564. "Paramount First to Cut Wages, Last to Agree to Postponement," *MPW,* 9 Jul 1927, 84. "Lasky Says Action of Studio Personnel Wins Wide Respect," *MPW,* 3 Sep 1927, 23. "New Production Policy Braring Fruit, Declares Lasky," *MPW,* 8 Oct 1927, pp. 369, 371. "Lasky Scoffs Report He'll Quit Paramount," *MPW,* 22 Oct 1927, 475–76.

Laslo, Lee [actor]. No data found. AMD, p. 208. "Hungarian Star Leaves Piermont," *MPW,* 16 Jul 1927, 185.

La Strange, Richard [actor] (b. Asheville NC, 27 Dec 1889–19 Nov 1963 [73]). BHD1, p. 612.

Laszlo, Aladar [scenarist] (b. Budapest, Hungary, 10 Oct 1896–16 Sep 1958 [61], Los Angeles CA). AS, p. 643.

Laszlo, Ernest [cinematographer] (b. Budapest, Hungary, 23 Apr 1896–6 Jan 1984 [87], Woodland Hills CA). m. Rosa. (Paramount.) "Ernest Laszlo, 85, Oscar-Winning Cameraman, Dies in Hollywood," *Variety,* 18 Jan 1984. AS, p. 643 (b. 1899). BHD2, p. 153 (b. 1898). Katz, p. 693 (b. 1906).

Latell, Lyle [actor] (*né* Lyle Zeiem, b. Elma IA, 5 Apr 1896–24 Oct 1967 [71], Los Angeles CA). AS, p. 643.

Latham, Fred G. [director] (b. England, 1853–31 Jan 1943 [89?], New York NY). BHD2, p. 153.

Latham, Joseph W., Sr. [actor] (b. 1890–10 Oct 1970 [80?], Valley Cottage NY). BHD, p. 225.

Latham, Woodville [devised the Pantoptikon projector, 1894; Latham loop, 1895] (b. 1837–1911 [73?]). Katz, p. 693. WWVC, pp. 78–79.

Latimer, Alice [actress] (d. 15 May 1930, Wynnewood PA). BHD, p. 225.

Latimer, Henry [actor] (b. 1876–25 Jan 1963 [86?], London, England). BHD, p. 225.

La Torre, Charles [actor] (b. New York NY, 15 Apr 1894–2 Feb 1990 [95], Los Angeles CA). BHD, p. 225.

Latte, Lilly [actress] (b. Germany, 1891–24 Nov 1984 [93?], Beverly Hills CA). m. **Fritz Lang** (d. 1976). AS, p. 644.

Laub, William B. [cameraman/scenarist/film editor]. No data found. AMD, p. 208. FDY, p. 491. "William Laub, Navy Cameraman," *MPW,* 28 Dec 1918, 1497.

Laucius, Juozapas [actor] (b. Utena, Lithuania, 23 Nov 1893–23 Jan 1985 [91], Kaunas, Lithuania). AS, p. 644.

Lauckner, Rolf [scenarist] (b. Germany, 1887–26 Apr 1954 [67?], Bayreuth, Germany). AS, p. 644.

Lauder, Harry (brother of actor Alec Lauder) [stage/radio/film actor/singer/composer] (b. Portobello, near Edinburgh, Scotland, 4 Aug 1870–26 Feb 1950 [79], Strathaven, Scotland; arterio-thrombosis and kidney ailment). m. Annie Vallance ("Nancy") (d. 1927). Sir Harry Lauder, *Roamin' in the Gloamin"* (Philadelphia: J.B. Lippincott Co., 1928). "Harry Lauder Dies After a Relapse; Noted Scottish Comedian and Singer, 79, Was Knighted in 1919 for His War Work," *NYT,* 27 Feb 1950, 1:2, 19:2 (d. 14 Aug). "Sir Harry Lauder," *Variety,* 177, 1 Mar 1950, 63 (d. 25 Feb, Lenarkshire, Scotland); Joe Laurie, "A Bonnie Laddie," pp. 2:4, 63:4 ("In 1914 the Palace [theater], N.Y., which never would pay Lauder his salary, ran his singing picture [a pioneer pic where he was synchronized with phonograph recordings]. They had three sheets in front of the theatre with Lauder's name in four-foot letterrs and in tiny print underneath 'Singing Picture.' The picture cost them $500 a week; Lauder would have cost $5,000."). AMD, p. 208. AS, p. 644 (d. 25 Feb). BHD, p. 225. IFN, p. 172. "Harry Lauder in Motion Pictures," *MPW,* 24 Jan 1914, 425. "Chaplin and Lauder Co-Star," *MPW,* 23 Feb 1918, 1103.

Laughlin, Anna [stage/film actress] (b. Sacramento CA, 11 Oct 1885–6 Mar 1937 [51], New York NY; suicide: found with head in oven). m. Dwight Van Monroe. "Anna Laughlin," *Variety,* 7 Apr 1937 (age 50). AMD, p. 208. AS, p. 644. BHD, p. 225. IFN, p. 172. SD, p. 742.. "Anna Laughlin Joins Reliance," *MPW,* 11 Oct 1913, 134. "Anna Laughlin," *MPW,* 29 May 1915, 1407.

Laughton, Charles [film/stage/TV actor/director] (b. Scarborough, England, 1 Jul 1899–15 Dec 1962 [63], Los Angeles CA; bone cancer). m. **Elsa Lanchester**, 1929. "Charles Laughton Is Dead at 63; Character Actor for 3 Decades," *NYT,* 17 Dec 1962, 15:6; "Charles Laughton [editorial]," 18 Dec 1962, 6:2 ("He was homely, loon-faced, fat and sloppy—and it did not mater in the slighest. He needed no prps, no handsome face, athletic figure or fashionable clothes. His career was based on the art of acting, and there have been few greater exponents of this art in our times."); "Laughton Is Hailed for Aid to U.S. Arts," CXII, 20 Dec 1962, 8:1 (eulogized by Christopher Isherwood at Forest Lawn, Hollywood Hills Cemetery; pallbearers included Raymond Massey, Lloyd Wright and Jean Renoir). "Charles Laughton," *Variety,* 229, 19 Dec 1962, 67:1 (AA for *The Private Life of Henry VIII,* 1933). AS, p. 644. BHD1, p. 317; BHD2, p. 154. IFN, p. 172.

Laugier, Germaine (daughter of **Louis Lugier**) [actress] (*née* Berthe Germaine Laugier, b. Louveciennes, France, 30 Jul 1902 [extrait de naissance no. 28/1902]-2 Oct 1982 [80], Paris, France). AS, p. 644.

Lasugier, Louis Pierre (father of **Germaine Lugier**) (b. Paris, France, 14 May 1864–1907 [43?], Louveciennes, France). AS, p. 644.

Launder, Frank Sydney [scenarist/producer/director] (b. Hitchin, Hertfordshire, England, 1905?–23 Feb 1997 [91], Princess Grace Hospital, Monte Carlo, Monaco). m. (2) actress Bernadette O'Farrell (b. 1926). "Frank Launder," *NYT,* 2 Mar 1997, 36. "Frank Launder," *Variety,* 3 Mar 1997, 82:4. "Frank Launder," *Pittsburgh Post-Gazette,* 70, 28 Feb 1997, A-20:3. Tom Vallance, "Frank Launder," *The Independent,* 24 Feb 1997, p. 16 (b. 1907; he worked at Elstree Studios as a title writer for silent films, starting with *Cocktail,* 1928). AS, p. 645 (b. 1907). BHD2, p. 154.

Laurel, Mae [actress] (b. Australia, 24 May 1886–1960 [74?], Sayville NY). BHD, p. 225.

Laurel, Stan (brother of Ted Jefferson, 1893–1933) [stage/film actor/director] (*né* Arthur Stanley Jefferson, b. Ulverston, England, 16 Jun 1890–23 Feb 1965 [74], Santa Monica CA). m. (1) Mae; (2) Lois Nielson (*née* Dixie Kay Nelson, b. Santa Fe NM, 15 Aug 1933); (3) three times to Virginia Roth; (4) Illeana (Vera Shuvalova); (5) Ida Kitaeva. John McCabe and Al Kilgore, *Laurel & Hardy* (NY: Bonanza Books, 1975). "Stan Laurel Dies; Movie Comedian; Teamed with Oliver Hardy in 200 Slapstick Films—Played 'Simple' Foil," *NYT,* 24 Feb 1965, 41:1. "Stan Laurel," *Variety,* 3 Mar 1965. AMD, p. 208. AS, p. 645. BHD1, p. 317; BHD2, p. 154. FSS, p. 175. IFN, p. 173. JS, p. 236 (made *Atollo K* in Italy in 1951).

Katz, pp. 695–97. SD. Truitt, p. 191. "Bernstein to Produce Comedies," *MPW,* 7 Jul 1917, 73 (as Stanley Jefferson; *Stanley Comdies* series). "Amalgamated Producing Co. Will Soon Present Stan Laurel to Public," *MPW,* 20 May 1922, 296. "Metro to Release Laurel Comedies," *MPW,* 30 Sep 1922, 379. "Pathé Signs Stan Laurel for Series of One-Reel Comedies," *MPW,* 3 Mar 1923, 93. "Stan Laurel Directing," *MPW,* 8 Aug 1925, 648. "Stan Laurel Directing," *MPW,* 27 Mar 1926, 278. "Stan Laurel on Roach Contract; Pathé Release," *MPW,* 14 May 1927, 121. Allan Hoffman, "Dick und Doof; The Twilight Years," Part I, *CFC,* 24 (Summer, 1969), 49; Part II, 25 (Fall, 1969), 54; Part III, 26, 58, 62. Peter Squarini, "Laurel and Hardy Bibliography," *CI,* 70 (Jul 1980), 61.

Laurell, Kay [actress] (b. Erie PA, 1889?–31 Jan 1927 [37], London, England; pneumonia). m. **Winfield R. Sheehan** (d. 1945). (Film debut: *The Brand,* Goldwyn, 1919.) "Kay Laurell Dead," *Variety,* 2 Feb 1927. AMD, p. 208. AS, p. 645 (b. Newcastle PA). BHD, p. 225 (b. New Castle Pa, 1890). IFN, p. 173. "Beach Engages Kay Laurell," *MPW,* 21 Dec 1918, 1338. "Paramount Engages Grace Darmond," *MPW,* 8 Mar 1919, 1318.

Laurence, Max [director] (*né* Friedrich Rudolf Maximilien Laurence, b. Berlin, Germany, 7 Aug 1852). AS, p. 645.

Laurente, Eugénie Joséphine [actress] (b. Saint-Priest-en-Jarez, France, 4 Aug 1882–13 Dec 1964 [82], Lyons, France). AS, p. 645.

Laurent, Marie Thérèse [actress] (b. Paris, France, 25 Jun 1825).

Laurie, Ed J. [film/stage actor] (d. 9 Jan 1919, London, England). (Mutual, Vogue Company.) BHD, p. 225. Cal York, "Plays and Players," *Photoplay,* Jul 1917, 110.

Laurie, John [actor] (b. Dumfries, Scotland, 25 Mar 1897–23 Jun 1980 [83], Chalfont St. Peter, England; emphysema). AS, p. 645.

Laurier, Jay [actor] (*né* Jay Chapman, b. Birmingham, England, 31 May 1879–15 Apr 1969 [89], Durban, South Africa). AS, p. 645.

Lauritzen, Lau [actor/driector] (b. Silkeborg, Denmark, 13 Mar 1878–2 Jul 1938 [60], Denmark). AS, p. 645. BHD2, p. 154.

Lauste, Eugène [inventor] (b. Paris, France, 1856–27 Jun 1935 [79?], Montclair NJ). AS, p. 645. BHD2, p. 154.

Lauterbock, Helene [actress] (b. Vienna, Austria, 16 Jan 1895–ca. 1956 [61?]). AS, p. 646.

Lavalliere, Eve [actress] (*née* Eugenie Marie Pascaline Fenoglio, b. Toulon, France, 1 Apr 1866–10 Jul 1929 [63], Thuillieres, France; cancer [extrait de décès no. 6]). AS, p. 646.

La Varnie, Laura [stage/film actress] (*née* Laura Anderson, b. Jefferson City MO, 2 Mar 1853–18 Sep 1939 [86], Los Angeles CA). (Biograph, 1909; K&E; retired 1931.) "Laura La Vernie [sic]," *Variety,* 27 Sep 1939 (age 85). AS, p. 630 (Laura La Vernie, b. 1854). BHD1, p. 317. IFN, p. 173 (b. 1854). Truitt, p. 192.

Lavelle, Kay [actress] (b. 1889–18 Nov 1965 [76?], Tujunga CA). AS, p. 646.

La Vere, June [actress] (*née* Gladys Fry, b. 1903–7 Feb 1991 [87], Woodland Hills CA). "June La Vere," *Variety,* 25 Feb 1991, p. 261. AS, p. 630. BHD1, p. 317.

Laverne, Dorothy [actress] (b. 1910–29 Dec 1940 [30], Los Angeles CA). AS, p. 646. BHD, p. 225. IFN, p. 173.

Laverne, Henri [actor] (*né* Henri Eugène Lavernhe, b. Boulogne-sur-Mer, France, 30 Dec 1890 [extrait de naissance no. 1277/1890]-4 Sep 1953 [62], Saint-Quay-Portrieux, France). AS, p. 646.

La Verne, Lucille [actress; voice of the Queen and the Witch in *Snow White and the Seven Dwarfs,* Disney, 1937] (b. Memphis TN, 8 Nov 1872–4 Mar 1945 [72], Culver City CA). "Lucille La Verne, Noted Actress, 72; Creator of Widow Cagle Role in 'Sun Up' Dies—Character Star in Many Movies," *NYT,* 7 Mar 1945, 21:3. "Lucille La Verne," *Variety,* 7 Mar 1945 (age 76). AS, p. 630. BHD1, p. 317 (b. 7 Nov 1869). FSS, p. 178. IFN, p. 173. Truitt, pp. 191–92 (b. Nashville TN).

Laverty, Jean [actress] (aka Jean Bary or Bery, *née* Gladys Louise Laverty, b. Bluelake CA, 3 Apr 1904–28 Sep 1973 [69], Pismo Beach, San Luis Obispo CA; cardio respiratory arrest; terminal cardiomatosis; carcinoma of tonsils; buried at Los Osos Memorial Park CA [County of San Luis Obispo Certificate of Death #84363]). m. William V. Muir. (MGM.) "Gladys [Jean] Muir," *Telegram Tribune,* 1 Oct 1993. Data supplied by a relative, Mr. Edward Costello, of Raleigh NC.

Lavigne, Maurice [actor] (b. 1887–24 Jun 1952 [65?], New York NY). AS, p. 646.

Lavner, Harry S. [publicist]. No data found. AMD, p. 208. "Lavner with Hodkinson Company," *MPW,* 7 Jun 1919, 1500. "Lavner Leaves Hodkinson," *MPW,* 19 Jun 1920, 1608.

La Volle, Kay [actress] (b. 1889–18 Nov 1965 [76?], Tujunga CA). BHD1, p. 317.

La Voy, Merl [cameraman] (b. 1886–6 Dec 1953 [67?], Johannesburg, South Africa). AMD, p. 208. AS, p. 646. "Merl LaVoy to Visit Battlefront," *MPW,* 1 Jun 1918, 1295. "Merl LaVoy Appointed Globe-Trotting Cameraman by Pathé," *MPW,* 7 May 1927, 43.

Law, Arthur [stage/film actor] (b. Northrepps, Norfolk, England, 22 Mar 1844–2 Apr 1913 [69], Parkstone, Dorset, England). "Arthur Law," *Variety,* 11 Apr 1913. AS, p. 646 (d. Bournemouth, England). SD, p. 744.

Law, Betty [actress] (*née* Betty Valentine, b. New York NY, 2 Mar 1882–3 Feb 1955 [72], Woodland Hills CA). AS, p. 646.

Law, Burton [actor] (b. Ouray CO, 22 Oct 1877–2 Nov 1963 [86], Los Angeles Co. CA). AS, p. 646. BHD, p. 225. IFN, p. 173.

Law, Donald [actor] (b. Tampa FL, 1920–5 Feb 1959 [38], Meadville PA). BHD, p. 225. IFN, p. 173.

Law, Rodman, "The Human Fly" [aviator/stuntman/actor] (b. MA, 1885?–14 Oct 1919 [34], Greenville SC; tuberculosis). "Rodman Law Dead; Parachute Jumper, Brother of Noted Aviatrix [Ruth Law], Dies of Consumption," *NYT,* 15 Oct 1919, 17:3. AMD, p. 208. AS, p. 647. BHD, p. 225. "Blows Up Balloon and Escapes; Rodman Law Shows Unparalleled Daring for Motion Picture Purposes," *NYDM,* 20 Nov 1912, 31:1 (rose 500 feet above the Hudson River in a balloon filled with superheated naphtha gas, then blew it up with dynamite and parachuted into the water. Filmed for *At the Risk of His Life,* 3 reels, International Film Co. "When it was all over Law was the coolest man in the party. He was not hurt in the least and merely remarked, 'I told you it could be done.'"). "Law Does Stunts for Reliance," *MPW,* 1 Feb 1913, 450. "Skyrocket Bursts with Man on Board; Law Near Death When He Attempts to Shoot Himself Far Through the Air; His Rocket 44 Feet Long; It Flies into a Thousand Pieces When Set Off, but Parachute Jumper Escapes Harm," *NYT,* 14 Mar 1913, 8:4 (previously jumped from the Brooklyn Bridge and from some skyscrapers; occurred on 13 Mar 1913 in Jersey City NJ. He had planned to shoot himself into Elizabeth NJ, 12 miles away. The skyrocket burst apart and projected Law about 30 feet from the scaffold. His hands and face were scorched. He explained that his mixing of the powder caused more rapid combustion than he had intended). "Coaxed Off Capitol Dome; Policeman Spies Rodman Law on Visit to Goddess of Liberty," *NYT,* 8 May 1913, 3:5 (on 7 May Law climbed the Capitol Dome "while a moving picture camera was focussed on him." Law evaded police by crawling through a window in the lanter [of the statue], but came down because the cornice of the statue was rusted.). "Law Hurt Flying for Films; Leaping into Water from Aeroplane, He Loses Senses," *NYT,* 19 Oct 1913, II, 5:3–8 (on 18 Oct Law attempted a jump from a plane for *Dare Devil Rescue* (Ryno Film Co.) at Midland Beach Pier, Staten Island NY. "Frederick Bennett, an actor in the film company's employ, was in the water dressed as a woman. He was supposed to be drowning. It was Law's role to jump after him and rescue him." However, Law turned over in the air and landed in the water on his back and became unconscious. Bennett, momemtarily shocked, brought Law ashore. Law suffered a badly strained tendon of the neck.). "Fall with Aeroplane; Daredevil Law and Aviator [Walter Edwards], Posing for Ryno Film, Meet with Accident," *NYDM,* 22 Oct 1913, 28:4 (Law suffered a dislocated right shoulder, a broken jaw and several other injuries. He refused to go to a hospital. The stunt was for *A Daredevil Rescue.*). "Two Jump from Bridge; Law and Miss Bennett Do a Parachute Stunt for Movies," *NYT,* 6 Feb 1914, 6:3 (both jumped from the Williamsburg Bridge, witnessed by startled people who at first did not notice a motion picture machine at work.). "'The Human Fly' Arrested; Picture Man Says Law Threatened to Kill Him," *NYT,* 7 Feb 1914, 3:1 (arrested on 6 Feb, NYC, for threatening Clarkson F. Ryttenberg for $30 owed to him for motion picture work. As a detective searched him, a knife fell from Law's sleeve; he was charged with attempted assault and concealment of a weapon. A Miss Constance Bennett and friends made a bail bond for him.). "Daredevil Rodman Law," *Variety,* 22 May 1914, p. 23. "To Operate on Rodman Law; Aviator Taken to Bellevue Hospital in Weekend Condition," *NYT,* 31 May 1917, 11:1 (arrived to submit to a minor operation so weak that he had to be carried into the hospital.). "Leaps from Airplane with a Parachute; French Aviator Makes Safe Descent from a Height of 800 Meters," *NYT,* 1 Aug 1918, 2:2 (appended to this item is a quip stating that Law jumped from a plane at Kelly Field, San Antonio TX).

Law, Walter [actor] (b. Dayton OH, 26 Mar 1876–8 Aug 1940 [64], Los Angeles CA). (Lubin.) "Walter Law," *NYT,* 10 Aug 1940, 13:6. "Walter Law," *Variety,* 14 Aug 1940. AMD, p. 208. AS, p. 647 (b. Farmersville OH; d. 9 Aug). BHD1, p. 317 (b. Farmersville). IFN, p. 173 (b. Farmersville). MH, p. 122 (b. 1878). Truitt, p. 192. "Law Deserts Villain Role to Be Detective for Perret," *MPW,* 15 Feb 1919, 887.

Lawes, Lewis E. [scenarist] (b. 1884–23 Apr 1947 [53?], Gasrrison NY). AS, p. 647. BHD2, p. 154.

Lawford, Betty (daughter of **Ernest Lawford**; cousin of Peter Lawford) [actress] (b. London, England, 1910–20 Nov 1960 [50?], New York NY). m. (1) **Monta Bell** (d. 1958); (2) Barry Buchanan. "Betty Lawford, Actress, Is Dead; Stage, Film and Television Performer Was Noted for Role in 'The Women,'" *NYT,* 21 Nov 1960, 29:5. "Betty Lawford," *Variety,* 30 Nov 1960. BHD1, p. 317. IFN, p. 173 (age 44). Truitt, p. 192.

Lawford, Ernest E. (father of **Betty Lawford**) [stage/film actor] (b. Yorkshire, England, 20 Apr 1870–26 Dec 1940 [70], New York NY). m. Janet Slater. "Ernest Lawford, Noted Actor, Dies; Abandoned Law in England for 50-Year Career on Stage—Is Stricken Here at 70; In Many Character Roles, Original Charley in 'Charley's Aunt' Played Polonius in Modern-Dress 'Hamlet,'" *NYT,* 28 Dec 1940, 15:1. "Ernest Lawford," *Variety,* 1 Jan 1941. AS, p. 647. BHD1, p. 317 (b. London). IFN, p. 173 (age 89).

Lawford, May [actress] (*née* May Summerville, b. England, 1900–23 Jan 1972 [71?], Monterey Park CA). AS, p. 647.

Lawford, Sydney (father of Peter Lawford, 1923–1984) [actor] (*né* Peter Sydney Erenst Lawford, b. England, 1866–15 Feb 1953 [86?], Los Angeles CA). AS, p. 647.

Lawler, Jerome [actor] (b. Canada, 13 Jul 1887–6 Jan 1974 [86], Santa Barbara CA). BHD1, p. 612.

Lawlor, Frank [stage/film actor] (b. Washington DC, 20 Aug 1869–15 Oct 1932 [63], New York NY). m. Vernie Conrad. "Frank Lalor," *Variety,* 18 Oct 1932. AS, p. 634 (Frank Lalor). BHD, p. 222. SD. Truitt, 1983.

Lawlor, Hoey [writer]. No data found. AMD, p. 208. "Lawlor Turns to Writing," *MPW,* 3 Jan 1925, 80.

Lawrence, Adelaide (daughter of **Edmund Lawrence**) [child actress] (b. ca. 1906). (Kalem.) AMD, p. 208. W. Stephen Bush, "The Screen Children's Gallery," *MPW,* 28 Feb 1914, 1066.

Lawrence, Ed [actor] (*né* Edwin Augustus Austin, b. Paris ID, 27 Aug 1866–2 Feb 1937 [70], Los Angeles CA). AS, p. 647.

Lawrence, Edmund [director] (b. Bridgeport CT, 1869–29 Jul 1944 [75?], Lake Secor NY). BHD2, p. 154.

Lawrence, Edmund "Eddy" (father of **Adelaide Lawrence**) [director/producer] (b. San Francisco CA, 1881?–5 Dec 1931 [50], San Diego CA; suicide by gas poisoning). (Kalem.) "Eddy Lawrence," *Variety,* 1 Dec 1931. AMD, p. 208. AS, p. 647. BHD, p. 225. IFN, p. 173. Truitt, p. 192. "Edmund Lawrence," *MPW,* 15 Aug 1914, 972. "Edmund Lawrence," *NYDM,* 19 Aug 1914, 22:1 (daughter Adelaide was 8 years old). "Gleichman Heads New Company," *MPW,* 6 Feb 1915, 806. "Lawrence to Direct for Ivan," *MPW,* 21 Jul 1917, 466. "Edmund Lawrence Re-engaged by Ivan," *MPW,* 10 Nov 1917, 863. "Lawrence to Stage Pearson Film," *MPW,* 25 May 1918, 1168. "Edmund Lawrence Assistant Metro Director," *MPW,* 20 Jul 1918, 378.

Lawrence, Florence, "Baby Flo, the Child Wonder Whistler" and "The Biograph Girl" (daughter of stage actress Charlotte "Lotta" Dunn, 18 Aug 1861–20 Aug 1929) [stage/film actress] (b. Hamilton, Ontario, Canada, 22 Sep 1886–28 Dec 1938 [52], Beverly Hills CA [Death Certificate #38–074416]; suicide by ingestion of ant paste [arsenic]). m. (1) **Harry [Lewis] Solter**, 30 Aug 1908, Elizabeth NJ (d. 1928); (2) Charles Bryne Woodring, 12 May 1921, SF CA—div. 20 Feb 1932; (3) Henry Bolton, 27 Nov 1933—div. ca. 1935. Kelly R. Brown, *Florence Lawrence, the Biograph Girl; America's First Movie Star* (Jefferson NC: McFarland, 1999). (Biograph, 1908; Imp; Victor.) "Florence Lawrence," *Variety,* 4 Jan 1939. AMD, p. 208. AS, p. 647. BHD1, p. 318 (b. 1 Jan 1890). FSS, p. 179. IFN, p. 173 (b. 1890). Katz, pp. 698–99. Spehr, p. 148. Truitt, p. 192 (b. 1888). "[Laemmle] Has Star Actress," *Variety,* XVI, 16 Oct 1909, 13:3. "The Imp Leading Lady," *MPW,* 2 Apr 1910, 517. "Florence Lawrence," *MPW,* 9 Apr 1910, 549. "Florence Lawrence," *MPW,* 7 Jan 1911, 26. Epes Winthrop Sargent, "Credit Where Credit Is Due," *MPW,* 14 Oct 1911, 106–07. "Florence Lawrence Joins Independents," *MPW,* 18 May 1912, 617. "The Return of Miss Lawrence," *MPW,* 9 Aug 1913, 620. "Florence Lawrence; Leading Woman with the Victor Company," *MPS,* 23 Jan 1914, 28. "Growing Up with the Movies," *MPW,* 26 Sep 1914, 1754. "Florence Lawrenc Seriously Ill," *MPW,* 7 Aug 1915, 972. "Florence Lawrence in Auto Accident," *MPW,* 4 Sep 1915, 1654. "Florence Lawrence to Return to the Screen," *MPW,* 11 Dec 1915, 1998. "Universal Gets Florence Lawrence," *MPW,* 1 Jan 1916, 86. "Universal Plans for Miss Lawrence," *MPW,* 8 Jan 1916, 232. "Florence Lawrence at Washington," *MPW,* 5 Feb 1916, 764. "Florence Lawrence Has Paris Gowns," *MPW,* 8 Apr 1916, 264. "Florence Lawrence Resigns," *MPW,* 22 Apr 1916, 631. "Voices from the Past," *MPW,* 3 Nov 1917, 686. "Producers Pictures Corporation Formed for Florence Lawrence, First Film Star," *MPW,* 27 Nov 1920, 462. Larry Lee Holland, "Florence Lawrence," *FIR,* Aug/Sep 1980, 385–94. Eve Golden, "Florence Lawrence; The First Movie Star," *CI,* 229 (Jul 1994), 14–16 (b. 1889). Death Certificate and Coroner's Register submitted by Mrs. Kelly Brown, Statesville NC. The Death Certificate lists Henry Bolton as the (former) husband. An autopsy was performed. The Coroner's Register (File No. 77915) gives Lawrence's age as 44 years, 11 months and 27 days; probable cause of suicide: ill health. George Lawrence, her brother from San Francisco, delivered the suicide note.

Lawrence, Frank [film editor]. No data found. m. **Viola**.

Lawrence, Gerald [actor] (b. London, England, 23 Mar 1873–16 May 1957 [84], London, England). AS, p. 647. BHD1, p. 318. IFN, p. 173.

Lawrence, Gertrude (mother of actress/painter Pamela Gordon) [stage/film actress/singer] (*née* Gertrude Alexandra Dagmar Klasen, b. London, England, 4 Jul 1898–6 Sep 1952 [54], New York Hospital, New York NY; infectious hepatitis, confirmed by an autopsy; buried at Upton MA). m. (1) Francis Gordon-Hawley, 1924–27; (2) Richard S. Aldrich, 1940. *A Star Danced* (NY: Doubleday, 1945). (Broadway debut: *Andre Charlot's Revue of 1924.*) "Gertrude Lawrence, Actress, Dies at 52," *NYT,* 7 Sep 1952, 1:2, 86:1 (b. 1900; age 52; half Danish, half Irish; admitted to the hospital on 16 Aug). "Gertrude Lawrence," *Variety,* 188, 10 Sep 1952, 56:4 (b. 1898; "She was an artist who made brilliant use of basically limited natural talents to achieve remarkable theatrical illusion."). BHD1, p. 318. IFN, p. 173.

Lawrence, Lillian (mother of **Ethel Grey Terry**) [actress] (b. Alexandria WV, 17 Feb 1868–7 May 1926 [58], Beverly Hills CA; heart attack). "Lillian Lawrence," *Variety,* 12 May 1926 and 4 Aug 1926 (age 56). AMD, p. 209. AS, p. 647. BHD, p. 225. IFN, p. 173. SD, p. 746. Truitt, p. 192 (b. 1870). "Obituary," *MPW,* 22 May 1926, 4.

Lawrence, Margaret [actress] (b. Trenton NJ, 2 Aug 1889–9 Jun 1929 [39], New York NY; murdered by **Louis Bennison**). AS, p. 647. "[Actress Margaret] Lawrence-Bennison Affair Ends in Killing and Suicide in New York," *Variety,* 12 Jun 1929. Joseph P. Eckhardt, "Louis Bennison Corrections [letter]," *CI,* 245 (Nov 1995), 6 (his suicide note read, "The sunset has a heart—look for us there.").

Lawrence, Maurice E. [composer] (b. 1888–16 Mar 1944 [56?], Los Angeles CA). AS, p. 647.

Lawrence, Paul [actor] (b. Cleveland OH). (Thanhouser; Metro.)

Lawrence, Raymond [actor] (*né* Raymond Francis Miles Atkinson, b. London, England, 8 Dec 1888–28 May 1976 [87], Los Angeles Co. CA). BHD1, p. 318. IFN, p. 173.

Lawrence, Rosina [vaudeville/film dancer/singer/actress: Our Gang, Little Rascals] (b. Westboro, Ontario, Canada, 30 Dec 1913–23 Jun 1997 [83], New York NY; cancer). m. (1) Juvenal P. Marchisio, 1939 (d. 1973); (2) John C. McCabe, 8 Jun 1987, NY NY (founder of the Laurel & Hardy Fan Club). (Film debut: *Lady of Quality,* Universal, 1923; Fox; Hal Roach.) Wolfgang Saxon, "Rosina Lawrence, 84, Is Dead; A Teacher in 'Our Gang' Films; Comedy and dancing were highlights of a brief, bright career," *NYT,* 6 Jul 1997, 19. Adam Goldworm, "Rosina Lawrence," *Variety,* 21 Jul 1997, 41:3. "Rosina Lawrence," *Pittsburgh Post-Gazette,* 70, 7 Jul 1997, A-11:6 (Rosina Marchisio-McCabe). AS, p. 647 (b. 1914). BHD1, p. 612. JS, p. 237 (her last film was *In campagna è caduta una stella,* Italy, 1939). John McCabe, "Rosina Lawrence," *CI,* 149 (Nov 1987), C26-C28, 61 (includes filmography).

Lawrence, Vincent S. [scenarist] (b. Boston MA, 1890–24 Nov 1946 [56?], Corpus Christi TX). AS, p. 648 (d. 24 Oct). BHD2, p. 154.

Lawrence, Viola [film editor] (*née?,* b. 1895?–20 Nov 1973 [78], Los Angeles CAl; cancer). m. **Frank Lawrence**. "Viola Lawrence," *Variety,* 28 Nov 1973. (Vitagraph, 1912; to Hollywood in 1917, at Universal, First National, Columbia, Goldwyn; retired 1961). AS, p. 648. BHD2, p. 154.

Lawrence, Walter [actor] (d. 18 Feb 1931, Lake Mohegan, Peekskill NY). "Walter Lawrence," *Variety,* 25 Feb 1931. AS, p. 648.

Lawrence, William [actor] (*né* William Lawrence Boehner, b. Nova Scotia, Canada-d. 17 Mar 1921, Boston MA). "William Lawrence," *Variety,* 25 Mar 1921. AS, p. 648. SD, p. 746.

Lawrence, William [actor] (b. Brooklyn NY?, 1880?–14 Jun 1914 [34], Bridgeport CT). "William Lawrence Dead," *Variety,* 19 Jun 1914. AS, p. 648.

Lawrence, William [playwright] (b. 1897?–4 Mar 1932 [35], New York NY; pneumonia). "William Lawrence," *Variety,* 8 Mar 1932.

Lawrence, William E[ffingham] "Babe" [actor] (b. Brooklyn NY, 22 Aug 1896–28 Nov 1947 [51], Los Angeles CA). (Griffith; Metro; Paramount.) AMD, p. 209. AS, p. 648. BHD, p. 225. IFN, p. 173. Truitt, p. 192. "Metro Engages

Lawrence," *MPW,* 28 Aug 1920, 1194:3 (in *Intolerance*).

Lawrence, Wingold [actor] (b. London, England, 1874–13 Mar 1938 [63?], London, England). BHD, "Addendum."

Lawson, Eleanor [actress] (*née* Eleanor Smith, b. IL, 23 Dec 1875–22 Mar 1966 [90], Pasadena CA; heart attack). AS, p. 648. BHD1, p. 319. Truitt, 1983.

Lawson, John [music hall sketch manager/film actor] (b. Hollingsworth, England, 9 Jan 1865–25 Nov 1920 [55], London, England; pneumonia). "John Lawson Dead," *Variety,* LXI, 3 Dec 1920, 2:3. BHD, p. 225. IFN, p. 173.

Lawson, John Howard [playwright/scenarist] (b. New York NY, 25 Sep 1894–11 Aug 1977 [82], San Francisco CA; complications from Parkinson's disease). m. (1) Kate Drain; (2) Susan Edmond. C. Gerald Fraser, "John Howard Lawson, 82, Writer Blacklisted by Hollywood in '47," *NYT,* 14 Aug 1977, 46:3. "John Howard Lawson," *Variety,* 17 Aug 1977. AS, p. 648. BHD2, p. 155 (b. 1895; d. 12 Aug). FDY, p. 491. IFN, p. 174 (age 80). SD.

Lawson, Kate Drain [actress] (b. Washington DC, 27 Jul 1894–19 Nov 1977 [83], Woodland Hills CA). AS, p. 648.

Lawson, Louise [actress] (d. 8 Feb 1924, New York NY). BHD, p. 226. IFN, p. 174.

Lawson, Stan [vaudeville/film actor] (b. 1909–17 Jul 1977 [68], Los Angeles CA). (Sennett.) "Stan Lawson," *Variety,* 287, 27 Jul 1977, 79:2 (in vaudeville as [Dewey] Barto & Lawson). AS, p. 648. BHD, p. 226. IFN, p. 174.

Lawson, Thomas W. [writer]. No data found. AMD, p. 209. "Lawson Sees 'Friday, the 13th,'" *MPW,* 30 Sep 1916, 2093.

Lawson, Wilfrid [actor] (*né* Wilfred Worsnop, b. Bradford, England, 14 Jan 1900–10 Oct 1966 [66], London, England). AS, p. 648.

Lawton, Frank [stage/film actor] (*né* Frank Mokeley, b. London, England, 30 Sep 1894?–10 Jun 1969 [74], London, England). m. (1) Virginia Earl (d. 1937); **Evelyn Laye**, 1934 (d. 1996). "Frank Lawton," *Variety,* 18 Jun 1969. AS, p. 648 (b. 1904). BHD1, p. 319 (b. 1904). IFN, p. 174 (b. 1904). SD (b. 1904).

Lawton, Mary [stage/film actress]. No data found. "Screen Acquires Mary Lawton," *NYDM,* 11 Aug 1915, 22:2 (to debut in an adaptation of Sutro's *John Glayde's Honor,* starring C. Aubrey Smith).

Lawton, Thais [stage/film actress] (b. Louisville KY, 18 Jun 1881–18 Dec 1956 [75], New York NY). m. Percy McDermott. "Thais Lawton, Stage Actress, Dies at 78; Played in Classical and Modern Works," *NYT,* 19 Dec 1956, 31:2. "Thais Lawton," *Variety,* 26 Dec 1956 (age 78). AS, p. 648. BHD, p. 226 (b. 1878). IFN, p. 174. Truitt, p. 192.

Lay, Irving T. [actor] (d. 15 Mar 1932, Seneca Falls NY; suicide by gas inhalation). (Goldwyn.) "Irving T. Lay," *Variety,* 29 Mar 1932 (weighed 400 lbs). AS, p. 648. BHD, p. 226. IFN, p. 174.

Laye, Evelyn [stage/film actress] (*née* Elsie Evelyn Lay, b. London, England, 10 Jul 1900–17 Feb 1996 [95], London, England). m. (1) **Sonny Hale**, 1926–31 (d. 1959); (2) **Frank Lawton** (d. 1969). "Evelyn Laye; Stage actress, favorite of Noel Coward," *Pittsburgh Post-Gazette,* 69, 19 Feb 1996, D-6:1. *The Daily Telegraph,* 19 Feb 1996. Ragan, *Who's Who in Hollywood,* p. 945. Richard Bebb, "Evelyn Laye," *The Independent,* 19 Feb 1996, p. 16. AMD, p. 209. AS, p. 648. BHD1, p. 319. "Myron Selznick Hails Evelyn Laye, English Actress, as Screen 'Find'; Possesses Exceptional Versatility," *MPW,* 11 Feb 1922, 611.

Layl, Ahmed [actor] (b. Egypt-d. 16 Jun 1929, Cairo, Egypt, heart attack). AS, p. 648.

Laymon, Gene [actor] (b. Michigan City IN, 25 Jul 1889–6 Jun 1946 [56], Los Angeles CA). AS, p. 648. BHD, p. 226. IFN, p. 174.

Lazar, Lajos [director] (b. Nagybanya, Hungary, 2 Dec 1885–2 Jun 1936 [50], Budapest, Hungary). AS, p. 648. BHD2, p. 155.

Lazarus, Paul N., Sr. (father of Ted R. Lazarus, Paramount advertising manager; grandfather of Tom Lazarus, adverstising coordinator for Seven Arts Pictures) [publicist/executive] (b. 4 May 1888–19 Feb 1965 [76], Sarasota FL). First wife d. 1945. (Began 1916 as publicity and advertising manager for Vitagraph Corp.; UA, 1919.) "Paul N. Lazarus, Sr.," *Variety,* 238, 24 Feb 1965, 79:1. AMD, p. 209. BHD2, p. 155. "Paul N. Lazarus," *MPW,* 26 Mar 1927, 311.

Lazarus, Sidney [title writer/scenarist] (b. Shelbyville KY, 1890?–4 Dec 1933 [43], Los Angeles CA; found dead in garage from monoxide poisoning). m. Maude. (WB; Universal; Pathé.) "Sid Lazarus and Wife Found Dead in Garage," *Variety,* 5 Dec 1933 (wrote "letters to numerous friends here informing them to notify the police"). AS, p. 648. BHD2, p. 155. FDY, p. 445.

Lazell, Ernest [cinematographer]. No data found. FDY, p. 461.

Lazslo, Josef [scenarist]. No data found. FDY, p. 491.

Lazurina, S.M. [scenarist]. No data found. FDY, p. 491.

Lazzeri, Tony [actor] (b. San Francisco CA, 6 Dec 1903–6 Aug 1946 [42], San Francisco CA). BHD, p. 226.

Lea, Flora [actress]. No data found. (Lubin.) "Flora Lea, A Lubin Ingenue," *NYDM,* 17 Mar 1915, 25:1 (photo).

Leach, John [actor] (b. 1853-Mar 1918 [64?], Chicago IL). BHD, p. 226.

Leahy, Agnes Brand [script girl/title writer/film editor/scenarist] (b. Portland OR, 18 Aug 1893–31 Mar 1934 [40], San Francisco CA). "Agnes Brand Leahy," *Variety,* 3 Apr 1934 (production manager at Paramount). AS, p. 651. BHD2, p. 155. FDY, p. 491.

Leahy, Eugene [actor] (b. Limerick, Ireland, 14 Mar 1883–25 Feb 1967 [83], London, England). AS, p. 651 (b. Newcastle West Co, Ireland; d. 17 Feb. BHD1, p. 319 (b. Newcastle, Ireland).

Leahy, Margaret [actress: Wampas Star, 1923] (b. London, England, 17 Aug 1902–17 Feb 1967 [64], Los Angeles CA). AMD, p. 209. AS, p. 651. BHD, p. 226. IFN, p. 174. "British Prize Winner Here to Make Productions with Norma Talmadge," *MPW,* 23 Dec 1922, 731.

Leal, Antonio [director/cinematographer] (b. Viana do Castelo, Portugal, 1876–1946 [70?], Rio de Jneiro, Brazil). AS, p. 651.

Leal, Milagros [actress] (b. Spain, 1902–1 Mar 1975 [73?], Madrid, Spain). AS, p. 651.

Learn, Alice (sister of **Bessie Learn**) [actress] (d. 23 Nov 1984, New York NY). (Edison.) BHD, p. 226.

Learn, Bessie (sister of **Alice Learn**) [stage/film actress] (b. San Diego CA, 30 Aug 1888–5 Feb 1987 [98], Burbank CA). m. J. Roy Prosser, 1913 (d. 1935); Arthur V. Robbins, 1947 (d. 1961). (Edison, 1911.) "Betsy Learn," *Variety,* 6 May 1987. AMD, p. 209. AS, p. 651. BHD, p. 226. "Fled from the War; Bessie Learn, of Edison, Returns After Harrowing Experiences in WAR Zone," *NYDM,* 26 Aug 1914, 32:3 (fled from Holland). "Bessie Learn in War Panic," *MPW,* 5 Sep 1914, 1353. "Bessie Learn Goes to Mirror Films," *MPW,* 25 Dec 1915, 2351. Billy H. Doyle, "Lost Players," *CI,* 151 (Jan 1988), C4-C5. James Trottier, "There's Something About Bessie: The Short, Fabulous Career [1911–16] of Bessie Learn," *CI,* 289 (Jul 1999), 26.

Learock, Gilbertie [actress] (*née?*). No data found. AMD, p. 209. "Mrs. Gilbertie Learock in 'In the Diplomatic Service,'" *MPW,* 21 Oct 1916, 420.

Leary, Gilda [stage/film actress] (b. London, England, 1896–17 Apr 1927 [31], New York NY; Addison's disease: progressive fatal anemia). "Gilda Leary," *Variety,* 20 Apr 1927, 55:4. BHD, p. 226.

Leary, Nolan [actor] (b. Rock Island IL, 26 Apr 1889–12 Dec 1987 [98], Los Angeles Ca). AS, p. 651 (b. NY NY). BHD1, p. 319.

Lease, Rex [actor/scenarist] (b. Central City WV, 11 Feb 1901–3 Jan 1966 [64], Los Angeles CA). m. **Charlotte Merriam** (d. 1972); Eleanor Hunt, 8 Apr 1931, Las Vegas NV. (MGM.) AMD, p. 209. AS, p. 651. BHD1, p. 320 (b. 1899). FDY, p. 491. FSS, p. 179. IFN, p. 174 (b. 1903). Katz, p. 701 (began 1924; b. 1901). Truitt, p. 192. "Rex Lease," *MPW,* 10 Sep 1927, 93. Nancy Pryor, "Rex Lease Parts from Bride; Domestic Tiffs Separate Cowboy Actor and Bride, Eleanor Hunt, After Few Brief Weeks of Wedded Bliss," *Movie Classic,* I, Sep 1931, 36.

Leavitt, Abe [actor] (*né* Douglas Leavitt, b. 1883–3 Mar 1960 [77?], Levittown PA). AS, p. 651.

Leavitt, Sam[uel] [cinematographer] (b. New York NY, 6 Feb 1904–21 Mar 1984 [80], Woodland Hills CA). AS, p. 651.

Le Bargy, Charles Gustave Auguste [actor] (b. La Chapelle, France, 28 Aug 1858–5 Feb 1936 [77], Nice, France [extrait de décès no. 442/1936]). AS, p. 649. BHD, p. 226. IFN, p. 174.

Le Baron, William [playwright/scenarist/director/producer] (b. Elgin IL, 16 Feb 1883–9 Feb 1958 [74], Los Angeles CA; heart attack). (Cosmopolitan, 1919–24; FP-L; FBO; RKO; TC-F.) m. Mabel H. Hollins (d. 1955). "William LeBaron, Film Producer, 74; Movie Maker from Silent Era to 1947 Is Dead—Successful Playwright," *NYT,* 10 Feb 1958, 23:2. "William Le Baron," *Variety,* 19 Feb 1958 (age 75). AMD, p. 209. AS, p. 649; p. 651 (William Lebaron). BHD2, p. 155. FDY, p. 491. IFN, p. 174 (age 75). Katz, p. 702. SD. "Scenarists Have Not Reached Development Attained by Magazine and Stage Play Writers," *MPW,* 17 Apr 1920, 390. "William LeBaron Now Director-=General of Cosmopolitan; Other Changes Made," *MPW,* 21 Jan 1922, 262. "Unique Offering from Paramount," *MPW,* 4 Sep 1926, 39. "LeBaron Leaves Paramount to Head F.B.O. Production," *MPW,* 9 Apr 1927, 536. "LeBaron Will Work Under Edwin King," *MPW,* 16 Apr 1927, 630. Tom Waller, "William LeBaron," *MPW,* 17

Sep 1927, 160–61. "LeBaron Discusses FBO's 1928 Plans," *MPW,* 31 Dec 1927, 26.

Lebedeff, Ivan Sergeevich [actor] (b. Uspoliai, Lithuania, 18 Jun 1894–31 Mar 1953 [58], Los Angeles CA). m. **Vera Engels** (b. c. 1904). (UFA; Griffith.) (Film debut: *King Frederick,* UFA, 1922.) "Ivan Lebedeff, Actor in Films for 25 Years," *NYT,* 2 Apr 1953, 27:4. "Ivan Lebedeff," *Variety,* 8 Apr 1953. AMD, p. 209. AS, p. 652. BHD1, p. 320. FSS, p. 179. IFN, p. 174. Katz, p. 702. SD. Truitt, p. 193. Paul Paige, "Close-Ups and Fade-Outs," *Paris and Hollywood,* Oct 1926, 96 ("Lebedeff was a member of the Russian nobility, but money, lands, and title were all swept away by the revolution...His father, before the war, was the ambassador to Austria-Hungay, and he himself was trained for the diplomatic service at a famous Russian school which each year admitted only ten boys chosen from the finest families in Russia."). "Griffith's Protége in DeMille Pictures," *MPW,* 9 Jul 1927, 96. Gladys Hall, "Sealed and Signed with Blood; Such, Ivan Lebedeff Says, Is His Past. And He Would Not Re-Open the Wound of Its Memory," *MPC,* Aug 1929, 45, 90–91.

Lebius, Aenderly [actor] (b. Tilsit, Russia, 6 Dec 1867–5 Mar 1921 [53], Berlin, Germany). BHD, p. 226 (b. Germany). IFN, p. 174.

Leblanc, Georgette [actress] (b. Tancarville, France, 6 Feb 1875–26 Oct 1941 [66], Cannes, France [extrait de décès no. 63/1941]). AS, p. 652. BHD, p. 226. IFN, p. 174.

Leblanc, Maurice [author: creator of Arsène Lupin] (*né* Marie Emile Maurice Leblanc, b. Rouen, France, 11 Dec 1864–6 Nov 1941 [76], Perpignan, France [extrait de décès no. 1305]). AS, p. 652.

Le Brandt, Gertrude Norris [actress] (b. 1863?–28 Aug 1955 [92], Los Angeles CA). "Gertrude N. Le Brandt," *Variety,* 31 Aug 1955. AS, p. 649. BHD, p. 226. IFN, p. 174. Truitt, p. 193.

Le Brandt, Joseph [scenarist] (b. 1864–5 Jun 1940 [76?], New York NY). AMD, p. 209. BHD2, p. 155. "LeBrandt—Special Scenario Writer," *MPW,* 6 Mar 1915, 1466.

Le Breton, Flora [actress] (b. Croydon, England, 1898). AS, p. 649. Susan Elizabeth Brady, "Thumbnail Sketches No. 1; Flora Le Breton; A Remarkable Young Woman," *MPC,* XX, Dec 1924, 68, 85.

Lebreton, Marcel [scenarist] (b. Paris, France, 22 Oct 1897). AS, p. 652.

Le Brun, Mignon [actress] (b. New York NY, 4 Jan 1888–20 Sep 1941 [53], Los Angeles CA). m. **Cullen Landis**—div. 1925 (d. 1981). AMD, p. 209. AS, p. 649. BHD, p. 226. IFN, p. 174. Truitt, p. 193. "Mignon LeBrun," *MPW,* 5 May 1917, 782. "Wife of Land Is Burned," *MPW,* 5 Mar 1921, 38 (dress caught fire from gas stove). "Another Film Baby," *MPW,* LIII, 10 Dec 1921, 685. "'Hoosegow' Looms for Cullen Landis," *MPW,* 17 Sep 1927, 163. "Landis Agrees to Pay," *MPW,* 24 Sep 1927, 227 ($100/month child support). June Lee, "Dan Cupid's Bulletin Board," *Paris and Hollywood Screen Secrets,* Oct 1927, 36 (Landis was put in jail for back alimony).

Le Claire, Blanche [actress]. No data found. AMD, p. 209. "New Girl Player," *MPW,* 6 Nov 1926, 2.

Leclerc, Joseph Pierre Alexndre [director] (b. Saint-Lo, France, 21 Dec 1900 [extrait de naissance no. 187]-5 May 1979 [78], Paris, France). AS, p. 652.

Leclerc, Louis Guillaume Augustin [director] (b. Pons, France, 5 Nov 1899 [extrait de naissance no. 74/1899]-10 Nov 1970 [71], Paris, France). AS, p. 652.

Leclercq, Paul [producer/scenarist] (b. Paris, France, 23 Mar 1897-ca. 1960 [63?]). AS, p. 652.

Lecourtois, Daniel Paul Henri [actor] (b. Paris, France, 25 Jan 1902–16 Jan 1985 [82], Challex, France [extrait de décès no. 1/1985]). AS, p. 653.

Lecuona, Ernesto [composer] (b. Cuba, 1895–29 Nov 1932 [37?], Santa Cruz de Tenerife, Spain). AS, p. 653.

Ledengast, Walter [actor] (b. Vienna, Austria, 4 Jul 1889). AS, p. 653.

Lederer, Francis [stage/film/TV actor/singer/dancer] (*né* Frantisek Lederer, b. Prague, Czechoslovakia [then part of Austria-Hungary], 6 Nov 1899–24 May 2000 [100], Palm Springs CA). m. (1) opera singer Ada Nejedly—div.; (2) María Marguerita Guadalupe Teresa Estela Bolado Castilla y O'Donnell (Margo), 1937–40; (3) Marion Irvine, 1941, Las Vegas NV. (Film debut: *Zu Flucht [Refuge]*, Germany; Hollywood debut: *A Man of Two Worlds,* RKO, 1934; final film: *Terror Is a Man,* 1959). Todd S. Purdom, "Francis Lederer Dies at 100; Actor Known for Suave Roles," *NYT,* 27 May 2000, A13. Doug Galloway, "Francis Lederer," *Variety,* 29 May 2000, 70:2 (d. 25 May). AS, p. 653 (b. Karlin, Czechoslovakia). Charles P. Mitchell, "Francis Lederer: A Man of Many Worlds," *CI,* 264 (Jun 1997), 20–26 ("Later I was engaged by RKO, and Thalberg wanted to negotiate a new contract with me, and he said, 'Francis, I'm going to make you a great star!' About two weeks later he got pneumonia and died."); "Dorothy Barrett on Francis Lederer," 26.

Lederer, George W., Jr. [publicist/producer] (b. Wilkes-Barre PA, 1861–8 Oct 1938 [76], Jackson Heights NY). m. (1) **Reine Davies,** 1907, Crown Point IN (d. 1938); (2) Adele Burt; (3) **Jessie Lewis** (d. 1971). "George Lederer, Producer, Is Dead; Called the Ziegfeld of His Day, Staged the Original 'Floradora'—Was 76; Began as Child Soprano; Starred Lillian Russell and Marie Dressler—Devised Modern Revue Technique," *NYT,* 9 Oct 1938, 44:8. "George W. Lederer, Dean of Musical Producers and Star-Maker, Dies at 76," *Variety,* 12 Oct 1938. AMD, p. 209. AS, p. 653. SD. "Lederer Forms New Producing Company," *MPW,* 11 Mar 1916, 1631. "Lederer Expands Film Interests," *MPW,* 27 Oct 1917, 526. "George W. Lederer, Jr., with Realart," *MPW,* 13 Dec 1919, 777.

Lederer, Gretchen [actress] (*née* Gretchen Mney, b. Cologne, Germany, 23 May 1891–20 Dec 1955 [64], Anaheim CA). m. **Otto Lederer** (d. 1965). AMD, p. 209. AS, p. 653. BHD, p. 226. IFN, p. 174. Truitt, p. 193. "Gretchen Lederer," *MPW,* 21 Jul 1917, 439.

Lederer, Maitland Rice [executive] (b. 1897–21 Jul 1934 [37?], Santa Monica CA). AS, p. 653. BHD2, p. 155.

Lederer, Otto [actor] (b. Prague, Czechoslovakia, 17 Apr 1886–3 Sep 1965 [79], Woodland Hills CA). m. **Gretchen** (d. 1955). (Vitagraph, 1913.) AMD, p. 209. AS, p. 653 (d. Prague). BHD1, p. 320. IFN, p. 174. "Six Years with Vitagraph," *MPW,* 14 Jun 1919, 1632 (as of 1 Jun 1919; began in 1913). "Otto Lederer," *MPW,* 13 Aug 1927, 456. George Katchmer, "Remembering the Great Silents," *CI,* 231 (Sep 1994), 48.

Lederer, Pepi [actress] (*née* Josephine Rose Lederer, b. Chicago IL, 18 Mar 1910–11 Jun 1935 [25], Los Angeles CA). AS, p. 653. BHD, p. 226.

Lederman, D[avid] **Ross** [actor/director/scenarist] (b. Lancaster PA, 12 Dec 1894–24 Aug 1972 [77], Los Angeles CA; heart attack). (Sennett, 1913; WB; MGM; Mascot.) "D. Ross Lederman," *Variety,* 30 Aug 1972 (age 76). AMD, p. 210. AS, p. 653 (b. 1895). BHD, p. 226; BHD2, p. 155 (b. 1895). FDY, p. 491. IFN, p. 174. Katz, pp. 703–704. "Gets Megaphone," *MPW,* 23 Jul 1927, 238. "Lederman Made Director," *MPW,* 6 Aug 1927, 399.

Ledoux, Fernand [stage/film actor] (*né* Jacques Joseph Félix Fernand Ledoux, b. Tienen, Belgium, 24 Jan 1897–21 Sep 1993 [96], Villerville, France [extrait de décès no. 10/1993]). (Began 1919; TC-F.) AS, p. 653. BHD1, p. 320. Waldman, p. 160.

Ledtke, Harry [actor] (b. Königsberg, Germany, 12 Oct 1881–28 Apr 1945 [63], Bad Saarow, Germany). Vittorio Martinelli, "Kino-Lieblinge," *Griffithiana,* 38/39 (Oct 1990), 58.

Lee, Alice [actress]. No data found. AMD, p. 210. "To Hold Up American Women to China," *MPW,* 15 Jun 1918, 1553–54.

Lee, Allen [actor] (b. OH, 1875?–5 Feb 1951 [76], New York NY). "Allen Lee," *NYT,* 7 Feb 1951, 29:2 (age 74). "Allen Lee," *Variety,* 7 Feb 1951. AS, p. 653. BHD1, p. 320. IFN, p. 174.

Lee, Annabelle [actress] (d. 8 Sep 1989, Santa Monica CA). BHD, p. 226.

Lee, Arthur [executive]. No data found. AMD, p. 210. "Lee-Bradford President Sounds Progressive Note," *MPW,* 16 Aug 1924, 577.

Lee, Auriol (descendant of Robert E. Lee; aunt of actress Virginia Field) [stage actress/director/producer] (b. London, England, 13 Sep 1880–2 Jul 1941 [60], near Hutchinson KS; auto accident when car skidded and left a highway). m. **Frederick W. Lloyd,** 1911—div. 1922 (d. 1949). (Stage debut: *The Price of Peace,* 14 Nov 1900, London.) "Auriol Lee Dies in Auto Accident; Stage Director and Actress Was Driving Through Kansas on Way from California; Burial at Place of Death; In Accordance with a Wish—A Veteran of the Theatre Here and in England," *NYT,* 4 Jul 1941, 16:4 (had left the ranch of playwright John van Druten at Thermal CA. In NYC she was to attend the wedding of Katherine Wiman, daughter of producer Dwight Deere Wiman. Her father was Dr. Rupert Lee. She was the first woman to fly across the equator.). "Auriol Lee," *Variety,* 143, 9 Jul 1941, 54:1. *Newsweek,* 18, 14 Jul 1941, 6. AS, p. 653. BHD1, p. 320. "Lee, Auriol," *Current Biography 1941,* p. 503. IFN, p. 174. *American Magazine,* Jun 1917, 83, 36. *Theatre World,* 18, Oct 1932, 187; 19, Jan 1933, 33; 20, Sep 1933, 141; 28, Sep 1937, 113. *Town and Country,* 86, 1 Jan 1932, 22. *Vanity Fair,* 43, Dec 1934, 34. *Who's Who. Who's Who in the Theatre.*

Lee, Bessie [actress] (b. Ogden UT, 8 Sep 1903–9 Nov 1931 [28], Los Angeles CA; cerebral hemorrhage). m. Billy Stewart. "Bessie Lee Dies at 27," *Variety,* 17 Nov 1931 (interred in Brigham UT). AS, p. 653. Truitt, 1983.

Lee, Bessie [actress] (b. 1906–28 Jun 1972 [66?], Pittsburgh PA). AS, p. 653. BHD1, p. 320.

Lee, Betsy [actress] (b. UT, 8 May 1907–19 Dec 1996 [89], Woodland Hills CA). BHD1, p. 612.

Lee, Carolyne [actress] (b. New York NY, 1860–11 Jan 1920 [59?], New York NY). "Carolyne Lee," *Variety,* 16 Jan 1920. AS, p. 654. BHD, p. 226. IFN, p. 175.

Lee, Charles T. [actor] (b. 1882?–14 Mar 1927 [45], Los Angeles CA; heart attack). (1st National.). "Charles T. Lee," *Variety,* 16 Mar 1927. AS, p. 654. BHD, p. 226. IFN, p. 175.

Lee, Dick *see* **Lee, Richard Lawrence**

Lee, Dixie [actress] (*née* Wilma Wyatt, b. Harriman TN, 4 Nov 1911–1 Nov 1952 [40], Holmby Hills CA). m. Bing Crosby, 1930. (Universal; Fox.) "Dixie Lee Crosby," *Variety,* 5 Nov 1952 (began 1928). AS, p. 654. BHD1, p. 321 (d. LA CA). IFN, p. 175. Truitt, p. 193.

Lee, Donald W. [scenarist/radio/TV network owner] (b. 1881?–30 Aug 1934 [53], Los Angeles CA; acute indigestion). m. (3) Geraldine May Jessup Timmons, 1934. "Don Lee Death Send Pickard on Coast Trip," *Variety,* 4 Sep 1934. FDY, p. 491.

Lee, Doris *see* **May, Doris**

Lee, Dorothy [actress] (*née* Marjorie Millsap, b. Los Angeles CA, 23 May 1911–24 Jun 1999 [88], San Diego CA). (RKO; final film: *Repent at Leisure,* 1941.) m. (1) Jimmie Fiedler; (2) John Bersbach, 9 Dec 1941; (3) Charles Calderini. "Dorothy Lee," *PP-G,* 72, 1 Jul 1999, B-6:1 (co-starred in 13 of the 21 RKO films popularized by the comedy team of Bert Wheeler and Robert Woolsey). (Began extra work around 1928; RKO; WB; Republic; Monogram; Universal.) Ragan 2, p. 952. Joe Collura, "Dorothy Lee: That Wheeler and Woolsey Girl," *CI,* 234 (Dec 1994), C14 *et passim* ("Lee" from maternal grandmother).

Lee, Duke R. [actor] (b. Prince Henry Co. VA, 13 May 1881–1 Apr 1959 [77], Los Angeles CA). m. Edith Louise. "Duke R. Lee," *Variety,* 8 Apr 1959 (age 78) (1st film: *Lure of the Circus,* 1915). AMD, p. 210. AS, p. 654. BHD1, p. 321 (b. 31 May). IFN, p. 175. Truitt, pp. 193–94. "Duke Lee Plans Personal Tour," *MPW,* 26 Aug 1922, 675 (*In the Days of Buffalo Bill*). George Katchmer, "Up-date—Forgotten Cowboys/Girls," *CI,* 179 (May 1990), 43.

Lee, Earl [actor] (b. 1886–2 Jun 1955 [69?], Redwood City CA). AS, p. 654.

Lee, Elizabeth Borders [actress] (b. 1892–1985 [93?], San Antonio TX). BHD, p. 226.

Lee, Etta [actress] (b. 1906?–27 Oct 1956 [50], Eureka CA). m. Frank Brown. "Etta Lee Brown," *Variety,* 31 Oct 1956. AS, p. 654. BHD1, p. 321. IFN, p. 175. Truitt, p. 194.

Lee, Florence D. [actress] (b. VT, 12 Mar 1888–1 Sep 1962 [74], Los Angeles CA). m. (1) Theodore Hayes; (2) **Dell Henderson** (d. 1956). (K&E.) "Florence Lee," *Variety,* 12 Sep 1962. AS, p. 654. BHD1, p. 321. IFN, p. 175. SD. Truitt, p. 194. George Katchmer, "Forgotten Cowboys and Cowgirls—Part V," *CI,* 177 (Mar 1990), C4. "Update—Forgotten Cowboys/Girls," *CI,* 179 (May 1990), 44.

Lee, Frank [actor] (*né* William H. Van Hoesen, d. 17 Aug 1923, Round Lake IL; apoplexy). m. "William H. Van Hoesen," *Variety,* 23 Aug 1923. AS, p. 654.

Lee, Frankie [actress/musical comedy star] (b. 1880?–12 Dec 1917 [37], New York NY). "Frankie Lee Prentice," *NYT,* 13 Dec 1917, 13:4. "Mrs. Franklin Lee Prentice (Frankie Lee)," *Variety,* 21 Dec 1917.

Lee, Frankie (brother of **Davy Lee**) [child actor] (b. UT, 31 Dec 1911–29 Jul 1970 [58], Los Angeles CA). BHD1, p. 612. George Katchmer, "Remembering the Great Silents," *CI,* 229 (Jul 1994), 39–40.

Lee, Frederick [vaudevillian] (b. 1871?–9 Feb 1932 [61], London, England). "Frederick Lee," *Variety,* 23 Feb 1932.

Lee, Georgia [stage/film actress] (*née* Willie Lee, b. Stewartson IL–d. 1 Apr 1915, Elizabeth NJ). m. George L. Brown. "Georgia Lee," *Variety,* 9 Apr 1915. SD.

Lee, Gwen [actress: Wampas Star, 1927] (*née* Gwendolyn Le Pinski, b. Hastings NB, 12 Nov 1904–20 Aug 1961 [56], Reno NV). (MGM.) AMD, p. 210. AS, p. 654 (d. LA CA). BHD1, p. 321. FSS, p. 180. IFN, p. 175. "Gwendolyn Lee in columbia Film," *MPW,* 19 Jun 1926, 622. "Gwendolyn Lee," *MPW,* 14 May 1927, 99.

Lee, Harry (brother of Tom and twin of **Richard Lee**) [actor/director/writer] (*né* William Henry Lee, b. Richmond VA, 1 Jun 1872–8 Dec 1932 [60], Los Angeles CA; suicide by leaping from fire escape of Roosevelt Hotel). m. Dorothy Pine. "Harry Lee," *Variety,* 12 Dec 1932. AMD, p. 210. AS, p. 654. BHD1, p. 321 (b. Brooklyn NY). IFN, p. 175. Truitt, p. 194. "The Kosmik Film Service," *MPW,* 25 Jul 1908, 63. "The Life of the World," *MPW,* 29 Jan 1910, 119–20. "In the Picture Studios," *NYDM,* 22 Sep 1915, 32:3 (Harry Lee had an important bit in *Ashton Kirke, Investigator,* then went with Brenon to Jamaica. Director Ashley Miller needed a retake and was able to use Richard Lee instead of Harry. Tom Lee was the sporting editor of the *Evening World.*).

Lee, Harry [scenarist] (b. 1874–20 Dec 1942 [68?], Plainfield NJ). BHD2, p. 156.

Lee, Jane (sister of **Katherine Lee**) [child actress] (b. Glasgow, Scotland, 1 Jun 1911–17 Mar 1957 [45], New York NY). m. (Fox.) "Jane Lee Is Dead at 45; Mrs. St. John Was Child Film Star Forty Years Ago," *NYT,* 20 Mar 1957, 37:4. "Jane Lee St. John," *Variety,* 27 Mar 1957 (began 1914). AMD, p. 210. AS, p. 654 (b. 1912). BHD, p. 227. IFN, p. 175. MSBB, p. 1038. Spehr, p. 148. Truitt, p. 295. "Jane Lee Recovering from Operation," *MPW,* 21 Dec 1918, 1330. "Jane and [K]atherine Lee Enter Producing Field," *MPW,* 28 Jun 1919, 1956. "Lee Kids to Star in Two Reelers," *MPW,* 4 Nov 1922, 56.

Lee, Jennie or **Jenny** [actress] (b. Sacramento CA, 1850?–4 Aug 1925 [75], Los Angeles CA). m. **William Courtright** (d. 1933). (Biograph, 1913.) "Jennie Lee, Actress, Is Dead," *NYT,* 7 Aug 1925, 15:7 (d. 5 Aug). "Jenny Lee," *Variety,* 12 Aug 1925. AMD, p. 210. AS, p. 654. BHD, p. 227. IFN, p. 175 (d. 3 May 1930 [75]). 1921 Directory, p. 228 (b. 1859). Truitt, p. 194. "Jennie Lee," *MPW,* 27 Jan 1917, 534. "Jennie Lee Supporting Eltinge," *MPW,* 27 Oct 1917, 544. "Jennie Lee Engaged by Universal," *MPW,* 28 Jun 1919, 1947. George Katchmer, "Jennie Lee," *CI,* 228 (Jun 1994), 43.

Lee, Joe [actor] (b. 1906?–11 Jul 1943 [37]). IFN, p. 175.

Lee, Katherine (sister of **Jane Lee:** child dancing and singing team) [stage/film child actress] (b. Glasgow, Scotland, 1904?–22 Oct 1968 [64], Flushing, Queens NY). m. boxer/referee Ray Miller (of New York), 1937. (Fox.) "Mrs. Ray Miller," *NYT,* 25 Oct 1968, 47:4. AMD, p. 210. Spehr, p. 148. "Katherine Lee," *MPW,* 16 Jan 1915, 375. "Jane and [K]atherine Lee Enter Producing Field," *MPW,* 28 Jun 1919, 1956. "Lee Kids to Star in Two Reelers," *MPW,* 4 Nov 1922, 56. *NYT* obituary supplied by James K. Foster, Minneapolis MN.

Lee, Leon L. [title writer/producer] (b. 1895?–11 Mar 1963 [68], Los Angeles CA; stroke). (Chadwick Films; Monogram; UA.) "Leon L. Lee," *Variety,* 20 Mar 1963 ("He turned out many of the Larry Semon and Oliver Hardy two-reelers..."). AS, p. 655. BHD2, p. 156. FDY, p. 445.

Lee, Lila [actress: Wampas Star, 1922] (*née* Augusta Appel, b. Union Hill NJ, 25 Jul 1895?–13 Nov 1973 [78?], Saranac Lake NY). m. (1) **James Kirkwood, Sr.** (d. 1963); (2) Jack R. Paine; (3) John E. Murphy. "Lila Lee, 68, Dies; Silent Film Star; Dark-Eyed Actress Caught Public's Fancy in the 20's," *NYT,* 14 Nov 1973, 48:1 (b. 1905). "Lila Lee," *Variety,* 21 Nov 1973 (age 68). AMD, p. 210. AS, p. 655 (b. 1902). BHD1, p. 321 (b. 1902). FFF, p. 19 (b. NYC, 1895). FSS, p. 180. IFN, p. 175 (b. 1905). Katz, pp. 705–706. MH, p. 122 (b. New York, 1895). SD. "Lila Lee," WBO1, pp. 108–109 (b. New York, 1901). WWS, p. 26 (b. New York). "Famous Players Announces a 'Find,'" *MPW,* 22 Jun 1918, 1701. "Lila Lee Now in California," *MPW,* 29 Jun 1918, 1823. "Seven Players New to Artcraft-Paramount," *MPW,* 6 Jul 1918, 57. "Famous Players-Lasky Plans Exploitation of Lila Lee," *MPW,* 27 Jul 1918, 568. Edward Weitzel, "Lila Lee's Screen Debut as Seen by a World Man," *MPW,* 28 Sep 1918, 1881. "Lila Lee, Juvenile Star, Files Suit Against Mrs. Edwards," *MPW,* 24 Apr 1920, 563 (her manager and guardian). "Lila Lee to Have New Guardian," *MPW,* 8 May 1920, 841. "Lila Lee's Contract Renewed with Famous Players-Lasky," *MPW,* 8 May 1920, 851. "Court Gives Lila Lee to Parents," *MPW,* 15 May 1920, 939. "Lile Lee Visits Home," *MPW,* 11 Dec 1920, 718 (in Chicago). "Lila Lee Vacations Here; Has Made Eighteen Films," *MPW,* 18 Dec 1920, 887. "Lee—Kirkwood," *MPW,* 18 Aug 1923, 548. "Hodkinson to Distribute Four Kirkwood-Lila Lee Features," *MPW,* 8 Dec 1923, 574. "Lila Lee and James Kirkwood at Home," *MW,* 3 May 1924, 6 (photo layout). Regina Cannon, "Is It Harder for a Girl to Win Screen Fame Than for a Man? 'Yes!' Says Lila Lee," *MW,* 10 May 1924, 11, 26. "Lila Lee," *MPW,* 12 Jul 1924, insert. "Lila Lee to Play Opposite Meighan," *MPW,* 29 Nov 1924, 438. Cover, *MPS,* 28 Jul 1925. Larry Lee Holland, "Lila Lee," *FIR,* Nov 1984, 530–39.

Lee, Lois (sister of **Virginia Lee**) [actress]. No data found. AMD, p. 210. "Lois Lee Signed by Fox," *MPW,* 6 Dec 1919, 687 (winner of 1917 "Beauty and Brains" contest). "Lois Lee Joins Torchy Comedies," *MPW,* 3 Dec 1921, 541.

Lee, Lolita [actress]. No data found. (1st National.) Paul Paige, "Close-Ups and Fade-Outs," *Paris and Hollywood,* Oct 1926, 93.

Lee, Manfred B. [publicist]. No data found. m. Betty Miller, 1927. AMD, p. 210. "'Manny' Lee Marries," *MPW,* 20 Aug 1927, 509. "Lee Leaving Sterling," *MPW,* 31 Dec 1927, 18.

Lee, Moe [actor] (b. 1884?–5 Jan 1966 [81], Chicago IL). "Moe Lee," *Variety,* 19 Jan 1966. AS, p. 655. BHD, p. 227.

Lee, Nancy [actress]. No data found. AMD, p. 210. "Nancy Pulls Through," *MPW,* 23 Apr 1927, 707.

Lee, Norma [actress] (b. Newport KY, 1899–12 Dec 1980 [81?], New York NY). m. **Elliott Nugent** (d. 1980). AS, p. 655. BHD1, p. 321.

Lee, Raymond [actor/writer] (b. Los Angeles CA, 1910?–26 Jun 1974 [64], Canoga Park CA, near Los Angeles; cancer). (Chaplin.) "Raymond Lee," *NYT,* 29 Jun 1974, 32:5 (in films 1915–27 and wrote about the movie business). "Raymond Lee," *Variety,* 7 Aug 1974. AS, p. 655. BHD, p. 227. IFN, p. 175. "Raymond Lee, Film Actor, Writer, Is Dead at 64," *Daily Variety,* 3 Jul 1974. Raymond Lee, "Lillian Gish: First Lady of the Screen," *CFC,* 16 (Fall, 1967), 27 (appeared in Fox Kiddie comedies).

Lee, Richard Lawrence (brother of Tom and twin of **Harry Lee**) [stage/film actor] (b. New York NY, 1 Jun 1870?–24 Jul 1931 [61], New York NY). m. Louise. "Dick Lee, of the Lee Twins, died recently in New York," *Variety,* 11 Aug 1931. AS, p. 655. BHD, p. 227 (b. 1872). IFN, p. 175. SD (b. 1872). "In the Picture Studios," *NYDM,* 22 Sep 1915, 32:3 (Harry Lee had an important bit in *Ashton Kirke, Investigator,* then went with Brenon to Jamaica. Director Ashley Miller needed a retake and was able to use Richard instead of Harry. Tom Lee was the sporting editor of the *Evening World.*).

Lee, Robert E[dwin] [art director] (b. Elyria OH, 15 Oct 1918).

Lee, Robert N[elson] (brother of **Rowland V. Lee**) [scenarist] (b. Butte MT, 12 May 1890–18 Sep 1964 [74], Los Angeles CA; heart attack). m. Betty. "Robert N. Lee," *Variety,* 23 Sep 1964. AS, p. 655. BHD2, p. 156. FDY, p. 491.

Lee, Rowland V[ance] [actor/director/scenarist] (brother of **Robert N. Lee**) (b. Findlay OH, 6 Sep 1891–21 Dec 1975 [84], Palm Desert CA). m. Eleanor. (Ince.) "Rowland V. Lee," *Variety,* 24 Dec 1975 (age 84). AMD, p. 210. AS, p. 655. BHD, p. 227; BHD2, p. 156. FDY, p. 491. IFN, p. 175. Katz, p. 706. SD. "Ince Signs Roland Lee," *MPW,* 3 Apr 1920, 143. "Rowland Lee Now Dirrector," *MPW,* 17 Jul 1920, 353. "Lee Returns to Fox," *MPW,* 23 Jun 1923, 642. Jim Tully, "Strictly a Family Affair," *MPC,* Feb 1925, 52, 79–80. "Lee Off for West Coast," *MPW,* 7 Mar 1925, 73. "Rowland Lee Has Contract with Famous," *MPW,* 15 Jan 1927, 199. Karl Wray, "Rowland V. Lee," *FIR,* Jan 1986, 2–14.

Lee, Sammy [dance director] (*né* Samuel Loy, b. New York NY, 26 May 1890–30 Mar 1968 [77], Woodland Hills CA). (Metro; Fox; Paramount.) "Sammy Lee," *Variety,* 10 Apr 1968. AS, p. 655 (d. 20 Mar). BHD2, p. 156. IFN, p. 175. *Green Encyclopedia of the Musical Film,* p. 166.

Lee, William [actor/producer] (b. 1863?–22 Sep 1913 [50?], Chicago IL; heart failure). AMD, p. 211. AS, p. 655. "American Adds Another Producer," *MPW,* 20 Jul 1912, 232. "William Lee, Deceased," *MPW,* 18 Oct 1913, 250.

Leeds, Arthur [scenario editor]. No data found. AMD, p. 211. "Arthur Leeds," *MPW,* 20 Mar 1915, 1777.

Leenhardt, Tony Albert Auguste (cousin of Roger Leenhardt, 1903–1985) [director] (b. Mauguio, France, 11 Sep 1906 [extrait de naissance no. 41/1906]-17 Feb 1982 [75], Grasse, France). AS, p. 656.

Leeson, Lois [scenarist]. No data found. FDY, p. 491.

Leezer, John W. [cameraman] (b. 1873?–6 Aug 1938 [65], Vista CA). "John Leezer," *Variety,* 17 Aug 1938. BHD2, p. 156. FDY, p. 461.

Le Faint, Jack [director]. No data found. m. **Eleanor Caines** (d. 1913).

Lefaur, André [actor] (*né* Alphonse André Lefaurichon, b. Paris, France, 25 Jul 1879–4 Dec 1952 [73], Paris, France). AS, p. 656 (b. 2 Jul). BHD, p. 227. IFN, p. 175.

Le Faure, G. [scenarist]. No data found. FDY, p. 491.

Lefcourt, A.E. [executive]. No data found. AMD, p. 211. "President Lefcourt, of Pioneer, Says Company Plans for Record Business," *MPW,* 29 Jan 1921, 545.

Lefebvre, Rene [actor/scenarist] (b. Nice, France, 6 Mar 1898–8 May 1991 [93]). BHD1, p. 322; BHD2, p. 156.

Lefeuvre, Guy [actor/director/scenarist] (b. Ottawa, Ontario, Canada, 7 Oct 1883–15 Feb 1950 [66], London, England). BHD2, p. 156.

Lefeuvre, Philip [actor] (b. 1871–23 Aug 1939 [68?], Arcadia CA). AS, p. 649.

Lefevre, René Paul Louis [actor/scenarist] (b. Nice, France, 6 Mar 1898 [extrait de naissance bno. 532]-23 May 1991 [93], Poissy, France; cancer [extrait de décès no. 308/1991]). AS, p. 656.

Leffingwell, George B. [actor] (b. Meadville PA, 18 May 1885–27 Apr 1934 [48], Downing CA). BHD, p. 227.

Leffler, Hermann [actor] (b. Quedlinburg, Germany, 3 Oct 1864–21 Nov 1929 [65]). BHD, p. 227. IFN, p. 176.

Leftwich, Alexander [actor] (b. Baltimore MD, 24 Dec 1885–13 Jan 1947 [61], Los Angeles CA; heart attack). AS, p. 656.

Legal, Ernst [actor/playwright/director] (*né* Ernst Otto Eduard Legal, b. Schlieben, Germany, 2 May 1881–29 Jun 1955 [74], Berlin, Germany). "Ernest Legal," *Variety,* 13 Jul 1955, p. 63:1. AS, p. 656. BHD, p. 227. IFN, p. 176.

Le Gallienne, Richard [writer]. No data found. AMD, p. 211. "Le Galliene for Screen; Literary Light Writes Feature [*The Chain Invisible*] for Production by Equitable Corporation," *NYDM,* 6 Oct 1915, 25:2. "Noted Author Writes for Equitable," *MPW,* 16 Oct 1915, 457.

Legault, Marie Françoise [actress] (b. Paris, France, 1 Jan 1858). AS, p. 656.

Le Gallot, Adrien [actor] (*né* Adrien Arthur Le Gallo, b. Paris, France, 15 Dec 1865–13 Jan 1936 [70], Paris, France [extrait de décès no. SN/1936]). AS, p. 649.

Legeay, Yvonne [actress] (*née* Yvonne Juliette Eugénie Charlot, b. Paris, France, 19 Mar 1892–11 Dec 1980 [88], Paris, France). AS, p. 656.

Leger, Fernand [director] (b. Argentan, France, 4 Feb 1881–17 Aug 1955 [74], Gif-sur-Yvette, France). AS, p. 657. BHD2, p. 156.

Legeret, Robert Eugène Ernest [director] (b. Vitry-le-Francois, France, 17 Oct 1899 [extrait de naissance no. 166]-9 Oct 1968 [68], Vitry-le-Francois, France). AS, p. 657.

Legneur, Charles [actor] (b. 1892–14 Feb 1956 [63?], Los Angeles CA). AS, p. 657.

Legrand, Camille [cameraman]. No data found. AMD, p. 211. "Pathé Cameraman Goes to Orient," *MPW,* 12 Oct 1918, 203. "Pathé Cameraman Commended," *MPW,* 26 Oct 1918, 532.

Legrand, H. André [scenarist] (*né* André Steigelmann, b. Paris, France, 10 Feb 1896-ca. 1962 [66?]). AS, p. 657.

Legrand, Jean-René [director] (b. Paris, France, 23 Jun 1899). AS, p. 657.

Le Grand, Lucienne [actress]. No data found. Rene de la Seine, "Latest Gossip from Paris," *Paris and Hollywood,* 2 (Oct 1926), 43 (she was "the amazing blonde with the perfect teeth who was a sensation in *Simone.*").

Legris, Roger [actor] (*né* Jean Roger Legris, b. Malakoff, France, 3 Jul 1898–22 May 1981 [82], Le Kremlin-Bicetre, France [extrait de décès no. SN/1981]). AS, p. 657.

Le Guere, George [stage/film actor] (b. Memphis TN, 17 Jul 1871?–21 Nov 1947 [76], New York NY). (McClure.) "George Leguere," *NYT,* 23 Nov 1947 (age 66; summer stock with Elitch's Gardens Co.). "George Le Guere," *Variety,* 26 Nov 1947. AMD, p. 211. AS, p. 650; p. 657 (George Leguere). BHD1, p. 322 (b. 1887). IFN, p. 176. "George LeGuere," *MPW,* 27 Nov 1915, 1649. "George LeGuere Still with Metro," *MPW,* 20 May 1916, 1358. "George LeGuere—McClure Pictures," *MPW,* 6 Jan 1917, 91. Al Ray, "Before the Stars Shone," *Picture-Play Masgazine,* Sep 1917, 93 (b. New Orleans LA). "George LeGuere with Brenon," *MPW,* 15 Dec 1917, 1622. "George LeGuere Signed by Bacon as Leading Man," *MPW,* 31 May 1919, 1351. "LeGuere to Combine Work," *MPW,* 13 Mar 1920, 1774.

Lehar, Franz [composer] (*né* Ferencz Lehar, b. Komarom, Austria, 30 Apr 1870–24 Oct 1948 [78], Bad Ischl, Austria). AS, p. 657.

Lehman, Gladys C. [scenarist; a founding member of the Screen Writers Guild] (*née* Gladys Collins, b. 24 Jan 1882?–7 Apr 1993 [101], Newport Beach CA; pneumonia). "Gladys Collins Lehman," *Variety,* 3 May 1993, 56:4. AS, p. 657 (b. 1894). BHD2, p. 156 (b. 1892). FDY, p. 491.

Lehman, Henry [actor] (b. 1883–30 Oct 1925 [42?], New York NY). AS, p. 657.

Lehman, W. [scenarist]. No data found. FDY, p. 491.

Lehmann, Beatrix [actress] (b. Bourne End, England, 10 Jul 1903–1 Aug 1979 [76], London, England). AS, p. 657.

Lehmann, Paul [executive] (b. 23 Aug 1884–14 Jun 1956 [71], Berlin, Germany). BHD2, p. 156.

Lehnberg, Jean [actress]. No data found. (Thanhouser.) "In the Picture Studios," *NYDM,* 4 Aug 1915, 27:1 (on the female baseball team at Thanhouser).

Lehr, Anna *see* **Dvorak, Ann**

Lehr, Anna [stage/film actress] (b. New York NY, 1885–8 Nov 1951 [66?], Los Angeles CA). (Triangle; FP-L.) "Anne Lehr," *Variety,* 14 Nov 1951 (no mention of films). AMD, p. 211 (aka Ann Dvorak is an error). AS, p. 657. BHD, p. 227. "Anna Lehr, New Figure in Triangle," *MPW,* 22 Apr 1916, 624:2 ("I was born in Austria, came to America when a child and in my stage career have supported many leading actors…"). "Anna Lehr Returns to Triangle," *MPW,* 14 Jul 1917, 270:2. "Anna Lehr Ill with Poisoning," *MPW,* 26 Jul 1919, 521 (she was replaced by Marguerite Courtot in *Teeth of the Tiger* because of ptomaine poisoning). George Katchmer, "Remembering the Great Silents," *CI,* 250 (Apr 1996), 50.

Lehr, Abraham [executive] (b. 13 Jul 1880–17 Oct 1952 [72], Los Angeles CA). BHD2, p. 156.

Lehr, Lew [stage/film actor/scenarist] (b. Philadelphia PA, 14 May 1895–6 Mar 1950 [54], Brookline MA). m. Anna Leonhardt (aka Nancy Belle), 1920. "Lew Lehr Is Dead; Dialect Comedian; Newsreel Commentator, 54, Was Former Vaudeville Actor—Once Gag Writer Here," *NYT,* 7 Mar 1950, 28:2 (noted for saying, "Monkeys is the cwaziest people"). "Lew Lehr," *Variety,* 8 Mar 1950. AS, p. 657. BHD2, p. 156. IFN, p. 176.

Lehrer, George J. [actor/director] (b. 1889–25 Aug 1966 [77?], Cleveland OH). AS, p. 658. BHD2, p. 156.

Lehrman, Henry "Pathé" [director/producer] (b. Vienna, Austria, 30 Mar 1886–7 Nov 1946 [60], Los Angeles CA; heart attack). (French Pathé; Biograph, 1910; Sennett; Imp; Kinemacoilor; Fox.) "Henry Lehrman, Film Veteran, 60; Producer and Director of Early Chaplin and Pickford Movies Dies—Worked for Fox," *NYT,* 9 Nov 1946, 17:4. "Henry Lehrman," *Variety,* 13 Nov 1946. AMD, p. 211. AS, p. 658. BHD, p. 227; BHD2, p. 157. IFN, p. 176. Katz, pp. 708–09. MSBB, p. 1046. 1921 Directory, p. 269. Truitt, p. 194. Kalton C. Lahue and Terry Brewer, *Kops and Custards; The Legend of Keystone Films* (Norman OK: University of Oklahoma Press, 1968), p. 28 *et passim.* "Lehrman Returns to Coast," *MPW,* 4 Dec 1915, 1811. "Henry 'Pathé' Lehrman," *MPW,* 6 Jan 1917, 95. "Lehrman Making Fox Copmedies," *MPW,* 3 Feb 1917, 698. Lehrman Pleases Fox," *MPW,* 10 Nov 1917, 894. "Henry Lehrman Talks Pointedly About Business of Comedy Making," *MPW,* 30 Aug 1919, 1279. "Lehrman to Direct Syd's Next," *MPW,* 5 Jun 1926, 459. "Roach Signs Up Henry Lehrman and L.J. Gasnier," *MPW,* 7 May 1927, 41.

Leibelt, Hans August Hermann [actor] (b. Volkmarsdorf, Germany, 11 Mar 1885–3 Dec 1974 [89], Munich, Germany). AS, p. 658.

Leiber, Fritz [stage/film actor] (b. Chicago IL, 31 Jan 1882–14 Oct 1949 [67], Pacific Palisades CA). m. Virginia Bronson. (Fox; MGM.) "Fritz Leiber Dies; Stage, Film Actor; Played Shakespearean Roles and Toured with Own Troupe—Entered Movies in '17," *NYT,* 15 Oct 1949, 15:1 (last role in *Devil's Doorway* for MGM). "Fritz Lieber," *Variety,* 19 Oct 1949. AS, p. 658. BHD1, p. 323. FSS, p. 181. IFN, p. 176. Truitt, p. 194.

Leiber, Robert [executive/President of First National Pictures] (b. 1870–12 Sep 1929 [59?], Indianapolis IN). AS, p. 658. BHD2, p. 157.

Leibrand, Leda Owens [scenarist]. No data found. m. **Marc Edmund Jones**, Nov 1917 (d. 1965). AMD, p. 211. "Scenario Writers Get Married," *MPW,* 15 Dec 1917, 1621.

Leicester, Ernest [actor] (b. 11 Jun 1866–5 Oct 1939 [73], London, England). BHD, p. 227.

Leidmann, Eva [scenarist] (d. 8 Feb 1938, Germany). BHD2, p. 157.

Leigh, Frank [stage/film actor] (b. London, England, 18 Apr 1876–9 May 1948 [72], Los Angeles CA). AS, p. 658. BHD1, p. 323. IFN, p. 176. Truitt, pp. 194–95. George Katchmer, "Remembering the Great Silents," *CI,* 248 (Feb 1996), 45–46 (began in England in 1912).

Leigh, Lisle [actress] (b. Salt Lake City UT, 1879?–18 May 1927 [48], New York NY). "Lisle Leigh," *Variety,* 25 May 1927. AS, p. 658. BHD, p. 227. IFN, p. 176.

Leigh, Philip [actor] (b. England, 1880–19 Jun 1935 [55?], New York NY). BHD, p. 227.

Leighton, Bert [composer] (*né* James A. Leighton, b. Beacher IL, 29 Dec 1877–10 Feb 1964 [86], San Francisco CA). AS, p. 658.

Leighton, Daniel [actor] (b. 1880–20 Jun 1917 [37?], Los Angeles CA; heart failure). AMD, p. 211. AS, p. 658. BHD1, p. 612. IFN, p. 176. Truitt, 1983. "Obituary," *MPW,* 7 Jul 1917, 72 (d. 21 Jun).

Leighton, Harry [actor] (b. New York NY, 14 Jun 1866–30 May 1926 [59], Bayshore, LI NY). m. Fannie Bernard. "Harry Leighton," *Variety,* 2 Jun 1926. AS, p. 658. BHD, p. 227. IFN, p. 176. SD, p. 758.

Leighton, Lillianne Brown [actress] (b. Auroraville WI, 17 May 1874–19 Mar 1956 [81], Woodland Hills CA). (Selig; E. & R. Jungle Film Company.) "Lillianne Leighton," *NYT,* 23 Mar 1956, 27:2. "Lillian Leighton," *Variety,* 28 Mar 1956 (age 82). AS, p. 658. BHD1, p. 323. IFN, p. 176. Truitt, p. 195. "Scenario and Comedian Added to E. and R. Staff," *MPN,* 25 Mar 1916, 1767. Billy H. Doyle, "Lost Players," *CI,* 177 (Mar 1990), 34–35. George A. Katchmer, "Forgotten Cowboys and Cowgirls—Part XIV," *CI,* 191 (May 1991), 25.

Leisen, Mitchell [actor/director/producer] (*né* James Mitchell Leisen, b. Menominee MI, 6 Oct 1898–29 Oct 1972 [74], Woodland Hills CA). m. Stella Seagar, Feb 1927; Sandra Gahle—1942. (FP-L; Paramount.) "Mitchell Leisen, Director, Dies; 'To Each His Own' Among Films," *NYT,* 1 Nov 1972, 48:1. "Mitchell Leisen," *Variety,* 8 Nov 1972 (d. 28 Oct). AMD, p. 211. AS, p. 658 (b. 3 Oct; d. 28 Oct). BHD2, p. 157 (b. 5 Oct). IFN, p. 176. Katz, p. 710. SD. "Leisen to Wed," *MPW,* 5 Feb 1927, 422.

Leister, Frederick [actor] (b. London, England, 1 Dec 1885–24 Aug 1966 [80]). AS, p. 658 (d. 1970). BHD1, p. 323.

Leiter, Karl Hans [director/scenarist] (b. Vienna, Austria, 9 Feb 1890–23 Aug 1957 [67], Vienna, Austria). AS, p. 658.

Leitner, Jules Louis Auguste [actor] (b. Paris, France, 13 Mar 1862). AS, p. 659.

Leitzbach, Adeline [playwright/scenarist]. No data found. AMD, p. 211. FDY, p. 491. "Miss Leitzbach Leaves Fox Films," *MPW,* 10 Aug 1918, 858.

Lekain, Tony [actor/director] (b. Paris, France, 5 Nov 1888–1966 [77?], Cannes, France). AS, p. 659.

Leloir, Louis Pierre [actor] (b. Paris, France, 5 Nov 1860–29 Nov 1909 [49], Paris, France). AS, p. 659.

Lely, Durward [actor/singer] (b. Arbroath County, Scotland, 2 Sep 1852–29 Feb 1944 [91], Glasgow, Scotland). "Durward Lely," *Variety,* 8 Mar 1944, p. 54:2 (d. 1 Mar, age 93; star of Gilbert & Sullivan operettas during the Victorian era). BHD, p. 227.

Lem, Betty [actress] (d. 10 Dec 1986, Los Angeles CA). BHD, p. 227.

Lemaire, Anna [actress] (*née* Johanna Cornelia Anken, b. Amsterdam, Holland, 26 Nov 1885–17 Nov 1964 [78], Amsterdam, Holland). AS, p. 659.

Le Maire, Charles [costume designer] (b. Chicago IL, 1897?–8 Jun 1985 [88], Palm Springs CA; heart attack). m. Beatrice Goetz. "Charles Le Maire, Costumer for Broadway and Hollywood," *NYT,* 11 Jun 1985, 26:4. "Charles Le Maire Dead at 88; Oscar-Winning Costume Designer," *Variety,* 12 Jun 1985. AS, p. 650. BHD2, p. 157. SD.

Le Maire, George (brother of **William Le Maire**) [actor/title writer/director] (b. Ft. Worth TX, 1884?–20 Jan 1930 [46], New York NY). m. Marie. (Pathé.) "George Le Maire Dies in Bed, Heart Victim," *Variety,* 22 Jan 1930. AS, p. 650. BHD1, p. 323; BHD2, p. 157. FDY, p. 445. IFN, p. 176. Truitt, p. 195.

Lemaire, Jan, Sr. (father of Jan Lemaire, Jr., 1906–1960) [actor] (*né* Johannes Joseph Petrus Lemaire, b. Amsterdam, Holland, 11 Mar 1884–6 Mar 1982 [97], Loosdrecht, Holland). AS, p. 659.

Le Maire, William (brother of **George Le Maire**) [actor] (b. Ft. Worth TX, 21 Dec 1892–11 Nov 1933 [40], Los Angeles CA; heart attack). m. Carol Ralston. "William Le Maire," *Variety,* 14 Nov 1933. AS, p. 650. BHD1, p. 323. IFN, p. 176. Truitt, p. 195.

Le Mans, Marcel [actor] (b. Antwerp, Belgium, 1897?–9 Jan 1946 [49], Lyons NJ). (Pathé, 1924.) "Marcel Le Mans," *Variety,* 16 Jan 1946. AS, p. 650. BHD, p. 228. IFN, p. 176. Truitt, p. 195.

Le March'Hadour, Yvon [actor] (b. France, 1898–7 Nov 1985 [87?], Paris, France). AS, p. 650.

Lemieux, Carrie [stage/film actress] (b. Quebec, Canada, 1881?–1 Oct 1925 [44]). m. **Ben Turpin**, 1907, Chicago IL. "Mrs. Turpin of Films Dies; Comedian Husband's Ten Months' Vigil at Sickbed Ended," *NYT,* 3 Oct 1925, 15:4. IFN, p. 176.

Lemonnier, Meg [actress] (*née* Marguerite Gabrielle Clarte, b. London, England, 15 May 1905–12 Jun 1988 [83], Paris, France [extrait de décès no. 563]). AS, p. 659.

Lemontier, Charles [actor] (*né* Louis Jean Eugène Charles, b. Toul, France, 21 Apr 1894 [extrait de naissance no. AC/73656]-28 May 1965 [71], Paris, France). AS, p. 660.

Le Moyne, Charles J. [actor] (*né* Charles J. Lemon, b. IL, 27 Jun 1880–13 Sep 1956 [76], Los Angeles CA). AS, p. 650. BHD1, p. 324. IFN, p. 176. Truitt, p. 195. George Katchmer, "Forgotten Cowboys and Cowgirls—Part VIII," *CI,* 180 (Jun 1990), 53.

Lemuels, William E. [actor] (b. 1891–21 Feb 1953 [61?], Los Angeles CA). AS, p. 660.

Lena, Al J. [assistant director]. No data found. AMD, p. 211. "Al J. Lena with Clara Kimball Young," *MPW,* 1 Dec 1917, 1303.

Lenard, Harry [actor/director] (b. 1875?–16 Nov 1915 [40], on train between Chicago IL and Plymouth IN). m. "Harry Lenard," *Variety,* 26 Nov 1915. AS, p. 660.

Lenci, Alfredo [cinematographer] (b. Rome, Italy, 1873). JS, p. 240 (in Italian silents from 1915).

Lender, Marcelle [actress] (b. Nancy, France, 17 Sep 1861 [extrait de naissance no. 897]). AS, p. 660.

Lengel, William C. [scenarist] (b. Durango, Mexico, 27 Jun 1888–11 Oct 1965 [77], New York NY). AMD, p. 211. BHD2, p. 157. "Lengel Now on Scenario Staff of Fox Company," *MPW,* 6 Dec 1919, 660.

Lenglen, Suzanne [actress/tennis champion] (b. Compiegne, France, 24 May 1899–4 Jul 1938 [39], Paris, France). AS, p. 660.

Lenkeffy, Ica [actress] (b. 1896–1955 [59?], Budapest, Hungary). BHD1, p. 612.

Leni, Paul A. [actor/art director/director]

(*né* Paul Jozef Leni, b. Stuttgart, Germany, 8 Jul 1885–2 Sep 1929 [44], Los Angeles CA; blood poisoning). (Universal.) "Paul Leni," *Variety,* 11 Sep 1929. AMD, p. 211. AS, p. 660. BHD2, p. 157. IFN, p. 177. Katz, p. 711 (began in Germany, 1914). Truitt, p. 195. Waldman, p. 161. Sumner Smith, "Leni Learns the Lingo," *MPW,* 29 Jan 1927, 326, 362.

Lennard, Arthur [actor] (b. Plumstead, England, 8 Mar 1867–14 Jan 1954 [86], Shoreham-by-Sea, England). BHD, p. 228.

Lennox, Lucille [actress] (b. Atlanta GA). AMD, p. 211. WWS, p. 273. "Lucille Lennox a Pathé Find," *MPW,* 15 May 1920, 962.

Lennox, Vera [actress] (b. Thornton Heath, England, 24 Nov 1904–7 Dec 1984 [80], London, England). BHD1, p. 324.

Leno, Dan (father of **Dan Leno, Jr.**) [actor] (b. London, England, 20 Dec 1860–31 Oct 1904 [43], London, England). BHD, p. 228. IFN, p. 177.

Leno, Dan, Jr. (son of **Dan Leno**) [vaudeville/film actor/writer] (*né* Sydney Paul Galvin, b. 1892–2 Jan 1962 [69?], London, England). "Dan Leno, Jr.," *Variety,* 17 Jan 1962, p. 79:1 (age 70). BHD, p. 228.

Lenor, Jacque [actor]. No data found. (Biograph, 1911).

Le Noir, Pass [actor] (b. 1873–12 Jun 1946 [73?], Los Angeles CA). AS, p. 650; p. 660 (Pass Lenoir).

Lenox, Fred [actor] (b. 1870?–28 Nov 1930 [60], New York NY; heart attack at funeral of a friend). "Fred Lenox," *Variety,* 10 Dec 1930 (age 60). AS, p. 660. BHD, p. 228 (b. 1864).

Lentz, Irene *see* **Irene**

Lenz, Andrew Francis [actor] (b. 1876–27 Apr 1946 [70?], New York NY). BHD, p. 228.

Lenz, Max Werner [actor/director] (*né* Max Russenberger, b. Kreuzlinge, Switzerland, 7 Oct 1887–31 Oct 1975 [88], Bssersdorf, Switzerland). AS, p. 661.

Leo, Jack G. [scenarist/executive] (b. 1887?–19 Feb 1968 [80], Stanford CT). (Fox, 1909, Brooklyn NY). "Jack G. Leo," *Variety,* 250, 21 Feb 1968, 78:3 (Vice President of Fox Film Corp., 1919–31; National Screen Service Corp., 1939–65. His sister married William Fox). AMD, p. 211. Jack G. Leno, "Greater Scenario Development," *MPW,* 21 Jul 1917, 381–82. "Leo Heads Fox Scenario Department," *MPW,* 21 Jul 1917, 431.

Leon, Connie [actress] (b. 1880–10 May 1955 [75?], Los Angeles CA). AS, p. 661.

Leon, Pedro [actor] (b. Tucson AZ, 29 Jun 1878–14 Jul 1931 [53]). AS, p. 661. BHD, p. 228. IFN, p. 177.

Leon, Valeriano [actor] (b. Collote-Oviado, Spain, 15 Dec 1892–13 Dec 1955 [62], Madrid, Spain). AS, p. 661. BHD1, p. 325.

Leonard, Barbara [actress] (b. San Francisco CA, 9 Jan).

Leonard, Benny [prizefighter/actor] (*né* Benjamin Leiner, b. New York NY, 7 Apr 1896–18 Apr 1947 [51], St. Nicholas Arena, New York NY). "Benny Leonard, 51, ex-Champion, Dies; Lightweight King from 1917 to 1925 Stricken While He Referees at St. Nicks," *NYT,* 19 Apr 1947, 15:1. AS, p. 661. BHD, p. 228. IFN, p. 177. David A. Balch, "Benny Leonard, Champion Lightweight, Becomes a Movie Star," *MW,* 28 Jun 1924, 4–5.

Leonard, Bonnie [actress]. No data found. (Essanay.)

Leonard, Eddie [actor] (b. Richmond VA, 1870–29 Jul 1941 [71?], New York NY). AS, p. 661.

Leonard, Foster A. [cinematographer] (b. 1892–3 Oct 1925 [33?], Los Angeles CA). BHD2, p. 157.

Leonard, Frank [cartoonist]. No data found. AMD, p. 211. "Leonard with Bray," *MPW,* 22 Aug 1925, 841.

Leonard, Gus [stage/film actor] (*né* Amédée Théodore Gaston Lerond, b. Marseilles, France, 8 Sep 1855 [extrait de naissance no. 412]–27 Mar 1939 [83], Los Angeles CA). (Lloyd, 1915.) "Gus Leonard; Stage and Screen Comedian, 80, Began with Tony Pastor," *NYT,* 28 Mar 1939, 24:3. "Gus Leonard," *Variety,* 29 Mar 1939. AS, p. 661. BHD1, p. 325 (b. 1859). IFN, p. 177. Truitt, p. 195.

Leonard, Harry [actor] (b. ca. 1857–1 Sep 1917 [60?], Los Angeles CA; suicide from self-inflicted wounds). "Harry Leonard Dead," *Variety,* 7 Sep 1917, p. 26 ("Los Angeles, Sept. 5. Harry Leonard, picture actor, who tried to kill Anneska Frolik, actress, by shooting and throwing vitriol at her, died from self-inflicted wounds."). AS, p. 661 (d. 5 Sep). BHD, p. 228.

Leonard, Henry W. [scenarist] (d. 21 Jan 1918). BHD2, p. 157.

Leonard, Jack [actor] (b. England-d. Oct 1921, Los Angeles CA). BHD, p. 228. IFN, p. 177.

Leonard, James [actor] (b. 1868?–4 Jul 1930 [62], Glendale CA). "James Leonard," *Variety,* 9 Jul 1930 (began 1928). AS, p. 661. BHD, p. 228. IFN, p. 177. Truitt, p. 195.

Leonard, Marion [actress] (b. OH, 9 Jun 1881–9 Jan 1956 [74], Woodland Hills CA). m. **Stanner E.V. Taylor** (d. 1948). (Biograph, 1908.) AMD, p. 211. AS, p. 661. BHD, p. 228. IFN, p. 177. Spehr, p. 148. Truitt, 1983 (b. 1880). "To Whom It May Concern—and It Concerns You!," *MPW,* 2 Dec 1911, 737. "Taylor and Leonard," *MPW,* 27 Jul 1912, 329. "Marion Leonard Joins Monopol Company," *MPW,* 7 Dec 1912, 988. "The Rachel of the Silent Drama," *MPW,* 1 Feb 1913, 454. "Warren, Taylor and Leonard with Warners," *MPW,* 23 Aug 1913, 851. "Marion Leonard Back with Warners," *MPW,* 14 Mar 1914, 1397. "Miss Leonard Back; After Siege of Illness, Screen Star Returns to Work on Feature," *NYDM,* 15 Apr 1915, 24:1 (involuntary retirement of seven months due to peritonitis and other ills. Working on *Mrs. Dane's Defense*). "Marion Leonard's Activities," *MPW,* 5 Jun 1915, 1616.

Leonard, Minnie [actress] (b. 1873–2 Jan 1940 [66], Los Angeles CA). AS, p. 661. BHD, p. 228. IFN, p. 177.

Leonard, Robert [stage/film actor] (b. Poland, 22 Feb 1888?–5 Jan 1948 [59], Brooklyn NY). m. Lillian. (Selig, 1907.) "Robert Leonard, A Stage Comedian; Actor Well Known in London for 'Potash and Perlmutter' Role Dies in Brooklyn," *NYT,* 6 Jan 1948, 23:3. "Robert Leonard," *Variety,* 14 Jan 1948. AS, p. 661 (b. 9 Jun). BHD, p. 228 (b. 1849).

Leonard, Robert Z[igler], "The Blond Giant of the Screen" (2nd cousin of **Lillian Russell**) [actor/director] (b. Chicago IL, 7 Oct 1889–27 Aug 1968 [78], Beverly Hills CA; aneurism). m. (1) **Mae Murray**, 1918–25; (2) **Gertrude Olmstead**, Jun 1926, Santa Barbara CA (d. 1975). (Selig-Polyscope; FP-L; Universal; Select; Equity; MGM.) "Robert Z. Leonard, 78, Director of Films for 40 Years, Is Dead; Began in Hollywood as Actor—Gave Greta Garbo First Screen Test on Coast," *NYT,* 29 Aug 1968, 35:2 (worked with Francis Boggs [Hollywood's first director]; in one-reelers in 1915). "Robert Z. Leonard," *Variety,* 4 Sep 1968. AMD, p. 212. AS, p. 661. BHD, p. 228; BHD2, p. 157. IFN, p. 177. JS, p. 249 (made *La donna più bella del mondo,* Italy, 1955). Katz, pp. 712–13 (began 1907). Truitt, pp. 195–96 (began with Selig in 1907). "Perry Signs Leonard," *MPW,* 8 Jan 1921, 163. Robert Z. Leonard, "Reconciling Art with the Dollar Sign Is the Motion Picture Director's Task," *MPW,* 31 Dec 1921, 1057. "Director and Miss Olmstead to Wed," *MPW,* 6 Mar 1926, 2. "Robert Leonard Weds Gertrude Olmstead," *MPW,* 26 Jun 1926, 682.

Leonardson, Edna S. [film editor] (b. 1885–6 Sep 1948 [63?], Los Angeles CA). BHD2, p. 158.

Leone, Henry [stage/film actor] (b. Vienna, Austria, 30 Mar 1857–9 Jun 1922 [65], Mt. Vernon NY; apoplexy). m. Anne Dale. "Henry Leone Dead," *NYT,* 10 Jun 1922, 11:5. "Henry Leone," *Variety,* 16 Jun 1922. AS, p. 661 (b. 1858). BHD, p. 228 (b. Constantinople, Italy, 1858). IFN, p. 177. SD. Truitt, 1983.

Leong, James B. [actor] (b. Shanghai, China, 18 Jan 1900–24 Oct 1963 [63], Los Angeles CA). AMD, p. 212. AS, p. 662. BHD1, p. 325 (b. 2 Nov 1889–16 Dec 1967 [78]). IFN, p. 177. "James B. Leong Heads Chinese Company," *MPW,* 17 Dec 1921, 829.

Leonidoff, Ileana [actress] (b. Crimea). JS, p. 241 (in Italian silents from 1916; she appeared naked in *Attila—flagello di Dio,* 1917).

Leonidoff, Olga [scenarist]. No data found. FDY, p. 491.

Leonidov, Leonid M. [actor] (b. Odessa, Russia, 3 Jun 1873–6 Aug 1941 [68], Moscow, Russia). BHD, p. 228. IFN, p. 177.

Lepanto, Victoria [actress] (*née* Vittorina Lepanto, b. Rome, Italy, 15 Feb 1885–31 May 1965 [80], Rome, Italy). AMD, p. 212. BHD1, p. 612. JS, p. 241 (in Italian silents from 1909). "Picture Personalities," *MPW,* 26 Feb 1910, 294.

Le Paul, Paul [actor] (*né* Paul Braden, b. 1901–8 Jun 1938 [37?], St. Louis MO). AS, p. 650.

Le Pearl, Harry [actor] (b. Danville IL, 1885–13 Jan 1946 [60?], Los Angeles CA). AS, p. 662.

Lepera, Alfred [composer/scenarist] (b. 1886–24 Jun 1935 [49?], Meddelin, Colombia; plane crash). AS, p. 662.

Le Picard, Marcel A. [cinematographer] (b. Le Havre, France, 17 Jan 1887–25 May 1952 [65], Los Angeles CA). BHD2, p. 158. FDY, p. 461.

Lepine, Charles [director] (b. Bordeaux, France, 3 Mar 1859–15 Jan 1941 [81], Turin, Italy). AS, p. 662.

Leprestre, Julien [actor] (*né* Julien François Le Prestre, b. Paris, France, 27 Apr 1864). AS, p. 662.

Le Prince, Louis Aimé Augustin [inventor] (b. Metz, France, 28 Aug 1841 [extrait de naissance no. 199/1841]–16 Sep 1890 [49], between Dijon and Paris; place unknown: disappeared). Christopher Rawlence, *The Missing Reel; The Untold Story of the Lost Inventor of Moving Pictures* (New York: Atheneum, 1990). AS, p. 662.

WWVC, pp. 82–83. Glenn Myrent, "100 Years Ago, the Father of Movies Disappeared," *NYT,* 16 Sep 1990, 28:1.

Leprince, René [actor/director] (b. Sathonay, France, 1876–20 May 1929 [53?], Saint Raphael, France). AS, p. 662 (d. 25 May). BHD2, p. 158.

Lerand, Léon [actor] (b. Paris, France, 1864). AS, p. 662.

Lerel, Max [actor/dancer/scenarist] (*né* Maurice Versel, b. Aigle, Switzerland, 8 Jan 1894–20 Dec 1962 [68], Lausanne, Switzerland). AS, p. 662.

Leriche, Augustine [actress] (b. Paris, France, 1860). AS, p. 662.

Leriche, Léon (brother of **Jeanne Cheirel**) [actor] (*né* Léon Balthazar-Leriche, b. Paris, France, 1865–4 Feb 1924 [58?], Paris, France). AS, p. 662.

Lerner, Jacques [actor] (b. Jitowir, Ukraine). AMD, p. 212. AS, p. 662 (appeared in French silents). "Lerner Arrives," *MPW,* 4 Sep 1926, 4.

Le Roy, Aimé John [inventor] (*né* Jean-Aimé Le Roy, b. Bedford KY, 5 Feb 1854–1944 [90?]). AS, p. 650.

Le Roy, Georges Daniel Eugène [actor] (b. Paris, France, 28 Feb 1885–3 Aug 1965 [80], Marly-de-Roi, France). AS, p. 650 (Le Roy); p. 663 (Leroy).

Le Roy, Mervyn (cousin of **Jesse Lasky**) [stage/film director/producer] (b. San Francisco CA, 15 Oct 1900–13 Sep 1987 [86], Beverly Hills CA; heart attack and Alzheimer's disease). m. (1) **Edna Murphy**, Dec 1927 (d. 1974); (2) Doris Warner, NY NY; (3) Kitty Spiegel, 1 Feb 1946. With Dick Kleiner, *Mervyn LeRoy: Take One* (New York: Hawthorn Books, Inc., 1974; debut: *Perils of Pauline*). (FP-L; WB; MGM.) Peter B. Flint, "Mervyn LeRoy, 86, Dies; Director and Producer," *NYT,* 14 Sep 1987, B16:1. Thomas M. Pryor, "Producer-Director Mervyn Le Roy Dead at 86; Worked 50 Years," *Variety,* 16 Sep 1987. AMD, p. 212. AS, p. 650. BHD, p. 228; BHD2, p. 158. Katz, pp. 714–15. "Will Direct Colleen," *MPW,* 16 Apr 1927, 630. "Personal Column," *Paris and Hollywood Screen Secrets Magazine,* May 1927, 8 (contract renewed with the Colleen Moore unit at First National. "LeRoy, who is 24, left vaudeville to enter motion pictures four years ago."). "Will Direct for Colleen Moore," *MPW,* 14 May 1927, 100. "Mervyn LeRoy Makes Hit with 'First,'" *MPW,* 1 Oct 1927, 291. "LeRoy—Murphy Wedding, About Dec. 15," *MPW,* 19 Nov 1927, 25.

Lerski, Helmar [cinematographer] (*né* Israel Schmukerski, b. Straatsburg, Germany, 18 Feb 1871–29 Sep 1956 [85], Zurich, Switzerland). AS, p. 663. BHD2, p. 158.

Lery, Maxime [actor] (b. France, 29 Dec 1884). AS, p. 663.

Le Saint, Edward J. [actor/director/producer] (b. Cincinnati OH, 13 Dec 1870–10 Sep 1940 [69], Los Angeles CA). m. **Stella Razetto**, 25 Dec 1913, San Diego CA (d. 1948). (Selig.) "Edward J. LeSaint," *NYT,* 12 Sep 1940, 25:4. "Edward J. Le Saint," *Variety,* 18 Sep 1940. AMD, p. 212. AS, p. 650. BHD1, p. 325; BHD2, p. 158. IFN, p. 177. 1921 Directory, p. 269. Truitt, p. 196. "The Film Actor and the Uniform," *MPW,* 11 Nov 1911, 480:2. "Edward J. LeSaint Joins the Universal," *MPW,* 25 Sep 1915, 2185. "LeSaint Takes a Rest," *MPW,* 27 May 1916, 1495. "Edward J. LeSaint Joins Lasky," *MPW,* 22 Jul 1916, 613. "Edward LeSaint Joins Realart on the Coast," *MPW,* 26 Nov 1921, 395. "C.B.C. Picks LeSaint," *MPW,* 8 Mar 1924, 107.

Le Saint, Stella R *see* **Razetto, Stella**

Leslie, Arthur [actor/writer/publicist] (b. England, 1902?–30 Jun 1970 [68], Cardigan, Holland). (Fox.) AMD, p. 212. AS, p. 663. IFN, p. 177. "Leslie Wins Again," *MPW,* 29 Aug 1914, 1222. "Leslie's Publicity Stunt Is Attracting Attention," *MPW,* 12 Jul 1919, 246.

Leslie, Edgar [lyricist] (b. Stamford CT, 31 Dec 1885–22 Jan 1976 [90], New York NY; heart ailment). C. Gerald Fraser, "Edgar Leslie, 90, Song Writer, Dies; Wrote 'Moon Over Miami'—Helped Found ASCAP," *NYT,* 24 Jan 1976, 30:5 (wrote *I'm a Yiddisher Cowboy; Why Ragtime Rosie Ragged the Rosary; All the Quakers Are Shoulder Shakers; Where Was Moses When the Lights Went Out?; Get Out and Get Under*). "Edgar Leslie," *Variety,* 28 Jan 1976 (wrote lyrics for *For Me and My Gal; Oh, What a Pal Was Mary; Lonesome*). AS, p. 663. BHD2, p. 158.

Leslie, Eleanor [actress] (b. London, England, 1874–14 Jun 1929 [54?], Glendale CA). AS, p. 663. BHD1, p. 325. IFN, p. 177 (Elinor).

Leslie, Fred [actor] (b. England, 29 Aug 1880–1 Jan 1945 [64], England). AS, p. 663.

Leslie, Gladys, "The Girl with the Million Dollar Smile" [actress] (b. New York NY, 5 Mar 1899–2 Oct 1976 [77], Boynton Beach FL). "Gladys Leslie Moore," *Miami Herald,* 7 Oct 1976. (Vitagraph, 1917.) AMD, p. 212. AS, p. 663. BHD, p. 228. IFN, p. 177. "Gladys Leslie," *MPW,* 17 Mar 1917, 1783. "Is Gladys Leslie a Star?," *MPW,* 14 Apr 1917, 300. Bert Adler, "Gladys Leslie—Soldiers' Samaritan," *Picture-Play Masgazine,* Sep 1917, 50 (established the Gladys Leslie Coffee Stand at the Long Island entrance to the Queensboro Bridge, NYC, when her brother, Richard, was called to service). Ethel Rosemon, "The Extra Girl Invades a Mimic Boarding-House; It's All in the Filming of Gladys Leslie's Latest Photoplay," *MPC,* Feb 1919, 56–57, 60. Billy H. Doyle, "Lost Players," *CI,* 147 (Sep 1987), 52–53.

Leslie, Helen [actress]. No data found. m. **Jacques Jaccard** (d. 1960). AMD, p. 212. "Helen Leslie," *MPW,* 28 Nov 1914, 1234. J. Van Cartmell, "Along the Pacific Coast," *NYDM,* 15 Sep 1915, 30:4 (cited as Jaccard's wife).

Leslie, James [actor] (b. England, 1863?–15 Nov 1918 [55], London, England; found dead in a ditch). "James Leslie," *Variety,* 22 Nov 1918. AS, p. 663.

Leslie, Lil[l]ie [stage/film actress] (b. Scotland, 1892–8 Sep 1940 [48], Los Angeles CA). (Lubin.) AMD, p. 212. AS, p. 663 (Lila Leslie). BHD1, p. 326. IFN, p. 178. "More Afraid of the Director Than of the Snakes," *MPW,* 25 Apr 1914, 519. "Lilie Leslie," *MPW,* 13 Jun 1914, 1522. Lester Sweyd, "What They Are Doing Now," *Motion Picture Magazine,* Feb 1918, 13 ("...is now on tour with one of the 'Experience' companies.").

Leslie, Margaret [actress]. No data found. (Equitable.) "Gossip of the Studios," *NYDM,* 13 Nov 1915, 33:1 (in a recent taxicab accident; "the cab ran into a hole in the pavement and overturned. Miss Leslie suffered severe contusions and a scalp wound which necessitated stitches."). *See* next entry.

Leslie, Marguerite [actress] (b. Ostersund, Sweden, 3 Apr 1884–1958 [74?]). BHD, p. 228. *See* previous entry.

Leslie, Noel [actor] (b. England, 1889–10 Mar 1974 [84?], New York NY). AS, p. 663.

Leslie, Robert (son of Richard Leslie) [child actor] (b. 17 May 1914). (Vitagraph.) *NYDM,* 8 Jul 1914.

LeSoir, George L. [director]. No data found. AMD, p. 212. LeSoir Back from New Orleans, LA," *MPW,* 18 May 1912, 639. "Four Directors for Premier Program," *MPW,* 18 Dec 1915, 2160.

Le Somptier, René Eugène [director/scenarist] (b. Caen, France, 12 Nov 1884 [extrait de naissance no. 764]–23 Sep 1950 [65], Paris, France). AS, p. 650.

Lesser, Myer [producer] (b. 1874–28 Jan 1954 [79?], Miami Beach FL). AS, p. 663.

Lesser, Sol [producer/executive] (b. Spokane WA, 17 Feb 1890–19 Sep 1980 [90], Los Angeles CA). Alfred E. Clark, "Sol Lesser, Pioneer Movie Producer, Dies at Age 90," *NYT,* 21 Sep 1980, 44:4. "Sol Lesser, 90, Predated Nearly All Industry Pioneers; 117 Features," *Variety,* 24 Sep 1980. AMD, p. 212. AS, p. 663. BHD2, p. 158. Katz, p. 715. "Sol Lesser Opens New York Office," *MPW,* 27 Dec 1913, 1528. "Sol Lesser, First National Official, Insists Organization Is Independent," *MPW,* 6 Feb 1926, 534–35 (Principal Pictures).

Lessey, George A. [stage/film actor/director/producer] (b. Amherst MA, 8 Jun 1879–3 Jun 1947 [67], Westbrook CT). m. **May Evers Abbey** (d. 1952). (Edison, 1912.) "George Lessey, Long in Broadway Shows," *NYT,* 4 Jun 1947, 27:4 ("the first actor to play Romeo in silent films"). AMD, p. 212. AS, p. 663. BHD1, p. 326; BHD2, p. 158. IFN, p. 178. SD. "Edison Touches Popular Chord," *MPW,* 3 Jan 1914, 28–29. "George A. Lessey," *MPW,* 22 Aug 1914, 1089. "Lessey Joins Eastern Film," *MPW,* 23 Oct 1915, 622. George Katchmer, "George Lessey," *CI,* 232 (Oct 1994), C23.

Lessing, Bruno [writer] (aka Rudolph Block) (b. 1870–29 Apr 1940 [70?], Tucson AZ). AMD, p. 212. BHD2, p. 158. "Bruno Lessing Goes East," *MPW,* 9 Sep 1916, 1678–79.

Lessley, Elgin [cinematographer]. No data found. AMD, p. 212. FDY, p. 461. "Elgin Lessley," *MPW,* 22 Jan 1927, 265.

L'Esteele, Eleanor Scott [actress] (b. England, 15 Apr 1881–25 Apr 1962 [81], Los Angeles CA). AS, p. 629 (L'Estelle). BHD1, p. 326.

Lester, Edward T. [sound director] (b. 1901?–15 Feb 1963 [61], Honolulu HI). (Columbia.) "Edward T. Lester," *Variety,* 27 Feb 1963. AS, p. 664. BHD2, p. 158 (d. 27 Feb).

Lester, Elliot [scenarist] (b. 1893–23 Feb 1951 [56?], Wyncote PA). AS, p. 664. BHD2, p. 158.

Lester, Kate [stage/film actress] (*née* Sarah Cody, b. Thorpe, Norfolk, England, 1857–12 Oct 1924 [67], Los Angeles CA; result of burns from a gas stove explosion). (FP-L; Fine Arts; Peerless; Selznick; Frohman; World.) "Kate Lester [Mrs. Sarah Cody] Dies of Burns; Noted Among Beautiful Women of Stage," *Variety,* 15 Oct 1924 (age 55). AMD, p. 212. AS, p. 664. BHD, p. 229. IFN, p. 178. MSBB, p. 1038. Truitt, 1983. "Obituary," *MPW,* 1 Nov 1924, 28.

Lester, Louise (mother of **Scott Beal**) [actress] (b. Milwaukee WI, 8 Aug 1867–17 Nov 1952

[85], Los Angeles CA). m. **Jack Richardson**, 13 May 1914, Santa Barbara CA (d. 1947); **Frank Beal** (d. 1934). (American.) "Louise Beal Dies at 85; Star of Calamity Ann Series Started Western Films," *NYT,* 19 Nov 1952, 29:3. "Louise L. Beal," *Variety,* 26 Nov 1952. AMD, p. 212. AS, p. 664 (d. 18 Nov). BHD1, p. 326. BR, pp. 51–52 (d. 18 Nov 1932). IFN, p. 178. Truitt, p. 196. "Louise Lester—'Calamity Jane,'" *MPW,* 18 Jan 1913, 254. "Richardson-Lester," *NYDM,* 10 Jun 1914, 50:2 (photo on p. 25). "Leading American Players," *MPW,* 11 Jul 1914, 240–42. "Louise Lester," *MPW,* 16 Oct 1915, 424. Billy H. Doyle, "Lost Players," *CI,* 152 (Feb 1988), C13. George A. Katchmer, "Forgotten Cowboys and Cowgirls—Part XIV," *CI,* 191 (May 1991), 20, 22.

Lester, William B. [actor/scenarist]. No data found. FDY, p. 491.

Lestina, Adolphe [stage/film actor]. No data found. m. Bessie Lee. (Biograph, 1909). SD.

Lestinguette, Pierre [scenarist]. No data found. FDY, p. 491.

L'Estrange, Dick [actor: Keystone Cop/director] (*né* Gunther von Strensch, b. Asheville NC, 27 Dec 1889–19 Nov 1963 [73], Burbank CA). m. Georgia. "Richard l'Estrange Dies; Movie-Television Official," *NYT,* 21 Nov 1963, 39:4. "Richard L'Estrange," *Variety,* 27 Nov 1963. AMD, p. 212. BHD, p. 229; BHD2, p. 158. IFN, p. 178. "L'Estrange Succeeds Cuneo," *MPW,* 3 Nov 1917, 683. "Dick L'Estrange Shifts Studios," *MPW,* 10 Jan 1920, 223. George A. Katchmer, "Forgotten Cowboys and Cowgirls—Part VIII," *CI,* 180 (Jun 1990), 58–59.

L'Estrange, Julian [actor] (b. Weston-super-Mare, Somersetshire, England, 6 Aug 1878–22 Oct 1918 [40], New York NY; pneumonia and influenza). m. **Constance Collier** (d. 1955). "Julian L'Estrange Dead; Prominent English Actor a Victim of Spanish Influenza," *NYT,* 23 Oct 1918, 13:2; "L'Estrange's Funeral Private," *NYT,* 24 Oct 1918, 13:2. "Julian L'Estrange," *Variety,* 25 Oct 1918 (age 38). AMD, p. 213. AS, p. 629. BHD, p. 229. IFN, p. 178. "Julian L'Estrange Emily Stevens' Leading Man," *MPW,* 8 Dec 1917, 1507. "Obituary," *MPW,* 9 Nov 1918, 651 (age 38).

L'Estrange, Richard [actor/director] (*né* Gunther von Strensch, b. Asheville NC, 27 Dec 1889–19 Nov 1963 [73], Burbank CA). AS, p. 629. BHD, p. 158.

Le Strange, Norman [actor] (b. France-d. 5 Jun 1936, London, England). AS, p. 650. BHD, p. 229. IFN, p. 178.

Le Sueur, Hal Hayes (brother of **Joan Crawford**) [actor] (b. San Antonio TX, 1903–3 May 1963 [60?], Los Angeles CA; peritonitis). AS, p. 650.

Letort, J. [cinematographer]. No data found. FDY, p. 461.

Lett, Robert [actor] (d. Mar 1916, West Orange NJ). BHD, p. 229.

Letta, Vin Sini [actor] (d. 4 May 1921, Chicago IL). BHD, p. 229.

Lettinger, Rudolf [actor] (b. 26 Oct 1865–21 Mar 1937 [71]). BHD, p. 229. IFN, p. 178.

Leubas, Louis [actor] (b. France, 1870–29 Aug 1932 [62], Digne-les-Bains, France; suicide). AS, p. 664. BHD, p. 229. IFN, p. 178.

Leudesdorff-Tormin, Philine [actress] (b. 1894–30 Apr 1924 [30?]). BHD, p. 229.

Leuthge, Bobby E. [scenarist] (b. Gleiwitz, Germany, 12 Sep 1892–11 Mar 1964 [71], Berlin, Germany). AS, p. 688. BHD2, p. 166.

Levall, G.E. [actor] (d. 7 Feb 1922, Coalinga CA). AS, p. 664 (O.E. Levall). BHD, p. 229.

Le Valle, Cleo [actress] (d. Aug 1925, Del Mar CA). BHD, p. 229.

Levaluoma, Eero Kullervo [actor] (b. Helsinki, Finland, 6 Jun 1896–18 Nov 1969 [73], Helsinki, Finland). AS, p. 664.

Levance, Cal [actor] (*né* Charles Waite, b. Canada-d. 6 Sep 1951, Toronto, Canada). AS, p. 664. BHD, p. 229. The Office of the Registrar General in Ontario, Canada, has no record of Levance's death (searched 1949–53).

Levant, Oscar [pianist/composer/actor] (b. Pittsburgh PA, 27 Dec 1906–14 Aug 1972 [65], Beverly Hills CA; heart attack). m. (1) Barbara Smith—div. 1938; (2) June Gale, 1939. *The Importance of Being Oscar; A Smattering Of Ignorance; Memoirs of an Amnesiac.* AS, p. 664. BHD1, p. 326; BHD2, p. 159.

Levasseur, Palmyre [actor] (*né* Palmyre Augustine Thion, b. Cuvergnon, France, 24 Dec 1888–4 Aug 1963 [74], Paris, France [extrait de décès no. SN/1963]). AS, p. 664.

Levee, M[ichael] **C.** [executive/producer/agent] (b. Baltimore MD, 19 Jan 1889–24 May 1972 [83], Palm Springs CA; cancer). m. Trudy. (Fox Films, 1917; Brunton; Paramount; UA; First National.) "Mike Levee," *Variety,* 31 May 1972. AS, p. 665. BHD2, p. 159.

Leventhal, Jacob Frank [animator/special effects] (aka L.F. Leventhal, b. St. Louis MO–d. 18 Jul 1953, New York NY). m. Elizabeth. "Jacob Leventhal, Movie Researcher; One of Earliest Developers of Animated Cartoon and 3-D Techniques Is Dead Here," *NYT,* 20 Jul 1953, 17:3 (early animated and 3-D cartoons). "Jacob F. Leventhal," *Variety,* 191, 22 Jul 1953, 63:2 ("credited with having produced one of the first animated shorts in 1917." Member of the American Optical Society and the Society of Motion Picture and Television Engineers. *Out of the Inkwell* series. Ives-Leventhal, "1st 3-D films [Plastigrams] in this country in 1934." With John A. Norling, produced *Audioscopics* for Metro.). AMD, p. 213. AS, p. 665. BHD2, p. 159. "Animated Drawings," *MPW,* 30 Jun 1917, 2078. "L.F. Leventhal," *MPW,* 21 Jul 1917, 397–98.

Le Veque, Edward [actor: Keystone Cop] (b. Juarez, Mexico, 1896?–28 Jan 1989 [92], Los Angeles CA). m. art titlist **Florence Gilbert**, 1927. (Griffith; Sennett.) "Eddie Le Veque Dead; A Keystone Kop," *NYT,* 1 Feb 1989, A19:3. "Edward Le Veque," *Variety,* 8 Feb 1989. AS, p. 651. BHD, p. 229. Eddie Le Veque, "The Last Keystone Kop," *CFC,* 28 (Fall, 1970), 25.

Leverett, George [sound engineer] (b. 1883?–20 Mar 1968 [85], Hemet CA). "George Leverett," *Variety,* 3 Apr 1968. BHD2, p. 159.

Levering, Jack [actor]. No data found. AMD, p. 213. "Jack Levering, Honored by King George, Is a Hero Both On and Off the Screen," *MPW,* 12 Jul 1919, 194.

Levering, James [stage/film actor] (b. Bristol, England, 1861). m. Cecelia Kitts. (Edison; Pathé; Solax; Lubin; Gaumont; Universal.) BHD, p. 229. MSBB, p. 1025.

Levering, Joseph [actor/producer/director]. No data found. (Solax; Blaché-American.) AMD, p. 213. "Solax Engages Levering," *MPW,* 9 Aug 1913, 641. "More Méliès Pictrures," *MPW,* 23 May 1914, 1122. "Levering, Knickerbocker Producer, in Paradise," *MPW,* 7 Aug 1915, 1018.

Levesque, Marcel [actor] (*né* Joseph Marcel Levesque, b. Paris, France, 6 Dec 1877–16 Feb 1962 [84], Pont-aux-Dames, France [extrait de décès no. 14/SN/1962]). AS, p. 665 (d. Paris, France). BHD1, p. 326. IFN, p. 178.

Levey, Ethel [actress] (b. San Francisco CA, 22 Nov 1881–27 Feb 1955 [73], New York NY). AS, p. 665.

Levey, Harry [producer]. No data found. AMD, p. 213. "Harry Levey Is Seeking a Modern Hercules for Industrial Productions," *MPW,* 4 Sep 1920, 70. "Levey Forms Company to Make Dramatic Productions; To Produce Eight a Year," *MPW,* 11 Sep 1920, 195. "Levey Sues Universal," *MPW,* 16 Oct 1920, 979. "Harry Levey Gets Medal from French Commission," *MPW,* 16 Oct 1920, 985. "Universal Files Answer to Harry Levey's Suit," *MPW,* 30 Oct 1920, 1230.

Levi-Leclerc, Claire [actress] (b. Paris, France, 27 May 1867). AS, p. 665.

Levien, Sonya [scenarist] (*née* Sonia Levica Levien, b. Moscow, Russia, 25 Dec 1888?–19 Mar 1960 [71], Los Angeles CA). m. Carl Hovey (d. 1956). "Sonya Levien, 71, Scenarist, Dead; Won Oscar for 'Interrupted Melody'—Had Worked on 'State Fair,' 'Quo Vadis,'" *NYT,* 20 Mar 1960, 86:8. "Sonya Levien," *Variety,* 23 Mar 1960. AMD, p. 213. AS, p. 665 (b. 1895). BHD2, p. 159 (b. 1889). FDY, p. 491 (Sonya Levin). IFN, p. 178. Katz, 1994 (b. 1895). "Joins Paramount," *MPW,* 17 Dec 1921, 788. Sonya Levien, "Diary of a Scenario Writer on Location with Alice Brady; Well-known movie author recounts adventures among Canadian wilds during out door filming of *The Snow Bride* [Part I]," *MW,* 12 May 1923, 13, 30; Part II, 19 May 1923, 21, 30; Part III, 26 May 1923, 21, 30; Part IV, 26 May 1923, 21, 30. "Miss Levien Busy," *MPW,* 12 Mar 1927, 114. "Scenarist's Contract," *MPW,* 9 Jul 1927, 103.

Le Vigan, Robert [actor] (*né* Robert Charles Alexandre Coquillaud, b. Paris, France, 7 Jan 1900 [extrait de naissance no. 192/1900]-12 Oct 1972 [72], Tandil, Argentina). AS, p. 651.

Levigard, Joseph [director] (b. Frankfurt, Germany, 5 Jun 1903–28 Apr 1931 [27]). BHD2, p. 159.

Levine, Harold Z. [publicist]. No data found. (Solax.) AMD, p. 213. F.J. Beecroft, "Publicity Men I Have Met…," *NYDM,* 14 Jan 1914, 48 (*see* Beecroft, Chester for full citation). Hugh Hoffman, "Levine Slated for London," *MPW,* 7 Mar 1914, 1247.

Levine, Max M. [publicist]. No data found. AMD, p. 213. "Levine with Associated," *MPW,* 17 Mar 1923, 359.

Levine, Nathaniel [executive] (b. New York NY, 26 Jul 1899–6 Aug 1989 [90], Woodland Hills CA). "Nathan Levine Dies; Film Executive Was 89," *NYT,* 13 Aug 1989, 36:4. "Nathaniel Levine," *Variety,* 16 Aug 1989, p. 96 (age 90; formed Mascot, 1927; Republic, 1935). AS, p. 665. BHD2, p. 159 (b. 1900). Mike Newton, *The Vanishing Legion: A History of Mascot Pictures 1927–35* [review]," *CI,* 259 (Jan 1997), 42.

Le Viness, Carl M. [actor/director/producer] (b. New York NY, 6 Jul 1885–15 Oct 1964 [79], Los Angeles CA; pneumonia). "Carl Le Viness," *Variety,* 21 Oct 1964. AMD, p. 213. AS, p.

651. BHD1, p. 327; BHD2, p. 159. IFN, p. 178. "Carm M. LeViness to Direct Sydney Ayres," *MPW,* 17 Jul 1915, 476. "More Horsley Play'rs," *MPW,* 2 Oct 1915, 62. "LeViness Directing for American," *MPW,* 18 Mar 1916, 1837. "LeViness Directing for American," *MPW,* 25 Mar 1916, 2019.

Le Vino, Albert Shelby [actor/scenarist] (b. Fredericksburg VA, 1878). m. **Margaret Prussing,** 29 Jun 1916, NYC (d. 1944). AMD, p. 213. BHD2, p. 159. FDY, p. 491. "LeVino Leaves Arrow," *MPW,* 22 Jan 1916, 573. "Albert Shelby LeVino Marries Miss Prussing," *MPW,* 22 Jul 1916, 615. "LeVino Goes to Coast for Metro," *MPW,* 12 Jan 1918, 208. "LeVino Completes the Cobb Scenario," *MPW,* 12 Feb 1927, 498.

Levinson, Nathan [producer] (b. New York NY, 1888–18 Oct 1952 [64?], Toluca Lake CA). AS, p. 665.

Levitsky, Aleksandr [cinematographer] (b. Russia). Yuri Tsivian, "Between the Old and the New: Soviet Film Culture in 1918–1924," *Griffithiana,* 55/56 (Sep 1996), 15–63.

Levy, E.A. [publicist]. No data found. AMD, p. 213. "Levy Premier's Publicity Man," *MPW,* 11 Dec 1915, 1985.

Levy, Ely [director/producer] (b. Smyrna, Turkey, 1889–16 Sep 1985 [96?], Los Angeles CA). AS, p. 666.

Levy, Herbert [producer] (b. Berlin, Germany, 24 Mar 1892–ca. 1954 [62?]). AS, p. 666.

Levy, Louis [composer] (b. London, England, 20 Nov 1894–18 Aug 1957 [62], Slough, England). AS, p. 666.

Levy, Melvin [scenarist] (b. 11 May 1902–1 Dec 1980 [78], Studio City CA). AS, p. 666. BHD2, p. 159. FDY, p. 491.

Levy-Strauss, Jean [producer] (b. France, 1898–30 Dec 1944 [46?], Santa Monica CA). AS, p. 666.

Lewin, Albert [scenarist/director/producer] (b. Brooklyn NY, 23 Sep 1894–9 May 1968 [73], New York NY; pneumonia). (Goldwyn; MGM; Paramount.) "Albert Lewin, 73, Filmmaker, Dies; Creator of Many Movies, Also Director and Author," *NYT,* 10 May 1968, 44:1. "Albert Lewin," *Variety,* 15 May 1968. AS, p. 666 (b. Newark NJ). BHD2, p. 160 (b. Newark NJ; d. 6 May). FDY, p. 491. IFN, p. 178. Katz, p. 717.

Lewis, Ada [stage/film actress] (b. New York NY, 1875–24 Sep 1925 [50?], Hollis, LI NY; following nervous breakdown in Jan. Interred in Calvary Cemetery). m. John W. Parr (d. 1901). (Rickette's "Flying A" Co.) "Ada Lewis," *Variety,* 30 SDep 1925, p. 48:4 (The 500 persons attending her funeral included Charles Dillingham, David Belasco, Nellie Revell, Oscar Shaw, Ernest Truex, Blanche Bates, Ina Claire and May Irwin). BHD, p. 229. "To Star Ada Lewis," *NYDM,* 13 May 1914, 36:4 (in the Heine-Katrina series).

Lewin, Ike [actor] (b. Chicago IL, 5 Jul 1889–10 Jun 1941 [51], Los Angeles CA). AS, p. 666.

Lewis, Albert E. [film/TV director/producer/scenarist] (b. Poland, 15 Mar 1884–5 Apr 1978 [94], Beverly Hills CA). Alfred E. Clark, "Albert Lewis at 93; Broadway Producer; Presented 'Cabin in the Sky,' 'Jazz Singer,' 'Banjo Eyes' and 'Rain'—Worked in Films and TV," *NYT,* 10 Apr 1978, B2:4. "Albert Lewis," *Variety,* 12 Apr 1978. AS, p. 666. BHD2, p. 160. IFN, p. 178.

Lewis, Barran [publicist]. No data found. AMD, p. 213. "Lewis Is Ad Chief," *MPW,* 13 Nov 1926, 3. "Barran Lewis," *MPW,* 26 Mar 1927, 311.

Lewis, Ben (brother of **Joseph H. Lewis**) [film editor] (d. 29 Dec 1970, Los Angeles CA). m. Doris. (Metro.) "Ben Lewis," *Variety,* 20 Jan 1971.

Lewis, Bertha [stage/film actress] (b. London, England, 12 May 1887–8 May 1931 [44], Cambridge, England; auto accident). m. Herbert Heyner. "Bertha Lewis," *Variety,* 13 May 1931. SD, p. 720.

Lewis, Charles H. [actor] (b. 1850–3 Nov 1928 [78?]). BHD, p. 229.

Lewis, Clifford [advertising] (b. Wabash IN, 27 Jan 1899–17 Dec 1969 [70], Beaverton OR). AMD, p. 213. BHD2, p. 160. "Rath Leaves Paramount; Clifford Lewis Succeeds Him," *MPW,* 22 Oct 1927, 479.

Lewis, Dorothy [actress] (b. 1870–16 Jun 1952 [82?], Los Angeles CA). AS, p. 667.

Lewis, Edgar [stage/film actor/producer/director] (b. Holden MO, 22 Jun 1872–21 May 1938 [65], Los Angeles CA). (Lubin; Solax; Reliance; Photoplay Prods. Co.; Life Photo; Rex Beach; Fox; Edgar Lewis Prods.) "Edgar Lewis," *Variety,* 25 May 1938. AMD, p. 213. AS, p. 667. BHD1, p. 327; BHD2, p. 160. IFN, p. 278. MSBB, p. 1046. Spehr, p. 148 (b. 1877). "Another Feature Company," *MPW,* 25 Apr 1914, 531. "Edgar Lewis Recuperating," *MPW,* 19 Sep 1914, 1658. "Edgar Lewis," *MPW,* 3 Oct 1914, 40. "Edgar Lewis Joins Box Office Attractions Co.," *MPW,* 10 Oct 1914, 205. "Bos Office Producers," *MPW,* 7 Nov 1914, 791. "Deal Kindly with the Director," *MPW,* 12 Dec 1914, 1503. "Make-Up as Important on Screen as on Stage," *MPW,* 30 Jan 1915, 681. "Edgar Lewis Gets a Horse," *MPW,* 17 Apr 1915, 375. "Lewis to Leave Fox," *MPW,* 29 May 1915, 1408. "Three New Stars for Essanay," *NYDM,* 1 Sep 1915, 28:1 (to appear in *In the Palace of the King,* to be released Oct 1915, with E.J. Radcliffe [sic] and Arline Hackett. "Five thousand extra people will be used, including over a hundred professioal dancing girls."). "Edgar Lewis Joins Lubin," *MPW,* 4 Sep 1915, 1653. "More Lubin Enterprise," *MPW,* 9 Oct 1915, 236. "Edgar Lewis," *MPW,* 8 Apr 1916, 271. "Edgar Lewis Will Direct 'The Barrier,'" *MPW,* 27 May 1916, 1494. "Producer Edgar Lewis at Liberty," *MPW,* 26 Aug 1916, 1415. "Edgar Lewis Producing," *MPW,* 3 Mar 1917, 1377. "Set Aside Attachments Against Edgar Lewis," *MPW,* 19 Apr 1919, 339. "Lewis to Produce in West," *MPW,* 17 Jan 1920, 397. "Edgar Lewis to Make Series of Five Big Features for Pathé Under New Agreement," *MPW,* 19 Jun 1920, 1608.

Lewis, Eloise M. [scenarist]. No data found. FDY, p. 491.

Lewis, Eric [actor] (b. Northampton, England, 23 Oct 1855–1 Apr 1935 [79], Margate, England). BHD, p. 229.

Lewis, Eugéne B. [scenarist]. No data found. AMD, p. 214. "New Scenario Editor for Universal," *MPW,* 24 Jun 1916, 2214.

Lewis, Eva [actress] (b. St. Louis MO, 1881–6 May 1939 [58], Los Angeles CA). AS, p. 667. BHD, p. 229. IFN, p. 178.

Lewis, Fred [actor] (b. Kingston-on-Thames, England, 23 Dec 1860–25 Dec 1927 [67], England). BHD, p. 229. IFN, p. 178.

Lewis, Frederick G. [actor] (b. Oswego NY, 14 Feb 1873–19 Mar 1946 [73], Amityville, LI NY). m. Charlotte Kauffman. "Frederick Lewis, Retired Actor, 73; A Principal in Repertory Group of Sothern and Marlowe Dies—Noted as Shakespearean," *NYT,* 21 Mar 1946, 25:4. "Frederick G. Lewis," *Variety,* 27 Mar 1946. AS, p. 667. BHD, p. 229. IFN, p. 179. SD.

Lewis, Gene [actor/director/scenarist] (b. Philadelphia PA, 3 Nov 1887–27 Mar 1979 [91], Woodland Hills CA). AS, p. 667 (b. 1888). BHD2, p. 160.

Lewis, George "Beetlepuss" [actor] (b. 1901?–8 Apr 1955 [54]). AMD, p. 214. AS, p. 667. IFN, p. 179.

Lewis, George J. [film/TV actor] (*né* Jorge Lewis, b. Guadalajara, Mexico, 10 Dec 1903–10 Dec 1995 [92], Rancho Santa Fe CA; stroke). m. Mary Louise Lohman, Mar 1928. (Began as an extra, 1923; Universal; Columbia; Paramount; Republic; made Spanish-language films in Hollywood.) AS, p. 667 (d. 29 Dec 1977). Waldman, p. 163. "George J. Lewis [obituary]," *CI,* 249 (Mar 1996), 58:2. BHD1, p. 327 (d. 8 Dec). "George Lewis for Collegiat4e Series," *MPW,* 22 May 1926, 301. "George Lewis to Star in 'The Collegians,'" *MPW,* 22 May 1926, 311. "George Lewis Rises to Cinema Fame at 'U' City," *MPW,* 5 Jun 1926, 462. "George Lewis," *MPW,* 23 Jul 1927, 240. Dorothy Manners, "The Perpetual Collegian; George Lewis Wonders If He'll Be a University Man All His Life," *MPC,* Jun 1929, 65, 82. Ken Law, "George J. Lewis," *CI,* 131 (May 1986), C22-C23, 63 (b. 1904). Chapter 13, "George Lewis," *BS,* pp. 172–90 (includes filmography). Blackie Seymour, "George J. Lewis: Now That's a Star!," *CI,* 302 (Aug 2000), 65–67.

Lewis, Gordon [actor] (b. Harrison AR, 1890–17 Mar 1933 [42], Tucson AZ; suicide by shooting). AS, p. 667. BHD, p. 229. IFN, p. 179.

Lewis, Harold C. [producer] (b. New York NY, 18 Feb 1901–28 Dec 1967 [66], Los Angeles CA; heart attack). "Harold Lewis," *Variety,* 10 Jan 1968. AS, p. 667. BHD2, p. 160.

Lewis, Harry [actor] (b. 1886?–18 Nov 1950 [64], Los Angeles CA). "Harry Lewis," *Variety,* 29 Nov 1950. AS, p. 667. BHD, p. 229. IFN, p. 179. Truitt, p. 196.

Lewis, Harry [artist]. No data found. AMD, p. 214. "Pathé Employs Large Staff of Art Experts," *MPW,* 29 Jun 1918, 1870.

Lewis, Ida [actress] (b. New York NY, 1848?–21 Apr 1935 [86], Los Angeles CA). "Ida Lewis," *Variety,* 24 Apr 1935. AS, p. 667 (b. 1871). BHD1, p. 327. IFN, p. 179. 1921 Directory, p. 229 (b. England). Truitt, p. 196 (b. 1871).

Lewis, James H. "Daddy" [actor] (b. 1850?–3 Nov 1928 [78], Pawtucket RI). "James H. Lewis," *Variety,* 7 Nov 1928. AS, p. 667. BHD, p. 229. IFN, p. 179. Truitt, p. 196. WWS, p. 196.

Lewis, Jeffreys [stage/film actress] (b. London, England, 1857?–29 Apr 1926 [69], New York NY). m. Harry Mainhall (d. 7 Nov 1902, LA CA). "Jeffreys Lewis, Actress, Dies at 69; Once Prominent Player Who Won Fame in 'Forget-Me-Not' and 'Diplomacy'; On the Stage Here at 16; Was Leading Woman at Wallack's Theatre and Later Won Great Success at Daly's," *NYT,* 29 Apr 1926, 23:3. "Jeffreys Lewis," *Variety,* 5 May 1926. AS, p. 667. BHD, p. 229.

Lewis, Jessica (or **Jessie**) [actress] (b. 1891?–6 Apr 1971 [80], Los Angeles CA). m. **George W. Lederer** (d. 1938). (World; in *The Pit* and *Trilby.*) "Jessica Lewis," *Variety,* 14 Apr 1971. AS, p. 667.

Lewis, Joe [actor] (*né* Joe Lewis Barrow, b. 1898–9 Oct 1938 [40?], Corning CA). AS, p. 667.

Lewis, Joseph H. (brother of **Ben Lewis**) [film/TV editor/director] (b. Brooklyn NY, 6 Apr 1900?–30 Aug 2000 [100?], St. John's Hospital, Santa Monica CA). m. (daughter Candy). (MGM; Mascot Films [which later became Republic Pictures]; LA Film Critics Association Lifetime Achievemenet Award, 1997, honoring his 38 films made between 1937 and 1958.) Lawrence Van Gelder, "Joseph H. Lewis, 93, Director Who Turned B-Movies into Art," *NYT,* 13 Sep 2000, B10 (age 93). Jon Thurber, "Joseph H. Lewis; Acclaimed director of B movies," *PP-G,* 17 Sep 2000, E-6:4 ("Mr. Lewis was believed to be 93, although some reference books list his birthday as April 6, 1900.... Born in New York City, Mr. Lewis came to Hollywood in the 1920s hoping to become an actor. His brother Ben, then a film editor at Metro Goldwyn Mayer, helped him get work at the studio as a camera loader. At a time when the industry was turning away from silent films, Mr. Lewis joined his brother in the editing room learning how to put sound with moving pictures.").

Lewis, Katherine [extra actress] (b. Newark NJ, 7 Nov 1906–25 Aug 1949 [42], Van Nuys CA). AMD, p. 214. BHD, addendum. Ragan 2, p. 972. "Katherine Lewis," *MPW,* 24 Mar 1917, 1929. Robert Donaldson, "Famous Extras," *MPC,* Feb 1927, 32 [photo]-33, 68, 80.

Lewis, Martin [stage/film/radio actor] (*né* Andrew Martin Lewis, b. London, England, 8 Sep 1888 [extrait de naissance no. 669]-15 Apr 1970 [81], Farnborough, Kent, England). "Martin Lewis," *Variety,* 15 Apr 1970, p. 63:2. AS, pp. 667–68. BHD1, p. 327 (b. Blackheath, England). IFN, p. 179.

Lewis, Mary [scenrist] (b. 1884–8 Nov 1942 [58?], Los Angeles CA). BHD2, p. 160.

Lewis, Mary [stage/film actress/singer] (*née* Mary Sybil Kidd, b. Hot Springs AR, 7 Jan 1900–31 Dec 1941 [41], New York NY). m. Michael Bohnen, 1927; Robert L. Hague (d. 1939). (Christie, 1920.) "Mary Lewis Dead; Ex-Star in Opera; Soprano Who Made Debut as Mimi in 'La Boheme' in 1926 at Metropolitan Was 41; Was in Church Choir at 8; Starred in Ziegfeld 'Follies'—Widow of Robert L. Hague, Standard Oil ex-Official," *NYT,* 1 Jan 1942, 25:1 (*née* Mary Sybil). "Mary Lewis," *Variety,* 7 Jan 1942. AS, p. 668. BHD, p. 229. IFN, p. 179. SD. Truitt, p. 196.

Lewis, Mitchell J. [actor] (b. Syracuse NY, 26 Jun 1880–24 Aug 1956 [76], Woodland Hills CA). m. (1) Nan Francis; (2) Rosabel Morrison. (Thanhouser; Universal; World; Kleine; Rex Beach Pictures; Edgar Lewis Prods.; Select; Metro.) "MItchell J. Lewis," *NYT,* 26 Aug 1956, 85:1. "Mitchell Lewis," *Variety,* 29 Aug 1956 (d. Hollywood CA, age 68). AMD, p. 214. AS, p. 668. BHD1, p. 327. FSS, p. 182. IFN, p. 179. MH, p. 122. MSBB, p. 1025 (b. 1884). SD. Truitt, pp. 196–97. WWS, p. 207. "'Mitch' Lewis Heap Big Chief," *MPW,* 8 Jul 1916, 239. "Edgar Lewis Signs Up Mitchell Lewis," *MPW,* 17 Feb 1917, 1028. "Mitchell Lewis," *MPW,* 5 May 1917, 781. "Mitchell Lewis Now a Select Star," *MPW,* 30 Nov 1918, 924. Fritzi Remont, "The Brownie Who Became a Star," *MPC,* Mar 1919, 31–32, 64. "Mitchell Lewis to Star for Metro," *MPW,* 6 Dec 1919, 669. "Nineteen Years on the Screen," *MPW,* 25 Jun 1927, 572. George Katchmer, "Remembering the Great Silents," *CI,* 209 (Nov 1992), 54–55.

Lewis, Philip S. [founded Chicago Film Exchange, 1904] (b. Poland, 1890?–28 Nov 1976 [86], Port Chester NY). "Philip S. Lewis," *Variety,* 15 Dec 1976.

Lewis, Ralph Percy [actor/producer] (b. Englewood IL, 28 Oct 1872–4 Dec 1937 [65], Los Angeles CA; from injuries sustained in an auto accident). (Reliance-Majestic, 1912; Griffith.) m. **Vera** (d. 1956). "Ralph Lewis," *Variety,* 8 Dec 1937. AMD, p. 214. AS, p. 668. BHD1, p. 327. FSS, p. 182. IFN, p. 179. KOM, pp. 144–45 (b. 16 Oct; d. 6 Dec). MH, p. 122. Truitt, p. 197. "William Fox Signs Ralph and Vera Lewis," *MPW,* 13 Jan 1917, 222. "Mayer Signs Ralph Lewis," *MPW,* 17 Jul 1920, 309. "Ralph Lewis B9uilds," *MPW,* 20 Aug 1921, 793 (Hollywood home). "Lewis Signs Again," *MPW,* 3 Dec 1921, 542. "Ralph Lewis on Crest of Stardom," *MPW,* 3 Nov 1923, 94. "Lewis to Produce," *MPW,* 1 Dec 1923, 498. "Sax Signs Ralph Lewis," *MPW,* 16 Jan 1926, 232. George Katchmer, "Remembering the Great Silents," *CI,* 251 (May 1996), p. 50.

Lewis, Randolph C. [publicist/scenarist] (b. 1862?–3 Sep 1934 [72]). AMD, p. 214. AS, p. 668. BHD2, p. 160. IFN, p. 179. "Lewis Joins Pathé Staff," *MPW,* 14 Sep 1918, 1571. "Pathé's Publicity Director Is Author of Blackton Special 'Forbidden Valley,'" *MPW,* 4 Sep 1920, 101. Arthur James, "A Word to and About Randolph Lewis," *MPW,* 13 May 1922, 160.

Lewis, Richard [actor] (b. 1869?–30 Apr 1935 [66], Los Angeles CA). "Richard Lewis," *Variety,* 8 May 1935. AS, p. 668. BHD, p. 229. IFN, p. 179. Truitt, p. 197.

Lewis, Sam [actor] (b. 1878–28 Apr 1963 [85], Los Angeles CA). BHD1, p. 328. IFN, p. 179.

Lewis, Sam [actor] (d. 11 Jan 1964, New York NY). "Sam Lewis," *Variety,* 22 Jan 1964. AS, p. 668.

Lewis, Sheldon [stage/film actor] (b. Philadelphia PA, 20 Apr 1868–7 May 1958 [89], San Gabriel CA). m. **Virginia Pearson** (d. 1958). (Pathé.) "Sheldon Lewis," *Variety,* 14 May 1958. AMD, p. 214. AS, p. 668. BHD1, p. 328 (b. 1869). FSS, p. 182. IFN, p. 179. Lowrey, p. 98. MH, p. 122. MSBB, p. 1025. Spehr, p. 148. Truitt, p. 197. "Sheldon Lewis with Pathé," *MPW,* 16 Jan 1915, 356. "Sheldon Lewis," *MPW,* 12 Aug 1916, 1121. "Sheldon Lewis," *MPW,* 28 Jul 1917, 621. "Sheldon Lewis to Return to Stage," *MPW,* 26 Jan 1918, 493. "Sheldon Lewis to Remain in Pictures," *MPW,* 9 Feb 1918, 798. "Sheldon Lewis to Star," *MPW,* 24 May 1919, 1160. George Katchmer, "Remembering the Great Silents," *CI,* 209 (Nov 1992), 55.

Lewis, Sinclair [actor/playwright/scenarist] (b. Sauk Centre MN, 7 Feb 1885–10 Jan 1951 [65], Rome, Italy; paralysis of the heart). m. (1) Grace Livingston Hegger, 15 Apr 1914; (2) Dorothy Thompson, 14 May 1928. (First novel: *Our Mr. Wrenn,* 1914.) "Sinclair Lewis, 65, Dies in Rome Clinic; First American to Win Nobel Prize for Literature Wrote 'Babbitt' and 'Main Street,'" *NYT,* 11 Jan 9151, 1:2, 25:2. AMD, p. 214. AS, p. 668. "Sinclair Lewis to Write 'New York' for Paramount," *MPW,* 29 Aug 1925, 929.

Lewis, Ted [actor/singer/bandleader/composer] (*né* Theodore Leopold Friedman, b. Circleville OH, 6 Jun 1891–25 Aug 1971 [80], New York NY). m. Adah Becker, 1915, Rochester NY. William M. Freeman, "Ted Lewis, Showman, Dies at 80; Top-Hatted Jazzman Made 'Is Ev'rybody Happy?' His Line," *NYT,* 26 Aug 1971, 40:1. "Ted Lewis, 'Top-Hatted Tragedian of Jazz,' Dies at 80 in New York Home," *Variety,* 1 Sep 1971. AS, p. 668. BHD1, p. 328 (b. 1890); BHD2, p. 160. IFN, p. 179.

Lewis, Tom [actor] (*né* Thomas Lewis Maguire, b. St. John, New Brunswick, Canada, 17 May 1864?–19 Oct 1927 [63], New York NY; cancer). "Tom Lewis, Veteran of the Stage, Dies; Comedian for Fifty Years Succumbs in Roosevelt Hospital After an Operation; Began His Career at 13; Appeared in Many New York Productions, Including Ziegfeld 'Follies' and 'Louie the 14th,'" *NYT,* 20 Oct 1927, 29:5 (no mention of films; stage debut in Boston). "Tom Lewis," *Variety,* 26 Oct 1927. AS, p. 668. BHD, p. 230 (b. 1867). IFN, p. 179. Truitt, p. 197. WWS, p. 197.

Lewis, Vera [actress] (*née?,* b. New York NY, 10 Jun 1873–8 Feb 1956 [82], Woodland Hills CA). m. **Ralph Lewis** (d. 1937). (Griffith, 1914.) "Vera Lewis," *Variety,* 15 Feb 1956 (age 72). AMD, p. 214. AS, p. 668. BHD1, p. 328. IFN, p. 179 (age 82). Truitt, p. 197. "William Fox Signs Ralph and Vera Lewis," *MPW,* 13 Jan 1917, 222.

Lewis, Walter L. [actor] (b. 1884?–1 Jun 1957 [73], Cedar Grove NJ). (Biograph, 1912.) "Walter L. Lewis," *NYT,* 4 Jun 1957, 35:5.

Lewis, Walter Pratt [stage/film actor] (b. Albany NY, 10 Jun 1866–30 Jan 1932 [65], New York NY). (Biograph; Pathé; Edison; FP-L; Metro; Goldwyn; World; Fox.) AMD, p. 214. AS, p. 668. BHD1, p. 328. IFN, p. 179. MSBB, p. 1025 (b. 1871). "Daughter Born to Walter Lewis," *MPW,* 18 Jul 1914, 421 (b. 21 Jun 1914).

Lewton, Nina [film editor] (b. Russia, 1874–26 Feb 1967 [92?], Woodland Hills CA). BHD2, p. 160.

Lewyn, Louis [producer] (b. Houston TX, 18 Dec 1891–24 May 1969 [77], Huntington Beach CA). m. **Marion Mack**, 1923, Monterey CA (d. 1989). AMD, p. 214. BHD2, p. 161. BHD2, p. 161. "Screen Snap Shots' Show Sidelights on Film Folk," *MPW,* XLIII, 28 Feb 1920, 1472.

Lexy, Edward [actor] (*né* Edward Gerald Little, b. London, England, 18 Feb 1897–ca. 1958 [61?]). AS, p. 668.

Leyton, George [stage/film singer/actor] (b. New Orleans LA, 24 Apr 1864–5 Jun 1948 [84], London, England). "George Leyton," *Variety,* 171, 23 Jun 1948, 40:1. AS, p. 668. BHD, p. 230.

Leyton, Harold B. [film editor] (b. 1894–15 Jan 1962 [67?], Los Angeles CA). BHD2, p. 161.

Leyva, Frank [actor] (b. 26 Oct 1897–25 Feb 1981 [83]). BHD, p. 230.

L'Herbier, Marcel [director/scenarist] (b. Paris, France, 23 Apr 1888–26 Nov 1979 [91], Paris, France). BHD2, p. 161.

Li, Ming-Wei [actor/director/scenarist] (b. Japan, 1893–1956 [63?], Hong Kong, China). AS, p. 669.

Libbert, Hervey W. [actor] (b. 1900?–23 Jun 1953 [53], Ventura CA). "Hervey W. Libbert," *Variety,* 1 Jul 1953. AS, p. 669.

Libbey, J. Aldrich [stage/film actor/singer] (b. 1872–29 Apr 1925 [53], San Francisco CA; heart failure while talking to his wife). (Began in Milwaukee WI, Mar 1893). "J. Aldrich Libbey," *Variety,* 6 May 1925, 54:4 (became famous for singing *After the Ball).* AS, p. 669. BHD, p. 230.

Libeau, Gustave [actor] (*né* Gustave Nicolas Libion, b. Schaerbeek, Belgium, 8 Nov 1877–15 Jan 1957 [79], Brussels, Belgium [extrait de décès no. 111/1957]). AS, p. 669. BHD1, p. 328.

Libson, Isaac "Ike" [exhibitor] (b. 1877?–24 Oct 1943 [66], Cincinnati OH; heart attack). "Libson, Pioneer Exhib, Dies of Heart Attack," *Variety,* 27 Oct 1943, 6:3 ("For several years up to 1909 Libson managed the nation's first nickelodeon in Pittsburgh for the late Senator John P. Harris." Opened the Bijou, Cincinnati, 1909, a five-cent movie.).

Licho, Edgar Adolph [actor] (*né* Edgard Adolph Schowetzert, b. Ukraine, Russia, 13 Sep 1876–11 Oct 1944 [68], Los Angeles CA). AS, p. 669. BHD, p. 230. IFN, p. 179.

Lichtman, Al[exander] [actor/producer] (b. Budapest, Hungary, 9 Apr 1885–20 Feb 1958 [72], Los Angeles CA). (Powers; Famous Players; Alco; Artcraft; UA; MGM.) "2 Film Vets Die Within One Week; Al Lichtman at 70, Louis K. Sidney 63 [studio and theater executive]," *Variety,* 26 Feb 1958). AMD, p. 214. AS, p. 669. BHD2, p. 161 (b. 1888). IFN, p. 179. W. Stephen Bush, "A Magnet for Quality," *MPW,* 14 Nov 1914, 935. "Alco Has Receiver for a Day," *MPW,* 5 Dec 1914, 1357. "Al Lichtman with the World Film," *MPW,* 26 Dec 1914, 1819. "Lichtman Opens Booking Office," *MPW,* 15 May 1915, 1076. Al Lichtman, "Advancing the Industry," *MPW,* 13 Jan 1917, 222. "Walter Greene Directs Paramount," *MPW,* 19 Jan 1918, 352. Al Lichtman, "Work Cut Out for the Distribution Department," *MPW,* 28 Jun 1919, 1923. Al Lichtman, "Pledges That Mean Profits to Exhibitors," *MPW,* 27 Jan 1923, 362. "Al Lichtman 'Surprise Banquet' Honor Guest," *MPW,* 3 Mar 1923, 72. "Lichtman Enthusiastic About Coming Pictures," *MPW,* 11 Aug 1923, 499. "Lichtman to Rest," *MPW,* 20 Oct 1923, 647. "Lichtman with Universal," *MPW,* 8 Dec 1923, 544. "Lichtman Recuperates," *MPW,* 19 Jan 1924, 184 (from the grippe). "Lichtrman Sells His Interest in Preferred," *MPW,* 23 Feb 1924, 6535. "Lichtman Back in N.Y.," *MPW,* 5 Apr 1924, 477. "Laemmle's 'One Price' Policy an Innovation in Sales Plans," *MPW,* 31 May 1924, 481. "No Election Slump in Field of Picturees, Says Lichtman," *MPW,* 5 Jul 1924, 20. "Honors Al Lichtman," *MPW,* 13 Sep 1924, 122 (Oct 1924 "Universal-Lichtman Month). "Lichtman Leaves Universal," *MPW,* 25 Oct 1924, 686. "Al Lichtman Is Suing Koplar in St. Louis for $75,000," *MPW,* 21 Mar 1925, 240. "Lichtman Plans Fall Activity," *MPW,* 30 May 1925, 522. "Koplars, St. Louis, Now Fefendants in 2 Actions," *MPW,* 30 May 1925, 526. "Lichtman Enters Production Field; 'Charley's Niece,' First Picture," *MPW,* 20 Feb 1926, 711. "Schenck Designates Lichtman to Hea Sales Division of United Artists Corporation," *MPW,* 27 Nov 1926, 213. Tom Waller, "Lichtman Given Presidency Week Before Abrams' Death," *MPW,* 27 Nov 1926, pp. 1, 2.

Liddy, James Robley [actor] (b. 1894?–18 Feb 1936 [41], New York NY). m. Esther Hicks. "James Robley Liddy," *Variety,* 26 Feb 1936. AS, p. 669. BHD, p. 230 (b. 1895). IFN, p. 179 (age 40).

Liddy, Lewis W. [scenarist] (b. 1882–7 Nov 1932 [50?], Los Angeles CA). AS, p. 669. BHD2, p. 161.

Lieb, Harry [film editor] (b. 1896?–8 Dec 1932 [36], No. Hollywood CA; pneumonia). (Began with Universal at Ft. Lee NJ studio.) "Harry Lieb," *Variety,* 13 Dec 1932. BHD2, p. 161.

Lieb, Herman [actor] (b. Chicago IL, 9 Mar 1873–9 Mar 1966 [93], Tucson AZ). m. Evelyn Wall. "Herman Lieb," *Variety,* 22 Jun 1966. AMD, p. 215. AS, p. 669 (b. 1871). BHD1, p. 328. Truitt, 1983. "Herman Lieb," *MPW,* 29 Dec 1917, 1931.

Lieber, Fritz [actor] (b. Chicago IL, 31 Jan 1882–14 Oct 1949 [67], Pacific Palisades CA). AS, p. 669.

Lieber, Robert [executive]. No data found. AMD, p. 215. "Robert Lieber Is Back After 3 Months in Europe," *MPW,* 26 Dec 1925, 754. "First National to Build World's Largest Studio, Announces Lieber," *MPW,* 6 Feb 1926, 540 (75 acres). "Lieber and Rowland in Conference," *MPW,* 28 Aug 1926, 529.

Lieberenz, Paul [director/producer] (b. Germany, 1893–31 Aug 1954 [61?], Berlin, Germany). AS, p. 669.

Lieberman, Jacob [actor] (b. 1879–16 Feb 1956 [77], Philadelphia PA). AS, p. 669. BHD, p. 230. IFN, p. 179.

Liebler, Theodore A[ugust], **3d** (father of playwright/scenarist **Theodore A. Liebler, Jr.**) [stage producer/scenarist] (b. New York NY, 1852?–23 Apr 1941 [89], Old Greenwich CT). m. Mildred Walther. (Vitagraph Liebler Feature Film Co.) "Theodore Liebler, Stage Producer [Liebler & Co.], 89; He Brought Duse, Rejane, Mrs. Patrick Campbell to U.S.—Dies in Old Greenwich; Presented 240 Plays; Left Lithographic Business to Be Partner of [producer] George [C.] Tyler—Gave Early Shaw Works," *NYT,* 24 Apr 1941 21:4 (interment in Greenwood Cemetery, Brooklyn NY). Scott Allen Nollen, Sir *Arthur Conan Doyle at the Cinema* (Jefferson NC: McFarland, 1996), p. 249.

Liebman, Robert [scenarist]. No data found. FDY, p. 491.

Liebmann, Hans H. [actor/dancer] (b. Leipzig, Germany, 1894–24 Jan 1960 [65?], Hannacroix NY). AS, p. 670.

Liedtke, Harry [actor] (b. Königsberg, Germany, 12 Oct 1882–28 Apr 1945 [62], Bad-Saarow-Pieskow, Germany). AS, p. 670. BHD1, p. 328. IFN, p. 179. Truitt, 1983 (b. 1881).

Ligero, Miguel [actor] (b. Madrid, Spain, 21 Oct 1897–20 Feb 1968 [70], Madrid, Spain). AS, p. 670. BHD1, p. 329.

Liggett, Louis [actor] (*né* Louis Ligaty, b. Hungary, 30 May 1884–27 Nov 1928 [44], Los Angeles CA; result of auto accident on 16 Nov). m. Amalia. "Louis Ligety," *Variety,* 5 Dec 1928 (age 47). AS, p. 670. BHD, p. 230. IFN, p. 179. Truitt, p. 198 (Louis Ligety, b. 1881).

Light, Ann Rork *see* **Rork, Ann**

Lighton, Louis Duryea [producer/scenarist] (b. Omaha NB, 25 Nov 1891?–1 Feb 1963 [71], Palma de Majorca, Spain; heart attack). "Louis D. Lighton, Producer of Films, Dies in Majorca," *NYT,* 4 Feb 1963, 8:8. AS, p. 670. BHD2, p. 161 (b. 1895). FDY, p. 491. IFN, p. 180.

Ligon, Grover G. [actor: Keystone Cop] (*né* Grover Liggon, b. Kerney MO, 1 Feb 1885–3 Mar 1965 [80], Los Angeles CA). (Biograph; Sennett.) "Grover Ligon," *Variety,* 10 Mar 1965. AS, p. 670. BHD1, p. 329. IFN, p. 180. Truitt, p. 198.

Lillard, Charlotte [actress] (b. New Orleans LA, 1884?–4 Mar 1946 [62], Los Angeles CA). (Edison; Vitagraph.) "Charlotte Lillard; Actress Appeared with Duncan Sisters in 'Topsy and Eva,'" *NYT,* 8 Mar 1946, 21:1. "Charlotte Lillard," *Variety,* 13 Mar 1946. AS, p. 670. BHD, p. 230 (b. 1893). IFN, p. 180. Truitt, p. 198 (b. 1844).

Lilley, Edward Clarke [actor/director] (b. Chester PA, 7 Aug 1888–3 Apr 1974 [85], Englewood NJ). AS, p. 670. BHD2, p. 161.

Lillford, Harry [actor] (d. 9 Jan 1931, New York NY). BHD, p. 230.

Lillie, Beatrice Gladys [stage/film actress] (*née* Constance Sylvia Munston, b. Toronto, Canada, 29 May 1894–20 Jan 1989 [94], Henley-on-Thames, Oxfordshire, England). m. Robert Peel. With James Brough, *Every Other Inch a Lady* (Garden City NY: Doubleday, 1972). Bruce Laffey, *Beatrice Lillie; The Funniest Woman in the World* (Wynwood Press, 1990). (MGM.) Albin Krebs, "Beatrice Lillie Dead at 94; A Clown with Acerbic Wit," *NYT,* 21 Jan 1989, 34:1. "Bea Lillie," *Variety,* 25 Jan 1989, p. 82. AS, p. 670. BHD1, p. 329. GSS, pp. 232–35. Waldman, p. 165. Beatrice Wilson, "Fannie [Brice] and Her English Rival," *Classic,* Jun 1924, 34–35. Paul Paige, *Paris and Hollywood,* Sep 1926, 93 (playing in *Charlot's Revue* in Los Angeles, she "succumbed to the lure of the movies," and will make *Taxi, Taxi* for Universal). Eleanor Ball, "Lady Peel Comes to the Movies; Beatrice Lillie, the Brilliant English Comedienne of 'Charlot's Revue,' Spent Her Vacation Making 'Exit Smiling,'" *Cinema Arts,* Dec 1926, 32–33.

Lillie, Major Gordon W. "Pawnee Bill" [actor] (b. Bloomington IL, 14 Feb 1860–3 Feb 1942 [81], Pawnee OK). m. May (d. 1936). "Pawnee Bill Dead; Western Showman; Frontiersman, Once Business Partner of Buffalo Bill, Stricken in Oklahoma; Had Many an Adventure; Organized 'Boomers,' Group that Rushed into Territory in 1893—Friend of Indians," *NYT,* 4 Feb 1942, 19:1; "Pawnee Bill's Ranch to Scouts," *NYT,* 10 Feb 1942, 17:1. "Pawnee Bill," *Variety,* 11 Feb 1942. AS, p. 670; p. 674 (Major Gordon W. Little). BHD1, p. 329.

Lilly, Lou [extra/animator/cartoon writer] (b. Henderson KY, 1909–9 Aug 1999 [90], Los Angeles CA). (Charles Mintz; WB.) Harris Lentz, III, "Lou Lilly [obituary]," *CI,* 292 (Oct 1999), C45.

Lince, John [actor] (b. London, England, 19 Feb 1862–21 Jun 1937 [75], Los Angeles CA. BHD1, p. 329. George Katchmer, "Remembering the Great Silents," *CI,* 250 (Apr 1996), 50.

Lincoln, Al [actor]. No data found. AMD, p. 215. "Al Lincoln Is Engaged for Lead in 'Determination,'" *MPW,* 6 Nov 1920, 32.

Lincoln, Caryl [actress: Wampas Star, 1929] (sister-in-law of Barbara Stanwyck) (b. Oakland CA, 16 Nov 1903–20 Feb 1983 [79], Woodland Hills CA). m. George Brown; Byron Stevens (brother of **Barbara Stanwyck**). (Fox; Christie; Roach.) BHD1, p. 329. BR, pp. 357–58. FSS, p. 183. "The Christie Comedy Girls," *Cinema Arts,* Nov 1926, 16 (photo). Cedric Belfrage, "As Nice as She Looks; Collegians and Cowboys Think Caryl Lincoln Is the Berries—And She Is," *MPC,* Aug 1928, 58, 86. George Katchmer, "Forgotten Cowboys and Cowgirls—Part VIII," *CI,* 180 (Jun 1990), 53; 203 (May 1992), 42.

Lincoln, Edward K[line] [stage/film actor/producer] (b. Johnstown PA, 8 Aug 1884–9 Jan 1958 [73], Los Angeles CA). (Vitagraph, 1912; E.K. Lincoln Players, MA.) AMD, p. 215. AS, p. 671. BHD, p. 230 (Edward Klink Lincoln). IFN, p. 180 (1884–1958). Lowrey, p. 100. MSBB, p. 1025 (owner of Lincoln motion picture studio,

Grantwood NJ). Spehr, p. 148 (1889–1952). "Stage Stars on the Screen; Views of One Screen Player [E.K. Lincoln] on the Ability of the Stage Star to Adapt Himself to the Screen," *NYDM,* 22 Apr 1914, 32:3 ("While I do not wish to decry the work of legitimate stars in any way...their appearance in motion pictures has impressed on me the fact that oftentimes a very smart person may not understand another's business.... ¶One great difference between motion-picture players and those of speaking stage is that the first must be primarily actors or actresses, while the latter ae often readers of lines.... [W]hen a player from the speaking stage comes to pictures where his silver throat does him no good, he is as handicapped as a whis player would be if his hand was stripped of all its trump cards."). "Another Feature Company," *MPW,* 25 Apr 1914, 531. "Finish Lincoln Films; Former Vitagraph Star Now Has Four Strong Productions Ready for the Market," *NYDM,* 9 Dec 1914, 28:1 (*The Final Settlement,* 4 reels; *The Lost Gauntlet* and '*Mid Berkshire Hills,* 2 reels each; and *The Silent Messenger,* 1 reel, dealing with moonshiners. "...Eddie says he succeeded in locating an actual still for the picture through visiting a jailed moonshiner."). "Lincoln Will Produce 'The Whistling Man,'" *MPW,* 17 Apr 1915, 403. "Lincoln Builds Studio," *NYDM,* 2 Jun 1915, 21:2 (a three-story, concrete studio and factory in Grantwood NJ). "Lincoln Studio at Grantwood," *MPW,* 19 Jun 1915, 1922. "Lincoln with Lubin," *MPW,* 11 Dec 1915, 1993. "E.K. Lincoln with World Film," *MPW,* 3 Jun 1916, 1704. "E.K. Lincoln," *MPW,* 7 Oct 1916, 80. "E.K. Lincoln," *MPW,* 13 Jan 1917, 234. "E.K. Lincoln," *MPW,* 3 Mar 1917, 1337. "E.K. Lincoln Entertains Press," *MPW,* 8 Sep 1917, 1544. "Lincoln Joins Cabanne," *MPW,* 9 Feb 1918, 831. "E.K. Lincoln in New War Picture," *MPW,* 20 Jul 1918, 378. "E.K. Lincoln Starred in Special S-L Pictures," *MPW,* 23 Nov 1918, 849. "Lincoln Makes Statement on Joining S-L Pictures," *MPW,* 30 Nov 1918, 977. "Star of 'S-L' Pictures a Well-Known Player," *MPW,* 21 Dec 1918, 1376. "E.K. Lincoln Meets with Accident," *MPW,* 21 Dec 1918, 1377. "Ralph Ince Gets Praise from E.K. Lincoln," *MPW,* 28 Dec 1918, 1547. "Eddie Lincoln Didn't Like These Court Room Settings," *MPW,* 1 Feb 1919, 622. "Lincoln Takes a Vacation," *MPW,* 8 Mar 1919, 1383. "Lincoln Is Much Pleasd with Zane Grey Pictures," *MPW,* 5 Apr 1919, 113. "E.K. Lincoln Denies Rumors," *MPW,* 14 Jun 1919, 1636. "E.K. Lincoln Signs with American Cinema to Appear in Four Special Features a Year," *MPW,* 23 Aug 1919, 1159. "Lincoln Files Suit Against Associated Pictures Company," *MPW,* 27 Mar 1920, 2092. "Lincoln Will Havce Lead in Arrow Film," *MPW,* 2 Dec 1922, 426. "E.K. Lincoln May Become Producer," *MPW,* 30 Dec 1922, 891. George Katchmer, *CI,* 227 (May 1994), 52:3.

Lincoln, Elmo [stage/film actor] (*né* Otto Elmo Linkenhelt, b. Rochester IN, 6 Feb 1889–27 Jun 1952 [63], Los Angeles CA; heart failure). m. (2) Ida Lee Tanchick, 1935. Marcia Lincoln Rudolph [daughter], *My Father Elmo Lincoln: The Original Tarzan* (2000). (Griffith, 1913; Fox; National.) "Elmo Lincoln Dies; First Film Tarzan; Screen Actor, Who Had Many Roles in 'Birth of a Nation,' Starred in 100 Movies," *NYT,* 28 Jun 1952, 20:5. "Elmo Lincoln," *Variety,* 2 Jul 1952. AMD, p. 215. AS, p. 671. BHD1, p. 329. FSS, p. 183. IFN, p. 180. Katz, pp. 720–21 (b. NY). Truitt, p. 198. "Henry McRae Starts New Serial," *MPW,* 1 Mar 1919, 1185. "Elmo Lincoln Has Attained Stardom by Sheer Merit," *MPW,* 10 May 1919, 812. "Lincoln Signs with Great Western," *MPW,* 14 Jun 1919, 1636. "Elmo Lincoln to Make a Personal Appearance Tour," *MPW,* 7 Jan 1922, 84. "Loew Signs Elmo Lincoln," *MPW,* 4 Feb 1922, 516. Roger Ferri, "Elmo Lincoln Proves Showmen's Claim That Personal Appearances Are Business Builders," *MPW,* 4 Feb 1922, 517. "Elmo Lincoln Ends His Tour," *MPW,* 15 Apr 1922, 739. Carlos de Paula Couto, "Elmo Lincoln, the Original Tarzan," *CFC,* 44 (Fall, 1974), 28, 33–35 (includes filmography). Gene Popa, "Five Tarzans: The Silent Apemen," *CI,* 264 (Jun 1997), 30–32, C1-C2.

Lind, Alfred [director] (*né* Sören Estrup Alfred Lind, b. Hoielt, Denmark, 27 Mar 1869–29 Apr 1959 [90], Glostrup, Denmark). AS, p. 671. JS, p. 243 (in Italy from 1914).

Lind, Myrtle [actress: Sennett Bathing Beauty]. No data found. AMD, p. 215. m. F.A. Gesell, 25 Feb 1920. (Universal). "New Leading Lady for King-Bee Films," *MPW,* 8 Jun 1918, 1456. "Sennett Beauty Marries," *MPW,* 17 Apr 1920, 69 ("Miss Lind declares she'll retire from the screen.").

Lindau, Rolf [actor] (b. Thale, Germany, 21 Aug 1904–27 Jul 1969 [64], Santa Monica CA). BHD, p. 230.

Lindberg, Per [director] (b. Stockholm, Sweden, 5 Mar 1880–7 Feb 1944 [63], Stockholm, Sweden). AS, p. 671. BHD2, p. 161.

Lindblom, Sadie [actress] (b. Sweden). W.E. Wing, "Along the Pacific Coast," *NYDM,* 19 May 1915, 24:3.

Linde, Rose [actress] (b. 1880–20 Jan 1929 [48?], Los Angeles CA). AS, p. 671.

Linden, Edwin "Eddie" G. [cinematographer] (b. Lake Geneva WI, 26 Aug 1891–15 Nov 1956 [65], Los Angeles CA; heart attack while working on *Circus Boy* for Columbia). m. Rockford IL, Dec? 1913. "Edwin G. Linden," *Variety,* 21 Nov 1956. AS, p. 671 (b. 1896). BHD2, p. 161. FDY, p. 461. "Gossip of the Studios," *NYDM,* 7 Jan 1914, 29:2.

Linden, Einar [actor] (b. Sweden, 26 Jun 1886–19 Oct 1954 [68], Los Angeles CA). (Fox.) AS, p. 671 (b. Copenhagen, Denmark, 3 Oct). BHD, p. 230.

Lindenburn, Henry [actor] (b. 1874–28 Mar 1952 [78?], Cincinnati OH). AS, p. 671.

Linder, Max [stage/film actor/director/scenarist] (*né* Gabriel Maximilien Leuvielle, b. Saint-Loubes, near Bordeaux, France, 16 Dec 1883–1 Nov 1925 [41], Paris, France; double suicide with wife [poison and slashed wrists; neurasthenia]. Extrait de décès no. 2027.) (Stage debut: Classic theatre, Bordeaux, ca. 1902; began with Pathé, 1905; Essanay.) Maud Linder [daughter], *The Man in the Silk Hat* (1983; VHS). m. Helene Peters, 1923. "Double Linder Suicide," *Variety,* 4 Nov 1925. AMD, p. 215. AS, p. 671. BHD, p. 230 (d. 31 Oct); BHD2, p. 161 (b. 1882). IFN, p. 180 (b. Saint Loubes, France). Katz, p. 721. Lowrey, p. 102. Truitt, p. 198. Waldman, p. 166. "Max Linder Returns," *MPW,* 4 May 1912, 432. "Linder Only Wounded; Pathe Star, Reported Killed in Battle, Phones That He Is Alive," *NYDM,* 7 Oct 1914, 25:1 (age given as 29. He made about $70,000 a year on his Pathé contract.). "Max Linder Reported Killed," *MPW,* 10 Oct 1914, 170. "Max Linder Denies He Is Dead," *MPW,* 17 Oct 1914, 316. "Max Linder Coming to America," *MPW,* 19 Aug 1916, 1220. "Max Linder, Celebrated Comnedian, Is Due," *MPW,* 18 Nov 1916, 987. "Max Linder Is Now with Us," *MPW,* 25 Nov 1916, 1144. "Max Linder Ready for Camera," *MPW,* 2 Dec 1916, 1340. "Complete Plans for Max Linder," *MPW,* 9 Dec 1916, 1477. "Linder Finishing First Comedy," *MPW,* 13 Jan 1917, 211. "Max Linder—The Film's First Comedian," *Photoplay,* Feb 1917, 98 ("In the battle of the Aisne, he was shot through the lung just above the heart. When recovered he joined the aeroplane service, but his lungs could not stand the change of air in rising to the necessary heights. He was honorably discharged."). Gordon Seagrove, "Max Linder Says: Through his efficient aide [M. Albert], the noted film artist, releases a few of his life thrills," *Photoplay Magazine,* XI (Feb 1917), 99–101 (he once killed a bull in Spain while filming a picture. Another time he was thrown 16 metres by a bullock, ending up in the hospital for fifteen days.). "Linder Goes to Coast," *MPW,* 24 Mar 1917, 1954. "Linder, Ill, Stops Work," *MPW,* 19 May 1917, 1129. "Max Linder Reported Improved," *MPW,* 26 May 1917, 1271. "Max Linder Leaves for France," *MPW,* 25 Aug 1917, 1225. "Max Linder Coming Back," *MPW,* 9 Feb 1918, 798. "Max Linder Coming Back to Us," *MPW,* 23 Mar 1918, 1640. "Linder Returns to Screen," *MPW,* 26 Jul 1919, 510. "Max Linder Back," *MPW,* 17 Jan 1920, 397. "Max Linder Making Five-Reeler," *MPW,* 7 Aug 1920, 727. "Max Linder Arrives from Coast wi Print of New Production, 'My Wife?,' *MPW,* 28 May 1921, 392. "Linder Is Honor Guest at A.M.P.A. Luncheon," *MPW,* 4 Jun 1921, 516. "Obituary," *MPW,* 14 Nov 1925, 118. Fritz Guttinger, "Max Linder," *CI,* 62 (Mar 1979), 42–44. Daniel W. Horton, "Max Linder; Father of Film Comedy," *CI,* 87 (Sep 1982), 11. Eve Golden, "A French Kiss for Max Linder," *CI,* 220 (Oct 1993), C2, C4, 59 (d. 21 Oct).

Lindley, Bert [actor] (b. Chicago IL, 3 Dec 1873–12 Sep 1953 [79], Los Angeles Co. CA). AS, p. 671. BHD1, p. 330. IFN, p. 180. George Katchmer, "Remembering the Great Silents," *CI,* 199 (Jan 1992), 15.

Lindlof, John [actor/director] (b. Sweden, 1878–1954 [76?], Sweden). AS, p. 671.

Lindner, Esther [publicist]. No data found. m. Ralph M. Haas, 1924. AMD, p. 216. "Esther Lindner Betrothed," *MPW,* LXVI, 16 Feb 1924, 559.

Lindo, Olga [actress] (b. London, England, 13 Jul 1899–7 May 1968 [68], London, England). AS, p. 671.

Lindon, Margaret [actress]. No data found. AMD, p. 216. "World Pictures Engages Australian Actress," *MPW,* 3 Aug 1918, 681.

Lindroth, Helen [actress] (b. Sweden, 3 Dec 1874–5 Oct 1956 [81], Boston MA). (Kalem; FP-L.) "Helen Lindroth," *NYT,* 12 Oct 1956, 29:3. AMD, p. 216. AS, p. 672. BHD, p. 230. IFN, p. 180. "Little Stories That Are True; Wherein Actors Are Not Always Welcome Guests," *Motion Picture Magazine,* Feb 1918, 80–81 (out West to make exteriors for an Indian picture, the troupe's automobile became stranded in the soft sand of a comparatively new road. a band of Italians helped dig them out. Arriving at the hotel where they were to change, the host informed them that she "didn't want no actor-folks round her place." The director met a man who said he had a medicine show ayonder. Blanket curtains were drawn and the players made up. Just as they finished the director said there was no light left and they would have to hot-foot it to the next town. With no water, they removed what makeup they could. At a dingy hotel, they were afraid of being accosted by the drinking and dancing clientele, but were not. "The next day we finished our scenes and returned home, the most bedraggled-looking 'location' party you could vainly strive to imagine."). "Helen Lindroth Signed," *MPW,* 25 Oct 1924, 670.

Lindsay, Earl [actor/director] (b. Philadelphia PA, 1894–12 May 1945 [51?], Miami Beach FL). AS, p. 672.

Lindsay, Howard [actor/director/playwright] (b. Waterford NY, 29 Mar 1889–11 Feb 1968 [78], New York NY). m. (1) Virginia Fralick—div. 1925; (2) Dorothy Stickney, 1927. "Howard Lindsay, Playwright, Star of 'Life with Father,' Dies," *NYT,* 12 Feb 1968, 1:5, 39:1; "Howard Lindsay Is Eulogized; 600 Attend Memorial Service," *NYT,* 16 Feb 1968, 37:1; "Howard Lindsay Will Filed," *NYT,* 24 Feb 1968, 26:8 (left estate of from $250,000 to $500,000 to widow). "Howard Lindsay," *Variety,* 14 Feb 1968. AS, p. 672. BHD2, p. 161 (b. Saratoga NY). IFN, p. 180. Truitt, p. 198.

Lindsay, James [actor] (b. London, England, 26 Feb 1869–9 Jun 1928 [59], Melbourne, Australia). AS, p. 672. BHD, p. 230. IFN, p. 180 (b. 1871).

Lindsay, Marguerita [actress] (b. 1883–26 Dec 1955 [82?], Los Angeles CA). AS, p. 672. BHD, p. 230.

Lindsey, Ben D. [scenarist]. No data found. AMD, p. 216. FDY, p. 491. "Judge Ben Lindsey in Pictures," *MPW,* 12 Apr 1913, 148.

Lindsey, Emily [actress] (b. 1887–3 Mar 1944 [57?], Los Angeles CA). AS, p. 672.

Ling, Richie [stage/film actor] (b. London, England, 1867?–5 Mar 1937 [70], New York NY). m. (1) Lotta Faust (d. 1909); (2) Rose Winter. "Richie Ling Dead; 50 Years on Stage; Prominent in the Cast of Many Broadway Successes, He Is Heart Stroke Victim; Veteran Equity Backer; With Jane Cowl in 'The Road to Rome'—Leading Man for Other Noted Actresses," *NYT,* 6 Mar 1937, 17:2. "Richie Ling," *Variety,* 10 Mar 1937. AMD, p. 216. AS, p. 672. BHD, p. 230. SD, p. 778. "Richie Ling in 'The Woman Next Door,'" *MPW,* 28 Aug 1915, 1484.

Lingham, Thomas G. [actor] (b. Indianapolis IN, 7 Apr 1870–19 Feb 1950 [79], Woodland Hills CA). m. **Katherine Goodrich**. (Kalem, 1913; PDC.) AMD, p. 216. AS, p. 672. BHD1, p. 330. IFN, p. 180. Truitt, p. 198. "Thomas G. Lingham, Heavy Leads, Signal," *MPN,* 21 Oct 1916, 222 (b. 1874). "Thomas G. Lingham," *MPW,* 10 Mar 1917, 1571. George A. Katchmer, "Update—Forgotten Cowboys/Girls," *CI,* 179 (May 1990), 43.

Lingheim, Emil A. [director] (*né* Emil A. Pehrsson, b. Sweden, 31 May 1898–21 Mar 1984 [85], Sweden). AS, p. 672.

Link, Adolph [actor] (b. Budapest, Hungary, 15 Sep 1851–23 Sep 1933 [82], New York NY). "Adolf Link," *Variety,* 26 Sep 1933. AS, p. 672 (d. 24 Sep). BHD, p. 230 (b. 1881). IFN, p. 180.

Link, William [actor] (b. 1867–17 Apr 1937 [70], Los Angeles CA). AS, p. 672. BHD, p. 231. IFN, p. 180.

Linley, Betty [actress] (b. Malmebury, England, 1889–9 May 1951 [62?], New York NY). AS, p. 672.

Linn, Kurt W. [executive] (b. Germany, 1878?–18 Sep 1928 [50], New York NY; dropsy). Bachelor. (Pathé, Paris, 1900; New Orleans, 1905; Laemmle, 1911). "Kurt W. Lynn," *Variety,* 17 Oct 1928 ("died recently"). "Kurt W. Linn Dead; Was General Manager of Universal Pictures of Delaware," *NYT,* 21 Sep 1928, 29:4. AMD, p. 216. AS, p. 673. "A Cosmopolitan Film Magnate; Mr. Kurt W. Linn, the Well-Known Globe Trotter, Locates in New York After an Extensive European Trip in Quest of Features," *MPW,* 21 Dec 1912, 1198.

Linow, Ivan [actor] (b. Latvia, 1888-d. after 1932). AS, p. 673. BHD, p. 231. Ragan 2, p. 983.

Linson, Harry [actor]. No data found. AMD, p. 216. "Harry Linson," *MPW,* 19 Sep 1914, 1624.

Lion, Jeanne [actress] (b. France, 1877–15 Oct 1969 [92?], Paris, France). AS, p. 673.

Lion, Leon M. [actor/manager/producer/playwright] (b. London, England, 12 Mar 1879–28 Mar 1947 [68], Brighton, England). (Began in *True Blue,* Olympic Theatre, 1895). "Leon M. Lion," *Variety,* 166, 2 Apr 1947, 49:2 (d. Sussex). AS, p. 673. BHD1, p. 330. IFN, p. 180.

Lion, Margo [actress] (*née* Marguerite Helène Constantine Barbe Elisabeth Lion, b. Constantinople, Turkey, 28 Feb 1899–25 Feb 1989 [89], Annecy-le-Vieux, France [extrait de décès no. 17/189/CF11037]). AS, p. 673.

Lion, Roger [director/scenarist] (d. 27 Oct 1934, France). BHD2, p. 162.

Lipizzi, Atilio [director/scenarist] (b. Italy, 1867-d. Argentina). AS, p. 673.

Lippert, William H. [scenarist]. No data found. AMD, p. 216. "William Lippert Joins Universal Scenario Staff," *MPW,* 26 Aug 1916, 1415.

Lips, Konrad [directror] (*né* Konrad Wilhelm Lips-Mattler, b. Bale, Switzerland, 3 Apr 1893–25 Jun 1970 [77], Bale, Switzerland). AS, p. 673.

Lipschultz, George M. [music director] (b. Chicago IL, 12 Dec 1884–24 Dec 1932 [48], Los Angeles CA). BHD2, p. 162.

Lipscomb, W[illiam] **P.** [actor/scenarist/playwright/director/producer] (b. Merton, Surrey, England, 1887–24 Jul 1958 [71], London, England). (Ealing Studios, 1947–51.) "William P. Lipscomb," *Variety,* 211, 30 Jul 1958, 127:1 (d. 25 Jul). AS, p. 673 (d. 25 Jul). BHD, p. 231; BHD2, p. 162. IFN, p. 180 (age 70).

Lipsitz, Harold [scenarist]. No data found. FDY, p. 492.

Lipson, Jack "Tiny" [actor] (b. CO, 17 Jan 1901–28 Nov 1947 [46]). IFN, p. 180.

Lipton, Lew L. [scenarist/gagman/director] (b. Chicago IL, 23 Feb 1893–27 Dec 1961 [68], New York NY). (MGM.) AMD, p. 216. BHD2, p. 162. IFN, p. 180. FDY, p. 493. "Lew Lipton to Direct 'The Three Twins' for M-G-M," *MPW,* 3 Apr 1926, 345. "Lipton with M-G-M," *MPW,* 25 Dec 1926, 556. "Lipton Signed," *MPW,* 1 Jan 1927, 40. Doris Denbo, "Their Kingdom for a Laugh," *Pictures,* Aug 1926, 36–37, 80–83.

Lipton, Sir Thomas [actor] (b. Glasgow, Scotland, 10 May 1850–2 Oct 1931 [81], London, England). BHD, p. 231.

Lisa, Mona [actress]. No data found. *Fl.* 1920. (Webb.)

Liserini, Gino *see* **Corey, Eugene**

Lissenko, Nathalie [actress] (*née* Anatalia Andrianovna Lissenko, b. Moscow, Russia, 18 Aug 1884–7 Jan 1969 [84], Paris, France). AS, p. 674. BHD1, p. 330.

Lissner, Ray [assistant director] (b. New York NY, 10 Jan 1903–28 Apr 1944 [41], Woodland Hills CA). (Cosmopolitan; Fox.) "Ray Lissner," *Variety,* 10 May 1944. AS, p. 674. BHD2, p. 162.

Lisson, Heinrich [actor/director/producer] (né Heinrich Nischwitz, b. Gebweiler, Germany, 18 Aug 1867–6 Jan 1933 [65], Berlin, Germany). AS, p. 674.

Lister, Francis (son of stage actor Francis Lister, Sr.) [actor] (b. London, England, 2 Apr 1899–28 Oct 1951 [52], London, England). "Francis Lister," *Variety,* 184, 31 Oct 1951, 63:1. AS, p. 674. BHD1, p. 331. IFN, p. 180.

Liston, Hudson [actor] (b. Belfast, Ireland, 1841–15 Sep 1929 [88?], Amityville NY). BHD, p. 231.

Liston, Millicent [actress] (b. 1859–20 Feb 1920 [60?], New York NY). BHD, p. 231.

Litson, Mason N. [actor] (b. New York NY, 1878–19 Dec 1949 [71?], Los Angeles CA). BHD, p. 231; BHD2, p. 162.

Littgow, David [baritone/actor]. No data found. (Universal.) "Studio Gossip," *NYDM,* 22 Apr 1914, 33:1.

Little, Anna [stage/film actress] (*née* Mary H. Brooks, b. Sisson CA, 7 Feb 1890–21 May 1984 [94], Los Angeles CA). m. **Allan Forrest**, 19 Aug 1916, Santa Barbara CA—div. 1918 (d. 1941). (Ince, 1911; Bison; NYMP; Universal; American; Mutual; Selznick; Metro; Paramount; Lasky.) "Ann Little," *Variety,* 20 Jun 1984. AMD, p. 216. AS, p. 674 (b. Mount Shasta CA). BHD, p. 231 (b. 1891). BR, pp. 52–55 (b. 1 Feb 1891). MH, p. 122. MSBB. p. 1038 (b. 1894). "Anna Little," *MPW,* 20 Dec 1913, 1397. "Anna Little Joins Universal," *MPW,* 21 Mar 1914, 1531. J. Van Cartmell, "Along the Pacific Coast," *NYDM,* 30 Oct 1915, 27:1 (on location for a film, Little sent the *NYDM* this postcard: "The gas isn't and the town ain't. The man who started this place went away the second day and forgot it."). "Marriage in Filmland," *NYDM,* 9 Sep 1916, 28 (*née* Mary Brooks). "Mary Brooks and Alan Fisher [Allan Forrest] Marry," *MPW,* 16 Sep 1916, 1807. "Matrimony Claims Anna Little," *MPW,* 30 Sep 1916, 2115. "Hooking Up in a Hurry," *MPW,* 23 Jun 1917, 1953. Neil G. Caward, "Screen Gossip," *Picture-Play Magazine,* Sep 1917, 110 (received a wire to become Harold Lockwood's leading lady in Under Handicap, filming in Arizona, and took a train there). "Anna Little," *MPW,* 8 Sep 1917, 1529. Adam Hull Shirk, "Ann Little and the Great Desire," *MPC,* Jan 1919, 36–37. Dr. F.C. MacKnight, "Ann Little and the 1980 Cinevent," *CI,* 86 (Aug 1982), 11, 19. Dr. Gerald Hamm, "Ann Little [letter]," *CI,* 87 (Sep 1982), 48. F.C. MacKnight, "Ann Little; 'She Could Do Anything,'" *CI,* 204 (Jun 1992), 10 *et passim;* Part II, *CI,* 20 (Jul 1992), 32, C2-C3, 63; Part III, *CI,* 206 (Aug 1992), 52–55, 59; Part IV, *CI,* 207 (Sep 1992), 46–47. Dr. Franklin C. MacKnight and William C. Wilson, "Braff's Filmographies; Corrections and Additional Film Credits for Anna Little," *CI,* 238 (Apr 1995), 43–44.

Little Billy [actor] (*né* Billy Rhodes, b. IL, 1 Feb 1894–24 Jul 1967 [73], Los Angeles CA). "Little Billy," *Variety,* 2 Aug 1967. AS, p. 674. IFN, p. 181. Truitt, p. 199.

Little, Chief Edward [actor] (b. 1868–10 Jan 1928 [59?], Detroit MI). BHD, p. 231.

Littlefield, Emma [actress] (b. New York NY, 12 Jan 1881?–23 Jun 1934 [53], Farmingdale NY). m. **Victor Moore** (d. 1962). "Emma Littlefield," *Variety,* 26 Jun 1934. AS, pp. 674–75. BHD, p. 231 (b. 1883).

Littlefield, Lucien L. [actor] (b. San Antonio TX, 16 Aug 1895–4 Jun 1960 [64], Los Angeles CA). m. Constance. (Film debut: *Rose on the Range.*) "Lucien Littlefield Is Dead at 64; Film Character Actor Since '13," *NYT,* 7 Jun 1960, 35:3. "Lucien Littlefield," *Variety,* 15 Jun 1960. AMD, p. 216. AS, p. 675. BHD, p. 231. FSS, p. 183. IFN, p. 181. Katz, pp. 723–24. MH, p. 122. 1921 Directory, p. 185 (b. Richmond VA). Truitt, p. 199. "Littlefield Cast for Role with Mary Pickford," *MPW,* 23 Jul 1927, 258. George Katchmer, "Remembering the Great Silents," *CI,* 200 (Feb 1992), C2, C4.

Litvak, Anatole Ivanovich [actor/director/producer/scenarist] (b. Kiev, Ukraine, Russia, 21 May 1902–15 Dec 1974 [72], Neuilly-sur-Seine, France). (Nordkino; Taliana, 1923; last film, *Lady in a Car,* 1970.) m. (1) Miriam Hopkins; (2) Sophie. "Anatole Litvak Dies at 72; Directed 'The Snake Pit'; Acclaimed Also for 'Long Night' in '47 and 'Sorry, Wrong Number,'" *NYT,* 17 Dec 1974, 40:1. "Anatole Litvak," *Variety,* 18 Dec 1974, 79:1. AS, p. 675 (d. 16 Dec). BHD2, p. 162. JS, p. 244 (made Russian and German silents and films in Italy from 1961–63).

Livadary, John P[aul] [sound engineer] (b. Constantinople, Turkey, 29 Apr 1889–7 Apr 1987 [97], Balboa Island CA). BHD2, p. 162.

Livesey, Barry (brother of **Jack** and **Roger Livesey**) [actor] (b. Barry, So. Wales, 1904). AS, p. 675.

Livesey, Jack (son of **Sam Livesey**; brother of **Barry** and **Roger Livesey**) [actor] (b. Barry, So. Wales, 11 Jun 1901–12 Oct 1961 [60], Burbank CA; aneurism). AS, p. 675. BHD1, p. 331.

Livesey, Roger (son of **Sam Livesey**; brother of **Barry** and **Jack Livesey**) [actor] (b. Barry, So. Wales, 25 Jun 1906–4 Feb 1976 [69], Watford, Hertfordshire, England). m. Ursula Jeans (d. 1973). "Roger Livesey," *Variety,* 11 Nov 1976, p. 83. Patrick Brock, "Roger Livesey," *CI,* 218 (Aug 1993), 12, 14. AS, p. 675. BHD1, p. 331. IFN, p. 181. SD, p. 782. Truitt, 1983.

Livesey, Sam (father of **Barry**, **Jack** and **Roger Livesey**) [stage/film actor] (b. Flintshire, Wales, 14 Oct 1873–7 Nov 1936 [63], London, England; following an operation). "Sam Livesey," *Variety,* 124, 11 Nov 1936, 62:2; 25 Nov 1936, 62:2. AS, p. 675 (b. Flintshire, England). BHD1, p. 331. IFN, p. 181.

Livingston, Charlotte [scenarist] (b. 1898–2 Apr 1934 [36?]). BHD2, p. 162.

Livingston, Crawford [executive]. No data found. AMD, p. 216. "Crawford Livingston Is Thanhouser Head," *MPW,* 30 Mar 1918, 1830.

Livingston, Ivy (sister of **Margaret Livingston**) [actress]. No data found.

Livingston, Jack [actor] (b. St. Albans VT). (Masterpiece.) AMD, p. 216. 1921 Directory, p. 185. W.E. Wing, "On the Pacific Coast," *NYDM,* 9 Dec 1914, 26:2 (birth of son). "Jack Livingston," *MPW,* 24 Feb 1917, 1197. "Jack Livingston," *MPW,* 2 Jun 1917, 1439.

Livingston, Margaret (sister of **Ivy Livingston**) [actress] (b. Salt Lake City UT, 25 Nov 1895–13 Dec 1984 [89], Warrington PA). m. **Paul Whiteman** (d. 1967). (Selig; Fox.) "Margaret Livingston," *NYT,* 16 Jan 1985, B5:3. "Margaret Livingston Whiteman," *Variety,* 9 Jan 1985. AMD, p. 216. AS, p. 675. BHD1, p. 331. FFF, p. 186. FSS, p. 184. Katz, 1994. MH, p. 123. "Actresses Ill," *MPW,* LIII, 10 Dec 1921, 685 (appendicitis). "Margaret Livingston," *MPW,* 12 Jul 1924, insert. "Fox Signs Miss Livingston," *MPW,* 30 May 1925, 574. "Margaret Livingston Signs Contract with Fox films," *MPW,* 5 Dec 1925, 459. Dorothy Cartwright, "Margaret Livingston Is the Man of Her Family," *Paris and Hollywood,* Oct 1926, 9–11, 74, 76 ("A vamp…is a girl with a lot of bills and no money to pay them…I have created the 'fun vamp.' She's just a good-time girl, full of snap and pep, but without a grain of malice in her make-up. She wants only a jolly good time—and if the man is married it doesn't matter if he takes his wife along." In 1919, after her fiance died, she allegedly got a film job after visiting the Selig Zoo and feeding a giraffe. She had four cousins to raise, but she left Utah for Hollywood when Selig wrote her to come, at $3.50 a day. A small part in *Bound in Morroco* was followed by better parts, especially one in the upcoming *A Trip to Tilsit.* She couldn't marry just yet because she was the man of the family.). "Margaret Livingston Returns to Hollywood," *MPW,* 22 Oct 1927, 492. Alice Dyer, "Band Leader Marries Movie Star; Paul Whiteman Weds Margaret Livingston after Long-Distance Courtship over 'Phone and Disproves Old Adage that Fat Men Are Not Great Lovers," *Movie Classic,* Nov 1931, 35.

Livingston, Robert (brother of **Jack Randall**) [stage/film actor] (*né* Robert E. Randall, Quincy IL, 9 Dec 1904–7 Mar 1988 [83], Tarzana CA; emphysema). m. Margaret Roach. (Republic; MGM.) "Robert Livingston, 83, an Actor in 100 Films," *NYT,* 10 Mar 1988, D22. "Robert Livingston," *Variety,* 16 Mar 1988 (b. 8 Dec). AS, p. 675 (b. 8 Dec). BHD1, p. 331. SD. John Cocchi, "The Western—3," *CI,* 147 (Sep 1987), 19.

Livingstone, Beulah [publicist/scenarist]. No data found. AMD, p. 216. "Will Write for Two Talmadges," *MPW,* XL, 17 May 1919, 1030. "Beulah Livingston Promoted," *MPW,* 17 Apr 1926, 489. Charles Edward Hastings, "Beulah Livingstone," *MPW,* 17 Apr 1926, 489. "Scenario Girl in Conference at West Coast," *MPW,* 18 Dec 1926, 494. "Gets West Coast Job," *MPW,* 28 May 1927, 252.

Livingstone, Frank H. [actor/director] (b. San Francisco CA, 1870–26 Nov 1932 [62], Oakland CA). AS, p. 675. BHD, p. 231; BHD2, p. 162. IFN, p. 181.

Llazena, Luis [actor/violinist/baritone] (b. Spain, 1877–1956 [79?]). (Pathé; Spanish-language films for Roach, MGM, Paramount; Joinville; Elstree.) Waldman, p. 168.

Llewellyn, Fewlass (b. Hull, Yorkshire, England, 5 Mar 1866–16 Jun 1941 [75], London, England). AS, p. 675 (b. 1886). BHD1, p. 331. IFN, p. 181.

Lloyd, Albert S. [vaudeville: Aneling & Lloyd/film actor] (b. 1884–10 Jul 1964 [80?], Los Angeles CA; heart attack). m. Dorothy Ceballos. "Al Lloyd," *Variety,* 235, 22 Jul 1964, 95:3. AS, p. 675. BHD, p. 231.

Lloyd, Alice (sister of **Marie Lloyd**) [actress] (b. London, England, 20 Oct 1873–16 Nov 1949 [76], London, England). AS, p. 675 (d. 17 Nov). BHD, p. 231. IFN, p. 181.

Lloyd, Alice [actress] (b. England, 1885–31 Jan 1981 [95?], Burbank CA). AS, p. 676.

Lloyd, Charles M. [actor] (b. VA, 1870?–4 Dec 1948 [78], Los Angeles CA; heart attack). m. Adeline. (Sennett; Roach.) "Charles M. Lloyd," *NYT,* 7 Dec 1948, 31:5 ("veteran actor of stage and screen"). "Charles M. Lloyd," *Variety,* 8 Dec 1948. AS, p. 676. BHD1, p. 331. IFN, p. 181. Truitt, p. 199.

Lloyd, Doris [actress] (*née* Hessy Doris Lloyd, b. Liverpool, England, 3 Jul 1896–21 May 1968 [71], Santa Barbara CA). (Film debut: *The Shadow Between,* 1920; final film: *Rosie,* 1967.) "Doris Lloyd," *Variety,* 29 May 1968. AMD, p. 216. AS, p. 676. BHD1, p. 331. IFN, p. 181. Katz, pp. 725–26. Truitt, pp. 199–200. Tom Waller, "Doris Lloyd," *MPW,* 9 Apr 1927, 544–45. George Katchmer, "Remembering the Great Silents," *CI,* 231 (Sep 1994), 50. Blackie Seymour, "Doris Lloyd," *CI,* 246 (Dec 1995), 22, 24.

Lloyd, Ethel Louise [stage/film actress] (b. Brooklyn NY–d. 12 Jan 1923, Brooklyn NY). m. Howard Noble Lewis. AMD, p. 217. AS, p. 676. BHD, p. 231. IFN, p. 181. SD. Truitt, 1983. "Ethel Louise Lloyd," *MPW,* 6 Feb 1915, 831.

Lloyd, Frank William G. [stage/film actor/director/producer/scenarist] (b. Glasgow, Scotland, 2 Feb 1887–10 Aug 1960 [73], Santa Monica CA). m. (1) Dorothy Cummings; (2) Alma Haller (d. 1952); (3) Virginia Kellogg. (Universal; Morosco-Pallas; Paramount; Fox.) "Frank Lloyd, Film Director, Dies; Winner of 3 Academy Awards," *NYT,* 11 Aug 1960, 18:1. "Frank Lloyd," *Variety,* 17 Aug 1960 (b. 1888). AMD, p. 217. AS, p. 676 (b. 1886). BHD, p. 231; BHD2, p. 163 (d. LA CA). IFN, p. 181 (b. 1888). Katz, p. 726. Lowrey, p. 104. SD. Spehr, p. 148. Truitt, 1983 (b. 1886). "Frank Lloyd Scores," *MPW,* 18 Dec 1915, 2158. E.V. Durling, "A Director with a Conscience; Lloyd, who told a tale of two towns [*A Tale of Two Cities*], willing to let Dickens share credit for his first big effort," *Photoplay,* Jul 1917, 91–92. "Lloyd West—Edwards East," *MPW,* 17 Nov 1917, 1010. "Frank Lloyd to Make Grey Stories," *MPW,* 4 May 1918, 682. "Frank Lloyd Returns to Coast," *MPW,* 30 Nov 1918, 965. "Lloyd Finishes 'For Freedom,'" *MPW,* 7 Dec 1918, 1104. "Lloyd to Become Independent Producer," *MPW,* 22 Mar 1919, 1628. "Director Frank Lloyd Signs with Goldwyn," *MPW,* 3 May 1919, 654. "Frank Lloyd Mob Expert," *MPW,* 12 Jul 1919, 215. "Director Lloyd Arraigns Exhibitors Who Cut Films," *MPW,* 10 Jan 1920, 260. "Frank Lloyd's Productions to Be Featured by Goldwyn," *MPW,* 4 Sep 1920, 62. "Lloyd to Produce," *MPW,* 13 Aug 1921, 700. "Schenck Signs Lloyd for Another Film," *MPW,* 10 Feb 1923, 588. "Frank Lloyd Signed by First National," *MPW,* 21 Apr 1923, 814. "Frank Lloyd Series for First National," *MPW,* 9 Jun 1923, 511 (b. England). "Lloyd Picks Sills," *MPW,* 12 Jan 1924, 100. "Frank Lloyd's Next," *MPW,* 11 Oct 1924, 499. "Four Lloyd Pictures for First National," *MPW,* 24 Jan 1925, 381. "Lloyd Denies Rumors," *MPW,* 20 Jun 1925, 848. "Frank Lloyd Signed by Paramount to Long Term Contract," *MPW,* 20 Feb 1926, 713. "Frank Lloyd Reported Returning to Wm. Fox," *MPW,* 17 Sep 1927, 159.

Lloyd, Frederick W. [stage/film/radio actor] (b. London, England, 15 Jan 1880–24 Nov 1949 [69], Hove, Sussex, England). m. **Auriol Lee** (d. 1941). "Frederick W. Lloyd," *Variety,* 176, 30 Nov 1949, 55:2. AS, p. 676. BHD1, p. 331. IFN, p. 181.

Lloyd, Gail [actress]. No data found. AMD, p. 217. "Gail Lloyd," *MPW,* 27 Nov 1926, 275. "Another 'Shooting Star' Reaches Up Into Film Heaven," *MPW,* 5 Feb 1927, 422.

Lloyd, Gaylord F[raser] (brother of **Harold Lloyd**; nephew of **William Fraser**) [assistant director/associaste producer/actor] (b. Burchard NB, 1888?–1 Sep 1943 [55], Beverly Hills CA; heart attack). m. (1) d. 1922; (2) Vera Webb (**Barbara Starr**), 17 Sep 1924 (age 20). (Pathé; *fl.* 1921.) "Gaylord E. Lloyd; Film Star's Brother Had Been in Movie Industry 20 Years," *NYT,* 2 Sep 1943, 19:4. "Gaylord Lloyd," *Variety,* 8 Sep 1943. AMD, p. 217. AS, p. 676. BHD, p. 231; BHD2, p. 163. IFN, p. 181. "Gaylord Lloyd to Be Featured in Coming Pathé Comedies," *MPW,* 20 Aug 1921, 826. "Gaylord Lloyd Film," *MPW,* 24 Sep 1921, 441. "Gaylord Lloyd to Resume Acting," *MPW,* 3 Oct 1925, 415. "Gaylor [sic] Lloyd Marries," *Variety,* 24 Sep 1924, 21. Garth Pedler, "Gaylord Lloyd; Harold's Brother," *CI,* 74 (Mar 1981), 11.

Lloyd, Gerrit [title writer/scenarist]. No data found. FDY, pp. 445, 492.

Lloyd, Harold Clayton (brother of **Gaylord E. Lloyd**; nephew of **William Fraser**) [stage/film actor/director/producer] (b. Burchard NB, 20 Apr 1893–8 Mar 1971 [77], Beverly Hills CA 90213; cancer). m. **Mildred Davis**, 10 Feb 1923 (d. 1969; son, Harold Lloyd, Jr., 1931–71; 1 daughter). Richard Schickel, *Harold Lloyd; The Shape of Laughter* (NY Graphic Society, 1974). Tom Dardis, *Harold Lloyd; The Man on the Clock* (New York: Viking Press, Inc., 1984). Annette M. D'Agostino, *Harold Lloyd; A Bio-Bibliography* (Westport CT: Greenwood Press, 1994). (Edison; Sennett; Rolin-Pathé; Universal.) "Harold Lloyd, Screen Comedian, Dead"; Murray Illson, "Horne-Rims His Trademark," *NYT,* 9 Mar 1971, 1:4, 40:1; "Lloyd Home to Be Museum," 13 Mar 1971, 26:3. "Harold Lloyd," *Variety,* 10 Mar 1971 (d. Hollywood CA). AMD, p. 217. AS, p. 676. BHD1, p. 332; BHD2, p. 163. FFF, p. 132. FSS, p. 184. HCH, p. 107. IFN, p. 181. Katz, p. 726–27. MH, p. 123. MSBB, p. 1025. Truitt, p. 200. WWS, p. 67. "Pathé's 'Lonesome Luke' Comedies Unique," *MPW,* 12 Feb 1916, 963. "Harold Lloyd," *MPW,* 10 Feb 1917, 847. "Harold Lloyd as 'Lonesome Luke,'" *MPW,* 7 Apr 1917, p. 101. "Get Roach Comedies from Pathé," *MPW,* 1 Sep 1917, 1405. "Harold Lloyd Visits New York," *MPW,* 30 Mar 1918, 1798. Robert C. McElravy, "Comedy Folks," *MPW,* 13 Apr 1918, 218–19. "Harold Looyd Returns," *MPW,* 13 Apr 1918, 255. "No Vacation for Harold Lloyd," *MPW,* 20 Jul 1918, 412. "Harold Lloyd Is Making Distinctive Comedies," *MPW,* 25 Jan 1919, 514. "Harold Lloyd in a 'Tight' Situation," *MPW,* 22 Mar 1919, 1626. "Pathé Pictures to Entertain President," *MPW,* 22 Mar 1919, 1635. "Harold Lloyd Put on Skates," *MPW,* 30 Aug 1919, 1298. "Harold Lloyd, Comedian, Injured by Explosion of Property Bomb," *MPW,* 6 Sep 1919, 1449 (24 Aug 1919, Witzel Photographers, LA CA). "Despite Accident, Harold Lloyd Multiples Will Be Released Monthlyu After November 2," *MPW,* 13 Sep 1919, 1628. "Harold Lloyd Opens New Era in Comedies with the Release of 'Bumping Into Broadway,'" *MPW,* 27 Sep 1919, 1940. "Lloyd Will Resume Work on New Series of Two Reel Comedies for Pathé Within a Month," *MPW,* 4 Oct 1919, 106. "Harold Lloyd 'Lamps' Broadway," *MPW,* 22 Nov 1919, 452. "Lloyd on Way to California," *MPW,* 6 Dec 1919, 661. "Harold Lloyd Signs with Pathé for Long Term and Large Salary," *MPW,* 20 Dec 1919, 971. "Hal Roach Receives Many Wires Praising New Harold Lloyd Comedy, 'Haunted Spooks,'" *MPW,* 10 Apr 1920, 277. James Fredericks, "Lloyd: Laughsmith," *MPW,* Apr/May 1920, pp. 38–39. "Harold Lloyd's Sixth Comedy Will Be 'An Eastern Westerner,' a Keen Satire," *MPW,* 17 Apr 1920, 449. "Lloyd Ready to Embark on Second Series of Comedies," *MPW,* 5 Jun 1920, 1340. Herbert J. Hoose, "We Have with Us To-Day," *MPW,* 26 Jun 1920, 1728. "Harold Lloyd in New York to Discuss Campaign Plans on Second Series of Comedies," *MPW,* 26 Jun 1920, 1738. "Harold Lloyd Becomes Associated Star; Pathé Continues as Releasing Agency," *MPW,* 3 Jul 1920, 67. "Lloyd's Seven Multiple Reelers in Year Show How Success Comes from Hard Work," *MPW,* 24 Jul 1920, 454. "Harold Lloyd Wins Fame on Two Sides of Continent with 'High and Dizzy,' His Latest," *MPW,* 31 Jul 1920, 630. "Lloyd the 'Life-Saver,'" *MPW,* 28 Aug 1920, 1191. "Lloyd vs. Chaplin," *MPW,* 18 Sep 1920, 336. "Lloyd Completes Last Comedy for Pathé; Starts Work for Associated Exhibitors," *MPW,* 30 Oct 1920, 1276. "Lloyd Starts on His First for Associated Exhibitors," *MPW,* 20 Nov 1920, 372. "Pathé Says Harold Lloyd's Contract with Associated Exhibitors Will Make Him World's Highest Paid Comedian," *MPW,* 11 Dec 1920, 748. "Lloyd's First for Associated Exhibitors Is Three-Reel Comedy Released March 13," *MPW,* 19 Feb 1921, 947. "Harold Lloyd in His First Three Reeler Makes Debut with Associated Exhibitors," *MPW,* 26 Feb 1921, 1078. "Picture House to Replace Harold Lloyd's Old Home," *MPW,* 2 Apr 1921, 500 (Pawnee City NB). Arthur James, "Harold Lloyd Puts It Over," *MPW,* 3 Dec 1921, 532. "Film Magazine [*Motion Picture Magazine*] Fans Vote Harold Lloyd 'Leading Comedian,'" *MPW,* 10 Dec 1921, 653. "Harold Lloyd Has Bought Him a Business Band Wagon for All Good Boys to Ride On," *MPW,* 21 Jan 1922, 256. "Harold Lloyd Signs Long Term Contract with Pathé; Brunet Frames Agreement," *MPW,* 4 Feb 1922, 480. "Pirates, After 'Grandma's Boy,' Are Foiled by Harold Lloyd," *MPW,* 29 Jul 1922, 349. "'Gag' Comedies Are Popular—Ed Lyons," *MPW,* 12 Aug 1922, 515. Herbert Howe, "Out of His Shell; Harold Lloyd Spectacularly Unrimmed," *Classic,* Oct 1922, 46–47, 90. Sumner Smith, "Harold Lloyd, a Real Showman, Discusses Comical Comedy," *MPW,* 25 Nov 1922, 316. "'Dr. Jack,' Second of Lloyd's Big Comedies," *MPW,* 2 Dec 1922, 421. "Denies Lloyd Story," *MPW,* 10 Feb 1923, 539. "Lloyd Marries Mildred Davis," *MPW,* 3 Mar 1923, 35. "Back from Honeymoon," *MPW,* 17 Mar 1923, 310. "Loses False Teech Laughing at Film," *MPW,* 7 Apr 1923, 666. Paul Rochester, "No Trick Photography in 'Safety Last,' Says Harold Lloyd," *MW,* 12 May 1923, 8, 29. "Harold Lloyd's Own Story of His Rise to Screen Fame; Famous film comedian tells how his screen success was a hard uphill fight in this, the first gripping instalment of his autobiography, *My Life in the Movies.* Written in collaboration with Lawrence Langdon," *MW,* 26 May 1923, 12–13, 30; "How My Screen Career Hung on the Toss of a Coin; Part II, 2 Jun 1923, 19, 29; Part III, "Go West, Young Man!," 9 Jun 1923, 12, 30; Part IV, "I Arrive in Hollywood," 16 Jun 1923, 13, 30; Part IV, 23 Jun 1923; Part V, "A Screen Star at Last—at Five Dollars a Week!," 23 Jun 1923, 12–13, 29; Part VI, 30 Jun 1923. "Lloyd and Roach Terminate Relations in Friendly Way," *MPW,* 7 Jul 1923, 52. "Lloyd and Bride Here," *MPW,* 7 Jul 1923, 54. "Lloyd to Start Independent Producing at Hollywood Studio," *MPW,* 21 Jul 1923, 209. "Pathé Holds Reception," *MPW,* 21 Jul 1923, 210. "'Why Worry,' Lloy's Next Comedy[,] Is Listed for Premiere," *MPW,* 28 Jul 1923, 320. "Says Report Is Untrue," *MPW,* 11 Aug 1923, 464. "Harold Lloyd's Latest Plans," *MPW,* 8 Sep 1923, 179. "Harold Lloyd Working on Antoher Big Comedy," *MPW,* 10 Nov 1923, 251. "Buys Studio Site," *MPW,* 8 Dec 1923, 540. "To Finish Film Soon," *MPW,* 29 Dec 1923, 793. "Lloyd's Tummy Precedes Him East," *MPW,* 9 Feb 1924, 451. "J.D. Wiliams Has Not Signed Harold Lloyd," *MPW,* 12 Apr 1924, 539. "Harold Lloyd a Father; Girl Born to Mildred Davis in Los Angeles Hospital," *NYT,* 23 May 1924, 2:6 (8 lbs.). Grace Kingsley, "Those Young Things; Their first baby is always a BIG EVENT...," *MW,* 16 Aug 1924, 12–13, 28. "No Jurisdiction," *MPW,* 23 Aug 1924, 640. Dorothy Donnell, "The Face on the Cutting-Room Floor," *MPC,* Sep 1924, 16–18, 76 (*Girl Shy* and other films are discussed). "Lloyd Denies Report," *MPW,* 6 Sep 1924, 65. Gladys Hall and Adele Whitely Fletcher, "We Interview Harold Lloyd; An Interview Playlet in One Act and Three Scenes," *MW,* 4 Oct 1924, 6–8, 21, 27–28. "Lloyd and Valentino to Distribute Their Pictures Through Paramount," *MPW,* 11 Oct 1924, 472. "Harold Lloyd First," *MPW,* 2 May 1925, 33 (favorite film actor of Fairmont WV). "Lloyd Given Big Reception on His Trip Across Country," *MPW,* 9 May 1925, 219. "Lloyd Party in New York," *MPW,* 23 May 1925, 410. "Harold Lloyd," *MPW,* 13 Jun 1925, 786. Frederick James Smith, "Inside Facts About Screen Salaries; What the Players Really Earn," *MPC,* Aug 1925, 16–17, 88 (Lloyd was allegedly the highest paid). Harry Carr, "The War of the Comedians; It's Comedy Year on the Screen," *MPC,* Aug 1925, 18–19, 76. Mark Queensberry, "The Big Dempsey-Lloyd Fight: Round by Round," *MPC,* Aug 1925, 34–35. "Harold Lloyd at Work," *MPW,* 1 Aug 1925, 568. Isabel Darrow, "The Freshman [novelization]," *MPC,* Oct 1925, 35–37, 74, 87. "Evolution of a Laugh," *MPC,* Apr 1926, 57. "The Low-Down on a Scenario's Fate," *MPW,* 3 Apr 1926, 322. "Not with Lloyd," *MPW,* 22 May 1926, 3. Frederick James Smith and Tamar Lane, "The Truth About Film Salaries," *MPC,* Jun 1926, 16–17, 70, 87 (Lloyd made $2 million a year). Robert Donaldson, "Local Boy Makes Good; Most of the Successes of Life Come from the Old Home Town—and the Movies Are No Exception," *MPC,* Nov 1926, 26–27, 67, 87 (re Lloyd, La Rocque, Robert Ames, Neil Hamilton, Dix, Gilbert, Buddy Rogers, Warner Baxter and Charles Farrell). Paul Paige, "Close-Ups and Fade-Outs," *Paris and Hollywood Screen Secrets Magazine,* May 1927, 66 (spectators may notice that Lloyd's *The Kid Brother* resembles *The White Sheep,* a Glenn Tryon picture of about three years ago made after Lloyd left Roach. Ted Wilde, J.A. Howe, and Tom Crizer, who wrote Lloyd's film, were members of the company that filmed the Tryon picture. The plot and theme of both films are the same, although some gags are new. Lloyd's film is a success, while Tryon suffered from being practically unknown at the time. "All of which goes to show the importance of box office names in the making of successful films."). "Lloyd Recovers," *MPW,* 11 Jun 1927, 406. "Lloyd Wins Popularity Poll Held by London Daily Mirror," *MPW,* 11 Jun 1927, 425. "Lloyd May Produce Abroad," *MPW,* 13 Aug 1927, 448. "Lloyd to Make Film in East," *MPW,* 20 Aug 1927, 518. "Harold Lloyd Discusses Comedies," *MPW,* 27 Aug 1927, 602. "Lloyd Starts Work on N.Y.

Exteriors," *MPW,* 3 Sep 1927, 10. "Harold Lloyd May Produce Two Pictures Yearly for Paramount," *MPW,* 26 Nov 1927, 10. "Want $200? Hel Lloyd," *MPW,* 10 Dec 1927, 49. "Lloyd Insures Glasses," *MPW,* 17 Dec 1927, 10 (with Lloyd's of London). "Paramount Stars Win in Popularity," *MPW,* 17 Dec 1927, 14. Harold Lloyd, "When They Gave Me the Air," *Ladies Home Journal,* 45:19, Feb 1928. Jim Beauchamp, "Harold Lloyd," *CFC,* 17 (Winter/Spring, 1967), 33, 35. William T. Leonard and Thomas Fullbright, "Woody Wise [Manager of the Lloyd Estate, 1225 Benedict Canyon Drive, Beverly Hills CA] Finds His Shangri-La," *CFC,* 39 (Summer, 1973), 8–9. Dr. F.C. MacKnight, "Schickel...on Lloyd," *CFC,* 49 (Winter, 1975), 33, 35. Gene Fernett, "Harold Lloyd; A Retrospective," *CI,* 93 (Mar 1983), 37–38. "Harold Lloyd," WBO2, pp. 24–25. *Harold Lloyd,* American Masters, Two Parts (Thames Television Production, 1989: Narrator, Lindsay Anderson; Writers and Producers, Kevin Brownlow and David Gill; Executive Producer, Susan Lacy). Annette M. D'Agostino, "Harold Lloyd: A Comic Genius Learns Comedy," *CI,* 238 (Apr 1995), 14–16, 24. Annette M. D'Agostino, "Silent Film Comedy, as Redefined by Harold Lloyd," *Films of the Golden Age,* Winter 1997/1998), 74–79.

Lloyd, Jack V. [actor/make-up artist] (b. 1887?–20 May 1933 [46], Los Angeles CA; fell dead of heart disease while working at studio). (Columbia.) "Jack V. Lloyd," *Variety,* 23 May 1933. BHD2, p. 163.

Lloyd, James Darsie [actor] (b. 1864–17 Dec 1947 [83?], Los Angeles CA). BHD, p. 231.

Lloyd, Marie (sister of **Alice Lloyd**) [stage/film actress/singer] (*née* Matilda Alice Victoria Lloyd, b. London, England, 12 Feb 1870–7 Oct 1922 [52], London, England). m. (2) Alec Henry; (3) Bernard Dillon. "Marie Lloyd," *Variety,* 13 Oct 1922, 8:5 ("In her day Marie Lloyd had no rival on either side of the water."). AS, p. 676. BHD, p. 232. IFN, p. 181.

Lloyd, Rollo de Leon [actor/director/scenarist] (b. Akron OH, 22 Mar 1883–24 Jul 1938 [55], Los Angeles CA). "Rollo de Leon Lloyd," *NYT,* 26 Jul 1938, 19:2. "Rollo Lloyd," *Variety,* 27 Jul 1938. AS, p. 676. BHD1, p. 332; BHD2, p. 163. IFN, p. 181.

Loback, Marvin Oscar [actor] (b. Tacoma WA, 21 Nov 1896–18 Aug 1938 [41], Los Angeles CA). "Marvin Loback," *Variety,* 24 Aug 1938 (age 42). AS, p. 676. BHD1, p. 332. IFN, p. 181. Truitt, p. 200.

Lobel, Léopold [inventor] (b. France, 19 May 1881–12 Mar 1952 [70], Paris, France). AS, p. 676.

Lobel, Malvine [actress]. No data found. AMD, p. 218. "Mme. Malvine Lobel," *MPW,* 17 Apr 1915, 383.

Locher, Félix Maurice [actor] (b. Switzerland, 16 Jul 1882–13 Mar 1969 [86], Sherman Oaks CA). AS, p. 677.

Lochers, Jens [director/scenarist] (b. Copenhagen, Denmark, 10 Mar 1889–22 Jun 1952 [63], Copenhagen, Denmark). AS, p. 677. BHD2, p. 163.

Locke, William J[ohn] [actor/director] (b. Barbados, British West Indies, 20 Mar 1863–15 May 1930 [67], Paris, France). BHD, p. 232; BHD2, p. 163.

Lockhart, Gene (father of June Lockhart) [stage/film actor/composer] (*né* Edwin Eugene Lockhart, b. London, Ontario, Canada, 18 Jul 1891 [birth certificate #024014]–31 Mar 1957 [65], Santa Monica CA). m. **Kathleen** Arthur (d. 1978). Art Ronnie, *Locklear: The Man Who Walked on Wings* (NY: A.S. Barnes, 1973). "Gene Lockhart of Stage, Screen; Actor of Supporting Roles in Films Dies—Had First Broadway Part in 1916," *NYT,* 1 Apr 1957, 25:3. "Gene Lockheart," *Variety,* 3 Apr 1957 (age 66). AS, p. 677. BHD1, p. 332; BHD2, p. 163. IFN, p. 181. Katz, p. 727. SD.

Lockhart, Kathleen [actress] (née Kathleen Arthur, b. 1894–17 Feb 1978 [83?], Los Angeles CA). m. **Gene Lockhart** (d. 1957). AS, p. 677.

Locklear, Ormer Leslie [aviator/stuntman] (b. Ft. Worth TX, 28 Oct 1891–2 Aug 1920 [28], Los Angeles CA; airplane accident while filming *The Skywayman* for Fox). m. Ruby Graves, 1915. "Locklear Buried with Honors," *NYT,* 7 Dec 1948, 31:5 (buried with full military honors). "Locklear's Death Film; Film Carrying Last Flight of Aviator Exhibited in Theatre," *Variety,* 13 Aug 1920. AMD, p. 219. AS, p. 677 (Omar Locklear). BHD, p. 232. IFN, p. 181. Truitt, p. 201. "Aviator Ormer Locklear Signs Up with Universal," *MPW,* 19 Jul 1919, 366. "Locklear, Who Jumps from Airplanes, Will Be Featured in Universal Five Reel Film," *MPW,* 26 Jul 1919, 514. "Locklear Does His Well-Known Quick Change Between Airplanes for Universal," *MPW,* 16 Aug 1919, 988. "Lieutenant Locklear Says He Is in Love with Picture Work," *MPW,* 13 Mar 1920, 1788. "Locklear, Daredevil of the Skies, Now Has Own Company," *MPW,* 3 Apr 1920, 75. "Obituary," *MPW,* 14 Aug 1920, 861 (age 27; his pilot, Milton Elliott, 24, was also killed). "Lieut. Locklear's Death Deeply Mourned in Chicago," *MPW,* 21 Aug 1920, 1007. "Fox to Release Locklear's Last Picture at Once and Give Families Percentage," *MPW,* 28 Aug 1920, 1199. "Louise Lovely Plays Opposite Locklear in Thrilling Fox film, 'The Skywayman,'" *MPW,* 4 Sep 1920, 59. Eldon K. Everett, "Death Met the Sky Man; Ormer Locklear and the Great Movie Stunt Pilots," *CFC,* 46 (Spring, 1975), 36–37 (b. 1893). Eve Golden, "Ormer Locklear: That Daring Young Man and His Flying Machine," *CI,* 214 (Apr 1993), C8, C10 (b. Greenville TX).

Lockwood, Harold A. [actor] (b. Newark NJ, 12 Apr 1887–19 Oct 1918 [31], New York NY [Death Certificate No. 32742, age 30]); influenza and double pneumonia). (Rex; Nestor; Bison; FP-L; American; Metro.) "Harold Lockwood," *Variety,* 25 Oct 1918 (b. Brooklyn NY; age 29). AMD, p. 219. AS, p. 677. BHD, p. 232 (b. Brooklyn). IFN, p. 181. "Harold A. Lockwood," *MPW,* XI, 6 Jan 1912, 48. "Harold A. Lockwood," *MPW,* 10 Oct 1914, 194. "How I Became a Photoplayer," *Motion Picture Magazine,* Feb 1915, 111. "Harold Lockwood Joins 'Flying A,'" *MPW,* 6 Mar 1915, 1433. "Harold A. Lockwood," *MPW,* 24 Jul 1915, 644. "New Metro Stars," *MPW,* 25 Mar 1916, 2013. "Metro Stars Not Married," *MPW,* 20 May 1916, 1348 (Lockwood and his co-star, May Allison). "Metro Players Marooned by Storm," *MPW,* 8 Jul 1916, 233. "Metro-Yorke Players Held as Spies," *MPW,* 8 Jul 1916, 258. "Harold Lockwood," *MPW,* 13 Jan 1917, 234. "Harold Lockwood Re-Signs with Metro-Yorke," *MPW,* 21 Apr 1917, 464. Harold Lockwood, "Getting Close to the Public," *MPW,* 21 Jul 1917, 424. "Harold Lockwood Entertains on Thanksgiving Day," *MPW,* 22 Dec 1917, 1774. "Obituary," *MPW,* 2 Nov 1918, 575. "Burial of Harold Lockwood," *MPW,* 9 Nov 1918, 651 (Woodlawn Cemeteryu NYC). "Metro Has Three Lockwood Pictures," *MPW,* 23 Nov 1918, 830. "Lockwood's Death Brings Heavy Call for His Work," *MPW,* 21 Dec 1918, 1368.

Lockwood, King [actor] (b. 8 Jul 1897–23 Feb 1971 [73], Encino CA; cerebral hemorrhage). AS, p. 677. BHD1, p. 333.

Loder, John [actor] (*né* John Muir Lowe, b. York, England, 3 Jan 1897–26 Dec 1988 [91], Selbourne, England). m. Hedy LaMarr, 1943; Sophie Kabel; Micheline Cheirel; Evelyn Carolyn Auffmordt; Alba Julia Lagomarsino, 1958. *Hollywood Hussar* (1977). (Film debut: *Madame Wants No Children,* Germany, Dec 1926). C. Gerald Fraser, "John Loder, 90, British Actor," *NYT,* 19 Jan 1989, B16:4. "John Loder," *Variety,* 25 Jan 1989. AS, p. 677 (b. London, England). BHD1, p. 333 (b. London, 1898). Katz, 1994. Cedric Belfrage, "From Pickles to Pictures; At Eton, John Loder Was Usually in One; In Germany He Made His Own," *MPC,* May 1929, 55, 75 (he had ten featured parts up to Mar 1928; while making a film in England, Jesse Lasky signed him up).

Lodge, Ben [actor] (d. 10 Jan 1927, Lond Island NY). BHD, p. 232.

Lodi, Theodore A ***see*** **Lodijensky, Theodore A.**

Lodijensky, Theodore A. [actor] (aka Theodore Lodi, b. Russia, 1876?–6 Mar 1947 [71], Great Neck, LI NY). "Gen. Lodijensky, 71, Fled Bolsheviki; Czarist Ex-Officer, Who with Wife, Was to Be Shot by Reds in Few Hours, Dies," *NYT,* 7 Mar 1947, 25:5. AS, p. 677. BHD1, p. 333. IFN, p. 182.

Loean, Clarence [title writer]. No data found. FDY, p. 445.

Loeb, Jacob Weil [executive] (b. 1865?–25 Jun 1957 [92], New York NY). "Jacob Loeb Dies at 92; Former Booking Manager Was a Partner of William Fox," *NYT,* 28 Jun 1957, 23:4 ("He was credited with helping William S. Hart, Theda Bara, William Farnum and George Jessel, among others, in their theatrical careers. He also was said to have originated the use of special music to accompany silent films in the nickelodeon era."). "Jacob W. Loeb," *Variety,* 3 Jul 1957. BHD2, p. 163.

Loeb, Philip [actor] (b. Philadelphia PA, 28 Mar 1894–1 Sep 1955 [61], New York NY; overdose of barbituates). AS, p. 677.

Loeb, Sophie Irene [writer]. No data found. AMD, p. 219. "Miss Loeb Writes Story for Jackie [Coogan]," *MPW,* 25 Feb 1922, 823.

Loeffler, Louis R. [film editor] (b. 1897?–22 Apr 1972 [75], Los Angeles CA). m. Florence. "Louis Loeffler," *Variety,* 10 May 1972 (edited *In Old Arizona; Laura; Carmen Jones; Anatomy of a Murder*). BHD2, p. 163.

Loew, Marcus [producer/executive/founder of Loew's Inc.] (b. New York NY, 7 May 1870–5 Sep 1927 [57], Glen Cove, LI NY; heart attack). m. Carrie Rosenheim (sons Arthur, 1897–1977, and David, 1897–1973). "Marcus Loew Dies Suddenly in Sleep; Head of Theatre Chain Long Ill, but End Comes Unexpectedly on Long Island Estate; Power in Film World; He Battled Up from Poverty and After Failures Got His Start with Penny Arcades," *NYT,* 6 Sep 1927, 1:5, 23:2. "Hollywood Is Stunned by Marcus Loew's Sudden Death"; "Marcus Loew Wept For; B'way Sad Over

Best Beloved; Outstanding Figure in All Theatredom Dies Suddenly on Monday Morning—Little Change Anticipated in Operation of Loew's Inc.—Best Organized Theatrical Circuit in U.S.; Services Tomorrow," *Variety,* 7 Sep 1927. AMD, p. 219. AS, p. 678. BHD2, p. 163. IFN, p. 182. Katz, p. 729. SD. Robert Grau, "A Modern M.P. Showman," *MPSM,* Sep 1912, 129. Hanford C. Judson, "Marcus Loew, a Real Showman," *MPW,* 6 Oct 1917, 78–79. Marcus Loew, "Marcus Loew, as Exhibitor and Producer, Predicts Metro Will Have Record Season," *MPW,* 4 Aug 1923, 392. "Loew Visits Los Angeles to View Coming Metro Pictures," *MPW,* 5 Jan 1924, 31. "Marcus Loew Names President of Metro-Goldwyn Corporation," *MPW,* 31 May 1924, 484. "Big Things Can Be Counted on to Come from Metro-Goldwyn-Mayer, Says Loew," *MPW,* 19 Jul 1924, 195. W. Stephen Bush, "Loew Asserts Much of 'Ben Hur' Could Have Been Made in U.S.," *MPW,* 2 Aug 1924, 348. "Loew Back, Enthusiastic Over 'Ben Hur'; Bought London Theatre for Premieres," *MPW,* 23 Aug 1924, 612. "Chance for Fame!," *MPW,* 25 Oct 1924, 708. "Loew in Hollywood," *MPW,* 8 Nov 1924, 118. "Loew Buys Mansion," *MPW,* 15 Nov 1924, 220 (Pembroke, Glen Cove NY, cost over $1,000,000). "Marcus Loew Tells About George Walsh and 'Ben Hur,'" *MPW,* 22 Nov 1924, 308 (Walsh was replaced by Ramon Novaroo). "Back from Coast, Marcus Loew Sees 1925 as Biggest Year," *MPW,* 20 Dec 1924, 708. Marcus Loew, "Metro-Goldwyn-Mayer Certai of Topping Its Record in 1925–1926," *MPW,* 13 Jun 1925, 791. "They Control Your Films!," *MPC,* Jan 1926, 26. "Marcus Loew Highly Compliments Studio Efficiency on Visit to Big M-G-M 'Lot,'" *MPW,* 2 Jan 1926, 68. "Loew and Hearst Honored at Striking Los Angeles Dinner," *MPW,* 9 Jan 1926, 131. "American Domination Misunderstood—Loew," *MPW,* 10 Jul 1926, 1. "Loew Honored," *MPW,* 28 Aug 1926, 2. "Marcus Loew Is Familiar by Now," *MPW,* 27 Nov 1926, 212. "Last Minute News Flashes," *MPW,* 29 Nov 1926, 4 (relapse of pneumonia). "Marcus Loew Expected to Be Up Soon," *MPW,* 4 Dec 1926, 337. "Marcus Loew Returns Improved in Health," *MPW,* 2 Apr 1927, 461. Merritt Crawford, "Marcus Loew Asked to Head Motion Picture Social Club," *MPW,* 18 Jun 1927, 473. Michawel Kavanagh, "Marcus Loew Sets Good-Will Highest of Theatre's Business Makers," *MPW,* 18 Jun 1927, 531–32. "Obituary," *MPW,* 10 Sep 1927, 77, 82. M. Crawford, "Marcus Loew Is Laid to Rest in Maimonides Cemetery; High and Low in Picture Industry Pa¥ Him Last Respects," *MPW,* 10 Sep 1927, 77, 82. "Whole Picture Industry Deplores Passing of Marcus Loew," *MPW,* 10 Sep 1927, 83. "Many Tributes Received from Prominent Men," *MPW,* 10 Sep 1927, 83. "Theatres Close Throughout Nation," *MPW,* 10 Sep 1927, 83. "Marcus Loew," *MPW,* 10 Sep 1927, 97. "Mourn Marcus Loew," *MPW,* 17 Sep 1927, 146. "Loew Will Gives All to Relatives," *MPW,* 24 Sep 1927, 216 (will dated 7 May 1912).

Loff, Jeanette [actress] (*née* Jeanette Lov, b. Orofino ID, 9 Oct 1906–4 Aug 1942 [35], Los Angeles CA; ammonia poisoning). m. Harry Rosenbloom—div. Oct 1929. "Jeanette Laff [sic]," *Variety,* 12 Aug 1942. AS, p. 632 (Jeannette Laff); p. 678 (Loff). BHD1, p. 333. IFN, p. 182. Truitt, p. 201.

Loftus, Cecilia [stage/film actress/singer] (*née* Mary Cecilia McCarthy, b. Glasgow, Scotland, 22 Oct 1876–12 Jul 1943 [66], New York NY [Death Certificate Index No. 16050]). m. (1) Justin H. M'Carthy (d. 1936); (2) A.H. Waterman. "Cissie Loftus, 67, Dies in N.Y. Hotel," *Variety,* 14 Jul 1943. AMD, p. 220. AS, p. 678. BHD1, p. 333. IFN, p. 182. SD. Truitt, p. 201. "Miss Loftus Fainted; Actress Collapsed While Playing in an Akron Theatre [in *Serio-Comic Governess*]," *NYT,* 7 Feb 1905, 1:6 (she fainted, was taken from the stage, and the audience was dismissed. "Physicians say her illness is nervous prostration, due to overwork."). "Cecilia Loftus Among Famous Players," *MPW,* 1 Nov 1913, 483. "Cecilia Loftus as a Famous Player," *MPW,* 27 Dec 1913, 1527. (Enrico Caruso once said, "Who is that lady with my voice in her throat?")

Loftus, William C. [actor] (b. 1862–11 Mar 1931 [68?], Los Angeles CA). AS, p. 678. BHD, p. 232.

Logan, Dorothy [actress] (*née* Yvonne Dorothy Logan, b. ca. 1916). m. Mr. Bramble. "Rare Logan Movie [*A Clouded Name,* Logan Company, 1922, with Norma Shearer] Found, To Be Shown," *Syracuse Herald-Journal,* 30 Dec 1974.

Logan, Jacqueline [stage/film actress: Wampas Star, 1922] (b. San Antonio TX, 30 Nov 1902–4 Apr 1983 [80], Melbourne FL). m. 3 times: Ralph James Gillespie, 4 Jun 1925. "Jacqueline Logan," *Variety,* 15 Jun 1983 (b. Corsicana TX; age 78). AMD, p. 220. AS, p. 678 (b. Corsicana TX, 1901). BHD1, p. 333 (b. Corsicana TX, 29 Nov 1904). FSS, p. 186. Katz, 1994 (b. 1901). MH, p. 123. "Jacqueline Logan," WBO2, pp. 156–57. "Dwan Gets Follies Girl," *MPW,* 8 Jan 1921, 178. "Jacqueline Logan Plays Opposite Thomas Meighan," *MPW,* 12 Feb 1921, 802. Ernest Powers, "Doves and Desires," *MPC,* Oct 1921, 32–33, 81. "Jacqueline Logan Makes Contract with Goldwyn," *MPW,* 12 Nov 1921, 163. "Miss Logan Signed by Paramount," *MPW,* 23 Sep 1922, 279. "Jacqueline Logan to Star in 'The House of Youth,'" *MPW,* 14 Jun 1924, 652. "Miss Logan Entertained," *MPW,* 26 Jul 1924, 287. "Logan Lead for Dix," *MPW,* 27 Sep 1924, 318. "Ince to Star Jacqueline Logan," *MPW,* 29 Nov 1924, 428. "Cross-Country Star," *MPW,* 31 Jan 1925, 485. "Jacqueline Logan Weds," *MPW,* 20 Jun 1925, 850. "Jacqueline Logan Signed," *MPW,* 17 Jul 1926, 4. Wilbert Wadleigh, "Cecil Bawled Her Out and Jackie Wouldn't 'Yes' Him; It Isn't Being Done—Not with De Mille—But the Logan Lady Got Away with It," *MPC,* Feb 1927, 20–21, 70, 81 (her bracelet slipped off during shooting and...). "Jacqueline Logan Ill; An Influenza Victim," *MPW,* 12 Nov 1927, 19. Weona Cleveland, "Star of Early Films Recalls Her Career," *CFC,* 53 (Winter, 1976), 59 (reprint). Ted Reinhart, "Jacqueline Logan," *CI,* 64 (Jul 1979), 23.

Logan, Lillie [actress]. No data found. AMD, p. 220. "Lillie Logan Joins Selig," *MPW,* 8 Feb 1913, 587.

Logan, Stanley [stage/film actor/director/producer/scenarist] (b. London, England, 12 Jun 1885–30 Jan 1953 [67], New York NY). m. Odette Myrtil. (Began in *Light O'London,* Theatre Royal, Middleborough, England, 1903; WB.) "Stanley Logan," *Variety,* 189, 4 Feb 1953, 63:1. AS, p. 678 (b. Earlsfield, England). BHD1, p. 333; BHD2, p. 163 (b. Earlsfield, England). IFN, p. 182 (b. Earlsfield).

Logue, Charles A. [scenarist/director] (b. Boston MA, 8 Feb 1889–2 Aug 1938 [49], Venice CA). (Began 1928; Universal; Columbia.) "Charles A. Logue," *NYT,* 4 Aug 1938, 17:4 (d. 3 Aug; age 51). "Charles A. Logue," *Variety,* 10 Aug 1938 (age 48). AMD, p. 220. AS, p. 678. BHD2, p. 164. FDY, p. 492. IFN, p. 182. "Charles Logue, Author, Becomes a Director," *MPW,* 27 Dec 1919, 1125. "Charles Logue Is Author of First Edward Jose Picture," *MPW,* 25 Sep 1920, 510. "Logue with Warner Bros." *MPW,* 7 Feb 1925, 595.

Lohman, Zalla [actress] (b. Yugoslavia, 1906?–17 Jul 1967 [61?], Los Angeles CA). AS, p. 678 (b. Croatia). BHD, p. 232. Truitt, p. 201.

Lohr, Marie [actress] (b. Hamburg, Germany, 12 Feb 1890–3 Jan 1953 [62], Berlin, Germany). BHD1, p. 334.

Lolli, Alberto Carlo [director] (b. Naples, 1876). AS, p. 678 (b. Florence, Italy). JS, p. 245 (in Italian silents from 1914).

Lomas, Herbert [actor] (*né* Herbert Charles angelo Kuchacevith ze Schluderpacheru, b. Burnley, England, 1887–11 Apr 1961 [74?], Devonshire, Bermuda). AS, p. 679.

Lombard, Carole (2nd cousin of **Howard Hawks**) [actress] (*née* Jane Alice Peters, b. Ft. Wayne IN, 6 Oct 1908–16 Jan 1942 [33], Table Mountain NV; plane crash). m. (1) **William Powell**, 1931–33 (d. 1984); (2) **Clark Gable**, 1939 (d. 1960). Warren G. Harris, *Gable and Lombard* (NY: Simon and Schuster, 1974). (Fox; Sennett.) "21 on a Lost Plane; Miss Lombard One; TWA Airliner Vanishes After Leaving Las Vegas—Blast Heard, Fire on Peak Seen," *NYT,* 17 Jan 1942, 1:2, 30:5 (*née* Carol Jane Peters, b. 1909). "Lombard's Tragic End; Saga of Small Town Girl Who Rose to Screen Heights," *Variety,* 21 Jan 1942 (b. 1909; age 32). AMD, p. 220. AS, p. 679. BHD1, p. 334. FSS, p. 186. IFN, p. 182 (b. 1909). Katz, pp. 730–31. Truitt, p. 201 (b. 1909). "One Girl in Cast," *MPW,* 11 Apr 1925, 595. Agnes O'Malley, "Scars that Glorified; Carol Lombard's Features Survived the Motor Crash; Her Soul Didn't," *MPC,* Jun 1929, 45, 92 ("Her upper lip was almost completely severed from her face."). Joan Standish, "William Powell Weds Carole Lombard; Famous Man of the World Tires of Bachelor's Freedom—Bill and Bride Plan Quiet Life," *Movie Classic,* Sep 1931, 37. Karen Burroughs Hannsberry, "Carole Lombard: Gone Too Soon," *CI,* 231 (Sep 1994), 12–14, 26.

Lombardi, Dillo [actor] (b. Rome, Italy, 10 Jan 1858–15 Jul 1935 [77], Civita Castellana, Italy). AS, p. 679 (b. Parma, Italy). BHD, p. 232 (b. Parma, Italy). JS, p. 246 (in Italian silents from 1912).

Lombardo, Gustavo [executive] (b. Naples, Italy, 1885-Mar 1951 [66?], Naples, Italy). m. **Leda Gys** (d. 1957; son, producer Goffredo Lombardo, b. Naples, 15 May 1920). (Founded Titanus studios in 1928.). AS, p. 679. JS, p. 246 (see entry under Lombardo, Goffredo).

Lommel, Ludwig Manfred (father of Ruth Lommel) [actor] (b. Jauer, Germany, 10 Jan 1891–19 Sep 1962 [71], Bad Nauheim, Germany). m. (daughter Ruth Irmgard Lommel, b. 6 May 1918). AS, p. 679.

London, Babe [actress] (*née* Jean London, b. Des Moines IA, 28 Sep 1901–29 Nov 1980 [79], Woodland Hills CA). AMD, p. 220. AS, p. 679. BHD1, p. 334. FSS, p. 187. "Babe London Cast," *MPW,* 26 Nov 1927, 10.

London, Jack [novelist/scenarist] (b. San Francisco CA, 12 Jan 1876–22 Nov 1916 [50], Glen Ellen CA; uremic poisoning). m. Charmion. "Jack London Dies Suddenly on Ranch; Novelist Is Found Unconcious from Uremia, and Expires

After Eleven Hours; Wrote His Life of Toil; His Experiences as Sailor Reflected in His Fiction—'Call of the Wild' Gave Him His Fame," *NYT,* 23 Nov 1916, 13:3; "London to Be Cremated; Author's Funeral to Be Held in Oakland Today—His Mother VERY Ill," 24 Nov 1916, 13:5 (died of "gastro-intestinal type of uremia." His mother, Mrs. Flora London, was not told of her son's death.). AMD, p. 220. AS, p. 679. BHD2, p. 164. W. Stephen Bush, "Jack London—Picture Writer," *MPW,* 31 Jan 1914, 547–48. "Jack London Loses," *MPW,* 13 May 1916, 1172. "Obituary," *MPW,* 9 Dec 1916, 1482. "Jack London Posed for Pictures," *MPW,* 16 Dec 1916, 1629 (3 days before death, in *Mutual Weekly #101*). "Buys Rights to Jack London Stories," *MPW,* 8 Mar 1919, 1323.

London, Tom [actor] (*né* Leonard T. Clapham, b. Louisville KY, 24 Aug 1889–5 Dec 1963 [74], No. Hollywood CA). m. Edith Stayart. (Universal.) "Tom London," *Variety,* 11 Dec 1963 (age 81; in *The Great Train Robbery*). AS, p. 680. BHD, p. 232 (d. LA CA). IFN, p. 182. Truitt, p. 202.

Lonergan, Elizabeth (sister of **Lloyd F.** and **Philip Lonergan**) [magazine writer/scenarist]. No data found. (Biograph; Kalem; Majestic.) AMD, p. 220. "Mrs. Thomas Lonergan Dead," *MPW,* 8 Jul 1916, 260 (mother, d. 19 Jun 1916, Brooklyn NY).

Lonergan, Lester (father of Lester Lonergan, Jr.) [actor] (b. Ireland, 28 Apr 1869–13 Aug 1931 [62], Lynn MA). m. (1) Alice Treat Hunt (d. 1908; son, Lester, Jr., 1894–1959); (2) Amy Ricard (d. 1937). (Thanhouser; Griffith.) "Lester Lonergan," *Variety,* 18 Aug 1931. AS, p. 680. BHD1, p. 334. IFN, p. 182. SD. Truitt, p. 202.

Lonergan, Lloyd F. (brother of **Elizabeth** and **Philip Lonergan**; brother-in-law of **Edward Thanhouser**) [writer/ journalist/scenarist/producer] (b. Chicago IL-d. 6 Apr 1937, New York NY). (Thanhouser.) "Lloyd Lonergan," *Variety,* 14 Apr 1937. AMD, p. 220. AS, p. 680. BHD2, p. 164. IFN, p. 182. "The Ever Important Picture," *MPW,* 22 Feb 1913, 759. "What the Picture Was," *MPW,* 1 Mar 1913, 869. Epes Winthrop Sargent, "The Photoplaywright," *MPW,* 4 Apr 1914, 55. John William Kellette, "Makers of Movies: The Lonergan's," *MPW,* 12 Sep 1914, 1497–98. "Mrs. Thomas Lonergan Dead," *MPW,* 8 Jul 1916, 260. Lloyd Lonergan, "How I Came to Write 'Continuity,'" *MPW,* 21 Jul 1917, 403. "Lonergan Retires," *MPW,* 22 Sep 1917, 1833 (wrote the first scenario for Thanhouser). Edward Azlant, "Screenwriting for the early silent film: forgotten pioneers, 1897–1911," *Film History,* 9 (1997), 241.

Lonergan, Philip (brother of **Elizabeth** and **Lloyd F. Lonergan**) [scenarist/chief of production] (b. Hackensack NJ, 18 May 1887?–8 Mar 1940 [52], Los Angeles CA). (Thanhouser; Majestic.) "Phil Lonergan Dead; Long a Film Writer; Was Newspaper Man and Critic Here Before Career on Coast," *NYT,* 10 Mar 1940, 48:7. "Phil Lonergan," *Variety,* 13 Mar 1940 (age 50). AMD, p. 220. AS, p. 680. BHD2, p. 164 (b. 1883). "Philip Lonergan to California," *MPW,* 25 Jul 1914, 406. John William Kellette, "Makers of Movies: The Lonergan"s," *MPW,* 12 Sep 1914, 1497–98. "Philip Lonergan Has New Job," *MPW,* 10 Oct 1914, 168. "Universal Gets Lonergan," *MPW,* 19 Dec 1914, 1691. "Mrs. Thomas Lonergan Dead," *MPW,* 8 Jul 1916, 260. "Lonergan Joins World Scenario Staff," *MPW,* 31 May 1919, 1350. "Philip Lonergan Selected to Write Continuity for First Gouveneur Morris-Goldwyn Picture," *MPW,* 6 Dec 1919, 661. "Philip Lonergan Compares Scenario Writer to Builder," *MPW,* 17 Apr 1920, 443.

Long, Alice M. [executive]. No data found. m. **Samuel Long** (d. 1915). AMD, p. 221. "Mrs. Long, Kalem Vice President," *MPW,* 1 Apr 1916, 95.

Long, Frederic J. [stage/film actor] (b. 1857–18 Oct 1941 [84], Los Angeles CA). "Frederic Long," *Variety,* 144, 29 Oct 1941, 54:2 (d. 18 Oct). AS, p. 680. BHD, p. 232.

Long, Lew [cinematographer]. No data found. FDY, p. 461.

Long, Louise [scenarist]. No data found. (Paramount.) FDY, p. 433.

Long, Luray [actress] (aka Luray Huntley, *née* Luray Roble, b. WI, 3 Dec 1890–2 Jan 1919 [28], Los Angeles CA; pneumonia and influenza). m. **Walter H. Long** (d. 1952). "Mrs. Luray Long," *Variety,* 10 Jan 1919. AMD, p. 221 (under Long, Walter). AS, p. 680. BHD, p. 232. "Wife of Walter Long Dies," *MPW,* 25 Jan 1919, 473 (d. 6 Jan). Billy H. Doyle, "Lost Players," *CI,* 139 (Jan 1987), 55.

Long, Melvin Harry [actor] (b. 1895–14 Nov 1940 [45?], Los Angeles CA). AS, p. 680.

Long, Nick, Jr. (son of **Nicholas Long, Sr.**) [actor] (b. Greenlawn NY, 1906?–31 Aug 1949 [43], New York NY; from injuries after a car accident). "Nick Long, Jr.," *Variety,* 7 Sep 1949. AS, p. 680. BHD1, p. 335. IFN, p. 182.

Long, Nicholas, Sr. (father of **Nick Long, Jr.**) [actor] (b. 1851–16 Apr 1926 [74?], New York NY). BHD, p. 232.

Long, Ray [scenarist] (b. 1878-Jul 1935 [57?], Beverly Hills CA). BHD2, p. 164.

Long, Sally [actress: Wampas Star, 1926] (b. Kansas City MO, 5 Dec 1901–12 Aug 1987 [85], Newport Beach CA). m. composer Jean Schwartz. AMD, p. 221. BHD1, p. 335. Ragan 2, p. 996. "Sally Long Goes to Hollywood," *MPW,* 20 Dec 1924, 762. "Sally Long Makes Film Debut," *MPW,* 14 Feb 1925, 708. George A. Katchmer, "Remembering the Great Silents," *CI,* 183 (Sep 1990), 46; *CI,* 184 (Oct 1990), 58.

Long, Samuel [a founder of Kalem] (b. 1875?–28 Jul 1915 [40], New York NY; typhoid fever). m. **Alice.** (American Mutoscope and Biograph, 1897; Kalem, 1907.) "Samuel Long Dead; President of Kalem [1907] Company Entered Film Business 18 Years Ago," *NYT,* 29 Jul 1915, 9:6. AMD, p. 221. BHD2, p. 164. "Kalem Company (Inc.)," *MPW,* 8 Jun 1907, 223. "Loving Cup for Samuel Long," *MPW,* 30 May 1914, 1241. "Film Notables Pay Tribute to Samuel Long, of Kalem; Prominent Men at Funeral of Film Pioneer—Was One of the Founders of General Film," *NYDM,* 4 Aug 1915, 21:2 ("His lovable disposition and energetic handling of the company's affairs endeared him to the workers in the Kalem factories and studios."). "Obituary," *MPW,* 7 Aug 1915, 972. W. Stephen Bush, "Samuel Long," *MPW,* 14 Aug 1915, 1132. "Funeral of Samuel Long," *MPW,* 14 Aug 1915, 1171. "Long Died a Millionaire," *MPW,* 4 Dec 1915, 1804 ($2 million estate). "Death's Toll for the Decade," *MPW,* 10 Mar 1917, p. 1528.

Long, Walter H. [stage/film actor] (b. Nashua NH, 5 Mar 1879–4 Jul 1952 [73], Los Angeles CA; heart attack). m. **Luray** Roble (d. 1919). (Began 1909.) "Walter H. Long," *NYT,* 6 Jul 1952, 48:7. "Walter H. Long," *Variety,* 9 Jul 1952. AMD, p. 221. AS, p. 680 (d. 5 Jul). BHD1, p. 335; BHD2, p. 164 (b. Milford NH). FSS, p. 188. IFN, p. 182. KOM, p. 145 (b. Milford, 1888). Truitt, p 202. "Walter Long," *MPW,* 21 Apr 1917, 427. "Stars in Wreck," *MPW,* 19? May 1917, 144. "Walter the Wicked; He expiates his screen crimes by taking up arms for the U.S.A.," *Photoplay,* Jul 1917, 67–68 (was a second lieutenant in the Pacific Coast Artillery). "Wife of Walter Long Dies," *MPW,* 25 Jan 1919, 473. Maude Cheatham, "A Bad Actor—and a Good One," *Classic,* Jul 1923, 36–37, 79–80. George A. Katchmer, "Remembering the Great Silents," *CI,* 231 (Sep 1994), 52.

Longden, John [actor] (b. West Indies, 11 Nov 1900–26 May 1971 [70], London, England). AS, p. 680 (b. Calcutta, India). BHD1, p. 335. IFN, p. 182.

Longen, Emil Arthur [actor/director/scenarist] (b. Pardubice, Slovakia, 29 Jul 1885–24 Apr 1936 [50], Beneschau, Germany). AS, p. 680.

Longenecker, Bert [cinematographer] (b. Tumwater WA, 16 Sep 1876–10 May 1940 [63], Los Angeles CA). "Bert Longnecker," *Variety,* 22 May 1940. BHD2, p. 164.

Longfellow, Malvina [actress] (b. VA, 30 Mar ca. 1890). BHD, p. 232.

Longfellow, Stephanie [actress]. No data found. (Biograph, 1909).

Longford, Raymond [actor/director/producer] (*né* John Walter Longford, b. Hawthorn, Victoria, Australia, 23 Sep 1878–2 Apr 1959 [80], Sydney, New South Wales, Australia). AS, p. 680. BHD, p. 232; BHD2, p. 164.

Longman, Edward G. [actor] (b. Brooklyn NY, 1881–14 Apr 1969 [88], Miami FL). m. "Edward Longman," *Variety,* 23 Apr 1969. AS, p. 680. BHD, p. 232. IFN, p. 182.

Longnecker, Bert [cinematographer]. No data found. FDY, p. 461.

Longworth, Edward O. [actor] (b. 1893–27 Nov 1927 [34?], Los Angeles CA; suicide). AS, p. 680. BHD, p. 232.

Lonsdale, Frederic [scenarist] (*né* Frederick Leonard, b. Jersey, Channel Islands, 5 Feb 1881–9 Apr 1954 [73], London, England). AS, p. 680. BHD2, p. 164.

Lonsdale, Harry G[ettus] [stage/film actor] (b. Worcester, England, 6 Dec 18—?–12 Jul 1923, Derby, England). m. Alice Lonnon (*née* Alice Lonnon Perkins). (American.) AMD, p. 221. AS, p. 680. BHD, p. 232. IFN, p. 182. SD, p. 989.. "Mr. Harry Lonsdale," *MPW,* 3 Aug 1912, 434. George Katchmer, "Remembering the Great Silents," *CI,* 200 (Feb 1992), C4, 63.

Loomes, Harry E. [actor] (d. 17 Mar 1946, Philadelphia PA). BHD, p. 233. IFN, p. 183.

Loomis, Margaret [actress]. No data found. (Paramount.) AMD, p. 221. "Margaret Loomis Signs Up with Famous Players-Lasky," *MPW,* 1 May 1920, 696. "Gilding the Lily; Demonstrating that, properly encouraged, the camera does lie, after all," *Photoplay,* Mar 1921, 70 (before and after pictures of the actress).

Loomis, Virginia [actress] (b. Kansas City KS, 1916–23 Aug 1934 [18?], New York NY). BHD1, p. 335.

Looney, Jerry [writer]. No data found. AMD, p. 221. "Looney Leaves F.B.O.," *MPW,* 15 Sep 1923, 272.

Loos, Anita E. [stage actress/dancer/title

writer/scenarist/novelist/director/producer] (*née* Corinne Anita Loos, b. Sissons [Mt. Shasta] CA, 26 Apr 1888–18 Aug 1981 [93], New York NY [Death Certificate Index No. 13582, age 92]). m. (1) composer Frank Pallma, Jr., 1915; (2) **John Emerson**, 15 Jun 1919, Bayside NY (d. 1956). *A Girl Like I* (1966); *Kiss Hollywood Good-by* (NY: The Viking Press, 1974). Alden Whitman, "Anita Loos Dead at 93; Screenwriter, Novelist," *NYT,* 19 Aug 1981, D19:1. "Anita Loos," *Variety,* 26 Aug 1981 (age 88). AMD, p. 221. AS, p. 681. BHD, p. 233 (b. 1889); BHD2, p. 164. FDY, pp. 433, 445. KOM, pp. 145–46 (b. 1893). SD. Spehr, p. 148 (b. 1893). W.E. Wing, "Along the Pacific Coast," *NYDM,* 10 Mar 1915, 27:1 ("Anita Loos, the child-wonder of photoplayland, made her semi-annual visit to Los Angeles, but failed to ring us up. We think this young miss is somewhat overrated anyway..."). William Lord Wright, "...Enter Anita Loos," *NYDM,* 19 May 1915, 30:1 ("To tell the truth, I don't think much of a woman's opinions anyway, and when I am called for one I generally go to the nearest man and borrow it."). W.E. Wing, "Popular Anita a Bride," *NYDM,* 30 Jun 1915, 25:2. B.F. Wilson, "Anita Loos Writes the Titles," *MPW,* 2 Dec 1916, 1337. "Anita Loos Ill," *MPW,* 7 Apr 1917, 104 (grippe). Julian Johnson, "The Soubrette of Satire," *Photoplay,* Jul 1917, 27–28, 148 ("She believes that man is the little Kaiser of creation, and, despising suffrage, avers that domesticity is the only plane of female existence; that a woman's first duty is to be lovable; her second to be loved, and that when she has made herself unlovely and unlovable she should be dead."). "Emerson and Loos Leave Fairbanks," *MPW,* 29 Dec 1917, 1948. "Emerson and Loos Go to Paramount," *MPW,* 26 Jan 1918, 492. "Anita Loos Goes to Los Angeles," *MPW,* 1 Jun 1918, 1296. Edward Weitzel, "Corralling Practical Experience," *MPW,* 8 Feb 1919, 737–38. "Emerson-Loos Go on Tour to Study Picture Conditions," *MPW,* 12 Apr 1919, 227. "Emerson and Anita Loos Make Permanent Alliance," *MPW,* 28 Jun 1919, 1955. "Anita Loos to Undergo Throat Operation," *MPW,* 29 Nov 1919, 527. "Husbands Take Note," *MPW,* 27 Dec 1919, 1136 (3 days of no talking after surgery). "Anita Loos Back form Palm Beach," *MPW,* 6 Mar 1920, 1601. "Emerson and Loos Find Screen Material in Europe," *MPW,* 28 Aug 1920, 1205. "Emerson and Loos Tell How They Write Their Scenarios," *MPW,* 25 Sep 1920, 465 (*How to Write Photoplays,* James A. McCann Co., 154 pp., $1.50). "Authors Prefer Royalties; Anita Loos Having Put Over the Blondes, We Ask—Why Not Brunettes?," *MPC,* Nov 1926, 16–17, 81. Warren Dow, "Do Gentlemen Really Prefer Blondes?; Ever Since Anita Loos Started the Argument by Telling the World that *They* Preferred 'Em, She's Got Everybody Choosing Sides. Peace Will Never Be Declared, for Some Like 'Em Dark—and Others Like 'Em Fair," *MPC,* Dec 1926, 30–31, 70. "Emerson-Loos to Retire?," *MPW,* 1 Oct 1927, 289.

Loos, Theodor [actor] (*né* August Konrad Loos, b. Zwingenberg, Germany, 18 May 1883–27 Jun 1954 [71], Stuttgart, Germany). AS, p. 681. BHD1, p. 335. Vittorio Martinelli, "Kino-Lieblinge," *Griffithiana,* 38/39 (Oct 1990), 59.

Lopez, Augustina [actress]. No data found. AMD, p. 221. "Lady Stick-to-It Wins After a Long Struggle," *MPW,* 22 Oct 1927, 498.

Lopez, Carlos (Chaflan) [actor] (b. Durango, Mexico, 4 Nov 1887–13 Feb 1942 [54], Tapachula, Mexico; accidentally drowned). AS, p. 681. BHD1, p. 335. IFN, p. 183.

Lopez, Don Carlos [cameraman] (b. 1900?–8 Oct 1975 [75], Los Angeles CA). "Don Carlos Lopez," *Variety,* 15 Oct 1975. BHD2, p. 164.

Lopez, John S. [scenarist]. No data found. FDY, p. 433.

Lopez, Tony [actor] (*né* Antonio Lopez Moreno, b. Mexico, 8 May 1902–23 Sep 1949 [47], Los Angeles CA). AS, p. 681.

Lopinski, Bruno [actor/director] (*né* Bronislaus Lopinski, b. Posen, Germany, 15 Nov 1877). AS, p. 681.

Lopokova, Lydia [actress] (b. St. Petersburg, Russia, 21 Oct 1892–8 Jun 1981 [88], Seaford, England). BHD1, p. 335.

Loraine, Oscar [actor] (b. Vienna, Austria, 11 Oct 1877–7 May 1955 [77], Los Angeles CA). AS, p. 681.

Loraine, Robert [actor] (b. Liscard, Cheshire, England, 14 Jan 1876–23 Dec 1935 [59], London, England). BHD1, p. 336 (b. New Brighton, England). IFN, p. 183.

Lorand, Daisy [actress in Italian silents]. No data found.

Lorant, Stefan [stills photographer/cameraman/editor/director/scenarist/publisher] (*né* István Lóránt, b. Budapest, Hungary, 22 Feb 1901–14 Nov 1997 [96], Rochester MN). Michael Hallett, "Stefan Lorant," *The Independent,* 17 Nov 1997, p. 16 (in 1919 he worked as first violinist in a silent movie house in Tetschen, Czechoslovakia. In Mar 1920 until the spring of 1925, he worked in the emerging silent movie industry in Austria and Germany. He went from being a stills photographer to a film director within one year. "His first film, *Mozart's Leben, Lieben und Leiden* [*Mozart's Life, Loves and Suffering*], established him as one of Europe's leading cameramen. He gave Marlene Dietrich her first film test and turned her down, and began his long friendship with Greta Garbo." He published *Picture Post* from Oct 1938, and other publications.). AS, p. 682.

Lorch, Theodore A. [stage/film actor] (b. Springfield IL, 29 Sep 1873?–11 Nov 1947 [64?], Camarillo CA). m. Jeannette. (1st National; WB; Metro; Universal.) "Theodore A. Lorch," *NYT,* 12 Nov 1947, 28:2 (age 68). "Theodore A. Lorch," *Variety,* 19 Nov 1947 (age 74). AS, p. 682 (b. 1880). BHD1, p. 336 (b. 1880). IFN, p. 183. Truitt, p. 203. George Katchmer, "Remembering the Great Silents," *CI,* 248 (Feb 1996), 46.

Lord, Dell [actor/director] (b. Grimsby, Ontario, Canada, 7 Oct 1894–23 Mar 1970 [75], Calabasas CA). AMD, p. 221. AS, p. 682. BHD, p. 233; BHD2, p. 164 (d. Vista CA). IFN, p. 183. "Lord Renews Contract," *MPW,* 16 Aug 1924, 527. "Del Lord Remains," *MPW,* 26 Sep 1925, 338. "Del Lord to Do New Film 'Bayo-Nuts,'" *MPW,* 15 Jan 1927, 202. "Del Lord," *MPW,* 9 Jul 1927, 86.

Lord, John [actor] (b. 1859?–21 Aug 1931 [72], Los Angeles CA). "John Lord," *Variety,* 1 Sep 1931. AS, p. 682.

Lord, Marion [actress] (b. 1882–25 May 1942 [60?], Los Angeles CA). AS, p. 682. BHD1, p. 336.

Lord, Pauline [actress] (b. Hanford CA, 8 Aug 1890–11 Oct 1950 [60], Alamogordo NM). AS, p. 682.

Lord, Phillip F[rancis] [actor] (b. 1879–25 Nov 1968 [89?], Chicago IL). AS, p. 682.

Lord, Phillips H. [actor/producer/radio writer] (b. Hartford VT, 13 Jul 1902–19 Oct 1975 [73], Ellsworth ME). "Phillips H. Lord," *Variety,* 22 Oct 1975, p. 167. AS, p. 682. BHD1, p. 336. IFN, p. 183.

Lord, Robert [producer/title writer/scenarist] (b. Chicago IL, 1 May 1900–5 Apr 1976 [75], Los Angeles CA; heart attack). m. (1) Martha; (2) Anna May (d. 1975). (WB; MGM.) "Robert Lord," *Variety,* 14 Apr 1976 (AA for *One Way Passage,* 1932). AMD, p. 221. AS, p. 682. BHD2, p. 164 (b. 1901). FDY, pp. 433, 445. IFN, p. 183. "Scenarist Rewarded," *MPW,* 3 Sep 1927, 17.

Lordier, Georges [producer] (*né* Georges Levy, b. Paris, France, 1883–7 Jan 1922 [38?], Paris, France). AS, p. 682. BHD2, p. 164.

Lorelle, William J. [actor]. No data found. AMD, p. 221. "With Cosmopolitan," *MPW,* 18 Nov 1922, 246.

Lorenz, John [vaudevillian] (d. 4 Aug 1921, Mt. Clemmons MI). "John Lorenz," *Variety,* 12 Aug 1921. AS, p. 682.

Lorenz, John A. [actor] (b. Buffalo NY, 1887?–30 Apr 1972 [85], Paramus NJ). m. Janet Rathbun. "John A. Lorenz," *Variety,* 14 Jun 1972. AS, p. 682. BHD, p. 233. IFN, p. 183.

Lorimer, Enid [actress] (b. England, 1888–15 Jul 1982 [94?], Sydney, Australia). AS, p. 682. BHD, p. 233.

Lorimor, Alec [publicist]. No data found. AMD, p. 221. Herbert J. Hoose, "We Have with Us Today," *MPW,* 1 May 1920, 667.

Loring, Hope [scenarist]. No data found. m. Louis R. Lighton, 1920. AMD, p. 221. FDY, p. 433. "And the Greatest of These Is Hope," *MPW,* 28 Jun 1919, 1965. "Recovers from Sleep Sickness," *MPW,* 31 Jan 1920, 716 (encephalitis lethargica). "Two Weddings in Filmland," *MPW,* 8 May 1920, 833.

Lorraine, Emily [actress] (b. England, 1878?–6 Jul 1944 [66], New York NY). "Emily Lorraine; Actress Appeared Here with Faversham and May Robson," *NYT,* 6 Aug 1944, 37:3. "Emily Lorraine," *Variety,* 9 Aug 1944. AS, p. 683. BHD, p. 233.

Lorraine, Harry [actor] (*né* Henry Herd, b. Brighton, England, 1880?–21 Aug 1934 [54], Astoria, LI NY). "Harry Lorraine," *Variety,* 28 Aug 1934. AS, p. 683 (b. 1886; d. 22 Aug). BHD, p. 233 (b. Brighton, England, 1866). IFN, p. 183 (age 44).

Lorraine, Jean [actress] (b. 1906?–24 Jan 1958 [51], Alameda Co. CA). AMD, p. 221. BHD1, p. 336. IFN, p. 183. "Jean Lorraine," *MPW,* 21 May 1927, 180.

Lorraine, Leota [actress] (*née* Leota Crider, b. Kansas City MO, 14 Mar 1899–9 Jul 1974 [75], Los Angeles CA). m. **Robert F. Lakenan, Jr.** (1 daughter, Nancy). AMD, p. 221. AS, p. 683 (b. 1893; d. 1975). BHD1, p. 336 (b. 1893). IFN, p. 183. Truitt 1983 (b. 1893). "Leota Lorraine," *MPW,* 5 May 1917, 782. June Lee, "Dan Cupid's Bulletin Board," *Paris and Hollywood,* Sep 1926, 96 (Lakenam named G.E. Munger as co-respondent in his divorce suit against Lorraine, and charged his wife "with cruel and inhuman treatment, and declares that she has taken a diamond ring, valued at $500. He asks for custody of their four-year-old daughter, Nancy Lorraine. Mrs. Lakenam some time ago filed a suit for divorce against her husband, which was later dismissed."). June Lee, "Dan Cupid's Bulletin Board," *Paris and Hollywood*, Oct 1926, 89 (in court over the custody of their four-year-old daughter).

Lorraine, Lillian [stage/film actress] (*née* Mary Ann Brennan, b. San Francisco CA, 1 Jan 1892–17 Apr 1955 [63], New York NY). m. (1) Frederick M. Gresheimer, 25 Apr 1913, Hoboken NJ; (2) Jack O'Brien, 1946. "Lillian Loraine Married, *NYDM*, 7 May 1913, 11. "Lillian Lorraine, Star of Ziegfeld 'Follies' [since 1907] and Other Broadway Musicals, Dead at 63," *NYT*, 21 Apr 1955, 29:2. "Lillian Lorraine," *Variety*, 27 Apr 1955. AMD, p. 221. AS, p. 683. BHD, p. 233. IFN, p. 183. "Lillian Lorraine, the New Picture Star," *MPW*, 7 Aug 1915, 1018. Herbert G. Goldman, *Fanny Brice; The Original Funny Girl* (NY: Oxford University Press, 1992), p. 228: appeared in *The Ziegfeld Follies of 1910*. Truitt, 1983 (*née* Eulallean de Jacques).

Lorraine, Louise [actress: Wampas Star, 1922] (aka Louise Fortune, *née* Louise Escovar, b. San Francisco CA, 1 Oct 1901–2 Feb 1981 [79], Sacramento CA). m. (1) **Art Acord** (d. 1931); (2) Chester J. Hubbard (d. 1963). (Began 1921, Century Studios; Ince; Universal; MGM.) "Louise Lorraine," *Variety*, 11 Feb 1981 (80s). AMD, p. 222. AS, p. 683. BHD1, p. 336. BR, pp. 175–78. "Equitable Secures Lillian Lorraine," *MPW*, 16 Oct 1915, 452. "Now in Westerns," *MPW*, 2 Apr 1921, 478. Gordon Gassaway, "Louise of the Lions," *MPC*, Jul 1922, 36–37, 79. "Louise Lorraine Personifies Youth," *MPW*, 3 Nov 1923, 94. "Louise Lorraine," *CI*, 75 (May 1981), 16. *See* CNW, p. 97. Kalton C. Lahue, "Continued Next Week: Louise Lorraine," *8mm Collector*, 13 (Fall/Winter, 1965), 5.

Lorraine, Marie [actress] (*née* Isobel McDonagh, b. Sydney, Australia, 1899–5 Mar 1982 [83?], London, England). AS, p. 683. BHD1, p. 336.

Lorraine, Oscar [actor[(b. 1878–10 May 1955 [77?], Los Angeles CA). AS, p. 683.

Lorraine, Tui (Tui Bow) (b. New Zealand, 19 Oct 1906–25 Mar 1993 [86], Alderly, Australia). BHD1, p. 336.

Lorre, Peter [actor] (*né* Laaszlo Lowenstein, b. Rosenburg, Hungary, 26 Jun 1904–23 Mar 1964 [59], Los Angeles CA; cerebral hemorrhage). (In German silents; *The Man Who Knew Too Much*, Gaumont-British, 1934.) m. (1) Cecilia Lovsky, 1933–45 (d. 1979); (2) Karen Verne, 1945; (3) Anna Brenning, 1952. "Rites for Peter Lorre," *NYT*, 27 Mar 1964, 27:4 (500 persons in attendance). AS, p. 683. BHD1, p. 337 (b. Ruzonberok, Slovenia). IFN, p. 183. JS, p. 248 (made *Il tesoro dell'Africa* in Italy in 1953). Ernest N. Corneau, "Peter Lorre—Master of the Unusual," *CFC*, 49 (Winter, 1975), 40, 49. Daphne Dicastri, "Peter Lorre; The Career of a Great Actor," *CI*, 72 (Nov 1980), 12–16 (father's name was Albis Lorant). Jim Burgess, "Peter Lorre," *CI*, 132 (Jun 1986), 9, C13, 62.

Lorsay, René [actor] (*né* René Le Vigan, b. France, 14 May 1898–10 May 1923 [24], France). AS, p. 683.

Lortac, Robert [director/producer] (*né* Robert Collard, b. Cherbourg, France, 19 Nov 1894-ca. 1960 [65?]). AS, p. 683.

Lorville, Armand [actor] (b. France, 1875–28 Sep 1955 [80?], Paris, France). AS, p. 683.

Lorys, Denise [actress] (b. France-d. 19 Nov 1930, Paris, France; suicide). AS, p. 683. BHD, p. 233. IFN, p. 183.

Lo Savio, Gerolamo [director]). JS, pp. 248–49 (in Italian silents from 1909).

Losee, Frank [stage/film actor] (b. Brooklyn NY, 12 Jun 1856–14 Nov 1937 [81], Yonkers NY; pulmonary embolism). m. stage actress Marion Elmore. (Film debut: *The Eternal City*, 1915—he played a corpse; Paramount; FP-L). "Frank Losee, 81, 50 Years on Stage; Had Appeared with John Drew, Clara Morris and Frances Starr—Dies in Yonkers; Also Had Screen Roles; Supported George Arliss in 'Disraeli,' Mary Pickford and Pauline Frederick," *NYT*, 15 Nov 1937, 23:4. "Frank Losee," *Variety*, 17 Nov 1937. AMD, p. 222. AS, p. 683. BHD1, p. 337. IFN, p. 183. MSBB, p. 1025. SD. Truitt, p. 203. WWS, p. 247. "Famous Players Sign Frank Losee," *MPW*, 13 Nov 1915, 1315. "Losee with F.P.; Will Play Denman Thompson Role in Production of 'The Old Homestead,'" *NYDM*, 20 Nov 1915, 31:1 (signed an exclusive contract). "Frank Losee Renews Contract with Famous Players," *MPW*, 21 Oct 1916, 401. "Losee Renews Contract with Famous Players," *MPW*, 10 Nov 1917, 846. C. Blythe Sherwood, "Richman, Poorman, Beggarman—!; They're All Frank Losee," *MPC*, May 1919, 44, 78. "Losee Renews Contract with Famous Players," *MPW*, 20 Sep 1919, 1837.

Lotinga, Ernest [actor/scenarist] (b. Sunderland, England, 1876–28 Oct 1951 [75?]). AS, p. 684. BHD1, p. 337.

Lott, H. Stokes, Jr. [director/scenarist] (b. Winston-Salem NC, 1899–18 May 1937 [38?], Switzerland). BHD2, p. 165.

Lotto, Claire [actress] (b. Mar 1898-Aug 1952 [54]). BHD, p. 233. IFN, p. 184 (age 59).

Lotto, Fred [actor/director] (b. England, 11 Oct 1854–10 Dec 1937 [83], Los Angeles CA). "Fred Lotto; Veteran Actor, 83, Had Directed Booth, Mantell and Goodwin," *NYT*, 11 Dec 1937, 19:5. "Fred Lotto," *Variety*, 15 Dec 1937. AS, p. 684. BHD1, p. 613. IFN, p. 184.

Loty, Maud [actress] (b. Paris, France, 1894–18 May 1976 [82?], Paris, France). AS, p. 684.

Louden, Thomas [actor] (b. Belfast, Ireland, 1874–15 Mar 1948 [74?], Los Angeles CA). AS, p. 684.

Loughborough, James [publicist]. No data found. AMD, p. 222. "James Loughborough Joins Metro," *MPW*, 28 Oct 1916, 530.

Louis, Maude [actress] (b. OR, 19 Feb 1884–14 Mar 1976 [92], Glendale CA). BHD, p. 233.

Louis, Willard [actor/scenarist/director/producer] (b. San Francisco CA, 19 Mar 1882–22 Jul 1926 [44], Glendale CA; typhoid pneumonia). (Began ca. 1914; Edison; Fox; 1st National; WB.) "Willard Louis," *Variety*, 28 Jul 1926. AMD, p. 222. AS, p. 684. BHD, p. 233. IFN, p. 184 (age 40). Truitt, p. 203. "Willard Louis," *MPW*, 29 May 1915, 1417. "Former Edison Director Joins Vim Company," *MPW*, 22 Jan 1916, 613. *MPN Studio Directory*, 21 Oct 1916, 29 (b. 1882). "Lubitsch Signs Players," *MPW*, 31 Jan 1925, 494. "Obituary," *MPW*, 7 Aug 1926, 1. "The Final Fade-Out," *MPC*, Oct 1926, 61.

Louise, Anita [actress] (*née* Anita Louise Fremault, b. New York NY, 9 Jan 1915–25 Apr 1970 [55], West Los Angeles CA; massive stroke). m. Buddy Adler, 1940; Henry L. Berger. "Anita Louise, 53, Movie Star, Dies; Actress in 70 Films Was in TV's 'My Friend Flicka,'" *NYT*, 27 Apr 1970, 33:2 (age 53). "Anita Louise," *Variety*, 29 Apr 1970 (age 53). AS, p. 684. BHD1, p. 337 (b. 1917). IFN, p. 184. Katz, p. 735. Truitt, 1983.

Lounatcharski, Anatoli [actor/scenarist] (b. Poltavia, Russia, 1875–26 Dec 1933 [58?], Menton, France [extrait de décès no. 264]). AS, p. 684.

Loundin, Aksel Frantsievich [director] (b. Ukraine, Russia, 1886–1943 [57?], Ukraine, Russia). AS, p. 684.

Lourie, Eugene [director/art director] (b. Kharkov, Ukraine, Russia, 8 Apr 1903–26 May 1991 [88], Woodland Hills CA). *My Work in Films* (NY: Harcourt Brace Jovanovich, 1985). AS, p. 684 (b. 1905). BHD2, p. 165.

Loury, Jane [actress] (*née* Antoinette Jeanne Lours, b. Paris, France, 26 Nov 1896 [extrait de naissance no. 6093]-16 Jul 1951 [54], Paris, France). AS, p. 684.

Louvigny, Jacques [actor] (*né* Jacques Charles de Louvigny, b. Bordeaux, France, 15 Feb 1884 [extrait de naissance no. SN/1884]-9 Feb 1951 [66], Paris, France). AS, p. 684.

Love, Bessie [actress: Wampas Star, 1922] (*née* Juanita Horton, b. Midland TX, 10 Sep 1898–26 Apr 1986 [87], Middlesex, London, England). m. William B. Hawks (d. 1969). *From Hollywood with Love* (N. Pomfret VT: David & Charles, 1977). (Griffith; Vitagraph; Triangle.) "Bessie Love, Actress, Dies; Got Oscar Nomination in '29," *NYT*, 28 Apr 1986, B6:6. "Silent Film Star Bessie Love Dies in London at 87," *Variety*, 30 Apr 1986. AMD, p. 222. AS, p. 684. BHD1, p. 337. FFF, p. 24. FSS, p. 188. Katz, p. 736. KOM, pp. 146, 149. MH, p. 123. MSBB, p. 1038 (b. LA CA). WWS, p. 202. "Bessie Love One Year in Pictures," *MPW*, 30 Dec 1916, 1948. "Bessie Love Sings in Grand Opera," *MPW*, 17 Feb 1917, 1014. "Bessie Love, New Pathé Star," *MPW*, 3 Nov 1917, 686. "Bessie Love May Form Own Company," *MPW*, 13 Apr 1918, 251. "Bessie Love Is Honored," *MPW*, 4 May 1918, 688. "Bessie Love Escapes Landslide," *MPW*, 3 May 1919, 675. "Bessie Love to Visit Gotham and Replenish Her Wardrobe," *MPW*, 26 Jun 1920, 1781. "Kane Holds Luncheon in Honor of Bessie Love," *MPW*, 17 Jul 1920, 307. Edward Weitze, "How a Los Angeles Reporter Startled the Guests at a Bessie Love Feast," *MPW*, 17 Jul 1920, 313. "Federated Exchanges Will Distribute Callaghan-Bessie Love Screen Plays," *MPW*, 28 Aug 1920, 1149. "Signs Bessie Love," *MPW*, 16 Sep 1922, 200. "Be True to Your Type; That's My Best Beauty Secret, Says Bessie Love," *MPC*, May 1925, 62, 88. "Bessie Love," *MPW*, 9 Jul 1927, 86. "Bessie Love Versatile Performer on the Air," *MPW*, 26 Nov 1927, 12. Gladys Hall, "Confessions of the Stars IX; Bessie Love Tells Her Untold Tale," *MPC*, Jun 1929, 20–21, 72. George Katchmer, "Remembering the Great Silents," *CI*, 251 (May 1996), 50.

Love, Cecil D. [special effects director] (b. 1898?–29 Mar 1995 [97], Studio City CA). (RKO.) BHD2, p. 165 (b. 2 Oct 1900-d. 26 Jan 1995). "Cecil D. Love," *CI*, 240 (Jun 1995), 58 (AA for creation of the Acme film printer).

Love, Joe [vaudevillian] (b. Pittsburgh PA, 1861?–24 Oct 1923 [62], Buffalo NY). m. Florence Emily. "Joe Love," *Variety*, 22 Nov 1923. AS, p. 685.

Love, Laurel [actress]. No data found. m. **Henry Belmar** (d. 1931). *Fl.* 1911 or before.

Love, Leonard [stage manager] (b. 1894?–15 Aug 1936 [42], Los Angeles CA; pneumonia). "Leonard Love," *Variety,* 19 Aug 1936. AS, p. 685.

Love, Mabel [stage/film actress] (*née* Mabel Watson, b. England, 16 Oct 1874–15 May 1953 [78], Weybridge, Surrey, England). "Mabel Love Dies at 78; One of London 'Gaiety Girls' of 90's Acted on Broadway," *NYT,* 16 May 1953, 19:6. "Mabel Love," *Variety,* 20 May 1953. AS, p. 685. BHD, p. 233. SD. Truit, 1983.

Love, Montagu[e] [stage/film actor] (b. Portsmouth, England, 15 Mar 1877–17 May 1943 [66], Beverly Hills CA). m. Gertrude, 1908–28; Marjorie Hollis, 1929. (Possible film debut: *The Suicide Club,* 1914; World.) "Montague Love, 62, of Stage and Screen; English-Born Actor Began His American Career in 1914," *NYT,* 18 May 1943, XCII, 23:3. "Montague Love," *Variety,* 19 May 1943 (age 62). AMD, p. 222. AS, p. 685. BHD1, p. 337. FSS, p. 189. GK, pp. 468–87. IFN, p. 184. Katz, p. 736. MH, p. 123 (b. Calcutta, India). MSBB, p. 1025. Spehr, p. 148 (b. Calcutta). Truitt, p. 204. "Montagu Love Re-Engaged by Brady," *MPW,* 17 Mar 1917, 1783. Randolph Bartlett, "Montagu Encounters a Capulet," *Photoplay,* Jul 1917, 95–96 (fractured his wrist during the filming of *The Brand of Satan,* World-Peerless, in a staged fight at the top of a staircase with actor Allan Hart. Says he was born in Calcutta in 1877, "He drifted into pictures through visiting a projection room where a friend's 'test film' was being shown to a director."). "Montagu Love Continues with World," *MPW,* 22 Sep 1917, 1829. "Montagu Love Entertains Sailors," *MPW,* 6 Jul 1918, 77. "Salaries Soundly Based, Declares Montagu Love," *MPW,* 2 Nov 1918, 584. "Screen Star Talks at Cambridge, Mass., House," *MPW,* 14 Feb 1920, 1112. "Montagu Love to Have Important Part in Geraldine Farrar's 'The Riddle: Woman,'" *MPW,* 5 Jun 1920, 1341. Margaret Werner, "'Craze for Youth Stifles American Film Art,' Says Montagu Love," *MW,* 22 Sep 1923, 20, 30. "Pages From an Artist's Sketch Book; Montague Love Being the Artist and Italy His Sketch Book," *Classic,* Jul 1924, 18–19. "Love Signed by Paramount," *MPW,* 18 Jul 1925, 352. Tom Waller, "Montagu Love," *MPW,* 6 Aug 1927, 378–80. George A. Katchmer, "What...Another Villain?; Montague Love," *CI,* 146 (Aug 1987), C3, C5-C6, C9. Richard E. Braff, "The Films of Montagu[e] Love," *CI,* 157 (Jul 1988), 59, C12; 158 (Aug 1988), 29, 57–58. R.E. Braff, "Additional Film Credits for Montagu Love," *CI,* 238 (Apr 1995), 44. George Katchmer, "Remembering the Great Silents," *CI,* 251 (May 1996), 51–52.

Lovely, Louise [stage/film actress] (*née* Nellie Louise Corbasse, b. Sydney, Australia, 28 Feb 1885–18 Mar 1980 [95], Hobart, Australia). m. Mr. Welch. (Australian Biograph Co.; Fox; Universal-Bluebird.) "Louise Lovely," *Variety,* 26 Mar 1980 (b. 10 Sep 1806 [sic]; age 84). AMD, p. 222. AS, p. 685. BHD, p. 233 (b. 1896). BR, pp. 55–56 (b. 1896). MSBB, p. 1038 (b. 1896). "Bluebird Creates New Film Star," *MPW,* 4 Mar 1916, 1476. "Louise Lovely," *MPW,* 20 Jan 1917, 373. "Louise Lovely," *MPW,* 9 Jun 1917, 1619. "Louise Lovely Back to Bluebirds," *MPW,* 23 Jun 1917, 1951. K. Owen, "The Lady of the Names; But Louise Lovely finally found one that no one could criticize and it remained," *Photoplay,* Jul 1917, 46–48 (says she was born in 1895; 5 ft. 2 in., 125 lbs.). "Fox Signs Louise Lovely to Star in Series of Own Films," *MPW,* 24 Jul 1920, 491. "Louise Lovely's Rise to Stardom Confirmed by Fox," *MPW,* 14 Aug 1920, 896. George A. Katchmer, "Update—Forgotten Cowboys/Girls," *CI,* 179 (May 1990), 43.

Loveridge, Mabel [actress]. No data found. (Biograph; Essanay; Bison.) "Greenroom Jottings," *MPSM,* Sep 1912, 108 (loaned by Biograph to Essanay "to fill the temporary absence of Vedah Bertram.").

Loveridge, Margaret *see* **Marsh, Marguerite**

Lovering, Otho [director/film editor/scenrist] (b. Philadelphia PA. 1 Dec 1888–25 Oct 1968 [79], Santa Monica CA; ruptured main artery). "Otho Lovering," *Variety,* 6 Nov 1968. AS, p. 685 (Otto Lovering). BHD2, p. 165 (b. MD, 1892). IFN, p. 184.

Lovett, Josephine [scenarist/film editor] (b. San Francisco CA-d. 17 Sep 1958, Rancho Santa Fe CA). m. **John Robertson** (d. 1964). BHD1, p. 613; BHD2, p. 165. FDY, p. 433. Faith Service, "The Tortures of Cutting," *MPC,* Nov 1924, 20, 86–87.

Lovett, Shaw [actor] (b. New York NY, 22 Mar 1896–27 Dec 1971 [75], Escondido CA). BHD, p. 233; BHD2, p. 165.

Lovsky, Celia [actress] (*née* Cecile Josefina Lvonsky, b. Prague, Czechoslovakia, 21 Feb 1897–12 Oct 1979 [82], Los Angeles CA). AS, p. 685.

Low, Jack [actor] (b. CO, 2 Aug 1897–21 Feb 1958 [60], Los Angeles CA). AS, p. 685.

Low, Warren [actor] (b. Pittsburgh PA, 12 Aug 1905–27 Jul 1989 [83], Woodland Hills CA). AS, p. 685 (b. Pittsburg TX). BHD, p. 234; BHD2, p. 165.

Lowe, Edmund S. [actor] (b. San Jose CA, 3 Mar 1890–20 Apr 1971 [81], Woodland Hills CA). (b. 3 Mar 1890). m. (2) **Lilyan Tashman**, 1 Sep 1925, SF CA (d. 1934); (3) Rita Kaufman; (4) Esther Miller. (Began ca. 1915.) "Edmund Lowe, Screen Star, Dead at 79; Screen Idol in the 20's," *NYT,* 23 Apr 1971, 40:1. "Edmund Lowe," *Variety,* 28 Apr 1971 (age 81). AMD, p. 222. AS, p. 685. BHD1, p. 338. FFF, p. 111. FSS, p. 189. IFN, p. 184. Katz, p. 737 (began 1917). MH, p. 123. Truitt, p. 204 (b. 1892). "New Leading Man for Norma Talmadge," *MPW,* 27 Dec 1919, 1130. "Jans Engages Edmund Lowe as Olive Tell's Leading Man," *MPW,* 21 Feb 1920, 1253. Ruth Mabrey, "'Mix a Little Brains with Your Beauty,' Advises Edmund Lowe," *MW,* 9 Jun 1923, 10. Louise Morgan, "A Day in the Studio with 'The Fool,'" *MW,* 28 Jun 1924, 12–13, 30. "'The Fool' Made Lowe a Fox Star," *MPW,* 9 Aug 1924, 479. "Lowe Starts on Second," *MPW,* 6 Sep 1924, 34. "Edmund Lowe," *MPW,* 3 Oct 1925, 411. "Edmund Lowe," *MPW,* 29 Oct 1927, 550. Renee Dorr, "Just One of the Boys; The Tip Off on Edmund Lowe," *MPC,* Nov 1927, 58, 90. Bill Wilson, "The Urban 'Rowdy,'" *CI,* 87 (Sep 1982), 15–16, 18 (includes filmography). Richard E. Braff and Bill Wilson, "The Films of Edmund Lowe," *CI,* 125 (Nov 1985), 58–60; 126 (Dec 1985), C9.

Lowe, Edward T., Jr. [title writer/scenarist] (b. Nashville TN, 29 Jun 1890–17 Apr 1973 [82], Los Angeles CA). m. Helen. (Essanay; Universal; Fox; Paramount; MGM.) "Edward T. Lowe," *Variety,* 23 May 1973 (age 83). AMD, p. 222. AS, p. 685. BHD2, p. 165. FDY, pp. 433, 445. Truitt, p. 184. "Photoplay Writer Joins Essanay," *MPW,* 28 Jun 1913, 1370. Edward T. Lowe, Jr., "Ideals and Realities," *MPW,* 21 Jul 1917, 407. "Joins Scenarist Staff," *MPW,* 1 May 1926, 46.

Lowe, James B. [actor] (b. GA, 12 Oct 1879–19 Mar 1963 [83], Los Angeles CA). "James B. Lowe," *Variety,* 29 May 1963 (d. 18 May). AS, p. 685. BHD, p. 234. IFN, p. 184. Truitt, p. 204.

Lowe, Sherman L. [scenarist] (b. 18 Oct 1894–23 Jan 1968 [73], Los Angeles CA). AS, p. 685. BHD2, p. 165.

Lowell, Helen [stage/film actress] (*née* Helen Lowell Robb, b. New York NY, 2 Jun 1866–28 Jun 1937 [71], Los Angeles CA; found dead). (WB.) "Miss Lowell, Film and Stage Actress; Comedienne Whose Career Had Extended Over Fifty Years Dies in Hollywood," *NYT,* 30 Jun 1937, 24:1 (began 1934). "Helen Lowell," *Variety,* 7 Jul 1937. AMD, p. 222. AS, p. 685. BHD1, p. 338 (b. 1865). IFN, p. 184. SD. "Capellani Engages Helen Lowell," *MPW,* 14 Jun 1919, 1643.

Lowell, Joan [actress/writer] (aka Helen Trask, b. Berkeley CA, 23 Nov 1902–7 Nov 1967 [64], Brasilia, Brazil; found dead). "Joan Lowell," *Variety,* 249, 6 Dec 1967, 55:5. AS, p. 685 (b. 1900). BHD1, p. 338. IFN, p. 184 (age 67).

Lowell, John [actor/director] (*né* John Lowell Russell, b. Pleasant Valley IA, 22 Apr 1875–19 Sep 1937 [63], Los Angeles CA). AS, p. 685. BHD2, p. 165.

Lowenthal, Benjamin [music director, composer] (b. Rochester, NY, 1869-Dec 1931 [62?], Rochester NY). AS, p. 678 BHD2, p. 165.

Lowery, William A. [actor] (b. St. Louis MO, 22 Jul 1885–15 Nov 1941 [56], Los Angeles Co. CA). (Began ca. 1915.) AS, p. 686. BHD, p. 234. IFN, p. 184. George Katchmer, "Remembering the Great Silents," *CI,* 254 (Aug 1996), 50.

Lowry, Ira M. [actor/producer/director/Treasurer/General Manager of Lubin) (b. Philadelphia PA, 1889?–31 Jul 1951 [62], Los Angeles CA). "Ira M. Lowry," *NYT,* 4 Aug 1951, 15:3 ("He produced films in which many of the early motion-picture stars found prominence."). "Ira M. Lowry," *Variety,* 8 Aug 1951. AMD, p. 222. AS, p. 686. BHD2, p. 165 (b. 2 Aug). "Lubin's Serial Releases," *MPW,* 27 Mar 1915, 1915. "'Big Four' [A.E. Smith, W.N. Selig, Lowry, George K. Spoor] Surprises Film Men; Vitagraph-Lubin-Selig-Essanay Combination Means Radical Departure by Motion Picture Pioneers—Exchange Managers Appointed and Preparations Under Way for Flying Start," *NYDM,* 21 Apr 1915, 24:2.

Lowry, Rudd [actor] (b. 1892–15 Dec 1965 [73?], New York NY). AS, p. 686.

Loy, Myrna [actress] (*née* Myrna Adele Williams, b. Helena MT, 2 Aug 1905–14 Dec 1993 [88], New York NY). m. (1) **Arthur Hornblow, Jr.**, 1936–42 (d. 1976); (2) John D. Hertz, Jr., 1942–44; (3) Gene Markey, 1946–50; (4) Howland H. Sergeant, 1951–60). With James Kolsilibas-Davis, *Myrna Loy; Being and Becoming* (NY: Donald I. Fine, Inc., 1988). (MGM.) Peter B. Flint, "Myrna Loy, Model of Urbanity in 'Thin Man' Roles, Dies at 88," *NYT,* 15 Dec 1993, B11:1. Richard Natale, "Myrna Loy," *Variety,* 27 Dec 1993, p. 76:1. AMD, p. 222. AS, p. 686 (b. Raidersburg MT). BHD1, p. 338 (b. Raidersburg MT). FSS, p. 190. Katz, pp. 737–38 (began 1925). Ragan 2, pp. 1006–1007. Dorothy Donnell, "The Lady That's Known as Loy; An Exotic Flower from Some Ancestral Tree," *MPC,* Aug 1927, 55, 83.

"Myrna Loy Lead in A.S. Roche Romance," *MPW,* 3 Sep 1927, 35. "Myrna Loy," *MPW,* 24 Sep 1927, 228. "Long Terms for McAvoy, Hyams," *MPW,* 24 Dec 1927, 10. "The Lady Known as Loy," *Cinema Arts,* Jun 1937, 27 ("got her fancy surname when her co-discoverers, Mrs. and Mrs. Rudolph Valentino [Natacha Rambova], convinced her she must go Oriental to get a break in Hollywood."). Stephen Harvey, "For Myrna Loy, a Late But Loving Tribute," *NYT,* Sec. II, 13 Jan 1985, 1, 19.

Loyd, Sam [puzzle writer]. No data found. AMD, p. 223. "Another Famous Personage in the Moving Picture Ranks," *MPW,* 2 Jul 1910, 34.

Loyer, Georgette [actress] (b. Paris, France, 1881). AS, p. 686.

Lubetty, Madeleine [actress] (d. Sep 1968, Miami FL). BHD, p. 234.

Lubin, Arthur [film and stage actor/film director/producer] (b. Los Angeles CA, 25 Jul 1898–12 May 1995 [96], Glendale CA [Autumn Hills nursing home]; cerebral thrombosis). (Universal.) Robert McG. Thomas, Jr., "Arthur Lubin, 96, the Director of '[Francis the] Talking Mule' Film Series," *NYT,* 14 May 1995, 38:1. AS, p. 686 (b. 1901). BHD1, p. 613; BHD2, p. 165. JS, p. 250 (b. 1901; made *Il ladro di Bagdad* in Italy in 1960). Katz, pp. 738–39.

Lubin, Barney [producer]. No data found. AMD, p. 223. "Barney Lubin at Head of Production Staff for A.P.C. [Associated Picture Corp.]," *MPW,* 28 Mar 1925, 380.

Lubin, Herbert [general manager/producer] (b. New York NY, 1 Jun 1886–29 Jan 1953 [66], Los Angeles CA). m. Mollie. (Metro, 1916; 1st National.) "Herbert Lubin Dies; Built Roxy Theatre," *NYT,* 30 Jan 1953, 22:6. "Herbert Lubin," *Variety,* 4 Feb 1953. AMD, p. 223. AS, p. 686. BHD2, p. 165. "Herbert Lubin," *MPW,* 24 Apr 1915, 558. "New Combination Outlines Project," *MPW,* 16 Nov 1918, 746. "Herbert Lubin Under Knife," *MPW,* 14 Dec 1918, 1184. "Herbert Lubin Recovers from Serious Operation," *MPW,* 4 Jan 1919, 110. "Lubin Points Out Features of First 'S-L' Production," *MPW,* 18 Jan 1919, 373. "Herbert Lubin to Make Trip to Pacific Coast," *MPW,* 23 Aug 1919, 1160.

Lubin, Sigmund "Pop" (uncle of **Edna Luby**) [executive] (*né* Siegmund Lubszynskis, b. Breslau, Silesia, Germany, 20 Apr 1851?–11 Sep 1923 [72], Atlantic City NJ; heart disease and pneumonia). Joseph P. Eckhardt and Linda Kowall, *Peddler of Dreams; Siegmund Lubin and the Creation of the Motion Picture Industry 1896–1916* (National Museum of American Jewish History, 1984). Joseph P. Eckhardt, *The King of the Movies; Film Pioneer Siegmund Lubin* (Madison WI: Farleigh Dickinson Univ. Press, 1998). "Sigmund Lubin Dies; Pioneer in Movies; Philadelphia Optician, Once a Producer, Succumbs to Heart Disease at 72," *NYT,* 11 Sep 1923, 15:3. "Sigmund Lubin," *Variety,* 13 Sep 1923. "Mrs. Sigmund Lubin," *Variety,* 4 Jun 1941 (d. 23 May 1941 [78], New York NY). AMD, p. 223. AS, p. 686 (d. 11 Sep). BHD2, p. 165 (b. Breslau [Wroclaw, Poland]). IFN, p. 184. Katz, p. 739. "Trade Notes," *MPW,* 6 Apr 1907, 69–70. "A New Synchronizing Device," *MPW,* 20 Mar 1909, 339. "Siegmund Lubin," *MPW,* 6 Nov 1909, 641. Louis Reeves Harrison, "Studio Saunterings," *MPW,* 30 Mar 1912, 1142–44. "Mr. Lubin's Birthday," *NYDM,* 24 Apr 1912 (Apr 20). "Siegmund Lubin Buys 4100,000 Estate," *MPW,* 31 Aug 1912, 864–65 (Brentwood, 250 acres, Philadelphia PA). "Lubin to Make Big Investment at 'Betzwood,'" *MPW,* 21 Sep 1912, 1163. "Lubin Gets Klein Plays," *MPW,* 8 Feb 1913, 552. "S. Lubin, Philosopher; Pen Picture of the Philadelphia Pioneer," *MPW,* 1 Mar 1913, 877. "Siegmund Lubin's Birthday," *MPW,* 17 May 1913, 694 (21 Apr). "'Pop' Lubin Off for Europe," *MPW,* 11 Apr 1914, 187. "'Pop' Lubin Back in Philadelphia," *MPW,* 23 May 1914, 1099. "Fire Sweeps Lubin Plant; Blaze Follows Explosion in Film Storage House at Indiana Avenue Plant—Films Valued at Close to Million Lost," *NYDM,* 17 Jun 1914, 29:1. W.S. Bush, "A Day with Siegmund Lubin," *MPW,* 11 Jul 1914, 209–10. "Siegmund Lubin," *MPW,* 24 Oct 1914, 506. "Dissolve M.P. 'Trust'; Government the Victor in Suit—Appeal May Be Taken to the Supreme Court," *NYDM,* 6 Oct 1915, 24:2 (Lubin said the case would be dropped. The Méliès Manufacturing Company was "excluded from the findings made and the petition as against it is dismissed."). George Blaisdell, "'Pop' Lubin Recovers from Recent Illness," *MPW,* 2 Sep 1916, 1513. Siegmund Lubin, "A Toast to Those Who Made Mistakes; Courage of These Men Made Present Eminence of Industry Possible, Says 'Pop' Lubin—One Weak Spot Yet," *MPW,* 10 Mar 1917, 1525 ("It is my belief that I have put my finger on one of the weakest spots in the structure [of the industry]." He had a plan for removing it but doesn't state it here.). "'Pop' Lubin Resumes Activities," *MPW,* 1 Jun 1918, 1262. "Lubin Looking Around," *MPW,* 22 Mar 1919, 1627. "Lubin Seriously Ill," *MPW,* 12 May 1923, 116 ("...reported dying..." at Atlantic City home). Robert E. Welsh, "The Editor's Views," *MPW,* 22 Sep 1923, 321. Epes Winthrop Sargent, "Siegmund Lubin," *MPW,* 22 Sep 1923, 326 (d. 11 Sep). "For Nine Years, Betzwood Was 'Film Capital,'" *CFC,* 27 (Spring/Summer, 1970), 11. Krist Laube and Lewis G. Krohn, "Lubin: The Peddler Who Founded an Empire," *CI,* 78 (Nov 1981), 20, 56. Linda Kowall, "Lights, Camera... Fire!," *CI,* 127 (Jan 1985), 33–37. Joseph P. Eckhardt, "The Toonerville Trolley Films of the Betzwood Studio," *Griffithiana,* 53, May 1995, 24–33. Joseph P. Eckhardt, "BargainFilms from Philadelphia," *Griffithiana,* 60/61 (Oct 1997), 201–207.

Lubin, Viola [actress] (b. 1898?). (Universal.) "Gossip of the Studios," *NYDM,* 19 May 1915, 26:1 (17-year-old daughter of theatrical manager, Al. Lubin).

Lubitsch, Ernst [actor/director/producer/wscenrist] (b. Berlin, Germany, 29 Jan 1892–30 Nov 1947 [55], Bel Air CA; heart attack). m. (1) Helene (Leni) Sonnet (or **Irni Kraus**), 23 Aug 1922-Jun 1931 (d. 1960); (2) Vivian Gaye (*née* Sanya Bezencenet), 27 Jul 1935, Phoenix AZ—div. 4 Aug 1944. (Berlin Bioscope; to USA, 2 Dec 1922; UA; WB; Paramount.) Herman G. Weinberg, *The Lubitsch Touch,* 3rd ed. (New York: Dover Publications, 1977). Scott Eyman, *Ernst Lubitsch; Laughter in Paradise* (New York: Simon & Schuster, 1993). "E. Lubitsch Dead; Film Producer, 55; Director and Actor Introduced Negri, Jannings on Screen—Was Noted for 'Touch,'" *NYT,* 1 Dec 1947, 21:1. "Ernst Lubitsch," *Variety,* 3 Dec 1947. AMD, p. 223. AS, p. 686 (b. 28 Jan). BHD1, p. 338; BHD2, p. 165 (b. 28 Jan). IFN, p. 184. Katz, pp. 739–40. Truitt, p. 205. "Lubitsch Due Here to Study American Methods," *MPW,* 31 Dec 1921, 1075. Sumner Smith, "Ernst Lubitsch Describes Novel Method of Preparing a Picture for Production," *MPW,* 7 Jan 1922, 53–54. "Likes Her Work [Marion Davies]," *MPW,* 27 Jan 1923, 379. "Ernst Lubitsch Will Produce Several Features for Warners," *MPW,* 30 Jun 1923, 746. "Lubitsch to Direct," *MPW,* 1 Sep 1923, 68. "Director Lubitsch Also Has an Eye for Business," *MPW,* 15 Sep 1923, 76. Alison Smith, "Movies and the Melting Pot; Four Foreign Personalities Who Herald a Renaissance on the American Screen," *CLassic,* Mar 1924, 38–39, 78 (the other three were Richard Ordynski, Svend Gade and Victor Seastrom). Earl Canning, "Hollywood Directors Jealous of Lubitsch," *MW,* 5 Apr 1924, 13, 29. "Lubitsch to Direct Pola Negri," *MPW,* 8 Mar 1924, 113. "Lubitsch to Direct One for F.P.L.," *MPW,* 31 May 1924, 449. "Twelfth Year for Lubitsch," *MPW,* 17 Jan 1925. "Star [Irene Rich] and Director Guests of the Warners in New York," *MPW,* 24 Oct 1925, 634. "Pay Visit to President," *MPW,* 7 Nov 1925, 52 (on 18 Oct 1925). "Lubitsch Seeks Citizenship," *MPW,* 14 Nov 1925, 124. "Lubitsch Plans Biggest Film; American Spectacle," *MPW,* 14 Nov 1925, 125. "Lubitsch Ill," *MPW,* 23 Jan 1926, 2 (kidney trouble). "Lubitsch to Make 'The Door Mat' for Warners," *MPW,* 30 Jan 1926, 441. "Unique Honor for Lubitsch," *MPW,* 6 Mar 1926, 2. "Lubitsch Star s Work on 'Revillon' for Warner Bros.," *MPW,* 10 Apr 1926, 427. "Lubitsch Recuperating," *MPW,* 10 Jul 1926, 3 (from kidney stone). Matthew Josephson, "Masters of the Motion Picture; There Is a Handful of Directors Who Have Developed a Complete Character of Their Own as an Art...," *MPC,* Aug 1926, 24–25, 66, 83. "Lubitsch Signs with Famous Players-Lasky," *MPW,* 14 Aug 1926, 2. "Warners Sell Balance of Lubitsch Contract," *MPW,* 4 Sep 1926, 3 (with M-G-M and Paramount). "Lubitsch Going Arrboad," *MPW,* 2 May 1927, 787. "Lubitsch to Go to Europe for Camera Shots," *MPW,* 2 May 1927, 829. Rob Wagner, "The Foreign Legion of Hollywood," *Screenland,* Sep 1927, 32–33, 88, 90 (Germans in Hollywood). Robert Grosvenor, "Ernst Lubitsch Looks at Life and the Cinema," *Cinema Arts,* Oct 1927, 16–17, 45. Paul Thompson, "It's Always Fair Weather; A Toast to *The Student Prince,*" *MPC,* Nov 1927, 28–29, 68. Herbert Cruikshank, "The Troubadour of Silent Song; Although Working with Modern Mechanisms Ernst Lubitsch Is a Mediœval Minstrel," *MPC,* Oct 1928, 33, 76 ("A quiet little brown man, unassuming as a mouse..."). Vittorio Martinelli, "Kino-Lieblinge," *Griffithiana,* 38/39 (Oct 1990), 60.

Luby, Edna (niece of **Sigmund Lubin**) [stage/film actress] (b. New York NY, 12 Oct 1891–1 Oct 1928 [36], New York NY). m. Samuel Thor. "Edna Luby (Thor)," *Variety,* 10 Oct 1928. AS, p. 686. BHD, p. 234. SD, p. 795.. Truitt, 1983. "Vaudeville; Edna Luby Again," *NYDM,* 30 Jun 1915, 15:3 (did six imitations, including one of Nazimova, at the Fifth Ave. Theatre).

Lucan, Arthur [actor] (*né* Arthur Towle, b. Boston, England, 1887–17 May 1954 [67?], Hull, England). AS, p. 686.

Lucas, Herman [actor] (b. Omaha NB). (Kolb and Dill; Fine Arts; Dixon; Morosco; Universal.) "Herman Lucas," *MPN,* 21 Oct 1916, 216.

Lucas, Jackie [actor] (b. 1920?). No data found. AMD, p. 223. "Jackie Lucas, Three-Year Old Comedian, Signed by Sennett," *MPW,* 28 Jul 1923, 325.

Lucas, Jimmie [actor/composer] (*né* James Lucas, b. 1887–21 Feb 1949 [61?], Los Angeles CA). AS, p. 687.

Lucas, Sam[uel Mildmay] [actor] (b. Washington DC, 7 Aug 1839?–10 Jan 1916 [76], New York NY). (World.) "Dean of Negro Actors Dead," *NYT,* 11 Jan 1916, 11:5 (he was "the first to play the part of Uncle Tom, in *Uncle Tom's Cabin*"). "Sam Lucas," *Variety,* 14 Jan 1916. AS, p. 687. BHD, p. 234. IFN, p. 185. SD. Spehr, p. 148.

Lucas, Wilfred [actor/director] (*né* Norman Wilfred Lucas, b. Ontario, Canada, 30 Jan 1871 [birth certificate 003474]–13 Dec 1940 [69], Los Angeles CA). m. **Bess Meredyth** (d. 1969). (Biograph, 1907; Sennett.) "Wilfred Lucas; Stage and Screen Actor Once Directed with D.W. Griffith," *NYT,* 14 Dec 1940, 17:6. "Wilfred Lucas," *Variety,* 28 Dec 1940 (d. Los Angeles CA). AMD, p. 223. AS, p. 687. BHD1, p. 338; BHD2, p. 165. FSS, p. 191. IFN, p. 185. Katz, pp. 740–41. KOM, pp. 149–50. Spehr, pp. 1449. Truitt, p. 205. "Doings at Los Angeles; Changes in Universal Directing Forces," *MPW,* 15 Mar 1913, 1090. "Stars for Criterion," *MPW,* 21 Feb 1914, 975. "Wilfred Lucas a Star," *MPW,* 8 Jan 1916, 249. "Wilfred Lucas Will Stage Bluebird Plays," *MPW,* 5 Jan 1918, 59.

Luce, Clare Boothe [actress/playwright/politician] (*née* Ann Clare Boothe, b. NY, 10 Apr 1903–9 Oct 1987 [84], Washington DC; cancer). m. (1) George Tuttle Brokaw, 1923—div. 1929; (2) Henry R. Luce, 1935. Sylvia Jukes Morris, *Rage for Fame: The Ascent of Clare Booth Luce* (NY: Random House, 1997) (appeared in *The Heart of a Waif,* Edison, 1915, and *Under the Red Robe,* Cosmopolitan, 1924). "Clare Boothe Luce, Playwright and Politician, Succumbs at 84," *Variety,* 14 Oct 1987.

Lucenay, Harry [actor] (b. Marseilles, France, 8 May 1887–28 May 1944 [60], Los Angeles CA). BHD, p. 234. IFN, p. 185 (age 57).

Luckett, Edith (adoptive mother of Nancy Davis Reagan) [stage/film actress] (aka Edith Luckett Davis, b. Washington DC, 16 Jul 1896–26 Oct 1987 [91], Phoenix AZ; stroke). m. (1) Kenneth Robbins; (2) Loyal Davis, 1929 (d. 1982). "Edith Luckett Davis," *Variety,* 329, 28 Oct 1987, 110. (Raver Film Corp.) AMD, p. 224. AS, p. 687. BHD, p. 234. "Edith Luckett," *MPW,* 4 Dec 1915, 1809 (on Broadway in 1912 with G.M. Cohan in *Broadway Jones*).

Lucoque [director] (d. 1925).

Lucy, Arnold [stage/film actor] (*né* Walter George Campbell, b. Tottenham, Middlesex, England, 8 Aug 1865–15 Dec 1945 [80]). AS, p. 687 (b. 1875). BHD1, p. 339. IFN, p. 185. SD, p. 796.

Lucyenne, Mademoiselle [actress] (*née* Lucienne Saunier, Paris, France, 1885). AS, p. 687.

Luddy, Barbara [film/radio actress] (b. Great Falls MT, 25 May 1908–1 Apr 1979 [70], Los Angeles CA). AMD, p. 224. BHD1, p. 339 (b. Helena MT, 1907). IFN, p. 185 (age 71). "Barbara Luddy on New Fox Contract," *MPW,* 27 Feb 1926, 796.

Luddy, Edward I. [scenarist/director]. No data found. AMD, p. 224. "Century's New Director," *MPW,* 5 Apr 1924, 494. "Luddy to Direct," *MPW,* 28 May 1927, 267. "Edward I. Luddy," *MPW,* 10 Sep 1927, 92.

Luden, Jack [actor] (*né* Jacob Benson Luden, b. Reading PA, 8 Feb 1902–15 Feb 1951 [49], San Quentin State Prison, San Quentin CA). m. Elizabeth Seltzer—div. 1934; Charlotte Eckerd, 1934; Jay L. Kumler, 30 Dec 1947, Yuma AZ—div. 1950. (Paramount; FBO; Columbia; TC-F; Republic; Monogram; PRC.) AMD, p. 224. AS, p. 687. BHD1, p. 339. FSS, p. 192. IFN, p. 185. "Paramount-Famous-Lasky Graduate Elevated; Now a Western Star," *MPW,* 14 May 1927, 115. "Jack Luden," *MPW,* 30 Jul 1927, 318. Dunham Thorp, "By Way of Cough Drops; Jack Luden Overcomes the Mentholated Silver Spoon," *MPC,* Jan 1928, 63, 83, 87. Luther Hathcock, "Whatever Happened to Cowboy Star Jack Luden?" *CI,* 145 (Jul 1987), C13-C16 (nephew of William Luden) (sent to prison for bouncing checks and heroin possession; "Jack Luden is the only star of his stature to die in prison.").

Ludlow, Patrick [actor] (b. London, England, 24 Mar 1903–27 Jan 1996 [92], London, England). AS, p. 688. BHD1, p. 339.

Ludwig, Edward [actor/director] (b. Russia, 1899?–20 Aug 1982 [83], Santa Monica CA). "Edward Ludwig," *Variety,* 1 Sep 1982 (began with 1- and 2-reelers). AS, p. 688 (b. 1895). BHD, p. 234; BHD2, p. 166 (b. 1895).

Luey, William Allen [director/producer] (b. 1883–16 Dec 1954 [71?], Norton CT). AS, p. 688. BHD2, p. 165.

Luff, William [actor/cinematographer] (b. London, England, 31 May 1872–15 Mar 1960 [87], England). AS, p. 688 (b. 1875). BHD, p. 234; BHD2, p. 166. IFN, p. 185 (age 84).

Lufkin, Sam [actor] (b. UT, 8 May 1891–19 Feb 1952 [60], Los Angeles CA). (Sennett.) "Sam Dufkin [sic]," *Variety,* 27 Feb 1952 ("Starting in silent film days, he played for several years with Mack Sennett's company."). AS, p. 688 (b. 1892). BHD1, p. 339 (b. 1892). IFN, p. 185.

Lugg, William [actor] (b. Portsmouth, England, 4 Jun 1852–1940 [88?]). AS, p. 688. BHD, p. 234.

Lugne-Poe, Aureelien-Marie [actor/producer] (b. San Francisco CA, 27 Dec 1869–19 Jun 1940 [70], Avignon, France). AS, p. 688 (b. Paris, France). BHD2, p. 166.

Lugosi, Bela [actor] (aka Arisztid Olt, *né* Béla Lugosi Ferenc Blasko, b. Lugos, Hungary, 20 Oct 1882–16 Aug 1956 [73], Los Angeles CA). m. (1) Ilona Szmik; (2) Ilona von Montagh; (3) Beatrice W. Weeks; (4) Lilian Arch; (5) Hope Lininger. Arthur Lenning, *The Count* (1974). Gary Don Rhodes, *Lugosi: His Life in Films, on Stage, and in the Hearts of Horror Lovers* (Jefferson NC: McFarland & Co.,, 1997). "Bela Lugosi Dies; Created Dracula; Portrayer of Vampire Role on Stage and Screen Was Star in Budapest," *NYT,* 17 Aug 1956, 19:3 (b. 1884 [71]). "Bela Lugosi," *Variety,* 22 Aug 1956 (age 72). AS, p. 688 (b. 29 Oct). BHD1, p. 339 (b. Lugoj, Romania). FSS, p. 192. IFN, p. 185. Katz, p. 741 (began 1915). SD. Truitt, p. 205. István Nemeskürty and Tibor Szántó, *A Pictorial Guide to the Hungarian Cinema [1901–1984]* (Budapest, Hungary: Révai Printing House, 1985), p. 28 ("The most popular actor of the time was Béla Lugosi, who also played under the name of Arisztid Olt…").

Lugrin, Clarence T. [photographer] (d. Feb 1930, St. John's, Newfoundland, Canada). BHD2, p. 166.

Luguet, André (father of Rosine Luguet, 1921–1981) [actor/director] (*né* André Maurice Jean Allioux-Luguet, b. Fontenay-sous-Bois, France, 15 May 1892–24 May 1979 [87], Cannes, France). (Began 1911; MGM; Paramount.) AS, p. 688. BHD1, p. 330. IFN, p. 185. Waldman, p. 170.

Luitz-Morat [producer] (b. Geneva, Switzerland, 1875–1928 [53?], Paris, France). AS, p. 688. BHD2, p. 166.

Lukas, Paul [stage/film actor] (*né* Paul Lukacs, b. Budapest, Hungary, 26 May 1894–15 Aug 1971 [77], Tangier, Morocco). m. (1) Gizella Benes (d. 1962); (2) Anna Driesens (widow). (Film debut: *Samson and Delilah,* Germany). "Paul Lucas, 1943 Oscar Winner, Dies," *NYT,* 17 Aug 1971, 38:3. "Paul Lukas," *Variety,* 18 Aug 1971 (age 76). AMD, p. 224. AS, p. 688 (b. 1887). BHD1, p. 339. IFN, p. 185. Katz, pp. 741–42. SD. "Lukas Arrives," *MPW,* 24 Sep 1927, 223. Edward R. Sammis, "Quaint People These Hungarians; Paul Lukas Is One of Them," *MPC,* Jun 1928, 58, 78 (What if "'American maidenhood demanded that you go on with romantic roles?' 'In that case,' he replied, 'I should pack up my grease paint and go home.'"). Truitt, p. 206. Gladys Hall, "Paul Lukas Is a Love Expert—That's Why Women Love Him," *Movie Classic,* I, Dec 1931, 59, 72. "Ask the Answer Man," *Photoplay,* Apr 1932, 82 (b. 1896).

Luke, Monte [director] (b. Geelong, Australia, 1885–1962 [77?], Sydney, Australia). AS, p. 688.

Lumière, Antoine [producer] (*né* Claude Antoine Lumière, b. Ormoy, France, 13 Mar 1840–15 Apr 1911 [71], Paris, France). AS, p. 689. BHD2, p. 166 (b. 1843).

Lumière, Auguste Marie Nicolas (brother of **Louis** and **Edouard Lumière**) [scientist/cinematographer/director/ producer] (b. Bensançon, France, 25 Oct 1862–10 Apr 1954 [91], Lyons, France). *The Illustrated History of the Cinema,* consultant ed., David Robinson; ed., Ann Lloyd (NY: Macmillan, 1986), pp. 13–14. "August Lumiere, Scientist, 92, Dies; Co-Inventor with Brother of Early Movie Camera Made Many Medical Discoveries," *NYT,* 11 Apr 1954, 87:1. "Auguste Lumiere," *Variety,* 14 Apr 1954 (age 92). AS, p. 689. BHD, p. 234; BHD2, p. 166 (b. 19 Oct). IFN, p. 185 (age 92). WWVC, pp. 86–87.

Lumière, Edouard (brother of **Auguste** and **Louis Lumière**) [exhibitor] (b. France-d. 1917; airplane accident). Cal York, "Plays and Players," *Photoplay,* Jul 1917, 114 ("…said to be the first man to exhibit a film in Europe.").

Lumière, Louis Aimé Augustin (brother of **Auguste** and **Edouard Lumière**) [scientist/producer/director] (b. Bensançon, France, 5 Oct 1864–6 Jun 1948 [83], Bandol, Var, the Riviera, France). m. Jeanne L. Winckler (d. 1925). Georges Sadoul, *Louis Lumière* (Paris: Editions Seghers, 1964). "Louis Lumiere, 83, A Screen Pioneer; Credited in France with the Invention of Motion Picture in 1894—Dies on Riviera," *NYT,* 7 Jun 1948, 19:3. "Louis Lumiere," *Variety,* 9 Jun 1948. AMD, p. 224. AS, p. 689. BHD2, p. 166. IFN, p. 185. SD. WWVC, pp. 82–83. John Wakeman, ed., *World Film Directors,* Vol. I, 1890–1945 (NY: The H.W. Wilson Company, 1987), pp. 700–710 (d. 1968). "Lumière Again a Producer," *MPW,* 17 Jul 1909, 87.

Lund, Bert [assistant director]. No data found. AMD, p. 224. "Assistant Keystone Director Lund Drafter," *MPW,* 27 Oct 1917, 511.

Lund, Oscar A.C. [actor/director/scenarist] (b. Stockholm, Sweden, ca. 1890–1963 [70?]). (Eclair.) AMD, p. 224. AS, p. 689 (b. 1885). BHD, p. 234' BHD2, p. 166. "O.A.C. Lund," *MPW,* 11 Apr 1914, 195. "O.A.C. Lund to Direct for Thanhouser," *MPW,* 9 Sep 1916, 1712. "O.A.C.

Lund Directing Sonia Markova," *MPW,* 3 Nov 1917, 681. "Oscar Lund Leaves for Europe," *MPW,* 13 Mar 1920, 1775.

Lund, Richard [actor] (b. Göteborg, Sweden, 1885–17 Sep 1960 [75], Sweden). AS, p. 689. BHD1, p. 340. IFN, p. 185.

Lunda, Elena [actress] (b. Palermo, Italy, 21 Feb 1901 [extrait de naissance no. V.427 N.863.1]–9 Dec 1947 [46], Rome, Italy). AS, p. 689. JS, p. 252 (in Italian silents from 1919).

Lundberg, Frans [director/producer] (b. Sweden, 1851–1922 [71?], Sweden). AS, p. 689.

Lundequist, Gerda [actress] (*née* Gerda Lundequist-Dahlstrom, b. Stockholm, Sweden, 14 Feb 1871–23 Oct 1959 [88], Sweden). AS, p. 689. BHD1, p. 340. IFN, p. 185.

Lundine, Walter [actor/cinematographer] (b. ca. 1894). (Frontier.) FDY, p. 461 (Walter Lundin). "Gossip of the Studios," *NYDM,* 9 Sep 1914, 27:2 (20 years old).

Lung, Charles [actor] (*né* Bernard Clerc Davey, b. England, 3 May 1897–22 Jun 1974 [77], London, England). AS, p. 689.

Lunt, Alfred Davis [stage/film actor] (b. Milwaukee WI, 19 Aug 1892–3 Aug 1977 [84], Chicago IL; cancer). m. **Lynn Fontanne**, 26 May 1922, NY (d. 1983). "Alfred Lunt, a Star of Broadway for Third of Century, Dies at 84"; Alden Whitman, "Always Working," *NYT,* 4 Aug 1977, 1:1, C16:1. Hobe Morrison, "Alfred Lunt Dies at 84 in Chi; Costarred with Lynn Fontanne," *Variety,* 10 Aug 1977. AMD, p. 224. AS, p. 689. BHD1, p. 340. FSS, p. 193. GSS, pp. 241–46. IFN, p. 185. Katz, p. 744. "Lunt to Lead in 'Backbone,'" *MPW,* 9 Dec 1922, 541. David A. Balch, "'Less Director—More Drama,' Says Alfred Lunt," *MW,* 16 Jun 1923, 8, 31. Susan Elizabeth Brady, "For Which Wise Men Pray," *MPC,* Jan 1925, 22–23, 83.

Lupi, Ignazio [actor] (b. Rome, Italy, 11 Dec 1867–14 Dec 1942 [75], Rome, Italy). (Cines-Kleine.) AMD, p. 224. JS, p. 252 (in Italian silents from 1912). "Cines-Kleine Players," *MPW,* 11 Jul 1914, 237–38 (he "has a strong personality that one instinctively feels. Hes the undefinable power called 'stage presence,' that most valuable quality without which no one can win lasting success in the drama or photodrama.").

Lupi, Ruggero [actor] (b. Ferrara, Italy, 13 Oct 1882–1 Jul 1933 [50], Milan, Italy). JS, p. 252 (in Italian silents from 1916).

Lupino, Barry (son of actor George Lupino; cousin of Ida Lupino [1918–1995]) [actor] (b. London, England, 7 Jan 1882–25 Sep 1962 [80], Brighton, England). m. 3 times. "Barry Lupino," *Variety,* 228, 3 Oct 1962, 79:1 (d. 26 Sep). AMD, p. 224. BHD1, p. 340. IFN, p. 185. "Beaumont Smith Engages Comedian Barry Lupino," *MPW,* 20 Sep 1919, 1834.

Lupino, Mark (brother of Stanley Lupino; cousin of **Lupino Lane**) [actor/director] (b. England, 1869–4 Apr 1930 [60?], London, England; after a brain operation). "Mark Lupino," *Variety,* 23 Apr 1930, 76:5 (age 36). AS, p. 690. BHD, p. 234.

Lupino, Wallace (brother of **Lupino Lane**; cousin of Ida Lupino) [actor] (*né* Wallace Lane, b. Edinburgh, Scotland, 23 Jan 1897–11 Oct 1961 [64], Ashford, Middlesex, England). (Began 1925.) "Wallace Lupino," *NYT,* 13 Oct 1961, 35:3. "Wallace Lupino," *Variety,* 18 Oct 1961 ("He made many films, including over 70 comedy shorts."). AMD, p. 224. AS, p. 690. BHD1, p. 340 (b. 1898). IFN, p. 185. "Lupino Lane's Brother," *MPW,* 2 Octr 1926, 292.

Lupo, Rino [director/scenarist] (*né* Cesare Rino Lupo, b. Rome, Italy, 15 Feb 1888). AS, p. 690.

Lupton, Marie Fanning [scenarist] (b. 1867–28 Sep 1924 [57?], New York NY). BHD2, p. 166.

Lupu-Pick [actor/director] (*né* Lupu Pick, b. Jassy, Rumania, 2 Jan 1886–7 Mar 1931 [45], Berlin, Germany; suicide with poison). m. **Edith Posca** (d. 1931). AS, p. 690.

Lurville, Armand [actor] (*né* Armand Barouch Josephson, b. Paris, France, 21 Mar 1875–25 Sep 1955 [80], Paris, France). AS, p. 690.

Lusk, Norbert [publicist/scenarist] (b. New Orleans LA, 1883?–23 Jul 1949 [66], Forest Hills NY). (Lubin; World.) *I Love Actresses!* (National Board of Review Magazine, 1948). "Norbert Lusk," *Variety,* 3 Aug 1949. AMD, p. 224. AS, p. 690. BHD2, p. 166. "Norbert Lusk," *NYDM,* 16 Oct 1915, 26:3. "Norbert Lusk," *MPW,* 16 Oct 1915, 456.

Luther, Anna, "The Poster Girl" [actress] (b. Newark NJ, 7 Jul 1893–16 Dec 1960 [67], Los Angeles CA; heart attack). m. Edward Gallagher. (Lubin; Selig; Keystone; Fox.) "Ann Luther," *Variety,* 28 Dec 1960. AMD, p. 224. AS, p. 690. BHD1, p. 340 (b. 1897). IFN, p. 185 (b. 1897). MSBB, 1038 (b. 1894). "Anna Luther," *MPW,* 28 Mar 1914, 1660. "Anna Luther Supporting Tom Terriss," *MPW,* 19 Dec 1914, 1686. "Anna Luther," *MPW,* 8 May 1915, 880. J. Van Cartmell, "Studio News from the Coast," *NYDM,* 4 Dec 1915, 27:2 (Fred Mace directing a 2-reel farce comedy at Keystone, *Crooked to the Death,* a Triangle release, with Ann Luther, "The Poster Girl."). "Abramson Signs Well-Known Favorites," *MPW,* 19 Jan 1918, 362. "General Film to Release Anna Luther's 'Her Moment,'" *MPW,* 22 Jun 1918, 1735. "Prominent Players to Be Featured in Pathé Serials for the Next Two Years," *MPW,* 19 Jul 1919. 377–78.

Luther, Lester [actor] (b. 18 Dec 1887–19 Jan 1962 [74], Los Angeles CA). AS, p. 690.

Luther, Mark Lee [writer]. No data found. AMD, p. 224. "Joins Writer Colony," *MPW,* 14 May 1921, 179.

Luttringer, Al [actor] (*né* Alfonse Luttringer, b. San Francisco CA, 16 Nov 1878–9 Jun 1953 [74], Los Angeles CA). "Alfonse (Al) Luttringer," *Variety,* 17 Jun 1953. AS, p. 690. IFN, p. 185.

Luxford, Nola [actress] (b. Hastings, New Zealand, 24 Dec 1895–10 Oct 1994 [99], Pasadena CA). m. Mr. Dolberg. (Universal, 1925.) "Nola L. Dolberg, 99, Silent-Film Actress," *NYT,* 13 Oct 1994, B16:6. "Nola Luxford," *Variety,* 17 Oct 1994, p. 166:3 (age 97). AMD, p. 224. AS, p. 691. BHD1, p. 341 (b. Hawkes Bay, New Zealand). "Wally's Lead," *MPW,* 4 Jun 1927, 348. George A. Katchmer, "Remembering the Great Silents," *CI,* 183 (Sep 1990), 46.

Lydecker, Howard C. [technical director] (b. 1883–11 Jul 1935 [52?], Los Angeles CA). BHD2, p. 166.

Lyel, Viola [actress] (b. Hull, Yorkshire, England, 9 Dec 1900–14 Aug 1972 [71], England). AS, p. 691. BHD1, p. 341. IFN, p. 186.

Lyell, Lottie [stage/film actress] (*née* Lottie Edith Cox, b. Sydney, Australia, 23 Feb 1890–21 Dec 1925 [35], Sydney, Australia; tuberculosis). (Film debut: *Captain Midnight, The Bush King,* 1911; last film: *The Sentimental Bloke.*) AS, p. 691. BHD, p. 235. (Lyell is widely regarded as Australia's first film star).

Lygo, Mary [stage/film actress] (*née* Irene Goodall, b. Akron IA, 1902?–1 Jun 1927 [25], Los Angeles CA; suicide with poison over millionaire Gordon Thorne). "Mary Lygo, 25, Kills Herself on Coast; Formerly of 'Follies,' Known on Screen as Rene Fuller," *Variety,* 8 Jun 1927. AMD, p. 224. AS, p. 419 (Rene Fuller); p. 691 (Mary Lygo). BHD, p. 236 (*née* Irene Fuller). IFN, p. 186. Truitt, p. 206. "Obituary," *MPW,* 25 Jun 1927, 574.

Lyle, Clinton [actor] (*né* Clarence Lyle, b. CA, 27 Aug 1883–26 Jun 1950 [66], Los Angeles CA). AS, p. 691. BHD, p. 235. IFN, p. 186.

Lyle, Edith [actress] (d. 8 Jan 1982, Los Angeles CA). AMD, p. 224. BHD, addendum. "Edith Lyle in Hollywood to Work in Big Production," *MPW,* 14 Sep 1918, 1572.

Lyle, Lyston [stage/film actor] (b. 1856–19 Feb 1920 [63?], London, England). "In London; Lyston Lyle," *Variety,* LVIII, 19 Mar 1920, 16:2 (d. 20 Feb). BHD, p. 235 (Lynston Lyle).

Lyle, Warren E. [actor]. No data found. (Nola Film Company).

Lyles, Aubrey [actor] (b. Jackson TN, 1884–28 Jul 1932 [48?], New York NY). BHD1, p. 341.

Lynch, Frank J. [actor] (d. 4 Dec 1932, Springfield MA). BHD1, p. 341.

Lynch, Frank T. [actor] (b. 1869–18 Dec 1933 [64], New York NY). m. Alice Laziere. "Frank T. Lynch," *Variety,* 9 Jan 1934. AS, p. 691. BHD1, p. 341. Truitt, 1983.

Lynch, Helen [actress: Wampas Star, 1923] (b. Billings MT, 6 Apr 1900–2 Mar 1965 [64], Miami Beach FL). m. **Carroll Nye** (d. 1974). AMD, p. 224. AS, p. 691. BHD1, p. 341. IFN, p. 186. "Miss Lynch with Hoot," *MPW,* 17 Jan 1925, 278. George A. Katchmer, "Forgotten Cowboys and Cowgirls—Part XV," *CI,* 192 (Jun 1991), 43 (d. 2 Mar 1974).

Lynch, Jim [actor] (b. Holyoke MA–d. 20 Apr 1916, Chicago IL). AS, p. 691. BHD, p. 235.

Lynch, John [scenarist] (b. New York NY, 1870?–3 Oct 1936 [66], Los Angeles CA). (Triangle; NYMP Co.) "John Lynch," *Variety,* 7 Oct 1936. AMD, p. 224. AS, p. 691. BHD2, p. 167. Lowrey, p. 106. "'Not Better Stories, But Better Productions,' Says John Lynch, Scenario Writer for Selznick Pictures," *MPW,* 9 Aug 1919, 854. "Ballin and Lynch Added to F.P.-L.'s Production Staff," *MPW,* 25 Jul 1925, 443. "To Write for M-G-M," *MPW,* 17 Jul 1926, 1. "Lynch at F.B.O.," *MPW,* 5 Feb 1927, 422.

Lyndon, Alice [actress] (b. 1874?–9 Jul 1949 [75], Woodland Hills CA). (Sennett.) "Alice Lyndon," *Variety,* 20 Jul 1949. AS, p. 691. BHD1, p. 341. IFN, p. 186. Truitt, p. 206.

Lynn, Charles [stage/film actor] (b. San Francisco CA, 16 Jul 1886). (Universal; Fox; Sennett.) MSBB, p. 1025.

Lynn, Emmett [actor] (b. Muscatine IA, 14 Feb 1897–20 Oct 1958 [61], Los Angeles CA; heart attack). (Biograph, 1913.) "Emmett Lynn," *Variety,* 29 Oct 1958 (made 500+ films). AS, p. 692. BHD1, p. 341. IFN, p. 186. Truitt, pp. 206–207.

Lynn, Emmy [actress] (b. Paris, France, 1888–8 Jun 1978 [90?], Paris, France). AS, p. 692. BHD1, p. 341.

Lynn[e], Ethel [stage/film actress]. m. **Fred Fishbeck**, 1919 (d. 1925). (Universal.) AMD, p. 225. No data found. J. Van Cartmell, "Live Wires from the West Coast," *NYDM,* 27 Nov 1915, 29:4 (from the musical-comedy stage, joined the Universal Nestor). "Comedienne Weds Director," *MPW,* 26 Jul 1919, 505–06.

Lynn, Hastings [actor] (b. England, 1878–30 Jun 1932 [54?], Elstree, England). AS, p. 692.

Lynn, Helen [actress]. No data found. (Diamond Film Company.) AMD, p. 224. "Miss Helen Lynn," *MPW,* XII, 22 Jun 1912, 1136.

Lynn, Ralph [actor] (b. Manchester, England, 18 Mar 1882–8 Aug 1962 [80], London, England). AS, p. 692.

Lynn, Sharon E. [actress] (*née* D'Auvergne Sharon Lindsey, b. Weatherford TX, 9 Apr 1910–26 May 1963 [53], Los Angeles CA). m. **Benjamin (Barney) Glazer** (d. 1956); John Sershen. (Fox.) "Sharon Lynn Dead; Movie Actress, 53," *NYT,* 28 May 1963, 37:2. "Sharon Lynn," *Variety,* 5 Jun 1963. AMD, p. 224. AS, p. 692 (b. 1907). BHD1, p. 342 (b. 1904). FSS, p. 194. IFN, p. 186. Truitt, p. 207 (b. 1904). WWS, p. 207 (b. 1904). "Sharon Lynn in F.B.O. Picture," *MPW,* 11 Jun 1927, 424. George A. Katchmer, "Forgotten Cowboys and Cowgirls—Part XV," *CI,* 192 (Jun 1991), 42.

Lynnwood, Percival L. [driector] (b. 1878–12 Jul 1927 [49?], Los Angeles CA). BHD2, p. 167.

Lyon, Ben [actor/executive] (b. Atlanta GA, 6 Feb 1901–22 Mar 1979 [78], aboard the Queen Elizabeth II, Pacific Ocean). m. **Bebe Daniels** (d. 1971); **Marian Nixon**, Apr 1972 (d. 1983). *Life with the Lyons* (London: Odhams, 1953); Jill Algood, *Bebe and Ben* (1976). (FP-L.) "Ben Lyon, 78, Silent-Screen Star Who 'Discovered' Marilyn Monroe," *NYT,* 26 Mar 1979, B13:2. "Ben Lyon," *Variety,* 28 Mar 1979. AMD, p. 225. AS, p. 692. BHD1, p. 342; BHD2, p. 167. FFF, p. 100. FSS, p. 194. HCH, p. 19. IFN, p. 186. Katz, p. 746. MH, p. 123. Truitt, 1983 (b. 1889 or 1901). "Ben Lyon," *MPW,* 8 Sep 1917, 1529. "Ben Lyon in Films," *MPW,* 8 Sep 1923, 184. Regina Cannon, "A Kleig Light Romeo," *MW,* 20 Dec 1924, 9–10, 30. Sara Redway, "Just Like Your Brother," *MPC,* Jan 1926, 56–57, 82, 85. "Sign Ben Lyon Again," *MPW,* 17 Apr 1926, 507. Gladys Hall, "One of 'The Sad Young Men,'" *Pictures,* Aug 1926, 33, 76–78. Harold R. Hall, "Blame It on the Ladies; Ben Lyon Is Sitting Pretty Now, for the Women Have Put Him Over," *MPC,* Feb 1927, 54–55, 83, 87. "Ben Lyon Injures Hand While Boxing at H.A.C. [Hollywood Athletic Club]," *MPW,* 5 Nov 1927, 37. "Lyon to Berlin," *MPW,* 19 Nov 1927, 25.

Lyon, Esther [actress] (b. 30 Oct 1869–15 Jul 1958 [88], New York NY). BHD, p. 235.

Lyon, Frank A. [stage/film actor] (b. Bridgeport CT, 17 Jan 1900–6 Jan 1961 [60], Gardner MA). "Frank Lyon, 60, Dies; Stage and Screen Actor Had Appeared in Ten Film Roles," *NYT,* 7 Jan 1961, 19:5. "Frank Lyon," *Variety,* 18 Jan 1961. AS, p. 692. BHD1, p. 342. IFN, p. 186.

Lyon, Harry W. [cameraman]. No data found. AMD, p. 225. "Filming the Land of the Rising Sun," *MPW,* 9 Jun 1917, 1615.

Lyon, Wanda [stage/film actress]. No data found. (Pathe.) AMD, p. 225. "Wanda Lyon Supports Max Linder," *MPW,* 1 May 1920, 722. "Wanda Lyon Back in America Is Told of the Success of Pathé's 'The Little Cafe,'" *MPW,* 17 Jul 1920, 359:2.

Lyonel, Emma [actress] (b. Lorient, France, 6 Aug 1888–ca. 1956 [68?]). AS, p. 692.

Lyonell, Joseph [actor] (b. England, 1883–26 Jan 1929 [45?], Irvington NJ). AS, p. 692.

Lyons, Chester A. [cinematographer] (b. Westfield NY, 26 May 1885–27 Nov 1936 [51], Los Angeles CA; heart attack). m. Katherine. "Chet Lyons Dies on Set," *Variety,* 2 Dec 1936. AMD, p. 225. AS, p. 692. BHD2, p. 167. FDY, p. 461. IFN, p. 186. "Cameraman Takes Real War Pictures," *MPW,* 12 Dec 1914, 1545. "Cameraman Chester Lyons to Stay with Charles Ray," *MPW,* 6 Mar 1920, 1658.

Lyons, Clifton (Tex) [actor/stuntman] (brother of Joseph Lyonell) (*né* Clifford William Lyons, b. SD, 4 Jul 1901–6 Jan 1974 [72], Los Angeles CA). AS, p. 692. BHD1, p. 342. IFN, p. 186.

Lyons, Eddie (brother of **Harry M. Lyons**) [stage/film actor/producer/director/scenarist] (b. Beardstown IL, 25 Nov 1886–30 Aug 1926 [40], Pasadena CA; brain tumor). m. **Virginia Kirtley**, Aug 1917 (d. 1956). (Biograph, 1911; Imp; Nestor; Arrow; Universal.) AMD, p. 225. AS, p. 692. BHD, p. 235. IFN, p. 186. Katz, pp. 746–47. MSBB, p. 1025. Truitt, 1983. "Marriages," *Variety,* 17 Aug 1917, p. 16 (m. Kirtley). "Eddie Lyons," *MPW,* 13 Jun 1914, 1549. "Eddie Lyons Director of New Nestor Co.," *MPW,* 12 Dec 1914, 1536. "Eddie Lyons," *MPW,* 21 Jul 1917, 450. Robert C. McElravy, "Comedy Folks," *MPW,* 13 Apr 1918, 218–19. Lyons and Moran Complete Their 250th Production," *MPW,* 17 May 1919, 1064. "Eddie Lyons and Lee Moran to Be Featured in Comedy-Drama Series," *MPW,* 27 Dec 1919, 1163. "Eddie Lyons and Lee Moran Stop Making Single Reelers," *MPW,* 29 May 1920, 1220. "Eddie Lyons to Star in Series of Two Reel Comedies forArrow," *MPW,* 22 Oct 1921, 925. "'Gag' Comedies Are Popular—Eddie Lyons," *MPW,* 12 Aug 1922, 515. "September Is Set as Arrow Month; Sign William Fairbanks and Lyons," *MPW,* 19 Aug 1922, 585. Bo Berglund, "Eddie Lyons at Biograph," *Griffithiana,* 60/61 (Oct 1997), 209–11.

Lyons, Edgar [cameraman] (b. 1894?–4 Apr 1950 [56], Los Angeles CA). (Republic; Disney.) "Edgar Lyons," *Variety,* 12 Apr 1950 ("Starting his career in the days of silent films, Lyons was an early cameraman with Nat Levine's Mascot Productions..."). AS, p. 692. BHD2, p. 167.

Lyons, Fred [actor] (*né* Fred F. Leyva, d. 16 Mar 1921; auto accident). (Universal.) "Fred Lyons," *Variety,* 25 Mar 1921. "Obituary," *MPW,* 2 Apr 1921, 477. AMD, p. 225. AS, p. 693. BHD, p. 235. Truitt, p. 207.

Lyons, Harry M. (brother of **Eddie Lyons**) [actor] (b. IL, 12 Nov 1879–13 Mar 1919 [39], Los Angeles CA; heart failure. Interred in Calvary Cemetery, LA CA). AMD, p. 225. AS, p. 693. BHD, p. 235. IFN, p. 186. "Obituary," *MPW,* 5 Apr 1919, 76.

Lyons, Isabel S. (half-sister of **J. Stuart Blackton**) [actress] (b. 1889?–18 May 1972 [81], Los Angeles CA). m. **Reginald E. Lyons**. (Vitagraph, 1910.) "Isabel S. Lyons," *Variety,* 7 Jun 1972. AS, p. 693.

Lyons, Lurline [actress]. No data found. (Clune.) *MPC,* Aug 1916, 8 (photo).

Lyons, Reginald E[dgar] [cameraman] (b. 1892?–10 Sep 1966 [74], Los Angeles CA). (Vitagraph.) m. **Isabel**. "Reginald E. Lyons," *Variety,* 21 Sep 1966. AS, p. 693. BHD2, p. 167. FDY, p. 461.

Lyr, René [scenarist] (*né* René Vanderhaeghe, b. Couvin, Belgium, 15 Nov 1887–ca. 1956 [68?]). AS, p. 693.

Lys, Lya [actress] (*née* Natalia Lyecht, b. France, 18 May 1908–2 Jun 1986 [78], Newport Beach CA). (MGM; Fox.) BHD1, p. 342 (b. Berlin, Germany). Waldman, p. 170.

Lyses, Charlotte [actress] (*née* Charlotte Augustine Hortense Lejeune, b. Paris, France, 17 May 1877–6 Apr 1956 [78], Saint-Jean-Cap-Ferrat, France). m. **Sacha Guitry** (d. 1957). AS, p. 693.

Lysle, Edmond [inventor] (b. 1885–28 Aug 1953 [68?], Norwalk CT). AS, p. 693.

Lytell, Bert (brother of **Wilfred Lytell**) [actor] (*né* Bertram Lytell, b. New York NY, 24 Feb 1885–28 Sep 1954 [69], New York NY [Death Certificate Index No. 20008, age 67]). m. (1) **Evelyn Vaughn**—div. MO; (2) **Claire Windsor**, 14 May 1925, Juarez, Mexico (d. 1972); **Grace Menken** (d. 1978). (Metro.) "Bert Lytell Dies; Stage, Film Star; Leading Man for 30 Years Succumbs After Operation—He Made Debut at 3," *NYT,* 29 Sep 1954, 31:1. "Bert Lytell, One of 1st Matinee Idols, Dies at 67," *Variety,* 29 Sep 1954 (age 67). AMD, p. 225. AS, p. 693. BHD1, p. 342. FFF, p. 37. FSS, p. 195. IFN, p. 186. Katz, p. 747. Lowrey, p. 108. MH, p. 123. MSBB, p. 1025. Truitt, p. 207. WWS, p. 57. *Bert Lytell, as He Is to Those Who Know Him* (NY: Ross Publishing Co., Inc, 1920). "Bert Lytell Signs Contract with Metro," *MPW,* 9 Mar 1918, 1359. "Leaves for Training Camp," *MPW,* 23 Nov 1918, 819. "Metro to Present Bert Lytell in Four Specials Produced in New York Studio," *MPW,* 10 Jul 1920, 220. Edward Weitzel, "Bert Lytell Talks about Stock Acting and Metro's 'The Price of Redemption,'" *MPW,* 31 Jul 1920, 569. Gladys Hall, "Is There Such a Thing as a One Man-Girl? 'No!' Says Bert Lytell," *MW,* 23 Jun 1923, 7, 30 ("Men and women of nearly the same age should not marry...because women age more quickly than men."). Alma Talley, "Bert," *MW,* 2 Aug 1924, 8, 29. "Lubitsch Signs Bert Lytell," *MPW,* 27 Dec 1924, 865. "Bert Lytell in Vitagraph's Newest Curwood Production," *MPW,* 18 Apr 1925, 702. "Lytell on Vaudeville Tour," *MPW,* 18 Sep 1926, 176. June Lee, "Dan Cupid's Bulletin Board," *Paris and Hollywood Screen Secrets,* Oct 1927, 35 (to divorce Windsor); 37 (Lytell "is said to have been unreasonably jealous, having complained bitterly against his wife's associations during his professional absence"). George Katchmer, "Remembering the Great Silents; Bert Lytell," *CI,* 169 (Jul 1989), C15–C16, 38, 46. Henry R. Davis, "The Films of Bert Lytell," *CI,* 171 (Sep 1989), 34.

Lytell, Wilfred (brother of **Bert Lytell**) [actor] (b. New York NY, 1892–10 Sep 1954 [62], Salem NY). m. Jessie Mueller, 2 Aug 1912, Thompsonville MA. (Poll Stock Co., Springfield MA.) "Wilfred Lytell," *Variety,* 15 Sep 1954. AMD, p. 225. AS, p. 693. BHD, p. 235. IFN, p. 186. Truitt, p. 207. "News of Stock Plays and Players; Schenley Players, Pittsburgh," *NYDM,* 25 Nov 1914, 10:2 (m. Mueller, Aug 1893, Sprinngfield). "Concerning Miss Jessie Mueller," *NYDM,* 9 Dec 1914, 11:1 (not married in Springfield, 1893, as previously reported). "Wilfred Lytell Doubles for Screen," *MPW,* 13 Jul 1918, 228. "Beck Signs Wilfred Lytell," *MPW,* 16 Aug

1919, 983. "Bert Lytell's Brother Plays Lead in New Metro Production," *MPW,* 29 May 1920, 1229.

Lytton, Doris [actress] (b. Manchester, England, 23 Jan 1893–3 Dec 1953 [60], London, England). BHD, p. 235.

Lytton, L. Rogers [actor] (*né* Oscar Legare Rogers, b. New Orleans LA, 1867–9 Aug 1924 [57], New York NY). AS, p. 693. BHD, p. 235. IFN, p. 186. Slide, p. 145.

Lytton, Margia [actress]. No data found. (Gene Gauntier Players.) "Gossip of the Studios," *NYDM,* 7 Jan 1914, 29:1-2.

Lyvenden, Lord [actor] (*né* Percy Vernon, b. Kettering, England, 29 Dec 1857–25 Dec 1926 [68], London, England). BHD, p. 235.

M

Maberry, Cecil E. [producer]. No data found. AMD, p. 225. "Maberry, Producer, to Film Novel Soon," *MPW,* 25 Nov 1922, 330.

MacAdams, Rhea [actress] (b. 1884–20 Jul 1982 [98?], Placerville CA). AS, p. 695. BHD, p. 235.

McAfee, Lucy Page [art director] (d. 18 Jun 1923, Beverly Hills CA). BHD2, p. 167.

MacAlarney, Robert Emmet [scenarist]. No data found. AMD, p. 225. "Lasky Engages Editor Robert Emmet MacAlarney," *MPW,* 22 Jul 1916, 619. "MacAlarney to Be Scenario Chief," *MPW,* 9 Jun 1917, 1617. Louis Reeves Harrison, "He's Treating 'Em Rough," *MPW,* 9 Nov 1918, 656.

McAlister, Mary [actress: Wampas Star, 1927] (b. Los Angeles CA, 27 May 1909–1 May 1991 [81], Del Mar CA). AS, p. 736. BHD1, p. 342. MH, p. 126. 1921 Directory, p. 248 (b. 1910). Ragan 2, p. 1092. Cover, *Motion Picture Magazine,* Feb 1918. Billy H. Doyle, "Obituaries," *FIR,* Sep/Oct 1991, 358.

McAllister, Paul [actor] (b. Brooklyn NY, 30 Jun 1875–8 Jul 1955 [80], Santa Monica CA). AMD, p. 226. AS, p. 736. BHD1, p. 342. "Famous Players Present Paul McAllister," *MPW,* 27 Jun 1914, 1831.

McAlpin, Jean [actress] (b. 1872?–25 Aug 1928 [56]). m. (2) Archie Lockridge. "Jean McAlpin," *Variety,* 29 Aug 1928. AS, p. 736 (d. 19 Oct 1947, Hollywood CA).

McAlpine, Jane [actress] (b. 1896?–19 Oct 1947 [51], Long Branch NJ). AS, p. 736. BHD, p. 235. IFN, p. 189.

Macario, Erminio [actor] (b. Turin, Italy, 27 May 1902–26 Mar 1980 [77], Turin, Italy). AS, p. 698.

McArthur, Arthur [producer/agent] (b. 1885–3 May 1948 [63?], Los Angeles CA). m. Mildred Yorba, 15 Sep 1926, Placentia CA. AMD, p. 226. BHD2, p. 167. "Arthur McArthur Weds Mildred Yorba," *MPW,* 25 Sep 1926, 215.

McAtee, Clyde [actor/President of SAG] (b. 1880?–20 Feb 1947 [66], Woodland Hills CA). (Griffith.) "Clyde M'Atee," *NYT,* 22 Feb 1947, 13:3 (32-year film career). "Clyde McAtee," *Variety,* 26 Feb 1947 (age 67). AS, p. 736. BHD1, p. 343 (d. Calabasas CA). IFN, p. 189. Truitt, p. 220.

Macauley, Charles R. [cartoonist/writer]. No data found. AMD, p. 226. "Charles R. Macauley Making Pictures," *MPW,* 17 Oct 1914, 315. "New Cartoon Film Firm," *NYDM,* 23 Oct 1915, 25:1 (he "has recently obtained a patent for a new method of making animated cartoons which is said to allow the artist to work at top speed, and does away entirely with the laborious method previously used." To release a series to be known as Epic Cartoons.). "Macauley to Make Peace Pictures," *MPW,* 20 Jan 1917, 352.

McAuley, P.W. [scenarist] (b. 1881–6 Apr 1929 [48?], Los Angeles CA; suicide). AS, p. 736. BHD2, p. 167.

McAvoy, Charles [actor] (b. New York NY, 2 Apr 1885–20 Apr 1953 [68], New York NY). AS, p. 736.

McAvoy, May [actress] (b. New York NY, 18 Sep 1901–26 Apr 1984 [82], Sherman Oaks CA). m. Maurice Cleary, 1929 (d. 1973). (Fox, 1917; Paramount.) Herbert Mitgang, "May McAvoy, Star of 20's Silent Films; Role in 'Jazz Singer,'" *NYT,* 3 May 1984, D26:3 (d. LA CA, age 83). "Silent Era's May McAvoy Dies; Never Broke the Sound Barrier," *Variety,* 9 May 1984. AMD, p. 226. AS, p. 737. BHD1, p. 343 (b. 8 Sep). FFF, p. 55 (b. 8 Sep 1891). FSS, p. 196. HCH, p. 69. MH, p. 126 (b. 8 Sep 1891). "May McAvoy," SOS, pp. 110–35. "Realart Says 'The Wonder Girl' Is a Fitting Appellation for May McAvoy," *MPW,* 9 Jul 1921, 187. "May McAvoy, Realart's Latest Star, Wins Honor by Brains as Well as Pulchritude," *MPW,* 27 Aug 1921, 904. "Inspiration Signs May McAvoy," *MPW,* 13 Oct 1923, 560. Regina Cannon, "Is Screen Beauty a Matter of Make-Up? 'Yes!' Says May McAvoy," *MW,* 29 Mar 1924, 21, 40. "Pickw May McAvoy," *MPW,* 20 Sep 1924, 209. "May McAvoy an Arrow Star," *MPW,* 9 May 1925, 225. Doris Denbo, "Can Mae [sic] Do It?," *MPC,* Dec 1926, 34, 85. "May McAvoy Signs Up as Warner Star," *MPW,* 15 Jan 1927, 200. "Long Terms for McAvoy, Hyams," *MPW,* 24 Dec 1927, 10. Dorothy Calhoun, "Her Scandaless Reputation; May McAvoy Has Never Known the Delights of Notoriety," *MPC,* Dec 1928, 37, 84 ("May McAvoy has been in the movies for twelve years, and she has never been gossiped about."). William M. Drew, *Speaking of Silents* (Vestal NY: Vestal Press, Ltd., 1989), pp. 110–35.

McBan, Mickey [child actor] (b. Spokane WA, 27 Feb 1919). AMD, p. 226. Ragan 2, p. 1093. "Add Child Actor," *MPW,* 12 Jun 1926, 547.

McBride, Carl [actor/director] (b. Sioux City IA, 1893?–17 Dec 1937 [44], Los Angeles CA). (WB.) "Carl McBride," *Variety,* 22 Dec 1937. AS, p. 737. BHD2, p. 167.

MacBride, Donald Hugh [stage/film/TV actor] (b. Brooklyn NY, 23 Jun 1889–21 Jun 1957 [68], Los Angeles CA). m. Esther. (Paramount; MGM; WB.) "Donald M'Bride, Actor, 63, Dead; Stage, Screen and Television Performer Was Noted for Many Character Roles," *NYT,* 23 Jun 1957, 84:3 (age 63). "Donald MacBride," *Variety,* 26 Jun 1957. AS, p. 695 (McBride); AS, p. 737 (McBride). IFN, p. 186 (b. 1893). Truitt, pp. 220–21.

McBride, Edith Ethel [actress] (d. 10 Dec 1926, New York NY). AS, p. 737. BHD, p. 235.

MacBride, Olivia [actress] (b. Hemet CA, 1896–27 Aug 1976 [80?], Anaheim CA). BHD, p. 236.

McCabe, George F. [stage/film actor] (b. Chicago IL, 1865?–17 Dec 1917 [52?], Bellview NY). "Obituary Notes," *NYT,* 18 Dec 1917, 15:5 ("GEORGE F. McCABE, a character actor who had appeared recently in motion pictures, died yesterday at his home, 570 West 180th Street."). "George F. McCabe," *Variety,* 21 Dec 1917, p. 21. AS, p. 737.

McCabe, Harry [actor] (b. Chicago IL, 1880–11 Feb 1925 [44], Los Angeles CA; complications after operations). m. Evelyn McKibben, 8 Feb 1925. (Selig.) "Harry McCabe," *Variety,* 18 Feb 1925. AS, p. 737. BHD, p. 236 (b. 1879). IFN, p. 189.

McCabe, John [actor] (b. Cheyenne WY, 1879?–19 Jun 1929 [50], Buffalo NY; acute alcoholism). (Reliance.) "John McCabe, Veteran, Found Dead in Buffalo," *Variety,* 26 Jun 1929. AMD, p. 226. AS, p. 737. BHD, p. 236. IFN, p. 189. Hugh Hoffman, "In the Catskills with Reliance," *MPW,* 24 Apr 1912, 751.

McCabe, May North [stage/film actress] (*née* May North, b. Indianapolis IN, 1873?–22 Jun 1949 [76], New York NY). m. Jack McCabe (d. 1917). "Miss May N. M'Cabe, Retired Actress, 76," *NYT,* 24 Jun 1949, 23:6. "May McCabe," *Variety,* 29 Jun 1949. BHD, p. 236. IFN, p. 189. SD. Truitt, p. 221.

McCall, Lizzie [stage/film actress] (b. Buffalo NY, 4 Jul 1857–18 Apr 1942 [84], Bronx NY). (Stage debut, 1877.) "Lizzie McCall," *Variety,* 22 Apr 1942. AS, p. 737 (b. 14 Jul). BHD, p. 236. 1983 WWOS.

McCall, William [actor] (b. Delavan IL, 19 May 1870–10 Jan 1938 [67], Los Angeles CA). "William McCall," *Variety,* 19 Jan 1938. AS, p. 737. BHD1, p. 343. IFN, p. 189. Truitt, p. 221 (b. 1879). George A. Katchmer, "Remembering the Great Silents," *CI,* 175 (Jan 1990), C5.

McCallum, Anson L. [producer] (d. 25 Oct 1920). BHD2, p. 168.

McCallum, John A. [actor] (b. England, 1 Mar 1863–19 Feb 1923 [59], Los Angeles CA). AS, p. 737. BHD, p. 236. IFN, p. 189.

McCann, Charles Andrew [actor] (b. Baltimore MD, 1874?–28 Sep 1927 [53], Paris, France; heart attack). "Charles Andrew McCann," *Variety,* 5 and 26 Oct 1927 (debuted in Theda Bara's *The Tiger Woman*). AS, p. 737. BHD, p. 236. Truitt, p. 221.

McCardell, Roy Larcom [journalist/writer/scenarist] (b. Hagerstown MD, 30 Jun 1870). (Biograph, 1898.) AMD, p. 226. AS, p. 737. BHD2, p. 168. Roy Larcom McCardell, "The Chorus Girl Deplores the Moving Pictures'

Triumph Over Drama," *MPW,* II, 11 Apr 1908, 321–22. "The First Photoplaywright," *MPW,* 14 Dec 1912, 1075. Epes Winthrop Sargent, "The Photoplaywright," *MPW,* 14 Feb 1914, 802–03. Epes Winthrop Sargent, "The Literary Side of Pictures," *MPW,* 11 Jul 1914, 199 (McCardell was hired as the first story editor at Biograph in 1898 at $150 a week). "McCardell Wins Another Prize," *MPW,* 14 Nov 1914, 942. "Roy L. McCardell; Famous Scenario Writer," *MPS,* 27 Nov 1914, 25 (McCardell was the first salaried scenario writer, with Mutoscope and Biograph, 1900–1901). "Picking the Winner," *MPW,* 29 May 1915, 1419–20. "Getting It Right," *MPW,* 19 Jun 1915, 1925. Roy Larcom McCardell, "Writing for the Screen," *MPW,* 14 Aug 1915, 1147–48. "Roy McCardell Visits New York," *MPW,* 21 Aug 1915, 1320. "Roy Larcom McCardell Objects," *MPW,* 6 Nov 1915, 1115. "McCardell to Write for Horsley," *MPW,* 18 Dec 1915, 2156. "Pictures to Tell Story of Fire Prevention," *MPW,* 1 Apr 1916, 109. Roy Larcom McCardell, "A Business Without Brains," *MPW,* 21 Jul 1917, 401–02. "Gaiety Signs Roy Larcom McCardell for the Taylor Holmes Shorts," *MPW,* 26 Feb 1927, 649. Edward Azlant, "Screenwriting for the early silent film: forgotten pioneers, 1897–1911," *Film History,* 9 (1997), 228–56 (In 1900 McCardell published a book of light verse, *Olde Love and Lavender & Other Verses,* dedicated to H.N. Marvin of the Biograph. "He brought to film concrete experience in the creation of comic strips, popular Broadway musicals and comedies, newspaper vignettes and serials, poetry, narrative photography, and popular fiction...In all this he is not only early, but also exemplary of the pioneer scenarist who has a composite of skills and interests related to popular culture.").

McCarey, Leo (brother of **Ray McCarey**) [director/producer/scenarist] (*né* Thomas Leo McCarey, b. Los Angeles CA, 30 Oct 1897?–5 Jul 1969 [71], Santa Monica CA; emphysema). m. Stella Martin. "Leo McCarey, Director, Is Dead; Won Oscars for 'Going My Way'; Was Also a Winner in 1937 of Academy Award for 'The Awful Truth,'" *NYT,* 6 Jul 1969, 45:1. "Leo McCarey," *Variety,* 9 Jul 1969. AMD, p. 226. BHD2, p. 168 (b. 1898). IFN, p. 189. SD. "Long Contract for McCarey," *MPW,* 27 Jun 1925, 991. "Leo McCarey Rewarded," *MPW,* 8 Aug 1925, 650. "An Irishman's Jewish Films," *MPW,* 9 Apr 1927, 573. "This Irishman Directs Roach's Jew Comedies," *MPW,* 23 Apr 1927, 736. "Supervising Director," *MPW,* 17 Sep 1927, 151. "Leo McCarey on Roach Contract," *MPW,* 31 Dec 1927, 26.

McCarey, Ray (brother of **Leo McCarey**) [director] (*né* Raymond Bennett McCarey, b. Los Angeles CA, 6 Sep 1898–1 Dec 1948 [50], Los Angeles CA). (Paramount, 1918; Pathé; RKO; Sennett.) "Ray McCarey," *Variety,* 8 Dec 1948. AS, pp. 738–39. BHD2, p. 168 (b. 1904). IFN, p. 189.

McCarger, Emery [studio musician] (b. 1891?–6 Feb 1926 [35], Los Angeles CA; brain tumor). "Emery M'Carger," *Variety,* 10 Feb 1926. AS, p. 738.

McCarroll, Frank [actor] (b. MN, 5 Sep 1892–9 Mar 1954 [61], Burbank CA). AS, p. 738.

McCarthy, Charles E. [publicist] (b. Wareham MA, 1 Apr 1891–4 Jun 1974 [83], Riuverside CA; heart failure). m. Mary. (Fox; FP-L.) "Charles E. McCarthy," *Variety,* 12 Jun 1974, p. 55:1. AMD, p. 226. BHD2, p. 168. "Charles E. McCarthy Joins Paramount-Briggs," *MPW,* 7 Jun 1919, 1500.

McCarthy, Earl [actor] (b. Ft. Wayne IN, 1906–28 May 1933 [27], Los Angeles CA; heart attack). AS, p. 738. BHD1, p. 343. IFN, p. 189.

McCarthy, Henry [scenarist/director] (b. San Francisco CA, 30 Jan 1881?–19 Jul 1954 [73], Los Angeles CA). "Henry McCarthy," *Variety,* 28 Jul 1954. AS, p. 738 (b. 1882). BHD2, p. 168 (b. 20 Jan 1882). FDY, p. 433.

McCarthy, John P. [director] (b. San Francisco CA, 17 Mar 1885–4 Sep 1962 [77], Pasadena CA; coronary thrombosis). (Griffith; 2nd National; Russell Productions; Columbia; Pathé; MGM; Monogram; Trem Carr Productions.) "John P. McCarthy," *Variety,* 12 Sep 1962 (age 78) (directed *Out of the Dust, Pals* and *Vanishing Hoofs*). AMD, p. 226. AS, p. 738. BHD1, p. 343; BHD2, p. 168. IFN, p. 189. "McCarthy to Remain," *MPW,* 18 Jun 1927, 512.

McCarthy, Joseph [lyricist] (*né* Thomas Joseph McCarthy, b. Summerville MA, 27 Sep 1885–18 Dec 1943 [58], New York NY). m. Dorothy. "Joseph M'Carthy, a Lyricist, 58, Dies; Ex-Director of ASCAP Wrote 'Alice Blue Gown,' Several Musicals and Films," *NYT,* 19 Dec 1943, 49:1 (belonged to the Lambs; wrote the lyrics for *You Made Me Love You; Chasing Rainbows; Happy Days; They Go Wild, Simply Wild Over Me; Polly Put the Kettle On; Crying; What Do You Want to Make Those Eyes at Me For?;* and *Ireland Must Be Heaven*). "Joseph McCarthy," *Variety,* 22 Dec 1943 (age 53). AS, p. 738 (b. Malden MA, 1895; d. 13 Dec). BHD2, p. 168 (b. Malden, 1890).

McCarthy, Justin Huntley [actor] (b. England, 1860–21 Mar 1936 [76?], Putney, England). AS, p. 738.

McCarthy, Lawrence J. [stage/film actor] (b. Roxbury MA, 1861?–15 Apr 1918 [57], Brookline MA). "Lawrence J. McCarthy," *Variety,* 26 Apr 1918. AS, p. 738. SD.

McCarthy, Lewis [executive] (d. 11 Feb 1921). BHD2, p. 168.

McCarthy, Lillian [stage/film actress] (b. Cheltenham, Gloucestershire, England, 22 Sep 1875–15 Apr 1960 [84], London, England). "Lilian McCarthy," *Variety,* 20 Apr 1960, p. 159:3. BHD, p. 236 (Lillah McCarthy).

McCarthy, Myles [actor/director/scenarist] (b. Toronto, Ontario, Canada, 27 Apr 1874–27 Sep 1928 [54], Los Angeles CA). m. Ada Wolcott. "Myles McCarthy," *Variety,* 10 Oct 1928. AMD, p. 226. AS, p. 738. BHD, p. 236; BHD2, p. 168. IFN, p. 189. Truitt, p. 221. "Picture Players' Insurance," *MPW,* 11 Dec 1915, 1998.

McCarthy, Thomas J. [director] (b. 1865–23 Mar 1918 [53?]). BHD2, p. 168.

McCauley, Edna [actress] (b. Detroit MI, 1890–28 Jan 1919 [28?], Rome, Italy; typhoid fever). (FP-L.) "Edna McCauley," *Variety,* 7 Feb 1919. AS, p. 738. BHD, p. 236. IFN, p. 189 (d. 1918).

McCauley, Jack [actor] (*né* John B. McCauley, b. NY, 1901–13 Jun 1980 [79?], Menlo Park CA). AS, p. 738. BHD, p. 236.

McCay, Neil (brother of James Halfpenny) (b. 1869?–10 Apr 1933 [64], Englewood NJ). "Neil McCay," *Variety,* 18 Apr 1933. BHD, p. 236.

McCay, Winsor Zenis [animator] (b. Spring Lake MI, 26 Sep 1871–26 Jul 1934 [62?], Sheepshead Bay, Brooklyn NY). m. Maude Buford (d. 1949). "Mrs. Winsor M'Cay," *NYT,* 1 Mar 1949, 25:3 (Mrs. Maude Buford McCay; d. 27 Feb 1949, Peekskill NY). AS, p. 738. BHD, p. 236; BHD2, p. 168 (b. 1872). John Canamaker, "Winsor McKay," *Film Comment,* Jan/Feb 1975, 44–47. Donald Crafton, *Before Mickey; The Animated Film 1898–1928* (Cambridge MA: The MIT Press, 1984), p. 90.

McClain, Billy [actor] (b. IN, 15 Sep 1857?–28 Jan 1950 [93], Los Angeles CA; in a fire). "Billy McClain," *Variety,* 1 Feb 1950. AS, pp. 738–39 (b. 1864). IFN, p. 189 (b. 1884).

McClary, Clyde [actor] (b. Minneaplis MN, 10 Jul 1888–30 Jun 1939 [50], Los Angeles CA; crushed by a tank while filming *In Old Monterey*). AS, p. 739 (b. 1894). BHD1, p. 344. George A. Katchmer, "Remembering the Great Silents," *CI,* 231 (Sep 1994), 49.

McClellan, Hurd [actor/stuntman] (d. 20 Apr 1933, Los Angeles CA; in an accident during filming). AS, p. 739.

McClellan, Robert Francis [actor] (b. 1888–20 Mar 1973 [84?]). BHD, p. 236.

McClelland, Donald [actor] (b. New York NY, 29 Sep 1903–15 Nov 1955 [52], New York NY). BHD, p. 236.

McClintic, Guthrie [director] (b. Seattle WA, 3 Aug 1893). AS, p. 739.

McCloskey, Elizabeth Hayward [actress] (b. 1870?–8 Jan 1942 [71?], Los Angeles CA). "Elizabeth H. McCloskey," *Variety,* 21 Jan 1942 (began ca. 1920). AS, p. 739. BHD, p. 236 (b. 1872). IFN, p. 189 (age 70). Truitt, p. 221.

McCloskey, Justin H. [assistant director] (b. Orange NJ, 1887–1 Aug 1935 [48?], Los Angeles CA). m. **Eileen Sedgwick** (d. 1991). BHD2, p. 168.

McCloskey, Lawrence [title writer/scenarist]. No data found. (Lubin.) AMD, p. 226. Edwin Arthur, "Wrinkles on Photoplay Writing; A Straight-from-the-Shoulder Talk, Full of Hints on the Formation and Expression of Photoplay Plots," *NYDM,* 14 Jan 1914, 53 (photos of McCloskey; Calder Johnstone, Universal; and Frank E. Wood, Mutual). "McCloskey to Title Pearson Film," *MPW,* 2 Aug 1919, 688.

McClosky, Helen [actress] (b.1901?–1927 [26]; jumped to her death). AMD, p. 226. "Actress Jumps to Death," *MPW,* 22 Oct 1927, 484.

McClung, Hugh C. [cinematographer/director] (b. Brenham TX, 16 Dec 1874–5 Jan 1946 [71], Los Angeles CA). BHD2, p. 168.

McClure, Bud [actor] (b. Ukiah CA, 21 Feb 1883–2 Nov 1942 [59], No. Hollywood CA). "Bud McClure," *Variety,* 11 Nov 1942. AS, p. 739 (b, 1886). BHD1, p. 344. IFN, p. 189.

McClure, Frank [actor] (b. 1895–23 Jan 1960 [64?], Los Angeles CA). BHD, p. 236.

McClure, Gladys (sister of Adrienne Ames and Linda March) [child actress] (b. Ft. Worth TX, 1915?–15 Dec 1933 [18], near San Francisco CA; car accident). IFN, p. 189. Ragan 2, p. 1098.

McClure, Irene [actress] (d. 4 Sep 1928, near Bakersfield CA; injuries from auto accident). "Irene McClure," *Variety,* 12 Sep 1928. AS, p. 739. BHD, p. 236. IFN, p. 190. Truitt, p. 221.

Maccollum, Barry [actor] (b. Ireland, 6 Apr 1889–22 Feb 1971 [81], West Los Angeles CA). AS, p. 701 (Macollum). BHD, p. 242.

McCollum, H.H. [actor] (b. Wilkes-Barre PA, 1887?–19 Dec 1938 [51?], New York NY). m. playwright Lottie M. Meaney (wrote *Pay Day*),

Little Church Around the Corner, NYC, 1916. (Kleine.) AMD, p. 226. BHD, p. 236. IFN, p. 190. "H.H. McCollum," *MPW,* 8 Apr 1916, 273. "H.H. McCollum Marries Authoress," *MPW,* 29 Apr 1916, 815:2.

McComas, Carroll [vaudeville/film actress] (b. Albuquerque NM, 27 Jun 1886–9 Nov 1962 [76], New York NY [Carroll Gunn, Death Certificate Index No. 23661]). m. (1) Walter Enright, 1922–28; (2) Selskarr M. Gunn. "Carroll McComas Dies at 76; Actress Began Career in 1907; Star of 'Miss Lulu Bett' Sang and Whistled in Vaudeville—Seen in 'Our Town,'" *NYT,* 10 Nov 1962, 25:4. "Carroll McComas," *Variety,* 14 Nov 1962. AMD, p. 226. AS, p. 739 (b. 1884). BHD1, p. 344. IFN, p. 190. Ragan 2, p. 809. SD. Truitt, p. 221. "Miss Carroll McComas," *NYDM,* 26 May 1915, 4:2 (photo; in *Inside the Lines* on stage). "Edison Has a House Warming," *NYDM,* 18 Dec 1915, 23:4 (performed a singing and whistling act in vaudeville and musical comedy). "Carroll McComas, Edison Star," *MPW,* 25 Dec 1915, 2377.

McComas, Francis [artist]. No data found. AMD, p. 226. "Francis McComas Joins Famous Players," *MPW,* 16 Jun 1923, 591.

McComas, Kendall (Breezy Brisbane) [actor] (b. Holton KS, 29 Oct 1916–15 Oct 1981 [64], Lake Isabella CA). BHD, p. 236.

McComas, Lilas [actress] (b. 1906–13 Jun 1936 [30?], Los Angeles CA; auto accident). AMD, p. 227. AS, p. 739 (Lila McComas). "Undergoes Operation," *MPW,* 23 Jul 1927, 239:2 ("the result of an accident during the filming of a picture a few months ago.").

McComas, Ralph C. [actor] (b. CA, 8 Sep 1889–13 Jul 1924 [34], San Francisco CA; heart attack). AS, p. 739 (d. San Luis Obispo CA). BHD, p. 236.

McComb, Kate [actress] (*née* Kathleen Barry Addison, b. 1871–15 Apr 1959 [88?], New York NY). AS, p. 739.

McConaughy, J.W. [title writer]. No data found. FDY, p. 447.

McConnell, Gladys [actress: Wampas Star, 1927] (b. Oklahoma City OK, 22 Oct 1905–4 Mar 1979 [73], Los Angeles CA). AMD, p. 227. AS, p. 739 (b. 1907). BHD1, p. 344 (b. 1907; d. Fullerton CA). BR, pp. 178–79. IFN, p. 190 (b. 1907). "Fox Films Signs Gladys McConnell," *MPW,* 6 Mar 1926, 31. "Langdon Selects New Leading Lady," *MPW,* 14 May 1927, 97.

McConnell, Guy W. [director/scenarist] (b. Wrightsville PA, 1878?–4 Feb 1948 [70], Washington DC). (Wholesome Films Corp., Chicago IL). "Guy W. M'Connell," *NYT,* 7 Feb 1948, 15:4. AMD, p. 227. AS, p. 739. BHD2, p. 168. "McConnell to Write Child Welfare Subject," *MPW,* 5 May 1917, 785. "New Wholesome Films Official," *Motography,* 11 Aug 1917, 298 (directed Ralph Morgan in *The Penny Philanthropist*). "Guy McConnell wi Wholesome Films," *MPW,* 18 Aug 1917, 1057.

McConnell, Lulu [stage/film/radio actress] (b. Kansas City MO, 8 Apr 1882–9 Oct 1962 [80], Los Angeles CA; cancer). m. **Grant M. Simpson** (d. 1932). "Lulu M'Connell, Comedienne, Dies; Actress, 80, Played in Radio—Was Vaudeville Star," *NYT,* 11 Oct 1962, 39:1. "Lulu McConnell," *Variety,* 17 Oct 1962 (m. Grant Simmons). AS, p. 739. IFN, p. 190.

McConnell, Mollie [stage/film actress] (stage pseudonym, Moddlie Sherwood, *nee?,* b. Chicago IL, 24 Sep 1865–9 Dec 1920 [55], Los Angeles CA). m. William A. McConnell, 1890 (d. 1905); **Sherwood McDonald** (d. 1968). (Universal, May 1913; Balboa, 1913; Metro.) "Molly M'Connell," *Variety,* 17 Dec 1920 (d. 10 Dec). AMD, p. 227. AS, p. 739. BHD, p. 236 (b. IN). IFN, p. 190 (b. IN). Jura, pp. 128–32. Truitt, p. 221. "Mrs. McConnell Playing with Metro," *MPW,* 8 Jun 1918, 1407. "Obituary," *MPW,* 1 Jan 1921, 93. Cal York, "Plays and Players," *Photoplay,* Mar 1921, 80 (died in Los Angeles "recently. She was a popular portrayer of 'mother' and grande dame roles."). Billy H. Doyle, "Lost Players," *CI,* 15 (Mar 1988), 53.

McConnell, Oviatt [scenarist] (b. 1898–5 Oct 1953 [55?], New York NY). AS, p. 739.

McConville, Bernard [scenarist]. No data found. AMD, p. 227. FDY, p. 433. KOM, pp. 152–53. "Bernard McConville with Universal," *MPW,* 8 Jun 1918, 1411. "Joins Universal," *MPW,* 1 Sep 1923, 35. "Bernard McConville Signed," *MPW,* 21 Mar 1925, 283.

McCord, Harold [film editor] (b. New York NY, 30 Jul 1893–3 Nov 1957 [64], Los Angeles CA; cerebral hemorrhage). "Harold McCord," *Variety,* 13 Nov 1957 (head of WB editing department). BHD2, p. 168.

McCord, Lewis [stage/film actor] (*né* Landis Wanbaugh, b. Bainbridge PA, 1868?–16 Feb 1911 [42], New York NY; Bright's disease). m. **Bertha** St. Clair (d. 1917). "Lewis McCord," *Variety,* 25 Feb 1911. AS, p. 739. SD.

McCord, Mrs. Lewis [stage/film actress] (*née* Bertha St. Clair?, b. Philadelphia PA–d. 24 Dec 1917, Harrisburg PA; pleuro pneumonia and diabetes). m. **Lewis McCord** (d. 1911). "Mrs. Lewis McCord," *Variety,* 28 Dec 1917 (character player). AS, p. 739. BHD, p. 236. IFN, p. 190.

McCord, Ted D. [cinematographer] (b. Sullivan County IN, 1900?–19 Jan 1976 [75], Glendale CA; cancer). m. Ethel. (Hobart Bosworth Studio; WB.) "Ted McCord, Cameraman, Was Nominated for 3 Oscars," *NYT,* 26 Jan 1976, 26:2 (AA nominations for *The Sound of Music; Two for the Seasaw;* and *Johnny Belinda*). "Ted McCord," *Variety,* 28 Jan 1976 (lensed *East of Eden*). AS, p. 739 (b. 1898). FDY, p. 461.

McCord, Vera [actress] (b. 1877–3 Mar 1949 [71?], New York NY). BHD, p. 236.

McCormack, Billie (daughter of **Hank Harvey**) [actress] (b. 1876?–31 Jan 1935 [58?], Santa Monica CA). "Billie McCormack [Mrs. Blanche E. Burke]," *Variety,* 5 Feb 1935. AS, p. 739 (d. 1 Feb). BHD1, p. 345.

McCormack, Frank [actor/director] (b. Washington DC, 1876?–22 May 1941 [65], CT). "Frank McCormack," *Variety,* 4 Jun 1941. AMD, p. 227. AS, p. 739. BHD1, p. 345. IFN, p. 190. "Frank McCormack Joins Powell," *MPW,* 10 Feb 1917, 850.

McCormack, John [actor/singer] (b. Athlone, Ireland, 14 Jun 1884–16 Sep 1945 [61], Booterstown, Ireland). AS, pp. 739–40.

McCormick, Alyce [stage/film actress] (aka Joy Auburn, *née* Alyce McCornick, b. Chicago IL, 13 Jan 1901–6 Jan 1932 [30], Los Angeles CA; pneumonia). (Pathé.) "Alyce McCormick Dies; Film and Stage Player Started as Street Singer in Omaha," *Variety,* 12 Jan 1932. AS, p. 740 (b. 8 Feb). BHD1, p. 345. IFN, p. 190. Truitt, p. 221. 1983 WWOS (b. 1904).

McCormick, F.J. [actor] (*né* Peter Judge, b. Skerries, Ireland, 1891–24 Apr 1947 [56?], Dublin, Ireland). AS, p. 740.

McCormick, John E. [general manager of First National] (b. 1894?–3 May 1961 [67], Los Angeles CA; heart attack). m. (1) **Colleen Moore**, 18 Aug 1923 (d. 1988); (2) Janet Gattis, Honolulu HI. "John McCormick," *Variety,* 10 May 1961 (began in 1914). AMD, p. 227. "Colleen Moore Marries," *MPW,* 1 Sep 1923, 57. "McCormick General Manager of First National on Coast," *MPW,* 1 Aug 1925, 504. "John McCormick to N.Y.," *MPW,* 18 Sep 1926, 157. "McCormick Is Pleased About the Big Merger," *MPW,* 19 Mar 1927, 181. John E. McCormick, "The Trend of Production," *MPW,* 9 Apr 1927, 554. Tom Waller, "McCormick Resigns from First National; Watterson Rothacker Slated for Position," *MPW,* 28 May 1927, 247, 255. Paul Paige, "Close-Ups and Fade-Outs," *Paris and Hollywood Screen Secrets Magazine,* Aug 1927, 98 (general manager for seven years, McCormick resigned after a convention of First National officials in Hollywood. "It is believed…that McCormack [sic] resented too much interference with his position as general manager. Restrictions imposed upon the Burbank studio upon the recent affiliation of eastern bankers with First National are also believed to have been a factor.").

McCormick, Merrill [actor] (*né* William Merrill McCormick, b. Denver CO, 5 Feb 1892–19 Aug 1953 [61], San Gabriel CA; heart attack). "William M. McCormack," *Variety,* 26 Aug 1953 (age 62; "pioneer screen actor"). AS, p. 740. BHD1, p. 345. IFN, p. 190. Truitt, p. 221. George Katchmer, "Remembering the Great Silents," *CI,* 206 (Aug 1992), 39–40.

McCormick, S. Barret [director/scenarist] (b. Dewitt MO, 1890?–28 Sep 1965 [75], Denver CO). "S. Barret McCormick," *Variety,* 6 Oct 1965. AS, p. 740. BHD2, p. 169.

McCosh, Rufus [title writer]. No data found. FDY, p. 447.

Macowan, Norman [actor] (b. St. Andres, Scotland, 2 Jan 1877–31 Dec 1961 [84], Hastings, England). AS, p. 701.

McCoy, Frank [producer] (b. 1888–16 Jan 1947 [58?], New York NY). AS, p. 740.

McCoy, George N. [scenarist] (b. Milwaukee WI, 1891–18 Mar 1939 [48?], Los Angeles CA; heart attack). AS, p. 740. BHD2, p. 169.

McCoy, Gertrude [actress] (*née* Gertrude Lyon, b. Sugar Valley GA, 30 Jun 1890–17 Jul 1967 [77], Atlanta GA). m. **Duncan McRae**, 1919 (d. 1931). (Edison.) "Gertrude McCoy," *Variety,* 26 Jul 1967 (modeled as a Gibson Girl, then did extra work in films). AMD, p. 227. AS, p. 740. BHD, p. 237. IFN, p. 190. 1921 Directory, p. 232 (b. Rome GA). Truitt, pp. 221–22. "Gertrude McCoy Meets with Accident," *MPW,* 19 Sep 1914, 1658. "Biographies of Popular Players," *Motion Picture Magazine,* Feb 1915, 108–09. "Gertrude McCoy," *MPW,* 13 Mar 1915, 1609. "Gertrude McCoy in Double Role," *MPW,* 1 May 1915, 734. "*Will* Head Plimpton Forces," *MPW,* 23 Oct 1915, 589. "Baltimore Has Gertrude McCoy Theater," *MPW,* 13 Nov 1915, 1284.

McCoy, Harry [actor: Keystone Cop; Hallroom Boys series/director/scenarist/composer] (b. Philadelphia PA, 10 Dec 1893–1 Sep 1937 [43], Los Angeles CA; heart attack). (Sennett.) "Harry M'Coy; Actor and Director in the Films Composed

'Pagan Love Song,'" *NYT,* 2 Sep 1937, 21:4 (was Mabel Normand's first leading man). "Harry McCoy," *Variety,* 8 Sep 1937. AMD, p. 227. AS, p. 740. BHD1, p. 345; BHD2, p. 169. FDY, p. 433. IFN, p. 190. Truitt, p. 222. "Younger Keystoners," *MPW,* 5 Feb 1916, 783. "Harry McCoy," *MPW,* 24 Feb 1917, 1183. "McCoy to Co-Star," *MPW,* 8 Dec 1923, 575.

McCoy, Horace [scenarist/novelist] (b. Pegram TN, 14 Apr 1897–16 Dec 1955 [58], Beverly Hills CA; heart ailment). "Horace McCoy," *Variety,* 21 Dec 1955, p. 55:2. AS, p. 740. BHD, p. 237; BHD2, p. 169 (b. 1903). IFN, p. 190.

McCoy, "Kid." *See* Selby, Norman.

McCoy, Ruby [actress]. No data found. AMD, p. 227. "Ruby McCoy in Comedy," *MPW,* 24 Sep 1927, 221.

McCoy, Tim [film/TV actor] (*né* Timothy John Fitzgerald McCoy, b. Saginaw MI, 10 Apr 1891–29 Jan 1978 [86], Nogales AZ). m. actress Agnes Miller (children: Gerald, b. 30 May 1918, Fort Riley KS, D'Arcy, and Rita); Inga Marie Arvad, 1947 (d. 1973). With Ronald McCoy, *Tim McCoy Remembers the West; An Autobiography* (Lincoln NB: University of Nebraska Press, 1988). (MGM; Universal; Columbia; Puritan Pictures; Victory Pictures; PRC; Monogram.) A.H. Weiler, "Col. Tim M'Coy, 86; Cowboy Movie Star; Real-Life Indian Expert, Cowhand and Soldier Appeared in More Than 80 Films in 45 Years," *NYT,* 31 Jan 1978, 30:3. "Tim McCoy," *Variety,* 1 Feb 1978. AMD, p. 227. AS, p. 740 (d. Fort Huachuca AZ). BHD1, p. 345. FSS, p. 197. IFN, p. 190. SD. Josephine MacDowell, "Colonel Tim McCoy, 'High Eagle'; A Former Calvary Officer Is Using Genuine American Indians in a Series of Films," *Cinema Arts,* V (Nov 1926), 32, 49, 51. "Tim McCoy to Get His 'Chance,'" *MPW,* 23 Jul 1927, 253. Charles Paton, "Heap Big Injun Make Much Hokum; Colonel Tim McCoy Defends the Red Man," *MPC,* Oct 1927, 38, 82. Kitty Hubert, "Making 'Wyoming,' *Screenland,* Dec 1927, 34–35, 100. Mike Newton, "Col. Tim McCoy: Man of Destiny," *CI,* 279 (Sep 1998), 34–37. Mike Newton, "Col. Tim McCoy: Man of Destiny," *CI,* 279 (Sep 1998), 34–37.

McCray, Roy H. [director]. No data found. AMD, p. 227. "McCray Director of Joker Company," *MPW,* 24 Apr 1915, 565.

McCrea, Joel [actor] (b. So. Pasadena CA, 5 Nov 1905–20 Oct 1990 [84], Woodland Hills CA). m. Frances Dee (b. 26 Nov 1907; son, Jody McCrea, b. 6 Sep 1934). Peter B. Flint, "Joel McCrea, Actor, Dies at 84; A Casual, Amiable Leading Man," *NYT,* 21 Oct 1990, 38:1. Joseph McBride, "Amiable Comedy, Western Star Joel McCrea Is Dead at 84," *Variety,* 29 Oct 1990, pp. 14–15. "Cowboy Actor Joel McCrea Dies at 84," *LA Times,* 21 Oct 1990, A1:4. AS, p. 740. BHD1, p. 345 (b. LA CA). J. Eugene Chrisman, "The Great Lover of Hollywood Is Fed Up with Fame," *Movie Classic,* Nov 1931, 19, 74. Jimmie Hicks, "Joel McCrea," Part 1, *FIR,* XLII, Oct 1991, 314–23; Part 2, Nov/Dec 1991, 392–403.

McCree, [Mr.] Junie [actor/lyricist/President of the White Rats, 1909–13] (*né* Gonzalvo Macrillo, b. Toledo OH, 15 Feb 1865–13 Jan 1918 [52], New York NY; apoplexy). "Junie McCree Dies; Actor and Writer of Lyrics Expires Suddenly in His Home Here," *NYT,* 14 Jan 1918, 11:4 (age 53). "Junie McCree," *Variety,* 18 Jan 1918. ASCAP 66, p. 491. BHD2, p. 169 (d. 13 Jun).

McCulley, Arthur Johnston [novelist/playwright/scenarist] (b. IL, 2 Feb 1883–23 Nov 1958 [75], Los Angeles CA). "Johnston McCulley," *Variety,* 26 Nov 1958, p. 79:3 (created "Zorro"). AMD, p. 227. AS, p. 740. BHD2, p. 169. "Johnston McCulley Praises Picture Version of His Story by Universal," *MPW,* 6 Dec 1919, 688. "McCulley Signed," *MPW,* 23 Apr 1927, 732 (wrote *The Mark of Zorro*).

McCulley, W.T. [actor]. No data found. George A. Katchmer, "Remembering the Great Silents," *CI,* 231 (Sep 1994), 49.

McCulloch, Campbell [publicist] (b. 1880–6 Mar 1941 [61?], Los Angeles CA). AMD, p. 227. BHD2, p. 169 (McCullogh). "Campbell MacCulloch with Triangle," *MPW,* 11 Sep 1915, 1810.

McCullough, E.J. [actor] (d. 9 Sep 1913, near Pittsburgh PA). "E.J. McCullough," *Variety,* 19 Sep 1913.

McCullough, Paul T. [actor] (b. Springfield OH, 1883–25 Mar 1936 [53?], Boston MA; suicide with a razor). AS, p. 740 (d. Medford MA). BHD1, p. 345.

McCullough, Philo M. [stage/film actor] (b. San Bernardino CA, 16 Jun 1893–5 Jun 1981 [87], Burbank CA). m. **Laura Anson** (d. 1968). "Philo McCullough," *Variety,* 17 Jun 1981. AS, p. 740 (b. 1890). BHD1, p. 345. MH, p. 126 (b. San Brendo CA). 1921 Directory, p. 270 (b. San Brendo CA). '83 WWOS (b. 1890). SD.

McCullough, Ralph [actor] (b. Laramie WY, 2 Sep 1895–25 Dec 1943 [48], Los Angeles CA). AS, p. 740. BHD1, p. 345. IFN, p. 190. George A. Katchmer, "Remembering the Great Silents," *CI,* 178 (Apr 1990), 58–59.

McCullum, Bartley [stage/film actor] (b. Portland ME?–d. 25 Mar 1916, St. John's Hospital, Philadelphia PA). (Lubin.) "Bartlet McCullum," *Variety,* 7 Apr 1916 ("He had been in pictures for four years."). AS, p. 740. BHD, p. 237 (Bartlett McCullum). "Two Lubin Players Dead," *MPW,* 15 Apr 1916, 431:2 (played in *Way Down East* for 10 years).

McCutcheon, George Barr [actor/scenarist] (b. Tippecanoe County IN, 26 Jul 1866–23 Oct 1928 [62], New York NY; heart attack). AS, p. 740. BHD, p. 237; BHD2, p. 169. "Film Famous Authors; Vitagraph Company Prepares Novel Series for Authors' League Benefit," *NYDM,* 28 Jan 1914, 30:4.

McCutcheon, Wallace [stage/film actor/cameraman] (b. New York NY, 23 Dec 1880?–27 Jan 1928 [47], Los Angeles CA; suicide by shooting). m. **Pearl White**, 1919–21 (d. 1938). "Wallace M'Cutcheon Suicide in Hollywood; Broadway Actor, World War Major and Former Husband of Pearl White," *NYT,* 28 Jan 1928, 8:8 (age 45). "Wallace M'Cutcheon Suicide by Shooting; 'Have a Drink' Note Found Under Gin Bottle in Hotel Room," *Variety,* 1 Feb 1928. AMD, p. 227. AS, p. 741. BHD, p. 237; BHD2, p. 169 (b. 1894). IFN, p. 190 (b. 1894). Truitt, p. 190. WWVC, p. 88. "Schenck Engages McCutcheon," *MPW,* 23 Aug 1919, 1112. "Wallace McCutcheon, Three Year War Veteran, Carries Important Part in 'The Black Secret,'" *MPW,* 20 Sep 1919, 1815. Ed Wyatt, "Was The Great Train Robbery Really the First Western?," *CI,* 287 (May 1999), 35 (suggests that *Kit Carson,* AB&N, Oct 1903, was the first western).

McCutcheon, Wallace, Jr. [actor] (b. NY, 23 Dec 1894–27 Jan 1928 [33], Los Angeles CA). BHD2, p. 169.

McDaniel, George M. [stage/film actor/singer] (b. Atlanta GA, 1886?–20 Aug 1944 [58], San Fernando CA). m. twice: Alice Lohr. "George M'Daniel, Film, Stage Actor; Star of 'Shepherd of Hills' Dies—Sang with Victor Herbert Light Opera Group Here," *NYT,* 21 Aug 1944, 15:6. "George McDaniel," *Variety,* 23 Aug 1944. AS, p. 741. BHD, p. 237 (b. 1885). IFN, p. 190. Truitt, p. 222. George Katchmer, "George McDaniel," *CI,* 230 (Aug 1994), 39.

McDaniel, Sam[muel] Rufus [actor] (b. Columbus KS, 28 Jan 1886–24 Sep 1962 [76], Woodland Hills CA). AS, p. 741.

McDermott, John W. [actor/director/scenarist] (b. Green River WY, 9 Sep 1892–22 Jul 1946 [53], Los Angeles CA). (Universal.) AMD, p. 227. AS, p. 695 (MacDermott); p. 741. BHD, p. 237; BHD2, p. 169. FDY, p. 433. IFN, p. 190. Truitt, p. 207. "Universal Signs McDermott," *MPW,* 30 Jan 1926, 455. Dorothy Donnell, "A Mad Hatter Builds a Mad House of Movie Props and Sets," *MPC,* Jul 1927, 24–25, 75.

McDermott, Joseph [actor] (b. 1890?–6 Mar 1923 [33], Los Angeles CA; suicide by gas inhalation). "Joe McDermott a Suicide," *Variety,* 8 Mar 1923 ("He left a note stating that he was taking the gas route because he could not make the grade."). AS, p. 741. BHD, p. 237.

McDermott, Louis [producer] (b. 1893–11 Aug 1936 [43?], San Francisco CA; heart attack). AS, p. 741. BHD2, p. 169.

MacDermott, Marc [vaudeville/stage/film actor] (b. Goulburn, New South Wales, Australia, 24 Jul 1881–5 Jan 1929 [47], Glendale CA; during an operation). m. **Miriam Nesbitt**, Apr 1916, Leonia NJ (d. 1954). (Edison, 1908; Vitagraph; Fox.) "Marc McDermott," *Variety,* 9 Jan 1929 (b. England; age 48). AMD, p. 227. AS, p. 741. BHD, p. 237. FSS, p. 197. IFN, p. 186. MH, p. 124 (b. London, England). MSBB, p. 1025–26 (b. London). Truitt, p. 222 (b. England). "Edison Players Return," *MPW,* 16 Nov 1912, 647. "Marc MacDermott Has Bad Mishap," *MPW,* 6 Dec 1913, 1134. "New Edison Series," *MPW,* 28 Mar 1914, 1665. "Marc MacDermott," *MPW,* 13 Mar 1915, 1612. "Briefs of Biography," *NYDM,* 6 Oct 1915, 33:1 (discusses his stock work in the interior of Australia: "Oh! those days of discomfort always and salary never."). "Marc MacDermott Joins Vitagraph," *MPW,* 22 Apr 1916, 607. "MacDermott in Fox Films," *MPW,* 14 Aug 1920, 894. "Robertson Engages Marc MacDermott," *MPW,* 26 Mar 1921, 392. "Movie Star's Wife Has Him Arrested; Miriam Nesbit, Who Played with Ada Rehan, Seeks Alimony [$10,000 temporary alimony] from MacDermott," *NYT,* 11 Aug 1922 (she charged cruelty and abandonment). "Wife Has Movie Actor Arrested; Mrs. MacDermott Charges He Intends to Start for California," *NY Herald,* 11 Aug 1922 (she quoted letters written to her husband from actress Helen Gilmore including, "Marcus, what a wonderful wooer you are."). Billy H. Doyle, "Lost Players; Miriam Nesbitt and Marc McDermott," *CI,* 184 (Oct 1990), C12-C13, 45–46.

McDermott, Vincent [director] (b. 1892–24 Mar 1925 [33?], Los Angeles CA). AS, p. 741. BHD2, p. 169.

Mcdona, Charles T. [actor] (b. Dublin, Ireland, 1860–15 Nov 1946 [86?], Brighton, England). BHD, p. 237.

MacDonald, Ballard [songwriter/scenarist/director] (b. Portland OR, 15 Oct 1882–17 Nov

1935 [52], Forest Hills NY). m. Elizabeth Chapin. "Ballard MacDonald, 52, Dies in New York After Brief Illness," *Variety,* 20 Nov 1935 (wrote *Indiana; Trail of the Lonesome Pine; Rose of Washington Square; Somebody Loves Me; Beautiful Ohio*). AS, p. 695. ASCAP 66, p. 460. BHD2, p. 169.

McDonald, Charles [actor/producer/scenarist] (b. 1876–7 Aug 1953 [77], Tucson AZ). AS, p. 741. BHD, p. 237; BHD2, p. 169. IFN, p. 190.

McDonald, Charles B. [actor/executive] (b. Springfield MA, 26 May 1886–29 Dec 1964 [78], Hollywood FL). (Essanay.) "Charles B. McDonald," *Variety,* 6 and 13 Jan 1965 (d. 26 Dec). AS, p. 741. BHD, p. 237; BHD2, p. 169. IFN, p. 191. Truitt, p. 222.

MacDonald, Donald [stage/film actor/director] (b. Denison TX, 13 Mar 1898–9 Dec 1959 [61], New York NY). m. actress Maudie Gifford; Ruth Hammond. "Donald MacDonald," *Variety,* 16 Dec 1959. AMD, P. 227. AS, p. 695. BHD1, p. 346. IFN, p. 186. "Donald MacDonald, New Powers Director," *MPW,* 6 Dec 1913, 1154. Mary Keane Taylor, "The Den of a Modern Villain; Donald MacDonald and His Hollywood Castle," *MPC,* Mar 1919, 22–23, 71–72.

McDonald, Francis J. [stage/film actor] (b. Bowling Green KY, 22 Aug 1891–18 Sep 1968 [77], Los Angeles CA). m. (1) **Mae Busch**, 12 Dec 1915, LA CA—div. 1922 (d. 1946); (2) Bella Roscoe; (3) Irene Mary Schuck. (Began 1912, Monopole; Universal.) "Francis McDonald," *Variety,* 2 Oct 1968. AMD, p. 227. AS, p. 741. BHD1, p. 346 (b. Erlanger KY, 1889). FSS, p. 197. GK, pp. 487–504. IFN, p. 191. MH, p. 126. Truitt, p. 222. "Francis McDonald Triangler," *MPW,* 21 Sep 1918, 1718. "Francis McDonald to Star in National Film Feature," *MPW,* 7 Feb 1920, 895. George Katchmer, "The Versatile, Yet Forgotten Francis McDonald," *CI,* 95 (May 1983), 53–55; II, 96 (Jun 1983), 36–38 (filmography). George Katchmer, "Remembering the Great Silents," *CI,* 251 (May 1996), 52.

McDonald, Harry [actor] (*né* John Henry McDonald, b. Barbados, 1869–2 Jun 1943 [74?], Los Angeles CA). AS, p. 741.

MacDonald, J[oseph] **Farrell** [actor/director] (b. Waterbury CT, 14 Apr 1875–2 Aug 1952 [77], Los Angeles CA). (Imp.) m. **Edith Bostwick** (d. 1943). "J. Farrell MacDonald," *Variety,* 6 Aug 1952. AMD, p. 228. AS, p. 695 (b. 6 Jun). BHD1, p. 346; BHD2, p. 169. FSS, p. 198. GK, pp. 504–25. IFN, p. 187. Katz, p. 752 (b. 6 Jun). Truitt, p. 208 (b. 6 Jun). 1921 Directory, p. 270. "Versatility of Director MacDonald," *MPW,* 4 Jan 1913, 57. "MacDonald Joins Oz Forces," *MPW,* 18 Jul 1914, 406. W.E. Wing, "On the Pacific Coast," *NYDM,* 9 Dec 1914, 26:2 (birth of son). "Biograph Directors," *MPW,* 8 Jul 1916, 243–44. "Fox Signs MacDonald," *MPW,* 20 Dec 1924, 741. "MacDonald in 'Lightnin',"" *MPW,* 4 Apr 1925, 486. "Star Achieving Fame," *MPW,* 24 Oct 1925, 631. "Farrell MacDonald Becomes a Fox Star," *MPW,* 24 Dec 1927, 25. George A. Katchmer, "Admired Lovable J. Farrell MacDonald," *CI,* 113 (Nov 1984), 19–20, C1. "J. Farrell MacDonald," *CI,* 228 (Jun 1994), 39.

McDonald, J.K. [director/producer] (b. 1885?–24 Jan 1953 [67], Stockton CA). m. Bertha. (1st National.) "J.K. M'Donald," *NYT,* 28 Jan 1953, 27:4. "J.K. McDonald," *Variety,* 4 Feb 1953 (produced *Penrod and Sam; Boy of Mine*). AMD, p. 228. AS, p. 741. BHD2, p. 169 (d. 31 Jan). "McDonald to Direct," *MPW,* 1 Mar 1924, 32.

MacDonald, Jack [actor] (b. San Francisco CA, 17 Sep 1880). BHD, p. 237. Ragan 2, p. 1104. George A. Katchmer, "Forgotten Cowboys and Cowgirls—Part XIV," *CI,* 191 (May 1991), 23; *CI,* 251 (May 1996), pp. 52–53.

McDonald, James [actor] (b. 1886–26 Dec 1952 [66?], Los Angeles CA). AS, p. 741.

McDonald, Joseph [actor] (b. 1861–27 Oct 1935 [74?], Redondo Beach CA). AS, p. 741 ("s'est noyé accidentellement lors d'une baignade"). BHD1, p. 346.

McDonald, Josephine [actress] (b. 1861?–27 Oct 1935 [74], Redondo Beach CA; drowned). "Josephine McDonald," *Variety,* 30 Oct 1935 ("film extra and bit player").

MacDonald, Katherine Agnew, "The American Beauty" (sister of **Mary McDonald McLaren**) [actress/executive] (b. Pittsburgh PA, 14 Dec 1881 or 1883–4 Jun 1956 [72?], Santa Barbara CA). m. John S. Johnson; Christian H. Holmes (nephew of Max Fleischman, the yeast "king"), 1928. "Katherine M'Donald, 64; 'American Beauty' of Silent Screen Dies on Coast," *NYT,* 5 Jun 1956, 35:3. "Katherine MacDonald," *Variety,* 6 Jun 1956 (age 62). AMD, p. 228. AS, p. 696 (b. 1891). BHD, p. 237; BHD2, p. 169 (b. 1891). IFN, p. 187 (age 64). MH, p. 124. 1921 Directory, p. 230. Truitt, p. 208. WWS, p. 88. "Paramount Engages New Leading Woman," *MPW,* 3 Nov 1917, 681. "The Katherine MacDonald Company," *MPW,* 1 Mar 1919, 1185. "Katherine MacDonald Heads Company," *MPW,* 14 Jun 1919, 1652. "First National to Distribute Productions Starring Katherine MacDonald—First Two Pictures Completed," *MPW,* 16 Aug 1919, 982. "Katherine MacDonald to Be Presented Only in Appealing and Human Stories," *MPW,* 2 Oct 1920, 676. "Schulberg Renews Katherine MacDonald Contreact for Two Years for $600,000," *MPW,* 26 Mar 1921, 370. "Miss MacDonald Signs New First National Contract," *MPW,* 9 Apr 1921, 590. "Miss MacDonald Signally Honored," *MPW,* 7 Jan 1922, 75 (only American of "Most Beautiful Women in the World" photo exhibit). Ruth Mabrey, "'No More Marriage for Me!' Says Katherine MacDonald," *MW,* 5 May 1923, 21. "Actress Marries," *MPW,* 2 Jun 1923, 380. "Katherine MacDonald in Two Domestic Dramas," *MPW,* 9 Jun 1923, 512. "Katherine MacDonald Returns to Screen," *MPW,* 17 Jan 1925, 284. "Ethel Clayton Returns," *MPW,* 24 Jan 1925, 380. Mary Dickson, "Famous Beauty of Silent Screen Seeks Divorce," *Movie Classic,* Oct 1931, 41 (husband beat her with a snake-skin walking cane and burned her with a cigarette). George Katchmer, "Remembering the Great Silents," *CI,* 231 (Sep 1994), 48–49.

McDonald, Kenneth [actor] (*né* Kenneth Dollins, b. Portland IN, 8 Sep 1901–5 May 1972 [70]). AS, p. 741. IFN, p. 187. George Katchmer, "Remembering the Great Silents," *CI,* 200 (Feb 1992), 32.

McDonald, Marion [actress]. No data found. AMD, p. 228. (Sennett.) "Marion McDonald 'Steps Out,'" *MPW,* 17 Oct 1925, 574. "Six Reasons Why Mack Sennett Comedies Are Popular," *Cinema Arts,* V (Aug 1926), 23 (photo). Photo, *Paris and Hollywood,* Oct 1926, 56.

MacDonald, Mary *see* **MacLaren, Mary**

MacDonald, Mary [actress]. No data found. AMD, p. 228. "Bluebird Has Another Mary MacDonald," *MPW,* 22 Sep 1917, 1826.

MacDonald, Norman [producer]. No data found. AMD, p. 228. "Norman MacDonald Making Change," *MPW,* 11 Apr 1914, 189.

MacDonald Packe [actor] (b. England, 1892–2 Jul 1960 [68?], London, England). AS, p. 696.

MacDonald, Sherwood [director] (b. New York NY, 30 Jun 1880–25 Jan 1968 [87], Canoga Park CA). m. **Mollie McConnell** (d. 1920). BHD1, p. 613; BHD2, p. 170.

MacDonald, Wallace [director/producer, stage/film actor: Keystone Cop/producer/story editor] (b. Mulgrave, Nova Scotia, Canada, 5 May 1891–30 Oct 1978 [87], Santa Barbara CA). m. **Doris May**, 5 May 1921, Los Angeles CA (d. 1984). George Katchmer, *Eighty Silent Film Stars* (Jefferson NC: McFarland & Co., 1993). (Keystone; Navajo Film Co.; American; FP-L; Vitagraph; Triangle.) "Wallace MacDonald," *Variety,* 8 Nov 1978. AMD, p. 228. BHD1, p. 346; BHD2, p. 170. FFF, p. 183. GK, pp. 526–35. IFN, p. 187. MH, p. 124. MSBB, p. 1026. Slide, p. 163. "Wallace MacDonald," *MPW,* 5 Dec 1914, 1366. "Wallace MacDonald," *MPW,* 17 Nov 1917, 1002. "Wallace MacDonald Signs Contract with Triangle," *MPW,* 5 Jan 1918, 57. "Wallace MacDonald to Join the Colors," *MPW,* 22 Jun 1918, 1721. "MacDonald Out of Service," *MPW,* 11 Jan 1919, 235. "Wallace MacDonald Playing with Viola Dana for Metro," *MPW,* 30 Oct 1920, 1272. "In Auto Crash," *MPW,* 16 Jul 1921, 311 (with wife, 29 Jun 1921, Pico and Arnnez Streets, LA CA). "Wallace MacDonald; The Man Who Had to Fight Twice for His Place on the Screen," *Picture Show,* 16 Oct 1926, p. 11. George A. Katchmer, "Wallace MacDonald," *CI,* 99 (Sep 1983), 10–11. Richard E. Braff, "An Index to the Films of Wallace MacDonald," *CI,* 198 (Dec 1991), 22–24, 52. George Katchmer, "Remembering the Great Silents," *CI,* 238 (Apr 1995), C11, 51. AS, p. 696.

McDonnnell, Claude [cinematographer]. No data found. FDY, p. 461.

McDonough, Joseph A. [director] (b. Portland ME-d. 11 May 1944, Los Angeles CA). (Universal.) "Joseph A. McDonough," *Variety,* 17 May 1944. AS, p. 741. BHD2, p. 170. IFN, p. 191.

McDonough, Michael [actor] (b. 1876–8 Aug 1956 [60?], Los Angeles CA). AS, p. 742.

MacDougal, Allan R[oss] [actor] (b. Scotland, 1894–19 Jul 1956 [62?], Paris, France). AS, p. 696.

MacDougal, James D. [actor] (b. Glasgow, Scotland-d. 15 May 1932, Los Angeles CA). AS, p. 696.

McDowell, Claire (daughter of actors Eugene A. McDowell and Fanny Reeves) [stage/film actress] (b. New York NY, 2 Nov 1877–23 Oct 1966 [88], Woodland Hills CA). m. **Charles Hill Mailes** (d. 1937). (Biograph, 1910; K&E; MGM.) "Claire McDowell," *Variety,* 2 Nov 1966. AMD, p. 228. AS, p. 742. BHD1, p. 347 (b. 1878). FSS, p. 198. IFN, p. 191. MH, p. 126. Truitt, p. 223. "Claire McDowell," *MPW,* 16 Jan 1915, 348. "Claire McDowell Joins Universal," *MPW,* 8 Jul 1916, 230. "The Autobiography of Claire McDowell," *MPC,* II, Jul 1916, 55–56, 68 (named after a part her mother played, Claire Ffolliott in *The Shaughraun*). "Fanny Reeves McDowell Dead," *MPW,* 3 Mar 1917, 1367 (death of mother). "Claire McDowell," *MPW,* 5 May 1917, 782. "Claire McDowell Cast," *MPW,* 7 Nov 1925, 41. Raymond Lee, "Mother Claire," *CFC,* 26 (Winter,

1970), 43. Buck Rainey, "Claire McDowell, 'Mother' Quintessence—Part 1," *CI*, 125 (Nov 1985), C14-C16; Part 2, 126 (Dec 1985), 23–25. R.E. Braff, "An Index to the Films of Claire McDowell," *CI*, 202 (Apr 1992), C6, 61 (partial). George Katchmer, "Remembering the Great Silents," *CI*, 251 (May 1996), pp. 53–54.

MacDowell, Dr. Edward Burton [cameraman/lecturer]. No data found. AMD, p. 228. "A Globe-Trotting Camera Man," *MPW*, 30 Mar 1912, 1147. "MacDowell Educational Pictures," *MPW*, 27 Feb 1915, 1275–76.

MacDowell, Melbourne [vaudeville/stage/film actor] (*né* William Melbourne MacDowell, b. Washington, South River NJ, 22 Nov 1856–18 Feb 1941 [84], Decoto [Oakland] CA; stroke). m. (1) actress Fanny Davenport, 18 May 1889 (d. 26 Sep 1898); (2) Nellie Irving (d. 1897); (3) actress Wilhelmina Marie Strauss, 15 Jun 1900, Newport News VA; ; Virginia Drew Trescott (*née* Virginia Drew Allen, d. 1911); Mrs. Caroline Wells Neff, 28 Sep 1917, Riverside CA. (Film debut: *The Flame of the Yukon*, 1917.) "Wm. M. M'Dowell, Noted Actor, Dies; Matinee Idol of '90s, Known as Melbourne MacDowell, Is Stricken on Coast at 84; Wed Fanny Davenport; Appeared with Famed Actress in Many Stage Plays—Was in Films for 17 Years," *NYT*, 20 Feb 1941. "Melbourne MacDowell," *Variety*, 26 Feb 1941 ("he played in films in the silent days"). "W.M. MacDowell, 84, Is Dead; Husband of Fanny Davenport; Chiseled Cross on Pavement Where He First Saw Her Boarding a Horse-Car," *NY Tribune*, 20 Feb 1941 (d. 19 Feb). "Virginia Drew Trescott," *NYT*, 2 Jan 1912, 11:6 (b. Marshalltown PA, 1870?–31 Dec 1911 [41], Flushing NY; after appendicitis operation). AMD, p. 228. AS, p. 696. BHD, p. 238 (b. 1857). IFN, p. 187. SD, p. 814. Truitt, p. 208 (Melbourne MacDonald). "Fanny Davenport's Will; By It Her Husband and Relatives All Get a Share of the Estate," [13 Sep (1898?); clipping at Lincoln Center] (will dated 2 Jun 1892. "To Miss Davenport's husband, Melbourne McDowell, is bequeathed her library of books at the home in Canton [PA], all her manuscript plays and the residue of the estate, both real and personal."). "House [Melbourne Hall] at South Duxbury [MA] in Which She Died Offered to the Highest Bidder; Her Jewels Long Gone, Husband Remarried and Shuns the Spot at Which the Actress Passed Happy Hours; Yachts Sold to Strangers; Even the Sardou Plays, in Which She Made Her Fame, Have Been Sold," *The World*, Sep 1900. "Melbourne M'Dowell in Jail, His Bride Seeking Divorce," *New York World*, 9 Sep 1900 (MacDowell was put in jail by his bride [Strauss] of three months because of intolerable cruelty. MacDowell "took his arrest coolly,..." Locked up, "he refused to be interviewed, saying he was too much unstrung to talk of his troubles." The affidavit alleged "acts of cruelty and infidelity, beginning almost immediately after the marriage ceremony.... On Sept. 5, the wife says, he actually seized her by the throat."). "Divorce for Mrs. M'-Dowell; Referee Finds in Her Favor Against the Actor; Reports that the Defendant, Who Was Once the Husband of Fanny Davenport, Acted Improperly with a Woman in Paris—Another Co-Respondent Said to Live in This City," [*NY World?*], 20 Dec 1900 [clipping]. "M'Dowell's Heart-Broken by Love; Desertion by Blanche Walsh Drove Actor to Drink; He Signed Away Rights; Declares He Was Tricked into Marriage and Accuses His Manager of Duplicity," [Jan] 1902 [clipping] (claimed his former manager, Clarence M. Brune, drugged him [liquor] and induced him to sign away the rights of five Sardou plays for $500 and a transfer of the executorship of the estate of Fanny Davenport MacDowell. Brune promised the return of Walsh to the MacDowell Co.). "MacDowell Wants Manuscripts of Fannie Davenport," *NY Review*, 19 Mar 1910 (in the fall of 1900, MacDowell stored trunks containing plays, manuscripts, costumes, etc., with Clarence M. Brune. Two years later he sued to get them back but could not locate them. On 12 Mar an article in the *NY Review* mentioned a "rare find" to go to the New Theatre, and MacDowell wanted to recover the contents of the trunks."). "Auction of Fanny Davenport's Effects," *NYDM*, 16 Jun 1915, 5:2 (the low bidding for her effects was most marked—"250 prompt books, interlined with Augustin Daly's stage instructions, were bought by a dealer for $42."; stage jewelry went for fancy prices, while legitimate trinkets, "ten times as valuable," went for a song; "Her $1,200 Steinway piano went for $140."; a file of her personal correspondence sold for $2; "So much for sentiment."). G.P. Von Harleman, "New of Los Angeles and Vicinity," *MPW*, 21 Apr 1917, 430:2 (MacDowell, "a new member of the Ince players," rehearsing in a film with Dorothy Dalton for Triangle Kay-Bee). "Melbourne MacDowell," *MPW*, 30 Jun 1917, 2111. "Hero of Stage Loves Weds; MacDowell Romance Bared; Matinee Idol of Years Agone Wooes [sic] and Wins Nurse Who Won Him Back to Health," *LA Examiner*, 9 Oct 1917 (m. Caroline Wells Neff). "'The Man Who Came Back' via the Picture Screen," *Theatre Magazine*, May 1918, 332. "Melbourne MacDowell's Wife Sues," *Variety*, 23? Apr 1919 (sued by Catherine MacDowell [*née* Caroline Wells Neff]. "She charges desertion."). George Katchmer, "Remembering the Great Silents," *CI*, 183 (Sep 1990), 46, 51.

McDowell, Nelson [actor] (b. Greenville MO, 14 Aug 1870–3 Nov 1947 [77], Los Angeles CA; suicide by shooting because of cancer). (Biograph.) "Nelson MacDowell," *Variety*, 5 Nov 1947. AS, p. 742. BHD1, p. 347 (b. Greenfield MO). GK, pp. 536–64. IFN, p. 191. Truitt, p. 223 (b. 18 Aug 1875).

McDuff, James [actor] (b. Providence RI, 1863?–31 Mar 1937 [74], Bayshore, LI NY). "James McDuff," *NYT*, 1 Apr 1937, 23:3. "James McDuff," *Variety*, 7 Apr 1937. AS, p. 742. BHD, p. 238. IFN, p. 191.

McDunnough, Walter S. [actor] (b. Montreal, Canada, 15 Dec 1863–1 Jul 1942 [78], Los Angeles CA). BHD1, p. 347. IFN, p. 191.

Mace, Fred[erick] [stage/film actor/director/producer] (b. Philadelphia PA, 22 Aug 1878–21 Feb 1917 [38], New York NY [Death Certificate No. 6856]; apoplexy and stroke; found dead at the Hotel Astor). m. Gertrude Emily Johnson (d. 1973). (Biograph, 1910; Imp; Keystone; Majestic; Gem; University; Apollo.) "Fred Mace Dies Suddenly; Film Comedian Who Was Formerly Prominent in Musical Plays," *NYT*, 22 Feb 1917, 11:5 (age 39). "Fred Mace," *Variety*, 2 Mar 1917 (died of *poison d'amour* over Marguerite Marsh). AMD, p. 228. AS, p. 698. BHD, pp. 47–49; 238; BHD2, p. 170. IFN, p. 194. Katz, p. 753 (b. 1872). SD. Spehr, p. 150. "Mace to Head an Imp Company," *MPW*, 29 Jun 1912, 1218. "Fred Mace," *MPW*, 2 Nov 1912, 447. "Mace's Prop List," *MPW*, 5 Apr 1913, 33. "Mace Quits Keystone," *MPW*, 5 Apr 1913, 33. "Fred Mace's Plans," *MPW*, 12 Apr 1913, 150. "Mace for Mayor," *MPW*, 19 Apr 1913, 283. "And the Phone Bell Rang!," *MPW*, 17 May 1913, 798. "'One-Round O'Brien' Is a Series," *MPW*, 30 Aug 1913, 965. "Majestic's 'Fighter' Dead," *MPW*, 13 Sep 1913, 1163 (death of "Bull" Young). "A Mace Picture in Record Time," *MPW*, 15 Nov 1913, 720. "Mace Back to California," *MPW*, 22 Nov 1913, 849. "Keystoners Reunited; Fred Mace Back in the Fold with the Keystone's Original 'Big Four,'" *NYDM*, 30 Jun 1915, 21:4 ("Mr. Mace left the Keystone Company to make pictures for himself, but disastrous business conditions soon put an end to this. The star then assisted in the negotiations that brought about Evelyn Nesbitt Shaw's debut on the screen.") "N.Y.M.P. and Keystone Stars," *MPW*, 10 Jun 1916, 316. "Obituary," *MPW*, 10 Mar 1917, 1550 (suicide by poison). Billy H. Doyle, "Lost Players," *CI*, 183 (Sep 1990), 30–31, 54.

Mace, Lloyd [actor]. No data found. AMD, p. 229. "Hospital at Universal Hollywood Studios," *MPW*, 10 Jan 1914, 182.

Mace, Wynn [actor] (b. So. Pasadena CA, 3 Aug 1890–15 Jan 1955 [64], Los Angeles Co. CA). AS, p. 698. BHD, p. 238. IFN, p. 194.

McEdward, Jack (father of Blake Edwards) [actor/director/producer] (b. 1897–9 Mar 1992 [94?], Los Angeles CA). AS, p. 742.

McElhern, James [actor]. No data found. *Fl.* 1923–25.

McElwaine, Donn [publicist/title writer] (b. Indianapolis IN, 24 Feb 1899–1 Sep 1958 [59], Los Angeles CA; heart attack). (Mutual's *The Screen Telegram;* Robertson-Cole; 1st National; Fox; Pathé.) "Don McElwaine," *Variety*, 10 Sep 1958, p. 151:1. AMD, p. 229. BHD2, p. 170. FDY, p. 447. "McElwaine Now Heads Fox Publicity Force," *MPW*, 5 Nov 1927, 10.

McEveety, Bernard F. [director] (b. New York NY, 14 Feb 1893–1 Apr 1971 [78], Los Angeles CA; heart attack). (Edison.) "Bernard Francis McEveety," *Variety*, 7 Apr 1971. BHD2, p. 170.

McEvoy, Dorothea [actress] (b. 1896–6 Feb 1976 [79], La Jolla CA). AS, p. 742. BHD1, p. 347. IFN, p. 191.

McEvoy, Ernest Simon [actor] (b. 1894?–14 Apr 1953 [59], Los Angeles CA). "Ernest Simon McEvoy," *Variety*, 22 Apr 1953. AS, p. 742. IFN, p. 191.

McEvoy, J.P. [humorist/scenrist] (b. New York NY, 10 Jan 1895–8 Aug 1958 [63], New York NY. Interred at Gethsemane Cemetery, Congress NY). m. 3 times. "J.P. McEvoy," *Variety*, 13 Aug 1958, p. 63:1 (motto in his home: "Let No Guilty Dollar Escape"). AMD, p. 229. BHD2, p. 170. "McEvoy with Famous Players; To Write for W.C. Fields," *MPW*, 6 Feb 1926, 540.

MacEvoy, Tom [writer] (b. Cortland NY, 1869?–7 Nov 1942 [73], Syracuse NY). m. Regina Nagle. (K&E.) "Thomas M'Evoy, 73, An Educator, Author; Wrote 'Methods in Teaching'—Taught at Several Colleges Here," *NYT*, 10 Nov 1942, 27:5.

McEwan, Isabelle [actress/singer] (b. Scotland, 1896–19 Feb 1963 [66?], Vancouver, Canada). AS, p. 742.

MacEwen, Walter [actor] (b. Ayr, Scotland, 23 Sep 1906–15 Apr 1986 [79], Woodland Hills CA). (Gainsborough Pictures; British-International; WB; Paramount.) m. "Walter MacEwen," *Variety*, 23 Apr 1986. BHD2, p. 170.

MacFadden, Bernarr A. [editor/writer/producer] (b. Mill Springs MO, 16 Aug 1868–12

Oct 1955 [87], Jersey City NJ). AMD, p. 229. AS, p. 696. BHD, p. 238. "MacFadden Screen Magazine," *MPW,* 17 Nov 1917, 1010. "Bernarr MacFadden," *MPW,* 16 Mar 1918, 1532. "MacFadden Starts Picture; Publisher Outlines Plans," *MPW,* 13 Jun 1925, 802. "MacFadden Tells How True Story Films Will Be Put on the Screen," *MPW,* 20 Jun 1925, 847.

McFadden, Gertrude (sister-in-law of **Jack Haley**) [stage/film actress] (b. 1900–3 Jun 1967 [67], Los Angeles CA; heart attack). m. Harry Dorman. "Gertrude 'Mickey' McFadden," *Variety,* 14 Jun 1967, p. 71:3 (in vaudeville with her sister Florence as The McFadden Sisters). AS, p. 696. BHD, p. 238.

McFadden, Ivor [actor] (*né* Charles Ivor McFadden, b. San Francisco CA, 6 Aug 1887–14 Aug 1942 [55], Los Angeles CA; cerebral hemorrhage). "Charles I. McFadden," *Variety,* 19 Aug 1942 (age 54). BHD1, p. 347; BHD2, p. 170 (Charles Ivor McFadden). AS, p. 742. IFN, p. 191. Truitt, p. 223. George A. Katchmer, "Forgotten Cowboys and Cowgirls—Part X," *CI,* 182 (Aug 1990), 38 (b. 1897). George Katchmer, "Remembering the Great Silents," *CI,* 213 (Jun 1993), 48–49.

McFarland, Carroll A. [stage/film actor] (b. 1885–1 Mar 1935 [50], Portland OR. Interred in Lincoln Memorial Park). (Selig.) "C.A. McFarland," *Variety,* 117, 13 Mar 1935, 62:1 (d. 4 Mar; Baker Stock Co.). BHD, p. 238.

MacFarlane, George [baritone/actor] (b. Montreal, Canada, 1877–22 Feb 1932 [55], Los Angeles CA; auto accident). (Fox.) "George MacFarlane," *Variety,* 1 Mar 1932. AS, p. 696. BHD1, p. 347. IFN, p. 187 (in *Union Depot,* WB).

MacFayden, Harry [director] (*né* Henry MacFayden, b. Milwaukee WI, 1881?–13 Nov 1940 [59], New York NY). m. Teris Loring. "Harry M'-Fayden; NBC Production Director, Once on the Stage, Dies Here at 59," *NYT,* 15 Nov 1940, 21:3 (began at Universal in 1929). "Harry MacFayden," *Variety,* 20 Nov 1940. BHD, p. 238; BHD2, p. 170 (b. 1875). AS, p. 696.

McGaffey, Elizabeth [scenarist] (b. 1884–13 Mar 1944 [60?], Los Angeles CA). AS, p. 742. BHD2, p. 170.

McGaffey, Kenneth [publicist] (b. 1881–2 Dec 1938 [57?], San Francisco CA). (Lasky.) AMD, p. 229. BHD2, p. 170. J. Van Cartmell, "Live Wires from the West Coast," *NYDM,* 27 Nov 1915, 29:1 (Lasky; returned from San Francisco where he worked with exhibitors at their convention). "McGaffey with Mary Pickford," *MPW,* 7 Feb 1920, 899.

McGann, William M. [director] (b. Pittsburgh PA, 5 Apr 1893–15 Nov 1977 [84], Woodland Hills CA). (1st National, 1915; WB; Republic; Paramount; TC-F.) "William McGann," *Variety,* 23 Nov 1977. AS, p. 742. BHD2, p. 170 (William H. McGann).

McGarry, Garry [actor] (b. Franklin PA, 17 Oct 1889–17 Oct 1927 [38], New York NY; pneumonia). (Vitagraph.) AMD, p. 229. AS, p. 742. BHD, p. 238. IFN, p. 191. "Garry McGarry," *MPW,* 18 Sep 1915, 1978.

McGaugh, Wilbur [actor] (aka Bill Mack, b. CA, 12 Mar 1895–31 Jan 1965 [69], Los Angeles CA; heart attack). "Wilbur McGaugh," *Variety,* 10 Feb 1965 (age 70). BHD, p. 238; BHD2, p. 170. AS, p. 742. IFN, p. 191. Truitt, p. 223. George A. Katchmer, "Remembering the Great Silents," *CI,* 175 (Jan 1990), C5; 178 (Apr 1990), 59; "Update—Forgotten Cowboys/Girls," 179 (May 1990), 43.

McGee, James L. [producer] (b. Brownsville NB, 7 Jun 1873–15 Feb 1936 [62], Los Angeles CA). "James McGee," *Variety,* 19 Feb 1936 ("pioneer picture producer" from 1908–23). AS, p. 742. BHD, p. 238; BHD2, p. 170. IFN, p. 191.

McGill, Bernard or **Barney** [cinematographer] (b. Salt Lake City UT, 30 Apr 1890–11 Jan 1942 [51], Los Angeles CA). (Fox; WB; TC-F.) "Bernard McGill," *Variety,* 21 Jan 1942. FDY, p. 461. IFN, p. 191.

McGill, Lawrence B. [director/producer] (b. Courtland MS, 1869). (Champion; Eclair-American; Pathé.) AMD, p. 229. AS, p. 743 (d. ca. 1916). Spehr, p. 150. "Larry McGill's Hunt for Hounds," *MPW,* 17 May 1913, 714. Louis Reeves Harrison, "Studio Saunterings," *MPW,* 30 Aug 1913, 937–39. "Metro Secures Two New Directors," *MPW,* 22 May 1915, 1277. "Catching a Steamboat in Rome," *MPW,* 5 Jun 1915, 1584. "Larry McGill Signed by Astra," *MPW,* 18 Aug 1917, 1064.

MacGill, Moyna (mother of Angela Lansbury and producers Edgar and Bruce Lansbury) [stage/film actress] (*née* Moyna McIldowie, b. Belfast, Ireland, 10 Dec 1895–25 Nov 1975 [79], Santa Monica CA). m. (1) stage/film director/writer **Reginald Denham**—div. (d. 1983); (2) Edgar Lansbury (d. 1935). (Broadway debut: *The Boy Friend,* 1954). "Moyna MacGill," *Variety,* 3 Dec 1975, p. 71:1 (age 80). AS, p. 696. BHD1, p. 347. IFN, p. 187.

McGiveney, Owen [actor] (b. England, 4 May 1884–31 Jul 1967 [83], Woodland Hills CA). AS, p. 743.

McGlynn, Frank, Jr. (son of **Frank McGlynn, Sr.**) [actor] (b. Marin Co. CA, 9 Jul 1904–29 Mar 1939 [34]). AMD, p. 229. AS, p. 743. BHD, p. 238. IFN, p. 191. "Frank McGlynn," *MPW,* 15 Aug 1914, 940. "Frank McGlynn," *MPW,* 4 Sep 1915, 1660.

McGlynn, Frank, Sr. (father of **Frank McGlynn, Jr.**) [stage/film actor/director] (b. San Francisco CA, 26 Oct 1866–18 May 1951 [84], Newburgh NY). m. Rose O'Byrne. (Edison.) "Frank M'Glynn, 84; Lincoln on Stage; Veteran Actor Who Scored Hit in '19 in Drinkwater's Play Dies—Appeared in Films," *NYT,* 19 May 1951, 15:3. "Frank McGlynn," *Variety,* 23 May 1951. AS, p. 743. BHD1, p. 348. IFN, p. 191. Truitt, p. 223. "Frank McGlynn," *MPW,* 12 Jul 1913, 408 "New Edison Directors; George Ridgewell Added to Staff and Frank McGlynn Raised to Directorship," *NYDM,* 29 Sep 1915, 31:3).

McGovern, Albert [director]. No data found. AMD, p. 229. "McGovern Goes to Powers," *MPW,* 13 Jan 1912, 111.

McGovern, Elmer J. [publicist]. No data found. AMD, p. 229. "Debut of a Press Agent," *MPW,* 11 Oct 1913, 143. "Elmer J. McGovern," *MPW,* 8 Jun 1918, 1458. "How McGovern Helped to Put 'Mickey' Over Big," *MPW,* 7 Sep 1918, 1422. "McGovern Resigns from W.H.," *MPW,* 4 Oct 1919, 95.

McGowan, J.H. [executive, Signal Film Corporation]. No data found.

McGowan, Jack [singer] (d. Sep 1919, Philadelphia PA; pneumonia). m. Frankie Durand. "Jack McGowan," *Variety,* 26 Sep 1919.

McGowan, James P. [producer/director]. No data found. AMD, p. 229. J.P. McGowan, "Around Madeira with the O'Kalems," *MPW,* 3 Feb 1912, 379–80. J.P. McGowan, "O'Kalem Returns to Ireland," *MPW,* 10 Aug 1912, 537. "You Can't Down McGowan," *MPW,* 23 Jan 1915, 520. "James P. McGowan," *MPW,* 9 Oct 1915, 234.

McGowan, John P. [playwright/scenarist/actor/director] (aka J.P. and Jack McGowan, b. Muskegon MI, 12 Jan 1892–28 May 1977 [85], New York NY). "John W. McGowan," *Variety,* 8 Jun 1977, p. 79:2 (age 81). AMD, p. 229. AS, p. 743 (b. 1896). BHD, p. 238; BHD2, p. 171. FDY, p. 433. "John P. McGowan Wins Popularity Contest," *MPW,* 3 Jun 1916, 1715. John P. McGowan, "Specialization the Keynote to Success," *MPW,* 21 Jul 1917, 416. "McGowan Signs Long Term Contract with Universal," *MPW,* 5 Jul 1919, 57. "John P. McGowan to Direct Sterling's 'Red Signals,'" *MPW,* 1 Jan 1927, 38.

McGowan, John P[aterson] [stage actor/film director/producer] (b. Terowie, south Australia, 24 Feb 1880–26 Mar 1952 [72], Los Angeles CA). m. **Helen Holmes** (d. 1950). (Kalem, 1909; Lasky; Universal; Signal Corp.) George Katchmer, *Eighty Silent Film Stars* (Jefferson NC: McFarland & Co., 1993). "John M'Gowan, 72, Dies in Hollywood; Veteran Actor and Producer, ex-Aide of Screen Directors Guild, in Films Since '09," *NYT,* 27 Mar 1952, 30:3. "John P. McGowan," *Variety,* 2 Apr 1952. AS, p. 743. BHD1, p. 348; BHD2, p. 171. GK, pp. 564–80. IFN, p. 191. MSB, p. 1046. Truitt, pp. 223–24. George Katchmer, "Incredible, Prolific J.P. McGowan," *CI,* 68 (Mar 1980), 33. Billy H. Doyle, "Lost Players," *CI,* 157 (Jul 1988), 23. Richard E. Braff, "An Index to the Films of J.P. McGowan," *CI,* 185 (Nov 1990), 30–32; Part II, 18 (Dec 1990), 57–59. George Katchmer, "Remembering the Great Silents," *CI,* 238 (Apr 1995), 52.

Mcgowan, Kenneth [publicist/stage/film actor/producer] (b. Winthrop MA, 30 Nov 1888–27 Apr 1963 [74], West Los Angeles CA). m. Edna Behre. (RKO; Paramount; TC-F.) "Kenneth Macgowan Dead at 74; Headed U.C.L.A. Theater Arts; Producer of 35 Broadway Plays and 45 Films—Was Close Friend of O'Neill," *NYT,* 29 Apr 1963, 31:4. "Kenneth McGowan," *Variety,* 1 May 1963. AMD, p. 229. AS, p. 743. IFN, p. 187. SD. "Kenneth Macgowan Is Mad eGoldwyn Advertising Head," *MPW,* XL, 12 Apr 1919, 210.

McGowan, Lucille [gown designer]. No data found. AMD, p. 229. "Designs Comedyart Gowns," *MPW,* 19 Jun 1920, 1607.

McGowan, Robert F. [director] (b. Denver CO, 11 Jul 1882–27 Jan 1955 [72], Santa Monica CA). "Robert F. McGowan," *Variety,* 2 Feb 1955. AMD, p. 229. AS, p. 743 (b. 1886). BHD2, p. 171. IFN, p. 191. "Signs New Contract," *MPW,* 11 Oct 1924, 500. "Finishes Thirty-eighth Comedy," *MPW,* 14 Feb 1925, 711. "Fifty Pictures in Four Years," *MPW,* 12 Jun 1926, 549. Armand Falnieres, "'Our Gang' Makes Up Its Own Scenarios; Director McGowan Pays Twenty-five Cents for Each Idea Furnished by the Young Comedians," *Cinema Arts,* V (Dec 1926), 46–47, 58.

McGowan, Roxanna [stage/film actress] (b. Chicago IL, 15 Mar 1897–22 Nov 1976 [79], Los Angeles CA). (Sennett). BHD1, p. 613. MSBB, p. 1038.

McGrail, Walter B. [actor] (b. Brooklyn NY, 19 Oct 1888–19 Mar 1970 [81], San Francisco

CA). (Vitagraph, 1914.) m. Miriam. "Movie Hero, McGrail, Dies; Rescued Pearl White in the 'Perils of Pauline,'" *Baltimore Sun,* 23 Mar 1970. "Walter B. McGrail," *Variety,* 8 Apr 1970 (age 81). AMD, p. 229. AS, p. 743. BHD1, p. 348. FFF, p. 139 (b. 1894). IFN, p. 191. MH, p. 126 (b. 1894). Slide, p. 163. Truitt, p. 224 (b. 1899). "McGrail to Play in Pathé Serial," *MPW,* 15 Feb 1919, 929. "Walter McGrail Signs with Selznick," *MPW,* 10 Jan 1920, 236.

McGrane, Thomas [actor]. No data found. AMD, p. 229. "Thomas McGrane," *MPW,* 30 Sep 1916, 2094.

McGrath, Blane [film editor]. No data found. AMD, p. 229. "To Edit Mutual Screen Telegram," *MPW,* 16 Feb 1918, 972.

McGrath, Dennis [actor] (b. 1875–1955 [80?], New York NY). AS, p. 743.

McGrath, Harold [scenarist] (b. Syracuse NY, 4 Sep 1871–30 Oct 1932 [61], Syracuse NY). m. Alma Kenyon, 1905. "Harold M'Grath, Novelist, Is Dead; Career of 33 Years in Writing Popular Fiction Ends in Syracuse at Age of 61; Also in Newspaper Work; "Arms and the Woman,' His First Book, Was Followed by 'Puppet Crown' and 'Man on the Box,'" *NYT,* 30 Oct 1932, 37:1. "Harold McGrath," *Variety,* 1 Nov 1932. AS, p. 696 (MacGrath); p. 743 (McGrath). BHD2, p. 171.

McGrath, Larry Joseph [actor] (b. New York NY, 28 Aug 1888–6 Jul 1960 [71], Los Angeles CA). AS, p. 743. BHD1, p. 348. IFN, p. 192.

McGrath, Thomas [stage/film actor] (b. Boston MA, 1858?–22 Apr 1937 [79], Ft. Wayne IN). "Thomas M'Grath; Veteran Actor Was in the Original 'Sherlock Holmes' Cast," *NYT,* 23 Apr 1937, 21:2. "Thomas McGrath," *Variety,* 28 Apr 1937. AS, p. 743. BHD, p. 238. IFN, p. 192.

McGraw, John J. [baseball manager/actor/writer] (b. Truxton NY, 7 Apr 1873–24 Feb 1934 [60], New York NY). AMD, p. 230. AS, p. 744 (d. New Rochelle NY). BHD, p. 238. "McGraw an Actor; Baseball Manager to Be Seen in Eclectic Three-Reel Feature," *NYDM,* 12 Aug 1914, 24:1 (in *Detective Swift,* Aug 1914. "McGraw Writes Pathéserial; Giants to Help Produce It," *MPW,* 18 Apr 1925, 698. "Play Ball," *MPW,* 30 May 1925, 580. "'Play Ball' New Serial," *MPW,* 7 Jun 1925, 977.

McGraw, Robert [actor]. No data found. AMD, p. 230. "Captain Robert McGraw," *MPW,* 8 Apr 1916, 273.

MacGregor, Dollie Sullivan [scenarist]. No data found. AMD, p. 230. "Mrs. Dollie Sullivan MacGregor Goldwyn's Eastern Scenario Head," *MPW,* 16 Jul 1927, 184.

MacGregor, Edward J. [director] (b. Rochester NY, 1879–1 Sep 1957 [78?], New York NY). AS, p. 696. BHD2, p. 171.

MacGregor, Harman B. [stage/film actor] (b. New York NY, 1878?–4 Dec 1948 [70], Marblehead MA). m. Eleanor. (Film debut: *The Tides of TIme,* Knickerbocker, 4 Aug 1915.) "Harmon B. M'Gregor," *NYT,* 6 Dec 1948, 25:3. "Harmon B. MacGregor," *Variety,* 8 and 15 Dec 1948 ("silent film star of the early 1900's"). AS, p. 696. BHD, p. 239 (b. 1889). IFN, p. 187. Truitt, p. 208. "Studio Gossip," *NYDM,* 4 Aug 1915, 31:2.

McGregor, John E. [actor] (b. Scotland–d. 25 Jan 1928, West Hampton, LI NY). "John E. McGregor," *Variety,* 1 Feb 1928. AS, p. 744.

McGregor, Malcolm [actor] (b. Newark NJ, 13 Oct 1892–29 Apr 1945 [52], Los Angeles CA; from burns sustained in a fire). "Malcolm McGregor," *Variety,* 2 May 1945 (age 53). AMD, p. 230. AS, p. 744. BHD1, p. 348. FFF, p. 27. FSS, p. 199. IFN, p. 192. MH, p. 126. Truitt, p. 224. "MacGregor Signed," *MPW,* 3 Jun 1922, 476. MacGregor to Enact Leading Role," *MPW,* 30 Sep 1922, 377. Constance Palmer, "Hardships—De Luxe; Malcolm McGregor didn't have to starve in casting directors' offices…," *Picture-Play Magazine,* Jun 1923, 32, 90. "MacGregor Signed," *MPW,* 11 Aug 1923, 500. "Plays Opposite Florence Vidor," *MPW,* 13 Dec 1924, 651. "Asher Engages MacGregor," *MPW,* 14 Feb 1925, 708. "Malcolm MacGregor Signed," *MPW,* 21 Mar 1925, 274.

MacGregor, Norval [director/actor] (b. River Falls WI, 3 Apr 1862–21 Nov 1933 [71], Santa Cruz CA). AMD, p. 230. AS, p. 697 (b. 1865). BHD, p. 239; BHD2, p. 171. "MacGregor, Lewis' Director, Knows Backwoodsmen," *MPW,* 15 Feb 1919, 929.

McGrew, Willis F. [scenarist] (b. 1890–13 Oct 1957 [67?], Menlo Park CA). AS, p. 744.

McGuinness, James Kevin [writer/producer/title writer/scenarist] (b. New York NY, 20 Dec 1893–4 Dec 1950 [56], New York NY; heart attack). (Fox; MGM.) "James McGuinness," *Variety,* 6 Dec 1950 (age 57). AMD, p. 230. AS, p. 744. BHD2, p. 171. FDY, p. 447. IFN, p. 192. "Fox Scenario by McGuinness," *MPW,* 7 May 1927, 36.

McGuire, Benjamin [actor] (b. 1875?–10 Apr 1925 [50?], New York NY; heart attack). (FP-L.) "Benjamin McGuire," *Variety,* 22 Apr 1925. AS, p. 744. BHD, p. 239. Truitt, p. 224.

McGuire, George A. [film editor] (b. New York NY, 5 Dec 1888–24 May 1966 [77], Glendale CA; heart ailment). "George A. McGuire," *Variety,* 1 Jun 1966 (head of editorial department at 1st National and MGM; "Among many innovations for which he is credited was the first film viewer, later known as the Moviola."). BHD2, p. 171.

McGuire, Kathryn [actress: Wampas Star, 1922] (b. Peoria IL, 6 Dec 1903–10 Oct 1978 [74], Los Angeles CA; pancreatic cancer). m. George Landy. (Sennett; Fox; Universal.) "Kathryn McGuire," *Variety,* 18 Oct 1978. AMD, p. 230. AS, p. 744. BHD1, p. 349. FFF, p. 137. FSS, p. 199. IFN, p. 192. MH, p. 127. "Kathryn McGuire in Thomas Pictures," *MPW,* 30 Jun 1923, 771. "Keaton Picks New Lead," *MPW,* 29 Dec 1923, 794. "Finishes Sea Film," *MPW,* 5 Dec 1925, 424. "Danced Her Way into the Films," *MPW,* 14 May 1927, 99. Betty Standish, "This Little Star Went to Market; Kathryn McGuire Set Out to Be Gloria Swanson and Became Mrs. Landy," *MPC,* Oct 1928, 58, 79, 85.

McGuire, Neil [special effects] (d. 8 Jan 1972, Santa Maria CA). (Universal.) "Neil McGuire," *Variety,* 16 Feb 1972. BHD2, p. 171.

McGuire, Tom [actor] (*né* Thomas Maguire, b. Milford CT, 1 Sep 1869–6 May 1954 [84], Los Angeles CA). "Tom McGuire," *Variety,* 19 May 1954. AS, p. 744 (b. England, 1873). BHD1, p. 349 (b. England). IFN, p. 192 (b. England, 1873). Truitt, p. 224.

McGuire, William Anthony [director/producer/scenarist] (b. Chicago IL, 9 Jul 1881?–16 Sep 1940 [59], Beverly Hills CA; uremia). m. Lulu I. Cation. "W.A. M'Guire Dies; Noted Playwright; Film and Stage Figure Long Associated in Productions of Florenz Ziegfeld; Famed Scenario Writer; Author of 'The Great Ziegfeld,' 'Lillian Russell' and 'The Three Musketeers,'" *NYT,* 17 Sep 1940, 23:1 (age 55). "Death of Bill McGuire Recalls His Broadway Writing Idiosyncracies," *Variety,* 18 Sep 1940. AS, p. 744 (d. 16 Aug). BHD2, p. 171 (b. 1885). SD, p. 817 (b. 1885).

McGuirk, Charles J. [actor/scenarist] (b. 1889–4 Dec 1943 [54?], Reno NV). BHD2, p. 171.

Machado, Xavier [producer] (b. 1888-Sep 1953 [65?], Mexico City, Mexico). BHD2, p. 171.

McHale, Martin [producer] (b. Stoneham MA, 30 Oct 1888–7 May 1979 [90], Hempstead NY). BHD2, p. 171.

Machard, Alfred [director/scenarist] (b. Paris, France, 1887–5 Dec 1962 [75?], France). AS, p. 699. BHD2, p. 171.

Machaty, Gustav [director] (b. Prague, Czechoslovakia, 9 May 1901–14 Dec 1963 [62], Munich, Germany). Wife d. 1950. (Assistant to D.W. Griffith; MGM.) AS, p. 699. BHD2, p. 171. IFN, p. 194. Waldman, p. 172.

Machin, Alfred [director] (b. Blendecques, France, 20 Apr 1877 [extrait de naissance no. 21]-24 Jun 1929 [52?], Nice, France). AS, p. 699 (d. 2 Jul 1919). BHD2, p. 171.

Machin, William [actor] (aka Alfred Mackin, b. Coventry, England, 12 Dec 1882–9 Sep 1928 [45], Los Angeles CA). AS, p. 699.

MacHue, Arthur [publicist]. No data found. AMD, p. 230. "Arthur MacHue with Moss," *MPW,* 4 Sep 1915, 1656.

McHugh, Mrs. Catherine Lucy (mother of **Frank, Kitty,** and **Matt McHugh**) [actress] (*née?,* b. MT, 1869?–28 Jun 1944 [74?], Los Angeles CA). "Mrs. Catherine McHugh," *Variety,* 5 Jul 1944. AS, p. 744. BHD, p. 239 (d. 25 Mar 1954, LA CA). IFN, p. 192 (d. 25 Mar 1954 [84]). SD, p. 818.

McHugh, Charles Patrick [actor] (b. Philadelphia PA, 20 Jul 1870–21 Oct 1931 [61], Los Angeles CA; heart attack). "C.P. McHugh Dead," *Variety,* 27 Oct 1931. AS, p. 744. BHD1, p. 349. IFN, p. 192 (age 62). Truitt, p. 224. George Katchmer, "Remembering the Great SIlents," *CI,* 254 (Aug 1996), 50–51.

McHugh, Edward A. [actor] (b. 1860–9 Oct 1935 [75?], Santa Monica CA). AS, p. 744.

McHugh, Frank (son of **Catherine McHugh**) [actor] (*né* Francis Curray McHugh, b. Homestead [Pittsburgh] PA, 23 May 1898–11 Sep 1981 [83], Greenwich CT). m. Dorothy Spencer, 1928. Carter B. Horsley, "Frank McHugh Is Dead at 83; A Veteran Supporting Actor," *NYT,* 13 Sep 1981, 52:4. "Frank McHugh," *Variety,* 16 Sep 1981. BHD1, p. 349. SD, p. 818.

McHugh, Grace [actress] (b. Golden CO, 1898?–1 Jul 1914 [16], near Canon City CO; drowned in the Arkansas River while filming *Across the Border*). (Colorado M.P. Company.) AMD, p. 230. AS, p. 744. BHD, p. 239 (b. 1888). "Obituary," *MPW,* 18 Jul 1914, 439. *MPW,* 15 Aug 1914. *Filmograph,* 8 Nov 1914. *The Colorado Transcript,* 2 Jul 1914 and 27 Aug 1914. *The Golden [CO] Globe,* 4 and 18 Jul 1914. "Film Ends Fatally; Two Members [McHugh and Owen Carter] of Colorado M.P. Company Drowned While Producing Picture," *NYDM,* 8 Jul 1914, 32:1 ("The accident happened while the company was at work on a picture and was the result of Miss McHugh's falling from a horse while attemping to ford the river.

Carter made an attempt to rescue her, but both were lost."). "Body of Grace McHugh Found," *NYDM*, 22 Jul 1914, 28:2 (spotted three miles east of Florence CO). John E. Thayer, "Movie First... and Second," *CFC*, 38 (Spring, 1973), 11.

McHugh, John [actor: Our Gang Comedies] (b. MT, 25 May 1913–13 Jan 1983 [69], Las Vegas NV; heart attack). (Roach; Fox; Darmour; Paramount; WB.) "John McHugh," *Variety*, 26 Jan 1983. AS, p. 744. BHD1, p. 349 (Jack McHugh).

McHugh, Kitty (daughter of **Catherine McHugh**, sister of **Frank** and **Matt McHugh**) [actress] (b. Homestead [Pittsburgh] PA, 1902–25 Mar 1954 [52?], Los Angeles CA). AS, p. 745.

McHugh, Matt (brother of **Frank** and **Kitty McHugh**; son of **Catherine McHugh**) [actor] (*né* Matthew O. McHugh, b. Connellsville PA, 22 Jan 1894–22 Feb 1971 [77], North Ridge CA; heart attack). AS, p. 745. BHD1, p. 349. IFN, p. 192.

McIlwain, William A. [actor] (b. 1863?–29 May 1933 [70], Los Angeles CA; heart attack). "William A. McIllwain [sic]," *Variety*, 6 Jun 1933. AS, p. 745. BHD1, p. 613. IFN, p. 192. Truitt, p. 224.

McInnis, John (Stuffy) [actor] (b. Gloucester MA, 19 Sep 1890–16 Feb 1960 [69], Ipswich MA). BHD, p. 239.

McIntosh Burr [actor] (*né* William McIntosh, b. Wellsville OH, 21 Aug 1862–28 Apr 1942 [79], Los Angeles CA; heart attack). m. Jean. "Burr M'Intosh, 79, Actor, Author, Dies; Lecturer and Photographer, 'The Cheerful Philosopher' of Radio, Stricken on Coast; Wrote of Santiago Siege; In Cuba for Leslie's Weekly as Reporter in '98—Appeared in 'Trilby'—Owned Film Firm," *NYT*, 29 Apr 1942, 21:3. "Burr McIntosh," *Variety*, 6 May 1942. AMD, p. 230. AS, p. 745. BHD1, p. 349. IFN, p. 192. SD. Truitt, p. 225. "Burr McIntosh Before the Camera," *MPW*, 22 Nov 1913, 877. "Burr McIntosh Film Corporation," *MPW*, 10 Apr 1915, 222. "Burr McIntosh in Pathé's 'Wallingford,'" *MPW*, 18 Sep 1915, 1973. "McIntosh 'At Home,'" *MPW*, 28 Aug 1915, 935. Cal York, "Plays and Players," *Photoplay Magazine*, Feb 1917, 89 ("recently filed a petition in bankruptcy"). "Burr McIntosh Returns," *MPW*, 14 Feb 1920, 1098.

MacIntosh, Louise [actress] (*née* Louise MacIntosh-Rogers, b. 1865?–1 Nov 1933 [68?], Beverly Hills CA). AS, p. 697. Truitt, p. 209.

McIntyre, A.H. (Hughie) [executive] (b. 1887-Apr 1922 [35?]). BHD2, p. 171.

McIntyre, Adeline [actress]. No data found. (Christie.) "Beauties Who Make the Comedies Attractive," *Cinema Arts*, Aug 1926, 21 (photo).

McIntyre, Frank [stage/film actor] (b. Ann Arbor MI, 25 Feb 1879–8 Jun 1949 [70], Ann Arbor MI). "Frank M'Intyre, Stage Actor, Dies; Veteran Broadway Star Played Captain Henry on 'Showboat' of Radio in 1934–36," *NYT*, 9 Jun 1949, 31:1 (age 71). "Frank McIntyre," *Variety*, 15 Jun 1949 (age 71). AMD, p. 230. AS, p. 745. BHD, p. 239. IFN, p. 192. Truitt, p. 225. '83 WWOS (b. 1878). "McIntyre in 'The Traveling Salesman,'" *MPW*, 4 Nov 1916, 711.

McIntyre, Hercules [executive] (b. 17 Jan 1890–22 Feb 1976 [85], Sydney, New South Wales, Australia). BHD2, p. 171.

McIntyre, Leila [actress] (b. New York NY, 20 Dec 1882–9 Jan 1953 [70], Los Angeles CA). AS, p. 745 (d. West Los Angeles CA). BHD1, p. 349.

McIntyre, Marion [actress] (*née* Marion Gray, b. 1885–19 Nov 1975 [90?], Woodland Hills CA). AS, p. 745.

McIntyre, Molly [actress] (b. Glasgow, Scotland, 1886?–29 Jan 1952 [65], New York NY). "Miss Molly M'Intyre, 'Kitty Mackay' [1914] Star," *NYT*, 5 Feb 1952, 29:3. "Molly McIntyre," *Variety*, 6 Feb 1952. AS, p. 745. BHD, p. 239. IFN, p. 192.

McIntyre, Robert B. [casting director] (b. Philadelphia PA, 1881–31 May 1952 [71?], Los Angeles CA). AMD, p. 230. BHD2, p. 172. "McIntyre Makes Record of Actors," *MPW*, 4 Jan 1919, 52. "Robert B. McIntyre in New York Selects New Actors for Goldwyn," *MPW*, 11 Feb 1922, 623. "Goldwyn Signs McIntyre," *MPW*, 10 Oct 1925, 467. "McIntyre Made Production Head," *MPW*, 17 Oct 1925, 556.

McIntyre-Pearce, Robert [producer] (b. 1880–13 Jul 1962 [82?], Los Angeles CA). AS, p. 745.

Maciste [actor] (*né* Ernesto Pagano, b. Italy). AMD, p. 230. AS, p. 699 (date of death is given as 15 Sep 1917, Bain Zassa Plateau, Italy; in combat). "Maciste Reported Killed in Action," *MPW*, 6 Oct 1917, 96. "Maciste, 'Cabiria' Samson, Coming in Screen Serial," *MPW*, 31 Aug 1918, 1283. "Recovering from Wounds, Maciste to Resume Work," *MPW*, 25 Jan 1919, 475. "'Maciste' Proves Popular in 'The Liberator' Serial," *MPW*, 15 Feb 1919, 938. "Maciste in Los Angeles," *MPW*, 15 May 1920, 937.

McIvor, Mary [actress] (*née* Mary McKeever, b. Barnesville OH, 31 Aug 1900?–28 Feb 1941 [40], Los Angeles CA; heart attack). m. **William Desmond**, 22 Mar 1919, Pasadena CA (d. 1949). (Triangle.) "Mrs. William Desmond," *NYT*, 1 Mar 1941, 15:3. "Mary McIvor Desmond," *Variety*, 5 Mar 1941. AMD, p. 230. AS, p. 745. BHD, p. 239 (b. 1904). IFN, p. 192. Truitt, p. 224. "Mary MacIvor," *MPW*, 23 Dec 1916, 1793. "Mary MacIvor to Support 'Smiling Bill' Parsons," *MPW*, 29 Jun 1918, 1865. "Bill Desmond Married," *MPW*, 12 Apr 1919, 218. "Recuperating," *MPW*, 16 Jul 1921, 297 (from the grippe). George Katchmer, "Remembering the Great Silents," *CI*, 254 (Aug 1996), 51.

Mack, A. Johnny [publicist]. No data found. AMD, p. 230. "Johnn¥ Mack to Direct All Exploitation on Equity Films," *MPW*, 19 Jun 1920, 1619. "A. Johnny Mack Resigns as Director of Exploitation for Equity," *MPW*, 9 Oct 1920, 776.

Mack, Andrew [stage/film actor] (aka Tom Le Mack, *né* William Andrew McAloon, b. Boston MA, 25 Jul 1863–21 May 1931 [67], Bayside, LI NY). m. (2) Katherine Humphrey (d. 1926). "Andrew Mack," *Variety*, 27 May 1931 (age 68). AMD, p. 230. AS, p. 699. BHD, p. 239. IFN, p. 187. SD. Truitt, p. 209. "Andrew Mack Joins Ranks," *MPW*, 27 Jun 1914, 1841.

Mack, Arthur [actor] (b. 1877–19 Jun 1942 [65?], Jamaica Plain MA; suicide stemming from inhalation of toxic gases in Belgium). AS, p. 699.

Mack, Betty [actress] (b. IL, 30 Nov 1901–5 Nov 1980 [78], Placerville CA). AS, p. 699 (b. Piquay). BHD1, p. 355 (d. Sacramento CA).

Mack, Bill [stage/film actor] (b. Sacramento CA-d. 27 Jan 1961, New York NY). "Bill Mack," *Variety*, 1 Feb 1961 (vaudeville performer). AS, p. 699. BHD1, p. 355. Truitt, p. 209.

Mack, Charles E. [(George) Moran & Mack, the "Two Black Crows"] [stage/film actor] (*né* Charles E. Sellers, b. White Cloud KS, 22 Nov 1887–11 Jan 1934 [46], near Mesa AZ; auto accident). m. (1) Marion Robinson, 1920–32; (2) Mrs. Myrtle Buckley, 1932. (MGM.) "Charles E. Mack," and "Charles Mack Killed When Auto Overturns," *Variety*, 16 Jan 1934. AS, p. 699. BHD1, p. 355. IFN, p. 187. SD. Truitt, p. 209.

Mack, Charles Emmett [stage/film actor] (*né* Charles Stewart McNerney, b. Scranton PA, 25 Nov 1900–17 Mar 1927 [26], Riverside CA; auto accident). (Film debut: *Dream Street*.) "Charles Emmett Mack," *Variety*, 23 Mar 1927 (age 27). AMD, p. 230. AS, p. 699. BHD, p. 239. IFN, p. 187. Truitt, p. 209. Alice L. Tildesley, "Prop Boy to Star; Griffith Made Charles Emmett Mack Into an Actor," *MPC*, Jul 1926, 54–55, 88–89. "Obituary," *MPW*, 26 Mar 1927, 274.

Mack, Mrs. Charles Emmett [actress] (*née*?). No data found. AMD, p. 230. "Mrs. Mack Cast," *MPW*, 2 Jul 1927, 19.

Mack, Charles W. [stage/film actor/costumer] (*né* Charles McGaughey, b. PA, 29 Oct 1878–29 Nov 1956 [78], Los Angeles CA). (WB.) "Charles Mack," *Variety*, 5 Dec 1956 (began 1919). AS, p. 699. BHD, p. 239; BHD2, p. 172. IFN, p. 187. Truitt, p. 209.

Mack, Dick [stage/film actor] (b. 1854–4 Feb 1920 [66], San Francisco CA). "Dick Mack," *Variety*, 20 Feb 1920, 25:1 ("Mr. Mack was well known in San Francisco, having appeared in stock before the fire."). AS, p. 699. BHD, p. 239.

Mack, Edward J. [stage/film actor] (b. 1870?–7 Sep 1929 [59], Canton OH). m. Annie Berlein (d. 1935). "Edward Mack," *Variety*, 11 Sep 1929. AS, p. 699. SD.

Mack, George E. [stage/film actor] (b. Boston MA, 1866?–20 May 1948 [82], Cheyenne WY). m. Mabel Strickland (d. 1 Nov 1947). "George E. Mack, 82, Long a Comedian," *NYT*, 24 May 1948, 19:2 (with Castle Square stock company in Boston). "George E. Mack," *Variety*, 26 May 1948. AS, p. 699. BHD, p. 239.

Mack, Harry [actor] (b. 1880?–25 Mar 1920 [40], CA). "Harry Mack," *Variety*, 23 Apr 1920. AS, p. 700.

Mack, Hayward [actor] (b. Albany NY, 1879?–24 Dec 1921 [42], Los Angeles CA). (Imp, 1910; Majestic; FP-L; Biograph; Progressive Motion Picture Co.; Universal.) AMD, p. 231. AS, p. 700. BHD, p. 239. IFN, p. 187. "Hayward Mack," *MPW*, 14 Aug 1915, 1162. George Katchmer, "Remembering the Great Silents," *CI*, 229 (Jul 1994), 38.

Mack, Helen [child actress at Ft. Lee NJ] (*née* Helen McDougall, b. Rock Island IL, 13 Nov 1913–13 Aug 1986 [72], Beverly Hills CA; cancer). m. Thomas McAvity (d. 1974). AS, p. 700. BHD1, p. 355. Katz, p. 757. "Helen Mack, 72, an Actress in Silent and Talking Movies," *NYT*, 16 Aug 1986, 28:3. "Helen Mack," *Variety*, 20 Aug 1986 (in *Zaza*). (Bit roles in a few silent films; not in AFI Catalog.)

Mack, Hughie [actor] (*né* Hugh McGowan, b. Brooklyn NY, 26 Nov 1884–13 Oct 1927 [43], Santa Monica CA; heart attack). (Vitagraph, 1912.) "Hughie Mack," *Variety*, 19 Oct 1927. AMD, p. 231. AS, p. 700. BHD, p. 239. IFN, p. 187. Truitt, p. 209. Mabel Condon, "Sans Grease Paint and Wig," *Motography*, 4 Jul 1914, 23–24 (was an undertaker whose establishment was near

Vitagraph). "Hughie Mack," *MPW,* 17 Oct 1914, 343. "In the Picture Studios," *NYDM,* 21 Jul 1915, 19:2 (one of the quartette [along with Kate Price, William Shea, and Flora Finch] working in Vitagraph's *A Night Out,* Mack confessed to weighing 344 pounds; the quartette weighed 834 pounds.). "Obituary," *MPW,* 22 Oct 1927, 497.

Mack, Irving [producer] (b. 1894–10 Nov 1983 [89?], Chicago IL). AS, p. 700.

Mack, James (Buck) [actor/scenarist] (b. PA, 17 Aug 1888–19 Sep 1959 [71], Los Angeles CA). "Buck Mack," *Variety,* 23 Sep 1959. AS, p. 700. BHD1, p. 355. FDY, p. 433. IFN, p. 187.

Mack, James T. [actor] (b. Chicago IL, 16 May 1871–12 Aug 1948 [77], Los Angeles CA). m. "James T. Mack," *Variety,* 18 Aug 1948. AS, p. 700. BHD1, p. 355. IFN, p. 187. Truitt, p. 209.

Mack, Joseph P. [actor] (b. Boleneva, Italy, 4 May 1878–8 Apr 1946 [67], Los Angeles CA). "Joe Mack," *Variety,* 17 Apr 1946 (age 68; began 1925). AS, p. 700. BHD1, p. 355. IFN, p. 187. Truitt, p. 209.

Mack, Marion [actress/scenarist/Sennett Bathing Beauty, 1920] (*née* Joey Marion McCreery, b. Mammoth UT, 9 Apr 1902–1 May 1989 [87], Costa Mesa CA). m. **Louis Lewyn**, 1923, Monterey CA (d. 1969). (Sennett; Universal.) "Marion Mack, 87, Silent-Film Actress, Dies," *NYT,* 15 May 1989, D10:1. "Marion Mack," *Variety,* 24 May 1989, p. 77 (began 1920). AS, p. 700. BHD1, p. 613. Paul Rochester, "Movie-Mad Girl's Own Story Provides Scenario; Marion Mack visits Hollywood and her hard luck experiences seeking employment form the plot of *Mary of the Movies,*" *MW,* 2 Jun 1923, 23. "Marion Marries Louis," *MW,* 22 Sep 1923, 25. "Marion Mack: Keaton Co-Star in 'The General,'" *LA Times,* 14 May 1989, 36:1. Michael G. Ankerich, "Marion Mack: Memories of 'The General,'" *CI,* 171 (Sep 1989), 10, 12. Chapter 14, "Marion Mack," *BS,* pp. 191–98 (includes filmography).

Mack, Max [director/actor/producer/writer] (*né* Moritz Myrthezweig, b. Halberstadt, Germany, 21 Oct 1884–18 Feb 1973 [88], London, England). "Max Mack," *Variety,* 270, 14 Mar 1973, 71:2 (producer of early German silents). AS, p. 700 (d. 6 Mar). BHD1, p. 356; BHD2, p. 172. IFN, p. 197.

Mack, Nila [stage/film/radio actress] (*née* Nila MacLoughlin, b. Arkansas City KS, 29 Oct 1891–20 Jan 1953 [61], New York NY; heart attack). m. **Roy Briant** (d. 1927). "Nila Mack," *Variety,* 21 Jan 1953. AS, p. 700. BHD, p. 235 (Nila Mac). IFN, p. 186 (age 62). SD.

Mack, Robert (Bobby) [actor/cameraman] (b. Jamaica NY, 1877–2 May 1949 [72], Jamaica NY). AS, p. 700 (b. Scotland). BHD1, p. 356; BHD2, p. 172 (b. Scotland). George A. Katchmer, "Remembering the Great Silents," *CI,* 231 (Sep 1994), 50.

Mack, Rose [actress] (b. 1866?–9 Oct 1927 [61], New York NY [Holyoke MA?]). "Rose Mack," *Variety,* 12 Oct 1927. AS, p. 700 (b. 1886). IFN, p. 187. Truitt, p. 209. WWS, p. 209.

Mack, Roy [director] (b. 1892–16 Jan 1962 [69?], Los Angeles CA). AS, p. 700. BHD2, p. 172.

Mack, Vera [actress]. No data found. AMD, p. 231. "Woman Rodeo Champion in Films," *MPW,* 3 Jan 1920, 107.

Mack, Wilbur [actor] (b. Binghampton NY, 29 Jul 1873–13 Mar 1964 [90], Los Angeles CA). m. Gertrude Purdy. "Wilbur Mack," *Variety,* 8 Apr 1964 (age 91). AS, p. 700. BHD1, p. 356. IFN, p. 188. Truitt, p. 209. George A. Katchmer, "Remembering the Great Silents," *CI,* 175 (Jan 1990), C7, C8 (m. Gertrude Purdy).

Mack, Willard McLaughlin [stage/film actor/director/writer] (*né* Charles Willard MacLaughlin, b. Morrisburg, Ontario, Canada, 18 Sep 1873–18 Nov 1934 [61], Brentwood Heights, Los Angeles CA). m. (1) Maude Leone (d. 1930); (2) **Marjorie Rambeau** (d. 1970); (3) **Pauline Frederick**, 1917–20 (d. 1938); (4) Beatrice Banyard. (Ince.) "Willard Mack," *Variety,* 20 Nov 1934 (age 56). AMD, p. 231. AS, p. 700. BHD1, p. 356; BHD2, p. 172 (b. 17 Sep 1877). IFN, p. 188. SD. Truitt, p. 209. "Willard Mack in Hospital," *NYDM,* 5 May 1915, 17:1 (held up and assaulted on 24 Apr at Bridgeport CT; robbed of a gold watch and $190 cash, beaten and left on the sidewalk; suffered brain concussion.). "Pauline Frederick to Release Through Goldwyn," *MPW,* 25 May 1918, 1153. "Mack Off for New York," *MPW,* 3 May 1919, 661. "Pauline Frederick Asks for Divorce from Willard Mack," *MPW,* 28 Aug 1920, 1148. "Willard Mack Engaged," *MPW,* 7 Mar 1925, 87.

Mack, William B. [stage/film actor] (*né* William B. McGillicuddy, b. New York NY, 8 Apr 1872–13 Sep 1955 [83], Islip, LI NY). "William B. Mack," *Variety,* 21 Sep 1955. AMD, p. 231. AS, p. 700. BHD, p. 240 (b. Bay City MI). IFN, p. 188. SD. Truitt, p. 209. "To Play Heavy Lead," *MPW,* 13 Jan 1923, 158.

Mackaill, Dorothy [stage/film actress: Wampas Star, 1924] (b. Hull, Yorkshire, England, 4 Mar 1903–12 Aug 1990 [87], Honolulu HI). m. (1) **Lothar Mendes**, Oct? 1926, Hollywood CA—div. 1928 (d. 1974); (2) Neil Albert Miller, 1931—1934, LA CA; (3) Harold Patterson, 1935–38. (Film debut: *The Face at the Window,* British, ca. 1921.) "Dorothy Mackaill, Actress, 87," *NYT,* 16 Aug 1990, B14:5. "Dorothy Mackaill," *Variety,* 22 Aug 1990, p. 88. Burt A. Folkart, "Dorothy Mackaill, 87; Went from Ziegfeld Follies to Film," *LA Times,* 15 Aug 1990, A18:1. AMD, p. 231. AS, p. 697. BHD1, p. 356. FFF, p. 185. FSS, p. 199. Katz, p. 757. MH, p. 124. "Praises Miss Mackaill," *MPW,* 19 Jan 1924, 187. "Dorothy Mackaill and George O'Brien Featured by Wm. Fox," *MPW,* 9 Aug 1924, 471. Harry Carr, "Miss Audacity of Hollywood," *MPC,* Dec 1924, 24–25, 86. Regina Cannon, "She Has a Fortune-Teller for a Maid," *MW,* 11 Apr 1925, 4–5, 32. "Beauty; To Be or Not to Be; For Blondes, for Blondes, Lead a Hard Life," *MPC,* Apr 1925, 45, 96. "Dorothy Mackaill Signed," *MPW,* 5 Sep 1925, 77. "Marriages," *MPW,* 27 Nov 1926, 3. "Dorothy Mackaill," *MPW,* 1 Jan 1927, 51. "Dorothy Mackaill," *MPW,* 25 Jun 1927, 573. *Variety,* 113, 20 Feb 1934, 52:5 (divorced Miller).

MacKay, Belva [actress]. No data found. m. **Richard Thorpe** (d. 1991).

MacKay, Charles Donald [actor] (b. Philadelphia PA, 15 Oct 1867–19 Nov 1935 [68], Englewood NJ; heart attack). m. Lillian Kemble. (Edison; Peerless; Paragon.) "Charles MacKay," *Variety,* 27 Nov 1935. AS, p. 697. BHD, p. 240 (d. Ft. Lee NJ). IFN, p. 188. Truitt, p. 209.

MacKay, Edward J. [stage/film actor/director] (b. Philadelphia PA, 1874?–26 Dec 1948 [74], Elizabeth NJ). m. (2) Alice Coon Brown. "E.J. Mackay Dies; Retired Actor, 74; Early Movie Director, Player Had Appeared on Stage Here in Many Leading Roles," *NYT,* 27 Dec 1948, 22:2. "Edward J. MacKay," *Variety,* 29 Dec 1948. AS, p. 697. BHD, p. 240. IFN, p. 188.

McKay, George W. [actor] (*né* George W. Reuben, b. Salt Lake City UT, 15 Apr 1880–3 Dec 1945 [65], Los Angeles CA). AS, p. 745.

McKay, James C. [director/film editor]. No data found.

MacKay, Leonard [actor] (b. England, 1874–4 Jan 1929 [54?], Elstree, England). AS, p. 700.

McKay, Windsor [director] (b. New York NY, 1886–26 Jul 1934 [48?], Sheepshead Bay NY). AS, p. 745.

Mackaye, Dorothy [actress] (b. 1898?–5 Jan 1940 [42?], Los Angeles CA; auto accident). AS, p. 700. BHD, p. 240. IFN, p. 188 (age 37).

McKee, Buck [actor] (b. Claremore OK, 1865?–1 Mar 1944 [79], Roseville CA). "Buck McKee," *Variety,* 8 Mar 1944. AS, p. 745. IFN, p. 192.

McKee, John [actor/director] (b. Belfast, Ireland–d. 28 Dec 1953 [80+], New York NY). "John M'Kee, Actor and Stage Director," *NYT,* 29 Dec 1953, 23:4. "John McKee," *Variety,* 30 Dec 1953. IFN, p. 192.

McKee, Lafayette "Lafe" [actor] (*né* Lafayette Stocking, b. Morrison IL, 23 Jan 1872–10 Aug 1959 [87], Temple City CA; arteriosclerosis). (Selig-Polyscope, 1912; Fox; Columbia; Majestic.) AS, p. 745. BHD1, p. 350. IFN, p. 192. Ed Wyatt, "Lafe McKee; Western Films' Grand Old Man," *Films of the Golden Age,* #1 (Summer 1995), 31–33 (partial filmography; in about 300 films).

McKee, Raymond E. [actor/director/scenarist] (b. IN, 7 Dec 1892–3 Oct 1984 [91], Long Beach CA; pneumonia. Buried in Riverside National Cemetery, Riverside CA). m. (1) Frances White, 1921; (2) **Marguerite Courtot**, 4 Apr 1923, NYC (d. 1986). (Edison; Pathé; Kalem; Goldwyn.) AMD, p. 231. AS, p. 745. BHD1, p. 350; BHD2, p. 172. FFF, p. 180. MH, p. 127. Luther Hancock, "Raymond McKee [obituary]," *CI,* 116 (Feb 1985), 13–14. Anthony Slide, *Silent Portraits* (Vestal NY: The Vestal Press, Ltd., 1989), p. 180. "Raymond McKee, Edison Comedian," *MPW,* 15 May 1915, 1053. "Raymond McKee Again with Metro," *MPW,* 21 Oct 1916, 394. "Raymond McKee," *MPW,* 31 Mar 1917, 2108. "Raymond McKee Recovered," *MPW,* 21 Aug 1920, 1050. "Surprise Weddings," *MPW,* 3 Dec 1921, 566. "Marguerite Courtot to Wed," *MPW,* 31 Mar 1923, 511. "Sennett Signs McKee," *MPW,* 21 Feb 1925, 815.

McKee, Scott A. [actor] (b. Glasgow, Scotland, 9 May 1881–17 Apr 1945 [63], Los Angeles Co. CA). AS, p. 745. BHD, p. 240. IFN, p. 192.

McKeen, Lawrence D. "Snookums," Jr. [actor] (b. 1 Sep 1924–2 Apr 1933 [8], Los Angeles CA; blood poisoning). "Lawrence D. McKeen, Jr. (Snookums)," *Variety,* 11 Apr 1933. AMD, p. 231. BHD, p. 240. IFN, p. 193. "Lawrence 'Sunny' McKeen," *MPW,* 28 May 1927, 275–76. "Lawrence 'Sunny' McKeen," *MPW,* 4 Jun 1927, 353. "Mayor Walker Extends Regal Welcome to 'Baby Snookums,'" *MPW,* 11 Jun 1927, 433. "Snookums, Stern Bros. Baby Star, Selectected for First Feature Role," *MPW,* 26 Nov 1927, 17.

McKeever, Elizabeth [actress] (b. 1886–10 Jan 1928 [41?], Chicago IL; pneumonia). AS, p. 745.

McKenna, Henry T[om] (brother of **Kenneth H. McKenna**) [actor] (b. Brooklyn NY, b.

1894?–17 Jun 1958 [64], Los Angeles CA; heart attack). "Harry Tom M'Kenna," *NYT*, 19 Jun 1958, 31:4. "Henry T. McKenna," *Variety*, 25 Jun 1958. AS, p. 746. IFN, p. 193.

MacKenna, Kate [actress] (*née* Edith C.N. Howe, b. 1877–14 Jun 1957 [80?], Los Angeles CA; cancer). AS, p. 697.

MacKenna, Kenneth H. (brother of **Henry T. McKenna**) [stage/film actor/director] (*né* Leo Mielziner, Jr., b. Canterbury NH, 19 Aug 1899–15 Jan 1962 [62], Santa Monica CA). m. (1) **Kay Francis**, 1931–33 (d. 1968); (2) Mary Philips (d. 1975; former wife of Humphrey Bogart). "Kenneth MacKenna Dead at 62; Actor and Former M-G-M Aide; Editorial Director of Studio Had Appeared in Movies and in Broadway Plays," *NYT*, 17 Jan 1962, 33:4. "Kenneth MacKenna (Leo Mielziner, Jr.)," *Variety*, 17 Jan 1962 (age 63). AS, p. 697. BHD1, p. 350; BHD2, p. 172 (d. LA CA). FSS, p. 200. IFN, p. 188. Katz, pp. 757–58 (began 1919). Truitt, p. 210.

Mackensie, Lady Grace E. [producer]. No data found. AMD, p. 231. "Lady Mackensie's Big Game Pictures," *MPW*, 22 May 1915, 1279. "Lady Grace E. Mackensie in Trouble," *MPW*, 28 Aug 1915, 1463.

MacKensie, John [cameraman]. No data found. AMD, p. 231. "Men Who Made Kinemacolor Possible," *MPW*, 18 Dec 1909, 875. "John MacKensie," *MPW*, 10 Oct 1914, 264.

McKentry, Elizabeth [actress] (b. 1899?–3 Sep 1920 [21], New York NY). AMD, p. 231. BHD, p. 240. IFN, p. 193. "Obituary," *MPW*, 18 Sep 1920, 348.

McKenzie, Aeneas [scenarist] (b. 1889–2 Jun 1962 [73?], Los Angeles CA). AS, p. 697. BHD2, p. 172.

MacKenzie, Alexander (son of **John MacKenzie**) [actor] (b. Scotland, 1885–2 Jan 1966 [80?], Glasgow, Scotland). AS, p. 700.

MacKenzie, Compton [actor/scenarist] (b. West Hartlepool, England, 17 Jan 1883–30 Nov 1972 [89], Edinburgh, Scotland). BHD2, p. 172.

McKenzie, Bob [scenarist]. No data found. AMD, p. 231. "McKenzie Scenario Head of Joe Rock Productions," *MPW*, 30 Jan 1926, 452.

MacKenzie, Donald [stage/film actor/producer/director] (b. Edinburgh, Scotland, 17 Apr 1879–21 Jul 1972 [93], Jersey City NJ). (First U.S. play: *A Country Girl*, 1903; Pathé.) "Donald MacKenzie," *NYT*, 24 Jul 1972, 30:4 (age 92). "Donald MacKenzie," *Variety*, 26 Jul 1972 (age 92). "Donald Mackenzie, 92; Jersey City Man Was British Actor," *Hudson Dispatch*, 22 Jul 1972. AMD, p. 231. AS, p. 697. BHD1, p. 350; BHD2, p. 172. IFN, p. 188. 1921 Directory, p. 270. Spehr, p. 150. "Donald MacKenzie," *MPW*, 2 May 1914, 647. "Donald MacKenzie Gives a Dinner," *MPW*, 26 Dec 1914, 1826. "Donald MacKenzie," *MPW*, 3 Apr 1915, 82. "Studio Gossip," *NYDM*, 16 Jun 1915, 20:4 (he was playing in a Pathé film when the director fell ill. Louis Gasnier asked him to direct; MacKenzie refused; Gasnier insisted. "You see, the smell of the grease paint had become a habit and I didn't want to give it up to become the man behind the screen instead of before it." But he did not regret the change.). "Donald MacKenzie a Director by Chance," *MPW*, 26 Jun 1915, 2108. "Pathé's 'Gold Rooster' Producers," *MPW*, 28 Aug 1915, 1485. "MacKenzie Making New Pathé Picture," *MPW*, 4 Dec 1915, 1815. "MacKenzie Returns to Astra-Pathé," *MPW*, 25 Aug 1917, 1202. "MacKenzie Is to Direct Helen Holmes in Serial," *MPW*, 28 Jun 1919, 1915. Donald MacKenzie, "'One Reel a Week' Is Not for Real," *CFC*, 27 (Spring/Summer, 1970), 9–10 (wherein he corrects errors).

McKenzie, Donald [British playwright] (b. 1903?–12 Aug 1932 [29], Beauvais, France; auto accident). "Donald McKenzie," *Variety*, 16 Aug 1932.

McKenzie, Ella "Lollie" (sister of **Ida Mae McKenzie**) [actress] (b. OR, 9 Apr 1905–23 Apr 1987 [82], No. Los Angeles CA). m. (1) **Billy Gilbert** (d. 1971); (2) Edward Sweeney. (Essanay.) "Ella McKenzie," *Variety*, 327, 20 May 1987, 111 ("As a child actress in the early days of Hollywood, she appeared in over 100 films, working with Charlie Chaplin, Edna Purviance, Ben Turpin and Will Rogers."). AS, p. 746. BHD1, p. 351 (b. 1911).

McKenzie, Eva B. (mother of Fay McKenzie) [actress] (*née* Eva Heazlit, b. Toledo OH, 5 Nov 1889–15 Sep 1967 [78?], Los Angeles CA). m. **Robert McKenzie** (d. 1949; daughter, Fay b. 19 Feb 1919). "Eva B. McKenzie," *Variety*, 27 Sep 1967 (began 1915; made 150+ films). AS, p. 746. BHD1, p. 351. Truitt, p. 225.

Mackenzie, Frank Robert [stage actor] (b. 1869?–3 Apr 1920 [51], Narragansett Pier MA; Bright's disease). "Frank Robert Mackenzie," *Variety*, 9 Apr 1920.

McKenzie, Ida Mae (sister of **Ella McKenzie**) [child actress] (*née* Ida Mae Sweeny, b. OR, 15 Jan 1911–29 Jun 1986 [74?], Los Angeles CA). AMD, p. 231. AS, p. 746. BHD1, p. 351 (d. Tarzana CA). "Chester Comedy Introduces Child Actress," *MPW*, 10 Jul 1920, 242. "Ida Mae McKenzie," *CI*, 134 (Aug 1986), 47.

MacKenzie, Jack [cinematographer]. No data found. FDY, p. 461.

MacKenzie, John (father of **Alexander MacKenzie**) [director/scenarist] (b. Glasgow, Scotland-d. 1943, Glasgow, Scotland; complications from the grippe). AS, p. 700.

MacKenzie, Murdock [actor] (d. 28 Oct 1923). BHD, p. 240.

McKenzie, Robert B. (father of Fay McKenzie) [actor/director] (b. Ballymania, No. Ireland, 22 Sep 1880–8 Jul 1949 [68], Manunuck RI; heart attack). m. **Eva** (d. 1967; daughter, Fay). (Essanay.) "Robert B. McKenzie," *Variety*, 13 Jul 1949. AS, p. 746 (b. Bellymania, Ireland, 1883). BHD1, p. 351; BHD2, p. 172. IFN, p. 193. Truitt, p. 225 (b. 1883). WWS, p. 225 (b. 1883). George A. Katchmer, "Forgotten Cowboys and Cowgirls—Part XV," *CI*, 192 (Jun 1991), 56. Joe Collura, "Fay McKenzie; Girl of the Golden West," *Films of the Golden Age*, No. 13 (Summer 1998), pp. 36–41.

McKeon, Sydney [editor]. No data found. AMD, p. 232. "Sydney McKeon Leaves International," *MPW*, 21 Oct 1916, 407.

McKeon, John Joseph [producer] (b. 1884–12 Jul 1949 [65?], New York NY; heart attack). AS, p. 746.

McKeown, John A. [assistant director] (b. 1892?–17 Jun 1967 [75], Portland IN). (DeMille.) "John A. McKeown," *Variety*, 28 Jun 1967. BHD2, p. 172.

Mackey, Edward [actor/director]. No data found. (Lasky; Crystal; FP-L; Ivan.) AMD, p. 232. "Edward Mackey," *MPW*, 14 Nov 1914, 946.

McKey, William [stage/film actor] (b. LA, 1861?–3 Jan 1918 [56], New York NY; acute indigestion). m. Evelyn Forbes. "William McKey," *Variety*, 11 Jan 1918. AS, p. 746. BHD, p. 240. SD.

McKim, Edward [director]. No data found. AMD, p. 232. "McKim, Another New Lubin Director," *MPW*, 28 Aug 1915, 1486. "More Lubin Enterprise," *MPW*, 9 Oct 1915, 236.

McKim, Robert [actor] (b. San Francisco CA, 26 Aug 1886–4 Jun 1927 [40], Los Angeles CA; cerebral hemorrhage). (Ince.) m. **Dorcas Matthews**. "Robert M'Kim," *Variety*, 8 Jun 1927. AMD, p. 232. AS, p. 746. BHD, p. 240 (b. San Jacinto CA). IFN, p. 193. MH, p. 127 (b. San Jacinto CA, 1887). Truitt, p. 225. 1921 Directory, p. 189. "Robert McKim in Hart's Next," *MPW*, 13 Oct 1917, 222. "Dorcas Matthews' Injury Becomes Serious," *MPW*, 13 Jul 1918, 185. "McKim a Goldwynite," *MPW*, 4 Jan 1919, 54. "McKim Baby No. 2," *MPW*, 10 Sep 1921, 169 (son b. 24 Aug 1921, Beverly Hills CA). "Obituary," *MPW*, 25 Jun 1927, 574.

McKim, Sam (father of **Ann Dvorak**) [director]. No data found. m. (daughter Ann). (Biograph.) Christopher Finch and Linda Rosenkrantz, Gone Hollywood (Garden City NY: Doubleday & Co., Inc., 1979), p. 228.

Mackin, John E. [actor]. No data found. m. Mrs. E.C. Caldwell, 1914. (Kalem.) AMD, p. 232. "Kalem Players Wed," *NYDM*, 29 Jul 1914, 24:3. "Mackin—Caldwell," *MPW*, 8 Aug 1914, 844. "Mackin Now with Fox," *MPW*, 13 Jan 1917, 210.

Mackin, William [actor] (b. Coventry, England, 12 Dec 1882?–9 Sep 1928 [45], Los Angeles CA). (Kalem; Lasky; Selig.) BHD, p. 240. IFN, p. 194.

McKinnell, Norman [actor] (b. Maxwelltown, New Brunswick, Canada, 10 Feb 1870–29 Mar 1932 [62], London, England; heart attack). "Norman McKinnell," *Variety*, 12 Apr 1932. AS, p. 746. BHD1, p. 351. IFN, p. 193. Truitt, p. 225–26 (b. England).

McKinnon, Alfred I. [actor/scenarist] (b. San Francisco CA-d. 11 Jan 1927, aboard ship to San Francisco CA). AS, p. 746. BHD2, p. 172, BHD, p. 240.

McKinney, Michael Grange [set designer] (b. Steubenville OH, 10 Aug 1895 [Delayed Birth Records, Probate Court, Jefferson County Court House, Steubenville OH, Case No. 414, Vol. 7, p. 591]-14 Aug 1962 [Death Certificate No. I.1821] [67], Long Beach CA). m. Vera Bowen, 1 Apr 1920, Redlands CA. His son, Grange, writes: "I am not aware of his name being on any film credits or appearing in any articles. He was at Universal for only a brief period, and did not resume this line of work (set design) after World War I."

Mackintosh, Louise [actress] (*née* Louise McIntosh-Rogers, b. Port Hastings, England, 24 Dec 1864–1 Nov 1933 [68], Beverly Hills CA). AS, p. 700 (d. London, England). BHD1, p. 356. IFN, p. 188.

Mackley, Arthur J[ames] [actor/director/scenarist] (b. Portsmouth, England, 3 Jul 1865–21 Dec 1926 [61], Los Angeles CA; pneumonia). AS, p. 701. BHD, p. 240. IFN, p. 194. "Doings at Los Angeles; Mr. Mackley Experimenting on Mr. Static," *MPW*, 15 Mar 1913, 1090 (b. Scotland). "Mackley in Essanay Chinese Pictures," *MPW*, 29 Mar 1913, 1323. "Arthur Mackley," *MPW*, 10 Jul 1915, 220. "A Lead, Director, and Two Heavies Join Universal," *MPW*, 26 Jul 1919, 512. "Obituary," *MPW*, 1 Jan 1927, 29 (age 67).

McKnight, Anna [actress] (b. 1908?–25 Mar 1930 [22], Los Angeles CA). AS, p. 746. BHD, p. 240. IFN, p. 193.

McKnight, Tom [actor/director/producer/scenarist] (b. 1900–22 Apr 1963 [63?], Oxnard CA). AS, p. 746.

Mackris, Orestes [actor] (b. Chalkis, Greece, 1899–30 Jan 1975 [75?], Athens, Greece). AS, p. 701.

McLaglen, Clifford [actor] (b. Capetown, So. Africa, 1892–7 Sep 1978 [86], Huddersfield, Yorkshire, England). AS, p. 746 (b. London, England, 1900). BHD1, p. 351. IFN, p. 193.

McLaglen, Cyril [actor] (b. London, England, 9 Sep 1889–11 Jul 1987 [97], Perris CA). AS, p. 746. BHD1, p. 351.

McLaglen, Kenneth [actor] (b. England, 1901–20 Jan 1979 [77?], London, England). AS, p. 747. BHD, p. 241.

McLaglen, Victor Andrew DeBeers (father of director Andrew V. McLaglen, b. 28 Jul 1920) [boxer/actor] (b. McLaglen Manor, London, England, 11 Dec 1886–7 Nov 1959 [72], Newport Beach CA; congestive heart failure). m. (1) Enid Lamont, 1918, London (d. 1942); (2) Suzanne Bruggeman, 1943; (3) Mrs. Margaret Pumphrey. *Express to Hollywood* (London: Jarrolds, Ltd., 1934). (Film debut: *The Call of the Road,* British, 1920; Fox.) "Victor M'Laglen, Screen Star, Dies; Won 1935 Oscar as 'The Informer'—Capt. Flagg in 'What Price Glroy?'; Appeared in 150 Films; Blustering Tough Guy for 'Lost Patrol,' 'Gunga Din' and Ford's 'Quiet Man,'" *NYT,* 8 Nov 1959, 88:1; "Service for M'Laglen; Donald Crisp Gives Eulogy at Rites on Coast for Actor," *NYT,* 11 Nov 1959, 35:3. "Victor McLaglen," *Variety,* 11 Nov 1959. AMD, p. 232. AS, p. 747. BHD1, p. 351 (b. Tunbridge Wells, Kent, England, 10 Dec). FSS, p. 200. GK, pp. 580–94. HCH, p. 67. IFN, p. 193. JS, p. 255 (filmed *Gli italiani sono matti,* Italy, 1958). Truitt, p. 226. "McLaglen Will Be Starred in Vitagraph's 'Beloved Brute,'" *MPW,* 16 Aug 1924, 529. "First National Adds Several to List of Contract Players," *MPW,* 18 Apr 1925, 713. Leatrice Hagen, "This Man McLaglen," *MPC,* Oct 1925, 53, 84. "Fox Contract for McLaglen," *MPW,* 10 Jul 1926, 86. Joseph Mattern, "Big Vic, a Soldier of Fortune; Victor McLaglen Had Led the Most Colorful Existence of Any Man in Pictures...," *MPC,* Oct 1926, 48–49, 72, 78. Tom Waller, "McLaglen—Adventurer, Globe-Trotter and Artist," *MPW,* 8 Jan 1927, 114–15. "McLaglen Exclusively in Fox Films," *MPW,* 9 Jul 1927, 104. Dorothy Spensley, "The Daddy of Baghdad; Oh, Those Days with Victor, the Arabian Knight!," *MPC,* Dec 1928, 43, 70, 82 ("A modern Arabian Knight in Hollywood fetters. A Baghdad daddy gone movie."). George A. Katchmer, "Victor McLaglen; The Gentle Brute," *CI,* 123 (Sep 1985), 29–31. Eric Niderost, "Victor McLaglen: Boxing to Box Office," *CI,* 190 (Apr 1991), 26 *et passim.*

MacLane, Barton [actor] (b. Columbia SC, 25 Dec 1902–1 Jan 1969 [66], Santa Monica CA; double pneumonia). m. Charlotte Wynters. (WB.) "Barton MacLane," *Variety,* 8 Jan 1969 (age 68; began 1924). AS, p. 697. BHD1, p. 351. IFN, p. 188. Katz, p. 759. Truitt, p. 210. '83 WWOS (b. 1900).

MacLane, Mary [writer/actress] (b. Winnipeg, Canada, 2 May 1881–6 Aug 1929 [48], Chicago IL; died in poverty and found dead). "Mary MacLane, Author, Found Dead; Writer Who Caused Sensation by Tales of Own Romances Reaches End in Penury; Reverses after Success; Forgotten by the Public for Several Years Before Death—A Recluse Recently," *NYT,* 8 Aug 1929, 25:5 (wrote *The Story of Mary MacLane* and *Men Who Have Made Love to Me;* "You can no more explain Mary MacLane than you can explain Charlotte Brontë. Shut up there in a bleak and lonely moor, she is the genius she proclaims herself."). "Mary MacLane Dies," *Variety,* 14 Aug 1929. AMD, p. 232. AS, p. 697. BHD, p. 241. "Mary MacLane Picture Finished," *MPW,* 8 Dec 1917, 1517.

MacLaren, Ian [actor] (b. Lynmouth, England, 1 May 1875–10 Apr 1952 [76], Woodland Hills CA). AS, p. 697 (d. London, England). BHD1, p. 351. IFN, p. 188.

MacLaren, Mary (sister of **Katherine MacDonald**) [stage/film actress] (*née* Mary MacDonald, b. Pittsburgh PA, 19 Jan 1896–9 Nov 1985 [89?], West Hollywood CA; pneumonia). m. Lt.-Col. George Herbert Young, Hollywood, 1924; (2) Robert S. Coleman. (Film debut, *Shoes,* 1915; Universal, 1916.) "Mary McLaren," *Variety,* 13 Nov 1985. AMD, p. 232. AS, p. 697. BHD1, p. 351. FSS, p. 201. MH, p. 124. MSBB, p. 1038. SD. Slide, p. 163. "Mary MacLaren, New Star in Bluebird," *MPW,* 10 Jun 1916, 1906. "Mary MacLaren Coming Back," *MPW,* 6 Jan 1917, 107. Grace Kingsley, "Sweet Sobber of the Celluloid; Chorus Girl of 15 Becomes a Film Star Over Night; And My! How She Can Weep," *Photoplay,* Feb 1917, 27–28, 142. "Mary MacLaren," *MPW,* 3 Feb 1917, 672. "David Horsley Engages Mary MacLaren," *MPW,* 16 Jun 1917, 1785. Mary MacLaren, "How I Happened," *MPW,* 21 Jul 1917, 427, 459. "Mary MacLaren Injured," *MPW,* 22 Sep 1917, 1836. "Mary MacDonald MacLaren Resumes Work," *MPW,* 29 Dec 1917, 1948. "Mary MacLaren Returns to the Universal," *MPW,* 16 Feb 1918, 972. "Film Star Loses Suit," *MPW,* 3 Aug 1918, 686. "Film Star Fattens Her Cook Book," *MPW,* 5 Oct 1918, 103. "Mary MacLaren Entertains," *MPW,* 5 Apr 1919, 54. "Added to Cast," *MPW,* 23 Sep 1922, 280. Tom Topie, "Silent Film Star Remembers When...," *CFC,* 44 (Fall, 1974), X4.

M[a]cLarnie, Thomas [stage/film actor] (b. No. Adams MA, 1871–1 Dec 1931 [60?], Brighton MA). (Bosworth-Morosco.) BHD, p. 241. "Studio Gossip," *NYDM,* 16 Jun 1915, 20:4 (on stage for 20 years).

McLaughlin, Gibb [actor] (b. Sunderland, England, 19 Jul 1884–1960 [76]). AS, p. 747. BHD1, p. 351. IFN, p. 193.

McLaughlin, Harry (Tex) [aviator/actor] (d. 21 Sep 1920, Syracuse NY; plane collision). AS, p. 747. BHD, p. 241.

McLaughlin, Robert H. [scenarist] (b. 1877?–16 Jan 1939 [61], Cleveland OH). "Robert H. M'Laughlin; Cleveland Theatre Manager Was Also Playwright and Producer," *NYT,* 17 Jan 1939, 22:4. "Robert H. McLaughlin," *Variety,* 18 Jan 1939. AMD, p. 232. AS, p. 747. BHD2, p. 173. "Robert McLaughlin Is a Dramatist of Note," *MPW,* 30 Aug 1919, 1350.

McLaughlin, William "Froggy" [actor] (d. 15 Jul 1957, Huntington Beach CA). BHD1, p. 352.

McLean, Barbara [film editor/producer] (*née* Barbara Pollut, b. Palisades Park NJ, 16 Nov 1903–28 Mar 1996 [92], Newport Beach CA). m. Gordon McLean. (TC-F.) Robert McG. Thomas, Jr., "Barbara McLean; Film editor won 'Wilson' [1944] bio Oscar," *Pittsburgh Post-Gazette,* 69, 7 Apr 1996, B-6:1 (began in the 1920s in Palisades Park NJ with her father Charles). BHD2, p. 173.

MacLean, Douglas [stage/film actor/producer/scenarist] (*né* Charles Douglas MacLean, b. Philadelphia PA, 10 Jan 1890–9 Jul 1967 [77], Beverly Hills CA; after a cerebral thrombosis). m. (1) Faith (Fay) Cole; (3) Barbara Barondess, 1938–46. (Film debut: *As Ye Sow,* 1914; Ince; Christie; 1st National; RKO; Paramount.) "Douglas MacLean, Movie Producer; Comedian Who Starred in Silent Films Dies; Broker Turned Actor," *NYT,* 11 Jul 1967, 37:4. "Douglas MacLean," *Variety,* 12 Jul 1967. AMD, p. 232. AS, p. 697 (b. 14 Jan). BHD1, p. 352; BHD2, p. 173. FFF, p. 30. FSS, p. 202. IFN, p. 188. Katz, pp. 759–60 (b. 14 Jan). MH, p. 124. Ragan 2, pp. 88–89. Truitt, p. 210. WWS, p. 37. "Thomas Ince to Present New Stars," *MPW,* XL, 31 May 1919, 1316. Grace Kingsley, "They're Wedded Only in Films; McLean-May Partnership Is Purely Artistic; Feminine Co-Star Has Had Real Proposals from Frans; A Sketch of Pyramus and Thisbe of Cinema," *LA Times,* 29 Feb 1920, III, p. 1. "Douglas McLean's Dad Will Show Movies in His Church," *MPW,* 3 Apr 1920, 133 (Rev. C.C. McLean, Pastor of Lincoln Road M.E. Church, Washington DC). "Ince Separates Team of McLean—May; To Present McLean as Star in His Own Right," *MPW,* 15 May 1920, 964. "Douglas McLean Joins Associated Exhibitors," *MPW,* 18 Nov 1922, 244. "Douglas McLean's Popularity on the Increase," *MPW,* 10 Nov 1923, 252. "Douglas McLean," *MPW,* 4 Oct 1924, 408. "Doug McLean Signs with Paramount for a Series," *MPW,* 28 Mar 1925, 376. Doris Curran, "The Boy Who Knew the President; Douglas MacLean Was the Son of a Minister," *MPC,* Sep 1925, 42–43, 77. Doris Denbo, "They've Gotten Doug's 'Goat'; This MacLean Fellow Wants a Dark Past 'Cause They're Calling Him Clean and Wholesome," *MPC,* Nov 1926, 57, 90. Eve Golden, "Douglas MacLean: The Man with the Million-Dollar Smile," *CI,* 262 (Apr 1997), 16–19 (includes filmography by R.E. Braff).

McLean, Grace [vaudeville/film actress] (*née* Grace Dryborough, d. 22 Aug 1980, Dumbarton, Scotland). m. actor Lex McLean (d. Mar 1975). "Grace McLean," *Variety,* 300, 3 Sep 1980, 86.

McLean, Jack [actor]. No data found. AMD, p. 232. "Players Engaged for 'When Man Betrays,'" *MPW,* 18 May 1918, 1019.

McLean, K.C. [cinematographer]. No data found. FDY, p. 461.

McLean, Larry [actor] (b. Cambridge MA, 18 Jul 1881–14 Mar 1921 [39], Boston MA). BHD, p. 241.

MacLean, Leola Maye [actress/scenarist] (b. 1891–17 Apr 1928 [37?], Glendale CA). BHD2, p. 173.

MacLean, Rezin D. [stage/film actor] (*né* Rezin Donald Shepherd, b. New Orleans LA, 7 Mar 1859–27 Jun 1948 [89], Los Angeles CA). m. Odette Tyler (*née* Elizabeth Lee Kirkland, d. 1936) "Rezin D. MacLean," *Variety,* 30 Jun 1948. AS, p. 697. BHD, p. 241. IFN, p. 188. SD. Truitt, p. 210.

McLean, Ronald D. [actor] (b. New Orleans LA, 7 Mar 1859–27 Jun 1948 [89], Los Angeles CA). BHD1, p. 352.

McLennan, Rodney [actor] (b. Melbourne, Australia, 28 Dec 1901–27 Nov 1973 [71], Miami FL). BHD1, p. 352. IFN, p. 193.

McLeod, Elsie [actress]. No data found. (Edison, 1911.) AMD, p. 232. BHD, p. 241 (b. ca. 1890). "Elsie MacLeod with Vim," *MPW,* 12 Feb

1916, 937. "Elsie MacLeod," *MPW,* 18 Mar 1916, 1847. James Trottier, "Elsie McLeod: Edison's Sweetheart," *CI,* 265 (Jul 1997), C4.

McLeod, Gordon [actor] (b. Ivybridge, England, 27 Dec 1890–1961 [71?]). AS, p. 747 (b. 1886). BHD1, p. 352.

MacLeod, Kenneth T. [actor] (b. MA, 6 Sep 1895–6 Dec 1963 [68], Los Angeles CA). "Kenneth T. MacLeod, 68, film actor, died Dec. 6 in Hollywood. Sister survives," *Variety,* 18 Dec 1963. AS, p. 697. IFN, p. 188.

McLeod, Norman Z[enos] [title writer/director] (b. Grayling MI, 20 Sep 1895?–27 Jan 1964 [68], Los Angeles CA). (Fox, 1928; Paramount.) "Norman M'Leod, 68, Screen Director," *NYT,* 28 Jan 1964, 31:5 ("Capitalizing on his flair for drawing, he got a $25-a-week job sketching quaint figures to illustrate Al Christie comedies. Eventually he became a top director at Paramount, Metro-Goldwyn-Mayer and Sam Goldwyn studios."). "Norman Z. McLeod," *Variety,* 29 Jan 1964 (drew line characters on title cards). AS, p. 747 (b. 1898). BHD2, p. 173 (d. 26 Jan). FDY, p. 447. *Green Encyclopedia of the Musical Film,* pp. 87–88 (b. 30 Sep 1898).

McLeod, Tex (Alexander) [actor] (b. Gonzales TX, 11 Nov 1889–12 Feb 1973 [83], Brighton, England; heart attack). AS, p. 747 (b. 1896). BHD1, p. 352.

MacLiammoir, Michael [actor] (*né* Alfred Willmore, b. Cork, Ireland, 25 Oct 1899–6 Mar 1978 [78], Dublin, Ireland). AS, p. 697. BHD1, p. 352.

McMackin, Archer [journalist/director/producer/writer]. No data found. AMD, p. 232. "Big 'U' Captures Archer McMackin," *MPW,* 20 Feb 1915, 1126. "Gossip of the Studios," *NYDM,* 14 Apr 1915, 23:2. Grace Kingsley, "Flashes; Thala Is Ousted; Comedy Studio Taken Over by Bible Makers," *LA Times,* 12 Mar 1920, III, p. 4 (the Historical Film Corp. bought the Rolin studio on Bunker Hill Avenue, and hired McMackin as director, Henry Christeen Warnack as editor and supervising director, and Clara Frazee as actress and costumer).

MacMahon, Henry [publicist]. No data found. AMD, p. 232. "Pressmen Versus Agencies," *MPW,* 26 Feb 1916, 1305. "Henry MacMahon Already Busy," *MPW,* 18 Mar 1916, 1813. "MacMahon Writes on Adapting Novels," *MPW,* 12 May 1917, 934. "Starts Literary Bureau," *MPW,* 20 Oct 1917, 393. "MacMahon's List Ready," *MPW,* 15 Dec 1917, 1658. Henry MacMahon, "Obstacles to Good Press Work," *MPW,* 20 Jul 1918, 343. "MacMahon to Handle Pathé Publicity in West Coast Studio," *MPW,* 1 Oct 1927, 279.

McMahon, John G. [actor] (b. LA, 18 Jul 1890–18 Aug 1968 [78]). AS, p. 748.

McManigal, E.T. [cinematographer]. No data found. FDY, p. 461.

McManus, Edward A. [executive]. No data found. AMD, p. 233. "McManus Now Serial Manager of Paramount," *MPW,* 4 Aug 1917, 771. Edward A. McManus, "Public Demands Realism in Pictures Instead of Overwrought Sentiment," *MPW,* 27 Dec 1919, 1121.

McManus, George [actor/cartoonist] (b. St. Louis MO, 23 Jan 1884–22 Oct 1954 [70], Santa Monica CA). AMD, p. 233. AS, p. 748. BHD1, p. 353. IFN, p. 193. "'The World Needs to Laugh,' Says Originator of 'Jiggs,'" *MPW,* 3 Apr 1920, 108.

MacMillan, Violet [actress] (b. Grand Rapids MI, 4 Mar 1887–28 Dec 1953 [66], Grand Rapids MI). m. (1) G.W. Bird; John H. Folger. "'Cinderella Girl' Dies; Violet MacMillan, ex-Actress, Was Famed for Tiny Feet," *NYT,* 30 Dec 1953, 23:5. "Violet MacMillan," *Variety,* 6 Jan 1954 (d. 28 Dec 1953). AMD, p. 233. AS, p. 697. BHD, p. 241. IFN, p. 188. SD. Truitt, p. 210. "Violet MacMillan," *MPW,* 13 Feb 1915, 992. Billy H. Doyle, "Lost Players," *CI,* 171 (Sep 1989), C2.

McMurphy, Charles [actor] (b. North Vernon IN, 31 Jul 1892–24 Oct 1969 [77], Los Angeles Co. CA). BHD1, p. 353 (b. 1894). IFN, p. 193.

McNab, Dorothy Cumming [actress] (b. 1899?–10 Dec 1983 [84]). (Played the Virgin in *The King of Kings.*) AS, p. 748.

McNamara, Edward C. [actor/singer] (b. Paterson NJ, 1887–10 Nov 1944 [57?], Boston MA). AS, p. 748.

McNamara, Ted [actor] (b. Australia, 1891?–3 Feb 1928 [36], Ventura CA; pneumonia). (Fox.) "Ted McNamara," *Variety,* 8 Feb 1928. AMD, p. 233. AS, p. 748. BHD, p. 241 (b. 1894, addendum). IFN, p. 193. Truitt, p. 226. WWS, p. 226. "Ted McNamara on Fox Contract," *MPW,* 18 Sep 1926, 157.

McNamara, Tom [director/author] (b. San Francisco CA, 7 May 1886–19 May 1964 [78], San Francisco CA). "Tom McNamara," *Variety,* 27 May 1964 (cartoonist of "Our Gang" comic strip; directed Mary Pickford in *Little Annie Rooney*). AMD, p. 233. AS, p. 748. BHD2, p. 173. IFN, p. 193. "Joins Scenario Department," *MPW,* 5 Feb 1921, 682. "Hal Roach Re-engages Tom McNamara," *MPW,* 21 Apr 1923, 867. "Tom McNamara Signed," *MPW,* 11 Apr 1925, 566. "McNamara Signed by F.B.O.," *MPW,* 5 Mar 1927, 10. "F.B.O. Gets 'Mac,'" *MPW,* 5 Mar 1927, 45.

McNamara, Thomas J. [vaudevillian] (d. 21 May 1953, Brooklyn NY). "Thomas J. McNamara," *Variety,* 27 May 1953 (in films with Marion Davies and the Pickfords). AS, p. 748.

MacNamara, Walter [director] (b. Ireland). AMD, p. 233. "Walter MacNamara to Direct for Imp," *MPW,* 1 Nov 1913, 500. "Walter McNamara, Director [Universal]," *MPW,* 8 Nov 1913, 613. George Blaisdell, "Irish History on the Screen," *MPW,* 29 Aug 1914, 1245. "Walter MacNamara Rejoins Universal," *MPW,* 1 Jan 1916, 56. "MacNamara Writes Universal Story," *MPW,* 8 Jan 1916, 225. "MacNamara with Mirror Films," *MPW,* 26 Feb 1916, 1275. "Walter MacNamara Off for Keystoneville," *MPW,* 24 Mar 1917, 1938.

McNamee, Donald [actor] (b. 1897?–17 Jul 1940 [43?], Los Angeles CA; skull fracture). m. Ada Lilly. "Donald McNamee," *Variety,* 24 Jul 1940. AS, p. 748. BHD1, p. 353. Truitt, p. 226.

McNamee, Graham [actor] (b. Washington DC, 10 Jul 1888–9 May 1942 [53], New York NY). BHD1, p. 353. IFN, p. 193.

McNaughton, Charles (brother of **Tom** and **Fred McNaughton**) [actor] (b. Walthamstow, Essex, England, 24 Apr 1878–4 Dec 1955 [77], Los Angeles Co. CA). AS, p. 748 (d. London, England). BHD1, p. 353. IFN, p. 193.

McNaughton, Fred (brother of **Charles** and **Tom McNaughton**) [actor] (b. Walthamstow, England, 1869–15 Feb 1920 [50?], London, England). AS, p. 748.

McNaughton, Gus [actor] (*né* Augustus Howardle Clerq, b. London, England, 18 Jul 1881–18 Nov 1969 [88], Castor, England). AS, p. 748.

McNaughton, Harry [stage/radio/film actor] (b. Surbiton, England, 29 Apr 1896–26 Feb 1967 [70], Amityville, LI NY). m. Marion Turpie. "Harry M'Naughton of Stage and Radio," *NYT,* 28 Feb 1967, 34:1. "Harry McNaughton," *Variety,* 1 Mar 1967. AS, p. 748. BHD1, p. 353. IFN, p. 193. SD.

McNaughton, Tom (brother of **Charles** and **Fred McNaughton**) [actor] (b. Walthamstow, England, 1 Jul 1867–28 Nov 1923 [56], St. Albans, England). (Lubin.) AMD, p. 233. AS, p. 749. BHD, p. 242. "McNaughton with Lubin; Eccentric Lubin Comedian to Be Seen with Marie Dressler on the Screen [in *Tillie's Tomato Surprise*]," *NYDM,* 16 Jun 1915, 21:4. "Tom McNaughton," *MPW,* 26 Jun 1915, 2075.

McNeil, Allen [film editor/scenarist]. No data found. FDY, p. 433.

McNeil, Everett [scenarist]. No data found. (Vitagraph.) "Briefs of Biography; A Friend of Young America," *NYDM,* 6 Oct 1915, 33:2 (his specialty was juvenile fiction).

McNeil, Frank A[shby] [actor/wardrobe man] (b. MO, 18 Nov 1867–27 Feb 1918 [50], Los Angeles CA; heart ailment). AMD, p. 233. AS, p. 698. BHD, p. 242. "Obituary," *MPW,* 30 Mar 1918, 1829 (d. 9 Mar).

McNeil, Norman [actor] (b. Charleston SC, 27 Oct 1891–17 Dec 1938 [47]). AS, p. 749. BHD1, p. 363. IFN, p. 194.

McNeill, James P. [assistant director] (b. Philadelphia PA, 1881–25 Aug 1944 [63?], Philadelphia PA). BHD2, p. 173.

McNish, Frank E. [actor] (b. Camden NY, 14 Dec 1853–27 Dec 1924 [71], Chicago IL; stroke). "Frank McNish," *Variety,* 7 Jan 1925. AS, p. 749 (d. 1925). BHD, p. 242.

McNulty, Harold [film/TV actor] (b. 16 Mar 1901–6 Jun 1978 [77], Los Angeles CA; found dead). (Began 1918.) "Howard [sic] McNulty," *Variety,* 291, 14 Jun 1978, 83:1 (multiple nerve damage from a heart attack restricted his movements and ended his career. Had been dead several days when found by a niece). AS, p. 749. BHD1, p. 354. IFN, p. 194.

MacNulty, William [technical/art director]. No data found. AMD, p. 233. "MacNulty with Famous Players," *MPW,* 8 Jun 1918, 1409.

McNutt, Patterson (brother of **William S. McNutt**) [actor/scenarist/producer] (b. Urbana IL, 30 Sep 1896–23 Oct 1948 [52], New York NY). AS, p. 749 (d. 22 Oct). BHD2, p. 173.

McNutt, William S[lavens] (brother of **Patterson McNutt**) [actor/producer/director/playwright/scenarist] (b. Urbana IL, 12 Sep 1885–25 Jan 1938 [52], La Canada CA; bronchial pneumonia and weakened heart). m. (1) Georgina McNally—div. 1927; (2) Mrs. Louise Tanner Glorius, 1927. (Paramount; RKO.) "William S. M'Nutt, Screen Scenarist; One of Most Successful Film Writers in Recent Years Dies in Hollywood; Former Magazine Author; Worked at Variety of Trades Throughout Country Before Turning to Fiction," *NYT,* 27 Jan 1938, 21:4. "William Slavens McNutt," *Variety,* 2 Feb 1938. AMD, p. 233. AS, p. 749. BHD2, p. 173. IFN, p. 194. "William Slavens McNutt Signed," *MPW,* 8 Aug 1925, 656.

Mcollum, Barry [actor] (b. Belfast, No. Ireland, 6 Apr 1889–22 Feb 1971 [81], Los Angeles CA). BHD1, p. 356.

McOrlan, Pierre [actor/scenarist] (*né* Pierre Dumarchey, b. Peronne, France, 26 Feb 1882–27 Jun 1970 [88], Saint-Cyr-sur-Morin, France). AS, p. 698.

MacPhail, Angus [title writerr/scenarist] (b. 8 Apr 1903–22 Apr 1962 [59], England). (Began 1926; Gaumont British; Ealing.) "Angus MacPhail," *Variety*, 226, 9 May 1962, 87:3. AS, p. 698. BHD2, p. 173. FDY, p. 433.

MacPherson, Harry Farnsworth [actor] (b. MA, 14 May 1882?–5 Aug 1951 [69], Sawtelle CA; result of auto accident). "Harry Farnsworth MacPherson," *Variety*, 15 Aug 1951. AS, p. 698. BHD, p. 242; BHD2, p. 173 (b. 1887).

MacPherson, James Gladstone [actor/scenarist] (d. 14 Dec 1932). BHD2, p. 173.

MacPherson, Jeanie [scenarist] (b. Boston MA, 29 Aug 1884–26 Aug 1946 [61], Los Angeles CA). (Biograph, 1908.) "Jeanie M'Pherson, Early Film Writer," *NYT*, 27 Aug 1946, 27:2. "Jeanie MacPherson," *Variety*, 28 Aug 1946 (age 59). AMD, p. 233. AS, p. 698. BHD, p. 242; BHD2, p. 173 (b. 18 May 1887). FDY, p. 433. IFN, p. 188. Katz, p. 761 (b. 1884). Lowrey, p. 110. Truitt, p. 210. "Stars for Criterion," *MPW*, 21 Feb 1914, 975. "Miss MacPherson Wrote Pickford Photoplay," *MPW*, 14 Jul 1917, 225. Jeanie MacPherson, "Development of Photodramatic Writing," *MPW*, 21 Jul 1917, 393. "Jeanie MacPherson in Nerw York," *MPW*, 27 Oct 1917, 545. "Jeanie MacPherson," *MPW*, 5 Jan 1918, 86. "Miss MacPherson Entertains Fairbanks," *MPW*, 23 Feb 1918, 1095. "Evolving Film Titles Aids Writing of Dialogue," *MPW*, 13 Dec 1919, 831. Edward Weitzel, "Jeanie MacPherson on Film Limits and the Joys of Unbounded Space," *MPW*, 17 Jan 1920, 401. "Jeanie MacPherson to Write Five More Years for DeMille," *MPW*, 10 Jul 1920, 212. "Jeanie MacPherson Going to Europe to Take First Vacation in Several Years," *MPW*, 19 Mar 1921, 258. Edward Weitzel, "Jeanie MacPherson Has a Great Ambition; Hopes to Fly Across the Ocean Some Day," *MPW*, 2 Apr 1921, 500. "Returns from Europe," *MPW*, L, 18 Jun 1921, 703. "Jeanie MacPherson Resigns," *MPW*, 22 Mar 1924, 268. "Miss MacPherson Recovers," *MPW*, 30 Jul 1927, 307 (from nervous breakdown). George Katchmer, "Remembering the Great Silents," *CI*, 229 (Jul 1994), 37.

McPherson, Quinton [actor] (b. England, 1871–2 Jan 1940 [68?], London, England). AS, p. 749.

McPherson, William [photographer] (b. 1873–15 Jun 1934 [61?], Westwood CA). BHD2, p. 173.

McPherson, William [actor] (b. 1890?–1 Mar 1920 [30], near Los Angeles CA; auto and train collision). (National film cowboy.) AMD, p. 233. "Obituary," *MPW*, 20 Mar 1920, 1963.

MacQuarrie, Albert [actor/makeup artist] (b. San Francisco CA, 8 Jan 1882–17 Feb 1950 [68], Los Angeles CA). "Albert MacQuarrie," *Variety*, 22 Feb 1950. AS, p. 698 (d. 26 Aug 1946). BHD, p. 242; BHD2, p. 173. IFN, p. 188. George A. Katchmer, "Remembering the Great Silents," *CI*, 231 (Sep 1994), 49–50 (began at the Alcazar Theater in SF CA in 1904).

MacQuarrie, Frank M[ichael] [actor] (b. San Francisco CA, 27 Jan 1875–25 Dec 1950 [75], Los Angeles CA). BHD, p. 242. IFN, p. 188. George Katchmer, "Remembering the Great Silents," *CI*, 229 (Jul 1994), 38.

MacQuarrie, George [actor]. No data found. AMD, p. 233. "Brady Featuring George MacQuarrie," *MPW*, 12 Jan 1918, 217.

MacQuarrie, Haven [actor/producer] (*né* Frank Haven MacQuarrie, b. MA, 10 Apr 1894–4 Aug 1953 [59], Los Angeles CA). "Haven MacQuarrie," *Variety*, 12 Aug 1953. AS, p. 698. IFN, p. 188.

MacQuarrie, Murdock J. [actor/director] (b. San Francisco CA, 25 Aug 1878–22 Aug 1942 [63], Los Angeles CA). "Murdock MacQuarrie," *Variety*, 26 Aug 1942. AS, p. 698. BHD1, p. 354; BHD2, p. 173. IFN, p.188. 1921 Directory, p. 270. Truitt, p. 210. "Lives of the Players; Murdock MacQuarrie," *MPS*, 11 Jul 1913, 29.

McQuillan, Ada [scenarist]. No data found. FDY, p. 433.

McQuoid, Buddy [actor] (*né* Edwin McQuoid, b. 1910–15 Jul 1950 [40], Los Angeles CA). BHD, p. 242. IFN, p. 194.

McQuoid, Rose Lee [actress] (b. AZ, 26 Oct 1886–4 May 1962 [75], Los Angeles CA). (Universal.) "Rose Lee McQuoid," *Variety*, 16 May 1962. AS, p. 749. BHD1, p. 354. IFN, p. 194. Truitt, p. 227.

McRae, Bruce [stage/film actor] (b. India, 15 Jan 1867–7 May 1927 [60], City Island [New York] NY; heart attack). m. Nellie. (FP-L; Pathé; Equitable; Ince.) "Bruce M'Rae, Actor, Dies at 60; One of the Most Popular Leading Men on the American Stage for Thirty Years; Had a Colorful Career; Began at 16 as a Rancher in New Zealand—With Alice Brady in 'Legend of Lenora' Recently," *NYT*, 8 May 1927, 29:4. "Bruce McRae," *Variety*, 11 May 1927. AMD, p. 233. AS, p. 749. BHD, p. 242. IFN, p. 194. Truitt, p. 227. "Bruce McRae to Famous Players," *MPW*, 2 May 1914, 655. "Bruce McRae to Famous Players," *MPW*, 9 May 1914, 795. "Bruce McRae," *MPW*, 12 Feb 1916, 960.

McRae, Duncan [actor/director] (nephew of **Sir Charles Wyndham**) (b. London, England, 1881–4 Feb 1931 [49?], London, England). m. **Gertrude McCoy**, 1919 (d. 1967). (Mutual; Edison; Pathé; Essanay; Metro.) "Duncan McRae Dies," *Variety*, 11 and 18 Feb 1931. AMD, p. 233. AS, p. 749. BHD, p. 242; BHD2, p. 174. IFN, p. 194. SD, p. 828. "McRae Now Directing," *NYDM*, 5 May 1915, 24:3 (*Through Turbulent Waters*, Edison 3-reeler, story by Gertrude McCoy). "Duncan McRae, Viola Dana's Lead," *MPW*, 27 May 1916, 1496.

McRae, Gordon [actor] (b. East Orange NJ, 12 Mar 1921–24 Jan 1986 [64], Lincoln NB). BHD, p. 242.

McRae, Henry A. [scenarist/director/producer] (b. Toronto, Ontario, Canada, 29 Aug 1876–2 Oct 1944 [68], Beverly Hills CA; heart attack). m. Margaret Oswald. (Universal, 1910.) "Henry McRae," *Variety*, 4 Oct 1944. AMD, p. 233. AS, p. 749. BHD2, p. 174. IFN, p. 194. "Henry McRae Joins Selig Staff," *MPW*, 7 Sep 1912, 957. "The Man Who Put the 'Biz' in Bisons," *MPW*, 27 Dec 1913, 1559. "Universal's New Director," *MPW*, 24 Jul 1915, 630. "McRae to Direct 101 Bison Films," *MPW*, 5 Feb 1916, 781. "Henry McRae Starts New Serial," *MPW*, 1 Mar 1919, 1185. "McRae to Produce for Circuit," *MPW*, 3 Jul 1920, 93. "U.S. Films Do More Than Diplomacy in Convincing Japan We Are Firendly," *MPW*, 10 Jul 1920, 241. "Ernest Shipman Signs Henry McRae to Supervise Direction of Dominion FilMs," *MPW*, 17 Jul 1920, 356. *Bangkok Daily Mail*, 25 Jun 1923 (wrote and directed the first feature-length film produced in Siam [Thailand], *Miss Suwanna of Siam* [*Nangsao Suwan*], American Motion Picture Co., 1923. Upon his death he was credited with these innovations: artificial light for interiors, the wind machine, double exposures, and shooting at night). "McRae Heads 'U' City Plant," *MPW*, 5 Dec 1925, 420.

McRae, Tom A. [actor] (d. 6 Jan 1931, Hollis, LI NY). m. Ann Clark. "Tom A. McRae," *Variety*, 21 Jan 1931. AS, p. 749.

McShane, Kitty [actress] (b. Dublin, Ireland, 1898–24 Mar 1964 [65?], London, England). AS, p. 750.

MacSweeney, John P. [actor] (b. Deptford, England, 1 Mar 1857–14 Oct 1937 [81], Amityville, LI NY). "John P. Mac-Sweeney; Retired Actor, Native of England, Dies in Amityville at 80," *NYT*, 16 Oct 1937, 19:4. AS, p. 698.

McTammany, Ruth [actress]. No data found. AMD, p. 234. "Ruth McTammany," *MPW*, 21 Apr 1917, 440.

McVeigh, John [vaudevillian] (b. 1875?–2 Jul 1914 [39], New York NY). "John McVeigh," *Variety*, 10 Jul 1914. AS, p. 750. BHD, p. 242.

McVey, Joseph Lee (nephew of **Sidney Drew** and **Lucille McVey**) [actor]. No data found. AMD, p. 234. "Debut of Third Drew Generation," *MPW*, 7 Jul 1917, 89.

McVey, Lucille (aunt of **Joseph Lee McVey**) [concert singer/actress] (aka Jane Morrow, *née* Lucille McVegh, b. Sedalia MO, 18 Apr 1890–3 Nov 1925 [35], Los Angeles CA; respiratory ailment). m. **Sidney Drew**, 29 Jul 1914, Little Church Around the Corner, NYC (d. 1919). (Vitagraph; Metro; Paramount.) "Mrs. Sidney Drew Dead; Film Actress, Actor's Widow, Dies in Los Angeles at 35," *NYT*, 4 Nov 1925, 23:4; "Services for Mrs. Sidney Drew," 6 Nov 1925, 23:5. "Mrs. Lucille McVey-Drew," *Variety*, 11 Nov 1925. AMD, pp. 103, 234. AS, p. 750; p. 790 (Jane Morrow). BHD, p. 154; BHD2, p. 72. IFN, p. 87. MSBB, p. 1034. Slide, p. 98. Truitt, pp. 93–94. WWS, p. 220. "Sidney Drew to Wed," *NYDM*, 22 Jul 1914, 22:1. "Lucille McVey," *MPW*, 10 Jul 1915, 310. "The Sidney Drews Celebrate Second Wedding Anniversary," *MPW*, 12 Aug 1916, 1089. "Lucille McVey," *MPW*, 27 Jan 1917, 522. "The Drew's 'On Vacation' in Florida," *MPW*, 23 Feb 1918, 1103. Edward Weitzel, "How 'Henry' Keeps Her Smiling," *MPW*, 21 Dec 1918, 1323–24. "The Drew's Welcome All Exhibitor' Suggestions," *MPW*, 8 Feb 1919, 791. "Mr. and Mrs. Sidney Drew Honored at Operators' Ball," *MPW*, 8 Mar 1919, 1334. "The Passing of Sidney Drew," *MPW*, 26 Apr 1919, 511–12. "American Legion Honors Memory of S. Rankin Drew [son]," *MPW*, 20 Sep 1919, 1808. "Pathé Signs Hobart Henley and Mrs. Sidney Drew; Paul Bruner Predicts Brilliant Future for Both," *MPW*, 27 Sep 1919, 1963. "Mrs. Drew Sues V.B.K. Film Corporation," *MPW*, 15 Nov 1919, 336. "Mrs. Sidney Drew Returns to Films in Third of Her Pathé Comedies," *MPW*, 28 Feb 1920, 1503. "Mrs. Sidney Drew Intends to Try Her Art at Tragedy," *MPW*, 29 May 1920, 1215. "Mrs. Drew Seized by Appendicitis," *MPW*, 5 Jun 1920, 1320. "Mrs. Sidney Drew Returns to Vitagrpah Studio as Director," *MPW*, 21 Aug 1920, 1057.

McVicker, Julius [actor] (b. 1855–11 Mar 1940 [85?], Beverly Hills CA). AS, p. 750.

McWade, Edward [actor] (b. Washington

DC, 14 Jan 1865–17 May 1943 [78], Los Angeles CA). "Edward McWade," *Variety,* 19 May 1943. AS, p. 750. BHD1, p. 355; BHD2, p. 174. IFN, p. 194. Truitt, p. 227.

McWade, Margaret [actress] (b. IL, 3 Sep 1872–1 Apr 1956 [83], Los Angeles CA). (Metro.) AMD, p. 234. AS, p. 750. BHD1, p. 355. IFN, p. 194. "Famous Actress Joins World Pictures," *MPW,* 8 Jun 1918, 1414. "Wife of Play Author," *LA Times,* 19 Feb 1920, III, p. 14 (her husband wrote and produced *Winchester* and was to become a director at Goldwyn. Her had just finished a role in *Shore Acres* for Metro.). "First Actress to Introduce Films Into Spoken Drama Has Part in Selig-Rork Pictures," *MPW,* 29 Oct 1921, 1066.

McWade, Robert, Jr. (son of **Robert McWade, Sr.**) [actor] (b. Buffalo NY, 17 Jun 1872–19 Jan 1938 [65], Culver City CA). "Final Scene Finished, M'Wade Dies on Set; Character Actor Completes Role in His Latest Film [M-G-M's *Benefits Forgot*], Then Succumbs to a Heart Attack," *NYT,* 20 Jan 1938, 19:3. "Robert McWade," *Variety,* 26 Jan 1938 (age 56). AS, p. 750. BHD1, p. 355. IFN, p. 194. Truitt, p. 227.

McWade, Robert, Sr. (father of **Robert McWade, Jr.**) [actor] (b. Long Sault Rapids, Canada, 25 Jan 1835–5 Mar 1913 [78], New York NY). (Vitagraph.) "Robert McWade, Sr.," *Variety,* 14 Mar 1913, p. 26. AMD, p. 234. AS, p. 750. BHD, p. 242. "Obituary," *MPW,* 22 Mar 1913, 1226.

McWatters, Arthur J. [actor] (b. 1871–16 Jul 1963 [92?], Freeport NY). AS, p. 750.

MacWilliams, Glen [title writer/cinematographer] (b. Saratoga CA, 21 May 1898–15 Apr 1984 [85], Seal Beach CA). BHD2, p. 174. FDY, pp. 447, 461.

Macy, Carleton [vaudevillian/stage/film actor] (b. New Brighton, SI NY, 1861?–17 Oct 1946 [85], Bay Shore, LI NY). m. Maude Hall (d. 1938). (Ivan.) "Carleton Macy, 85, Veteran of Stage; Character Actor Who Played More than 500 Roles Dies—Also in Vaudeville," *NYT,* 18 Oct 1946, 23:5. "Carleton Macy," *Variety,* 23 Oct 1946. AS, p. 701 (d. 18 Oct). BHD1, p. 356. IFN, p. 194.

Macy, Jack [actor] (b. 1886–2 Jul 1956 [70?], heart attack on an airplane traveling between Los Angeles and Chicago). AS, p. 701.

Macy, Maud Hall [actress] (b. 1881–1 May 1938 [57?], Liberty NY). BHD, p. 242.

Madalena, Batiste [poster artist] (b. Italy, 12 Jan 1902–28 Nov 1988 [86], Rochester, Monroe NY 14619). *Movie Posters: The Paintings of Batiste Madalena* (NY: Harry N. Abrams, Inc., 1986).

Madame Simone [actress] (*née* Simone Benda, b. Paris, France, 3 Apr 1877–18 Oct 1985 [108], Bayonne, France). AS, p. 701.

Madan, J[amjetji] **F**[ramji] [director/producer] (b. India, 1856–1923 [67?], India). AS, p. 701.

Madd, Pierrette [actress] (*née* Paulette Poggionovo, b. Charenton, France, 9 Aug 1893–22 Aug 1967 [74], Cannes, France [extrait de décès no. 767/1967]). AS, p. 701.

Madden, Edward M. [composer] (b. New York NY, 17 Jul 1878–11 Mar 1952 [75], Los Angeles CA). "Edward Madden," *NYT,* 12 Mar 1952, 27:1 (age 74; wrote *Daddy's Little Girl; By the Light of the Silvery Moon;* and *Moonlight Bay*). "Edward Madden," *Variety,* 19 Mar 1952. AS, p. 701. ASCAP 66, p. 464. BHD2, p. 174.

Madden, Golda [actress] (b. NB, 17 Jul 1886–26 Oct 1960 [74], Los Angeles CA). BHD, p. 242.

Madden, Jerry [child actor] (b. ca. 1923). (Fox.) Ruth Tildesley, "Hollywood Night's Entertainment," *Paris and Hollywood Screen Secrets Magazine,* III (Oct 1927), 92 (celebrated his fourth birthday party).

Maddie, Ginette [actress] (*née* Marcelle Claudine Taride, b. Paris, France, 6 Jan 1897–31 Aug 1984 [87], Boulogne-Billancourt, France [extrait de décès no. 1/390/AA05599]). AS, p. 701.

Maddock, C.B. [producer] (b. 1881–17 Jun 1974 [93?], Los Angeles CA). BHD2, p. 174.

Madison, Cleo [actress/scenarist/director] (b. Chicago IL, 26 Mar 1884–10 Mar 1964 [79], Burbank CA; heart attack). m. Don Peake, Riverside CA, 25 Nov 1916. (Universal, 1913.) "Cleo Madison," *Variety,* 18 Mar 1964. AMD, p. 234. AS, p. 701 (b. Bloomington IL; d. 11 Mar). BHD, p. 242; BHD2, p. 174 (b. Bloomington). IFN, p. 195. MH, p. 124 (b. Bloomington). Slide, *Early Women Directors* (NY: A.S. Barnes and Co., 1977), pp. 52–54 (b. Bloomington). Truitt, p. 211. "Cleo Madison," *MPW,* 4 Apr 1914, 43. "Cleo Madison Has Narrow Escape," *MPW,* 8 Aug 1914, 846. "Cleo Madison Back from Vacation," *MPW,* 21 Nov 1914, 1064. "Cleo Madison and Ray Hanford Stricken with Pneumonia," *MPW,* 3 Jul 1915, 67. J. Van Cartmell, "Along the Pacific Coast," *NYDM,* 13 Nov 1915, 31:1 (injured while making *A Man, a Maid and a Liar;* 'A fall from a treacherous position resulted in cuts about the head and face so serious as to cause her removal to a Los Angeles hospital."). "Cleo Madison, a Bride," *MPW,* 23 Dec 1916, 1789. Cal York, "Plays and Players," *Photoplay Magazine,* Feb 1917, 86 (married Peake). "Cleo Madison," *MPW,* 7 Apr 1917, 100. "Cleo Madison Organizes Company," *MPW,* 3 May 1919, 661. Buck Rainey, "Cleo Madison; A Gal Who Could Be Counted On to Do Her Job in a Workmanlike Manner," *CI,* 143 (May 1987), 17–20.

Madison, Harry [actor] (b. 1877?–8 Jul 1936 [59], Los Angeles CA; pneumonia). "Harry Madison," *Variety,* 15 Jul 1936. AS, p. 701. BHD, p. 242. IFN, p. 195. Truitt, p. 211.

Madison, James [writer/scenarist] (*né* Charles Aronstein, b. San Francisco CA, 1870–27 Mar 1943 [73?], New York NY). AMD, p. 234. AS, p. 701. "Madison Signed by Fox," *MPW,* 17 Jul 1926, 1. "Fox Signs Madison," *MPW,* 21 Aug 1926, 3.

Madriguera, Enric [actor/composer] (b. Brazil, 1902–7 Sep 1973 [71?], Brazil). AS, p. 702.

Madsen, Harald [actor/Madsen and Schenstrom] (b. Silkeborg, Denmark, 20 Nov 1890–13 Jul 1949 [58], Copenhagen, Denmark). AS, p. 702. BHD1, p. 357. IFN, p. 195.

Madsen, Holger [actor/director] (b. Denmark, 1878–1943 [65?], Denmark). AS, p. 702.

Mae, Jimsey [actress] (*née* Charlotte Rawley, b. Spokane WA, 1893–10 Apr 1968 [74], Jackson OR). AS, p. 702 (b. 1878–d. LA CA). IFN, p. 195. Truitt, p. 211.

Maedler, Richard W. [title writer/insert photographer] (b. 20 Feb 1890-Dec 1985 [95], FL 33516).

Maertens, Willy [actor] (*né* Wilhelm Hermann August Maertens, b. Brunswick, Germany, 30 Oct 1893–28 Nov 1967 [74], Hamburg, Germany). AS, p. 702.

Maeterlinck, Maurice [poet/playwright/scenarist] (b. Ghent, Belgium, 29 Aug 1862–6 May 1949 [86], Château d'Orlamonde, near Nice, French Riviera; heart attack). m. (1) Georgette Leblanc; (2) actress Renée Dahon, 1919. *Blue Bubbles.* "Maeterlinck Dies; Noted Poet, Was 86; 'Belgian Shakespeare' Stricken at Villa on French Riviera—Wrote of Spiritual World; Won a Nobel Prize in 1911; Two of His Works, 'Blue Bird' [1910] and 'Pelleas et Melisande,' Later Stories for Operas," *NYT,* 7 May 1949, 13:1 ("He went to California, too, to write for the motion-picture interests, and this resulted in still another legal suit against the Goldwyn Corporation at Culver City."); "Maugham's Ashes Buried in England," 23 Dec 1965, 28:8.. "[Count] Maurice Maeterlinck," *Variety,* 11 May 1949, p. 55:1. AMD, p. 234. Louis Reeves Harrison, "Creative Methods—Maeterlinck," *MPW,* 14 Oct 1916, 208. "Ruth Clifford Entertains Maeterlinck at Luncheon," *MPW,* 14 Feb 1920, 1052. "Maurice Maeterlinck, Belgian Poet, to Write Annual Story for Goldwyn," *MPW,* 14 Feb 1920, 1075. "Maeterlinck on Way to Goldwyn's Coast Plant; To Study Film Technique," *MPW,* 21 Feb 1920, 1279. "Maeterlinck Finishes First Screen Story for Goldwyn," *MPW,* 2 Oct 1920, 607. "Maurice Maeterlinck Now with Metro-Goldwyn-Mayer," *MPW,* 14 Feb 1925, 713.

Maffeis, Narciso [cinematographer] (b. Turin, Italy, 1878–29 May 1938 [59?], Turin, Italy). JS, p. 256 (in Italian silents from 1915).

Magana, Delia [actress] (b. Mexico City, Mexico, 2 Feb 1903–31 Mar 1996 [93], Mexico City, Mexico). BHD1, p. 357.

Magee, Harriett [actress] (b. 1878?–19 Apr 1954 [76], Los Angeles CA). "Harriett Magee," *Variety,* 28 Apr 1954. AS, p. 702. BHD1, p. 357. IFN, p. 195. Truitt, p. 211.

Maggi, Luigi (father of **Rina Maggi**) [actor/director] (b. Turin, Italy, 21 Dec 1867–22 Aug 1946 [78], Turin, Italy). AS, p. 702. BHD, p. 242; BHD2, p. 174. JS, pp. 256–57 (in Italian silents from 1906).

Maggi, Rina (daughter of **Luigi Maggi**) [actress] (aka Kathryn Berg, *née* Caterina Maggi, b. Turin, Italy). JS, p. 257 (in Italian silents from 1917).

Magidson, Herb[ert] [lyricist] (b. Braddock PA, 7 Jan 1906–2 Jan 1986 [79], Beverly Hills CA). "Herbert Magidson," *Variety,* 15 Jan 1986 (AA for *The Continental,* with Con Conrad; also wrote film scores/lyrics for *Gone with the Wind; Music Maestro Please; Enjoy Yourself (It's Later Than You Think); A Pink Cocktail for a Blue Lady*). AS, p. 702. ASCAP 66, p. 466. BHD2, p. 174.

Magnani, Anna [singer/actress/scenarist] (b. Rome, Italy, 11 Apr 1908–26 Sep 1973 [65], Rome Italy; pancreatic cancer). m. **Goffredo Alessandrini**, 1935–annulled 1950 (d. 1978). Matilde Hochkofler, *Anna Magnani* (Rome: Gremese, 1984); Patrizia Carrano, *La Magnani* (Milan: Rizzoli, 1986). (Film debut: *Scampolo,* Germany, 1928; AA, *The Rose Tattoo,* 1955.) "Anna Magnani, the Actress, Dies at 65," *NYT,* 27 Sep 1973, 42:1 (b. 7 Mar). "Anna Magnani Lifted Int'l Stature of Italo Films, Dies in Rome at 65," *Variety,* 3 Oct 1973. AS, p. 702 (b. Alexandria, Egypt, 7 Mar 1908). AS, p. 702 (b. Alexandria, 7 Mar. BHD1, p. 357; BHD2, p. 174 (b. Alexandria). IFN, p. 195. JS, pp. 257–58. Katz, pp. 763–64 (b. Alexandria, 7 Mar). Waldman, p. 175. Magnani denied being born in Egypt.

Magnier, Pierre Frédéric [actor] (b. Paris, France, 22 Feb 1869–15 Oct 1959 [90], Clichy-la-Garenne, France). AS, p. 703. BHD1, p. 357.

Magnolia [actress]. No data found. AMD, p. 234. "Mack Sennett Has Signed Magnolia," *MPW*, 12 Nov 1927, p. 16.

Magnusson, Charles [producer/executive] (b. Gothenburg, Sweden, 26 Jan 1878–18 Jan 1948 [69], Stockholm, Sweden). (Svenska-Bio). AMD, p. 234. AS, p. 703 (b. 28 Jan). BHD2, p. 174. "Films Teach Swedes to Think Like Americans, Says Producer," *MPW*, 21 Nov 1925, 222.

Magri, Count Primo [midget actor] (b. 1849–31 Oct 1920 [71?], Middleboro MA). m. **Violet Howard** (formerly Mrs. Tom Thumb). AS, p. 703 (d. 21 Oct). BHD, p. 242. "First Headline Comedy [*Pee-Wee's Courtship*]," *NYDM*, 23 Jun 1915, 21:2.

Magrill, George [actor] (b. Brooklyn NY, 5 Jan 1900–31 May 1952 [52], Los Angeles CA). m. Ramona. "George Magrill," *NYT*, 3 Jun 1952, 29:4 (began 1924). AS, p. 703. BHD1, p. 357. IFN, p. 195. Truitt, p. 211 (b. NY NY). George A. Katchmer, "Update—Forgotten Cowboys/Girls," *CI*, 179 (May 1990), 43.

Maguire, Charles J. [actor] (b. 1882?–22 Jul 1939 [57], No. Hollywood CA). m. Janet Sully. "Charles J. Maquire," *Variety*, 26 Jul 1939. AS, p. 703. IFN, p. 195.

Maguire, Edward [actor] (b. 1867–10 Apr 1925 [58], New York NY). AS, p. 703. BHD, p. 243. IFN, p. 195.

Maguire, Tom [actor] (b. Milford CT, 7 Sep 1869–21 Jun 1934 [63], No. Hollywood CA). "Tom Maguire," *Variety*, 26 Jan 1934 (b. NY). AS, p. 703. BHD1, p. 357 (d. LA CA). IFN, p. 195 (b. 1870). Truitt, p. 211.

Magyari, Imre [actor] (b. Debrecen, Hungary, 10 Sep 1894–27 Apr 1940 [45], Budapest, Hungary). AS, p. 703.

Mahan, Vivian L. [actress] (b. 1902–13 Oct 1933 [31?], Los Angeles CA; suicide). AS, p. 703. BHD1, p. 357.

Mahieddine [actor/composer] (né Bachtarzi Mahieddine, b. Algeria, 15 Dec 1897). AS, p. 703.

Mahieu, Charles [actor] (b. Brussels, Belgium, 23 Feb 1894–2 Oct 1964 [70], Brussels, Belgium). AS, p. 703.

Mahler, Gustav [composer] (b. Kalischt, Czechoslovakia, 7 Jul 1860–18 May 1911 [50], Vienna, Austria. AS, p. 703.

Mahon, John [actor] (aka John Mayon, d. 22 Dec 1935, Jersey City NJ). "John Mahon," *Variety*, 25 Dec 1935. AS, p. 704.

Mahoney, Wilkie [gag writer/actor/scenarist] (b. San Miguel CA, 25 Jun 1897–30 Jul 1976 [79], Los Gatos CA). "Wilkie Mahoney," *Variety*, 284, 18 Aug 1976, 78:4. AS, p. 704. BHD, p. 243; BHD2, p. 174.

Mahoney, Will [stage/film actor] (b. Helena MT, 5 Feb 1894–9 Feb 1967 [73], Melbourne, Australia). m. (1) Iva Willis, 1917 (d. 1920); (2) Lillian "Sue" Wilson, 1924–32; (3) Evie Hayes, 1938. Leonard Traube, "Will Mahoney, Top Comedian for Half Century, Dies in Melbourne at 73," *Variety*, 245, 15 Feb 1967, 50:1 (d. 8 Feb). AS, p. 704 (d. 8 Feb 1966). BHD1, p. 358. IFN, p. 195.

Maierhofer, Ferdinand [actor] (b. Graz, Austria, 9 Apr 1881–6 Jun 1960 [79], Vienna, Austria). AS, p. 704.

Maigne, Charles M. [actor/scenarist/producer] (b. Richmond VA, 11 Nov 1879–28 Nov 1929 [50], San Francisco CA; pneumonia). m. (2) **Ann Cornwall** (d. 1980). (FP-L; 1st National; MGM.) "Charles M. Maigne," *Variety*, 4 Dec 1929 (age 50). AMD, p. 234. AS, p. 704. BHD, p. 243; BHD2, p. 174 (b. 1881). FDY, p. 433. IFN, p. 195 (b. 1881). "Maigne Wrote It," *MPW*, 13 May 1916, 1136. "Sign Maigne as Producer of Special Paramount Pictures," *MPW*, 7 Aug 1920, 714. "Charles Maigne to Direct Alice Brady for Realart," *MPW*, 19 Feb 1921, 949.

Mailes, Charles Hill [actor] (b. Halifax, Nova Scotia, Canada, 25 May 1870–17 Feb 1937 [66], Los Angeles CA). m. **Claire McDowell** (d. 1966). (Biograph, 1909; Universal.) "Charles Mailes," *Variety*, 24 Feb 1937 (age 67). AMD, p. 234. AS, p. 704. BHD1, p. 358. IFN, p. 195. Truitt, p. 211. "Charles Hill Mailes," *NYDM*, 6 Jan 1915, 25:4 (left Biograph). "Charles Hill Mailes," *MPW*, 16 Jan 1915, 347. "Mailes a Screen Perennial," *MPW*, 4 Nov 1916, 717. "Charles Hill Mailes," *MPW*, 7 Jul 1917, 90. George Katchmer, "Remembering the Great Silents," *CI*, 218 (Aug 1993), 41–42.

Maines, Don [actor] (b. 1868?–2 Jan 1934 [65], Los Angeles CA; heart attack). "Don Maines," *Variety*, 9 Jan 1934. AS, p. 704. BHD, p. 243. IFN, p. 195.

Mainwaring, Bernerd [director/producer] (b. Shropshire, England, 1897–30 Jul 1963 [66?], England). AS, p. 704. BHD2, p. 174.

Maiori, Antonio [actor] (b. 1869–30 Jul 1938 [69?], Brooklyn NY). BHD, p. 243.

Maire, Edward John [actor] (b. Hoboken NJ, 2 Jul 1892–24 Dec 1947 [55], Long Beach CA). AS, p. 704.

Maisch, Herbert Karl Adolf [actor/director] (b. Nurtingen, Germany, 10 Dec 1890–10 Oct 1974 [83], Cologne, Germany). AS, p. 704. BHD2, p. 174.

Maison, Edna [actress] (b. San Francisco CA, 17 Aug 1892–11 Jan 1946 [53], Los Angeles CA). m. Beverly Griffith, Dec? 1917, Los Angeles CA (d. 1970). (Universal.) "Edna Maison," *NYT*, 14 Jan 1946, 19:4. "Edna Maison," *Variety*, 16 Jan 1946. AS, p. 704. BHD, p. 243. IFN, p. 195. Truitt, p. 211. Richard Willis, "Edna Maison; Playing Leads with the Nestor Company," *MPS*, 19 Feb 1915, 25. "Marriages," *Variety*, 14 Dec 1917, p. 9.

Maisse, Louis [actor] (*né* Louis Maiss, b. Lille, France, 17 Aug 1899). AS, p. 704.

Maitland, Arthur [actor] (b. 1873–23 May 1959 [86?], New York NY). AS, p. 705.

Maitland, Gertrude [stage/film actress] (aka Gertrude Valentine, *née* Gertrude Horrigan, b. Boston MA, 1880?–28 Dec 1938 [58], New York NY). m. **Jefferson Hall** (d. 1945). (McAuliffe's Repertory Co., Lynn MA.) "Gertrude Maitland, Actress Many Years; Had Played on Broadway—Also Toured in 'Student Prince,'" *NYT*, 29 Dec 1938, 19:4 (Broadway debut: *The Brat*, 1916). "Gertrude Maitland," *Variety*, 4 Jan 1939. AS, p. 705. BHD, p. 243. SD, p. 834.

Maitland, Lauderdale [actor] (b. London, England, 1877–28 Feb 1929 [52], London, England). AS, p. 705. BHD, p. 243. IFN, p. 195.

Maitland, Richard [actor]. No data found. AMD, p. 235. Tom Waller, "Richard Maitland," *MPW*, 2 May 1927, 790–91.

Maitland, Ruth [actress] (*née* Ruth Erskine, b. London, England, 3 Feb 1880–12 Mar 1961 [81], Dorking, England). AS, p. 705.

Maja, Zelma [actress] (b. Sweden, 11 Feb 1883–28 May 1972 [89], Palo Alto CA). BHD, p. 243.

Majer, Vladimir [actor/director] (b. Czechoslovakia, 21 Feb 1894–5 Nov 1957 [63], Czechoslovakia). AS, p. 705.

Majerone, Achille [actor] (aka Achille Maieroni, b. Syracuse, Italy, 24 Aug 1881-ca. 1963 [82?]). AS, p. 705. JS, p. 259 (in Italian silents from 1913).

Majeroni, George [stasge/film actor] (*né* Giorgio Majeroni, b. Melbourne, Australia, 11 Jan 1877–5 Aug 1924 [47], Saranac Lake NY). "Giorgio Majeroni, Actor," *NYT*, 9 Aug 1924, 11:6 (age 49; began on stage in 1905). AS, p. 705. BHD, p. 243. IFN, p. 195.

Majeroni, Mario [actor] (b. New York NY, 1870?–18 Nov 1931 [61], New York NY; heart attack). "Mario Majeroni," *Variety*, 24 Nov 1931. AMD, p. 235. AS, p. 705. BHD, p. 243. IFN, p. 195. Truitt, p. 211. "Majrio Majeroni in Metro Feature," *MPW*, 28 Jul 1917, 636.

Majerova, Marie [director] (b. Uvaly, Czechoslovakia, 1 Feb 1882). AS, p. 705.

Majo, Fred [scenarist]. No data found. FDY, p. 433.

Major, Sam Collier (father of **Cleve** and **Colleen Moore**) (b. 1881?–31 Jul 1955 [74], Houston TX). "Sam Collier Major," *Variety*, 10 Aug 1955. AS, p. 705.

Majorana, Totò [actor] (*né* Antonio Majorana Di Militello di Militello da Valsavoja, b. Catania, Italy, 1862). JS, p. 259 (in Italian silents from 1913).

Makarenko, Daniel [actor] (b. 1879–6 Mar 1957 [77?], Philadelphia PA). BHD1, p. 358.

Makarov, Georgy Avetisovich [director] (b. St. Petersburg, Russia, 7 Sep 1894–16 Feb 1976 [81], St. Petersburg, Russia). AS, p. 705.

Makeham, Eliot [actor] (b. London, England, 22 Dec 1882–8 Feb 1956 [73], London, England). AS, p. 705.

Makowska, Helena [actress] (*née* Helena Makowska, b. Russia, 2 Mar 1893–22 Aug 1964 [71], Rome, Italy). BHD1, p. 613. JS, pp. 259–60 (b. 1895; in Italian silents from 1914).

Malachard, Noel [cameraman] (d. 1912; drowned on the *Titanic*). (Pathé Frérès Weekly.) "Lost on the Titanic," *NYDM*, 24 Apr 1912 (he "secured negatives of the sailing of the ship, all of which were of course lost also.").

Malan, William [actor] (b. New York NY, 2 Nov 1867–13 Feb 1941 [73], Los Angeles CA). (Sennett.) "William Malan," *Variety*, 19 Feb 1941 ("vet film comic of the pie-throwing days"). AS, p. 706. BHD1, p. 358. IFN, p. 195. Truitt, p. 212.

Malandrinos, Andrea Basil [actor] (b. Greece, 1888). AS, p. 706.

Malaparte, Curzio [director/scenarist/composer] (né Kurt Erich Suckert, b. Prato, Italy, 9 Jun 1898–19 Jul 1957 [59], Rome, Italy; cancer). AS, p. 706.

Malasomma, Nunzio [director] (b. Caserta, Italy, 4 Feb 1894–12 Jan 1974 [79], Rome, Italy). AS, p. 706. JS, p. 260 (in Italian silents from 1923).

Malatesta, Frederic M. [actor/director] (b. Naples, Italy, 18 Apr 1889–8 Apr 1952 [62], Burbank CA; complications after surgery). "Fred Malatesta," *Variety,* 16 Apr 1952 (age 64; began 1915). AMD, p. 235. AS, p. 706. BHD1, p. 358; BHD2, p. 175. IFN, p. 195. Truitt, p. 212. "Malatesta in Cast of First Drury Lane Play by Metro," *MPW,* 4 Oct 1919, 70. George Katchmer, "Remembering the Great Silents," *CI,* 206 (Aug 1992), 39.

Malavasi, Renato [actor] (b. Verona, Italy, 8 Aug 1904). JS, p. 260 (in Italian silents from 1928).

Malcolm, Reginald [actor] (b. Nottingham, England, 1884?–20 Jan 1966 [82], Ottawa, Canada). "Reginald Malcolm," *Variety,* 9 Feb 1966. AS, p. 706. IFN, p. 195.

Malena, Lena [actress] (b. Berlin, Germany). (Ufa.) "Lena Goes Domestic," *MPC,* Apr 1928, 64. (Social Security Death Benefit Records show a Lena Malena, b. 14 Apr 1900-Apr 1986, OH 45439;)

Maley, Denman (brother of Patrick A. and Stephen Maley) [actor] (b. Holyoke MA, 1877?–22 May 1927 [50], Collingswood NJ). m. "Denman Maley," *Variety,* 1 Jun 1927. AS, p. 706. BHD, p. 243.

Malinovskaya, Anna [actress]. No data found. AMD, p. 235. "Anna Malinovskaya," *MPW,* 31 Jul 1926, 280.

Malins, Geoffrey [director/scenarist] (b. Boston MA, 1887). AS, p. 706.

Malinverni, Silvia [actress] (b. Rome, Italy). JS, p. 261 (in Italian silents from 1913).

Malitz, Felix [executive/managing director] (b. Brandenburg, Germany, 10 Jan 1876). AMD, p. 235. "Pathe's Guiding Spirit; Felix Malitz, the Little-Known Film Man, Who Is Holding the Reins at Pathe Exchange, Inc.," *NYDM,* 3 Mar 1915, 24:1. "Felix Malitz," *MPW,* 13 Mar 1915, 1583. "Malitz Makes Statement," *NYDM,* 25 Aug 1915, 24:4 (discriminated against because of his German ancestry in spite of his application for U.S. citizenship). "English War Films Coming," *MPW,* 25 Aug 1917, 1192. "Malitz Heads Piedmont Corporation," *MPW,* 1 Sep 1917, 1393. "Felix Malitz Is Arrested," *MPW,* 19 Jan 1918, 346 (for smuiggling rubber into Germany; arraigned 3 Jan 1918). "Malitz and Engler Out of Piedmont," *MPW,* 26 Jan 1918, 480. "Felix Malitz Again in Toils," *MPW,* 2 Mar 1918, 1221. "Malitz's Appeal for Lower Bail Refused," *MPW,* 16 Mar 1918, 1480. "Malitz and Engler Sentenced to Prison," *MPW,* 25 May 1918, 1123 (2-year term, $5,000 fine).

Maljan, Abdul (Terrible Turk) [actor] (b. 1882–7 Sep 1944 [62?], Los Angeles CA). BHD1, p. 358. IFN, p. 196.

Malkames, Don [inventor/cinematographer] (b. Hazleton PA, 1904–24 Nov 1986 [82?], Yonkers NY). AS, p. 706.

Mallalieu, Aubrey [actor] (b. Liverpool, England, 8 Jun 1873–28 May 1948 [74], England). AS, p. 707.

Malle, Beatrice [actress]. No data found. (Edison.) "Beatrice Malle Recovered [from appendicitis]," *NYDM,* 11 Mar 1914, 32:2.

Malleson, Miles [actor/writer] (*né* William Miles Malleson, b. Croyden, England, 25 May 1888–15 Mar 1969 [80], London, England). AS, p. 707. BHD1, p. 359; BHD2, p. 175. IFN, p. 196.

Mallet-Stevens, Robert [scenarist]. No data found.

Mallon, Catherine [actress] (b. 9 Mar 1906–13 Feb 1929 [22], Los Angeles CA). AS, p. 707. BHD, p. 243. IFN, p. 196.

Malloy, John J. [actor] (b. Dover DE, 1898?–9 Feb 1968 [70?], Los Angeles CA; heart attack). AS, p. 707. BHD, p. 243. Truitt, p. 212.

Malone, Dudley Field [actor] (b. 1882–5 Oct 1950 [68?], Culver City CA). AS, p. 707.

Malone, Florence [actress] (d. 4 Mar 1956, Lyons NY). "Florence Malone," *Variety,* 14 Mar 1956. AS, p. 707. BHD, p. 243. Truitt, p. 212.

Malone, Molly [actress] (*née* Edith Roberts, b. WI, 7 Dec 1888–14 Feb 1952 [63], Los Angeles CA). m. (1) Forrest Cornett, Jul 1917–18; **William Grothers**—div. 1927; George Evans Greaves. (Christie; Universal.) "Mrs. Edith Greaves," *Variety,* 20 Feb 1952. AMD, p. 235. AS, p. 707 (b. Denver CO; d. 15 Feb). BHD, p. 243 (*née* Edith Greaves, b. 1889). BR, pp. 179–82 (b. 2 Feb 1897). FFF, p. 141. Katz, p. 768. MH, p. 124. MSBB, p. 1038 (b. Denver CO). Truitt, p. 212. WWS, p. 213. "Actress Sues for Divorce," *MPW,* 7 Sep 1918, 1396 (from Cornett). "Molly Malone Signed for Supreme Comedies," *MPW,* 6 Dec 1919, 661. "Petite Molly Malone Signs to Smile in Goldwyn Films," *MPW,* 19 Jun 1920, 1626. "Molly Malone Signs Contract," *MPW,* 27 Jun 1925, 993. "Molly Malone," *MPW,* 24 Apr 1926, 595. "Divorce Follows Trial Separation," *MPW,* 3 Sep 1927, 21 (from Grothers). "Molly Malone," *MPW,* 15 Oct? 1927, 1690. Buck Rainey, "Molly Malone: Many a Boy's First Experience with Unrequited Love," *CI,* 132 (Jun 1986), 38–39 (b. Denver CO, 2 Feb 1897). Billy H. Doyle, "Which Molly Malone? [letter]," *CI,* 135 (Sep 1986), C14 (b. Denver CO, 1897?). George Katchmer, "Remembering the Great Silents," *CI,* 200 (Feb 1992), 32, C2.

Maloney, Leo Daniel [actor/director/scenarist] (b. Santa Rosa CA, 1885?–2 Nov 1929 [44], New York NY; acute and chronic alcoholism [Death Certificate No. 26420; autopsy]). (Mutual; Ince; Pathé; Helen Holmes Signal Company.) "Film Director Dies in Hotel Room Here; L.D. Maloney of Hollywood Expires in Presence of Several Friends; Drinking Party Denied; Determination of Direct Cause of Death Awaits Report of the Toxicologist Today," *NYT,* 3 Nov 1929, 26:3 (b. 1888; age 42). "Leo D. Maloney," *Variety,* 6 Nov 1929. AMD, p. 235. AS, p. 707. BHD1, p. 359; BHD2, p. 175 (b. San Jose CA, 1888). FDY, p. 433. FSS, p. 202. IFN, p. 196 (age 41). Truitt, p. 212 (b. 1888). 1921 Directory, p. 187 (b. San Jose). "Studio Gossip," *NYDM,* 11 Aug 1915, 26:2 (he and Pat Chriseman injured in a screen fight). "Leo D. Maloney, Leading Man, Signal," *MPN,* 21 Oct 1916, 222 (b. San Jose, 1888). "Leo Maloney Ill," *MPW,* 17 Nov 1917, 1027. "Villain Receives Real Stab," *MPW,* 7 Jun 1919, 1492. "Pathé to Handlke Series of Two Reelers Starring Leo D. Maloney," *MPW,* 22 Jul 1922, 282. "Maloney Returns to Pathé in New Series," *MPW,* 27 Mar 1926, 3. Eldon K. Everett, "Ford Beebe Recalls Leo Maloney," *CI,* 68 (Mar 1980), 12–13. Mario DeMarco, "Leo Maloney," *CI,* 203 (May 1992), 7.

Maltby, Henry F. [actor/scenarist] (b. Ceres, South Africa, 25 Nov 1880–25 Oct 1963 [82], Hove, England). AS, p. 707. BHD1, p. 359; BHD2, p. 175.

Malvern, Paul [vaudevillian/stuntman/producer] (b. Portland OR, 28 Jan 1901–29 May 1993 [92], No. Hollywood CA). "Paul Malvern Is Dead; Former Stunt Man, 91," *NYT,* 4 Jun 1993, A23:2. AS, p. 708. BHD2, p. 175 (d. LA CA).

Maly, Walter [actor] (b. 11 Feb 1896-Mar 1978 [82], TX 77801). George A. Katchmer, "Forgotten Cowboys and Cowgirls—Part XIII," *CI,* 190 (Apr 1991), C6, C8.

Malyon, Eily [actress] (*née* Eily Sophie Lees-Craston, b. London, England, 30 Oct 1879–26 Sep 1961 [81], Los Angeles CA). AS, p. 708.

Mamelock, Emil [actor] (b. Zurich, Switzerland, 12 Sep 1882-May 1954 [81], Lucerne, Switzerland). BHD1, p. 613.

Mandel, Mrs. Frances Wakefield [actress] (*née?,* b. 1891–26 Mar 1943 [52], Batavia NY). AS, p. 708. BHD, p. 243. IFN, p. 196.

Mandelbaum, E. [executive]. No data found. AMD, p. 235. "Booming Feature Films," *MPW,* 23 Dec 1911, 995. "Twist Gives Gabfest," *MPW,* 8 Nov 1913, 615. "Mandelbaum Retires from World Film Corp.," *MPW,* 27 Jun 1914, 1814.

Mandell, Daniel M. [vaudeville acrobat/film editor] (b. New York NY, 13 Aug 1895–8 Jun 1987 [91], Huntington Beach CA). m. Leone. (Universal.) "Hollywood Film Editor Daniel Mandell," *LA Times,* 13 Jun 1987, p. 31:1 (age 92; AA for *The Pride of the Yankees,* 1942; *The Best Years of Our Lives,* 1946; and *The Apartment,* 1960). BHD2, p. 175. '94 Katz.

Mander, Miles [actor/scenarist/director] (*né* Lionel Mander, b. Wolverhampton, England, 14 May 1888–8 Feb 1946 [57], Los Angeles CA; heart attack). (Korda; British International; Gaumont; last appearance as actor, *Murder, My Sweet.*) "Miles Mander," *Variety,* 161, 13 Feb 1946, 54:4. AS, p. 708. BHD1, p. 359; BHD2, p. 175. IFN, p. 196.

Mandeville, William C. [stage/film actor] (b. Louisville KY, 1866–19 Apr 1917 [50], New York NY). m. Frances Calver. "William C. Mandeville," *Variety,* 27 Apr 1917 ("After playing leading parts in musical productions, he joined the screen forces."). "William C. Mandeville," *Dramatic Mirror,* 28 Apr 1917, 10:1. AS, p. 708. BHD, p. 243. IFN, p. 196. SD.

Mandy, Jerry [actor] (*né* Gerard Mandia, b. Utica NY, 5 Jun 1892–1 May 1945 [52], Los Angeles CA; heart attack). (Roach.) "Jerry Mandy," *Variety,* 9 May 1945. AMD, p. 235. AS, p. 708. BHD1, p. 359. IFN, p. 196. Truitt, p. 213. "Jerry Mandy Signed by Hal Roach-Pathé," *MPW,* 17 Apr 1926, 535.

Manes, Gina [actress] (*née* Blanche Moulin, b. Paris, France, 7 Apr 1893–6 Sep 1989 [96], Toulouse, France [extrait de décès no. 1570/2/1989]). AS, pp. 708–09. BHD1, p. 359.

Manetti, Lido [actor] (aka Arnold Kent, b. Florence, Italy, 21 Jan 1899–28 Sep 1928 [29], Los Angeles CA; auto accident). AMD, p. 192. AS, p. 603 (Arnold Kent, d. 29 Sep); p. 709 (Lido Manetti, b. Querceto, Italy; d. 29 Sep). BHD, p. 217 (Arnold Kent). IFN, p. 163. JS, p. 263 (in Italian and U.S. silents from 1917; "He was about to act in a Mary Pickford film when he died, as the result of an auto accident."). Truitt, pp. 180–81. WWS, p. 180. "Kent's Contract," *MPW,* 23 Jul 1927, 253.

Mangus, Saul [scenarist] (b. 1887–15 Nov 1936 [49?], Los Angeles CA). BHD2, p. 175.

Mankers, Roy L. [scenarist] (d. 5 Nov 1926, Los Angeles CA). BHD2, p. 175.

Mankiewicz, Herman J[acob] (brother of **Joseph L. Mankiewicz**) [title writer/scenarist/

playwright] (b. New York NY, 7 Nov 1897–5 Mar 1953 [55], Los Angeles CA; uremic poisoning). m. Sara Aaronson, 1 Jul 1920. "H.J. Mankiewicz, Screen Writer, 56; Winner of Academy Award in 1941 [for *Citizen Kane*] Dies—Playwright Was Former Newspaper Man," *NYT*, 6 Mar 1953, 23:3 (joined writing staff of Paramount LI studio in 1926. "Later he went to Hollywood, first as a writer of titles for silent films, and then as a writer and producer of silent and talking pictures."). "Herman J. Mankiewicz," *Variety*, 11 Mar 1953 (wrote *The Road to Mandalay*, 1926). AMD, p. 235. AS, p. 709. BHD2, p. 175. FDY, pp. 433, 447. IFN, p. 196. "Mankiewicz Added," *MPW*, 3 Apr 1926, 4. "Joins Paramount," *MPW*, 24 Apr 1926, 594.

Mankiewicz, Joseph L[eo] (brother of **Herman J. Mankiewicz**) [scenarist] (b. Wilkes-Barre PA, 11 Feb 1909–5 Feb 1993 [83], Mount Kisco NY; heart failure). m. (1) Elizabeth Young—div. 1937; (2) Rosa Stradner (d. 1958); (3) Rosemary Matthews, 1962. (AA, 1949 and 1950.) Peter B. Flint, "Joseph L. Mankiewicz, Literate Skeptic of the Cinema, Dies at 83," *NYT*, 6 Feb 1993, 10:1 (translated silent-film intertitles in Berlin, 1928). Lawrence Cohn, "Joseph L. Mankiewicz," *Variety*, 15 Feb 1993, p. 99:1 (d. Bedford NY). AS, p. 709 (d. Bedford Village NY). BHD2, p. 175.

Manley, Charles "Daddy" or "Pop" [stage/film actor] (b. Ireland, 25 Sep 1829–26 Feb 1916 [86], Los Angeles CA; arteriosclerosis). (Universal.) "Charles 'Daddy' Manley," *Variety*, 3 Mar 1916. AMD, p. 235. AS, p. 709 (b. 1830). BHD, p. 243 (b. 1830). IFN, p. 196. '83 WWOS (b. 1830). P.M. Powell, "Doings at Los Angeles; News Briefs," *MPW*, 12 Apr 1913, 152. "The World's Oldest Actor," *Pictures and the Picturegoer*, 22 May 1915, 139 (84 years old). "Daddy Manley Dead; Smiling Veteran of the Drama, Both Stage and Screen, Dies in Harness," *NYDM*, 11 Mar 1916, 26. "Obituary," *MPW*, 18 Mar 1916, 1841. "Funeral of 'Daddy' Manley," *MPW*, 1 Apr 1916, 94 (on 29 Feb 1916).

Manley, Dave [actor] (b. Paris, France, 25 Dec 1883–8 Jun 1943 [59], Los Angeles CA). AS, p. 709.

Mann, Alice [actress]. No data found. *Fl.* 1917–23.

Mann, Bertha [actress] (b. Atlanta GA, 21 Oct 1893–20 Dec 1967 [74], Los Angeles CA). AS, p. 709. BHD1, p. 360. IFN, p. 196.

Mann, Cato [actor] (b. 1887–14 Dec 1977 [90], Belleaire Bluffs FL). BHD, p. 244. IFN, p. 196.

Mann, Frances "Frankie" [actress] (b. 1901?–23 Jun 1969 [68], New York NY). m. Murdock Pemberton. "Frances Mahan Pemberton," *Variety*, 2 Jul 1969. AMD, p. 235. AS, p. 709. "Frances Mann, the New Ivan Vampire," *MPW*, 14 Oct 1916, 252. "Frances Mann," *MPW*, 17 Feb 1917, 1014. "Prominent Players to Be Featured in Pathé Serials for the Next Two Years," *MPW*, 19 Jul 1919, 377. "Frances Mann Signed by Beck," *MPW*, 2 Aug 1919, 697.

Mann, Hank [actor: Keystone Cop] (*né* David W. Lieberman, b. New York NY, 28 May 1887–24 Nov 1971 [84], So. Pasadena CA). (Keystone; Fox.) "Hank Mann, 84, Member of Keystone Kops, Dead," *NYT*, 27 Nov 1971, 34:2. "Hank Mann," *Variety*, 1 Dec 1971. AMD, p. 235. AS, p. 710. BHD1, p. 360. IFN, p. 196. Katz, pp. 772–73. Truitt, p. 213 (d. 25 Nov). "Hank Mann Has Own Company," *MPW*, 6 Jan 1917, 61. "Hank Mann Ill," *MPW*, 2 Oct 1920 (nervous breakdown). "Hank Mann Is Not Ill," *MPW*, 9 Oct 1920, 778. "Christie's Gag Men," *MPW*, 12 Jul 1924, 127.

Mann, Louis [actor] (b. New York NY, 20 Apr 1865–15 Feb 1931 [65], New York NY; intestinal illness). m. Clara Lipman. "Louis Mann," *Variety*, 18 Feb 1931. AS, p. 710. BHD1, p. 360. IFN, p. 196.

Mann, Margaret [actress] (b. Aberdeen, Scotland, 4 Apr 1868–4 Feb 1941 [72], Los Angeles CA; cancer). (Fox; in *Four Feathers*.) AS, p. 710. BHD1, p. 360. IFN, p. 197.

Mann, Ned H. [actor, 1920/director/special effects director] (b. Redkey IN, 1893?–1 Jul 1967 [74], La Jolla CA). m. Cora. AS, p. 710. BHD1, p. 360; BHD2, p. 176. IFN, p. 197. "Ned H. Mann," *Variety*, 247, 12 Jul 1967, 63:4. "Hank Mann," *CFC*, 19 (Fall/Winter, 1967), 59.

Mann, Stanley [actor/scenarist] (b. Liverpool, England, 30 Aug 1883–10 Aug 1953 [69], Los Angeles CA). "Stanley Mann," *Variety*, 19 Aug 1953 ("He started his motion picture [career] in silent films"). AS, p. 710. BHD1, p. 360; BHD2, p. 176. IFN, p. 197. Truitt, p. 213.

Mannering, Lewin [actor] (b. Poland, 19 Jan 1879–7 Jun 1932 [53], London, England). "Lewin Mannering," *Variety*, 21 Jun 1932. AS, p. 710 (b. 1876). BHD1, p. 360 (b. 1876). IFN, p. 197. Truitt, p. 213. '83 WWOS (b. 1876).

Manners, Lady Diana [actress] (b. London, England, 29 Aug 1892–16 Jun 1986 [93], London, England). AMD, p. 235. AS, p. 710. BHD, p. 244. "Lady Diana Manners, English Beauty, to Appear in Blackton-Made Productions," *MPW*, 27 Nov 1920, 505. "Kane Distributing Blackton Films Featuring Lady Diana Manners," *MPW*, 12 Feb 1921, 809. "The Lure of Lovely Hands; Lady Diana Manners and other Famous Women Make Up their Hands as Carefully as they do their Faces—and here we tell you *How* and *Why*," *MPC*, May 1925, 43, 83.

Manners, Dorothy [actress/gossip columnist] (b. TX, 1903?–24 Aug 1998 [95], Palm Springs CA). m. (1) Walter Ramsey; (2) John Haskell, 1947 (d. 1977). (DeMille; Fox; Universal.) "Dorothy Manners Haskell," *Variety*, 7 Sep 1998, 84:1. Harris Lentz, III, "Dorothy Manners," *CI*, 280 (Oct 1998), 55.

Manners, Dorothy [vaudevillian/actress] (d. 5 Jul 1949, Kennebunkport ME; heart ailment). m. Jim Kelly. "Dorothy Manners," *Variety*, 13 Jul 1949 (Kelly & Kent, with husband). AS, p. 710. IFN, p. 197.

Manners, J[ohn] **Hartley** [actor/playwright] (b. London, England, 10 Aug 1870–19 Dec 1928 [58], New York NY). m. **Laurette Taylor** (d. 1946). "Hartley Manners," *Variety*, 26 Dec 1928 (wrote *Peg o' My Heart*). AS, p. 710. SD, p. 838. "Denial by J. Hartley Manners," *NYDM*, 1 Sep 1915, 26:4 (quashed rumors that *Peg O' My Heart* would be filmed. "Furthermore, he most emphatically states that he has given no authority to any one to produce his play in pictures, and does not intend doing so.").

Mannes, Florence Vensen [actress] (*née* Vensen?, b. 1896?–30 Oct 1964 [68], Los Angeles CA; heart attack). m. Max Mannes. "Florence V. Mannes," *Variety*, 4 Nov 1964. AS, p. 710. BHD1, p. 360. IFN, p. 197. Truitt, p. 213.

Mannheim, Lucie [actress] (b. Berlin, Germany, 30 Apr 1895–28 Jul 1976 [81], Braunlage, Germany). AS, p. 710. BHD1, p. 360.

Manning, Aileen [actress] (b. Boulder CO, 20 Jan 1886–25 Mar 1946 [60], Los Angeles CA). (Fox.) "Aileen Manning," *Variety*, 3 Apr 1946 ("screen actress in the silent era"). AS, p. 710. BHD1, p. 360. IFN, p. 197. Truitt, p. 213 (b. Denver CO).

Manning, Ambrose (son of stage actor John Manning) [stage/film actor] (b. 1861–22 Mar 1940 [79], Brixham, So. Devon, England). "Ambrose Manning, Noted Actor, Dies; Appeared on Stage for Seven Decades—Was with Wilson Barrett 24 Years [1880–1904]; Here as Lately as 1934; Had a Part at Center Theatre in 'The Great Waltz'—Once in Sothern's Company," *NYT*, 25 Mar 1940, 16:2. "Ambrose Manning," *Variety*, 138, 27 Mar 1940, 47:1 ("Fond of collecting antiques, he was considered an authority upon period furniture."). BHD, p. 244. IFN, p. 197.

Manning, Bruce [producer/director/scenarist] (b. Cuddbackville NY, 15 Jul 1902–3 Aug 1965 [63], Encino CA). AS, p. 710 (b. 1900). BHD2, p. 176.

Manning, Jack [actor] (b. 1880–18 Jun 1938 [58?], Yonkers NY). BHD, p. 244.

Manning, Joseph [actor] (b. 1870?–30 Jul 1946 [76], Santa Monica CA; heart attack). "Joseph Manning," *NYT*, 1 Aug 1946, 23:4. "Joseph Manning," *Variety*, 7 Aug 1946. AS, p. 710. BHD1, p. 613 (d. LA CA). IFN, p. 197. Truitt, p. 213.

Manning, Marjorie [actress] (b. 1898–3 Jun 1922 [24?], Los Angeles CA). AS, p. 710. BHD, p. 244.

Manning, Mary Lee [actress] (d. 7 Dec 1937, Los Angeles CA). AS, p. 710.

Manning, Mildred [actress]. No data found. AMD, p. 235. "Mildred Manning," *MPW*, 31 Mar 1917, 2115. "Mildred Manning," *MPW*, 28 Apr 1917, 629.

Manning, Phillip Gustav Valère [actor/director] (b. Lewisham, England, 23 Nov 1869–11 Apr 1951 [81], Baden, Germany). AS, p. 710 (d. 9 Apr, Waldshut, Germany). BHD1, p. 360.

Manning, Tom [actor] (b. 1880–10 Oct 1936 [56?], Los Angeles CA). AS, p. 710.

Manning, W.H. [actor/stuntman] (b. 1899–10 Sep 1933 [34?], Chicago IL). AS, p. 710.

Mannini, Giorgio [director]. No data found. JS, p. 265 (in Italian silents from 1920).

Mannix, Eddie [executive/producer] (*né* Edgar J. Mannix, b. Fort Lee NJ, 1891?–30 Aug 1963 [72], Beverly Hills CA; cerebral hemorrhages). "Edgar J. Mannix, 72, Is Dead; Retired M-G-M Vice President," *NYT*, 31 Aug 1963, 17:1. "Eddie Mannix, 72, Vet Metro Topper, Dies in Beverly Hills After Long Illness," *Variety*, 4 Sep 1963. AS, p. 711. BHD2, p. 176.

Mannon, Hamilton W. [executive] (d. 1927; shot to death). AMD, p. 235. "Obituary," *MPW*, 13 Aug 1927, 453 (shot in "love tangle").

Manon, Marcia [actress] (*née* Camille Ankewich, b. CA, 28 Oct 1896–12 Apr 1973 [76], Loma Linda CA). (FP-L.) AMD, p. 236. BHD1, p. 361. "Talented Marcia Manon in Barrymore Support," *MPW*, 15 Feb 1919, 893. Frederick James Smith, "A Dreamer of Dreams; You Get Just What You Dream About, Is Marcia Manon's Philosophy," *MPC*, May 1919, 18–19, 65 ("Really, I can[']t see why I am being interviewed. I haven't accomplished anything yet."). "Has Leading Role in Frothingham Film," *MPW,* 12 Nov 1921, 213. Truman B. Handy, "Behind the Mask," *MPC,* Jul 1922, 24, 84–85 (real name: Camille Harrison).

Manoussi, Jean [producer] (b. Marseilles, France, 1889–23 Dec 1929 [40?], Paris, France). AS, p. 711 (b. Greece, 1879)). BHD2, p. 176.

Manse, Jean Jules [author/scenarist] (b. Marseilles, France, 19 Nov 1899 [extrait de naissance no. 769]-25 Aug 1967 [67], Marseilles, France). AS, p. 711.

Mansfield, Alice [actress] (b. 1858–17 Feb 1938 [79?]). BHD, p. 244.

Mansfield, Ann-Eve [actress]. No data found. AMD, p. 236. "Ann-Eve Mansfield," *MPW,* 1 May 1915, 730.

Mansfield, Duncan [film editor/scenarist/director/producer] (b. AL, 17 Sep 1897–15 Sep 1971 [73], Los Angeles CA). (Sennett; Lloyd.) "Duncan Mansfield," *Variety,* 22 Sep 1971. AS, p. 711. BHD1, p. 613; BHD2, p. 176. IFN, p. 197.

Mansfield, Lucille [actress] (*née* Pauline Daly, b. 1890–14 Aug 1981 [91?], Santa Monica CA). BHD, p. 244.

Mansfield, Margaret [stage/film actress]. No data found. (At Biograph at age 7.) "Personal; Mansfield," *NYDM,* 1 Sep 1915, 5:1 (with photo).

Mansfield, Martha [photographic model/stage/film actress] (aka Martha Early, *née* Martha Ehrlich, b. Mansfield OH, 14 Jul 1899–30 Nov 1923 [24], San Antonio TX; from burns sustained when a lit cigarette ignited her dress the day before during location shooting for *The Warrens of Virginia*). (Essanay, 1916; Metro; World; Selznick; Fox; FP-L.) "Martha Mansfield," *Variety,* 6 Dec 1923. AMD, p. 236. AS, p. 711. BHD, pp. 49–51; 244. IFN, p. 197 (age 23). Truitt, p. 214 (b. 1900; d. 20 Nov). "Martha Mansfield," *MPW,* 14 Jul 1917, 229. "Flashes; [Ziegfeld] Follies Beauty Coming," *LA Times,* 24 Jan 1920, 7. "Martha Mansfield with American Cinema," *MPW,* 1 May 1920, 680. "Myron Selznick Signs Martha Mansfield to Long Term Contract for Photoplays," *MPW,* 15 May 1920, 969. "Martha Mansfield and Conway Tearle Are Announced as Stars by Lewis J. Selznick," *MPW,* 25 Dec 1920, 1004. Courtenay Marvin, "Can a Woman Marry Any Man She Wants? 'Yes!,' Says Martha Mansfield," *MW,* 22 Sep 1923, 9. "Martha Mansfield Dying," *MPW,* 8 Dec 1923, 543. "Obituary," *MPW,* 15 Dec 1923, 604. James Craig Gordon, "Life Is Just Like That; In a curling plume of thin, grayish smoke passed Martha Mansfield, former 'Follies' girl and motion picture star—*Movie Weekly* mourns her untimely end," *MW,* 5 Jan 1924, 3. Louise Morgan, "Does a Grim Spectre Hover Over the Lives of Movie Stars?," *MW,* 5 Apr 1924, 4–5 (discusses Mansfield and Reid, Bunny, W.D. Taylor, Olive Thomas and Harold Lockwood). Billy H. Doyle, "Lost Players," *CI,* 146 (Aug 1987), 31. Eve Golden, "Brief Shining Star: The Career of Martha Mansfield," *CI,* 268 (Oct 1997), C2-C4 (includes filmography).

Mangussen, Fritz [director] (b. Copenhagen, Denmark, 13 Sep 1878–14 Apr 1920 [41], Denmark). AS, p. 703.

Manso, Juanita [actress] (*née* Juanita Ramirez Fernandez, b. Madrid, Spain, 1872–25 Feb 1957 [84?], Madrid, Spain). AS, p. 711.

Manson, Héléna [actress] (*née* Elena Eugénia Manson, b. Caracas, Venezuela, 18 Aug 1898–14 Sep 1994 [96], Neuilly-sur-Seine, France [extrait de décès no. 729/1994]). AS, p. 711.

Mantell, Ethel [actress] (d. 2 Sep 1942). BHD1, p. 361.

Mantell, Robert Bruce [stage/film actor] (b. Irvine, Ayrshire, Scotland, 7 Feb 1854–27 Jun 1928 [74], Atlantic Highlands NJ). m. (1) Ms. Hudson; (2) Charlotte Behrens (d. 1898); (3) Marie Sheldon (*née* Marie Shand, d. 1939); (4) **Genevieve Hamper**, 1916 (d. 1971). (Film debut: *The Blindness of Devotion,* Fox, 1915.) "Robert B. Mantell, Famous Actor, Dies; Player of Shakespearean and Romantic Roles Succumbs After a Break-Down; Born in Scotland in 1854; First Won Fame in America with Fanny Davenport in 'Fedora'—His Funeral Tomorrow," *NYT,* 28 Jun 1928, 25:3 (stage debut in *Romeo and Juliet,* Albany NY, 1878). "Robert B. Mantell," *Variety,* 4 Jul 1928. AS, p. 711. BHD, p. 244. IFN, p. 197. SD. Truitt, p. 214. WWS, p. 214. "Mantell Refuses Ince [of NYMP Co.]; Had Offered $10,000 for the Famous Actor to Play 'Richelieu' Before Camera," *NYDM,* 14 Jan 1914, 56:1 ("...the star for the sixth time refused to appear anywhere but on the legitimate stage until he has finally retired from actual screen life."). "Film Flashes," *Variety,* 23 Jan 1914, 14:2 ("The N.Y. Motion Picture Co. offered Robert Mantell $10,000 for a series of Shakespearean film productions. Offer refused."). Photo of Genevieve Hamper, *NYT,* 7 Feb 1915, Photogravure Section, Part I, n.p. "Mantell's Son to Wed," *NYDM,* 15 Sep 1915, 9:1 (Robert Shand Mantell to marry Marion Marsh, 18 Sep 1915, NYC. First wife, Mabel Lansing, d. 1911.).

Mantle, Burns [drama critic] (*né* Robert Burns Mantle, b. Watertown NY, 23 Dec 1873–9 Feb 1948 [74], Forest Hills, LI NY). m. Lydia Sears, 1903. "Burns Mantle, 74, Drama Critic, Dies; Dean of Reviewers Here, Noted as Anthologist of Best Plays, Served The News 21 Years," *NYT,* 10 Feb 1948, 23:1. "Burns Mantle Dead at 74," *Variety,* 11 Feb 1948. AMD, p. 236. BHD2, p. 176. SD. "Burns Mantle to Write Talmadge Films' Titles," *MPW,* 20 Nov 1920, 376.

Mantzius, Karl [actor/director] (b. Copenhagen, Denmark, 20 Feb 1860–17 May 1921 [61], Frederiksberg, Denmark). AS, p. 712.

Manz, Adolf [actor] (b. Meilen, Switzerland, 10 Oct 1885–23 Apr 1949 [63], Zurich, Switzerland). AS, p. 712.

Manzi, Alfredo [art director]. JS, pp. 265–66 (in Italian silents from 1914).

Manzini, Italia Almirante [actress] (b. Taranto, Italy, 3 Oct 1890–15 Oct 1941 [51], São Paulo, Brazil). (Kleine.) AS, p. 712. BHD, p. 244. IFN, p. 197.

Mapes, Agnes [actress]. No data found. (Kalem.) AMD, p. 236. "A Kalem Girl in Ireland," *MPW,* 15 Jul 1911, 31. "Miss Agnes Mapes in 'Il Trovatore,'" *MPW,* 11 Jul 1914, 259.

Mara, Lya [actress] (b. Riga, Latvia, 1 Aug 1897). AS, p. 712.

Marais, Mario [actor/director/scenarist] (b. Livorno, Italy, 1859–1 Mar 1922 [63?], Turin, Italy). AS, p. 712.

Marano, Mario [actor]. No data found. AMD, p. 236. "Brazil Makes Screen Contrib[ution]," *MPW,* 7 May 1927, 25.

Marba, Joseph [actor] (b. Peabody MA, 19 Oct 1879–7 Sep 1938 [58]). AS, p. 712. BHD1, p. 361. IFN, p. 197.

Marbe, Fay [actress]. No data found. Alma Talley, "She Gave Up Society for a Career; Fay Marbe, famous dancer and recent star in movies, tells why she chose hard work of theatrical profession in preference to life of social butterfly," *MW,* 7 Jun 1924, 3, 26.

Marble, John S. (son of actor Ben Marble) [stock/film actor] (b. Buffalo NY, 18 May 1844–23 Jun 1919 [75], New York NY). "John S. Marble, Comedian," *NYT,* 24 Jun 1919, 13:4. "Deaths; John Marble," *Variety,* LV, 27 Jun 1919, 15:4. AS, p. 712. BHD, p. 244. IFN, p. 197 (age 74).

Marble, Scott [actor/scenarist] (d. 5 Apr 1919, New York NY). BHD2, p. 176.

Marburgh, Bertram [stage/film actor] (b. New York NY, 17 May 1875–22 Aug 1956 [81], Woodland Hills CA). (Wharton.) AS, p. 713. BHD1, p. 361. IFN, p. 197. MSBB, p. 1026.

Marceau, Emily [actress]. No data found. AMD, p. 236. "Actress Says Director Left her Suspended in Air While He Lunched," *MPW,* 11 Sep 1920, 201.

Marcel-Vibert [actor] (b. Paris, France, 2 Nov 1888-ca. 1960 [72?]). AS, p. 713.

Marceline [stage/film actor] (*né* Marceline Orbes, b. Zaragoza, Spain, 15 May 1873–5 Nov 1927 [54], New York NY; suicide by shooting). m. Ada. "Marceline, Clown, Ends Life by Shot; Famous Hippodrome Figure for Many Years Is Found Dead in Narrow Hotel Bedroom; Had $6 and Pawn Ticket [pawned his ring for $15]; His Money Believed Lost in Business Ventures—Began Career Abroad at Age of 7," *NYT,* 6 Nov 1927, 1:2, 25:1 (he was an "august," i.e., his make-up was the misfit, evening clothes and not the baggy, ruffled pantaloons of the orthodox clown). "Marceline Kills Self," *Variety,* 9 Nov 1927, 29:2 (age 50; "...placed a gun against his right temple and sent a bullet into his brain."). BHD, p. 244.

Marcellus, Irene [actress]. No data found. AMD, p. 236. "Marshall Neilan Signs Irene Marcellus to Star in Terhune's 'The Lotus Eater,'" *MPW,* 30 Oct 1920, 1222.

Marcet, L.J. [actor]. No data found. AMD, p. 236. "American Actor Victim of Boy Bandits," *MPW,* 23 Aug 1913, 850.

March, Fredric [stage/film actor] (*né* Ernest Frederick McIntyre Bicgel [March was his mother's maiden name], b. Racine WI, 31 Aug 1897–14 Apr 1975 [77], Los Angeles CA; cancer). m. **Florence Eldridge**, 1927, Mexico (d. 1988). (Film debut: *Paying the Piper,* 1921; extra; AA, 1931–32 and 1946.) Albin Krebs, "Fredric March Dies of Cancer; Stage and Screen Actor Was 77," *NYT,* 15 Apr 1975, 11:6; Laurie Johnston, "Notes on People," *NYT,* 26 Apr 1975, 23:1 (will probated; left estate of over $830,000 to widow). Theo Wilson, "Fredric March Dies at 77; Won 2 Oscars, Starred on Stage," *The Daily News,* 56, 15 Apr 1975, 4. "Frederic March, Double Oscar Winner, Dies at 77 of Cancer," *Variety,* 16 Apr 1975. AS, p. 713. BHD1, p. 362. IFN, p. 197. Katz, p. 774 (*né* Bikel). Barton Boone, "Is Fredric March Barrymore's Talkie Twin?," *Screenland,* Feb 1931, 50–51, 127. "Ex-Banker: Fred Bickel," *Cinema Arts,* Sep 1937, 61.

Marchal, Arlette [model/actress] (*née* Lucienne Marie Marchal, b. Paris, France, 29 Jan 1902 [extrait de naissance no. 6/327]–11 Feb 1984 [82], Paris, France [extrait de décès no. 16/257]). m. **Marcel de Sano** (suicide, 1939). (Film debut: *L'Image,* 1923; Universal; MGM.) "Arlette Marchal,"

Variety, 22 Feb 1984. AMD, p. 236. AS, p. 713. BHD1, p. 362 (d. 9 Feb). JS, p. 267. Katz, pp. 774–75. Waldman, p. 178. "She Was the Queen of Naples," *MPC,* Dec 1925, 55, 80. Gladys Hall, "The Prize Parisienne; The Story of Arlette Marchal, the Latest Charmer to Be Imported to Our Shores," *MM,* Mar 1926, 29, 128–29. "Marchal Signs New Contract," *MPW,* 28 Aug 1926, 542. Paul Paige, "Close-Ups and Fade-Outs," *Paris and Hollywood,* Sep 1926, 91 (to play the lead in *Fortune River*).

Marchand, Henri François Jean André [actor] (b. Mainvilliers, France, 28 Aug 1898–22 May 1959 [60], Paris, France). AS, p. 713.

Marchand, Léopold [actor/scenarist] (b. Paris, France, 5 Feb 1891–25 Nov 1952 [61], Paris, France). AS, p. 713.

Marchant, Jay [director]. No data found. AMD, p. 236. "Marchant Holding Directorial Rank," *MPW,* 28 Jul 1923, 318.

Marche, Gazelle [actress] (b. Utica NY, 1892–26 Feb 1935 [42?], New York NY). AMD, p. 236. BHD, p. 245. "Gazelle Marche," *MPW,* 26 Feb 1916, 1302.

Marcilly [actor/director] (*né* Rodolphe Gaëtan Marcilly, b. Saint-Servan, France, 29 Jun 1898 [extrait de naissance no. 171]-27 Mar 1976 [77], Paris, France). AS, p. 714.

Marcin, Max [writer/scenarist/director] (b. Ponznan, Poland, 5 May 1879–30 Mar 1948 [68], Tucson AZ). m. Clara May Mings. "Max Marcin Dead; Wrote Mysteries; Stage, Screen and Radio Crime Author Turned Out Many Short Stories, Serials," *NYT,* 1 Apr 1948, 1 Apr 1948, 26:2. "Max Marcin," *Variety,* 7 Apr 1948. AS, p. 714 (b. 6 May). BHD2, p. 177. FDY, p. 433. IFN, p. 198. SD.

Marco, Raoul [actor] (*né* Maurice Raoul Mayzaud, b. Paris, France, 22 Nov 1892 [extrait de naissance no. 5202]-3 Apr 1971 [78], Paris, France [extrait de décès no. SN/1971]). AS, p. 714.

Marcotti, Margaret [actress] (b. Los Angeles CA, 1913–8 Apr 1985 [72?], San Diego CA). BHD, p. 245.

Marcoux, Vanni [actor/singer] (*né* Jean Emile Diogéne Vanni-Marcoux, b. Turin, Italy, 12 Jun 1870–21 Oct 1962 [92], Paris, France). AS, p. 714. BHD1, p. 362.

Marcus, James A. [actor] (b. New York NY, 21 Jan 1867–15 Oct 1937 [70], Los Angeles CA; heart attack). m. Lillian. "James A. Marcus; Veteran Actor Had Been Playing Father Roles in Recent Films," *NYT,* 16 Oct 1937, 19:5 (began 1916). "James Marcus," *Variety,* 20 Oct 1937 (age 69; began 1916). AS, p. 714. BHD1, p. 362. IFN, p. 198. Truitt, p. 214 (b. 1868). George Katchmer, "James Marcus," *CI,* 214 (Apr 1993), 51.

Marcyl, Cécyl [actress] (*née* Marie Cécile Frédérique Sesboue, b. Argentre, France, 6 Jul 1890 [extrait de naissance no. 47]-10 Feb 1960 [69], Paris, France). AS, p. 714.

Mardayn, Christl [actress] (*née* Anna Christine Maria Mardein, b. Vienna, Austria, 8 Dec 1896–10 Jul 1971 [74], Vienna, Austria). AS, p. 714.

Mardiganian, Aurora [actress] (*née* Aurora Mardigian, d. 6 Feb 1994, Los Angeles CA). (Made 1 film, *Ravished Armenia,* Selig, 1919.) Ravished Armenia *and the Story of Aurora Mardiganian,* comp. Anthony Slide (Scarecrow Press: Lnham MD, 1997) (to America from Oslo, Norway, 5 Nov 1917). AMD, p. 236. "Falls Fifteen Feet," *MPW,* 28 Dec 1918, 1496. Cover, *The American Weekly,* 12 Jan 1919.

Mardo, Estelle [actress]. No data found. (Vitagraph.) AMD, p. 236. "Gossip of the Studios," *NYDM,* 9 Sep 1914, 27:1 (changed professional name from Estelle Mardo Coffin to Estelle Mardo). "Estelle Mardo, Mirror Star," *MPW,* 5 Feb 1916, 750.

Mardzyanizvili, Kote [director] (b. Kvarli, Georgia, 28 May 1872–17 Apr 1933 [60], Moscow, Russia). AS, p. 714.

Maretskaya, Vera Petrovana [actress] (b. Moscow, Russia, 31 Jul 1906–17 Aug 1978 [72], Moscow, Russia). AS, p. 714. BHD1, p. 362. IFN, p. 198.

Marey, Etienne-Jules [physiologist/inventor] (b. Beaune, France, 5 Mar 1830–16 May 1904 [74], Paris, France). *The Illustrated History of the Cinema,* consultant ed., David Robinson; ed. Ann Lloyd (NY: Macmillan, 1986), pp. 11–12 (applied photography to his work contemporaneously with Eadweard Muybridge. 1882: contrived a photographic gun (*fusil photographique*) which took 12 individual photographs per second. 1888: Marey's Chronophotographe "used a continuous strip of paper film to record a sequence of individual photographs"; he used George Eastman's celluloid roll-film after 1889). AS, p. 715.

Margetson, Arthur [actor] (b. London, England, 27 Apr 1897–12 Aug 1951 [54], London, England). AS, p. 715.

Margolis, Charles "Doc" [stage manager/film actor] (b. 1874?–22 Sep 1926 [52?], Glendale CA; from a tropical illness). "Charles Margolis," *Variety,* 29 Sep 1926. AS, p. 715. BHD, p. 245.

Marguerite, Babe [singer/actress] (d. 12 Mar 1921, Galesburg IL). "Mrs. Babe Sterling (Marguerite)," *Variety,* 18 Mar 1921. BHD, p. 245.

Mari, Febo [director/actor] (*né* Alfredo Rodriguez, b. Messina, Sicily, Italy, 18 Jan 1884–6 Jun 1939 [55], Rome, Italy). AS, p. 715. BHD, p. 245; BHD2, p. 177. IFN, p. 198. JS, p. 269 (in Italian silents from 1911).

Mari, Sergio [actor] (b. 1895–1925 [30?], Berlin, Germany). BHD1, p. 613.

Marian, Edna *see* **Marion, Edna**

Marian, Ferdinand [actor] (*né* Ferdinand Haschowec, b. Vienna, Austria, 14 Aug 1902–7 Aug 1946 [43], Durneck, Germany). AS, p. 715.

Marievsky, Josef [actor] (b. Russia, 1 Jan 1888–27 Apr 1971 [83], Los Angeles CA). BHD1, p. 363. IFN, p. 198.

Marin, H.N. [general manager]. No data found. AMD, p. 236. "Distinctive Plans Busy Year; A.S. Friend Issues Statement," *MPW,* 13 Jan 1923, 123.

Marin, Ned [producer; VP of Famous Artists Corp.] (b. 1896?–11 Nov 1955 [59], Los Angeles CA; after brain tumor surgery). (Universal, 1920; Metro; TC-F; 1st National.) "Ned Marin," *NYT,* 14 Nov 1955, 27:4 (age 60). "Ned Marin," *Variety,* 16 Nov 1955. AS, p. 716. BHD2, p. 177.

Marinoff, Fania [stage/film actress] (b. Odessa, Ukraine, Russia, 20 Mar 1890–17 Nov 1971 [81], Englewood NJ). m. Carl Van Vechten, Nov? 1914. (World.) "Fania Marinoff, Actress, 81, Dead; Carl Van Vechten's Widow, a Noted Bohemian in '20's," *NYT,* 17 Nov 1971, 51:1. "Fania Marinoff," *Variety,* 24 Nov 1971. AS, p. 716 (d. 16 Nov). BHD, p. 245. IFN, p. 198. Truitt, p. 214. "Critic Marries Actress; Carl Van Vechten, Late of the Press and Times, Weds Fania Marinoff," *NYDM,* 11 Nov 1914, 17:2. "Fania Marinoff," *MPW,* 24 Apr 1915, 544. "Fania Marinoff," *NYDM,* 5 May 1915, 24:1 (with photo). "Fania Marinoff's Portrait," *MPW,* 22 May 1915, 1262. "Fania Marinoff with World Film," *MPW,* 25 Dec 1915, 2340.

Marion, Don [child actor] (b. 1915?). (Sennett.) *Fl.* 1920–30.

Marion, Edna [actress: Wampas Star, 1926] (*née* Edna Hannam, b. Chicago IL, 12 Dec 1906–2 Dec 1957 [50], Los Angeles CA). (Charlie Chase comedies.) "Edna Marion Naisbitt," *Variety,* 11 Dec 1957. AMD, p. 236. AS, p. 716. BHD1, p. 363. IFN, p. 198. Truitt, p. 214 (b. 1908). "Julius and Abe Stern Pick Four Century Comedy Stars," *MPW,* 13 Dec 1924, 652. "Edna Marion Steps Up," *MPW,* 18 Jul 1925, 354. "Beauties Who Make the Comedies Attractive," *Cinema Arts,* V (Aug 1926), 21 (Edna Marian; photo). Photo, *MPC,* Aug 1926, 42. "Edna Marion Chosen by Wampas," *MPW,* 16 Oct? 1926, 233. "Edna Marion to Continue in Her Comedies," *MPW,* 15? Jan 1927, 203. "Hal Roach has Edna Marion Under Contract," *MPW,* 21 May 1927, 199. George A. Katchmer, "Forgotten Cowboys and Cowgirls—Part XIV," *CI,* 191 (May 1991), 22.

Marion, Frances [actress/scenarist/director] (*née* Frances Marion Owens, b. San Francisco CA, 18 Nov 1886?–12 May 1973 [86], Los Angeles CA). m. (1) Robert Dixon Pike—div. Jan 1918; (2) **Fred Thomson**, Nov 1919 (d. 1928); (3) **George William Hill** (d. 1934). *Off with Their Heads!; A Serio-Comic Tale of Hollywood* (The Macmillan Co., Inc., 1972); Cari Beauchamp, *Without Lying Down: Frances Marion and the Powerful Women of Early Hollywood* (NYL Scribner, 1997); *Without Lying Down; Frances Marion and the Power of Women in Hollywood* (Turner Classic Movies documentary, directed by Bridget Terry). "Frances Marion Dies on Coast; Screenwriter Won Two Oscars," *NYT,* 14 May 1973, 34:4 (d. 13 May, age 80). "Frances Marion," *Variety,* 16 May 1973. AMD, p. 236. AS, p. 716 (b. 1887). BHD1, p. 363; BHD2, p. 177 (b. 1888). FDY, p. 433. IFN, p. 198 (b. 1888). Katz, pp. 776–77 (b. 1887). Spehr, pp. 150–51. "Frances Marion," *MPW,* 18 Mar 1916, 1813. "Frances Marion Engaged by Famous Players-Lasky," *MPW,* 26 May 1917, 1297. "Miss Marion at Lasky Studios," *MPW,* 7 Jul 1917, 73. "Little Whisperings from Everywhere in Playerdom," *Motion Picture Magazine,* Feb 1918, 144 (divorced Pike, who said that "the fair Marion had deserted him for a career."). "Frances Marion Signs Year's Contract," *MPW,* 29 Jun 1918, 1856. "Scenario Writer Off for France," *MPW,* 24 Aug 1918, 1101. "Frances Marion to Do War Work," *MPW,* 28 Sep 1918, 1860. "Frances Marion Returns to Task," *MPW,* 22 Feb 1919, 1013. "Picturizing Women War Workers," *MPW,* 5 Apr 1919, 75. "Frances Marion Ill," *MPW,* 12 Apr 1919, 219 (with grippe). "Frances Marion Writes Official Film," *MPW,* 10 May 1919, 830. "Marion Writing Pickford Scenario," *MPW,* 20 Sep 1919, 1799. "Frances Marion Off to Europe," *MPW,* 17 Apr 1920, 384. "Frances Marion to Direct Mary's Next Two Pictures," *MPW,* 4 Sep 1920, 71. "Frances Marion to Direct Mary," *MPW,* 4 Sep 1920, 89. "Frances Marion Signs a Long-Term Contract to Direct Mary Pickford," *MPW,* 16 Oct 1920, 973. "Frances Marion Directs Hubby

[Fred Thomson] in Newest Film," *MPW,* 3 Dec 1921, 539. "Frances Marion Now with Goldwyn," *MPW,* 23 Dec 1922, 738. "Warners Sign Frances Marion for 'Beau Brummel,'" *MPW,* 19 May 1923, 245. Harry Carr, "The Most Envied Girl in Hollywood," *MPC,* Sep 1924, 20–21, 87–88. "Frances Marion, Producer, in Munroe-DeMille Group," *MPW,* 7 Mar 1925, 84. "First Marion Production," *MPW,* 25 Apr 1925, 803. "To Write Continuity," *MPW,* 18 Jul 1925, 357. "Frances Marion Completes Her First Big Production," *MPW,* 24 Oct 1925, 628. "Frances Marion Preparing 'Calamity Jane' for Screen," *MPW,* 26 Dec 1925, 758. "Frances Marion to Devote All Time to Goldwyn Productions," *MPW,* 16 Jan 1926, 225. "Miss Marion Joins Goldwyn," *MPW,* 6 Feb 1926, 538. "Frances Marion Signs," *MPW,* 11 Sep 1926, 3. "Frances Marion Now with M-G-M," *MPW,* 29 Oct 1927, 551. Slide, *Early Women Directors* (NY: A.S. Barnes and Co., 1977), pp. 83–91 (b. 1890). Marsha McCreadie, "Pioneers," *FIR,* Nov/Dec 1994, 40–53. Carl Beauchamp, "Frances Marion and Mary Pickford; Two Powerful Women of Early Hollywood," *CI,* 262 (Apr 1997), C4-C6. "Original Documentary 'Without Lying Down' to Headline Women Film Pioneers on TCM in August," *CI,* 301 (Jul 2000), 17 (television premiere of the only existing film directed by Marion, *The Love Light,* 1921, and the two films for which she won Academy Awards, *The Big House,* 1930, and *The Champ,* 1931). Julie Salamon, "Women Wielding Power in a Wide-Open Hollywood," *NYT,* 3 Aug 2000, E5 (review of Without Lying Down. ("In the picture business you can spend your life searching for a man to look up to without lying down.").

Marion, Frank J[oseph] [a founder of Kalem/scenarist/producer] (b. 1870?–28 Mar 1963 [93], Stamford CT). (Kalem.) "Movie Producer Is Dead [Frank Joseph Marion]," *NYT,* CXII, 29 Mar 1963, 7:1. AMD, p. 237. AS, p. 716. BHD2, p. 177. "Kalem Company (Inc.)," *MPW,* 8 Jun 1907, 223. "Notes of the Trade," *MPW,* V, 2 Oct 1909, 447. "Kalem Sends Company to the Orient," *MPW,* 16 Dec 1911, 880. "Marion Digs Up Some Facts," *MPW,* 5 Sep 1914, 1356. "Aplaud Freedom of Screen," *MPW,* 8 May 1915, 872–73. William Lord Wright, "For Photoplay Authors, Real and Near; He Wrote the First One," *NYDM,* 19 May 1915, 30:1 (he was a pioneer photo-playwright and editor from Kalem's inception to ca. 1911.). "'The General Film Company Reorgtanized," *MPW,* 20 Nov 1915, 1458. "Marion Praises Co-operation of Creel," *MPW,* 1 Dec 1917, 1295. "Honors for Marion," *MPW,* 8 Dec 1917, 1471. "Opportunities in Spain, Says Marion," *MPW,* 19 Jan 1918, 355. Frank Joseph Marion, "Kalem Chief Writes of Spain as a Market," *MPW,* 23 Feb 1918, 1070. "Frank Marion Returns to United States," *MPW,* 22 Jun 1918, 1691–92. "Marion Says Trade Follows Films," *MPW,* 5 Apr 1919, 53–54. "Marion Sues Hodkinson, Collins, Duell and Bawley for $500,000 Over Disposal of Stock Holdings," *MPW,* 21 Jan 1922, 260. "Frank Joseph Marion," *MPW,* 2 May 1927, 794.

Marion, George F., Jr. (son of **George Marion, Sr.**) [title writer/scenarist/librettist/author] (b. Boston MA, 30 Aug 1899–25 Feb 1968 [68], New York NY; heart attack). m. Dorothy Maldeis. "George Marion, a Librettist, 68; Author of Guy Lombardo's 'Arabian Nights' Dies," *NYT,* 27 Feb 1968, 39:3 ("He wrote subtitles for the silent movies *Mantrap, It, Irene* and *Ella Cinders,* with Clara Bow [sic], and *The Son of the Sheik* and *The Eagle* with Rudolph Valentino."). "George F. Marion Jr.," *Variety,* 28 Feb 1968. AMD, p. 237. AS, p. 716. BHD2, p. 177. FDY, p. 447. "Marion, Jr., with F.B.O.," *MPW,* 8 Mar 1924, 108. "Marion, Jr., Titling," *MPW,* 3 May 1924, 72. "Marion's Titles," *MPW,* 21 May 1927, 190.

Marion, George F., Sr. (father of **George Marion, Jr.**) [actor/director/producer] (b. San Francisco CA, 16 Jul 1860–30 Nov 1945 [85], Carmel CA; heart attack). "George Marion, 85, Ziegfeld Aide, Dies; Staged and Appeared in Many of His Productions—Played Captain in 'Anna Christie,'" *NYT,* 2 Dec 1945, 46:3. "George F. Marion," *Variety,* 5 Dec 1945. AMD, p. 237. AS, p. 716. BHD1, p. 363. FSS, p. 202. IFN, p. 198. Truitt, p. 214. "Rork and Roth Unite as Producers; Sign George Marion and Buy 'Isobel,'" *MPW,* 28 Aug 1920, 1188. "Marion Himself," *MPW,* 28 Jul 1923, 324.

Marion, Oskar [actor/producer] (b. Brno, Czechoslovakia, 2 Apr 1896-Mar 1986 [89]). AS, p. 716 (b. Koningsfeld, Germany, 4 Feb...). BHD1, p. 363; BHD2, p. 177.

Marion, Sidney [actor] (b. MA, 14 Sep 1900–29 Jun 1965 [64], Los Angeles CA; heart attack). "Sid Marion," *Variety,* 7 Jul 1965 (age 65). AS, p. 716. IFN, p. 198.

Marion, William [actor] (b. CA, 12 Jan 1880–3 Jan 1957 [76], Los Angeles Co. CA). AS, p. 716. BHD, p. 245 (b. 1878). IFN, p. 198. '83 WWOS (b. 1878).

Mariotti, Frédéric [actor] (b. Marseilles, France, 1 Apr 1883 [extrait de naissance no. 216/1883]-22 Feb 1971 [87], Paris, France). AS, p. 716.

Maris, Lya [actress] (*née* Livia Marracci). No data found. JS, p. 270 (in Italian silents from 1926).

Maris, Mona [actress] (*née* María Rose Amita Capdevielle, b. Buena Aires, Argentina, 7 Nov 1903–23 Mar 1991 [87], Buenos Aires, Argentina). (Film debut: England, 1925; Ufa; Fox Spanish- and French-language films in Hollywood.) "Mona Maris," *CI,* Oct 1991. AS, p. 716 (d. Lima, Peru). BHD1, p. 363. '94 Katz. Waldman, p. 179. Elisabeth Goldbeck, "Not at All Bad; Marconi Persuaded Mona Maris' Mother That an Actress Could Be Good," *MPC,* Mar 1930, 70, 82.

Marischka, Ernst Josef (brother of **Hubert Marischka**) [director] (b. Vienna, Austria, 2 Jan 1893–15 Jun 1963 [70], Coire, Switzerland). AS, p. 716.

Marischka, Hubert Josef (brother of **Ernst Marischka**) [actor/director/scenarist] (b. Vienna, Austria, 2 Jan 1893–15 May 1963 [70], Chur, Switzerland). AS, p. 716 (b. 27 Aug 1882; d. 4 Dec 1959). BHD2, p. 177.

Maritza, Sari [actress] (b. Tianjin, China, 17 Mar 1910-Jul 1987 [77], Virgin Islands). AS, p. 716 (d. China). BHD1, p. 363.

Marjal [actor] (*né* Marius Soulie, b. Paris, France, 1886–1 Mar 1940 [54?], Paris, France). AS, p. 717.

Marjan, David Samoulovich [director/scenarist] (b. Ukraine, 1892–1937 [45?], Ukraine). AS, p. 717.

Mark, Michael [actor] (*né* Maurice L. Schulmann, b. Russia, 15 Mar 1886–3 Feb 1975 [88], Woodland Hills CA; heart failure). "Michael Mark," *Variety,* 12 Feb 1975. AS, p. 717. BHD1, p. 364. IFN, p. 198.

Mark, Mitchell H. [producer] (b. Greenville SC, 1861–19 Mar 1918 [57?], Buffalo NY). BHD2, p. 177.

Marke, Sidney [actor/assistant director] (b. 1896–30 May 1985 [89?], Pittsburgh PA). AS, p. 717. BHD, p. 245; BHD2, p. 177.

Marken, Jane [actress] (*née* Jeanne Berthe Adolphine Crabbe, b. Paris, France, 13 Jan 1895–1 Dec 1976 [81], Neuilly-sur-Seine, France [extrait de décès no. 825]). AS, p. 717. BHD1, p. 364.

Markey, Enid Virginia [actress] (b. Dillon CO, 22 Feb 1890?–15 Nov 1981 [91], Bay Shore, LI NY [Death Certificate Index No. 33]). (Ince; Fox; National.) m. George W. Cobb, Jr. C. Gerald Fraser, "Enid Markey, Actress, Dead; Starred in First Tarzan Film," *NYT,* 16 Nov 1981, B18:3. "Enid Markey," *Variety,* 18 Nov 1981. AMD, p. 237. AS, p. 717 (b. 1896. BHD1, p. 364. FSS, p. 203. MSBB, p. 1038 (b. 1896) SD, p. 345 (b. 1896). "Enid Markey," *MPW,* 20 Mar 1915, 1773. "Enid Markey in New Company," *MPW,* 24 Nov 1917, 1206.

Markey, Gene [title writer/scenarist/producer] (b. Jackson MI, 11 Dec 1895–1 May 1980 [84], Miami Beach FL). AS, p. 717. BHD2, p. 177. FDY, p. 447.

Marks, Clarence J. [production assistant/scenarist] (b. 25 Dec 1893–22 Mar 1972 [78], Woodland Hills CA). "Clarence Marks," *Variety,* 29 Mar 1972 (gag writer in 1920s; "Marks worked at Universal with William Wyler in director's early days..."). AS, p. 717. BHD2, p. 177.

Marks, George [film cutter] (b. 1900?–Feb 1933 [32], Azusa CA; car accident). (At WB for 26 years.) "George Marks Killed in Crash," *Variety,* 7 Feb 1933.

Marks, Joe E. [actor] (b. New York NY, 15 Jun 1891–14 Jun 1973 [81], New York NY). AS, p. 717.

Marks, Lou [actor] (b. 1895–11 Dec 1987 [92?], Little Neck NY). AMD, p. 237. BHD1, p. 364. "Lou Marks in Slapstick Series," *MPW,* 28 Jul 1917, 664.

Marks, Maurice [scenarist] (b. New York NY–d. 3 Nov 1952, New York NY). m. Rita Weiman. "Maurice Marks," *NYT,* 4 Nov 1952, 29:5. "Maurice Marks," *Variety,* 5 Nov 1952. AS, p. 718. BHD2, p. 177.

Marks, Percy [writer]. No data found. AMD, p. 237. "Percy Marks in New York," *MPW,* 30 May 1925, 580.

Marks, Tom [actor] (b. Canada, 1854–10 May 1936 [82?], Christy's Lake, Canada). AS, p. 718.

Marks, Willis [actor] (b. Rochester MN, 20 Aug 1865–6 Dec 1952 [87], Los Angeles CA). AS, p. 718. BHD1, p. 364. IFN, p. 198.

Markson, Benjamin [scenarist]. No data found. FDY, p. 433.

Markus, Laszlo [director] (b. Szentes, Hungary, 19 Nov 1882–28 Apr 1948 [65], Budapest, Hungary). AS, p. 718.

Marlborough, Helen [actress] (b. CA, ca. 1867–17 Aug 1955 [88?], Pasadena CA). BHD1, p. 613.

Marlborough, Leah [actress] (b. 1869–21 Dec 1953 [84?]). BHD, p. 245.

Marle, Arnold [actor] (b. Berlin, Germany, 15 Sep 1887–21 Feb 1970 [82], London, England). AS, p. 718.

Marley, J. Peverell [cinematographer] (b. San Jose CA, 14 Aug 1901–2 Feb 1964 [62], Santa Barbara CA). (FP-L; WB; MGM; TC-F.) m. (1) **Lina Basquette** (d. 1994); (2) Virginia Ruth McAdoo; (3) Linda Darnell, 1943–52. "J. Peverell Marley Is Dead; Hollywood Cameraman, 62," *NYT,* 4 Feb 1964, 33:3. "J. Peverell Marley," *Variety,* 5 Feb 1964. AMD, p. 237. AS, p. 718. BHD2, p. 177. FDY, p. 461. IFN, p. 199. Katz, pp. 778–79. "New Head Cameraman," *MPW,* 21 Jun 1924, 708 (24 years old). Hal K.Wells, "A Young Man Grinds Out a Good Job; Peverel Marley Turns the Crank on 'The King of the Kings' and Wins High Praise From Cecil," *MPC,* Jun 1927, 20–21, 68. Charles West, "Pev Marley Offers You a Job," *Screenland,* Oct 1927, 48–49, 101 (contest).

Marlo, George M. [actor/founded Marlo Music] (b. New York NY, 1884?–5 Feb 1970 [86], New York NY). "George Marlo," *Variety,* 11 Feb 1970. BHD, p. 245.

Marlow, Brian [actor/scenarist] (b. Boston MA, 1893–9 Apr 1949 [56?], Woodland Hills CA). BHD2, p. 178.

Marlowe, James C. [actor] (b. 1865–4 Sep 1926 [61?], New York NY). BHD, p. 245.

Marlowe, Julia [stage/film actress] (b. 1865??–12 Nov 1950 [85], Hotel Plaza, New York NY). m. (1) Robert S. Taber, 1895–1900; (2) **E.H. Sothern**, 1911 (d. 1933). (Stage debut: *Ingomar,* New London CT, 1887.) "Julia Marlowe," *Variety,* 15 Nov 1950, p. 71:1 ("In 1929 Miss Marlowe r eceived a gold-medal award of the American Academy of Arts and Letters for good diction on the stage, 'for clarity and melody in the use of the English language.'"). AMD, p. 237. "Her Stage Days Over; Ill Health Prevents Julia Marlowe from Ever Appearing on Stage Again," *NYDM,* 11 Aug 1915, 7:4 (announced by Sothern at Litchfield CT. "She has completely broken down."). "Frank Currier Engaged by Metro," *MPW,* 14 Oct 1916, 237.

Marlowe, June [actress: Wampas Star, 1925] (*née* Gisela Valaria Goetten, b. St. Cloud MN, 6 Nov 1902–10 Mar 1984 [81], Burbank CA; San Fernando Mission Cemetery). m. Rodney S. Sprigg, 2 Jul 1933 (d. 1982). (Film debut: *Fighting Blood,* FBO, 1923; 2-reel shorts.) "June Marlowe," *Variety,* 25 Apr 1984 (age 81). AMD, p. 237. AS, p. 718. BHD1, p. 364 (b. 1903). FFF, p. 240. FSS, p. 203. Katz, p. 778 (b. 1903). MH, p. 125 (b. 1905). "Sol Lesser Signs Unknown Beauty," *MPW,* 16 Jun 1923, 590. "New Warner Star Young and Clever," *MPW,* 2 Aug 1924, 380. "Artist Chooses June Marlowe," *MPW,* 27 Dec 1924, 864. "June Marlowe," *MPW,* 13 Feb 1926, 631. Scott Johnson, "June Marlowe," *CI,* 129 (Mar 1986), 10–11, 63 (b. 1903); 130 (Apr 1986), 34–36, 63. Scott Johnson, "June Marlowe; Filmography," *CI,* 131 (May 1986), C8-C9.

Marlowe, Mercedes [actress] (b. 1915–10 Nov 1987 [72?], San Diego CA). BHD1, p. 364.

Marmont, Percy [stage/film actor/director] (b. Denville Hall, London, England, 25 Nov 1883–3 Mar 1977 [93], Denville Hall, London, England). m. Dorothy Stewart-Dawson. AMD, p. 237. AS, p. 719. BHD1, p. 365. FFF, p. 35. IFN, p. 199. Katz, pp. 778–79. MH, p. 125. SD, p. 847. Slide, p. 163. WWS, p. 41. Faith Service, "Living Down the Name of Percy," *MPC,* May 1919, 31, 72 ("...I don[']t know that I can ever *quite* forgive my parents. They named me Percy. *Percy,* conceive of it! Do you think I can ever live it down? *Do* you?"). "Marmont Returns to Screen," *MPW,* 31 May 1919, 1318. "Marmont Signs Contract as Support to Alice Brady," *MPW,* 14 Jun 1919, 1624. "Song Dedicated to Marmont and Brady," *MPW,* 28 Jun 1919, 1950 (*I Cannot Believe I Lost You*). "Percy Marmont to Play Lead," *MPW,* 17 Jun 1922, 619. "In Leading Part," *MPW,* 30 Jun 1923, 759. "Marmont Is Lead in Metro Feature," *MPW,* 6 Oct 1923, 508. "Percy Marmont," *MPW,* 12 Jul 1924, insert. "Denial That Marmont Has Filed Charges with Academy," *MPW,* 24 Sep 1927, 231. Frances Breedlove, "Percy Marmont, A Reluctant Martyr," *Cinema Arts,* Dec 1927, 23, 49. Robert A. Evans, "Evans' 1977 Chronicle," *FIR,* Mar 1978, 147. John C. Tibbetts, "Percy Marmont; Leading man to 'more stars than are in heaven,'" *FIR,* Sep/Oct 1995, 9–19 (includes filmography).

Marnac, Jeanne [actress] (*née* Jane Fernande Mayer, b. Brussels, Belgium, 8 Feb 1892–2 Dec 1976 [84], Paris, France). AS, p. 719. BHD1, p. 365 (1896–1976).

Marodon, Pierre [director] (b. Paris, France, 2 May 1873–5 Apr 1949 [75], Ain Temouchent, Algeria). AS, p. 719.

Maroto, Eduardo G. [actor/director] (b. Jaen, Spain, 14 Dec 1905–27 Nov 1989 [83], Madrid, Spain). AS, p. 719.

Marquand, Rube [actor] (b. Cleveland OH, 1889–2 Jun 1980 [91?], Baltimore MD). AS, p. 719. BHD, p. 245.

Marquet, Mary [actress] (*née* Micheline Marie Marguerite Delphine Marquet, b. St. Petersburg, Russia, 14 Apr 1894–29 Aug 1979 [85], Paris, France; heart attack [extrait de décès no. 18/1490]). m. **Victor Francen** (d. 1077). AS, p. 719. BHD1, p. 365 (b. 1895).

Marquis, Don [writer]. No data found. AMD, p. 237. "Don Marquis's 'The Old Soak' to Be Produced by Universal," *MPW,* 16 May 1925, 363.

Marquis, Joseph P. [actor]. No data found. AMD, p. 238. "Joseph P. Marquis Joins Adolf Philipp. Corporation," *MPW,* 26 Jul 1919, 498.

Marr, Hans [actor] (*né* Johann Julius Richter, b. Breslau, Poland, 22 Jul 1878–30 Mar 1949 [70], Vienna, Austria). BHD1, p. 365. IFN, p. 199.

Marr, Kenneth Archibald [aviator/assistant director] (b. Oakland CA, 10 Jun 1885–28 Dec 1963 [78], Palo Alto CA; arteriosclerosis). m. actress Alice Ward, 1928. (Paramount.) Dennis Gordon, *Lafayette Escadrille Pilot Biographies* (Missoula MT: The Doughboy Historical Society, 1991), pp. 177–79.

Marr, Paula (mother of **Buster Collier**) [actress] (b. 1875–22 Dec 1960 [85?], Glendale CA). m. **William Collier, Sr.** (d. 1944). AS, p. 719.

Marr, William [actor] (*né* William Dobie, b. San Francisco CA, 1892–15 May 1960 [67], New York NY). "William Marr," *Variety,* 25 May 1960 (1st film: *Men of Steel,* 1916, with Milton Sills). AMD, p. 238. AS, p. 719. BHD, p. 245. IFN, p. 199. Truitt, p. 215. "William Marr Joins Fox," *MPW,* 31 Mar 1917, 2092.

Marret, Georges [producer] (d. 9 May 1937). BHD2, p. 178.

Marriot[t], Charles [stage/film actor] (b. London, England, 1859–12 Dec 1917 [58?], Los Angeles CA; tuberculosis). "Charles Marriot Dies," *Variety,* 14 Dec 1917 ("a pioneer stage and screen actor"). AS, p. 719. BHD, p. 245. SD, p. 868.

Marriott, Moore [stage/film actor] (*né* George Thomas Moore-Marriott, b. West Drayton, England, 14 Sep 1885–11 Dec 1949 [64], London, England). (Possible film debut: *Dick Turpin's Ride to York,* 1906.) AS, p. 719. BHD1, p. 365. IFN, p. 199. Kip-Xool, "Moore Marriott: 'The Lovable Old Codger,'" *CI,* 293 (Nov 1999), 25–26.

Marro, Alberto [director] (b. Barcelona, Spain, 1878–1956 [78?], Barcelona, Spain). AS, p. 720.

Mars, Séverin [actor] (*né* Armand-Jean de Malafayde, b. Bordeaux, France, 1873–17 Jul 1921 [48?], Paris, France). AS, p. 720. BHD, p. 245.

Marsac, Jean [actor] (*né* Henri Delanglade, b. Marseilles, France, 6 Jul 1894–20 Jun 1976 [81], Paris, France). AS, p. 720.

Marsh, Della [vaudeville/film actress] (d. 6 May 1973, Ithaca NY). m. Walter Fischter. (Vitagraph/Vitaphone films.) "Della Marsh," *Variety,* 271, 16 May 1973, 127:1 (a "Buster Brown" girl. Survived by a daughter, 3 grandchildren, 6 great-grandchildren, and a great-great-grandson). BHD, p. 245. IFN, p. 199.

Marsh, Frances (sister of **Mae Marsh**) [film editor] (b. 1897?–3 Mar 1958 [61], Hollywood CA). (Paramount.) "Frances Marsh," *Variety,* 12 Mar 1958.

Marsh, George E. [film editor] (b. 1904?–5 Nov 1967 [63], Los Angeles CA). "George E. Marsh," *Variety,* 22 Nov 1967.

Marsh, J. [cinematographer]. No data found. FDY, p. 461.

Marsh, Joan (daughter of **Charles Rosher**) (aka Dorothy Rosher, *née* Nancy Ann Rosher, b. Porterville CA, 10 Jul 1913–10 Aug 2000 [87], near Ojai CA). m. (1) scenarist Charles Belden (d. 1954); (2) John D.W. Morrill, 1943. (Appeared in *The Little Princess,* 1917; *Daddy Long Legs,* 1919; and *Pollyanna,* 1920; MGM; Universal; final film: *Follow the Leader,* 1944.) "Joan Marsh, 85, a Movie Star in Two Eras," *NYT,* 25 Aug 2000, C21. Myrna Oliver, "Joan Marsh; Child actress turned blond [sic] bombshell," *PP-G,* 26 Aug 2000, C-3:1 ("Weighing only 95 pounds, Ms. Marsh was said to have the smallest feet in Hollywood—wearing a size 2AAA, the smallest shoes in Paramount Pictures' vast wardrobe department of the 1930s.'). Katz, p. 779.

Marsh, Mae [actress] (sister of **Frances, Marguerite, Mildred** and **Oliver Marsh**) (*née* Mary Warne [mother's maiden name] Marsh, b. Madrid NM, 9 Nov 1895–13 Feb 1968 [72], Hermosa Beach CA; heart attack). m. Louis Lee Arms, 2 Sep 1918, NYC. (Biograph, 1911; Kalem; Reliance-Majestic; Fine Arts; Goldwyn.) "Mae Marsh, Sister in 'Birth of a Nation,' Is Dead; Actress, Star of Silent Films for Griffith, Appeared in Character Roles Later," *NYT,* 14 Feb 1968, 51:1. "Mae Marsh," *Variety,* 21 Feb 1968. AMD, p. 238. AS, p. 720. BHD1, p. 365. FSS, p. 203. IFN, p. 199. Katz, p. 779. KOM, pp. 150–51. MH, p. 125 ("May" Marsh, b. NY NY). MSBB, p. 1038 (b. 1897). Spehr, p. 152 (b. 1897). Truitt, p. 215. WWS, p. 121. "New Kalem Leading Lady," *MPW,* 13 Jul 1912, 132. "Mae Marsh at Work," *MPW,* 11 Dec 1915, 1985. Benjamin Zeidman, "The Poppy of the Films," *MPC,* Oct 1916, 42–43, 69. "Griffith Bids Mae Marsh Godspeed," *MPW,* 23 Dec 1916, 1787. "Mae Marsh," *MPW,* 15 Sep 1917, 1679. "Crowds See Moving Pictures Made," *MPW,* 8 Dec 1917, 1493. "Mae Marsh a Modeler in Clay," *MPW,* 29 Dec 1917, 1970. "No Blackberry Lips for

Mae Marsh," *MPW,* 12 Jan 1918, 230. "Mae Marsh Doll Brings $231," *MPW,* 9 Feb 1918, 810. "Mae Marsh Speaks at Baltimore," *MPW,* 13 Apr 1918, 236. "Mae Marsh, Philosopher," *MPW,* 22 Jun 1918, 1726. "Mae Marsh Arrives," *MPW,* 16 Nov 1918, 727. "Mae Marsh Married," *MPW,* 4 Jan 1919, 72. "Will Not Renew Goldwyn Contract," *MPW,* 22 Feb 1919, 1019–20. "A Sheldon Play for Stage Debut," *MPW,* 15 Mar 1919, 1473–74. "Gasnier Signs Mae Marsh," *MPW,* 15 Nov 1919, 335. "Me Marsh, Star in 'Little 'Fraid Lady' for Robertson-Cole Release in December," *MPW,* 4 Dec 1920, 630. "Mae Marsh Forms Company," *MPW,* 15 Jan 1921, 296. Cal York, "Plays and Players," *Photoplay,* Mar 1921, 122 ("Will Mae Marsh return to the Griffith fold?..." She left Griffith to become a star but her "stellar pictures did not do her justice; and whether or not her new pictures since her come-back from private life will be any better, remains to be seen."). "Joins Griffith," *MPW,* 30 Dec 1922, 884. Paul Rochester, "Why My Baby Has Made Me a Better Actress," *MW,* 5 May 1923, 10. Grace Kingsley, "How to Raise a 'System' Baby,"*MW,* 8 Dec 1923, 13, 29. "Vitagraph Signs Mae Marsh," *MPW,* 14 Feb 1925, 718. June Lee, "Dan Cupid's Bulletin Board," *Paris and Hollywood,* Sep 1926, 95 (already the mother of Mary, 6 years old, she just had a boy. Arms was a former sports writer in Kansas City. Their home was in Flintridge, near Pasadena CA.). Harold Dunham, "Mae Marsh," *FIR,* Jun/Jul 1958, 306–21.

Marsh, Marguerite Clarice (sister of **Frances, Mae, Mildred** and **Oliver Marsh**) [stage/film actress] (aka Marguerite Loveridge and Lovey Marsh, b. Lawrence KS, 18 Apr 1888–8 Dec 1925 [37], New York NY; broncho-pneumonia after nervous breakdown [Death Certificate No. 29470]). (Biograph, 1912; Essanay; Eastern Majestic; Reliance; Fine Arts; B.A. Rolfe Prods.) "Marguerite Marsh, Film Actress," *NYT,* 9 Dec 1925, 27:4. AMD, p. 238. AS, p. 720. BHD, p. 246 (b. 1892). IFN, p. 199. MSBB, p. 1038 (b. 1892). Ragan 2, p. 1064. Truitt, p. 215. "Margaret Loveridge," *MPW,* 12 Apr 1913, 166. "Margarita Loveridge Joins Selig," *MPW,* 26 Apr 1913, 389. J. Van Cartmell, "Along the Pacific Coast," *NYDM,* 14 Jul 1915, 323:1 (stage name of Loveridge changed to Marsh, "she being a sister of the well-known Mae Marsh."). "Marguerite Marsh Undergoes Operation," *MPW,* 9 Jun 1917, 1579. "Rolfe Signs Director and Prominent Players," *MPW,* 10 Aug 1918, 868. "Marguerite Marsh Has Lead in 'The Eternal Magdelene,'" *MPW,* 19 Apr 1919, 350. "Marguerite Marsh to Star in Her Own Two Reelers," *MPW,* 10 May 1919, 795. "Grossman Star Has Narrow Escape," *MPW,* 21 Feb 1920, 1254. "Marguerite Marsh Is Signed by Fox," *MPW,* 18 Mar 1922, 262. "Obituary," *MPW,* 19 Dec 1925, 639.

Marsh, Mildred (sister of **Frances, Mae, Marguerite** and **Oliver Marsh**) [actress] (b. 1902?). m. Ygnacio John Forest, LA CA, ca. 1921. (Mutual, 1918.) AMD, p. 238. "A Younger Marsh on the Screen," *MPW,* 28 Sep 1918, 1902 (16 years old). Cal York, "Plays and Players," *Photoplay,* Mar 1921, 80 (married recently).

Marsh, Mitzi (Mother) [actress] (d. 22 Feb 1928, Los Angeles CA). BHD, p. 246.

Marsh, Myra [actress] (b. 29 Oct 1894–29 Oct 1964 [70], Los Angeles CA). AS, p. 720.

Marsh, Oliver T. (brother of **Frances, Mae, Marguerite** and **Mildred Marsh**) [cinematographer] (b. Kansas City MO, 30 Jan 1892–5 May 1941 [49], Los Angeles CA). m. Elizabeth. (Griffith.) "Oliver Marsh," *NYT,* 6 May 1941, 21:1. "Oliver Marsh," *Variety,* 7 May 1941. AS, p. 720 (b. 1902; d. 1942). BHD2, p. 178. FDY, p. 461. IFN, p. 199. "He's Mae Marsh's Brother," *MPC,* Dec 1925, 35, 71.

Marshall, Betty [actress]. No data found. AMD, p. 238. "Recover from Effects of Accident," *MPW,* 10 Jul 1915, 330.

Marshall, Boyd [actor] (b. Port Clinton OH, 1884–10 Nov 1950 [66], Jackson Heights [Queens] NY [Death Certificate Index No. 9777]). m. musical comedy star Marishka "Mitzi" Hajos (b. Budapest, Hungary, 1891), 1920. "Boyd Marshall," *NYT,* 12 Nov 1950, 94:7. "Boyd Marshall," *Variety,* 15 Nov 1950. AMD, p. 238. AS, p. 720. BHD, p. 246. IFN, p. 199 (b. 1885). Truitt, p. 215. "Who the 'Princess' Man Is," *MPW,* 15 Nov 1913, 745. "Boyd Marshall Denies," *MPW,* 14 Feb 1914, 822. "Boyd Marshall, Thanhouser Leading Man," *MPW,* 4 Nov 1916, 713.

Marshall, George E. [actor/director] (b. Chicago IL, 29 Dec 1891–17 Feb 1975 [83], Los Angeles CA; pneumonia). m. **Corinne Griffith** (d. 1979). (Universal, 1912; Pathé; Fox.) Robert McG. Thomas, Jr., "George Marshall, Film Director, 84; Hollywood Figure 62 Years Dies—Made 400 Movies," *NYT,* 18 Feb 1975, 32:4. "George Marshall, 84, Dies Shortly After Film Trade Honoring," *Variety,* 19 Feb 1975. AMD, p. 238. AS, p. 721. BHD, p. 246; BHD2, p. 178. IFN, p. 199. JS, p. 271. Katz, 780. 1921 Directory, p. 270. SD. "George Marshall Wins His Promotion," *MPW,* 10 Jun 1916, 1894. "Supervises All Fox Comedies," *MPW,* 3 Oct 1925, 418. George Marshall, "The Comedy Angle of Fox Films," *MPW,* 9 Jan 1926, 169. "Marshall Discusses Comedy Players," *MPW,* 7 Aug 1926, 363.

Marshall, Herbert Brough Falcon [actor] (b. London, England, 23 May 1890–22 Jan 1966 [75], Beverly Hills CA; heart attack). m. (1) Lee Russell; (2) **Edna Best** (d. 1974; 2 sons, 1 daughter); (3) Molly Maitland; (4) Boots Mallory; (5) Dee Anne Kahmann. "Herbert Marshall," *Variety,* 241, 26 Jan 1966, 70:1. AS, p. 721 (d. 21 Jan). BHD1, p. 366. IFN, p. 199.

Marshall, Nini [actress] (*née* Marina Esther Traverso, b. Buenos Aires, Argentina, 1 Jun 1902–18 Mar 1996 [93], Buenos Aires, Argentina). AS, p. 721.

Marshall, Oswald [actor] (b. Newcastle-upon-Tyne, England, 1884–19 Apr 1954 [70?], New York NY). AS, p. 721.

Marshall, Tina [stage/film actress] (*née* Christina Marsh, b. 1883–30 Dec 1980 [97?], Los Angeles Co. CA). (Universal.) BHD1, p. 366. "In the Picture Studios," *NYDM,* 8 Sep 1915, 36:4 (one of the stage actresses at Universal).

Marshall, Tully [stage/film actor] (*né* William Phillips, b. Nevada City CA, 13 Apr 1864–10 Mar 1943 [78], Encino CA; heart attack). m. **Marion Fairfax** (d. 1970). (All-Star; Fine Arts; FP-L; Art Craft; Select.) "Tully Marshall, Screen Star, Dies; Character Actor Whose Career Spanned 60 Years Stricken in California at 79; Forsook Stage in 1915; Seen in More Than 100 Films, Including 'Covered Wagon' and 'Tale of Two Cities,'" *NYT,* 11 Mar 1943, 21:1. "Tully Marshall," *Variety,* 17 Mar 1943 (d. 9 Mar). AMD, p. 238. AS, p. 721. BHD1, p. 366. FFF, p. 182. FSS, p. 204. GK, pp. 595–613. IFN, p. 199. Katz, p. 781 (began 1914). KOM, pp. 151–52. Lowrey, p. 112. MH, p. 125. MSBB, p. 1026. Truitt, p. 216. WWS, p. 182. "Tully Engaged by Reliance," *MPW,* 10 Jul 1915, 327. "Bosworth and Marshall Join Lasky Forces," *MPW,* 28 Oct 1916, 527. "Tully Marshall's Birthday," *MPW,* 2 May 1925, 33. George A. Katchmer, "2 Unforgettable Character Actors; Tully Marshall and Russell Simpson," *CI,* 14 (Jun 1987), 14–16, C24, C40. Richard E. Braff, "An Index to the Films of Tully Marshall," *CI,* 187 (Jan 1991), 24, 26, 30–31; Part II, 188 (Feb 1991), 52–55. George Katchmer, "Remembering the Great Silents," *CI,* 240 (Jun 1995), 44–45.

Marshall, Virginia [actress]. No data found. *Fl.* 1925–26. George Katchmer, "Remembering the Great Silents," *CI,* 209 (Nov 1992), 55–56.

Marshall, William C. [cinematographer]. No data found. FDY, p. 461.

Marshek, Archie F. [film editor]. No data found.

Marson, R.D. [manufacturer]. No data found. AMD, p. 238. "Marson Organizes Picrture Company," *MPW,* 7 Dec 1912, 986.

Marstini, Rosita (or **Rosetta**) [actress] (b. Nancy, France, 19 Sep 1887–24 Apr 1948 [60], Los Angeles CA). "Rosita Marstini," *Variety,* 28 Apr 1948 (age 54). AS, p. 721. BHD1, p. 366. IFN, p. 199. 1921 Directory, p. 231. Truitt, p. 216 (b. 1894).

Marston, Mrs. A.C. [actress]. No data found. (K&E.)

Marston, Lawrence [director]. No data found. (K&E; Selig.) AMD, p. 238. Lawrence Marston, "How I Made 'The Star of Bethlehem,'" *MPW,* 28 Dec 1912, 1305. Lawrence Marston, "A Critique of Granville Barker," *MPW,* 12 Sep 1914, 1498. "Marston Joins Selig," *MPW,* 20 Feb 1915, 1145:1 (succeeded Giles R. Warren at the Chicago Selig studio). "Lawrence Marrston Joins Mirror," *MPW,* 4 Dec 1915, 1820.

Marston, Mrs. Lawrence [actress] (*née?*). No data found. m. **Lawrence Marston**. AMD, p. 238. "Mrs. Marston a Regular Lamb," *MPW,* 5 Jul 1913, 56.

Marston, Theodore [stage actor/film director]. (Pathé; Kinemacolor; Edison; Universal; Vitagraph.) AMD, p. 239 (and Marsden, p. 238). MSBB, p. 1046 (produced over 200 films up to 1918). "Theodore Marston, a Director of Big Scenes," *MPW,* 22 Jan 1916, 604. "McClure Pictures Engages Theodore Marston," *MPW,* 7 Oct 1916, 93. "Marston Directs 'Greed,'" *MPW,* 4 Nov 1916, 719. "Marston Returns to Pathé," *MPW,* 7 Apr 1917, 103. "Marsden Directing Earle Williams," *MPW,* 16 Aug 1919, 949.

Marta, John "Jack" [cameraman] (b. 1910?–26 Jun 1991 [81]). (Republic.) "Jack A. Marta," *CI,* Aug 1991. FDY, p. 461.

Martell, Alphonse [actor/director/scenarist] (b. Strasbourg, France, 27 Mar 1890–18 Mar 1976 [85], San Diego CA). AS, p. 722 (d. LA CA). BHD1, p. 366; BHD2, p. 178. IFN, p. 199.

Martell, Harry [actor/acrobat/showman] (*né* Herman H. Wallum, b. 1858?–11 Jan 1920 [61], Brooklyn NY). "Harry Martell," *Variety,* 16 Jan 1920.

Martelli, Otello [assistant cameraman/cinematographer] (b. Rome, Italy, 10 May 1902–21 Feb 2000 [98], Rome, Italy). JS, p. 271 (in Italian silents from 1919). David Rooney, "Otello Martelli," *Variety,* 28 Feb 2000, 96:1. Harris Lentz III, "Otello Martelli, 98," *CI,* 298 (Apr 2000), 58). AS, p. 722 (d. ca. 1964).

Marten, Helen [actress]. AMD, p. 239. *Photoplay Arts Portfolio* (Eclair; Lubin). "A New Lubin Leading Lady," *MPW,* 13 Jan 1912, 116. "Helen Marten," *MPW,* 4 Jul 1914, 42.

Martens, Fernand [actor] (b. Brussels, Belgium, 25 Dec 1904–2 Nov 1970 [65], Paris, France). BHD1, p. 613.

Martenson, Mona [actress] (b. Stockholm, Sweden, 4 May 1902–Jul 1956 [54], Stockholm, Sweden). (Sweden; MGM.) BHD1, p. 613.

Martin, Agnes [stage/film actress]. No data found. AMD, p. 239. "Agnes Martin," *MPW,* 23 Mar 1918, 1678. "Agnes Martin, Stage Favorite, Is Seen in New Torchy Comedy," *MPW,* 23 Oct 1920, 1142.

Martin, Albert [title writer] (b. 1896?–10 Oct 1971 [75], Los Angeles CA; emphysema). "Al Martin," *Variety,* 20 Oct 1971 ("Starting in silent pix, he wrote subtitles for an average of 200 pix annually for 10 years before swinging over to talking pix at beginning of the sound era."). AMD, p. 239. AS, p. 722. FDY, p. 447. "Martin Will Title 'Newlyweds,'" *MPW,* 6 Nov 1926, 30. "Al Martin Has New Contract with Christies," *MPW,* 11 Jun 1927, 431.

Martin, Beth (daughter of Metropolitan opera star Riccardo Martin) [actress]. No data found. AMD, p. 239. "Beth Martin in New Joyce Picture," *MPW,* 16 Oct 1920, 981.

Martin, Chris-Pin [actor] (*né* Ysabel Ponciana Chris-Pin Martin Piaz, b. Tucson AZ, 19 Nov 1893–27 Jun 1953 [59], Los Angeles CA; heart attack). (Began 1911.) "Chris-Pin Martin," *Variety,* 191, 1 Jul 1953, 55. AS, p. 722. BHD1, p. 366. IFN, p. 199.

Martin, Duke [actor]. No data found. *Fl.* 1927–30.

Martin, Eddie [actor] (b. London, England, 1 Jan 1880–22 Feb 1964 [84], London, England). AS, p. 722.

Martin, Ernest J. [scenic artist] (b. 1869–26 Jul 1938 [69?]). BHD2, p. 178.

Martin, Erwin K. [art director] (b. 1880–10 Jan 1925 [44?], Los Angeles CA). BHD2, p. 178.

Martin, Frank Wells [actor/director] (b. 1880?–9 Aug 1941 [61], Los Angeles CA). "Frank Wells Martin," *Variety,* 13 Aug 1941 ("film actor and director of silents"). BHD, p. 246; BHD2, p. 178.

Martin, Glenn L. [actor] (b. Marksburg IA, 17 Jan 1886–4 Dec 1955 [69], Baltimore MD). BHD, p. 246.

Martin, H. Kinley [cinematographer]. No data found. FDY, p. 461.

Martin, Irvin J. [art director] (d. 10 Jan 1925, Los Angeles CA). AMD, p. 239. BHD2, p. 178. "New Title Artist for Selznick," *MPW,* 17 Jan 1920, 404.

Martin, Jack [actor] (b. 1866–18 Aug 1916 [50?], Brownsville WI). BHD1, p. 613.

Martin, Jacques [actor/stage manager] (b. 1853–15 Aug 1917 [64?], New York NY; following an operation at the New York Eye and Ear Hospital). m. "Jacques Martin," *Variety,* 24 Aug 1917, 201. BHD, p. 246.

Martin, Mrs. Jacques [actress] (*née?,* b. 1863–11 Jul 1936 [73?], New York NY). m. **Jacques Martin** (d. 1917). BHD, p. 246.

Martin, John E. [actor] (b. Philadelphia PA, 1855?–22 Nov 1933 [78], New York NY). "John E. Martin," *Variety,* 28 Nov 1933 (age 77). AS, p. 723. BHD, p. 246. IFN, p. 200. Truitt, p. 216.

Martin, Karl Heinz [director] (b. Freiburg, Germany, 6 May 1886–13 Jan 1948 [61], Berlin, Germany). AS, p. 723. BHD2, p. 178.

Martin, Katherine [actress]. No data found. AMD, p. 239. "Join Burr Forces," *MPW,* 24 Feb 1923, 811.

Martin, Knut [actor/director] (b. Sweden, 1899–9 Jun 1959 [60?], Sweden). AS, p. 723.

Martin, Mary [child actress] (b. Waetherford TX, 1 Dec 1913–4 Nov 1990 [76], Rancho Mirage CA; cancer). AS, p. 723.

Martin, May [actress] (b. England, 1877–8 Jun 1948 [71?], Sandwich, England). AS, p. 723 (*née* Lady Playfair).

Martin, Owen [actor] (b. 1888–4 May 1960 [72?], Saranac Lake NY). AS, p. 723. BHD1, p. 367.

Martin, Paul [actor/director] (b. Maiolana, Hungary, 8 Feb 1899–26 Jan 1967 [67], Berlin, Germany). AS, p. 723.

Martin, Pete [actor] (*né* Peter Halfpanny, b. Scotland, 1899–15 May 1973 [74?], Glasgow, Scotland). AS, p. 723.

Martin, Rae [actress]. No data found. AMD, p. 239. "Miss Rae Martin Playing Opposite 'Budd' Ross," *MPW,* 1 Jan 1916, 62.

Martin, Rhea [film/stage actress]. No data found. (Biograph.) Lester Sweyd, "What They Are Doing Now," *Motion Picture Magazine,* Feb 1918, 13 ("...was with Blanche Ring at the beginning of the season in 'Broadway and Buttermilk.'").

Martin, Robert [cinematographer] (aka Tom Kuyl, *né* Anton Jacobus Kuyl, Batavia, Netherlands Indies, 24 Sep 1921). FDY, p. 461.

Martin, Silver Moon [actor] (*né* Michael James Martin, b. 1891–20 Jan 1969 [77?], Comanche OK). AS, p. 723. BHD, p. 246.

Martin, Tony [actor] (d. 15 Feb 1932, New York NY). AS, p. 724.

Martin, Townsend [author/actor/scenarist] (b. New York NY, 1896?–22 Nov 1951 [55], New York NY). (FP-L.) "Townsend Martin, Scenarist, 55, Dies; Stage and Film Writer Had Received French, American Medals for Heroism in '17," *NYT,* 24 Nov 1951, 11:1 (founded Film Guild with Dwight Deere Wiman, 1924. "Subsequently, he was supervisor for Famous Players and acted briefly in movies. ¶As a motion-picture scenario writer he wrote for films that starred Gloria Swanson, Richard Dix, Thomas Meighan and Bebe Daniels."). "Townsend Martin," *Variety,* 28 Nov 1951. AS, p. 724. BHD, p. 246. IFN, p. 200.

Martin, Vallie Belasco [actress]. No data found. AMD, p. 239. "Vallie Belasco Martin Appears in Truex Comedy," *MPW,* 26 Jul 1919, 533.

Martin, Vivian [stage/film actress] (*née* Louise Martin, b. Sparta [near Grand Rapids] MI, 22 Jul 1893–16 Mar 1987 [93], New York NY). m. (1) **William Winter Jefferson,** 1913 (d. 1946); (2) Arthur W. Samuels, 1926. (World, 1914; FP-L, 1917; Gaumont [U.S.], 1920; Graham; Fox; Morosco-Pallas; Goldwyn.) "Vivian Martin," *Variety,* 8 Apr 1987 (age 95). AMD, p. 239. AS, p. 724. BHD1, p. 367. Lowrey, p. 114. MSBB, p. 1038. Spehr, p. 152. WWS, p. 75. "Vivian Martin," *MPW,* 10 Oct 1914, 200. "Vivian Martin," *MPW,* 27 Feb 1915, 1296. "Vivian Martin Renews Paramount Contract," *MPW,* 15 Jun 1918, 1557. "Goldwyn to Distribute Vivian Martin Films Produced by Messmore Kendall," *MPW,* 2 Oct 1920, 674. "Vivian Martin Pictures Sued for Studio Rent," *MPW,* 9 Jul 1921, 192. "Vivian Martin Pictures Asks Dismissal of Suit," *MPW,* 8 Oct 1921, 630. Billy H. Doyle, "Lost Players," *CI,* 147 (Sep 1987), 52–53.

Martindel, Edward B. [stage/film actor] (b. Hamilton OH, 8 Jul 1873–4 May 1955 [81], Woodland Hills CA). "Edward B. Martindel," *Variety,* 11 May 1955. AMD, p. 239. AS, p. 724. BHD1, p. 367. IFN, p. 200 (b. 1873). Truitt, p. 217. "Martindel Makes Metro Debut," *MPW,* 6 May 1916, 978. "Martindale Has Big Role," *MPW,* 12 Jun 1920, 1487. Milton Howe, "Famous at Fifty," *MPC,* Apr 1926, 31, 87–88.

Martinelli, Alfredo [actor] (b. Siena, Italy, 1893-ca. 1966 [73?]). AS, p. 724. JS, pp. 272–73 (in Italian silents from 1917).

Martinelli, Arthur (uncle of **Enzo Martinelli**) [cameraman] (b. Italy, 29 Apr 1881–7 Sep 1967 [86], Los Angeles CA). "Arthur Martinelli," *Variety,* 20 Sep 1967. AS, p. 724. BHD2, p. 179.

Martinelli, Enzo (nephew of **Arthur Martinelli**) [film/TV cinematographer] (b. 1907?–5 Feb 1997 [89], Jackson TN). m. Valerie. (Paramount; WB.) "Enzo Martinelli," *Variety,* 17 Feb 1997, p. 81:1 (assistant cameraman on *Street of Sin*). AS, p. 724. BHD2, p. 179. Enzo Martinelli, "Photographing 'The Invisible Man,'" *American Cinematographer* (Jul 1975).

Martinelli, Giovanni [actor] (b. Montagnana, Italy, 24 Oct 1885–2 Feb 1969 [83], New York NY). AMD, p. 239. BHD1, p. 368. "Martinelli Surprises Himself," *MPW,* 13 Nov 1926, 77. "Vitaphone Sings Martinelli," *MPW,* 12 Feb 1927, 474.

Martinengo, Nino [director]. No data found. JS, p. 273 (in Italian silents from 1916).

Martinez, Eduardo L. [actor] (*né* Luis Eduardo Ortiz Martinez, b. Mexico, 11 Sep 1900–31 Oct 1968 [68], San Antonio TX). AS, p. 724.

Martinez, Paco (father of **Jose Martinez Griffell**) [actor] (*né* Francisco Martinez, b. Valencia, Spain, 17 Mar 1871–20 Feb 1956 [84], Mexico City, Mexico; heart attack and pneumonia). m. **Prudencia Griffell** (d. 1970). AS, p. 724.

Martin-Harvey, John (father of **Muriel Martin-Harvey**) [actor] (b. Wyvenboe, England, 22 Jun 1863–14 May 1944 [80], London, England). AS, p. 724.

Martin-Harvey, Muriel (daughter of **John Martin-Harvey**) [actress] (b. London, England, 1891–15 Dec 1988 [97?], Northwood, England). AS, p. 724.

Martin-Harvey, Sir John (father of actress Muriel Martin-Harvey) [actor] (b. Wyvenhoe, Essex, England, 22 Jun 1867–14 May 1944 [76], London, England). "Sir John Martin-Harvey," *Variety,* 154, 17 May 1944, 46:1 (age 81; knighted, 1921). AS, p. 724 (b. 1863). BHD1, p. 367. IFN, p. 200 (age 80).

Martin-Harvey, Michael [actor] (d. 30 Jun 1975). BHD1, p. 367.

Martini, Ferdinand [actor] (b. Munich, Germany, 1 Sep 1870–23 Dec 1930 [60], Munich, Germany). AS, p. 724.

Martini, Ferdinando Antonio [cinematographer] (b. Milan, Italy–d. 1 Apr 1937,

Rome, Italy). JS, p. 273 (in Italian silents from 1915).

Martinoff, M.I. [actor] (d. 1928, Koslov, Russia). "M.I. Martinoff," *Variety*, 18 Apr 1928. BHD, p. 246.

Martinson, Mona [actress]. No data found. AMD, p. 239. "New M-G-M Girl Star Arrives from Sweden," *MPW*, 13 Aug 1927, 444.

Martoglio, Nino [director] (b. Catania, Italy, 3 Dec 1870–15 Sep 1921 [50], Catania, Sicily, Italy). AS, p. 725 (b. Belpasso, Italy). BHD2, p. 179 (b. Belpasso). JS, p. 274 (made five films from 1913 to 1918, all lost since 1945).

Marton, Aletia [actress] (b. TX, 15 Sep 1894–4 Jun 1972 [77], Dallas TX). AMD, p. 239. BHD, addendum. "Two Prize Winners on Selznick Program," *MPW*, 11 Nov 1916, 857.

Marton, Andrew [director/producer] (*né* Endre Marton, b. Budapest, Hungary, 26 Jan 1904–7 Jan 1992 [87], Santa Monica CA; pneumonia). m. Lacerta. *Andrew Marton* (Scarecrow Press, 1992). (Universal, 1926; MGM.) William H. Honan, "Andrew Marton, 83, a Director of Films Featuring Action Scenes," *NYT*, 9 Jan 1992, D23:5. "Andrew Marton," *Variety*, 24 Feb 1992, p. 266. AS, p. 725. BHD2, p. 179. JS, p. 274 (in the U.S.A. from 1923). Katz, p. 783 (began in Vienna, 1922).

Marton, Hilda (mother of Peter Stone) [screenwriter] (*née* Hilda Hess, b. Sierra Mojoda, Mexico, 1905–4 Mar 1992 [86], Los Angeles CA). m. (1) **John Stone** (d. 1961). AS, p. 725. BHD2, p. 179. "Hilda Marton [obituary]," *CI*, 205 (Jul 1992), 61.

Marty, Marthe [actress/singer] (*née* Marthe Antoni, b. Marseilles, France, 21 Sep 1895–3 Feb 1968 [72], Marseilles, France). AS, p. 725.

Marvin, Arthur M. (brother of **Harry Norton Marvin**) [inventor] (b. Warners NY, 1857?–18 Jan 1911 [53], Los Angeles CA). "Arthur Marvin Dead," *MPW*, 4 Feb 1911, 251. AS, p. 725. Spehr, p. 152. WWVC, pp. 91–92.

Marvin, Arthur W. [cinematographer] (b. 1861–28 Jan 1912 [50?]). BHD2, p. 179.

Marvin, Harry Norton (brother of **Arthur M. Marvin**) [inventor/Vice Presidentof Biograph] (b. Jordan NY, 1863?–12 Jan 1940 [77], Treasure Island [Sarasota] FL). "Harry N. Marvin, Invented Biograph; Made First Motion Pictures of Royalty and Headed Film Firm—Dies in Florida; An Associate of Edison; Aided Installation of City's First Electric Light Plant—Perfected Radio Device," *NYT*, 13 Jan 1940, 15:3. "Marvin, Pic Pioneer, Inventor, Dies at 77," *Variety*, 17 Jan 1940. AMD, p. 239. AS, p. 725. Spehr, p. 152. WWVC, p. 92. "Facts Concerning the New Arrangement of the Principal Factors of the Motion Picture Manufacturing Interests in America," *MPW*, 26 Dec 1908, 519. "Lost on the Titanic," *NYDM*, 24 Apr 1912 (Daniel [also referred to as David] Marvin; had been married 12 Mar).

Marvin, Jack [actor] (b. MI, 16 Apr 1884–17 Oct 1956 [72], Los Angeles CA). AS, p. 725.

Marwille, Suzanne Schüllerova [actress] (b. Zizkov, Czechoslovakia, 11 Jul 1895). AS, p. 725.

Marx, Chico (brother of **Groucho**, **Gummo**, **Harpo** and **Zeppo Marx**; nephew of **Al Shean**) [stage/film/TV actor/musician] (*né* Leonard Marx, b. New York NY, 22 Mar 1887–11 Oct 1961 [74], Beverly Hills CA; heart attack). m. (2) actress Mary Dee. Wes Gehring, *The Marx Brothers: A Bio-Bibliography*. "Chico Marx Dies at 70; Will Still Be 'Active' in SG Cartoon Series [Screen Gem Cartoons]," *Variety*, 234, 18 Oct 1961, 4:2, 20:4 (joshed about "chasing chicks," he became "Chicko," then Chico). AS, p. 725. BHD1, p. 368. "Marx Brothers in New Comedy Series [Caravel Comedies Company]," *MPW*, 16 Apr 1921, 738 (*Comedies Without Custards*). Chico Marx and his brothers financed and appeared in *Humorisk*, 1920 (made at Ft. Lee NJ), a film withdrawn after the previews, it was so bad.

Marx, Groucho (brother of **Chico**, **Gummo**, **Harpo** and **Zeppo Marx**; nephew of **Al Shean**; father of writer Arthur Marx) [stage/film/TV actor/scenarist/singer/novelist] (*né* Julius Henry Marx, b. New York NY, 2 Oct 1890–19 Aug 1977 [86], Los Angeles CA; pneumonia after hip surgery). m. (1) Ruth Johnson; (2) Catherine Mavis Gorcey (former wife of Leo Gorcey); (3) Edith HJartford—div. (Began on stage, 1906; Paramount.) "Groucho Marx Dies at 86; Vaude Grad Spent 67 Yrs. as Flip Comic," *Variety*, 288, 24 Aug 1977, 2:4, 62 (on *You Bet Your Life*, NBC, for 14 years). AS, p. 725 (d. West Hollywood CA). BHD1, p. 368; BHD2, p. 179.

Marx, Gummo (brother of **Chico, Groucho, Harpo** and **Zeppo Marx**; nephew of **Al Shean**) [actor] (*né* Milton Marx, b. New York NY, 23 Oct 1892–21 Apr 1977 [84], Palm Springs CA; cancer). AS, p. 725.

Marx, Harpo (brother of **Chico**, **Groucho**, **Gummo** and **Zeppo Marx**; nephew of **Al Shean**) [stage/film/TV actor/musician] (*né* Adolph Arthur Marx, b. Yorkville, New York NY, 23 Nov 1888–28 Sep 1964 [75], Los Angeles CA; during open heart surgery). m. actress Susan Fleming, 1936. (Broadway debut: *I'll Say She Is*, 1924 revue.) *Harpo Speaks* (Bernard Geis Associates, 1961). "Harpo Marx, the Silent Comedian, Is Dead at 70; Blond-Wigged Horn-Tooting Star Scored on Stage and in Films with Brothers," *NYT*, 29 Sep 1964, 1:2 (age 70); "Harpo Marx Left $1 Million," *NYT*, 6 Oct 1964, 78:6 (age 75; widow was sole beneficiary). "Harpo Marx," *Variety*, 236, 30 Sep 1964, 63:1. AS, p. 725. BHD1, p. 368. IFN, p. 200. Truitt, p. 217.

Marx, Max [actor] (d. 1925, Universal City CA; in an accident). AS, p. 725. BHD, p. 246. Truitt, p. 217.

Marx, Samuel (father of the **Marx Brothers**) [actor] (b. 1861–11 May 1933 [72?], Los Angeles CA; heart attack). AS, p. 725.

Marx, Zeppo (brother of **Chico**, **Groucho**, **Gummo**, and **Harpo Marx**; nephew of **Al Shean**) [stage/film actor] (*né* Herbert Marx) (b. New York NY, 25 Feb 1901–30 Nov 1979 [78], Palm Springs CA; cancer). AS, p. 725. BHD1, p. 368.

Maryon, Carmen [actress]. (Crystal Film Co.) AMD, p. 239. "Miss Carmen Maryon," *MPW*, 9 Aug 1913, 643.

Mascagni, Pietro [composer] (b. Leghorn, Italy, 7 Dec 1863–2 Aug 1945 [81], Rome, Italy). BHD2, p. 179.

Masi, Philip W. [actor/assistant director] (b. Norfolk VA, 1888–12 Dec 1922 [34?], New York NY). AMD, p. 239. BHD, p. 246; BHD2, p. 179. "Obituary," *MPW*, 30 Dec 1922, 838 (d. 10 Dec).

Mason, A.E.W. pwriter]. No data found. AMD, p. 239. "Major Mason, English Author, Spends Day Inspecting the Famous Players Studio," *MPW*, 20 Nov 1920, 379.

Mason, Ann [actress] (b. VA, 1897?–6 Feb 1948 [50], New York NY; of burns sustained in a fire). m. (1) Thomas A. Chelis (aka Paul Gordon); (2) Philip Pepper. "Ann Mason," *Variety*, 18 Feb 1948. AS, p. 726. BHD, p. 246. IFN, p. 200. '83 WWOS (b. 1889).

Mason, (Smiling) Billy [actor/vaudevillian] (b. 1887?–24 Jan 1941 [53], Orange NJ). (Essanay.) "'Smiling Billy' Mason," *Variety*, 29 Jan 1941. AMD, p. 239. IFN, p. 200. "Billy Mason Now with Wharton, Inc.," *MPW*, 8 Aug 1914, 842. "'Smiling Billy' Mason Will Try a Comeback in Two-Reel Comedies," *MPW*, 8 Jul 1922, 162.

Mason, Buddy C. [actor/stuntman] (*né* Bruce Cameron Mason, b. PA, 30 Oct 1902–15 Apr 1975 [72], Woodland Hills CA). AS, p. 726. BHD1, p. 369. IFN, p. 200.

Mason, C. Post [director] (b. Australia-d. 4 Dec 1918, San Francisco CA). AS, p. 726.

Mason, Charles A. [actor] (d. 21 Mar 1918, Mt. Clemens MI). "Charles A. Mason," *Variety*, 29 Mar 1918. AS, p. 726.

Mason, Dan [stage/film actor/scenarist] (*né* Dan Grassman, b. Syracuse NY, 9 Feb 1853–6 Jul 1929 [76], Baersville NY; pneumonia). m. Millie La Fonte (d. 1919). (Edison.) "Dan Mason," *Variety*, 10 Jul 1929. AMD, p. 239. AS, p. 726. BHD, p. 246 (b. 1857). IFN, p. 200 (age 72). SD. Truitt, p. 217. "Dan Mason an Author," *NYDM*, 28 Jan 1914, 31:2 (wrote scenario based on his janitor character, as in *The Thrifty Janitor* and *The Janitor's Quiet Life*). "Biographies of Popular Players," *Motion Picture Magazine*, Feb 1915, 112. "Swain Star Featured in 12 New Rural Comedies," *MPW*, 22 Dec 1923, 716. George Katchmer, "Dan Mason," *CI*, 232 (Oct 1994), C26.

Mason, Eliza [actress] (b. England-d. 21 Jan 1925, New York NY). BHD, p. 246.

Mason, Evelyn M. [actress] (b. 1892?–29 Oct 1926 [34?], Los Angeles CA; after operation for ptomaine poisoning). "Evelyn Mason," *Variety*, 3 Nov 1926 ("colored actress"). AS, p. 726. BHD, p. 246. Truitt, p. 217.

Mason, Gregory [actor] (b. 1889–29 Nov 1968 [79?], Greenwich CT). AS, p. 726. BHD, p. 246.

Mason, Haddon [actor/agent] (b. London, England, 21 Feb 1898–30 Apr 1966 [68], London, England). AS, p. 726. BHD1, p. 369; BHD2, p. 179. IFN, p. 200.

Mason, Harry [cinematographer]. No data found. FDY, p. 463.

Mason, Herbert [actor/director/producer] (b. Moseley, England, 1891–20 May 1960 [69?], London, England). AS, p. 726.

Mason, James Neville [actor] (b. Paris, France, 3 Feb 1889–7 Nov 1959 [70], Los Angeles CA; heart attack). "James Mason," *Variety*, 11 Nov 1959. AS, p. 726. BHD1, p. 369. IFN, p. 200. Truitt, p. 217.

Mason, John B. [stage/film actor] (b. Orange NJ, 28 Oct 1857–12 Jan 1919 [61], Stamford CT; Bright's disease). m. (1) Marion Manola (d. 1914); (2) Katherine Grey (*née* Katherine Best, d. 1950). "John Mason," *Variety*, 17 Jan 1919 (age 60). AMD, p. 240. AS, p. 726. BHD, p. 247 (b. 1858). IFN, p. 200. SD. "Famous Players Secures John Mason," *MPW*, 19 Dec 1914, 1684. "Abramson Signs Well Known Favorites," *MPW*, 19 Jan 1918, 362.

Mason, Leroy [actor] (b. Larimore ND, 2

Jul 1903–13 Oct 1947 [44], Van Nuys CA; heart attack on the set of Republic's *California Firebrand*). m. **Rita Carewe**, 1928 (d. 1955). (Fox; MGM, Republic.) "Leroy Mason," *NYT*, 15 Oct 1947, 27:4. "Leroy Mason," *Variety*, 15 Oct 1947. AS, p. 726. BHD1, p. 369 (d. LA CA). IFN, p. 201. Truitt, pp. 217–18. Gladys Hall, "'I'm Going to Be Diff'runt'; In Resolving This, Anita Page and LeRoy Mason Are Exactly Alike," *MPC*, Sep 1928, 28–29, 85. Nick Nicholls, "Leroy Mason," *CI*, 152 (Feb 1988), 56 (includes filmography).

Mason, Lesley (or **Leslie**) [title writer/scenarist] (b. Roselle NJ, 1887–24 Mar 1964 [77?], Laguna CA). AMD, p. 240. BHD2, p. 179. FDY, p. 447. "Lesley Mason to Do Editing, Titling and Film Reconstruction," *MPW*, 27 May 1922, 376. "Lesley Mason Scores Success; A Leader Among Title Writers," *MPW*, 29 Jan 1927, 354.

Mason, Lew [casting director] (d. 19 May 1924, Los Angeles CA). BHD2, p. 180.

Mason, Louis [actor] (b. Danville KY, 1 Jun 1888–12 Nov 1959 [71], Los Angeles CA). AS, p. 727. BHD, p. 247. IFN, p. 201.

Mason, Margery Land [actress] (d. 21 Nov 1968, Tucson AZ). AS, p. 727 (d. LA CA). BHD, p. 247.

Mason, Mary [actress] (*née* Betty Ann Jenks, b. Pasadena CA, 1911–13 Oct 1980 [69?], New York NY). AS, p. 727. BHD1, p. 369.

Mason, Reginald [stage/film actor] (b. San Francisco CA, 27 Jun 1875–10 Jul 1962 [87], Hermosa Beach CA). "Reginald Mason Is Dead at 80; Actor Made Stage Debut in '03," *NYT*, 14 Jul 1962, 21:4 (b. 1882). "Reginald Mason," *Variety*, 1 Aug 1962 (age 80). AS, p. 727. BHD1, p. 369. IFN, p. 201. Truitt, p. 218 (b. 1882).

Mason, Sarah Y. [scenarist] (b. Puma AZ, 31 Mar 1896–28 Nov 1980 [84], Los Angeles CA). m. **Victor Heerman**, 1921, Hollywood CA (d. 1977). AMD, p. 240. AS, p. 727. BHD2, p. 180. FDY, p. 433. "Sarah Y. Mason on Metro Scenario Staff," *MPW*, 17 Apr 1920, 453. "Sarah T. Mason Visits Chicago," *MPW*, 3 Jul 1920, 74. "Sarah Y. Mason Renews Her Contract to Write Selznick Continuities," *MPW*, 1 Jan 1921, 58. "Weds Scenario Writer," *MPW*, 7 May 1921, 55. "Scenarist at Work," *MPW*, 10 Sep 1927, 93.

Mason, Shirley [stage/film actress] (sister of **Viola Dana** and **Edna Flugrath**) (*née* Edith Flugrath, b. Brooklyn NY, 6 Jun 1900 [Birth Certificate Index No. 9851]–27 Jul 1979 [79], Los Angeles CA). m. **Sidney Lanfield**, Feb 1927 (d. 1972). (Edison; Paramount; Columbia.) "Shirley Mason, 79, Was Actress in 'Vanity Fair' and Other Silents," *NYT*, 31 Jul 1979, B4:4. "Shirley Mason," *Variety*, 8 Aug 1979. AMD, p. 240. AS, p. 727. BHD1, p. 369 (b. 1901). FFF, p. 90. FSS, p. 205. IFN, p. 201. Katz, 786 (began 1914). Lowrey, p. 116. MH, p. 125. MSBB, p. 1038 (b. 1901). WWS, p. 209. "Shirley Mason—McClure Pictures," *MPW*, 30 Dec 1916, 1970. Shirley Mason, "Our Little Sister of the Screen," *MPW*, 21 Jul 1917, 387. "Seven Players New to Artcraft-Paramount," *MPW*, 6 Jul 1918, 57. "Shirley Mason Leads for Washburn," *MPW*, 1 Mar 1919, 1196. Hazel Shelley, "At the Fountain," *MPC*, Oct 1921, 48–49. "Shirley Mason and Mary Carr Are on a Personal Appearance Tour in South," *MPW*, 10 Dec 1921, 656. Helen Carlisle, "The Girl Who Refused Stardom," *MW*, 4 Jul 1925, 9–10. Adrian Falnieres, "A Chat With Shirley Mason; Having Just Completed 'Sin Cargo,' Miss Mason Talks Over Her Likes and Dislikes," *Cinema Arts*, Jan 1927, 24–25. "Not a Fox Trot," *MPW*, 4 Nov 1922, 52. "Shirley Mason," *MPW*, 29 Jan 1927, 341. "Two Columbia Stars Staged Surprise Weddings Last Week," *MPW*, 19 Feb 1927, 568. June Lee, "Dan Cupid's Bulletin Board," *Paris and Hollywood Screen Secrets Magazine*, May 1927, 51–52 (Mason and Lanfield honeymooned in Coronado CA). "Shirley Mason," *MPW*, 11 Jun 1927, 420. DeWitt Bodeen, "Where Did All the Fun Go?," *FIR*, Mar 1976, 141–65. George Katchmer, "Remembering the Great Silents," *CI*, 229 (Jul 1994), 42–43.

Mason, Sidney L. [actor] (b. Paterson NJ, 1886–1 Mar 1923 [36], New York NY). AMD, p. 240. BHD, p. 247. IFN, p. 201. "Sidney Mason with United," *MPW*, 6 Jun 1914, 1622. "Sidney Mason," *MPW*, 22 Jan 1916, 614. "First Hemmer Superior Film Features Popular Stage Star," *MPW*, 21 Aug 1920, 1049.

Mason, Sydney [actor] (b. 1905?–11 Apr 1976 [71], Los Angeles CA; heart attack). AS, p. 727. IFN, p. 201.

Mason, William C. "Smiling Billy" [vaudeville/film actor] (b. SD, 1887?–26 Jan 1941 [53], Orange NJ). (Essanay; Edison.) "William C. Mason," *NYT*, 26 Jan 1941, 36:1. "'Smiling Billy' Mason," *Variety*, 29 Jan 1941. AS, p. 727. BHD, p. 247. IFN, p. 200. Truitt, p. 218.

Massell, Sonia [actress]. No data found. AMD, p. 240. "Sonia Massell," *MPW*, 23 Oct 1915, 593.

Massi, Philip [assistant director/actor] (d. 12 Dec 1922, New York NY). (Biograph.) "Philip Massi," *Variety*, 15 Dec 1922.

Massine, Leonide [actor] (b. Moscow, Russia, 8 Aug 1895–16 Mar 1979 [83], Cologne, Germany). BHD1, p. 369.

Massingham, Richard [actor/director/producer/scenarist] (b. England, 1898–1 Apr 1953 [55?], Biddenden, England). AS, p. 727.

Massolle, Joseph [inventor] (b. Germany, 1888–1 Apr 1957 [68?], Hohengatow, Germany). AS, p. 727.

Masson, Tom L. [actor] (b. Essex CT, 21 Jul 1866–18 Jun 1934 [67], Glen Ridge NJ). AS, p. 727. BHD, p. 247.

Masters, E.L. [advertising]. No data found. E.L. Masters, "Service Must Precede National Advertising," *MPW*, 4 Dec 1915, 1819.

Masters, Harry [actor] (b. 1894–12 May 1974 [80?], Los Angeles CA). AS, p. 728.

Masters, Rene "Peewee" [actress/director] (*née?*, b. 1901?–16 Jan 1930 [28], Brooklyn NY; appendicitis). m. Frank Masters. "Rene Masters," *Variety*, 29 Jan 1930. AS, p. 728.

Masterson, Bat [actor] (*né* William Barclay Masterson, b. Iroquois Co. IL, 24 Nov 1853–25 Oct 1921 [67], New York NY). AS, p. 728.

Mastripietri, Augusto [actor] (b. Rome, Italy). JS, p. 27 (in Italian silents from 1913).

Mastrocinque, Camillo [stage set designer/film director] (aka Thomas Miller, b. Rome, Italy, 11 May 1901–23 Apr 1969 [67], Rome, Italy). AS, p. 728. JS, pp. 277–78 (worked on *Ben Hur*, 1925).

Maté, Rudolph [cinematographer/director] (*né* Rudolf Mathéh, b. Cracow, Poland, 21 Jan 1898–27 Oct 1964 [66], Beverly Hills CA; heart attack). "Rudolph Mate," *Variety*, 4 Nov 1964. AS, p. 728. BHD2, p. 180. IFN, p. 201. JS, pp. 279–80 (in U.S.A. from 1935). Katz, pp. 787–88 (began in Hungary, 1919).

Mateos, Hector [actor] (*né* Hector Alfonso Mateos Ortiz, b. Mexico, 18 Apr 1901–13 Feb 1957 [55], Mexico City, Mexico). AS, pp. 728–29.

Mathe, Edouard [actor] (b. Australia, 1886–1934 [48], Brussels, Belgium). AS, p. 729. BHD, p. 247. IFN, p. 201.

Mather, Aubrey [stage/film actor] (b. Minchinhampton, England, 17 Dec 1885–15 Jan 1958 [72], Strathmore, England). "Aubrey Mather, Character Actor, Dies; Briton Was in Films and on Broadway," *NYT*, 22 Jan 1958, 27:2 (stage debut, 1905). "Aubrey Mather," *Variety*, 22 Jan 1958. AS, p. 729. BHD1, p. 370 (d. Stanmore, England). IFN, p. 201. Truitt, p. 218.

Mather, Sydney [actor] (b. England, 1876?–18 Apr 1925 [49], New York NY; chronic nephritis). "Sydney Mather," *Variety*, 22 Apr 1925. AS, p. 729. BHD, p. 247.

Mathes, Allen [actor] (b. 1885–13 Aug 1934 [49?], New York NY). BHD, p. 247.

Matheson, George [executive] (b. 1876–23 Jul 1952 [76?], Brisbane, Queensland, Australia). BHD2, p. 180.

Mathews, Dorothy [actress/TV producer] (b. New York NY, 13 Feb 1912–18 May 1977 [65], Los Angeles CA; cerebral thrombosis). m. playwright Donald David, 1926–30.

Mathews, George H. [actor] (b. 1877?–7 Jun 1952 [75], Woodland Hills CA). "George H. Mathews," *Variety*, 18 Jun 1952. AS, p. 729.

Mathewson, Christy [baseball player/actor] (*né* Christopher Mathewson, b. Factoryville PA, 12 Aug 1880–7 Oct 1925 [45], Saranac Lake NY). AMD, p. 240. AS, p. 729. BHD, p. 247. "Christy Mathewson Signs with Universal," *MPW*, 18 Jul 1914, 443.

Mathewson, Tracy [cameraman]. No data found. AMD, p. 240. "Hearst Man with Pershing in Mexico," *MPW*, 8 Jul 1916, 239.

Mathis, June [stage actress/director/scenarist] (*née* June Beulah Hughes, b. Leadville CO, Jan 1887–26 Jul 1927 [40], New York NY; heart attack at a theatre performance). m. **Sylvano Balboni**, 6 Dec 1924, Mission of St. Cecilia, Riverside CA. (B.A. Rolfe Co.; Metro; 1st National; FP-L.) "June Mathis Dies While at Theatre [*The Squall*]; Her Scream, 'Mother, I'm dying!' Interrupts Performance at 48th Street Playhouse; Won Fame as Scenarist; At 35 She Was Screen's Highest-Paid Woman Executive—Discovered Valentino," *NYT*, 27 Jul 1927, 1:6, 3:5. "June Mathis," *Variety*, 3 Aug 1927. "Obituary," *MPW*, 30 Jul 1927, 307. AMD, p. 240 (b. 30 Jun 1899). AS, p. 729. BHD2, p. 180 (b. 1892). FDY, p. 433. IFN, p. 201 (age 38). Katz, p. 788. Lowrey, p. 118. ("Mathis" was her step-father's name.) "Edwin Carewe to Direct June Mathis," *MPW*, 18 Dec 1915, 2163. June Mathis, "Tapping the Thought Wireless," *MPW*, 21 Jul 1917, 409. "June Mathis Is Now Screen Classics' Chief Scenarist," *MPW*, 9 Aug 1919, 815–16., Edward Weitzel, "Talking 'Shop' with June Mathis Brings Out 'Nothing But the Truth,'" *MPW*, 27 Dec 1919, 1141. "June Mathis Confers with Ibanez on 'Four Horsemen of Apocalypse,'" *MPW*, 17 Jan 1920, 431. "June Mathis Completes Four Scenarios in Four Months," *MPW*, 8 May 1920, 850. "Film Folk Purchase Homes," *MPW*, 14 May 1921, 179 (in the Hollywood Hills). "Writing Continuity," *MPW*, 17 Sep 1921, 306. "Mathis Engaged," *MPW*,

23 Sep 1922, 256. "June Mathis Heads Goldwyn Department," *MPW,* 2 Dec 1922, 420. "June Mathis Will Assist Brabin," *MPW,* 13 Oct 1923, 595. "June Mathis Sails for Rome to Aid in Making 'Ben-Hur,'" *MPW,* 16 Feb 1924, 559. Gladys Hall, "A Maker of Young Men," *Classic,* Mar 1924, 22, 85. "June Mathis with Rudy," *MPW,* 6 Sep 1924, 36. "Signed by First National," *MPW,* 20 Sep 1924, 227. "June Mathis Weds Balboni," *MPW,* 20 Dec 1924, 712. "'Sinners in Paradise' First June Mathis for First National," *MPW,* 17 Apr 1926, 506. "June Mathis Now in Field of Free Lance," *MPW,* 13 Nov 1926, 85. "Miss Mathis Resigns," *MPW,* 20 Nov 1926, 4. "June Mathis Now Writing for M-G-M," *MPW,* 1 Jan 1927, 33. "Report June Mathis Signed with United," *MPW,* 26 Feb 1927, 633. "June Mathis Buried Near Valentino in Crypt of Hollywood Mausoleum," *MPW,* 13 Aug 1927, 454. "Contest Waged on Mathis Will; Bears No Date," *MPW,* 3 Sep 1927, 23. Marsha McCreadie, "Pioneers," *FIR,* Nov/Dec 1994, 40–53. Thomas J. Slater, "June Mathis; A Woman Who Spoke Through Silents," *Griffithiana,* 53, May 1995, 132–69 (includes filmography).

Mathot, Léon [actor/director] (b. Roubaix, France, 5 Mar 1886–6 Mar 1968 [82], Paris, France). "Leon Mathot," *NYT,* 7 Mar 1968, 43:3. "Leon Mathot," *Variety,* 13 Mar 1968 (appeared in 50 silents, 1914–25; directed 30 more, 1927–52). AMD, p. 241. AS, p. 729. BHD1, p. 370; BHD2, p. 180. IFN, p. 201. Truitt, p. 218. "French Star Coming," *MPW,* 22 Jan 1921, 425.

Matiesen, Otto [stage/film actor] (b. Klampenborg, Denmark, 27 Mar 1893–19 Feb 1932 [38], Safford AZ; auto accident). m. Isabelle. (In Hollywood, 1920; MGM.) "Matieson Killed," *Variety,* 23 Feb 1932 (age 40) (accompanied by Duncan Renaldo; had just completed *Grand Hotel*). AMD, p. 241. AS, p. 730 (b. 1873). BHD1, p. 370 (b. Copenhagen; d. Pima AZ). IFN, p. 201. Truitt, p. 218. "Noted Addition to Cast of 'The Happy Warrior,'" *MPW,* 25 Apr 1925, 808. Franchon Royer, "Otto Matiesen—A Viking in Hollywood; This Brilliant Character Actor Blazed the Trail for a Host of His Scandinavian Compatriots—His Own Story Is One of Struggle Against Indifference and Ignorance in the Days Before the Foreign Invasion," *Cinema Arts,* VI (Nov 1927), 16.

Matos, Maria [actress] (*née* Maria da Conceicao de Matos de Silva, b. Silva, Portugal, 29 Sep 1891–18 Sep 1952 [60], Lisbon, Portugal). AS, p. 730.

Matray, Ernst [actor/director] (b. Budapest, Hungary, 27 May 1891–12 Nov 1978 [87], Los Angeles CA). AS, p. 730. BHD, p. 247; BHD2, p. 180 (Ernst Matry). IFN, p. 201.

Matson, Thomas [actor] (b. 1888–1 Feb 1978 [89?], Woodland Hills CA). AS, p. 730 (d. 2 Feb). BHD, p. 247.

Matsui, Suisei [actor] (*né* Seiei Ioi, b. Tokyo, Japan, 5 Apr 1900–1 Aug 1973 [73], Kamakura, Japan; pancreatic cancer). AS, p. 730.

Matthews, A[lfred] **E**[dward] **"Matty"** [stage/film/TV actor] (b. Bridlington, Yorkshire, England, 22 Nov 1869–25 Jul 1960 [90], Bushey Heath, London, England). *Matty* (1953). "A.E. Matthews, Actor, 90, Dies; On the British Stage Since 1877; Witty and Dapper Player Appeared in 300 Roles—Also in TV and Films," *NYT,* 22 Jul 1960, 29:4. "A.E. Matthews," *Vasriety,* 219, 3 Aug 1960, 54:4 ("He was a great stage personality more than a great actor." He once remarked, "I pick up The Times every mornnng and, if I'm not in the obituary list then I go to work."). AS, p. 730. BHD1, p. 370. IFN, p. 201.

Matthews, Arthur W. [actor]. (Lubin.) No data found.

Matthews, Beatrice [actress] (b. 1890–10 Nov 1942 [52?], Los Angeles CA). AS, p. 730.

Matthews, Billy [actor/singer] (b. Cornwall, England, 1894–4 Apr 1985 [90?], Bramley, South Africa). AS, p. 730.

Matthews, Dorcas [actress] (b. England, 5 Nov 1890–24 Jan 1969 [78], Berkeley CA). m. **Robert McKim** (d. 1927). BHD, p. 247. Ragan 2, p. 1083. "Los Angeles Studio Shots," *MPW,* 22 May 1920, 1093 (birth of son, 4 May 1920).

Matthews, Dorothy [stage/film actress/TV producer] (b. New York NY, 13 Feb 1912–18 May 1977 [65], Los Angeles CA; following a stroke). m. playwright Donald Davis. (WB.) "Dorothy Matthews," *Variety,* 287, 25 May 1977, 94:3. BHD1, p. 370. IFN, p. 201.

Matthews, H.W. [director]. No data found. AMD, p. 241. "A New Powers Director," *MPW,* 30 Mar 1912, 1151.

Matthews, Harold Clarke [director] (d. 15 Sep 1933). BHD2, p. 180.

Matthews, Jean D. [actress] (*née* Jean Javalt Darnell, b. Sherman TX, 1889–20 Jan 1961 [71?], Dallas TX). "Jean D. Matthews," *Variety,* 8 Feb 1961. AS, p. 730. BHD1, pp. 143 (Jean Darnell); 371 (Jean D. Matthews). IFN, p. 73 (Jean Darnell). Truitt, p. 219. "Jean Darnell Ill," *MPW,* 13 Dec 1913, 1270. "Jean Darnell Thanks Friends," *MPW,* 21 Feb 1914, 953.

Matthews, Jessie Margaret [actress/singer/dancer] (b. London, England, 11 Mar 1907–19 Aug 1981 [74], London, England; cancer). AS, p. 730. BHD1, p. 371.

Matthews, Junius Conyers [actor] (b. IL, 12 Jun 1890–18 Jan 1978 [87], Los Angeles CA). AS, p. 731 (d. 17 Jan). BHD1, p. 371. IFN, p. 201.

Matthews, Lester [actor] (b. Nottingham, England, 3 Dec 1900–6 Jun 1975 [74], England). AS, p. 731.

Matthison, Edith Wynne [stage/film actress] (b. Birmingham, England, 23 Nov 1872?–23 Sep 1955 [83], West Los Angeles CA). m. playwright Charles Rann Kennedy. (Film debut: *The Governor's Lady,* Paramount, 1915.) "Edith Matthison, Actress, 83, Dead; On U.S. Stage 1902–18—Led College Drama Fetes with Husband C.R. Kennedy," *NYT,* 25 Sep 1955, 93:2. "Edith Wynne Matthison," *Variety,* 28 Sep 1955. AMD, p. 241. AS, p. 731. BHD, p. 247 (b. 1875). IFN, p. 202. SD, p. 861. '83 WWOS (b. 1875). "New Lasky Star; Edith Wynne Mathison to Appear in Adaptation of 'The Governor's Lady,'" *NYDM,* 6 Jan 1915, 28:2. "Lasky Gets Famous Star," *MPW,* 16 Jan 1915, 372. "Edith Wynne Matthison Not with Rolfe, Says Lasky," *MPW,* 10 Apr 1915, 244.

Mattison, Frank S. [director] (b. Minneapolis MN, 9 Jul 1894). AS, p. 731.

Mato, Sisto [actor] (*né* Sisto Mata, b. Durango, Mexico, 6 Aug 1894–20 Feb 1934 [39], Los Angeles CA). AS, p. 731.

Mattoli, Mario Raffaello Eugenio [director] (b. Tolentino, Italy, 30 Nov 1898 [extrait de naissance no. 416]-23 Feb 1980 [81], Ronciglione, Italy). AS, p. 731.

Mattox, Martha [actress] (b. Natchez MS, 19 Jun 1879–2 May 1933 [53], Sidney NY; heart disease). "Martha Mattox," *Variety,* 9 May 1933 (age 54). AMD, p. 241. AS, p. 731. BHD1, p. 371. IFN, p. 202 (age 54). MH, p. 125. Truitt, p. 219. "Cody Engages Martha Mattox," *MPW,* 6 Dec 1919, 678. "Martha Mattox," *CI,* 228 (Jun 1994), 40.

Mattraw, Scotty [actor] (b. Evans Mills NY, 19 Oct 1880–9 Nov 1946 [66], Los Angeles CA). "Scott Mattraw," *Variety,* 20 Nov 1946 (500+ films). AS, p. 731. BHD1, p. 371. IFN, p. 202. Truitt, p. 219. George Katchmer, "Scotty Mattraw," *CI,* 232 (Oct 1994), C26, 40.

Mattwir, Scot [actor]. No data found (but see preceding entry). AMD, p. 241. "Fat Man in Serial," *MPW,* 17 Jul 1926, 167.

Maturin, Eric [actor] (b. Kinai Tawl, India, 30 May 1883–17 Oct 1957 [74], London, England). AS, p. 731 (b. Ninaitawl, Himalayas)). BHD, p. 247. IFN, p. 202.

Matus, Kalman [actor]. (Vitagraph.) No data found.

Matzen, Madeline [scenarist]. No data found. FDY, p. 433.

Matzenauer, Margarete [actress/singer] (b. Temesvar, Hungary, 1 Jun 1881–19 Mar 1963 [81], Van Nuys CA). AS, p. 731.

Maude, Arthur [director/actor/writer/scenarist] (b. Pontefract, Yorkshire, England, 1881). (Ince; Universal.) AMD, p. 241. AS, p. 731 (b. 1894–d. ca. 1946). BHD, p. 248. "Arthur Maude Joins David Horsley," *MPW,* 9 Oct 1915, 276. "Arthur Maude in Big 'U' Film," *MPW,* 9 Aug 1919, 817. "Arthur Maude Is Preparing Scenario for Bert Lytell," *MPW,* 4 Sep 1920, 94.

Maude, Beatrice [actress] (b. London, England, 21 Jul 1892–14 Oct 1984 [92], Los Angeles CA). BHD1, p. 371.

Maude, Charles R[aymond] [actor] (b. England, 1882–14 Nov 1943 [61]). AS, p. 731 (d. 15 Nov). BHD, p. 248. IFN, p. 202.

Maude, Cyril (father of **Margery Maude**; cousin of Joan Maude, d. 1999) [stage/film actor] (b. London, England, 24 Apr 1862–20 Feb 1951 [88], Torquay, London, England). m. (1) Winifred Emery, 1888 (d. 1924); (2) Mrs. Beatrice M. Trew, 1927. "Cyril Maude Dead; British Stage Star; Light Comedy Actor Appeared in 'Grumpy' 1,300 Times—Managed London Theatres," *NYT,* 21 Feb 1951, 27:1. "Cyril Maude," *Variety,* 28 Feb 1951. AMD, p. 241. AS, p. 731. BHD1, p. 371. IFN, p. 202. "Morosco Signs Maude; Star of 'Grumpy' Starts for Coast Studios to Make Film Debut," *NYDM,* 26 May 1915, 22:2. "Morosco Secures Cyril Maude," *MPW,* 5 Jun 1915, 1585. "First Maude Film," *NYDM,* 16 Jun 1915, 24:1 (to debut in *As the Years Go By* for the Oliver Morosco Photoplay Co.; with Lenore Ulrich). Cover, *NYDM,* 11 Aug 1915 (with Marie Tempest, Francis Wilson, and Graham Browne, all Frohman stage players). "Three New Stars; Morosco Captures Blanche RIng, Cyril Maude and Charlotte Greenwood," *NYDM,* 11 Aug 1915, 22:4. "Gossip of the Studios," *NYDM,* 1 Sep 1915, 32:2 (on the steamship *Philadelphia,* escaped death when "two bombs were discovered timed to explode the next day, placed on board by Frank Holt, the man who attempted to assassinate J.P. Morgan."). "Maude Opposes Maude; Actor Appearing in 'Grumpy' at Empire Will Have Himself as Rival in 'Peer Gynt' at B'way," *NYDM,* 15 Sep 1915, 11:2 ("This will be the first time in New York that a prominent actor has thus played in opposition to himself.... Throughout the country motion picture exhibitors have shown a tendency to challenge the legitimate theater managers in the most direct way possible. In whatever city a well known star is engaged to appear the motion picture people in the city arrange for his screen appearance at the same time."). "Mrs. Cyril Maude Dies; Winifred Emery Toured This Country with Henry Irving," *NYT,* 16 Jul 1924, 17:5 (b. Manchester, England, 1862–15 Jul 1924 [62?], Bexhill, England).

Maude, Margery (daughter of **Cyril Maude**) [actress] (b. Wimbledon, England, 29 Apr 1889–7 Aug 1979 [90], Cleveland OH). AS, p. 731.

Maudru, Charles Emile (father of **Pierre Maudru**) [director] (b. Asnieres-sur-Seine, France, 1858). AS, p. 732.

Maudru, Pierre (son of **Charles Maudru**) [director/scenarist] (b. Asnieres-sur-Seine, France, 24 Apr 1892–1 Mar 1992 [99], Paris, France). AS, p. 732.

Maugham, W[illiam] **Somerset** [writer/playwright/actor/scenarist] (b. Paris, France, 25 Jan 1874–16 Dec 1965 [91], Villa La Mauresque, French Riviera; after falling and suffering a stroke). m. Mrs. Syrie Barnardo Wellcome, 1917–27 (d. 1955). *The Summing Up.* "Somerset Maugham Is Dead at 91; Novelist, Short Story Writer, Playwright Succumbs in Nice," *NYT,* 16 Dec 1965, 1:3, 50:1 (wrote 30 plays, 21 novels, 120 short stories; *Of Human Bondage,* 1915). AMD, p. 241. AS, p. 732. BHD2, p. 180 (d. Nice, France). "Maugham to Write for Famous Players-Lasky," *MPW,* 16 Jun 1917, 1766. Neil G. Caward, "Screen Gossip," *Picture-Play Magazine,* Sep 1917, 108–09 (to write for FP-L). "W. Somerset Maugham, English Author, Joins Writing Staff of Famous Players-Lasky," *MPW,* 15 Jan 1921, 300. "Maugham to Visit Strange Corners of World in Search of Paramount Stories," *MPW,* 19 Mar 1921, 262.

Mauloy, Georges [actor] (b. France, 1879–1942 [63?]). AS, p. 732. (Began 1919; Paramount, Joinville; MGM.) Waldman, p. 185.

Maupi, [Ernest] **Marcel** [actor] (*né* Marcel Louis Alexandre Barberin, b. Marseilles, France, 6 Nov 1881–4 Jan 1949 [67], Cap d'Antibes, France [extrait de décès no. 6/1949]). AMD, p. 241. AS, p. 732. BHD1, p. 371. IFN, p. 202. "Ernest Maupain [sic]," *MPW,* 26 Feb 1916, 1279. Ernest Maupain, "Simplicity and Impressionability," *MPW,* 21 Jul 1917, 380–81.

Maupin, Clifton [cinematographer]. No data found. FDY, p. 463.

Maur, Meinhart [actor] (b. Hajdúnanás, Hungary, 18 Aug 1891–1964 [73?], London, England). AS, p. 732. BHD1, p. 371.

Maurer, Georges [producer] (b. Mulhouse, France, 3 Mar 1874–5 Feb 1940 [65], Perigueux, France). BHD2, p. 180.

Maurer, John [cinematographer] (d. 5 Dec 1912, Chicago IL). BHD2, p. 180.

Maurette, Marc (father of Claude Mauriac, b. 25 Apr 1914) [director/scenarist] (*né* Joseph Mandel, b. Geneva, Switzerland, 7 Nov 1880 [extrait de naissance no. 1301]-5 May 1957 [76]). AS, p. 732.

Mauriac, François [author/scenarist] (*né* Charles François Mauriac, b. Bordeaux, France, 11 Oct 1885–1 Sep 1970 [84], Paris, France). AS, p. 732.

Maurice *see* **Mouvet, Maurice**

Maurice, Clément [director/producer] (*né* Clément Gratioulet, b. Aiguillon, France, 22 Mar 1853–15 Jul 1933 [80], Sanary-sur-Mer, France [extrait de décès no. 40]). AS, p. 732.

Maurice, Mrs. Mary Birch [actress] (*née* Mary Birch, b. Morristown OH, 15 Nov 1844–30 Apr 1918 [73], Port Carbon PA). (Vitagraph, 1910.) AMD, p. 241. AS, p. 732. BHD, p. 248. IFN, p. 202. Slide, p. 45. "Mother Maurice's Anniversaries," *NYDM,* 27 Nov 1915, 25:2 (71 years old on 15 Nov and her 50th anniversary as an actress, having played with F.S. Chanfrau, John T. Raymond, Edwin Booth, Lawrence Barrett, Joseph Jefferson, and Robert Mantell). "Mary Maurice," *MPW,* 4 Dec 1915, 1820. "'Mother' Mary Maurice Ill in Hospital," *MPW,* 27 Apr 1918, 545. "Obituary," *MPW,* 18 May 1918, 986 (d. 31 Apr, age 74).

Maurice, Newman [actor] (d. 11 Sep 1920, London, England). BHD, p. 248.

Mauricet [actor] (*né* Georges Maurice Renut, b. Paris, France, 19 May 1888–25 Feb 1968 [79], Paris, France [extrait de décès no. 18/569/1968]). AS, p. 732.

Mauries [actor] (*né* Auguste Mourre, b. Marseilles, France, 30 Aug 1883–16 Feb 1956 [72], Marseilles, France). AS, p. 732.

Mauro, Humberto [Brazilian actor/director/scenarist] (b. Minas Geraes, Brazil, 30 Apr 1897–6 Nov 1983 [86], Volta Grande, Brazil; heart attack after pneumonia). AS, p. 733. BHD2, p. 180 (b. Volta Grande, Brazil).

Maurois, André [author/scenarist] (*né* Emile Salomon Wilhelm Herzog, b. Elbeuf, France, 26 Jul 1885 [extrait de naissance no. 369]-9 Oct 1967 [82], Neuilly-sur-Seine, France). AS, p. 733.

Maurstad, Alfred [actor/director] (b. Nordfjord, Norway, 26 Jul 1896–5 Sep 1967 [71], Oslo, Norway). AS, p. 733.

Maurus, Gerda [stage/film actress] (*née* Gertrud Maria Pfeil, b. Vienna Austria, 25 Aug 1903–25 Aug 1968 [65], Düesseldorf, Germany). "Gerda Maurus," *Variety,* 252, 28 Aug 1968, 63:3 (b. Dusseldorf, Germany). AS, p. 733. BHD1, p. 372 (b. Croatia, 1909). IFN, p. 202.

Maury, Willy [actor] (b. Brussels, Belgium, 1887–1 Aug 1955 [68?], Brussels, Belgium). AS, p. 733.

Mawson, Edward R[obert] [actor] (b. 1861–20 May 1917 [55], New York NY). "Edward Robert Mawson," *Variety,* 25 May 1917. AS, p. 733. BHD, p. 248. IFN, p. 202.

Max, Jean [actor] (*né* Jean Max Marie Mehouas, b. Paris, France, 16 Feb 1895–7 Dec 1970 [75], Paris, France [extrait de décès no. 7/1299/1970]). AS, p. 733.

Max, Madeleine [actress]. No data found. Rene de la Seine, "Moviettes from Gay Paree," *Paris and Hollywood Screen Secrets Magazine,* Aug 1927, 94 ("...a tragedienne, very dark and very pretty...").

Maxam, Louella Modie [actress] (b. St. Augustine FL, 10 Jun 1896–3 Sep 1970 [74], Burbank CA). (Triangle.) "Louella Modie Maxam," *Variety,* 16 Sep 1970 (d. 4 Sep). AS, p. 733. BHD, p. 248. BR, pp. 56–57. IFN, p. 202.

Maxim, Hudson [actor] (b. Orneville ME, 3 Feb 1853–6 May 1927 [74], Hopatocong NJ). BHD, p. 248; BHD2, p. 181.

Maximilian, Max [actor] (d. 25 Jun 1930, Berlin, Germany). AS, p. 733. BHD1, p. 372 (Maximillan).

Maximilian, Robert [actor]. No data found. (Betzwood Film Co., PA).

Maximilienne [actress] (*née* Henriette Adeline Genty, b. Paris, France, 28 Nov 1884–29 Aug 1978 [93], Nice, France []extrait de décès no. 3871/1978). AS, p. 733.

Maximov, Vladimir Vasilevich [actor] (b. Moscow, Russia, 27 Jul 1880–22 Mar 1937 [56], Moscow, Russia). AS, p. 733. BHD, p. 248.

Maxudian [actor] (*né* Max Agop Maxudian, b. Smyrna, Turkey, 12 Jun 1881–20 Jul 1976 [95], Boulogne-Billancourt, France [extrait de décès no. SN/1976]). AMD, p. 241. AS, p. 733. AS, p. 733. "Noted European Actors in Rex Ingram's 'The Arab,'" *MPW,* 9 Feb 1924, 466.

Maxwell, Edwin [actor/director] (b. Dublin, Ireland, 9 Feb 1886–13 Aug 1948 [64], Falmouth MA; cerebral hemorrhage). AS, p. 733 (d. 12 Aug). BHD1, p. 372.

Maxwell, Everett C. [writer]. No data found. AMD, p. 241. FDY, p. 433. "Everett C. Maxwell with National," *MPW,* 4 Oct 1919, 137.

Maxwell, Jane [actress] (b. 1851–12 Aug 1924 [73?], Wilmington CA). AS, p. 733. BHD, p. 248.

Maxwell, John [executive] (b. 1877–3 Oct 1940 [63?], London, England). BHD2, p. 181.

Maxwell, Joseph A. [director] (b. 1871?–27 Jun 1930 [59], New York NY; acute indigestion). m. twice. "Joseph A. Maxwell," *Variety,* 2 Jul 1930. AS, p. 733.

Maxwell, Vera [Ziegfeld Follies, 1910–15; film actress/dancer] (b. New York NY, 1892?–1 May 1950 [58], New York NY). (Ziegfeld Follies, 1911–13; retired 1928.) "Vera Maxwell," *NYT,* 2 May 1950, 29:5 (member of the Ziegfeld Club—former stars as well as chrous girls of the Follies). "Vera Maxwell," *Variety,* 178, 3 May 1950, 63:1 ("Miss Maxwell, w.k. as a looker, was acclaimed the world's most beautiful woman by the French portrait artist, Paul Helleu, in 1914. However, this was contested by Sir Philip Bourse-Jones, a British artist, who felt that actress Gladys Cooper deserved that honor."). BHD, p. 248.

Maxwell-Wilshire, Gerard [actor] (b. 1893–3 Apr 1947 [53?], London, England). BHD, p. 248. IFN, p. 202.

May, Alyce [dancer/Lana Turner's stand-in for 30 years] (b. Los Angeles CA, 21 Aug 1905–31 Dec 1980 [75], Rosa Rito Beach, Baja, Mexico; heart attack). (WB; MGM.) "Alyce May," *Variety,* 28 Jan 1981 ("...she danced as a child in the silent pictures, 'Twinkle Toes' and 'The Phantom of the Opera'..."). AS, p. 734. BHD1, p. 372 (b. 1911).

May, Ann [actress] (b. Cincinnati OH, 25 Nov 1899–26 Jul 1985 [85], Los Angeles CA). m. **C. Gardner Sullivan** (d. 1965). AMD, p. 241. AS, p. 734. BHD, p. 248. MH, p. 125. MSBB, p. 1038. (Keeney Pictures.) "Recovers from Injuries, Only to Face Hospital Set," *MPW,* 14 Dec 1918, 1238. "She Rose—by Any Other Name," *MPW,* 21 Dec 1918, 1374. "Anna May to Stay in Pictures," *MPW,* 1 May 1920, 709. Lillian Montanye, "Ann Ascends," *Motion Picture Classic,* Dec 1920, 36–37, 72. George Katchmer, "Remembering the Great Silents," *CI,* 200 (Feb 1992), 32.

May, Betty [actress]. No data found. AMD,

p. 241. "Betty May Leading for Century," *MPW,* 26 Aug 1922, 668.

May, Doris [actress] (aka Doris Lee, *née* Helen Garrett, b. Seattle WA, 15 Oct 1899?–12 May 1984 [85], Camarillo CA; heart attack). m. **Wallace MacDonald**, 5 May 1921, Los Angeles CA (d. 1978). (Film debut: *His Mother's Boy,* Ince, 1917; FP-L.) "Doris May," *Variety,* 28 Nov 1984 (d. Camarillo CA, age 82). AS, p. 654 (Doris Lee); p. 734 (b. 1902). BHD, p. 248 (b. 1902). MH, p. 125. WWS, p. 19 (b. 1902). Grace Kingsley, "They're Wedded Only in Films; [Douglas] M[a]cLean-May Partnership Is Purely Artistic; Feminine Co-Star Has Had Real Proposals from Frans; A Sketch of Pyramus and Thisbe of Cinema," *LA Times,* 29 Feb 1920, III, p. 1 ("Even though they are lovers, everything sweet that happens between 'em must happen between the hours of 9:30 a.m. and 5 p.m.!"). "Doris May's Seven Rivals in Love; The wife of Wallace MacDonald has learned how to be seven different women, to offset the studio wiles of Pola Negri and company," *MPC,* Jun 1925, 34–35, 90. Billy H. Doyle, "Lost Players," *CI,* 173 (Nov 1989), 28. George Katchmer, "Remembering the Great Silents," *CI,* 240 (Jun 1995), 46.

May, Edith [actress]. No data found. AMD, p. 241. "Mayflower's National Beauty Contest Won by Miss Edith May of Wisconsin," *MPW,* 23 Oct 1920, 1129. "Edith May, Mayflower Star, May Be Welcomed by Mayor," *MPW,* 6 Nov 1920, 83.

May, Edna [stage/film actress] (*née* Edna May Pettie, b. Syracuse NY, 2 Sep 1875–2 Jan 1948 [72], Lausanne, Switzerland; heart attack). m. (1) Frederick Titus (d. 1918); (2) Oscar Lewisohn, Jun 1907 (d. 1917). (Vitagraph.) "Edna May, Starred on London Stage; American Actress Who Won Fame for 'Belle of New York' Role Dies at 69," *NYT,* 3 Jan 1948, 13:5 (age 69). "Mrs. Lewisohn's Will Filed," *NYT,* 9 Oct 1948, 11:2 (the estate totaled $94,852). "Edna May," *Variety,* 7 Jan 1948 (age 69). AMD, p. 241 (*née* Edna May Van Velzer). AS, p. 734. BHD, p. 248. IFN, p. 202. SD. Truitt, p. 219. "Edna May," *MPW,* 5 Jun 1915, 1581. "Edna May," *MPW,* 14 Sep 1915, 1835. "Edna May to Act for Vitagraph; Former Comic Opera Favorite to Work in One Picture for Benefit of Red Cross," *MPW,* 4 Dec 1915, 1835 (her alleged $100,000 salary was to be turned over to the Red Cross. She was rich from her marriage to Lewisohn and didn't need the money.). "Edna May in Elaborate Picture," *MPW,* 18 Dec 1915, 2158. "Johnny Hines Picks Edna May for Lead; Girl Gets Contract," *MPW,* 8 Oct 1927, 356. "Edna May," *MPW,* 12 Nov 1927, 23.

May, Eva (daughter of Maria May, Austrian film star) [actress] (b. Vienna, Austria, 29 May 1901–11 Sep 1924 [23], Vienna, Austria; shot herself). "Eva May, 23, a Suicide; German Actress Shoots Herself Because of Love Affair," *Variety,* 24 Sep 1924. BHD, p. 248 (d. Baden, Austria).

May, Hans [actor/composer] (*né* Johannes Mayer, b. Vienna, Austria, 11 Jul 1886–31 Dec 1958 [72], London, England). AS, p. 734.

May, Harold R. [actor] (b. 1903?–16 Sep 1973 [70], Los Angeles CA). (Sennett.) "Harold R. May," *Variety,* 26 Sep 1973. AS, p. 734. BHD, p. 248.

May, James C. [actor] (b. Dundee, Scotland, 8 Apr 1857–25 Aug 1941 [84], Los Angeles CA). AS, p. 734.

May, Joe [producer/director/scenarist] (*né* Joseph Otto Mandel, b. Vienna, Austria, 7 Nov 1880–29 Apr 1954 [73], Los Angeles CA). m. Hermine Pfleger (**Mia May**). (Ufa, 1917.) AS, p. 734. BHD2, p. 181. IFN, p. 202. Waldman, p. 185.

May, Leola [actress] (b. 1891?–17 Apr 1928 [37], Glendale CA; in a sanitarium). m. (1) Howard Elder; (2) Victor McLean. "Leola [Maye] McLean," *Variety,* 25 Apr 1928. AS, p. 734.

May, Margaret [actress] (b. Pittsburgh PA, 1895?–21 Feb 1994 [98], Paterson NJ). m. Samuel Gibler. AS, p. 734 (b. 1893). BHD, p. 178. Billy H. Doyle, "Obituaries," *FIR,* Sep/Oct 1994, p. 55. "Margaret May Gibler," *CI,* 288 (Jun 1994), 58:2 (lived in Mendham NJ).

May, Mia [actress] (*née* Hermine Pfleger, b. Vienna, Austria, 2 Jun 1884–28 Nov 1980 [96], Los Angeles CA). m. **Joe May** (d. 1954). (Film debut: *In der Tiefe des Schachtes,* 1912.) AS, p. 734. BHD1, p. 372. Vittorio Martinelli, "Kino-Lieblinge," *Griffithiana,* 38/39 (Oct 1990), 18.

Mayakovsky, Vladimir [actor/scenarist/poet] (b. Bagdadi, Georgia, 19 Jul 1893–14 Apr 1930 [36], Moscow, Russia; suicide). AS, p. 734. BHD, p. 248.

Mayall, Herschel [stage/film actor] (b. Bowling Green [Warren Co.] KY, 12 Jul 1863–10 Jun 1941 [78], Detroit MI; cerebral hemorrhage). (NYMP Co.; Ince; Fox.) "Hershell Mayall," *NYT,* 11 Jun 1941, 21:6. "Hershell Mayall," *Variety,* 18 Jun 1941. AS, p. 734. BHD1, p. 372. IFN, p. 202. MH, p. 126. Truitt, p. 219. George Katchmer, "Remembering the Great Silents," *CI,* 229 (Jul 1994), 41–42.

Mayberry, Mary [actress] (aka Mary Mabery). No data found. George A. Katchmer, "Forgotten Cowboys and Cowgirls—Part XIV," *CI,* 191 (May 1991), 20.

Maydoch, John [actor] (b. 1894-Jan 1918 [23?], New York NY). BHD, p. 248.

Maye, Jimsy [actor] (b. Spokane WA, 1893–10 Apr 1968 [74?], Jackson OR). AS, p. 734. BHD, p. 248.

Maye, Leola [actress] (b. 1891–17 Apr 1928 [36?], Glendale CA). BHD, p. 248.

Mayer, Arthur L. [director] (b. New York NY, 1886–14 Apr 1981 [95?], New York NY). AS, pp. 735–36.

Mayer, Carl [producer/scenarist] (b. Graz, Austria, 20 Feb 1894–1 Jul 1944 [49], London, England). "Carl Mayer; British Film Writer, Co-Producer—Did Script for 'Sunrise,'" *NYT,* 4 Jul 1944, 19:4 (wrote *Variety, Tartuffe*). "Carl Mayer," *Variety,* 155, 12 Jul 1944, 42:2 (wrote *The Last Laugh, The Cabinet of Dr. Caligari, Sunrise*). AS, p. 735. BHD2, p. 181. FDY, p. 433. IFN, p. 202 (d. 3 Jul).

Mayer, Edwin Justus [playwright/title writer/scenarist] (b. New York NY, 8 Nov 1896–11 Sep 1960 [63], New York NY). m. Mrs. Frances O'Neill McIntyre, 1927–27. *A Preface to Life* (1923; written at age 25). (Goldwyn, 1919.) "Edwin Justus Mayer, 63, Dead; Playwright and Movie Scenarist," *NYT,* 12 Sep 1960, 29:2 (a founder of the Screen Writers Guild). "Edward Justus Mayer," *Variety,* 21 Sep 1960. AMD, p. 241. AS, p. 735. BHD2, p. 181. FDY, p. 447. IFN, p. 202. Edwin Justus Mayer, "Screen Fright," *MPS,* 13 May 1921, 25 (some who had it when there were strangers on the set: Tom Moore, Will Rogers, Irene Rich, Pauline Frederick. "Onlookers, on the studio stage, are close to the actor; there is no sheen of light between to create the illusion of distance. But there is another sort of light—the glare of the Kliegs and other powerful light paraphernalia, and this is often trying to the most experienced screen actor's temper."). "Mayer to Write Titles for Goldwyn," *MPW,* 22 Oct 1921, 921. "Named Title ditor," *MPW,* 6 Nov 1926, 3.

Mayer, Hy [animator/director] (b. Worms-on-Rhine, Germany, 1868?–27 Sep 1954 [86], So. Norwalk CT). "Hi Mayer," *Variety,* 29 Sep 1954 ("From 1909–16, Mayer drew the cartoons for his 'Animated Weekly,' a film short"). AMD, p. 242. AS, p. 735. BHD2, p. 181 (b. 1886). "Hy Mayer's 'Travelaugh,'" *MPW,* 13 Oct 1917, 264. "Hy Mayer to Illustrate Serial Stories," *MPW,* 1 Feb 1919, 665. "Pathé Has World Rights to Hy Mayer's Travelaughs; To Add to Screen Magazine," *MPW,* 26 Jun 1920, 1781. "Abandons Pen to Direct," *MPW,* 15 Sep 1923, 280. "Hy Mayer with Pathé for 'Sketch Book' Series," *MPW,* 8 May 1926, 167. "Hy Mayer's New Sketch Book for Pathé," *MPW,* 10 Jul 1926, 116.

Mayer, J.H. [publicist]. No data found. AMD, p. 242. "Mayer Succeeds Rice as Universal's Publicity Head," *MPW,* 21 Feb 1920, 1230.

Mayer, Louis B[urt] [executive] (*né* Eliezer [Lazar] Mayer, b. Demre, Vilna, Russia, 4 Jul? 1885–29 Oct 1957 [72], Los Angeles CA; leukemia). m. (1) Margaret Schenberg; (2) Lorena Z. Danker, Dec 1948. Bosley Crowther, *Hollywood Rajah* (1960). (Alco; Metro; MGM.) "Louis B. Mayer, Film Maker, Dies; Former Production Chief of M-G-M [1924–51], 72, Built Movies Around Leading Stars; Guided Garbo to Fame; Highest Paid Executive in U.S. for 7 Years Resigned from Studio in 1951," *NYT,* 30 Oct 1957, 29:1 (b. Minsk, Russia, and the disputed birth date of 4 Jul 1885). "Mayer Dies 'In Exile' from Films; Once 'King of Hollywood' and a Power in National Politics Succumbs to Leukemia," *Variety,* 30 Oct 1957 (b. Minsk, Russia; d. Hollywood CA). AMD, p. 242. AS, p. 735 (b. Demre, Lithuania). BHD2, p. 181. IFN, p. 202. Katz, p. 792 (b. Minsk, Russia). SD. "Louis B. Mayer Undergoes Operation," *MPW,* 6 Feb 1915, 841. "Back to First Principles," *NYDM,* 28 Apr 1915, 21:4, 28:4 (directors of the Metro Corp. were announced as Richard A. Rowland, Joseph W. Engel, Mayer, Otto N. Davies, George Grombacher, James A. Fitzgerald, and James B. Clarke). "Combine to Aid Extras; Producers in East to Take Hiring Out of the Agents' Hands," *NYDM,* 1 Sep 1915, 28:2 (agents took 40 to 75 cents of the extra's humble salary. An employment agency at 126 W. 46th St., NYC, "would secure extras for all of the companies in the agreement." The companies included Equitable, Peerless, World, Paramount, Triangle, Wizard Studio, and Metro.). "Vitagraph Seeks Injunction," *MPW,* 22 Sep 1917, 1349–50. "Metro Enjoins Mayer," *MPW,* 10 Nov 1917, 864. "Select Pictures' New England Manager," *MPW,* 15 Dec 1917, 1623. "Mayer Returns to Old Position," *MPW,* 23 Feb 1918, 1103. "Louis Mayer Gets Rights to Plays," *MPW,* 27 Apr 1918, 545. "Mayer Goes West to Rest and to Visit His Company," *MPW,* 25 Jan 1919, 481. "Louis Mayer Talks About Anita Stewart's Pictures," *MPW,* 19 Apr 1919, 364. "Mayer's Daughter Ill," *MPW,* 12 Jul 1919, 364. A.H. Giebler, "Mayer Explains 'Three Hundred PerCent Film," *MPW,* 9 Aug 1919, 827. "Mayer Buys Twelve Curwood Stories," *MPW,* 30 Aug 1919, 1289. "Picture Industry Steadily Developing, Not Disintegrating, Says Louis Mayer," *MPW,* 5 Feb

1921, 700. T.S. daPonte, "Mayer Sees Prosperity Ahead; Praises Hays and Zukor; Calls Them Unselfish," *MPW,* 17 Jun 1922, 617. "Mayer Sees San Francisco as New FIlm Production Center," *MPW,* 8 Dec 1923, 540. "Louis B. Mayer Has Huge Studios Going at Full Speed for Metro-Goldwyn-Mayer," *MPW,* 19 Jul 1924, 196. "West Is Pedrmanent Center for Production, Says Louis Mayer," *MPW,* 26 Jul 1924, 288. "Must Depend on Exhibitors to Learn Public's Taste, Says Mayer," *MPW,* 4 Oct 1924, 404. "Mayer Off to Europe," *MPW,* 11 Oct 1924, 494. "Million for Production Not Excessive When Art Is Achieved, Mayer Declares," *MPW,* 20 Dec 1924, 708. "Metro Production Is Speeding on Coast, Says Mayer, Here for Meet," *MPW,* 2 May 1925, 83. "Mayer Gives Details of 1925–26 Plans and Annoucces Four New M-G-M Stars," *MPW,* 6 Jun 1925, 669 (Shearer, Rovarro, Gilbert Chaney). "Present Gold Cup to Louis Mayer," *MPW,* 27 Jun 1925, 947. "Mayer Signs New Contract; Henley Remains with Metro," *MPW,* 19 Dec 1925, 661. "Studio Equipment Plays Big Part in Upholding M-G-M's High Quality," *MPW,* 2 Jan 1926, 104–05. "Metro-Goldwyn-Mayer Studios Make Equipment Help Quality," *MPW,* 9 Jan 1926, 183. Louis B. Mayer, "Pictures Like of Which Never Before Attempted," *MPW,* 1 May 1926, 33. "Louis B. Mayer Asserts Motion Pictures Will Spell End of Vaudeville Theatres," *MPW,* 29 May 1926, 401. "Louis B. Mayer Outlines 1927 Plans for M-G-M Production," *MPW,* 15 Jan 1927, 195, 198. "Mayer Professes Disbelief in M-G-M—United Artists Merger," *MPW,* 12 Feb 1927, 473. "Mayer Arrives in New York for Preoduction Conferences," *MPW,* 12 Feb 1927, 493. "Mayer Asserts M-G-M Will Develop Stars and Authors," *MPW,* 28 May 1927, 267. "Tiffany-Stahl Denies Louis B. Mayer Affiliation," *MPW,* 17 Dec 1927, 12. Eric Niderost, "The Ultimate Mogul: Louis B. Mayer," *CI,* 263 (May 1997), 24–27. Maurice Rapf, *Back Lot; Growing Up with the Movies* (Lanham MD: Scarecrow Press, 1999), p. 17 ("...Mayer was a junk dealer in Nova Scotia...The best line I know about a B'nai Birth funeral is attributed to producer Sam Goldwyn, who, on seeing the large turnout for the funeral of his not-very-popular rival, Louis B. Mayer, said, 'The reason so many people showed up was to make sure he was dead.'").

Mayhew, Kate [actress] (b. Indianapolis IN, 2 Sep 1853–16 Jun 1944 [90], New York NY). (Film debut: *Hazel Kirke,* 1915.) "Kate Mayhew Dies; Actress 79 Years; She Enacted More than 500 Roles and Appeared with Nation's Top Stage Stars," *NYT,* 18 Jun 1944, 35:1 (age 91). "Kate Mayhew," *Variety,* 21 Jun 1944 (age 90; began in *Hazel Kirke* [1915]). AS, p. 735. BHD, p. 248. IFN, p. 202. Truitt, p. 220.

Mayhew, Stella [stage/film producer] (b. 1875?–2 Apr 1934 [59], New York NY; blood poisoning. Interred at Mt. Kensico Cemetery). m. Billie Taylor. "Stella Mayhew," *Variety,* 114, 8 May 1934, 62:1 (cause of death was a cut suffered in subway three weeks ago when her foot was jammed between train and the platform. Erysipelas developed and then septicemia."). AMD, p. 243. "Stella Mayhew to Produce Two-Reel Comedies," *MPW,* 15 Nov 1919, 360.

Maynard, Harry [actor] (b. 1898–23 Jul 1976 [78], Saratoga CA). BHD, p. 248. IFN, p. 203.

Maynard, Ken (brother of **Kermit Maynard**) [actor] (b. Vevay IN, 21 Jul 1895–23 Mar 1973 [77], Woodland Hills CA; died alone, suffering from malnutrition). m. (2) Jeanne Knudson, 14 Feb 1923; (3) Mary [Lapeer?] (b. 1899), near Arrowhead Lake CA, 1926–39; (4) Bertha Rowland Denham, tightrope walker from Cole Brothers Circus, 1939 (d. Oct 1968). (Film debut: *Janice Meredith,* 1924.) "Ken Maynard of Westerns Dies; Bashful and Wholesome," *NYT,* 25 Mar 1973, 71:1 (b. Mission TX); 13 Apr 1973, 41:7 (correction of birthplace: b. Vevay IN). "Ken Maynard," *Variety,* 28 Mar 1973 (d. 23 Mar). AMD, p. 243. AS, p. 735. BHD1, p. 373. FSS, p. 205. GK, pp. 613–25. IFN, p. 203. Katz, pp. 792–93. Matthew Josephson, "The Wild, Wild West Is Coming Strong; Whoopee for the Open Spaces! A Flood of Outdoor Celluloid Threatens, But 'Twill Be Something New and Different," *MPC,* Dec 1926, 22–23, 68, 77 (discusses Maynard, Jones, Gibson, McCoy, Mix, Hart and Acord). "Ken Maynard," *MPW,* 13 Aug 1927, 455. Dorothy Wooldridge, "A Big Lot of Whoopee; Ken Maynard Has to Be Reckoned With When It Comes to Ridin' a Hoss," *MPC,* May 1928, 55, 84. Herbert Cruikshank, "Ken Carries On; He's the Last and Lone Champion of the Legend of Our West," *MPC,* Jun 1929, 60, 91 ("...let's give thanks for Ken Maynard, who keeps the movies safe for America against the encroaching invasion of foreign stars and foreign stories."). George A. Katchmer, "Ken Maynard: Dr. Jeckyll or Mr. Hyde?," *CI,* 102 (Dec 1983), 49–51, 77. Mario DeMarco, "Ken Maynard: A Champion in His Own Right," *CI,* 214 (Apr 1993), 10. Mike Newton, "'So You're the Rattler'—Ken Maynard Comes to Mystery Mountain," *CI,* 225 (Mar 1994), 28, 30. (The Vevay Public Library, 210 Ferry Street, Vevay IN 47043, collects material on Maynard.)

Maynard, Kermit Roosevelt "Tex" (brother of **Ken Maynard**) [stage/film/TV actor/stuntman] (b. Vevay IN, 20 Sep 1897–16 Jan 1971 [73], No. Hollywood CA). m. Edith Jessen 23 Feb 1924 (son William, b. 10 May 1943). (Film debut: *Wild Bull of the Campus,* FBO, 1926; final film, *Tarus Bulba,* UA, 1962.) "Kermit Maynard," *Variety,* 27 Jan 1971 (age 73). AS, p. 735. BHD1, p. 373. IFN, p. 203. Katz, p. 793 (b. 1902). SD. Truitt, p. 200 (b. 1902). Nick Williams, "Kermit Maynard as Western Star and Stunt Man," *Filmograph,* II, No. 1 (1971), 24–37. John Cocchi, "The 2nd Feature; A History of the B Movies; The Western—4," *CI,* 148 (Oct 1987), 23.

Mayne, Clarice [actress] (b. London, England, 6 Feb 1886–16 Jan 1966 [79], London, England). AS, p. 735 (b. 1890; d. 17 Jan). BHD, p. 248.

Mayne, Eric [actor] (b. Dublin, Ireland, 28 Apr 1865–9 Feb 1947 [81], Los Angeles CA). (World.) "Eric Mayne, Shakespearean Actor a Veteran of Films in Hollywood," *NYT,* 12 Feb 1947, 25:5. "Eric Mayne," *Variety,* 12 Feb 1947. AS, p. 735. BHD1, p. 373. IFN, p. 203. Truitt, p. 220. "A Specialist in Dignity," *MPC,* Mar 1926, 54, 82 (to U.S.A. in 1913).

Mayne, Ernie [actor] (b. 1874–15 May 1937 [63?], Brighton, England). BHD, p. 249.

Mayo, Albert [actor] (b. 1887?–20 May 1933 [46], Los Angeles CA; heart attack). m. Hilda Twogood, 1916. (Reliance; Thanhouser; Lubin.) "Albert Mayo," *Variety,* 30 May 1933. AS, p. 735. BHD, p. 249. IFN, p. 203. Truitt, p. 220. "Al Mayo a Benedict," *NYDM,* 25 Mar 1916, 24 (re marriage).

Mayo, Archie L. [writer/director] (*né* Archibald L. Mayo, b. New York NY, 29 Jan 1891–4 Dec 1968 [77], Guadalajara, Mexico; cancer). m. Lucille (d. 1945). (WB; Christie.) "Archie Mayo," *Variety,* 11 Dec 1968. "Mrs. Archie Mayo," *NYT,* 27 Feb 1945, 19:4 (d. 24 Feb 1945, Santa Monica CA). AMD, p. 243. AS, p. 735. BHD, p. 249; BHD2, p. 181. "Mayo with Christie," *MPW,* 15 Mar 1924, 193. "Archie Mayo Gets Warner Contract," *MPW,* 9 Jul 1927, 97.

Mayo, Christine [actress]. No data found. AMD, p. 243. "Christine Mayo," *MPW,* 11 Jul 1914, 232. "Christine Mayo," *MPW,* 4 May 1918, 684. "Christine Mayo Engaged with Marshall Neilan," *MPW,* 24 Jan 1920, 583.

Mayo, Edgar C. [actor/director] (*né* Jean Jordan, b. 1858?–21 Jun 1944 [86], Detroit MI). (Selznick; Universal.) "Edgar C. Mayo," *Variety,* 5 Jul 1944. AS, p. 735. BHD2, p. 181. IFN, p. 203. SD.

Mayo, Edna [actress] (*née* Lane, b. Philadelphia PA, 23 Mar 1895–5 May 1970 [75], San Francisco CA). m. Mr. Royce; Mr. White, SF CA, 1930. AMD, p. 243. AS, p. 735. BHD, p. 249. IFN, p. 203. "Favorite Pla¥ers Signs Edna Mayo," *MPW,* 29 Aug 1914, 1229. "Edna Mayo," *MPW,* 27 Feb 1915, 1267. Cover, *NYDM,* 14 Jul 1915 ("Leading Woman with Essanay"). Margaret I. MacDonald, "Getting to See Edna Mayo," *MPW,* 4 Dec 1915, 1811. "Edna Mayo," *MPW,* 20 Jan 1917, 373. R.R. Maskell, "What Happened to Edna Mayo?," *CFC,* 34 (Spring, 1972), 29. '83 WWOS (b. 1893).

Mayo, Frank L. [actor/director] (b. New York NY, 28 Jun 1886–9 Jul 1963 [77?], Laguna Beach CA; heart attack). (Selig; Balboa.) m. Joyce Eleanor—div. Oct 1921; **Dagmar Godowsky,** Tia Juana, Mexico, 1921—annulled 1928 (d. 1975). "Frank Mayo, Actor in Films Since 1915," *NYT,* 10 Jul 1963, 35:4 (age 74). "Frank Mayo," *Variety,* 17 Jul 1963 (age 74). AMD, p. 243. AS, p. 735. BHD1, p. 373; BHD2, p. 181 (b. 1889; d. Long Beach CA). FFF, p. 156. GK, pp. 625–37. IFN, p. 203 (age 74). MH, p. 126. Truitt, p. 220. WWS, p. 235. "Frank Mayo," *MPW,* 1 Jan 1916, 57. "Frank Mayo Signs Contract with World," *MPW,* 11 May 1918, 862. "Mayo Answers Wife; Says Charge of Friendship for Film Actress Caused Him Anguish," *LA Times,* 20 Feb 1920, III, p. 4 (in his cross-complaint to the separate maintenance suit of Joyce Eleanor Mayo, Mayo said that "his wife caused him mental suffering by her accusations connecting his name with film actresses. He says his wife has no cause for suspicion in his associations with Miss Dagmar Godowsky. The latter has pending a $16,000 suit for libel against Mrs. Mayo. Mr. Mayo says his wife is unreasonably jealous. He alleges he did not spend large sums of money entertaining the members of the film company with which he is connected."). "Mayo Gets Decree," *MPW,* 15 Oct 1921, 746. Marion Lake, "The Third Generation," *MPC,* Dec 1921, 60–61, 86. "Goldwyn Signs Mayo," *MPW,* 24 Feb 1923, 766. Full-page photograph, *MPS,* 26 Aug 1924, 35. George Katchmer, "Frank Mayo of the Acting Mayos," *CI,* 94 (Apr 1983), 23–25.

Mayo, George [actor] (b. 1891–21 Dec 1950 [59?], Los Angeles CA). AS, p. 735.

Mayo, Harry A. [actor] (*né* Ray Simpson, b. Helena MT, 11 Mar 1898–6 Jan 1964 [65], Woodland Hills CA; cadio-vascular ailment). (Griffith.) "Harry Mayo," *Variety,* 15 Jan 1964 ("leading man in silent pix"). AS, p. 735. BHD1, p. 373. IFN, p. 203. Truitt, p. 220.

Mayo, Margaret [playwright] (*née* Lillian Slatten, b. near Brownsville IL, 19 Nov 1882–25 Feb 1951 [68], Ossining NY). m. **Edgar Selwyn** (d. 1944). (Goldwyn.) "Margaret Mayo, Playwright, Dies; Her 'Baby Mine,' 'Twin Beds' and 'Polly of the Circus' Won Acclaim as Comedy Hits," *NYT,* 26 Feb 1951, 23:1. "Margaret Mayo," *Variety,* 28 Feb 1951. AMD, p. 243. AS, p. 736. BHD, p. 249. "Edgar Selwyn and Margaret Mayo in 'The Arab,'" *MPW,* 13 Feb 1915, 999. "Margaret Mayo Out of Goldwyn Position," *MPW,* 16 Mar 1918, 1487.

Mayo, Melvin [actor]. (Lubin.) No data found. AMD, p. 243. "Melvin Mayo," *MPW,* 19 May 1917, 1119.

Mayo, Rose [actress] (b. 1877?–25 Jul 1936 [59], Atlantic City NJ). "Rose Mayo," *Variety,* 29 Jul 1936. AS, p. 736. BHD, p. 249.

Mayring, Lothar [actor/director] (b. Wurzburg, Germany, 19 Sep 1879–6 Jul 1948 [68], Leipzig, Germany). AS, p. 736. BHD2, p. 181.

Mazaletti, Collette [actress]. No data found. (Christie.) "Beauties Who Make the Comedies Attractive," *Cinema Arts,* Aug 1926, 21.

Mazza, Desdemona [actress] (b. Castel San Pietro, Italy, 3 Oct 1901). AS, p. 736. JS, p. 282 (b. Bologna, Italy; made *I naufraghi della vita,* 1918; went to Paris after World War I).

Mazzolotti, Pier Angelo [director/scenarist] (b. Lentà, Italy, 29 Dec 1890–5 Apr 1972 [81], Turin, Italy). AS, p. 736. JS, p. 282 (in Italian silents from 1914).

Mdivani, David [actor] (*né* David Manor, b. Batumi, Georgia, 4 Feb 1904–5 Aug 1984 [80], Los Angeles CA). m. **Mae Murray**, Beverly Hills CA, 27 Jun 1926—div. 1933 (d. 1965). BHD, p. 249.

Mead, Anna [actress]. No data found. AMD, p. 243. "Little Picture Actress Saves Mother," *MPW,* 1 Sep 1917, 1356. "Anna Mead to Return to Pictures," *MPW,* 29 Jun 1918, 1848.

Mead, Lydia [actress]. No data found. (Thanhouser.) "In the Picture Studios," *NYDM,* 4 Aug 1915, 27:1 (on Thanhouser's frmale baseball team, along with Peggy Burke, Eleanor Brown, Janet Henry, Violet Hite, Ethlye Benham, Winifred Lane, Jean Lehberg, Ruth Elder, and Fan Gregory).

Meade, Charles A. [actor] (b. Rutland VT, 1876–14 Sep 1949 [73?], New York NY). BHD, p. 249.

Meade, Claire [actress] (*née* Marguerite Fields, b. NJ, 2 Apr 1883–14 Jan 1968 [84], Encino CA). AS, p. 750.

Meade, Mildred [actress] (b. 1879?–20 Jul 1951 [72], Woodland Hills CA). m. **Thomas R. Mills** (d. 1953). "Mildred Meade," *NYT,* 22 Jul 1951, 61:2. AS, p. 750.

Meader, George [actor] (b. Minneapolis MN, 6 Jul 1888–17 Dec 1963 [75]). AS, p. 750.

Meador, J.E.D. (Jack) [producer] (b. 1885–7 Mar 1940 [55?], New York NY). AMD, p. 243. AS, p. 750. BHD2, p. 181. "Meador Joins Producers' Ranks; Resigns from Metro-Goldwyn," *MPW,* 4 Apr 1925, 444.

Meagher, Edward J. [scenarist]. No data found. FDY, p. 433.

Meakin, Charles W. [actor] (b. Ogden, UT, 2 Oct 1879–17 Jan 1961 [81], Los Angeles CA). m. **Ruth** (d. 1939). "Charles Meakin," *Variety,* 25 Jan 1961 (appeared in some 3,000 films). BHD1, p. 374. IFN, p. 203. Truitt, p. 227.

Meakin, Ruth [actress] (*née* Ruth Eldredge, b. 1879?–3 Nov 1939 [60], Los Angeles CA). m. **Charles W. Meakin** (d. 1961). "Ruth Meakin," *Variety,* 8 Nov 1939. AS, p. 750. BHD, p. 249.

Meakins, Charles J. [actor] (b. Canada, 1880–5 May 1951 [71?], Elora, Canada). AS, p. 750.

Meaney, Donald A. [publicist/casting director]. No data found. (Essanay.) AMD, p. 243. F.J. Beecroft, "Publicity Men I Have Met...," *NYDM,* 14 Jan 1914, 48 (*see* Beecroft, Chester for full citation). "Meaney's Song Popular; Exhibitors Awake to Possibilities of 'Broncho Billy' Songin Publicity Work," *NYDM,* 28 Jan 1914 (wrote the song with H. Tipton Steck and Arthur A. Penn. To be sold to movie patrons for 10¢ a copy). "Meaney Leaves Essanay; Popular Advertising Man Succeeded by Victor Eubank, Chicago Newspaper Man," *NYDM,* 15 Jul 1914, 25:3. Don Meaney, "Go East, Film Men, Go East; Horacve Greeley's Advice Is Reversed by Picture Man Who Gives Reasons Why Producers Should Go East—'Pictures as Good; Cost Is Less,' He Says," *NYDM,* 6 Oct 1915, 25:1 (a) a picture company must get a permit to take a scene in a public park, which takes 1/2 to 2 hours, and is good only on the day it is issued; 2) exteriors of saloons are forbidden to be filmed so must be built; 3) the fire department withdrew the use of its extra equipment, such as chemical wagons, engines, and hose carts; 4) the police may not work in pictures when off duty; 5) costumes, props, and furniture are difficult to secure; and 6) costs of filming exteriors of homes on the West is high: $1 to $10; in addition to rainy days and problems with natural light. *See* rebuttal to this article under Horkheimer, H.M., *NYDM,* 13 Nov 1915.). "Meaney Now Casting Director for Ince," *MPW,* 8 Dec 1917, 1465.

Meano, Cesare [director/scenarist] (b. Turin, Italy, 22 Dec 1899–24 Nov 1957 [57], Palermo, Sicily, Italy). AS, p. 750.

Mears, Benjamin S. [vaudeville actor/playwright] (b. 1872–27 Jan 1952 [80], Cliffside Park NJ). (Stage, 1890.) "Benjamin S. Mears, Actor, Playwright," *NYT,* 31 Jan 1952, 27:1 (known as Stannard Mears on the stage, "[h]e was seen in early moving pictures with Pearl White and other 'big names' of the pioneer days, and also was a vaudeville headliner in a team with his wfe and others, some of whom later became famous as stars." He collaborated with Hugh Stanislaus Stange, as on the stage vrsion of Tarkington's *Seventeen,* produced in 1918.). "Benjamin S. Mears," *Variety,* 185, 6 Feb 1952, 63:2. AS, p. 750. BHD, p. 249. IFN, p. 203.

Mears, John Henry [producer] (b. 1878–26 Jul 1956 [78?], Los Angeles CA). BHD2, p. 182.

Measor, Adele [actress] (b. Ireland, 2 Sep 1890–9 Jun 1933 [42]). BHD, p. 249.

Medbury, John P. [scenarist] (b. 1893–29 Jun 1947 [54?], Laguna Beach CA). AS, p. 751. BHD2, p. 182.

Medcraft, Russell G[raham] (playwright/scenarist/teacher) (b. 1897–28 Sep 1962 [65], New York NY; result of a fire in the Dorchester cooperative building, 57th Street). "Playwright Killed Here as Fire Hits Apartment," *NYT,* 30 Sep 1962, 40:1 ("According to the police, a cigarette fell into a television and hi-fi cabinet and caused the fire." His white poodle survived and was taken to an A.S.P.C.A. shelter. Also survived by Charles Medcraft, of Hollywood.). "Russell Graham Medcraft," *Variety,* 228, 10 Oct 1962, 71:3. AS, p. 751. BHD, p. 249; BHD2, p. 182.

Medin, Gastone [art director] (b. Spalato, Dalmatia, 6 Jul 1905). JS, pp. 282–83 (in Italian silents from 1929).

Medina, José [director] (b. Sorocaba, Brazil, 1894–1980 [86?], Sao Paulo, Brazil). AS, p. 751.

Meech, Edward Raymond [actor] (b. 1892–2 Mar 1952 [60], Findlay OH). AS, p. 751. BHD, p. 249. IFN, p. 203.

Meech, George T. [stage/film actor] (b. Chicago IL, 1866–29 Mar 1941 [75], Jamaica, LI NY). m. Anna B. "George T. Meech; Queens Realty Man Appeated on the Stage for Forty Years," *NYT,* 30 Mar 1941, 48:7; death notice, p. 48:6 (funeral on 31 Mar). "George T. Meech," *Variety,* 142, 2 Apr 1941, 46:2 (age 75). BHD, p. 249.

Meehan, Elizabeth (mother of actress Frances Meehan) [Ziegfeld girl/drammatist/scenarist] [actress/scenarist] (b. 1905–24 Apr 1967 [62?], New York NY). "Betty Williams [stage name]," *Variety,* 17 May 1967. BHD2, p. 182. FDY, p. 433.

Meehan, George B. [cameraman] (b. 1891?–10 Feb 1947 [55], Los Angeles CA). "George B. Meehan," *Variety,* 26 Feb 1947. BHD2, p. 182. FDY, p. 463.

Meehan, J[ames] **Leo** [director/scenarist/studio policeman] (d. 21 Apr 1936, Los Angeles CA). (Paramount.) AMD, p. 243. FDY, p. 433. "James Meehan," *Variety,* 29 Apr 1936. "Director Weds," *MPW,* 30 Jun 1923, 775. "Her Father's Daughter," *MPW,* 14 Mar 1925, 171. "Gene Stratton Porter's 'Her Father's Daughter,'" *MPW,* 18 Apr 1925, 701. "James Leo Meehan," *MPW,* 18 Dec 1926, 491. "Leo Meehan to Direct Valli," *MPW,* 16 Apr 1927, 633. "Boy Born to Meehan's," *MPW,* 22 Oct 1927, 485.

Meehan, Jeannett Porter [title writer]. No data found. FDY, p. 447.

Meehan, John [author/actor/director] (b. Lindsay, Ontario, Canada, 8 May 1890–12 Nov 1954 [64], Woodland Hills CA). m. (1) **Kay Francis** (d. 1968); (2) Bernice. "John Meehan," *Variety,* 17 Nov 1954. AS, p. 751. BHD2, p. 182. IFN, p. 203. Katz, p. 794. SD.

Mehan, Leo [director] (b. 1888–8 Nov 1943 [55?], San Francisco CA). AS, p. 751. BHD2, p. 182.

Meehan, Lew [actor] (*né* James Lew Meehan, b. MN, 7 Sep 1890–10 Aug 1951 [60], Los Angeles Co. CA). AS, p. 751. BHD1, p. 374. IFN, p. 203.

Meehan, William E. [actor] (b. New York NY, 1885?–23 Mar 1920 [35], Kingsbridge NY; hasty consumption). m. Violet Pearl. "William E. Meehan," *Variety,* 26 Mar 1920. AS, p. 751. BHD, p. 249.

Meek, Donald [stage/film actor] (b. Glasgow, Scotland, 14 Jul 1878–18 Nov 1946 [68], Los Angeles CA; acute leukemia). m. Belle Walken, 1909, Boston MA. "Donald Meek Dies; Character Actor; Stage, Screen Veteran Had Built Up Following by Taking Milquetoast Roles for Years," *NYT,* 19 Nov 1946, 31:1 (b. 1880; began 1928). "Donald Meek," *Variety,* 20 Nov 1946 (age 66). AS, p. 751. BHD1, p. 374. IFN, p. 203. Truitt, p. 227 (b. 1880).

Meek, Kate [stage/film actress] (b. New York NY, 1838?–4 Sep 1925 [87], New York NY).

"Kate Meek, Actress, Dies at 87 Years; Supported the Old Tragic Stars and in Later Years Drew, Skinner and Maude Adams," *NYT,* 5 Sep 1925, 13:6. "Kate Meek," *Variety,* 9 Sep 1925. BHD, p. 249. IFN, p. 203.

Meeker, George [stage/film actor] (b. Brooklyn NY, 6 Jul 1883–17 Dec 1963 [80], Brooklyn NY). (Universal; MGM; WB; Paramount; Goldwyn; TC-F; PRC; Monogram; Columbia; UA.) AS, p. 751 (b. 1888). IFN, p. 203 ("Meader"). Truitt, p. 228. Robert C. Achorn, "George Meeker; Not Even a Footnote," *CI* (Nov 1996), C14-C15 (b. 1889; d. 1958 [69]; one of the 3 Yankee officers playing cards with Gable in *Gone with the Wind*). George Meeker, , was b. 5 Mar 1904-Aug 1984 [80], CA); George Meador, , was b. 6 Jul 1883-Dec 1963 [80], CA).

Meeker, George [actor] (b. Brooklyn NY, 5 Mar 1904–19 Aug 1984 [80], Carpinteria CA). BHD1, p. 374 (d. Santa Barbara CA).

Meeker, George R. [editor]. No data found. AMD, p. 243. "Pictograph Editor Takes Vacation [at Palm Beach]—Why Not?; From Paramount Picture Corporation Press Department, Chas. E. Moyer," *MPW,* 25 Mar 1916, 1985:2.

Megargee, Lon [artist/titler]. No data found. "Secure Cowboy Artist; Noted Western Painter to Do Art Titles for [Arbuckle's] 'Round-Up,'" *LA Times,* 23 Jan 1920, II, 9.

Megrue, Roi Cooper [playwright/scenarist] (b. New York NY, 12 Jun 1882–27 Feb 1927 [44], New York NY). "Roi Cooper Megrue, Playwright, Dies; Author of 'Under Cover' and 'Under Fire' Began His Career in a Play Brokerage Office," *NYT,* 28 Feb 1927, 19:4. "Roi Cooper Megrue," *Variety,* 2 Mar 1927. AMD, p. 243. BHD2, p. 182. SD, p. 868. "Famous Players Signs Roi Cooper Megrue and Nina Wilcox Putnam to Write Original Plays," *MPW,* 9 Aug 1919, 828.

Mehaffey, Blanche [stage/film actress: Wampas Star, 1924] (aka Joan Alden and Janet Morgan, *née* Blanche Mehaffey Collins, b. Cincinnati OH, 28 Jul 1908–31 Mar 1968 [59], Los Angeles CA). m. Ralph Light. (Universal.) BR, pp. 372–74 (b. 1907; d. LA CA). AMD, p. 243. AS, p. 752. BHD1, p. 374. FSS, p. 206. IFN, p. 203. Ragan 2, p. 1185. '83 WWOS (b. 1907). SD. "Blanche Mehaffey," *Variety,* 21 Nov 1913, 7:2 (toured the Orpheum circuit as a soprano; in vaudeville with Herbert Cyril. "Miss Mehaffey makes a stunning appearance and wears gowns that make the feminine portion of the audience gasp."). "Blanche Mehaffey with Universal," *MPW,* 30 Jan 1926, 416.

Mehnert, Lothar [actor] (b. Berlin, Germany, 21 Feb 1875–30 Nov 1926 [51]). BHD, p. 249. IFN, p. 203.

Mehra, Lal Chand [actor] (b. Amritsar, India, 14 Aug 1897–21 Oct 1980 [83], Los Angeles Co. CA). AS, p. 752 (b. 8 Jun). BHD1, p. 374.

Mehrmann, Helen Alice [stage/film actress] (b. Oakland CA, 14 Jan 1894–23 Sep 1934 [40], Oakland CA). "Helen Alice Mehrmann, *Variety,* 2 Oct 1934. AS, p. 752. BHD1, p. 374. IFN, p. 201.

Mehta, G.K. [director] (b. Lahore, India, 8 Jul 1899). AS, p. 752.

Mei, Lan-Fang [actor] (b. Beijing, China, 1894–8 Aug 1961 [67?], China). AS, p. 752.

Mei, (Lady) Tsen [actress]. No data found. (Goldwyn.) AMD, p. 243. "Lady Mei's Vaudeville Tour Favorably Affects Her Films," *MPW,* 29 Mar 1919, 1825.

Meighan, King (brother of **Thomas Meighan**) [actor]. No data found. AMD, p. 243. "King Meighan Hops Screenward; Columbia Signs Tom's Brother," *MPW,* 13 Feb 1926, 645.

Meighan, Thomas (brother of **King Meighan**) [stage/film actor] (b. Pittsburgh PA, 9 Apr 1879–8 Jul 1936 [57], Great Neck, LI NY; buried in Calvary Cemetery, Queens NY). m. Frances Ring, Jersey City NJ, 1909 (d. 5 Jan 1951). (Began 1914; FP-L; Select; Paramount.) "Thomas Meighan, Movie Actor, Dies; Star of the Silent Pictures Succumbs at Home in Great Neck at Age of 57; Began Career on Stage; 'The Miracle Man' His Greatest Success—Had Appeared in Scores of Roles," *NYT,* 9 Jul 1936, 21:1. "Thomas Meighan," *Variety,* 15 Jul 1936. AMD, p. 243. AS, p. 752. BHD1, p. 375. FFF, p. 127 (b. 1887). FSS, p. 206. GK, pp. 637–50. IFN, p. 204. Katz, p. 795. MH, p. 127. MSBB, p. 1026. Truitt, p. 228. WWS, p. 18. "Thomas Meighan with Lasky," *MPW,* 1 Apr 1916, 70. "Thomas Meighan Continues with Famous Players-Lasky," *MPW,* 22 Sep 1917, 1828. "Two Screen Players Hear Themselves Talk," *MPW,* 22 Dec 1917, 1818. "Thomas Meighan," *MPW,* 6 Jul 1918, 64. "Thomas Meighan to Star in Barrie's 'Admirable Crichton,'" *MPW,* 21 Jun 1919, 1762. "Meighan to Lead in Artcraft Films," *MPW,* 26 Jul 1919, 488. "Meighan Advocates Stage Stock Work as Best Field for Screen Training," *MPW,* 27 Dec 1919, 1178. "Meighan Rescues Pretty Ones at Cleveland Fire," *MPW,* 19 Jun 1920, 1571. "Tom Meighan Visits Chicago; Popular? Yes, But Bashful," *MPW,* 28 Aug 1920, 1169. "Panamans Honor Meighan," *MPW,* 0 Jan 1923, 220. "Meighan Coming Back from Panama," *MPW,* 24 Feb 1923, 808. Charles L. Gartner, "The Kind of Woman I Could Love," *MW,* 1 Mar 1923, 7. "Meighan Corrects Rumor," *MPW,* 14 Apr 1923, 721. Aline O'Brien, "Tommy's Great Gift," *MW,* 9 May 1923, 6–7. Vincent de Sola, "Meighan's Old-Fashioned Morality Makes Him Popular," *MW,* 9 Jun 1923, 18, 29. "Meighan's Father Diess," *MPW,* 17 Nov 1923, 294. Alma Talley, "Those Dangerous Forties," *MW,* 30 Aug 1924, 6–7, 26 (mentions Meighan, Eugene O'Brien, Menjou, Tearle, Sills, Lewis Stone, Tellegen, Fairbanks, Barrymore). "Thumbnail Sketches, No. VI; Thomas Meighan—A Serious-Minded Irishman," *MPC,* May 1925, 36, 83. "Meighan Signs New Contract," *MPW,* 8 Aug 1925, 662. "Thomas Meighan Goes to Ireland to Make Picture," *MPW,* 15 Aug 1925, 765. "Thomas Meighan Receives tirring Ovation in Film," *MPW,* 29 Aug 1925, 934. "Thomas Meighan," *MPW,* 12 Sep 1925, 193. "Thomas Meighan Gives $1,000 Check to Jewish Drive," *MPW,* 14 Nov 1925, 110. Gladys Hall, "He's Tommie to Them All; A Miniature of Meighan—Who's Everybody's Favorite—A Good Mixer and a Regular Fellow," *MPC,* Dec 1926, 53, 81, 83. "Tommy Meighan Back on Coast," *MPW,* 14 May 1927, 98. Robert Grosvenor, "Tom Meighan, Realist," *Cinema Arts,* Nov 1927, 17, 46 ("I find it difficult to get a rôle that I can believe in."). "Meighan to Quit Paramount?," *MPW,* 5 Nov 1927, 7. "Meighan for U.A.?," *MPW,* 26 Nov 1927, 8. "Meighan All Set with Caddo Productions," *MPW,* 10 Dec 1927, 26. DeWitt Bodeen, "Thomas Meighan, 1879–1936," *FIR,* Apr 1974, 193–210. George A. Katchmer, "Dependable Thomas Meighan," *CI,* 118 (Apr 1985), 19–20, 22, C1. Richard E. Braff, "An Index to the Films of Thomas Meighan," *CI,* 191 (May 1991), 47, 56. George A. Katchmer, "Remembering the Great Silents," *CI,* 229 (Jul 1994), 43.

Meinert, Rudolf [director] (b. Vienna, Austria, 28 Sep 1882-ca. 1945 [63?], England). AS, p. 752. BHD2, p. 182.

Meinhard, Carl [actor] (b. Iglau, Germany, 28 Nov 1875–12 Feb 1949 [73], Buenos Aires, Argentina). AS, p. 752.

Meins, Gus[tav] [director/scenarist] (b. Germany, 1893–4 Aug 1940 [47?], Los Angeles CA; suicide). AS, p. 752 (d. La Crescenta CA). BHD2, p. 182.

Meirelkhold, Vsevolode Emilievitch [actor/director] (b. Moscow, Russia, 9 Feb 1874–2 Feb 1940 [], Moscow, Russia). AS, p. 752 ("décédé dans une prison stalinienne").

Meister, Carl [cinematographer] (b. 1898–18 Apr 1934 [36?], Los Angeles CA). BHD2, p. 182.

Meister, Otto L. [actor] (b. 1869?–10 Jul 1944 [75?], Milwaukee WI). (Sennett.) "Otto L. Meister," *Variety,* 19 Jul 1944 (age 73; only film: *Droppington's Family Tree,* Sennett, 1914]. AS, p. 752. BHD, p. 249. Truitt, p. 228.

Melato, Maria [actress] (b. Reggio Emilia, Italy, 16 Oct 1885–24 Aug 1950 [64], Vittoria Apuana a Forte dei Marmi, near Lucca, Italy). JS, p. 283 (in Italian silents from 1914).

Melbourne-Cooper, Arthur [producer[(b. England, 1871–28 Nov 1961 [90?], Cambridge, England). AS, p. 753.

Melchior, Georges [actor] (b. France, 1888). AS, p. 753.

Melchior, Lauritz Lebrecht Hommel [actor/singer] (b. Copenhagen, Denmark, 20 Mar 1890–18 Mar 1973 [82], Santa Monica CA). AS, p. 753.

Mele, Luigi [actor/director] (b. Naples, Italy-d. 1921). JS, p. 284 (in Italian silents from 1913).

Melesh, Alex [actor] (*né* Alexander Melesher, b. Kiev, Ukraine, Russia, 28 Oct 1890–4 Mar 1949 [58], Los Angeles CA). (Columbia.) "Alex Melesh," *Variety,* 16 Mar 1949. AS, p. 753 (b. 21 Oct). BHD1, p. 375. IFN, p. 204. Truitt, p. 228.

Melford, Austin [stage/film actor/scenarist] (b. Alverstoke, England, 24 Aug 1884–19 Aug 1971 [86], London, England). AS, p. 753. BHD, p. 249; BHD2, p. 182. IFN, p. 204.

Melford, George H. [actor/director] (*né* George H. Knauff, b. Rochester NY, 19 Feb 1877–25 Apr 1961 [84], Los Angeles CA; heart attack). m. **Diana Miller** (d. 1927); **Louise** (d. 1942). (Kalem, 1909; FP-L; Paramount.) "George Melford," *Variety,* 3 May 1961. AMD, p. 244. AS, p. 753. BHD2, p. 182. BHD1, p. 375. IFN, p. 204. Katz, pp. 796 (b. 1889). 1921 Directory, p. 271. Spehr, p. 152. Truitt, p. 228. "George Melford with Lasky," *MPW,* 21 Nov 1914, 1054. "Neilan and Melford Continue with Lasky," *MPW,* 12 May 1917, 984. "Melford Rounds Out Three Years," *MPW,* 24 Nov 1917, 1157. "Melford Coming to New York," *MPW,* 5 Oct 1918, 66. "Melford to Make Special Paramount-Artcraft Plays," *MPW,* 27 Dec 1919, 1183. "Melford Discusses Alluring Titles; To Use 'The Cat That Walked Alone,'" *MPW,* 14 Jan 1922, 160. "Melford Signed for Series," *MPW,* 27 Jun 1925, 977. "Diana Miller Dead," *MPW,* 24 Dec 1927, 8. Billy H. Doyle, "Lost Players," *CI,* 157 (Jul 1988), 23.

Melford, Jack [actor/producer] (b. London, England, 5 Sep 1899–22 Oct 1972 [73], London, England). AS, p. 753.

Melford, Louise Leroy [actress] (*née?*, b. 1880?–15 Nov 1942 [62], No. Hollywood CA). m. **George Melford** (d. 1961). (Kalem.) "Louise Melford," *Variety,* 25 Nov 1942. AS, p. 753. BHD, p. 249. IFN, p. 204. Truitt, p. 228.

Melford, Mark [actor/author/playwright] (d. 4 Jan 1914, London, England). "Mark Melford Dead; By Marconi Transatlantic Wireless Telegraph to The New York Times," *NYT,* 5 Jan 1914, 9:6. "Mark Melford," *Variety,* 23 Jan 1914, p. 4. BHD, p. 249.

Melgarejo, Jesus [director] (*né* Jesus Melgarejo Martinez, b. Mexico, 23 Feb 1876–29 Dec 1941 [65], Mexico City, Mexico; auto accident). AS, p. 753. BHD2, p. 182.

Méliès, Gaston (brother of **Georges Méliès**) [executive] (d. Isle of Corsica, Apr 1915). m. (2) **Jeanne D'Alcy** (d. 1956). "Obituary," *MPW,* 24 Apr 1915, 532. AMD, p. 244. BHD2, p. 182. "Valuable Prizes for Scenarios," *MPW,* 31 Jul 1909, 153. "Gaston Méliès in New York," *MPW,* 4 Nov 1911, 368. "A California Fish Story," *MPW,* 11 Nov 1911, 455. "Mr. Gaston Méliès," *MPW,* 27 Jul 1912, 334. "Doings at Los Angeles;...Melies on Trip Around World," *MPW,* 3 Aug 1912, 438. "Méliès Off for the South Seas," *MPW,* 17 Aug 1912, 647. Hanford C. Judson, "Méliès Globe Trotters Reach Tahiti Islands," *MPW,* 24 Aug 1912, 774. Doré Hoffman, "Méliès in the South Seas," *MPW,* 14 Dec 1912, 1061–62. Doré Hoffman, "Picture Making in the South Seas," *MPW,* 28 Dec 1912, 1281–82. Doré Hoffman, "Méliès in New Zealand," *MPW,* 8 Feb 1913, 553–54. Doré Hoffman, "Méliès in Australia," *MPW,* 17 May 1913, 687–88. Doré Hoffman, "The Méliès Company in Java," *MPW,* 21 Jun 1913, 1234–35. "Méliès Makes Categorical Denial," *MPW,* 9 Aug 1913, 613. "Death's Toll for the Decade," *MPW,* 10 Mar 1917, p. 1528.

Méliès, Georges (brother of **Gaston Méliès**) [inventor/producer/actor/director] (*né* Marie Georges Jean Méliès, b. Paris, France, 8 Dec 1861–21 Jan 1938 [76], Orly, France). "Georges Melies; French Motion Picture Producer a Pioneer in Industry," *NYT,* 23 Jan 1938, II, 9:2 (age 77). "Stop Camera Pioneer Discoverer, Melies, Dies Broke in Paris," *Variety,* 26 Jan 1938. AMD, p. 244. AS, p. 753. BHD, p. 249; BHD2, p. 182 (d. Paris). IFN, p. 204. Katz, pp. 796–98. WWVC, pp. 94–95. "Burglars Break in and Steal," *MPW,* 25 May 1907, 188. "Mr. Gaston Méliès's Burglary," *MPW,* 8 Jun 1907, 211. "The Méliès Competitions," *MPW,* 21 Aug 1909, 250. "Georges Méliès"'s Scenario Contest," *MPW,* 25 Sep 1909, 409. "Georges Méliès's Scenario Contest," *MPW,* 2 Oct 1909, 444. "Melies' Suit Near Trial," *Variety,* 16 Oct 1909, 13:1 (against the Motion Picture Patents Co. in the U.S. court at Jersey City NJ).

Méliés, Paul [manufacterer]. No data found. AMD, p. 244. "Paul Méliès Goes to California," *MPW,* 6 Jan 1912, 31.

Meller, Raquel [actress] (*née* Francisca Romana Marques-Lopez, b. Madrid, Spain, 10 Mar 1888–26 Jul 1962 [74], Barcelona, Spain). m. (1) writer Gomez Carillo—div. 1923 (d. 1927); (2) Edmond Salac. "Raquel Meller, Singer, 74, Dead; Spanish Personality in '30's Won International Fame," *NYT,* 27 Jul 1962, 25:1; "Raquel Meller Rites Held," *NYT,* 28 Jul 1962, 19:6 (attended by 100,000 people). "Raquel Meller," *Variety,* 1 Aug 1962. "Gomez Carillo Dead; Noted Parisian Writer Was Former Husband of Raquel Meller," *NYT,* 30 Nov 1927, 25:4 (b. Guatemala–d. 29 Nov 1927 [53], Paris, France). "Raquel's Ex-Mate Dies; Carillo, Divorced Husband, Brought Chanteuse Out," *Variety,* 7 Dec 1927 (age 56). AS, p. 754 (b. Tarazona, Spain). BHD1, p. 375. IFN, p. 204. Truitt, p. 228. W. Adolphe Roberts, "Beautiful Spanish Screen Star Takes Paris by Storm—Will Soon Visit America," *MW,* 19 May 1923, 4–5, 27. Clement Douglas, "Raquel Meller; A New Screen Personality," *MPC,* Jan 1925, 39, 80 (made *Violetas Imperiales* in France).

Mellish, Fuller, Jr. (son of **Fuller Mellish, Sr.**) [actor] (b. London, England, 1895?–8 Feb 1930 [35], Forest Hills, LI NY; cerebral hemorrhage). m. Olive Reeves-Smith. (Paramount.) "Fuller Mellish, Jr.," *Variety,* 12 Feb 1930. AS, p. 754. BHD1, p. 375. IFN, p. 204. Truitt, p. 229.

Mellish, Fuller, Sr. (father of **Fuller Mellish, Jr.**) [stage/film actor] (*né* Harold Arthur Fuller, b. London, England, 3 Jan 1865–7 Dec 1936 [71], New York NY; heart attack). m. Eliza A. Buckley. "Fuller Mellish," *Variety,* 9 Dec 1936. AS, p. 754. BHD1, p. 375. IFN, p. 204. SD, p. 869. Truitt, p. 229.

Mellish, Vera Fuller [stock/stage/film actress] (b. England). (Kalem.) AMD, p. 244. "Briefs of Biography; A Kalem 'Broadway Favorite,'" *NYDM,* 23 Jun 1915, 24:1 ("In speaking of her motion picture debut, Miss Mellish laughingly mentioned the fact that several of her friends had advised her against entering the photoplay field. 'They predicted all sorts of dire things,' the actress laughingly declared. 'I, however, thought of the geneeral stampede on the part of legitimate players to enter the silent drama and decided that if they had no hesitation about accepting motion picture engagements, why should I?'"). "Vera Fuller Mellish," *MPW,* 26 Jun 1915, 2100.

Mellot, Marthe Paul Geneviève [actress] (b. Cosne-sur-Loire, France, 16 Feb 1870 [extrait de naissance no. 24]-14 Aug 1947 [77], Paris, France). AS, p. 754.

Melnati, Umberto [actor] (*né* Raimondo Malnatt, b. Livorno, Italy, 17 Jun 1897–30 Mar 1979 [81], Rome, Italy). AS, p. 754. JS, p. 284 (in Italian silents from 1919).

Melrack, Louis [actor] (*né* Louis Marie Auguste Rossignol, b. Le Mans, France, 12 Dec 1890 [extrait de naissance no. 1052]-24 Apr 1960 [69], Le Mans, France). AS, p. 754.

Melrose, Rhoda [actress] (*née* Rhoda Monasch, b. 1892–25 Feb 1985 [92?], Los Angeles CA). AS, p. 754. BHD1, p. 375.

Mels, Edgar [publicist]. No data found. AMD, p. 244. "Edgar Mels with Lubin," *NYDM,* 14 Jul 1915, 22:3 (as publicity manager). "Mels Is Lubin Publicity Man," *MPW,* 24 Jul 1915, 656.

Melville, Emilie [stage/film actress] (b. Philadelphia PA, 1849–20 May 1932 [82], San Francisco CA). m. Thomas Derby. "Emilie Melville," *Variety,* 24 May 1932 (age 80). AS, p. 754 (b. 1849). BHD1, p. 376 (b. 1852). IFN, p. 204. SD, p. 871 (b. 1852).

Melville, Frederick [actor] (b. Swansea, Wales, 1876–5 Apr 1938 [62?], Shoreham, England). BHD, addendum.

Melville, George Donald [actor] (b. Valparaiso IN, 1857–20 May 1917 [60?], Jersey City NJ). m. Mamie Conway. "George Donald Melville," *Variety,* 25 May 1917. AS, p. 754.

Melville, Rose [stage/film actress] (*née* Rose Smock?, b. Terre Haute IN, 30 Jan 1873–8 Oct 1946 [73], Lake George NY). m. **Frank Minzey,** 1910 (d. 1939); (2) Frank Melville (*né* Frank J. Donald, d. 1908). "Rose Melville, 68, Stage Star, Dead; Played Role of Sis Hopkins More Than 5,000 Times in Course of 18-Year Run," *NYT,* 9 Oct 1946, 27:1. "Rose Melville," *Variety,* 16 Oct 1946. AMD, p. 244. AS, p. 754. BHD, p. 250. IFN, p. 204. SD. Truitt, p. 229. "'Sis Hopkins' for the Screen," *NYDM,* 18 Dec 1915, 25:1 (lured out of retirement, she said, for the fun of leaving the filmed version for future generations. She began her stage career with her sister, Ida Melville, in E.E. Rice's *Little Christopher, Jr.*) "'Sis Hopkins' a Kalem Star," *MPW,* 25 Dec 1915, 2338. "Death Notice," *NYDM,* 8 Jan 1916, p. 8 (of her brother, Alexander Smock). "Sis Hopkins' Experiences," *MPW,* 22 Jan 1916, 585. "Goldwyn Buys 'Sis Hopkins' as Vehicle for Miss Normannd," *MPW,* 23 Nov 1918, 848.

Melville, Capt. Wilbert [director/producer] (b. 6 Nov 1892–15 Nov 1965 [73], Villas, Cape May NJ 08251). (data from NYFHC). (Lubin, LA CA.) AMD, p. 244. AS, p. 754. "Melville Joins Lubin," *MPW,* 23 Sep 1911, 879. "Wilbert Melville," *MPW,* 4 May 1912, 432. "Studio Efficiency," *MPW,* 9 Aug 1913, 624. W.E. Wing, "Xmas on the Coast; News Notes of Activity in Los Angeles Film Circles," *NYDM,* 31 Dec 1913 (constructing permanent studios at 4560 Pasadena Avenue, "in the beautiful arroyo district."). "Efficiency in the Studio," *NYDM,* 16 Sep 1914, 23:4.

Menahan, Jean [actress] (b. 1905–18 May 1963 [58?], Washington DC). AS, p. 754. BHD, p. 250.

Menant, Paul [actor] (b. France, 1891–27 Apr 1934 [43?], Paris, France). AS, p. 754.

Mendaille, Daniel Henri Elie [actor] (b. Tours, France, 17 Nov 1885–17 May 1963 [77], Couilly-Pont-aux-Dames, France [extrait de décès no. 10/1963]). (French-language films in Hollywood; last film: *Lola Montes,* 1955.) AS, p. 755. Waldman, p. 186.

Mendel, Jules [stage/film actor] (aka Jewel Mendel, b. 1875?–17 Mar 1938 [63], Los Angeles CA). m. Teddy La Due. "Jules Mendel," *Variety,* 23 Mar 1938. AS, p. 755. IFN, p. 204.

Mendelssohn, Eleonora (daughter of the composer) [actress] (b. Berlin, Germany, 1899–24 Jan 1951 [50?], New York NY; overdose of barbituates). AS, p. 755.

Mendes, Lothar [actor/producer/director] (b. Berlin, Germany, 19 May 1894–25 Feb 1974 [79], London, England). m. **Dorothy Mackaill,** Oct? 1926, Hollywood CA—div. 1928 (d. 1990). (Essanay; Paramount, Joinville; 1st National; MGM.) AMD, p. 244. AS, p. 755. BHD, p. 250; BHD2, p. 183. IFN, p. 204. Waldman, p. 187. "New German Director Arrives; Reports to Mr. Kane," *MPW,* 3 Apr 1926, 336. "Marriages," *MPW,* 27 Nov 1926, 3. "Mendes Directing," *MPW,* 22 Jan 1927, 275. Harold R. Hall, "Camera Angles—The Bunk; They're Nothing But Trick Photography and Hokum—and Not So New After All," *MPC,* Feb 1927, 18–19, 66, 79.

Mendez, Lucila [actress]. No data found. AMD, p. 244. "Lucila Mendez," *MPW,* 24 Sep 1927, 229.

Mendoza, David [composer] (b. New York NY, 13 Mar 1894–23 May 1975 [81], New York NY). AS, p. 755. BHD2, p. 183.

Ménessier, Henri [art director/director]. (Began 1904; Solax; World; Selznick; Paramount, Joinville.) Spehr, p. 152. Waldman, p. 187.

Menhart, Alfred [actor] (*né* Alfred Mehlhart, b. Munich, Germany, 24 Feb 1899–14 Nov 1955 [56], Munich, Germany; complications from an operation). AS, p. 755.

Menichelli, Dora (sister of **Pina Menichelli,** cousin of **Italia Almirante Manzini**) [actress] (b. Monteleone Calabro, near Catanzaro, Italy, May 1888). m. **Armando Migliari**. JS, p. 285 (in Italian silents from 1914).

Menichelli, Pina (sister of **Dora Menichelli**; cousin of **Italia Almirante Manzini**) [actress/producer] (*née* Giuseppina Menichelli, b. Messina, Sicily, Italy, 10 Jan 1890–29 Aug 1984 [94], Milan, Italy). AMD, p. 245. AS, p. 755 (b. Messina, Italy). BHD1, p. 613. JS, p. 285 (in Italian silents from 1913; "She was the first diva to break away from the "grand gesture' school of acting and use a more naturalistic style."). "Leading Italian Female Star to Produce Four Films Yearly for Audiences Here," *MPW,* 25 Jun 1921, 822.

Menjou, Adolphe Jean (brother of **Henri Menjou**) [actor] (b. Pittsburgh PA, 18 Feb 1890–29 Oct 1963 [73], Beverly Hills CA; chronic hepatitis). With M.M. Misselman, *It Took Nine Tailors* (NY: Whitlessey House, 1948). m. Katherine Tinsley, 20 Apr 1920; (2) **Kathryn Carver**, 1927–33 (d. 1947); (3) Verree Teasdale, 1934 [1904–1987]. (Arrived in the U.S. on 13 May 1912, according to "Yeah?," *Film Fun,* Apr 1926, 49.) "Adolphe Menjou Is Dead at 73; Suave and Debonair Film Star; Mustached Actor Was Known for His Sartorial Elegance—Active in G.O.P. Politics," *NYT,* 30 Oct 1963, 39:2. "Adolph Menjou," *Variety,* 30 Oct 1963. AMD, p. 245. AS, p. 755. BHD1, p. 376. FFF, p. 105. FSS, p. 207. HCH, p. 63. IFN, p. 205. Katz, p. 799. MH, p. 127. Truitt, p. 229. "Lasky Signs Menjou," *MPW,* 8 Mar 1924, 111. Adolphe Menjou, "Why I'm Glad I'm a 'Ladys Man!,'" *MW,* 12 Apr 1924, 13. Mary Winship, "A Man of Pittsburg[h]; A delightful personality sketch of the worldly wise bachelor of 'A Woman of Paris,'" *Photoplay Magazine,* May 1924, 74, 140. Faith Service, "Adolphe Menjou Tallks About Women; Read It and Weep!," *Classic,* Jun 1924, 41, 76. Gladys Hall, "Mrs. Menjou Talks About Adolphe," *MW,* 25 Oct 1924, 10–11, 25–26. "New Stories for Menjou," *MPW,* 25 Jul 1925, 442. "Adolphe Menjou Comes East," *MPW,* 5 Sep 1925, 89. "Menjou Chosen for Role of Satan in Coming Griffith Film [*The Sorrows of Satan*]," *MPW,* 30 Jan 1926, 448:2 (after a six-weeks' search and film tests of "a dozen of the best known actors in America considered suitable for the part..."). Sara Redway, "Women; Adolphe Menjou declares that he really knows nothing about women," *MPC,* Mar 1926, 18–19, 74, 84. Faith Service, "This Love Stuff," *Pictures,* Jun 1926, 55–56, 117–18. "Most Popular," *MPW,* 19 Jun 1926, 2. Gladys Hall, "Adolphe the Elegant; An Impressionable Pen Picture of Menjou, the Master of the Sophisticated Shrug and the Emotional Eyebrow," *MPC,* Sep 1926, 53, 87. "Plans Shaping for Adolphe Menjou," *MPW,* 18 Sep 1926, 176. Elizabeth Fontron, "This Menjou Habit; A short sketch of an actor who is fast becoming an obsession with American movie audiences," *Cinema Arts,* Jun 1927, 21. "Menjou Follows Academy"s Suggestion," *MPW,* 30 Jul 1927, 330.

Menjou, Henri Arthur (brother of **Adolph Menjou**) [actor] (b. Pittsburgh PA, 2 Jun 1891–27 Jan 1956 [64], Sawtelle CA). m. **Fran Pallay** (d. 1981). "Menjou's Brother, 74, Dies," *NYT,* 30 Jan 1956, 27:3. AMD, p. 245. AS, p. 755. BHD, p. 250 (d. West Los Angeles CA). IFN, p. 205. "Another Menjou," *MPW,* 29 Jan 1927, 352.

Menken, Grace [actress] (b. 1892–14 Aug 1978 [86?], New York NY). m. **Bert Lytell** (d. 1954). AS, p. 755.

Menzel, Gerhard [actor/scenarist] (b. Waldenburg, Germany, 1894). AS, p. 755.

Menzies, William Cameron [stage/film art director/director/producer] (b. New Haven CT, 29 Jul 1896–5 Mar 1957 [60], Beverly Hills CA). m. Mignon. "William C. Menzies," *NYT,* 7 Mar 1957, 29:2 (d. Beverly Hills CA). "William C. Menzies," *Variety,* 13 Mar 1957. AS, p. 756. BHD2, p. 183. IFN, p. 205. Katz, pp. 799–800. SD.

Mera, Edith [actress] (*née* Edith Claire Zeibert, b. Bozen, Italy, 7 Jan 1905–24 Feb 1935 [30], Paris, France; liver infection). AS, p. 756.

Mercanton, Jean Louis Georges (son of **Louis Mercanton**) [actor] (b. La Roque d'Atherton, France, 17 May 1920–4 Nov 1947 [27], Neuilly-sur-Seine, France; poliomyelitis [extrait de décès no. 769/1947]). AS, p. 756. BHD1, p. 376. IFN, p. 205.

Mercanton, Louis Samuel Eugène (father of **Jean Mercanton**) [actor/director/scenarist] (b. Switzerland, 1879–29 Apr 1932 [53?], Paris, France; heart attack). AS, p. 756. BHD2, p. 183.

Mercer, Beryl [stage/film actress] (b. Seville, Spain, 13 Aug 1882–28 Jul 1939 [56], Santa Monica CA). m. (1) Maitland S. Pasley; (2) **Holmes Herbert** (d. 1956). "Beryl Mercer, 57, A Noted Actress; Stage and Screen Character Delineator Who Starred in Barrie Playlets Dies; Began Career as Child; British Favorite Made Debut Here in 1906—Mrs. Midget in 'Outward Bound,'" *NYT,* 29 Jul 1939, 15:5 (age 57. "Beryl Mercer," *Variety,* 2 Aug 1939 (age 57; began in *Mother's Boy,* Pathé, 1929). AS, p. 756. BHD1, p. 376. IFN, p. 205. Katz, p. 800. SD. Truitt, p. 229.

Mere, Charles [director/producer/scenarist] (*né* Auguste Charles alexandre Mere, b. Marseilles, France, 29 Jan 1883 [extrait de naissance no. 551/1883]-2 Oct 1970 [87], Paris, France). AS, p. 757.

Meredith, Anne [actress] (d. 8 Jan 1961, London, England). BHD, p. 250.

Meredith, Charles H. [stage/film actor/director] (b. Knoxville TN, 27 Aug 1894–28 Nov 1964 [70], West Los Angeles CA). m. Melba Melsing, Mar 1920, Riverside CA; Mary Blair (d. 1947); Margaret Muse. (FP-L.) "Charles H. Meredith, Director and Early Screen Actor, Dies," *NYT,* 3 Dec 1964, 45:3. "Charles H. Meredith," *Variety,* 9 Dec 1964. AMD, p. 245. AS, p. 757 (b. Knoxville PA). BHD1, p. 377 (b. Knoxville PA). IFN, p. 205. SD. Truitt, pp. 229–30. "Wedding in Filmland," *MPW,* 3 Apr 1920, 69.

Meredith, Joan [actress] (b. 1885–15 Feb 1945 [59?], New York NY). AMD, p. 245. BHD, p. 250. "Joan Meredith in Walsh Film," *MPW,* 16 May 1925, 348. "Joan Me0

redith Signed," *MPW,* 22 Aug 1925, 831. "Meredith with Walsh," *MPW,* 30 Jan 1926, 450.

Meredith, Lois [stage/film actress] (b. 1898). (General Film Co. [Knickerbocker Star Features]; Morosco-Paramount; Lasky.) AMD, p. 245. MSBB, p. 1038, 1040. "Morosco Producing 'Help Wanted,'" *MPW,* 27 Mar 1915, 1905. "Rolfe Gets Stars; Lois Meredith and Max Figman Among Latest Signed by Metro Ally," *NYDM,* 21 Apr 1915, 22:1. "Lois Meredith with Balboa," *MPW,* 4 Mar 1916, 1456. "Lois Meredith Heads Own Company," *MPW,* 30 Jun 1917, 2096. "Lois Meredith Supports Barrymore," *MPW,* 22 Jun 1918, 1733.

Meredyth, Bess [stage/film actress/scenarist] (*née* Helen MacGlashan, b. Buffalo NY, 12 Feb 1889–13 Jul 1969 [80], Woodland Hills CA). m. **Wilfred Lucas** (d. 1940); **Michael Curtiz** (d. 1962). (Biograph.) "Bess Meredyth," *Variety,* 16 Jul 1969. AMD, p. 245. AS, p. 757. BHD, p. 250; BHD2, p. 183. FDY, p. 433. IFN, p. 205 (age 79). Katz, p. 801. SD. Truitt, p. 230 (d. 6 Jul). "Series of Comedy-Dramas for Miss Meredyth," *MPW,* 6 Jun 1914, 1419. Tom Waller, "Bess Meredyth," *MPW,* 2 Jul 1927, 14–15.

Meredyth, Joan [actress: Wampas Star, 1925] (d. 1980 [70s]). Ragan 2, p. 1134 *see* **Meredith, Joan**

Merelle, Claude [actress] (*née* Lise Henriette Marie Laurent, b. Bois-Colombe, France, 17 Apr 1888 [extrait de naissance no. E090]). AS, p. 757.

Meriel [actor] (*né* Paul Lornier, b. London, England, 1875). AS, p. 757.

Merivale, Bernard [scenarist] (b. Newcastle-upon-Tyne, England, 15 Jul 1882–12 May 1939 [56], London, England). BHD2, p. 183.

Merivale, Philip [stage/film actor] (b. Rehutia, Manickpur, India, 2 Nov 1880–12 Mar 1946 [65], Los Angeles CA; heart ailment). m. (1) Viva Birkett; **Gladys Cooper**, 1937, Chicago (d. 1971). "Philip Merivale, Noted Actor, Dies; Star of Stage and Screen on 2 Continents, 59—Named 2nd Most Handsome Man in U.S.," *NYT,* 14 Mar 1946, 25:1 (age 59). "Philip Merivale," *Variety,* 20 Mar 1946 (age 59). AS, p. 757 (b. 1886). BHD1, p. 377 (b. 1886). IFN, p. 205 (b. 1886). Truitt, p. 230.

Merkel, Una [stage/film actress/stand-in for **Lillian Gish**] (b. Covington KY, 10 Dec 1903–2 Jan 1986 [82], Los Angeles CA). m. Ronald L. Burla. (Film debut: *The Fifth Horseman,* 1924; Griffith.) "Una Merkel Dies at Age of 82; From Silent Films to a Tony," *NYT,* 5 Jan 1986, 24:4. "Una Merkel," *Variety,* 15 Jan 1986. AS, p. 757. BHD1, p. 377. Katz, p. 801. SD.

Merkel, Louis [stage/film midget actor] (b. ca. 1878). No other data found. "Midget Won by Jiu-Jitsu; Chorus Girl Hales Him to Court—Then Forgives Merkel," *NYT,* 4 Mar 1905, 24:6 (47 inches tall; age 27. Beatrice Wilson and other chorus girls were taunting and cuddling Merkel until he leaped on Wilson's shoulders and struck her several blows in the face. He was dragged from her and soothed before the play could go on. She thought she was the victim of jiu-jitsu. "Merkel, she added, had aimed a stage cannon at her the night before." The Lilliputian apologied to her in court; "Miss Wilson bent down and accepted it, and the Magistrate dismissed the matter."). "First Headline Comedy [*Pee-Wee's Courtship*]," *NYDM,* 23 Jun 1915, 21:2.

Merkert, Delbert (Bert) [actor] (b. 1875–28 Jun 1953 [78?], North East PA). BHD, p. 250.

Merkle, Fred [actor] (b. Watertown WI, 10

Dec 1888–2 Mar 1956 [67], Daytona Beach FL). BHD, p. 250.

Merky [actor] (*né* Pierre Charpy, b. Paris, France, 8 Jan 1889–ca. 1960 [71?]). AS, p. 757.

Merkyl, Wilmuth [actor] (aka John Merkyl, b. IA, 2 Jun 1885–1 May 1954 [68], Los Angeles CA; coronary occlusion). AMD, p. 245. AS, p. 757. BHD1, p. 377. IFN, p. 205. "Kalem's Star Series; Wilmuth Merkyl Added to List of Stars to Be Seen in 'Broadway Favorites,'" *NYDM*, 14 Apr 1915, 22:4. "New Stars for Kalem," *MPW*, 24 Apr 1915, 560. "Wilmuth Merkyl, New Petrova Leading Man," *MPW*, 26 Feb 1916, 1305.

Merland, Henry J. [actor/cinematographer] (b. OH, 7 Aug 1892–9 Dec 1955 [63], Los Angeles CA). (Paramount, 1920.) "Henry J. Merland," *Variety*, 14 Dec 1955. AS, p. 757 (b. 1882). BHD2, p. 183.

Merlo, Anthony J. [actor] (b. Italy, 1 Oct 1886–25 Apr 1976 [89], Woodland Hills CA). AS, p. 758. BHD1, p. 377. IFN, p. 205. Barry Brown, "Letter," *FIR*, Oct 1977, 507.

Merollo, Ralph [cinematographer] (b. 1880–23 Jan 1943 [62?], Los Angeles CA). BHD2, p. 183.

Merrall, Mary [actress] (*née* Mary Lloyd, b. Liverpool, England, 5 Jan 1890–31 Aug 1973 [83], London, England). AS, p. 758. BHD1, p. 377.. IFN, p. 205.

Merriam, Charlotte [actress] (b. Fort Sheridan IL, 5 Apr 1906–10 Jul 1972 [66], Studio City CA). m. **Rex Lease** (d. 1966). (Began at age 13; Vitagraph; Christie.) AMD, p. 245. AS, p. 758. BHD1, p. 377 (b. 1904). Ragan 2, p. 1136. "Charlotte Merriam in 'The Honey Bee,'" *MPW*, 1 May 1920, 698. "Charlotte Merriam," *MPW*, 25 Apr 1925,801. "The Christie Comedy Girls," *Cinema Arts*, Nov 1926, 16 (photo).

Merriam, Harold A. [actor] (b. 1876–21 Dec 1937 [61], Elmsford NY). BHD, p. 250. IFN, p. 205.

Merrick, George [film editor/scenarist] (b. 1884?–16 Dec 1964 [80], Los Angeles CA). "George Merrick," *Variety*, 23 Dec 1964. BHD2, p. 183. FDY, p. 433.

Merrick, Leonard [scenarist] (b. 1864–7 Aug 1939 [75?], London, England). BHD2, p. 183.

Merrick, Tom [actor] (b. Hanford CA, 1895?–26 Apr 1927 [32], Los Angeles CA; shot by wife). "Hollywood's 2d Killing Within Week; Tom Merrick Shot by Wife—Gin Basis of Jealous Rage," *Variety*, 4 May 1927. AS, p. 758 (b. 1892). BHD, p. 250 (b. 1894; d. 24 Apr).

Merrill, Frank [actor] (b. Newark NJ, 21 Mar 1893–12 Feb 1966 [72], Los Angeles CA). "Frank Merrill," *Variety*, 23 Feb 1966. AS, p. 758. BHD, p. 250. IFN, p. 205. Truitt, p. 230. Dorothy Donnell, "Poverty Row; Poverty Row is the land of the free producers, home of the brave-hearted, the independents, the states righters, the little 'uns," *MPC*, Apr 1925, 16–17, 78–79, 91–92 (some of the actors who worked on Poverty Row include Merrill, Fay Wray, Violet La Plante and William Lowrey).

Merrill, Richard [actor/scenarist] (b. 1923?–13 Sep 1998 [75], Southbury CT). m. actress Jan Miller, ca. 1963. "Other Deaths; Richard Merrill," *PP-G*, 26 Sep 1998, A-11:1.

Merrill, Walter (Wally) [actor] (b. Bangor PA, 22 Apr 1906–10 Jan 1985 [78], Los Angeles CA). AMD, p. 245. BHD1, p. 378. "Merrill Goes West," *MPW*, 12 Jun 1926, 541. "Walter Merrill Signed by Warner," *MPW*, 7 Aug 1926, 339.

Merritt, George [actor] (b. London, England, 10 Dec 1890–27 Aug 1977 [86], London, England). AS, p. 758. AS, p. 758.

Merry, Eleanor [actress] (b. 11 Jun 1906–28 Aug 1991 [85], Santa Monica CA). m. **Tom Moore** (d. 1955). (Columbia; Fox.) "Eleanor Moore," *Variety*, 30 Sep 1991, p. 83. AS, p. 758. BHD1, p. 378.

Mersereau, Claire [actress] (sister of **Violet Mersereau**) (b. New York NY, 25 Aug 1894 [Birth Certificate Index No. 43124 (Clara M. Mersereau)]-26 Jun 1982 [87], Cloisters of Mission Hills, San Diego CA; bronchial pneumonia). m. Mr. Krieger. (Nestor.) AMD, p. 245. AS, p. 758. BHD1, p. 613 (b. 20 Sep). Spehr, p. 152. "Clare Mersereau," *MPW*, 1 Jul 1911, 1500. (Her death certificate has 20 Sep 1894 as a birth date.)

Mersereau, Verna [stage/film dancer/actress]. No data found. AMD, p. 245. "Competes with Herself; Mlle. Mersereau in Vaudeville Act, Opposed by Kalem Film [*The Dance of Death*] in Which She Appears," *NYDM*, 6 May 1914, 31:2. "Two New Universalites," *MPW*, 29 Sep 1917, 1971.

Mersereau, Violet, "The Child Wonder" (sister of **Claire Mersereau**) [stage/film actress] (b. New York NY, 2 Oct 1892–12 Nov 1975 [83], Plymouth MA). (Biograph, 1909; Horsley; Nestor; Imp; Bison; FP-L; Universal; Fox; Lee-Bradford.) AMD, p. 245. AS, p. 758 (1894–1961, NYC). BHD1, p. 613. MSBB, p. 1038. Spehr, p. 152. "Violet Mersereau," *MPW*, 1 Jul 1911, 1500. "Violet Mersereau—Imp Star," *MPW*, 26 Dec 1914, 1852. "Gossip of the Studios," *NYDM*, 19 May 1915, 26:1 (corrected the printed report that it was Claire Mersereau, not she, "who recently sued the Solax Company successfully."). "Violet Mersereau," *MPW*, 27 Nov 1915, 1641. "Mersereau and Van Loan to Lead March," *MPW*, 17 Mar 1917, 1784. "Violet Mersereau Renews Contract," *MPW*, 16 Jun 1917, 1806. "Big Receptions Greet Miss Mersereau," *MPW*, 21 Jul 1917, 462. "Violet Mersereau Honored," *MPW*, 18 Jan 1919, 330. "Violet Mersereau Leads in Contest," *MPW*, 22 Mar 1919, 1648. "Violet Mersereau Claims the Honors," *MPW*, 12 Apr 1919, 228 (popularity contest). "Violet Mersereau Signs with H&H," *MPW*, 7 Jun 1919, 1480. "Violet Mersereau Denies Report," *MPW*, 29 May 1920, 1218. "Fox Actress Comments on Work Abroad," *MPW*, 4 Feb 1922, 503. 'C.C. Burr Signs Diminutive Star," *MPW*, 18 Nov 1922, 240. John E. Thayer, "Elsie Albert," *CFC*, 56 (Fall 1977), 56 (died in 1961?).

Merson, Billy [actor] (*né* William Henry Thompson, b. Nottingham, England, 29 Mar 1881–25 Jun 1947 [66], London, England). "Billy Merson," *Variety*, 2 Jul 1947, p. 55. AS, p. 758. BHD1, p. 378. IFN, p. 205.

Merson, Isabel [actress] (b. 1883–19 May 1952 [69?], New York NY). AS, p. 758.

Merton, Collette (sister of dancer Mona Merton) [actress] (née Colette Helene Mazzoletti, b. New Orleans LA, 7 Mar 1907–24 Jul 1968 [61], Los Angeles CA; found dead). (Universal's two-reel *Collegians* series.) "Collette Merton," *Variety*, 251, 7 Aug 1968, 63:3. AS, p. 758. BHD1, p. 378. IFN, p. 205.

Merwin, Anne [scenarist] (*née?*). No data found. m. **Bannister Merwin** (d. 1922). Edward Azlant, "Screenwriting for the early silent film: forgotten pioneers, 1897–1911," *Film History*, 9 (1997), 244.

Merwin, Bannister (brother of **Samuel Merwin**) [director/scenarist] (d. 22 Feb 1922, London, England). m. **Anne**. AMD, p. 245. BHD2, p. 183. Epes Winthrop Sargent, "The Photoplaywright," *MPW*, 23 May 1914, 1109. "Bannister Merwin to Produce," *MPW*, 23 Sep 1916, 1975. "Obituary," *MPW*, 1 Apr 1922, 458.

Merwin, Samuel (brother of **Bannister Merwin**) [writer]. No data found. AMD, p. 245. "Samuel Bannister Lauds Vignola for Picturization of Story," *MPW*, 28 Aug 1920, 1154. "Samuel Merwin, Newest Paramount Author, Finds Films Great Story-Telling Medium," *MPW*, 12 Feb 1921, 802.

Mery, Andrée [actress] (*née* Andrée Meriaux, b. France, 28 Dec 1876). AS, p. 758.

Merzbach, Paul [director/producer/scenarist] (b. Austria, 27 Nov 1888–1947 [58?], Austria). AS, p. 759. FDY, p. 433.

Mescall, John J. [cinematographer] (b. Litchfield IL, 10 Jan 1899). AMD, p. 245. AS, p. 759. FDY, p. 463. Katz, p. 802. "DeMille Signs Mescal," *MPW*, 7 Aug 1926, 2.

Mesguich, Felix [cinematographer] (b. Algeria, 16 Sep 1871–25 Apr 1949 [77], Paris, France). AS, p. 759. BHD2, p. 183.

Messinger, Buddy (brother of **Gertrude Messinger**) [actor/assistant director] (*né* Melvin Joe Messinger, b. San Francisco CA, 26 Oct 1907–25 Oct 1965 [57], Los Angeles CA). AMD, p. 246 (Messenger). AS, p. 759. BHD1, p. 378. IFN, p. 205. MH, p. 127. Truitt, p. 230 (b. 1909). "Buddy Messenger Signed," *MPW*, 18 Nov 1922, 270. "Buddy Messenger's Comeback at 'U,'" *MPW*, 11 Jun 1927, 431. Billy H. Doyle, "Lost Players," *CI*, 174 (Dec 1989), C12.

Messinger, Frank [unit manager at Metro] (b. 1891?–19 Dec 1939 [48], Hollywood CA; self-inflicted bullet wound; "despondent over ill health"). "Frank Messinger," *Variety*, 27 Dec 1939.

Messinger, Gertrude (sister of **Buddy Messinger**) [actress] (b. Spokane WA, 28 Apr 1911–9 Nov 1995 [84], Woodland Hills CA). (Universal, 1915; Fox; RKO.) AS, p. 759. BHD1, p. 378. BR, pp. 378–82. Ragan 2, p. 1137. Ray Nielsen, "Gertrude Messinger of 'Anne of Green Gables,'" *CI*, 207 (Sep 1992), 44–45.

Messinger, Josephine [actress] (b. 1885–3 Mar 1968 [82?], Los Angeles CA). AS, p. 759. BHD, p. 250.

Messinger, Marie [actress] (b. Coeur D'Alene ID, 27 Nov 1905–4 Apr 1987 [81], Woodland Hills CA). AS, p. 759. BHD1, p. 613.

Messiter, Eric [actor] (b. England, 1892–13 Sep 1960 [68?], London, England; heart attack). AS, p. 759.

Messlein, John [actor] (b. 1899–25 Aug 1920 [21], Weehawken NJ; auto accident). AS, p. 759. BHD, p. 251. IFN, p. 205.

Messmer, Otto [animator/creator of Felix the Cat, 1919] (b. Union City NJ, 16 Aug 1892–28 Oct 1983 [91], Holy Name Hospital, Teaneck NJ; heart attack). m. Anne Mason (daughters Doris and Jeanne). (Universal, 1915.) Douglas C. McGill, "Otto Messmer Is Dead at 91; Created 'Felix the Cat' Films," *NYT*, 29 Oct 1983, 32 ("In 1915, he went to work for the Universal Film Manufacturing Company in Fort Lee as a scenery painter. His drawings soon came to the attention of Mr. [Pat]

Sullivan [d. 1933], and at the producer's New York studio, Felix the Cat was born and thrived."). AS, p. 759. BHD2, p. 183. John Canemaker, "Otto Messmer and Felix the Cat," *CFC,* 55 (Summer, 1977), 20–22.

Messter, Oskar Edward [inventor/director/producer] (b. Berlin, Germany, 21 Nov 1866–7 Dec 1943 [77], Tegernsee, Germany). AS, p. 759.

Mestayer, Harry [stage/film actor] (b. San Francisco CA, 29 Feb...). AMD, p. 246. AS, p. 759. (Selig.) "Harry Mestayer," *MPW,* 30 Jan 1915, 676. "Mestayer Signs with Selig," *NYDM,* 17 Mar 1915, 24:3 (to appear in *The Millionaire's Baby,* Selig-Polyscope). "Harry Mestayer to Leave Selig," *MPW,* 15 Apr 1916, 425.

Mestel, Jacob [actor/scenarist] (b. Poland, 1884–5 Aug 1958 [74?], New York NY). AS, p. 759.

Metcalfe, Earl Keeney [actor/director] (b. Newport KY, 11 Mar 1889–26 Jan 1928 [38], Burbank CA; fall from a plane). (Lubin.) "Earl Metcalf," *Variety,* 1 Feb 1928. AMD, p. 246. AS, p. 759 (b. 3 Feb). BHD, p. 251; BHD2, p. 183 (b. 1890). IFN, p. 205. MH, p. 127. Truitt, p. 230. "Earl Metcalfe," *MPW,* 31 Jan 1914, 533. "Earl Metcalfe's Mother Dies," *NYDM,* 8 Jul 1914, 22:4 (Mrs. Cora B. Metcalfe, d. 21 Jun 1914 [56], Cincinnati OH). "Earl Metcalfe Loses His Mother," *MPW,* 18 Jul 1914, 443. "Earl Metcalfe," *MPW,* 28 Nov 1914, 1214. "In the Studios," *NYDM,* 5 May 1915, 21:2 (suffered cuts and bruises in a screen fight with Joseph Kaufman while filming *Darkness Before Dawn,* Lubin). "Earl Metcalfe," *MPW,* 7 Oct 1916, 89. "The Roll of Honor," *MPW,* 15 Sep 1917, 1676. "Earl Metcalfe to Direct Paramount-Flagg Comedies," *MPW,* 1 Mar 1919, 1178. "Metcalfe Receives Citation," *MPW,* 5 Jul 1919, 62. "Earl Metcalfe to Play Leading Role in 'Battler,'" *MPW,* 2 Aug 1919, 693. George Katchmer, "Remembering the Great Silence," *CI,* 200 (Feb 1992), 32.

Metcalfe, Edward [actor] (b. 1867?–2 Apr 1951 [84], Brentwood, LI NY). "Edward Metcalfe," *Variety,* 4 Apr 1951. AS, p. 759. BHD1, p. 378. IFN, p. 206.

Metcalfe, Lyne S. [scenarist]. No data found. AMD, p. 246. "Metcalfe Now Goldwynn-Bray Industrial Scenario Writer," *MPW,* 10 Apr 1920, 287.

Methling, Svend [actor/director/scenarist] (b. Copenhagen, Denmark, 1 Oct 1891). AS, p. 760.

Metz, Albert [actor] (b. 1886–20 Aug 1940 [54], North Hollywood CA). AS, p. 760. BHD1, p. 378. IFN, p. 206.

Metzetti, Otto [stuntman/actor] (b. 1891–31 Jan 1949 [57?], Los Angeles CA). AS, p. 760. BHD1, p. 378. IFN, p. 206.

Metzetti, Victor [actor] (b. 1895–21 Aug 1949 [54?], Los Angeles CA). AS, p. 760. BHD1, p. 378.

Metzler, Fred L. [executive] (b. 1887–4 Nov 1964 [77?], Los Angeles CA). BHD2, p. 183.

Metzner, Erno [director] (b. Szabadka, Hungary, 25 Feb 1892–25 Sep 1953 [61], Los Angeles CA). AS, p. 760.

Meusel, Bob [actor] (b. San Jose CA, 19 Jul 1896–28 Nov 1977 [81], Downey CA). BHD1, p. 378.

Meusel, Emil (Irish) [actor] (b. Oakland CA, 9 Jun 1893–1 Mar 1963 [69], Long Beach CA). BHD1, p. 378.

Meyer, Frank [executive] (b. St. Louis MO, 1877–16 Aug 1956 [79?], Bronxville NY). BHD2, p. 184.

Meyer, George W. [composer] (*né* Joseph-Louis Mundviller, b. Boston MA, 1 Jan 1885–28 Aug 1959 [74], New York NY; from burns and suffocation; fell asleep while smoking). m. (1) Grace; (2) Kathleen. "'For Me and My Gal' [1917, with Edgar Leslie] Composer Dies in a Fire in His Hotel Room; George W. Meyer Was 74—Parade of Hits Began in 1909 with 'Lonesome' [1909]," *NYT,* 29 Aug 1959, 38:2. "George W. Meyer," *Variety,* 2 Sep 1959 (wrote *Everything Is Peaches Down in Georgia; Mandy, Make Up Your Mind; Red Hot Hannah from Savannah*). BHD2, p. 184.

Meyer, Greta [actress] (b. Germany, 7 Aug 1883–8 Oct 1965 [82], Gardena CA). BHD1, p. 379.

Meyer, Hyman [actor] (b. San Francisco CA, 1875?–7 Oct 1945 [70?], Los Angeles CA). "Hyman Meyer," *Variety,* 10 Oct 1945. BHD1, p. 379. Truitt, p. 231.

Meyer, Johannes [actor/director] (b. Brieg, Silesia, Poland, 13 Aug 1888–25 Jan 1976 [87], Marburg-Lahn, Germany). "Johannes Meyer," *Variety,* 3 Mar 1976, p. 94. BHD1, p. 378 (b. Brzeg, Poland); BHD2, p. 184. IFN, p. 206.

Meyer, Joseph [composer] (b. Modesto CA, 1893–22 Jun 1987 [93?], New York NY). AS, p. 760. BHD2, p. 184.

Meyer, Otto [stage/film actor] (b. Germany, 1851–8 Nov 1921 [70], Jamaica, LI NY). "Otto Meyer," *Variety,* 18 Nov 1921, 20:5. AMD, p. 246. BHD, p. 251. "Méliès' Cowboy a Contest Winner," *MPW,* 6 Apr 1912, 54. "Otto Meyer," *MPW,* 4 May 1912, 424.

Meyer, Torben [actor] (b. Copenhagen, Denmark, 1 Dec 1884–22 May 1975 [90], Woodland Hills CA; bronchial pneumonia). (Began in mid-1920s). "Torben Meyer," *Variety,* 28 May 1975. AS, p. 761. BHD, p. 251. IFN, p. 206.

Meyerkhold, Vsevolod Emil [actor/director] (b. Penza, Russia, 9 Feb 1874–2 Feb 1942 [67], Moscow, Russia). AS, p. 761 (d. 1940). BHD2, p. 184.

Meyers, Maurice [publicist]. No data found. AMD, p. 246. "Maurice Meyers with Rogers," *MPW,* 19 Jul 1919, 372.

Meyroos, Emily [theater pianist] (b. 1863?–7 Mar 1963 [100], Chicago IL). m. John Meyroos. "Emily Meyroos," *Variety,* 230, 13 Mar 1963, 70:3 ("In 1898, Mrs. Meyroos played at the Paris Nickelodeon at Harrison and State streets, where she accompanied the firstrun of 'The Great Train Robbery.'").

Miano, Andrea [actor/producer/director/cinematographer] (b. Genoa, Italy, 22 May 1909–22 Jul 1987 [78], Genoa, Italy [extrait de décès no. 2838]). AS, p. 761. JS, p. 288 (in Italian silents from 1924).

Michaels, Edna [publicist]. No data found. AMD, p. 246. "Edna Michaels Regains Health," *MPW,* 22 May 1920, 1056.

Michaud, André [actor] (b. Paris, France, 6 Oct 1892). AS, p. 761.

Micheaux, Oscar Devereaux [writer/director/producer] (b. Metropolis, near Cairo IL, 2 Jan 1884–1 Apr 1951 [67], Charlotte NC). m. twice: Alice B. Russell, 1929. (Micheaux Book and Film Co., Chicago IL.) Donald Bogle, *Toms, Coons, Mulattoes, Mammies, & Bucks; An Interpretive History of Blacks in American Films* (NY: Continuum, 1989), pp. 109–16. AS, p. 762. BHD2, p. 184. Richard Gehr, "One-Man Show," *American Film,* May 1991, 34–39. Wheeler W. Dixon, *The "B" Director; A Biographical Directory* (Metuchen NJ: The Scarecrow Press, Inc., 1985), pp. 366–67 (d. 1952). Charlene Regester, "The misreading and rereading of African American filmmaker Oscar Micheaux; A crititical review of Micheaux scholarship," *Film History,* VII (Winter 1995). Karen Burroughs Hannsberry, "Oscar Micheaux: Race Movie Pioneer," *CI,* 248 (Feb 1996), C4. J. Ronald Green, "Micheaux v. Griffith," *Griffithiana,* 60/61 {Oct 1997), 33–49. Monica L. Haynes, "Looking back at black films; Movies from another era unreel from the archives for series on cable," *PP-G,* 30 Jun 1998, E1–E2 (a 29-film series beginning 1 Jul 1998 on the Turner Classic Movie Channel. To include *The Symbol of the Unconquered,* 1921, recently discovered in a Belgium film archive.). Ervin Dyer, "Filmmaker Micheaux countered stereotypes of black America," *Pittsburgh Post-Gazette,* 2 Feb 2000, E1–E2 (film festival of Micheaux' films to be shown in Pittsburgh PA).

Michel, Gaston [actor] (b. France, 1856–15 Nov 1921 [65?], Lisbon, Portugal). AS, p. 762. BHD, p. 251.

Michel, Germaine [actress] (b. Paris, France, 7 Nov 1892–9 Jan 1976 [83], Clichy-la-Garenne, France [extrait de décès no. 17/63/1976]). AS, p. 762.

Michelena, Beatriz (sister of **Vera Michelena**) [soprano/actress] (b. New York NY, 22 Feb 1890–10 Oct 1942 [52], San Francisco CA). m. **George E. Middleton** (d. 1967). For a discussion of her career, *see* Geoffrey Bell, *The Golden Gate and the Silver Screen* (NY: Cornwall Books, 1984). "Beatriz Michelena," *NYT,* 12 Oct 1942, 17:4. "Beatrice Michelena," *Variety,* 21 Oct 1942. AMD, p. 246. AS, p. 762. BHD, p. 251. IFN, p. 206. Truitt, p. 231. "Prima Donna Film Star; Beatriz Michelena to Be Featured in California Company Pictures," *NYDM,* 11 Feb 1914, 32? "Beatriz Michelena," *MPW,* 28 Feb 1914, 1071 (signed by the California Motion Picture Corporation). "A Prima Donna of the Screen; An Interview with Beatriz Michelena, a Picture Recruit from the Operatic Stage," *NYDM,* 1 Jul 1914, 25:1. "Picture Player Has Narrow Escape," *MPW,* 29 Aug 1914, 1216. Cover of *NYDM,* 9 Dec 1914. "Michelena Rejects Big Offer," *NYDM,* 10 Feb 1915, 26:2 (Her film *Mignon* was shown at the St. Francis Hotel, SF CA, and the audience prevailed upon her to sing. She was asked to appear with the film for a week but her commitment to the California Motion Picture Corp. required her presence to film *Lily of Poverty Flat.*) "Beatriz Michelena Returns to Work," *MPW,* 13 Feb 1915, 998. "Screen Star in Accident," *NYDM,* 16 Jun 1915, 22:2 (she was thrown from a bucking horse. The back of her head hit a large rock; she was unconscious for an hour, sustaining only an ugly bruise. A mere three scenes more were needed to complete *A Phyllis of the Sierras;* "Realizing the exigencies of the case, the injured star, with the proverbial pluck of her profession, insisted on returning to work in the afternoon, and the picture was done before evening."). "A Closeup of Beatriz Michelena," *MPW,* 4 Sep 1915, 1656. "Beatriz Michelena Studies Hypnotism," *MPW,* 16 Oct 1915, 471. "Beatriz Fights Fake Schools," *MPW,* 13 May 1916, 1143. "Miss Michelena Leaves California Corporation," *MPW,* 13 Jan 1917, 211. Margaret I. MacDonald, "Beatriz

Michelena Speaks," *MPW,* 7 Apr 1917, 105. "Beatriz Michelena Heads Own Company," *MPW,* 11 Aug 1917, 961. "Michelena Back in Big Attraction," *MPW,* 22 Mar 1919, 1633. "Michelena Has Two More Films and Plans for Three," *MPW,* 29 Mar 1919, 1796. George Katchmer, "Remembering the Great Silents," *CI,* 240 (Jun 1995), 46–47.

Michelena, Vera (sister of **Beatriz Michelena**) [stage/film actress] (b. New York NY, 16 Jun 1884–26 Aug 1961 [77], Bayside, LI NY [Death Certificate Index No. 9977; M.E. Case No. 2806]). m. Paul Schindler—div. Oct 1917, Brooklyn NY; **Harry Spingler** (d. 1953); Fred Hillebrand. "Vera Michelena," *NYT,* 27 Aug 1961, 85:1 (originated Balling the Jack dance). "Vera Michelena," *Variety,* 30 Aug 1961. AMD, p. 246. AS, p. 762. BHD, p. 251. IFN, p. 206. Ragan 2, p. 879. SD. Truitt, p. 231. "Vera Michelena with Ocean Film," *MPW,* 18 Dec 1915, 2190. "Miss Michelena Has Divorce," *Variety,* 19 Oct 1917, p. 7.

Michell, A. Danson [publicist]. No data found. AMD, p. 246. "Mr. Michell Goes to Excelsior," *MPW,* 18 Jul 1914, 435.

Michin, Boris Alexandrovich [director[(b. Russia, 1881–11 Apr 1963 [81?], Russia). AS, p. 762.

Micon, Sabino Antonio [director] (Bilbao, Spain, 1890). AS, p. 762.

Middlemass, Robert M. [playwright/scenarist] (b. New Britain CT, 3 Sep 1883–11 Sep 1949 [66], Los Angeles CA). "Richard M. Middlemass," *Variety,* 21 Sep 1949 (d. 10 Sep; age 65). AMD, p. 246. AS, p. 762 (d. 10 Sep). BHD1, p. 379. IFN, p. 206. "Middlemass Supports Hale Hamilton," *MPW,* 21 Sep 1918, 1726 (b. Boston MA).

Middleton, Charles B. [actor] (b. Elizabethtown KY, 3 Oct 1878–22 Apr 1949 [70], Los Angeles CA; heart attack). m. **Leora** Spellmeyer (d. 1954). (Film debut: *A Man of Peace,* 1928, short.) "Charles B. Middleton," *NYT,* 25 Apr 1949, 23:2. "Charles B. Middleton," *Variety,* 27 Apr 1949. AS, p. 762. BHD1, p. 379 (b. 7 Oct 1874). IFN, p. 206 (b. 7 Oct 1879). Truitt, p. 231. Alan P. Spater, "Charles B. Middleton; The Screen's Most Awesome Villain Remembered," *CI,* 104 (Feb 1984), C8; 104 (Mar 1984), 33–35 (filmography); 105 (Apr 1984), 60–61. Alan P. Spater, "Charles B. Middleton," *CI,* 126 (Dec 1985), C17-C18 (includes more filmography).

Middleton, Edwin [director/scenarist]. No data found. AMD, p. 246. "Director Middleton to Make Masterpictures," *MPW,* 15 Jan 1916, 400. "Edwin Middleton Directing 'The Sorceress,'" *MPW,* 12 Feb 1916, 961. "Edwin Middleton to Direct Gaumont's Three-Act Plays," *MPW,* 10 Jun 1916, 1860.

Middleton, George E. [playwright/director/scenarist] (b. Paterson NJ, 27 Oct 1880–23 Dec 1967 [87], Washington DC). m. Fola La Follette, 1911; **Beatriz Michelena** (d. 1942). (FP-L; Fox.) *These Things Are Mine—The Autobiography of a Journeyman Playwright* (1947). "George Middleton, A Playwright, 87; Former Head of Dramatists' Guild, 87, Is Dead," *NYT,* 24 Dec 1967, 49:1. "George Middleton," *Variety,* 27 Dec 1967. AMD, p. 246. AS, p. 762. BHD2, p. 184. "George E. Middleton," *MPW,* 17 Jun 1916, 2044. "George Middleton Contributing to Famous Players-Lasky," *MPW,* 26 May 1917, 1271.

Middleton, Jack [title writer]. No data found. FDY, p. 447.

Middleton, Josephine [actress] (b. Nashville TN, 2 Sep 1886–8 Apr 1971 [84], England). AS, p. 762.

Middleton, Leora [actress] (*née* Leora Spellmeyer, b. 1891?–4 Sep 1945 [54], Los Angeles CA). m. **Charles B. Middleton** (d. 1949). "Leora Middleton," *Variety,* 12 Sep 1945. AS, p. 763. IFN, p. 206.

Midermoth, Marc. No data found. (Edison.) Gene Fernett, "The Edison Studios," *CI,* 102 (Dec 1983), 39–41 (photo on p. 40).

Midgley, Fanny [actress] (*née* Fanny B. Frier, b. Cincinnati OH, 26 Nov 1879–4 Jan 1932 [52], Los Angeles CA). (NYMP Co.) AS, p. 763. BHD1, p. 380. IFN, p. 206. George A. Katchmer, "Forgotten Cowboys and Cowgirls—Part XIV," *CI,* 191 (May 1991), 22. '83 WWOS (b. 1877).

Midgley, Florence [actress] (b. 1890?–16 Nov 1949 [59], Los Angeles CA). "Florence Midgley," *Variety,* 23 Nov 1949 (began 1918). AS, p. 763. BHD1, p. 380. IFN, p. 206. Truitt, p. 231.

Mierendorff, Hans [actor/director] (*né* Johannes Reinhold Mierendorff, b. Rostock, Germany, 30 Jun 1878–26 Dec 1955 [77], Eutin, Germany). AS, p. 763 (b. 1882; d. Holstein, Germany). Vittorio Martinelli, "Kino-Lieblinge," *Griffithiana,* 38/39 (Oct 1990), 61 (began 1911).

Migliar, Adelqui [actor/director] (*né* Adelqui Migliar Icardi, b. Concepcion, Chili, 5 Aug 1891–6 Aug 1956 [65], Santiago, Chili). AS, p. 763.

Migliari, Armando Giambattista [actor] (b. Frosinone, Italy, 19 Jun 1887 [extrait de naissance no. 139]-15 Jun 1976 [88], Italy). m. **Dora Menichelli**. AS, p. 763. JS, p. 289 (b. 29 Apr; in Italian silents from 1916).

Mihalesco, Alexander [actor] (*né* Alexander Mihalescu, b. Bucharest, Romania, 19 Oct 1883–28 Dec 1974 [91], Paris, France). AS, p. 763.

Mihhoels, Salomon [actor] (b. Daugavpils, Latvia, 1890–1948 [58?], Moscow, Russia). BHD1, p. 380.

Milaine, Amille [stage/film actress] (b. CA, ca. 1908). Merton, "He'll Help You Get in the Movies!," *Paris and Hollywood Screen Secrets Magazine,* May 1927, 22–25 (age 19; discovered by George Beban).

Milani, Chef Joseph [actor] (*né* Joseph Leopoldo Milani, b. Naples, Italy, 5 Jan 1892–30 Nov 1965 [73], Los Angeles CA). AS, p. 764.

Milar, Adolph [actor] (b. Germany, 19 Apr 1886–25 May 1950 [64], Santa Clara Co. CA). AS, p. 764. BHD1, p. 380. IFN, p. 206.

Milasch, Robert E. [actor] (b. New York NY, 18 Apr 1885–14 Nov 1954 [69], Woodland Hills CA). (Edison Co., 1900.) "Robert E. Milasch," *NYT,* 18 Nov 1954, 33:5. "Robert E. Milasch," *Variety,* 24 Nov 1954. AS, p. 764. BHD1, p. 380. IFN, p. 206. Truitt, p. 231.

Milcinovic, Adela [scenarist] (b. 1884–18 Jun 1968 [84?], New York NY). BHD2, p. 184.

Milcrest, Howard M. [actor/director] (b. 1892?–23 Nov 1920 [28], Huachuca Mountains AZ; trampled by a horse on location). (Griffith; Marshall Neilan Company.) "Howard Milcrest," *Variety,* 3 Dec 1920. AS, p. 764. BHD, p. 251; BHD2, p. 184. IFN, p. 206. Truitt, p. 231.

Milder, Max [executive] (b. Zanesville OH, 1891–1 Aug 1948 [57?], England). BHD2, p. 184.

Miles, David [actor/director/producer] (b. Milford CT, 1871–28 Oct 1915 [44?], New York NY; stricken on street and died in the hospital; interment at Milford MA). m. **Anita Hendry** (or Hendrie) (d. 1940). (Kinemacolor; Biograph; Klaw & Erlanger.) AMD, p. 246. AS, p. 764. BHD, p. 251; BHD2, p. 184. "David Miles," *MPW,* 10 Feb 1912, 485. "David Miles Leaves Majestic," *MPW,* 4 May 1912, 437. "Taking Pictures Under Difficulties," *MPW,* 15 Mar 1913, 1083. "First David Miles Comedy Arrives," *MPW,* 28 Nov 1914, 1243. "David Miles Dead," *NYDM,* 6 Nov 1915, 24:2 (member of the Screen Club). "Obituary," *MPW,* 6 Nov 1915, 1122.

Miles, Henry J. (brother of **Herbert Miles**) [executive] (d. 1 Jan 1908). AMD, p. 246. "Obituary," *MPW,* 4 Jan 1908, 4.

Miles, Herbert (brother of **Henry J. Miles**) [manufacturer]. No data found. AMD, p. 246. (Biograph, 1908). "Trade Notes," *MPW,* I, 4 May 1907, 136. "Trade Notes," *MPW,* I, 3 Aug 1907, 342. "Moving Picture Exhibitors' Association," *MPW,* 7 Sep 1907, 420. "Chats with the Interviewer," *MPW,* 11 Apr 1908, 317–18. "Herbert Miles—A Picture Pioneer," *MPW,* 19 Mar 1910, 416–17. "Herbert Miles Resigns," *MPW,* 14 Oct 1911, 136. "MIles After Automobile Race Pictures," *MPW,* 2 Dec 1911, 734. "Miles Brothers, Pioneers," *MPW,* 10 Jul 1915, 248.

Miles, Joseph R. [director] (b. 1881–3 Mar 1929 [48?], New York NY). AS, p. 764.

Miles, Lotta [actress] (*née* Florence Court, b. 1899–25 Jul 1937 [38?], Los Angeles CA; heart attack). AS, p. 764.

Miles, Gen. Nelson A[ppleton] [actor] (b. Westminster MA, 8 Aug 1839–15 May 1925 [85], Washington DC; heart attack). AS, p. 764. BHD, p. 251.

Milestone, Lewis [director/producer/scenarist] (*né* Leiba Milstein, b. Chisinau near Odessa, Ukraine, Russia, 30 Sep 1895–25 Sep 1980 [84], Los Angeles CA; complications after surgery). Peter B. Flint, "Lewis Milestone, 84, Director of Films; Received Oscars for 'All Quiet on the Western Front' and 'Two Arabian Knights [1929–30],'" *NYT,* 27 Sep 1980, 16:3. "Milestone, 84, Started in '20s; Credited with Mobility of Talkies," *Variety,* 1 Oct 1980. AMD, p. 247. AS, p. 764. BHD1, p. 380; BHD2, p. 184. JS, p. 289. Katz, p. 807. "Lloyd's Director," *MPW,* 5 Jun 1926, 2 (of *The Kid Brother*). John Roberts, "Lewis Milestone—Remembered by Few," *CI,* 180 (Jun 1990), 18.

Miley, Jerry [actor]. No data found. *Fl.* 1927–32. AMD, p. 247. "Jerry Miley," *MPW,* 27 Aug 1927, 589.

Milford, Arthur Eugene [stuntman/title writer/actor] (b. Lamar CO, 1902–23 Dec 1991 [89], Santa Monica CA; pneumonia). m. Dorothy. (RKO; Columbia; Republic; Rank.) "Arthur Milford, 89, Film Editor, Is Dead; Winner of 2 Oscars [for *Lost Horizon* and *On the Waterfront*]," *NYT,* 7 Jan 1992, B7:5 (began in silents as stuntman and title writer). "Gene Milford," *Variety,* 6 Jan 1992, p. 99. AS, p. 764. BHD, p. 251. FDY, p. 447.

Milford, Bliss [actress] (b. ca. 1890). (Edison). AMD, p. 247. BHD, p. 251. "This Week's Crop of Accidents," *MPW,* 19 Jul 1913, 306 (sore eyes). "Bliss Milford," *MPW,* 24 Oct 1914, 504. "Bliss Milford with August," *MPW,* 26 Dec 1914, 1845. "Bliss Milford with Pathé," *MPW,* 22 May 1915, 1270.

Milford, Mary Beth [actress]. No data found. AMD, p. 247. "Just Comes Natural for Mary," *MPW,* 3 Nov 1923, 102. "Chosen as Leading Woman," *MPW,* 14 Feb 1925, 717. George

Katchmer, "Remembering the Great Silents," *CI,* 248 (Feb 1996), 48–49.

Milhaud, Darius [actor/composer] (b. Aix-en-Provence, France, 4 Sep 1892–22 Jun 1974 [81], Geneva, Switzerland). AS, p. 765.

Miljan, John [actor] (b. Lead City SD, 9 Nov 1892–24 Jan 1960 [67], Los Angeles CA). m. Victoire Lowe (d. 31 Mar 1965; former wife of Creighton Hale). "John Miljan, Actor, Dies at 67; Was a Villain in Many Movies," *NYT,* 25 Jan 1960, 27:2. "John Miljan," *Variety,* 10 Feb 1960 (age 67). AMD, p. 247. AS, p. 765. BHD1, p. 380 (b. 8 Nov). FSS, p. 208. IFN, p. 206 (b. 8 Nov 1893). Katz, p. 807. Truitt, pp. 231–32. "John Miljan," *MPW,* 2 Jul 1927, 18.

Millar, Adelqui [stage/film actor/director] (b. Concepcion, Chile, 5 Aug 1891–5 Aug 1956 [65], Santiago, Chile). AMD, p. 247. BHD, p. 251; BHD2, p. 185 (d. 7 Aug). JS, p. 290 (in silents from 1910). "Noted European Actors in Rex Ingram's 'The Arab,'" *MPW,* 9 Feb 1924, 466.

Millar, Lee C. [actor/voice of Disney's Pluto] (b. Oakland CA, 20 Feb 1888–24 Dec 1941 [53], Glendale CA; heart attack). m. **Verna Felton** (d. 1966). "Lee Millar," *Variety,* 31 Dec 1941. AS, p. 765. IFN, p. 207.

Millard, Evelyn [actress] (b. London, England, 18 Sep 1869–9 Nov 1941 [72], London, England). BHD, p. 251.

Millarde, Harry E. [stage/film actor/director] (b. Springfield OH, 12 Nov 1884–2 Nov 1931 [46], New York NY; heart attack). m. **June Caprice** (d. 1936). AMD, p. 247. AS, p. 765 (b. 1885). BHD, p. 252; BHD2, p. 185 (b. Cincinnati, 1885). IFN, p. 207 (age 46). 1921 Directory, p. 271. SD. Spehr, p. 152. Truitt, p. 232. "Millarde with Kalem," *MPW,* 15 Apr 1916, 410. "Millarde Directs Teare Comedies," *MPW,* 6 May 1916, 951. "Thalberg Signs Millarde," *MPW,* 30 Jan 1926, 448:2. "To Direct 'Little Journey,'" *MPW,* 27 Mar 1926, 254. Billy H. Doyle, "Lost Players," *CI,* 147 (Sep 1987), 52.

Millefleurs, Lina [variety/film actress] (aka Clara Losy, b. France). JS, p. 290 (in Italian films from 1915; returned to the variety theater in 1920).

Millen, Frank H. [actor] (b. 1861–26 Dec 1931 [70], Albuquerque NM). BHD, p. 252. IFN, p. 207.

Miller, Alice Duer [author/actress/scenarist] (b. New York NY, 28 Jul 1874–22 Aug 1942 [68], New York NY). m. Henry Wise Miller, 1899. "Alice Duer Miller Dies at Home Here; Author of 'The White Cliffs' [1940], Poem That Sold 300,000 Copies, Stricken at 68; Defender of Hollywood; Said Film Folk Aided Writers—Novelist and Playwright a Trustee of Barnard," *NYT,* 23 Aug 1942, 42:1 (wrote *Come Out of the Kitchen,* 1912); "Alice Duer Miller [editorial]," 24 Aug 1942, 14:3; "Alice Duer Miller Buried in Jersey; Persons Well Known in Many Fields Pay Tribute to the Novelist and Poet; Rites at Her Home Here; Rev. J. Brett Langfstaff, Rector of St. Edmund's Church [a cousin of Henry Wise Miller], Reads the Episcopal Service," 25 Aug 1942, 24:2 (the Lunts, Berlins and others attended. Burial in Evergreen Cemetery, Morristown NJ). AS, p. 765. BHD2, p. 185. IFN, p. 207.

Miller, Alice Duer G. [scenarist] (b. Milwaukee WI, 1894?–24 Jul 1985 [91], Woodland Hills CA). (Griffith, 1919.) "Alice Duer G. Miller," *Variety,* 31 Jul 1985 (this may be the daughter of Alice Duer Miller, above—the obituary confuses the two by attributing *The White Cliffs* to her). AMD, p. 247. AS, p. 765. BHD2, p. 185. FDY, p. 433. "Continuity Writers Improve Rather Than Impair Her Stories, Says Alice Miller," *MPW,* 21 Aug 1920, 1063. "Alice Duer Miller Joins Group of Goldwyn Authors," *MPW,* 2 Apr 1921, 482. "Signs Contract," *MPW,* 17 Oct 1925, 552.

Miller, Arthur C[harles] [cinematographer] (b. New York NY, 8 Jul 1895–13 Jul 1970 [75], Los Angeles CA; tuberculosis). Fred J. Balshofer & Miller, *One Reel a Week* (Berkeley CA: University of California Press, 1967). (TC-F.) "Arthur C. Miller," *Variety,* 15 Jul 1970. AS, p. 765 (b. Roslyn, LI NY). BHD2, p. 185 (b. Roslyn). FDY, p. 463. IFN, p. 207. Katz, pp. 808–809 (b. Roslyn). Spehr, p. 154.

Miller, Ashley [actor/director/producer/writer] (b. Cincinnati OH, 11 Aug 1867–19 Nov 1949 [82], New York NY). (Edison.) m. **Ethel Browning**. (Edison, 1909.) "Ashley Miller," *Variety,* 23 Nov 1949 ("appeared in several films in the early days of the motion picture industry"). AMD, p. 247. AS, p. 765. BHD, p. 252; BHD2, p. 185 (b. 1877). IFN, p. 207. SD, p. 882 (b. 1877). Truitt, p. 232. "Edison Players Return," *MPW,* 16 Nov 1912, 647. "Ashley Miller," *NYDM,* 1 Jul 1914, 22:4. "Miller a Free Lance; Dean of Edison Producers Drops Regular Work to Develop New Plan," *NYDM,* 19 May 1915, 22:4 (to write scripts: "The day of the creative writer is coming."). "Miller Offers Innovation," *NYDM,* 30 Oct 1915, 25:4 (he invented a new process that would do away with the much overworked fade out. "Mr. Miller has invented a mat or vignette which cuts out the corners of the main scene and permits their use for the showing of those events which the character is telling about without the character leaving the screen." To be seen for the first time in *Ashton Kirke, Investigator.*). "Film Producer Writes a Play," *MPW,* 30 Oct 1915, 806. Quip, *NYDM,* 11 Dec 1915, 29:4 (he and his wife purchaed a plot of land in College Point; their houseboat, the *Arkady,* could then enable the Sound to come up to their prospective door). "In the Picture Studios," *NYDM,* 18 Dec 1915, 34:4 (finished a film on child labor with his wife). Ashley Miller, "Miller Speaks for Better Scenarios," *MPW,* 12 Feb 1916, 962. "Ashley Miller to Direct O. Henrys," *MPW,* 24 Nov 1917, 1156. "Ashley Miller," *MPW,* 16 Mar 1918, 1522. "'Silent Bill' Haddock Is Assistant to Miller," *MPW,* 15 Oct 1927, 419.

Miller, Bertha [actress]. No data found. *Fl.* 1912 (Bison).

Miller, C.C. [stage manager/actor]. No data found. "Additions to Lubin Western," *NYDM,* 26 May 1915, 22:3 (he and Dorothy Barrett were signed by Capt. Wilbert Melville at Lubin).

Miller, Carl [actor] (*né* Charlton or Carlton Miller, b. Wichita Falls TX, 9 Aug 1893–14 Feb 1979 [85], Honolulu HI). AMD, p. 247. AS, p. 765. BHD1, p. 381. IFN, p. 207. '83 WWOS. "Miller with Nazimova," *MPW,* 13 Dec 1924, 649. George Katchmer, "Carl Miller," *CI,* 232 (Oct 1994), C23.

Miller, Charles A. (nephew of actor Henry Miller) [actor/director/producer/scenarist] (b. Saginaw MI, 1857?–14 Nov 1936 [79], New York NY [Death Certificate Index No. 24731]). (Ince.) "Charles Miller," *Variety,* 18 Nov 1936 (does not cite film career). AMD, p. 247. AS, p. 765. FDY, p. 433. Lowrey, p. 120. J. Van Cartmell, "Film News from the Coast...," *NYDM,* 20 Nov 1915, 35:2 (nephew of Henry Miller; to direct at the New York Motion Picture Co.). "Charles Miller Directs Norma Talmadge," *MPW,* 8 Sep 1917, 1533. "Charles Miller New Director for Norma Talmadge," *MPW,* 15 Sep 1917, 1686. "Director Miller Becomes Producer," *MPW,* 19 Apr 1919, 372. "Realart to Release Service Tales Made by Director Charles Miller," *MPW,* 28 Feb 1920, 1487.

Miller, Charles B. [actor] (b. CA, 16 Mar 1891–5 Jun 1955 [64], Los Angeles CA; suicide or murder). AS, p. 765.

Miller, Diana [actress] (*née* Diana Moreland, b. Seattle WA, 18 Mar 1902–18 Dec 1927 [25], Monrovia CA; triple hemorrhage of lungs). m. **George Melford,** 1925 (d. 1961). "Diana Miller," *Variety,* 21 Dec 1927. AMD, p. 244 (under Melford, George H.). AS, p. 766. BHD, p. 252. IFN, p. 207. "Diana Miller Dead," *MPW,* 24 Dec 1927, 8 (age 24). George A. Katchmer, "Forgotten Cowboys and Cowgirls—Part XIII," *CI,* 190 (Apr 1991), C8.

Miller, Edward G[eorge] [actor] (b. Eastbourne, England, 22 Dec 1881–1 Dec 1948 [66], Los Angeles Co. CA). (Griffith.) "Edward G. Miller," *Variety,* 15 Dec 1948. AS, p. 766. BHD, p. 252. IFN, p. 207. Truitt, p. 232.

Miller, Ernest W. [cimnematographer] (b. Los Angeles CA, 7 Mar 1885–23 Apr 1957 [72], Los Angeles CA). BHD2, p. 185. FDY, p. 463.

Miller, Ernest [jazz player] (b. 1896?–4 Dec 1971 [75], New Orleans LA; emphysema). "Ernest (Punch) Miller, 75, Early Jazz Trumpeter, Dies," *NYT,* 5 Dec 1971, 87:1. "Ernest (Punch) Miller," *Variety,* 15 Dec 1971.

Miller, Ernie [cameraman]. No data found. AMD, p. 247. "Ernie Miller," *MPW,* 15 Jan 1927, 191.

Miller, Flournoy Eakin [actor] (b. Columbia TN, 14 Apr 1887–6 Jun 1971 [84], Los Angeles CA; heart attack). AS, p. 766.

Miller, Frank [actor] (b. London, England, 1891-ca. 1950 [59?], England). AS, p. 766. BHD1, p. 381; BHD2, p. 185.

Miller, Gilbert [director] (b. New York NY, 3 Jul 1884–2 Jan 1969 [84], New York NY). BHD2, p. 185.

Miller, George F. "Lefty" [baseball player/actor/manager/producer/publicist] (d. 4 Jul 1952 [60s], Queens, New York NY). m. Caroline Ryan Green, 24 Sep 1915, Jersey City NJ. (Pathé Frérès.) "George 'Lefty' Miller," *Variety,* 187, 9 Jul 1952, 55:2. AMD, p. 247. "Here and There," *NYDM,* 29 Sep 1915, 31:1 (former pitcher of the St. Louis Nationals). "Mother of George Miller Dead," *MPW,* 25 Dec 1915, 2368 (d. 14 Dec 1915).

Miller, Gertie [actress] (b. Bradford, Yorkshire, England, 21 Feb 1879–25 Apr 1952 [73], Chiddingford, England). "Gertie Miller," *Variety,* 30 Apr 1952. AS, p. 766. BHD, p. 252. SD, p. 881.

Miller, Gordon [actor] (né Luke Aloysius Miller, b. PA, 18 May 1882–9 Apr 1962 [79], Encino CA). AS, p. 766.

Miller, Harold A[tison] [actor] (*né* Harold Edwin Kammermeyer, b. Redondo Beach CA, 31 May 1894–18 Jul 1972 [78], Los Angeles CA). AS, p. 766. BHD1, p. 381.

Miller, Henry, Sr. (father of **Jack Miller**) [stage/film actor] (b. London, England, 1 Feb 1858?–9 Apr 1926 [68], Baltimore MD; lobular pneumonia). m. Helen Heron. "Henry Miller Dies; Veteran of Stage; Noted Actor-Manager Succumbs at 66 to Pneumonia in New York Hospital;

Began His Career at 18 [in *Amy Robsart*]; First Won Fame as Leading Man of Empire Theatre Stock Company—His Notable Successes," *NYT,* 10 Apr 1926, 1:4 (b. 1860–d. NYC). "Henry Miller," *Variety,* 14 Apr 1926. AS, p. 766. SD, p. 883.

Miller, Hugh J. (father of actress Barbara Heller) [actor] (b. 1902–11 May 1956 [54], Los Angeles CA). "Hugh J. Miller," *Variety,* 202, 16 May 1956. AS, p. 766. BHD1, p. 381. Truitt, p. 232.

Miller, Hugh L[orimer] [stage/film actor] (*né* Hugh Lorimer Miller, b. Berwick-on-Tweed, England, 22 May 1889–1 Nov 1976 [87], London, England). m. Olga Katzin. AS, p. 766. BHD1, p. 381 (b. 1880). IFN, p. 207. SD, p. 883.

Miller, J[ohn] **Clarkson** [scenarist] (b. 1889–13 Oct 1966 [77?], Dunn Loring VA). BHD2, p. 185. FDY, p. 433.

Miller, Jack (son of **Henry Miller, Sr.**) [actor] (b. England-1 Apr 1927, Mexico City, Mexico; drug overdose). AS, p. 766.

Miller, Jack [actor] (b. 1888?–25 Sep 1928 [40], San Diego CA). m. Dell. "Jack Miller," *Variety,* 3 Oct 1928, p. 58. AS, p. 766. BHD, p. 252. IFN, p. 207. Truitt, p. 232. WWS, p. 232.

Miller, Jack [actor] (b. 1894–28 Feb 1941 [46], Burbank CA). AS, p. 766.

Miller, Jack [director] (b. 1895?–25 Jan 1969 [73], Blackheath, England). "Jack Miller," *Variety,* 5 Feb 1969. AS, p. 766.

Miller, Jane [actress] (d. 20 Sep 1936, New York NY). m. Charles A. Smylie. "Jane Miller," *Variety,* 30 Sep 1936. AMD, p. 247. AS, p. 766. BHD, p. 252. "Something About Jane Miller," *MPW,* 9 Nov 1918, 682. George Katchmer, "Remembering the Great Silents, *CI,* 229 (Jul 1994), 40.

Miller, John F. [producer] (b. 1872–24 May 1939 [67?], Sawtelle CA). BHD2, p. 185.

Miller, Josephine [actress]. No data found. AMD, p. 247. "Picture Personalities," *MPW,* 3 Sep 1910, 512.

Miller, Juanita [actress] (b. 1880?–9 Apr 1970 [90?], Oakland CA). AS, p. 766. BHD, p. 252. Truitt, p. 232.

Miller, Katherine B. [writer] (b. 1859?–24 Mar 1960 [101], Berkeley CA). "Katherine B. Miller," *Variety,* 30 Mar 1960. AS, p. 767.

Miller, Leslie [title writer]. No data found. FDY, p. 447.

Miller, Marilyn [stage/film dancer/actress] (*née* Mary Lynn Reynolds, b. Findlay OH, 1 Sep 1898–7 Apr 1936 [37], New York NY; toxic poisoning). m. (1) **Frank Carter**, 1919 (killed in auto crash in 1920); (2) **Jack Pickford**, 31 Jul 1922 (d. 1933); (3) Chester (Chet) O'Brien. (The Five Columbians, 1903; 1st legitimate play on Broadway, *The Passing Show of 1914,* Winter Garden, NYC). "Marilyn Miller Dies in New York at 38," *Variety,* 122, 8 Apr 1936, 1:5, 54:3 (b. Evansville IN. "At various times she had told friends she did not care to live beyond the age of 40."). AMD, p. 247. AS, p. 767 (b. Evansville IN). BHD1, p. 382 (b. Evansville IN). IFN, p. 207. "'Passing Show,' June 6; Annual Summer Production at the Winter Garden Promises to Be a Big Affair," *NYDM,* 3 Jun 1914, 9:4. On cover of *NYDM,* 16 Dec 1914. "Marilyn Miller and Pickford to Co-Star in Screen Play," *MPW,* 5 May 1923, 74. June Lee, "Dan Cupid's Bulletin Board," *Paris and Hollywood Screen Secrets Magazine,* III (Aug 1927), 35 (her divorce from Pickford is confirmed).

Miller, Martin [actor] (*né* Rudolph Muller, b. Kremsier, Czechoslovakia, 2 Sep 1899–26 Aug 1969 [69], Innsbruck, Austria). AS, p. 767.

Miller, Mary Louise [child actress] (b. Los Angeles CA, 15 Jan 1924). "Behind the Cameras," *Cinema Arts,* Dec 1926, 34 (photo from *The Third Degree*).

Miller, Max [actor] (*né* Thomas Sargent, b. Brighton, England, 1895–7 May 1963 [68?], Brighton, England). AS, p. 767.

Miller, Max O. [cameraman/producer]. No data found. AMD, p. 247. "Progress in Photography," *MPW,* 9 May 1925, 227 (stereoscopic camera).

Miller, Morris *see* **DeCosta, Morris**

Miller, Patsy Ruth (sister of **Winston Miller**) [film/stage actress: Wampas Star, 1922/writer] (*née* Patricia Ruth Miller, b. St. Louis MO, 17 Jan 1904–16 Jul 1995 [91], Palm Desert CA; heart failure). m. (1) **William Boyd**, 1921 (d. 1972); (2) **Tay Garnett**, Sep 1929–33 (d. 1977); (3) John Lee Mahin, 1937–47 (son, Timothy); (3) Effingham S. Deans, 1951 (d. 1986). *My Hollywood; When Both of Us Were Young; The Memories of Patsy Ruth Miller* (Brigantine NJ: Magic Image Filmbooks, 1988). (Discovered by director Douglas Gerrard; film debut: *One a Minute,* Ince/Paramount, Jun 1921; final film, *Quebec,* Parmount, Mar 1951.) "Patsy Ruth Miller, Movie Actress, 91, an Early Esmeralda [1923]," *NYT,* 19 Jul 1995, D20:1. "Patsy Ruth Miller, *Variety,* 24 Jul 1995, 80:2. AMD, p. 247. AS, p. 767. BHD1, p. 382 (b. 22 Jun). FFF, p. 45 (b. 22 Jun 1905). FSS, p. 209. Katz, p. 809 (b. 22 Jun 1905). MH, p. 127. "Patsy Ruth Miller," SOS, pp. 136–59. "Film Players Wed," *MPW,* 15 Oct 1921, 756 (m. Boyd). Winston Miller, "Patsy Ruth's Number; By One Who Has It!," *Classic,* Aug 1923, 41, 79 (Winston Miller was PRM's 12-year-old brother). "Patsy Ruth Miller," *MPW,* 12 Jul 1924, insert. "Miss Miller Remains," *MPW,* 31 Jan 1925, 489. "Patsy Ruth Miller Signed," *MPW,* 21 Mar 1925, 286. Dorothy Spensley, "The High Cost of Stardom," *MW,* 22 Aug 1925, 10–12, 43. "Patsy Ruth Miller," *MPW,* 25 Sep 1926, 214. Carol Johnston, "Always a Bride-to-Be, Never a Bride; A Close-Up of Patsy Ruth Miller," *MPC,* Jun 1928, 51, 83. "Patsy Ruth Miller," WBO1, pp. 160–61 (b. 1905). Adele Whitely Fletcher, "The Flapper Who Grew Up," *MW,* 8 Nov 1924, 11–12. "Patsy Miller at Universal," *MPW,* 7 May 1927, 35. "Patsy Ruth Miller," *MPW,* 8 Oct 1927, 359. Murray Summers, "The Film Career of Patsy Ruth Miller," Part I, *Filmograph,* II, No. 1 (1971), 2–17; Part II, No. 2 (1971), 2–21 (includes filmography; wrote *That Flannigan Girl* [NY: Wm. Morrow & Co.], 1939). Joy Rubin, "Patsy Ruth Miller," *CFC,* 41 (Winter, 1973), 12–14. Michael G. Ankerich, "Reel Stars," *CI,* 165 (Mar 1989), 7, 20, 22. William M. Drew, *Speaking of Silents* (Vestal NY: Vestal Press, Ltd., 1989), pp. 136–59. Chapter 15, "Patsy Ruth Miller," *BS,* pp. 199–211 (includes filmography).

Miller, Phoebe M. [scenarist] (b. 1880-Nov 1942 [62?], St. Louis MO). BHD2, p. 185.

Miller, Ranger Bill (adopted son of Buffalo Bill) [actor] (*né* William Joseph Miller, b. Kutztown PA, 5 Mar 1878–12 Nov 1939 [61], Los Angeles CA). (Bill Miller Productions, 1922.) "'Ranger Bill' Miller, Early Film Cowboy; Rode 'King, the Wonder Horse' of Buffalo Bill—Dies at 61," *NYT,* 14 Nov 1939, 23:5. "Ranger Bill Miller," *Variety,* 15 Nov 1939 ("film cowboy of the early silents"). AS, p. 767. BHD, p. 252 (b. 1887). IFN, p. 207 (b. 1887). Truitt, p. 232. Edgar Wyatt, "Ranger Bill Miller," *CI,* 280 (Oct 1998), C-7.

Miller, Rube [director]. No data found. AMD, p. 247. "Rube Miller with Kriterion," *MPW,* 13 Mar 1915, 1621. "Ruibe Miller, Vogue Director," *MPW,* 15 Jan 1916, 417. "Rube Miller to Direct Vogue," *MPW,* 24 Mar 1917, 1934.

Miller, Ruby [actress] (b. London, England, 14 Jul 1889–2 Apr 1976 [86], Chichester, England). AMD, p. 248. AS, p. 767. BHD1, p. 382. IFN, p. 207. "Ruby Miller Buys 'Fools for Luck,'" *MPW,* 15 Sep 1923, 271.

Miller, Ruth [actress] (b. 1903?–13 Jun 1981 [78], Santa Monica CA). m. Ryan Hayes. (Began at age 12 at Samuelson Studios in England; Sennett; De Mille; MGM.) "Ruth Miller," *Variety,* 24 Jun 1981. AS, p. 767. BHD, p. 252.

Miller, Seton I. [producer/scenarist/actor] (b. Chehalis WA, 3 May 1902–29 Mar 1974 [71], Woodland Hills CA; emphysema). m. Ann Evers [1914–1987]. (WB; TC-F; Paramount.) "Seton I. Miller," *Variety,* 10 Apr 1974 ("entered motion pictures as an actor in 1926 in 'Brown of Harvard'"; AA for script of *Here Comes Mr. Jordan* (1941). AS, p. 767. BHD, p. 252; BHD2, p. 185. FDY, p. 433. IFN, p. 207.

Miller, Tom [actor] (b. 6 Dec 1872–6 Dec 1942 [70], Los Angeles CA). AS, p. 767.

Miller, Victor [cameraman]. No data found. AMD, p. 248. "Packing a Camera," *MPW,* 15 Mar 1913, 1094. 'In a Post of Danger," *MPW,* 6 Dec 1913, 1155. "Victor Miller Talks of the Congo," *MPW,* 27 May 1916, 1499–1500. "Miller Goes to Rockies," *MPW,* 12 Aug 1916, 1105. "Vic Miller, Cinematographer," *MPW,* 10 Mar 1917, 1538.

Miller, Virgil E. [cinematographer] (b. Coffeen IL, 20 Dec 1886–5 Oct 1974 [87], Los Angeles CA). (Universal, 1912; WB; Paramount; TC-F.) "Virgil Miller," *Variety,* 16 Oct 1974. AS, p. 767. BHD2, p. 185. FDY, p. 463.

Miller, Walter C[orwin] [stage/film actor] (b. Dayton OH, 9 Mar 1892–30 Mar 1940 [48], Los Angeles CA; heart attack as a result of a screen fight in *Gaucho Serenade,* Republic, 1940). m. Lillian Louise Coffin; Eileen Schofield. (Reliance, 1910; Biograph, 1912; Pathé; Victor; Universal.) "Walter C. Miller," *Variety,* 3 Apr 1940 (age 47). AMD, p. 248. AS, p. 767. BHD1, p. 382. FSS, p. 209. GK, pp. 650–62. IFN, p. 207. *MPN Studio Directory,* 21 Oct 1916 (b. Atlanta GA). Sue Roberts, "Where Have They Gone?; Vanished Stars Discovered and Meteorits Unearthed," *Motion Picture Magazine,* Feb 1918, 132, 134, (Roberts found out the whereabouts of Walter Miller, who had been off the screen for about two years. At the Hotel Remington, NYC, Mrs. Miller [Coffin], related what happened. He made 3 films in Jamaica with Robert Mantell for Fox. She "contracted the tumor the necessitated our removal to Florida." He accepted a film job there, but the picture was never made. When she felt better, they returned to New York, where he worked for the Art Dramas Company and Metro.). "Miller Proud Papa," *MPW,* 6 Nov 1926, 3. George Katchmer, "Walter Miller; King of the Serials," *CI,* 116 (Feb 1985), 17–19. Frank Dolven, "Walter Miller; The All-Around Actor," *CI,* 223 (Jan 1994), C2, C4 (b. 3 Mar 1893). George Katchmer, "Remembering the Great Silents," *CI,* 252 (Jun 1996), 38 (Walter Corwin Miller); *CI,* 253 (Jul 1996), 48–49.

Miller, W[illiam] **Christy** [stage/film actor]

(b. Dayton OH, 10 Aug 1843–23 Sep 1922 [79], Staten Island NY [Death Certificate No. 1470; b. NY]; cerebral hemorrhage). m. Jennie Towell. (Biograph, 1909.) "William C. Miller," *Variety*, 29 Sep 1922. AS, p. 767. BHD, p. 252 (b. NY NY). IFN, p. 207. SD. Spehr, p. 154. P.M. Powell, "Doings at Los Angeles," *MPW*, 12 Apr 1913, 152 (elected to the Photoplayers Club; one of the oldest actors in films).

Miller, William [cinematographer]. No data found. FDY, p. 463.

Miller, William J[oseph] *see* **Miller, Ranger Bill**

Miller, Winston (brother of **Patsy Ruth Miller**) [actor/TV producer/writer] (b. St. Louis MO, 22 Jun 1910–21 Jun 1994 [83], Los Angeles CA). AS, p. 767. BHD, addendum.

Millet, Arthur Nelson [actor] (b. Pittsfield ME, 21 Apr 1874–24 Feb 1952 [77], Los Angeles Co. CA). AS, p. 768. BHD1, p. 382. IFN, p. 208. George Katchmer, "Remembering the Great Silents," *CI*, 209 (Nov 1992), 56.

Millhauser, Bertram [scenarist/director] (b. New York NY, 25 Mar 1892–1 Dec 1958 [66], Los Angeles CA; heart attack). (De Mille.) "Bertram Millhauser," *Variety*, 10 Dec 1958. AMD, p. 248. AS, p. 768. BHD2, p. 185. IFN, p. 208. "Millhauser Directing Juanita Hansen," *MPW*, 7 Feb 1920, 935. "Millhauser Joins Big 'U,'" *MPW*, 31 Mar 1923, 508. "Millhauser Engaged," *MPW*, 2 Feb 1924, 388. "Millhauser Story for F.B.O.," *MPW*, 15 Mar 1924, 184. "Engages Millhauser," *MPW*, 29 Mar 1924, 371.

Milligan, Mary [actress] (b. Ireland, 1882–10 Mar 1966 [83?], Belfast, Ireland). AS, p. 768.

Milliken, Conrad [producer]. No data found. AMD, p. 248. "E.K. Lincoln Starred in Special S-L Pictures," *MPW*, 23 Nov 1918, 849.

Millman, Bird (b. 1895–5 Aug 1940 [45?], Canon City CO). BHD, p. 252.

Millman, William L'Estrange [stage/film actor] (b. Toronto, Canada, 7 May 1883 [birth certificate #025605, no. 71]–19 Jul 1937 [54], Los Angeles CA). "William Millman; Stage and Screen Actor Succumbs in Hollywood at 54," *NYT*, 20 Jul 1937, 23:1 (began 1934). "William Millman," *Variety*, 21 Jul 1937. AS, p. 768. IFN, p. 208.

Millner, Marietta [actress] (b. Vienna, Austria, 1907–7 Jul 1929 [22?], Badenweiler, Germany; consumption). (Ufa.) "Marietta Millner Dies," *Variety*, 17 Jul 1929. AS, p. 768. BHD, p. 252 (d. 26 Jun). IFN, p. 208 (d. Jul 1929).

Mills, Alyce [actress] (b. Pittsburgh PA, 16 Feb 1899–27 Apr 1990 [91], Ft. Lauderdale FL). (Fox; FP-L.) AMD, p. 248. BHD, p. 252. Ruth Mabrey, "'I Shall Not Depend on Beauty to Win Screen Fame!,' Says Contest Winner," *MW*, 16 Jun 1923, 10, 31. "Alyce Mills Engaged," *MPW*, 13 Sep 1924, 121. "Miss Mills Engaged," *MPW*, 18 Oct 1924, 4595. "Alyce Mills," *MPW*, 14 Feb 1925, 711. "Plans for Alyce Mills," *MPW*, 4 Jul 1925, 81. David Balch, "A Blonde from Pittsburgh," *MPC*, Jul 1926, 31, 77 (won a beauty contest in Pittsburgh). Henriette, "From Hollywood to You," *MPS*, 1 Mar 1927, 7, 31 (was to elope but a friend told, and "several carloads of sightseers tried to accompany her thither. Matrimony was foregone for the time." Mills vowed to sneak away when nobody was looking.) Anthony Slide, *Silent Portraits* (Vestal NY: The Vestal Press, Ltd., 1989), p. 184.

Mills, Bob [actor] (b. Detroit MI, 1898–16 Oct 1934 [36?], CO). BHD, p. 252.

Mills, Edwin [actor] (b. Washington DC, 8 Mar 1918–19 May 1981 [63], Los Angeles CA). AS, p. 768 (b. 1917; d. 23 May). BHD1, p. 383.

Mills, Frank [actor] (b. Kendal MI, 1870–11 Jun 1921 [51], MI; insane asylum). "Frank Mills," *Variety*, 17 Jun 1921. AMD, p. 248. AS, p. 768 (d. NY NY). BHD, p. 252. IFN, p. 208. "Frank Mills, Metro Leading Man," *MPW*, 20 Jul 1918, 378. "Mills Prefers Screen to Stage," *MPW*, 21 Dec 1918, 1369.

Mills, Frank C. [actor] (b. WA, 26 Jan 1891–18 Aug 1973 [82], Los Angeles CA; arteriosclerosis). AS, p. 768 (b. Kalamazoo MI). BHD1, p. 383. IFN, p. 208.

Mills, Guy [actor/stuntman] (b. England, 1898–15 Oct 1962 [64?], Chichester, England). AS, p. 768.

Mills, John, Sr. [actor/singer] (b. Bellefonte PA, 11 Feb 1882–8 Dec 1967 [85], Bellefontaine OH). AS, p. 768.

Mills, Joseph S. [actor] (*né* Joseph Stapleton Mills, b. 1875?–19 Oct 1935 [60], Los Angeles CA). "Jos. S. Mills," *Variety*, 23 Oct 1935. AS, p. 768. BHD1, p. 383. IFN, p. 208. Truitt, p. 233.

Mills, Marlyn [actress] (*née* Mary Cecilia Brunning, b. 16 Nov 1904). m. J. Charles Davis. BR, p. 182. George A. Katchmer, "Remembering the Great Silents," *CI*, 175 (Jan 1990), C8; "Update—Forgotten Cowboys/Girls," 179 (May 1990), 43.

Mills, Thomas R. [actor/director] (b. England, 28 Jun 1878–29 Nov 1953 [75], Woodland Hills CA). m. **Mildred Meade** (d. 1951). (Vitagraph.) "Thomas R. Mills," *Variety*, 9 Dec 1953 ("in pictures for 35 years"). AS, p. 768. BHD1, p. 383; BHD2, p. 185. IFN, p. 208. Truitt, p. 233. "Studio Gossip," *NYDM*, 7 Jul 1915, 41:1 (saved Arline Pretty from drowning while filming *Sis*).

Millsfield, Charles A. (Monsieur Pompon) [actor] (b. Netherlands, 6 Nov 1876–18 Sep 1962 [85], Los Angeles Co. CA). BHD1, p. 383. IFN, p. 208.

Milne, Margaret [actress]. No data found. AMD, p. 248. "Margaret Milne Joins Van Dyke Co.," *MPW*, 25 Nov 1916, 1147.

Milne, Minnie [actress] (b. Syria, 1872–9 Apr 1932 [60?], New York NY). BHD, p. 253.

Milne, Peter [title writer/scenarist] (b. New York NY, 15 Aug 1896–29 Mar 1968 [71], Los Angeles CA). AMD, p. 248. BHD2, p. 186. FDY, p. 433. "Milne Assumes New Duties," *MPW*, 5 Feb 1921, 669. "Peter Milne to Do Continuity on New Film," *MPW*, 19 Feb 1927, 565.

Milner, Victor [cinematographer] (b. New York NY, 15 Dec 1893–29 Oct 1972 [78], Los Angeles CA). AS, p. 769. BHD2, p. 186. FDY, p. 463. Katz, p. 811.

Milnor, Mary [actress]. No data found. AMD, p. 248. "Northern Girl Wins the Lead in Pathé Baseball Serial," *MPW*, 16 May 1925, 314.

Milo, Ruth [actress]. No data found. AMD, p. 248. "Ruth Milo," *MPW*, 18 Dec 1926, 491.

Milowanoff, Sandra [actress] (*née* Alexandrine Milowanoff, b. St. Petersburg, Russia, 10 Jun 1892–8 May 1957 [64], Paris, France [extrait de décès no. 321]). m. Nikitine; Maurice de Moolek; Joseph Mejinsky. AS, p. 769 (b. 1896). BHD1, p. 614 (b. 23 Jun). Garth Pedler, "Sandra Milowanoff in 'Nene' (1924)," *CI*, 130 (Apr 1986), C3-C4.

Miltern, John [actor] (*né* John E. Sheehan, b. New Britain CT, 13 Jul 1870–15 Jan 1937 [66], Los Angeles CA; hit by car while walking with **Basil Rathbone**). "John Miltern," *Variety*, 20 Jan 1937 (age 67). AS, p. 769. BHD1, p. 383. IFN, p. 208. Truitt, p. 233.

Milton, Billy [actor] (b. London, England, 8 Dec 1905–22 Nov 1989 [83], Northwood, England). AS, p. 769. BHD1, p. 383 (d. London).

Milton, Ernest [actor] (b. San Francisco CA, 10 Jan 1890–24 Jul 1974 [84], London, England). AS, p. 769. BHD1, p. 383.

Milton, Georges [actor] (*né* Georges Désiré Michaud, b. Puteaux, France, 20 Sep 1886–17 Oct 1970 [84], Antibes, France [extrait de décès no. 581/1970]). AS, p. 769.

Milton, Glenn [actress]. No data found. AMD, p. 248. "Glenn Milton in Callahan Comedies," *MPW*, 17 Sep 1921, 300.

Milton, Harry [actor] (b. London, England, 26 Jun 1900–8 Mar 1965 [64], London, England). m. **Chili Bouchier**, 28 Sep 1929. *Shooting Star; The Last of the Silent Film Stars; Chili Bouchier* (London: Atlantis, 1995). AS, p. 769. Michael Grantside, "Chili Bouchier; Britain's 'It' Girl," *CI*, 276 (Jun 1998), 20–22.

Milton, Maud [stage/film actress] (*née* Kate Maud Milton, b. Gravesend, England, 24 Mar 1859–19 Nov 1945 [86], Ryde, Isle of Wright, England). m. Mr. Butler. AS, p. 769 (d. London, England). BHD, p. 252. IFN, p. 208. SD, p. 886.

Milton, Robert D[avidor] [actor/director/scenarist] (b. Dinaburgh, Russia, 24 Jan 1885–13 Jan 1956 [70], Calabasas CA). AS, p. 769 (d. Woodland Hills CA). BHD2, p. 186 (b. 1886). IFN, p. 208.

Milward, Dawson [actor] (b. London, England, 13 Jul 1870–15 May 1926 [55], London, England). AS, p. 769 (b. Woolwich, England, 1866). BHD, p. 252. IFN, p. 208 (age 60).

Minciotti, Esther [actress] (*née?*, b. Italy, 18 Mar 1888–15 Apr 1962 [74], New York NY). m. **Silvio Minciotti** (d. 1961). AS, p. 769.

Minciotti, Silvio [actor] (b. Naples, Italy, 1882–2 May 1961 [79?], Elmhurst NY). m. **Esther** (d. 1962). AS, p. 769.

Mindil, Philip Kearny [publicist] (b. Philadelphia PA, 3 Aug 1874–22 Oct 1920 [46], New York NY; dropsy). m. Rosemonde West. (Mutual Film Co.) "Phil Mindil," *Variety*, 29 Oct 1920, p. 6:3. AMD, p. 248. BHD2, p. 186. F.J. Beecroft, "Publicity Men I Have Met...," *NYDM*, 14 Jan 1914, 48 (*see* **Beecroft, Chester** for full citation). Philip Mindil, "Publicity for the Pictures," *MPW*, 11 Jul 1914, 217. "Phil Mindil Resigns from Mutual," *MPW*, 11 Jul 1914, 287. "Mindil Has Publicity Office," *MPW*, 15 Aug 1914, 935.

Mineer, Afton [actress: understudy for Margarita Fisher]. No data found. (Beauty Co.) "Gossip of the Studios," *NYDM*, 4 Nov 1914, 29:2.

Miner, Daniel [stage/film actor] (b. 1880?–24 Jun 1938 [58], Los Angeles CA). "Daniel Miner," *Variety*, 6 Jul 1938 ("stage and screen actor for 40 years"). AS, p. 769 (b. 1879). BHD1, p. 384 (b. 1879). IFN, p. 208. Truitt, p. 233.

Minetti, Maria [actress] (d. 9 Dec 1971, London, England). BHD1, p. 384.

Minevitch, Borrah [actor/producer] (b.

Kiev, Ukraine, 5 Nov 1902–26 Jun 1955 [52], Neuilly-sur-Seine, France [extrait de décès no. 459]). AS, p. 770.

Ming, Moy Luke [actor] (b. Canton, China, 10 Jan 1863–16 Aug 1964 [101], Granada Hills CA). AS, p. 770.

Minium, Arthur [actor]. No data found. (Lubin.)

Mino, Frank [actor]. No data found. AMD, p. 248. "Karper Signs Juvenile," *MPW,* 27 Aug 1927, 581.

Minotti, Felice [actor] (b. Milan, Italy, 19 Nov 1887). JS, pp. 291–92 (in Italian silents from 1908).

Minter, Mary Miles (daughter of **Charlotte Shelby**; sister of **Margaret Shelby**) [stage/film actress] (*née* Juliet Reilly, b. Shreveport LA, 1 Apr 1902–5 Aug 1984 [82], Santa Monica CA; heart attack). m. Brandon O. Hildebrandt, 1957 (d. 1965). (American; Frohman; Metro.) "Silent Film Actress Mary Miles Minter Succumbs at 82," *Variety,* 15 Aug 1984. AMD, p. 248. AS, p. 770. BHD, p. 253. Katz, pp. 812–13. Lowrey, p. 122. MH, p. 128. MSBB, p. 1038. WWS, p. 79. "William L. Sherrill," *MPW,* 20 Feb 1915, 1145:2 (Sherrill, vice-president of the Frohman Amusement Co., spoke of its first production of *The Fairy and the Waif* ["that you would be glad to take your sister and mother to"], starring Minter, of *The Little Rebel* stage fame, in her debut film. The director, George Irving, said of her: "I think she is the most beautiful girl I have ever seen on the screen."). "Mary Miles Minter," *NYDM,* 19 May 1915, 32:1. "Mary Miles Minter, Metro's Latest Star," *MPW,* 7 Aug 1915, 1003. "Mary Miles Minter Gets Ovation in Canada," *MPW,* 1 Apr 1916, 91. Cal York, "Plays and Players," *Photoplay Magazine,* Feb 1917, 89 (in an automobile accident in December while en route from Los Angeles to Santa Barbara. Mrs. Shelby was driving when the car skidded and turned over in a ditch. "Mrs. Shelby sustained a broken arm, her sister was badly cut and bruised and Miss Minter suffered suffered severe cuts from broken glass."). "Mary Miles Minter," *MPW,* 8 Sep 1917, 1529. "Honors for Mary Miles Minter," *MPW,* 29 Dec 1917, 1948. "Miss Minter Christens Plane," *MPW,* 20 Apr 1918, 412. "Mary Miles Minter Makes Flight," *MPW,* 18 May 1918, 1011. "Mary Miles Minter to REemain with American," *MPW,* 7 Sep 1918, 1404. "Mary Miles Minter Realart Star," *MPW,* 28 Jun 1919, 1940. "Mary Minter and Zukor Join Forces," *MPW,* 19 Jul 1919, 368. "Mary Miles Minter Begins Work on Her First Realart," *MPW,* 9 Aug 1919, 848 (directed by William Desmond Taylor). "Mary Miles Minter Makes Personal Appearance in England," *MPW,* 6 Sep 1919, 1465. "Director William Taylor Saves Mary Minter Party," *MPW,* 3 Jan 1920, 94. "Mary Minter to Move," *LA Times,* 9 Jan 1920, III, 4 ("...will pack up her make-up box, her professional poor-little-girl rags, and her pet canary bird and move to the Lasky studio..."). "Mary Miles Minter Is Honor Guest at Luncheon," *MPW,* 21 Feb 1920, 1243. "Miss Minter Appears on Stage," *MPW,* 17 Apr 1920, 451. "Mary Miles Mintejr's Age Is Shown by Decision of Court," *MPW,* 26 Jun 1920, 1778 (b. 1 Apr 1902). Mary Miles Minter, "Good, Wholesome Pictures Is What the Public Wants," *MPW,* 10 Jul 1920, 236. "Miss Minter to Buy Aeroplane," *MPW,* 7 Aug 1920, 774. "Mary Miles Minter to Take First Vacation in a Year," *MPW,* 28 Aug 1920, 1192. "Actress Gets Invitation," *MPW,* 18 Sep 1920, 354 (to the 284th Anniversary of the Signing of the Dedham Covenant by Jonathan Fayerbanks on 11 Sep 1636). "Mary Miles Minter Values Criticism of Children Gained by Theatre Visits," *MPW,* 8 Jan 1921, 168. "Film Folk Purchase Homes," *MPW,* 14 May 1921, 179 (Laughlin Park). "Honor Guest at Dinner," *MPW,* 18 Jun 1921, 701. "Miss Minter Speaks," *MPW,* 25 Feb 1922, 818 (on Taylor murder). "Did Hoeffler Ban Mary Miles Minter? No, He Dared Critics and Won Praise," *MPW,* 4 Mar 1922, 45. "The Official Facts," *MPW,* 8 Apr 1922, 616. "Miss Minter in New Picture; Has Her First Grown Up Part," *MPW,* 22 Jul 1922, 282. "Mary Miles Minter Sued," *MW,* 21 Jun 1924, 21. "On the Set and Off," *MW,* 7 Mar 1925, 33 (asked court to compel her mother to give a rendering of the money she earned as a minor; her mother spent $700,000 of it). "On the Set and Off," *MW,* 5 Sep 1925, 45 (took her mother to court again). "On the Set and Off," *MM,* II, Mar 1926, 83 (Mrs. Charlotte Shelby answered her daughter's suit, alleging that she was entitled to her daughter's earnings as a minor). Henriette, "From Hollywood to You," *MPS,* 1 Mar 1927, 7 (reconciled with her mother "after years of bitter feud," and living with her in Paris where "both refuse to discuss their making-up."). Paul Paige, "Close-Ups and Fade-Outs," *Paris and Hollywood Screen Secrets Magazine,* Aug 1927, 98 (Mrs. Isabelle Spencer, daughter of an English lord, "charges that her husband [Captain Harold Sherwood Spencer] went abroad for a four weeks' trip last winter, but that his stay lengthened into six months. This time, she asserts, he spent in a Paris apartment with Mary Miles Minter ['the screen star of yesterday'], who was supposedly there to nurse him through an illness."). Aydelott Ames, "Mary Miles Minter Was the Creation, and Victim, of a Dominating Mother," *FIR,* Oct 1969, 473–95, 501. Robert K. Klepper, "Mary Miles Minter: Beauty Wronged," *CI,* 265 (Jul 1997), C6-C11.

Minter, W[illiam] **F**[red] [actor] (b. 1892?–13 Jul 1937 [45], Los Angeles CA). "W.F. Minter," *Variety,* 21 Jul 1937 (in pictures 15 years). AS, p. 770. BHD1, p. 384. IFN, p. 208. Truitt, p. 234.

Mintz, Charles B. [animator/producer] (b. York PA, 1889–30 Dec 1939 [50?], Beverly Hills CA). AMD, p. 249. AS, p. 770. BHD2, p. 186. "Mintz Re-signs with Paramount," *MPW,* 17 Dec 1927, 17.

Mintz, Jack [actor: Keystone Cop] (b. 1895–19 Jan 1983 [88?], Woodland Hills CA). AS, p. 770 (b. 1893). BHD, p. 253.

Mintz, Sam [gag man/scenarist] (b. MA, 12 Jul 1898–13 Sep 1957 [59], Oakland CA). "Sam Mintz," *Variety,* 18 Sep 1957. AMD, p. 249. AS, p. 770. BHD2, p. 186. FDY, p. 433. "Comedy Constructionist Works with McDermott," *MPW,* 24 Apr 1926, 600.

Minzey, Frank [stage/film actor] (b. MA, 1879?–12 Nov 1949 [70], Lake George NY). m. **Rose Melville**, 1910 (d. 1946). (Kalem; Biograph; Keystone [LI NY]; Fox; Goldwyn.) "Frank Minzey, 70, On-Stage-Hit Team; With His Wife, Rose Melville, He Appeared in 'Sis Hopkins' 5,000 Times—Dies Up-State," *NYT,* 14 Nov 1949, 27:2. AS, p. 770. BHD, p. 253. IFN, p. 209. Truitt, p. 234.

Miranda, Carmen (sister of Aurora Miranda, 1905–1982) [film/TV singer/actress] (*née* Maria do Carmo Miranda da Cunha, b. Marco de Canavezes, Portugal, 9 Feb 1909–5 Aug 1955 [46], Beverly Hills CA; heart attack). m. David Alfred Sebastian, 17 Mar 1947, Beverly Hills CA. Martha Gil-Montero, *Brazilian Bombshell; The Biography of Carmen Miranda* (NY: Donald I. Fine, Inc., 1989). Aline Mosby, "Carmen's Last Dance; Film Shows Fatal Attack," *Pittsburgh Press,* 13 Oct 1955 (Miranda faltered during taping of a show with Jimmy Durante for NBC-TV the previous August; "A few hours later she was dead of a heart attack at her home."). (Extra, 1926; film debut: *O Carnaval Cantado No Rio;* TC-F; last film: *Scared Stiff,* 1953.) AS, p. 771. Warren Hoge, "A Museum in Rio Recalls Days of Carmen Miranda," *NYT,* 22 Apr 1979 (the Carmen Miranda Museum wqs built in Rio de Janeiro in 1976 to house her outfits). Stephen Holden, "Tragic Figure Beneath a Crown of Fruit," *NYT,* 5 Jul 1995, C11-C12 (review of documentary, *Carmen Miranda: Bananas Is My Business.* International Cinema, Inc., 1995). John J. O'Connor, "One Woman's Tragedy, Playing the Latin Clown," *NYT,* 6 Oct 1995, D18:5 (review of documentary). Eve Golden, "The Lady in the Tutti-Fruitti Hat: The Short, Dazzling Career of Carmen Miranda," *CI,* 274 (Apr 1998), 20–24 (includes filmography).

Miranda, Thomas N. [scenarist/title writer/publicist] (b. Warren Co. OH, 10 May 1886–17 Dec 1962 [76], Los Angeles CA). "Tom Miranda," *Variety,* 26 Dec 1962. AMD, p. 249. AS, p. 771. BHD2, p. 186. FDY, p. 447. "Miranda with World Film," *MPW,* 27 May 1916, 1524. "Miranda to Title 'Amateur Gentleman,'" *MPW,* 17 Jul 1926, 152. "Inspiration Signs Miranda," *MPW,* 7 Aug 1926, 339.

Mirande, Yves [director/scenarist] (*né* Charles Anatole Le Guerrec, b. Bagneux, France, 8 Mar 1875–20 Mar 1957 [82], Paris, France). AS, p. 771. BHD2, p. 186.

Miss Beautiful [actress]. No data found. AMD, p. 249. "'Miss Beautiful' Accepts a Dare," *MPW,* 11 Apr 1914, 222.

Mister, Cato [actor] (*né* Cato Mann, b. 1887–14 Dec 1977 [90?], Belleaire Bluffe FL). AS, p. 771.

Mistinguett [music hall/film actress/dancer] (*née* Jeanne Florentine Bourgeois, b. Enghiten-les-Bains, Val-d'Oise, [12 miles north of Paris], France, 17 Dec 1872–5 Jan 1956 [83], Bougival, near Paris, France; double pneumonia after a cerebral hemorrhage on 24 Dec 1955 [extrait de décès no. 1]). *Toute Ma Vie* (Paris: Rene Julliard, 1954). Mintinguett, *Mistinguett; Queen of the Paris Night,* trans. Lucienne Hill (London: Elek Books, 1954). *Mistinguett and Her Confessions,* trans. and ed., Hubert Griffith (London: Hurst & Blackett, Ltd., 1938). David Bret, *The Mistinguett Legend* (London: Biddles, Ltd., 1990). "Mistinguett Dies at Age of 82; Starred in French Music Halls; Singer and Dancer Between Wars Was Known for Her 'Million Dollar Legs,'" *NYT,* 6 Jan 1956, 23:2 (performed Apache dance with Maurice Chevalier at the Folies Bergère, 1911). "Mistinguett," *Variety,* 11 Jan 1956, 70:1; "Passing of Mistinguett at 82 Recalls Colorful French Music Hall Era," p. 63:3–64:4 ("Her famous gams, reportedly insured for millions of dollars, her flamboyant private life and her raucous but taking nature endeared her to generations of house fans."). AS, p. 771 (b. 3 Apr 1875). BHD, p. 253 (b. 5 Aug 1875). JS, p. 293 (in *La doppia ferita,* Italy, 1915).

Mitchell, Abbie [actress/singer] (b. Baltimore MD, 1884?–16 Mar 1960 [76], New York NY). m. Will Marion Cook (d. 1944). "Abbie

Mitchell; Actress, Is Dead; Singer [soprano] Was Widow of Composer," *NYT,* 20 Mar 1960, 86:4 (Broadway debut, 1898). "Abbie Mitchell," *Variety,* 23 Mar 1960. AS, p. 772. BHD, p. 253.

Mitchell, Belle [stage/film actress] (b. MI, 24 Sep 1889–12 Feb 1979 [89], Woodland Hills CA). (Paramount; Republic; MGM; Universal.) "Belle Mitchell," *Variety,* 21 Feb 1979. AS, p. 772. BHD1, p. 385. IFN, p. 209 (age 90).

Mitchell, Bruce [actor/director/scenarist] (*né* James Bruce Mitchell, b. Freeport IL, 16 Nov 1880–26 Sep 1952 [71], Los Angeles CA). "Bruce Mitchell," *Variety,* 1 Oct 1952 (age 70; "pioneer film director"). AS, p. 772. BHD, p. 253; BHD2, p. 186. FDY, p. 433. IFN, p. 209. Truitt, p. 234 (b. 1883).

Mitchell, Charles J. [actor] (b. New York NY, 17 May 1879–13 Dec 1929 [50], Los Angeles CA; suicide). "Charles Mitchell," *Variety,* 18 Dec 1929 (age 45). AS, p. 772. BHD, p. 253. IFN, p. 209. Truitt, p. 234.

Mitchell, Charles Mason [actor] (b. 1859?–16 Jun 1930 [71], New York NY). "Charles M. Mitchell," *Variety,* 25 Jun 1930. AS, p. 772. IFN, p. 209.

Mitchell, Claude H. [director] (b. Melbourne, Victoria, Australia, 18 Mar 1891–22 Nov 1967 [76], Los Angeles CA). BHD2, p. 186.

Mitchell, Dodson L[omax] [stage/film actor] (b. Memphis TN, 23 Jan 1868–2 Jun 1939 [71], New York NY). "Dodson Mitchell; On Stage 53 Years; Appeared with Alla Nazimova, Julia Marlowe and John Drew—Dies at 71; Made Debut Here in 1885; He Played in 'Ben-Hur,' 'Hedda Gabler'—Final Performance with Hampden in 1938," *NYT,* 3 Jun 1939, 15:4. "Mitchell Dodson," *Variety,* 7 Jun 1939. AS, p. 772. BHD, p. 253. IFN, p. 209.

Mitchell, Doris [actress]. No data found. AMD, p. 249. "New Stars with Essanay," *MPW,* 9 Aug 1913, 617.

Mitchell, Earle [stage/film actor] (b. La Platte MO, 1881?–17 Feb 1946 [64], New York NY [Death Certificate Index No. 4520]). "Earle Mitchell, Retired Actor, 64; Thespian Who Had 325 Roles in 276 Plays Dies—Appeared Under Noted Producers Here," *NYT,* 18 Feb 1946, 21:3. "Earle Mitchell," *Variety,* 20 Feb 1946. AS, p. 772.

Mitchell, Edmund [scenarist] (b. Glasgow, Scotland, 1861–31 Mar 1917 [56?], New York NY). BHD2, p. 186.

Mitchell, George A. [inventor of the camera which carries his name] (b. TN, 1889–16 Apr 1980 [90?], Pasadena CA). AS, p. 772.

Mitchell, Grant [stage/film actor] (*né* John Grant Mitchell, b. Columbus OH, 17 Jun 1874–1 May 1957 [82], Los Angeles CA; cerebral thrombosis). "Grant Mitchell, Actor, 82, Dead; Stage and Screen Performer for 45 Years Was Known for Character Roles," *NYT,* 2 May 1957, 31:3. "Grant Mitchell," *Variety,* 8 May 1957 (age 74; to Hollywood in 1933). AS, p. 772 (b. 17 Jan). BHD1, p. 385. IFN, p. 209. Katz, p. 814. SD. Truitt, p. 234.

Mitchell, Howard M. [actor/director] (b. Pittsburgh PA, 11 Dec 1883–9 Oct 1958 [75], Los Angeles CA). m. **Mary Land**, 22 Apr 1911, Jersey City NJ. "Howard Mitchell," *Variety,* 22 Oct 1958. AMD, p. 249. AS, p. 773 (b. 1887). BHD1, p. 385; BHD2, p. 186 (b. 1887; d. 4 Oct). IFN, p. 209 (d. 4 Oct). 1921 Directory, p. 271 (b. 1883). Truitt, p. 234. "Photoplayers Marry," *MPW,* 2 Dec 1911, 734. "Howard Mitchell at Thanhouser's," *MPW,* 18 Sep 1915, 1998.

Mitchell, [James] **Irving** [actor] (b. OR, 18 Mar 1891–3 Aug 1969 [78], Los Angeles CA; heart attack). "James I. Mitchell," *Variety,* 13 Aug 1969. AS, p. 773. BHD1, p. 385. IFN, 209.

Mitchell, Julien [actor] (b. Glossop, England, 13 Nov 1888–4 Nov 1954 [61], London, England). AS, p. 773.

Mitchell, Leslie Harold "Lee" [actor: Keystone Cop] (b. near Brandon, Manitoba, Canada, 1885–25 Oct 1965 [80], Vancouver, Canada). (Sennett, 1911.) "Leslie H. Mitchell," *Variety,* 240, 17 Nov 1965, 70:5 ("Bothered by klieg lights, he left film work in 1918."). AS, p. 773. BHD, p. 253. IFN, p. 209.

Mitchell, Millard [actor] (b. Havana, Cuba, 14 Aug 1900–13 Oct 1953 [53], Santa Monica CA). AS, p. 773.

Mitchell, Pell [editor/news director]. No data found. AMD, p. 249. "Second Year for Editor Mitchell," *MPW,* 17 Jun 1916, 2056. "Editor of Mutual Weekly on Vacation," *MPW,* 3 Feb 1917, 673. "Pell Mitchell Added to Staff of Fox News Weekly," *MPW,* 23 Aug 1919, 1110. "Pell Mitchell Organizes Free Lance Film Agency," *MPW,* 21 Aug 1920, 1045.

Mitchell, Rhea "Ginger" [actress] (b. Portland OR, 10 Dec 1890–16 Sep 1957 [66], Los Angeles CA; murdered by strangulation). (NYMPC.) "Rhea (Ginger) Mitchell," *Variety,* 18 Sep 1957 (age 52). AMD, p. 249. AS, p. 772 (Ginger Mitchell, b. 1893). BHD1, p. 385 (b. 1893). BR, pp. 57–58 (b. 1893). IFN, p. 209 (b. 1893). Truitt, p. 235. "Edeson-Mitchell-Hart," *MPW,* 19 Dec 1914, 1682. "Rhea Mitchell," *MPW,* 29 May 1915, 1411. "Rhea Mitchell," *MPW,* 15 Jul 1916, 417. "New Company for Rhea Mitchell," *MPW,* 13 Jan 1917, 215. "Rhea Mitchell Joins Paralta," *MPW,* 29 Sep 1917, 1980. "Rhea Mitchell to Play Opposite Bert Lytell," *MPW,* 13 Jul 1918, 227. Billy H. Doyle, "Lost Players," *CI,* 175 (Jan 1990), 38–39.

Mitchell, Sager J. [executive] (b. 1867–13 Oct 1952 [85?], Blackburn, England). BHD2, p. 186.

Mitchell, Sidney D. [lyricist] (b. Baltimore MD, 15 Jun 1888–25 Feb 1942 [53], Los Angeles CA). "Sidney D. Mitchell," *Variety,* 4 Mar 1942 (wrote lyrics for *You Turned the Tables on Me; I've Taken a Fancy to You*). AS, p. 773. ASCAP 66, p. 515. BHD2, p. 186.

Mitchell, Thomas [stage/film actor/director/producer] (b. Elizabeth NJ, 11 Jul 1892–17 Dec 1962 [70], Beverly Hills CA; cancer). m. Anne S. Brewer; Susan. (Columbia; MGM; AA, 1939.) "Thomas Mitchell, Actor Dead; Star of Stage and Screen, 70; Actor's Career in the Movies and in Theater Spanned a Half Century," *NYT,* 18 Dec 1962, 4:6 (began in *Cloudy with Showers,* 1934). "Thomas Mitchell," *Variety,* 19 Dec 1962. AS, p. 773. BHD1, p. 386. IFN, p. 209. Katz, p. 814. SD. Truitt, p. 235 (b. 1895).

Mitchell, Yvette [actress]. No data found. George A. Katchmer, "Forgotten Cowboys and Cowgirls—Part V," *CI,* 177 (Mar 1990), C6.

Mitsoras, Demetrius J. [actor] No data found. (Universal.)

Mittler, Leo [scenarist] (b. Vienna, Austria, 18 Dec 1893–16 May 1938 [44], Berlin, Germany). AS, p. 774.

Mitzer, Wilson [scenarist] (b. Benicia CA, 19 May 1876–3 Apr 1933 [66], Los Angeles CA; heart attack after pneumonia). AS, p. 774.

Mix, Art *see* **Dixon, Denver**

Mix, Ruth Jane (daughter of **Tom Mix** and **Olive M. Stokes**) [actress] (b. Dewey OK, 13 Jul 1912–21 Sep 1977 [65], Corpus Christi TX; buried in Brownsville TX). m. (1) Douglas Gilmore, Jun 1930, Yuma AZ; annulled; (2) John A. Guthrie, 1938; (3) William Hickman Hill (d. 1976). AS, p. 774. BHD1, p. 386. BR, pp. 384–86. GK, pp. 662–67. IFN, p. 209. George A. Katchmer, "Ruth Mix; A Chip Off the Old Block," *CI,* 100 (Oct 1983), 34, X1-X2. George Katchmer, "Remembering the Great Silents," *CI,* 245 (Nov 1995), 44–45.

Mix, Tom (father of **Ruth Mix**) [actor/scenarist/director] (*né* Thomas Hezikiah Mix, b. Mix Run [Dubois], Clearfield Co. PA, 6 Jan 1880–12 Oct 1940 [60], 18 miles south of Florence AZ; car accident). m. (1) Grace I. Allin, 18 Jul 1902, Louisville KY; (2) Kitty Jewell Perrine, 20 Dec 1905, Oklahoma City OK; (3) **Olive M. Stokes** [mother of Ruth Jane Mix, 1912–1977], 19 Jan 1909, Medora ND—div. 1917 (d. 1972); (4) **Victoria Forde** (*née* Hannaford), May 1918, Riverside CA—div. 24 Dec 1930 (d. 1964); (5) Mabel Hubbard Ward, 15 Feb 1932, Mexicali, Mexico. John H. Nichols, *Tom Mix; Riding Up to Glory* (Kansas City MO: The Lowell Press, Inc., 1980); *Tom Mix; Portrait of a Superstar; A Pictorial and Documentary Anthology* (Hershey PA: Keystone Enterprises, 1991); Paul E. Mix, *Tom Mix; A Heavily Illustrated Biography of the Western Star; with a Filmography* (Jefferson NC: McFarland & Co., Inc, 1995). (Selig-Polyscope, 1910; Fox; FBO; Universal.) "Tom Mix, Rider, Dies Under Auto; Circus and Screen Equestrian, Cowboy Idol of Youth, Killed in Arizona Car Upset," *NYT,* 13 Oct 1940, 1:6, 48:6 (began 1909; 370 features in 24 years). "Tom Mix One of the Screen's Fabulous Figures; Cowboy Star Earned $4,000,000," *Variety,* 16 Oct 1940 (age 69). AMD, p. 249. AS, p. 774. BHD1, p. 386; BHD2, p. 187. FFF, p. 43 (b. TX). FSFM, p. 265 (b. El Paso TX, 6 Jan 1880). FSS, p. 210. HCH, p. 115. IFN, p. 209 (b. DuBois PA). Katz, p. 815–16. MH, p. 128 (b. TX). MSBB, p. 1026. SD. Truitt, p. 235 (b. El Paso). WWS, p. 181 (b. El Paso). "Tom Mix Married," *Variety,* 10 May 1918, p. 44. "Tom Mix as a Thriller," *MPW,* 28 Jun 1913, 1345. "Tom Mix, Actor, Author," *MPW,* 20 Sep 1913, 1286. James S. McQuade, "Chicago Letter," *MPW,* 17 Jan 1914, 270. "Las Vegas' Welcome to Mix," *MPW,* 24 Jul 1915, 630. "Tom Mix," *MPW,* 18 Mar 1916, 1832. "Tom Mix," *MPW,* 20 May 1916, 1306. "Tom Mix Joins Fox Films," *MPW,* 6 Jan 1917, 61. Cal York, "Plays and Players," *Photoplay Magazine,* Feb 1917, 89 ("His latest mishap took the form of an injury in an automobile wreck near Los Angeles. And as a sort of painkiller, Tom was pinched for reckless driving."). "Tom Mix in Features," *MPW,* 20 Oct 1917, 368. "Mix Has Made Hit in Fox Pictures," *MPW,* 10 Aug 1918, 823. "Reynolds Talks of Mix, Range and Screen Cowboy," *MPW,* 14 Sep 1918, 1554. "X-Ray Reveals Bullets in Tom Mix's Leg," *MPW,* 23 Nov 1918, 848. "Tom Mix Begins Work," *MPW,* 7 Dec 1918, 1096. "Selig Polyscope Sells All Tom Mix Negatives," *MPW,* 7 Dec 1918, 1107. "Shoots Bullete Under Mix's Tie," *MPW,* 1 Mar 1919, 1195–96. "Mix Injured in Staging Fight," *MPW,* 29 Mar 1919, 1798. "Mix Writes Waltz in Memory of Horse," *MPW,* 12 Apr 1919, 230 (*Old Blue Waltz*). "Tom Mix," *MPW,* 19 Jul 1919, 357–58. "Tom Mix Wins Auto Race," *MPW,*

9 Aug 1919, 853. "Oil Discovered on Tom Mix Ranch," *MPW,* 31 Jul 1920, 610. "Fox Advises Those Who Would Sign Tom Mix His Contract Does Not Expire Until 1924," *MPW,* 4 Sep 1920, 101. "Tom Mix Is Acclaimed Everywhere on His First Visit to New York City," *MPW,* 9 Jul 1921, 210. "Tom Mix and Tony, Fiolm Star and Pony, Meet Guests at Hotel Astor Luncheon," *MPW,* 16 Jul 1921, 298. "Mix in Lawsuit," *MPW,* 24 Sep 1921, 421. "Mix Wins Auto Case," *MPW,* 1 Oct 1921, 536. "Wants to Regain Child," *MPW,* 26 Nov 1921, 425 (9-year-old daughter from marriage to Stokes). "Mix a Playwright," *MPW,* 4 Nov 1922, 58. "A Home for Tony," *MPW,* 30 Jun 1923, 755 (his horse). "Plan Varied Roles for Speedy Tom Mix," *MPW,* 30 Jun 1923, 756. "Tom Mix Appearing in a New Type of Role," *MPW,* 17 Nov 1923, 332. "Tom Mix Starts His Fiftieth Starring Vehicle for Fox," *MPW,* 14 Jun 1924, 653. "Zane Grey and Tom Mix Are Real Box Office Combination," *MPW,* 9 Aug 1924, 479. "Tom Mix Renews Contract with Fox Film Corporation," *MPW,* 31 Jan 1925, 491. "Tom Mix," *MPW,* 18 Apr 1925, 680. "Tom Mix," *MPW,* 23 May 1925, 456. Gladys Hall and Adele Whitely Fletcher, "We Interview Tom Mix," *MW,* 23 May 1925, 8–10, 33. "Tom Mix," *MPW,* 30 May 1925, 515. "Tom Mix," *MPW,* 6 Jun 1925, 683. "Tom Mix," *MPW,* 20 Jun 1925, 906. Don Ryan, "The Centaur of the Cinema; Tom Mix Is the Last of the Vanishing Americans," *MPC,* Jul 1926, 22–23, 64, 82–84. "Tom Mix," *MPW,* 11 Jul 1925, 194. "Tom Mix," *MPW,* 8 Aug 1925, 658. "Tom Mix," *MPW,* 3 Apr 1926, 326. "Tom Gives the Wife Some Spending Money," *MPW,* 2 May 1927, 787 (Forde). "Tom Mix Is Best News Story of Week on Coast," *MPW,* 25 Jun 1927, 571. "Tom Mix," *MPW,* 22 Oct 1927, 496. "Tom Mix and Wm. Fox Will Part Company, March 24, 1928," *MPW,* 26 Nov 1927, 19. Cedric Belfrage, "Just Him and Tony; Tom Mix Can't Make Out Why His Wife and Thomasina Left Him," *MPC,* Feb 1929, 55, 86 ("Gosh, I feel lonesome up here in this big place without my wife and Thomasina."). Mike Gaffney, "The Films of Tom Mix," *CFC,*47 (Summer, 1975), 56. Eldon K. Everett, "The Tom Mix Chronicles," *CI,* 67 (Jan 1980), 32–34 (filmography); 68 (Feb 1980), 26–27; 69 (Mar 1980), 21.; 70 (Jul 1980), 30–31; 71 (Sep 1980), 50–51; 72 (Nov 1980), 32–34; 73 (Jan 1981), 46–47; 74 (Mar 1981), 46–49. William Wilson, "Mix Myths [letter]," *CI,* 76 (Jul 1981), 58 (AWOL, Oct 1902; declared a deserter in Nov 1902). Eldon K. Everett, "Tom Mix's Love Life," *CI,* 112 (Oct 1984), 14–15 (account of marriages to Stokes and Forde). Buck Rainey, "Tom Mix's Selig Films," *CI,* 145 (Jul 1987), 50–51. Bud Norris, "New Tom Mix Revelations," *CI,* 201 (Mar 1992), 46–48. Tom Gibb, "Tom Mix Legend Alive at Birthplace," *Pittsburgh Post-Gazette,* 10 Jul 1994, pp. D-1, D-4 (re Tom Mix Comes Home Museum in Cameron County. "Tom Mix was a hero to a lot of people."). Gene Bell, "Who The Hell Is Tom Mix; Part II," *CI,* 251 (May 1996), 36; Part III, *CI,* 253 (Jul 1996), C10-C11; Part IV, *CI,* 255 (Sep 1996), 32; Part V, *CI,* 257 (Nov 1996), C6; Part VI, *CI,* 258 (Dec 1996), 40–41; Part VII, *CI,* 263 (May 1997), 40; Part VIII, *CI,* 264 (Jun 1997), C10-C11; Part IX, *CI,* 265 (Jul 1997), 38–39; Part X, *CI,* 266 (Aug 1997), 42–43; Part XI, *CI,* 270 (Dec 1997), C8-C9; Part XII, *CI,* 271 (Dec 1997), 42–43; Part XIII, *CI,* 272 (Feb 1998), C8-C9; Conclusion, *CI,* 273 (Mar 1998), C10-C13. Bud Norris, "Tom Mix Stamp Debuts Soon," *CI,* 251 (May 1996), 38.

Miyagawa, Kazuo [cinematographer] (b. Kyoto, Japan, 25 Feb 1908–7 Aug 1999 [91], Kyoto, Japan; kidney failure). m. Kazuko (2 sons, 1 daughter). (Nikkatsu Corp., 1926.) "Kazuo Miyagawa, 'Rashomon [1950]' Cinematographer, 91," *NYT,* 10 Aug 1999, C20. "Other Deaths; Kazuo Miyagawa," *PP-G,* 9 Aug 1999, C-4:5 (also filmed *Ugetsu,* 1953).

Mizner, Wilson [playwright/scenarist] (b. Benicia CA, 19 May 1876–3 Apr 1933 [57], Los Angeles CA). m. Mrs. Charles T. Yerkes. "Wilson Mizner, Dramatist, Dead; Colorful Career from Klondike to Hollywood Ends on West Coast at Age of 58; Married Widow of Yerkes; Author of 'The Deep Purple' Won and Lost Fortune in a Life of Adventure," *NYT,* 4 Apr 1933, 17:3. "Wilson Mizner," *Variety,* 11 Apr 1933 (age 56). AMD, p. 250. AS, p. 774. BHD2, p. 187. SD. "Wilson Mizner Doing More Playlets…," *NYDM,* 13 Nov 1915, 20:2 ("Mizner is one of the most interesting men on Broadway to-day. His gift of original, incisive speech is all his own, and he uses Anglo-Saxon like a sickle to cut down upstarts."). "Mizner Turns Writer," *MPW,* 21 May 1927, 171. Frances Gilmore, "He's Done Very Well by Himself; Wilson Mizner Is Broadway's Pride; He's Won and Lost Fortunes; It's All in the Game," *MPC,* Mar 1928, 25, 66.

Mizoguchi, Kenji [director/producer/scenarist] (b. Tokyo, Japan, 16 May 1898–24 Aug 1956 [58], Kyoto, Japan). AS, p. 774.

Moberg, Vilhelm [actor/director] (b. Sweden, 1899–8 Aug 1973 [74?], Stockholm, Sweden). AS, p. 774.

Modeen, Thor [actor/dancer/director] (b. Kingsor, Sweden, 22 Jan 1898–28 May 1950 [52], Stockholm, Sweden). AS, p. 775.

Modi, Sohrab [actor/director/producer] (*né* Sorhab Meherwanji, b. Bombay, India, 2 Nov 1897–28 Jan 1984 [86], Bombay, India). AS, p. 775.

Modjeska, Felix B. [actor] (b. Omaha NB, 6 Aug 1887–29 Mar 1940 [52], Newport Beach CA). BHD, p. 253.

Modley, Albert [actor] (b. England, 1891–23 Feb 1979 [87?], Morecambe, England; heart attack). AS, p. 775.

Modot, Gaston Victor [actor/scenarist] (b. Paris, France, 30 Dec 1887–19 Feb 1970 [82], Le Raincy, France [extrait de décès no. 51]). AS, p. 775 (b. 31 Dec). BHD1, p. 386; BHD2, p. 187. IFN, p. 210.

Moehring, Kansas [actor] (*né* Carl F. Moehring, b. OH, 9 Jul 1897–3 Oct 1968 [71], Los Angeles Co. CA). (Universal.) AS, p. 775 (d. 1969). BHD1, p. 386. IFN, p. 210. George Katchmer, "Remembering the Great Silents," *CI,* 248 (Feb 1996), 46–47.

Moeller, Philip [director] (b. New York NY, 1880–26 Apr 1958 [78?], New York NY). BHD2, p. 187.

Moen, Lars [producer/director]. No data found. AMD, p. 250. "Moen Victim of Kleig Eyes," *MPW,* 10 Sep 1927, 84. "Moen's Direction Wins Him GERMan Assignment," *MPW,* 17 Sep 1927, 147.

Moerman, Ernest [director/scenarist] (b. Belgium, 1897–1943 [46?], Belgium). AS, p. 775.

Moeschlin, Felix [director/scenarist] (b. Bale, Switzerland, 31 Jul 1882–4 Oct 1969 [88], Bale, Switzerland). AS, p. 775.

Moest, Hurbert [director] (*né* Richard Hubert Moest, b. Cologne, Germany, 3 Dec 1877–5 Dec 1953 [76], Berlin, Germany). AS, p. 775.

Moffat, Margaret [actress] (b. Scotland, 11 Oct 1883–19 Feb 1942 [58], Los Angeles CA). AS, p. 775.

Moffatt, Edward S. [actor/scenarist] (b. NJ, 1876–8 Jun 1944 [68?], Los Angeles CA). AS, p. 775.

Moffett, Cleveland [scenarist] (b. 1863–Oct 1926 [53?], Paris, France). BHD2, p. 187.

Moffitt, Jefferson [scenarist] (b. CA, 17 Dec 1887–8 Apr 1954 [66], Los Angeles CA). BHD2, p. 187. FDY, p. 433.

Moglia, Linda [actress in Italian silents]. No data found.

Moguy, Léonide [director] (*né* Léonide Maguilewsky, b. Odessa, Ukraine, Russia, 14 Jul 1898–20 Apr 1976 [77], Paris, France). AS, p. 775.

Mohan, Earl John [actor] (b. Pueblo CO, 1889?–15 Oct 1928 [39], Los Angeles CA). "Earl Mohan," *Variety,* 17 Oct 1928. AS, p. 775. BHD, p. 253. IFN, p. 210.

Moholy-Nagy, Laszlo [director/scenarist] (b. Bacs-Bodrog, Hungary, 20 Jul 1895–24 Nov 1946 [51], Chicago IL). AS, p. 775.

Mohr, Hal [cinematographer/director] (b. San Francisco CA, 2 Aug 1894–10 May 1974 [79], Santa Monica CA). m. Evelyn Venable. "Hal Mohr, Winner of 2 Oscars, Dies; Cameraman for First Sound Film, 1927 'Jazz Singer,'" *NYT,* 12 May 1974, 51:4. "Hal Mohr," *Variety,* 15 May 1974. AMD, p. 250. AS, p. 775. BHD2, p. 187. FDY, p. 463. IFN, p. 210. Katz, 818. "Crack Cameraman to Warner Bros.," *MPW,* 18 Dec 1926, 498.

Moisant, Bertin [cinematographer] (b. 1891–4 Dec 1933 [42?]). BHD2, p. 187.

Moissi, Alexander (father of Bettina Moissi) [stage/film actor] (b. Austrian Trieste, Italy, 2 Apr 1879–22 Mar 1935 [55], Vienna, Austria; pneumonia). m. (daughter Bettina, b. Berlin, Germany, 14 Oct 1923). (Began 1913; made the German-language *The Royal Box,* WB, 1929.) AS, p. 776 (d. Lugano, Switzedrland). BHD1, p. 387. JS, p. 295 (appeared in *Lorenzino de' Medici,* Italy, 1934). Waldman, p. 195. Vittorio Martinelli, "Kino-Lieblinge," *Griffithiana,* 38/39 (Oct 1990), 62.

Moisson, Charles Clément [director] (b. Chateau-Gontier, France, 8 Aug 1864–1 Oct 1943 [79], Paris, France). AS, p. 776.

Moja, Hella [actress/scenarist] (*née* Helene Gertrud Muyzyscyzck, b. Königsberg, Germany, 18 Jan 1896–15 Jan 1937 [40], Charlottenburg, Germany). m. Erich Morawsky. *Nie wieder in meinem Leben.* AS, p. 776 (*née* Moyzyscyck). BHD1, p. 387. Vittorio Martinelli, "Kino-Lieblinge," *Griffithiana,* 38/39 (Oct 1990), 19.

Mojica, José [opera tenor/stage/film actor/singer] (*né* Francisco Mojica, b. San Gabriel, Mexico, 14 Sep 1899–20 Sep 1974 [75], Lima, Peru; heart attack). *I, a Sinner* (1963); sold 3,000,000 copies in Spanish. "Jose Mojica, Mexican Film Star Who Became a Friar [Fray José], Dies at 78," *NYT,* 22 Sep 1974, 57:1; William M. Freeman, "Sang at the Met," 57:1 (entered a monastery in 1942 following the death of his mother). "Jose Mojica," *Variety,* 276, 25 Sep 1974, 62:3 (age 78; ordained a priest in 1948). AS, p. 776 (b. San Miguel de Allende, Mexico). BHD1, p. 387. IFN, p. 210 (b. 1896, San Miguel de Allende, Mexico).

Molander, Gustaf (brother of **Olaf Molander**) [actor/scenarist/director] (*né* Gustav Molander, b. Helsinki, Finland, 18 Nov 1888–19 Jun 1973 [84], Stockholm, Sweden). AS, p. 776. BHD2, p. 187.

Molander, Karin [actress] (*née* Karin Edwertz, b. Stockholm, Sweden, 20 May 1889–1978 [89?], Vardinge/Stockholm, Sweden). AS, p. 776. BHD, p. 254.

Molander, Olaf (brother of **Gustaf Molander**) [actor/director] (aka Olaf Morel, b. Helsinki, Finland, 18 Oct 1892–26 May 1966 [73], Stockholm, Sweden). AS, p. 776. BHD1, p. 387; BHD2, p. 187.

Molina, Joe [actor] (b. AZ, 23 May 1899–16 Dec 1977 [78], Woodland Hills CA). AS, p. 776. BHD1, p. 387. IFN, p. 210.

Molinari, Aldo [director] (b. Rome, Italy, 1885–31 May 1959 [74?], Rome, Italy). AS, p. 776.

Molinari, Luciano [actor] (b. Garlasco, Italy, 1878–26 Jul 1940 [62?], Turin, Italy; alone and forgotten in a hospital bed). JS, p. 296 (in Italian silents from 1913).

Mollison, Clifford [actor] (b. London, England, 1896–5 Jun 1986 [90?], Cyprus). AS, p. 776.

Molnar, Ferenc [actor/scenarist/playwright] (b. Budapest, Hungary, 12 Jan 1878–1 Apr 1952 [74], New York NY). m. (2) Lili Darvas. "Ferenc Molnar," *Variety,* 186, 2 Apr 1952, 79:1 (his *Liliom* inspired *Carousel*). AMD, p. 250. AS, p. 776. BHD1, p. 387; BHD2, p. 187. "Ferenc Molnar to Write for M-G-M," *MPW,* 31 Oct 1925, 710.

Molter, Bennett A. [scenarist/actor/assistant director]. (Pathé; Kalem; Universal; Metro.) AMD, p. 250. "Henry Otto's Assistant Made Deputy Sheriff," *MPW,* 12 Aug 1916, 1122 (LA county). "Molter Off to War; Picture Man to Join American Ambulance Corps Somewhere in France," *MPW,* 28 Oct 1916, 566.

Molyneaux, Eileen (cousin of dress designer Edward Molyneux) [stage/film actress/dancer] (b. Pietermaritzburg, Natal, South Africa, 26 Aug 1893–13 Apr 1962 [68], Bryn Mawr PA). (Stage debut: *London Calling,* London.) "Eileen Molyneaux," *Variety,* 226, 25 Apr 1962, 63:3 (ca. 60). BHD, p. 254.

Momand, Arthur [cartoonist]. No data found. AMD, p. 250. "Arthur Momand's Cartoons," *MPW,* 11 Sep 1915, 1809.

Mon, Arturo S. [director] (b. La Plata, Argentina, 2 Dec 1893).

Moncao, Eitel [producer] (b. Rome, Italy, 1902–4 Feb 1989 [86?], Rome, Italy). AS, p. 777.

Monaco, James V. [songwriter] (b. Fornici, Italy, 3 Jan 1885–16 Oct 1945 [60], Beverly Hills CA; heart attack). "James V. Monaco; Composer of Numerous Popular Songs Dies on Coast," *NYT,* 18 Oct 1945, 23:3 (wrote *Madam Lasonga; Pocketful of Dreams; Mr. Dream Man; Only Forever*). "James V. Monaca," *Variety,* 24 Oct 1945 (wrote *You Made Me Love You; Row, Row, Row*). AS, p. 777. ASCAP 66, p. 517. BHD2, p. 187.

Mona-Dol [actress] (*née* Amélie Alice Gabrielle Delbart, b. Lille, France, 28 May 1901–29 Dec 1990 [89], Paris, France). AS, p. 777.

Monahan, Joseph A., Sr. [actor/assistant director] (b. 1882–9 Nov 1931 [49?], Teaneck NJ). BHD, p. 254; BHD2, p. 187.

Monaldi, Gastone [actor/director] (b. Passignano sul Trasimento, Italy, 9 Jun 1882–1 Jan 1932 [49], Sarteano, Italy). m. **Fernanda Batiferri**. JS, p. 296 (in Italian silents from 1911).

Monberg, George [actor] (b. IL, 9 Aug 1890–7 Mar 1925 [34]). BHD, p. 254. IFN, p. 210.

Monca, Georges [actor/director] (b. France, 1888–15 Jan 1940 [51?], France). AS, p. 777.

Moncrieff, Murray [actor] (d. 21 May 1949). BHD, p. 254.

Moncries, Edward [actor] (aka Edward Moncrief, b. Brooklyn NY, 1859?–22 Mar 1938 [79], Los Angeles CA). (Chaplin.) "Edward Moncries," *Variety,* 30 Mar 1938. AS, p. 777. BHD, p. 254. IFN, p. 210.

Mondose, Alex [actor/singer] (*né* Alexandre Marie Michel Onsmonde, b. Liege, Belgium, 28 Nov 1893–27 Jan 1972 [78], Schaerbeek, Belgium). AS, p. 777.

Mong, William V. [actor/director/scenarist] (b. Chambersburg PA, 25 Jun 1875–11 Dec 1940 [65], Studio City CA). m. Esme Ward. "William V. Mong; ex-Actor Made Screen Debut in 'Connecticut Yankee' in 1910," *NYT,* 14 Dec 1940, 17:4 (age 63). "William V. Mong," *Variety,* 18 Dec 1940. AMD, p. 250. AS, p. 777 (d. 10 Dec). BHD1, p. 387; BHD2, p. 187. IFN, p. 210. MH, p. 128. SD. Truitt, pp. 235–36. "Mong Writing Scenario," *MPW,* 24 Sep 1921, 426. George Katchmer, "Remembering the Great Silents," *CI,* 229 (Jul 1994), 40–41.

Monica, A.G. Maria [dancer/actress] (*née* Maria Antonia Modica, b. Palermo, Sicily, Italy, 19 May 1899–29 Oct 1991 [92], Las Vegas NV). "Maria A.G. Monica," *Variety,* 11 Nov 1991, p. 71. AS, p. 777 (b. 27 Aug). BHD, p. 254 (Marcia Monica). (She danced with Valentino in a stage show that toured the U.S.)

Monkman, Phyllis [stage/film actress/dancer] (*née* Phyllis Harrison, b. London, England, 8 Jan 1892–2 Dec 1976 [84], London, England). m. (widowed, 1937). "Phyllis Monkman," *Variety,* 285, 29 Dec 1976, 63:4. AS, p. 777. BHD1, p. 387. IFN, p. 210.

Monroe, Frank [stage/film actor] (b. Jersey City NJ, 1864?–19 Jul 1937 [73], Bay Shore, LI NY). m. Viola B. Miles (d. 1915). "Frank Monroe, Long a Character Actor; Detective in the Original Cast of 'Alias Jimmy Valentine' Began Career in 1884—Dies at 73," *NYT,* 20 Jul 1937, 23:2. "Frank Monroe," *Variety,* 21 Jul 1937. AS, p. 778. BHD, p. 254. SD.

Monson, Beatrice Bee [actress]. No data found. (Mermaid Comedies.) In *April Fool* with Lloyd Hamilton (*MPW,* 30 Oct 1920, p. 1230).

Montagne, Edward J. [scenarist/director/producer] (b. London, England, 1885?–15 Sep 1932 [47], Los Angeles CA). (Paramount; RKO.) "E.J. Montagne," *Variety,* 20 Sep 1932. AS, p. 778. BHD2, p. 187. FDY, p. 433.

Montagu, E.H. [executive]. No data found. AMD, p. 250. E.H. Montagu, "The Motion Picture Trade in Europe," *MPW,* 11 Jul 1914, 192.

Montague, Fred[erick] [actor] (b. London, England, 1864–2 Jul 1919 [55], Los Angeles CA; intestinal obstruction). m. **Rita** (d. 1962). (Universal.) "Frederick Montague," *Variety,* 25 Jul 1919 (age 52). AMD, p. 250. AS, p. 778 (d. 3 Jul). BHD, p. 254. IFN, p. 211 (d. 3 Jul). "Frederick Montague Appears in 'The Bait,'" *MPW,* 8 Jan 1916, 220. "Obituary," *MPW,* 26 Jul 1919, 505 (d. 4 Jul, age 58). George Katchmer, "Remembering the Great Silents," *CI,* 234 (Dec 1994), 41.

Montague, Harry E. [actor] (d. 5 Nov 1944).

Montague, Monte [actor] (*né* Walter Montague, b. Somerset KY, 23 Apr 1891–6 Apr 1959 [67], Burbank CA). AS, p. 778. BHD1, p. 388. IFN, p. 211.

Montague, Rita [actress] (*née?,* b. IL, 16 May 1883–5 May 1962 [78], Los Angeles CA). m. **Frederick Montague** (d. 1919). "Rita Montague," *Variety,* 23 May 1962 ("in motion pictures in the teens"). AS, p. 778. BHD, p. 254. IFN, p. 211. Truitt, p. 236.

Montague, Walter [actor] (b. 1892?–Apr? 1959 [47], Burbank CA). "Walter Montague," *Variety,* 22 Apr 1959 ("appeared in early westerns, with such stars as Buck Jones, Tom Mix and Hoot Gibson. He was in the first 'Tarzan' film, with Elmo Lincoln.").

Montague, Walter [scenarist] (b. Kent, England, 1855–15 Jan 1924 [68?], San Francisco CA). AS, p. 778. BHD2, p. 188.

Montalvan, Celia [actress] (*née* Celia Montalvan Romero, b. Agosto, Mexico, 1899–10 Jan 1958 [58?], Mexico City, Mexico). AS, p. 779.

Montana, Bill *see* **Church, Fred**

Montana, Bull [actor] (*né* Luigi Montagna, b. Vogliera, Italy, 16 May 1887–24 Jan 1950 [62], Los Angeles CA; lombar thrombosis). m. (2) Mary Mathews—div. 1931. "Bull Montana Dead; Actor and Wrestler," *NYT,* 25 Jan 1950, 27:1. "Lewis (Bull) Montana," *Variety,* 25 Jan 1950 (age 64). AMD, p. 250. AS, p. 779. BHD1, p. 388. IFN, p. 211. Truitt, p. 236. "'Bull' Montana to Coach Sailors," *MPW,* 15 Jun 1918, 1570. "Quick-Thinking Actor Escapes from the Snare of the Fowler and Shows a Way to Beat Cops," *MPW,* 29 May 1920, 1176. "Wants to Be an American," *MPW,* 17 Sep 1921, 293. "'Bull' Ties Up with a 'Tartar,'" *MPW,* 23 Sep 1922, 280. Jack Wooldridge, "Yea! Bo!! The *Bull* Has His Mash Notes Too," *MPC,* Apr 1928, 40, 83, 87. George Katchmer, "Remembering the Great Silents," *CI,* 234 (Dec 1994), 41–42.

Montano, A. [actor] (b. Barbados, West Indies-d. 6 Sep 1914, Long Island NY). AS, p. 779. BHD, p. 254.

Monteiro, Pilar [actress] (b. Portugal, 1876–15 Dec 1962 [86?], Lisbon, Portugal). AS, p. 779.

Montel, Blanche [actress] (*née* Rose Blanche Jeanne Montel, b. Tours, France, 14 Aug 1902–31 Mar 1998 [95], Luzarches, France [extrait de décès no. 14]). AS, p. 779.

Montenegro, Conchita [actress] (b. San Sebastian, Spain, 1912). m. actor/singer/director Raúl Roulien. (Began in Spain, 1927; made foreign-language films in Hollywood; last film: Lola Montès, 1944.) Waldman, p. 198.

Monterey, Carlotta [stage/film actress] (*née* Hazel Neilson Taasinge, b. San Francisco CA, 28 Dec 1888–18 Nov 1970 [82], Westwood NJ). m. (3) Ralph Barton; (4) playwright Eugene O'Neill, 1929, Paris, France; M.C. Chapman. "Carlotta Monterey O'Neill," *Variety,* 25 Nov 1970 (age 75). AS, p. 779. BHD, p. 254. SD, p. 896.

Montes, Gina [actress] (b. Florence, Italy). JS, p. 299 (in Italian silents from 1914).

Montgomery, Baby Peggy *see* **Baby Peggy**

Montgomery, Betty [actress] (d. 1 Jan 1922). BHD, p. 254. IFN, p. 211.

Montgomery, David C. [stage/film actor] (b. St. Joseph MO, 21 Apr 1870–20 Apr 1917 [46], Chicago IL; after illness and operation). Unmarried. "David C. Montgomery," *Variety,* XLVI, 27 Apr 1917, 14:3 (age 47; vaudeville team of Montgomery and Stone, formed 19 Apr 1895; made $150 a week, "an enormous salary for those days."). BHD, p. 254.

Montgomery, Earl Triplett [actor] (b. Santa Cruz CA, 24 May 1894–28 Oct 1966 [72], Los Angeles Co. CA; cancer). (Vitagraph.) AMD, p. 250. AS, p. 779 (b. 24 Mar). BHD1, p. 388. IFN, p. 211. "Father of Comedian Dead," *MPW,* 17 May 1919, 1026 (d. in Juneau AK). "Vitagraph to Star Separetely Earl Montgomery and Joe Rock," *MPW,* 20 Mar 1920, 1992.

Montgomery, Frank E. [actor/director] (b. Petrolia PA, 14 Jun 1877–18 Jul 1944 [67], Los Angeles CA). m. **Mona Darkfeather** (d. 1977). (Bison; Universal; Kalem.) "Frank Montgomery," *Variety,* 26 Jul 1944. AMD, p. 250. AS, p. 780. BHD1, p. 388; BHD2, p. 188. "Secrets of Success," *MPW,* 7 Sep 1912, 982. "Montgomery's Own Co.; Producer of Indian Features Has Now Formed Company for Comedies and Dramas," *NYDM,* 23 Sep 1914, 25:2 (temporarily at Edendale CA). "'Monty' and 'Darkfeather' Features," *MPW,* 3 Oct 1914, 45. "Montgomery Now Producing Darkfeather Series," *MPW,* 17 Oct 1914, 318. "Montgomery to Direct for Liberty," *MPW,* 13 Feb 1915, 1003. "Horsley Engages Frank Montgomery," *MPW,* 28 Aug 1915, 1457. "Staging African STOries," *MPW,* 9 Oct 1915, 265. "Montgomery Hard at Work in Spokane," *MPW,* 25 May 1918, 1129. Billy H. Doyle, "Lost Players," *CI,* 157 (Jul 1988), 23.

Montgomery, Jack Travers (father of **Baby Peggy**) [extra/stuntman] (b. Omaha NB, 14 Nov 1891–21 Jan 1962 [70], Los Angeles CA; cancer). m. **Marian** Baxter, 16 Jun 1915, Lancaster WI (d. 1977). Diana Serra Cary [daughter], *The Hollywood Posse* (Boston: Houghton Mifflin Co., 1975; rpt. Norman OK: Univ. of OK, 1996). "Jack Montgomery," *Variety,* 31 Jan 1962. AS, p. 780. BHD1, p. 388. IFN, p. 211. Truitt, p. 236.

Montgomery, James H. [scenarist] (b. 1888?–17 Jun 1966 [78], New York NY). m. Constance Montague (widow). (MGM.) "J.H. Montgomery, Author of Comedies," *NYT,* 19 Jun 1966, 84:8. "James H. Montgomery," *Variety,* 29 Jun 1966. BHD2, p. 188.

Montgomery, James S. [stage/film actor] (b. 1898?–9 Nov 1955 [57], Phildelpha PA; heart attack). AS, p. 780. (Ince.) IFN, p. 211. J. Van Cartmell, "Along the Pacific Coast," *NYDM,* 13 Nov 1915, 31:1 (hired by Ince).

Montgomery, Mabel [actress] (b. Brooklyn NY–d. 20 Jul 1942, Honolulu HI; result of nervous shock suffered during bombing of Pearl Harbor on 7 Dec 1941). m. twice: (2) James Mooney. "Mabel Montgomery; Ex-Actress Dies in Hawaii—Was Victim of Japanese Raid," *NYT,* 24 Jul 1942, 19:4. "Mabel Montgomery," *Variety,* 29 Jul 1942. AS, p. 780. BHD, p. 254.

Montgomery, Marian (mother of **Baby Peggy**) [extra] (*née* Marian Baxter, b. Milwaukee WI, 2 Jul 1896–7 Feb 1977 [79], Woodland Hills CA). m. **Jack Montgomery**, 16 Jun 1915, Lancaster WI (d. 1962). Diana Serra Cary [daughter], *The Hollywood Posse; The Story of a Gallant Band of Horsemen Who Made Movie History* (rpt., Norman OK: Univ. of Oklahoma, 1996.) AS, p. 780 (under Peggy Montgomery). BHD1, p. 389 (b. 3 Jul; d. 5 Feb). IFN, p. 211. George A. Katchmer, "Remembering the Great Silents [Marion Baxter]," *CI,* 172 (Oct 1989), C12; "Update—Forgotten Cowboys/Girls," *CI,* 179 (May 1990), 43. George Katchmer, "Remembering the Great Silents," *CI,* 249 (Mar 1996), 46–47. Her daughter, Mrs. Diana Serra Cary (Baby Peggy), writes: "Mother's birthdarte was always a bit beclouded, but to my best knowledge it was July 2, 1897. She used to fudge the year and later even changed the date to the 4th of July out of a sense of patriotism. But I remember she celebrated her 32nd birthday in July of 1929 and that squares with the above date." (letter to author, 12 May 1997).

Montgomery, Peggy [actress] (b. Rock Island IL, 1907). AMD, p. 251. BR, pp. 182–83. "Wins Beauty Contest," *MPW,* 13 Sep 1924, 116.

Montgomery, Robert (father of Elizabeth Montgomery) [stage/film/radio/TV actor/director/producer/SAG president, 1935–37] (*né* Henry Montgomery, Jr., b. Beacon NY, 21 May 1904–27 Sep 1981 [77], New York NY; cancer). (Broadway debut: *The Mask and the Face,* 10 Sep 1924; film debut: *College Days,* 1926; MGM.) m. (1) Elizabeth Bryan Allen, 1928–50 (son, Robert, Jr.; daughter, Elizabeth, 1933–95); (2) Elizabeth Grant Herkness, 1950. David Bird, "Robert Montgomery, Actor, Dies at 77," *NYT,* 28 Sep 1981, B6:1. Todd McCarthy, "Robert Montgomery, Stage, Screen and Radio-TV Talent, Dies at 77," *Variety,* 30 Sep 1981. AS, p. 780. BHD1, p. 389; BHD2, p. 188. John Roberts, "Robert Montgomery: A Man of Many Parts," *CI,* 297 (Mar 2000), 6–9 (includes filmography).

Monthyl, Marcelle [actress] (*née* Marcelle Madeleine Montalenti, b. Monaco, Principality of Monaco, 8 Jun 1892–8 Nov 1950 [58], Paris, France [extrait de décès no. 1993/1950]). AS, p. 780.

Monti, Carlotta [actress] (b. 20 Jan 1907–3 Dec 1993 [86], Woodland Hills CA). AS, p. 780. BHD1, p. 389 (d. 8 Dec).

Montori, Alfredo [art director] (b. Rome, Italy, 17 Feb 1893). JS, p. 300 (worked on *Ben Hur,* 1925, and other Italian silents).

Montoya, Maria Tereza [actress] (*née* Maria Teresa Montoya Pardave, b. Mexico City, Mexico, 17 Jun 1885–1 Aug 1974 [89], Mexico; heart attack). AS, p. 780.

Montranez, Rita [actress] (*née* Rita Montanez de los Perez, b. Guanabacoa, Cuba, 22 May 1900). AS, p. 779.

Montrose, Belle [actress] (b. 1886–25 Oct 1964 [78?], Los Angeles CA). AS, p. 780.

Montt, Christina [actress] (b. Chile, 1897?–22 Apr 1969 [72], Los Angeles CA; heart attack). (Paramount.) "Cristina Montt," *Variety,* 30 Apr 1969. AS, p. 780. BHD1, p. 389. IFN, p. 211. Truitt, p. 236.

Montuori, Carlo Luigi (father of cinematographer Mario Montuori, b. 1920) [cinematographer] (b. Casacalenda, Italy, 3 Aug 1883 [extrait de naissance no. 231]-4 Mar 1968 [82], Rome, Italy [extrait de décès no. 479/1968]). AS, p. 780 (b. 1883). BHD2, p. 188 (Carlo Montueri, b. 1885). JS, pp. 300–01 (in Italian silents from 1914).

Moody, William Vaughn [scenarist] (b. Spencer IN, 8 Jul 1869–17 Oct 1910 [41], Colorado Springs CO). BHD2, p. 188.

Moody, Mrs. William Vaughn [scenarist] (*née?,* d. 22 Feb 1932, Chicago IL). m. **William Vaughn Moody** (d. 1910). BHD, p. 254; BHD2, p. 188.

Mooers, De Sacia (sister of **Ruth Saville**) [actress/writer] (b. MI, 19 Nov 1888–11 Jan 1960 [71], Los Angeles CA). m. Harry L. Lewis. "De Sacia Mooers Dead; Star of Silent Films Was 72—Tom Mix' Leading Lady," *NYT,* 13 Jan 1960, 47:3 (age 72; in 100+ films). "De Sacia Mooers," *Variety,* 20 Jan 1960 (age 72). AMD, p. 251. AS, p. 781 (b. Allessandro, Mojave Desert CA). BHD1, p. 389. IFN, p. 211. Truitt, p. 236 (b. Alessandro, Mojave Desert CA). "Bruenner and Persons Star Miss Mooers, Blond Vampire," *MPW,* 28 Aug 1920, 1146. "Rock and Miss Mooers Lose Receivership Application," *MPW,* 3 Dec 1921, 550.

Moomaw, Lewis H. [director/scenarist] (b. Baker OR, 5 May 1889–22 Aug 1980 [91], San Diego CA). AMD, p. 251. BHD2, p. 188. "Notes of the Trade," *MPW,* 8 May 1909, 586. "New Moomaw Picture," *MPW,* 4 Jul 1925, 83.

Moon, Arthur M[orse] [actor] (b. Garden City KS, 1889–17 Oct 1918 [29?], Helena MT; influenza). m. **Donna** Drew (d. 1918). (Mutual; Universal; Vogue.) AMD, p. 251 (Arthur Morris Moon). AS, p. 781. BHD, p. 255. "Obituary," *MPW,* 16 Nov 1918, 727. Billy H. Doyle, "Lost Players," *CI,* 139 (Jan 1987), 55.

Moon, Donna [stage/film actress] (*née* Donna Drew, d. 24 Oct 1918, Helena MT; influenza). m. **Arthur M. Moon** (d. 1918). AMD, p. 251. AS, p. 781. BHD, p. 254. Ragan 2, p. 1171. SD. "Obituary," *MPW,* 16 Nov 1918, 727. Billy H. Doyle, "Lost Players," *CI,* 139 (Jan 1987), 55.

Moon, George [actor] (b. London, England, 1886–4 Jun 1967 [81?], London, England). AS, p. 781.

Moon, Lorna [scenarist] (*née* Helen Nora Lorna Leonore Flora MacDonald Wilson Cameron-Cameron of Flassiefern and Erracht, b. Sicken, Aberdeenshire, Scotland, 1895?–1 May 1930 [35], Albuquerque NM). (Paramount; MGM.) "Lorna Moon," *Variety,* 7 May 1930. AMD, p. 251. AS, p. 781. BHD2, p. 188. FDY, p. 433. IFN, p. 211. "Lorna Moon Joins Realart," *MPW,* 20 Aug 1921, 819. "Lorna Moon, the Authoress, Added to Writing Staff of Realart Corporation," *MPW,* 27 Aug 1921, 906. "Trade Notes," *Paris and Hollywood,* 2 (Oct 1926), 62 ("The woman with the longest name in the world…").

Moon, Virginia B. [extra] (b. 1844?–11 Sep 1925 [81], New York NY [Death Certificate Index No. 22451]). (FP-L.) Appeared in *The Spanish Dancer* (1923); *Robin Hood.* She and her sister, Charlotte Moon, were spies for the Confederacy during the Civil War. AS, p. 781.

Mooney, Martin [scenarist/producer] (b. 17 Apr 1896–21 Jan 1967 [70], Los Angeles CA). AS, p. 781. BHD2, p. 188.

Mooney, Paul C. [executive] (b. 1878–9 Jul 1972 [94?], New York NY). BHD2, p. 188.

Moor, Robert [actor] (*né* Robert Jean Alexandre Mouret, b. Rouen, France, 17 Jul 1889–23 Dec 1972 [83], Suresnes, France [extrait de décès no. 17/1857]). AS, p. 781.

Moore, Alice [assistant art director]. No data found. AMD, p. 251. "Alice Moore with Triangle," *MPW,* 11 Aug 1917, 923.

Moore, Bin [director]. No data found. AMD, p. 251. "Bin Moore Joins Fox," *MPW,* 14 Jun 1919, 1646.

Moore, Carlyle, Jr. (son of **Carlyle Moore, Sr.**) [actor] (b. New York NY, 5 Jan 1909–3 Mar 1977 [68], Sun Valley ID). BHD1, p. 389. IFN, p. 211.

Moore, Carlyle, Sr. (father of **Carlyle Moore, Jr.**) [playwright] (b. Oakland CA, 17 Jun 1875–26 Jun 1924 [49], Milford PA; suicide). m. Ethelyn Palmer (d. 1906). "Carlyle Moore a Suicide," *Variety,* 2 Jul 1924. AS, p. 781. BHD2, p. 188 (b. 1879). SD, p. 898.

Moore, Charles R. [actor] (b. Chicago IL, 23 Apr 1893–20 Jul 1947 [54], Los Angeles CA). BHD1, p. 389.

Moore, Cleve (son of **Sam Collier Major**; brother of **Colleen Moore**) [actor] (*né* Cleve Morrison, b. Port Huron MI, 10 Jun 1904–25 Jan 1954 [49], Miami FL). AS, p. 781 (b. 1904). BHD1, p. 389 (b. 1901). IFN, p. 211.

Moore, Colleen (daughter of **Sam Collier Major**; sister of **Cleve Moore**) [actress: Wampas Star, 1922] (*née* Kathleen Morrison, b. Port Huron MI, 19 Aug 1900–25 Jan 1988 [87], Paso Robles CA). *Silent Star* (Garden City NY: Doubleday & Co., Inc., 1968). m. (1) **John E. McCormick**, 18 Aug 1923 (d. 1961); (2) Albert Parker Scott; (3) Homer Hargrave, 1937 (d. 1967); (4) Paul Maginot, Switzerland. (1st National.) Glenn Fowler, "Colleen Moore, Ultimate Flapper of the Silent Screen, Is Dead at 87," *NYT,* 27 Jan 1988, D23:1. "Colleen Moore, 85, Silent-Screen Star, Succumbs on Coast," *Variety,* 27 Jan 1988 (b. 1902; d. Templeton CA). AMD, p. 251. AS, p. 781. BHD1, p. 389 (d. Templeton). FFF, p. 17 (b. 12 Aug 1902). FSS, p. 211. HCH, p. 17. Katz, p. 824. MH, p. 128. "Colleen Moore," SOS, pp. 160–85. "Colleen Moore," WBO2, pp. 120–21 (b. 1902). WWS, p. 240. William M. Drew, *Speaking of Silents* (Vestal NY: Vestal Press, Ltd., 1989), pp. 160–85 (b. 1902). "Colleen Moore," *MPW,* 20 Jan 1917, 384. Cal York, "Plays and Players," *Photoplay,* Jul 1917, 112 (caption under photo: "...She is seventeen, was educated in a convent in Tampa, and practiced weeping to and from school until she could weep at will." Then Griffith found her; "he proposes to utilize her extensively."). "Colleen Moore," *MPW,* 8 Sep 1917, 1512. "Colleen Moore with Christie," *LA Times,* 28 Jan 1920, II, 11 ("This reverses the procedure by which comedy stars usually go into the drama."). "Neilan Engages Colleen Moore," *MPW,* 15 May 1920, 960. "Neilan Announces Another 'Find' in Colleen Moore," 29 May 1920, 1182. Clodagh Saurin, "The Wearing of the Green," *Photoplay,* Mar 1921, 31, 76 (re Moore, Pat O"Malley, and Mickey Neilan). "Colleen Moore Defends Motion Picture Folk in Talk Broadcasted by Wireless," *MPW,* 8 Apr 1922, 606. "Universal Engages Colleen Moore," *MPW,* 30 Sep 1922, 374. "Miss Moore to Play in 'The Huntress,'" *MPW,* 12 May 1923, 171. "Colleen Moore to Star in Series for First National," *MPW,* 9 Jun 1923, 510. "Colleen Moore Marries," *MPW,* 1 Sep 1923, 57. "Colleen Honored," *MPW,* 27 Oct 1923, 725. "Richard Rowland and Colleen Moore Are Godparents," *MPW,* 3 Jan 1925, 25. "Colleen Moore," *MPW,* 21 Feb 1925, 819. "Colleen Moore Goes Abroad," *MPW,* 16 May 1925, 286. "Colleen Moore," *MPW,* 27 Jun 1925, 987. "Colleen Moore," *MPW,* 18 Jul 1925, 352. "Colleen Moore," *MPW,* 25 Jul 1925, 449. Colleen Moore, "The True Story of My Life," *MW,* 5 Sep 1925, 10–12, 44; 12 Sep 1925, 12–14, 42; 19 Sep 1925, 12–14, 44–45; 26 Sep 1925, 21–22, 38. Colleen Moore and John McCormick, "The Trying Years; Confidences of Married Life," *MM,* Oct 1925, 27–28, 95–96. "Colleen Moore," *MPW,* 20 Nov 1926, 143. "Colleen Moore Is Voted Leading Box Office Name," *MPW,* 29 Nov 1926, 280. "Colleen Returns to First National Family," *MPW,* 16 Jul 1927, 157. James Haviland, "The Movies Call the Comic Strip; The Funnies Are No Longer Greeted with Scorn. The Great American Public Has Fallen So Hard for These Comic Characters That It Demands Them Brought to Life on the Screen," *MPC,* Dec 1926, 32–33, 74, 86. "Colleen Moore; The Girl on the Cover," *Cinema Arts,* Dec 1926, 37, 57. Gladys Hall, "One of the Little People; An Impression of Colleen Moore—Who Is Irish and Irresistible," *MPC,* Feb 1927, 53, 87. "Flashes from Filmland," *Paris and Hollywood Screen Secrets Magazine,* Aug 1927, 10 (she and McCormack walked out of their contract with 1st National over her unwillingness to play in *When Irish Eyes Are Smiling*). Dorothy Pownall, "Limericks; A Peek at the Stars in Rhythm," *Paris and Hollywood Screen Secrets Magazine,* Aug 1927, 19 ("The Super-Flapper. The screen has its flappers galore,/Their brave nonchalance we adore./It's not, we confess,/ That we love others less,/It's just that we love Colleen Moore."). Paul Paige, "Close-Ups and Fade-Outs," *Paris and Hollywood Screen Secrets,* III (Oct 1927), 24 (Moore ended her troubles with 1st Natioal. She was to make 4 and not 5 pictures under her old contract, and the scenario, *When Irish Eyes Are Smiling,* to which she objected, was eliminated from her schedule. She will also receive $50,000 more per picture, or $700,000 a year, "which makes her the second highest paid feminine star," Swanson being the highest paid at $875,000 with UA.). Don Juan, "So This Is Hollywood; Want Colleen Back," *Paris and Hollywood Screen Secrets,* Oct 1927, 62 (1st National began legal action against Moore in NYC to get her back to Burbank). "Colleen Will do U.A. Films," *MPW,* 24 Dec 1927, 6. Gladys Hall, "Are Vampires Children?; Colleen Moore Believes That for the Wild Women of the World, Love Springs Paternal," *MPC,* Nov 1928, 40, 72. George Katchmer, "Remembering the Great Silents," *CI,* 251 (May 1996), p. 54.

Moore, Eva [actress] (b. Brighton, England, 9 Feb 1870–27 Apr 1955 [85], Maidenhead, England). AS, p. 781. BHD1, p. 390. IFN, p. 211.

Moore, Fayette T[homas] [producer/scenarist] (b. 1880–21 May 1955 [75?], Los Angeles CA; suicide). AS, p. 781 (b. 1885). BHD2, p. 188.

Moore, Florence E. (sister of **Frank F. Moore**) [stage/film actress] (b. Philadelphia PA, 13 Nov 1885–23 Mar 1935 [49], Darby PA; complications after surgery). m. Jules I. Schwob; William Montgomery; John Ogden Kerner. "Florence Moore," *Variety,* 27 Mar 1935 (d. 9 Mar). AS, p. 782. BHD, p. 255 (b. 1886). IFN, p. 211. SD. Truitt, p. 237.

Moore, Frank F. (brother of **Florence Moore**) [actor] (b. Philadelphia PA, 15 Nov 1880–28 May 1924 [43], Los Angeles CA). m. Grace. "Frank F. Moore," *Variety,* 4 Jun 1924. AS, p. 782. BHD, p. 255. IFN, p. 211. SD, p. 899. Truitt, p. 237.

Moore, Frederick Ernest [stage/film actor/manager] (b. Memphis TN, 1872?–11 Dec 1924 [52], Atlantic City NJ). m. Eleanor Gates—div. (d. 1951). "Frederick E. Moore," *NYT,* 12 Dec 1924, 21:3 (vaudeville partner of Al Jolson). "Frederick Ernest Moore," *Variety,* 17 Dec 1924. SD. George Katchmer, *CI,* 225 (Mar 1994), 45:1.

Moore, Gladys C. [actress] (b. 1864–5 Sep 1937 [73?], Jackson Heights NY). BHD, p. 255.

Moore, Hilda (mother of Churton Fairman) [stage/film actress] (b. England, 1886–18 May 1929 [43], New York NY; throat infection; interred in Kensico cemetery). m. **Austin Fairman** (son Austin Churton, b. 15 Nov 1924–24 Apr 1997). "Hilda Moore," *Variety,* 22 May 1929, 69:1. AS, p. 782. BHD, p. 255. IFN, p. 212.

Moore, Ida [actress] (b. Newark NJ, 1 Mar 1882–26 Sep 1964 [82], Los Angeles CA). AS, p. 782. BHD1, p. 390 (b. Newark OH). IFN, p. 212. Katz, p. 825 (b. Altoona KS, 1883). Truitt, p. 237.

Moore, Joseph [actor] (brother of **Mary, Matt, Owen** and **Tom Moore**) [actor] (b. County Meath, Ireland, 1895–22 Aug 1926 [30], Santa Monica CA; drowned). m. **Grace Cunard**, 1917 (d. 1967). AMD, p. 251. AS, p. 782. BHD, p. 255. IFN, p. 212. "Joe Moore Drowned; Brother of Tom and Matt Stricken by Heart Attack While Bathing," *Variety,* 25 Aug 1926. "Grace Cunard Married to Joseph Moore," *MPW,* 10 Feb 1917, 854. "Moore with C.B.C.," *MPW,* 17 Feb 1923, 706. "Joseph Moore Dies From Heart Failure," *MPW,* 11 Sep 1926, 97. George A. Katchmer, "The Four Moore Brothers; Matt and Joe," *CI,* 155 (May 1988), 34–37, 63.

Moore, Kathryn [actress] (b. 1887?–14 Oct 1983 [96], Woodland Hills CA). (Began 1918; MGM.) "Kathryn Moore," *Variety,* 26 Oct 1983. AS, p. 782.

Moore, Lola [scenarist/agent] (b. 1891–26 Jan 1985 [93?], Burbank CA). BHD2, p. 188. FDY, p. 433.

Moore, Lucia [actress] (b. LA, 1867-Apr 1932 [64?], New York NY). BHD, p. 255.

Moore, Marcia [actress]. No data found. (Universal.) AMD, p. 251. J. Van Cartmell, "Along the Pacific Coast," *NYDM,* 23 Oct 1915, 30:4. "Marcia Moore Joins Universal," *MPW,* 1 Jan 1916, 86.

Moore, Marjorie [actress]. No data found. AMD, p. 251. "Marjorie Moore Cast," *MPW,* 12 Nov 1927, 16.

Moore, Mary [actress] (b. London, England, 3 Jul 1861–6 Apr 1931 [70], London, England). BHD, p. 255. IFN, p. 212.

Moore, Mary (sister of **Joseph, Matt, Owen** and **Tom Moore**) [actress] (d. 15 Jan 1919, France; influenza). "Mary Moore," *Variety,* 14 Feb 1919. AMD, p. 251. AS, p. 782. BHD, p. 255. IFN, p. 212 (d. 1918). "Mary Moore in Bushman Company," *MPW,* 15 Apr 1916, 470. "Obituary," *MPW,* 1 Mar 1919, 1186 (while in Red Cross service). "Buried with Military Honors," *MPW,* 29 Mar 1919, 1794. Billy H. Doyle, "Lost Players," *CI,* 139 (Jan 1987), 55.

Moore, Matt (brother of **Joseph, Owen, Mary** and **Tom Moore**) [actor/director] (b. Fordstown Crossroads, County Meath, Ireland, 8 Jan 1888–20 Jan 1960 [72], Los Angeles CA). m. Alice Miller. (Universal; Artcraft; Selznick.) "Matt Moore," *Variety,* 27 Jan 1960. AMD, p. 252. AS, p. 782. BHD1, p. 390; BHD2, p. 188. FSS, p. 212. IFN, p. 212. Katz, p. 825 (began 1913). Spehr, p. 154. Truitt, p. 237. "Matt Moore, Universal Star," *MPW,* 15 May 1915, 1083. "Matt Moore," *MPW,* 23 Sep 1916, 1952. "Matt Moore a Selig Leading Man," *MPW,* 9 Mar 1918, 1354. "Matt Moore Is

Leading Man in Blanche Sweet Company," *MPW,* 31 Aug 1918, 1283. "Matt Moore," *MPW,* 12 Jul 1924, insert. Dorothy Donnell, "His Mother and Father Were Irish—And He Is Irish, Too; Our Dorothy finds that Matt Moore has a sense of humor that laughs at the world—including himself," *MPS,* 24 Feb 1925, 20–21, 28–29. "Matt Moore," *MPW,* 17 Dec 1927, 32. George A. Katchmer, "The Four Moore Brothers; Matt and Joe," *CI,* 155 (May 1988), 34–37, 63.

Moore, Mickey (brother of **Pat Moore**) [child actor] (b. ca. 1916). "Stage and Film News," *LA TImes,* 25 Jan 1920, III, 13. "'Picture Show' Chat," *Picture Show,* VI, 5 Nov 1921, p. 3 (quip with photograph).

Moore, Mildred [actress]. No data found. AMD, p. 252. BR, pp. 58–59. "Lyons and Moran Increase Staff," *MPW,* 15 Feb 1919, 887. George A. Katchmer, "Forgotten Cowboys and Cowgirls—Part V," *CI,* 177 (Mar 1990), C6.

Moore, Milton [cinematographer]. No data found. m. **Laura Oakley** (d. 1957). FDY, p. 463.

Moore, Nora [actress]. No data found. AMD, p. 252. "Arnold Daly Finds a Star," *MPW,* 1 Jan 1916, 67.

Moore, Owen (brother of **Joseph**, **Tom**, **Mary** and **Matt Moore**) [stage/film actor] (b. Fordstown Crossroads, County Meath, Ireland, 12 Dec 1886–9 Jun 1939 [52], Beverly Hills CA). m. (1) **Mary Pickford**, 7 Jan 1911–3 Mar 1920 (d. 1979); (2) **Kathryn Perry**, 1921 (d. 1983). (Biograph, 1908; Reliance-Majestic; Fine Arts; FP-L; Victor; Goldwyn.) "Owen Moore Found Dead in California; First Husband of Mary Pickford Brooded Over Lack of Work," *NYT,* 10 Jun 1939, 36:2. "Owen Moore," *Variety,* 14 Jun 1939. AMD, p. 252. AS, p. 782. BHD1, p. 390. FFF, p. 181. FSS, p. 213. IFN, p. 212. Katz, pp. 825–26. MH, p. 128. MSBB, p. 1026. Spehr, p. 154. Truitt, p. 237. WWS, p. 130. "Owen Moore and Little Mary with Majestic," *MPW,* 21 Oct 1911, 217. "Majestic Enterprise," *MPW,* 4 Nov 1911, 389. "Moore and Colley Join Reliance," *MPW,* 24 Jan 1914, 423. "Owen Moore Sues; Wants Damages from Independent Moving Picture Company for Loss of Employment," *NYDM,* 15 Apr 1914, 33:1 ("for $2,000 damages, alleging a violation of contract that caused him the loss of fourteen weeks' employment. The cause of the suit dates back to December of 1910…[when he was employed] at $150 a week."). "Owen Moore to Appear with Fritzi Scheff," *MPW,* 13 Feb 1915, 997. "Owen Moore with Famous Players," *MPW,* 24 Jun 1916, 2215. "Owen Moore Is Engaged by Selznick Pictures," *MPW,* 28 Jun 1919, 1918. "Owen Moore to Produce Soon," *MPW,* 2 Aug 1919, 686. "Mary Pickford Gets Divorce from Owen Moore in Nevada," *MPW,* 13 Mar 1920, 1759. "Owen Moore Recovering," *MPW,* 5 Mar 1921, 74 (from inflammatory rheumatism). "Moore Leaves Hospital," *MPW,* 12 Mar 1921, 170 (in NY). "Moore Better," *MPW,* 26 Mar 1921, 394. "Owen Moore Will Soon Resume Work," *MPW,* 2 Jul 1921, 66. "Owen Moore Charges Secretary with Theft," *MPW,* 1 Oct 1921, 534. Lillian Montanye, "Honeymoon Unlimited," *MPC,* Dec 1921, 34–35, 85. "Moore Bros. on Same Program," *MPW,* 27 Jun 1925, 990. "Owen Moore Signs Long-Term Contract with Metro," *MPW,* 6 Feb 1926, 542. George A. Katchmer, "The Four Moore Brothers; Owen," *CI,* 154 (Apr 1988), 30, 32, C1-C2.

Moore, Pat (brother of **Mickey Moore**) [child actor] (b. ca. 1914). "Stage and Film News; Pat Moore with Salisbury," *LA Times,* 25 Jan 1920, III, 13 (lists his films). "'Picture Show' Chat," *Picture Show,* 5 Nov 1921, p. 3 (quip with photograph).

Moore, Patti [actor] (*née* Patricia Moore, b. 1901–26 Nov 1972 [71?], Los Angeles CA; cancer). AS, p. 782. BHD1, p. 390.

Moore, Percy [stage/film actor/Executive Secretary of Episcopal Actors Guild since 1927] (b. Montreal, Canada, 1878–8 Apr 1945 [67], New York NY). m. "Percy Moore," *Variety,* 158, 11 Apr 1945, 46:1. AS, p. 782. BHD, p. 255. IFN, p. 212.

Moore, Rex [actor] (b. 26 Feb 1900–21 Apr 1975 [75], Los Angeles Co. CA). BHD, p. 255.

Moore, Ruth Hart *see* **Hart, Ruth**

Moore, Scott [actor] (b. 1889–18 Dec 1967 [78], Miami Beach FL). AS, p. 782 (d. 14 Dec). BHD, p. 255. IFN, p. 212.

Moore, Tim [actor] (*né* Thomas J. Moore, b. County Meath, Ireland, 1 May 1883–12 Feb 1955 [71], Santa Monica CA). AS, p. 782.

Moore, Tom (brother of **Joseph**, **Mary**, **Matt** and **Owen Moore**) [stage/film actor/director/scenarist] (*né* Thomas J. Moore, b. Fordstown Crossroads, County Meath, Ireland, 1 May 1883–12 Feb 1955 [71], Santa Monica CA). m. **Alice Joyce**, 11 May 1914, Jacksonville FL (d. 1955); **Renée Adorée**–div. 1926 (d. 1933); **Eleanor Merry** (d. 1991). (Biograph, 1908; Kalem; Paramount; Goldwyn.) "Tom Moore, 71, Veteran Actor; Silent Screen Player Dies—Brothers Matt and Owen Also Movie Figures," *NYT,* 14 Feb 1955, 19:4. "Tom Moore," *Variety,* 16 Feb 1955. AMD, p. 252. AS, p. 782. BHD1, p. 390; BHD2, p. 188. FFF, p. 46. FSS, p. 213. IFN, p. 212. Katz, p. 826 (b. 1885; began 1912). MH, p. 128. MSBB, p. 1026. Spehr, p. 154. Truitt, p. 237 (b. 1885). WWS, p. 134. "Alice Joyce Weds; Kalem Star the Bride of Tom Moore In Jacksonville, Fla.," *NYDM,* 20 May 1914, 29:1. "Alice Joyce Marries Tom Moore," *MPW,* 30 May 1914, 1238. "Tom Moore Gives Banquet to Famous Players," *MPW,* 13 Jun 1914, 1543. Clarence L. Linz, "'Tom' Moore, Moving Picture King," *MPW,* 4 Jul 1914, 78. "Tom Moore with Lubin," *MPW,* 4 Dec 1915, 1808. "Tom Moore," *MPW,* 8 Jan 1916, 251. Roberta Courtland, "Mr. and Mrs. Tom Moore at Home," *MPC,* Aug 1916, 35–36, 70. "Tom Moore with Constance Talmadge," *MPW,* 7 Jul 1917, 82. "Tom Moore," *MPW,* 19 Jan 1918, 348. "Tom Moore," *MPW,* 25 May 1918, 1146. "In 'Just for Tonight,' Tom Moore Makes Debut as Star," *MPW,* 29 Jun 1918, 1866. "Tom Moore to Continue with Goldwyn," *MPW,* 29 Mar 1919, 1788. "Tom Moore, Goldwyn Star, Finishing Filming of A.C. Gunther's Noted Play, 'Mr. Barnes, of New York,'" *MPW,* 25 Dec 1920, 1062. "Mayer Signs Tom Moore," *MPW,* 31 May 1924, 454. "Moore Bros. on Same Program," *MPW,* 27 Jun 1925, 990. "Tom Moore Lead in Phyllis Haver's 'Wise Wife,'" *MPW,* 23 Jul 1927, 254. George A. Katchmer, "The Four Moore Brothers," *CI,* 153 (Mar 1988), 40–43, 61. Henry R. Davis, "The Films of Tom Moore," *CI,* 157 (Jul 1988), C32. George Katchmer, "Tom Moore," *CI,* 225 (Mar 1994), 45:1.

Moore, Unity [actress] (b. Galway, Ireland, 27 Jul 1894-Feb 1981 [86], London, England). BHD, p. 255.

Moore, Victor Frederick [stage/film actor] (b. Hammonton NJ, 24 Feb 1876–23 Jul 1962 [86], East Islip, LI NY [Pine Acres, actors' home]; heart attack). m. (1) **Emma Littlefield** (d. 1934); (2) Shirley Paige, 1942. (Film debut: *Snobs,* FP-L, 1915; Klever Komedies; Paramount.) "Victor Moore, 86, Comedian, Is Dead; Actor 65 Years Was Known for Throttlebottom Role in 'Of Thee I Sing,'" *NYT,* 24 Jul 1962, 27:1. "Celebrities Attend Victor Moore Rites," *NYT,* 27 Jul 1962, 25:1. "Victor Moore," *Variety,* 25 Jul 1962. AMD, p. 252. AS, p. 782. BHD1, p. 390. IFN, p. 212. Katz, p. 826 (began 1915). MSBB, p. 1026. SD. Truitt, p. 238. "Lasky Gets Moore; Star of Cohan Plays Will Be Seen in Feature Screen Production Soon," *NYDM,* 20 Jan 1915, 24:1 (to debut in *Snobs*). "'Snobs' with Victor Moore," *MPW,* 3 Apr 1915, 87. "Victor Moore with Lasky," *MPW,* 30 Jan 1915, 650. "Cannot Act in Pictures; United Booking Office After Actors Who Encroach on Other Fields," *NYDM,* 14 Jul 1915, 12:3 (engagement at Keith's Theater, Washington, cancelled because his film, *Chimmie Fadden,* was being shown.). Walter Kingsley, "U.B.O. Claims Film Appearances of Stars Injure Variety Value; Victor Moore Cancelled in Washington Because Another Theater Offered Him in Feature Photoplay," *NYDM,* 14 Jul 1915, 17:2. "Screen Only for Moore; Victor Moore Forsakes Legitimate and Vaudeville to Be Lasky Star," *NYDM,* 1 Sep 1915, 27:1 (2nd film, *Chimmie Fadden;* 3rd film, *Chimmie Fadden Out West*). "Victor Moore to Become Lasky Star," *MPW,* 11 Sep 1915, 1810. "Paramount Gets Klever Komedies," *MPW,* 2 Dec 1916, 1347. VIctor Moore, "Victor Moore's Comedies," *MPW,* 6 Jan 1917, 66. "Victor Moore," *MPW,* 3 Feb 1917, 691. "Moore to Increase His Klever Komedies," *MPW,* 30 Jun 1917, 2125.

Moore, Victoria [scenarist]. No data found. FDY, p. 433.

Moore, Vin [actor/director] (b. Mayville NY, 1878?–5 Dec 1949 [71], Los Angeles CA). "Vin Moore," *Variety,* 14 Dec 1949 ("pioneer film director" from 1917). AS, p. 783. BHD1, p. 390; bHD2, p. 188. IFN, p. 212. Truitt, p. 238.

Moore, W. Eugene [actor/director]. (Thanhouser.) AMD, p. 252. "Moore an Actor Once More," *MPW,* 9 Aug 1913, 615. "W. Eugene Moore," *MPW,* 29 May 1915, 1436. "Moore to Produce Independently," *MPW,* 29 Mar 1919, 1786.

Moor[e]head, Natalie [actress] (*née* Nathalia Messner, b. Pittsburgh PA, 27 Jul 1898–6 Oct 1992 [94], Montecito CA). m. (1) **Alan Crosland** (d. 1936); Raymond Phillips, Jul 1929-Jan 1930; (3) Juan G. Torena. "Natalie Moorehead Torena," *Variety,* 7 Dec 1992, 84:3. AS, p. 783. BHD1, p. 391 (b. 1901). Ragan 2, p. 1179 (b. 7 Jul 1901). "Natalie Moorhead," *CI,* 210 (Dec 1992), 59.

Moorehouse, Bert [actor] (b. IL, 20 Nov 1894–26 Jan 1954 [59], Los Angeles CA; suicide with gun). "Bert Moorhouse," *Variety,* 3 Feb 1954. BHD1, p. 390. IFN, p. 212. Truitt, p. 238.

Moorhouse, S.A. [actor]. No data found. AMD, p. 252. "Comedian Suffers Injuries," *MPW,* 31 May 1919, 1333.

Morais, Mario [director/writer/actor] (b. Livorno, Italy, 1859–1 Mar 1922 [62?], Turin, Italy). JS, p. 302 (in Italian silents from 1911).

Moran, Byron [scenarist]. No data found. FDY, p. 433.

Moran, Frank Charles [actor/boxer] (b. OH, 18 Mar 1887–14 Dec 1967 [80], Los Angeles CA). AS, p. 783. BHD1, p. 391. IFN, p. 212.

Moran, George [actor/scenarist] (*né* George Searcy, b. Elwood KS, 3 Oct 1881–1 Aug 1949 [67], Oakland CA; cerebral hemorrhage). m.

Claire White, 1928–38. "George Moran, Comedian, Is Dead; Partner of Charles E. Mack in Famous 'Two Black Crows' Act from 1921 to 1934," *NYT,* 2 Aug 1949, 19:1. "George Moran," *Variety,* 3 Aug 1949. AS, p. 783. BHD1, p. 391. FDY, p. 433. IFN, p. 212. Truitt, p. 238.

Moran, Lee [stage/film actor/director] (b. Chicago IL, 23 Jun 1888–24 Apr 1961 [72], Woodland Hills CA; heart attack). (Nestor, 1912.) "Lee Moran," *Variety,* 3 May 1961. AMD, p. 252. AS, p. 783. BHD1, p. 391 (b. 1887). IFN, p. 212. Katz, p. 827 (began 1909). MSBB, p. 1026 (b. 1887). Truitt, p. 238. "Lives of the Players; Lee Moran," *MPS,* I, 24 Jan 1913, 31. Richard Willis, "Lee Moran; Universal Leading Man," *MPS,* 4 Dec 1914, 25. "Lee Moran's Many Roles," *MPW,* 25 Dec 1915, 2396. "Lee Moran Ill with Pneumonia," *MPW,* 16 Dec 1916, 1645. Robert C. McElravy, "Comedy Folks," *MPW,* 13 Apr 1918, 218–19. "Lyons and Moran COmplete Their 250th Production," *MPW,* 17 May 1919, 1064. "Eddie Lyons and Lee Moran to Be Featured in Comedy-Drama Series," *MPW,* 27 Dec 1919, 1163. "Eddie Lyons and Lee Moran Stop Making Single Reelers," *MPW,* 29 May 1920, 1220. "Lee Moran Engaged to Make Century Comedies," *MPW,* 29 Oct 1921, 1020. "'You Know Me, Al,' Says Lee Moran," *MPW,* 30 Dec 1922, 837. "Jack White Signs Lee Moran," *MPW,* 15 Sep 1923, 280. "Moran to Direct," *MPW,* 5 Jan 1924, 65. "Moran Starred 14 Years Ago," *MPW,* 2 Jul 1927, 18.

Moran, Leo D. [actor] (b. 1889?–8 Mar 1927 [37?], Tucson AZ; tuberculosis). AS, p. 783 (d. 3 Mar). BHD, p. 255.

Moran, Lois [stage/film actress] (*née* Lois Darlington Dowling, b. Pittsburgh PA, 1 Mar 1908–13 Jul 1990 [82], Sedona AZ; cancer). (Film debut: France, 1924; *Stella Dallas,* 1925; last film: *West of Broadway,* MGM, 1931.) m. Col. Clarence M. Young (d. 1973). Donatella Lorch, "Lois Moran Young Dead at 81; Musical Star and Movie Actress," *NYT,* 15 Jul 1990, A22:1. "Lois Moran," *Variety,* 18 Jul 1990, p. 92 (age 81). "Lois Moran [obituary]," *CI,* 183 (Sep 1990), 60–61 (includes filmography by Henry R. Davis). AMD, p. 253. AS, p. 783. BHD1, p. 391 (b. 1907). FSS, p. 214. Katz, p. 827 (in French silents). "Lois Moran," *MPW,* 23 Jan 1926, 315. Cal York, "The Girl on the Cover," *Photoplay Magazine,* Jun 1926, 94. "Lois Moran," *MPW,* 3 Sep 1927, 25. "Flashes from Filmland," *Paris and Hollywood Screen Secrets Magazine,* Aug 1927, 10 (Fox elevated Moran to the rank of star by giving her a long-term contract and *I Don't Want to Marry* as her first film for the company. "A change in the screen persoanality of the new star is also expected, the most startling move being the bobbing of her hair."). Mary Sharon, "Just a Sweet Kid; Lois Moran Dared Paris to Rob Her of Her Winsomeness," *Paris and Hollywood Screen Secrets Magazine,* III (Aug 1927), 31, 89 ("...it is distinctly refreshing in this city of ego to find someone who is unspoiled enough to talk of the virtues and talents of others."). Carol Johnston, "The Girl Without 'It'; A Study of Lois Moran," *MPC,* Jan 1928, 51, 86. Dorothy Donnell, "Little Miss Wolf of Wall Street; Lois Moran Got Rich by Following Ford Instead of Franklin," *MPC,* Mar 1929, 22, 94–95. Michael G. Ankerich, "Reel Stars," *CI,* 162 (Dec 1988), 55–56. Chapter 16, "Lois Moran," BS, pp. 212–23 (includes filmography). R.E. Braff, "Braff's Filmographies; The Films of Lois Moran," *CI,* 241 (Jul 1995), 44. Richard P. Buller, "Lois Moran; From Goldwyn to Gershwin," *Films of the Golden Age,* #1 (Summer 1995), pp. 34–44.

Moran, Percy [actor] (b. Ireland, 1886–1958 [72?]). AS, p. 783. BHD, p. 255; BHD2, p. 188.

Moran, Polly [stage/film actress] (*née* Pauline Therese Moran, b. Chicago IL, 28 Jun 1883–25 Jan 1952 [68], Los Angeles CA; heart attack). m. Martin T. Malone. "Polly Moran, 66, Veteran of Films; Comedy Teammate of the Late Marie Dressler for Years Dies—Began with Mack Sennett," *NYT,* 26 Jan 1952, 13:3. "Polly Moran," *Variety,* 30 Jan 1952 (d. 24 Jan, Hollywood CA). AMD, p. 253. AS, p. 783. BHD1, p. 391. IFN, p. 212. FSS, p. 214. Katz, pp. 827–28 (b. 1884). SD. Truitt, p. 238. "Polly Moran Joins Fox Comedy Forces," *MPW,* 5 Jul 1919, 79. "Polly Moran Engaged by DeMille for Comedy Bit in 'Affairs of Anatol,'" *MPW,* 22 Jan 1921, 454. "Polly Moran in Pathé Comedies," *MPW,* 19 Feb 1927, 573.

Moran, Priscilla [child actress]. No data found. AMD, p. 253. "New Company to Star Baby Priscilla Moran," *MPW,* LXV, 8 Dec 1923, 569. "Wrangle Over Child Actress Ends," *MPW,* 23 Jul 1927, 238.

Moran, Tommy [actor] (d. 23 Oct 1931, Chicago IL). "Tommy Moran," *Variety,* 3 Nov 1931.

Moran, William F. [actor] (b. New Orleans LA, 2 Oct 1888–6 Jan 1972 [83], Los Angeles CA). BHD1, p. 391.

Morand, M.R. [actor] (b. 1861–5 Mar 1922 [60?]). BHD, p. 255.

Morand, Paul [actor] (b. Paris, France, 13 Mar 1888–1976 [88?], Vevey, Switzerland). AS, p. 783.

Morange, Edward A. [scenic artist/set designer] (b. Cold Spring NY, 1865?–19 May 1955 [90], Torrington CT). "E.A. Morange, 90, Designer of Sets; Member of Noted Firm [Gates & Morange] Did Work for Many Shows—Dies in Torrington, Conn.," *NYT,* 20 May 1955, 25:5. "Edward A. Morange," *Variety,* 25 May 1955.

Morano, Gigetta [actress] (*née* Luigia Morano, b. near Turin, Italy, 1886). JS, p. 302 (in Italian silents from 1909).

Morante, Joseph [actor] (b. 1853?–13 Apr 1940 [87], Los Angeles CA). "Joseph Morante," *Variety,* 17 Apr 1940. AS, p. 784.

Morante, Milburn M. Charles [actor/director/producer] (b. San Francisco CA, 6 Apr 1887–28 Jan 1964 [76], Pacoima CA). (Keystone-Triangle.) AS, p. 784. BHD1, p. 391; BHD2, p. 188 (d. 1965). IFN, p. 212. Katz, p. 828 (began 1913). George A. Katchmer, "Forgotten Cowboys and Cowgirls—Part IX," *CI,* 181 (Jul 1990), 55.

Morat, Luitz [director] (b. Geneva, Switzerland, 1875–1928 [53?], Paris, France). AS, p. 784.

Morawsky, Erich [producer] (b. Berlin, Germany, 25 Oct 1890–3 Mar 1958 [67], Ascona, Switzerland). BHD2, p. 188.

Mordant, Edwin [stage/film actor] (b. Baltimore MD, 22 Dec 1868–16 Feb 1942 [73], Los Angeles CA). m. **Grace Atwell** (d. 1952); (2) Virginia Stuart. "Edwin Mordant; Former Stage Actor Appeared in Many Films Since 1932," *NYT,* 7 Feb 1942, 21:2. "Edwin Mordant," *Variety,* 18 Feb 1942 (age 74). AS, p. 784. BHD1, p. 391. IFN, p. 212. SD. Truitt, p. 238.

Mordant, Grace *see* **Atwell, Grace**

More, Unity [actress] (b. Galway, Ireland, 27 Jul 1884–17 Feb 1981 [96], London, England). AS, p. 784.

Moreau, Gabriel [actor/director] (b. France). JS, p. 303 (began 1904).

Moree, Maxfield [actor]. No data found. AMD, p. 253. "Maxfield Moree in Kleine's 'Musty Suffer,'" *MPW,* 13 May 1916, 1160.

Morel, Dene (b. England, 17 Jan 1901-Oct 1928 [27]). BHD, p. 255.

Morena, Erna [actress] (*née* Erna Fuchs, b. Aschaffenburg, Bavaria, Germany, 24 Apr 1885–23 Jul 1962 [77], Munich, Germany). (Film debut: *Die Sphinx,* 1912.) BHD1, p. 392 (b. 1892; d. 21 Jul). Vittorio Martinelli, "Kino-Lieblinge," *Griffithiana,* 38/39 (Oct 1990), 20.

Morena, Gene [director] (b. 1896–5 Dec 1925 [29?], New York NY; suicide). AS, p. 784.

Morena, Sena [actress] (b. 1896–5 Dec 1925 [29?], Los Angeles CA). AS, p. 784.

Moreno, Antonio [stage/film actor] (*né* Antonio Garride Monteagudo Moreno, b. Madrid, Spain, 26 Sep 1886–15 Feb 1967 [80], Beverly Hills CA). m. Daisy Canfield Danziger. (Biograph, 1912; Vitagraph, 1914.) "Antonio Moreno, Silent-Film Star; Portrayer of Latin Lovers in Many Movies Dies," *NYT,* 16 Feb 1967, 35:3 (age 78). "Antonio Moreno," *Variety,* 22 Feb 1967. AMD, p. 253. AS, p. 785. BHD1, p. 392 (b. 1887). FFF, p. 115 (b. 1888). FSS, p. 215. GK, pp. 667–80. IFN, p. 213 (b. 1887). Katz, p. 829 (b. 1887). MH, p. 128 (b. 1888). MSBB, p. 1026 (b. 1888). SD. Slide, p. 145 (b. 1887; d. Beverly Hills CA). Spehr, p. 154. Truitt, p. 238 (b. 1888). WWS, p. 94 (b. 1888). "Antonio Moreno Denies Knowledge of Girl's Disappearance," *MPW,* 15 Apr 1916, 420. "Antonio Moreno a Gold Rooster Star," *MPW,* 16 Jun 1917, 1791. "Moreno to Support Mrs. Castle," *MPW,* 14 Jul 1917, 221. "Little Stories That Are True; Under the Wheels of Death," *Motion Picture Magazine,* Feb 1918, 78–79 (was to hang from a railroad trestle to escape thieves while a train passed for a film. Next morning, waiting for the hired train to arrive, Moreno walked out onto the testle to inspect it. When he got to the middle of it, a train approached and he actually hung from the side of the trestle till it passed. The actual filming of the scene was comparatively tame.). "Moreno's Contract with Vitagraph Is Extended," *MPW,* 24 May 1919, 1182. "Moreno in New York from Coast," *MPW,* 23 Aug 1919, 1154. "Moreno to Forsake Serials for Leading Role in Features," *MPW,* 11 Sep 1920, 182. "Moreno Signs to Act for Paramount," *MPW,* 14 Oct 1922, 572. "Paramount Signs Moreno," *MPW,* 10 Feb 1923, 542. Regina Cannon, "'No One Can Take Valentino's Place,' Says Antonio Moreno," *MW,* 19 May 1923, 10. Harry Carr, "A Spanish Cavalier," *Classic,* May 1923, 36–37, 78. Antonio Moreno, "The True Story of My Life," *MW,* 8 Nov 1924, 4–6, 27–28; Part II, 15 Nov 1924, 9–10, 25; Part III, 22 Nov 1924, 11–12, 28; Part IV, 29 Nov 1924, 16–17, 29; Part V, 6 Nov 1924, 17–18, 26; Part VI, 13 Dec 1924, 17–18, 30. Robert Keene, "Ramon Novarro Discloses a Secret About Antonio Moreno," *MW,* 27 Dec 1924, 8–9. "Elinor Glyn Selects Antonio Moreno to Head Cast," *MPW,* 3 Apr 1926, 343. Daisy Moreno [wife], "The Portrait of a Man," *Pictures,* II, Aug 1926, 67, 102–04. Gladys Hall, "The Regular Guy; A Miniature of Moreno, a Nice, Young Chap—and Normal, Too," *MPC,* Nov 1926, 53, 86. "Moreno Will Become an American Citizen," *MPW,* 29 Oct

1927, 551. George A. Katchmer, "Antonio Moreno; The Latin Lover," *CI*, 79 (Jan 1982), 22–23. Richard E. Braff, "An Index to the Films of Antonio Moreno," *CI*, 179 (May 1990), 34, 57; Part II, 18 (Jun 1990), 52, 59. George Katchmer, "Antonio Moreno," *CI*, 225 (Mar 1994), 45:3.

Moreno, Gabriel Garcia [founder of Azteca Pictures] (b. Mexico, 17 Jan 1880–24 Jan 1943 [63], Mexico City, Mexico). AS, p. 785.

Moreno, Marguerite [stage/film actress] (*née* Lucie Marie Marguerite Monceau, b. Paris, France, 15 Sep 1871–14 Jul 1948 [76], Touzac, Lot, France [extrait de décès no. 3]). m. Marcel Schwob (d. 1905). (Stage debut: Comédie Française, 1890; Paramount, Joinville). "Mme. Marguerite Moreno," *Variety*, 171, 21 Jul 1948, 55. AS, p. 785. BHD1, p. 392. IFN, p. 213. Waldman, p. 202 (stage debut, 1908).

Moreno, T[homas] **B. (Skyball)** [actor/stuntman] (b. 1890–25 Oct 1938 [48?], Los Angeles CA). AS, p. 785 (b. 1895). BHD, p. 256. IFN, p. 213 (age 43).

Moret, Neil [composer] (*né* Charles N. Daniels, b. 1878–23 Jan 1943 [64?], Compton CA). AS, p. 785. BHD2, p. 189.

Moretti, Raoul [composer] (b. Marseilles, France, 10 Aug 1893–6 Mar 1954 [60], Saint-Paul-de-Vence, France). AS, p. 785.

Morey, Harry T[emple] [actor] (b. Charlotte MI, 1873?–24 Jan 1936 [63], Brooklyn NY [Death Certificate Index No. 2140]). (Vitagraph, 1909.) "Harry T. Morey," *Variety*, 29 Jan 1936. AMD, p. 253. AS, p. 785. BHD1, p. 392. FFF, p. 253. IFN, p. 213. MH, p. 128. MSBB, p. 1026. Slide, p. 163. Truitt, p. 239. WWS, p. 69. "Morey Is Elephant Shy," *MPW*, 21 Sep 1912, 1178. "Harry T. Morey," *MPW*, 3 Feb 1917, 691. Harold Bennett, "Caught in Dressing Room No. 10," *MPC*, Mar 1919, 48–49, 71. "Morey Recovers from Illness," *MPW*, 10 Jan 1920, 260. "Harry Morey Leaps Into Bay and Saves Drowning Player," *MPW*, 17 Apr 1920, 442 (Webster Campbell). "Morey Resigns from Vitagraph," *MPW*, 10 Jul 1920, 194.

Morey, Henry A. [actor] (b. 1848?–8 Jan 1929 [81], Astoria NY; heart attack). (Paramount.) "Henry A. Morey," *Variety*, 16 Jun 1929. AS, p. 785. BHD, p. 256. IFN, p. 213. Truitt, p. 239.

Morgan, Boyd F. "Red" [actor/stuntman] (b. Waurika OK, 1915?–8 Jan 1988 [72], Tarzana CA; heart attack). BHD, p. 256. Nick Nicholls, "Boyd 'Red' Morgan," *CI*, 20 (Mar 1992), 9.

Morgan, Byron [scenarist] (b. Carthage MO, 24 Oct 1889–22 May 1963 [74], Los Angeles CA). "Byron Morgan," *Variety*, 29 May 1963. AMD, p. 253. AS, p. 785. BHD, p. 256; BHD2, p. 189. IFN, p. 213. "Byron Morgan Signs Contract," *MPW*, 28 Feb 1920, 1443. "Byron Morgan Continues as a Paramount Author," *MPW*, 1 Jan 1921, 91.

Morgan, Charles L[angbridge] [writer] (b. Kent, England, 22 Feb 1894–6 Feb 1958 [63], London, England). m. Hilda Vaughan. "Charles Morgan, Novelist, Is Dead; British Author, Playwright Was London Times Drama Critic from 1926 to 1939," *NYT*, 7 Feb 1958, 21:1 (age 64). "Charles Morgan," *Variety*, 12 Feb 1958.

Morgan, Fitzroy [actor] (b. England–d. 25 Oct 1912). BHD, p. 256.

Morgan, Frank (brother of **Ralph Morgan** [actor] (*né* Francis Phillip Wupperman, b. New York NY, 1 Jun 1890 [Birth Certificate Index No. 16428]–18 Sep 1949 [59], Beverly Hills CA). m. Alma. (Vitagraph; Goldwyn; Select; MGM.) "Frank Morgan, 59, Noted Actor, Dies; Stage, Screen and Radio Star for Years—Family Controlled Angostura Bitters Firm," *NYT*, 19 Sep 1949, 23:1; "Frank Morgan Funeral; 30 Friends of Actor at Rites in Beverly Hills Church," *NYT*, 21 Sep 1949, 31:4. "Frank Morgan," *Variety*, 21 Sep 1949. AMD, p. 253. AS, p. 785. BHD1, p. 392. FSS, p. 216. IFN, p. 213. Katz, p. 830. Spehr, p. 154. Truitt, p. 239 (b. 1 Jul). "Caprice's New Cast," *MPW*, 16 Dec 1916, 1648.

Morgan, Gene [actor] (*né* Eugene Schwartzkopf, b. Racine WI, 12 Mar 1893–15 Aug 1940 [47], Santa Monica CA; heart attack). (Pathé; Roach; Fox; Columbia.) "Gene Morgan," *NYT*, 16 Aug 1940, 15:5 (*né* Eugene Kenney; b. Montgomery AL). "Gene Morgan," *Variety*, 21 Aug 1940 (d. 13 Aug; age 48). AMD, p. 253. AS, p. 785 (d. 13 Aug). BHD1, p. 392. IFN, p. 213. Truitt, p. 239 (d. 13 Aug). "Gene Morgan Supports Star in Roach Comedy," *MPW*, 12 Nov 1927, 15.

Morgan, George [scenarist/director] (b. 1854?–8 Jan 1936 [81], Philadelphia PA). "George Morgan Dies," *Variety*, 15 Jan 1936. AMD, p. 253. AS, p. 785. FDY, p. 433. "Biograph Directors," *MPW*, 10 Jul 1915, 243–44.

Morgan, Harry "Swifty" [actor] (*né* Harry Nor, b. Russia, 1885–19 Sep 1975 [90?], Los Angeles CA). AS, p. 786.

Morgan, Helen [singer/actress] (*née* Helen Riggins, b. Danville IL, 2 Aug 1900–8 Oct 1941 [41], Chicago IL; 2 weeks after a kidney operation). m. (1) Maurice (Buddy) Maschke, Jr., 1933–35; (2) Lloyd Johnson, 27 Jul 1941. Jack Pulaski, "Helen Morgan, Top Torcher of the Dry Era, Des Broke in Chicago at 41," *Variety*, 144, 15 Oct 1941, 48:1. AMD, p. 253. AS, p. 786. BHD1, p. 392. IFN, p. 213. "Helen Morgan in Fox Film," *MPW*, 30 Jun 1923, 769.

Morgan, Henry R[ichard] **"Cy"** [baseball player/actor] (b. Pomeroy OH, 10 Nov 1877–28 Jun 1962 [84], Wheeling WV). "Harry Cy Morgan," *NYT*, 30 Jun 1962, 19:4. BHD, p. 256 (b. 1878). *The Baseball Bug* (Thanhouser ad), *MPW*, 11 Nov 1911, 514. "Who They Are; Some Handy Data on the Champion Ball Players Who Became Picture Players," *MPW*, 18 Nov 1911, 558.

Morgan, Horace A. "Kewpie" [actor]. No data found. George A. Katchmer, "Forgotten Cowboys and Cowgirls—Part IX," *CI*, 181 (Jul 1990), 55–56.

Morgan, Howard E. [scenarist]. No data found. FDY, p. 433.

Morgan, Ira H. [cinematographer] (b. Fort Ross CA, 2 Apr 1889–10 Apr 1959 [70], San Rafael CA). (Essanay; Monogram.) "Ira H. Morgan," *Variety*, 22 Apr 1959. AS, p. 786. BHD2, p. 189. FDY, p. 463. IFN, p. 213.

Morgan, Jane [actress] (b. England, 6 Dec 1880–1 Jan 1972 [91], Burbank CA). AS, p. 786.

Morgan, Jackie [actor] (b. Aberdean SD, 7 Jul 1916–25 Jul 1981 [65], Brea CA). BHD, p. 256.

Morgan, Jeanne (mother of scenarist Douglas Grant) [actress] (aka Jeanne Fenwick and Jeanne Fenwick Morgan, b. Trinidad, British West Indies, 1907). AMD, p. 253. "Jeanne Morgan Under Contract as F.B.O. Star," *MPW*, 5 Feb 1927, 427.

Morgan, Joseph [cinematographer]. No data found. FDY, p. 463.

Morgan, John A. [commercial artist] (b. Coventry, England, 1878?–1 Oct 1965 [87], Union NJ; struck by a truck). "John A. Morgan," *NYT* [strike paper], 11 Oct 1965, 61:3 (d. Roselle Park NY; "Mr. Morgan was responsible for Leo the Lion, trademark of Metro-Goldwyn-Mayer movies"). "John A. Morgan," *Variety*, 13 Oct 1965.

Morgan, Lee [actor] (*né* Raymond Lee Morgan, b. TX, 12 Jun 1902–30 Jan 1967 [64], Los Angeles CA; cardio-vascular disease). AS, p. 786. IFN, p. 213.

Morgan, Margaret [actress] (b. Ontario, Canada, 1895–29 Aug 1926 [31?], Glendale CA). BHD, p. 256. IFN, p. 213.

Morgan, Margo [actress] (*née* Marguerite Rockwood, b. KY, 27 Jan 1897–16 May 1962 [65], Los Angeles CA). (Metro.) "Margo Morgan," *Variety*, 30 May 1962. AS, p. 786.

Morgan, Myrtis [actress]. No data found. AMD, p. 253. "Myrtis Morgan Returns from France," *MPW*, 12 Apr 1919, 233.

Morgan, Paul [actor] (*né* Paul Morgenstern, b. Vienna, Austria, 1 Oct 1886–10 Dec 1938 [52], Camp Buchenwald, Germany; pulmonary congestion). (MGM.) AS, p. 786. BHD1, p. 393. IFN, p. 213. Waldman, p. 203.

Morgan, Ralph (brother of **Frank Morgan**; father of Claudia Morgan) [stage/film actor; helped to found the Screen Actors Guild [SAG] n 1933] (*né* Raphael Kuhner Wupperman, b. New York NY, 6 Jul 1883–11 Jun 1956 [72], New York NY [Death Certificate Index No. 12858]). m. Grace Arnold (daughter, Claudia). "Ralph Morgan, 72, Actor, Dies Here; Stage and Screen Performer Was Seen in 'Rasputin' Film and in 'Strange Interlude,'" *NYT*, 13 Jun 1956, 37:1. "Ralph Morgan," *Variety*, 20 Jun 1956. AS, p. 786. BHD1, p. 393. IFN, p. 213. Katz, p. 831. Blackie Seymour, "Ralph Morgan: Quite the Fighter," *CI*, 301 (Jul 2000), 60–61.

Morgan, Ruth [actress] (b. Columbus OH–d. 28 Jun 1917, Venice CA). BHD, p. 256.

Morgan, Sidney [director/scenarist] (b. London, England, 1872–15 Jun 1946 [74?], London, England). AS, p. 786.

Morgan, Sidney [actor] (b. Dublin, Ireland, 21 Oct 1885–5 Dec 1931 [46], London, England). AS, p. 786.

Morgan, Tommy [actor] (b. Bridgeton, Glasgow, Scotland, 1898?–28 Nov 1958 [60], Glasgow, Scotland). "Tommy Morgan," *Variety*, 3 Dec 1958.

Morgan, William [actor] (b. 1851–2 Jan 1944 [92?], Los Angeles CA). (Bison.) AS, p. 786. IFN, p. 213.

Morhange, Jacqueline [actress]. No data found. AMD, p. 253. "Jacqueline Morhange," *MPW*, 28 Aug 1915, 1460.

Moriarity, Bernard A. [producer] (b. Springfield MA, 1889–7 Oct 1937 [48?], Los Angeles CA). AS, p. 787.

Moriarity, Marcus [actor] (d. 21 Jun 1916, New York NY). AS, p. 787. BHD, p. 256. IFN, p. 213.

Morin, Alberto [actor] (b. San Juan, Puerto Rico, 26 Nov 1902–7 Apr 1989 [86], Los Angeles CA; coronary thrombosis). AS, p. 787. BHD1, p. 393.

Morin, Pilar [actress]. No data found. AMD, p. 253. "Mlle. Pilar Morin in a New Edison Film,"

MPW, VI, 15 Jan 1910, 55. "The Future of the Silent Drama," *MPW,* 22 Jan 1910, 84–85. Pilar Morin, "Silent Drama Music," *MPW,* 30 Apr 1910, 676. Bernard C. Cook, "Making Moving Pictures Popular," *MPW,* 28 May 1910, 876–77. "Pilar Morin," *MPW,* 24 Sep 1910, 682. "Pilar Morin," *MPW,* 18 Mar 1911, 591.

Morison, Lindsay [actor] (b. Newcastle-on-Tyne, England-d. 22 Feb 1917, New Rochelle NY). BHD, p. 256. IFN, p. 213.

Moriss [actor] (*né* Frédéric Edouard Maurice Boyer, b. Nimes, France, 3 May 1874 [extrait de naissance no. 644]-ca. 1951 [77?]). AS, p. 787.

Morlas, Laurent [actor] (b. France, 1888–1942 [54?], France). AS, p. 787.

Morlay, Gaby [stage/film actress] (aka Gaby de Morlaix, *née* Blanche Pauline Fumoleau, b. Angers, France, 8 Jun 1893–4 Jul 1964 [71], Nice, France; cancer [extrait de décès no. 239.6.1964]). (Stage debut, 1912; first film of seventy films, 1914.) "Gaby Morlay," *Variety,* 235, 8 Jul 1964, 63:2. AS, p. 787. BHD1, p. 393 (b. Biskra, Algeria). IFN, p. 213.

Morlet, Jeanne [actress/singer] (b. Paris, France, 1883-ca. 1956 [73?]). AS, p. 787.

Morley, Christopher [actor/scenarist] (b. 4 May 1890). AS, p. 787.

Morley, Jay [actor] (b. Port Orange FL, 14 Jul 1890–9 Nov 1976 [86], Santa Monica CA). (Lubin.) AMD, p. 253. AS, p. 787. BHD1, p. 393. IFN, p. 213. "Jay Morley, Lubin Player," *MPW,* 15 May 1915, 1079. George A. Katchmer, "Forgotten Cowboys and Cowgirls—Part V," *CI,* 177 (Mar 1990), C4, C6; "Update," *CI,* 179 (May 1990), 44.

Morley, Robert James [actor] (b. 1892?–29 Aug 1952 [60], Los Angeles CA). "Robert James Morley," *Variety,* 10 Sep 1952. AS, p. 787 (b. 1901; d. 30 Aug). IFN, p. 214 (age 51).

Morne, Maryland [actress] (*née* Mary Morne, b. England, 1900?–18 Jul 1935 [35], Los Angeles CA). m. Eugene Strong. "Maryland Strong," *Variety,* 24 Jul 1935. AS, p. 787. BHD1, p. 393. IFN, p. 214.

Morosco, Oliver (father of **Walter Morosco**) [producer] (*né* Oliver Morosco Mitchell, b. Logan UT, 20 Jun 1875–25 Aug 1945 [69], Los Angeles CA; struck by streetcar). m. (1) Annie T. Cockrell; (2) **Selma Paley**; (3) Helen Mitchell; Dorothy. "Oliver Morosco Killed in Hollywood Accident," *Variety,* 29 Aug 1945. (Oliver Morosco Photoplay Co.) AMD, p. 253. AS, p. 787. IFN, p. 214. SD, p. 905. "Morosco in Film Field; Forms New Company with Garbutt to Release Through Paramount," *NYDM,* 11 Nov 1914, 24:1 (with partners, Garbutt [head of Bosworth M.P. Co.], Charles Eyton, and Ruth Garbutt; 1st star: Lenore Ulrich). "Morosco and Cort Enter Picture Field," *MPW,* 21 Nov 1914, 1093. "Oliver Morosco's Views," *NYDM,* 2 Dec 1914, 22:3. "Morosco Preparing Plays for Screen," *MPW,* 9 Jan 1915, 224. "Oliver Morosco," *MPW,* 10 Jul 1915, 330. "Morosco Makes Denial," *MPW,* 7 Oct 1916, 52. "Another Combination of Picture Companies," *MPW,* 21 Oct 1916, 376. "Morosco, Producer of 300 Stage Plays, Finishes First Film, 'The Half Breed,'" *MPW,* 23 Apr 1921, 832. "Mrs. Morosco's Suit Against Husband Temporarily Checked," *MPW,* 28 Aug 1920, 1143 (Selma Paley). "Morosco and WIfe Discontinue Suits; Basis of Settlement Is Not Disclosed," *MPW,* 24 Sep 1921, 406.

Morosco, Walter (son of **Oliver Morosco**) [director/producer] (b. San Francisco CA, 1899?–30 Dec 1948 [49], Coronado CA). m. **Corinne Griffith**, 1933–34 (d. 1979); Shirley Listenwalter; Marie O'Keefe. "Walter Morosco, Film Producer, 49; Twentieth Century-Fox Aide for Ten Years, Son of Late Impresario, Dies on Coast," *NYT,* 31 Dec 1948, 15:2. "Walter Morosco," *Variety,* 5 Jan 1949. AMD, p. 254. AS, p. 787. BHD, p. 256; BHD2, p. 189. IFN, p. 214. "Walter Morosco to Direct Warner Bros. Productions," *MPW,* 6 Feb 1926, 544.

Moroso, John A. [scenarist] (b. 1874–6 Jun 1957 [83?], New Rochelle NY). BHD2, p. 189.

Morrell, George [actor] (b. CA, 10 Apr 1872–28 Apr 1955 [83], Los Angeles CA). "George Morrell," *Variety,* 4 May 1955 (age 82). AS, p. 788. BHD1, p. 394. IFN, p. 214. Truitt, p. 240.

Morrell, Louis [actor] (*né* Louis Kasforff, b. 1873?–11 Jul 1945 [72], Elgin IL). "Louis Morrell," *Variety,* 18 Jul 1945. AS, p. 788. BHD, p. 256. IFN, p. 214.

Morriarity, Bernard A. [producer] (d. 6 Oct 1937, Los Angeles CA). BHD2, p. 189.

Morris, Adrian M. [actor] (brother of **Chester** and **Gordon Morris**) [actor] (*né* Michael Morris, b. Mt. Vernon NY, 12 Jan 1907–30 Nov 1941 [34], Los Angeles CA). AS, p. 787. BHD1, p. 394. IFN, p. 214.

Morris, Chester (son of **William Morris**; brother of **Adrian** and **Gordon Morris**) [stage/film actor] (*né* John Chester Brooks Morris, b. New York NY, 16 Feb 1901 [Birth Certificate Index No. 19455]–11 Sep 1970 [69], New Hope PA; overdose of barbituates). m. (1) Suzanne Kilborn; (2) Lili Kenton. "Chester Morris Is Dead at 69; Created Role of Boston Blackie; In Hollywood, He Made Over 85 Films—Last Stage Part Was Capt. Queeg," *NYT,* 12 Sep 1970, 27:3. "Chester Morris," *Variety,* 16 Sep 1970. AS, p. 788. BHD1, p. 394. IFN, p. 214. Katz, p. 833. SD. Truitt, p. 240. Herbert Cruikshank, "Alias Chester Morris; McGann's Slayer Posing as Movie Actor, Is Unmasked by a Lot of Tripe," *MPC,* l 1929, 43, 82. "Buck Rainey's Filmographies; Chester Morris," *CI,* 170 (Aug 1989), 42–45.

Morris, Clara [stage/film actress] (*née* Clara La Montagne, b. Toronto, Canada, 17 Mar 1848–19 Nov 1925 [77], New Canaan CT). m. Frederick C. Harriot (d. 1914). "Clara Morris Rites in the 'Little Church'; Famous Actress's Body Lies in State in Mortuary Chapel—Services Tomorrow at 4," *NYT,* 22 Nov 1925, 9:1 (age 80). "Clara Morris," *Variety,* 25 Nov 1925. AMD, p. 254. AS, p. 788. SD. Truitt, p. 240 (b. Omaha NB, 1897). "New Reliance Studio," *MPW,* 26 Jul 1913, 433. "Famous Stage Name Gets Into Pictures," *MPW,* 5 Oct 1918, 101.

Morris, Corbet [actor] (*né* Louis McClanahan Thompson, b. CO, 31 Dec 1881–10 Mar 1951 [69], Los Angeles CA). AS, p. 788.

Morris, Dave [actor] (b. Middlesbrough, England, 1897?–8 Jun 1960 [63], Blackpool, England). (K&E.) "Dave Morris," *Variety,* 22 Jun 1960. AMD, p. 254. AS, p. 788. IFN, p. 214. Richard V. Spencer, "Los Angeles," *MPW,* 20 May 1911, 1125. "Dave Morris Joins L-KO," *MPW,* 8 Dec 1917, 1506.

Morris, Diana [actress] (b. CA, 21 Jul 1906–19 Feb 1961 [54], Los Angeles CA; throat cancer). m. Stanley Opegez. "Diana Morris," *Variety,* 222, 8 Mar 1961, 79:2 (one of the original Wampas Baby Stars). AS, p. 788. BHD, p. 256. IFN, p. 214.

Morris, Frank [cameraman]. No data found. AMD, p. 254. "Frank Morris Joins California M.P. Corp.," *MPW,* 20 Dec 1913, 1414.

Morris, Gordon (brother of **Chester** and **Adrian Morris**) [stage/film actor/scenarist] (b. 1899–7 Apr 1940 [41], Los Angeles CA). "Gordon Morris," *Variety,* 138, 10 Apr 1940, 46:5. AS, p. 788. BHD, p. 256; BHD2, p. 189. IFN, p. 214.

Morris, Gouverneur [writer] (b. NY, 1876?–14 Aug 1953 [77], Gallup NM). m. Ruth Wrightman. "Gouverneur Morris, Novelist, Ex-Banker," *NYT,* 24 Dec 1940, 15:4. "Mrs. Gouverneur Morris," *NYT,* 20 Apr 1939, 23:3 (d. 19 Apr 1939 [43], Alameda NM). AS, p. 788.

Morris, Jack J[ulius] [actor: The Keystone Cops] (*né* Jack Maurice, b. 1904–21 Apr 1990 [85?], Sherman Oaks CA). AMD, p. 254. BHD, p. 256. "Bull's Eye to Star 'A Human Fly,'" *MPW,* 6 Sep 1919, 1522 (16 years old).

Morris, Johnnie (or **Johnny**) [vaudevillian/actor] (*né* John Morris Erickson, b. New York NY, 15 Jun 1886–7 Oct 1969 [83], Los Angeles CA). "Johnny Morris," *Variety,* 15 Oct 1969. AS, p. 788. BHD1, p. 394 (b. 1887). IFN, p. 214 (age 82).

Morris, Lee [actor] (b. MO, 23 Jun 1863–6 Feb 1933 [69], Los Angeles CA). AS, p. 788. BHD, p. 256. IFN, p. 214.

Morris, Margaret [actress: Wampas Star, 1924] (b. Minneapolis MN, 7 Nov 1898–7 Jun 1968 [69], Los Angeles CA). AMD, p. 254. AS, p. 788. BHD1, p. 394. BR, pp. 183–85 (b. 1903). IFN, p. 214. "Margaret Morris," *MPW,* 18 Dec 1926, 491. George A. Katchmer, "Remembering the Great Silents," *CI,* 178 (Apr 1990), 40–41.

Morris, Percy [actor/director] (b. 1879–24 Apr 1941 [62?], Los Angeles CA). BHD2, p. 189.

Morris, Phyllis [actress] (b. London, England, 18 Jul 1894–9 Feb 1982 [87], Northwood, England). AS, p. 789.

Morris, Reginald (actor/scenarist/gag writer) (*né* James Reginald Morris, b. New York NY, 26 Jun 1886?–16 Feb 1928 [41], Los Angeles CA; heart attack). (K&E; Keystone.) "Reginald Morris," *Variety,* 22 Feb 1928. AMD, p. 254. AS, p. 789. BHD, p. 257; BHD2, p. 189 (b. NJ, 25 Jun). FDY, p. 433. IFN, p. 214. *MPN Studio Directory,* 21 Oct 1916 (b. 1890). "New Christie Director Announced," *MPW,* 31 Jan 1920, 754. "Special Signs Reggis Morris," *MPW,* 7 Aug 1920, 728.

Morris, Richard [actor] (*né* W. Richard Stuart Morris, b. Boston MA, 1861–11 Oct 1924 [63?], Los Angeles CA). AS, p. 789. BHD, p. 257.

Morris, Sam [general manager]. No data found. AMD, p. 254. Merritt Crawford, "Presenting Sam Morris of Warner Brothers," *MPW,* 13 Nov 1926, 75.

Morris, Mrs. Steven *see* **Edith Ritchie**

Morris, Virginia [publicist]. No data found. AMD, p. 254. "Miss Morris with Fox," *MPW,* 12 Dec 1925, 534. "Miss Morris with Warners," *MPW,* 5 Mar 1927, 12.

Morris, William (father of **Chester Morris**) [actor] (b. Boston MA, 1 Jan 1861–11 Jan 1936 [75], Los Angeles CA). m. Etta Hawkins. "William Morris," *Variety,* 15 Jan 1936 (age 70). AS, p. 789. BHD1, p. 394. IFN, p. 214.

Morris, William, "Dean of the Golden Age of Vaudeville" [stage/film actor] (b. Schwartzenau,

Germany, 1 May 1873–1 Nov 1932 [59], New York NY). m. Emma Berlinghoff. "William Morris," *Variety,* 8 Nov 1932. AS, p. 789. SD, p. 947.

Morris, William E. [actor] (b. NY, 1878?–21 Sep 1948 [70], East Islip NY). m. Ella Clary. "William E. Morris," *NYT,* 23 Sep 1948, 29:4. "William E. Morris," *Variety,* 29 Sep 1948. AS, p. 789. IFN, p. 214.

Morrison, Adrienne (mother of the **Bennett** sisters) [stage/film actress] (*née* Mabel Adrienne Morrison, b. New York NY, 1 Mar 1883–20 Nov 1940 [57], New York NY). m. **Richard Bennett**, 1903–25 (d. 1944); Eric S. Pinker, 1927. "Miss A. Morrison, Retired Actress; Mother of Constance, Joan and Barbara Bennett Dies Here of a Heart Ailment; On Stage at 6 Months; Literary Agent Had Appeared in 'Hamlet,' 'Squaw Man' and 'Damaged Goods,'" *NYT,* 21 Nov 1940, 29:3. "Adrienne Morrison," *Variety,* 27 Nov 1940. AMD, p. 254. AS, p. 789. BHD, p. 257. SD. Truitt 3, p. 524 (b. 1878). "Adrienne Morrison Wins Recognition," *MPW,* 18 Nov 1916, 989.

Morrison, Anna Marie [actress] (*née?,* b. 1884?–5 Jul 1972 [88], Los Angeles CA). m. **Chick Morrison** (d. 1924; one son). "Anna Marie," *Variety,* 267, 19 Jul 1972, 103:2. AS, p. 789. BHD, p. 257. IFN, p. 214.

Morrison, Anne [actress] (d. 7 Apr 1967, Los Angeles CA). BHD, p. 257.

Morrison, Arthur [actor] (b. St. Louis MO, 1 May 1877–20 Feb 1950 [72], Los Angeles CA). AS, p. 789. BHD1, p. 395. IFN, p. 214. Truitt, p. 241 (b. 1880). George A. Katchmer, "Forgotten Cowboys and Cowgirls—Part XIV," *CI,* 191 (May 1991), 24.

Morrison, Carl (brother of **Chick** and **Peter Morrison**) [actor]. No data found. (American.)

Morrison, Charles P. [actor] (b. 1863?–25 Mar 1934 [71], New York NY). m. Henrietta Lee. "Charles P. Morrison," *Variety,* 3 Apr 1934. AS, p. 789.

Morrison, Chick (brother of **Carl** and **Peter Morrison**) [actor] (*né* Charles Pacific Morrison, b. Mt. Morrison CO, 3 Apr 1878–20 Jun 1924 [46], Los Angeles CA; from injuries after falling off a horse). m. **Ann Marie** (d. 1972). (American.) AS, p. 789. BHD, p. 257 (C.P. [Chick] Morrison). IFN, p. 214. Truitt, p. 241. Tom Reeves, "Rex, King of Wild Horses," *MPC,* Sep 1924, 62, 83–84 (Morrison was killed before publication of this article). George Katchmer, "Chick Morrison," *CI,* 225 (Mar 1994), 46:1.

Morrison, Chris [actor]. No data found. AMD, p. 254. "Horse Drags Actor Many Feet," *MPW,* 5 Jul 1919, 76.

Morrison, Ernest W. [executive] (b. 1892?–4 Jan 1940 [47], Atlanta GA). "Ernest W. Morrison," *NYT,* 5 Jan 1940, 20:3.

Morrison, Ernie "Sunshine Sammy" [actor: Our Gang Comedies] (*né* Frederick Ernest Morrison, b. New Orleans LA, 20 Dec 1912–24 Jul 1989 [76], Lynwood CA; cancer). AMD, p. 254. AS, p. 789. BHD1, p. 395. "'Smiling Sammy' a Near-Star," *MPW,* 27 Jul 1918, 570.

Morrison, Florence [actress] (b. 1871?–8 May 1928 [57?], New York NY). BHD, p. 257.

Morrison, Florence [actress] (*née* Mary Florence Horne, b. 1887?–15 Jun 1942 [55], Denison TX). m. **Priestley Morrison** (d. 1938). "Florence Morrison," *Variety,* 24 Jun 1942. AS, p. 789.

Morrison, Helen S. [actress] (*née* Helen Stewart, b. 1896–6 May 1961 [65?], New York NY). AS, p. 789.

Morrison, James Woods [actor] (b. Mattoon IL, 15 Nov 1888–15 Nov 1974 [86], New York NY [Death Certificate Index No. 20255]). (Vitagraph, 1910.) "James W. Morrison," *NYT,* 23 Nov 1974, 42:4. AMD, p. 254. AS, p. 789. BHD, p. 257. IFN, p. 214. Lowrey, p. 124. FFF, p. 184. MH, p. 128. Slide, pp. 145–46. "The Actologue," *MPW,* 18 Jul 1908, 45. "Several Vitagraph Artists Close," *MPW,* 29 Mar 1913, 1319. "Brief Biographies of Popular Players," *Motion Picture Magazine,* Feb 1915, 107. "James Morrison, Versatile Vitagrapher," *MPW,* 6 May 1916, 978. "James Morrison Joins Ivan," *MPW,* 14 Oct 1916, 217. "Personal and Otherwise," *MPW,* 8 Mar 1919, 1323. "James Morrison Is Signed by Jans to Appear in Support of Olive Tell," *MPW,* 17 Jan 1920, 426. "Morrison Is Engaged for 'Man Next Door,'" *MPW,* 24 Mar 1923, 464. Billy H. Doyle, "Lost Players," *CI,* 162 (Dec 1988), 44.

Morrison, John [actor/singer] (b. Ireland, 1877–16 Feb 1923 [45?], Tacoma WA; pneumonia). AS, p. 789.

Morrison, Joseph [actor]. No data found. AMD, p. 254. "Marshal Foch's Double Is Captain Morrison, Who Plays in 'Mystery of the Yellow Room,'" *MPW,* 13 Sep 1919, 1642. "Captain Morrison in New Brady Film," *MPW,* 8 Nov 1919, 244. "Capt. Morrison to Appear on the American Stage," *MPW,* 5 Feb 1921, 681. "Foxh Meets Foch as Marshal Docks on His First Visit Here," *MPW,* 31 Dec 1921, 1073.

Morrison, Leo [press agent/talent manager] (b. 1899?–19 Apr 1974 [75], New York NY). (Griffith; Zukor.) m. Marjorie Booth. "Leo Morrison Dies; Film Star, Agent, 75," *NYT,* 21 Apr 1974, 53:4. "Leo Morrison," *Variety,* 1 May 1974. AS, p. 790.

Morrison, Lindsay [actor/director] (b. Newcastle-upon-Tyne, England-d. 22 Feb 1917, New Rochelle NY). BHD2, p. 189.

Morrison, Louis [actor] (b. Portland ME, 8 Feb 1866–22 Apr 1946 [80], Los Angeles CA). AS, p. 790. BHD1, p. 395. IFN, p. 214 (b. Portland MD).

Morrison, Meta [actress] (b. 1892?–28 Nov 1982 [90], Chicago IL). (Essanay, 1917.) "Meta Morrison," *Variety,* 8 Dec 1982 ("actress in silent films when they were made in Chicago"). AS, p. 790. BHD, p. 257.

Morrison, Pete (brother of **Carl** and **Chick Morrison**) [actor] (*né* George D. Morrison, b. Denver CO, 8 Aug 1890–5 Feb 1973 [82], Los Angeles CA). (American; Universal.) "Pete Morrison," *Variety,* 14 Feb 1973. "George Morrison Dies; Silent Movie Cowboy," *The Evening Bulletin* [Philadelphia], 8 Feb 1973 (grandfather founded Morrison CO in 1859). AMD, p. 254. BHD1, p. 395. GK, pp. 680–91. IFN, p. 214. "Universal to Star Pete Morrison," *MPW,* 6 Oct 1923, 507. George A. Katchmer, "The Kids Also Loved Peter Morrison," *CI,* 152 (Feb 1988), 22–24, 61.

Morrison, Priestly [stage director/actor] (*né* Howard Priestley Morrison, b. Baltimore MD, 5 Jul 1871–26 Jan 1938 [66], Kew Gardens, Queens NY). m. (1) Fanny Young (d. 1908); (2) Mary Florence Horne [**Florence Morrison**], 1901 (d. 1942). "Priestly Morrison of Stage, 66, Dead; Director of Scores of Plays on Broadway Had Been an Actor as Well; Had Trained Many Stars; Former Head of Stock Troupe in Des Moines, Where Noted Performers Got Start," *NYT,* 27 Jan 1938, 21:1. "Priestly Morrison," *Variety,* 2 Feb 1938. AS, p. 790. BHD, p. 257; BHD2, p. 189. Ragan 2, p. 908. SD.

Morrison, Mrs. Priestly *see* **Morrison, Florence**

Morrissey, Betty [actress] (*née* Elizabeth Morrisey, b. Brooklyn NY, 1907–20 Apr 1944 [36], New York NY). AS, p. 790. BHD1, p. 395. IFN, p. 215. Truitt, p. 241.

Morrissey, Edward [director]. No data found. AMD, p. 254. "Biograph Directors," *MPW,* 10 Jul 1915, 243–44. "From College Professor to Film Director," *MPW,* 22 Jan 1916, 613.

Morrissey, Will [actor/song writer/sketch writer/stage producer] (b. New York NY, 19 Jun 1887–16 Dec 1957 [70], California Hotel, Santa Barbara CA). m. 7 times. "Will Morrissey, 72, Actor, Producer," *NYT,* 18 Dec 1957, 35:1. Abel, "Morrissey Closes Out Era; 'I Stranded Better Actors Than Shuberts Starred,'" *Variety,* 209, 25 Dec 1957, 1:2 (age 72). AS, p. 790. BHD, p. 257.

Morrow, Jane [actress] *see* **McVey, Lucille**

Morrow, Jane [scenarist] (b. 1874–9 Jan 1914 [39?], New York NY). BHD2, p. 189.

Morse, Beatrice [scenarist]. No data found. AMD, p. 255. "Scenario Writers Join World Film," *MPW,* 9 Mar 1918, 1349. "Beatrice NMorse, World Pictures Scenarioist," *MPW,* 13 Jul 1918, 188. "Munsey Engages Scenarist," *MPW,* 28 Jun 1919, 1952.

Morse, Karl [actor] (b. 1888–22 Jan 1936 [48], Los Angeles CA). AS, p. 790. BHD, p. 257. IFN, p. 215.

Morse, N. Brewster [writer/director] (b. New York NY, 29 May 1903). AMD, p. 255. AS, p. 790 (b. 19 May). "N. Brewster Morse Has Signed for Three Years with Fanark," *MPW,* 2 Oct 1920, 634.

Morse, Salmi [dramatist/producer] (d. ca. 1913; suicide). BHD, p. 257. Edward Azlant, "Screenwriting for the early silent film: forgotten pioneers, 1897–1911," *Film History,* 9 (1997), 228–56 (dramatized the *Passion Play,* mounted by David Belasco at the Grand Opera House, San Francisco CA, on 3 Mar 1879. Rich G. Hollaman produced a film version based on Morse's script which premiered at the Eden Musee on 30 Jan 1898, directed by L.J. Vincent, photography by William C. Paley, with Frank Russell as the Christus.).

Morse, Terrell (Terry) O. [film editor/director] (b. St. Louis MO, 30 Jan 1906–19 May 1984 [78], Newhall CA). "Terry O. Morse," *Variety,* 13 Jun 1984 ("entered the film business as a film wrapper at First National in 1921."). BHD2, p. 189.

Morse, William [actor] (b. 1887?–23 Sep 1918 [31], New York NY; pneumonia). "William Morse," *Variety,* 27 Sep 1918. AS, p. 790.

Mortelle, Louis [actor]. (Lubin.) No data found.

Mortimer, Charles [actor] (b. England, 1885–1 Apr 1964 [79?], London, England). AS, p. 790.

Mortimer, Dorothy [actress] (b. 1898–15 Feb 1950 [52], New York NY). BHD, p. 257. IFN, p. 215.

Mortimer, Edmund [actor/director/scenarist] (b. New York NY, 1875–21 May 1944 [69], Los Angeles CA). (Universal; Selznick.) "Edmund Mortimer," *NYT,* 25 May 1944, 21:6. "Edmund Mortimer," *Variety,* 31 May 1944. AS, p. 791 (b. 1874). BHD1, p. 395; BHD2, p. 189 (b. 1880). IFN, p. 215. 1921 Directory, p. 271. Spehr, p. 154. Truitt, p. 241.

Mortimer, Henry [actor] (*né* John O'-Donohoe Rennie, b. Toronto, Ontario, Canada, 14 Aug 1882 [birth certificate #042175, no. 1895]–20 Aug 1952 [70], Whitby, Ontario, Canada). "Henry Mortimer," *Variety,* 27 Aug 1952 ("silent screen actor"). AS, p. 791 (b. 1875). BHD1, p. 395. IFN, p. 215. SD, p. 910.

Morton, Charles S. [actor] (*né* Carl Mudge, b. Vallejo CA, 28 Jan 1907–26 Oct 1966 [58], No. Hollywood CA; cardiovascular ailment). (1st bit at Astoria: an angel in *Sorrows of Satan;* Fox.) AS, p. 791. BHD1, p. 395 (b. IL). IFN, p. 215. Katz, pp. 834–35. Cedric Belfrage, "Forbidden to Fall; His Contract Won't Permit Charles Morton to Lose His Heart," *MPC,* Jun 1929, 24, 78 ("I may have avoided the early extra work days in Hollywood, but I've certainly known most of the struggles for a place in the sun than most movie actors.").

Morton, Clive [actor] (b. London, England, 16 Mar 1904–24 Sep 1975 [71], London, England). AS, p. 791.

Morton, Drew [actor] (b. 1855–4 Sep 1916 [61?], New York NY). AS, p. 791. BHD, p. 257; BHD2, p. 190.

Morton, Howard E. [scenarist] (b. 1878–23 Dec 1938 [60?], New York NY; heart attack). AS, p. 791.

Morton, James C. [actor] (b. Helena MT, 1884–24 Oct 1942 [58?], Reseda CA). AS, p. 791.

Morton, Maxine [actress] (*née* Katherine West, b. 1883–26 Sep 1936 [53?], Los Angeles CA). AS, p. 791.

Morton, Walter [actor/director]. No data found. AMD, p. 255. "Walter Morton Reaches France," *MPW,* 9 Nov 1918, 678.

Morway, Jacques [actor] (b. Hungary, 1843–6 May 1914 [71?]). BHD, p. 257.

Moschini, Giacomo [actor] (aka Aldo Moschino, b. Padua, Italy, 16 Apr 1896–1945 [49?]). JS, p. 307 (in Italian silents from 1928).

Moscovitch, Maurice [actor] (*né* Morris Maaskoff, b. Odessa, Ukraine, Russia, 23 Nov 1871–18 Jun 1940 [68], Los Angeles CA). AS, p. 791.

Moscowitz, Mrs. Jennie [stage/film actress] (*née?,* b. Romania, 1868?–26 Jul 1953 [85], Bronx NY). m. **Max Moscowitz**, 1888 (d. 1947). "Jennie Moscowitz, Jewish Actress, 85; Performer Known for Mother Roles Is Dead—Made Her Debut in Rumania at 13," *NYT,* 27 Jul 1953, 19:5. "Mrs. Jennie Moscowitz," *Variety,* 29 Jul 1953. AS, p. 791. BHD1, p. 396. IFN, p. 215. NNAT NEZ, p. 439 (b. Jassy, Armenia).

Moscowitz, Max [actor/producer] (b. Romania, 1858?–11 Jan 1947 [88], New York NY). m. **Jennie**, 1888 (d. 1953). "Max Moscowitz, 88, Ran Variety Houses," *NYT,* 13 Jan 1947, 21:5. "Max Moscowitz," *Variety,* 15 Jan 1947. AS, p. 791.

Moser, Frank [animator/producer] (b. 1886–30 Sep 1964 [78?], Dobbs Ferry NY). AS, p. 791 (founder of Terry Toons). BHD2, p. 190.

Moser, Hans [actor] (*né* Johann Julier, b. Vienna, Austria, 6 Aug 1880–19 Jun 1964 [83], Vienna, Austria; cancer). AS, p. 791. BHD1, p. 396.

Moses, Alan [cinematographer] (b. 1895–Jun 1929 [34?], Redondo Beach CA). BHD2, p. 190.

Moses, Alfred H., Jr. (cameraman]. No data found. AMD, p. 255. "Alfred H. Moses, Jr.," *MPW,* 7 Aug 1915, 1008.

Moses, Vivian M. [publicist]. No data found. AMD, p. 255. "Vivian M. Moses Joins Goldwyn," *MPW,* 17 Feb 1917, 1020. Vivian M. Moses, "With Art as Her Handmaiden," *MPW,* 21 Jul 1917, 383–87. "Vivian Moses with Selznick," *MPW,* 18 Aug 1917, 1078. "Moses Vists the Old Home Town," *MPW,* 8 Jun 1918, 1440 (Sumter SC). VIvian M. Moses, "Where Do We Go from Here?," *MPW,* 20 Jul 1918, 345. "Publicity Manager on Vacation," *MPW,* 16 Nov 1918, 723. "Vivian M. Moses Leaves Select to FOrm Partnership with Empey," *MPW,* 30 Aug 1919, 1303. "William Fox Appoints VIvian M. Moses Director of Publicity and Advertising," *MPW,* 3 Jul 1920, 66. Vivian M. Moses, "Star Comedies ESsential for Complete Program; Add Relish to Entertainment," *MPW,* 2 Dec 1922, 431. "Vivian M. Moses," *MPW,* 26 Mar 1927, 311.

Mosheim, Greta [actress] (b. Berlin, Germany, 8 Jan 1905–29 Dec 1986 [81], New York NY). AS, p. 791. BHD1, p. 396.

Mosjoukine, Ivan Illich (father of Romain Gary) [actor/director] (aka Ivan Moskin, b. Penza, Russia, 28 Sep 1888–17 Jan 1939 [50], Neuilly-sur-Seine, France; hemoptysis [extrait de décès no. SN/1939]). (Began 1911.) "Ivan Mosjoukine; Franco-Russian Actor Starred in Silent Film Days," *NYT,* 19 Jan 1939, 19:4 (age 50). "Ivan Mosjoukine," *Variety,* 25 Jan 1939 (age 50). AS, p. 791 (b. 26 Sep 1893). BHD1, p. 396; BHD2, p. 190 (b. 26 Sep 1887; d. 18 Jan). IFN, p. 215. JS, p. 307 (appeared in *Le avventure di Casanova,* Italy, 1927). Katz, p. 837 (b. 1889; began in Russia; single Hollywood film: *Surrender,* 1927). Truitt, p. 242. Waldman, p. 205. Garth Pedler, "The Russian Season in New York, 1917–1918," *CI,* 88 (Oct 1982), 18, 46. Garth Pedler, "Ivan Mosjoukine in 'The House of Mystery' (1922)," *CI,* 203 (May 1992), 34–35, 57; Part II, 204, Jun 1992, 36–38. Garth Pedler, "Ivan Mosjoukine in 'Prince of Adventurers' (or 'Casanova') (1927)," *CI,* 222 (Dec 1993), C2 *et passim.*

Moskvin, Andrei Nikolaevic [director of photography] (b. St. Petersburg, Russia, 14 Feb 1901–1961 [60?], Leningrad, Russia). AS, p. 792.

Moskvin, Ivan M[ikhailovitch] [stage/film actor/director] (b. Moscow, Russia, 18 Jun 1874–16 Feb 1946 [71], Moscow, Russia). "Ivan M. Moskvin, Russian Actor, 72; Stage and Screen Star Dies—Supreme Soviet Member Was Hailed on U.S. Visits [1923 and 1924]," *NYT,* 18 Feb 1946, 21:5 ("In 1943 Mr. Moskvin was one of a number of Soviet artists to be honored in the distribution of more than 5,000,000 rubles on Premier Stalin's birthday." His widow was to receive 25,000 rubles and a lifetime pension of 150 rubles a month.). "Ivan M. Moskvin," *Variety,* 161, 20 Feb 1946, 54:1. AS, p. 792. BHD1, p. 396 (Iva Moskvin); BHD2, p. 190. IFN, p. 215.

Mosley, Fred [actor] (*né* Frederick Charles Mosley, b. 1854?–9 Mar 1927 [73], Staten Island NY). m. May Kritzer. "Fred Mosley," *Variety,* 16 Mar 1927. AS, p. 792. BHD, p. 258. IFN, p. 215. Truitt, p. 242.

Mosquini, Marie [actress] (b. Los Angeles CA, 3 Dec 1899–21 Feb 1983 [84], Los Angeles CA). m. (1) Ray Harlow; (2) **Lee De Forest**, Oct 1930 (d. 1961). De Forest, *Father of Radio.* "Marie Mosquini," *Variety,* 30 Mar 1983. AS, p. 792. BHD, p. 258 (b. 1902). MH, p. 129 (b. 1899). WWS, p. 255. Willis Goldbeck, Interview, *Motion Picture Classic,* Nov 1920, 60. Willis Goldbeck, "Facing Facts; Concerning the New Faces in Hollywood," *Motion Picture,* Jul 1922, 43–45, 117–19. Harry Carr, "They Call Her 'The Wop,'" *Classic,* XVI, Jul 1923, 35. June Lee, "Dan Cupid's Bulletin Board," *Paris and Hollywood Screen Secrets Magazine,* May 1927, 52 (divorced Harlow. "Many of those who knew Marie around the studio didn't even know she was married in the first place."). Miracles in Trust, The Penham Foundation, 101 First Street, Suite 394, Los Altos CA 94022, holds the memorabilia of the De Forests.

Moss, Benjamin S. [exhibitor/theater builder/producer] (b. 1878?–12 Dec 1951 [73], New York NY). m. Estelle Dreyfuss. "B.S. Moss, Active in Theatre World; Builder and Operator of Film Houses Is Dead—Once with Albee in Vaudeville Chain," *NYT,* 13 Dec 1951, 33:2. "Benjamin S. Moss," *Variety,* 19 Dec 1951 (produced *Three Weeks* and *Boots and Saddles*). AMD, p. 255. AS, p. 792. BHD2, p. 190. "About B.S. Moss; Some Information about the Last Addition to the Film Producers' Ranks," *NYDM,* 21 Oct 1914, 32:2 (1st production: Elinor Glyn's *Three Weeks,* 6 reels, 280-odd scenes, produced for $53,000). "Moss to Make Pictures," *MPW,* 31 Jul 1915, 798. "B.S. Moss Enters the Production Field," *MPW,* 29 Jul 1916, 771. "B.S. Moss to Produce Again," *MPW,* 21 Sep 1918, 1699.

Moss, Howard S. [director/animator]. No data found. AMD, p. 255. "Funny Face Does His Bit for Uncle's Liberty Loan," *MPW,* 14 Sep 1918, 1546.

Moss, Stewart [cinematographer]. No data found. FDY, p. 463.

Motard, Lucien Auguste [director/producer] (b. Nogent-sur-Oise, France, 30 Sep 1893–7 Oct 1963 [70], Fontenay-aux-Roses, France [extrait de décès no. 107/1963]). AS, p. 792.

Mouezy-Eon, André [actor/scenarist] (*né* André Marie Joseph Mouezy, b. Chantenay, France, 9 Jun 1880 [extrait de naissance no. SN/880]–23 Oct 1967 [87], France). AS, p. 792.

Moulan, Frank [actor] (b. New York NY, 24 May 1872?–13 May 1939 [67], New York NY). m. Maude Lilian Berri, 1900, Chicago—div. 1911; Beatrice Mershon—div. 1924, NYC; Elsie. "Frank Moulan, 67, Comedy Star, Dies; Former Member of Roxy Gang Staged and Played Leads in Savoy Operettas," *NYT,* 14 May 1939, III, 6:7. "Frank Moulan," *Variety,* 17 May 1939. AS, p. 792 (b. 1871). BHD1, p. 396 (b. 24 Jul 1875). IFN, p. 215. SD, p. 914 (b. 1876). Truitt, p. 242.

Moulton, Buck [actor] (*né* Edwin Moulton, b. New York NY, 8 Apr 1891–7 May 1959 [68], Los Angeles Co. CA). AS, p. 793. BHD1, p. 396. IFN, p. 215. George A. Katchmer, "Forgotten Cowboys and Cowgirls—Part XIII," *CI,* 190 (Apr 1991), C8.

Mounet, Lily [actress] (*née* Emilie Renée Louise Mounet, b. Cannes, France, 9 Feb 1895 [extrait de naissance no. 63/1895]–2 Oct 1978 [83], Paris, France). AS, p. 793.

Mounet-Sully, Jean [stage/film actor/playwright] (b. Dordogne Department, Bergerac,

France, 27 Feb 1841 [extrait de naissance no. 38]–1 Mar 1916 [75], Paris, France). "Mounet-Sully Dies in His Paris Home; Famous Tragedian Served with Distinction in the Franco-Prussian War; Toured America in 1894; Dean of the Comedie Francaise and a Knight of the Leghion of Honor," *NYT,* 4 Mar 1916, 11:3 (d. 3 Mar, aged 76. He was the male Bernhardt of France.). "Jean Mounet-Sully," *Variety,* 10 Mar 1916, 11:4. AMD, p. 255. AS, p. 793. BHD, p. 258. "Obituary," *MPW,* 18 Mar 1916, 1831 (d. 23 Mar).

Mountford, Harry [scenarist] (b. Dublin, Ireland, 1871–4 Jun 1950 [79?], New York NY). BHD2, p. 190.

Mouries [actor] (*né* Auguste Mourre, b. Marseilles, France, 30 Aug 1883–16 Feb 1956 [72], Marseilles, France). AS, p. 793.

Mouse, Mickey [cartoon character] (*né* Mortimer Mouse, b. CA, 18 Nov 1928–1950's [but periodically revived]). Created by Walt Disney and Ub Iwerks. Allegedly m. Minnie Mouse on date of birth. E.M. Forster, "Mickey and Minnie," *The American Animated Cartoon; A Critical Anthology,* edd. Danny Peary and Gerald Peary (NY: E.P. Dutton, 1980), pp. 238–40. "Walt Disney," in Leonard Maltin, *Of Mice and Magic; A History of American Animated Cartoons* (NY: New American Library, 1980), pp. 34–36. (Film debut: *Plane Crazy,* 1927). John Canemaker, "An American Icon Scampers in for a Makeover," *NYT,* Sec. II, 6 Aug 1995, 9, 20 (at 67, appeared in *Runaway Brain,* his first short since *The Simple Things,* 1953).

Moussinac, Léon [historian/critic] (b. Migennes, France, 19 Jan 1890–15 Mar 1964 [74], Paris, France). AS, p. 793.

Moussy, Mathieu [pioneer of French cinema] (b. Lyon, France, 12 Jun 1873–15 Aug 1927 [54], Lyon, France; auto accident). AS, p. 793.

Mouvet, Maurice O.L. [dancer/actor] (b. Chelsea, New York NY, 17 Mar 1887–18 May 1927 [40], Lausanne, Switzerland; tuberculosis). m. (1) Florence Walton—div. 1920; (2) Eleanora Ambrose, Apr 1926, Paris, France. (Appeared in *The Quest of Life,* FP-L, 1916.) "Maurice, Dancer, Is Dying; He Is at Lausanne, Switzerland, in Last Stages of Consumption," *NYT,* 13 May 1927, 29:2 ("...the bracing air [at St. Mauritz] failed to purge his lungs of the infection that has wracked him for years."). "Hope to Save Maurice by Change in Air; Physicians Plan to Take Dancer Higher into Alps If He Survives Crisis," *NYT,* 16 May 1927, 25:2. "Maurice Sinking Rapidly; Dancer Not Expected to Live More Than 24 Hours, Brother Reports," *NYT,* 18 May 1927, 29:2. "Maurice Is Dead; Famed as Dancer; Succumbs to Tuberculosis in Switzerland, with Wife and Brother at Bedside; Was Born in New York; Appeared Before All Monarchs of Europe Except One [the Emperor of Germany]—Had Many Partners and Married Two," *NYT,* 19 May 1927, 27:5 [his dancing partner before Ambrose was Barbara Bennett). "Rites for Maurice Monday; Dancer to Be Buried in Montparnasse Cemetery, Paris," *NYT,* 20 May 1927, 19:3. "Maurice," *Variety,* 25 May 1927, 48:2 (danced with Joan Sawyer, as did Valentino. Three pioneers of ballroom dancing had died: Valentino, Muris, and Maurice.). AS, p. 732 (Maurice. b. 1888). BHD, pp. 248, 258. IFN, p. 215 (age 41). "Dancer's Widow Is Here," *NYT,* 11 Jun 1927, 25:2 (Mrs. Eleanora Ambrose Maurice [sic] arrived in New York City and said that her husband "did not die of tuberculosis but of an infection. He was conscious to the end and asked her to retain his name in all her professional engagements."). "Maurice's Will [six paragraphs long, made in Oct 1926] Is Filed; Dancer's Widow to Share Estate with His Brother [Oscar Mouvet, Jr.]," *NYT,* 7 Jul 1927, 27:4. "Maurice Left $25,622; Dancer's Wife and Brother Share Equally in the Estate," *NYT,* 26 Apr 1928, 14:4 (the estate included cash, jewelry, securities and "147 Imperial Russian bonds, dated in 1916, for 100 rubles each...worth a total of only $29.40.").

Mowbray, Henry [actor] (*né* Harry E. Sweeney, b. Australia, 5 Sep 1882–9 Jul 1960 [77], Woodland Hills CA; arteriosclerosis). AS, p. 793. BHD1, p. 397. IFN, p. 215.

Mower, Jack [actor] (b. Honolulu HI, 5 Sep 1890–6 Jan 1965 [74], Los Angeles CA). "Jack Mower," *Variety,* 13 Jan 1965 (in films 50 years). AMD, p. 255. AS, p. 793. BHD1, p. 397 (b. CA). IFN, p. 215. MH, p. 129. Truitt, p. 242. "Two New Universalites," *MPW,* 29 Sep 1917, 1971. "Mower to Star in Two-Reel Westerns," *MPW,* 13 Oct 1923, 597.

Moya, Mariana [actress]. No data found. AMD, p. 255. "Signs Austrian Actress," *MPW,* 4 Oct 1924, 402.

Moyea, John W. [actor] (d. Aug 1912). BHD, p. 258.

Moyer, Charles E. [publicist]. No data found. AMD, p. 255. "Reading Newspaperman Joins Paramount," *MPW,* 25 Sep 1915, 2159. "Charles E. Moyer," *MPW,* 26 Mar 1927, 311.

Moylan, Catherine [actress] (b. Dallas TX, 4 Jul 1904–9 Sep 1969 [65], Fort Worth TX). BHD1, p. 397.

Moyles, Daniel [actor] (b. 1873?–25 Sep 1933 [60], New York NY). "Daniel Moyles," *Variety,* 3 Oct 1933. AS, p. 793. BHD, p. 258.

Moynihan, John H. [publicist] (b. 1903–29 Jun 1956 [53?], San Jose CA). AMD, p. 255. BHD2, p. 190. "Contest Winner Arrives," *MPW,* 8 Oct 1927, 343 (won 8-week F.B.O. publicity job at $30 a week in *Screenland* magazine).

Mozart, George [musician/vaudeville/film actor] (b. Great Yarmouth, England, 15 Feb 1864–10 Dec 1947 [83], London, England). "George Mozart," *NYT,* 11 Dec 1947, 33:5 ("He was featured in several British movies..."). "George Mozart," *Variety,* 169, 17 Dec 1947, 63:2. AS, p. 793 (d. 10 Dec). BHD1, p. 397. IFN, p. 215.

Mozzato, Umberto Luigi [actor/director] (b. Bologna, Italy, 28 Aug 1879 [extrait de naissance no. 2277/1879]-6 Nov 1947 [68], Turin, Italy [extrait de décès no. 1777/1947]). JS, p. 308 (in Italian silents from 1913).

Mudd, E. Virginia [actress] (b. 1893–21 May 1979 [86?], San Antonio TX). BHD, p. 258. IFN, p. 215 (E. Virginia Mudd Klumker).

Mudie, Leonard [stage/film actor] (*né* Leonard Mudie Cheetham, b. Manchester, England, 11 Apr 1883–14 Apr 1965 [82], Los Angeles CA; cardiovascular ailment). m. (1) Beatrice Terry; (2) Gladys Lennox. "Leonard Mudie," *Variety,* 28 Apr 1965. AS, p. 794. BHD1, p. 397 (b. Cheetham, England). IFN, p. 215. SD. Truitt, pp. 242–43 (b. 1884).

Mueller-Eingen, Hans [scenarist] (b. Austria, 1882–9 Mar 1950 [68?], Thoune, Switzerland). AS, p. 794. BHD2, p. 190.

Mueller-Schloesser, Hans [scenarist] (b. Germany, 1884–25 Apr 1956 [72?], Dusseldorf, Germany). AS, p. 794.

Muerling, A.E. [scenarist] (b. 1869-Dec 1925 [56?], Los Angeles CA). BHD2, p. 190.

Muethel, Lothar [actor/director] (b. 1895–8 Sep 1964 [69?], Frankfurt, Germany). BHD2, p. 190.

Mugeli, Jean [director] (b. France, 1890–1954 [64?], France). AS, p. 794.

Muguet, Livia [actress in Italian silents]. No data found.

Muir, Esther (mother of actress Jacqueline Coslow) [stage/film actress] (b. Andes NY, 11 Mar 1903–1 Aug 1995 [92?], Mt. Kisco NY). m. (1) Busby Berkeley—div. 1931; (2) **Sam Coslow**—div. 1948 (d. 1989). Katz, p. 837 (b. 1895). "Esther Muir, 92, Character Actress," *NYC,* 9 Aug 1995, D20:5. "Esther Muir," *Variety,* 14 Aug 1995, 69:5 (b. in 1895?). Michael G. Ankerich, "Reel Stars," *CI,* 182 (Aug 1990), 8; Part II, *CI,* 183 (Sep 1990), 8, 26, C3.

Muir, Florabel [scenarist] (b. Rock Springs WY, 1889–27 Apr 1970 [81?], Los Angeles CA). AS, p. 794 (b. Laramie WY; d. Cheviot Hills CA). BHD2, p. 190.

Muir, Helen [actress] (b. 1864?–2 Dec 1934 [70], Los Angeles CA). (Griffith.) "Helen Muir," *Variety,* 11 Dec 1934. AS, p. 794. BHD, p. 258. IFN, p. 216. Truitt, p. 243.

Mulcaster, George H. [stage/film actor] (b. London, England, 27 Jun 1891–19 Jan 1964 [72], London, England). (Began on stage in Brighton, 1910; West End debut: *The Promised Land,* 1917.) "G.B. Mulcaster," *Variety,* 233, 29 Jan 1964, 79:3. AS, p. 794 (George B. Mulcaster). BHD1, p. 397. IFN, p. 216.

Muldoon, William [actor] (b. 25 May 1845–3 Jun 1933 [88], Purchase NY). BHD, p. 258.

Mulgrew, Thomas G. [actor] (b. Providence RI, 1889?–3 Dec 1954 [65], Providence RI). (Eastern Film Co.) "Thomas Mulgrew," *NYDM,* 5 Mar 1913, 12. "Thomas G. Mulgrew," *Variety,* 15 Dec 1954. AS, p. 794. BHD, p. 258. IFN, p. 216. Truitt, p. 243.

Mulhall, Jack [stage/film actor] (*né* John Joseph Francis Mulhall, b. New York NY, 7 Oct 1887–1 Jun 1979 [91], Woodland Hills CA; congestive heart failure). m. (1) Bertha Vuillot (d. shortly after marriage); (2) **Laura Burton**, 1914 (chloroform suicide, 6 Jun 1921); (2) Evelyn Mary Williams, 1924 (d. 1959). (Edison; Biograph, 1 Jan 1914.) "Jack Mulhall," *Variety,* 13 Jun 1979. AMD, p. 255. AS, p. 794 (b. Wappingers Falls NY). BHD1, p. 397 (b. Wappingers Falls). FFF, p. 230. FSS, p. 216 (d. 1977). GK, pp. 692–713. HCH, p. 99. IFN, p. 216 (b. Wappingers Falls). Katz, p. 838 (b. Wappingers Falls). MH, p. 129 (b. 1898). SD. WWS, p. 21. "Jack Mulhall Joins Universal," *MPW,* 10 Jun 1916, 1897. "Mulhall Back to Paramount," *MPW,* 5 Oct 1918, 96. "Famous Players-Lasky Puts Mulhall Under Long Contract," *MPW,* 10 Apr 1920, 286. "Mrs. Mulhall Ends Life," *MPW,* 25 Jun 1921, 807. "Jack Mulhall," *MPW,* 15 Jan 1927, 198. "Jack Muilhall," *MPW,* 21 May 1927, 180. "Jack Mulhall," *MPW,* 29 Oct 1927, 1994. Eleanor Barnes, "Meet the Missus; Jack Mulhall Through the Eyes of his Best Friend, the Little Woman!," *Screenland,* Aug 1929, 54–55, 111. "Jack Mulhall Turns 90," *CFC,* 57 (Winter, 1977), 32. George A. Katchmer, "Jack Mulhall," *CI,* 117 (Mar 1985), 25–26, C3. Richard E. Braff, "An Index to the Films of Jack Mulhall; Part I," *CI,* 196 (Oct 1991), 24–26; Part II, 197 (Nov 1991), 12,

14, 16. George Katchmer, "Jack Mulhall," *CI*, 225 (Mar 1994), 46:2 (b. Wappinger Falls).

Mulhauser, James [actor] (b. Brooklyn NY, 31 Oct 1889–15 Jun 1939 [49], Beverly Hills CA; heart attack). (Universal.) "James Mulhauser," *Variety*, 21 Jun 1939). AS, p. 794 (b. 1889). BHD1, p. 397; BHD2, p. 190 (b. 1890). IFN, p. 216. Truitt, p. 243.

Mull, Edward A. [assistant director] (b. 1902–27 Aug 1959 [57?], Los Angeles CA). BHD2, p. 190.

Mull, William E. [assistant director] (b. 1900–26 Nov 1964 [64?], Los Angeles CA). BHD2, p. 190.

Mullaly, Don [scenarist] (b. 1885–1 Apr 1933 [48?], Duarte CA). AS, p. 795. BHD2, p. 190.

Mullally, Jode [actor] (b. New Orleans LA, 19 Nov 1886–23 Dec 1918 [32], Philadelphia PA). BHD, p. 258.

Mullally, Joseph T. [actor] (b. New Orleans LA, 1888?–29 Dec 1918 [30], Philadelphia PA; influenza). (Lasky.) "Joseph T. Mullaly," *Variety*, 10 Jan 1919. AS, p. 795.

Mullaney, Rose [casting director]. No data found. AMD, p. 255. "Rose Mullaney Is Appointed Selznick Casting Director," *MPW*, 29 May 1920, 1216. William J. Reilly, "We Have with Us To-Day," *MPW*, 3 Jul 1920, 63.

Mulle, Ida [stage/film actress] (b. Boston MA, 1863?–5 Aug 1934 [71], New York NY; from injuries after a fall). m. Ben Tuttle. "Ida Mulle," *Variety*, 14 Aug 1934 ("played in a few silent pictures"). AS, p. 795. IFN, p. 216. SD, p. 916. Truitt, p. 243.

Mullen, Edward B. [publicist]. No data found. AMD, p. 255. "Ed Mullen Universal's Publicity Manager," *MPW*, 28 Apr 1917, 626.

Mullen, Gordon M. [coach of aquatic stars] (b. 1890?–10 Jul 1949 [59], Glenside PA). m. Martha. "Gordon M. Mullen," *NYT*, 13 Jul 1949, 27:4.

Mullens, Willy [director] (*né* Willibrordus Mullens, b. Weesp, Holland, 4 Oct 1880–21 Apr 1952 [71], Amsterdam, Holland). AS, p. 795.

Müller, Hildegard [German actress] (sister of **Lotte Müller**). No data found. (Film debut: *Ein Unglück in der Kinderstube*, 1910.) Vittorio Martinelli, "Kino-Lieblinge," *Griffithiana*, 38/39 (Oct 1990), 21.

Müller, Lotte [German actress] (sister of **Hildegard Müller**). No data found. (Film debut: *Ein Unglück in der Kinderstube*, 1910.) Vittorio Martinelli, "Kino-Lieblinge," *Griffithiana*, 38/39 (Oct 1990), 21.

Muller, Robert [actor/scenarist] (b. Vienna, Austria, 29 Mar 1879–1 Feb 1968 [88], Berlin, Germany). AS, p. 795. BHD2, p. 190.

Müller-Lincke, Anna [actress] (*née* Anna Waltmüller, b. Berlin, Germany, 8 Apr 1869–24 Jan 1935 [65], Berlin, Germany. m. composer Paul Lincke. BHD1, p. 398. Vittorio Martinelli, "Kino-Lieblinge," *Griffithiana*, 38/39 (Oct 1990), 22.

Mullin, Eugene [scenarist/director] (b. Brooklyn NY, 1890?). (Vitagraph, 1912.) AMD, p. 255. Lowrey, p. 126. 1921 Directory, p. 291. "*Alixe* [Vitagraph, 1913; review]," *MPW*, 19 Apr 1913, 279. "Studio Gossip," *NYDM*, 7 Jul 1915, 41:1 (made a director at Vitagraph. "The title of his first picture sounds like a jinx…'One Performance Only.'"). "Eugene Mullin to Write and Direct for VItagraph," *MPW*, 13 Nov 1915, 1328. "Eugene Mullin Engaged by Universal as Scenario Head," *MPW*, 5 Apr 1919, 64. "Eugene Mullin Joins Gibraltar," *MPW*, 22 May 1920, 1098.

Mundin, Herbert [actor] (b. St. Helens, England, 21 Aug 1898–4 Mar 1939 [40], Van Nuys CA; auto accident). AS, p. 796.

Mundviller, Joseph [director of photography] (*né* Joseph-Louis Mundviller, b. Mulhouse, France, 10 Apr 1896-ca. 1937 [41?]). AS, p. 796.

Munier, Ferdinand [actor] (b. San Diego CA, 3 Dec 1889–27 May 1945 [55], Los Angeles CA; heart attack). m. Charlotte Treadway. (Preferred.) "Ferdinand Munier, Character Actor, 55," *NYT*, 29 May 1945, 15:6 (weighed 287 lbs. in '32). "Ferdinand Munier," *Variety*, 30 May 1945. AS, p. 796. BHD1, p. 398. IFN, p. 216.

Munro, Douglas [actor] (b. London, England-d. 27 Jan 1924, Birmingham, England; double pneumonia). AS, p. 796. BHD, p. 258. IFN, p. 216.

Munson, Audrey [actress]. No data found. (American.)

Munson, Audrey [actress]. No data found. AMD, p. 256. "Audrey Munson in Canada; Can't Get U.S. Passport," *MPW*, 17 May 1919, 1035. "Audrey Munson and Her Manager Arrested," *MPW*, 15 Oct 1921, 748. "Court Frees Audrey Munson ad Manager in St. Louis," *MPW*, 22 Oct 1921, 892.

Munson, Byron [actor] (b. Chicago IL, 29 Jun 1900–28 Jul 1989 [89], Burbank CA). (Universal.) BHD1, p. 398.

Munson, Ona [stage/film actress] (*née* Ona Wolcott, b. Portland OR, 16 Jun 1903–11 Feb 1955 [51], New York NY; suicide with sleeping pills). m. **Edward "Eddie" Buzzell** (d. 1985); Stewart McDonald; Eugène Berman, 1950, Beverly Hills CA. "Ona Munson Dead, a Note at Bedside; 'Don't Follow Me,' Actress Wrote, 'This Is Only Way I Know to Be Free Again,'" *NYT*, 12 Feb 1955, 16:1 (age 48). "Ona Munson," *Variety*, 16 Feb 1955. AS, p. 796. BHD1, p. 398 (b. 1906). IFN, p. 216 (b. 1906). Katz, p. 840 (b. 1906). SD. Truitt, p. 243. Brian Herbert, "The Munson Line," *Screenland*, Feb 1931, 82–83, 119.

Murari, Lina [film/stage actress]. No data found. JS, p. 309 (in Italian silents from 1919; "[l]eft the cinema for what turned out to be an unsuccessful stage career.").

Murat, Jean Robert Edouard [actor] (b. Perigueux, France, 13 Jul 1888–4 Jan 1968 [79], Aix-en-Province, France; myocardial infarction [extrait de décès no. 17/1968]). AS, p. 796. BHD1, p. 398 (d. 5 Jan).

Murata, Minoru [director] (b. Tokyo, Japan, 2 Mar 1894–26 Jun 1937 [43], Tokyo, Japan; pleurisy). AS, p. 796.

Muratore, Lucien [singer/actor] (b. Marseilles, France, 29 Aug 1878–16 Jul 1954 [75], Paris, France). m. (1) **Marguerite Bériza**; (2) **Lina Cavalieri**, 1913 (d. 1944); (3) Marie Louise Brivaud. "Lucien Muratore, Opera Singer, Dies; French Tenor Had Starred in Chicago," *NYT*, 4 Aug 1954, 21:1 (age 76). "Lucien Muratore," *Variety*, 11 Aug 1954. AS, p. 796 (b. 1876). BHD, p. 258. IFN, p. 216.

Murdock, Ann [stage/film actress] (*née* Irene Coleman, b. Port Washington NY, 10 Nov 1890–22 Apr 1939 [48], Lucerne, Switzerland). m. (1) Harry C, Powers; (2) Hallam K. Williams; (3) Leone Colleoni. (Essanay; Edison; McClure; Empire All-Star.) AMD, p. 256. AS, p. 796. BHD, p. 258. IFN, p. 216. MSBB, p. 1038. SD. "Ann Murdock with Metro," *MPW*, 8 May 1915, 873. "And Still They Come; Metro Secures Services of More Stage Luminaries and Adds to Plays," *NYDM*, 30 Jun 1915, 24:1 (to debut in *A Royal Family*). "Ralph Herz with Metro," *MPW*, 3 Jul 1915, 69. "Ann Murdock in 'Captain Jinks,'" *MPW*, 25 Dec 1915, 2351. "Ann Murdock," *MPW*, 1 Jan 1916, 59. "Ann Murdock with Mutual," *MPW*, 17 Feb 1917, 1009. "Ann Murdock," *MPW*, 26 May 1917, 1296. Neil G. Caward, "Screen Gossip," *Picture-Play Magazine*, Sep 1917, 102.

Murdock, Henry T. [drama critic] (b. Philadelphia PA, 1902?–20 Apr 1971 [69], Philadelphia PA). "Henry T. Murdock," *Variety*, 28 Apr 1971.

Murdock, J[ohn] **J.** [vaudville actor/managing director, American Talking Pictures Co.] (d. 8 Dec 1948 (ca. 85], Los Angeles CA; St. Erne Sanitorium). m. stage actress Grace Akaas. Joe Laurie, Jr., "John J. Murdock (The Last of a Great Tradition)," *Variety*, 173, 15 Dec 1948, 2:4, 18:4 (Edison threw him out of the ATP Co and changed the name to the Edison Kinetophone Co. in 1913). AMD, p. 256. Sumner Smith, "Pathé Recapitalizes for P.D.C. Merger; J.J. Murdock to Be Elected President," *MPW*, 23 Apr 1927, 701–02.

Murdock, Perry H. [actor] (b. OK, 18 Sep 1901–19 Apr 1988 [86], Van Nuys CA). BHD1, p. 398; BHD2, p. 191. George Katchmer, "Perry Murdock," *CI*, 232 (Oct 1994), C23.

Murdock, Russell [actor/scenarist] (b. New York NY, 1896–6 Jun 1943 [47?], New York NY). AS, p. 796.

Murfin, Jane [actress/scenarist/producer/director] (b. Quincy MI, 27 Oct 1892–10 Aug 1955 [62], Brentwood CA). m. **Donald Crisp**, 1932–44 (d. 1974). (FP-L; RKO; Metro; U-I.) "Jane Murfin," *Variety*, 17 Aug 1955. AS, p. 797. BHD2, p. 191. FDY, p. 433. IFN, p. 216. Katz, p. 840.

Murnane, Allan L. [actor/director] (b. Philadelphia PA, 1882–2 Apr 1950 [67], New Rochelle NY). AS, p. 797. BHD, p. 258; BHD2, p. 191. IFN, p. 216.

Murnau, F.W. [actor/director] (*né* Friedrich Wilhelm Plumpe, b. Murnau, Westphalia, 28 Dec 1888–11 Mar 1931 [42], Santa Barbara CA; auto accident). Lotte H. Eisner, *Murnau* (Los Angeles: University of CA Press, 1973). (Ufa; Fox.) "F.W. Murnau," *Variety*, 18 Mar 1931. AMD, p. 256. AS, p. 797 (b. Bielefeld, Germany). BHD, p. 258; BHD2, p. 191 (b. Bielefeld). IFN, p. 216 (b. Bielefeld). Katz, pp. 840–41 (b. Bielefeld). Waldman, p. 206. "Fox Gets F.W. Murnau, Who Directed 'The Last Laugh,'" *MPW*, 4 Apr 1925, 474. "Murnau to Produce for Fox Film Corp.," *MPW*, 2 Jan 1926, 69. "Dr. Murnau Here," *MPW*, 10 Jul 1926, 4. "Murnau Now Rushing Work on 'Sunrise,'" *MPW*, 20 Nov 1926, 150. "Murnau Will Become Fixture at Fox Studios," *MPW*, 12 Mar 1927, 102. "Murnau Insists Camera Angles Shall Be 'Dramatic,' If Anything," *MPW*, 2 Apr 1927, 490. Herbert Cruikshank, "Murnau or Never; An Intrepid Interviewer Trails the Red-Headed German Director to His Lair," *MPC*, Jul 1928, 33, 80. Heinrich Fraenkel, "Murnau, Maker of 'The Last Laugh,' Speaks; He Is Coming to America to Make a Single Picture," *MPC*, Jan 1926, 24–25, 80. Matthew Josephson, "F.W. Murnau Comes to America; The German Genius of the Films Talks of Movies and Men," *MPC*, Oct 1926, 16–17, 84. Paul Thompson, "Murnau's Trip to Hollywood Brings Sunrise to the Screen," *MPC*, Jul 1927, 36–37, 74, 86. Anne Sterling, "Herr Murnau Will Not Compromise," *Cinema Arts*, Dec 1927, 22, 43. Garth Pedler, "Murnau's 'Faust' (1926)," *CI*, 139 (Jan 1987), C13-C15.

Muro, Henri [actor] (b. France, 13 Jul 1884–12 Dec 1967 [73], Los Angeles CA). AS, p. 797.

Murphy, Ada [actress] (b. England, 6 Jan 1887–25 Aug 1961 [74], Encino CA). AS, p. 797. BHD1, p. 398. IFN, p. 216. Truitt, p. 243.

Murphy, Alma [actress] (b. 1889–10 Dec 1978 [89?], Los Angeles CA). AS, p. 797.

Murphy, Catherine T. (sister of actress Rosemary Murphy). No data found.

Murphy, Charles B[ernard] [stage/film actor] (b. Independence MO, 12 Dec 1881–11 Jun 1942 [60], Bakersfield CA; crushed under an overturned wagon during filming of Paramount's *Lost Canyon*). "Charles Murphy," *Variety*, 17 Jun 1942 (age 58). (Began 1907; Selig; Kalem; Pathé; Universal; Paralta; Vitagraph; Paramount.) AS, p. 797. BHD1, p. 399. IFN, p. 217. MSBB, p. 1026 (Dublin, Ireland). Truitt, p. 244 (b. 1884).

Murphy, Dudley [scenarist/cinematographer/director] (b. Winchester MA, 10 Jul 1895–22 Feb 1968 [72], Mexico City, Mexico). AS, p. 797. BHD2, p. 191 (d. 23 Feb, LA CA). FDY, p. 433.

Murphy, Eddie [actor] (b. Nincock NY, 2 Oct 1891–21 Feb 1969 [77], Dunmore PA). BHD, p. 259.

Murphy, Edna [actress] (*née* Elizabeth Edna Murphy, b. New York NY, 17 Nov 1899–3 Aug 1974 [74], Santa Monica CA). m. **Mervyn LeRoy**,Dec 1927 (d. 1987). AMD, p. 256. AS, p. 797. BHD1, p. 399. FFF, p. 161. IFN, p. 217. MH, p. 129. Slide, p. 164 (b. 1904). "Edna Murphy to Star in Pathé's Novel Serial 'Dangerous Paths,'" *MPW*, 26 May 1923, 337. Henriette, "From Hollywood to You," *MPS*, 1 Mar 1927, 31 (won a cup for excelling in the Black Bottom. Henriette wrote, "I've seen so much of this extremely ugly dance and it seems to me it would be a good idea to bestow a whole dinner service on somebody who would invent a beautiful and graceful movement and make a fad of it."). "Shearer-Thalberg Nuptials Soon," *MPW*, 27 Aug 1927, 590. "LeRoy—Murphy Wedding, About Dec. 15," *MPW*, 19 Nov 1927, 25.

Murphy, "Senator" Francis [actor] (*né* Samiel Letrravnik, b. Russia, 1888?–26 Oct 1961 [73], Los Angeles CA). "'Senator' Francis Murphy," *Variety*, 1 Nov 1961.

Murphy, Jack [John A.] [vaudevillian/stage/film actor] (*né* Joseph D. Galloway, b. Philadelphia PA, 1861?–21 Jul 1947 [86], Englewood NJ). m. Eloise Willard. "John A. Murphy, 86, Long in Vaudeville," *NYT*, 22 Jul 1947, 23:2 (theatrical debut: *The Log Cabin Varieties*, 1876). "Jack Murphy," *Variety*, 23 Jul 1947. AS, p. 797.

Murphy, Jimmy [actor] (b. San Francisco CA, 1894–15 Sep 1924 [30?], Syracuse NY). BHD, p. 259.

Murphy, John Daly [stage/film actor] (*né* John Daly Conlon?, b. County Kildare, Ireland, 5 Feb 1873–20 Nov 1934 [61], New York NY; heart attack). "John Daly Murphy," *Variety*, 27 Nov 1934. AMD, p. 256. AS, p. 797. BHD, p. 259 (b. Chicago IL). IFN, p. 217. SD, p. 919. Truitt, p. 244. "Gaumont Secures John Daly Murphy," *MPW*, 13 Nov 1915, 1276.

Murphy, John L. [producer] (b. 1894?–26 Jul 1976 [82], Woodland Hills CA). "John L. Murphy," *Variety*, 4 Aug 1976 (production manager for Harold Lloyd Productions, 1918–66). AMD, p. 256. AS, p. 797. BHD2, p. 191. Sumner Smith, "The Low-Down on a Scenario's Fate," *MPW*, 3 Apr 1926, 322.

Murphy, John T. [actor] (b. Helena MT, 24 Aug 1879–7 Jul 1955 [75], Los Angeles Co. CA). BHD, p. 259. IFN, p. 217.

Murphy, Joseph [stage/film actor] (b. Brooklyn NY, 16 May 1832–31 Dec 1915 [83], New York NY). m. (1) Martha Shattuck (d. 1908); (2) Mary Fermier, 1909. "Joseph Murphy," *Variety*, 7 Jan 1916. AS, p. 797. SD.

Murphy, Joseph J. [actor: Keystone Cop] (b. CA, 16 May 1877–31 Jul 1961 [84], San Jose CA). m. (Sennett.) "Joseph J. Murphy," *Variety*, 2 Aug 1961. AS, p. 797. BHD, p. 259. IFN, p. 217. Truitt, p. 244.

Murphy, Maurice [actor: Our Gang] (b. Seattle WA, 3 Oct 1913–23 Nov 1978 [65], Los Angeles CA). (Began 1921.) AS, p. 797. BHD1, p. 399. IFN, p. 217. "Maurice Murphy," *CI*, 63 (May 1979), 57.

Murphy, Ralph R. [actor/director] (b. Rockville CT, 1 May 1895–10 Feb 1967 [71], Los Angeles CA). AS, p. 797. BHD2, p. 191.

Murphy, Robert [actor] (*né* Duke Foster Dunnell, b. Webster NY, 9 Mar 1889–6 Aug 1948 [59], Santa Monica CA; pneumonia). AS, p. 797.

Murphy, Steve [actor]. No data found. George Katchmer, "Steve Murphy," *CI*, 232 (Oct 1994), C24.

Murphy, Tim [actor] (b. Rupert VT, 1861–11 Jan 1929 [67?], New York NY; heart attack). AS, p. 797.

Murray, B. Franklin [title writer]. No data found. FDY, p. 447.

Murray, Bobby [actor] (*né* Robert Hayes Murray, b. St. Albans VT, 4 Jul 1898–4 Jan 1979 [80], Nashua NH). AS, p. 798. BHD1, p. 399.

Murray, Charlie [actor/Keystone Cop] (*né* Charles Murray, b. Laurel IN, 22 Jun 1872–29 Jul 1941 [69], Los Angeles CA; pneumonia). m. Nellie B.; Boe Hamilton, May 1911. (Biograph.) "Charlie Murray, Film Comedian, 69; Actor Served Half-Century on Stage and Screen—Dies in Hollywood Home; One-Time 'Keystone Cop'; Made 'The Cohens and Kellys' Series—Last Work Was Group of Shorts," *NYT*, 30 Jul 1941, 17:3. "Charlie Murray," *Variety*, 30 Jul 1941. "Mrs. Charlie Murray," *NYT*, 19 May 1942, 20:2 (Mrs. Nellie B. Murray, b. 1877?–17 May 1942 [65], Hollywood CA; m. Murray ca. 1906). AMD, p. 256. AS, p. 798. BHD1, p. 399. FSS, p. 217. IFN, p. 217. Katz, p. 842. MH, p. 129. Truitt, p. 244. WWS, p. 193 (b. Laurel MD). "Actor Murray Injured," *MPW*, 24 May 1913, 798. "Murray Will Not Return to Stage," *MPW*, 22 Feb 1919, 1055. "Twenty-Four Silk Shirts Gone," *MPW*, 5 Apr 1919, 75. "Murray Does Detective Stunt," *MPW*, 12 Apr 1919, 218. "Charles Murray's Father Dead," *MPW*, 6 Mar 1920, 1638 (Isaac Murray, d. 12 Feb 1920 [82], LA CA). "Burr Signs Charles Murray and Others," *MPW*, 9 Sep 1922, 125. "First National Adds Several to List of Contract Players," *MPW*, 18 Apr 1925, 713. "Charles Murray," *MPW*, 10 Apr 1926, 427. "Charles Murray," *MPW*, 18 Jun 1927, 483. George A. Katchmer, "Remembering the Great Silents; Everyone's Favorite Comedian, Charlie Murray," *CI*, 170 (Aug 1989), C12-C14 (b. 22 Jun 1872); Part II, *CI*, 171 (Sep 1989), 42–44.

Murray, David Mitchell [actor] (b. 1853?–20 Oct 1923 [70?], Brooklyn NY). "David Mitchell Murray," *Variety*, 25 Oct 1923. AS, p. 798. BHD, p. 259 (d. Long Island NY). Truitt, p. 244.

Murray, Edgar [actor] (b. 1865?–31 Oct 1932 [67], Los Angeles CA). "Edgar Murray," *Variety*, 8 Nov 1932. AS, p. 798. BHD1, p. 399. Truitt, p. 244.

Murray, Edgar [actor] (b. 1892–16 Oct 1959 [67], Los Angeles CA; heart attack). m. Nadia Popkova. (Vitagraph.) "Edgar Murray," *Variety*, 28 Oct 1959. BHD, p. 259. IFN, p. 217. Truitt, p. 244.

Murray, Elizabeth M. [stage/film actress] (*née?*, b. 25 Apr 1870–27 Mar 1946 [75], Philadelphia PA). "Mrs. Elizabeth M. Murray; Former Broadway Comedienne a Star in Keith's, Philadelphia," *NYT*, 29 Mar 1946, 23:1. "Elizabeth M. Murray," *Variety*, 3 Apr 1946. AS, p. 798. BHD1, p. 399 (b. 1871). IFN, p. 217. Truitt, p. 244.

Murray, J. Harold [stage/film actor] (*né* Harry Roulon, b. South Berwick ME, 17 Feb 1891–11 Dec 1940 [49], Killingworth CT). m. Dolly Hackett. "J. Harold Murray, ex-Star of Stage; Scored His Greatest Success in 'Rio Rita' for Ziegfeld—He Succumbs at 49; Sang for Hammerstein—Made Debut at Winter Garden in 1920—Also Seen in Films—Head of Brewing Company [New England Brewing Co.]," *NYT*, 13 Dec 1940, 23:3. "Harold Murray, Lately a Brewer, Dies at 49," *Variety*, 18 Dec 1940 (began 1929). AS, p. 798. BHD1, p. 399. IFN, p. 217. Truitt, p. 244.

Murray, Jack [actor/scenarist/director] (*né* John W.B. Murray, b. Bronx NY-d. 1 May 1941, Bronx NY). AMD, p. 256. AS, p. 798. FDY, p. 433. IFN, p. 217. Truitt 3, p. 531. "Jack Murray, Director and 'Dare Devil,'" *MPW*, 18 Mar 1916, 1840.

Murray, James [stage/film actor] (b. New York NY, 9 Feb 1901–11 Jul 1936 [35], New York NY; fell off a pier into the Hudson River and drowned). (Began in films in New York, 1923; MGM.) "James Murray," *Variety*, 15 Jul 1936. AMD, p. 256. AS, p. 798. BHD1, p. 399. FSS, p. 218. IFN, p. 217. Katz, p. 843 (b. Bronx NY). Truitt, p. 244. "Actor, Seeking a 'Lift,' Is Signed by King VIdor," *MPW*, 8 Jan 1927, 124. "'Lady Luck' Smiles on James Murray," *MPW*, 6 Aug 1927, 381. "James Murray in 'Rose Marie,'" *MPW*, 5 Nov 1927, 12. Robert Grosvenor, "One's an Extra, Two's a 'Crowd'; Alone, James Murray Was Just One of the Extras on the Lot Waiting for Fate to Happen, but When King Vdor Discovered Him They Took Fate by the Forelock," *Cinema Arts*, Sep 1927, 22–23, 44.

Murray, James Sylvester [actor] (b. England, 1862–17 Oct 1939 [77?], Bronx NY). BHD, p. 259.

Murray, James V. [cinematographer] (b. 1896–5 Dec 1955 [59?], Los Angeles CA). AS, p. 798. BHD2, p. 191. FDY, p. 463.

Murray, John "Red" [actor] (b. Arnot PA, 4 Mar 1884–4 Dec 1958 [74], Sayre PA). BHD, p. 259.

Murray, John T. [actor] (b. Melbourne,

Australia, 28 Aug 1886–12 Feb 1957 [70], Woodland Hills CA). m. **Vivien Oakland** (d. 1958). (1st National.) "John T. Murray," *Variety*, 20 Feb 1957 (age 71). AMD, p. 256. AS, p. 798. BHD1, p. 399. IFN, p. 217. Truitt, p. 244. "John T. Murray Engaged," *MPW*, 24 Jan 1925, 371.

Murray, Julian "Bud" [actor/dance director] (b. New York NY, 21 Nov 1888–1 Nov 1952 [63], Sawtelle CA; cerebral hemorrhage). (Metro; Fox; Paramount.) "Julian (Bud) Murray," *Variety*, 12 Nov 1952 (age 61). AS, p. 798. BHD2, p. 191.

Murray, Louise [actress]. No data found. AMD, p. 256. "Louise Murray," *MPW*, 19 Aug 1916, 1227.

Murray, Mae, "The Gardenia of the Screen" or "The Girl with the Bee Stung Lips" [stage/film dancer/actress] (*née* Marie Antoinette [or Adrienne] Koenig, b. Portsmouth VA, 10 May 1883?–23 Mar 1965 [81?], Woodland Hills CA; heart attack). m. (1) William Schwenker, Jr., ca. 1906; (2) Jay O'Brien, 19 Dec 1916; (3) **Robert Z. Leonard**, Jun 1918—div. 26 May 1925 (d. 1968); (4) **Prince David Mdivani**, Beverly Hills CA, 27 Jun 1926—div. 1933. Jane Kesner Ardmore, *The Self-Enchanted Mae Murray; Image of an Era* (NY: McGraw-Hill, 1959). (Film debut: *To Have and to Hold*, 1916, FP-L; Universal; MGM.) "Mae Murray, Silent Screen Star, Dies in Actors' Home on Coast; Ex-Actress, 75, Was Known for 'Merry Widow' Role—In Ziegfeld 'Follies,'" *NYT*, 24 Mar 1965, 43:2 (b. 1889; age 75). "Mae Murray," *Variety*, 31 Mar 1965 (age 75). AMD, p. 256. AS, p. 798 (b. 7 May 1885). BHD1, p. 400 (b. 1889). FFF, p. 61 (b. 9 May). FSS, p. 218. IFN, p. 217 (b. 1889). Katz, p. 843 (b. 1885; began 1916). MH, p. 129. MSBB, p. 1038. SD. Truitt, pp. 244–45. WWS, pp. 11, 82. Frederick James Smith, "Vaudeville," *NYDM*, 25 Mar 1914, 21:2 (made dancing debut with Clifton Webb at the Palace). "Mae Murray in Lasky Productions," *MPW*, 4 Dec 1915, 1807. "Lasky Star Marooned," *MPW*, 12 Feb 1916, 957. "Mae Murray Marries Jay O'Brien," *MPW*, 13 Jan 1917, 212. "Mae Murray Signs Again with Lasky," *MPW*, 21 Apr 1917, 455. "Mae Murray," *MPW*, 4 Aug 1917, 808. "Mae Murray Saved by a Hair," *MPW*, 1 Dec 1917, 1311. "Film Star Obtains Divorce," *MPW*, 31 Aug 1918, 1239 (separated from O'Brien on 3 Jan 1917). Alice Bennett, "Mae Murray Makes-Believe," *MPC*, Feb 1919, 25–26. "International Signs Mae Murray," *MPW*, 8 Nov 1919, 235. "Mae Murray's Address Wins Clubwomen as Opponents of Legalized Censorship," *MPW*, 3 Apr 1920, 133. "Mae Murray to Go to Europe," *MPW*, 14 Aug 1920, 882 (m. Leonard). Edward Weitzel, "Why Mae Murray's First Serious Role May Not Prove to Be a Blunder After All," *MPW*, 28 Aug 1920, 1161. "Mae Murray Signs as Paramount Star; Robert Leonard to DIrect Her," *MPW*, 9 Oct 1920, 815. "Associated Exhibitors Will Release Four Mae Murray Specials; Work to Start in East," *MPW*, 19 Mar 1921, 264. Mae Murray, "Mae Murray's Life History [Part I]," *Picture Show*, 5 Nov 1921, 7. "Metro to Handle Mae Murray Pictures; 'Peacock Alley' First; Four in a Year," *MPW*, 17 Dec 1921, 809. "Metro Entertains Mae Murray at Lunch in Celebration of Releasing Contract," *MPW*, 24 Dec 1921, 931. "Cuban Papers Record Triumphal Entry of Mae Murray into Havana," *MPW*, 21 Jan 1922, 277. "Mae Murray Brings Spain Here in Picturizing 'Fascination,'" *MPW*, 4 Mar 1922, 49. "Mae Murray Denies Her Films Will Be Independently Released," *MPW*, 12 May 1923, 125. Gladys Hall, "The Greatest Thing Money Can Buy; Dainty screen star tells *Movie Weekly* what life has brought her and what she deems its greatest treasure," *MW*, 9 Jun 1923, 3, 28. Grace Kingsley, "The Home Life of the Hollywood Stars; An intimate glimpse into the home life of Mae Murray and her director-husband, Bob Leonard," *MW*, 8 Mar 1924, 9. Alma Talley, "Mae Murray as Herself," *MW*, 18 Oct 1924, 12–13. "On the Set and Off," *MW*, 12 Sep 1925, 45 (Murray feuded with von Stroheim on the set of *The Merry Widow;* here, she could not get along with von Sternberg while making *The Masked Bride;* he was fired.). "Mae Murray Signs M-G-M Contract," *MPW*, 20 Mar 1926, 2. "Mae Murray Weds," *MPW*, 17 Jul 1926, 3 (m. Mdivani; best man, Valentino; maid of honor, Negri). "Mae Murray; The Girl on the Cover," *Cinema Arts*, Aug 1926, 42. Paul Paige, "Close-Ups and Fade-Outs," *Paris and Hollywood*, Sep 1926, 88 (purchased a Spanish residence in Hollywood, adjoining a country club, for $65,000, equipped with a pipe organ and a set of French antique furniture. "Mae has now set about building a five-room addition to the residence."). Don Juan, "So This Is Hollywood," *Paris and Hollywood*, Oct 1926, 16 (Murray said that Mdivani, age 27, owned oil wells. "Officials of the Harry Sinclair Oil Company, however, came forth heartlessly with the information that seven years ago the prince was a laborer in their Oklahoma oil fields, receiving for his hire $125 each month."). "Lya Joins P.D.C.; Miss Murray and M-G-M in Break," *MPW*, 8 Jan 1927, 95. "Mae Murray Breaks with M-G-M—Temperament," *MPW*, 8 Jan 1927, 116. "Mae Murray Launches Su[i]t Over Antiques," *MPW*, 2 Apr 1927, 481. "Donovans File Complete Denial of Mae Murray Suit," *MPW*, 30 Jul 1927, 320. "English Producers Seek Mae Murray," *MPW*, 17 Sep 1927, 163. "Mae Murray Gets 9 Weeks on Publix," *MPW*, 3 Dec 1927, 8. Eric Minton, "Mae Murray, Star," *Filmograph*, I, No. 3 (1970), 35–42 (includes filmography). Eve Golden, "Mae Murray: The Golden Dragonfly," *CI*, 208 (Oct 1992), 28, 32, 57. Jimmy Bangley," Mae Murray: 'The Girl with the Bee Stung Lips,'" *CI*, 254 (Aug 1996), 14–18, 20–25 (b. 1889; includes filmography).

Murray, Marion [actress] (b. 1885?–11 Nov 1951 [66], New York NY). m. **Jed Prouty** (d. 1956). (Essanay.) "Marion Murray," *Variety*, 14 Nov 1951. AS, p. 798. BHD1, p. 400. IFN, p. 217. Truitt, p. 245.

Murray, Raymond B. [Director of U.S. Army Motion Picture Service] (b. 1896?–3 Jan 1945 [48], Washington DC). "Raymond B. Murray; Director of Army Film Service Dies While Driving His Car," *NYT*, 4 Jan 1945, 19:5. "Raymond B. Murray," *Variety*, 10 Jan 1945.

Murray, Tom [stage/film actor] (b. Stone foot IL, 8 Sep 1874–27 Aug 1935 [60], No. Hollywood CA; heart attack). m. Louise Spilger (**Louise Carver**, d. 1956). "Tom Murray," *Variety*, 4 Sep 1935. AS, p. 798. BHD1, p. 400. IFN, p. 217. SD. Truitt, p. 245.

Murray, Walter [actor]. (Biograph, 1913.) No data found.

Murray, Will [actor/producer] (b. Liverpool, England, 1878–17 Mar 1955 [77?], New Brighton, England). AS, p. 799.

Murrillo, Mary [writer]. No data found. AMD, p. 257. "Mary Murillo," *MPW*, 16 Mar 1918, 1525. "Mary Murillo Added to Talmadge Staff," *MPW*, 6 Sep 1919, 1472.

Murth, Florence [actress] (b. Boswell PA, 20 Jan 1897–30 Mar 1934 [37], Duarte CA). (Sennett; Christie.) "Florence Murth," *Variety*, 3 Apr 1934 (age 32). AS, p. 799. BHD, p. 259. IFN, p. 217. Truitt, p. 245 (b. 1902).

Musco, Angelo [stage/film actor] (b. Catania, Italy, 18 Dec 1871–6 Oct 1937 [65], Milan, Italy). JS, p. 309 (in Italian silents from 1918; Rossano Brazzi starred in his life story in 1953).

Muse, Clarence Edward [actor/scenarist] (b. Baltimore MD, 15 Oct 1889–13 Oct 1979 [89], Perris CA; cerebral hemorrhage). m. 3 times: Irene Ena. "Clarence Muse, 89; Acted in 219 Films; First Black to Star in a Movie—Also Directed on Broadway," *NYT*, 17 Oct 1979, D23:1 (wrote *When It's Sleepy Time Down South*). "Clarence Muse," *Variety*, 24 Oct 1979 (219 film credits). AS, p. 799. BHD1, p. 400; BHD2, p. 192 (b. 14 Oct). IFN, p. 217. SD.

Musgrave, William F. [actor] (b. Toledo OH). (Began 1912; Rolin; Universal.) AMD, p. 256. "William F. Musgrave," *MPW*, 21 Apr 1917, 427.

Musidora, Juliet [Folies-Bergere/French films, 1911/ballerina/singer/actress/director] (*née* Jeanne Roques, b. Paris, France, 23 Feb 1889–7 Dec 1957 [68], Paris, France [extrait de décès no. 14/261.5062]). "Jeanne Roques," *Variety*, 18 Dec 1957. AMD, p. 257. AS, p. 799. BHD1, p. 400 (d. 11 Dec). JS, p. 309 (in *La vagabonda*, Italy, 1917; "she was the first vamp of French films"). "Juliet Musidora," *MPW*, 11 Nov 1916, 861.

Muskov, George [assistant director/producer] (b. Kharkov, Russia, 1894–6 Aug 1970 [76?], Los Angeles CA). BHD2, p. 192.

Muslili, Boots (b. 1916–23 Sep 1967 [51?], Norfolk MA). BHD, p. 259.

Mussett[e], Charles [actor/theater manager] (b. London, England, 1876–6 Dec 1939 [63], Bernardsville NJ). m. Victoria. "Charles Mussett; One-Time Actor and Theatrical Manager Dies at 63," *NYT*, 11 Dec 1939, 23:1. AS, p. 799. BHD, p. 259. IFN, p. 217 (d. 8 Dec). Ragan 2, p. 1211.

Mussey, Francine [actress] (b. 1901–26 Mar 1933 [32?], Paris, France; suicide with poison swallowed 3 days previously). "Francine Mussey," *Variety*, 110, 11 Apr 1933, 54:3 ("unable to recover from the shock of he death of her 7-year-old son in Paris." She had come from Berlin only to witness his death. Succeeded on her third attempt.). AS, p. 799. BHD1, p. 400. IFN, p. 217.

Mussiere, Lucien [actor] (*né* Luien Meurisse, b. Belgium, 1890–23 Dec 1972 [82], Brussels, Belgium). AS, p. 799.

Mussolini, Benito [dictator/actor] (b. Dovia di Predappio, Italy, 29 Jul 1883–28 Apr 1945 [61], Como Province, Italy). m. (son, Vittorio Mussolini, 1916–12 Jun 1997). BHD, p. 259.

Musson, Bennet [actor/scenarist] (b. Cairo IL, 1866?–17 Feb 1946 [80], Amityville, LI NY). (Universal; FP-L.) "Bennet Musson," *NYT*, 19 Feb 1946, 25:3. "Bennett Musson," *Variety*, 20 Feb 1946. AMD, p. 257. AS, p. 799. BHD, p. 259. IFN, p. 217. Truitt, p. 245. "Musson Becomes Scenario Editor for Hart," *MPW*, 15 Nov 1919, 332.

Mustacchi, Amedeo [director] (b. Piedmont, Italy). JS, p. 310 (in Italian silents from 1915).

Mustin, Burt [actor] (*né* Burton Mustin, b. Pittsburgh PA, 8 Feb 1882–28 Jan 1977 [94], Glendale CA). AS, p. 799.

Musuraca, Nicholas [cinematographer]

(b. Riace, Italy, 28 Oct 1892–3 Sep 1975 [82], Los Angeles CA). (Vitagraph; RKO.) AS, p. 799 (Musaraco). BHD2, p. 192 (b. 25 Oct). FDY, p. 463 (Nick Mesarouka); p. 465 (Nicholas Musuraca). Katz, p. 844.

Muth, Russell [cameraman]. No data found. AMD, p. 257. "Cameraman Has a Narrow Escape Filming Volcano," *MPW,* 25 Mar 1922, 353. "Fox Cameraman Injured," *MPW,* 24 Mar 1923, 422.

Mutio, Ricardo [actor] (*né* Ricardo Mutio Levy, b. Mexico City, Mexico, Apr 1882–2 Apr 1957 [74?], Mexico City, Mexico). AS, p. 800.

Muybridge, Eadweard [photographer] (*né* Edward James Muggeridge, b. Kingston-on-Thames, Surrey, England, 4 Apr 1830–8 May 1904 [74], Kingston-on-Thames, England). *The Illustrated History of the Cinema,* consultant ed., David Robinson; ed., Ann Lloyd (Macmillan, 1986), p. 11 (in 1878 he photographed an animal or person with a battery of cameras to record movement). AS, p. 800. Katz, pp. 844–45. Spehr, p. 154. WWVC, pp. 99–100 (b. 9 Apr). *Who Was Who in America,* Vol. I. Jay Pridmore, "Muybridge's Photos Set Stage for Movies," *Chicago Tribune,* 16 Feb 1996, VII, 4.

Mycroft, Walter C[harles] [director/scenarist] (b. London, England, 1891–14 Jun 1959 [68?]). AS, p. 800. BHD2, p. 192.

Myers, Carmel (daughter of **Isadore Myers**; sister of **Zion Myers**) [actress] (b. San Francisco CA, 9 Apr 1900–9 Nov 1980 [80], Los Angeles CA; heart attack). (Carmel Schwalberg). m. (1) Isadore Benjamin Kornblum (b. 1895), 16 Jul 1919—div. 5 Jul 1923; (2) Ralph H. Blum, 9 Jun 1929, LA CA (d. ca. 1932); (3) Alfred W. Schwalberg (: b. 8 Aug 1898-Dec 1973 [75], NY). (Triangle; Metro; Universal.) Josh Barbanel, "Carmel Myers, Silent Movie Star Who Played Wicked Women, 80," *NYT,* 19 Nov 1980, A31:5. "Carmel Myers," *Variety,* 19 Nov 1980. AMD, p. 257. AS, p. 800. BHD1, p. 400 (b. 1899). FFF, p. 75. FSS, p. 219. Katz, p. 845 (b. 4 Apr 1899). KOM, p. 153 (b. 1901). MH, p. 127 (entries under "Meyers" and "Myers"). MSBB, p. 1038 (b. 1901). 1921 Directory, p. 233 (b. 1901). SD. WWS, p. 314. "Carmel Myers, New Griffith Protége," *MPW,* 11 Nov 1916, 862. "Carmel Myers to Support Harold Lockwood," *MPW,* 12 May 1917, 951. "Carmel Myers," *MPW,* 26 May 1917, 1309. "Carmel Myers with Jewel," *MPW,* 15 Sep 1917, 1686. "Carmel Myers in Bluebird's Flock," *MPW,* 13 Oct 1917, 217. "Carmel Myers Under Universal Contract," *MPW,* 13 Jul 1918, 186. "Carmel Myers to Visit Cantonments," *MPW,* 20 Jul 1918, 357. "Carmel Myers May Desert Screen," *MPW,* 24 Aug 1918, 1101. "Two Years More of Pictures," *MPW,* 11 Jan 1919, 195. "Carmel Myers Signs to Star in Universal Productions," *MPW,* 17 Apr 1920, 454. "Carmel Myers Signs to Make Eight Pictures for Universal," *MPW,* 26 Jun 1920, 1740. "Carmel with Vitagraph," *MPW,* 13 Aug 1921, 700. Carmel Myers, "Is There Any Difference Between a Real Kiss and a Reel Kiss?," *MW,* 29 Mar 1924, 25. "Carmel Myers Assigned," *MPW,* 29 Aug 1925, 942. "Death of Mother," *MPW,* 20 Aug 1927, 516 (Mrs. Isador Myers, d. at 60). Charles Dunn, "The Loves and Hates of Carmel Myers," *Screenland,* May 1929, 56, 109.

Myers, Harry C. [actor/director] (b. New Haven CT, 5 Sep 1882–25 Dec 1938 [56], Los Angeles CA; pneumonia). m. **Rosemary Theby**, ca. 1924, San Francisco CA (d. 1973). (Biograph, 1908; Lubin.) "Harry Myers," *NYT,* 26 Dec 1938, 23:3. "Harry Myers," *Variety,* 28 Dec 1938. AMD, p. 257. BHD1, p. 400; BHD2, p. 192. FSS, p. 219. IFN, p. 217. Katz, p. 845. Truitt, p. 245 (b. 1886). "Harry C. Myers," *MPW,* 3 Jan 1914, 51. "Universal Gets Lubin Players," *MPW,* 15 Aug 1914, 972. "Harry C. Myers; Victor Leading Man and Director," *MPS,* 20 Nov 1914, 25 (b. New Haven, 1882). "Harry C. Myers," *MPW,* 20 Mar 1915, 1772. "Myers Gets Letter from the Trenches," *MPW,* 26 Jun 1915, 2073. "Harry Myers in New 'Vim' Series," *MPW,* 6 May 1916, 949. "Harry Myers," *MPW,* 12 May 1917, 971. Maude Cheatham, "The Darkest Hour," *Classic,* Mar 1923, 66, 86.

Myers, Rabbi Isadore (father of **Carmel** and **Zion Myers**) [technical advisor on *Intolerance*] (b. Suwalki, Russian Poland, 15 Feb 1856–25 Apr 1922 [66], Los Angeles CA). m. Anna Jacobson.

Myers, Kay [actress] (b. 1884–14 Mar 1954 [70?], Los Angeles CA). AS, p. 800.

Myers, Kathleen [actress] (b. New York NY, 1905?). (Vitagraph; Universal; Fox; 1st National.) AMD, p. 257. "New Leading Woman," *MPW,* 12 Mar 1921, 168. "Kathleen Myers in Lead Role," *MPW,* 13 Jun 1925, 786. George A. Katchmer, "Forgotten Cowboys and Cowgirls—Part X," *CI,* 182 (Aug 1990), 41.

Myers, Ray [actor] (b. 1884?–14 Mar 1954 [69], Los Angeles CA). (Ince; Kalem.) "Ray Myers," *Variety,* 17 Mar 1954.

Myers, Zion (son of **Isadore Myers**; brother of **Carmel Myers**) [scenarist/director] (b. San Francisco CA, 26 Jun 1898–24 Feb 1948 [49], Los Angeles CA). (Century.) AMD, p. 257. BHD2, p. 192. "Davis for Century," *MPW,* 27 Jan 1923, 385:4 (assistant director to Jim Davis on *Brownie* for Century). "To Supervise Comedies," *MPW,* 25 Jul 1925, 436. "To DIrect Comedies," *MPW,* 10 Jul 1926, 117.

Mygatt, Gerald [publicist]. No data found. AMD, p. 257. "Mygatt Joins Hodkinson Corporation," *MPW,* 15 Feb 1919, 897. "Gerald Mygatt Writes Article in Praise of Verne H. Porter," *MPW,* 11 Feb 1922, 619.

Myles, Mary [actress/singer] (b. Mattawa, Canada, 1891–23 Nov 1984 [93?], Los Angeles CA). AS, p. 800.

Myles, Norbert A. [actor] (b. Wheeling WV, 29 Aug 1887–15 Mar 1966 [78], Los Angeles CA). AMD, p. 257. BHD1, p. 401. "Norbert Myles," *MPW,* 18 Jul 1914, 436. "Norbert Myles," *MPW,* 26 Jun 1915, 2104.

Myles, Roland [actor] (b. Cape Colony, 1884). Edith Nepean, "Gossip about British Players," *Picture Show,* 5 Nov 1921, 19.

Myll, Louis [director/producer]. No data found. (Kleine-Edison.) AMD, p. 257. "Louis Myll, Comedy Producer," *MPW,* 1 Apr 1916, 63.

Mylong-Munz, Jack [actor] (*né* Adolf Heinz Munz, b. Vienna, Austria, 27 Sep 1893–8 Sep 1975 [81], Beverly Hills CA). AS, p. 800.

Myral, Nina [actress/dancer/singer] (*née* Eugénie Hortense Gruel, b. Paris, France, 26 Jun 1884 [extrait de naissance no. 2862]-30 Mar 1975 [90], Draveil, France). AS, p. 800.

Myrtile, Odette [actress/singer] (b. Paris, France, 28 Jun 1898–18 Nov 1978 [80], Doylestown PA; apoplexy). AS, p. 800. BHD1, p. 401.

Myton, Frederick K[ennedy] [scenarist] (b. Garden City KS, 1887?–6 Jun 1955 [68], Los Angeles CA). AMD, p. 257. BHD2, p. 192. FDY, p. 433. IFN, p. 218. "Myton Made Scenario Editor," *MPW,* 9 May 1925, 220.

N

Nabarro, Max [actor] (*né* Mozes Numes Nabarro, b. Amsterdam, Holland, 17 Jan 1889–8 Jan 1977 [87], Amsterdam, Holland). AS, p. 801.

Nadel, Joseph H. [assistant director/production manager/producer/executive] (b. 1893?–20 Nov 1950 [57], Los Angeles CA; after heart attack on 17 Nov). "Joseph H. Nadel," *NYT,* 21 Nov 1950, 31:2. "Joseph H. Nadel," *Variety,* 22 Nov 1950 (began in 1915 as a property boy). AS, p. 801. BHD2, p. 192.

Nadherny, Ernst Julius Johann Franz [actor/director] (b. Vienna, Austria, 28 Dec 1885–24 Feb 1966 [80], Austria). AS, p. 801.

Nagahara, Yukimo [actress]. No data found. AMD, p. 258. "Japanese Girl Engaged for 'Beatrice Fairfax,'" *MPW,* 16 Sep 1916, 1836.

Nagel, Beth [actress] (*née* Elizabeth Heckor, b. Chicago IL, 9 Apr 1877–29 Oct 1936 [59], Beverly Hills CA). AS, p. 801. BHD, p. 260. IFN, p. 218.

Nagel, Conrad [vaudeville/legitimate stage/film/radio/TV actor/director] (b. Keokuk IA, 16 Mar 1897–24 Feb 1970 [72], New York NY [Death Certificate Index No. 4381]). m. (1) Ruth E. Helms, 24 Jun 1919—div. 1935; (2) Lynn Merrick, 1945; (3) Michele Coulson Smith, 1955. (Peerless Stock Co., 1914; Broadway: *Forever After,* 1916; film debut: *Little Women,* 1919; Vitagraph; FP-L; WB.) Autobiography in Bernard Rosenberg and Harry Silverstein, eds., *The Real Tinsel* (1970). "Conrad Nagel, Actor, Dies at 72; Star of Stage and Silent Pictures; Made Transition in Talkies—Radio and TV Host Helped Found Academy Awards," *NYT,* 25 Feb 1970, 47:2. "Conrad Nagel," *Variety,* 4 Mar 1970. AMD, p. 258. AS, p. 801. BHD1, p. 401; BHD2, p. 193. FFF, p. 23. FSS, p. 220. GK, pp. 713–28. HCH, p. 75. IFN, p. 218. Katz, p. 846. Lowrey, p. 128. MH, p. 129. Truitt, p. 245. WWS, p. 34. "Conrad Nagel [photo]," *NYDM,* 30 Oct 1915, 5 (appearing in

The Natural Law at the Lexington Theatre). C. Blythe Sherwood, "Emergency Nagel," *MPC,* Mar 1919, 26, 80. "Conrad Nagel to Play Leads in Paramount-Artcraft Films," *MPW,* 1 May 1920, 711. "Conrad Nagel a Father," *MPW,* 20 Nov 1920, 318 (Ruth, b. 29 Oct 1920). "Mrs. Nagel Dies," *MPW,* 17 Dec 1921, 829 (mother, Frances Nagel, d. LA CA). "Goldwyn Signs Nagel," *MPW,* 17 Feb 1923, 645. "Aileen Pringle and Nagel Chosen," *MPW,* 25 Aug 1923, 665. Grace Kingsley, "The Home Life of Conrad Nagel," *MW,* 10 May 1924, 7, 31. "Nagel with Two Firms," *MPW,* 31 Dec 1927, 25. Larry Lee Holland, "Conrad Nagel," *FIR,* 1979. Robert A. Armour, *DAB,* Supp. 8 (1988), pp. 459–60 (formed AMPAS in 1927 with Mayer and Niblo; President in 1932—resigned 20 Apr 1933).

Nagel, George H. [propety man] (b. 1898–22 Oct 1977 [79?]). AMD, p. 258. BHD2, p. 193 (cinematographer). "Life Photo Engages George H. Nagel," *MPW,* 17 Apr 1915, 396.

Nagiah, V. [actor/producer/singer/director] (b. Chithoor, India, 28 Mar 1904–30 Dec 1973 [69], Madras, India). AS, p. 801. BHD1, p. 401.

Nagle, George [cinematographer]. No data found. FDY, p. 465.

Nagrom, Hugh [scenarist]. No data found. FDY, p. 433.

Nagy, Anton [cameraman] (b. Hungary, 6 Dec 1869–1 Jul 1956 [86], Los Angeles Co. CA). AMD, p. 258. BHD2, p. 193. "Anton Nagy," *MPW,* 29 Nov 1926, 275.

Nainby, Robert [actor] (b. Dublin, Ireland, 14 Jun 1869–17 Feb 1948 [78], England). AS, p. 802. BHD1, p 401.

Nairn, Ralph [actor] (b. Scotland, 1873–Dec 1934 [61?], London, England). BHD, p. 260.

Naish, J. Carrol [film/radio actor] (*né* Joseph Patrick Carrol Naish, b. New York NY, 21 Jan 1897–24 Jan 1973 [76], La Jolla CA). m. Gladys Heaney, 1929. "J. Carrol Naish, Actor, 73, Dead; Master of Dialects Starred in Radio 'Life with Luigi,'" David A. Andelman, "Man of Many Parts," *NYT,* 27 Jan 1973, 32:1 (age 73). "J. Carroll Naish," *Variety,* 31 Jan 1973 (age 73). AS, p. 802. BHD1, p. 401. IFN, p. 218. Katz, p. 846 (b. 1900; extra work in middle '20s).

Naldi, Nita [stage/film actress] (*née* Anita Donna Dooley, b. New York NY [Hungary?], 1 Apr 1895–17 Feb 1961 [65], New York NY [Death Certificate Index No. 3985]). m. J. Searle Barclay. (Paramount; Ufa.) (Film debut: *Dr. Jekyll and Mr. Hyde.*) "Nita Naldi of Silent Films Dies; Won Fame Opposite Valentino; Starred with Him in 'Blood and Sand' and 'Cobra'—Had Roles on Broadway," *NYT,* 18 Feb 1961, 19:3. "Nita Naldi," *Variety,* 22 Feb 1961. AMD, p. 258. AS, p. 802. BHD, p. 260 (b. 1897). FFF, p. 57 (b. 2 Apr). IFN, p. 218 (b. 1897). Katz, p. 847 (b. 1899). MH, p. 129 (b. 2 Apr). SD. Spehr, p. 154 (b. 1899). Truitt, p. 246 (b. 1899). "Robertson Engages Nita Naldi," *MPW,* 27 Dec 1919, 1169. "To Play in Experience," *MPW,* 19 Mar 1921, 290. Lillian Montanye, "As by Fire," *MPC,* Jul 1921, 22–23, 87. "Nita Naldi a Star," *MPW,* 29 Jul 1922, 352. Regina Cannon, "What I Learned About Men from the Movies," *MW,* 3 May 1924, 3. "Studio News Notes," *MW,* 31 May 1924, 27 (FP-L notified Naldi that she must reduce 15 lbs.). Gladys Hall and Adele Whitely Fletcher, "We Interview Nita Naldi; An Interviewer Playlet in One Act and Three Scenes," *MW,* 5 Jul 1924, 6–7, 31. "Jackie Coogan Back with Lots of Toys;...Valentino Returns from Spain," *NYT,* 11 Nov 1924, 20:3 (on the *Leviathan* with Coogan and Valentino and his wife aboard; to be in his new Ritz-Carlton film). "Questions and Answers," *Photoplay,* Sep 1926, 94 (b. 1899). Cedric Belfrage, "Why Stars Leave Home; Once in a While Europe Puts in a Call for American Stars to Decorate Her Pictures—Which Accounts for Hollywood's Sending Its Quota to Have a Holiday Abroad," *MPC,* Dec 1926, 56–57, 82. Alan Brock, "Nita Naldi," *CI,* 90 (Dec 1982), 58 (written in 1940).

Nally, William G. [actor] (d. Mar 1929, New York NY). BHD, p. 260. IFN, p. 218. Ragan 2, p. 1215.

Namara, Marguerite [opera singer/actress] (*née* Marguerite Banks, b. Cleveland OH, 19 Nov 1888–3 Nov 1974 [86], Marbella, Spain). m. **Guy Bolton** (d. 1979). AMD, p. 258. AS, p. 802. BHD1, p. 401. IFN, p. 218. SD. "Namara to Star on Second Feature," *MPW,* 3 Jul 1920, 67 (debut, *Stolen Moments*). "Namara to Continue Screen Work," *MPW,* 25 Sep 1920, 512.

Nankivell, Frank A. [cartoonist/animator] (b. Australia, 1870?–4 Jul 1959 [89], Florham Park NJ). m. twice. "Frank Nankivell, an Artist, Was 89; Ex-Newspaper Illustrator Is Dead—Puck Cartoonist Had Works in Museums," *NYT,* 8 Jul 1959. AMD, p. 258. "Nankivell Cartoons for Dra-Ko," *MPW,* 15 Apr 1916, 470. "Dra-Ko Will Show Christmas Picture on November 11," *MPN,* 4 Nov 1916, 2836.

Nanook [actor] (b. Alaska-d. Nov 1925). BHD, p. 260. IFN, p. 218.

Nansen, Betty [stage/film actress] (*née* Betty Anna-Marie Muller, b. Copenhagen, Denmark, 19 Mar 1873–15 Mar 1943 [69], Copenhagen, Denmark; pneumonia). (U.S. debut: *The Celebrated Scandal,* Fox, 1915). "Betty Nansen; Danish Tragedienne, on Stage for 51 Years, Dies at 67," *NYT,* 16 Mar 1943, 19:4. "Betty Nansen," *Variety,* 17 Mar 1943 (age 67). AMD, p. 258. AS, pp. 802 03. BHD, p. 260. IFN, p. 218 (b. 1873). Katz, p. 847 (U.S. films in 1915). "New Great Northern Favorite," *MPW,* 9 Aug 1913, 641. "Betty Nansen Here; Danish Actress Arrives to Appear in Pictures for William Fox," *NYDM,* 30 Dec 1914, 24:1. "Betty Nansen Coming to America," *MPW,* 2 Jan 1915, 79. "Betty Nansen Likes America," *MPW,* 16 Jan 1915, 377. "Personal," *NYDM,* 3 Feb 1915, 5:2 (friend and interpreter of Ibsen).

Napier, Diana [actress] (*né* Molly Ellis, b. Bath, England, 31 Jan 1904–12 Mar 1982 [78], London, England; heart attack). m. **Richard Tauber** (d. 1948). AS, p. 803 (b. 1906; d. Windlesham, England). BHD1, p. 402.

Napierkowska, Stacia [actress/dancer] (*née* Stanislawa Napierkowska, b. Paris, France, 16 Dec 1886–11 May 1945 [58], Paris, France). AS, p. 803. BHD, p. 260. JS, p. 311 (in Italian silents from 1915).

Narcita [actress]. No data found. AMD, p. 258. "Mlle. Narcita Engaged for Picture," *MPW,* 2 Dec 1922, 424.

Nardelli, George [actor] (*né* Achille Nardelli, b. France, 21 Oct 1895–16 Sep 1973 [77], Los Angeles Co. CA). AS, p. 803 (d. 15 Sep. France). BHD1, p. 402. IFN, p. 218.

Nares, Anna [actress] (b. 1870–19 Dec 1915 [46], Flushing NY). BHD, p. 260. IFN, p. 218.

Nares, Owen [stage/film actor] (*né* Owen Nares Ramsay, b. Maiden Erleigh, Berkshire, England, 11 Aug 1888–30 Jul 1943 [54], Brecon, Wales). m. Marie Polini. *Myself and Some Others* (1925). "Owen Nares, Star of British Stage; Actor Who Made Debut in 1909 at Haymarket Dies in Wales on Tour of Army Camps," *NYT,* 2 Aug 1943, 15:4. "Owen Nares," *Variety,* 4 Aug 1943 (age 55). AS, p. 803. BHD1, p. 402. IFN, p. 218. Katz, p. 847. SD. Truitt, p. 246.

Narvaez, Sara [actress] (b. Nicaragua-d. 14 Dec 1935, Mexico City, Mexico). AS, p. 803.

Nash, Eugenia (mother of **Ted Healy**) [actress] (b. 1866?–8 Apr 1937 [71], Culver City CA). "Eugenia Nash," *Variety,* 14 Apr 1937. AS, p. 803. Truitt, p. 246.

Nash, Florence (step-daughter of **Philip Nash**; sister of **Mary Nash**) [stage/film actress] (*née* Florence Ryan, b. Troy NY, 2 Oct 1888–2 Apr 1950 [61], Los Angeles CA; heart attack). "Florence Nash, 60, Stage Comedienne; Retired Actress Who Scored First Hit in 'Within the Law' in 1912 Dies in Hollywood," *NYT,* 3 Apr 1950, 23:2 (stage debut, 1907). "Florence Nash," *Variety,* 5 Apr 1950 (age 60). AMD, p. 258. AS, p. 803. BHD1, p. 402. IFN, p. 218. Truitt, p. 246. "Florence Nash," *MPW,* 19 Dec 1914, 1700. Cover (with Alice Brady), *NYDM,* 5 May 1915 (appearing in play, *Sinners*).

Nash, George Frederick [stage/film actor] (b. Philadelphia PA, b. 1873?–30 Dec 1944 [71], Amityville LI NY). m. Julia Hay, 1910 (d. 1937). "George F. Nash; 80, Veteran of Stage; Retired Actor, on Broadway for 50 Years, Dies—Debut Here in 1888 in 'The Rivals,'" *NYT,* 1 Jan 1945, 21:5 (age 80; stage debut, 1886). "George Frederick Nash," *Variety,* 10 Jan 1945. AMD, p. 258. AS, p. 803 (d. 31 Dec). BHD1, p. 402. IFN, p. 218. SD, p. 926. Truitt, p. 246. "Engage Popular Players," *MPW,* 26 Apr 1924, 735.

Nash, John E. [producer] (b. England, 1864?–5 Nov 1934 [70], Los Angeles CA). m. Lil Hawthorne. "John E. Nash," *Variety,* 13 Nov 1934. AS, p. 803. BHD2, p. 193. W.E. Wing, "Nash Now Producing; Nash M.P. Company to Produce Animal Features—Strong Organization," *NYDM,* 3 Jun 1914, 32:2.

Nash, June [actress] (b. 1911?–8 Oct 1979 [68], Hampton Bays, LI NY). (Paramount.) "June Nash," *Variety,* 17 Oct 1979. AS, p. 803. BHD1, p. 402. IFN, p. 218.

Nash, Mary (step-daughter of **Philip Nash**; sister of **Florence Nash**) [stage/film actress] (*née* Mary Ryan, b. Troy NY, 15 Aug 1884?–3 Dec 1976 [92], Brentwood CA). m. **José Ruben** (d. 1969). "Mary Nash Dead; Character Actress of Stage and Film," *NYT,* 8 Dec 1976, IV, 22:4. "Mary Nash," *Variety,* 15 Dec 1976 (1st film, *Come and Get It,* 1936. Step-father's name was Nash). AMD, p. 258. AS, p. 803 (b. 1885). BHD1, p. 402 (b. 1885). IFN, p. 218. "Mary Nash Signs with Knickerbocker," *MPW,* 10 Jul 1915, 312. "Mary Nash with World Film," *MPW,* 13 Jan 1917, 203.

Nash, Mary Evelyn [actress] (b. 1889?–28 Jun 1965 [76], Paramus NJ). "Rites Held for Mary Nash; Former Actress Was 76," *NYT,* 3 Jul 1965, 19:2. AS, p. 803. Spehr, p. 154 (b. Troy NY, 1885–1966). Truitt, p. 246.

Nash, Percy [director] (b. 1869–1958 [89?]). AS, p. 804 (b. 1880). BHD2, p. 193.

Nash, Philip K. (stepfather of **Mary** and **Florence Nash**) [general office manager of United Booking Offices] (b. Pottsville PA, 1859?–4 Oct 1914 [55], New York NY; acute indigestion). "Phillip K. Nash," *Variety,* 10 Oct 1914, 15:4 (age

56; interred at St. Agnes Cemetery, Albany NY). "Death of Philip Nash; General Office Manager of the United Booking Offices Dies Suddenly," *NYDM,* 7 Oct 1914, 20:1.

Nash, Tom [director]. No data found. AMD, p. 258. "Selig Veterans Join Universal Forces," *MPW,* 6 Jul 1918, 51.

Naskova, Ruzena [actress] (*née* Ruzena Noskova, b. Prague, Czechoslovakia, 28 Nov 1884). AS, p. 804.

Nassiet, Henry Bernard [actor] (b. Begles, France, 24 Feb 1895–16 Apr 1977 [82], Paris, France). AS, p. 804.

Nat, Lucien [actor] (*né* Lucien Maurice Natte, b. Paris, France, 11 Jan 1895–23 Jul 1972 [77], Clichy-la-Garenne, France [extrait de décès no. 1219/1972]). AS, p. 804.

Natge, Hans Karl Heinrich [director/author] (b. Berlin, Germany, 16 Jul 1893). AS, p. 804.

Nathan, Perry [scenarist]. No data found. FDY, p. 433.

Natheaux, Louis [actor] (aka Louis Natho, *né* Louis F. Natho, b. Pine Bluff AR, 10 Dec 1894–23 Aug 1942 [47], Los Angeles CA). m. (2) Billy. (De Mille.) AMD, p. 258. AS, p. 804. BHD1, pp. 402; 614. IFN, p. 218. Truitt, p. 246 (b. 1898). "Two Talented Players Signed for DeMille Stock Company," *MPW,* 18 Apr 1925, 698. "DeMille Renews with Three Featured Players," *MPW,* 22 May 1926, 4. "Villain Roles Hard on Nose," *MPW,* 16 Apr 1927, 633. Elisabeth Greer, "A Kiss and a Contract," *Pictures,* Jul 1926, 65, 74, 76.

Natho, Louis *see* **Natheaux, Louis**

Natol, Florence [stage/film actress]. No data found. (Vitagraph.) "Florence Natol," *MPW,* 25 Sep 1915, 2189. "In the Picture Studios," *NYDM,* 16 Oct 1915, 39:2.

Natteford, John Francis [scenarist] (b. Wahoo NB, 27 Nov 1894–7 Jan 1970 [75], Los Angeles CA). BHD2, p. 193. FDY, p. 435.

Natwick, Myron "Grim" [animator] (b. WI, 16 Aug 1890–7 Oct 1990 [100], Santa Monica CA; pneumonia and heart attack). "Myron Natwick, 100; Animated Betty Boop," *NYT,* 10 Oct 1990, B24:6. "Grim Natwick," *Variety,* 15 Oct 1990, p. 90. AS, p. 804. BHD2, p. 193. John Canemaker, "Grim Natwick," *Film Comment,* Jan/Feb 1975, 57–61.

Nau, Mary [actress]. No data found. AMD, p. 258. "Apfel's Questions to Actress Mary Nau Uncover Romance of Belgium and of War," *MPW,* 7 Sep 1918, 1392.

Naughton, Charlie [actor] (b. Glasgow, Scotland, 1887–11 Feb 1976 [88?], London, England). AS, p. 804.

Naulty, J.N. [general manager]. No data found. AMD, p. 258. "Triangle Appoints a General Manager," *MPW,* 21 Aug 1915, 1303.

Navarre, René [actor/director] (*né* Victor René Navarre, b. Limoges, France, 8 Jul 1877–8 Feb 1968 [90], Azay-sur-Cher, France [extrait de décès no. 151/1968]). AS, p. 805.

Navarrete, Rodolfo [actor] (*né* Rodolfo Navarette de la Torre, b. Mexico, Jul 1884–6 Nov 1959 [75], Mexico City, Mexico; cancer). AS, p. 805.

Navarro, Anita [actress]. No data found. AMD, p. 259. "Anita Navarro," *MPW,* 18 Dec 1915, 2157.

Navarro, Mary *see* **Anderson, Mary**

Nawn, Tom [actor] (b. Scotland, 11 Jan 1863–8 Feb 1949 [86], Norwalk CA). BHD1, p. 614.

Nazarro, Cliff[ord] [actor] (b. New Haven CT, 31 Jan 1904–18 Feb 1961 [57], Ventura County CA). AS, p. 805 (d. LA CA). BHD1, p. 403.

Nazimova, Alla (aunt of Val [Vladimir] Lewton) [stage/film actress/producer/scenarist] (*née* Adelaide Leventon, b. Yalta, Crimea, Russia, 22 May 1879–13 Jul 1945 [66], Los Angeles CA). m. **Charles E. Bryant** (d. 1948). (Brenon-Selznick.) "Alla Nazimova, 66, Dies in Hollywood; Stage and Screen Star 45 Years Was Well Known for Roles in Ibsen Plays," *NYT,* 14 Jul 1945, 11:5 (b. 4 Jun 1879). "Alla Nazimova," *Variety,* 18 Jul 1945. AMD, p. 258. AS, p. 805 (*née* Alla Lavendera Orleney Nazimov). BHD1, p. 403 (b. 4 Jun 1878); BHD2, p. 193 (b. 4 Jun 1879). FFF, p. 74. FSS, p. 220. IFN, p. 219. Katz, pp. 848–49 (b. 4 Jun). Lowrey, p. 130. MH, p. 130. MSBB, p. 1040. Spehr, p. 154. Truitt, p. 246. WWS, p. 61. Walter J. Kingsley, "Laurette Taylor Gets Vaudeville Offer...," *NYDM,* 2 Jun 1915, 17:3 (offered "$30,000 cash to do two motion pictures in Los Angeles."). "Nazimova with Metro," *MPW,* 28 Jul 1917, 622. "To Cooperate on Plays," *MPW,* 16 Mar 1918, 1539. "Nazimova Talks About Metro's 'Eye for Eye,'" *MPW,* 14 Sep 1918, 1568. "Nazimova to Work for Screen Throughout 1919," *MPW,* 4 Jan 1919, 52. "Nazimova Signs a Metro Contract for Two Years," *MPW,* 14 Jun 1919, 1620. "Nazimova Selects Seven Vehicles," *MPW,* 9 Aug 1919, 810–811. "Nazimova Bruised While Acting for 'The Brat,'" *MPW,* 16 Aug 1919, 963. "Nazimova, as Adapter and Star, Spent Five Months on 'The Brat'; Six Weeks Devoted to Filming," *MPW,* 23 Aug 1919, 1134. "Nazimova at Work on Ninth Picture for Metro," *MPW,* 24 Apr 1920, 555. "Nazimova Spends Fortune for Gorgeous Gowns in 'Camille,'" *MPW,* 16 Apr 1921, 744. "Nazimova Contract with Metro Films Ends," *MPW,* 7 May 1921, 55. Edward Weitzel, "Nazimova Follows the Tragedy of 'Camille' with a Comedy Performance of Fine Humor," *MPW,* LII, 8 Oct 1921, 651. "Nazimova Signs a Contract to Release Her Films Through United Artists," *MPW,* 8 Oct 1921, 656. Maude Cheatham, "The Darkest Hour, III," *Classic,* Sept 1922, 47, 97. "The Revival of a Decadent Drama; Nazimova and Natsacha [sic] Rambova Conceive a Weird Salomé That Out-Beardsley's Aubrey Himself," *Classic,* Oct 1922, 48–49. "First National Signs Nazimova," *MPW,* 7 Jun 1924, 565. "Signs Nazimova," *MPW,* 8 Nov 1924, 179. Helen Starr, "How the Picture Stars Invest Their Savings; Modern Actors Are No Suckers; Today's Thespian Possesses Canny Business Head. Real Estate Gossip Is Chief Source of Conversation," *Paris and Hollywood,* Oct 1926, 26–29, 91 ("Nazimova is perhaps one of the shrewdest investors among the stars. He beautiful Hollywood home, fronting as it does a block square on Sunset Boulevard, a business artery, has just been leased for 99 years at an enormous rental and will be remodeled for a smart hotel."). "Alla Seeks Citizenship," *MPW,* 2 May 1927, 781. In *Madam Valentino* (1991), Michael Morris states that Nazimova and Bryant "posed as man and wife, although no record of their marriage exists" (p. 66). Eve Golden, "Alla Nazimova: Mother Russia Goes Hollywood," *CI,* 236 (Feb 1995), C4-C18.

Neal, Lex [scenarist] (*né* Alexander Neal, b. 1894?–4 Jul 1940 [46], Los Angeles CA). m. Eleanore. "Lex Neal," *NYT,* 5 Jul 1940, 13:6 (gag writer for Harold Lloyd and Buster Keaton "during the days of the silent pictures."). "Lex Neal," *Variety,* 10 Jul 1940 (gag writer for Lloyd, Keaton and Lloyd Hamilton). AMD, p. 259. AS, p. 805. BHD2, p. 193. FDY, p. 435. "Warner Engages Neal," *MPW,* 16 Sep 1922, 200.

Neal, Lloyd [actor] (b. MI, 20 Oct 1861–19 Aug 1952 [90], Los Angeles Co. CA). BHD, p. 260. IFN, p. 219.

Neame, Elwin (father of Ronald Neame) [cinematographer/producer] (b. England, 1887–14 Aug 1923 [36?], London, England). m. (son Ronald b. 23 Apr 1911). AS, p. 805. BHD2, p. 193.

Neason, Hazel [stage/film/scenarist actress] (b. Pittsburgh PA, 16 Aug 1892–24 Jan 1920 [27], New York NY). (Vitagraph; Kalem, 1912). m. **Albert E. Smith** (d. 1958). AS, p. 805. BHD, p. 260. IFN, p. 219. Photo, 9; "Chats with the Players; Hazel Neason, of the Kalem Company," *MPSM,* Sep 1912, 131–32.

Nebenzal, Seymour [actor/producer] (*né* Seymour Nebenzahl, b. New York NY, 22 Jul 1899–25 Sep 1961 [62], Munich, Germany). AS, p. 805.

Nedell, Alice B[lakeney] [actress] (b. 1894–21 Oct 1959 [65?], Los Angeles CA). AS, p. 805 (her maiden name may have been Olive Blakeney; *see* next entry).

Nedell, Bernard Jay [actor] (b. New York NY, 14 Oct 1893–23 Nov 1972 [79], Los Angeles CA). m. Olive Blakeney (*see* previous entry). "Bernard Nedell," *Variety,* 29 Nov 1972. AS, p. 805. BHD1, p. 403. IFN, p. 219.

Neely, Neil [actor]. No data found. AMD, p. 259. "Neil Neely Gets Important Role," *MPW,* 5 Nov 1927, 13.

Neff, Johnnie [actor/minstrel] (b. Waterbury CT, 1882?–30 May 1925 [43], New York NY; pneumonia). m. Carrie Starr. "Johnnie Neff," *Variety,* 10 Jun 1925. AS, p. 806 (b. 1872).

Neff, M.A. [general manager/producer] (b. 1860?–6 Oct 1915 [55], New York NY). AMD, p. 259. "M.A. Neff Dies; Long President of the Exhibitors League, He Was Ill But Short Time," *NYDM,* 16 Oct 1915, 33:2) produced *The Battle of the Ballots*). "Neff Now a Producer," *MPW,* 19 Jun 1915, 1916.

Neff, Pauline [actress] (b. Altoona PA, 17 Apr 1885–3 Jul 1951 [66], Los Angeles CA). BHD1, p. 403.

Neff, Wolfgang [director] (b. Prague, Czechoslovakia, 8 Sep 1875). AS, p. 806 (made films in Germany).

Negin, Koliz [actor] (b. Kiev, Ukraine, Russia, 1885–4 Mar 1947 [62?], San Francisco CA). AS, p. 806.

Negri, Mario [director] (b. Naples, Italy, 28 Jun 1890). AS, p. 806. JS, p. 313 (in Italian silents from 1918).

Negri, Pola [stage/film actress] (*née* Barbara Apollonia Chalupiec, b. Lipno, Poland [or Janova, Russian Poland], 31 Jan 1897?–1 Aug 1987 [90], San Antonio TX; brain tumor and pneumonia). Sergei Mdivani, 14 May 1927, France. *Memories of a Star* (Garden City NY: Doubleday & Co., Inc., 1970). (Film debut: *Niewolnica Zmyslow* [*Love and Passion*], 1914; Sphinx Co., Poland; Paramount; Ufa.) m. "Pola Negri, a Vamp of the Silent Screen, Dies at 88," *NYT,* 3 Aug 1987, D11:1. "Femme Fatale Silent Film Star Pola Negri Succumbs in

Texas," *Variety,* 5 Aug 1987 (b. Lipno or Janowa, Poland, 31 Dec 1899; age 87). AMD, p. 259. AS, p. 806 (b. 3 Jan 1897). BHD1, p. 403 (b. 31 Dec 1894). FFF, p. 33. FSS, p. 221. Katz, p. 851 (b. 1894; began in Poland, 1914). MH, p. 130 (b. Bromberg, Poland, 3 Jan). SD. "Pola Negri," WBO1, pp. 36–37 (*née* Chalupec). Waldman, p. 211. "Pola Negri Coming to America to Make a Special Production for Paramount," *MPW,* 15 Jul 1922, 206. "Miss Negri a Surprise," *MPW,* 23 Sep 1922, 254. "On Way to Coast," *MPW,* 30 Sep 1922, 358. Rose Shulsinger, "The Uncertainty of Certainty," *Classic,* Oct 1922, 18–19, 74, 77. "Extensive Publicity Tour for Paramount Star," *MPW,* 14 Apr 1923, 775. Thomas Tarrington, "'Hollywood Is a Spotless Town!' Declares Pola Negri," *MW,* 10 May 1924, 6, 31. Grace Kingsley, "Pola Negri at Home," *MW,* 31 May 1924, 10–11, 30. "Negri to Live in U.S.," *MPW,* 22 Nov 1924, 307. Helen Carlisle, "Why We Love Them," *MW,* 21 Feb 1925, 6–8. "Pola Negri Plans a Brief Visit to Europe's Capitals," *MPW,* 14 Mar 1925, 178. "Dinner to Pola Negri," *MPW,* 11 Apr 1925, 549. Helen Carlisle, "The Never-Very-Happy Pola," *MW,* 16 May 1925, 7–8, 31. "On the Set and Off," *MW,* 5 Aug 1925, 32 (Negri was attached by the government for failing to declare jewels she brought into the country). Paul Bern: Her Director, "What America Has Done to Pola," *MM,* Jan 1926, 49, 84–85. Paul Paige, "Close-Ups and Fade-Outs," *Paris and Hollywood,* Oct 1926, 67 ("A few more pictures like those she has been putting out [most recently, *Good and Naughty*] and Pola may as well retire to private life."). "Berlin Concern Sues Pola Negri for Cash," *MPW,* 5 Feb 1927, 420. Henriette, "From Hollywood to You," *MPS,* 1 Mar 1927, 7 (Margraf & Company of Berlin asking legal relief because "Negri hasn't paid for jewels purchased from them, so they say." She says she "returned the emerald ring…because they misrepresented the amount of duty payable and the suit is without merit."). "Pola Negri Marries," *MPW,* 21 May 1927, 172 (Mdvani). Richard Coyle, "No You Needn't Yes 'Em; They're Talking Back to Their Bosses," *MPC,* Aug 1927, 33, 78 (re Negri, Goudal, McAvoy, Hoot Gibson *et al.*). Paul Paige, "Close-Ups and Fade-Outs," *Paris and Hollywood Screen Secrets Magazine,* Aug 1927, 40–41 ("Pola…was unable to present a birth certificate to the French marriage registrars, resulting in a number of frantic wires being sent to the little Polish village were Pola came into the world as the daughter of a wine shop keeper." Finally, a civil ceremony was arranged. Prince Mdivani's sister Roussadana, his brother Alexander, and his brother David and his wife Mae Murray did not attend. "Mae declared that she was not interested in Pola's marriage." Her husband said, "Mae and I have made an appointment to kill a lot of animals in Africa, and we are going." At the ceremony, "Pola appeared extremely pale, but her lips were a bright cerise. She wore the huge diamond that involved her recently in unpleasantness with the New York customs inspectors, two diamond bracelets studded with emeralds bigger than hickory nuts, and giant pearl earrings. It was observed that the prince perspired profusely throughout the ceremony." "'I did love my husband, Count Domski,' she says. 'I adored Valentino. I became very fond of Mr. Chaplin, but Serge means more than all o me. Serge has decided to give up everything for me, his title and heritage if necessary. He asks me to give up nothing. He realizes that I have a great career and belong to my art."). Rene de la Seine, "Movieettes from Gay Paree," *Paris and Hollywood Screen Secrets Magazine,* Aug 1927, 65–67 ("…the Mdiviani title is Georgian and there hasn't been a ruling family in Georgia [part of Transcaucasia] since George XIII, last of the Bagradid dynasty [founded in 1008 A.D.], abandoned his throne to the Russian Tsar in 1801." Georgians says that Russian princes and grand dukes are not entitled to their titles since 1917 when the Czar abdicated. "Hollywood picture queens would be well-advised to look into the antecedents of such princes [whose] name ends in 'sky' or 'i.' But if the name ends in 'of' or 'ine,' "grab him before someone else does, for you have met a real, live member of the last ruling dynasty in Russia, the Romanofs."). James Bagley, "The Truth About Pola's Prince [Serge Mdivani]," *MPC,* Oct 1927, 20–21, 67. "Negri Sells Home," *MPW,* 19 Nov 1927, 25. "Paramount Offers Pola $125,000 Per," *MPW,* 3 Dec 1927, 8. "Negri Cancels Trip to New York," *MPW,* 3 Dec 1927, 21. Gladys Hall, "What Hollywood Did to Pola; Her Five American Years Find Her Still Imperial, Yet Not Unchanged," *MPC,* Aug 1928, 21, 68, 77 ("And the new importation, Lucy Doraine, was being rumored about as the Negri successor. They didn't even wait for the body to cool."). Reg Mortimer, "Pola Puts It Over; She's the First to Win Bernard Shaw's Consent to Film a Play of His [*Caesar and Cleopatra*]," *MPC,* Apr 1929, 53, 79, 85. Eve Golden, "The Opportunist: Pola Negri on Her (More or Less) Centenary," *CI,* 270 (Dec 1997), C4-C6 (with filmography by Richard E. Braff).

Negri-Pouget, Fernanda [actress] (*née* Fernanda Negri, b. Rome, Italy, 28 Mar 1899–17 Feb 1955 [55], Rome, Italy). m. **Armand Pouget**. AS, p. 806 (b. 1889). JS, pp. 313–14 (in Italian films from 1911).

Negroni, Baldassare [director] (b. Rome, Italy, 21 Jan 1877–18 Jul 1948 [71], Rome, Italy). m. **Hesperia**, 1923 (d. 1959). AS, p. 806 (d. 1945). BHD2, p. 194. JS, p. 314 ("From a noble family, he himself was a count"; in Italian films from 1912).

Neher, Carola [actress] (*née* Caroline Neher, b. Munich, Germany, 2 Nov 1900–28 Jun 1942 [41], Solyletsk, Russia). AS, p. 806.

Nehles, R[ichard] **R.** [publicist/general manager of American/producer] (b. Chicago IL, 29 Mar 1875–9 Mar 1966 [], Los Angeles Co. CA). (American [Chicago].) AMD, p. 259. BHD2, p. 194. "Richard R. Nehls," *MPW,* 11 Nov 1911, 487. F.J. Beecroft, "Publicity Men I Have Met…," *NYDM,* 14 Jan 1914, 48 (*see* Beecroft, Chester for full citation). "With the Film Men; R.R. Nehls [sic]," *NYDM,* 13 May 1914, 36:2.

Neice, Alice [actress]. No data found. AMD, p. 259. "Alice Neice," *MPW,* 23 Dec 1916, 1793.

Neiiendam, Nicolai [actor] (b. Copenhagen, Denmark, 21 Mar 1865–15 Mar 1945 [79], Copenhagen, Denmark). BHD1, p. 614.

Neilan, Marshall A. "Mickey" [actor/director] (b. San Bernardino CA, 11 Apr 1891–26 Oct 1958 [67], Woodland Hills CA; cancer). m. **Gertrude Bambrick**, 21 Dec 1913, Hoboken NJ—div. Mar 1921; **Blanche Sweet**, 1922–29 (d. 1986). (Biograph, 1913; American; Rex; Kalem; Universal; Artcraft; K&E; Selig.) "Marshall Neilan of Silent Movies; Director of Films with Top Performers of Era Dies—Had Been Leading Actor," *NYT,* 28 Oct 1958, 35:3. "Marshall Neilan," *Variety,* 29 Oct 1958. AMD, p. 259. AS, p. 806. BHD1, p. 403; BHD2, p. 194. IFN, p. 219. Katz, pp. 851–52. Lowrey, p. 134. MSBB, p. 1046. Spehr, pp. 154–55. Truitt, p. 246. WWS, p. 131. "Marshall Neilan Returns to Kalem," *MPW,* 27 Dec 1913, 1529. "Marshall 'Mickey' Neilan," *MPW,* 23 May 1914, 1118. "Newsy Week on the Coast; Marshall Neilan and Gertrude Bambrick Wed…," *NYDM,* 27 May 1914, 27:1 (kept marriage a secret for six months). "Neilan to Selig?; Reported on Coast That Director and Leading Man Will Make Change," *NYDM,* 14 Apr 1915, 22:1. "Marshall Neilan with Selig," *MPW,* 12 Jun 1915, 1762. "Famous Players Secures Marshall Neilan," *MPW,* 28 Aug 1915, 1483. "Marshall Neilan Now a Lasky Director," *MPW,* 23 Sep 1916, 1956. "Neilan and Melford Continue with Lasky," *MPW,* 12 May 1917, 984. "Marshall Neilan Signs Up with Garson as Supervising Director of Production," *MPW,* 7 Sep 1918, 1417. "Neilan to Start for Circuit June 1," *MPW,* 17 May 1919, 1028. "Continuity Writers the Great Need," *MPW,* 14 Jun 1919, 1620. "Marshall Neilan Discontinues Purchasing of Supplies form Los Angeles Merchants," *MPW,* 26 Jul 1919, 484. "At Last the Day of the Director Has Arrived, Says Marshall Neilan," *MPW,* 13 Dec 1919, 787. "Marshall Neilan Leases 'Big Four' Western Studio," *MPW,* 27 Dec 1919, 1132. "Neilan Talks of Next Year's Plans; Will Have No Set Release Schedule," *MPW,* 27 Dec 1919, 1133. "Marshall Neilan Promises Special Exploitation Service to Exhibitors," *MPW,* 3 Jan 1920, 86. "Public Now Shops in Newspapers, Marshall Neilan Tells Exhibitors," *MPW,* 24 Jan 1920, 587. "Marshall Neilan Asks Directors to Oppose 'Snipe' Advertising," *MPW,* 31 Jan 1920, 752. "Marshall Neilan Company Is Now Established in New Home," *MPW,* 20 Mar 1920, 1982. "Marshall Neilan Plans Novel Stunts for Exploitation of Next Three Films," *MPW,* 27 Mar 1920, 2163. "Neilan to Produce in Europe; To Take Entire Company Abroad, Remaining Six Months," *MPW,* 3 Apr 1920, 117. "Marshall Neilan and Albert Kaufman Form Cooperative Producing Alliance," *MPW,* 10 Apr 1920, 223. "Neilan Warns of Alleged Attempts to Sell His Productions on Series Basis," *MPW,* 18 Sep 1920, 383. "Neilan in Formation of Own Company Realized Consummation of His Ideals," *MPW,* 25 Dec 1920, 1018. Marshall Neilan, "Producers Produce (and Exhibit); Exhibitors Exhibit (and Produce); and the Peace Dove Flies Over All," *MPW,* 29 Jan 1921, 531. Clodagh Saurin, "The Wearing of the Green," *Photoplay,* Mar 1921, 31, 76 (re Neilan, Colleen Moore, and Pat O'Malley). "Mrs. Neilan Gets Divorce; Blanche Sweet 'Other Woman'; Mother of Movie Star's Estranged Wife Blames the Husband for Causing Break," *Toledo Blade,* 18 Mar 1921. "Neilan Stops Work on Los Angeles Plant Because of Local Censorship Agitation," *MPW,* 15 Oct 1921, 762. Kenneth McGaffey, "The Entertainer," *MPC,* Dec 1921, 50, 88. Marshall Neilan, "'Mickey' Writes to Santa Claus," *MPW,* 31 Dec 1921, 1082. "Marshall Neilan Will Work in Conjunction with Goldwyn Company," *MPW,* 29 Apr 1922, 921. "Marshall Neilan Sails; Signs Goldwyn Contract," *MPW,* 6 May 1922, 36. "Neilan Made Member of Goldwyn Company's Board of Directors," *MPW,* 20 May 1922, 308. "'No Program Films from Me,' Neilan Promises Exhibitors," *MPW,* 15 Jul 1922, 213. Marshall Neilan, "'The Eternal Three' Neilan's Work," *MPW,* 4 Aug 1923, 409. Paul Rochester, "Can You Buy Your Way into the Movies?," *MW,* 22 Sep 1923, 3. "Mickey Neilan to Be Operated Upon," *MPW,* 7 Jun 1924, 535. "'Tess of d'Urbervilles' His

Best, Neilan Thinks," *MPW,* 28 Jun 1924, 819. "Director Neilan Praised," *MPW,* 16 Aug 1924, 556. "Neilan Buys Garson Studios," *MPW,* 9 May 1925, 136. "Neilan Signs with Flinn for Producers Dist. Corp.," *MPW,* 29 Aug 1925, 935. "Neilan Tells Why 'The Sky Rocket' Shouild Be One of Year's Biggest Plays," *MPW,* 7 Nov 1925, 39. "Neilan to Make Specials for Paramount," *MPW,* 2 Jan 1926, 79. "Neilan to Direct Series of Specials for Paramount," *MPW,* 27 Mar 1926, 262. "Neilan Produces Story He Wrote," *MPW,* 4 Sep 1926, 20. Jack Spears, *Hollywood: The Golden Era* (NY: A.S. Barnes & Co., 1971), p. 282.

Neill, James [actor/director] (b. Savannah GA, 29 Sep 1860–16 Mar 1931 [70], Glendale CA; heart attack). m. **Edythe Chapman** (d. 1948). "James Neill," *Variety,* 18 Mar 1931. AMD, p. 260. AS, p. 806. BHD1, p. 403 (d. 15 Mar, LA CA). IFN, p. 219. Truitt, pp. 246–47. "James Neill to Direct for Universal," *MPW,* 6 Sep 1913, 1073. "Add Neill and Chapman to Goldwyn Repertory Players," *MPW,* 27 Sep 1919, 1974. George Katchmer, "Remembering the Great Silents," *CI,* 201 (Mar 1992), 38–39.

Neill, Richard R. [stage/film actor] (b. Philadelphia PA, 12 Nov 1875–8 Apr 1970 [94], Woodland Hills CA). AMD, p. 260. AS, p. 806. BHD1, p. 404; BHD2, p. 194. IFN, p. 219. MSBB, p. 1026. Truitt, p. 247. "Richard R. Neill with McIntosh," *MPW,* 8 May 1915, 902. "Thanhouser Signs Richard R. Neill," *MPW,* 3 Mar 1917, 1367. George A. Katchmer, "Remembering the Great Silents," *CI,* 178 (Apr 1990), 41–42.

Neill, Roy William [producer/director] (*né* Roland de Gostrie, b. Queenstone Harbor, Ireland, 4 Sep 1887–14 Dec 1946 [59], London, England; heart attack). (Ince; Universal.) "Roy William Neill; Hollywood Producer and Director Dies in London at Age of 59," *NYT,* 17 Dec 1946, 38:4. "Roy William Neill," *Variety,* 18 Dec 1946. AMD, p. 260. AS, p. 806. BHD, p. 261; BHD2, p. 194. IFN, p. 219. Katz, p. 852. Lowrey, p. 132. 1921 Directory, p. 272. "Neill Signed by Dietrich, Is Handler of Woman Stars," *MPW,* 19 Jul 1919, 387. "Director R. William Neill Now Cutting 'The Bandbox,'" *MPW,* 20 Sep 1919, 1802. "Sax Signs R. William Neill to Direct Gotham Pictures," *MPW,* 1 Oct 1927, 287.

Neilson, Julia *see* **Neilson-Terry, Julia**

Neilson, Lois [actress] (b Tulare CA, 1898–9 Jul 1990 [92?]). BHD, p. 261.

Neilson-Terry, Dennis (son of Fred and **Julia Neilson**; brother of **Phyllis Neilson-Terry**; nephew of **Ellen Terry**; cousin of Sir **John Gielgud**) [stage/film actor/producer/manager] (b. London, England, 21 Oct 1895–14 Jul 1932 [36], Bulawaya, So. Rhodesia; double pneumonia). m. **Mary Glynne** (d. 1954). "Dennis Neilson-Terry," *Variety,* 107, 26 Jul 1932, 47:1 (d. 12 Jul, age 37. "There being no son, this means the last of the Terrys, one of the oldest theatrical families in England."). AS, p. 806. BHD1, p. 404 (d. Bulawayo, Zimbabwe). IFN, p. 219.

Neilson-Terry, Julia (mother of **Dennis** and **Phyllis Neilson-Terry**; grandmother of Hazel Terry) [stage/film singer/actress] (b. London, England, 12 Jun 1868–27 May 1957 [88], Hempstead, London, England). m. actor Fred Terry, brother of Ellen Terry (d. 1933). (Stage debut: *Pygmalion and Galatea,* 1888.) "Julia Neilson Terry, 88; Well-Known Actress on Stage in Britain, 1888–1944, Dies," *NYT,* 28 May 1957, 34:2. "Julia Neilson-Terry," *Variety,* 206, 29 May 1957, 75:1. AS, p. 806. BHD, p. 261.

Neilson-Terry, Phyllis (daughter of **Fred Terry** and **Julia Neilson-Terry**; sister of **Dennis Neilson-Terry**; mother of Hazel Terry; niece of **Ellen Terry**; cousin of Sir **John Gielgud**) [stage/film/vaudeville/TV actress] (b. London, England, 15 Oct 1892–25 Sep 1977 [84], near London, England). m. (2) Heron Carvic. (Stage debut: *Henry of Navarre,* Blackpool, England, 1909.) "Phyllis Neilson-Terry," *Variety,* 288, 5 Oct 1977, 98:2. AS, p. 806. BHD1, p. 404. IFN, p. 219.

Neitz, Alvin J *see* **James, Alan**

Nekut, Max [director] (b. Vienna, Austria, 9 Apr 1883). AS, p. 806.

Nelson, Berta [actress in Italian silents]. No data found.

Nelson, Bill [actor] (d. 2 Jun 1992). BHD1, p. 404.

Nelson, Eddie "Sunkist" [actor] (b. 1894?–5 Dec 1940 [46], Los Angeles CA; heart attack). "Eddie Nelson," *Variety,* 11 Dec 1940. AMD, p. 260. AS, p. 807. IFN, p. 219. Truitt, p. 247. "New Faces in Comedies," *MPW,* 6 Jun 1925, 682.

Nelson, Evelyn [actress] (b. Chloride AZ, 13 Nov 1899–16 Jun 1923 [23], Los Angeles CA; suicide by gas asphyxiation). (Fox; Christie; Century; Roach.) AS, p. 807. BHD, p. 261. BR, p. 185. IFN, p. 219. George A. Katchmer, "Forgotten Cowboys and Cowgirls—Part IX," *CI,* 181 (Jul 1990), 56. George A. Katchmer, "Remembering the Great Silents," *CI,* 203 (May 1992), 41.

Nelson, Florence Irene [actress] (b. 1886–3 Aug 1929 [44?], Denver CO; complications during an operation). AS, p. 807.

Nelson, Frances M. [actress] (b. St. Paul MN, 1892). (Metro, 1917.) AMD, p. 260. "Frances M. Nelson," *MPW,* 24 Oct 1914, 503. "Frances M. Nelson; Leading Lady with the Imp Company," *MPS,* 11 Dec 1914, 26 (age 22). "Frances Nelson in Metro Feature Play," *MPW,* 4 Nov 1916, 711.

Nelson, Frank [actor] (b. 1872?–27 Nov 1932 [60], CA). (Selig.) AS, p. 807 (b. 1972). BHD1, p. 404. IFN, p. 219. George Katchmer, "Remembering the Great Silents," *CI,* 248 (Feb 1996), 47.

Nelson, Harold [actor] (b. Boston MA, 26 Aug 1864–26 Jan 1937 [72], Los Angeles CA; pneumonia). AS, p. 807 (d. 1947). BHD1, p. 404. IFN, p. 219. Truitt, p. 247.

Nelson, Hilda [actress] (b. 1880?–Jan 1919 [38], Bellevue Hospital, New York NY; pneumonia. Interment in Actors' Fund park on Staten Island NY). "Hilda Nelson," *Variety,* 10 Jan 1919, 25:1 (member of Film Players' Club). BHD, p. 261.

Nelson, Jack [actor/director/scenarist] (b. Memphis TN, 1885?–10 Nov 1948 [63], North Bay, Ontario, Canada). (Pathé; Regal Films.) "Jack Nelson," *Variety,* 17 Nov 1948. AMD, p. 260. AS, p. 807 (b. Scranton PA). BHD, addendum (b. 1882). FDY, p. 435. WWE, p. 200 (b. Scranton PA). *MPN Studio Directory,* 21 Oct 1916 (Jack Nellson, b. Memphis TN, 15 Oct 1882; Selig; Ince; Universal). "Jack Nelson with Horsley," *MPW,* 6 May 1916, 976. "Jack Nelson to Direct MacLean-May Features," *MPW,* 28 Feb 1920, 1518. "Nelson and Poland Under Contract," *MPW,* 12 Jun 1920, 1434.

Nelson, Jenny [actress] (b. Copenhagen, Denmark). *Fl.* 1912 (Lubin). AMD, p. 260. "Jenny Nelson," *MPW,* 15 Jun 1912, 1025.

Nelson, Lottie (mother of **Sam Nelson**) [actress] (*née* Lottie O. Tompkins, b. CA, 13 Mar 1875–8 May 1966 [91], Los Angeles CA; pulmonary embolism). "Lottie Nelson," *Variety,* 25 May 1966 (active mostly as bit player in silents). AS, p. 807. IFN, p. 220. Truitt, p. 247.

Nelson, Otto [actor]. No data found. George Katchmer, "Remembering the Great Silents," *CI,* 210 (Dec 1992), 51.

Nelson, Sam (son of **Lottie Nelson**) [actor/assistant director] (b. Whittier CA, 11 May 1896–1 May 1963 [66], Los Angeles CA). (Columbia.) "Sam Nelson," *Variety,* 8 May 1963 (age 67). AS, p. 808. BHD1, p. 404 (b. 31 May). IFN, p. 220. George A. Katchmer, "Remembering the Great Silents," *CI,* 178 (Apr 1990), 42.

Nelson-Ramsey, John [actor] (d. 5 Apr 1929, London, England). BHD, p. 261. IFN, p. 220.

Nemetz, Max [actor] (b. 18 Oct 1884–2 Jul 1971 [86]). BHD1, p. 614.

Ne Moyer, Frances E. [stage/film actress] (b. Westfield NY). (Anson Gilmore Stock Co..) AMD, p. 260. "Almost Another Picture Accident," *MPW,* 10 Aug 1912, 530. "Chats with the Players," *MPSM,* Sep 1912, 134.

Ne Moyer, Marguerite [actress]. No data found. AMD, p. 260. "Marguerite NeMoyer," *MPW,* 4 Jul 1914, 46.

Nepoti, Alberto [actor/director] (b. Piedmonte, Italy). JS, p. 314 (in Italian films from 1909).

Nerking, Hans [actor/director] (b. Darmstadt, Germany, 10 Dec 1888–24 Apr 1964 [75], Berlin, Germany). AS, p. 808.

Nero, Curtis [actor] (b. Muskogee OK, 3 Apr 1906–28 Jan 1942 [35], Los Angeles Co. CA). BHD1, p. 405. IFN, p. 220.

Neroni, Nicola Fausto [director/scenarist] (b. Rome, Italy, 12 Dec 1896). AS, p. 808. JS, p. 315 (in Italian films from 1920).

Nervig, Conrad (film editor). No data found. (MGM.)

Nervo, Jimmy [actor] (*né* James Holloway, b. London, England, 2 Jan 1898–5 Dec 1975 [77], London, England). AS, p. 808. BHD1, p. 405.

Nesbit, Evelyn, "The Girl in the Red Velvet Swing" [artist's model/vaudeville/stage/film actress/*femme fatale*] (*née* Florence Evelyn Nesbit, b. Tarentum PA, 25 Dec 1884–17 Jan 1967 [82], Santa Monica CA). m. **Harry K**[endall] **Thaw**, 4 Apr 1905, Pittsburgh PA—div. 1916 (d. 1947); **Jack Clifford** (Virgil Montani), 1916–19 (d. 1956). *The Story of My Life,* 1914; *Prodigal Days: The Untold Story,* 1934. Michael MacDonald Mooney, *Evelyn Nesbit and Stanford White* (1976). (Fox.) "Evelyn Nesbit, 82, Dies in California," *NYT,* 19 Jan 1967, 1:3; "Evelyn Nesbit Buried," *NYT,* 21 Jan 1967, 31:3 (buried at Holy Cross Cemetery, Inglewood CA). Robert J. Landry, "Evelyn Nesbit, of Thaw Case, Dies," *Variety,* 25 Jan 1967 ("Her talent was negligible, as true of more than a few showgirls who had looks period."). AMD, p. 260. AS, p. 808. BHD, p. 261. IFN, p. 220. MSBB, p. 1040. Spehr, p. 156. Truitt, p. 323. "Thaw Weds Miss Nesbit; Marriage Takes Place in Pittsburg[h]—Bridegroom's Mother Present," *NYT,* 5 Apr 1905, 1:6 (she became the sister-in-law of the Countess of Yarmouth. The couple arrived in East Liberty, Pittsburgh, on the 7:10 a.m. train; Nesbit went to her mother's home on Oakland Avenue). "Evelyn

Thaw Defiant; Actress in Performance Against Mayor's Order—Dismissal Follows Arrest," *NYDM,* 18 Feb 1914, 10:3 (arrested in Richmond VA at the Academy of Music on 10 Feb not having proceeded beyond her first dance; arrested because her public performance was "'a detriment to public morals.' The result was that a capacity audience witnessed her performance later in the vening." The charge was dismissed because there was no law to hold her.) "Vaudeville; Evelyn Nesbit Returns," *NYDM,* 30 Oct 1915, 18:1 (appearing at the Palace with Jack Clifford. Her singing, "if better than last season, isn't up to her dancing."). "Evelyn Thaw to Fight Divorce; Wife of White's Slayer Will Contest Suit 'for Little Son's Sake'; Wants Him to Share Wealth; Actress Retains Lawyer, Thus Contradicting Assertions She Would Put Up No Defense," *The [NY] Morning Telegraph,* 19 Dec 1915, 14:5 (she was charged with infidelity). "Evelyn Nesbit to Make Series of Fox Pictures," *MPW,* 7 Sep 1918, 1423. Edward Weitzel, "Tonneau Talk with Evelyn Nesbit," *MPW,* 21 Sep 1918, 1702–03. Ethel Rosemon, "The Extra Girl Becomes a Village Belle; An Evelyn Nesbit Feature in the Filming," *MPC,* Apr 1919, 52–53, 78, 87–88. "Dedicate Song to Evelyn Nesbit," *MPW,* 24 May 1919, 1176 (*Fallen Idols*). Patricia Scollard Painter, "Nesbit, Evelyn Florence," *DAB,* Supp. 8 (1988), pp. 460–62 (met Stanford White in Aug 1901. Later on, she dined alone with him and after abundant champagne she woke "in terror to find herself naked and no longer a virgin." In 1902 she "began an affair with 22-year-old John Barrymore. In Apr 1903 she was hospitalized with appendicitis, though rumors abounded. She convalesced with Harry K. Thaw in Paris, accompanied by her mother. He allegedly beat her with a dog whip which did not prevent her marrying him. He shot White three times in the head on 25 Jun 1906 in NYC. His trial began on 23 Jan 1907. She divorced him and her next husband and became a heroin addict.). Stephanie Savage, "Evelyn Nesbit and the film(ed) histories of the Thaw-White Scandal," *Film History,* 8, 1996, 159–175 (filmography lists ten films).

Nesbit, Pinna [actress]. No data found. m. Lt. Frederic H. Cruger, N.G.U.S., Sep 1917. "Marriages," *Variety,* 21 Sep 1917, p. 10.

Nesbitt, Cathleen [actress] (*née* Kathleen Mary Nesbitt, b. Liscard, England, 24 Nov 1888–2 Aug 1982 [93], Chelsea, England; cardiac arrest). m. **Cecil Ramage**, 1922—div. (d. 1988). *A Little Love and Good Company,* 1977. Carol Lawson, "Cathleen Nesbitt, British Character Actress, Dead," *NYT,* 4 Aug 1982, B6:2. "Noted Actress Cathleen Nesbitt, 93, Dies at Her London Home," *Variety,* 11 Aug 1982. AS, p. 808 (b. 29 Nov). BHD1, p. 405 (b. Cheshire, England, 1889).

Nesbitt, Miriam [stage/film actress] (*née* Miriam Anne Schancke, b. Chicago IL, 14 Sep 1873–11 Aug 1954 [80], Los Angeles CA). m. **Marc McDermott**, Apr 1916, Leonia NJ (d. 1954). (Edison.) AMD, p. 261. AS, p. 808. BHD, p. 261. IFN, p. 220. "Edison Players Return," *MPW,* 16 Nov 1912, 647. "Miss Nesbitt Directs; Leading Woman Will Stage Novel Edison Feature [*A Close Call*] on Journey Across the Continent," *NYDM,* 28 Jul 1915, 25:4 (first woman to direct at Edison). "Miriam Nesbitt, Director," *MPW,* 7 Aug 1915, 976. "Wright to Direct Miss Nesbitt," *MPW,* 20 Nov 1915, 1470. Miriam Nesbitt, "In the World of Make-Believe," *Motion Picture Magazine,* Feb 1918, 77–78 ("began my dramatic career as the leading-lady of James K. Hackett, in 1908."). Billy H. Doyle, "Lost Players; Miriam Nesbitt and Marc McDermott," *CI,* 184 (Oct 1990), C12-C13, 45–46.

Nesbitt, Thomas, Jr. [actor] (b. England, 1890–31 Mar 1927 [36], Johannesburg, So. Africa). AS, p. 808. BHD, p. 261. IFN, p. 220.

Nesler, Lloyd [film editor]. No data found. AMD, p. 261. Lloyd Nesler, "Film Editing," *MPW,* 26 Mar 1927, 408.

Nesmith, Ottola [stage/film actress] (*née* Ottola Nesmith D'Usseau, b. Washington DC, 12 Dec 1889–7 Feb 1972 [82], Los Angeles CA). (FP-L.) AMD, p. 261. AS, p. 808. BHD1, p. 405. IFN, p. 220. "Miss Ottola Nesmith," *NYDM,* 6 Nov 1915, 7:4. "Raver Engages Ottala Nesmith," *MPW,* 18 Dec 1915, 2163.

Ness, Ole M. [actor] (b. Philadelphia PA, 12 Mar 1888–19 Jul 1953 [65], No. Hollywood CA). m. Nine Garnett. "Ole Ness," *Variety,* 29 Jul 1953. AS, p. 808. BHD1, p. 405. IFN, p. 220. Truitt, p. 247.

Nestell, Bill [actor] (b. Los Angeles CA, 3 Mar 1893–18 Oct 1966 [73], Bishop CA; heart attack). (Republic; Universal.) "Bill Nestell," *Variety,* 26 Oct 1966 (age 71). AS, p. 808. BHD1, p. 405. IFN, p. 220. Truitt, p. 247. Geo. Katchmer, "Remembering the Great Silents," *CI,* 210 (Dec 1992), 51.

Nettlefold, Arch [producer] (b. 1870–1 Dec 1944 [74?], London, England). BHD2, p. 194.

Neu, Oscar F. [actor/director] (b. Buffalo NY, 22 Jun 1886–26 Aug 1957 [71], Crestwood NY). m. Adelaide. (Mutual Girl series, 1911–12.) "Oscar F. Neu, 71, Dead; Headed Movie, Radio and TV Equipment Concern," *NYT,* 28 Aug 1957, 27:5. "Oscar Neu," *Variety,* 4 Sep 1957. AS, p. 808. BHD, p. 261; BHD2, p. 194. IFN, p. 220. Truitt, p. 247.

Neufeld, Max [director] (b. Gunersdorf, Germany, 13 Feb 1887–1967 [80?], Vienna, Austria). AS, p. 808. BHD2, p. 194.

Neumann, Alfred [actor] (b. Germany, 1896–3 Oct 1952 [56?], Lugano, Switzerland). AS, p. 809.

Neumann, Harry C. [cameraman] (b. 11 Feb 1891?–14 Jan 1971 [79], Los Angeles CA). m. Eva. (Selig, 1913.) "Harry C. Neumann," *Variety,* 20 Jan 1971. BHD2, p. 194. FDY, p. 465. IFN, p. 220.

Neumann, Lotte [actress] (b. Berlin, Germany, 5 Aug 1889–26 Feb 1977 [87], Bavaria, Germany). (Film debut: *Die Launender Schicksal,* 1912.) AS, p. 809 (b. 1896). BHD, p. 261; BHD2, p. 195 (b. 1899). Vittorio Martinelli, "Kino-Lieblinge," *Griffithiana,* 38/39 (Oct 1990), 24.

Neumann-Viertel, Elisabeth [actress] (*née* Elisabeth Neumann, b. Vienna, Austria, 5 Apr 1900–24 Dec 1994 [94], Vienna, Austria). AS, p. 809.

Neuss, Alwin [actor] (*né* Carl Alwin Heinrich Neuss, b. Cologne, Germany, 17 Jun 1879–30 Oct 1935 [56], Berlin, Germany). AS, p. 809. Vittorio Martinelli, "Kino-Lieblinge," *Griffithiana,* 38/39 (Oct 1990), 63.

Nevaro [actor/acrobat] (*né* Otto Willkomm, b. 1887–13 Nov 1941 [54?], Milwaukee WI). AS, p. 809.

Nevelli, Amlette [actor] (b. Italy-d. 17 Mar 1924, Rome, Italy; heart attack). AS, p. 809.

Neville, George [actor] (b. Boston MA, 17 Oct 1865–18 Aug 1932 [66], New York NY). "George Neville," *Variety,* 23 Aug 1932. AS, p. 809. BHD, p. 261. IFN, p. 220.

Neville, Harry [actor] (b. Launceston, Australia, 24 Mar 1867–25 Jan 1945 [77], Hempstead, LI NY). "Harry Neville; Veteran Actor, Recently Played Here in 'Embezzled Heaven,'" *NYT,* 27 Jan 1945, 11:4 (d. Rockeville Centre LI NY). "Harry Neville," *Variety,* 31 Jan 1945. AS, p. 809. BHD1, p. 405 (d. Rockeville Centre). IFN, p. 220.

Neville, John Thomas [scenarist]. No data found. FDY, p. 435.

Nevius, B.A. [actor] (d. Aug 1928, Leon IA). BHD, p. 261.

New, Clarence Herbert [scenarist/film editor] (b. Brooklyn NY, 14 Nov 1862–8 Jan 1933 [70], Brooklyn NY). BHD2, p. 195.

Newall, Guy [actor/director] (b. Isle of Wight, England, 25 May 1885–25 Feb 1937 [51], Hampstead [London] England). m. (2) Ivy Duke; (3) Dorothy Batley. (London Film Co., 1912.) "Guy Newall Dead; English Actor 51; Active on Stage and Screen, He Once Toured in U.S.—Served His Country During War," *NYT,* 28 Feb 1937, II, 9:2. "Guy Newall," *Variety,* 3 Mar 1937. AMD, p. 261. AS, p. 809. BHD1, p. 405; BHD2, p.195 (b. Newport, England). IFN, p. 220. Katz, pp. 854–55. Truitt, p. 247. T.S. daPonte, "Guy Newall Talks About the Film Industry in England and America," *MPW,* 10 Dec 1921, 675.

Newburg, Frank [or **Francis**] **A.** [actor] (b. PA, 9 Oct 1866–4 Nov 1969 [83], Woodland Hills CA). m. **Laura Oakley** (d. 1957); **Jane Novak** (d. 1990). (Selig; K&E.) "Frank Newburg," *Variety,* 19 Nov 1969. AS, p. 809. BHD, p. 261. IFN, p. 220. Truitt, p. 247.

Newcomb, Mary [stage/film actress] (b. North Adams MA, 24 Aug 1893–26 Dec 1966 [73], Dorchester, England). m. (1) **Robert Edeson** (d. 1931); (2) Alexander H. Higginson. AS,p. 809 (b. 2 Aug 1897). BHD1, p. 405. IFN, p. 220. SD, p. 933 (b. 20 Aug 1897). Truitt, p. 247 (b. 1894-Jan 1967).

Newcombe, Caroline [actress] (b. Shreveport LA, 1872–17 Dec 1941 [69], New York NY). BHD, p. 261. IFN, p. 220.

Newcombe, Jessamine [actress] (b. London, England, 1885–15 Mar 1961 [75?], Los Angeles CA). AS, p. 809.

Newcombe, Robert E. [actor] (b. 1867?–27 Aug 1921 [54], New York NY; plural pneumonia). "Robert E. Newcombe," *Variety,* 9 Sep 1921. AS, p. 809.

Newcombe, Warren A. [producer/art director]. No data found. m. Hazel Lindsley, 14 Jun 1924. AMD, p. 261. "Producer to Wed Star," *MPW,* 9 Feb 1924, 448. "Signed by Griffith," *MPW,* 19 Apr 1924, 650. "Newcombe Marries," *MPW,* 26 Jul 1924, 287.

Newell, David [actor/makeup artist] (b. Carthage MO, 23 Jan 1905–25 Jan 1980 [75], Los Angeles CA). (Paramount.) "David Newell," *Variety,* 13 Feb 1980 (early film: *The Hole in the Wall,* 1929). AS, p. 809. BHD1, p. 405; BHD2, p. 195. IFN, p. 220.

Newell, Willard [producer]. No data found. AMD, p. 261. "A New Producer in Chicago," *MPW,* 30 Aug 1913, 947.

Newhard, Robert S. [cinematographer] (b. Allentown PA, 28 Apr 1884–20 May 1945 [61], Los Angeles CA). BHD2, p. 195. FDY, p. 465.

Newland, Anna Dewey [actress] (b. 1881?–24 Jun 1967 [86], Los Angeles CA; pneumonia). "Anna Dewey Newland," *Variety,* 5 Jul 1967. AS, p. 810. Truitt, p. 247.

Newman, Albert E. [actor/singer] (b. 1885?–26 Sep 1952 [67], Wasoga Beach, near Toronto, Canada). m. "Albert E. Newman," *Variety,* 1 Oct 1952. AS, p. 810.

Newman, E.M. [producer] (b. 1869–16 Apr 1953 [84?], Los Angeles CA). AMD, p. 261. AS, p. 810. BHD2, p. 195. "E.M. Newman Goes Abroad," *MPW,* 25 May 1918, 1144. "Newman Hunts Out the Remote Spots," *MPW,* 15 Jun 1918, 1579.

Newman, Horace [actor] (b. 1863–13 Nov 1947 [84?], New York NY). BHD, p. 262.

Newman, John K[och] [actor] (b. 1864?–2 Mar 1927 [63], New York NY). AS, p. 810. BHD, p. 262. IFN, p. 221. Truitt, p. 247.

Newman, Lu Barden [actress] (d. 1 Dec 1918, New York NY). AS, p. 810 (Lur Barden Newman). BHD, p. 262.

Newman, Nell [actress] (b. 1881?–6 Aug 1931 [50], Los Angeles CA; pneumonia). (Nazimova Productions.) "Nell Newman," *Variety,* 25 Aug 1931. AS, p. 810. BHD, p. 262. IFN, p. 221. Truitt, p. 247.

Newman, Widgey R. [director] (b. Bedford, England, 1900–15 Jul 1944 [44?], England). AS, p. 811.

Newmark, Lucille [title writer]. No data found. FDY, p. 447.

Newmeyer, Fred C. [director/scenarist] (*né* Fred Richard Newmeyer, b. Central City CO, 9 Aug 1888–24 Apr 1967 [78], Woodland Hills CA). (Universal.) AMD, p. 261. AS, p. 811. BHD, p. 262; BHD2, p. 195. Katz, p. 856. "Fred Newmeyer Directs New Chadwick Comedy," *MPW,* 12 Dec 1925, 548. "Newmeyer Back on Coast; Infected Leg Still Bothers Him," *MPW,* 15 May 1926, 240. "Mildred Davis in Paramount Crook Story," *MPW,* 8 Jan 1927, 124. Tom Waller, "Fred Newmeyer: Box Office Director," *MPW,* 26 Mar 1927, 272–73. "Newmeyer Re-Signed," *MPW,* 30 Jul 1927, 311. "Fred Newmeyer," *MPW,* 17 Sep 1927, 166.

Newton, Charles Lindner [actor] (b. Rochester NY, 1874–1926 [52?]). m. **Dorrit Ashton** (d. 1936). (Universal.) AS, p. 811. BHD, p. 262. IFN, p. 221. Truitt, p. 248. George Katchmer, "Remembering the Great Silents," *CI,* 201 (Mar 1992), 39.

Newton, Irving (Fig) [actor] (b. 1898–13 Jun 1980 [82?], Sherman Oaks CA; heart attack). AS, p. 811. BHD1, p. 406.

Newton, Mabel D. (sister of Broadway producer Charles B. Dillingham) [actress] (*née* Mabel Dillingham, d. 29? Dec 1937, Hartford CT). "Mrs. Mabel D. Newton," *NYT,* 31 Dec 1937, 16:2.

Newton, Marie [actress]. No data found. (Biograph; K&E.) "The Great Cast Contest," *Photoplay,* Apr 1915, 125.

Ney, Marie [actress] (*née* Marie Fix, b. London, England, 18 Jul 1895–11 Apr 1981 [85], London, England). AS, p. 811. BHD1, p. 406.

Neyra, Rodney [actor/producer] (*né* Rederico Neyra, b . Havana, Cuba, 1896–15 Mar 1962 [66?], Mexico City, Mexico). AS, p. 811.

Nezval, Viteslaw [scenarist] (b. Biskupic, Czechoslovakia, 26 May 1900–6 Apr 1958 [57], Prague, Czechoslovakia). AS, p. 811.

Niblo, Fred, Sr. (father of scenarist Fred Niblo, Jr.) [actor/director] (*né* Federico Nobile, b. York NB, 6 Jan 1874–11 Nov 1948 [74], New Orleans LA; pneumonia). m. (1) Josephine Cohan (b. Providence RI, 1876), 1901 (d. Jul 1916, NYC; son, Fred, Jr., 1903–1973); (2) **Enid Bennett**, Apr 1918, LA CA—div. 1920 (d. 1969). (Ince.) "Fred Niblo Dead; Leader in Films; Noted Director in Silent Era Handled Movies Starring Valentino and Gilbert," *NYT,* 12 Nov 1948, 23:1. "Fred Niblo, Sr.," *Variety,* 17 Nov 1948. "Josephine Cohan," *Variety,* 14 Jul 1916. AMD, p. 261. AS, p. 811. BHD1, p. 406; BHD2, p. 195. IFN, p. 221. Katz, pp. 857–58. Lowrey, p. 136. Truitt, p. 248. "Theatrical Notes," *NYT,* 9 Feb 1915, 9:2 (Mrs. and Mrs. Niblo starred in Australia for the past three years under the management of J.C. Williamson & Co., Ltd., and were to "return to America in June, to appear in a new play under the direction of Cohan & Harris."). "Niblo-Bennett," *MPW,* 23 Mar 1918, 1645. "Niblo Makes Enviable Mark as Ince Director," *MPW,* 14 Feb 1920, 1096. "Read Signs Niblo," *MPW,* 12 Feb 1921, 803. "Niblo to Direct," *MPW,* 26 Mar 1921, 402. "Little Miss Niblo," *MPW,* 27 Aug 1921, 888 (daughter b. 8 Aug 1921). Kenneth McGaffey, "Doug's Director," *MPC,* Oct 1921, 60–61, 88. "Niblo to Form Company," *MPW,* 22 Oct 1921, 900. "Fred Niblo with L.B. Mayer," *MPW,* 29 Oct 1921, 1034. "Niblo Signs with Paramount for Series of Valentino Films," *MPW,* 15 Apr 1922, 724. "Director Niblo to Screen Metro's 'Capt. Applejack,'" *MPW,* 26 Aug 1922, 663. "Niblo Hopes to Complete Metro's 'Ben-Hur' in Spring," *MPW,* 24 Jan 1925, 386. "No Labor Troubles Hindered 'Ben Hur,' Declares Niblo," *MPW,* 21 Feb 1925, 775. Fred Niblo, "Making 'Ben Hur,'" *MPW,* 7 Mar 1925, 69. "Fred Niblo Joins Rank of Master Directors as a Result of Splendid Work in 'Ben Hur,'" *MPW,* 16 Jan 1926, 228. "Fred Niblo Renews with M-G-M," *MPW,* 12 Jun 1926, 539. "To Direct Valentino," *MPW,* 10 Jul 1926, 2. "Predicts Fred Niblo…," *MPW,* 11 Sep 1926, 2. "Fred Niblo Signs Director Contract with Jos. Schenck," *MPW,* 8 Jan 1927, 97.

Nicholls, Norma [actress]. No data found. AMD, p. 261. BHD2, p. 196. "Norma Nicholls with Kalem Forces," *MPW,* 1 Apr 1916, 95. "Norma Nicholls Joins Ruth Roland Company," *MPW,* 3 Apr 1920, 126.

Nichols, Anne [writer/stage actress/scenarist] (b. Dales Mill GA, 26 Nov 1891–15 Sep 1966 [74], Cliff House Nursing Home, Englewood Cliffs NJ; heart attack. Buried at Kensico Cemetery, Valhalla NY). m. actor/producer Henry Duffey, 1915—div. 1924 (1 son, Henry). *Such Is Fame.* "Ann Nichols Is Dead at 75; Auhtor of 'Abie's Irish Rose'; Play Panned by Critics Ran 5 Years Here [22 May 1922–22 Oct 1927; 2,327 performances] and Became Film and Radio Show," *NYT,* 18 Sep 1966, 37:2 ("In 1929, Miss Nichols sued the Universal Pictures Corporation for $3-million. She charged that its film, 'The Cohens and the Kellys' was stolen from 'Abie's Irish Rose.'" She lost the case, the Romeo and Juliet plot deemed too prevalent by then.). "Anne Nichols, 75, Author of 'Abie,' Dies in a Home," *Variety,* 244, 21 Sep 1966, 64:3. BHD, p. 262; BHD2, p.196.

Nichols, Dudley [director/producer/scenarist/composer] (b. Wapakoneta OH, 6 Apr 1895–4 Jan 1960 [64], Los Angeles CA; cancer). AS, p. 812. BHD2, p. 196.

Nichols, George, Jr. (son of **George O. Nichols, Sr.**) [actor/director] (b. San Francisco CA, 5 May 1897–13 Nov 1939 [42], Los Angeles CA; auto accident). AS, p. 812. BHD, p. 262; BHD2, p. 196. IFN, p. 221. Truitt, p. 248.

Nichols, George O., Sr. (father of **George Nichols, Jr.**) [actor/director] (b. Rockford IL, 1864–20 Sep 1927 [62], Los Angeles CA). (Biograph, 1908.) "George Nichols," *Variety,* 28 Sep 1927. "Obituary," *MPW,* 1 Oct 1927, 295. AMD, p. 261. AS, p. 812. BHD, p. 262. IFN, p. 221. Truitt, p. 248. WWS, p. 248. "George Nicholls with Bison," *MPW,* 25 May 1912, 737. "George Nicholls Leaves Gem," *MPW,* 12 Oct 1912, 151. "George Nicholl's New Auto," *MPW,* 24 May 1913, 797. "George Nicholls Joins Sterling Co.," *MPW,* 20 Jun 1914, 1671. Tom Waller, "Nicholls—The Man Who Does Things," *MPW,* 5 Mar 1927, 28–29. George Katchmer, "Remembering the Great Silents," *CI,* 201 (Mar 1992), 40, 58.

Nichols, Guy [actor] (b. 1862?–23 Jan 1928 [66?], Hempstead, LI NY). "Guy Nichols," *Variety,* 25 Jan 1928. AS, p. 812. BHD, p. 262.

Nichols, Mabel [singer/actress] (*née* Mabel Hutchings, b. 1875?–17 Aug 1929 [54], Centreport, LI NY). "Mabel Nichols," *Variety,* 28 Aug 1929. AS, p. 812.

Nichols, Margaret [actress] (*née* Marguerite Nichols, b. Los Angeles CA, 1900?–17 Mar 1941 [41], Los Angeles CA; pneumonia). m. **Hal Roach** (d. 1992). "Mrs. Hal Roach," *Variety,* 19 Mar 1941. "Obituary," *MPW,* 1 Oct 1927, 295. BHD, p. 262. IFN, p. 221. Truitt, p. 248.

Nichols, Nellie V. [actress] (b. NJ, 5 May 1885–16 Jul 1971 [86], Los Angeles CA). AS, p. 812.

Nicholson, John [stage/film actor] (b. Charleston IL, 1873?–24 Jun 1934 [61], New York NY). m. Letta Vance. "John Nicholson," *Variety,* 3 Jul 1934. AS, p. 812. BHD, p. 262. IFN, p. 221. SD.

Nicholson, Kenyon [scenarist] (b. Crawfordsville IN, 21 May 1894-Dec 1986 [92], Trenton NJ). BHD2, p. 196.

Nicholson, Leo [director] (b. Winnipeg, Manitoba, Canada, 1895-Oct 1947 [52?], Vancouver, British Columbia, Canada). BHD2, p. 196.

Nicholson, Lillian [actress] (b. 1881–31 Mar 1949 [68], Los Angeles Co. CA). BHD1, p. 407. IFN, p. 221.

Nicholson, Meredith [writer]. No data found. AMD, p. 261. "Wins Film Rights," *MPW,* 26 Jan 1924, 286.

Nicholson, Nora [actress] (b. Leamington Spa, England, 7 Dec 1889–18 Sep 1973 [83], London, England). AS, p. 812.

Nicholson, Paul [actor] (b. Orange NJ, 23 Mar 1876–2 Feb 1935 [58], Santa Monica CA; influenza). (American Mutoscope and Biograph Co., 1897.) "Paul Nicholson," *Variety,* 5 Feb 1935. AS, p. 812. BHD1, p. 407. IFN, p. 221. Truitt, p. 248.

Nickolaus, John M. [cameraman]. No data found. AMD, p. 261. "John M. Nickolaus," *MPW,* 4 Dec 1926, 339.

Nickols, Walter [actor] (b. 1853?–25 Dec 1927 [74], New York NY; heart attack). "Walter Nickols," *Variety,* 28 Dec 1927. AS, p. 812. BHD, p. 262. IFN, p. 221.

Nicol, John [actor/dancer] (b. 1880–7 Apr 1960 [80?], New York NY). AS, p. 812.

Nicol, Joseph E. [actor] (b. 1856?–31 May 1926 [70?], Bernardsville NJ). m. Irene Wentworth. "Joseph E. Nicol," *Variety*, 9 Jun 1926. AS, p. 812 (d. 1 Jun). BHD, p. 262. Truitt, p. 248.

Nicolle, André [actor] (b. Paris, France, 1 Jun 1885–25 Feb 1945 [59], Paris, France). AS, p. 813.

Niebuhr, Walter F. [executive]. No data found. m. Bennett Johnstone, 16 Sep 1920, NYC. AMD, p. 262. "E.K. Lincoln Signs with American Cinema to Appear in Four Special Features a Year," *MPW*, 23 Aug 1919, 1159. "President of American Cinema Is Wed to Bennett Johnstone," *MPW*, 2 Oct 1920, 619. "American Cinema Again Elects Walter Niebuhr," *MPW*, 12 Feb 1921, 796.

Niederaur, Lillian [actress]. No data found. AMD, p. 262. "Lillian Niederaur," *MPW*, 16 Oct 1915, 456.

Nielsen, Asta, "Die Asta" [actress/producer] (*née* Asta Sofie Amalie Nielsen, b. Copenhagen, Denmark, 11 Nov 1881–24 May 1972 [90], Copenhagen, Denmark). m. 3 times: (1) Urban Gad; (3) 1970. *Die schweigende Muse* (*The Silent Muse*, 1946). (Film debut: *Afgrunden* [*The Abyss*], Sep 1910; Union Co.; Saturn Film Co.) Made 73 silents and 1 sound film (quit films in 1926). "Asta Nielsen," *Variety*, 28 Jun 1972. "Asta Nielsen, Silent Film Star, Dies," *Washington Post*, 26 May 1972. AMD, p. 262. AS, p. 813. BHD1, p. 407; BHD2, p. 196 (b. 11 Sep; d. Frederiksberg, Denmark). IFN, p. 221. Katz, pp. 859–60. "The Asta Nielsen Pictures," *MPW*, 23 Mar 1912, 1054–55. J.A. Fleitzer, "German Trade Notes," *MPW*, 15 Apr 1916, 431:2 (signed with Saturn Film Co.). "Asta Nielsen," *MPW*, 1 Sep 1917, 1350. "Copenhagen Theatre Honors Asta Nielsen," *MPW*, 19 Nov 1921, 297. Marguerite Engberg, "The Erotic Melodrama in Danish Silent Films 1910–1918," *Film History*, 1 Nov 1993, 63–67.

Niemeyer, Bernhardt [stage/film actor]. No data found. (Pathé; Lubin; Kalem; Kinemacolor.) "Gossip of the Studios," *NYDM*, 11 Feb 1914, 40:1.

Niemeyer, Joseph H. [actor/dancer] (b. TX, 14 Jun 1887–27 Sep 1965 [78], Santa Monica CA). AS, p. 813.

Niepce, Joseph-Nicéphore (uncle of **Abel Niepce de Saint-Victor**) [physician/inventor] (b. Chalon-sur-Saone, France, 7 Mar 1765–5 Jul 1833 [68], Saint-Loup-de-Varennes, France). AS, p. 813.

Niepce de Saint-Victor, Abel (nephew of **Joseph-Nicéphore Niepce**) [inventor] (b. Chalon-sur-Saone, France, 1805–1870 [65?], Paris, France). AS, p. 813.

Nieto, José García [actor] (b. Murcie, Spain, 3 May 1902–9 Aug 1982 [80], Huelva, Spain). (Fox.) AS, p. 813. Waldman, p. 213.

Nigh, William S. [stage/film director/producer] (*né* Emil Kreuske, b. Berlin WI, 12 Oct 1881–27 Nov 1955 [74], Burbank CA). (Sennett; Majestic; California Motion Picture Co.; Metro; Columbia; MGM.) AMD, p. 262. AS, p. 813. BHD, p. 262; BHD2, p. 196. IFN, p. 221. Katz, p. 860. "And Still They Come; Metro Secures Services of More Stage Luminaries and Adds to Plays," *NYDM*, 30 Jun 1915, 24:1 (directorial debut at Metro, *A Royal Family*). "William Nigh, Metro Director," *MPW*, 11 Dec 1915, 2021. "Roosevelt Screen Biography Ready," *MPW*, 4 Jan 1919, 60. "William Nigh Directed Lybarger's 'Democracy,'" *MPW*, 24 Apr 1920, 561. "Nigh Expounds on Merits and Appeal of 'School Da¥s,'" *MPW*, 10 Dec 1921, 663. "Exhibitor's Education One of Screen's Most Vital Problems, Says William Nigh," *MPW*, 31 Dec 1921, 1065. "William S. Nigh Gives His Version of Timely Picture," *MPW*, 4 Feb 1922, 520. "William Nigh Will Title All Feature Pictures," *MPW*, 30 Sep 1922, 368. "Will Nigh Arrives at M-G-M Studios on Coast," *MPW*, 3 Apr 1926, 327. "William Nigh," *MPW*, 8 Jan 1927, 113. "Personal Column," *Paris and Hollywood Screen Secrets Magazine*, May 1927, 8 (first attracted attention with his handling of *My Five Years in Germany*). Linda Arvidson, *When the Movies Were Young* (NY: Dover, 1969), p. 9 (for real name). George Katchmer, "William Nigh," *CI*, 226 (Apr 1994), 40.

Night, Harry A. [actor] (b. 1847?–24 Apr 1930 [83?], Los Angeles CA). "Harry A. Night," *Variety*, 30 Apr 1930 (Hank Knight on screen). AS, p. 813. BHD, p. 262. Truitt, p. 248.

Nightingale, Virginia [actress]. No data found. "Wouldn't Stand For It," *LA Times*, 27 Feb 1920, III, p. 4 (playing in William Duncan's Vitagraph serial, *The Silent Avenger*, Nightingale "isn't speaking to her leading man. The reason is that he called her by the same name she used in her comedy days. That name was 'Nightie.'").

Nijinsky, Romola [dance director] (b. Budapest, Hungary, 1892–8 Jun 1978 [86?], Paris, France). BHD2, p. 196.

Nile, Grace Dunbar [actress] (d. 14 Nov 1958, Lakewood CO). BHD, p. 262.

Nillan, M.A. [actor]. No data found. AMD, p. 262. "American Hires More Actors," *MPW*, 1 Jun 1912, 816.

Nillson, Carlotta [actress[(b. Stockholm, Sweden, 1878?–30 Dec 1951 [73], New York NY). "Carlotta Nillson," *Variety*, 9 Jan 1952. AS, p. 814 (d. 31 Dec). BHD, p. 262. IFN, p. 222. SD, p. 245.

Nilsen, Hans Jacob [director] (b. Fredrikstad, Norway, 8 Nov 1897). AS, p. 814.

Nilsson, Anna Q[uirentia] [actress] (b. Ystad, Sweden, 30 Mar 1888–11 Feb 1974 [85], Riverside Co., Hemet CA; heart attack). m. John Marshall Gunnerson, 1923; div. 1925 Emigrated to U.S. in 1905. (Began 1909; Kalem; Fox; Kleine; World; Arrow-Pathé; Ivan; Art Dramas; Selznick; Select.) "Anna Q. Nilsson, Swedish Star in Many Early Films, Dies at 65," *NYT*, 13 Feb 1974, 42:4. "Anna Q. Nilsson," *Variety*, 27 Feb 1974. "Anna Q. Nilsson, Star of Silent Movies, Dies at 55; Career Cut by Accident [thrown from horse, breaking hip, in 1928]," *Los Angeles Times*, 12 Feb 1974. AMD, p. 262. AS, p. 814. BHD1, p. 408. FFF, p. 50. FSS, p. 222. IFN, p. 222. Katz, pp. 860–61. MH, p. 130. MSBB, p. 1040. *Photoplay Arts Portfolio* (Kalem) (b. Mariestadt, Sweden). "Anna Q. Nilsson," *MPW*, 5 Feb 1916, 762. "Anna Nilsson in Pathé's 'Who's Guilty?,'" *MPW*, 29 Apr 1916, 805. "Anna Q. Nilsson Joins Ivan," *MPW*, 2 Sep 1916, 1551. "Anna Q. Nilsson," *MPW*, 31 Mar 1917, 2108. "Director Works Nutty Idea," *MPW*, 14 Sep 1918, 1590. "Stolen Automobile Recovered," *MPW*, 19 Oct 1918, 363. "Three Stars Form Companies," *MPW*, 9 Aug 1919, 807. "Anna Q. Nilsson Incorporates," *MPW*, 17 Jul 1920, 327. "Anna Q. Nillson Finds the Heroine in Metro's 'Temple Dusk' a Weird Being," *MPW*, 15 Jan 1921, 292. Regina Cannon, "The Men That Girls Forget," *MW*, 26 Apr 1924, 3, 29. "Rork Starts Production," *MPW*, 4 Oct 1924, 405. Helen Carlisle, "There's No One Like Her; Anna Nilsson Occupies a Unique Position on the Screen," *MW*, 11 Oct 1924, 7, 27–28. "Nilsson Coming East," *MPW*, 1 Nov 1924, 58. Gladys Hall and Adele Whitely Fletcher, "We Interview Anna Q. Nilsson," *MW*, 3 Jan 1925, 9–11, 29. "Signs Anna Q. Nilsson," *MPW*, 18 Apr 1925, 708. Anna Q. Nilsson, "The True Story of My Life," *MW*, 13 Jun 1925, 16–17, 46; 20 Jun 1925, 22–23, 45 (Querentia means "The Ever Seeking"); 27 Jun 1925, 20–21, 44; 4 Jul 1925, 14–15, 46; 11 Jul 1925, 19–20, 45; 18 Jul 1925, 16–17, 44–45; 25 Jul 1925, 23, 41. "On the Set and Off," *MW*, 12 Sep 1925, 45 (a cable fell on Nilsson's foot and an amputation was threatened). "Anna Q. Leaves First National," *MPW*, 21 May 1927, 175. Gladys Hall, "Confessions of the Stars VI; Anna Q. Nilsson Tells Her Untold Tale," *MPC*, Mar 1929, 16–17, 68, 77. Sue Dibble, "Anna Q. Nilsson Fights Her Way Back to Health; Blonde Actress Recovers from Injury that Made Her an Invalid for Three Years—Many Months of Which Were Spent in Plaster Cast," *Movie Classic*, Nov 1931, 38. Stig Dahlin-Steinhielm, letter, *CI*, 78 (Nov 1981), 14, 60.

Ninchi, Annibale (brother of **Carlo Ninchi**; cousin of actress Ave Ninchi, 1915–1997) [actor] (b. Corfù, Italy, 20 Nov 1887–16 Jan 1967 [79], Pesaro, Italy [extrait de décès no. 13/1]). AS, p. 814 (b. Bologna, Italy). JS, p. 317 (in Italian silents from 1909).

Ninchi, Carlo (brother of **Annibale Ninchi**) [actor] (b. Bologna, Italy, 31 May 1897–29 Apr 1974 [76], Milan, Italy). AS, p. 814.

Niska, Adolf [actor/director] (b. Viipuri, Finland, 17 Feb 1884–3 Mar 1960 [76], Stockholm, Sweden). AS, p. 814.

Nissen, Greta [Ziegfeld girl/actress] (*née* Grethe Ruzt-Nissen, b. Oslo, Norway, 30 Jan 1906–17 May 1988 [82], Montecito CA; Parkinson's disease). (Film debut: *In the Name of Love*, Paramount, 1924.) m. (1) Weldon Heyburn; (2) Stuart D. Eckert. "Greta Nissen," *Variety*, 17 Aug 1988. AMD, p. 262. AS, p. 814 (d. 15 May). BHD1, p. 408 (b. 1905). FSS, p. 222. HCH, p. 109. Katz, p. 861. SD. Dorothy Calhoun, "The Viking's Daughter; From the Danish Royal Ballet to Hollywood Comes Greta Nissen," *MPC*, Jul 1925, 32–33, 77–78. "The Belle of Oslo," *MPC*, Mar 1926, 57. "On the Set and Off," *MM*, May 1926, 90 (her contract with FP-L was broken because of her "pyrotechnical behavior on the set of *A Social Celebrity*"). "On the Set and Off," *Pictures*, Jun 1926, 93 (she moved to Universal.—"her Lasky pictures were failures..."). Ramon Romeo, "Reeling Down Broadway; Greta Nissen in 'No Foolin,'" *Paris and Hollywood*, Oct 1926, 54 (returned to the stage in Ziegfeld's show in an act written by herself, *Lady Bluebeard*. "Greta will return to pictures this fall, bigger and better, or perhaps it is fairer and wiser!"). Lars Moen, "'Flirting—But No More Vam-ping,' Have You Wondered Why Greta Nissen Hasn't Done So Well on the Screen? It's Because They Cast Her as a Vamp Instead of a Comedienne," *MPC*, Nov 1926, 40–41, 80. "Greta Nissen Signed by Caddo Productions," *MPW*, 19 Nov 1927, 25.

Nissen, Helga [actress] (b. 5 Sep 1871–5 Oct 1926 [55], Copenhagen, Denmark). BHD1, p. 614.

Nitter, Erna [actress] (b. Berlin, Germany, 28 Aug 1888–17 Jun 1986 [97], Hamburg, Germany). BHD1, p. 408.

Nivoix, Paul [director/scenarist] (b. Saint-

Denis, France, 24 Dec 1894–1958 [63?], France). AS, p. 814.

Nixon, Charles E. [scenarist/publicist]. No data found. (Selig Polyscope Co.) AMD, p. 262. "Charles E. Nixon Now a Selig Editor," *MPW,* 28 Sep 1912, 1269. F.J. Beecroft, "Publicity Men I Have Met...," *NYDM,* 14 Jan 1914, 48 (*see* Beecroft, Chester for full citation). "Turns to Writing; Charles Nixon, Selig Publicity Man, Resigns to Devote All His Time to Scenarios," *NYDM,* 15 Jul 1914, 25:3 (wrote Selig's *The Coming of Columbus,* "one of the greatest historical films made in America,").

Nixon, Marian [actress: Wampas Star, 1924] (*née* Marion Nixon, b. Superior WI, 20 Oct 1904–13 Feb 1983 [78], Los Angeles CA; complications after open-heart surgery). m. (1) prizefighter Joe Benjamin, 4 Aug 1925-Oct 1926; (2) Edward Hillman, Jr., 11 Aug 1929-Mar 1933; (3) **William A. Seiter**, 16 Aug 1934 (d. 1964; 3 children); (4) **Ben Lyon**, Apr 1972 (d. 1979). (Film debut: bits; *Rosita,* 1923.) "Marian Nixon, 78, Actress; Tracy's First Leading Lady," *NYT,* 17 Feb 1983, D23:5 (d. Hollywood). "Marian Nixon," *Variety,* 23 Feb 1983. AMD, p. 262. AS, p. 815. BHD1, p. 408. BR, pp. 185–88. FSS, p. 223. Katz, p. 862. MH, p. 130 (b. Superior WI). "New Leading Lady in 'Big Dan,'" *MPW,* 20 Oct 1923, 683. Ramon Romeo, "Reeling Down Broadway," *Paris and Hollywood,* Sep 1926, 59–60 (Joe Benjamin was offered the lead in *Is Zat So?* He will "get so tired of fighting behind the ropes that he won't want to fight at home! Some marriages have advantages!"). "Marian Nixon Signed," *MPW,* 11 Dec 1926, 419. "Marian Nixon," *MPW,* 14 May 1927, 100. Helen Carlisle, "Nix-On Matrimony—Maybe; Marian Has Her Say on the Marital Problems," *MPC,* Mar 1928, 55, 81. Murray Summers, "Marion Nixon Talkes About Her Films," *Filmograph,* V, No. 1 (1976), 30–37. Buck Rainey, "Marion Nixon; Innocence Was Her Forte," *CI,* 127 (Jan 1986), 27–28; 128 (Feb 1985), C10-C12. George Katchmer, "Forgotten Cowboys and Cowgirls—Part IX," *CI,* 181 (Jul 1990), 56.

Noa, Julian [actor] (b. Boston MA, 1879–26 Nov 1958 [79?], New York NY). AS, p. 815. BHD, p. 262.

Noa, Manfred [actor/director] (b. Berlin, Germany, 22 Mar 1893–5 Dec 1930 [37], Berlin, Germany; appendectomy). "Manfred Noa," *Variety,* 10 Dec 1930. AS, p. 815 (b. 22 Sep-d. 8 Dec). BHD1, p. 614; BHD2, p. 196. IFN, p. 222.

Nobello, Arnold *see* **Toto**

Noble, John W. [actor/director/producer] (b. Albemarle County VA, 24 Jun 1880). (Goldwyn.) AMD, p. 262. AS, p. 815. BHD2, p. 196. Lowrey, p. 138. 1921 Directory, p. 272. Spehr, p. 156. "Jack Noble Goes Mutual," *MPW,* 27 Dec 1913, 1556. "John W. Noble," *MPW,* 17 Apr 1915, 371. "Noble Likes Work of Valli Valli," *MPW,* 24 Apr 1915, 572. "John Noble Finishes 'One Million Dollars,'" *MPW,* 16 Oct 1915, 422. "Bushman and Bayne Have New Director," *MPW,* 18 Dec 1915, 2157. "Noble to Produce Independently," *MPW,* 7 Jul 1917, 100. "Noble Back Again," *MPW,* 24 Nov 1917, 1194. "Noble Becomes a Vitagraph Director," *MPW,* 2 Aug 1919, 697.

Nobles, Dolly (sister of opera singer Lora Belline) [vaudeville/stage/film actress] (*née* Dolly Woolvine, b. Cincinnati OH, 1863–6 Oct 1930 [67], 139 First Place, Brooklyn NY; heart ailment). m. Milton Nobles, ca. 1880 (d. ca. 1925). "Dolly Nobles," *Variety,* 100, 15 Oct 1930, 68:5. BHD, p. 262. IFN, p. 222.

Nobles, Milton, Jr. (son of **Milton Nobles, Sr.**) [actor] (b. Brooklyn NY, 1892?–22 Feb 1925 [32], Chester PA; suicide by poison). m. Norma Farnsworth. "Milton Nobles, Jr.," *Variety,* 25 Feb 1925. AS, p. 815. BHD, p. 262. SD, p. 940.

Nobles, Milton, Sr. (father of **Milton Nobles, Jr.**) [actor/playwright] (*né* Milton Tamey, b. Almont MI, 28 Sep 1847–14 Jun 1924 [76], Brooklyn NY; apoplexy). m. Dollie Woolwine, Jun 1881. "Milton Nobles, Actor; Had Been Playing Up to Friday, in 'She Stoops to Conquer,'" *NYT,* 15 Jun 1924, 23:2. "Milton Nobles," *Variety,* 18 Jun 1924 (b. 1844; stage debut: *Hamlet,* 13 Apr 1867, Cincinnati OH). AS, p. 815 (b. Cincinnati OH, 15 Dec 1843). AS, p. 815 (b. Cincinnati OH, 15 Dec 1843). BHD, p. 262. IFN, p. 222. SD. Truitt, p. 248.

Nobles, William W. [cameraman]. No data found. AMD, p. 262. FDY, p. 465. "William W. Nobles," *MPW,* 26 Feb 1927, 635.

Noda, Kogo [scenarist] (b. Hakodate, Japan, 17 Nov 1893–23 Sep 1968 [74], Tokyo, Japan; myocardial infarction). AS, p. 815.

Noe, Yvan [director/producer] (*né* Marie Edgar Jean Noetinger, b. Nancy, France, 18 May 1895–7 Jul 1963 [68], Nice, France). m. **Pierrette Caillol** (d. 1991). AS, p. 815.

Noel, Billy [actor] (b. Canada, 1885–13 Aug 1969 [84?], New Rochelle NY). BHD, p. 262.

Noel, Lelia [actress]. No data found. (California Motion Picture Manufacturing Co.) Richard V. Spencer, "With the Western Producers," *MPW,* 8 Jul 1911, 1576 (joined the CMPM Co. at Long Beach CA).

Noel, Mason [director]. No data found. (Universal.)

Noel, Robert [actor] (b. Bourges, France, 24 Dec 1899). AS, p. 815.

Noel, Rose F. [scenarist] (b. 1882–16 Jun 1950 [68?], Santa Monica CA). AS, p. 815.

Noel-Noel [actor/director/scenarist] (*né* Lucien Edouard Noel, b. Paris, France, 9 Aug 1897–5 Oct 1989 [92], Nice, France [extrait de décès no. 4532/1989]). AS, p. 815 (d. 4 Oct). BHD2, p. 196.

Noemi, Lea [actress] (b. 1883–6 Nov 1973 [90?], New York NY). AS, p. 816.

Noges, Nettie [stage/film actress]. No data found. (Began 1911; Centaur.) AMD, p. 262. "Horsley's Latest Star," *NYDM,* 16 Sep 1914, 31:2. "Nettie Noges," *MPW,* 26 Sep 1914, 1758.

Nolan, Alice [stage/film actress] (b. 1888–24 Nov 1930 [42?], Harbor Sanitarium, New York NY; cerebral hemorrhage brought on by grippe and other complications). m. stage producer Sam H. Harris. (Stage debut: *Little Johnny Jones,* 1904, NYC.) "Mrs. Sam H. Harris," *Variety,* 100, 26 Nov 1930, 68:2. BHD, p. 193.

Nolan, Harry T. [producer] (b. Chicago IL, 25 Jul 1871–1 Jul 1944 [72], Denver CO). BHD2, p. 197.

Nolan, Mary [actress] (*née* Mary Imogene Robertson, aka Imogene "Bubbles" Wilson, b. Louisville KY, 18 Dec 1905–31 Oct 1948 [42], Los Angeles CA; found dead). "Mary Nolan Dies; Won Follies Fame; Former Bubbles Wilson, 42, Was Ill of Malnutrition Recently in Hollywood," *NYT,* 1 Nov 1948, 29:2. "Mary Nolan," *Variety,* 3 Nov 1948. AMD, p. 262. AS, p. 816. BHD1, p. 409. FSS, p. 223. IFN, p. 222. Katz, p. 863 (began in Germany, 1925). Truitt, pp. 248–49. "Mary Nolan Transfers Contract to Universal," *MPW,* 22 Oct 1927, 497. DeWitt Bodeen, "The Hard Luck Girl," *FIR,* May 1980, 273–82. Cliff Howe, "Mary Nolan; A Real Battler," *CI,* 114 (Dec 1984), C12.

Nolan, Robert. (K&E). No data found.

Nolan, William C. [animator] (b. 1894–6 Dec 1954 [60?], Sawtelle CA; during surgery). AS, p. 816. BHD2, p. 197 (d. 1956). Adrien Falnieres, "Making the Cartoons Move," *Cinema Arts,* Nov 1926, 26–27, 47–48.

Nolbandov, Sergei [director/producer/scenarist] (b. Russia, 1895–1971 [76?], England). AS, p. 816.

Noldan, Svend [director] (*né* Heinrich August Noldan, b. Bad Nauheim, Germany, 25 Apr 1893–1978 [85?], Germany). AS, p. 816.

Noll, Karel [actor] (b. Duetschbrod, Czechoslovakia, 4 Nov 1880–29 Feb 1928 [47], Prague, Czechoslovakia). "Karl Noll," *Variety,* XC, 28 Mar 1928, 57:3 ("Karl Noll, Czech picture actor, died at Prague."). AS, p. 816 (Karl Noll). BHD1, p. 614 (Karl Noll). IFN, p. 222.

Noll, Louise M. [actress] (b. 1884–1 Nov 1944 [60?], Los Angeles CA). AS, p. 816.

Nomis, Leo [stuntman] (b. IN, 5 May 1892–5 Feb 1932 [39], Los Angeles CA). "Stunt Flyer Killed; Leo Nomis Dies Filming 'Sky Bride' for Par," *Variety,* 9 Feb 1932. AS, p. 816. BHD1, p. 409. IFN, p. 222.

Nonguet, Lucien [director] (b. France, 1868). AS, p. 816.

Noon, Paisley [actor] (b. Los Angeles CA, 1897?–27 Mar 1932 [35], Los Angeles CA; complications after an appendectomy). (Universal.) "Paisley Noon," *Variety,* 5 Apr 1932. AS, p. 816. BHD, p. 409. IFN, p. 222. Truitt, p. 249.

Noonan, Patrick [actor] (b. Dublin, Ireland, 9 Jan 1887–19 May 1962 [75], Wokingham, England). AS, p. 816. BHD1, p. 409.

Noonan, William [makeup artist] (b. 1896–25 Apr 1941 [45?], Los Angeles CA). BHD2, p. 197.

Norbert, René [actor/producer] (*né* Raoul Ottavi, b. Algiers, 1889). AS, p. 816.

Norcross, Frank M. [stage/film actor] (b. Boston MA, 10 Jul 1857–12 Sep 1926 [69], Glendale CA). (K&E.) "Frank Norcross," *Variety,* 22 Sep 1926 (age 70; "veteran character actor"). "Obituary," *MPW,* 2 Oct 1926, 2. AMD, p. 262. AS, p. 816. BHD, p. 263. IFN, p. 222. MSBB, p. 1026. Truitt, p. 249.

Norcross, Hale [actor] (b. San Francisco CA, 1877?–15 Oct 1947 [70], New York NY; pneumonia). m. Florence Simmons, 1903 (d. 1941). "Hale Norcross, 70, Veteran of Stage," *NYT,* 17 Oct 1947, 21:2. "Hale Norcross," *Variety,* 22 Oct 1947. AS, p. 816. IFN, p. 222.

Nord, Hilda [actress]. No data found. AMD, p. 262. "Hilda Nord," *MPW,* 31 Mar 1917, 2084.

Norden, Virginia [actress]. No data found. AMD, p. 262. "Virginia Norden Now with Vitagrpah," *MPW,* 12 Feb 1916, 963. "Virginia Norden Joins Balboa," *MPW,* 15 Apr 1916, 420.

Nordensskiold, Sten [director] (b. Sweden, 21 Sep 1889). AS, p. 817.

Nordhaus, Gosta [director] (b. Dusseldorf, Germany, 8 Jan 1899). AS, p. 817.

Nordhoff, Charles [actor/scenarist] (b. London, England, 1887–11 Apr 1947 [60?], Montecito CA). AS, p. 817.

Nordlinger, Victor [casting director]. No data found. AMD, p. 263. "Victor Nordlinger," *MPW,* 10 Sep 1927, 92.

Nordqvist, Gustav Lazarus [composer] (b. Stockholm, Sweden, 12 Feb 1886–28 Jan 1949 [62], Stockholm, Sweden). AS, p. 817.

Nordstrom, Clarence A. [actor] (b. Chicago IL, 13 Mar 1893–13 Dec 1968 [75], East Orange NJ). m. Maude Posner. "Clarence Nordstrom, 75; Retired Actor and Comic," *NYT,* 15 Dec 1968, 86:3. "Clarence Nordstrom," *Variety,* 18 Dec 1968. AS, p. 817. BHD1, p. 409. IFN, p. 222. Truitt, p. 249 (d. 1 Dec).

Nordstrom, Frances [scenarist]. No data found. FDY, p. 435.

Nores, Gaston [actor] (b. France, 1895). AS, p. 817.

Noriega, Manuel [actor/director] (*né* Manolo Noriega Ruiz, b. Mexico, 24 Jul 1880–12 Aug 1961 [81], Mexico City, Mexico). AS, p. 817 (Manolo Noriega). IFN, p. 222. Waldman, p. 214.

Norman, Amber [actress] (b. UT, 6 Jun 1901–21 Oct 1972 [71], Los Angeles CA). (Hal Roach.) AS, p. 817. BHD1, p. 409. IFN, p. 222.

Norman, George [producer] (b. 1887–19 May 1943 [56?], Los Angeles CA). AS, p. 817. BHD2, p. 197.

Norman, Gertrude [actress] (b. London, England, 19 May 1848–20 Jul 1943 [95], Los Angeles CA). "Gertrude Norman," *Variety,* 28 Jul 1943. AMD, p. 263. AS, p. 817. BHD1, p. 409. IFN, p. 222. Truitt, p. 249. "In Auto Accident," *MPW,* 1 Jan 1921, 93. "'Mother' of Early Stars Is Film Grandma Now," *The Arizona Daily Star,* 29 Jul 1935 (age 83).

Norman, Josephine [actress] (*née* Josephine Arrich, b. Vienna, Austria, 12 Nov 1904–24 Jan 1951 [46], Roslyn, LI NY). m. **Herbert Rawlinson** (d. 1953). "Mrs. Josephine Rawlins," *Variety,* 31 Jan 1951. AMD, p. 263. BHD, p. 263. IFN, p. 222. Truitt, p. 249. "DeMille Signs New Beauty," *MPW,* 20 Jun 1925, 894.

Norman, Karin (sister of **Lillian Walker**) [actress] (*née* Karin Walker). No data found. (Vitagraph.) "In the Picture Studios; Karin Walker Norman [with photo]," *NYDM,* 18 Dec 1915, 34:4 (in films from 1911. "Very shortly her present contract with the Vitagrpah company expires, and as yet she has not decided definitely on any future plans for picture work.").

Norman, Richard E. [filmmaker] (b. 1891–1961). Matthew Bernstein and Dana F. White, "'Scratching Around' in a 'Fit of Insanity': The Norman Film Manufacturing Company and the Race Film Business in the 1920s," *Griffithiana,* 62/63 (May 1998), pp. 81–127.

Norman, Rolla [actor] (*né* Edouard Charles Normand, b. Paris, France, 24 Jun 1889–18 Nov 1971 [82], Buc, France). (MGM; 1st National; WB.) AS, p. 817. Waldman, p. 215.

Normand, Claire [actress] (b. Paris, France, 1891). BHD, p. 263.

Normand, Mabel Ethelreid [actress/director] (aka Mabel Fortescue, b. Staten Island NY, 9 Nov 1892–23 Feb 1930 [37], Monrovia CA; tuberculosis). m. **Lew Cody** (d. 1934). Betty Harper Fussell, *Mabel* (New Haven: Ticknor & Fields, 1982), p. 21. William Thomas Sherman, *Mabel Normand: A Source Book to Her Life and Films* (Seattle WA: Cinema Books, 1994). (Biograph; Vitagraph; Keystone; Goldwyn.) "Mabel Normand, Film Star, Dead; The Comedienne Succumbs to Tuberculosis in California Sanitarium; Conscious to the Last; Began Career as Artists' Model, Intending to Study Art—Went into Movies by Chance," *NYT,* 24 Feb 1930, 1:7, 21:4 (b. 10 Nov 1897, age 33). "Mabel Normand," *Variety,* 26 Feb 1930 (b. Quebec, Canada, 10 Nov 1894; age 35). AMD, p. 263. AS, p. 817 {b. Boston MA, 10 Nov 1894). BHD, p. 263. FFF, p. 179 (b. Boston MA, 10 Nov 1894). IFN, p. 222 (b. Boston, 1894). Katz, p. 864. Lowrey, p. 140 (b. Atlanta GA). MH, p. 130 (b. Staten Island NY, 10 Nov). MSBB, p. 1040 (b. Boston). 1921 Directory, p. 234 (b. Boston). SD. Spehr, p. 156 (b. Boston, 1894). Truitt, p. 249 (b. Boston, 10 Nov 1894). WWS, p. 145 (b. Atlanta). "Miss Normand, Director," *MPW,* 13 Dec 1913, 1289. "Mabel Normand, Key to Many Laughs in Keystone Comedies," *MPW,* 11 Jul 1914, 239. "Gossip of the Studios," *NYDM,* 12 Aug 1914, 27:2 (she denied she was married: "Not a wedding bell in the whole city of Los Angeles or any other city ever struck a note in my behalf."). W.E. Wing, "Along the Pacific Coast," *NYDM,* 14 Apr 1915, 26:2 (a local newspaper published her "marriage [!] and the Keystone star immediately accumulated strenuous thoughts of homicide. Mabel is a good fellow but she wishes to do her own marrying if the time ever comes."). "Mabel Normand Seriously Ill," *MPW,* 9 Oct 1915, 274. J. Van Cartmell, "Along the Pacific Coast," *NYDM,* 6 Nov 1915, 3:3 ("fully recovered from her recent illness," vacationing in San Francisco). J. Van Cartmell, "Film News from the Coast...," *NYDM,* 20 Nov 1915, 32:4 ("recently recovered from the effects of an almost fatal accident and who has been enjoying a vacation at the San Francisco Exposition during her convalescence," was to leave for New York for a series of pictures directed by Fatty Arbuckle, accompanied by Ferris Hartman, Al St. John, and others.) "Fatty and Mabel's New Year," *MPW,* 8 Jan 1916, 251. "Mabel Normand in Wider Field," *MPW,* 8 Apr 1916, 273. "Mabel Normand Leaves for Culver City," *MPW,* 29 Apr 1916, 8C6. "Mabel Normand Will Have Studio of Her Own," *MPW,* 13 May 1916, 1151. "Mabel Normand Back at Work," *MPW,* 3 Jun 1916, 1693–94. "Mabel Normand Has New 'Dressing Table,'" *MPW,* 11 Nov 1916, 882. "Her Day of Rest," *MPW,* 18 Nov 1916, 995. "Mabel Normand," *MPW,* 3 Mar 1917, 1355. "Goldwyn Seeks to Enjoin Mabel Normand," *MPW,* 21 Jul 1917, 468. "Goldwyn and Mabel Normand Good Friends Again," *MPW,* 11 Aug 1917, 925. "Congratulations Follow Normand Engagement," *MPW,* 18 Aug 1917, 1094. "Crowds See Moving Pictures Made," *MPW,* 8 Dec 1917, 1493. "Goldwyn Again Signs Mabel Normand," *MPW,* 25 May 1918, 1126. "Mabel Normand on Song Cover," *MPW,* 10 May 1919 (*Kentucky Dream*). "Mabel Normand Renews Contract," *MPW,* 22 Nov 1919, 451. "Mabel Normand Wins in Contest," *MPW,* 6 Mar 1920, 1663. "Mabel Normand Pictures Are Limited to Three a Season; 'Slim Princess' Ready," *MPW,* 19 Jun 1920, 1608. "Mabel Normand Quits Goldwyn for Sennett," *MPW,* 12 Feb 1921, 797. "Evades Greeters," *MPW,* 12 Nov 1921, 163. "Sennett Closes Deal wi Associated to Distribute Mabel Normand Series," *MPW,* 11 Aug 1923, 465. "Mabel Normand Likes Her Part," *MPW,* 18 Aug 1923, 579. "Mabel Normand Scales New Artistic Heights," *MPW,* 10 Nov 1923, 250. "Two Movie Stars See C.S. Dines Shot; Edna Purviance and Mabel Normand in His Apartment When Oil Operator Is Wounded; Chauffeur Admits Firing; Declares He Wanted to Get Miss Normand, His Employer, Away and Feared Attack by Dines," *NYT,* 2 Jan 1924, pp. 1–2 (Courtland S. Dines, 35, was shot by H.A. Kelly, alias R.C. Greer, at 9:30 p.m. A .25 calibre bullet lodged in his chest but did not puncture either lung. "After the shooting, Miss Purviance and Miss Normand were taken to the Central Police Station, where they wept copiously until their release after questioning."). "Blame Jealousy for Dines Shooting; Los Angeles Police Think the Chauffeur Was Infatuated with Miss Normand; She Contradicts His Story; Breaks Down from Excitement and Goes to Hospital—Dines Develops Pneumonia," *NYT,* 3 Jan 1924, pp. 1–4 (Normand claimed that she was in another room when shots were fired, helping to hook up Purviance's evening gown. She ridiculed the theory that Greer was infatuated with her: "Impossible!' she exclaimed. "The man must have been insane. He was only one of my servants and was treated like one..." Normand was to have had her appendix out this day. The bullet had pierced a lung after all. Dines: "...and then in walks this moron hop-head. He must be a hop, and what's all the shooting for?"); "[Will] Hays Leaves for Pacific; But Denies Return Has Anything to Do with Dines Shooting," p. 4:3; "Normand Family Shocked; Actress's Father and Mother, in Staten Island, Regret Notoriety," p. 4:3. "Miss Normand Rests After an Operation; She Goes Under Knife for Appendicitis—Dines, in Same Hospital [Good Samaritan], Is Expected to Recover," *NYT,* 4 Jan 1924, 7:5 (Greer was charged with "assault with a deadly weapon, with intent to kill." He denied using habit-forming narcotics. Will Hays was not going to ignore the Mabel Normand-Edna Purviance-Courtland-Dines escapade: "...I am going to California—forthwith—and I have my chin out."). "Miss Normand Asks Public for Fair Play; Wants Censors to Withhold Judgment Until the Truth Is Told," *NYT,* 5 Jan 1924, 3:1 (Greer was arraigned with a hearing set for 11 Jan. Bonds were placed at $10,000, "and he was removed to the County Jail."). "Courtland Dines Better; Mabel Normand Is Also Reported to Be "Doing Nicely,'" *NYT,* Sec. II, 5:2 (the MPPDA would take no action on Normand's pictures because "[t]he producers of Mabel Normand pictures are not members of the producers' organization."). "No Ban on Normand Films; New York Commission Also Refuses to Bar Miss Purviance," *NYT,* 8 Jan 1924, 25:6 ("...public sentiment here did not warrant any action."). "Ohio Bars Normand Films; Massachusetts Theatres Ask Ban—Kansas Governor Halts Censors," *NYT,* 10 Jan 19224, 18:1 (Purviance's films were also banned). "Miss Normand Collapses; Unable to Testify at Hearing in Dines Shooting Case," *NYT,* 19 Jan 1924, 10:2 (Purviance insisted she never saw Greer. Greer's bail was reduced to $5,000). "Mabel Normand Defiant on Stand; Insists on 'Telling All' at Hearing on Shooting of C.S. Dines by Her Chauffeur," *NYT,* 22 Jan 1924, 21:6 (she failed to identify her own gun). "Judge Raps Evidence of shooting on Dines; Declares There Seems to Be a Conspiracy to Keep Facts from the Court," *NYT,* 23 Jan 1924, 21:7. "Public Sentiment, After Outcry, Rallies to Defend Normand Films," *MPW,* 26 Jan 1924, 273. "Court Orders Inquiry into Dines's Disability; Anonymous Letters Tell Judge That Victim of Shooting Is Not as Ill as Reported," *NYT,* 7 Feb

1924, 19:4. "Miss Normand in East," *MPW,* 22 Mar 1924, 287. T. Howard Kelly, "'Would I Have Been Happier If I'd Been Married?,' Asks Mabel Normand," *MV,* 19 Apr 1924, 4–5. "On the Set and Off," *MW,* 15 Sep 1924, 19, 26 (Normand filed a $500,000 libel suit against Mrs. Norman W. Church, whose husband she met in a hospital the previous year). "On the Set and Off," *MW,* V, 21 Feb 1925, 34 (Normand was exonerated of the charges brought by Mrs. Norman W. Church). "Mabel Normand," *MPW,* 27 Mar 1926, 273. "Hal Roach Signs Mabel Normand," *MPW,* 15 May 1926, 247. "Mabel Normand and Lew Cody," *MPW,* 2 Oct 1926, 280 (married). "Mabel Normand Explains Title," *MPW,* 18 Dec 1926, 510. "Miss Normand Recovering," *MPW,* 26 Feb 1927, 617. "Flashes from Filmland," *Paris and Hollywood Screen Secrets Magazine,* Aug 1927, 10 ("Mabel Normand crashed into the studio limelight again the other day, but this time only as a visitor. Her host was her husband, Lew Cody. Cameramen were on hand to help greet this once famous star."). "Mabel Normand's Condition Improving," *MPW,* 13 Aug 1927, 449. Sam Peeples, "Madcap; The Story of Mabel Normand," *CFC,* 26 (Winter, 1970), 7–10, 15; Part 2, 27, 24–27; Part 3, 28, 21–24; Part 4, 29, 26–29 (includes filmography). Bruce Long, "The Battle of Mack and Mabel," *CI,* 116 (Feb 1985), 56–58. William T. Sherman, "Love and Courage: A Look at the Films and Career of Mabel Normand," *CI,* 185 (Nov 1990), 48–52, 58; Part II, 186 (Dec 1990), 7 ff.; Part III, 187 (Jan 1991), 40–44; Part IV, Filmography (with Don Schneider), 188 (Feb 1991), 38, 40–42; "Filmography Update," 205 (Jul 1992), 36–38, 57; "Filmography Update; The Films of Mabel Normand, Part II," 206 (Aug 1992), 36–37, 59. Robert Edwards, "A Movie Lover's Guide to Cemeteries of Los Angeles," *Films of the Golden Age,* #1 (Summer 1995), pp. 56–60 (Normand was buried in Calvary Cemetery in East Los Angeles; other stars' burial places are cited). Tony Crnkovich," *Molly O'*: Lost Film Found [at Gosfilmofond, Russia]," *CI,* 255 (Sep 1996), 5; "Mabel N. and *Molly O',*" *CI,* 255 (Sep 1996), 5- 6. Stephen Burstin, "Mabel Normand's Remaining Effects Examined," *CI,* 267 (Sep 1997), 22–23 (discusses personal effects of the star bought at an auction.). Ben Brantley, "Pie Fights, Keystone Kops and Pain; A stormy love story from the era of silent movies," *NYT,* 3 Jul 1999, B19 (review of revived play, *Mack and Mabel* [1974], book by Michael Stewart revised by his sister, Francine Pascal, directed by Julianne Boyd. "And for a work about creating comedy, it is almost never funny.").

Normanly, James P. [producer] (b. 1894–10 May 1947 [53?], Los Angeles CA). BHD2, p. 197.

Noro, Line [actress] (*née* Aline Simonne Noro, b. Houdelaincourt, France, 22 Feb 1900–4 Nov 1985 [85], Paris, France). AS, p. 817.

Norr, Roy M. [publicist] (b. 1886–18 Mar 1962 [76?], New York NY). BHD2, p. 197.

Norrie, Claude [actor] (b. Scotland, 1872–10 May 1916 [44?], Chicago IL). BHD, p. 263. IFN, p. 222.

Norris, Anna [actress] (*née* Anna Petterson, b. Stockholm, Sweden, 1860-Jul 1957 [97?]). AS, p. 818 (Anna Norrie). BHD, p. 263.

Norris, Charles G. [writer]. No data found. AMD, p. 263. "Author of 'Brass' Discusses Novel adaptation for Screen," *MPW,* 8 Apr 1922, 634.

Norris, Kathleen [writer]. No data found. AMD, p. 263. "Kathleen Norris Praises Screen Version of Story," *MPW,* 7 Feb 1920, 919. "Kathleen Norris Signed to Write for Goldwyn," *MPW,* 12 Mar 1921, 166.

Norris, William [stage/film actor] (*né* William Norris Block, b. New York NY, 15 Jun 1870–20 Mar 1929 [58], West Bronxville NY). m. Mabel Mordaunt. "William Norris," *Variety,* 27 Mar 1929 (age 57). AS, p. 818. BHD, p. 263. IFN, p. 222. SD. Truitt, pp. 249–50.

North, Bob [actor] (*né* Harold Young, b. Decatur IL, 11 Sep 1885–18 Mar 1936 [50], Los Angeles CA; suicide by inhaling gas). "Bob North," *Variety,* 25 Mar 1936 ("Inability to find work said by police to have prompted his act"). AS, p. 818. BHD1, p. 409. IFN, p. 222.

North, Joseph B. [actor] (b. England, 27 Dec 1873–8 Jan 1945 [71], Woodland Hills CA). "Joseph B. North," *Variety,* 17 Jan 1945. AS, p. 818. BHD1, p. 409. IFN, p. 222. Truitt, p. 250.

North, Robert [actor/producer] (aka Bobby North, b. New York NY, 2 Feb 1884–13 Aug 1976 [92], Los Angeles CA; heart attack). m. Stella Maury. "Robert North," *Variety,* 25 Aug 1976. AS, p. 818. BHD, p. 263; BHD2, p. 197. IFN, p. 222.

North, Tom [producer] (b. Hamilton OH, 1875–22 May 1951 [76?], Chicago IL). AS, p. 818.

North, Wilfred (or Wilfrid) [stage/film actor/director/scenarist] (*né* Wilfrid Northcroft, b. London, England, 16 Jan 1863–3 Jun 1935 [72], Los Angeles CA). (Vitagraph, 1915.) "Wilfrid North," *Variety,* 12 Jun 1935. AMD, p. 263. AS, p. 818. BHD1, p. 409; BHD2, p. 197. IFN, p. 223. Lowrey, p. 142. MSBB, p. 1046. 1921 Directory, p. 272. SD. Slide, p. 146. Truitt, p. 250 (b. 1853). "North Recovering," *MPW,* 27 Sep 1913, 1372. "Wilfred North Out of Danger," *MPW,* 11 Oct 1913, 134. "North Will Play J.R. Wallingford," *MPW,* 16 Apr 1921, 748. "Noted Additions to Cast of 'The Happy Warrior,'" *MPW,* 25 Apr 1925, 808. George Katchmer, "Remembering the Great Silents," *CI,* 248 (Feb 1996), 47.

Northcote, Sidney W. [director] (b. 3 Nov 1897–15 May 1968 [70], London, England). BHD2, p. 197.

Northpole, John [actor] (*né* John Kovacevich, b. Yugoslavia, 23 Dec 1892–26 Feb 1964 [71], Los Angeles Co. CA). BHD, p. 263. IFN, p. 223.

Northrup, Harry S[tabo] [stage/film actor] (*né* Henri Stabo Wallace Northrup, b. Paris, France, 31 Jul 1875–2 Jul 1936 [60], Los Angeles CA). m. **Merceita Esmonde** (d. 1929). (Vitagraph; Metro; Edison; FP-L; Artcraft.) AMD, p. 263. AS, p. 818. BHD1, p. 409. IFN, p. 223. MH, p. 130. MSBB, p. 1026. Slide, pp. 146–47. "Harry S. Northrup," *MPW,* 8 Aug 1914, 825. "Harry Northrup," *Motion Picture Magazine,* Jan 1915, 117 (b. 1877). "Harry S. Northrup," *MPW,* 24 Feb 1917, 1165. "Harry S. Northrup," *MPW,* 25 May 1918, 1149. George Katchmer, "Harry S. Northrup," *CI,* 226 (Apr 1994), 40.

Norton, Barry [actor] (*né* Alfredo Carlos de Birben, b. Buenos Aires, Argentina, 16 Jun 1905–25 Aug 1956 [51], Los Angeles CA; heart attack). (Fox; Paramount.) "Barry Norton," *Variety,* 5 Sep 1956 (d. 24 Aug). AS, p. 818 (d. 24 Aug). BHD1, p. 409 (b. 1909). FSS, p. 224. IFN, p. 223 (b. 1909). Katz, p. 865 (b. 1905). Truitt, p. 250. Madeline Matzen, "A Young Blood from the Pampas," *MPC,* May 1927, 63, 91.

Norton, Cecil A. [actor/TV scriptwriter] (b. 1895?–30 Nov 1955 [60], Los Angeles CA). "Cecil A. Norton," *Variety,* 7 Dec 1955 ("vet motion picture actor and TV writer"). AS, p. 818. BHD, p. 263; BHD2, p. 197. IFN, p. 223. Truitt, p. 250.

Norton, Edgar [actor] (*né* Harry Mills, b. London, England, 11 Aug 1868–6 Feb 1953 [84], Woodland Hills). AS, p. 818. BHD1, p. 409. IFN, p. 223.

Norton, Elda [actress] (b. Ontario, Canada, 21 Apr 1891–15 Apr 1947 [55], Los Angeles CA). "Elda Norton," *Variety,* 23 Apr 1947 (age 56). AS, p. 818. BHD, p. 263. IFN, p. 223.

Norton, Fletcher [actor] (b. San Francisco CA, 4 Aug 1877–3 Oct 1941 [64], Los Angeles CA; heart attack). "Fletcher Norton," *Variety,* 8 Oct 1941 (began ca. 1926). AS, p. 818. BHD1, p. 410. IFN, p. 263. IFN, p. 223. Truitt, p. 250.

Norton, Frederick [actor/singer] (b. Manchester, England, 1875–15 Dec 1946 [71?]). AS, p. 818. BHD, p. 263; BHD2, p. 197. IFN, p. 223.

Norton, Henry Field [actor] (b. Jeffersonville IN, 12 Dec 1891–10 Aug 1945 [53], Los Angeles CA; complications after surgery). "Henry Field Norton," *Variety,* 15 Aug 1945 (a founder of Screen Extras Guild). AS, p. 818.

Norton, Jack [actor] (*né* Mortimer J. Naughton, b. Brooklyn NY, 2 Sep 1889–15 Oct 1958 [69], Saranac Lake NY [Will Rogers Hospital]; complications from respiratory problems). m. Lucille Healy. "Jack Norton, Comedian, Is Dead at 69; Played 'Lovable Drunk' in 200 Films," *NYT,* 16 Oct 1958, 37:2. "Jack Norton," *Variety,* 22 Oct 1958. AS, p. 818. IFN, p. 223.

Norton, Lucille [actress] b. 1894–17 Jun 1959 [65?], Beverly Hills CA). AS, p. 818.

Norton, Captain Richard [director/executive] (b. London, England, 2 Apr 1892–12 Jul 1954 [62], London, England). BHD2, p. 197.

Norton, Stephen B. [cinematographer] (b. Palmyra NY, 13 Oct 1877–14 Mar 1951 [73], Los Angeles CA). BHD2, p. 197. FDY, p. 465.

Norwood, Eille [actor] (*né* Anthony Brett, b. Yorkshire, England, 11 Oct 1861–24 Dec 1948 [87], London, England). AS, p. 819. BHD, p. 263. IFN, p. 223.

Norworth, Jack [actor/composer] (b. Philadelphia PA, 5 Jan 1879–1 Sep 1959 [80], Laguna Beach CA; heart attack). m. Nora Bayes, 1907–13; Dorothy Adelphi; **Louise Dresser** (d. 1965); (5) Mrs. Amy Swor. "Jack Norworth, Song Writer, Dies; Ex-Actor Composed 'Take Me Out to the Ball Game,' 'Shine On Harvest Moon' [1907]," *NYT,* 2 Sep 1959, 29:1. "Jack Norworth," *Variety,* 9 Sep 1959. AMD, p. 263. AS, p. 819. BHD1, p. 410. IFN, p. 223. Truitt, p. 250. "Jack Norworth to Star in 'Crooked Dagger' Serial," *MPW,* 26 Jul 1919, 504. "Norworth Writes Film Song," *MPW,* 9 Aug 1919, 830 (for *The Crooked Dagger*).

Norworth, Ned [actor] (b. 1889?–12 Feb 1940 [51], New York NY). m. (1) Josephine Bennett; (2) Wanda Nash. "Ned Norworth," *Variety,* 14 Feb 1940. AS, p. 819. BHD, p. 263.

Nosher, Edith [actress] (b. 1894–13 Jul 1929 [35]). BHD, p. 263. IFN, p. 223.

Nosler, Lloyd [actor] (b. Portland OR, 13 Mar 1900-Sep 1985 [85], CA). AS, p. 819.

Nosler, Ned [actor] (b. 1889–12 Feb 1940 [50?], New York NY). AS, p. 819.

Nosseck, Martin [actor] (b. 1903–29 Nov 1981 [78?], Los Angeles CA). AS, p. 819.

Nosseck, Max [actor/director/producer/scenarist] (*né* Alexander M. Norris, b. Nakel, Poland, 19 Sep 1902–29 Sep 1972 [70], Bad Wiesse, Germany). m. Dietland. (Ufa.) "Max Nosseck," *Variety,* 268, 11 Oct 1972, 71:3. AS, p. 819. BHD, p. 263; BHD2, p. 197. IFN, p. 223.

Notari, Eduardo [actor] (b. Naples, Italy, 1 Jan 1903–1986 [83]). BHD1, p. 614.

Notari, Guido [actor/cinematographer/director] (b. Asti, Italy, 10 May 1893–21 Jan 1957 [63], Rome, Italy). AS, p. 819. BHD1, p. 410. JS, p. 319 (in Italian films from 1914).

Notter, Harriet [actress]. (Essanay.) No data found.

Nova, Hedda [stage/film actress] (*née* Hedwiga Peonie Kuszewiski, b. Odessa, Russia, ca. 1890). m. **Paul C. Hurst**, 4 Nov 1919, Santa Ana CA (d. 1953). AMD, p. 263. BHD, p. 263. 1921 Directory, p. 234. "Weddings," *MPW,* 22 Nov 1919, 422 (age 24). June Lee, "Dan Cupid's Bulletin Board," *Paris and Hollywood Screen Secrets Magazine,* Aug 1927, 37 (Nova filed a divorce complaint against Hurst. "In her complaint the Russian actress asserts that her husband has continually shown preference for other women, was frequently intoxicated, used violent language to her, and made such a disturbance at home occasionally that neighbors have called in the police to quiet him."). George Katchmer, "Remembering the Great Silents," *CI,* 201 (Mar 1992), 38.

Novak, Eva (sister of **Jane Novak**) [actress] (b. St. Louis MO, 11 Apr 1898–17 Apr 1988 [90], Woodland Hills CA; pneumonia). m. William Reid. (Film debut: *The Speed Maniac,* Fox, 1919.) "Eva Novak Dies at 90; Starred with Tom Mix," *NYT,* 20 Apr 1988, B9:1. "Eva Novak," *Variety,* 27 Apr 1988. AMD, p. 263. AS, p. 819 (b. 14 Feb). BHD1, p. 410 (b. 14 Feb). BR, pp. 188–90 (b. 1899). FSS, p. 224. "Eva Novak and Vernon Steele Signed for C.B.C.'s 'Temptation,'" *MPW,* 24 Feb 1923, 797. "Eva Novak Signed by Hal Roach," *MPW,* 8 May 1926, 167. June Lee, "Dan Cupid's Bulletin Board," *Paris and Hollywood Screen Secrets Magazine,* May 1927, 53 (returned to Sydney, Australia with her husband). Buck Rainey, "Eva Novak," *CI,* 115 (Jan 1985), 18–19 (includes filmography).

Novak, Jane (sister of **Eva Novak**) [actress] (b. St. Louis MO, 12 Jan 1896–1 Feb 1990 [94], Woodland Hills CA). m. **Frank Newburg**, 1915 (d. 1969). (Began 1913 at Kalem.) "Jane Novak," *Variety,* 14 Feb 1990. Burt A. Folkart, "Jane Novak; Film Star in Hollywood's Early Years," *LA Times,* 3 Feb 1990, A32:1. AMD, p. 264. AS, p. 819 (d. 6 Feb). BHD1, p. 410 (d. 1 Feb). BR, pp. 190–94 (d. 6 Feb). FFF, p. 178. FSS, p. 224. MH, p. 130. "Jane Novak in First Fox Picture," *MPW,* 4 Aug 1917, 807. "Marshall Neilan Engages Jane Novak," *MPW,* 22 Nov 1919, 444. "Jane Novak to Star in F.B.O. Picture for Release July 9," *MPW,* 8 Jul 1922, 96. "From the Convent to the Film Studios," *MPW,* 3 Nov 1923, 102. Dorothy Donnell, "Gentle Jane; An Interview with Jane Novak," *Classic,* Apr 1924, 36–37, 77. "Jane Novak," *MPW,* 4 Jul 1925, 84. "Jane Novak," *CI,* 179 (May 1990), 60–61 (d. 6 Feb, but *see* Billy H. Doyle, "Letter," *CI,* 179 (May 1990), 50 (d. 3 Feb, not 1 Feb). Tom Fullbright, "Jane Novak; The Golden Trail," *CFC,* 20 (Spring, 1968), 4–5; Part II, 21, 4–5, 48, 54; Part III, 22, 12–13, 50; "The Films of Jane Novak," 23, 6–7. Buck Rainey, "Jane Novak; Undoubtedly One of the Best Known and Gifted of Sagebrush Ingenues," *CI,* 93 (Mar 1993), 56–57; Part II, 94 (Apr 1993), 34–35.

Novak, Joe [cinematographer] (b. 1892–19 Aug 1958 [66?], Los Angeles CA). AS, p. 819. BHD2, p. 197.

Novak, Maurixio [director/producer] (b. Athens, Greece, 1897). AS, p. 819.

Novan, René [actor] (*né* Adolphe Louis Avon, b. Marseilles, France, 1895). AS, p. 819.

Novarro, Ramon (second cousin of **Dolores Del Rio**) [actor/singer/director/scenarist] (*né* José Ramon Gil Samaniegos, b. Durango, Mexico, 6 Feb 1899–31 Oct 1968 [69], Los Angeles CA; bludgeoned to death). Single. Allan R. Ellenberger, *Ramon Novarro; A Biography of the Silent Film Idol, 1899–1968; With a Filmography* (Jefferson NC: McFarland & Co. Inc., 1999) p. 70 ("[Dolores] Del Rio, who was a second cousin to Novarro, first met him after his success with *Ben-Hur.* A bond developed between them that lasted until Novarro's death. Dolores would prove to be someone he could confide in about everything, including his homosexuality."). (MGM.) "Ramon Novarro Slain on Coast; Starred in Silent Film 'Ben-Hur,'" *NYT,* 1 Nov 1968, 1:2, 43:3; "Novarro Left $500,000 to 7 Relatives [4 sisters, 2 brothers] and Aide [secretary Eugene J. Weber]," 15 Nov 1968, 47:2. "Ramon Novarro, 69, Dies of Blows; Slayer Unknown [but later two men were caught]," *Variety,* 6 Nov 1968. AMD, p. 264. AS, p. 819. BHD1, p. 410; BHD2, p. 197. FFF, p. 98 (b. 20 Sep 1901). FSS, p. 225. HCH, p. 39. IFN, p. 223. Katz, p. 866. MH, p. 130 (b. 20 Sep 1901). Truitt, p. 250. "Ramon Novarro," WBO1, pp. 178–79. "Coogan, Keaton and Novarro Are New Metro Stars," *MPW,* 27 Jan 1923, 317. Nanette Kutner, "Why I Like American Girls Best," *MW,* 12 Apr 1924, 19. Herbert Howe, "A Prediction," *Photoplay Magazine,* May 1924, 51–52, 131. "The Deciding Pictures Which Gave 'Ben Hur' to Ramon Novarro," *MW,* 9 Aug 1924, 18. "Will Ramon Novarro Desert the Screen for the Opera?," *MW,* 8 Nov 1924, 13, 30. Robert Keene, "Ramon Novarro Discloses a Secret About Antonio Moreno," *MW,* 27 Dec 1924, 8–9. Adele Whitely Fletcher, "Considering Ramon Novarro as He Strummed a Guitar and Sang Mexican Folk-Songs at a Casual Teaparty," *MW,* 7 Mar 1925, 8–9. "Metro to Star Ramon Novarro," *MPW,* 28 Mar 1925, 391. Ramon Novarro, "Ramon Novarro Tells of His Screen Loves," *MW,* 25 Apr 1925, 4–5, 32 (they included Terry, La Marr, Enid Bennett, McAvoy and Carmel Myers). "Novarro's Next Will Have Annapolis for Background," *MPW,* 6 Jun 1925, 676. Harry Carr, "What Is the Mystery of Ramon Novarro? Has the Aztec Civilization Reached to Him Across the Chasm of the Ages?; Does the Young Actor Echo the Long Dead Memories of a Thousand Years Ago?," *MPC,* Oct 1925, 22–23, 72, 76. Louise Helen Johnson, "When Realist and Idealist Meet; A Captivating Study at Close Range of Two Opposite Types—John Gilbert and Ramon Novarro," *Cinema Arts,* Sep 1926, 22, 55. Ramon Romeo, "Reeling Down Broadway; Ramon Novarro and Matrimony," *Paris and Hollywood,* Sep 1926, 82 ("A few weeks ago the headlines announced that Ramon was about to take the fatal plunge into the rocky sea of matrimony, and Ramon promptly announced that it was all applesauce in search of a plate. So far as he was concerned Cupid could pick up his arrows and be on his way."). Gladys Hall, "He Walks with Quiet Feet; The Sensitive Ramon Is a Dreamer Apart from the Crowd," *MPC,* May 1927, 53, 89. "Novarro to Be King Instead of a Monk," *MPW,* 3 Sep 1927, 10. Jon Varga, "Ramon Novarro: Memory of a Legend," *CI,* 201 (Mar 1992), 10, 12, 14; Part II, *CI,* 202 (Apr 1992), 26, 28–30.

Novelli, Amleto [actor] (b. Bologna, Italy, 18 Oct 1885–16 Apr 1924 [38], Turin, Italy). "Deaths Abroad," *Variety,* 21 May 1924, 2:3 ("He held a lead in the big production 'Quo Vadis.'"). AS, p. 819 (b. 1881). BHD, p. 264. JS, p. 320 (in Italian silents from 1908).

Novelli, Anthony *see* **Novelli, Ermete**

Novelli, Enrico (son of **Ermete Novelli**) [actor/director/scenarist] (*nom de plume,* Yambo; b. Pisa, Italy, 5 Jun 1874–30 Dec 1943 [69], Florence, Italy). AS, p. 819. JS, p. 320 (in Italian silents from 1914).

Novelli, Ermete (father of **Enrico Novelli**) [stage/film actor] (aka Anthony Novelli, b. Lucca, Italy, 5 May 1851–30 Jan 1919 [67], Rome, Italy). m. (Stock in Naples; Cines-Kleine, 1911.) "Ermete Novelli," *Variety,* 7 Feb 1919, p. 18. AMD, p. 264. AS, p. 819 (d. 29 Jan, Naples, Italy). BHD, p. 264. "Ermete Novelli in Pictures," *MPW,* 22 Mar 1913, 1233. "Cines-Kleine Players," *MPW,* 11 Jul 1914, 237–38 ("He maintains bachelor apartments in the Appian Way, a short distance from the Cines Studio.... He is emphatically Cines-Kleine's leading man, but the difficult roles given him entitle him to the distinction of 'character man' as well.").

Novello, Ivor [stage/film actor/scenarist/composer] (*né* David Ivor Davies [son of musician Clara Novello Davies], b. Cardiff, Wales, England, 15 Jan 1893–6 Mar 1951 [58], London, England; coronary thrombosis). (Film debut: *Call of the Blood,* France, 1919; U.K., *Carnival,* 1921; U.S. films, 1921; Gainsborough Pictures, Islington, 1925; last film *Autumn Crocus,* 1934; stage debut: *Deburau,* Nov 1921, London West End.) "Ivor Novello Dies; British Stage Star; Composer and Producer Played in Many Musical Comedies—Once Appeared Here," *NYT,* 6 Mar 1951, 27:1 (age 57). "7,000 Mourn Novello; Stage Stars at Rites in London for Noted Actor Novello," *NYT,* 13 Mar 1951, 31:5 ("...women outnumbered men by fifty to one" at services for the matinée idol). "Ivor Novello," *Variety,* 7 Mar 1951 (age 57). AMD, p. 264. AS, p. 820 (d. 5 Mar). BHD1, p. 410; BHD2, p. 197. GSS, pp. 292–94. IFN, p. 223. Katz, pp. 866–67. Truitt, p. 250. Waldman, p. 215. "Griffith Signs Novello," *MPW,* 20 Jan 1923, 218. Freda Novello, "Ivor Novello; The Perennial Matinee Idol," *CI,* 260 (Feb 1997), 28–32 (at Oxford, 1903–09; includes filmography).

Novello, Jay [film/TV actor] (b. Chicago IL, 22 Aug 1904–2 Sep 1982 [78], No. Hollywood CA; cancer). m. Patricia. "Jay Novello, Character Actor; Mayor in TV 'McHale's Navy,'" *NYT,* 4 Sep 1982, 15:6 ("veteran of hundreds of movies and television roles"; interred at San Fernando Mission Cemetery). AS, p. 820. BHD1, p. 410.

Novello, Roselle [actress/wardrobe mistress] (b. 1896–16 Jan 1992 [95], Los Angeles CA). (Columbia.) "Roselle Novello," *Variety,* 27 Jan 1992, p. 67. AS, p. 820. BHD, p. 264.

Novin, Joseph A. [makeup artist] (b. 1883–10 Oct 1954 [71?]). BHD2, p. 197.

Novinsky, Alex[ander] [actor] (b. St. Petersburg, Russia, 1 Jul 1878–30 Jan 1960 [81], Russia). AS, p. 820 (b. 2 Jul). BHD1, p. 410.

Nowell, Wedgwood [stage/film actor] (b. Portsmouth NH, 14 Jan 1878–17 Jun 1957 [79], Philadelphia PA; heart attack). m. Claire Colwell. "Wedgwood Nowell," *Variety,* 26 Jun 1957. AS, p. 820. BHD1, p. 410. IFN, p. 223. MH, p. 131 (Wedgewood Nowell). SD. Truitt, p. 251. WWS, p. 144. "Wedgwood Nowell," *NYDM,* 6 Oct 1915, 26:4.

Nowlan, Phillip Frances [author/scenarist; creator of Buck Rogers] (b. 1887–17 Jun 1957 [70?], Philadelphia PA). AS, p. 820.

Nowland, Eugene [actor/director]. No data found. (Edison-Kleine; Thanhouser.) AMD, p. 264. "Thrills Under Difficulties," *MPW,* 29 May 1915, 1412. "Eugene Nowland Leaves Edison," *NYDM,* Sep 1915, 27:4. "Thanhouser Engages Notable Players," *MPW,* 18 Sep 1915, 2015. "Nowland Engaged by Van Dyke," *MPW,* 23 Jun 1917, 1945.

Nox, André [actor] (*né* André Nonnez, b. Paris, France, 1872–12 Feb 1946 [73?], Paris, France). AS, p. 820.

Noy, Wilfred [stage actor/director/scenarist] (b. Kensington, England, 24 Dec 1882–ca. 1939 [56?]). (Clarendon Film Co., London, 1909; British Actors Film Co.; Master Films; Progress Films: 150 European films; 1st American film as director: *Lost Chord,* for Whitman Bennett.) AMD, p. 264. AS, p. 820. BHD2, p. 197. Ragan 2, p. 1248 (b. 1883). "Wilfred Noy Is Directing Alice Lake in 'The Fast Pace,'" *MPW,* 27 Dec 1924, 858. "Noy Entered Industry 1909 After Ten Years on Stage," *MPW,* 14 Feb 1925, 725:1 ("The Daily Sketch of London in reviewing one of Mr. Noy's pictures said: 'Wilfred Noy has in one film raised the level of British pictures from dull mediocrity to brilliant artistry.'"). "Bennett Signs Noy," *MPW,* 2 May 1925, 75.

Noyes, Joseph "Skeets" [actor] (b. New Orleans LA, 19 Sep 1868–17 Apr 1936 [67], Los Angeles CA; run down by auto). "Joseph Noyes," *Variety,* 22 Apr 1936. AS, p. 820. BHD, p. 264. IFN, p. 223.

Noyes, Newbold [scenarist] (b. 1892–16 Apr 1942 [50?], Washington DC). BHD2, p. 197.

Nucci, Laura (sister of Carlo Lodovici, b. 1912) [actress] (*née* Maria Laura Lodovici, b. Carrara, Itlay, 26 Feb—-?). JS, pp. 320–21 (in Italian silents from 1928).

Nuemann, Charles [actor] (b. 1883–16 Jul 1927 [44], Glendale CA). AS, p. 820. BHD, p. 264. IFN, p. 223.

Nugent, Edward "Eddie" [stunt man/prop boy/actor/director/producer] (b. New York NY, 7 Feb 1904–3 Jan 1995 [90], New York NY). (Film debut: *Our Dancing Daughters;* Vitagraph; MGM.) AS, p. 820. BHD1, p. 411; BHD2, p. 197. Ragan 2, p. 1248. "Edward 'Eddie' Nugent," *CI,* 246 (Dec 1995), 59:3. Grace Kingsley, "Eddie Props Up; Young Mr. Nugent Achieves an Actor's Estate," *MPC,* Aug 1928, 63, 90.

Nugent, Elliott (son of **J.C. Nugent**) [actor/scenarist/director/producer] (b. Caval, Dover OH, 20 Sep 1896–9 Aug 1980 [83], New York NY). m. **Norma Lee**, 1921 (d. 1980). *Events Leading Up to the Comedy* (New York: Trident Press, 1965). (Paramount.) Les Ledbetter, "Elliott Nugent, 83, Actor-Writer, Dies; 'The Male Animal' Was His Biggest Hit—Director and Producer of Both Films and Plays," *NYT,* 11 Aug 1980, D9:5. "Elliott Nugent," *Variety,* 13 Aug 1980. AS, p. 820. BHD1, p. 411; BHD2, p. 198 (b. 1897). Katz, p. 867 (b. 1899). John Roberts, "Elliott Nugent," *CI,* 217 (Jul 1993), 42–43.

Nugent, J[ohn] **C**[harles] (father of **Elliott Nugent**) [playwright/stage/film actor/director/scenarist] (b. Niles OH, 6 Apr 1868–21 Apr 1947 [79], New York NY; stroke). m. Grace Fertig. (MGM, 1929.) "J.C. Nugent Dead; Actor, Playwright; Veteran of Legitimate Stage and Vaudeville Collaborated on Plays with Son, Elliott," *NYT,* 22 Apr 1947, 27:1. "J.C. Nugent Dies; Vet Actor-Author," *Variety,* 23 Apr 1947. AS, p. 820. BHD1, p. 411; BHD2, p. 198. IFN, p. 223. SD.

Nugent, Moya (stage/film child/adult actress] (b. 1901–26 Jan 1954 [52?], London, England; collapsed during a rehearsal of *All Night Sitting*). "Moya Nugent, 52, British Actress," *NYT,* 27 Jan 1954, 27:2. "Moya Nugent," *Variety,* 193, 3 Feb 1954, 75:4. BHD, p. 264.

Numes, Armand Juda [actor] (b. France, 1857–2 May 1933 [76?], Paris, France). AS, p. 821.

Numes, fils [actor] [*né* André Numes, b. Paris, France, 9 Nov 1896–7 Jan 1972 [75], Asnieres-sur-Seine, France). AS, p. 821.

Nungesser, Charles [actor] (b. 1857–8 May 1927 [70?]; auto accident). AS, p. 821.

Nunn, Wayne [actor] (*né* Shephard Wayne Nunn, b. IN, 1881?–17 Dec 1947 [66], New York NY). m. (1) **Grace Valentine** (d. 1964); (2) Zoe Barnett. "Shephard Wayne Nunn," *Variety,* 24 Dec 1947. AS, p. 821. BHD1, p. 411. IFN, p. 223.

Nye, Carroll [actor] (b. Canton OH, 4 Oct 1901–17 Mar 1974 [72], No. Hollywood CA; heart attack). (MGM.) m. Dorothy; **Helen Lynch** (d. 1965). "Carroll Nye," *Variety,* 27 Mar 1974. AS, p. 821. BHD1, p. 411 (d. Encino CA). IFN, p. 224.

Nye, G. Raymond [actor] (b. Tamaqua PA). (Began in *Is Any girl Safe?,* 1916). BHD, p. 264. George Katchmer, "Remembering the Great Silents," *CI,* 216 (Jun 1993), 49.

Nye, Ned [actor/scenarist] (*né* Edgar Wilson Nye, b. 1871?–11 Dec 1924 [53], Los Angeles CA; found dead). m. Caroline Greenfield. "Edgar Wilson Nye (Ned Nye)," *Variety,* 17 Dec 1924. AMD, p. 264. AS, p. 821 (d. 1 Dec). BHD, p. 264; BHD2, p. 198. "Obituary," *MPW,* 3 Jan 1925, 22 (d. of pneumonia).

Nystrom, Ulrica [actress] (b. France-d. Nov 1923, France). "Ulrica Nystrom," *Variety,* 22 Nov 1923, 3:4 ("Mme. Ulrica Nystrom, cinematographic actress, died recently."). BHD, p. 264.

O

Oaker, John [actor] (b. Ottawa, Canada, 9 Oct 1893). (Bosworth; Horsley, 1915.) *MPN Studio Directory,* 21 Oct 1916. BHD, p. 264. AS, p. 829.

Oakie, Jack (son of teacher/actress Mary **Evelyn Offield**) [stage/film/TV actor] (*né* Lewis Delaney Offield, b. Sedalia MO, 12 Nov 1903–23 Jan 1978 [74], Northridge CA; aortic aneurysm). m. (1) Venita Varden, 1936-div. 1938 (d. 1948); (2) Victoria Horne, 1950. *Jack Oakie's Double Takes,* 1980. (Film debut: *His Children's Children,* Paramount, 1923.) Richard F. Shepherd, "Jack Oakie, Film Buffoon, Is Dead; Played Napolini in 'Great Dictator,'" *NYT,* 24 Jan 1978, 34:1. "Jack Oakie," *Variety,* 25 Jan 1978. AS, p. 829 (b. Sedalia MT). BHD1, p. 411 (d. LA CA). AS, p. 829. IFN, p. 224. Ruth Biery, "O.K. with Oakie; Joan Crawford Is Still the World's Only Girl to Jack," *MPC,* Jan 1929, 40, 73. Eve Golden, "An Oakie from Missouri," *CI,* 260 (Feb 1997), C12-C15, 34 (includes "An Index to the Films of Jack Oakie," by Richard E. Braff).

Oakland, Ethelmary [child actress]. No data found. (World.) AMD, p. 264. "Ethelmary Oakland," *MPW,* 2 Oct 1915, 66. "Thanhouser Child Actress," *MPW,* 9 Sep 1916, 1669.

Oakland, Vivien [actress] (*née* Vivian Anderson, b. Oakland CA, 20 May 1895–1 Aug 1958 [63], Los Angeles CA). m. **John T. Murray** (d. 1957). "Vivien Oakland," *Variety,* 20 Aug 1958. AS, p. 829. BHD1, p. 411. IFN, p. 224. Katz, pp. 868–69. Truitt, p. 251.

Oakland, Will [singer/actor] (*né* Herman Hinrichs, b. Jersey City NJ, 1883–15 May 1956 [73], Bloomfield NJ). "Will Oakland, Ballad Singer, Dies at 73; Operated Many Night Clubs Here in '20s," *NYT,* 16 May 1956, 35:2. Leonard Traube, "Will Oakland's Uphill (& Down) Show Biz Saga," *Variety,* 23 May 1956. AS, p. 829. Truitt, p. 251.

Oakley, Annie [circus performer/actress] (*née* Phoebe Annie Oakley Mozee, b. Patterson Township OH, 13 Aug 1860–4 Nov 1926 [66], Greenville OH). m. Frank E. Butler. "Annie Oakley Dies; Noted Rifle Shot; Markswoman Who Astounded Circus Crowds Was Born in an Ohio Log Cabin; Won Plaudits of Kings; Began Her Career at 16 Years and Performed Wonderful Shooting Feat at 62," *NYT,* 5 Nov 1926, 21:3. "Annie Oakley (Mrs. Frank Butler)," *Variety,* 10 Nov 1926. AS, p. 829 (d. 3 Nov 1936). BHD, p. 264. IFN, p. 224.

Oakley, Florence [actress] (b. MO, 21 Dec 1890–25 Sep 1956 [65], Los Angeles CA). m. **Lewis Stone** (d. 1953). AS, p. 829. BHD1, p. 411. IFN, p. 224.

Oakley, Laura [actress] (b. Oakland CA, 10 Jul 1879–30 Jan 1957 [77], Altadena CA; heart attack). m. **Milton Moore; Frank Newburg** (d. 1969). (Universal.) AS, p. 829. BHD, p. 264. IFN, p. 224.

Oakman, Wheeler [actor] (*né* Vivian Eichelberger, b. Washington DC, 21 Feb 1890–19 Mar 1949 [59], Van Nuys CA; heart attack). m. 3 times: **Priscilla Dean**, 10 Jan 1920, Reno NV (d. 1987). (Lubin, 1911; Selig.) "Wheeler Oakman,"

NYT, 20 Mar 1949, 76:3. "Wheeler Oakman," *Variety,* 23 Mar 1949. AMD, p. 264. AS, p. 829. BHD1, p. 411. FSS, p. 225. IFN, p. 224. MH, p. 131. Truitt, p. 251 (b. VA). WWS, p. 123. "Wheeler Oakman," *MPW,* 4 Sep 1915, 1646. "Wheeler Oakman Opposite Miss Storey," *MPW,* 15 Dec 1917, 1620. "Metro Has Engaged Wheeler Oakman," *MPW,* 19 Jan 1918, 355. "Wheeler Oakman Enlists as Private," *MPW,* 16 Mar 1918, 1501. "'Grizzly' Hero to Appear in New Viola DAna Picture," *MPW,* 22 Mar 1919, 1646. "Annette Kellerman's Lead Will Be Wheeler Oakman," *MPW,* 21 Feb 1920, 1252. "Oakman—Dean Marriage Announced," *MPW,* 17 Apr 1920, 421 (m. SF CA). Jack Oakman and Bill Wilson, "Wheeler Oakman; The Heroic Villain," *CI,* 96 (Jun 1983), 19–20; 97 (Jul 1983), 68–70 (filmography); Part II, 98 (Aug 1983), 45–47; Part III, 99 (Sep 1983), 25.

Oates, Cicely [actress] (b. England, 1889–23 Dec 1934 [45?], England). AS, p. 829.

Obal, Max [scenarist/director] (*né* Max David Gotthelf Stroke, b. Brieg, Germany, 4 Sep 1881–17 May 1949 [67], Berlin, Germany). AS, p. 829. FDY, p. 435.

Obeck, Ferd[inand] [actor/director] (b. Philadelphia PA, 1882?–31 Jan 1929 [46], Los Angeles CA; heart attack). "Fred Obeck," *Variety,* 6 Feb 1929. AS, p. 829. BHD, p. 264; BHD2, p. 198. IFN, p. 224. Truitt, p. 251.

Obellona, Carlos [actor] (*né* Carlos Ovellaira Martinez, b. Mexico, 28 Dec 1900–24 Jan 1960 [59], Mexico). AS, p. 829.

Obenaus, Richards A. [actor] (*né* Richard Bernard, b. 1875–17 Dec 1941 [66?], Kingston NY). BHD, p. 264.

Ober, Mrs. Adelaide D. [actress/scenarist] *née* Adelaide Power, b. 1841–8 Feb 1922 [80?], Hastings-on-Hudson NY). m. **George Ober** (d. 1912). BHD, p. 264; BHD2, p. 198.

Ober, George [stage/film actor] (b. Baltimore MD, 1849?–17 Nov 1912 [63], Hastings-on-Hudson NY; pneumonia). m. **Adelaide** Power (d. 1922). "George Ober Dead; Actor-Producer Played Here for Many Years Under Hoyt," *NYT,* 18 Nov 1912, 11:4. "George Ober," *Variety,* 22 Nov 1912. AMD, p. 264. AS, p. 829 (d. 16 Nov). BHD, p. 264. SD. "George Ober Is Dead," *NYDM,* 20 Nov 1912, 31:3 (first member of the Screen Club to die). "George Ober, Veteran Actor, Dead," *MPW,* 30 Nov 1912, 858 (d. 16 Nov). Willard Holcomb, "A Pioneer Picture Player; George Ober the Original Out-Door 'Rip an Winkle,'" *MPW,* 14 Dec 1912, 1070.

Ober, Kirt [actor] (b. Huntington Beach CA, 1875?–1 Jun 1939 [64], Huntingdon Beach CA). "Kirt Ober," *Variety,* 7 Jun 1939. AS, p 829. BHD, p. 264 (d. 31 May). IFN, p. 224.

Ober, Robert Howard [stage/film actor] (b. Bunker Hill IL, 3 Sep 1881–7 Dec 1950 [69], New York NY). m. (1) **Maude Fulton** (d. 1950); **Mabel Taliaferro** (d. 1979). AS, p. 829. BHD1, p. 412; BHD2, p. 198. IFN, p. 224. SD. Truitt, p. 251 (b. St. Louis MO).

Oberle, Florence [stage/film actress] (*née?,* b. Tarrytown NY, 1870?–10 Jul 1943 [73], No. Glendale CA). (Essanay, 1915; Keystone; Triangle, FP-L.) "Mrs. Florence Oberle; Stage and Screen Actress Dies on Coast at Age of 73," *NYT,* 11 Jul 1943, 34:7. "Florence Oberle," *Variety,* 14 Jul 1943. AS, p. 829. BHD, p. 264 (d. LA CA). IFN, p. 224. Truitt, p. 251.

Obey, André Alexis [author/scenarist] (b. Douai, France, 8 May 1892–11 Apr 1975 [82], Montsoreau, France). AS, p. 829.

O'Brien, Barry [stage manager/actor/agent/producer] (b. London, England, 23 Dec 1893–25 Dec 1961 [68], London, England). Unmarried. "Barry O'Brien," *Variety,* 225, 17 Jan 1962, 65:3 (age 69). BHD, p. 265.

O'Brien, Daniel J. [actor] (b. 1874–12 Oct 1933 [59?], San Francisco CA). BHD, p. 265.

O'Brien, Duncan [assistant director] (b. 1885–6 Jan 1935 [49?], Los Angeles CA). BHD2, p. 198.

O'Brien, Eugene [stage/film actor] (b. Boulder CO, 14 Nov 1880–29 Apr 1966 [85], Los Angeles CA; bronchial pneumonia). "Eugene O'Brien, Actor, 85, Dead; Starred as a 'Great Lover' in Films of Silent Era," *NYT,* 1 May 1966, 89:1. "Eugene O'Brien," *Variety,* 4 May 1966. (FP-L; Metro; World; Artcraft; Select.) AMD, p. 264. AS, p. 823. BHD, p. 265. FFF, p. 95 (b. 1884). IFN, p. 224. Katz, p. 870. MH, p. 131 (b. 1884). MSBB, p. 1026 (b. 1884). Truitt, p. 252 (b. 1882). WWS, p. 157. "Eugene O'Brien with the World Film," *MPW,* 15 May 1915, 1088. "Eugene O'Brien Mary Pickford's New Leading Man," *MPW,* 4 Aug 1917, 784. "Eugene O'Brien," *MPW,* 22 Dec 1917, 1792. "Keeney Engages Players," *MPW,* 16 Feb 1918, 954. "O'Brien to Return to Stage in Fall," *MPW,* 3 Aug 1918, 685. "Eugene O'Brien Signs with Famous," *MPW,* 5 Oct 1918, 66. "Eugene O'Brien Second Selznick Star," *MPW,* XL, 3 May 1919, 670. "Selznick Takes Big Insurance on O'Brien," *MPW,* XL, 31 May 1919, 1311 ($1 million). "Eugene O'Brien Finishes Contract with Selznick," *MPW,* 1 Apr 1922, 462. Patty Doyle, "Oh, Where Is the Hero?," *MPC,* Jul 1922, 63, 85–86 ("Do you like women?"..."But of course I like them...Women are the best friends in the world."). "Actor Brings Suit," *MPW,* 5 Feb 1927, 421. Henriette, "From Hollywood to You," *MPS,* 1 Mar 1927, 7 (bringing suit agfainst DeMille "because that eminent producer didn't let him play the leading male rôle in 'Nobody's Widow' opposite Leatrice Joy. He "entered into a contract with DeMille last August...but when the time came to make the picture nobody said a word to him and another actor was signed. He is asking $20,000 damages."). "Eugene O'Brien Has Accident," *MPW,* 23 Jul 1927, 241. "Eugene O'Brien Robbed," *MPW,* 29 Oct 1927, 543. "Burglars Ransack Gene O'Brien's Home," *MPW,* 5 Nov 1927, 42 (691 Whitley Terrace NY).

O'Brien, George [actor] (b. San Francisco CA, 19 Apr 1899–4 Sep 1985 [86], Franciscan Villa, Broken Arrow OK). m. Marguerite Churchill, 1933–49 (1 son, Darcy; 1 daughter). (Fox; RKO; last film: *Cheyenne Autumn,* 1964.) "George O'Brien, Movie Actor," *NYT,* 6 Sep 1985, B6:5. "George O'Brien," *Variety,* 11 Sep 1985 (b. 1900; age 85). AMD, p. 265. AS, p. 823. BHD1, p. 412. FFF, p. 250. FSS, p. 226. Katz, pp. 870–71. MH, p. 131 (b. 1900). "Dorothy Mackaill and George O'Brien Featured by Wm. Fox," *MPW,* 9 Aug 1924, 471. "George O'Brien," *MPW,* 13 Dec 1924, 659. Joan Cross, "Once a Cameraman—Now a Star," *MW,* 21 Mar 1925,8–9, 30. "George O'Brien," *MPW,* 27 Jun 1925, 997. Dorothy Donnell, "A Child of the Frisco Earthquake Is George O'Brien," *MPC,* Aug 1925, 24–25, 81. Scott Pierce, "The O'Brien Boy Gets a Kick Out of Life," *MPC,* Aug 1926, 56, 86. Henriette, "From Hollywood to You," *MPS,* 1 Mar 1927, 7 (accused his valet of theft. "...the Filipino who used to take care of George got $40 worth of pawn tickets for them [gold watches and diamond rings] and he is now out on bail awaiting trial."). Lewis Kelton, "Stunting to Stardom," *MPC,* Oct 1927, 42, 84, 89. Mario de Marco, "George O'Brien, Seafaring Cowboy," *CI,* 62 (Mar 1979), 19 (b. 1900). Robert Cotton, "George O'Brien...Fadeout," *CI,* 124 (Oct 1985), 40–41. John Cocchi, "The 2nd Feature; A History of the B Movies," *CI,* 146 (Aug 1987), 23. Maury Daly, "George O'Brien," *FIR,* May/Jun 1994, 50–52. George Katchmer, "Remembering the Great Silents," *CI,* 248 (Feb 1996), 47–48. Amelia Hart, "Darcy O'Brien," *Variety,* 4 May 1998, 97P:4 (b. 1939–2 Mar 1998 [58], Tulsa OK; heart attack).

O'Brien, Gypsy [actress]. No data found. AMD, p. 265. "Gypsy O'Brien with Metro," *MPW,* 12 Feb 1916, 980. "Gypsy O'Brien Joins Vitagraph Company," *MPW,* 3 Jun 1916, 1674. "Gypsy O'Brien a Vitagraph Player," *MPW,* 30 Aug 1919, 1289.

O'Brien, Jack [actor]. No data found. (Essanay.) "The Essanay Company Out West," *MPW,* 4 Dec 1909, 801–02 (filming *The Heart of a Cowboy;* "a handsome young actor, who does the 'heavies'"). *See* next entry.

O'Brien, John [actor] (b. 1890?–19 Jun 1923 [33], Alpena MI; suicide: drank poison, slashed throat with a razor and jumped into Thunder Bay). "John O'Brien," *Variety,* 28 Jun 1923. AMD, p. 265. AS, p. 823. "Cabanne Engages O'Brien," *MPW,* 31 Jul 1920, 601.

O'Brien, John B. [actor/director] (b. Richmond VA, 1885?–15 Aug 1936 [51], Los Angeles CA; complications after surgery). (Ince.) "John B. O'Brien," *Variety,* 19 Aug 1936. AMD, p. 265. AS, p. 823. BHD2, p. 198. KOM, p. 154. 1921 Directory, p. 272. "John B. O'Brien, Director," *MPW,* 14 Dec 1912, 1091 (with Circle Ranch Film Company in Los Angeles CA). "New Directors for Famous Players," *MPW,* 15 Jan 1916, 397. "Director John B. O'Brien with Metro," *MPW,* 7 Oct 1916, 83. "John B. O'Brien Joins Thanhouser," *MPW,* 11 Nov 1916, 867. "John B. O'Brien, Director," *MPW,* 17 Nov 1917, 1010. "Director O'Brien Gets Detail," *MPW,* 22 Dec 1917, 1820. George Katchmer, "Remembering the Great Silents," *CI,* 210 (Dec 1992), 51.

O'Brien, Joseph [cinematographer/editor] (b. New York NY, 1900?–29 Mar 1945 [45], New York NY). m. Helen. "Joseph O'Brien, 45, Newsreel Editor; Head of Universal Since 1938 Dies—Ex-Cameraman for the Navy Once with Biograph," *NYT,* 30 Mar 1945, 15:3 (..."Mr. O'Brien at the age of 14 got his first job in the screen industry working as a developer for the old American Biograph Company."). "Joseph O'Brien," *Variety,* 4 Apr 1945.

O'Brien, Lt. Pat [aviator/actor] (b. CA, 1880–18 Dec 1920 [40?], Los Angeles CA; suicide by shooting). AS, p. 823. BHD, p. 265.

O'Brien, Pat (son of **William J. O'Brien**) [actor] (*né* William Joseph Patrick O'Brien, b. Milwaukee WI, 11 Nov 1899–15 Oct 1983 [83], Santa Monica CA; heart attack). m. Eloise Taylor, 23 Jan 1931, CA. *Wind on My Back* (1963). C. Gerald Fraser, "Pat O'Brien, Movies' All-American, Is Dead," *NYT,* 16 Oct 1983, 36:1. Bill Edwards, "Pat O'Brien Is Dead at 83; His Career Spanned 60 Years," *Variety,* 19 Oct 1983. AS, p. 823. BHD1, p. 412. Katz, p. 871. "Actor Saves 2 Children; Pat

O'Brien Rescues Young Son and Daughter in Surf," *NYT,* 18 Aug 1942, 21:6 (pulled to safety Mavourneen, 6, and Shawn, 5, from "a deep hole in the ocean surf near the family's home [San Diego CA] last night.").

O'Brien, Terrence [stage/film actor] (b. Dublin, Ireland, 25 Oct 1887–13 Oct 1970 [82], Welwyn, Hertfordshire, England). (Stage: London, 1909.) "Terrence O'Brien," *Variety,* 260, 11 Nov 1970, 63:3. BHD, p. 265. IFN, p. 224.

O'Brien, Thomas E[verett] [actor] (b. San Diego CA, 25 Jul 1890–8 Jun 1947 [56], Los Angeles CA). (Griffith; Ince.) "Thomas O'Brien," *Variety,* 18 Jun 1947. AMD, p. 265. AS, p. 823 (d. 9 Jun). BHD1, p. 412. IFN, p. 224. Truitt, p. 252 (b. 1891). "O'Brien Signs with M-G-M," *MPW,* 24 Jul 1926, 217. George Katchmer, "Remembering the Great Silents," *CI,* 201 (Mar 1992), 38.

O'Brien, William J. (father of **Pat O'Brien**) [actor] (b. 1871?–24 Apr 1939 [68], Los Angeles CA). m. Margaret. "Pat O'Brien's Father Dies," *NYT,* 25 Apr 1939, 23:2. "William O'Brien," *Variety,* 26 Apr 1939. AS, p. 823.

O'Brien, Willis H[arold] [producer/cinematographer] (b. Oakland? CA, 2 Mar 1886–8 Nov 1962 [76], Los Angeles CA). m. Darlyne. (*The Dinosaur and the Missing Link,* Edison; Manikin Films.) "Willia O'Brien, Film Man, 76, Dies; Producer Created King Kong and Mighty Joe Young," *NYT,* 12 Nov 1962, 29:2. "Willis H. O'Brien," *Variety,* 228, 14 Nov 1962, 71:3 (d. 10 Nov). AMD, p. 265. AS, p. 823 (d. 10 Nov). IFN, p. 224. "Willis H. O'Brien Now with Rothacker," *MPW,* 9 Aug 1919, 844.

Obrock, Herman [cameraman]. No data found. AMD, p. 265. "A Daring Cameraman," *MPW,* 16 Mar 1912, 960. "Obrock Has Adventure," *MPW,* 5 Oct 1912, 51.

O'Byrne, Patsy [actress] (b. KS, 28 Jul 1884–18 Apr 1968 [83], Woodland Hills CA). (Hal Roach.) "Patsy O'Byrne," *Variety,* 24 Apr 1968 (age 82). AS, p. 823. BHD1, p. 412 (b. 1886). IFN, p. 224. Truitt, p. 252.

O'Casey, Sean [scenarist] (b. Dublin, Ireland, 30 Mar 1880–18 Sep 1964 [84], Torquay, England). AS, p. 824.

O'Connell, Hugh [actor] (b. New York NY, 4 Aug 1898–19 Jan 1943 [44], Los Angeles CA). AS, p. 824.

O'Connell, L. William [cinematographer]. No data found. FDY, p. 465.

O'Connor, Charles F. [actor] (b. 22 Sep 1897–7 Nov 1979 [82], New York NY). BHD1, p. 412.

O'Connor, Edward [stage/film actor] (b. Dublin, Ireland, 20 Feb 1862–14 May 1932 [70], New York NY). (Edison.) AMD, p. 265. AS, p. 824. BHD, p. 265. IFN, p. 224. 1921 Directory, p. 193. "Edward O'Connor," *MPW,* 14 Mar 1914, 1368:2 ("This jovial Edison player has the gift of humor so phenomenally developed that he might well be accused of having the Blarney stone as his birthstone.... O'Connor has won a well-deserved place among the foremost funny men of photoplaydom. His popularity with the public is steadily growing and he numbers his loyal friends to-day by the thousands."). Lester Sweyd, "What They Are Doing Now," *Motion Picture Magazine,* Feb 1918, 12 ("Bald-headed Ed O'Connor...has reason to be proud of his success as Mike in that charming stage play, 'Old Lady 31.'").

O'Connor, Frank [actor/director/writer] (b. New York NY, 11 Apr 1882–22 Nov 1959 [77], Los Angeles CA). (FP-L.) "Frank O'Connor," *Variety,* 25 Nov 1959 (age 78; "veteran director, writer and actor"). AMD, p. 265. AS, p. 824. BHD1, p. 413; BHD2, p. 199 (b. 1881). IFN, p. 224. "O'Connor to Direct 'Hearts and Spangles,'" *MPW,* 6 Feb 1926, 539. "Frank O'Connor," *MPW,* 11 Dec 1926. 407.

O'Connor, Harry M. [actor] (b. Chicago IL, 27 Apr 1873–10 Jul 1971 [98], Woodland Hills CA; pneumonia). AS, p. 824. BHD1, p. 413. IFN, p. 224. Truitt, p. 252. George Katchmer, "Remembering the Great Silents," *CI,* 210 (Dec 1992), 51–52. George Katchmer, "Remembering the Great Silents," *CI,* 248 (Feb 1996), 48.

O'Connor, John [actor] (b. 1874?–10 Sep 1941 [67?], Santa Monica CA). "John O'Connor," *Variety,* 17 Sep 1941. AS, p. 824. BHD, p. 265. Truitt, p. 252.

O'Connor, Kathleen [actress] (b. Dayton OH, 7 Jul 1894–25 Jun 1957 [62], Los Angeles CA). m. **Lynn F. Reynolds** (d. 1927). AMD, p. 265. AS, p. 824. BHD, p. 265. BR, pp. 194–95. IFN, p. 224. MH, p. 131. 1921 Directory, p. 234 (b. 1897). Truitt, p. 252. "Kathleen O'Connor Engaged by Rolin," *MPW,* 28 Jul 1917, 635. "Another Filmland Wedding," *MPW,* 25 Jun 1921, 807. "Reynolds' Suicide Leaves Job Open," *MPW,* 5 Mar 1927, 31. Billy H. Doyle, "1957 Film Necrology [letter]," *FIR,* Mar 1958, 156 (d. 1957, age 60). George A. Katchmer, "Forgotten Cowboys and Cowgirls—Part X," *CI,* 182 (Aug 1990), 41–42.

O'Connor, Kathryn Kennedy [actress] (*née?,* b. Cortland NY, 1894?–16 Nov 1965 [71], Albuquerque NM). m. Jimmy O'Connor. (Pathé.) "Kathryn O'Connor," *Variety,* 24 Nov 1965. AS, p. 824. BHD, p. 265. IFN, p. 225.

O'Connor, L. William [cameraman]. No data found. AMD, p. 265. "O'Connor in Cinematography School," *MPW,* 20 Jul 1918, 386.

O'Connor, Louis J. [actor] (b. Providence RI, 28 Jun 1879–7 Aug 1959 [80], Los Angeles CA). AS, p. 824. BHD1, p. 413. IFN, p. 225. Truitt, p. 252. George Katchmer, "Remembering the Great Silents," *CI,* 210 (Dec 1992), 52.

O'Connor, Loyola [actress] (b. St. Paul MN, ca. 1880). BHD, p. 265.

O'Connor, Mary H[amilton] [scenarist/film editor] (b. St. Paul MN). (Griffith; FP-L.) AMD, p. 265. KOM, p. 154. Margaret I. MacDonald, "Mary O'Connor Illuminates Studio System While Angling for New Ideas," *MPW,* 26 Jun 1920, 1737. "Mary O'Connor Will Now Give Scenarios Entire Attention," *MPW,* 25 Sep 1920, 514 (wrote many Fine Arts originals for the Gish sisters, Bessie Love, and others. Retired as scenario and film editor [succeeded by Lee Daugherty] to write scenarios full-time). "Quits Continuity for Creative Writing," *MPW,* 2 Oct 1920, 635. "Miss O'Connor Joining MacAlarney in London," *MPW,* 15 Jan 1921, 292.

O'Connor, Robert Emmett [actor] (b. Milwaukee WI, 18 Mar 1885–4 Sep 1962 [77], Los Angeles CA; from burns received when clothing caught fire from a book of matches). (MGM.) "Robert O'Connor, Screen Actor, 77; Player Well Known for His Portrayals of Police Dies," *NYT,* 7 Sep 1962, 29:2. "Robert E. O'Connor," *Variety,* 12 Sep 1962 (began 1925). AS, p. 824. BHD1, p. 413. IFN, p. 225. Truitt, p. 252.

O'Connor, Una [actress] (*née* Agnes Teresa McGlade, b. Belfast, Ireland, 23 Oct 1880–4 Feb 1959 [78], Nw York NY). AS, p. 824.

O'Dare, Peggy *see* **O'Day, Peggy**

O'Davoren, Vesey [actor] (b. Ireland, 8 Dec 1888–30 May 1989 [100], Los Angeles CA). AS, p. 824. BHD1, p. 413.

O'Day, Alice [actress] (b. England-d. 7 Dec 1937). BHD1, p. 413.

O'Day, Allan [actor]. No data found. Renee Van Dyke, "Paragraphs Pertaining to Plays and Players," *Cinema Arts,* V (Oct 1926), 53 (O'Day was added to the cast of *The Rough Riders*).

O'Day, Dawn *see* **Shirley, Anne**

O'Day, Molly (sister of **Kitty Kelly** and **Sally O'Neil**) [actress: Wampas Star, 1928] (*née* Suzanne Noonan, b. Bayonne NJ, 16 Oct 1909–15 Oct 1998 [89], Los Angeles CA; cancer). m. Jack Durant (d. 1984). (1st National.) *The International Guardian,* 29 Oct 1998. Liebman, *From Silents to Sound,* pp. 226–27. AMD, p. 265. AS, p. 825 (d. 1987). FSS, p. 226. Katz, p. 872. Ragan, p. 1285. "Molly Finishes First Big Part," *MPW,* 11 Jun 1927, 409. Ann Cummings, "O'Neil! O'Day! O' Boy!!," *MPC,* Oct 1927, 48–49, 75. Lewis Yablonsky, *George Raft* (San Francisco CA: Mercury House, rpt. 1989) ("I began to date Molly.... She was doing pretty well in films but she loved to overeat and that weight proved to be her downfall. She tried some weird plastic surgery, where she paid quack doctors a fortune for an operation in which they tried to cut the fat off her body. When they sewed her up she had seam scars running up the sides of her formerly beautiful body. The operation ruined her health, her career, and damn near killed her. It was the first time I realized what some people would do to make it and to stay on top in Hollywood," pp. 57–58.). "Molly O'Day Information [letter]," *CI,* 211 (Jan 1992), 10. Tony Villecco, "Molly O'Day: Hollywood's Four Leaf Clover," *CI,* 261 (Mar 1997), 18–19 (includes filmography).

O'Day, Nell [actress] (b. Prairie Hill TX, 22 Sep 1909–3 Jan 1989 [79], Los Angeles CA; heart attack). AS, p. 825 (b. 1910). BHD1, p. 413. BR, pp. 391–94.

O'Day, Patricia [actress]. No data found. m. Dr. Clement R. Joynt—div. 1936. "News From the Dailies," *Variety,* 124, 4 Nov 1936, 62:2 (Patsy O'Day, "screen actress, granted divorce in L.A. from Dr. Clement R. Joynt.").

O'Day, Peggy [actress] (*née* Peggy Reis or Aarup, aka Peggy O'Dare, b. Youngstown OH, 19 Jun 1900–25 Nov 1964 [64], Santa Monica CA). m. Gordon Courtney (d. 1964). (Christie; L-KO; Universal; Metro; De Mille.) "Peggy O'Day," *Variety,* 9 Dec 1964 ("injured while leaping a horse for one of the Christie comedies in silent days and was forced to abandon her career as a performer"). AMD, p. 265. AS, p. 825. BHD, p. 265 (b. NY NY). BR, pp. 195–96. IFN, p. 225. SD. Truitt, p. 253. WWS, p. 259 (b. NY NY). "'Secret Servide' Series," *MPW,* 18 Apr 1925, 715.

O'Day, Thomas [director] (d. Nov 1923, Niles CA). BHD2, p. 199.

O'Day, William [actor/minstrel] (b. 1862?–14 May 1926 [64], Bernardsville NJ). "William O'Day," *Variety,* 19 May 1926. AS, p. 825. BHD, p. 265.

O'Dea, Jimmy [actor] (b. England, 1899–7 Jan 1965 [65], Dublin, Ireland). AS, p. 825.

O'Dell, Edna [actress] (b. 1896–11 Jun 1987 [91?], Woodland Hills CA). AS, p. 825. BHD, p. 265.

O'Dell, Garry (or **Gerry**) [actor]. No data found. (Universal.) George Katchmer, "Remembering the Great Silents," *CI,* 248, 48.

O'Dell, George [actor]. No data found. AMD, p. 265. "Hoxie and O'Dell with Universal," *MPW,* 13 Oct 1917, 217.

O'Oell, Georgia [actress] (b. 1893–6 Sep 1950 [57], Los Angeles Co. CA). BHD1, p. 413. IFN, p. 225.

Odell, Maude [stage/film actress] (b. Beaufort SC, 10 Nov 1871–27 Feb 1937 [65], New York NY; heart attack—died in dressing room while awaiting call to appear in *Tobacco Road*). m. A. Hagemann. "Sister Bessie of 'Tobacco Road' Dies in Dressing Room [Forrest Theatre], but the Play Goes On," *NYT,* 28 Feb 1937, 1:4. "Maude Odell's Estate $5,000," *NYT,* 3 Mar 1937. "Maude Odell," *Variety,* 3 Mar 1937. AS, p. 830. BHD, p. 265. IFN, p. 225. SD.

Odell, Robert A. [art director] (b. Los Angeles CA, 4 May 1896–20 Feb 1984 [87], Los Angeles CA). (Paramount.) "Robert A. Odell," *Variety,* 28 Mar 1984. AS, p. 830. BHD2, p. 199.

O'Dell, Seymour H. [actor] (b. Ireland, 1863?–3 Apr 1937 [74], Los Angeles CA). "Seymour H. O'Dell," *Variety,* 7 Apr 1937. IFN, p. 225.

O'Dell, Shorty [actor] (*né* Solomon Schwartz, b. 1874?–11 Nov 1924 [50?], New York NY). "'Shorty' O'Dell," *Variety,* 12 Nov 1924. AS, p. 825. BHD, p. 265. Truitt, p. 253.

Odemar, Fritz Otto Emil [actor] (b. Hanover, Germany, 31 Jan 1890–3 Jun 1955 [65], Munich, Germany; cancer). AS, p. 830. BHD, p. 265. IFN, p. 225.

Odette, Mary [actress] (*née* Marie Goimbault, b. Dieppe, France, 10 Aug 1901 [extrait de naissance no. 426]). AS, p. 830.

O'Doherty, Mignon [actress] (b. Brisbane, Australia, 30 Jan 1890–12 Mar 1961 [71], London, England). AS, p. 825.

O'Donahue, J.T.L. [scenarist] (b. 1898?–15 Aug 1928 [30], Los Angeles CA; found dead in his bathtub of heart disease). "J.T.L. O'-Donahue," *Variety,* 29 Aug 1928. AS, p. 825.

O'Donnell, Bob [actor] (*né* Robert J. O'-Donnell, b. Chicago IL, 1891–10 Nov 1959 [68?], Dallas TX). AS, p. 825.

O'Donnell, Charles H. [actor] (b. 1886?–10 Sep 1962 [76], Pompano Beach FL). m. Ethel Blair. "Charles H. O"Donnell," *Variety,* 3 Oct 1962. AS, p. 825. BHD1, p. 414. IFN, p. 225.

O'Donnell, George J. [stage/film actor] (d. 30 Jan 1930, Brooklyn NY). m. Josephine Henderson (d. 1927). "George J. O'Donnell," *Variety,* 12 Feb 1930. AS, p. 825. SD.

O'Donnell, John Thomas *see* **Ward, Hap**

O'Donnell, Walter "Spec" [actor] (b. Fresno CA, 9 Apr 1911–14 Oct 1986 [75], Woodland Hills CA). BHD1, p. 414.

O'Donohue, James T. [scenarist]. No data found. FDY, p. 435.

O'Donovan, Frank [actor/composer] (b. Ireland, 1900–28 Jun 1974 [74?], Majorque, Spain). AS, p. 825.

O'Donovan, Fred [actor] (b. Dublin, Ireland, 14 Oct 1889–19 Jul 1952 [62], London, England). AS, p. 825 (d. 21 Jul). BHD, p. 266.

O'Dunn, Irvin [actor] (b. 1898?–1 Jan 1933 [34], New York NY; fell from a window accidentally). m. Bernice Frankel. "Irvin O'Dunn," *Variety,* 10 Jan 1933 (age 29; "child actor in the pictures"). AS, p. 825. IFN, p. 225.

Oelze, Charles F. [director] (b. Brooklyn NY, 24 Nov 1885–2 Aug 1949 [63], Culver City CA). BHD2, p. 199.

Oertel, Curt Franz Albert [director/producer/scenarist] (b. Osterfeld, Germany, 10 May 1890–1 Jan 1960 [69], Wiesbaden, Germany; auto accident). AS, p. 830. BHD2, p. 199 (d. Limburg, Germany).

Oes, Ingvald C. [general manager]. No data found. AMD, p. 265. "Ingvald C. Oes," *MPW,* 28 Mar 1908, 261. "The Moving Picture Outlook in America," *MPW,* 1 May 1909, 550. "Oes Returns," *MPW,* 23 Sep 1911, 882. "Great Northern Announcement," *MPW,* 6 Nov 1915, 1148.

Oettel, Walter (Wally) [actor] (b. 17 Aug 1891–21 Jul 1980 [88], Woodland Hills CA). BHD, p. 266.

Oettly, Paul Emile [actor/singer] (b. Constantine, Algeria, 24 Jun 1890–17 Mar 1959 [68], Cliousclat, France). AS, p. 830.

O'Farrell, Mary [actress] (b. London, England, 27 May 1892–10 Feb 1968 [75], London, England). AS, p. 825.

O'Fearna, Edward [assistant director] (brother of **Francis** and **John Ford**) (b. Cape Elisabeth ME, 1889–15 Jan 1969 [79], Los Angeles CA). (Fox.) "Edward O'Fearna," *Variety,* 22 Jan 1969. AS, p. 825. BHD2, p. 199.

Offerman, George, Jr. (son of **Marie** and **George Offerman, Sr.**) [actor] (b. Chicago IL, 14 Mar 1917–14 Jan 1963 [45], New York NY). "George Offerman," *Variety,* 6 Feb 1963. BHD1, p. 414. IFN, p. 225. Truitt, p. 253.

Offerman, George, Sr. (father of **George Offerman, Jr.**) [actor] (b. Hoboken NJ, 29 Apr 1879–5 Mar 1938 [58], Los Angeles CA). m. **Marie** (d. 1950). "George Offerman," *Variety,* 9 Mar 1938. AS, p. 830. BHD1, p. 414.

Offerman, Marie (mother of **George Offerman, Jr.**) [actress] (*née?,* b. 1894?–14 May 1950 [56], Los Angeles CA). m. **George Offerman, Sr.** (d. 1938); Mr. Bestar. "Marie Offerman [Mrs. Marie Offerman Bestar]," *Variety,* 24 May 1950. AS, p. 830. BHD1, p. 414.

Offield, Evelyn (mother of Jack Oakie) [actress] (*née* Mary Evelyn Offield, b. 1880–28 Feb 1939 [58?], Los Angeles CA). AS, p. 830.

O'Flynn, Paddy [actor] (b. Pittsburgh PA, 19 Jan 1896–11 Dec 1961 [65], Los Angeles CA). BHD1, p. 414.

O'Fredericks, Aline [actress/director] (b. Goteborg, Sweden, 8 Sep 1900–18 Feb 1968 [67], Sweden). AS, p. 825.

Ogden, M.L. [publicity]. No data found. AMD, p. 265. "Miss Ogden Joins World Film," *MPW,* 21 Sep 1918, 1717.

Ogden, Vivia (or **Vivian**) [actress] (b. 21 Mar...–d. 22 Dec 1952, Los Angeles CA). AMD, p. 265. AS, p. 830. BHD, p. 266. IFN, p. 225. "Called from the Ranks," *MPW,* 28 Feb 1925, 917.

Ogle, Charles Stanton [actor] (b. Steubenville [Morgan County] OH, 5 Jun 1865–11 Oct 1940 [75], Long Beach CA). (Biograph, 1909; Edison.) AMD, p. 266. AS, p. 830. BHD, p. 266. FFF, p. 249. IFN, p. 225. MH, p. 131. "Charles Ogle," *MPW,* 17 Oct 1914, 352. George A. Katchmer, "Remembering the Great Silents," *CI,* 184 (Oct 1990), 57. Laura Ernide, "Author has a monster hit on his hands," *The Herald-Mail Antietam Advertiser,* 19 Aug 1997, 1–2 (Alois F. Dettlaff, Sr., from Wisconsin, found a unique copy of Edison's 15-minute *Frankenstein* [1910] in a batch of films he bought ca. 1957 for $40. Writer Fred Wiebel, of Hagerstown, wrote a book about the film. "Ogle had a large part in designing the first Frankenstein monster costume, influencing all later portrayals of the monster.... In the film, Frankenstein concocts his monster in a vat of chemicals and powders.").

O'Grady, Monty [film/TV actor: Our Gang comedies] (*né* Montgomery O'Grady, b. CA, 6 Mar 1916–8 Mar 2000 [84], Woodland Hills CA). (Began ca. 1925.)

O'Grady, Tom [actor] (*né* Thomas R. Atchinson, b. 1901?–1 Sep 1942 [41], Los Angeles Co. CA). "Thomas R. Atchinson," *NYT,* 2 Sep 1942, 23:2 ("motion-picture character actor known also as Tom O'Grady"). AS, p. 826. BHD1, p. 414 (d. 31 Aug). IFN, p. 225.

O'Hara, Fiske [actor] (b. 1878–2 Aug 1945 [67?], Los Angeles CA). AS, p. 826.

O'Hara, George [film editor/assistant director/scenarist/actor] (b. ID, 22 Feb 1899–16 Oct 1966 [67], Los Angeles CA; cancer). AMD, p. 266. AS, p. 826. BHD1, p. 414. FDY, p. 435. IFN, p. 225. "O'Hara Knows How to Save His Face," *MPW,* 3 Nov 1923, 102. Harry Carr, "Dining with George and Alberta," *MPC,* Dec 1924, 24–25, 80.

O'Hara, Joe [title writer]. No data found. FDY, p. 447.

O'Hara, John [actor] (b. 1859–15 Jul 1929 [70], St. Kilda, Australia). "John O'Hara," *Variety,* 10 Jul 1929, 37:5 ("On his last trip to Australia, Mr. O'Hara's wife died and that shock helped to undermine his health. She had been an invalid for many years."). BHD, p. 266.

O'Hara, Kenneth Anthony [publicist] (b. Brooklyn NY, 22 Aug 1891–24 Oct 1935 [44], Los Angeles CA). AMD, p. 266. AS, p. 826. BHD2, p. 199. "Kenneth O'Hara, Regular Writer," *MPW,* 18 Nov 1916, 990.

O'Hara, Mary [scenarist] (*née* Mary Alsop, b. 1885–15 Oct 1980 [95?], Chevey Chase MD). AMD, p. 266. AS, p. 826. FDY, p. 435. "To Write DeMille Scripts," *MPW,* 2 May 1925, 76.

O'Hara, Neal [journalist/title writer] (b. Boston MA, 1893?–4 Oct 1962 [69], Boston MA). "Neal O'Hara," *Variety,* 17 Oct 1962. BHD2, p. 199. Neal O'Hara and Paul Thompson, "O'Hara of Harvard in Person; Not a Motion Picture," *MPC,* Aug 1927, 39, 77, 87 (wrote titles for *One Minute to Play* and *Kosher Kitty Kelly*). Not in AFI catalog.

O'Hara, Shirley [actress] (*née* Shirley O'Hara-Nolan, b. New York NY, 23 May 1910–5 May 1979 [68], Los Angeles CA; cancer). AMD, p. 266. AS, p. 826. BHD1, p. 415. IFN, p. 225. "Shirley O'Hara," *MPW,* 23 Jul 1927, 240.

Oh Gran, Gilbert [actor] (*né* Justo Masso, b. Spain, 1886–12 Sep 1971 [85?], Barcelona, Spain). AS, p. 831.

O'Higgins, Harvey [writer]. No data

found. AMD, p. 266. "Harvey O'Higgins Joins Galaxy of Film Authors," *MPW,* 9 Apr 1921, 589.

Ohnet, Dolly [actress]. No data found. (Universal.) J. Van Cawrtmell, "Along the Pacific Coast," *NYDM,* 11 Aug 1915, 26:1 (filming *Too Many Smiths*).

Ojeda, Jesus "Chucho" [actor] (*né* Jesus Arturo Ojeda Fernandez, b. Mexico, Oct 1892–13 Nov 1943 [51], Mexico City, Mexico; heart attack). AS, p. 831.

Okazaki, Bob [actor] (b. 1902–28 May 1985 [83?], Los Angeles CA). BHD, p. 266.

O'Keefe, Arthur J. [actor] (b. 1874–29 Mar 1959 [85], Los Angeles CA). AS, p. 826. BHD1, p. 614. IFN, p. 225.

O'Keefe, Dennis [scenarist/actor/director] (*né* Edward Vincent Flanagan, Jr., b. Fort Madison IA, 28 Mar 1908–31 Aug 1968 [60], Los Angeles CA; lung cancer). m. Stephanie Berindey (actress Steffi Duna [1904–1992]). "Dennis O'Keefe," *Variety,* 4 Sep 1968, p. 55 (middle name, "Vanes"). AS, p. 826 (b. 29 Mar; d. Santa Monica CA); p. 395 (Ed Flanagan, b. 21 Mar; d. Santa Monica CA). BHD1, p. 415; BHD2, p. 200 (b. 29 Mar). IFN, p. 225. WWS, p. 254 (wrote scripts under the pen name of Jonathan Ricks). Frank Dolven, "The Talented Irishman Dennis O'Keefe Made It the Hard Way in Hollywood," *The Big Reel* (Nov 1993), p. 130 (wrote *Our Gang* scripts at age 16 and appeared as an extra in over 200 films).

O'Keefe, Lawrence V[incent] [actor] (b. New York NY, 28 Oct 1883–23 Jan 1950 [66], Los Angeles CA). AS, p. 826. BHD1, p. 614.

O'Keefe, Loraine [actress] (b. KS, 23 Nov 1894–12 Sep 1924 [29], Los Angeles CA). AS, p. 826. BHD, p. 266. IFN, p. 225 (age 25).

O'Keefe, Walter [songwriter] (b. Hartford CT, 18 Aug 1900–26 Jun 1983 [82], Torrance CA; congestive heart failure). "Walter O'Keefe," *Variety,* 29 Jun 1983 (wrote *I Wanna Dance wid Da Guy What Brung Me; Henry's Made a Lady Out of Lizzie*). AS, p. 826.

Okey, Jack [art director] (b. CA, 3 Jun 1889–8 Jan 1963 [73], Los Angeles CA). (RKO.) "Jack Okey," *Variety,* 16 Jan 1963 (scenic artist in 1910). AS, p. 831. BHD2, p. 200.

Okochi, Denjiro [actor] (aka Muromachi Jiro, *né* Masuo Obe, b. Fukuoka, Japan, 5 Feb 1898–18 Jul 1962 [64], Kyoto, Japan). AS, p. 831.

Oland, Warner [stage/film actor] (*né* Jonah Werner Ohlund, b. Umea, Vester-bötten, Sweden, 3 Oct 1880–6 Aug 1938 [57], Stockholm, Sweden; bronchial pneumonia). m. **Edith Shearn** (d. 1968). (World; Pathé.) "Warner Oland, 57, Screen Star, Dies; 'Charlie Chan' of Films Victim of Pneumonia on Visit to Sweden, His Homeland; Began Career on Stage; Film Debut with Theda Bara—Was the Villain in Pearl White's 'Perils of Pauline,'" *NYT,* 7 Aug 1938, 32:5 (*né* John Warner Oland). "Warner Oland's Funeral; Ashes of Charlie Chan of the Films Buried in Stockholm," *NYT,* 31 Aug 1938, 15:3 (Nils Asther and 200 friends attended). "Warner Oland," *Variety,* 10 Aug 1938. AMD, p. 266. AS, p. 831. BHD1, p. 415. FSS, p. 227. GK, pp. 728–41. IFN, p. 225. Katz, p. 874 (began 1912). MH, p. 131. Spehr, p. 156. Truitt, p. 254. WWS, p. 125. "Warner Oland," *MPW,* 21 Apr 1917, 408. "Warner Oland Engaged by Astra," *MPW,* 12 May 1917, 972. "Warner Oland to Appear with World," *MPW,* 8 Jun 1918, 1417. Janet Service, "The Interesting Life; Warner Oland Leads It—Or Rather, Mr. and Mrs. Oland, for They Work, Play, Dream and Plan Together," *MPC,* Feb 1919, 22–23, 71. "Prominent Players to Be Featured in Pathé Serials for the Next Two Years," *MPW,* 19 Jul 1919, 377. "Oland's Leaving Causes Surprise," *MPW,* 6 Aug 1921, 624. "Oland Definitely Quits Serial Work," *MPW,* 13 Aug 1921, 728. "Warner Oland Sues Pathé for $6,000," *MPW,* 26 Nov 1921, 395 (breach of contract). "Warner Oland on Way to Hollywood," *MPW,* 24 Dec 1921, 946. "A Free Lancer Joins Warners," *MPW,* 2 May 1927, 795. Tom Waller, "Warner Oland," *MPW,* 19 Nov 1927, 22–23. R.E. Braff, "An Index to the Films of Warner Oland," *CI,* 201 (Mar 1992), C6, C8, 54. George Katchmer, "Remembering the Great Silents," *CI,* 210 (Dec 1992), 52–53. Charles P. Mitchell, "A Guide to Charlie Chan Films; Part One—Warner Oland and the First Chans," *CI,* 267 (Sep 1997), 28-C-1 (includes filmography).

Olcott, Peggene [scenarist]. No data found. FDY, p. 435.

Olcott, Sidney [stage actor/film director/director//scenarist] (*né* John Sidney Alcott, b. Toronto, Ontario, Canada, 20 Sep 1872–16 Dec 1949 [77], Los Angeles CA; in the home of **Robert Vignola**). (Mutoscope, 1904; Kalem; Olcott Prods.; Powers; Universal; Majerstic; FP-L; Metro; Triangle.) "Sidney Olcott, 76, Film Pioneer, Dies; Director Who Joined Industry in '05 Worked with Stars of Silent Screen Days," *NYT,* 18 Dec 1949, 88:5. "Sidney Olcott," *Variety,* 21 Dec 1949. AMD, p. 266. AS, p. 831. BHD, p. 266; BHD2, p. 200 (b. 20 Jan). IFN, p. 226. Katz, pp. 874–75. Lowrey, p. 144. MSBB, p. 1046. Spehr, p. 156 (b. 1873). Truitt, p. 254. "Notes and Comments," *MPW,* 5 Dec 1908, 447. "The Sunny South in Motion Pictures," *MPW,* III, 19 Dec 1908, 498. "Kalem Sends Stock Company to Ireland," *MPW,* 3 Jun 1911, 1242. "Kalem Players Go South," *MPW,* 18 Nov 1911, 560. "New Picture Making Company," *MPW,* 10 Jan 1914, 181. George Blaisdell, "Sidney Olcott in Traveltalk," *MPW,* 17 Jan 1914, 272–73. "Sid Olcott Is Back from Florida," *MPW,* 23 May 1914, 1098. "Sid Olcott Going Abroad," *MPW,* 13 Jun 1914, 1519. "Olcott's Company Reaches London," *MPW,* 11 Jul 1914, 231. "Sidney Olcott and Players in Ireland," *MPW,* 18 Jul 1914, 576. "Olcott Players Attracts Tourists," *MPW,* 15 Aug 1914, 950. "Olcott in the Gap of Dunloe," *MPW,* 22 Aug 1914, 1078. "Sidney Olcott Back, Too," *MPW,* 12 Sep 1914, 1518. "Sidney Olcott Engaged by Famous Players!," *MPW,* 24 Apr 1915, 534. "Olcott to Direct Mary Pickford," *MPW,* 24 Jul 1915, 666. "Olcott Leaves Famous Players," *MPW,* 30 Sep 1916, 2118. "Olcott May Submit to Operation," *MPW,* 24 Nov 1917, 1193 (fallen arches). "Film Division Names Director Advisors," *MPW,* 20 Jul 1918, 363–64. "Jewel Carmen, Under Keeney Contract, Will Be Directed by Sidney Olcott," *MPW,* 7 Sep 1918, 1403. "Sidney Olcott Signed to Direct for Goldwyn," *MPW,* 7 Feb 1920, 923. "Paramount Signs Olcott," *MPW,* 15 Sep 1923, 233. Regina Cannon, "How I Cope with 'Artistic Temperament,'" *MW,* 22 Mar 1924, 7, 24. "Olcott Signs New Contract," *MPW,* 30 Aug 1924, 717. George Mitchell, "Sidney Olcott; He Was the First American Director to Go on Location Abroad," *FIR,* Apr 1954, 175–81. George Geltzer, "Letters," *FIR,* May 1954, 251 (b. 1873).

Oldfield, Barney [film editor/writer]. No data found. "Mother of Barney Oldfield," *Variety,* 19 Sep 1979 (d. 9 Sep 1979 [92], Lincoln NB).

Oldfield, Barney [auto racer/actor] (*né* Berna Eli Oldfield, b. Wausson OH, 29 Jan 1878–4 Oct 1946 [68], Beverly Hills CA; apparent heart attack in bed). m. (1) 1905–24; (2) Bessie Gooby—div. Apr 1940; (3) Mrs. Hulda Rae Braden—div. 1945; (4) remarried Bessie Gooby, 1946. "Barney Oldfield, ex-Racer, Is Dead; Pioneer Auto Driver Was First to Travel a Mile a Minute [15 Jun 1903]—Retired from Track in 1918," *NYT,* 5 Oct 1946, 17:1 (began racing in 1902). AS, p. 831. BHD1, p. 415 (b. York Township OH). "Mrs. Oldfield Dead; Widow of the Famous Racing Driver Succumbs on Coast," *NYT,* 7 Nov 1955, 29:1.

Oldham, Derek [actor/singer] (*né* John Stephens Oldham, b. Accrington Lanes, England, 29 Mar 1892–20 Mar 1968 [75], England). AS, p. 831.

"Old Marie" [actress] (d. May 1927, New York NY; asphyxiation). "'Old Marie' Found Dead," *Variety,* 25 May 1927.

Oldring, Reuban "Rube" Henry [baseball player/actor] (b. New York NY, 30 May 1884–9 Sep 1961 [77], Bridgeton NJ). m. Hanna. "Rube Oldring," *NYT,* 11 Sep 1961, 27:4 (age 76). AS, p. 832. BHD, p. 266. *The Baseball Bug* (Thanhouser ad), *MPW,* 11 Nov 1911, 514. "Who They Are; Some Handy Data on the Champion Ball Players Who Became Picture Players," *MPW,* 18 Nov 1911, p. 558.

O'Leary, Bill [actor] (*né* William J. O'Leary, b. New York NY, 24 Aug 1887–24 Jan 1954 [66], Los Angeles CA). AS, p. 826.

Olgium, Maria Ciprinna Lobato [actress] (b. Castel Blanco, Portugal, 26 Apr 1894–1984 [90?], Lisbon, Portugal). AS, p. 832.

Olive, Dorothy [actress]. No data found. AMD, p. 266. "Dorothy Olive Wins Applause," *MPW,* 22 Apr 1922, 842.

Olive, Edyth [actress] (b. Newton Abbott, England, 1872–7 Nov 1956 [84?], London, England). BHD, p. 266.

Oliver, David [cameraman]. No data found. AMD, p. 266. "Cameraman for Air Work," *MPW,* 14 Aug 1926, 419.

Oliver, Edna May (descendant of John Quincy Adams) [stage/film actress] (*née* Edna May Cox-Nutter, b. Malden MA, 9 Nov 1883–9 Nov 1942 [59], Cedars of Lebanon Hospital, Los Angeles CA; intestinal disorder; cremated). m. stock broker David Welford Pratt, 24 Jan 1928, NY NY—div. 1933. (Film debut: *Wife in Name Only,* 1921; RKO; Universal; MGM; TC-F; last film: *Lydia,* UA, 1941.) "Edna May Oliver Dies in Hollywood; Character Comedienne of the Stage and Screen Stricken on 59th Birthday; Started as an Amateur; Appearance in 'Show Boat' Attracted Film Scouts—Also Scored as Tragedienne," *NYT,* 10 Nov 1942, 28:2. "Edna May Oliver Left $156,000," *NYT,* 27 Apr 1943, 18:3. "Edna May Oliver," *Variety,* 11 Nov 1942. AMD, p. 266. AS, p. 832; p. 734 (May Oliver, Edna). BHD1, p. 415. FSS, p. 228. IFN, p. 226. Katz, p. 875. Truitt, p. 254. "Enda May Oliver in Burr Film," *MPW,* 27 Oct 1923, 751. DeWitt Bodeen, "The Four Dowagers of MGM," *Focus on Film,* No. 24, Spring 1976, 26–32 (b. NY NY, 12 Jan 1885; includes filmography). Charles Stumpf, "Edna May Oliver; One and Only," *Films of the Golden Age,* No. 13 (Summer 1998), pp. 42–49 (in 1931 she legally changed her name to Oliver. "No woman named 'Nutter' would ever get anywhere in the theater or films.").

Oliver, Guy [actor] (b. Chicago IL, 25 Sep 1875?–1 Sep 1932 [56?], Los Angeles CA; cancer). (Lubin; Eclair; Kinemacolor; Selig.) "Guy Oliver," *Variety,* 6 Sep 1932 (age 54; began 1908 and made over 600 films). AS, p. 832. BHD1, p. 415 (b. 1878). IFN, p. 226 (b. 1878). Truitt, pp. 254–55 (b. 1875).

Oliver, Harry [art director] (*né* Harold G. Oliver, b. Hastings MN, 1888?–5 Jul 1973 [85], Woodland Hills CA; cancer). "Harry Oliver, Oscar Winner for Art Direction [for *Seventh Heaven* (1928) and *Street Angel* (1929)], Is Dead," *NYT,* 6 Jul 1973, 26:2. "Harry Oliver," *Variety,* 11 Jul 1973 ("gave up film work to become a desert hermit" in 1946 in the Coachella Valley desert). AMD, p. 266. AS, p. 832. "Harry Oliver Designs Sets for Fox Film [*7th Heaven*]," *MPW,* 29 Jan 1927, 349:1. "Oliver Designs Spanish 'Sets' for 'Carmen,'" *MPW,* 2 Apr 1927, 483.

Oliver, I. [executive]. No data found. AMD, p. 266. "I. Oliver a Newcomer in Picture Industry," *MPW,* 22 Mar 1919, 1694.

Oliver, Joseph A. [actor] (b. 1848?–1911 [63?]). (Pathé.) AMD, p. 266. "Joseph A. Oliver," *MPW,* 1 Jul 1911, 1516 (age 63). Richard V. Spencer, "With the Western Producers," *MPW,* 8 Jul 1911, 1576 (James A. Oliver).

Oliver, Olive [actress] (b. 1871–7 Nov 1961 [90?], San Francisco CA). AS, p. 832.

Oliver, Ted [actor] (*né* Virgil Kinley Oliver, b. KY, 2 Feb 1892–30 Jun 1957 [65], Los Angeles CA). AS, p. 832. BHD1, p. 415. IFN, p. 226. Truitt, p. 255 (b. 1895).

Oliver, Virgil, Jr. [actor: Our Gang comedies] (b. 5 Sep 1915–3 Jun 1988 [72], Baton Rouge LA). AS, p. 832. BHD1, p. 614.

Oliver, William Elwell [scenarist] (b. England–d. 28 Nov 1964, Los Angeles CA). AMD, p. 266. AS, p. 832. "Sign Scenario Contest Winner," *MPW,* 17 Apr 1926, 503.

Olivette, Marie [actress] (b. 1892?–15 Mar 1959 [67], New York NY; burns from lighted cigarette). m. John Riker Ditmars. "Widow Dies in Fire; Former Actress, 66, Found in Sutton Place Home," *NYT,* 18 Mar 1959, 17:4. "Mrs. John Riker Ditmars," *Variety,* 25 Mar 1959 ("silent film actress"). AS, p. 833. BHD, p. 266.

Olivier, Claire Louise Georgette [actress] (b. Vallon-sur-Gee, France, 13 Mar 1892–28 Mar 1974 [82], Limeil-Brevannes, France). AS, p. 833.

Olivier, Paul [actor] (*né* François Hilarion Paul Olivari, b. Marseilles, France, 10 Feb 1876–10 Jun 1948 [72], Paris, France). AS, p. 833.

Ollendorff, Julian [artist]. No data found. AMD, p. 267. "Now Sketching for Kinograms," *MPW,* 29 Apr 1922, 941.

Olmstead, Gertrude [actress] (b. Chicago IL, 13 Nov 1904–18 Jan 1975 [70], Beverly Hills CA). m. **Robert Z. Leonard** (d. 1968). "Gertrude Olmstead," *Variety,* 29 Jan 1975. AMD, p. 267. AS, p. 833. BHD1, p. 416. BR, pp. 196–98 (b. 10 Nov). FFF, p. 163. FSS, p. 229. IFN, p. 226. Katz, p. 876 (b. 1897). MH, p. 131. "Carl Laemmle's Offer to Star Winner Helped Chicago Elks' Beauty Contest," *MPW,* 3 Jul 1920, 73. "Gertrude Olmstead Voted Most Popular," *MPW,* 24 Dec 1921 (in Brooklyn NY contest). "Signs with Metro," *MPW,* 13 Sep 1924, 127. "Gertrude Olmstead Signed," *MPW,* 4 Jul 1925, 83. "Director Leonard and Miss Olmstead to Wed," *MPW,* 6 Mar 1926, 2. "Robert Leonard Weds Gertrude Olmstead," *MPW,* 26 Jun 1926, 682. "M-G-M Gives Miss Olmstead New Contract," *MPW,* 15 Jan 1927, 199. George A. Katchmer, "Forgotten Cowboys and Cowgirls—Part IX," *CI,* 181 (Jul 1990), 56. Anthony Slide, *Silent Portraits* (Vestal NY: The Vestal Press, Ltd., 1989), p. 207 (b. 1897).

Olmsted, Stanley [writer] (b. 1877?–8 Nov 1939 [62], Arlington VA). "Stanley Olmsted," *Variety,* 15 Nov 1939.

Olonova, Olga [actress]. No data found. AMD, p. 267. "Olga Olonova," *MPW,* 12 Aug 1916, 1121.

O'Loughlin, John Carr [actor] (b. Dublin, Ireland, 1886). BHD, p. 266.

Olsen, Lauritz [actor] (b. Copenhagen, Denmark, 10 Aug 1872–9 May 1955 [82]). BHD, p. 266. IFN, p. 226.

Olsen, Ole [producer] (b. Tangemose, Denmark, 5 May 1863–4 Oct 1943 [80], Copenhagen, Denmark). AS, p. 833. BHD2, p. 200.

Olsen, Ray [cinematographer] (*né* Raider Olsen, b. 1895–11 Apr 1980 [85?], Woodland Hills CA). AS, p. 833. BHD2, p. 200. FDY, p. 465.

Olson, Ivy [actress] (*née* Ivan Massie Olson, b. Kansas City MO, 14 Oct 1885–1 Sep 1965 [79], Inglewood CA). AS, p. 834.

O'Madigan, Isabel [actress] (b. St. Louis MO, 16 Oct 1871–23 Jan 1951 [79], Culver City CA sanitarium). (Selznick.) "Isabel O'Madigan," *NYT,* 25 Jan 1951, 25:2. "Isabel O'Madigan," *Variety,* 31 Jan 1951. AS, p. 826. BHD1, p. 416 (d. LA CA). IFN, p. 226.

O'Malley, Charles E. (brother of **Pat O'Malley**) [actor] (b. PA, 12 Apr 1897–29 Jul 1948 [51], Los Angeles CA). AS, p. 826 (d. 1958). BHD1, p. 416; BHD2, p. 200 (d. 1958). George Katchmer, "Charles O'Malley," *CI,* 226 (Apr 1994), 40.

O'Malley, David [publicist/producer] (b. Boston MA, 11 Feb 1887–16 Oct 1948 [61], New York NY). BHD2, p. 200.

O'Malley, Grania [actress/singer] (b. Ireland, 1888–14 Jun 1973 [85?], New York NY). AS, p. 826.

O'Malley, Pat (brother of **Charles O'Malley**) [actor] (*né* Patrick H. O'Malley, Jr., b. Dublin, Ireland [or Forest City PA], 3 Sep 1890–21 May 1966 [75], Van Nuys CA; heart attack at home while dining). m. Lillian Wilkes, Jul 1915 (d. 1976; 3 daughters, Sheila, Eileen, and Mary Kathleen). (Edison, 1907; Universal.) "Pat O'Malley," *Variety,* 25 May 1966. AMD, p. 267. AS, p. 827. BHD1, p. 416. FFF, p. 177. FSS, p. 229. IFN, p. 226 (b. Forest City PA). Katz, p. 877. MH, p. 132. Truitt, p. 255. "Patrick O'Malley in Edison Stock," *MPW,* 19 Dec 1914, 1688. "In the Picture Studios," *NYDM,* 21 Jul 1915, 19:2 (O'Malley quietly left the [Edison] studio one day "last week" and "[a]t 12 o'clock he was at the altar and at 1.30 back at the studio with make-up on acting in a picture and incidentally making ardent love to another woman, in the play, of course."). "Patrick O'Malley Rides to Fame," *MPW,* 4 Aug 1917, 801. "Patrick O'Malley Is Enbgaged for Neilan-First National Film," *MPW,* 3 Apr 1920, 53. Clodagh Saurin, "The Wearing of the Green," *Photoplay,* Mar 1921, 31, 76 (re O'Malley, Colleen Moore, and Mickey Neilan). Grace Kingsley, "Pat; He's the Head of His House," *MW,* 13 Sep 1924, 17–18. Hubert V. Coryell, "Pat O'Malley; Fighting Irishman," *MW,* 11 Jul 1925, 16–17. Ralph Sutter, "Standing Pat with O'Malley; They Called Him a Type Actor, But Being Irish, He's Showing 'Em How," *MPC,* Oct 1926, 58–59, 87. Alice Barrows, "Alice in Movieland," *Paris and Hollywood,* Oct 1926, 50 (family portrait with wife and 3 daughters).

O'Malley, Rex [stage/film actor] (*né* Sean Rex Patrick O'Malley, b. London, England, 2 Jan 1901–1 May 1976 [75], Mary Manning Walsh Home, New York NY). "Rex O'Malley Dies; Stage, Film Actor," *NYT,* 2 May 1976, 52:1. "Rex O'Malley," *Variety,* 283, 12 May 1976, 468:3. AS, p. 827. BHD1, p. 416. IFN, p. 226.

O'Malley, Thomas E. [actor] (b. Boston MA, 1856?–5 May 1926 [70], Brooklyn NY). "Thomas E. O'Malley," *Variety,* 12 May 1926. AS, p. 827. BHD, p. 266. IFN, p. 226. Truitt, p. 256.

O'Meara, Joseph [actor] (b. 1874?–15 Jan 1921 [47], Norwood [Cincinnati] OH; apoplexy). "Joseph O'Meara," *Variety,* 28 Jan 1921. AS, p. 827.

Omegna, Roberto [cinematographer/documentary filmmaker] (b. Turin, Italy, 28 May 1876–19 Nov 1948 [72], Turin, Italy). AS, p. 834. BHD2, p. 200. JS, p. 323 (in Italian silents from 1901; possibly Italy's first cameraman).

Ommos, Pio [actor/stuntman] (b. Mexico, 8 Jan 1899–24 May 1965 [66], Guanajato, Mexico). AS, p. 834.

O'Moore, Barry *see* **Yost, Herbert A**

Ondra, Anny [actress] (*née* Anna Sophia Ondrakova, b. Tarnów, Poland, 15 May 1903–28 Feb 1987 [83], Hamburg, Germany; cerebral thrombosis). AS, p. 834. BHD1, p. 417.

O'Neal, Ann [actress] (*née* Patsy Ann Epperson, b. MO, 23 Dec 1893–24 Nov 1971 [77], Woodland Hills CA). AS, p. 827.

O'Neal, Zelma [actress] (*née* Zelma Schroeder, b. Rock Falls IL, 28 May 1903–3 Nov 1989 [86], Largo FL). AS, p. 827. BHD1, p. 417.

O'Neil, Barry [stage/film actor/director] (*né* Thomas J. McCarthy, b. New York NY, 24 Sep 1864–23 Mar 1918 [53], New York NY). m. stage actress Nellie Walters (b. Glasgow, Scotland–d. 21 Nov 1915, NYC). AMD, p. 267. AS, p. 827. BHD2, p. 200 (b. 1865). IFN, p. 226. SD. "Barry O'Neil," *MPW,* 3 Oct 1914, 47. "The Late Mrs. Barry O'Neil," *NYDM,* 4 Dec 1915, 25:1 (funeral services were held 23 Nov at the Church of the Transfiguration; honorary pallbearers were George D. McIntyre, Peter M. Lang, Gerald Griffin, Joseph W. Smiley, George Soule Spencer, and William Norton). "Death of Mrs. Barry O'Neil," *MPW,* 4 Dec 1915, 1822. "Funeral of Mrs. Barry O'Neil," *MPW,* 4 Dec 1915, 1843 (23 Nov 1915).

O'Neil, Colette [actress] (*née* Constance Annesley, b. Glasgow, Scotland, 1895–6 Oct 1975 [80?], London, England). AS, p. 827.

O'Neil, Frank [actor] (d. 8 Dec 1917, New York NY). (Biograph.) AS, p. 827. BHD, p. 267.

O'Neil, George [scenarist] (b. St. Louis MO, 1898?–24 May 1940 [42], Los Angeles CA; cerebral hemorrhage). (Universal.) "George O'Neil, 42, Coast Scenarist; Collaborator on 'Magnificent Obsession' and Author of 'Only Yesterday' Dies; A Dramatist and Poet; Wrote Keats Biography and Had Play, 'American Dream,' Produced Here in 1933," *NYT,* 25 May 1940, 17:4. "George O'Neil," *Variety,* 29 May 1940. AS, p. 827. BHD2, p. 200. IFN, p. 226.

O'Neil, Helen [actress]. No data found. AMD, p. 267. "Helen O'Neil to Have Important

Part in 'Torchy's Frame Up,'" Now Being Filmed," *MPW,* 23 Apr 1921, 830.

O'Neil, Nance [stage/film actress] (*née* Gertrude Lamson, b. Oakland CA, 8 Oct 1874–7 Feb 1965 [90], Englewood NJ). m. **Alfred D. Hickman**, 11 Aug 1916 (d. 1931). (Lubin; Fox; Selznick.) "Nance O'Neil, 90, Tragedienne of Stage in Early 1900's, Dead," *NYT,* 8 Feb 1965, 25:2 (stage name from Nance Oldfield and Eliza O'Neil). "Nance O'Neil," *Variety,* 10 Feb 1965. AMD, p. 267. AS, p. 827. BHD1, p. 417. FSS, p. 230. IFN, p. 226. Spehr, p. 156 (b. 1875). Truitt, p. 256. "New Lubin Star; Nance O'Neil Signs Contract for Series of Appearances in Features," *NYDM,* 30 Oct 1915, 25:3. "Nance O'Neil in Lubin Play," *MPW,* 4 Dec 1915, 1818. Carolyn Lowrey, "Nance O'Neil, Lubin Star, in a Reminiscent Mood," *The [NY] Morning Telegraph,* 12 Dec 1915, VI, 4:1. "Nance O'Neil Engaged by Metro," *MPW,* 26 Aug 1916, 1412. "Nance O'Neil Marries Alfred Hickman," *MPW,* 26 Aug 1916, 1416. "Nance O'Neil Acting for McClure Pictures," *MPW,* 21 Oct 1916, 413.

O'Neil, Peggy [stage/film actress] (*née* Margaret O'Neill, b. Greeveguilla, County Kerry, Ireland, 16 Jun 1898–7 Jan 1960 [61], London, England). Unwed. "Peggy O'Neil Dies; Ex-Stage Star, 61; Musical Comedy Actress Inspired the Popular Song That Was Named for Her," *NYT,* 8 Jan 1960, 23:1. "Peggy O'Neil," *Variety,* 13 Jan 1960. AS, p. 827 (b. Ireland, 1899). BHD, p. 267 (b. Buffalo NY, 1897). SD, p. 957.

O'Neil, Sally (sister of **Kitty Kelly** and **Molly O'Day**) [actress: Wampas Star, 1926] (*née* Virginia Louise Concepta Noonan, b. Bayonne NJ, 23 Oct 1910–18 Jun 1968 [57], Galesburg IL; pneumonia). m. Stewart S. Battles. "Sally O'Neill, 55, ex-Movie Actress; Star of 'The Brat' and First Talkie in Color Dies," *NYT,* 20 Jun 1968, 45:4 (b. 1912; d. Bayonne, age 55). "Sally O'Neil," *Variety,* 26 Jun 1968. AMD, p. 267. AS, p. 827. BHD1, p. 417 (b. 1908). FSS, p. 230. IFN, p. 226 (b. 1910). Katz, p. 878 (b. 1908). Truitt, p. 256. "Sally O'Neil, New to Screen, Had Lead in Neilan's 'Patsy,'" *MPW,* 21 Mar 1925, 274. Doris Curran, "She's Irish—and No Mistake," *MPC,* Sep 1925, 60, 81. "Discovered in L.A. Ballroom," *MPW,* 23 Apr 1927, 715. Ann Cummings, "O'Neil! O'Day! O' Boy!!," *MPC,* Oct 1927, 49, 75.

O'Neil, Suzanne [actress]. No data found. AMD, p. 267. "New Players Starting Work," *MPW,* 4 Jul 1925, 78.

O'Neill, Alice [stage name: Ethel Dante] (b. 1862?–30 Mar 1954 [92], Nottingham, England; from burns). "Alice O'Neill," *Variety,* 14 Apr 1954. AS, p. 827.

O'Neill, Edward [actress] (b. Bombay, India, 1867). BHD, p. 267.

O'Neill, Henry Joseph [actor] (b. Orange NJ, 10 Aug 1891–18 May 1961 [68], Los Angeles CA). AS, p. 827.

O'Neill, Jack [actor/director/scenarist] (b. Philadelphia PA, 28 Jun 1883–20 Aug 1957 [74], Los Angeles CA). (Lubin, 1905; U-I.) "Jack O'Neill," *Variety,* 28 Aug 1957. AS, p. 828. BHD, p. 267; BHD2, p. 200. IFN, p. 227. Truitt, p. 256.

O'Neill, James (father of Eugene O'Neill) [stage/film actor] (b. Thomastown, County Kilkenny, Ireland, 14 Oct 1847–10 Aug 1920 [72], New London CT; stomach cancer). m. Ellen Quinlan. (Stage debut: 1868, Cincinnati OH.) "James O'Neil Dies After Long Illness; Famous Romantic Actor a Victim of Cancer of the Stomach in His 71st Year; Monte Cristo 6,000 Times; His Roles Included d'Artagnan, Virginius and Julius Caesar—Associate of Booth and Cushman," *NYT,* 11 Aug 1920, 9:1 (b. 15 Nov 1849). AMD, p. 267. AS, p. 828. BHD, p. 267 (b. 15 Nov). GSS, pp. 300–301. IFN, p. 227. Truitt, p. 256 (d. 8 Oct 1938: *see* next entry). "'Virginius' in Vaudeville; James O'Neill and Louis James Both to Produce Part of It," *NYT,* 22 Apr 1905, 11:2 (producer F.F. Proctor to produce the play at the 23rd St. Theatre, 1 May; to include James O'Neill, Jr., and 50 supernumeraries). "O'Neill Seeks to Enjoin 'Monte Cristo,'" *MPW,* 28 Dec 1912, 1282. "James O'Neill Wins Suit Against General Film Company," *MPW,* 25 Jan 1913, 452. "James O'Neill," *MPW,* 25 Jul 1914, 588. "O'Neil [sic] Wins Suit; Court Upholds His Right to 'Count of Monte Cristo' and Grants Injunction," *NYDM,* 14 Apr 1915, 24:1 (wanted an accounting of the profits of the General Film version. He had acquired the Fechter version of Alexander Dumas's novel in 1885. Played the part onstage over 5,000 times. His lawyers contended the film included incidents not in the novel and only found in Fechter.). "James O'Neill Injured by Northwest Sled Dogs," *MPW,* 21 Feb 1920, 1237:1 (filming Vitagraph's *The Courage of Marge O'Doone,* O'Neill was bitten by sled dogs who had been starved for three days in order to attack Neill, playing Mukoki, an Indian guide. Raw meat and fish had been hidden in the actor's clothing. "Mr. O'Neill was unconscious by the time the dogs had been driven away." The O'Neill mentioned here may be the next entry.).

O'Neill, James "Tip" [stage/film actor] (b. Philadelphia PA, 1 Jul 1863–8 Oct 1938 [75], Los Angeles CA). (Solax; U.S. Amusement Co.) "James O'Neill," *Variety,* 12 Oct 1938 ("veteran vaude actor, and in pictures for the past 20 years"). AS, p. 828. BHD1, p. 417. IFN, p. 227. Spehr, p. 156.

O'Neill, James Cornelius [stage/film actor] (b. Philadelphia PA, 1876?–27 Nov 1944 [68], New York NY [Death Certificate Index No. 25164]). "James O'Neill Dies; Actors Equity Aide; Member of Staff for 2 Decades Retired in '39—Ex-Manager Was on Stage Many Years," *NYT,* 29 Nov 1944, 23:1. "Jimmy O'Neill, 68, Dies; Vet Equity Exec," *Variety,* 29 Nov 1944 (acted at Universal in Fort Lee NJ). AS, p. 828.

O'Neill, Johnny P. [actor] (b. 1852–14 Sep 1930 [78], Sydney, Australia). BHD, p. 267. IFN, p. 227.

O'Neill, Joseph Jefferson [publicist/scenarist]. No data found. AMD, p. 267. FDY, p. 435. "Joseph Jefferson O'Neill Writing," *MPW,* 29 Jan 1927, 322. "Joe O'Neill Now Writing Scenarios," *MPW,* 25 Jun 1927, 573. "Joe O'Neill Is Only Writer Left on FBO Staff," *MPW,* 13 Aug 1927, 454.

O'Neill, Maire [actress] (*née* Maire Allgood, b. Dublin, Ireland, 12 Jan 1885–2 Nov 1952 [67], London, England). AS, p. 828.

O'Neill, Mickey [actor/director] (*né* Clarence J. H. Dion, b. Modesto CA, 1902–14 May 1932 [29], near Atascadero CA; auto accident). "Mickey O'Neill," *Variety,* 24 May 1932. AS, p. 828. BHD2, p. 200. IFN, p. 227.

Ong, Dana De Moss [actor] (b. Richmond OH, 3 Jul 1874–31 Dec 1948 [74], Los Angeles CA). AS, p. 834. BHD, p. 267. IFN, p. 227.

Ongley, Amy [actress] (b. Roanoke VA, 1886–4 Dec 1926 [40?], New York NY). BHD, p. 267.

Onno, Ferdinand [actor] (*né* Ferdinand Onowotschek, b. Czarnowitz, Russia, 19 Oct 1881–1970 [89]). BHD, p. 267. IFN, p. 227.

Onoe, Matsunosuke [actor] (b. Okoyama, Japan, 12 Sep 1875–11 Sep 1926 [50], Kyoto, Japan). AS, p. 834.

Opp, Julie (mother of Philip Faversham) [stage/film actress] (b. New York NY, 28 Jan 1871–8 Apr 1921 [50], Post Graduate Hospital, New York NY; following an operation). m. (1) Robert Lorraine; (2) **William Faversham**, 1902 (d. 1940). "Julie Opp, Actress, Dies After Operation; Wife of William Faversham Was Native New Yorker, Who First Won Success in London," *NYT,* 9 Apr 1921, 11:6. "Julie Opp," *Variety,* 15 Apr 1921, 17:4. AS, p. 834. BHD, p. 267. IFN, p. 227. "Personal; Opp," *NYDM,* 6 Nov 1915, 5:2 (returned to home in East Seventeenth St., NYC, suffering from a nervous breakdown).

Opperman, Frank [actor]. No data found. (Biograph, 1912; K&E; NYMPC.)

O'Ramey, Georgia [stage/film actress] (b. Mansfield OH, 31 Dec 1886–2 Apr 1928 [41], New Haven CT; heart attack). m. Robert Griffith, 1912. (Biograph; Progressive Film Co.) "Georgia O'Ramey, Stage Star, Is Dead; Expires Suddenly in New Haven When About to Open in 'Nize Girl'; Noted as Comedienne; Play Is Abandoned for the Present and Presentation Here May Be Delayed," *NYT,* 3 Apr 1928, 32:2. "Georgia O'Ramey Died as Show Due to Open; New Production of 'Nize Girl' Farce Built Around Comedienne—Died in New Haven," *Variety,* 4 Apr 1928. AS, p. 828 (d. 1 Apr). BHD, p. 267. IFN, p. 227. "Gossip of the Studios," *NYDM,* 15 Jul 1914, 23:1.

Orbach, Duke [publicist]. No data found. AMD, p. 267. "Duke Orbach Qualifies as a 'King-Maker,'" *MPW,* 2 Apr 1927, 480.

Orbal [actor] (*né* Gaston Etienne Phgilippe Labro, b. Montpellier, France, 22 Nov 1898 [extrait de naissance no. 1460]-31 Jan 1983 [84], Largentiere, France). AS, p. 835.

Ordynski, Ryszard [producer] (*né* Ryszard Blumenfeld, b. Kraków [Warsaw], Poland, 3 Oct 1878–13 Aug 1953 [75], Warsaw, Poland). "Richard Ordynski, Producer, 75, Dies; Former 'Met' Stage Director Worked with Max Reinhardt—Teacher, Drama Critic," *NYT,* 16 Aug 1953, 77:1. "Ryszard Ordynski," *Variety,* 19 Aug 1953. AMD, p. 267. AS, p. 835 (b. Makov, Austria). BHD, p. 267' BHD2, p. 201 (b. 5 Oct). "Will Soon Be Director," *MPW,* 27 Jan 1923, 324 (former stage director of Metropolitan Opera).

O'Reilly, Tex [actor] (*né* Edward O'Reilly, b. TX, 1880–8 Dec 1946 [66?], Summount NY). BHD, p. 267.

Orellana, Carlos [actor] (*né* Carlos Orellana Martinez, b. Mexico, 28 Dec 1901–24 Jan 1960 [58], Mexico City, Mexico). AS, p. 835.

Orla, Ressel [actress] (b. 12 Dec 1898–23 Jul 1931 [32], Berlin, Germany). BHD, p. 267. Vittorio Martinelli, "Kino-Lieblinge," *Griffithiana,* 38/39 (Oct 1990), 25.

Orlamond, Fritz [technical director]. No data found. AMD, p. 267. "Fritz Orlamond," *MPW,* 2 Octr 1915, 58.

Orlamond, Madge B. [actor] (b. St. Charles MN, 15 Jan 1861–22 Jun 1947 [86], Los Angeles CA). BHD, p. 267.

Orlamond, William H. [actor] (b. Copenhagen, Denmark, 1 Aug 1867–23 Apr 1957 [89], Los Angeles CA). m. Ruth. (Lubin, 1912.) AS, p. 835 (d. Copenhagen). BHD, p. 267. IFN, p. 227. George Katchmer, "Remembering the Great Silents," *CI*, 254 (Aug 1996), 49.

Orlandini, Lia [actress] (b. Milan, Italy, 12 Jan 1892). JS, p. 324 (in Italian silents from 11912).

Orlando, Guido [actor] (b. Italy, 1907–22 May 1988 [81?], Los Angeles CA). BHD, p. 267.

Orloff, Madame [actress]. No data found. AMD, p. 267. "Madame Orloff," *MPW*, 22 Nov 1913, 853.

Orlov, Dimitri Nicolaievich [actor] (b. Spassk, Russia, 8 May 1892–19 Dec 1955 [63], Moscow, Russia). AS, p. 835.

Orlova, Lyubov Petrovna [actress] (b. Svenigorod, Russia, 29 Jan 1902–26 Jan 1975 [72], Moscow, Russia). AS, p. 835.

Orlova, Vera Georgievna [actress] (b. Moscow, Russia, 27 May 1894–28 Sep 1977 [83], Moscow, Russia). AS, p. 835.

Orman, Felix [actor/scenarist] (*né* Gus Abraham, b. 1884?–15 Jan 1933 [49?], Nashville TN). "Felix Orman," *Variety*, 24 Jan 1933. AS, p. 835. BHD2, p. 201. Truitt, p. 256.

Ormonde, Eugene [actor] (b. Boston MA–d. 16 Jul 1922, Saratoga Springs NY). AS, p. 836. BHD, p. 267. Billy H. Doyle, "Lost Players," *CI*, 134 (Aug 1986), 53.

Ormont, James [journalist/scenarist] (*né* James T. Goldberg, b. 1880?–28 Aug 1962 [82], Santa Monica CA; cancer). "Jerry Lester's Father Dies," *NYT*, 30 Aug 1962, 29:5. "James Ormont," *Variety*, 5 Sep 1962. BHD2, p. 201.

Ormston, Frank D. [technical director] (b. Baltimore MD, 16 Sep 1883–14 Aug 1973 [89], No. Hollywood CA). AMD, p. 267. BHD2, p. 201. "Ormston Now Technical Director," *MPW*, 28 Aug 1915, 1488.

Ornitz, Samuel [scenarist] (b. New York NY, 15 Nov 1890–10 Mar 1957 [66], Los Angeles CA). AS, p. 836. BHD2, p. 201.

Oro, Juan Bustillo [director/scenarist/editor] (b. Mexico City, Mexico, 2 Jun 1904–10 Apr 1989 [84?], Mexico). *Juan Bustillo Oro* (Mexico: Vida cinematografía, 1981). (In Mexican silents from1927.) AS, p. 836 (d. 1998).

Orol, Juan [actor/director/producer] (*né* Juan Orol Garcia, b. La Corogne, Spain, 3 Nov 1897–26 May 1988 [90]). AS, p. 836.

O'Rourke, Brefni [actor] (*né* Brefni O'Rorke, b. Dublin, Ireland, 26 Jun 1889–11 Nov 1946 [57], Ireland). AS, p. 828.

O'Rourke, Eugene [actor] (b. New York NY, 28 Jul 1863–30 Oct 1917 [54], Washington DC). "Eugene O'Rourke," *Variety*, 2 Nov 1917. AS, p. 828. BHD, p. 267. SD, pp. 961–62.

O'Rourke, Jean [child actress]. No data found. AMD, p. 267. "'Baby' Jean with Selig, Gains Fame in Her First Film Part," *MPW*, 9 Oct 1920, 796.

O'Rourke, Thomas P. [actor] (b. 1872?–16 Oct 1958 [86], Queens NY). (Fox.) "Thomas O'Rourke Dies; Actor in Silent Films, 86, Had Been Stage Coach Driver," *NYT*, 19 Oct 1958, 87:1. "Thomas O'Rourke," *Variety*, 22 Oct 1958. AS, p. 828. BHD1, p. 418. IFN, p. 227. Truitt, p. 257.

Orr, Anna [stage/film actress] (b. Piqua OH). No other data found. AMD, p. 268. "Briefs of Biography; A Piquant Miss from Piqua," *NYDM*, 18 Aug 1915, 24:3 (in *The Masked Dancer*, Kalem, 30 Aug 1915). "Anna Orr," *MPW*, 28 Aug 1915, 1461.

Orr, Gertrude [scenarist]. No data found. AMD, p. 268. FDY, p. 435. "Gertrude Orr Is Crack Film Author," *MPW*, 1 Jan 1927, 51.

Orr, Stanley W. [actor] (b. Canada, 7 Apr 1887–19 May 1968 [81], Los Angeles County CA). AS, p. 836. BHD1, p. 614. IFN, p. 227.

Orry-Kelly [costume designer] (*né* John Kelley, b. Sydney, New So. Wales, Australia, 31 Dec 1897–26 Feb 1964 [67], Los Angeles CA; cancer). (WB.) "Orry-Kelly Dies; Movie Designer; Won 2 Oscars for Costumes [*An American in Paris* and *Les Girls*]—With Warners and Fox," *NYT*, 27 Feb 1964, 31:3 (b. Kiama, Australia; drew subtitles for silent movies). "Orry-Kelly," *Variety*, 4 Mar 1964. AS, p. 836 (*né* Walter Orry-Kelly, b. Kiama, Australia). BHD2, p. 201. Katz, p. 880.

Orsini, Silvio [actor] (b. Naples, Italy). JS, p. 324 (in Italian silents from 1922).

Orska, Maria [actress] (b. Nikolajeff, Russia, 16 Mar 1893–16 May 1930 [37], Vienna, Austria). BHD, p. 267.

Ortega, Arthur A. [actor] (b. San Jose CA, 9 Feb 1890–24 Jul 1960 [70], Burbank CA). m. Billie Mack, 26 Jun 1917, Luna Park CA. (Bison.) AS, p. 836. BHD1, p. 419 (Ortego). IFN, p. 227. *MPS*, I, 28 Mar 1913, 14. "Marriages," *Variety*, 29 Jun 1917, p. 13 ("Art A. Ortega and Billie Mack, cowboy and cowgirl with the Wild West at Luna Park, principals in an old-fashioned western ceremony, made part of the performance Tuesday afternoon.").

Ortes, Armand F[rancis] [actor] (b. France, 1880?–20 Nov 1948 [68?], San Francisco CA; auto accident). "Armand F. Ortes," *NYT*, 21 Nov 1948, 88:4 ("Hollywood screen actor of the silent days"). AS, p. 836. Truitt, p. 257.

Orth, Dorothy [actress]. No data found. AMD, p. 268. "Christie Promotes Tiny Dorothy Orr," *MPW*, 2 Jul 1921, 66 (87 lbs.).

Orth, Frank [actor] (b. Philadelphia PA, 21 Feb 1880–17 Mar 1962 [82], Los Angeles CA). AS, p. 836.

Orth, George [actor/director] (b. New York NY, 24 Mar 1894). AMD, p. 268. AS, p. 836. 1921 Directory, p. 272. "Orth Returns to New York," *MPW*, 18 Nov 1916, 1026.

Orth, Louise [actress] (b. Denver CO, 1890?). (K&E; Christie.) AMD, p. 268. AS, p. 836. BHD, p. 267. Agnes Kessler, "Moving Picture Actresses' Fashions," *MPS*, 18 Jun 1915, p. 29 (with photo). "Louise Orth," *MPW*, 22 Jan 1916, 612. "New Christie Beauty," *MPW*, 3 Jul 1920, 109.

Orth, Marion [scenarist]. No data found. AMD, p. 268. FDY, p. 435. "Enlarges Scenario Staff," *MPW*, 24 Mar 1923, 422. "To Collaborate on 'Corporal Kate,'" *MPW*, 5 Jun 1926, 462.

Ortin, Leopoldo "Chato" [actor] (*né* Leopolodo Ortin Salas, b. Lima, Peru, 23 Dec 1893–2 Aug 1953 [59], Acapulco, Mexico). AS, p. 836.

Ortin, Miguel [actor] (b. Spain, 1891–10 May 1978 [87?]). BHD, p. 267.

Ortiz, Mecha [actress] (*née* Maria Mercedes Valera, b. Buenos Aires, Argentina, 1900–20 Dec 1987 [87?], Buenos Aires, Argentina; heart attack). AS, p. 836.

Ortiz, Thula [actress] (b. 1894–30 Jul 1961 [67?], New York NY). AS, p. 837.

Orton, John [scenarist/director] (*né* Major John Orton, b. London, England-d. Apr/May 1943). AS, p. 837. FDY, p. 435.

Orval, Claude [director/scenarist] (*né* Gaston Emile Jean Farragut, b. Paris, France, 1 Nov 1897–24 Apr 1963 [65], Paris, France [extrait de décès no. 18/715/1963]). AS, p. 837.

Ory, Kid [actor/musician] (*né* Edward Ory, b. La Place LA, 25 Dec 1886–23 Jan 1973 [86], Honolulu HI). AS, p. 837.

Orzazewski, Kasia [actress] (b. PA, 16 Oct 1888–17 Jul 1936 [47], Los Angeles CA). AS, p. 837.

Osborne, George (son of **Herbert Standing**) [actor] (b. 1884–11 Aug 1916 [32?], San Francisco CA). (Ince.) BHD, p. 267. "Actors in Trolley Crash; Herbert Standing, His Daughter, and George Osborses' Lives Endangered in [Santa Monica] California," *NYDM*, 7 Jan 1914, 8:2.

Osborne, Hubert [actor/author/scenarist] (b. Kingston, Canada, 26 Jun 1881–25 Oct 1958 [77], Nancy, France [extrait de décès no. 1823/1958]). AS, p. 837.

Osborne, Jefferson [actor] (*né* J.W. Schroeder, b. Bay City MI, 1871–11 Jun 1932 [61], Hondo CA; cerebral hemorrhage). "Jefferson Osborne," *Variety*, 28 Jun 1932. AS, p. 837 (Jefferson Osbourne). AMD, p. 268. BHD, p. 267 (b. Saginaw MI, 1872). IFN, p. 228. Truitt, p. 257. "New Players for MinA," *MPW*, 5 Jun 1915, 1614.

Osborne, Lennie "Bud" [actor/producer] (aka Miles Osborne, b. Knox Co. TX, 20 Jul 1881–2 Feb 1964 [82], Los Angeles CA). (Ince.) "Lennie Osborne," *Variety*, 12 Feb 1964 (age 79). AMD, p. 268. AS, p. 837. BHD, p. 267 (b. 1884). IFN, p. 228 (b. OK, 1884). Katz, pp. 880–81. Truitt, p. 257. "Bud Orborne to Produce," *MPW*, 24 Sep 1921, 421.

Osborne, Osborne H[emley] [founder of Negro Art theatre] (b. 1906?–15 Jan 1934 [27], New York NY; pneumonia). "Osborne H. Osborne," *Variety*, 23 Jan 1934.

Osborne, Ro[w]land [actor] (b. Fulton NY, 1874–19 Apr 1920 [45], New York NY). AS, p. 837. BHD, p. 267. IFN, p. 228.

Osborne, Vivienne [actress] (b. Des Moines IA, 10 Dec 1896–10 Jun 1961 [64], Los Angeles CA). AS, p. 837. BHD1, p. 419 (d. Malibu CA). IFN, p. 228. Katz, p. 881 (began 1920).

Osborne, William Hamilton [lawyer/short story writer/novelist/scenarist]. No data found. AMD, p. 268. "Another Pathe Serial; 'Neal of the Navy,' from the Pen of William Hamilton Osborn [sic], to Be the Next," *NYDM*, 16 Jun 1915, 24:1. "William Hamilton Osborne Writes Pathé Play," *MPW*, 26 Jun 1915, 2074.

Oscar, Henry [actor/director] (né Henry Oscar Wale, b. Hornsey, England, 14 Jul 1891–28 Dec 1969 [78], London, England). AS, p. 837.

Oscar, Martin [actor] (b. Sweden, 28 Dec 1879–25 Apr 1921 [40], Stockholm, Sweden). BHD1, p. 614.

O'Shea, Danny [actor] (b. Philadelphia PA, 1900–ca. 1988 [88?]). (FBO.) AS, p. 828.

O'Shea, James [actor]. No data found. AMD, p. 268. "O'Shea Returns to the Universal," *MPW*, 10 May 1919, 809.

O'Shea, Oscar [actor] (b. 8 Oct 1881–6 Apr 1960 [78], Los Angeles CA). AS, p. 828.

Osman, Sadie Frances [child actress]. No data found. (Essanay.) Photo, *MPSM*, Sep 1912, 2.

Osmun, Leighton Graves [playwright/scenarist] (b. Newark NJ, 1881?–12 Jun 1929 [48], La Jolla CA; tried to save a youngster from drowning). "Leighton Graves Osmun," *Variety*, 19 Jun 1929. AMD, p. 268. BHD2, p. 202. "Leighton Osmun Writing for Metro," *MPW*, 9 Mar 1918, 1374.

Osso, Adolphe [producer] (b. Saffed, Israel, 8 Sep 1894–15 Sep 1961 [67], Paris, France). AS, p. 837.

Osten, Franz [actor/director] (*né* Franz Ostermayr, b. Munich, Germany, 23 Dec 1876–2 Dec 1956 [79], Bad Aibling, Germany). AS, pp. 837–38. BHD2, p. 202.

Osterman, Kathryn (aunt of **Marguerite Risser**) [stage/film actress] (b. Toledo OH, 5 May 1871–25 Aug 1956 [85], New York NY [Death Certificate Index No. 18033]). m. J.J. Rosenthal. "Kathryn O. Rosenthal," *Variety*, 29 Aug 1956. AMD, p. 268. AS, p. 838 (b. 1883). BHD, p. 267 (b. 1883). "Miss Dressler's Troubles; 'Frisco Managers Prevent Her Performance of 'The Merry Gambols' by Force," *NYDM*, 4 Feb 1914, 6:2 (Rosenthal was angry because Osterman was denied a part in the play). "J.J. Rosenthal Out; George M. Anderson Transfers Manager of Gairety to Morosco Theater in Los Angeles," *NYDM*, 25 Feb 1914, 14:2. "Kathryn Osterman a World Star," *NYDM*, 3 Feb 1915, 29:1. "Kathryn Osterman," *MPW*, 13 Feb 1915, 987. "Kathryn Osterman," *MPW*, 31 Jul 1915, 828.

Ostermann, Willy [composer] (b. Mulheim-Rhein, Germany, 1876–6 Aug 1936 [60?]). BHD2, p. 202.

Ostermayr, Ottmar [producer] (b. Munich, Germany, 1886–15 Dec 1958 [72?], Munich, Germany). AS, p. 838. BHD2, p. 202.

Ostermayr, Peter [director/producer] (b. Muhldorf, Germany, 18 Jul 1882–7 May 1967 [84], Munich, Germany). AS, p. 838. BHD2, p. 202.

Ostland, Louis G. [cameraman] (d. 9 Sep 1918, Los Angeles CA; appendicitis). m. Natalie. (World Pictures.) "Louis Ostland," *Variety*, 20 Sep 1918. "Obiturary," *MPW*, 28 Sep 1918, 1855. "Death Benefit Paid for World Film Man," *MPW*, 12 Oct 1918, 237 ($600 to widow). AMD, p. 268. BHD2, p. 202.

Ostriche, Muriel [actress] (*née* Muriel Henrietta Oestrich, b. New York NY, 24 Mar 1896 [Birth Certificate Index No. 14409]–3 May 1989 [93], St. Petersburg FL; cardiac arrest). m. Frank A. Brady, 1918; Charles W. Copp, Jr. Q. David Bowers, *Muriel Ostriche; Princess of Silent Films* (Vestal NY: The Vestal Press, Ltd., 1987). (Thanhouser; Vitagraph; Equitable.) "Muriel Ostriche," *Variety*, 14 Jun 1989. "Muriel Ostriche [obituary]," *CI*, 168 (Jun 1989), 59. AMD, p. 268. AS, p. 838. BHD, p. 268. Spehr, p. 156 (b. 1897). "Muriel Ostriche; Leading Ingenue with the Thanhouser Co.," *MPS*, 3 Oct 1913, 29. "Miss Ostriche Will Be Heard, Too," *MPW*, 7 Mar 1914, 1226. "Brief Biographies of Popular Players," *Motion Picture Magazine*, Feb 1915, 108. "Muriel Ostrich with 'Vita,'" *NYDM*, 31 Mar 1915, 25:2 ("More recently work under over-powerful studio lights resulted in her being stricken blind, and for a time it was feared that she would not recover her sight, but the pretty star is now prepared for active work."). "Muriel Ostriche," *MPW*, 3 Apr 1915, 77. "Muriel Ostriche Joins Vitagraph Players," *MPW*, 10 Apr 1915, 215. "Muriel Ostriche for Equitable," *NYDM*, 1 Sep 1915, 26:4. "Muriel Ostriche with Equitable," *MPW*, 4 Sep 1915, 1627. Muriel Ostriche, "Director and Actor," *MPW*, 30 Oct 1915, 807. "Emily Stevens and Muriel Ostriche to Be Seen in Schomer's Latest Film, 'The Sacred Flame,'" *MPW*, 27 Sep 1919, 1983. "Salient Signs Muriel Ostriche for Series of Ten Five-Reelers," *MPW*, 5 Feb 1921, 719. Michael G. Ankerich, "Reel Stars; Muriel Ostriche, Princess of the Silent Films," *CI*, 164 (Feb 1988), 7, 10. Chapter 18, "Muriel Ostriche," *BS*, pp. 237–48 (includes filmography).

O'Sullivan, Anthony (Tony) [actor/director] (d. 4 Jul 1920, Bronx NY). m. Ida Cavanagh. (Biograph, 1908; Sennett.) "Tony O'Sullivan," *Variety*, 9 Jul 1920 and 23 Jul 1920. AMD, p. 268. AS, p. 829 (d. 5 Jul). BHD, p. 268. IFN, p. 228. Truitt, p. 258. "In the Catskills with Reliancce," *MPW*, XIII, 24 Aug 1912, 748–51. "Tony Sullivan Returns to Biograph," *MPW*, 16 Nov 1912, 653. "Tony O'Sullivan in California," *MPW*, 26 Apr 1913, 360. "Obituary," *MPW*, 24 Jul 1920, 472.

Oswald, Emma K. [producer]. No data found. AMD, p. 268. "Emma K. Oswald, Picture Maker," *MPW*, 22 Apr 1916, 635.

Oswald, Margaret [actress]. m. Henry McRae. (Universal.)

Oswald, Marianne [actress/singer/producer] (*née* Sarah Alice Bloch, b. Sarreguemines, France, 9 Jan 1901 [extrait de naissance no. 16/1901]-25 Feb 1985 [84], Limeil-Brevannes, France). AS, p. 838.

Oswald, Richard [actor/director/producer/scenarist] (*né* Richard W. Ornstein, b. Vienna, Austria, 5 Nov 1880–11 Sep 1963 [82], Dusseldorf, Germany). AS, p. 838. BHD2, p. 202.

Oswalda, Ossi [actress/producer] (*née* Oswalda Stäglich, b. Pankow, Prague, Czechoslovakia, 2 Feb 1895–17 Jul 1947 [52], Prague, Czechoslovakia). (Began 1915.) AS, p. 838 (b. Berlin, Germany, 1897). BHD1, p. 420 (b. 1899; d. 1 Jan 1948, Berlin, Germany). Vittorio Martinelli, "Kino-Lieblinge," *Griffithiana*, 38/39 (Oct 1990), 26.

Otani, Takejiro [producer] (b. Kyoto, Japan, 13 Dec 1877–27 Dec 1969 [92], Kyoto, Japan). AS, p. 838.

Otho, Henry [actor] (*né* Henry Otho Wright, b. Brooklyn NY, 10 Aug 1888–6 Jun 1940 [51], Los Angeles CA). AS, p. 838.

Otis, Elita Proctor [actress] (b. Cleveland OH, 1851?–10 Aug 1927 [76], Pelham NY). "Elita Proctor Otis," *Variety*, 17 Aug 1927 (d. 13 Aug). AS, p. 838. BHD, p. 268. IFN, p. 228.

Ott, Frederick P. [a member of Edison's scientific staff, not an actor] (b. 1860–24 Oct 1936 [76], West Orange NJ). "Frederick P. Ott," *Variety*, 28 Oct 1936. AS, p. 838. BHD, p. 268; BHD2, p. 202. IFN, p. 228. Spehr, p. 156. WWVC, p. 103.

Ott, Jackie [child actor]. No data found. AMD, p. 268. "Baby Ott Signed," *MPW*, 21 Jun 1924, 730.

Ottani, Nino [director/producer] (b. Udine, Italy, 4 Aug 1894–12 Feb 1949 [54], Rome, Italy). AS, p. 838.

Otte, Henri Rolf [actor] (b. 1879?–17 Dec 1930 [51], San Francisco CA). "Henri Rolphe Otte," *Variety*, 24 Dec 1930 (age 50). AS, p. 838. BHD, p. 268. IFN, p. 228.

Ottenheimer, Adolph [actor] (b. 1876–20 Aug 1937 [61?], Los Angeles CA). AS, p. 838.

Ottiano, Rafaela [stage/film/radio actress] (b. Venice, Italy, 4 Mar 1888–18 Aug 1942 [54], E. Boston MA; heart attack). "Rafaela Ottiano, Actress, Is Dead; Player of Stage, Screen and Radio, Who Made Debut at 18, Stricken in Boston; Appeared with Notables; Had Character Roles in Films of Greta Garbo and John and Lionel Barrymore," *NYT*, 18 Aug 1942, 22:2 (in Mae West's *Diamond Lil*, 1928). AS, p. 838. BHD1, p. 420. IFN, p. 228. Truitt, p. 258 (b. 1894).

Otto, Arthur [actor] (d. 17 Jan 1918, Tacoma WA). AS, p. 838. BHD, p. 268.

Otto, Henry [operatic stage/stock/film actor/director] (b. St. Louis MO, 8 Aug 1877–3 Aug 1952 [74], Los Angeles CA). (Selig; Balboa; American; Nestor-Universal.) "Henry Otto," *NYT*, 5 Aug 1952, 19:3. "Henry Otto," *Variety*, 6 Aug 1952. AMD, p. 268. AS, p. 839. BHD1, p. 420; BHD2, p. 202. IFN, p. 228. 1921 Directory, p. 272. Truitt, p. 258 (b. 1878). "Henry Otto," *NYDM*, 17 Mar 1915, 24:1. "Henry Otto Near Injury," *NYDM*, 12 May 1915, 24:4 (he helped Winifred Greenwood down a cliff on location for *The Guiding Light*, lost his balance, and fell on the rocks below. Fortunately, the waves had just gone out; he received bruises and scratches). "Henry Otto Leaves American [for Universal]," *NYDM*, 1 Sep 1915, 27:1. "Henry Otto with Universal," *MPW*, 11 Sep 1915, 1838. "Laemmle Sends Otto to New York," *MPW*, 5 Feb 1916, 766. "Henry Otto, Now a Metro Director," *MPW*, 27 May 1916, 1494. "Henry Otto with New Company," *MPW*, 16 Jun 1917, 1785–86. "Otto to Be Lockwood Co-Director in Yorke-Metro," *MPW*, 24 Aug 1918, 1140. "Otto to Direct May Allison," *MPW*, 25 Jan 1919, 454. "Henry Otto Felt Call of Footlights at an Early Age," *MPW*, 15 Mar 1919, 1479. "Karger Engages Directors for Three Plays to Be Filmed by Screen Classics," *MPW*, 19 Jul 1919, 352. Billy H. Doyle, "Lost Players," *CI*, 152 (Feb 1988), C13.

Otto, Paul [actor/director] (b. Berlin, Germany, 8 Feb 1878–30 Nov 1943 [65], Berlin, Germany; suicide). BHD, p. 268 (d. 25 Nov); BHD2, p. 202. Vittorio Martinelli, "Kino-Lieblinge," *Griffithiana*, 38/39 (Oct 1990), 64 (began 1910).

Otton, William G. [actor] (b. England, 1852–7 May 1930 [78], New York NY). BHD, p. 268. IFN, p. 228.

Otvos, A. Dorian [scenarist] (b. Budapest, Hungary, 11 Oct 1893–27 Aug 1945 [51], Los Angeles CA). BHD2, p. 202.

Oudart, Félix Charles [actor] (b. Lille, France, 8 Jun 1881–10 Aug 1956 [75], Suresnes, France). AS, p. 839.

Ouida [author/scenarist] (*née* Marie-Louise de la Ramee, b. France, 1839–1908 [69?], France). AS, p. 839.

Oukrainsky, Serge [actor] (b. Odessa, Ukraine, Russia, 3 Dec 1885–1 Nov 1972 [86], Los Angeles CA). BHD1, p. 614.

Oursler, Fulton [actor/scenarist] (*né* Charles Fulton Oursler, b. Baltimore MD, 22 Jan 1893–24 May 1952 [59], New York NY; heart attack). AS, p. 839. BHD2, p. 202.

Ouspenskaya, Maria [stage/film actress] (b. Tula, Russia, 29 Jul 1876–3 Dec 1949 [73], Woodland Hills CA; burn injuries suffered from smoking in bed on 1 Dec). "Mme. Ouspenskaya, Actress, 73, Is Dead; Veteran of Character Roles in

Plays and Films Succumbs to Burn Injuries on Coast," *NYT,* 4 Dec 1949, 108:6. "Maria Ouspenskaya," *Variety,* 176, 7 Dec 1949, 63:3. AS, p. 839. BHD, p. 268. IFN, p. 228 (b. 1887).

Outcault, Richard F[elton] (uncle of **William S. Rising**) [artist/producer] (b. Lancaster OH, 14 Jan 1863–25 Sep 1928 [65], Flushing, LI NY [Death Certificate No. 5757; cardiac exhaustion and cirrhosis of the liver]). "Richard Outcault, Noted Artist, Dead; Father of the Modern Comic Newspaper Supplement Succumbs at 65; Creator of Buster Brown; Son Was the Original—'The Yellow Kid' Another of His Many Characters," *NYT,* 26 Sep 1928, 27:5. AMD, p. 269. AS, p. 839. *See* Musser, pp. 267–71. "Buster Brown's Pup Sure Cure for Blues; Outcault Cartoons Transferred to the Stage; Two Chief Figures Funny; Create Enough Laughter to Atone for the Sins of the So-Called Musical Comedy [*Buster Brown*]," *NYT,* 25 Jan 1905, 9:3 (starring George Ali as Tige). "Outcault in Motion; Celebrated Cartoonist Embarks in the Picture Business with 'Buster Brown' and Others," *MPW,* 27 Dec 1913, 1551.

Ouvrard, Gaston Emile [actor/singer] (b. Bergerac, France, 10 Mar 1890–26 Nov 1981 [91], Caussade, France [extrait de décès no. 108/1981]). AS, p. 839.

Ouyang, Yu-Chen [actor]director] (*né* Li-Yuan Ouyang, b. Liuyang CO, China, 1889–1962 [73?], Peking, China). AS, p. 839.

Overbaugh, Roy F. [cameraman] (b. 14 Nov 1882–6 Feb 1966 [83], Los Angeles Co. CA). AMD, p. 269. BHD2, p. 202. FDY, p. 465. "Overbaugh Seriously Ill," *MPW,* 10 Jan 1920, 230.

Overholt, Miles [title writer]. No data found. AMD, p. 269. "Overholt to Write Titles for Triangle," *MPW,* 11 May 1918, 866.

Overman, Lynne [actor] (b. Marysville MO, 19 Sep 1887–19 Feb 1943 [55], Santa Monica CA). m. Emily Drange. AS, p. 839.

Overton, Evart Emerson [actor] (b. Osborne OH, 5 Aug 1889–27 Jan 1949 [59], New York NY [Death Certificate Index No. 2236]). (Vitagraph.) "Evart E. Overton," *NYT,* 29 Jan 1949, 13:4 (does not cite film career). AMD, p. 269. AS, p. 839. BHD, p. 268 (d. Riverdale NY). Slide, p. 147. "Evart Emerson Overton," *MPW,* 19 Jun 1915, 1928. Billy H. Doyle, "Lost Players," *CI,* 134 (Aug 1986), 53.

Ovey, George [stage/film actor] (*né* George Overton Odell, b. Trenton MO, 13 Dec 1870–23 Sep 1951 [80], Los Angeles CA). m. Louise Horner. (Horsley, 1915.) AMD, p. 269. AS, p. 839. BHD1, p. 421. IFN, p. 228. Katz, p. 884 (b. Kansas City MO). MSBB, p. 1026 (b. Kansas City MO). SD. "New Players for MinA," *MPW,* 5 Jun 1915, 1614. "George Ovey," *MPW,* 10 Jul 1915, 285. "Ovey Remains with Horsley," *MPW,* 18 Sep 1915, 2001. "George Ovey, Comedian, Horsley," *MPN,* 21 Oct 1916, 187 (b. Kansas City KS). "Horsley Re-Engages Ovey," *MPW,* 31 Mar 1917, 2116. "George Ovey," *MPW,* 12 May 1917, 971. "George Ovey," *MPW,* 3 Nov 1917, 684. "George Ovey Leaves Horsley," *MPW,* 29 Dec 1917, 1947–48. Billy H. Doyle, "Lost Players," *CI,* 169 (Jul 1989), C15-C16, 38, 46.

Owen, Catherine Dale [stage/film actress] (b. Louisville KY, 28 Jul 1903–7 Sep 1965 [62], New York NY). m. H.P. Metzger. "Catherine Owen, Actress, 62, Dies; She Played Leading Roles on Stage and in Films," *NYT,* 8 Sep 1965, 47:1. "Catherine Dale Owen," *Variety,* 15 Sep 1965. AMD, p. 269. AS, p. 839. BHD1, p. 421. IFN, p. 228. Katz, p. 884. SD. Truitt, p. 258. "Stage Star Signed," *MPW,* 1 Oct 1927, 287.

Owen, Cecil [actor/director/casting director] (b. London, England, 2 Jun 1873–15 Jul 1928 [55], Rockville Centre, LI NY). m. Florence. "Cecil Owen," *Variety,* 18 Jul 1928. AMD, p. 269. AS, p. 839. BHD, p. 268' BHD2, p. 202. SD, p. 964. "Cecil Owen Now Casting Director," *MPW,* 9 Apr 1921, 618.

Owen, Dale *see* **Heller, William**

Owen, Garry [actor] (b. Brookhaven MI, 18 Dec 1897–1 Jun 1951 [53], Los Angeles CA). AS, p. 839.

Owen, Louise [actress]. No data found. AMD, p. 269. "Louise Owen, Vogue 'Heavy,'" *MPW,* 15 Apr 1916, 450. "Lillian Owen Joins Universal," *MPW,* 11 Nov 1916, 873.

Owen, Reginald [actor/writer] (*né* John Reginald Owen, b. Wheathampstead, Hertfordshire, England, 5 Aug 1887–5 Nov 1972 [85], Boise ID; heart attack). m. (1) Lydia Bilbrooke (*née* Lydia Macbeth); (2) Mrs. Harold Austin; (3) Barbara Haveman. "Reginald Owen Is Dead at 85; Star of the Stage and Screen; Roles Ranged from 'Forum' to Shakespeare—Wrote Novel and Two Plays," *NYT,* 7 Nov 1972, 38:1. "Reginald Owen," *Variety,* 15 Nov 1972. AS, p. 840. BHD1, p. 421. IFN, p. 229. Katz, pp. 884–85.

Owen, Ruth Bryan (daughter of William Jennings Bryan) [producer]. No data found. AMD, p. 269. "Bryan's Daughter to Produce Films," *MPW,* 13 Aug 1921, 713.

Owen, Seena [stage/film actress/scenarist] (*née* Signe Aüen, b. Spokane WA, 14 Nov 1894–15 Aug 1966 [71], Los Angeles CA). m. **George Walsh**, Feb 1916–24 (d. 1981). (Kalem, 1914; Reliance-Majestic; Fine Arts; Artcraft.) "Seena Owen," *NYT,* 19 Aug 1966, 33:4. "Seena Owen," *Variety,* 24 Aug 1966. AMD, p. 269. AS, p. 840. BHD1, p. 421; BHD2, p. 202. FFF, p. 157 (b. 1896). FSS, p. 231. IFN, p. 229. Katz, p. 885. KOM, pp. 154–56. MSBB, p. 1040. Truitt, p. 259. "Two Stars United," *MPW,* 1 Jul 1916, 81. "Fox Signs Seena Owen," *MPW,* 11 Aug 1917, 942. "Three Stars Form Companies," *MPW,* 9 Aug 1919, 807. "Seena Owen Is Leading Woman for Lytell in Metro Picture," *MPW,* 10 Apr 1920, 281. George Katchmer, "Seena Owen," *CI,* 226 (Apr 1994), 42.

Owen, Tudor [actor] (b. Wales, 20 Jan 1898–13 Mar 1979 [81], Los Angeles Co. CA). AS, p. 840 (b. 30 Jan). BHD, p. 268. IFN, p. 229.

Owens, Lela [actress]. No data found. m. Marc Edmund Jones, Nov 1917. (Pathé.) "Marriages," *Variety,* 30 Nov 1917, p. 9.

Owens, William [actor] (b. New NY, 1863?–20 Aug 1926 [63], Chicago IL). "William Owens," *Variety,* 25 Aug 1926. AS, p. 840. BHD, p. 268. IFN, p. 229. Truitt, p. 259.

Owsley, Monroe [stage/film actor] (b. Atlanta GA, 11 Aug 1900–7 Jun 1937 [36], Belmont CA; heart attack). "Monroe Owsley, Hollywood Actor; Suave Villain of Many Films with Wide Popularity Is Dead on Coast; Formerly on Stage Here; Made Broadway Debut in 'Young Blood' with Helen Hayes After Playing in Stock," *NYT,* 9 Jun 1937, 25:5 (related to Ethan Allan on the paternal side). "Monroe Owsley," *Variety,* 9 Jun 1937 (d. SF CA). AS, p. 840. BHD1, p. 421 (d. SF CA). IFN, p. 229. Truitt, p. 259.

Oxford, Burleigh Fritz [scenarist]. No data found. FDY, p. 435.

Oxilia, Nino [director] (*né* Angelo Agostino Adolfo Oxilia, b. Turin, Italy, 13 Nov 1889–18 Nov 1917 [28], Mt. Tomba in Monte Grappa, Italy; hit by an Austrian grenade). AS, p. 840. JS, p. 326 (in Italian silents from 1913).

Oya, Ichijiro [actor] (b. Tokyo, Japan, 11 Feb 1894–28 May 1972 [78], Tokyo, Japan; cancer). AS, p. 840.

Ozanne, Robert Achille [actor] (b. Limeil Brevannes, France-d. 14 Sep 1941, France). AS, p. 840.

Ozenne, Jean Marcel [actor] (b. Paris, France, 13 Feb 1898–27 Jan 1969 [70], Paris, France). AS, p. 840.

Ozep, Fedor Aleksandrovich [director/scenarist] (b. Moscow, Russia, 9 Feb 1893–20 Jun 1949 [56], Beverly Hills CA). m. **Anna Sten**—div. (d. 1993). AS, p. 840. BHD2, p. 202 (b. 1895).

Ozores, Frances Mriano [actor] (b. Madrid, Spain, 17 Oct 1890). AS, p. 840.

Ozu, Yasujiro [director/scenarist] (b. Fukagano, Japan, 15 Dec 1903–12 Dec 1960 [56], Tokyo, Japan; cancer). Nora Sayre, "The Visual Poetry of a Japanese Master," *NYT,* 21 Jan 1994, C1:5, C14, C15. AS, p. 840 (b. Fukagawa, Japan; d. 1963). BHD2, p. 202 (d. 1963). SD.

P

Pabst, G.W. [actor/producer/scenarist/director] (*né* Georg Wilhelm Pabst, b. Raudnitz, Bohemia, 27 Aug 1885–29 May 1967 [81], Vienna, Austria; cerebral hemorrhage). "G.W. Pabst, Maker of Films Abroad; Early Viennese Producer and Director Dies at 82," *NYT,* 31 May 1967, 43:1. "G.W. Pabst," *Variety,* 7 Jun 1967. AS, p. 841. BHD, p. 268; BHD2, p. 203. IFN, p. 229. JS, p. 326 (made films in Italy in 1952 and 1954). Katz, pp. 886–87. Waldman, p. 223.

Pacchioni, Italo [director/cinematographer/writer] (b. Mirandola di Modena, Italy, 29 Mar 1872–11 Jul 1940 [68], Milan, Italy). JS, p. 326 ("In 1895 he became the first Italian to organize a moving picture show, in a store in Porta Genova." One of his films, *La gabbia dei matti* [1896], starred his son Achille, his brother Enrico, his cousin Ettore, and a parrot).

Packard, Clayton L[incoln] [actor] (b. Washington DC, 6 Mar 1887–7 Sep 1931 [44], San Diego CA; complications after surgery). (DeMille.) "Clayton L. Packard," *Variety,* 15 Sep 1931 (age 43). AS, p. 841 (d. 6 Sep). BHD, p. 268. IFN, p. 229. Truitt, p. 259.

Packard, Frank L. [writer]. No data found. AMD, p. 269. "Packard Pays Great Tribute to Fox's 'The White Moll,'" *MPW,* 21 Aug 1920, 1055. "Author's Rights Upheld," *MPW,* 5 Jan 1924, 32.

Packnell, George [cinematographer]. No data found. FDY, p. 465 (Packnell and Pocknall).

Padden, Sarah [stage/film actress] (b. London, England, 16 Oct 1881–4 Dec 1967 [86], London, England). (Film debut: *Obey the Law,* Columbia, 5 Nov 1926.) AMD, p. 269. AS, p. 841. BHD1, p. 422 (d. LA CA). BR, pp. 394–98. IFN, p. 229. "Fox Signs Up Sarah Padden, Stage Actress," *MPW,* 7 May 1927, 40. Buck Rainey, "Sarah Padden," *CI,* 122 (Aug 1985), C4-C5; 123 (Sep 1985), 57; 124 (Oct 1985), C7.

Paddock, Charles [world champion sprinter/actor] (b. Gainesville TX, 8 Nov 1900–22 Jul 1943 [43], Sitaka AL; killed in a plane crash). AS, p. 841. BHD, p. 268 (d. Sitka AK). IFN, p. 229. Joseph Jackson, "Things I Have Seen," *Paris and Hollywood,* 2 (Sep 1926), 50 (Paddock signed to appear in *The College Flirt* with Bebe Daniels. The director, Clarence Badger, expected great things of him; Paddock was a "good-looking blond with a wonderful smile." 'I don't expect to rival John Barrymore, but I may give Rin-Tin-Tin a run,' says the genial Paddock.").

Padilla, Emma [actress] (*née* Emma Padilla Rosales, b. Mexico City, Mexico, 8 Mar 1900–2 Jul 1966 [66], Mexico City, Mexico; diabetes). (In Mexican silents from at least 1917.) AS, p. 841. BHD, p. 268. IFN, p. 229.

Padjen, Jack [actor] (aka Jack Duane, b. MT, 14 Dec 1887–1 Feb 1960 [72], Riverside Co. CA). m. "Prairie Rose" Henderson. AS, p. 841. BHD1, p. 422. IFN, p. 229. Robert Donaldson, "Famous Extras," *MPC,* Feb 1927, 32–33 [photo], 68, 80.

Padula, Vincent [actor] (b. Argentina, 14 Jul 1898–16 Jan 1967 [68], Glendale CA; peritonitis). AS, p. 841 (b. 1893). BHD1, p. 422. IFN, p. 229 (age 67).

Pagano, Bartolomeo [actor] (b. Sant'Ilario Ligure, near Nervi, Genoa, Italy, 22 Sep 1878–24 Jun 1947 [68], Sant'Ilario Ligure, Italy). m. Camilla Balduzzi. AS, p. 841. BHD, p. 269 (b. 27 Sep). IFN, p. 229 (b. Nerva). JS, p. 327 (in Italian films from 1914; "discovered" by Roberto Roberti to play Maciste in *Cabiria* [1914] at 20 lire a day. He left films after 1928 because of a serious diabetic condition.).

Pagano, Ernest S. [producer/scenarist] (b. Florence CO, 16 Jan 1900–29 Apr 1953 [53], Beverly Hills CA; heart attack). (RKO; Metro; Paramount; Columbia; Universal; U-I.) "Ernest S. Pagano," *NYT,* 1 May 1953, 21:5. "Ernest S. Pagano," *Variety,* 6 May 1953. AS, p. 841. BHD2, p. 203. IFN, p. 229.

Pagay, Sofie [actress] (b . Berlin, Germany, 22 Apr 1857–23 Jan 1937 [79], Berlin, Germany). BHD1, p. 422. IFN, p. 229.

Pagden, Leonard [actor] (b. 1862–24 Mar 1928 [66]). BHD, p. 269. IFN, p. 229.

Page, Bob *see* **Page, Robert**

Page, Earle [actor] (b. Denver CO, 2 May 1890). (Keystone; Universal.) AS, p. 841.

Page, Izola Forrester [scenarist] (b. 1879–6 Mar 1944 [65?], Keene NH). BHD2, p. 203.

Page, James E. [actor] (b. London, England, 1 Jun 1870–26 Mar 1930 [59], London, England). "J.E. Page," *Variety,* 9 Apr 1930, 76:3 ("J.E. Page, 60, actor, died London hospital, March 27. For 20 consecutive years he played every Christmas in the London revivals of 'Charley's Aunt' and it is doubtful if he ever appeared in any other play."). AS, p. 842. IFN, p. 229.

Page, Mann [playwright/scenarist] (b. 1890?–15 Mar 1961 [71], Keene NH). "Mann Page," *NYT,* 18 Mar 1961, 23:3. "Mann Page," *Variety,* 22 Mar 1961. AS, p. 841. BHD2, p. 203. FDY, p. 435.

Page, Norman [actor] (b. Nottingham, England, 1876–4 Jul 1935 [59], London, England). BHD, p. 269. IFN, p. 229.

Page, Robert [actor] (b. 1886–23 Jul 1943 [57]). BHD, p. 269. IFN, p. 229.

Paget, Alfred [actor] (b. England, 1880?–1925 [45?], Los Angeles CA). (Biograph, 1910; Mutual; K&E.) AS, p. 841. BHD, p. 269. Katz, p. 888. William E. Wing, "Along the Pacific Coast," *NYDM,* 8 Apr 1915, 24:2 (recently lost his wife and new-born baby the same night). George Katchmer, "Alfred Paget," *CI,* 235 (Jan 1995), 40.

Paget, Doriel [actress] (b. 1897-Aug 1991 [94?], England). BHD, p. 269.

Pagnol, Marcel [director/producer/scenarist] (b. Aubagne, France, 28 Feb 1895–18 Apr 1974 [79], Paris, France). BHD2, p. 203.

Pahle, Ted [cinematographer] (*né* Theodore J. Pahle, b. 1899–9 Jan 1979 [79?], New York NY). BHD2, p. 203. FDY, p. 465.

Paige, Jean [actress] (*née* Lucile Beatrice O'Hair, b. Paris IL, 3 Jul 1895–15 Dec 1990 [95], Los Angeles CA). m. **Albert E. Smith**, Paris IL, Dec 1920 (d. 1958). (Film debut: *The Discounters of Money,* Vitagraph, 1917.) "Jean Page," *Variety,* 24 Dec 1990, p. 54. AMD, p. 269. AS, p. 841 (b. 1897). BHD, p. 269. Slide, p. 111 (b. 1896). WWS, p. 106 (b. 1898). "Jean Paige Signs Vitagraph Contract," *MPW,* 13 Jul 1918, 216. "Jean Paige Signs a New Contract with Vitagrpah," *MPW,* 12 Jul 1919, 236. "Joe Ryan and Jean Paige Will be Co-Starred in New Vitagraph Serial," *MPW,* 3 Jan 1920, 105. "Vitagraph Will Star Jean Paige in 'Black Beauty,'" *MPW,* 11 Sep 1920, 240. "Albert E. Smith, Vitagraph President, Weds Jean Paige, Popular Screen Star," *MPW,* 25 Dec 1920, 989. Cal York, "Plays and Players," *Photoplay,* Mar 1921, 88 (wed Smith).

Paige, Mabel [actress] (*née* Mabel Roberts, b. New York NY, 19 Dec 1880–8 Feb 1954 [73], Van Nuys CA). m. Charles Ritchie. "Mabel Paige Dead; Actress 7 Decades," *NYT,* 10 Feb 1954, 29:2 (age 74; 1st film: *Young and Willing,* 1942). "Mabel Paige," *Variety,* 17 Feb 1954 (age 73). AS, p. 841. BHD1, p. 422. IFN, p. 230. Katz, p. 889. SD. Truitt, p. 259.

Paige, Patsy *see* **Brill, Patti**

Paigne, Eva Marius [actress]. No data found. AMD, p. 269. "Eva Marius Paigne with Associated," *MPW,* 30 Oct 1915, 807.

Pal, George [illustrated titles for silents; Puppetoons] (*né* Gyula Gyorgy Marczinczak, b. Cegled, Hungary [near Budapest], 1 Feb 1908–2 May 1980 [72], Beverly Hills CA; heart attack). m. Zsoka ca. 1929. (Hunnia Films, Budapest; Ufa, Germany; Paramount.) AS, p. 843. BHD2, p. 203 (b. Gegled, Hungary). Chris Buchman, Jr.,"George Pal," *CI,* 70 (Jul 1980), 46–47.

Palasthy, Alexander [actor] (b. Hungary, 1877–16 Mar 1948 [71], Los Angeles Co. CA). BHD1, p. 423. IFN, p. 230.

Palermi, Amleto [director/producer] (b. Rome, Italy, 11 Jul 1889–20 Apr 1941 [51], Rome, Italy). AS, p. 843. BHD2, p. 203. JS, pp. 328–29 (in Italian films from 1914).

Palermi, Mimmo (b. Italy, 1917–1925 [8?]). BHD, p. 269.

Paley, Selma [actress]. No data found. m. **Oliver Morosco** (d. 1945). AMD, p. 269. "Mrs. Morosco's Suit Against Husband Temporarily Checked," *MPW,* 28 Aug 1920, 1143. "Morosco and Wife Discontinue Suits; Basis of Settlement Is Not Disclosed," *MPW,* 24 Sep 1921, 406.

Paley, William Daley [cameraman] (b. Lincolnshire, England, 1843?–2? Jun 1924 [81?], Hollywood CA; complications after an amputation). Wife d. 8 Dec 1913. (Nestor.) "W.D. Paley Dead; Succumbs at Hollywood—Perfected First News Camera," *Variety,* 4 Jun 1924 (b. 1857). AMD, p. 269 (William A. Paley). AS, p. 843 (b. 1857). "William Paley in Hard Lines," *MPW,* 30 Nov 1912, 860. "William Paley Relief Fund," *MPW,* 7 Dec 1912, 988. "William A. Paley Loses Foot," *MPW,* 28 Dec 1912, 1273. "Paley Relief Fund," *MPW,* XV, 4 Jan 1913, 65. "Fund Established for Unfortunate Cameraman," *MPW,* 11 Jan 1913, 142. "Paley Relief Fund Grows," *MPW,* 1 Feb 1913, 454. *MPW,* 5 Apr 1913, 34 (states age as over 70). "Who Will Help?," *MPW,* 10 Jan 1914, 179 (wife died). "Paley Getting Around Again," *NYDM,* 11 Feb 1914, 34:2 (recently lost a leg; helped financially by a subscription from Vitagraph which "has enabled him to purchase a cork leg for himself, and justr as soon as it is delivered by the manufacturer he will be able to get about again and help himself."). "William Paley Wants a Job," *MPW,* 9 May 1914, 801. Paul H. Dowling, "He's Sixteen Years Ahead of All War Photographers," *Photoplay Magazine,* Mar 1917, 122–23. *See* Robert C. Allen, "Contra the Chaser Theory," in *Film Before Griffith,* ed. John L. Fell (Berkeley CA: University of California Press, 1983), p. 111.

Palfi, Lotte [actress] (*née* Lotte Mosbacher, b. Bochum, Germany, 28 Jul 1903–8 Jul 1991 [87], New York NY). AS, p. 843. BHD, p. 269.

Pallay, Fran [actress] (b. Atlanta GA, 1904–6 Nov 1981 [77?], Brentwood CA). m. **Henri Menjou** (d. 1956). AS, p. 843. BHD, p. 269.

Pallen, Dr. Condé B[enoist] [writer/editor/executive] (b. St. Louis MO, 5 Dec 1858–26 May 1929 [70], New York NY). m. Georgianna McDougall Adams, 1886. "Conde B. Pallen, Noted Editor, Dies; He Had Been Head of Roman Catholic Publications for Many Years; Wrote Novels and Poetry; Honored by Two Popes—He Occupied the Chair of Philosophy in St. Louis University," *NYT,* 27 May 1929, 25:3. AMD, p. 270. AS, p. 843. "Catholic Film Association," *MPW,* 29 Aug 1914, 1246.

Pallenberg, Max [actor] (b. Vienna, Austria, 18 Dec 1877–20 Jun 1934 [56], Karlevy Vary, Czechoslovakia). AS, p. 844. BHD1, p. 423. IFN, p. 230.

Pallette, Eugene W. [actor] (*né* Eugene Phelps, b. Winfield KS, 8 Jul 1889–3 Sep 1954

[65], Los Angeles CA; lung cancer). m. **Phyllis Gordon**; Marjorie Cagnacci, Sep 1932. "Eugene Pallette, Actor, Dies at 65; Popular Character Player Was Known for His Ample Girth and Foghorn Voice," *NYT,* 4 Sep 1954, 11:3; "Pallette Will Is Probated," *NYT,* 9 Sep 1954, 36:8. "Eugene Pallette," *Variety,* 8 Sep 1954 (d. Hollywood). AMD, p. 270. AS, p. 844. BHD1, p. 423. FSS, p. 231. GK, pp. 742–62. IFN, p. 230. Katz, p. 890. KOM, pp. 156–57. Truitt, pp. 259–60. WWS, p. 269. "Gene Pallette Waits for Air Call," *MPW,* 8 Jun 1918, 1418. "Pallette on Trip to New York," *MPW,* 26 Jun 1920, 1762. George A. Katchmer, "Rotund Eugene Pallette," *CI,* 148 (Oct 1987), 29–31. Richard E. Braff, "An Index to the Films of Eugene Pallette," *CI,* 173 (Nov 1989), 54–56; *CI,* 174 (Dec 1989), 54–56. R.E. Braff, "Additional Film Credits for Eugene Pallette," *CI,* 238 (Apr 1995), 41.

Palma, Mona [actress]. No data found. AMD, p. 270. "Mona Palma Chosen," *MPW,* 11 Sep 1926, 118.

Palmarini, Umberto [actor] (b. Macerata, Italy, 1883–31 Dec 1934 [51?], Milan, Italy). m. **Mercedes Brignone**. JS, p. 330 (in Italian silents from 1914).

Palmentola, Paul V. [art director] (b. Italy, 18 Feb 1888–19 Apr 1966 [78], Woodland Hills CA). BHD2, p. 203.

Palmer, Corliss [actress] (*née* Corliss Martin, b. near Macon [Edison?] GA, 25 Jul 1902–27 Aug 1952 [50], Carmarillo CA state hospital for the mentally insane). m. (1) **Eugene V. Brewster**, 1926 (d. 1939); (2) stuntman William Taylor. (Film debut: *The Sailmaker;* Paramount.) AMD, p. 270. AS, p. 844. BHD1, p. 423 (b. 1909). "Corliss Palmer Begins Her Climb to Stardom," *MPW,* 19 Mar 1921, 260. Lillian Montanye, "The Girl with the Eyes of Mystery," *MPC,* Oct 1921, 44–45, 90–91. Paul Paige, "Close-Ups and Fade-Outs," *Paris and Hollywood,* 2 (Sep 1926), 56 (theater owners held a convention in Los Angeles. The independents felt strapped in by the big studios, which control 10,000 of 17,000 theaters. The owners wanted to investigate the report that Eugene V. Brewster "had ordered his editors to favor Metro-Goldwyn in publicity, because this company is said to have given a contract to Corliss Palmer, Mr. Brewster's sweetheart." Brewster and Palmer had been engaged for about six years, but he has "been unable to marry her because of an insurmountable difficulty, his wife. The theatre owners think they should take action to discourage the featuring of Miss Palmer. To be consistent, they should discourage the featuring of Marion Davies," who is also over-publicized.). Billy H. Doyle, "Lost Players," *CI,* 167 (May 1989), 45.

Palmer, Ernest G. [cinematographer] (b. Kansas City MO, 6 Dec 1885–22 Feb 1978 [92], Pacific Palisades CA). "Ernest Palmer," *Variety,* 1 Mar 1978 (filmed *Ivanhoe,* 1912). AS, p. 844. BHD2, p. 203. FDY, p. 465. IFN, p. 230. Katz, p. 891. Richard Koszarski, "Ernest Palmer on Frank Borzage and F.W. Murnau," *Griffithiana,* 46 (Dec 1992), 115–20.

Palmer, Fred[erick] **B.** [scenarist] (b. Belmont NY, 31 May 1881). AMD, p. 270. BHD2, p. 203. "Fred B. Palmer Will Write Keystone Comedies," *MPW,* 24 Nov 1917, 1157.

Palmer, Harry [writer/cartoonist/animator]. No data found. AMD, p. 270. "Horsley Adds to His Forces," *MPW,* 8 Aug 1914, 821. "Palmer War Sketches for Centaur," *MPW,* 5 Sep 1914, 1385. "Kriterion Komic Kartoon," *MPW,* 20 Feb 1915, 1155. "Cartoonists Go to Court," *MPW,* 24 Apr 1915, 532. "Mutual's Animated Cartoons," *NYDM,* 8 Sep 1915, 26:3 ("Keeping Up with the Joneses," a syndicated newspaper cartoon feature, to be animated by Palmer; released by Gaumont on the Mutual programme). "Harry Palmer Writes Comedy for 'Budd' Ross," *MPW,* 8 Jan 1916, 221. "Harry Palmer Making News Cartoons," *MPW,* 18 Mar 1916, 1842. "The Place of the Animated Cartoon," *MPW,* 22 Jul 1916, 638.

Palmer, Inda [actress] (*née* Independence Palmer, b. 4 Jul 1853–16 Apr 1923 [69], near Ridgewood NJ; found dead). "Inda Palmer Dead; Skeleton Found Near Ridgewood N.J.—Disappeared Last April," *Variety,* 15 Nov 1923 (Mrs. Independence Palmer Guard). AS, p. 844. BHD, p. 269. IFN, p. 230 (d. 10 Nov).

Palmer, Jack F. [actor] (b. Toronto, Canada, 27 Apr 1866–27 Sep 1928 [62], Los Angeles CA). AS, p. 844. BHD, p. 269. IFN, p. 230.

Palmer, Kyle D. [publicist]. No data found. AMD, p. 270. "Palmer on Famous Players Press Staff," *MPW,* 6 Dec 1919, 660.

Palmer, Lorle [stage/film actress] (b. 1878–21 Jul 1952 [74], New York NY). m. stage actor Alfred G. Swenson. "Lorle Palmer," *Variety,* 187, 30 Jul 1952, 79:2. AMD, p. 270. BHD, p. 269. "Lorle Palmer," *MPW,* 20 Feb 1915, 1151.

Palmer, Lorna [actress] (b. Chicago IL, 1907–14 Jun 1928 [21?], Los Angeles CA; pneumonia). AS, p. 844 (Palmar). BHD, p. 269.

Palmer, Nancy [actress]. No data found. AMD, p. 270. "Christy Model for World Pictures," *MPW,* 4 May 1918, 678.

Palmer, Patricia *see* **Gibson, Margaret**

Palmer, Robert [cinematographer] (b. 1891–10 Jan 1988 [98?], Woodland Hills CA). BHD2, p. 203.

Palmer, Shirley [actress]. No data found. AMD, p. 270. "Samuel Goldwyn Has New Star: Shirley Palmer," *MPW,* 16 Apr 1927, 648.

Palmer, Violet [actress]. AMD, p. 270. "World Pictures Announces 'Ginger' as a May Release," *MPW,* 29 Mar 1919, 1829. George Katchmer, "Violet Palmer," *CI,* 227 (May 1994), 52:1.

Palmeri, Mimi [actress] (b. New York NY). AMD, p. 270. MH, p. 132. "Mrs. Arthur Friend Finds a Movie Star," *MPW,* 31 Mar 1923, 569. David A. Balch, "Must a Girl Pay a Price for Screen Fame? 'No!' Says Mimi Palmeri," *MW,* 26 May 1923, 3, 29.

Palmi, Bruno Emanuel [actor] (b. Rome, Italy, 18 Feb 1890). JS, p. 331 (in Italian silents from 1916).

Palombi, Augusto [actor] (d. 5 Feb 1924, Rome, Italy). BHD, p. 269.

Palsikar, Nana [actress] (b. 1907–1 Jun 1984 [77?], Bombay, India). AS, p. 845. BHD1, p. 424.

Panacci, Charles [actor] (b. Sea Bright NJ, 1903–16 Mar 1927 [24?], Long Branch NJ; complications from pneumonia). AS, p. 845.

Pangborn, Franklin [stage/film actor] (b. Newark NJ, 23 Jan 1889–20 Jul 1958 [69], Santa Monica CA). "Franklin Pangborn, Actor, Dies; Noted for Harassed Clerk Roles; Comedian in Many Movies and in Television Starred with Nazimova on Stage," *NYT,* 21 Jul 1958, 21:2. "Franklin Pangborn," *Variety,* 23 Jul 1958 (age 65). AMD, p. 270. AS, p. 845. BHD1, p. 424. IFN, p. 230. Katz, p. 892. Truitt, p. 260 (b. 1894). "Pangborn Is Signed as P.D.C. Comedian," *MPW,* 5 Feb 1927, 424. "Franiklin Pangborn," *MPW,* 23 Jul 1927, 240. "Starred by DeMille," *MPW,* 20 Aug 1927, 517. *CI,* 244 (Oct 1995). R.E. Braff, "A Filmography of Franklyn (Franklin) Pangborn," *CI,* 253 (Jul 1996), C22-C24, C34-C38. Richard Finegan, "Additional Films of Franklin Pangborn," *CI,* 272 (Feb 1998), C19-C20.

Pann, Peter [actor] (b. Hamburg, Germany, 1872?–29 Dec 1948 [76], New York NY). "Peter Pann," *NYT,* 31 Dec 1948, 16:2. "Peter Pann," *Variety,* 5 Jan 1949. AS, p. 845. BHD, p. 269. IFN, p. 230.

Pannaci, Charles [actor] (b. 1904?–15 Feb 1927 [23], Long Branch NJ; pneumonia). "Charles Pannaci," *Variety,* 16 Mar 1927. BHD, p. 269. IFN, p. 230. Truitt, p. 260.

Panzer, Paul [actor] (b. 1867?–11 Apr 1937 [70?], New York NY; heart attack). (Vitagraph, 1905–09; Pathé.) "Paul Panzer," *Variety,* 14 Apr 1937. AS, p. 845. BHD, p. 269. Spehr, p. 156 (1867–1937). Truitt, p. 260.

Panzer, Paul W. [actor] (*né* Paul Wolfgang Panzerbeiter, b. Wurtzberg, Bavaria, Germany, 3 Nov 1871?–15 Aug 1958 [86?], Los Angeles CA). (Edison, 1905.) "Paul Panzer," *NYT,* 17 Aug 1958, 85:2. "Paul W. Panzer," *Variety,* 20 Aug 1958 (age 86). AMD, p. 270. AS, p. 845. BHD1, p. 424 (b. 1872). FSS, p. 232. IFN, p. 230 (b. 1872). Katz, p. 892 (in films in 1904). Slide, p. 147 (b. 1872). Truitt, p. 260 (b. 1872). "Paul W. Panzer on Tour," *MPW,* 22 Nov 1913, 874. "No Pathe Stock; All But Three Players [Panzer, Pearl White and Crane Wilbur] Let Out—Will Engage Actors as Pictures Are Put On," *NYDM,* 22 Jul 1914, 22:1 (Jersey CIty NJ company. Eclair had recently dropped its Eastern production.). "Gossip of the Studios; Paul Panzer," *NYDM,* 22 Jul 1914, 23:1 (it was reported that Panzer's manager, M. Krauss, had had M.K. Jerome [Watterson, Berlin & Snyder] write a song, *The Moving Picture Man,* about Panzer. But *see* Wilbur, Crane, *NYDM,* 29 Jul 1914). "Paul Panzer Goes on Tour," *MPW,* 2 Jan 1915, 81. "Paul Panzer Popular," *MPW,* 13 Mar 1915, 1620. "Paul Panzer Back from Lecture Trip," *MPW,* 1 May 1915, 733. "Paul W. Panzer," *MPW,* 27 Nov 1915, 1642. "A New Actor: Paul Panzer, Jr.," *MPW,* 22 Jul 1916, 642 (son born). "Paul W. Panzer," *MPW,* 17 Feb 1917, 1010. Paul Panzer, "The Actor in the Early Days," *MPW,* 10 Mar 1917, 1509–10. "What Became of Paul Panzer?," *MW,* 28 Oct 1922, 15, 26. "Panzer Plays 3 Roles," *MPW,* 2 Feb 1924, 373. "Paul Panzer, One of the Pioneers, Is with Pathé," *MPW,* 30 Jul 1927, 331. George Katchmer, "Paul Panzer," *CI,* 226 (Apr 1994), 43 (began in *Stolen by Gypsies,* 1904).

Paola, Dria [actress] (*née* Etra Pitteo, b. Rovigo, Italy, 21 Nov 1909). AS, p. 845. JS, p. 333 (in Italian silents from 1929; retired in 1941).

Paoli, Evelina [actress] (*née* Eveline Paoli Papa, b. Florence, Italy, 30 Mar 1878). JS, p. 333 (in Italian silents from 1915).

Paoli, Raoul [actor] (b. Ajaccio, Corsica, Italy). AMD, p. 270. AS, p. 846. "Paoli in Cast," *MPW,* 9 Jul 1927, 101.

Pape, Edward Lionel [actor] (b. Brighton, England, 17 Apr 1877–21 Oct 1944 [67], Woodland Hills CA). AMD, p. 270. AS, p. 846. BHD1, p. 424 (d. Calabassas CA). IFN, p. 230 (b. 1877).

Truitt, p. 260. "Lionel Pape," *MPW,* 16 Jan 1915, 379.

Papke, Billy [actor] (b. Spring Valley IL, 17 Sep 1886–26 Nov 1936 [50], Newport Beach CA). BHD, p. 269.

Paquet, Jacqueline Paule [actress] (b. Namur, Belgium-d. 18 Sep 1955). m. **Kenneth Gibson**, 1926 (d. 1972). AS, p. 846. June Lee, "Dan Cupid's Bulletin Board," *Paris and Hollywood,* Sep 1926, 96 (recently married Gibson).

Paradisi, Olga [actress] (b. Naples, Italy). JS, p. 335 (in Italian silents from 1915).

Paradisi, Umberto Mario Lodovico (brother of Clelia Paradisi [**Paola Grey**]) [director] (b. San Giorgio di Lomellina, Italy, 29 Jun 1878 [extrait de naissance no. 8/1878]-21 Jun 1933 [55], Turin, Italy [extrait de décès no. 1081/2/1933]). AS, p. 846. JS, p. 335 (in Italian silents from 1913).

Paramore, Edward E., Jr. [poet/playwright/journalist/scenarist] (b. Manchester MA, 17 Sep 1895–1 May 1956 [60], Shreveport LA; fractured skull in auto accident). "Edward E. Paramore, Jr., Screen Writer, Dies in Shreveport, La., After Accident," *NYT,* 2 May 1956, 31:1 (he sued Mack Sennett for $5,000 for using his *Ballad of Yukon Jake* [1921] in "the silent film comedy 'Yukon Jake.'"). "Edward E. Paramore, Jr.," *Variety,* 9 May 1956. AS, p. 846. BHD2, p. 204. IFN, p. 230.

Paranjpe, Raja [actor/director/producer] (*né* Rajabhau Dattatraya Paranjpe, b. India, 1909–9 Feb 1979 [70?], Poona, India). AS, p. 846. BHD1, p. 424.

Pardee, C.W. (Doc) [actor] (b. 6 Jan 1885–17 Jul 1975 [90], Glendale AZ). AS, p. 846 (d. Glendale CA). BHD1, p. 424. IFN, p. 230.

Parish, Guido [director] (aka Guido Schamberg, b. Rome, Italy). AS, p. 847. JS, pp. 335–36 (in Italian silents from 1919—retired 1927; "discovered" **Marcella Albani**).

Park, Custer B. [actor] (b. MO, 4 Nov 1899–25 Sep 1955 [55], Los Angeles CA). BHD, p. 270.

Park, Ida May [director] (b. Los Angeles CA, 28 Dec 1879–13 Jun 1954 [74], Los Angeles CA). m. **Joseph de Grasse**, 1920 (d. 1940). (Directorial debut: *The Flashlight,* Bluebird, 1917.) AMD, p. 270. AS, p. 847. BHD2, p. 204. IFN, p. 230. 1921 Directory, p. 272. "Ida May Park's Latest—'The Full Cup,'" *MPW,* 25 Mar 1916, 1991. "Ida May Park, Director," *MPW,* 14 Jul 1917, 222. "Ida May Park Director," *MPW,* 3 Nov 1917, 701.

Park, Josephine [stage/film actress] (b. Glen Falls NY-d. 12 Jan 1931, Glen Falls NY). m. **Conway Tearle** (d. 1938). AS, p. 847. BHD, p. 270. IFN, p. 230. SD.

Park, Lester [producer]. No data found. AMD, p. 270. "Lil Walker Pictures to Be Made on the Coast," *MPW,* 7 Sep 1918, 1436. "Industry Needs Ideas, Says Hodkinson Producers," *MPW,* 14 Sep 1918, 1572.

Park, Post [actor/stuntman] (*né* Custer B. Park, b. MO, 4 Nov 1899–18 Sep 1955 [55], Hollywood CA; heart attack). "Custer B. Park," *Variety,* 28 Sep 1955 ("western film actor and stuntman for 28 years"). AS, p. 847 (d. 25 Sep). BHD1, p. 425. IFN, p. 230. Truitt, p. 261.

Park, Samuel J. [actor/scenarist] (b. Birmingham AL, 2 Sep 1892–15 Jan 1960 [67], Keansburg NJ). BHD2, p. 204.

Parke, Mrs. Alice Harrington *see* **Harrington, Alice**

Parke, William [stage/film actor/director] (b. Bethlehem PA, 1873–28 Jul 1941 [68], New York NY [Death Certificate Index No. 15766]; heart attack). "Wm. Parke Dies; Veteran of Stage; As Mr. Witherspoon He Took Here Nightly Last Laugh in 'Arsenic and Old Lace'; Had Played with Sothern; Appeared in 'If I Were King'—Subsequently Was Manager for Richard Mansfield," *NYT,* 29 Jul 1941, 15:1. "William Parke," *Variety,* 30 Jul 1941. AMD, p. 271. BHD, p. 270; BHD2, p. 204. IFN, p. 230. Lowrey, p. 146. 1921 Directory, p. 272. Truitt, p. 261. "Thanhouser Engages Notable Players," *MPW,* 18 Sep 1915, 2015. "Directors with Dramatic Instinct Needed," *MPW,* 16 Sep 1916, 1809. "William Parke," *MPW,* 24 Mar 1917, 1937. "'Business' Counts, Says Picture Producer," *MPW,* 21 Jul 1917, 379. "Parke to Direct Ruth Roland," *MPW,* 28 Jun 1919, 1916. "Parke Goes to Goldwyn," *MPW,* 20 Sep 1919, 1832.

Parker, Adele [actress] (b. Plainsfield NJ, 1885–20 Jan 1966 [80?], Cleveland OH). BHD, p. 270.

Parker, Agnes Gust [dancer/actress] (d. 1935). IFN, p. 230.

Parker, Albert [director] (b. Brooklyn NY, 1887?–10 Aug 1974 [87], London, England). m. (1) Margaret Green; (2) Margaret Johnston. "Albert Parker, 87, Director and Actors' Representative," *NYT,* 14 Aug 1974, 36:5. "Albert Parker," *Variety,* 21 Aug 1974. AMD, p. 271. BHD, p. 270; BHD2, p. 204. IFN, p. 230. "Parker Engaged by Fairbanks," *MPW,* 5 Oct 1918, 63. "Albert Parker Will Make Specials for J.M. Schenck Starring Norma Talmadge," *MPW,* 25 Dec 1920, 1028. Dunham Thorp, "How Fairbanks Took the Color Out of Color; The Man who made 'The Black Pirate' explains how the Menace of Color was met and overcome," *MPC,* May 1926, 28–29, 87–89. "Albert Parker Will Direct Gloria Swanson's Second Opus," *MPW,* 9 Apr 1927, 570.

Parker, Austin [scenarist] (b. Great Falls MT, 11 Sep 1892–20 Mar 1938 [45], Los Angeles CA). BHD2, p. 204.

Parker, Barnett [stage/film actor] (*né* William Barnett Parker, b. Batley, Yorkshire, England, 11 Sep 1886–5 Aug 1941 [54], Los Angeles CA). "Barnett Parker; Screen Character Actor Had Played Also on Stage Here," *NYT,* 6 Aug 1941, 17:2. AMD, p. 271. AS, p. 848. BHD1, p. 425. IFN, p. 231. "Barnett Parker, Thanhouser Leading Man," *MPW,* 28 Oct 1916, 565.

Parker, Cecil [stage/film actor] (*né* Cecil Schwabe, b. Hastings, Sussex, England, 3 Sep 1897–20 Apr 1971 [73], Brighton, England). "Cecil Parker, 73, a British Actor; Star of Stage and Film, Who Played Gentlemen, Dies," *NYT,* 22 Apr 1971, 45:1. "Cecil Parker," *Variety,* 28 Apr 1971. AS, p. 848 (d. 21 Apr). BHD1, p. 425. IFN, p. 231. Katz, p. 894. Truitt, p. 261.

Parker, Dorothy [writer] (*née* Dorothy Rothschild, b. West End NJ, 22 Aug 1893–7 Jun 1967 [73], New York NY [Death Certificate Index No. 11687]). m. (1) Robert Walter Fennell, 22 Jul 1917 (d. ca. 1920); (2) Edward P. Parker II; (3) **Alan Campbell** (d. 1963). "Dorothy Parker, 73, Literary Wit, Dies," 1:2; "Dorothy Parker, Short-Story Writer, Poet, Critic, Sardonic Humorist and Literary Wit Dies at Age 73," *NYT,* 8 Jun 1967, 38:1; 10 Jun, 33:1; Morris Kaplan, "Dorothy Parker's Will Leaves Estate of $10,000 to Dr. King," 27 Jun 1967, 22:2. "Dorothy Parker," *Variety,* 14 Jun 1967. AS, p. 848. BHD2, p. 204. Katz, p. 895. SD. "News of the Dailies," *Variety,* 20 Feb 1920, 27:1 (Parker contested the will of Fennell who left $300,000 "and cut her off without a penny.").

Parker, Emma Jean [actress]. No data found. AMD, p. 271. "Emma Jean Parker," *MPW,* 9 Jun 1917, 1586.

Parker, Flora [actress] (b. Perth Amboy NJ, 1 Sep 1883–9 Sep 1950 [67], Los Angeles CA). m. **Carter DeHaven** (d. 1977). (Film debut: *The College Orphan,* Universal, 1915.) AMD, p. 271. AS, p. 300 (Flora De Haven); p. 848 (Flora Parker, b. 1893). BHD, p. 147. IFN, p. 77. WWS, p. 287. "The DeHavens with 'Smiling Bill' Parsons," *MPW,* 25 Jan 1919, 516. "The Carter DeHavens to Appear in Capitol Comedies," *MPW,* 19 Apr 1919, 375. "DeHavens Emphasize Teamwork," *MPW,* 30 Aug 1919, 1268. "Mr. and Mrs. Carter DeHaven Affiliate with Arthur S. Kane," *MPW,* 26 Jun 1920, 1777.

Parker, Sir Gilbert [writer/scenarist] (b. Camden East, Ontario, Canada, 1863–6 Sep 1932 [69?], London, Canada; heart attack). AMD, p. 271. AS, p. 848. BHD2, p. 204 (d. London, England). "Sir Gilbert Parker Guest of Commodore Blackton," *MPW,* 22 Sep 1917, 1830. "Sir Gilbert Parker Sails for England," *MPW,* 13 Oct 1917, 220. "Blackton Talks of Parker's Works," *MPW,* 24 Nov 1917, 1202. "Sir Gilbert Parker Signs Contract to Write Original Stories for Paramount," *MPW,* 9 Oct 1920, 825.

Parker, Harry B. [director] (b. 1891–1 Oct 1947 [56?], Van Nuys CA). BHD2, p. 204.

Parker, Lemuel B. [director/producer/scenarist] (b. 1865?–3 Apr 1928 [63], Amarillo TX; heart trouble). m. stage actress Minnie Dixon. "Lemuel Parker," *Variety,* 11 Apr 1928, p. 58. AMD, 58:5. BHD2, p. 204 (d. Temple TX). "Parker Goes to California," *MPW,* 28 Sep 1912, 1259.

Parker, Lucy [actress] (b. 1863?–21 Mar 1947 [84], New York NY). "Lucy Parker," *Variety,* 26 Mar 1947. AS, p. 848. BHD, p. 270. IFN, p. 231.

Parker, Marion [actress] (d. Nov 1920, Venice CA; heart failure). m. **Billy Armstrong** (d. 1924). AMD, p. 271. BHD, p. 270. IFN, p. 231. "Obituary," *MPW,* 20 Nov 1920, 318.

Parker, Max [art director]. No data found. AMD, p. 271. "Parker on Vacation," *MPW,* 7 Apr 1923, 614. "Cecil B. DeMille Secures Max Parker as Art Director for His Productions," *MPW,* 4 Jul 1925, 73.

Parker, Norton S. [producer/novelist/scenarist] (b. 1901?–5 Jul 1969 [68], Jackson Heights, Queens NY; heart attack). m. Kallie Foutz. "Norton Parker, A Producer, Dead; Led the Writers Branch of Army Pictorial Center," *NYT,* 8 Jul 1969, 39:3 (began in early 1920's in Hollywood; wrote *The Lady from Hell,* with Blanche Sweet and Roy Stewart). "Norton S. Parker," *Variety,* 16 Jul 1969. AS, p. 848. BHD2, p. 204. IFN, p. 231.

Parker, Vivien [actress] (b. 1896–2 Feb 1974 [77], Bronx NY; pulmonary embolism). AS, p. 849. BHD, p. 270. IFN, p. 231.

Parker, Watt L. [publicity]. No data found. AMD, p. 271. "Parker to Handle Selznick Advertising; Bartlett Goes Over to Famous Players," *MPW,* 11 Feb 1922, 611. "Warner Bros. Advertising Head Lauds Tour of Radio Station," *MPW,* 12 Jun 1926, 545.

Parker, William [scenarist] (b. Walla Walla WA, 17 Sep 1886). AMD, p. 271. BHD2, p. 205. "Newspaperman Writes Scenario," *MPW,* 25 Mar 1916, 2039. "William Parker Joins U. Scenario Staff," *MPW,* 19 Aug 1916, 1258.

Parkes, Edward [actor] (b. New York NY, 1893–24 Jul 1985 [92?], Los Angeles CA). BHD1, p. 425.

Parkhurst, Frances [actress] (d. 31 Dec 1969, Caldwell NJ). AS, p. 849. BHD, p. 270. IFN, p. 231. Truitt, p. 261.

Parkington, Beulah [actress] (b. 1899?–7 Nov 1958 [59], Los Angeles CA; heart attack). "Beulah Parkington," *Variety,* 26 Nov 1958 (in films over 30 years). AS, p. 849. BHD1, p. 426 (b. Szczecin, Poland). IFN, p. 231. Truitt, p. 261.

Parkinson, Harry B. [director/producer] (b. Blackburn, England, 1884-Aug 1970 [86?], England). BHD2, p. 205.

Parlo, Dita [actress] (*née* Gerthe Gerda Kornstaedt, b. Stettin, Germany, 4 Sep 1906–13 Dec 1971 [65], Paris, France [extrait de décès no. 790]). m. Frank Guetal, 1949. (Ufa; Paramouont, Joinville; last film: *La Dame de Pique,* 1965.) "Dita Parlo," *Variety,* 265, 12 Jan 1972, 77:5 (last film: *Queen of Spades*). AS, p. 849 (b. 1908). BHD, p. 270. IFN, p. 231 (b. 1907). JS, p. 336 (made *La signora di Montecarlo,* Italy, 1938). Waldman, p. 225 (b. 1907).

Parmalee, Philip [actor] (b. ca. 1913). BHD, p. 270.

Parmer, Devore [actor]. No data found. (Edison; Nestor; Biograph; Cosmos Features, Crystal, Harvard; Metro; Arrow; Triangle; Erbograph.) AMD, p. 271. "Devore Palmer with Triangle," *MPW,* 30 Oct 1915, 981. "Devore Parmer," *MPW,* 18 Dec 1915, 2161.

Parpagnoli, Mario [actor] (b. Rome, Italy). JS, p. 336 (in Italian silents from 1917; one in Argentina, 1927).

Parr, Charles Theodore [actor/stage manager] (b. 1843?–3 Nov 1923 [80], New York NY). "Charles Theodore Parr," *Variety,* 8 Nov 1923. AS, p. 849. BHD, p. 270.

Parr, Peggy [actress]. No data found. AMD, p. 271. "Jans Signs Peggy Parr," *MPW,* 17 Jan 1920, 428.

Parr, Thelma [actress]. No data found. (Paramount.) *MW,* 25 Jul 1925, cover painting. Paul Paige, "Close-Ups and Fade-Outs," *Paris and Hollywood Screen Secrets Magazine,* Aug 1927, 98 (won a Miss Massachusetts beauty contest and a place in the Paramount Picture School, "and she has risen steadily in the esteem of that studio ever since.").

Parr, Walter [actor] (b. 1913). BHD, p. 270.

Parravicini, Florencio [actor/director/scenarist] (b. 1874–25 Mar 1941 [67?], Buenos Aires, Argentina). BHD2, p. 205.

Parrish, Beverly [actress] (b. 10 May 1919–27 Feb 1930 [10], Los Angeles CA). BHD1, p. 615.

Parrish, Helen [film/TV actress] (b. Columbus GA, 12 Mar 1924–22 Feb 1959 [34], Los Angeles CA; cancer). m. (1) Charles Lang, 1942–54; (2) John Guedel, 1956. (Film Debut: *When Babe Comes Home* [at age 2]). "Helen Parrish Dead; Film Actress Since Age of 2 Had TV Show on Coast," *NYT,* 23 Feb 1959, 23:1 (age 35). "Helen Parrish," *Variety,* 25 Feb 1959 (age 35). AS, p. 849. BHD1, p. 426 (b. 1923). BR, pp. 403–06. IFN, p. 231. Katz, pp. 896–97 (b. 1922). Truitt, p. 261. Buck Rainey, "Helen Parrish; Her 21-Year Film Career Was Superseded by That New Medium, TV," *CI,* 131 (May 1986), 31, C16, 50.

Parrish, Laura Reese [actress] (b. 1887–15 Aug 1977 [90], Los Angeles CA). AS, p. 850. BHD1, p. 426. IFN, p. 231.

Parrish, Robert B. [actor/film editor/director/writer] (b. Columbus GA, 4 Jan 1916–4 Dec 1995 [79], Southampton, LI NY; heart attack). m. Kathleen Thompson. *Growing Up in Hollywood* (NY: Harcourt Brace Jovanovich, 1976); *Hollywood Doesn't Live Here Anymore* (Boston: Little, Brown & Co., 1988). Lawrence Van Gelder, "Robert Parrish, 79, Film Editor-Director, Dies," *NYT,* 6 Dec 1995, B17:1 (in *City Lights,* 1931; AA with Francis Lyon as editor of *Body and Soul,* 1947). AS, p. 850. BHD1, p. 426.

Parrish, Mary Catherine [actress] (b. 1873–13 Sep 1951 [78], Los Angeles Co. CA). BHD, p. 270. IFN, p. 231.

Parrot, Charles *see* **Chase, Charley**

Parrot, James (brother of **Charley Chase**) [actor/scenarist/director] (aka Poll Parrott, *né* Paul James Chase, b. Baltimore MD, 2 Aug 1892–10 May 1939 [46], Los Angeles CA; heart attack). (Pathé.) "James Parrott," *Variety,* 17 May 1939 (age 42). AMD, p. 271. AS, p. 850 (b. 1898). BHD, p. 270; BHD2, p. 205. IFN, p. 231 (b. 1898). Katz, p. 897 (b. 1892). Truitt, p. 261 (b. 1892). "James Parrot to Direct," *MPW,* 10 Jul 1926, 117. "Directing Chase," *MPW,* 28 May 1927, 267.

Parry, Harvy [stuntman/Keystone Cop] (b. CA, 23 Apr 1900–18 Sep 1985 [85], Sherman Oaks CA; heart attack). "Harvey Parry," *Variety,* 25 Sep 1985. AS, p. 850. BHD, p. 270.

Parry, Lee [actress] (*née* Mathilde Benz, b. Munich, Germany, 14 Jan 1901–24 Jan 1977 [76], Bad Tolz, Germany). AS, p. 850. BHD1, p. 615.

Parsons, Carola [actor] (d. 18 Dec 1958, New York NY). BHD, p. 270.

Parsons, Donovan [lyricist/scenarist] (b. 1888–10 Jan 1980 [91?], Brighton, England). BHD2, p. 205.

Parsons, Harriet, "Baby Parsons" (daughter of **Louella O. Parsons**) [actress/producer/scenarist] (*née* Harriet McCaffrey, b. Burlington IA, 23 Aug 1906–2 Jan 1983 [76], Santa Monica CA; cancer). m. King Kennedy (d. 1974). (Film debut: *The Magic Wand,* ca. 1912.) "Harriet Parsons, Film Maker; Daughter of Louella Parsons," *NYT,* 4 Jan 1983, D18:6 (d. Hollywood). "Harriet Parsons," *Variety,* 5 Jan 1983. AS, p. 850 (b. Burlington KY). BHD, p. 270; BHD2, p. 205. SD.

Parsons, Louella O. [mother of **Harriet Parsons**] [scenario editor/scenarist/actress/columnist] (*née* Louella Rose Oettinger, b. Freeport IL, 6 Aug 1881–9 Dec 1972 [91], Santa Monica CA nursing home; arteriosclerosis). m. (1) John McCaffrey, Jr. (from Vicksburg MS), 1905 (d. 1911); (2) Dr. Harry Martin (d. 1951). (Essanay.) Murray Illson, "Louella Parsons, Gossip Columnist, Dies; Hollywood Her World," *NYT,* 10 Dec 1972, 85:1. "Parsons Rites Wednesday," *NYT,* 11 Dec 1972, 42:3. AS, p. 850. BHD2, p. 205 (b. 1884). IFN, p. 231. "Mass for Louella Parsons Attended by Stars on Coast," *NYT,* 14 Dec 1972, 50:4 (at Good Shepherd Roman Catholic Church. Pallbearers: Ben Lyon; Harry Brand [publicist]; Louis Collins [butler]; Dr. Rexford Kennamer [personal physician]; King Kennedy [former son-in-law]; and Gordon Maynard [cousin]. Attendees included Bob Hope, Danny Thomas, George Burns, Jack Benny, Dorothy Lamour, Irene Dunne, Cesar Romero, and David Janssen.). "Gossip of the Studios," *NYDM,* 20 Jan 1915, 33:2. William Lord Wright, "For Photoplay Authors, Real and Near," *NYDM,* 7 Apr 1915, 30:3 (Luella [sic] O. Parsons has been appointed Editress of the Chicago *Herald Photoplay Page,* and is also editing a scenario page in that newspaper. She knows her business."). William Lord Wright, "For Photoplay Authors, Real and Near; About the Photoplay," *NYDM,* 14 Jul 1915, 30:2 ("well-known editress and authoress of photoplays," expounds on the progress of recent scenario writing.).

Parsons, P[ercy] **Allen** [publicist] (b. Newbury MA, 12 Jun 1878–3 Oct 1944 [66], England). (Pathé Frérès.) AMD, p. 271. AS, p. 850. BHD1, p. 426 (b. Louisville KY). F.J.B., "With the Film Men; P.A. Parsons," *NYDM,* 2 Dec 1914, 25:1. "Parsons to Give Whole Time to Advertising," *MPW,* 6 Apr 1918, 71. P.A. Parsons, "Doping It Out for the Papers," *MPW,* 20 Jul 1918, 327–28. "P.A. Parsons Tells A.M.P.A. That Simple, Direct Words Do Most to Help Sales Talks Hit the Bull's Eye," *MPW,* 5 Mar 1921, 36. P.A. Parsons, "A History of Motion Picture Advertising," *MPW,* 26 Mar 1927, 301, 304–05, 308–09. "P.A. Parsons," *MPW,* 26 Mar 1927, 311. *See* Beecroft, Chester for citation.

Parsons, William "Smiling Bill" [actor/producer/founded National Film Company of America] (b. New York NY, 14 Aug 1878–29 Sep 1919 [41], Los Angeles CA; diabetic coma). m. **Billie Rhodes** (d. 1988). "Bill Parsons' Death," *Variety,* 3 Oct 1919. AMD, p. 272. AS, p. 850. BHD, p. 270; BHD2, p. 205 (b. Middletown NY). IFN, p. 231. Katz, p. 897. "Parsons Making Comedies for Goldwyn; Producer of 'Tarzan of the Apes' to Issue Twenty-six Two-Reelrs in the Next Year," *MPW,* 23 Feb 1918, 1096:1. "Billy Parsons Strong for Settings," *MPW,* 11 May 1918, 871. "Parsons Makes Speech to Strand Audience," *MPW,* 20 Jul 1918, 379. "Parsons Ends His Eastern Vacation," *MPW,* 17 Aug 1918, 971. "Parsons in New Comedies," *MPW,* 28 Dec 1918, 1495. "What Ho! Ye Darkest Africa Vamps," *MPW,* 18 Jan 1919, 344. "The DeHavens with 'Smiling Bill' Parsons," *MPW,* 25 Jan 1919, 516. "Smiling Billy a Benedict," *MPW,* 22 Mar 1919, 1628. "Parsons Renews Contract with Goldwyn," *MPW,* 12 Apr 1919, 235. "Parsons Seriously Begins Serials," *MPW,* 16 Aug 1919, 941.

Pascal, Ernest [art director/title writer/scenarist] (b. London, England, 11 Jan 1896–4 Nov 1966 [70], Bernardsville NJ). (Paramount, 1923.) "Ernest Pascal," *Variety,* 9 Nov 1966 (d. 24 Oct 1966 [71]; AA for *Sunset Boulevard* [1950]; *Samson and Delilah* [1950]; *Frenchman's Creek* [1944]). AS, p. 850. BHD2, p. 205 (d. LA CA). FDY, p. 447. IFN, p. 231.

Pascal, Gabriel [director/producer] (b. Arad, Romania, 4 Jun 1894–6 Jul 1954 [60], New York NY). BHD2, p. 205.

Pasha, Kalla [wrestler/actor] (*né* Joseph T. Rickard, b. New York NY, 1877?–10 Jun 1933 [56?], Talmage CA). (Sennett.) "Joseph T. Rickard," *Variety,* 13 Jun 1933 (age 50). AMD, p. 272. AS, p. 851. BHD1, p. 426 (b. 1879). IFN, p. 232 (b. Paris, France, 1879). Truitt, pp. 261–62. "Sennett Renews Contract with Pasha," *MPW,* 6 Dec 1919, 679.

Pasquali, Alberto Vittorio Antonio [actor] (b. Turin, Italy, 24 Aug 1882 [extrait de naissance no. 2351]-15 Feb 1929 [46], Milan, Italy). AS, p. 851. JS, pp. 337–38 (in Italian silents from 1915).

Pasquali, Ernesto Maria [head of Pasquali Films/scemarist/director/producer] (b. Montù Beccaria, near Pavia, Italy, 1883–9 May 1919 [35?], Turin, Italy [extrait de décès no. 1103/1/1919]). AS, p. 851. BHD2, p. 205. JS, p. 339 (in Italian silents from 1909).

Pastore, Pietro [soccer player/actor] (b. Padua, Italy, 3 Mar 1903). JS, pp. 338–39 (in Italian silents from 1928).

Pastrone, Giovanni [director/producer] (*né* Piero Fosco, b. Montechiaro d'Asti, Italy, 13 Sep 1882–29 Jun 1959 [76], Turin, Italy). Paolo Cherchi Usai, *Giovanni Pastrone* (Florence, Italy: La Nuova italia, 1985). AS, p. 851. BHD2, p. 206 (b. 13 Sep; d. 27 Jun). IFN, p. 232. JS, p. 339 (b. 11 Sep 1883-d. 27 Jun; in Italian films from 1909; invented the *carrello* ["dolly"], for tracking shots).

Patch, Wally [stage/film actor] (*né* Walter Vinicombe, b. Willesden, England, 26 Sep 1888–27 Oct 1970 [82], London, England). "Wally Patch," *Variety,* 18 Nov 1970 ("in films since 1919"). AS, p. 852. BHD1, p. 427 (b. London). IFN, p. 232. SD.

Paterson, Elinor [actress]. No data found. AMD, p. 272. "Elinor Paterson, 'Miracle' Nun, Signed to 'U' Picture Contract," *MPW,* 12 Mar 1927, 113. "Elinor Paterson to Quit Pictures," *MPW,* 10 Sep 1927, 85.

Pates, Gwendolyn [actress] (b. TX, 1893). m. actor/producer **William Crew**. (Pathé Fréŕes; Selig.) BHD, p. 270. *MPW,* 9 Aug 1913, 1227. "Miss Pates with Selig," *NYDM,* 1 Apr 1914, 34:4. Lester Sweyd, "What They Are Doing Now," *Motion Picture Magazine,* Feb 1918, 12 ("Miss Pates is now delighting vaudeville audiences in her playlet, 'Solitaire,' in which she is supported by her husband, Wm. Grew [sic], who was formerly a Selig player.").

Pates, Vivian [actress]. No data found. m. James S. Kirkbride, 1 Feb 1914. (Lubin; Pathé.) "Studio Gossip," *NYDM,* 29 Apr 1914, 29:1.

Pathé, Charles Morand (brother of **Emile Pathé**) [executive/producer/Pathé Frères, 1896] (b. Chevry-Cossigny, France, 25 Dec 1863–25 Dec 1957 [94], Monte Carlo, Monaco). "Charles Pathe, Film Pioneer, Dies; Founder of Newsreel Known by Crowing Rooster Was Expert in Distribution," *NYT,* 27 Dec 1957, 19:1. "Charles Pathe, 94, Dies in Monaco," *Variety,* 1 Jan 1958. AMD, p. 272. AS, p. 852. BHD2, p. 206. IFN, p. 232. Katz, p. 900. WWVC, pp. 106–07. "Pathé Signs Contracts with Dramatists," *MPW,* 25 Apr 1908. W. Stephen Bush, "Charles Pathé's Views," *MPW,* 24 Jan 1914, 390–91. "Charles Pathé Shoulders Camera," *MPW,* 19 Sep 1914, 1630. "Charles Pathé," *MPW,* 14 Nov 1914, 904–05. "Pathé Sails for Europe," *MPW,* 16 Jan 1915, 342. "Charles Pathé the Guiding Spirit," *MPW,* 27 Mar 1915, 1914h. "The Romance of a Great Business," *MPW,* 1 Jan 1916, 55. Charles Pathé, "Special Writers Needed," *MPW,* 16 Dec 1916, 1644. Charles Pathé, "Passing Through Crisis, Says Pathé," *MPW,* 28 Apr 1917, 593–94. "Monopoly Impossible, Says Pathé," *MPW,* 24 May 1919, 1143–44. "Pathé Chief Honored by Friends," *MPW,* 21 Jun 1919, 1753–54. "Leaving for Europe, Charles Pathé Predicts Expansion of Industry," *MPW,* 13 Dec 1919, 817. "Paul Bruner Succeeds Charles Pathé as President of Great Film Organization," *MPW,* 25 Sep 1920, 457.

Pathé, Emile (brother of **Charles Pathé**) [producer] (b. Paris, France, 12 Feb 1860 [extrait de naissance no. 242/1860]-3 Apr 1937 [77], Pau, France). AS, p. 852. BHD2, p. 206 (d. 5 Apr).

Pathe, Polly [actress] (*née* Grace Wheeler Green). No data found. AMD, p. 272. "Polly Pathe," *MPW,* 18 Sep 1915, 2001.

Patin, M. Claude [secretary]. No data found. AMD, p. 272. "Answers Call to Colors," *MPW,* 29 Aug 1914, 1249. "Claude Patin Back from France," *MPW,* 20 Feb 1915, 1116.

Paton, Charles [actor] (b. London, England, 31 Jul 1873–10 Apr 1970 [97]). BHD1, p. 427. IFN, p. 232.

Paton, Stuart [actor/director] (b. Glasgow, Scotland, 23 Jul 1883–16 Dec 1944 [61], Woodland Hills CA). m. **Ethel Patrick** (d. 1944). (Universal, 1912.) "Stuart Paton; Early Film Director Made Hit, '20 Thousand Leagues,' in 1916," *NYT,* 18 Dec 1944, 19:1 (began 1912). "Stuart Paton," *Variety,* 20 Dec 1944 (age 59). AMD, p. 272. AS, p. 852. BHD, p. 270; BHD2, p. 206. IFN, p. 232. "Stuart Paton Returns," *MPW,* 19 Feb 1916, 1147. "Paton's Wooden Wedding," *MPW,* 8 Apr 1916, 272. "Son of Director Paton Dies," *MPW,* 12 Aug 1916, 1084 (1-year-old son George).

Patrick, Ethel [actress] (b. London, England, 1887?–18 Sep 1944 [57], Woodland Hills CA). m. **Stuart Paton** (d. 1944). "Ethel Patrick," *Variety,* 20 Sep 1944. AS, p. 852. BHD, p. 270. IFN, p. 232.

Patrick, Jerome [stage/film actor] (b. New Zealand, 1883–26 Sep 1923 [39], New York NY). m. Grey Brunelle. "Jerome Patrick Dead; Prominent Leading Man a Victim of Heart Disease at 39 Years," *NYT,* 28 Sep 1923, 7:3. "Jerome Patrick," *Variety,* 4 Oct 1923 (age 40). AS, p. 852. BHD, p. 270. IFN, p. 232. Truitt, p. 262.

Patrick, John [actor/scenarist] (*né* John Patrick Goggan, b. Louisville KY, 17 May 1905–7 Nov 1995 [90], Del Ray Beach FL; suicide). m. Mildred Legaye, May? 1925. (1st National.) AMD, p. 272. AS, p. 852. BHD2, p. 206. "Warners Signs John Patrick" *MPW,* 7 Nov 1925, 45.

Patricola, Tom (brother of Isabelle Patricola) [stage/film actor] (b. New Orleans LA, 22 Jan 1891–1 Jan 1950 [58], Pasadena CA; after an operation). m. Dorothy Daly. "Tom Patricola, Star of Vaudeville Days," *NYT,* 2 Jan 1950, 23:3 (age 59; for 15 years on the old Keith-Orpheum Circuit). AS, p. 852. BHD1, p. 427. IFN, p. 232. "Miss Patricola Dies; Vaudeville Star, 79," *NYT,* 25 May 1965, 41:4 (d. 23 May 1965 [79], Manhasset NY; stroke. m. Walter A. Morris. Keith-Orpheum and Pantages vaudeville circuits.).

Patry, Albert [actor/director] (b. Elblag, Poland, 29 Feb 1864–26 Nov 1938 [74], Berlin, Germany). BHD1, p. 615; BHD2, p. 206 (b. Elbing, Germany).

Patterson, Elizabeth [actress] (*née* Mary Elizabeth Patterson, b. Savannah TN, 22 Nov 1875–31 Jan 1966 [90], Los Angeles CA). "Elizabeth Patterson Dies at 90; Well Known Character Actress; Was Said to Have 'Played Mother of About Every Star in Hollywood,'" *NYT,* 1 Feb 1966, 35:1. "Elizabeth Patterson," *Variety,* 2 Feb 1966. AS, p. 853. BHD1, p. 427 (b. 1874). IFN, p. 232. Katz, p. 901 (b. 1874). Truitt, p. 262.

Patterson, Joy W. [actress] (b. 1906?–23 Mar 1959 [53], Santa Ana CA). AS, p. 853. BHD1, p. 428. IFN, p. 232. Truitt, p. 262.

Patterson, Starke [actor] (b. 1899-May 1951 [52?], Jonesboro AR). BHD, p. 270.

Patterson, Walter [actor]. No data found. George Katchmer, "Walter Patterson," *CI,* 232 (Oct 1994), C24.

Patton, William P. [stage/film actor] (b. Amarillo TX, 2 Jun 1894–12 Dec 1951 [57], Los Angeles Co. CA). m. **Jessie Ralph** (d. 1944). AMD, p. 272. AS, p. 853. BHD1, p. 428. IFN, p. 232. SD. "Bill Paton Recovers," *MPW,* 21 May 1927, 179.

Patullo, George [writer]. No data found. AMD, p. 272. "Well Known Story Writer to Aid on Script for Next Arbuckle Film," *MPW,* 5 Feb 1921, 700.

Paul, Albert [actor] (b. Berlin, Germany, 2 Feb 1856–5 Aug 1928 [72], Dresden, Germany). BHD, p. 271.

Paul, Edward F. [cameraman/assistant director] (b. New York NY, 1900?–23 Mar 1946 [46], Bronx NY). "Dr. Edward F. Paul; Retired Physician, 46, Former Assistant Film Director," *NYT,* 24 Mar 1946, 46:3 (worked with the Whitman Bennett Studios in Yonkers, "where he photographed Douglas Fairbanks Sr., Francis X. Bushman, Beverly Bayne and other stars. Later he was in Hollywood, Calif., before turning to medicine."). AS, p. 853. BHD2, p. 206.

Paul, Elliot [scenarist] (b. 1890–7 Apr 1958 [68?], Providence RI). BHD2, p. 206.

Paul, Fred [actor] (b. Lausanne, Switzerland, 1880). BHD, p. 271. AS, p. 853.

Paul, Heinz [director] (b. Munich, Germany, 13 Aug 1893–14 Mar 1983 [89], Germany). BHD2, p. 206.

Paul, Logan [actor] (b. Ayr, Scotland, 1848?–15 Jan 1932 [83], Brooklyn NY). (Vitagraph.) "Death Takes Logan Paul," *Variety,* 19 Jan 1932. AS, p. 854. BHD, p. 271. IFN, p. 232.

Paul, Richard Holmes [art director] (b. Norwich, England, 1882). AMD, p. 272. BHD2, p. 206. "Art Director Paul with Paralta," *MPW,* 16 Jun 1917, 1791.

Paul, Robert W[illiam] [pioneer British film exhibitor/instrument maker/director/producer] (b. Highbury, England, 3 Oct 1869–28 Mar 1943 [73], London, England). "Robert Paul," *Variety,* 21 Apr 1943 ("He was first to make and show films of any kind in the United Kingdom and earlier made peepshow pix machines.... [H]e shot and showed the 1896 Derby"; invented the Bragg-Paul Pulsometer, with Sir William Bragg, used for respiratory paralysis). AS, p. 854 (d. 27 Mar). BHD2, p. 206 (d. 27 Mar). *The Illustrated History of the Cinema,* consulting ed., David Robinson; ed. Ann Lloyd (NY: Macmillan, 1986), p. 14.

Paul, Val[entine] [actor/director] (b. Denver CO, 10 Apr 1886–23 Mar 1962 [75], Los Angeles CA). m. May Foster,1914. (Universal.) AMD, p. 272. AS, p. 854. BHD, p. 271; BHD2, p. 206. IFN, p. 232. "Val Paul, Bison, Takes a Wife," *MPW,* 11 Jul 1914, 273. "Val Paul Becomes Proud Father," *MPW,* 5 Feb 1916, 782. "A Lead, Director, and Two Heavies Join Universal," *MPW,* 26 Jul 1919, 512. "Val Paul Signed," *MPW,* 18 Jul 1925, 309. George Katchmer, "Val Paul," *CI,* 226 (Apr 1994), 40–41.

Paulder, Maria [actress] (b. Tetschon-Bodenbach, Germany, 20 Jun 1903–17 Aug 1990 [87], Munich, Germany). BHD1, p. 428.

Paulig, Albert [actor/singer] (b. Stollberg,

Germany, 14 Jan 1873–19 Mar 1933 [60], Berlin, Germany; heart attack). AS, p. 854. BHD1, p. 428 (b. Saxony, Germany). Vittorio Martinelli, "Kino-Lieblinge," *Griffithiana*, 38/39 (Oct 1990), 65.

Pauline, J. Robert [hypnotist/actor] (b. 1874–11 Nov 1942 [68?], Rochester NY). AMD, p. 272. BHD, p. 271. "Hypnotism, Not Mysterious Power, Says Scientist and Picture Star," *MPW*, 7 Feb 1920, 929. "Pauline in 'Mystery Mind' Makes Debut as an Actor," *MPW*, 6 Mar 1920, 1641. "Pauline, Skilled Showman, to Help Exploit 'Mystery Mind,'" *MPW*, 7 Aug 1920, 772. "Dr. J. Robert Pauline to Make Series of Comedy Dramas," *MPW*, 26 Feb 1921, 1076.

Paull, Townsend D. [actor] (b. 1898–3 Dec 1933 [35?], Los Angeles CA; murdered). AS, p. 854 (died "a été assassiné"). BHD1, p. 428.

Paulowla, Magda [actress] (*née* Countess Magda Solomonesco, b. Bucharest, Rumania). JS, p. 359 (in Italian films from 1917).

Paulsen, Harald Johannes David [actor/director] (b. Elmshorn, Germany, 26 Aug 1895–4 Aug 1954 [58], Hamburg, Germany; heart attack). AS, p. 854. BHD, p. 271. IFN, p. 232.

Paulsen, Lina [actress] (b. Germany-d. 17 Nov 1932). BHD, p. 271. IFN, p. 232.

Paulton, Edward Antonio [actor/scenarist/director/lyricist] (b. Glasgow, Scotland, 23 Mar 1867–20 Mar 1939 [72], Los Angeles CA). m. actress Jessie Storey. "Edward Paulton, a Playwright, 73; Writer for Films and the Stage Began His Career as British Actor—Dies in California; Served in Field 45 Years; Had Part in Creating 'The Royal Vagabond' and Many Other Musical Offerings," *NYT*, 21 Mar 1939, 23:3. AS, p. 854. BHD2, p. 206 (b. 1877).

Paumier, Alfred [actor] (*né* Alfred Hodgson, b. Liverpool, England, 14 Nov 1870–25 Jan 1951 [80]). BHD, p. 271.

Pauncefort, Claire [actress] (b. England-d. 23 Nov 1924, Worthing, England). BHD, p. 271.

Pauncefort, George [stage/film actor] (b. San Francisco CA, 24 Nov 1869–25 Mar 1942 [72], Los Angeles CA). BHD1, p. 428. IFN, p. 232. SD.

Pauquette, Myron [scenarist] (b. 1900–27 Nov 1935 [35?], Los Angeles CA). BHD2, p. 206.

Pavanelli, Livio Cesare [actor/director/producer] (b. Copparo, Italy, 7 Sep 1881–29 Apr 1958 [76], Rome, Italy). AS, p. 854. BHD1, p. 428. JS, pp. 339–40 (in Italian silents from 1913).

Pavese, Luigi [actor] (brother of Nino Pavese [1904–1979], b. Asti, Italy, 25 Oct 1897–13 Dec 1969 [72], Rome, Italy). AS, p. 854. BHD1, p. 428. JS, p. 340 (in Italian silents from 1916).

Pavlenko, Peter [actor/director/scenarist] (b. 1899–16 Jun 1951 [52?], Moscow, Russia). BHD2, p. 206.

Pavlowa, Anna [stage/film actress] (*nee* Tatiana Tereschenko [Anna Matvejevna Pavlowa?], b. St. Petersburg, Russia, 31 Jan 1882–23 Jan 1931 [48], Gravenvenhague, Netherlands; pleurisy). m. Victor d'Andrè, 1924 (widower). (Film debut: *The Dumb Girl of Portici*, Universal, 1915.) "Anna Pavlowa Dies at Height of Fame; Succumbs to Pleurisy at The Hague After an Illness of Only Three Days; World's Premier Dancer; Operation Fails to Aid Her and Vaccine Comes Too Late—Husband at Bedside," *NYT*, 23 Jan 1931, 1:4, 16:2 (b. 1885). "Pavlowa Dies Suddenly on Last Tour of World," *Variety*, 28 Jan 1931 (age 42). AMD, p. 273. AS, p. 855 (b. 3 Jan 1885). BHD, p. 271 (b. 1881). IFN, p. 233. JS, p. 341 (b. Bjeloplavici, Ukraine; in Italian films from 1919). Truitt, p. 262 (b. 3 Jan 1885). "Mme. Pavlova with Universal," *MPW*, 19 Jun 1915, 1920. "Special Studio for Pavlova," *MPW*, 17 Jul 1915, 468. "Pavlowa's Quick Decision," *NYDM*, 6 Nov 1915, 31:4 (for over a year, "the greatest living dancer" refused film offers, but with the war and all capitulated at Universal, naming an 8-reel adaptation of Auder's Grand Opera, 'Masiniello,' as her initial vehicle. Her impresario, Max Rabinoff, named a sum of money to be guaranteed to his client. "The sum has never been published and neve will be because Pavlowa stipulated that she was to be spared such undignified exploitations."). "Estimating Salaries in Seconds," *MPW*, 11 Dec 1915, 2020. "Anna Pavlova Visits Universal Office," *MPW*, 18 Dec 1915, 2162. "Mme. Pavlova Five Years in America," *MPW*, 30 Jun 1917, 2129. "Pavlova Enthuses," *MPW*, 23 Feb 1924, 638.

Pàvlova, Tatiana [actress] (b. Bjeloplavici, Ukraine, 10 Dec 1893). JS, p. 341 (in Italian silents from 1919; "Ram away from home at 15 to become an actress, soon becoming famous. She fled the Bolshevik revolution, and arrived in Italy in 1919.").

Pawar, Lalita [stuntwoman/actress] (*née* Ambika Sagun, b. Indore, India, 1914–24 Feb 1998 [83?], Pune, India). m. (1) director Ganpatrao Pawar; (2) director Raj Kumar Gupta. (Began 1921 in Pune, India; final film, *Bhal* [*Brother*], 1990). Kuldip Singh, "Lalita Pawar," *The Independent*, 6 Mar 1998, p. 21 (appeared in 600 films). AS, p. 855.

Pawle, Lennox [stage/film actor] (*né* John Lennox Pawle, b. London, England, 27 Apr 1872–22 Feb 1936 [63], Los Angeles CA; intestinal hemorrhage). m. Dorothy Parker (not the American writer). "Lennox Pawle," *Variety*, 26 Feb 1936. AS, p. 855. BHD1, p. 428. IFN, p. 233. SD. Truitt, p. 263.

Pawn, Doris [actress] (b. Norfolk VA, 29 Dec 1894–30 Mar 1988 [93], La Jolla CA). m. **Rex Ingram** (d. 1950). (Film debut: *The Trey o' Hearts*, Universal; Fox Film Co.) AMD, p. 273. BHD1, p. 615 (b. Norfolk NE). 1921 Directory, p. 235. *Munsey*, Nov 1915, 271 (portrait). "Doris Pawn Returns to Fox," *MPW*, 10 Mar 1917, 1584. John E. Thayer, "Stars in View—1922," *CI*, 61 (Summer, 1978), 36–38. George Katchmer, "Remembering the Great Silents," *CI*, 211 (Jan 1992), 43.

Paxton, George [stage/film actor] (b. England, 1862–19 Feb 1914 [51?], Fort Lee NJ.) (Solax.) AS, p.855. BHD, p. 271. IFN, p. 233. SD. Spehr, p. 156.

Paxton, Sidney [actor] (*né* Sydney Oughton Paxton Hood, b. London, England, 25 Jun 1860–13 Oct 1930 [70], Montauk NY). m. Lilie Leicester (d. 1884). AS, p. 855. BHD, p. 271. IFN, p. 233. SD. Truitt, p. 263.

Payne, B. Iden [director] (b. Newcastle-upon-Tyne, England, 5 Sep 1881–6 Apr 1976 [94], Austin TX). BHD2, p. 206.

Payne, Douglas [actor] (b. England, 1875?–3 Aug 1965 [90], England). "Douglas Payne," *Variety*, 18 Aug 1965. AS, p. 855. BHD1, p. 429. IFN, p. 233.

Payne, Edmund [actor] (b. London, England, 1865–1 Jul 1914 [49?], London, England). BHD, p. 271.

Payne, Edna [stage/film actress] (b. Mt. Vernon NY, 5 Dec 1891–31 Jan 1953 [61], Los Angeles CA). m. **Jack Rollens**, 22 Aug 1917, NYC (d. 1955). (Eclair.) AMD, p. 273. AS, p. 855 (b. NY NY). BHD, p. 271 (b. NY NY). IFN, p. 233 (b. NY NY). "Edna Payne," *MPW*, 17 Feb 1912, 566. "Edna Payne," *MPW*, 18 Jul 1914, 440. "Edna Payne; Ingénue Lead of the Eclair Company," *MPS*, 15 Jan 1915, 26 (b. NYC). "Marriages," *Variety*, 31 Aug 1917, p. 15. Lester Sweyd, "What They Are Doing Now," *Motion Picture Magazine*, Feb 1918, 13 ("...was starred last season in 'Dora Deane.'"). Billy H. Doyle, "Lost Players," *CI*, 144 (Jun 1987), C58.

Payne, Herbert [executive]. No data found. AMD, p. 273. "Western Picturemen in Town," *MPW*, 21 Nov 1914, 1093.

Payne, Louis [actor] (*né* William Louis Payne, b. Elmira NY, 13 Jan 1873–14 Aug 1953 [80], Woodland Hills CA). m. **Mrs. Leslie Carter**, 1906 (d. 1937). "William 'Lou' Payne," *Variety*, 19 Aug 1953, p. 63 (member of the Lambs). AS, p. 855 (b. NY NY). BHD1, p. 429. IFN, p. 233 (b. PA). Truitt, p. 263 (b. NY NY, 1876).

Payne, Will [writer]. No data found. AMD, p. 273. "Will Payne Joins Realart on Coast," *MPW*, LIII, 3 Dec 1921, 530.

Payne, William Louis *see* **Payne, Louis**

Paynter, Corona [actress] (b. Canada, 1898–29 Jul 1986 [88?], Los Angeles CA). BHD, p. 271.

Payre, Andree [aviatrix/actess]. No data found. AMD, p. 273. "Mlle. Payre in Witwer Picture," *MPW*, 5 Nov 1921, 88. "Pathé Engages Andree Payre to Play in Ruth Roland Serials," *MPW*, 1 Apr 1922, 474.

Payson, Blanche [actress] (b. Santa Barbara CA, 20 Sep 1881–4 Jul 1964 [82], Los Angeles CA). (Sennett.) "Blanche Payson," *Variety*, 15 Jul 1964 (age 83). AMD, p. 273. AS, p. 855 (d. 3 Jul). BHD1, p. 429. IFN, p. 233. Truitt, p. 263. "Blanche Payne," *MPW*, 22 Jan 1927, 277.

Payton, Claude Duval [actor] (b. Centerville IA, 30 Mar 1882–1 Mar 1955 [72], Los Angeles CA). m. **Lucy** (d. 1969). AS, p. 855. BHD1, p. 429. IFN, p. 233. George A. Katchmer, "Remembering the Great Silents," *CI*, 175 (Jan 1990), C8.

Payton, Corse, "America's Best Bad Actor" (brother of actress Mary Gibbs Spooner; uncle of **Cecil** and **Edna May Spooner**) [stage/film actor/producer] (b. Centerville IA, 18 Dec 1867–23 Feb 1934 [66], Greenpoint Hospital, Brooklyn NY; chronic heart disease). m. (1) actress Etta Reed (d. 1915); (2) Henrietta Browne (d. 1958). (Stage debut: *Dora, or a Farmer's Iron Will.*) "Corse Payton Dies in Brooklyn at 66; Billed Himself in '10–20–30' Melodramas as 'America's Best Bad Actor'; His Wit Became Legend; Many Stars Began Career in His Theatre—Produced Revivals in Jamaica [NY] Up to September," *NYT*, 24 Feb 1934, 13:4 (b. 1868; his father served under Gen. John M. Corse of Iowa in the Civil War. "Mary Pickford, the Gish sisters, Bert Lytell, Fay Bainter, Mary Miles Minter, Richard Bennett, Ernest Truex and many others served their apprenticeships in his company." He owned Payton's Lee Avenue Theatre in Brooklyn and earned close to $100,000 a year in his heyday: a matinee idol in the Nineties. He lived at 72 Tompkins Avenue, Brooklyn. In

1925 he was suspended by Actors Equity for trying to appear in *The Gorilla* in burlesque.). "Corse Payton," *Variety,* 113, 27 Feb 1934, 62:1 ("The advent of the picture theatres was the first blow dealt the actor.... He made several tries to come back, and sought in vain to break into talking pictures. He has been practically destitute for some time." Interred in Centerville OH). "Etta Reed Payton Dead; Wife of Corse Payton Was a Popular Stock Player in Brooklyn," *NYT,* 12 Oct 1915, 11:4 (d. 11 Oct 1915, Hampden Hospital, Springfield MA. Had suffered a paralytic stroke in her dressing room at the Lee Avenue Theatre Mar 1907.). "Mrs. Corse Payton," *NYT,* 29 Nov 1958, 21:5 (d. 28 Nov 1958 [80], Kings County Hospital, NYC. Actress in stock/vaudeville/radio; lived at 171 Stockton St., Brooklyn NY.). BHD, p. 271. "May Take Lee Ave.," *Variety,* 23 Jan 1914, 16:3 (William A. Mortimer, a former ally of Payton, sought to lease the Lee Avenue Theatre, "a dead one since the golden days, when the Corse Payton Co., headed by Etta Reed Payton, used to turn 'em away."). "Corse Payton and His Stock Company (Springfield MA)," *NYDM,* 28 Jul 1915, 10:2 (photo with caption). "Stock Beats the Pictures," *NYDM,* 4 Aug 1915, 10:1 (his company beat out four large theaters nearby and a dozen smaller ones with its productions). "Death of Etta Reed Payton," *NYDM,* 23 Oct 1915, 9:3 (d. 11 Oct 1915 [44], Hampden Hospital, Springfield MA).

Payton, Gloria [actress] (b. New York NY, 2 Aug 1897–1 Aug 1989 [91], Louisiana MO). AMD, p. 273. BHD, p. 271. "Gloria Payton," *MPW,* 17 Mar 1917, 1778. "Gloria Payton to Lead for Lewis," *MPW,* 28 Jun 1919, 2010.

Payton, Lucy [actress] (*née*?, b. KS, 12 Oct 1877–15 Jan 1969 [91], Louisiana MO). m. **Claude Payton** (d. 1955). BHD, p. 271. Ragan 2, p. 1312.

Peacock, Kim [journalist/stage/film/radio/TV actor] (b. Watford, Hertfordshire, England, 24 Mar 1901–26 Dec 1966 [65], Emsworth, Hants., England; heart attack). Bachelor. "Kim Peacock," *Variety,* 245, 11 Jan 1967, 70:2. AS, p. 856. BHD1, p. 429. IFN, p. 233.

Peacock, Lillian [actress] (b. Scottsdale PA, 23 Oct 1890–18 Aug 1918 [27], Los Angeles CA; from injuries after a fall). AMD, p. 273. AS, p. 856. BHD, p. 271 (b. 1889). IFN, p. 233. "Obituary," *MPW,* 14 Sep 1918, 1549 (age 28; film-related auto accident).

Peacocke, Capt. Leslie T. [magazine writer/vaudeville sketches/playwright/actor/scenarist] (b. Bangalore, India). No other data found. (Universal, 1913.) AMD, p. 273. "Leslie T. Peacocke," *MPW,* 11 Jul 1914, 238:1 (produced 338 scenarios to date. Appeared in *His Neighbor's Wife,* FP-L, with Lily Langrty.). "Leslie T. Peacocke," *MPW,* 31 Oct 1914, 648. "Captain Peacocke with Venus Film Corporation," *MPW,* 1 May 1915, 734. "Peacocke with California Co.," *MPW,* 11 Mar 1916, 1627. "Captain Peacocke Returns to Screen," *MPW,* 2 Jun 1917, 1462. Captain Leslie T. Peacocke, "Original Photoplays—Versus Adaptations," *Photoplay,* Jul 1917, 127–130. "Three Authors Added to Universal Forces," *MPW,* 20 Oct 1917, 364.

Pearce, George C. [stage/film actor] (b. New York NY, 26 Jun 1865–13 Aug 1940 [75], Los Angeles CA). (Biograph). "George C. Pearce; Actor More Than 50 Years—Created Nanky Poo Role Here," *NYT,* 14 Aug 1940, 19:6 (stage debut, 1889; in *The Birth of a Nation*). "George C. Pearce," *Variety,* 21 Aug 1940. AMD, p. 273. AS, p. 856. BHD1, p. 429. IFN, p. 233. Truitt, p. 263. "George C. Pearce Joins Universal," *MPW,* 14 Oct 1916, 258. George Katchmer, "George Pearce," *CI,* 226 (Apr 1994), 41.

Pearce, Peggy *see* **Barry, Viola**

Pearce, Vera [actress] (b. Broken Hill, Australia, 1896–21 Jan 1966 [69?], London, England). m. Frederick Wilmot Smith, Sep? 1917, All Soul's Church, NYC. "Marriages," *Variety,* 5 Oct 1917, p. 10. AMD, p. 273. BHD1, p. 429 (d. 18 Jan). AS, p. 856. "Vera Pearce a Metro Actress," *MPW,* 15 Apr 1916, 419.

Pearl, Jack [stage/film/radio actor] (*né* Jake Perlman, b. New York NY, 29 Oct 1894 [Birth Certificate Index No. 48212]–25 Dec 1982 [88], New York NY [Death Certificate Index No. 20661]). m. Winifred Desborough. (In early 1920's sound tests.) "Jack Pearl, 88, Comedy Star of Radio and Stage," *NYT,* 26 Dec 1982, 36:3. "Jack Pearl," *Variety,* 29 Dec 1982. AS, p. 856. "Who's Who in Pictures," *NYT,* 29 Oct 1933, 4:4 (b. 1895). "Jack Pearl," WBO2, pp. 188–89.

Pearson, Albert H. (Bert) [executive] (b. 1870–29 Nov 1955 [85?], Leeds, England). BHD2, p. 207.

Pearson, George [director] (b. London, England, 1875–8 Feb 1973 [97?]). BHD2, p. 207.

Pearson, Humphrey [scenarist] (b. 1894–25 Feb 1937 [42?], Palm Springs CA; gunshot wound). m. Rive King. "Pearson's Death Still a West Coast Mystery," *Variety,* 3 Mar 1937. BHD2, p. 207.

Pearson, Molly [stage/film actress] (b. Edinburgh, Scotland, 1876–26 Jan 1959 [83], Newton CT). m. actor Ethelbert Hales. "Molly Pearso, 83, Ex-Stage Actress," *NYT,* 30 Jan 1959, 27:4. "Molly Pearson," *Variety,* 213, 4 Feb 1959, 79:2. (*Carmen,* Pittsburgh PA, 1906; last stage work: *Ladies in Retirement*). AMD, p. 273. AS, p. 856. BHD, p. 272. IFN, p. 233. "Molly Pearson to Make Screen Debut," *MPW,* 1 Dec 1917, 1312.

Pearson, Virginia [stage/film actress] (b. Louisville KY, 7 Mar 1886?–6 Jun 1958 [72], Los Angeles CA; uremic poisoning). m. **Sheldon Lewis** (d. 1958). (FP-L; Vitagraph, 1915; Thanhouser; Fox; Chadwick; MGM; Pathé; Universal.) "Virginia Pearson Dies; Actress, 72, Had Appeared in Many Silent Films," *NYT,* 10 Jun 1958, 33:3. "Virginia Pearson," *Variety,* 11 Jun 1958 (age 70). AMD, p. 273. AS, p. 856 (b. 1888). BHD1, p. 430 (b. 1888); 272. FSS, p. 233. IFN, p. 233 (b. Louisville KY). Lowrey, p. 148. MH, p. 132 (b. Louisville, 1888). MSBB. p. 1040 (b. 1888). Truitt, p. 263 (b. 1888). "Virginia Pearson's Mother Dead," *NYDM,* 7 Jan 1914, 8:2 (d. 1 Jan 1914, Louisville KY). "Actress in Tilt; Virginia Pearson No Longer with Louisville Players—Wanted Electric Sign," *NYDM,* 14 Jan 1914 (theater manager Fred Hilton refused her request to erect an electric sign bearing her name [in her hometown]. "...he upbraided me for alleged interference in his business.... Later I received word from him telling me that I must cancel my engagement. He made the excuse that I did not know my lines..."). "Miss Pearson to Pathe; Legitimate Star to Appear Under Direction of Frank Powell," *NYDM,* 8 Apr 1914, 36:1 (to debut in *The Stain*). "Virginia Pearson," *MPW,* 8 May 1915, 878. "Personal; Pearson," *NYDM,* 23 Oct 1915, 5:1 ("Virginia Pearson, Vitagraph Star," on cover; the *NYDM* began publication on Saturday instead of Wednesday with this issue). "Virginia Pearson," *NYDM,* 23 Oct 1915, 27:2 (hired by Vitagraph). "Virginia Pearson Plans Poe Monument," *MPW,* 4 Dec 1915, 1802. "Virginia Pearson," *MPW,* 26 May 1917, 1295. "Virginia Pearson Speaks for Orphans," *MPW,* 30 Jun 1917, 2109. "Virginia Pearson May Head Own Company," *MPW,* 28 Jul 1917, 630. "Virginia Pearson Two Years with Fox," *MPW,* 23 Feb 1918, 1122. "Virginia Pearson to Be Independent," *MPW,* 9 Nov 1918, 679. "Virginia Pearson Forms an Independent Company," *MPW,* 14 Dec 1918, 1184. "Tells Plans of Pearson Photoplays," *MPW,* 22 Feb 1919, 1014. "Pathé Will Distribute Virginia Pearson Pictures," *MPW,* 22 Mar 1919, 1648. "To Distribute 20,000 Pictures of Virginia Pearson," *MPW,* 29 Mar 1919, 1829. "Virginia Pearson to Write a Book," *MPW,* 17 May 1919, 1039 (*The Art of Motion Pictures*). "Virginia Pearson Appears Personally at Port Henry," *MPW,* 19 Jul 1919, 379. "Clothng Shortage on East Side, Thinks Miss Pearson," *MPW,* 10 Jan 1920, 256. "Deacons Veto Minister's Request That Actress Speak from Pulpit; Big Congregation Waits in Vain," *MPW,* 6 May 1922, 44. "Virginia Pearson in New Borzage Film," *MPW,* 16 Jun 1923, 591. Virginia Pearson, "The True Story of Her Long Absence from the Screen Is Revealed for the First Time," *MW,* 26 Sep 1925, 8–9, 42 (her chauffeur drove her car into a telegraph pole almost ending her life; her face was cut and battered, requiring a long period of plastic surgery). Billy Doyle, "Lost Players; Virginia Pearson," *CI,* 199 (Jan 1992), 38.

Pearsons, W. Blaine [actor/scenarist] (b. KY, 21 Mar 1892–6 Nov 1918 [26], Los Angeles CA; influenza). AMD, p. 273. AS, p. 856. BHD2, p. 207. "Obituary," *MPW,* 30 Nov 1918, 938. Billy H. Doyle, "Lost Players," *CI,* 139 (Jan 1987), 55.

Peck, Charles Mortimer [scenarist] (b. NY, 28 Jul 1872–4 Nov 1941 [69], Los Angeles CA). BHD2, p. 207.

Peck, Richard K. [cinematographer]. No data found. FDY, p. 465.

Peckham, Frances Miles [actress] (b. 1893?–7 Jun 1959 [66], New York NY [Death Certificate Index No. 13013). "Mrs. Frances Peckham," *NYT,* 9 Jun 1959, 37:2 (made silents in Chicago IL). "Frances Miles Peckham," *Variety,* 10 Jun 1959 (She "appeared in early films made in Chicago"). AS, p. 857. BHD, p. 272. IFN, p. 233.

Peer, Heinrich [actor] (b. Vienna, Austria, 25 Nov 1867–13 May 1927 [59]). BHD, p. 272. IFN, p. 233 (age 60).

Peer, Helen [actress/actress] (b. New York NY, 1898?–6 May 1942 [44], New Rochelle NY). (Edison.) "Helen Peer," *Variety,* 13 May 1942. AS, p. 857. BHD, p. 272. IFN, p. 233. Truitt, p. 263.

Peerless Annabelle *see* **Annabelle**

Peers, Joan [actress] (b. Chicago IL, 19 Aug 1909–11 Jul 1975 [65], San Francisco CA). AS, p. 857. BHD1, p. 430. IFN, p. 233.

Peers, Victor [director/producer/scenarist] (b. Warwick, England, 1891–18 Sep 1971 [80?]). BHD2, p. 207.

Pegg, Vester House [actor] (b. Appleton City MO, 23 May 1889–19 Feb 1951 [61], Los Angeles CA; stroke). AS, p. 857. BHD1, p. 430. IFN, p. 233.

Peil, Edward, Jr *see* **Jones, Johnny**

Peil, Edward J., Sr. (father of **Edward J. Peil, Jr.**) [actor] (*né* Charles Edward Peil, b. Racine WI, 18 Jan 1882–29 Dec 1958 [76], Los Angeles CA). (Lubin.) "Edward Piel," *Variety,* 7 Jan 1959.

AS, p. 857 (b. 1883). BHD1, p. 430 (b. 1883). IFN, p. 234. Truitt, p. 264. "Motography's Gallery of Picture Players," *Motography*, 27 Jun 1914, 477. George A. Katchmer, "Remembering the Great Silents," *CI*, 178 (Apr 1990), 42.

Peile, Kinsey [actor] (b. Allahabad, India, 20 Dec 1862–13 Apr 1934 [71]). BHD, p. 272. IFN, p. 234.

Peirce, Charlotte [actress] (b. New Bedford MA, 1883?–24 Jul 1950 [77], New Bedford MA). (Universal.) "Miss Charlotte Peirce," *NYT*, 26 Jul 1950, 25:3. AS, p. 857. George A. Katchmer, "Forgotten Cowboys and Cowgirls—Part XIV," *CI*, 191 (May 1991), 23–24.

Pelissier, H[arry] **G**[abriel] [actor] (b. Finchley, England, 1874–25 Sep 1913 [39?], London, England). m. **Fay Compton** (d. 1978). AS, p. 858.

Pellegrinetti, Margot [actress] (*née* Margherita Pellegrinetti, b. Massa Carrara, Italy, 1897). JS, p. 342 (in Italian silents from 1916).

Pellegrini, Lina [actress]. m. **Giovanni Zannini**. JS, p. 343 (in Italian silents from 1916).

Pelley, William Dudley [scenarist] (b. Lynn MA, 12 Mar 1890–30 Jun 1965 [75], Noblesville IN). *The Door to Revelation; An Autobiography* (Asheville NC: Pelley Publishers, 1939). "William Dudley Pelley, 75, Dies; Founded Fascist Silver Shirts," *NYT*, 2 Jul 1965, 27:1 (imprisoned in 1942 for publishing seditious, inflammatory material supporting the enemies of the U.S.; released in 1950. "He switched careers [from author to politician], he wrote, when he 'died and went to heaven' for seven minutes in 1928." He ran for president on the Christian Party ticket in 1936. In Washington, the only state that allowed him on the ballot, he received 1,500 plus votes.). AMD, p. 273. AS, p. 858. "Hold 'Em Down," *MPW*, 12 Jan 1924, 112. "Pelley to Aid Directors," *MPW*, 19 Jan 1924, 198. "Pelley a Busy Writer," *MPW*, 9 Feb 1924, 456. Arthur Graham, "Crazy Like a Fox; Pelley of the Silver Shirts," *The New Republic*, 18 Apr 1934, pp. 264–66. (Data supplied by Vance Pollock.)

Pelton, James B. [cinematographer] (b. 1886–9 Nov 1928 [42?], Los Angeles CA). BHD2, p. 207.

Peman, Jose Maria [scenarist] (b. Cadiz, Spain, 1896–19 Jul 1981 [85?], Cadiz, Spain). BHD2, p. 207.

Pemberton, Henry W. [actor] (b. Richmond VA, 1875?–26 Jul 1952 [77?], Orlando FL). (Gaumont [LI NY].) "Henry W. Pemberton," *Variety*, 6 Aug 1952. AS, p. 858. BHD, p. 272. IFN, p. 234. Truitt, p. 264.

Pemberton, Max [scenarist] (b. 1863–22 Feb 1950 [86?], London, England). BHD2, p. 207.

Pemberton, Patricia [actress] (d. 9 Mar 1929). BHD, p. 272. IFN, p. 234.

Pembleton, Georgia Bess [acrtress]. No data found. AMD, p. 273. "Another New Baby Star," *MPW*, 19 Oct 1918, 362.

Pembroke, Scott [actor/director/scenarist] (b. 1889?–21 Feb 1951 [61], Pasadena CA; cerebral hemorrhage). m. **Gertrude Short** (d. 1968). (Rayart; Universal; Republic.) "Scott Pembroke," *Variety*, 21 Mar 1951. AMD, p. 274. AS, p. 858. BHD2, p. 207. "Cohn Signs Scott Pembroke to Direct Columbia's Comedy Films," *MPW*, 9 Jul 1927, 99.

Peña, Julio [actor] (*né* Julio Peña Munhoz, b. Madrid, Spain, 18 Jun 1912–22 Jul 1972 [60], Marbella, Spain; heart attack). AS, p. 858. BHD1, p. 431.

Penbrook, Harry [extra] (b. 1887?–14 Sep 1960 [73?], Los Angeles CA). "Harry Penbrook," *Variety*, 21 Sep 1960 ("active from 1908 to 1953"). AS, p. 858. BHD1, p. 431. Truitt, p. 264.

Pendleton, Edna [actress]. No data found. m. **Johnny Powers**, the Church Around the Corner, NYC, Nov 1915. (Universal.) AMD, p. 274. "Johnny Powers—Edna Pendleton," *MPW*, 4 Dec 1915, 1803.

Pendleton, Gaylord [actor] (aka Steven Pendleton, b. New York NY, 16 Sep 1908–3 Oct 1984 [76], Los Angeles CA). BHD1, p. 431.

Pendleton, Nat [actor] (*né* Nathaniel Greene Pendleton, b. Davenport IA, 9 Aug 1895–11 Oct 1967 [72], San Diego CA; heart attack). "Nat Pendleton, Movie Actor, 72, Portrayer of Simpletons in Many Films Is Dead," *NYT*, 13 Oct 1967, 39:4 (d. La Jolla CA). "Nat Pendleton," *Variety*, 18 Oct 1967 (d. 12 Oct, La Jolla). AS, p. 858. BHD1, p. 431 (d. La Jolla). IFN, p. 234. Katz, p. 904. Truitt, p. 264.

Penman, Lea [actress] (b. Red Cloud NB, 1895?–12 Oct 1962 [67], Los Angeles CA). AS, p. 858. BHD, p. 272. IFN, p. 234. Truitt, p. 264.

Penn, Arthur A. [publicist] (b. 1875–6 Feb 1941 [65?], New London CT). BHD2, p. 207.

Penn, M.O. [singer/actor] (b. U.S.A., 1870). (Pathé Frères.) AMD, p. 274. Spehr, p. 156. "M.O. Penn," *NYDM*, 8 Jul 1914, 24:4. "M.O. Penn," *MPW*, 18 Jul 1914, 413.

Pennell, Richard O. [actor] (b. Jersey City NJ, 21 Feb 1866–22 Mar 1934 [68], Los Angeles CA). (Lasky.) "Richard O. Pennell," *Variety*, 27 Mar 1934 (b. Chester, England; age 73). AS, p. 859. BHD1, p. 431. IFN, p. 234. Truitt, 264.

Pennick, Jack [actor] (*né* Ronald Jack Pennick, b. Portland OR, 7 Dec 1895–16 Aug 1964 [68], Manhattan Beach CA). (Fox.) "Jack Pennick, 69, Dies; Character Actor in Films," *NYT*, 19 Aug 1964, 37:4. "Jack Pennick," *Variety*, 26 Aug 1964. AS, p. 859 (d. Hollywood CA). BHD1, p. 431. IFN, p. 234. Truitt, pp. 264–65. George Katchmer, "Jack Pennick," *CI*, 226 (Apr 1994), 41–42.

Pennington, Ann "Tiny" [dancer/actress] (*née* Anna Pennington, b. Wilmington DE, 23 Dec 1893–4 Nov 1971 [77], New York NY [Death Certificate Index No. 21653]). (Popularized the "Black Bottom" [from Nashville TN] in 1926.) William M. Freeman, "Ann Pennington, Dancing Star, Dies," *NYT*, 5 Nov 1971, 46:1 (age 77). "Rites for Ann Pennington," *NYT*, 6 Nov 1971, 34:3. "Ann Pennington," *Variety*, 10 Nov 1971. AMD, p. 274. AS, p. 859 (b. Camden NJ, 21 Dec). BHD1, p. 431 (b. 1892). FSS, p. 233. IFN, p. 234 (b. 1894). SD, p. 987. Truitt, p. 265. WWS, p. 265. "Famous Players Engage Ann Pennington," *MPW*, 13 May 1916, 1158. "Ann Pennington Comes Back to Screen," *MPW*, 28 Apr 1917, 594. "Ann Pennington Signed," *MPW*, 30 May 1925, 579. "In 'Little Eva' Role," *MPW*, 18 Jul 1925, 348. Stuart Oderman, "Ann Pennington, the Girl with the Dimpled Knees," *CFC*, 50 (Spring, 1976), 31–33; II, 51 (Summer, 1976), 25–28 (b. Wilmington DE).

Pennington, Edith Mae [actress] (d. 16 May 1964, Shreveport LA). AS, p. 859 (d. 1924). BHD, p. 272.

Penrod, A[lexander] **G.** [cinematographer] (d. Mar 1931, Newfoundland, Canada, Antarctic; in an explosion). AS, p. 859. BHD2, p. 207 (Arthur E. Penrod). FDY, p. 465.

Penwarden, Duncan [actor] (b. Halifax, Nova Scotia, Canada, 9 Feb 1880–13 Sep 1930 [50], Jackson Heights, New York NY). AS, p. 859. BHD1, p. 431. IFN, p. 234.

Peon, Ramón Garcia [actor/director] (b. Hvana, Cuba, 5 Jun 1897). (Estudios Golden Sun Pictures, Havana, Cuba.) AS, p. 859. Waldman, p. 226.

Peple, Edward [writer]. No data found. AMD, p. 274. "Another Feature Company," *MPW*, 25 Apr 1914, 531.

Pepper, Helsey James [actor] (b . 1874–9 Sep 1928 [54?], Los Angeles CA). BHD, p. 272.

Percival, C. Harold [art director] (d. 14 Dec 1918, Los Angeles CA; flu). m. (Ince.) "C. Harold Percival," *Variety*, 20 Dec 1918. "Obituary," *MPW*, 11 Jan 1919, 196. AMD, p. 274. BHD2, p. 207.

Percival, Walter C. [actor/writer] (*né* Charles David Lingenfelter, b. Chicago IL, 1887?–28 Jan 1934 [46], Los Angeles CA). m. Kate Campbell. "Walter C. Percival," *Variety*, 30 Jan 1934. AMD, p. 274. AS, p. 860. BHD1, p. 432. IFN, p. 234. Truitt, p. 265. "Percival to Make Screen Debut," *MPW*, 13 Jul 1918, 186. "Emmy Wehlen's New Leading Man," *MPW*, 5 Oct 1918, 105.

Percy, Edward [scenarist] (b. 1890–28 May 1968 [78?], England). BHD2, p. 207.

Percy, Eileen (sister of **Thelma Percy**) [actress] (b. Belfast, Ireland, 21 Aug 1900–29 Jul 1973 [72], Beverly Hills CA; cancer). m. (1) Ulrich Busch, 1919 (grandson of Adolphus Busch, founder of the brewery; 1 son); (2) Harry Ruby. (Film debut: *Wild and Woolly*, Artcraft, 1917.) "Eileen Percy," *Variety*, 8 Aug 1973. AMD, p. 274. AS, p. 860. BHD1, p. 432. FFF, p. 175. FSS, p. 233. IFN, p. 234. Katz, p. 905 (b. 1 Aug 1899). MH, p. 132. WWS, p. 205. "Eileen Percy," *MPW*, 28 Apr 1917, 630. "Eileen Percy Playing for Metro," *MPW*, 31 Aug 1918, 1232. "Eileen Percy Is Engaged to Appear with Hayakawa," *MPW*, 31 May 1919, 1315. "Eileen Percy Deser s Screen for Some Time," *MPW*, 16 Aug 1919, 980. "Eileen Percy Is Married to Ulrich Busch, St. Louis," *MPW*, 16 Aug 1919, 987. "Eileen Percy to Be Leading Woman to Tom Mix in Fox Film, 'The Untamed,'" *MPW*, 3 Apr 1920, 127. "Fox Signs Eileen Percy to Long-Term Contract as Star," *MPW*, 1 May 1920, 701. "Eileen Percy to Star in Fox Features; Producer Purchases Two Stories for Her," *MPW*, May 1920, 1072. "Eileen Percy Signs with C.B.C. Films," *MPW*, 16 Jun 1923, 589. June Lee, "Dan Cupid's Bulletin Board," *Paris and Hollywood*, Oct 1926, 88 (expecting in December). June Lee, "Dan Cupid's Bulletin Board," *Paris and Hollywood Screen Secrets Magazine*, May 1927, 53 (birth of a boy). George Katchmer, "Remembering the Great Silents," *CI*, 201 (Mar 1992), 38.

Percy, Fred [actor] (b. London, England, 1852–15 Jul 1926 [84?], Brixton, England). BHD, p. 272.

Percy, Thelma (sister of **Eileen Percy**). No data found. m. W.A. Brady, Jr., 27 Oct 1920. AMD, p. 274. "Thelma Percy Is Featurd," *MPW*, 31 Jul 1920, 613. "Thelma Percy Engaged for Leads in Mermaid Comedies," *MPW*, 9 Oct 1920, 827. "Weds W.A. Brady, Jr.," *MPW*, 13 Nov 1920, 212.

Percyval, T. Wigney [actor/writer]. No data found. AMD, p. 274. "T. Wigney Percyval," *MPW,* 8 Sep 1917, 1517.

Perdue, Derleys [actress: Wampas Star, 1923] (b. Kansas City MO, 22 Mar 1902–30 Sep 1989 [87], Los Angeles CA). AMD, p. 274. AS, p. 860. BHD, p. 272. "Derlys Perdue Danced to Stardom," *MPW,* 3 Nov 1923, 100. George A. Katchmer, "Forgotten Cowboys and Cowgirls—Part VIII," *CI,* 180 (Jun 1990), 53–58.

Pereda, Ramón [actor/director/producer] (b. Spain, 1897–1986 [89?]). Waldman, p. 228.

Perego, Eugenio [director]. JS, p. 344 (in Italian silents from 1913).

Pereira, Arthur [cinematograher] (b. 1871–Jun 1961 [90?], Glebelands, England). BHD2, p. 208.

Peres, Marcel [actor] (*né* Marcel Jean Peal Laurent Farenc, b. Castelsarrasin, France, 24 Jan 1898 [extrait de naissance no. 14/1898]–28 Jun 1974 [76], Chalette-sur-Loing, France). AS, p. 860.

Perese, Thomas [singer/actor] (b. 1861–7 Apr 1920 [59?], Venice CA). AS, p. 860.

Perestiani, Ivan [director] (b. Russia, 13 Apr 1870–14 May 1959 [89], Moscow, Russia). BHD2, p. 208.

Perez, Paul E. [publicist/title writer]. No data found. AMD, p. 274. FDY, p. 447. "Paul Perez Leaves to Assume Important Position in London," *MPW,* 20 Sep 1924, 234. "Paul Perez to Title," *MPW,* 11 Jun 1927, 403. "Perez Enjoys Title Writing," *MPW,* 18 Jun 1927, 483.

Periolat, George E. [actor] (b. Chicago IL, 1875?–20 Feb 1940 [64], Los Angeles CA; found dead under mysterious circumstances, perhaps suicide with arsenic). (Essanay.) "Periolat Is Found Dead; Veteran Film Actor Had Been Ill Three Years in Hollywood," *NYT,* 21 Feb 1940, 12:5 (age 65). "George Periolat," *Variety,* 28 Feb 1940. AMD, p. 274. AS, p. 860. BHD1, p. 432 (b. 1873). IFN, p. 234. Truitt, p. 265. "George E. Periolat," *MPW,* 10 Jun 1911, 1304. "Prominent Star on a Recreation Tour," *MPW,* 7 Dec 1912, 968. "George E. Periolat," *MPW,* 4 Jul 1914, 39. "George E. Periolat," *MPW,* 5 Jun 1915, 1580. "George E. Periolat," *MPW,* 15 Sep 1917, 1690. "Periolat to Go on Tour," *MPW,* 15 Dec 1917, 1637. George Katchmer, "George Periolat," *CI,* 232 (Oct 1994), C24.

Periot, Arthur [stuntman] (b. 1899–24 Feb 1929 [30], Monterey CA). BHD, p. 272. IFN, p. 234.

Perkins, Bert P. [publicist]. No data found. AMD, p. 274. "Perkins Resigns," *MPW,* 13 Sep 1924, 144.

Perkins, David [actor/scenarist] (b. 1885?–31 Dec 1962 [77], New York NY [Death Certificate Index No. 27988]). m. "David Perkins," *Variety,* 16 Jan 1963. BHD2, p. 208.

Perkins, Dr. James M. [actor] (b. Farmington MO, 1863–28 Oct 1926 [63?], Denver CO). BHD, p. 272.

Perkins, Jean Edward "Daredevil" [stuntwoman] (b. 1899?–24 Dec 1922 [23?], Riverside CA; died while filming *The Eagle's Talons,* released in 1923). AS, p. 861. BHD, p. 272. IFN, p. 234.

Perkins, Kenneth [scenarist] (b. 1890–8 Jun 1951 [61?], Los Angeles CA). BHD2, p. 208.

Perkins, Osgood (father of Anthony Perkins) [stage/film actor] (*né* James Ridley Osgood Perkins, b. West Newton MA, 16 May 1892–21 Sep 1937 [45], Washington DC). m. Janet Esselstyn Rane, 1922. Laura Kay Palmer, *Osgood and Anthony Perkins: A Comprehensive History of Their Work in Theatre, Film and Other Media, with Credits and an Annotated Bibliography* (Jefferson NC: McFarland, 1991). (Film Guild.) "Osgood Perkins, Stage Star, Dies; Stricken After Premiere of 'Susan and God,' in Which He Was Leading Man; Also Appeared in Films; Made Broadway Debut in 1924 in 'Beggar on Horseback'—Noted for Versatility," *NYT,* 22 Sep 1937, 27:1. "Osgood Perkins Dies of Heart Attack," *Variety,* 22 Sep 1937. AS, p. 861. BHD1, p. 432. IFN, p. 235. SD. Truitt, p. 265.

Perkins, Walter E[ugene] [stage/film actor] (b. Biddeford ME, 1870?–3 Jun 1925 [55], Brooklyn NY). "Walter E. Perkins," *NYT,* 5 Jun 1925, 17:5. "Walter E. Perkins," *Variety,* 10 Jun 1925. AS, p. 861. BHD, p. 273. IFN, p. 235. SD. Truitt, p. 265.

Perl, Lloyd [actor] (b. CA, 15 Jan 1909–14 Mar 1993 [84], Los Angeles CA). BHD1, p. 615.

Perley, Mrs. Anna [actress] (*née?,* b. 1848?–20 Jan 1937 [88], Santa Ana CA). "Mrs. Anna Perley," *Variety,* 27 Jan 1937. AS, p. 861. BHD, p. 273 (d. LA CA). IFN, p. 235.

Perley, Charles G. [actor] (b. Los Angeles CA, 1886–10 Feb 1933 [47], Santa Ana CA; heart attack). m. Louise Hall. (Biograph; K&E; Kinemacolor.) "Charles Perley," *Variety,* 14 Feb 1933. AS, p. 861. BHD, p. 273. IFN, p. 235. Truitt, p. 265. "Lives of the Players; Charles Perley," *MPS,* 11 Jul 1913, 29.

Perojo, Benito [actor/director/producer] (*né* Benito Perojo Gonzalez, b. Madrid, Spain, 14 Jun 1894–11 Nov 1974 [80], Madrid, Spain). (Began directing in 1913; Ufa; Fox, 1931; last film as director, *Sangre en Castilla,* 1950; last film as producer, *Pan, amor y Andalucia,* 1974.) "Benito Perojo," *Variety,* 277, 27 Nov 1974, 87:2. AS, p. 861. BHD2, p. 208. IFN, p. 235. Waldman, p. 228.

Perrault, Oliver [cinematographer] (b. 1894–21 Nov 1941 [47?], Los Angeles CA). BHD2, p. 208.

Perret, Léonce [vaudeville/film actor/writer/producer/director] (b. Niort, France, 13 May 1880–14 Aug 1935 [55], Niort, France). (Europe's first director of five-reel films; World; Pathé; Metro.) AMD, p. 274. AS, p. 862 (b. 14 Mar; d. Paris). BHD, p. 273; BHD2, p. 208. IFN, p. 235. Katz, p. 907 (began 1907). Spehr, p. 156. Waldman, p. 229. "Léonce Perret," *MPW,* 23 Feb 1918, 1097. "Perret at Work on First Production," *MPW,* 15 Jun 1918, 1550. "Léonce Perret Says Title Must Be Born Out of Film," *MPW,* 30 Nov 1918, 975. "Employ Returned Soldiers, Advocates Léonce Perret," *MPW,* 30 Nov 1918, 976. "Perret Predicts Future of Educationals," *MPW,* 11 Jan 1919, 207. "Mr. Perret Discusses Mystery Play," *MPW,* 22 Mar 1919, 1640. "Léonce Perret Prepares Second Super Production," *MPW,* 8 Jan 1921, 184. "Simmons Brings Suit for $7,750 Against Perret," *MPW,* 13 Aug 1921, 700. "Perret to Direct," *MPW,* 23 Aug 1924, 638.

Perrin, Dwight S. [publicist]. No data found. AMD, p. 274. Dwight S. Perrin, "What Can Advertising Accomplish?," *MPW,* 20 Jul 1918, 335–36. "Dwight S. Perrin Resigns as Goldwyn's Publicist," *MPW,* 8 Mar 1919, 1318.

Perrin, Jack [actor] (aka Jack Gable and Richard Terry, b. Three Rivers [St. Joseph Co.] MI, 25 Jul 1896–17 Dec 1967 [71], Los Angeles CA; heart attack). m. (1) **Josephine Hill**, 17 Sep 1920–1937 (D. 1989); (2) Ethel Compton, 1943 (d. 6 Oct 1993 [96], Lopez Island WA). (Keystone, 1917; Triangle; Arrow; Universal.) "Jack Perrin," *Variety,* 27 Dec 1967. Luther Hathcock, "Ethel Compton Perrin, 96," *CI* [obituary], 224 (Feb 1994), 59:3. AMD, p. 275. AS, p. 862. BHD1, p. 432. FSS, p. 234. GK, pp. 763–82. IFN, p. 235. Truitt, pp. 265–66. "Jack Perrin Engaged by Universal," *MPW,* 12 Jul 1919, 234. "Universal Introduces Two New Western Actors," *MPW,* 2 Aug 1919, 694. "Two Weddings in Filmland," *MPW,* 8 May 1920, 833 (m. Hill). "Jack Perrin," *MPW,* 31 Jan 1925, 495. Carlos de Paulo Couto, "Jack Perrin and *The Lion Man,*" *CFC,* 42 (Spring, 1974), 14–15, X8. John Cocchi, "The 2nd Feature; A History of the B Movies," *CI,* 146 (Aug 1987), 26, 28. George A. Katchmer, "The Kids Loved Jack Perrin," *CI,* 149 (Nov 1987), 13–14, 17. Richard E. Braff, "An Index to the Films of Jack Perrin," *CI,* 192 (Jun 1991), 18 *et passim.* R.E. Braff, "Additional Film Credits for Jack Perrin," *CI,* 238 (Apr 1995), 41–42. George Katchmer, "Remembering the Great Silents," *CI,* 247 (Jan 1996), 43–44.

Perrine, Ruth [actress]. No data found. AMD, p. 275. "Chicago Girl Wins Chance in Comedies," *MPW,* 11 Dec 1926, 427.

Perrins, Leslie [stage/film/radio actor] (b. Moseley, England, 7 Oct 1902–13 Dec 1962 [60], Esher, England). (Stage debut: *The Rattlesnake,* Shaftesbury Theatre, London, 1922.) "Leslie Perrins," *Variety,* 229, 19 Dec 1962, 79:2. BHD1, p. 432 (b. Birmingham, England). IFN, p. 235.

Perry, Albert H. [actor] (b. Detroit MI, 1869–6 May 1933 [63], St. George, Staten Island NY). "Albert H. Perry," *Variety,* 9 May 1933. AS, p. 862.

Perry, Anna Day [actress] (b. 1853–28 Oct 1928 [75?], Peak Island ME). BHD, p. 273.

Perry, Antoinette [stage/film actress] (b. Denver CO, 27 Jun 1888–28 Jun 1946 [58], New York NY; heart attack). m. Frank W. Frueauff, 1909 (d. 1922). (Stage debut, 1905.) "Antoinette Perry, Directed Hit Plays; Stager of 'Harvey' and Other Pemberton Successes Dies—Leader in Theatre Wing," *NYT,* 29 Jun 1946, 19:3. "Antoinette Perry Dies at 58 of Heart Attack; Star Stage Director," *Variety,* 3 Jul 1946. AS, p. 862. BHD, p. 273. Truitt, p. 266.

Perry, Charles Emmett [actor] (b. New York NY, 26 Dec 1901–26 Feb 1967 [65], Los Angeles CA; heart attack). AS, p. 862. BHD1, p. 432. IFN, p. 235.

Perry, Fayette [actress] (b. NB, ca. 1895). (Gaumont; Mutual; Universal; Lasky, Pathé, Kinemacolor.) AMD, p. 275. "Fayette Perry," *MPW,* 30 Oct 1915, 794.

Perry, Frederick [actor]. No data found. (Debut: *Dr. Rameau,* Fox, 1915.)

Perry, Harry [cinematographer] (b. KS, 2 May 1888–9 Feb 1985 [96], Woodland Hills CA). (FP-L, 1918; Preferred Pictures, 1922.) "Harry Perry," *Variety,* 20 Feb 1985. AS, p. 862. BHD2, p. 208. FDY, p. 465.

Perry, Ida [actress] (b. Berlin, Germany, 16 Feb 1877–21 Jun 1966 [89], Berlin, Germany). BHD1, p. 433. IFN, p. 235.

Perry, Jack [actor] (d. 7 Oct 1971). BHD1, p. 433. IFN, p. 235.

Perry, [Mr.] Jean [actor]. No data found. George Katchmer, "Remembering the Great Silents," *CI,* 247 (Jan 1996), 47.

Perry, Jessie [actress] (b. Aurora IN, 1 Sep 1876–6 Jul 1944 [67], Los Angeles Co. CA). BHD1, p. 433. IFN, p. 235.

Perry, Joseph [pioneer of Australian cinema] (b. Engeland, Australia, 1862–15 Apr 1943 [81?], Sydney, Australia). AS,p. 862.

Perry, Kathryn [actress] (b. New York NY, 5 Jan 1897–14 Oct 1983 [86], Woodland Hills CA). m. **Owen Moore**, 16 Jul 1921 (d. 1939). AMD, p. 275. AS, p. 862. BHD1, p. 433. "Katherine Perry to Play 'Leads' with Owen Moore," *MPW,* 30 Oct 1920, 1280. "Kathryn Was in Ziegfeld Band," *MPW,* 21 May 1927, 181.

Perry, Orrie [actor] (*né* Orizaba Perry, b. Australia, 1887–1950 [63?], Australia). AS, p. 862.

Perry, Paul P. [cinematographer] (b. Demver CO, 13 Dec 1891–24 Oct 1963 [71], Los Angeles CA). "Paul Perry," *Variety,* 30 Oct 1963. AS, p. 862. BHD2, p. 208. FDY, p. 465.

Perry, Pauline [actress] (b. 1882–7 Sep 1985 [103?], San Diego CA). BHD, p. 273.

Perry, Reginald Harry [actor/rep for Universal in So. Australia from 1920–62] (b. Australia, 1890?–13 Jun 1981 [91], Adelaide, Australia; stroke). "Reginald Perry," *Variety,* 1 Jul 1981 (may have been born in 1885; his father, Joseph Perry, made *Soldiers of the Cross* in 1900, "which has been claimed to be the first feature film in history.").

Perry, Robert E. [actor] (b. New York NY, 26 Dec 1878–8 Jan 1962 [83], Los Angeles CA). "Robert E. Perry," *Variety,* 17 Jan 1962. AS, p. 862. BHD1, p. 433. IFN, p. 235. Truitt, p. 266. George Katchmer, "Robert (Bob) Perry," *CI,* 232 (Oct 1994), C25.

Perry, Walter L. [actor] (b. San Francisco CA, 14 Sep 1868–22 Jan 1954 [85], Los Angeles Co. CA). AS, p. 862. BHD1, p. 433. IFN, p. 235. George Katchmer, "Walter Perry," *CI,* 232 (Oct 1994), C25-C26.

Pershing, Marcella [actress]. BR, pp. 198–99. George A. Katchmer, "Forgotten Cowboys and Cowgirls—Part V," *CI,* 177 (Mar 1990), C6. (In *Until They Get Me,* 1917.)

Persons, Thomas A. [studio manager]. No data found. AMD, p. 275. "Persons with DeLuxe Pictures," *MPW,* 5 Oct 1918, 73.

Persse, Thomas [actor/opera singer] (b. Lembrick, Ireland, 4 Sep 1862–17 Apr 1920 [57], Venice CA). "Thomas Persse," *Variety,* 23 Apr 1920 (age 59). BHD, p. 273. IFN, p. 235. Truitt, p. 266.

Pertwee, Roland [actor/playwright/title writer/scenarist] (b. Brighton, England, 15 May 1885–26 Apr 1963 [77], London, England). (WB.) "Roland Pertwee, Playwright, Dies; Film Writer and Novelist Studied Art with [John Singer] Sargent," *NYT,* 28 Apr 1963, 88:4 (age 78). "Roland Pertwee," *Variety,* 230, 1 May 1963, 84:2 (wrote *Interference*). AS, p. 863. BHD1, p. 433; BHD2, p. 208. FDY, p. 447. IFN, p. 235.

Pescatori, Lilla (mother of Olga Pescatore) [actress] (*née* Lilla Manichelli). m. actor Nicola Pescatori (d. 1936). JS, p. 345 (in Italian silents from 1913).

Pesce, Franco [director of photography from 1942; actor] (aka Frank Oliveras, b. Naples, Italy, 11 Aug 1890). AS, p. 863. JS, p. 345–46 (in Italian silents as an assistant cinematographer, 1910).

Petacci, Emilio [actor] (b. Rome, Italy, 25 Jan 1886). JS, p. 346 (in Italian silents from 1913).

Peter the Great [dog star] (d. Jun 1926, Hollywood CA; gunshot wound). AMD, p. 275. "Obituary," *MPW,* 26 Jun 1926, 683.

Peters, Fred[erick] [actor] (*né* Frederick P. Tuite, b. Waltham MA, 30 Jun 1884–23 Apr 1963 [78], Los Angeles CA). AMD, p. 275. AS, p. 863. BHD1, p. 433. IFN, p. 235. Truitt, p. 266. "Fred Peters Is Signed by Universal," *MPW,* 2 Apr 1927, 480.

Peters, George [cameraman] (b. Chicago IL, 1890–17 Oct 1935 [45?], Los Angeles CA). AMD, p. 275. BHD2, p. 208. FDY, p. 465. "New Cameraman Shooting Hines' 'The Brown Derby,'" *MPW,* 1 May 1926, 41. "George Peters," *MPW,* 12 Mar 1927, 101.

Peters, George W. [aviator/cameraman] (d. 17 Oct 1935). (Biograph; FP-L; Selig; Keystone.) "George Peters, former cameraman, died Oct. 17 in Los Angeles General hospital," *Variety,* 23 Oct 1935. AMD, p. 275. "George W. Peters Joins American Forces," *MPW,* 8 Jun 1912, 946. "Up in Air Again; Flying Camera-man Joins Popular Plays and Players," *NYDM,* 29 Jan 1916, p. 54 ("...first man to make motion pictures from an aeroplane."). "Aviator Peters with Metro," *MPW,* 5 Feb 1916, 762. "Peters to Photograph Burr FEature Productions in 1922," *MPW,* 31 Dec 1921, 1096.

Peters, House, Sr., "The Star of a Thousand Emotions" (father of House Peters, Jr.; brother of **Page E. Peters**) [stage/film actor] (*né* Robert House Peters, b. Bristol, Gloucestershire, England, 12 Mar 1880–7 Dec 1967 [87], Woodland Hills CA). m. Mae King (*née* House), 1914, San Francisco CA (d. Apr 1985, aged 95; son, House Peters, Jr., b. 2 Jan 1916). (Stage debut: *Robbery Under Arms;* film debut: *The Bishop's Carriage,* FP-L, 1913; World; Ince.) "House Peters," *Variety,* 13 Dec 1967 (age 88). AMD, p. 275. AS, p. 863. BHD1, p. 434. FFF, p. 170 (b. 1888). GK, pp. 782–91. IFN, p. 235. Katz, p. 908. MH, p. 132. Spehr, p. 156 (b. 1880). Truitt, p. 266. "House Peters Goes to California," *MPW,* 9 May 1914, 800. "House Peters Married," *MPW,* 5 Sep 1914, 1377. "House Peters," *MPW,* 23 Oct 1915, 624. "House Peters with Paragon," *MPW,* 4 Mar 1916, 1451. "Morosco-Pallas Sign House Peters," *MPW,* 28 Oct 1916, 552. Allen Corliss, "The Wandering House," *Photoplay,* Jul 1917, 24–25 (quoted as saying he was born in Hong-Kong). "House Peters in Two Hodkinson Releases," *MPW,* 1 Mar 1919, 1230. "House Peters Incorporates," *MPW,* 24 Jul 1920, 447. "House Peters Has Been Signed for Five Years by Baumann," *MPW,* 31 Mar 1923, 558. "House Peters to Make 6 for Universal," *MPW,* 17 May 1924, 271. George A. Katchmer, "He-Man House Peters," *CI,* 121 (Jul 1985), 19–20, C8. "House Peters Addendum," *CI,* 127 (Jan 1986), 55, 61. Richard E. Braff, "An Index to the Films of House Peters, Sr.," *CI,* 168 (Jun 1989), C4.

Peters, Capt. John [actor] (b. Germany–d. 21 Oct 1940, Santa Rosa CA). "Capt. John Peters," *Variety,* 6 Nov 1940. AS, p. 864. BHD, p. 273. Truitt, p. 266.

Peters, John S[ylvester] [actor/military technical adviser] (b. OH, 31 Dec 1894–7 Nov 1963 [68], San Fernando CA). "Capt. John S. Peters," *Variety,* 20 Nov 1963. AS, p. 864. BHD1, p. 434. IFN, p. 235.

Peters, Lloyd T. [actor] (b. Spokane WA, 2 Mar 1902–11 Apr 1988 [86], Spokane WA). BHD1, p. 615.

Peters, Page E. (brother of **House Peters, Sr.**) [actor] (b. 1889?–22 Jun 1916 [26], Hermosa Beach CA; drowned). "Page Peters Drowned," *Variety,* 30 Jun 1916. AMD, P. 275. AS, p. 864. BHD, p. 273. IFN, p. 235. "Page Peters with Morosco Company," *MPW,* 18 Dec 1915, 2160. "Week of Deaths and Injury," *MPW,* 15 Jul 1916, 441. "Obituary," *MPW,* 15 Jul 1916, 465.

Peters, Rollo [actor/assistant director] (b. Paris, France, 25 Sep 1892–21 Jan 1967 [74], Monterey CA). BHD2, p. 208.

Peters, Thomas Kimmwood [cameraman]. No data found. AMD, P. 275. "Will Take Camera Around the World," *MPW,* 9 Oct 1915, 280.

Peters, William Frederick [composer/violinist] (b. Sandusky OH, 9 Aug 1871?–1 Dec 1938 [67], Englewood NJ; heart disease). "William F. Peters, Composer for Films; Musical Director for Belasco and Maude Adams Dies," *NYT,* 2 Dec 1938, 24:2 (He was "the first composer to write an original score for the movies. Notable examples of his compositions were the scores for *Way Down East, Orphans of the Storm, When Knighthood Was in Flower, Under the Red Robe, The Four Feathers,* and *Little Old New York.*"). "William F. Peters," *Variety,* 7 Dec 1938. ASCAP 66, p. 569 (b. 1876). AS, p. 864. BHD2, p. 209.

Petersen, Ernst [actor] (b. 1860–26 Mar 1930 [70?]). BHD, p. 273.

Peterson, Gustave C. [cinematographer] (b. San Francisco CA, 19 Jul 1893–17 Dec 1969 [76], Woodland Hills CA). BHD2, p. 209.

Petit, Wanda *see* **Hawley, Wanda**

Petley, Frank E. [actor] (b. Old Charlton, England, 28 Mar 1872–12 Jan 1945 [72]). BHD1, p. 434. IFN, p. 236.

Petra, Hortense [actress] (b. 1910–8 Jul 1982 [72?], Los Angeles CA; heart attack). AS, p. 865 (Petro). BHD1, p. 434.

Petroff, Paul [actor] (b. Denmark, 1908–27 Apr 1981 [73?], Antwerp, Belgium). BHD, p. 273.

Petrolini, Ettore [actor] (b. Rome, Italy, 13 Jan 1886–29 Jun 1936 [50], Rome, Italy). AS, p. 865. JS, p. 347 (in Italian films from 1913).

Petrova, Olga [stage/film actress/writer] (*née* Muriel Harding, b. Liverpool, England, 10 May 1884?–30 Nov 1977 [93?], Clearwater FL). m. Boris Petrov; John D. Stewart; **Lewis Willoughby** (d. 1968). *Butter with My Bread* (NY: The Bobbs-Merrill Co., 1942). (Lasky; Metro; Petrova Pictures.) "Olga Petrova, Actress and Playwright, Was 93," *NYT,* 7 Dec 1977, II, 14:1. "Olga Petrova," *Variety,* 14 Dec 1977 (*née* Muriel Harding). AMD, P. 275. AS, p. 865. BHD, p. 273. IFN, p. 236 (b. England). Katz, p. 909 (b. England, not Warsaw, Poland). MSBB, p. 1040 (b. Warsaw). SD, p. 992. Spehr, p. 158 (b. 1886). "Olga Petrova," *MPW,* 12 Dec 1914, 1507. "Petrova Likes Screen; Signs Contract for Two Years with the Popular Plays and Players Company," *NYDM,* 7 Apr 1915, 32:1 (to make 12 films released on the Metro programme—"a Petrova picture every eight weeks.") "Olga Petrova," *MPW,* 1 May 1915, 730. "Olga Petrova in Frank Mood," *MPW,* 24 Jul 1915, 656. "Petrova with Popular Players," *MPW,* 25 Dec 1915, 2354. "Popular Plays and Players Active," *MPW,* 22 Jan 1916, 573. "Mme. Olga Petrova

Becomes Lasky Star," *MPW*, 6 Jan 1917, 93. Cal York, "Plays and Players," *Photoplay Magazine*, Feb 1917, 89 (The "high voltage vamp of the Metro organization" was dickering with the Lasky company. "Mme. Petrova, according to advices, asks the paltry pittance of 4,000 *pesos oro* per week, which is quite some wages."). "Petrova Has Own Company," *MPW*, 25 Aug 1917, 1203. "Petrova on First National Circuit," *MPW*, 6 Oct 1917, 67. "Madame Petrova Purchases Home at Great Neck, L.I.," *MPW*, 29 Dec 1917, 1925. "Olga Petrova," *MPW*, 29 Dec 1917, 1933. "Olga Petrova to Return to Screen," *MPW*, 16 Nov 1918, 752. Gladys Hall, "Why Is Petrova Barred from the Screen???; Famous stage star, who was formerly a prime movie favorite, cannot obtain a place in films—What is the reason for her exclusion from the silver sheet," *MW*, 7 Jun 1924, 4–5, 28. Gladys Hall, "Why? Ask the Readers; Some experts from the innumerable letters, which, with generous praise for Madame Petrova as an individual and artist, repeat our question, 'Why is Petrova barred from the screen?,'" *MW*, 16 Aug 1924, 21, 30. Alan Brock, "Madame Olga Petrova," *CFC*, 58 (Spring, 1978), 6, 10, 35.

Petrovich, Ivan [actor] (b. Novi Sad, Serbia, 1 Jan 1894–12 Oct 1962 [68], Munich, Germany). (Universal.) AMD, p. 275. AS, p. 865. BHD1, p. 434. Waldman, p. 231. "Ivan Petrovitch, Ingram 'Find,' Medal Winner," *MPW*, 12 Mar 1927, 115.

Petschler, Erik [actor/director] (b. Göteborg, Sweden, 2 Sep 1881–10 Dec 1945 [64], Stockholm, Sweden). AS, p. 865. BHD1, p. 615; BHD2, p. 209.

Pettingell, Frank [actor] (b. Liverpool, England, 1 Jan 1891–17 Feb 1966 [75], London, England). m. Ethel Till. "Frank Pettingell," *Variety*, 23 Feb 1966. AS, p. 865. BHD1, p. 435. IFN, p. 236.

Peukert, Leo [actor/director] (*né* Leonhard Peukert, b. Munich, Germany, 26 Aug 1885–6 Jan 1944 [58], Tiengen, Germany). m. **Sabine Impekoven** (d. 1970). AS, p. 866. BHD1, p. 435. IFN, p. 236.

Peukert-Impekoven, Sabine (sister of Toni Impekoven) [actress] (*née* Sabine Impekoven, b. Germany, 1890–5 May 1970 [80], Frankfurt, Germany). m. **Leo Peukert** (d. 1944). "Sabine Peukert-Impekoven," *Variety*, 259, 27 May 1970, 63:4. AS, p. 866. BHD, p. 273. IFN, p.236.

Peyton, Lawrence Ross [actor] (b. Hartford KY, 1895–15 Oct 1918 [23?], France; killed in action). (Universal.) "Serg. Lawrence R. Peyton," *Variety*, 18 Oct 1918. AMD, P. 275. AS, p. 866. BHD1, p. 615. IFN, p. 236 (d. Nov). "Lawrence Ross Peyton," *MPW*, 30 Jun 1917, 2081. "Lawrence Ross Peyton," *MPW*, 15 Sep 1917, 1676.

Pezzana, Giacinta [actress] (b. Turin, Italy, 28 Jan 1841–4 Nov 1919 [78], Aci Castello, Italy). m. novelist Luigi Gualtieri. JS, p. 347 ("Nini Martoglio pressed her into making her only film, *Teresa Raquin*, 1915.").

Pezzinga, Giovanni [director]. JS, p. 347 (in Italian silents from 1919).

Phalke, D[hurdiraj] **G**[ovind] [film pioneer/director/producer] (b. Trimbackeshwar, India, 30 Apr 1870–15 Feb 1944 [73], Nazik, India). AS, p. 866. BHD2, p. 209.

Phelps, Buster [actor] (*né* Silas V. Phelps, Jr., b. Los Angeles CA, 5 Nov 1926–10 Jan 1983 [56], Los Angeles CA). AS, p. 866. BHD1, p. 435.

Phelps, Francher, Sr. [actor] (b. 1898–2 Nov 1972 [74]). BHD, p. 274. IFN, p. 236.

Phelps, Lee [character actor] (*né* Napoleon Bonaparte Ku-Kuck, b. PA, 15 May 1893–19 Mar 1953 [59], Culver City CA). "Lee Phelps," *Variety*, CII, 21 Mar 1953, 17:5. AS, p. 866. BHD1, p. 435. IFN, p. 236. Truitt, p. 267.

Philbin, Mary [actress: Wampas Star, 1922] (b. Chicago IL, 16 Jul 1903–7 May 1993 [89], Huntington Beach CA; Alzheimer's disease). Bachelorette. (Universal.) (Film debut: *The Blazing Trail*, 1921.) "Mary Philbin, Phantom's Silent Singer, Dead at 89," *New York Post*, 22 May 1993. "Mary Philbin," *Variety*, 14 Jun 1993, p. 64:2. AMD, p. 276. AS, p. 866. BHD1, p. 435. FFF, p. 220. FSS, p. 234. HCH, p. 117. Katz, p. 910. MH, p. 132 (b. 1904). "Mary Philbin to Make Four Jewel Pictures," *MPW*, 7 Jul 1923, 87. Harry Carr, "A Bashful Little Bernhardt," *MPC*, Feb 1925, 40–41, 93. Dorothy Donnell, "The Girl Who Had No Childhood; Mary Philbin Is a Star—But She Never Has Time to Play," *MPC*, Oct 1925, 40–41, 85–86. Paul Paige, "Close-Ups and Fade-Outs," *Paris and Hollywood*, Sep 1926, 57 (it "is whispered about the lots that Mary Philbin is a victim of tuberculosis and plays less and less in her own films. A young Miss Stodgill so closely resembes [her] that she is kept on the lot continually at $30 a day, and of late, has even done that star's crying scenes and other emotional work. Miss Philbin poses for the actual close-ups, and her work and her hours are shortened as much as possible."). Selma Robinson, "Mary of the Moods; Mary Philbin of the Chameleon Personality Is the Favorite of Artists and Directors. Like an Emotional Violin, She's Not a Movie Star, But an Actress," *MPC*, Dec 1926, 54–55, 76. "Estelle Taylor May Not Renew Contract with U-A," *MPW*, 27 Aug 1927, 587. Frances Gilmore, "The World Is Her Convent; Mary Philbin Is the Mystery Girl of the Screen," *MPC*, Apr 1928, 42, 84 ("When Mary Philbin comes onto a set, all vulgar talk is silenced."). Jimmy Bangley, "My Friend, Mary Philbin; Unmasking the Phantom," *CI*, 282 (Dec 1998), 6, 8.

Philbrick, William H. [actor] (d. 20 Oct 1955, Chelsea MA). "William H. Philbrick," *Variety*, 26 Oct 1955. BHD1, p. 435. IFN, p. 236.

Philby, Alex [actor] (d. 16 Aug 1912, Chicago IL; from injuries sustained in a fall from a horse on 6 Aug). AMD, p. 276. BHD1, p. 615. "'Flying A' Player Is Given Unique Cowboy Funeral," *MPW*, 31 Aug 1912, 887.

Philipp, Adolf [stage/film actor/producer/composer] (aka Jean Briquet, *né* Adolph Phillip, b. Hanover, Germany, 29 Jan 1864–30 Jul 1936 [72], New York NY). "Adolf Philipp," *Variety*, 5 Aug 1936. AMD, p. 276. AS, p. 866. BHD, p. 274 (b. Hamburg, Germany). IFN, p. 236 (d. 1937). "Adolf Phillip Collects," *Variety*, 15 Dec 1916, 30:4 (won $2,700 from the Peerless Feature Film Producing Co. for breach of contract. A scenario of his stage piece, *The Corcer Grocer*, was made but not produced). "Adolf Philipp with World Film," *MPW*, 15 Jan 1916, 404. "Adolf Philipp Ready with Musical Comedy Photoplays," *MPW*, 13 Sep 1919, 1676. "Adolf Philipp Is Brother and Not Father of Paul," *MPW*, 27 Sep 1919, 1993.

Philley, Virginia [actress] (b. 1890–10 Feb 1980 [89?], Ft. Wayne IN). BHD, p. 274.

Phillips, Albert [stage/film actor] (b. Edwardsville IN, 1875?–24 Feb 1940 [65], New York NY). m. Leila Shaw. "Albert Phillips, 65, Played in 'Lincoln'; Actor Had Stephen A. Douglas Role in Sherwood Drama Here," *NYT*, 26 Feb 1940, 15:2. "Albert Phillips," *Variety*, 28 Feb 1940. AS, p. 867. BHD, p. 274,.

Phillips, Alex, Sr. [actor/cameraman] (*né* Alec Phillips, b. Renfrew, Canada, 1900?–14 Jun 1977 [77], Mexico City, Mexico). (Christie.) "Alex Phillips, Sr.," *Variety*, 29 Jun 1977. AS, p. 867. BHD, p. 274; BHD2, p. 209. FDY, p. 465 (Alec Phillips).

Phillips, Alexandra [stage/film actress/short story writer/scenarist/director] (b. Scotland, 1876–22 Jun 1936 [60?], Los Angeles CA). m. **Milton H. Fahrney**, 12 Jan 1911 (d. 1941). (Nestor.) AMD, p. 276. BHD1, p. 615; BHD2, p. 209. "Alexandra Phillips," *NYDM*, 28 Feb 1912, 29:2. "Horsley Adds to His Forces," *MPW*, 8 Aug 1914, 821.

Phillips, Augustus [actor] (b. Rensselaer IN, 1 Aug 1874). Fl. 1915–20. AMD, p. 276. BHD, p. 274. "Augustus Phillips, Pioneer," *MPW*, 27 Feb 1915, 1293. "Universal Gets Augustus Phillips," *MPW*, 5 Feb 1916, 765. "Augustus Phillips Joins Metro," *MPW*, 28 Oct 1916, 552.

Phillips, Carmen [actress] (b. Chicago IL, 10 Jan). George Katchmer, "Carmen Phillips," *CI*, 226 (Apr 1994), 42.

Phillips, Charles [actor] (b. 1904–25 May 1958 [54], Los Angeles CA). AS, p. 867. BHD1, p. 435. IFN, p. 236.

Phillips, Clement K. [stuntman] (b. 1900?–4 Oct 1928 [28], Castro Valley [near Oakland] CA). "Stunt Flyer Killed on Way for Film Scenes," *Variety*, 10 Oct 1928. AS, p. 867. BHD, p. 274 (d. Hayward CA). IFN, p. 236. Truitt, p. 267. WWS, p. 267.

Phillips, Coles [artist]. No data found. AMD, p. 276. "Some Coles Phillips Pictures," *MPW*, 17 Oct 1914, 349.

Phillips, Dorothy [stage/film actress] (*née* Dorothy Gwendolyn Strieble, b. Baltimore MD, 30 Oct 1889–1 Mar 1980 [90], Woodland Hills CA; pneumonia). m. **Allen J. Holubar**, 1912, Wildwood NJ (d. 1923). (Film debut: *The Rosary*, Essanay, 1911; Imp; Universal, May 1914; Principal; Trueart; Fox; PDC.) AMD, p. 276. AS, p. 867. BHD1, p. 435. Katz, p. 910. Lowrey, p. 150. MH, p. 132. WWS, p. 260. "Dorothy Phillips Signs with Universal," *MPW*, 11 Jul 1914, 267. "Dorothy Phillips," *MPW*, 11 Dec 1915, 2020 (b. 1892). "Dorothy Phillips as Tournament Herald," *MPW*, 30 Dec 1916, 1948–49 (in Pasadena CA). "Dorothy Phillips," *MPW*, 5 May 1917, 778. "Dorothy Phillips Renews Contracts," *MPW*, 23 Jun 1917, 1963. "Dorothy Phillips [photo]," *Photoplay*, Jul 1917, 13. "Dorothy Phillips," *MPW*, 4 Aug 1917, 786. "DOrothy Phillips Has Narrow Escape," *MPW*, 13 Oct 1917, 244. "Another Super-Drama for Dorothy Phillips, *MPW*, 22 Mar 1919, 1685. Fritzi Remont, "Dorothy, Alan and Gwen [their 4-year-old daughter]," *MPC*, Apr 1919, 34–35, 70. "Dorothy Phillips to Continue with 'U,'" *MPW*, 12 Apr 1919, 231. "Phillips and Holubar Leave Universal," *MPW*, 10 Jan 1920, 234. "Carl Laemmle Threatens to Sue Dorothy Phillips," *MPW*, 24 Jan 1920, 548. "Dorothy Phillips Believes It Unfair to Demand Picture a Month from Stars," *MPW*, 9 Oct 1920, 832. "Sacarcity of Good Productions Is Due to Lack of Good Actors, Says Big Star," *MPW*, 18 Dec 1920, 856. T.S. daPonte, "Dorothy Phillips Speaks of Herself and About 'Man-Woman-Marriage,' Too," *MPW*, 22 Jan 1921, 403–04. "Makes

Serial Debut," *MPW,* 28 Nov 1925, 348. "Dorothy Phillips Returns," *MPW,* 13 Feb 1926, 636. "Dorothy Phillips," *MPW,* 20 Feb 1926,712. Dorothy Phillips, "I Had to Come Back to Pictures," *MPC,* Dec 1926, 48–49, 84 (gave up career when husband died). "Miss Phillips Free," *MPW,* 5 Feb 1927, 423. Richard Morrissey [grandson], "Dorothy Phillips [letter]," *CI,* 86 (Aug 1982), 15, 46. Billy H. Doyle, "Lost Players; Dorothy Phillips and Allen J. Holubar," *CI,* 186 (Dec 1990), 36–37.

Phillips, Edna (mother of **Phillips Holmes**) [actress] (b. Canada, 26 Feb 1878–26 Feb 1952 [74], Los Angeles CA). m. **Taylor Holmes** (d. 1959). "Edna Phillips," *NYT,* 27 Feb 1952, 27:5. AS, p. 867. BHD, p. 274. IFN, p. 236. Truitt, p. 267.

Phillips, Edward N. [child actor/film editor] (b. Philadelphia PA, 14 Aug 1899–22 Feb 1965 [65], No. Hollywood CA; struck by car). m. Lee. (MGM.) "Edward N. Phillips," *Variety,* 3 Mar 1965 (age 66). AMD, p. 276. AS, p. 867. BHD1, p. 435. IFN, p. 236. Truitt, p. 267. "Edward Engaged," *MPW,* 18 Nov 1922, 251. "Edward N. Phillips," *MPW,* 2 Jul 1927, 19. George Katchmer, "Eddie Phillips," *CI,* 232 (Oct 1994), C24-C25.

Phillips, Edwin R. [stage/film actor/director] (b. Providence RI–d. 29 Aug 1915, New York NY; pneumonia). (Vitagraph, 1905; played Uncle Tom in *Uncle Tom's Cabin,* Vitagraph, 1910.) "Edwin R. Phillips," *Variety,* 3 Sep 1915 (d. Coney Island NY; with Vitagraph, 1908). AMD, p. 276. AS, p. 867 (d. 20 Aug). BHD, p. 274 (d. Coney Island NY). IFN, p. 236. Slide, p. 147. "Inquiries; H.K.," *MPW,* 15 Jun 1912, 1029. "Film Pioneer Dies; Edward Phillips, Member of Original Vitagraph Stock, Succumbs to Heart Trouble," *NYDM,* 15 Sep 1915, 27:1 ("Mr. Phillips brought the late John Bunny into the Vitagraph fold…"). "Obituary," *MPW,* 18 Sep 1915, 2000.

Phillips, Festus (Dad) [actor/makeup artist: organized The Association of Makeup Artists & Hair Stylists] (b. 1872–5 Sep 1955 [83], Los Angeles CA). m. (3 sons, 1 daughter). (Griffith; Columbia.) "Festus Phillips," *Variety,* 200, 14 Sep 1955, 71:2 ("…he was persuaded to become an actor by David W. Griffith."). AS, p. 867. BHD, p. 274. IFN, p. 236.

Phillips, Helena [actress] (aka Helena Evans, b. MA, 21 May 1875–24 Jul 1955 [80], Santa Monica CA; heart attack). m. Charles E. Evans. "Mrs. Helena Phillips Evans," *Variety,* 3 Aug 1955. AS, p. 370 (Helena Phillips Evans); p. 867. BHD1, p. 435 (Helene Phillips). IFN, p. 98. Truitt, p. 104.

Phillips, Henry Albert [writer] (b. Brooklyn NY, 28 Jan 1880–28 Jan 1951 [71], Stamford CT). m. Margaret Wheeler Shepard, 1908. "H.A. Phillips Dies; Author and Editor; World Wide Traveler Wrote and Lectured on Experiences—Published Many Books," *NYT,* 29 Jan 1951, 19:3 (editor of *Motion Picture Magazine,* 1910). AMD, p. 276. BHD2, p. 209. "Author Appears in Person," *MPW,* 31 Mar 1917, 2084.

Phillips, Joseph H. [stage/film actor] (b. 1888?–10 Dec 1966 [78], New York NY [Death Certificate Index No. 25631; M.E. Case No. 0697]). "Joe Phillips," *Variety,* 28 Dec 1966 (in vaudeville). AMD, p. 276. AS, p. 867. "Joseph H. Phillips," *MPW,* 7 Apr 1917, 100.

Phillips, Kate [actress] (b. Essex, England, 28 Jul 1856–9 Sep 1931 [75], London, England). BHD, p. 274.

Phillips, Kember (Tubby) [actor] (b. Bloemfontein, South Africa, 1884–26 Apr 1930 [46?], London, England; auto accident). AS, p. 868 (d. 15 Apr). BHD, p. 274. IFN, p. 236.

Phillips, Minna [actress] (b. Sydney, Australia, 1 Jun 1871–17 Jan 1963 [91], New Orleans LA; heart attack). AMD, p. 276. AS, p. 868. BHD1, p. 436 (b. 1885). IFN, p. 236. "Minna Phillips Makes Her Photoplay Debut," *MPW,* 8 Jan 1916, 236.

Phillips, Miriam [actress] (b. Philadelphia PA, 1899–24 Oct 1997 [98?], Englewood NJ; Alzheimer's disease). AS, p. 868. BHD, p. 615.

Phillips, Norma S., "The Mutual Girl" [actress] (b. Baltimore MD, 1893?–12 Nov 1931 [38], New York NY [Death Certificate No. 26364; age 34]; cancer). m. **Robert P. Gleckler**—div. 1929 (d. 1939). (Mutual.) "Norma Phillips Dies; Was 'Mutual Girl,'" *Variety,* 17 Nov 1931. AMD, p. 276. AS, p. 868. BHD, p. 274 (d. 11 Nov). IFN, p. 236. Truitt, p. 267. "Norma Phillips; Leading Woman with the Reliance Company," *MPS,* 5 Sep 1913, 30. "Mutual Girl Series," *MPW,* 27 Dec 1913, 1525. "Mutual Girl Entertains Broadway," *MPW,* 31 Jan 1914, 523.

Phillips, Norman, Sr. [actor] (b. 1892?–11 Feb 1931 [39], Culver City [MGM studios] CA; heart attack). "Norman Phillips," *Variety,* 18 Feb 1931 (began 1930?). AS, p. 868. BHD, p. 274. IFN, p. 236. Truitt, p. 267.

Phillips, Richard [actor] (b. 1826?–4 May 1941 [115], Los Angeles CA). "Richard Phillips," *Variety,* 28 May 1941. AS, p. 868. BHD1, p. 436. IFN, p. 236. Truitt, p. 267.

Phillips, Sam [actor/stage manager] (b. England, 1848?–26 Feb 1918 [70], Cincinnati OH). "Samuel Phillips," *Variety,* 1 Mar 1918). AS, p. 868.

Phillips, William [actor] (b. Washington DC, 1 Jun 1908–27 Jun 1957 [49], Los Angeles Co. CA). BHD1, p. 436. IFN, p. 236.

Phipps, Sally [actress: Wampas Star, 1927] (*née* Byrnece Beutler, b. San Francisco CA, 25 May 1909–17 Mar 1978 [69], LI New York NY). m. Benedict Gimbel, Jr., 1931–1935; Alfred M. Harned, 1941. (Began 1915; Fox.) "Sally Phipps, 67, Star of the Silent-Movie Era," *NYT,* 21 Mar 1978. "Sally Phipps," *Variety,* 29 Mar 1978. AMD, p. 276. AS, p. 868. BHD1, p. 436 (b. 24 May). IFN, p. 237. "Sally Phipps," *MPW,* 3 Sep 1927, 25. "The Answer Man," *MPC,* Mar 1928, 74 (b. 1909). Dorothy Manners, "Kute and Kool and Kalm; Twenty Years from Now Sally Phipps Might Take Pictures Seriously," *MPC,* Oct 1928, 42, 77 ("I studied to be a lawyer…Frank [Borzage] asked me to make a test and I did and then they offered me a contract. That's how I got in pictures."). John Roberts, "Sally Phipps," *CI,* 113 (Nov 1984), 57, 63.

Physioc, Lewis W. [cinematographer/director/producer] (b. Columbia SC, 30 Jun 1879–16 Jan 1972 [92], Los Angeles CA). BHD2, p. 209. FDY, p. 465.

Physioc, Wray Bartlett [set designer/director] (b. Columbia SC, 23 Nov 1890). (Pathé Frères; Ramo; World.) AMD, p. 276. AS, p. 868. BHD2, p. 209. 1921 Directory, p. 273. Spehr, p. 158. "Ramo Remarks," *MPW,* 28 Jun 1913, 1371. "Physioc to Fight; Former Ramo Head to Claim Trade Mark and Demand an Accounting," *MPW,* 19 Jul 1913, 306. "Biograph's Director," *MPW,* 10 Jul 1915, 243–44. "Wray Physioc Engaged by Pioneer," *MPW,* 20 Sep 1919, 1854.

Piazza, Ben [casting director] (b. Hazlehurst MS, 1886–22 Jul 1955 [69?], Los Angeles CA). BHD2, p. 209.

Pica, Tina (daughter of actor Giuseppe Pica) [actress] (*née* Concetta Annunziata Pica, b. Naples, Italy, 31 Mar 1884–16 Aug 1968 [84], Naples, Italy). AS, p. 868. BHD1, p. 436. JS, p. 348 (in Italian silents from 1916).

Picart, José [cinematographer]. No data found. FDY, p. 465.

Picasso, Lamberto [actor] (b. La Spezia, Italy, 21 Oct 1883). JS, pp. 348–49 (in Italian silents from 1914).

Picha, Hermann [actor] (*né* Hermann August Karl Picher, b. Charlottenburg, Germany, 20 Mar 1865–7 Jan 1936 [70], Berlin, Germany). AS, p. 869 (d. 7 Jun, Tempelhof, Germany). BHD1, p. 436. IFN, p. 237.

Pichel, Irving [director/actor/scenarist] (b. Pittsburgh PA, 24 Jun 1891–13 Jul 1954 [63], La Canada CA; heart attack. m. Violette Wilson. (MGM; Fox; Paramount; RKO; Universal.) "Irving Pichel, 63, Actor, Director; His 'Martin Luther' Acclaimed Last Year—Community Theatre Leader Dies," *NYT,* 14 Jul 1954, 27:3. "Irving Pichel," *Variety,* 17 Jul 1954 (age 60). AS, p. 869. BHD1, p. 436; BHD2, p. 209. IFN, p. 237. Katz, pp. 911–12.

Pick, Lupu [director/actor] (b. Jassy, Romania, 2 Jan 1886–7 Mar 1931 [45], Berlin, Germany; due to poisoning). m. actress Edith Posa. "Lupe Pick," *Variety,* 102, 25 Mar 1931, 69:3 (directed *Scherben,* "…considered one of the best silent pictures ever produced." Had just finished directing *Gassenhauer,* his first talkie.). BHD, p. 274; BHD2, p. 210. IFN, p. 237.

Pickard, Helene [actress] (b. Handsworth, England, 13 Oct 1899–27 Sep 1959 [59], Birmingham, England). m. **Cedric Hardwicke** (d. 1964). AS, p. 869 (b. Sheffield, England, 1900; d. Oxfordshire, England). BHD1, p. 436.

Picker, Sylvia [actress] (*née* Sylvia McGraw, b. New Yotk NY, 11 Apr 1912–25 Sep 1981 [69], Los Angeles CA). AS, p. 869. BHD1, p. 437.

Pickert, Elizabeth W. [actress/director/scenarist] (*née?,* b. 1865?–16 Mar 1937 [72], Miami FL). m. Willis A. Pickert. "Mrs. Elizabeth Pickert; Former Actress and One of Miami's First Residents," *NYT,* 17 Mar 1937, 25:3 ("She once was character actress in a New York stock company managed in the early 1900's by her husband, the late Willis A. Pickert."). "Elizabeth W. Pickert," *Variety,* 24 Mar 1937. AMD, p. 276. AS, p. 869. FDY, p. 435. Tom Waller, "Elizabeth Pickett," *MPW,* 17 Dec 1927, 28–29.

Pickett, Bill [actor] (b. 1870–2 Apr 1932 [62?], OK). BHD1, p. 615.

Pickett, Ingram B. "Seven Foot" [actor: Keystone Cop] (b. 1898–14 Feb 1963 [64], Santa Fe NM). "Ingram B. Pickett," *Variety,* 6 Mar 1963 (6' 10 1/2" high). AS, p. 869. BHD, p. 274. IFN, p. 237. Truitt, p. 268.

Pickford, Charlotte (mother of **Jack, Lottie** and **Mary Pickford**; grandmother of **Mary Pickford Rupp**; aunt of **Isabelle Sheridan**) [actress] (*née* Elsie Charlotte Printer, b. Toronto, Canada, 1873–22 Mar 1928 [54?], Los Angeles CA). AMD, p. 276. AS, p. 1012 (Charlotte Smith). BHD, p. 274. "Mary Pickford's Mother in Hospital," *MPW,* 23 Dec 1916, 1332. "Mrs. Pickford Heads Two Companies," *MPW,* 1 Feb 1919, 621.

Pickford, Jack (son of **Charlotte Pickford**; brother of **Mary** and **Lottie Pickford**; uncle of **Mary Pickford Rupp**; cousin of **Isabelle Sheridan**) [stage/film actor/director] (*né* John Charles Smith, Jr., b. Toronto, Ontario, Canada, 18 Aug 1896–3 Jan 1933 [36], Paris, France; multiple neuritis). m. **Olive Thomas**, May 1917, NJ (d. 1920); **Marilyn Miller**, 31 Jul 1922 (d. 1936); Mary Mulhern. (Biograph, 1909; Pathé; Mutual; FP-L; Selig; Paramount.) "Jack Pickford, 36, Is Dead in Paris; Mary's Brother, Who Was Film Star and Producer, Had Long Been Ill; Career Colorful, Tragic; His First Wife, Olive Thomas, Died of Poisoning—Marilyn Miller, Second Wife, Divorced Him," *NYT,* 4 Jan 1933, 17:1. "Jack Pickford," *Variety,* 10 Oct 1933. AMD, p. 277. AS, p. 869. BHD1, p. 437; BHD2, p. 210. FFF, p. 173. FSS, p. 235. IFN, p. 237. Katz, p. 912. MH, p. 133. MSBB, p. 1026. Spehr, p. 158. Truitt, p. 268. WWS, p. 133. "Selig Has a Pickford," *NYDM,* 15 Sep 1915, 25:1 (19-year-old Pickford to work for Selig on the Pacific coast). "In the Picture Studios," *NYDM,* 23 Oct 1915, 31:1 (to make his Selig debut in *The Making of Crooks,* 2 reels). "Lottie and Jack Pickford Rejoin Famous Players," *MPW,* 2 Sep 1916, 1518. "Jack Pickford Now a Censor," *MPW,* 13 Apr 1918, 255 (enlisted in Navy). "Jack Pickford Signs Up with the First National," *MPW,* 14 Dec 1918, 1220. "Jack Pickford Undergoes Operation," *MPW,* 25 Jan 1919, 474. "Presents Wife with $9,000 Car," *MPW,* 1 Feb 1919, 616. "Jack Pickford in New Home," *MPW,* 8 Feb 1919, 754. "Jack Pickford Will Fly to Location," *MPW,* 8 Mar 1919, 1335. "Pickford Denies He Was Dishonorably Discharged," *MPW,* 17 May 1919, 1006. "Jack Pickford Signs Long Contract with Goldwyn," *MPW,* 30 Aug 1919, 1327 (b. 15 Aug). "Jack Pickford Has Name Legally Changed as He Becomes Citizen of United States," *MPW,* 21 Aug 1920, 1009. "Jack Pickford Has Bronchial Pneumonia," *MPW,* 5 Mar 1921, 29. "Pickford Ready to Start on Next Film," *MPW,* 24 Feb 1923, 805. "Marilyn Miller and Pickford to Co-Star in Screen Play," *MPW,* 5 May 1923, 74. "Jack Pickford's Latest," *MPW,* 20 Oct 1923, 682. Irene Martin, "On a Wedding Anniversary," *MW,* 20 Sep 1924, 16–17 (married to Marilyn Miller). "Schenck Signs Pickford on Long Term Contract," *MPW,* 2 Jan 1926, 81. June Lee, "Dan Cupid's Bulletin Board," *Paris and Hollywood Screen Secrets Magazine,* Aug 1927, 35 (divorce from Miller confirmed). Stuart Oderman, "In My Sister's Shadow and Other Private Hells of Jack Pickford," *CFC,* 58 (Spring, 1978), 22–24. George Katchmer, "Jack Pickford," *CI,* 228 (Jun 1994), 42. Stuart Oderman, "Jack Pickford and Olive Thomas; Scandalous goings-on for Mary's little brother," *FIR,* Nov/Dec 1995, 86–97.

Pickford, Lottie (daughter of **Charlotte Pickford**; mother of **Mary Pickford Rupp**; sister of **Mary** and **Jack Pickford**; cousin of **Isabelle Sheridan**) [actress] (*née* Charlotte Smith, b. Toronto, Canada, 9 Jan 1895–9 Dec 1936 [41], Brentwood CA; heart attack). m. (1) Albert George Rupp; (2) **Allan Forrest**, 8 Jan 1922—div. 1928 (d. 1941). "Lottie Pickford," *Variety,* 16 Dec 1936. AMD, p. 277. AS, p. 869. BHD, p. 274 (b. 9 Jun). IFN, p. 237. Truitt, p. 268. "Lottie Pickford with the Pilot Company," *MPW,* 14 Jun 1913, 1125. Edna Wright, "Lottie Pickford, of the Famous Players," *Motion Picture Magazine,* Feb 1915, 92–94. "Lottie Pickford," *MPW,* 1 May 1915, 718. "Lottie and Jack PIckford Rejoin Famous Players," *MPW,* 2 Sep 1916, 1518. "Lottie Pickford Seriously Ill," *MPW,* 9 Nov 1918, 668. "Lottie Pickford to Make Pictures," *MPW,* 6 Dec 1919, 650 (filed for divorce from Rupp in late 1919; action withdrawn). "Lottie Pickford Is Playing Lead in Playgoers Picture," *MPW,* 23 Jul 1921, 427. "Lottie Pickford Divorced; Film Actress Got Decree Against Allan Forrest in Paris 7 Months Ago," *NYT,* 17 Feb 1928, 25:4.

Pickford, Mary (daughter of **Charlotte Pickford**; sister of **Jack** and **Lottie Pickford**; aunt of **Mary Pickford Rupp**; cousin of **Isabelle Sheridan**) [stage/film actress/producer/executive] (aka Dorothy Nicholson, *née* Gladys Louise Smith, b. Toronto, Ontario, Canada, 8 Apr 1892 [Birth certificate #040680, no. 1935, daughter of John Smith and Elsie Charlotte Printer]–29 May 1979 [87], Santa Monica CA; cerebral hemorrhage). m. **Owen Moore**, 7 Jan 1911–2 Mar 1920 (d. 1939); **Douglas Fairbanks, Sr.**, 28 Mar 1920, LA CA (d. 1939); **Charles "Buddy" Rogers** (d. 1999). *Sunshine and Shadow* (Garden City NY: Doubleday & Co., Inc., 1955). Scott Eyman, *Mary Pickford; America's Sweetheart* (NY: Donald I. Fine, Inc., 1990). Cari Beauchamp, *Without Lying down: Frances Marion and the Powerful Women of Early Hollywood* (Scribner, 1997). Eileen Whitfield, *Pickford: The Woman Who Made Hollywood.* (Biograph, 1909; AA, 1928–29.) Alden Whitman, "Mary Pickford Is Dead at 86; 'America's Sweetheart' of Films," *NYT,* 30 May 1979, 1:1, C20:1 (b. 9 Apr 1893). "Mary Pickford Dies at 86; Biggest of Silent Stars, Co-Founder of UA," *Variety,* 30 May 1979 (b. 1893). AMD, p. 277. AS, p. 869 (b. 1893). BHD1, p. 437; BHD2, p. 210. FFF, p. 103 (b. 1893). FSFW, p. 264 (b. 1893). FSS, p. 235. HCH, p. 29. IFN, p. 237 (b. 1893). Lowrey, p. 152. MH, p. 133 (b. 1893). MSBB, p. 1040. Spehr, p. 158. WWS, p. 87 (b. 1893). "Mary Pickford," *MPW,* 24 Dec 1910, 1462. "Mary Pickford," *MPW,* 7 Jan 1911, 26. "Owen Moore and Little Mary with Majestic," *MPW,* 21 Oct 1911, 217. "Majestic Enterprise," *MPW,* 4 Nov 1911, 389. "Our 'Little Mary' Makes a Hit," *MPW,* 18 Jan 1913, 276. "Little Mary Holds Daily Reception," *MPW,* 8 Feb 1913, 585. "A New Picture by 'Little Mary,'" *MPW,* 17 May 1913, 689. "'Little Mary' Again in Pictures," *MPW,* 17 May 1913, 707. "Mary Pickford with Famous Players," *MPW,* 29 Nov 1913, 1015. George Blaisdell, "'Little Mary' and Her Correspondents," *MPW,* 11 Jul 1914, 280–81. "Fine Portrait of Mary Pickford," *MPW,* 18 Jul 1914, 447. "Mary Pickford Announcement Misleading," *MPW,* 8 Aug 1914, 818. "Concerning 'Little Mary,'" *MPW,* 29 Aug 1914, 1224. "Mary Pickford; Playing with the Famous Players Company," *MPS,* 18 Sep 1914, 26. "Miss Pickford Has Not Signed New Contract," *MPW,* 26 Dec 1914, 1822. "Little Mary Remains with Famous Players," *MPW,* 2 Jan 1915, 47. "'Little Mary' Wins; Polls Over a Million Votes in Contest Held by 'Ladies' World,'" *NYDM,* 17 Mar 1915, 24:1 (followed by Alice Joyce, Mary Fuller, Blanche Sweet, Clara Kimball Young, and Norma Phillips). "A Pickford Family Reunion," *NYDM,* 12 May 1915, 24:4 (the first time the three Pickford siblings appeared together, in *Fanchon the Cricket*). W.E. Wing, "Los Angeles News," *NYDM,* 12 May 1915, 29:1 (landlady sued Pickford "because Mary's cute, darling doggie slept on expensive stuff in the rented bungalow. There was also a claim for rent." Pickford, on the witness stand, "indignantly denied injuring the place. In fact, she told how she personally scrubbed the floors and otherwise fought to keep up the appearance of the 'old house.' Then she looked up into the face of the kind-hearted judge with quivering lip, and it was all off for the plaintiff, who didn't get a single cent." Pickford's cost was $200.). Cover, *NYDM,* 20 Nov 1915 (in *Madame Butterfly,* FP-L). "Famous Players—Mary Pickford Co.," *MPW,* 15 Jan 1916, 394. "Miss Pickford Still with Famous," *MPW,* 8 Apr 1916, 232. "Toronto, Canada, Claims Birthplace of 'Little Mary,'" *MPW,* 15 Jul 1916, 394. "Mary Pickford a Producer," *MPW,* 26 Aug 1916, 1376. "Mary Pickford in Dangerous Accident," *MPW,* 2 Dec 1916, 1332. "Mary Pickford's Mother in Hospital," *MPW,* 23 Dec 1916, 1805. "Mary Pickford," *MPW,* 10 Mar 1917, 1550. "Pickford and Fairbanks Most Popular," *MPW,* 10 Mar 1917, 1558. "Mary Pickford Has New Home," *MPW,* 17 Mar 1917, 1783. "Future Plans for Mary Pickford," *MPW,* 19 May 1917, 1149. "Mary Pickford Doing Her 'Bit,'" *MPW,* 7 Jul 1917, 65. "Miss Pickford Gets Police Guard," *MPW,* 8 Sep 1917, 1558. "Mary Pickford Adopts 600 Soldiers," *MPW,* 20 Oct 1917, 392. "Mary Pickford, Autobiographer," *MPW,* 23 Feb 1918, 1080. "Mary Pickford to Pay Heavy Income Tax," *MPW,* 2 Mar 1918, 1218 ($200,000-$250,000). "Mary Pickford to Begin Work," *MPW,* 28 Sep 1918, 1869. "First National Signs Mary Pickford," *MPW,* 23 Nov 1918, 816. Edward Weitzel, "'Glad' Tidings for Pickford Fans," *MPW,* 30 Nov 1918, 929. "Mary PIckford Ill," *MPW,* 18 Jan 1919, 313. "United Artists Association Formed," *MPW,* 25 Jan 1919, 455. "Star Combination Was Unexpected," *MPW,* 1 Feb 1919, 619. "Pikford Buys Beach Site for Home," *MPW,* 17 May 1919, 1026 (100' by 200' lot, Adelaide Drive, Santa Monica CA). "Paint Little Mary's Portrait," *MPW,* 28 Jun 1919, 1928 (Matteo Sandona, artist). "Mary Pickford Wins Before Juery," *MPW,* 6 Dec 1919, 641. "'Exhibitor' Shocked When $50 Didn't Buy a Pickford," *MPW,* 6 Dec 1919, 641. "Mary Pickford Is Again Sued by Mrs. Wilkening," *MPW,* 13 Dec 1919, 777. "Mary Pickford's Attorney Answers Alleged Interview," *MPW,* 3 Jan 1920, 58. "Mary Pickford's Grandmother Dies," *MPW,* 10 Jan 1920, 219 (Mrs. Sarah Smith, d. 19 Dec 1919, Toronto). "Wilkening-Pickford Suit May Be Heard This Month," *MPW,* 10 Jan 1920, 238. "Mary Pickford to Tour WOrld and Make Pictures in Various Lands," *MPW,* 21 Feb 1920, 1282. "Pickford-Wilkening Suit Again," *MPW,* 28 Feb 1920, 1449. "May Name Town After Little Mary," *MPW,* 6 Mar 1920, 1676 (Grand Rapids WI). "Mary Pickford Gets Divorce from Owen Moore in Nevada," *MPW,* 13 Mar 1920, 1759 (on grounds of desertion). "Pickford-Fairbanks Wedding Celebrated in Los Angeles," *MPW,* 10 Apr 1920, 214. "Thousands Greet Mary and Doug on Arrival in England," *MPW,* 3 Jul 1920, 72. "Mary and Doug Headed Home After Trip Through Europe," *MPW,* 31 Jul 1920, 617. "England Cannot Have Our Mary," *MPW,* 7 Aug 1920, 699. "Doug and Mary Paraded on Return to America," *MPW,* 7 Aug 1920, 757. "'Ambassadress of Sunshine' Is the Way Bottomley, M.P., Describes Our Mary; Asks Her to Stay and Enter Parliament," *MPW,* 7 Aug 1920, 758. "Mary Pickford Asks Damages from Publishers of Music," *MPW,* 2 Oct 1920, 604 ($2,000 from Watterson, Berlin & Snyder). Edward Weitzel, "Mary Pickford Admits She DId Not See the Funny Side of the Joke Herself," *MPW,* 29 Oct 1921, 1020. "Mary Pickford Wins Suit," *MPW,* 11 Mar 1922, 154. "Miss Pickford Sure of Better 'Tess of the Storm Country,'" *MPW,* 6 May 1922, 55. Billie Blenton, "Welcome Home to 'Mary & Doug,'" *MW,* 7 Jan 1922, 4–5. "Mary Pickford to Make 'Faust,'" *MPW,* 20 Jan 1923, 219. "Mary Pickford Chosen," *MPW,* 14 Jul 1923, 132. B.F. Wilson, "The Golden Scourge;

A discussion of the strange, yet logical reason why a golden crown may become a crown of thorns," *Classic,* Aug 1923, 18–20, 80–81. "Mary Pickford Engages Two New Directors," *MPW,* 8 Sep 1923, 189. "Mary and Doug, New York Visitors, Hope for End of Internal Discord," *MPW,* 1 Mar 1924, 31. "Mary and Doug to Talk to Picture Fans Over Radio," *MPW,* 15 Mar 1924, 190. David A. Balch, "Doug and Mary in New York," *MW,* 29 Mar 1924, 8–9. T. Howard Kelly, "If Your Income Was $500,000 a Year Would You Punch a Time Clock Every Morning?; That's What Mary Pickford Does," *MW,* 26 Apr 1924, 4–5, 28. "Douglas and Mary Unknown as They Try to See Danish King," *NYT,* 8 May 1924, 21:2. "Hiram Abrams Denies Mary Pickford Will Make 'Peter Pan,'" *MPW,* 24 May 1924, 365. Helen Jameson, "I Believe in the Conventions," *MW,* 19 Jul 1924, 11–12. Mary Pickford, "The Lillian Gish I Know," *MW,* 24 Jan 1925, 5–6. "Mary Pickford," *MPW,* 28 Feb 1925, 919. "Mary Pickford to Make Three Productions for United Artists," *MPW,* 9 May 1925, 212. Harry Carr, "The Most Successful Wife in the World," *MPC,* Jul 1925, 16–17, 79. "On the Set and Off," *MW,* 29 Aug 1925, 34 (three men were charged with conspiring to kidnap Pickford for $200,000 ransom); 5 Sep 1925, 45 (kidnappers arrested on May 30th). "On the Set and Off," *MW,* 12 Sep 1925, 46 (two men who conspired to kidnap Pickford were sentenced to 10 to 50 years in San Quentin). William J. Reilly, "Get a Mary Pickford, 'J.D.,'" *MPW,* 31 Oct 1925, 689. "Mary and Doug May Co-Star Soon in Film," *MPW,* 7 Nov 1925, 42. Gladys Hall and Adele Whitely Fletcher, "We Interview Mary and Doug," *Pictures,* Jul 1926, 31–32, 76, 78–80. Paul Paige, "Close-Ups and Fade-Outs," *Paris and Hollywood,* Oct 1926, 92 ("The papers are announcing that Mary Pickford is returning and will begin work on a new picture. It is too bad that some one hasn't the courage to tell her that her days as the Mary of old are over. *Little Annie Rooney* was beyond contradiction one of the worst pictures ever produced. *Sparrows* was no better. Her desperate striving to be a little girl again was painful..."). "Mary Pickford," *MPW,* 1 Jan 1927, 29, 33. "Mary Pickford Made Defendant in Plagiarism-Copywright Suit," *MPW,* 25 Jun 1927, 564. "Attempts to Kidnap Mary May Be Bunk," *MPW,* 25 Jun 1927, 571. John Deming, "What Is the Age of Screen Stars," *MPC,* Dec 1927, 27, 85 (Pickford and other women were in the thirty or older class; men averaged twenty-eight but most were in their thirties). "Solona Beach 'Pickfair' Site," *MPW,* 24 Dec 1927, 23. Gladys Hall, "Mary and Doug Will Never Be Divorced!," *Movie Classic,* I, Oct 1931, 20–22, 80–81. Richard Griffith and Arthur Mayer, *The Movies* (NY: Simon & Schuster, 1957), p. 57. Rosemary McKittrick, "Antiques; Sweetheart of a doll; Famous prototype turns up at auction," *Pittsburgh Post-Gazette,* 21 Jun 1996, 17 (a unique Pickford bisque-head model doll sculpted by Lilly Baitz in Germany was sold on 18 May at Theriault's for $34,000. Pickford dropped the project). John C. Tibbetts, "*Coquette:* Mary Pickford Finds a Voice," *FIR,* Jan/Feb 1997, pp. 61–66. Judie Glave, "New authors give [Little] Orphan Annie a cool makeover," *PP-G,* 12 Jun 2000, D-5 ("Created by Harold Gray [d. 1968], the strip first appeared in *The Daily News* [on] 5 Aug 1924. Annie is said to have been inspired by silent screen star Mary Pickford.").

Picon, Molly [actress] (b. New York NY, 28 Feb 1898–5 Apr 1992 [94], Lancaster PA; Alzheimer's disease). m. **Jacob Kalich** (d. 1975). AS, p. 869. BHD1, p. 437.

Pidgeon, Edward E. [publicist]. No data found. AMD, p. 279. "Edward E. Pidgeon," *MPW,* 16 Mar 1912, 943.

Pidgeon, Walter Davis [actor] (b. St. John, New Brunswick, Canada, 23 Sep 1897–25 Sep 1984 [87], Santa Monica CA; apoplexy). (MGM.) Joseph Berger, "Walter Pidgeon, Actor, Dies at 87, Hollywood Star Five Decades—Best Known for Roles in 40's with Greer Garson," *NYT,* 26 Sep 1984, B8:1. Todd McCarthy, "Walter Pidgeon, 87, Gentlemanly Leading Man, Dies in California," *Variety,* 3 Oct 1984. AMD, p. 279. AS, p. 870 (b. East St. John, Canada). BHD1, p. 437. FSS, p. 237. Katz, pp. 913–14. "Walter Pidgeon Scores Seven," *MPW,* 16 Oct 1926, 441. "Walter Pidgeon," *MPW,* 29 Oct 1927, 550.

Piel, Edward *see* **Peil, Edward**

Piel, Harry [director/actor] (*né* Heinrich Piel, b. Düsseldorf, Germany, 12 Jul 1892–27 Mar 1963 [70], Munich, Germany). AS, p. 870 (d. 23 Mar). BHD1, p. 437; BHD2, p. 210. IFN, p. 237. Vittorio Martinelli, "Kino-Lieblinge," *Griffithiana,* 38/39 (Oct 1990), 66.

Pierade, Jean Pierre [actor] (b. Charleroi, Belgium-d. 28 Aug 1937, Paris, France). BHD1, p. 437.

Pierce, Adele [scenarist] (d. Nov 1923, Santa Monica CA). BHD2, p. 210.

Pierce, Edith Adele [vaudeville/film actress] (b. 1899?). No other data found. (Lubin.) "In the Picture Studios," *NYDM,* 4 Aug 1915, 27:1 (16 years old).

Pierce, Evelyn [actress: Wampas Star, 1925] (b. Del Rio TX, 5 Feb 1908–9 Aug 1960 [52], Oyster Bay NY). m. Robert Allen; Theodore Baehr. AMD, p. 279. AS, p. 870. BHD1, p. 437. IFN, p. 237. Truitt, p. 268. "Evelyn Pierce a Baby Star," *MPW,* 28 Feb 1925, 920. George Katchmer, "Remembering the Great Silents," *CI,* 254 (Aug 1996), 49.

Pierce, Frances [actress] (d. 25 Nov 1913, Los Angeles CA). BHD, p. 275. IFN, p. 237.

Pierce, George C. [vaudevillian: Russell & Pierce and Pierce & Armstrong] (b. 1895?–7 Mar 1965 [70], Miami FL). "George Pierce," *Variety,* 31 Mar 1965. AS, p. 870.

Pierce, Jack P. [actor/cinematographer/assistant director/makeup artist] (b. Greece, 5 May 1889–19 Jul 1968 [79], Burbank CA). (Universal.) "Jack P. Pierce," *Variety,* 31 Jul 1968. AS, p. 870 (b. NY NY). BHD1, p. 437; BHD2, p. 210. IFN, p. 237.

Pierce, James H. [actor: played Tarzan] (b. Freedom IN, 8 Aug 1900–12 Nov 1983 [83], Apple Valley CA). m. Joan Burroughs. AMD, p. 279. AS, p. 870. BHD1, p. 437. "New Personalities in F.B.O.'s 'Tarzan' Film," *MPW,* 16 Oct 1926, 421.

Piercy, Samuel W. [producer] (b. San Francisco CA, 1883–11 Oct 1960 [77?], San Francisco CA). BHD2, p. 210.

Piergiovanni, Ettore [actor/director]. No data found. JS, p. 350 (in Italian silents from 1916).

Pieri, Vittorio [actor] (b. Turin, Italy, 1854–21 May 1926 [72?], Turin, Italy [extrait de décès no. 1110/1/1926]). AS, p. 870. BHD, p. 275. JS, p. 350 (b. 1856; in Italian silents from 1916).

Pierlot, Francis [actor] (b. MA, 15 Jul 1875–11 May 1955 [79], Hollywood CA; heart attack). "Francis Pierlot," *NYT,* 13 May 1955, 25:4. "Francis Pierlot," *Variety,* 18 May 1955. AS, p. 870 (b. 15 Jun). BHD1, p. 437. IFN, p. 237.

Pierozzi, Giuseppe [actor] (b. Rome, Italy, 8 Mar 1883). JS, p. 351 (in Italian silents from 1919).

Pierre, Anatole [actor] (d. 17 Feb 1926, New Orleans LA). "Anatole Pierre," *Variety,* 17 Feb 1926 ("colored minstrel show comedian" in *Uncle Tom's Cabin*). AS, p. 870. BHD, p. 275. Truitt, p. 268.

Pierson, Arthur [actor/director] (b. Oslo, Norway, 6 Jun 1891–1 Jan 1975 [83], Santa Monica CA). m. Ruth Matteson. "Arthur Pierson," *Variety,* 15 Jan 1975. AS, p. 870. BHD2, p. 210 (b. 16 Jun). IFN, p. 237.

Pierson, Carl L. [actor] (b. 1891–11 Feb 1977 [85?], Los Angeles Co. CA). AS, p. 870. BHD2, p. 210.

Pierson, Leo O. [actor] (b. Abilene KS, 25 Dec 1888–2 Oct 1943 [54], Los Angeles CA). (Universal.) BHD, p. 275.

Pigott, Tempe [actress] (b. England, 2 Feb 1884–6 Oct 1962 [78], Woodland Hills CA). "Tempe Pigott," *Variety,* 24 Oct 1962 (d. 13 Oct). AS, p. 871 (d. 13 Oct). BHD1, p. 438. IFN, p. 237. Truitt, p. 268.

Pike, Charlie [theatrical agent/film actor]. (Film debut: *A Man's Man.*) "Coast Picture News," *Variety,* 19 Oct 1917, p. 28.

Pike, Harry J. [actor] (b. New York NY, 1873–18 Dec 1919 [46?], New York NY). AS, p. 871. BHD, p. 275. IFN, p. 237.

Pike, Samuel [scenarist] (b. 1891–10 Feb 1938 [46?], Bakersfield CA). BHD2, p. 210.

Pike, William [actor] (b. Birmingham, England, 1889?–1 Apr 1959 [70], New York NY [Death Certificate Index No. 7509; M.E. Case No. 2874; age 69]). "William Pike," *Variety,* 8 Apr 1959. AS, p. 871. BHD, p. 275 (b. Salt Lake City UT, ca. 1888).

Pila, Maximo [actor] (b. Santanda, Spain, 30 Jan 1885–2 Aug 1939 [54], Los Angeles CA). "Maximo Pila," *Variety,* 9 Aug 1939 ("He had been in pictures 14 years"; age 53). AS, p. 871. BHD1, p. 438. IFN, p. 237.

Pilcer, Harry [stage/film actor] (b. New York NY, 29 Apr 1885–14 Jan 1961 [75], Cannes, France). m. **Gaby Deslys** (d. 1920). "Harry Pilcer, 75, an Entertainer; Dancer Who Was Partner of Mistinguett, Deslys Dies—Well Known in Paris," *NYT,* 16 Jan 1961, 27:5. "Harry Pilcer," *Variety,* 18 Jan 1961. AS, p. 871. BHD1, p. 438. IFN, p. 237. SD.

Pilcher, Jay [scenarist]. No data found. AMD, p. 279. "Heroism Rewarded," *MPW,* 2 Aug 1924, 356.

Pilkington, Paul [actor] (b. 1877–26 Jan 1918 [40]). BHD, p. 275. IFN, p. 237.

Pillsbury, Helen [actress]. No data found. (Vitagraph.)

Pilotto, Camillo [actor] (b. Rome, Italy, 6 Feb 1890–27 May 1963 [73], Rome, Italy). BHD1, p. 438. JS, pp. 351–52 (in Italian silents from 1916).

Piltz, William [cinematographer] (b. 1875–2 Nov 1944 [69?], Los Angeles CA). BHD2, p. 210.

Pinchot, Rosamond [actress] (b. New York NY, 26 Oct 1904–24 Jan 1938 [33], Old

Brookville NY; suicide by inhaling carbon monoxide). AS, p. 871. BHD1, p. 438. IFN, p. 238.

Pine, Ed [actor] (b. 1904?–9 May 1950 [46], Woodland Hills CA). "Ed Pine," *Variety,* 17 May 1950 ("film actor for 27 years"). AS, p. 871. BHD1, p. 438. IFN, p. 238.

Pine, F.A.E. [scenarist]. No data found. FDY, p. 435.

Pine, William H. [director/producer] (b. NY, 15 Feb 1896–29 Apr 1955 [59], Los Angeles CA). BHD2, p. 210.

Pinero, Arthur Wing [actor/playwright] (b. London, England, 24 May 1855–23 Nov 1934 [79], London, England; after an operation). m. actress Myra Holme, 1883 (d. 1919). (Began with *£200 a Year,* 1877, one-act play.) "SIr Arthur Pinero, Dramatist, 79, Dies; 'Enfante Terrible of Nineties' Produced 37 Plays in 32 Years—Actor at 19; Knighted by King Edward [1909]; Was Author of 'The Second Mrs. Tanqueray' and 'Trelawny of the Wells'—Also Lectured," *NYT,* 24 Nov 1934, 15:1. "Sir Arthur Wing Pinero," *Variety,* 116, 27 Nov 1934, 62:1 (wrote *The Notorious Mrs. Ebbsmith, Letty, Mid-Channel, The Mind-the-Paint Girl,* and others). AS, p. 872. BHD, p. 275.

Pingree, Earl M. [actor] (*né* Galan Galt, b. IL, 4 Mar 1887–12 Jul 1958 [71], Los Angeles Co. CA). BHD1, p. 438. IFN, p. 238.

Pini, Linda [actress] (aka Gery Land, b. Milan, Italy, 1896). JS, p. 352 (discovered in a fashion shop by Soava Gallone; in Italian silents from 1916).

Pinson, Lucile [actress] (b. Ramsey IL, 1 Jun 1900–12 Jan 1977 [76], Van Nuys CA). BHD1, p. 438. IFN, p. 238.

Pinto, Giuseppe [director]. JS, p. 352 (in Italian silents from 1914).

Piovani, Pina [actress] (b. Rome, Italy, 1897–2 Jan 1955 [57?], Rome, Italy). m. Giulio Battiferri. JS, p. 353 (in Italian silents from 1928).

Piperno, Ugo [actor] (b. Livorno, Italy, 1862–4 May 1922 [59?], Casalecchio, Italy). JS, p. 353 (in Italian silents from 1914).

Pirandello, Luigi [playwright: Nobel Prize winner, 1934/story consultant] (b. Grigenti, Agrigento, Italy, 28 Jun 1867–10 Dec 1936 [69], Rome, Italy; enlargement of the heart). (Novel Prize winner for literature in 1934.) "Pirandello's Death Ends Secret Deal with Metro; Shubert Suits," *Variety,* 16 Dec 1936 (was to play himself in *Six Characters in Search of an Author* for WB; lawsuits were to be filed against the Shuberts which claimed U.S. rights to his plays from a 1932 agreement.). JS, p. 353 (he suggested scenes and episodes for *Papà mio, mi piaccion tutti,* Italy, 1918).

Piscator, Erwin [director/producer] (b. Ulm, Germany, 17 Dec 1893–30 Mar 1966 [72], Starnberg, Germany). BHD2, p. 210.

Pittaluga, Stefano [producer] (b. Campomotone, Genoa, Italy, 2 Feb 1887–5 Apr 1931 [44], Rome, Italy). JS, pp. 354–55 (began as a small distributor in Liguria; formed Società Anonima Stefano Pittaluga [S.A.S.P.] in 1914. Produced Italy's first sound film, *La canzione dell'amore,* 1930). AS, p. 873. JS, pp. 354–55 (in Italian films from 1914 in Turin, Italy; produced Italy's first sound film, *La canzone dell'amore,* 1930).

Pitti, Ben [actor] (b. MO, 27 Aug 1892–26 Jul 1955 [62], Culver City CA). AS, p. 873. BHD1, p. 439. IFN, p. 238.

Pitts, ZaSu [film/stage actress] (*née* Eliza Susan Pitts, b. Parsons KS, 3 Jan 1898–7 Jun 1963 [65], Los Angeles CA; cancer). (MGM.) m. (1) **Tom Gallery**, 24 Jul 1920, Santa Ana CA—div. 27 Apr 1932 (d. 1993); (2) John Edward Woodall, 8 Oct 1934, Minden NV. "ZaSu Pitts, Actress, Dies at 63; Talkies Turned Her to Comedy; Quavering Drawl Barred Her from Drama—Silent Role in 'Greed' Won Acclaim," *NYT,* 8 Jun 1963, 25:2 (b. 1900, age 63). "ZaSu Pitts," *Variety,* 12 Jun 1963 (age 63). AMD, p. 279. AS, p. 873. BHD1, p. 439. FFF, p. 174 (b. 1898). FSS, p. 239. IFN, p. 238. Katz, p. 915. MH, p. 133. SD. Truitt, p. 269. Quip, *MPW,* 14 Jul 1917, 270:2 (she and Milburn Moranti supported William Franey and Lillian Peacock in the 1-reel *A Jungle Cruise* at Universal). "Smith Syndicate Signs ZaSu Pitts; To Start First Picture in Spring," *MPW,* 31 Jan 1920, 740. "ZaSu Pitts Signs New Contract," *MPW,* 6 Mar 1920, 1637. "ZaSu Pitts a Bride," *MPW,* 14 Aug 1920, 903 (m. 23 Jul; both age 21). "ZaSu Pitts to Lead in Goldwyn Picture," *MPW,* 24 Mar 1923, 464. "ZaSu Pitts," *MPW,* 12 Jul 1924, insert. "ZaSu Pitts," *MPW,* 4 Jun 1927, 332. DeWitt Bodeen, "ZaSu Pitts," *FIR,* Jun/Jul 1980, 321–42 (b. 1900). Alan Marsh, "Zasu Pitts; Comedienne Extraordinaire," *CFC,* 59 (Summer, 1978), 34, 40, 57.

Pittschau, Werner [actor] (b. Germany, 1903–28 Oct 1928 [25], Spandau, Germany; auto accident). AS, p. 873 (d. 28 Nov). BHD, p. 275. IFN, p. 238.

Pivar, Ben [editor/writer/producer] (b. Manchester, England, 2 Mar 1901–28 Mar 1963 [62], Los Angeles CA). (Universal.) "Ben Pivar," *Variety,* 10 Apr 1963. AS, p. 873. BHD2, p. 210. IFN, p. 238.

Pivar, Maurice [film editor] (b. Manchester, England, 11 Oct 1894–14 Jun 1982 [87], Los Angeles CA; heart attack). (Universal; Columbia.) "Maurice (Murray) Pivar," *Variety,* 23 Jun 1982. BHD2, p. 210.

Pixley, Gus [actor] (*né* Gus Shea, b. ca. 1864–2 Jun 1923 [58?], Saranac Lake NY). m. Mary Malatesta. (K&E.) "Gus Pixley," *Variety,* 7 Jun 1923 (age ca. 58); 9 Aug 1923 (age 49). AS, p. 873. BHD, p. 275.

Pizor, Irwin (son of **William M. Pizor**) [child actor/producer/executive] (b. 1917–7 May 1997 [80], Boca Raton FL; heart attack from complications of diabetes). Samuel M. Sherman, "Irwin Pizor [son]," *CI,* 266 (Aug 1997), 58:1 (appeared in *Lunches and Punches,* 1924, with Sid Smith. President of Screen Guild Productions, 1957.).

Pizor, William M. [actor] (father of **Irwin Pizor**) [producer/distributor] (d. 1957). (Imperial Pictures.)

Plaisetty, René [director/producer] (b. Chicago IL, 7 Mar 1889–4 Jan 1955 [65], New York NY). AMD, p. 279. "New Southern Film Company," *MPW,* 30 Jan 1915, 651. "Plaisetty with Blache," *MPW,* 19 Jun 1915, 1920. "Gossip of the Studios," *NYDM,* 6 Nov 1915, 32:3 (as a Lubin director, he worked with a whistle in his big ensemble scenes). "In the Picture Studios," *NYDM,* 11 Dec 1915, 34:4 (finished with a street erected for the big fire scene in the Raymond Hitchcock feature *The Wonderful Wager* at Betzwood PA, and off to the Philadelphia Lubin plant with his stars, Raymond and Marion Sunshine).

Planer, Franz F. [cameraman] (b. Karlsbad, Germany, 29 Mar 1894–10 Jan 1963 [68], Los Angeles CA; cancer). "Franz Planer," *Variety,* 16 Jan 1963. AS, p. 874. BHD2, p. 210 (b. Karlovy Vary, Czechoslovakia).

Plank, Eddie [actor] (b. Gettysburg PA, 31 Aug 1875–24 Feb 1926 [50], Gettysburg PA). BHD, p. 275.

Plannette, Dean [title writer/scenarist]. No data found. FDY, pp. 435, 447 (Jean Planette).

Plateau, Joseph Antoine [inventor of the phenakistiscope in 1932] (b. Brussels, Belgium, 14 Oct 1801–15 Sep 1883 [81], Ghent, Belgium). AS, p. 874.

Platen, Karl [actor] (b. 6 Mar 1877–4 Jul 1952 [75]). BHD1, p. 439. IFN, p. 238.

Platt, George Foster [producer/director]. No data found. AMD, p. 279. "Thanhouser's Triple Coup," *MPW,* 17 Apr 1915, 374. "Directed by Vibration," *MPW,* 23 Nov 1918, 819 (Helen Keller in *Deliverance*).

Platt, J.T. [scenarist]. No data found. AMD, p. 279. "Two Scenario Men Killed," *MPW,* 27 May 1916, 1515 (only survivor).

Platt, William [magician] (b. 1884?–1 Dec 1950 [66], New York NY). "William Platt," *Variety,* 6 Dec 1950.

Platte, Rudolf Antonius Heinrich [actor] (b. Dortmund, Germany, 12 Feb 1904–18 Dec 1984 [80], Berlin, Germany). AS, p. 874 (d. 17 Dec). BHD1, p. 439.

Plaut, I.S. [executive]. No data found. AMD, p. 279. "I.S. Plaut to Retire," *MPW,* 20 Nov 1915, 1461.

Playfair, Nigel [actor] (b. London, England, 1 Jul 1874–19 Aug 1934 [60], London, England). "Sir Nigel Playfair," *Variety,* 21 Aug 1934, p. 54. AS, p. 874. BHD1, p. 439. IFN, p. 238.

Playter, Wellington [actor/director] (b. Rawcliffe, England, 9 Dec 1879–15 Jul 1937 [57], Oakland CA). M. Dorothy Reynolds. AMD, p. 279. AS, p. 874. BHD, p. 275. IFN, p. 238. 1921 Directory, p. 195 (b. 1883). "Wellington Playter," *MPW,* 20 Nov 1915, 1473. "Playter Arrives with Bride," *MPW,* 26 Oct 1918, 498.

Pledath, Werner [actor] (b. 26 Apr 1898–5 Dec 1965 [67], Berlin, Germany). BHD1, p. 615.

Pleschkoff, M.M. [military film assistant]. No data found. "Pleschkoff to Aid with 'Resurrection,'" *MPW,* 30 Oct 1926, 547.

Plimmer, Rev. Walter J. (son of vaudevillians Walter Plimmer, Sr., and Rose Linden) [stage/film actor] (b. 1901–18 Sep 1968 [67], Lexington KY). "Rev. Walter J. Plimmer Is Dead; Broadway Actor Trned Priest," *NYT,* 19 Sep 1968, 47:3 (life member of The Lambs; ordained on 26 May 1934). "Rev. Walter J. Plimmer," *Variety,* 252, 25 Sep 1968, 79:1 ("He gave up the lead role in 'Hello, Yourself' in 1930 to enter the priesthood." Ordanied in Jun 1934.). BHD, p. 275.

Plimpton, Horace "Harry," Sr. (father of **Horace G. Plimpton, Jr.**) [cameraman/Edison studio manager/producer]. No data found. (Edison, 1909.) AMD, p. 279. "Picture Personalities," *MPW,* 3 Sep 1910, 512–13. "Fire Sweeps Edison Studio [Bronx NY]; Loss Heavy, But Films, Scenarios, Etc., Are Saved. No Interruption in Release Schedule," *NYDM,* 1 Apr 1914, 32:1 (Plimpton was at the dock for a trip to Europe when studio officials picked him up. "A stateroom banked high with flowers is making the ocean trip without its intended occupant…"). Horace G. Plimpton, "The Development of the Motion

Picture," *MPW,* 11 Jul 1914, 197–98. "Plimpton Resigns; Leonard McChesney Now Manager of Edison Company's Studio—No Change in Policy," *NYDM,* 11 Aug 1915, 24:4 (at Edison for six years). "Plimpton Prophetic," *MPW,* 28 Aug 1915, 1456. "Plimpton Epic Pictures," *MPW,* XXV, 4 Sep 1915, 1652. "Plimpton to Release Through Authors," *MPW,* 2 Oct 1915, 60. "Plimpton Epics to Expand," *MPW,* 16 Oct 1915, 422.

Plimpton, Horace G., Jr. (son of **Horace "Harry" Plimpton, Sr.**) No data found. m. **Marie LaManna**, Church of the Ascension, 117th St. & msterdam, NYC, 11 Sep 1915. (Edison.) "Edison Actress Marries; Marie La Manna Becomes Mrs. Horace Plimpton Jr., as Culmination of Romance," *NYDM,* 15 Sep 1915, 33:2. "Plimpton—LaManna," *MPW,* 25 Sep 1915, 2186.

Plisnier, Charles [scenarist] (b. 1895–17 Jul 1952 [57?], Brussels, Belgium). BHD2, p. 211.

Plues, George L. [actor] (b. Washington DC, 12 Jun 1895–16 Aug 1953 [58], Woodland Hills CA). "George L. Plues," *Variety,* 26 Aug 1953. AS, p. 875 (d. Calabassas CA). BHD1, p. 439. IFN, p. 238.

Plumb, E. Hay [actor/director] (b. England, 1883–1960 [77?]). BHD1, p. 439; BHD2, p. 211.

Plummer, Lincoln [actor] (b. MD, 28 Sep 1875–14 Feb 1928 [52], Los Angeles CA; heart attack). "Lincoln Plummer," *Variety,* 22 Feb 1928. AS, p. 875. BHD, p. 275. IFN, p. 238 (Plumer). Truitt, p. 269. WWS, p. 269 (b. 1876).

Plunkett, Joseph [executive] (b. New York NY, 1884?–17 Dec 1960 [76], New York NY [Death Certificate Index No. 27101]). "Joseph Plunkett," *Variety,* 28 Dec 1960. AS, p. 875. BHD2, p. 211.

Plunkett, Walter [stage actor/costume designer] (b. Oakland CA, 5 Jun 1902–8 Mar 1982 [79], Santa Monica CA). (FBO, 1926.) AS, p. 875. BHD, p. 275; BHD2, p. 211. Pamela Pratt Forbes, "The Men Behind the Gowns," *Cinema Arts,* Jun 1937, 74–75 ("While touring in legitimate productions, he met Ruth St. Denis, who prevailed upon him to design her costumes.").

Plympton, George Holcombe [scenarist] (b. Brooklyn NY, 2 Sep 1889–11 Apr 1972 [82], Bakersfield CA). BHD2, p. 211. FDY, p. 435.

Podesta, Maria Esther [actress/singer] (b. Uruguay, 1896–18 Sep 1983 [87?], Buenos Aires, Argentina; cerebral thrombosis). AS, p. 875. BHD1, p. 439.

Poff, Lon [actor] (*né* Alonzo M. Poff, b. Bedford IN, 8 Feb 1870–8 Aug 1952 [82], Los Angeles Co. CA). (Fox.) AS, p. 875. BHD1, p. 439. IFN, p. 239. George Katchmer, "Remembering the Great Silents," *CI,* 201 (Mar 1992), 40.

Pogany, Willy [set decorator] (b. Szeged, Hungary, 24 Aug 1882–30 Jul 1955 [72], New York NY). BHD2, p. 211.

Poggioli, Augusto [actor] (b. Rome, Italy). JS, p. 356 (in Italian films from 1915).

Pohl, Max [actor] (b. 10 Dec 1885–7 Apr 1935 [49]). BHD1, p. 440.

Pointner, Anton [stage/film actor] (b. Salzburg, Austria, 8 Dec 1890–8 Sep 1949 [58], Munich, Germany). (German-language films in Hollywood.) AS, p. 876. BHD1, p. 440. Waldman, p. 232.

Poirer, Leon [director/scenarist] (b. Paris, France, 25 Aug 1884–26 Jun 1968 [83], Urval, France). BHD2, p. 211.

Pokrass, Sam [composer/lyricist] (b. Kiev, Ukraine, Russia, 1893–15 Jun 1939 [46?], New York NY). BHD2, p. 211.

Pola, Isa [actress] (*née* Maria Luisa Betti di Montesano, b. Bologna, Italy, 19 Dec 1909–15 Dec 1984 [74], Milan, Italy). AS, p. 876. BHD1, p. 440. JS, p. 357 (in Italian silents from 1927).

Polaire, Mme. [actress]. No data found. AMD, p. 279. "Mme. Plaire in Pictures," *MPW,* 25 Oct 1913, 387.

Polaire, Pauline (niece of **Hesperia**) [actress] (b. 1905). JS, p. 357 (in Italian silent films from 1919).

Poland, Joseph Franklin [scenarist] (b. Waterbury CT, 4 Sep 1892–23 Mar 1962 [69], Los Angeles CA). (Vitagraph; Metro; Ince; 1st National; Universal.) AMD, p. 279. BHD2, p. 211. FDY, p. 435. "Poland Becomes Free Lance," *MPW,* 3 Mar 1917, 1356. "Poland Writing for American," *MPW,* 21 Dec 1918, 1328. "Joseph Franklin Poland Author of Many Screen Plays," *MPW,* 24 May 1919, 1160. "Poland to Write for Universal," *MPW,* 28 Jun 1919, 1959. "Ince Engages Writer," *MPW,* 21 Feb 1920, 1250. "Nelson and Poland Under Contract," *MPW,* 12 Jun 1920, 1434. "Joseph Franklin Poland Talks to Amateur Scenario Writers," *MPW,* 4 Sep 1920, 70. "Joins Fox Staff," *MPW,* LVI, 17 Jun 1922, 619. "Poland Signed by Universal," *MPW,* 18 Sep 1926, 156. "Joe Poland Busy," *MPW,* 2 Oct 1926, 280. Tom Waller, "Joseph Franklin Poland," *MPW,* 25 Jun 1927, 568–69.

Polanski, Goury [actor] (b. Russia, 1893–17 Oct 1976 [83], Los Angeles CA; cancer). m. "Goury Polanski," *Variety,* 284, 27 Oct 1976, 95:4 (doubled for John Barrymore and John Gilbert). AS, p. 876 (Youry Polanski). BHD1, p. 440. IFN, p. 239.

Polgar, Alfred [scenarist] (b. Vienna, Austria, 17 Oct 1873–24 Apr 1955 [81], Zurich, Switzerland). BHD2, p. 211.

Polglase, Van Nest [art director] (b. Brooklyn NY, 25 Aug 1898–20 Dec 1968 [70], Los Angeles CA; cigarette set his robe afire). (FP-L [NY]; Paramount; RKO; Columbia.) "Van Nest Polglase," *Variety,* 8 Jan 1969 (age 70). AMD, p. 279. BHD2, p. 211. Katz, pp. 919–20. "New Art Director with Paramount," *MPW,* 24 Dec 1927, 22.

Polidor (father of Wanda Guillaume) [actor] (aka, Tontolino, *né* Ferdinando Guillaume, b. Bayonne, France, 19 May 1887 [extrait de naissance no. 186/1887]–3 Dec 1977 [90], Viareggio, Luca, Italy). AS, p. 876. BHD1, p. 440. IFN, p. 239. JS, pp. 358–59 (in Italian silents from 1910).

Polini, Emelie [stage/film actress] (d. 31 Jul 1927, England). AMD, p. 279. BHD, p. 276. "Emelie Polini on Screen," *NYDM,* 15 Sep 1915, 25:4 (to be in *The Little Church Around the Corner* for World). "Emelie Polini," *MPW,* 25 Sep 1915, 2158. "In the Picture Studios," *NYDM,* 23 Oct 1915, 31:1 (discusses debut film).

Polito, Sol [cinematographer] (*né* Salvador Polito, b. Palermo, Sicily, Italy, 12 Nov 1892 [extrait de naissance no. 4965]–23 May 1960 [68], Los Angeles CA). "Sol Polito," *Variety,* 1 Jun 1960. AS, p. 877. BHD2, p. 211. FDY, p. 465. IFN, p. 239. Katz, p. 920.

Polla, Isa [actress] (b. Italy, 1909?–15 Dec 1984 [75], Los Angeles CA). (Began ca. 1924.) AS, p. 877.

Polla, Pauline M. [actress/singer] (aka Paula Depolla, *née?,* b. 1868?–9 Apr 1940 [72], Albany NY). m. William C. Polla (d. Dec 1939). (FP-L.) "Mrs. Pauline M. Polla; Actress of Silent Screen, 72, Had Been Light Opera Singer," *NYT,* 10 Apr 1940, 25:2. "Pauline M. Polla," *Variety,* 17 Apr 1940 ("former player in silent pictures who also sang in operetta"). AS, p. 877. BHD, p. 276. IFN, p. 239. Truitt, p. 269.

Pollack, Ben [actor] (b. Chicago IL, 22 Jun 1903–7 Jun 1971 [67], Palm Springs CA; suicide by hanging). AS, p. 877. BHD1, p. 440.

Pollack, Joseph [producer] (b. 1882–12 Sep 1945 [63?]). BHD2, p. 211.

Pollack, Lew [songwriter] (b. New York NY, 16 Jun 1895–18 Jan 1946 [50], Los Angeles CA; heart attack). (TC-F; RKO.) "Lew Pollack, 50, Noted for Songs; Composer of Scores for Films Since 1928 Dies on Coast—Author of 'Charmaine,'" *NYT,* 19 Jan 1946, 13:3 ("He entered show business in 1918 as a piano player from the William von Tilzer Music Company."; wrote *Diane* [from *Seventh Heaven*]; *Miss Annabelle Lee; Angela Mia; Little Mother* [from *Four Sons*]; *Two Cigarettes in the Dark*). "Lew Pollack," *Variety,* 23 Jan 1946. AS, p. 877. ASCAP 66, p. 575. BHD2, p. 211.

Pollack, Max [title writer/scenarist]. No data found. FDY, pp. 435, 447.

Pollak, Adolph [producer] (b. Hungary, 8 Apr 1891). BHD2, p. 211.

Pollar, Gene [actor] (*né* Joseph C. Pollar, b. New York NY, 1892–20 Oct 1971 [79], Ft. Lauderdale FL; heart attack). AMD, p. 279. AS, p. 877. BHD, p. 276. IFN, p. 239. "The Greatest Thrill of All," *MPW,* 20 Mar 1920, 1986 (son b. 3 Mar 1920).

Pollard, Bud [actor/writer/editor/director/1st President of Screen Directors Guild] (b. 12 May 1886–16 Dec 1952 [66], Culver City CA; heart attack). "Bud Pollard," *NYT,* 18 Dec 1952, 29:3. "Bud Pollard," *Variety,* 24 Dec 1952 ("pioneer filmite"; in industry 42 years; age 65). BHD2, p. 212. IFN, p. 239.

Pollard, Daphne (sister of **Harry "Snub" Pollard**) [stage/film actress] (*née* Daphne Trott Fraser, b. Melbourne, Australia, 19 Oct 1890–22 Feb 1978 [87], Los Angeles CA). AMD, p. 280. AS, p. 877. BHD1, p. 440 (b. 1892). IFN, p. 239 (age 85). Photo, *NYDM,* 7 Jul 1915, 4 (from *The Passing Show of 1915*). "Sennett Signs Daphne Pollard," *MPW,* 2 Jul 1927, 35.

Pollard, Harry A. [actor/director] (b. Republic City KS, 23 Jan 1879–6 Jul 1934 [55], Pasadena CA; cancer). m. **Margarita Fischer** (d. 1975). (Selig.) "Harry Pollard," *Variety,* 10 Jul 1934. AMD, p. 280. AS, p. 877. BHD, p. 276; BHD2, p. 212 (b. 1882). IFN, p. 239. Katz, p. 920. 1921 Directory, p. 273. Truitt, p. 270. "Leading American Players," *MPW,* 11 Jul 1914, 240–42. "How I Became a Photoplayer," *Motion Picture Magazine,* Feb 1915, 111–12. "Lederer Forms New Producing Company," *MPW,* 11 Mar 1916, 1631. "Harry Pollard Busy," *MPW,* 1 Apr 1916, 59. "Pollard Players Marooned," *MPW,* 22 Apr 1916, 604. "Pollard Renews 'U' Contract," *MPW,* 10 Oct 1925, 475. Don Juan, "So This Is Hollywood," *Paris and Hollywood,* Oct 1926, 19 (was to have directed *Uncle Tom's Cabin,* "but while he was in New York he had a tooth pulled; the dentist broke his jaw in the process, and now poor old Harry is spending the autumn months in the Good Samaritan Hospital." Lois Weber got the job.). "Harry Pollad to Be

Director of "Show Boat,'" *MPW,* 12 Mar 1927, 99. "High Pay for Pollad," *MPW,* 26 Mar 1927, 267. Billy H. Doyle, "Lost Players; Margarita Fisher and Harry Pollard," *CI,* 185 (Nov 1990), C4-C5.

Pollard, Harry "Snub" (brother of **Daphne Pollard**) [actor: Keystone Cop] (*né* Harold Fraser, b. Melbourne, Australia, 9 Nov 1889–19 Jan 1962 [72], Burbank CA; heart attack). m. Elizabeth Brown. (Sennett; Roach.) "Snub Pollard, 72, Film Comic, Dead; Dead-Pan Actor Was One of the Keystone Kops," *NYT,* 21 Jan 1962, 88:1. "Harry (Snub) Pollard," *Variety,* 24 Jan 1962. AMD, p. 280. AS, p. 877 (b. 1886). BHD1, p. 440. FSS, p. 240. IFN, p. 239. Katz, pp. 920–21. Truitt, p. 270 (b. 1886). "Harold Lloyd Is Making Distinctive Comedies," *MPW,* 25 Jan 1919, 514. "Pollard Plays Without Mustache," *MPW,* 6 Nov 1920, 73. "Pollard Finishes One Hundredth Comedy for Pathé," *MPW,* 21 Jan 1922, 281. "Full Stardom for Pollard; New Pathé Kiddie Comedies," *MPW,* 5 Aug 1922 (re *Our Gang*). "Artclass Signs Snub," *MPW,* 5 Jun 1926, 479. Bo Berglund, "Charlie Chaplin and Snub Pollard," *CI,* 89 (Nov 1982), 36–39.

Pollarrd, Wilfred A. [actor] (b. England, 1887–18 Jun 1950 [63?], Los Angeles CA). BHD1, p. 440.

Pollet, Albert [actor] (b. France, 15 Feb 1889–24 Jul 1979 [90], Los Angeles CA). BHD1, p. 440.

Pollock, Alice [scenarist] (b. New York NY, 1881–6 Sep 1957 [76?], Philadelphia PA). BHD2, p. 212.

Pollock, Channing [playwright/scenarist] (b. Washington DC, 4 Mar 1880–17 Aug 1946 [66], Shoreham LI NY). m. Anna Marble, 1906 (d. Mar 1946). "Channing Pollock, Playwright, Dead; Author of More Than 30 Works, Including 'The Fool,' 'Enemy' and 'The House Beautiful'; Wrote Several Books; Crusaded in Lectures Against State Censorship Boards and Flimsy Plagiarism Suits," *NYT,* 18 Aug 1946, 47:3. "Channing Pollock Dies on L.I. at 66," *Variety,* 21 Aug 1946. AMD, p. 280. BHD2, p. 212. "Pollock's Career Basis of Success on Stage and Screen," *MPW,* 10 Apr 1920, 289.

Pollock, Ellen C. [actress] (b. Heidelberg, Germany, 29 Jun 1903–24 Mar 1997 [93], London, England). AS, p. 877 (d. Northwood, England). BHD1, p. 615.

Pollock, Gordon W. [Broadway producer] (d. 15 Apr 1956; plane accident). "Rites Tomorrow for Pollock," *NYT,* 2 Aug 1956, 25:5 (to be held on 3 Aug; "Mr. Pollock and his wife were killed on April 15 while he was flying his private plane over Lake Erie.").

Pollock, Helen [actress]. No data found. AMD, p. 280. "Helen Pollock," *MPW,* 25 Sep 1915, 2185.

Polo, Eddie [actor] (*né* Edward Wyman, b. San Francisco CA, 1 Feb 1875–14 Jun 1961 [86], Los Angeles CA; heart attack at a restaurant). m. (1) Alice Finch; (2) Pearl Grant, Los Angeles CA, 2 Mar 1908—div. LA, Oct 1923. (Began 1913; Universal.) "Eddie Polo, Actor, Film Daredevil, 86," *NYT,* 15 Jun 1961, 43:3. "Eddie Polo," *Variety,* 21 Jun 1961. AMD, p. 280. AS, p. 877. BHD1, p. 441 (b. LA CA). FSS, p. 240. GK, pp. 791–800. IFN, p. 239. Katz, p. 921. Truitt, p. 270. Anthony Slide, *Early American Cinema* (New York: A.S. Barnes & Co., 1970), p. 168. "Eddy Polo," *MPW,* 21 Jul 1917, 450. Lillian Conlon, "The Prowess of Polo," *Motion Picture Magazine,* Feb 1918, 47–49. "Eddie Polo in New York," *MPW,* 30 Nov 1918, 936. "Eddie Polo Pays Chicago Brief Visit," *MPW,* 30 Nov 1918, 943. "Eddie Polo Received by Large Crowds in Mid-West," *MPW,* 28 Dec 1918, 1546. "Polo Now Directing Himself," *MPW,* 17 Jan 1920, 397. "Eddie Polo Incorporates His Own Serial Company," *MPW,* 28 Jan 1922, 380. "Eddie Polo to Make Six Serials; Explains State Rights Program," *MPW,* 25 Mar 1922, 375. "Eddie Polo Quits Krellberg; Brandt-Cohn Buy Latter Out," *MPW,* 1 Apr 1922, 528. Carlos de Paulo Couto, "Serial King!," *CFC,* 40 (Fall, 1973), 31–33 (b. Italy, *né* Edward Wyman; buried at Valhalla Memorial Park, 10621 Victory Blvd., No. Hollywood; includes filmography). George Katchmer, "Eddie Polo; The Mighty Mite," *CI,* 105 (Mar 1984), 38–41 (*né* Edward Wyman). R.E. Braff, "An Index to the Films of Eddie Polo," *CI,* 200 (Feb 1992), 28.

Polo, Sam [actor] (b. CA, 7 Nov 1872–3 Oct 1966 [93], Woodland Hills CA). AS, p. 878. BHD, p. 276. IFN, p. 239.

Polotskova, Garda [actress]. No data found. AMD, p. 280. "War Adds Another Recruit," *MPW,* 29 Apr 1916, 787.

Pomeroy, Roy J. [director] (b. Darjeeling, India, 20 Apr 1892–3 Sep 1947 [56], Los Angeles CA). AS, p. 878. BHD2, p. 212.

Pommer, Erich [producer/director] (b. Hildesheim, Germany, 20 Jul 1889–8 May 1966 [76], Los Angeles CA). (Gaumont; Ufa; Paramount; MGM.) "Erich Pommer," *Variety,* 242, 11 May 1966, 79:1. AMD, p. 280. AS, p. 878. BHD2, p. 212. IFN, p. 239. Waldman, p. 233. "Pommer in M-G-M," *MPW,* 5 Mar 1927, 11.

Poncela, Enrique Jardiel [playwright/scenarist/novelist] (b. Madrid, Spain, 1901–18 Feb 1952 [50], Madrid, Spain; heart attack). (Began in Spain, 1927; in Hollywood, 1926–32; Spanish-language films for Fox.) "Enrique Jardiel Poncela," *Variety,* 185, 5 Mar 1952, 79:2. AS, p. 878. Waldman, p. 146 (under Jardiel).

Ponder, Jack [actor] (b. Shreveport LA, 20 Nov 1903–5 Aug 1970 [66], Los Angeles Co. CA). BHD, p. 276. IFN, p. 239. George Katchmer, "Remembering the Great Silents," *CI,* 220 (Oct 1993), 42.

Ponting, Herbert George [cinematographer] (b. Wiltshire, England, 1870-Feb 1935 [64?], London, England). BHD2, p. 212.

Ponto, Erich Johannes Bruno [stage/film/radio actor] (b. Lübeck, Germany, 14 Dec 1884–4 Feb 1957 [72], Stuttgart, Germany). (Began acting in 1908.) "Erich Ponto," *Variety,* 205, 13 Feb 1957, 95:1. AS, p. 878. BHD1, p. 441. IFN, p. 239.

Pope, Frank T. [executive] (b. 1871–8 Nov 1954 [83?]). BHD2, p. 212.

Pope, Unola B. [actress] (*née* Blanche Pope, b. Palermo, Italy, 1884?–1 Feb 1938 [53?], Fremont OH). AS, p. 878. BHD, p. 276. Truitt, p. 270; Truitt 3, p. 586 (b. Fremont OH).

Popov, Alexi Dimitrievitch [actor/directorscenarist] (b. Nikolajevsk, Russia, 24 Mar 1892–18 Aug 1961 [69], Russia). AS, p. 879. BHD2, p. 212. FDY, p. 435.

Poppe, Harry H., Sr. [scenarist/producer] (b. OH, 3 May 1890–25 Aug 1976 [86], Los Angeles CA). (Began 1915; Metro; Pathé; DeMille.) "Harry H. Poppe, Sr.," *Variety,* 1 Sep 1976. AMD, p. 280. AS, p. 879. BHD2, p. 212. "Harry H. Poppe at Liberty," *MPW,* 29 Apr 1916, 816. "Poppe Manages Horsley Publicity," *MPW,* 2 Dec 1916, 1332. "Harry Poppe Goes to Camp Upton," *MPW,* 13 Oct 1917, 239. "Poppe Back on Job," *MPW,* 20 Oct 1917, 362. "Harry H. Poppe Resigns from Fischer to Write Scenarios," *MPW,* 8 May 1920, 802.

Porcasi, Paul [actor] (b. Palermo, Sicily, Italy, 1 Jan 1879–8 Aug 1946 [67], Los Angeles CA). (Paramount, 1920.) "Paul Porcasi," *Variety,* 14 Aug 1946 (age 66). AS, p. 879. BHD1, p. 441. IFN, p. 239. Truitt, p. 270.

Porchet, Arthur [director] (b. Neuchatel, Switzerland, 11 May 1879–1 Feb 1956 [76], Lausanne, Switzerland). BHD2, p. 212.

Porten, Franz [director] (b. 23 Aug 1859–May 1932 [72]). BHD2, p. 212.

Porten, Henny [actress/producer] (*née* Henny Frieda Ulricke Porten, b. Madgeburg, Germany, 7 Jan 1890–15 Oct 1960 [70], Berlin, Germany). m. (1) Kurt Stark; Dr. Wilhelm Kaufmann-Asser, 1921. "Henny Porten, 70, German Actress," *NYT,* 17 Oct 1960, 29:4. "Henny Porten," *Variety,* 19 Oct 1960 and 2 Nov 1960 (age 71). AS, p. 879. BHD1, p. 441; BHD2, p. 212 (b. 1888). IFN, p. 239. Katz, p. 923 (b. 7 Apr 1888). Truitt, p. 270.

Porter, Caleb [actor] (b. London, England, 1 Sep 1867–13 Mar 1940 [72], London, England). BHD1, p. 441. IFN, p. 239.

Porter, Edward D. [actor] (b. Columbus IN, 26 May 1881–29 Jul 1939 [58], Los Angeles CA; pulmonary embolism). "Edward D. Porter," *Variety,* 2 Aug 1939 ("stage and screen actor," in Hollywood since 1927). AS, p. 880 (b. 1884). BHD, p. 276. IFN, p. 239 (b. 1884). Truitt, p. 270.

Porter, Edwin S[tanton] [director/producer] (b. Connellsville [Fayette County] PA, 21 Apr 1870–30 Apr 1941 [71], New York NY [Death Certificate Index No. 9703 (Edward S. Porter)]). m. Caroline. Charles Musser, *Before the Nickelodeon; Edwin S. Porter and the Edison Manufacturing Company* (Berkeley CA: University of California Press, 1991). "Edwin S. Porter, 71, Pioneer in Films; Collaborator with Edison on Invention of Motion-Picture Camera Dies in Hotel; Once Partner of Zukor; Ex-Head of Simplex Projector Company Was Producer of 'Great Train Robbery,'" *NYT,* 1 May 1941, 23:5 (b. Pittsburgh PA). "Edwin S. Porter," *Variety,* 7 May 1941 (b. Pittsburgh). AMD, p. 280. AS, p. 880. BHD2, p. 212 (b. 1869). IFN, p. 240. Katz, pp. 923–25 (b. 1869). SD. Spehr, p. 160 (b. 1864). WWVC, pp. 112–13 (Edward Stanton Porter). "Rex," *MPW,* 4 Feb 1911, 251. "The First Rex Release," *MPW,* 4 Mar 1911, 463–64. "Edwin S. Porter," *MPW,* 22 Apr 1911, 878. "The Rex Director; Mr. Edwin S. Porter, the Man Behind the Camera and the Product of the Rex Studios," *MPW,* 24 Feb 1912, 674. "Edwin S. Porter Resigns from Universal," *MPW,* 2 Nov 1912, 441. George Blaisdell, "Edwin S. Porter; A Sketch of the Treasurer and Director of the Famous Players—His New Studio," *MPW,* 7 Dec 1912, 961 (cites Fayette County PA as his birthplace). Louis Reeves Harrison, "Studio Saunterings," *MPW,* 4 Jan 1913, 26–28. "Two Producers Go Abroad," *MPW,* 16 May 1914, 975. "Send-Off Porter and [Hugh] Ford," *MPW,* 23 May 1914, 1096. Edwin S. Porter, "Evolution of the Motion Picture," *MPW,* 11 Jul 1914, 206. "Porter and Ford Retrun Home," *MPW,* 1 Aug 1914, 681. "Anniversary for F.P.; Famous Players Organization Celebrates Third Birthday—A Review of Its Career," *NYDM,*

14 Apr 1915, 24:2 (formed FP-L with Adolph Zukor and Daniel Frohman). "A 'Famous' Birthday Party," *MPW,* 8 May 1915, 909. "Stereoscopic Films Shown," *NYDM,* 16 Jun 1915, 21:2 (Porter and William E. Waddell sponsored an exhibition of stereoscopic films on 11 Jun. Two lenses captured images on film, which was separated the distance of a normal pair of eyes. The films were tinted red and green; the spectator wore a pair of similar glasses. Scenes from *Jim the Penman,* FP-L, were shown. Review of the film on p. 28:3.) "Stereoscopic Pictures Screened," *MPW,* 26 Jun 1915, 2072. "Porter Sells Famous Players Holdings," *MPW,* 20 Nov 1915, 1468. "Porter Returns from South America," *MPW,* 25 Mar 1916, 1991.

Porter, Fred L. [producer]. No data found. AMD, p. 280. "Porter Heads Production," *MPW,* 14 Feb 1925, 705.

Porter, Gene Stratton [noveliest/scenarist/producer] (*née* Geneva Grace Stratton, b. Wabash County IN, 17 Aug 1868–6 Dec 1924 [56], Los Angeles CA; injuries from auto accident). m. Charles Darwin Porter, 22 Apr 1886. "Gene Stratton Porter," *Variety,* 10 Dec 1924. "Obituary," *MPW,* 20 Dec 1924, 715 (d. 7 Dec). AS, p. 880. *The National Cyclopædia of American Biography,* Vol. 15 (1916), pp. 242–43. AMD, p. 280. BHD2, p. 212. *Twentieth Century Authors,* pp. 117–18. "Her Father's Daughter," *MPW,* 14 Mar 1925, 171 (more of her stories produced by her son-in-law, Leo Meehan). "Gene Stratton Porter's 'Her Father's Daughter,'" *MPW,* 18 Apr 1925, 701.

Porter, Harold B. [actor/cinematographer] (b. Waterbury CT, 15 Jul 1897–30 Jul 1939 [42], Los Angeles CA). BHD2, p. 212.

Porter, Paul, Sr. [actor] (b. 1886–17 Oct 1957 [71], New York NY). BHD, p. 276. IFN, p. 240.

Porter, Verne Hardin [writer] (b. 1889–29 Nov 1942 [53?], Los Angeles CA). AMD, p. 280. BHD2, p. 212. "Photoplaywright's Wife Dies," *MPW,* 12 Oct 1918, 207 (d. 19 Sep 1918, Venica CA). "William LeBaron Now Director-General of Cosmopolitan; Other Changes Made," *MPW,* 21 Jan 1922, 262. "Gerald Mygatt Writes Article in Praise of Verne Hardin Porter," *MPW,* 11 Feb 1922, 619. "Appointed Editor-in-Chief," *MPW,* 2 Jan 1926, 80. "Porter in Hollywood," *MPW,* 6 Feb 1926, 533.

Porter, Viola Adele [actress] (b. 1879?–29 Dec 1942 [63], Hollywood CA). "Viola Adele Porter," *Variety,* 6 Jan 1943. AS, p. 880. IFN, p. 240.

Posca, Edith [actress] (b. Germany, 4 Nov 1892–28 Jun 1931 [38], Berlin, Germany). m. **Lupu-Pick** (d. 1931). AS, p. 880.

Posner, George A. [writer/scenarist]. No data found. (Edison; Kinemacolor; Biograph; Reliance; Kalem; American; Universal.) *NYDM,* 4 Feb 1914, 15:3.

Post, Charles A[shbrook] **"Buddy"** [stage/film actor] (b. Salt Lake City UT, 3 Nov 1897–20 Dec 1952 [55], Los Angeles Co. CA). (1st National.) AMD, p. 281. AS, p. 880. BHD1, p. 442; BHD2, p. 213. IFN, p. 240. "Flashes; Tall Comedian a Star," *LA Times,* 11 Mar 1920, III, p. 4 (L.V. Jefferson writing a series of 26 2-reelrs at First National for the altitudinous comedian, 6 feet, 6 inches, 325 pounds). "Buddy Post and Lucille Rubey Will Star in National Series," *MPW,* 27 Mar 1920, 2140. "Some Hair Dye, Presto! Career!," *MPW,* 23 Apr 1927, 714.

Post, Charles J. [writer/publicist]. No data found. AMD, p. 281. "Charles J. Post with Triangle," *MPW,* 27 May 1916, 1495.

Post, G.O. [cinematographer]. No data found. FDY, p. 467.

Post, Guy Bates [stage/film actor] (b. Seattle WA, 22 Sep 1875–16 Jan 1968 [92], Los Angeles CA). m. (1) stage actress Jane Peyton—annulled 1915 (d. 1946); (2) Adele Ritchie (d. 1930); (3) Sarah Truax (d. 1958); (4) Lily Kemble-Cooper. "Guy Bates Post, 92, an Actor Since '93," *NYT,* 18 Jan 1968, 39:4. "Guy Bates Post," *Variety,* 24 Jan 1968. AS, p. 880. BHD1, p. 442. IFN, p. 240. Truitt, p. 271. Harry Carr, "'From Harmony, from Heavenly Harmony,'" *Classic,* Dec 1922, 40–41, 76. "Jane Peyton," *Variety,* 164, 11 Sep 1946, 62:1 (d. 7 Sep 1946, Auburn NY).

Post, William, Jr. [stage/film actor] (b. Montclair NJ, 19 Feb 1901–26 Sep 1989 [88], Oklahoma City OK; pulmonary embolism). "William Post Jr., 88; Film and Stage Actor;" *NYT,* 29 Sep 1989, B7:2. "William Post Jr.," *Variety,* 25 Oct 1989, p. 85. AS, p. 880. BHD1, P. 442,

Post, Wilmarth H. [actor/writer/director] (d. 25 Aug 1930, Rutherford NJ; heart attack). (Paramount.) "Wilmarth H. Post," *Variety,* 27 Aug 1930. AS, P. 880. BHD, p. 276; BHD2, p. 213. Truitt, p. 271.

Postance, William C.F. [actor/director/producer] (b. High Holborn, London, England, 4 Jun 1874–14 Apr 1953 [78], Hoboken NJ). m. Sybil Campbell, 1902. "W.C. Postance Dies; Producer, Actor, 78; Veteran of 167 Plays Joined The Times in 1943—Staged 'Sherlock Holmes' Here," *NYT,* 15 Apr 1953, 31:1. "Wm. C.F. Postance," *Variety,* 15 Apr 1953. AS, p. 880 (b. High Holbom, England). BHD, p. 276 (b. 1875). IFN, p. 240.

Potamkin, Harry Alan [director] (d. 1933). BHD2, p. 212.

Potechina, Lydia Semenovna [actress] (b. 5 Sep 1883–7 Apr 1934 [50], Moscow, Russia). AS, p. 880. BHD1, p. 615.

Potel, Victor A[lfred] [actor: Keystone Cop/scenarist] (b. Lafayette IN, 12 Oct 1889–8 Mar 1947 [57], Los Angeles CA). m. Mildred Pam, Nov 1914, SF CA. (Essanay, 1910; Universal; Keystone; Sunshine Comedies.) "Victor Potel; Veteran Film Actor Was One of Original Keystone Cops," *NYT,* 10 Mar 1947, 21:5. "Victor Potel," *Variety,* 12 Mar 1947. AMD, p. 281. AS, p. 880. BHD1, p. 442. FDY, p. 435. IFN, p. 240. MSBB, p. 1026. Truitt, p. 271. "Some Prominent Essanay Photoplayers," *MPW,* 11 Jul 1914, 234–35. "Two Players Wed," *NYDM,* 2 Dec 1914, 24:1. "Victor Potel Company," *MPW,* 10 Apr 1920, 248. "Potel Com pleting First Comedy," *MPW,* 5 Jun 1920, 1321. "Victor Potel to Direct," *MPW,* 29 Jan 1927, 322. Billy H. Doyle, "Lost Players," *CI,* 155 (May 1988), 26.

Potter, Billy [actor] (b. 1874–2 Apr 1961 [86?], New York NY). BHD, p. 276.

Potter, H[enry] **C**[odman] [stage/film director] (b. New York NY, 13 Nov 1904–31 Aug 1977 [73], New York NY). m. Lucilla Wylie. Dena Kleiman, "H.C. Potter, Director of Plays and Films; An Urban Wit Characterized His Work in Both Forms—Staged 'A Bell for Adano' in '44," *NYT,* 1 Sep 1977, C2:4. BHD2, p. 213. IFN, p. 240.

Potter, Paul M[eredith] [playwright/scenarist] (*né* Walter Arthur MacLean, b. Brighton, England, 3 Jun 1853–7 Mar 1921 [67], New York NY). "Paul M. Potter, Playwright, Dead; Dramatist of 'Trilby' Stricken in His Room in Murray Hill Baths in His 68th Year," *NYT,* 8 Mar 1921, 11:4 (age 68). "Paul M. Potter," *Variety,* 11 Mar 1921 (age 68). AMD, p. 281. BHD2, p. 213. SD. "Potter Writes for Ramo," *MPW,* 27 Jun 1914, 1813.

Potts, Hank [actor] (b. 26 May 1896–1 Apr 1980 [83], Los Angeles CA). BHD1, p. 442.

Potts, Walter L. [actor] (b. 1873–25 Feb 1943 [70], Indianapolis IN). BHD, p. 276. IFN, p. 240.

Pouctal, Henri [director] (b. Ferte-sous-Jouarre, France, 1856–3 Feb 1922 [65?], Paris, France). BHD2, p. 213.

Pouget, Armando [astor] (*né* Armand Pouget, b. France). m. **Fernanda Negri**. JS, p. 362 (in Italian silents from 1911).

Poulsen, Adam [actor] (b. Copenhagen, Denmark, 19 Nov 1879–30 Jan 1969 [89], Grinsted, Denmark). BHD1, p. 615.

Poulsen, Olaf [actor] (b. 26 Apr 1849–26 Mar 1923 [73]). BHD1, p. 615.

Poulton, Mabel [actress] (b. London, England, 13 Apr 1901–21 Dec 1994 [93], London, England). m. Richard Phillips, Baghdad, 1939. (Film debut: *Nothing Else Matters,* 1920.) Kevin Brownlow, "Mabel Poulton," [London] *Independent,* 30 Dec 1994, p. 28. AS, p. 881 (b. 29 Jul 1903). BHD1, p. 442 (b. 29 Jul). Garth Pedler, "Mabel Poulton Attends 1928 Re-Screening," *CI,* 114 (Dec 1984), C11.

Pounds, Charles Courtice (son of singer Mary Courtice; brother of actress Louie [sic] Pounds) [actor/singer] (b. London, England, 30 May 1862–21 Dec 1927 [65], Kingston, England; heart disease). (Stage debut: *Patience,* Savoy, 1881.) "Courtice Pounds, Opera Star, Dies; Famous Portrayer of Gilbert and Sullivan Roles Succumbs in London at 65 Years; Church Singer as Child; Appeared Here in 'The Mikado,' 'Ruddigore,' 'Princess Ida,' and 'The Dutchess of Dantzig,'" *NYT,* 22 Dec 1927, 23:5. "Courtice Pounds," *Variety,* 11 Jan 1928, 57:2 (Arthur Sullivan wrote *Take a Pair of Sparkling Eyes* for him for *The Goldoliers*). BHD, p. 276.

Pouree, M. [title writer/scenarist/cinematographer]. No data found. FDY, pp. 435, 447, 467.

Pouyet, Eugène [actor] (b. France, 23 Aug 1883–22 May 1950 [66], Alameda Co. CA). BHD, p. 276. IFN, p. 240.

Powell, A. Van Buren [scenarist] (b. Macon GA, 31 Mar 1886). BHD2, p. 213.

Powell, Baden [actor]. No data found. (Biograph, 1911.)

Powell, David [stage/film actor] (b. Glasgow, Scotland, 17 Dec 1883–16 Apr 1925 [41], New York NY; broncho-pneumonia [Death Certificate No. 10823]). (FP-L.) "David Powell," *Variety,* 22 Apr 1925 (b. Wales). AMD, p. 281. AS, p. 881. BHD, pp. 60–62 (b. 1894); 276. FFF, p. 176. IFN, p. 240 (age 40). MH, p. 133. Truitt, p. 271 (b. Wales). WWS, p. 27. "Madame Critic," *NYDM,* 9 Dec 1914, 4:1 (Onstage for ten years. In anti-war playlet, *Across the Border,* Princess Theater; hasn't recovered from his "ovbernight" fame). Julian Johnson, "Powell, The Military Heart-Burglar," *Photoplay Magazine,* Jun 1917, 78–79. "David Powell," *MPW,* 25 Aug 1917, 1203. "Keeney Engages

Players," *MPW,* 16 Feb 1918, 954. "Powell Signs with Goldwyn," *MPW,* 16 Nov 1918, 749. "David Powell to Be Featured in Paramount British Films," *MPW,* 9 Oct 1920, 778. "Distinctive Signs Powell for Big Role," *MPW,* 26 May 1923, 331. "Obituary," *MPW,* 2 May 1925, 33.

Powell, Dick [stuntman] (b. Philadelphia PA, 28 Nov 1901–26 Sep 1948 [46], Hales Corner WI; plane crash). AS, p. 881 (b. 1911). BHD1, p. 442. IFN, p. 240.

Powell, Frank E. [director/producer] (b. Hamilton, Ontario, Canada). m. Jane Miller, 14 Oct 1915. (Biograph, 1908; Pathé Frérès; Fox; Powers; 1st film directed: *All on Account of the Milk,* Biograph, ©J137280, 15 Jan 1910.) AMD, p. 281. AS, p. 881. BHD2, p. 213. 1921 Directory, p. 273. Spehr, p. 160. "Frank Powell Joins Powers," *MPW,* 27 Apr 1912, 305. "Frank Powell," *MPW,* 29 Jun 1912, 1231. "Frank Powell," *NYDM,* 16 Sep 1914, 26:1. "Frank Powell," *MPW,* 19 Sep 1914, 1648. "Box Office Producers," *MPW,* 7 Nov 1914, 791. "Powell Buys Large Estate," *NYDM,* 23 Oct 1915, 26:2 (bought the Teller estate, a 12-room house, on Bradish Avenue, Bayside Park, Bayside Long Island). "Powell Buys Large Estate," *MPW,* 30 Oct 1915, 766. "Equitable Gets Frank Powell," *MPW,* 20 Nov 1915, 1473. "Powell a Benedict," *MPW,* 27 Nov 1915, 1673. "Frank Powell as a Director," *MPW,* 25 Mar 1916, 2018. Lynde Denig, "Powell Favors Advanced ARt," *MPW,* 8 Jul 1916, 229. "Powell MAy Visit Screen Clubs," *MPW,* 29 Jul 1916, 771. "Powell to Produce for Mutual," *MPW,* 9 Dec 1916, 1513. Edward Weitzel, "Plenty of Room for Expansion," *MPW,* 28 Sep 1918, 1867.

Powell, Paul M[ahlon] [journalist/director/actor//scenarist] (b. Peoria IL, 6 Sep 1881–2 Jul 1944 [62], Pasadena CA; interred at Forest Lawn Cemetery, Glendale CA). m. Valerie (1 daughter, Janice). (Lubin, 1911; Mutual; Triangle; FP-L.) "Paul M. Powell," *Variety,* 5 Jul 1944. AMD, p. 281. AS, p. 881. BHD2, p. 213. FDY, p. 435. IFN, p. 240. KOM, p. 157. "Paul Powell to Direct," *MPW,* 15 Nov 1924, 262. Craig A. Williams, "Paul Powell: Outspoken Innovator of Silent Film," *CI,* 270 (Dec 1997), 32, C1-C3.

Powell, [J.] **Russell** [actor] (b. Indianapolis IN, 16 Sep 1875–28 Nov 1950 [75], Woodland Hills CA; arteriosclerosis). AS, p. 881. BHD1, p. 442. IFN, p. 240.

Powell, Soldene (b. 1860–12 Apr 1915 [54?], New York NY). BHD, p. 277.

Powell, W. Templer [actor] (d. 29 Jun 1949, Los Angeles CA). AMD, p. 281. AS, p. 882. BHD, p. 277. IFN, p. 240. "Templar Powell Is Member of Cast of Melford Special," *MPW,* May 1920, 851.

Powell, William Horatio [stage/film actor] (b. Pittsburgh PA, 29 Jul 1892–5 Mar 1984 [91], Palm Springs CA; heart attack). m. (1) Eileen Wilson; **Carole Lombard**, 1931–33 (d. 1942); Diana Lewis. Peter B. Flint, "William Powell, Film Star, Dies at 91," *NYT,* 6 Mar 1984, B11:1. Todd McCarthy, "William Powell, 91, Sophisticated Leading Man, Dies in California," *Variety,* 14 Mar 1984. AMD, p. 281. AS, p. 882. BHD1, p. 442. FSFM, p. 287 (b. 1893). FSS, p. 240. Katz, pp. 926–27. SD. "William Powell," WBO2, pp. 188–89. "To Support Ferguson," *MPW,* 14 Oct 1922, 569. "Powell to Be in New Cosmopolitan Film," *MPW,* 12 May 1923, 171. "Lasky Signs William Powell," *MPW,* 6 Dec 1924, 551. Gladys Hall, "Evil as You and I; An Unprotected Girl, Hoping for the Worst, Interviews William Powell," *MPC,* Oct 1928, 37, 74 ("...I had a talking test the other day and I came out *lisping*...Buster Collier made a test and didn't lisp. And *he* does."). Joan Standish, "William Powell Weds Carole Lombard," *Movie Classic,* Sep 1931, 37.

Powelson, Arthur S. No data found. m. Kate L.—div. 7 Jan 1920. "'Nude' Figures in Court," *LA Times,* 8 Jan 1920, III, 3 ("by reason of his being a confirmed liar." He also "associated with girls and women unknown to herself, and exhibited to the court...photographs of a young woman in the nude." And a Lora Sherman was asserted to have written Powelson love letters. Powelson's declared disinclination to work and support her won Mrs. Powelson a divorce.).

Power, John [stage/film actor] (b. Sydney, Australia, 1874?–25 Sep 1951 [77], Culver City CA). m. Clara Reid. "John Power," *Variety,* 3 Oct 1951 ("stage and screen actor for half a century"). AS, p. 882. BHD, p. 442. IFN, p. 240 (Powers).

Power, Nicholas, "The Grand Old Man of the Movies" [actor/inventor] (b. New York NY, 22 Oct 1854–7 Feb 1921 [67], Palm Beach FL; heart ailment). AMD, p. 281. AS, p. 882 (d. Miami FL). "Honor Nicholas Power; Staff and Friends at Banquet to Welcome Inventor Back Home," *NYDM,* 22 Apr 1914, 37:1. "Uphold Power Patent; Framing Device and Fire Valve Patents, Secured by Nicholas Power, Are Sustained," *NYDM,* 28 Apr 1915, 29:2. "Here and There," *NYDM,* 30 Oct 1915, 25:1 (61 years old on Friday, 22 Oct). "Making Films Steady; The Man Who Took the Flicker Out of Pictures was Nicholas Power," *NYDM,* 27 Nov 1915, 30:3 (kept his patents in his own control. "...it was Mr. Power who devoted years of his life to taking the 'flicker' out of the film and conserving the eyesight of his own generation and for generations to come."). "Nicholas Power," *NYDM,* 29 Jan 1916, 48:1 (promoted the Peerlesscope [1902], which became the Cameragraph. "It is generally recognized that the success of the moving picture machine industry and the high standard attained by projection is largely due to the unceasing labors and inventive ability of Nicholas Power." Premature obituary?) "Obituary," *MPW,* 19 Feb 1921, 912.

Power, Paul [actor] (*né* Luther Vestergard, b. Chicago IL, 7 Dec 1902–5 Apr 1968 [65], No. Hollywood CA). AS, p. 882. BHD1, p. 443. IFN, p. 240. Truitt, p. 272.

Power, Tyrone, Sr. (uncle of **Crane Wilbur**) [stage/film actor] (*né* Frederick Tyrone Edmond Power, b. London, England, 2 May 1869–30 Dec 1931 [62], Los Angeles CA; heart attack). m. **Edith Crane** (d. 1912); Patia Reaume (**Mrs. Tyrone Power** [d. 1959]; son, Tyrone Power, Jr. [1913–1958]). (Selig.) William Winter, *Tyrone Power* (New York: Moffat, Yard and Co., 1913). Hector Arce, *The Secret Life of Tyrone Power* (New York: William Morrow and Co., Inc., 1979), pp. 17 ff. "Tyrone Power Dies Suddenly on Coast; Actor of the 'Old School' Who Was Appearing in Film at Hollywood Was 62; Mrs. Fiske's Leading Man; He Had Played Also with Henry Irving and Beerbohm Tree in a Notable Stage Career," *NYT,* 31 Dec 1931, 19:1. "Tyrone Power Death Due to Heart Spasm," *Variety,* 5 Jan 1932. AMD, p. 281. AS, p. 882. BHD1, p. 443. FSS, p. 242. IFN, p. 240. Katz, p. 927. Truitt, p. 272. "Tyrone Power in 'Aristocracy,'" *NYDM,* 11 Nov 1914, 29:1 (his debut film, with Marguerite Skirvin). "Tyrone Power in Selig; 'A Texas Steer' Being Filmed in Chicago by [director] Giles Warren," *NYDM,* 2 Dec 1914, 24:4. "Tyrone Power in Selig Productions," *MPW,* 5 Dec 1914, 1389. "Tyrone Power in 'Mizpah,'" *MPW,* 3 Jul 1915, 72. "Tyrone Power," *MPW,* 25 Sep 1915, 2157. "Tyrone Power Now with Universal," *MPW,* 15 Jan 1916, 445. "Pneumonia Threatens Tyrone Power," *MPW,* 24 Mar 1917, 1924. "Tyrone Power Signs with Marine," *MPW,* 30 Jun 1917, 2106. "Power and Trimble Prepare for Work," *MPW,* 13 Apr 1918, 232. George A. Katchmer, "Forgotten Cowboys and Cowgirls—Part XV," *CI,* 193 (Jun 1991),43, 56.

Power, Mrs. Tyrone [actress] (*née* Helen Emma Reaume, b. KY-d. 29 Sep 1959, Canterbury NH). m. **Tyrone Power, Sr.** (d. 1931). AS, p. 906 (Patia Reaume; d. 1 Nov 1924). BHD, p. 277.

Powers, Francis [actor/director/scenarist] (b. Marner VA, 4 Jun 1865–10 May 1940 [74], Santa Monica CA). (Fox.) "Francis Powers," *NYT,* 12 May 1940, 48:8. "Francis Powers," *Variety,* 15 May 1940. AMD, p. 281. AS, p. 882. BHD1, p. 443; BHD2, p. 213. IFN, p. 240. "Francis Powers to Direct for Reliance," *MPW,* 23 Aug 1913, 823.

Powers, John [actor] (b. 1874?–25 Sep 1951 [77]). AS, p. 882. IFN, p. 240 *see* **Powers, Johnny**

Powers, John H. [actor] (b. 1885?–17 Jan 1941 [56?], New York NY). (Griffith.) "John H. Powers," *Variety,* 22 Jan 1941. AS, p. 882. BHD1, p. 443. Truitt, p. 272.

Powers, Johnny [assistant director]. No data found. m. **Edna Pendleton**, the Church Around the Corner, NYC, Nov 1915. (Universal.) AMD, p. 281. "Johnny Powers—Edna Pendleton," *MPW,* 4 Dec 1915, 1803:2. Note: *See* Powers, John.

Powers, Jule [actress] (b. Portland OR-d. 14 Feb 1932, Los Angeles CA). m. Edwards Davis. (The girl in *Gloria's Romance,* 1916.) "Jule Powers," *Variety,* 23 Feb 1932. BHD, p. 277 (Jule Power). IFN, p. 240. Truitt, p. 272.

Powers, Len [cinematographer] (b. Rodney IA, 12 Dec 1894–25 Jan 1965 [70], Los Angeles CA). BHD2, p. 213.

Powers, Lucille [actress] (b. San Antonio TX, 18 Nov 1911–11 Sep 1981 [69], El Monte CA). BHD1, p. 443.

Powers, Maurine [actress] (b. 1904?). No data found. AMD, p. 281. "Maurine Powers Is Raised to Star," *MPW,* 26 Feb 1921, 1042 (16 years old). "William Nigh Film Stars Miss Powers," *MPW,* 19 Mar 1921, 299.

Powers, May [actress] (d. 24 Jul 1961, Louisville KY). BHD, p. 277. IFN, p. 240.

Powers, Patrick A. "Pat" [executive] (b. Waterford, Ireland, 1869?–30 Jul 1948 [79], New York NY [Death Certificate Index No. 17195]). "Patrick A. Powers, Film Official, Dead," *NYT,* 1 Aug 1948, 57:2. "Pat Powers," *Variety,* 4 Aug 1948 (age 78). AMD, p. 281. AS, p. 882. BHD2, p. 213. "'Picture Plays' and Their Production," *MPW,* 23 Apr 1910, 636–37. "P.A. Powers and His Staff of Managers," *MPW,* 27 Jul 1912, 329 (photograph only). "P.A. Powers Resigns from Universal; Carl Laemmle and William H. Swanson Purchase His Entire Holdings—No Change in Universal Program," *MPW,* 22 Feb 1913, 793 (resigned on 13 Feb 1913). "Warners Celebrates Anniversary," *MPW,* 3 Oct 1914, 70. "Powers Opposes High Admission," *MPW,* 2 Jan 1915, 61.

Powers, Tom [stage/film actor] (b. Owensboro KY, 7 Jul 1890–9 Nov 1955 [65], Manhattan

Beach CA; heart ailment). m. Anita Janney. "Tom Powers Dies; Stage, Film Actor; Performer Won Praise for Roles in Shaw and O'Neill Plays—Rode Movie Range," *NYT,* 10 Nov 1955, 35:1 ("For ten years he was 'the' Tom Powers who chased robbers and Indians across Staten Island as the star of Vitagraph's Western films."). "Tom Powers," *Variety,* 16 Nov 1955. AMD, p. 282. AS, p. 882. BHD1, p. 443. IFN, p. 240. Slide, pp. 147–48. Truitt, p. 272. "Several Vitagraph Artists Close," *MPW,* 29 Mar 1913, 1319.

Powers, Tom [cartoonist]. No data found. AMD, p. 282. "Tom Powers, Cartoonist," *MPW,* 8 Jan 1916, 251.

Powley, Bryan [actor] (b. Reading, England, 16 Sep 1871-Dec 1962 [91], London, England). BHD1, p. 443. IFN, p. 240.

Poynter, Beulah [stock/film actress/director] (b. St. Joseph MO, 6 Jun 1886). m. George Leffler (d. 1951). In *Lena Rivers* (Cosmos Feature Corp., 1914). AMD, p. 279 (Pointer). BHD, p. 277. SD, p. 1013. "Poynter Co. Liked; Birmingham Welcomes Permanent Stock Co.—Matinees for Asylum Children," *NYDM,* 4 Feb 1914. "Beulah Pointer with Hector Film Corp.," *MPW,* 4 Jul 1914, 80. "Beulah Poynter in 'School Bells,'" *NYDM,* 23 Oct 1915, 26:1. George Hall and Margarita Lorenz, "'Pirates of the Plains' [Colorado Motion Picture Co., Oct 1913; 3 reels] and Beulah Poynter's 'Lena Rivers' [Cosmos Feature Film Co., 15 Oct 1914; 5 reels]—Lost Films Found," *CI,* 235 (Jan 1995), 31–32.

Pradot, Marcelle [actress] (*née* Marcelle Marie Claire Penicaut, b. Montmorency, France, 27 Jul 1901–24 Jun 1982 [80], Neuilly-sur-Seine, France [extrait de décès no. 379/1982]). m. Marcel L'Herbier (d. 1979). AS, p. 883. BHD1, p. 443.

Prager, Benjamin A. [executive]. No data found. AMD, p. 282. "President of Mayflower Champions Idea of Conferring Full Power on Director," *MPW,* 18 Sep 1920, 344.

Prager, Wilhelm [director] (b. Augsburg, Germany, 6 Sep 1876–20 Apr 1955 [78]). BHD2, p. 213.

Pratchett, Arthur [executive] (b. Liverpool, England, 1881–15 Aug 1964 [83?], Mexico City, Mexico). BHD2, p. 213.

Pratt, Gilbert W[alker] [actor/scenarist/director] (b. Providence RI, 16 Feb 1892–15 Dec 1954 [62], Los Angeles CA). (Rolin Film Co.) AMD, p. 282. AS, p. 883. BHD, p. 277; BHD2, p. 213. FDY, p. 435. "Gil Pratt Signed," *MPW,* 20 Nov 1926, 148.

Pratt, John H. [director] (b. St. John, New Brunswick, Canada, 12 Jan 1878–24 Dec 1938 [60], Los Angeles CA). AMD, p. 282. AS, p. 883. BHD1, p. 443; BHD2, p. 213 (Jack Pratt). IFN, p. 241. "John Pratt," *MPW,* 28 Aug 1915, 1469. George Katchmer, "Remembering the Great Silents," *CI,* 175 (Jan 1990), C8.

Pratt, Lynn [actor] (b. Sylvan Center MI, 18 Jan 1863–9 Jan 1930 [67], New York NY). "Lynn Pratt," *Variety,* 29 Jan 1930. BHD, p. 277. IFN, p. 241. Truitt, p. 272.

Pratt, Purnell B. [actor] (b. Bethel IL, 20 Oct 1885–25 Jul 1941 [55], Los Angeles CA). (Metro.) "Purnell Pratt," *Variety,* 6 Aug 1941 (b. CA). AS, p. 883. BHD1, p. 443. IFN, p. 241. Truitt, p. 272 (b. 1886).

Pratt, Thomas P. [film editor] (b. 1899?–4 Aug 1973 [74], Holland; stroke). (Began 1916.) "Thomas P. Pratt," *Variety,* 15 Aug 1973. BHD2, p. 213.

Pray, Anna M. [stage/film actress] (*née?,* b. 1891?–30 Jun 1971 [80], New York NY [Death Certificate Index No. 12062; M.E. Case No. 5091]). m. **Fleming Ward** (d. 1962). "Anna M. Pray," *Variety,* 14 Jul 1971 ("actress in silent films and on Broadway"). AS, p. 883. BHD, p. 277. IFN, p. 241.

Prazsky, Beda [actress] (b. 15 Jun 1914–6 Aug 1975 [61]). BHD, p. 277.

Preer, Evelyn [actress] (b. Chicago IL, 26 Jul 1896–17 Nov 1932 [36], Los Angeles CA; pneumonia). m. Edward Thompson. "Evelyn Preer," *Variety,* 22 Nov 1932 ("the foremost dramatic actress of the colored race"). AS, p. 883 (b. Vicksburg MS). BHD1, p. 444. IFN, p. 241. Truitt, p. 272. Dorothy Manners, "Enter the Dixies; Casts of a Chocolate Cast Find Opportunity in the Talkies," *MPC,* Feb 1929, 63, 88.

Prejean, Albert [actor] (b. Paris, France, 27 Oct 1893–1 Nov 1979 [86], Paris, France; heart attack [b. Pantin, France, 1894; extrait de décès no. 16/1632/1979]). AS, p. 884. BHD1, p. 444. IFN, p. 241.

Preobrazhenskaya, Olga Ivanovna [actress/director] (b. Moscow, Russia, 24 Jul 1881–31 Oct 1971 [90], Moscow, Russia). AS, p. 884. BHD, p. 277; BHD2, p. 214.

Presbrey, Eugene [playwright/scenarist] (b. New York NY, 1853?–9 Sep 1931 [78?], Los Angeles CA). m. (1) **Annie Russell** (d. 1936); (2) Alice L. (Paramount.) "Eugene Presbrey," *Variety,* 15 Sep 1931, p. 62. AMD, p. 282. AS, p. 884. BHD2, p. 214. "Metro Installs Eugene Presbrey," *MPW,* 19 Jun 1920, 1582.

Prescott, Vivien [actress] (b. Genoa, Italy). (Biograph, 1910). AMD, p. 282. "Crystal Secures Two New Stars," *MPW,* 21 Mar 1914, 1537. *NYDM,* 2 Dec 1914, p. 24. "Vivian Prescott Nursing Husband," *MPW,* 6 Jan 1917, 64.

Pressburger, Arnold [producer/director] (b. Bratislava, Slovakia, 27 Aug 1885–17 Feb 1951 [65], Hamburg, Garmany; stroke). "Arnold Pressburger," *Variety,* 181, 21 Feb 1951, 53:1 (became American citizen in 1942). AS, p. 884. BHD2, p. 214 (b. Hungary). IFN, p. 241. Waldman, p. 236.

Prestelle, Mae [actress] (b. IA, 4 Jul 1878–29 Apr 1952 [73], Los Angeles CA). BHD, p. 277.

Preston, Edna [stage/film actress] (*née* Edna Pew, b. 1892?–18 Aug 1960 [68], New York NY [Death Certificate Index No. 17703 (Edna Coots); M.E. Case No. 6560]). m. James Coots. "Edna Preston Dies; Actress 50 Years," *NYT,* 20 Aug 1960, 19:3. "Edna Preston," *Variety,* 24 Aug 1960 (began acting at age 18). AS, p. 884. IFN, p. 241. SD.

Preston, Madeline [actress]. No data found. AMD, p. 282. "Madeline Preston," *MPW,* XXIII, 27 Mar 1915, 1935.

Pretty, Arline [stage/film actress] (b. Washington DC, 5 Sep 1885–14 Apr 1978 [92], Los Angeles CA). (Vitagraph; Imp; Universal; Pathé.) AMD, p. 282. AS, p. 885. BHD, p. 277. IFN, p. 241. MH, p. 133. MSBB, p. 1040 (b. 1893). 1921 Directory, p. 236. Slide, p. 148 (b. Philadelphia). "Arline Pretty; Leading Woman with the Imp Co.," *MPS,* III, 26 Jun 1914, 25. "Arline Pretty," *MPW,* 26 Jun 1915, 2078. "Studio Gossip," *NYDM,* 7 Jul 1915, 41:1 (while filming *Sis,* Pretty "was nearly drowned when she miscalculated in diving into a lake and was carried to the bottom, running her arms into the soft mud up to the elbows. When she came to the surface she fainted and it took the combined efforts of Thomas Mills, who is playing the opposite role, and the camera man, Len Smith, to save her. After it was all over some one discovered that the scene was number thirteen."). "Arline Pretty Leading Lady to Fairbanks," *MPW,* 17 Mar 1917, 1750. Gary Dowling, "Arline Pretty Was Born That Way," *Photoplay Magazine,* Jun 1917, 74 (b. 1893). "Arline Pretty," *MPW,* 2 Jun 1917, 1439. "Arline Pretty Is Engaged to Star in the Williamsons' Serial 'A Woman in Grey,'" *MPW,* 23 Aug 1919, 1144. "Arline Pretty on Way West," *MPW,* 4 Jun 1921, 491.

Prevert, Pierre André Marie (brother of Jacques Prevert) [actor] (b. Neuilly-sur-Seine, France, 26 May 1906–5 Apr 1988 [81], Joinville-le-Pont, France; pneumonia). AS, p. 885. BHD1, p. 444 (b. and d. in Paris, France).

Prevost, Margery (Peggy) (sister of **Marie Prevost**) [actress] (b. Denver CO, 22 Apr 1904–6 Mar 1965 [60], San Diego CA). (Metropolitan.) BHD1, p. 615 (Peggy Prevost).

Prevost, Marie (sister of **Margery Prevost**) [actress: Sennett Bathing Beauty] (*née* Marie Bickford Gunn, b. Sarnia, Ontario, Canada, 8 Nov 1892?–20? Jan 1937 [44?], Los Angeles CA; of possible acute alcoholism; found dead after 2 days). m. (1) H.C. Gerke; **Kenneth Harlan**, 24 Oct 1924, LA CA—div. 21 Nov 1927 (d. 1967). (Sennett, 1917; Universal; Metropolitan; PDC.) "Marie Prevost Dies Alone in Her Home; Screen Actress Is Found Fully Clad on Bed in Hollywood Apartment; No Evidence of Violence; But the Rooms of the Former Sennett Bathing Beauty Were in Disarray," *NYT,* 24 Jan 1937, 25:1; "Marie Prevost Left Only $300," *NYT,* 20 Feb 1937, 8:4. "Marie Prevost," *Variety,* 27 Jan 1937. AMD, p. 282. AS, p. 885. BHD1, p. 444 (b. 6 Nov 1899). FFF, p. 106 (b. 1902). FSS, p. 242. HCH, p. 125. IFN, p. 241 (age 37). Katz, p. 931. MH, p. 133 (b. 1902). SD. Truitt, p. 273. WWS, p. 189. Alfred A. Cohn, "The 'Follies' of the Screen," *Photoplay Magazine,* Jun 1917, 84–90 (photos of Prevost and Mary Thurman). "Marie Prevost Will Be Featured in Comedy Dramas by Universal," *MPW,* 21 May 1921, 312. "Marie Prevost and Hoot Gibson Are to Star in Universal Attractions," *MPW,* 4 Jun 1921, 521. "Warners Signs Marie Prevost," *MPW,* 29 Jul 1922, 370. Alma M. Talley, "Finger Printing the Stars to Foil Impostors; Movie company on west coast employs a unique device to safeguard players against fraudulent misrepresentation," *MW,* 9 Jun 1923, 13. "Harlan Finishes Role," *MPW,* 25 Oct 1924, 685 (m. 14 Oct). "Marie Prevost," *MPW,* 17 Jan 1925, 278. "Marie Prevost's Contract," *MPW,* 24 Jan 1925, 378. "Stars in Wreck," *MPW,* 9 May 1925, 144. "Metropolitan Pictures Signs Marie Prevost," *MPW,* 23 Jan 1926, 321. "Mrs. Prevost Killed," *MPW,* 20 Feb 1926, 4 (mother d. 5 Feb 1926, car accident in LA). "Signs Long Term Contract," *MPW,* 5 Mar 1927, 12. "Rift in Harlan-Prevost Family," *MPW,* 4 Jun 1927, 330. "Marie Prevost," *MPW,* 9 Jul 1927, 97. Cover and "Who's Who in Hollywood; Marie Prevost," *Paris and Hollywood Screen Secrets Magazine,* Aug 1927, 61, 93 (was a bathing beauty at $3 a day). Tom Waller, "Marie Prevost," *MPW,* 20 Aug 1927, 512–13. "Prevost Sues Harlan," *MPW,* 22 Oct 1927, 484 (for divorce). Dorothy Wooldridge, "—and the Jinx Is Sure to Follow," *MPC,* Nov 1927, 38, 80, 91. Dorothy Donnell, "Marie-and-Ken;

They're in Again; These Two Married People Simply Couldn't Make a Success of Divorce," *MPC,* Oct 1928, 26, 80. Eve Golden, "Marie Prevost: The Beautiful and the Damned," *CI,* 234 (Dec 1994), 22, 32.

Prevost, Peggy *see* **Prevost, Margery**

Price, Adda [actress]. No data found. AMD, p. 282. "No Trained Gold Fish for Adda; She Wins by Talent," *MPW,* 10 Jan 1920, 230.

Price, Alonzo [actor/director] (b. MA 4 Feb 1884–4 Jun 1962 [78], Los Angeles CA). BHD2, p. 214.

Price, Ann [scenarist]. No data found. FDY, p. 435.

Price, Burr [publicist]. No data found. AMD, p. 282. "Friend Appoints Price," *MPW,* 13 Jan 1923, 125.

Price, Helen [actress]. No data found. AMD, p. 282. "Society Girl in 'Moral Suicide,'" *MPW,* 9 Mar 1918, 1380.

Price, Kate (sister of **Jack Duffy**; aunt of **Mary Charleson**) [actress] (*née* Katherine Duffy, b. Cork, Ireland, 13 Feb 1872–4 Jan 1943 [70], Woodland Hills CA). m. Joseph Price Ludwig. (Vitagraph, 1902.) "Kate Price; Screen Actress for 36 Years Seen in 'Cohens and Kellys,'" *NYT,* 6 Jan 1943, 25:5. "Kate Price [Mrs. Joseph Price Ludwig]," *Variety,* 13 Jan 1943. AMD, p. 282. AS, p. 885. BHD1, p. 444. IFN, p. 241 (Katherine Duffy Ludwig). MH, p. 133. Slide, p. 148. Truitt, p. 273 (*née* Kate Duffy). "In the Picture Studios," *NYDM,* 21 Jul 1915, 19:2 (as a member of "Vitagrpah's Big Comedy Four" [along with Hughie Mack, William Shea, and Flora Finch], she weighed 227 lbs.). "Kate Price Now a Vim Star," *MPW,* 14 Oct 1916, 245. "Kat e Price," *MPW,* 6 Jan 1917, 78. "Kate Price in Comedy Series," *MPW,* 29 Sep 1917, 1991.

Price, Mark [actor] (b. Ireland–d. 31 Mar 1917, New York NY). m. Clara Babbitt (d. 1941). "Mark Price, Actor," *NYT,* 1 Apr 1917, 19:2. "Mark Price," *Variety,* 6 Apr 1917. BHD, p. 277. IFN, p. 241. SD.

Price, Nancy (actress/writer] (*née* Lilian Nancy Bache Price, b. Kinver, Worcestershire, England, 3 Feb 1880–31 Mar 1970 [90], Worthing, England). m. Charles Maude (d. 1943). "Nancy Price," *Variety,* 8 Apr 1970 (wrote 19 books, most of them about birds). AS, p. 885 (*née* Lillian Nancy Maude). BHD1, p. 445; BHD2, p. 214. IFN, p. 241. SD.

Price, Oscar A. [executive: 1st President of UA] (b. 1873?–17 Apr 1931 [58], New York NY; heart trouble). "Oscar Price," *Variety,* 102, 22 Apr 1931, 69:5, 71:4 (founded Associated Producers, composed of Sennett, Dwan, Ince, Tourneur, and Neilan). AMD, p. 282. BHD2, p. 214. "President Price Meets Trade Paper Editors," *MPW,* 10 May 1919, 809. "Announce New Era in Film Rental," *MPW,* 24 May 1919, 1149–50. "Oscar A. Price at Head of Parthenon Pictures Corp.," *MPW,* 27 Dec 1924, 861.

Price, Stanley L. [actor] (b. KS, 31 Dec 1892–13 Jul 1955 [62], Los Angeles CA; heart attack). "Stanley L. Price," *NYT,* 15 Jul 1955, 21:3. AS, p. 885. BHD1, p. 445. IFN, p. 241. Truitt, p. 273 (b. 1900).

Price, Ted [actor] (b. 1882–13 Mar 1928 [45?], Newhall CA; murdered). AS, p. 885. BHD, p. 277.

Priest, Janet [publicist]. No data found. AMD, p. 282. "Janet Priest Joins Metro Publicity Staff," *MPW,* 20 May 1916, 1326.

Priest, Robert W. [publicist]. No data found. AMD, p. 282. "New 'Civilization' Press Agent," *MPW,* 9 Sep 1916, 1701. "Son of Robert W. Priest Dies," *MPW,* 23 Sep 1916, 1957 (Robert Rendall, aged 3, d. 4 Sep 1916 of infantile paralysis).

Prieur, R. [executive]. No data found. AMD, p. 282. "Manufacturers Balk at Sales Company," *MPW,* 28 May 1910, 893. "R. Prieur Returns," *MPW,* 4 Oct 1913, 31.

Prim, Suzy [actress] (*née* Suzanne Mariette Arduini, b. Paris, France, 11 Nov 1895–7 Jul 1991 [95], Boulogne, Billancourt, France; suicide [extrait de décès no. 761]). AS, p. 886 (b. 11 Oct 1896). BHD1, p. 445. JS, p. 365 (in silents from 1898; in Italian films from 1919).

Primrose, Daisy [actress] (b. 1889–19 Nov 1927 [38], Los Angeles CA). BHD, p. 278. IFN, p. 241.

Prince, Adelaide [actress] (b. London, England, 14 Dec 1859?–4 Apr 1941 [81], Shawnee-on-Delaware PA). m. Creston Clark, 1895 (nephew of Edwin Booth; d. 1910). "Adelaide Prince Clark," *Variety,* 9 Apr 1941. BHD, p. 278 (b. 1866).

Prince, Arthur [actor] (b. London, England, 17 Nov 1881–14 Apr 1948 [66], London, England). BHD, p. 278.

Prince, Charles H. [actor] (b. Maisons-Lafite, France, 1872–18 Jul 1933 [61?], Paris, France). AMD, p. 283. BHD, p. 278. "Charles H. Prince," *MPW,* 22 Jan 1916, 605.

Prince, John T. [actor] (b. Boston MA, 11 Sep 1871–23 Dec 1937 [66], Los Angeles CA). (Film debut?: *Mission Bells,* 1913.) "John T. Prince," *Variety,* 12 Jan 1938. BHD1, p. 445. IFN, p. 241. Truitt, p. 273. George Katchmer, "Remembering the Great Silents," *CI,* 211 (Jan 1992), 43–44.

Principi, Mirra [stage/film actress] (b. Locarno, Switzerland, 26 Dec 1871). JS, p. 364 (in Italian films from 1908; retired from the stage in 1924).

Pringle, Aileen [actress] (aka Aileen Savage, *née* Aileen Bisbee, b. San Francisco CA, 23 Jul 1895–16 Dec 1989 [94], New York NY). m. (1) Charles McK. Pringle; (2) James M. Cain. "Aileen Pringle, Actress in 60 Films, Dies at 94," *NYT,* 18 Dec 1989, D13:1. "Aileen Pringle," *Variety,* 20 Dec 1989 (began 1919). AMD, p. 283. AS, p. 886. BHD1, p. 445. FFF, p. 15. FSS, p. 243. Katz, pp. 932–33. MH, p. 133. "Aileen Pringle," WBO2, pp. 174–75. "Aileen Pringle Signed," *MPW,* 6 Jan 1923, 33. "Aileen Pringle and Nagel Chosen," *MPW,* 25 Aug 1923, 665. "Signs Aileen Pringle," *MPW,* 25 Oct 1924, 675. Gladys Hall, "'I Want to Be Human,' Says Aileen Pringle," *MW,* 21 Feb 1925, 10–11, 31. Patricia Cork Dugan, "A Charming Queen of Hearts; Aileen Pringle does her luring in the grand manner, and scorns the name of vamp," *MPC,* Jun 1925, 38–39. Alice L. Tildesley, "'She Has IT!'; So Spoke Elinor Glyn of Aileen Pringle," *MPC,* Jan 1926, 32–33, 70–71. "Aileen Pringle," *MPW,* 25 Dec 1926, 580. Katherine Albert, "Sophisticated Aileen; With too much of a sense of humor to be a vampire, and too much individuality to become a 'type,' Aileen Pringle still manages to be just what we all want—Aileen Pringle," *Cinema Arts,* V (Feb 1927), 20, 41. Elizabeth Goldbeck, "For Men Only; Aileen Pringle's Parties Are the Envy of Every Other Woman in Hollywood," *MPC,* Nov 1928, 43, 88. Gladys Hall, "Confessions of the Stars V; Aileen Pringle Tells Her Untold Tale," *MPC,* Feb 1929, 16–17, 68, 72 ("I was born with a clubfoot, a crossed eye, convulsions, yellow jaundice, and a head like a squashed egg.").

Pringle, Della "Jolly" [stage/film actress]. (Keystone.) No data found. "'Rah Della Pringle; Jolly Actress Strikes into New Field of Enterprise with an 'Automobile Show [letter],'" *NYDM,* 15 Sep 1915, 6:3 (her troupe of five played in Idaho via auto, making 2- and 3-night stands, booking them by telephone, and enjoying the outdoors). Cal York, "Plays and Players," *Photoplay Magazine,* Feb 1917, 88.

Pringle, Jack [set architect]. No data found. AMD, p. 283. "Jack Pringle, Former Clown, Becomes Architect for Fox," *MPW,* 25 Sep 1920, 509.

Pringle, John (father of **John Gilbert**) [stage actor/film extra] (surname originally Preigle, b. 1862?–12 Aug 1929 [67], Los Angeles CA). m. Ida Adair Apperly. "John Pringle," *Variety,* 14 Aug 1929. AS, p. 886. BHD, p. 278. IFN, p. 241. Truitt, p. 273. Carolyn Dawson, "Ask Dad—He Knows; John Gilbert's Father Stalks Out of the Past to Release a Flood of Memories," *MPC,* Jan 1928, 23, 82.

Printy, Florence [actress]. No data found. AMD, p. 283. "Florence Printy Will Support Wilbur," *MPW,* 8 Sep 1917, 1512.

Printzlau, Olga [scenarist] (b. Philadelphia PA, 1893?–8 Jul 1962 [69], Los Angeles CA; heart attack). m. **Hal C. Clements**. (Edison; American; Majestic; Ince; Fox; Preferred; FP-L; Universal.) "Olga Printzlau," *Variety,* 18 Jul 1962. AMD, p. 283. AS, p. 886. BHD2, p. 214. FDY, p. 435. IFN, p. 242. "Olga Printzlau to Write for Famous Players Corporation," *MPW,* 11 Sep 1920, 183. "Olga Printzlau Signed," *MPW,* 18 Dec 1920, 855. "Warners Engage Noted Scenarioist," *MPW,* 29 Jul 1922, 370. "Renews Contract," *MPW,* 8 Dec 1923, 570:1 (with B.P. Schulberg for Preferred Pictures). "Writing Screen Version," *MPW,* 16 Aug 1924, 529. "Columbia Signs Olga Printzlau," *MPW,* 30 Jul 1927, 334.

Prior, Herbert [stage/film actor] (aka Herbert Pryor, b. London, England, 2 Jul 1867–3 Oct 1954 [87], Los Angeles CA). m. **Mabel Trunnelle** (d. 1981). (Biograph, 1909.) AMD, p. 283. AS, p. 886 (d. 2 Oct). BHD1, p. 445 (b. Oxford, England). IFN, p. 242. "Herbert Prior, An Early Recruit from the Legitimate, Now Firmly Established as a Leading Photoplayer," *MPW,* 17 Jan 1914, 273. "Persudaing Actors Into Pictures," *MPW,* 10 Mar 1917, 1516.

Prior, Peggy [scenarist]. No data found. FDY, p. 435.

Prisco[e], Albert [actor]. No data found. George Katchmer, "Remembering the Great Silents," *CI,* 211 (Jan 1992), 44.

Pritchard, Charles C. [cameraman] (d. 1925, Dayton OH; hit by car). AMD, p. 283. "Obituary," *MPW,* 15 Aug 1925, 707 (was covering Scopes trial for Pathé).

Pritchard, Curtis C. [cinematographer] (b. 1884–23 Jul 1925 [41?], Chicago IL). BHD2, p. 214.

Pritchard, Walter [cinematographer]. (Centaur; Nestor.) AMD, p. 283. "Walter Pritchard—Cameraman," *MPW,* 8 Nov 1913, 718. "Walter Pritchard—Cameraman," *MPW,* 15 Nov 1913, 718.

Prival, Lucien [stage/film actor] (b. Germany, 14 Jul 1901–3 Jun 1994 [92], Daly City CA). (1st National; UA.) AMD, p. 283. AS, p. 887 (b. NYC, 1900). BHD1, p. 445. "Rowland Signs Lucien Prival; Young Player," *MPW,* 22 Jan 1927, 272. "Lucien Prival," *MPW,* 8 Oct 1927, 358. Murray Irwin, "A Ham Among the Yeggs; Lucien Prival Lived a Gangster's Life in Order to Be Able to Portray It," *MPC,* Sep 1928, 55, 77.

Probert, George [actor]. No data found. (Pathé.) "Probert in Two Gold Roosters [*The Spender* and *Nedra*]," *NYDM,* 29 Sep 1915, 24:4.

Proctor, George Dubois [scenarist]. No data found. m. Eileen Alanna, 3 Jul 1916, NYC. AMD, p. 283. "Proctor Scenario Editor for GAUmont," *MPW,* 6 Nov 1915, 1116. "George Proctor Marries Miss Curran," *MPW,* 22 Jul 1916, 638. "Another Hard-Boiled Egg Cracked," *MPW,* 13 Oct 1917, 222. "Proctor with Pathé Staff," *MPW,* 8 Dec 1917, 1471. "Proctor to Write for World Film," *MPW,* 16 Mar 1918, 1504. "George DeBois Proctor Will Write Broadwell Continuity," *MPW,* 28 Aug 1920, 1184.

Promio, Alexandre (brother of **Georges Promio**) [director] (*né* Jean Alexandre Louis Promio, b. Lyon, France, 9 Jul 1868–26 Dec 1926 [58], Asnieres-sur-Seine, France). AS, p. 887.

Promio, Georges (brother of **Alexandre Promio**) [inventor/director] (b. Lyon, France, 1870–1927 [57?], Paris, France). AS, p. 887.

Prout, Evebelle [actress]. No data found. *Fl.* 1911–12. (Essanay.) "Evebelle Prout [photo only]," *NYDM,* 15 May 1912, 25:2.

Prouty, Jed [actor/singer/dancer] (b. Boston MA, 6 Apr 1879–10 May 1956 [77], New York NY). m. **Marion Murray** (d. 1951). "Jed Prouty," *Variety,* 16 May 1956. AS, pp. 887–88. BHD1, p. 446. IFN, p. 242. Katz, pp. 935–36. Truitt, p. 273.

Provost, Minnie (Minnie Ha-Ha) [actress]. No data found.

Prussing, Louise [actress] (b. Chicago IL, 11 Jan 1895–27 Mar 1994 [99], Los Angeles CA). AS, p. 888. BHD1, p. 446.

Prussing, Margaret [actress/scenarist] (b. Highland IL, 29 Mar 1890–13 Jan 1944 [53], Los Angeles Co. CA). m. **Albert Shelby LeVino,** 29 Jun 1916, NYC. (Eclair; Selig; Kalem; Edison, 1914). AMD, p. 283. BHD, p. 278; BHD2, p. 215. IFN, p. 178 (LeVino, Margaret Prussing). Ragan 2, p. 1368. "Margaret Prussing," *MPW,* 13 Sep 1913, 1155. "Margaret Prussing," *MPW,* 20 Mar 1915, 1779. "Edison Stars in Narrow Escape," *NYDM,* 22 Sep 1915, 25:4 (Prussing and Edward Earle were filming *The Land of Adventure* for Edison; the script called for a hold-up. A man, "his wits dulled by soothing wine," awoke just as Earle pointed a gun through a door. "Thinking it was a real holdup the semi-intoxicated Southerner let loose with his own gun narrowly missing both Earle and Miss Prussing. Lack of ammunition kept him from doing serious damage."). "Albert S. LeVino Marries Miss Prusser," *MPW,* 22 Jul 1916, 615 (she then retired).

Pryce, Col. C. Rhys [actor/director] (d. Feb 1915, Europe). "C. Ryse Pryce," *Variety,* 12 Feb 1915, 21:4 (killed on the European battlefield, "soldier of fortune and well known as a former movie director."). BHD, p. 278; BHD2, p. 215.

Pryor, Arthur [musician] (father of Roger Pryor, husband of Ann Sothern) (b. St. Joseph MO, 22 Sep 1870–18 Jun 1942 [71], West Long Branch NJ). m. Maude Russell, 1895. "Arthur Pryor, 71, Bandmaster, Dies; Played 10,000 Trombone Solos for Sousa Before Heading Own Troupe for 30 Years; Composer of 300 Works; Had Toured Many Countries—Heard by Edward VII and Russia's Last Czar," *NYT,* 19 Jun 1942, 23:1. "Arthur Pryor," *Variety,* 24 Jun 1942. AS, p. 888.

Psilander, Valdemar [actor] (b. Copenhagen, Denmark, 9 May 1884–16 Mar 1917 [32], Copenhagen, Denmark). AMD, p. 283. AS, p. 888. BHD, p. 278. IFN, p. 242. "Valdemar Psilander," *MPW,* 5 Jun 1915, 1585.

Pucci, Giovanni [cinematographer] (b. Rome, Italy, 13 Aug 1903). JS, p. 365 (in Italian silents from 1921).

Pudovkin, Vsevolod [director/actor] (b. Penza, Saratov, Russia, 28 Feb 1893–30 Jun 1953 [60], Moscow, Russia). "Vsevolod Pudovkin, Soviet Film Director," *NYT,* 2 Jul 1953, 23:4 (wrote *Film Technique* and *Film Acting*). "Vsevolod Pudovkin," *Variety,* 191, 8 Jul 1953, 71:2. BHD, p. 278; BHD2, p. 215. IFN, p. 242.

Puffy, Charles H. [actor] (*né* Karoly Huszar, b. Budapest, Hungary, 3 Nov 1884–1942 [57], Tokyo, Japan). (Universal.) AMD, p. 283. AS, p. 889 (d. 1940). BHD, p. 278. IFN, p. 242. "Laemmle Signs Charles H. Puffy," *MPW,* 18 Apr 1925, 711.

Puglia, Frank [actor] (b. Linguaglossa, Italy, 9 Mar 1892–25 Oct 1975 [83], So. Pasadena CA). "Frank Puglia," *Variety,* 5 Nov 1975. "Frank Puglia," obituary reprinted in *CFC,* 49 (Winter, 1975), X5. AS, p. 889. BHD1, p. 446 (b. Catania, Italy). IFN, p. 242. Katz, p. 937.

Pujol, René [scenarist] (b. Bordeaux, France, 18 Aug 1888–21 Jan 1942 [53], Paris, France). BHD2, p. 215.

Pullian, Pauline [actress]. No data found. m. Earl V. Shanks, 25 Feb 1920. AMD, p. 283. "Manager [Special Pictures Corp.] Weds Screen Actress; Misplacing License Reveals Marriage of Film People," *LA Times,* 29 Feb 1920, III, p. 1 ("Handing the marriage license by accident with other official papers to a file clerk in the company's offices for filing gave away the marriage that had been quietly performed."). "Shanks—Pullian," *MPW,* 13 Mar 1920, 1824.

Pupilli, Piero [cinematographer] (b. 23 Aug 1900). JS, p. 366 (in Italian silents from 1920).

Purcell, Ruth M. [beauty contest winnner/actress]. No data found. W.E. Wing, "Pick the Prize Beauty; Capitol City Girl Adjudged Winner of Universal's Big Contest," *NYDM,* 16 Jun 1915, 21:2 (from Washington DC; "will appear in Universal pictures.").

Puron, Lenore [actress]. No data found. "Gossip of the Studios," *NYDM,* 14 Apr 1915, 23:1 ("...the American danseuse, can be seen as the boy magician on the trailer of the Kriterion releases.").

Purviance, Edna Olga [amateur theatricals/film actress] (b. Lovelock, Paradise Valley NV, 21 Oct 1894–13 Jan 1958 [63], Woodland Hills CA). m. John P. Squire. (Essanay; Lone Star Mutual; 1st National.) "Edna Purviance, Actress, 61, Dies; Chaplin's Leading Lady in Early Comedies Starred in 'A Woman of Paris,'" *NYT,* 16 Jan 1958, 29:1 (b. Reno NV). "Edna Purviance," *Variety,* 22 Jan 1958 (age 61). AMD, p. 283. AS, p. 890. BHD1, p. 447 (b. 1896). IFN, p. 242 (b. 1896). Katz, p. 938 (began 1915). MH, p. 133 (b. Reno). MSBB, p. 1040 (b. 1895). SD. Truitt, p. 274 (b. Reno). "Edna Purviance's Illness Delays 'The Adventurer,'" *MPW,* 29 Sep 1917, 1968. "Edna Purviance in New York," *MPW,* 15 Dec 1917, 1640. "Film Star in Accident," *MPW,* 21 Dec 1918, 1327. "Barely Escapes Asphyxiation," *MPW,* 15 Mar 1919, 1474. "Edna Purviance Injured," *MPW,* 1 May 1920, 697. "Only a Scratch," *MPW,* 8 May 1920, 833. "Edna Purviance Returns to Screen in 'Sea Gull,'" *MPW,* 27 Mar 1926, 259.

Putnam, Nina Wilcox [writer] (b. New Haven CT, 28 Nov 1888–8 Mar 1962 [73], Cuernavaca, Mexico). AMD, p. 283. BHD2, p. 215. "Famous Players Signs Roi Cooper Megrue and Nina Wilcox Putnam to Write Original Plays," *MPW,* 9 Aug 1919, 828.

Pye, Merrill [art director] (b. 14 Aug 1901–17 Nov 1975 [73], Los Angeles CA). (MGM.) "Merrill Pye," *Variety,* 26 Nov 1975. AS, p. 890. BHD2, p. 215 (d. 1957).

Pyper, George W. [scenarist] (b. Salt Lake City UT, 6 Apr 1886–18 Jan 1965 [78], Van Nuys CA). BHD2, p. 215. FDY, p. 435.

Q

Quadreny, Ramon [actor/director] (*né* Ramon Quatreny Orellano, b. Barcelona, Spain, 5 Apr 1892). AS, p. 891.

Quaranta, Isabella Maria Rosa Teresa (sister of **Lydia** and twin of **Letizia Quaranta**) [stage actress] (b. Turin, Italy, 30 Dec 1892 [extrait de naissance no. 24/1893]–3 Apr 1975 [82], Milan, Italy). AS, p. 891.

Quaranta, Letizia Beatrice Giuseppina Angela (sister of **Lydia Quaranta** and twin of **Isabella Quaranta**) [actress] (aka Laetitia Quaranta, b. Turin, Italy, 30 Dec 1892 [extrait de naissance no. 24/1893]–9 Jan 1977 [84], Rome, Italy). m. **Carlo Campogalliani,** 1921. AS, p. 891. JS, pp. 366–67 (in Italian silents from 1909).

Quaranta, Lydia (sister of **Isabella** and **Letizia Quaranta**) [actress] (*née* Lidia Gemma Mattia Quaranta, b. Turin, Italy, 6 Mar 1891 [extrait de renaissance no. 772]–5 Mar 1928 [36], Turin, Italy [extrait de décès no. 430/1928]). AS, p. 891. BHD, p. 278. JS, p. 367 (in Italian silents from 1910).

Quarberg, Lincoln [publicist]. No data found. AMD, p. 283. "Quarberg Handling Caddo's Publicity," *MPW,* 19 Nov 1927, 25.

Quartermaine, Charles [actor] (b.

Richmond, England, 30 Dec 1877-Aug 1958 [80]). AS, p. 891. BHD, p. 278. IFN, p. 243.

Quartermaine, Leon [actor] (b. Richmond, Surrey, England, 24 Sep 1876–25 Jun 1967 [90], Salisbury, England). m. (1) Aimee de Burgh; (2) **Fay Compton** (d. 1978); (3) Barbara Wilcox. "Leon Quartermaine of London Stage, 90," *NYT,* 28 Jun 1967, 45:5. "Leon Quartermaine," *Variety,* 5 Jul 1967 (age 91). AS, p. 891. BHD1, p. 447. IFN, p. 243.

Quartero, Nena (or **Gladys**) [actress] (*née* Gladys Quartaro, b. New York NY, 17 Mar 1910–23 Nov 985 [75], Woodland Hills CA). m. (1) John C. Outhet, 1934; (2) Joseph C. Shea, 6 Mar 1937—div. Jul 1939. AMD, p. 284. BHD1, p. 447. BR, pp. 409–11. Ragan 2, p. 1372 (age 77). David A. Balch, "The Youngest Vamp on the Screen; Dainty little Gladys Quartero, who is a protege of D.W. Griffith, says that men who let themselves be 'vamped' are silly—Hear her views on the subject," *MW,* 3 May 1924, 7. "Nena Quartaro Signed for Cruze-DeMille Role," *MPW,* 29 Oct 1927, 549. "Nena Quartero [photo and quip]," *MPC,* Jul 1928, 11.

Quattrociocchi, Nicky [actor] (b. Palermo, Sicily-d. Apr 1968, Palermo, Sicily). BHD, p. 278.

Queeny, Mary [actress/producer] (b. Egypt, 1901). AS, p. 891.

Querio, Isa [actress] (b. 1893–1976 [83?]). BHD, p. 278.

Questiau, Georges Maurice [actor] (b. Aubervilliers, France, 23 Oct 1900 [extrait de naissance no. 775/1900]-15 Jul 1977 [76], Creteil, France [extrait de décès no. 1678/1977]). AS, p. 892.

Quick, Evelyn *see* **Carmen, Jewel**

Quignon, Roland Jean [director] (b. Paris, France, 19 Dec 1897). AS, p. 892.

Quill, Tom [manufacturer/general manager]. No data found. AMD, p. 284. "Tom Quill Enters Educational Field," *MPW,* 10 Feb 1912, 469.

Quillan, Eddie (son of **Joseph F.** and **Sarah Quillan**) [actor] (*né* Edward Quillen, b. Philadelphia PA, 31 Mar 1907–19 Jul 1990 [83], Burbank CA; cancer). (Sennett.) "Eddie Quillan, Actor, 83," *NYT,* 25 Jul 1990, 18:1. "Eddie Quillan," *Variety,* 25 Jul 1990. AMD, p. 284. AS, p. 892. BHD1, p. 447. Katz, pp. 939–40 (began 1926). O&W, pp. 228–29. "Eddie Quillan," *MPW,* 10 Sep 1927, 93. Stephanie Stassel, "Eddie Quillan; Acting Career Spanned 60 Years," *Los Angeles Times,* CIX, 24 Jul 1990, A20:1. Joe Collura, "Eddie Quillan: Mr. Personality," *CI,* 142 (Apr 1987), 29–31. Michael G. Ankerich, "Reel Stars; A Double Take with Eddie Quillan," *CI,* 170 (Aug 1989), 8, 10. Chapter 19, "Eddie Quillan," *BS,* pp. 249–62 (includes filmography).

Quillan, John [actor] (b. Philadelphia PA, 25 Jun 1906–27 Aug 1985 [79], Los Angeles CA). AS, p. 892 (b. 1905). BHD1, p. 447.

Quillan, Joseph [actor] (b. 1916–6 Apr 1961 [45?], Los Angeles CA; heart attack). AS, p. 892. BHD, p. 278.

Quillan, Joseph F. (father of **Eddie Quillan**) [actor] (b. Glasgow, Scotland, 27 Jul 1884–16 Nov 1952 [68], Los Angeles CA). m. **Sarah** Owens (d. 1969). "Joseph F. Quillan," *Variety,* 19 Nov 1952. AS, p. 892. BHD1, p. 447. IFN, p. 243.

Quillan, Mrs. Sarah (mother of **Eddie Quillan**) [actress] (*née* Sarah Owen, b. Scotland, 17 Jan 1888–3 Aug 1969 [81], Van Nuys CA). m. **Joseph F. Quillan** (d. 1952). AS, p. 892 (b. 1879). BHD1, p. 448.

Quimby, Cassius C. [actor] (b. 1873–12 Feb 1944 [70?], Bridgeport CT). BHD, p. 279.

Quimby, Fred[erick C.] [animator/producer] (b. Minneapolis MN, 1886?–16 Sep 1965 [79], Santa Monica CA). (Pathé; MGM; TC-F.) "Fred Quimby," *Variety,* 22 Sep 1965. AMD, p. 284. AS, p. 892. BHD2, p. 215. IFN, p. 243. "Frederick C. Quimby Leaves Associated Exhibitors to Become a Producer; Will Star Jack Dempsey in Serial," *MPW,* 30 Oct 1920, 1273. "Quimby and Richard Are Fined for Transporting Fight Films to New York," *MPW,* 6 Aug 1921, 585 ($1,000 each). "Frederick Quimby Joins Universal as Manager of Short Subjects," *MPW,* 2 Feb 1924, 417.

Quimby, Margaret [stage dancer/film actress] (b. Minneapolis MN, 1905?–26 Aug 1965 [60], Minneapolis MN). AMD, p. 284. AS, p. 892. BHD1, p. 448. IFN, p. 243. "Opposite Dempsey," *MPW,* 6 Sep 1924, 34. "MArgaret Quimby SIgned," *MPW,* 3 Jan 1925, 73. James F. Taggart, "Rebuilding Noses for the Screen," *Paris and Hollywood Screen Secrets,* Oct 1927, 41–43 (photos show before and after pictures of her nose job).

Quinlan, Gertrude [actress] (b. Boston MA, 25 Feb 1875–29 Nov 1963 [88], New York NY). AMD, p. 284. BHD, p. 279. "Making Her Debut," *MPW,* 2 Dec 1922, 423.

Quinn, Alan J. [actor] (b. 1889?–23 Jan 1944 [55], Philadelphia PA). (Lubin; Vitagraph.) "Alan J. Quinn," *Variety,* 2 Feb 1944. AS, p. 893. BHD1, p. 615. IFN, p. 243. Truitt, p. 274.

Quinn, Jack [dancer] (d. 10 Dec 1929, New York NY). BHD, p. 279. IFN, p. 243.

Quinn, James [actor] (b. 1884?–30 Nov 1919 [35], New York NY; gas jet accident). "James Quinn Asphyxiated," *Variety,* 5 Dec 1919. AS, p. 893. BHD, p. 279. IFN, p. 243.

Quinn, James T. [actor] (b. New Orleans LA, 17 Jul 1885–21 Aug 1940 [55], Los Angeles CA). (Universal; MGM.) "James Quinn," *NYT,* 23 Aug 1940, 15:6 (was filming *Little Nancy Kelly*). "James Quinn," *Variety,* 28 Aug 1940 (began 1919). AS, p. 893 (d. 22 Aug). BHD1, p. 448. IFN, p. 243. Truitt, p. 274.

Quinn, Joe [vaudeville stage/film/TV actor] (b. 1899–20 May 1974 [75], Los Angeles CA; emphysema). m. Bessie. "Joe Quinn," *Variety,* 275, 29 May 1974, 62:5. AS, p. 893. BHD, p. 279. IFN, p. 243.

Quinn, John M. [general manager] (b. 1886–4 Feb 1924 [37?], Los Angeles CA; heart ailment). (Vitagraph.) AMD, p. 284. BHD2, p. 215 (d. 5 Feb). "Obituary," *MPW,* 16 Feb 1924, 564. "Quinn Buried in Chicago," *MPW,* 23 Feb 1924, 633 (on 12 Feb 1924, Mt. Carmel Cemetery).

Quinn, John P[hilip] [actor] (b. St. Louis MO, 1851–18 Apr 1916 [64?], Philadelphia PA). AS, p. 893. BHD, p. 279.

Quinn, Paul [actor] (b. 1870–20 Apr 1936 [66?], Los Angeles CA). AS, p. 893.

Quinn, Regina [actress]. No data found. AMD, p. 284. "Regina Quinn Is New Leading Woman for Walsh," *MPW,* 13 Sep 1919, 1662.

Quinn, Tony [actor] (b. Naas, Ireland, 27 Jun 1899–1 Jun 1967 [67], London, England). AS, p. 893.

Quinn, William J. [actor]. No data found. George Katchmer, "William Quinn," *CI,* 214 (Apr 1993), 51–52.

Quintaro, Anna [actress]. No data found. AMD, p. 284. "Famous Camera Actress in America," *MPW,* 3 Apr 1909, 397.

Quintela, Francisco A[ntonio] [producer] (b. Portugal, 1901–12 Jan 1952 [51?], Oporto, Portugal). AS, p. 893.

Quirk, James Robert [editor] (b. Boston MA, 1883?–1 Aug 1932 [49], Los Angeles CA; pneumonia and heart disease). m. **May Allison** (d. 1989). "J.R. Quirk, Editor and Publisher, Dies; Half Million Movie 'Fans' Were Readers of His Once Little Known Photoplay Magazine; Formerly Was a Reporter; Had Owned Several Magazines During Career—Husband of May Allison, Film Actress," *NYT,* 2 Aug 1932, 17:1. "James R. Quirk Dies Suddenly on Coast," *Variety,* 2 Aug 1932 (age 48). AS, p. 893.

Quirk, Josephine [scenarist]. No data found. AMD, p. 284. FDY, p. 435. "Miss Quirk Signs," *MPW,* 25 Sep 1926, 2.

Quirk, William A. "Billy" [actor/director] (b. Jersey City NJ, 29 Mar 1873–20 Apr 1926 [53], Los Angeles CA). (Biograph, 1909; Pathé; Solax.) "Billy Quirk," *Variety,* 28 Apr 1946 (b. Hollywood CA). AMD, p. 284. AS, p. 893. BHD, p. 279; BHD2, p. 215. IFN, p. 243. Katz, p. 941 (b. 1881). 1921 Directory, p. 273. Spehr, p. 160 (b. 1881). Truitt, p. 274 (b. 1881). "Solax Engages Billy Quirk," *MPW,* 30 Dec 1911, 1078. "Billy Quirk with the VItagraph," *MPW,* 14 Feb 1914, 813. George Blaisdell, "At the Sign of the Flaming Arcs," *MPW,* 28 Feb 1914, 1103. "Universal Answers Suit; Declares It Had Cause for Discharging Quirk, Who Sued for Salary," *NYDM,* 22 Apr 1914, 30:1 (long-term contract at $75 a week. "...Quirk was discharged with cause, since he failed to abide by the rules of the studio concerning rehearsals, being frequently late and often failing to appear."). "Billy Quirk Goes to Harvard," *MPW,* 2 Oct 1915, 85. "Billy Quirk Screeners New Head," *MPW,* 16 Oct 1915, 424. "Quirk Again Heads Screen Club," *MPW,* 21 Oct 1916, 404. "Billy Quirk," *MPW,* 14 Jul 1917, 229. Billy H. Doyle, "Lost Players," *CI,* 160 (Oct 1988), 30. George Katchmer, "Billy Quirk," *CI,* 235 (Jan 1995), 37.

Quiroz, Salvador [actor] (b. Cuautla, Mexico, 2 Nov 1892–23 Nov 1956 [64], Mexico City, Mexico). AS, p. 893.

R

Rabagliati, Alberto [singer/actor] (*né* Alberto Rabagliati-Vinata, b. Milan, Italy, 26 Jun 1906–7 Mar 1974 [67], Rome, Italy; cerebral thrombosis). AS, p. 895 (d. 8 Mar). BHD1, p. 448. JS, p. 368 (in *Street Angel*, US, 1928).

Rabaud, Henri [composer] (b. Paris, France, 10 Nov 1873–11 Sep 1949 [75], Paris, France). AS, p. 895.

Rabier, Benjamin [actor] (b. Paris, France, 1864–1939 [75?], Paris, France). AS, p. 895.

Rabinovitch, Gregor [producer] (b. Kiev, Ukraine, Russia, 2 Apr 1889–12 Nov 1953 [64], Munich, Germany). AS, p. 895. BHD2, p. 216.

Raboch, Alfred [director]. No data found. AMD, p. 284. "Alfred Raboch a Director," *MPW*, 4 Jul 1925, 85. "Goldwyn Engages Raboch," *MPW*, 30 Jul 1927, 334 (Rabach).

Rachlitz, Violet [actress] (b. 1908-ca. 1926 [18?]). BHD, p. 279.

Rachmaninof, Sergei Vassilievich [composer] (b. Semionovo, Russia, 1 Apr 1873–28 Mar 1943 [69], Beverly Hills CA; cancer and pneumonia). AS, p. 895.

Racy, Charles [actor]. (Essanay.) No data found.

Radcliffe, Jack [actor] (*né* Charles Smith, b. Cleland, Scotland, 18 Sep 1900–26 Apr 1967 [66], Glasgow, Scotland; cancer). "Jack Radcliffe," *Variety*, 3 May 1967. AS, p. 895.

Radcliffe, Minnie [stage/film actress] (b. Albany NY, 1868?–1 Oct 1918 [50], New York NY). m. M.R. Williams. "Minnie Radcliffe," *Variety*, 4 Oct 1918. AS, p. 895. SD.

Radcliffe, Violet [child actress] (b. Niagara Falls NY, 1908–1926 [18?], New York NY). *Fl.* 1910–18. (Pathé; Fine Arts; Fox.) AS, p. 895. BHD, p. 279. F.E. Hasty, "The Children Are Promoted," *NYDM*, 8 Sep 1915, 37:2 (age 6).

Rader, William E. [actor] (b. St. Louis MO, 12 Aug 1890–7 Feb 1947 [56], Los Angeles CA). BHD, p. 279.

Radford, Basil [actor] (b. Chester, England, 22 Jun 1897–20 Oct 1952 [55], London, England; heart attack). AS, p. 896. BHD1, p. 448.

Radin, Nicolai Mariusovich [actor] (*né* Nicolai Mariusovich Ravin, b. St. Petersburg, Russia, 15 Dec 1872–24 Aug 1935 [62], St. Petersburg, Russia). AS, p. 896.

Rae, Alice *see* **Houghton, Alice**

Rae, Claire [actress] (b. 1889? 7 Jul 1938 [49], Canton OH; leukemia). "Claire Rae," *Variety*, 13 Jul 1938 (Mrs. Claire Rae Trostler). AS, p. 896. BHD, p. 279. IFN, p. 243. Truitt, p. 275 (b. 1899).

Rae, Jack [stage/film actor] (*né* Alton Sampley, b. 1899?–3 May 1957 [58], Los Angeles CA; heart attack). m. Teresa. "Jack Rae," *Variety*, 8 May 1957 ("vet stage and screen actor"). AS, p. 896. IFN, p. 241.

Rae, Lawrence [actor] (d. 24 Aug 1913, New York NY). AS, p. 896.

Rae, Zoe [child actress] (*née* Zoe Rae Palmiter Bech, b. 13 Jul 1910). AMD, p. 284. "Little Zoe Bech," *MPW*, 20 Nov 1915, 1459. "Zoe Bech, Child Actres, with Universal," *MPW*, 19 Feb 1916, 1102. "Zoe Rae," *MPW*, 4 Aug 1917, 786.

Raffaelli, Dino [actor] (b. Florence, Italy, 5 Dec 1899). JS, p. 369 (in Italian silents from 1925).

Rafferty, George W., Sr. [actor] (b. 1882–11 Jan 1973 [90?], St. Louis MO; pulmonary embolism). AS, p. 896.

Rafferty, Patrick C. [actor] (d. Apr 1935, Utica NY). BHD, p. 279.

Raffetto, Michael [actor] (*né* Elwyn Creighton Raffetto, b. Placerville CA, 30 Dec 1898–31 May 1990 [91], Berkeley CA; heart attack). AS, p. 896. BHD1, p. 449.

Raffles, Bill [actor] (*né* Andreas Aglassinger, b. Braunau, Austria, 1895–21 Feb 1940 [44?], Berlin, Germany; stomach hemorrhage). AS, p. 896.

Raft, George [extra in silents] (*né* George Ranft, b. New York NY, 26 Sep 1895–24 Nov 1980 [85], Los Angeles CA; emphysema). m. Grayce Mulrooney, 1923 (d. 1970). Lewis Yablonsky, *George Raft* (NY: McGraw-Hill Book Co., Inc., 1974) ("His interest in the making of movies led him to take the 129th Street ferry across the Hudson to Fort Lee, New Jersey, where many of the early silents were films." Virginia Pearson once let him watch filming on the lot [p.10]. "...an opportunity arose in 1927 when Texas Guinan, about to leave for Hollywood to supervise the filming of her life story [*Queen of the Night Clubs*, 1929], offered Raft a part in her movie. He had had a few minor roles in New York films...," p. 56). "Film Tough George Raft, 85, Dies; Succumbs to Emphysema; in 105 Movies," *NY Daily News*, 25 Nov 1980. AS, p. 896 (b. 27 Sep). BHD1, p. 449. JS, p. 369 (made films in Italy in 1951, 1953, and 1967).

Raglan, James [stage/film/TV actor] (b. Redhill, Surrey, England, 6 Jan 1901–15 Nov 1961 [60], London, England). (Broadway debut: *Insult*, 1930.) "James Raglan," *Variety*, 6 Dec 1961, p. 71:3. AS, p. 897. BHD1, p. 449. IFN, p. 243.

Ragland, John Calvin [executive] (b. Petersburg VA, 11 Nov 1883–19 Jan 1933 [49], Los Angeles CA). BHD2, p. 216.

Rahm, Knute Olaf [actor/cameraman] (b. Sweden, 20 Mar 1876–23 Jul 1957 [81], Los Angeles CA; heart attack). AS, p. 897. BHD, p. 279; BHD2, p. 216. IFN, p. 243.

Rahn, Bruno [actor/director/scenarist] (b. Berlin, Germany, 24 Nov 1897–12 Sep 1929 [31], Berlin, Germany). AS, p. 897. BHD2, p. 216 (d. 15 Sep 1927).

Raicevich, Giovanni [wrestler/actor] (b. Trieste, Italy, 10 Jun 1881–1 Nov 1957 [76], Rome, Italy). m. Bice Raicevich, 1916 (his niece). JS, p. 369 (from 1907–30 he was greco-wrestling world champion ; in Italian silents from 1920).

Raikh, Zinaide Naumovna [actress] (b. Moscow, Russia, 18 Apr 1893–5 Dec 1935 [42], Moscow, Russia). AS, p. 897.

Raimu, Jules [stage/film actor] (*né* Jules Auguste Muraire, b. Toulon, France, 17 Dec 1883–20 Sep 1946 [62], American Hospital, Neuilly-sur-Seine, Paris, France; heart attack [extrait de décès no. 629/1946]). (Began in films in 1929.) "Jules Raimu, Star of French Theatre; Comic Actor of Stage, Films Is Dead—Won Praise Here for Role in 'Baker's Wife' [1940]," *NYT*, 21 Sep 1946, 15:5 (b. Bandol, near Marseilles; had been seriously hurt in a car accident several weeks previously). "Jules Raimu," *Variety*, 164, 25 Sep 1946, 62:1. AS, p. 897 (b. 18 Dec). BHD1, p. 449. IFN, p. 244.

Raine, Adelaide [actress] (b. 4 Jan 1894–20 Jan 1978 [84], Drexel Hills PA). BHD, p. 279.

Raine, Jack [actor] (b. London, England, 18 May 1897–30 May 1979 [82], So. Laguna Beach CA). AS, p. 897.

Raine, William MacLeod [writer]. No data found. AMD, p. 284. "Famous Authors with Universal," *MPW*, 5 Sep 1914, 1356.

Rainer, Robert Richard [actor] (b. 1889–25 Aug 1960 [71?], West Los Angeles CA). BHD, p. 279.

Rainey, Norman [actor] (*né* William Morrison, b. Ireland, 28 Apr 1888–10 Sep 1960 [72], Los Angeles CA). AS, p. 898.

Rainey, Paul J. [explorer/producer/cameraman] (b. 1877?–Sep 1923 [46], on his way to Africa; buried at sea 18 Sep 1923). AMD, p. 284. BHD2, p. 216. "Paul Rainey Pictures for State Rights," *MPW*, 8 Nov 1913, 619. "Obituary," *MPW*, 6 Oct 1923, 479.

Rains, Claude (son of **Frederick Rains**; father of Jennifer Rains) [stage/film/TV actor] (*né* William Claude Rains, b. London, England, 10 Nov 1889–30 May 1967 [77], Lakes Region Hospital, near Sandwich NH; intestinal hemorrhage). (1) Isabel Jeans, 1926; (2) Marie Hemingway; (3) Beatrix Lindsay Thomas; (4) Frances Propper (mother of Jennifer); (5) Agi Jambor; (6) Rosemary Clark, 1960, West Chester PA (d. 1964). (Stage debut: *Sweet Nell of Old Drury*, ca. 1901; last film: *Lawrence of Arabia*, 1962.) "Claude Rains, Film Star, Dead; Began Career on London Stage; 'Caesar and Cleopatra' and 'The Invisible Man' Were Among Actor's Hits," *NYT*, 31 May 1967, 43:2 (b. 1890. Received $1 million for *Caesar and Cleopatra;* nominated for AA four times.). "Claude Rains," *Variety*, 247, 7 Jun 1967, 71:1 (d. Laconia NH; became U.S. citizen in 1938). "Mrs. Claude Rains [Rosemary Clark] Is Dead; Wife of the Actor Was 47," *NYT*, 1 Jan 1965, 19:5 (d. 31 Dec 1965, Sandwich NH). AS, p. 898 (d. Laconia, England). BHD1, p. 449 (d. Laconia NH). IFN, p. 244.

Rains, Frederick William (father of **Claude Rains**) [stage/film actor/director] (b. London, England, 1860–3 Dec 1945 [85], London, England). AS, p. 898. BHD1, p. 449. IFN, p. 244 (age 85).

Rainsford, William H. [executive] (b. 1873–16 Sep 1916 [43?]). BHD2, p. 216.

Raisa, Rosa [actress] (*née* Rose Burchstein, b. Vladivostok, Russia, 30 May 1893–28 Sep 1963 [70], Los Angeles CA). AS, p. 898 (b. Bialystock, Poland; d. 31 Jul 1984, Santa Monica CA). BHD1, p. 450.

Raisbeck, Kenneth [scenarist]. No data found. FDY, p. 437.

Raizman, Yuli Jakovlevich [actor/director] (b. Rize, Russia, 15 Dec 1903–13 Dec 1994 [90],

Moscow, Russia). AS, p. 898. BHD1, p. 615; BHD2, p. 216 (b. Moscow, Russia).

Rajas, Louis [actor] (d. Mar 1921, Redondo Beach CA). BHD, p. 279.

Raker, Lorin [actor] (b. Joplin MO, 8 May 1891–25 Dec 1959 [68], Woodland Hills CA; cancer). AS, p. 898. BHD1, p. 450. IFN, p. 244.

Rale, Michael W. [actor] (*né* Michael W. Israle, b. Russia, 28 Mar 1877–8 Jul 1940 [63], Englewood NJ). "Michael W. Rale," *NYT,* 9 Jul 1940, 21:4. "Michael W. Rale," *Variety,* 10 Jul 1940 (age 73). AS, p. 898. BHD, p. 279 (b. 25 Mar).

Raleigh, Mrs. Cecil [stage/film actress] (*née* Isabel Ellisen, b. England, 1866–22 Aug 1923 [57?], London, England). m. Cecil Raleigh (d. 1914). "Saba Raleigh," *Variety,* 6 Sep 1923. "Cecil Raleigh Dead; Author of 'The Whip' and Other Drury Lane Melodramas," *NYT,* 11 Nov 1914, 13:6 (*né* Cecil Rowlands, b. England, 27 Jan 1856–10 Nov 1914 [58], London, England). BHD, p. 279. SD, p. 1031.

Raleigh, Sarah [actress] (*née* Isabel Elliss, b. England, 1866–22 Aug 1923 [57?], London, England). AS, p. 898.

Ralli, Paul [actor/author] (b. Cyprus, Greece, 2 Mar 1903–4 Sep 1953 [50], Van Nuys CA). "Paul Ralli," *NYT,* 7 Sep 1953, 19:6. AMD, p. 284. AS, p. 898 (d. 2 Sep). BHD1, p. 450 (d. LA CA). IFN, p. 244. Truitt, p. 275 (b. 29 Dec 1905). "Paul Ralli," *MPW,* 20 Aug 1927, 517.

Ralph, Hanna [actress] (b. 25 Sep 1885–25 Mar 1978 [93], Berlin, Germany). BHD1, p. 450.

Ralph, Jessie [stage/film actress] (*née* Jessie Ralph Chambers, b. Gloucester MA, 5 Nov 1864–30 May 1944 [79], Gloucester MA). m. **William Patton** (d. 1951). "Jessie Ralph, 79, of Stage, Screen; Character Actress Is Dead in Gloucester—Played with Jane Cowl in 'Romeo and Juliet,'" *NYT,* 31 May 1944, 19:3. "Jessie Ralph," *Variety,* 7 Jun 1944. AS, p. 898 (b. 1876). BHD1, p. 450. IFN, p. 244. Katz, p. 945. Truitt, p. 275. "Studio Gossip," *NYDM,* 4 Aug 1915, 31:2 (to debut in *The Galloper,* Pathé). DeWitt Bodeen, "The Four Dowagers of MGM," *Focus on Film,* No. 24, Spring 1976, 32–38 (includes filmography).

Ralph, Louis [actor/director] (*né* Ludwig Musik, b. Graz, Austria, 17 Aug 1884-Sep 1952 [68?], Lichterfelde, Germany). AS, p. 898. BHD2, p. 216 (d. Berlin, Germany).

Ralston, Bradford [actor] (b. 3 Oct 1906–17 Apr 1991 [84], Phoenix AZ). BHD1, p. 615.

Ralston, Esther, "The American Venus" (sister of **Howard Ralston**) [actress] (aka Jane Carlton, b. Bar Harbor ME, 17 Sep 1902–14 Jan 1994 [91], Ventura CA; heart attack). m. (1) **George Webb** Frey, 12 Dec 1925–33 (d. 1943); (2) Will Morgan, 1934–38; (3) Ted Lloyd, 1939–54. *Some Day We'll Laugh; An Autobiography* (Metuchen NJ: The Scarecrow Press, Inc., 1985). (Paramount; MGM; Universal; Monogram; Republic; Mascot.) (Film debut: *Deep Purple,* 1916; extra work.) Glenn Collins, "Esther Ralston, 91, A Featured Actress of Silent-Film Era," *NYT,* 27 Jan 1994, D21:1. "Esther Ralston," *Variety,* 7 Feb 1994, 62:5. AMD, p. 284. AS, p. 898. BHD1, p. 450. BR, pp. 199–202. FSS, p. 243. HCH, p. 105. Katz, p. 945. "Esther Ralston," SOS, pp. 186–211. "Esther Ralston," WBO2, pp. 206–207. "Esther Ralston in 'Mutiny of the Elsinore,'" *MPW,* 12 Jun 1920, 1462. "Signs Esther Ralston," *MPW,* 18 Oct 1924, 609. "Esther Ralston Marries," *MPW,* 9 Jan 1926, 129 (m. Frey). Carol White, "Eight Years a Leading Woman But Never a Star; Esther Ralston Struggled Onward—And 'Peter Pan' Made Her Overnight," *MPC,* Dec 1925, 24–25, 73. Faith Service, "Can a Star Be Herself?," *MM,* I, Jan 1926, 45–46, 97–98. "Esther Ralston," *MPW,* 27 Mar 1926, 262. "Esther Ralston," *MPW,* 17 Apr 1926, 502. "Esther Ralston," *MPW,* 11 Jun 1927, 423. "Honor for Star," *MPW,* 17 Dec 1927, 27. Faith Service, "It Cost Esther Ralston $100,000 to Have Her Baby," *Movie Classic,* I, Dec 1931, 35. Jay Rubin, "Esther Ralston," *CFC,* 42 (Spring, 1974), 10–13 (credited as "Jane Carlton" in *The Spy Ring,* 1938). Buck Rainey, "Esther Ralston," *CI,* 111 (Sep 1984), 23–24 (includes filmography); 112 (Oct 1984), 31. Michael G. Ankerich, "Reel Stars; Esther Ralston," *CI,* 161 (Nov 1988), 7–8. MH, p. 134. William M. Drew, *Speaking of Silents* (Vestal NY: Vestal Press, Ptd., 1989), pp. 186–211. Eve Golden, "The American Venus; A Conversation with Silent Film Star Esther Ralston," *CI,* 207 (Sep 1992), 16, 18, C15 (the family name of North was changed to Ralston ca. 1904). Chapter 20, "Esther Ralston," *BS,* pp. 263–76 (includes filmography).

Ralston, Howard (brother of **Esther Ralston**) [actor] (b. 7 Apr 1909–1 Jun 1992 [83], Los Angeles CA). (FP-L.) *The Play's the Thing* (Fithian Press, 1988). (Film Debut: *Huckleberry Finn,* 1919.) "Howard Ralston," *Variety,* 20 Jul 1992, 76:3–4. AS, p. 898. BHD, p. 280 (b. 25 Jul 1904).

Ralston, Jobyna [actress: Wampas Star, 1923] (*née* Jobyna Lancaster Raulston, b. So. Pittsburg TN, 21 Nov 1900–22 Jan 1967 [66], Woodland Hills CA; pneumonia). m. **Richard Arlen,** 28 Jan 1927, Riverside CA-45 (d. 1976). (Cuckoo Comedies, 1919.) "Jobyna Ralston, 66, ex-Screen Actress," *NYT,* 23 Jan 1967, 43:3. "Jobyna Ralston," *Variety,* 1 Feb 1967. "Jobyna Ralston, Silent Screen Actress, 66," *NY World-Journal Tribune,* 23 Jan 1957. AMD, p. 285. AS, p. 898. BHD1, p. 450. FSS, p. 244. IFN, p. 244. Katz, pp. 945–46 (b. 24 Nov 1902). Truitt, p. 275 (b. 1904). "Jobyna Ralston to Lead for Lloyd," *MPW,* 13 Jan 1923, 160. Myrtle Gebhart, "Job Had the Patience to Wait," *Picture-Play Magazine,* Jun 1923, 64–65, 99. "In Lloyd Comedies," *MPW,* 1 Sep 1923, 70. "Cast Complete for Lloyd's First Paramount Picture," *MPW,* 5 Sep 1925, 90. Alice L. Tildesley, "Joby from the Tennessee Hills; Miss Ralston Has Been Harold Lloyd's Leading Woman for Four Years," *MPC,* May 1926, 38–39, 74, 86. Paul Paige, "Close-Ups and Fade-Outs," *Paris and Hollywood,* 2 (Sep 1926), 91 (suffered from an attack of Klieg eyes "because of the strain of rushing [a] picture through." Loaned by Harold Lloyd to DeMille.). "Miss Ralston to Wed," *MPW,* 9 Oct 1926, 343. "Miss Ralston Leading Lady for Ed. Cantor," *MPW,* 15 Jan 1927, 199. "Arlen—Ralston," *MPW,* 12 Feb 1927, 475. "Son Born to Mrs. Richard Arlen," *NYT,* 19 May 1933. "Ex-Actress Divorced from Richard Arlen," *N.Y. Daily News,* 1945 (charged desertion; "just packed up all his clothes and said he was leaving"). Ivar Lohman, "Jobyna Ralston," *CI,* 98 (Aug 1983), 17–18; 99 (Sep 1983), 28–29, 65 (includes filmography). Scott Johnson, "Jobyna Ralston," *CI,* 198 (Dec 1991), 12, 14, 16 (b. 1901).

Ramage, Cecil Beresford [actor] (b. Edinburg, Scotland, 17 Jan 1895–22 Feb 1988 [93], Glasgow, Scotland). m. **Cathleen Nesbitt,** 1922–div. (d. 1982). AS, pp. 898–99.

Rambeau, Marjorie [stage/film actress] (b. San Francisco CA, 15 Jul 1889–7 Jul 1970 [80], Palm Springs CA). m. (1) **Willard Mack** (d. 1934); (2) Hugh Dillmer; (3) Francis A. Gudger. "Marjorie Rambeau Dies at 80; Broadway and Screen Actress," *NYT,* 8 Jul 1970, 43:3. "Marjorie Rambeau," *Variety,* 15 Jul 1970. AMD, p. 285. AS, p. 899. BHD1, p. 450. IFN, p. 244. Katz, p. 946. SD. Truitt, pp. 275–76. "Powell to Produce for Mutual," *MPW,* 9 Dec 1916, 1513. "Marjorie Rambeau, Mutual's New Star," *MPW,* 20 Jan 1917, 346. C. Blythe Sherwood, "Sliding Down the Banisters to Success," *MPC,* Feb 1919, 20–21, 80. DeWitt Bodeen, "Marjorie Rambeau; 1889–1970," *FIR,* Mar 1978, 129–42.

Rambova, Natacha [actress/scenarist/costumer] (*née* Winifred Kimball Shaughnessy [adopted by Richard Hudnut], b. Salt Lake City UT, 19 Jan 1897–5 Jun 1966 [69], Pasadena CA; complications from stomach ulcers). Michael Morris, *Madam Valentino; The Many Lives of Natacha Rambova* (New York: Abbeville Press, 1991). m. (1) **Rudolph Valentino,** 13 May 1922 in Mexicali, Mexico; re-wed, 14 Mar 1923, Crown Point IN—div. 19 Jan 1926, Paris (d. 1926); (2) Alvaro de Urzáiz, ca. 1932, re-wed 6 Aug 1934, Palma, Spain—annulled, ca. 1957). "Miss Rambova, 69, Film Figure, Dead; 2d Wife of Valentino—Was Ballerina and Columnist," *NYT,* 8 Jun 1966, 47:1; "Miss Rambova Left $368,000," *NYT,* 6 Aug 1966, 15:8 (d. 3 Jun). "Natacha Rambova," *Variety,* 15 Jun 1966. AMD, p. 285. AS, p. 899 (b. 9 Jan). BHD2, p. 216. FDY, p. 437. IFN, p. 244. Truitt, p. 276. "Natacha Rambova," *MPW,* 14 Nov 1925, 129. "Natacha Rambova," *MPW,* 21 Nov 1925, 223. "Chatter," *Variety,* 151, 25 Aug 1943, 46:3 ("Natacha Rambova, once wife of Valentino, bought mountain home near Phoenix, Arizona. Writes for *Harper's Bazaar* and other mags on occult themes.").

Rameau, Emil [actor] (b. Berlin, Germany, 13 Aug 1888–9 Sep 1957 [69], Berlin, Germany). BHD1, p. 450. IFN, p. 244 (b. 1878).

Ramirez, Pepita [actress] (b. New York NY, 1902–27 Dec 1927 [25], Los Angeles CA; auto accident). "Pepita Ramirez," *Variety,* 11 Jan 1928. AS, p. 899. BHD, p. 280. IFN, p. 244. Truitt, p. 276. WWS, p. 276.

Ramirez, Rosita [actress]. No data found. AMD, p. 285. "Beautiful Cuban in 'Mare Nostrum,'" *MPW,* 3 Oct 1925, 418.

Ramon, Vida [actress]. No data found. Richard V. Spencer, "Los Angeles," *MPW,* 20 May 1911, 1125.

Ramos, José Manuel [director] (b. Mexico). (In Mexican silents from 1917.)

Ramos, Silvano [composer] (b. Mexico, 6 Mar 1888–2 Mar 1943 [54], Celaya, Mexico). AS, p. 899.

Ramsay, Frank Morris [actor/writer] (d. 4 Nov 1917, NJ). "Frank Morris Ramsay," *Variety,* 9 Nov 1917. AS, p. 899.

Ramsaye, Terry [publicist/writer] (b. Tonganoxie KS, 2 Nov 1885–19 Aug 1954 [68], Norwalk CT). m. **Betty Shannon,** May? 1916, Philadelphia PA. *A Million and One Nights* (1926). (Mutual Film Corp.) "T. Ramsaye Dies; A Film Historian; Former Official of the Motion Picture Herald Was Editor in Chief of Pathe News," *NYT,* 20 Aug 1954, 19:3. "Terry Ramsaye," *Variety,* 25 Aug 1954. AMD, p. 285. AS, p. 899. BHD2, p. 216. "Terry Ramsaye," *MPW,* 11 Sep 1915, 1812.

"Terry Ramsaye Marries Betty Shannon," *MPW,* 27 May 1916, 1524. "Farewell Luncheon for Terry Ramsaye," *MPW,* 16 Sep 1916, 1809 (relocation to Mutual's Chicago office). "Terry Ramsaye in Town," *MPW,* 27 Jan 1917, 509. Terry Ramsaye, "Function of Advertising in Distribution," *MPW,* 20 Jul 1918, 324–25. "Ramsaye Joins Rothapfel," *MPW,* 23 Nov 1918,824. "Terry Ramsaye Resigns as Publicity Director," *MPW,* 3 May 1919, 637. William J. Reilly, "Keeping Up with Terrible Terry," *MPW,* 19 Jul 1919, 367–68. Terry Ramsaye, "The Romantic History of the Motion Picture [Part I]," *Photoplay Magazine,* May 1924, 71, 132–140.

Ramsey, Alicia [playwright] (d. 1933). m. **Rudolph deCordova**, 14 Sep 1916, NYC (d. 1941). AMD, p. 285. "Alicia Ramsey Weds Rudolph deCordova," *MPW,* 30 Sep 1916, 2127. "Metro Gets Another Alicia Ramsey Play," *MPW,* 16 Mar 1918, 1501.

Ramsey, James A. [cameraman]. No data found. AMD, p. 285. "Cameraman Missing," *MPW,* 18 Sep 1920, 351.

Ramsey, John Nelson [actor] (b. London, England, 1863–5 Apr 1929 [66?], London, England). AS, p. 899.

Ramsey, Hill C.S. [actor] (*né* Cyril Seyes Ramsay-Hill, b. British Guyana, 30 Nov 1890–3 Feb 1976 [85], Van Nys CA; cystic fibrosis). AS, p. 899.

Ramsey, Ray [cinematographer]. No data found. FDY, p. 467.

Ranaldi, Frank [child actor/casting director] (b. 1905?–2 May 1933 [28], Los Angeles CA). (MGM.) "Frank Ranaldi," *Variety,* 9 May 1933. AS, p. 900. BHD, p. 280; BHD2, p. 216.

Ranalow, Frederick [actor] (b. Dublin, Ireland, 7 Nov 1873–8 Dec 1953 [80], London, England). BHD1, p. 451.

Rand, Ayn [actress/novelist/scenarist] (b. St. Petersburg, Russia, 2 Feb 1905–6 Mar 1982 [77], New York NY). AS, p. 900. BHD, p. 280; BHD2, p. 216.

Rand, John F. [actor] (b. New Haven CT, 19 Nov 1871–24 Jan 1940 [68], Los Angeles CA). (Essanay.) AS, p. 900 (d. 25 Jan). BHD1, p. 451. IFN, p. 244. Truitt, p. 276.

Rand, Sally [stage/film dancer/actress: Wampas Star, 1927] (*née* Helen Gould Beck, b. Hickory County MO, 2 Jan 1903–31 Aug 1979 [76], Glendora CA; pulmonary congestion). m. (1) Thurkel Greenough; (2) Harry Finkelstein; (3) Frederick Lalla. "Sally Rand of Fan Dance Fame Dies at 75; Last Performed in May," *Variety,* 5 Sep 1979 (age 75). AMD, p. 285. AS, p. 900. BHD1, p. 451 (b. 3 Apr 1904). IFN, p. 244 (b. 1904). Katz, p. 946 (Hickory Co., MO). SD. "DeMille Renews with Three Featured Players," *MPW,* 22 May 1926, 4. "Sally Rand," *MPW,* 18 Jun 1927, 484. Cover, *MPS,* 1 Mar 1927. Alan Brock, "Sally Rand; Behind the Fan!," *CI,* 223 (Jan 1994), 30, 32.

Randall [actor] (*né* André Randall, b. Bordeaux, France, 9 Dec 1893). AS, p. 900.

Randall, Bernard "Barney" [stage/film actor] (b. Odessa, Russia, 4 Jul 1884–17 Dec 1954 [70], New York NY). (In Thanhouser's first film, *She Wanted to Marry a Hero;* MGM.) AMD, p. 285. AS, p. 900. BHD1, p. 451. IFN, p. 244. MSBB, p. 1026. Truitt, p. 276. "Bernard Randall Engaged as Heavy," *MPW,* 9 Aug 1919, 848.

Randall, Fred [actor] (b. 1899–15 Aug 1933 [34?], Los Angeles CA). AS, p. 900.

Randall, Harry [actor] (b. 1860–18 May 1932 [72?], London, England). BHD, p. 280.

Randall, Jack [actor] (*né* Addison Owen Randall, b. San Fernando CA, 12 May 1906–16 Jul 1945 [39], Conoga Park CA; fell from his horse while making a western thriller at Canoga Park, his first day on the film). m. (1) Louise Stanley; (2) Barbara Bennett, 1941. "Addison (Jack) Randall," *Variety,* 159, 18 Jul 1945, 63:5 (age 38. "While he was riding his horse at break-neck speed past the cameras, The actor's hat blew off and, in an attempt to grab it, he lost his balance and fell, striking a tree). AS, p. 900 (b. 1907). BHD, p. 280. IFN, p. 244.

Randall, Mon [art director] (b. San Francisco CA, 1891–21 Jul 1935 [44?], Riverside CA). BHD2, p. 217.

Randall, Rae [actress: double for Greta Garbo] (*né* Sigrum Salvason, b. Sweden, 1909–7 May 1934 [25], Los Angeles CA; suicide). AS, p. 900. BHD1, p. 451 (b. Canada, 5 Dec 1897; d. 4 May). IFN, p. 244. Truitt, p. 276.

Randall, William [actor] (b. Rochester NY, 1877?–22 Apr 1939 [62], Elizabeth NJ). (Pathé.) "William Randall; Retired Actor of Stage and Screen Dies in Elizabeth at 62," *NYT,* 23 Apr 1939, III, 7:1 ("He appeared in early motion pictures"). "William Randall," *Variety,* 26 Apr 1939. AS, p. 900. BHD, p. 280 (d. Elizabeth NY). IFN, p. 244. Spehr, p. 160. Truitt, p. 276.

Randax, Georges [actor] (*né* Georges Colin, b. Belgium, 1897–30 Jan 1979 [81?], Molenbeek-Saint-Jean, Belgium; heart attack). AS, p. 900.

Randell, Charles [artist/titler]. No data found. (Ince.) J. Van Cartmell, "Studio News from the Coast," *NYDM,* 4 Dec 1915, 27:2 (to make "decorative sub-titles for each of his plays," *i.e.,* 4 to 10 distinct backgrounds upon which the lettering will be printed).

Randle, Frank [actor] (*né* Arthur McEvoy, b. Wigan, England, 1901–7 Jul 1957 [56?], Blackpool, England). AS, p. 900.

Randolf, Anders [stage/film actor] (b. Viborg, Denmark, 18 Dec 1869–3 Jul 1930 [60], Los Angeles CA; complications after an operation). (Vitagraph, 1911; Petrova; Ivan; Buffalo Motion Picture Corp.) "Anders Randolph," *Variety,* 9 Jul 1930. AMD, p. 285. AS, p. 900. BHD1, p. 451 (b. 1870). FSS, p. 244. IFN, p. 244 (age 59). MH, p. 134 (b. 1875). MSBB, p. 1026, 1028 (b. 1875). Truitt, p. 276. "Anders Randolf," *MPW,* 9 Oct 1915, 264. "Anders Randolf in Cast of 'The Cinema Murder,'" *MPW,* 26 Jul 1919, 502.

Randolf, Rolf [actor/director] (*né* Rudolf Zambauer, b. Vienna, Austria, 15 Jan 1878–29 Jun 1941 [63], Vienna, Austria). AS, p. 900. BHD2, p. 217.

Randolph, Amanda [actress] (b. Louisville KY, 22 Sep 1896–24 Aug 1967 [71], Duarte CA). AS, p. 900.

Randolph, Dorothy [actress] (*née* Dorothy Cohan, d. 10 Mar 1918, Atlanta GA). (Triangle.) "Dorothy Cohan Mathewson," *Variety,* L, 29 Mar 1918, 18:1. AS, p. 900. BHD, p. 280.

Randolph, Elsie [actress/dancer] (b. London, England, 9 Dec 1901–15 Oct 1982 [80], London, England). AS, p. 900.

Randolph, Isabel [actress] (b. IL, 4 Dec 1889–11 Jan 1973 [83], Burbank CA; cancer). AS, p. 900. BHD1, p. 451.

Randolph, Louise [actress] (b. Fort Leavenworth KS, 12 Mar 1870–2 Nov 1953 [83], Port Chester NY). "Louise Randolph," *Variety,* 11 Nov 1953, p. 71. BHD, p. 280.

Randolph, May [actress] (b. 1872–13 Apr 1936 [64?], Los Angeles CA). AS, p. 901.

Ranevskaja, Fania Georgievna [actress] (b. Taganrog, Russia, 27 Aug 1896–19 Jul 1984 [87], Moscow, Russia). AS, p. 901.

Rangel, Arturo Soto [actor] (b. Leon, Mexico, 12 Mar 1882–25 May 1965 [83], Mexico City, Mexico). AS, p. 901.

Ranier, Richard Robert [actor] (b. CA, 6 Nov 1889–25 Aug 1960 [70], Los Angeles CA; arthritis). AS, p. 901. BHD, p. 280. IFN, p. 245.

Ranin, Helge [actor] (b. Sweden, 1896–15 Apr 1952 [56?], Stockholm, Sweden). AS, p. 901.

Rankin, Arthur L. [actor/writer] (son of **Harry Davenport** and **Phyllis Rankin**; nephew of **Sidney Drew**) (*né* Arthur Rankin Davenport, b. New York NY, 30 Aug 1896–22 Mar 1947 [51?], Los Angeles CA; cerebral hemorrhage). m. Marian. "Arthur Rankin, 50, Actor and Writer," *NYT,* 24 Mar 1947, 25:5. "Arthur Rankin," *Variety,* 26 Mar 1947 (d. 23 Mar 1947, Hollywood, age 51). AMD, p. 285. AS, p. 901 (d. 23 Mar). BHD1, p. 452 (b. 1895). IFN, p. 245. SD, p. 1034. Truitt, p. 276. WWS, p. 237. "F.B.O. Signs Rankin," *MPW,* 10 May 1924, 203.

Rankin, Arthur McKee [actor] (b. 1841–17 Mar 1914 [73?], San Francisco CA). AS, p. 901.

Rankin, Caroline "Spike" [actress] (b. Pittsburgh PA, 22 Aug 1880–2 Feb 1953 [72], Los Angeles Co. CA). AS, p. 901. BHD1, p. 452. IFN, p. 245.

Rankin, Doris [stage/film actress] (b. ca. 1880-ca. 1946 [66?], Washington DC). m. (1) **Lionel Barrymore**, 19 Jun 1904, NYC (d. 1954); (2) Malcolm R. Mortimer. AS, p. 901. BHD1, p. 452. SD.

Rankin, Herbert [actor] (b. Chicago IL, 27 Feb 1876–16 Jul 1946 [70], Los Angeles CA). AS, p. 901.

Rankin, Phyllis (mother of **Arthur Rankin**, Kate and **Dorothy Davenport**) [stage/film actress] (b. New York NY, 31 Aug 1874–17 Nov 1934 [60], Canton PA; paralysis). m. **Harry Davenport** (d. 1949). AS, p. 901. SD, p. 1034.

Ranous, William V. [actor/writer/director/producer] (b. New York NY, 12 Mar 1857–1 Apr 1915 [58], Santa Monica CA). m. Doris Knowlton Thompson (d. 1916). (Vitagraph.) "William P. Ranous [sic]," *Variety,* 19 Apr 1915 (age 68). "Obituary," *MPW,* 17 Apr 1915, 366 (d. 3 Apr). Ball, pp. 308–309. AMD, p. 285. AS, p. 901 (d. 7 Apr). BHD, p. 280; BHD2, p. 217. IFN, p. 245. SD. Slide, p. 149. "Director Ranous Dead," *NYDM,* 7 Apr 1915, 32:4. *Photoplay,* Jun 1915, 137 (first director employed by Vitagraph; age 50).

Ransom[e], Edith [actress] (b. 1904?–26 Jan 1933 [28], Seattle WA; overdose of sleeping powders). "Edfith Ransome," *Variety,* 31 Jan 1933, 62:1 ("Notes in her room indicated that the act was deliberate." In 1929 she obtained a $20,000 judgment against Thomas Wilkes, Inc., Wilkes as an individual, and Lionel Samuels, claiming they ousted her from the play, *White Cargo.*). BHD, p. 280.

Ranson, Nellie Crawford [actress] (b. 1876–16 Nov 1964 [88]). BHD, p. 280. IFN, p. 245.

Ransone, John W. [actor] (b. 1860?–12 Aug 1929 [69], New York NY). m. Margaret. "John W. Ransone," *Variety,* 14 Aug 1929. AS, p. 901.

Rapee, Erno [conductor] (b. Budapest, Hungary, 4 Jun 1891–26 Jun 1945 [54], New York NY; heart attack). m. Mariska. (Ufa; 1st National; WB.) "Erno Rapee Dies; Noted Musician; Head of Orchestra at Radio City Music Hall—Composer of Song Hits in Films," *NYT,* 27 Jun 1945, 19:3. "Erno Rapee Dies at 55 of a Heart Attack," *Variety,* 27 Jun 1955 (pioneer in the presentation of music to screen productions). AS, p. 901 (d. 1955). BHD2, p. 217.

Rapf, Harry (father of Maurice Rapf) [producer] (b. New York NY, 16 Oct 1880–6 Feb 1949 [68], Los Angeles CA). m. Clementine Uhlfelder, 1911 (son Maurice b. 19 May 1914). "Harry Rapf Dead; Film Producer, 68; M-G-M Executive Since 1941, Movie Maker for 28 Years, Once with Gus Edwards," *NYT,* 7 Feb 1949, 19:1. "Harry Rapf," *Variety,* 9 Feb 1949. AMD, p. 285. AS, p. 896 (Harry Raff); p. 901 (b. 1882). BHD2, p. 217 (b. Denver CO). SD. "Harry Rapf—A Man of Constructive Capacity," *MPW,* 29 Dec 1917, 1964. "Warner Discusses Industry's CHief Need While Harry Rapf Forecasts Coming Winners," *MPW,* 31 Dec 1921, 1061. "Harry Rapf Will Produce Four Features by September 1; 'Rags to Riches' Is the First," *MPW,* 22 Apr 1922, 859. Harry Rapf, "The Independent Producer," *MPW,* 8 Jul 1922, 138. Harry Rapf, "'Good Star-Director Scarce,' Says Rapf," *MPW,* 10 Mar 1923, 177. "Harry Rapf Is Supervising 8 Metro-Goldwyn Productions," *MPW,* 11 Oct 1924, 502. "Rapf Recuperating," *MPW,* 1 Nov 1924, 26. "Harry Rapf to 'Scat About' for Material in New York," *MPW,* 6 Dec 1924, 549. Sumner Smith, "New Blood Needed in Picture Industry; Harry Rapf Offers Young Men a Chance," *MPW,* 27 Dec 1924, 811. "Rapf Host at a Novel Screen Party in Los Angeles," *MPW,* 22 Aug 1925, 803. Sumner Smith, "M-G-M Still Seeks Youths with Imagination, Says Rapf," *MPW,* 28 Nov 1925, 316.

Rapf, Joe [wardrobe] (b. New York NY, 12 Feb 1882–29 Jan 1939 [56], Murietta Springs CA). BHD2, p. 217.

Rappé, Virginia [bit actress] (*née* Virginia Rapp, b. New York NY, 1894–9 Sep 1921 [26?], San Francisco CA; rupture of the bladder; acute peritonitis; alleged manslaughter). AMD, p. 285. AS, p. 902. BHD, p. 280 (b. Chicago IL, 1896). IFN, p. 245 (age 22). Truitt, p. 277. Andy Edmonds, *Frame-Up! The Untold Story of Roscoe "Fatty" Arbuckle* (NY: William Morrow and Co., Inc., 1990), p. 155 (b. 1894); a photograph of her death certificate is on p. 122 (b. 1895). "Exhibitors Withdraw Arbuckle Comedies, Awaiting Court Action on Murder Charge," *MPW,* 24 Sep 1921, 382. "First National Witholds Virginia Rappe Films," *MPW,* 24 Sep 1921, 395 (*The Punch of the Irish; Wet and Warmer; Kick in High Life; Twilight Baby; Game Lady*).

Rappoport, Guebert [director] (b. Russia-1926, Russia; ruptured aorta). AS, p. 902.

Rapport, Helena [actress] (b. 1884–5 Dec 1954 [70], New York NY). BHD, p. 280. IFN, p. 245.

Raquello, Edward [actor] (b. Warsaw, Poland, 14 May 1900–24 Aug 1976 [76], New York NY). AS, p. 902 (d. LA CA). BHD1, p. 452. IFN, p. 245.

Rasch, Albertina [actress/dancer] (b. Vienna, Austria, 19 Jan 1896–2 Oct 1967 [71], Woodland Hills CA). m. Dmitri Tiomkin [1899–1979]. AS, p. 902 (b. 1891). BHD1, p. 452.

Rasilov, Sasha [actor] (*né* Vaclare Rasch, b. Prague, Czechoslovakia, 6 Sep 1891–4 May 1955 [63], Zbraslv, Czechoslovakia). AS, p. 902.

Rasmussen, Maurine [actress] (b. IL, 16 May 1883–5 May 1962 [78], Los Angeles CA). BHD, p. 281.

Rasoumnich, Alexndr Yefimovich [director/scenarist] (b. Yelisavetgrad, Ukraine, Russia, 1891–1972 [81?], Moscow, Russia). AS, p. 902.

Rasp, Fritz Heinrich [actor] (b. Båyreuth, Germany, 13 May 1891–30 Nov 1976 [85], Graefelfing, Germany; cancer). AS, p. 902. BHD1, p. 452 (d. Munich). IFN, p. 245.

Rastrelli, Amadee [actor]. No data found. AMD, p. 286. "Comedian Is War Hero," *MPW,* 8 Dec 1917, 1505.

Rasumny, Mikhail [actor] (b. Odessa, Ukraine, Russia, 13 May 1890–17 Feb 1956 [65], Los Angeles CA). AS, p. 903.

Ratcliffe, E[dward] **J.** [stage/film actor] (b. London, England, 10 Mar 1863–28 Sep 1948 [85], Los Angeles CA). m. Eleanor L'Estelle. AMD, p. 286. AS, p. 903. BHD, p. 452. IFN, p. 245. SD. "Three New Stars for Essanay," *NYDM,* 1 Sep 1915, 28:1 (to appear in *In the Palace of the King,* to be released Oct 1915, with E.J. Radcliffe [sic], Arline Hackett, and Edgar Lewis. "Five thousand extra people will be used, including over a hundred professioal dancing girls."). "Metro Engages E.J. Ratcliffe for 'Love, Honor and Obey,'" *MPW,* 22 May 1920, 1098. George Katchmer, "Remembering the Great Silents," *CI,* 211 (Jan 1992), 44.

Rath, Frederick [scenarist/publicist]. No data found. AMD, p. 286. "Frederick Rath Apollo Scenario Editor," *MPW,* 21 Apr 1917, 409. "Rath Goes to Yaphank," *MPW,* 15 Sep 1917, 1675. "Rath Leaves Paramount; C. Lewis Succeeds Him," *MPW,* 22 Oct 1927, 479.

Rathbone, Basil [stage/film actor] (*né* Philip St. John Basil Rathbone, b. Johannesburg, Transvaal, South Africa, 13 Jun 1892–21 Jul 1967 [75], New York NY; heart attack [Death Certificate Index No. 14857]). *In and Out of Character* (Garden City NY: Doubleday, 1962). m. (1) Marion **Ethel Foreman**—div. (d. 1976); (2) **Ouida Bergère** (d. 1974). "Basil Rathbone, 75, Dies at Home Here," *NYT,* 22 Jul 1967, 1:1, 25:4; "Rathbone Rites Attended by 350; Cornelia Otis Skinner Reads Actor's Favorite Poems," *NYT,* 26 Jul 1967, 39:4; "Rathbone Will Filed," *NYT,* 19 Aug 1967, 22:3. "Basil Rathbone," *Variety,* 26 Jul 1967. AS, p. 903. BHD1, p. 453. IFN, p. 245. JS, p. 372 (appeared in *Ponzio Pilato,* Italy, 1961). Katz, pp. 948–49. SD. Truitt, p. 277. Blackie Seymour, "Pentagram Revues; Basil Rathbone," *CI,* 236 (Feb 1995), C20–34, 36–37.

Rathbone, Guy B. [actor] (b. Liverpool, England, 28 May 1884–21 Apr 1916 [31]). BHD, p. 281.

Ratner, Anna [actress] (b. 1892?–2 Jul 1967 [75], Chicago IL). (Essanay.) AS, p. 903. BHD, p. 281. IFN, p. 245. Truitt, p. 277.

Rattenberry, Harry L. (brother of **William A. Rattenberry**) [actor/singer] (*né* Harry Rattenbury, b. Sacramento CA, 14 Nov 1857–9 Dec 1925 [68], Los Angeles CA). "Harry Rattenberry," *Variety,* 23 Dec 1925. AS, p. 903 (d. 10 Dec). BHD, p. 281. IFN, p. 245. Truitt, p. 277 (b. 1860). George Katchmer, "Harry Rattenberry," *CI,* 235 (Jan 1995), 38.

Rattenberry, William A. (brother of **Harry L. Rattenberry**) [stage [as Bill White]/film actor] (b. Sacramento CA, 26 Apr 1856–21 Apr 1933 [76], Los Angeles CA). AS, p. 903.

Rau, William [producer] (b. 1893–28 Sep 1925 [32?], Los Angeles CA; hemorrhaged ten days earlier). m. (Universal.) "William Rau," *Variety,* 7 Oct 1925, 53:5. BHD, p. 281; BHD2, p. 217.

Raucourt, Jules [actor] (b. Brussels, Belgium, 8 May 1890–30 Jan 1967 [76], Los Angeles CA). AMD, p. 286. AS, p. 903. BHD1, p. 453. IFN, p. 245. "Jules Raucourt," *MPW,* 4 Aug 1917, 786.

Raulet, Georges [director] (b. Paris, France, 18 Jan 1886–1954 [68?], France). AS, p. 903.

Rausch, Russell [stunt flyer]. No data found. (Paramount.) AMD, p. 286. "Stunt Flyer Hurt," *MPW,* 12 Nov 1927, 19.

Rauscher, William [actor] (d. ca. 1962, Mount Vernon NY). BHD, p. 281.

Ravel, Gaston [director/producer] (*né* Gaston Levar, b. Paris, France, 28 Oct 1878–23 Feb 1958 [79], Nice, France). AS, p. 903. BHD1, p. 453; BHD2, p. 217. JS, p. 372 (in Italian films from 1919).

Ravel, Maurice Joseph [composer] (b. Ciboure, Basses-Pyrenees, France, 7 Mar 1875–28 Dec 1937 [62], Paris, France). AS, p. 903. BHD2, p. 217.

Ravenscroft, Ralph [actor] (b. 1871–18 May 1934 [63], Rochester IN). BHD, p. 281. IFN, p. 245.

Raver, Harry R[ush] [executive/producer] (b. 1880?–14 Sep 1941 [61], Los Angeles CA; result of beating by a burglar two weeks previously). (Began 1899.) "Harry R. Raver," *Variety,* 24 Sep 1941. AMD, p. 286. "Putting It Over Us," *MPW,* 1 Oct 1910, 758. "A Nameless Picture and a Prize," *MPW,* 14 Dec 1912, 1085. "Raver Stays with Film Supply," *MPW,* 1 Feb 1913, 475. "Raver After Pirates," *MPW,* 22 Nov 1913, 881. "'The Man of the Hour'; Harry R. Raver's Interesting Career—From Fifty-Foot Subjects Down to the Twelve-Reel 'Cabiria,'" *NYDM,* 12 Aug 1914, 26:2. "Harry R. Raver," *MPW,* 15 Aug 1914, 943. "Raver Issues Denial—World Film Rumors Ridiculous, He Says—Busy Enough with Itala Company," *NYDM,* 3 Mar 1915, 25:3 (denied that he was replacing Lewis J. Selznick at World Film, adding that "if the use of my name will prove of benefit to others at any time, I shall offer no serious objection, providing it isn't spelled incorrectly."). Harry R. Raver, "The Cure for Censorship," *NYDM,* 17 Mar 1915, 22:3. "Itala Company's Plans," *MPW,* 31 Jul 1915, 800. Raver Film Corporation," *MPW,* 23 Oct 1915, 589. "Raver Has Studio on Staten Island," *MPW,* 6 Nov 1915, 1148. "Raver Sells British Rights," *MPW,* 20 Nov 1915, 1462. "Raver Thinks His Policy Best," *MPW,* 22 Jan 1916, 631. "Raver Has a Studio," *MPW,* 1 Apr 1916, 60. "Raver Forms New Company," *MPW,* 20 May 1916, 1346. "Raver Moves to Rockville Cent[re]," *MPW,* 24 Jun 1916, 2251. "Raver Comes Back," *MPW,* 23 Dec 1916, 1793. "Raver Heads Art Dramas," *MPW,* 10 Mar 1917, 1554. "Prize Offered for Trade Mark," *MPW,* 12 May 1917, 985 ($25.00). "Raver Resigns as Art Dramas Head," *MPW,* 8 Sep 1917, 1518. "Apollo Pictures, Incorporated, Not Sued," *MPW,* 27 Oct 1917, 514. "Raver Has Energetic Plans for 1918,"

MPW, 29 Dec 1917, 1966. Harry Raver, "Why Pick on the Poor Adjective?," *MPW,* 8 Feb 1919, 743–44. "'Maciste' Proves Popular in 'The Liberator' Serial," *MPW,* 15 Feb 1919, 938. "Author Aids in Filming of First Four Star Feature," *MPW,* 5 Apr 1919, 117. "Raver Leaves Four-Star Combination," *MPW,* 9 Aug 1919, 820.

Rawlins, John [stuntman/actor/film editor/film/TV director] (b. Long Beach CA, 9 Jun 1902–20 May 1997 [94], Arcadia CA; pneumonia). m. Lisa. (Columbia.) "John Rawlins," *Variety,* 26 May 1997, 89:3 (stuntman/actor in the 20s). AS, p. 904. BHD2, p. 217.

Rawlinson, Herbert [stage/film actor/director] (b. Brighton, East Sussex, England, 15 Nov 1885–12 Jul 1953 [67], Los Angeles CA; lung cancer). m. Roberta Arnold, ca. 1917—div. ca. 1923; Loraine Abigail Long, 1 Jan 1924, Detroit MI—div. 1927; **Josephine Norman** (d. 1951). (Film debut: *The Novice,* Selig, 17 Jun 1911; Bosworth; Universal; Vitagraph.) "H. Rawlinson Dies; Film, Stage Actor; Character Player Scored in Movies After Having Lead Roles in Broadway Plays," *NYT,* 14 Jul 1953, 27:1. "Herbert Rawlinson," *Variety,* 15 Jul 1953. AMD, p. 286. AS, p. 904. BHD1, p. 453. FFF, p. 245. FSS, p. 245. GK, pp. 800–21. IFN, p. 245. Katz, p. 950 (began 1911). MH, p. 134. MSBB, p. 1028. Truitt, p. 277. "Herbert Rawlinson," *MPW,* 30 May 1914, 1266. "Herbert Rawlinson," *MPW,* 28 Apr 1917, 619. "Irving Cummings Busy," *MPW,* 26 Jan 1924, 282. George A. Katchmer, "Herbert Rawlinson; The Man with the Smile," *CI,* 107 (May 1984), 38–40. George A. Katchmer, "Herbert Rawlinson [letter]," *CI,* 108 (Jun 1984), C5, C15. R.E. Braff and William C. Wilson, "An Index to the Films of Herbert Rawlinson," *CI,* 115 (Jan 1985), C7, 63; Part II, 116 (Feb 1985), 52–53; Part III, 117 (Mar 1985), C10-C11. R.E. Braff, "Herbert Rawlinson Filmography; Additions," *CI,* 132 (Jun 1986), 54, 63. George Katchmer, "Herbert Rawlinson," *CI,* 235 (Jan 1995), 38–39. R.E. Braff, "Additional Film Credits for Herbert Rawlinson," *CI,* 238 (Apr 1995), 42.

Rawlston, Zelma [stage/vaudeville/film actress] (b. Germany, 1868–30 Oct 1915 [47], New York NY). "Zelma Rawlston," *Variety,* 5 Nov 1915, 8:4 (d. 31 Oct; "The deceased is reported to have left considerable property."). BHD, p. 281.

Ray, Adele [actress] (*née* Evelyn Prevost). No data found. AMD, p. 286. "Society Girl in Films?," *MPW,* 31 May 1913, 898.

Ray, Al (cousin of **Charles Ray**) [stage/film actor/director/scenarist] (b. New Rochelle NY, 28 Aug 1894–8 Feb 1944 [49], Los Angeles CA). (On stage at age 7; Biograph as a child actor; Federal Film Co.; Pathé; General Film; 1st National; Educational.) AMD, p. 286. BHD, p. 281; BHD2, p. 218 (b. 1897). "Al Ray Produces Federal Special," *MPW,* 18 Sep 1915, 2012:2 (produced *The Waiter Who Waited,* Federal, 2 reels, with Harry La Pearl and Gertrude Bambrick [Mrs. Marshall Neilann]. "Mr. Ray has many surprises in this film, among them being a brand new way of introducing his characters."). "Al Ray with Astor Company," *MPW,* 30 Oct 1915, 989:2. "Al. Ray at Vim Studios," *MPW,* 15 Apr 1916, 416:2 (22 years old; with photo)."William Fox Engages Two Bright Youngsters [Ray and Elinor Fair]," *MPW,* 15 Feb 1919, 887. "Ray and Fair," *MPW,* 19 Jul 1919, 360. "Many Prominent Picture Players in the Cast of 'The Honey Bee,'" *MPW,* 28 Feb 1920, 1492. "Al Ray Is Signed by Jack White to Head His Scenario Department," *MPW,* 6 Oct 1923, 515:1 (wrote *The Courtship of Miles Standish* for his cousinn Charles). "To Direct Again," *MPW,* 8 Dec 1923, 570:4 (first directing in four years).

Ray, Albert [actor] (b. Haverhill MA, 28 Aug 1883–5 Feb 1944 [60], Los Angeles CA). (Fox.) AMD, p. 286. AS, p. 904. IFN, p. 245.

Ray, Allene [actress] (*née* Allene Burch, b. near San Antonio TX, 2 Jan 1901–5 May 1979 [78], Temple City CA; cancer). m. (1) Larry Wheeler, Mexico, 1925. (Metro; Fox; Pathé; Paramount.) AMD, p. 286. AS, p. 904. BHD1, 453. BR, pp. 202–05. FFF, p. 153 (b. 1903). FSS, p. 245. Katz, p. 950. LD, pp. 245–49. MH, p. 134 (b. 1903). "Miss Ray Goes to Texas," *MPW,* 8 Aug 1925, 648. "On the Set and Off," *MW,* V, 29 Aug 1925, 44 (married Wheeler). "Allene Ray," *MPW,* 24 Oct 1925, 640. "Allene Ray Will Essay Long Swim," *MPW,* 18 Sep 1926, 3. "Allene Ray," *MPW,* 5 Feb 1927, 419. Billy H. Doyle, "Lost Players," *CI,* 167 (May 1989), 45–46. George A. Katchmer, "Forgotten Cowboys and Cowgirls—Part IX," *CI,* 181 (Jul 1990), 56–57.

Ray, Ben H. [actor] (d. 14 Apr 1974, Los Angeles CA). "Ben H. Ray," *Variety,* 1 May 1974. AS, p. 904.

Ray, Bernard B. (brother of **Robert Ray**) [director] (b. 1898–11 Dec 1964 [66?], Los Angeles CA). AS, p. 904. BHD2, p. 218.

Ray, Carl [actor/producer] (b. 1877–22 Jul 1949 [72?], Los Angeles CA). AS, p. 904. BHD2, p. 218.

Ray, Charles Edward, Jr. (cousin of **Al Ray**) [actor/director/producer] (*né* Charles Edward Alfred Ray, b. Jacksonville IL, 15 Mar 1891–23 Nov 1943 [52], Los Angeles CA; throat infection). m. Clara Grant. (Ince-Paramount, Dec 1912; NYMP Co.; Triangle.) *Hollywood Shorts; Compiled from Incidents in the Everyday Life of Men and Women Who Entertain in Pictures* (LA: Ca. Graphic Press, 1935). "Charles Ray, 52, Silent-Film Star; Noted Portrayer of Shy Youth Dies in Hollywood—Lost Fortune as Producer," *NYT,* 24 Nov 1943, 21:3. "Charles Ray," *Variety,* 24 Nov 1943. AMD, p. 286. AS, p. 904. BHD1, p. 453; BHD2, p. 218. FFF, p. 85. FSS, p. 245. IFN, p. 246. Katz, p. 950. MSBB, p. 1028. Truitt, p. 278. "Charles Ray," *NYDM,* 12 Aug 1914, 24:4. "Charles Edward Ray, Jr.," *MPW,* 3 Oct 1914, 53. "Charles Edward Ray, Jr.," *MPW,* 27 Jan 1917, 509. "Charles Edward Ray, Jr.," *MPW,* 2 Jun 1917, 1439. "Ray Not to Leave Ince," *MPW,* 21 Sep 1918, 1721. "Ray Putting on Baseball Picture," *MPW,* 14 Dec 1918, 1239. "Arthur S. Kane Signs Charles Ray; First National to Release Pictures," *MPW,* 7 Feb 1920, 926. "Charles Ray Completes Final Picture for Tom Ince; Star Now on Vacation," *MPW,* 14 Feb 1920, 1069. "Charles Ray Soon to Start Work on 'Forty-Five Minutes from Broadway,'" *MPW,* 28 Feb 1920, 1445. "Charles Ray's New Studio at Hollywood Completed; Tank Under Stage a Feature," *MPW,* 3 Jul 1920, 99. "Arthur S. Kane, Back from Coast, Says Charles Ray Will Be Revelation in 1921," *MPW,* 25 Dec 1920, 1003. "Charles Ray Says That Titles and Sub-titles Are Very Important," *MPW,* 12 Feb 1921, 841. "Takes Hand at Directing," *MPW,* 12 Mar 1921, 166. Maude Cheathem, "The Bashful Boy," *MPC,* Jul 1921, 18–19, 75. "Ray Injured," *MPW,* 30 Jul 1921, 512. "Ray Coming East for First Time in Career," *MPW,* 22 Oct 1921, 890. "Charles Ray Enjoying New York Visit After Formal Welcome by Mayor Hylan," *MPW,* 10 Dec 1921, 676. Sumner Smith, "Charles Ray Stands the Acid Test of Praise at Luncheon for Newspapermen," *MPW,* 17 Dec 1921, 783. "Rousing Welcome to Charles Ray in City of Beans and Dignity," *MPW,* 24 Dec 1921, 948. "Charles Ray Signs with United Artists; Plans to Make Fewer and Better Pictures; To Remain an Independent Producer," *MPW,* 11 Feb 1922, 612. "Ray May Leave Screen," *MPW,* 6 Jan 1923, 34. "Charles Ray Enterprises to Build Elaborate Studio," *MPW,* 14 Jul 1923, 128. "Charles Ray Achieves Ambition of His Career," *MPW,* 10 Nov 1923, 252. David A. Balch, "The Most Human Note in the Movies; Charles Ray, famous delineator of youth on screen, reveals method whereby he climbed to the top of the ladder," *MW,* 8 Dec 1923, 7, 29. "Charles Ray Signs for Series Under Old Director, Tom Ince," *MPW,* 29 Mar 1924, 368. Clement Douglas, "'Just a Real Nice Boy'; Charles Ray Says What He Thinks of 'The Courtship of Miles Standish' in an Honest Confession-Is-Good-for-the-Soul Sort of Story," *Classic,* Jun 1924, 20, 81–82. "On the Set and Off," *MW,* 6 Sep 1924, 29:2 (First National Pictures sued Ray). "Charlie with Home for a Backdrop and Mrs. Ray as Leading Lady," *MW,* 13 Sep 1924, 10–11. "Chadwick Signs Charles Ray," *MPW,* 28 Feb 1925, 909. "Ray Remains with Chadwick," *MPW,* 15 Aug 1925, 764. "Ray to Return to Chadwick," *MPW,* 19 Sep 1925, 268. Helen Perrin, "The Tragedy of Charlie Ray," *MPC,* Oct 1925, 49, 73. "As We Go to Press," *MM,* Nov 1925, 102–103 (threatened foreclosure on his Beverly Hills home). "Ray Signs with M-G-M," *MPW,* 7 Nov 1925, 41. "Charles Ray Bankrupt," *MPW,* 12 Dec 1925, 535. Joan Cross, "The Tragedy of Charlie Ray," *Pictures,* Jul 1926, 38–39, 105–06. "Ray Going Abroad," *MPW,* 11 Dec 1926, 405. "Charles Ray," *MPW,* 8 Jan 1927, 113. "Posed as Charles Ray's Brother," *MPW,* 20 Aug 1927, 515. Nemo, "Hollywood Day by Day," *The New Movie Magazine,* Oct 1934, 17 (at a preview Ray received a round of applause when he appeared in a small part in Paramount's *Ladies Should Listen,* but when he made it he had holes in his shoes and was driving an ancient flivver). Mike Kornik, "Hayseed," *CFC,* 23 (Spring, 1969), 14–15; Part II, 8–9, 58–59. Mike Kornick, "The Films of Charles Ray," *CFC,* 25 (Fall, 1969), 38–39. Lewis G. Krohn, "The Tragic Figure of Charles Ray," *CI,* 70 (Jul 1980), 20–23, 48; 71 (Sep 1980), 54–55 (filmography). Gene Fernett, "The Country Bumpkin Establishes His Own Studio," *CI,* 113 (Nov 1984), C16-C17. Lewis Krohn and Chris Laube, "What Goes Up; Charles Ray," *CI,* 154 (Apr 1988), C19-C20. George Katchmer, "Charles Ray," *CI,* 235 (Jan 1995), 39.

Ray, Emma [vaudeville/film actress[(*née* Emma Sherwood, b. 1871–3 Jan 1935 [64], Los Angeles CA; heart ailment; cremated). m. actor **Johnny Ray** (d. 1926). (Last film: *The Old-Fashioned Way,* Paramount.) "Emma Ray," *Variety,* 117, 8 Jan 1935, 63:4 (outstanding moneymaker in vaudeville with husband: *A Hot Time*). AMD, p. 287. AS, p. 904. BHD1, p. 453. IFN, p. 246. "Ray Comedies," *MPW,* 20 May 1916, 1344. "Emma Ray," *MPW,* 9 Jun 1917, 1638.

Ray, Estelle Goulding [actress] (b. 1888?–1 Aug 1970 [82], Los Angeles CA; result of a fall). AS, p. 904. BHD, p. 281. IFN, p. 246. Truitt, p. 278.

Ray, Helen [actress] (b. Fort Stockton TX, 1879?–2 Oct 1965 [86], Wolfboro NH). m. Homer Miles. (Griffith.) "Helen Ray," *Variety,* 6 Oct 1965. AS, p. 904. BHD, p. 281. IFN, p. 246. Truitt, p. 278.

Ray, Jack [vaudeville/film actor: "Freckles" in Our Gang] (b. 10 Apr 1917–31 Oct 1975 [58], Montclair CA). m. Marion. "Jack Ray," *Variety,* 281, 12 Nov 1975, 70:3. AS, p. 904. BHD1, p. 453. IFN, p. 246.

Ray, Joe [actor] (b. New York NY, 24 Feb 1885). AS, p. 904. Billy H. Doyle, "Lost Players," *CI,* 154 (Apr 1988), 52. George Katchmer, "Joe Ray," *CI,* 235 (Jan 1995), 39–40.

Ray, Johnny [actor] (*né* John Matthews, b. Wales, United Kingdom, 1859?–4 Sep 1927 [68], Los Angeles CA; stroke). m. **Emma** Sherwood, ca. 1889 (d. 1935). (MGM.) "Johnny Ray," *Variety,* 7 Sep 1927. AMD, p. 287. AS, p. 904. BHD, p. 281. IFN, p. 246. Truitt, p. 278. "Ray Comedies," *MPW,* 20 May 1916, 1344. "Johnny Ray," *MPW,* 9 Jun 1917, 1638. "Johnny Ray Making Comedies," *MPW,* 16 Jun 1917, 1767. "Obituary," *MPW,* 17 Sep 1927, 163.

Ray, Katherine [actress]. No data found. AMD, p. 287. "Katherine Ray Signed," *MPW,* 24 Oct 1925, 634.

Ray, Marjorie [actress] (b. 1890?–22 Jul 1924 [34], San Diego CA; tetanus [lockjaw]). "Marjorie Ray," *Variety,* 6 Aug 1924 (age 24). AMD, p. 287. AS, p. 904. BHD, p. 281. IFN, p. 246. Truitt, p. 278 (b. 1900). "L-KO Fun Makers," *MPW,* 20 Jan 1917, 382.

Ray, Naomi [actress] (b. 1893–13 Mar 1966 [73], New York NY). AS, p. 904. BHD, p. 281. IFN, p. 246.

Ray, Rene [actress] (*née* Irene Creese, b. London, England, 22 Sep 1911–28 Aug 1993 [82], Jersey, Channel Islands). AS, p. 905 (b. 1912). BHD1, p. 453.

Ray, Robert (brother of **Bernard B. Ray**) [assistant director/scenarist] (b. 1900?–26 Mar 1957 [57], Los Angeles CA; heart attack). "Robert Ray," *Variety,* 3 Apr 1957. AS, p. 905. FDY, p. 437.

Rayburn, Donald [scenarist] (b. 1891?–20 Jun 1916 [25], Los Angeles CA; auto accident). (American.) AMD, p. 287. "Killed in Auto Crash, Donald Rayburn, American Film Scenario Editor, Meets Death in Los Angeles," *NYDM,* 1 Jul 1916, p. 38. "Donald Rayburn," *MPW,* 15 Jul 1916, 441.

Rayford, Alma [actress] (b. Muskogee OK, 24 Mar 1903–14 Feb 1987 [83], Muskogee OK). AMD, p. 287. BHD1, p. 454 (d. El Paso TX). BR, pp. 205–07. "Alma Rayford," *MPW,* 4 Dec 1926, 354.

Raymaker, Herman C. [actor: Keystone Cop/director] (b. Oakland CA, 22 Jan 1893–6 Mar 1944 [51], Oceanside CA). (Sennett; WB.) "Herman Raymaker," *NYT,* 9 Mar 1944, 17:1. AMD, p. 287. AS, p. 905 (b. Fruitvale CA; d. 7 Mar). BHD2, p. 218. IFN, p. 246 (age 47). "Stern Reengages Raymaker," *MPW,* 10 Feb 1923, 595. "How Raymaker Became a Picture Director," *MPW,* 13 Oct 1923, 586. "Raymaker Directs Aubrey," *MPW,* 1 Nov 1924, 81. "Warners Sign Raymaker," *MPW,* 18 Apr 1925, 712. "Raymaker to Direct 'The Sap,'" *MPW,* 15 Aug 1925, 761. "Raymaker Is Signed," *MPW,* 30 Oct 1926, 4. "Jack-of-All Studio Trades," *MPW,* 16 Apr 1927, 632. Tom Waller, "Herman Raymaker," *MPW,* 21 May 1927, 176–77. "Directing Monty Banks," *MPW,* 30 Jul 1927, 333.

Raymond, Charles [actor/director] (b. London, England, 1858–1930 [72?], London, England). AS, p. 905. BHD, p. 281; BHD2, p. 218.

Raymond, Cyril [actor] (b. Bowley, Regis, England, 1897–21 Mar 1973 [75], London, England). AS, p. 905 (b. 1895). BHD1, p. 454 (b. 1895). IFN, p. 246.

Raymond, Frances (Frankie) [stage/film actress] (*née* Mary Frances Raymond, b. Selma MA, 24 May 1869–18 Jun 1961 [92], Los Angeles CA). m. David Henderson. "Frankie Raymond, Actress in Nineties," *NYT,* 22 Jun 1961, 31:3 (stage debut, 1890; began in Hollywood, 1920). "Frances Raymond," *Variety,* 28 Jun 1961 (in films 1915–50). AMD, p. 287. AS, p. 905 (23 Apr 1899). BHD1, p. 454. IFN, p. 246. Truitt, p. 278. "Original Players in 'Secret Service,'" *MPW,* 10 May 1919, 925.

Raymond, Helen [stage/film actress] (b. Philadelphia PA, 1885?–26 Nov 1965 [80?], New York NY [Death Certificate No. 24614; age 77]). "Helen Raymond Is Dead; A Broadway Comedienne," *NYT,* 29 Nov 1965, 35:2. "Helen Raymond," *Variety,* 1 Dec 1965. AS, p. 905. BHD, p. 281. Truitt, p. 278.

Raymond, Jack [actor/director/producer] (b. Wimborne, England, 1886–20 Mar 1953 [67?], London, England). AS, p. 905. BHD1, p. 454; BHD2, p. 218.

Raymond, Jack [actor] (b. England, 1892–7 Jul 1942 [50?], Los Angeles CA). (1st National; FP-L.) AS, p. 905. BHD, p. 281. "Fresh from Bond Street," *MPW,* 9 Apr 1927, 549:1.

Raymond, Jack [actor/cinematographer/assistant director] (*né* George Feder, b. Minneapolis MN, 14 Dec 1901–5 Dec 1951 [49], Santa Monica CA; heart attack). "Jack Raymond," *Variety,* 12 Dec 1951 (age 50). BHD1, p. 454; BHD2, p. 218 (b. 1902). IFN, p. 246 (b. 1902). Truitt, p. 278.

Raymond, Peter [actor] (b. Minneapolis MI, 1871–19 Apr 1927 [55?], New York NY). AS, p. 905 (d. 30 Mar).

Raymond, Ray [actor] (b. 1894?–19 Apr 1927 [33], Los Angeles CA); beaten to death by **Paul Kelly** on 15 Apr 1927). m. Dorothy MacKaye. "Ray Raymond," *Variety,* 27 Apr 1927. AMD, p. 288. AS, p. 905. IFN, p. 246. "Actor's Death Sends Kelly to Jail," *MPW,* 23 Apr 1927, 703.

Raymond, Roma [actress]. No data found. AMD, p. 288. "Roma Raymond in New Metro Picture," *MPW,* 26 Aug 1916, 1376.

Raymond, Whitney [actor]. No data found. (Essanay). AMD, p. 288. "Mr. Whitney Raymond," *MPW,* 24 Feb 1912, 691.

Raymond, William Miner [actor] (b. 1873?–30 Oct 1960 [87], New York NY [Death Certificate Index No. 23091]). "William M. Raymond," *NYT,* 1 Nov 1960, 39:4. "William Miner Raymond," *Variety,* 16 Nov 1960 (d. 6 Nov). AS, p. 905. IFN, p. 246 (d. 2 Nov 1960).

Raymone [actress] (*née* Raymone Jeanne Augustine Duchateau, b. Gardanne, France, 11 Aug 1896 [extrait de naissance no. 42]-15 Mar 1986 [89], Geneva, Switzerland). AS, p. 905.

Rayner, Minnie [actress] (b. London, England, 2 May 1869–13 Dec 1941 [72], London, England). AS, p. 906. BHD1, p. 454. IFN, p. 246.

Raynor, William E. [executive] (b. 1883–13 Dec 1944 [61?], Jamaica NY). BHD2, p. 218.

Razetto, Stella [actress] (b. San Francisco CA, 17 Dec 1880–21 Sep 1948 [67], Malibu Beach CA). m. **Edward J. Le Saint**, 25 Dec 1913, San Diego CA (d. 1940). (Majestic; Kinemacolor; Selig.) "Stella R. Le Saint," *Variety,* 29 Sep 1948. AMD, p. 288. AS, p. 906. BHD1, p. 454 (b. San Diego CA, 1881). IFN, p. 177 (b. San Diego, 1881). 1921 Directory, p. 269. Truitt, p. 196 (Stella R. Le Saint). "Producer and Leading Lady Married," *MPW,* 17 Jan 1914, 291. "Director Le Saint's Bride; Attractive Selig Leading Lady Who Recently Became Bride of Los Angeles Producer," *NYDM,* 28 Jan 1914. "Stella Razetto," *MPW,* 14 Feb 1914, 818. "Stella Razetto," *MPW,* 26 Sep 1914, 1787. "Cats, Gardening and Pictures [Stella Razeto]," *Pictures and the Picturegoer,* 2 Aug 1915, 398. George Katchmer, "Stella (Razetto) Razeto," *CI,* 235 (Jan 1995), 40.

Razumny, Aleksandre Efimovich [director] (b. Yelisavetgrad, Russia, 1 May 1891–18 Nov 1972 [81], Moscow, Russia). AS, p. 906. Yuri Tsivian, "Between the Old and the New: Soviet Film Culture in 1918–1924," *Griffithiana,* 55/56 (Sep 1996), p. 21 (Razumny was also an expert caricaturist).

Rea, Isabel [stage/film actress]. No data found. (Imp; Biograph; K&E; Universal.) AMD, p. 288. "Isabel Rea," *MPW,* 13 Jan 1912, 133. Lester Sweyd, "What They Are Doing Now," *Motion Picture Magazine,* Feb 1918, 12 ("When last heard of, fair-haired Isabel Rea [Biograph], was appearing in vaudeville, supporting Adele Blood.").

Read, Didde [actress] (b. Australia, 1899–6 Feb 1932 [33], Los Angeles CA). AS, p. 906. BHD, p. 282. IFN, p. 246.

Read, J. Parker, Jr. [director/producer] (b. 1885–22 Aug 1942 [57?], Beverly Hills CA; heart attack). AMD, p. 288. AS, p. 906. BHD2, p. 218. "Dyreda—New Producing Company," MPW, 3 Oct 1914, 69. "J. Parker Read, Jr., Is Now with Ince," *MPW,* 23 Oct 1915, 603. "Thomas H. Ince and J. Parker Read, Jr., Are Welcomed at Luncheon in New York," *MPW,* 6 Mar 1920, 1604. "John Parker Read, Jr., Announces His Plans for Twelve Special Productions in 1920," *MPW,* 6 Mar 1920, 1677. "'Love,' Starring Louise Glaum, Produced by J. Parker Read, Jr., Reaches New York," *MPW,* 4 Dec 1920, 593. "John Parker Read, Jr., Names Winners of Successful Scenario Writers' Contest," *MPW,* 9 Jul 1921, 216.

Read, Jack [cameraman]. No data found. AMD, p. 288. "Read Took Togo Pictures," *MPW,* 23 Sep 1911, 883.

Read, Lillian [actress]. No data found. AMD, p. 288. "Lillian Read," *MPW,* 29 Jul 1916, 780.

Read, Opie [author/scenarist] (b. Nashville TN, 22 Dec 1852–2 Nov 1939 [86], Chicago IL). m. Ada Benham (d. 24 Jul 1928). "Opie Read Is Dead; Famous Humorist; Arkansas Traveler's Founder Wrote More than 50 Books, Many Best-Sellers; Epigrams Amused Nation; Friend of Mark Twain and Eugene Field Still Writing Shortly Before Death at 87," *NYT,* 3 Nov 1939, 21:3. "Opie Read," *Variety,* 8 Nov 1939 ("pioneer American humorist"; age 81). AMD, p. 288. BHD, p. 282; BHD2, p. 218. "Opie Read Will Write for Mirror," *MPW,* 30 Oct 1915, 980.

Reader, Ralph [actor] (b. Crewkerne, Somerset, England, 25 May 1903–13 May 1982 [78], London, England). AS, p. 906. BHD, p. 282; BHD2, p. 218 (dance director).

Readick, Frank M. [actor] (b. 1861–26 Aug 1924 [63], New York NY; heart attack). AS, p. 906. BHD, p. 282. IFN, p. 246.

Ready, Mike [actor] (b. Troy NY, 21 Aug 1858–26 Mar 1936 [77], Los Angeles CA). BHD, p. 282. IFN, p. 246.

Reals, Grace [stage/film actress] (d. 30 Aug 1925, New York NY). "Grace Reals, Actress, Dies; Had Played Leading Roles with Sothern, Hackett and Lackaye," *NYT,* 2 Sep 1925, 23:4. AS, p. 906. BHD, p. 282.

Reardon, Edmund H. (Ned) [stage/film actor] (b. Boston MA?–d. 4 Feb 1916, St. Luke's Hospital, New York NY; pneumonia). (Universal, 1914–16.) "Obituary," *MPW,* 4 Mar 1916, 1476. "Edmund H. Reardon," *Variety,* 11 Feb 1916, 8:4. "Edmund H. Reardon," *NYDM,* 19 Feb 1916, p. 6. AMD, p. 288. AS, p. 906. BHD, p. 282. IFN, p. 246.

Reardon, James [actor/director] (b. England, 1885). AS, p. 906.

Reardon, Mildred, "The Girl with the Brown Eyes" [actress]. No data found. (Paramount.) AMD, p. 288. 1921 Directory, p. 237. WWS, p. 266. "Diando Annexes 'Folly' Beauty," *MPW,* 27 Jul 1918, 572.

Reaume, Helen *see* **Power, Mrs. Tyrone**

Reaume, Patia *see* **Power, Mrs. Tyrone**

Rector, Enoch [inventor] (b. 1873–26 Jan 1957 [83?], New York NY). AS, p. 907.

Redding, Eugene [actor] (b. Montreal, Canada, 20 May 1870-Apr 1937 [66], Montreal, Canada). BHD, p. 282.

Redding, Harry [actor] (b. 1882–9 Mar 1949 [66?], New York NY). BHD, p. 282.

Reddy, George (brother of **Joe Reddy**) [publicist]. No data found. AMD, p. 288. "Pathé Contact Man in West Coast Job," *MPW,* 28 May 1927, 249.

Reddy, Joe (brother of **George Reddy**) [publicist]. No data found. AMD, p. 288. Edward Weitzel, "An Ever-Ready Pathé Publicity Man; or Interviewing James Young by Proxy," *MPW,* 23 Apr 1921, 825. "Joe Reddy, Jr., Arrives," *MPW,* 1 Jan 1927, 13 (son b. 25 Dec 1926).

Redgrave, Roy (father of Michael Redgrave; grandfather of Vanessa and Lynn Redgrave) [actor] (b. 1872–25 May 1922 [50?], Sydney, Australia). AS, p. 907 (d. 15 May, Melbourne, Australia). AS, p. 907. BHD, p. 282.

Redman, Frank E. [property man] (b. New York NY, 1879?–24 Jul 1940 [61], Englewood NJ). m. Wilhelmina. (FP-L; Paramount.) "Frank E. Redman," *NYT,* 25 Jul 1940, 17:2. "Frank E. Redman," *Variety,* 31 Jul 1940 ("chief property man for the Famous-Lasky studio at Fort Lee, N.J., in the pioneer days of the industry"). AS, p. 907. BHD, p. 282; BHD2, p. 219.

Redman, Minna [actress] (aka Minna Ferry). No data found. George Katchmer, "Remembering the Great Silents," *CI,* 202, Apr 1992, 6.

Redmond, Elmer E. [actor/assistant director] (b. PA, 5 May 1887–18 Jul 1955 [68], Los Angeles Co. CA). BHD, p. 282; BHD2, p. 219. IFN, p. 246.

Redmond, Harry A. [actor] (b. Cincinnati OH, 1881?–4 Nov 1966 [85], Canoga Park CA). (1st National; Pathé; RKO; Goldwyn; Universal.) "Harry A. Redmond," *Variety,* 9 Nov 1966. AS, p. 907. BHD2, p. 218.

Redway, Eddie [actor/director] (*né* Percy Saylor, b. Pittsburgh PA, 1870?–9 Apr 1919 [49], Reading PA). m. Katherine Pearl. "Eddie Redway," *Variety,* 18 Apr 1919. AS, p. 907. BHD, p. 282; BHD2, p. 218 (Eddie Reddway).

Red Wing, Princess (reputed aunt of **Rodd Redwing**) [actress] (*née* Winona Redwing or Princess Lillian Red Wing St. Cyr, b. Winnebago Reservation NB, 13 Feb 1873–13 Mar 1974 [101], New York NY [Death Certificate Index No. 4816, age 90]). m. **James Young Deer** (d. 1946). (Bison; Pathé.) "Red Wing, 90, Star in 1913 'Squaw Man,'" *NYT,* 14 Mar 1974, 40:3. "Red Wing," *Variety,* 20 Mar 1974 (age 90). AS, p. 907; p. 1025 (Lillian St. Cyr, b. 1884). BHD, p. 282 (b. 1884; d. 12 Mar). BR, pp. 59–61 (b. 1884). IFN, p. 321. Spehr, p. 160. "Princess Redwing," *MPW,* 8 Jun 1912, 914. George A. Katchmer, "Forgotten Cowboys/Girls—Part VIII," *CI,* 180 (Jun 1990), 61.

Redwing, Rodd (reputed nephew of **Princess Red Wing**) [stage/film actor/gun coach] (*né* Roderick Redwing, b. NY, 24 Aug 1904–30 May 1971 [66], Los Angeles CA; heart attack; stricken on a plane from London). m. Erika. "Rodd Redwing," *Variety,* 263, 9 Jun 1971, 54:5, 63:1 (full-blooded Chickasaw Indian; had just filmed *The Red Sun* in Spain). AS, p. 907 (d. London, England). BHD, p. 282. IFN, p. 246.

Ree, Max [artist/art director/cinematographer] (b. Copenhagen, Denmark, 1889?–7 Mar 1953 [64], Los Angeles CA; cancer). (MGM; RKO.) "Max Ree," *NYT,* 8 Mar 1953, 89:5. "Max Ree," *Variety,* 11 Mar 1953 (AA for *Cimarron,* 1931). AMD, p. 288. AS, p. 907. BHD2, p. 219. "F.N. Signs Max Ree," *MPW,* 19 Feb 1927, 542.

Reed, Arthur [cinematographer]. No data found. FDY, p. 467.

Reed, Bob [actor] (b. 1869–27 Sep 1927 [58?], London, England). BHD, p. 282.

Reed, Dave [vaudeville stage: The Seven Reed Birds/film actor/composer] (b. New York NY, 30 Jul 1872–11 Apr 1946 [73], New York NY). m. Florence. (FP-L.) "Dave Reed, Composer and ex-Vaudevillian," *NYT,* 12 Apr 1946, 27:4 (wrote lyrics for *Love Me and the World Is Mine,* 1906). "Dave Reed," *Variety,* 17 Apr 1946. AS, p. 908. ASCAP 66, p. 513. BHD1, p. 455. IFN, p. 247. Truitt, p. 278. "In the Picture Studios," *NYDM,* 8 Sep 1915, 36:4.

Reed, Donald [actor] (*né* Ernesto Avila Guillen, b. Mexico City, Mexico, 23 Jul 1901–27 Feb 1973 [71], Los Angeles CA). AS, p. 908. BHD1, p. 455 (d. 28 Feb, Westwood CA). FSS, p. 246. IFN, p. 247. Katz, p. 955.

Reed, Florence (daughter of actor Roland Reed) [stage/film actress] (b. Philadelphia PA, 10 Jan 1883–21 Nov 1967 [84], East Islip, LI NY [Death Certificate Index No. 33; age 85]). m. **Malcolm Williams**, 12 Nov 1915, Philadelphia PA (d. 1937). (Stage debut: *If I Were King,* 1909; film debut: *The Dancing Girl,* Paramount, 11 Jan 1915; Pathé; Brenon; Today Film Corp.; Harry Rapf.) "Florence Reed, Actress, 84, Dies; Star of 'Shanghai Gesture' Also in 'Skin of Our Teeth,'" *NYT,* 22 Nov 1967, 47:1. "Florence Reed," *Variety,* 29 Nov 1967. AMD, p. 288. AS, p. 908. BHD1, p. 455. IFN, p. 247. Lowrey, p. 154. MSBB, p. 1040. Truitt, p. 279. "Florence Reed on Screen," *NYDM,* 30 Dec 1914, 28:4 (to appear in *The Dancing Girl*). "Florence Reed Marries," *NYDM,* 20 Nov 1915, 7:1 ("The couple are now playing a motion picture engagement."). "Florence Reed in Pathé's 'The Woman's Law,'" *MPW,* 8 Apr 1916, 265. "Roland Reed's Daughter—Florence," *Photoplay,* Jul 1917, 93. Hazel Simpson Naylor, "It's Great to Be a Star; Being an Interview with that Shining Satellite, Florence Reed," *Motion Picture Magazine,* Feb 1918, 30–33 (disliked making movies but will continue making them, not for the money, but to discover what is fascinating aboutjthem. She was opening in *Chu Chin Chow* at the Manhattan Opera House that week. She would get up at 7:30, go to the studio at 8, play in pictures from 10 to 4, rehearse for her play 4 days a week, and arrive home at 7 for dinner "'One of the things I object to so much in pictures, besides the limited scope of the camera [I dont like being hemmed in by a six-foot camera range], is the attention one has to pay to fine details...My method which had been so effective on the stage didn't even register on the screen. Naturally I am volcanic, dynamic, and I found that I had to learn to be negative, quiet. I had to learn reserve, poise.' During all this time, Florence Reed gave me the impression of leashed electricity...It was plain to be seen that it was a positive effort for her to sit still for any length of time."). Aileen St. John-Brenon, "Florence, the Oriental," *MPC,* Jan 1919, 20–21, 69. Ethel Rosemon, "The Extra Girl Invades Another Courtroom," *MPC,* May 1919, 48–49, 80, 88. "Tribute Sues Ziegfeld Over Miss Florence Reed," *MPW,* 20 Nov 1920, 326.

Reed, George E. [musical comedy star] (b. 6 May 1890?–11 Jun 1952 [62], Camden NJ). m. Alice Lucey, 1923. "George E. Reed," *NYT,* 14 Jun 1952, 15:5. "George E. Reed," *Variety,* 18 Jun 1952. AS, p. 908. BHD, p. 282. IFN, p. 247. Truitt, p. 279.

Reed, George H[enry] [actor] (b. Macon GA, 27 Nov 1866–6 Nov 1952 [85], Woodland Hills CA; arteriosclerosis). (Paramount; FBO.) AS, p. 908. BHD1, p. 455. IFN, p. 247. George Katchmer, "Remembering the Great Silents," *CI,* 201 (Mar 1992), 39–40. Ed Wyatt, "George Reed: Early Black Actor in Western Films," *CI,* 203 (May 1992), C20.

Reed, Gus [actor] (*né* Harold Nelson, b. 1880–17 Jul 1965 [85?], Cherry Valley CA). AS, p. 908.

Reed, Ione [actor]. No data found. (Universal.) AMD, p. 288. BR, pp. 207–08. "Barsky Signs Reed," *MPW,* 17 Jul 1926, 152.

Reed, J. Theodore [director/producer] (b. Cincinnati OH, 1887–22 Feb 1959 [72], San Diego CA). (UA; Paramount; Columbia.) "J. Theodore Reed," *Variety,* 4 Mar 1959 (began 1918). AS, p. 908. Katz, p. 956 (began 1918).

Reed, Julian (nephew of **Roland Reed**) [actor] (b. 1864–28 May 1934 [70?], Englewood NJ). m. Mrs. Mary Darcey Goodwin, 29 Aug 1915, Jersey City NJ. (Edison.) AMD, p. 288. BHD, p. 282. IFN, p. 247 (age 74). "Marriages," *NYDM,* 15 Sep 1915, 6:4. "Julian Reed, Edison Actor, Married," *MPW,* 18 Sep 1915, 1978.

Reed, Leslie [stage/film actor] (b. England-d. Dec 1915, Santa Inez River CA; died while performing a stunt). AMD, p. 288. "Death of Leslie Reed," *MPW,* 4 Dec 1915, 1839. "Accidental Death of Leslie Reed," *NYDM,* 11 Dec 1915, 24:1 (he was to jump from a bridge into a river for *The Ride for Life,* Flying A. He failed to clear the rocks below, "and their jagged edges caused almost instant death.").

Reed, Luther A. [director/scenarist] (b. Berlin WI, 14 Jul 1888–16 Nov 1961 [73], New York NY [Death Certificate Index No. 24867]). m. 3 times: (2) **Naomi Childers** (d. 1964); (3) Jocelyn Lee. (FP-L; Metro; Ince; Cosmopolitan;

Paramount.) "Luther Reed Dies; Ex-Film Director; Writer for Marion Davies, 73, Worked on 'Rio Rita' Movie," *NYT,* 17 Nov 1961, 35:1 (began in Hollywood in 1916). "Luther Reed," *Variety,* 22 Nov 1961. AMD, p. 288. AS, p. 908. BHD2, p. 219. IFN, p. 247. Katz, p. 956. Lowrey, p. 156. "Luther A. Reed Joins Lasky Staff," *MPW,* 25 Dec 1915, 2334. "Luther Reed Joins Metro's Scenario Staff," *MPW,* 19 Jan 1918, 348. "Quickly Breaks into Officer's School; Luther Reed, Metro Scenarioist, Is Yanked Out of Yaphank Within Twenty-four Hours," *MPW,* 31 Aug 1918, 1252:1 (was drama critic of the *New York Herald*). "Lieutenant Luther Reed Again a Metro Scenarist," *MPW,* 15 Feb 1919, 888. "Reed Is Ince Scenarist," *MPW,* 12 Jul 1919, 248. "Reed with Paramount," *MPW,* 7 Feb 1925, 594. "Promoted to Directors," *MPW,* 8 May 1926, 144.

Reed, R. Ralston [writer]. No data found. AMD, p. 288. "Dr. Reed Guest of Lasky Company," *MPW,* 9 Sep 1916, 1711 (won Columbia University Prize Play Contest, "Witchcraft").

Reed, Roland (uncle of **Julian Reed**) [producer] (b. New York NY, 7 Jul 1894–15 Jul 1972 [78], Los Angeles CA). BHD2, p. 219.

Reed, Theodore [director/producer/scenarist] (*né* J. Theodore Reed, b. Cincinnati OH, 1887–22 Feb 1959 [71?], San Diego CA). AS, p. 908. BHD2, p. 219.

Reed, Tom [film publicist/title writer/scenarist] (b. Shelton WA, 24 Dec 1901–17 Aug 1961 [59], Long Beach CA; cancer). (Ince.) "Tom Reed," *Variety,* 23 Aug 1961. AS, p. 908. BHD2, p. 219 (producer). FDY, p. 447. IFN, p. 247.

Reed (Reid?), Violet B. [actress]. No data found. (K&E.) AMD, p. 289. "Violet Reed in Support of Petrova," *MPW,* 30 Dec 1916, 1939.

Reed, Vivian [calendar girl/stage/film actress] (b. Chicago IL, 17 Apr 1894–19 Jul 1989 [95], Woodland Hills CA). m. **Alfred E. Green** (d. 1960; 3 sons). (Selig.) "Vivian Reed," *Variety,* 2 Aug 1989, 83:5 ("...portrayed Glinda, the good witch, in the first film version of 'The Wizard of Oz.'"). AMD, p. 289. BHD, p. 282. "The Girl on the Caldendar; That is, she was there once, but now she smiles only for the movie camera," *Photoplay,* Feb 1917, 33. "Vivian Reed," *MPW,* 17 Feb 1917, 1010.

Reed, Walter Finnigan [scenarist]. No data found. AMD, p. 289. "Famous Irish Comedian with Arbuckle," *MPW,* 2 Mar 1918, 1231.

Reed, William H. [assistant director] (b. 1893?–7 Jan 1944 [50], W. Los Angeles CA). "William Reed," *Variety,* 12 Jan 1944. AS, p. 909. BHD2, p. 219 (d. Sawtelle CA).

Reehm[s], George E. [actor/director]. No data found. (Lubin.) AMD, p. 289. "George Reehm [photo only]," *NYDM,* 28 Feb 1912, 29:2. "Inquiries," *MPW,* 11 May 1912, 526 ("one of the oldest photoplayers in the business"). "George E. Reehms," *MPW,* 18 Apr 1914, 346. "Biograph Directors," *MPW,* 10 Jul 1915, 243–44.

Reel, Frederick, Jr. [scenarist]. No data found. FDY, p. 437.

Rees[e], William [actor/producer] (b. Newcastle, South Wales, 1904?–1 Oct 1961 [57], Melbourne, Australia). "William Reese," *Variety,* 11 Oct 1961. AS, p. 909 (d. LA CA).

Reeve, Ada [actress] (b. London, England, 3 Mar 1874–25 Sep 1966 [92], London, England). AS, p. 909.

Reeve, Arthur B. [writer/producer] (b. Patchogue NY, 1880–9 Aug 1936 [56?], Trenton NJ). AMD, p. 289. BHD2, p. 219. "Arthur B. Reeve Signs with Goldwyn to Produce Craig Kennedy Stories," *MPW,* 21 Feb 1920, 1264. "'Why Let Poor Cutting Ruin a Good Production?,' Says Arthur B. Reeve," *MPW,* 28 Feb 1920, 1471.

Reeve, Winifred Eaton [writer]. No data found. AMD, p. 289. "Universal Engages New Story Editor," *MPW,* 15 May 1926, 232. "M-G-M Signs Miss Reeve," *MPW,* 1 Jan 1927, 14.

Reeves, Alfred [executive] (b. London, England, 2 Dec 1876–6 Apr 1946 [69], Playa del Ray CA). AS, p. 909. BHD2, p. 219.

Reeves, Arthur E[dward] [cameraman] (b. 1892?–10 Oct 1954 [62], Los Angeles CA). "Arthur Edward Reeves," *Variety,* 20 Oct 1954. BHD2, p. 219. FDY, p. 467.

Reeves, Billy [vaudevillian/acrobat/pantomimist/actor] (b. No. Ixworth, near Bury St. Edmunds, Suffolk, England, 1864?–29 Dec 1943 [79], No. Ixworth, near Bury St. Edmunds, Suffolk, England). (Lubin.) "Billy Reeves, Comedian, Dies," *NYT,* 30 Dec 1943, 17:4. "Billy Reeves," *Variety,* 5 Jan 1944. AMD, p. 289. AS, p. 909 (d. No. Ixworth). BHD, p. 282. IFN, p. 247. Truitt, p. 279. "Reeves with Lubin [at Jacksonville FL]; Popular Stage Comedian Signed for Series of Lubin Comedies," *NYDM,* 31 Mar 1915, 24:4. "Billie Reeves with Lubin," *MPW,* 10 Apr 1915, 212. "Billie Reeves in 'Out for a Stroll,'" *MPW,* 29 May 1915, 1436. "Reeves Sticks to Screen," *NYDM,* 6 Oct 1915, 24:4 (had a tempting offer to return to vaudeville but signed with Lubin for six more months. Known as King of Inebriates, the Purveyor of Boozed Comedy, The Knight of Drunken Swells, and the Scream of the Screen.). Roberta Courtlandt, "One of the Three 'Original Chaplins,'" *MPC,* May 1916, 27–28.

Reeves, Edith [actress]. No data found. AMD, p. 289. J. Van Cartmell, "Along the Pacific Coast," *NYDM,* 4 Aug 1915, 33:1 ("Miss Reeves is a direct descendant of Colonel Samuel Paynter, who was Governor of Delaware in 1827."). "Edith Reeves," *MPW,* 15 Apr 1916, 448.

Reeves, Kynaston P. [stage/film actor] (*né* Philip Kynaston Reeves, b. London, England, 29 May 1893–10 Dec 1971 [78], London, England.). "Kynaston Reeves," *Variety,* 5 Jan 1972 (began 1919). AS, p. 909. BHD1, p. 456. IFN, p. 247. SD. Truitt, p. 279.

Reeves, Myrtle [actress] (b. Atlanta GA, 1897–18 Jan 1983 [85?], Garden Grove CA). m. **Oliver Hardy**, 24 Nov 1921, Thanksgiving Day (d. 1983). (Universal.) AMD, p. 289. BHD, p. 282. "Hardy Married," *MPW,* 17 Dec 1921, 829.

Reeves, Robert Jasper [actor] (b. Marlin TX, 28 Jan 1892–13 Apr 1960 [68], Los Angeles CA; heart attack). (Film debut: *Elmo the Mighty,* Universal, 1919; FBO; Rayart.) AS, p. 909 (d. 12 Apr). BHD1, p. 456. IFN, p. 247. Truitt, p. 279 (b. 2 Apr). Ed Wyatt, "Big Bob Reeves: Born to the Saddle," *CI,* 268 (Oct 1997), 37–39 (includes filmography).

Reeves-Smith, H[arry] [stage/film actor] (b. Scarborough, England, 17 May 1862–29 Jan 1938 [75], Elwell, Surrey, England; heart attack). m. Clara White. (London debut, 1879.) "H. Reeves-Smith, Stage Star, Dies; English Actor, a Favorite in American Theatre for More than 40 Years, Was 75; First Seen Here in 1881; Created Such Notable Roles as Capt. Jinks and Juvenile of 'Charlie's Aunt,'" *NYT,* 30 Jan 1938, II, 9:1. "H. Reeves-Smith," *Variety,* 2 Feb 1938. AS, p. 909 (b. 1862). BHD1, p. 456 (b. 1852). IFN, p. 247. SD. Truitt, p. 279.

Regan, Edgar J. [actor] (b. San Francisco CA, 1880–21 Jun 1938 [58], San Francisco CA; heart attack). AS, p. 909. BHD, p. 283. IFN, p. 247.

Regan, Joseph [lyric tenor/actor] (b. Boston MA, 1896?–9 Nov 1931 [35?], New York NY; cerrebral hemorrhage). m. Alberta Curlis. "Joseph Regan Dies in Bed in Hotel Room," *Variety,* 17 Nov 1931 (no mention of films). AS, p. 909. Truitt, p. 279.

Regas, George (brother of **Pedro Regas**) [actor] (aka Jorge Regas, b. Sparta, Greece, 9 Nov 1890–13 Dec 1940 [50], Los Angeles CA; complications after an operation). m. **Reine Douras** (sister of Marion Davies, d. 1938). (1st National.) "George Regas," *NYT,* 14 Dec 1940, 17:5. "George Regas," *Variety,* 18 Dec 1940. AS, p. 909. BHD1, p. 456. IFN, p. 247. Truitt, p. 279. George Katchmer, "Remembering the Great Silents," *CI,* 233 (Nov 1994), 38.

Regas, Pedro [actor] (brother of **George Regas**) (*né* Panagiotis Regas, b. Sparta, Greece, 12 Apr 1882–10 Aug 1974 [92], Los Angeles CA; heart attack in his sleep). AS, p. 909. BHD1, p. 456 (b. 18 Apr 1897).

Reginald [actor] (b. Brussels, Belgium, 29 Dec 1881–29 Oct 1951 [69], Brussels, Belgium). AS, p. 910.

Regis, Colette [actress] (*née* Yvonne Artigues, b. Brive-la-Gaillarde, France, 23 Oct 1893 [extrait de naissance no. 306/1893]–23 Oct 1978 [85], Paris, France). AS, p. 910.

Regno, Ugo Del [actor] (b. 1897–14 Jun 1981 [84?]). BHD, p. 283.

Rehan, Mary [stage/film actress] (b. Chippewa Falls MN, 1887?–28 Aug 1963 [76], Rochester MN). (Gaumont.) "Mary Rehan, a Tariff Lawyer and a Former Actress, Is Dead; Stage and Film Performer Changed Careers in '20's—Founded Legal Firm," *NYT,* 30 Aug 1963, 21:1. "Mary Rehan," *Variety,* 4 Sep 1963. AS, p. 910. BHD, p. 283. IFN, p. 247. Truitt, p. 279.

Rehfeld, Curt [actor/director] (b. Dresden, Germany, 11 Feb 1881–24 Mar 1934 [53], Germany). AS, p. 910. BHD1, p. 457; BHD2, p. 219 (d. CA). IFN, p. 247.

Rehg, Wally [actor] (*né* Walter Phillip Rehg, b. Summerfield IL, 31 Aug 1888–5 Apr 1946 [57], Burbank CA). AS, p. 910.

Rehkopf, Paul [actor] (b. Brunswick, Germany, 21 May 1872–29 Jun 1949 [77], Berlin, Germany). BHD1, p. 457. IFN, p. 247.

Reichart, Marie [actress]. No data found. AMD, p. 289. "Marie Reichart in Metro Production," *MPW,* 18 Nov 1916, 1023.

Reichenbach, Harry L. [publicist]. No data found. AMD, p. 289. "Harry Reichenbach Is Watched," *MPW,* 27 Jun 1914, 1834. "The Irrepressible Reichenbach," *MPW,* 14 Aug 1915, 1136. "Harry Reichenbach Entertains," *MPW,* 21 Aug 1915, 1290. "Reichenbach Joins Frohman," *MPW,* 26 Aug 1916, 1385. "Reichenbach Becomes Free Lance," *MPW,* 23 Dec 1916, 1811. Harry L. Reichenbach, "Putting Over Features on Broadway," *MPW,* 20 Jul 1918, 346–47. "Goes to Paramount," *MPW,* 14 Jan 1922, 163. "Reichenbach with Chadwick," *MPW,* 29 Aug 1925, 941. "Harry L.

Reichenbach," *MPW,* 26 Mar 1927, 311. Harry Reichenbach, "Press Books Then and Now," *MPW,* 26 Mar 1927, 318.

Reicher, Ernst [actor/director] (*né* Ernst Erwin Preichert, b. Berlin, Germany, 19 Sep 1885–1935 [50?], Prague, Czechoslovakia). AS, p. 910 (d. 1936). Vittorio Martinelli, "Kino-Lieblinge," *Griffithiana,* 38/39 (Oct 1990), 67.

Reicher, Frank (half-brother of **Hedwiga Reicher**) [stage/film actor/director/scenarist] (*né* Franz Reichert, b. Munich, Germany, 2 Dec 1875–19 Jan 1965 [89], Playa del Rey CA). (World; Paramount; Metro.) "Frank Reicher of Films Is Dead; Former Stage Director Was 89," *NYT,* 23 Jan 1965, 25:2 (d. Inglewood CA). "Frank Reicher," *Variety,* 27 Jan 1965. AMD, p. 289. AS, p. 910. BHD1, p. 457; BHD2, p. 219. IFN, p. 247. Katz, 958. 1921 Directory, p. 273 (b. 1875). Spehr, p. 162. Truitt, pp. 279–80. "Reicher with Lasky; Former Stage Director for Henry [B.] Harris Turns to Screen Work," *NYDM,* 19 May 1915, 22:3. "Frank Reicher to Be Lasky Director," *MPW,* 29 May 1915, 1437. "Frank Reicher Joins Metro Staff," *MPW,* 6 Oct 1917, 65. "Director Reicher Back in New York," *MPW,* 8 Jun 1918, 1418. "Frank Reicher Engaged by World," *MPW,* 27 Jul 1918, 561. "Reicher to Lecture World Cameramen," *MPW,* 3 Aug 1918, 690. Blackie Seymour, "Pentagram Profiles; Frank Reicher: Is There a Doctor in the House?," *CI,* 299 (May 2000), 72–74.

Reicher, Hedwiga (half-sister of **Frank Reicher**) [stage/film actress] (b. Oldenburg, Germany, 12 Jun 1884–2 Sep 1971 [87], Los Angeles CA). AS, p. 910. BHD1, p. 457. IFN, p. 248. SD.

Reichers, Helene [stage/film actress] (b. Germany, 1869–24 Jul 1957 [88?], Berlin, Germany). "Helene Riechers," *Variety,* 207, 7 Aug 1957, 63:3 (65 years on the stage). BHD, p. 285.

Reichert, Catherine "Kittens" [actress] (*née* Catherine Alma Reichert, b. Yonkers NY, 3 Mar 1910–11 Jan 1990 [79], Louisville KY; interred at Fort Knox KY). m. Mr. Lundy. (Fox; Blaché; Metro; FP-L; Universal; Ivan; Vitagraph; U.S. Amusement Co.; Paramount.) AS, p. 910. BHD, pp. 64–65; 283. Spehr, p. 162 (b. 1911). Billy H. Doyle, "Lost Players," *CI,* 179 (May 1990), 30–31.

Reichert, Heinz [scenarist] (b. 1878–16 Nov 1940 [62?], Los Angeles CA). BHD2, p. 219.

Reid, Billy (son of **Dorothy Davenport** and **Wallace Reid**) [child actor]. No data found. Henriette, "From Hollywood to You," *MPS,* 1 Mar 1927, 6 (photo from *Young Hollywood,* Pathé, with Eillen O'Malley, Erich von Stroheim Jr., and Billy Reid).

Reid, Hal (father of **Wallace Reid**) [actor/scenarist/director/producer] (*né* James Halleck Reid, b. St. Omer IN, 14 Apr 1860–22 May 1920 [60], West New York NJ). m. (1) Marcelle F.; (2) **Bertha** Westbrook (d. 1979). "Hal Reid," *Variety,* 28 May 1920 (d. 23 May). "Hal Reid Joins Universal," *MPW,* 4 Jan 1919, 59. "Obituary," *MPW,* 5 Jun 1920, 1302 (d. at West New York NJ, age 57). AMD, p. 289. AS, p. 911 (b. Red Bank NJ). BHD, p. 283 (b. Cedarville OH, 1862; d. NY NY). IFN, p. 248. Katz, p. 958. SD. Slide, p. 149 (under "Wallace Reid"). "Another Three-Reel Vitagraph Life Portrayal Coming," *MPW,* 24 Jun 1911, 1429. "Hal Reid Joins Reliance," *MPW,* 30 Mar 1912, 1180. "Hal Reid—Actor, Author, Director," *MPW,* 4 May 1912, 414. "Hal Reid Leaves Reliance," *MPW,* 8 Jun 1912, 911. "Hal Reid with Universal," *MPW,* 27 Jul 1912, 357 (conducted Universal's scenario department). "Universal Disclaims Connection with Hal Reid—Republican Film," *MPW,* 14 Oct 1916, 244.

Reid, Mrs. Hal [actress] (*née* Bertha Westbrook, d. 18 Jul 1979, New York NY). m. **Hal Reid** (d. 1920). BHD, p. 283.

Reid, James Halleck [actor/director/scenarist] (b. St. Omer IN, 14 Apr 1862–22 May 1920 [58], Red Bank NJ). BHD2, p. 220.

Reid, Jane [actress] (b. Chicago IL, 2 Jul 1909). AS, p. 911.

Reid, Leslie [actor] (b. Canada-d. 1917). BHD, p. 283. IFN, p. 248.

Reid, Marguerite [actress]. No data found. (Vitagraph.)

Reid, Mary [actress] (b. Gibraltar, 29 Aug 1895–18 Jul 1979 [83], New York NY; apoplexy). AS, p.911. BHD, p. 283. IFN, p. 248.

Reid, Peggie [actress]. *Fl.* 1913 (Majestic). "Peggie Reid; Majestic Leading Lady," *MPW,* 18 Jan 1913, 244 (photo only).

Reid, Wallace, Mrs *see* **Davenport, Dorothy**

Reid, Wallace (son of **Hal Reid**; father of **Billy** and **Wallace Reid, Jr.**) [stage/film actor/cameraman/director/ producer/scenarist] (*né* William Wallace Reid, b. St. Louis MO, 15 Apr 1891 [or New York NY, 15 Apr 1890]–18 Jan 1923 [32], Los Angeles CA; nervous breakdown after drug addiction). m. **Dorothy Davenport**, 13 Oct 1913, Christ Episcopal Church, LA CA (d. 1977). (Selig, 1910; Vitagraph; Universal; FP-L.) "Wallace Reid Dies in Fight on Drugs; Motion-Picture Star Expires at Hollywood After Nervous Breakdown; He Had Held Out Gamely; Told His Wife He Was Winning—Gained Screen Fame After Stage Career," *NYT,* 19 Jan 1923, 17:5. "Obituary," *MPW,* 17 Jan 1923, 316. "The Lesson of Reid's Death," *Variety,* 25 Jan 1923; "Reid Left $40,000; Waltman Joins Pal; Dead Screen Star's Estate Appraised—Claude Tynan Waltman Commits Suicide," *Variety,* 8 Feb 1923. AMD, p. 290. AS, p. 911. BHD, p. 283; BHD2, p. 220. IFN, p. 248 (b. 1891). Katz, pp. 958–59. Lowrey, p. 158. MSBB, p. 1028. Slide, p. 149. Truitt, p. 280. WWS, p. 13. "W. Wallace Reid Joins Producing Staff of American," *MPW,* 14 Dec 1912. "Universal Film Director Marries Leading Woman," *MPW,* 29 Nov 1913, 993. "Ince Seriously Injured...," *NYDM,* 28 Apr 1915, 22:3 (Reid, with Reliance-Majestic, "is out on bail while the authorities are investigating an auto crash which killed a man and injured two others." Reid crashed into the car, upsetting it, and asserted that "the accident was unavoidable, as the other machine shot in front of him."). W.E. Wing, "Along the Pacific Coast," *NYDM,* 19 May 1915, 24:1 (Reid "was exonerated by the justice court at the preliminary hearing and released from bond. The coroner's jury had already returned a verdict of unavoidable accident."). "W. Wallace Reid," *MPW,* 23 Oct 1915, 591. "Cleo Ridgley and Wallace Reid Co-Stars," *MPW,* 27 Nov 1915, 1666. Roberta Courtlandt, "Introducing Mr. and Mrs. Wallace Reid," *MPC,* Jul 1916, 30–32. "Wallace Reid Coming East," *MPW,* 1 Dec 1917, 1305. "Wallace Reid in New York," *MPW,* 29 Dec 1917, 1973. "Reid Company in Wreck," *MPW,* 15 Mar 1919, 1474. "Reid Signs New Contract with Famous Players-Lasky," *MPW,* 16 Aug 1919, 936. "Paramount Stars Lead in Rio de Janeiro Contest," *MPW,* 17 Apr 1920, 439 (most popular actor). "Wallace Reid Back in Hollywood," *MPW,* 29 May 1920, 1223. "Norma Talmadge and Wallace Reid Win National Star Popularity Contest," *MPW,* 19 Mar 1921, 247. "Wallace Reid Given Ovation at Opening of Vancouver Theater," *MPW,* 26 Mar 1921, 402. "Reid Does Not Think All-Star Casts Hurt Individual Player's Popularity," *MPW,* 30 Jul 1921, 495. "Paramount Stars Win in Contest," *MPW,* 29 Oct 1921, 1066 (favorite of Scandinavians). "Convention Wires Condolence," *MPW,* 3 Feb 1923, 434. Myrtle Gebhart, "Some Memories of Wallace Reid," *Picture-Play Magazine,* May 1923, 26–29, 90. Nina Goodelman, "A Memorial to Wallace Reid; The Proposed Bay in the Cathedral of St. John the Divine Will Keep Alive the Memory of One of the Most Universally Beloved of Cinema Stars," *Cinema Arts,* Oct 1927, 34. "The Wallace Reid Memorial," *Cinema Arts,* Dec 1927, 45. DeWitt Bodeen, "Wallace Reid...Was an Idol in the Age of Innocence with Feet of Clay," *FIR,* Apr 1966, 205–30. Sam Peeples, "The Forgotten Idol," *CFC,* 25 (Fall, 1969), 6–9, 51. Sam Peeples, "Wallace Reid: A Filmography," *CFC,* 26 (Winter, 1970), 12–13. George Katchmer, "Wallace Reid," *CI,* 227 (May 1994), 49:3–50:1.

Reid, Wallace, Jr. (son of **Wallace Reid**; grandson of **Hal Reid**) [actor] (*né* William Wallace Reid, Jr., b. Los Angeles CA, 18 Jun 1917–26 Feb 1990 [72?], Santa Monica CA). AS, p. 911. BHD1, p. 457.

Reiger, Marjorie [actress]. (Essanay.) No data found.

Reilley, Frank D. [actor] (d. 17 May 1919, Chicago IL). "Frank D. Reilley," *Variety,* 23 May 1919. AS, p. 811.

Reiman, Johannes [actor/director/scenarist] (*né* Eugene Johannes Reimann, b. Berlin, Germany, 31 May 1887–8 Oct 1959 [72], Konstanz, Germany). AS, p. 911.

Reimers, Georg [actor] (b. 1870–15 Apr 1936 [65?], Vienna, Austria). BHD, p. 283.

Reimers, Henry [cameraman] (b. 1873?–30 May 1916 [43], New York NY). AMD, p. 290. BHD2, p. 220. "Obituary," *MPW,* 17 Jun 1916, 2049 ("...not only the first cameraman, but one of the very best.").

Reinach, Edward [actor] (d. 2 Aug 1936, Beverly Hills CA). BHD, p. 283; BHD2, p. 220.

Reineck, Willard N. [actor] (b. 6 Nov 1891-Dec 1964 [73]).

Reiner, Fritz [actor] (b. Budapest, Hungary, 19 Dec 1888–15 Nov 1963 [74], New York NY). AS, p. 911.

Reiner, Robert [director] (b. 1872-Oct 1928 [56?]). BHD2, p. 220.

Reinert, Robert [scenarist/director/producer] (near Vienna, Austria, 22 Apr 1872–30 Aug 1928 [56], Berlin, Germany; heart attack). (Ufa.) FDY, p. 437 (Reinhart). Jan-Christpher Horak, "Robert Reinert: Film as Metaphor," *Griffithiana,* 60/61 (Oct 1997), 181–89 (includes filmography).

Reinhardt, F.L. [scenarist]. No data found. FDY, p. 437.

Reinhardt, John [actor/director/scenarist] (b. Vienna, Austria, 1901?–6 Aug 1953 [52], Berlin, Germany; heart attack). "John Reinhardt," *NYT,* 12 Aug 1953, 31:4. "John Reinhardt," *Variety,* 19 Aug 1953. AMD, p. 290. AS, p. 911. BHD1, p. 458; BHD2, p. 220. FDY, p. 437. IFN, p. 248. "John Reinhardt," *MPW,* 28 Aug 1915, 1458.

Reinhardt, Max (father of WB producer Wolfgang Reinhardt) [stage/film director/producer] (*né* Maximilian Goldmann, b. Baden, Austria, 8 Sep 1873–31 Oct 1943 [70], New York NY; pneumonia which followed paralysis). m. **Helene Thimig** (d. 1974; son, Wolfgang, 1910–1985). "Max Reinhardt," *Variety,* 152, 3 Nov 1943, 46:1. AMD, p. 290. AS, p. 911. BHD2, p. 220. Waldman, p. 242. "Engaged to Direct Marion Davies," *MPW,* 2 Feb 1924, 391. "Schenck Signs Reinhardt," *MPW,* 27 Aug 1927, 583.

Reinold, Bernard [actor] (*né* Major Bernard Adolph Reinold, b. 1860–24 Mar 1940 [80?], East Islip LI NY). AS, p. 912.

Reinwald, Hanni [actress] (b. Degerloch, Germany, 24 Aug 1903–1978 [75?]). BHD, p. 283.

Reinwald, Otto [actor] (b. Konstanz, Germany, 23 Aug 1889-Jun 1968 [79?]). BHD1, p. 458.

Reis, Irving [director/scenarist] (b. New York NY, 7 May 1906–3 Jul 1953 [47], Woodland Hills CA; cancer). m. Vanessa Idu. "Irving Reis Dies; Film Director, 47; Recently Finished 'Fourposter'—He Founded the Columbia Workshop Radio Program," *NYT,* 4 Jul 1953, 11:3 ("He was preparing to direct 'The Library,' which was to have marked the return to acting of Mary Pickford, when the project was canceled."). "Irving Reis," *Variety,* 8 Jul 1953. BHD2, p. 220. IFN, p. 248.

Reisner, Charles (Chuck) F[rancis] [scenarist/director/actor] (b. Minneapolis MN, 14 Mar 1887–24 Sep 1962 [75], La Jolla CA; heart attack). (Keystone; Vitagraph; Century; Chaplin; Universal; Metro; WB; Eagle-Lion.) "Charles F. Riesner, Movie Director, 75," *NYT,* 26 Sep 1962, 39:3. "Charles F. Riesner," *Variety,* 3 Oct 1962. AMD, p. 290. AS, p. 912; p. 922 (Charles F. Riesner). BHD, p. 283. FDY, p. 437. IFN, p. 251 (Riesner). JS, pp. 377–78 (co-directed *L'ultima cena,* Italy, 1949). Katz, pp. 960–61. Truitt, p. 280. "Charles Reisner Is Directing Bull Montana Film for Metro," *MPW,* 12 May 1923, 177. "Reisner to Direct Syd's Next," *MPW,* 31 Jul 1926, 279. "Reisner Wants a Larger Check," 14 May 1927, 98. "Reisner May Leave Warners," *MPW,* 21 May 1927, 181. "Chuck Reisner Continues with Bussr Keaton," *MPW,* 2 Jul 1927, 29.

Reiter, Carlo [actor] (b. Naples, Italy). JS, p. 373 (in Italian silents from 1923).

Reithe, Aloise D. [actor/director] (b. Los Angeles CA, 1890?–5 Sep 1943 [53], Monte Nido CA). "Aloise D. Reithe," *NYT,* 7 Sep 1943, 23:5. AS, p. 912. BHD, p. 283 (d. LA CA). IFN, p. 248.

Réjane, Gabrielle [actress] (*née* Gabrielle Charlotte Réju, b. Paris, France, 6 Jun 1856–14 Jun 1920 [64], Paris, France; heart attack). m. Paul Porel (d. 1917). "Mme. Rejane," *Variety,* 18 Jun 1920. AMD, p. 290. AS, p. 912. BHD, p. 283 (b. 1857). IFN, p. 248. SD. Truitt, p. 280. "Bernhardt and Réjane," *MPW,* 10 Feb 1912, 468. W. Steven Bush, "Bernhardt and Réjane in Pictures," *MPW,* 2 Mar 1912, 760.

Relander, Sven Runar Alarik [actor] (b. Helsinki, Finland, 24 May 1897–13 Aug 1956 [50], Helsinki, Finland). AS, p. 912.

Relkin, Edwin A. [actor/producer] (b. 1881–11 Oct 1952 [71?], New York NY). AS, p. 912.

Relly, Gina [actress] (b. Lyon, France, 1897). AMD, p. 290. AS, p. 912. "Gina Relly Sails for France," *MPW,* 14 Aug 1920, 898. "Gina Relly Makes American Screen Debut in Fox Film," *MPW,* 20 Nov 1920, 357 (*The Face at Your Window*).

Relph, George (father of Michael Relph) [stage/film actor] (b. Cullercoats, England, 27 Jan 1888–24 Apr 1960 [72], London, England). m. (1) Deborah Hanson; (2) **Mercia Swinburne**. (London stage debut, 1909.) "George Relph, Actor, Dies at 72; Noted for Shakespearean Roles," *NYT,* 25 Apr 1960, 29:2. "George Relph," *Variety,* 27 Apr 1960 (in Hollywood silents). AS, p. 912. BHD1, p. 458. IFN, p. 248. SD.

Remauge, Adrien [producer] (b. Trilport, France, 25 May 1890 [extrait de naissance no. 22]-13 Jul 1966 [76], Cabourg, France). AS, p. 912.

Remley, Ralph McHugh [actor] (b. Cincinnati OH, 24 May 1885–26 May 1939 [54], Sawtelle CA). "Ralph M'Hugh Remley; Character Actor in Films Was Captain in France During War," *NYT,* 28 May 1939, III, 6:5. "Ralph McHugh Remley," *Variety,* 31 May 1939. AS, p. 913 (d. LA CA). IFN, p. 248.

Remongin, Emile Charles Marie [actor] (b. Nantes, France, 27 Feb 1876 [extrait de naissance no. 102/1876]-15 Dec 1962 [86], Draveil, France). AS, p. 913.

Remont, Pierre [director/producer/scenarist] (b. Paris, France, 23 Jan 1897). AS, p. 913.

Remus, Romola [actress] (d. 17 Feb 1987, Chicago IL). BHD, p. 283.

Remy, Constant [actor/director] (b. Paris, France, 20 May 1882–16 Aug 1957 [75], Cannes, France [extrait de décès no. 432/1957]). AS, p. 913. BHD2, p. 220 (b. 1884).

Remy, Dick, Sr. [actor/director] (b. 1873?–1 Jun 1947 [74?], Los Angeles CA; heart attack). AS, p. 913. BHD, p. 283; BHD2, p. 220. Truitt, p. 280.

Ren, Pengnian [director] (b. Shanghai, China, 1892–1968 [76?], Hong Kong, China). AS, p. 913.

Renaldo, Duncan [actor] (*né* Renault Renaldo Duncan, b. Valladolid, Spain, 23 Apr 1904–3 Sep 1980 [76], Santa Monica CA; lung cancer). m. Audrey. (MGM.) "Duncan Renaldo, Movie Actor, Dies; Played in 'Bridge of San Luis Rey' and 'Trader Horn'—Was the Cisco Kid on TV," *NYT,* 4 Sep 1980, D19:4 (b. Rumania). "Duncan Renaldo," *Variety,* 10 Sep 1980. AS, p. 913 (b. Camden NY; d. Goleta CA). BHD, p. 283 (d. Santa Barbara CA). Katz, p. 962. SD. "Buck Rainey's Filmographies; Duncan Renaldo—Part I," *CI,* 178 (Apr 1990), C5-C7, C9; Part II, *CI,* 179 (May 1990), 54–55.

Renard, Ervin [or **Irvin**] [actor]. No data found. (Began 1925?) George Katchmer, "Remembering the Great Silents," *CI,* 211 (Jan 1992), 44–45.

Renaud, Madeline [actress] (*née* Lucie Madeleine Renaud, b. Paris, France, 21 Feb 1900–23 Sep 1994 [94], Neuilly-sur-Seine, France [extrait de décès no. 753/1994]). m. Jean-Louis Barrault (d. 1994). AS, p. 913. BHD1, p. 458.

Renavent, George [actor] (*né* Georges de Cheux, b. Paris, France, 23 Apr 1894–2 Jan 1969 [74], Guadalajara, Mexico). m. **Selena Royle** (d. 1983). AS, p. 913. BHD1, p. 458 (b. 1893). IFN, p. 248. Truitt, p. 281.

Renfro, Rennie [actor/stuntman] (*né* James Leige Renfro, b. Denison TX, 30 Sep 1892–2 Mar 1962 [69], Redding CA; heart attack). AS, p. 913. BHD1, p. 458. IFN, p. 248.

Renick, Ruth [stage/film actress] (b. Galveston TX, 23 Sep 1892–7 May 1984 [91], Los Angeles CA). (Began late 'teens.) "Ruth Renick," *Variety,* 20 Jul 1984 ("silent screen actress"). AMD, p. 290. AS, p. 913. BHD1, p. 459 (b. 1893). "Ruth Renick Plays a Leading Role in 'What's a Wife Worth?,'" *MPW,* 2 Apr 1921, 503. "When Life Was Strenuous," *MPS,* 13 May 1921, 24–25 (age given as 20; graduated from Phoenix [AZ] High School. Renick was present in Galveston TX during the disaster of 1907, where "all we had to do was to hurry away out of town," but she had to endure the hardships of filming *The Golden Snare* "in the frigid heart of the Canadian Rockies.").

Renieri, Bianca [actress in Italian silents]. No data found.

Rennahan, Ray[mond] [cinematographer] (b. Las Vegas NM, 1 May 1896–19 May 1980 [84], Tarzana CA). (National Film Corp., 1916; Sennett; Christie; winner of two Academy Awards.) "Ray Rennahan," *Variety,* 28 May 1980 (photographed *The Toll of the Sea* [1921]). AS, p. 914. BHD2, p. 221. Katz, p. 962.

Rennie, James Urban [actor] (b. Toronto, Canada, 18 Apr 1889 [birth certificate #044927, no. 2530]–31 Jul 1965 [76], New York NY [Death Certificate Index No. 16032]). m. **Dorothy Gish**, 26 Dec 1920, CT?—div. 1935 (d. 1969); Sara Eldon McConnell. "James Rennie, Actor, Dies at 76; Long a Broadway Leading Man," *NYT,* 1 Aug 1965, 77:2. "James Rennie," *Variety,* 4 Aug 1965. AS, p. 914 (b. 1890). BHD1, p. 459 (b. 1890). IFN, p. 248 (b. 1890). Truitt, p. 281.

Renoir, Jean (son of Impressionist painter Pierre-Auguste Renoir [d. 1919]; brother of Charles and **Pierre** and uncle of Claude Renoir [1913–1993) [actor/scenarist/director] (b. Montmartre, Paris, France, 15 Sep 1894–12 Feb 1979 [84], Los Angeles CA; heart attack). m. (1) Catherine Hessling (*née* French actress Andrée Madeleine Heuschling [1900–1979]), 1920; (2) Dido Freire, 1944. *My Life and My Films* (1974); Ronald Bergan, *Jean Renoir; Projections of Paradise* (NY: The Overlook Press, 1994). Paul Montgomery, "Jean Renoir, Director of 'Grand Illusion' Film Dies," *NYT,* 14 Feb 1979, D19:1. Todd McCarthy, "Jean Renoir, a Colossus Among Cinema Directors, Dies at 84," *Variety,* 21 Feb 1979. (Prix Louis Delluc in 1937.) AS, p. 914. BHD, p. 459 (d. Beverly Hills CA); BHD2, p. 221. IFN, p. 248. JS, p. 374 (made films in Italy in 1953 and 1956).

Renoir, Pierre (brother of Claude and **Jean Renoir** and father of Claude Renoir [1913–1993]) [actor] (b. Paris, France, 21 Mar 1885–11 Mar 1952 [66], Paris, France; uremic poisoning [extrait de décès no. SN/9/1952]). m. **Vera Sergine** (d. 1946). AS, p. 914. BHD1, p. 459.

Requa, Charles [actor] (b. New York NY, 20 Mar 1892–11 Dec 1967 [75], Los Angeles Co. CA). AS, p. 914. BHD1, p. 459. IFN, p. 248.

Rescher, Jay [cameraman] (b. Bayonne NJ, 1 Jan 1893–11 Aug 1973 [80], Ft. Lauderdale FL). m. Jean Tolley, 1923. "Jay Rescher," *Variety,* 22 Aug 1973. BHD2, p. 221.

Reticker, Hugh [director]. No data found. AMD, p. 290. "Four Directors for Premier Program," *MPW,* 18 Dec 1915, 2160.

Reumert, Elith (b. Copenhagen, Denmark, 9 Jan 1855–24 Jun 1934 [79], Copenhagen, Denmark). BHD1, p. 615.

Reumert, Poul [actor] (b. Copenhagen, Denmark, 26 Mar 1883–19 Apr 1968 [75], Copenhagen, Denmark). BHD1, p. 615.

Reuter-Eichberg, Adele [actress] (b. Germany-d. 4 Oct 1928). BHD, p. 284.

Reuver, Germaine Jeanne Françoise [actress] (b. Paris, France, 20 Nov 1885 [extrait de naissance no. 5259]-22 Jul 1959 [73], Sandillon, France). AS, p. 914.

Reval, Else [actress] (*née* Else Langer, b. Berlin, Germany, 14 Jun 1893–25 Jan 1978 [84], Berlin, Germany). AS, p. 914.

Revalles, Flora [dancer/actress]. No data found. AMD, p. 290. "Mme. Flora Revalles Signs to Play in 'Earthbound,'" *MPW,* 27 Dec 1919, 1140.

Revel, Maurice [actor] (b. 7 Mar 1875). AS, p. 915.

Revel, Mollie [actress] (b. 1848–31 Dec 1932 [84]). BHD, p. 284. IFN, p. 249.

Revell, Nellie [publicist/agent/title writer] (b. 1873?–11 Aug 1958 [85], New York NY). m. (2) Joe Revell; (3) Arthur J. Kellar. "Nellie Revell," *Variety,* 20 Aug 1958. AMD, p. 290. "Nellie Revell Titling Films," *MPW,* 2 Jul 1927, 34.

Revelle, Hamilton [stage/film actor/photographer] (*né* Arthur Hamilton Engstrom, b. Gibraltar, Spain, 31 May 1872–11 Apr 1958 [85], Nice, France). "Hamilton Revelle," *NYT,* 28 May 1958, 31:5 (stage matinee idol). (Ambrosio; Metro.) AMD, p. 290. AS, p. 915 (d. 11 Aug). BHD, p. 284. IFN, p. 249. SD, p. 1056. "Metro Signs Three New Stars," *NYDM,* 22 Sep 1915, 35:1 (Martha Hedmann, Lionel Barrymore, and Revelle). "Personal; Revelle," *NYDM,* 6 Oct 1915, 5:3 (American film debut: *DuBarry*). "Personal; Revelle," *NYDM,* 13 Nov 1915, 5:2 (on cover as "The Latest Metro Star"). "Revelle's Photo Exhibition," *NYDM,* 27 Nov 1915, 35:2 (on the stage in *Fair and Warmer,* began work on a Rolfe-Metro unnamed feature after signing to make 5 films. An expert photographer, he was to exhibit 60 of his prints at the Allison & Hadaway art gallery on Fifth Avenue during the frist two weeks in December. "He has received five gold medals for exhibitions he gave in Paris and London. Among the prints he will show are studies of New York streets and many artisitc prints made in Italy, where he was starring in the big Ambrosio productions until Italy went to war."). "Hamilton Revelle," *MPW,* 29 Dec 1917, 1933. "Hamilton Revelle," *MPW,* 9 Feb 1918, 832.

Revier, Dorothy, "Queen of Poverty Row" [actress: Wampas Star, 1925] (*née* Doris Valegra, b. San Francisco CA, 18 Apr 1904–19 Nov 1993 [89], Los Angeles CA). m. (1) **Harry J. Revier**—div. 1926 (d. 1957); (2) Charles S. Johnson, 1929; (3) William Pelayo, 1950–64; (4) Charles S. Johnson (d. 1976). (Film debut: *The Broadway Madonna,* 1922). "Dorothy Revier Dead; Silent-Film Actress, 89," *NYT,* 25 Nov 1993, D19:3. "Dorothy Revier to Rewed; Reported Engaged to C.S. Johnson—Both Await Divorces," *NYT,* 24 Jul 1927, 24:5. "Dorothy Revier," *Variety,* 13 Dec 1993, p. 88:4. AMD, p. 290. AS, p. 915. BHD1, p. 459. BR, pp. 208–11 (b. Oakland CA). FSS, p. 246. Katz, pp. 967–68 (*née* Doris Velegra). "Columbia Signs Wampas Star; Miss Revier the Lucky Girl," *MPW,* 4 Apr 1925, 473. "Beautiful Dorothy Revier's First Waldorf Production," *MPW,*18 Jul 1925, 310. Gladys Hall, "She Has Both Feet on the Ground; Dorothy Revier Doesn't Know What It's All About, But She's Learning Fast Enough," *MPC,* May 1928, 42, 89. Michael G. Ankerich, "Dorothy Revier; The Queen of Poverty Row," *CI,* 171 (Sep 1989), 7–8. Henry R. Davis, "The Films of Dorothy Revier," *CI,* 173 (Nov 1989), 41, 58. Chapter 21, "Dorothy Revier," *BS,* pp. 277–88 (includes filmography).

Revier, Harry J. [director] (b. Philadelphia PA, 16 Mar 1889–13 Aug 1957 [68], Winter Park FL). m. **Dorothy**—div. 1926 (d. 1993). AS, p. 915. BHD2, p. 221. Katz, p. 968 (began in Italy).

Reville, Alma (mother of Patricia Hitchcock) [film cutter/continuity girl/scenarist] (b. London, England, 13 Aug 1899–6 Jul 1982 [82], Bel Air CA). m. **Alfred Hitchcock**, 1926 (d. 1980). (Film cutter, London Film Cutter, 1915; FP-L, London; UFA, Berlin.) "ALma Reville Hitchcock," *Variety,* 21 Jul 1982, p. 78:3 (born one day after Hitchcock). AS, p. 915 (b. 14 Aug). BHD, p. 284; BHD2, p. 221 (b. 14 Aug). FDY, p. 437.

Revol, Max [actor] (*né* Maxime Louis Revol, b. Grenoble, France, 21 Aug 1894 [extrait de naissance no. 456]-23 Dec 1967 [73], Paris, France). AS, p. 915.

Revueltas, Sylvestra [composer] (b. 1900–5 Oct 1940 [40?], Mexico City, Mexico). BHD2, p. 221.

Revy, Richard Aton Robert Felix [actor/director] (b. Foherczeglack, Hungary, 13 Sep 1885–22 Dec 1965 [80], Los Angeles CA). AS, p. 915.

Rex, "King of the Wild Horses" (b. so. CO). Mated with Lady (from Kentucky). Trained by Rex Jackson. Tom Reeves, "Rex, King of Wild Horses," *MPC,* Oct 1924, 62, 83–84 (Chick Morrison died before publication of this article). Tom Reeves, "Rex and Lady; A Love Story," *MW,* 25 Jul 1925, 21, 44. Hal K. Wells, "The Story of Rex," *MPC,* Jul 1926, 28–29, 65 (appeared in *Rex, King of the Wild Horses; Black Cyclone; The Devil Horse*).

Rex, Eugen [actor/director] (b. Berlin, Germany, 8 Jul 1884–21 Feb 1943 [58], Berlin, Germany). AS, p. 915. BHD1, p. 459.

Rex, Will [actor/writer/director] (b. 1892-d. 12 May 1916 [24?]; septic spinal meningitis). AMD, p. 291. BHD, p. 284. "Obituary," *MPW,* 27 May 1916, 1520.

Rey, Florian [actor/director] (*né* Antonio Martinez del Castillo, b. Saragossa, Spain, 25 Jan 1894–11 Apr 1962 [68], Alicante, Spain). AS, p. 915. BHD2, p. 221.

Rey, Harry [actor] (b. 1878-Jul 1910 [32?]; suicide [neurasthenia]). (Pathé; Gaumont.) "Harry Rey," *Variety,* 16 Jul 1910, 10:4. BHD, p. 284.

Rey, Roberto [actor] (*né* Roberto Colas Iglesias, b. Valparaiso, Chile, 15 Feb 1905–30 May 1972 [68], Madrid, Spain). (Spain, 1924.) AS, p. 915. IFN, p. 249. JS, p. 375 (in Spain since 1921; made films in Italy in 1939 and 1940). Waldman, p. 245.

Reyher, Ferdinand [scenarist] (b. Philadelphia PA, 26 Jul 1891-Oct 1967 [76], Cambridge MA). BHD2, p. 221.

Reynaud, Emile [director/inventor] (*né* Charles Emile Reynaud, b. Montreul-sous-Bois, France, 8 Dec 1844–9 Jan 1918 [73], Ivry-sur-Seine, France [extrait de décès no. 43/1918]). AS, pp. 915–16.

Reynaud, Jean-Charles [scenarist/author] (*né* Jules Jean Charles Reynaud, b. Lyon, France, 18 Nov 1893 [extrait de naissance no. 1739]-15 Oct 1957 [63], Nice, France). AS, p. 916.

Reynolds, Abe [actor] (b. 1884–25 Dec 1955 [71], Los Angeles CA). AS, p. 916.

Reynolds, Adeline De Walt [actress] (b. Benton Co. IA, 19 Sep 1862–13 Aug 1961 [98], Los Angeles CA). AS, p. 916.

Reynolds, Ben[jamin F.] [cameraman] (b. 1887–28 Jan 1950 [62?], Los Angeles CA). m. Sarah (d. 1967). (Universal; MGM; FP-L; WB; Paramount.) "Jersey Woman [Mrs. Sarah Reynolds] Dies at 104," *NYT,* 11 Feb 1967, 29:3 (b. 1863?–8 Feb 1967 [104], Madison NJ). AMD, p. 291. AS, p. 916 (listed as an actor). BHD2, p. 221 (b. 1891-d. 14 Feb 1968). FDY, p. 467. Katz, p. 969. "Ben Reynolds with M-G-M," *MPW,* 9 Jan 1926, 159. "Cameraman Renews with M-G-M," *MPW,* 31 Jul 1926, 278.

Reynolds, Carrie [stage/film actress] (b. Philadelphia PA). (Lubin.) "Carrie Reynolds in Movies," *NYDM,* 20 Nov 1915, 30:4 (light opera and musical comedy prima donna soubrette. Supporting Billy Reeves and David L. Don. "Miss Reynolds is one of the few blondes who register faithfully upon the screen, which is a valuable asset to those pictures requiring the services of a blonde.").

Reynolds, E. Vivian [actor] (b. London, England, 24 Jun 1866–13 May 1952 [85]). BHD1, p. 460. IFN, p. 249.

Reynolds, Edna [actress] (b. New York NY, 10 Feb 1888). BHD, p. 284.

Reynolds, Genevieve [actress] (b. Ireland, 1852–15 Oct 1919 [67?], Christchurch, New Zealand). AS, p. 916.

Reynolds, Genevieve [actress/singer] (b. New York NY-d. 25 Jan 1922, Chicago IL). "Genevieve Reynolds," *Variety,* 3 Feb 1922. BHD, p. 284.

Reynolds, Harry [actor] (b. 1896?–21 Sep 1972 [76], Los Angeles CA; heart attack). AS, p. 916. IFN, p. 249.

Reynolds, Harrington [actor] (b. Ireland, 1852?–15 Oct 1919 [67], Christchurch, New Zealand). m. Blanche Douglas. (Ince.) "Harrington Reynolds," *Variety,* 2 Jan 1920. BHD, p. 284. W.E. Eing, "...Gossipy Coast Notes," *NYDM,* 28 Jan 1914, 35:1.

Reynolds, Harrington "Harry" [film editor] (*né* Harrington Ford Reynolds, b. CA, 4 Apr 1901–22 Dec 1971 [70], Los Angeles CA; emphysema). "Harrington Reynolds," *Variety,* 29 Dec 1971 (edited *Ben-Hur,* 1925). BHD2, p. 221.

Reynolds, Lake [actor] (b. 1888–9 Feb 1952 [63?], Los Angeles CA). AS, p. 916.

Reynolds, Lynn F. [director/scenarist] (b. Harlan IA, 7 May 1891–25 Feb 1927 [35], Los Angeles CA; suicide by shooting). m. **Kathleen O'-Connor**, 1921 (d. 1957). (Selig, 1910; Fox.) "L.A. Guessing on Reynolds Suicide; Director Threatened Wife and Guests Before Turning Gun on Himself," *Variety,* 2 Mar 1927 (age 36). AMD, p. 291. AS, p. 916. BHD, p. 284; BHD2, p. 221 (b. Harlem IA). FDY, p. 437. IFN, p. 249. "A New Arrival in Filmdom," *MPW,* 22 Dec 1917, 1783 (birth of son). "Reynolds Talks of Mix, Range and Screen Cowboy," *MPW,* 14 Sep 1918, 1554. "Lynn Reynolds Back with Fox; Now Making Tom Mix Feature," *MPW,* 3 Jul 1920, 116. "Another Filmland Wedding," *MPW,* 25 Jun 1921, 807. "Reynolds to Direct for FIrst National," *MPW,* 5 May 1923, 75. "Able Directors Behind FIrst National Pictures," *MPW,* 9 Jun 1923, 510. "Obituary," *MPW,* 5 Mar 1927, 31. "Reynolds to Direct 'Show Boat'; Irvin Willat to Do 'The Big Gun,'" *MPW,* 12 Mar 1927,

108. Dorothy Donnell, "Are the Movies to Blame for Hollywood Suicides?," *MPC*, Oct 1927,18–19, 70 ("In the last three months more than thirty suicides, or attempted suicides have taken place among movie people.").

Reynolds, Marjorie [film/TV actress] (aka Marjorie Moore, *née* Marjorie Goodspeed, b. Buhl ID, 12 Aug 1917–1 Feb 1997 [79], Manhattan Beach CA; congestive heart failure). m. (1) scenarist Jack Reynolds, 1936–53; (2) film editor John M. Haffen (d. 1985). (*Scaramouche*, 1923; last film: *The Silent Witness*, 1962; Paramount.) "Marjorie Reynolds, 79, Actress in Classic Films and on Television," *NYT*, 16 Feb 1977, 51. Doug Galloway, "Marjorie Reynolds," *Variety*, 10 Feb 1997, p. 70:4 (b. 1921). Myrna Oliver, "Marjorie Reynolds; 'Holiday Inn' love interest, wife in 'Riley' [1953–58]," *Pittsburgh Post-Gazette*, 14 Feb 1997, D-6:3. AS, p. 916. BHD1, p. 460 (d. Redondo Beach CA). BR, pp. 411–13. Katz, p. 970. Buck Rainey, "Marjorie Reynolds; Value Received for Your Saturday Matinee Quarter," *CI*, 139 (Jan 1987), 23–26. Laura Wagner, "Marjorie Reynolds: Sassy and Smart," *CI*, 263 (May 1997), 6 (b. 1916).

Reynolds, Noah [actor] (b. 1908?–19 Sep 1948 [40], No. Philadelphia PA). (Lubin; McCardy Film Co.) "Noah Reynolds," *NYT*, 22 Sep 1948, 31:2 (began 1907?). AS, p. 916. BHD, p. 284. IFN, p. 249. Truitt, p. 281.

Reynolds, Robert Rice [actor] (b. Asheville NC, 18 Jun 1884–13 Feb 1963 [78], Asheville NC). Married 5 times. "Robert R. Reynolds Dies; In Senate for 12 Years [1933–45]," *NYT*, 15 Feb 1963, 9:8. AS, p. 916. BHD, p. 284. Billy H. Doyle, "Lost Players," *CI*, 137 (Nov 1986), C24.

Reynolds, Steve [writer]. No data found. AMD, p. 291. "Reynolds, Globe Trotting Author, to Write for Fox," *MPW*, 20 Mar 1920, 1985.

Reynolds, Tom [actor] (b. London, England, 9 Aug 1866–25 Jul 1942 [75]). BHD1, p. 460. IFN, p. 249.

Reynolds, Vera Norma [actress: Sennett Bathing Beauty/Wampas Star, 1926] (b. Richmond VA, 25 Nov 1899–22 Apr 1962 [62], Woodland Hills CA). m. Carl T. Montgomery; **Robert Ellis** (d. 1935). (Christie; Sennett.) "Vera Reynolds," *Variety*, 9 May 1962. AMD, p. 291. AS, p. 916. BHD1, p. 460. FFF, p. 169. FSS, p. 247. IFN, p. 249. Katz, p. 970. MH, p. 134. 1921 Directory, p. 249. Truitt, p. 281. "Vera Reynolds Another DeMille Screen Find," *MPW*, 7 Jun 1924, 562. "Vera Reynolds," *MPW*, 27 Mar 1926, 260. "Vera Reynolds Wins New DeMille Contract," *MPW*, 31 Jul 1926, 3. "Vera Reynolds," *MPW*, 11 Jun 1927, 408.

Reynolds, Wilson [actor/director] (b. Louisville KY, 1870?–10 Apr 1938 [68], Ossining NY). m. Nellie Mark (d. 1912). "Wilson Reynolds, 68, Actor and Director; Artist Who Appeared in Many Broadway Plays Dies," *NYT*, 12 Apr 1938, 23:3. "Wilson Reynolds," *Variety*, 13 Apr 1938. AS, p. 916. BHD, p. 284. SD.

Rhein-Schrading, Otto Franz [actor] (d. 30 Apr 1952, Milwaukee WI). BHD, p. 284. IFN, p. 249.

Rhodes, Billie, "The Nestor Girl" [stage/film actress] (*née* Levita Axelrod, b. San Francisco CA, 15 Aug 1894–12 Mar 1988 [93], Los Angeles CA). m. **William "Smiling Bill" Parsons**, 1919 (d. 1919); **G. Pat Collins** (d. 1959). (Film debut: *The Perils of the Sea*, Kalem, 1913; Universal; Strand-Mutual; Christie; National.) "Billie Rhodes," *Variety*, 18 May 1988 (*née* Levita Axelrod). AMD, p. 291. AS, p. 917. BHD, p. 284. Katz, p. 970. "Billie Rhodes," *MPW*, 21 Apr 1917, 456. Betty Shannon, "The Devil's Little Daughter," *Photoplay*, Jul 1917, 97 (5 ft. tall, 106 lbs.). Elizabeth Peltret, "Billie Rhodes—Circus Girl," *MPC*, Jan 1919, 26–27, 74 ("In the springtime of her youth Billie Rhodes has deserted two-reel comedies and become a star."). "Smiling Billy a Benedict," *MPW*, 22 Mar 1919, 1628. Grace Kingsley, "Flashes; Billie Rhodes to Resume," *LA Times*, 11 Mar 1920, III. p. 4 (in retirement since the death of her husband, Rhodes "is shortly to enter the picture field again."). "Billie Rhodes to Be Featured in Full Length Specials," *MPW*, 21 Jul 1923, 238. Stuart Oderman, "Billie Rhodes: The Nestor Girl Re-Visited," *CFC*, 53 (Winter, 1976), 6–7; II, 54 (Spring, 1977), 17–20.

Rhodes, Little Billy [actor] (b. IL, 1 Feb 1894–24 Jul 1967 [73], Los Angeles CA). AS, p. 917. BHD1, p. 461.

Rhodes, Eugene M[anlove] [rancher/writer] (b. Tucumseh NB, 19 Jan 1869–27 Jun 1934 [65], Pacific Beach CA). m. May Louise Davison, 9 Aug 1899, Apalachin NY. May Louise Davison, *The Hired Man on Horseback* (1938). "Eugene M. Rhodes," *Variety*, 3 Jul 1934. "Mrs. Eugene M. Rhodes," *NYT*, 21 Mar 1957, 31:4 (b. 1872?–20 Mar 1957 [85], Apalachian NY). AMD, p. 291. "Famous Authors with Universal," *MPW*, 5 Sep 1914, 1356. "Rhodes, Eugene Manlove," *The National Cyclopœdia of American Biography*, Vol. 45 (1967), p. 433.

Rhodes, Percy W. [actor] (b. 1871-Nov 1956 [85?]). BHD, p. 284.

Rhudin, Fridolf [actor] (b. Munkfors, Sweden, 10 Oct 1895–6 Mar 1935 [40], Stockholm, Sweden; tumor). AS, p. 917. BHD1, p. 461. IFN, p. 249.

Rhys, Noel [scenarist]. No data found. FDY, p. 437.

Rial, Louise [actress] (*née?*, b. 1850?–9 Aug 1940 [90], New York NY). m. Jay Rial. "Louise Rial; Actress, 90, Made Debut in 'Uncle Tom's Cabin' in 1878," *NYT*, 11 Aug 1940, 31:2 (age 91). "Louise Rial," *Variety*, 14 Aug 1940. AS, p. 917. BHD, p. 284.

Riaume, Helen [actress] (b. KY-d. 1 Nov 1924, Cincinnati OH). AS, p. 917. BHD1, p. 616. IFN, p. 249.

Ribemont-Dessaignes, Georges Victor Jules Léon [actor/scenarist] (b. Montpellier, France, 19 Jun 1884 [extrait de naissance no. 633]–9 Jul 1974 [90], Saint-Jeannet, France). AS, p. 917.

Ricci, Giorgio [cinematographer/director] (b. Rome, Italy). JS, p. 376 (in Italian silents from 1913).

Riccioni, Enzo [director of photography] (b. Italy). JS, pp. 376–77 (in Italian and French silents from 1918).

Rice, Andy [burlesque/vaudeville actor/gag man/vaudeville sketch author/scenarist] (b. 1880?–17 Feb 1963 [82], Dallas TX). "Andy Rice," *Variety*, 230, 27 Feb 1963, pp. 60:3, 71:1. AS, p. 918. BHD2, p. 222. FDY, p. 437.

Rice, Burton [artist]. No data found. AMD, p. 291. "Burton Rice Going Abroad," *MPW*, 23 Dec 1916, 1808. "Burton Rice Returns," *MPW*, 25 Aug 1917, 1198. "Posters for Rialto Film Designed by Burton Rice," *MPW*, 8 Jun 1918, 1456.

Rice, Edward E[verett] [producer] (b. Brighton MA, 21 Dec 1847–16 Nov 1924 [76], New York NY). m. Clara E. Rich. "Edward E. Rice, Composer, Is Dead; Producer of 'Evangeline' and '1492' Dies in the Polyclinic Hospital at 75 Years; 'The Father of Burlesque'; His Productions of Long Ago Include 'Adonis,' 'Hiawatha' and 'Conrad the Corsair,'" *NYT*, 17 Nov 1924, 19:5. "Edward E. Rice Buried; Prominent Thespians at Rites for Pioneer Producer in Little Church," *NYT*, 20 Nov 1924, 23:3. "Edward R. Rice," *Variety*, 19 Nov 1924. AMD, p. 291. AS, p. 918 (b. 1849; d. 19 Nov). SD, p. 1053 (b. 1848). *A Genealogical Register of Edmund Rice Descendants* (Tuttle, 1970), p. 991. "Edward E. Rice to Film Former Successes," *MPW*, 27 Sep 1913, 1394.

Rice, Emmit B. [actor/executive] (b. 1884–23 Mar 1939 [54?], Los Angeles CA). AS, p. 918. BHD, p. 284; BHD2, p. 222. IFN, p. 250.

Rice, Fanny [stage/film actress] (b. Lowell MA, 4 Feb 1859–10 Jul 1936 [77], Bronx NY). m. G.W. Purdy. "Fanny Rice," *Variety*, 15 Jul 1936. AMD, p. 291. AS, p. 918. BHD, p. 284. SD, p. 1053 (b. 1863). "Fanny RIce, Comedienne, Signed for Blackton Film," *MPW*, 24 May 1919, 1160.

Rice, Frank Thomas [actor] (b. Muskegon MI, 13 May 1892–9 Jan 1936 [43], Los Angeles CA; neuritis and hepatitis). AS, p. 918. BHD1, p. 461. IFN, p. 250. SD.

Rice, Grantland (father of Florence Rice) [writer] (*né* Henry Grantland Rice, b. Murfreesboro TN, 1 Nov 1880–13 Jul 1954 [73?], New York NY; cerebral hemorrhage). m. Katherine Hollis, 1906 (d. 1966; daughter Florence, 1907–1974). "Grantland Rice Dies at Age of 73; Veteran Sports Writer and Authority Suffers Stroke While Working in Office; Popular for His Verse; Author of Sportlight Column and Books on Golf Selected All-America Football Teams," *NYT*, 14 Jul 1954, 27:1. "Sports Notables Attend Rice Rites; Heroes of 'Golden Age' Are Among 400 to Pay Tribute to 'Dean' of Writers in Field," *NYT*, 17 Jul 1954, 13:4. AMD, p. 291. AS, p. 918. BHD1, p. 461; BHD2, p. 222. Truitt, p. 282. Paul Thompson, "Grantland Rice Puts the Spotlight on Every Light-O-Sport," *MPC*, Jun 1917, 24–25, 67. "Grantland Rice Making Series of One-Reel Sport Films for Pathé," *MPW*, 10 Nov 1923, 256.

Rice, Harry [publicist]. No data found. AMD, p. 291. "Harry Rice, Publicity Man of Universal, Hurt in Auto Crash," *MPW*, 30 Aug 1919, 1287–88. "Harry Rice Made 'Big U' Publicity Director," *MPW*, 8 Nov 1919, 238. "New York Mournes but Harry Rice Does Not," *MPW*, 14 Feb 1920, 1083 (resigned from Universal). "Mayer Succeeds Rice as Universal's Publicity Head," *MPW*, 21 Feb 1920, 1230.

Rice, Herbert [midget actor] (b. 1888-Jul 1938 [50?], Chicago IL). (Headline Amusement Co.) BHD, p. 284. "First Headline Comedy [Pee-Wee's Courtship]," *NYDM*, 23 Jun 1915, 21:2.

Rice, Ivy [actress] (b. 1898–8 Nov 1962 [64?], Los Angeles CA). BHD, p. 284.

Rice, Jack Clifford [actor] (b. Grand Rapids MI, 14 May 1893–14 Dec 1968 [75], Woodland Hills CA). AS, p. 918.

Rice, John C. [stage/film actor] (*né* John C. Hilburg, b. Sullivan County NY, 7 Apr 1858–5 Jun 1915 [57], Hotel Majestic, Philadelphia PA; Bright's disease). m. Sally Cohen. (Edison.) "John C. Rice Dead; Widely Known Comedian Expires While Preparing to Pose in a Movie," *NYT*, 6 Jun

1915. "John C. Rice," *Variety,* 11 Jun 1915. AS, p. 918. BHD, p. 285. IFN, p. 250. SD. Spehr, p. 162. "In the Vaudeville Spotlight," *NYDM,* 9 Jun 1915 (in Philadelphia to appear with Marie Dressler in a Lubin comedy).

Rice, Marion [actress]. No data found. AMD, p. 291. "Yoiung Chicago Beauty Signed by Universal," *MPW,* 15 May 1926, 239.

Rice, Roy Hiram [actor] (*né* Roy S. Munroe, b. New York NY, 4 Apr 1887–29 Dec 1966 [79], Visalia CA). m. (1) Mary Werner (d. 1957). "Roy Rice," *Variety,* 18 Jan 1967. AS, p. 918. AS, p. 918. BHD1, p. 461. IFN, p. 250.

Rice, Sam [actor] (*né* George Samuel O'Hanlon, b. 1873–12 Mar 1946 [74?], Burbank CA). AS, p. 918.

Rich, Carl [actor]. No data found. AMD, p. 291. "Carl Rich," *MPW,* 21 Jul 1917, 446.

Rich, H. Thompson [scenarist]. No data found. AMD, p. 291. "Rich to Write for Screen," *MPW,* 5 Apr 1919, 78. "RIch Joins Metro's Scenario Staff," *MPW,* 3 Jan 1920, 137.

Rich, Helen [stage/film actress] (b. Pittsburgh PA, 9 Mar 1897–28 Aug 1963 [66], New York NY [Death Certificate Index No. 18701]). "Helen Rich, Stage Beauty of '20's, and Businesswoman, 66, Dies," *NYT,* 30 Aug 1963, 21:4. AS, p. 918. BHD, p. 285. IFN, p. 250.

Rich, Irene [actress] (*née* Irene Luther, b. Buffalo NY, 31 Oct 1891–22 Apr 1988 [96], Hope Ranch CA; heart attack). m. (1) Elvo Deffenbaugh; (2) Charles Rich; (3) George H. Clifford; David Blankenhorn. (WB.) Peter B. Flint, "Irene Rich, Silent-Screen Actress and Radio Personality, Dies at 96," *NYT,* 25 Apr 1988, D12:1. "Irene Rich," *Variety,* 27 Apr 1988 (b. 13 Oct; d. Santa Barbara CA). AMD, p. 291. AS, p. 918. BHD1, p. 462 (d. Santa Barbara). BR, pp. 211–14 (b. 13 Oct). FFF, p. 64 (b. 13 Oct 1898). FSS, p. 247. HCH, p. 101. IFN, p. 250. MH, p. 134 (b. 13 Oct). Katz, p. 971. SD. "Irene Rich," WBO1, pp. 190–91. "Irene Rich SIgns Contract to Appear in Goldwyn Pictures," *MPW,* 13 Mar 1920, 1833. "Hard Work Made Irene RIch Star," *MPW,* 2 Aug 1924, 384. Helen Carlisle, "She's the Man of the Family," *MW,* 30 May 1925, 8–9, 33. Dorothy Donnell, "The Lady of Tears; From Tropic Tragedy to Screen Success," *MPC,* Sep 1925, 38–39, 72. "Signs New Contract," *MPW,* 26 Jun 1926, 3. Beatrice Browning, "A Siren's Off Hours; After she has hung up her vamp costume in the studio, Irene Rich goes home to play with her children and mess about in the garden," *Cinema Arts,* Feb 1927, 17, 36. "Two Film Weddings," *MPW,* 16 Apr 1927, 632. Henry B. Davis, "Films of Irene Rich," *CI,* 157 (Jul 1988), 14. George Katchmer, "Remembering the Great Silents," *CI,* 197 (Nov 1991), 50.

Rich, John [actor] (d. 27 Aug 1912, New York NY). BHD, p. 285.

Rich, Lillian [actress] (b. Herne Hill, London, England, 1 Jan 1900–5 Jan 1954 [54], Woodland Hills CA). m. Leo Nicholson. "Lillian Rich," *Variety,* 13 Jan 1954. AMD, p. 291. AS, p. 918. BHD1, p. 462. FSS, p. 248. IFN, p. 250. Katz, p. 971. Truitt, p. 282. "Selects Lillian Rich," *MPW,* 25 Oct 1924, 708. "Lillian RIch," *MPW,* 11 Dec 1926, 407. George A. Katchmer, "Forgotten Cowboys and Cowgirls—Part IX," *CI,* 181 (Jul 1990), 57–58.

Rich, Vivian [vaudeville/film actress] (b. Philadelphia PA, 26 May 1893–17 Nov 1957 [64], Los Angeles CA; auto accident). m. J.W. Jesson. (Lux; Nestor; American; Fox; Pathé.) AMD, p. 292. AS, p. 919. BHD1, p. 462. BR, pp. 61–64. IFN, p. 250. MSBB, p. 1040 (b. in the South). "Vivian Rich; Playing Leads with the American Co.," *MPS,* II, 3 Oct 1913, 29 ("born on the high seas"; began 1911). "Leading American Players," *MPW,* 11 Jul 1914, 240–42. "Vivian Rich with Universal," *MPW,* 15 Sep 1917, 1686. "VIvian Rich Made a Star by Fox; Will Act in 'Would You Forgive?,'" *MPW,* 21 Feb 1920, 1282. June Lee, "Dan Cupid's Bulletin Board," *Paris and Hollywood,* Oct 1926, 88 (birth of a son). Billy H. Doyle, "Lost Players," *CI,* 152 (Feb 1988), C13.

Richard, Albert J. [actor] (b. Bordeaux, France, b. 1890?–13 Feb 1963 [73], Atlanta GA). "Albert J. Richard," *Variety,* 27 Feb 1963. AS, p. 919.

Richard, Frieda [actress] (*née* Fredericke Raithel, b. Vienna, Austria, 1 Nov 1873–12 Sep 1946 [72], Salzburg, Austria). (Began 1909.) AS, p. 919. BHD1, p. 462. Vittorio Martinelli, "Kino-Leiblinge," *Griffithiana,* 38/39 (Oct 1990), 27.

Richard, Fritz [actor] (b. Vienna, Austria, 17 Nov 1869–9 Feb 1933 [63], Berlin, Germany). BHD1, p. 462.

Richard, Henri [actor] (b. Marseilles, France, 19 Sep 1883-ca. 1952 [79?]). AS, p. 919.

Richard, Philippe [actor] (*né* Auguste Philippe Richard, b. Saint-Etienne, France, 24 Jun 1891–24 Dec 1973 [82], Paris, France [extrait de décès no. 4738/1973]). AS, p. 919.

Richards, Addison Whitaker [actor] (b. Zenesville OH, 20 Oct 1887–22 Mar 1964 [76], Los Angeles CA). AS, p. 919.

Richards, Charles [casting director] (b. Indianapolis IN, 16 Dec 1899–29 Jul 1948 [48], Los Angeles CA). "Charles Richards," *Variety,* 4 Aug 1948 (age 51). AS, p. 919. BHD, p. 285. Truitt, p. 282.

Richards, Cicely [actress] (b. London, England, 1850–8 Apr 1933 [83], London, England). BHD, p. 285. IFN, p. 250.

Richards, Tom [actor]. No data found. AMD, p. 292. "Tom Richards," *MPW,* 27 Mar 1915, 1943.

Richards, Gordon [actor] (b. Gillingham, England, 27 Oct 1893–13 Jan 1964 [70], Los Angeles CA). AS, p. 919.

Richards, Viola [actress] (b. Canada, ca. 1910). AMD, p. 292. "Mystery Girl Is Viola Richards," *MPW,* 19 Feb 1927, 575. Don Juan, "So This Is Hollywood," *Paris and Hollywood Screen Secrets Magazine,* May 1927, 32, 76 (Hal Roach signed a long-term contract with "the seventeen-year-old Canadian girl whom he will begin featuring in his comedies presently.").

Richardson, Dorothy [scenarist] (b. 1872–27 Mar 1955 [83?], New Haven CT). BHD2, p. 222.

Richardson, Frank "Daddy" Atwood [actor] (b. New York NY, 1892–14 Feb 1913 [21?], Murietta Hot Springs CO). AMD, p. 292. AS, p. 919. BHD, p. 285 (d. 29 Jan 1913, Murrieta Springs CA). (Selig, 1907–1913). "Daddy Richardson, of Selig Players, Recovers," *MPW,* 13 Jul 1912, 158. *MPS,* 28 Mar 1913, 31.

Richardson, Frank C. [wardrobe] (b. 1899?–19 Aug 1971 [72], Los Angeles CA). (Paramount, 1916.) "Frank C. Richardson," *Variety,* 8 Sep 1971.

Richardson, Frankie Joseph [singer/actor] (b. Philadelphia PA, 6 Sep 1898–30 Jan 1962 [63], Philadelphia PA; heart attack). "F.J. Richardson, 63, ex-Singer in Films," *NYT,* 1 Feb 1962, 31:3. AS, p. 920. BHD1, p. 462. IFN, p. 250. Truitt, p. 283.

Richardson, Jack [actor] (*né* John Howard Richardson, b. New York NY, 18 Nov 1883–17 Nov 1957 [74], Santa Barbara CA). m. **Florence Stone** (d. 1950); **Louise Lester**, 13 May 1914, Santa Barbara CA (d. 1952). (American.) AMD, p. 292. AS, p. 920. BHD1, p. 462. IFN, p. 250. "Richardson Refuses to Be Buried," *MPW,* 17 Feb 1912, 584. "Richardson—Lester," *NYDM,* 10 Jun 1914, 50:2 (photo on p. 25). "Jack Richardson and Louise Lester, of the American Company forces, at Santa Barbara, California, were married recently," *Motography,* 27 Jun 1914, 494. "American Features; Kentucky Story a Forthcoming 'Flying A'—Jack Richardson Seen in Character," *NYDM,* 15 Jul 1914, 22:3 (in *Their Worldly Goods*). "Jack Richardson Joins Universal," *MPW,* 11 Nov 1916, 877. "Jack Richardson Joins Triangle," *MPW,* 23 Jun 1917, 1919. "Frohman Engages Three Stars to Appear with Texas Guinan," *MPW,* 29 Mar 1919, 1786. "Jack Richardson Re-Engaged," *MPW,* 19 Jul 1919, 405. "Gets His WIsh," *MPW,* 7 Apr 1923, 668. Nick C. Nicholls, "Jack Richardson," *CI,* 142 (Apr 1987), 61.

Richardson, Leander [playwright/publicist] (b. 1855?–2 Feb 1918 [62], New York NY; pneumonia). (World Film Corp.) "Leander Richardson," *Variety,* 8 Feb 1918, p. 10. AMD, 10:3. BHD2, p. 222. "Richardson Joins Ince Publicity Staff," *MPW,* 8 Jul 1916, 231. "Obituary," *MPW,* 16 Feb 1918, 953.

Richardson, William [actor] (b. 1886–8 Nov 1937 [51?], Los Angeles CA). AS, p. 920.

Richebe, Roger [director/producer] (b. Marseilles, France, 3 Dec 1897–10 Jul 1989 [91], Paris, France). AS, p. 920. BHD2, p. 222.

Richepin, Jean [scenarist] (b. Medeah, Algeria, 4 Feb 1849–12 Dec 1926 [77], Paris, France). BHD, p. 285; BHD2, p. 222.

Richer, Donna [publicist]. No data found. AMD, p. 293. "Miss Risher with R-C," *MPW,* 15 Oct 1921, 748.

Ri[t]chie, Ethel [actress]. No data found. AMD, p. 292. "Ethel Richie Engaged by Universal," *MPW,* 24 May 1919, 1151.

Richman, Al [actor] (b. New Orleans LA, 21 May 1885–20 Apr 1936 [50], Los Angeles CA; heart attack). "Al Richman," *Variety,* 29 Apr 1936. AS, p. 920. BHD, p. 285. IFN, p. 250 (age 51).

Richman, Arthur [scenarist] (b. 1886–8 Sep 1944 [58?], New York NY). BHD2, p. 222.

Richman, Charles J. [stage/film actor] (b. Chicago IL, 12 Jan 1865–1 Dec 1940 [75], Bronx NY [Death Certificate Index No. 11072]). m. Jane Grey. (Lasky; Fox; Vitagraph.) "Charles Richman, Noted Actor, Dead; Leading Man for Ada Rehan, Lily Langtry Scored Hit in 'Bought and Paid For'; Last Seen Here in 1936; Played Grandfather Role in 'And Stars Remain'—He Had Appeared in Pictures," *NYT,* 2 Dec 1940, 23:3 (age 70). "Charles Richman," *Variety,* 4 Dec 1940 (age 70). AMD, p. 292. AS, p. 920. BHD1, p. 463 (b. 1870). IFN, p. 250 (b. 1870). MSBB, p. 1028. SD. Slide, p. 149. Truitt, p. 283 (b.1870). "More Lasky Stars," *MPW,* 22 Aug 1914, 1107. "Charles J. Richman," *MPW,* 13 Nov 1915, 1314. "Charles Richman Suffering from Eye Strain," *MPW,* 15 Jan 1916, 397. "Charles

Richman Returns to Screen in 'Half an Hour,'" *MPW,* 14 Feb 1920, 1074.

Richmond, Al [actor] (*né* Al Raetznab). No data found. (*Fl.* 1924–28 in westerns; Approved Pictures, 1924; Sierra Pictures; Universal.) Ed Wyatt, "Al Richmond Info," *CI,* 280 (Oct 1998), 16.

Richmond, Hazel [actress] (aka Mrs. Hazel Craig). No data found. AMD, p. 292. "Hazel Richmond in Will Suit," *MPW,* 6 Sep 1919, 1456.

Richmond, Joseph A. [director]. No data found. AMD, p. 292. "Premier Director Breaks Arm," *MPW,* 27 Nov 1915, 1646. "Four Directors for Premier Program," *MPW,* 18 Dec 1915, 2160. "Dra-Ko DIrector Fully Recovered," *MPW,* 8 Jan 1916, 251.

Richmond, Warner P. [actor] (b. Racine WI, 11 Jan 1886–19 Jun 1948 [62], Los Angeles CA; stroke). "Warner Richmond," *Variety,* 23 Jun 1948 (age 53). AS, p. 920. BHD1, p. 463. IFN, p. 250. Truitt, p. 283 (b. Culpepper Co. VA, 1895). George Katchmer, "Remembering the Great Silents," *CI,* 211 (Jan 1992), 45.

Richter, Ellen [actress] (b. Vienna, Austria, 21 Jul 1893-d. Baden-Baden, Germany). m. Dr. Willi Wolff, 1923. (Film debut: *Das Gesetz der Mine,* 1915.) AS, p. 920. BHD, p. 463 (d. ca. 1969, Düsseldorf, Germany). "Idols of Berlin," *MPC,* Feb 1926, 41. Vittorio Martinelli, "Kino-Leiblinge," *Griffithiana,* 38/39 (Oct 1990), 28.

Richter, Friedrich [actor] (*né* Friedrich Rosenthal, b. Brunn, Germany, 5 Jun 1894–3 Mar 1984 [89], Berlin, Germany). AS, p. 920.

Richter, Hans [actor/artist/director/producer/scenarist] (b. Berlin, Germany, 6 Feb 1888–1 Feb 1976 [87], Locarno, Switzerland). *Dada: Art and Anti-Art,* 1964. "Hans Richter," *Variety,* 281, 4 Feb 1976, 71:1. AS, p. 920. BHD1, p. 463; BHD2, p. 222. IFN, p. 251.

Richter, Paul Martin Edward [actor] (b. Vienna, Austria, 1 Apr 1895–30 Dec 1961 [66], Vienna, Austria). m. **Aud Egede-Nissen** (d. 1974). "Paul Richter," *Variety,* 17 Jan 1962 (b. Germany; age 65). AS, p. 921. BHD1, p. 463 (b. 16 Apr 1887). IFN, p. 251. Truitt, p. 283.

Rickard, George L. (Tex) [actor] (b. Sherman TX, 2 Jan 1870–5 Jun 1929 [59], Miami Beach FL; complications from peritonitis). AS, p. 921. BHD, p. 285.

Rickelt, Gustav [actor] (b. Dortmund, Germany, 21 Jun 1862–26 Jun 1946 [84], Germany). BHD1, p. 463.

Ricker, Maurice G. ["réalisateur [director] pour l'Armée américaine] (b. 1870–9 Sep 1952 [82?], Washington DC). AS, p. 921.

Ricketts, Josephine *see* **Ditt, Josephine**

Ricketts, Thomas V. [actor/director] (b. London, England, 15 Jan 1853–19 Jan 1939 [86], West Hollywood CA; pneumonia). (Began 1906; Nestor; Essanay; Universal; American; MGM.) m. **Josephine Ditt** (d. 1939). "Thomas Ricketts, Pioneer of Movies; Man Who Directed the First Hollywood Picture Dies in Dire Straits at 86; Developed Early Stars; J.W. Kerrigan, Ethel Clayton and Bryant Washburn Were Among His 'Discoveries,'" *NYT,* 21 Jan 1939, 15:3. "Thomas Ricketts," *Variety,* 25 Jan 1939 (d. Hollywood CA). AMD, p. 292. AS, p. 921 (d. 20 Jan). BHD1, p. 463; BHD2, p. 222. IFN, p. 251. Spehr, p. 162. Truitt, p. 283. "Tom Ricketts Back with American," *MPW,* 12 Jul 1913, 190; photo, p. 209. "Tom Ricketts, Feature Director with American," *NYDM,* 13 Nov 1915, 26:1. Thomas Ricketts, "Importance of Quality," *MPW,* 21 Jul 1917, 460. "Christie Secures Thomas Ricketts," *MPW,* 31 May 1919, 1335. "Aged Character Man Is Signed by Columbia," *MPW,* 19 Dec 1925, 648.

Ricks, Archie [actor] (b. CA, 29 Feb 1896–10 Jan 1962 [65], Los Angeles CA). AS, p. 921. BHD1, p. 463. IFN, p. 251.

Ricksen, Lucille [actress: Wampas Star, 1924] (*née* Lucille Ericksen, b. Chicago IL, 22 Aug 1907?–13 Mar 1925 [17], Los Angeles CA; tuberculosis). "Lucille Ricksen, Young Film Star," *NYT,* 15 Mar 1925, 26:5. (Essanay, 1913; Goldwyn; Universal; Fox; FBO; Metro-Goldwyn, 1925.) AMD, p. 292. AS, p. 921 (b. 1910; d. NY NY). BHD, pp. 65–66; 285 (b. 1909). IFN, p. 251 (b. 1910). Truitt, p. 283 (b. 2 Sep 1907). Billy H. Doyle, "Lost Players," *CI,* 146 (Aug 1987), 31 (b. 1910). FFF, p. 172. "Lucille Ricksen to Be in New Film," *MPW,* 21 Oct 1922, 676. "On the Set and Off," *MW,* 25 Feb 1925, 34 (had a complete nervous breakdown). "On the Set and Off," *MW,* V, 25 Apr 1925 (her father, Soren Ericksen, inherited his daughter's $50,000 life insurance. She was reported to be 16 at her death but before she died she petitioned Rupert Hughes and Conrad Nagel to be her brother's guardians; after her death her father wanted to be his guardian). Norman Bruce, "What Price Glory; How the Stars Have Paid for Success in Diet, Heartache and Tears," *MPC,* Jul 1925, 54–55, 89.

Ricksen, Marshall [actor] (b. IL, 19 Dec 1907–16 Jan 1975 [67], Oakland CA). BHD, p. 285.

Rickson, Joseph [actor] (b. Clear Creek MT, 6 Sep 1880–8 Jan 1958 [77], Los Angeles CA). (Vitagraph; Bison; Victor; Bluebird; Gold Sea; Nestor; Pathé.) AS, p. 921. BHD1, p. 463. IFN, p. 251. Nick C. Nicholls, "Joe Rickson," *CI,* 145 (Jul 1987), 59 (b. 1882). George A. Katchmer, "Forgotten Cowboys and Cowgirls—Part IX," *CI,* 181 (Jul 1990), 58.

Rico, Mona [actress: Wampas Star, 1929] (*née* Maria Enriqueta Valenzuela, b. Mexico City, Mexico, 15 Jul 1906–26 Aug 1994 [88], Los Angeles CA). AS, p. 921 (b. 1909). BHD1, p. 463.

Riddell, George [actor] (b. England, 1864–19 Mar 1944 [80?], New York NY). BHD, p. 285.

Rider, Lillian [actress] (b. Danville PA, 16 Oct 1896–13 Aug 1969 [72], Torrence CA). BHD1, p. 616.

Ridge, Walter J. [actor] (b. PA, 28 Dec 1898–20 Sep 1968 [69], Glendale CA). AS, p. 921.

Ridgely, Cleo, "The Continental Girl" [actress] (*née?,* b. New York NY, 12 May 1894–18 Aug 1962 [68], Glendale CA). m. (1) J.M. Ridgley—div. ca. 1917; **James W. Horne** (d. 1942). "Cleo Ridgely," *Variety,* 29 Aug 1962. AMD, p. 292. AS, p. 921. BHD1, p. 464. IFN, p. 251. Truitt, p. 283. *MPW,* 30 Mar 1912, 1164 (with Rex). "Cleo Ridgely on Long Contract," *NYDM,* 7 Jul 1915, 24:4. "Cleo Ridgely Engaged by Lasky," *MPW,* 17 Jul 1915, 499. "Cleo Ridgely and Wallace Reid Co-Stars," *MPW,* 27 Nov 1915, 1666. Pearl Gaddis, "The Girl Who Rode Across the Continent—Cleo Ridgely," *MPC,* Aug 1916, 33–34 (b. 1893). Cal York, "Plays and Players," *Photoplay Magazine,* (Feb 1917), 89 (at her trial for divorce from director J.M. Ridgley in Los Angeles, she claimed that he "had not treated her as a dutiful wife should be treated."). Billy H. Doyle, "Lost Players," *CI,* 15 (Jul 1988), 23.

Ridgely, Richard [stage/film actor/scenarist/director] (*né* Richard Peckover, b. KY?, 1869?–30 Nov 1949 [80], Bay Shore, LI NY). (Edison, 1912.) "Richard Ridgely, 80, Restauranteur, Actor," *NYT,* 2 Dec 1949, 29:2. "Richard Ridgely," *Variety,* 7 Dec 1949. AMD, p. 292. AS, p. 921. BHD2, p. 222. "Briefs of Biography; Keep Your Eye on Him," *NYDM,* 7 Jul 1915, 39:1 (while still a scenarist, he finished a film when the director became ill and turned to directing. The secret of his success "is his ability to get the best out of the player, for no one is quicker to commend really worth while work."). "Richard Ridgeley," *MPW,* 16 Oct 1915, 445.

Ridges, Stanley C[harles] [actor] (b. Southampton, England, 17 Jul 1891–22 Apr 1951 [59], Westbrook CT). "Stanley C. Ridges," *Variety,* 25 Apr 1951. AS, p. 921. BHD1, p. 464 (b. Westchester, England, 1892). IFN, p. 251. Truitt, p. 284.

Ridgeway, Fritzie [actress] (b. Missoula MT, 8 Apr 1898–29 Mar 1961 [62], Edwards AFB, Lancaster CA; heart attack). m. Mr. Baekaelinikoff, ca. 1926. "Fritzi Ridgeway," *Variety,* 5 Apr 1961. AMD, p. 292. AS, p. 921 (b. Butte MT). BHD1, p. 464. BR, pp. 214–15. IFN, p. 251. Truitt, p. 250. "Fritzi Ridgeway Will Star in Series of Twelve Two Reel Productions for Capital Film Company," *MPW,* 28 Aug 1920, 1167. "Fritzi Ridgeway to Make Series of Five-Reel Films for Capital," *MPW,* 26 Feb 1921, 1039. June Lee, "Dan Cupid's Bulletin Board," *Paris and Hollywood,* 2 (Oct 1926), 89 (recently married a motion picture orchestra leader. "It was Miss Ridgeway's hopes to return to pictures, but it seems practically impossible to come back after any appreciable absence. The public soon forgets."). "Fritzi Ridgeway," *MPW,* 12 Nov 1927, 22.

Ridgwell, George [comic opera and dramatic actor/scenarist/director] (b. Woolwich, England, 1870–1935 [65?], England). (Edison, Vitagraph.) AMD, p. 292. AS, p. 921. BHD2, p. 222. "Studio Gossip," *NYDM,* 7 Jul 1915, 41:1 (filming *Sis*). "Ridgwell a Vitagraph Director," *MPW,* 10 Jul 1915, 273. "New Edison Directors; George Ridgwell Added to Staff and Frank McGlynn Raised to Directorship," *NYDM,* 29 Sep 1915, 31:3. "George Ridgwell," *MPW,* 9 Oct 1915, 257.

Ridley, Arnold [actor/director/scenarist] (b. Bath, England, 7 Jan 1896–12 Mar 1984 [88], London, England). AS, p. 921.

Ridley, Robert [actor/a founder of the Screen Extras Guild] (b. 1901?–19 Nov 1958 [57], Los Angeles CA). "Robert Rid-ley," *Variety,* 3 Dec 1958. AS, p. 921. IFN, p. 251.

Riechers, Helene [actress] (b. Hamburg, Germany, 6 Jun 1869–15 Jul 1957 [88], Berlin, Germany). AS, p. 921.

Rieck, Arnold [actor] (b. 22 Jun 1876–7 Nov 1924 [48], Leipzig, Germany). BHD, p. 285.

Rieck, Johnnie H. [actor] (b. Denmark, 20 Nov 1880–26 Oct 1956 [75], Greenville SC). BHD, p. 285.

Riegal, Charles Henry [actor] (b. 1857–21 Oct 1935 [78?], Briarcliff NY). BHD, p. 286.

Riemann, Johannes [stage/film singer/actor/director/scenarist] (b. Berlin, Germany, 31

May 1887–30 Sep 1959 [72], Konstanz, Germany). (Mexico; Universal.) "Johannes Riemann," *Variety,* 216, 28 Oct 1959, 71:3. BHD1, p. 464; BHD2, p. 222. IFN, p. 251. Waldman, p. 246.

Riemers, Henry [cameraman] (b. 1873?–15 Jun 1916 [43], New York NY). (Selig [Chicago]; Diamond Feature Film Co.) "Father of Cameraman Dead," *Variety,* 16 Jun 1916. AS, p. 922.

Riento, Virgilio [actor] (*né* Virgilio d'Armiento, b. Rome, Italy, 26 Nov 1889–7 Sep 1959 [69], Civitavecchia, Italy). AS, p. 922.

Riera, Albert Charles Joseph [director/scenarist] (b. Banyuls-sur-Mer, France, 28 Jan 1895 [extrait de naissance no. 23]-14 Dec 1968 [73], Paris, France). AS, p. 922.

Ries, Irving G. [special effects cameraman] (b. Akron OH, 15 Jan 1890–20 Aug 1963 [73], Los Angeles CA). (MGM.) "Irving G. Ries," *Variety,* 28 Aug 1963. AS, p. 922. BHD2, p. 222. FDY, p. 467.

Ries, Ray[mond] [cameraman] (b. 1894–23 Aug 1977 [83?], Los Angeles Co. CA). BHD2, p. 222. FDY, p. 467.

Ries, William J. [actor] (b. 1895–16 Nov 1955 [60], Los Angeles CA). AS, p. 922. BHD1, p. 464. IFN, p. 251.

Riesenfeld, Dr. Hugo [composer/conductor] (b. Vienna, Austria, 26 Jan 1879–10 Sep 1939 [60], Los Angeles CA). (Paramount; UA.) m. Mabel Gertrude Dunning, 1912. "Hugo Riesenfeld, Music Conductor; Concert Master of Manhattan Opera Company, 1907–11, Dies in Los Angeles at 60; Directed Theatres Here; Developed Film Presentation While at Rivoli, Rialto and Criterion from 1917–25," *NYT,* 11 Sep 1939, 19:3. "Dr. Hugo Riesenfeld, Pioneer in De Luxe Presentations, Dies at 60," *Variety,* 13 Sep 1939. AS, p. 922 (b. 1878). ASCAP 66, p. 603. BHD2, p. 222 (b. 1883). B.F. Wilson, "The Motion-Picture Palaces of New York," *MPC,* Jun 1925, 24–25, 79.

Riesner, Charles F. (Chuck) [actor/director/producer/scenarist] (b. Minneapolis MN, 14 Mar 1887–24 Sep 1962 [75], La Jolla CA). BHD2, p. 223.

Riethof, Peter ["pionnier français du doublage des films"] (b. Czechoslovakia, 1905–22 Aug 1994 [89?], Paris, France). AS, p. 922.

Rietti, Vittorio [actor/producer] (b. Ferrara, Italy, 29 Feb 1888 [extrait de naissance no. 179]-4 Dec 1963 [75], London, England; heart attack). AS, p. 922.

Rifkin, Herman [executive] (b. Russia, 1884–14 Jan 1966 [81?], Boston MA). BHD2, p. 223.

Riga, Nadine [actress] (*née* Nadine Evans, b. 13 Aug 1896–11 Dec 1968 [72], Los Angeles CA; cerebral hemorrhage). m. Phil Evans. "Nadine Evans," *Variety,* 25 Dec 1968 (age 59). AS, p. 922 (b. 1909). BHD, p. 286 (b. 1909). IFN, p. 251. Truitt, p. 284.

Rigal, André [director/producer] (b. Paris, France, 18 Feb 1898). AS, p. 922.

Rigas, George [actor] (b. Sparta, Greece, 9 Nov 1890–13 Dec 1940 [50], Los Angeles CA). BHD1, p. 464.

Rigaux, Lucien (father of Jean Rigaux) (b. director/producer] (b. Paris, France, 1885–1954 [69?], Paris, France). m. (son, Jean, 1909–1991). AS, p. 922.

Rigby, Arthur [actor] (b. 2 Jul 1870–17 Apr 1944 [73], London, England). BHD2, p. 223.

Rigby, Arthur [actor] (*né* Arthur Turner, b. London, England, 27 Sep 1900–25 Apr 1971 [70], Worthing, England; cerebral hemorrhage). AS, p. 922. BHD1, p. 464; BHD2, p. 223. IFN, p. 251.

Rigby, Edward [actor] (*né* Edward Coke, b. Ashford, Kent, England, 5 Feb 1879–5 Apr 1951 [72], London, England). AS, p. 922. BHD1, p. 464. IFN, p. 251.

Rigby, L. Gordon [scenarist]. No data found. FDY, p. 437.

Riggs, Bettie or Betty *see* **Brent, Evelyn**

Riggs, Lynn [scenarist] (b. Claremore OK, 1899–30 Jun 1954 [55?], New York NY). BHD2, p. 223.

Righelli, Gennaro Salvatore [director] (b. Salerno, Italy, 12 Dec 1885 [extrait de naissance no. 1917]-6 Jan 1949 [63], Rome, Italy). m. actress **Maria**. AS, p. 923. BHD2, p. 223 (b. 1886). JS, p. 378 (in Italian silents from 1910).

Righelli, Maria [actress]. No data found. m. **Gennaro Righelli** (d. 1949). JS, p. 379 (in Italian silents from 1911).

Rightmire, William H. [actor] (b. 1856?–14 Jan 1933 [76], Long Beach NY; heart attack). "William H. Rightmire," *Variety,* 17 Jan 1933. AS, p. 923.

Rigot, Fernand Mary Louis Eugène [director/producer] (b. Lennick-St.-Quentin, Belgium, 16 Feb 1894–22 Jul 1981 [87], Anderlecht, Belgium). AS, p. 923.

Riley, Edna Goldsmith [playwright/scenarist] (b. 1880?–3 May 1962 [82], New York NY [Death Certificate No. 9995; M.E. Case No. 3934; age 81]). m. Edward P. Riley. "Edna Goldsmith Riley," *Variety,* 16 May 1962. AMD, p. 292. AS, p. 923. "Edna G. Riley," *MPW,* 24 Feb 1917, 1188.

Riley, George [vaudeville/film/TV actor] (b. Rochester NY, 3 Dec 1897–30 May 1972 [74], Memorial County Hospital, Los Angeles CA). "George Riley," *Variety,* 267, 7 Jun 1972, 63:2 (age 72; with Helene Heller as Heller & Riley). AS, p. 923. BHD1, p. 465 (d. 20 May). IFN, p. 251.

Riley, Jack (Slim) [actor] (b. 1895–9 Jul 1933 [38], Newhall CA). AS, p. 923. BHD, p. 286. IFN, p. 251.

Riley, James Whitcomb [actor] (b. Greenfield IN, 7 Oct 1853–22 Jul 1916 [62], Indianapolis IN). BHD, p. 286.

Riley, Jean [actress]. No data found. AMD, p. 292. "Jean Riley Hurt," *MPW,* 13 Aug 1921, 699.

Riley, Mack [actor] (*née* Maynard Cyril Stokes, b. TN, 15 Feb 1886–29 Aug 1963 [77], Los Angeles CA). AS, p. 923. IFN, p. 251.

Rilla, Walter Wilhelm Karl Ernst [actor/scenarist] (b. Neunkirchen, Germany, 22 Aug 1894–21 Nov 1980 [86], Rosenheim, Germany). AS, p. 923. BHD1, p. 465.

Rimsky, Nicolas [director] (b. Russia, 1886–1941 [55?], France). AS, p. 923.

Rinaldo, Alice [actress]. No data found. AMD, p. 293. "Alice Rinaldo Retained by Horsley," *MPW,* 15 Apr 1916, 411.

Rinehart, Mary Roberts [writer/scenarist] (*née* Mary Roberts, b. Allegheny [now North Side], Pittsburgh PA, 12 Aug 1876–22 Sep 1958 [82], New York NY; heart attack). m. Dr. Stanley Marshall Rinehart (d. 1932). (First published book: *The Circular Staircase,* Bobbs-Merrill, 1908; Goldwyn.) Biography by Jan Cohn. "Mary Roberts Rinehart Is Dead; Author of Mysteries and Plays," *NYT,* 23 Sep 1958, 1:6, 33:2. "Rinehart Funeral Tomorrow," *NYT,* 24 Sep 1958, 27:5 (buried at Arlington National Cemetery beside her husband). AMD, pp. 291 (Rhinehart), 293 (Rinehart). BHD2, p. 223. "Mrs. Rhinehart Admires Pictures," *MPW,* 4 Sep 1915, 1661. "Mrs. Rinehart Visits Lasky Studio," *MPW,* 30 Mar 1918, 1821. Gretta Palmer, "I Had Cancer," *Ladies Home Journal,* Jul 1947. Stuart McIver, "Essentially Pittsburgh; Taking the Mystery Out of Breast Cancer; Author Mary Roberts Rinehart helped bring her illness out of the shadows," *Pittsburgh Post-Gazette,* 15 Oct 1995, G-4:1.

Ring, Blanche (sister of **Cyril** and **Frances Ring**) [stage/film actress] (b. Boston MA, 24 Apr 1871–13 Jan 1961 [89], Santa Monica CA). m. (1) Walter F. MacNichol; (2) James Walker, Jr.; (3) Edward Wentworth; (4) Frederic E. McKay—div. ca. 1908; (5) **Charles Winninger**, 8 Nov 1912 (d. 1969). "Blanche Ring, 89, Stage Star, Dies; Musical Comedy Entertainer Introduced 'I've Got Rings on My Fingers' in 1912," *NYT,* 15 Jan 1961, 86:1. "Blanche Ring," *Variety,* 18 Jan 1961 (age 82). AMD, p. 293. AS, p. 923. BHD1, p. 465 (b. 1877). IFN, p. 251 (b. 1878). SD. Truitt, p. 285 (b. 1876). "Blanche Ring Remarried; Musical Comedy Star Will Continue Under Management of Her Ex-Husband [McKay]," *NYDM,* 20 Nov 1912, 17:1. "Three New Stars; Morosco Captures Blanche Ring, Cyril Maude and Charlotte Greenwood," *NYDM,* 11 Aug 1915, 22:4. "Blanche Ring to Appear in Former Success," *MPW,* 28 Aug 1915, 1486. Tarleton Winchester, "The Motion Picture as Blanche Ring Sees It," *MPC,* Feb 1916, 53.

Ring, Cyril (brother of **Blanche** and **Frances Ring**) [actor] (b. Boston MA, 5 Dec 1892–17 Jul 1967 [74], Los Angeles CA). m. **Charlotte Greenwood**, 24 Jul 1915, LA CA [d. 1978); Molly Green. (WB.) "Cyril Ring," *Variety,* 19 Jul 1967. AS, p. 923. BHD1, p. 465. IFN, p. 252. Truitt, p. 285. "Weds Charlotte Greenwood," *NYDM,* 28 Jul 1915, 7:3.

Ring, Frances (sister of **Blanche** and **Cyril Ring**) (b. New York NY, 4 Jul 1882–15 Jan 1951 [68], Los Angeles CA). m. **Thomas Meighan** (d. 1936). "Frances Ring Meighan," *Variety,* 17 Jan 1951. AS, p. 923. SD, p. 1061 (b. Boston MA).

Rinne, Jalmari Ivar (brother of **Joel Rinne**) [actor] (b. Asikkala, Finland, 13 Nov 1893–24 Oct 1985 [91], Helsinki, Finland). AS, p. 924.

Rinne, Joel (brother of **Jalmari Rinne**) [actor] (*né* Toivo Joel Rinne, b. Asikkala, Finland, 6 Jun 1897–25 Aug 1970 [73], Helsinki, Finland). AS, p. 924.

Rin-tin-tin [dog actor owned by Lee Duncan] (b. Metz, France, 12 Sep 1918–8 Aug 1932 [13], Los Angeles CA). (Film debut: *Where the North Begins,* 1923; WB.) AMD, p. 292. AS, p. 923. BHD, p. 286. FSS, p. 248. IFN, p. 252. "Rin Tin Tin on World Tour Following Success in Films," *MPW,* 20 Dec 1924, 765. "Warner's Rin Tin Tin Is Very Much Alive," *MPW,* 14 Feb 1925, 706 (rumored dead). "Rin Tin Tin, Warner's Dog Srar, Pays Visit to N.Y.," *MPW,* 17 Apr 1926, 512 (5 Apr 1926). Van Powell, "'I'm No Pup-licity Hound' Says Pup-ular Rin Tin Tin," *MPW,* 24 Apr 1926, 579. "Rin Tin Tin Departs for Pittsburgh and Other Cities," *MPW,* 15 May 1926, 228. Beatrice Browning, "Rin-Tin-Tin Grants an Interview; This Famous German Police Dog Was Picked Up as a Pup by an American Soldier in 1918, Somewhere Near the Hindenburg Line," *Cinema Arts*, Jan 1927, 22–23. "More Blue Ribbons for Rin Tin Tin," *MPW*, 5 Feb 1927, 425. Ruth Biery, "It's a Dog's Life," *MPC*, Dec 1927, 63, 89. Cedric Belfrage, "The Love Secrets of Rex and Rinty; 'A Jug of Water, a Meat Loaf and Thou,' says Rin-Tin-Tin; 'A Dog Need Not Flirt and Stay Out Nights to Enjoy Life,'" *MPC*, Mar 1929, 31, 76 ("Rin-Tin-Tin held out a paw. 'Delighted you dropped in,' he said."). Ken Law, "Rin-tin-tin: Wonder Dog of the Silver Screen," *CI*, 90 (Dec 1982), 34.

Ripley, Arthur D[eWitt] [scenarist/director] (b. New York NY, 1895–13 Feb 1961 [65], Los Angeles CA; cancer). (Kalem [NYC], 1909; Vitagraph, 1912; Universal; Fox; Metro; Sennett; Langdon; RKO; Wanger.) AMD, p. 293. AS, p. 924. BHD2, p. 223 (b. Townshend VT). FDY, p. 437. "Arthur Ripley, 66, Wrote for Movies," *NYT*, 15 Feb 1961, 35:4 (age 66). "Arthur Ripley," *Variety*, 22 Feb 1961. Katz, p. 974. "Ripley Made a Director; Will Direct Bert Lytell," *MPW*, 27 Dec 1919, 1162. "Arthur Ripley Is Made Scenario Editor for Sennett," *MPW*, 15 Nov 1924, 222. "Ripley Heads Langdon Scenario Department," *MPW*, 24 Jul 1926, 217.

Ripley, Raymond [stage/film actor] (b. 1891?–7 Oct 1938 [47], Los Angeles CA). "Raymond Ripley," *Variety*, 12 Oct 1938 (began 1918). AMD, p. 293. AS, p. 924. BHD, p. 286. IFN, p. 253. Truitt, p. 285. "Ray Ripley, Broadway Star, Joins Universal," *MPW*, 30 Aug 1919, 1327. George Katchmer, "Remembering the Great Silents," *CI*, 233 (Nov 1994), 38.

Ripley, Robert L[eroy] [actor] (b. Santa Rosa CA, 25 Dec 1893–27 May 1949 [55], New York NY). AS, p. 924.

Rippert, Otto [actor/director] (b. Offenbach, Germany, 1869–15 Jan 1940 [70], Berlin, Germany). AS, p. 924.

Riscoe, Arthur [actor] (b. Berburn in Elmet, England, 19 Nov 1896–6 Aug 1954 [57], London, England). AS, p. 924 (b. Sherburn-in-Elmet, England). BHD1, p. 465.

Risdon, Elizabeth [stage/film actress] (*née* Elizabeth Evans, b. London, England, 26 Apr 1887–20 Dec 1958 [71], Santa Monica CA; cerebral hemorrhage). m. (1) **George Loane Tucker** (d. 1921); (2) Brandon Evans. "Elizabeth Risdon Dies; Retired Actress Starred in Several Plays by Shaw," *NYT*, 23 Dec 1958, 2:6. AMD, p. 293. AS, p. 924. BHD1, p. 465 (b. Wandsworth, England). IFN, p. 252 (b. 1888). Katz, pp. 974–75. Truitt, p. 285. "Simultaneously on Screen and Stage," *MPW*, 1 Dec 1917, 1346. "Elizabeth Risdon," *MPW*, 29 Dec 1917, 1933. "Star Appears in Picture and Play at Same TIMe," *MPW*, 30 Mar 1918, 1840. "George Loane Tucker Dies in Los Angeles," *MPW*, 2 Jul 1921, 31. Blackie Seymour, "Pentagram Revues; Elizabeth Risdon," *CI*, 197 (Nov 1991), 48–49.

Rishell, Myrtle [actress] (b. Portland OR, 12 Sep 1877–12 Sep 1942 [65], Los Angeles CA; cancer). AS, p. 924. BHD, p. 286.

Risi, Fernando (brother of Dino Risi, b. 23 Dec 1916, and director Nelo Risi, b. 21 Apr 1920) [cinematographer] (b. Rome, Italy, 20 Oct 1890). JS, p. 380 (in Italian films from 1922).

Rising, William S. (nephew of **Richard F. Outcault**) [actor/producer] (b. 1860?–5 Oct 1930 [70], New York NY; heart attack [Death Certificate No. 22953]). "William S. Rising," *Variety*, 8 Oct 1930. AMD, p. 293. AS, p. 924. BHD, p. 286; BHD2, p. 223 (b. 1851). IFN, p. 252. Truitt, p. 285. "Will S. Rising the Dean of Moving Picture Actors," *MPW*, 1 Nov 1913, 484 (photograph only). "Songs of All Nations by Rising," *MPW*, 28 Feb 1914, 1105. "An Old Timer," *MPW*, 31 Oct 1914, 652. "Past Performances," *MPW*, 3 Jul 1915, 54. "Will Rising's Mother Dies," *MPW*, 30 Oct 1915, 948. *See* Ramsaye, p. 492.

Riskin, Everett [actress] (b. 1895–27 Mar 1982 [86?], Beverly Hills CA). AS, p. 924. BHD2, p. 223.

Risser, Marguerite (niece of **Kathryn Osterman**) [actress] (b. 1897?). AMD, p. 293. "The Girl of Today; Marguerite Risser of Pathe Included in the Favored List [of *NYT* contest]," *MPW*, 27 Dec 1913, 1555 ("just turned sixteen"); photograph, 1565. "Marguerite Risser," *MPW*, 6 Feb 1915, 842.

Rissone, Giuditta [actress] (b. Genoa, Italy, 29 Aug 1895–31 May 1977 [81], Rome, Italy). m. **Vittorio de Sica** (d. 1974). AS, p. 925.

Rist, Preben [actor/director] (b. Copenhagen, Denmark, 10 Jan 1885). AS, p. 925.

Ristelhueber, Joseph H. [actor] (b. 1847–28 Feb 1943 [96], Los Angeles CA). AS, p. 925. BHD, p. 286. IFN, p. 252.

Ritchard, Cyril Trimnel [actor] (b. Sydney, Australia, 1 Dec 1897–18 Dec 1977 [80], Chicago IL; heart attack). AS, p. 925. BHD1, p. 466.

Ritchey, J.V. [producer]. No data found. AMD, p. 293. "Reliance Under New Management," *MPW*, 14 Oct 1911, 135.

Ritchey, William M. [scenarist] (b. Evansville IL, 1882?–14 Jan 1937 [55], Pasadena CA; heart attack). (Paramount; Metro.) "William M. Ritchey; One-Time Scenarist of Silent Films; Former Journalist," *NYT*, 16 Jan 1937, 17:4. "William M. Ritchey," *Variety*, 20 Jan 1937. AMD, p. 293. AS, p. 925. BHD2, p. 223. FDY, p. 437. IFN, p. 252. "William Ritchey, Serial Writer," *MPW*, 16 Jun 1917, 1790. "William M. Ritchey Writing for Pathé," *MPW*, 14 Jul 1917, 249. "William Ritchey Takes Charge at San Barbara," *MPW*, 22 Dec 1917, 1787. "New Editor for American Scenario Department," *MPW*, 29 Dec 1917, 1949. "Quits Writing," *MPW*, 9 Jul 1921, 211.

Ritchie, Billy [actor] (aka Willie Munro, b. Glasgow, Scotland, 14 Sep 1877–6 Jul 1921 [43], Los Angeles CA; from internal injuries from an ostrich attack two years previously). (L-KO, Jul 1914?) "Billie Ritchie," *Variety*, 15 Jul 1921 (age 42). "Obituary," *MPW*, 23 Jul 1921, 413. AMD, p. 293. IFN, p. 252. AS, p. 925. BHD, p. 286 (b. 1878). IFN, p. 252 (b. 1878). Katz, p. 975 (began 1914). Truitt, p. 285 (b. 1879). "Billy Ritchie, the Original 'Drunk,'" *MPW*, 13 Feb 1915, 991. "Billy Ritchie; Star of the L-Ko Comedy Company," *MPS*, 19 Mar 1915, 27 (b. 1877). "Screen Comedians; Billie Ritchie, Universal Film Company," *MPS*, 18 Jun 1915, 26–27 (b. England, 1877). "Billy Ritchie's New Home," *MPW*, 28 Sep 1918, 1880 (in Laurel Canyon CA).

Ritchie, Charles [actor] (d. 25 May 1931, Chattanooga TN). BHD, p. 286.

Ritchie, Edith [actress] (d. 24 Mar 1916, Bryn Mawr Hospital, Philadelphia PA). m. Steven Morris. (Lubin.) AMD, p. 293. IFN, p. 252. BHD, p. 286. "Edith Ritchie," *MPW*, 27 Mar 1915, 1937. "Two Lubin Players Dead," *MPW*, 15 Apr 1916, 431:2 (secured employment at Lubin because of financial reverses. "Later she became secretary of a booking concern, and it is believed that hard work in that position brought on a nervous ailment which resulted in her death, leaving a husband and invalid daughter to mourn her loss.").

Ritchie, Ethel *see* **Richie, Ethel**

Ritchie, Franklin [actor] (b. Ritchie PA, 26 Jun 1865–25 Jan 1918 [52], Los Angeles CA; auto accident). m. Esther Bamberg, 1916. (K&E; Ince; American.) "Franklin Ritchie Killed Under Auto," *NYT*, 27 Jan 1918, 17:2 (in *The Gentle Intruder* and *Beloved Rogues*). "Franklin Ritchie," *Variety*, 1 Feb 1918. AMD, p. 293. AS, p. 925. BHD, p. 286. IFN, p. 252. SD, p. 1062. "Franklyn Ritchie," *MPW*, 16 Feb 1918, 948.

Ritchie, John B. [scenarist]. No data found. AMD, p. 293. "Ritchie Made Script Head," *MPW*, 11 Dec 1920, 718.

Ritchie, Perry V. [actor] (b. KS, 23 Nov 1887–27 Jul 1918 [30], Los Angeles CA; suicide over "the refusal of a picture actress to marry him"). "Picture Actor Commits Suicide," *Variety*, 9 Aug 1918. AS, p. 925. BHD, p. 286. IFN, p. 252.

Ritchie, Robert Welles [scenarist]. No data found. AMD, p. 293. FDY, p. 437 (Wells Ritchie). "Robert Welles Ritchie," *MPW*, 22 Jul 1916, 646.

Rittau, Gunther [cameraman/director] (b. Koningshutte, Germany, 7 Aug 1893–6 Aug 1971 [77], Munich, Germany). AS, p. 925 (director). BHD2, p. 223. FDY, p. 467.

Ritter, Esther [actress] (b. IL, 30 Mar 1902–30 Dec 1925 [23], Los Angeles CA; appendicitis). m. **Cuyler Supplee** (d. 1944). "Esther Ritter Supplee," *Variety*, 13 Jan 1926. AS, p. 925. BHD, p. 286. IFN, p. 252. Truitt, p. 285. WWS, p. 285.

Ritter, George [actor] (d. 15 Dec 1919, New York NY). AS, p. 925. BHD, p. 286. IFN, p. 252.

Ritter, Karl [director/scenarist] (b. Wurzburg, Germany, 7 Nov 1888–7 Apr 1977 [88], Buenos Aires, Argentina). AS, p. 925. AS, p. 223.

Ritter, Paul J. [actor/producer] (d. 27 Apr 1962, Dacca, Pakistan). "Paul J. Ritter," *Variety*, 30 May 1962. AS, p. 925. AS, p. 223. IFN, p. 252.

Ritterband, Gerhard [actor/producer] (b. Berlin, Germany, 8 May 1904–29 Sep 1959 [54], Berlin, Germany). AS, p. 925. BHD, p. 286. IFN, p. 252.

Rittner, Rudolf [actor] (b. Weissbach, Germany, 30 Jun 1869–4 Feb 1943 [73], Germany). BHD1, p. 466. IFN, p. 252.

Ritz, Al [stage/film actor] (*né* Alfred Joachim or Joaquim, b. Newark NJ, 27 Aug 1901–22 Dec 1965 [64], New Orleans LA; heart attack). m. Annette. "Al Ritz, Comedian, Dies at 62; Oldest Member of Brother Act; Clowned Way to Fame, with Jimmy and Harry, in 30's—Victim of Heart Attack," *NYT*, 23 Dec 1965, 28:1 (age 62; 1st film, *Sing, Baby, Sing*). "Al Ritz," *Variety*, 29 Dec 1965 (age 62). AS, p. 925. BHD1, p. 466. IFN, p. 252 (b. 1903).

Ritzler, Robert [scenarist] (b. 1894–27 Nov 1936 [42?], Canton OH). BHD2, p. 223.

Rivas, José M[aria] **L**[inares] [actor] (b. Madrid, Spain, 17 Mar 1901–13 Apr 1955 [54], Mexico City, Mexico). AS, p. 926.

Rive, Joseph (father of **Ken Rive**) [cinematographer]. No data found.

Rivel, Charlie [actor/clown] (*né* José Andreu y Laserre, b. Cubellas, Spain, 23 Apr 1896–26 Jul 1983 [87], Barcelona, Spain). AS, p. 926.

Rivelles, Rafael [actor] (*né* Rafael Rivelles Guillen, b. Valencia, Spain, 1898–1971 [73?]). IFN, p. 252 (b. 1899; d. Nov 1966, age 67). Waldman, p. 246.

Rivero, Julian [actor] (b. San Francisco CA, 25 Jul 1890–24 Feb 1976 [85], Los Angeles CA). m. **Isabel Thomas** (d. 1948). "Julian Rivero," *Variety,* 3 Mar 1976. BHD1, p. 466 (b. 1891). AS, p. 926. BHD2, p. 223 (b. 1891). IFN, p. 252. George A. Katchmer, "Remembering the Great Silents," *CI,* 175 (Jan 1990), C8.

Rivers Cadet (brother of **Fernand Rivers**) [ctor] (*né* Jean-Maurice Large, b. Paris, France, 1 Mar 1892–1 Nov 1968 [76], Issy-les-Moulineaux, France [extrait de décès no. 721]). AS, p. 926.

Rivers, Fernand (brother of **Cadet Rivers**) [actor/producer/director/distributor] (*né* Fernand Large, b. Saint-Lager, France, 6 Sep 1879–12 Sep 1960 [81], Nice, France). m. "Fernand Rivers," *Variety,* 220, 7 Sep 1960, 63:3 ("Originally an actor, he first appeared in early slapstick silent films."). AS, p. 926. BHD, p. 286; BHD2, p. 223 (b. 1882-d. Aug 1960). IFN, p. 252.

Rives, Amelie *see* **Troubetzkoy, Princess Youcca**

Riviere, Fred "Curly" [actor] (b. England, 1875?–6 Nov 1935 [60], Los Angeles CA; heart attack). "Fred Riviere," *Variety,* 13 Nov 1935 ("cowboy film actor"). AS, p. 926. BHD1, p. 466. IFN, p. 252. Truitt, p. 286.

Rix, Felice [child actress] (b. 1911). "She Admits It Herself," *NYDM,* 20 Nov 1915, 33:3 (4 1/2 years old, in *The Unwritten Law,* California Motion Picture Co. "She quite frankly admits that she is the star of the cast.").

Rizzoli, Angelo [producer] (b. Milan, Italy, 31 Oct 1889–24 Sep 1970 [80], Milan, Italy). AS, p. 926. BHD2, p. 223.

Rizzotto, Giulia [actress] (b. Sicily, Italy). m. **Alfonso Cassini.** JS, p. 85 (in Italian silents from 1912).

Roach, Bert [actor] (*né* Egbert Roach, b. Washington DC, 21 Aug 1891–16 Feb 1971 [79], Los Angeles CA). (Christie, Universal; Sennett.) AMD, p. 293. AS, p. 926 (b. 1890). BHD1, p. 466. IFN, p. 252. MH, p. 134. "Roach with Century," *MPW,* 27 Sep 1924, 313. "Bert Roach Assigned," *MPW,* 15 Aug 1925, 748. "It's a Gift," *MPW,* 24 Dec 1927, 13. George Katchmer, "Remembering the Great Silents," *CI,* 239 (May 1995), C5.

Roach, Charles H. [executive] (b. Alexandria County VA, 28 Mar 1860–27 May 1936 [76], Culver City CA). BHD2, p. 224.

Roach, Hal E. [director/producer/scenarist/executive/Rolin Film Company] (*né* Harold Eugene Roach, b. Elmira NY, 14 Jan 1892–2 Nov 1992 [100], Bel-Air CA; pneumonia). m. (1) **Margaret Nichols** (d. 1941; son, Hal Roach, Jr., 1921–1972; daughter, Margaret, 1921–1964); (2) Lucille Prin (said she was 29), 31 Aug 1942, LA CA. (Began 1912; Universal; Essanay.) Peter B. Flint, "Hal Roach Is Dead at 100; A Pioneer in Film Comedy," *NYT,* 3 Nov 1992, B8:1. Judy Brennan, "Hal Roach," *Variety,* 9 Nov 1992, 78:1. "'Rascals' Creator Hal Roach Dies at 100," *New York Post,* 191, 3 Nov 1992, 2:1. AMD, p. 293. AS, p. 926. BHD, p. 286; BHD2, p. 224 (b. 19 Jan). Katz, pp. 977–78 (began 1912). "Hal Roach of Rolin Married," *MPW,* 25 Nov 1916, 1173. "Rolin Company's Rise," *MPW,* 2 Jun 1917, 1426. "Hal Roach in New York, " *MPW,* 22 Sep 1917, 1838. "Hal Roach Buys Whiting's Interest in Rolin," *MPW,* 4 May 1918, 681. "Harold Lloyd, Comedian, Injured by Explosion of Property Bomb," *MPW,* 6 Sep 1919, 1449. "Hal Roach Receives Many WIres Praising New Harold Lloyd Comedy, 'Haunted Spooks,'" *MPW,* 10 Apr 1920, 277. "Hal E. Roach Invests Large Amount in Studios to Meet Growing Business Needs," *MPW,* 7 May 1921, 51. "Roach Pays Brunet Annual Visit; Says Studio Resources Utilized to Limit to Keep Pace with Pathé Distribution," *MPW,* 14 Jan 1922, 155. "Pathé Signs for Three Year Output of Hal Roach Studios," *MPW,* 18 Feb 1922, 724. "Hal Roach Studios to Devote All Their Time to Comedies," *MPW,* 8 Apr 1922, 619. "Hal Roach Calls Forces Together; Emphasizes Cleanliness in Films," *MPW,* 17 Jun 1922, 619. "Roach Buys Film Ranch to Meet Demand for More Studio Space," *MPW,* 17 Mar 1923, 308. "Lloyd and Roach Terminate Relations in a Friendly Way," *MPW,* 7 Jul 1923, 52. "Pathé Confirms Report," *MPW,* 11 Aug 1923, 465 ("School for Directors"). "Roach Joins Hays," *MPW,* 18 Aug 1923, 548. "Hal Roach's Ninth Year with Pathé," *MPW,* 8 Sep 1923, 182. "Hal Roach to Amplify Pathé's Feature Production Activities," *MPW,* 17 Nov 1923, 321. "Roach to Cruise," *MPW,* 12 Jul 1924, 124. Annie Hamilton Donnell, "Our Gang; A Story About the Smallest Private School in the World," *MW,* 1 Nov 1924, 3–4, 28–29. "New Harold Roach-Pathé Contract Involves $15,000,000 in Pictures," *MPW,* 4 Apr 1925, 444. "Mack Sennett Perfects 1925-'26 Plans; Harold Roach's Huge Program for Pathé," *MPW,* 18 Apr 1925, 682. "Don't Crowd, Girls," *MPW,* 6 Jun 1925, 689. Hal Roach, "A New Day a New Policy," *MPW,* 9 Jan 1926, 173. "At Last—Here's Something New in Pictures," *MPW,* 30 Jan 1926, 475. Hal Roach, "The New Trend in Short Comedies," *MPW,* 3 Apr 1926, 352. "Hal Roach Discusses Comedy Production," *MPW,* 29 May 1926, 413. "Roach to Open Location Camp," *MPW,* 31 Jul 1926, 299. "'Drop in Houses' for the Cities," *MPW,* 30 Oct 1926, 539. "Roach Remodels," *MPW,* 30 Oct 1926, 3. "Hal Roach Describes Short Subject Theatre," *MPW,* 6 Nov 1926, 22–24. "Roach Admits He Desires D.W. Griffith," *MPW,* 4 Dec 1926, 337. "Reincorporation by Roach Adds Power to Strong Unit," *MPW,* 29 Jan 1927, 355. "Roach Tells of News Reel Plan for Mr. Hearst," *MPW,* 5 Mar 1927, 33. "Roach Changes Short Subject Theatre Plans," *MPW,* 7 May 1927, 23. "Big Box Office Names to Adorn Billings of Roach Two-Reelrs," *MPW,* 24 Sep 1927, 217–18. "Hal Roach Dissects Vote on 'Presentations,'" *MPW,* 8 Oct 1927, 368, 371. "Roach-West Coast Tie-Up for 'Gang' Talent," *MPW,* 26 Nov 1927, 8. Nicholas Niles, "Hal Roach of 'Our Gang' Fame," *Cinema Arts,* Dec 1927, 20, 49. "Hal Roach Supports Contest to Find 'Our Gang' Member," *MPW,* 24 Dec 1927, 23. "[Major] Hal Roach Takes Bride; 'Our Gang' Comedy Originator Marries Miss Lucille Prin," *NYT,* 1 Sep 1942, 23:4. "Centenarian Hal Roach Tours Berlin Studio, Too Tired to Take Award," *CI,* 201 (Mar 1992), 4. Richard M. Roberts, "Their Gangs; A Look at the Our Gang Spinoff Comedies of the 1920s," *CI,* 267 (Sep 1997), 26–40.

Roach, Jack [cinematographer]. No data found. FDY, p. 467.

Roach, John B. [assistant director] (b. Elmira NY, 15 Sep 1889–8 Nov 1979 [90], San Diego CA). BHD2, p. 224.

Roach, Joseph Anthony [scenarist]. No data found. m. **Ruth Stonehouse,** 1914, St. Louis MO (d. 1941). (Essanay.) AMD, p. 294. FDY, p. 437. "An Essanay Elopement; Joseph Roach and Ruth Stonehouse Are Married in St. Louis," *NYDM,* 4 Feb 1914, 30:2. "Roach on 24-Hour Notice," *MPW,* 27 Oct 1917, 544.

Roache, Viola [actress] (b. England, 3 Oct 1885–17 May 1961 [75], Los Angeles CA). AS, p. 927.

Roan, Tom [scenarist]. No data found. FDY, p. 437.

Roanne, André [actor] (*né* André Albert Louis Rahou, b. Paris, France, 22 Sep 1896–6 Sep 1959 [63], Cannes, France [extrait de décès no. 470/1859]). AS, p. 927. BHD1, p. 466. IFN, p. 253.

Roanne, Gabrielle [actress] (*née* Gabrielle Pollefeyt, b. Brussels, Belgium, 26 Oct 1888). AS, p. 927.

Roark, C[harles] **F**[rancis] **(Counsellor)** [actor] (b. IN, 26 Apr 1860–15 Nov 1929 [69]). BHD, p. 286. IFN, p. 253.

Roasio, Maria [actress] (b. Milan, Italy). JS, p. 383 (in Italian silents from 1917; "One of the last of Ambrosio's divas.").

Robards, Jason Nelson, **Sr.** [stage/film/TV actor] (father of Jason Robards, Jr., b.1922; grandfather of Jason Robards III, b. 1949) (b. Hillsdale MI, 31 Dec 1892–4 Apr 1963 [70], Sherman Oaks CA; heart attack). m. Agnes Lynch. "Jason Robards Sr., 70, Dead; Stage, TV and Screen Actor; Made Broadway Debut in '17—Resumed Career in 1957 After 8 Years of Blindness," *NYT,* 6 Apr 1963, 19:1. "Jason Robards Sr.," *Variety,* 10 Apr 1963. AMD, p. 294. AS, p. 927. BHD1, p. 467. FSS, p. 249. IFN, p. 253. Katz, p. 978. SD. Truitt, p. 286. Truitt, p. 286. "Jason Robards Working in Two Warner Films," *MPW,* 29 Jan 1927, 347. "Jason Robards," *MPW,* 18 Jun 1927, 484.

Robards, Willis Lewis [actor/producer/director/writer] (b. TX, 1 Jan 1873–3 Nov 1921 [48], Los Angeles CA; heart disease). (Universal.) AMD, p. 294. AS, p. 927. BHD, p. 287; BHD2, p. 224. IFN, p. 253. "Director Robards Happy," *MPW,* 9 Mar 1912, 881. "Enter—Willis Lewis Robards, III," *MPW,* 24 Aug 1912, 758 (birth of son). "Willis Lewis Robards with Frontier," *MPW,* 20 Sep 1913, 1291. "Willis Lewis Robards," *MPW,* 27 Jun 1914, 1833. "Finishes Part, Then Dies," *MPW,* 26 Nov 1921, 425.

Robbins, Edwina [actress] (*née* Edwina Mercier, b. 18 Jan 1886). AMD, p. 294. "Edwina Robbins," *MPW,* 5 Jun 1915, 1607.

Robbins, Elmer W. [film editor] (b. 1889?–3 Mar 1920 [30], Laguna Beach CA). AMD, p. 294. "Obituary," *MPW,* 20 Mar 1920, 1963 (founded *Camera* magazine).

Robbins, Herman [executive] (b. 1888–31 Jul 1963 [75?], New York NY). BHD2, p. 224.

Robbins, J. Edwin [director] (b. 1897?–18 Jul 1940 [43], Hermosilla, Mexico; heart attack). "J. Edwin Robbins," *Variety,* 24 Jul 1940 ("film director in the silent days"). AS, p. 927. BHD2, p. 224.

Robbins, J.J. [cameraman]. No data found. (Essanay, 1909 or earlier.) "The Essanay Company Out West," *MPW,* 4 Dec 1909, 801–02 (photographed *The Heart of a Cowboy*).

Robbins, Jean, "The Girl with Possibilities" [actor] (b. 1904?–20 Jun 1977 [73], No. Bergen NJ; apoplexy). "Jean Robbins," *Variety,* 29 Jun 1977 (female impersonator). AS, p. 927.

Robbins, Jesse J. [director] (b. Dayton OH, 30 Apr 1886–11 Mar 1973 [86], Los Angeles CA). AMD, p. 294. BHD2, p. 224. "New Director for Aubrey Comedies," *MPW,* 28 Feb 1920, 1494. "Signs Robbins," *MPW,* 1 Nov 1924, 63.

Robbins, Marcus B. [actor/scenarist] (*né* Mercus B. Robbins, b. 3 Jan 1868–5 Apr 1931 [63], Los Angeles CA). (American.) AMD, p. 295. AS, p. 927 (d. 7 Apr). BHD, p. 287; BHD2, p. 224. IFN, p. 253. Truitt, p. 286 (d. Apr 7). "Robbins Resigns from Fox," *MPW,* 19 Jul 1919, 364. "Robbins Joins Metro Writing Staff," *MPW,* 29 May 1920, 1194. George Katchmer, "Mark Robbins," *CI,* 227 (May 1994), 49:1.

Robbins, Roy "Skeeter Bill" [actor] (*né* Roy Robert Robbins, b. Glen Rock WY, 16 Jul 1887–28 Nov 1933 [46], Los Angeles CA; auto accident). AS, p. 928 (d. 29 Nov 1923, Mint Acton Canyon CA). BHD1, p. 467. George Katchmer, "Remembering the Great Silents," *CI,* 233 (Nov 1994), 38.

Robbins, Tod [scenarist]. No data found. FDY, p. 437.

Robbins, Walter [actor] (b. Chicago IL, 18 Oct 1888–13 Jul 1965 [76], Reseda CA). AS, p. 928 (b. NY NY). BHD1, p. 467. George Katchmer, "Walt Robbins," *CI,* 227 (May 1994), 49:2. George Katchmer, "Remembering the Great Silents," *CI,* 233 (Nov 1994), 38–39.

Robert, Mr. [cinematographer]. No data found. AMD, p. 295. "Pictrures of Fighting in Madeconia," *MPW,* 25 Oct 1913, 359.

Robert, Alfredo [director/actor] (b. Fucecchio, Italy, 5 Apr 1877). AS, p. 928 (b. Florence, Italy, 7 Apr). JS, p. 383 (in Italian silents from 1911).

Robert, Camille [composer] (b. France, 1871–29 Mar 1957 [85?], Paris, France). AS, p. 928.

Robert, Jacque [actor/director] (*né* Jacque Robert Kneubuhler, b. Switzerland, 1890–15 Jan 1928 [37?], France). AS, p. 928. BHD2, p. 224 (d. 16 Jan).

Roberti, Roberto (father of director Sergio Leone) [stage actor/film director] (*né* Leone Roberto Roberti, b. Torella dei Lombardi, near Avellino, Italy, 27 Apr 1869–9 Jan 1959 [89], Torella dei Lombarti, Italy [extrait de décès no. 1/1/1959]). m. Bice Valorian. AS, p. 928 (b. 1879). JS, p. 383 (in Italian silents from 1913).

Roberts, Albert G. [actor/cinematographer] (b. Blackfoot ID, 11 Oct 1902–30 May 1941 [38], No. Hollywood CA; suicide by shooting). m. **Peggy Shannon**, Oct 1940 (d. 1941). "Albert G. Roberts," *Variety,* 4 Jun 1941. AS, p. 928. BHD2, p. 224. IFN, p. 253. Truitt, p. 286.

Roberts, Anna [actress] (d. 15 Nov 1915, Quebec, Canada). "Actress Reported Dead," *Variety,* 3 Dec 1915, 20:4 (Roberts, "a one-time film queen, is reported dead in Quebec. Her father here [Los Angeles CA] received word this week to that effect."). AS, p. 928. BHD, p. 287.

Roberts, Arthur [actor/executive] (b. London, England, 21 Sep 1852–27 Feb 1933 [80], London, England). "Arthur Roberts," *Variety,* 7 Mar 1933. AMD, p. 295. AS, p. 928. BHD, p. 287. IFN, p. 253. "Arthur Roberts," *MPW,* 24 May 1913, 795.

Roberts, Arthur [film editor]. No data found. AMD, p. 295. "Arthur Roberts Joins Lehrman," *MPW,* 8 Nov 1919, 228.

Roberts, Beryl [actress]. No data found. AMD, p. 295. "Prize Beauty Wins," *MPW,* 2 Oct 1926, 284.

Roberts, Bob [cinematographer]. No data found. FDY, p. 467.

Roberts, Charles B. (Jack) [actor] (d. 14 Sep 1927, Los Angeles CA). BHD, p. 287. IFN, p. 253.

Roberts, Charles E. (Chuck) [comedian/scenarist/director] (b. 1894?–10 Nov 1951 [57], Los Angeles CA). (Griffith, 1914; Educational; RKO.) "Charles E. Roberts," *NYT,* 12 Nov 1951, 25:5 (wrote and directed Lloyd Hamilton comedies). "Charles E. Roberts," *Variety,* 14 Nov 1951. AS, p. 928. BHD2, p. 224.

Roberts, Desmond [actor] (b. London, England, 5 Feb 1894–11 Jan 1968 [73], London, England). AS, p. 928 (d. LA CA). BHD1, p. 468. IFN, p. 253.

Roberts, Edd J. [actor] (*né* Edward J. Roberts, b. 1892–23 Jan 1953 [60], Fort Worth TX). AS, p. 928.

Roberts, Edith Josephine [stage/film actress] (b. New York NY, 17 Sep 1898–20 Aug 1935 [36], Los Angeles CA; complications during the birth of her son). m. Harold Carter; Earl Snokes; William A. Duncan. (Universal, 1914.) "Edith Roberts," *Variety,* 28 Aug 1935. AMD, p. 295. AS, p. 928. BHD, p. 287 (b. 1899). FFF, p. 152. FSS, p. 249. IFN, p. 253. Katz, p. 980. MH, p. 135. SD. Truitt, p. 286. WWS, p. 229. "Here's the Real Youngest Star!," *MPW,* 12 Feb 1916, 964. "Edith Roberts Joins L-KO Forces," *MPW,* 3 May 1919, 641. "Universal Signs Contract with Little Edith Roberts," *MPW,* 10 Jan 1920, 293. "Universal Star Deserts Studio One Night to Be Hit by Revue," *MPW,* 19 Mar 1921, 304. "Edith Roberts in Leading Role in DeMille Play," *MPW,* 17 Sep 1921, 317. "Edith Roberts in Cast," *MPW,* 26 Aug 1922, 665. "Distinctive Pictures Signs Edith Roberts," *MPW,* 2 Dec 1922, 422. George Katchmer, "Remembering the Great Silents," *CI,* 254 (Aug 1996), 49–50 (b. 1899).

Roberts, Evelyn [actor] (b. Reading, Berkshire, England, 28 Aug 1886–30 Nov 1962 [76], London, England). AS, p. 928 (b. 1896). BHD, p. 287. IFN, p. 253.

Roberts, Florence [stage/film actress] (b. Frederick MD, 16 Mar 1861–6 Jun 1940 [79], Los Angeles CA). m. Walter Gale. (Film debut: *Grandma's Girl,* Sennett.) "Florence Roberts, Screen Actress, 79; Veteran of Character Parts Took Role of Grandma in 'Jones Family' Films; Began on Stage When 19; Made First Appearance at the Brooklyn Opera House—Got Film Start with Sennett," *NYT,* 7 Jun 1940, 23:4 (b. Isle of Man). "Florence Roberts," *Variety,* 12 Jun 1940. AS, p. 929. BHD1, p. 468. IFN, p. 253. Truitt, p. 287.

Roberts, Florence (cousin of **Theodore Roberts**) [actress] (b. New York NY, 14 Feb 1871–17 Jul 1927 [56], Los Angeles CA; after emergency surgery). m. (1) Lewis Morrison (d. 1906); (2) **Fredrik Vogeding** (d. 1942). "Florence Roberts," *Variety,* 20 Jul 1927. AMD, p. 295. AS, p. 928. BHD, p. 287. IFN, p. 253. SD. Truitt, p. 287. "Florence Roberts," *MPW,* 9 Aug 1913, 645. "Back in Pictures," *MPW,* 17 Dec 1921, 793. "Obituary," *MPW,* 30 Jul 1927, 317.

Roberts, Frances [actress] (b. Furnas County? NB, 19 Oct 1886–16 Oct 1971 [84], Palmdale CA). m. **Raymond Hatton,** 17 Apr 1909, Vancouver WA (resided in Portland OR at the time; d. 1971). AS, p. 929. BHD, p. 195. IFN, p. 136. Truitt, p. 146 (b. 1888). Photocopy of Marriage Certificate supplied by Charles R. Roberts, Steilacoom WA.

Roberts, Fred [actor] (b. London, England, 15 Jun 1850–28 Aug 1930 [80], Brooklyn NY). m. Fanny V. Reynolds. "Fred Roberts," *Variety,* 3 Sep 1930. AS, p. 929.

Roberts, George [actor/playwright] (b. England, 1845–25 Apr 1930 [85?], London, England; months after fracturing a leg in a fall). "George Roberts (English)," *Variety,* 14 May 1930, 76:1. AS, p. 929. BHD, p. 287.

Roberts, Hans [actor] (b. 1874–2 May 1954 [80?], Jamaica NY). BHD, p. 287.

Roberts, J[ohn] **H**[enry] [stage/film actor] (b. London, England, 11 Jul 1884–1 Feb 1961 [76], London, England). m. Beatrice Smith. "J.H. Roberts," *Variety,* 1 Mar 1961. AS, p. 929. BHD1, p. 468. IFN, p. 253. SD.

Roberts, Joseph [actor] (b. 1870?–28 Oct 1923 [53], Los Angeles CA). AMD, p. 295. AS, p. 929. BHD, p. 287. IFN, p. 253. "Buster Keaton as a Duffer Linesman Promises Laughs to Devotees to Golf," *MPW,* 25 Sep 1920, 472.

Roberts, Leona [actress] (b. 1880–30 Jan 1954 [73], Santa Monica CA). AS, p. 929.

Roberts, Lynne (daughter of film extra May Roberts) [extra in silents/vaudeville/film/radio/stage/TV actress] (aka Lynn Roberts and Mary Hart, *née* Theda Mae Roberts, b. El Paso TX, 22 Nov 1922–1 Apr 1978 [55], LA USC Medical Center, Los Angeles CA; respiratory failure due to an intercranial hemorrhage as a result of a fall in the bathroom when she hit her head on the tiles on 16 Dec 1977; buried at Forest Lawn Memorial Park on 4 Apr 1978 alongside her mother). m. (1) William Englebert, Jr., 5 Jan 1941—div. 14 Dec 1944 (son, William Englebert III, b. 6 Apr 1942); (2) Louis John Gardella, 16 Dec 1944—div. 1951; (3) Hyman B. Samuels, 6 Jun 1953, Ontario CA (daughter Peri Margaret, b. 1955)—div. 4 Aug 1958; remarried—div. 1961; (4) Don Sebastian, 1971. (Republic; TC-F; Monogram; last film: *Port Sinister,* RKO, 1953.) AS, p. 929 (b. 1919). BHD1, p. 468. Barrie Roberts, "Lynne Roberts: 'Bette Davis, I'm Not!,'" *CI,* 290 (Aug 1999), 8–13 (includes filmography. She was named after Theda Bara, her mother's favorite film star).

Roberts, Merrill [actor] (b. 1885–2 Dec 1940 [55?], Los Angeles CA). AS, p. 929.

Roberts, Nancy [actress] (*née* Annette Finlay, b. St. Asaph, Wales, 1882–25 Jun 1962 [80?], London, England). AS, p. 929 (b. Luban, England, 1892). BHD1, p. 468.

Roberts, R.B. [executive]. No data found. m. Frankie Aldrich, 1915. AMD, p. 295. "R.B. Roberts Married," *MPW,* 4 Dec 1915, 1810.

Roberts, Ralph Arthur [actor/director/scenarist] (*né* Robert Arthur Schonherr, b. Meerane, Germany, 2 Oct 1886–12 Mar 1940 [53], Berlin, Germany). AS, p. 929 (b. 1884). BHD1, p. 468; BHD2, p. 224 (b. 1884). IFN, p. 254 (b. 1884).

Roberts, Sara Jane ["Our Gang" child actress and Liberace's secretary] (b. NB, 8 Mar 1923–19 Aug 1968 [45], Los Angeles CA). "Sara

Jane Roberts," *Variety,* 28 Aug 1968. AS, p. 929. BHD1, p. 468. IFN, p. 254. Truitt, p. 287.

Roberts, Stephen R. [actor/director] (b. Summerville MA, 23 Nov 1895–17 Jul 1936 [40], Beverly Hills CA; heart attack). "Stephen Roberts," *Variety,* 22 Jul 1936 (age 41). AMD, p. 295. AS, p. 929. BHD, p. 287; BHD2, p. 224 (b. Summerville WV). Katz, p. 980. "Lion Cub Claws Director," *MPW,* 23 Oct 1926, 493. "Stephen Roberts," *MPW,* 27 Aug 1927, 588.

Roberts, Theodore, "The Grand Duke of Hollywood" (cousin of **Florence Roberts**) [stage/film actor] (b. San Francisco CA, 8 Oct 1861–14 Dec 1928 [67], Los Angeles CA; uremic poisoning). m. Lucy C., 1890, NYC; **Florence Smythe**, Oct 1917 (d. 1925); Ms. Harron. (Began 1910; FP-L; Paramount.) "Theodore Roberts, Screen Star, Dead; Veteran Actor, Well Known on the Stage, Found Chief Success in the Films; Motion Picture Pioneer Starting Life on Boards at 18; He Later Tried Studio as Experiment—Played Many Leads," *NYT,* 15 Dec 1928, 19:5. "Theodore Roberts," *Variety,* 19 Dec 1928. AMD, p. 295. AS, p. 929 (b. 2 Oct). BHD1, p. 468. FFF, p. 26. FSS, p. 250. IFN, p. 254. Katz, pp. 980–81. MH, p. 135. SD. Truitt, p. 287. "More Lasky Stars," *MPW,* 22 Aug 1914, 1107. "Theodore Roberts Re-Engaged by Lasky," *MPW,* 22 May 1915, 1235. "Sues for Alimony," *NYDM,* 18 Aug 1915, 13:1 (Lucy C. sued Roberts, of FP-L, for back alimony. Granted a legal separation in 1912 by the Supreme Court of NY accompanied by an order to pay her $50 a week alimony during her life. She asserted that about $3,000 was paid and now demanded what she claimed was still due her.). Kenneth McGaffey, "Busting the Hair Trust; Theodore Roberts grows his own foilage, and has never been bald out for a poor crop," *Photoplay,* Jul 1917, 35–36 (re Roberts' ingenuity with hair pieces). "Doesn't Want Final Divorce," *Variety,* 12 Oct 1917, p. 12 ("LA, Oct. 10. Mrs. Lucy C. Roberts, granted recently an interlocutory decree of divorce…to refrain from making a final decree against her husband…"). "Theodore Roberts Remarries," *Variety,* 19 Oct 1917, p. 13 (married Smythe, who was corespondent in divorce action). "Theodore Roberts Renews Famous Players Contract," *MPW,* 6 Sep 1919, 1468. Hazel Simpson Naylor, "His Dream House and Himself," *MPC,* Dec 1921, 48, 95. Maude Cheatham, "The Darkest Hour, VI," *Classic,* Dec 1922, 43. "Theodore Roberts Given Big Ovation by Hollywood Folk," *MPW,* 7 Jun 1924, 540. "Theodore Roberts," *MPW,* 23 Jul 1927, 239:1 (finished a 42-week vaudeville engagement; ill for 3 1/2 years, he used a crutch and cane). Dorothy Calhoun, "Alive and Sticking; Theodore Roberts, the Dean of the Screen, Lights a Fresh Stogie," *MPC,* Oct 1928, 22, 78 ("Neither he nor his cigar has lost its drawing power.").

Roberts, Theodore Goodridge [actor] (b. 1877?–23 Feb 1953 [75], Digby, Nova Scotia). "Theodore G. Roberts," *NYT,* 25 Feb 1953, 27:3 (age 75). AS, p. 929. WWS, p. 14.

Roberts, Thomas Benton [actor] (d. 11 May 1987, Los Angeles CA). BHD, p. 287.

Roberts, Walter C. [actor] (d. 21 Mar 1926, South Haven MI). BHD, p. 287.

Robertshaw, Jerrold [actor] (b . Allerton, York, England, 28 Mar 1866–14 Feb 1941 [74], London, England). AS, p. 929 (b. Albertson, England). BHD1, p. 469. IFN, p. 254. SD, p. 1067. Truitt, p. 287.

Robertson, Agnes [Kelly] [stage/film actress] (b. Edinburgh, Scotland, 25 Dec 1832–6 Nov 1916 [83], London, England). m. **Dion Boucicault** (d. 1929). "Agnes Robertson Dead; Once Famous Actress, the Widow of Dion Boucicault, Dies at 83," *NYT,* 7 Nov 1916, 11:4 (age 83). "Mrs.Dion Boucicault," *Variety,* 10 Nov 1916 (age 82). AS, p. 929. SD.

Robertson, Clifford [casting director]. No data found. AMD, p. 295. "Robertson Engaged as Casting Director by M-G-M," *MPW,* 3 Apr 1926, 327.

Robertson, Sir J. Forbes *see* **Forbes-Robertson, Johnston**

Robertson, James Francis [actor] (b. Weymouth, England, 1868?–18 May 1942 [74], Nyack NY). "James F. Robertson," *NYT,* 19 May 1942, 19:5 (age 73). "James Francis Robertson," *Variety,* 20 May 1942. AS, p. 930. BHD1, p. 469.

Robertson, James (Scotty) [actor] (b. 1859?–13 Nov 1936 [77], Los Angeles CA). (Paramount.) "James Robertson," *Variety,* 18 Nov 1936 ("oldest employe in point of service at the studio"). BHD1, p. 469. IFN, p. 254.

Robertson, Jean [actress] (b. Australia, 1894?–15 Aug 1967 [73], Sydney, Australia). "Jean Robertson," *Variety,* 30 Aug 1967 ("Miss Robertson also starred in several silent films"). AS, p. 930. BHD, p. 287. IFN, p. 254. Truitt, p. 287.

Robertson, John S[tewart] [actor/director] (b. London, Ontario, Canada, 14 Jun 1878 [Birth certificate #018165, no. 201]–5 Nov 1964 [86], Escondido CA). m. **Josephine Lovett** (d. 1958). (Vitagraph.) "John Robertson, 86, of Early Film Days," *NYT,* 8 Nov 1964, 88:6 (began 1915). "John S. Robertson," *Variety,* 18 Nov 1964 ("film pioneer who was one of the top silent screen directors"; d. 7 Nov). AMD, p. 295. AS, p. 930 (d. 7 Nov). BHD, p. 287; BHD2, p. 224. IFN, p. 254. Katz, p. 981. Truitt, p. 287. "With Inspiration," *MPW,* 18 Nov 1922, 246. Susan Elizabeth Brady, "Little Great Heart," *Classic,* Mar 1923, 18–19 (Robertson discusses Pickford). "John Robertson Sees Higher Standard in Acting," *MPW,* 9 Jun 1923, 507. Faith Service, "The Tortures of Cutting," *MPC,* Nov 1924, 20, 86–87. "Meador Signs Robertson to Direct Trucraft Specials," *MPW,* 25 Jul 1925, 454. "Robertson to Make Pictures for M-G-M," *MPW,* 20 Mar 1926, 168. Robert Grosvenor, "John S. Robertson, His Opinions and Personality; Known as the 'Best-Liked Director in Hollywood,' He Combines the Enthusiasm of an Amateur With the Practical Sense of One of the Most Experienced Men in the Industry," *Cinema Arts,* Dec 1927, 21, 47.

Robertson, Lolita [stage/film actress] (b. CA, ca. 1890). m. **Max Figman** (d. 1952). AMD, p. 295. BHD, p. 287. SD. "New Lasky Picture Stars," *MPW,* 16 May 1914, 953. "Figman—Robertson Comedies for Metro," *MPW,* 8 Jul 1916, 241.

Robertson, Orie O. [stuntman/actor] (b. IL, 9 Jan 1881–14 Apr 1964 [83], Los Angeles CA; cancer). "Orie O. Robertson," *Variety,* 22 Apr 1964 ("early-day cowboy actor and stuntman"). AS, p. 930. BHD, p. 287. IFN, p. 254. Truitt, p. 287.

Robertson, Willard [actor] (b. Runnels TX, 1 Jan 1886–5 Apr 1948 [62], Los Angeles Co. CA). AS, p. 930. BHD1, p. 469. IFN, p. 254. Katz, p. 981.

Robeson, Paul [singer/stage and film actor] (*né* Paul Leroy Bustill Robeson, Sr., b. Princeton NJ, 9 Apr 1898–23 Jan 1976 [77], Philadelphia PA; severe cerebral vascular disorder, from stroke on 28 Dec 1975). m. Eslanda Cardozo Goode, 1921 (b. WA 1896-d. 13 Dec 1965 [68], NYC). *Here I Stand* (NY: Othello, 1958); Martin Bauml Duberman, *Paul Robeson* (NY: Knopf, 1988); Dorothy Butler Gilliam, *Paul Robeson: All American* (Washington DC: NY Republic Book Co., 1976; Shirley Graham, *Paul Robeson: Citizen of the World* (NY: Julian Messner, 1948). (Film debut: *Body and Soul,* 1924.) Alden Whitman, "Paul Robeson Dead at 77; Singer, Actor and Activist," *NYT,* 24 Jan 1976, 1:5, 30:1 (Stalin Peace Prize, 1953); "Robeson Funeral Tuesday [27 Jan], 25 Jan 1976, 44:2; Charlayne Hunter, "Mourners, at the Chapel, 'Go Tell It' to Robeson," 27 Jan 1976, 34:1; Charlayne Hunter, "5000 at Robeson's Funeral in Harlem," 28 Jan 1976, 36:3; "Notes on People," 4 Feb 1976, 65:7 (left 3/4 of his $150,000 estate to his son, Paul Robeson, Jr., and the rest to his sister Marion Forsythe, with whom he lived in Philadelphia. Will entered for probate on 3 Feb 1976); "Rutgers Memorial Service Pays Homage to Robeson," 6 Feb 1976, 32:2 (Rutgers was his alma mater). "Paul Robeson," *Variety,* 28 Jan 1976. "Eslanda Goode Robeson Is Dead; Writer and Wife of Singer, 68," *NYT,* 14 Dec 1965, 43:4 (wrote *Paul Robeson, Negro* [1930] and *African Journey* [1945]). AS, p. 930. BHD1, p. 469. IFN, p. 254. Wheeler Winston Dixon, "Compromise and Triumph: The Films of Paul Robeson," *CI,* 305 (Nov 2000), 67–72.

Robey, George [stage/film actor] (*né* George Edward Wade, b. London, England, 20 Sep 1869–29 Nov 1954 [85], Saltdean, Sussex, England). m. (1) Ethel Haydon; (2) Blanche Littler (d. 1981). "Sir George Robey, Music Hall Comic; 'Prime Minister of Mirth,' 85, a Practitioner of 'Honest Vulgarity,' Dies in England," *NYT,* 30 Nov 1954, 29:2. "Sir George Robey," *Variety,* 1 Dec 1954. AS, p. 930. BHD1, p. 469. IFN, p. 254. SD.

Robin, Leo [lyricist] (*né* Leon Robin, b. Pittsburgh PA, 6 Apr 1895–29 Dec 1984 [89], Woodland Hills CA; heart failure). m. Cherie. (Paramount.) "Leo Robin, a Lyricist, Is Dead," *NYT,* 3 Jan 1985, B8:4 (AA for *Thanks for the Memory*). "Leo Robin," *Variety,* 9 Jan 1985. AS, p. 930 (b. 1899). BHD2, p. 224 (b. 1889).

Robinne, Gabrielle Anna Charlotte [actress] (b. Montlucon, France, 1 Jul 1886 [extrait de naissance no. 345]-18 Dec 1980 [94], Saint-Cloud, France). AS, p. 930. BHD, p. 288.

Robins, Edward H. [actor] (b. Shamokin PA, 15 Oct 1880–27 Jul 1955 [74], Paramus NJ). AS, p. 930.

Robinson, Bill "Bojangles" [dancer/actor] (*né* Luther Robinson, b. Richmond VA, 25 May 1878–25 Nov 1949 [71], New York NY; heart attack). m. (1) Fannie S. Clay; (2) Elaine Dash. "Bill (Bojangles) Robinson Dies; 'King of the Tap Dancers' Was 71," *NYT,* 26 Nov 1949, 1:2, 10:3. "Bill Robinson," *Variety,* 30 Nov 1949 (age 71). AS, p. 930. BHD1, p. 469. IFN, p. 254. Katz, p. 982. SD. Truitt, p. 287. Zan Turner, "The Tap Dancing King—'Bo Jangles,'" *CI,* 181 (Jul 1990), 45; 182 (Aug 1990), 26 *et passim.*

Robinson, Carlyle [publicist]. No data found. m. Maurie Newell, 16 Jan 1920, LA CA. AMD, p. 295. "Flashes; Another Filmdom Wedding," *LA Times,* 17 Jan 1920, II, 7. "Back with Chaplin," *MPW,* 22 Oct 1927, 481.

Robinson, Casey [title writer/scenarist/actor/director] (*né* Kenneth Casey Robinson, b. Logan UT, 17 Oct 1903–6 Dec 1979 [76], Sydney, Australia). m. (1) Audray Dale; (2) Tavara Toumanova (1917–1996); (3) Joan Potts. "Casey Robinson," *Variety,* 12 Dec 1979. AS, p. 931. BHD2, p. 225. FDY, p. 447. IFN, p. 254.

Robinson, Daisy O. [actress] (b. New York NY, 26 Apr 1889–3 Jun 1967 [78], Los Angeles CA). (UA.) BHD1, p. 616.

Robinson, Dewey [actor] (b. New Haven CT, 17 Aug 1898–11 Dec 1950 [52], Las Vegas NV). AS, p. 930.

Robinson, Edward G. [actor] (*né* Emanuel Goldenberg or Rabinowich, b. Bucharest, Romania, 12 Dec 1893–26 Jan 1973 [79], Los Angeles CA; cancer). (Film Debut: *Bright Shawl.*) m. (1) Gladys Lloyd [1896–1971], 1927–55 (son, Edward G. "Manny" Robinson, Jr. [1933–1974]); (2) Jane Bodenheimer ("Jane Arden"). "Edward G. Robinson, 79, Dies, His 'Little Caesar' Set a Style"; Alden Whitman, "Man of Great Kindness," *NYT,* 27 Jan 1973, 1:7, 32:3. "Ed. G. Robinson, 79; Long and Notable Thesping Career," *Variety,* 31 Jan 1973 (*né* Goldenberg). AS, p. 931. BHD1, p. 469. IFN, p. 254. Katz, p. 983. Christoher Finch and Linda Rosenkrantz, *Gone Hollywood* (Garden City NY: Doubleday & Co., Inc., 1979), p. 42 (overindulged by his parents, Manny Robinson was sent to a military school. "Manny became increasingly disturbed, feeling that his father worked so hard that they had no time together. The only thing that seemed to unite the family was crises, and so Manny, in his early teens, began to manufacture them. There were joy rides in stolen cars, traffic violations and crashes, and before long, Manny's old friends in the Beverly Hills police department were getting to know him in a new way."). Eric Niderost, "Edward G. Robinson: The Classic Gangster," *CI,* 215 (May 1993), 20 *et passim.*

Robinson, Forrest [stage/film actor] (b. NY, 2 Aug 1858–6 Jan 1924 [65], Los Angeles CA). m. (1) Eugenie Blair; (2) Mabel Burt. "Forrest Robinson," *NYT,* 8 Jan 1924, 23:3 ("for many years an actor in motion pictures and on the stage"). "Forest Robinson," *Variety,* 10 Jan 1924. AS. p. 931. BHD, p. 288. IFN, p. 254. Truitt, p. 288.

Robinson, Frances [actress] (*née* Marion Frances Ladd, b. Fort Wadsworth NY, 26 Apr 1916–16 Aug 1971 [55], Los Angeles CA; heart attack). AS, p. 931 (d. 15 Aug). BHD1, p. 470. IFN, p. 254.

Robinson, Francis De Groat [cinematographer] (b. 1878–7 Feb 1941 [62?], Altadena CA). BHD2, p. 225.

Robinson, George H. [cinematographer] (b. CA, 2 Apr 1890–30 Aug 1958 [68], Los Angeles CA). (Universal.) BHD2, p. 225. FDY, p. 467. Halliwell 12, p. 353. Katz, pp. 983–84.

Robinson, George K. [producer] (b. 1865-Nov 1923 [58?], Newark NJ). BHD2, p. 225.

Robinson, Gertrude R. [actress] (b. New York NY, 1891–19 Mar 1962 [71], Woodland Hills CA). m. **James Kirkwood, Sr.**, 30 Sep 1916, Santa Barbara CA (d. 1963). (Biograph, 1909; K&E; Reliance.) "Gertrude R. Kirkwood," *Variety,* 28 Mar 1962 ("early silent pix actress"). AMD, p. 295. AS, p. 931. BHD, p. 288. IFN, p. 254. SD. Truitt, p. 288. "In the Catskills with Reliance," *MPW,* 14? Aug 1912, 748–51. "Kirkwood—Robinson," *MPW,* 21 Oct 1916, 412.

Robinson, Harry T. [actor] (b. Des Moines IA, 1 Jun 1872–8 Sep 1946 [74], Los Angeles CA). BHD, p. 288. IFN, p. 254.

Robinson, Henry S. [vaudevillian] (d. 20 Dec 1918, New York NY). "Henry S. Robinson," *Variety,* 27 Dec 1918. AS, p. 931 (Harry S.).

Robinson, J.A. [actor] (b. 1891–15 May 1936 [45?], Phoenix AZ). BHD, p. 288.

Robinson, Legal W. [actor] (b. 1877-Jan 1919 [41?], New York NY). BHD, p. 288. IFN, p. 254.

Robinson, Lloyd [publicist]. No data found. (Edison.) AMD, p. 295. F.J. Beecroft, "Publicity Men I Have Met...," *NYDM,* 14 Jan 1914, 48 (*see* Beecroft, Chester for full citation). "Lloyd Robinson Joins Famous Players," *MPW,* 18 Sep 1915, 1972. "Lloyd Robinson on the Honor Roll," *MPW,* 17 Nov 1917, 1005.

Robinson, Percy [journalist/dramatist/title writer/scenarist/actor] (b. 1889?–Jul? 1967 [78], England). m. (Stage debut: *Abraham Lincoln,* London, 1919.) "Percy Robinson,"247, *Variety,* 19 Jul 1967, 63:2. BHD2, p. 225. FDY, p. 447.

Robinson, Ruth A. [actress] (b. KS, 18 Aug 1887–17 Mar 1966 [78], No. Hollywood CA). AS, p. 931. BHD, p. 288. IFN, p. 254.

Robinson, Spike [actor] (*né* W.C. Robinson, b. 1884–13 Jul 1942 [58?], Maywood CA). AS, p. 931.

Robinson, Walter C. [cinematographer] (b. 1894–1 Nov 1958 [64?], Los Angeles CA). BHD2, p. 225.

Robinson, Walter Charles "Spike" [actor] (b. 1884?–13 Jul 1942 [58], Maywood CA; heart attack). (K&E.) AMD, p. 295. AS, p. 931. BHD, p. 288. IFN, p. 255 (Robison). Truitt, p. 288. "Death of Mother of 'Spike' Robinson," *MPW,* 9 Oct 1915, 271. "Walter Charles Robinson with Fox," *MPW,* 24 Mar 1917, 1925. "Spike' Robinson Breaks Collar Bone," *MPW,* 2 Jun 1917, 1420.

Robinson, Walter Charles [actor] (b. England, 1872–1942 [70?]). BHD, p. 288.

Robison, Arthur [director] (b. Chicago IL, 25 Jun 1883–20 Oct 1935 [52], Berlin, Germany; heaqrt attack). (Germany, 1916; MGM.) "Arthur Robison," *Variety,* 6 Nov 1935. AS, p. 931 (b. 1888). BHD2, p. 225. IFN, p. 255 (age 47). Katz, p. 984 (began in Germany, 1914). Waldman, p. 247 (b. 1888).

Robson, Andrew [actor] (b. Hamilton, Ontario, Canada, 1867?–26 Apr 1921 [52], Los Angeles CA; heart attack). (Goldwyn.) "Andrew Robson," *Variety,* 6 May 1921 (age 54). AMD, p. 295. AS, p. 932. BHD, p. 288. IFN, p. 255. Truitt, p. 288. "Obituary," *MPW,* L, 14 May 1921, 179 (b. Toronto, Canada; age 55). George Katchmer, "Remembering the Great Silents," *CI,* 239 (May 1995), C5.

Robson, May (mother of **Stuart Robson, Jr.**) [stage/film/radio actress] (*née* Mary Jeanette Robison, b. Melbourne, Australia, 19 Apr 1858–20 Oct 1942 [84], Beverly Hills CA). m. (1) E.H. Gore; (2) Dr. Augustus H. Brown (d. 1922). (Film debut: *How Molly Malone Made Good,* Photo Drama Co., 1915.) "May Robson Dies in Beverly Hills; Beloved Actress of the Stage, Screen and Radio Was a Trouper for 58 Years; Made Film Debut in 1927; Began Career in Gaslight Era in Brooklyn—Was Long Under Chas. Frohman Management," *NYT,* 21 Oct 1942, 21:1 (b. 1864). "May Robson," *Variety,* 21 Oct 1942 (b. 1864). AMD, p. 295. AS, p. 932. BHD1, p. 470 (d. LA CA). IFN, p. 255. Katz, p. 985. Truitt, p. 288. "May Robson for Vitagraph," *NYDM,* 2 Jun 1915, 21:4 (to be in a feature based on her play, *A Night Out*). "May Robson Signed by DeMille," *MPW,* 12 Jun 1926, 539. Renee Van Dyke, "Paragraphs Pertaining to Players and Pictures," *Cinema Arts,* Aug 1926, 53 (announces Robson's screen debut [an error] in *Pals in Paradise,* Metropolitan). "May Robson in DeMille Opus," *MPW,* 15 Jan 1927, 200. "May Robson," *MPW,* 9 Apr 1927, 550. DeWitt Bodeen, "The Four Dowagers of MGM," *Focus on Film,* No. 24, Spring 1976, 39–45 (includes filmography).

Robson, Philip [stage/film actor] (b. Edinburg, Scotland, ca. 1850–6 May 1919 [69?], New York NY). AS, p. 932. BHD, p. 288. IFN, p. 255. SD, p. 1072.

Robson, Robert [actor] (b. Neenah WI, 1870–3 Jun 1947 [77?], New York NY). BHD, p. 288.

Robson, Mrs. Stuart [actress] (*née* May Waldron, b. Hamilton, Ontario, Canada, 1 Nov 1861?–22 Dec 1924 [63], Louisville KY). m. Stuart Robson (d. 1903). "Mrs. Stuart Robson," *NYT,* 23 Dec 1924, 19:4 (age 56). "Mrs. Stuart Robson," *Variety,* 24 Dec 1924 (b. 1868; age 56). AS, p. 932. BHD, p. 288 (b. 1868; d. Louisville LA). IFN, p. 307 (May Waldron).

Robson, Stuart, Jr. (son of stage actor Stuart Robson and **May Robson**) [actor] (d. 21 Aug 1946, New York NY). m. Yvette Ledoux, 7 Jan 1920, City Hall, NYC. AMD, p. 296. BHD, p. 288. "Robson—Ledoux," *MPW,* 17 Jan 1920, 400. "Stuart Robson Sues Metro and Others Over Picturization of 'The Henrietta,'" *MPW,* 4 Sep 1920, 94. "Stuart Robson Files Amended Complaint in Suit Against Playwright and Metro," *MPW,* 2 Oct 1920, 614. "Judge Denies Demurrer in Smith-Robson Suit," *MPW,* 9 Jul 1921, 186. Appeared in *The Harvest Moon* (Hodkinson, 1920).

Robyns, William [actor] (b. St. Louis MO, 1855?–22 Jan 1936 [80], Verdugo Hills [Glendale] CA). (Paramount.) "William Robyns," *Variety,* 29 Jan 1936 (age 81). AS, p. 932. BHD1, p. 470 (d. LA CA). IFN, p. 255. Truitt, p. 288.

Rocca, Gino [writer] (b. Mantova, Italy, 22 Feb 1891–13 Feb 1941 [49], Milan, Italy). JS, p. 384 (in Italian silents from 1928).

Roccardi, Albert [actor] (b. Rome, Italy, 9 May 1864–14 May 1934 [70], Paris, France). (Vitagraph.) AMD, p. 296. AS, p. 932 (b. Paris, France). BHD1, p. 470. IFN, p. 255. "The Man with a Thousand Faces," *MPC,* Jan 1916, 60. "Albert Roccardi's Novel Medicine," *MPW,* 8 Aug 1914, 823. "Albert Roccardi," *MPW,* 12 Dec 1914, 1512.

Rochal, Grigori Lyovich [director] (b. Kislovodsk, Russia, 21 Oct 1898–11 Jan 1983 [84], Moscow, Russia). AS, p. 932.

Roche, Arthur Somers [writer/playwright/scenarist] (b. Somerville MA, 27 Apr 1883–17 Feb 1935 [51], Villa Bellaria, Palm Beach FL; heart ailment and pneumonia). m. (1) Ethel Kirby Rowell, 1910, New Castine ME (d. 1915); (2) author Ethel Pettit, 28 Sep 1917, NYC. (First book: *Loot,* 1916.) "Arthur S. Roche, 61, Novelist, Is Dead; Heart Ailment and Pneumonia Fatal After Two Weeks' Illness in Florida; Was Author of 23 Books; Popular and Proficient Writer, Former Reporter, Also Tried Hand at Two Plays," *NYT,* 18

Feb 1935, 15:1. AMD, p. 296. AS, p. 932. "Houdini Story by Roche," *MPW,* 5 May 1917, 822. "Roche to Write Series of Original Stories for Warners," *MPW,* 6 Feb 1926, 552. "Roche, Arthur Somers," *National Cyclopædia of American Biography,* Vol. 35 (1953), pp. 35–36 (wrote under thirteen *noms-de-plume*).

Roche, John C. [actor] (b. Penn Yan NY, 6 Feb 1893–10 Nov 1952 [59], Los Angeles CA; stroke). "John C. Roche," *Variety,* 19 Nov 1952. AMD, p. 296. AS, p. 932. BHD1, p. 470 (b. 6 May). IFN, p. 255. Truitt, p. 288 (b. 1896). "Warner Brothers Sign John Roche," *MPW,* 2 Aug 1924, 383.

Roche, Madge [actress]. No data found. m. weight lifter Rigolot. Rene de la Seine, "Moviettes from Gay Paree," *Paris and Hollywood Screen Secrets Magazine,* Aug 1927, 66 (photo).

Rocher, Pierre Armand Asther [writer/scenarist] (b. Alencon, France, 29 Oct 1898 [extrait de naissance no. 223]–22 May 1963 [64], Nice, France). AS, p. 932.

Rochin, Paul [actor] (b. Poland, 9 May 1890–5 May 1964 [73], Los Angeles CA). "Paul Rochin," *Variety,* 20 May 1964 (age 75). AS, p. 932. IFN, p. 254.

Rock, Allan [publicist/founder of the Press Service Bureau]. No data found. AMD, p. 296. "Allan Rock," *MPW,* 20 Jul 1918, 351. "Allan Rock with Affiliated," *MPW,* 7 Sep 1918, 1399.

Rock, Charles "Old Bill" [actor] (*né* Charles Rock de Fabeck, b. Vellore, East Indies, 30 May 1866–12 Jul 1919 [53], London, England). (Began on stage in 1885.) "Charles Rock, English Actor," *NYT,* 13 Jul 1919, 22:4. "Charles Rock Dead," *Variety,* 18 Jul 1919, 4:4 (age 54; "appeared in picturres as 'Old Bill.'"). AS, p. 933. BHD, p. 288. IFN, p. 255.

Rock, John B. (son of **William T. 'Pop' Rock**) [general manager]. No data found. AMD, p. 296. "John B. Rock Is General Manager of Vitagraph; A.V. Smith, Assistant," *MPW,* 1 Mar 1924, 39. "John B. Rock on Coast," *MPW,* 26 Apr 1924, 740. "Rock in Hollywood," *MPW,* 7 Jun 1924, 564. "John Rock, 'Rolling Stone,' Visits 100 Houses in 2 Weeks," *MPW,* 9 Aug 1924, 440. John B. Rock, "True Talk," *MPW,* 20 Sep 1924, 203. "A. Victor Smith Lauds Work of John B. Rock for Vitagraph," *MPW,* 8 Nov 1924, 161. "Vitagraph Drive Planned in 'John B. Rock' Month," *MPW,* 15 Nov 1924, 264.

Rock, Joseph P. [actor/stuntman/producer/managing director of Rock Studios, Elstree] (b. New York NY, 19 Dec 1890–5 Dec 1984 [93], Sherman Oaks CA). (Vitagraph.) "Joe Rock," *Variety,* 12 Dec 1984. AMD, p. 296. AS, p. 933. BHD, p. 288 (b. 25 Dec 1892); BHD2, p. 225 (b. 25 Dec). MH, p. 135. Slide, p. 165. "Vitagraph to Star Separately Earl Montgomery and Joe Rock," *MPW,* 20 Mar 1920, 1992. "Joe Rock Forms Producing Company," *MPW,* 3 Jul 1920, 93. "Rock SIgns with Standard; To Make Comedies for F.B.O.," *MPW,* 25 Jul 1925, 439. "Short Subjects in Demand; Says Rock, Comedy Producer," *MPW,* 14 Nov 1925, 692. "Joe Rock to Hollywood," *MPW,* 19 Dec 1925, 692. "Rock May Align Himself as Executive for Some Company," *MPW,* 19 Feb 1927, 561.

Rock, William "Billy" [vaudeville stage/film dancer/director/producer] (b. Bowling Green KY, 1875–27 Jan 1922 [46?], Philadelphia PA; stomach ailment). m. Helen Ebey. (In vaudeville as Rock & Fulton, with Maude Fulton, and as Rock & White, with Frances White, who married Frank Fay.) "William Rock, Dancer," *NYT,* 28 Jun 1922, 15:6. "Billy Rock," *Variety,* 30 Jun 1922, 17:4 (age 47; to be buried at Bowling Green). BHD, p. 288.

Rock, William T. "Pop" (father of **John B. Rock**) [executive] (b. Birmingham, England, 31 Dec 1853–27 Jul 1916 [62], Oyster Bay, LI NY; heart attack). "W.T. Rock Dies Suddenly; Founder of Vitagraph Company Was Ill from Overwork," *NYT,* 28 Jul 1916, 11:7 (age 63); "Rock, Film Producer, Leaves $4,000,000; Bequest of $50,000 to Housekeeper, Who Files Petition Saying She Is Widow; Agrees Not to Fight Will; The Bulk of the Fortune Goes to a Son of the Testator by His First Marriage," *NYT,* 3 Aug 1916, 11:5. "William T. ('Pop') Rock," *Variety,* 4 Aug 1916. AMD, p. 296. AS, p. 933. BHD, p. 288; BHD2, p. 225. WWVC, pp. 122–123. "Interviews with Manufacturers," *MPW,* 8 Feb 1908, 95. "Wedding Bells," *MPW,* 15 Feb 1908, 117 (daughter May m. Carl Willatrowski, 6 Feb 1908). "Phonographic Song Selections," *MPW,* 28 Mar 1908, 255. "William T. 'Pop' Rock," *MPW,* II, 28 Mar 1908, 260. "'Pop' Rock Is Sixty—Goes Like Forty," *MPW,* 10 Jan 1914, 181 (b. 30 Dec). "Vitagraph Opens Additional Brooklyn Studio," *NYDM,* 21 Jan 1914, 27. "'Pop' Rock at Palm Beach," *MPW,* 19 Feb 1916, 1114 (on 5 Feb 1916). "'Pop' Rock Convalescing," *MPW,* 17 Jun 1916, 2049. "Obituary," *MPW,* 12 Aug 1916, 1078. "Death of a Pioneer," *MPW,* 19 Aug 1916, 1220. "Pop Rock's Fortune Was $1,436,677," *MPW,* 27 Apr 1918, 526.

Rockenfeller, Theo [director] (d. Duisburg, Germany, 17 May 1894). AS, p. 933.

Rockett, Al[bert] **L.** [producer] (b. Vincennes IN, 24 Sep 1889–30 Aug 1960 [70], Los Angeles CA). m. Laura (Lottie). (1st National; Fox.) "Al Rockett," *Variety,* 7 Sep 1960. AS, p. 933. BHD2, p. 225. IFN, p. 255. Laurence Reid, "The Picture of the Month (*The Dramatic Life of Abraham Lincoln*)," *Classic,* Apr 1924, 46, 93.

Rockett, Frederick K. [executive] (b. 1883–2 Oct 1958 [75?], Los Angeles CA; heart attack). AS, p. 933.

Rockwell, Florence [stage/film actress] (*née* Grace Atherton, b. St. Louis MO, 9 Jul 1887–24 Mar 1964 [76], Stamford CT). m. Howard F. Smith. (Pathé.) "Florence Rockwell, 76, Dies; Former Broadway Actress," *NYT,* 26 Mar 1964, 35:2. AMD, p. 296. AS, p. 933. BHD, p. 288. IFN, p. 255. SD. "Knickerbocker Signs Noted Star," *NYDM,* 11 Aug 1915, 22:4. "Miss Rockwell with Knickerbocker," *MPW,* 14 Aug 1915, 1171. "Florence Rockwell with Frohman Co.," *MPW,* 28 Aug 1915, 1483. "Morosco's New Star; Florence Rockwell Engaged for Screen Appearances by Oliver Morosco Co.," *NYDM,* 6 Nov 1915, 26:1 (to be in *He Fell in Love with His Wife*). Hector Ames, "Florence Rockwell (Knickerbocker)," *MPC,* Dec 1915, 56.

Roden, Edelaine [actress] (b. 1901–26 Mar 1989 [88?], Los Angeles CA). BHD, p. 288.

Roden, Robert F. [scenarist/composer] (d. 27 Nov 1934, Los Angeles CA; apoplexy). AMD, p. 296. AS, p. 933. "Roden Resigns from Universal," *MPW,* 5 Jun 1920, 1305.

Roderick, Leslie [dancer/actress] (b. 1907–16 Aug 1927 [20], Los Angeles CA; pneumonia). AS, p. 933. BHD, p. 288. IFN, p. 255.

Rodgers, Eugene [actor] (b. 1867–9 Mar 1919 [52], Los Angeles CA). AMD, p. 297. BHD, p. 288. IFN, p. 255. "Obituary," *MPW,* 29 Mar 1919, 1793 (funeral arranged by Charlie Murray).

Rodgers, Walter L. [actor] (b. OH, 31 Aug 1886–24 Apr 1951 [64], Los Angeles CA; stroke). (Began 1916.) AS, p. 933. BHD1, p. 471. IFN, p. 255. Truitt, p. 289. George Katchmer, "Walter Rodgers," *CI,* 233 (Nov 1994), 39–40.

Rodman, Victor [actor] (b. AR, 6 Aug 1892–29 Jun 1965 [72], Los Angeles CA). AS, p. 933. BHD1, p. 471. IFN, p. 255.

Rodney, Earle [actor/director/scenarist] (*né* Earle Rodney Hupp, b. Toronto, Ontario, Canada, 4 Jun 1888–16 Dec 1932 [44], Los Angeles CA; pneumonia). (Reliance-Majestic; Selig; Keystone; Griffith; Christie.) "Earl Rodney," *Variety,* 20 Dec 1932 (age 41). AMD, p. 297. AS, p. 933. BHD1, p. 471; BHD2, p. 225. FDY, p. 437. IFN, p. 255. Truitt, p. 289 (b. 1891). "Rodney Former Keystone 'Kop,' with Sennett," *MPW,* 12 Feb 1927, 499.

Rodney, Lynne [actress] (d. 15 Sep 1937, Los Angeles CA; auto accident). AS, p. 933.

Rodolfi, Eleuterio [actor/director] (b. Bologna, Italy, 28 Jan 1876–19 Dec 1933 [57], Brescia, Italy). AS, p. 933.

Rodriguez, Endre [director] (b. Budapest, Hungary, 28 Apr 1899–5 Aug 1975 [76], Munich, Germany). AS, p. 934.

Rodwell, S. [cinematographer]. No data found. FDY, p. 467.

Roe, Bassett [actor] (b. Folkestone, Kent, England, 10 Sep 1860–2 Nov 1934 [74]). BHD, p. 289.

Roebuck, Earle [scenarist]. No data found. FDY, p. 437.

Roels, Marcel [actor] (*né* Oscar August Roels, b. Antwerp, Belgium, 12 Jan 1894–27 Dec 1973 [79], Brussels, Belgium). AS, p. 934 (b. 1 Jan). BHD1, p. 471. IFN, p. 255.

Roemheld, Heinz Eric [composer] (b. Milwaukee WI, 1 May 1901–11 Feb 1985 [83], Huntington Beach CA; pneumonia). "Heinz Eric Roemheld Dies; Hollywood Film Composer," *NYT,* 14 Feb 1985, B12:1. "Heinz Eric Roemheld," *Variety,* 20 Feb 1985. AS, p. 934. ASCAP 66, p. 614. BHD2, p. 225.

Rogan, Rita [actress] (b. 1916?). AMD, p. 297. "Rita Rogan in Important Part," *MPW,* L, 14 May 1921, 189 (5 years old).

Rogell, Albert S. [director/producer] (b. Oklahoma City OK, 21 Aug 1901–7 Apr 1988 [86], Los Angeles CA; cancer aggravated by diabetes). m. Irma Warner (d. 1982). (1st National; FBO; Universal; Tiffany.) "Albert S. Rogell, 86, Director of Dozens of B-Pictures, Dies," *Variety,* 13 Apr 1988. "Death Notices; Rogell, Albert S.," *LA Times,* 9 Apr 1988, 28:5 (entered industry, 1916, with Washington Motion Picture Company, Spokane WA; began in Hollywood as assistant to George Loane Tucker). AMD, p. 297. AS, p. 934. BHD2, p. 225. Katz, p. 986. "Rogell Leaves Universal," *MPW,* 5 Dec 1925, 424 ("...lack of opportunity...").

Rogell, Irma S. [actress] (*née ?,* b. 12 Nov 1893–3 Aug 1982 [88], Los Angeles CA). m. **Jack L. Warner** (d. 1978). "Irma S. Rogell," *Variety,* 11 Aug 1982. AS, p. 934 (b. 1899).

Rogell, Sid [producer] (b. St. Joseph MO, 16 Jan 1900–15 Nov 1973 [73], Los Angeles CA). BHD2, p. 225.

Roger, Odette [actress/singer] (*née* Thérèse

Marie Louise Vin, b. Marseilles, France, 1 Jan 1900–24 Aug 1985 [85], La-Penn-sur-Huveaune, France). AS, p. 934.

Rogers, Andrew [actor]. No data found. AMD, p. 297. "Rogers with Nola on Associated Program," *MPW,* 18 Dec 1915, 2163.

Rogers, Bessie [actress] (b. 1884–5 Mar 1930 [46], Venice Beach CA). BHD, p. 289. IFN, p. 255.

Rogers, Bogart [scenarist/producer] (b. Los Angeles CA, 1897–24 Jul 1966 [69?], Burbank CA). BHD2, p. 225.

Rogers, Carl D. [child actor] (b. 1898–2 Mar 1965 [66?], Houston TX). m. (1 son, 2 daughters.) (Sennett.) "Carl Rogers," *Variety,* 238, 10 Mar 1965, 79:3. AS, p. 935 (b. 1901; d. 3 Mar). BHD, p. 289. IFN, p. 256 (age 63). Truitt, p. 289 (d. Humble TX).

Rogers, Charles A. [scenarist/director] (b. Birmingham, England, 15 Jan 1887–20 Dec 1956 [69], Los Angeles CA). AS, p. 935 (b. 1900). BHD, p. 289; BHD2, p. 226. IFN, p. 256.

Rogers, Charles Edward "Buddy" [bandleader/vaudeille/radio/stage/film actor/producer] (b. Olathe KS, 13 Aug 1904 [at 224 South Cherry Street]–21 Apr 1999 [94], Rancho Mirage CA). m. (1) **Mary Pickford**, 1936 (d. 1979); (2) Beverly Ricono, 1981. (Film debut?: bit in *So's Your Old Man,* Paramount; Jean Hersholt Humanitarian Award, 1985.) Lawrence Van Gelder, "Buddy Rogers, Star of 'Wings' and Band Leader, Dies at 94; 'Wings' won the first Academy Award, and its handsome star won Mary Pickford's heart," *NYT,* 23 Apr 1999, A23. Myrna Oiver, "Buddy Rogers; Actor, married 42 years to movie star Mary Pickford," *PP-G,* 25 Apr 1999, E-5:3 ("...Pickford—who divorced Douglas Fairbanks in 1936 and married Mr. Rogers the next year—soon threatened to divorce him if he didn't give up the band and stay home. ¶'I couldn't blame her. I was away to much. But she really took my band away from me,' Mr. Rogers recalled with his usual wry grin."). AMD, p. 297. AS, p. 935 (Budd Rogers). FSS, p. 250. HCH, p. 43. Katz, p. 986. "Rogers Loaned to Pickford," *MPW,* 7 May 1927, 23. "Charles 'Buddy' Rogers," *MPW,* 9 Jul 1927, 86. Carol Johnston, "Don't Call Him Buddy; A Close-Up of Charles Rogers," *MPC,* Aug 1928, 51, 85 9received 17,862 fan letters one month). John Engstead, "He's the Harmony Kid!," *Screenland,* May 1929, 70–71, 109. Dorothy Donnell, "B.H. Rogers' Boy; That's All Buddy Is to His Home-Townsmen in Olathe, Kansas," *MPC,* Jun 1929, 36–37, 80. Helen Louise Walker, "Will Buddy Rogers Rival Rudy Vallee?," *Movie Classic,* Oct 1931, 16–17, 78, 80.

Rogers, Charles R. [producer] (b. New York NY, 15 Jul 1892–29 Mar 1957 [64], Los Angeles CA; from auto accident on 18 Feb 1957). (Pathé; Universal.) "Charles Rogers, Producer, 64, Dies; Ex-Official at Universal Had Filmed 'My Man Godfrey' and '100 Men and a Girl,'" *NYT,* 31 Mar 1957, 38:7 ("Earlier Mr. Rogers made films starring Corinne Griffiths [sic] at the old First National Studios."). "Charles R. Rogers," *Variety,* 3 Apr 1957. AMD, p. 297. AS, p. 935. BHD2, p. 226. IFN, p. 256. "Charles Rogers Offers Radios to Hospitals," *MPW,* 20 Aug 1927, 511.

Rogers, Eugene [opera singer/film actor] (b. 1867–10 Mar 1919 [52?], Los Angeles CA; heart attack brought on by alcoholism; destitute). "Eugene Rogers Found Dead," *Variety,* 14 Mar 1919. AS, p. 935 (d. 9 Mar).

Rogers, Howard Emmett [scenarist] (b. New York NY, 13 Jul 1890–16 Aug 1971 [81], Los Angeles CA). (Began 1924; MGM.) "Howard Emmett Rogers," *Variety,* 1 Sep 1971. AS, p. 935. BHD2, p. 226 (d. 7 Aug). FDY, p. 437. IFN, p. 256.

Rogers, Jim (son of **Will Rogers**; brother of **Will Rogers, Jr.**) [actor/rancher] (*né* James Blake Rogers, b. New York NY, 20 Jul 1915 [Birth Certificate Index No. 37732]–28 Apr 2000 [84], Bakersfield CA; cancer). "Other Deaths; Jim Rogers," *PP-G,* 5 May 2000, B-6:6. Harris Lentz, III, "Jimmy Rogers, 84," *CI,* 300 (Jul 2000), p. 57 (d. Claremore OK). WWS, p. 215. Bob Pontes, "Interview with Jimmy Rogers," *CI,* 152 (Feb 1988), 41–42, 44–46 (1st film: *Just Call Me Jim*).

Rogers, Joseph [actor] (b. Lebanon, Syria, 10 Apr 1871–27 Dec 1942 [71], Los Angeles CA). AS, p. 935. BHD, p. 289. IFN, p. 256.

Rogers, Lora [actress] (b. Lathrop MA, 1874?–23 Dec 1948 [74], Providence RI). "Miss Lora Rogers, 74, a Character Actress," *NYT,* 24 Dec 1948, 17:2. "Lora Rogers," *Variety,* 29 Dec 1948. AS, p. 935. BHD, p. 289. IFN, p. 256.

Rogers, Louise Mackintosh [stage/film actress] (b. 1865–1 Nov 1933 [68], Beverly Hills CA). (Fox.) "Louise MacKintosh," *Variety,* 112, 7 Nov 1933, 62:3. BHD, p. 289.

Rogers, Lucretia Harris [actress] (d. Aug 1923, Los Angeles CA). BHD, p. 289.

Rogers, Mildred [actress] (b. NB, 14 Apr 1899–14 Apr 1973 [74], Los Angeles CA). AS, p. 935. BHD1, p. 472. IFN, p. 256.

Rogers, Rena [actress] (b. IL, 7 Jun 1900–19 Feb 1966 [65], Los Angeles CA). m. **Frank Borzage** (d. 1962). (Vogue comedies.) AMD, p. 297. AS, p. 935 (d. Santa Monica CA). BHD, p. 289. IFN, p. 256. Truitt, p. 289. "Rena Rogers," *MPW,* 23 Jan 1915, 520. Cal York, "Plays and Players," *Photoplay,* Jul 1917, 112 (back in films after her marriage to Borzage).

Rogers, Robert M. [vaudeville/stage/film actor] (b. 1863?–15 Dec 1916 [54?], New York NY; dropped dead at stage entrance of Fulton Theatre). m. Louise McIntyre. "Robert M. Rogers," *Variety,* 22 Dec 1916, 25:3 ("Mrs. Rogers was with him" when he died). AS p. 935. BHD, p. 289.

Rogers, Rod [actor] (d. 23 Feb 1983, Tamarac FL). AS, p. 935. BHD1, p. 472.

Rogers, Will (father of **Will Rogers, Jr.**, and **Jimmy Rogers**) [stage/film actor/scenarist] (*né* William Penn Adair Rogers, b. Claremont OK [Indian Territory], 4 Nov 1879–15 Aug 1935 [55], near Point Barrow AK). m. Betty Blake. *The Autobiography of Will Rogers* (Boston: Houghton Mifflin, 1949); Peter C. Rollins, *Will Rogers; A Bio-Bibliography* (Westport CT: Greenwood Press, 1984); Ben Yagoda, *Will Rogers* (New York: Alfred A. Knopf, 1993); Richard J. Maturi and Mary Buckingham Maturi, *Will Rogers, Performer; An Illustrated Biography with a Filmography* (Jefferson NC: McFarland, 1999). "Will Rogers, Wiley Post Die in Airplane Crash in Alaska; Nation Shocked by Tragedy; 10-Minute Hop Their Last; Engine Fails on a Take-Off for Final 15 Miles to Point Barrow; Landed to Get Bearings; Startled Eskimos See Huge Bird Plunge to Bank from 50 Feet Above Water; One Runs 3 Hours to Tell; Humorist Revealed as Financing a Trip Around the World with Famous Pilot," *NYT,* 17 Aug 1935, 1:6, 4:4; "Adventure Marked Life of Humorist; Born in Indian Territory on 4 Nov 1879, He Rose to Become 'Envoy of World'; Often Acclaimed Abroad; Became a Familiar Figure to Broadway at Hammerstein's and the Follies," 6:1 [and more coverage]. "Will Rogers," *Variety,* 21 Aug 1935 (age 56). AMD, p. 297. AS, p. 935 (b. 16 Aug). BHD1, p. 472; BHD2, p. 226 (b. Oologah OK). FSFM, p. 310. FSS, p. 251. HCH, p. 103. IFN, p. 256 (b. Ologah OK). Katz, pp. 987–88. MH, p. 135. SD. Truitt, p. 289. WWS, p. 147. "Will Rogers Coming to the Screen," *MPW,* 10 Aug 1918, 811. "Goldwyn Signs Rogers, and Screen Is Winner," *MPW,* 28 Dec 1918, 1505. "Ford Weekly Gets 'WISe Cracks,'" *MPW,* 8 Mar 1919, 1318. "Goldwyn Ready for Rogers to Begin Contract June 1," *MPW,* 8 Mar 1919, 1344. "Will Rogers Declares President Stole His Act," *MPW,* 15 Mar 1919, 1468. "Gaumont Graphic Features the Sayings of Will Rogers," *MPW,* 17 May 1919, 1067. "Will Rogers Ready for Culver City," *MPW,* 31 May 1919, 1380. "Will Rogers Leaves for Goldwyn's Coast Studios," *MPW,* 14 Jun 1919, 1641. "Will Rogers Is Developing New Screen Type," *MPW,* 15 Nov 1919, 331. "Will Rogers's Son Dead," *MPW,* 3 Jul 1920, 56 (Frederick Rogers, d. 17 Jun 1920, aged 3, from diphtheria). "Will Rogers Discovered by Rex Beach, Proves His Stellar Worth to Goldwyn," *MPW,* 1 Jan 1921, 52. "Rogers in Two-Reelers," *MPW,* 30 Jul 1921, 491. "Popularity Contest Enters Final Week; Madge Kennedy and Will Rogers Lead," *MPW,* 13 May 1922, 155. "Praises Film Actors," *MPW,* 28 Oct 1922, 760. "Rogers to Star in Thirteen Two-Reel comedies for Pathé," *MPW,* 17 Feb 1923, 706. "Rogers Impersonates Stars of Screen," *MPW,* 24 Nov 1923, 419. "Rogers the Satirist," *MPW,* 26 Jan 1924, 279. "Will Rogers," *MPW,* 1 Jan 1927, 32. "A Message to *You* from Will Rogers," *MPW,* 26 Feb 1927, 642. "Rogers Loses Gall Stones," *MPW,* 25 Jun 1927, 571. Dorothy Donnell, "Will Rogers CHEWS to Run for President; *Classic* Hopes He May Be Ropin the White House," *MPC,* Apr 1928, 21, 66. George Katchmer, "Remembering the Great Silents," *CI,* 216 (Jun 1993), 48. Margo Jefferson, "A Serious Look at a Humorous Man," *NYT,* 29 Sep 1993, C20:3; review of Yagoda's book. John J. O'Connor, "A Man of the People, A Symbol of His Time," *NYT,* 30 Nov 1994, C18:5: review of *American Masters; Rediscovering Will Rogers,* PBS, produced and directed by Stephan Chodorov, Nov 1994.

Rogers, Will, Jr. (son of **Will Rogers**; brother of **Jim Rogers**) [actor] (*né* William Rogers, b. New York NY, 20 Oct 1912–9 Jul 1993 [80], Tubac AZ). AS, p. 935 (b. 1911). BHD1, p. 472.

Rognoni, Raymond [actor] (*né* Roch Raymond Rognoni, b. Paris, France, 16 Aug 1892–26 Sep 1965 [73], Paris, France [extrait de décès no. SN/1965]). AS, p. 935.

Rogoz, Zvonimir [actor/producer] (b. Zagreb, Croatia, 10 Oct 1887–6 Feb 1988 [100], Zegreb, Croatia). AS, p. 935.

Rohig, Walter [art director] (b. Germany, 1897–1945 [48?]). BHD2, p. 226.

Rohlfs, John [production manager] (b. Germany-d. 9 Feb 1942, Yonkers NY). "John Rohlfs," *NYT,* 11 Feb 1942, 22:2.

Rohmer, Sax [actor/scenarist] (*né* Arthur Sarsfield Warde, b. England, 1883–1 Jun 1959 [76?], London, England). AS, p. 936.

Roitfeld, Jacques [producer] (b. Akkerman, Russia, 19 Jan 1889–1956 [67], Paris, France). AS, p. 936.

Roland, Frederick [actor] (b. Toronto,

Canada, 12 Nov 1885–2 Jun 1936 [50], Los Angeles CA). "Frederick Roland," *Variety,* 3 Jun 1936. AS, p. 936. BHD1, p. 472. IFN, p. 256.

Roland, Gilbert (brother of Julio Alonso and Chico Day) [actor] (name taken from John Gilbert and Ruth Roland; *né* Luis Antonio Dámaso de Alonso, b. Ciudad Juárez, Mexico, 11 Dec 1905–15 May 1994 [88], Beverly Hills CA; cancer). m. (1) **Constance Bennett** (d. 1965); (2) Guillermina Cantú, 1954. Peter B. Flint, "Gilbert Roland Is Dead at 88; Actor from Silent Films to TV," *NYT,* 18 May 1994, B8:1. "Film's Gilbert Roland, 88, Played Dashing Characters," *Pittsburgh Post-Gazette,* 17 May 1994, C6:2. "Gilbert Roland," *Variety,* 23 May 1994, 60:1. AMD, p. 297. AS, p. 936. BHD1, p. 472. FSS, p. 252. "Schulberg Signs Another Star in Gilbert Roland," *MPW,* 8 Aug 1925, 659. "Gilbert Roland," *MPW,* 18 Jun 1927, 484. Dunham Thorp, "Lady Luck Presents the Breaks," *MPC,* Nov 1927, 36, 79, 85. Michael R. Pitts, "Gilbert Roland; The Most Virile Actor in Movies," *CFC,* 32 (Fall, 1971), 4–5; 33 (Winter, 1971), 56–57 (with filmography); corrections, 36 (Fall, 1972), 13.

Roland, Ruth, "Queen of the Thriller Serials" [stage/film actress] (b. San Francisco CA, 26 Aug 1892–22 Sep 1937 [45], Los Angeles CA; cancer). m. Lionel T. Kent, 16 May 1917, St. Paul's Episcopal Church, LI, New York NY; **Ben Bard** (aka Benjamin F. Greenburg), 1929 (d. 1974). (Film debut: *A Chance Shot,* Kalem, 1911; Pathé; Balboa, 1914; one sound film: *Reno,* ca. 1930.) "Ruth Roland Dies; Former Film Star; 'Queen' of Thriller Serials of 20 Years Ago Succumbs in Hollywood at 39; Made Fortune in Realty; Investments in California Land Said to Have Raised One of Biggest Coast Estates," *NYT,* 23 Sep 1937, 27:1. "Ruth Roland," *Variety,* 29 Sep 1937 (age 39). "Ruth Roland, Heroine of the Silent Screen, Dies on Coast; Entered Movies in 1912, Won Fortune with Real Estate," *Arizona Daily Star* [Tucson], 22 Sep 1937 (A realty development took place on her property, which "was converted from wide waste areas of Beverly Hills into what has been known as 'the miracle mile,' of business property on Wilshire boulevard, housing skyscrapers."). AMD, p. 297. AS, p. 936. BHD1, p. 472. BR, pp. 215–19. CNW, pp. 34, 119. FFF, p. 80 (b. 26 Aug). FSS, p. 253. GK, pp. 822–32. IFN, p. 256 (b. 1894). Jura, pp. 119–24. Katz, p. 989. Lowrey, p. 160. MH, p. 135. MSBB, p. 1040. Spehr, p. 162. Truitt, p. 289. WWS, p. 110. "Ruth Roland," *MPW,* 4 Nov 1911, 361. "Ruth Roland," *MPW,* 30 Dec 1911, 1059. "Ruth Roland," *MPW,* 7 Mar 1914, 1215. "Ruth Roland, Kalem Girl Who Does Things," *MPW,* 11 Jul 1914, 263. "Ruth Roland; Playing Leads with Kalem Co.," *MPS,* 28 Aug 1914, 25 (cites birthdate as 26 Aug 1892). "A New Kalem Star," *MPW,* 5 Dec 1914, 1374. "Ruth Roland Goes to Balboa," *MPW,* 19 Dec 1914, 1682. Albert Levin Roat, "The Real Mission of the Movies; The Personal Viewpoint of Miss Ruth Roland, 'The Kalem Girl,'" *Motion Picture Magazine,* Feb 1915, 51. "Ruth Roland, Star of 'Who Pays?,'" *MPW,* 5 Jun 1915, 1583. "Ruth Roland," *MPW,* 24 Jul 1915, 639–40. "Ruth Roland," *MPW,* 17 Jun 1916, 2068. "Ruth Roland," *MPW,* 28 Apr 1917, 619. "Ruth Roland Is a Bride," *MPW,* 9 Jun 1917, 1579. Neil G. Caward, "Screen Gossip," *Picture-Play Magazine,* Sep 1917, 106 ("said 'Yes' to the bashful proposal of one Lionel T. Kent of Los Angeles"). "Little Stories That Are True; Leaving It to Central," *Motion Picture Magazine,* Feb 1918, 79–80 (to get up for a 6 a.m. call to work on The Neglected Wife serial, she wound her clock so tightly that it broke. Determined to get up at 6 a.m. on sheer will, she fell asleep, but found herself up at 2 a.m. trying to get into her car in her bedclothes. She then called Information and had the phone company wake her up at 6.). "Ruth Roland Goes with Douglas Film," *MPW,* 6 Apr 1918, 82. "Hospital Wins Ruth Roland's $300 Award," *MPW,* 27 Jul 1918, 559. "Ruth Roland Hurt," *MPW,* 14 Sep 1918, 1571. "Ruth Roland in New York," *MPW,* 7 Jun 1919, 1489. William J. Reilly, "Ruth Roland Is the 'One' Girl," *MPW,* 14 Jun 1919, 1619–20. "Ruth Roland Returns to Coast," *MPW,* 21 Jun 1919, 1770. "Prominent Players to Be Featured in Pathé Serials for the Next Two Years," *MPW,* 19 Jul 1919, 377–78. "Ruth Roland Is Executive," *MPW,* 20 Sep 1919, 1833. "Dedicate Song to Ruth Roland," *MPW,* 13 Dec 1919, 840 (*Romantic Ruth*). "Ruth Roland, Pathé Star, Is in New York to Spend Short Vacation and to 'Shop,'" *MPW,* 29 Jan 1921, 556. "Ruth Roland, Pathé Star, Extends Her Vacation," *MPW,* 5 Feb 1921, 678. "Pathé Star Takes Plane to Attend a Luncheon," *MPW,* 30 Apr 1921, 952. "Begins New Serial," *MPW,* 30 Apr 1921, 953. "Ruth Roland Injured," *MPW,* 5 Nov 1921, 51. "Roland Serial Breaks Records; Episode Ttitles Up to Twelfth," *MPW,* 17 Dec 1921, 798. David A. Balch, "Young People Don't Take Marriage Seriously Enough, Says Ruth Roland," *MW,* 9 Jun 1923, 7, 28. Paul Paige, "Close-Ups and Fade-Outs," *Paris and Hollywood,* Oct 1926, 95 (to return in *The Masked Woman,* her first film in several years, costumed by Cora McGeachy, former Ziegfeld Follies designer. "Ruth's entire time of late has been occupied by the management of her large real estate holdings."). Eldon K. Everett, "Ruth Roland, Queen of the Cliffhangers," *CFC,* 42 (Spring, 1974), 54–55. Alan Brock, "A Treasured Meeting with Ruth Roland," *CFC,* 49 (Winter, 1975), 10. George A. Katchmer, "Ruth Roland; The Screen Girl of Action," *CI,* 123 (Oct 1985), 23–26. R.E. Braff, "An Index to the Films of Ruth Roland," *CI,* 199 (Jan 1992), 22–24.

Rolands, George K. [title writer]. No data found. FDY, p. 447.

Rolfe, Alfred [actor/director] (*né* Alfed Roker, b. Australia, 1862–9 Sep 1943 [81?], USA). AS, p. 936. BHD2, p. 226.

Rolfe, Benjamin A[lbert] [director/stage producer/conductor] (b. 1880?–23 Apr 1956 [76], Walpole MA). m. Edna Britton. "B.A. Rolfe Dead; Band Leader, 76; Conductor of Original Lucky Strike Dance Orchestra Won Fame on Radio," *NYT,* 24 Apr 1956, 31:1. "B.A. Rolfe," *Variety,* 25 Apr 1956. AMD, p. 298. AS, p. 936. BHD2, p. 226. "Rolfe's Film Plans; Former Vaudeville Producer Enters Picture Field—To Release Through Alco," *NYDM,* 7 Oct 1914, 25:3 (1st film: *Satan Sanderson*). "B.A. Rolfe," *MPW,* 31 Oct 1914, 643. "Rolfe Makes Deal with Fiske," *MPW,* 26 Dec 1914, 1858. "Fiske Not to Produce Pictures," *MPW,* 2 Jan 1915, 52. "Rolfe Re-Enters Manufacturing Field," *MPW,* 20 Jul 1918, 382. "Jan Pictures, Inc., Signs B.A. Rolfe as Director," *MPW,* 27 Dec 1919, 1175.

Rollan, Henri Martine [actor/director] (b. Paris, France, 23 Mar 1888–23 Jun 1967 [79], Paris, France). AS, p. 936. BHD, p. 289. IFN, p. 256.

Rolland, Edna [vaudeville/film actress] (b. Neenah WI–d. 26 Nov 1915, Colorado Springs CO; hemorrhage of the stomach). m. Harry Ellis. (Pikes Peak Photoplay Co.) "Edna Rolland (Mrs. Harry Ellis)," *Variety,* 10 Dec 1915, 10:4. BHD, p. 289.

Rollens, Jacques (or **Jack Rollins**) [vaudevillian/film actor/director/scenarist] (b. Chicago IL, 13 Oct 1902–19 Mar 1955 [52], Los Angeles CA). m. **Edna Payne**, 22 Aug 1917, NYC (d. 1953). (Fox.) "Marriages," *Variety,* 31 Aug 1917, p. 15. BHD1, p. 472; BHD2, p. 226. George Katchmer, "Jack Rollins," *CI,* 233 (Nov 1994), 40.

Rolli, Torello [director] (b. Rome, Italy, 1891–1 Mar 1927 [35?], Paris, France). AS, p. 937. JS, pp. 385–86 (in Italian silents from 1920).

Rollins, David Jerome [actor] (b. Kansas City MO, 2 Sep 1907–25 May 1997 [89], Encinatas CA; cremated). (Universal extra; Fox.) "David Rollins [obituary]," *CI,* 267 (Sep 1997), 58:2. AMD, p. 298. BHD1, p. 616. Truitt, p. 289 (b. 1908). "Boy Wins Contract," *MPW,* 3 Sep 1927, 24. "David Rollins," *MPW,* 17 Dec 1927, 32. Chapter 22, "David Rollins," *BS,* pp. 289–97 (includes filmography).

Rollow, Preston J. [actor] (b. Fredericksburg VA, 1871?–20 May 1947 [76], New York NY). "Preston J. Rollow," *Variety,* 28 May 1947. AS, p. 937 (d. 15 May). BHD, p. 289. IFN, p. 256. Truitt, p. 289.

Roma, Enrico [actor/director] (b. Rome, Italy, 1888-Nov 1941 [53?], Rome, Italy). JS, p. 386 (in Italian silents from 1916).

Romaine, George E. [actor/director] (b. Bordeaux, France, 1878?–7 May 1929 [51?], Philadelphia PA; heart attack during performance of *Chinese O'Neill* at the Walnut Street Theatre). "George Romain," *Variety,* 8 May 1929. AS, p. 937. BHD, p. 289; BHD2, p. 226. IFN, p. 256.

Romaine, Mildred [title writer/scenarist]. No data found. FDY, pp. 437, 447.

Romains, Jules [scenarist] (*né* Louis Henri Jean Farigoule, b. Saint-Julien-Chapteuil, France, 26 Aig 1885 [extrait de naissance no. 38]-14 Aug 1972 [86], Paris, France). AS, p. 937.

Roman, Benjamin [producer] (b. 1885–10 Dec 1972 [87?], Miami FL). AS, p. 937.

Roman, Frank [actor] (b. Granada, Spain, 25 Sep 1908–23 Mar 1987 [78], Santa Monica CA). BHD1, p. 473.

Romano, Nina [actress] (*née* Isabel Craven Dilworth). No data found. m. **Lou Tellegen**, 17 Dec 1923, Rutherford NJ (d. 1934). AMD, p. 298. "Mrs. Lou Tellegen in Gotham Picture," *MPW,* 18 Sep 1926, 175.

Romanoff, Constantine [wrestler/actor]. No data found. AMD, p. 298. "Cast Complete for Lloyd's First Paramount Picture," *MPW,* 5 Sep 1925, 90. "All Roles in Lloyd Film Filled," *MPW,* 7 Aug 1926, 338.

Romanoff, Michaël [actor] (*né* Prince Michaël Alexandrovitch Dimitri Oblensky Romanoff, b. Vilnious, Lithuania, 21 Feb 1890–1 Sep 1971 [81], Los Angeles CA). AS, p. 937.

Romanos, Lola [actress]. No data found. JS, p. 387 (in Italian silents from 1920).

Romanov, Natasha Galitzine (b. Moscow, Russia, 1906?–28 Mar 1989 [82], Woodside CA). "Natasha Romanov," *NYT,* 7 Apr 1989, D21:5. AS, p. 937. BHD, p. 289 (d. Menlo Park CA).

Romberg, Sigmund [composer/scenarist] (b. Nagykaniza, Hungary, 29 Jul 1887–9 Nov 1951

[64], New York NY; cerebral hemorrhage). m. Lillian Harris, 1925. "Sigmund Romberg, Composer, Dies, 64; Victim of Stroke in His Suite at Ritz Towers—Came Here From Coast a Week Ago; Writer of 78 Musicals; 'The Student Prince,' 'Blossom Time' Among Successes—Produced 2,000 Songs," *NYT,* 10 Nov 1951, 17:1 (also wrote *The Desert Song* and *New Moon;* 1st published song, *Memories,* 1911; 1st musical show, *The Midnight Girl;* songs: *When I Grow Too Old to Dream; Zing, Zing, Zoom, Zoom*); "Romberg Left $428,167," *NYT,* 16 Jan 1957, 36:3 (estate tax appraisal; wife was the principal beneficiary). "Sigmund Romberg, Last of Operetta Triumvirate, Dies Suddenly in N.Y. at 64," *Variety,* 14 Nov 1951 (adapted operettas for films). AS, p. 938. BHD2, p. 226 (b. Szeged, Hungary). SD.

Rome, Bert [actor] (b. 1887–25 Aug 1946 [59], Chelan WA). BHD1, p. 473. IFN, p. 256.

Rome, Betty [actress] (b. 2 Nov 1892–12 Feb 1973 [80], Los Angeles Co. CA). BHD, p. 289.

Rome, Stewart [stage/film actor] (*né* Septimus Wernham Ryott, b. Newbury, Berkshire, England, 30 Jan 1886–26 Feb 1965 [79], Newbury, Berkshire, England). m. Grace Miller. (Hepworth, 1906.) "Stewart Rome," *Variety,* 10 Mar 1965 (age 78). AS, p. 938. BHD1, p. 473. IFN, p. 256. Katz, pp. 989–90. SD. Truitt, pp. 289–90 (Septimus Wernham Ryott).

Romee, Marcelle [actress] (*née* Marcelle Arbant, b. Neuilly-sur-Seine, France, 7 Feb 1903–3 Dec 1932 [29], Paris, France; suicide by jumping into the Seine [extrait de décès no. 356/1932]). AS, p. 938.

Romeo, Ramon [writer]. No data found. AMD, p. 298. "Romeo Attributes Success to the Prayers of His Friends," *MPW,* 26 Feb 1927, 637.

Romer, Leila [actress] (*née* Leila Tyler Romer, b. 18 Sep 1878–10 Feb 1944 [65], Los Angeles CA; heart attack). AS, p. 938. BHD1, p. 473. Truitt, p. 290.

Romero, Manuel [director] (b. Buenos Aires, Argentina, 21 Sep 1891–3 Oct 1954 [63], Buenos Aires, Argentina). AS, p. 938. BHD2, p. 226.

Romero, Ramon [scenarist] (b. Jacksonville FL, 25 Dec 1904–5 Jul 1981 [76], Los Angeles CA). m. **Gloria Grey** (d. 1947). AS, p. 938. BHD, p. 289; BHD2, p. 226. FDY, p. 437 (photo and ad, p. 419).

Romine, Freeda Hartzell (daughter of scenarist/actress Mary Hartzell) [actress]. No data found. "Paul J. Eisloeffel and Andrea I. Paul, "Hollywood on the Plains; Nebraska's Contribution to Early American Cinema," *Journal of the West,* 33 (Apr 1994), 13–19 (Hartzell starred as Calamity Jane in *In the Days of '75 and '76* [Black Hills Feature Film Co. (Chadron NB), 24 Sep 1915]).

Ronceray, Janine [actress] (*née* Anne Marie Marguerite Jeanne Girard, b. Lauzerte, France, 21 Nov 1899 [extrait de naissance no. 26]–17 Jul 1987 [87], Boulogne-Billancourt, France). AS, p. 938.

Roncoroni, Mario [director]. JS, p. 387 (in Italian silents from 1915).

Ronet, Emile [actor] (*né* Emile Robinet, b. Paris, France, 11 Jul 1884). AS, p. 938.

Rooke, Irene [stage/film actress] (b. Bridgeport, Dorset, England, 1878?–14 Jun 1958 [80], Chesham, Buckinghamshire, England). m. **Milton Rosmer** (d. 1971). AS, p. 938. BHD1, p. 473. IFN, p. 256.

Room, Avram Matreevich [director/scenarist] (b. Vilnius, Lithuania, 28 Jun 1894–26 Jul 1967 [73], Moscow, Russia). AS, p. 938. BHD2, p. 226 (Abram M. Room, d. 28 Jul).

Roomanoff, Michael [scenarist] (b. 1891–14 Dec 1934 [43?], Los Angeles CA). BHD2, p. 226.

Roome, Alfred Wallace [film editor/director/producer] (b. London, England, 22 Dec 1908–19 Nov 1997 [88], Gerrards Cross, Buckinghamshire, England). m. actress Janice Adair, 1929 (d. 1996; 1 daughter, 1 son [killed 1987]). (Assistant property man, Elstree, 1927; Gainsborough.) Tony Sloman, "Alfred Roome," *The Independent,* 12 Dec 1997, p. 17. AS, p. 938.

Rooner, Charles [actor/director] (*né* Ernest R. Pruster, b. Vienna, Austria, 1901–22 Nov 1964 [63?], Mexico City, Mexico). AS, p. 938. BHD2, p. 226.

Rooney, Pat[rick] James, Sr. [dancer/songwriter] (b. New York NY, 4 Jul 1880–9 Sep 1962 [82], New York NY [Death Certificate Index No. 18996]; cerebral hemorrhage). m. (1) **Marion Bent**, 10 Apr 1903, Boston (d. 1940); (2) Janet Reade (*née* Helen Rulon), 1942 (d. 1943); Carmen Schaffer, 1943. "Pat Rooney Dies; Dancer 72 Years; Ex-Vaudeville Performer, at 82, Was Still on Stage," *NYT,* 11 Sep 1962, 33:1 (master of the waltz-clog). "200 Attend Rites for Pat Rooney; Dancer Is Called 'Husband, Father, Friend' of Theatre," *NYT,* 13 Sep 1962, 37:2 (buried at Evergreen Cemetery, Brooklyn). "Pat Rooney, 72 Years in Show Biz and Symbol of Vaudeville, Dies at 82," *Variety,* 12 Sep 1962. AS, p. 939. BHD1, p. 473. IFN, p. 256. SD. "Rooney and Bent Comedy," *NYDM,* 28 Apr 1915, 28:3 (appeared with Marion Bent and Pat Rooney, Jr., in *The Busy Bell Boy,* Lubin, released 8 May—their screen debut). J. Van Cartmell, "Live Wires from the West Coast," *NYDM,* 27 Nov 1915, 29:1 (Orpheum headliner who has stepped from before the footlights to appear in the "shivering tintypes." To appear in *The Bell Hopper* for Universal, 2-reel Joker comedy, directed by Roy Clements, with Victor Potel and Lillian Hamilton). George Katchmer, "Pat Rooney," *CI,* 227 (May 1994), 50:2.

Rooney, Pat [actor] (*né* Fred E. Ratsch, b. 1890?–15 Jan 1933 [42], Los Angeles CA; lung cancer). m. **Grace Darling**. (Essanay.) "Pat Rooney," *Variety,* 17 Jan 1933. AMD, p. 298. AS, p. 939. BHD, p. 290 (d. 15 Jun). IFN, p. 256. Truitt, p. 290. "Pat Rooney with Universal," *MPW,* 18 Dec 1915, 2212.

Rooney, Pat, III [actor] (b. 1 Apr 1909–5 Nov 1979 [70], South Sutton MA). AS, p. 939 (d. 6 Nov, Lake Blaisdell NH). BHD1, p. 473. IFN, p. 257.

Rooney, Patricia *see* **Bent, Marion**

Roope, Fay [actress] (b. 1893–13 Sep 1961 [68?], Port Jefferson NY). AS, p. 939.

Roos, Charles G. [cinematographer/director] (b. Canada, 1882). BHD2, p. 226.

Roos, Len H. [cinematographer]. No data found. FDY, p. 467.

Roosevelt, Andre (b. Paris, France, 1879–Jul 1962 [83?], Port-au-Prince, Haiti). BHD2, p. 227.

Roosevelt, Buddy [actor] (*né* Kent Sanderson, b. near Meeker CO, 25 Jun 1898–6 Oct 1973 [75, Meeker CO]). AS, p. 939. BHD1, p. 474. IFN, p. 257. Ed Wyatt, "Buddy Roosevelt Rides Again," *CI,* 135 (Sep 1986), 32 (b. near Meeker OK). George Katchmer, "Buddy Roosevelt," *CI,* 227 (May 1994), 50:3.

Roosevelt, Theodore [actor] (b. New York NY, 27 Oct 1858–6 Jan 1919 [60], Oyster Bay NY). BHD, p. 290.

Root, Wells [title writer/.scenarist] (b. Buffalo NY, 21 Mar 1900–8 Mar 1993 [92], Woodland Hills CA). AS, p. 939. BHD2, p. 227. FDY, p. 447.

Roper, Jack [actor/boxer] (b. MS, 25 Mar 1904–28 Nov 1966 [62], Woodland Hills C; cancer). AS, p. 939. BHD1, p. 474. IFN, p. 257.

Roquemore, Henry [actor] (b. Marshall TX, 13 Mar 1886–30 Jun 1943 [57], Beverly Hills CA; heart attack). (MGM.) "Henry Roquemore," *Variety,* 7 Jul 1943. AS, p. 939. BHD1, p. 474 (b. 1888). IFN, p. 257. Truitt, p. 290. George Katchmer, "Remembering the Great Silents," *CI,* 249 (Mar 1996), 48–49.

Roques, Jeanne *see* **Musidora**

Roquever, Noël [actor] (*né* Noël Louis Raymond Benevent, b. Doue-la-Fontaine, France, 18 Dec 1892–6 Nov 1973 [80], Douarmenez, France; heart attack [extrait de décès no. 163/1973]). (American film debut: The Three Must-Get-Theirs, 1922; Fox.) AS, p. 939. BHD1, p. 474 (d. 5 Nov, Paris, France). IFN, p. 257 (Roquevert). Waldman, p. 248.

Rork, Ann [actress] (b. Darien CT, 12 Jun 1908–23 Jan 1988 [79], Nashville TN). m. J. Paul Getty. AS, p. 670 (Ann Rork Light). BHD, p. 290. "Ann Rork Light, Former Actress, 79," *NYT,* 25 Jan 1988, B9:5. Anthony Slide, *Silent Portraits* (Vestal NY: The Vestal Press, Ltd., 1989), p. 234.

Rork, Sam[uel] **E.** [actor/executive] (b. Albany NY, 1870?–24 Jul 1933 [63], Los Angeles CA; complications after an operation for appendicitis). (Fox; Sennett; 1st National.) "Sam Rork Dies; Veteran Showman and Producer Succumbs to Operation," *Variety,* 1 Aug 1933. AMD, p. 298. AS, p. 939. BHD2, p. 227 (b. 1874–31 Jul). "Rork and [Eugene] Roth Unite as Producers; SIgn George Marion and Buy 'Isobel,'" *MPW,* 28 Aug 1920, 1188.

Rorke, Hayden (son of **Margaret Hayden Rorke**) [film/stage/TV actor] (b. New York NY, 23 Oct 1910–19 Aug 1987 [76], Toluca Lake CA; cancer). "Hayden Rorke, Actor in Film, Plays and TV," *NYT,* 21 Aug 1987, B7:6. "Hayden Rorke," *Variety,* 26 Aug 1987. AS, p. 939 (b. Brooklyn NY).

Rorke, Ina [actress] (b. Portugal, 1868–23 Apr 1944 [76], Morristown NJ). BHD, p. 290. IFN, p. 257.

Rorke, Kate (sister of actress Mary Rorke) [stage/film actress] (b. London, England, 22 Feb 1866–31 Jul 1945 [79], Little Hadham, Hertfordshire, England). m. (1) Edward Gardiner (d. 1899); (2) Dr. Douglas Cree (d. 1932). "Kate Rorke, Star of British Drama; Actress, Retired Since 1917, Played Here with Wyndham and Beerbohm Tree," *NYT,* 1 Aug 1945, 19:4 (age 81). "Kate Rorke," *Variety,* 159, 8 Aug 1945, 46:4 (age 81). BHD, p. 290.

Rorke, Margaret Hayden (mother of **Hayden Rorke**) [actress] (b. 1884?–2 Mar 1969 [85?], Los Angeles CA). "Margaret Hayden Rorke," *Variety,* 12 Mar 1969. AS, p. 939. Truitt, p. 290.

Rorke, Mary [actress] (b. London, England, 14 Feb 1858–12 Oct 1938 [80], London, England). AS, p. 939. BHD, p. 290.

Rosa, Silvio Laurenti [director] (b. Viterbo, Italy, 21 Feb 1892–24 Dec 1965 [73], Rome, Italy). AS, p. 645 (Laurenti Rosa, Silvio); p. 939. JS, p. 236 (in Italian silents from 1920).

Rosai, Claretta [actress] (aka Claretta Rosaj, b. Rome, Italy, 1893). JS, p. 388 (in Italian silents from 1918).

Rosanova, Rosa [actress] (b. Odessa, Ukraine, Russia, 23 Jun 1869–29 May 1944 [74], Santa Monica CA). AS, p. 939 (d. LA CA). BHD1, p. 474. IFN, p. 257. MH, p. 135.

Rosapina, Carlo [actor] (b. Italy-d. 18 Jan 1929, Rome, Italy). AS, p. 939.

Rosar, Annie [actress] (*née* Anna Rosar, b. Vienna, Austria, 17 May 1888–1 Aug 1963 [75], Vienna, Austria; heart attack). AS, p. 939. BHD1, p. 474. IFN, p. 257.

Rosas, Enrique [director/producer] (b. Puebla, Mexico, 1877–9 Aug 1920 [43?], Mexico City, Mexico). AS, p. 939.

Rosay, Françoise [film/stage/TV singer/actress/scenarist] (*née* Françoise Gilberte Chauvin, b. Paris, France, 19 Apr 1891–28 Mar 1974 [82], Montgeron, France). m. **Jacques Feyder**, 26 Jul 1917 (d. 1948). (Film debut: *Falstaff*, 1913; final film, *The Pedestrians*, 1973.) "Francoise Rosay, Actress, 82, Dies; Star of 100 Films and Many Plays Was Resistance Hero," *NYT*, 30 Mar 1974, 34:2 ("...the film people are nice and keep me busy. They think of me as being only tragic and strong. But I can be very, very comic—maybe something like Marie Dressler."). "Francoise Rosay," *Variety*, 274, 3 Apr 1974, 71:1. AS, pp. 939–40. BHD1, p. 474. IFN, p. 257. Waldman, p. 249.

Rosca, Gabriel [actor/director] (*né* nGabriel Calbours, b. France, 1895–1943 [48?], France). AS, p. 940. JS, p. 388 (in Italian silents from 1914; also filmed in France, Great Britain and Rumania).

Roscoe, Albert [stage/film actor] (*né* John A. Rascoe, b. Nashville TN, 23 Aug 1888–8 Mar 1933 [44], Los Angeles CA; cancer). m. Violet May Rose [**Barbara Bedford**], 1922–1930 (d. 1981); remarried. (Essanay, Chicago, 1915; 1st National; FBO; Columbia; Paramount; Metro; Radio.) "Alan Roscoe," *Variety*, 14 Mar 1933 ("one of the early players in pictures"). AS, p. 940 (b. 28 Aug; d. 1925). BHD1, p. 474. GK, pp. 833–42. IFN, p. 257. MH, p. 135 (b. 1887). Truitt, p. 290. George A. Katchmer, "Albert Roscoe; The Good Indian," *CI*, 92 (Feb 1983), 20–21 (includes filmography). R.E. Braff, "Additional Film Credits for Allan Roscoe," *CI*, 238 (Apr 1995), 42. George Katchmer, "Remembering the Great Silents," *CI*, 247 (Jan 1966), 46. Billy Doyle, "Albert Roscoe—Barbara's Leading Man," *CI*, 253 (Jul 1996), C2.

Rose, Berthold [actor] (b. Germany, 30 Mar 1870–8 Mar 1925 [54]). BHD, p. 290.

Rose, Billy [composer/showman] (*né* William Samuel Rosenberg, b. 4 Sep 1899–10 Feb 1966 [66], Montego Bay, Jamaica, West Indies; lobar pneumonia). m. 5 times: (1) **Fanny Brice**, 9 Feb 1929, New York NY—div. 1 Oct 1938 (divorce complaint) (d. 1951); Eleanor Holm; Doris Warner; Joyce Matthews. Herbert G. Goldman, *Fanny Brice; The Original Funny Girl* (New York: Oxford University Press, 1992). "Billy Rose Is Dead; Showman Was 66," *NYT*, 11 Feb 1966, 1:7, 30:1. "Billy Rose's Will [22 Nov 1965] Aids Foundation; It Gets Bulk of Estate and 2 Ex-Wives [Holm and Matthews] Are Named," *NYT*, 12 Feb 1966, 16:2. "Billy Rose's Rites Held in Theater Named for Him," *NYT*, 14 Feb 1966, 35:5. Abel Green, "2 in 1 Week: Sophie Tucker Dies at 82; Billy Rose Succumbs at 66," *Variety*, 16 Feb 1966 (wrote *Rainbow 'Round My Shoulder; Only a Paper Moon*). AS, p. 940. BHD2, p. 227 (b. 6 Sep).

Rose, Blanche [actress] (*née* Blanche Starr, b. Detroit MI, 1878?–5 Jan 1953 [75], Los Angeles CA). "Blanche Rose," *NYT*, 6 Jan 1953, 29:4 (Mrs. Blanche Starr; age 72). "Blanche Rose," *Variety*, 14 Jan 1953. AS, p. 940. BHD1, p. 474. IFN, p. 257. Truitt, p. 290.

Rose, Bob [stuntman] (*né* Robert Theodore Rose, b. Jones County TN, 4 Feb 1902–8 Mar 1993 [91], Montrose CO). (Ince, 1917.) AS, p. 940. BHD1, p. 474. Luther Hancock, "Bob Rose; Hollywood Stuntman," *CI*, 149 (Nov 1987), 51–53, 60. Luther Hancock, "Remembering Bob Rose," *CI*, 215 (May 1993), 53.

Rose, David E. [general manager for Douglas Fairbanks] (b. Kansas City MO, 1896?–21 Aug 1992 [96], Phoenix AZ). "David E. Rose," *Variety*, 31 Aug 1992, p. 92. AS, p. 940. BHD2, p. 227.

Rose, Harry [actor] (b. 1892–10 Dec 1962 [70?], Los Angeles CA; heart attack). AS, p. 940.

Rose, Helen Gerould [actress]. No data found. (Betzwood Film Co. [PA]).

Rose, Jack [actor] (b. England, 1884?–29 May 1926 [38 or 42], Riverdale NJ; lost his mind after operation for cancer). "Jack Rose," *Variety*, 2 Jun 1926. AS, p. 940.

Rose, Jackson J. [cameraman] (b. Chicago IL, 29 Oct 1886–23 Sep 1956 [69], Los Angeles CA). (Essanay [Chicago], 1910.) "Jackson Rose," *Variety*, 26 Sep 1956. AMD, p. 298. AS, p. 940. BHD2, p. 227. FDY, p. 467. "'U' Cameraman Tries New One with Success," *MPW*, 21 May 1927, 196.

Rose, Norman S. [publicist]. No data found. m. Eloise DeMontford, 10 Jun 1916. AMD, p. 298. "Rose—DeMontford," *MPW*, 24 Jun 1916, 2243.

Rose, Robert [actor] (b. 1868–1 Jun 1936 [68], Los Angeles CA). BHD1, p. 474. IFN, p. 257.

Rose, Ruth [actress] (b. 16 Jan 1896–8 Jun 1978 [82], Santa Monica CA). BHD, p. 290.

Rose, Selma [actress] (*née* Bertha Merkel, b. 1873?–21 Nov 1933 [60?], Los Angeles CA; heart attack). m. **Reginald Barlow** (d. 1943). "Mrs. Bertha Barlow," *Variety*, 28 Nov 1933. AS, p. 940. Truitt, p. 290.

Roseleigh, Jack [actor] (b. TN, 1887?–5 Jan 1940 [53?], Los Angeles CA; heart attack). m. **Velma Whitman**. "Jack Roseleigh," *Variety*, 17 Jan 1940. AS, p. 940. BHD, p. 290. IFN, p. 257. "In the Picture Studios," *NYDM*, 4 Dec 1915, 31:2 (leading man of the Hudson Players at Union Hill NJ).

Roselle, William [stage/film actor] (b. New York NY, 1878?–1 Jun 1945 [67], Bronx NY). m. Rose Winter. "William Roselle; Actor Had Appeared for Many of the Leading Producers Here," *NYT*, 2 Jun 1945, 15:6. "William Roselle," *Variety*, 6 Jun 1945. AMD, p. 298. AS, p. 940. BHD, p. 290. IFN, p. 257. Truitt, p. 290. "William Roselle," *MPW*, 9 Oct 1915, 257.

Roseman, Edward F. [actor]. No data found. George Katchmer, *CI*, 227 (May 1994), 51:1.

Rosemond, Clinton C. [actor] (b. SC, 1 Nov 1882–10 Mar 1966 [83], Los Angeles CA; pneumonia). AS, p. 940.

Rosen, Jimmy [midget actor] (*né* James Rosen, b. Russia, 1885–1 Jun 1940 [55], New York NY). (Headline Amusement Co.) AS, p. 940. BHD1, p. 475. IFN, p. 257. "First Headline Comedy [Pee-Wee's Courtship]," *NYDM*, 23 Jun 1915, 21:2 (Jimmie Rosen).

Rosen, Philip E. [cameraman/director/producer] (b. Marienburg, Germany, 8 May 1888–22 Oct 1951 [63], Los Angeles CA). (Edison, 1912; Universal; Fox; MGM.) "Phil Rosen," *Variety*, 31 Oct 1951. AMD, p. 298. AS, p. 940. BHD2, p. 227. IFN, p. 257. Katz, p. 993. 1921 Directory, p. 273 (b. Machias ME). Spehr, p. 162. Wheeler W. Dixon, *The "B" Director; A Biographical Directory* (Metuchen NJ: The Scarecrow Press, Inc., 1985), pp. 413–16. "Another Feature Company," *MPW*, 25 Apr 1914, 531. "Philip Rosen with Goldwyn," *MPW*, 28 Apr 1917, 626. "Philip Rosen Signs," *MPW*, 21 Feb 1925, 809. "Rosen Begins His First for M-G-M," *MPW*, 9 Jan 1926, 153. "Philip Rosen Signed by M-G-M," *MPW*, 9 Jan 1926, 160. "Direcrtor Rosen Ill," *MPW*, 12 Nov 1927, 9.

Rosenbach, Arthur [executive] (b. 1885?–11 Mar 1965 [80]). "Ed Rosenbaum," *Variety*, 1 Mar 1965, p. 103. "Mrs. Ed Rosembaum," *Variety*, 24 May 1932, p. 79 (d. 20 Mar 1932 [75]). AMD, p. 298. "Rosenbach Joins Reliance," *MPW*, 16 Jan 1915, 374.

Rosenbaum, Ed, Jr. (son of theatrical manager Edward Rosenbaum, Sr., and actress Rosa Lee) [publicist] (b. 1885?–11 Mar 1965 [80], Philadelphia PA). "Ed Rosenbaum," *Variety*, 238, 17 Mar 1965, 103:1 ("personal rep for cowboy star Tom Mix"). AMD, p. 298. BHD2, p. 227. "He Crowned the King-Bees," *MPW*, 8 Dec 1917, 1505. "Rosenbaum Sees Great Possibilities," *MPW*, 20 Jul 1918, 333. "Rosenbaum Writes a March," *MPW*, 7 Sep 1918, 1390.

Rosenberg, Sarah [actress] (b. Poland, 1 Jul 1874–16 Jun 1964 [89], Los Angeles CA). AS, p. 941. BHD1, p. 475. IFN, p. 257. Truitt, p. 290.

Rosenblatt, Cantor Josef [actor] (b. New York NY, 9 May 1882–19 Jun 1933 [51], Jerusalem, Israel; heart attack). m. Traube Kaufmann (had 5 sons, 3 daughters). (Amiercan-Palestine Fox Film Co.) "Josef Rosenblatt, Noted Cantor, Dies; Succumbs to Heart Attack in Jerusalem After a Busy Day Making Film; Won World-Wide Fame; Exiled from Russia as Boy, He Began Career in Austria and Achieved a Reputation Here," *NYT*, 19 Jun 1933, 15:4 (b. Biala-Cierkew, Russia. Invested in a Jewish weekly in 1922; bankrupted in 1926, $150,000. "He resigned his position with Ohab Zedek to earn money on the stage to pay his creditors, and at last reports had paid off most of it. ¶Cantor Rosenblatt never shaved. He once refused an offer of $3,000 a night to sing in 'The Jewess' with the Chicago Opera Company because the role would have required him to shave his beard."). "Josef Rosenblatt," *Variety*, 20 Jun 1933, 46:1. AS, p. 941. BHD1, p. 475.

Rosener, George M. [actor/writer] (b. Brooklyn NY, 23 May 1879–29 Mar 1945 [65], Los Angeles Co. CA). BHD, p. 290; BHD2, p. 227. IFN, p. 257.

Rosenfeld, Israel [producer] (b. Germany-d. 28 Mar 1956, Berlin, Germany; auto accident). AS, p. 941. BHD2, p. 227.

Rosenfield, Sydney [scenarist] (b. 1856–13 Jun 1931 [75?], New York NY). BHD2, p. 227.

Rosenthal, Barney [executive] (b. 1884–3 May 1948 [64?], St. Louis MO). BHD2, p. 227.

Rosenthal, Caroline [scenarist]. No data found. AMD, p. 298. "Caroline Rosenthal Joins Metro," *MPW,* 15 May 1920, 965.

Rosenthal, Edward (b. 1852-Jul 1914 [62?]). BHD2, p. 227.

Rosenthal, J. [cinematographer]. No data found. AMD, p. 298. "A Much Travelled Cinematographer," *MPW,* 8 May 1909, 591.

Rosher, Charles A. [cinematographer] (father of **Joan Marsh**) (b. London, England, 17 Nov 1885–15 Jan 1974 [88], Lisbon, Portugal; result of a fall). "Charles A. Rosher," *Variety,* 30 Jan 1974 (age 89). AMD, p. 298 (Charles G. Rosher). AS, p. 941. BHD2, p. 228. Brownlow, p. 226. FDY, p. 467. IFN, p. 257 (age 89). Katz, p. 994. "No Cameras Going to the Front," *MPW,* 12 Sep 1914, 1487. "Neilan Signs Charles Rosher to Head Photographic Staff," *MPW,* 21 Aug 1920, 1045. "Mary's Cameraman," *MPW,* 24 Sep 1921, 421. "Charles Rosher Joins Williams in England," *MPW,* 14 Aug 1926, 4.

Rosing, Bodil [actress] (*née* Bodil Hammerich, b. Copenhagen, Denmark, 27 Dec 1877–31 Dec 1941 [64], Los Angeles CA; heart attack). *The NYT Obituary Index* lists an obituary on 3 Jan 1942, p. 32:4, but it is missing on the microfilm. AS, p. 941. BHD1, p. 475. IFN, p. 257. Truitt, p. 291.

Roskam, Edward M. [executive]. No data found. AMD, p. 298. "Edward Roskam to Be a Manufacturer," *MPW,* 7 Sep 1912, 967. "World Series Pictures Successful," *MPW,* 1 Nov 1913, 503. "Roskam's Narrow Escape; Life-Photo Company President in Automobile That Skids on Palisade Cliff," *NYDM,* 21 Oct 1914, 28:4 (unhurt). "Roskam in Auto Accident," *MPW,* 31 Oct 1914, 643. "Roskam's Film Hospital," *NYDM,* 22 Sep 1915, 35:2 (at 220 West 42nd Street, he "will 'cure' pictures.that have been placed on the shelf because of poor construction, weak titling, dragginess, lack of continuity, poor photography, or any of the hundred and one reasons that put pictures on the sick list.").

Rosley, Adrian [stage/vaudeville/film actor] (b. Rumania, 28 Oct 1888–5 Mar 1937 [48], Hollywood Hills, Los Angeles CA; heart ailment). m. "Adrian Rosley Dies; Screen Actor, 47; Appeared in 'The Garden of Allah'—Played in Several Stage Successes on Broadway," *NYT,* 6 Mar 1937, 17:5 (b. so. France; age 47; member of the Masquers and the Lambs Club). "Adrian Rosley," *Variety,* 125, 10 Mar 1937, 62:1 (age 47). AS, p. 941 (b. Marseille, France, 28 Mar). BHD1, p. 475. IFN, p. 257.

Rosmer, Milton [stage/film/radio/TV actor] (*né* Arthur Milton Lunt, b. Southport, Lancastershire, England, 4 Nov 1882–7 Dec 1971 [89], Chesham, Buckinghamshire, England). m. **Irene Rooke** (d. 1958). "Milton Rosmer," *Variety,* 15 Dec 1971, 62:5. AS, p. 941 (b. 1881). BHD1, p. 475; BHD2, p. 228. IFN, p. 257. 1921 Directory, p. 199. "The Expressions of Milton Rosmer; A British Star on Stage and Screen," *Picture Show,* VI, 5 Nov 1921, 9 (with seven photographs). George A. Katchmer, "Forgotten Cowboys and Cowgirls—Part IX," *CI,* 181 (Jul 1990), 58–59.

Rosmino, Gian Paolo [actor/director] (aka Paolo Gian, *né* Giovanni Rosmino, b. Turin, Italy, 2 Jul 1888–20 Jul 1982 [94], Rapallo, Italy [extrait de décès no. 118/201/B/1982]). AS, p. 941. BHD1, p. 475; BHD2, p. 228 (d. 19 Jul). JS, p. 389 (b, 1890; in Italian silents from 1913).

Ross, Arthur S. [actor] (b. 1880?–17 Feb 1955 [75], Los Angeles Co. CA; of injuries sustained in an auto accident). "Arthur S. Ross," *Variety,* 23 Feb 1955. AS, p. 941. BHD, p. 291. IFN, p. 257.

Ross, Betty C *see* **Clark[e], Betty Ross**

Ross, Blanche [actress] (b. 1890–29 May 1969 [79?], Paris, France). BHD, p. 291.

Ross, Bob [actor] (b. Vancouver, Canada, 1925–17 Apr 1982 [57?], Vancouver, Canada). AS, p. 942. BHD, p. 291.

Ross, Charles J. [actor] (*né* Charles J. Kelly, b. Montreal, Canada, 18 Feb 1859–15 Jun 1918 [59], No. Asbury Park NJ). m. Ada Toune (aka **Mabel Fenton**; d. 1931). "Charles J. Ross," *Variety,* 21 Jun 1918 (age 58). AMD, p. 298. AS, p. 942. BHD, p. 291. IFN, p. 258. "New Equitable Stars," *MPW,* 11 Sep 1915, 1813.

Ross, Churchill [actor] (*né* Ross Weighr, b. Lafayette IN, 29 Jan 1901–23 May 1962 [61], Los Angeles CA). AS, p. 942. BHD1, p. 475. IFN, p. 258.

Ross, Colin [scenarist]. No data found. FDY, p. 437.

Ross, Corinne Heath Summer [actress] (b. IL, 15 Jun 1879–21 Jun 1965 [86], Los Angeles CA). AS, p. 942.

Ross, David [actor] (b. New York NY, 1891–12 Nov 1975 [84?], New York NY). AS, p. 942.

Ross, Earle [actor] (b. IL, 29 Mar 1888–21 May 1961 [73], No. Hollywood CA). AS, p. 942.

Ross, Frances A. [actor] (b. Chicago IL). AMD, p. 298. WWS, p. 156. "Engaged by Ross," *MPW,* 8 Jul 1923, 317.

Ross, Frank [actor/director/producer/scenrist] (b. Boston MA, 12 Aug 1904–18 Feb 1990 [85], Los Angeles CA; after an operation for a tumor). AS, p. 942. BHD1, p. 476.

Ross, Herbert [actor/director] (b. Calcutta, India, 3 Oct 1865–18 Jul 1934 [68], England; complications during an operation). AS, p. 942.

Ross, James B. [actor]. No data found. (Pathé.) "Film Player Sues; Thrown by Horse, Player Now Seeks Damages from Pathe," *NYDM,* 2 Dec 1914, 26:4 (sought to secure $15,000 "for alleged injuries resulting from an accident while he was working on a picture at Staten Island. The plaintiff asserts that the defendants knew that a horse which was provided for him had a vicious disposition.").

Ross, Kewpie. (Sunshine Comedies.) No data found.

Ross, Marion (aka Marion Roland, b. 1898?–23 Jul 1966 [68?], Seattle WA; cancer). "Marion Ross," *Variety,* 3 Aug 1966. AS, p. 942. BHD1, p. 476. Truitt, p. 291.

Ross, Milton L. [actor/director] (*né* Arthur Milton Lunt, b. San Francisco CA, 1881). AS, p. 942.

Ross, Nat[athaniel R.] [director] (b. San Francisco CA, 13 Jul 1902–24 Feb 1941 [38], Los Angeles CA; rifle shot through the heart). m. actress Audrene Brier. (Universal; Columbia.) "Nat Ross Slain by Discharged Worker," *Variety,* 26 Feb 1941. AMD, p. 298. AS, p. 942. BHD2, p. 228. "Nat Ross," *MPW,* 16 Jul 1927, 156.

Ross, Robert [actor/director] (b. Port Colborne, Ontario, Canada, 1901?–23 Feb 1954 [52], New York NY). m. Margalo Gilmore. "Robert Ross Dies; Actor, Director; He Left Cast of 'Kind Sir' on Feb. 17—His Wife, Margalo Gillmore, Also Was in Play," *NYT,* 25 Feb 1954, 31:1. "Robert Ross," *Variety,* 3 Mar 1954. AS, p. 942. IFN, p. 258.

Ross, Samuel [stage producer/actor] (b. Russia, 1872?–22 Jun 1943 [71], Irvington NJ). m. Rose Eisenberg. "Samuel Ross; Theatrical Producer and Actor Traveled with Russian Troupe," *NYT,* 23 Jun 1943, 21:4. "Samuel Ross," *Variety,* 30 Jun 1943. AS, p. 942.

Ross, Thomas W. [stage/film actor] (b. Boston MA, 22 Jan 1873?–14 Nov 1959 [86], Torrington CT). (All Star Feature Corp.) "Thomas Ross, 86, Stage Actor, Dies; Played Mr. Webb in Original Production of 'Our Town'—In 'Your Uncle Dudley,'" *NYT,* 15 Nov 1959, 86:6. "Thomas Ross," *Variety,* 18 Nov 1959. AMD, p. 298. AS, p. 942 (b. 1875). BHD1, p. 476 (b. 1875). IFN, p. 258 (b. 1875). Truitt, p. 299. "Thomas W. Ross," *MPW,* 9 May 1914, 809. "Thomas Ross Latest Stage Star to Enter Pictures; Is Playing in Metro Subject," *MPW,* 15 May 1920, 958.

Rossak, Frank Ward [director] (b. Vienna, Austria, 1897–1957 [60?], Vienna, Austria). AS, p. 942.

Rosse, Hermann [art director] (b. Amsterdam, Netherlands, 1886–13 Apr 1965 [79?], Nyack NY). BHD2, p. 228.

Rossi, Gilberto [director/producer] (b. Livorno, Italy, 2 Mar 1882 [extrait de naissance no. 508]-1971 [89?], Sao Paulo, Brazil). AS, p. 943.

Rossi-Pianelli, Vittorio [actor/director] (b. Italy, 1869–1953 [83?], Rome, Italy). AS, p. 943. JS, pp. 391–92 (in Italian silents from 1913).

Rossiter, Ralph J. [publicist]. No data found. AMD, p. 299. "Succeeds Miss Lindner," *MPW,* 23 Feb 1924, 643.

Rossito, Angelo Salvatore [dwarf actor] (b. 18 Feb 1908–21 Sep 1991 [83], Los Angeles CA; complications after surgery). AS, p. 943. BHD1, p. 476. Ragan 2, p. 1465.

Rossman, Earl [producer]. No data found. AMD, p. 299. "Rossman on the Air," *MPW,* 8 Aug 1925, 651 (WOR Radio).

Rosson, Arthur H. (brother of **Harold** and **Richard Rosson**) [director] (b. London, England, 24 Aug 1886?–17 Jun 1960 [73], Los Angeles CA). (Triangle.) "Arthur H. Rosson, Film Director, 73," *NYT,* 19 Jun 1960, 88:5. "Arthur H. Rosson," *Variety,* 13 Jul 1960. AMD, p. 299. AS, p. 943. BHD, p. 291; BHD2, p. 228 (b. 1887). IFN, p. 258. Katz, p. 998. Truitt, p. 291 (b. 1889). "Art Rosson New William Fox Director," *MPW,* 15 Feb 1919, 894. "Arthur Rosson Directing Johnny Hines," *MPW,* 5 May 1923, 59. "Death of Mrs. Rosson," *MPW,* 23 Apr 1927, 737 (mother d. in Hollywood).

Rosson, Ethel "Queenie" [actress] (b. 24 Feb 1889–19 Dec 1978 [89], West Palm Beach FL). AS, p. 943. BHD, p. 291.

Rosson, Harold G. [actor/cinematographer] (brother of **Arthur** and **Richard Rosson**) (b. New York NY, 1895–6 Sep 1988 [93], Palm Beach FL; heart attack). m. **Jean Harlow,** 1933–34 (d. 1937). (Vitagraph, 1908; MGM.) "Harold G. Rosson, 93, 'Oz' Cinematographer," *NYT,* 9 Sep 1988, D18:6. "Top Lenser Hal Rosson Dead at 93; Four Decades of Films," *Variety,* 14 Sep 1988. Burt A. Folkart, "Hal Rosson; Pioneer Film Cameraman," *LA Times,* 8 Sep 1988, I, 33:1. AS. p. 943.

BHD, p. 291; BHD2, p. 228. FDY, p. 467. Katz, p. 998.

Rosson, Helene [actress] (b. Newport RI, 14 Jun 1897–5 May 1985 [87], Palm Beach FL). m. **Ashton Dearholt** (d. 1942). AMD, p. 299. AS, p. 943. BHD, p. 291. "Universal Films' Youngest Star Ever," *MPW,* 27 Sep 1913, 1394. "Helene Rosson, Designer," *MPW,* 4 Mar 1916, 1446. "Helene Rosson," *MPW,* 16 Sep 1916, 1839. George A. Katchmer, "Remembering the Great Silents," *CI,* 175 (Jan 1990), C8.

Rosson, Richard (brother of **Arthur** and **Harold Rosson**) [actor/director] (b. New York NY, 4 Apr 1893–31 May 1953 [60], Pacific Palisades CA; suicide over illness; found dead in car from carbon monoxide fumes). m. **Vera Sisson** (d. 1954). (Vitagraph, 1914; Ince; Universal; Paramount.) "Richard Rosson," *Variety,* 3 Jun 1953 (d. LA CA). AMD, p. 299. AS, p. 943 (Dick Rosson). BHD, p. 291 (d. LA CA); BHD2, p. 228 (b. 1892). IFN, p. 258. Katz, p. 998. "Promoted to Directors," *MPW,* 8 May 1926, 144. "Death of Mrs. Rosson," *MPW,* 23 Apr 1927, 737 (mother d. in Hollywood). "Richard Rosson," *MPW,* 17 Dec 1927, 32. George Katchmer, "Remembering the Great Silents," *CI,* 239 (May 1995), C5–6.

Rostand, Edmund [actor] (b. Marseilles, France, 1 Apr 1868–2 Dec 1918 [50], Paris, France). AS, p. 943.

Rosvaenge, Helge [actor] (*né* Helge Anton Rosenvinge Hansen, b. Copenhagen, Denmark, 29 Aug 1897–17 Jun 1972 [74], Munich, Germany). AS, p. 943.

Roswell, Elena [actress]. No data found. JS, p. 392 (in Italian silents from 1919).

Roth, Albert A. [actor] (b. Hungary, 1898?–24 Nov 1969 [71], Houston TX). "Albert A. Roth," *Variety,* 3 Dec 1969. AS, p. 944.

Roth, Ann [actress] (b. 1913-Jan 1979 [65?]). BHD1, p. 476.

Roth, Elliott [actor]. No data found. AMD, p. 299. "Roth Finishes Work in Big Special," *MPW,* 4 Aug 1923, 413.

Roth, Eugene [producer]. No data found. AMD, p. 299. "[Sam E.] Rork and Roth Unite as Producers; Sign George Marion and Buy 'Isobel,'" *MPW,* 28 Aug 1920, 1188.

Roth, Eva May [actress/wardrobe mistress]. No data found. AMD, p. 299. "Eva May Roth to Play in Pictures," *MPW,* 3 Sep 1921, 91.

Roth, Lillian [singer/actress] (*née* Lillian Rutstein, b. Boston MA, 13 Dec 1910–12 May 1980 [69], New York NY). m. (1) William Scott; (2) Ben Shalleck; (3) Mark Harris; (4) Edward Leeds; (5) Burt McGuire. With Gerold Frank, *I'll Cry Tomorrow* (NY: Frederick Fell, Inc.,1954). (Film debut: 1916.) AS, p. 944. BHD1, p. 476. Les Ledbetter, "Lillian Roth, Actress and Singer, Dies," *NYT,* 13 May 1980, III, 20:1. "Lillian Roth," *Variety,* 14 May 1980 (first name from Lillian Russell). Katz, p. 999. SD. *Stars of the Photoplay* (Chicago: Photoplay Publishing Co., 1930) ("At the age of five, Lillian Roth played in motion pictures.").

Roth, Murray [director/title writer/scenarist] (b. NY, 1894?–17 Feb 1938 [44], Los Angeles CA). (Fox, 1921; Universal; WB.) "Murry Roth," *Variety,* 23 Feb 1938 (d. 16 Feb). AS, p. 944. BHD2, p. 228. FDY, pp. 437, 447. IFN, p. 258.

Roth, Sandy [assistant film director] (*né* Sanford L. Roth, b. 1889?–4 Nov 1943 [54], Beverly Hills CA; heart attack). "'Sandy' Roth," *Variety,* 10 Nov 1943. AS, p. 944. BHD, p. 291; BHD2, p. 228. IFN, p. 258. Truitt, p. 291.

Rothacker, Watterson R. [executive/producer] (b. Chicago IL, 1884?–25 Jan 1960 [75], Santa Monica CA; cancer). "W.R. Rothacker, ex-Film Producer; Retired Paramount Aide Dies—Publisher Was Pioneer in Educational Movies," *NYT,* 27 Jan 1960, 33:5. "Watterson R. Rothacker," *Variety,* 3 Feb 1960. AMD, p. 299. AS, p. 944. BHD2, p. 228. "Chicago Notes," *MPW,* 8 Oct 1910, 808. Watterson R. Rothacker, "Commercial Use of Motion Pictures," *MPW,* 11 Jul 1914, 215–16. "Watterson R. Rothacker," *MPW,* 5 Dec 1914, 1390. Watterson R. Rothacker, "The Rothacker Film Manufacturing Co.," *MPW,* 3 Jun 1916, 1720. Watterson R. Rothacker, "Action of Industry Fast and Furious," *MPW,* 10 Mar 1917, 1500. Watterson R. Rothacker, "Industrials as Entertainment," *MPW,* 21 Apr 1917, 465. "Rothacker Gets Big Order," *MPW,* 10 Nov 1917, 865–66. "W.H. O'Brien Now with Rothacker," *MPW,* 9 Aug 1919, 844. Sumner Smith, "Rothacker Finds That English Film Men Are Sprinters and Promise Competition," *MPW,* 11 Sep 1920, 187. "'Lost World' Makes Rothacker Debut in Amusement Field," *MPW,* 23 Aug 1924, 633. Tom Wallter, "McCormick Resigns from FIrst National; Watterson Rothacker Slated for Position," *MPW,* 28 May 1927, 247, 255. Carol Stafford, "Paragraphs Pertaining to Players and Pictures," *Cinema Arts,* VI (Sep 1927), 41 (founded Rothacker Film Manufacturing Co., 1910; elected VP of First National Productions). Tom Wallter, "Watterson Rothacker," *MPW,* 3 Sep 1927, 18–19. "Rothacker to Coast," *MPW,* 26 Nov 1927, 6.

Rothafel, Samuel Lionel "Roxy" [exhibitor] (*né* Samuel Rothapfel, b. Stillwater MN, 9 Jul 1882–13 Jan 1936 [53], New York NY). "S.L. Rothafel Dies; 'Roxy' of Theatre; Transformed Movie Theatres from Dingy Halls to Now Customary Palaces; Gained Fame Over Radio; Innovator of Modern Screen and Stage Effects Stricken in Sleep at Hotel," *NYT,* 14 Jan 1936, 21:1. Joe Bigelow, "Roxy, Films' No. 1 Exhibitor, Pioneer in Cinema Standards, Dies at 53," *Variety,* 15 Jan 1936. AMD, p. 299. AS, p. 944. "Tribute to Rothapfel," *MPW,* 10 Jul 1915, 288–89. "Samuel Rothapfel, Program Producer," *MPW,* 22 Feb 1919, 1048. Gladys Hall, "He Makes the World at Home," *Classic,* Aug 1923, 25, 84. Dunham Thorp, "Roxy Builds His Dream; S.L. Rothapfel, Who Once Showed Pictures in a Shed, Had a Vision to Preside Over the World's Largest Theater and Present the Last Word to De Luxe Entertainment. His Dream Has Come True," *MPC,* Dec 1926, 16–17, 73, 83. Rosa Reilly, "Roxy; The Story of the Man—The Theatre—and The Gang!," *Screenland,* May 1929, 46–47 *et passim.*

Rothauser, Edouard [actor] (b. Budapest, Hungary, 8 Dec 1876–24 Jan 1956 [79], Barcelona, Spain). BHD1, p. 477.

Roth-de Markus, Albert [director/scenarist] (*né* Arthur Samuel Roth-de Markus, b. Vevey, Switzerland, 5 Dec 1861–22 Oct 1927 [65], Huttwil, Switzerland). AS, p. 944.

Rothe, Anita [stage/film actress] (b. Alexandria VA, 1866?–9 Jan 1944 [77], Bronx NY). m. James Kearney. "Miss Anita Rothe; Retired Actress, Made Debut Here in 1890's, Dies at 77," *NYT,* 11 Jan 1944, 19:4. "Anita Rothe," *Variety,* 12 Jan 1944. AS, p. 944. BHD, p. 291 (b. 1867). IFN, p. 258.

Rothgardt, Wanda [actress] (b. Stockholm, Sweden, 12 Mar 1905–1950 [45?], Göteborg, Sweden). BHD1, p. 616.

Rothier, Leon [actor] (b. Rheims, France, 1875–6 Dec 1951 [76?], New York NY). BHD, p. 291.

Rothstein, Nat G. [publicist]. No data found. AMD, p. 299. "Striking Example of Film Advertising," *MPW,* 18 Dec 1915, 2159. Nat Rothstein, "Campaign Books for Motion Pictures," *MPW,* 20 Jul 1918, 330–31. "Nat Rothstein Tries Out Gas Sedan," *MPW,* 24 Aug 1918, 1092. "Nat Rothstein," *MPW,* 26 Mar 1927, 311. "Nat Rothstein Broadcasts on 'Shield of Honor,'" *MPW,* 26 Nov 1927, 12 (WGBS Radio, NYC, for Gimbel Bros.). "Nat Rothstein to Air 'Uncle Tom' on Dec. 15," *MPW,* 3 Dec 1927 (WPCH Radio, NYC). "Nat Rothstein on 'Uncle Tom's Cabin,'" *MPW,* 17 Dec 1927, 8.

Rothwell, Mary Nettie [actress] (b. Windsor, Canada, 24 Jul 1869–15 Sep 1926 [57], Neuilly-sur-Seine, France [extrait de décès no. 536/1826]). m. **Charles Burkhardt** (d. 1925). AS, p. 944.

Rotmund, Ernst [actor] (b. Torun, Poland, 26 Nov 1886–2 Mar 1955 [68], Munich, Germany). AS, p. 944 (b. Thorn, Germany). BHD1, p. 477.

Rottmacker, Watterson R. [producer] (b. 1884–25 Jan 1960 [75?], Santa Monica CA). AS, p. 944.

Rottman, Victor [actor]. No data found. AMD, p. 299. "Kalem Signs Victor Rottman," *MPW,* 6 May 1916, 976.

Roubert, Matty [child actor] (b. New York NY, 22 Jan 1907–17 May 1973 [66], Honolulu HI). AMD, p. 299. BHD1, p. 477. Ragan 2, p. 1467. W. Stephen Bush, "The Screen Children's Gallery," *MPW,* 28 Feb 1914, 1066. "'Universal Boy' Series Beginning," *MPW,* 11 Jul 1914, 290. "The Universal Boy," *MPW,* 25 Jul 1914, 585. "Chinese Humor Seems the Real Thing," *MPW,* 8 Aug 1914, 813. "Matty Roubert, Boy Star of 'The Waif,'" *MPW,* 25 Dec 1915, 2368. "Reelcraft Producing a Series of Two-Reel Boyhood Stories with Matty Roubert as Star," *MPW,* 5 Jun 1920, 1324.

Roudenko, Nicolas [actor] (b. Nice, France, 1 May 1909–23 Aug 1976 [67], Paris, France). BHD1, p. 616.

Rouer, Germaine Joséphine [actress] (b. Paris, France, 2 Nov 1897–26 Dec 1994 [97], Paris, France [extrait de décès no. 4/552/1884]). AS, p. 944.

Rouffe, Alida [actress] (*née* Joséphine Marie Rouffe, b. Bordeaux, France, 20 Mar 1874–21 Nov 1949 [75], Marseilles, France [extrait de décès no. 773/1949]). AS, p. 944.

Rough, John W. [scene painter]. No data found. (Property boy, *The Emerald King,* 1868; Edison, Bronx NY.) "Scene Painting for Pictures," *NYDM,* 14 Oct 1914, 26:3.

Roughwood, Owen [actor] (b. London, England, 9 Jun 1876–30 May 1947 [70]). BHD, p. 291. IFN, p. 258 (b. 1870).

Rouleau, Raymond [actor/author/director] (*né* Edgard Marie Raymond Rouleau, b. Brussels, Belgium, 4 Jun 1904–11 Dec 1981 [77], Paris, France [extrait de décès no. 7/1075/1981]). AS, p. 945. BHD1, p. 477; BHD2, p. 229.

Rousel, Jeanne [actress]. No data found. Rene de la Seine, "Moviettes from Gay Paree,"

Paris and Hollywood Screen Secrets Magazine, Aug 1927, 67 (photo).

Rouse, Hallock [actor] (b. 1897–2 Jan 1930 [32?], Pacific Ocean; plane crash). AS, p. 945.

Rouskaya, Norka [actress]. No data found. AMD, p. 300. "Norka Rouskaya," *MPW,* 6 Apr 1918, 76. "Baroness Rouskaya to Make Pictures," *MPW,* 9 Oct 1920, 818.

Rousse, Dolores [actress]. No data found. *Fl.* 1923–25. AMD, p. 300. "Dolores Rousse Signs Fox Contract," *MPW,* 8 Sep 1923, 190. George Katchmer, "Remembering the Great Silents," *CI,* 239 (May 1995), 54.

Rousseau, Gladys [designer] (b. 1899?–21 May 1975 [76], Fountain Valley CA). "Gladys Rousseau, 76, Designer of Swimsuits for Sennett, Dies," *NYT,* 22 May 1975, 42:4. AS, p. 945.

Rousseau, Victor [sculptor/scenarist] (b. 1866?–16 Mar 1954 [88], Brussels, Belgium). "Victor Rousseau," *NYT,* 18 Mar 1954, 31:4. FDY, p. 437.

Roussel, Arthur [executive] (b. 1880?–Dec 1914? [34]; bronchial pneumonia). AMD, p. 300. BHD2, p. 229. "Arthur Roussel," *MPW,* 11 Apr 1914, 197. "Mr. Roussel of Pathé Seriously Ill," *MPW,* 19 Sep 1914, 1633. "Mr. Roussel's Health Improving," *MPW,* 26 Sep 1914, 1762. "Obituary," *MPW,* 2 Jan 1915, 51.

Roussel, Henri [actor/director] (b. Bayonne, France, 1875–1946 [71?], Paris, France). AS, p. 945.

Roussillon, Marcelle [actress]. No data found. AMD, p. 300. "Newcomer from Paris," *MPW,* 12 Jan 1918, 211.

Routh, George [actor]. (Lubin.) No data found.

Rouverol, Aurania [scenarist] (b. 1886–23 Jun 1955 [69?], Palo Alto CA). AS, p. 945. BHD2, p. 229.

Roux, Antonio [actor] (b. Mexico, 7 May 1901–9 Nov 1976 [75], Woodland Hills CA). BHD, p. 291. IFN, p. 258.

Rouzilley, Yvonne [actress/singer] (*née* Marie Yvonne Gilberte Rouzille, b. Commentry, France, 5 Jan 1900 [extrait de naissance no. 4]-1 Dec 1985 [85], Grasse, France). AS, p. 946.

Rovensky, Josef [actor/director] (b. Prague, Czechoslovakia, 17 Apr 1894–5 Nov 1937 [43], Prague, Czechoslovakia). AS, p. 946. BHD2, p. 229.

Roveri, Ermanno [actor] (b. Milan, Italy, 5 Oct 1903–28 Dec 1968 [65], Milan, Italy). BHD1, p. 477. IFN, p. 258. JS, p. 394 (in Italian silents as a child from 1913).

Row, Arthur [stage/film actor]. No data found. (Edison.) "In the Picture Studios," *NYDM,* 28 Jul 1915, 29:2 (to debut in *Vanita Fair*).

Rowan, Ernest [actor] (b. 1886?–30 Sep 1960 [74], Hampton VA). "Ernest Rowan, 74, an Actor 35 Years," *NYT,* 3 Oct 1960, 31:3. AS, p. 946. BHD, p. 291. IFN, p. 258. Truitt, p. 291.

Rowe, George [actor] (b. 1871?–Nov? 1923 [52]). "Georges Roux," *Variety,* 15 Nov 1923.

Rowland, Adele [stage/film actress] (b. Washington DC, 10 Jul 1883–8 Aug 1971 [88], Los Angeles CA). m. **Charles Ruggles**, 4 Mar 1914, Jersey City NJ (d. 1970); **Conway Tearle** (d. 1938). AS, p. 946. IFN, p. 258. "Marriages," *NYDM,* 25 Mar 1914, 15:2 (married Ruggles). Cover, *NYDM,* 16 Jun 1915 (with Lawrence Grossmith, onstage in *Nobody Home*).

Rowland, (Baby) Helen [child actress] (b. ca. 1919). "Consult Mystic Myra," *MPS,* 28 Jul 1925, 24 ("She is now six years old and is acting regularly in pictures.").

Rowland, Richard A. [executive] (b. Pittsburgh PA, 8 Dec 1880–12 May 1947 [66], New York NY [Death Certificate Index No. 11110]). (1st National.) "R.A. Rowland Dies; Pioneer in Films; Founder of Old Metro Picture Corp., a Former Paramount, First National Executive," *NYT,* 13 May 1947, 25:1. "Richard A. Rowland," *Variety,* 14 May 1957. AMD, p. 300. AS, p. 946. BHD2, p. 229. IFN, p. 258. "Decision Reserved," *MPW,* 8 Mar 1913, 981. "Metro Controls Productions," *MPW,* 20 Mar 1915, 1745. "Going Direct to the Public," *MPW,* 27 Nov 1915, 1639. "Rowland Refused Injunction," *MPW,* 22 Jan 1916, 572. "Metro Has Election," *MPW,* 4 Mar 1916, 1453. "Metro's First Birthday," *MPW,* 8 Apr 1916, 237. "Rowland Laughs at Mergers," *MPW,* 15 Apr 1916, 411. "Metro Will Pay Its Soldiers' Salaries," *MPW,* 8 Jul 1916, 257. Manley, "Pittsburgh, Pa., Has a Record Date for 'Store Shows'; Rowland and [James B.] Clark Take a Hand,"*MPW,* 15 Jul 1916, 405–06. "Star System Folly, Says Rowland," *MPW,* 4 Jan 1919, 53. "Rowland Leaves for the Coast," *MPW,* 5 Apr 1919, 54. "Metro Will Make Announcement o Rowland's Return from Europe," *MPW,* 9 Aug 1919, 809–10. "Rowland on Way Home from Europe," *MPW,* 16 Aug 1919, 973. "Richard Rowland Gets Information and Secures Plays on Trip Abroad," *MPW,* 30 Aug 1919, 1265–66. "Richard Rowland Places Metro Output for England in All the Jury Theatres," *MPW,* 6 Sep 1919, 1455. "Rowland Predicts Best Year of All for Fast-Expanding Metro Organization," *MPW,* 27 Sep 1919, 1948. "Richard A. Rowland Pleased with Improvements and Progress at Metro's Hollywood Studios," *MPW,* 15 Nov 1919, 326. "Entry of Big Business Means New Blood, System, and Death of Waste," *MPW,* 27 Dec 1919, 1124. "Rowland Denies Loew Is Interested in or Affiliated with Any Other Firm," *MPW,* 10 Apr 1920, 221. Richard A. Rowland, "Says Public Will Not Tolerate Any But the Best Kind of Picture Entertainment," *MPW,* 1 May 1920, 712. "Metro Is in Its Best Position in Its History to Accomplish Big Things During Coming Year, Says Rowland," *MPW,* 10 Jul 1920, 215. "Rowland Considers Buster Keaton a Real Screen Comedy Sensation; Metro Finds Films Book Rapidly," *MPW,* 11 Dec 1920, 751. Richard A. Rowland, "New Theatres Springing Up Reflect Growth of Moving Picture Industry," *MPW,* 25 Dec 1920, 1015. "Rowland Resigns Presidency of Metro; Effective After Return from Continent," *MPW,* 1 Oct 1921, 526. Arthur James, "A Word About Richard A. Rowland," *MPW,* 1 Oct 1921, 528. "Richard Rowland Will Distribute," *MPW,* 22 Apr 1922, 852. "Richard A. Rowland Joins the Executive Forces of First Natioal," *MPW,* 3 Jun 1922, 460. "'Dick' Rowland Says—," *MPW,* 16 Sep 1922, 182. "Rowland Urges More Attention Be Given Continuity Writing," *MPW,* 21 Oct 1922, 656. "Williams Resigns from First National; Rowland Appointed General Manager," *MPW,* 11 Nov 1922, 142. Richard A. Rowland, "First National May Enter Production Field," *MPW,* 18 Nov 1922, 232. "Richard A. Rowland Warns Against Reduction of Admission Price," *MPW,* 17 Feb 1923, 641. "Industry in State of Evolution, Says Rowland; Sees New Class of Pictrure," *MPW,* 21 Apr 1923, 813. Richard A. Rowland, "First National Slogan for New Season 'Big Time Product Only,'" *MPW,* 9 Jun 1923, 501. "Rowland Highly Pleased with 4 First Nationals Just Completed," *MPW,* 15 Sep 1923, 274. "Finds Producers Have Wrong Idea of Gross Business on Their Pictures," *MPW,* 13 Oct 1923, 557. "Rowland Viewing Specials in West; May Split His Production Forces," *MPW,* 19 Jan 1924, 179. "First National Maintaining High Standard, Says Rowland," *MPW,* 1 Mar 1924, 43. "Richard Rowland Organizes First National Productions," *MPW,* 8 Mar 1924, 118. "Richard Rowland and Colleen Moore Are Godparents," *MPW,* 3 Jan 1925, 25 (to John Francis Dillon, Jr.). "Rowland Announces Another Big Million Dollar Special," *MPW,* 21 Feb 1925, 809. "Rowland Urges Theatres' Support on Radio," *MPW,* 4 Apr 1925, 436. "Rowland Says First National's Prospects Were Never So Bright as They Are Today," *MPW,* 15 Aug 1925, 750. William J. Reilly, "Personalities—Pictures—Positions," *MPW,* 7 Nov 1925, 25. "They Control Your Films!," *MPC,* Jan 1926, 26. Richard A. Rowland, "First National's Hollywood Plant Making Explosive Sales Ammunition," *MPW,* 30 Jan 1926, 436. Covarrubias, "Distinguished Picture People," *MPW,* 20 Feb 1926, 696. "First National Builds 'The Finest,'" *MPW,* 20 Mar 1926, 209–10. "Lieber and Rowland in Conference," *MPW,* 28 Aug 1926, 529. "Rowland Returns with Noted European Stars," *MPW,* 20 Nov 1926, 150. "Rowland Upholds the Star System," *Cinema Arts,* Jan 1927, 19. "Mr. Rowland Says:," *MPW,* 26 Mar 1927, 318. "Resignation of Rowland Doubted in Studio Circles," *MPW,* 1 Oct 1927, 291. "Rowland Back from W.C. Gives Glowing Review of F.N. Releases," *MPW,* 24 Dec 1927, 8. "F.N. Month Is Dedicated to Richard A. Rowland," *MPW,* 31 Dec 1927, 18. James D. Van Trump, "The Rowland [theater]: Elegant Ghost; Could Be Restored," *Wilkinsburg [PA] Gazette,* 77, 30 Apr 1975, 1, 3.

Rowlands, Art [actor] (b. Oakland CA, 26 Aug 1897–25 May 1944 [46], Los Angeles CA). m. Betty. (WB.) "Art Rowlands," *Variety,* 31 May 1944 (stuntman for 28 years). AS, p. 946. BHD1, p. 477. IFN, p. 258.

Rowson, Simon [executive] (b. Manchester, England, 1877–28 Jun 1950 [73?], London, England). BHD2, p. 229.

Roxa, Lina [actress] (*née* Raymonde Duconget, b. Maisons-Lafitte, France, 24 Sep 1902 [extrait de naissance no. 120]-30 Nov 1995 [93], Argenteul, France). AS, p. 946.

Roy, Charu [director] (b. Berthampore, India, 6 Sep 1890–28 Sep 1971 [81], India). AS, p. 946.

Roy, Prafulla Kumar [director] (b. Kustia, Bengali, 1 Jan 1892). AS, p. 947.

Royal, Charles E. [actor/scenarist] (b. OR, 27 Jan 1880–26 Jul 1955 [75]). BHD2, p. 229.

Royce, Arthur [art director] (b. 1891–29 Jan 1943 [51?], Los Angeles CA). BHD2, p. 229.

Royce, Brigham [actor] (b. Memphis TN, 1864–7 Mar 1933 [68?], Baltimore MD). BHD, p. 291. IFN, p. 259 (age 66).

Royce, Edward [dance director] (b. 1870–15 Jun 1964 [94?], London, England). BHD2, p. 229.

Royce, Edward William "Teddy." *See* Royce, Teddy.

Royce, Julian [actor] (*né* Julian Gardener, b. Bristol, England, 26 Mar 1870–10 May 1946 [76], London, England). AS, p. 947. BHD1, p. 478. IFN, p. 259.

Royce, Lionel [actor] (aka Leo Brandhofer, b. Dolina, Poland, 30 Mar 1891–1 Apr 1946 [55], Manila, Philippines). AS, p. 947.

Royce, Riza [actress] (b. Lancaster PA, 18 Jul 1903–20 Oct 1980 [77], Los Angeles CA; heart attaack). AMD, p. 301. AS, p. 947 (b. 1908). BHD1, p. 478. "Radio Debut of Riza Royce," *MPW,* 15 Aug 1925, 764. "Riza Royce in First Film," *MPW,* 5 Sep 1925, 85.

Royce, Ruth [actress] (b. Versailles MO, 6 Feb 1893–7 May 1971 [78], Los Angeles CA). AS, p. 947. BHD, p. 291. BR, p. 220. IFN, p. 259. George Katchmer, "Forgotten Cowboys and Cowgirls—Part VIII," *CI,* 180 (Jun 1990), 53.

Royce, Teddy [stage/film actor] (*né* Edward William Royce, b. 1840–24 Jan 1926 [85], London, England). "Edward William "Teddy" Royce," *Variety,* 10 Feb 1926, 2 ("Some years ago he boasted he was the oldest working actor in London. ¶Royce was the last of the famous Gaiety 'stars' who made history under the management of John Hollingshead. The others were Kate Vaughan, who died in 1903; Nellie Farren in 1904, and Edward Terry in 1912."). BHD, 291.

Royce, Virginia [actress]. No data found. m. James Fidler. AMD, p. 301. "Razz Causes Rift," *MPW,* 14 May 1927, 97 (formerly Mrs. James Fidler).

Royer, Franchon [extra/producer] (b. Des Moines IA, 1903?). m. Raymond Cannon, 1921? Ruth Tildesley, "The Girl Producer; Franchon Royer Crashed That Gate," *Screenland,* Jan 1929, 40–41, 100–01.

Royer, Harry "Missouri" [actor] (b. MO, 6 Oct 1889–1 Aug 1951 [61], Los Angeles CA; heart attack). "Harry Royer," *Variety,* 8 Aug 1951 (age 62; "pioneer film cowboy," began 1918). AS, p. 947 (b. 1890). BHD, p. 291. IFN, p. 259 (b. 1890). Truitt, p. 292.

Royle, Edwin Milton [actor/novelist/playwright] (b. 1862?–16 Feb 1942 [79], New York NY). m. **Selena** Fetter (d. 1983). "Edwin Milton Royle," *Variety,* 145, 18 Feb 1942, p. 46:1 (wrote *The Squaw Man,* 1905.). AMD, p. 301 (Edward Milton Royle). W. Stephen Bush, "Edward Milton Royle," *MPW,* 21 Feb 1914, 930.

Royle, Selena [stage/film actress] (*née* Selena Fetter, b. New York NY, 6 Nov 1904–23 Apr 1983 [78], Guadalajara, Mexico). m. (1) **Edwin Milton Royle** (d. 1942); (2) **Earle Larimore** (d. 1947); (3) **George Renavent** (d. 1969). AS, p. 947. BHD1, p. 478. Katz, p. 1001. SD.

Royle, William [actor] (b. Rochester NY, 22 Mar 1887–9 Aug 1940 [53], Los Angeles CA). AS, p. 947.

Royston, Julius [actor] (b. England, 1870–1 Jul 1935 [65?], Johannesburg, So. Africa; bronchopneumonia). AS, p. 947.

Royston, Roy [actor] (b. London, England, 5 Apr 1889–7 Oct 1976 [87], Kingston-upon-Thames, England). BHD1, p. 478. IFN, p. 259 (age 77).

Rozenberg, Lucien [actor] (b. France, 1874–1947 [73?], France). AS, p. 947.

Rub, Christian [actor] (b. Passau, Germany, 13 Apr 1886–14 Apr 1956 [70], Santa Barbara CA). AS, p. 947 (b. 1887). BHD1, p. 478.

Ruben, J. Walter [actor/scenarist/director/producer] (b. New York NY, 14 Aug 1899–4 Sep 1942 [43], Los Angeles CA; heart ailment). m. (1) Mildred S.; (2) **Virginia Bruce**, 1937 (d. 1982). (MGM.) "J. Walter Ruben, 43, Film Producer, Dies; Also Was a Director for MGM—Husband of Virginia Bruce," *NYT,* 5 Sep 1942, 13:5 and 6 Sep 1942, 31:2 ("Mr. Rubin...began writing for the films in 1924."). "J. Walter Ruben," *Variety,* 9 Sep 1942. AS, p. 947. BHD1, p. 478; BHD2, p. 229. FDY, p. 437. SD, p. 1088.

Ruben, José [stage/film actor] (b. Paris, France, 8 Dec 1886–28 Apr 1969 [82], New York NY [Death Certificate No. 09141]). m. **Mary Nash** (d. 1976). (K&E.) "Jose Ruben," *Variety,* 7 May 1969. AS, p. 947. BHD, p. 291 (b. 1889). IFN, p. 259. SD. Truitt, p. 292.

Rubennstein, Leon J. [publicist/producer]. No data found. AMD, p. 301. "Rubenstein Re-Enters Producing Field," *MPW,* 17 Jun 1916, 2051.

Rubens, Alma [actress] (*née* Alma Smith, b. San Francisco CA, 19 Feb 1897–21 Jan 1931 [33], Los Angeles CA; drug addiction). m. (1) **Franklyn Farnum**, ca. 1915, Los Angeles CA—1918 (d. 1929); (2) Dr. **Daniel Goodman**, 12 Aug 1923–28 Jan 1925 (d. 1957); (3) Jacob Krantz (**Ricardo Cortez**), 30 Jan 1926 (d. 1977). (Vitagraph; Triangle.) "Alma Rubens Dies; Former Film Star; Actress Succumbs to Pneumonia After Uphill Fight to Regain Her Health; Was in Coma Three Days; Victim of Narcotic Habit, She Made Several Futile Attempts to Return to the Stage," *NYT,* 22 Jan 1931, 23:2. "Alma Rubens Ends Her Long Battle Against Drug Habit; Death Comes to Actress After Many Hours of Coma When Double Pneumonia Proves Too Much for Young Motion Picture Star in Los Angeles," *The Arizona Daily Star,* 31 Jan 1931. "Alma Rubens," *Variety,* 28 Jan 1931. AMD, p. 301. AS, p. 947. BHD1, p. 478. FFF, p. 171. FSS, p. 254. IFN, p. 259. Katz, p. 1002. KOM, p. 158; *née* Alma Rueben, d. 23 Jan). MH, p. 135. MSBB, p. 1040. Truitt, p. 292. WWS, p. 119. "Alma Rubens, Triangle Favorite," *MPW,* 17 Feb 1917, 1017. "Alma Rubens," *MPW,* 21 Apr 1917, 429. "Alma Rubens," *MPW,* 14 Jul 1917, 229. "Operated on for Appendicitis," *MPW,* 12 Oct 1918, 207 (attack on 15 Sep 1918). "Alma Rubens at Head of Her Own Company," *MPW,* 4 Jan 1919, 59. "Recurrence of Old Trouble," *MPW,* 19 Apr 1919, 360. "Pathé Contracts for Ruben—Goodman Plays," *MPW,* 10 May 1919, 794. Regina Cannon, "Observation Is the Best Training for the Screen," *MW,* 12 May 1923, 11. "Alma Rubens to Play Lead," *MPW,* 1 Dec 1923, 498. Alma Talley, "'I Want to Die in the Last Reel!,' Says Alma Rubens," *MW,* 19 Apr 1924, 3. Regina Cannon, "The Dark Lady of the Screen," *MW,* 5 Jul 1924, 7. "Alma Rubens Signed by Fox," *MPW,* 27 Dec 1924, 867. Cover, *MPS,* 30 Dec 1924. "Alma Rubens a Dancer," *MPW,* 10 Oct 1925, 475. "Alma Rubens Stays with Fox Films; In Big Roles," *MPW,* 30 Jan 1926, 452. "Alma Rubens to Close Relations with Wm. Fox," *MPW,* 19 Feb 1927, 557. "Alma Rubens Shows Gain; Hospital Head Says She Responds to Narcotic Treatment Satisfactorily," *NYT,* (date?), 22:6 (committed to State Narcotic Hospital, Spadra, LA Co., by mother and husband, Ricardo Cortez). "Alma Rubens Leaves Hospital," *NYT,* 17 Apr 1929, 56:8 (released from Spadra, State Narcotic Hospital; committed in February; paroled on 15 Apr 1929). "Alma Rubens in Asylum; Committed to California State Hospital on New Outburst," *NYT,* 17 May 1929, 29:2 (on 16 May Rubens was removed to the City Psychopathic Ward after a call from Mrs. Theresa Rubens, "who said her daughter had attacked her nurse and threatened to commit suicide. She stood the officers off for three hours before being overpowered." Removed to Southern California State Hospital for the Insane at Patton). "Questions Alma Rubens; Narcotic Agent Says She Described Hollywood Drug Traffic," *NYT,* 25 May 1929, 2:6 ("...Miss Rubens made admissions which would be of material aid in an investigation of conditions in the film capital."). "Alma Rubens Recovers; California Authorities Plan Her Release from Narcotic Hospital," *NYT,* 16 Nov 1929, 24:2 (she was to be released from Patton State Hospital after four months. "Miss Rubens will be taken to a mountain retreat for thirty days...after which she must report to the hospital. If the report is satisfactory, she will be formally discharged."). "Alma Rubens Released; Actress Drug Addict Reported Cured in California Asylum," *NYT,* 22 Dec 1929, II, 2:2 ("Previous attempts to treat her at private institutions and at Spadra, an institution for men, but nearer to her home than Patton, in which she was placed by special dispensation, failed. She escaped from the Spadra institution." She wrote her friends: "I am coming out of the hospital a new Alma Rubens. I shall devote all of my time to the work of going back on the stage and screen a better actress."). "Alma Rubens Coming Here; Actress, Recovered, on Way to Resume Her Career," *NYT,* 10 Feb 1930, 19:5 (paused in Chicago on her way to NYC. "After the sanitarium restrictions the smallest pleasures are exciting, even my breakfast cup of coffee."). "Alma Rubens to Take Lead; Former Film Actress to Replace Edith Broden in 'With Privileges,'" *NYT,* 8 Oct 1930, 29:2 (at the Belmont Theatre—her first Broadway appearance). Sam Peeples, "The Girl with the Beautiful Eyes; The Tragedy of Alma Rubens," *CFC,* 37 (Winter, 1972),16–19, 44, 53. George Katchmer, "Remembering the Great Silents," *CI,* 239 (May 1995), 38, 53. Eve Golden, "Alma Rubens: 'A Red Rose in an Onyx Vase,'" *CI,* 247 (Jan 1966), 34–35 (*née* Genevieve Driscoll).

Rubenstein, Ida [actress/dancer] (b. Charkov, Ukraine, Russia, 5 Oct 1885–20 Sep 1960 [74], Saint-Paul-de-Vence, France). AS, p. 948.

Rubenstein, Ida [actress/dancer] (b. St. Petersburg, Russia, 1883–20 Sep 1960 [77], Paris, France). BHD, p. 292. IFN, p. 259 (b. Kharkov, Russia). JS, p. 394 (b. Kharkhov, Russia; d. Vence, France; appeared in only two films, *San Giorgio,* 1919, and *La nave,* 1920, both made in Italy).

Rubenstein, Irving [cinematographer] (b. New York NY, 1892–16 Jan 1954 [61?], New York NY). BHD2, p. 229.

Rubenstein, Lillian M. [Lubin bulletin editor/scenarist]. No data found. (Lubin.) *MPN,* 3 Feb 1912, p. 22 ("Lillaim M. Rubenstein, former associate editor of the Lubin Manufacturing Co. Bulletins, has recently succeeded Giles R. Warren as scenario editor of the firm. Miss Rubenstein is a successful newspaper and magazine writer and is the author of numerous photoplays...").

Rubey, Lucille [actress]. No data found. AMD, p. 301. "Fire Singes Actors; Considerable Damage [$3,000] Done by the Flames on Movie Stage," *LA Times,* 7 Feb 1920, II, p. 9 (at National Film Corp. of America, Santa Monica, on 6 Feb. Also hurt was Neal Burns. "A flash pistol used in the picture sent sparks toward the cloth covering the set, which was quickly consumed by the flames...the studio fire department extinguished the flames. The loss is covered by insurance."). "Buddy Post and Lucille Rubey Will Star in National Series," *MPW,* 27 Mar 1920, 2140.

Rubin, Benny [stage/film actor] (b. Boston MA, 2 Feb 1899–15 Jul 1986 [87], Los Angeles CA; heart attack after a prostrate operation). "Benny Rubin, an Actor and Vaudeville Comic," *NYT,* 17 Jul 1986, D21:5 (1st film: *Naughty Baby;* last film, *Won Ton Ton—The Dog Who Saved Hollywood*). "Benny Rubin," *Variety,* 23 Jul 1986 (Rubin & [Jack] Haley). AS, p. 948. BHD1, p. 478; BHD2, p. 229. SD.

Rubin, J. Robert [executive] (b. Syracuse NY, 1882–10 Sep 1958 [76], New York NY [Death Certificate Index No. 19191). "J. Robert Rubin of Loew's Is Dead; Retired Vice President and General Counsel Brought Popular Plays to Screen," *NYT,* 11 Sep 1958, 33:1. "J. Robt. Rubin Dies at 76; Long a Link with Loew-Mayer," *Variety,* 17 Sep 1958. AS, p. 948. BHD2, p. 229.

Ruby, Herman [composer/executive] (b. NY, 15 Mar 1891–30 Jul 1959 [68], Beverly Hills CA; heart attack). (WB.) "Herman Ruby [no relation to Harry Ruby], 68, Wrote Hit Songs; Composer and Lyricist Dies—Author of 'Cecilia' and 'My Sunny Tennessee,'" *NYT,* 31 Jul 1959, 24:3 (signed with WB in 1929). "Herman Ruby," *Variety,* 5 Aug 1959. AS, p. 948. ASCAP 66, p. 629. BHD2, p. 229.

Ruby, Mary [actress] (aka Mary Rubin Orkin, b. Brooklyn NY, 1894–18 Feb 1987 [92?], New York NY). AS, p. 948 (d. LA CA). BHD, p. 292. Ragan 2, p. 1472.

Rucker, Joseph T. [cameraman] (b. Atlanta GA, 1887–21 Oct 1957 [70?], San Francisco CA). (Oscar winner.) AMD, p. 301. AS, p. 948 (b. Atlanta LA). BHD2, p. 229. "Joseph T. Rucker," *MPW,* 18 Dec 1915, 2194. "Universal 'Peace' Cameraman Back," *MPW,* 26 Feb 1916, 1273.

Rudami, Rosa [actress] (b. NY, 1899?–2 Feb 1966 [67], Albany NY). AMD, p. 301. AS, p. 948. BHD, p. 292. IFN, p. 259. Truitt, p. 292. "Neapolitan Beauty Signed," *MPW,* 20 Jun 1925, 898.

Ruddman, Walter [cinematographer]. No data found. FDY, p. 467.

Ruddock, John [actor] (b. Lima, Peru, 20 May 1897). AS, p. 948 (English actor).

Rudhyar, Dane [actor/composer] (*né* Daniel de Chenneviere, b. Paris, France, 23 Mar 1895–15 Sep 1985 [90], San Francisco CA). AS, p. 948. BHD, p. 292; BHD2, p. 229.

Rudolph, Oscar [actor/assistant director] (b. Cleveland OH, 2 Apr 1911–1 Feb 1991 [79], Encino CA; cerebral thrombosis). AS, p. 948. BHD1, p. 478; BHD2, p. 230.

Rudulph, Gerald K. [publicist] (b. Bowling Green OH, 1877–14 May 1957 [80?], Buffalo NY). BHD2, p. 230.

Rufart, Carlos [actor/singer] (b. Spain, 1886–3 Apr 1957 [71?], Madrid, Spain). AS, p. 948.

Ruffini, Sandro [actor] (b. Rome, Italy, 21 Sep 1889–29 Nov 1954 [65], Rome, Italy; cerebral thrombosis). m. actress **Lina Tricerri**. JS, pp. 394–95 (in Italian silents from 1913).

Ruffo, Titta [actor/singer] (*né* Ruffo Capero Titta, b. Pisa, Italy, 9 Jun 1877–5 Jul 1953 [76], Florence, Italy). AS, p. 949.

Rufini, Giulio [cinematographer] (b. Albano Laziale, Italy, 14 Apr 1892). JS, p. 395 (in Italian silents from 1916).

Ruge, Billy [actor] (b. NY, 1885). BHD, p. 292.

Ruggeri, Telemaco [actor/director] (b. Narni, Italy, 15 Sep 1876–15 Oct 1957 [81], Rome, Italy). AS, p. 949. JS, p. 395 (in Italian silents from 1913; "One of the first to dub foreign films into Italian.").

Ruggieri, Ruggero [actor] (b. Fano, Italy, 14 Nov 1871–20 Jul 1953 [81], Milan, Italy). AS, p. 949. JS, p. 395 (in Italian silents from 1914).

Ruggles, Charles (brother of **Wesley Ruggles**) [stage/film actor] (*né* Charles Sherman Ruggles, b. Los Angeles CA, 8 Feb 1886–23 Dec 1970 [84], Santa Monica CA; cancer). m. **Adele Rowland**, 4 Mar 1914, Jersey City NJ (d. 1971). "Charles Ruggles, Actor, Dies," *NYT,* 24 Dec 1970, 24:1. "Charles Ruggles," *Variety,* 30 Dec 1970. AMD, p. 301. AS, p. 949. BHD1, p. 479. IFN, p. 259. Katz, p. 1002. Truitt, p. 292 (b. 1890). "Marriages," *NYDM,* 25 Mar 1914, 15:2. "Ruggles to Make Specials for Famous," *MPW,* 14 Jul 1923, 170. Charles Ruggles, "Looking at the Ladies; In Which a Famous Stage Comedian Makes his Debut as an Author and his Bow to his New Public. He Writes about Ladies First!," *Screenland,* Aug 1929, 68–69.

Ruggles, Wesley H. (brother of **Charles Ruggles**) [actor: Keystone cop/film editor/director/producer] (b. Los Angeles CA, 11 Jun 1889–8 Jan 1972 [82], Santa Monica CA; stroke). m. Arline Judge (1912–1974). "Wesley Ruggles," *Variety,* 12 Jan 1972. AMD, p. 301. AS, p. 949. BHD, p. 292; BHD2, p. 230. IFN, p. 259. Katz, pp. 1002–1003. 1921 Directory, p. 274. "Lieut. Ruggles Back from War," *MPW,* 26 Apr 1919, 531. "Ruggles Busy on New Alice Joyce Film," *MPW,* 5 Jul 1919, 112. "Selznick SIgns Wesley H. Ruggles," *MPW,* 16 Aug 1919, 976. "Morosco SIgns Ruggles," *MPW,* 4 Jun 1921, 501. "Ruggles to Direct Reid's Next," *MPW,* 25 Nov 1922, 327. "Signed by Paramount," *MPW,* 3 Mar 1923, 35. "Ruggles to Make Specials for Famous," *MPW,* 14 Jul 1923, 170. Dorothy Donnell, "From Hollywood to You," *MPS,* 12 Aug 1924, p. 30 (Mrs. Doris, Ruggles's mother, was shot by Doris as he and a Mr. Meyers argued over money matters). "Wesley Ruggles Signed to Direct for B.P. Schulberg," *MPW,* 1 Aug 1925, 560. "Ruggles to Direct 'Collegians,'" *MPW,* 18 Sep 1926, 179. "Wesley H. Ruggles," *MPW,* 6 Aug 1927, 384. Herbert Cruikshank, "No Hits, No Errors; But Wesley Ruggles Has Given Everybody Plenty of Runs for His Money," *MPC,* Jul 1929, 33, 84 (discovered George Lewis and Jack Oakie).

Ruiz, Federico [composer] (*né* Federica Ruiz Martinez, b. Galicia, Spain, 11 Nov 1889–15 Nov 1961 [], Mexico City, Mexico). AS, p. 949.

Ruiz, José Rivero [actor, "apparu dans le premier film parlant espagnol"] (b. Spain, 1896–27 Dec 1949 [53?], Madrid, Spain). AS, p. 949.

Rullier, Gaston François Marie [actor/author] (b. Libourne, France, 19 May 1882 [extrait de naissance no. 124/1882]-16 Oct 1972 [90], Bagnolet, France). AS, p. 949.

Ruman, Sig [actor] (*né* Siegfried Albon Rumann, b. Hamburg, Germany, 11 Oct 1884–14 Feb 1967 [82], Julian CA; heart attack). m. Clara. "Sig Ruman, Actor, Dead at 82; Sgt. Schultz in 'Stalag 17' Film; German-Born Performer Was in 150 Movies—Soviet Envoy in 'Ninotchka,'" *NYT,* 16 Feb 1967, 35:1. "Sig Ruman," *Variety,* 22 Feb 1967. AS, p. 949 (d. Julian NB). BHD1, p. 479. IFN, p. 259. Katz, p. 1003. Truitt, pp. 292–93.

Runnel, Albert F. [vaudeville/circus/film actor/scenic constructor] (b. St. Paul MN, 27 Apr 1891–4 Jan 1974 [82], Belleair-Clearwater FL; heart ailment). m. Ernestine. (Albert F. Runnel Studios, Detroit MI, 1946.) "Albert F. Runnel," *Variety,* 30 Jan 1974, 62:2 ("...in movies produced at the Biograph Studios."). AS, p. 949. BHD1, p. 615.

Runyon, Damon [writer/actor/scenarist] (*né* Alfred Damon Runyon, b. Manhattan KS, 4 Oct 1884–10 Dec 1946 [62], New York NY; throat cancer). AS, p. 949 (b. Manhattan NY). BHD1, p. 479; BHD2, p. 230.

Rupp, Mary Pickford (daughter of **Lottie Pickford**; niece of **Jack** and **Mary Pickford**; granddaughter of **Charlotte Pickford**) [actress] (b. 10 Mar 1916). AMD, p. 302. "Mary Pickford II Enters the Films," *MPW,* 7 Apr 1917, 115. "Birthday Party for Mary Pickford Rupp," *MPW,* 29 Mar 1919, 1793. "Grandmother Adopts Mary Pickford II," *MPW,* 14 Aug 1920, 903 (new name, Mary Pickford).

Rush, Dick [director]. No data found. AMD, p. 302. "Dick Rush to Join the Anzaks," *MPW,* 5 Oct 1918, 56.

Rushton, Roland [actor] (b. Australia-d. 11 Oct 1925, New York NY; pneumonia). "Roland Rushton," *Variety,* 11 Nov 1925. AS, p. 950. BHD, p. 292.

Ruskin, Harry [scenarist/producer] (b. Cincinnati OH, 30 Nov 1894–16 Nov 1969 [74], Burbank CA). BHD2, p. 230.

Ruskin, Jacob [actor] (b. 1886–6 Nov 1962 [76?], New Rochelle NY). BHD, p. 292.

Ruskin, Shimen [stage/film actor] (b. Vilnius, Poland, 25 Feb 1907–23 Apr 1976 [69], Los Angeles CA; cancer). m. Kay. (Child actor in Vilna, Poland; Broadway debut: *Having a Wonderful Time,* 1937.) m. (1 son). "Shimen Ruskin, Yiddish Actor Who Went to Hollywood, Dead," *NYT,* 4 May 1976, 40:4 (Lee J. Cobb charged him as belonging to a Communist group, which resulted in his being blacklisted. In 1965, he and ten scenarists shared an $80,000 out-of-court settlement that had charged the Motion Picture Association of America [MPAA, excepting UA] with maintaining a blacklist.). "Shimen Ruskin," *Variety,* 282, 5 May 1976, 191:1 (blacklisted by HUAC). AS, p. 950 (b. Vilnius, Lithuania, 4 Oct 1884). BHD1, p. 479 (b. Vilnius, Lithuania). IFN, p. 259.

Russ, Paula [actress] (*née* Pauline Ignatiev Russ, b. 1885–14 Mar 1966 [81?], Los Angeles CA). AS, p. 950.

Russell, Albert (son of stage actress Sarah Russell; brother of **William Russell**) [actor/director] (*né* Albert Lerche, b. New York NY, 2 Aug 1890–4 Mar 1929 [38], Los Angeles CA; pneumonia). m. **Vola Vale** (d. 1970). "Albert Russell," *Variety,* 6 Mar 1929, 59:2 (directed serials from 1910–20 "with such old timers as Ruth Gibson, Eddie Polo and Art Acord."). AS, p. 950. BHD, p. 292; BHD2, p. 230. IFN, p. 259.

Russell, Annie [stage/film actress] (b. 1863?–16 Jan 1936 [72], Winter Park FL). "Annie Russell," *Variety,* 121, 22 Jan 1936, 70:1 ("Essentially feminine, she scored a mild sensation in one play by smoking a cigar."). m. (1) **Eugene Presby**; (2) **Osward Yorke** (d. 1943). (First stage success: *Esmeralda,* 1881; London debut, 1898.) AMD, p. 302. "Annie Russell as Jinny [at the Park Theatre, Boston]; She Creates the Title Role in Israel Zangwill's New Play," *NYT,* 21 Feb 1905, 7:2 (Oswald Yorke was in the cast. "The play was well received,

Miss Russell responding to repeated curtain calls."). "Annie Russell's Career Guarantee for Cavell Role," *MPW,* 2 Nov 1918, 605.

Russell, Bob [executive]. No data found. AMD, p. 302. "Russell's Monarch Feature Ready," *MPW,* 30 Sep 1916, 2094.

Russell, Byron [actor] (*né* Patrick Joseph Russell, b. Clonmel, Tipperary, Ireland, 1884?–4 Sep 1963 [79], New York NY [Death Certificate Index No. 19253]). m. Helene Veola (d. 17 Aug 1963). "Byron Russell, 79, a Character Actor," *NYT,* 7 Sep 1963, 19:2. "Byron Russell," *Variety,* 18 Sep 1963. AS, p. 950. BHD1, p. 479. IFN, p. 260. Truitt, p. 293.

Russell, Dan [actor] (b. Birmingham, England, 1875–19 Mar 1925 [50?], Dallas TX). AMD, p. 302. BHD, p. 292. "L-KO Fun Makers," *MPW,* 20 Jan 1917, 382.

Russell, Edd X. [vaudeville/musical comedy/film actor] (b. NY, 27 May 1878–17 Nov 1966 [88], Los Angeles CA). m. "Edd X. Russell," *Variety,* 23 Nov 1966, 70:3 (joined a circus in 1892 at age 14; an extra himself, helped to organize the Screen Extras Guild; stand-in for Robert Benchley). AS, p. 950. BHD, p. 292. IFN, p. 260.

Russell, Ethel [playwright/scenarist] (*née* Ethel Harriman, d. 4 Jul 1953, New York NY). m. Henry Potter Russell, 1918–25. (RKO; MGM.) "Ex-Envoy's Daughter Dies; Mrs. Harriman Russell, Former Scenarist, Was A.E.F. Nurse," *NYT,* 5 Jul 1953, 49:2. "Ethel Bordon [pseudonym]," *Variety,* 8 Jul 1953 (Mrs. Ethel Harriman Russell). AS, p. 950.

Russell, Evangeline [actress] (b. New York NY, 18 Aug 1902–22 Feb 1966 [63], Los Angeles Co. CA). m. C. Harrison De Rippeteau, 1927. AS, p. 950. BHD, p. 292. IFN, p. 260. June Lee, "Cupid's Bulletin Board," *Paris and Hollywood Screen Secrets Magazine,* May 1927, 53 (m. De Rippeteau).

Russell, Frank [actor] (b. 1857–12 Aug 1925 [68?], New York NY). BHD, p. 292.

Russell, Hattie (sister of actress Ada Rehan [d. 1916]) [stage/film actress] (*née* Hattie Crenan, b. 1850–12 Aug 1918 [68], Long Branch NJ). "Hattie Russell," *Variety,* LI, 16 Aug 1918, 33:4. BHD, p. 292.

Russell, J[ames] **Gordon** [actor] (b. Piedmont AL, 11 Jan 1883–21 Apr 1935 [52], Los Angeles CA; heart attack). (Vitagraph; FBO.) "J. Gordon Russell," *Variety,* 1 May 1935. AS, p. 950. BHD1, p. 480. IFN, p. 260. Truitt, p. 293. George A. Katchmer, "Forgotten Cowboys and Cowgirls—Part IX," *CI,* 181 (Jul 1990), 59.

Russell, Jean [bit player] (d. 8 Jul 1922, New York NY; suicide with bichloride tablets). "Ann Duane," *Variety,* 21 Jul 1922 (both Duane and Russell committed suicide in a hospital; "Miss Russell at times did picture bits"). AS, p. 950. BHD, p. 292. Truitt, p. 293.

Russell, Jimmy [actor] (b. England, 1886–27 Oct 1963 [77?], Bognor Regis, England). AS, p. 949.

Russell, John [scenarist] (b. Davenport IA, 1885?–6 Mar 1956 [71], Santa Monica CA; heart attack). m. (2) Lili Hilson. "John Russell, 71, Author, Scenarist," *NYT,* 8 Mar 1956, 29:4. "John Russell," *Variety,* 14 Mar 1956. AMD, p. 302. AS, p. 950. BHD2, p. 230. FDY, p. 437. IFN, p. 260. "John Russell Has Gone to Hollywood to Join the Metro Literary Organization," *MPW,* 18 Dec 1920, 899.

Lowell, John Lowell [actor] (b. Pleasant Valley IA, 22 Apr 1875–20 Sep 1937 [62], Los Angeles CA). BHD1, p. 616. AS, p. 951 (d. 19 Sep, West LA CA). BHD1, p. 338; BHD2, p. 230. IFN, p. 260. Truitt, p. 205. George A. Katchmer, "Update—Forgotten Cowboys/Girls," *CI,* 179 (May 1990), 43.

Russell, L. Case [writer/director]. No data found. AMD, p. 302. "Mrs. Russell, Authoress of 'Title,'" *MPW,* Feb 1918, 836 (*The Light Within*). "L. Case Russell Directing Last 'Blazed Trail' Films," *MPW,* 14 Feb 1920, 1058.

Russell, Lillian (sister of **Susan Westford**; mother of Dorothy Russell; 2nd cousin of **Robert Z. Leonard**) [stage/film actress] (*née* Helen Louise "Nellie" Leonard, b. Clinton IA, 4 Dec 1861–6 Jun 1922 [60], Pittsburgh PA; mausoleum at Allegheny Cemetery). m. (1) **Harry Braham** (d. 1923); (2) Edward "Teddy" Solomon; (3) John Healy Chatterton (aka Signor Perugini onstage), 1894, Hoboken NJ (d. 1914); (4) Alexander P. Moore. Armond Fields, *Lillian Russell: A Biography of "America's Beauty"* (Jefferson NC: McFarland, 1998). (Made one film, *Wildfire,* World, 1915.) "Lillian Russell Dies of Injuries; Noted Stage Beauty of Years Ago Succumbs at Age of 61 After 10 Days of Illness; Hurt on Trip from Europe; Had Long Career in Comic Opera, Beginning in 1879—Married Four Times," *NYT,* 6 Jun 1922, 1:4, 2:5. "Only Near Friends to View Lillian Russell; Famous Actress's Request to Be Obeyed—Statesmen Among Pallbearers—White House Roses," *NYT,* 8 Jun 1922, 19:4. "Lillian Russell," *Variety,* 9 Jun 1922 (age 61). AMD, p. 302. AS, p. 951. BHD, p. 292. IFN, p. 260. Spehr, p. 162. Truitt, p. 293. "A.L. Einstein Locked Up; Lillian Russell's Daughter Says Husband Threatened to Kill Her," *NYT,* 5 Feb 1905 [Sunday], 1:6 (Einstein was detained at the Harrison St. Police Station on 4 Feb. He threatened Dorothy Russell on the street; she signed a "criminal complaint charging [Abbott Lewis] Einstein with threats to kill her." He was arrested half an hour later and jailed until Monday unless bail was posted. Hearing on Monday.). "Wife Unjust, Einstein Says; Could Quickly Prove She Is Mistaken—Denies Charges," *NYT,* 5 Feb 1905, 1:6 (Dorothy Russell left Chicago for St. Louis to appear in vaudeville. Einstein said "the trouble had been caused by his wife's attorneys, and that he loved her dearly and had been everything a husband should be."). "Miss [Dorothy] Russell Breaks Down; Leaves St. Louis Stage [Columbia Theatre] in Middle of Song [*She Reads the New York Papers Every Day*]—Husband Freed," *NYT,* 7 Feb 1905, 1:4 (she told the audience that she lost her voice in Chicago the week before, "due to worriment over her troubles with her husband, Abbott L. Einstein. In Chicago, she failed to appear in court against him, whom she had charged with threatening to kill her. Case dismissed, but her suit for divorce was still pending.). "Lillian Russell in Pictures," *MPW,* 15 Mar 1913, 1107. "Lillian Russell in 'Wildfire,'" *MPW,* 12 Dec 1914, 1534. "Says Lillian to Lewis," *MPW,* 19 Dec 1914, 1697. "Lillian Russell's 10," *Variety,* 24 Nov 1916, 3:4 ("Pittsburgh, Nov. 22. Notwithstanding a handsome home and a wealthy husband, Lillian Russell has again listened to the lure of the vaudeville dollar. She will start picking up $2,500 weekly for 10 weeks on the big time, opening Jan. 8.").

Russell, Martha [stage/film actress]. No data found. m. Charles C. Pyle. (Essanay; Satex Co.) AMD, p. 302. "Miss Martha Russell's Tour of Moving Picture Theaters," *MPW,* 3 Feb 1912, 390. "Montgomery Likes Miss Russell," *MPW,* 10? Feb 1912, 683. "Miss Russell Back with Essanay," *MPW,* 27 Apr 1912, 338. "Essanay's Leading Lady Saves Life of Youth," *MPW,* 3 Aug 1912, 425. "Miss Martha Russell's Lecture Tour," *MPW,* 12 Oct 1912, 128. James S. McQuade, "Chicago Letter," *MPW,* 14 Dec 1912, 1066–67. "Miss Martha Russell; Leading Lady of the Satex Film Company, Associated with Warner's Features," *MPW,* 8 Mar 1913, 1005 (photograph only). Lester Sweyd, "What They Are Doing Now," *Motion Picture Magazine,* Feb 1918, 13 (Russell, "who played opposite Francis Bushman when he first joined the Essanay Company, is appearing in vaudeville.").

Russell, Raymond [actor] (b. 1887?–Aug? 1918 [31], NY). No data found. (Keystone.) AMD, p. 302. AS, p. 951. "Actor's Body Brought to Los Angeles for Burial," *MPW,* 10 Aug 1918, 829.

Russell, Reb [actor/circus performer] (*né* Lafayette H. Russell, b. Oswatomie KS, 31 May 1905–16 Mar 1978 [72], Coffeyville KS). m. (1) (daughter, Betty); (2) Julia Stevens, 1943 (adopted son, Jimmie). "Reb Russell," *Variety,* 3 Jan 1979 (age 72). AS, p. 951. IFN, p. 260. Bill G. (Buck) Rainey, "Reb Russell, His Interlude as Western Star," *Filmograph,* III, No. 3 (1973), 32–37, 43 (cites *The All-American,* Universal, 1932, as his first film. His horse was named Rebel.). "A (Provisional) Filmography of Reb Russell," *Filmograph,* III, No. 4 (1973), 6, 42–44. Chuck Anderson, "The Tape Trail," *CI,* 145 (Jul 1987), C2-C3 (*né* Charles Franklin Russell; "Rebel"); Part II, 146 (Aug 1987), 33.

Russell, W.K. [property man/actor]. No data found. (Essanay, 1909.) "The Essanay Company Out West," *MPW,* 4 Dec 1909, 801–02 (worked on *The Heart of a Cowboy* as "property man and assistant hero and villain").

Russell, William F. (son of stage actress Sarah Russell; brother of **Albert Russell**) [vaudevillian/stage/film actor/producer] (*né* William Lerche, b. New York NY, 12 Apr 1886–18 Feb 1929 [42], Beverly Hills CA; pneumonia). m. **Charlotte Burton**, May 1917—div. 1921 (d. 1942); **Helen Ferguson**, 1925, LA CA (d. 1977). (Began Biograph, 1909; Thanhouser; FP-L; American; Pathé; William Russell Productions.) "William Russell," *Variety,* 20 Feb 1929 (age 40). AMD, p. 302. AS, p. 951. BHD1, p. 480 (b. 1884). FSS, p. 254. GK, pp. 843–54. IFN, p. 260. Katz, p. 1003 (b. Bronx NY, 1884; began 1912). Lowrey, p. 162 (b. Bronx NY). MH, p. 135. MSBB, p. 1028. Truitt, p. 293. WWS, p. 210. "[Thomas Ince] Has Yacht and Steward," *MPW,* 26 Jul 1913, 407. "William Russell Goes to Biograph," *MPW,* 13 Dec 1913, 1265. "Newsy Notes," *NYDM,* 23 Jun 1915, 20:4 (while "broncho busting," Russell's horse backed up against a barb wire fence, one of the prongs piercing Russell's arm severely. Blood poisoning set in, but he rallied.). "William Russell Gets Birthday Party," *MPW,* 20 May 1916, 1348. "William Russell May Go on Stage," *MPW,* 30 Sep 1916, 2112. "William Russell Is Re-Signed by Amnerican," *MPW,* 25 Nov 1916, 1174. "William Russell," *MPW,* 27 Jan 1917, 522. "Russell—Burton," *MPW,* 9 Jun 1917, 1614. "'Bill' Russell Entertains Press," *MPW,* 26 Jan 1918, 491. "Russell Forms Producing Company," *MPW,* 2 Mar 1918, 1213. "William Russell Back on the Job," *MPW,* 9 Mar 1918, 1352. "Santa Barbara to Be Russell's Home," *MPW,* 16 Mar 1918, 1487. "William Fox Signs William Russell," *MPW,* 12 Jul 1919, 236. "William Russell,"

MPW, 19 Jul 1919, 355. "More Than 30 Productions Are Listed by Russell's 5 Companies," *MPW,* 1 Nov 1924, 32. Don Juan, "So This Is Hollywood; Bill Russell's Comeback," *Paris and Hollywood,* Oct 1926, 21 (at age 18 he was a victim of a hip disease that withered his leg. After surgery and exercise, he was cured at age 19.). June Lee, "Dan Cupid's Bulletin Board," *Paris and Hollywood,* Oct 1926, 86 (celebrated his first anniversary with Ferguson). "Went on Stage at Age of Nine," *MPW,* 2 Jul 1927, 18. Buck Rainey, "Ask the Answer Man," *Photoplay,* Dec 1931, 112 (*né* Lerche). George Katchmer, "William Russell: Forgotten?," *CI,* 98 (Aug 1983), 52–53. "William Russell; A Long Forgotten Cowboy Star," *CI,* 144 (Jun 1987), C3-C7. Richard E. Braff, "An Index to the Films of William Russell," *CI,* 181 (Jul 1990), 34–36, 61. George Katchmer, "Remembring the Great Silents," *CI,* 254 (Aug 1996), 51–52 (*né* Leach).

Rutan, Charles Hart [actor] (b. Brookyn NY, 6 Jul 1892–17 Jul 1968 [76], Los Angeles Co. CA). BHD, p. 292. IFN, p. 260.

Ruth, George Herman "Babe" [baseball player/actor] (*né* George Herman Ruth, b. Baltimore MD, 6 Feb 1895–16 Aug 1948 [53], New York NY; throat cancer). m. Claire. Murray Schumach, "Babe Ruth, Baseball Idol, Dies at 53 After Lingering Illness; Famous Diamond Star Fought Losing Battle Against Cancer for 2 Years—End Comes Suddenly After Encouraging Rally," *NYT,* 17 Aug 1948, 1:4, 15:5 (more coverage on pp. 15–16). AMD, p. 302. AS, p. 951. BHD, p. 292. IFN, p. 260. Truitt, p. 293. "'Babe' Ruth to Star in Baseball Movie," *MPW,* 29 Nov 1919, 565. "Kessel and Baumann Come Back with Home-Run Babe Ruth's 'Headin' Home,'" *MPW,* 7 Aug 1920, 716. " Bebe [Daniels] Auctions Baseball Autographed by Babe Ruth," *MPW,* 14 Aug 1920, 923 (for $110.00). "'Babe' Ruth to Finish 'Headin' Home' in Short TIme, Says Kessel & Baumann," *MPW,* 21 Aug 1920, 1008. "'Babe' Ruth's 'Headin' Home' Promises Box Office Records," *MPW,* 4 Sep 1920, 62. "'Babe' Ruth Would Restrain Educational from Releasing Films of Him in Action," *MPW,* 11 Sep 1920, 182. "Educational Retaliates by Suing 'Babe' Ruth Company," *MPW,* 18 Sep 1920, 332. "Ruth Loses in Court," *MPW,* 25 Sep 19230, 478 a"...moving pictures of 'Babe' Ruth are news..."). "Educational to Press Suit for ¢250,000 Against Ruth," *MPW,* 2 Oct 1920, 679. "'Babe' Ruth Sues W.A. Shea and H.D. Yudkin for $35,000," *MPW,* 23 Oct 1920, 1134. "'Babe' Ruth Fails to Stop Exhibition of 'Headin' Home,' Losing Court Case," *MPW,* 6 Nov 1920, 38. "'Babe' Ruth Appeals," *MPW,* 20 Nov 1920, 357. "'Babe' Loses Again," *MPW,* 27 Nov 1920, 490. "Educational Films Amended Complaint in Suit Against Ruth and Yankee Co.," *MPW,* 25 Dec 1920, 1052. "Appeal Denied Ruth," *MPW,* 12 Feb 1921, 786. "Wesley Meets "Babe,'" *MPW,* 3 Sep 1921, 42. "'Babe' Ruth Helps Exploit 'In the Name of the Law' During Second Week of Run," *MPW,* 29 Jul 1922, 352. "Babe Ruth," *MPW,* 7 May 1927, 19. "Babe Ruth in Vocafilm," *MPW,* 16 Jul 1927, 143. Frank Clements, "Babe Now Batting for Kleig," *MPC,* Nov 1927, 54, 81, 90.

Ruth, Marshall [actor] (b. Marshalltown IA, 24 Dec 1898–19 Jan 1953 [54], Los Angeles CA). AS, p. 951. BHD1, p. 480. IFN, p. 260. Truitt, p. 293.

Rutherford, Jack [actor] (b. England, 12 Apr 1893–21 Aug 1982 [89], Tucson AZ). "Jack Rutherford," *Variety,* 15 Sep 1982. AS, p. 951. BHD1, p. 480 (d. Patagonia AZ).

Ruthven, Madeleine [title writer/scenarist]. No data found. FDY, pp. 437, 447.

Rutland, Belle [actress]. No data found. AMD, p. 303. "Belle Rutland," *MPW,* 21 Feb 1914, 958.

Rutland, Jeannette [actress]. No data found. AMD, p. 303. "Jeannette Rutland," *MPW,* 24 Apr 1915, 562.

Rutledge, Dorothy [actress]. No data found. AMD, p. 303. "Screen Career," *MPW,* 8 Oct 1927, 359.

Ruttenberg, Joseph [cinematographer] (b. St. Petersburg, Russia, 4 Jul 1889–1 May 1983 [93], Los Angeles CA). (Fox, 1915; Paramount; MGM; winner of four Oscars.) Eleanor Blau, "Joseph Ruttenberg, Winner of 4 Oscars as Cinematographer," *NYT,* 5 May 1983, D21:3. "Joseph Ruttenberg, 4-Time Oscar Winning Lenser, Is Dead at 93," *Variety,* 11 May 1983. AS, p. 950. BHD2, p. 230. Katz, p. 1006. Spehr, p. 164. Scott Eyman, "Joseph Ruttenberg Interview," *Focus on Film,* No. 24, Spring 1976, 46–49.

Rutter, Louise [stage/film actress] (b. Baltimore MD). No other data found. (Pathé.) AMD, p. 303. "Another Thanhouser Star," *NYDM,* 19 May 1915, 22:1 (to debut at New Rochelle studio). "Thanhouser Signs Louise Rutter," *MPW,* 22 May 1915, 1236. "Louise Rutter in Arnold Daly's Pathé Pictures," *MPW,* 30a Oct 1915, 989:1 ("the reputation for charm which Southern girls possess does not suffer at her hands.").

Ruttmann, Walter [director] (b. Frankfort, Germany, 28 Dec 1887–15 Jul 1941 [54], Russia). BHD2, p. 230.

Ryal, Nina [actress] (b. Paris, France, 26 Jun 1892). AS, p. 952.

Ryan, Annie [actress] (b. 1865?–14 Feb 1943 [78], Los Angeles CA). AS, p. 952. BHD, p. 292 (b. 1863). IFN, p. 260. Truitt, p. 293.

Ryan, Bennett [scenarist] (b. Kansas City MO, 1891–5 Jul 1968 [77?], Leonia NJ). BHD2, p. 230.

Ryan, Chet (brother of **Joe Ryan**) [actor] (b. Spearfish SD, 17 May 1889–20 Jan 1943 [53], Los Angeles Co. CA). AS, p. 952. BHD, p. 292. IFN, p. 260. George A. Katchmer, "Forgotten Cowboys and Cowgirls—Part IX," *CI,* 181 (Jul 1990), 59.

Ryan, Donald [dance team of Ryan & Laidlaw/title writer/director/producer]. No data found. (McHenry Film Corp., Akron OH.) AMD, p. 303. FDY, p. 447. "Ryan Making Amateur Photoplays," *MPW,* 15 Jul 1916, 371.

Ryan, Edith [publicist/scenarist] (b. Appleton WI-d. 5 Oct 1955, Los Angeles CA). "Edith Ryan," *Variety,* 12 Oct 1955. AS, p. 952. BHD2, p. 230.

Ryan, James [casting director]. No data found. AMD, p. 303. "James Ryan Is Chief Casting Director," *MPW,* 11 Aug 1923, 505. "Casting Expert Picks Winners," *MPW,* 14 May 1927, 100. "Big Executive Berth for F-N Casting Expert," *MPW,* 28 May 1927, 255.

Ryan, James Thurston [scenarist] (b. 1880–13 Apr 1953 [73?], Los Angeles CA). AS, p. 1070 (Thurston Ryan, James).

Ryan, Joe (brother of **Chet Ryan**) [actor] (b. Crook County WY, 23 May 1887–23 Dec 1944 [57], Riverside Co. CA). m. **Helene Marjorie Ingersoll,** Oct? 1918, Merced CA. (Eclair; Colorado M.P. Co.; Vitagraph; Columbia.) AMD, p. 303. AS, p. 952. BHD, p. 293. IFN, p. 260. Slide, p. 165. WWS, p. 98. "Colorado Star Injured; Joe Ryan Injured When Horse Falls and Others Ride Over Him," *NYDM,* 25 Feb 1914, 31:2 (his horse stumbled and fell during filming). "Gossip of the Studios," *NYDM,* 11 Mar 1914, 29:2 (to be released from the hospital soon). "Joe Ryan Married," *MPW,* 2 Nov 1918, 595. "Joe Ryan and Jean Paige Will Be Co-Starred in New Vitagraph Serial," *MPW,* 3 Jan 1920, 105. "Maddened Steer Injures Joe Ryan, Delaying Exciting Vitagraph Serial," *MPW,* 28 Feb 1920, 1507. "Ryan Recovers from Injuries by Steer; To Fight a Shark," *MPW,* 27 Mar 1920, 2103. Nick Nicholls, "Joe Ryan," *CI,* 116 (Feb 1985), p. 11 (includes filmography). Ed Wyatt, "Joe Ryan; From Extra to Serial Star," *Films of the Golden Age,* No. 13 (Summer 1998), 90–93 (includes partial filmography).

Ryan, Marsh Ellis [scenarist] (b. 1866–11 Jul 1934 [68?], Los Angeles CA). BHD2, p. 230.

Ryan, Martha Ellis [writer]. No data found. AMD, p. 303. "Famous Players to Screen Ryan Novel," *MPW,* 29 Mar 1919, 1787 (*Told in the Hills*).

Ryan, Mary E. [stage/film actress] (b. New York NY, 11 Nov 1880?–2 Oct 1948 [68], Cranford NJ). m. Sam Forrest, 1908 (d. 1944). "Mary Ryan, 65, Widow of Sam Forrest, Dies," *NYT,* 3 Oct 1948, 67:4 (age 65). "Mary Ryan," *Variety,* 6 Oct 1948. AMD, p. 303. AS, p. 952. BHD, p. 293 (b. Brooklyn NY, 1885). SD, p. 1084 (b. 1885). "Kleine Signs Star; Mary Ryan, Scoring in 'On Trial,' to Appear in 'Stop Thief' on Screen," *NYDM,* 25 Nov 1914, 25:4. "Mary Ryan," *MPW,* 6 Feb 1915, 810.

Ryan, Maurice [actor]. No data found. *Fl.* 1922–27.

Ryan, Mildred [actress]. No data found. AMD, p. 303. "Mildred Ryan Chosen," *MPW,* 18 Jul 1925, 357.

Ryan, Robert [actor] (*né* Robert Bushnell Ryan, b. Chicago IL, 11 Nov 1909–11 Jul 1973 [63], New York NY; lymphatic cancer). AS, p. 952.

Ryan, Robert J. [actor] (b. Pipestone MN, 16 Apr 1896–27 Nov 1958 [62], Los Angeles Co. CA). BHD1, p. 481. IFN, p. 260. Ragan 2, p. 1483.

Ryan, Samuel J. [editor and publisher of Appleton WI *Crescent*] (b. 1860?–4 Apr 1939 [79], Monrovia CA). (Pathé.) "Samuel J. Ryan," *NYT,* 5 Apr 1939, 25:2 (no mention of films). "Motography's Gallery of Picture Players," *Motography,* 11 Jul 1914, 53.

Ryan, Tim[othy] [actor] (b. Bayonne NJ, 5 Jul 1899–22 Oct 1956 [57], Los Angeles CA). AS, p. 952. BHD2, p. 230 (b. 27 Jul).

Ryan, Tommy [boxer/actor] (*né* Joseph Youngs, b. Redwood NY, 1870?–3 Aug 1948 [78], Granada Hills, Los Angeles CA; influenza). "Tommy Ryan, Held Two Ring Titles, 78; Winner of Welter Crown in 76-Round Bout Dead on Coast—Retired Undefeated in '07," *NYT,* 4 Aug 1948, 21:4. AS, p. 952.

Ryckman, Chester [actor] (b. 1897–6 Nov 1918 [21?], Fort Rosecrans CA; influenza). "Chester Ryckman," *Variety,* 15 Nov 1918 ("in pictures"). AMD, p. 303. AS, p. 952. BHD, p. 293. "Obituary," *MPW,* 30 Nov 1918, 938 (d. 8 Nov). Billy H. Doyle, "Lost Players," *CI,* 139 (Jan 1987), 55.

Ryder, Edwin L. [actor/producer] (b. Syracuse NY-d. 22 Jun 1929, Onondaga NY). AS, p. 953. BHD2, p. 230.

Ryder, Loren L. [sound director] (b. Pasadena CA, 9 Mar 1900–28 May 1985 [85], Monterey CA). "Loren L. Ryder, an Engineer in Sound-Recording for Film," *NYT,* 31 May 1985, D19:5 (d. Carmel CA). "Loren L. Ryder," *Variety,* 5 Jun 1985. BHD2, p. 230.

Ryder, Philip [actor] (b. 1881?–22 Oct 1958 [77], New York NY [Death Certificate Index No. 22261]). "Philip Ryder," *Variety,* 29 Oct 1958. AS, p. 953.

Rydquist [director] (b. Sweden, 1893–1965 [], Sweden). AS, p. 953.

Rye, Stellan [director] (b. Randers, Denmark, 4 Jul 1880–14 Nov 1914 [34], Hopital De Guerre, France; in battle at Ypres, Belgium). AS, p. 953 (German director). BHD2, p. 231.

Ryerson, Florence [scenarist] (b. Glendale CA, 20 Sep 1894–8 Jun 1965 [70], Mexico City, Mexico). BHD2, p. 231. FDY, p. 437.

Ryle, Fred C. [make-up artist] (b. 1899?–3 Mar 1960 [61], New York NY). "Fred C. Ryle," *NYT,* 4 Mar 1960, 25:1.

Ryley, Phil [actor] (d. Oct? 1937, Los Angeles CA). m. Daisy Leighton. "Phil Ryley," *Variety,* 27 Oct 1937. BHD1, p. 481.

Ryno, William "Bill" H. [actor] (b. New York NY, 8 Oct 1864–3 Dec 1939 [75]). (MinA; Rex; Fox; Universal; FBO.) AMD, p. 303. AS, p. 953 (d. Hollywood CA). BHD1, p. 481. IFN, p. 261. "Dolly Larkin with MinA," *MPW,* 5 Jun 1915, 1628. George A. Katchmer, "Forgotten Cowboys and Cowgirls—Part IX," *CI,* 181 (Jul 1990), 59.

Ryskind, Morrie [title writer/scenarist] (*né* Morris Ryskind, b. Brooklyn NY, 20 Oct 1896–24 Aug 1985 [88], Washington DC; cerebral hemorrhage). AMD, p. 303. AS, p. 953. BHD2, p. 231. "Titles by Morrie Ryskind," *MPW,* 12 Jun 1926, 554.

Ryu, Chishu [actor] (b. Kumamotoken, Japan, 13 May 1904–16 Mar 1993 [88], Yokohama, Japan; cancer). "Chisku Ryu," *The London Times,* 14 Apr 1993. "Chishu Ryu," *Variety,* 22 Mar 1993, p. 63:5 (in Yasujiro Ozu's 2nd film in 1928). AS, p. 953 (b. Kumamoto, Japan). BHD1, p. 481.

S

Sabatini, Ernesto [actor] (b. Padua, Italy, 8 Sep 1878–6 Oct 1954 [76], Milan, Italy). AS, p. 955.

Sabatini, Rafael [writer] (b. Italy, 29 Apr 1875–13 Feb 1950 [75], Adelboden, Switzerland). m. Christine Dixon, 1935. "Rafael Sabatini, Author, Dies at 76; Creator of Captain Blood [1922] Won Fame with 'Scaramouche [1921],' 'Sea Hawk [1915]' and 'The Snare [1917],'" *NYT,* 14 Feb 1950, 25:1 ("Arriving here on a visit in 1931, Mr. Sabatini said that he was 'out of touch with the modern world' as he preferred to live mentally in the past, although he was grateful for today's physical comforts."). AMD, p. 303. AS, p. 955. BHD2, p. 231. "Vitagraph to Film Sabatini's Latest," *MPW,* 10 Nov 1923, 244 (*Captain Blood*). "A Volume to Cherish," *MPW,* 20 Dec 1924, 769. "Adolph Zukor's $10,000 Prize Award Goes to Rafael Sabatini," *MPW,* 3 Jan 1925, 30.

Sabato, Alfredo [actor/director] (b. Italy, 23 Mar 1894–10 Feb 1956 [61], Los Angeles Co. CA). AS, p. 955 (d. Italy). BHD1, p. 481; BHD2, p. 231. IFN, p. 261.

Sabbatini, Ernesto [actor] (b. Padua, Italy, 8 Sep 1878–5 Oct 1954 [76], Milan, Italy; heart attacl). m. Lena Adani (sister of Laura Adani). AS, p. 955. BHD, p. 481. JS, p. 398 (in Italian silents from 1914).

Sabbatini, Marcella [child actress] (b. 1915). JS, p. 398 (in Italian silents from 1919; one sound film: *Perchè no?,* 1930).

Sabel, Josephine [actress] (*née* Josephine Saint-Clair, b. Lawrence MA, 1866–24 Nov 1945 [79?], Patchogue NY). AS, p. 955.

Sabin, Mrs. Catherine J[erome] [actress] (*née?,* b. 1889–19 May 1943 [54], New York NY). AS, p. 955. BHD, p. 293. IFN, p. 261.

Sablon, Germaine Berthe (sister of **Jean Sablon**) [actress/singer] (b. Le-Perreux-sur-Marne, France, 19 Jul 1899–17 Apr 1885 [85], Saint-Raphael, France [extrait de décès no. 141/1985]). AS, p. 955.

Sablon, Jean Georges (brother of **Germaine Sablon**) [actor] (b. Nogent-sur-Marne, France, 25 Mar 1906–24 Feb 1994 [87], Cannes-la-Bocca, France [extrait de décès no. 4]). AS, p. 955.

Sablon, Loulette [actress] (b. Le-Perreux-sur-Marne, 16 Jul 1897–21 Oct 1970 [73], France). AS, p. 955.

Saburi, Shin [actor/director] (aka Gen Shimazu, b. Hokkaido, Japan, 17 Feb 1909–22 Sep 1982 [73], Japan; cancer). AS, p. 955. BHD1, p. 482.

Sacchietto, Rita [dancer/actress] (b. München, Germany, 1879–18 Jan 1959 [79], Nervi, Italy). AMD, p. 303. "Rita Sacchetto," *MPW,* 27 Sep 1913, 1373. "Rita Sacchetto," *MPW,* 30 Oct 1915, 799. Vittorio Martinelli, "Kino-Lieblinge," *Griffithiana,* 38/39 (Oct 1990), 29 (taught dancing to Anita Berber, Lore Sello, Valeska Gert).

Sack, Nathaniel [actor] (b. Libau, Russia, 15 Jul 1880–2 Jul 1966 [85], New York NY [Death Certificate Index No. 14161; M.E. Case No. 5814]). "Nathaniel Sack, 84, Actor in 'Student Prince' 25 Years," *NYT,* 5 Jul 1966, 37:3. "Nathaniel Sack," *Variety,* 6 Jul 1966. AS, p. 956 (b. 1882). BHD, p. 293. IFN, p. 261 (age 84).

Sackville, Gordon [actor] (b. Petersborough, Ontario, Canada, 1880–6 Aug 1926 [46], Los Angeles CA; apoplexy). (Film debut: *The Best Man Wins,* 1911.) "Gordon Sackville," *Variety,* 11 Aug 1926. AMD, p. 303. AS, p. 956. BHD, p. 293. IFN, p. 261. Truitt, p. 294. "Gordon Sackville," *MPW,* 16 Dec 1911, 908. George Katchmer, "Remembering the Great Silents," *CI,* 212 (Feb 1993), 34.

Saddler, Harvey Walter [actor] (aka John Johnson) (b. 1848?–30 Sep 1918 [70], Hollywood CA). AMD, p. 303. "The Hermit of the Screen," *MPW,* 26 Oct 1918, 497.

Sadler, Charles R[obert] [stuntman/actor] (b. 1875?–23 Mar 1950 [75], Los Angeles CA). m. Violet. "Charles R. Sadler," *NYT,* 24 Mar 1950, 26:2 (began 1910; posed for Norman Rockwell's painting, *The Old Swiss Watchmaker*). "Charles R. Sadler," *Variety,* 29 Mar 1950 ("pioneer motion picture stunt man"). AS, p. 956. BHD1, p. 482. IFN, p. 261.

Sadler, Josie [actress] (b. New York NY, ca. 1871-ca. 1933 [62?]). (Vitagraph; World.) BHD, p. 293. Slide, pp. 149–50.

Sadler, William [Irish comedian]. No data found. "Mrs. William Sadler," *Variety,* 1 May 1909 (d. 27 Apr 1909 [34], Buffalo NY).

Saenz, Antoine (brother of **John** and **Josephine Saenz**) [actor] (b. Indianapolis IN, 5 May 1840–7 May 1905 [65], Los Angeles CA). AS, p. 956.

Saenz, John (brother of **Antoine** and **Josephine Saenz**) [actor] (b. Indianapolis IN, 28 Jun 1844–4 May 1930 [85], Los Angeles CA). AS, p. 956.

Saenz, Josephine (sister of **Antoine** and **John Saenz**) [actress] (b. Indianapolis IN, 26 Jan 1843–9 Nov 1926 [83], Los Angeles CA). AS, p. 956.

Saffo-Momo, Irene [actress] (*née* Countess Irene Saffo-Momo Federici di Martorano). JS, pp. 398–99 (in Italian silents from 1916; "she belonged to a cadet branch of an ancient noble Roman family.").

Sagan, Léontine [actress/director] (*née* Léontine Schlesinger, b. Vienna, Austria, 13 Feb 1899–20 May 1974 [75], Johannesburg, So. Africa). AS, p. 957 (b. Budapest, Hungary-d. Pretoria, South Africa; worked in Germany). BHD2, p. 231.

Sagarra, José [author/scenarist] (*né* José Maria de Sagarra y Castellarnau, b. Spain, 1894–12 Nov 1961 [67?], Barcelona, Spain). AS, p. 957.

Sage, G. Byron [child actor] (b. KS, 31 Jul 1915–14 Jan 1974 [58], Los Angeles CA). AS, p. 957. BHD1, p. 482.

Sage, Stuart [actor] (b. Sioux Falls SD, 1893–4 Mar 1926 [32?], New York NY). AS, p. 957. BHD, p. 293. 1921 Directory, p. 199. Billy H. Doyle, "Lost Players," *CI,* 137 (Nov 1986), C24.

Saharet [dancer/actress in German films] (b. Sydney, Australia). Vittorio Martinelli, "Kino-Lieblinge," *Griffithiana,* 38/39 (Oct 1990), 30.

Saidreau, Robert [producer] (*né* Robert Saidreau-Reymont, b. France, 1877–5 Dec 1925 [48?], Paris, France; pneumonia). AS, p. 957 (b. 1882). BHD2, p. 231.

Saillard, Georges Augustin Eugène [actor] (b. Besancon, France, 5 Jul 1877 [extrait de naissance no. 682]–11 Sep 1967 [90], Versailles, France [extrait de décès no. 1049/1967]). AS, p. 957.

Sainati, Alfredo [actor] (b. Sestri Ponente, Italy, 28 Feb 1868–10 Jan 1936 [67], Bertinoro, Italy). JS, p. 399 (in Italian silents from 1911).

Sainpolis, John *see* **St. Polis, John**

St. Audrie, Stella [actress] (b. 1876–11 May 1925 [49?]). BHD, p. 293.

St. Clair, Eric (brother of **Malcolm St. Clair**) [actor]. No data found. AMD, p. 304. "Dorothy Devore and St. Clair Sign Warner Bros. Contracts," *MPW,* 23 Aug 1924, 520.

St. Clair, Jacques [actor] (d. Apr 1929). BHD, p. 293.

St. Clair, Malcolm (brother of **Eric St. Clair**) [director/actor/scenarist] (b. Los Angeles CA, 17 May 1897–1 Jun 1952 [55], Pasadena CA). (Sennett, 1915.) "Malcolm St. Clair," *NYT,* 3 Jun 1952, 29:4 (age 54). Ruth Anne Dwyer, *Malcolm St. Clair; His Films, 1915–1948* (Lanham MD: Scarecrow Press, Inc.,1996). "Malcolm St. Clair," *Variety,* 4 Jun 1952. AMD, p. 304. AS, p. 1025. BHD2, p. 231. IFN, p. 261. Katz, p. 1009. "Keaton Signs St. Clair," *MPW,* 26 Feb 1921, 1070. "Mal St. Clair Signs with F.B.O.," *MPW,* 15 Dec 1923, 643. "Film Without Sets," *MPW,* 12 Jul 1924, 123. "Mal St. Clair Will Direct," *MPW,* 28 Feb 1925, 909. "Sign Malcolm St. Clair," *MPW,* 15 Aug 1925, 764. "St. Clair to Produce 'The Show-Off' in East," *MPW,* 15 May 1926, 222. Peter Milne, "The Keystone Kop Who Became a Director; Mal St. Clair Has Made Big Strides Since His Keystone and Cartoon Days...," *MPC,* Oct 1926, 34–35, 81. "Cartooned Way Into Pictures," *MPW,* 11 Jun 1927, 409. "St. Clair Signs with Paramount," *MPW,* 30 Jul 1927, 306. "Change Plans for Mal St. Clair," *MPW,* 27 Aug 1927, 599.

St. Claire, Adah [actress] (b. New York NY, 1854?–16 Aug 1928 [74], Amityville, LI NY). m. Frederick Cobb. "Adah St. Claire," *Variety,* 22 Aug 1928 (Mrs. Frederick Cobb). AS, p. 1025. BHD, p. 293. IFN, p. 261. Truitt, p. 294.

St. Denis, Ruth [dancer/actress] (*née* Ruth Dennis, b. Newark NJ, 20 Jan 1878–21 Jul 1968 [90], Los Angeles CA; heart attack). m. **Ted Shawn** (d. 1972). *An Unfinished Life; An Autobiography* (Brooklyn NY: Dance Horizons, 1939). "Ruth St. Denis, Pioneer of Modern Dance, Is Dead; Paved Way for a Free New Art in 7-Decade Career," *NYT,* 22 Jul 1968, 1:1, 35:1. "Ruth St. Denis," *Variety,* 24 Jul 1968. AS, p. 1025. BHD1, p. 483. Truitt, p. 294. WWVC, p. 126.

St. Elmo, Boyce [scenarist] (b. 1899–30 Sep 1930 [31?], Los Angeles CA; suicide). AS, p. 1025.

St. Gaudens, Homer [director] (b. 1879–8 Dec 1958 [79?], Miami FL). AMD, p. 304. BHD2, p. 231. "Homer St. Gaudens, Prominent Stage Director, Now with Whitman Bennett," *MPW,* 16 Oct 1920, 978.

St. George, Jenny (d. 15 Apr 1938, Freehold NJ). BHD, p. 293.

St. Germaine, Marie [actress] (b. Mattawa, Canada, 1891–23 Nov 1984 [93?], Los Angeles CA). BHD1, p. 483.

St. Granier [actor/singer/composer] (*né* Jean Granier de Cassagnac, b. Paris, France, 27 May 1888–25 Jun 1976 [88], Paris, France). AS, p. 958.

St. Helier, Ivy [actress/composer] (*née* Ivy Atchinson, b. St. Helier, Jersey, Channel Islands-d. 8 Nov 1971, London, England). AS, p. 1025. BHD1, p. 483.

St. James, William H. [actor] (b. 1876?–23 Jul 1931 [55], New York NY). m. Rhea Bacon. "Will St. James," *Variety,* 28 Jul 1931 (age 53). AS, p. 1025. BHD, p. 293. IFN, p. 261 (age 55).

St. John, Al "Fuzzy" (nephew of **Roscoe Arbuckle**) [actor] (*né* Alfred St. John, b. Santa Ana CA, 10 Sep 1892–21 Jan 1963 [70], Vidalia GA; heart attack). m. June Price Pearce, 30 Jun 1926. (Keystone, 1913; Paramount; Fox; Educational; WB.) "Actor in Westerns Is Dead," *NYT,* 23 Jan 1963, 7:5. "Al St. John," *Variety,* 30 Jan 1963. AMD, p. 304. AS, p. 1025. BHD1, p. 483 (d. Lyons GA). FSS, p. 255. IFN, p. 261. Katz, p. 1011. MH, p. 137. Spehr, p. 164 (b. 1893). WWS, p. 111. Truitt, p. 294 (b. 1893). "Al St. John in Triangle Comedy," *MPW,* 13 May 1916, 1173. "Why Not Try a Number on the Screen?," *MPW,* 9 Mar 1918, 1361. "Producers of Comedies Must Have Much Nerve and Some Conscience," *MPW,* 13 Dec 1919, 839. "Al St. John Is Now Engaged in Work on the Films of the Fox Sunshine Comedies," *MPW,* 20 Nov 1920, 371. "Hal Roach to Co-Feature Well-Known Fun Makers," *MPW,* 16 May 1925, 356. "Al St. John Re-Signed by Educational for Mermaids," *MPW,* 19 Jun 1926, 628. "St. John—Pearce," *MPW,* 17 Jul 1926, 3. June Lee, "Dan Cupid's Bulletin Board," *Paris and Hollywood,* Oct 1926, 87 (married Pearce). "Buck Rainey's Filmographies; Al St. John, from Keystone Kop to Cowboy Sidekick, Part I," *CI,* 155 (May 1988), C3-C4, C7; Part II, 156 (Jun 1988), 33–37. P.A. Carayannis, "Additions and Corrections to the Al St. John Filmography," *CI,* 159 (Sep 1988), C1. George Katchmer, "Remembering the Great Silents," *CI,* 213 (Mar 1993), 48.

St. John, Howard [actor] (b. Chicago IL, 9 Oct 1905–13 Mar 1974 [68], New York NY; heart attack). AS, p. 1025. BHD1, p. 483.

St. John, Mrs. Jane Lee *see* **Lee, Jane**

St. John, Marguerite [stage/film actress] (b. London, England, 17 May 1861–16 Oct 1940 [79], New York NY). m. George Murray Wood. "Marguerite St. John; Actress Who Made Her American Debut 40 Years Ago Dies," *NYT,* 17 Oct 1940, 25:2. "Marguerite St. John," *Variety,* 23 Oct 1940. AS, p. 1025. IFN, p. 261.

St. Johns, Adela Rogers [actress/writer/scenarist] (*né* Adela Rogers, b. Los Angeles CA, 20 May 1894–10 Aug 1988 [94], Arroyo Grande CA). *The Honeycomb* (Garden City NY: Doubleday, 1969). Eric Pace, "Adela R. St. Johns, 94, Journalist, Novelist, Teacher and Scriptwriter," *NYT,* 11 Aug 1988, D20:4. "Adela Rogers St. Johns," *Variety,* 17 Aug 1988. AMD, p. 304. AS, p. 1025. BHD1, p. 483; BHD2, p. 231. FDY, p. 437. "Writing for Tom Mix," *MPW,* 26 Dec 1925, 767.

St. Leo, Leonard [actor] (b. England, 1 May 1894–9 Feb 1977 [82], Los Angeles Co. CA). BHD1, p. 483. IFN, p. 262.

St. Lou, Maurice [director/scenarist] (b. Paris, France, 24 Oct 1897). AS, p. 958.

St. Luc, André Raymond Léopold Charles [actor] (b. Bordeaux, France, 6 Jun 1901 [extrait de naissance no. 30]-25 Dec 1987 [86], Couilly-Pont-aux-Dames, France). AS, p. 958.

St. Marc, René [actor] (b. Bordeaux, France, 1880-ca. 1960 [80?]). AS, p. 958.

St. Ober [actor] (*né* Emile Louis Saintober, b. La Madeleine, France, 6 Oct 1882 [extrait de naissance no. 382]-26 Sep 1962 [79], Ville-Neuve-Saint-Georges, France). AS, p. 958.

St. Pagano, Ernest [scenarist]. No data found. FDY, p. 437.

St. Pierre, Clara [actress] (b. Canada, 1866?–30 Jan 1942 [76], Santa Monica CA). "Clara St. Pierre," *Variety,* 11 Feb 1942 ("entered films 20 years ago"). AS, p. 1025. BHD1, p. 483. IFN, p. 262. Truitt, p. 295.

St. Polis, John [actor] (aka John Sainpolis, b. New Orleans LA, 24 Nov 1873–8 Oct 1946 [72], Los Angeles CA). (Goldwyn.) AMD, p. 304. AS, p. 1025. BHD1, p. 483. IFN, p. 262. "World Gets Sainpolis to Support June Elvidge," *MPW,* 27 Sep 1919, 1990. "John Sainpolis Back," *MPW,* 18 Jun 1921, 731.

St. Saens, Camille ["compositeur français de la première musique pour un film en 1908"] (*né* Charles-Camille Saint-Saens, b. Paris, France, 9 Oct 1835–16 Dec 1921 [86], Algiers, Algeria). AS, p. 958.

Saintsbury, H.A. [stage/film actor/playwright] (b. Chelsea, London, England, 18 Dec 1869–19 Jun 1939 [69], London, England). (First stage appearance: *Masks and Faces,* Opéra Comique Theatre, 1887.) "H.A. Saintsbury, 69, Actor, Playwright; Had Role of Sherlock Holmes 1,404 Times—Dies in London," *NYT,* 20 Jun 1939, 21:4. "H.A. Saintsbury," *Variety,* 135, 21 Jun 1939, 54:1 (broke a leg one month previously). BHD, p. 293. IFN, p. 262.

Sais, Marin [vaudeville/film actress] (*nee?,* b. San Rafael [Marin County] CA, 2 Aug 1890–31 Dec 1971 [81], Woodland Hills CA; cerebral arteriosclerosis). m. **Jack Hoxie**, 1921 (d. 1965). (Vitagraph, 1909; Kalem; Universal.) AMD, p. 304. AS, p. 958. BHD1, p. 483. BR, pp. 64–69 (b. 1887). FSS, p. 255. IFN, p. 262. Katz, pp. 1010–11 (b. 1888). MSBB, p. 1040. "Marin Sais to Form Polo Team," *MPW,* 1 Jul 1916, 70. Cecilia Mount, "Marin 'Versatile' Sais,' *MPC,* Sep 1916, 55–56, 68. "Marin Sais to Be Hayakawa's Leading Woman," *MPW,* 11 May 1918, 866–67. "Marin Sais Plays Opposite to Star in 'Bonds of Honor,'" *MPW,* 8 Feb 1919, 738. "Surprise Weddings," *MPW,* 3 Dec 1921, 566.

Saito, Tastuo [actor] (b. Tokyo, Japan, 10 Jun 1902–2 Mar 1968 [65], Tokyo, Japan; stomach cancer). AS, p. 958.

Sakall, S.Z. "Cuddles" [actor] (*né* Jeno Gero Szakall, aka Szöke Szakall, b. Budapest, Hungary, 2 Feb 1883–12 Feb 1955 [72], Beverly Hills CA; heart attack). m. Boszi. (Began 1916.) "S.Z. (Cuddles) Sakall Dies on Coast; Widely Known Film Character Actor," *NYT,* 14 Feb 1955, 19:2. "S.Z. Sakall," *Variety,* 16 Feb 1955. AS, p. 958. BHD1, p. 483. IFN, p. 262. JS, p. 399 (*né* Eugen Gerö Szakall; worked in Italy *[Maria Bashkirtseff,* 1935], Berlin and Vienna). Katz, p. 1011. Truitt, p. 295 (b. 1884).

Saker, Annie [stage/film actress] (b. 13 Mar 1882–8 Oct 1932 [50], Essex, England). "Annie Saker," *Variety,* 108, 25 Oct 1932, 55:2. BHD, p. 293.

Sala, Franz [actor] (b. Alessandria (Piedmonte), Italy, 17 Dec 1886-Nov 1952 [65], Rome, Italy). JS, p. 399 (in Italian silents from 1912).

Salacrou, Armand Camille [writer/scenarist] (b. Rouen, France, 9 Aug 1899 [extrait de naissance no. 1356/1899]-23 Nov 1989 [90], Le Havre, France). AS, p. 959.

Salas, Caritad [actress] (b. Havana, Cuba, 1893–8 Apr 1930 [37?], Havana, Cuba). AS, p. 958.

Salas, Paco [actor] (*né* Francisco Lago Severino, b. Cuba, 1875–24 Dec 1964 [89], Havana, Cuba). AS, p. 958.

Sale, Charles "Chic" [stage/film actor] (*né* Charles Partlow Sale, b. Huron SD, 25 Aug 1885–7 Nov 1936 [51], Los Angeles CA; lobar pneumonia). "Chic Sale Is Dead; Noted Comedian; Succumbs at 51 on Coast to Lobar Pneumonia—Often Played G.A.R. Veteran; Wanted to Be Cartoonist; Talent as Mimic Manifested in Early Youth—Man of 80 Was Long His Vaudeville Role," *NYT,* 8 Nov 1936, B8:6 (d. Hollywood CA). "Charles 'Chic' Sale," *Variety,* 11 Nov 1936. AMD, p. 304. AS, p. 959. BHD1, p. 483. IFN, p. 262. Truitt, p. 295. WWS, p. 140. "Charles Sale Signed for Robertson-Cole Pictures," *MPW,* 6 Dec 1919, 652. "So Is Chic Sale [with Christie]," *LA Times,* 28 Jan 1920, II, 11 (to debut in *The Smart Aleck,* 5 reels). "Sale, Burr Star, to Go on Stage," *MPW,* 27 Oct 1923, 751.

Sale, Frances *see* **Adams, Frances Sale**

Sale, Virginia [actress] (b. Urbana IL, 20 May 1899–23 Aug 1992 [93], Woodland Hills CA; heart attack). m. **Sam Wren** (d. 1962). "Virginia Sale, 93, Actress in Hundreds of Character Roles," *NYT,* 25 Aug 1992, B8:3 (began 1927). "Virginia Sale-Wren," *Variety,* 31 Aug 1992, p. 92 (b. 1900). AS, p. 959 (b. 1900). BHD1, p. 484.

Salfner, Heinz [actor] (b. Munich, Germany, 31 Dec 1877–13 Oct 1945 [67]). BHD, p. 294. IFN, p. 262.

Salisbury, Edward A. [cameraman/producer]. No data found. AMD, p. 304. "Wild Life in Films," *MPW,* 6 Mar 1915, 1462–63. "A Successful Educational Series," *MPW,* 22 May 1915, 1239. "Cameras to Explore Tropical Wilds," *MPW,* 6 Nov 1915, 1108. "Salisbury Back After Remarkable Trip," *MPW,* 27 Jan 1917, 502–03. "Salisbury Returning from China," *MPW,* 15 Sep 1917, 1664.

Salisbury, Monroe [stage/film actor] (b. Angola [Erie Co.] NY, 8 May 1876–7 Aug 1935 [59], San Bernardino CA; from injuries after a fall). "Monroe Salisbury," *Variety,* 14 Aug 1935 (d. 7 Aug). (Lasky; Fine Arts; Mutual; Universal; Fox; Morosco.) AMD, p. 304. AS, p. 959. AS, p. 959. BHD1, p. 484. IFN, p. 262. Lowrey, p. 164 (b. Buffalo NY). MSBB, p. 1028. Truitt, p. 295. "Monroe Salisbury Joins Bluebird," *MPW,* 6 Oct 1917, 77. "Film Star Really Aids Red Cross," *MPW,* 5 Oct 1918, 102. "Salisbury to Form Own Company," *MPW,* 23 Aug 1919, 1119. "Salisbury at Work Again," *MPW,* 30 Jul 1921, 497. George A. Katchmer, "Remembering the Great Silents," *CI,* 164 (Feb 1988), 50–52 (b. Lake Erie [Buffalo] NY); 240 (Jun 1995), 45–46.

Salmi, Albert [actor] (b. Coney Island, New York NY, 11 Mar 1928–22 Apr 1990 [62], Spokane WA; murder-suicide by gunshot). m. actress Peggy Ann Garner, 1953–56 (d. 1984), Roberta. "Albert Salmi, Actor, 62, Is Found Shot to Death in Home with Wife," *NYT,* 25 Apr 1990, D29. AS, p. 960 (d. 23 Apr). BHD1, p. 484. Katz, p. 1012.

Salmonova, Lyda [actress/dancer] (b. Prague, Czechoslovakia, 14 Jul 1889–18 Nov 1968 [79], Prague, Czechoslovakia). m. **Paul Wegener** (d. 1948). AS, p. 960. BHD, p. 294. Vittorio Martinelli, "Kino-Lieblinge," *Griffithiana,* 38/39 (Oct 1990), 31.

Saloman, A.M. (Doc) [executive] (b. Heidelberg, Germany, 15 Jan 1891-Jul 1944 [53], England). BHD2, p. 232.

Salou, Louis Vincent Goulven [actor] b. Oissel, France, 23 Apr 1902–21 Oct 1948 [46], Fontenay-aux-Roses, France; suicide with an overdose of barbituates [extrait de décès no. 84/1948]). AS, p. 960. BHD1, p. 484 (b. Quimper, France; d. Paris, France). IFN, p. 262.

Salter, Harold "Hal" or "Harry" [actor] (b. Atlanta GA, 8 Apr 1886–19 May 1928 [42], Los Angeles CA; influenza). m. **Florence Lawrence** (d. 1938). (Biograph, 1908; Universal.) "Harold Salter," *Variety,* 23 May 1928. AS, p. 960. BHD, p. 294. IFN, p. 262. Slide, p. 164 (d. 1920). Spehr, p. 164. Truitt, p. 295. "Harry Salter on Vacation," *MPW,* 28 Sep 1912, 1265. "Obituary," *MPW,* 3 Apr 1920, 54 (a Harry Solter d. 3 Mar 1920, El Paso TX. Not Harry Salter). George Katchmer, "Remembering the Great Silents," *CI,* 212 (Feb 1993), 34.

Salter, Harry L. [producer] (b. 1880?–2 Mar 1920 [40?], El Paso TX [Death Certificate #1779D]; hemiplegia from cerebral hemorrhage. Buried at Baltimore MD, 18 Mar 1920.). BHD, p. 294.

Salter, Joe [actor] (b. Los Angeles CA, 5 Dec 1847–26 Nov 1913 [65], Washington DC). AS, p. 960.

Salter, Thelma [extra/child actress] (b. Los Angeles CA, 1909–17 Nov 1953 [44?], No. Hollywood CA). m. Edward Kaufman. (Ince.) "Mrs. Thelma Kaufman," *Variety,* 25 Nov 1953 ("she performed as a child actress in silent films"). AMD, p. 304. AS, p. 960. BHD, p. 294 (d. LA CA). IFN, p. 262. Truitt, p. 295. "New Horsley Player," *MPW,* 20 May 1916, 1357. "Thelma Salter in 'The Crab,'" *MPW,* 6 Jan 1917, 95. "Joe Knight Trains a Substitute," *Photoplay,* Jul 1917, 98 (photo). Robert Donaldson, "Famous Extras," *MPC,* Feb 1927, 32 [photo]–33, 68, 80. "Thelma Salter with Lupino Lane," *MPW,* 8 Oct 1927, 348. Billy H. Doyle, "Lost Players," *CI,* 179 (May 1990), 30.

Saltykov, Nicolay Aleksndrovich [actor/director] (b. Russia, 1886–1928 [42?], Russia). AS, p. 960.

Salvador, Jaime [scenarist/director] (b. Barcelona, Spain, 1901–1976 [75?]). (Gaumont, Paris, 1922; Barcelona Films.) Waldman, p. 254.

Salvatori, Fausto [scenarist/director] (b. Rome, Italy, 20 Jan 1870–3 Jun 1929 [59], Rome, Italy). JS, p. 401 (in Italian silents from 1915).

Salvatori, Jack [actor/director] (*né* Giovanni Salvatori Manners, b. Rome, Italy, 1901). AS, p. 960. JS, p. 401 (in silents in Hollywood after WWI).

Salven, Edward [assistant director] (b. 1904–22 Jan 1955 [50?], Los Angeles CA). AS, p. 960.

Salvi, Alberto [director] (b. Foligno, Italy, 10 Dec 1890–17 Feb 1946 [55], Rome, Italy). AS, p. 960. JS, p. 402 (in Italian silents from 1913).

Salvini, Alessandro [actor] (b. Pisa, Italy, 6 Aug 1890–24 Jul 1955 [64], Rome, Italy). AS, p. 960 (Sandro Salvini). BHD1, p. 484. IFN, p. 262. JS, p. 402 (in Italian silents from 1917).

Salvini, Guido (son of **Gustavo Salvini**; brother of **Sandro Salvini**) [director] (b. Florence, Italy, 12 May 1893–4 May 1965 [71], Florence, Italy). AS, p. 960.

Salvini, Gustavo (son of stage actor Tommaso Salvini; father of **Guido** and **Sandro Salvini**) [actor] (b. Civitavecchia, Italy, 24 May 1859–18 Dec 1930 [71], Marina di Pisa, Italy). m. Ida Bertini (son, Guido, b. Florence, Italy, 12 May 1893; son, Alessandro). AS, p. 960. JS, p. 402 (in Italian silents from 1918).

Salvini, Sandro (son of **Gustavo Salvini**; brother of **Guido Salvini**) [actor] (*né* Alessandro Salvini, b. Pisa, Italy, 6 Aug 1890–24 Jul 1955 [64], Rome, Italy). AS, p. 960. JS, p. 402 (in Italian silents from 1917).

Salzedo, Carlos [composer] (*né* Charles Moise Leon Salzedo, b. Arcachon, France, 6 Apr 1885 [extrait de naissance no. 60/1885]-17 Aug 1961 [76], Waterville ME; heart attack). AS, pp. 960–61.

Samama, Albert [director] (b. Tunis, Tunisia, 1872–1934 [62?]). AS, p. 961.

Samana-Chicly [director] (b. Tunia, Tunisia, 24 Jan 1872–1950 [78?], Tunisia). AS, p. 961.

Samberg, Arnold *see* **Gregg, Arnold**

Sambucini, Kally [actress] (*née* Calliope Sambucini, b. Rome, Italy, 18 Aug 1892). AS, p. 961. JS, p. 402 (in Italian silents from 1915).

Samoloff, Leonid [actor]. No data found. AMD, p. 304. "Leonid Samoloff," *MPW,* 16 Jan 1915, 376.

Sampson, Teddy [actress] (b. New York NY, 8 Aug 1898–24 Nov 1970 [72], Woodland Hills CA; cancer). m. **Ford Sterling** (d. 1939). (Griffith; Christie.) AMD, p. 305. AS, p. 961. BHD, p. 294. IFN, p. 262. 1921 Directory, p. 238 (b. 2 Jun 1895). WWS, p. 230. "Teddy Sampson," *MPW,* 29 May 1915, 1412. "Teddy Sampson with Equitable," *MPW,* 27 Nov 1915, 1637. "Selznick Signs Teddy Sampson," *MPW,* 30 Oct 1920, 1230.

Samson, Ivan [actor] (b. Brighton, England, 28 Aug 1894–1 May 1963 [68], London, England). "Ivan Samson," *Variety,* 8 May 1963. AS, p. 961. BHD1, p. 484. IFN, p. 262. Truitt, p. 295 (b. London, England).

Samuel, Andrew [actor: Our Gang] (b. Los Angeles CA, 10 Apr 1909–5 Mar 1992 [82], Colton CA). (Roach.) "Andrew Samuel," *Variety,* 16 Mar 1992, p. 76. AS, p. 961. BHD, p. 294.

Samuels, Maurice [actor/scenarist] (b. Bucharest, Romania, 13 Jan 1885–1 Aug 1964 [79], Los Angeles CA). AS, p. 961. BHD2, p. 232.

Samuelson, G[eorge] **B**[erthold] [director] (b. Birmingham, England, 6 Jul 1888–24 Apr 1947 [58], Staffordshire, England). (Samuelson Film Productions; British Lion Films.) "G.B. Samuelson," *NYT,* 20 Apr 1947, 60:2 (began 1910). "G.B. Samuelson," *Variety,* 30 Apr 1947 ("took the first British film company to Hollywood"). AS, p. 961. BHD2, p. 232 (d. 17 Apr).

Sanberg, Gus [actor] (*né* Gustave E. Sanberg, b. Long Island City NY, 23 Feb 1896–3 Feb 1930 [33], Los Angeles CA). AS, p. 961. BHD1, p. 484.

Sand, Henrietta [actress] (b. Indianapolis IN, 23 Sep 1842–9 Apr 1922 [79], Antwerp, Belgium). AS, p. 962.

Sandberg, A[nders] **W**[ilhelm] [actor/director] (b. Viborg, Denmark, 22 May 1887–27 Mar 1938 [50], Bad Nauheim, Germany). m. Ruth Jacobsen. (Tobias; Terra.) "A.W. Sandberg," *Variety,* 130, 27 Apr 1938, 62:1 ("As a talker director he was not popular, costing producers extra monies because of retakes."). AMD, p. 305. AS, p. 962. BHD2, p. 232. "Sandberg, Danish Director, Now in 1st National-Zelnik Scheme," *MPW,* 25 Jun 1927, 565.

Sandberg, Olof [actor] (b. Göteberg, Sweden, 30 Apr 1884–26 Mar 1965 [80], Stockholm, Sweden). AS, p. 962.

Sandberg, Robert Albert [actor] (b. Chicago IL, 6 Oct 1887). BHD, p. 294.

Sandberg, Sergei [director/producer] (b. Kouno, Lithuania, 23 Nov 1879–15 Feb 1981 [101], Paris, France). AS, p. 962.

Sande, Earle H. [actor] (b. Groton SD, 13 Nov 1898–19 Aug 1968 [69], Jacksonville OR). BHD, p. 294.

Sanderson, Julia [actress] (*née* Julia Sackett, b. Springfield MA, 20 Aug 1887–27 Jan 1975 [87], Springfield MA; cardiac arrest in her sleep). m. (1) James T. Sloane; (2) Bradford Burnette; (3) Frank Cromit. "Julia Sanderson," *Variety*, 12 Feb 1975. AMD, p. 305. AS, p. 962. BHD, p. 294. IFN, p. 262. "Capellani to Direct Miss Sanderson," *MPW*, 23 Jun 1917, 1946. "Julia Sanderson," *MPW*, 25 Aug 1917, 1198. "Julia Sanderson in 'The Runaway,'" *MPW*, 29 Sep 1917, 2018.

Sanderson, Lynn [actress]. No data found. George Katchmer, "Remembering the Great Silents," *CI*, 202 (Apr 1992), 6.

Sanderson, Zack [scenarist]. No data found. AMD, p. 305. "Enlarges Scenario Staff," *MPW*, 24 Mar 1923, 422.

Sandford, Stanley J. (Tiny) [actor] (*né* Stanely J. Sandford, b. Osage IA, 26 Feb 1894–29 Oct 1961 [67], Los Angeles CA). AS, p. 962. BHD1, p. 485. IFN, p. 263.

Sandmeier, Julius [director/scenarist] (b. Germany, 1881–1941 [60?], Germany). AS, p. 963.

Sando, Teralv [director/scenarist] (b. Serflatager, Norway, 6 Apr 1899). AS, p. 962.

Sandow, Eugene [bodybuilder] (b. Königsberg, East Prussia, 10 Apr 1867–14 Oct 1925 [58], London, England; cerebral hemorrhage). David L. Chapman, *Sandow the Magnificent: Eugen Sandow and the Beginnings of Bodybuilding* (Univ. of Illinois Press, 1994). "Sandow, Famous Strong Man, Dead; Bursting of Blood Vessel in His Brain Attributed to Strain of Lifting a Motor Car; Injured Some Time Ago; Death of Professor of Physical Culture to King George Closely Follows That of [Sigmund] Breitbart," *NYT*, 15 Oct 1925, 23:5. "Eugene Sandow," *Variety*, 21 Oct 1925. AS, p. 963. BHD, p. 294. IFN, p. 262. SD, p. 1103.

Sandrock, Adele [actress] (b. Rotterdam, Holland, 19 Aug 1863–30 Aug 1937 [74], Berlin, Germany). AS, p. 963 (b. 1864). BHD1, p. 485. IFN, p. 262.

Sands, Charles S. [cinematographer] (b. 1865-Jul 1943 [78?], Coral Gables FL). BHD2, p. 232.

Sandten, Thea [German and Italian actress]. No data found. (Retired in the early 1920's.) m. actress Hanne Brinkmann. Vittorio Martinelli, "Kino-Lieblinge," *Griffithiana*, 38/39 (Oct 1990), 32.

Sanford, Albert "Bert," Jr. [actor] (b. New York NY, 1893?–10 Feb 1953 [60], New York NY). (Biograph; General Film Co.; Pathé.) "Albert Sanford," *Variety*, 18 Feb 1953. AS, p. 963. BHD, p. 294. IFN, p. 263. Truitt, p. 295.

Sanger, Bert [actor: Keystone Cop] (b. 1894?–31 Aug 1968 [74], Blackpool, England). "Bert Sanger," *Variety*, 11 Sep 1968. AS, p. 963. BHD, p. 294. IFN, p. 263. Truitt, p. 296 (d. Sep 1969).

Sanger, Eugene B. [producer] (b. 1875–24 Feb 1946 [70?], Amityville NY). BHD2, p. 232.

Sanger, Gerald [director] (b. Surbiton, England, 23 May 1898). AS, p. 963.

Sangro, Elena [actress] (*née* Maria Antonietta Barroli Avveduti, b. Vasta d'Aimone, Italy, 5 Sep 1896–26 Jan 1969 [72], Rome, Italy). AS, p. 963. JS, pp. 404–05 (b. 1901; in Italian silents from 1917; stage name bestowed on her by Gabriele D'Annunzio).

Sangster, Margaret E. [scenarist] (b. 1892–23 Oct 1981 [89?], Valatie NY). AS, p. 963.

Sanin, Alexander Akimovich [actor/director] (b. Russia, 1866–7 May 1956 [90?], Rome, Italy). AS, p. 963.

Sanisvili, Nicholay Consantinovich [actor/director] (b. Koetaisi, Georgia, 24 Dec 1902). AS, p. 964.

Sankey, Bessie M. [actress] (d. 10 Aug 1970?, Stanislaus Co. CA). AS, p. 964. "Bits for Fans," *MPW*, 22 Mar 1913, 1206.

San Martin, Carlos [actor]. No data found. AMD, p. 305. "Spanish Actor Succumbs to Lure of the Pictures," *MPW*, 17 Jan 1920, 388.

Sannom, Emilie [actress] (b. Copenhagen, Denmark, 1886–30 Aug 1931 [47?]). BHD1, p. 616.

Sansberry, Hope [actress] (*née* Virginia Staunton, b. 19 Jun 1894–14 Dec 1960 [66], Laguna Hilla CA; heart attack in her sleep). AS, p. 964 (*née* Virginia Staunders, b. 1896-d. 1990). BHD1, p. 485.

Santana, Vasco Antonio Rodriguez [actor] (b. Lisbon, Portugal, 28 Jan 1898–13 Jun 1958 [59], Lisbon, Portugal; heart attack). AS, p. 964. BHD1, p. 485.

Santana, William [actor] (b. Portugal, 1878–18 Jan 1958 [79?], Lisbon, Portugal; heart attack). AS, p. 964.

Santell, Alfred Allen [scenarist/actor/director/producer] (*né* Alfred Samuelson, b. San Francisco CA, 14 Sep 1894–19 Jun 1981 [86], Salinas CA). m. Jane Neave (d. 1944). (Lubin; Kalem; American; World; Sennett; 1st National.) "Alfred A. Santell," *Variety*, 29 Jul 1981. AMD, p. 305. AS, p. 964 (b. 1895). BHD2, p. 233 (b. 1895). Katz, p. 1015. "Mrs. Al Santell," *NYT*, 15 Sep 1944, 19:5 (b. Kansas City KS, 1908?–13 Sep 1944 [36], Los Angeles CA). "Al Santell Directs Kolb and Dill," *MPW*, 30 Dec 1916, 1943. "Santell Retuns to Universal," *MPW*, 12 Apr 1919, 215. "Santell Reassigned," *MPW*, 8 Sep 1923, 190. "Santell Re-Engaged," *MPW*, 11 Oct 1924, 496. Herbert Cruikshank, "Old Doc Santell; Al Keeps Falling Stars from Falling," *MPC*, Jun 1929, 35, 79, 81 (helped the careers of Corinne Griffith, Richard Barthelmess, Vilma Banky and Alice White).

Santley, Frederic (brother of **Joseph Santley**) [actor/scenarist] (*né* Frederic Mansfield, b. Salt Lake City UT, 20 Nov 1887–14 May 1953 [65], Los Angeles CA). m. Marion Simpson (d. 1913). "Frederic Santley," *NYT*, 16 May 1953, 19:2 (age 64). "Frederic Santley," *Variety*, 20 May 1953. AMD, p. 305. AS, p. 964 (b. 1888). BHD1, p. 485 (b. 1888). FDY, p. 437. IFN, p. 263. Truitt, p. 296. "Pictures and Personality," *MPW*, 9 Dec 1911, 795. "Fred Santley with Cosmopolitan," *MPW*, 25 Nov 1922, 329.

Santley, Joseph (brother of **Frederic Santley**) [stage/film actor/writer/director] (*né* Joseph [aka Eugene] Mansfield, b. Salt Lake City UT, 10 Jan 1889–8 Aug 1971 [82], West Los Angeles CA). m. Ivy Sawyer, 22 Jun 1917, Greenpoint, LI NY. "Joseph Santley, Stage Veteran, 81; 'Greatest Boy Actor' at the Turn of the Century Dies," *NYT*, 10 Aug 1971, 34:1. "Joseph Santley," *Variety*, 18 Aug 1971 (age 81; Eugene Santley was his stepfather). AS, p. 964. BHD, p. 294; BHD2, p. 233. IFN, p. 263. Katz, p. 1015. Truitt, p. 296. "Marriages," *Variety*, 29 Jun 1917, p. 13.

Santley, Laurence [actor] (b. 1868–22 Sep 1933 [65?], Los Angeles CA). AS, p. 964 (Laurene Santley). BHD, p. 294.

Santon, Celia [actress]. No data found. m. Earl W. Arnold, ca. Jan 1918. (Universal.) AMD, p. 305. "Celia Santon New Horsley Star," *Motography*, 23 Oct 1915, 838. "Arnold—Santon," *MPW*, 26 Jan 1918, 509 (former leading lady to Crane Wilbur).

Santoncha, Maria [actress/singer] (b. Spain, 1873–17 Apr 1958 [85?], Madrid, Spain). AS, p. 964.

Santoni, Dante [producer]. No data found. JS, p. 406 ("Co-founder of the Albertoni-Santoni Company, Italy's first film studio. It was built in Roma, and became Cines in 1906.").

Santoro, Jack (brother of actor John and uncle of Tony) [actor] (b. New York NY, 18 Apr 1898–23 Oct 1980 [82], Los Angeles CA; stroke). "Jack Santoro," *Variety*, 29 Oct 1980 ("appeared in many Warners Bros. silents, including numerous 'Rin-Tin-Tin' pictures"). AS, p. 964. BHD1, p. 485.

Santos, Carmen [actress/director/producer] (b. Vila Flor, Portugal, 1904–1952 [48?], Rio de Janeiro, Brazil). AS, p. 964.

Santos, Edmundo [actor/composer] (*né* Edmundo Santos Arteaga, b. Mexico, ca. 1902–3 Aug 1977 [75?], Mexico). AS, p. 964.

Santos, Enrique [set/decoratordirector] (b. Valencia, Spain-d. 1924, Spain). AMD, p. 305. AS, p. 964 (d. 1925). JS, pp. 406–07 (in Italian silents from 1912). William J. Reilly, "Making the Eagle Scream a la Santos," *MPW*, 16 Oct 1920, 923, 952.

Santschi, Thomas [stage/film actor/director] (*né* Paul William Santschi, b. Luzerne, Switzerland, 24 Oct 1878–9 Apr 1931 [52?], Los Angeles CA). m. Lois. (Began 1906; Selig; Pioneer Film Co.; Universal.) "Tom Santschi," *Variety*, 15 Apr 1931 (age 50). AMD, p. 305. AS, p. 965 (b. 1880). BHD1, p. 485; bHD2, p. 233 (b. MO, 1880). FFF, p. 135. FSS, p. 255. GK, pp. 854–70. IFN, p. 263 (b. MO, 1880). Katz, pp. 1015–16 (b. 14 Oct). MH, p. 136. MSBB, p. 1028. Truitt, p. 296. "Thomas Santschi," *MPW*, 10 Jan 1914, 180. "Thomas Santschi's Guide to Success," *MPW*, 30 May 1914, 1251. "Santschi Now Producer," *Motography*, 27 Jun 1914, 478 (b. Switzerland). "Thomas Santschi," *MPW*, 4 Jul 1914, 44. "Thomas Santschi," *MPW*, 5 Feb 1916, 788. "Thomas Santschi," *MPW*, 3 Mar 1917, 1355. Thomas Santschi, "Playing Pictures Difficult," *MPW*, 21 Jul 1917, 418. "Same Actor for Universal's 2," *MPW*, 8 Sep 1923, 170. George A. Katchmer, "One of the Best; Tom Santschi," *CI*, 70 (Jul 1980), 56–57 (*né* Paul). Billy H. Doyle, "Lost Players," *CI*, 189 (Mar 1991), 7–8. Richard E. Braff, "An Index to the Films of Tom Santschi," *CI*, 175 (Jan 1990), C10-C12; *CI*, 176 (Feb 1990). George Katchmer, "Remembering the Great Silents," *CI*, 241 (Jul 1995), 33–34 (b. 14 Oct 1876).

Sanyasi, Rajarishi Bala [director/producer] (b. Bengali, 16 Mar 1877). AS, p. 965.

Sarbel, Marthe [actress] (*née* Marthe Pauline Sansonnet, b. Paris, France, 16 Aug 1884 [extrait de naissance no. 3667]-10 Aug 1976 [91], Saint-Jean-d'Angely, France). AS, p. 965.

Sarda, Pierre [actor] (b. Paris, France, 28 Nov 1895). AS, p. 965.

Sarecky, Barney [producer] (b. New York NY, 7 May 1895–10 Aug 1968 [73], Los Angeles CA). BHD2, p. 233.

Sarecky, Louis A. [producer] (b. Odessa, Ukraine, Russia, 26 Jan 1888–4 May 1946 [58], Los Angeles CA). m. Helen (d. 1942). BHD2, p. 233.

Saredo, Enna [actress] (b. Naples, Italy). JS, p. 407 (in Italian silents from 1913).

Sargeantson, Kate [actress] (b. Wales-d. 16 Feb 1918, New York NY). BHD, p. 294.

Sargent, Alfred Maxwell [actor] (b. 1861–15 Jan 1949 [87?], Kalamazoo MI; pneumonia). AS, p. 966 (b. 1881). BHD, p. 294. IFN, p. 263 (age 68).

Sargent, Epes Winthrop, VI, "Chicot" [writer/scenarist] (b. Nassau, Bahamas, 31 Aug 1872–6 Dec 1938 [66], Brooklyn NY [Death Certificate Index No. 23547]). (Sold scenarios to Vitagraph, 1898; Lubin; Imp; Edison.) "Epes W. Sargent, Critic on Variety; Member of Magazine's Staff When It Was Organized in 1905 Dies at 66; Former Scenario Writer; Wrote Under Name of Chicot—Had Served as Reviewer for Several Papers," *NYT*, 8 Dec 1938, 27:3. "Epes Sargent, 'Chicot,' Dies at 66," *Variety*, 14 Dec 1938. AS, p. 966. BHD2, p. 233. "All But the 'Movies,'" *MPW*, 20 Dec 1913, 1403. "Copyright Bill Introduced; Text of Representative Willis's Bill to Include Photoplays in Townsend Law," *NYDM*, 8 Apr 1914, 37:3 (Sargent "first blazed the trail for copyright agitation when he visited Washington two years ago and conferred with the Register of Copyrights..."). Edward Azlant, "Screenwriting for the early silent film: forgotten pioneers, 1897–1911," *Film History*, 9 (1997), 246–48.

Sargent, George L[ewis] [writer/director/producer/President of Sargent & Co., 1928] (b. 1863?–5 Feb 1944 [81], New Haven CT). m. Alice Bessie Forbes (d. 1902); Margaret Berrien Motte, 1911 (widow). "G. Sargent, ex-Head of Lock Firm, Dies; Son of Former Mayor of New Haven, Tennis Star at Yale," *NYT*, 6 Feb 1944, 42:4 (no mention of films). AMD, p. 305. "Ed-Au Club on Psychology," *MPW*, 28 Nov 1914, 1241. "Sargent Declares for the Draco," *MPW*, 6 Feb 1915, 831.

Sargent, Lewis [actor] (b. Los Angeles CA, 19 Aug 1903–19 Nov 1970 [67], Los Angeles CA). AS, p. 966 (b. 1904). BHD, p. 295; BHD2, p. 233. MH, p. 136 (b. 1904). (Began in films at age 10 in 1914 with Jesse Lasky; Fox.) Edwin Schallert, "He's a King in Boyville; Lewis Sargent's Ambition Is Soaring Kind; He Began His Career at the Psychological Time; Selected as Hero of Mark Twain's Famed Story [*Huckleberry Finn*]," *LA Times*, 8 Feb 1920, III, pp. 1, 8 (age 16. He said he aspired to be a director, "a part of the preserve where is biggest game is.").

Sargent, Margherita [stage/film actress] (b. Bedford MA, 1883?–10 Sep 1964 [81], Wilton CT). m. Augustin Duncan. (Broadway debut, 1907.) "Margherita Sargent Dies; Mother of Angus Duncan," *NYT*, 11 Sep 1964, 33:2. "Margherita Sargent," *Variety*, 16 Sep 1964. AS, p. 966 (d. 1954). SD, p. 1105.

Sarkka, Toïvo Jalmari [director/producer] (b. Mikkelin, Finland, 20 Nov 1890–9 Feb 1975 [84], Helsinki, Finland). AS, p. 966. BHD2, p. 233.

Sarment, Jean [actor] (*né* Jean gaston Bellemere, b. Nantes, France, 13 Jan 1897 [extrait de naissance no. 13/1897]-29 Mar 1976 [79], Boulogne-Billancourt, France). AS, p. 966.

Sarno, Hector V. [actor] (b. Naples, Italy, 24 Apr 1880–16 Dec 1953 [73], Pasadena CA). (Biograph; K&E; Vitagraph.) "Hector V. Sarno," *NYT*, 18 Dec 1953, 29:2 ("stage and film actor who appeared in early silent pictures"). "Hector V. Sarno," *Variety*, 23 Dec 1953. AMD, p. 305. AS, p. 966. BHD1, p. 486. IFN, p. 296. Truitt, p. 263. "Sarno Joins Edwin Carewe," *MPW*, 25 Mar 1922, 375. George Katchmer, "Hector V. Sarno," *CI* (May 1994), 51:3.

Sarony, Gilbert [burlesque/vaudeville/film actor] (d. 15 Dec 1910, Pittsburgh PA; acute indigestion). "Obituary; Gilbert Sarony," *Variety*, 24 Dec 1910, 13:2 ("Sarony was one of the first female impersonators of the old maid type. He was considered one of the funniest men in the show business."). BHD, p. 295.

Sarony, Leslie [actor/composer] (*né* Leslie Frye, b. Surbiton, England, 26 Jan 1897–12 Feb 1985 [87], London, England). AS, p. 966.

Sarrade, Henri Alexandre [actor/director] (b. Asnieres-sur-Seine, France, 26 Feb 1898 [extrait de naissance no. 89/1898]-16 Jan 1985 [86], Lagny-sur-Marne, France [extrait de décès no. 40/1985]). AS, p. 966.

Sartene, Raymonde [actress] (b. Paris, France, 8 May 1898). AS, p. 966.

Sartorio, G[iulio] **A**[ristide] [director/art director] (b. Rome, Italy, 11 Feb 1860–3 Oct 1932 [72], Rome, Italy). AS, p. 966. JS, p. 407 (in Italian silents from 1919).

Sartov, Hendrik C. [cinematographer] (b. 14 May 1885–21 Mar 1970 [84], Glendale CA). AMD, p. 305. BHD2, p. 233 (Henrik Sartov). FDY, p. 467. "Sartov Signed [by] M-G-M," *MPW*, 1 Aug 1925, 556.

Sarver, Charles [scenarist] (b. Leechburg PA, 1871?–9 Nov 1944 [73], New York NY). m. Lucy. "Charles Sarver, 73, News Copy Desk Dean," *NYT*, 11 Nov 1944, 13:6 (wrote scenarios from 1916 on the West Coast). AMD, p. 305. AS, p. 967. BHD2, p. 233. "Charles Sarver, New World Scenario Man," *MPW*, 2 Mar 1918, 1251. "How Works of Old Writers Reappear in a New Form," *MPW*, 12 Oct 1918, 210. "Charles Sarver, World Scenarist, Sees Author Assuming Director's Importance," *MPW*, 19 Jul 1919, 342.

Sarvil, René [actor] (*né* René Ernest Antoine Crescenzo, b. Toulon, France, 18 Jan 1901 [extrait de naissance no. SN/1901]-31 Mar 1975 [73], Marseilles, France). AS, p. 967.

Sass, Edward [actor] (b. 1858–15 Nov 1916 [58?], New Malden, Surrey, England). BHD, p. 295.

Satie, Erik Alfred Leslie [actor/composer] (b. Honfleur, France, 17 May 1866–1 Jul 1925 [59], Paris, France). AS, p. 967. BHD, p. 295.

Satterthwaite, Lucille [actress]. No data found. AMD, p. 305. "Lucille Satterthwaite," *MPW*, 6 Apr 1918, 75.

Sattomayor, Carlos [actor] (b. Fortaleza, Brazil, 8 Jun 1901). AS, p. 967.

Satz, Ludwig [actor/director] (b. Lemberg, Poland, 1891–31 Aug 1944 [53?], New York NY). AS, p. 967 (b. Lemburg, Germany). BHD2, p. 233.

Sauber, Harry [scenarist] (b. Russia, 16 Apr 1882–21 Sep 1967 [85], Los Angeles CA). BHD2, p. 233.

Sauer, Fred [director] (*né* Alfred Sauer, b. Graz, Austria, 14 Jul 1886–17 Sep 1952 [66], Berlin, Germany). AS, p. 967. BHD2, p. 233.

Sauerman, Carl [actor] (b. Stockholm, Sweden, 1868?–9 Apr 1924 [56], Brooklyn NY). AS, p. 967. BHD, p. 295. IFN, p. 263.

Saule, Phyllis [actress]. No data found. (Sennett.) "Six Reasons Why Mack Sennett Comedies Are Popular," *Cinema Arts*, Aug 1926, 23 (photo).

Saum, Clifford P. [actor/director] (b. Columbus OH, 18 Dec 1882–5 Mar 1943 [60], Glendale CA). "Clifford Saum," *Variety*, 17 Mar 1943 (character actor). AS, p. 967. BHD1, p. 486; BHD2, p. 233. IFN, p. 263. Truitt, p. 296.

Saunders, Alice [actress] (b. Holyoke MA, 4 Sep 1872–25 Jul 1953 [80], Los Angeles Co. CA). AS, p. 967. BHD, p. 295. IFN, p. 263.

Saunders, Claud [stage/film publicist/general manager] (b. La Porte IN, 17 Apr 1880–1 Mar 1942 [61], Cheyenne WY; heart attack). "Claud Saunders," *Variety*, 146, 11 Mar 1942, 54:1 (buried in LA CA). AMD, p. 305. BHD2, p. 233 (d. LA CA). "Claud Saunder Resigns as Famous Exploitation Head," *MPW*, 26 Dec 1925, 752.

Saunders, Ed (brother of **Jackie Saunders**) [assistant director]. No data found. "Briefs of Biography," *NYDM*, 18 Aug 1915, 24:3 (worked under Henry King).

Saunders, Florence [actress] (b. Valparaiso, Chile, 1890–24 Jan 1926 [35?], London, England, in a nursing home). m. actor John Laurie. "Florence Saunders," *Variety*, 10 Feb 1926, 45:1. BHD, p. 295.

Saunders, Hortense [publicist]. No data found. AMD, p. 305. "Hortense Saunders Joins Selznick," *MPW*, 3 Jan 1920, 138.

Saunders, Jackie, "The Maid of Long Beach" (sister of **Ed Saunders**) [stage/film actress] (*née* Anna Jackal, b. Philadelphia PA, 6 Oct 1892–14 Jul 1954 [61], Cedars of Lebanon Hospital, Palm Springs CA; cancer; buried in Wellwood Cemetery, Palm Springs CA). m. (1) **Elwood D. Horkheimer**, 1916—div. ca. 1920 (d. 1966; daughter Jacqueline, b. 1 Sep 1917); (2) J. Ward Cohen, 29 Jun 1927, El Mirasol Hotel, Santa Barbara CA (daughter actress Mary Ann Gibson, b. 29 Jun 1927; d. 1950). (Biograph; Universal; Balboa, Dec 1913; WB.) "Jackie Saunders, 56, former stage and screen actress, died July 14 in Palm Springs, Cal.," *Variety*, 21 Jul 1954. AMD, p. 305. AS, p. 967. BHD1, p. 487. IFN, p. 263 (b. 1897). Jura, pp. 112–19. Truitt, p. 296 (b. 1898). "Jacqueline Saunders," *MPW*, 26 Sep 1914, 1793. "Jacqueline Saunders," *MPW*, 19 Dec 1914, 1764. "Jacqueline Saunders in Pathé Gold Rooster Play," *MPW*, 30 Oct 1915, 767. B., "Colored Film Liked; Pathe Presents Jackie Saunders in Artistic Foreign-Colored Film...," *NYDM*, 13 Nov 1915, 32:3 (*The Adventures of a Madcap*, 4 reels, released 2 Nov 1915, with Frank Mayo, Corenne Grant, and Philo McCullough. "After seeing this picture it is hard to understand why the colored picture is not more often seen."). Mae Tinee, *Life Stories of the Movie Stars*, Vol. I (Hamilton OH: The Presto Publishing Co., 1916), p. 50. "Jacqueline Saunders," *MPW*, 6 Jan 1917, 78. Pearl Gaddis, "Jackie's Stolen Day," *Motion Picture Magazine*, Feb 1918, 68–69 (she and her collie, Laddie, spent time in a cabin in the mountains after getting 60 days' vacation from her studio). "Jacqueline Saunders Engaged to Appear in 'Dad's Girl,'" *MPW,* 30 Aug 1919, 1332. "Metro Engages Jacqueline Saunders," *MPW,* 4 Dec 1920, 631. Billy H. Doyle, "Lost Players," *CI,* 153 (Mar 1988), 53.

Saunders, John Monk [scenarist] (b. Hinckley MN, 22 Nov 1895?–11 Mar 1940 [44?], Ft. Myers FL; suicide by hanging). m. **Fay Wray,** 1928–39. "John Monk Saunders," *Variety,* 13 Mar 1940 (age 42). AS, p. 967 (b. 1897). BHD2, p. 233 (b. 1897-d. 10 Mar). FDY, p. 437. Katz, p. 1017 (b. 1897).

Saunders, John Root [actor] (b. 1860–1 Feb 1929 [68?], Los Angeles CA). AS, p. 967.

Saunders, Lucille [actress] (d. 8 Jun 1919, San Francisco CA). BHD1, p. 616.

Saunders, Nellie Peck [actress] (b. Saginaw MI, 1870–3 Mar 1942 [71], Greenwood SC). "Nellie Peck Saunders," *Variety,* 11 Mar 1942 (age 71). AS, p. 967. BHD1, p. 487 (b. 1869). IFN, p. 263. Truitt, p. 296.

Savage, Henry W. [playwright/theatrical producer/film director/producer/realtor] (b. New Burham NH, 21 Mar 1859–29 Nov 1927 [68], Boston MA). m. Louise Batchelor. (Paramount.) "Henry W. Savage, Producer, Is Dead; First Impresario to Present Grand Opera in English Succumbs at 68; He Staged 50 Successes; 'Prince of Pilsen' and 'Merry Widow' Among His Offerings—Was Long a Real Estate Man," *NYT,* 30 Nov 1927, 25:3. "Henry W. Savage," *Variety,* 7 Dec 1927. AMD, p. 305. AS, p. 968. BHD2, p. 234. "Henry W. Savage Allies with Famous Players," *MPW,* 21 Feb 1914, 955. "Savage's Screen Entry; Maclyn Arbuckle in 'The County Chairman,' the First Famous Players-Savage Release," *NYDM,* 7 Oct 1914, 25:3. "Pathé Acquires Savage's Plays," *MPW,* 18 Dec 1915, 2187.

Savage, Mary [actress]. No data found. AMD, p. 305. "Mary Savage Heads Her Own Firm, CAPItalized at $100,000," *MPW,* 7 Aug 1920, 722.

Savage, Nellie [stage/film actress]. No data found. AMD, p. 306. "Nellie Savage in Leading Role," *MPW,* 10 Jan 1925, 159. Ramon Romeo, "Reeling Down Broadway," *Paris and Hollywood Screen Secrets Magazine,* III (May 1927), 61–62 (filming *The Broadway Drifter.* Valentino discovered her when she was in Lowell Sherman's stage production of *Casanova;* he gave her a role in *Monsieur Beaucaire.* Griffith used her as the symbolic figure of Sin in *The Sorrows of Satan,* and should he make *The Holy Grail* he will award her an important role. This girl properly handled and photographed has the possibilities of becoming another Greta Garbo.").

Savage, Turner [actor]. George Katchmer, "Remembering the Great Silents," *CI,* 212 (Feb 1993), 34.

Savarin [actor]. No data found. AMD, p. 306. "Notes of the Trade," *MPW,* 16 Jan 1909, 65.

Savchenko, Chikly [director] (b. Tunis, Tunisia, 24 Jan 1872–1950 [78?], France). AS, p. 968.

Savelli, Alba [actress] (*née* Luigina Lapini, b.Subbiano, Italy). JS, p. 409 (in Italian silents from 1922).

Savelli, Rebecca [actress] (b. Indianapolis IN, 2 Jun 1846–7 Jul 1908 [62], Los Angeles CA). AS, p. 968.

Saville, Gus C. [actor] (b. Peekskill NY, 1857–25 Mar 1934 [77], Los Angeles CA). m. Mrs. Jessie Tate. "Gus Saville," *Variety,* 3 Apr 1934. AS, p. 968. BHD1, p. 487. IFN, p. 263. Truitt, p. 296. George Katchmer, "Remembering the Great Silents," *CI,* 212 (Feb 1993), 34–35.

Saville, Ruth (sister of **De Sacia Mooers**) [actress] (b. Mojave Desert [Alessandro] CA, 1892–31 Mar 1985 [92], Los Angeles CA). m. Mr. Connors. (Essanay, 1913.) "Ruth Saville," *Variety,* 10 Apr 1985. AS, p. 968. BHD, p. 295 (b. 1893).

Saville, Victor [director/producer/scenarist] (b. Birmingham, England, 25 Sep 1895–8 May 1979 [83], London, England). (Last film: *The Greenngage Summer,* English, 1961.) C. Gerald Fraser, "Victor Saville, 83, Film Producer, Dies; Briton Made 'Goodbye Mr. Chips,' 'Evergreen,' 'The Citadel' and 'Dr. Jekyll and Mr. Hyde,'" *NYT,* 10 May 1979, IV, 23:3. "Victor Saville," *Variety,* 16 May 1979. "Victor Saville," *CI,* 64 (Jul 1979), 68. AS, p. 968 (b. 1897). BHD2, p. 234. FDY, p. 437. IFN, p. 263. Waldman, p. 255 (b. 1897).

Savini, Robert M. [executive] (b. 29 Aug 1886–29 Apr 1956 [69], New York NY). BHD2, p. 234.

Savo, Jimmy [stage/film actor] (b. Bronx NY, 31 Jul 1895–6 Sep 1960 [65], Terni, Umbria, Italy; heart attack while on vacation). m. Lina Farina Vecchi. "Jimmy Savo Dead; Comedian Was 64; Mime Noted for Baggy-Pants Routines Starred in Revues, Night Clubs and Films," *NYT,* 7 Sep 1960, 41:1 (right leg amputated above knee on 11 Sep 1946). "Savo Left $3,000; Will of Pantomimist Names Wife as Beneficiary," *NYT,* 4 Nov 1960, 7:7. "Jimmy Savo," *Variety,* 7 Sep 1960. AMD, p. 306. AS, p. 969 (b. 1896). BHD1, p. 487. IFN, p. 263. Truitt, p. 296. "Jimmie Savo," *MPW,* 11 Dec 1926, 407.

Savoir, Alfred [scenarist] (b. 1883–26 Jun 1934 [51?], Paris, France). BHD2, p. 234.

Sawamura, Kunitaro (father of actors Kiroyuki Nagato and Masahiko Tsugawa; brother of actor Daisuke Kato and actress Sadako Sawamura) [stage/film actor] (*né* Tomoichi Kato, b. Tokyo, Japan, 15 Jun 1905–26 Nov 1974 [69], Tokyo, Japan; stroke). "Kunitarso Sawamura," *Variety,* 25 Dec 1974, 47:3 (bedridden from a cerebral hemorrhage in 1960). AS, p. 969. BHD1, p. 487. IFN, p. 263.

Sawyer, Arthur H. [producer/President of Kinemacolor] (b. Portland ME, 8 Mar 1877–24 Jun 1966 [89], Keene NH). "Arthur Sawyer," *NYT,* 26 Jun 1966, 73:1 ("He produced silent films in Hollywood, then became associated with Mr. [William E.] Atkinson in building the Roxy Theater in 1927 and operating it. The theater was torn down in 1960."). "Arthur Sawyer," *Variety,* 29 Jun 1966. AMD, p. 306. AS, p. 969 (b. 1977). BHD2, p. 234. Emmet Roberts, "'Prosperity' Is the Prophecy; A Business Forecast by A.H. Sawyer, Who Sees a Banner Year for the Wise Men and a Weeding Out of the Inefficient," *NYDM,* 14 Jan 1914, 47. "Sawyer, Incorporated," *MPW,* 16 May 1914, 977. "New Combination Outlines Project," *MPW,* 16 Nov 1918, 746. "Sawyer Announces Plans of New S-L Pictures," *MPW,* 30 Nov 1918, 975. "Sawyer the Director," *MPW,* 6 Sep 1924, 28.

Sawyer, Joan [stage/film dancer/actress] (b. El Paso TX, 1884). (Film debut: *Love's Law,* Fox, 1917.) AMD, p. 306. "Jeannette Gilder Writes for Joan Sawyer," *MPW,* 9 May 1914, 797. "Madame Critic," *NYDM,* 15 Jul 1914, 4:1 (dancing with Nigel Barrie). "She's the Spirit of the Dance; 'I Wouldn't Want to Change Places with Anyone Else in the World,'" *NYDM,* 29 Jul 1914, 18:2. *Photoplay Magazine,* Mar 1917, 176. *Biographical Dictionary of Dance,* pp. 795–96/

Sawyer, Laura [actress/scenarist] (b. 3 Feb 1885–7 Sep 1970 [85], Matawan NJ). m. Charles F. Wolff. (Edison.) "Mrs. Charles F. Wolff, 85, Had Leads in Early Films," *NYT,* 10 Sep 1970, 47:4. "Laura Sawyer," *Variety,* 16 Sep 1970. AMD, p. 306. AS, p. 969. BHD, p. 295. IFN, p. 263. Spehr, p. 164. Truitt, p. 296. "Laura Sawyer," *MPW,* 26 Apr 1913, 386. "Laura Sawyer Joins Famous Players," *MPW,* 30 Aug 1913, 965. Lester Sweyd, "What They Are Doing Now," *Motion Picture Magazine,* Feb 1918, 12 (wrote *The Valentine Girl* for Marguerite Clark).

Sax, Carroll M. [producer] (b. Chicago IL, 1885?–30 Sep 1961 [76], New York NY). "Carol M. Sax Dies; Theatrical Producer Was 76—Ex-Professor of Art," *NYT,* 2 Oct 1961, 31:5. "Carol M. Sax," *Variety,* 4 Oct 1961. AS, p. 969 (b. 1880; d. 2 Jan 1962, Hollywood CA). BHD2, p. 234 (b. 1883–24 May 1969).

Sax, Samuel [producer/founded Gotham Pictures] (b. Russia, 1880?–2 Jan 1962 [81], Los Angeles CA). m. Lulu. (Universal, 1913; Robertson-Cole; Metro; WB.) "Sam Sax," *Variety,* 17 Jan 1962. AMD, p. 306. BHD2, p. 234. "To Make Series of Six," *MPW,* 28 Jun 1924, 784. "Sax Will Make 12 Gothams as Scheduled; Last 4 in Work," *MPW,* 14 Nov 1925, 122. "Sax Has Production Plans for Next Season," *MPW,* 5 Dec 1925, 436. "Sam Sax Denies Gotham's Farce Goes Elsewhere," *MPW,* 19 Mar 1927, 188.

Saxe, Templar [opera singer/stage/film actor] (*né* Templer William Edward Edevein, b. Redhill, Surrey, England, b. 22 Aug 1865–17 Apr 1935 [70], Cincinnati OH). (Stage debut, 1888; Vitagraph.) AMD, p. 306. AS, p. 969. BHD, p. 295. IFN, p. 264. MSBB, p. 1028. "Templar Saxe," *MPW,* 30 Oct 1915, 982.

Saxon, Hugh A. [actor] (b. New Orleans LA, 14 Jan 1869–14 May 1945 [76], Beverly Hills CA). "Hugh A. Saxon," *Variety,* 23 May 1945 (acted 29 years). AS, p. 969. BHD1, p. 487. IFN, p. 264. Truitt, p. 296. George Katchmer, "Remembering the Great Silents," *CI,* 249 (Mar 1996), 49.

Saxton, Charles [title writer]. No data found. AMD, p. 306. "Charles Saxton Does Cartoon Titles," *MPW,* 21 Aug 1926, 466.

Saylor, Syd [actor] (*né* Leo Sailor, b. Chicago IL, 24 May 1895–21 Dec 1962 [67], Los Angeles CA; heart attack). "Syd Saylor," *Variety,* 2 Jan 1963 (in more than 1,000 films; began in silents in 1929). AMD, p. 306. AS, p. 969. BHD1, p. 487. IFN, p. 264. Katz, p. 1019. Truitt, pp. 296–97. "Stern Brothers Sign Sid Saylor," *MPW,* 10 Apr 1926, 454. Ken Law, "Syd Saylor; Sidekick, Comedian, Character Actor," *CI,* 107 (May 1984), 58–59.

Sayres, Margaret [actress] (b. 1868–17 Apr 1937 [69?], Asheville NC). BHD, p. 295. IFN, p. 264.

Sazanov, Panteleymon Petrovich [director of animated films] (b. Russia, 28 May 1895–3 Oct 1950 [55], Russia). AS, p. 969.

Scaduto, Joseph [actor] (b. New York NY, 28 May 1898–19 Oct 1943 [45], Los Angeles CA). AS, p. 970. BHD1, p. 488. IFN, p. 264. Truitt, p. 297.

Scalenghe, Giuseppe Angelo [cinematographer] (b. Turin, Italy, 1886–18 Sep 1916 [30?], Turin, Italy). JS, p. 412 (in Italian silents from 1911).

Scanlan, Edward [actor] (b. New York NY, 1883–31 Aug 1949 [66?], Weehawken NJ). BHD, p. 295.

Scannell, John J. [actor] (b. 1887–18 Feb 1926 [38?], Jackson Heights NY). BHD, p. 295.

Scarano, Tecla [actress] (*née* Tecla Moretti, b. Naples, Italy, 20 Aug 1894). m. composer Franco Langella. AS, p. 970. JS, p. 412 (in Italian silents from 1919).

Scarborough, George M. [title writer/scenarist] (d. 16 Dec 1951, Mt. Kisco NY). "Mrs. G. Scarborough," *NYT,* 17 Dec 1951, 31:3 9 (discovered Lenore Ulric). AMD, p. 306. BHD2, p. 234. FDY, p. 447. "Fox Strengthens Scenario Staff," *MPW,* 12 May 1917, 958.

Scardon, Paul [actor/director] (b. Melbourne, Victoria, Australia, 6 May 1874–17 Jan 1954 [79], Fontana CA; heart attack). (World.) m. **Betty Blythe** (d. 1972). "Paul Scardon," *NYT,* 20 Jan 1954, 27:4. "Paul Scardon," *Variety,* 27 Jan 1954. AMD, p. 306. AS, p. 970. BHD1, p. 488; BHD2, p. 234. IFN, p. 264. Lowrey, p. 166. Slide, p. 150. Spehr, p. 164 (1878–1961). Truitt, p. 297 (b. 1878). "Popular Paul Scardon to Join the Reliance Company," *MPW,* 19 Apr 1913, 285. "Enter 'Miss Scardon,'" *MPW,* 26 Apr 1913, 370 (birth of daughter). "Paul Scardon," *MPW,* 23 Jan 1915, 498. "Meeting the War Tax in the Studio," *MPW,* 22 Dec 1917, 1796. "Paul Scardon Joins Goldwyn's Culver City Directors Staff," *MPW,* 13 Mar 1920, 1835.

Scarpetta, Vincenzo [actor/scenarist] (b. Naples, Italy, 17 Jun 1876–3 Aug 1952 [76], Naples, Italy; after a heart attack). AS, p. 970. JS, p. 413 (in Italian silents from 1910).

Scates, Walter [executive] (d. Jul 1929). BHD2, p. 234.

Scatizzi, Enrico [actor] (b. Siena, Italy). JS, p. 413 (in Italian silents from 1919).

Scelzo, Filippo Francesco Luigi [actor] (b. Ivrea, Italy, 19 Apr 1900 [extrait de naissance no. 66/1900]-3 Oct 1980 [80], Genoa, Italy [extrait de décès no. 142/PII/1980]). AS, p. 970.

Scey, Georges [actor] (*né* Georges Camus, b. Paris, France, 23 Oct 1876-ca. 1961 [85?]). AS, p. 970.

Schable, Robert [actor/director] (b. Hamilton OH, 31 Aug 1873–3 Jul 1947 [73], Los Angeles CA). m. **Wilda Bennett** (d. 1967). "Robert Schable, 74, character actor, died in Hollywood July 7," *Variety,* 16 Jul 1947. AMD, p. 306. AS, p. 970 (d. 7 Jul). BHD1, p. 488; BHD2, p. 234. IFN, p. 264. MH, p. 136. Truitt, p. 297. WWS, p. 43. "Schable to Play Lead," *MPW,* 20 Nov 1920, 354. "Schable Very Ill," *MPW,* 18 Dec 1920, 893 (ptomaine poisoning).

Schacht, Gustav [actor] (b. 1876–8 Oct 1943 [67], New York NY). BHD1, p. 488. IFN, p. 264.

Schade, Betty Marie [actress] (b. Berlin, Germany, 22 Nov 1894). m. **Ernest W. Shields**, Church of the Angels, LA CA, Easter Sunday, 1917 (d. 1944). (Essanay [Chicago IL]; American, Universal; FP-L; Fox; Selig.) AMD, p. 306. AS, p. 970. 1921 Directory, p. 238. "Betty Schade Joins Universal," *MPW,* 29 Nov 1913, 1020. "Betty Schade, Ingenue, Universal," *MPN,* 21 Oct 1916, 229. "A Demure War Bride," *MPN,* 5 May 1917, 2824 (married a sergeant in the Hollywood Coast Artillery). Cal York, "Plays and Players," *Photoplay,* Jul 1917, 111 (married Shields). George Katchmer, "Remembering the Great Silents," *CI,* 240 (Jun 1995), 47.

Schade, Fritz [actor] (b. Germany, 1880–17 Jun 1926 [46], Los Angeles CA). BHD, p. 295. IFN, p. 264.

Schaefer, Albert John [actor: Our Gang Comedies] (b. Galveston TX, 1 May 1916–26 Oct 1942 [26], Los Angeles CA). "Albert Schaefer," *Variety,* 4 Nov 1942. BHD, p. 295. AS, p. 970. IFN, p. 264. Truitt, p. 297.

Schaefer, Anne (aunt of **Jane Novak**) [actress] (b. St. Louis MO, 10 Jul 1870–3 May 1957 [86], Los Angeles CA). (Vitagraph.) AMD, p. 306. AS, p. 970. BHD1, p. 488. IFN, p. 264. Slide, p. 150. "Miss Schaefer on Vacation," *MPW,* 14 Sep 1912, 1060. "In Corinne's Cast," *MPW,* 11 Dec 1926, 419. George Katchmer, "Remembering the Great Silents," *CI,* 220 (Oct 1993), 41.

Schaefer, Fred [writer/publicist/title writer]. No data found. AMD, p. 306. "Fred Schaefer with VItagraph," *MPW,* 6 May 1916, 964. "Fred Schaefer Quits General," *MPW,* 22 Mar 1919, 1634. "Schaefer Doing Much Titling and Editing," *MPW,* 5 Jun 1920, 1356. Fred Schaefer, "Uses of the Motion Picture Subtitle," *MPW,* 29 Jan 1921, 552.

Schaeffer, Charles N *see* **Schafer, George N.**

Schaeffer, Chester W. [film editor] (nephew of **William Russell**; 1st cousin of **William Beaudine**) (b. New York NY, 9 Sep 1902–5 Jan 1992 [89], Santa Clara CA). "Chester W. Schaeffer," *Variety,* 27 Jan 1992, p. 66.

Schaeffer, Freddie [technical director]. No data found. AMD, p. 306. "Arbuckel and Schaeffer Part," *MPW,* 15 Jul 1916, 447.

Schaeffer, Otis [actor] (b. 1907–8 Jun 1962 [55?], Norwalk CT). BHD, p. 296.

Schafer, George N. [actor] (b. 12 Feb 1863–5 Feb 1939 [75], Los Angeles CA). "George N. Schaefer," *Variety,* 15 Feb 1939 (began in 1909). AS, p. 970 (d. 5 Jan). BHD1, p. 488 (Charles N. Schaefer). IFN, p. 264. Truitt, p. 297. George Katchmer, "Remembering the Great Silents," *CI,* 233 (Nov 1994), 40.

Schaffner, Glenn H. [actor]. m. Pearl. "Naughty Cowboy," *Variety,* 13 Jul 1917, p. 19 ("Glenn H. Schaffner, film cowboy, is being sued for divorce by Pearl Schaffner, who charges cruelty.").

Schaffner, Lillian [actress] (b. 1862 8 Jan 1930 [67?], Los Angeles CA). AS, p.971.

Schamoni, Victor [actor/director] (b. Berlin, Germany, 1901–1942 [41?], Berlin, Germany). AS, p. 971.

Schang, Wally [actor] (b. South Wales NY, 22 Aug 1889–6 Mar 1985 [95], St. Louis MO). BHD, p. 296.

Scharpegge, Ernie [actor] (b. 1898?–11 Mar 1940 [42], Milwaukee WI). BHD, p. 296. IFN, p. 264.

Schauffuss, Hans Joachim [actor] (b. Germany, 28 Dec 1918–27 Oct 1941 [22]). BHD, p. 296. IFN, p. 264 (b. 1919).

Schaumer, Adolph [1st assistant director] (b. CA, 12 Apr 1898–6 Apr 1977 [78], Pacific Palisades CA). (Fox; TC-F.) "Adolph Schaumer," *Variety,* 13 Apr 1977. AS, p. 971 (b. 1905). BHD2, p. 234.

Schayer, E. Richard [publicist/scenarist] (b. Washington DC, 13 Dec 1880?–15 Mar 1956 [75], Los Angeles CA). (MGM.) "Richard Schayer," *Variety,* 21 Mar 1956. AMD, p. 306. AS, p. 971 (b. 1882). BHD2, p. 234 (b. 1882). FDY, p. 437. IFN, p. 264 (age 75). Katz, p. 1021 (b. 1882). "Schayer Retires from Selznick Staff," *MPW,* 23 Jun 1917, 1922. "Honeymooners Begin World Tour," *MPW,* 1 Sep 1917, 1393. "Schayer to Write for Mix," *MPW,* 15 Feb 1919, 895. "New Contract for Schayer from M-G-M," *MPW,* 25 Dec 1926, 582. "Writer May Be Chosen Director," *MPW,* 14 May 1927, 100.

Scheff, Fritzi [stage/film actress] (b. Vienna, Austria, 30 Aug 1879–8 Apr 1954 [74], New York NY; heart attack). m. (1) Baron Fritz von Bardeleben; (2) John Fox, Jr.; (3) George Anderson. "Fritzi Scheff," *Variety,* 14 Apr 1954 (made 1 film: *The Pretty Mrs. Smith*). "Fritzi Scheff, 74, Star in Operettas; Noted Fifi of 'Mlle. Modiste' Dies Here—Began Her U.S. Career in 1901 at 'Met,'" *NYT,* 9 Apr 1954, 23:3. "Scheff Estate Less than $1,000," *NYT,* 14 May 1954, 16:3 (famous for singing *Kiss Me Again*). "Fritzi Scheff Left $476; Singing Star's Estate Mostly Momentoes of Stage Glories," *NYT,* 4 Feb 1955, 16:8 (actually, $476.75; peak of fame in 1904). AMD, p. 306. AS, p. 971. BHD1, p. 488. IFN, p. 264. Truitt, p. 297. "Fritzi Scheff as Twins; Sings Dual Role in Revival of Girofie-Girofia [an opera bouffe, Paris, 1873]," *NYT,* 1 Feb 1905, 9:5 ('Miss Scheff was in good voice, having completely recovered from her late illness…"). "Fritzi Scheff Is Screened by Universal," *MPW,* 23 May 1914, 1095. "Fritzi Scheff Signed; Will Appear Under Bosworth Banner in 'The Pretty Mrs. Smith,'" *NYDM,* 6 Jan 1915, 24:4. "Fritzi Scheff's Belongings Seized," *NYDM,* 13 Jan 1915, 7:1 (on 8 Jan her belongings were attached to satisfy a judgment obtained by Henri Bendel, a New York costumer. "When the writ was served Miss Scheff was in bed, so that her French *robe du nuit* is all she has left, and a deputy sheriff stood guard at her door to prevent her leaving."). "Miss Scheff Closes," *NYDM,* 13 Jan 1915, 7:4 (closed *Pretty Mrs. Smtih* in St. Louis on 9 Jan. "A film version of the musical comedy is contemplated."). W.E. Wing, "Mack Sennett's Forces," *NYDM,* 3 Feb 1915, 23:3 (she declared "that it was a 'refreshing' experience for her [to appear in pictures] after years of rehearsals, long performances and rushing about the country. Fritzi has not proven shy on wardrobe since appearing here, despite of the night-robe story….").

Scheibe, George H. [cinematographer] (b. Plymouth WI, 1880–17 Nov 1948 [68?], Los Angeles CA; auto accident). AS, p. 971. BHD2, p. 235.

Scheim, Freddy [director] (*né* August Ferdinand Scheim, b. Biel, Switzerland, 26 Dec 1892–5 Dec 1957 [64], Zurich, Switzerland). AS, p. 971.

Schell, Margarete (mother of Maria and Maximilian Schell) [actress] (*née* Noe von Nordberg, b. Vienna, Austria, 2 Jun 1905–25 Nov 1995 [90], Kaernten, Austria). m. (daughter Margarete Schell [Maria Schell], b. 15 Jan 1926; son, Marimilian Schell [Maximilian Konrad Maria Immaculata Schell], b. 8 Dec 1930). AS, p. 972.

Schellinger, Rial B. [cameraman] (b. 1877?–23 Apr 1954 [77], Yonkers NY). m. Marguerite. (Fox.) "Early Camera Man Dies; Rial B.

Schellinger, 77, Took [Jack] Johnson-[Jess] Willard Fight Films," *NYT,* 25 Apr 1954, 87:2. "Rial B. Schellinger," *Variety,* 28 Apr 1954. BHD2, p. 235.

Schenck, Earl O. [actor/writer] (b. Columbus OH, 13 May 1889). AMD, p. 306. AS, p. 972. BHD, p. 296. "Champion Crown Princer Is Earl Schenck, Metro," *MPW,* 8 Feb 1919, 736. Ragan 2, p. 1507.

Schenck, George [executive] (b. 1873–10 Feb 1962 [88?], Los Angeles CA). BHD2, p. 235.

Schenck, Harry W. [director/producer/scenarist] (b. Brookfield MO, 24 Jul 1885–26 Mar 1953 [67], Los Angeles CA). AMD, p. 307. BHD2, p. 235. "Mexican War in Solax Features," *MPW,* 4 Jul 1914, 80.

Schenck, Joseph M. (brother of **Nicholas M. Schenck**) [executive] (b. Rybinsk, Russia, 25 Dec 1877–22 Oct 1961 [83], Beverly Hills CA; heart attack). m. **Norma Talmadge**, Oct 1916, Stamford CT—div. 1934 (d. 1957). "Joseph M. Schenck, 82, Is Dead; A Pioneer in the Movie Industry," *NYT,* 23 Oct 1961, 1:2, 29:3 (b. 25 Dec 1878; age 82). "Joseph M. Schenck," *Variety,* 25 Oct 1961 (d. 20 Oct 1961). AMD, p. 307. AS, p. 972. BHD2, p. 235 (b. 1887). IFN, p. 264. Katz, p. 1022. Spehr, p. 164 (b. 1878). "Norma Talmadge and Joe Schenck Marry," *MPW,* 18 Nov 1916, 986. "Joseph M. Schenck in Los Angeles," *MPW,* 6 Jan 1917, 85. "Schenck Shifts to First Natioal," *MPW,* 21 Dec 1918, 1333. "Neither Norma Nor Constance Talmadge Intend to Quit Circuit, Says Schenck," *MPW,* 17 Apr 1920, 384. "Joseph Schenck in France Finds Picture Business Several Years Behind Our Standard in America," *MPW,* 2 Oct 1920, 680. "Schenck Buys United," *MPW,* 10 Feb 1923, 538. "Costume Play a Success If Drama Is Real, Says Schenck," *MPW,* 28 Apr 1923, 904. Joseph M. Schenck, "Cut in Schedules for the Talmadges Means Films of Even Higher Quality," *MPW,* 9 Jun 1923, 504. "Schenck Is President," *MPW,* 2 Feb 1924, 389 (Motion Picture Producers' Association, elected 22 Jan 1924). "Schenck Ignorant of Mayer Severance Rumor," *MPW,* 25 Oct 1924, 706. "Schenck Relinquishes Loew Interests," *MPW,* 8 Nov 1924, 122. "Schenck–United Merger Has Expansion Budget," *MPW,* 15 Nov 1924, 218. "United Artists to Continue," *MPW,* 6 Dec 1924, 513. "Joseph M. Schenck Honored by Producers of California," *MPW,* 12 Dec 1925, 530. "They Control Your Films!," *MPC,* Jan 1926, 26. "Must Have O.K. by Schenck to 'Shoot' Streets," *MPW,* 19 Feb 1927, 561. Joseph M. Schenck, "Human Interest Makes Pictures," *MPW,* 26 Mar 1927, 408. "Joseph M. Schenck Elected to Head United Artists," *MPW,* 9 Apr 1927, 537. "SChenck Signs Brenon for U.A.; 'Sorrell and Son' First Opus," *MPW,* 9 Apr 1927, 565. "Schenck Gives Up Position as Street Arbiter," *MPW,* 2 May 1927, 793. "Schenck Denies Annoying Rumor," *MPW,* 20 Aug 1927, 531. "Commissioner Schenck Goes to Work," *MPW,* 3 Sep 1927, 21 (California State Highway Commissioner). "Roosevelt Hotel Formally Opened," *MPW,* 5 Nov 1927, 42. "Schenc Flays Vaudeville, Calls 5000 Seaters Scourge," *MPW,* 3 Dec 1927, 7, 14. "Schenck to Coast," *MPW,* 17 Dec 1927, 5. "Banquet for Joseph M. Schenck," *MPW,* 31 Dec 1927, 26.

Schenck, Joseph T[homas] [stage/film actor] (b. Brooklyn NY, 1891?–28 Jun 1930 [39], Detroit MI; heart attack). m. (1) Amelia-1923; (2) Lillian Broderick. "Joseph Schenck, Entertainer, Dies; Partner, Gus Van, with Him, Filling Vaudeville Engagement in Detroit Theatre; He Had Played Day Before; Two Singers, Early in Life, Were Motorman and Conductor on Brooklyn Street Car," *NYT,* 29 Jun 1930, II, 6:1 (age 38). "Joseph T. Schenck," *Variety,* 2 Jul 1930. AS, p. 972. BHD1, p. 489. IFN, p. 264.

Schenck, Nicholas M., "The General" (brother of **Joseph M. Schenck**) [executive] (b. Rybinsk, Russia, 14 Nov 1881–4 Mar 1969 [87], Miami Beach FL; pulmonary embolism). "Nicholas M. Schenck, 87, Dead; Was Head of M-G-M and Loew's; Ruled Film Empire Without Flamboyance for 30 Years," *NYT,* 5 Mar 1969, 47:1. "Nick Schenck, L.B. Mayer's Boss, Dies Three Days After [Joe] Vogel," *Variety,* 5 Mar 1969. AS, p. 972. BHD2, p. 235 (d. 3 Mar). IFN, p. 265. Katz, p. 1022. Spehr, pp. 164–65.

Schenstrom, Carl [actor] (b. Copenhagen, Denmark, 13 Nov 1881–10 Apr 1942 [60], Copenhagen, Denmark). AS, p. 972. BHD1, p. 489. IFN, p. 265.

Scherer, Charles A. [cinematographer] (b. Aug 1918). BHD2, p. 235.

Scherer, James A.D. [writer]. No data found. AMD, p. 307. "Dr. Scherer Leaves California 'Tech' to Join Staff of Famous Players-Lasky," *MPW,* 25 Sep 1920, 512.

Schertzinger, Victor L. [composer/director/scenarist] (b. Mahanoy City PA, 8 Apr 1890–26 Oct 1941 [51], Los Angeles CA; heart attack). (MGM; Ince.) "Schertzinger Dies; A Film Director, 52; Pioneer in Making of Musicals Composed 'Marcheta' Which Sold 4,000,000 Copies; Boy Violinist with Sousa; First to Handle Color Pictures—Was an Early Director of Valentino and Ray," *NYT,* 27 Oct 1941, 17:3. "Victor Schertzinger," *Variety,* 29 Oct 1941 (age 52). AMD, p. 307. AS, p. 972 (b. Mahanoy City WI). BHD2, p. 235. IFN, p. 265. Katz, p. 1022 (b. 1880). "Ince Builds Music Studio," *MPW,* 25 Mar 1916, 1989. "Victor L. Schertzinger to Direct in Films," *MPW,* 3 Mar 1917, 1364. "Victor Schertzinger an Ince Director," *MPW,* 7 Dec 1918, 1083. "Director Loses Father," *MPW,* 7 Jun 1919, 1491 (Charles F. Schertzinger, d. 15 May 1919, LA CA). "Schertzinger's Mother Dies," *MPW,* 6 Mar 1920, 1637 (d. Feb 1920). "Engage Schertzinger to Direct Special," *MPW,* 17 Mar 1923, 363. "To Direct Coogan's First," *MPW,* 5 May 1923, 79. "Mary Pickford's Choice," *MPW,* 15 Mar 1924, 193. "Schertzinger to Direct," *MPW,* 22 Mar 1924, 287. "Will Direct 'Bread,'" *MPW,* 29 Mar 1924, 360. "On the Set and Off," *MW,* 3 Jan 1925, 23:2 (Fred C. Beers sued Schertzinger for $250,000 for his alleged involvement with Mrs. Beers, which he denied. Mrs. Beers: "I am dearly in love with Mr. Schertzinger and I think he is a wonderful man."). "Fox Signs Schertzinger," *MPW,* 21 Mar 1925, 277. "Writes Musical Score," *MPW,* 25 Apr 1925, 812 (*Zander the Great,* with Marion Davies). "Schertzinger Has All-Russian Staff to Aid Him in 'Siberia,'" *MPW,* 30 Jan 1926, 438. "Rise of Victor Schertzinger as Director Covers Ten Years Unmarred by Failure," *MPW,* 1 Jan 1927, 47. "Schertzinger to Begin Work at Lasky Studios," *MPW,* 1 Oct 1927, 289.

Scheurich, Victor H. [cameraman] (b. 1889?–10 Oct 1962 [73], Los Angeles CA). "Victor Scheurich," *Variety,* 24 Oct 1962. BHD2, p. 235.

Schiavone, Saul [scenic artist]. No data found. AMD, p. 307. "Saul SChiavone," *MPW,* 2 Oct 1915, 63.

Schiffrin, Simon [director/producer] (b. Bakou, Azerbaidjan, 29 Sep 1894–22 Jul 1985 [90], Paris, France). AS, p. 972.

Schildkraut, Joseph (son of **Rudolph Schildkraut**) [actor] (b. Vienna, Austria, 22 Mar 1895 [extrait de naissance no. 1690]–21 Jan 1964 [69], New York NY [Death Certificate Index No. 1690]; heart attack). m. (1) **Elise Bartlett** (d. 1944); (2) Mary McKay; (3) Leonara Rogers. *My Father and I* (1959). (AA, 1937.) "Joseph Schildkraut, Actor, Dies; Played Father of Anne Frank; Praised for Stage and Film Portrayals—Won Oscar in '38 as Capt. Dreyfus," *NYT,* 22 Jan 1964, 37:1. "Joseph Schildkraut," *Variety,* 29 Jan 1964. AMD, p. 307. AS, p. 972. BHD1, p. 489. FSS, p. 256. IFN, p. 265. Katz, p. 1023. Truitt, p. 297. Faith Service, "The Genius of Desire; An Observation," *Classic,* Sep 1923, 35, 77–78. "DeMille Signs Schildkraut," *MPW,* 16 May 1925, 347. "Joseph Schildkraut," *MPW,* 12 Sep 1925, 182. "Joseph Schildkraut Wins New Contract," *MPW,* 15 Jan 1927, 195. Michael Grantside, "Chili Bouchier; Britain's 'It' Girl," *CI,* 276 (Jun 1998), p. 21 (starring with Chili Bouchier in *Carnival,* he "was determined to seduce her, but any chance he had of interesting Chili was lost when he caught his most tender member in a chest of drawers one morning and had to cry off shooting. The whole studio knew.").

Schildkraut, Rudolph (father of **Jospeh Schildkraut**) [stage/film actor] (b. Constantinople, Turkey, 27 Apr 1862–15 Jul 1930 [68], Los Angeles CA; heart attack). m. Erna Weinstein. (Ufa; Paramount.) "R. Schildkraut Dies from Heart Attack; Noted Stage and Screen Actor Succumbs at Son's Home in Hollywood; Had Played in 3 Languages; Performed Leading Roles in Berlin, on Yiddish Stage and in English Here and in Talkies," *NYT,* 16 Jul 1930, 23:3 (b. Wallachia; age 65). "Rudolph Schildkraut," *Variety,* 16 Jul 1930 (age 65). AMD, p. 307. AS, p. 972. BHD1, p. 489 (b. Istanbul). IFN, p. 265. Truitt, p. 297. "Schildkraut Says American Films Popular in Vienna," *MPW,* 16 Oct 1920, 919. "Sign Rudolph Schildkraut to Appear Exclusively in DeMille Films," *MPW,* 6 Mar 1926, 29. "Rudolph Schildkraut," *MPW,* 15 May 1926, 235. "Rudolph Schildkraut," *MPW,* 18 Sep 1926, 157. "Slang Comes Easy," *MPW,* 11 Dec 1926, 421.

Schiller, Fanny [actress] (b. Mexico City, Mexico, 3 Aug 1897). AS, p. 973.

Schiller, Paul [director] (b. Prague, Czechoslovakia, 1885). AS, p. 973.

Schipa, Carlo [actor/director/scenarist] (b. Italy, 11 Oct 1899–25 Aug 1988 [88], Los Angeles CA). BHD1, p. 489; BHD2, p. 235.

Schipa, Tito [actor] (*né* Raffaele Attilio Amedeo Schipa, b. Lecchia, Italy, 2 Jan 1887–16 Dec 1965 [78], New York NY). AS, p. 973.

Schipper, Anna [actress] (b. 1888–16 Oct 1978 [90?], Woodland Hills CA). AS, p. 973.

Schlank, Morris R. [producer] (b. Omaha NB, 1876?–29 Jun 1932 [56], Murietta Hot Springs CA). m. Bess. (Premier Pictures Corp.) "Morris Schlank," *Variety,* 5 Jul 1932 (produced 1-reelers with Charley Chase in 1920). AS, p. 973. BHD2, p. 235 (b. 1885).

Schlettow, Hans Adelbert [actor] (*né* Hans Adelbert Droescher von Schlettow, b. Frankfurt, Germany, 11 Jun 1888–30 Apr 1945 [56], Berlin, Germany). AS, p. 973. BHD1, p. 489.

Schley, Edna R. [scenarist]. No data found. AMD, p. 307. "Edna R. Schley Joins Universal Staff," *MPW,* 30 Dec 1916, 1936.

Schliepper, Carlos [director] (b. Buenos Aires, Argentina, 23 Sep 1902–11 Apr 1957 [54], Buenos Aires, Argentina). AS, p. 973.

Schmid, Alfred [cinematographer] (b. Germany, 1889–21 Jun 1982 [93?], Culver City CA). AS, p. 973. BHD2, p. 235.

Schmid, August [director] (b. Diessenhofen, Switzerland, 1877–19 Jan 1955 [77?], Zurich, Switzerland). AS, p. 973.

Schmid, Paul [director] (b. Berne, Switzerland, 11 Apr 1886–13 Apr 1970 [84], Berne, Switzerland). AS, p. 973.

Schmid, Pete [publicist]. No data found. AMD, p. 308. "Pete Schmidt," *MPW,* 20 Jul 1918, 331.

Schmidt, Albert [cameraman]. No data found. AMD, p. 308. "Police Interfering with Cameramen," *MPW,* 13 Nov 1915, 1279.

Schmidt, Erich [director] (b. Maxen, Germany, 13 Aug 1892–6 Sep 1971 [79]). AS, p. 974.

Schmidt, Walter [producer] (b. Stuttgart, Germany, 5 Sep 1896). AS, p. 974.

Schmidt-Gentner, Willy Gerhardt [composer/director] (b. Neustadt, Germany, 6 Apr 1884–12 Feb 1964 [79], Vienna, Austria). AS, p. 974 (b. 1894). BHD2, p. 235.

Schmidt-Habler, Walter [director/scenarist] (b. 1 Jul 1864–4 Dec 1923 [59]). BHD2, p. 235.

Schmitt, Joseph [actor] (b. 1871?–25 Mar 1935 [64], Los Angeles CA). "Joseph Schmitt," *Variety,* 3 Apr 1935 ("He had been in pictures since 1912."). AS, p. 974. BHD1, p. 489. IFN, p. 265. Truitt, p. 298.

Schmitz, Ludwig Joseph [actor] (b. Cologne, Germany, 28 Jan 1884–28 Jun 1954 [70], Munich, Germany). AS, p. 974.

Schmitz, Sybille Mariz Christina [actress] (b. Düren, Germany, 2 Dec 1909–13 Apr 1955 [45], Munich, Germany; suicide with an overdose of barbituates). AS, p. 974. BHD1, p. 489.

Schmole, Otto Siegfried [actor] (b. Frankfurt, Germany, 23 Jan 1890–12 Apr 1968 [78], Mondsee, Austria). AS, p. 974.

Schnall, Ida [swimmer/actress] (d. 14 Feb 1973, Los Angeles CA). AS, p. 974. BHD, p. 296. "Ida Schnall; One of the Champion Swimmers and Divers of the Films," *MPC,* Sep 1916, 21 (photos).

Schnedler-Sorenson, Edward [director] (b. Denmark, 22 Sep 1886–30 Sep 1947 [61], Denmark). AS, p. 974.

Schneevoigt, George [actor/director] (b. Copenhagen, Denmark, 23 Dec 1893–6 Feb 1961 [67], Copenhagen, Denmark). AS, p. 974. BHD2, p. 236.

Schneider, James [actor: Keystone cop/director] (b. NY, 15 Dec 1881–14 Feb 1967 [85], Los Angeles CA). (Sennett.) "James Schneider," *Variety,* 22 Feb 1967. AS, p. 974. BHD, p. 296; BHD2, p. 236. IFN, p. 265. Truitt, p. 298.

Schneider, Max [actor] (b. Eisleven, Germany, 20 Jul 1875–5 May 1967 [91], Halle, Germany).

Schneider-Edenkoben, Richard [director/scenarist] (b. Germany, 1899). AS, p. 974.

Schneiderman, George [cinematographer] (b. NY, 20 Sep 1894–19 Nov 1964 [70], Van Nuys CA). AS, p. 975 (d. 22 Jan 1951, Beverly Hills CA). BHD2, p. 236. FDY, p. 467. IFN, p. 265.

Schnell, Georg Heinrich [actor] (b. China, 11 Apr 1878–31 Mar 1951 [72], Berlin, Germany). BHD1, p. 490.

Schnitzer, Joseph I. [executive] (b. Pittsburgh PA, 14 Mar 1887–20 Jul 1944 [57], Beverly Hills CA). BHD2, p. 236.

Schoedsack, Ernest B[eaumont] [cinematographer/director/producer] (b. Council Bluffs IA, 8 Jun 1893–23 Dec 1979 [86], CA). AS, p. 975. BHD2, p. 236. FDY, p. 467. *World Film Encyclopedia,* p. 204 (b. 1889).

Schoenbaum, Charles Edgar [actor] (b. Los Angeles CA, 28 Apr 1893–22 Jan 1951 [57], Beverly Hills CA). (FP-L, 1916; MGM.) "Charles Schoenbaum," *Variety,* 31 Jan 1951. AS, p. 975. BHD2, p. 236. FDY, p. 467.

Schoenberg, Arnold [composer] (*né* Arnold Franz Schonberg, b. Vienna, Austria, 13 Sep 1874–13 Jul 1951 [76], Los Angeles CA). AS, p. 975.

Schoenborn, Lili Anna Maria [actress] (b. Berlin, Germany, 31 Mar 1898–4 May 1987 [89], Berlin, Germany). AS, p. 975.

Schoenfelder, Erich Eduard Josef [actor/director] (b. Frankfurt, Germany, 23 Apr 1885–14 May 1933 [48], Berlin, Germany). AS, p. 975 (also listed under Schonfelder). BHD2, p. 236.

Schoenhals, Albrecht Moritz Josef Karl [actor] (b. Mannheim, Germany, 7 Mar 1888–4 Dec 1978 [90], Baden-Baden, Germany). AS, p. 975.

Schofield, Johnnie [actor] (b. London, England, 10 Mar 1889–9 Sep 1961 [72], London, England). AS, p. 975.

Schofield, Paul [scenarist]. No data found. AMD, p. 308. FDY, p. 437. "Schofield Signed by Paramount," *MPW,* 18 Apr 1925, 714. Tom Waller, "Paul Schofield," *MPW,* 16 Jul 1927, 152–53.

Scholander, Sven [actor] (b. Stockholm, Sweden, 21 Apr 1860–14 Dec 1936 [76], Sweden). BHD1, p. 616.

Scholl, Olga Lunck [writer]. No data found. "Olga Scholl Returns," *MPW,* 22 Jan 1921, 453.

Scholz, Robert [actor] (b. 1886–10 Oct 1927 [41?], Berlin, Germany). BHD, p. 296.

Schomburgk, Hans Hermann [director/scenarist/historian] (b. Hamburg, Germany, 28 Oct 1880–26 Jul 1967 [86], Berlin, Germany). AS, p. 975.

Schomer, Abraham S. [playwright/director] (b. Minsk, Russia, 1876?–16 Aug 1946 [70], Los Angeles CA). "Abraham S. Schomer, Led Jewish Congress," *NYT,* 17 Aug 1946, 13.7. "Abraham S. Schomer," *Variety,* 21 Aug 1946. AMD, p. 308. AS, p. 975. BHD2, p. 236. "Abraham S. Schomer, Playwright and Director, Completes 'The Scarlet Flame' for S.-Ross Concer[n]," *MPW,* 13 Sep 1919, 1641.

Schon, Margarethe [actress] (b. 7 Apr 1895–26 Dec 1985 [90]). BHD1, p. 616.

Schonberg, Alexander [actor] (b. 1886–1 Oct 1945 [59?], Los Angeles CA). AS, p. 975.

Schonberg, Ib [actor] (b. Copenhagen, Denmark, 23 Oct 1902–24 Sep 1955 [52], Copenhagen, Denmark). AS, p. 976.

Schopp, Herman [actor/cinematographer] (b. 1899?–8 Aug 1954 [55]). BHD2, p. 236 (d. 1958). FDY, p. 469 (Shoop). IFN, p. 265.

Schorcht, Kurt [executive] (b. Erfurt, Germany, 26 Feb 1890–18 Sep 1957 [67], Munich, Germany; heart attack). AS, p. 976. BHD2, p. 236.

Schott, Frederic J. [scenic designer] (b. 1864–4 Nov 1936 [72?], Los Angeles CA). BHD2, p. 236.

Schram, Violet [actress] (b. San Antonio TX, 1 Dec 1898–20 Mar 1987 [88], Pasadena CA). BHD1, p. 490. George Katchmer, "Remembering the Great Silents," *CI,* 233 (Nov 1994), 40.

Schramm, Karla [actress] (b. Los Angeles CA, 1 Feb 1891–17 Jan 1980 [88], Los Angeles CA). (Griffith; retired in 1924; returned.) (Christie.) "Karla Schramm," *Variety,* 27 Feb 1980. AS, p. 976. BHD, p. 296. IFN, p. 266.

Schreck, Max[imilian] [actor] (b. Berlin, Germany, 6 Sep 1879–19 Feb 1936 [56], Munich, Germany). AS, p. 976 (also listed under Max Screck). BHD1, p. 490. IFN, p. 266.

Schreiber, Elsa [actress] (b. Vienna, Austria, 1900–9 Jan 1982 [81?], Los Angeles CA; heart attack). AS, p. 976.

Schrock, Raymond L. [scenarist/general manager] (b. Goshen IN, 1892?–12 Dec 1950 [58], Los Angeles CA; heart attack). "Raymond L. Schrock," *Variety,* 20 Dec 1950. AMD, p. 308. AS, p. 976. BHD2, p. 236. FDY, p. 437. IFN, p. 266. "Schrock Joins Universal Staff," *MPW,* 3 Apr 1915, 52. "Wray Resigns as Head of Universal City; Schrock Succeeds," *MPW,* 21 Mar 1925, 242. "Schrock to Remain at 'U' City," *MPW,* 21 Nov 1925, 218. "Raymond L. Schrock, The Man Who Makes Hebrew Comedies," *MPW,* 1 Jan 1927, 50. "Schrock Quits Warner Post to Join Paramount," *MPW,* 5 Feb 1927, 421. "M-G-M Signs Schrock," *MPW,* 5 Mar 1927, 12. "Schrock Contract Awaits Signing," *MPW,* 24 Dec 1927, 21.

Schroder, Arthur [actor] (b. 20 Nov 1892–4 Feb 1986 [93], Berlin, Germany). BHD1, p. 490.

Schroeder, Doris [scenarist]. No data found. FDY, p. 437.

Schroff, William [actor/stuntman] (b. Stuttgart, Germany, 25 Feb 1889–5 Dec 1964 [75], Los Angeles CA). AS, p. 976.

Schroth, Heinrich August Franz [actor] (b. Pirmasens, Germany, 21 Mar 1871–13 Jan 1945 [73], Berlin, Germany). AS, p. 976.

Schubert, Georg Hermann [director] (b. Berlin, Germany, 14 Jun 1879). AS, p. 977.

Schuenzel, Reinhold (father of actress Marianne Stewart) [stage/film actor/director] (b. Hamburg, Germany, 7 Nov 1886–11 Sep 1954 [67], Munich, Germany; heart attack). (Stage, Berlin, 1915.) "R. Schuenzel, 65, Actor, Director; Movie and Stage Artist Who Made Hollywood Films Dies—Won West German Prize," *NYT,* 14 Sep 1954, 27:3 (he was "forced to suspend his acting career twice under orders from the regimes headed by Kaiser Wilhelm II and Adolf Hitler, whom he once described as 'persons of recognized authority and the worst possible dramatic taste.'" U.S. citizen, 1943.). "Reinhold Schuenzel," *Variety,* 196, 15 Sep 1954, 63:1 (age 65). BHD2, p. 237. IFN, p. 266.

Schuessler, Fred [casting director]. No data found. AMD, p. 308. "Schuessler Succeeds Datig," *MPW,* 3 Oct 1925, 415. "Schuessler Casting," *MPW,* 25 Sep 1926, 4. Fred Schuessler, "Present-Day Casting Methods," *MPW,* 26 Mar 1927, 409. "Fred Schuessler," *MPW,* 6 Aug 1927, 383.

Schüfftan, Eugen [cinematographer] (aka Eugene Shuftan, b. Breslau, Germany, 21 Jul 1893–6 Sep 1977 [84], New York NY). AS, p. 977 (b. Breslau, Poland). BHD2, p. 237. JS, p. 415.

Schuhmacher, Ewald Mathias [director] (b. Dusseldorf, Germany, 22 Jul 1893). AS, p. 977.

Schuitema, Paul [director] (*né* Geert Paul H. Schuitema, b. Groningen, Holland, 27 Feb 1897–25 Oct 1973 [76], Wassenaar, Holland). AS, p. 977.

Schukin, Boris [actor] (b. Russia, 1894–7 Oct 1939 [45?], Moscow, Russia). AS, p. 977.

Schulberg, B[enjamin] **P**[ercival] [publicist/scenarist/producer] (b. Bridgeport CT, 19 Jan 1892–25 Feb 1957 [65], Key Biscayne FL; heart attack in his sleep). m. (1) Adeline Jaffe, 14 Jun 1913; (2) Helen M. Keebler. (Rex; FP-L; Universal; Paramount.) "B.P. Schulberg, 65, ex-Film Producer; Executive of Paramount Who Discovered Many Stars Dies—Father of Novelist," *NYT,* 27 Feb 1957, 27:3. "B.P. Schulberg Dies in His Sleep at 65; Headed Par Prod," *Variety,* 27 Feb 1957. AMD, p. 308. AS, p. 977. BHD2, p. 237. IFN, p. 267. Katz, p. 1026. "With the Famous Players; B.P. Schulberg," *MPW,* 18 Jan 1913, 257 (script editor for Rex and Imp). "Schulberg—Jaffe," *MPW,* 21 Jun 1913, 1259. F.J. Beecroft, "Publicity Men I Have Met...," *NYDM,* 14 Jan 1914, 48 (*see* Beecroft, Chester for full citation). "Schulberg Is Paramount's General Manager," *MPW,* 24 Feb 1917, 1196. "Abrams and Schulberg on Tour," *MPW,* 20 Oct 1917, 393. "Famous Players Creates Administrative Bureau," *MPW,* 23 Feb 1918, 1073. "Seymour Schulberg Has a Sister," *MPW,* 16 Mar 1918, 1483 (daughter, Sonia Gladys, b. 20 Feb 1918). "Two Zukor Men Start New Company," *MPW,* 28 Dec 1918, 1492 (*see MPW,* 25 Sep 1920). "Ben Schulbrg Leaves United Artists," *MPW,* 12 Apr 1919, 216. "Ben Schulberg Still Claims London Will Be Film 'Hub,'" *MPW,* 7 Jun 1919, 1464. "Ben Schulberg Sues Hiram Abrams; Alleging Partnership Agreement Broken," *MPW,* 25 Sep 1920, 510 (*see MPW,* 28 Dec 1918). "Schulberg to Produce at the Mayer Studios," *MPW,* 15 Apr 1922, 718. "Schulberg Says Need of Screen Is Proper Handling of Story," *MPW,* 26 Aug 1922, 664. "Ben P. Schulberg Successfully Launches Cooperative Plan," *MPW,* 21 Oct 1922, 686. Ben P. Schulberg, "Pictures That Showmen Want—And Why," *MPW,* 27 Jan 1923, 364–65. "Schulberg Here to Discuss Plans for Big Program for Preferred," *MPW,* 31 Mar 1923, 508. "Schulberg Offers $10,000 a Word for Picture Titles," *MPW,* 7 Apr 1923, 612. "Movie Magnate [Schulberg] Was Once Cartoonist's [R.L. 'Rube' Goldberg] Office Boy," *MW,* 5 May 1923, 8, 29. "Schulberg Acquires Selig Studios," *MPW,* 8 Sep 1923, 130. "Watch for New Talent—Schulberg," *MPW,* 22 Sep 1923, 362. "Schulberg Says Preferred Tests Each Story Before Purchasing," *MPW,* 27 Oct 1923, 756. "Lull in Production Will Mean Better Casts, Says Schulberg," *MPW,* 1 Dec 1923, 499. "Schulberg Wants Some Good Juvenile Actors," *MPW,* 22 Dec 1923, 719. "Schulberg Argues Against Eastern Production Center," *MPW,* 5 Jan 1924, 33. "Schulberg Studio Busy," *MPW,* 23 Feb 1924, 630. "Schulberg and Bachmann Discuss 1925 Productions," *MPW,* 27 Dec 1924, 867. "'Give New Players a Chance,' Schulberg Urges Producers," *MPW,* 4 Apr 1925, 487. "Literary Leaders Contribute Stories for Ben P. Schulberg," *MPW,* 2 May 1925, 73. "Schulberg Pictures Plan to Discourage Censorship," *MPW,* 4 Jul 1925, 83. "Schulberg Files Bankruptcy Paper," *MPW,* 31 Oct 1925, 696. "Ben P. Schulberg Joins Paramount; Will Produce in the Lasky Studio," *MPW,* 7 Nov 1925, 32. "Schulberg Must Remain at Paramount Studios," *MPW,* 16 Jul 1927, 155, 157.

Schultz, Abe [scenarist/cinematographer]. No data found. FDY, pp. 437, 469.

Schultz, Fritz [actor/director] (b. Karlsbad, Germany, 25 Apr 1896–9 May 1972 [76], Zurich, Switzerland). AS, p. 977. BHD2, p. 237.

Schultz, Harleigh [publicist] (b. 1883–22 Oct 1958 [75?], Los Angeles CA). BHD2, p. 237.

Schultz, Harry [actor] (*né* Alexander Heinberg, b. Germany, 11 Mar 1883–4 Jul 1935 [52], Los Angeles CA). AS, p. 977 (d. 5 Jul). BHD1, p. 490. IFN, p. 266. Truitt, p. 298.

Schultz, Joseph [actor] (b. 1866–1 Oct 1916 [50?], Chicago IL). BHD, p. 296.

Schulze, John (Jack) D[ucasse] [art director] (b. 1876?–18 Jun 1943 [67], Los Angeles CA; heart ailment). (Began at the turn of the century; Edward Small Productions, Inc.) "John Ducasse Schulze," *NYT,* 19 Jun 1943, 13:1 (worked on *The Last of the Mohicans, Man in the Iron Mask,* and *Cheers for Miss Bishop*). AMD, p. 308. BHD2, p. 237 (d. 17 Jun). "Mayer Signs Art Director, *MPW,* 11 Dec 1920, 724.

Schumaker, Ida C. [actress] (d. 25 Aug 1969, Los Angeles Co. CA). BHD1, p. 490.

Schumann-Heink, Ernestine (mother of **Ferdinand Schumann-Heink**) [singer/actress] (*née* Ernestine Roessler, b. Lieben, near Prague, Czechoslovakia, 15 Jun 1861–17 Nov 1936 [75], Los Angeles CA; leukemia). m. (1) Ernest Heink; (2) Paul Schumann (d. 1904); (3) George Rapp, Jr., May 1904–14. (Film debut: *Here's to Romance.*) "Schumann-Heink, Great Singer, Dead; Native of Bohemia, She Won World-Wide Acclaim in Opera and Concerts; Sang at Baireuth in 1896; Joined Metropolitan in 1898—in War Work for U.S.—Lately in Films," *NYT,* 18 Nov 1936, 1:2, 22:3 (stage fright on MGM movie set). AS, p. 977. BHD1, p. 491. IFN, p. 266. Truitt, p. 298.

Schumann-Heink, Ferdinand (son of **Ernestine Schumann-Heink**) [actor/scenarist] (b. Hamburg, Germany, 9 Aug 1893–15 Sep 1958 [65], Los Angeles CA; heart attack). "Schumann-Heink's Son Dies," *NYT,* 17 Sep 1958, 323:6. AMD, p. 308. AS, p. 977. BHD1, p. 491; BHD2, p. 237. IFN, p. 266. Truitt, p. 298. "Ferdinand Schumann-Heink," *MPW,* 27 Aug 1927, 589.

Schumann-Heink, Henry [actor] (b. Hamburg, Germany, 24 Jun 1886–28 Mar 1951 [64], Los Angeles CA). BHD, p. 296.

Schumm, Hans [actor] (b. Stuttgart, Germany, 2 Apr 1896–2 Feb 1990 [93], Los Angeles CA). AS, p. 977.

Schumm, Harry W. [actor] (b. Chicago IL, 27 Sep 1877–4 Apr 1953 [75], Los Angeles CA). AS, p. 977. BHD, p. 296. IFN, p. 266. Truitt, p. 298.

Schünzel, Reinhold [actor/director] (b. Hamburg, Germany, 7 Nov 1886–11 Sep 1954 [67], Munich, Germany). Vittorio Martinelli, "Kino-Lieblinge," *Griffithiana,* 38/39 (Oct 1990), 68. AS, p. 978 (b. 1888). BHD1, p. 491. IFN, p. 266. Truitt, p. 298. Waldman, p. 258 (b. 1888).

Schur, Willi [actor] (b. Breslau, Poland, 22 Aug 1888–1 Nov 1940 [52], Berlin, Germany). AS, p. 978.

Schurr, William F. [cameraman] (b. NY, 15 Aug 1902–5 Dec 1962 [60], Los Angeles CA). (WB.) BHD2, p. 237. FDY, p. 469.

Schuster, Harold D. [actor/cameraman/film editor/director] (b. Cherokee IA, 1 Aug 1902–19 Jul 1986 [83], Westlake Village CA). (Fox.) "Harold Schuster," *Variety,* 30 Jul 1986. AS, p. 978. BHD, p. 296; bHD2, p. 237.

Schutz, Maurice [actor] (*né* Paul Maurice Schutzenberger, b. Paris, France, 4 Aug 1866–22 Mar 1955 [88], Clichy-la-Garenne, France). AS, p. 978.

Schuyler, Philip L[ansing] [actor] (b. 1877?–6 Jan 1962 [84], Brockton MA). m. Gertrude Alger. "Philip L. Schuyler, Army Colonel, 84," *NYT,* 7 Jan 1962, 89:1. AS, p. 978.

Schwab, Laurence [director/producer/scenarist] (b. Boston MA, 1893–29 May 1951 [58?], Southampton NY). AS, p. 978.

Schwab, Rose Marie [actress] (b. Los Angeles CA, 24 Jan 1844–14 Mar 1922 [78], Los Angeles CA). AS, p. 978.

Schwab, Sam [actor] (b. Los Angeles CA, 17 May 1847–4 Jul 1903 [56], Susalito CA). AS, p. 978.

Schwaiger, Franz [actor] (b. Germany, 1880–2 Dec 1926 [46?]). BHD, p. 296.

Schwannecke, Ellen [actress] (b. Berlin, Germany, 11 Aug 1906–16 Jun 1972 [65], Zurich, Switzerland). AS, p. 978. BHD1, p. 491.

Schwartz, Albert Richman [actor] (b. New Orleans LA, 21 May 1885–20 Apr 1936 [50], Los Angeles CA). AS, p. 978.

Schwartz, Gare [film editor] (b. 1890–18 Mar 1961 [70?], Santa Monica CA). BHD2, p. 237.

Schwartz, Harold [assistant director] (b. 1896?–8 May 1951 [55], Los Angeles CA). (Paramount.) "Harold O. Schwartz," *Variety,* 16 May 1951. AS, p. 978.

Schwartz, Harold L. [director/scenarist] (b. Los Angeles CA, 1896–8 May 1951 [55?], Los Angeles CA). BHD2, p. 237.

Schwartz, Maurice [actor/director] (b. Russia, 18 Jun 1890–10 May 1960 [69], Jerusalem, Israel). BHD2, p. 237.

Schwartz, Maurice [stage/film actor] (b. Sedikov, Ukraine, Russia, 18 Jun 1890–10 May 1960 [69], Petah Tikva, near Tel Aviv, Israel; heart attack). m. Anne Bordofsky. "Maurice Schwartz, Actor, Dead; Founder of Yiddish Art Theatre; Genre's Leading Figure Was Noted for Broad Style—Set Up Company in Israel," *NYT,* 11 May 1960, 39:2. "Schwartz Funeral Today," *NYT,* 13 May 1960, 41:6. "Maurice Schwartz," *Variety,* 18 May 1960. AS, p. 978. BHD1, p. 491. IFN, p. 266. Katz, p. 1027. Truitt, p. 298.

Schwarz, Hanns [director/scenarist] (aka Harold Sheldon, b. Vienna, Austria, 19 Feb 1889–15 Nov 1945 [56], Los Angeles CA). m. **Lissy Arna** (d. 1964). AS, p. 978. BHD2, p. 237 (d. 20 Jul 1949). Waldman, p. 259.

Schwarzer, Johann [founder of Vienna's Saturn Films, producer of erotic films, 1906–1910] (b. Javornik, Silesia, 30 Aug 1880–10 Oct 1914 [34], an early causalty of WWI). m. Olga Jarosch-Stehlik, 14 Jun 1914. Michael Achenbach and Paolo Caneppele, "Born Under the Sign of Saturn: The Erotic Origins of Cinema in the Austro-Hungarian Empire," *Griffithiana,* 65 (Oct 1999), 127–139

("As he himself wrote, Schwarzer founded his company to cater to public wishes, supplying the greatest demand, which was for erotic movies. His movies bridged the gap between [reasonably chaste] products originating in France, and explicitly pornographic movies. In his Saturn films, the female models are completely naked, allowing Schwarzer to offer distributors and audiences a far more explicit and desirable product than French imports, though still, by his own definition, 'artistic.'").

Schwarzwald, Milton [producer] (b. 1891–2 Mar 1950 [58?], Los Angeles CA). AS, p. 978 (composer). BHD2, p. 237.

Schwed, Blanche [actress] (b. 1906–4 Jul 1983 [77?], New York NY). BHD, p. 297.

Schweid, Mark [actor] (b. 1891–2 Dec 1969 [78?], New York NY). BHD1, p. 491.

Schweikart, Hans [director] (b. Berlin, Germany, 1 Oct 1895–1 Dec 1975 [80], Munich, Germany). BHD2, p. 237.

Schwelkart, Hans [actor/director] (b. Berlin, Germany, 1 Oct 1895–1 Dec 1975 [80], Munich, Germany). AS, p. 978.

Schwenzen, Harald [actor/director] (b. Gluchsberg, Norway, 18 May 1895–1954 [59?], Norway). AS, p. 978.

Schwerin, Hermann [producer] (b. Berlin, Germany, 1902–2 Oct 1970 [68?], Bad Tolz, Germany; auto accident). m. **Grethe Weiser** (d. 1970). AS, p. 978–79.

Sciamengo, Carlo [director/executive]. No data found. AMD, p. 309. "Carlo Sciamengo," *MPW,* 1 Oct 1910, 745. "Head of Itala Film Company Sails," *MPW,* 31 Aug 1912, 868.

Scize, Pierre [scenarist/author/journalist] (*né* François Michel Piot, b. Pont-de-Cheruy, France, 17 Feb 1894 [extrait de naissance no. 10]–10 Dec 1956 [62], Melbourne, Australia). AS, p. 979.

Scofield, Eileen [actress]. No data found. m. Walter Miller. AMD, p. 309. "Miller Proud Papa," *MPW,* 6 Nov 1926, 3.

Scott, Betty [actress] (b. New York NY, 25 Jul 1846–5 May 1904 [57], Chicago IL). AS, p. 979.

Scott, Blanche Stuart [aviatrix/actress/scenarist] (b. Rochester NY?, 1892?–12 Jan 1976 [84], Rochester NY). (Champion.) "Blanche Stuart Scott, 84, Dies; Made First Solo Flight in 1910 [Sep 5th]; Feat Followed Cross-Country Drive—Later Toured as Daredevil Flier; Accidentally Took Flight," *NYT,* 12 Jan 1976. BHD, p. 297 (b. 1885; d. 1970). "Champion Aviation Pictures," *MPW,* 23 Dec 1911, 994.

Scott, Carrie [actress/vocalist] (b. 1870–18 Dec 1928 [58], New York NY). m. James P. Smith. "Carrie Scott," *Variety,* 19 Dec 1928. AS, p. 979. BHD, p. 297. IFN, p. 266.

Scott, Cyril [stage/film actor] (b. Bambridge, County Down, Ireland, 9 Feb 1866–16 Aug 1945 [79], Flushing, Queens NY). m. Louise Eissing. (Universal.) "Cyril Scott Dead; On Stage 53 Years; Actor in Companies of Minnie Maddern Fiske, Mansfield and Hopper Made Debut in 1883," *NYT,* 18 Aug 1945, 11:5. "Cyril Scott," *Variety,* 22 Aug 1945. AMD, p. 309. AS, p. 979. BHD, p. 297. IFN, p. 266. Truitt, p. 298. "Cyril Scott as Famous Player," *MPW,* 17 Jan 1914, 300. "Cyril Scott," *MPW,* 4 Dec 1915, 1808.

Scott, Edgar [film editor]. No data found. AMD, p. 309. "Edgar Scott, 'Decapitator,'" *MPW,* 5 Feb 1916, 791.

Scott, Ewing [director/producer/scenarist] (b. Omaha NB, 3 Sep 1897–5 Aug 1971 [74], San Diego CA). AS, p. 979 (b. LA CA). BHD2, p. 238.

Scott, Fred Leedon [actor] (b. Fresno CA, 14 Feb 1902–15 Dec 1991 [89], Palm Springs CA). (Sennett.) AS, p. 979 (d. LA CA). BHD1, p. 491 (b. LA CA; d. 16 Dec). Katz, p. 1029. "Fred Scott," *Classic Images,* Jan 1992.

Scott, Frederick T. [actor] (b. Staten Island NY, 1863?–22 Feb 1942 [78], South Beach, Staten Island NY [Death Certificate Index No. 410]). "Frederick T. Scott," *NYT,* 24 Feb 1942, 21:1. "Frederick T. Scott," *Variety,* 25 Feb 1942. AS, p. 979. BHD1, p. 491. IFN, p. 266. Truitt, p. 299.

Scott, George [cinematographer] (b. 1874–11 Jan 1929 [54?], Los Angeles CA). BHD2, p. 238.

Scott, Gertrude [actress] (b. Sevenoaks, Kent, England-d. 23 Dec 1951, England). AS, p. 980. BHD, p. 297.

Scott, Gregory [actor] (b. Sandy, England, 15 Dec 1879). (Broadwest Film Co.) BHD, p. 297. "His Dearest Possession; Screen Hero Tells the Story of the Tunic that was the Joy of His Army Life," *The Picture Show,* 12 Jul 1919, 3 (just returned from the war).

Scott, Harold [actor] (b. Kensington, England, 21 Apr 1891–15 Apr 1964 [72], London, England). AS, p. 980.

Scott, Homer [actor]. No data found. AMD, p. 309. "Scott Narrowly Escapes Death When Trapped in DIver's Bell," *MPW,* 10 Jul 1920, 238.

Scott, Howard [stage/film actor]. No data found. (Selig.) W.E. Wing, "Along the Pacific Coast," *NYDM,* 19 May 1915, 24:1 (in Selig's *The Isle of Content*).

Scott, Ivy [actress] (b. Sydney, Australia, 10 Feb 1885–3 Feb 1947 [61], New York NY). AS, p. 980.

Scott, Leroy [journalist/writer] (b. Fairmount IN, 11 May 1875–21 Jul 1929 [54], Merrill NY; drowned in Lake Chateaugay). m. Miriam Finn, 24 Jun 1904 (d. 1944). BHD2, p. 238. "Mrs. Miriam Scott Consultant on Parent and Child Relationship, Author's Widow," *NYT,* 7 Jan 1944, 17:5 (d. 6 Jan). *National Cyclopedia of American Biography,* Vol. 26, p. 243.

Scott, Lester F. [director] (b. 1883–16 Apr 1954 [71?], Mesa AZ; auto accident). AS, p. 980.

Scott, Lester F., Jr. [director] (b. Los Angeles CA, 14 Mar 1892–10 Sep 1958 [66], South Pasadena CA). (Fox; WB.) BHD2, p. 238.

Scott, Lewis James [director] (b. 1885–30 Jun 1952 [67?], Los Angeles CA). AS, p. 980. BHD2, p. 238.

Scott, Lois [actress] (d. Aug? 1924, Hollywood CA). m. Alfred A. Mulford, Mar 1924 (d. Jul? 1924; auto accident). "Lois Scott-Mulford Dies of Broken Heart," *Variety,* 3 Sep 1924. BHD, p. 297 (d. Sep 1924).

Scott, Mabel Julienne (sister of **William Scott**) [stage/film acrress] (b. Minneapolis MN, 2 Nov 1892–1 Oct 1976 [83], Los Angeles CA). (Film debut: *The Lash of Destiny,* 1916; Edgar Selwyn prods.; Abramson; International.) "Mabel Julienne Scott," *Variety,* 2 Feb 1977. AMD, p. 309. AS, p. 980. BHD1, p. 492. IFN, p. 266. MH, p. 136. MSBB, p. 1040. WWS, p. 218. "Mabel Julienne Scott," *MPW,* 21 Apr 1917, 427. "Mabel Julienne Scott," *MPW,* 13 Apr 1918, 261. "Mabel Scott Engaged for 'Ashes of Love,'" *MPW,* 20 Jul 1918, 415. George Katchmer, "Remembering the Great Silents," *CI,* 240 (Jun 1995), 47.

Scott, Markie [actor] (b. 1873?–4 Jul 1958 [85], Los Angeles CA). "Markie Scott," *Variety,* 9 Jul 1958 ("former silent film cowboy" with Hart and Mix). AS, p. 980. BHD, p. 297 (Markle Scott). IFN, p. 266. Truitt, p. 299.

Scott, Peggy [actress] (b. 1901–26 Aug 1926 [25?], London, England). BHD, p. 297. IFN, p. 267.

Scott, Randolph [actor] (*né* George Randolph Crane Scott, b. Orange County VA, 23 Jan 1898–2 Mar 1987 [89], Bel Air CA; heart attack in his sleep). AS, p. 980. BHD1, p. 492.

Scott, Robert C. [scenarist] (d. 4 Jul 1923, Los Angeles CA). BHD2, p. 238.

Scott, Virtus R. [journalist/director] (b. New York NY). No other data found. AMD, p. 309. "Scott Scouts for Belmore," *NYDM,* 27 Nov 1915, 35:2 (formerly with Biograph, Famous Players, NYMP Co., Equitable, and other companies, now assistant director for Lionel Belmore at Quality-Metro on Bushman-Bayne films. He was a former newspaperman.). "Scott to Direct for Metro," *MPW,* 27 Nov 1915, 1666.

Scott, Wallace "Wally" [actor] (b. Australia, 18 Sep 1905–8 May 1970 [64], Australia). AS, p. 981. IFN, p. 267.

Scott, Walter F. [actor/cinematographer/director] (b. Baltimore MD, 1879?–5 Mar 1940 [61], New York NY). "Walter F. Scott," *NYT,* 6 Mar 1940, 23:2. "Walter F. Scott," *Variety,* 13 Mar 1940. AS, p. 981. BHD1, p. 492. FDY, p. 469. IFN, p. 267 "Mrs. Walter F. Scott," *NYT,* 18 Jan 1953, 92:6 (b. 1874?–16 Jan 1953 [78], Taberg NY).

Scott, Walter K. [actor/cinematographer/producer] (d. 9 Apr 1958, Washington DC). AS, p. 981. BHD, p. 297; BHD2, p. 238.

Scott, William (brother of **Mabel Julienne Scott**) [actor] (aka Billy Scott). No data found. (Selig.) George Katchmer, "Remembering the Great Silents," *CI,* 212 (Feb 1993), 35. Ragan 2, p. 1518.

Scott-Gatty, Alexander [stage/film/radio actor] (b. Ecclesfield, Yorkshire, England, 3 Oct 1876–6 Nov 1937 [61], London, England). "Alexander Scott-Gatty," *Variety,* 128, 10 Nov 1937, 62:3 (close friend of Johnston Forbes-Robertson who died on the same day). AS, p. 981. BHD1, p. 492. IFN, p. 267.

Scotto, Giovana [actress] (*née* Giovanna Piana-Canova, b. Turin, 26 Aug 1897). JS, p. 418 (in Italian silents from 1921).

Scotto, Vincent [actor/composer] (b. Marseilles, France, 22 Apr 1874–15 Nov 1952 [78], Paris, France). AS, p. 981.

Scowcroft, Albert [executive]. No data found. AMD, p. 309. "Scowcroft Reaches New York," *MPW,* 24 Nov 1917, 1194.

Scull, George Francis [lawyer] (b. Camden NJ, 1874?–10 Dec 1942 [68], Montclair NJ). "George F. Scull, 68, Patent Attorney; Senior Partner of Firm Here, an Expert in His Field, Dies in Hospital in Montclair; Once Worked for Edison; Graduated from Rutgers as an Engineer—Got Law

Degree While in U.S. Office," *NYT*, 12 Dec 1942, 15:4. AMD, p. 309. "Facts Concerning the New Arrangement of the Principal Factors of the Motion Picture Manufacturing Interests in America," *MPW*, 26 Dec 1908, 519.

Scully, Frank (son of **Mary Alice Scully**) [scenarist] (b. 1892–23 Jun 1964 [72?], Palm Springs CA). BHD2, p. 238.

Scully, Mary Alice [mother of W.A. Scully, sales manager for Universal and John and **Frank Scully**) [scenarist] (d. 15 Mar 1940, Brookline MA). "Mrs. Mary Scully," *NYT*, 17 Mar 1940, 51:3. FDY, p. 437.

Scully, William J. [production and assistant director] (b. New York NY, 1889?–1 May 1949 [60], Los Angeles CA). m. Evelyn M. (Biograph, 1914; Hollywood, 1925; De Mille; Metro; TC-F; FP-L; Universal.) "William J. Scully, a Movie Official, 60," *NYT*, 3 May 1949, 25:4. "William J. Scully," *Variety*, 4 May 1949. AMD, p. 309. AS, p. 981. BHD2, p. 238 (b. Green Island NY). "Scully Made a Director," *MPW*, 17 Jul 1920, 354.

Seabury, Forrest [actor] (b. 1875?–15 Feb 1944 [68], Los Angeles Co. CA). AS, p. 981. BHD, p. 297. IFN, p. 267.

Seabury, Ynez, "The Biograph Baby" [actress] (b. OR, 26 Jun 1907–11 Apr 1973 [65), Sherman Oaks CA). m. V. Keith White. "Ynez Seabury," *Variety*, 25 Apr 1973. AS, p. 981. BHD1, p. 493. IFN, p. 267.

Seadler, Silas F. (Si) [art directorpublicist] (b. New York NY, 31 Aug 1897–19 Feb 1981 [83], East Stroudsburg PA). m. Dora A. Gelbin, 24 Nov 1920, NYC. AMD, p. 309. BHD2, p. 238. "Frank Shallebarger Succeeds Silas F. Seadler at Kane Offices," *MPW*, 3 Jul 1920, 111. "Seadler of Kane Pictures Weds Dora A. Gelbin," *MPW*, 15 Jan 1921, 317. "Silas F. Seadler," *MPW*, 26 Mar 1927, 311.

Seagram, Wilfrid [actor] (b. England, 1884–28 May 1938 [54], Medical Arts Center Hospital, New York NY; following abdominal operation). m. Rita Otway (son and daughter). (Stage debut, 1910.) "Wilfrid Seagram, Actor, Dies Here; Last Appeared with Ina Claire in 'Once Is Enough,' Which Closed Few Weeks Ago; Was Native of England; Toured with George Arliss in 'Disraeli'—Made Debut in 1910 in 'The Islander' [Appollo Theatre]," *NYT*, 29 May 1938, II, 6:6 (member of The Players). "Wilfred Seagram," *Variety*, 1 Jun 1938, 54:1. BHD, p. 297.

Sealy, Lewis A. [stage/film actor] (*né* William Armiger Sealy Lewis, b. Dublin, Ireland, 1850–19 Mar 1931 [80], New York NY). "Lewis Sealy," *Variety*, 25 Mar 1931, 69:2 (interred in Actors' Fund plot in Kensico cemetery). AS, p. 981 (b. London, England). BHD, p. 297. IFN, p. 267. SD, p. 1119. WWVC, p. 128. "Lewis Sealy, English Pioneer Picture-Maker," *MPW*, 2 Sep 1916, 1547 ("One of the first three producers of motion pictures in England...').

Sealey, Sybil [actress]. No data found. (MGM.) m. **Jules Furthman**, ca. Jun 1920 (d. 1966). AMD, p. 309. A.H. Giebler, "Los Angeles News Letter; Furthman—Sealey," *MPW*, 26 Jun 1920, 1753.

Seaman, Marjorie [actress] (b. PA, 21 Jun 1900–9 Mar 1923 [22], Los Angeles CA). BHD, p. 297. IFN, p. 267.

Searl, Veta [actress]. No data found. AMD, p. 309. "Veta Searl," *MPW*, 9 Sep 1916, 1714.

Searle, Josef [director] (b. Germany, 7 Mar 1879). AS, p. 981.

Searle, Kamuela C. [actor] (*né* Samuel Cooper Searle, b. HI, 29 Aug 1890–14 Feb 1924 [33], Los Angeles CA; from injuries during a shooting). AS, p. 981. BHD, p. 297. IFN, p. 267.

Searle, Leon A. [newspaper cartoonist/animator with International Film Service] (b. Kansas City MO, 1881?–27 Jan 1919 [37], Flushing, LI NY; acute indigestion). m. Victoria F. (International Film Service, 1916.) "Obituary Notes," *NYT*, 29 Jan 1919, 13:4 ("Leon A. Searl, a cartoonist and contributor of animated pictures for the moving pictures, died at his home in flushing, L.I., on Monday at the age of 37 years..."; d. 27 Jan). "Leon A. Searl," *Variety*, 31 Jan 1919, p. 54. BHD2, p. 238. Peter Hastings Falk, ed., *Who Was Who in American Art*, 1985, p. 556.

Searles, Cora B. [actress] (b. 1859–4 Mar 1935 [75?], Los Angeles CA). AS, p. 981 (b. 1861). BHD, p. 297. IFN, p. 267 (age 73).

Sears, Allan D. [actor] (*né* Alfred Sears, b. San Antonio TX, 9 Mar 1887–18 Aug 1942 [55], Los Angeles CA). "Allan D. Sears," *NYT*, 21 Aug 1942, 19:2 ("leading man in the early days of moving pictures and later a character actor"). "Allan Sears," *Variety*, 26 Aug 1942. AMD, p. 309. AS, p. 981. BHD1, p. 493. IFN, p. 267. Truitt, p. 299. "Allan Sears in 'Blue Blood,'" *MPW*, 6 Oct 1917, 94. George Katchmer, "Rembering the Great Silents," *CI*, 252 (Jun 1996), 42; *CI*, 253 (Jul 1996), 49–50.

Sears, Mrs. Blanche [actress] (b. Waterford PA, 29 Aug 1870–7 Aug 1939 [68], Los Angeles CA). AS, p. 982.

Sears, Grad [executive] (b. 1897–21 Nov 1956 [69?], New York NY). AS, p. 982 ("fut président de United Artists").

Sears, Richard "Dick" [cameraman]. No data found. AMD, p. 309. "Police Interferring with Cameramen," *MPW*, 13 Nov 1915, 1279. "Richard Sears, Vet News Man, Goes to Pathé," *MPW*, 23 Apr 1927, 735.

Sears, Zelda [stage/film actress/playwright/scenarist] (*née* Zelda Lewis Paldi, b. near Brockway MI, 21 Jan 1873–19 Feb 1935 [62], Los Angeles CA). m. (1) Herbert E. Sears; (2) Louis C. Wiswell (widower). (De Mille; Metro.) "Zelda Sears Dies; Writer, Actress; Author of Several Shows and Scenarios Once Newspaper Woman in Chicago; Raised Chickens 10 Years; First Job Was in Department Store at $3 a Week—Stage Career Inspired by Bernhardt," *NYT*, 20 Feb 1935, 19:1. "Zelda Sears," *Variety*, 27 Feb 1935. AMD, p. 309. AS, p. 982. BHD1, p. 493 (b. 1874). FDY, p. 437. IFN, p. 267. Truitt, p. 299. "To Collaborate on 'Corporal Kate,'" *MPW*, 5 Jun 1926, 462.

Seastrom, Dorothy [actress] (b. Dallas TX, 16 Mar 1903–31 Jan 1930 [26], Dallas TX). m. Francis Corby. (1st National.) AS, p. 982 (d. 31 Jul). BHD1, p. 616. IFN, p. 267. Verne Kibbe, "The Girl Who Smiles; Dorothy Seastrom Was on the Threshold of Success; Today She Is Fighting for Life [from tuberculosis] in the Hills Above Hollywood," *MPC*, Feb 1926, 33, 72.

Seastrom, Victor (son of actress Elisasbeth Hartmann; nephew of Swedish actor Viktor Hartman) [stage/film director/actor] (*né* Viktor David Sjöström, b. Silbodal, Varmland, Sweden, 20 Sep 1879–3 Jan 1960 [80], Stockholm, Sweden). m. (1) Sascha Stjagoff, 1900; (2) **Lily Beck**—div. 1916 (d. 1939); (3) actress **Edith Erastoff** (1887–1945). Hans Pensel, *Seastrom and Stiller in Hollywood* (NY: Vantage Press, 1969); Bengt Forslund, *Victor Sjöström; His Life and His Work* (NY: Zoetrope, 1988.) *Victor Sjostrom* [video] (Sweden, 1981, 65 mins., director: Gosta Werner). (Hired at Svenska Biograf Studio [became Svensk Filmindustri in 1919] on 1 Jun 1912; first film as actor, *Vampyren,* 1912; first as director, *Tradgardsmastern,* 1912.) "Victor Seastrom of Swedish Films; Actor, 80, Last Seen Here in 'Wild Strawberries,' Is Dead—Also Was Director," *NYT*, 4 Jan 1960, 29:3. "Victor Seastrom," *Variety*, 13 Jan 1960. AMD, p. 309. AS, p. 1008 (Victor Sjostrom, b. 21 Sep). BHD1, p. 493; BHD2, p. 238. FDY, p. 437. IFN, p. 267. Katz, pp. 1063–64. Truitt, p. 299. Waldman, p. 269. "Swedish Actor-Director Adopts 'Proxy Playing,'" *MPW*, 17 Jan 1920, 428. "Prominent Swedish Director to Produce Goldwyn Specials," *MPW*, 10 Feb 1923, 544. "Seastrom Begins on His FIrst Here," *MPW*, 23 Jun 1923, 680. Jim Tully, "The Greatest Director in the World," *Classic*, Apr 1924, 17–18, 85. "To Direct Lillian Gish," *MPW*, 26 Dec 1925, 758. Charles Paton, "What Sense Censorship?; Public Opinion's Moral Code Operates Everywhere—Even in Sweden According to Seastrom," *MPC*, Nov 1926, 58, 72. "Seastrom Will Again Direct for Lillian Gish," *MPW*, 18 Dec 1926, 506. Robert Herring, "Film Imagery: Seastrom," *Close Up* (Jan 1929), 14–27. Charles L. Turner, "Victor Seastrom," *FIR*, Part I (May 1960), 273; Part II (Jun-Jul 1960). Raymond Bellour and Jean-Jacques Brochier, "Victor Seastrom," *Dictionnaire du cinema* (Paris: Editions Universitaires, 1966), p. 631.

Seaton, Frederick R. [actor] (d. 1914). AMD, p. 309. "Obituary," *MPW*, 29 Aug 1914, 1248.

Seaton, Scott [actor] (*né* Horace Scott Seaton, b. Sacramento CA, 11 Mar 1871–3 Jun 1968 [97], Los Angeles CA). (Universal.) "Scott Seaton," *Variety*, 19 Jun 1968 (began 1926). AS, p. 982. BHD1, p. 493. IFN, p. 267. Truitt, p. 299 (b. 1878).

Seaton, Walter [director] (b. England, 1872–12 Aug 1952 [80?], Hornsea, England). AS, p. 982. BHD2, p. 238.

Seay, Charles M. [stage/film actor/scenarist/director/producer] (b. Atlanta GA). (Edison, 1909; World.) AMD, p. 309. "What the DIrector Is Up Against," *MPW*, 19 Apr 1913, 266. "Edison Touches Popular Chord," *MPW*, 3 Jan 1914, 28–29. "Seay Writes About Pictures," *MPW*, 21 Mar 1914, 1531. "Briefs of Biography," *NYDM*, 6 May 1914, 27:3. "Charles M. Seay," *MPW*, 14 Nov 1914, 905. "Seay's Unique Record," *NYDM*, 14 Apr 1915, 34:1 (made the shortest and longest [*Fantasma*] films ever made at Edison.) "Charles Seay Joins Equitable," *MPW*, 7 Aug 1915, 1007. "Briefs of Biography; Seay of the Southland," *NYDM*, 11 Aug 1915, 24:2. "In the Picture Studios," *NYDM*, 4 Dec 1915, 31:1 (Seay—"the only original owner of the name that is spelled with the 'y' and pronounced without it"—was peeved at an actor with the same name in the Union Hill Stock company. "Mr. Seay means to s[e]ay that if he had time he would cross an arm of the sea[y] to see the other Seay and see 'Who Seay?'—See?").

Sebastian, Charles E. [mayor of Los Angeles CA/actor]. No data found. "Only in Los Angeles Could This Happen; How the Chief Executive of Screenland's Capital Became a Film Actor," *Photoplay*, XII (Jul 1917), 78 (in *The Downfall of a Mayor.* "Sebastian was really ousted as mayor a few months ago, although his resignation was ascribed to ill health.").

Sebastian, Dorothy [stage/film actress] (b. Birmingham AL, 26 Apr 1903–9 Apr 1957 [54?], Woodland Hills CA). m. (1) Al Stafford; (2) **William Boyd** (d. 1972); (3) Herman Shapiro (d. 1978). (Film debut: *Sackcloth and Scarlet;* MGM.) "Dorothy Sebastian Is Dead at 51; Starred in Many Silent Movies; Former Wife of William Boyd Appeared in 'George White's Scandals' on Stage in 1924," *NYT,* 10 Apr 1957, 33:2. "Dorothy Sebastian," *Variety,* 10 Apr 1957 (d. Hollywood CA, age 52). AMD, p. 309. AS, p. 982. BHD1, p. 493 (b. 1906). FSS, p. 257. IFN, p. 267. Katz, pp. 1032–33. Truitt, p. 299. Norma Johnstone, "She's from Alabam'," *MPC,* Jul 1926, 35, 78. Peggy Snow, "Dorothy Sebastian 'Just Walks into Good Parts,'" *Paris and Hollywood,* Sep 1926, 48, 85 (jobs came easy to her. She asked to test for Henry King's *Sackcloth and Scarlet* and won a role, later getting a contract from MGM). "Cast in Three Separate Films," *MPW,* 23 Apr 1927, 715. "Conway Tearle and Dorothy Sebastian Escape Injury," *MPW,* 13 Aug 1927, 454.

Sebastian, Malcolm "Big Boy" [child actor] (b. 1923?). AMD, p. 41. "Big Boy," *MPW,* 23 Apr 1927, 709 (Malcolm Sabiston). "Four Candles Lighted on His Birthday Cake," *MPW,* 12 Nov 1927, 15.

Sebastian, Malcolm [actor: Our Gang Comedies] (b. 1924). (Began as the baby in *Three Weeks;* Educational.) Robert G. Blackburn, "A Star Who Can't Read His Fan Mail; Directing two-year-old 'Big Boy' is largely a matter of coaxing, teasing, begging and threatening," *Cinema Arts,* Nov 1926, 30.

Sechan, André [actor] (d. 1924, France). AS, p. 982.

Sedan, Rolfe [film/TV actor] (b. New York NY, 21 Jan 1896–16 Sep 1982 [86], Pacific Palisades [Santa Monica] CA). "Rolfe Sedan, Character Actor on TV and in Films Since '16," *NYT,* 24 Sep 1982, D19:6. "Rolfe Sedan," *Variety,* 22 Sep 1982. AS, p. 982 (b. 20 Jan; d. 15 Sep). BHD, p. 297 (b. 20 Jan). "Rolfe Sedan," *CI,* 89 (Nov 1982), 18. Jordan Young, "Rolfe Sedan in Over 300 Films [letter]," *CI,* 92 (Feb 1983), 11.

Seddon, Margaret [actress] (*née* Marguerite Hungerford Whiteley Sloan, b. Washington DC, 18 Nov 1872–17 Apr 1968 [95], Philadelphia PA). (MGM.) AS, p. 982. BHD1, p. 494. IFN, p. 267.

Sedgwick, Edward M. (brother of **Eileen** and **Josie Sedgwick**) [film/TV actor/writer/director] (b. Galveston TX, 7 Nov 1892–7 May 1953 [60], No. Hollywood CA; heart attack). m. Ebba Havez. (MGM.) "Edward Sedgwick, Film Director, 60; Officer of Desilu Productions Dies—Pioneer in Hollywood Discovered Mix, Gibson," *NYT,* 8 May 1953, 25:3. "Edward M. Sedgwick," *Variety,* 13 May 1953 [text missing]. AMD, p. 309. AS, p. 982. BHD, p. 298; BHD2, p. 239 (b. 1889-d. LA CA). IFN, p. 267. Katz, p. 1033 (began 1915). Kathleen Brady, *Lucille; The Life of Lucille Ball* (NY: Hyperion, 1994), p. 214. "Ed Sedgwick Joins the Lubin Co.," *MPW,* 28 Mar 1914, 1682. "Sedgwick to Write for Walsh," *MPW,* 28 Jun 1919, 1953. "Signs Sedgwick for Gibson," *MPW,* 7 Apr 1923, 673. "Edward Sedgwick with Universal," *MPW,* 26 May 1923, 331. "Ed Sedgwick Joins M-G-M," *MPW,* 3 Apr 1926, 334. 'Edward Sedgwick," *MPW,* 2 Apr 1927, 477.

Sedgwick, Eileen (sister of **Edward** and twin of **Josie Sedgwick**) [actress] (aka Greta Yoltz, b. Galveston TX, 17 Oct 1895–15 Mar 1991 [95], Marina del Ray CA). m. **Justin H. McCloskey** (d. 1935). (Lubin, 1914; Universal.) "Eileen Sedgwick," *Variety,* 6 May 1991. AMD, p. 310. AS, p. 982 (d. Hollywood). BHD, p. 298 (b. 1898). BR, pp. 220–24 (b. 1899). Katz, pp. 1033–34. MH, p. 136. "Eileen Sedgwick," *MPW,* 7 Jul 1917, 90. Eileen Sedgwick, "Viewpoint of the Actress," *MPW,* 21 Jul 1917, 418. "Eileen Sedgwick Divorced," *LA Times,* 29 Mar 1920, II, p. 12 (supposed to have been divorced from vaudevillian Chic Lloyd. *See* next citation.). "Another Eileen," *LA Times,* 31 Mar 1920, III, p. 4 (Sedgwick was married to McCloskey, so couldn't have been divorced from Lloyd in Reno.). "Pacific Signs Eileen Sedgwick," *MPW,* 3 Apr 1920, 57. "Actor Seeks Damages for Eileen's Realism," *MPW,* 2 Jul 1927, 13. Buck Rainey, "Eileen Sedgwick; Always in Merciless Clutches and the Path of Doom, She Survived to Reign as One of Filmdom's Greatest Serial Queens," *CI,* 129 (Mar 1986), 17–18 (b. 1897).

Sedgwick, Josie (Josephine) (sister of **Edward** and twin **Eileen Sedgwick**) [actress] (b. Galveston TX, 17 Oct 1895–30 Apr 1973 [77], Santa Monica CA; cerebral hemorrhage). m. Bill Gettinger (**Bob Steele**), 12 Oct 1919 (d. 1966); Justin H. McCloskey. (Lubin; Universal; Triangle; Metro.) "Josie Sedgwick," *Variety,* 9 May 1973. AMD, p. 310. AS, p. 982. BHD1, p. 494 (b. 13 Mar 1896). BR, pp. 224–26. Katz, p. 1034 (b. 1895). MSBB, p. 1042 (b. 1896). "Josie Sedgwick Now with Universal," *MPW,* 3 May 1919, 641. "Josie Sedgwick Weds Argonne Hero," *MPW,* 8 Nov 1919, 255. "M-G-M Signs Star," *MPW,* 23 Apr 1927, 729.

Sedley, Henry [stage/film actor] (b. NY). (Triangle; FP-L; Keeney; Goldwyn.) AMD, p. 310. MSBB, p. 1028. "Henry Sedley Appears in First Hemmer Production," *MPW,* 31 Jul 1920, 586.

See, Edward [actor] (b. New York NY, 1855–17 Feb 1923 [67?], New York NY). BHD, p. 298.

Seeber, Guido [cinematographer] (b. Chemmitz, Germany, 22 Jun 1879–1940 [61?], Berlin, Germany). AS, p. 982. BHD2, p. 239. FDY, p. 469.

Seeck, Adelheid [actress] (b. Berlin, Germany, 3 Nov 1899–17 Feb 1973 [73], Germany). AS, p. 983.

Seed, David [actor] (b. New York NY, 8 Jul 1888–3 Nov 1960 [72], Brooklyn NY). BHD, p. 298. IFN, p. 267.

Seegar, Miriam [actress] (b. Greenwood IN, 1 Sep 1909). AS, p. 983. Ragan 2, p. 1523. *World Film Encyclopedia.*

Seelbach, James [cinematographer] (b. 1899–21 Jan 1936 [36?]). BHD2, p. 239.

Seeley, James L. (son of actress Jane Kendrick) [stage/film actor] (b. Rushville IL, 1867?–15 Feb 1943 [76], New York NY). "James Seeley; Veteran Character Actor Was in Many Plays on Broadway," *NYT,* 16 Feb 1943, 19:1. "James L. Seeley," *Variety,* 17 Feb 1943. AS, p. 983 (d. 14 Feb). BHD, p. 298.

Seeley, Walter Hoff [executive]. No data found. AMD, p. 310. W. Stephen Bush, "A Magnet for Quality," *MPW,* 14 Nov 1914, 935. "Alco Has Receiver for a Day," *MPW,* 5 Dec 1914, 1357.

Seeling, Charles R. [cameraman/director/producer] (b. Perth Amboy NJ, 1895?–13 Oct 1951 [56], Pasadena CA). (Sennett.) "Charles R. Seeling," *NYT,* 16 Oct 1951, 31:3. "Charles R. Seeling," *Variety,* 17 Oct 1951. AS, p. 983. BHD2, p. 239.

Seelos, Annette [actress] (*née* Blanche Wallis, b. San Francisco CA, 1891–23 Oct 1918 [27?], New York NY; influenza). m. Al Kaufman. (Essanay; World.) "Annette Seelos," *Variety,* 1 Nov 1918. AS, p. 983. BHD, p. 298. Billy H. Doyle, "Lost Players," *CI,* 139 (Jan 1987), 55.

Seely, Sybil [actress] (b. 2 Jan 1900–26 Jun 1984 [84], Culver City CA). BHD, p. 298.

Segal, A.B. [director] (b. Russia, 5 May 1897–18 Oct 1950 [53], Russia). AS, p. 983.

Segal, George [director] (b. 23 Jun 1847–7 May 1920 [72], Los Angeles CA). AS, p. 983.

Segal, John [director] (b. Los Angeles CA, 24 Jun 1847–7 May 1936 [88], Los Angeles CA). AS, p. 983.

Segarra, Consuelo [actress] (*née* Consuelo Segarra Martinez, b. Mexico, Nov 1875–28 Apr 1946 [70], Mexico City, Mexico). AS, p. 983.

Seger, Lucia Backus [actress] (b. 1873?–17 Jan 1962 [88], Queens NY [Death Certificate Index No. 751 (Lucy Seger)]). (Paramount.) "Lucia Backus Seger," *Variety,* 7 Feb 1962. AS, p. 983. BHD1, p. 494. IFN, p. 268. Truitt, p. 299.

Seidewitz, Marie [actress] (*née* Marie Bussey, d. 27 Dec 1929], Baltimore MD). "Marie Seidewitz [Marie Bussey Duffy Seidewitz]," *Variety,* 1 Jan 1930. AS, p. 983. IFN, p. 268. Truitt, p. 299.

Seidl, Lea [actress] (*née* Caroline Mayrseidl, b. Vienna, Austria, 1895–4 Jan 1987 [91?], London, England). AS, p. 984.

Seidner, Irene [actress] (b. Vienna, Austria, 10 Dec 1880–17 Nov 1959 [78], Los Angeles CA). AS, p. 984.

Seigel, Bernard *see* **Siegel, Bernard**

Seiler, Lewis [director] (b. New York NY, 1891–8 Jan 1964 [73], Los Angeles CA). "Lewis Seiler," *Variety,* 22 Jan 1964 ("pioneer film director"). AS, p. 984. BHD2, p. 239. IFN, p. 268. Katz, pp. 1034–35.

Seiter, Robert [actor/editor/cameraman] (b. NY, 15 Nov 1905–12 Jan 1986 [80], St. Petersburg FL. "Robert Seiter," *Variety,* 26 Feb 1986. AS, p. 984. BHD, p. 298; BHD2, p. 239. Ragan 2, p. 1524.

Seiter, William A. [actor: Keystone Cop/director] (b. New York NY, 10 Jun 1892–26 Jul 1964 [72], Beverly Hills CA; heart attack). m. **Laura La Plante**, 14 Nov 1926–32 (d. 1996); **Marian Nixon**, 1934 (d. 1983). (Sennett.) "William A. Seiter, 72, Dies; A Movie and TV Director," *NYT,* 28 Jul 1964, 29:5. "William A. Seiter," *Variety,* 29 Jul 1964. AMD, p. 310. AS, p. 984. BHD1, p. 984; BHD2, p. 239 (b. 1890). IFN, p. 268. Katz, p. 1035. Truitt, p. 299. "Seiter Engaged to Direct Jesters," *MPW,* 29 Jun 1918, 1875. "National Director Grew Up with Firm," *MPW,* 21 Feb 1920, 1254. "Seiter Signed by Ince," *MPW,* 20 Nov 1920, 280. "William A. Seiter," *MPW,* 27 Nov 1926, 209. "Directs Wife?," *MPW,* 30 Jul 1927, 312 (La Plante). Tom Waller, "Bill and Laura," *MPW,* 10 Sep 1927, 86–87. "Denny—Seiter Reported Out," *MPW,* 31 Dec 1927, 25. Herbert Cruikshank, "A Bill in a China Shop; Mr. Seiter Cut Loose Early from the Cut-Glass Profession and Stampeded to Hollywood," *MPC,* Aug 1928, 33, 80.

Seitz, Franz [director/scenarist] (b. Munich, Germany, 1888–7 Mar 1952 [64?]). BHD2, p. 239.

Seitz, George B[rackett] (brother of **John F. Seitz**) [actor/stage manager/illustrator/writer/director/scenarist/producer] (b. Boston MA [73 Center St.; MVRB, Vol. 387, p. 239], 3 Jan 1888–8 Jul 1944 [56], Los Angeles CA). (Pathé.) "George Seitz Dies; Film Director, 56," *NYT,* 9 Jul 1944, 35:3. "George B. Seitz," *Variety,* 12 Jul 1944. AMD, p. 47 (Brackett, George); p. 310. AS, p. 984. BHD, p. 298; BHD2, p. 239. IFN, p. 268. Katz, p. 1035. Spehr, p. 166. Truitt, p. 299. WWS, p. 108. "Seitz to Write New Pathé Series," *MPW,* 9 Oct 1915, 239. "Truth Beats the Screen; George Brackett Seitz's Experience Stranger than His Wildest Fiction," *NYDM,* 11 Dec 1915, 29:4 (five years ago, Seitz pawned a worn suit for 75¢ so that he could eat for the first time in several days in his dreary rooms at Washington Square, New York City. Now, as scenario editor for the Pathé Exchange, he makes between $30,000 and $40,000 a year and is married with one child. "Before becoming a scenario writer he was an actor and stage-manager, and had some success in writing magazine stories and vaudeville sketches. He has also studied painting, and for one year was an illustrator."). "They Built 'The House of Hate,'" *MPW,* 16 Feb 1918, 978. "Prominent Players to Be Featured in Pathé Serials for the Next Two Years," *MPW,* 19 Jul 1919, 377. "George B. Seitz Directs Himself in 'Bound and Gagged,'" *MPW,* 30 Aug 1919, 1303. "Seitz, Scenarist, Plays in 'Bound and Gagged,'" *MPW,* 13 Sep 1919, 1645. Edward Weitzel, "SIzing Up George 'Serial' Seitz," *MPW,* 27 Sep 1919, 1941–42. "George Seitz to Direct Features; Resigns from Pathé," *MPW,* 11 Apr 1925, 542. "Seitz Gets New Contract," *MPW,* 7 Aug 1926, 3. "Seitz Directing Another Thriller," *MPW,* 7 May 1927, 25.

Seitz, John F. (brother of **George B. Seitz**) [cinematographer] (b. Chicago IL, 23 Jun 1892?–27 Feb 1979 [86], Woodland Hills CA). "John F. Seitz," *Variety,* 7 Mar 1979. AS, p. 984. BHD2, p. 239. FDY, p. 469. Katz, pp. 1035–36 (b. 1893).

Seixas, Claude [actor]. No data found. AMD, p. 310. "Italian Comedian in Pictures," *MPW,* 6 Dec 1913, 1158.

Sekely, Steve [director] (*né* Istvan Szekely, b. Budapest, Hungary, 25 Feb 1889–9 Mar 1979 [90], Palm Springs CA; stomach cancer). AS, p. 984.

Selander, Leslie [film/TV director] (b. Los Angeles CA, 26 May 1900–5 Dec 1979 [79], Los Alamitos CA). (Universal; Paramount; Republic; RKO; TC-F; Allied Artists.) "Leslie Selander," *Variety,* 12 Dec 1979. AS, p. 984. BHD2, p. 239. IFN, p. 268.

Selbie, Evelyn, "The Bronco Billy Girl" [stage/film actress] (b. Louisville KY, 6 Jul 1871–6 Dec 1950 [79], Woodland Hills CA; heart attack). "Evelyn Selbie, Actress; Stage and Screen Star During 25-Year Career Dies at 79," *NYT,* 9 Dec 1950, 15:3. "Evelyn Selbie," *Variety,* 20 Dec 1950. AMD, p. 310. AS, p. 984 (d. 7 Dec). BHD1, p. 494. BR, pp. 69–71 (b. 1882). IFN, p. 268. Ragan 2, p. 1524. Truitt, p. 300 (b. Louisville KY, 1882). "Notes from the Essanay Western Company at Niles," *MPW,* 9 Nov 1912, 555. "Gossip for the Fans," *MPW,* 15 Mar 1913, 1106. "Evelyn Selbie a Versatile Player," *MPW,* 21 Sep 1918, 1745. George A. Katchmer, "Forgotten Cowboys and Cowgirls—Part X," *CI,* 182 (Aug 1990), 42 (d. 6 Sep).

Selby, Gertrude B. [actress]. No data found. (Universal.) AMD, p. 310. "Gertrude Selby," *MPW,* 15 May 1915, 1080. "Gertrude Selby," *MPW,* 15 Jan 1916, 430. "Gertrude Selby," *MPW,* 23 Jun 1917, 586.

Selby, Norman "Kid McCoy" [pugilist/actor] (b. Rushville, Rush Co. IN, 13 Oct 1873–18 Apr 1940 [66], Detroit MI; suicide). m. 9 times. AS, p. 984. BHD1, p. 495. IFN, p. 268. "Friends Aiding Kid McCoy; Pathetic Sigh in Prison. Mrs. Mors Reported Having Taken Oath to Former Husband to Break Away from Fighter—'Life Against Me—Drew a Blank,' Says the Kid," *Variety,* 20 Aug 1924, 20 (charged with murdering Mrs. Teresa Mors, a wealthy antique shop owner, who was to become his tenth wife).

Selden, Edgar [scenarist] (b. 1868–14 Jun 1924 [56?], Bellmore NY). AS, p. 984. BHD2, p. 239.

Selig, Al [publicist] (b. 1885?–28 Jul 1946 [61], New York NY; incurable ailment). (Fox; Tiffany; Columbia; RKO; Universal; TC-F.). "Al Selig," *Variety,* 163, 31 Jul 1946, 54:1. AMD, p. 310. BHD2, p. 239. "Tiffany's Advertising and Publicity Chief Is Newspaperman of Twenty Years' Experiencee," *MPW,* 25 Jun 1927, 586.

Selig, August [producer] (b. 1870–3 Jul 1943 [73?], Chicago IL). BHD2, p. 239.

Selig, Col. William N[icholas] [executive, Selig Polyscope Company] (b. Chicago IL, 14 Mar 1864–16 Jul 1948 [84], Los Angeles CA). m. Mary H. Pinkham. "William N. Selig, Pioneer in Films; Early Producer and Developer of Industry Dies—Fought with Edison on Patents," *NYT,* 17 Jul 1948, 15:3. "William N. Selig," *Variety,* 21 Jul 1948. AMD, p. 310. AS, p. 984. BHD2, p. 239. IFN, p. 268. Katz, p. 1037. WWVC, p. 129. "Notes of the Trade," *MPW,* 8 May 1909, 586. "A Notable Film Producer," *MPW,* 12 Jun 1909, 792. "Selig's—The Great Moving Picture Plant of the West," *MPW,* 21 Aug 1909, 247–48. James S. McQuade, "Selig Entertains," *MPW,* 9 Sep 1911, 701–02. "The Los Angels Tragedy," *MPW,* 11 Nov 1911, 455 (shot by Frank Minnematsu, 27 Oct 1911; director Francis Boggs killed). "A Kangaroo for Pictures," *MPW,* 20 Jul 1912, 245. "Startling and Pleasant Surprise for Wm. N. Selig," *MPW,* 14 Dec 1912, 1067. "A Roster of Selig Players," *MPW,* 22 Mar 1913, 1199. "New Blood in Selig Studio," *MPW,* 16 Aug 1913, 728. "Selig Buys Two Giraffes," *MPW,* 8 Nov 1913, 590. "William N. Selig Goes West," *MPW,* 15 Nov 1913, 743. James S. McQuade, "Chicago Letter," *MPW,* 6 Jun 1914, 1416. William N. Selig, "Present Day Trend in Film Lengths," *MPW,* 11 Jul 1914, 181–82. James S. McQuade, "Wm. N. Selig Near Scene of War," *MPW,* 19 Sep 1914, 1649. "A Master Stroke by Wm. N. Selig," *MPW,* 30 Jan 1915, 650. "A Motion Picture Pioneer," *NYDM,* 31 Mar 1915, 22:3 (illustrated with first photo of Selig other than a snapshot. "So strongly was he impressed [with the possibilities of the new form of amusement] that 1887 found him a full fledged producer of motion pictures with a studio in Chicago—one of the first three men to undertake the manufacture of motion pictures in America."). "'Big Four' [A.E. Smith, Selig, Ira Lowry, George K. Spoor] Surprises Film Men; Vitagraph-Lubin-Selig-Essanay Combination Means Radical Departure by Motion Picture Pioneers—Exchange Managers Appointed and Preparations Under Way for Flying Start," *NYDM,* 21 Apr 1915, 24:2. "Short Films Important; 'Don't Overlook the One, Two and Three-Reelers,' Is William N. Selig's Advice," *NYDM,* 26 May 1915, 22:4. George Blaisdell, "Great Selig Enterprise," *MPW,* 10 Jul 1915, 227–30. "Our Apologies to Col. William N. Selig," *MPW,* 17 Jul 1915, 464. "Selig and Mutual in Suit," *NYDM,* 29 Sep 1915, 24:1 (Selig sued Mutual for their production of *The House of a Thousand Scandals,* alleging the title infringed on his right to Meredith Nicholson's *The House of a Thousand Candles.* Asked $25,000 and an injunction against Mutual and American.). Quip, *NYDM,* 30 Oct 1915, 27:2 (Selig Polyscope's application for the registration of the Red Seal trademark was granted by the U.S. Patent office). G.P. von Harleman, "A VIsit to the Selig Zoo," *MPW,* 10 Jun 1916, 1857. "Selig Pinned Faith to Short Subjects," *MPW,* 22 Jul 1916, 642. "Selig Returns from Coast; Talks of New Pictures," *MPW,* 19 Aug 1916, 1257. "'Nothing to Rumors,' Says Selig," *MPW,* 9 Sep 1916, 1707. "Diamond Trade Mark Is Selig's," *MPW,* 11 Nov 1916, 864. "Selig Predicts a Good Year," *MPW,* 6 Jan 1917, 93. "William N. Selig Reminded of the Twenty-First Birthday of the Selig Polyscope Company," *MPW,* 5 May 1917, 799. "Twenty-One Years in the Business," *MPW,* 12 May 1917, 948–49. "Selig to Release Through Capital," *MPW,* 1 Jun 1918, 1275. "Selig Tells How 'Hoosier Romance' Came to Be Filmed," *MPW,* 31 Aug 1918, 1285. "William N. Selig to Make SIx Features Starring Franklyn Farnum; Cannon Will Distribute," *MPW,* 22 May 1920, 1079. "'Jungle Goddess,' Last Selig Serial; Export-Import Selling Territories," *MPW,* 11 Feb 1922, 631. "Selig Continues Production," *MPW,* 22 Sep 1923, 343. Connie Lauerman, "Hollywood East; At the dawn of the movie age, Chicago had its place in the sun," *Chicago Tribune,* 19 Mar 1995, pp. 9, 22 ("Selig and Essanay were the main Chicago companies...").

Selk, George W. [actor] (b. 15 May 1893–22 Jan 1967 [73], Montrose CA). AS, p. 985.

Sell, Henry G *see* **Gsell, Henry**

Seller, Robert [actor] (b. Paris, France, 1 Aug 1889 [extrait de naissance no. 3839]–17 Aug 1967 [78], Frejus, France [extrait de décès no. 2316]). AS, p. 985.

Sellers, Ollie (Oliver) L. [producer]. No data found. AMD, p. 311. "It Freezes Nights in Los Angeles," *MPW,* 1 Mar 1919, 1188.

Sellier, Georges Eugène [actor] (b. Paris, France, 25 Feb 1893–11 Sep 1988 [95], Clamart, France [extrait de décès no. 749/588]).

Sellon, Charles S. [actor] (b. Boston MA, 24 Aug 1870–26 Jun 1937 [66], La Crecenta CA; cancer). m. (1 son). AS, p. 985. BHD1, p. 495 (d. LA CA). IFN, p. 268. Truitt, p. 300. George A. Katchmer, "Forgotten Cowboys and Cowgirls—Part X," *CI,* 182 (Aug 1990), 40. Dorothy Donnell, "From Hollywood to You," *MPS,* 29 Jul 1925, 14 (he lived with Louise Arthur, who committed suicide by poison in a Hollywood hotel. His wife had come to Hollywood a week before to give him the divorce he wanted, "but now—oh, I can't help hoping that he will come back to us." His son was 14.).

Selman, David [director]. No data found. AMD, p. 311. "David Selman to Direct Newest Columbia Film," *MPW,* 5 Mar 1927, 40.

Selten, Morton [actor] (*né* Morton Richards Stubbs, b. Marlborough, England, 6 Jan 1860–27 Jul 1939 [79], London, England). AS, p. 985. BHD1, p. 495.

Selwyn, Arch [producer] (b. 1877–21 Jun 1959 [82?], Los Angeles CA). AS, p. 985.

Selwyn, Edgar [actor/producer/author] (*né* Edgar Simon, b. Cincinnati OH, 20 Oct 1875–13 Feb 1944 [68], Los Angeles CA; cerebral hemorrhage). m. (1) **Margaret Mayo** (d. 1951); (2) Ruth Wilcox (d. 1954). (All-Star Feature Films Co., 1912.) "Edgar Selwyn, 68, Producer Is Dead; Leader of Stage and Films Had Been Star of Own Plays—Started as Usher Here," *NYT,* 14 Feb 1944, 17:1. Jack Pulaski, "Edgar Selwyn's Death Recalls Prominence as Author-Producer-Actor," *Variety,* 16 Feb 1944. AMD, p. 311. AS, p. 984 (Seldwyn); p. 985. BHD, p. 298; BHD2, p. 240. IFN, p. 268. Katz, p. 1047. Spehr, p. 166. "Edgar Selwyn and Maragaret Mayo in 'The Arab,'" *MPW,* 13 Feb 1915, 999. "DeMille Grabs Selwyn Stage Plot for Screen," *MPW,* 18 Jan 1919, 314. "Goldwyn Capital Now $20,000,000," *MPW,* 9 Aug 1919, 785.

Selwynne, Clarissa [stage/film actress] (*née* Clarissa Schultz, b. London, England, 26 Feb 1886–13 Jun 1948 [62], Los Angeles CA). (World; Selig; Pallas; Metro; Universal.) AMD, p. 311. AS, p. 985 (d. West Hollywood). BHD1, p. 495. IFN, p. 268. MSBB, p. 1042. "Clarissa Selwyn," *MPW,* 27 Nov 1915, 1641. "Clarissa Selwyn Back to Films with 'U,'" *MPW,* 3 Sep 1927, 35.

Selznick, David O[liver] (son of **Lewis J. Selznick**; brother of Howard and **Myron Selznick**; father of Jeffrey L. Selznick) [producer] (b. Pittsburgh PA, 10 May 1902–22 Jun 1965 [63], Los Angeles CA; heart attack). m. (1) Irene Mayer; (2) Jennifer Jones. "David O. Selznick, 63, Producer of 'Gone with the Wind,' Dies," *NYT,* 23 Jun 1965, 1:4, 38:1; "Selznick Funeral Tomorrow," *NYT,* 24 Jun 1965, 35:1. "Producer D.O. Selznick Dies in Hollywood at 63; Had Two Heart Attacks," *Variety,* 23 Jun 1965. AMD, p. 311. AS, p. 985 (b. Pittsburg TX, 22 May). BHD2, p. 240. IFN, p. 268. JS, p. 419 (co-produced *Stazione Termini,* Italy, 1953). Katz, p. 1038. Spehr, p. 166. "David Selznick Reports His Plans for Reorganizing Department of Publicity," *MPW,* 10 Jul 1920, 247.

Selznick, Lewis J. (father of **David**, Howard and **Myron Selznick**) [executive] (*né* Lewis Zeleznik, b. Kiev, Ukraine, Russia, 2 May 1870–25 Jan 1933 [62], Beverly Hills CA; heart attack). m. Florence Sachs. (Universal; World; Select.) "L.J. Selznick Dies; A Film Pioneer; Retired Producer, 62, Was Once Head of the World Sales Corporation," *NYT,* 26 Jan 1933, 17:3. "Lewis J. Selznick," *Variety,* 31 Jan 1933. AMD, p. 311. AS, p. 985. BHD2, p. 240. IFN, p. 268. Spehr, pp. 166, 168. "Selznick Entertains," *MPW,* 3 Oct 1914, 66. "Lewis J. Selznick's Idea," *MPW,* 31 Oct 1914, 617. "Says Lillian to Lewis," *MPW,* 19 Dec 1914, 1697. Lewis J. Selznick, "Behind the Scenes; Not in the Studio But in the Business Office—Inside Facts That Tell You What It Means to Develop an Idea into a Two Million Dollar Organization," *NYDM,* 27 Jan 1915, 44:1. "World Film's Profits; Report for First Fiscal Year Shows Up Well—Commendation for Selznick," *NYDM,* 4 Aug 1915, 23:2 (a profit for the parent corporation and its producing allies amounted to $329,025.08. Selznick was V-P and general manager of World.). "Sellznick Highly Endorsed," *MPW,* 7 Aug 1915, 1007. "Selznick Reviews Year's Work," *MPW,* 11 Sep 1915, 1838. Harry L. Reichenbach, "Two Sides of Selznick," *MPW,* 2 Oct 1915, 64. "Selznick on Distribution," *MPW,* 25 Dec 1915, 2344. "Berst Leaves General Film," *MPW,* 22 Jan 1916, 574. "Selznick Forms New Company," *MPW,* 12 Feb 1916, 931. "James Young Sues Selznick," *MPW,* 19 Feb 1916, 1103. "Selznick Goes West," *MPW,* 25 Mar 1916, 2021. "Selznick Leases Suite of Offices," *MPW,* 20 May 1916, 1319 (49th and 7th Avenue, NYC). "Selznick Closes Two Big Deals," *MPW,* 20 May 1916, 1348. "Busy Days for Selznick," *MPW,* 3 Jun 1916, 1701. Lewis J. Selznick, "Selznick Likes Programs—Admits It," *MPW,* 14 Apr 1917, 252. "Clara Kimball Young Sues Selznick," *MPW,* 9 Jun 1917, 1580. "Selznick Would Enjoin Miss Young," *MPW,* 16 Jun 1917, 1761. "Selznick on Tour," *MPW,* 15 Sep 1917, 1674. Lewis J. Selznick, "Selznick Backs Up Crandall," *MPW,* 16 Feb 1918, 972. "Mrs. Selznick to Join Sons," *MPW,* 1 Mar 1919, 1192. "Selznick Pictures a Family Affair," *MPW,* 15 Mar 1919, 1477. "Lewis J. Selznick Now Sole Owner of Select," *MPW,* 19 Apr 1919, 340. "Elsie Janis Becomes Selznic Star," *MPW,* 28 Jun 1919, 1913. "Selznick Wins Second Point in Suit Involving 'Eyes of Youth,'" *MPW,* 13 Dec 1919, 783. "Lewis J. Selznick's FIrst Stage Play Will Be 'Bucking the Tiger,'" *MPW,* 13 Dec 1919, 829. "You Have It on he Word of Selznick That Women Want Their Stars Just So," *MPW,* 27 Dec 1919, 1114. "Hour Is Here for Big Readjustment Between Exhibitor and Producer," *MPW,* 27 Dec 1919, 1123. "Selznick Reviews and Anticipates in Considering Two Active Years," *MPW,* 27 Dec 1919, 1184. "Howard Selznick Marriage Announced," *MPW,* 1 May 1920, 676 (m. Mildred Schneider, Jan 1920). "'For the First Time I Believe the Exhibitor to Be Earnest'—Selznick," *MPW,* 12 Jun 1920, 1426. "Selznick Scores N.A.M.P.I.'s Bulletin Dealing with Gov. Collidge's Candidacy," *MPW,* 3 Jul 1920, 53. "Selznick Wins in Suit from Equity," *MPW,* 11 Dec 1920, 707. Lewis J. Selznick, "'Everything's Going Great' Is the Optimistic Slogan of Lewis J. Selznick," *MPW,* 25 Dec 1920, 1017. "Selznick Advocates Getting Together for Centralized Distribution System," *MPW,* 6 Aug 1921, 615. "'World' Has Greatly Aided Industry—Selznick," *MPW,* 11 Mar 1922, 154. "Ten Years Ago Selznick Was 'Radical' Because He VIsualized Long Features," *MPW,* 20 May 1922, 310. "Star Series Production Plan Abandoned by Selznick, Who Explains Capitulation," *MPW,* 1 Jul 1922, 23. "Selznick Places His Sons in Control of His Enterprises," *MPW,* 6 Jan 1923, 33. "Suit Against Selznick," *MPW,* 20 Jan 1923, 218. "Lewis J. Selznick Heads Radio Company; Keeps Film Interests," *MPW,* 10 May 1924, 208.

Selznick, Myron (son of **Lewis J. Selznick**; brother of Howard and **David Selznick**) [producer/agent/executive] (b. Pittsburgh PA, 5 Oct 1898–23 Mar 1944 [45], Santa Monica CA; portal thrombosis after 8 blood transfusions). m. **Marjorie Daw**, 1929–42 (d. 1979). "Myron Selznick, 45, Actors' Agent, Dies; Outstanding Figure in Screen World Represented Host of Well Known Stars," *NYT,* 24 Mar 1944, 20:2 (general manager of Norma Talmadge Film Corp.). "Myron Selznick's Career as Colorful as Scripts He Sold; Agent Dies at 45," *Variety,* 29 Mar 1944. AMD, p. 312. AS, p. 985 (b. Pittsburg TX). BHD2, p. 240. "Myron Selznick to Produce," *MPW,* 14 Dec 1918, 1187. "'Selznick Pictures' Again in Field," *MPW,* 18 Jan 1919, 316. "Myron Selznick Working on Big Exploitation Plan," *MPW,* 22 Mar 1919, 1688. "California Gets Another Rude Blow," *MPW,* 26 Apr 1919, 521. "Owen Moore Is Engaged by Selznick Pictures," *MPW,* 28 Jun 1919, 1918. "Myron Selznick Is Made Vice-President Select Pictures," *MPW,* 8 May 1920, 850. "Myron Selznick Tells of His Efficiency Production Methods," *MPW,* 22 May 1920, 1103. Myron Selznick, "New Output to Consist of Star Series and Specials," *MPW,* 31 Dec 1921, 1052. T.S. daPonte, "England Not Suitable for Production Purposes, Says Myron Selznick; English Would Like to See Sweden Succeed America as World's Film Center," *MPW,* 28 Jan 1922, 375.

Semels, Harry [actor] (b. New York NY, 20 Nov 1887–2 Mar 1946 [58], Los Angeles CA). m. Jean. "Harry Semels," *Variety,* 13 Mar 1946. AS, p. 985 (d. 3 Mar). BHD1, p. 495. IFN, p. 268. George Katchmer, "Remembering the Great Silents," *CI,* 249 (Mar 1996), 49–50.

Semmler, Gustav Adolf [actor] (b. 14 Mar 1885–24 Feb 1968 [82], Berlin, Germany). BHD, p. 298.

Semon, Larry (son of vaudeville comedian Zera the Great, d. 1903) [newspaper cartoonist/stage/vaudeville/film actor/ director/scenarist] (known as Ridolini in Italy; *né* Lawrence Semon, b. West Point MS, 16 Jul 1889–8 Oct 1928 [39], Garcelon Ranch, near Victorville CA; lobar pneumonia after nervous breakdown). m. **Lucille Carlisle**; **Dorothy Dwan**, 22 Jan 1925 (d. 1980). (Vitagraph, 1915; Universal; Palace Players.) "Film Comedian Larry Semon Dies; Succumbs to Pneumonia, Following a Nervous Break-Down, at a California Ranch; His Salary Once Million; Died a Bankrupt as a Producer—Left Job as Cartoonist for Slapstick Comedy," *NYT,* 9 Oct 1928, 31:3. "Larry Semon," *Variety,* 10 Oct 1928. AMD, p. 312. AS, p. 985. BHD, p. 298; BHD2, p. 240 (b. 19 Feb 1890). FFF, p. 87. IFN, p. 268. Katz, pp. 1038–39. MH, p. 136. MSBB, p. 1028. 1921 Directory, p. 274. Slide, pp. 102–105 (b. 16 Jul 1889). Truitt, p. 300. WWS, p. 70. "Larry Semon Renews Vitagraph Contract," *MPW,* 15 Nov 1919, 333. "Larry Semon Renews His Contract with VItagraph," *MPW,* 6 Dec 1919, 655. "Vitagraph Sues Larry Semon, Comedian, for $400,000, Charging Waste of Money," *MPW,* 18 Sep 1920, 348. "Semon Again Ill," *MPW,* 4 Jun 1921, 503. "Semon Gets Front-Page Space Fighting Fire in California," *MPW,* 3 Sep 1921, 72. "Signing of Semon Gives Independents a Big Comedy Bet," *MPW,* 9 Jun 1923, 496. "Semon Making Four More for VItagraph," *MPW,* 16 Jun 1923, 597. "Work Begun on First Semon Feature Comedy," *MPW,* 6 Oct 1923, 507. "Chadwick Signs Larry Semon for Series of Five-Reel Comedies," *MPW,* 17 May 1924, 303. "To Supply Comic Strip," *MPW,* 20 Sep 1924, 211. "Larry Semon Discards Clown Clothes in 'Her Boy Friend,'" *MPW,* 11 Oct 1924, 475. "Larry Semon," *MPW,* 22 Aug 1925, 845. "Semon Uses School Kids," *MPW,* 31 Oct 1925, 710. "Not with Lloyd," *MPW,* 22 May 1926, 3 (as a director). "F.P. Signs L.S.," *MPW,* 11 Dec 1926, 3. "Larry Semon to Build Own Studio," *MPW,* 23 Jul 1927, 238. "Larry Semon," *MPW,* 27 Aug 1927, 589. Sam Gill, "The Funny Men: Larry Semon," *8mm Collector,* No. 10 (Winter, 1964), 12–13. Herb Gordon, "The Comedian's Comedian," *CI,* 71 (Sep 1980), 62, 68. George A. Katchmer, "Remembering the Great Silents," *CI,* 165 (Mar 1989), C20-C21, C23-C24; *CI,* 166 (Apr 1989), 57–59. Richard M. Roberts, "Larry Semon: The Cartoonist as Comic; Part I," *CI,* 286 (Apr 1999), C3-C6 (Semon was a cartoonist on the *New York Sun* and *Telegraph* newspapers)p; "Heyday," Part II, *CI,* 292 (Oct 1999), 13–16; Part III, *CI,* 301 (Jul 2000), 6–14, 59 (states that Dorothu Dwan died in 1980).

Sen, Hirabal [director] (b. Bakjuri, India, 15 Aug 1899–29 Oct 1917 [18], India). AS, p. 986.

Senarens, Louis Philip [scenarist] (b. Brooklyn NY, 1863–26 Dec 1939 [76?], New York NY). BHD2, p. 240.

Senger, Victor Alexander Ludwig [actor/director] (b. Germany, 11 Aug 1870). AS, p. 986.

Sennett, Mack [actor/director/producer/scenarist/executive] (*né* Michael [Mikall] Sinnott, b. Danville [Richmond], Quebec, Canada, 17 Jan 1880–5 Nov 1960 [80], Woodland Hills CA; heart attack). Bachelor. Davide Turconi, *Mack Sennett; il "re delle comiche"* (Rome, Italy: Edizioni dell'Ateneo, 1961). With Cameron Shipp, *King of Comedy* (rpt. 1990; San Francisco: Mercury House, Inc., 1954). (Biograph, 1908; Keystone.) "Mack Sennett, 76, Film Pioneer Who Developed Slapstick, Dies; Keystone Kops, Custard Pies and Bathing Beauties Were Symbols of His Movies," *NYT,* 6 Nov 1960, 1:3, 88:1 (b. 1884). "King of the Piefaces Dies at 80, Mack Sennett Created a Metier," *Variety,* 9 Nov 1960. AMD, p. 312. AS, p. 986. BHD1, p. 495; BHD2, p. 240. FDY, p. 437. IFN, p. 268. Katz, pp. 1039–41. Spehr, p. 168. Truitt, p. 300. "Keystone Pictures Out," *MPW,* 19 Oct 1912, 234. "Sennett and Mace Meet a Bear," *MPW,* 26 Oct 1912, 331. "Sennet Making 'Comedy-Melodramas,'" *MPW,* 26 Apr 1913, 366. "Sennett to Act; Originator of Keystone Comedies Will in Future Appear in All His Plays," *NYDM,* 4 Mar 1914, 30:1. "Ince and Sennett Comning East," *MPW,* 1 Aug 1914, 686. "Mack Sennett Talks of His Work," *MPW,* 15 Aug 1914, 968. W.E.W., "Mack Sennett, of Keystone," *NYDM,* 27 Jan 1915, 43:3. "The Psychology of a Laugh," *MPW,* 10 Jul 1915, 236. "Sennett Sends East for Circus DIving Horse," *MPW,* 11 Mar 1916, 1636. "'More Keystones,' Says Sennett," *MPW,* 18 Mar 1916, 1831. George Blaisdell, "Mack Sennett in the East," *MPW,* 29 Jul 1916, 767. "Interviewing Mack Sennett," *MPW,* 28 Oct 1916, 557. "Ince and Sennett Continue in Triangle," *MPW,* 10 Feb 1917, 827. Mack Sennett, "Slim Days in Keystone Beginnings," *MPW,* 10 Mar 1917, 1535. "Sennett Withdraws from Triangle," *MPW,* 7 Jul 1917, 63. "Sennett, Too, Goes with Paramount," *MPW,* 14 Jul 1917, 216. "Mack Sennett Off for the Pacific Coast," *MPW,* 21 Jul 1917, 437. Neil G. Caward, "Screen Gossip," *Picture-Play Magazine,* Sep 1917, 101–02 (Sennett and Ince resigned from Triangle). "Sennett's Evaluation of 'Mickey,'" *MPW,* 9 Feb 1918, 836. "Sennett Talks on Changes," *MPW,* 16 Mar 1918, 1532. "Action Drama Succeeding Artificial, Says Sennett," *MPW,* 4 Jan 1919, 62. "Sennett's Water Nymphs on Tour," *MPW,* 10 May 1919, 827. "Mack Sennett, the Laugh King, Oddly Enough Has a Horror of Having His Picture Taken," *MPW,* 20 Sep 1919, 1828. "Clowning Not All—Sennett," *MPW,* 22 Nov 1919, 444. "Mack Sennett Says Great Popularity of Short Subjects Is Year's Most Important Development," *MPW,* 20 Dec 1919, 966. "Miniature Madterpieces Much in Demand, Says Mack Sennett, Relating His Plans," *MPW,* 27 Mar 1920, 2164. "Mack Sennett Soliloquizes on Marriage in Discussing 'Love, Honor and Behave,'" *MPW,* 2 Oct 1920, 677. "[Charles O. Baumann] Sues Sennett for $22,000 and Percentage of Comedy Profits," *MPW,* 30 Oct 1920, 1270. "Mack Sennett wi 'Heartbalm' to Make Debut as Creator of Romantic Pictures," *MPW,* 20 Nov 1920, 328. "Baumann Serves Papers on Mack Sennett; Claims $122,579 Due on an Old Contract," *MPW,* 18 Dec 1920, 903. "Supreme Court Releases Mack Sennett Pictures," *MPW,* 22 Jan 1921, 456. Mack Sennett, "Sennett Views New Year with Optimism; Pledges Features as Well as Comedies," *MPW,* 31 Dec 1921, 1063. Mack Sennett, "New Year to See Further Stabilization and Economy," *MPW,* 31 Dec 1921, 1054. "Sennett Praises 'World's' Service to the Industry," *MPW,* 11 Mar 1922, 141. "City Officials Greet Sennett Upon Arrival in Philadelphia," *MPW,* 8 Apr 1922, 618. "Sennett Closes with Associated to Distribute Mabel Normand Series," *MPW,* 11 Aug 1923, 465. "Mack Sennett Studio Speeds Up to Meet Requirements of Pathé," *MPW,* 24 Nov 1923, 411. "Sennett Sees Good Resulting from Economic Readjustments," *MPW,* 5 Jan 1924, 28. "Sennett in Cast," *MPW,* 1 Mar 1924, 37. Charles F. Berry, "How Mack Sennett Picks His Bathing Beauties," *MW,* 24 May 1924, 4–5. Alma Talley, "When They Refuse to Laugh—in the Movies," *MW,* 5 Jul 1924, 11, 28. "Mack Sennett Perfects 1925-'26 Plans; Hal Roach's Hugh Program for Pathé," *MPW,* 18 Apr 1925, 682. "Mack Sennett Says, 'Laugh Is Only Universal Idea,'" *MPW,* 22 Aug 1925, 845. Harry Carr, "What Makes You Laugh on the Screen; Mack Sennett Tells a Few Secrets of Making Film Comedies," *MPC,* Sep 1925, 18–19, 81–82. "Pathé and Mack Sennett Sign Contract Involving Big Two-Reel Comedy Schedule," *MPW,* 16 Jan 1926, 254–55. Mack Sennett, "A Good Comedy Covers the Whole World," *MPW,* 6 Feb 1926, 568. Charles Edward Hastings, "Mack Sennett," *MPW,* 8 May 1926, 168. Bert Ennis, "How the Keystone Kops Happened; Mack Sennett's famous comedy Policemen developed from a chance Purchase in a New York second-hand Store," *MPC,* Jun 1926, 34–35, 74 (Ennis bought costumes for Sennett at Harry Guttenberg's store on Sixth Avenue, which specialized in cast-off theatrical wardrobes. He sent some police uniforms to the Keystone studio and Sennett liked their oversized look on his actors.). "Sennett's S.O.S.: 'Bathing Girls Wanted,'" *MPW,* 17 Jul 1926, 167. "Mack Sennett to Distribute Through Pathé," *MPW,* 4 Jun 1927, 329. "Sennett to Build on Ventura Blvd., Starting New Boom," *MPW,* 25 Jun 1927, 565. Dunham Thorp, "Mack Sennett University Give Them Good Degrees," *MPC,* Aug 1927, 23, 72 (Alice Day, Phyllis Haver, Marie Prevost, *et al.* are discussed). "Mack Sennett at Megaphone; Goulding Ill," *MPW,* 3 Sep 1927, 21. "Sennett an Inventor," *MPW,* 17 Dec 1927, 10 (submarine camera). "Sennett Reported Supervising All Pathé Comedies; Banks' Mugs Clipped," *MPW,* 17 Dec 1927, 31. Joe Adamson, "*Smith's Restaurant;* A Case Study in the Sennett Method," *Griffithiana,* 53, May 1995, 4–23. Ben Brantley, "Pie Fights, Keystone Kops and Pain; A stormy love story from the era of silent movies," *NYT,* 3 Jul 1999, B19 (review of revived play, *Mack and Mabel* [1974], book by Michael Stewart revised by his sister, Francine Pascal, directed by Julianne Boyd. "And for a work about creating comedy, it is almost never funny.").

Sepulveda, Carl [actor]. No data found. George Katchmer, "Remembering the Great Silents," *CI,* 233 (Nov 1994), 40, 42.

Sequeyro, Adela Garcia [actress/director] (aka Perlita, *née* Adela Sequeyro Haro, b. Vera Cruz, Mexico, 11 Mar 1901–24 Dec 1992 [91]; cancer). Alfaro Vega, Eduardo de la y Patricia Torres San Martín, *Adela Sequeyro* (Mexico: University of Guadalajara and University of Vera Cruz, 1997; ISBN 968-895-741-0. "Esta monografía rinde tributo a quien fuera la única directora de cine en los años del establecimiento de esta industria en [Mexico]."). (In Mexican silents from 1923.) AS, p. 986 (d. 15 Mar 1996, Mexico City, Mexico).

Seragnoli, Oreste [actor] (b. Italy, 10 Jul 1883–13 Apr 1965 [81]). BHD1, p. 495. IFN, p. 268.

Serda, Julia [stage/film actress] (b. Vienna, Austria, 6 Apr 1875–3 Nov 1965 [90], Dresden, East Germany). "Julia Serda," *Variety,* 240, 17 Nov 1965, 71:3. AS, p. 986. BHD1, p. 495. IFN, p. 268.

Serena, Gustavo [actor/director] (*né* Marquis Gustavo Serena, b. Naples, Italy, 5 Oct 1881–16 Apr 1970 [88], Rome, Italy). AS, p. 986. BHD1, p. 616. JS, p. 421 (in Italian silents from 1911).

Sergine, Vera [actress] (*née* Marguerite Aimée Roche, b. France, 18 Aug 1884–22 Feb 1946 [61], Paris, France). m. **Pierre Renoir** (d. 1952). AS, p. 987.

Sergis, Simone [actress] (d. 12 Jul 1971, Los Angeles Co. CA). BHD1, p. 495.

Sergius [actor] (b. Paris, France, 22 Nov 1878–30 Oct 1966 [87], France). AS, p. 987.

Sergyl, Yvonne [actress] (b. Constantine, Algeria, 1896). AS, p. 987.

Seroe, George [actor] (b. France, 1897–27 Oct 1929 [32?], France). AS, p. 987.

Serra, Domenico [actor], b. Crescentino, Italy, 19 Sep 1899). JS, p. 422 (in Italian silents from 1916).

Serrano, Georges [actor] (*né* Georges Serrano de Mulder, b. Antwerp, Belgium, 18 Aug 1890–ca. 1961 [71?]). AS, p. 987.

Serrano, Vincent [actor] (b. New York NY, 17 Feb 1866–10 Jan 1935 [68], New York NY; heart attack). "Vincent Serrano," *Variety,* 15 Jan 1935. AMD, p. 313. AS, p. 987. BHD, p. 298. IFN, p. 269. Truitt, pp. 300–301. "Vincent Serrano Engaged by Famous Players," *MPW,* 18 Dec 1915, 2156. "Vincent Serrano Joins Thanhouser," *MPW,* 9 Sep 1916, 1704. "Vincent Serrano," *MPW,* 30 Sep 1916, 2125.

Serrurier, Iwan [inventor] (b. 1878–31 Jan 1953 [74], Los Angeles CA). AS, p. 987.

Sersen, Fred [special effects] (b. Czechoslovakia, 24 Feb 1890–11 Dec 1962 [72], Glendale CA). (Winner of 2 Academy Awards.) AS, p. 987. BHD2, p. 240.

Serta, Mary [stage/film actress]. No data found. (Monat.) Rene de la Seine, "Latest Gossip from Paris; Foreign Stars Look to Hollywood," *Paris and Hollywood,* Oct 1926, 43 (appeared in *Le Marchand de Bonheur* [*The Merchant of Happiness,* Monat, 1926. "She has the peculiar type of mobile beauty which the screen most demands, and she has youth and personality on her side.").

Sertel, Neela [actress] (b. Turkey, 1901–15 Dec 1969 [68?], Tanbul, Turkey). AS, p. 987.

Sertz, Franz [director/producer] (b. Munich, Germany, 1888–7 Mar 1952 [64?], Germany). AS, p. 987.

Servaes, Dagny [actor] (b. Berlin, Germany, 10 Mar 1897–10 Jul 1961 [64], Vienna, Austria). AS, p. 987 (b. 1894). BHD1, p. 496. IFN, p. 269.

Serventi, Luigi [actor/director] (b. Rome, Italy, 31 Jul 1885–1976 [91?]). BHD, p. 298. JS, p. 423 (in Italian silents from 1914).

Service, Robert W. [actor] (b. Preston, England, 16 Jan 1874–12 Sep 1958 [84], France). BHD1, p. 496.

Servoss, Mary [actress] (b. Washington DC, 2 Jun 1887–20 Nov 1968 [81], Los Angeles CA). AS, p. 987.

Sessions, Almira [actress] (b. Washington DC, 16 Sep 1888–3 Aug 1974 [85], Los Angeles CA). AS, pp. 987–88.

Sesti, Claire [actress] (b. New York NY, 23 May 1913–29 Jan 1990 [76], Boynton Beach FL). BHD, p. 298.

Sestier, Marius Ely Joseph [director] (b. Suzet, France, 8 Sep 1861–8 Nov 1928 [67], Sauzet, France). AS, p. 988.

Settle, Joseph [cameraman] (b. 1889?–20 Jan 1938 [48], Canada Lake NY). "Joseph Settle," *Variety*, 26 Jan 1938. BHD2, p. 241.

Severi, Elisa [actress] (b. Ravenna, Italy, 6 Apr 1872–26 Aug 1930 [58], Rome, Italy). AS, p. 988.

Severin, Gaston Léon [actor] (b. Paris, France, 8 Aug 1879 [extrait de naissance no. 1090]–22 Dec 1962 [83], Clichy-la-Garenne, France). AS, p. 988.

Severin-Mars, M. [actor/director/scenarist] (*né* Armand Jean Malafayde, b. Bordeaux, France, 21 Feb 1873 [extrait de naissance no. 316/1873]–17 Jul 1921 [48], Courson, France; heart attack). AS, p. 988. BHD, p. 298. IFN, p. 269.

Sevor, Alfred [actor] (b. 1891?–26 Mar 1953 [62], New York NY). "Alfred Sever," *Variety*, 1 Apr 1953 (in silents at Ft. Lee NJ "in the pre-sound era"). AS, p. 988 (listed under Sever and Sevor). BHD, p. 298. IFN, p. 269. Truitt, p. 301.

Seward, Edmond [scenarist] (b. 1891–12 Feb 1954 [62?], Los Angeles CA). BHD2, p. 241.

Sewall, Lucille [actress] (b. 1888–15 Dec 1976 [88], Los Angeles CA). AS, p. 988. BHD1, p. 496. IFN, p. 269.

Seward, Edmond [scenarist] (b. 1890–12 Feb 1954 [63?], Los Angeles CA; heart attack). AS, p. 988.

Sewall, Allen D[evereaux] [actor] (b. MA, 23 Jul 1882–20 Jan 1954 [71], Los Angeles CA). AS, p. 988.

Sewell, Allen D[evereaux] [actor] (b. MA, 23 Jul 1882–20 Jan 1954 [71], Los Angeles CA; heart attack). m. Lucille. (DeMille; U-I.) "Allen D. Sewell," *Variety*, 27 Jan 1954. AS, p. 988. BHD1, p. 496. IFN, p. 269. Truitt, p. 301.

Sewell, Blanche [film editor] (b. 1899?–3 Feb 1949 [49], Burbank CA). "Blanche Sewell," *Variety*, 9 Feb 1949. BHD2, p. 241.

Sewell, George Harold [director] (b. London, England, 1899). AS, p. 988.

Seyawetz, Alphonse ["chimiste française, pionnier du cinéma"] (b. Lyon, France, 14 Mar 1869–21 Aug 1940 [71], Bron, France). AS, p. 988.

Seybolt, Eleanor [actress] (b. 1885–17 Sep 1947 [62?], New York NY). BHD, p. 299.

Seyler, Athene [actress] (*née* Athene Hannen, b. London, England, 31 May 1889–12 Sep 1990 [101], London, England). AS, p. 988. BHD, p. 299.

Seylis, Emile [actor] (*né* Emile de Neve, b. Arras, France, 21 Nov 1881 [extrait de naissance no. 486/1881]–20 Mar 1963 [81], Paris, France). AS, p. 988.

Seymour, Clarine E. [actress] (b. Brooklyn NY, 9 Dec 1898 [Birth Certificate Index No. 18495]–25 Apr 1920 [21], New York NY [Death Certificate No. 14962]; pneumonia). "Clarine E. Seymour, Film Actress," *NYT*, 26 Apr 1920, 13:4. "Clarine E. Seymour," *Variety*, 30 Apr 1920. AMD, p. 313. AS, p. 989. BHD, p. 299. IFN, p. 269 (age 20). Truitt, p. 301. "Clarine Seymour in Toto Comedies," *MPW*, 20 Oct 1917, 366. "Clarine Seymour Very Ill," *MPW*, 1 May 1920, 672. Harrison Haskins, "The Last Interview," *MPC*, Jul 1920, 51, 83. Eve Golden, "Clarine Seymour: The First Flapper," *CI*, 224 (Feb 1994), 38–39.

Seymour, Harry [actor/composer] (b. New York NY, 22 Jun 1891–11 Nov 1967 [76], Los Angeles CA; heart attack). m. **Myna Cunard** (d. 1978). (TC-F; WB.) "Harry Seymour," *Variety*, 22 Nov 1967 (age 77). AS, p. 989. BHD1, p. 496; BHD2, p. 241. IFN, p. 269. Truitt, p. 301.

Seymour, James (brother of actors **John** and Anne Seymour) [scenarist] (b. 1895?–29 Jan 1976 [80], London, England; heart attack). (RKO; WB.) "James Seymour," *Variety*, 4 Feb 1976. AS, p. 989. BHD2, p. 241 (d. LA CA).

Seymour, John (brother of Anne and **James Seymour**) [actor] (b. Boston MA, 1898–10 Jul 1986 [88?], New York NY). AS, p. 989.

Shackelford, Floyd [actor] (*né* Flord Schackelford, b. IA, 7 Sep 1905–17 Dec 1972 [67], Dockweller CA). AS, p. 989 (d. LA CA). BHD1, p. 497. George Katchmer, "Remembering the Great Silents," *CI*, 212 (Feb 1993), 35.

Shade, Jamesson [actor] (b. New York NY, 23 Nov 1895–17 Apr 1956 [60], Los Angeles CA). AS, p. 989.

Shadow, Bert [actor] (b. Boston IL, 1890–12 Nov 1936 [46?], Los Angeles CA). AS, p. 989.

Shadur, Arthur E. [producer]. No data found. AMD, p. 313. "Arthur E. Shadur to Supervise 'U' Production," *MPW*, 2 Apr 1927, 485.

Shafer, Molly B. [actress] (b. CA, 1872?–19 Nov 1940 [68], Los Angeles CA). AS, p. 989. BHD, p. 299. IFN, p. 269. Truitt, p. 301.

Shaffner, Mrs. Lillian [actress] (b. 1860?–10 Jan 1930 [69], Los Angeles CA). AS, p. 989. BHD, p. 299 (b. 1862). IFN, p. 269.

Shah, Chandulal [director/producer/scenarist] (*né* Chandeulal J. Shah, b. Jamnagar, India, 13 Apr 1898–25 Nov 1975 [77], Bombay, India). AS, p. 989.

Shaiffer, Howard C[harles] **(Tiny)** [actor] (b. 1917–24 Jan 1967 [49?], Burbank CA). AS, p. 990. BHD, p. 299.

Shain, John Howard [actor/producer] (b. 22 Jun 1903–6 Dec 1979 [76], Bryn Mawr PA). AS, p. 990. BHD, p. 299; BHD2, p. 241. IFN, p. 269.

Shairp, Mordaunt [scenarist] (b. 1887–18 Jan 1939 [51?], Hastings, England). BHD2, p. 241.

Shallebarger, Frank L. [publicist] (b. 1878?–25 Jan 1926 [47], Plainfield NJ; heart disease and asthma). AMD, p. 313. "Frank Shallebarger Succeeds S.F. Seadler at Kane Offices," *MPW*, 3 Jul 1920, 111. "Obituary," *MPW*, 6 Feb 1926, 4.

Shallenberger, W[ilbert] **Edgar** [executive] (d. Mar 1935, Chicago IL). AMD, p. 313. BHD2, p. 241. "W. Edgar Shallenberger," *MPW*, 3 Jul 1915, 68. "Shallenberger on Western Tour," *MPW*, 3 Mar 1917, 1338. "Independents to Win as Money Interests Fight," *MPW*, 27 Dec 1919, 1119. W. Edgar Shallenberger, "The Past Year One of Achievement for Arrow with Greater Promise for 1921," *MPW*, 25 Dec 1920, 1011. "W. Edgar Shallenberger, President of Arrow, Predicts Greatest Year for Independents," *MPW*, 8 Jul 1922, 113. "Dr. W. Edgar Shallenberger on Status of Independents," *MPW*, 22 Jul 1922, 302. W. Edgar Shallenberger, "Dr. W. Edgar Shallenberger Looks Forward to a Record Year," *MPW*, 26 Aug 1922, 692. W. Edgar Shallenberger, "How Independent Leaders See New Season," *MPW*, 8 Sep 1923, 158. W. Edgar Shallenberger, "Arrow Pictures Corp. Enters Tenth Year," *MPW*, 24 Jan 1925, 339. "Shallenberger Sounds Appeal," *MPW*, 14 Mar 1925, 171. "Shallenberger Sees Success of the Independent Movement," *MPW*, 1 Aug 1925, 507. "Shallenberger Quotes 'Informant' on Activities of Atlanta Board," *MPW*, 15 Aug 1925, 704. "Mrs. Shallenberger Hurt," *MPW*, 14 May 1927, 90 (broken ankle).

Shamroy, Leon [cinematographer] (b. New York NY, 16 Jul 1901–7 Jul 1974 [72], Woodland Hills CA). m. Mary Anderson. (Fox, 1920; Pathé.) "Leon Shamroy Dies at 72; Cameraman Won 4 Oscars," *NYT*, 10 Jul 1974, 40:5 (nominated for an AA 21 times: won for *The Black Swan* [1942]; *Wilson* [1944]; *Leave Her to Heaven* [1945]; and *Cleopatra* [1961]. "In 1920 he joined the Fox Film Corporation's film laboratory and four years later began camera work."). "Leon Shamroy," *Variety*, 17 Jul 1974. AS, p. 990. BHD2, p. 241. FDY, p. 469 (Shamray). IFN, p. 269.

Shane, Maxwell [publicist/scenarist/producer] (b. Paterson NJ, 26 Aug 1905–25 Oct 1983 [78], Woodland Hills CA). AMD, p. 314. AS, p. 990 (director/producer/scenarist). BHD2, p. 241. "Maxwell Shane with Harry Langdon Unit," *MPW*, 17 Jul 1926, 152.

Shane, Theodore [scenarist]. No dasta found. m. author Margaret Woodward Smith (pseudonym of Woodward Boyd; d. 3 Sep 1965). "Mrs. Theodore Shane," *NYT*, 5 Sep 1965, 57:3. FDY, p. 437.

Shanley, Lila [stuntwoman] (b. Los Angeles CA, 28 Nov 1909–15 Nov 1996 [86], Santa Monica CA; heart attack). AS, p. 990.

Shannon, Alexander K. [actor] (b. Le Havre, France, 1862?–7 Mar 1932 [70], New York NY). "Alex K. Shannon," *Variety*, 15 Mar 1932. AS, p. 990. BHD, p. 299.

Shannon, Betty [publicist]. No data found. m. **Terry Ramsaye**, May? 1916, Philadelphia PA (d. 1954). AMD, p. 314. "Terry Rams[aye] Marries Betty Shannon," *MPW*, 27 May 1916, 1524.

Shannon, Cora [actress] (b. IL, 30 Jan 1869–27 Aug 1957 [88], Woodland Hills CA; cancer). AS, p. 990. BHD1, p. 497. IFN, p. 269.

Shannon, Mrs. Dale [actress] (*née?*, d. 1 Jun 1923, New York NY). (Lubin.) "Mrs. Dale Shannon," *Variety*, 7 Jun 1923. AS, p. 990. BHD, p. 299. IFN, p. 269. Truitt, p. 301.

Shannon, Effie [stage/film actress] (b. Cambridge MA, 13 May 1867–24 Jul 1954 [87], Bay Shore, LI NY). m. (1) Henry Guy Carleton (d. 1922); **Herbert Kelcy** (d. 1917). (Film debut: *After the Ball*, Photo Drama Co., 1914.) "Effie Shannon, 87, Actress, Is Dead; Her 68-Year Career Took in Such Roles as Little Eva to Part in 'Arsenic' in 1942," *NYT*, 25 Jul 1954, 69:1. "Effie Shannon," *Variety*, 28 Jul 1954. AMD, p. 314. AS, p.990. BHD1, p. 497. IFN, p. 269. Truitt, p. 301. "Kelcey and Shannon Sign for Pictures," *MPW*, 20 Jun 1914, 1671. "Effie Shannon Engaged for New Graphic Film," *MPW*, 3 Aug 1918, 707.

Shannon, Ethel [actress: Wampas Star, 1923/scenarist] (b. Denver CO, 22 May 1898–10 Jul 1951 [53], Los Angeles CA). m. Robert J. Cary; **Joseph Jackson** (d. 1932). AMD, p. 314. AS, p. 990. BHD1, p. 497; BHD2, p. 133 (Ethel Shannon Jackson). IFN, p. 269. Truitt, p. 301 (d. 14 Jul). "Ethel Shannon Signed," *MPW,* 2 May 1925, 75. "Ethel Shannon," *MPW,* 21 Nov 1925, 236. "Ethel Shannon Signed to Big Contract by Sax," *MPW,* 20 Feb 1926, 712. Allen Prewitt, "Red Hair and a Piano; A tale of a Denver Gal who sold the family piano, and got a job as a shipping clerk," *Photoplay Magazine,* Jun 1926, 70, 117. George A. Katchmer, "Forgotten Cowboys and Cowgirls—Part VIII, *CI,* 180 (Jun 1990), 61.

Shannon, Frank Connolly [actor] (b. Ireland, 27 Jul 1874–1 Feb 1959 [84], Los Angeles CA). (First feature: *Perjury,* Fox, 1921.) "Frank Connolly Shannon," *Variety,* 4 Feb 1959. AS, p. 990. BHD1, p. 497. IFN, p. 269. Truitt, pp. 301–302. Alan P. Spater, "Frank Shannon; Flash Gordon's Original Zarkov," *CI,* 128 (Feb 1986), 57–59.

Shannon, Jack [actor/stuntman] (*né* Jack L. Tyler, b. OH, 31 Aug 1892–27 Dec 1968 [76], Los Angeles CA). m. **Grace Cunard** (d. 1967). AS, p. 990. BHD1, p. 497. IFN, p. 270. Truitt, p. 302.

Shannon, Peggy [stage/film actress] (*née* Winona Shannon, b. Pine Bluff AR, 10 Jan 1907–11 May 1941 [34], No. Hollywood CA; found dead of acute alcoholism). m. (1) Alan Davis; (2) **Albert G. Roberts**, Oct 1940 (widower, d. 1941). (Paramount.) "Peggy Shannon Is Dead; Husband Finds Actress's Body in Hollywood Home," *NYT,* 12 May 1941, 17:3 (age 31). "Peggy Shannon," *Variety,* 14 May 1941 (age 31). AS, p. 990 (*née* Winona Simmon). BHD1, p. 497 (d. LA CA). IFN, p. 270. Katz, p. 1045. Truitt, p. 302 (b. 1909). F.J.B., "With the Film Men," *NYDM,* 10 Mar 1915, 24:3 (appeared in *The Birth of a Nation*). Elisabeth Goldbeck, "A New Redhead Succeeds Clara Bow," *Movie Classic,* Sep 1931, 50, 75 (replaced Bow in *The Secret Call* and replaced Mary Brian in *Silence.* "If you develop an unwanted pound of flesh somewhere, they do everything but send out bulletins").

Shannon, Ray [actor] (b. 12 Aug 1894–1 Jan 1971 [76], Cincinnati OH). "Ray Shannon, Comic of Stage and Radio," *NYT,* 4 Jan 1971, 35:1 (teamed with Stan Laurel for 3 years). "Ray Shannon," *Variety,* 13 Jan 1971. AS, p. 990.

Shanor, Peggy [actress] (b. WV, 1896?–30 May 1935 [39], New York NY). (Pathé.) "Peggy Shanor," *Variety,* 5 Jun 1935. AMD, p. 314. AS, p. 991. BHD, p. 299. IFN, p. 270. Truitt, p. 302. "Peggy Shanor, Baby Vampire," *MPW,* 13 Apr 1918, 224.

Shapiro, Irvin [distributor] (b. WA, 1906?–1 Jan 1989 [82], New York NY [Death Certificate Index No. 45]). "Irvin Shapiro, 82, Distributor of Films by Foreign Directors," *NYT,* 6 Jan 1989, D15:4. AS, p. 991.

Shapiro, Victor M. [publicist] (b. NY, 1892–31 Mar 1967 [75?], Los Angeles CA). AMD, p. 314. BHD2, p. 241. "'Vic' Shapiro Moves," *MPW,* 16 Feb 1924, 555. Merritt Crawford, "Spotting a Comer," *MPW,* 19 Feb 1927, 553. "Victor M. Shapiro," *MPW,* 26 Mar 1927, 311. "Victor M. Shapiro Returns, After Studying United Artists Plans," *MPW,* 11 Jun 1927, 424. Victor Shapiro, "United Artists to Wage War on Bunk Picture Production," *MPW,* 16 Jul 1927, 189–90. "'Vic' Pulls New One," *MPW,* 8 Oct 1927, 348.

Sharkey, Tom (Sailor) [actor] (b. Dundalk, Ireland, 26 Nov 1873–17 Apr 1953 [79], San Francisco CA). AS, p. 991. BHD1, p. 498.

Sharland, Reginald [actor] (b. Southend-on-Sea, England, 19 Nov 1886–21 Aug 1944 [57], Loma Linda CA). AS, p. 991.

Sharman, Harry [producer] (b. 1885–25 Sep 1952 [67?], Los Angeles CA). AS, p. 991.

Sharon, Elaine [actress] (b. Indianapolis IN, 9 Jun 1845–6 Jun 1900 [54], Los Angeles CA). AS, p. 991.

Sharp, Henry [stage/film actor] (*né* Henry Schacht, b. Riga, Latvia, 19 Feb 1887–10 Jan 1964 [76], Brooklyn NY [Death Certificate Index No. 803]). m. Effie Thomas. (Griffith.) "Henry Schacht, Actor, Teacher; Stage and Screen Player as Henry Sharp Dies at 77," *NYT,* 11 Jan 1964, 23:5. "Henry Sharp," *Variety,* 22 Jan 1964. AS, p. 991 (b. NY NY). BHD1, p. 498. IFN, p. 270 (age 77). Truitt, p. 302.

Sharp, Henry T. [cinematographer] (b. New York NY, 13 May 1894–6 Aug 1966 [72], Los Angeles CA). AMD, p. 314. BHD2, p. 241. FDY, p. 469. Katz, p. 1046. "Cameraman Sharp Promoted," *MPW,* 7 Feb 1920, 933. "Doug Chooses New Cameraman," *MPW,* 7 Feb 1925, 597. "Henry Sharp," *MPW,* 2 Apr 1927, 477.

Sharp, Len [actor] (b. England, 1890–24 Oct 1958 [68?], Waterford, England). AS, p. 991.

Sharp, Ramona [actress] (*née* Ramona Smith, b. Longwood MO, 9 May 1901–26 Apr 1941 [39], Glendale CA). AS, p. 992. BHD, p. 299. IFN, p. 270.

Sharp-Bolster, Anita [actress] (b. Glenlohan, Ireland, 28 Aug 1900–1985 [85?]). BHD1, p. 616.

Sharpe, David Hardin [actor/director] (b. St. Louis MO, 2 Feb 1910–30 Mar 1980 [70], Altadena CA; Parkinson's disease). (Film debut: *The Thief of Bagdad,* 1924, at age 7; Fox; Paramount; Roach.) AS, p. 992 (b. 1917). BHD1, p. 498; BHD2, p. 241. Ken Law, "Dave Sharpe; Crown Prince of Daredevils," *CI,* 109 (Jul 1984), C5-C6, C16.

Sharpe, Lester [actor] (*né* Lester Scharff, b. New York NY, 21 May 1895–30 Nov 1962 [67], Los Angeles CA). AS, p. 992. BHD1, p. 498.

Shattuck, Truly [actress] (*née* Clarice Etrulia de Burcharde, b. San Miguel CA, 27 Jul 1876–6 Dec 1954 [78], Woodland Hills CA). m. Stephen A. Douglas. (Ince.) "Truly Shattuck," *NYT,* 10 Dec 1954, 27:1. "Truly Shattuck," *Variety,* 15 Dec 1954. AS, p. 992. BHD1, p. 498. IFN, p. 270. Truitt, p. 302.

Shaw, Anna [suffragette/actress]. No data found. AMD, p. 314. "Anna Shaw and Jane Addams in Pictures," *MPW,* 18 May 1912, 617.

Shaw, Brinsley [actor]. No data found. AMD, p. 314. "Universal Gets Lubin Players," *MPW,* 15 Aug 1914, 972. George Katchmer, "Remembering the Great Silents," *CI,* 212 (Feb 1993), 35–57.

Shaw, Bud [actor] (b. CA, 30 Apr 1906–29 Aug 1976 [70], Los Angeles CA). "Buddy Shaw," *Variety,* 20 Occt 1976 (child actor at age 5). AS, p. 992. BHD1, p. 498 (b. 29 Mar 1907). IFN, p. 270.

Shaw, C[harles] **Montague** [stage/film actor] (b. Adelaide, So. Australia, 23 Mar 1882–6 Feb 1968 [85], Woodland Hills CA). (Film debut: *The Blue Boy,* 2 reels, 1926.) "Montague Shaw," *Variety,* 14 Feb 1968. AS, p. 992. BHD1, p. 498. IFN, p. 270. Truitt, p. 302 (b. 1884). Blackie Seymour, "C. Montague Shaw...The English Professor Type," *CI,* 296 (Feb 2000), 60 (b. 1884).

Shaw, Frank M. [actor] (b. 1894?–7 May 1937 [43], Kansas City MO). "Frank M. Shaw," *Variety,* 19 May 1937. AS, p. 992. IFN, p. 270.

Shaw, G. Harold [actor/director] (*né* George Arnold Shaw, b. England, 1887–3 Jan 1926 [38?], Los Angeles CA). AS, p. 992.

Shaw, George Bernard [playwright/scenarist] (b. Dublin, Ireland, 26 Jul 1855–2 Nov 1950 [95], Ayot St. Lawrence, England). AS, p. 992 (b. 1856; d. 1 Nov). BHD, p. 299; BHD2, p. 241 (b. 1856).

Shaw, Harold M[arvin] [actor/director] (b. England, 3 Nov 1877–30 Jan 1926 [48], Los Angeles CA; auto accident). m. **Edna Flugrath**, Jan 1917, Johannesburg, South Africa (d. 1966). (Edison, 1909; Imp.) "G. Harold Shaw Killed," *Variety,* 3 Feb 1926. AMD, p. 314. AS, p. 992. BHD, p. 299; BHD2, p. 242 (b. TN). IFN, p. 270 (b. TN, 3 Nov 1877). Katz, pp. 1046–47 (b. TN). "Harold Shaw to Direct in London," *MPW,* 24 May 1913, 821. "Praise for Harold Shaw," *MPW,* 23 May 1914, 1101. "Shaw Joins English Army," *MPW,* 10 Apr 1915, 245. "Edna Flugrath Weds Harold Shaw," *MPW,* 31 Mar 1917, 2113. "Harold Shaw Will Direct Metro Film," *MPW,* 16 Jun 1923, 591. "Shaw to Direct Metro Film," *MPW,* 8 Sep 1923, 166. "Shaw Gets Chance to Cash in on Experience," *MPW,* 29 Sep 1923, 435. "Obituary," *MPW,* 13 Feb 1926, 4.

Shaw, Lewis [actor] (b. London, England, 6 May 1910–13 Jul 1987 [77], London, England). BHD1, p. 498.

Shaw, Oscar [stage/film actor/dancer] (*né* Oscar Schwartz, b. Philadelphia PA, 11 Oct 1887–6 Mar 1967 [79], Little Neck, Queens NY [Death Certificate Index No. 3135]). m. Louise Gale. (MGM.) "Oscar Shaw Dies; Singer and Dancer in Broadway Shows," *NYT,* 8 Mar 1967, 45:3. "Oscar Shaw," *Variety,* 15 Mar 1967. AS, p. 992. BHD1, p. 498. IFN, p. 270 (age 76). SD, p. 1129. Truitt, p. 302.

Shaw, Peggy [actress] (b. Pittsburgh PA?). AMD, p. 314. "Fox Signs Peggy Shaw," *MPW,* 3 Feb 1923, 436. "Peggy Shaw Goes on the Air," *MPW,* 28 Aug 1926, 550. George Katchmer, "Remembering the Great Silents," *CI,* 220 (Oct 1993), 41.

Shawn, Ted [dancer/actor] (*né* Edwin Myers Shawn [originally Von Schaun], b. Kansas City MO, 21 Oct 1891–9 Jan 1972 [80], Orlando FL). m. **Ruth St. Denis** (d. 1968). "Ted Shawn Is Dead; Led Modern Dance to Stature as Art," *NYT,* 10 Jan 1972, 1:1; McCandlish Phillips, "Overcame Paralysis of Legs," 36:2. "Ted Shawn," *Variety,* 12 Jan 1972. AS, p. 992.

Shawqi, Farid [actor/scenarist/producer] (b. Cairo, Egypt, 3 Jul 1920–27 Jul 1998 [78], Cairo, Egypt). "Other Deaths; Farid Shawqi," *PP-G,* 1 Aug 1998, A-9:6 ("appeared in more than 400 films during the golden days of Egyptian moviemaking'; age 76). AS, p. 993.

Shay, Larry [actor/composer] (b. 1897–22 Feb 1988 [90], Newport Beach CA). "Larry Shay, 90, Dies; Composer and Coach," *NYT,* 23 Feb 1988, D26:6. "Larry Shay," *Variety,* 9 Mar 1988. AS, p. 993.

Shay, William E. [actor]. No data found.

AMD, p. 314. "Shay to Play Opposite Florence Reed," *MPW,* 11 Nov 1916, 878.

Shayer, Richard [scenarist] (b. 1880–13 Mar 1956 [76?], Los Angeles CA). AS, p. 993.

Shayne, Konstantin [actor] (b. Russia, 29 Nov 1888–15 Nov 1974 [85], Los Angeles CA). AS, p. 993.

Shdanoff, Elsa Schreiber [actress] (b. Vienna, Austria, 1900–8 Jan 1982 [81?], Los Angeles CA). BHD, p. 299.

Shea, Billy [film editor]. No data found. AMD, p. 314. "Billy Shea Goes to Louis Mayer," *MPW,* 19 Jul 1919, 375.

Shea, Bird [actress] (b. 1893–23 Nov 1924 [31?], Los Angeles CA). m. William Hartman. "Bird Shea [Mrs. Lavon Hartman]," *Variety,* 26 Nov 1924. AS, p. 993. BHD, p. 299. IFN, p. 270. Truitt, p. 302.

Shea, Cornelius [short story writer for *Wild West Weekly*/scenarist] (b. near Tottenville, Staten Island NY, 1863). (Selig Polyscope.) "Successful Scenario Writers; Cornelius Shea," *MPS,* 18 Jun 1915, 30 (began 1912).

Shea, Daniel [branch man] (b. 1869–7 May 1924 [55?], Baltimore MD). BHD2, p. 242.

Shea, James Joseph [scenarist] (d. 22 Jul 1935, Los Angeles CA). BHD2, p. 242.

Shea, Louis [actor] (b. 1870–13 Jul 1925 [55?], New York NY). BHD, p. 300.

Shea, Thomas E. [stage/film actor] (b. E. Cambridge MA, 1861?–23 Apr 1940 [79], Cambridge MA). m. Nellie Burkett, 1892. "Thomas E. Shea, 79, Veteran of Stage; Headed Successful Stock Troupe—Jekyll-Hyde Roles Noted," *NYT,* 24 Apr 1940, 23:5. "Thomas E. Shea," *Variety,* 1 May 1940. AS, p. 993. BHD, p. 300.

Shea, William J[ames] [actor] (b. Dumfries, Scotland, 1862–6 Nov 1918 [56], 348 Lafayette Avenue, Brooklyn NY [Death Certificate No. 28165, age 55; angina pectoris]). (Vitagraph.) AMD, p. 314. AS, p. 993. BHD, p. 300 (b. 1861). IFN, p. 270. Slide, pp. 150–51. George Blaisdell, "At the Sign of the Flaming Arcs," *MPW,* 19 Apr 1913, 288 (Shea reminisced about actors shunning the early flickers). "In the Picture Studios," *NYDM,* 21 Jul 1915, 19:2 (as a member of "Vitagraph's Big Comedy Four [with Hughie Mack, Kate Price, and Flora FInch]," he wighed 163 lbs.). "Obituary," *MPW,* 23 Nov 1918, 840 (d. 5 Nov). Shea, "the oldest moving picture actor in the country in years of service, and the first comedian of the Vitagraph Company, died suddenly of heart disease, at his Brooklyn residence," *Theatre Magazine,* Dec 1918, 392 (age 56).

Shean, Al (uncle of the **Marx brothers**) [stage/film actor/composer] (*né* Alfred Schoenberg, b. Dornum, Germany, 12 May 1868–12 Aug 1949 [81], New York NY). m. Johanna. "Al Shean, 81, Dies; Veteran Trouper; Teamed with Ed Gallagher for Vaudeville Circuits in '20's—Also Stage and Film Star," *NYT,* 13 Aug 1949, 11:1. "Al (Positively) Shean Passes, Recalling Anew Roaring '20s Refrain," *Variety,* 17 Aug 1949 (*né* Schonberg). AMD, p. 314. AS, p. 993. BHD1, p. 499; BHD2, p. 242. IFN, p. 270. Truitt, pp. 302–303. "Wm. Fox SIgns Gallagher and Shean as Stars in Big Special Picture," *MPW,* 30 Jun 1923, 759. "Mr. Gallagher and Mr. Shean at Work," *MPW,* 21 Jul 1923, 246. "Fox Suing Comedians," *MPW,* 4 Dec 1926, 4. "Mrs. Al Shean; Wife of Vaudeville and Film Actor Dies in Hollywood, 73," *NYT,* 28 Jun 1944, 23:6 (b. 1871?–26 Jun 1944 [73], Hollywood CA).

Shearer, Athole (sister of **Douglas** and **Norma Shearer**) [actress] (b. Montreal, Canada, 20 Nov 1900–17 Mar 1985 [84], Los Angeles CA). m. **Howard Hawks** (d. 1977). BHD, p. 300.

Shearer, Douglas (brother of **Athole** and **Norma Shearer**) [sound director] (b. Westmount, Quebec, Canada, 17 Nov 1899–5 Jan 1971 [71], Culver City CA). "Douglas Shearer, M-G-M Sound Chief; Winner of 12 Oscars Dies—At Studio 41 Years," *NYT,* 9 Jan 1971, 30:1 (age 70). "Doug Shearer Dies; Understood 'Sound' When Nobody Did," *Variety,* 13 Jan 1971. AS, p. 993. BHD2, p. 242. IFN, p. 270 (age 70). Katz, p. 1048.

Shearer, Edith F. [actress] (b. Canada, 1873–2 Jul 1958 [85?], Garden Grove CA). BHD, p. 300.

Shearer, Norma (sister of **Athole** and **Douglas Shearer**) [actress] (*née* Edith Norma Shearer, b. Westmount [Montreal] Canada, 11 Aug 1902–12 Jun 1983 [80], Woodland Hills CA; bronchial pneumonia). m. (1) **Irving Thalberg**, 6 Oct 1927 (d. 1936); (2) Martin Arrouge. Gavin Lambert, *Norma Shearer; A Life* (NY: Alfred A. Knopf, 1990). (Metro; MGM; AA, 1929.) Eric Pace, "Norma Shearer, Film Star Two Decades, Is Dead," *NYT,* 14 Jun 1983, B8:1. Todd McCarthy, "Norma Shearer, 80, Ultimate Leading Lady, Dies in California," *Variety,* 15 Jun 1983 (b. 15 Aug). AMD, p. 315. AS, p. 993. BHD1, p. 499. FFF, p. 81. FSFW, p. 286 (b. 1904). FSS, p. 257. HCH, p. 89. Katz, p. 1048–49. MH, p. 136 (b. 1903). "Norma Shearer," WBO1, pp. 176–77. "Norma Shearer in Chief Female Role in Eugene O'Brien Film," *MPW,* 17 Dec 1921, 818. Norma Shearer, "Should a Girl Be Chaperoned in Hollywood?," *MW,* 22 Mar 1924, 6. "In Leading Role," *MPW,* 10 May 1924, 202. David A. Balch, "How Some Screen Stars Are Made; A Close-up of the McFadden Studio, which has served as a stepping stone to many a girl seeking screen fame," *MW,* 21 Jun 1924, 19 (posed for photos that appeared in *True Story Magazine*). Gladys Hall, "O! Don't You Wish You Were Me?," *MW,* 27 Dec 1924, 21, 30. "Wins Popularity Contest," *MPW,* 28 Feb 1925, 912. "Shearer Voted Princeton's Favorite," *MPW,* 6 Jun 1925, 668. Alice Tildesley, "Love and Other Things According to Norma Shearer," *MW,* 1 Aug 1925, 15–16. Doris Curran, "A Close-Up of Fame," *MPC,* Nov 1925, 38–39, 72. Lucille Arms, "A Haughty and Reserved Young Lady," *Pictures,* Jul 1926, 49, 111–12. "Norma Shearer on the Air," *MPW,* 9 Oct 1926, 346. "Norma Wins," *MPW,* 22 Jan 1927, 269. "Shearer—Thalberg Nuptials Soon," *MPW,* 27 Aug 1927, 590. "Shearer—Thalberg Nuptials," *MPW,* 1 Oct 1927, 289. Dunham Thorp, "The Love Interest; Norma Shearer Is Now Doubling in a Marital Role," *MPC,* Dec 1927, 37, 79, 84. "Favor Barrymore, Shearer," *MPW,* 10 Dec 1927, 14. Fredrick Santon, "How MGM Kept Norma Shearer After Irving Thalberg's Death," *CI,* 233 (Nov 1994), 37, 44.

Shearn, Edith [actress] (b. 1870–14 May 1968 [98], Los Angeles CA). m. **Warner Oland** (d. 1938). "Mrs. Warner Oland," *Variety,* 22 May 1968. AS, p. 994. Truitt, p. 303.

Sheehan, John J. [stage/film actor] (b. Oakland CA, 22 Oct 1885–15 Feb 1952 [66], Calabasas CA; heart ailment). m. Blanche Roberts. (Began acting in San Francisco in 1906; NY stage debut, 1909; began in films, 1914; American.) "John J. Sheehan, 66, Stage, Film Actor; Player on Boards and Screen for 42 Years Dies—Appeared Here in 'School for Brides,'" *NYT,* 16 Feb 1952, 13:4. "John J. Sheehan," *Variety,* 20 Feb 1952. AS, p. 994 (d. LA CA). BHD, p. 300 (d. LA CA). IFN, p. 270. Truitt, p. 303 (b. 1890). Lester Sweyd, "What They Are Doing Now," *Motion Picture Magazine,* Feb 1918, 13 ("...has joined the Wilkes stock in Seattle, where he has become quite a favorite.").

Sheehan, Perley Poore [scenarist/director] (b. Cincinnati OH, 11 Jun 1875–30 Sep 1943 [68], Sierra Madre CA). m. Virginia Pont, 1902. (FP-L; Goldwyn; Universal.) "Perley P. Sheehan, ex-Editor, Author; Executive of Paris Herald in 1905–07, Novelist, Scenario Writer, Dies in California," *NYT,* 2 Oct 1943, 13:5. AS, p. 994. BHD2, p. 242 (b. 1884). IFN, p. 271 (age 69).

Sheehan, Tess [actress] (*née* Maria Theresa Sheehan, b. 1888–29 Oct 1972 [], Detroit MI). AS, p. 994.

Sheehan, Winfield Richard [producer] (b. Buffalo NY, 24 Sep 1883–25 Jul 1945 [61], Los Angeles CA; complications after an operation). m. (1) **Kay Laurel**, 1922 (d. 1927); (2) Maria Jeritza, 1935 (widow). (Fox, 1914.) "Winfield Sheehan, Film Producer, 61; Creator of 'Calvacade,' 'What Price Glory' Dies—Husband of Jeritza, Opera Star," *NYT,* 26 Jul 1945, 19:3. Arthur Ungar, "Winfield Sheehan, Film Pioneer, Dies After Devoting 31 Years to Industry," *Variety,* 1 Aug 1945 (age 62). AMD, p. 315. AS, p. 994 (b. 21 Sep). BHD2, p. 242. IFN, p. 271. Katz, p. 1049. Spehr, p. 168. "The New Rental Basis," *MPW,* 17 Oct 1914, 316. "Sheehan Tours the West," *MPW,* 26 Dec 1914, 1852. Blaisdell, "Sheehan Helps Boost Prices; Uses Practical Methods of Impressing Exhibitors with Need for Higher Admissions," *MPW,* 22 May 1915, p. 1238:1 ("instructed the local Fox management to supply no more films to houses charging 5 cents admission"). "Motion Pictures Entering New Era in Opinion of Winfield R. Sheehan," *MPW,* 12 Jun 1926, 561. "Hollywood Too Cramped for Winfield R. Sheehan," *MPW,* 16 Oct 1926, 422. Sumner Smith, "Star-Making Competitor to Sheehan Appears, Fades Out," *MPW,* 20 Nov 1926, 1, 2. "Winfield R. Sheehan Predicts a New Era in Film Stories," *MPW,* 19 Feb 1927, 565. Don Juan, "So This Is Hollywood; Original Production Scrapped," *Paris and Hollywood Screen Secrets,* Oct 1927, 60–61 (*The Secret Studio,* directed by Harry Beaumont, cost Fox $125,000 to produce. Sheehan disliked it, got three writers to work on it with a new director, Victor Schertzinger. Fox poured $75,000 more into the film; it was finished in less than a month. "The original production was scrapped and he present one, from present indications, is expected to gross upward of $1,000,000.").

Sheer, William A. [actor] (b. Birmingham, England–d. 10 Jul 1933, New York NY). AMD, p. 315. AS, p. 994. BHD, p. 300. IFN, p. 271. "William Sheer, of 'The Regeneration' Fame, Again with Fox," *MPW,* 18 Nov 1916, 1031.

Sheerer, William E. [actor] (d. 24 Dec 1915, Yonkers NY). AMD, p. 315. AS, p. 994. BHD, p. 300. IFN, p. 271. "Will E. Sheerer," *MPW,* 8 Aug 1914, 818.

Sheffield, Leo [actor] (b. Malton, England, 15 Nov 1873–3 Sep 1951 [77]). BHD1, p. 500.

Sheffield, Reginald (father of Johnny Sheffield) [actor] (*né* Matthew Reginald Sheffield-Cassan, b. London, England, 18 Feb 1901–8 Dec 1957 [56], Pacific Palisades CA). m. Louise.

"Reginald Sheffield, 56; Actor Since 1913, Long in Movies, Dies on Coast," *NYT,* 9 Dec 1957, 35:3. AS, p. 994. BHD1, p. 500. IFN, p. 271. Katz, p. 1049. Truitt, p. 303.

Shelby, Charlotte (mother of **Margaret Shelby** and **Mary Miles Minter**) [stage actress] (*née* Lily Pearl Miles, b. Shreveport LA, 19 Dec 1877–13 Mar 1957 [79], Santa Monica CA). m. AS, p. 994. BHD, p. 300. Robert S. Klepper, "Mary Miles Minter: Beauty Wronged," *CI,* 265 (Jul 1997), C6-C11 (surname of Shelby came from her family; d. at age 85).

Shelby, Jeanne [stage/film actress] (b. 1889?–1 Nov 1964 [75], New York NY [Death Certificate Index No. 22925]). "Jeanne Shelby, 71, Actress Was Featured in Musicals," *NYT,* 3 Nov 1964, 31:1. "Jeanne Shelby," *Variety,* 18 Nov 1964. AS, p. 994.

Shelby, Margaret (daughter of **Charlotte Shelby**; sister of **Mary Miles Minter**) [actress] (*née* Margaret Reilly, b. San Antonio TX, 16 Jun 1900–21 Dec 1939 [39], Los Angeles CA; chronic alcoholism). m. **Emmett J. Flynn** (d. 1937); grandson of President Millard Fillmore. (American.) AS, p. 994. BHD, p. 300. IFN, p. 271.

Sheldon, E. Lloyd [scenarist]. No data found. AMD, p. 315. FDY, p. 437. "Sheldon Says His Best Play Is 'Wolves of the Night,'" *MPW,* 10 May 1919, 925. "Movie Fans in China Are Permitted to Assail Screen Villain, Says Sheldon," *MPW,* 31 Jul 1920, 586. "Sheldon Has Influenza," *MPW,* 10 Mar 1923, 144.

Sheldon, Forrest K. [scenarist]. No data found. FDY, p. 437.

Sheldon, Harry S[ophos] [actor/playwright/scenarist] (b. Copenhagen, Denmark, 1877?–18 Mar 1940 [63], New York NY; suicide with gas). "Harry S. Sheldon," *Variety,* 20 Mar 1940. BHD2, p. 242. SD, p. 131.

Sheldon, James M. [executive]. No data found. AMD, p. 315. "James M. Sheldon," *MPW,* 18 Aug 1917, 1057. "Freuler Resigns as Mutual's President," *MPW,* 18 May 1918, 971. "Screen Telegram Comes to New York," *MPW,* 20 Jul 1918, 379. "Sheldon Negotiating for More Players," *MPW,* 27 Jul 1918, 560. "Elinor FIeld to Star in One-Reel Strands," *MPW,* 27 Jul 1918, 572.

Sheldon, Jerome [actor] (b. OH, 13 Aug 1890–15 Apr 1962 [71], Los Angeles CA). (Universal.) Jerome Sheldon," *Variety,* 25 Apr 1962. AS, p. 994. BHD, p. 300. IFN, p. 271. Truitt, p. 303.

Sheldon, Kathryn [actress] (b. Cincinnati OH, 22 Sep 1879–25 Dec 1975 [96], Los Angeles Co. CA). AS, p. 994. BHD1, p. 500. IFN, p. 271.

Sheldon, Mrs. Marion W. [actress] (*née?,* b. Cambridge MA, 3 May 1885–28 Feb 1944 [58], Los Angeles CA). "Mrs. Marion W. Sheldon," *Variety,* 8 Mar 1944 (began 1917). AS, p. 994. BHD, p. 300. IFN, p. 271. Truitt, p. 303.

Sheldon, Orlo [makeup artist]. No data found. AMD, p. 315. "Has Knack for Clever Make-Up," *MPW,* 7 May 1927, 24.

Sheldon, Suzanne [actress] (b. Rutland VT, 24 Jan 1875–21 Mar 1924 [49], London, England; pneumonia). (Stage debut: *The Medicine Man,* Lyceum Theatre, London, 1898.) "Syuzanne Sheldon Is Dead; London Actress a Victim of Pneumonia—Was Native of Vermont," *NYT,* 24 Mar 1924, 15:4. "Suzanne Sheldon Dies," *Variety,* 26 Mar 1924, 3:2 (d. 22 Mar; her grandfather was Charles Sheldon, a pioneer in development of the Vermont marble quarries). BHD, p. 300.

Sheldon, William [assistant film director/TV director] (b. 1906?–31 Dec 1998 [92], Santa Monica CA; cardiac arrest). (MGM; awarded the Frank Capra Achievement Award for the Directors Guild of America in 1993.) Harris Lentz, III, "William Sheldon," *CI,* 285 (Mar 1999), 48.

Shelton, George [actor] (b. 1883–12 Feb 1971 [87?], New York NY; burned in a fire). AS, p. 995.

Shelton, Howard [director/producer] (né Hans Schwartz, b. Germany, 1890–27 Oct 1945 [55?], Los Angeles CA). AS, p. 995.

Shelton, James [actor/composer/lyricist/comedy writer for Jackie Gleason] (b. Paducah KY, 1913–2 Sep 1975 [62], Miami Heart Institute, Miami FL; heart attack). "James Shelton," *Variety,* 10 Sep 1975, 87:3 (in *Over the Hill* and other silents). AS, p. 995. BHD1, p. 500. IFN, p. 271.

Shelton, Marie [actress] (*née* Betty Marie Shelton, b. Muskogee OK, 1904–13 Mar 1949 []45?, Los Angeles CA). AS, p. 995. BHD, p. 300 (b. Atlanta GA).

Shenton, William [cinematographer]. No data found. FDY, p. 469.

Shepard, Burt [minstrel] (d. 15 Apr 1913, London, England). "Burt Shepard," *Variety,* 25 Apr and 2 May 1913. AS, p. 995.

Shepard, H.J. [publicist]. No data found. AMD, p. 315. H.J. Shepard, "Must Satisfy the Showman," *MPW,* 20 Jul 1918, 336.

Shepard, Iva [stage/film actress] (b. Cincinnati OH, 23 Apr 1886–26 Jan 1973 [86], Arcadia CA). (Selig; Universal.) m. **Joseph Singleton**; Lyle Clement, 2 Feb 1918, Fitchburg MA. AMD, p. 315. AS, p. 995. BHD, p. 300. Richard V. Spencer, "Los Angeles," *MPW,* 4 Mar 1911, 466 (rejoined Selig Co. in 1911). "This Week's Crop of Accidents," *MPW,* 19 Jul 1913, 306 (engaged to Joseph Edward Victor Fairfield Daveran Singleton). "Universal Actors Engaged to Wed," *MPW,* 19 Jul 1913, 332. "Engagement Note a Joke," *MPW,* 16 Aug 1913, 727. "Iva Shepard," *MPW,* 4 Jul 1914, 77. "Iva Shepard in Gaumont Stock," *MPW,* 6 May 1916, 947. "Marriages," *Variety,* 8 Feb 1918, p. 9 (to Clement).

Shepard, Pearl [actress]. No data found. "Auburn-Haired Beauty Wins at Ball," *MPW,* 18 Mar 1916, 1833.

Shepherd, Leonard [actor] (b. London, England, 13 Apr 1872–17 Apr 1958 [86], Enfield, Middlesex, England). BHD1, p. 500. Data supplied from St. Catherine's House by Mrs. Janice Healey of London.

Shepherd, William H. [actor/film editor] (b. 1894–10 Jul 1979 [85?], Sydney, New South Wales, Australia). AS, p. 995. BHD2, p. 242.

Shepley, Ruth [stage/film actress] (b. Providence RI, 29 May 1892–16 Oct 1951 [59], New York NY). m. (1) George Sarre, 1920–32; (2) Dr. Beverly C. Smith, 1932 (widower). "Ruth Shepley, 59, a Retired Actress; Former Star for U.S.O. Had Many Leading Roles Here—Dies After Long Illness," *NYT,* 17 Oct 1951, 31:2. "Ruth Shelpley," *Variety,* 24 Oct 1951. AMD, p. 315. AS, p. 995. BHD, p. 300. IFN, p. 271. Truitt, p. 303 (b. NY, 1889–5 Oct 1951). "Ruth Shepley," *MPW,* 30 Jan 1915, 674.

Sheppard, Bert [actor] (b. Australia, 1882?–18 Aug 1929 [47], Cassopolis MI; during a nervous breakdown). AS, p. 995. BHD, p. 300. IFN, p. 271.

Sheppard, Mabel G[ordon] [actress] b. 1879–5 Sep 1963 [84?], Philadelphia PA). AS, p. 995.

Sherek, Frank [actor] (b. Los Angeles CA, 19 Mar 1840–5 Jun 1903 [63], Los Angeles CA). AS, p. 995.

Sherek, Harold [actor] (b. Los Angeles CA, 21 Jul 1841–5 Jun 1913 [71], Los Angeles CA). AS, p. 995.

Sherek, Harry [actor] (b. Inglewood NJ, 18 May 1844–25 Jun 1931 [87], Los Angeles CA). AS, p. 995.

Sheridan, Andrew W. [assistant director] (b. 1885–25 Apr 1949 [64?], New York NY). BHD2, p. 242.

Sheridan, Ann, The "Oomph Girl" [film/TV actress] (aka Gloria Heller, *née* Clara Lou Sheridan, b. Denton TX, 21 Feb 1915–21 Jan 1967 [51], Los Angeles CA; cancer). m. (1) S. Edward Norris, Aug 1936–Oct 1937; (2) George Brent, 5 Jan 1942–42; (3) Scott McKay, Jun 1966 (widower). (Lasky; Paramount; WB.) "Ann Sheridan, Actress, 51, Dies; Career Spanned 33-Year Period; 'Man Who Came to Dinner' and 'Kings Row' Among Her Many Films," *NYT,* 22 Jan 1967, 77:1. "Funeral for Ann Sheridan Takes Place on the Coast [in No. Hollywood CA]," *NYT,* 23 Jan 1967, 43:4. "Ann Sheridan," *Variety,* 25 Jan 1967. AS, p. 996. BHD1, p. 501. IFN, p. 271. Katz, pp. 1050–51. Don Juan, "So This Is Hollywood," *Paris and Hollywood Screen Secrets Magazine,* May 1927, 31–32 (16 years old; filming *Casey at the Bat*). George A. Katchmer, "Remembering the Great Silents," *CI,* 183 (Sep 1990), 46.

Sheridan, Frank [stage/film actor] (b. Boston MA, 11 Jun 1869–24 Nov 1943 [74], Los Angeles CA). m. Edna M. Carrol. "Frank Sheridan Dies; Actor for 62 Years; Stage and Screen Veteran Made Debut at 12—Dies in Hollywood," *NYT,* 28 Nov 1943, 68:7. "Frank Sheridan," *Variety,* 1 Dec 1943 (in *Fast Life,* 1st National, 1929). AMD, p. 315. AS, p. 996. BHD1, p. 501. IFN, p. 271. Truitt, p. 303. "Sheridan in Klein's 'The Money Master,'" *MPW,* 11 Sep 1915, 1815.

Sheridan, Isabelle (cousin of **Jack, Lottie** and **Mary Pickford**; niece of **Charlotte Pickford**) [actress]. No data found. AMD, p. 315. "Mary Pickford's Cousin in Cast," *MPW,* 25 Jun 1927, 592.

Sherman, Evelyn [actress] (b. IA, 13 Dec 1882–19 Apr 1974 [92], Los Angeles Co. CA). AS, p. 996. BHD1, p. 501. IFN, p. 271. George Katchmer, "Remembering the Great Silents," *CI,* 202 (Apr 1992), 6.

Sherman, Harry A. "Pop" [producer] (b. Boston MA, 5 Nov 1884–25 Sep 1952 [67], Los Angeles CA). m. Florence Gardner—div. 1942. (Hollywood, 1916; Pathé; MGM.) "Harry Sherman, 67, 'Hopalong' Producer," *NYT,* 27 Sep 1952, 17:2. "Harry Sherman," *Variety,* 1 Oct 1952. AMD, p. 315. AS, p. 996. BHD2, p. 242. IFN, p. 271. "Harry A. Sherman Enters Producing Ranks," *MPW,* 16 Jun 1917, 1783.

Sherman, Joseph C. [scenarist] (b. Chicago IL, 1892–19 Dec 1944 [52?], Tucson AZ). AS, p. 995. BHD2, p. 243.

Sherman, Lowell J. [stage/film actor/director] (b. San Francisco CA, 11 Oct 1885–28 Dec 1934 [49], Los Angeles CA; pneumonia). m. Evelyn Booth; **Helene Costello** (d. 1957); **Pauline Garon** (d. 1965). (Griffith.) "Lowell Sherman Dies on the Coast; Actor and Film Director Who Had Many Successes on Broadway Was 49," *NYT,* 29 Dec 1934, 15:1. "Lowell Sherman," *Variety,* 1 Jan 1935. AMD, p. 315. AS, p. 996. BHD1, p. 501; BHD2, p. 243 (b. 1888). FSS, p. 258. IFN, p. 271 (b. 1888). Katz, p. 1051. Truitt, pp. 303–304. "Joins Sennett," *MPW,* 28 May 1921, 422. Horace T. Jenkins, "How a Screen Star's Cold Cost $10,000 a Day; Blemish on lip of Lowell Sherman causes suspension in production plans at Famous Players-Lasky studio—Star is screenically *hors d'-combat,*" *MV,* 26 Apr 1924, 14, 26 (during filming of *Monsieur Beaucaire*). "Warners Sign Lowell Sherman," *MPW,* 28 Feb 1925, 925. Nanette Kutner, "The Wickedest Man on the Screen," *MM,* Mar 1926, 47–48, 88–89.

Sherman, Mary [actress] (*née* Ida Sherman, b. Russia, 1887–13 Aug 1980 [93?], Santa Monica CA). AS, p. 996. BHD1, p. 501.

Sherman, Sam [title writer]. No data found. FDY, p. 447.

Sherriff, R[obert] **C**[edric] [scenarist] (b. Kingston-on-Thames, England, 6 Jun 1896–13 Nov 1975 [79], London, England). AS, p. 995.

Sherrill, Jack [stage/film actor] (b. Atlanta GA, 14 Apr 1898–26 Nov 1973 [75], Honolulu HI). (Arthurs Film Co.; Frohman; Mutual.) AMD, p. 315. AS, p. 997. BHD, p. 300. MSBB, p. 1028. 1921 Directory, p. 200. WWS, p. 128. "Jack Sherrill," *MPW,* 25 Mar 1916, 2012. "Jack Sherrill Is Off to California," *MPW,* 13 May 1916, 1145. Jack Sherrill, "As It Was in the Beginning," *MPW,* 21 Jul 1917, 461–62. "Jack Sherrill in Author's Film Subject," *MPW,* 25 Aug 1917, 1203. "Sherrill Talks of His Coming Picture," *MPW,* 1 Sep 1917, 1361. "Jack Sherrill Will Star in Serial," *MPW,* 13 Sep 1919, 1677. "Jack Sherrill Jumps from Airplane in Serial Scene," *MPW,* 7 Feb 1920, 895.

Sherrill, William L. [executive: vice-president of the Frohman Amusement Co.] (b. Macon GA, 1866?–5 Dec 1940 [74], Van Nuys CA). "William L. Sherrill," *Variety,* 11 Dec 1940. AMD, p. 316. AS, p. 997. BHD2, p. 243. "William L. Sherrill," *MPW,* 20 Feb 1915, 1145:2 (first production at Frohman: *The Fairy and the Waif,* with Mary Miles Minter and Percy Helton). "Sherrill on the Fence," *MPW,* 14 Oct 1916, 245. "Sherrill Gives Views on Open Market," *MPW,* 21 Oct 1916, 407. "Sherrill Tells His Plans," *MPW,* 30 Dec 1916, 1943. "Sherrill Withdraws from Art Dramas," *MPW,* 3 Mar 1917, 1334. "William L. Sherrill Talks," *MPW,* 21 Jul 1917, 469. "Sherrill Talks of His Coming Picture," *MPW,* 1 Sep 1917, 1361. "Sherrill to Make Two-Reel Westerns," *MPW,* 1 Feb 1919, 602. "Sherrill Has Some Do's and Dont's," *MPW,* 1 Mar 1919, 1201. "Jack Sherrill Will Star in Serial," *MPW,* 13 Sep 1919, 1677. William L. Sherrill, "'Wildcat' Independent Operators to Be Wiped Out and Stability to Be Served by Industry," *MPW,* 27 Dec 1919, 1119. "Sherrill Has Increased Capital Stock of Frohman Corporation," *MPW,* 10 Jan 1920, 224. William L. Sherrill, "Gain for Producer and Buyer Seen in Closer Co-Operation by Exchange Men," *MPW,* 6 Mar 1920, 1653. John G. Holme, "Film-Flamming the Public; Exposing some further activities of those who prey on the public faith in the Motion Picture," *Photoplay,* XIX (Mar 1921), 60, 120–21 (he announced a contract with Lillian Gish last summer. She was to receive $3,500 per week with yearly increases and other perks. "To finance his star, Sherrill ran big stock-selling advertisements in papers throughout the country and carried on an aggressive stock selling campaign by mail." However, war-time prosperity was on the ebb and in Sep 1920 he gave up the effort to float himself. He then proposed to form a small syndicate to finance two films starring Gish and Ruth Clifford; he stated that the money was pledged. Clifford sued and there was a countersuit. Then the Gish project was halted. "Jesse J. Goldberg, general manager of the Frohman Company, announced his resignation, and finally came the receivership proceedings.").

Sherry, J. Barney [stage/film actor] (*né* J. Barney Sherry Reeves, b. Germantown, Philadelphia PA, 4 Mar 1871–22 Feb 1944 [72], Philadelphia PA). "J. Barney Sherry, Veteran Actor, 72; Stage and Screen Figure Dies in Pennsylvania—Known for Portrayal of General Lee," *NYT,* 23 Feb 1944, 19:4. "J. Barney Sherry," *Variety,* 1 Mar 1944. AMD, p. 316. AS, p. 997. BHD1, p. 501 (b. 1874). IFN, p. 271. Lowrey, p. 168. MH, p. 136. Truitt, p. 304. "Picture Players Arrested for Assault," *Variety,* 38, 16 Apr 1915, 17:4 (On 14 Apr 1915, Barney Sherry, Harry Woodruff and Harry Clark were "arrested for attacking William Faber at the Venice Dance Pavillion." Released on bond.) "J. Barney Sherry," *MPW,* 26 May 1917, 1296.

Sherwin, Louis [scenarist]. No data found. AMD, p. 316. "Louis Sherwin Now on Goldwyn Scenario Staff," *MPW,* 26 Apr 1919, 513. "Louis Sherwin, ex-Critic, Becomes Goldwyn Scenarist," *MPW,* 16 Aug 1919, 988. "Play for Fox," *MPW,* 23 Jun 1923, 678.

Sherwood, Arthur W. [actor] (b. Los Angeles CA-d. 14 Mar 1986, Joplin MO). BHD, p. 301.

Sherwood, Clarence L. [actor] (b. Shiloh LA, 5 Jan 1884–15 Jan 1941 [57], Los Angeles Co. CA). AS, p. 997. BHD1, p. 501. IFN, p. 271.

Sherwood, Clifford [scenarist] (b. 1884–20 Jun 1933 [49?], Los Angeles CA). BHD2, p. 243.

Sherwood, Lydia [actress] (*née* Lily Shavelson, b. London, England, 5 May 1906–20 Apr 1989 [82], London, England). AS, p. 997. BHD1, p. 501 (b. 1903).

Sherwood, Millige G. [actor] (b. Los Angeles CA, 24 Apr 1876–12 Nov 1958 [82], Los Angeles CA). AS, p. 997.

Sherwood, William "Billy" [stage/film actor] (b. New Orleans LA, ca. 1896–24 May 1918 [ca. 22], Washington DC; result of a three-storey fall onto concrete). (Kleine.) AMD, p. 316. AS, p. 997 (Billy Sherwood). BHD, pp. 66–67; 301. "Billy Sherwood Joins Kalem Forces," *MPW,* 6 Nov 1915, 1123. "Billy Sherwood at Work with Edison," *MPW,* 1 Jan 1916, 73. "'Billy' Sherwood, Metro Juvenile Lead," *MPW,* 3 Jun 1916, 1700. "'Billy' Sherwood, Versatile Player," *MPW,* 23 Sep 1916, 1950. "Sherwood to Play Opposite Mabel Taliaferro," *MPW,* 21 Jul 1917, 489. Billy H. Doyle, "Lost Players," *CI,* 134 (Aug 1986), 53.

Sherwood, Yorke [actor] (b. England, 14 Dec 1873–27 Sep 1958 [84], Los Angeles CA). (Sennett.) "Yorke Sherwood," *Variety,* 8 Oct 1958 (age 85). AS, p. 997. BHD1, p. 501. IFN, p. 272. Truitt, p. 304.

Shields, Arthur [actor] (b. Dublin, Ireland, 15 Feb 1896–27 Apr 1970 [74], Santa Barbara CA; emphysema). AS, p. 997. BHD1, p. 502.

Shields, Ella [actress] (b. Baltimore MD, 26 Sep 1879–5 Aug 1952 [72], Lancaster, England). BHD1, p. 502.

Shields, Ernest W. [actor] (b. Chicago IL, 5 Aug 1884–13 Dec 1944 [60], Los Angeles CA)). m. **Betty Schade**, Church of the Angels, Los Angeles CA, Easter Sunday, 1917. (Universal.) AS, p. 997 (b. 1897). BHD1, p. 502. Cal York, "Plays and Players," *Photoplay,* Jul 1917, 111 (married Schade).

Shields, Russell G. [film editor] (b. Kensington PA, 1889?–3 May 1947 [58], New York NY). m. Valeska Weidig. (Lubin; Fox.) "Russell G. Shields; Was Twentieth Century-Fox Film Editor—In Field 35 Years [since 1912]," *NYT,* 6 May 1947, 27:3. "Russell Shields," *Variety,* 7 May 1947 (age 55).

Shields, Sandy [actor] (b. 1873?–3 Aug 1923 [50], New York NY). "Sandy Shields," *Variety,* 9 Aug 1923. AS, p. 997. BHD, p. 301. IFN, p. 272. Truitt, p. 304.

Shields, Sydney [actress] (b. New Orleans LA, 1888?–19 Sep 1960 [72], Queens, New York NY). m. Edward H. Robins. (Interstate Feature Film Co.) "Sydney Shields, 72, Long an Actress," *NYT,* 21 Sep 1960, 37:1. "Sydney Shields," *Variety,* 28 Sep 1960. AS, p. 997. BHD, p. 301. IFN, p. 272. Truitt, p. 304.

Shildkert, K. [scenarist]. No data found. FDY, p. 437.

Shilkret, Nathaniel [composer] (b. New York NY, 25 Jan 1895–18 Feb 1982 [87], Franklin Square, New York NY). AS, p. 998 (b. 1 Jan). ASCAP 66, p. 670. BHD2, p. 243 (b. 1 Jan).

Shimazu, Yasujiro [director] (b. Tokyo, Japan, 3 Jun 1897–18 Sep 1945 [48], Tokyo, Japan; stomach cancer). AS, p. 998.

Shine, John L. [actor/playwright/producer] (b. Manchester, England, 28 May 1854–16 Oct 1930 [76], New York NY; Bright's disease). m. Annie L. Maccabe. "John L. Shine Dead; On Stage 55 Years; Was Actor, Playwright and Producer During Career that Began in England; In One Play 2,000 Times; Toured All Over the World in Boucicault's 'The Shaughraum'—American Debut 20 Years Ago," *NYT,* 17 Oct 1930, 23:5. AS, p. 998. BHD, p. 301.

Shine, Wilfred [burlesque/comic opera/stage/film/TV actor/radio writer] (b. Manchester, England, 12 Jul 1863–14 Mar 1939 [75], Kingston, Surrey, England). "Wilfred Shine," *Variety,* 134, 22 Mar 1939, 62:2 (age 76). AS, p. 998 (1864). BHD1, p. 502. IFN, p. 272 (b. 1864).

Shingleton, Barney (brother of **Betty Shingleton**) [actor] (b. Indianapolis IN, 11 Aug 1844–6 Oct 1902 [58], Los Angeles CA). AS, p. 998.

Shingleton, Betty (sister of **Barney Shingleton**) [actress] (b. Indianapolis IN, 17 Mar 1843–25 Sep 1928 [85], Los Angeles CA). AS, p. 998.

Shinn, Everett P. [artist] (b. Woodstown NJ, 1873–1 May 1953 [79], New York NY). m. (1) Florence Scovel, 1898; (2) Corinne Baldwin, 1913; (3) Gertrude McManus Chase, 1924; (4) Paula Downing, 1933. "Everett Shinn, 79, Noted Artist, Dies; One of '8 Men of Rebellion' Who Introduced Modernism to U.S. Was an Eclectic; Armory Show Sponsor; Painting of Theatre Subjects Inspired His Production of Vaudeville Melodramas," *NYT,* 3 May 1953, 89:1 (produced *Myrtle Clayton, Wronged from the Start; Hazel Weston, or More Sinned Against than Usual;* and *Lucy Moore, the Prune Hater's Daughter*). "Everett Shinn," *Variety,* 6 May 1953. AMD, p. 316. AS, p. 998.

"Everitt Shinn with Goldwyn Staff," *MPW,* 26 May 1917, 1289. "The Art of Everitt Shinn," *MPW,* 1 Dec 1917, 1302.

Shipman, Alfred [producer] (b. 1889–28 May 1956 [67?], London, England). AS, p. 998.

Shipman, Barry (son of **Nell Shipman**) [actor] (b. So. Pasadena CA, 24 Feb 1912–12 Aug 1994 [82], San Bernardino CA). BHD1, p. 502; BHD2, p. 243.

Shipman, Edna (niece of **Ernest Shipman**) [actress] (b. 15 Nov 1901). AMD, p. 316. "Edna Shipman, FIlm Actress, Is Given Surprise Party on Her Eighteenth Birthday," *MPW,* 29 Nov 1919, 547. "Edna Shipman Loaned to Winnipeg," *MPW,* 7 Aug 1920, 716.

Shipman, Ernest (uncle of **Edna Shipman**) [producer] (b. Ottawa, Ontario, Canada-d. 7 Aug 1931, New York NY). m. **Nell**, 1911–20. AMD, p. 316. BHD2, p. 243. "Ernest Shipman Resigns from Universal," *MPW,* 24 Apr 1915, 534. "Ernest Shipman's Mother Dies," *MPW,* 10 Apr 1920, 231 (Mrs. M.A.B. Shipman, d. at 67, Pasadena CA). "Ernest Shipman Will Exploit Fourteen Big Attractions for the Coming Season," *MPW,* 28 Aug 1920, 1162. "Shipman Writes of Italian Market," *MPW,* 4 Jun 1921, 497. "Ernest Shipman Negotiates Contracts for Series of International Pictures," *MPW,* 18 Jun 1921, 695. "Ernest Shipman Joins Ranks of W.W. Hodkinson Corporation," *MPW,* 24 Feb 1923, 766. "Shipman Has Exclusive Rights to the Tut-Ankh-Amen Pictures," *MPW,* 31 Mar 1923, 510. "Ernest Shipman Will Produce a Series of Pictures in the South," *MPW,* 20 Oct 1923, 646. "Production Possibilities in South Stir Ernest Shipman," *MPW,* 15 Dec 1923, 604. "Independent Studios Soon Will Dot Florida, Shipman Predicts," *MPW,* 2 Feb 1924, 389.

Shipman, Gertrude [actress]. No data found. (Champion.) Spehr, p. 168.

Shipman, Nell (mother of **Barry Shipman**) [stage/film actress/scenarist] (*née* Helen Foster-Barham, b. Victoria, British Columbia, Canada, 25 Oct 1892–23 Jan 1970 [77], Cabazon CA). m. (1) **Ernest Shipman**, 1911–div. 1920 (d. 1931); Charles Austin Ayers, 1925 (d. 1964). *The Silent Screen & My Talking Heart; An Autobiography* (2nd ed., 1990; Boise ID: Boise State Univ., 1987). (First professional stage engagement, *At Yale,* 1906; Fox; Vitagraph.) AMD, p. 316. AS, p. 998. BHD, p. 301. BR, pp. 71–74. FDY, p. 437. IFN, p. 273. MSBB, p. 1042. 1921 Directory, p. 239. "Egan Contest Award," *MPW,* 21 Dec 1912, 1198 (cited as an experienced scenarist). "Nell Shipman Busy; Charming Writer, Who Appears on 'Mirror' Cover, One of Busiest Persons in Filmland," *NYDM,* 31 Mar 1915, 25:1. "Nell Shipman Returns East," *MPW,* 4 Nov 1916, 682. "Nell Shipman Returns from West Indies," *MPW,* 7 Jul 1917, 99. "Nell Shipman Independent," *MPW,* 8 Sep 1917, 1558. "Nell Shipman, Australian Favorite," *MPW,* 29 Jun 1918, 1831. "Nell Shipman Leaves Vitagraph," *MPW,* 9 Nov 1918, 669. "Curwood and Nell Shipman Form Producing Company," *MPW,* 9 Nov 1918, 678. "Star Loses Mother," *MPW,* 28 Dec 1918, 1496 (Mrs. Rose Barham, d. 7 Dec 1918, GLendale CA). "Nell Shipman Heads New Company," *MPW,* 4 Sep 1920, 89. "Nell Shipman Enters Production Field with Company of Her Own," *MPW,* 9 Oct 1920, 802. Tom Fullbright, "Nell Shipman: Queen of the Dog Sleds," *CFC,* No. 25 (Fall, 1969), 30–31, 39. "Something New," *The Big Reel,* #222, Nov 1992, 127. Mike Newton, "Nell Shipman: 'The Girl from God's Country,'" *CI,* 210 (Dec 1992), C6.

Shirart, Georgia [actress] (b. 1861–26 Feb 1929 [67?], Los Angeles CA; stomach cancer). (Lubin, 1913; Universal; Triangle.) "Georgia Shirart," *Variety,* 20 Feb 1929. AS, p. 998 (d. 10 Feb). BHD1, p. 300 (Sherart); 616. IFN, p. 271 (Sherart). Truitt, p. 304.

Shirk, Adam Hull [editor of *New York Dramatic Mirror*/scenarist] (b. 1887?–27 Jul 1931 [44], Lanrescenta CA). "Adam Hull Shirk," *Variety,* 28 Jul 1931. AMD, p. 316. BHD2, p. 243 (b. 1881). FDY, p. 437. "Shirk Now Lasky Publicity Head," *MPW,* 18 Jan 1919, 329.

Shirley, Anne [actress] (aka Dawn O'Day, *née* Dawn Evelyeen Paris, b. New York NY, 17 Apr 1918–4 Jul 1993 [75], Los Angeles CA; lung cancer). m. (1) John Payne, 22 Aug 1937–43 (d. 1989; daughter Julia); (2) Adrian Scott, 10 Feb 1945–49 (d. 1972); (3) Charles Lederer, 10 Oct 1949 (d. 1976; son, Daniel). (RKO.) "Anne Shirley," *Daily News,* 75, 7 Jul 1993, 47:1 (age 74). (Began ca. 1921.) "Anne Shirley Is Dead; Film Actress Was 74," *NYT,* 8 Jul 1993, D18:5. AMD, p. 265 (Dawn O'Day). AS, p. 825 (Dawn O'Day); p. 998. BHD, p. 265 (Dawn O'Day); BHD1, p. 502. Katz, p. 1054 (began 1922). "Century Signs Baby Dawn O'Day," *MPW,* 17 Nov 1923, 333. James Bawden, "Sketching the Film Careers of Dawn O'Day and Anne Shirley," *Filmograph,* IV, No. 3 (1975), 21–40 (includes filmography). George Katchmer, "Remembering the Great Silents," *CI,* 210 (Dec 1992), 52 (changed name in 1934; retired, 1945).

Shirley, Arthur [actor/writer] (b. London, England, 17 Feb 1853–22 Aug 1925 [72], London, England). m. Florence Hay-Allen. "Arthur Shirley, Dramatist, Dead; Prolific Writer of Thrilling Melodramas Dies in London at 72 Years; A Collaborator of Sims; 'Strangers of Paris,' 'Two Little Vagabonds' and 'Tommy Atkins' Among His Best Known Plays," *NYT,* 23 Aug 1925, II, 7:3. "Arthur Shirley Dead," *Variety,* 26 Aug 1925. AS, p. 998. IFN, p. 272. "Australia Calls Arthur Shirley," *NYDM,* 27 Nov 1915, 35:1 (an Australian promoter offered to provide funds and a studio if Shirley, the lead in *The Fall of a Nation,* were to return to "his native land," Australia. "However, Shirley seems to be pretty well pelased with his present place in Los Angeles.").

Shirley, Arthur [actor/director/producer/scenarist] (b. Hobart, Tasmania, 31 Aug 1886–1967 [80?], Sydney, New South Wales, Australia). AS, p. 998. BHD1, p. 616; BHD2, p. 243.

Shirley, Bobbie [actor] (d. 13 Feb 1970). AS, p. 999. BHD, p. 301.

Shirley, Florence [actress] (b. New York NY, 5 Jun 1892–12 May 1967 [74], Los Angeles CA). AS, p. 999.

Shirley, Jessie [actress] (b. 1886–30 May 1918 [32?], Spokane WA). m. Harry W. Smith. "Jessie Shirley," *Variety,* 14 Jun 1918. AS, p. 999. BHD, p. 301.

Shirley, Tom [actor] (*né* Thomas P. Shirley, b. Chicago IL, 1899?–23 Jan 1962 [62], New York NY [Death Certificate Index No. 1857]). "Tom Shirley, Actor on Stage and TV, 62," *NYT,* 25 Jan 1962, 31:2. "Tom Shirley," *Variety,* 7 Feb 1962. AS, p. 999. BHD, p. 301 (b. 1900; d. 24 Jan). IFN, p. 272. Truitt, p. 304.

Shirley, Winona (cousin of **Buster Keaton**) [actress]. No data found. AMD, p. 316. "Beauties Added," *MPW,* 24 Oct 1925, 644.

Shoemaker, Ann [actress] (b. Brooklyn NY, 10 Jan 1891–18 Sep 1978 [87], Los Angeles CA; cancer). AS, p. 999. BHD1, p. 502.

Shooting Star [actor] (b. 1889–4 Jun 1966 [77?], Los Angeles CA; cerebral thrombosis). AS, p. 999.

Shore, Viola Brothers [lyricist/title writer/scenarist] (*née* Viola Brothers?, b. New York NY, 26 May 1890–29 Mar 1970 [79], New York NY; heart attack; found dead). (Viola Shore). m. 3 times: (1) William J. Shore. "Viola Shore, Wrote Stories and Movies," *NYT,* 31 Mar 1970, 41:3 ("...she wrote titles for silent films and scripts for sound movies, including the first pictures starring Clara Bow."). "Viola Shore," *Variety,* 1 Apr 1970. AS, p. 999. BHD2, p. 243. FDY, p. 447.

Shores, Lynn [director/scenarist] (b. Binghamton NY, 22 Sep 1893–28 Dec 1949 [56], Los Angeles CA). AS, p. 999. BHD2, p. 243 (b. PA). FDY, p. 437.

Shorr, Lester [cameraman] (b. Brooklyn NY, 11 Apr 1907–28 Jul 1992 [85], Los Angeles CA; cancer). m. Rosalind. (Columbia.) "Lester Shorr," *Variety,* 10 Aug 1992, p. 67. AS, p. 999. BHD2, p. 243.

Short, Antrim (son of **Lewis Short**; brother of **Gertrude** and **Florence Short**; cousin of **Blanche Sweet**) [actor] (*né* Mark Antrim Short, b. Cincinnati OH, 11 Jul 1900–24 Nov 1972 [72], Woodland Hills CA; emphysema). m. actress Frances Morris. (Biograph, 1912.) "Antrim Short," *Variety,* 29 Nov 1972. AMD, p. 317. AS, p. 999 (d. 23 Nov). BHD1, p. 503; BHD2, p. 243. FSS, p. 259. IFN, p. 272. "Antrim Short Signed," *MPW,* 28 Feb 1925, 912. "Antrim Short," *MPW,* 6 Jun 1925, 672. George Katchmer, "Antrim Short," *CI,* 214 (Apr 1993), 52.

Short, Don [actor] (d. 1 Apr 1949, Hollywood CA; suffocated in apartment fire with wife). m. **Faith Hampton** (d. 1949). "Faith Hampton," *Variety,* 6 Apr 1949. AS, p. 999 (d. 1 Apr).

Short, Florence (daughter of **Lewis Short**; sister of **Gertrude** and **Antrim Short**; cousin of **Blanche Sweet**) [actress] (b. Springfield MA, 19 May 1889–10 Jul 1946 [57], Los Angeles CA). "Florence Short," *Variety,* 17 Jul 1946. AMD, p. 317. AS, p. 999 (b. Cincinnati OH). BHD1, p. 503. IFN, p. 272. Truitt, p. 304. "Florence Short," *MPW,* 15 Sep 1917, 1699. "Florence Short," *MPW,* 6 Apr 1918, 73.

Short, Gertrude (daughter of **Lewis Short**; sister of **Antrim** and **Florence Short**; cousin of **Blanche Sweet**) [actress] (*née* Carmen Gertrude Short, b. Cincinnati OH, 6 Apr 1900–31 Jul 1968 [68], Los Angeles CA). m. **Scott Pembroke** (d. 1951). (Film debut: *Rent Free,* Paramount; Edison.) "Gertrude Short," *Variety,* 7 Aug 1968. AMD, p. 317. AS, p. 999 (b. 1902). BHD1, p. 503. IFN, p. 272 (b. 1902). Truitt, p. 305. "Miss Short Cast," *MPW,* 31 Jan 1925, 495. "Fitzgerald Engages Short," *MPW,* 1 Aug 1925, 554. "Gertrude Short," *MPW,* 3 Apr 1926, 354. "'Comedy Girl' Choen to Play 'Tragic' Child Role," *MPW,* 4 Dec 1926, 352. George Katchmer, "Remembering the Great Silents," *CI,* 202 (Apr 1992), 6 (began in 1913 in *Uncle Tom's Cabin*).

Short, Harry [vaudeville/stage/film/radio actor] (b. 1876–17 Aug 1943 [67], House of Cavalry, Bronx NY). "Harry Short Dies; Stage Comedian, 67; Actor, Long with the Ziegfeld Follies, Later Was in Radio," *NYT,* 19 Aug 1943, 19:2 (member of the Lambs Club). "Harry Short,"

Variety, 151, 25 Aug 1943, 46:4. AS, p. 999. BHD1, p. 503. IFN, p. 272.

Short, Hassard [actor/director] (*né* Hubert Hassard-Short, b. Edington, Lincolnshire, England, 15 Oct 1877–7 Oct 1956 [78], Nice, France). Bachelor. "Hassard Short, Director, Dead; Staged 50 Broadway Shows—Made Many Innovations in Lighting and Designing," *NYT,* 10 Oct 1956, 39:1. "Memorial Service for Short," *NYT,* 21 Nov 1956, 27:4. "Hassard Short," *Variety,* 17 Oct 1956. AS, p. 999 (d. 1936). BHD, p. 301 (d. 9 Oct). IFN, p. 272.

Short, Lewis W. [actor] (father of **Gertrude, Florence** and **Antrim Short**) (b. Dayton OH, 14 Feb 1875–26 Apr 1958 [83], Los Angeles CA). (Biograph, 1910; Universal.) "Lewis W. Short," *Variety,* 30 Apr 1958. AS, p. 999. BHD1, p. 503. IFN, p. 272. Truitt, p. 305.

Shostakovich, Dmitri [composer/scenarist] (b. St. Petersburg, Russia, 25 Sep 1906–9 Aug 1975 [68], Moscow, Russia). Laurel E. Fay, *Shostakovich: A Life* (NY: Oxford Univ. Press, 2000). BHD2, p. 243.

Shotter, Winifred [actress] (b. London, England, 5 Nov 1904–4 Apr 1996 [91], Montreaux, Switzerland). AS, p. 999. BHD, p. 503.

Shotwell, Marie [actress] (b. New York NY, 1880?–18 Sep 1934 [54], Long Island City NY). "Marie Shotwell," *Variety,* 25 Sep 1934. AMD, p. 317. AS, p. 999. BHD, p. 301 (b. 1886). IFN, p. 272. "Marie Shotwell Joins Thanhouser," *MPW,* 5 Aug 1916, 930. "Hallmark Secures Marie Shotwell," *MPW,* 22 Nov 1919, 416.

Shrewbury, Lillian [actress] (b. Talladega AL, 28 Oct 1888–15 Jun 1979 [90], Los Angeles CA). AS, p. 1000.

Shtraukh, Maxim Maximovich [actor] (b. Russia, 23 Feb 1900–3 Jan 1974 [73], Moscow, Russia). AS, p. 1000 (b. 24 Feb. BHD1, p. 503.

Shub, Esther [director] (b. Chernigovsky, Ukraine, Russia, 3 Mar 1894–ca. 1959 [65?]). AS, p. 1000.

Shubert, Eddie [actor] (b. Milwaukee WI, 11 Jul 1898–23 Jan 1937 [38], Los Angeles CA). AS, p. 1000.

Shubert, Lee (brother of Jacob J. and Samuel S. Shubert [d. 11 May 1905]) [director/producer/executive] (b. Syracuse NY, 15 Mar 1870?–25 Dec 1953 [83?], New York NY; cerebral hemorrhage and complete failure of the circulatory system). m. Marcella Swanson—div. 1948; remarried 1949. Jerry Stagg, *The Brothers Shubert.* "Lee Shubert Dies in Hospital; Long Ruled Theatre Empire; Producer and Owner for Fifty Years Succumbs—Fought Erlanger," *NYT,* 26 Dec 1953, 1:4, 13:2 (successfully fought the monopoly of Klaw & Erlanger. In 1950, the Shubert brothers were charged by the government with monopolistic practices in the legitimate theatre). "Far-Reaching Legit Changes Likely as Result of the Shubert Passing," *Variety,* 193, 30 Dec 1953, 63:1 (b. ca. 1870). AMD, p. 317. "Lee Shubert Home, Ill of Grief," *NYT,* 1 Jun 1905, 11:4 (arrived 31 May on the Oceanic from Europe. Prostrate with grief over the death of his brother, "[h]e was too ill last evening to talk of his plans."). "All to Lee Shubert; His Brother's Will Directs That He Provide for Mother and Sisters," *NYT,* 6 Jun 1905, 9:4 (will dated 25 Jun 1903 "directs that after the payment of his debts and funeral expenses, all his property be turned over to his brother, Lee Shubert, with whom he was associated in business." He made the provision "well knowing, and directing that he will act fairly and honorably toward our sisters and mother, and that he shall never leave them in want, but will maintain them in the proper station and sphere of life."). "Goldwyn Capital Now $20,000,000," *MPW,* 9 Aug 1919, 785.

Shuford, Andy [actor] (b. Helena AR, 16 Dec 1917–19 May 1995 [77], Monteagle TN). BHD1, p. 503.

Shuftan, Eugen [cinematographer] (b. Breslau, Germany, 21 Jul 1886–6 Sep 1977 [91], New York NY). AS, p. 1000 (b. Wroclaw, Poland, 1893–15 Sep). BHD2, p. 243.

Shulkin, Esther [scenarist]. No data found. FDY, p. 437.

Shulsinger, Rose [publicist] (d. 26 Sep 1924, Lake Placid NY). (Cosmopolitan; FP-L.) "Rose Shulsinger," *Variety,* 1 Oct 1924, 26:5. AMD, p. 317. "Rose Shulsinger Appointed," *MPW,* 25 Sep 1920, 522.

Shultz, Harry [actor] (b. 1883–4 Jul 1935 [52?], Los Angeles CA). BHD1, p. 503.

Shumate, Harold [title writer/scenarist/radio announcer] (b. 1912?–20 Mar 1950 [38], near Harlingen TX; airplane crash). "Hal Shumate," *Variety,* 29 Mar 1950. FDY, pp. 437, 447.

Shumate, Harold M. [scenarist] (b. Austin TX, 7 Sep 1893–5 Aug 1983 [89], Thousand Oaks CA). BHD2, p. 244.

Shumway, Lee (Leonard) C. [actor] (b. Salt Lake City UT, 4 Mar 1884–4 Jan 1959 [74], Los Angeles CA). (Lubin; Universal.) AMD, p. 317. AS, p. 1000. BHD1, p. 503. IFN, p. 272. "L.C. Shumway," *MPW,* 8 May 1915, 873. "In the Picture Studios," *NYDM,* 14 Jul 1915, 27:1 ("...has been forced to take to his bed for several days in order to recoup his energy. It is feared that he will have to give up work for several months to entirely regain his health.").

Shumway, Walter George [actor] (b. Cleveland OH, 26 Aug 1884–13 Jan 1965 [80], Woodland Hills CA; heart attack). AS, p. 1000. BHD1, p. 503. IFN, p. 272. George Katchmer, "Remembering the Great Silents," *CI,* 202 (Apr 1992), 6.

Sibirskaia, Nadia [actress] (aka Jeanne Brunet, *née* Germaine Marie Joseph Lebas, b. Redon, France, 11 Sep 1900 [extrait de naissance no. 99]–14 Jul 1980 [79], Dinard, France). AS, p. 1001.

Sibley, Lucy [actress] (d. 30 Dec 1945). BHD, p. 301.

Sibley, Richard E. [art director]. No data found. AMD, p. 317. "Sibley Signs with Mayer," *MPW,* 21 Feb 1920, 1271.

Sidman, Sam [actor] (b. Austria-Hungary, 1871?–3 Jan 1948 [77], Pinewald NJ). "Sam Sidman," *NYT,* 4 Jan 1948, 52:3. "Sam Sidman," *Variety,* 14 Jan 1948. AS, p. 1001. BHD, p. 301.

Sidney, Aurelio [director] (b. Austria-d. 1920, Sitges, Spain). AS, p. 1001.

Sidney, George [stage/film actor/director] (brother **Louis K. Sidney**; uncle of director George Sidney) (*né* Samuel Greenfield, b. Nagynichal, Hungary, 15 Mar 1876–29 Apr 1945 [69], Los Angeles CA). m. Carey Weber (d. ca. 1940). (Kelly & Cohen series; Potash & Perlmutter series; Universal; MGM.) "George Sidney, 68, Stage, Screen Actor," *NYT,* 30 Apr 1945, 19:2. "George Sydney," *Variety,* 2 May 1945 (age 68). AMD, p. 317. AS, p. 1001. BHD1, p. 503 (b. 1877). FSS, p. 259. IFN, p. 273 (b. 1877). Katz, p. 1055 (b. NYC; began 1924). Truitt, p. 305. "'Busy Izzy' in PIctures," *MPW,* 25 Sep 1915, 2160. "George Sidney," *MPW,* 16 Jan 1926, 240.

Sidney, Louis K. (brother of **George Sidney**; father of George Sydney. b. 1911) [producer] (b. New York NY, 1884–22 Feb 1958 [73?], Los Angeles CA). AS, p. 1001.

Sidney, Mabel [actress] (b. 1884–18 Oct 1969 [85?], New York NY). AS, p. 1001.

Sidney, Scott [actor/director] (*né* Harry Scott Siggins, b. Philadelphia PA, 1872?–20 Jul 1928 [56], London, England heart attack). m. **Julia Williams** (d. 1936). (Christie; Ince.) "Scott Sidney," *Variety,* 25 Jul 1928 ("...at his death owned 25 per cent of Christie Comedies"; age 55). AMD, p. 317. AS, p. 1001 (b. England). BHD, p. 302 (d. Elstres, England; BHD2, p. 244). IFN, p. 273. Truitt, p. 305. "Kalem Infuses New Blood," *MPW,* 10 Mar 1917, 1598. "Scott Sidney, Director," *MPW,* 7 Apr 1917, 103. Scott Sidney, "Would Rather Direct Comedy Productions," *MPW,* 20 Sep 1924, insert. "Scott Sidney Gives Close-Up of Unique, Oldtime Theatre," *MPW,* 18 Jul 1925, 257. "Scott Sidney Loaned to 'U,'" *MPW,* 14 Aug 1926, 401. "Scott Sidney Will Direct 'No Control,'" *MPW,* 28 Aug 1926, 529.

Siebel, Peter [actor] (b. 1884–4 Mar 1949 [64?], Long Beach CA). AS, p. 1001. BHD, p. 302.

Siegel, Bernard [actor] (aka Beigel and Segel, b. Lemberg, Poland, 19 Apr 1868–9 Jul 1940 [72], Los Angeles CA; heart attack). (Lubin.) AS, p. 983 (Seigel); p. 1001 (b. Austria). BHD1, p. 503 (b. Lwów, Ukraine). IFN, p. 273 (b. Austria). George Katchmer, "Remembering the Great Silents," *CI,* 213 (Mar 1993), 48–49.

Siegel, Max [stage/film/TV producer/general manager/assistant to Thalberg in 1925] (b. 1901?–16 Nov 1958 [57], Mt. Sinai Hospital, New York NY). m. Pauline (1 daughter). "Max Siegel, 57, Theatrical Aide; Co-Producer of Plays Dies—Worked with Liebman on Several TV Shows," *NYT,* 17 Nov 1958, 31:6. "Max Siegel," *Variety,* 19 Nov 1958, p. 79. BHD2, p. 244.

Siegel, Morris J. [executive] (b. New York NY, 1901?–28 Aug 1948 [47]; heart attack on a train near Winslow AZ). "M.J. Siegel, ex-Head of Republic Pictures," *NYT,* 31 Aug 1948, 23:4. "Morris J. Siegel," *Variety,* 1 Sep 1948. AS, p. 1001. BHD2, p. 244.

Siegler, Allen [cameraman]. No data found. AMD, p. 317. FDY, p. 469. "Al Siegler," *MPW,* L18 Dec 1926, 491.

Siegmann, George A. [actor/director] (b. New York NY, 8 Feb 1882–22 Jun 1928 [46], Los Angeles CA; pernicious anemia). (Biograph, 1909; Edison; Reliance.) "George Siegmann," *Variety,* 27 Jun 1928. AMD, p. 317. AS, p. 1001. BHD, p. 302. IFN, p. 273. MH, p. 136. Truitt, p. 305. Hugh Hoffman, "In the Catskills with Reliance," *MPW,* 24 Aug 1912, 751. "George Siegmann," *MPW,* 6 Sep 1913, 1070. W.E. Wing, "Along the Pacific Coast," *NYDM,* 30 Jun 1915, 22:2 (in an auto accident with Elmer Booth, who was killed, and Tod Browning. Siegmann suffered three broken ribs and internal complications.). "George Siegmann Chosen by 'Doug' for 'Porthos,'" *MPW,* 26 Mar 1921, 373. "Siegman Signed by 'U,'" *MPW,* 9 Jan 1926, 156. "Siegmann Improves," *MPW,* 2 Oct 1926, 280 (from nervous breakdown). Doris Denbo, "What's a Man to Do?; They're Speaking All Languages in Hollywood Now—But George

Siegmann Should Worry! He's Always in Demand," *MPC,* Jan 1927, 35, 87. "George Siegmann," *MPW,* 15 Oct 1927, 431. George Katchmer, "Remembering the Great Silents," *CI,* 233 (Nov 1994), 42.

Sielanski, Stanley [actor] (*né* Stanislaw Nasielski, b. Lodz, Poland, 8 Aug 1899–23 Apr 1955 [55], New York NY). AS, p. 1001.

Sievers, William [treasurer]. No data found. AMD, p. 317. "ALco Has Receiver for a Day," *MPW,* 5 Dec 1914, 1357.

Sifter, Magnus [actor] (b. Vienna, Austria, 23 Jan 1878–8 Sep 1943 [65], Vienna, Austria). BHD1, p. 616.

Siggins, Scott *see* **Sidney, Scott**

Signoret, Gabriel Augustin Marius (brother of **Jean Signoret**) [actor] (b. Marseilles, France, 15 Nov 1878 [extrait de naissance no. 585]–16 Mar 1937 [58], Neuilly-sur-Seine, France). AS, p. 1002. BHD, p. 302. IFN, p. 273 (age 64).

Signoret, Jean Jules Marius (brother of **Gabriel Signoret**) [actor] (b. Marseilles, France, 13 Dec 1886 [extrait de naissance no. 695]-10 Oct 1923 [38], Paris, France; fever). "Deaths Abroad; Jean Signoret," *Variety,* 25 Oct 1923, 2:5. AS, p. 1002. BHD, p. 302. IFN, p. 273 (b. Cavaillon, France).

Sigueiros, Placido [actor] (b. Sinaloa, Mexico, 10 Oct 1861–19 Dec 1946 [85]). AS, p. 1002.

Sikla, Ferry (b. Hamburg, Germany, 11 Mar 1865–8 Feb 1932 [66], Dresden, Germany). BHD1, p. 611.

Silbert, Jacob [actor] (b. 1870–19 Apr 1937 [67?], New York NY). BHD, p. 302.

Silbert, Lisa [Yiddish theater//film/TV actress] (*né* Lisa Rosenblum, b. Rumania, 1880–29 Nov 1965 [85], Miami FL). m. actor Jacob Silbert, 1897, 1 son, 2 daughters (d. 1937). "Lisa Silbert Is Dead at 85; Actress in Yiddish Theater," *NYT,* 30 Nov 1965, 41:2. "Lisa Silbert," *Variety,* 241, 1 Dec 1965, 71:3 (to U.S. in 1900). AS, p. 1002. BHD1, p. 504. IFN, p. 273.

Siletti, Mario G. [actor] (b. Sestri Ponente, Italy, 22 Jul 1901–19 Apr 1964 [62], Los Angeles CA; auto accident). AS, p. 1002. JS, pp. 424–25 (b. 1903; "In the U.S.A. from 1921.").

Sills, Milton [stage/film actor] (b. Chicago IL, 12 Jan 1882–15? Sep 1930 [48], Santa Monica CA; angina pectoris; dropped dead while playing tennis). m. **Gladys Wynne** (Gweldys Edith Wynne), 1910, London—div. 1925 (d. 1964); **Doris Kenyon,** 12 Oct 1926, Adirondacks (d. 1979; 1 son). (World; Selznick-Select; Pathé.) (Film debut: *The Pit,* 2 Jan 1915; Fox; Pathé.) "Milton Sills Drops Dead at Tennis Game," *Variety,* 17 Sep 1930. AMD, p. 317. AS, p. 1002. BHD1, p. 504 (d. LA CA). FFF, p. 227. FSS, p. 260. GK, pp. 870–81. HCH, p. 79. IFN, p. 273. Katz, pp. 1057–58 (began 1914). Lowrey, p. 170. MH, p. 137. MSBB, p. 1028. Spehr, p. 168. Truitt, p. 306. "Milton Sills Joins Ivan," *MPW,* 21 Jul 1917, 470. "Milton SIlls Leading Man for Farrar," *MPW,* 27 Jul 1918, 547. "Returns to Goldwyn," *MPW,* 19 Apr 1919, 358. "Metro Engages Milton Sills," *MPW,* 31 Jan 1920, 764. "Signs New Contract," *MPW,* 18 Oct 1924, 574. Ruth Mabrey, "Milton Sills Tells How 'The Sea Hawk' Was Made," *MW,* 26 Apr 1924, 12, 26. Ann Storm, "Why Milton Sills Became an Actor," *MW,* 29 Nov 1924, 11–12, 30. "Milton Sills," *MPW,* 21 Mar 1925, 284. "On the Set and Off," *MW,* V, 26 Sep 1925, 30 (Gladys E. Sills charged that her husband deserted her in Aug 1924, "when he came to New York to make pictures." She also asked custody of their fourteen-year-old daughter). Carol Bird, "A Man of Talents; Student, actor, artist, philosopher, linguist—Milton Sills is a seeker of beauty in life," *Photoplay Magazine,* Jun 1926, 41, 78. "Sills—Kenyon," *MPW,* 25 Sep 1926, 2. "Sills Elected President," *MPW,* 2 Oct 1926, 280. "Niagara Falls!," *MPW,* 30 Oct 1926, 2. "Sills Speaks at Harvard," *MPW,* 14 May 1927, 113. "Milton Sills," *MPW,* 28 May 1927, 257. June Lee, "Dan Cupid's Bulletin Board," *Paris and Hollywood Screen Secrets Magazine,* Aug 1927, 36 (birth of son). George A. Katchmer, "Milton Sills, the Intellect," *CI,* 129 (Mar 1986), 13–15, 60.

Silton, Eddie [casting agent/producer]. No data found. AMD, p. 317. "Eddie Silton to Produce," *MPW,* 14 Feb 1925, 722.

Silva, Antonio Joao [actor] (b. Portugal, 1869–30 Jan 1954 [84?], Lisbon, Portugal). AS, p. 1002.

Silvain, Eugène Charles Joseph [actor] (b. Bourg-en-Bresse, France, 17 Jan 1851–1930 [79?], Marseilles, France). AS, p. 1003.

Silvaney, Elsie [actress] (b. 10 Feb 1898–22 Aug 1983 [85], Toowoomba, Australia). BHD1, p. 504.

Silvani, Aldo [actor] (b. Turin, Italy, 21 Jan 1892–12 Nov 1964 [72], Milan, Italy). AS, p. 1003.

Silver, Abner [composer/author] (b. New York NY, 28 Dec 1899–24 Nov 1966 [66], New York NY; phlebitis inflammation). "Abner Silver," *Variety,* 30 Nov 1966 (wrote *There Goes My Heart; Rocket to the Moon; How Green Was My Valley*). AS, p. 1002. ASCAP 66, p. 675.

Silver, Christine [stage/film/TV actress] (b. London, England, 17 Dec 1883–23 Nov 1960 [76], London, England). (Began on the stage in 1902.) "Christine Silver," *Variety,* 221, 7 Dec 1960, 87:3. AS, p. 1002 (b. 1885). BHD1, p. 504. IFN, p. 273.

Silver, Marcel [director] (b. Bordeaux, France, 4 Oct 1891). AS, p. 1003. BHD2, p. 244.

Silver, Pauline [actress] (b. SD, 13 Feb 1888–2 Jan 1969 [80], West Hollywood CA; murdered). AS, p. 1002. BHD, p. 302. IFN, p. 273. Truitt, p. 306.

Silvera, Carlos [actor]. No data found. "Carlos Silvera," *Classic Images,* Mar 1996.

Silverman, Sidney [title writer]. No data found. FDY, p. 447.

Silverman, Sime [publisher] (b. Cortland NY, 19 May 1872–23 Sep 1933 [61], Los Angeles CA found dead of a lung hemorrhage). m. Hattie Freeman, ca. 1897. "Sime Silverman, Publisher, Dead; Familiar Figure on Broadway Succumbs Unattended in Los Angeles Hotel; Owned Weekly, Variety; Unique Editorial Policy Won a Large Following in Theatre and Night Club Life," *NYT,* 23 Sep 1933, 15:1 (started *Variety* in 1905 with $1,500. "His paper was Variety, the handbook, guidebook, directory of Broadway, as well as the glossary to its argot." His 96-year-old mother was still alive when he died.).

Silvernail, Clarke White [actor/director/scenarist] (b. PA, 31 Jan 1893–22 Sep 1930 [37], Los Angeles CA). AS, p. 1003. BHD1, p. 505; BHD2, p. 244.

Silvers, Louis [composer] (b. New York NY, 6 Sep 1889–26 Mar 1954 [64], Los Angeles CA; heart attack). m. Betty. (Metro; Columbia; FP-L.) "Louis Silvers, 64, Composer [*April Showers*], Is Dead; Music Director in Hollywood and on Broadway Received 'Oscar' in '34 for Scoring," *NYT,* 28 Mar 1954, 88:3. "Louis Silvers," *Variety,* 31 Mar 1954. AS, p. 1003. ASCAP 66, p. 676. BHD1, p. 505; BHD2, p. 244.

Silverstein, David F. [scenarist] (b. Pittsburgh PA, 13 Jun 1896-Jul 1944 [48], Staten Island NY). BHD2, p. 245.

Silverwood, Don [actor] (d. 10 Jan 1928, Reno NV). BHD, p. 302. IFN, p. 273.

Silvey, Ben [assistant director/producer] (b. 1895?–7 Feb 1948 [53], Los Angeles CA; heart attack). m. Vivien. (Cosmopolitan; Fox at Fort Lee NJ; WB; 1st National, 1925; TC-F.) "Ben Silvey," *NYT,* 8 Feb 1948, 60:2 (age 54). "Ben Silvey," *Variety,* 11 Feb 1948. AMD, p. 317. AS, p. 1003. BHD2, p. 245. "Silvey to Assist Brabin," *MPW,* 24 Jul 1926, 216.

Sima, Oskar Michael [actor] (b. Hobenau, Austria, 31 Jul 1900–24 Jun 1969 [68], Hobenau, Austria). AS, p. 1003 (b. 1896). BHD1, p. 505. IFN, p. 273.

Simmons, Earl [director] (b. 20 Aug 1915, Concord NH). BHD2, p. 245.

Simmons, Earl [actor/writer] (b. 1888?–10 Jan 1934 [45], New York NY; suicide by gas inhalation). m. (4) Catherine Prince. "Earl Simmons," *Variety,* 16 Jan 1934. AS, p. 1004. BHD, p. 302; BHD2, p. 245 (b. 1889).

Simmons, Joseph [producer] (b. 1882–8 Aug 1945 [63?], Los Angeles CA; heart attack). AS, p. 1004.

Simon, Jules Adolpohe [actor/director/scenarist] (b. Saint-Josse-Ten-Noode, Belgium, 30 Aug 1872–16 Oct 1958 [86], Paris, France [extrait de décès no. 654]). AS, p. 1004.

Simon, Michel (son of François Simon) [stage/film actor/producer] (*né* François Joseph Simon, b. Geneva, Switzerland, 9 Apr 1895–30 May 1975 [80], hospital near Paris, France; pulmonary embolism [extrait de décès no. 210/1975]). m. (1 son, actor François). (Acrobatic dancer, 1911.) Alden Whitman, "Michel Simon, Actor, 80, Dead; Acclaimed for 'Two of Us' Film," *NYT,* 31 May 1975, 30:6 ("Never make me do a scene over. I am not an actor," he said. "I live a scene as a moment, and once it's dead, God himself could not revive it." ¶"For many years he lived in the country with four apes and a parrot."). "Michel Simon," *Variety,* 4 Jun 1975, 63:1 ("His career was interrupted for several years in 1957 when makeup for a role in 'Un Certain Monsieur Jo' upset his central nervous system, finally coming back to acting in 'The Two of Us.'"). AS, p. 1004 (d. Bry-sur-Marne, France). BHD1, p. 505; BHD2, p. 245. IFN, p. 273.

Simon, Sol S. [actor] (b. Sacramento CA, 15 Dec 1864–24 Apr 1940 [75], Los Angeles CA). "Sol Simon," *NYT,* 27 Apr 1940, 15:5 (age 76; began 1919). AS, p. 1004. BHD1, p. 505. IFN, p. 273. Truitt, p. 306. George Katchmer, "Sol S. Simon," *CI,* 233 (Nov 1994), 42.

Simon, Walter Cleveland [composer] (b. Cincinnati OH [or Lexington KY], 27 Oct 1884–5 Mar 1958 [73], New York NY [Death Certificate Index No. 5883]). AS, p. 1004. *The ASCAP Biographical Dictionary of Composers, Authors and Publishers* (NY: ASCAP, 1966), p. 579.

Simon-Girard, Aimé [actor] (*né* Aimé Max Simon, b. Paris, France, 20 Mar 1889 [extrait de naissance no. 1446/1889]-15 Jun 1950 [61], Paris, France). AS, p. 1004. BHD1, p. 505. IFN, p. 273.

Simone, Charles [Nestor Co. business manager/director] (b. Castellana, Italy, 18 Nov 1879). AMD, p. 317. BHD2, p. 245 (b. 1874). Spehr, p. 168. "Simone Revives Centaur," *MPW,* 5 Apr 1913, 62. "Charles Simone Is at Liberty," *MPW,* 6 Sep 1913, 1073. "Charles Simone," *MPW,* 5 Dec 1914, 1393. "Simone Leaves Centaur," *MPW,* 12 Jun 1915, 1760.

Simoneschi, Carlo (father of Lidia Simoneschi) [actor/director] (b. Rome, Italy, 25 Aug 1878). m. (daughter, Lidia, b. Rome, Italy, 4 Apr 1908). AS, p. 1005. JS, p. 427 (in Italian silents from 1912).

Simoni, Renato [writer//scenaristfilm and theater director] (b. Verona, Italy, 5 Nov 1875–5 Jul 1952 [76], Milan, Italy). AS, p. 1005. JS, p. 427 (in Italian silents from 1917).

Simons, L.J. [cameraman]. No data found. AMD, p. 318. "Cameraman with Taft Party," *MPW,* 4 Jan 1913, 55. "Mr. Taft's Party Returns from Panama," *MPW,* 11 Jan 1913, 140.

Simpson, Al[l]an [actor]. No data found. *Fl.* 1923–27. (Paramount).

Simpson, Earl [actor]. No data found. m. Tillie Elwood, 1927. (Paramount.) June Lee, "Dan Cupid's Bulletin Board," *Paris and Hollywood Screen Secrets,* Oct 1927, 36 (wed Elwood().

Simpson, Fanny [actress] (d. 17 Oct 1961, Woodstock NY). (Solax). "Alma Harding Dean," *Variety,* 1 Nov 1961. BHD, p. 302. IFN, p. 273. Spehr, p. 168.

Simpson, George E. [executive] (d. 22 Dec 1925, Rochester NY). BHD2, p. 245.

Simpson, Grant M. [actor] (b. Sioux Falls SD, 1884?–5 Jan 1932 [47], Asheville NC). m. **Lulu McConnell** (d. 1962). "Grant Simpson Dead; Husband of Lulu McConnell," *Variety,* 12 Jan 1932 (d. 8 Jan). AS, p. 1005 (d. 8 Jan). BHD, p. 302 (b. 1885). IFN, p. 273.

Simpson, Ivan [stage/film actor] (b. Glasgow, Scotland, 4 Feb 1875–12 Oct 1951 [76], New York NY). "Ivan Simpson Dead; Veteran Actor, 76; Character Performer in Plays and Movies Won Success in Support of George Arliss," *NYT,* 14 Oct 1951, 89:1 (b. Hargate, England). "Ivan Simpson," *Variety,* 17 Oct 1951. AS, p. 1005. BHD1, p. 506. IFN, p. 273. SD, p. 1140 (b. Margate, Kent, England). Truitt, p. 306.

Simpson, John [actor] (d. 17 Jun 1918, New York NY). BHD, p. 302.

Simpson, Reginald [actor/scenarist] (b. 1896–12 Nov 1964 [68?], Windsor, England). BHD1, p. 506; BHD2, p. 245.

Simpson, Russell [stage/film actor] (b. Danville CA, 17 Jun 1878?–12 Dec 1959 [81], Los Angeles CA). m. Gertrude Aller, 1910. (Film debut: *The Barrier,* 27 Jan 1917.) World; Select; Edison; Metro; Goldwyn.) "Russell Simpson Dies; Actor 60 Years Was Seen on Stage, in Silent Movies," *NYT,* 13 Dec 1959, 86:4. "Russell Simpson," *Variety,* 16 Dec 1959. AS, p. 1005 (b. 1880). BHD1, p. 506 (b. SF CA, 1880). GK, pp. 881–99. IFN, p. 274 (b. 1880). Truitt, pp. 306–307 (b. San Francisco CA, 1880). 1921 Directory, p. 201 (b. San Francisco CA, 1880). Herbert Cruikshank, "Curth You, Jack Dalton!; More Dirty Work at the Crothwoads, Thayth Russell Simpson, Ith What Movieth Need," *MPC,* 60, 94 (b. 1880). "2 Unforgettable Character Actors: Tully Marshall and Russell Simpson—2," *CI,* 145 (Jul 1987), 31 *et passim.* George Katchmer, "Remembering the Great Silents," CI, 252 (Jun 1996), 42, 44; *CI,* 253 (Jul 1996), 50 (b. 1880).

Sims, George R. [director/scenarist] (b. England, 1847–4 Sep 1922 [75?], England). AS, p. 1005.

Sinaberg, Milton [scenarist] (d. 2 Dec 1918, Los Angeles CA). BHD2, p. 245.

Sinaz, Guglielmo [actor] (*né* Guglielmo Zanasi, b. Rome, Italy, 20 Nov 1885–5 Feb 1947 [61], Rome, Italy). AS, p. 1005.

Sinclair, Arthur [actor] (*né* Arthur McDonnell, b. Dublin, Ireland, 3 Aug 1883–14 Dec 1951 [68], Belfast, Ireland). AS, p. 1005.

Sinclair, Daisy [actress] (*née* Margaret Sinclair, b. New York, 1877–14 Jan 1929 [51], New York NY; heart attack). m. John Edwards. "Daisy Sinclair (Mrs. Margaret Edwards)," *Variety,* 16 Jan 1929. AS, p. 1006. BHD, p. 302 (b. 1878). IFN, p. 274. Truitt, p. 307. "No Naked 'Truth'; Boston's Mayor Insists Upon Draping Truth in Bosworth's 'Hypocrites,'" *NYDM,* 14 Apr 1915, 24:4 (Mayor Curley strenously objected to an undraped Margaret Edwards after viewing 1 3/4 reels.).

Sinclair, Horace [actor] (b. Sheffield, England, 1883–19 Feb 1949 [65?], New York NY). AS, p. 1006.

Sinclair, John W. [actor/stuntman] (b. Memphis TN, 6 Jan 1900–13 Feb 1945 [45], Los Angeles CA). m. **Thelma Hill** (d. 1938). AS, p. 1006.

Sinclair, Richard C. [actor] (d. 16 Sep 1926, Brooklyn NY). BHD, p. 302.

Sinclair, Ruth *see* **Cummings, Ruth Sinclair**

Sinclair, Upton Beall [writer/scenarist] (b. Baltimore MD, 20 Sep 1878–25 Nov 1968 [90], Somerset Valley Nursing Home, Bound Brook NJ). m. (1) Meta H. Fuller, 1900—div. 1911 (son, Dr. David Sinclair); (2) Mary Craig Kimbrough, 1913 (d. 26 Apr 1961, St. Luke's Hospital, Pasadena CA); (3) Mary Elizabeth Willis, Oct 1961, Claremont CA. (Pulitzer Prize for *Dragon's Teeth,* 1943.) "Upton Sinclair, Author, Dead; Crusader for Social Justice, 90; 90 Books, Including 'Oil!' [1927] and 'The Jungle' [1906], Caused Many to Join His Protests," *NYT,* 26 Nov 1968, 1:6, 34:4; Alden Whitman, "Rebel With a Cause," 1:6. "Mrs. Upton Sinclair, Novelist's Wife, 78," *NYT,* 27 Apr 1961, 21:2 (wrote biography, *Southern Belle,* 1958). "Mrs. Upton Sinclair, Wife of Author, Is Dead at 85," *NYT,* 21 Dec 1967, 37:2 (Mary Elizabeth Willis, d. 18 Dec 1967 [85], Washington DC). AS, p. 1006. BHD, p. 302; BHD2, p. 245.

Sindelar, Charles [actor] (d. Los Angeles CA, 15 May 1947). BHD1, p. 617.

Sindelar, Pearl [actress/minister] (b. Virginia City NV, 5 Feb 1887–9 Jul 1958 [71], Glendale CA). AMD, p. 318. BHD1, p. 617. "Pearl Sindelar; Playing Leads with the Pathé Company," *MPS,* 3 Apr 1914, 26 (b. Virginia City NV). "Pearl Sindelar," *MPW,* 4 Apr 1914, 44.

Sinding, Leif [director] (b. Oslo, Norway, 19 Nov 1895). AS, p. 1006.

Singer, Benny [casting directorr]. No data found. AMD, p. 318. "Singer Casting for Metro," *MPW,* 24 Jul 1920, 495.

Singer, Marian [actress] (b. England, 1851–21 Nov 1924 [73?], Long Island NY). (Universal.) BHD, p. 302.

Singh, Bhogwan [actor] (b. India, 22 Sep 1883–6 Mar 1962 [78], Woodland Hills CA; cerebral thrombosis). AS, p. 1006. BHD1, p. 506.

Singh, Sarain [actor] (b. India, 1887–14 Apr 1952 [65?], Los Angeles CA). AS, p. 1006.

Singh, Suchet [producer]. No data found. AMD, p. 318. "Will Make Photo Dramas in Bombay," *MPW,* 21 Dec 1918, 1326.

Singhi, Ferdinand [Vice President of Lubin). No data found.

Singleton, Joseph [actor] (*né* Joseph Edward Victor Fairfield Daveran Singleton, b. Australia, 1881). m. **Iva Shepard**, 1913 (d. 1973). AMD, p. 318. BHD, p. 302. "This Week's Crop of Accidents," *MPW,* 19 Jul 1913, 306 (engaged to Shepard). "Universal Actors Engaged to Wed," *MPW,* 19 Jul 1913, 332. "Engagement Note a Joke," *MPW,* 16 Aug 1913, 727. George Katchmer, "Remembering the Great Silents," *CI,* 240 (Jun 1995), 45.

Sini'letta, Vic [actor] (*né* Victor A. Smith, d. 4 May 1921, Chicago IL; dropsy and heart attack). AS, p. 1006. BHD, p. 302. Truitt, p. 307.

Sinimberghi, Aldo [actor]. m. actress Fernanda. JS, p. 428 (in Italian silents from 1911).

Sinoel [actor] (*né* Jean Léonis Bies, b. Sainte-Terre, France, 13 Aug 1868–30 Aug 1949 [81], Paris, France). AS, p. 1006.

Sintzenich, Harold [cameraman]. No data found. AMD, p. 318. "Taking Pictures in Africa," *MPW,* 26 Jun 1915, 2102.

Siodmak, Curt (brother of Robert Siodmak) [extra actor/director/scenarist/novelist] (b. Dresden, Germany, 10 Aug 1902–2 Sep 2000 [98], Three Rivers CA). Harris Lentz, III, "Curt Siodmak, 98," *CI,* 304 (Oct 2000), 61–62 (appeared as an extra in *Metropolis,* 1927).

Sipperly, Ralph [actor] (b. 1890?–9 Jan 1928 [38], Bangor ME; grief-stricken over the death of his wife). m. Gladys (d. 1928). "Ralph Sipperley," *Variety,* 18 Jan 1928. AMD, p. 318. AS, p. 1007. BHD, p. 302. IFN, p. 274. "Ralph Sipperly Signed," *MPW,* 12 Jun 1926, 540.

Sipple, Crete (b. MO, 18 Nov 1882–20 Feb 1972 [89], Los Angeles CA). BHD1, p. 507.

Sissle, Noble Lee [actor/composer] (b. Indianapolis IN, 10 Jul 1889–17 Dec 1975 [86], Tampa FL). AS, p. 1007. BHD1, p. 507.

Sisson, Vera [actress] (b. Salt Lake City UT, 31 Jul 1891–6 Aug 1954 [63], Carmel CA; overdose of barbituates). m. **Richard Rosson** (d. 1953). (General; Biograph, 1915; Universal; Metro; Maxwell Films.) AS, p. 1007. BHD, p. 302 (b. CO; d. Salinas CA). IFN, p. 274 (b. CO). MSBB, p. 1042 (b. 1895). 1921 Directory, p. 239. "Vera Sisson," *NYDM,* 13 Nov 1915, 27:1.

Sitgreaves, Marion [actress] (d. 2 Feb 1961, East Islip NY). BHD, p. 302.

Sittenham, Fred W. [director]. No data found. AMD, p. 318. "Sittenham Is Becoming a Psychic Director," *MPW,* 28 Feb 1920, 1480. "Fred Sittenham Is Again on List of Metro Directors," *MPW,* 17 Jul 1920, 348.

Sjeljabuezjky, Yuri Andreyevich [director/scenarist] (b. Russia, 1888–1956 [68?], Russia). AS, p. 1183.

Sjöberg, Alf [stage/film director/scenarist] (*né* Sven Erik Alf Sjöberg, b. Stockholm, Sweden, 21 Jun 1903–17 Apr 1980 [76], Stockholm, Sweden; traffic accident). "Alf Sjoberg," *Variety,* 30 Apr 1980 ("Along with Greta Garbo, Sjoberg in 1920 passed his entrance test to the Dramaten Drama School…"). AS, p. 1007. BHD2, p. 246 (b. 1902).

Sjoeb, Esfir Ilinitsjna [director] (aka Esther Schub, b. Ukraine, 16 Mar 1894–21 Sep 1959 [65], Moscow, Russia). AS, p. 1008.

Skala, Lilia [actress] (b. Vienna, Austria, 28 Nov 1896–18 Dec 1994 [98], Bay Shore NY). AS, p. 1008.

Skands, Lauritz [director/scenarist] (b. Jutland, Denmark, 4 May 1885–1935 [50?], Denmark). AS, p. 1008.

Skavlan, Olaf [actor] (b. Oslo, Norway, 1885–2 Jun 1949 [64?], San Francisco CA). BHD, addendum.

Skelly, Hal [actor] (*né* Joseph Harold Skelly, b. Allegheny PA, 31 May 1891?–16 Jun 1934 [43], near West Cornwall CT; grade-crossing accident). "Hal Skelly Killed in Train-Car Crash," *Variety,* 19 Jun 1934 (age 42). AS, p. 1008. BHD1, p. 507. IFN, p. 274. Paul Cates, "Take It or Leave It; Hall Skelly Told Hollywood That and Hollywood Took," *MPC,* Aug 1929, 24, 74.

Skelton, Patricia [actress] (b. Los Angeles CA, 19 Mar 1843–18 Jun 1921 [78], Los Angeles CA). AS, p. 1008.

Skinner, Cornelia Otis (daughter of **Otis Skinner**; cousin of **Harold Otis Skinner**) [actress] (b. Chicago IL, 30 May 1901–9 Jul 1979 [78], New York NY [Death Certificate Index No. 10932 (Cornelia O. Blodget); age 80]). m. Alden Sanford Blodgett, 2 Oct 1928 (d. 1964). Alden Whitman, "Cornelia Otis Skinner, Actress and Author, Dies," *NYT,* 10 Jul 1979, D15:1. "Cornelia Otis Skinner," *Variety,* 11 Jul 1979. AS, p. 1008. BHD1, p. 507. IFN, p. 274.

Skinner, George F. [executive: President of Educational Film Co.] (b. 1871?–20 Dec 1935 [64], New York NY). "George F. Skinner," *Variety,* 121, 25 Dec 1935, 55:1. AMD, p. 318 (George A. Skinner). E.T. Keyser, "Putting the Educational on the Map; George A. [sic] Skinner, President of Educational, Tells of His Company's Plans and Preparations," *MPW,* 25 Jan 1919, 468:1.

Skinner, Harold Otis (nephew of **Otis Skinner**; cousin of **Cornelia Otis Skinner**) [actor] (b. 1889?–14 Sep 1922 [33], San Diego CA). m. Evelyn Farrar. "Harold Otis Skinner," *Variety,* 22 Sep 1922. AS, p. 1008. BHD, p. 303.

Skinner, Olive [actress]. No data found. AMD, p. 318. "Olive Skinner in Pictures," *MPW,* 25 Jan 1913, 353.

Skinner, Otis (father of **Cornelia Otis Skinner**; uncle of **Harold Otis Skinner**) [actor] (b. Cambridge MA, 28 Jun 1858–4 Jan 1942 [83], New York NY [Death Certificate Index No. 363]). m. Maude Durbin, 21 Apr 1895, Corning NY (d. 1936). "Otis Skinner Dies; Famous Actor, 83; Stricken While Attending 'Wookey' Performance Dec. 7; On Stage Nearly 60 Years; Appeared with Drew, Booth, Rehan, Modjeska—Father of Cornelia Otis Skinner," *NYT,* 5 Jan 1942, 17:1. "Otis Skinner Rites to Be Held Today; Funeral of Noted Actor at 'Little Church Around Corner,'" *NYT,* 6 Jan 1942, 24:3. "Otis Skinner; Estate May Total $500,000; Was Sagacious Actor," *Variety,* 14 Jan 1942. AMD, p. 318. AS, p. 1008. BHD1, p. 507 (b. 1857). GSS, pp. 352–54. IFN, p. 274. Truitt, p. 307 (b. 1857). WWS, p. 126. "Otis Skinner Visits Selig Plant," *MPW,* 16 Nov 1912, 664. "Otis Skinner Praises Moving Pctures," *MPW,* 11 Jan 1913, 141. "California Signs Otis Skinner," *MPW,* 4 Mar 1916, 1453. "Otis Skinner Inspects the Camera," *MPW,* 3 Jun 1916, 1675. "Otis Skinner Secured by Waldorf to Star in 'Kismet,' Edward Knoblauch's Masterpiece," *MPW,* 20 Sep 1919, 1829. "Waldorf Insures Otis Skinner for Big Sum but He Balks at Algeria for His Location," *MPW,* 13 Dec 1919, 832 ($1,250,000, Aetna insurance). "Otis Skinner Signed by Robertson-Cole to Appear in His Role of Hajj in 'Kismet,'" *MPW,* X20 Mar 1920, 1948. "'Kismet,' with Otis Skinner Is Now Nearing Completion," *MPW,* 21 Aug 1920, 996. "Otis Skinner's FInal Appearance in 'Kismet' Will Be for Robertson-Cole," *MPW,* 28 Aug 1920, 1156. "Otis Skinner Returns to Screen for Exceptional Pictures in 'Mister Antonio,'" *MPW,* 10 Dec 1921, 655.

Skipworth, Alison [actress] (*née* Alison Mary Elliott Margaret Groom, b. London, England, 25 Jul 1863–5 Jul 1952 [88], New York NY). m. (1) Frank Markham Skipworth. (Began in 1915.) "Alison Skipworth, Actress, Dies at 88; London-Born Performer Won Praise for Characterizations on the Stage and Screen," *NYT,* 7 Jul 1952, 21:3. "Alison Skipworth," *Variety,* 9 Jul 1952. AS, p. 1008. BHD1, p. 507. IFN, p. 274. Katz, pp. 1064–65 Truitt, p. 307.

Skirvin, Marguerite [stage/film actress] (aka Edna Earl). No data found. m. Robert J. Adams, 1920, NYC. (Universal.) AMD, p. 318. "Marguerite Skirvin," *NYDM,* 10 Mar 1915, 10:2 ("She retired from the Famous Players' Film Company to accept" an engagement in *Rebecca of Sunnybrook Farm,* Poli's Theater, Hartford CT). "Marguerite Skirvin in 'The Quitter,'" *MPW,* 10 Jun 1916, 1862. "Edna Earl," *LA Times,* 29 Mar 1920, II, p. 12 (m. Adams; "the pretty young actress … formerly with Universal, but whose papa's millions made it unnecessary for her to work…" Her father was William H. Skirvin, an oil magnate and hotel owner from Oklahoma City OK, who convinced her to give up her career.).

Skladanowsky, Max [inventor; predecessor of Louis Lumiere] (b. Berlin, Germany, 30 Apr 1863–30 Nov 1939 [76], Berlin, Germany). AS, p. 1008.

Sladdin, Spencer G. [publicist]. No data found. AMD, p. 318. "Sladdin Starts Advertising Campaign," *MPW,* 9 Sep 1916, 1709. "Sladdin Back from Business Trip," *MPW,* 16 Dec 1916, 1648. "Sladdin Returns from West," *MPW,* 20 Jan 1917, 350.

Slater, George [actor] (b. Indianapolis IN, 8 Jul 1847–4 Jun 1932 [84], Los Angeles CA). AS, p. 1009.

Slater, Robert S[amuel] **(Bob)** [stage, Slater and (Bert) Murphy/film actor] (b. New Orleans LA, 22 Jun 1869–20 Jun 1930 [61], Presbyterian Hospital, New York NY; complication of diseases; interment in Yonkers NY). m. (1 son, 1 daughrter). "Robert Slater," *Variety,* 25 Jun 1930, 258:4 (founded the Colored Vaudeville Benevolent Association). AS, p. 1009. BHD, p. 303. IFN, p. 274.

Slattery, Nell [actress]. (Biograph). AMD, p. 318. "Popular Picture Personalities," *MPW,* 14 Apr 1917, 279.

Slaughter, Tod [actor] (*né* N. Carter Slaughter, b. Newcastle-upon-Tyne, England, 19 Mar 1885–19 Feb 1956 [70], Derby, England). AS, p. 1010.

Slavin, John C. [stage/vaudeville/film actor] (b. New York NY, 1869?–27 Aug 1940 [71], New York NY). "John C. Slavin, 71, Former Comedian; Retired Stage and Vaudeville Actor Began Career at 10," *NYT,* 29 Aug 1940, 19:2. "John C. Slavin," *Variety,* 4 Sep 1940. AS, p. 1010. BHD, p. 303. IFN, p. 275.

Slavinsky, Jevgeny [director/cameraman] (né Jevgeny Josefovich Stavinsky, b. Moscow, Russia, 24 Jan 1877–23 Sep 1950 [73], Moscow, Russia). AS, p. 1010.

Slavinsky, Vladimir [actor/director/scenarist] (*né* Oskar Vladimir Pitrman, b. Dolni Stepanice, Czechoslovakia, 26 Sep 1890–16 Aug 1949 [58], Prague, Czechoslovakia). AS, p. 1010.

Sleeman, Philip [actor] (b. England, 28 Feb 1891–19 Sep 1953 [62], Los Angeles Co. CA). AS, p. 1010. BHD1, p. 508. IFN, p. 275.

Sleeper, Martha [stage/film actress: Wampas Star, 1927] (b. Lake Bluff IL, 24 Jun 1904–25 Mar 1983 [78], Beaufort SC; heart attack). m. (1) **Hardie Albright**, 1934–40 (d. 1975). (Roach.) David Bird, "Martha Sleeper Is Dead at 72; Star of Films and Broadway," *NYT,* 7 Apr 1983, D26:1. "Martha Sleeper," *Variety,* 20 Apr 1983 (age 72). AMD, p. 318. AS, p. 1010. BHD1, p. 508. FSS, p. 260. Katz, pp. 1065–66 (b. 1907). "New Leading Lady," *MPW,* 16 Feb 1924, 591.

Slevin, James [cameraman/writer]. No data found. AMD, p. 318. "Slevin to Film the Pope," *MPW,* 4 Oct 1913, 39. "A Motion Picture Triumph," *MPW,* 31 Oct 1914, 614–15.

Slezak, Leo (father of **Walter Slezak**) [actor/singer] (b. Maehrisch-Schvenberg, Germany, 18 Aug 1873–1 Jun 1946 [72], Rottach-Egern, Germany). AS, p. 1010.

Slezak, Margarete [actress] (b. Breslau, Poland, 9 Jan 1901–30 Aug 1953 [52], Rottach-Egern, Germany). AS, p. 1010.

Slezak, Walter Leo (son of **Leo Slezak**) [actor] (b. Vienna, Austria, 3 May 1902–22 Apr 1983 [80], Flower Hill, LI NY; suicide by shooting). m. Johanna Van Rijn. Leo Slezak, *What Time's the Next Swan?* (1962). (Began ca. 1923.) "Walter Slezak," *Variety,* 27 Apr 1983. AS, p. 1010 (d. 21 Apr). BHD1, p. 508. JS, p. 428 (in the Italian silent *Addio, giovinezza!,* 1927). SD, p. 1145 (b. 31 Jun 1902).

Sloan, Tod [actor] (*né* James F. Sloan, b. Bunker Hill IN, 10 Aug 1874–21 Dec 1933 [59], Los Angeles CA). AS, p. 1010. BHD1, p. 508.

Sloane, Olive (Baby Pearl) [stage, Jeffrey's Juggling Girls/film actress] (b. London, England, 16 Dec 1896–28 Jun 1963 [66], London, England). (First West End appearance, 1912.) "Olive Sloane," *Variety,* 231, 17 Jul 1963, 87:3 (age 67). AS, p. 1010. BHD1, p. 508. IFN, p. 275 (age 67).

Sloane, Paul H. [scenarist/director/producer] (b. New York NY, 16 Apr 1893–15 Nov 1963 [70], Santa Monica CA; heart attack). (Edison; Fox; Metro; Paramount.) "Paul H. Sloane," *Variety,* 27 Nov 1963. AMD, p. 318. AS, p. 1010. BHD2, p. 246. FDY, p. 437. IFN, p. 275. Katz, p. 1066. "Paul H. Sloane of Fox Pens Plays for Walsh," *MPW,* 7 Feb 1920, 915. "New Fox Picture by Sloane," *MPW,* 23 Sep 1922, 279. "DeMille Signs Paul Sloane to Direct Rod LaRocque," *MPW,* 4 Apr 1925, 493.

Sloan[e], William H[ope] [actor] (b. 1863?–12 Jan 1933 [69], Amityville, LI NY). (K&E.) "William H. Sloan," *Variety,* 17 Jan 1933. AS, p. 1010. IFN, p. 275.

Slocum, Cy "Tex" [stunt double] (*né* Lyle

Asher, b. 1897?–18 Jan 1963 [65?], Concord CA; heart attack). "Tex Slocum," *Variety*, 6 Feb 1963. AS, p. 1010. BHD1, p. 508 (b. 1901). IFN, p. 275 (age 61).

Sloman, Edward "Ted" (son of English concert singer, Isaac Sloman) [stage actor/film director] (b. Bayswater [London], England, 19 Jul 1886–29 Sep 1972 [86], Calabasas Park, Los Angeles CA 91364). (b. 19 Jul 1886). m. **Hylda** Hallis (d. 1961). AMD, p. 318. AS, p. 1010 (b. 1883; d. Woodland Hills CA); p. 1011 (Ted Sloman). BHD, p. 303 (b. 1885); BHD2, p. 246 (b. 1883).. IFN, p. 275. Katz, pp. 1066–67. 1921 Directory, p. 275. "Edward Sloman, New American Diiector," *MPW*, 25 Mar 1916, 2019. "Edward Sloman to Direct Amercans," *MPW*, 8 Apr 1916, 289. Edward Sloman, "Glaring Flaws in Careless Directon," *MPW*, 21 Jul 1917, 377. "Edward Sloman," *MPW*, 15 Sep 1917, 1690. "Sloman to Direct 'The Westerners,'" *MPW*, 22 Mar 1919, 1695. "Ted Sloman in a Nutshell," *MPW*, 24 May 1919, 1234. "Edward Sloman Becomes a B.B. Features Director," *MPW*, 6 Dec 1919, 654. "Director for London Stories," *LA Times*, 25 Jan 1920, 13:3 (related to David Belasco on his mother's side). "Railway Strike Holds Up Edward Sloman," *MPW*, 2 Sep 1922, 43. "Edward Sloman tto Direct Story by Andrew Soutar," *MPW*, 27 Mar 1926, 261. "Edward Sloman at Megaphone for 'Lea Lyon,'" *MPW*, 26 Feb 1927, 645. "Edward Sloman Directs Scenes in New York Harbor," *MPW*, 2 Jul 1927, 32. "The Lost Work of Edward Sloman," Brownlow, p. 156–63 (b. 1883).

Sloman, Hylda Hallis [actress] (b. PA, 10 Jul 1891–9 Dec 1961 [70], Los Angeles CA). m. **Edward Sloman** (d. 1972). AS, p. 1010. IFN, p. 275.

Slott, Nate David [actor/assistant director] (b. Chicago IL, 22 Apr 1902–26 Sep 1963 [61], Los Angeles CA). AS, p. 1011. BHD1, p. 508; BHD2, p. 246. IFN, p. 275 (age 58).

Small, Edna [vaudeville/film actress] (*née* Edna Ellis?, b. 1898–14 Jul 1917 [19], General Hospital, Cincinnati OH; convulsions). m. **Edward Small** (2 sons, Robert and Bernard [Bud]; d. 1977). "Edna Small (Mrs. Edna Small Ellis)," *Variety*, 20 Jul 1917, 20:4 (separated from husband after three weeks. "Mrs. Ellis told a friend that she had formerly acted in pictures with Charlie Chaplin and about a year ago she and another girl bet $1,000 with the famous comedian that they could walk from Los Angeles to New York, without funds. They left California, selling papers to obtain money for food and lodging." They got as far as Montana.). AS, p. 1011. BHD, p. 303.

Small, Edward [actor/independent producer] (b. Brooklyn NY, 1 Feb 1891–25 Jan 1977 [85], Los Angeles CA; cancer). m. **Edna** (2 sons, Robert and Bernard [Bud]; d. 1917). "Edward Small," *Variety*, 285, 26 Jan 1977, 95:1. AS, p. 1011. BHD, p. 303; BHD2, p. 246. IFN, p. 275.

Smalley, Phillips Wendell [actor/director/producer] (b. Brooklyn NY, 7 Aug 1865–2 May 1939 [73], Los Angeles CA). m. (1) **Lois Weber**, 1905 (d. 1939). (Rex.) "Wendell P. Smalley," *Variety*, 10 May 1939. AMD, p. 319. AS, p. 1011. BHD1, p. 508; BHD2, p. 246. IFN, p. 275. Katz, p. 1067. 1921 Directory, p. 275. Truitt, p. 308 (b. 1875). "Ready to Resume," *MPW*, 12 Oct 1912, 129. George Blaisdell, "Phillips Smalley Talks," *MPW*, 24 Jan 1914, 399. "The Smalleys Joins Bosworth," *MPW*, XX, 13 Jun 1914, 1550. "Smalleys Back with Universal," *MPW*, 3 Apr 1915, 76. "George W. Smalley Dies," *MPW*, 13 May 1916, 1156 (death of father). "Smalley Added to 'Temptation' Cast," *MPW*, 3 Mar 1923, 78. Billy H. Doyle, "Lost Players," *CI*, 154 (Apr 1988), 53.

Smallwood, Arthur N. [producer]. No data found. AMD, p. 319. "Smallwood Comes Back," *MPW*, 15 Sep 1917, 1699.

Smallwood, Ray[mond] **C.** [cameraman/director] (b. New York NY, 19 Jul 1887–23 Feb 1964 [76], Woodland Hills CA). m. **Ethel Grandin**, 1912 (d. 1988). "Ray Smallwood," *Variety*, 4 Mar 1964. AMD, p. 319. AS, p. 1011. BHD2, p. 246. IFN, p. 275. 1921 Directory, p. 275. Slide, *Aspects*, p. 28. "Ray C. Smallwood," *MPW*, 14 Sep 1912, 1066. "^The Smallwoods in New York," *MPW*, 21 Jun 1913, 1237. "Ray Smallwood Becomes a Director," *MPW*, 13 Dec 1913, 1285. "Smallwood and Grandin Leave Universal," *MPW*, 20 Jun 1914, 1706. "George Kleine Engages New Director," *MPW*, 7 Aug 1915, 983. "Smallwood Heads Metro's Camera Force," *MPW*, 16 Feb 1918, 955. "Ray Smallwood in California," *MPW*, 11 Jan 1919, 203. "Smallwood Mourns Father," *MPW*, 12 Jul 1919, 208 (d. Cincinnati OH, aged 65). "Ray C. Smallwood Selected by Maxwell Karger to Direct Drury Lane Dramas for Screen Classics," *MPW*, 23 Aug 1919, 1157. "Ray C. Smallwood Has Had Wide Directorial Experience," *MPW*, 27 Dec 1919, 1183. "Now Is the Time to Do Heavy Advertising, Says Smallwood," *MPW*, 4 Jun 1921, 530. James Trottier, "Ethel Grandin: The IMP Girl," *CI*, 275 (May 1998), 34–35.

Smart, H.F. [actor] (*né* Ray Archer, b. England, 1845?–22 Jul 1923 [78], Los Angeles CA). BHD, p. 303. IFN, p. 275.

Smart, Josephine [actress] (b. Los Angeles CA, 23 Nov 1842–19 Apr 1934 [91], Los Angeles CA; pneumonia). AS, p. 1011.

Smart, William G. [technical director]. No data found. AMD, p. 319. "Smart Returns from Vacation," *MPW*, 18 Nov 1916, 993.

Smeraldo, Ida [actress] (b. Rome, Italy, 18 Feb 1898–20 Sep 1964 [66], Los Angeles CA). AS, p. 1011.

Smiley, Charles A. [actor] (b. 1856?–22 Jun 1925 [69], Los Angeles CA). "Charles A. Smiley," *Variety*, 1 Jul 1925. AS, p. 1011. BHD, p. 303 (b. 1855).

Smiley, Frank [actor]. (Lubin.) No data found.

Smiley, Joseph W. [stage/film actor/director] (b. Boston MA, 18 Jun 1870–2 Dec 1945 [75], New York NY). m. Lilie Leslie, 1914. (Imp; Eclair.) "Joseph W. Smiley; Actor, on Stage for 52 Years, Last in 'Skin of Our Teeth,'" *NYT*, 4 Dec 1945, 30:2. "Joseph W. Smiley," *Variety*, 5 Dec 1945 (age 64). AMD, p. 319. AS, p. 1011. BHD, p. 303; BHD2, p. 246 (b. 1881). IFN, p. 275 (age 64). Spehr, p. 168 (1881–1945). Truitt, p. 308 (b. 1881). "Joseph W. Smiley," *MPW*, 30 Nov 1912, 871. "Smiley Has a Birthday," *MPW*, 5 Jul 1913, 50. "Joseph W. Smiley," *MPW*, 24 Jan 1914, 395. *NYDM*, 1 Jul 1914, p. 21. "Joseph Smiley's Birthday Party," *MPW*, 4 Jul 1914, 51. "Smiley an Educational Factor," *MPW*, 18 Dec 1915, 2161.

Smirnova, Dina [actress] (b. Russia, 24 Feb 1889–16 Jan 1947 [57]). BHD1, p. 509. IFN, p. 275.

Smith, A. Victor (brother of **Albert E.** and **David Smith**) [assistant general manager]. No data found. AMD, p. 319. "J.B. Rock Is General Manager of Vitagraph; A. Victor Smith, Assistant," *MPW*, 1 Mar 1924, 39. "Vitagraph's Optimistic," *MPW*, 14 Jun 1924, 646. "A. Victor Smith Lauds Work of John B. Rock for Vitagraph," *MPW*, 8 Nov 1924, 161. "A. Victor Smith Recovering," *MPW*, 2 May 1925, 28.

Smith, Albert E[dward] (brother of **A. Victor** and **David Smith**) [inventor/director/producer/executive/founder of Vitagraph] (b. Faversham, Kent, England, 4 Jun 1875–1 Aug 1958 [83], Los Angeles CA). m. **Hazel Neason** (d. 1920); **Jean Paige**, Paris IL, Dec 1920 (d. 1990); Lucille. "Albert Smith, 83, Film Pioneer Dies; Inventor of Vitagraph Was Co-Founder of Firm that Achieved Early Success," *NYT*, 3 Aug 1958, 80:3. "Albert E. Smith," *Variety*, 6 Aug 1958. AMD, p. 319. AS, p. 1011. BHD, p. 303; BHD2, p. 246 (b. 1878). IFN, p. 275. WWVC, pp. 134–35. "Interviews with Manufacturers," *MPW*, 8 Feb 1908, 95. "'Big Four' [Smith, W.N. Selig, Ira Lowry, George K. Spoor] Surprises Film Men; Vitagraph-Lubin-Selig-Essanay Combination Means Radical Departure by Motion Picture Pioneers—Exchange Managers Appointed and Preparations Under Way for Flying Start," *NYDM*, 21 Apr 1915, 24:2. "Scope of the 'V-L-S-E,'" *MPW*, 1 May 1915, 703–04. "Vitagraph Plans," *MPW*, 4 Dec 1915, 1802. "General Film Company in No Danger of Receiver," *MPW*, 1 Jul 1916, 64. "School of Pantomime for Screen Aspirants Planned," *MPW*, 23 Nov 1918, 824. A.E. Smith, "Screen Set for Photoplay's Ibsen," *MPW*, 1 Feb 1919, 603–04. "Albert E. Smith Goes West to Attend Family Reunion," *MPW*, 22 Mar 1919, 1624 (in Santa Barbara CA). "Entire Vitagraph Plant Will Move to Los Angeles," *MPW*, 19 Apr 1919, 359. "Albert E. Smith Reviews Trade History," *MPW*, 26 Apr 1919, 535. "Mrs. Albert Smith Dies," *MPW*, 7 Feb 1920, 914 (d. 24 Jan 1920, pneumonia). "Albert E. Smith Returns East After Trip to Vitagraph's Western Studio," *MPW*, 2 Oct 1920, 681. "Albert E. Smith, Vitagraph President, Weds Jean Paige, Popular Screen Star," *MPW*, 25 Dec 1920, 989. "Albert E. Smith Says 1921 Is to Be a Very Successful Year for Vitagraph," *MPW*, 25 Dec 1920, 1008. Cal York, "Plays and Players," *Photoplay*, Mar 1921, 88 (wed Paige). "Albert E. Smith Goes to Look Over Conditions in Europe," *MPW*, 27 Oct 1923, 725. "'Captain Blood' Screen Rights Bought by Smith," *MPW*, 15 Dec 1923, 634. Albert E. Smith, "A Christmas Warning Against Pessimism and Extravagance," *MPW*, 29 Dec 1923, 798. "Vitagraph Head Personally Editing 'Captain Blood,'" *MPW*, 30 Aug 1924, 725. "Vitagraph Exchanges Receive a Wire from President Smith," *MPW*, 13 Dec 1924, 655. "President Albert E. Smith Reviews Vitagraph's Record," *MPW*, 24 Jan 1925, 379. "Vitagraph Quits Hays Organizaton, Quoting 'Live and Let Live' Belief," *MPW*, 7 Feb 1925, 547. "M.P.T.O.A. Congratulates Albert Smith and VItagraph," *MPW*, 14 Feb 1925, 654. "Vitagraph to Release 30 Productions, President Albert E. Smith Announces," *MPW*, 11 Apr 1925, 587.

Smith, Albert J[ones] [actor] (b. Chicago IL, 15 Feb 1894–11 Apr 1939 [45], Los Angeles CA). "Albert Smith," *Variety*, 19 Apr 1939. AS, p. 1011. BHD1, p. 509. IFN, p. 275 (in westerns for 25 years). Truitt, p. 308 (b. NY NY). George A. Katchmer, "Remembering the Great Silents," *CI*, 178 (Apr 1990), 42–43; *CI*, 217 (Jul 1993), 55 (d. 11 Mar).

Smith, Albert R. [producer] (b. 1875–7 Aug 1943 [68?], Los Angeles CA). AS, p. 1011. BHD2, p. 247.

Smith, Arlene [actress] (b. Arena WI, 1892–12 Jan 1984 [91?], Los Angeles CA). BHD, p. 303.

Smith, Art [stage/film actor] (*né* Arthur Gordon Smith, b. 1900?–24 Feb 1973 [73], West Babylon, LI NY; heart attack). "Art Smith, Stage Actor, Dead; Won Acclaim in Play by Odets," *NYT,* 28 Feb 1973, 44:2. "Art Smith," *Variety,* 7 Mar 1973. AS, p. 1012. IFN, p. 275.

Smith, Arthur T. [actor] (b. 1879?–14 Apr 1958 [79]). (Essanay.) IFN, p. 275. "The Essanay Company Out West," *MPW,* V, 4 Dec 1909, 801–02 (appeared in *The Heart of a Cowboy,* 1909, as a chasracter actor; I assume this is the Smith listed in the *IFN.*).

Smith, Beatrice Lieb [stage/film actress] (b. 1862?–6 Aug 1942 [80], Los Angeles CA). "Beatrice Lieb Smith," *Variety,* 12 Aug 1942 ("one-time stage and film actress"). AS, p. 1012. IFN, p. 275.

Smith, Beaumont [producer] (b. Adelaide, South Australia, ca. 1881–3 Jan 1950 [68?], Sydney, New South Wales, Australia). AS, p. 1012. BHD2, p. 247.

Smith, Bruce [agent/vaudevillian] (b. 1880?–17 Dec 1942 [62], New York NY). "Bruce Smith," *Variety,* 23 Dec 1942.

Smith, C[harles] **Aubrey** [stage/film actor] (b. London, England, 21 Jul 1863–20 Dec 1948 [85], Beverly Hills CA; double pneumonia). m. Isobel Mary Wood, Aug 1896. (Film debut: *The Builder of Bridges,* World, 1915.) "C. Aubrey Smith, Noted Actor, Dies; Screen's Aristocratic Englishman Knighted in '44 at 80—Began 0n Stage in 1892," *NYT,* 21 Dec 1948, 25:1. "C. Aubrey Smith," *Variety,* 22 Dec 1948. AMD, p. 320. AS, p. 1012. BHD1, p. 509 (b. Brighton, England). IFN, p. 275. Katz, p. 1068. Spehr, p. 168. Truitt, p. 308. "C. Aubrey Smith," *MPW,* 29 May 1915, 1420. "C. Aubrey Smith—Doctor, Cricketer, Actor," *MPW,* 25 Sep 1915, 2200. "A Regular Toff," *Photoplay,* Feb 1917, 29 (toured the U.S. on the stage in 1896). Eric Niderost, "Image of Empire: Sir C. Aubrey Smith; Hollywood's English Gentleman," *Films of the Golden Age,* No. 4, Spring 1996, pp. 72–77.

Smith, Charles H. [actor] (b. Washington IL, 3 Oct 1865–11 Jul 1942 [76], Los Angeles CA). m. Lillian Ashley. "Charles H. Smith," *Variety,* 22 Jul 1942. AS, p. 1012. BHD, p. 303. IFN, p. 275. Truitt, p. 308.

Smith, Charlotte *see* **Pickford, Charlotte**

Smith, Clara Reynolds [actress]. No data found. AMD, p. 320. "Well Known Dramatic Woman Joins Essanay Eastern Stock Company," *MPW,* 14 Jun 1913, 1116.

Smith, Clifford S. [actor/director/producer] (b. Richmond IN, 22 Aug 1886–17 Sep 1937 [51], Los Angeles CA; peritonitis following appendectomy). (Triangle; Ince; Vitagraph; Biograph; Universal.) "Clifford Smith; Directed William S. Hart in Many Early Western Films," *NYT,* 18 Sep 1937, 19:1. "Clifford S. Smith," *Variety,* 22 Sep 1937. AMD, p. 320. AS, p. 1012. BHD, p. 303; BHD2, p. 247 (b. 1894). IFN, p. 275 (age 51). Katz, p. 1068 (b. 1894). "Clifford Smith Starts Work," *MPW,* 11 Aug 1917, 937. "Clifford Smith Breaks Two Ribs," *MPW,* 27 Apr 1918, 567. "Clifford Smith, Cowboy Director, to Direct Mix," *MPW,* 8 Nov 1919, 236. "Smith Seriously Ill," *MPW,* 27 Sep 1924, 324.

Smith, Courtland [producer] (b. 1884–9 Aug 1970 [86?], Santa Fe NM). BHD2, p. 247.

Smith, Cyril [actor] (*né* Cyril Bruce-Smith, b. Peterhead, Scotland, 4 Apr 1892–5 Mar 1963 [70], London, England). m. actress Anne Rendall. (Stage debut, 1900; in 500 films.) "Cyril Smith," *Variety,* 230, 13 Mar 1963, 70:3. AS, p. 1012. BHD1, p. 509. IFN, p. 275.

Smith, David (aka David Divad) [cinematographer]. No data found. FDY, p. 469.

Smith, David (brother of **A. Victor** and **Albert E. Smith**) [director/producer] (b. England-d. 25 Apr 1930, Santa Barbara CA). AMD, p. 320. BHD2, p. 247. "David Smith Praises 'Man from Brodney's,'" *MPW,* 6 Oct 1923, 511. "Smith Ties Up Traffic," *MPW,* 24 Nov 1923, 412. "David Smith Chosen," *MPW,* 1 Mar 1924, 36. "David Smith Busy," *MPW,* 12 Apr 1924, 536.

Smith, Dick [actor/director/scenarist] (b. 1887–7 Feb 1937 [49?], Los Angeles CA). BHD, p. 303; BHD2, p. 247.

Smith, Dwight [actor] (b. Vevay IN, 1857?–30 May 1949 [92], Monsey NY). "Dwight Smith," *NYT,* 1 Jun 1949, 32:4. "Dwight Smith," *Variety,* 8 Jun 1949 ("in silent films with the late William S. Hart"). AS, p. 1012. BHD, p. 303. IFN, p. 275. Truitt, p. 309.

Smith, Edward I. "Gunboat" [boxer/actor] (b. Philadelphia PA, 17 Feb 1887–6 Aug 1974 [87], Leesburg FL). Pete Heller, *In This Corner* (NY: Simon & Schuster, 1973). (Paramount; FBO; Universal; Rayart.) AS, p. 1012 (Gunboat Smith). BHD, p. 303 (b. 1887). IFN, p. 276 (b. 12 Dec 1887–15 Feb 1934 [46]). Luther Hathcock, "Gunboat Smith, White Hope Heavyweight Champion [1915] of the World," *CI,* 130 (Apr 1986), 44–45.

Smith, Ernest [cinematographer]. No data found. FDY, p. 469.

Smith, Ernest [actor] (b. New York NY, 28 Apr 1844–6 May 1931 [87], Chicago IL). AS, p. 1012.

Smith, Frank [actor/scenarist/director] (b. Paris KY, 1860). AMD, p. 320. AS, p. 1012. "Frank Smith; Student of the Silent Drama, Assistant Director and First Character Man of the Imp Company," *MPW,* 10 Jan 1914, 158.

Smith, Frederick W[ilson] (actor] (b. Ft. Madison IA, 1880?–13 Jul 1944 [64], Miami FL). m. Bernice Parker. "Frederick W. Smith," *NYT,* 14 Jul 1944, 13:5. "Frederick W. Smith," *Variety,* 19 Jul 1944. AS, p. 1012. IFN, p. 276.

Smith, G[eorge] **Albert** [actor/producer] (b. Louisville KY, 1898?–3 Sep 1959 [61], New York NY [Death Certificate Index No. 19370]). m. Nathalie. "G. Albert Smith, Actor, Dead; Seen in Many Character Roles," *NYT,* 4 Sep 1959, 21:2. "G. Albert Smith," *Variety,* 23 Sep 1959. AMD, p. 320. AS, p. 1012. "Smith Is Named Assistant to Zecca," *MPW,* 13 Apr 1918, 230. "Smith to Distribute War Pictures," *MPW,* 4 May 1918, 688.

Smith, George Albert [inventor/director/producer] (b. London, England, 4 Jan 1864–17 May 1959 [95], Brighton, England). AMD, p. 320. AS, p. 1012 (b. Brighton, England). Katz, p. 1068 (patented Kinemacolor in 1906). WWVC, pp. 135–36 (moved to Brighton after death of his father). "Cinematography in Natural Colors," *MPW,* 12 Sep 1908, 197. "Color Kinematography," *MPW,* 14 Nov 1908, 375. George A. Smith, "Animated Photographs in Natural Colors," *MPW,* 2 Jan 1909, 6–9. Thomas Bedding, "Moving Pictures in Natural Colors," *MPW,* 9 Jan 1909, 30–31. "Notes and Comments," *MPW,* 20 Mar 1909, 335. "Kinemacolor," *MPW,* 18 Dec 1909, 873–74. "Men Who Make Kinemacolor Possible," *MPW,* 18 Dec 1909, 875. "The Kinemacolor Demonstration," *MPW,* 25 Dec 1909, 912–13. "Kinemacolor," *MPW,* 25 Dec 1909, 913–15. Burton H. Albee, "Impressions of Kinemacolor Films," *MPW,* 25 Dec 1909, 915–16.

Smith, George W. [actor] (b. 1897–18 Nov 1947 [49], Chicago IL; stroke). m. Claire. "G.W. Smith, Once Aide of George Abbott, 48," *NYT,* 19 Nov 1947, 27:2. "George W. Smith," *Variety,* 26 Nov 1947. AS, p. 1012. IFN, p. 276 (age 48).

Smith, Gerald [actor] (b. Indianapolis IN, 17 May 1844–6 May 1932 [87], Los Angeles CA). AS, p. 1012.

Smith, Gerald Oliver [actor] (b. London, England, 26 Jun 1892–28 May 1974 [81], Woodland Hills CA). "Gerald Smith," *Variety,* 12 Jun 1974. AS, p. 1012. BHD1, p. 509. IFN, p. 276.

Smith, Gertrude [actress] (b. Indianapolis IN, 16 Dec 1842–8 May 1923 [80], Los Angeles CA). AS, p. 1012.

Smith, Hamilton [scenarist/director] (b. Muskegon MI, 22 Oct 1887–29 Oct 1941 [54], Los Angeles CA). (Kalem.) "Hamilton Smith, 54, Producer of Films; Noted as Scenarist and Director—Author of 1,000 Stories," *NYT,* 30 Oct 1941, 23:4. "Hamilton Smith," *Variety,* 5 Nov 1941. AMD, p. 320. AS, p. 1012. BHD2, p. 247 (d. Newhall CA). Spehr, p. 168. "Hamilton Smith in New Kalem Series," *MPW,* 9 Oct 1915, 281. "Kalem Author-Director Becomes Executive," *MPW,* 23 Oct 1915, 589. "Three Scenario Writers for World," *MPW,* 16 Apr 1918, 73. "Hamilton Smith Joins Universal," *MPW,* 17 May 1919, 1038.

Smith, Harry James [actor/assistant director] (b. New Britain CT, 24 May 1880–16 Mar 1918 [37], New Westminster, B.C., Canada; auto accident). "Harry J. Smith Dies in Auto Accident; Author of 'Tailor-Made Man' Was in British Columbia on Red Cross Mission; An Authority on Sphagnum; Volunteered to Get a Supply of the Moss for Surgical Dressings in the Army," *NYT,* 18 Mar 1918, 13:3. "Harry James Smith," *Variety,* 22 Mar 1918. AS, p. 1012.

Smith, Harry Nelson [cinematographer] (b. 1888–10 Apr 1931 [43?], Los Angeles CA). BHD2, p. 247.

Smith, Herbert (brother of Sam Smith [d. 1945]) [executive] (b. England, 13 Jun 1901–1986 [84]). m. Pav. (Began 1916; Ruffles Imperial Bioscope; Southall Studios; British Lion.) AS, p. 1012 (b. 30 Jun). Peta Levi, "Herbert Smith; One of the Early Film Moguls," *CI,* 135 (Sep 1986), 10–11.

Smith, Howard I. [stage/film actor/scenarist] (b. Attleboro MA, 12 Aug 1894–10 Jan 1968 [73], Los Angeles CA; heart attack). m. Lillian Boardman (d. 1953, NYC). "Howard Smith, 73, an Actor, Is Dead; Performed for 50 Years in Vaudeville and on Air," *NYT,* 11 Jan 1968, 33:1. "Howard I. Smith," *Variety,* 17 Jan 1968. AS, pp. 1012–13. BHD1, p. 509. FDY, p. 437. IFN, p. 276. Truitt, p. 309.

Smith, J.R. "Jay" [actor]. No data found. AMD, p. 320. "'Our Gang' Increased," *MPW,* 17 Oct 1925, 575.

Smith, J. Sebastian [actor] (b. Southwell,

Nottinghamshire, England, 3 Oct 1869–15 Jan 1948 [78]). BHD, p. 304.

Smith, Jack C. [composer/singer/actor] (b. 1896?–14 Jan 1944 [48], Los Angeles CA). m. Ruth. "Jack C. Smith; Song Writer, Singer, and Actor Once Was with Irving Berlin," *NYT,* 17 Jan 1944, 19:5 (in Mickey McGuire series with Mickey Rooney). AS, p. 1013. BHD, p. 304. IFN, p. 276. Truitt, p. 309.

Smith, James [vaudevillian] (b. 1877?–6 Oct 1951 [74], Rahway NJ). "James Smith," *Variety,* 24 Oct 1951. AS, p. 1013.

Smith, Jess [actor/producer] (b. Pittsburgh PA, 9 Mar 1897–11 Apr 1965 [68], Los Angeles CA; heart attack). AMD, p. 320. AS, p. 1013. BHD, p. 304; BHD2, p. 247. IFN, p. 276. "Jess Smith Is Laugh Gleaner," *MPW,* 28 May 1927, 257.

Smith, John [cinematographer]. No data found. FDY, p. 469.

Smith, John T. [playwright] (b. Saratoga Springs NY, 1855?–24 Sep 1923 [68], New York NY). "Rev. Father John T. Smith," *Variety,* 4 Oct 1923.

Smith, Joseph C. [dancer/actor] (b. Philadelphia PA, 1882?–22 Dec 1932 [50], New York NY?; struck by truck). m. Frances Demorest. "Joseph C. Smith," *Variety,* 27 Dec 1932. AS, p. 1013.

Smith, Len [cameraman] (*né* Leonard Smith, b. Brooklyn NY, 1894?–20 Oct 1947 [53], Beverly Hills CA; heart attack). "Len Smith," *Variety,* 168, 22 Oct 1947, 63:3 (AA for *The Yearling*). (Metro.) AS, p. 1013. "Studio Gossip," *NYDM,* 7 Jul 1915, 41:1 (saved Arline Pretty from drowning while filming *Sis*).

Smith, Leonard L. [actor] (b. 1883–14 May 1942 [59?], Los Angeles CA). AS, p. 1013.

Smith, Leonard R. [director/actor] (b. 1889?–9 Jul 1958 [69], San Antonio TX). (Sennett.) "Col. Leonard R. Smith," *Variety,* 23 Jul 1958. AS, p. 1013. BHD, p. 304; BHD2, p. 247. IFN, p. 276. Truitt, p. 309.

Smith, Margaret M. [actress] (b. England, 9 Jul 1881–9 Dec 1960 [79], Los Angeles CA). "Margaret M. Smith," *Variety,* 21 Dec 1960 ("silent screen character actress"). AS, p. 1013. BHD, p. 304. IFN, p. 276. Truitt, p. 309.

Smith, Mark [stage/film/radio actor] (b. New York NY, 16 Apr 1886–10 May 1944 [58], New York NY; cirrhosis of the liver). m. Annabelle. "Mark Smith, Actor and Radio Artist; Appeared in 70 Theatres Here, and, 2,000 Programs on Air," *NYT,* 10 May 1944, 19:4 (b. 1887). "Mark Smith," *Variety,* 17 May 1944. AS, p. 1013. BHD, p. 304 (b. 1887). IFN, p. 276.

Smith, May [actress] (*née* Mary Niemeyer, b. 1871–5 Dec 1928 [57?], Los Angeles CA). AS, p. 1013.

Smith, Noel Mason [director] (aka Noel Mason, b. Rockland ME, 22 May 1895–20 Sep 1955 [60], Los Angeles CA). m. **Louise Fazenda**, 1917–26 (d. 1962). (L-KO; Fox; Sunshine Comedies; Sennett; WB; Associated Studios, Inc.) AMD, p. 320. AS, p. 1013 (b. 1890). Katz, p. 1069. "Drives Motorcycle Through WIndow," *MPW,* 7 Feb 1920, 880. "Noel Smith to Direct for Century," *MPW,* 5 May 1923, 82. "Noel Smith Directs," *MPW,* 20 Oct 1923, 683. "Noel Smith Busy," *MPW,* 8 Mar 1924, 146.

Smith, Oscar [actor] (b. Topeka KS, 28 Oct 1885–18 Mar 1956 [70], Los Angeles Co. CA). AS, p. 1013. BHD1, p. 510. IFN, p. 276.

Smith, Paul Gerard [director/scenarist] (b. Omaha NB, 14 Sep 1894–4 Apr 1968 [73], San Diego CA). m. Mary Alice. "Paul Gerrard Smith," *Variety,* 10 Apr 1968. AS, p. 1014. BHD, p. 304; BHD2, p. 247. IFN, p. 276.

Smith, Pete [publicist/actor/producer] (*né* Peter Schmidt, b. Brooklyn NY, 4 Sep 1892–12 Jan 1979 [86], Santa Monica CA; suicide by jumping off the roof of a nursing home). Thomas M. Pryor, "Pete Smith Suicide at 86; Probably First Studio Publicist Paid $1,000 Weekly—Became a Hit with His Comic Shorts," *Variety,* 17 Jan 1979. AMD, p. 320. AS, p. 1014. BHD1, p. 510; BHD2, p. 247. IFN, p. 276. Katz, p. 1069. Arthur H. Lewis, *It Was Fun While It Lasted* (New York: Trident Press, 1973), pp. 182–197 (b. Brooklyn NY). "Pete Smith Is Neilan's Special Publicity Man," *MPW,* 27 Sep 1919, 1934. "Before Leaving for the West, Pete Smith Issues Statement," *MPW,* 3 Jul 1920, 111. "Pete Smith Joins Metro," *MPW,* 25 Apr 1925, 762. "Pete Smith Recovering," *MPW,* 19 Jun 1926, 617.

Smith, Pleasant [heavyweight wrestling champion, 1913–19/actor] (*né* Tommy Lee Pleasant Jimmy Dee Smith, b. 1886?–12 Mar 1969 [83], Las Vegas NV). "Pleasant Smith," *Variety,* 19 Mar 1969 ("appeared in a number of silent pix"). AS, p. 1014. BHD, p. 304. IFN, p. 276. Truitt, p. 309.

Smith, R. Cecil [scenarist] (b. Parkersburg WV, 1880–17 Dec 1922 [42?], Los Angeles CA). AMD, p. 320. BHD2, p. 247. "Author Smith on Ince Staff," *MPW,* 10 Nov 1917, 843. "Smith Joins Selznick's Staff," *MPW,* 23 Aug 1919, 1146.

Smith, Richard H. [scenarist] (b. Cleveland OH, 17 Sep 1886–7 Feb 1937 [50], Los Angeles CA). AS, p. 1014. BHD2, p. 247.

Smith, Robert C[ecil] [cameraman] (b. 1901?–11 Apr 1945 [44], Los Angeles CA; on the set of WB's *A Stolen Life*). "Robert C. Smith," *Variety,* 18 Apr 1945 ("in pictures 20 years"). AMD, p. 321. AS, p. 1014. BHD2, p. 247. "Metro Engages Robert C. Smith, Photographer," *MPW,* 13 May 1916, 1156. "Cameraman Smith Back on Old Job," *MPW,* 16 Sep 1916, 1836.

Smith, Roy [actor/stuntman] (b. Poland, 30 Oct 1889–12 Dec 1944 [55], London, England). AS, p. 1014.

Smith, Russell E. [scenarist/publicist]. No data found. AMD, p. 321. "Newspaper Man Joins Picture," *MPW,* 20 Dec 1913, 1419. "Russell Smith with Triangle," *MPW,* 17 Jun 1916, 2050. "Russell Smith Joins Army," *MPW,* 10 Aug 1918, 814.

Smith, Samuel Wolf [executive] (b. 1888–8 Oct 1945 [57?], London, England). BHD2, p. 248.

Smith, Sebastian [actor] (b. Southwell, England, 3 Oct 1869–15 Jun 1948 [78]). BHD1, p. 617.

Smith, Sidney C. [cartoonist/actor] (b. Faribault MN, 28 Feb 1891–4 Jul 1928 [36], Los Angeles CA; effects of bad liquor). m. Ruth Beckman, Mar 1915. (Christie; Selig.) "Sidney Smith," *Variety,* 11 Jul 1928. AMD, p. 321. AS, p. 1014. BHD, p. 304 (b. 1893). IFN, p. 276. Truitt, p. 309. "Sidney Smith's Cartoons in Selig Films," *MPW,* 5 Jul 1913, 56 (*Doc Yak*). W.E. Wing, "Along the Pacific Coast," *NYDM,* 7 Apr 1915, 32:2. "Sidney Smith to Be Starred in a Series of Comedies," *MPW,* 4 Oct 1919, 136. Mary Keely, "Every Home Has Its Andy and Its Min, Says Sidney Smith, Creator of 'Gumps,'" *MPW,* 19 Jun 1920, 1626. "Sid Smith Signed for Cameo Comedies," *MPW,* 22 Dec 1923, 724.

Smith, Solly G. [actor] (b. 1876–28 Aug 1933 [57?], Culver City CA). AS, p. 1014.

Smith, Stanley [actor] (*né* Joseph Stanley Smith, b. Kansas City MO, 6 Jan 1903–13 Apr 1974 [71], Pasadena CA; cancer). AS, p. 1014 (d. 13 Mar). BHD1, p. 510. IFN, p. 276.

Smith, Stephen, Jr. [cinematographer]. No data found. FDY, p. 469.

Smith, Thomas C. [actor] (b. 1892–3 Dec 1950 [58?], Los Angeles CA). AS, p. 1014.

Smith, Tom [actor] (*né* Thomas C. Smith, b. OK, 10 Sep 1892–23 Feb 1976 [83], Los Angeles CA). AS, p. 1014.

Smith, Vernon [scenarist]. No data found. FDY, p. 437.

Smith, Vina [actress] (b. 1895–22 Mar 1949 [54?], New York NY). AS, p. 1014.

Smith, Vola *see* **Vale, Vola**

Smith, Wallace [novelist/title writer/scenarist] (b. Chicago IL, 30 Dec 1888–31 Jan 1937 [48], Los Angeles CA). "Wallace Smith Dies in California at 48; Novelist, Magazine Writer and Illustrator—'Gay Desperado' Among His Screen Plays," *NYT,* 1 Feb 1937, 19:4 (also wrote the screenplay of *Two Arabian Knights*). "Wallace Smith," *Variety,* 3 Feb 1937. AS, p. 1014. BHD2, p. 248. FDY, pp. 437, 447. IFN, p. 276.

Smith, William J. [actor] (b. 1868?–1 Apr 1933 [65], Wilkes-Barre PA). "William J. Smith," *Variety,* 4 Apr 1933. AS, p. 1014.

Smith, Winchell [actor/playwright/scenarist] (b. Hartford CT, 5 Apr 1871–10 Jun 1933 [62], Farmington CT). m. Grace F. Spencer. "Winchell Smith," *Variety,* 13 Jun 1933. AMD, p. 321. AS, p. 1014. BHD2, p. 248 (b. 1872). IFN, p. 276 (age 61). "Winchell Smith Joins Metro Authors; 'New Henrietta' to Be His First Film," *MPW,* 13 Mar 1920, 1829 (renamed *The Saphead*). "Winchell Smith Believs Screen Offers Greater Creative Field for Dramatist," *MPW,* 27 Mar 1920, 2132. "Walter, Veiller and Smith, Prominent Dramatists, Turn Talents to Metro Screen," *MPW,* 24 Apr 1920, 557.

Smith, Wingate [actor/assistant director] (b. Washington DC, 2 Dec 1894–22 Jul 1974 [79], Los Angeles CA). BHD2, p. 248.

Smithson, Frank [actor/director/producer] (b. Ireland, 1860?–15 Jan 1949 [88], New York NY). (Edison; Sennett.) "Frank Smithson," *Variety,* 173, 19 Jan 1949, 55:1 (life member of The Lambs). AMD, p. 321. AS, p. 1014. BHD2, p. 248. "Smithson with Edison; Well Known Theatrical Man Appointed Director General at Bronx Studio," *NYDM,* 6 Nov 1915, 24:2 (acted in England). "Edison's New Director General," *MPW,* 6 Nov 1915, 1110.

Smithson, Laura [actress] (b. Stockton-on-Tees, England, 14 Feb 1885–20 Dec 1963 [78], London, England). AS, p. 1014 (d. Barnet, England). BHD1, p. 511. IFN, p. 276.

Smitterick, Grover [actor] (d. Sep 1914, New York NY; drowned during filming). AS, p. 1014. BHD, p. 304.

Smoller, Dorothy [actress] (b. Memphis TN, 1901?–9 Dec 1926 [25], New York NY; suicide by swallowing liquid shoe polish). "Dorothy Smoller," *Variety,* 15 Dec 1926. AS, p. 1015. BHD, p. 304. IFN, p. 277. Truitt, p. 309.

Smythe, Alvord H. [composer] (b. Plymouth IN, 1876–3 Jun 1931 [55?], Wilkes-Barre PA). AS, p. 1015.

Smythe, Florence [actress] (b. San Francisco CA, 19 Apr 1878–29 Aug 1925 [47], Los Angeles CA; heart attack). m. **Theodore Roberts**, Oct 1917 (d. 1928). (FP-L.) "Florence Smythe Roberts," *Variety*, 2 Sep 1925. AS, p. 1015. BHD, p. 304. IFN, p. 277.

Snegoff, Leonid [actor] (b. Russia, 15 May 1883–22 Feb 1974 [90], Los Angeles CA; arteriosclerosis and heart attack). AS, p. 1015. BHD1, p. 511. IFN, p. 277.

Snell, Anita [actress]. No data found. AMD, p. 321. "Anita Snell," *MPW*, 15 Jan 1916, 432.

Snell, Earle [scenarist] (b. Santa Ana CA, 23 May 1886–6 May 1965 [78], Los Angeles CA; cancer). (1st National; WB; Universal; Republic.) "Earle Snell," *Variety*, 12 May 1965 ("screenwriter since 1923"). AMD, p. 321. AS, p. 1015. BHD2, p. 248. FDY, p. 437. IFN, p. 277. "Author Earle Snell Gets High Praise from Middleton," *MPW*, 31 May 1919, 1392.

Snell, Mina Sloane [scenarist] (b. 1882–24 Jan 1953 [70?], Los Angeles CA). AS, p. 1015. BHD2, p. 248.

Snelling, Minnette N. [actress] (b. 1878?–19 Dec 1945 [67], Los Angeles CA). (Sennett.) "Minnette Snelling," *Variety*, 26 Dec 1945. AS, p. 1015 (Ninette Snelling). BHD, p. 304. IFN, p. 277. Truitt, p. 309.

Snodgrass, Smythe [actor] (b. 1887–3 Oct 1921 [34?], Bayonne NJ). BHD, p. 304. IFN, p. 277.

Snow, Henry A. [cinematographer/producer] (b. Santa Cruz CA, 1870–28 Jul 1927 [57?], Oakland CA; tropical fever contracted in Africa). AS, p. 1015. BHD2, p. 248.

Snow, Herman Berry [scenarist] (b. 1878–6 Jan 1922 [43?], Brooklyn NY). BHD2, p. 248.

Snow, Marguerite [stage/film actress] (b. Savannah GA, 9 Sep 1889–17 Feb 1958 [69], Woodland Hills CA; kidney failure). m. **James Cruze**—div. 1923 (d. 1942); (2) Robert A. Smart; (3) **Neely Edwards** (d. 1965). (Thanhouser; Wharton; Ivan; Artcraft; Pathé.) "Marguerite Snow," *Variety*, 26 Feb 1958. AMD, p. 321. AS, p. 1015. BHD, p. 304 (b. Salt Lake City UT). IFN, p. 277. Katz, p. 1070 (began 1911). MSBB, p. 1042 (b. 1892). Truitt, p. 309. *Life Stories of the Movie Stars* (b. 1892). "Thanhouser Players Have Narrow Escape," *MPW*, 8 Jun 1912, 934. "Marguerite Snow's Return," *MPW*, 6 Dec 1913, 1158. "Thanhouser's Leading Woman Back Again," *MPW*, 17 Jan 1914, 292. "Frans Start 'Peggy' Snow Club," *MPW*, 15 Aug 1914, 966. "Sign Marguerite Snow; Metro Secures 'Million Dollar Mystery' Star to Play Opposite Bushman," *NYDM*, 5 May 1915, 24:1. "Marguerite Snow with Metro," *MPW*, 15 May 1915, 1078. Cover, *NYDM*, 23 Jun 1915. "Marguerite Snow Recovering from Injury," *MPW*, 4 Mar 1916, 1455. "Marguerite Snow Joins Ivan," *MPW*, 17 Jun 1916, 2046. "Marguerite Snow, Ivan Star," *MPW*, 15 Jul 1916, 467. "Marguerite Snow Opposite George M. Cohan," *MPW*, 13 Jan 1917, 221. "Marguerite Snow Makes Southern Tour," *MPW*, 22 Sep 1917, 1826. "Miss Snow Sells Bonds in Boston," *MPW*, 3 Nov 1917, 673. "King Baggot's Leading Woman," *MPW*, 8 Dec 1917, 1505. "Giving Marguerite Her Say," *MPW*, 16 Mar 1918, 1492. June Lee, "Dan Cupid's Bulletin Board," *Paris and Hollywood*, Sep 1926, 94 (recently married Smart, a wealthy mineowner of Goldfield NV. She divorced Cruze in 1923 "charging him with beating her and verbal abuse. Rumor at one time declared that she and Neely Edwards, vaudeville actor, were engaged as the result of an ardent long-distance telephone courtship.").

Snow, Mary [actress: the little girl in *The Great Train Robbery*, Edison, 1903] (*née*?). Stuart Oderman, "Mary Snow—The Girl at the Train Station!," *CFC*, 47 (Summer, 1975), 15 (in *The Great Bank Robbery* and *The Little Songbird*).

Snow, Mortimer [actor] (b. Brighton City UT, 19 Nov 1868–20 Jun 1935 [66], East Islip NY). m. Adelaide Warren (d. 1907). AS, p. 1015 (d. Hollywood CA). BHD, p. 304. IFN, p. 277. Truitt, p. 309.

Snow, Phoebe [actress] (aka Marion Murray, b. 11 May 1882–3 Aug 1967 [85], Flushing NY). AS, p. 1015.

Snow, Sidney A. [cinematographer/producer] (b. 1899–26 Aug 1959 [60?], Oakland CA). BHD2, p. 248. FDY, p. 469.

Snowden, Caroline [or **Carolynne**] [dancer/actress] (b. Oakland CA, 1900–6 Sep 1985 [85], Los Angeles CA). AMD, p. 321. BHD, p. 304. "Miss Snowden Cast," *MPW*, 24 Sep 1927, 220. Ragan 2, p. 1580.

Snyder, Earl "Spanky" [actor: Our Gang] (b. 1907?–16 Jan 1973 [65], Phoenix AZ; cancer). m. Maxine. (Began 1916.) "Earl 'Spanky' Snyder," *Billboard*, 30 Jan 1973. AS, p. 1015.

Snyder, Edward J. "Ed" [cinematographer]. No data found. (Pathé.) AMD, p. 321. FDY, p. 469. Spehr, p. 168. "Edward J. Snyder," *MPW*, 5 Feb 1927, 419.

Snyder, Matt B. [actor] (b. 22 Mar 1835–17 Jan 1917 [81], San Francisco CA). "Matt B. Snyder," *Variety*, 26 Jan 1917 (age 80). "Obituary," *MPW*, 10 Feb 1917, 819, 852. AMD, p. 321. AS, p. 1015. BHD, p. 304. IFN, p. 277 (age 81).

Snyder, Ray [film editor] (b. 1905?–10 Aug 1957 [52], Los Angeles CA; heart attack). "Ray Snyder," *Variety*, 21 Aug 1957.

Sobler, Albert W. [publicist]. No data found. AMD, p. 321. "Sobler Joins Mayflower's Advertising-Publicity Staff," *MPW*, 3 Apr 1920, 114.

Sodders, Carl [actor] (d. 18 Dec 1958, Dayton OH). (Griffith.) "Carl Sodders," *Variety*, 24 Dec 1958. AS, p. 1016. BHD, p. 304. IFN, p. 277. Truitt, p. 309.

Soderholm, Oscar [actor/director] (b. Sweden, 1875–1936 [61?], Sweden). AS, p. 1016.

Soderling, Walter [actor] (b. CT, 13 Apr 1872–10 Apr 1948 [75], Los Angeles CA). AS, p. 1016.

Sofaer, Abraham [actor[(b. Rangoon, Burma, 1 Oct 1896–21 Jan 1988 [91], Woodland Hills CA). AS, p. 1016.

Sohnker, Hans Albert Edmund [actor] (b. Kiel, Germany, 11 Oct 1903–20 Apr 1981 [77], Berlin, Germany). AS, p. 1016. BHD1, p. 511.

Sojin [stage/film actor] (*né* Sojin Kamiyama, b. Sendai, near Matsushima Bay, Japan, 30 Jan 1884–28 Jul 1954 [70], Tokyo, Japan). (U.S. film debut: *The Thief of Bagdad*.) "Sojin Kamiyama," *NYT*, 30 Jul 1954, 17:6. "Sojin Kamiyama," *Variety*, 4 Aug 1954. AS, p. 589 (Sojin Kamiyama); p. 1016 (Sojin, b. 1891). BHD1, p. 511 (b. 1891). FSS, p. 261. IFN, p. 159. Truitt, p. 175. Onoto Watanna (Winifred Reeve), "Honorable Movie Takee Sojin," *MPC*, Mar 1928, 37, 72.

Sokoll, Mike [actor] (b. Poland, 1891–24 Aug 1991 [100?]). BHD, p. 304.

Sokoloff, Vladimir [actor] (*né* Vladimir Nikolaevich Sokoloff, b. Moscow, Russia, 24 Dec 1889–15 Feb 1962 [72], Los Angeles CA; cerebral hemorrhage after a fall from a horse). Wife d. 1948. "Vladimir Sokoloff Dead at 72; Character Actor for 50 Years; Film Veteran Portrayed 35 Nationalities—Associate of Stanislavski, Reinhardt," *NYT*, 16 Feb 1962, 27:1. "Vladimir Sokoloff," *Variety*, 21 Feb 1962 (began 1937). AS, p. 1016 (d. 14 Feb). BHD1, p. 511. IFN, p. 277. Katz, p. 1070. Truitt, p. 309.

Solbelli, Olga, "Sunbeauty" [actress] (*née* Anna Olga Solbelli, b. Verghereto, Italy, 11 May 1898–1976 [78?]). AS, p. 1016; p. 1045 (Olga Sunbeauty). JS, pp. 429–30. Dr. Vittorio Martinelli, "Letter," *FIR*, Aug/Sep 1977, 448.

Soler, Andres (brother of **Domingo**, **Fernando**, and **Julian Soler**) [actor] (*né* Andres Diaz Pavia, b. Saltillo, Mexico, 18 Nov 1898–26 Jul 1969 [70], Mexico City, Mexico). AS, p. 1017.

Soler, Domingo (brother of **Andres**, **Fernando**, and **Julian Soler**) [actor] (*né* Domingo Diaz Pavia, b. Guererro, Mexico, 17 Apr 1902–13 Jun 1961 [59], Acapulco, Mexico; heart attack). AS, p. 1017.

Soler, Fernando (brother of **Andres**, **Domingo**, and **Julian Soler**) [actor/director] (*né* Fernando Diaz Pavia, b. Saltillo Coahuila, Mexico, 24 Mar 1896–24 Oct 1979 [83], Mexico City, Mexico). AS, p. 1017.

Soler, Julian (brother of **Andres**, **Domingo**, and **Fernando Soler**) [actor/director] (*né* Julian Diaz Pavia, b. Ciudad Jimenez, Mexico, 17 Feb 1905–5 May 1977 [72], Mexico City, Mexico). AS, p. 1017.

Soler, Vicente [actor] (b. Valence, Spain, 16 Apr 1903). AS, p. 1017.

Solidor, Suzy [actress/singer] (*née* Suzanne Louise Rocher, b. Saint-Servan-sur-Mer, France, 18 Dec 1900–30 Mar 1983 [82], Cagnes-sur-Mer, France [extrait de décès no. 6/1983]). AS, p. 1017.

Solntseva, Youlia Ippolitovna [actress/director] (b. Odessa, Ukraine, Russia, 7 Aug 1901–1989 [88?], Moscow, Russia). AS, p. 1017.

Solomon, Julian M., Jr. [publicist]. No data found. AMD, p. 321. Julian M. Solomon, "Service Department and the Exhibitor," *MPW*, 20 Jul 1918, 349. "Julian Solomon's Father Dies," *MPW*, 14 Feb 1920, 1087 (Julian Solomon, Sr., d. 21 Jan 1920, Philadelphia PA; apoplexy). "Solomon Joins Columbia," *MPW*, 13 Feb 1926, 636.

Solovitch, Don [actor] (d. 6 Jan 1928, Manti UT). BHD, p. 304. IFN, p. 277.

Solow, Sidney P. [film pioneer] (b. Jersey City NJ, 15 Sep 1910–2 Jan 1984 [73], Los Angeles CA; heart attack). AS, p. 1017.

Solser, Adrienne (sister of **Lion** and **Louis Solser**) [actress/producer] (*née* Engelina Adriana Solser, b. Rotterdam, Netherlands, 18 Feb 1873–29 Nov 1943 [70], Doetinchem, Netherlands). AS, p. 1017.

Solser, Lion (brother of **Adrienne** and **Louis Solser**) [actor] (*né* Abraham Lion Solser, b. Rotterdam, Netherlands, 6 Feb 1877–3 Aug 1915 [38], Rotterdam, Netherlands). AS, p. 1017.

Solser, Louis Johan (brother of **Adrienne** and **Lion Solser**) [actor] (b. Beverwijk, Netherlands, 15 Aug 1868–28 Jan 1944 [75], Auschwitz, Poland). AS, p. 1017.

Soltz, Rose Posner [actress] (b. Austria, 6 Mar 1902–18 Sep 1973 [71], Austria). AS, p. 1018.

Somborn, Herbert K. [executive] (b. 1880?–2 Jan 1934 [53], Beverly Hills CA). m. **Gloria Swanson**, 20 Dec 1919, Alexandria Hotel, LA CA—div. 1922 (d. 1983). "Herbert K. Somborn," *Variety,* 113, 9 Jan 1934, 54:1 (organized the Brown Derby with Wilson Mizner). AMD, p. 321. BHD2, p. 248. "Somborn—Swanson," *MPW,* 10 Jan 1920, 233. "Gloria Swanson Somborn," *MPW,* 23 Oct 1920, 1129 (daughter b. 7 Oct 1920, LA CA).

Somerset, Pat [actor] (*né* Patrick Holme-Sumerset, b. London, England, 28 Feb 1897–20 Apr 1974 [77], Apple Valley CA; arterial hemorrhage). m. (1) Margaret Bannerman; (2) **Edith Day**—div. 1927 (d. 1971); (3) Shelby Worrall; (4) Barbara Todd. AS, p. 1018. BHD1, p. 512. IFN, p. 277. SD, p. 1156. Lewis Richmond, "Crash! Another Romance on the Rocks!," *Paris and Hollywood Screen Secrets Magazine,* May 1927, 46–48 (named as co-respondent by Richard "Skeets" Gallagher, married to Irene Martin).

Somerville, Roy [writer/scenarist]. No data found. KOM, p. 158. J. Van Cartmell, "Film News from the Coast…," *NYDM,* 20 Nov 1915, 35:1 (contributor to *New York Magazine* and *Blue Book Magazine,* to write scripts for the Fine Arts Film Co.).

Somlay, Arthur [actor] (b. Budapest, Hungary, 28 Feb 1883–11 Nov 1951 [68], Budapest, Hungary). AS, p. 1018.

Somlo, Josef [producer] (b. Papa, Hungary, 1885–29 Nov 1973 [88?], Locarno, Switzerland). AS, p. 1018. BHD2, p. 248.

Sondermann, Emil [actor] (b. Germany, 1861–29 Aug 1927 [65?]). BHD, p. 304.

Sondes, Walter [actor] (b. England, 4 Jul— —d. 1941). BHD1, p. 513.

Sonja, Magda [actress] (*née* Magda Sonja Vesela, b. Vienna, Austria, 1895-ca. 1957 [62?]). AS, p. 1018.

Sontag, Jocelyne [actress] (b. New York NY, 16 Feb 1846–8 Jun 1907 [61], Denver CO). AS, p. 1018.

Sorel, Cécile [actress] (*née* Céline Emilie Seurre, b. Paris, France, 7 Sep 1873 [extrait de naissance no. 1552]-3 Sep 1966 [92], Trouville-sur-Mer, France; heart attack). AS, p. 1018.

Sorenson, Arthur A. [cinematographer] (b. 1894–2 Oct 1959 [65?], Brooklyn NY). BHD2, p. 249 (also listed under Arthur Sorsen).

Sorenson, B. [cinematographer]. No data found. FDY, p. 469.

Sorrelle, William J. [actor] (d. 30 May 1944, Tuolumne Co. CA). (Edison.) AS, p. 1019.

Sorter, Irma [actress] (b. CO, 3 Nov 1904–3 Sep 1968 [63], Santa Clara Co. CA). AS, p. 1019. BHD, p. 304. IFN, p. 278.

Sosso, Pietro [actor] (b. Italy, 20 Nov 1869–25 Apr 1961 [91], San Francisco CA). AS, p. 1019 (d. LA CA). BHD1, p. 513. IFN, p. 278.

Soster, William C. [director] (b. 1881–17 Jan 1923 [41?], Los Angeles CA). BHD2, p. 249.

Sothern, E[dward] **H**[ugh] Stewart (uncle of **Harry Sothern**) [stage/film actor] (b. New Orleans LA, 6 Dec 1859–28 Oct 1933 [73], New York NY; pneumonia [Death Certificate Index No. 28108, age 93]). m. (1) Virginia Harned; (2) **Julia Marlowe**, 1911 (d. 1950). "E.H. Sothern Dies of Pneumonia at 73; Julie Marlowe at Deathbed of Famous Actor in Their Hotel Suite Here; He Was Ill a Fortnight; Co-Stars of Shakespearean Stage Had Recently Come from Abroad for Visit," *NYT,* 30 Oct 1933, 1:2, 12:2. "E.H. Sothern," *Variety,* 31 Oct 1933. AS, p. 1019. BHD, p. 305. GSS, pp. 263–65. IFN, p. 278. Truitt, p. 309. "Personal," *NYDM,* 6 Nov 1915, 5:2 (his reminiscences to be published in *Scribner's Magazine,* Jan 1916).

Sothern, Ethel [actress] (b. 1881–20 Feb 1957 [75?], Los Angeles CA). AS, p. 1019.

Sothern, Harry (nephew of **E.H. Sothern**) [stage/film actor] (b. London, England, 26 Apr 1883–22 Feb 1957 [73], New York NY [Death Certificate Index No. 4202]). "Harry Sothern, Long an Actor, 73; Supporting Player, Nephew of Shakespearean Star, Dies—Ex-Production Manager," *NYT,* 23 Feb 1957, 17:4. "Harry Sothern," *Variety,* 27 Feb 1957. AMD, p. 321. AS, p. 1019. BHD, p. 305 (d. Ft. Lee NJ). IFN, p. 278. Truitt, p. 310. "Harry Sothern Has Signed for Long Term with Fox," *MPW,* 18 Sep 1920, 377 (b. 1882).

Sothern, Hugh [stage/film actor] (stage name: Roy Sutherland, b. Anderson County KS, 20 Jul 1881–13 Apr 1947 [65], Los Angeles CA). "Hugh Sothern," *Variety,* 23 Apr 1947. AS, p. 1019. BHD1, p. 513 (b. MO). IFN, p. 278.

Sothern, Jean [actress] (*née* Jean Brannen, b. Richmond VA, 1895–8 Jan 1924 [29], Chicago IL; cancer). m. Beverly S. Chew, 1917. "Jean Sothern," *Variety,* 10 Jan 1924. AMD, p. 322. AS, p. 1019. BHD, p. 305 (b. Philadelphia PA). IFN, p. 278 (age 25). Truitt, p. 310. "Psychologist Selects Screen Star," *MPW,* 6 May 1916, 943. Cal York, "Plays and Players," *Photoplay,* Jul 1917, 111 (married Chew. "Mrs. Chew will quit the screen, it is said.").

Sothern, Sam [actor] (*né* George Evelyn Augustus Townley Sothern, b. London, England, 1865?–21 Mar 1920 [55], Los Angeles CA; cancer). m. Janet Mullinger. AS, p. 1019. BHD, p. 305. IFN, p. 278. Truitt, p. 310 (Sam Southern).

Soto, Roberto, "El Panzon" [actor] (*né* Roberto Soto Mejia, b. Mexico, Apr 1888–18 Jul 1960 [72], Mexico City, Mexico; heart attack). AS, p. 1020.

Sotomayor, José [comedy theater/film actor] (*né* José Sotomayor Flores, b. Mexico, Sep 1904–24 Jan 1967 [62], Mexico City, Mexico; heart attack). (Film debut: *Juan Soldado,* 1919.) "Jose Sotomayer," *Variety,* 8 Feb 1967, 63:3 (founded ANDA, Mexican Artists Union). AS, p. 1020. BHD1, p. 513. IFN, p. 278.

Soto Rangel, Arturo [actor (b. Leon, Mexico, 12 Mar 1882–1 Jun 1965 [83], Mexico City, Mexico). AS, p. 1020.

Soule, Mrs. Leona Cardona [actress] (*née?,* b. 1864–15 Feb 1928 [65?], New York NY). BHD, p. 305.

Souper, G. Kay [actor] (d. 2 Jan 1947). BHD1, p. 513. IFN, p. 278.

Souplex, Raymond [actor] (*né* Raymond Guillermain, b. Paris, France, 1 Jun 1901 [extrait de naissance no. 5/193/1661]–22 Nov 1972 [71], Paris, France). AS, p. 1020.

Sourza, Jane [actress] (*née* Jeanne Elise Sourzat, b. Paris, France, 1 Dec 1902–3 Jun 1969 [66], Paris, France [extrait de décès no. 309/1969]). AS, p. 1020.

Souskevich, Boris Michailovich [actor/director/scenarist] (b. St. Petersburg, Russia, 1887–1946 [59?], Russia). AS, p. 1020.

Soussanin, Nicholas (father of actors Nicholas Saunders and Lanna Saunders) [actor/cinematographer] (b. Yalta, Ukraine, Russia, 16 Jan 1889–27 Apr 1975 [86], New York NY; cardiac arrest). m. **Olga Baclanova** (d. 1974). (Began 1923.) "Nicholas Soussanin," *Variety,* 30 Apr 1975. AS, p. 1020. BHD1, p. 513. FDY, p. 469. IFN, p. 278.

Soutar, Andrew [scenarist] (b. 1880–24 Nov 1941 [61?], Cornwall, England). AS, p. 1020 (d. 15 Nov, St. Austell, England). BHD2, p. 249.

Southard, Bennett [actor]. No data found. AMD, p. 322. "Bennett Southard," *MPW,* 15 Jan 1916, 400.

Southard, Harry D. [stage/film actor] (*né* Harry D. Weill, b. Buffalo NY, 1881?–27 Apr 1939 [58], New York NY). m. Emily Johnson. "Harry D. Southard, 30 Years on Stage; Former Member of New York Yankees Was an Alumnus of Cornell—Dies at 58; Engaged in Oil Business; Associated with Father—He Was Born in Buffalo as Harry D. Weill," *NYT,* 29 Apr 1939, 17:6. "Harry D. Southard," *Variety,* 3 May 1939. AS, p. 1020. BHD1, p. 513 (b. 1880). IFN, p. 278. Truitt, p. 310.

Southard, J. Irving [actor] (b. 1862?–8 May 1932 [70], New York NY). m. Nellie R. "J.I. Southard," *Variety,* 10 May 1932. AS, p. 1020.

Southern, Eve [actress] (b. TX, 1898). AMD, p. 322. AS, p. 1020. FSS, p. 261. "With Samuel Goldwyn," *MPW,* 4 Oct 1924, 402. Frances Gilmore, "Nordic Poise and Latin Passion; A Study of Temperaments," *MPC,* Sep 1927, 55, 90 (that she is like Lupe Velez; commits suicide in Chaplin's *The Woman from the Sea*).

Southwick, Albert P. [actor] (b. 1876–19 Jan 1929 [53], New York NY). BHD, p. 305. IFN, p. 278.

Southwick, Dale [actor: Our Gang) (b. Long Beach CA, 1913–29 Apr 1968 [55], Long Beach CA). m. (2 daughters). "Dale Southwick," *Variety,* 250, 8 May 1968, 263:2 ("He preceded Spanky McFarland as the chubby member of moppet two-reel series…"). AS, p. 1020 (d. Compton CA). BHD, p. 305. IFN, p. 278.

Sovern, Clarence [stunt cowboy] (b. MO, 16 Sep 1899–13 Mar 1929 [29], Burbank CA; heart attack). "Clarence Sovern," *Variety,* 30 Mar 1929. AS, p. 1021. BHD1, p. 617. IFN, p. 278. Truitt, p. 310.

Sowards, George A[lbert] [actor] [brother of **Len Sowards**] (b. MO, 27 Nov 1888–20 Dec 1975 [87], Los Angeles Co. CA). m. **Edna E. Zilke**, 1914. (Pathé.) "Real Wild West Wedding," *Variety,* 24 Apr 1914, 19:3 (Soward [sic] and Zilke "were wed in open air here. The guests rode horses and wore clothes of the plains."). AS, p. 1021. BHD1, p. 513.

Sowards, Len [stuntman/film/TV actor] (brother of **George A. Sowards**) (*né* James Len Sowards, b. MO, 17 Oct 1892–20 Aug 1962 [69], Sawtelle CA). m. (Began 1920.) "Len Sowards," *Variety,* 228, 29 Aug 1962, 55:4. AS, p. 1021. BHD1, p. 514. IFN, p. 278.

Sowers, Dan [actor]. No data found. AMD, p. 322. "Dan Sowers, a New Screen Heavyweight, Guided Pompous Parties Along Fake Fronts in France," *MPW,* 4 Oct 1919, 111.

Spacey, John Graham [actor] (b. England, 1894–2 Jan 1940 [45?], Los Angeles CA; heart attack). AS, p. 1021.

Spada, Marcello [actor] (b. Florence, Italy, 16 Jan 1895). JS, p. 433 (b. 1905; in Italian silents from 1927).

Spadaro, Odoardo [actor/singer] (b. Florence, Italy, 16 Jan 1895–26 Jun 1965 [71], Florence, Italy). AS, p. 1021.

Spalding, Albert [actor] (b. Chicago IL, 15 Aug 1888–26 May 1953 [64], New York NY). BHD1, p. 514.

Spanelly, Georges [actor] (b. Paris, France, 25 Dec 1898). AS, p. 1021.

Spanuth, Hans A. [producer/executive]. No data found. AMD, p. 322. "Spanuth Gets a Roosevelt Picture," *MPW,* 28 Sep 1912, 1287. "Hans A. Spanuth," *MPW,* 31 Jul 1915, 829. "Spanuth Denies Zukor Produced First Feature," *MPW,* 1 Apr 1922, 461.

Sparkhul, Theodor [cinematographer] (b. Hanover, Germany, 7 Oct 1894–13 Jun 1946 [51], Santa Fe NM; following a heart attack). (Began 1912; Ufa; Paramount; final film: *Blood on the Sun,* with Cagney.) "Theodor Sparkhul," *Variety,* 163, 19 Jun 1946, 49:5. AS, p. 1021 (d. 1945, LA CA). BHD2, p. 249. FDY, p. 469.

Sparks, Ned [stage/film actor] (*né* Arthur Edward Sparkman, b. Guelph, Ontario, Canada, 19 Nov 1883 [Birth certificate #037131, no. 5]–3 Apr 1957 [73], Apple Valley VA; intestinal blockage). m. Mercedes Caballero, 1931. (Film debut: *The Golden Girl.*) "Ned Sparks Dead; Comedian Was 73; Stage and Screen Performer Was Noted for Rasping Voice and Dour Mien," *NYT,* 4 Apr 1957, 33:5 (d. Victorville CA. In strike against stage producers in 1918; later blacklisted on Broadway). "Rites for Ned Sparks; John Charles Thomas Sings at Comedian's Funeral," *NYT,* 7 Apr 1957, 89:2. "Ned Sparks," *Variety,* 10 Apr 1957 (d. Victorville CA). AS, p. 1021. BHD1, p. 514 (d. Victorville CA). IFN, p. 278. Katz, p. 1079. Truitt, p. 310.

Spaulding, George D. [actor] (b. CO, 6 Jul 1881–23 Aug 1959 [78], Los Angeles CA). m. Geraldine Wood. "George Spaulding," *Variety,* 2 Sep 195. AS, p. 1021. BHD1, p. 514. IFN, p. 278.

Spaulding, Mrs. Nellie Parker (*née?,* b. Machias ME, 4 Aug 1870–18 Jun 1945 [74], Glendale CA). BHD, p. 305.

Speak, Jimmy (Jean) [sound recorder] (b. 1893?–27 Jun 1965 [72], Los Angeles CA). "Jimmy (Jean) Speak," *Variety,* 21 Jul 1965. AS, p. 1021. BHD2, p. 249.

Speaker, Tris [actress] (b. Hubbard TX, 4 Apr 1888–8 Dec 1958 [70], Whitney TX). BHD, p. 305.

Spear, Harry [actor] (b. Los Angeles CA, 25 Dec 1912–11 Feb 1969 [56], Los Angeles CA). AS, p. 1022 (d. 10 Feb). BHD1, p. 514. IFN, p. 278. Truitt, p. 310.

Spear, Harry A. [actor/director] (d. 13 Jun 1914, Los Angeles CA). BHD2, p. 249.

Spear, Rita [actress] (d. 9 Nov 1968, Los Angeles CA). BHD, p. 305.

Spearing, James O. [scenarist/director/title writer] (b. New Orleans LA–d. 9 Jan 1937, New York NY). AMD, p. 322. BHD2, p. 249. FDY, p. 447. "Spearing Made Director," *MPW,* 9 Jan 1926, 158. "Spearing's Titles," *MPW,* 26 Feb 1927, 647.

Spearman, Frank [novelist/playwright] (b. 1859?–29 Dec 1937 [78], Hollywood CA). "Frank Spearman," *Variety,* 129, 5 Jan 1938, 202:4. AMD, p. 322. "Author Sees His Story Before Camera," *MPW,* 10 Nov 1917, 891.

Spector, Harold H. [assistant general manager]. No data found. AMD, p. 322. "Harold H. Spector," *MPW,* 3 Jul 1915, 68.

Spedon, Samuel M. [publicist/scenarist] (b. New York NY, 1860?–7 Dec 1920 [60?], Atlanta GA; heart failure). (Vitagraph.) "Sam Spedon Drops Dead," *Variety,* 10 Dec 1920. AMD, p. 322. BHD2, p. 249 (d. Nov 1920). Slide, p. 151. "An Interesting Vitagraph Booklet," *MPW,* 28 Dec 1912, 1304. "Two Well-Known Publicity Men; Samuel M. Spedon, Publicity Manager of the Vitagraph Co.," *MPS,* 17 Oct 1913, 28. F.J. Beecroft, "Publicity Men I Have Met…," *NYDM,* 14 Jan 1914, 48 (see Beecroft, Chester for full citation. "His is one of the most important positions in the film industry, as the Vitagraph Company is one of the two largest advertisers in the business."). F.J.B., "With the Film Men; S.M. Spedon, Head of Vitagraph Publicity Department [photo only]," *NYDM,* 15 Apr 1914, 38:2. "Samuel Spedon," *MPW,* 5 Dec 1914, 1396. "San Francisco Convention," *MPW,* 31 Jul 1915, 790–94. Sam Spedon, "Sam Spedon Still on the Coast," *MPW,* 4 Sep 1915, 1655. "Sam Spedon to Represent Vitagraph," *MPW,* 8 Jul 1916, 233. "Spedon Returns to New York," *MPW,* 18 Nov 1916, 995. "Sam Spedon Joins M.P. World Staff," *MPW,* 6 Jan 1917, 51–52. "Ten Years of Film Publicity; Sam Spedon Relates His Experience as an Organizer of Advertising Stunts," *MPW,* 10 Mar 1917, 1528. Sam Spedon, "Business Healthy Around Newark," *MPW,* 21 Dec 1918, 1355–56. "Obituary," *MPW,* 16 Oct 1920, 835–36, 837, 842 (d. 8 Dec, aged 65). Sam Spedon, "Keeping in Personal Touch," *MPW,* 18 Dec 1920, 846 (last of his weekly columns). "Telegrams and Letters from Many Testify to Widespread Sorrow at the Death of KIndly Sam Spedon," *MPW,* 25 Dec 1920, 990.

Speelmans, Hermann Maria Louise [actor] (b. Urdingen, Germany, 14 Aug 1904–9 Feb 1960 [55], Gruenwald, Germany). AS, p. 1022 (b. Krefeld, Germany, 1902). BHD, p. 305 (d. Berlin). IFN, p. 278.

Speers, R. [title writer]. No data found. FDY, p. 447.

Speicher, Ann Drew [actress] (b. New York NY, 1888–6 Feb 1974 [85?], Miami FL). AS, p. 1022.

Speight, Nina [actress]. No data found. AMD, p. 322. "Nina Speight," *MPW,* 2 Jun 1917, 1439.

Speiro, Gerald B. [publicist]. No data found. AMD, p. 322. "Speiro Is Off for Spartanburg," *MPW,* 22 Jun 1918, 1723.

Spellman, Leora [actress] (aka Josephine Middleton, *née* Leora Spellmeyer, b. 1891–4 Sep 1945 [54?], Los Angeles CA; heart attack). AS, p. 1022. BHD1, p. 514.

Spence, Eulalie [scenarist] (b. 11 Jun 1894). BHD2, p. 249.

Spence, J.N. (Essanay.) No data found.

Spence, Ralph H. [actor/title writer/scenarist] (b. Key West FL, 4 Nov 1890–21 Dec 1949 [59], Woodland Hills [Calabasas] CA; heart attack). "Ralph Spence," *NYT,* 22 Dec 1949, 23:2 ("best known for the witty subtitles in the heyday of silent pictures"). "Ralph Spence," *Variety,* 28 Dec 1949 (age 60). AMD, p. 322. AS, p. 1022. BHD1, p. 514; BHD2, p. 249 (b. 1889). FDY, p. 447. IFN, p. 278. Truitt, p. 310. "Spence Promoted by Fox," *MPW,* 28 Jul 1917, 620. "Spence to Write Walsh Comedy-Dramas," *MPW,* 15 Dec 1917, 1617. "Screen Musical Comedy Ready for Lee Kids," *MPW,* 23 Nov 1918, 857. "Spence Will Title New Harold Lloyd Comedy [*The Freshman*]," *MPW,* 4 Apr 1925, 478. "Laemmle Buys Spence Stories," *MPW,* 18 Apr 1925, 714. "Spence Signed by Rock," *MPW,* 13 Jun 1925, 746. "Ralph Spence Busy," *MPW,* 31 Jul 1926, 279 (highest-paid title writer in the world at $5/word). "Look Where They Put Ralph Spence," *MPW,* 2 Apr 1927, 481. "Spence to N.Y.," *MPW,* 20 Aug 1927, 517. "Ralph Spence Quits Pictures for Stage," *MPW,* 27 Aug 1927, 581.

Spencer, Baldwin [director] (*né* Walter Baldwin Spencer, b. Engeland, Australia, 1860–1929 [69?], Australia). AS, p. 1022.

Spencer, Fred [actor] (*né* Fred Spencer Bretherton, b. Pueblo CO, 1901?–13 Oct 1952 [51], Los Angeles CA). (Sennett.) AS, p. 1022. BHD1, p. 515. IFN, p. 279. Truitt, p. 310.

Spencer, George Soule [actor] (b. WI, 25 Sep 1874–7 Aug 1949 [74], Los Angeles Co. CA). (Lubin.) AMD, p. 322. AS, p. 1022. BHD, p. 305. IFN, p. 279. "George Soule Spencer," *MPW,* 25 Jul 1914, 580.

Spencer, Helen [actress]. No data found. AMD, p. 322. "Helen Spencer with King-Bee," *MPW,* 20 Oct 1917, 404.

Spencer, James P. [actor] (b. Honolulu HI, 2 Jan 1893–28 Jul 1943 [50], Los Angeles CA). AS, p. 1022. BHD1, p. 515. IFN, p. 279.

Spencer, Marvelle [actress]. No data found. (Eclair.) AMD, p. 322. "Marvelle Spencer, Ideal Ingenue," *MPW,* 5 Jun 1915, 1580. "Along the Pacific Coast," *NYDM,* 7 Jul 1915, 26:1. "More Horsley Stars," *MPW,* 2 Oct 1915, 62.

Spencer, Richard V. [scenarist]. No data found. AMD, p. 322. "Richard V. Spencer," *MPW,* 14 Sep 1912, 1059. "Richard V. Spencer," *MPW,* 7 Dec 1912, 973. "Richard V. Spencer in East on Vacation," *MPW,* 5 Sep 1914, 1383.

Spender, Robert [actor] (d. 18 Sep 1993). BHD1, p. 515.

Spencer, Robert [actor] (b. 1900–4 Sep 1939 [39?], New York NY). BHD1, p. 515.

Spencer, Sophie [actress] (b. Los Angeles CA, 2 Jul 1872–5 Aug 1932 [60], Los Angeles CA). AS, p. 1022.

Spencer, Terry [actor/director] (b. 1895–3 Oct 1954 [59?], Los Angeles CA; heart attack). AS, p. 1022.

Spencer, Walter [actor] (b. Murray UT, 17 Sep 1882–8 Sep 1927 [44], Long Beach CA). AS, p. 1022. BHD, p. 305. IFN, p. 279.

Spender, Katherine [actress] (b. Cincinnati OH). John E. Thayer, "Stars in View—1922," *CI,* 61 (Winter, 1978), 36–38.

Sperani, Esperia [radio/film actress] (*née* Esperia Messa, b. Milan, Italy, 29 Jan 1903). JS, p. 434 (in Italian silents from 1917).

Spere, Charles [actor] (b. Lincoln NB, 17 Jul 1897–20 Apr 1945 [47], Los Angeles CA). AMD, p. 323. BHD, p. 305. "Charles Spere Is Leading Man," *MPW,* 30 Aug 1919, 1289.

Spero, Joseph [executive]. No data found. AMD, p. 323. "Another Feature Film Company," *MPW,* 6 Apr 1912, 26–27.

Speyer, Eva [actress] (*née* Eva Stöckl Speyer, b. Berlin, Germany, 1895). Vittorio Martinelli,

"Kino-Lieblinge," *Griffithiana,* 38/39 (Oct 1990), 33.

Speyer, Jaap [director] (b. Amsterdam, Netherlands, 29 Nov 1891–18 Sep 1952 [60], Germany). AS, p. 1022 (d. 17 Sep). BHD2, p. 250.

Speyer, Wilhelm [scenarist] (b. Germany, 1887–1 Dec 1952 [65?], Basel, Switzerland). AS, p. 1022. BHD2, p. 250.

Spiegel, Arthur H. [President of Equitable Motion Pictures Corp.—succeeded by William A. Brady] (b. 1885?–7 Apr 1916 [31], New York NY; pneumonia and grippe). "Arthur H. Spiegel Dies; Film Official and Chicago Merchant [the Spiegel-May-Stern Co. mail-order house] a Victim of Pneumonia," *NYT,* 8 Apr 1916, 15:7. AMD, p. 323. AS, p. 1022. BHD2, p. 250. "Spiegel Outlines Equitable Plant," *MPW,* 9 Oct 1915, 261. "Penny-a-Liners Won't Do," *MPW,* 30 Oct 1915, 979. "'Give Us Better Stories'; So Says Arthur Spiegel, of Equitable, Who Declares 'The Penny-a-Liners Won't Do,'" *NYDM,* 6 Nov 1915. 31:1 ("'The pennny-a-liner,' to quote Mr. Spiegel, 'who writes for the yellow-back novel, the cheap magazine and the boiler plate newspaper at so much a line, without consideration of the matter he is writing, who simply compiles laboriously a flow of rhetoric because he is getting so much for so much, is of no earthly use to the film world. We need, ever so badly, more brain power in the story department, and we have decided to get it, if we have to exhume the dead masters' bodies and get their "mark" on a contract. ¶'We need the unconventional denouement.... Our weakness is the finish of the stories.... ¶'Unconventionality—new business, less trickery, less double exposure, more straight dramatic work with more deductional power required from the audiences is what is wanted...'"). "Arthur H. Spiegel Dead; Wm. A. Brady Succeeds as President of Equitable and Gen. Man. of the World," *NYDM,* 15 Apr 1916, 24. "Obituary," *MPW,* 22 Apr 1916, 599. "Death's Toll for the Decade," *MPW,* 10 Mar 1917, p. 1528.

Spier, Martha [actress]. No data found. AMD, p. 323. "Essanay Acquires Talented Leading Lady," *MPW,* 23 Apr 1910, 643.

Spinelly [actress] (*née* Elisa Fournier, b. Paris, France, 1 May 1890–25 Jul 1966 [76], Bidart, France [extrait de décès no. 23/1966]). AS, p. 1023.

Spingler, Harry [actor/director] (b. Buffalo NY, 3 Aug 1889–22 Apr 1953 [63], Woodland Hills CA). m. **Vera Michelena** (d. 1961). (Fox.) "Harry Spingler," *Variety,* 29 Apr 1953. AMD, p. 323. AS, p. 1023. BHD, p. 305. IFN, p. 279. Truitt, p. 311. "New Ivan Player," *MPW,* 26 Aug 1916, 1382. "Los Angeles Studio Shots," *MPW,* 17 Jul 1920, 327 (started divorce proceedings against Michelena).

Spingold, Nate B. [executive] (b. Chicago IL, 6 Mar 1886–14 Jun 1958 [72], New York NY). BHD2, p. 250.

Spink, George [vaudeville composer/actor/scenarist] (b. 1873?–27 May 1936 [63], East Providence RI). Ellen Tate. (Lubin.) "George Spink," *Variety,* 122, 3 Jun 1936, 54:1 (composed *Bill Simmons* and "songs brought into popularity by Eva Tanguay, Blanche Ring, Trixie Friganza, Nora Bayes and Andrew Mack."). AS, p. 1023. BHD2, p. 250. "Spink Joins Lubin Staff," *NYDM,* 30 Oct 1915, 25:2.

Spira, Camilla [actress] (b. Hamburg, Germany, 1 Mar 1906–25 Aug 1997 [91], Berlin, Germany). AS, p. 1023. BHD1, p. 617.

Spitz, Leo [executive] (b. Chicago IL, 30 Jun 1888–16 Apr 1956 [67], Los Angeles CA). BHD2, p. 250.

Spitzer, Nat [executive]. No data found. (President, Bullseye Film Corp.) Grace Kingsley, "Flashes; New Film Concern; Reelcraft Latest to Enter Cinema Realm," *LA Times,* 11 Mar 1920, III, p. 4.

Spivey, Thomas [special effects] (b. 1873–27 Mar 1954 [81?], Los Angeles CA). BHD2, p. 250.

Spoerl, Heinrich [actor/scenarist] (b. Germany, 1887–24 Aug 1955 [68?], Rottach-Egern, Germany). AS, p. 1023.

Spofford, (Baby) Charles S. Van Norman [actor] (b. West Los Angeles CA, 10 Dec 1915–29 Sep 1935 [19], Los Angeles CA). AS, p. 1023. BHD, p. 305. IFN, p. 279.

Spong, Hilda [stage/film actress] (*née* Hilda Frances Spong, b. London, England [Melbourne, Australia?], 14 May 1875–16 May 1955 [80], Norwalk CT). (World.) "Miss Hilda Spong, Actress 65 Years; Stage Star Noted for Comedy Roles Dies at 80—Made American Debut in 1898," *NYT,* 17 May 1955, 29:4. "Hilda Spong," *Variety,* 18 May 1955. AMD, p. 323. AS, p. 1024. BHD, p. 305. IFN, p. 279. Truitt, p. 311. "Hilda Spong," *MPW,* 21 Aug 1915, 1293.

Spooner, Cecil (daughter of Sprague and Mary Gibbs Spooner; sister of **Edna May Spooner**; niece of Corse Payton) [actress] (b. New York NY, 29 Jan 1874–13 May 1953 [78], Sherman Oaks CA; heart attack). m. **Charles E. Blaney**, 1909 (d. 1944). (Edison.) AMD, p. 323. AS, p. 1024. BHD, p. 306 (b. 1875). IFN, p. 280. SD, p. 1161. "Cecil Spooner on the Moving Picture Stage," *MPW,* 28 Aug 1909, 277. "Cecil Spooner and Ed Barry in Wilson-Federated Comedy," *MPW,* 22 Jul 1922, 300 (fifteen years in films).

Spooner, Edna May (daughter of Sprague and Mary Gibbs Spooner; sister of **Cecil Spooner**; niece of **Corse Payton**) [stage/film actress] (b. Centerville IA, 10 May 1873–14 Jul 1953 [80], Sherman Oaks CA; heart attack). m. actor Arthur J. Waley, 1912—div. 1921. "Miss Edna May Spooner," *NYT,* 16 Jul 1953, 21:3 (age 78). "Edna May Spooner," *Variety,* 191, 22 Jul 1953, 63:2 (age 78). AS, p. 1024 (b. 1893). BHD, p. 306. IFN, p. 279.

Spooner, Franklin E[dward] [actor] (b. Centerville IA, 16 Apr 1860–14 Jan 1943 [82], Monterey Park CA; heart attack). AS, p. 1024. BHD, p. 306.

Spoor, George K. (brother of **Mary Spoor**) [inventor/director/producer/executive] (b. Highland Park IL, 1872?–24 Nov 1953 [81], Chicago IL). "George K. Spoor, 81, Film Pioneer, Dies; Head of Old Essanay Concern in Chicago Devised a 3-D Picture Process in 1923," *NYT,* 25 Nov 1953, 23:1. "George K. Spoor," *Variety,* 2 Dec 1953. AMD, p. 323. AS, p. 1024. BHD2, p. 250. IFN, p. 279. WWVC, p. 138. "Trade Notes," *MPW,* 3 Aug 1907, 342. "Notes and Comments," *MPW,* 23 Jan 1909, 91. "Essanay Will Release Two Reels," *MPW,* 6 Nov 1909, 538. "English Appreciation of George K. Spoor," *MPW,* 20 Nov 1909, 717. "A Trick of the Film Producer," *MPW,* 15 Jan 1910, 51. "Mr. Spoor Back from Europe," *MPW,* 2 Jul 1910, 22. "Essanay Company in Flourishing Condition," *MPW,* 1 Oct 1910, 742. "Photoplay," *MPW,* 15 Oct 1910, 858. George K. Spoor, "Remarkable Growth of Motion Picture Industry," *MPW,* 11 Jul 1914, 191. "'Big Four' [A.E. Smith, W.N. Selig, Ira Lowry, Spoor] Surprises Film Men; Vitagraph-Lubin-Selig-Essanay Combination Means Radical Departure by Motion Picture Pioneers—Exchange Managers Appointed and Preparations Under Way for Flying Start," *NYDM,* 21 Apr 1915, 24:2. "Spoor Talks on Features; Essanay's President Speaks of Organization of V-L-S-E and of Essanay's Plans for Future," *NYDM,* 12 May 1915, 25:1 ("In 1895, when I was first making pictures, anything that would move on the screen would pass. Moving pictures were a novelty and everything was accepted. Then was conceived the 1,000-foot film with some connecting idea, though loosely constructed, and the motion picture was born. This gave way to the photoplay of the present..."). "George Spoor Talks," *MPW,* 22 May 1915, 1235. "Spoor on 'Sermonizing,'" *MPW,* 31 Jul 1915, 825. "Realism on the Screen," *NYDM,* 18 Aug 1915, 22:3 ("Essanay, in its aim for realism, is seeking for truth to detail, truth to the things as it [sic] exists and truth to our conception of life."). "Spoor Adds Orchestra," *MPW,* 30 Oct 1915, 805. George K. Spoor, "Smaller Theaters Must Have Variety," *MPW,* 15 Jul 1916, 437. George K. Spoor, "Pictures in Schools and Churches," *MPW,* 26 Aug 1916, 1377. "Spoor Comments on New Service," *MPW,* 23 Sep 1916, 1955. "Spoor Outlines Essanay's Activities," *MPW,* 11 Nov 1916, 869. George K. Spoor, "The Turning of the Ways," *MPW,* 10 Mar 1917, 1515–16. "Spoor Would Exchange Suggestions," *MPW,* 14 Jul 1917, 265. "Perfection Pictures Announces Plans," *MPW,* 29 Sep 1917, 1977–78. "Spoor Helps [Herbert S.] Hoover [U.S. Food Administration]," *MPW,* 17 Nov 1917, 1025. "Essanay Busy on 'Young America,'" *MPW,* 11 May 1918, 863. "Mrs. Spoor Presents Flag to Essanay Unit," *MPW,* 20 Jul 1918, 386. "Spoor Perfects Processing Machine," *MPW,* 9 Nov 1918, 677. James S. McQuade, "Spoor-Thompson Processing Machine," *MPW,* 30 Nov 1918, 965. "George K. Spoor Increases Sales and Factory Forces," *MPW,* 22 Mar 1919, 1608. Gunnar Lundquist, "The Father Figure of the Western Film; Broncho Billy Anderson; They All Rode in His Tracks," *CI,* 144 (Jun 1987), 21. Michael Wilmington, "August 10, 1907; Lights! Cameras! Where action was for one brief decade, Essanay Studios, a pioneering movie studio turned Chicago into Hollywood-on-the-prairie," *Chicago Tribune,* 13 Apr 1997, IV, 2:1.

Spoor, Marvin K. [cinematographer] (b. 1893–3 Dec 1951 [58?], Evanston IL). AS, p. 1024. BHD2, p. 250.

Spoor, Mary (sister of **George K. Spoor**) [designed Indian Head trademark of Essanay] (b. 1887?–18 Oct 1985 [98]).

Spottswood, James C. [stage/film/radio actor] (b. Washington DC, 1882–11 Oct 1940 [58], New York NY; heart attack). (Paramount.) "James Spottswood, Actor, Dead at 58; Descendant of Colonial Official of Virginia [Alexander Spottswood, Lt.-Gov. of the Colony of Virginia in 1710] Had Appeared in Many Comedies; Also in Films and Radio; Heard on Air with Edward G. Robinson and Fannie Brice—Was Trained as a Lawyer," *NYT,* 12 Oct 1940, 17:3. "James Spottswood," *Variety,* 16 Oct 1940. AS, p. 1024. BHD1, p. 515. IFN, p. 279. Truitt, p. 311.

Sprague, Alvin [stage hand/actor] (b. New York NY-d. 15 Aug 1928, Riverside CA; from injuries after a fall backstage at a Riverside house performance of *Wings*). "Alvin Sprague," *Variety,* 29 Aug 1928. AS, p. 1024.

Sprague, Chandler [director/scenarist] (b. Haverhill MA, 26 May 1886–15 Nov 1955 [69], Sacramento CA). (UA; Paramount; MGM.) "Chandler Sprague," *NYT,* 16 Nov 1955, 35:4. "Chandler Sprague," *Variety,* 23 Nov 1955. AS, p. 1024. BHD2, p. 250. FDY, p. 437.

Springer, Norman [title writer/scenarist]. No data found. FDY, pp. 437, 447.

Sprotte, Bert[hold] [actor] (b. Chemnitz, Saxony, Germany, 9 Dec 1870–30 Dec 1949 [79], Los Angeles Co. CA). AS, p. 1024. BHD1, p. 515. IFN, p. 279. George A. Katchmer, "Forgotten Cowboys and Cowgirls—Part X," *CI,* 182 (Aug 1990), 40 (m. Alma Ruzena); 203, May 1992, 43.

Sprunck, Paul G. [technical director]. No data found. AMD, p. 323. "C.B. DeMille Signs Technical Expert," *MPW,* 4 Jul 1925, 79.

Squire, Ronald [stage/film actor] (*né* Ronald Lancelot Squirl, b. Tiverton, Devonshire, England, 25 Mar 1886–16 Nov 1958 [72], London, England). (Began on stage in Eastbourne, England, 1909.) m. (1 daughter). "Ronald Squire, British Actor, 72; Stage and Screen Comedian Dies—Seen Here in Two Plays and Many Films," *NYT,* 17 Nov 1958, 31:5. "Ronald Squire," *Variety,* 212, 19 Nov 1958, 79:1. AS, p. 1024. BHD1, p. 516. IFN, p. 279.

Squires, Jack [actor] (b. New York NY, 1894–21 Jun 1938 [44?], New York NY). BHD1, p. 516.

Staby, Oscar C. [executive] (b. 1886–23 Oct 1927 [41?], Los Angeles CA). BHD2, p. 250.

Stack, William [actor] (b. Baker OR, 5 Mar 1882-ca. 1934 [52?]). AS, p. 1025.

Stafford, H.C. [scenarist]. No data found. AMD, p. 323. "Dr. H.C. Stafford Author of Villon Series," *MPW,* 1 Aug 1914, 715.

Stafford, Harry Frank [scenarist] (d. 8 Sep 1917, New Rochelle NY). BHD2, p. 250.

Stafford, John Alvin [director] (b. Kehoka MO, 5 May 1889–15 Apr 1961 [71], Glendale CA). BHD2, p. 250.

Stagg, Clinton Holland [scenarist] (b. NJ-d. 3 May 1916, Santa Monica CA; auto accident). AMD, p. 323. BHD2, p. 250 (d. LA CA). "New Thanhouser Writers," *MPW,* 25 Sep 1915, 2185. "Obituary," *MPW,* 27 May 1916, 1515.

Stagno-Bellincioni, Bianca (daughter of **Gemma Bellincioni**) [actress/soprano opera singer] (b. Budapest, Hungary, 23 Jan 1888). JS, p. 436 (in Italian silents from 1916).

Stahl, John M[alcolm] [director/producer] (b. New York NY, 21 Jan 1886–12 Jan 1950 [63], Los Angeles CA; heart attack). "John Stahl Dies; Film Director, 63, Supervised 'Keys of Kingdom,' 'Father Was a Fullback'—Entered Industry in '13," *NYT,* 14 Jan 1950, 15:3. "John M. Stahl," *Variety,* 18 Jan 1950. AMD, p. 323. AS, p. 1026. BHD2, p. 250. IFN, p. 279. Katz, p. 1082 (began 1913). 1921 Directory, p. 275. "Stahl to Direct Mollie King," *MPW,* 31 May 1919, 1346. "Stahl to Direct Mollie King," *MPW,* 2 Aug 1919, 660. "Stahl Arrives in Los Angeles," *MPW,* 3 Jan 1920, 94. "John Stahl Is to Direct Mildred Harris Chaplin," *MPW,* 14 Feb 1920, 1075. "Stahl Near Death When Auto Skids," *MPW,* 21 Oct 1922, 677. "Signs John M. Stahl," *MPW,* 15 Mar 1924, 189. "Stahl Renews Contract," *MPW,* 6 Dec 1924, 556.

Stahl, Walter O. [actor] (b. Bonn, Germany, 3 Jul 1884–6 Aug 1943 [59], Los Angeles CA; heart attack). m. Irene Rohan. "Walter D. Stahl," *Variety,* 11 Aug 1943. AS, p. 1026.

Stahl, Walter Richard [writer/director]. No data found. AMD, p. 323. "Walter Richard Stahl," *MPW,* 23 Jun 1917, 1922. "Walter Stahl to Wed Miss Lorraine," *MPW,* 7 Jul 1917, 101.

Stahl-Nachbaur, Ernst [actor] (*né* Ernst Julius Emil Guggenheimer, b. Munich, Germany, 6 Mar 1886–13 May 1960 [74], Berlin, Germany). AS, p. 1026.

Stall, Karl [actor] (b. Cincinnati OH, 1870–14 Jun 1947 [77?], New York NY). AS, p. 1026.

Stallard, Ernest [actor] (b. 1864–18 Oct 1929 [65?], Chicago IL). BHD, p. 306.

Stallings, Charles P. [assistant director] (b. 1893?–26 Sep 1960 [67], Los Angeles CA). "Charles P. Stallings," *Variety,* 5 Oct 1960. AMD, P. 323. AS, p. 1026. BHD2, p. 251. "Charles P. Stallings Assistant to Henry Otto," *MPW,* 23 Sep 1916, 1987.

Stallings, Laurence Tucker [writer/scenarist] (b. Macon GA, 25 Nov 1894–28 Feb 1968 [73], Pacific Palisades CA). m. (1) Helen Potest, 1919–36; (2) Louise St. Leger Vance. *The Plumes* (1924). "Laurence Stallings Dead at 73; 'What Price Glory?' Co-Author; Collaborated with Maxwell Anderson—Wrote of War in Novels and Plays," *NYT,* 29 Feb 1968, 37:1 (lost leg in WWI; "When a writer drops out he just drops out, and it's better to let it go at that. I was just lucky the first time. Like a lot of writers, I had just one thing to say and I said it. There wasn't any more."; wrote screenplay for *The Big Parade*). " Laurence Stallings," *Variety,* 6 Mar 1968. AMD, p. 324. AS, p. 1026. BHD2, p. 251. IFN, p. 279. "Laurence Stallings Engaged," *MPW,* 2 Jan 1926, 67. "Stallings to Write for M-G-M," *MPW,* 2 Apr 1927, 475.

Stammers, Frank M. [playwright] (d. 27 Jun 1921], New York NY; typhoid-pneumonia). "Frank Stammers, Composer," *NYT,* 4 Jul 1921, 9:7. "Frank M. Stammers," *Variety,* 1 Jul 1921.

Stamper, Dave [composer] (b. New York NY, 10 Nov 1883–18 Sep 1963 [79], Poughkeepsie NY). "Dave Stamper Is Dead at 79; Composer for 'Ziegfeld Follies' [1905–32]," *NYT,* 19 Sep 1963, 27:5 (wrote, among others, *Daddy Has a Sweetheart,* and the music for "the first operetta produced in sound film, 'Married in Hollywood.'") "Dave Stamper," *Variety,* 25 Sep 1963. AS, p. 1026.

Stamper, F. Pope [actor] (b. Richmond, Surrey, England, 20 Nov 1880–12 Nov 1950 [69]). BHD1, p. 516. IFN, p. 280.

Stamper, Dave [composer] (b. New York NY, 10 Nov 1883–18 Sep 1963 [79], Poughkeepsie NY). AS, p. 1026.

Stamp-Taylor, Enid [stage/film actress] (b. Monkseaton, England, 12 Jun 1904–13 Jan 1946 [41], London, England; of injuries after a fall in her apartment). m. 1929 (1 daughter). "Enid Stamp-Taylor," *Variety,* 16 Jan 1946, 62:2. AS, p. 1026 (b. Whitley Bay, England). BHD1, p. 516.

Stander, Lionel Jay [actor/organizer of SAG] (b. Bronx NY, 11 Jan 1908–30 Nov 1994 [86], Brentwood, Los Angeles CA; lung cancer). m. (6) Stephana. Lawrence Van Gelder, "Lionel Stander Dies at 86; Actor Who Defied Blacklist," *NYT,* 2 Dec 1994, D20:4. As, p. 1026. Katz, p. 1083.

Standing, Gordon H. (nephew of **Herbert Standing**; cousin of **Guy**, **Jack** and **Wyndham Standing**) [actor] (b. London, England, 24 Nov 1887–21 May 1927 [39], Los Angeles CA; attacked by a lion at the Selig Zoo). "Actor Dies as Result of Studio Lion's Attack," *Variety,* 25 May 1927. AMD, p. 324. AS, p. 1026. BHD, p. 306. IFN, p. 280. Truitt, p. 311. "Stamding, Noted Actors, Planning Family Reunion," *MPW,* 20 Nov 1920, 1025. "Obituary," *MPW,* 28 May 1927, 247.

Standing, Sir Guy (son of **Herbert Standing**; father of **Guy Standing, Jr.**; brother of **Jack** and **Wyndham Standing**) [actor] (b. London, England, 1 Sep 1873–24 Feb 1937 [63], Apple Valley CA; heart attack). m. (1) Isabel Urquehart; (2) Blanche Burton; (3) Dorothy Hammond. "Sir Guy Standing Drops Dead at 63; Actor Collapses in Hollywood After Telling Garage Man He 'Never Felt Better'; Knighted for War Work; Spent Most of Life in America and Was in Many Plays Here—with Movies Since 1933," *NYT,* 25 Feb 1937, 23:1. "Sir Guy Standing," *Variety,* 3 Mar 1937. AS, p. 1026. BHD1, p. 517 (d. LA CA). IFN, p. 280. "Guy Standing," *MPW,* 15 Aug 1914, 966. "Famous Players Postpone 'Silver King,'" *MPW,* 22 Aug 1914, 1102. "Standing Writes Zukor; Stage Star, Who Was to Have Appeared in Famous Players' Film [*The Silver King*], Now in British Navy," *NYDM,* 9 Sep 1914, 32:3.

Standing, Guy, Jr. (son of **Sir Guy Standing**) [actor] (b. New York NY, 12 Apr 1904–14 Nov 1954 [50], Reseda CA). AS, p. 1026. BHD1, p. 517. IFN, p. 280.

Standing, Herbert, Jr. (father of **Joan Standing**; son of **Herbert Standing, Sr.**; brother of **Wyndham** and **Guy Standing**) [stage/film actor] (b. London, England, 1884–23 Sep 1955 [71], New York NY). m. Dulcie I.F. Clayton, 1931. "Herbert Standing, Retired Actor, Dies; Member of Noted English Stage Family," *NYT,* 24 Sep 1955, 19:2. "Herbert Standing," *Variety,* 28 Sep 1955. AS, p. 1027. BHD, p. 306. IFN, p. 280. Truitt, p. 311. "Actors in Trolley Crash; Herbert Standing, His Daughter, and George Osbornes' Lives Endangered in [Santa Monica] California," *NYDM,* 7 Jan 1914, 8:2 ("Standing sustained a broken knee cap and cuts; Osborne was painfully injured about the shoulders; Joan Standing, Mr. Standing's ten-year-old daughter, was bruised and cut by flying glass.").

Standing, Herbert, Sr. (father of **Guy**, **Jack** and **Wyndham Standng**; uncle of **Gordon Standing**) [actor] (*né* James Herbert Crellin Standing, b. Peckham, England, 13 Nov 1846–5 Dec 1923 [77], Los Angeles CA). m. Emilie Brown. AMD, p. 324. AS, p. 1027. IFN, p. 280. W.E. Wing, "Along the Pacific Coast," *NYDM,* 14 Apr 1915, 26:2 (cites Standing as the father of 7 sons and 5 daughters). "Gordon Standng Now a Commander," *MPW,* 13 Jul 1918, 190. "Herbert Standing a Goldwynite," *MPW,* 17 May 1919, 1016. "Standing Struck by Streetcar," *MPW,* 22 May 1920, 1093 (on 1 May 1920). "Standing Brings Suit," *MPW,* 3 Jul 1920, 93 (against Pacific Electric Co. for $27,000).

Standing, Jack, Jr. (son of **Jack Standing, Sr.**; grandson of **Herbert Standing**; nephew of **Guy** and **Wynndham Standing**; cousin of **Gordon Standing**) [actor] (b. 1914?). AMD, p. 324. "Jack Standing, Jr., Makes Debut," *MPW,* 20 Apr 1918, 407 (4 Years old).

Standing, Jack, Sr. (son of **Herbert Standing**; father of **Jack Standing, Jr.**; brother of Gregory, **Percy** and **Wyndham Standing**; grandson of **Herbert Standing**; cousin of **Gordon Stading**) [stage/film actor] (b. London, England, 10 Feb

1886–25 Oct 1917 [31], Los Angeles CA). (Pathé Frères; Fox.) "Jack Standing Dies," *Variety*, 2 Nov 1917, p. 51. "Jack Standing," *The Billboard*, 3 Nov 1917, p. 66. AMD, p. 324. AS, p. 1027 (d. 26 Oct). BHD, p. 306. IFN, p. 280. Spehr, p. 168. "Jack Standing with Lubin," *MPW*, 15 May 1915, 1087. Billy H. Doyle, "Lost Players," *CI*, 172 (Oct 1989), 36.

Standing, Joan (daughter of **Herbert Standing, Jr.**) [actress] (b. London, England, 21 Jun 1902–3 Feb 1979 [76], Houston TX; cancer). AS, p. 1027 (b. 1903). BHD1, p. 517 (b. 1903). IFN, p. 280.

Standing, Percy D. (son of **Herbert Standing**; brother of **Jack**, Gregory and **Wyndham Standing**) [actor] (b. England, ca. 1882). BHD, p. 306. Ragan 2, p. 1596. "First View of the Creature," *NYDM*, 20 Nov 1915, 36:4 (cited as the brother of Guy Standing, he played Frankinstein [sic] in *Life Without Soul*, Ocean Film Corp., released 21 Nov at the Candler Theater. The Frankenstein legend was adapted to modern Georgia.).

Standing, Wyndham (son of **Herbert Standing**; brother of **Guy** and **Jack Standing, Sr.**; cousin of **Gordon Standing**; uncle of **Jack Standing, Jr.**) [stage/film actor] (*né* Charles Wyndham Standing, b. London, England, 23 Aug 1880–1 Feb 1963 [82], Los Angeles CA). (Began 1915; Universal; Triangle-Ince; FP-L.) AMD, p. 324. AS, p. 1027 (b. 24 Aug). BHD1, p. 517 (b. 1881). Finch, p. 281. IFN, p. 280 (b. 1881). MH, p. 137. MSBB, p. 1028. "Metro SIgns Standing," *MPW*, 28 Aug 1920, 1210. Susan Elizabeth Brady, "Wyndham Standing on the Art of Pantomime," *Classic*, Sep 1922, 61, 92. "Standing with Chadwick," *MPW*, 23 May 1925, 460.

Standish, Joseph W. [actor] (b. 1865?–27 Oct 1943 [78], Cleveland OH). m. Gertrude Bailey. "Joseph W. Standish; Ohio Loew's Theatres Official Former Actor and Manager," *NYT*, 28 Oct 1943, 23:4. "Joseph Standish," *Variety*, 10 Nov 1943. AS, p. 1027. BHD, p. 306. IFN, p. 280.

Stanelli [actor] (*né* Edward de Groot, b. Dublin, Ireland, 1895–12 Feb 1961 [65?], Datchett, England). AS, p. 1027.

Stanford, Arthur [actor] (b. Philadelphia PA, 24 Aug 1878–21 Jul 1917 [38], New Bedford MA). BHD, p. 306.

Stanford, Henry B. [actor] (b. Ramleh, Egypt, 22 Feb 1872–18 Feb 1921 [49], Great Kills, Staten Island NY; heart attack). m. Laura Burt. "Henry Stanford Dead; English Actor of Romantic Roles Dies at His Home in Great Kills," *NYT*, 19 Feb 1921, 11:5 (home estate: Appletree Cottage). "Henry Stanford," *Variety*, 25 Feb 1921. AS, p. 1027 (d. Great Hills NY). BHD, p. 306 (b. 22 Jan). SD, p. 1164.

Stange, Stanislaus [director] (b. 1862–4 Jan 1917 [54?], New York NY). BHD2, p. 251.

Stanlaws, Penrhyn [portrait painter/playwright/director] (*né* Penrhyn Stanley Adamson, b. Dundee, Scotland, 19 Mar 1877–18 May 1957 [80], Los Angeles CA; burned to death). m. Jean Pughsley, 30 Apr 1913. (FP-L, 1921.) "Studio Fire Kills Stanlaws, Artist; Originator of Magazine Girl Killed at 80 on Coast—Active in Recent Years," *NYT*, 20 May 1957, 20:2 ("Firemen said he apparently had fallen asleep while smoking in an upholstered chair."; directed *The Little Minister*). AMD, p. 324. AS, p. 1027 (b. 1923). BHD2, p. 251. *Who Was Who in America*, Vol. 3,1951–60 (Chicago: Marquis, 1960), p. 812:2. "Penryhn Stanlaws Gives Up Painting to Become Future Famous Players Director," *MPW*, 12 Jun 1920, 1485. "Penrhynn Stanlaws to Direct Films," *MPW*, 5 Mar 1921, 41. "Penryhn Lays Aside Brush and Easel," *MPW*, 7 Jan 1922, 61.

Stanley, Edwin [actor] (b. Chicago IL, 22 Nov 1880–25 Dec 1944 [64], Los Angeles CA). m. Maude Moller (d. 1922). "Edwin Stanley," *Variety*, 3 Jan 1945 (d. 24 Dec). AS, p. 1027 (d. 24 Dec). BHD1, p. 517. IFN, p. 280. Truitt, p. 311.

Stanley, Forrest [actor] (b. New York NY, 21 Aug 1889–27 Aug 1969 [80], Los Angeles CA; from injuries after a fall). m. Marion Hutchins. AMD, p. 324. AS, p. 1027. BHD1, p. 517. FFF, p. 234. IFN, p. 280. MH, p. 137. "Forrest Stanley Joins Morosco," *MPW*, 28 Aug 1915, 1487. "Forrest Stanley," *MPW*, 23 Oct 1915, 594. "Forrest Stanley Is Cecil DeMille's New Leading Man; Succeeds Meighan and Dexter," *MPW*, 3 Jul 1920, 53. "Forrest Stanley," *MPW*, 28 Feb 1925, 914. June Lee, "Dan Cupid's Bulletin Board," *Paris and Hollywood Screen Secrets*, Oct 1927, 37 (his wife "ran a half-page ad in one of the Los Angeles papers advertising the sale of her house and furnishings as the means of announcing that her twelve years of married life have drawn to a close. She has gone to Paris for the customary divorce proceedings, and declares that she will make Europe her permanent home. This is Stanley's second divorce.").

Stanley, Fred [scenarist/title writer] (b. Derby, England, 1891?–26 May 1949 [58], Los Angeles CA; heart attack). m. Alice May Burke. (1st National, 1923.) "Fred Stanley, Wrote for Papers, Films, 58," *NYT*, 28 May 1949, 15:6 (began with 1st National in 1923). "Fred Stanley," *Variety*, 1 Jun 1949. AS, p. 1027. FDY, p. 437.

Stanley, Frederic [actor]. No data found. AMD, p. 324. "Kalem Sends Stock Company to Ireland," *MPW*, 3 Jun 1911, 1242.

Stanley, George C. [actor] (b. San Francisco CA, 29 Jan 1875). AMD, p. 324. BHD, p. 306. "George Stanley," *MPW*, 2 May 1914, 654. George Katchmer, "Remembering the Great Silents," *CI*, 233 (Nov 1994), 42–43.

Stanley, Henry [actor] (b. New York NY, 25 Jan 1864). (Star Film; Balboa, 1914–16.) AMD, p. 324. AS, p. 1027 (Harry Stanley). BHD, p. 306. Jura, p. 104. "Henry Stanley," *MPW*, 10 Oct 1914, 205. Billy H. Doyle, "Lost Players," *CI*, 153 (Mar 1988), 53.

Stanley, Imogene [scenarist] (b. Denton TX, 1894–6 Jan 1962 [67], San Antonio TX). AS, p. 1027 (b. 1899). BHD2, p. 251.

Stanley, Martha M. [scenarist] (b. 1867–15 Jan 1950 [82?], Los Angeles CA). BHD2, p. 251.

Stanley, Minnie [actress] (b. 1874–1 Apr 1948 [74?], New York NY). BHD, p. 306.

Stanley, S. Victor [actor] (b. Clun, England, 17 Feb 1892–29 Jan 1939 [46], London, England). AS, p. 1027.

Stanmore, Frank [actor] (*né* Francis Henry Pink, b. London, England, 10 Mar 1877–15 Aug 1943 [66], Gravesend, England). AS, p. 1027 (b. 1878). BHD1, p. 517. IFN, p. 280.

Stannard, Eliot [scenarist]. No data found. FDY, p. 437.

Stanton, Ernie [actor] (b. London, England, 23 Aug 1890–6 Feb 1944 [53], Oakland CA). BHD1, p. 517.

Stanton, Frederick R. [actor] (*né* Frederick R. Schwerd, b. 1881?–27 May 1925 [44], Los Angeles CA; stomach cancer). AS, p. 1027. BHD, p. 307. IFN, p. 280. Truitt, p. 312. George Katchmer, "Remembering the Great Silents," *CI*, 233 (Nov 1994), 43–44.

Stanton, Larry T. [actor] (b. OH, 22 Oct 1893–9 May 1955 [61], Los Angeles CA; heart attack). AS, p. 1028. BHD1, p. 518. IFN, p. 280. Truitt, p. 312.

Stanton, Paul [actor] (b. IL, 21 Dec 1884–9 Oct 1955 [70], Los Angeles Co. CA). AS, p. 1028. BHD1, p. 518. IFN, p. 280.

Stanton, Richard S. [actor/director/producer]. No data found. (Ince; Fox.) AMD, p. 324. "RIchard Stanton Joins Universal," *MPW*, 9 Oct 1915, 254. "Richard Stanton Working on 'Graft,'" *MPW*, 4 Dec 1915, 1812. "Stanton Takes Vacation," *MPW*, 10 Jun 1916, 1986. "Richard Stanton Directs Production of 'Checkers,'" *MPW*, 16 Aug 1919, 994. "Richard Stanton Completes the First Serial for Fox Company," *MPW*, 22 May 1920, 1057. "Stanton Wants Exhibitors to Collaborate with Producers," *MPW*, 29 May 1920, 1223. "Stangton Going to Europe to Make Feature Productions," *MPW*, 26 Jun 1920, 1784. "Stanton Decries Screen Waste," *MPW*, 10 Jul 1920, 198. "Stanton Invents Method to Cut Production Costs in Half," *MPW*, 24 Jul 1920, 430. "Stanton Going to Europe to Study Habits of Its Peoples," *MPW*, 28 Aug 1920, 1198.

Stanton, Sanford [publicist]. No data found. AMD, p. 325. "New Triangle Publicity Man," *MPW*, 3 Jun 1916, 1697.

Stanton, Will [actor] (*né* William Stanley Stanton, b. London, England, 18 Sep 1885–18 Dec 1969 [84], Santa Barbara CA; bronchial pneumonia). AS, p. 1028. BHD1, p. 518 (d. LA CA). IFN, p. 280.

Stanwood, Rita [actress] (*née* Marguerite L. Stanwood, b. Salem MA, 15 Jan 1888–15 Nov 1961 [73], Los Angeles CA). m. **H.B. Warner**, 3 May 1915, Chicago IL (d. 1958). "Rita S. Warner," *Variety*, 22 Nov 1961. AS, p. 1028. BHD, p. 307. IFN, p. 280. WWS, p. 305. "Warner Weds Miss Stanwood," *NYDM*, 12 May 1915, 7:2 (age given as 26).

Stanwyck, Barbara (sister of Byron E. Stevens, 1905–1964) [actress] (*née* Ruby Stevens, b. Brooklyn NY, 16 Jul 1907–20 Jan 1990 [82], Santa Monica CA; pulmonary congestion). m. (1) Frank Fay, 26 Aug 1928, St. Louis MO-9 Nov 1935; (2) Robert Taylor, 13 May 1939-Feb 1952. (Columbia; WB.) (Film debut: *Broadway Nights*, 1927.) Axel Madsen, *Stanwyck* (NY: Harper Collins, 1994). Peter B. Flint, "Barbara Stanwyck, Actress, Dead at 82," *NYT*, 22 Jan 1990, D11:1. "Barbara Stanwyck, 4-Time Oscar Nominee, Is Dead; The 4-Time Oscar Nominee and 3-Time Emmy Winner Was the Consummate Pro," *Variety*, 24 Jan 1990. AS, p. 1028. BHD1, p. 518 (d. LA CA). Aljean Harmetz, "Barbara Stanwyck: 'I'm a Tomorrow Woman,'" *NYT*, 22 Mar 1981, II, 1:5, 12:1. Joan Standish, "Barbara Stanwyck to Give Up Career for Husband? Friends say star prefers to leave screen rather than be parted from Frank Fay," *Movie Classic*, Oct 1931, 39. "Barbara Stanwyck Beaten in Bedroom," *New York Post*, 29 Oct 1981. Katz, pp. 1083–84. Stanwyck's papers are in the American Heritage Center, University of Wyoming, P.O. Box 3924, Laramie WY 82071; general information, 766-2570.

Star, Janusz [director] (b. Klonowic, Poland, 12 Dec 1896). AS, p. 1028.

Starace-Sainati, Bella [actress] (b. Naples, Italy, 2 Jun 1878–4 Aug 1958 [80], Bologna, Italy; in an actors' nursing home). JS, p. 437 (in Italian silents from1911).

Starewicz, Wladyslaw [director] (b. Vilnius, Lithuania, 6 Aug 1892–28 Feb 1965 [73], Fontenay-sous-Bois, France [extrait de décès no. 76/1965). AS, p. 1028 (Ladislas Starewicz, b. Moscow, Russia). BHD2, p. 251.

Stark, Audaine [actress]. No data found. AMD, p. 325. W. Stephen Bush, "The Screen Children's Gallery," *MPW,* 6 Jun 1914, 1413.

Stark, Dick *see* **Stark, Richard S.**

Stark, Kurt [actor/director] (d. 1916). AS, p. 1028. BHD, p. 307; BHD2, p. 251.

Stark, L.R. [scenarist]. No data found. AMD, p. 325. "L.R. Stark Joins Metro Scenario Staff," *MPW,* 13 May 1916, 1139.

Stark, Leighton I. [actor] (d. 20 Jul 1924, Mawasquoia NJ). "Leighton I. Stark," *Variety,* 20 Aug 1924. AS, p.1028. BHD, p. 307. IFN, p. 280.

Stark, Mabel [actress] (b. 1889?–29 Apr 1968 [79?], Thousand Oaks CA; heart attack). AS, p. 1028. BHD1, p. 518. Truitt, p. 312.

Stark, Marie [actress]. No data found. m. **Donald Crisp,** 1917/18, San Juan Capistrano CA (d. 1974). "Donald Crisp Takes a Bride," *MPW,* 19 Jan 1918, 365.

Stark, Richard S[alisbury] [actor] (b. Grand Rapids MI, 1911–12 Dec 1986 [75?], Sotogrande, Spain; heart attack). AS, p. 1028. BHD, p. 307.

Starke, Pauline [actress: Wampas Star, 1922] (b. Joplin MO, 10 Jan 1900–3 Feb 1977 [77], Santa Monica CA). m. **Jack White,** 4 Sep 1927, SF CA (d. 1984); George Sherwood, 1932; (3) John H. Jay. (In *The Birth of a Nation* as a child crying on the widow's knee; MGM.) "Pauline Starke [Sherwood]," *Variety,* 9 Feb 1977 (b. 1901; age 76). AMD, p. 325. AS, p. 1028. BHD1, p. 518. FFF, p. 67. FSS, p. 262. IFN, p. 280. Katz, pp. 1084–85. KOM, p. 159 (b. 1901; d. LA CA). MH, p. 137. "Orientals Visit Pauline Starke," *MPW,* 30 Mar 1918, 1845. "Warners SIgn Pauline Starke," *MPW,* 18 Nov 1922, 240. "Signs Pauline Starke," *MPW,* 4 Oct 1924, 384. "The Truth About Chorus Girls...Their Temptations...and Stage Door Johnnies Is Told by Pauline Starke Who Masqueraded for a Week as 'The Girl on the End, Front Row,'" *MM,* Nov 1925, 29–30, 76–77. Alice Tildesley, "The Girl to Whom Nothing Ever Happened; How Pauline Starke Won Silverscreen Prominence Thru Hard Work," *MPC,* Feb 1926, 30–31, 77. Creighton Peet, "Pauline Starke; The Heroine of 'Love's Blindness' Sends Up a Cheer Because She No Longer Has to Wear Old Clothes," *Cinema Arts,* Nov 1926, 20. "Pauline Starke Joins the Free Lance Ranks," *MPW,* 16 Apr 1927, 632. "Starke—White Wed; Mary Astor Next," *MPW,* 10 Sep 1927, 89. Carol Stafford, "Paragraphs Pertaining to Players and Pictures," *Cinema Arts,* Nov 1927, 41 (re marriage to White). George A. Katchmer, "Forgotten Cowboys and Cowgirls—Part XV," *CI,* 192 (Jun 1991), 42.

Starkey, Bert [stock/carnival/minstrel/vaudeville/film actor] (*né* Buckley Starkey, b. Manchester, England, 10 Jan 1880–10 Jun 1939 [59], Los Angeles CA; heart attack). (Eclair, 1910; World.) AMD, p. 325. AS, p. 1028. BHD1, p. 518. IFN, p. 280. Truitt, p. 312. "Briefs of Biography; From Rags to Riches," *NYDM,* 23 Jun 1915, 24:1. "Buckley Starkey," *MPW,* 7 Apr 1917, 100.

Starling, Lynn [scenarist] (b. Hopkinsville KY, 13 Sep 1888–25 Feb 1955 [66], Los Angeles CA). AS, p. 1028 (d. 17 Mar). BHD2, p. 251.

Starr, Barbara [actress] (*née* Vera Webb, b. 1904?). m. **Gaylord Lloyd,** 17 Sep 1924 (d. 1943). "Gaylor [sic] Lloyd Marries," *Variety,* 24 Sep 1924, p. 21. George A. Katchmer, "Forgotten Cowboys and Cowgirls—Part V," *CI,* 177 (Mar 1990), C6.

Starr, Frederick [actor] (b. San Francisco CA, 1878–20 Aug 1921 [43], Los Angeles CA). AMD, p. 325. AS, p. 1028. BHD, p. 307. IFN, p. 281. Truitt, p. 312. "Frederick Starr," *MPW,* 10 Sep 1921, 169. George Katchmer, "Remembering the Great Silents," *CI,* 233 (Nov 1994), 44 (in films from at least 1914).

Starr, Helen [publicist/scenarist]. No data found. AMD, p. 325. "Helen Starr with Universal," *MPW,* 9 Oct 1915, 255. "Universal Seeking Regular Scripts," *MPW,* 3 Jun 1916, 1704.

Starr, Henry (brother of Belle Starr) [actor/outlaw] (d. 23 Feb 1921, Harrison OK; of gunshot wounds received while robbing a bank four days earlier). "Slain Outlaw Once Tried Picture Game; Henry Starr Attempted to Rival W.S. Hart," *Variety,* 4 Mar 1921. AS, p. 1028. BHD, p. 307 (Harry Starr). Gene Fernett, "The Historic Film Studios; They Went That-a-Way; The Studios at Tulsa," *CI,* 148 (Oct 1987), 16. Ed Wyatt, "Henry Starr: *Outlaw Turned Actor Turned Outlaw,*" *CI,* 260 (Feb 1997), 27 (appeared in *Debtor of the Law,* 1919; servved four years in prison to 1919; d. 22 Feb).

Starr, James A. [actor/title writer/scenarist] (b. Clarksville TX, 2 Feb 1902–13 Aug 1990 [88], Phoenix AZ). m. (1 son). *365 Nights in Hollywood,* 1926. "Jimmy Starr," *Variety,* 22 Aug 1990, p. 89:4 ("Early in his career he wrote the titles for silents 'Smith's Candy Shop' and 'Lumber a La Carte,' Mack Sennett comedies starring Raymond McKee.'). AS, p. 1028 (b. 1904). BHD2, p. 251. FDY, pp. 437, 447.

Starr, Sally [stage/film actress] (b. Pittsburgh PA, 23 Jan 1910). "Grandmother of Sally Starr," *Variety,* 8 Jan 1936 ("Burial from family home in Pittsburgh."). AS, p. 1029.

Starrett, Charles [stage/film actor] (b. Athol MA, 28 Mar 1903–22 Mar 1986 [82], Borrego Springs CA; cancer). m. Mary. (Columbia.) (Film debut: *The Quarterback,* 1926; extra.) "Charles Starrett Dies at 82; Actor on Stage and Screen [The Durango Kid]," *NYT,* 26 Mar 1986, B4:5. "Charles Starrett," *Variety,* 2 Apr 1986 (age 82). AS, p. 1029. BHD1, p. 518. Katz, p. 1085. Ralph Roberts, "Charles Starrett (1903–1986); 'The Durango Kid,'" *CI,* 131 (May 1986), 51, 55. John Cocchi, "The 2nd Feature; A History of the B Movies," *CI,* 146 (Aug 1987), C19, 34. Mike Newton, "Charles Starrett: Columbia's Action Ace," *CI,* 245 (Nov 1995), 24, 26.

Statter, Arthur F. [scenarist]. No data found. AMD, p. 325. FDY, p. 437. "Statter to Take Charge," *MPW,* 4 Feb 1922, 488.

Staudte, Fritz [actor/scenarist] (b. Sipirol, India, 19 Apr 1883–1958 [75?], Holland). AS, p. 1029.

Steadman, Lincoln *see* **Stedman, Lincoln**

Steadman, Monte [cinematographer]. No data found. FDY, p. 469.

Steadman, Vera [actress] (b. Monterey CA, 23 Jun 1900–14 Dec 1966 [66], Long Beach CA). m. Jackie Taylor. AMD, p. 325. AS, p. 1029. BHD1, p. 518 (b. 21 Jun). IFN, p. 281 (b. 21 Jun). MH, p. 137. Truitt, p. 312. "Vera Steadman Joins Universal," *MPW,* 5 Apr 1919, 85. "Twin Girls," *MPW,* 29 Oct 1921, 1026 (Frances and Marie). "Stork Favors Stars," *MPW,* 3 Dec 1921, 566. "Twin Baby Dies," *MPW,* 10 Dec 1921, 685 (Frances d. at six weeks). "Vera Steps Up," *MPW,* 14 Feb 1925, 722.

Stearns, Myron Morris [scenarist/producer] (b. Hartford CT, 19 May 1884–19 Apr 1963 [78], Palm Beach FL; cancer). "Myron Morris Stearns," *Variety,* 15 May 1963. AS, p. 1029. BHD2, p. 251.

Stechan, Hans O. [scenarist] (b. Indianapolis IN, 4 Apr 1879–8 Oct 1944 [65], Altadena CA). BHD2, p. 251.

Steck, Harry Tipton [actor/title writer/scenarist] (b. Chicago IL, 1889?–3 Jun 1953 [64], Bel Air CA). (Essanay, Chicago IL, 1918; Ince; Universal; WB.) "Harry Tipton Steck," *Variety,* 10 Jun 1953. AMD, p. 325. AS, p. 1029. BHD2, p. 251. FDY, pp. 437, 447. H. Tipton Steck, "Doing My Bit," *MPW,* 21 Jul 1917, 408–09. "Steck to Write for Louise Glaum," *MPW,* 2 Oct 1920, 663.

Stecker, A[lgernon] **S.** [actor] (b. 1892–23 Jun 1924 [32?], Los Angeles CA). BHD, p. 307.

Stedler, Allen [cinematographer]. No data found. FDY, p. 469.

Stedman, Charles Frohman [actor]. No data found. "Stedman Not Nephew of Charles Frohman," *MPW,* 3 Aug 1918, 669.

Stedman, Lincoln (son of **Marshall** and **Myrtle Stedman**) [actor/producer] (b. Denver CO, 18 May 1906–22 Mar 1948 [41], Los Angeles CA). m. Carol. "Lincoln Stedman," *NYT,* 23 Mar 1948, 25:5 ("child actor in silent motion pictures"). "Lincoln Stedman," *Variety,* 24 Mar 1968. AS, p. 1029 (b. 1907). BHD1, p. 518. IFN, p. 281. Truitt, p. 312.

Stedman, Marshall (father of **Lincoln Stedman**) [actor/director] (b. Bethel ME, 1874–16 Dec 1943 [69], Laguna Beach CA). m. **Myrtle Stedman,** 1900, Chicago IL (d. 1938). "Marshall Stedman," *Variety,* 22 Dec 1943. AMD, p. 325. AS, p. 1029. BHD, p. 307; BHD2, p. 251. IFN, p. 281. Truitt, p. 312. "Marshall Stedman Visits Denver," *MPW,* 18 Nov 1916, 1032. "Stedman Applies for Divorce," *MPW,* 19 Apr 1919, 360 (from Myrtle). Billy H. Doyle, "Lost Players," *CI,* 154 (Apr 1988), 53.

Stedman, Myrtle (mother of **Lincoln Stedman**) [stage/film actress] (*née* Myrtle Lincoln, b. Chicago IL, 3 Mar 1885–8 Jan 1938 [52], Los Angeles CA; heart attack). m. **Marshall Stedman,** 1900, Chicago IL (d. 1943). (Selig.) "Myrtle Stedman, 50, Film Actress, Dead; Had Played Character Parts in Pictures Since 1913—Was in Light Opera Earlier," *NYT,* 9 Jan 1938, 42:4. "Myrtle Stedman," *Variety,* 12 Jan 1938 (age 50). AMD, p. 325. AS, p. 1029. BHD1, p. 518. BR, pp. 74–78. FFF, p. 252 (b. 1888). FSS, p. 262. IFN, p. 281. MH, p. 137. Truitt, p. 312 (b. 1889). "Convicts Make Present for Miss Stedman," *MPW,* 21 Sep 1912, 1187. "Myrtle Stedman at Liberty," *MPW,* 1 Nov 1913, 500. "Myrtle Stedman," *MPW,* 10 Oct 1914, 201. "Myrtle Stedman Gets Valuable RIng," *MPW,* 22 May 1915, 1276. "Myrtle Stedman Appears in Person," *MPW,* 24 Jul 1915, 671. "Stars Added to Horsley's Array," *MPW,* 25 Sep 1915, 2187. "Myrtle Stedman Still with Morosco," *MPW,*

16 Oct 1915, 429. "Myrtle Stedman Making Hit on Tour," *MPW*, 20 Oct 1917, 377. "[Marshall] Stedman Applies for Divorce," *MPW*, 19 Apr 1919, 360. "Read Engages Myrtle Stedman," *MPW*, 15 Nov 1919, 337. "Laugh Your Way to Beauty; Plenty of Exercise and Eight Hours Sleep Will Help, Too, Says Myrtle Stedman," *MPC*, Jun 1925, 68, 86. Buck Rainey, "Myrtle Stedman; Always Beautiful and Appealing, She Made the West More Alluring," *CI*, 109 (Jul 1984), 14–15, C16; 110 (Aug 1984), 41–42. Billy H. Doyle, "Lost Players," *CI*, 154 (Apr 1988), 53–54.

Steele, Agnes [actress] (b. 1882–3 Mar 1949 [67], Los Angeles Co. CA). BHD1, p. 519. IFN, p. 281.

Steele, Bill [actor/stuntman] (*né* William A. Gettinger, b. San Antonio TX, 28 Mar 1889–13 Feb 1966 [76], Los Angeles CA). m. **Josie Sedgwick**, 12 Oct 1919 (d. 1973). (Universal.) "Bill Steele," *Variety*, 2 Mar 1966. AS, p. 1029. AMD, p. 134. BHD1, p. 519 (William Steele). IFN, p. 281. Truitt, p. 312. "Gettinger Goes to Camp Lewis," *MPW*, 22 Dec 1917, 1787. "Josie Sedgwick Weds Argonne Hero," *MPW*, 8 Nov 1919, 255.

Steele, Bob (son of **Robert E. Bradbury** and twin of William) [actor] (*né* Robert Adrian Bradbury, Jr., b. Pendleton OR, 23 Jan 1906–21 Dec 1988 [82], Burbank CA; heart attack). (FBO; Monogram; PRC; WB.) "Bob Steele, 82, Actor in 'F-Troop' and Films," *NYT*, 23 Dec 1988, A28:6 (d. 22 Dec 1988). "Bob Steele," *Variety*, 28 Dec 1988. AMD, p. 325. AS, p. 1029. BHD1, p. 519 (b. Portland OR, 1907). Burt A. Folkart, "Bob Steele; Prolific Star of Dozens of Western Films," *LA Times*, 23 Dec 1988, I, 26:1. FSS, p. 262. Katz, p. 1086. "Bob Steele," *MPW*, 10 Dec 1927, 48. John Cocchi, "The 2nd Feature; A History of the B Movies; The Western," *CI*, 145 (Jul 1987), 17–21, 52; "Bob Steele," 19–20 (b. 1907). Nick C. Nicholls, "Bob Steele," *CI*, 154 (Apr 1988), 56 (b. 1906). F.M. Dolven, "A Tribute to Bob Steele," *CI*, 164 (Feb 1989), 28, C6 (b. 1907). Grady Franklin, "The Western Film," *CI*, 200 (Feb 1992), 48 (*né* Robert Adrian Bradbury, b. 1907). Bobby J. Copeland, "Remembering 'Battling' Bob Steele," *CI*, 248 (Feb 1996), C6.

Steele, Clifford [actor] (b. 1878?–5 Mar 1940 [62], Los Angeles CA). "Clifford Steele," *Variety*, 13 Mar 1940 ("For 25 years he had played minor roles in pictures"). AS, p. 1029. BHD1, p. 519. IFN, p. 281. Truitt, p. 312.

Steele, John [title writer]. No data found. FDY, p. 447.

Steele, Minnie [actress] (*née* Minnie Steele Brinkman, b. Australia, 1881?–5 Jan 1949 [68], Los Angeles CA; stroke). (Christie.) "Minnie Steele," *Variety*, 12 Jan 1949. AS, p. 1029. BHD, p. 307. IFN, p. 281. Truitt, p. 312.

Steele, Rufus [producer] (b. 1877–24 Dec 1935 [58?], Boston MA). BHD2, p. 251.

Steele, Vernon [actor] (*né* Vernon Antonietti, b. Santiago, Chile, 18 Sep 1882–23 Jul 1955 [72], Los Angeles CA; heart attack). (World; Goldwyn.) "Vernon Steele," *NYT*, 25 Jul 1955, 19:6 (b. England). "Vernon Steele," *Variety*, 27 Jul 1955. AMD, p. 325. AS, p. 1029. BHD1, p. 519. IFN, p. 281. Spehr, p. 168 (b. 1883). Truitt, p. 312. "Eva Novak and Vernon Steele Signed for C.B.C.'s 'Temptation,'" *MPW*, 24 Feb 1923, 797.

Steele, William *see* **Steele, Bill**

Steelman, Henry Paul (Hank) [actor] (b. 1902–30 Jan 1939 [36?], Atascadero CA). BHD, p. 307.

Steelman, Hosea E. [actor] (b. Cincinnati OH, 31 Mar 1876–4 Jul 1953 [77], Los Angeles Co. CA). AS, p. 1030. BHD, p. 307. IFN, p. 281.

Steene, E. Burton [cinematographer] (b. 1885–21 Apr 1929 [44?], Los Angeles CA). BHD2, p. 251.

Steers, Larry [actor] (*né* Lawrence Steers, b. Chicago IL, 14 Feb 1881?–15 Feb 1951 [70?], Woodland Hills CA). "Larry Steers," *Variety*, 21 Feb 1951 (age 60; began 1917). AS, p. 1030 (b. 1888). BHD1, p. 518 (b. IN, 1888). IFN, p. 281 (b. IN, 1888). Truitt, p. 312. George Katchmer, "Remembering the Great Silents," *CI*, 264 (Aug 1996), 48–49 (b. IN, 1888).

Steger, Julius [actor/director/executive, head of Fox in NY, 1920–23] (b. Vienna, Austria, 4 Mar 1870–25 Feb 1959 [88], Vienna, Austria). "Julius Steger," *NYT*, 3 Mar 1959, 33:5. "Julius Steger," *Variety*, 4 Mar 1959. AMD, p. 325. AS, p. 1030. BHD, p. 307; BHD2, p. 252. "Steger on Screen; Will Be Presented by World Film in 'The Fifth Commandment,'" *NYDM*, 17 Mar 1915, 24:3. "Julius Steger," *MPW*, 17 Apr 1915, 378. "Julius Steger [photo]," *NYDM*, 21 Apr 1915, 22:4. "Julius Steger Joins Metro," *MPW*, 27 Nov 1915, 167749. "Steger to Direct Norma Talmage," *MPW*, 27 Jan 1917, 510. "Steger Resigns," *MPW*, 27 Oct 1917, 546. "Steger May Succeed Brady," *MPW*, 16 Feb 1918, 953. "Julius Steger Joins International," *MPW*, 30 Mar 1918, 1829.

Steib, Art [cinematographer/photographer] (b. 1894–7 Aug 1945 [51?], Los Angeles CA). BHD2, p. 252.

Steichen, Edward [photographer/director] (b. 1878–27 Mar 1973 [94?], West Redding CT). BHD2, p. 252.

Steidl, Robert [actor] (b. Germany, 1861–24 Apr 1927 [65?]). BHD, p. 307.

Stehli, Edgar [actor] (b. Lyon, France, 12 Jul 1884–25 Jul 1973 [89], Upper Montclair NJ). AS, p. 1030.

Stein, Abe M. [stage/film actor] (aka Sol Aiken, b. 1853?–27 Mar 1920 [67], New York NY). "Abe M. Stein," *Variety*, 26 Mar 1920.

Stein, Al [assistant director] (d. 9 Oct 1921, Los Angeles CA). BHD2, p. 252.

Stein, Geoffrey C. [stock/stage/actor] (b. Washington DC, 1869–28 May 1930 [61?], Brunswick Home, Amityville NY). "Geoffrey C. Stein," *Variety*, 4 Jun 1930, 77:4 (age 60). BHD, p. 307.

Stein, Lotte [actress] (b. Berlin, Germany, 12 Jan 1894–20 Sep 1982 [88], Munich, Germany) BHD1, p. 519.

Stein, Paul L[udwig] [director] (b. Vienna, Austria, 1 Feb 1892–1959 [67?], London, England). m. Ollie Kuntze, 26 Oct 1926, Hollywood CA. AMD, p. 325. AS, p. 1030 (d. 1951). BHD2, p. 252 (d. 1951). "Director Stein Weds," *MPW*, 13 Nov 1926, 4.

Steinbicker, Reinhart [director] (b. 1905–Aug 1935 [30?], Berlin, Germany). BHD2, p. 252.

Steiner, Elio (son of Countess Elena Lupati) [actor] (b. Strà, Venice, Italy, 9 Mar 1904–6 Dec 1965 [61], Rome, Italy). AS, p. 1030 (b. Stroa, Italy). BHD1, p. 519 (b. 1905). JS, p. 438 (in Italian silents from 1927).

Steiner, Sigfrit [actor] (*né* Siegfried Albert Steiner, b. Bale, Germany, 31 Oct 1906–21 Mar 1988 [81], Munich, Germany). AS, p. 1030 (b. Bale, Switzerland). BHD1, p. 519 (b. Basel, Switzerland).

Steiner, William [producer]. No data found. AMD, p. 326. "William 'Bill' Steiner in Bermuda," *MPW*, 11 Mar 1911, 518. "Steiner to Take a Vacation," *MPW*, 26 Aug 1916, 1411. "William Steiner at Saratoga," *MPW*, 9 Sep 1916, 1665. "'Stars Supporting Star' Idea Proves a Winner, Says Steiner," *MPW*, 14 Feb 1925, 707.

Steinhoff, Hans [director/scenarist] (b. Pfaffenhofen, Germany, 10 Mar 1882–20 Apr 1945 [63], Luckenwalde, Germany; plane accident). AS, p. 1030 (b. Marienburg, Germany). BHD2, p. 252.

Steinke, Hans [actor] (b. Germany, 1892–26 Jun 1971 [79?], Chicago IL; stomach cancer). AS, p. 1030.

Steinruck, Albert [actor] (*né* Albert Steinrueck, b. Wettenburg, Walkdeck, Germany, 20 May 1872–2 Feb 1929 [56], Berlin, Germany). AS, p. 1031. BHD, p. 308 (Steinrueck). IFN, p. 281.

Stelli, Jean [director/scenarist] (b. Lille, France, 6 Dec 1894-ca. 1961 [66?]). AS, p. 1031.

Stembridge, J[ames] **S**[idney] [actor] (b. Milledgeville GA, 9 Feb 1869–31 Oct 1942 [73], Los Angeles Co. CA). AS, p. 1031. BHD, p. 308.

Sten, Anna [actress] (*née* Annel "Anyuschka" Stenskaya Sudakevich, b. Kiev, Ukraine, Russia, 1 Dec 1908–12 Nov 1993 [84], New York NY; cardiac arrest). m. (1) **Fedor Ozep**—div. (d. 1949); (2) director/producer Eugene Frenke [b. 1907]. Eric Pace, "Anna Sten Is Dead; Film Actress Touted as Another Garbo," *NYT*, 15 Nov 1993, D14:1. "Anna Sten," *Variety*, 29 Nov 1993, p. 69:3. AS, p. 1031. BHD1, p. 520 (b. 3 Dec). Ragan 2, p. 1606 (b. 3 Dec 1908). Waldman, p. 275.

Stengler, Mack [composer/film and TV cinematographer] (b. 1895?–27 May 1962 [67], Los Angeles CA; heart attack). "Mack Stengler," *Variety*, 6 Jun 1962. AS, p. 1031. BHD2, p. 252. FDY, p. 469.

Stepanek, Karel [actor] (b. Brno, Czechoslovakia, 29 Oct 1889–25 Dec 1980 [91], Los Angeles CA). AS, p. 1031 (b. Brno, Moravia). BHD1, p. 520. JS, p. 439 (in Germany from 1923 to 1939).

Stepanek, Zdenik [actor] (b. Benesov, Czechoslovakia, 22 Sep 1896–20 Jun 1968 [73], Prague, Czechoslovakia). AS, p. 1031.

Stephen, Isabel [publicist]. No data found. AMD, p. 326. "Isabel Stephen Joins Arrow Publicity Force," *MPW*, 7 Feb 1920, 933.

Stephen, Pierre [actor] (*né* Piette Trambouze, b. Paris, France, 28 Apr 1890–3 Jun 1980 [90], Paris, France [extrait de décès no. 1092]). AS, p. 1031.

Stephens, Jud [actor] (b. 1888?–18 Apr 1935 [47], New York NY). "Jud Stephens," *Variety*, 24 Apr 1935 ("former western film actor and studio construction boss"). AS, p. 1031. IFN, p. 281.

Stephenson, Henry [stage/film actor] (*né* Henry Stephenson Garroway, b. Grenada, British West Indies, 16 Apr 1871–24 Apr 1956 [85], San Francisco CA). m. (2) Dorothy (actress Ann Dorothea Shoemaker) [d. 1978]). (NY debut: *The Man from Blankley's*, Garrick Theatre, 7 Oct 1901.) "Stephenson Dead; Stage, Film Actor; Performer Noted for Roles as Suave Farceur Was 85—Made Debut Here in '01," *NYT*, 25 Apr 1956, 35:3. "Henry Stephenson," *Variety*, 2 May 1956. AS, p.

1032. BHD1, p. 520. IFN, p. 281. Katz, p. 1088. Truitt, p. 313.

Stephenson, James [actor] (b. Yorkshire, England, 14 Apr 1899–29 Jul 1941 [42], Pacific Palisades CA; heart attack). AS, p. 1032.

Steppling, John C. [stage/film actor] (b. Essen, Germany, 8 Aug 1870–5 Apr 1932 [62], Los Angeles CA). (Edison, FP-L.) "John C. Steppling," *Variety*, 12 Apr 1932. AMD, p. 326. AS, p. 1032. BHD1, p. 520 (d. 6 Apr). IFN, p. 282 (b. 1870). Truitt, p. 313. "Steppling Still with Essanay," *MPW*, 21 Sep 1912, 1183. "John Steppling to Support Mrs. Fiske," *MPW*, 21 Jun 1913, 1233. *MPW*, 6 Sep 1913, 1071 (to leave pictures for stock work in San Francisco). George Blaisdell, "At the Sign of the Flaming Arcs," *MPW*, 20 Dec 1913, 1420. "John Steppling Again a Universalite," *MPW*, 12 Aug 1916, 1090.

Sterler, Fritz [actor] (b. 12 Apr 1886–24 Apr 1920 [34]). BHD, p. 308.

Sterling, Edythe [actress] (*née* Edith May Kessinger, b. Leavenworth KS, 29 Oct 1892–5 Jun 1962 [69], Los Angeles CA). m. **Art Acord**, Jul 1913–19 (d. 1931); Clifford Younger. (St. Louis Motion Picture Co.) "Edythe Sterling," *Variety*, 13 Jun 1962. AMD, p. 326. AS, p. 1032 (b. Kansas City KS, 1886; d. 4 Jun). BHD, p. 308. BR, pp. 78–79. IFN, p. 282. Truitt, p. 313. "Edith Sterling," *MPW*, 20 Feb 1915, 1122. "Edythe Sterling," *MPW*, 2 Oct 1915, 66. "Edythe Sterling and Murdock MacQuarrie Join Signal Forces," *MPW*, 22 Jan 1916, 603. George A. Katchmer, "Remembering the Great Silents," *CI*, 178 (Apr 1990), 42 (married to Acord from July, 1913–1916); 203 (May 1992), 43 (b. 10 Oct 1884). Grange McKinney, San Clemente CA, writes that her birth was recorded in the City Clerk's Office, Leavenworth KS, on 14 Nov 1892, and that the date of birth and names of her parents agree with those given on her death certificate.

Sterling, Ford [actor] (*né* George Ford Stich, b. La Crosse WI, 3 Nov 1880–13 Oct 1939 [58], Los Angeles CA; heart attack). m. **Teddy Sampson** (d. 1970). (Biograph; Keystone.) "Ford Sterling, 55, Movie Comic, Dies; 'Chief of Keystone Police,' Contemporary of Chaplin and Gloria Swanson; In Mabel Normand Films; Survivor of Custard Pie Days Lost Left Leg Last Year Through an Operation," *NYT*, 14 Oct 1939, 19:1. "Ford Sterling," *Variety*, 18 Oct 1939. AMD, p. 326. AS, p. 1032 (b. 1883). BHD1, p. 520. FSS, p. 263. IFN, p. 282 (*né* Stich, b. 1884). Katz, p. 1089. MH, p. 137. Spehr, p. 168 (b. 1883). Truitt, p. 313 (b. 1880). WWS, p. 194. "Ford Sterling Using Vaudeville Stunts," *MPW*, 26 Apr 1913, 361. "Ford Sterling a Universal Star," *MPW*, 14 Mar 1914, 1391. "'Sterling' Adopted as Universal Brand," *MPW*, 11 Apr 1914, 223. "Ford Sterling; Leading Comedian with the Universal," *MPS*, 17 Apr 1914, 25 (b. 1880). "Impersonated Ford Sterling—'Pinched,'" *MPW*, 17 Jun 1916, 2015. "Ford Sterling s Latest Comedy Star to Be Acquired by Special Pictures," *MPW*, 4 Sep 1920, 64. "On the Set and Off," *MW*, IV, 13 Sep 1924, 30 (Sterling's mother suffered an attack of apoplexy in a court room listening to her son's divorce story and died a few hours later in a Los Angeles hospital). Sara Redway, "Passing of the Brown Derby; The Last of the Old Slapstick Gang Goes in for the Fairly Polite Drama," *MPC*, Jan 1926, 30–31, 72. "Ford Sterling Signs to Stay with Famous," *MPW*, 1 Jan 1927, 35. "Sterling Burned," *MPW*, 12 Nov 1927, 16. "Ford Sterling Resumes Work," *MPW*, 17 Dec 1927, 31.

Sterling, Gene [actor] (b. TX, 1920). (Republic.) Nick Nicholls, "Gene Sterling," *CI*, 129 (Mar 1986), 25 (began 1926).

Sterling, Jane [actress] (b. New York NY, 1866–30 Dec 1956 [90?], Middlebury VT). BHD, p. 308.

Sterling, Merta [actress] (b. 1883?–14 Mar 1944 [61], Los Angeles CA). (Fox.) "Merta Sterling," *Variety*, 22 Mar 1944 ("retired actress of silent films"). AS, p. 1032. BHD, p. 308. IFN, p. 282. Truitt, p. 314.

Sterling, Richard [stage/film actor] (*né* Albert G. Leggett, b. New York NY, 30 Aug 1880–15 Apr 1959 [78], Douglaston, Queens NY [Death Certificate Index No. 4644; age 86 (Richard Sterling); he is also listed under "Albert Leggett" with the same data]; heart attack). (Eclair.) (Stage debut: 27 Sep 1897, Boston MA.) "Richard Sterling, Actor, Dead; Created 'Life with Father' Role," *NYT*, 16 Apr 1959, 33:2. "Richard Sterling," *Variety*, 22 Apr 1959. AMD, p. 326. AS, p. 1032. BHD, p. 308; BHD2, p. 252. IFN, p. 282. "Richard Sterling to Direct Atlas," *MPW*, 15 Dec 1917, 1636.

Stern, D. [title writer]. No data found. FDY, p. 447.

Stern G.B. [scenarist] (b. London, England, 17 Jun 1890–1973 [83?]). BHD2, p. 252.

Stern, Julius [general manager]. No data found. AMD, p. 326. "Stern Back from California," *MPW*, 13 Apr 1912, 141. "Universal European Company Home," *MPW*, 15 Nov 1913, 720. "Stern Supervises Victor Work," *MPW*, 12 Sep 1914, 1488.

Stern, Louis [vaudeville/film actor] (b. New York NY, 10 Jan 1860–15 Feb 1941 [81], Los Angeles CA). m. Peggy Ward. (Ft. Lee NJ; Hollywood, 1926.) "Louis Stern; Character Actor on the Screen Once Was in Vaudeville," *NYT*, 17 Feb 1941, 15:4. "Louis Stern," *Variety*, 19 Feb 1941 ("pioneer character actor"). AS, p. 1032. BHD, p. 308. IFN, p. 282. Truitt, p. 314.

Stern, René [actor] (b. Bordeaux, France, 6 Feb 1890–27 Nov 1952 [62], Paris, France). AS, p. 1032.

Stern, Samuel [executive] (b. 1875–4 Sep 1963 [88?], Philadelphia PA). BHD2, p. 252.

Sterne, Elaine [scenarist]. No data found. (Vitagraph; Universal.) AMD, p. 326. "Elaine Sterne, Sun-Vitagraph Winner," *MPW*, 27 Jun 1914, 1840. "Elaine Sterne Series; Photo-playwright Signed to Wrtie One Feature a Month for Mary Fuller," *NYDM*, 6 Jan 1915, 28:1. "Universal Engages Elaine Sterne," *MPW*, 16 Jan 1915, 389. "Remarkable Record of Young Author," *MPW*, 28 Aug 1915, 1487. "Elaine Stern Still Winning," *MPW*, 18 Dec 1915, 2156. "Miss Sterne Writes 'Sonny Jim' Book," *MPW*, 9 Sep 1916, 1711 (Boston: W.A. Wilde & Co., 1 Sep 1916, 314 pp.). "Elaine Sterne a Real Story Teller," *MPW*, 23 Sep 1916, 1956. "Elaine Sterne Writes a Novel," *MPW*, 28 Apr 1917, 600 (*The Road to Ambition*, Britton Publishing Co.). "Elaine Sterne Is Author of Many Scripts and Books," *MPW*, 7 Sep 1918, 1390.

Sterni, Giuseppe [director/actor] (b. Bologna, Italy, 27 Dec 1883-Jul 1952 [68], Rome, Italy). JS, p. 439 (in Italian silents from 1916).

Sternroyd, Vincent [stage/film actor] (b. Highgate, London, England, 8 Oct 1857–3 Nov 1948 [91], London, England). m. Beatrice Coleman. (Stage debut: 1879; NY debut: 10 Nov 1885.) "V. Sternroyd, 91, British Actor, Dies; Stage Veteran of Half Century Played with Sir Henry Irving and Many Other Notables," *NYT*, 4 Nov 1948, 30:2 (film debut: *The Marriage of Corbal*, 1935). AS, p. 1033. BHD1, p. 520. IFN, p. 282.

Sterrett, Lee [director] (b. Erie PA-d. 3 Jan 1927, Erie PA). BHD2, p. 252.

Steven, Boyd [actress/singer] (b. Scotland, 1875–15 Dec 1967 [92?], Glasgow, Scotland). AS, p. 1033.

Stevens, Charles (grandson of Apache warrior Geronimo) [actor] (b. Solomonsville AZ, 26 May 1893–22 Aug 1964 [71], Los Angeles CA). (Griffith.) "Charles Stevens," *Variety*, 16 Sep 1964. AS, p. 1033. BHD1, p. 521. FSS, p. 263. IFN, p. 282. Truitt, p. 314.

Stevens, Charlotte [actress] (b. Chicago IL). (Selig; Christie.) AMD, p. 326. "Completes Arrangements to Engage Miss Stevens," *MPW*, LI, 6 Aug 1921, 593 (beauty contest winner; won part in Christie comedy). "Beauty Contest Winner in F.B.O. Film," *MPW*, 30 Jul 1927, 330. George A. Katchmer, "Forgotten Cowboys and Cowgirls—Part VIII," *CI*, 180 (Jun 1990), 61.

Stevens, Edwin [stage/film actor/director] (b. San Francisco CA, 16 Aug 1860–1 Jan 1923 [62], Los Angeles CA; pleurisy). (Universal; 1st National.) "Edwin Stevens Dead," *Variety*, 5 Jan 1923. AMD, p. 326. AS, p. 1033 (b. LA CA; d. 3 Jan). BHD, p. 308. IFN, p. 282. "Edwin Stevens Joins Universal," *MPW*, 31 Jul 1915, 804. "In the Picture Studios," *NYDM*, 8 Sep 1915, 36:4. "How Would You Like to Be Known as 'The Devil,'" *MPW*, 9 Sep 1916, 1708. "Stevens Director for Bluebird," *MPW*, 27 Jan 1917, 501. "Edwin Stevens with Goldwyn," *MPW*, 22 Mar 1919, 1637.

Stevens, Emily (daughter of **Robert E. Stevens**; sister of **Robert B. Stevens**; niece of **Minnie Maddern Fiske**) [stage/film actress] (b. New York NY, 27 Feb 1882–2 Jan 1928 [45], New York NY; accidental? suicide with sedatives). (Stage debut: 8 Oct 1900, Bridgeport CT.) "Emily Stevens Dies; Was Found in Coma; Medical Examiner Lays Death to Overdose of Drug, but Her Doctor Blames Pneumonia; Autopsy to Be Held Today; Actress, 45, Who Was a Cousin of Mrs. Fiske, Had Been Under Neurologist for Year," *NYT*, 3 Jan 1928, 10:2 (her mother, Emma Madden, was sister to Mrs. Fiske's mother). "Emily Stevens," *Variety*, 11 Jan 1928. AMD, p. 326. AS, p. 1033. BHD, p. 308. IFN, p. 282. MSBB, p. 1042. Truitt, p. 314. "Emily Stevens," *MPW*, 3 Apr 1915, 50. "Ralph Herz with Metro," *MPW*, 3 Jul 1915, 69. "Emily Stevens Improving After Operation," *MPW*, 15 Jul 1916, 465. "Emily Stevens Recovering," *MPW*, 5 Aug 1916, 929. "Emily Stevens," *MPW*, 31 Mar 1917, 2081. "Emily Stevens Postpones Stage Engagement," *MPW*, 25 Aug 1917, 1203. "Emily Stevens Starred in First Schomer-Ross Production Entitled 'The Sacred Flame,'" *MPW*, 13 Sep 1919, 1679. "Emily Stevens and Muriel Ostriche to Be Seen in SChomer's Latest Film, 'The Sacred Flame,'" *MPW*, 27 Sep 1919, 1983. "Emily Stevens in Hospital," *MPW*, 30 Oct 1920, 1285 (nervous breakdown due to dieting). "Emily Stevens Leaves Hospital," *MPW*, 20 Nov 1920, 327 (31 Oct 1920, St. Agnes Hospital, Baltimore MD).

Stevens, Evelyn [actress] (b. Brooklyn NY, 1891?–28 Aug 1938 [47], New York NY). AS, p. 1033. BHD, p. 308. IFN, p. 282. Truitt, p. 314.

Stevens, Fred [cinematographer]. No data found. FDY, p. 469.

Stevens, George, Sr. (father of George

Stevens, Jr.) [cinematographer/director/producer/scenarist] (b. Oakland CA, 18 Dec 1904–8 Mar 1975 [70], Lancaster CA; heart attack). m. (1) Yvonne Stevens, 1 Jan 1930—div. 1947 (son George, Jr., b. 3 Apr 1932); (2) Joan. Donald Richie, *George Stevens; An American Romantic* (NY: Garland Publishing, Inc., 1985). (Roach; RKO; Universal; Oscars in 1951 and 1956.) "George Stevens, Film Director, Dies"; A.H. Wheeler, "Solid and Business-Like," 32:3, *NYT,* 10 Mar 1975, 32:3. Myrna Oliver, "Oscar-Winning Director George Stevens, 70, Dies; His Films Included 'Shane,' 'Giant,' and 'A Place in the Sun,'" *Los Angeles Times,* 10 Mar 1975. "George Stevens, 70, Dies on the Coast," *Variety,* 12 Mar 1975. AS, p. 1033. BHD1, p. 521; BHD2, p. 252. FDY, p. 469. IFN, p. 282. Katz, pp. 1091–92 (began 1921).

Stevens, George S. [actor] (*né* George S. Chapple, b. London, England, 1860?–20 Aug 1940 [80], Brooklyn NY). m. Katherine L. "George S. Stevens," *NYT,* 22 Aug 1940, 20:3. "George S. Stevens," *Variety,* 28 Aug 1940. AMD, p. 326. AS, p. 1033. BHD, p. 308. "George S. Stevens," *MPW,* 31 Jan 1920, 760.

Stevens, Gosta [director/scenarist] (b. Stockholm, Sweden, 1 Feb 1897–1964 [67?], Sweden). AS, p. 1033. BHD2, p. 252.

Stevens, Jack [cinematographer]. No data found. FDY, p. 469.

Stevens, Jessie [actress] (d. Jun 1922, Palmyra NY). (Edison.) AMD, p. 326. BHD, p. 308. "Jessie Stevens," *MPW,* 10 Apr 1915, 222.

Stevens, Josephine [actress]. No data found. m. **Edward Ellis**, 5 Apr 1917 (d. 1952). AMD, p. 327. "Josephine Stevens," *MPW,* 21 Apr 1917, 433. "Edward Ellis and Josephine Stevens," *MPW,* 28 Apr 1917, 600.

Stevens, K.T *see* **Wood, Baby Gloria**

Stevens, Landers [actor] (father of George and Jack Stevens) (*né* John Landers Stevens, b. San Francisco CA, 17 Feb 1877–19 Dec 1940 [63], Los Angeles CA; heart attack during an appendectomy). m. Georgie Cooper (widow). "Landers Stevens," *NYT,* 21 Dec 1940, 17:4. "Landers Stevens," *Variety,* 25 Dec 1940. AS, p. 1033. BHD1, p. 521. IFN, p. 282. Truitt, p. 314.

Stevens, Louis [title writer/scenarist] (b. 1900?–29 Sep 1963 [63], Los Angeles CA). (Ince; Paramount; Universal; RKO.) "Louis Stevens," *Variety,* 2 Oct 1963. AMD, p. 327. AS, p. 1033. BHD2, p. 252. FDY, pp. 437, 447. IFN, p. 282. "Ince Signs Two More Writers," *MPW,* 12 Jun 1920, 1434.

Stevens, Lynn [actor] (*né* Franklin Feeney, b. 1898?–28 Mar 1950 [52], Worcester MA). "Lynn Stevens," *Variety,* 5 Apr 1950. AS, p. 1033. BHD, p. 308. IFN, p. 282. Truitt, p. 314.

Stevens, Morton L[yman] [film/stage/TV actor] (b. Marlboro MA, 30 Sep 1887 [MA Birth Cetificate, Vol. 1870, p. 134]-5 Aug 1959 [71], Marlboro MA [MA Death Certificate, Vol. 1926, p. 108]; heart disease). m. Dr. Coryne (Foree) Lockhart, 1955, NY. "Morton L. Stevens of Stage and Films," *NYT,* 6 Aug 1959, 27:6 (in *Perils of Pauline;* 7th generation American). "Prominent Television, Movie and Stage Star Morton Stevens Dies," *Marlboro Enterprise,* 6 Aug 1959, pp. 1–2. AS, p. 1034 (b. 1890). BHD1, p. 521 (b. 1890). IFN, p. 282.

Stevens, Robert B. (son of **Robert E. Stevens**; brother of **Emily Stevens**; nephew of **Minnie Maddern Fiske**) [actor/assistant director] (b. 25 Jan 1880?–19 Dec 1963 [83?], Lauderdale-by-the-Sea FL). (Metro.) "Robert Stevens," *Variety,* 1 Jan 1964. AMD, p. 327. AS, p. 1034. BHD2, p. 253 (b. 1882). Truitt, p. 314. "Stevens Added to Metro's Staff," *MPW,* 24 Aug 1918, 1104.

Stevens, Robert E. (father of **Emily** and **Robert B. Stevens**) [stage manager] (b. Philadelphia PA, 1837?–21 Jul 1918 [81], New York NY). m. Emma Maddern. "Robert E. Stevens," *NYT,* 21 Dec 1940, 17:4 (age 80). "Robert E. Stevens," *Variety,* 26 Jul 1918. AS, p. 1034.

Stevens, Vi[iolet] [actress] (b. Islington, England, 1891–22 Mar 1967 [75?], London, England). AS, p. 1034.

Stevenson, Charles A[lexander] [actor] (b. Dublin, Ireland, 6 Nov 1851–2 Jul 1929 [77], New York NY). m. **Kate Claxton** (d. 1924). "C.A. Stevenson, Actor, Dies at 77; Former Leading Man for Mrs. Leslie Carter Was Oldest Elected Member of Lambs; Appeared Here Last in 1918; For Eight Years He Had Been Playing in Movies in Hollywood—His Latest Film [*The Insidious Dr. Fu Manchu*] Not Yet Shown," *NYT,* 3 Jul 1929, 21:3 (wrote memoirs). "Charles A. Stevenson," *Variety,* 10 Jul 1929. AMD, p. 327. AS, p. 1034. BHD, p. 308. IFN, p. 282. Truitt, p. 314. "Charles Stevens and Louis Bennison Signed," *MPW,* 10 Dec 1921, 657.

Stevenson, Charles E. [actor] (*né* Charles Edward Hafner, b. Sacramento CA, 13 Oct 1887–4 Jul 1943 [55], Palo Alto CA). (Vitagraph; Fox; Select; 1st National; Hal Roach; Paramount.) "Charles E. Stevenson," *Variety,* 14 Jul 1943. AMD, p. 327. AS, p. 1034. BHD1, p. 521. IFN, p. 282. Truitt, p. 314. "Fox Signs Stevenson," *MPW,* 24 Jul 1926, 4.

Stevenson, Douglas [actor] (b. Versailles KY, 1885–31 Dec 1934 [49?], Versailles KY). (Stage, 1903.) "Douglas Stevenson," *Variety,* 117, 8 Jan 1935, 63:4 (nervous breakdown in 1930; age 52). AMD, p. 327. AS, p. 1034 (b. 1883). BHD, p. 308. "Engage Popular Players," *MPW,* 26 Apr 1924, 735.

Stevenson, George U. [publicist]. No data found. AMD, p. 327. "Universal Publicity Staff," *MPW,* 26 Sep 1914, 1756–57. "George Universal Stevenson Back," *MPW,* 21 Aug 1915, 1303. "George U. Stevenson in Hospital," *MPW,* 27 Nov 1915, 1646. "George Stevenson in France," *MPW,* 8 Jun 1918, 1420.

Stevenson, Hayden [actor] (b. Georgetown KY, 2 Jul). (Universal.) AMD, p. 327. MH, p. 138. "Hayden Stevenson," *MPW,* 17 Sep 1927, 167.

Stevenson, Houseley, Sr. (father of Onslow Stevens) [actor] (b. London, England, 30 Jul 1879–6 Aug 1953 [74], Los Angeles CA). "Houseley Stevenson, Sr.," *Variety,* 12 Aug 1953. AS, p. 1034 (b. Liverpool, England). IFN, p. 282.

Stevenson, John [actor] (b. NY, 1884?–10 Aug 1922 [38], New York NY; during the filming of *Plunder*). "'Stunt Man' Killed; Acrobat Doubling for Pearl White Makes Fatal Leap," *Variety,* 18 Aug 1922. AS, p. 1034. BHD, p. 308. IFN, p. 282. Truitt, p. 315.

Stevenson, Kate E *see* **Claxton, Kate**

Steward, Manyon [actor] (b. 1880–25 Dec 1932 [52]). BHD, p. 309. IFN, p. 282.

Stewart, Aileen [actress] (b. 1887–7 Feb 1931 [42?], Los Angeles CA). AS, p. 1034.

Stewart, Anita (sister of **George** and **Lucille Lee Stewart**) [actress] (*née* Ann E. Stewart, b. Brooklyn NY, 24 Apr 1895 [Birth Certificate Index No. 17322]–4 May 1961 [66], Beverly Hills CA; heart attack). m. (1) **Rudolph C**[ameron] Brennan (d. 1958); (2) George P. Converse. (Vitagraph, 1911; Metro; 1st National; Anita Stewart Pictures; she appeared in a sound short in the early 30's.) "Anita Stewart, Silent-Film Star, Actress, 65, Dies on Coast—Won Fame in 'Goddess,'" *NYT,* 5 May 1961, 29:3; "150 at Anita Stewart Rites," *NYT,* 10 May 1961, 45:2 (present were Vivian Duncan, Barbara Shields, Claire Windsor, Laura La Plante, May McAvoy and Mae Murray). "Anita Stewart," *Variety,* 10 May 1961 (age 63). AMD, p. 327. AS, p. 1034. BHD1, p. 617 (b. 17 Feb). FFF, p. 44. IFN, p. 282 (b. 17 Feb). Katz, pp. 1093–94. Lowrey, p. 177. MH, p. 137 (b. 17 Feb). MSBB, p. 1042 (b. 1896). Slide, p. 151 (b. 7 Feb). Truitt, p. 315. WWS, p. 95. "Anita Stewart," *MPW,* 1 Aug 1914, 711. "Anita Stewart; The Vitagraph Leading Lady," *MPS,* 14 Aug 1914, 25 (cites birthdate of 17 Feb 1895). "In the Picture Studios," *NYDM,* 23 Oct 1915, 31:1 (Stewart "has purchased a plot of ground next to her brother-in-law, Ralph W. Ince, at Brightwaters, Long Island, and is building a house to cost $30,000.". Tom Bret, "The Most Beautiful 'Good Woman' in the Movies; Great Girl Within Inspires a Charming Character Which Exudes Joy in Volumes—An Ardent Jap Captivated by Her Figure But No Wedding Bells for Anita Stewart," *MPC,* Apr 1916, 43–45. "Anita Stewart Makes Her Debut as a Songster," *MPW,* 5 Aug 1916, 964. "Anita Stewart Convalescent," *MPW,* 23 Sep 1916, 1952. "Anita Stewart in New Company," *MPW,* 15 Sep 1917, 1668. "Vitagraph Seeks Injunction," *MPW,* 22 Sep 1917, 1835. "Little Whisperings from Everywhere in Playerdom," *Motion Picture Magazine,* Feb 1918, 144 ("Anita Stewart sought to have the injunction which restrains her from acting for any other corporation than Vitagraph set aside by the Appellate Division of the Supreme Court, New York, but that court affirmed the injunction previously granted by the Supreme Court, and the fair Anita must make up all lost time. Her contract with Vitagraph called for $1,000 a week and royalties guaranteed not to be less than $75,000 a year—and yet she wishes to break it! 'Oh,Girl!'"). "Anita Stewart's Marriage Revealed in Court," *MPW,* 9 Feb 1918, 834. "Vitagraph Wins Anita Stewart Suit," *MPW,* 6 Apr 1918, 58. "Anita Stewart Again at Work," *MPW,* 11 May 1918, 864. "Vitagraph Settles Anita Stewart Case," *MPW,* 3 Aug 1918, 667. "Stewart Pictures Go to First National," *MPW,* 10 Aug 1918, 819. "Film Men Talk Big Figures While at Luncheon," *MPW,* 16 Nov 1918, 750. "Lois Weber to Direct Anita Stewart," *MPW,* 7 Dec 1918, 1056. "Anita Stewart Talks Entertainingly," *MPW,* 7 Dec 1918, 1065. "Anita Stewart Helps the Poor," *MPW,* 28 Dec 1918, 1501. "Anita Stewart Is Thanked by President in Telegram," *MPW,* 12 Jul 1919, 242. "Star's Diamonds Stolen," *MPW,* L, 7 May 1921, 55 (valued at $20,000). "Film Folk Purchase Homes," *MPW,* 14 May 1921, 179 (Franklin and Vista Streets, Hollywood). Goldbeck, "The Star at Evening," *MPC,* Jul 1921, 24–25, 85. "Anita Stewart Signs," *MPW,* 3 Mar 1923, 38. Carolyn Carter, "Can a Wife Protect Her Home from a Love Pirate? 'Yes!,' Says Anita Stewart," *MW,* 28 Jun 1924, 7. "Anita Stewart Returns to Vitagraph for 'Baree' Film," *MPW,* 21 Feb 1925, 814. "Anita Stewart Kept Busy,"

MPW, 28 Feb 1925, 909. "Sebastian Signs Anita Stewart," *MPW,* 16 May 1925, 351. "Anita Stewart," *MPW,* 5 Dec 1925, 438. "Anita Stewart Signed by Fox to Play in Big Production," *MPW,* 13 Mar 1926, 97.

Stewart, Athole [actor] (b. Ealing, England, 24 Jun 1879–22 Oct 1940 [61], Buckinghamshire, England). AS, p. 1034.

Stewart, Danny Kalauawa [actor/musician] (b. Hawaii, 1906–15 Apr 1962 [55], Honolulu HI; heart attack). AS, p. 1035. BHD1, p. 522. IFN, p. 283.

Stewart, Donald Ogden [stage/TV actor/scenarist/playwright] (b. Columbus OH, 30 Nov 1894–2 Aug 1980 [85], London, England; heart attack). m. (1) Beatrice Ames; (2) Lenore W. Steffens; (3) Ella Winter. AMD, p. 327. AS, p. 1035. BHD2, p. 253. Dorothy Donnell, "Hollywood Thru a Humorist's Eyes; Donald Ogden Stewart Says the Studios Inspired Him in Writing His New Book, 'The Crazy Fool,'" *MPC,* Aug 1925, 52–53, 86. "Author to Adapt for Screen," *MPW,* 1 Aug 1925, 554.

Stewart, Etta [actress] (d. 23 Apr 1929). BHD, p. 309. IFN, p. 283.

Stewart, Fred [actor/director] (b. Atlanta GA, 7 Dec 1906–5 Dec 1970 [63], New York NY). "Fred Stewart," *Variety,* 9 Dec 1970. AS, p. 1035.

Stewart, George (brother of **Anita** and **Lucille Lee Stewart**) [actor] (b. New York NY, 27 Jun 1888?–25 Dec 1945 [57], Beverly Hills CA; in a sanitarium for 20 years). (Film debut: *Virtuous Wives,* Anita Stewart Prdns, 1918.) "George Stewart," *Variety,* 2 Jan 1946. AMD, p. 327. AS, p. 1035. BHD, p. 309 (b. Brooklyn NY; d. 24 Dec). IFN, p. 283. Truitt, p. 315. "George Stewart Is New Christie Star," *MPW,* 18 Mar 1922, 263. June Lee, "Dan Cupid's Bulletin Board," *Paris and Hollywood,* Sep 1926, 22 (reportedly engaged to stage actress Marie Callahan).

Stewart, Grant [actor] (b. Scotland, 18 Apr 1866–18 Aug 1929 [63], Woodstock NY). m. Helen. "Grant Stewart," *Variety,* 21 Aug 1929. AS, p. 1035 (b. England). BHD, p. 309 (b. England).

Stewart, Hamilton [actor] (d. 15 May 1924, Oxford, England). BHD, p. 309.

Stewart, Julia [actress] (b. Edinburgh, Scotland, ca. 1880-ca. 1940 [ca. 60], Philadelphia PA). BHD, p. 309.

Stewart, Katherine [stage/film actress] (b. Sandwich, England, 1867?–24 Jan 1949 [81], Bronx NY). "Katherine Stewart," *NYT,* 26 Jan 1949, 25:2 (veteran character actress on stage). "Katherine Stewart," *Variety,* 26 Jan 1949. AS, p. 1035. BHD, p. 309.

Stewart, Lemuel L. [executive] (d. Mar 1938, Long Beach CA). BHD2, p. 253.

Stewart, Lowell (or **Loel**) (daughter of **Maurice** and **Mrs. Maurice Wilcov Stewart**) [child actress] (b. 20 Jan 1914). (Biograph.) "Studio Gossip," *NYDM,* 21 Jan 1914, 36:1 ("Loel Stewart[,] of the three Biograph babies, celebrated her fourth birthday yesterday.").

Stewart, Lucille Lee [stage/film actress] (sister of **Anita** and **George Stewart**) (b. Brooklyn NY, 25 Dec 1889–8 Jan 1982 [92], Hemet CA). m. **Ralph Ince**—div. 1925 (d. 1937). (Biograph, 1910; Vitagraph, 1912; Metro; Fox.) AMD, p. 327. AS, p. 1035. BHD, pp. 67–69; 309. "Lucille Stewart, New Vitagraph Player," *MPW,* 26 Feb 1916, 1276. "Lucille Lee Stewart," *MPW,* 18 Mar 1916, 1811. "Lucille Lee Stewart in Metro Pictures," *MPW,* 6 Jul 1918, 42. Billy H. Doyle, "Lost Players," *CI,* 159 (Sep 1988), 22.

Stewart, Maurice (father of **Lowell Stewart**) [actor]. No data found.

Stewart, Mrs. Maurice Wilcox Stewart (mother of **Lowell Stewart**) [stage/film actress] (*née* Wilcox). m. **Maurice Stewart**. No data found. "Studio Gossip," *NYDM,* 28 Jan 1914, 31:2 ("Mrs. Maurice Wilcox Stewart, whose stage name was Myrtle Hass, of *Brown of Harvard* fame, has joined the forces of the Biograph Company with her three Biograph Stewart Babies.").

Stewart, Melville [singer/actor] (*né* Theodore Rettich, b. London, England, 17 Feb 1869–5 Aug 1915 [46], Sea Gate NY). m. Genevieve Findley. "Melville Stewart," *Variety,* 20 Aug 1915. AMD, p. 327. BHD, p. 309. "Another Pathe Star; Clifton Crawford Signed by Pathe [in NJ] to Play in Production of 'The Gallopers,'" *NYDM,* 30 Jun 1915, 20:1 (supported Crawford). "Another Big Star for Pathé," *MPW,* 24 Jul 1915, 633.

Stewart, Nellie [actress/singer] (b. Melbourne, Australia, 1859–20 Jun 1931 [72?], Sydney, Australia). AS, p. 1035. BHD, p. 309.

Stewart, Richard [actor] (d. ca. 1938). AS, p. 1035. BHD, p. 309.

Stewart, Roy [actor] (*né* John Roy Stewart, b. San Diego CA, 17 Oct 1883–26 Apr 1933 [49], Los Angeles CA; heart attack). (Film debut: *The Trail of the Lonesome Star,* 19 Oct 1913, Flying A). "Roy Stewart," *Variety,* 2 May 1933 (age 44). AMD, p. 327. AS, p. 1035. BHD1, p. 522 (b. 1884; d. Westwood CA). FSS, p. 264. IFN, p. 283 (b. 1883). MH, p. 138. Truitt, p. 315 (b. 1889). "Roy Stewart," *MPW,* 23 Dec 1916, 1791. "Roy Stewart Wrtes a Western," *MPW,* 20 Jul 1918, 411. "Casting Coinncidence," *LA Times,* 7 Mar 1920, III, p. 16 (on 19 Oct 1919, Stewart was cast in B.B. Hampton's Desert Wheat; on the same day, Joe Dowling was given a part in it. He subsequently discovered that both he and Dowling made their film debuts on 19 Oct 1913, in *The Trail of the Lonesome Star,* Flying A at San Diego). "Roy Stewart Is Star of Brandt's Big Special 'Heart of the North,'" *MPW,* 18 Jun 1921, 724. Louise Kirk, "Sans Horse and Sombrero," *MPC,* Jul 1921, 26, 78. "Posing as Stewart," *MPW,* 3 Mar 1923, 41. Buck Rainey, "Roy Stewart; A Page from the Past!," *CFC,* 56 (Fall, 1977), 30 *et passim* (b. 1884; includes filmography).

Stewart-Slager, R.W. [assistant director] (b. 1886–21 Dec 1959 [73?], Los Angeles CA). BHD2, p. 253.

Stiebner, Hans Friedrich Wilhelm Georg Paul [actor/director] (b. Vetschay, Germany, 19 Nov 1896–27 Mar 1958 [61], Baden-Baden, Germany). AS, p. 1035.

Stiller, Mauritz [stage/film actor/director/scenarist] (*né* Mowscha or Mosché Moise Stiller, b. Helsingfors, Grand Duchy of Finland, 17 Jul 1883 or b. Lvov, Poland, 21 May 1882–8 Nov 1928 [45?], Helsingfors, Finland; infectious pleurisy). (Began as film actor in 1912; MGM; Paramount.) Gösta Werner, *Mauritz Stiller och hans filmer; 1912–1916* (Stockholm: PA Norstedt & Söners förlag, 1969). "Mauritz Stiller," *Variety,* 14 Nov 1928 (d. Stockholm, no date). AMD, p. 327. AS, p. 1036 (d. Stockholm). BHD, p. 309; BHD2, p. 253 (b. 17 Jul 1883; d. Stockholm, Sweden). FDY, p. 437. IFN, p. 283. Katz, pp. 1095–96 (began in Sweden, 1912). Waldman, p. 275 (But suffering from lung cancer, he committed suicide."). "Mauritz Stiller Here," *MPW,* 26 Sep 1925, 344 (with Greta Garbo).

Stindt, Bruno [cinematographer] (b. 1887–25 Jan 1958 [70?], Berlin, Germany). BHD2, p. 253.

Stine, Charles J. [actor] (b. 1865?–5 Jan 1934 [69], Bay Shore, LI NY). "Charles J. Stine," *Variety,* 9 Jan 1934. AS, p. 1036. BHD, p. 309 (b. 1869). IFN, p. 283 (age 65).

Stinson, Mortimer E. [actor] (b. New York NY, 25 Dec 1871–20 Jul 1927 [55], Los Angeles CA). AS, p. 1036. BHD, p. 309. IFN, p. 283.

Stirling, Edward [actor] (b. Birmingham, England, 26 May 1892–12 Jan 1948 [55], Paris, France). AS, p. 1036.

Stites, Frank [actor] (b. IN, 28 Feb 1882–15 Mar 1915 [33], Universal City CA; airplane crash). AS, p. 1036. BHD, p. 309.

Stockdale, Carl[ton] [actor] (b. Worthington MN, 19 Feb 1874–15 Mar 1953 [79], Woodland Hills CA; heart attack). (Essanay.) AMD, p. 328. AS, p. 1036. BHD1, p. 523. IFN, p. 283. "Bill Russell Engages Carl Stockdale," *MPW,* 6 Apr 1918, 71.

Stockdale, Franklin E. [actor] (b. 1870–31 Dec 1950 [80?], Los Angeles CA). AS, p. 1036.

Stockfield, Betty [stage/film actress] (*née* Elizabeth Stockfield, b. Sydney, Australia, 15 Jan 1905–26 Jan 1966 [61], Surrey, London, England; cancer). "Betty Stockfield, Actress of British Stage and Films," *NYT,* 29 Jan 1966, 27:2. "Betty Stockfield," *Variety,* 241, 2 Feb 1966, 63:3 (d. 27 Jan). AS, p. 1036. BHD1, p. 523. IFN, p. 283.

Stocklin, Sally [actress] (b. Indianapolis IN, 22 Feb 1843–5 Aug 1925 [82], Los Angeles CA). AS, p. 1036.

Stocklin, Sam [actor] (b. 21 Jul 1864–3 Aug 1932 [68], Los Angeles CA). AS, p. 1036.

Stockwell, Winifred [actress] (b. 1894?–8 Feb 1981 [86], New Hope MN). m. Andrew Hilger. (Began 1920.) "Winifred S. Hilger," *Variety,* 25 Feb 1981. "Winifred S. Hilger," *CI,* 75 (May 1981), 16 ("acted in numerous silent films in the early 1920's"). AS, p. 1036. BHD, p. 309.

Stoddard, Belle (sister-in-law of **Frank Mayo**) [stage/film actress] (b. Remington OH, 13 Sep 1869–13 Dec 1950 [81], Los Angeles CA). m. Paul Menifee Johnstone. "Belle Stoddard, Veteran Actress; Broadway Stage Star of Half a Century Ago Dies on Coast—Played in Silent Films," *NYT,* 14 Dec 1950, 35:4. "Belle Stoddard," *Variety,* 20 Dec 1950. AS, p. 1036. BHD1, p. 523. IFN, p. 283. Ragan 2, p. 835. Truitt, p. 315.

Stoddard, Betsy [actress] (*née* Elizabeth Stoddard, b. 1884–7 Sep 1959 [75?], Los Angeles CA). AS, p. 1036.

Stoeckel, Joe [stage/film actor/director] (*né* Joseph Stockel, b. Munich, Germany, 27 Sep 1894–14 Jun 1959 [64], Munich, Germany; circulatory ailment). m. (1 daughter). "Joe Stoeckel," *Variety,* 215, 24 Jun 1959, 127:1 (began in silents with Peter Ostermayr, 1916). AS, p. 1036. BHD1, p. 523. IFN, p. 283.

Stoffer, Josephine [actress] (b. Baltimore MD-d. 25 Oct 1922, New York NY). BHD, p. 309.

Stoker, H[ew] **G**[ordon] Dacre [actor] (b.

Dublin, Ireland, 2 Feb 1885–2 Feb 1966 [81], England). AS, p. 1037.

Stokes, Olive M. [actress] (b. OK, 10 Apr 1887–1 Nov 1972 [85], Los Angeles Co. CA). m. **Tom Mix**, 19 Jan 1909, Medora ND—div. 1917 (d. 1940; 1 daughter, Ruth Jane, 1912–1977). (Selig, 1911). AS, p. 1037. BHD, p. 309. IFN, p. 283.

Stokes, Sylvanus [actor]. No data found. Don Juan, "So This Is Hollywood," *Paris and Hollywood Screen Secrets Magazine,* Aug 1927, 56, 95 (Stokes was a "millionaire youth…well known in Newport and Washington soceity. ¶He will appear with Irene Rich in their Warner production, *Dearie.*").

Stoll, Oswald [producer] (b. Mebourne, Victoria, Australia, 26 Jan 1866-Jan 1942 [75?], Putney, England). BHD2, p. 253.

Stoloff, Ben[jamin] [director/producer] (b. Philadelphia PA, 1895–7 Sep 1960 [64], Los Angeles CA). (Fox.) "Ben Stoloff," *Variety,* 14 Sep 1960. AS, p. 1037. BHD2, p. 253. IFN, p. 283. Katz, p. 1097.

Stoltz, Arnold Theodore [actor] (b. Germany, 1902–11 May 1986 [84?], Melbourne, Australia). AS, p. 1037.

Stone, Arthur Taylor [actor/makeup artist] (b. St. Louis MO, 28 Nov 1883–4 Sep 1940 [56], Los Angeles CA). m. **Dorothy Westmore**, 1927. (Sennett.) "Arthur Taylor Stone," *NYT,* 6 Sep 1940, 21:1 (age 54). AMD, p. 328. AS, p. 1037. BHD1, p. 523. IFN, p. 284. Truitt, p. 316. "Arthur Stone Signed on Long Term Contract by First National," *MPW,* 15 May 1926, 234. "Arthur Stone," *MPW,* 23 Jul 1927, 240. "Dan Cupid Chalks Up Two Weddings," *MPW,* 3 Sep 1927, 23. George A. Katchmer, "Remembering the Great Silents," *CI,* 183 (Sep 1990), 51.

Stone, Dorothy (daughter of **Fred Stone**) [stage/film actress] (b. Brooklyn NY, 3 Jun 1905–24 Sep 1974 [69], Montecito CA). "Dorothy Stone," *Variety,* 276, 2 Oct 1974, 78:3 (Dorothy Stone Collins). AS, p. 1037. BHD1, p. 523. IFN, p. 284.

Stone, Florence [actress] (b. 1880?–25 Aug 1950 [70], Los Angeles CA). m. Dick Ferris; **Jack Richardson** (d. 1957). "Florence Stone," *NYT,* 27 Aug 1950, 89:3. "Florence Stone," *Variety,* 30 Aug 1950. AS, p. 1037. BHD1, p. 523. IFN, p. 284.

Stone, Fred (father of Pamela and **Dorothy Stone**) [stage/film actor] (*né* Alfred Andrew Stone, b. in log cabin near Longmont CO, 19 Aug 1873–6 Mar 1959 [85], No. Hollywood CA; heart attack). m. Allene Crater (d. 13 Aug 1957). *Rolling Stones* (1945). (Film debut: *The Goat,* FP-L, 1918; Artcraft.) "Fred Stone, Actor, Dead at 85; Won Fame in 'The Wizard of Oz'; Creator of Scarecrow Role in 1903 Was Top Comedian—Played in 'Chin Chin,'" *NYT,* 7 Mar 1959, 1:3, 21:4 (began 1917). "Fred Stone Dies at 85; Versatile and Perennial, Career Spanned 64 Yrs.," *Variety,* 11 Mar 1959. AMD, p. 328. AS, p. 1037. BHD1, p. 523 (d. LA CA). FSS, p. 264. IFN, p. 284. Katz, p. 1097 (b. Denver CO). MSBB, p. 1028 (b. Denver CO). Truitt, p. 316. "Paramount Secures Fred Stone," *MPW,* 29 Dec 1917, 1949. "Fred Stone Starts for West Coast," *MPW,* 15 Jun 1918, 1559. "Seven Players New to Artcraft-Paramount," *MPW,* 6 Jul 1918, 57. "Fred Stone Invades Canada and Resumes Camera Acting,"' *MPW,* 5 Jul 1919, 80. "Fred Stone Will Be Guest at Wyoming Frontier Day," *MPW,* 2 Aug 1919, 686. "Movie History in the Making Ten Years Ago," *Paris and Hollywood Screen Secrets,* Oct 1927, 93 (debuted in *Under the Top,* a circus story).

Stone, Gene [actor] (*né* Eugene Stone, b. Budapest, Hungary, 15 Jun 1892–21 Feb 1947 [54], Los Angeles CA). BHD1, p. 523. IFN, p. 284. Ragan 2, p. 1621.

Stone, George [vaudeville/film actor] (*né* George Stonseifer, b. 1890?–17 Jul 1928 [38], New York NY; pneumonia). m. Dooley Ioleen, 30 Jun 1920. "George Stone," *Variety,* 18 Jul 1928. AS, p. 1037 (d. 9 Aug 1966).

Stone, George [child actor] (b. 1909?). No data found. (Majestic.) F.E. Hasty, "The Children Are Promoted," *NYDM,* 8 Sep 1915, 37:2 (age 6; Majestic Juvenile Co. member to appear in 2-reel features, Reliance brand).

Stone, George E. [actor] (*né* George Edward Stein, b. Lodz, Poland, 18 May 1903–26 May 1967 [64], Woodland Hills CA; cerebral thrombosis). (Film debut: *Seventh Heaven,* 1927.) "George E. Stone, Character Actor; Performer Known for Roles in Gangster Films Dies," *NYT,* 29 May 1967, 25:2 (extra at Ft. Lee NJ). "George E. Stone," *Variety,* 31 May 1967. AS, p. 1037 (b. 1904). BHD1, p. 523. IFN, p. 284. Katz, pp. 1097–98 (b. 23 May). Truitt, p. 316.

Stone, Mrs. George S. [actress/writer] (b. 1875?–9 Aug 1966 [91], Kensington MD). (Lubin [Philadelphia PA]). "Mrs. George S. Stone," *Variety,* 17 Aug 1966. AS, p. 1037.

Stone, Gerald [actor] (b. Indianapolis IN, 22 Apr 1844–6 May 1931 [87], Los Angeles CA). AS, p. 1037.

Stone, Henry "Buddy" Lewis [stuntman] (b. Lynn MA, 28 Jan 1899). Bachelor. (Began in 1921.) AS, p. 1037. Ernest N. Corneau, "The Biggest Little Daredevil in the Movies," *CFC,* 38 (Spring, 1973), 32–33, 44.

Stone, Jack [actor] (b. London, England, 26 Nov 1906–8 Apr 1962 [55], Mt. Kisko NY). BHD1, p. 523.

Stone, John (father of scenarist Peter Stone) [scenarist/director/producer] (*né* Jack Strumwasser, b. New York NY, 12 Sep 1888–3 Jun 1961 [72], Los Angeles CA). m. Lucille; Hilda Hess (*see* **Marton, Hilda**). (Fox, 1919; Columbia; 1944.) "John Stone, Film Writer, Dies; Did 30 Charlie Chan Movies," *NYT,* 4 Jun 1961, 86:7. "John Stone," *Variety,* 14 Jun 1961 ("early-day western director"). AMD, p. 328. AS, p. 1037. BHD2, p. 254. FDY, p. 437. IFN, p. 284. "Stone Tells How to Write for Pictures," *MPW,* 1 Jan 1927, 33. "Left the Little Red Schoolhouse," *MPW,* 25 Jun 1927, 572.

Stone, Joseph E. [producer] (b. 1880–17 Nov 1948 [68?], Los Angeles CA). AS, p. 1038. BHD2, p. 254.

Stone, Leroy [film editor] (b. San Francisco CA, 1894?–15 Sep 1949 [55], Santa Monica CA). (Ince, 1916.) "Leroy Stone," *Variety,* 20 Sep 1949. BHD2, p. 254 (b. 1896-d. 18 Sep).

Stone, Lewis Shepard [stage/film actor] (b. Worcester MA, 15 Nov 1879–13 Sep 1953 [73], Los Angeles CA; heart attack). m. (1) Margaret Langham, 1907; (2) **Florence Oakley** (d. 1956); Hazel Woof, 1930. (Essanay; World; Ince; MGM.) (Film debut: *Honor's Altar,* 1915.) "Lewis Stone Dies; Stage, Screen Star; Stricken on Sidewalk—Actor, 73, Won Fame for Portrayal of 'Judge Hardy' in Films," *NYT,* 13 Sep 1953, 84:4. "Lewis Stone," *Variety,* 16 Sep 1953. AMD, p. 328. AS, p. 1038. BHD1, p. 523. FFF, p. 117. FSS, p. 264. GK, pp. 900–16. IFN, p. 284. Katz, p. 1098 (began 1915). MH, p. 138. Spehr, p. 168. Truitt, p. 316. "Lewis H. [sic] Stone," *MPW,* 10 Jun 1916, 1868. "Lewis S. Stone Makes Screen Debut in 'Man's Desire,'" *MPW,* 16 Aug 1919, 970. "Lewis Stone Returns to Screen," *MPW,* 7 Feb 1920, 919. "Lewis Stone Signed by Paramount," *MPW,* 19 Aug 1922, 578. "In Leading Role," *MPW,* 21 Apr 1923, 862. Malcolm H. Oetinger, "The Age of Discretion," *Picture-Play Magazine,* Jun 1923, 22–23, 96. Lewis Stone, "This Cosmic Urge," *Classic,* May 1924, 24, 84. "Lewis Stone Signed by First National for Long Term," *MPW,* 25 Jul 1925, 451. Helen Perrin, "He Won Fame in Spite of Himself; Lewis Stone Is a Shrinking Favorite Who Has Never Come to Like Notoriety," *MPC,* Dec 1925, 40–41, 72. Joseph Henry Steele, "The Stone Age as Represented by One of Its Regulars," *MPC,* Apr 1928, 23, 77. Dorothy Manners, "A Hairpin and Two Tickets; Do These Mean that Lewis Stone Has a New and Hidden Romance?," *MPC,* Apr 1929, 39, 82. George A. Katchmer, "Dignified Actor Lewis Stone," *CI,* 134 (Aug 1986), 24–27, 51.

Stone, Maxine [actress] (b. 1910?–20 Nov 1964 [54], Hollywood CA). m. Benny Ross, 1929. (Early Vitaphone shorts.) "Maxine Stone," *Variety,* 25 Nov 1964. AS, p. 1038. BHD1, p. 523. IFN, p. 284. Truitt, p. 317.

Stone, Melville [scenarist] (d. Jan 1918, Pasadena CA). BHD2, p. 254.

Stone, Michael J. [producer] (b. 1883–17 Nov 1948 [65?], Los Angeles CA). BHD2, p. 254.

Stone, Phil [actor] (b. 1893?–20 Feb 1967 [74], Oxford MS). "Phil Stone, 74, a Lawyer, Gave Early Aid to Faulkner," *NYT,* 22 Feb 1967, 29:2. AS, p. 1038.

Stone, Mrs. Robert E. [actress] (d. 5 Nov 1916). AS, p. 1038. BHD, p. 310.

Stonehouse, Ruth [vaudeville/film actress] (b. Denver CO or Elkhart IN, 28 Sep 1892–12 May 1941 [48], Los Angeles CA). m. **Joseph Anthony Roach** (or Roche), 1914, St. Louis MO; Felix Hughes, 1 Oct 1927. (Film debut: *Sunshine,* Essanay [Chicago], 1911 [$12 per week]; Universal; B.A. Rolfe Prods.) "Ruth Stonehouse," *Variety,* 21 May 1941. AMD, p. 328. AS, p. 1038. BHD, p. 310. IFN, p. 284. Katz, pp. 1098–99. MH, p. 138 (b. Denver CO, 1894). MSBB, p. 1042 (b. 1894). Truitt, p. 317 (b. 1893). "Essanay Players Favorably Mentioned," *MPW,* 14 Sep 1912, 1068 (cites Victor CO as her hometown). "Miss Stonehouse Resumes Work," *MPW,* 5 Apr 1913, 51. "An Essanay Elopement; Joseph Roach and Ruth Stonehouse Are Married in St. Louis," *NYDM,* 4 Feb 1914, 30:2 ("The couple stole away to Milwaukee [braving the new Wisconsin eugenics law]," but there was a five-day residency requirement. So they hopped a train to St. Louis, where "the law was not so cantankerous" and got married. Francis X. Bushman, appearing at the Hippodrome, announced the event to the audieence and "brought down the house."). "Some Prominent Essanay Photoplayers," *MPW,* 11 Jul 1914, 234–35. "Ruth Stonehouse in Denver," *MPW,* 18 Jul 1914, 407. "Ruth Stonehouse," *MPW,* 5 Feb 1916, 764. "Ruth Stonehouse," *MPW,* 21 Apr 1917, 427. "Ruth Stonehouse to Have Own Company," *MPW,* 15 Dec 1917, 1637. "Rolfe Signs Director and Prominent Players," *MPW,* 10 Aug 1918, 868. "Stonehouse in Radio Talk," *MPW,* 13 Dec 1924, 658. Nanette Kutner, "Knowing Gloria When…," *Pictures,* Sep 1926, 49, 99–101. "Starke—White Wed; Mary Astor Next," *MPW,* 10 Sep 1927, 89 (wed

Hughes). George A. Katchmer, "Remembering the Great Silents," *CI*, 178 (Apr 1990), 43.

Stopp, Gerald D. [actor] (b. 1894–30 Apr 1931 [37?], New York NY). AS, p. 1038.

Stora, Edgar [actor] (b. New York NY, 1 Jun 1840–5 May 1903 [62], New York NY). AS, p. 1038.

Storey, Edith "Billie" (sister of **Richard Storey**) [stage/film actress] (b. New York NY, 18 Mar 1892–9 Oct 1967 [75], Northport NY). Unmarried. (Vitagraph, 1908; Méliès; Metro; Haworth; Robertson-Cole.) AMD, p. 328. AS, p. 1038 (d. 23 Sep 1955). BHD, pp. 69–60; 310. IFN, p. 284 (d. 23 Sep 1955, age 63). Katz, p. 1100. Lowrey, p. 174 (b. NYC). MSBB, p. 1042. Slide, p. 151 (b. NYC, 18 Mar 1892). WWS, p. 117. Cover, *NYDM*, 25 Aug 1915 (in *Dust of Egypt*). "Edith Storey's New Home Ready," *MPW*, 2 Sep 1916, 1519. "Film Star Given Ovation," *MPW*, 21 Oct 1916, 400. "Edith Storey," *MPW*, 3 Feb 1917, 691. "Edith Storey Goes to Metro," *MPW*, 7 Jul 1917, 63. "Edith Storey Completes First Production for Metro," *MPW*, 6 Oct 1917, 57. "Edith Storey Has the Aeroplane Feveritis," *MPW*, 27 Apr 1918, 569. "Edith Storey Finished with War Work, Returns to Screen," *MPW*, 13 Sep 1919, 1653. "First Edith Storey Picture to Be November Release," *MPW*, 20 Sep 1919, 1790. Billy H. Doyle, "Lost Players," *CI*, 195 (Sep 1991), p. 20. George Katchmer, "Remembering the Great Silents," *CI*, 229 (Jul 1994), 37.

Storey, Fred [actor] (b. London, England, 20 Jun 1861–4 Dec 1917 [56], London, England). BHD, p. 310.

Storey, Helen [actress] (b. 1903–26 Apr 1935 [32?], Chicago IL). BHD, p. 310.

Storey, Richard (brother of **Edith Storey**) [assistant director]. No data found. AMD, p. 328. "Richard Storey Joins Ice," *MPW*, 29 May 1920, 1209.

Storm, Jerome V. [stage/film actor/director] (b. Denver CO, 11 Nov 1890–10 Jul 1958 [67], Desert Hot Springs CA). m. Mildred Richter, 19 Mar 1921, Beverly Hills CA (at the home of Robert McKim). (Broncho; Domino; Ince; KB; 1st National; Fox; Paramount; Chadwick.) AMD, p. 328. AS, p. 1039. BHD, pp. 70–72; 310; BHD2, p. 254. "Jerome Storm Resignss as Director of Charles Ray," *MPW*, 26 Jun 1920, 1784. "Sherrill Signs Jerome Storm to Direct First Lillian Gish Feature for Frohman," *MPW*, 28 Aug 1920, 1185. "Sherrill Signs Jerome Storm to Direct Miss Lillian Gish," *MPW*, 4 Sep 1920, 72. "Storm Is Ready to Work on First Gish-Frohman Picture," *MPW*, 11 Sep 1920, 233. "[James] Rennie Will Have Male Lead 'World Shadows,'" *MPW*, 6 Nov 1920, 73. "Jerome Storm Advocates Collaboration of Author and Director During Production," *MPW*, 4 Dec 1920, 629. Jerome STOrm, "Threat of Business DEPression Is of Benefit to Films, Says Jerome Storm," *MPW*, 25 Dec 1920, 1010. "Wedding in Filmland," *MPW*, 9 Apr 1921, 589. "Jerome Storm Engaged as New Director for Little Jackie Coogan," *MPW*, 12 Nov 1921, 166. "Jerry Storm Likes Ray Production," *MPW*, 17 Feb 1923, 699. "Storm Back with Fox," *MPW*, 13 Sep 1924, 124. "Storm to Direct Ray," *MPW*, 14 Mar 1925, 173. "Jerome Storm Signed by Hal Roach," *MPW*, 24 Apr 1926, 604. "Storm to Direct FBO Picture," *MPW*, 13 Aug 1927, 465. "Jerome Storm," *MPW*, 12 Nov 1927, 22. Billy H. Doyle, "Lost Players," *CI*, 160 (Oct 1988), 30.

Storm, Olaf [actor] (b. Frederiksberg, Denmark, 10 Jan 1894-Mar 1931 [36]). BHD1, p. 617.

Stormont, Leo [actor] (d. 28 Jan 1923). BHD, p. 310.

Stossel, Ludwig [actor] (b. Lockenhaus, Austria, 12 Feb 1883–29 Jan 1973 [89], Beverly Hills CA). AS, p. 1039.

Stothart, Herbert [composer/music director] (b. Milwaukee WI, 11 Sep 1885–1 Feb 1949 [63], Los Angeles CA). m. Mary Wolfe. (MGM.) "H. Stothart Dies; Films Composer; Collaborator with Gershwin, Youmans, Friml Got Academy Award for 'Wizard of Oz,'" *NYT*, 2 Feb 1949, 27:1. "Herbert Stothart," *Variety*, 9 Feb 1949. AS, p. 1039. BHD2, p. 254 (Stothard). IFN, p. 284.

Stout, Archibald J. [cinematographer] (b. Renwick IA, 30 Mar 1886–10 Mar 1973 [86], Los Angeles CA). (Keystone, 1914.) AMD, p. 328. AS, p. 1039 (d. 1965). BHD2, p. 254. FDY, p. 469. Katz, p. 1101. "New Head Cameraman," *MPW*, 21 Jun 1924, 708.

Stowe, Leslie [actor] (b. Homer LA, 1886?–16 Jul 1949 [63], Englewood NJ). "Leslie Stowe," *NYT*, 19 Jul 1949, 29:1 (age 82). "Leslie Stowe," *Variety*, 20 Jul 1949. AS, p. 1039. BHD1, p. 524. IFN, p. 284.

Stowell, Clarence W[arner] [actor] (b. 1878–26 Nov 1940 [62?], Paterson NJ). AS, p. 1039.

Stowell, William H. [stage/film actor] (b. Boston MA, 13 Mar 1885–24 Nov 1919 [34], Belgian Congo [near Elizabethville], South Africa; train wreck). (Selig, 1909; American; Universal, 1917; Jewel.) "William Stowell," *Variety*, 5 Dec 1919. AMD, p. 329. AS, p. 1039 (d. 9 Dec). BHD, pp. 72–73; 310. IFN, p. 284. "Stowell Joins Universal," *MPW*, 20 Jan 1917, 382. "William H. Stowell," *MPW*, 7 Jul 1917, 90. "William Stowell VIsits Windy City," *MPW*, 12 Jul 1919, 203. "Traveler's Club Honors Stowell," *MPW*, 16 Aug 1919, 951. "Obituary," *MPW*, 13 Dec 1919, 777 (d. 3 Dec). "Ashes of Bill Stowell Should Rest in Chicago," *MPW*, 20 Dec 1919, 956. "Stowell Leaves Estate of $17,000 to His Aunt," *MPW*, 3 Jan 1920, 134. "Stowell's Body to Be Sent Home [to Los Angeles]," *MPW*, 17 Jan 1920, 398. "Story of Bill Stowell's Death in Belgian Congo," *MPW*, 28 Feb 1920, 1475–76. Billy H. Doyle, "Lost Players," *CI*, 143 (May 1987), C6-C7, 40. George Katchmer, "Remembering the Great Silents," *CI*, 238 (Apr 1995), 51–52.

Stradling, Harry (father of Harry Stradling, Jr.) [cinematographer] (b. Newark NJ, 1 Sep 1901–14 Feb 1970 [68], Los Angeles CA). "Harry Stradling," *Variety*, 18 Feb 1970. AS, p. 1039 (d. 15 Feb). BHD2, p. 254 (b. England). FDY, p. 469. Katz, p. 1101.

Stradling, Walter E. [cameraman/actor] (b. 1859–5 Jul 1918 [59?], New York NY; pneumonia). (FP-L [Neilan]). "Walter Stradling Dead," *Variety*, 12 Jul 1918. AMD, p. 329. AS, p. 1039. BHD2, p. 254. "Obituary," *MPW*, 20 Jul 1918, 384 (d. 6 Jul).

Strand, Paul [cinematographer/director/producer] (b. New York NY, 16 Oct 1890–31 Mar 1976 [85], Orgeval, France). AS, p. 1039. BHD2, p. 254.

Straner, John [actor] (b. 1846-Jul 1912 [66?], St. Louis MO). BHD, p. 310.

Strange, Robert [actor] (b. New York NY, 26 Nov 1881–22 Feb 1952 [70], Los Angeles CA). AS, p. 1039.

Strassberg, Morris [film/stage/TV actor] (b. 18 Apr 1897–8 Feb 1974 [76], South Laguna CA). m. (2 daughters). "Morris Strassberg; A Character Actor," *NYT*, 10 Feb 1974, 51:4 ("His hobby was modeling actors in clay, and his art has been acquired by the Jewish Museum and exhibited at the Jewish Scientific Institute."). "Morris Strassberg," *Variety*, 274, 13 Feb 1974, 95:3. AS, p. 1040. BHD1, p. 525. IFN, p. 284.

Stratton, Eugene [actor] (b. Buffalo NY, 8 May 1861–15 Sep 1918 [57], London, England). BHD, p. 310.

Stratton, Gene [actor] (b. 1915–16 Aug 1966 [51?], Los Angeles CA). BHD, p. 310.

Straub, Agnes [stage/film actress] (b. Munich, Germany, 2 Apr 1890–8 Jul 1941 [51], Berlin, Germany). Vittorio Martinelli, "Kino-Lieblinge," *Griffithiana*, 38/39 (Oct 1990), 34.

Straub, Mary E. [actress] (b. 1884–7 Nov 1951 [67?], Los Angeles CA). AS, p. 1040.

Straus, Clement [actor] (b. NY, 27 Sep 1886–8 Aug 1915 [28], Los Angeles CA; found dead). "Clement Straus," *Variety*, 20 Aug 1915, 7:4 ("was found dead in a bathroom at his home in Hollywood. Hemorrhages of the lungs were responsible."). AS, p. 1040. BHD, p. 310.

Straus, Oscar [composer] (b. Vienna, Austria, 6 Mar 1870–11 Jan 1954 [83], Vienna, Austria). AS, p. 1040. BHD2, p. 254.

Strauss, Clement [actor] (b. New York NY, 27 Sep 1886–18 Aug 1915 [29], Los Angeles CA). AS, p. 1040.

Strauss, Malcolm [producer/artist] (b. New York NY, 1878–10 Apr 1936 [58?], New York NY). AMD, p. 329. BHD2, p. 254. "Strauss to Produce Series of Comedies," *MPW*, 22 Mar 1919, 1695.

Strauss, Robert W. [actor] (b. 1885–10 Nov 1940 [55?], Cold Spring-on-the-Hudson NY; suicide by carbon monoxide gas). AS, p. 1040.

Strauss, William H. [actor] (b. New York NY, 13 Jun 1885–5 Aug 1943 [58], Los Angeles CA; heart attack). AS, p. 1040. BHD1, p. 525. IFN, p. 284. Truitt, p. 317.

Strawn, Eve [actress]. No data found. (Pallas.) *Motion Picture Magazine*, Sep 1916 (photo).

Strayer, Frank R. [actor/director] (b. Altoona PA, 7 Sep 1891–3 Feb 1964 [72], Los Angeles CA; cancer). (Columbia.) "Frank R. Strayer," *Variety*, 12 Feb 1964. AMD, p. 329. AS, p. 1040. BHD, p. 310; BHD2, p. 254. IFN, p. 284. Katz, p. 1102. "New Director Making Good," *MPW*, 28 Nov 1925, 335. "Strayer Loaned," *MPW*, 1 Jan 1927, 39.

Street, George A. [actor] (b. Montreal, Canada, 1868–30 May 1956 [88?], Weston-super-Mare, England). AS, p. 1040.

Street, Julian [actor] (b. Chicago IL, 1880–19 Feb 1947 [66?], Lakeville CT; cerebral hemorrhage). AS, p. 1040. BHD, p. 310.

Streeter, Coolidge [scenarist] (d. 30 Nov 1924, New York NY). BHD2, p. 254.

Streyckmans, Hector J. [publicist/writer/executive]. No data found. m. Della Musselman, 21 Mar 1913. AMD, p. 329. "The Internatioal Projecting and Producing Company," *MPW*, 20 Feb 1909, 197. "Has Streyckmans Resigned?," *MPW*, 31 Jul 1909, 155. "Brand New Job for Streyckmans," *MPW*, 14 Sep 1912, 1090. "Streyckmans—Musselman," *MPW*, 5 Apr 1913, 24. "Streyckmans

Resigns from Mutual," *MPW,* 16 Aug 1913, 748. "Streyckmans Out of Pasquali American Co.," *MPW,* 11 Oct 1913, 162. "Streyckmans with Pilot," *MPW,* 25 Oct 1913, 361. "Beulah Pointer with Hector FIlm Corp.," *MPW,* 4 Jul 1914, 80. "Streyckmans Out of Mirror," *MPW,* 20 May 1916, 1312. "Streyckmans a Broker," *MPW,* 7 Oct 1916,. 50 (left films to become a motor securities broker). "Streychmans, Recovered, with Artcraft," *MPW,* 20 Oct 1917, 393.

Stribolt, Oscar [actor] (b. Copenhagen, Denmark, 12 Feb 1873–27 May 1927 [54], Copenhagen, Denmark). AS, p. 1041.

Strickland, Edith [costumer] (b. 1883?–8 Oct 1918 [35], Chicago IL; influenza). "Edith Strickland," *Variety,* 11 Oct 1918. AS, p. 1041. BHD2, p. 254.

Strickland, Helen [stage/film actress] (b. Boston MA, 12 Sep 1863–11 Jan 1938 [75], New York NY). m. Robert Conness. "Helen Strickland, 60 Years on Stage; Taken Ill at Rehearsal, Dies on Opening Night of Her Show, 'Borrowed Time'; Had Appeared with Stars; With Francis Wilson, James K. Hackett, Ann Harding and Tallulah Bankhead," *NYT,* 15 Jan 1938, 15:4. "Helen Strickland," *Variety,* 19 Jan 1938. AS, p. 1041. BHD1, p. 525. IFN, p. 285.

Strickland, Hugh [actor] (b. 1885–2 May 1941 [56?], Los Angeles CA). BHD, p. 310.

Strickland, Mabel [actress] (b. 1897–3 Jan 1976 [78?]). AS, p. 1041. BHD, p. 310.

Strickling, Howard [press agent] (b. St. Mary's WV, 25 Aug 1899–14 Jul 1982 [82], Upland CA). BHD2, p. 254. Arthur H. Lewis, *It Was Fun While It Lasted* (NY: Trident Press, 1973), pp. 169–81.

Striker, Joseph [stage/film actor] (b. New York NY, 23 Dec 1898–24 Feb 1974 [75], Livingston NJ). m. Beatrice Smith. (MGM.) "Joseph Striker, Actor, 74, Played [John the Baptist] in 'King of Kings' [1927]," *NYT,* 27 Feb 1974, 42:2. "Joseph Striker," *Variety,* 6 Mar 1974. AMD, p. 329. AS, p. 1041. BHD1, p. 525. IFN, p. 285. "Joseph Striker Wins DeMille Long Contract," *MPW,* 23 Jul 1927, 260.

Stringer, Arthur John Arbuthnott [novelist/playwright/poet/scenarist] (b. Chatham, Ontario, Canada, 26 Feb 1874–14 Sep 1950 [76], Mountain Lakes NJ). m. (1) **Jobyna Howland**, 1900 (d. 1936); (2) Margaret, 1914 (his first cousin by whom he had 3 sons). (Hollywood, 1923.) "Arthur Stringer, Poet, Novelist, 76; Shakespearen Scholar Who Wrote for Stage and Films Dies at Home in Jersey," *NYT,* 15 Sep 1950, 25:3 (wrote 50 novels, 12 books of poetry, etc.). Stanley Kunitz and Howard Haycraft, *Twentieth Century Authors* (NY: H.W. Wilson, 1956), pp. 1361–62. Stanley Kunitz, *Twentieth Century Authorss: First Supplement* (NY: H.W. Wilson, 1959). p. 967. AMD, p. 329. AS, p. 1041. BHD2, p. 255. "Famous Authors with Universal," *MPW,* 5 Sep 1914, 1356.

Strippentow, Oscar [director] (b. Graudenz, Germany, 4 Apr 1877). AS, p. 1041.

Stromberg, Hunt [publicist/producer] (b. Louisville KY, 12 Jul 1894–23 Aug 1968 [74], Santa Monica CA; stroke). m. Katherine Kerwin (d. 1951). (MGM; UA.) "Hunt Stromberg, Filmmaker, Dead; Producer Was Among Big 4 [with Mayer, Thalberg and Rapf] of Early Days at M-G-M," *NYT,* 25 Aug 1968, 88:6. "Hunt Stromberg Dies at 74; Prolific Producer One of Metro's 'Big Four,'" *Variety,* 28 Aug 1968. AMD, p. 329. AS, p. 1041. BHD2, p. 255. IFN, p. 285. Katz, p. 1105. "Mrs. Hunt Stromberg," *NYT,* 16 Mar 1951, 31:2 (b. Arcadia MO–d. 15 Mar 1951 [57], LA CA). "New Director of Publicity at Ince," *MPW,* 17 Jan 1920, 397. "Hunt Stromberg Productions," *MPW,* 3 Nov 1923, 82. "Chadwick Gets Stromberg," *MPW,* 21 Jun 1924, 700. "Hunt Stromberg Joins Executive Staff Of the Metro-Goldwyn-Mayer Studios," *MPW,* 19 Sep 1925, 265.

Strong, Austin [scenarist] (b. 1881–17 Sep 1952 [71?], Nantucket MA). AS, p. 1041. BHD2, p. 255.

Strong, Eugene K. [actor/producer] (b. WI, 9 Aug 1893–25 Jun 1962 [68], Los Angeles CA). AMD, p. 329. AS, p. 1041. BHD1, p. 525; BHD2, p. 255. IFN, p. 285. "Eugene Strong," *MPW,* 29 Jul 1916, 772. "Eugene Strong," *MPW,* 21 Oct 1916, 399. "Strong to Support Lois Meredith," *MPW,* 21 Jul 1917, 482.

Strong, Fred [actor] (d. 1938). BHD, p. 310.

Strong, Jay [actor/assistant director] (b. Cleveland OH, 1896?–1 Dec 1953 [57], New York NY). "Jay Strong," *Variety,* 9 Dec 1953. AS, p. 1041. BHD, p. 310; BHD2, p. 255. IFN, p. 285. Truitt, p. 317.

Strong, Malcolm W. [scenarist] (b. NY, 1883–3 May 1916 [33?], Santa Monica CA: car accident). AMD, p. 329. BHD2, p. 255 (d. LA CA). "Obituary," *MPW,* 27 May 1916, 1515.

Strong, Nat [publicist] (d. 6 Feb 1919). BHD2, p. 255.

Strong, Porter [actor] (b. St. Joseph MO, 1879?–11 Jun 1923 [44], New York NY; of natural causes). (Griffith.) (Last film: *One Exciting Night.*) "Porter Strong, Actor, Found Dead," *NYT,* 12 Jun 1923, 19:2. "Porter Strong," *Variety,* 14 Jun 1923. AS, p. 1041. BHD, p. 310. IFN, p. 285.

Strong, Robert Glenn [cinematographer] (d. 25 Jul 1935, San Miguel Island CA). BHD2, p. 255.

Strongheart [dog] (b. Germany.) Trained by Larry Trimble. Laurence Trimble, "Strongheart," *Classic,* Jul 1923, 20, 82, 84. Charles F. Berry, "Is Your Dog a Second Strongheart?," *MW,* IV, 8 Mar 1924, 13, 30. Catherine Brady, "If You Are Curious to Know How They Make the Animals Do All Those Amazing Things Read 'FOUR-FOOTED STARS,'" *MW,* 11 OCT 1924, 3–4, 25 (discusses Strongheart, Rin-tin-tin, Rex, Jiggs, Peter the Great, Joe Martin [the orangoutang]).

Strongheart, Nipo [actor] (b. Yakima Reservation WA, 15 May 1891–30 Dec 1966 [75], Los Angeles CA). BHD1, p. 526. IFN, p. 285.

Struss, Karl [actor/cinematographer] (b. New York NY, 30 Nov 1886–16 Dec 1981 [95], Santa Monica CA). (Griffith; Paramount.) "Karl Struss, 95, Cinematographer; Film Pioneer Who Won Oscar for His Work on the 1925 Version of 'Ben Hur,'" *NYT,* 19 Dec 1981, 50:4. "Karl Struss," *Variety,* 23 Dec 1981. AMD, p. 329. AS, p. 1042. BHD2, p. 255. FDY, p. 469. Katz, p. 1106. "Karl Struss," *MPW,* 7 May 1927, 19.

Stryker, Gustave [actor] (b. Chicago IL, 1866?–3 Jun 1943 [77], New York NY). "Gustave Stryker; Actor, 77, Supported Richard Mansfield—Recently in Films," *NYT,* 4 Jun 1943, 21:3. "Gustave Stryker," *Variety,* 9 Jun 1943. AS, p. 1042. BHD, p. 310. IFN, p. 285.

Stuart, Aimee [scenarist] (b. Glasgow, Scotland, 1885–17 Apr 1981 [95?], Brighton, England). BHD2, p. 255.

Stuart, Charles (son of **J. Stuart Blackton**; brother of **Violet Stuart**) [actor]. No data found. AMD, p. 329. "Blackton Children Play French Refugees," *MPW,* 17 Aug 1918, 964.

Stuart, Donald [actor] (b. London, England, 2 Dec 1898–22 Feb 1944 [45], Los Angeles CA; heart attack). "Donald Stuart," *Variety,* 1 Mar 1944 (age 46; in Hollywood, 1925). AS, p. 1042. BHD1, p. 526. IFN, p. 285. Truitt, p. 317.

Stuart, Iris [actress: Wampas Star, 1927] (b. 2 Feb 1903–21 Dec 1936 [33], New York NY). AMD, p. 329. AS, p. 1042. BHD, p. 310. "Girl with the 'Perfect Hands' Gets Big Role," *MPW,* 29 Nov 1926, 284. Don Juan, "So This Is Hollywood," *Paris and Hollywood Screen Secrets Magazine,* May 1927, 31–32 (filming *Casey at the Bat*).

Stuart, Jean [actress] (*née* Margaret Elizabeth Leisenring, b. Vallejo CA, 13 Jul 1904–23 Nov 1926 [22], Los Angeles CA; from injuries sustained after a horse fell on her). "Jean Stuart," *Variety,* 1 Dec 1926. AMD, p. 329. AS, p. 1042. BHD, p. 310 (b. 1906). IFN, p. 285 (b. 1906). Truitt, p. 317. "Obituary," *MPW,* 4 Dec 1926, 346.

Stuart, John [actor] (*né* John Alfred Louden Croall, b. Edinburgh, Scotland, 18 Jul 1898–17 Oct 1979 [81], London, England; heart attack in his sleep). AS, p. 1042 (d. 18 Oct). BHD1, p. 526. IFN, p. 185.

Stuart, Julia [actress] (b. Edinburgh, Scotland). *Photoplay Arts Portfolio.* "Julia Stuart; Playing Character Leads with Eclair Company," *MPS,* 22 May 1914, 25.

Stuart, Leslie [composer] (*né* Thomas Augustine Barrett, b. Southport, Lancashire, England, 15 Mar 1862–27 Mar 1928 [66], Richmond, Surrey, England [age confirmed in the registration district of Richmond by Mrs. Janice Healey]). "Leslie Stuart, 64, Dies; Last Opera Unproduced," *Variety,* 28 Mar 1928. AS, p. 1042 (b. 1864). SD, p. 1184 (b. 1866).

Stuart, Leslie [actor] (d. 3 Apr 1977, Los Angeles Co. CA). BHD1, p. 526.

Stuart, Nick [actor] (*né* Niczulae Pratzu, b. Abrud, Romania, 10 Apr 1903–7 Apr 1973 [69], Biloxi MS; cancer). m. **Sue Carol**, Jul 1929 (d. 1982); Martha Burnett, 1942 (widow). (Fox; Columbia.) "Nick Stuart, 69, 30's Movie Star; Actor Who Played in College Stories Dies—Led Band [from 1936]," *NYT,* 8 Apr 1973, 81:3. "Nick Stuart," *Variety,* 11 Apr 1973. "Nick Stuart Taken by Death; Biloxi Clothier Actor During Thirties," *New Orleans Times Picayune,* 9 Apr 1973 (*né* Prada). AMD, p. 329. AS, p. 1042 (b. 1904). BHD1, p. 525. FSS, p. 265. IFN, p. 285. Katz, pp. 1106–07. "Nick Stuart," *MPW,* 20 Aug 1927, 516. Dorothy Wooldridge, "You Show 'Em, Nick; The Stuart Boy Answers the Maidens' Prayers for Someone Young and Lively," *MPC,* Mar 1928, 26, 88. Walter Ramsey, "Strange Interview; With Apologies to Eugene O'Neill and Nick Stuart," *MPC,* Jul 1929, 63, 97.

Stuart, Ralph, Sr. (father of **Ralph, Jr.**, Kenneth and Donald Stuart) [stage/film actor] (d. 12 Sep 1915, 200 Manhattan Avenue, New York NY; apoplexy). m. Edith Ramsey (d. 1915). "Death of Ralph Stuart," *NYDM,* 15 Sep 1915, 11:2.

Stuart, Ralph Ramsey, Jr. (son of **Ralph Stuart, Sr.**) [actor] (b. 1890?–4 Nov 1952 [62], New York NY). m. Doris Rich. "Ralph R. Stuart," *NYT,* 5 Nov 1952, 27:3. "Ralph R. Stuart," *Variety,* 12 Nov 1952. AMD, p. 329. AS, p. 1042. BHD, p. 310. IFN, p. 285. Truitt, p. 317. "Ralph Stuart a Picture Star," *MPW*, 4 Apr 1914, 72. "Ralph Stuart in Pictures," *MPW*, 15 May 1915, 1084.

Stuart, Simeon (b. 15 May 1864–1939 [75?]). BHD1, p. 526.

Stuart, Violet (daughter of **J. Stuart Blackton**; sister of **Charles Stuart**) [actress]. No data found. AMD, p. 329. "Blackton Children Play French Refugees," *MPW*, XXXVII, 17 Aug 1918, 964.

Stuart, William [James Clinton] [playwright] (b. 1853?–16 Feb 1937 [84], Washington DC). Bachelor. (First produced play: *A Woman of the Temple*, 1880's.) "William Stuart, Playwright, Dies; Successful Author of 1880's Succumbs in Obscurity in Washington," *NYT*, 18 Feb 1937, 21:5. "William Stuart," *Variety*, 24 Feb 1937.

Stubbs, Harry Oakes [actor/scenarist] (b. England, 7 Sep 1874–9 Mar 1950 [75], Woodland Hills CA; cancer and heart attack). AS, p. 1042. BHD1, p. 526; BHD2, p. 254. IFN, p. 285. "Rockefeller Aids Equity Players; John D. Jr. Becomes 'Founder' on Pledging to Give $1,000 Toward Permenant Theatre; Plans Told at Dinner; Organization Aims to Open Houses Also in Chicago and San Francisco," *NYT*, 28 Jan 1924, 17:3 (Macklyn Arbuckle was toastmaster; Stubbs was master of ceremonies).

Studiford, Grace [actress] (b. 1877–21 Oct 1947 [70?], Long Beach NY). BHD, p. 311.

Steuwe, Hans *see* **Stuwe, Hans**

Stull, Walt [actor]. No data found. AMD, p. 329. "Pokes and Jabs," *MPW*, 11 Sep 1915, 1811.

Stumar, Charles J. (brother of **John S. Stumar**) [cinematographer] (b. Budapest, Hungary, 1891?–29 Jun 1935 [44], near Triunfo CA; plane crash). (Lubin, 1908; Universal.) "Charles Stumar," *Variety*, 3 Jul 1935. AS, p. 1042. BHD2, p. 255. FDY, p. 469. IFN, p. 285.

Stumar, John S. (brother of **Charles J. Stumar**) [cinematographer] (b. Budapest, Hungary, 30 May 1892–27 Oct 1962 [70], Los Angeles Co. CA). BHD2, p. 255. FDY, p. 469.

Sturgeon, Rollin S. [director] (b. Rock Island IL, 25 Aug 1877–10 May 1961 [83], Santa Monica CA). m. Edna Levi (**Edna Foster**], 26 Sep 1912, LA CA (b. 1893]. (Vitagraph.) AMD, p. 330. AS, p. 1042. BHD2, p. 255. 1921 Directory, p. 275. "Miss Schaefer on Vacation," *MPW*, 14 Sep 1912, 1060. P.M. Powell, "Doings at Los Angeles," *MPW*, 12 Oct 1912, 130. "Sturgeon Leaves Vitagraph; Future Plans Not Announced...," *NYDM*, 25 Feb 1914, 33:1. "Rollin Sturgeon Joins Universal," *MPW*, 29 Mar 1919, 1774. "Sturgeon to Direct for Universal," *MPW*, 31 May 1919, 1318.

Sturges, Preston [actor/director/producer/scenarist/composer] (*né* Edwin Preston Biden, b. Chicago IL, 29 Aug 1898–6 Aug 1959 [60], New York NY [Death Certificate Index No. 17341]; heart attack). m. (1) Estelle Mudge; (2) Eleanor Hutton; (3) Louise S. Tevis. "Preston Sturges, Scenarist, 60, Dies; Winner of Academy Award Was Director and Producer—Also Had Stage Hits," *NYT*, 7 Aug 1959, 23:1; "Preston Sturges Rites; Service for Writer Heard by Friends in Entertainment," *NYT*, 9 Aug 1959, 88:5. Leonard L. Levinson, "Preston Sturges Dies at 60; Had Colorful Career," *Variety*, 12 Aug 1959. AS, p. 1042. BHD2, p. 255. IFN, p. 285.

Sturgis, Edwin [actor/director] (*né* Josef Edwin Sturgis, b. Washington DC, 22 Oct 1881–13 Dec 1947 [66], Los Angeles CA; heart attack). AS, p. 1042. BHD1, p. 526; BHD2, p. 255 (Joseph E. Sturgis). IFN, p. 285.

Sturz, Louis [actor] (b. 1885–13 Feb 1958 [72?], FL). BHD, p. 311.

Stuwe, Hans Karl [actor] (b. Marnitz/Meckl, Germany, 14 May 1901–13 May 1976 [74], Berlin, Germany). AS, p. 1043 (b. Halle, Germany). BHD1, p. 526 (Hans Stuewe). IFN, p. 285.

Styan, Arthur [actor] (d. Jan 1926, Melbourne, Australia). BHD, p. 311.

Styers, Amma [actress]. No data found. AMD, p. 330. "Beauties Added," *MPW*, 24 Oct 1925, 644. "Amma Styers," *MPW*, 25 Dec 1926, 573.

Styles, Edwin [actor] (b. London, England, 13 Jan 1899–20 Dec 1960 [61], London, England). AS, p. 1043.

Subject, Evelyn [stage/film actress] (b. Chicago IL–d. 22 Apr 1975, Temple City CA). (Essanay, Chicago IL; Vitagraph.) "Evelyn Subject," *Variety*, 278, 30 Apr 1975, 71:3 ("Surviving is a nephew, Harold A. Powell, who said that the name 'Subject' was a shortened version of a Czech family name."). AS, p. 1043. BHD, p. 311. IFN, p. 285.

Suffell, Madeleine Blanche [actress] (b. Paris, France, 26 Nov 1899–11 Apr 1974 [74], Paris, France [extrait de décès no. 411/1974]). AS, p. 1043.

Suffield, Donald [inventor] (b. England, 1891–27 Jul 1991 [100?], Nelson, New Zealand). AS, p. 1043.

Sulky, Leo [actor] (*né* Leo Bernstein, b. Cincinnati OH, 6 Dec 1874–3 Jun 1957 [82], Los Angeles Co. CA). AS, p. 1044. BHD1, p. 527. IFN, p. 285.

Sullivan, Anne [actress] (b. Feeding Hills MA, 11 Apr 1866–20 Oct 1936 [70], New York [Queens] NY). BHD, p. 311.

Sullivan, Billy *see* **Sullivan, William A. (Billy)**

Sullivan, C. Gardner [actor/title writer/scenarist] (b. Stillwater MN, 18 Sep 1884–5 Sep 1965 [80], Los Angeles CA; heart attack in his sleep). m. **Ann May** (d. 1985). (Ince.) "C. Gardner Sullivan," *Variety*, 8 Sep 1965. AMD, p. 330. AS, p. 1044 (b. 1879). BHD2, p. 256 (d. 4 Sep). FDY, pp. 437, 447. IFN, p. 285. Katz, p. 1109 (b. 1879). "Sullivan to Novelize 'Civilization,'" *MPW*, 8 Jul 1916, 230. "C. Gardner Sullivan Returns to Culver City," *MPW*, 13 Jan 1917, 219. "C. Gardner Sullivan Writes Comedy Success," *MPW*, 12 May 1917, 950. "Sullivan Writes for Hart," *MPW*, 9 Mar 1918, 1392. William J. Reilly, "We Have with Us To-Day," *MPW*, 10 Apr 1920, 235. "C. Gardner Sullivan, Screen Author, Elected Associated Producers Member," *MPW*, 27 Nov 1920, 455. "Sullivan Again with Ince," *MPW*, 10 Sep 1921, 169. "To Supervise Pictures," *MPW*, 15 Mar 1924, 188. "Sullivan to Write Four," *MPW*, 26 Jul 1924, 287. "An Independent Producer," *MPW*, 27 Sep 1924, 314. "DeMille Signs Sullivan," *MPW*, 30 Jan 1926, 441.

Sullivan, Charles B. [actor] (b. LA, 24 Apr 1899–25 Jun 1972 [73], Los Angeles Co. CA). AS, p. 1044. BHD1, p. 527. IFN, p. 285.

Sullivan, Charles E. [executive] (b. Quincy MA, 2 Mar 1890–22 Oct 1943 [53], Quincy MA). BHD2, p. 256.

Sullivan, Daniel J. [actor] (b. 1874–23 Feb 1937 [62?], New York NY). BHD, p. 311.

Sullivan, Denis J. [executive]. No data found. AMD, p. 330. "Sullivan Retires from Mutual," *MPW*, 27 Jul 1918, 560.

Sullivan, Edward [actor] (b. New York NY, 1834?–8 Dec 1919 [85], New York NY). "Edward Sullivan," *Variety*, 19 Dec 1919. AS, p. 1044.

Sullivan, Edward Dean [scenarist] (b. 1889–4 Apr 1938 [49?], Los Angeles CA). BHD2, p. 256.

Sullivan, Edward P. [stage/film actor] (d. 15 Dec 1940, Tampa FL; auto accident). "Edward P. Sullivan," *Variety*, 25 Dec 1940 (no mention of films). AMD, p. 330. AS, p. 1044. "E.P. Sullivan in Kalem Feature," *MPW*, 16 Oct 1915, 452. "Kalem's 'Black Crook'; Feature Will Tell Complete Story of Famous Offering for First Time, Says Star," *NYDM*, 6 Nov 1915, 26:3.

Sullivan, Frederick R. [actor] (b. London, England, 18 Jul 1872–24 Jul 1937 [65], Los Angeles CA; heart attack). AMD, p. 330. AS, p. 1044. BHD1, p. 527; BHD2, p. 256. IFN, p. 286. Truitt, p. 318. "Frederic R. Sullivan Joins Reliance," *MPW*, 15 Mar 1913, 1093. "Thanhouser's Triple Coup," *MPW*, 17 Apr 1915, 374. "Frederic Sullivan Signs to Direct for Christie," *MPW*, 27 Dec 1919, 1173. "A Director of Big Productions: Frederic Sullivan," *MPW*, 22 Sep 1923, 345.

Sullivan, Helene [actress]. No data found. AMD, p. 330. "Complete Roster Announced for Cecil B. DeMille Studio," *MPW*, 25 Apr 1925, 814.

Sullivan, James E., "The Polite Lunatic" [actor] (b. 1864?–1 Jun 1931 [67?], Los Angeles CA). "James E. Sullivan," *Variety*, 3 Jun 1931. AS, p. 1044. BHD, p. 311. SD, p. 1187 (d. NY NY). Truitt, p. 318.

Sullivan, John Maurice [actor] (b. Washington DC, 24 Sep 1875–8 Mar 1949 [73], Los Angeles CA; heart attack). AS, p. 1044. BHD, p. 311; BHD2, p. 256. IFN, p. 286.

Sullivan, Lillian [actress]. No data found. AMD, p. 330. "Lillian Sullivan," *MPW*, 10 Feb 1917, 859.

Sullivan, Margaret C. [actress]. No data found. AMD, p. 330. "Margaret Sullivan with Cosmopolitan," *MPW*, 23 Jun 1923, 680.

Sullivan, Maurice [scenarist] (b. 1894–31 Jan 1935 [40?], Loma Linda CA). BHD2, p. 256.

Sullivan, Pat[rick] [animator; created Felix the Cat] (b. Sydney, New South Wales, Australia, 1887–15 Feb 1933 [45], New York NY; pneumonia). "Pat Sullivan," *Variety*, 21 Feb 1933. AMD, p. 330. AS, p. 1045. BHD2, p. 256. Katz, p. 1109. "Pat Sullivan in Cartoon Field," *MPW*, 22 Jan 1916, 583. "Pat Sullivan's Cartoons Score," *MPW*, 29 Apr 1916, 813. "Cartoonist Pat Sullivan Signs Contract with Famous Players," *MPW*, 20 Mar 1920, 1927. "Pat Sullivan on Advisory Board," *MPW*, 17 Jul 1926, 168.

Sullivan, Ruth [actress]. No data found. m. **Dick Curtis** (d. 1952).

Sullivan, William A. (Billy) (grandnephew of John L. Sullivan) [actor] (aka Arthur Sullivan, b. Worcester MA, 1890–23 May 1946 [55], Great Neck, LI NY). m. Edith. (Pathé.) (Film debut: *Perils of Pauline*, 1914; Astra Film Corp.; Universal; Rayart; Sterling Pictures; Pathé; Cameo; last film, *Big Brown Eyes*, Paramount, 1936.) "William A. Sullivan; Former Film Actor, Director, Script Writer Dies at 55," *NYT*, 25 May 1946, 15:4. AMD, p. 330. AS, p. 1044. BHD1, p.527. IFN, p. 285. "Billy Sullivan to Star in New

'Leather Pushers' for Universal," *MPW,* 22 Sep 1923, 363. Ed Wyatt, "Billy Sullivan: The Mystery Cowboy," *CI,* 277 (Jul 1998), C8-C9 (nephew of Sullivan; includes filmography).

Sul-Te-Wan, Madame (grandmother of Dorothy Dandridge) [actress] (*née* Nellie Conley, b. Louisville KY, 7 Mar 1873–1 Feb 1959 [85], Woodland Hills CA). (Griffith.) AS, p. 1044; p. 1128 (Wan, Sul Te [Mrs.], b. 12 Sep). BHD, p. 316. IFN, p. 285. KOM, p. 159. Truitt, p. 341.

Sulzer, William [actor] (b. NJ, 18 Mar 1883–6 Nov 1941 [58], New York NY). BHD, p. 311. *NYT,* 21 Nov 1913, 9:4 (film debut).

Summers, Edna Lee [extra] (b. Little Rock AL, 12 Dec 1895–1 Nov 1989 [93], San Diego CA). *Fl.* late teens and early 20's. m. Norman Polkinhorn. (Goldwyn; appeared in Lloyd's *Get Out and Get Under* as a bridesmaid.) AS, p. 1045. BHD, p. 311.

Summers, Leonora [vaudeville/stage/film actress] (*née* Lillian Hill, b. 12 Dec 1897–29 Jun 1976 [78], Woodland Hills CA). m. juggler Jack Hanley; boxer Mushy Callahan. (Sennett.) "Lillian Hill Le Callahan," *Variety,* 283, 7 Jul 1976, 124:3. AS, p. 1045. BHD, p. 311. IFN, p. 286.

Summers, Walter [actor/director/scenarist] (b. Barnstaple, England, 2 Sep 1896–1973 [77?]). AS, p. 1045. BHD2, p. 256.

Summerville, Amelia [stage/film actress] (*née* Amelia M. Shaw, b. County Kildare, Ireland, 15 Oct 1862–21 Jan 1934 [71], New York NY). m. Frederick Rummels; (2) Max E. Stepan. (Select.) "Miss Summerville, Comedienne, Dead; Succumbs at 71 to Effects of Recent Fall [on 3 Jan]—Began Stage Career at 7 in Operetta; Dancer in 'Black Crook'; Starred in 'Adonis' with Dixey—Played in Movies and Was Voice Coach for Talkies," *NYT,* 22 Jan 1934, 15:3 ("despite her 250 pounds, she was pretty and winsome"; she later lost 150 lbs.). "Amelia Summerville," *Variety,* 23 Jan 1934 (age 70). AS, p. 1045. BHD, p. 311. IFN, p. 286.

Summerville, Slim [actor: Keystone Cop/director/scenarist] (*né* George J. Summerville, b. Albuquerque NM, 10 Jul 1892–5 Jan 1946 [53], Laguna Beach CA; stroke). m. (1) Gertrude M. Roell; (2) Eleanor Brown. (Sennett, 1913; Fox; FBO; Universal.) "Slim Summerville, Movie Actor, Dead; An Original Keystone Cop, 50, Tall Comedian Won Fame in 'All Quiet on Western Front,'" *NYT,* 7 Jan 1946, 19:1. "Slim Summerville," *Variety,* 16 Jan 1946 (age 50). AS, p. 1045. BHD1, p. 528; BHD2, p. 256. FDY, p. 437. FSS, p. 266. GK, pp. 536–64. IFN, p. 286. Katz, pp. 1109–10. Richard E. Braff, "The Films of Slim Summerville," *CI,* 160 (Oct 1988), 34, 36–38. R.E. Braff, "Additional Film Credits for Slim Summerville," *CI,* 238 (Apr 1995), 42.

Sumner, Frederick [vaudeville/legitimate/film actor] (b. 1875?–11 Jan 1942 [66], New York NY). m. stage actress Maydel Turner. "Fred Sumner," *Variety,* 145, 21 Jan 1942, 54:2. BHD1, p. 528.

Sumner, Verlyn [actress] (b. Lakefield MN, 7 Jun 1897–10 Feb 1935 [37], Bremerton WA). AS, p. 1045 (d. 10 Apr). BHD, p. 311.

Sun, Todd [actor] (b. 14 Apr 1887–14 May 1950 [63], Los Angeles CA). AS, p. 1045.

Sun, Uta [actress] (b. Indianapolis IN, 11 Nov 1845–3 Mar 1901 [55], Los Angeles CA). AS, p. 1045.

Sunada, Komako [actress]. No data found. AMD, p. 330. "Japanese Star Here," *MPW,* 21 May 1927, 175.

Sunderland, John [actor]. No data found. m. **Claire Whitney**, Dec 1917 (d. 1969). (Clara Kimball Young.) "Marriages," *Variety,* 21 Dec 1917, p. 9 ("Sunderland is a flight officer in the English aviation corps..."). AMD, p. 330. "'Shirley Kaye' Lovers Are Married," *MPW,* 5 Jan 1918, 58. "Sunderland a War Veteran," *MPW,* 9 Nov 1918, 682.

Sunshine, Baby [child actress] (*née* Pauline Flood, b. CA, 1 Dec 1915–19 Oct 1917 [1], Los Angeles CA). BHD, p. 311.

Sunshine, Marion [actress/songwriter] (*nee?,* Mary Tunstall Ijames, b. Louisville KY, 15 May 1894–25 Jan 1963 [68], New York NY [Death Certificate Index No. 2225 (Mary Azpiazu)]). m. Eusebio S. Azpiazu (aka Mario Antobal). (Biograph, 1908.) "Marion Sunshine," *Variety,* 30 Jan 1963 (composed under name of Mary Tunstall Ijames; age 66). AMD, p. 330. AS, p. 1046. ASCAP 66, p. 719. BHD1, p. 528. Katz, p. 1110. Truitt, p. 318. "Sunshine and Tempest," *MPW,* 25 Sep 1915, 2184.

Supplee, Cuyler C. [actor] (b. Germantown PA, 13 Feb 1894–3 May 1944 [50], Los Angeles CA). m. **Esther Ritter** (d. 1925). AS, p. 1046. BHD1, p. 528. IFN, p. 286. George A. Katchmer, "Forgotten Cowboys and Cowgirls—Part XIII," *CI,* 190 (Apr 1991), C6.

Suratt, Valeska [actress] (b. Terre Haute IN, 28 Jun 1882–2 Jul 1962 80], Washington DC). (Film debut: *The Immigrant,* Paramount, 1915.) AMD, p. 330. AS, p. 1046 (d. LA CA). BHD, p. 311. IFN, p. 286 (d. 1962). Spehr, p. 168. "Valeska Suratt Signed; Lasky Company to Present Star in a Series of Modern Plays," *NYDM,* Nov 1914, 25:1 (Lasky gained her services until 30 Nov 1916. One of the "highest-salaried stars secured for the screen," Suratt had it written into her conntract that she select her own wardrobe and supporting players). "Lasky Secures Valeska Suratt," *MPW,* 21 Nov 1914, 1092. "Gives Week's Salary to Red Cross," *MPW,* 21 Jul 1917, 438. "Suratt Action Stirs DeMille; $1,000,000 Suit Names Many," *MPW,* 17 Sep 1927, 168.

Susini, Enrique T. [director] (b. Buenos Aires, Argentina, 31 Jan 1891–4 Jul 1972 [81], Buenos Aires, Argentina). BHD2, p. 256.

Sutch, Herbert [actor] (b. London, England, 29 Jun 1884–22 Jan 1939 [54], London, England). AS, p. 1046. BHD1, p. 528. IFN, p. 286.

Sutherland, A[lbert] **Edward** [actor/director/producer] (nephew of **Charlotte Greenwood** and **Thomas Meighan**) (b. London, England, 5 Jan 1895–31 Dec 1973 [77], Palm Springs CA; cancer). m. (1) **Marjorie Daw**, 1921—div. 1925 (d. 1979); (2) **Louise Brooks**, 1926–28 (d. 1985); (3) Edwina. (Keystone; Paramount.) "Albert E. Sutherland, 76, Director of Silent Films," *NYT,* 5 Jan 1974, 30:6 (d. 4 Jun 1974 [76]). "A. Edward Sutherland," *Variety,* 2 Jan 1974 (d. 1 Jan 1974. AMD, p. 330. AS, p. 1046. BHD1, p. 529 (b. 1897); BHD2, p. 256. IFN, p. 286 (b. 1897). Katz, p. 1111. "Sutherland Gets Contract," *MPW,* 30 May 1925, 576. June Lee, "Dan Cupid's Bulletin Board," *Paris and Hollywood,* Oct 1926, 31–32 (married Brooks). "Sutherland to Build Another Comedy Team," *MPW,* 29 Jan 1927, 348.

Sutherland, Anne [stage/film actress] (b. Washington DC, 1 Mar 1867–22 Jun 1942 [75], Brentwood, LI NY). m. Charles Harding. (Stage debut: 1881, Chicago IL.) "Anne Sutherland, Actress, Dies at 75; Veteran Trouper, on Stage Nearly 60 Years, Began Career in 'Pinafore'; Played in 'Craig's Wife'; She Toured with Jefferson in 'Rip Van Winkle' and Had Supported Mrs. Carter," *NYT,* 24 Jun 1942, 19:1. "Anne Sutherland," *Variety,* 24 Jun 1942. AS, p. 1046. BHD1, p. 529. IFN, p. 286.

Sutherland, Anthony [director] (b. 5 Feb 1877–17 Aug 1945 [68], Los Angeles CA). AS, p. 1046.

Sutherland, Delos [title writer]. No data found. FDY, p. 447.

Sutherland, Dick [actor] (*né* Archie Thomas Johnson, b. Benton KY, 23 Dec 1881–3 Feb 1934 [52], Los Angeles CA; kidney illness). m. Verba Hutchinson (3 sons, Harry, Everett, and Lester). "Dick Sutherland," *Variety,* 13 Feb 1934. AMD, p. 330. AS, p. 1046. BHD1, p. 529. IFN, p. 286. Truitt, p. 318. Dorothy Donnell, "Getting in by the Back Door," *MPS,* 26 Aug 1924, 20–21, 31 "Dick Sutherland used to drive a brewery truck about the streets of Los Angeles. His tremendous hands won him a place on the screen when one of his customers happened to be a director."). "Strong Cast," *MPW,* 7 Nov 1925, 46. George Katchmer, "Remembering the Silents," *CI,* 215 (May 1993), 48–49. Greg Travis, "Dick Sutherland; Tough Looks Catapulted Him to Silent Screen Stardom," *The Tribune Courier* [Benton KY], 13 Apr 1994, p. 9A.

Sutherland, E. Loew [title writer]. No data found. FDY, p. 447.

Sutherland, Edward *see* **Sutherland, Albert Edward**

Sutherland, John [actor] (b. Scotland, 1845?–31 Aug 1921 [76], So. Brooklyn NY; apoplexy). m. Laura Alberts. "John Sutherland, Actor," *NYT,* 2 Sep 1921, 13:3. "John Sutherland," *Variety,* 9 Sep 1921. AS, p. 1046. BHD, p. 311.

Sutherland, Pat [title writer]. No data found. FDY, p. 447.

Sutherland, Victor [stage/film actor] (b. Paducah KY, 28 Feb 1889–29 Aug 1968 [79], Los Angeles CA). m. **Pearl White**, 1907–14 (d. 1938); Linda Barrett. (Victor; Fox; Rex Beach; Edgar Lewis Prods.) "Victor Sutherland," *Variety,* 11 Sep 1968. AMD, p. 330. AS, p. 1047. BHD1, p. 529. IFN, p. 286. MSBB, p. 1028. Truitt, p. 318. "Sutherland Supporting Virginia Pearson," *MPW,* 20 Apr 1918, 378.

Sutton, Bradley [actor] (b. 1863?–19 Aug 1932 [69], Richmond, SI NY; nephritis). "Brad Sutton," *Variety,* 23 Aug 1932. AS, p. 1047. BHD, p. 312.

Sutton, Charles [actor] (b. 1856?–20 Jul 1935 [79], Englewood NJ). "Charles Sutton," *Variety,* 24 Jul 1935. AMD, p. 330. AS, p. 1047. BHD, p. 312. "Charles Sutton," *MPW,* 30 Oct 1915, 970.

Sutton, Grady Harwell [film/TV actor] (b. Chattanooga TN, 5 Apr 1906?–17 Sep 1995 [89], Woodland Hills CA; natural causes). (Extra work; early film: *The Freshman,* 1924; last film: *Rock 'n' Roll High School,* 1979.) "Grady Sutton, 89, a Comic Foil to Fields, Hepburn and Lombard," *NYT,* 28 Sep 1995, D22:1. "Grady Harwell Sutton," *Variety,* 2 Oct 1995, 200:2. "Grady Sutton; Supporting Actor in Films, Foil for W.C. Fields," *Pittsburgh Post-Gazette,* 29 Sep 1995, D6:3. AS, p. 1047 (b. 1908). BHD1, p. 529. Katz, p. 111 (b. 1908).

Sutton, Susie [actress] (d. 2 Feb 1956, New York NY). BHD, p. 312.

Sutton, William, "The Great Fontonelle" [actor] (b. 1877?–10 Sep 1955 [78], West Los Angeles CA). AS, p. 1047. BHD, p. 312. IFN, p. 286. Truitt, p. 319.

Svab-Malostransky, Josef [actor] (b. Prague, Czechoslovakia, 16 Mar 1860–30 Apr 1932 [72], Prague, Czechoslovakia). AS, p. 1047.

Svetozarov, Boris Fedeodorovich [director/scenarist] (b. Russia, 22 Mar 1892–22 Jul 1968 [76], Russia). AS, p. 1047.

Swain, Mack M. [actor: Keystone Cop] (b. Salt Lake City UT, 16 Feb 1876–25 Aug 1935 [59], Tacoma WA; heart attack). (Keystone, 1913; L-KO.) "Mack Swain," *Variety,* 28 Aug 1935. AMD, p. 331. AS, p. 1047. BHD1, p. 529. FSS, p. 266. IFN, p. 286. Katz, p. 1112. Truitt, p. 319 (b. 16 Feb 1876). "Mack Swain," *MPW,* 10 Feb 1917, 847. "Mack Swain Joins Billy West," *MPW,* 22 Mar 1919, 1640. "Sherrill Signs Mack Swain for a Series of Comedies," *MPW,* 29 Mar 1919, 1798. "Mack Swain Has Finished First Two Poppy Comedies," *MPW,* 10 May 1919, 890. "Mrs. Swain Dies," *MPW,* 10 Dec 1921, 685 (mother, Mrs. Mary Swain, d. Salt Lake City UT, aged 82, survived by four sons). "Mack Swain Must Stay Fat," *MPW,* 23 Oct 1926, 486. Sam Gill, "The Funny Men: Mack Swain," *8mm Collector,* 13 (Fall/Winter, 1965), 32–33. Herb Gordon, "The Original Big Mack," *CFC,* 60 (Fall, 1978), 30, 63 (b. 1875).

Swallow, Ernest [actor] (b. SD, 24 Dec 1886–13 Dec 1967 [80], Los Angeles Co. CA). BHD, p. 312.

Swan, Billy [circus/vaudeville performer: Swan & Branford] (b. 1869?–16 Oct 1944 [75], New York NY). "Bill Swan," *Variety,* 1 Nov 1944.

Swan, Mark [scenarist]. No data found. AMD, p. 331. "More Lubin Enterprise," *MPW,* 9 Oct 1915, 236.

Swan, Paul, "The Most Beautiful Man in the World" [actor] (b. Ashland IL, 6 Jun 1883–1 Feb 1972 [88], Bedford Hills NY). m. Helen Gavit. "Paul Swan, Artist-Dancer, Dies; Also Had Career in the Movies," *NYT,* 2 Feb 1972, 42:4. "Paul Swan," *Variety,* 9 Feb 1972. AMD, p. 331. AS, p. 1047. BHD1, p. 529. IFN, p. 286. "Goldwyn Engages Paul Swan," *MPW,* 22 Nov 1919, 437.

Swanson, Gloria [film/stage/TV actress] (*née* Gloria May Swenson, b. Chicago IL, 27 Mar 1899–4 Apr 1983 [84], New York NY [Death Certificate Index No. 5651, age 84]; complications during open-heart surgery). (b. CA, 27 Mar 1899; d. Birmingham, Oakland MI 48010). *Swanson on Swanson* (NY: Random House, 1980). m. 6 times: (1) **Wallace Beery**, 1913–19 (d. 1949); (2) **Herbert K. Somborn**, 20 Dec 1919, Alexandria Hotel, LA CA (d. 1934); (3) **Marquis Jacques Henri de Falaise de la Coudray** (d. 1972); (4) F. Michael Farmer; (5) William N. Davey. (Essanay, 1913; Keystone; Paramount.) Peter B. Flint, "Gloria Swanson Dies; 20's Film Idol," *NYT,* 5 Apr 1983, D27:1 (b. 17 Mar). "Gloria Swanson, 84, Star of Motion Pictures, Dies in N.Y.," *Variety,* 6 Apr 1983 (b. 1898, but age as 84). AMD, p. 331. AS, p. 1047. BHD1, p. 529. FFF, p. 77 (b. 1898). FSFW, p. 308 (b. 1898). FSS, p. 267. HCH, p. 61. JS, p. 443 (*Mio figlio Nerone,* Italy, 1956). Katz, pp. 1112–13 (b. 1897). MH, p. 138. MSBB, p. 1042 (age 19). Harry C. Carr, "An Interview in Great Danish," *Photoplay,* Jul 1917, 29 (photos with Swanson from *Teddy at the Throttle*). "Gloria Swanson Back on Keystone Lot," *MPW,* 2 Feb 1918, 678. Edward Weitzel, "Gloria Swanson's Greatest Thrill Came to Her in 'Male and Female,'" *MPW,* 13 Dec 1919, 827. "Somborn—Swanson," *MPW,* 10 Jan 1920, 233. "Gloria Swanson Continues with Famous; DeMille to Further Develop Her Gifts," *MPW,* 12 Jun 1920, 1442. "Gloria Swanson Somborn," *MPW,* 23 Oct 1920, 1129 (b. 7 Oct 1920, LA CA). "Gloria Swanson Made a Paramount Star; Exhibitors Highly Appreciate Her Work," *MPW,* 19 Feb 1921, 960. "Two Stars Ill," *MPW,* 6 Aug 1921, 591. "Gloria Swanson Coming to New York," *MPW,* 13 Aug 1921, 712. "Is Gloria Swanson the Victim of a Plot?," *MW,* 7 Jan 1922, 3, 30. Maude Cheatham, "The Darkest Hour," *Classic,* Oct 1922, 52. Regina Cannon, "Why I Want My Daughter to Do as She Pleases," *MW,* 16 Jun 1923, 7. Jeffery Carter, "At Lunch with Gloria," *Classic,* Jun 1923, 32–34, 75. J.M. Jerauld, "How Gloria Swanson Became a Salesgirl for a Day [for *Manhandled*]," *MW,* 10 May 1924, 5, 30. Carolyn Carter, "The Most Misunderstood Woman on the Screen," *MW,* 17 May 1924, 3–4. T. Howard Kelly, "Who Is Mysteriously Circulating the Report of Gloria Swanson's Death?," *MW,* 31 May 1924, 4–5. "The Discovery of Gloria," *Photoplay Magazine,* May 1924, 113 (quip). "Gloria Swanson Buys; Will Occupy Forty-Acre Estate [a colonial farmhouse] at Croton [-on-the-Hudson NY] as Summer Home," *NYT,* 8 Jun 1924, 23:4. "Gloria Swanson Will Produce 'Madame Sans-Gene' in Paris," *MPW,* 2 Aug 1924, 361. "Gloria Off to France," *MPW,* 20 Sep 1924, 212. "Belgians Honor Swanson," *MPW,* 22 Nov 1924, 310. Lois Wilson, "The Gloria Swanson I Know," *MW,* 28 Feb 1925, 8–9, 31. "Gloria Swanson Recovering," *MPW,* 7 Mar 1925, 38. "Gloria Swanson," *MPW,* 11 Apr 1925, 598. "Gloria and the Marquis; As They Appeared to Fellow Voyagers on the *S.S. Paris,*" by Julanne Johnston (Who Was One of Them), *MW,* 25 Apr 1925, 6–7, 34. Clement Douglas, "Gloria Swanson, America's Own Marquise," *MPC,* May 1925, 49–52, 82, 94. "Brilliant Gathering at Dinner Given Gloria Swanson," *MPW,* 2 May 1925, 32. "On the Set and Off," *MW,* 6 Jun 1925, 36 (Swanson adopted a boy). Anne Jordan, "Gloria Plans Her Future," *MM,* Oct 1925, 40–42, 84–86. Mrs. F. Vance de Revere, "How Will Gloria's Marriage End?," *MPC,* Nov 1925, 25, 84–85. Carol White, "Just the Victim of Publicity," *MPC,* Feb 1926, 52–53, 70 ("...the price of fame is just one lawsuit after another."). "Gloria Now with United Artists," *MPW,* 15 May 1926, 3. Gloria Swanson, "What My Experiences Have Taught Me; The Star Talks Frankly of Her Marriages, Her Career and the Criticism of Newspapers," *MPC,* Jul 1926, 18–19, 85–87. "Gloria Swanson's First for United Artists," *MPW,* 24 Jul 1926, 4. Nanette Kutner, "Knowing Gloria When...She Was Merely a Simple Little Extra Girl, Minus Fancy, Elaborate Clothes, and Who Always Seemed Just a Bit Slower Than the Rest of the Girls," *Pictures,* Sep 1926, 49, 99–101 (related by Ruth Stonehouse). Dunham Thorp, "Gloria Sings the Battle-Cry of Freedom; The Swanson Lady Becomes Philosopher and Argues for Realities and New Ideas," *MPC,* Jan 1927, 25–26, 74. "Gloria Swanson," *MPW,* 29 Jan 1927, 351. "Swanson Co. Renamed," *MPW,* 5 Mar 1927, 10. "Gloria Swanson," *MPW,* 4 Jun 1927, 332. Gordon R. Silver, "My Contract Won't Let Me," *MPC,* Sep 1927, 63, 91 (and discusses other stars). Don Juan, "So This Is Hollywood," *Paris and Hollywood Screen Secrets,* Oct 1927, 58–59 (dining at the Crillon Hotel in NYC, Swanson and de la Coudray dined next to Adolph Zukor. "This was the first time Gloria and Adolph had been in close proximity since the star had piqued her erstwhile employer by turning down his offer of $25,000 per week for three years in favor of an arrangement with the Joe Schenck organization." Zukor tried to ignore her.). "Gloria Sells Seals," *MPW,* 24 Dec 1927, 12. Gladys Hall, "Will Gloria Swanson Marry Again?; If she does, it will be the fourth time...," *Movie Classic,* Nov 1931, 50, 76. Herb Gordon, "Speaking of Silents," *CI,* 95 (May 1983), 19, 50. Stuart Oderman, "Swanson; That Fabulous Face," *CI,* 96 (Jun 1983), 22–23. John McGee, "Swanson; Big as a Minute, But Larger than Life," *CI,* 96 (Jun 1983), 34.

Swanson, William H. [producer]. No data found. AMD, p. 331. "P.A. Powers Resigns from Universal," *MPW,* 22 Feb 1913, 793. "Obituary," *MPW,* 1 Jul 1922, 14.

Swanstrom, Arthur [composer] (b. 1888–4 Oct 1940 [52?], Scarsdale NY). BHD2, p. 256.

Swanstrom, Karin [actress/director/producer] (b. Norrkoping, Sweden, 13 Jun 1873–5 Jul 1942 [69], Stockholm, Sweden). AS, p. 1047. BHD1, p. 529. IFN, p. 286.

Swarts, Sara [actress] (b. 1899?–30 Mar 1949 [50], Woodland Hills CA). (Universal.) "Sara Swarts," *Variety,* 6 Apr 1949 ("in pictures for 31 years"). AS, p. 1048 (Swartz. d. 31 Mar). BHD1, p. 529. IFN, p. 287 (Swartz). Truitt, p. 319 (Swarts).

Swayne, Marion [actress] (b. Philadelphia PA). (Solax; Blaché-American.) AMD, p. 331. Spehr, p. 168. "Solax Enlarging Studios," *MPW,* 4 Nov 1911, 386. "Marian Swayne," *MPW,* 16 Dec 1911, 893. "Marian Swayne in Stock," *MPW,* 18 May 1912, 638. "Marian Swayne Sold Programs," *MPW,* 10 May 1913, 602. "Marian Swayne Joins United Film," *MPW,* 30 Jan 1915, 654. "Marian Swayne Joins Arrow Company," *MPW,* 16 Sep 1916, 1812. "Marian Swayne," *MPW,* 30 Sep 1916, 2085.

Sweatnam, Willis P. [stage/film actor] (b. Zanesville OH, 1854?–25 Nov 1930 [76], New York NY, at Lamb's Club). "Willis P. Sweatnam," *Variety,* 3 Dec 1930. AS, p. 1048. BHD, p. 312. IFN, p. 287.

Sweeney, Daniel J[immy] [minstrel man] (d. Aug? 1929, Boston MA). "Daniel J. Sweeney," *Variety,* 21 Aug 1929.

Sweeney, Jack [actor] (b. 1889?–12 Apr 1950 [61?], Los Angeles CA). AS, p. 1048. BHD, p. 312. IFN, p. 287. Truitt, p. 319.

Sweeney, James R. [film editor] (b. 1902?–11 Mar 1957 [55], Los Angeles CA; heart attack). "James R. Sweeney," *Variety,* 20 Mar 1957. BHD2, p. 256.

Sweeney, Joseph [actor] (b. 26 Jul 1884–25 Nov 1963 [79], New York NY). AS, p. 1048. BHD1, p. 530. IFN, p. 287.

Sweet, Blanche (cousin of **Florence Antrim** and **Gertrude Short**) [stage/film actress] (*née* Sarah Blanche Sweet, aka Blanche Alexander as a child, aka Daphne Wayne, b. Chicago IL, 18 Jun 1895–6 Sep 1986 [90], New York NY; cerebral hemorrhage). m. **Marshall Neilan**, 1922–29 (d. 1958); **Raymond Hackett**, 1936 (d. 1958). (Edison; Biograph, 1909; FP-L; Garson.) George James, "Blanche Sweet, Film Actress," *NYT,* 7 Sep 1986, A42:4. "Blanche Sweet," *Variety,* 10 Sep 1986. AMD, p. 331. AS, p. 1048. BHD1, p. 530 (b.

1896). BR, pp. 79–84 (b. 1896). FFF, p. 60. FSS, p. 269. Lowrey, p. 178. Katz, p. 1115. MH, p. 138. MSBB, p. 1042. Spehr, p. 168. "Blanche Sweet," SOS, pp. 212–45 (b. 1905). "Blanche Sweet," WBO1, pp. 82–83 (b. 1895). WWS, p. 73. "Blanche Sweet with Mutual," *MPW,* 27 Dec 1913, 1524. "Griffith on the Job," *MPW,* 28 Feb 1914, 1096. "Blanche Sweet Engaged by Lasky," *MPW,* 5 Dec 1914, 1365. J. Van Cartmell, "Film News from the Coast...," *NYDM,* 20 Nov 1915, 32:3 ("On account of the persistent rumors, the Jesse L. Lasky Company wish to emphatically state that there is no intention of Miss Blanche Sweet severing her connection with that organization."). "Blanche Sweet Re-Engaged by Lasky," *MPW,* 25 Dec 1915, 2351. Sue Roberts, "Where Have They Gone?," *Motion Picture Magazine,* Feb 1918, 136, 138 (Roberts heard that Sweet was at the Knickerbocker Hotel, NYC, with Edna Purviance [and Adele Rowland]. She was on a shopping spree. She had been ill since last December, when she felt the strain of working hard for six years in a row in films.). Edward Weitzel, "Blanche Sweet Shops in Fifth Avenue," *MPW,* 24 Aug 1918, 1104. "Blanche Sweet Blows into Town," *MPW,* 21 Dec 1918, 1332. "Blanche Sweet Signs Contract with Pathé," *MPW,* 12 Jul 1919, 210. "Blanche Sweet Unhurt in Railroad Wreck in West," *MPW,* 13 Dec 1919, 844. "Fourth Blanche Sweet Film in Year Shown at Broadway," *MPW,* 4 Sep 1920, 105. "Mrs. Neilan Gets Divorce; Blanche Sweet 'Other Woman'; Mother of Movie Star's Estranged Wife Blames the Husband for Causing Break," *Toledo Blade,* 18 Mar 1921. "Miss Sweet Names for Lead in Film," *MPW,* 3 Feb 1923, 491. "Sol Lesser Signs Blanche Sweet," *MPW,* 10 Mar 1923, 239. "Miss Sweet in New York," *MPW,* 14 Jun 1924, 646. Joan Cross, "What Life Has Taught Blanche Sweet," *Pictures,* Aug 1926, 55, 109–10. Margaret Ettinger, "An Impression of Blanche Sweet," *Cinema Arts,* Sep 1926, 42–43. "Miss Sweet with Fox," *MPW,* 16 Oct 1926, 3. Gladys Hall, "Confessions of a Star; Blanche Sweet Tells Her Untold Tale," *MPC,* Oct 1928, 16–17, 70, 87. "Jay Rubin Interviews Blanche Sweet," *CFC,* 47 (Summer, 1975), 4–7, X11, 33. Steve Higgins, "A Survey: The Blanch[e] Sweet Griffith Biographs," *CFC,* 55 (Summer, 1977), X2-X5. "Buck Rainey's Filmographies," *CI,* 167 (May 1989), 32, 50, 54; *CI,* 168 (Jun 1989), 36–37, 48 (b. 1896). William M. Drew, *Speaking of Silents* (Vestal NY: Vestal Press, Ltd., 1989), pp. 212–45. Jeffrey M. Rolick, "Blanche Sweet; Silent Screen Legend Looks Back," *CI,* 252 (Jun 1996), 34, 36.

Sweet, Harry [Keystone Cop/actor/director/scenarist] (b. Palo Alto CA, 1901–18 Jun 1933 [32], near Big Bear Lake CA; plane accident). (Sennett; Pathé; RKO.) m. "Harry Sweet, Harold Danitt [writer] and Woman [Claudette Ford (*née* Vera Williams, actress)] Killed in Calif. Plane Crash," *Variety,* 20 Jun 1933. AMD, p. 331. AS, p. 1048. BHD1, p. 530; BHD2, p. 256 (b. CO, 1900). FDY, p. 437. IFN, p. 287. "Harry Sweet Has Appeared in Even Dozen Century Comedies," *MPW,* 13 Aug 1921, 725.

Sweigart, Fred [actor]. No data found. AMD, p. 331. "Who Wants This 'I.W.W.,'" *MPW,* 3 Apr 1915, 45.

Swenson, Alfred G. [actor] (b. Salt Lake City UT, 1882–28 Mar 1941 [58], Great Kills, Staten Island NY; heart attack). m. Lorle Palmer. "Alfred G. Swenson," *NYT,* 29 Mar 1941, 15:1. "Alfred G. Swenson," *Variety,* 2 Apr 1941. AMD, p. 331. AS, p. 1048. BHD1, p. 530. IFN, p. 287. "Alfred Swenson Joins Kriterion," *MPW,* 6 Mar 1915, 1457.

Swerling, Joseph [scenarist] (b. Russia, 18 Apr 1893–23 Oct 1964 [71], Los Angeles CA). AS, p. 1048 (b. 8 Apr 1897-d. ca. 1961). BHD2, p. 256.

Swete, Lyall [stage/film actor/producer] (*né* Edward L. Swete, b. Warrington, England, 25 Jul 1865–19 Feb 1930 [64], London, England). (Stage, 1887.) "Edward L. Swete," *Variety,* 5 Mar 1930, 66:5 (age 65). BHD, p. 312.

Swickard, Charles F. (brother of **Joseph Swickard**) [actor/director] (b. Colblenz, Germany, 21 Mar 1861?–12 May 1929 [68?], Fresno CA; appendicitis attack). AMD, p. 331. AS, p. 1048 (b. 1868). BHD, p. 312 (b. 1868). IFN, p. 287 (b. 1868). Truitt, p. 319. "Swickard Is a Metro Director," *MPW,* 24 Aug 1918, 1141. "Swickard Rejoins Metro; WIll Direct Alice Lake," *MPW,* 24 Jul 1920, 494.

Swickard, Joseph (brother of **Charles F. Swickard**) [actor] (*né* Josef Swickard, b. Coblenz, Germany, 26 Jun 1866–1 Mar 1940 [73], Los Angeles CA). m. **Margaret Campbell** (d. 1939). "Joseph Swickard; Western Screen Actor, 73, Had Roles in Many Productions," *NYT,* 3 Mar 1940, 44:6. "Joseph Swickard," *Variety,* 6 Mar 1940 (d. 29 Feb, age 74). AS, p. 1048. BHD1, p. 530. IFN, p. 287. MH, p. 138. Slide, p. 166 (b. 1867). Truitt, p. 319 (b. 1886; d. 29 Feb). George Katchmer, "Forgotten Cowboys & Cowgirls—Part IV," *CI,* 175 (Jan 1990), C8-C9.

Swinburne, Mercia [actress] (b. England, 2 Feb 1900). m. **George Relph** (d. 1960). AS, p. 1048.

Swinburne, Nora [stage/film/TV dancer/actress] (b. Bath, Somerset, England, 24 Jul 1902–1 May 2000 [97], London, England). m. (1) Francis Lister, son of Cissie Loftus (1 son; d. 1951)—div.; (2) Edward Ashley, 1946—div.; (3) blind actor Esmond Knight (d. 1987). (Film debut: *Branded,* 1921.) Hugo Vickers, "Nora Swinburne," *Independent Review,* 16 May 2000, p. 6. Harris Lentz, III, "Nora Swinburne, 97," *CI,* 300 (Jul 2000), p. 58. AS, p. 1048.

Swinley, Ion [stage/film/radio actor/playwright] (b. Barnes, Surrey, England, 27 Oct 1891–16 Sep 1937 [45], London, England). (Stage debut: *A Midsummer Night's Dream,* His Majesty's Theatre, 16 Apr 1911.) "Ion Swinley, Star of British Drama; Fine Quality of Voice Won Him Many Shakespearean Roles—Dies at 45 in London; Screen and Radio Actor; Had Part in Open-Air Production of 'Comedy of Errors' at Death—Wrote Number of Plays," *NYT,* 17 Sep 1937, 25:5 (wrote *The Aspirations of Archibald, The Lifting of the Dark, The Man in the Chair,* and *The Lonely Piper*). "Ion Swinley," *Variety,* 128, 22 Sep 1937, 62:1; 128, 29 Sep 1937, 61:2. AS, p. 1048. BHD1, p. 530. IFN, p. 287.

Swor, Bert (brother of **John Swor**) [actor] (b. Paris TN, 7 Apr 1878–30 Nov 1943 [65], Tulsa OK; heart attack in a hotel room). AS, p. 1049. BHD1, p. 530.

Swor, John (brother of **Bert Swor**) [actor] (b. Paris TN, 7 Apr 1883–15 Jul 1965 [82], Dallas TX). AS, p. 1049.

Sydmeth, Louise [stage/film actress] (b. London, England, 1868–26 Nov 1938 [70], New York NY). "Louise Sydmeth; Retired Actress Who Was Seen in Many Plays Here Is Dead," *NYT,* 27 Nov 1938, 48:5 (to U.S. in 1890. "...she made a brief appearance in vaudeville with Anita Stewart."). "Louis Sydmeth," *Variety,* 30 Nov 1938, p. 54. BHD, p. 312.

Sydney, Aurele [British silent actor] (d. 15 May 1920, London, England; smallpox). *Fl.* 1915–17. "Aurele Sydney Dead," *Variety,* 28 May 1920. AS, p. 1049. BHD, p. 312 (d. Madrid, Spain). Ragan 2, p. 1643.

Sydney, Basil [film/TV actor] (*né* Basil Sidney Nugent, b. St. Osyth, Essex, England, 23 Apr 1894–10 Jan 1968 [73], London, England; pleurisy). m. (1) Doris Keane; (2) Mary Ellis; (3) Joyce Howard. (Film debut: *Romance,* 1920.) "Basil Sydney, 73, Character Actor; Briton Acclaimed Here in '61 for TV 'Antigone' Dies," *NYT,* 11 Jan 1968, 33:3. "Basil Sydney," *Variety,* 17 Jan 1968. AS, p. 1049. BHD1, p. 530. IFN, p. 287. Katz, p. 1116. Truitt, p. 320.

Sydney, Bruce [actor] (b. 1889–18 Oct 1942 [53?], Los Angeles CA). AS, p. 1049.

Sykes, Ethel [actress]. No data found. (MGM.) "We Nominate as Famous Figures of Filmland," *Paris and Hollywood,* 2 (Sep 1926), 38 (photo; appeared in small parts as in *Sally, Irene, and Mary*).

Sylva, Marguerite [opera singer/actress] (*née* Marguerite Alice Hélène Smith, b. Brussels, Belgium, 10 Jul 1875–21 Feb 1957 [81], Glendale CA; result of auto accident a year before). m. (1) William D. Mann; (2) Bernard L. Smith, 1915. (Kleine.) "Mme. Sylva, 81, ex-Opera Singer; Noted Carmen Early in the Century Is Dead—Revived Role at 'Met' in 1910," *NYT,* 22 Feb 1957, 21:5. "Marguerite Sylva," *Variety,* 27 Feb 1957. AMD, p. 331. AS, p. 1049. BHD, p. 312. IFN, p. 287. "Marguerite Sylva in Film," *NYDM,* 20 May 1914, 29:1. "Birth Notice," *NYDM,* 26 Feb 1916, p. 6 (child born to Sylva and naval lieutenant Bernard L. Smith). "Prominent Belgian Artiste Starred in American Film," *MPW,* 3 Jan 1920, 131. "Mme. Sylva Latest Diva to Enter Screen Work," *MPW,* 14 Feb 1920, 1093. "Many Prominent Picture Players in the Cast of 'The Honey Bee,'" *MPW,* 28 Feb 1920, 1492.

Sylvaine, Vernon [scenarist] (b. 1897–22 Nov 1957 [60?], Sussex, England). BHD2, p. 257.

Sylvani, Gladys [actress] (*née* Gladys McCornick-Goodhart, b. England, 1885–20 Apr 1953 [68?], Alexandria VA). m. (1 son, 1 daughter). "Gladys Sylvani," *Variety,* 190, 22 Apr 1953, 63:1 (Mrs. Gladys McCormick-Goodhart. "She was the first British screen player to receive a term contract."). AS, p. 1049 ("l'une des premières stars du film muet anglais"). BHD, p. 312. IFN, p. 287.

Sylvano, Wanda [actress] (b. Paris, France-d. 8 Apr 1926, Paris, France). BHD, p. 312.

Sylvester, Frank L. [actor] (b. MA, 3 Apr 1869–17 Dec 1931 [62], Los Angeles CA; heart attack). "F.L. Sylvester Dead," *Variety,* 22 Dec 1931. AS, p. 1049 (d. 15 Dec). BHD1, p. 530. IFN, p. 287. Truitt, p. 320.

Sylvester, Henry [actor] (b. MO, 2 Sep 1881–8 Jun 1961 [79], Los Angeles CA). AS, p. 1049.

Sylvester, Josephine [actress]. No data found. (Essanay.)

Sylvia, Gaby [actress] (*née* Gabriele Zignani, b. Cesena, Italy, 24 Mar 1920–26 Jul 1980 [60], Chamalieres, France; cerebral hemorrhage [extrait de décès no. 84/1980]). AS, p. 1049. JS, p. 443 (in France from 1923; *Wanda la peccatrice,* Italy, 1952).

Sylvie [actress] (*née* Louise Pauline Mainguene, b. Paris, France, 3 Jan 1883–6 Jan 1970 [87], Compiegne, France [extrait de décès no. 19/1970]). AS, p. 1049. BHD1, p. 531 (d. 5 Jan, Paris, France).

Sym, Igo [actor] (*né* Karl Julius Sym, b. Innsbruck, Austria, 3 Jul 1896–7 Mar 1941 [44], Warsaw, Poland). AS, p. 1049. BHD, p. 312. IFN, p. 287.

Symon, Burk [actor/director] (b. Pittsburgh PA, 18 Nov 1888–20 Feb 1950 [61], Woodland Hills CA). "Burk Symon," *NYT,* 22 Feb 1950, 29:3. "Burk Symon," *Variety,* 1 Mar 1950. AS, p. 1049. BHD2, p. 257. IFN, p. 287.

Symonds, Augustin [actor] (b. Newcastle, England, 24 Nov 1868–14 Jul 1944 [75], England). AS, p. 1049.

Symonds, Henry Roberts [scenarist]. No data found. FDY, p. 437.

Szaro, Henryk [director] (b. Warsaw, Poland, 21 Oct 1900–1942 [42?], Warsaw, Poland). AS, p. 1049.

Szekely, Steven [director] (b. Budapest, Hungary, 25 Feb 1889–9 Mar 1979 [90], Palm Springs CA). BHD2, p. 257.

Szigeti, Joseph [actor] (b. Budapest, Hungary, 5 Sep 1892–20 Feb 1973 [80], Lucerne, Switzerland). AS, p. 1050.

Szucs, Ladislaus [director] (b. Budapest, Hungary, 23 Jan 1895). AS, p. 1050.

T

Taber, Richard [stage/film/TV actor/writer] (b. Long Branch NJ, 31 Oct 1884–16 Nov 1957 [73], New York NY [Death Certificate Index No. 24512; M.E. Case No. 8937]). m. Mary Ellen Hanley. "Richard Taber, 72, Broadway Actor; Co-Author of 'Is Zat So?,' a Hit in Twenties [1925], Dies—Had Screen, TV Roles," *NYT,* 8 Nov 1957, 31:3. "Richard Taber," *Variety,* 20 Nov 1957. AS, p. 1051 (b. 1885). BHD1, p. 531 (b. 1885). IFN, p. 287 (age 72).

Tabler, P[erce] **Dempsey** [actor] (b. TN, 23 Nov 1876–7 Jun 1956 [79], San Francisco CA). (Paramount.) AS, p. 1051. BHD, p. 313. IFN, p. 287.

Tabor, Rose [actress] (b. 1890?–19 Sep 1925 [35], Chicago IL). BHD, p. 313. IFN, p. 287.

Taft, Lucille [actress]. No data found. AMD, p. 332. (Gaumont.) "Lucille Taft," *MPW,* 15 Jan 1916, 395. "'Loop-the-Loop' Lucille," *MPC,* Apr 1916, 18.

Taggart, Ben L. [actor] (b. Ottawa, Canada, 5 Apr 1889–17 May 1947 [58], Santa Monica CA). AMD, p. 332. AS, p. 1051. BHD1, p. 531 (b. NY NY). IFN, p. 288. "Taggart in Kleine's 'Woman Next Door,'" *MPW,* 24 Jul 1915, 631.

Taillon, Gus [actor] (*né* Angus D. Taillon, b. Ontario, Canada, 11 Oct 1887–6 May 1953 [65], Los Angeles CA; heart attack). AS, p. 1052.

Tainguy, Lucien [cinematographer] (b. Paris, France, 10 Aug 1881-Feb 1971 [89], Baychester NY). BHD2, p. 257.

Tairraz, Georges [director of photography] (b. Chamonix-Montblanc, France, 20 Mar 1900 [extrait de naissance no. 20/1900]-1 Jun 1975 [75], Chamonix-Montblanc, France). AS, p. 1052.

Tait, Robert B[laikie] [actor] (b. Canada, 30 Jan 1900–28 May 1950 [50], Woodland Hills CA). AS, p. 1052.

Takada, Kokichi [film/stage actor] (*né* Takeichi Kaijura, b. 1911–19 May 1998 [86], Kyoto, Japan; pneumonia). (Film debut, Shochiku Co., 1926.) "Kokichi Tanada," *CI,* 277 (Jul 1998), 58.

Takada, Minoru [actor] (b. Akita, Japan, 20 Dec 1899–28 Dec 1977 [78], Tokyo, Japan; cancer). AS, p. 1052. BHD1, p. 532. IFN, p. 288.

Takagi, Taku [actress]. No data found. AMD, p. 332. "N.Y. World Interviews Jap Actress," *MPW,* 28 Sep 1912, 1286.

Talamo, Gino Michele Ulwis [actor/editor/director] (*né* Luigi Talamo, b. Taranto, Italy, 13 Dec 1895 [extrait de naissance no. 1891]). AS, p. 1052. JS, p. 444 (in Italian silents from 1920 after *Mascamor,* France, 1918).

Talazac, Odette Pauline [actress] (b. Paris, France, 6 May 1883–29 Mar 1948 [64], France [extrait de décès no. 638/1948]). AS, p. 1052. BHD1, p. 532.

Talbot, Earl [stock/legitimate/film actor] (b. 1892–13 Feb 1914 [22], New York NY; pneumonia). "Earl Talbot Dies," *Variety,* 20 Feb 1914, 10:2 ("His life was but short just at the time he was getting a chance to blossom forth in his chosen line."). AS, p. 1052. BHD1, p. 617.

Talbot, Hayden [scenarist]. No data found. AMD, p. 332. FDY, p. 439. "Hayden Talbot with Paralta," *MPW,* 28 Jul 1917, 617. "New Triangle Acquisition," *MPW,* 24 Nov 1917, 1182. "Talbot to Write for Metro," *MPW,* 24 Jul 1920, 493. "M-G-M Retains Hayden Talbot," *MPW,* 26 Feb 1927, 643.

Talbot, Joseph B. (Slim) [actor] (b. Hamilton IL, 1895–25 Jan 1973 [77], Boulevard CA). BHD, p. 313. IFN, p. 288.

Talbot, Mae [actress] (b. 1869?–4 Aug 1942 [73], Glendale CA; heart attack). (Universal.) "Mae Talbot," *Variety,* 12 Aug 1942. AS, p. 1052. BHD, p. 313. IFN, p. 288.

Talbot, Rowland [producer] (d. 1917). BHD2, p. 256.

Talbot, Stella [actress]. No data found. AMD, p. 332. "Stella Talbot Appearing in Six Southern Cities," *MPW,* 24 May 1919, 1177.

Taliaferro, Edith (sister of **Mabel Taliaferro**; cousin of **Bessie Barriscale**) [stage/film actress] (b. Richmond VA, 21 Dec 1893–2 Mar 1958 [64], Newtown CT). m. (1) Earle Brown; (2) House B. Jameson. (Film debut: *Young Romance,* Paramount, 1915.) "Edith Taliaferro of Stage, Was 64; Star of the Early Nineteen Hundreds Is Dead—Made Her Debut at Age of 2," *NYT,* 3 Mar 1958, 27:3. "Edith Taliaferro," *Variety,* 5 Mar 1958. AMD, p. 332. AS, p. 1053. BHD, p. 313. IFN, p. 287. Truitt, p. 320. "Edith Taliaferro with Lasky," *MPW,* 31 Oct 1914, 646. "Edith Taliaferro Again on the Screen," *MPW,* 15 Nov 1919, 359. "Rapid Sale of Equity Feature Shows Wide Popularity of Edith Taliaferro," *MPW,* 4 Sep 1920, 73.

Taliaferro, Hal *see* **Alderson, Floyd T.**

Taliaferro, Mabel, "The Sweetheart of American Movies" (sister of **Edith Taliaferro**; cousin of **Bessie Barriscale**) [actress] (*née* Maybelle Evelyn Taliaferro, b. New York NY, 21 May 1887–24 Jan 1979 [91], Honolulu HI). m. (1) Frederick W. Thompson (d. 1919); (2) **Thomas J. Carrigan** (d. 1941); (3) Joseph O'Brien, 1920; (4) **Robert Ober** (d. 1950). (Selig, 1911.) "Mabel Taliaferro, 91, Star of Silent Screen Acted in 100 Plays," *NYT,* 3 Feb 1979, 24:4. "Mabel Taliaferro," *Variety,* 7 Feb 1979. AMD, p. 332. AS, p. 1053. BHD1, p. 532. FSS, p. 270. IFN, p. 288. Katz, p. 1118. "Mabel Taliaferro on New Years," *NYDM,* 13 Dec 1911, 29. Ashton Stevens, "Mabel Taliaferro Talks About Pictures," *MPW,* 23 Dec 1911, 971. "Rolfe Signs Mabel Taliaferro," *MPW,* 14 Nov 1914, 920. "Mabel Taliaferro," *MPW,* 28 Nov 1914, 1220. "Metro Signs Mabel Taliaferro," *MPW,* 20 Nov 1915, 1474. "Mabel Taliaferro Joins Metro," *MPW,* 11 Dec 1915, 2014. "Mabel Taliaferro Gives a 'Rag Party,'" MPW, 6 Jan 1917, 66. "Mabel Taliaferro to Work on Stage," *MPW,* 7 Apr 1917, 122. "Mabel Taliaferro," *MPW,* 14 Apr 1917, 279. "Miss Taliaferro Returns to Screen," *MPW,* 2 Jun 1917, 1462. "Mabel Taliaferro Weds," *LA Times,* 28 Jan 1920, 11 (remarried O'Brien, by whom she had a daughter). "Mabel Taliaferro Engaged for 'Sentimental Tommy,'" *MPW,* 9 Oct 1920, 780. Billy H. Doyle, "Lost Players," *CI,* 161 (Nov 1988), C19.

Tallents, Stephen [actor] (b. England, 20 Oct 1884–1958 [74?], England). AS, p. 1053.

Talley, Truman H. [director] (b. Rockport MO, 1891–18 Jan 1942 [50?], New York NY). AMD, p. 332. BHD2, p. 257. "Vivid Stories of News Reel Exploits Told at Opening of Fox News Cameramen's College," *MPW,* 12 Dec 1925, 566.

Tallier, Armand [actor] (b. Marseilles, France, 15 Mar 1887–1 Mar 1958 [70]). AS, p. 1053.

Tallroth, Konrad [actor/director] (b. Sweden, 1872–1926 [54?], Sweden). AS, p. 1053.

Tally, Thomas Lincoln [producer] (b. TX, 1861?–22 Nov 1945 [84], Beverly Hills CA). "Thomas L. Tally, Film Pioneer, Dies; Producer First Signed Mary Pickford, Chaplin—A Founder of First National Pictures," *NYT,* 25 Nov 1945, 50:4. "Thomas Lincoln Tally," *Variety,* 28 Nov 1945. AMD, p. 332. AS, p. 1053. BHD2, p. 257. "Griffith Has Not Signed with Circuit, Says Tally," *MPW,* 8 Feb 1919, 731.

Talma, Zolya (d. 26 Nov 1983, Los Angeles Co. CA). BHD, p. 313.

Talmadge, Constance Alice (daughter of **Margaret L. Talmadge**; sister of **Norma** and **Natalie Talmadge**) [actress] (b. Brooklyn NY, 19 Apr 1897–23 Nov 1973 [76], Los Angeles CA; pneumonia). m. (1) John Pialoglou, Greenwich CT, 26 Dec 1920—div. 1 Jun 1922; (2) Capt. Alistair W.

Mackintosh, Feb 1926–15 Oct 1927; (3) Townsend Netcher; (4) Walter M. Giblin. Anita Loos, *The Talmadge Girls; A Memoir* (NY: The Viking Press, 1978). (Griffith; Vitagraph; Triangle; Selznick; UA.) "Constance Talmadge, 73, Dead; A Film Star of the Silent Era," *NYT,* 26 Nov 1973, 34:4. "Constance Talmadge," *Variety,* 28 Nov 1973. AMD, p. 332. AS, p. 1053. BHD, p. 313 (b. 1900). FFF, p. 110 (b. 1900). IFN, p. 288 (b. 1900). Katz, p. 1118 (began 1914). KOM, pp. 159–60 (b. 1899). MH, p. 138 (b. 1900). MSBB, p. 1042 (b. 1900). WWS, p. 77. "Constance Talmadge," WBO1, pp. 184–85 (b. 1900). "Constance Talmadge," *MPW,* 6 Feb 1915, 839. "Constance Talmadge," *MPW,* 5 May 1917, 782. "Constance Talmadge New Selznick Star," *MPW,* 23 Jun 1917, 1941. "Another Star Is Added," *Picture-Play Magazine,* Sep 1917, 94 (another star on the background of the flag. She "has just been made a full-fledged star, for the first time in her life, by Lewis J. Selznick. She has starred in a few pictures before, but never regularly."). "Features Select Player on Cover of Sheet Music," *MPW,* 1 Mar 1919, 1235 (*Then You'll Come Back to Me*). "Constance Talmadge with First National, Is Rumor," *MPW,* 3 May 1919, 637. "Circuit Signs Constance Talmadge," *MPW,* 10 May 1919, 796. "Flashes; Connie's to Wed; Report Says She's Engaged to Irving Berlin," *LA Times,* 24 Jan 1920, 7. Edward Weitzel, "Constance Talmadge, Sister Natalie and Marie the Haughty Understudy," *MPW,* 14 Feb 1920, 1029. "Neither Norma Nor Constance Talmadge Intend to Quit Circuit, Says Schenck," *MPW,* 17 Apr 1920, 384. "Schenck Renews First National Contract for Norma and Constance Talmadge," *MPW,* 27 Nov 1920, 461. "New York and Vicinity Votes Norma and Constance Talmadge Leading Favorites," *MPW,* 18 Dec 1920, 858. "Norma Talmadge Looking for Plays Which Will Offer Strong, Dramatic Emotional Roles, While Constance Wants to Play in Subtle Comedies," *MPW,* 25 Dec 1920, 1025. "They're Married!; The double romance and marriage of Constance Talmadge and Dorothy Gish," *Photoplay,* Mar 1921, 59, 113 (Pialoglo was a "wealthy young Greek importer and exporter of cigars and cigarettes"). "Constance Divorced," *MPW,* 10 Jun 1922, 545. Harry Carr, "Connie Becomes a Chink; ...in order to lend verisimilitude to her characterization in 'East Is West,'" *Classic,* Sep 1922, 52–53, 94. "Talmadge Biography," *MPW,* 28 Oct 1922, 762 (Mrs. Margaret Talmadge, *The Talmadge Sisters,* Henry Bee Co.). "New Films for the Talmadge Sisters," *MPW,* 13 Jan 1923, 163. Constance Talmadge, "Beauty; My Pep—And How I Keep It Up," *MPC,* Apr 1925, 24, 77. "Fred Talmadge Dies," *MPW,* 28 Nov 1925, 316 (father). Constance Talmadge, "What I Think of Norma," *MM,* Apr 1926, 33, 85–86. Paul Paige, "Close-Ups and Fade-Outs," *Paris and Hollywood,* Oct 1926, 67, 92 (Mackintosh, whom she recently married, was born in Inverness, Scotland, in Dec 1889). "Constance Talmadge Covers Big Fights for 800 Papers," *MPW,* 16 Oct 1926, 422. Constance Talmadge, "Rire et Faire Rire," *Cinema Arts,* Nov 1926, 44–45. Cover, *Paris and Hollywood Screen Secrets Magazine,* Oct 1927. "Connie Finishes Last for F-N," *MPW,* 2 Jul 1927, 19. Ann Dickson, "What About Mother-in-Law?," *MPC,* Aug 1927, 58, 81, 87 (re Mrs. Frederick "Peg" Talmadge; Mrs. Charlotte Pickford *et al.*). "Constance Talmadge as an 'Extra,'" *MPW,* 17 Sep 1927, 155. "'Connie' Divorced," *MPW,* 22 Oct 1927, 484 (from MacIntosh). Gladys Hall, "Confessions of the Stars, II—Constance Talmadge Reveals the Untold Truth About What She Has Been, What She Is, and What She Wants to Be," *MPC,* Nov 1928, 18–19, 70, 83. "A Very Square Peg; Rough-Hewn, But Clean-Grained and Sturdy, Is the Woman Who Is More Than the Talmadge Sisters' Mother," *MPC,* Dec 1928, 26, 74 ("She has been accused of supplying many of the wise cracks for 'Gentlemen Prefer Blondes.'"). Eve Golden, "Constance Talmadge: Jazz Baby * Smart Cookie," *CI,* 231 (Sep 1994), 18, 26.

Talmadge, Margaret L. (Peg) (mother of **Constance**, **Natalie** and **Norma Talmadge**) [actress] (*née?,* d. 28 Sep 1933, Los Angeles CA). m. Frederick Talmadge (d. 1925). BHD, p. 313.

Talmadge, Natalie (daughter of **Margaret L. Talmadge**; sister of **Norma** and **Constance Talmadge**) [actress] (b. Brooklyn NY, 29 Apr or 17 Jun 1898–19 Jun 1969 [71], Santa Monica CA). m. **Buster Keaton**, 1921–33 (d. 1966). "Natalie Talmadge, Silent Screen Star," *NYT,* 21 Jun 1969, 27:3. "Natalie Talmadge, ex-Film Star, Dies," *LA Times,* Sec. III, 21 Jun 1969, p. 7 (b. 1899; buried in Hollywood Cemetery). "Natalie Talmadge," *Variety,* 25 Jun 1969. AMD, p. 333. AS, p. 1053 (b. 29 Apr 1899). BHD, p. 313 (b. 1899). IFN, p. 288. Truitt, p. 320. WWS, p. 80. "Dorothy Gish Saves Natalie Talmadge from Drowning," *MPW,* 29 Jul 1916, 775. "Natalie Talmadge with Arbuckle," *MPW,* 23 Feb 1918, 1117. Edward Weitzel, "Constance Talmadge, Sister Natalie and Maria the Haughty Understudy," *MPW,* 14 Feb 1920, 1029. "Keaton and Bride Arrive," *MPW,* 25 Jun 1921, 807. "Fred Talmadge Dies," *MPW,* 28 Nov 1925, 316 (father).

Talmadge, Norma (daughter of **Margtaret L. Talmadge**; sister of **Constance** and **Natalie Talmadge**) [actress] (b. Jersey City NJ, 26 May 1895–24 Dec 1957 [62], Las Vegas NV; pneumonia and cerebral hemorrhage). (Modeled for illustrated slides; film debut: *A Four-Footed Pest,* Vitagraph, 1910.) m. (1) **Joseph M. Schenck**, Oct 1916—div. 1934 (d. 1961); (2) **George Jessel** (d. 1981); (3) Dr. Carvel James, 1946. Margaret L. Talmadge, *The Talmadge Sisters; Norma, Constance, Natalie; An Intimate Story of the World's Most Famous Screen Family* (Philadelphia: J.B. Lippincott Co., 1924) (b. Niagara Falls, p. 17). (Vitagraph; Triangle; Selznick.) "Norma Talmadge, Film Star, Dead; Noted Actress of the Silent Screen, 1911–1930–Made Her Movie Debut at 14," *NYT,* 25 Dec 1957, 31:1 (age 60). "Norma Talmadge," *Variety,* 1 Jan 1958 (age 61). AMD, p. 333. AS, p. 1053. BHD1, p. 532 (b. 1897). FFF, p. 72 (b. Niagara Falls NY, 2 May 1897). FSS, p. 270. HCH, p. 73. IFN, p. 288 (b. Niagara Falls, 1897). Katz, pp. 1118–19. KOM, pp. 160–61 (b. 1897). Lowrey, p. 180 (b. Niagara Falls). MH, p. 138 (b. Niagara Falls, 2 May 1897). MSBB, p. 1042 (b. 1896, Niagara Falls). 1921 Directory, p. 241 (b. Niagara Falls). Slide, p. 152 (b. 1897). Spehr, p. 158 (b. Niagara Falls, 1897). Truitt, p. 320 (b. Niagara Falls, 1897). WWS, p. 76 (b. Niagara Falls). "Norma Talmadge; Playing Leads with the Vitagraph Co.," *MPS,* 4 Sep 1914, 25 (age 19). "National Engages Norma Talmadge," *MPW,* 10 Jul 1915, 312. "Norma Talmadge, Selznick Star," *MPW,* 21 Oct 1916, 410. "Norma Talmadge and Joe Schenck Marry," *MPW,* 18 Nov 1916, 986. "The Company on the Cover; Norma Talmadge, Inc.," *Photoplay Magazine,* Feb 1917, 84–85 (cover painting). "Norma Talmadge Off for Plam Beach," *MPW,* 17 Mar 1917, 1753. "Norma Talmadge," *MPW,* 24 Mar 1917, 1929. "Miss Talmadge Uses Home as Location," *MPW,* 30 Jun 1917, 2126. "Norma Talmadge," *MPW,* 21 Jul 1917, 390. "Norma Talmadge Wants Book Plays," *MPW,* 1 Sep 1917, 1360. "Norma Talmadge to Remain with Select," *MPW,* 18 May 1918, 973. "Norma Talmadge Quits 'Personal Appearances,'" *MPW,* 5 Oct 1918, 74. Edward Weitzel, "Roast Dog and Alligator Steak," *MPW,* 4 Jan 1919, 61. "Norma Talmadge Company Buys Additional Building," *MPW,* 18 Jan 1919, 314. "Select to Release for 1919 All Norma Talmadge Output," *MPW,* 25 Jan 1919, 208. "Norma Talmadge to Aid Loan Drive," *MPW,* 26 Apr 1919, 515. "Dedicates Song in Honor of Norma Talmadge, Select Star," *MPW,* 17 May 1919, 1065 (*Norma*). "Dedicates Song to Norma Talmadge," *MPW,* 28 Jun 1919, 1958 (*The New Moon,* by Irving Berlin). "Norma Talmadge Visits Cuba," *MPW,* 24 Jan 1920, 612. "Neither Norma Nor Constance Talmadge Intend to Quit Circuit, Says Schenck," *MPW,* 17 Apr 1920, 384. "Her First Vitagraph Check," *MPW,* 25 Sep 1920, 509. "Schenck Renews FIrst National Contract for Norma and Constance Talmadge," *MPW,* 27 Nov 1920, 461. "New York and Vicinity Votes Norma and Constance Talmadge Leading Favorites," *MPW,* 18 Dec 1920, 858. "Norma Talmadge Looking for Plays Which Will Offer Strong, Dramatic EMotional ROles, While Constance Wants to Play in Subtle Comedies," *MPW,* 25 Dec 1920, 1025. "Norma Talmadge and Wallace Reid Win National Star Popularity Contest," *MPW,* 19 Mar 1921, 247 (37,156 votes). Adele Whitely Fletcher, "Girl—Woman," *MPC,* Dec 1921, 20–21. "A Star in the Making," *Classic,* Oct 1922, 20–21. "Crowds Welcome Norma Talmadge," *MPW,* 10 Dec 1921, 686. Harry Carr, "Slumbering Fires; ...two of the most expensive words in the English language: 'Norma Talmadge,'" *Classic,* Dec 1922, 32–33, 77. "New Films for the Talmadge Sisters," *MPW,* 13 Jan 1923, 163. "Norma Starts Run of Her Ten-Reeler," *MPW,* 18 Aug 1923, 580. "Lead in Contest," *MPW,* 22 Sep 1923, 355. "Borzage to Direct Norma Talmadge," *MPW,* 27 Oct 1923, 754. "Greetings to My Friends the Fans," *MW,* 14 Jun 1924, 3 (she edited this issue). David A. Balch, "The Emotional Queen of the Screen," *MW,* 14 Jun 1924, 8–9, 26. "How It Feels to Grow Old—on the Screen," *MW,* 14 Jun 1924, 10, 26. "At the Home of Norma Talmadge," *MW,* 14 Jun 1924, 6. "If I Were You; Norma Talmadge Stands Ready to Put Herself in Your Place," *MW,* 26 Jul 1924, 3, 31 (she was to write a future advice column). "Schenck Reports Plans," *MPW,* 13 Dec 1924, 615. Adele Whitely Fletcher, "Norma...a Woman...a Paradox...a Riddle! (This Is Not an Interview!)," *MW,* 28 Feb 1925, 18–19, 33. Harry Carr, "The Millionaire Actress; Norma Talmadge Can Afford the Luxury of Being Natural," *MPC,* Jul 1925, 42, 71. "Fred Talmadge Dies," *MPW,* 28 Nov 1925, 316 (father). Norma Talmadge, "What I Think of Constance," *MM,* Apr 1926, 32, 86–88. "Norma Talmadge Novelizes 'Kiki,'" *MPW,* 25 Dec 1926, 583. Norma Talmadge, "Close-Ups," *The Saturday Evening Post,* 12 Mar 1927, pp. 6–7, 115–16, 121–22. Gladys Hall, "Just Like Your Next Door Neighbor; Near and Real to the People—That's Norma Talmadge," *MPC,* Jun 1927, 58, 89. Nancy Pryor, "Is Norma Talmadge Heading for Divorce?," *Movie Classic,* Dec 1931, 42. Jack Spears, "Norma Talmadge; Made a Career and a Fortune Out of Sobs and Smiles," *FIR,* Jan 1967, 16–40 (b. 1897 from Mrs. Peggy Talmadge). Eve Golden, "The Life of Brooklyn Tragedienne Norma Talmadge," *CI,* 215 (May 1993), C12-C13.

Talmadge, Richard [actor/assistant director] (*né* Sylvester Metz; aka Silvio Metzetti, b.

Switzerland, 3 Dec 1892–25 Jan 1981 [88], Carmel CA; cancer). m. Madeleine Francis Allen, 1917 (d. 1929); Mammy. (Began ca. 1917.) "Richard Talmadge," *Variety,* 25 Mar 1981 (*né* Sylvester Metzetti). AMD, p. 333 (b. Munich, Germany). AS, p. 1053 (b. Munich). BHD1, p. 532 (b. Munich, 1896). FSS, p. 271. GK, pp. 916–24. Katz, p. 1119 (b. Munich, 1896). "Phil Goldstone Sued by Dick Talmadge," *MPW,* 7 Apr 1923, 658. "Richard Talmadge Signed by Truart for Feature Series," *MPW,* 14 Jul 1923, 161. "Injured Stars Betters," *MPW,* 20 Sep 1924, 209. "Richrd Talmadge Signs F.B.O. Starring Contract," *MPW,* 28 Feb 1925, 931. "Richard Talmadge Is Guest of Honor at F.B.O. Luncheon," *MPW,* 24 Oct 1925, 622. "Talmadge Sues Magazine," *MPW,* 26 Dec 1925, 745. "'Dick' Signed," *MPW,* 3 Apr 1926, 4. "Dick Talmadge with 'U,'" *MPW,* 29 Jan 1927, 324. "Richard Talmadge Free Agent, to Find Another Distributor," *MPW,* 15 Oct 1927, 430. George A. Katchmer, "Richard Talmadge; He Floats on Air," *CI,* 100 (Oct 1983), 63–65.

Tamara [actress] (*née* Tamara Swann, b. Russia, 1910–22 Feb 1943 [32?], Lisbon, Portugal; airplane crash). AS, p. 1053. BHD1, p. 532 (Tamara Drasin). IFN, p. 288.

Tamarez, Tom [actor] (*né* Gaber Tanos, b. Syria, 27 Feb 1901–25 Oct 1963 [62], Los Angeles Co. CA). (Fox.) AS, p. 1053. BHD1, p. 532. IFN, p. 288.

Tamberlani, Carlo [actor] (*né* Francesco Paolo Carlo Tamberlani, b. Salice Salentino, Italy, 11 Mar 1899 [extrait de naissance no. 24]-5 Aug 1980 [81], Subiaco, Italy). AS, p. 1053.

Tamberlani, Nando [actor] (*né* Ferdinando Tamberlani, b. Campi Salentino, Italy, 15 Jan 1896–11 Mar 1967 [71], Milan, Italy). AS, p. 1053.

Tambour, Clara [actress] (*née* Claire Eugénie Germain, b. Paris, France, 19 Feb 1891 [extrait de naissance no. 834]-24 Jun 1982 [91], Dinard, France [extrait de décès no. 93/1982]). AS, p. 1053.

Tams, Irene [actress]. No data found. AMD, p. 333. MSBB, p. 1033 (photo). "Irene Tams Is to Head Own Company," *MPW,* 16 Apr 1921, 750.

Tanaka, Eizo [director] (b. Tokyo, Japan, 3 Nov 1886–13 Jun 1968 [81], Tokyo, Japan). AS, p. 1054.

Tanaka, Kinuyo [actress] (b. Shimonoseki, Japan, 29 Dec 1909–21 Mar 1977 [66], Tokyo, Japan). m. Hiroshi Shimizu [1903–1966]. AS, p. 1054. BHD1, p. 533 (b. Tokyo, Japan, 29 Nov 1910).

Tanaka, Michiko [actress/singer] (b. Tokyo, Japan, 15 Jul 1909–18 May 1968 [58], Tokyo, Japan). m. **Viktor De Kowa** (d. 1973). AS, p. 1054.

Tanaka, Shoji [actor] (b. Japan, 1886–19 Oct 1918 [32?], New York NY; influenza). AS, p. 1054 (d. 20 Oct). BHD, p. 313. Billy H. Doyle, "Lost Players," *CI,* 139 (Jan 1987), 55.

Tanguay, Eva [stage/film dancer/singer/actress] (b. Marbleton, Quebec, Canada, 1 Aug 1878–11 Jan 1947 [68], Los Angeles CA; heart attack and cerebral hemorrhage). m. (1) John W. Ford; (2) Roscoe Ails; (3) Alexander Booke. (Promotional film, *Energetic Eva,* Tanguay Films, 1916; debut: *The Wild Girl,* Selznick, 1917.) "Eva Tanguay Dies in Hollywood, 68; Famed for 'I Don't Care,' She First Sang on Broadway in 'Chaperones of 1904'; Starred for Ziegfeld; Made Her Screen Debut at 8—Spent Several Fortunes but Lost Last in 1929 Crash," *NYT,* 12 Jan 1947, 59:1. Ed Barry, "Eva Tanguay—'I Don't Care' Girl—Slips Away, Taking an Era with Her," *Variety,* 15 Jan 1947. AMD, p. 333. AS, p. 1054. BHD, p. 313. IFN, p. 288. Spehr, p. 170. Truitt, p. 321. "'I Do Care!' Says Eva Tanguay; 'I Want So Much to Be Understood,'" *NYDM,* 27 Jan 1915, 30:1 (had been in vaudeville for seven years; song, *I Don't Care,* from *The Sambo Girl*). "Tanguay Would Stop Film," *NYDM,* 7 Jul 1915, 32:3 (sought an injunction against the reissue of *Success* "alleging that the crude work of seven years ago would be detrimental to her if shown before the public today."). "Eva Tanguay Makes a Picture," *MPW,* 8 Jul 1916, 256. "Eva Tanguay Comes to the Screen," *MPW,* 14 Jul 1917, 249. "Eva Tanguay Shows Her Speed," *MPW,* 1 Dec 1917, 1355.

Tannehill, Frank H. (father of **Muriel** and **Myrtle Tannehill**) [stage/film actor/playwright] (b. 1859?–5 Feb 1932 [72], New York NY; fell or jumped 8 floors from the solarium at the Elks Club). m. (1) (mother of Muriel and Myrtle); (2) Anna Ray. "Frank H. Tannehill Plunges to His Death," *Variety,* 105, 9 Feb 1932, 55:1. J. Van Cartmell, "Along the Pacific Coast," *NYDM,* 13 Nov 1915, 31:1 (Tennahill [sic] hired by Ince).

Tannehill, Muriel (daughter of **Frank H. Tannehill**; half-sister of **Myrtle Tannehill**) [actress] (b. Jersey City NJ, 1893?–13 May 1989 [96], Ossining NY). m. Jean Dansereau. "Muriel Tannehill Dansereau," *Variety,* 12 Jul 1989. AS, p. 1054.

Tannehill, Myrtle (daughter of **Frank H. Tannehill**; half-sister of **Muriel Tannehill**) [stage/film actress] (b. 18 May 1886–25 Jul 1977 [91], Yorktown Heights NY). m. **Hale Hamilton** (d. 1942); Mr. Nichols. "Myrtle Tannahill," *Variety,* 3 Aug 1977. AMD, p. 333. AS, p. 1054. BHD, p. 313. "New Stars for Kalem," *MPW,* 24 Apr 1915, 560. "Myrtle Tannehill; In Kalem's Broadway Favorites, 'When the Mind Sleeps,'" *NYDM,* 2 Jun 1915, 25:1 (to be released 14 Jun). "Myrtle Tannehill," *MPW,* 5 Jun 1915, 1618. "Grace La Rue Sued," *LA Times,* 11 Feb 1920, II, p. 7 (sued in New York for alienation of the affections of Hamilton. La Rue "denied that she lured Mr. Hamilton away from his wife.").

Tannen, Julius [actor] (b. Chicago IL, 16 May 1880–3 Jan 1965 [84], Los Angeles CA; cerebral thrombosis). AS, p. 1054.

Tannenbaum, Harold J. [cinematographer] (b. 1897–16 Apr 1943 [46?]). BHD2, p. 257.

Tanner, Fred [actor] (*né* Albert T. Tanner, b. Ruschlikon, Switzerland, 12 Sep 1885–27 Oct 1982 [97], Zurich, Switzerland). AS, p. 1054.

Tanner, Jack J. [actor] (b. 1872–3 Apr 1934 [62?], Los Angeles CA). AS, p. 1054.

Tanner, James J. [actor] (b. 1873–3 Apr 1934 [61?], Los Angeles CA). AS, p. 1054 (Jack Tanner). BHD1, p. 533. IFN, p. 288 (Jack Tanner).

Tanner, Marion [actress] (b. Buffalo NY, 1891–30 Oct 1985 [94?], New York NY). BHD, p. 313.

Tannura, Philip [cinematographer/actor] (b. New York NY, 28 Mar 1897–7 Dec 1973 [76], Los Angeles CA). AS, p. 1054. BHD, p. 313; BHD2, p. 257. FDY, p. 469. *Filmlexicon degli autori e delle opere,* Vol. 7 (Rome: Bianco e Nero, 1967).

Tansey, Mrs. Emma (mother of **Robert Emmett Tansey**) [actress] (*née?,* b. Louisville KY, 12 Sep 1870–23 Mar 1942 [71], Los Angeles CA). "Mrs. Emma Tansey," *Variety,* 1 Apr 1942 (age 58). AMD, p. 334 (Emma Tausey). AS, p. 1054. BHD1, p. 533. IFN, p. 288. Truitt, p. 321 (b. 1884). "Blame the Actress," *MPW,* 17 Sep 1921, 278.

Tansey, John Foster [actor/director] (b. New York NY, 8 Oct 1901–28 Apr 1971 [69], No. Hollywood CA). (Biograph, 1908.) AMD, p. 333. AS, p. 1054 (b. 1904). BHD1, p. 533; BHD2, p. 257. "Noted Boy Actor Engaged by Metro," *MPW,* 27 Nov 1915, 1641. "John Tansey," *MPW,* 23 Feb 1918, 1074. "John Tansey Returns," *MPW,* 12 Jul 1924, 102.

Tansey, Robert Emmett (son of **Emma Tansey**) [director/producer/scenarist] (b. Brooklyn NY, 28 Jun 1897–17 Jun 1951 [53], Los Angeles CA; heart attack). "Robert Tansey," *Variety,* 27 Jun 1951 (age 52). AS, p. 1055. BHD, p. 314; BHD2, p. 257 (b. 29 Jun). FDY, p. 439. IFN, p. 289.

Tansey, Sheridan (Sherry) James [actor] (b. New York NY, 29 Jul 1906–12 Apr 1961 [54], Sacramento CA). (Early film: *Destruction,* 1915.) BHD1, p. 533. George Katchmer, "Remembering the Great Silents," *CI,* 220 (Oct 1993), 41.

Tantlinger, Verne [actor] (b. 1863–27 Feb 1939 [75?], Los Angeles CA). BHD, p. 314.

Tapley, Rose E[lizabeth] [stage/film actress] (b. Petersburg VA, 30 Jun 1881–23 Feb 1956 [74], Woodland Hills CA). m. Frank E. Holaban, 30 Mar 1906. (Edison.) (Film debut: *Wanted Wife,* Edison, 1905; last film, *Resurrection,* 1931.) "Rose Tapley, 74, Dies; First Heroine of Silent Films Left Career on Stage," *NYT,* 26 Feb 1956, 88:4. "Rose Tapley," *Variety,* 29 Feb 1956. AMD, p. 334. AS, p. 1055. BHD1, p. 533. IFN, p. 289 (b. MA). Slide, p. 152. Truitt, p. 321 (b. 1883). "Rose Tapley," *MPW,* 19 Sep 1914, 1632 (daughter Rosemary b. 18 Jan 1907). "Rose Tapley Has Busy Week in Chicago and Evanston," *MPW,* 24 May 1919, 1166. "Rose Tapley Returns in American Cinema Film," *MPW,* 13 Nov 1920, 199. "Rose Tapley Returns," *MPW,* 18 Nov 1922, 251. "English Actress's Debut Here in 'Redeeming Sin,'" *MPW,* 6 Dec 1924, 555. George Katchmer, "Remembering the Great Silents," *CI,* 213 (Mar 1993), 49.

Taptuka, Clarence S. [actor] (b. 1898–8 Nov 1967 [69?], Albuquerque NM). AS, p. 1055. BHD, p. 314.

Tarasova, Alla Konstantinovna [actress] (b. Kiev, Ukraine, Russia, 25 Jan 1898–5 Apr 1973 [75], Moscow, Russia). AS, p. 1055.

Tarbell, Ida M. [writer]. No data found. "Film Famous Authors; Vitagraph Company Prepares Novel Series for Authors' League Benefit," *NYDM,* 28 Jan 1914, 30:4. "Film Ida Tarbell's Stories," *NYDM,* 11 Feb 1914, 32:1.

Tarbell, James [actor]. No data found. AMD, p. 334. "Tarbell Signed," *MPW,* 26 Jun 1926, 706.

Tarbutt, Fraser [actor/assistant director] (b. Toronto, Ontario, Canada, 1896–16 Jun 1918 [22?], France; plane crash). "Fraser Tarbutt Killed," *Variety,* 19 Jul 1918, p. 42 ("Fraser Tarbutt from pictures was killed in action while flying his machine back of the German lines in France June 16. He was of the Royal Flying Corps."). AS, p. 1055. BHD, p. 314; BHD2, p. 258 (Frazer Tarbutt).

Taritsj, Jury Vokorovich [director] (b. Polotsk, Ukrain, Russia, 24 Jan 1885–21 Feb 1967 [82], Moscow, Russia). AS, p. 1055.

Tarkington, Booth [author/playwright] (*né* Newton Booth Tarkington, b. Indianapolis IN, 29 Jul 1869–19 May 1946 [76], Indianapolis IN; bronchial obstruction). m. (1) Laurel Louise Fletcher—div. 1911; (2) Mrs. Temple Robinson (Susanah Robinson). Asa Don Dickinson, *Booth Tarkington; A Gentleman from Indiana* (Garden City NY: Doubleday, 1914). Robert Cortes Holliday, *Booth Tarkington* (Garden City NY: Doubleday, 1918). James Leslie Woodress, *Booth Tarkington; Gentleman from Indiana* (Philadelphia: Lippincott, 1955). "Booth Tarkington, Novelist, 76, Dead; Creator of Penrod and Other Beloved Characters Twice Won Pulitzer Prizes [for *The Magnificent Ambersons,* 1918, and *Alice Adams,* 1921]; Also Was a Playwright; Author of 'The Gentleman from Indiana' [1899] Working on New Book Though Nearly Blind," *NYT,* 20 May 1946, 23:1. "Booth Tarkington Rites Today," *NYT,* 21 May 1946, 23:3. "Rites for Tarkington; Indianapolis Pastor Lauds the Novelist's 'Greatness of Heart,'" *NYT,* 22 May 1946, 21:3 (wrote 40 novels, including *Monsieur Beaucaire,* and 20 plays; "He wrote of things we know and love, because he knew and loved them, too."). "Tarkington Will Filed; Estate Is Bequeathed to Widow—Riley Portrait to Library," *NYT,* 28 May 1946, 23:3 (income from his property was to go to Mrs. Tarkington for life). AMD, p. 334. BHD2, p. 258. "Booth Tarkington and the Indiana Literary Bacillus; Blames Lew Wallace and James Whitcomb Riley for the Epidemic in Hoosierdom—How 'Monsieur Beaucaire' Was Written Around a Picture—A Good Story About the Family Coachman," *NYT,* 7 May 1905, III, 3 ("[A]ccording to vital statistics the Stawte of Indiana has produced more literature than any other State in the Union." Tarkington used to sketch cartoons for a magazine that failed. One left-over sketch "represented a little man in a peruque, sitting disconsolately at a table, while in front of him stood a big tall man in a uniform that I concluded was English. The little man looked to me like a Frenchman, and the other one was big enough to be a Duke. So I began to write around the sketch, and the result was 'Monsieur Beaucaire.'"). "Film Famous Authors; Vitagraph Company Prepares Novel Series for Authors' League Benefit," *NYDM,* 28 Jan 1914, 30:4 (also included were Ida M. Tarbell, Princess Troubetzkoy, Ellis Parger Butler, George Ade, Rex Beach, George Barr McCutcheon, and Louis Joseph Vance). "Famous Authors with Universal," *MPW,* 5 Sep 1914, 1356. "Booth Tarkington to Furnish Goldwyn with Twelve Two-Reel Comedies on American Youth," *MPW,* 8 Nov 1919, 255. "Tarkington, Goldwynite," *MPW,* 20 Dec 1919, 995. "Booth Tarkington to Write Scenarios for His Cousin," *MPW,* 10 Apr 1920, 215. "Booth Tarkington to Write Photoplays for Goldwyn; Liked Handling of 'Edgar,'" *MPW,* 26 Jun 1920, 1733. "Meighan to Star in Booth Tarkington Story," *MPW,* 4 Nov 1922, 58. "Tarkington Stories Are Ideal Screen Material," *MPW,* 24 Nov 1923, 412. "Approved by Tarkington," *MPW,* 20 Dec 1924, 760.

Tarlarini, Mary Cléo [actress] (*née* Maria Cleofe Tarlarini, b. Milan, Italy, 22 Apr 1878–22 Oct 1954 [76], Rome, Italy). JS, p. 447 (in Italian silents from 1908).

Tarleau, Lisa Y. [scenarist] (b. 1878–9 Oct 1952 [74?], Kew Gardens NY). AS, p. 1055.

Tarride, Abel Anatole [actor] (b. Niort, France, 18 Apr 1865 [extrait de naissance no. 137]-3 Feb 1951 [85], Lyon, France [extrait de décès no. 97]). AS, p. 1056.

Tarron, Elsie Maud [actress: Sennett Bathing Beauty] (b. 30 Sep 1903–24 Oct 1990 [87], Los Angeles CA). m. **Andy Clyde** (d. 1967). BHD, p. 314.

Tarshis, Harold E. [title writer]. No data found. FDY, p. 447.

Tarver, J.G. [actor]. No data found. (Fox.) "'Fee Fi Fo Fum'—You're Right! Finish It!," *Photoplay,* Jul 1917, 94 (photo of the giant actor on the set of *Jack and the Beanstalk*).

Tashman, Kitty [actress] (b. 1887–6 Nov 1931 [44?], Los Angeles CA). AS, p. 1056.

Tashman, Lilyan [stage/film actress] (*née* Lillian Tashman, b. Brooklyn NY, 23 Oct 1899–21 Mar 1934 [34], New York NY; cancer. Buried in Washington Cemetery, Brooklyn NY). m. (1) Al Lee, 1914–21; (2) **Edmund S. Lowe**, 1 Sep 1925, SF CA (d. 1971). (FIlm debut: *Experience,* Paramount, 1921; MGM.) "Lilyan Tashman Dies in Hospital; 'Best Dressed Woman' in Films Succumbs at 34 After an Operation Performed Here; Wife of Edmund Lowe; Native of Brooklyn, She Began Career in Ziegfeld Show—Mourned in Hollywood," *NYT,* 22 Mar 1934, 21:4. "Lilyan Tashman," *Variety,* 27 Mar 1934. AMD, p. 334. AS, p. 1056. BHD1, p. 533. FSS, p. 272. IFN, p. 289. Katz, p. 1121 (began 1921). Truitt, p. 321 (b. 1900). "Signs Lilyan Tashman," *MPW,* 18 Jul 1925, 297. "Lilyan Tashman Signed," *MPW,* 8 Aug 1925, 656. "Lilyan Tashman to Wed," *MPW,* 12 Sep 1925, 137. "From Follies to Free Lance," *MPW,* 7 May 1927, 24. Gladys Hall, "New Fashions in Vamps; The Wiggle as a *Yoo-Hoo* Device Is Definitely *Passe,* Lilyan Tashman Says," *MPC,* Feb 1929, 48–49, 70 ("Lilyan further says that sin, today, has acquired a sense of humor."). Faith Service, "I'm Going to Have a Baby!," *Movie Classic,* Nov 1931, 23, 80. Eve Golden, "Lilyan Tashman: Show Girl in Hollywood," *CI,* 266 (Aug 1997), 20–23 (includes filmography).

Tasin, Georgy Nicolaievich [director/scenarist] (b. Russia, 22 Mar 1895–6 May 1956 [61], Ukraine). AS, p. 1056.

Tasker, Robert Joyce [scenarist] (b. 1898–7 Dec 1944 [46?], Mexico City, Mexico; overdose of barbituates). AS, p. 1056. BHD2, p. 258.

Tata, Paul M., Sr. [actor/fencer] (b. 1883?–30 Mar 1962 [79], Memphis TN). "Paul M. Tata Sr.," *NYT,* 2 Apr 1962, 31:5 (taught fencing to Douglas Fairbanks, Sr., Ramon Novarro and Errol Flynn). AS, p. 1056. BHD, p. 314. IFN, p. 289. Truitt, p. 321.

Tate, Cullen B. [director] (b. Paducah KY, 10 Mar 1896–12 Oct 1947 [51], Los Angeles CA; stroke). m. Bess. (DeMille.) "Cullen D. Tate," *Variety,* 22 Oct 1947 (Cullen D. Tate; began 1915). AMD, p. 334. AS, p. 1056. BHD, p. 314; BHD2, p. 258. IFN, p. 289. "Tate to Assist James Cruze," *MPW,* 3 May 1919, 642. "Where's Tate's Dog?," *MPW,* 15 Sep 1923, 266 ("Harmonica").

Tate, Harry [actor] (*né* Ronald MacDonald Hutchinson, b. Scotland, 4 Jul 1872–14 Feb 1940 [67], London, England; during an air raid). AS, p. 1056 (b. England; d. 1941). BHD1, p. 534. IFN, p. 289.

Tate, Ralph [actor]. No data found. AMD, p. 334. "Ralph Tate," *MPW,* 20 Nov 1926, 143.

Tate, Reginald [actor] (b. Garforth, England, 13 Dec 1896–23 Aug 1955 [58], London, England). AS, p. 1056.

Tatum, Buck [actor] (b. 1897–2 Oct 1941 [44?], Santa Monica CA). AS, p. 1056.

Taube, Mathias [actor] (b. Lindesberg, Sweden, 1876–1934 [60?], Sweden). AS, p. 1056. BHD1, p. 534.

Tauber, Richard Seiffert Ernst [actor/composer/singer] (b. Linz, Austria, 16 May 1892–8 Jan 1948 [55], London, England). m. **Diana Napier** (d. 1982). AS, pp. 1056–57.

Tauchert, Arthur [actor] (b. Sydney, Australia, 11 Aug 1878–27 Nov 1933 [55]). BHD1, p. 617.

Taurog, Norman (uncle of **Jackie Cooper**) [actor/director] (b. Chicago IL, 23 Feb 1899–7 Apr 1981 [82], Rancho Mirage CA). m. (1) Julie Leonard; (2) Susan Ream, 1944. (Imp; Ince; Vitagraph; Educational; MGM; Paramount; Oscar, 1930–31.) "Norman Taurog, 82, Child Actor and Long Reign Director, Dies," *Variety,* 15 Apr 1981. AMD, p. 334. AS, p. 1057. BHD, p. 314; BHD2, p. 258. Katz, p. 1122. "Taurog—Leonard," *MPW,* 13 Jun 1925, 747. "Norman Taurog," *MPW,* 25 Dec 1926, 573. "Norman Taurog," *MPW,* 24 Sep 1927, 229.

Tauszky, D. Anthony [artist/portrait painter]. No data found. AMD, p. 334. "Painter Tauszky Will Enhance Art in Metro Subjects," *MPW,* 14 Sep 1918, 1592.

Tavano, C[harles] **F**[élix] [director/producer/scenarist] (b. Nice, France, 19 Apr 1887–29 May 1963 [76], Chatel-de-Neuvre, France [extrait de décès no. 4/1963]). AS, p. 1057.

Tavares, Arthur [actor] (*né* Arturo Tavares, b. CA, 10 Jan 1884–27 May 1954 [70], Los Angeles Co. CA). AS. p. 1057. BHD1, p. 534. IFN, p. 289.

Tavernier, Albert [actor] (b. 1859–3 Nov 1929 [70?], Los Angeles CA). AS, p. 1057. BHD, p. 314 (d. Boston MA).

Taylor, Al [actor] (b. 1882–10 Oct 1947 [65]). AS, p. 1057. IFN, p. 289. George Katchmer, "Remembering the Great Silents," *CI,* 202 (Apr 1992), 6, 63.

Taylor, Albert [actor] (b. Montgomery AL, 8 Apr 1868–9 Apr 1940 [72], Los Angeles CA). AS, p. 1057 (d. 10 Apr). BHD1, p. 534.

Taylor, Alma Louise [actress] (b. London, England, 1 Mar 1895–23 Jan 1974 [78], London, England; stroke [death certificate no. QDX 149392]). m. Leonard Avery. (Appeared in over 200 films.) AMD, p. 334. AS, p. 1057 (b. 3 Jan-d. 29 Jan). BHD1, p. 534. IFN, p. 289. "Alma Taylor," *MPW,* 14 Feb 1914, 824.

Taylor, Arthur [director] (d. 19 May 1955, Birmingham, England). BHD2, p. 258.

Taylor, Avonne [stage/film dancer/actress] (b. Springfield OH, 12 Feb 1899–20 Mar 1992 [93], Cleveland OH). AMD, p. 334. BHD1, p. 534. "M-G-M SIgns Stage Dancer," *MPW,* 7 May 1927, 39.

Taylor, Beth [actress] (*née* Elizabeth C. Ownes, b. 1889–1 Mar 1951 [62], Los Angeles CA). AS, p. 1057. BHD, p. 314. IFN, p. 289.

Taylor, Billy [actor] (*né* William H. Taylor, b. Brownsville TX, 9 Jul 1829–26 Nov 1930 [101], Los Angeles CA). AS, p. 1057.

Taylor, Charles A[lonzo] [playwright/-

scenarist] (b. So. Hadley MA?, 1864?–21 Mar 1942 [78], Glendale CA). m. (1) Emma McKenna (d. 1888); (2) Laura Cooney [**Laurette Taylor**], 1900 (d. 1946). "Charles A. Taylor, Playwright, Dead; 'Master of Melodrama' Wrote 'From Rags to Riches' for His Ex-Wife, Laurette Taylor; Once a Train Conductor; Action in Wreck Won Him Job from Senator Hearst—Had 5 Hits on Stage at Once," *NYT,* 22 Mar 1942, 48:8. "Charles A. Taylor," *Variety,* 25 Mar 1942. AMD, p. 334. AS, p. 1057. BHD2, p. 258 (b. Greenfield MA, 1888-d. 20 Mar). FDY, p. 439. "Charles A. Taylor with Metro," *MPW,* 8 Apr 1916, 271. "Taylor to Address Authors' League," *MPW,* 29 Apr 1916, 813. "Charles A. Taylor Write Pathé Story," *MPW,* 17 Feb 1917, 1049.

Taylor, Clarence [actor]. No data found. AMD, p. 334. "How One Fellow Got Work in Pictures," *MPW,* 18 Apr 1914, 341.

Taylor, E. Forrest [actor] (b. Bloomington IL, 29 Dec 1883–19 Feb 1965 [81], Garden Grove CA). (Selig; Kalem; American.) AMD, p. 334. AS, p. 1057 (d. LA CA). BHD1, p. 534. IFN, p. 289. "E. Forrest Taylor Joins Kalem," *MPW,* 17 Jun 1916, 2048. Nick C. Nicholls, "Forrest Taylor," *CI,* 141 (Mar 1987), 34.

Taylor, Edward C. [stage/film director]. No data found. (Edison.) AMD, p. 334. "Edward C. Taylor," *MPW,* 12 Jun 1915, 1752. "Three New Edison Directors," *MPW,* 24 Jul 1915, 632.

Taylor, Elberton [stage manager]. No data found. AMD, p. 334. "New Stage Manager for Edison," *MPW,* 6 Feb 1915, 818.

Taylor, Eric [actor] (b. New York NY, 14 Feb 1848–4 Aug 1910 [62], New York NY). AS, p. 1057.

Taylor, Eric [scenarist] (b. 1897–8 Sep 1952 [55?], San Francisco CA; heart attack). AS, p. 1057. BHD2, p. 258.

Taylor, Estelle [actress] (*née* Estelle Boylan, b. Wilmington DE, 20 May 1894–15 Apr 1958 [63], Los Angeles CA; cancer). m. (1) Kenneth Malcolm Peacock, Wilmington DE at age 14; (2) **Jack Dempsey**, 7 Feb 1925, San Diego CA—div. 1931 (d. 1983); (3) Paul Small, 1943–45. (Film debut: *While the City Sleeps.*) "Estelle Taylor, Actress, 58, Dies; ex-Wife of Jack Dempsey Played Supporting Roles in Hollywood Movies," *NYT,* 16 Apr 1958, 33:1. "Estelle Taylor," *Variety,* 23 Apr 1958 (age 58). AMD, p. 334. AS, p. 1058. BHD1, p. 534. FFF, p. 36 (b. 1903). FSS, p. 273. IFN, p. 289. Katz, pp. 1123–24. MH, p. 139 (b. 1903). Truitt, p. 322 (b. 1899). "Fox Actress Is Chosen as [football] Mascot," *MPW,* 7 Jan 1922, 74. "Two New Stars Signed by C.B.C.," *MPW,* 11 Aug 1923, 494. Alma Talley, "How Styles in Movie Love Making Have Changed," *MW,* 3 May 1924, 9. Gladys Hall and Adele Whitely Fletcher, "We Interview Jack Dempsey and Estelle Taylor," *MW,* 13 Jun 1925, 9–10, 43. "Miss Taylor Signed," *MPW,* 9 Oct 1926, 4. "Estelle Taylor Better," *MPW,* 13 Aug 1927, 455. "Estelle Taylor May Not Renew Contract with U-A," *MPW,* 27 Aug 1927, 5. "Columbia Signs Estelle Taylor," *MPW,* 31 Dec 1927, 16. Joan Standish, "Is Jack Dempsey Broke?; Manassa Mauler Is Said to Have Created Huge Trust Funds for Himself. But All Estelle Taylor Asks Is His Purchase of Their $100,000 Hollywood Home," *Movie Classic,* Nov 1931, 43.

Taylor, Genevieve [extra actress]. No data found. Paul Paige, "Close-Ups and Fade-Outs," *Paris and Hollywood Screen Secrets,* Oct 1927, 22 (attempting suicide, she "slashed her wrist with a razor blade").

Taylor, George M. [producer] (d. 17 Aug 1920, Schenectady NY; pneumonia). AS, p. 1058. BHD2, p. 258.

Taylor, Grant [actor] (b. England, 1917–1971 [54?], Melbourne, Australia). AS, p. 1058.

Taylor, James O. [cinematographer]. No data found. FDY, p. 469.

Taylor, Josephine [actress] (*née* Josephine Motz, b. 1891?–26 Nov 1964 [73], Calumet City IL). (Essanay [Chicago IL].) "Josephine Taylor," *Variety,* 9 Dec 1964. AS, p. 1058. BHD, p. 314. IFN, p. 289. Truitt, p. 322.

Taylor, Julia [stage/film actress] (b. 20 Sep 1878–4 Dec 1976 [98], Los Angeles CA). m. **Wallace A. Worsley, Sr.** (d. 1944; 1 son, Wallace Worsley, Jr.). "Julia Taylor Worsley," *Variety,* 285, 22 Dec 1976, 107:1. AS, p. 1058. BHD, p. 314.

Taylor, Lark [actor] (*né* John Lark Taylor, b. Nashville TN, 1881–26 Mar 1946 [65?], Nashville TN). BHD, p. 314.

Taylor, Laurette [stage/film actress] (*née* Laura Cooney, b. New York NY, 1 Apr 1884–7 Dec 1946 [62], New York NY; stroke). m. **Charles A. Taylor** (d. 1942); (2) **J**[ohn] **Hartley Manners** (d. 1928). Marguerite Courtney [daughter], *Laurette* (New York: Atheneum, 1968). "Laurette Taylor, Stage Star, Dies; Actress, 62, Hailed in 1912 as 'Peg o' My Heart'—Last Seen in 'Glass Menagerie,'" *NYT,* 8 Dec 1946, 78:2. "Laurette Taylor," *Variety,* 11 Dec 1946. AMD, p. 334. AS, p. 1058 (*née* Helen Laura Magdelene Cooney). BHD, p. 314. GSS, pp. 369–71 (d. 17 Dec 1946). IFN, p. 289. Katz, p. 1124. Truitt, p. 322 (*née* Laurette Cooney). "Laurette Taylor to Star in Film," *MPW,* 17 Jun 1922, 620. "Begins Acting," *MPW,* 15 Jul 1922, 232. "Luck Leaves from Laurette Taylor," *MPW,* 2 Jun 1923, 393. "Metro Signs Laurette Taylor," *MPW,* 4 Aug 1923, 414. "Vidor Directing Laurette Taylor," *MPW,* 24 Nov 1923, 413. Harry Carr, "Laurette Does Her Stuff [in *Happiness*]," *Classic,* Aug 1924, 24–25.

Taylor, Loren E. [cinematographer] (b. NB, 1881?–21 Feb 1956 [74], Los Angeles Co. CA). "Loren E. Taylor," *Variety,* 29 Feb 1956. BHD2, p. 258.

Taylor, Marie [stage/radio actress] (*née?,* b. 1857?–23 Dec 1947 [90], West Philadelphia PA). "Marie Taylor," *NYT,* 25 Dec 1947, 21:1 (Mrs. Emma Taylor Johnson). "Marie Taylor," *Variety,* 31 Dec 1947.

Taylor, Mrs. Mary McKetrick [actress] (*née?,* b. 1888?–20 Jun 1963 [75], Cheverly MD). "Mrs. Mary McKetrick Taylor," *Variety,* 10 Jul 1963.

Taylor, Matt [scenarist] (b. 1897?–11 Sep 1966 [69], Port Chester NY). m. Marion Baxter. (TC-F; Paramount; Universal.) "Matt Taylor Dead; Fiction Writer, 69," *NYT,* 12 Sep 1966, 45:5. AMD, p. 335. AS, p. 1058. FDY, p. 439. "Taylor Goes West," *MPW,* 6 Nov 1926, 2. "Taylor Joins F.P.," *MPW,* 29 Nov 1926, 4.

Taylor, May [actress/dancer] (*née* Mag Waggoner, d. 22 Jul 1945, New York NY). m. (1) Jack Taylor. "May Taylor Waggoner," *Variety,* 1 Aug 1945. AS, p. 1058. SD, p. 1202.

Taylor, Mrs. May A. (mother of **Julia Taylor Weber**) (*née?,* b. 1844?–30 Jul 1913 [69], Philadelphia PA). "Mrs. Mary A. Taylor," *Variety,* 8 Aug 1913. AS, p. 1058.

Taylor, Ray [director] (b. Perham MN, 1 Dec 1888–15 Feb 1952 [63], Los Angeles CA). (Fox; Universal.) "Ray Taylor," *Variety,* 27 Feb 1952. AS, p. 1058. BHD2, p. 258. IFN, p. 289. Katz, p. 1124.

Taylor, Rex [scenarist] (b. Des Moines IA, 1 Nov 1889–27 Dec 1968 [79], San Pedro CA). AMD, p. 335. BHD2, p. 258. FDY, p. 439. "Taylor Fashions Funny Films," *MPW,* 12 Jan 1918, 250.

Taylor, Robert [actor] (b. 1873–9 Dec 1936 [63?], Santa Monica CA; cancer). AS, p. 1058.

Taylor, Ruth Lee [actress: Wampas Star, 1928] (b. Grand Rapids MI, 13 Jan 1908–12 Apr 1984 [75], Palm Springs CA). "Ruth Taylor," *Variety,* 30 Apr 1969. AMD, p. 335. AS, p. 1058 (d. London, England). BHD1, p. 535 (b. 1907). "Ruth Taylor Steps Up," *MPW,* 26 Jun 1926, 707. "Pick 'Lorelei,'" *MPW,* 27 Aug 1927, 579. "Ruth Taylor," *MPW,* 10 Sep 1927, 95. Ann Cummings ("*Classic's* Own *Lorelie Lee*"), "The Blonde Preferred," *MPC,* Nov 1927, 33, 88, 89 (Taylor wins the role of Lorelei Leed in *Gentlemen Prefer Blondes*).

Taylor, Sam[uel] **J.** [director/producer/scenarist] (b. New York NY, 13 Aug 1895–6 Mar 1958 [62], Santa Monica CA; heart attack). m. Olive. (Kalem, 1916; Vitagraph.) "Sam Taylor," *NYT,* 8 Mar 1958, 17:3. "Sam Taylor," *Variety,* 12 Mar 1958. AMD, p. 335. AS, p. 1058. BHD2, p. 258. FDY, p. 439. IFN, p. 289. Katz, p. 1125 (began 1916). "Sam Taylor Joins Vitagraph Staff," *MPW,* 22 Mar 1919, 1611. "Joins Roach Comedy Forces," *MPW,* 12 Mar 1921, 186. "Taylor Signed," *MPW,* 15 Apr 1922, 723. "Sam Taylor Signed to Direct First Lloyd-Paramount Film," *MPW,* 4 Apr 1925, 442. "Taylor Leaves Lloyd," *MPW,* 20 Mar 1926, 4.

Taylor, Sidney [film salesman] (b. 1908?–Jan? 1965 [56], London, England). "Sidney Taylor," *Variety,* 13 Jan 1965.

Taylor, Stanley [actor] (b. Campbell MI, 3 Mar 1891–27 Nov 1980 [89], Inglewood CA). AS, p. 1058. BHD1, p. 535 (b. 1900). George Katchmer, "Remembering the Great Silents," *CI,* 213 (Mar 1993), 49.

Taylor, Stanner E[dward]**V**[arley] [writer/director] (b. St. Louis MO, 28 Sep 1877–23 Nov 1948 [71], Los Angeles CA). m. **Marion Leonard** (d. 1956). (Biograph, 600 scenarios; Reliance; Rex; Edison; Vitagraph; Kalem: ca. 1,000 scripts in all.) AMD, p. 335. AS, p. 1058. BHD2, p. 258. IFN, p. 290. 1921 Directory, p. 275. "Taylor and Leonard," *MPW,* 27 Jul 1912, 329. "Warren, Taylor and Leonard with Warners," *MPW,* 23 Aug 1913, 851. "Stanner Taylor's Record; Marion Leonard Producer Has Unusually Successful Photoplaywright Record," *NYDM,* 8 Apr 1914, 36:1 ("Mr. Taylor was probably the first photoplaywright to receive a regular salary as such and a much higher fee than customary for his output, both of which were given him by the Biograph and continued for several years."). "Knickerbocker Star Features Successful," *MPW,* 25 Sep 1915, 2189. "Stanner E.V. Taylor," *MPW,* 9 Oct 1915, 266. "Stanner E.V. Taylor, Noted Playwright, Adapted New Taylor Holmes Pictures," *MPW,* 28 Feb 1920, 1512. "Taylor Signs with Woody; 'The Lone Wolf' His First," *MPW,* 19 Jan 1924, 188. "Taylor Starts Production on Associated's 'Miracle of Life,'" *MPW,* 30 May 1925, 567.

Taylor, William Desmond [actor/director] (*né* William Cunningham Deane-Tanner, b. Mallows County Cork, Ireland, 26 Apr 1872–1 Feb

1922 [49], Los Angeles CA; shot to death by unknown assailant). m. Ethel Kay. Samuel Anthony Peeples, *The Man Who Died Twice: A Novel About Hollywood's Most Baffling Murder* (NY: Putnam, 1976). Sidney D. Kirkpatrick, *A Cast of Killers* (NY: E.P. Dutton, 1986). Robert Giroux, *A Deed of Death; The Story Behind the Unsolved Murder of Hollywood Director William Desmond Taylor* (NY: Alfred A. Knopf, 1990). Bruce Long, *William Desmond Taylor: A Dossier* (Metuchen NJ: Scarecrow Press, 1991) (includes filmography). "Re-Enacts Murder of Film Director; District Attorney Goes to Taylor's Home to Determine Circumstances; Miss Normand Recalled; Actress Who Was the Last to See the Movie Director Alive Is Again Examined," *NYT,* 11 Feb 1922, 1:4, 8:4; "Miss Normand Issues Statement," 8:4 ("Please tell the public that I know absolutely nothing about this terrible happening and that Mr. Taylor and I did not quarrel."). "7,000 Hollywood Rumors Dissolve as Police Flop in Taylor Murder; Dead Director Well Thought Of—No Philanderer—Opinion on Coast No Women Involved—Reformers Active as Usual," *Variety,* 20 Feb 1922. AMD, p. 335. AS, p. 1059 (b. Carlow, Ireland). BHD, p. 314 (b. 26 Mar); BHD2, p. 258 (b. 1867). IFN, p. 290 (b. 26 Mar). Katz, p. 1125. Truitt, p. 322 (b. 1877). "William Desmond Taylor," *MPW,* 3 Oct 1914, 44. "William Desmond Taylor," *MPW,* 31 Oct 1914, 647. "William Desmond Taylor with the Favorite Players," *MPW,* 28 Nov 1914, 1245. "William Desmond Taylor," *MPW,* 4 Sep 1915, 1654. "Pallas Pictures Secure William Desmond Taylor," *MPW,* 30 Oct 1915, 772. "William Desmond Taylor Signs with Famous-Lasky," *MPW,* 5 Jan 1918, 63. "Director Taylor Prefers the West," *MPW,* 22 Nov 1919, 425. "Director William Taylor Saves Mary Minter Party," *MPW,* 3 Jan 1920, 94. "Taylor to Make Four Super-SPecial Pictures for Realast; 'Soul of Youth' Is the First," *MPW,* 10 Jul 1920, 232. "William Desmond Taylor Calls His Realart Contract 'A Chance to "Go the Limit,"'" *MPW,* 10 Jul 1920, 236. "Memorial Service for Dead Film Stars," *MPW,* 9 Oct 1920, 783 (delivered eulogy for Olive Thomas, Robert Harron, Frank Elliott, Clarine Seymour and Ormer Locklear). "Taylor Praises Technical Men for 'Movies' Advance," *MPW,* 30 Oct 1920, 1230. William Desmond Taylor, "Films Coming to Be Recognized as Best Advertising Medium for Books and for Successful Stage Productions," *MPW,* 25 Dec 1920, 1020. "Taylor for e Directors Urges Quick Organization," *MPW,* 5 Mar 1921, 35. William Desmond Taylor, "Motion Picture DIrectors Against Extravagant Prologues and Extras," *MPW,* 17 Dec 1921, 776. "Riesenfeld Agrees with Taylor That Must Must Be Subservient to Picture; Terms It as an Opiate," *MPW,* 14 Jan 1922, 164. "Obituary," *MPW,* 11 Feb 1922, 598 (b. 1877; clues to robbery as motive). "Crowds Storm Church at Taylor Funeral; Police Seek Sands, Butler and Secretary," *MPW,* 18 Feb 1922, 715. "Los Angeles Film People, Maligned, Demard Fair Play of General Public," *MPW,* 25 Feb 1922, 813. "The Official Facts," *MPW,* 8 Apr 1922, 616. Bruce Long, "The William Desmond Taylor Murder Case," *CFC,* 57 (Winter, 1977), 24–32. Douglas J. Whitton, "The Career of William Desmond Taylor; Part I," *CI,* 92 (Feb 1983), 42–45; Part II, No. 93 (Mar 1983), 46–49. Robert S. Birchard, "Disputed Titles [letter]," *CI,* 96 (Jun 1983), 30; Doug Whitton, "More Taylor [letter]," 31.

Taylor, William H. (Billy) [actor] (b. Brownsville TX, 9 Jul 1829–26 Dec 1930 [101], Los Angeles CA). BHD, p. 314. IFN, p. 290 (age 103).

Taylor, Wilton [actor] (b. 1869–24 Jan 1925 [56]). AS, p. 1059. BHD, p. 314. IFN, p. 290.

Tayo, Lyle [actor] (b. Elmdale KS, 19 Jan 1889–2 May 1971 [82], Los Angeles CA). BHD1, p. 535.

Tchaikovsky, Boris Vitaljevich [actor/director] (b. Russia, 1888–5 Nov 1924 [36?], Russia). AS, p. 1059.

Tchardynin, Petr Ivanovich [director] (b. Tcherdyne, Russia, 1873–1934 [61?], Odessa, Russia). AS, p. 1059.

Tchekoff, Michael Pablovich [actor] (b. St. Petersburg, Russia, 18 Aug 1891–17 Apr 1955 [63], Los Angeles CA). AS, p. 1059.

Tchiaourelli, Mikhail Yedisjerovich [actor/director] (b. Tbilissi, Georgia, 25 Jan 1894–15 Nov 1974 [80], Tbilissi, Georgia). AS, p. 1059.

Tchouchounava, Alekander [director] (b. Russia, 28 Jan 1881–25 Oct 1955 [74], Russia). AS, p. 1059.

Teachout, H. Arthur [actor] (b. 1887–5 Mar 1939 [52?], Cedar Rapids IA). AS, p. 1059.

Tead, Phil[lips] [actor] b. Somerville MA, 29 Sep 1893–9 Jun 1974 [80], Pomona CA). AS, p. 1060. BHD1, p. 535. IFN, p. 290.

Teare, Ethel [actress] (*née* Ethel O. Risso, b. Phoenix AZ, 11 Jan 1894–4 Mar 1959 [65], San Mateo CA). (Kalem.) AMD, p. 335. AS, p. 1060. BHD, p. 315. IFN, p. 290. Truitt, p. 322. "New Kalem Comedies," *MPW,* 12 Feb 1916, 934. Cecilia Mount, "Ethel Teare—And That Flirtatious Way," *MPC,* Apr 1916, 25–26, 68. "Kalem Ham Comedy Company," *MPN,* 21 Oct 1916, 197.

Tearle, Conway (son of Ormsby Tearle and Minnie Conway; half-brother of **Godfrey** and **Malcolm Tearle**) [stage/film actor] (*né* Frederick Conway Levy, b. New York NY, 17 May 1878–1 Oct 1938 [60], Los Angeles CA; heart attack). m. (1) Josephine Park (d. 1931); (2) Mrs. Roberta Menges Corwen-Hill; (3) **Adele Rowland** (d. 1971). (FP-L; Selznick; Paramount; 1st National.) "Conway Tearle, 60, Dies on the Coast; Stage and Screen Actor Is the Victim of Heart Attack—Ill Only a Few Weeks; Made His Debut in 1892; His Last Film Appearance Was in 'Romeo and Juliet'—A Native of New York," *NYT,* 2 Oct 1938, 48:6. "Conway Tearle," *Variety,* 5 Oct 1938. AMD, p. 335. AS, p. 1060. BHD1, p. 536. FFF, p. 62 (b. 1880). FSS, p. 273. GK, pp. 925–38. IFN, p. 290. Katz, p. 1126 (began 1914). MH, p. 139 (b. 1880). MSBB, p. 1028. Spehr, p. 170 (b. 1880). Truitt, pp. 322–23. WWS, p. 267 (b. 1880). "Stage Notes," *NYDM,* 9 Jun 1915, 7:2 (Roberta Menges Tearle granted a discharge from bankruptcy; petition of 25 Apr 1914; liabilities of $11,669 and no assets.). "Conway Tearle, Lead for Miss Young," *MPW,* 19 Aug 1916, 1222. "Conway Tearle Screen Star Over Night," *MPW,* 14 Oct 1916, 261. Hazel Simpson Naylor, "Hard Luck Tearle," *MPC,* May 1919, 20–21. "Conway Tearle Will Be Starred in Forthcoming Equity Special Picture," *MPW,* 24 Jan 1920, 600. "Lewis J. Selznick Announces Conway Tearle as Star for National Picture Theatres, Inc.," *MPW,* 26 Jun 1920, 1778. "Conway Tearle Will Star in Six National Films Yearly," *MPW,* 10 Jul 1920, 230. "Tearle to Make Debut as Author," *MPW,* 27 Nov 1920, 493. "Martha Mansfield and Conway Tearle Are Announced as Stars by Lewis J. Selznick," *MPW,* 25 Dec 1920, 1004. "Conway Tearle to Be Shubert Star on Stage," *MPW,* 5 Nov 1921, 79. "Selznick Signs Conway Tearle for Two Special Productions," *MPW,* 15 Jul 1922, 216. "Tearle Signs with Schenck Once More," *MPW,* 30 Jun 1923, 773. Harry Carr, "Il Est Très Difficile," *Classic,* Apr 1923, 36–37, 78–79. Grace Kingsley, "'Cake-Eaters No Longer Popular with Flappers!,' Says Conway Tearle," *MW,* 26 Apr 1924, 9, 29–30. Regina Cannon, "It's His Job," *MW,* 26 Jul 1924, 15–16. Gladys Hall and Adele Whitely Fletcher, "We Interview Conway Tearle," *MW,* 6 Dec 1924, 4–6, 25. "Conway Tearle's Name on Metro-Goldwyn Contract," *MPW,* 21 Feb 1925, 813. "Columbia Signs Three Stars of the First Magnitude," *MPW,* 30 Jul 1927, 331. "Conway Tearle and Dorothy Sebastian Escape Injury," *MPW,* 13 Aug 1927, 454. "Denial that Marmont Has Filed Charges with Academy," *MPW,* 24 Sep 1927, 231. George A. Katchmer, "Anyone Remember Conway Tearle?," *CI,* 151 (Jan 1988), 19–20, 23, 34.

Tearle, Godfrey (brother of **Malcolm Tearle**; half-brother of **Conway Tearle**) [stage/film actor] (b. New York NY, 12 Oct 1884–8 Jun 1953 [68], London, England). m. (1) Mary Malone (2) Stella Freeman; (3) Barbara Palmer. "Godfrey Tearle, British Actor, 68; 'Greatest Othello,' Who Was Knighted in 1951, Is Dead—Made Debut in 1893," *NYT,* 10 Jun 1953, 29:5 ("His first appearance in pictures was in 1906 when he played Romeo. He appeared in many silent and talking pictures.") "Sir Godfrey Tearle," *Variety,* 10 Jun 1953. AS, p. 1060. BHD1, p. 536. IFN, p. 290. Katz, p. 1126. Truitt, p. 323.

Tearle, Malcolm (brother of **Godfrey Tearle**; half-brother of **Conway Tearle**) [actor] (b. 1888?–8 Dec 1935 [47?], London, England; suicide). m. Roma Lynette. "Malcolm Tearle," *Variety,* 25 Dec 1935. AS, p. 1060. Truitt, p. 323.

Teddy [dog star] (b. ca. 1915). (Keystone.) Harry C. Carr, "An Interview in Great Danish," *Photoplay,* Jul 1917, 29 (photos with Gloria Swanson from *Teddy at the Throttle*).

Tedeschi, Carlo [actor]. No data found. JS, p. 448 (in Italian silents from 1921).

Tedmarsh, William J. [actor] (b. London, England, 3 Feb 1876–10 May 1937 [61]). (American.) AS, p. 1060. BHD, p. 315. IFN, p. 290.

Tedro, Henrietta [actress] (b. 1885–25 Jul 1948 [63], Los Angeles CA). BHD, p. 315. IFN, p. 290.

Teitel, Albert [executive]. No data found. AMD, p. 336. "Teitel Leaves Ideal Studios," *MPW,* 21 Oct 1916, 394.

Teje, Tora [actress] (b. Stockholm, Sweden, 17 Jan 1893–30 Apr 1973 [80], Stockholm, Sweden). AS, p. 1060. BHD, p. 315.

Telde, Tilde [actress] (b. Milan, Italy, 14 Apr 1878). JS, p. 448 (in Italian silents from 1914).

Tell, Alma (sister of **Olive Tell**) [stage/film actress] (b. New York NY, 27 Mar 1898–29 Dec 1937 [39], San Fernando CA). m. **William S. Blystone** (d. 1956). "Alma Tell, Actress on Stage and Screen; Retired Player Had Appeared in 'Main Street' and 'Peg o' My Heart'—Dies at 39," *NYT,* 1 Jan 1938, 19:4. "Alma Tell," *Variety,* 5 Jan 1938 (d. 30 Dec 1937, San Fernando CA). AS, p. 1060. BHD1, p. 536. FSS, p. 274. IFN, p. 290. MH, p. 139. Truitt, p. 323 (b. 1892). WWS, p. 39. David A. Balch, "'Reform the Daughter by Reforming the Mother,' Declares Alma Tell," *MW,* 19 May 1923, 7.

Tell, Olive (sister of **Alma Tell**) [stage/film

actress] (b. New York NY, 27 Sep 1894–8 Jun 1951 [56], New York NY). m. Henry M. Hobart. (World; Selznick; Empire All-Star Mutual; Metro.) "Olive Tell, Appeared on Stage and Screen," *NYT,* 9 Jun 1951, 19:4 (age 55). "Olive Tell," *Variety,* 13 Jun 1951 (age 55). AMD, p. 336. AS, p. 1060 (b. 26 Sep-6 Jun). BHD1, p. 536 (d. 6 Jun). FSS, p. 274. IFN, p. 290 (d. 6 Jun, age 55). MH, p. 139. MSBB, p. 1042. Spehr, p. 170. Truitt, p. 323. WWS, p. 236. "Olive Tell," *MPW,* 21 Apr 1917, 403. "Olive Tell," *MPW,* 21 Apr 1917, 439. "Olive Tell," *MPW,* 8 Sep 1917, 1518. "Olive Tell," *MPW,* 3 Nov 1917, 684. "Metro Engages Two Stars; Each Will Head Company," *MPW,* 20 Jul 1918, 408. Edward Weitzel, "Olive Tell Introduced to 'Secret Strangers,'" *MPW,* 27 Jul 1918, 559. "Olive Tell Signed by Jans; B.A. Rolfe to Be Director," *MPW,* 3 Jan 1920, 64. "Olive Tell Has Been Engaged to Play in a Selznick Picture with Eugene O'Brien," *MPW,* 20 Nov 1920, 362.

Tellegen, Lou- [stage/film actor/director] (*né* Isadore Louis Bernard van Dommelem, b. St. Oedenrode, south Holland, 26 Nov 1881?–29 Oct 1934 [52?], Los Angeles CA; suicide by stabbing with scissors because of incurable cancer). m. **Geraldine Farrar**, 8 Feb 1916, NY NY—1923 (d. 1967); Isabel Craven Dilworth [aka **Nina Romano**], 17 Dec 1923, Rutherford NJ. *Women Have Been Kind; The Memoirs of Lou Tellegen* (NY: Vanguard Press, 1931). (Early U.S. film: *The Explorer,* Paramount, 1915.) "Tellegen's End in Poverty Contrasts with Thrifty State of Newer Stars," *Variety,* 6 Nov 1934 (age 51). AMD, p. 336. AS, p. 1061 (b. 20 Nov 1883; d. 28 Oct). BHD1, p. 536; BHD2, p. 258 (b. 1883). FSS, p. 274. IFN, p. 290 (age 50). Katz, p. 1127 (*né* Isidor Van Dameler). Truitt, p. 323 (b. 1884; d. 1 Nov). "Lou Tellegen with Famous Players," *MPW,* 30 Jan 1915, 690. "Lou Tellegen in Court," *NYDM,* 12 May 1915, 7:2 (appeared in Yorkville Court on 5 May "to answer charges of participating in an alleged immoral production [*Taking Chances* at the Thirty-ninth Street Theater]. Mr. Tellegen was arrested upon the complaint of Howard Clark Barber, superintendent of the Society for the Suppression of Vice," who claimed that in the second act Tellegen, as Count De Lasta, "invades the bedroom of the wife of the Minister of police during the midnight hours...subversive to public morals." Case postponed until 14 May.). "Lou Tellegen to Appear on Screen," *MPW,* 19 Jun 1915, 1916. "Lou Tellegen with Lasky Company," *MPW,* 8 Jul 1916, 242. "Lou Tellegen to Return to Stage," *MPW,* 14 Oct 1916, 247. "Lou Tellegen Quits Screen to Become a Director," *MPW,* 24 Mar 1917, 1936. "Lou Tellegen to Star with Farrar," *MPW,* 17 May 1919, 1010. "Blackton Signs Lou Tellegen," *MPW,* 13 Oct 1923, 559. "Tellegen Starts Fourth Vitagraph Film in Year," *MPW,* 15 Nov 1924, 263.

Tellegen, Mike [actor] (b. Russia, 20 Apr 1885–16 Aug 1970 [85], Los Angeles Co. CA). BHD1, p. 536. IFN, p. 290.

Tello, Alfonso Sanchez [actor/director/producer] (b. Mexico, 8 Mar 1905–18 Apr 1979 [74], La Jolla CA). BHD, p. 315; BHD2, p. 259. IFN, p. 290.

Telzlaff, Teddy (b. 1883-d. 1929 [46?], Santa Ana CA). BHD1, p. 617.

Temary, Elza [actress] (b. Germany, 12 Feb 1905–16 Feb 1968 [63], Tucson AZ). BHD1, p. 536.

Temerson, Jean [actor] (*né* Lucien Jean Temersohn, b. Paris, France, 12 Jun 1898–9 Aug 1956 [58], Paris, France [extrait de décès no. 20]). AS, p. 1061.

Tempest, Florence [vaudeville: Tempest & Sunshine/film actress]. No data found. (World.) AMD, p. 336. "Gossip of the Studios," *NYDM,* 14 Apr 1915, 23:2. "Florence Tempest Appears in Pictures," *MPW,* 17 Apr 1915, 401. "Sunshine and 'Tempest,'" *MPW,* 25 Sep 1915, 2184.

Tempest, Marie [stage/film actress] (*née* Marie Susan Etherington, b. Marylebone Road, London, England, 15 Jul 1862–13? Oct 1942 [80], Westminster, London, England). m. (1) Alfred E. Izard; (2) Cosmo Stuart (d. 1921); (3) **W. Grahame Browne**, 1921 (d. 1937). "Marie Tempest, 78, Stage Star, Dies; Dame of British Empire Had Delighted Americans Here, in England for 55 Years; Home Razed by Bombs; Fortune Gone with the War, Her Retort to Nazis: 'You Can't Live on Regret,'" *NYT,* 16 Oct 1942, 19:1 (states that she made 1 film in 1936, but she also made *Mrs. Plumb's Pudding* [Universal, 1915] and others). "Marie Tempest," *Variety,* 21 Oct 1942 (d. 15 Oct 1942). AS, p. 1061 (b. Westminster, England-d. 15 Oct). BHD1, p. 536 (d. 15 Oct). Blum, p. 92. GSS, pp. 374–77. IFN, p. 290 (b. 1862). Truitt, p. 323 (d. 15 Oct). "Marie Tempest Arrives; Her Company Brought ver for Run in 'The Freedom of Suzanne,'" *NYT,* 16 Apr 1905, 5:3 (15 Apr, on the *Lucania* from Liverpool; to play at the Empire Theatre from 19 Apr to 12 May. "'I am most enthusiastic over Mr. Frohman's plan of placing two theatres at my disposal one on each side of the Atlantic,' said Miss Tempest, 'and although at first I had a little horror of the voyage, for I am a wretched sailor, now that it is over I am anticipating a delightful four weeks in New York."). Cover, *NYDM,* 11 Aug 1915 (with Cyril Maude, Francis Wilson, and Graham Browne, all Frohman stage players).

Tempest, Tom [actor] (b. 1874?–14 Dec 1955 [81], Skowhegan ME). "Tom Tempest," *Variety,* 21 Dec 1955. AS, p. 1061. BHD, p. 315 (b. 1876). IFN, p. 290.

Temple, Elaine (sister of **Jennifer Temple**) [actress] (b. Indianapolis IN, 12 Mar 1846–6 Jun 1905 [59], Los Angeles CA). AS, p. 1061.

Temple, Jennifer (sister of **Elaine Temple**) [actress] (b. Indianapolis IN, 20 Sep 1848–17 May 1903 [54], Los Angeles CA). AS, p. 1061.

Temple, Richard, Jr. [stage/film/TV actor] (b. England, 1873?–14 Oct 1954 [81], New York NY). m. Evie Green. "Veteran Actor, 81, Dead; Richard Temple Was on TV and Played for Shuberts," *NYT,* 17 Oct 1954, 87:3. "Richard Temple," *Variety,* 20 Oct 1954. AS, p. 1061. BHD, p. 315.

Templeton, Fay [actress] (b. Little Rock AR, 25 Dec 1865–3 Oct 1939 [73], San Francisco CA). AS, p. 1061.

Templeton, Olive [actress] (*née* Olive MacMackin, b. 1883?–29 May 1979 [96], New York NY [Death Certificate Index No. 8713 (Olive T. Flannery); age 95]). m. John L. Flannery, 1919 (d. 1937). (Edison.) "Olive Templeton," *Variety,* 6 Jun 1979. AS, p. 1061. BHD, p. 315. IFN, p. 290.

Templey, Marguerite Anne Marie [actress] (b. Nantes, France, 2 Mar 1880–24 Mar 1944 [64], Vals-les-Bains, France [extrait de décès no. SN/1944]). AS, p. 1061.

Tenbrook, Harry [actor/assistant director] (*né* Henry Olaf Hansen, b. Oslo, Norway, 9 Oct 1887–14 Sep 1960 [72], Woodland Hills CA; lung cancer). AS, p. 1061. BHD1, p. 536; BHD2, p. 259. IFN, p. 290. George A. Katchmer, "Forgotten Cowboys and Cowgirls—Part X," *CI,* 182 (Aug 1990), 39.

Ten Eyck, Lillian [actress] (b. NJ, 22 Apr 1886–6 Dec 1966 [80], Los Angeles Co. CA). BHD, p. 315. IFN, p. 290.

Tengroth, Birgit [actress] (b. Stockholm, Sweden, 13 Jul 1915–21 Sep 1983 [68], Stockholm, Sweden). AS, p. 1061. BHD1, p. 537.

Tennant, Barbara [actress] (b. London, England, 19 May 1892). (Eclair.) AMD, p. 336. AS, p. 1061. BHD, p. 315. Spehr, p. 170. "A New Star with Eclair," *MPW,* 11 May 1912, 540. Hugh F. Hoffman, "Miss Barbara Tennant; New Eclair Leading Lady an Acquisition to the Photoplay Field. How She Hypnotized Charles Frohman," *MPW,* 22 Jun 1912, 1121. "Miss Barbara Tennant," *MPW,* 9 Aug 1913, 615. "Eclair Players Out—Company Discontinues Eastern Aggregation—Players Go to Peerless Ranks," *NYDM,* 15 Jul 1914, 25:1 (others affected were Oscar Lund, Alec Francis, Bert Starkey, and Stanley Walpole. Clara Horton was transferred to the Tucson AZ company.).

Tennant, Dorothy [stage/film actress] (b. San Francisco CA, 10 Jul 1865–3 Jul 1942 [76], West Palm Beach FL). "Dorothy Tennant," *NYT,* 4 Jul 1942, 17:3 ("former stage and screen actress"). AS, p. 1061. BHD, p. 315. IFN, p. 290.

Tennyson, Gladys [actress: Sennett Bathing Beauty] (b. TX, 2 Nov 1894–27 Apr 1983 [88], Yuba City CA). BHD, p. 315.

Terhune, Albert Payson (son of author Virginia Hawes Terhune; pseudonym: Marion Harland) [actor/writer/scenarist] (b. Newark NJ, 21 Dec 1872–18 Feb 1942 [69], Pompton Lakes NJ; heart ailment). m. Anice Stockton, 1901 (d. 1964). *Now That I'm Fifty; To the Best of My Memory.* "Albert P. Terhune, Noted Author, Dies; Writer of Stories About Dogs Stricken at Pompton Lakes—His Kennel Famous; Once Did Screen Work; Published 'Lad: A Dog,' First in Canine Series, in 1919—Reporter on The World," *NYT,* 19 Feb 1942, 19:1 (wrote 64 books; "In 1900 he collaborated with William C. De Mille in writing the libretto of 'Nero,' a comic opera."). "Terhune Will Aids Dogs; Writer Directs Some Be Sold into 'Good Homes in Country,'" *NYT,* 5 Mar 1942, 25:7. "Mrs. Albert Terhune," *NYT,* 10 Nov 1964, 47:3 (d. 9 Nov 1964 [91]). "Albert P. Terhune," *Variety,* 25 Feb 1942. AMD, p. 336. AS, p. 1061. BHD, p. 315; BHD2, p. 259. FDY, p. 439. "To Novelize Chapin Subject," *MPW,* 16 Feb 1918, 955.

Terrell, Maverick [scenarist] (b. 1875–16 Aug 1943 [68?], Los Angeles CA). AS, p. 1062. BHD2, p. 258.

Terribili-Gonzales, Gianna [actress] (*née* Giovanna Terribili-Gonzales). JS, p. 449 (in Italian silents from 1908; from a family of counts).

Terriss, Ellaline (sister of **Tom Terriss**) [actress] (*née* Ellaline Lewin, b. Port Stanley, Falkland Islands, 13 Apr 1871–16 Jun 1971 [100], London, England). m. **E. Seymour Hicks**, 1893 (d. 1949). "Ellaline Terriss," *Variety,* 23 Jun 1971. AS, p. 1062. BHD1, p. 537 (d. Richmond, England). IFN, p. 291. SD, p. 1206. Truitt, p. 323.

Terriss, Tom (son of actor William Terriss; brother of **Ellaline Terriss**) [stage/film actor/scenarist/director/producer] (*né* Herbert Thomas Lewin, b. London, England, 28 Sep 1872–8 Feb 1964 [91], New York NY). m. Mildred Devere (*née* Mildred Smith; b. Olean NY, 1883?–3 Jan 1964 [80], NY NY). (World; Vitagraph; Paramount.)

"Mildred Devere, 80, Dies; A 'Ziegfeld Follies' Girl," *NYT,* 4 Jan 1964, 23:4 (Mrs. Mildred Smith Terriss). AMD, p. 336. AS, p. 1062. BHD, p. 315; BHD2, p. 259 (b. 1874). FDY, p. 439. IFN, p. 291. MSBB, p. 1028 (b. 1877). "Terriss Not with Gibraltar Co.," *MPW,* 31 Oct 1914, 643. "August and Terriss Join Forces," *MPW,* 12 Dec 1914, 1536. "Tom Terriss Heading Own Company," *MPW,* 20 Mar 1915, 1768. "First Terriss Picture Soon," *MPW,* 3 Apr 1915, 76. "Picture Playhouse Gets Terriss," *MPW,* 17 Apr 1915, 377. "Jamaica Likes Picture People," *MPW,* 1 May 1915, 733. "Jamaica as a Producer's Field," *MPW,* 26 Jun 1915. "In the Picture Studios," *NYDM,* 23 Oct 1915, 31:1 ("Tom Terriss has just discovered that being a moving picture actor also has its drawbacks. When he went to take out some additional life insurance recently, he found that his occupation was classed as extra hazardous along with that of steeplejacks."). "Terriss Film Barred In Penn," *NYDM,* 6 Nov 1915, 25:1 (*Flame of Passion* was banned in the Keystone state. Since the National Board of Review passed the film in its entirety without an adverse comment, Terriss planned a stiff court battle, guessing that the title brought down the wrath of the censors, since the complaint was not detailed.). "Terriss Joins Vitagraph," *MPW,* 29 Sep 1917, 1990. "Tom Terriss Starts on Thirteenth Joyce Picture," *MPW,* 8 Mar 1919, 1328. "Exhibitor and Director Must Understand Each Other Better," *MPW,* 15 Nov 1924, 258. "Terriss Made Dean of School," *MPW,* 30 May 1925, 576 (Paramount Picture School, Inc., Long Island NY). "Terriss to Direct for Famous Attractions, Says Bachmann," *MPW,* 15 May 1926, 226.

Terry, Alice Frances [actress] (*née* Helen Taaffe, b. Vincennes IN, 24 Jul 1900–22 Dec 1987 [87], Burbank CA; pneumonia). m. **Rex Ingram**, 1921, Pasadena CA (d. 1950). (Triangle, 1916.) "Alice Terry," *Variety,* 30 Dec 1987. AMD, p. 336. AS, p. 1062 (b. 1899). BHD1, p. 337 (b. 1899). Katz, p. 1128. MH, p. 139 (b. 1901). 1921 Directory, p. 241 (b. Nashville). Slide, p. 166 (b. 1896). FFF, p. 28 (b. 1901). Maude Cheathem, "The Waking Beauty," *MPC,* Jul 1921, 32–33, 74. "Surprise Weddings," *MPW,* 3 Dec 1921, 566. "Alice Terry," *MPW,* 19 Jul 1924, 199. "Alice Terry's Plans," *MPW,* 15 Nov 1924, 255. Helen Carlisle, "The Remote Alice and Her Protégée," *MW,* 14 Feb 1925, 17–18, 28. Alice Terry, "The True Story of My Life," *MW,* 16 May 1925, 4–5, 32; 23 May 1925, 12–13, 34; 30 May 1925, 14–15, 31; 6 Jun 1925, 12–13, 41; 13 Jun 1925, 28, 43. "Alice Terry Returning," *MPW,* 12 Sep 1925, 189. Certificate of Birth, Knox County Health Dept., 624 Broadway Street, Vincennes IN 47591 (Book No. CH-1, Vol. 1, p. 39; filed 18 Aug 1900; copy supplied by Gene Shaw, NYC).

Terry, Don [actor] (*né* Donald Loker, b. Natick MA, 8 Aug 1902–6 Oct 1988 [86], Oceanside CA; stroke). (Film debut: *Me, Gangster,* 1928.) "Don Terry," *Variety,* 332, 19 Oct 1988; 511:5. AS, p. 1062. BHD1, p. 537.

Terry, Ellen Alice (mother of **Edward Gordon Craig**; aunt of **Dennis Neilson-Terry**; great-aunt of **John Gielgud**) [actress] (b. Coventry, Warwickshire, England, 27 Feb 1848–21 Jul 1928 [80], Small Hythe, Kent, England; cerebral hemorrhage). m. (1) George F. Watts; (2) Charles Kelly (d. 1885); (3) **James Carew** (d. 1938). "Ellen Terry," *Variety,* 25 Jul 1928. AMD, p. 336. AS, p. 1062. BHD, p. 315. GSS, pp. 379–83. IFN, p. 291. Truitt, p. 323 (b. 1848). WWS, p. 323. "Ellen Terry Featured on the Screen," *MPW,* 9 Aug 1919, 848.

Terry, Ethel Grey (daughter of Lillian Lawrence) [actress] (b. Oakland CA, 2 Oct 1882?–6 Jan 1931 [48], Los Angeles CA). m. Carl Gerrard. "Ethel Grey Terry," *Variety,* 14 Jan 1931 (age 48). AS, p. 1062. BHD, p. 315 (b. 1891). FFF, p. 154 (b. 1898). IFN, p. 291 (b. 1891). MH, p. 139 (b. 1898). Slide, p. 166 (d. 1931). Truitt, p. 323. WWS, p. 242. "Ethel Grey Terry," *NYDM,* 1 Jul 1914, 11:2. George Katchmer, "Remembering the Great Silents," *CI,* 222 (Dec 1993), C15.

Terry, Fred (related to **Ellen Terry**) [actor] (b. London, England, 9 Nov 1863–17 Apr 1933 [69], London, England). m. (1 son, 1 daughter). (Stage debut, 1890.) "Fred Terry," *Variety,* 110, 25 Apr 1933, 62:2 (age 68). AS, p. 1062. BHD, p. 316. IFN, p. 291.

Terry, Jessie [actress]. (Lubin.) No data found.

Terry, John C. [director of animated films] (b. 1880–23 Feb 1934 [53?], Coral Gables FL). AS, p. 1062.

Terry, John S. (Jack) [actor] (b. 1864?–9 Oct 1940 [76], Belmont Hill MA). m. Mabel. "John S. (Jack) Terry," *Variety,* 16 Oct 1940. AS, p. 1062 (b. 1869).

Terry, Paul H[olton] [animator] (b. San Francisco CA, 19 Feb 1887–25 Oct 1971 [84], New York NY [Death Certificate Index No. 20800]). m. Irma (d. 1969). (Terrytoons.) "Paul H. Terry," *Variety,* 27 Oct 1971. "Mrs. Paul Terry," *NYT,* 8 Jan 1969, 44:1 (d. 7 Jan 1969, Port Chester NY). AMD, p. 336. AS, p. 1062. BHD2, p. 259. IFN, p. 291. Katz, p. 1128 (b. San Mateo CA). "Paul Terry, the Artist, Gives Talk on How Cartoons Are Made," *MPW,* 6 Feb 1926, 565. Adrien Falnieres, "Making the Cartoons Move," *Cinema Arts,* Nov 1926, 26–27, 47–48. "Students in P.T.M.T.S. [Publix Theatre Managers' Training School] Study Cartoon Art with Paul Terry," *MPW,* 11 Jun 1927, 421.

Terry, Tex [actor] (*né* Edward Earl Terry, b. Terre Haute IN, 22 Aug 1902–18 May 1985 [82], Terre Haute IN). (Began 1922.) AS, p. 1062. BHD1, p. 537.

Terry-Lewis, Mabel [actress] (b. London, England, 28 Oct 1872–29 Nov 1957 [85]). BHD1, p. 538.

Terwilliger, George W. [director] (b. NY, 27 Feb 1882–12 Dec 1970 [88], Hialeah FL). (Lubin; Vitagraph.) AMD, p. 336. BHD2, p. 259. "In the Catskills with Reliance," *MPW,* 24 Aug 1912, 748–51. "George Terwilliger Leaves Reliance," *MPW,* 31 Aug 1912, 863. "George Terwilliger Can Swim?," *MPW,* 16 Aug 1913, 723. "Some Doctor—What?," *MPW,* 29 Nov 1913, 1015 (was a former physician). "Terwilliger Doesn't Want Misplaced Credit," *MPW,* 28 Feb 1914, 1090. "Terwilliger Takes Lubin Players to Cuba," *MPW,* 23 Jan 1915, 523. "Terwilliger Back with Plays," *MPW,* 17 Apr 1915, 401. "George Terwilliger," *MPW,* 18 Mar 1916, 1843. "Terwilliger with Vitagraph," *MPW,* 13 Sep 1919, 1641.

Terzano, Massimo [actor/cinematographer] (b. Turin, Italy, 23 Apr 1892–18 Oct 1947 [55], Rome, Italy). FDY, p. 469. JS, pp. 449–50 (in Italian silents from 1915).

Tessier, Valentine Anne [actress] (b. Paris, France, 5 Aug 1892–11 Aug 1981 [89], Vallauris, France [extrait de décès no. 92/1982]). AS, p. 1063.

Testa, Dante (father of **Eugenio Testa**) [actor/director] (b. Turin, Italy, 1861–3 Mar 1923 [61?], Turin, Italy). JS, p. 451 (in Italian silents from 1912).

Testa, Eugenio Valentino Mario Ernesto (son of **Dante Testa**) [director] (*né* Giusto Entea, b. Turin, Italy, 6 Oct 1892 [extrait de naissance no. 2937]–11 Oct 1957 [65?], Turin, Italy [extrait de décès no. 1934]). AS, p. 1063. JS, p. 451 (in Italian silents from 1913; from 1942 to 1956 he lived in Barcelona, Spain).

Tetzlaff, Ted (Theodore) [former world's champion automobile racing driver/cinematographer/director] (b. Los Angeles CA, 3 Jun 1903–9 Dec 1929 [26], Santa Ana CA; "...to complications from a spine injury received in an accident during a road race in 1911."). "Tetzlaff, Race Driver, Dies," *NYT,* 9 Dec 1929, 39:1 (d. Artesia CA). AS, p. 1060 (Ted Tedzlaff); p. 1063. BHD, p. 316 (b. 1883); BHD2, p. 259 (d. 7 Jan 1995, Fort Baker CA). FDY, p. 469. Katz, p. 1129.

Teuber, Arthur Georg Karl [director] (b. Neisse, Germany, 5 Aug 1878). AS, p. 1063.

Thalasso, Arthur [actor] (b. OH, 26 Nov 1883–13 Feb 1954 [70], Los Angeles Co. CA). (Fox.) AS, p. 1063. BHD1, p. 538. IFN, p. 291.

Thalberg, Irving Grant [production executive] (b. Brooklyn NY, 30 May 1899–14 Sep 1936 [37], Santa Monica CA; lobular pneumonia). m. **Norma Shearer**, 6 Oct 1927 (d. 1983). Samuel Marx, *Mayer and Thalberg; The Make-Believe Saints* (New York: Random House, 1975). (Universal; MGM.) "I.G. Thalberg, Dies; Film Producer, 37; 'Boy Wonder' of Hollywood Was Called Most Brilliant Figure in His Field; Regarded as Pacemaker; Made Succession of Hits and Had Developed Many Stars—Husband of Norma Shearer," *NYT,* 14 Sep 1936, 29:3. "Regard Irving Thalberg's Passing as a World Loss in Entertainment," *Variety,* 16 Sep 1936. AMD, p. 337. AS, p. 1063. BHD2, p. 259. IFN, p. 291. Katz, p. 1129–30. "Thalberg Resigns," *MPW,* 17 Feb 1923, 645. "Women Are Real Censors, Says Irving Thalberg to Delegates," *MPW,* 26 Jul 1924, 256. "Thalberg Supervising 9 Metro-Goldwyn Specials," *MPW,* 4 Oct 1924, 406. "Thalberg Visits New York for Series of Conferences," *MPW,* 31 Jan 1925, 495. "Thalberg Tells Metro Formula of Making Box-Office Pictures," *MPW,* 7 Feb 1925, 607. "Thalberg Returns to West Coast; Has New Scripts; Signs Goulding," *MPW,* 14 Feb 1925, 716. "Thalberg, Recovering from Flu, Is Given Surprise Party," *MPW,* 11 Jul 1925, 151. "Thalberg Returns to Studios,"' *MPW,* 1 Aug 1925, 508. "Thalberg Back at Studio Following Weeks of Illness," *MPW,* 19 Dec 1925, 650. "Thalberg Due in New York," *MPW,* 13 Feb 1926, 640. "Thalberg Arrives in East for Conference with M-G-M Officials," *MPW,* 20 Feb 1926, 715. Covarrubias, "Distinguished Picture People," *MPW,* 27 Feb 1926, 782. "Original Stories to Predominate Next Season, Says Irving THalberg," *MPW,* 8 May 1926, 140. June Lee, "Dan Cupid's Bulletin Board," *Paris and Hollywood,* Sep 1926, 96 (to be an engagement announcement between Thalberg and Rosabelle Laemmle). "Shearer—Thalberg Nuptials Soon," *MPW,* 27 Aug 1927, 590. "Shearer—Thalberg Nuptials," *MPW,* 1 Oct 1927, 289. "Hollywood Weddings Interest Colony," *MPW,* 8 Oct 1927, 360.

Thanhouser, Edwin [executive/producer] (b. Baltimore MD, 11 Nov 1865?–21 Mar 1956 [90], New York NY [Death Certificate Index No. 6404]). m. **Gertrude** Homan (d. 1951). "Edwin Thanhouser Dies; Movie Producer Who Formed Company in 1909 Was 90," *NYT,* 23 Mar 1956, 27:4. "Edwin Thanhouser," *Variety,* 28 Mar 1956

(b. 1880, but age 90). AMD, p. 337. AS, p. 1064. BHD2, p. 260. IFN, p. 291. "New Independent Mannufacturer," *MPW,* 5 Feb 1910, 177. "Thanhouser Company: A New Film Producer," *MPW,* 12 Mar 1910, 374. "Messrs. Hite and Thanhouser Together," *MPW,* 11 May 1912, 522. Louis Reeves Harrison, "Studio Saunterings," *MPW,* 6 Jul 1912, 123–26. "Thanhouser Advocates Natural-Length Films," *MPW,* 5 Oct 1912, 47. "Edwin Thanhouser Here," *MPW,* 21 Jun 1913, 1235. "Edwin Thanhouser," *MPW,* 27 Sep 1913, 1370. "The Thanhousers in Egypt," *MPW,* 14 Feb 1914, 789. Hanford C. Judson, "Edwin Thanhouser Home from Europe," *MPW,* 12 Sep 1914, 1523. "Edwin Thanhouser," *MPW,* 6 Mar 1915, 1451. "A Day with Thanhouser," *MPW,* 24 Apr 1915, 563. "Screen Will Dominate Drama," *MPW,* 23 Oct 1915, 595. "Does Not Advocate the Nude," *MPW,* 20 Nov 1915, 1465. "Thanhouser Won't Quit," *MPW,* 18 Mar 1916, 1855. "Thanhouser Talks on Sunday Pictures," *MPW,* 30 Dec 1916, 1934. "Thanhouser Compliments Trade Journals," *MPW,* 13 Jan 1917, 209. "Thanhouser in Retrospection; Head of Thanhouser Film Corporation Also Talks About 1917 Product," *MPW,* 13 Jan 1917, 252:1 (the reception given to Thanhouser-Pathé Gold Rooster "plays" during 1916 justified the results of his policy of "five-reel features with top-notch stars in expertly developed stories adequately directed and staged."). Edwin Thanhouser, "Reminiscences of Picture's Babyhood Days; Interesting Details of Difficulties Under Which Manufacturers Labored—Shoveling Snow from Stage and Making Locale Fit the Clime," *MPW,* 10 Mar 1917, 1524–25 (in Nov 1909 there was difficulty in getting glass for the roof of the first New Rochelle studio, but filming commenced with a big stove and a few screen lean-tos for dressing rooms. If it snowed, locations were changed [as with *In Siberia*]. When the stove and the sun melted the scenery there was a scene shift to "Later—A Warmer Clime." One advantage was a fully-developed scenario department, early for the times. The first release was *The Actor's Children,* a 1-reel subject with "heart interest." One of only five independents [from the Patents Co.], he sold his films to scattered exchanges; usually one-half of the copies sent out were returned. With his second film, *St. Elmo* (also playing on the stage), he had a hit, and exchanges also bought copies of *The Actor's Children.* His 2-reel *Romeo and Juliet* was too much for exhibitors, so it was sent out one reel at a time, as was the 3-reel *David Copperfield.* "Early in the moving picture business I made a statement that the time was coming when one moving picture would provide a whole evening's entertainment. I was ridiculed for this, and that was only seven or eight years ago.... The idea in the early days was that motion pcutres should have as much motion as possible—never mind the acting." "T. Co," the company logo, was used freely—"We...put the largest sized trade-mark we dared in the most conspicuous place in every set." Exchangemen were mistrustful of the ability of manufacturers to make pictures. "There was no stability in the business, and many of us would not look more than thirty days ahead for the permanency of our business life."). "Thanhouser Favors Stars," *MPW,* 12 May 1917, 986. "Thanhouser Sticks to Advance Showings," *MPW,* 2 Jun 1917, 1455. "Edwin Thanhouser Retires," *MPW,* 2 Mar 1918, 1230.

Thanhouser, Gertrude [actress/scenarist] (*née?,* b. Beauvoir MS, 23 Apr 1880–29 May 1951 [71], Glen Cove NY). m. **Edwin Thanhouser** (d. 1956). "Mrs. Edwin Thanhouser," *NYT,* 31 May 1951, 27:5. "Gertrude H[oman] Thanhouser," *Variety,* 6 Jun 1951. BHD, p. 316; BHD2, p. 260.

Tharp, Norman [actor] (b. England-d. 2 Apr 1921, London, England). BHD, p. 316.

Thatcher, Evelyn "Eva" [actress] (b. Omaha NB, 14 Mar 1862–28 Sep 1942 [80], Los Angeles CA). (Sennett; Mutual.) "Evelyn Thatcher," *Variety,* 30 Sep 1942 ("early silent film comedienne"). AS, p. 1064. BHD, p. 316. IFN, p. 291. Truitt, p. 323. George Katchmer, "Remembering the Great Silents," *CI,* 213 (Mar 1993), 49, 59.

Thatcher, Heather Mary [actress] (b. London, England, 3 Sep 1896–15 Jan 1987 [90], Hiddington, England). AS, p. 1064. BHD1, p. 538.

Thaw, Evelyn Nesbit *see* **Nesbit, Evelyn**

Thaw, Harry K[endall] (father of **Russell William Thaw**) [producer] (b. Pittsburgh PA, 1 Feb 1871–23 Feb 1947 [76], Miami Beach FL; coronary thrombosis). m. Florence **Evelyn Nesbitt**, 4 Apr 1905, Pittsburgh PA—div. 1916 (d. 1967). (Kenilworth Productions.) "Harry K. Thaw, 76, Is Dead in Florida; Coronary Thrombosis Fatal for Former 'Playboy' Who Shot Stanford White [a *crime passionel*]in 1906 [25 Jun 1906, NYC]," *NYT,* 23 Feb 1947, 53:1 ("The verdict [of second trial, 1908] was 'not guilty,' on the ground that Thaw had been insane at the time he committed the crime." Committed to the Matteawan State Hospital for the Criminal Insane. Escaped 17 Aug 1913. Finally acquitted and freed on 16 Jul 1915. Charged in 1916 with horsewhipping Fred Gump, Jr. Found in Philadelphia with a self-inflicted slash on his throat on 11 Jan 1917. Committed to an asylum again until April, 1924). "Thaw Weds Miss Nesbitt; Marriage Takes Place in Pittsburg[h]—Bride's Mother Present," *NYT,* 5 Apr 1905, 1:6 (there were four witnesses: Mrs. William Thaw, "who is said to have told her son never to cross her threshold again if he persisted in his attentions to the model"; Josiah Copley Thaw, his brother, and Mr. and Mrs. Charles Holman, stepfather and mother of the bride. The couple arrived in East Liberty, Pittsburgh, on the 7:10 a.m. train; Nesbitt went to her mother's home on Oakland Avenue. "It is conceded that Harry Thaw, whose allowance had been cut to $2,500 a year, will now enjoy his full allowance of $80,000 annually."). "Thaw Drops Effort to Get Out on Bail; Enters Plea of Not Guilty to Conspiracy Charge and Trial Set for Feb. 23; Will Be Held in Tombs; No Attempt Will Be Made to Send Him Back to Matteawan Pending Trial," *NYT,* 28 Jan 1915, 5:3. "Harry K. Thaw Making Pictures; Squabbles Feature First Effort," *MPW,* 7 May 1927, 11–12. "Thaw Completes Two Comedies; Begins Plans for Big Feature," *MPW,* 4 Jun 1927, 323. Cedric Belfrage, "Thaw Starts Shooting in a Big Way; Harry K. Allows the Camera Is Mightier than the Gun," *MPC,* Mar 1928, 23, 70 (produced three films in 1927, one allegedly called *Not So Good,* with Wilfred Lytell and Muriel Kingston; promoted 17-year-old actresses Anita Rivers and Susan Hughes).

Thaw, Russell William [actor/aviator] (son of **Evelyn Nesbitt** and **Harry K. Thaw**) (b. Germany, 25 Oct 1910–6 May 1984 [73], Lompoc [Santa Barbara] CA). m. Barbara. "Russell W. Thaw," *Lompoc Record,* 8 May 1984, p. 3 (interred at McDermott-Crockett Mortuary, 1903 State St., Santa Barbara CA). BHD1, p. 618.

Thayer, Otis B. [director/producer] (b. Richland Center WI). AMD, p. 337. BHD2, p. 260. "Pike's Peak Film Company," *MPW,* 19 Dec 1914, 1703. "Thayer a Master Hand at Mountain Pictures," *MPW,* 30 Jan 1915, 688. "Otis B. Thayer in New York," *MPW,* 11 Dec 1915, 2036. "Franklyn Farnum Signed for Art-O-Graf Feature," *MPW,* 1 Mar 1919, 1237. "Thayer Nearly Drowned," *MPW,* 17 Jul 1920, 334.

Thayer, Tiffany [actor/scenarist] (b. Freeport IL, 1902–23 Aug 1959 [57?], Nantucket MA). BHD2, p. 260.

Thea [actress] (b. Rome, Italy, 1898). JS, p. 451 (in Italian silents from 1917; retired in 1920 after marrying a rich Roman businessman).

Theby, Rosemary (sister of **Mary Charleson**) [stage/film actress] (*née* Rosemary Masing, b. St. Louis MO, 8 Apr 1892–10 Nov 1973 [81], Los Angeles CA). m. **Harry C. Myers**, San Francisco CA, 1924 (d. 1938). (Vitagraph; Reliance; Lubin; Universal; Vim; Pathé; Bluebird Photoplays; Artcraft; Ince; Triangle; Metro; Elk Photoplays; Pioneer; Selznick; Fox; Francis Ford Prods.) AMD, p. 337. AS, p. 1064 (b. 1885). BHD1, 618. FSS, p. 274. MH, p. 139. MSBB, p. 1042 (b. 1892). Slide, p. 152 (b. 8 Apr). WWS, p. 251. "Miss Rosemary Theby," *MPW,* 13 Apr 1912, 123. "The Reliance to Star Rosemary Theby," *MPW,* 21 Jun 1913, 1238. "Lives of the Players; Rosemary Theby; Playing Leads in Reliance Films," *MPS,* 1 Aug 1913, 30. "Rosemary Theby," *MPW,* 22 Nov 1913, 875. "Rosemary Theby," *MPW,* 25 Apr 1914, 499. "Universal Gets Lubin Players," *MPW,* 15 Aug 1914, 972. "Rosemary Theby," *MPW,* 16 Jan 1915, 374. "Rosemary Theby; Leading Lady with the Imp Company," *MPS,* 12 Mar 1915, 27. "Rosemary Theby," *MPW,* 13 Mar 1915, 1613. "Rosemary Theby," *MPW,* 27 Jan 1917, 522. "Rosemary Theby Returns to Universal," *MPW,* 1 Sep 1917, 1360. "Rosemary THeby's Vampire Parts Belie Quaint Name," *MPW,* 8 Mar 1919, 1346. "Rosemary Theby a Star," *MPW,* 25 Sep 1920, 479. Billy H. Doyle, "Lost Players," *CI,* 170 (Aug 1989), 51–52. George Katchmer, "Remembering the Great Silents," *CI,* 234 (Dec 1994), 40.

Theiss, John Henry [cinematographer] (b. New Haven CT, 1881–23 Nov 1950 [69?], St. Lucie River FL). BHD2, p. 260.

Thery, Jacques Edmond [scenarist] (b. Paris, France, 6 Apr 1881–29 Sep 1970 [89], Beausoleil, France [extrait de décès no. 24/1970]). AS, p. 1064 (b. 1899). BHD2, p. 260.

Thery, Maurice Frédéric [director/scenarist] (b. Laon, France, 28 Mar 1898 [extrait de naissance no. 96]-7 Dec 1974 [76], Clichy-la-Garenne, France). AS, p. 1064.

Thesiger, Ernest [stage/film actor/painter] (b. London, England, 15 Jan 1879–14 Jan 1961 [82], London, England). m. Janette M.F. Rankin. *Practically True.* "Ernest Thesiger, Actor, 82, Is Dead; Stage and Film Performer in Britain Since 1909—Had Paintings Displayed," *NYT,* 15 Jan 1961, 86:6. "Ernest Thesiger," *Variety,* 25 Jan 1961. AS, p. 1064. BHD1, p. 538. IFN, p. 291. Katz, p. 1130. Truitt, p. 323.

Thew, Harvey F. [scenarist] (b. Vernon Center MO, 4 Jul 1883–6 Nov 1946 [63], Los Angeles CA). (*Death on the Diamond,* MGM, 1934.) AMD, p. 337. BHD2, p. 260. FDY, p. 439 (Harry Thew). "Thew Joins Famous Players-Lasky," *MPW,* 9 Sep 1916, 1670. "Scenario Department

Again Expanded," *MPW,* 21 Oct 1916, 412. "Thew to Write for Fox," *MPW,* 17 Sep 1927, 154.

Theyer, Hans [cinematographer]. No data found. FDY, p. 469.

Thibaud, Anna [actress] (*née* Marie-Louise Thibaudet, b. France, 1891–1936 [45?], France). AS, p. 1064.

Thiele, William J. [director/actor/title writer] (*né* Wilhelm J. Thieleiser-Sohn, b. Vienna, Austria, 10 May 1890–7 Sep 1975 [85], Woodland Hills CA). m. (2 sons, John and Fred; 1 daughter, writer Doris Rush). (Ufa; MGM.) "William J. Thiele," *Variety,* 280, 17 Sep 1975, 86:3 (to U.S. in 1934). AS, p. 1065. BHD, p. 316; BHD2, p. 260. FDY, p. 447. IFN, p. 291. Waldman, p. 281.

Thimig, Helene [actress] (b. Vienna, Austria, 5 Jun 1889–7 Nov 1974 [85], Vienna, Austria; heart attack). m. **Max Reinhardt** (d. 1943). AS, p. 1065. BHD2, p. 1065.

Thimig, Hermann Friedrich August [actor] (b. Vienna, Austria, 3 Oct 1890–7 Jul 1982 [91], Vienna, Austria). AS, p. 1065. BHD1, p. 539.

Thirard, Armand Henri Julien [actor/producer] (b. Nantes, France, 25 Oct 1895–12 Nov 1973 [78], Colombes, France). AS, p. 1065.

Thom, Norman [actor] (b. Greenup KY, 19 Oct 1877–24 May 1931 [53]). BHD, p. 316. IFN, p. 292.

Thomas, A.E. [novelist/scenarist] (b. 1873?–18 Jun 1947 [74], Wakefield RI). "A.E. Thomas," *Variety,* 167, 25 Jun 1947, 55:1 (wrote *Come Out of the Kitchen,* produced 1916, with Ruth Chatterton). AMD, p. 338. IFN, p. 292. "Thomas Owns Title 'Her Husband's Wife,'" *MPW,* 7 Oct 1916, 91.

Thomas, Abel C. [executive] (d. 21 Feb 1945, New York NY). BHD2, p. 260.

Thomas, Al F. [stage/film actor] (b. NY). (Began 1912; Metro; Popular Players; Federal; Fox; Equitable.) MSBB, p. 1028.

Thomas, Albert [actor/scenarist] (b. Chester MA, 16 Sep 1872–18 Jun 1947 [74], Wakefield RI). BHD2, p. 260.

Thomas, Alfred [actor] (b. Hohenlimburg, Germany, 1 Mar 1905–3 Oct 1976 [71], Los Angeles CA). AS, p. 1065. BHD1, p. 539. IFN, p. 292.

Thomas, Augustus [writer] (b. St. Louis MO, 8 Jan 1857–12 Aug 1934 [77], Nyack NY). m. Lisle Colby. "Augustus Thomas," *Variety,* 14 Aug 1934. AMD, p. 338. AS, p. 1065. BHD2, p. 260. SD, p. 1211. W. Stephen Bush, "Augustus Thomas Joins the M.P.'s," *MPW,* 9 Aug 1913, 618. W. Stephen Bush, "Augustus Thomas Retrospective," *MPW,* 11 Jul 1914, 282. "Raver to Picturize Six Augustus Thomas Plays," *MPW,* 29 Mar 1919, 1833. "Author Aids in Filming First Four Star Feature," *MPW,* 5 Apr 1919, 117. "Screen Verson of Play Pleases Augustus Thomas," *MPW,* 12 Apr 1919, 258. "Co-Operative Plans of the Four Star Pleases Thomas," *MPW,* 12 Apr 1919, 264. "Augustus Thomas Is Pleased with Picturization of 'The Copperhead,'" *MPW,* 17 Jan 1920, 433. "Thomas Sues Artco," *MPW,* 19 Mar 1921, 264 (for $50,000, from 25 Jul 1915 scenario contract). "Augustus Thomas Now Member of M.P.D.A.," *MPW,* 1 Oct 1921, 530.

Thomas, Calvin L. [stage/film actor] (b. Kansas City KS, 1885?–26 Sep 1964 [79], Caldwell NJ). m. Delia (widow). "Calvin L. Thomas, Actor, Dies at 79; Played in Character Roles on Broadway 50 Years," *NYT,* 27 Sep 1964, 87:1. "Calvin L. Thomas," *Variety,* 30 Sep 1964. AS, p. 1065. BHD1, p. 618.

Thomas, Edward [actor] (b. Red Bank NJ, 20 Dec 1884–29 Dec 1943 [59], Los Angeles CA). AS, p. 1066. BHD1, p. 539. IFN, p. 292.

Thomas, Edward C. [publicist] (b. 1887–9 Oct 1960 [73?], Los Angeles CA). BHD2, p. 260.

Thomas, Faith [scenarist]. No data found. FDY, p. 439.

Thomas, Frank M. [stage/film/TV actor] (b. St. Joseph MO, 13 Jul 1889–25 Nov 1989 [100], Tujunga CA; cardiac arrest in his sleep). m. actress Mona Bruns. (RKO.) "Frank M. Thomas," *Variety,* 31 Jan 1990. AS, p. 1066. BHD1, p. 539.

Thomas, George H. [publicist] (b. West Liberty IA, 1888–16 Sep 1962 [74?], Monrovia CA). BHD2, p. 260.

Thomas, Gretchen [actress] (b. 1897?–1 Nov 1964 [67], Los Angeles CA). "Gretchen Thomas," *Variety,* 11 Nov 1964. AS, p. 1066. BHD, p. 316. IFN, p. 292.

Thomas, Gus[tave] [actor] (b. Toronto, Canada, 1865?–3 May 1926 [61?], Everett WA). AS, p. 1066. BHD, p. 316. Truitt, p. 324.

Thomas, Isobel [actress: Sennett Bathing Beauty] (b. Liverpool, England, 25 Sep 1903–23 Oct 1948 [45], Los Angeles CA). m. **Julian Rivero** (d. 1976). BHD1, p. 618.

Thomas, Jameson [stage/film actor/director/scenarist] (b. London, England, 24 Mar 1888–10 Jan 1939 [50], Sierra Madre CA; tuberculosis). m. Dorothy Dix. (Gaumont; British International.) (Film Debut?, *Chu Chin Chow,* Germany, 1920, with Betty Blythe]; 1st Hollywood film, *Body and Soul,* 1931). "Jameson Thomas, Hollywood Actor; Londoner, Who Entered Films After Career on Stage, Is Dead at 45; Served Also as Director; Appeared in Pictures Made in Many Countries and Took Chief Roles in Some," *NYT,* 11 Jan 1939, 19:3 (age 45). "Jameson Thomas," *Variety,* 11 Jan 1939. AS, p. 1066. BHD1, p. 539; BHD2, p. 260 (d. LA CA). IFN, p. 292. Truitt, p. 324.

Thomas, Jane [actress] (b. Chicago IL?). (Fox.) AMD, p. 338. "Jane Thomas to Appear in 'Trimmed with Red,'" *MPW,* 21 Feb 1920, 1273. Alma M. Talley, "'Vampire Roles Are Outlets for Suppressed Desires,' Says Jane Thomas," *MW,* 19 May 1923, 9. John E. Thayer, "Stars in View—1922," *CI,* 61 (Winter, 1978), 36–38.

Thomas, John [writer]. No data found. AMD, p. 338. "Joins Paramount Scenario Staff," *MPW,* 25 Jun 1927, 594.

Thomas, John Charles [stage/film/radio/actor/singer] (b. Meyersdale PA, 6 Sep 1889–13 Dec 1960 [71], Apple Valley CA; intestinal cancer). m. Dorothy May Koehler. (Cosmopolitan.) "John Charles Thomas Dies at 69; Concert, Opera and Radio Star; Popular Baritone Performed in Musicals and Operettas—Noted as Showman," *NYT,* 14 Dec 1960, 39:3 (age 69; "He took a fling at the movies but didn't care much for the medium"). "John Charles Thomas' Rites," *NYT,* 18 Dec 1960, 84:1 (age 68; Mountain View Cemetery, San Bernardino CA). "John Charles Thomas," *Variety,* 21 Dec 1960 (age 68). AMD, p. 338. AS, p. 1066 (b. Baltimore MD). BHD1, p. 539. IFN, p. 292. Truitt, p. 324 (b. Baltimore MD, 1887). Cover, *NYDM,* 11 Dec 1915. "Makes Picture Debut," *MPW,* 31 Mar 1923, 564. Nanette Kutner, "What Qualities in a Woman Lure a Man Most?; John Charles Thomas Tells," *MW,* 2 Jun 1923, 8, 29.

Thomas, Juanita [actress]. No data found. "Prize Beauty Comes to N.Y.," *MPW,* 10 Sep 1921, 207.

Thomas, Madoline [actress] (b. Abergaveny, Wales, 2 Jan 1890–30 Dec 1989 [99], Weston-super-Mare, England). AS, p. 1066.

Thomas, Nona [actress]. No data found. (Triangle.) *MPC,* Oct 1916, 11 (photo).

Thomas, Olive [stage/film actress] (*née* Oliveretta Elaine Duffy, b. Charleroi PA, 20 Oct 1894–10 Sep 1920 [25], Neuilly, Paris, France; suicide stemming from ingestion of bichloride of mercury). m. (1) Kenneth Krough, 1 Apr 1911, Pittsburgh PA; (2) Bernard Krug [Carew?] Thomas, 1912—div. 1913; (3) **Jack Pickford,** May 1917, NJ (d. 1933). (FP-L; Ince-Triangle; Selznick.) "Olive Thomas's Funeral; Service for Film Star in St. Thomas's Church Tuesday Morning," *NYT,* 25 Sep 1920, 13:4 (cites death from "mercurial poisoning"). "Olive Thomas," *Variety,* 17 Sep 1920 (d. 9 Sep 1920, age 26). AMD, p. 338. AS, p. 1066 (b. 1898; d. 9 Sep). BHD, p. 316 (b. 1894). IFN, p. 292 (b. 16 Oct 1898). Katz, p. 1132 (b. 1884). MSBB, p. 1042 (b. 1898). Spehr, p. 170. Truitt, p. 324 (b. 29 Oct 1884). WWS, p. 132. "Olive Thomas, One of the Chief Reasons for the Appeal of Mr. Ziegfeld's 'Follies,'" *NYDM,* 8 Sep 1915, 5:2 (photo only). "Olive Thomas Has Big Ambition," *MPW,* 14 Oct 1916, 252. "Olive Thomas with Triangle," *MPW,* 21 Apr 1917, 433. J. B., Waye, "An Alluring Call to Arms,"*Picture-Play Masgazine,* Sep 1917, 70 (worked at a recruiting station for the war effort). "Olive Thomas," *MPW,* 23 Mar 1918, 1642. "'Selznick Pictures' Again in Field," *MPW,* 18 Jan 1919, 316. "[Jack Pickford] Presents Wife with $9,000 Car," *MPW,* 1 Feb 1919, 616. "Stars' Cars Hit Boys," *MPW,* 22 Mar 1919, 1628. Sue Roberts, "An Olive from Sunny California," *MPC,* Apr 1919, 37–38. Edward Weitzel, "Olive Thomas Has Narrow Escape from an Embarrassment of Actors," *MPW,* 6 Mar 1920, 1646. "Obituary," *MPW,* 25 Sep 1920, 471 ("Those who really knew Olive Thomas resented the stories that she had committed suicide."). "'Screen Snapshots' Shows Stars," *MPW,* 2 Oct 1920, 654 ("...last motion pictures of..."). "Women and Girls Storm Church to Attend Funeral of Olive Thomas; Many Tears in the Vast Audience," *MPW,* 9 Oct 1920, 827. "Olive Thomas Left No Will," *MPW,* 16 Oct 1920, 980. "Film Gives Public Chance to Pay Tribute to Olive Thomas," *MPW,* 23 Oct 1920, 1122. "Olive Thomas Estate Reported at $37,094," *MPW,* 29 Jul 1922, 341 (left to mother, Mrs. Lorena VanKirke). "Ask the Answer Man," *Photoplay,* Dec 1931, 112 (b. 29 Oct 1898). Eve Golden, "Olive Thomas: The Midnight Frolics Girl," *CI,* 238 (Apr 1995), 30, 32. Ann Eichholtz, "Celebrity Neighbor [letter]," *CI,* 240 (Jun 1995), 6 (re marriage to Carew Thomas). (Her birth certificate is located in the Clerk of Otphan's Court in Washington PA. The Prothonotary of Allegheny County has her first marriage certificate. A parental consent for an underage marriage was signed by [step]father Laurence Van Kirk and mother Sourena Van Kirk. Data supplied by Jonathan C. Pettit, Appleton WI).

Thomas, Queenie [actress] (*née* Marjorie Violet Queenie Thomas, b. Willesden, England, 18 Jun 1898 [extrait de naissance no. 62/1898]–11 Oct 1977 [79], Sweeninghill, England; bronchial pneumonia [extrait de décès no. 29]). AS, p. 1066.

Filmarama, Vol. I, p. 250; Vol. II, p. 522 (filmographies).

Thomas, Suzette [actress]. No data found. Rene de la Seine, "Moviettes from Gay Paree," *Paris and Hollywood Screen Secrets Magazine,* Aug 1927, 67 (photo).

Thomas, Virginia [actress] (d. 12 Jan 1955, Los Angeles CA). BHD1, p. 539.

Thomas, Walter [actor] (b. England, 1867–21 Mar 1917 [49?], New York NY). BHD, p. 316.

Thomashefsky, Boris (father of script writer, Theodore Thomas; brother of **Max Thomashefsky**; uncle of Paul Muni) [stage/film actor] (b. Kiev, Russia, 12 May 1868–9 Jul 1939 [71], New York NY). m. (1) Bessie, 1891; (2) Rebecca Zuckersberg (widow). "Thomashefsky, 71, Yiddish Actor, Dies; He Introduced the Theatre to His People on the East Side Delighting Packed Houses; Shakespeare Enthusiast; Had Bard's Works Translated—Wrote 500 Plays—Brought Bertha Kalich to America," *NYT,* 10 Jul 1939, 19:3. "Boris Thomashefsky, Yiddish Legit Vet, Dies at 71 in N.Y.," *Variety,* 12 Jul 1939. "Mrs. B. Thomashefsky," *NYT,* 8 Jul 1962, 65:2 (d. 7 Jul 1962 [88], Hollywood CA). AMD, p. 338. AS, p. 1067. BHD1, p. 540. "Trade Notes," *MPW,* 29 Jun 1907, 263. "Producing Primarily for the Jews," *MPW,* 6 Feb 1915, 809.

Thomashefsky, Max (brother of **Boris Thomashefsky**) [actor] (b. 1872–24 Jul 1932 [60?], New York NY). AS, p. 1067. BHD1, p. 540.

Thompson, Al[bert] [actor] (b. PA, 21 Sep 1884–1 Mar 1960 [75], Los Angeles Co. CA). BHD, p. 316. IFN, p. 292.

Thompson, Allan [cinematographer]. No data found. FDY, p. 469.

Thompson, Blackie [actor] (*né* Clarence Bergen, b. 1877–17 May 1936 [59?], Los Angeles CA). BHD, p. 316.

Thompson, Clarence [publicist] (b. New Haven CT, 1876?–3 May 1945 [69], New York NY). m. Katherine Robie. "Clarence Thompson, Political Publicist," *NYT,* 4 May 1945, 19:2 (worked for Lee De Forest). AS, p. 1067.

Thompson, David H. [actor/agent] (b. Liverpool, England, 4 May 1884–20 May 1957 [73], Los Angeles CA). (Edison; Thanhouser.) "David H. Thompson," *Variety,* 29 May 1957 (age 73). AMD, p. 338. AS, p. 1067. BHD2, p. 261 (b. NY NY). BHD, p. 316 (b. NY NY, 1886). IFN, p. 292. *Photoplay Arts Portfolio* [Thanhouser] (b. 1886). Truitt, p. 324 (b. NY NY, 1886). "Dave Thompson," *MPW,* 17 Jan 1914, 273. "Dave THompson Back with THanhouser," *MPW,* 12 Sep 1914, 1527.

Thompson, Donald C. [cameraman]. No data found. AMD, p. 338. "Paramount Photo-News Man," *MPW,* 6 Nov 1915, 1114. "Donald C. Thompson Home from War," *MPW,* 25 Dec 1915, 2375. "Donald C. Thompson Injured," *MPW,* 1 Apr 1916, 95. "Donald Thompson, War Photographer," *MPW,* 4 Nov 1916, 710. "Thompson Lectures at Rialto," *MPW,* 11 Nov 1916, 868. "War Photographer Thompson Forms Company," *MPW,* 2 Dec 1916, 1334. "Photographer of Russian Riots Here," *MPW,* 17 Nov 1917, 1005.

Thompson, Duane [stage/radio/film actress: Wampas Star, 1925] (b. Red Oak IA, 28 Jul 1903–15 Aug 1970 [67], Studio City CA). AMD, p. 338. AS, p. 1067 (b. 1905-d. LA CA). BHD, p. 316. BR, p. 226–27. "Dancing Won Her First Movie Part," *MPW,* 7 May 1927, 24. George Katchmer, "Remembering the Great Silents," *CI,* 202 (Apr 1992), 6.

Thompson, Ebba [actress]. No data found. *Fl.* 1913. (Great Northern.)

Thompson, Frances (great-granddaughter of Gen. John Bell Hood) [stage/film actress] (b. VA). (Film debut: *The Other Girl,* 1915–16.) AMD, p. 338. "Artist Selects Raver Star for Model," *MPW,* 20 Nov 1915, 1464. "In the Picture Studios," *NYDM,* 18 Dec 1915, 34:3.

Thompson, Frank [actor] (b. Los Angeles CA, 10 Jul 1840–1907 [67?], Los Angeles CA). AS, p. 1067.

Thompson, Frank C. [actor] (b. 1867?–5 Dec 1919 [52], Los Angeles CA; struck by car). AMD, p. 338. "Obituary," *MPW,* 27 Dec 1919, 1148.

Thompson, Fred [composer/scenarist] (b. London, England, 24 Jan 1884–10 Apr 1949 [65], London, England). m. (1) Elizabeth Edmonds; (2) Cecile A. Bentham; (3) Clarice E. Rudge. "Fred Thompson, Wrote Musicals; Author of 'Rio Rita' and 'Lady Be Good' Is Dead in London—Turned Out 50 Shows," *NYT,* 12 Apr 1949, 29:6. "Fred Thompson," *Variety,* 13 Apr 1949. BHD2, p. 261. SD, p. 1214.

Thompson, Frederick A. "Bing" [stage/film actor/director] (b. Montreal, Quebec, Canada, 7 Aug 1869–23 Jan 1925 [55], Los Angeles CA; heart attack). (Edison, 1907; Vitagraph; Selig-Polyscope; Pathé.) "Frederick A. Thompson," *Variety,* 28 Jan 1925. AMD, p. 338. AS, p. 1067. BHD, p. 317; BHD2, p. 261. IFN, p. 292. Slide, p. 153. Truitt, p. 324. "Frederick A. Thompson," *MPW,* 1 May 1915, 732. "New Directors in Famous Players," *MPW,* 15 Jan 1916, 397. "Frederick 'Bing' Thompson Returns to Vitagraph," *MPW,* 17 Jun 1916, 2041. "Frank Thompson to Direct Bessie Love," *MPW,* 22 Dec 1917, 1815. Ed Wyatt, "The Other Fred Thom[p]son," *CI,* 259 (Jan 1997), 32 (includes filmography).

Thompson, Garfield [scenarist]. No data found. AMD, p. 339. "Garfield Thompson," *MPW,* 7 Aug 1915, 1010.

Thompson, George C. [actor] (b. IA, 25 Mar 1868–29 May 1929 [61], Los Angeles CA; complications during an operation for a stomach infection). AS, p. 1067. BHD1, p. 540.

Thompson, Grace [double for Mary Pickford/actress]. No data found. J. Van Cartmell, "Live Wires from the West Coast," *NYDM,* 27 Nov 1915, 29:1 (to appear in *Love Thine Enemy,* 5 reels, directed by Joseph DeGrass). J. Van Cartmell, "Studio News from the Coast," *NYDM,* 4 Dec 1915, 27:2 (to film scenes in San Francisco for Universal's *Love Thine Enemy,* by Ida May Park).

Thompson, Hal [actor] (b. New York NY, 1894–3 Mar 1966 [71?]). AS, p. 1067. BHD1, p. 540.

Thompson, Hallett [actor] (*né* Frank Hallett Thompson, b. Gloucester MA, 1871?–13 Aug 1938 [67], New York NY; self-inflicted cuts of wrist arteries). m. (1) Irma La Pierre (d. 1951); Josephine Foy. "Hallett Thompson," *Variety,* 17 Aug 1938. AS, p. 1067.

Thompson, Harlan [scenarist/director/producer/landscape photographer] (b. Hannibal MO, 24 Sep 1890–29 Oct 1966 [76], New York NY). m. **Marian S.** Spitzer (d. 1983). "Harlan Thompson of Broadway, 76; Producer Is Dead—Wrote 'Little Jesse James' [opened in Aug 1923 at the Longacre Theatre, with Miriam Hopkins]," *NYT,* 30 Oct 1966, 88:5 (to Hollywood in 1928. Wrote "dialogue for Fox's first all-talking picture, 'The Ghost Talks,' with Helen Twelvetrees." Supervised the production of 1,200 Army training films at the Signal Corps Photographic Center in Astoria, Queens.). "Harlan Thompson," *Variety,* 2 Nov 1966. AS, p. 1067. ASCAP 66, p. 731. BHD2, p. 261.

Thompson, Hugh E. [stage/film actor] (b. Los Angeles CA, 20 May 1882). (Appeared in *The Old Sin,* Essanay, 5 Oct 1915; 3 reels.) AMD, p. 339. AS, p. 1067. BHD, p. 317 (b. St. Louis MO, 1887). Ragan, p. 1673. "Hugh Thompson Supports Miss WHelan," *MPW,* 1 Jun 1918, 1296. "Hugh Thompson Likes Picture Work More Than the Stage," *MPW,* 24 May 1919, 1176.

Thompson, John [actor] (b. 1844?–10 Mar 1929 [85], New York NY). "John Thompson," *Variety,* 13 Mar 1929. AS, p. 1067.

Thompson, John [actor] (d. May 1917). BHD, p. 317.

Thompson, Keene [actor/scenarist] (b. 1886?–11 Jul 1937 [51], Los Angeles CA; pneumonia). (Paramount.) "Keene Thompson," *Variety,* 14 Jul 1937. AMD, p. 339. AS, p. 1067. BHD, p. 317; BHD2, p. 261. FDY, p. 439. IFN, p. 292. "Keene Thompson with Fairbanks," *MPW,* 22 Sep 1917, 1831.

Thompson, Kenneth [scenarist] (b. FL, 6 Nov 1841–17 Feb 1918 [76], Hartford CT). AS, p. 1067. FDY, p. 439.

Thompson, Lotus [actress] (b. Sydney, Australia, 22 Aug 1906–19 May 1963 [56], Burbank CA). BHD1, p. 540. BR, p. 227. "On the Set and Off," *MW,* 7 Mar 1925, 34 (Thompson gave herself a nitric acid bath from the hips down in an effort to destroy the beauty of her legs, which producers insisted upon filming. She would not be scarred). George A. Katchmer, "Forgotten Cowboys and Cowgirls—Part V," *CI,* 177, Mar 1990, C6. "Update—Forgotten Cowboys/Girls," *CI,* 179 (May 1990), 44.

Thompson, Maravene [writer]. No data found. AMD, p. 339. "Mrs. Thompson Writes for World Pictures," *MPW,* 2 Mar 1918, 1220. "World Produces Maravene Thompson Story," *MPW,* 22 Jun 1918, 1726.

Thompson, Margaret [actress] (b. Trinidad CO, 26 Oct 1889–26 Dec 1969 [80], Los Angeles CA). m. **E.H. Allen,** 1914. (Ince.) AS, p. 1067. BHD, p. 317. IFN, p. 292. W.E. Wing, "On the Pacific Coast," *NYDM,* 25 Nov 1914, 28:3. Billy H. Doyle, "Lost Players," *CI,* 175 (Jan 1990), 38. George Katchmer, "Remembering the Great Silents," *CI,* 239 (May 1995), 35.

Thompson, Marian S. [author/scenarist] (*née* Marian Spitzer, b. 1895–18 Jul 1983 [88?], New York NY). m. **Harlan Thompson** (d. 1966). AS, p. 1067.

Thompson, May [actress] (b. Birmingham, England, 1890–18 Nov 1978 [88?], Devon PA). BHD, p. 317.

Thompson, Molly [actress/casting director for Hal Roach] (b. 1878?–14 Feb 1928 [49], Culver City CA; cerebral hemorrhage). "Molly Thompson," *Variety,* 22 Feb 1928. AS, p. 1067. BHD, p. 317. IFN, p. 292. Truitt, p. 324. WWS, p. 324 (b. 1879).

Thompson, Nick J. [actor] (b. Galveston TX, 11 Sep 1889–22 Apr 1980 [90], Los Angeles CA). AS, p. 1067. BHD1, p. 540 (b. Houston TX). George Katchmer, "Remembering the Great Silents," *CI,* 204 (Jun 1992), 42.

Thompson, Philip E. [journalist/publicist] (b. Norwich CT, 1882?–9 Apr 1924 [42], New York NY). m. Lillian Fair, 1908. "Philip E. Thompson; Was Newspaper Man and Publicity Agent for Circuses," *NYT,* 10 Apr 1924, 23:4.

Thompson, Polly [actress] (*née* Hippolita Thompson, d. 8 Mar 1933, New York NY; suicide by gas inhalation). AS, p. 1068.

Thompson, Ray[mond] [actor] (b. 1898?–29 Jun 1927 [29], Cooper River, Abercrombie Canyon, 50 miles from Cordova AK; drowned during filming of *The Trail of '98,* MGM). "3 Men [Thompson, Joseph Bautin, 34, and F.H. Daughters, 23] Drowned in Alaskan Icy Film Scene," *Variety,* 6 Jul 1927. AS, p. 1068. BHD, p. 317. IFN, p. 292. George Katchmer, "Remembering the Great Silents," *CI,* 234 (Dec 1994), 41.

Thompson, Raymond L. [actor] (b. Salt Lake City UT, 14 Aug 1894–9 Dec 1937 [43]). AS, p. 1068. IFN, p. 292.

Thompson, Therese (sister of **Trixie Friganza**) [actress] (*née* Therese O'Callaghan, b. Anna IL, 1876?–16 Sep 1936 [60?], Los Angeles CA). AS, p. 1068 (b. Grenola KS; d. 17 Sep 1938). BHD, p. 317. Truitt, p. 324.

Thompson, Ulu M. [actress] (b. 1873–13 Apr 1957 [84?], Los Angeles CA). AS, p. 1068.

Thompson, Walker [actor] (b. Lexington KY, 1888?–19 Sep 1922 [34], Chicago IL). AS, p. 1068. BHD, p. 317. IFN, p. 292.

Thompson, William C. [publicist] (b. 1872?–23 Sep 1918 [46], Chicago IL; pneumonia). AMD, p. 339. "Obituary," *MPW,* 12 Oct 1918, 219.

Thompson, William C[reevy] [cameraman]. No data found. FDY, p. 469 (Bill Thompson).

Thompson, William H. [stage/film actor] (b. Glasgow, Scotland, 24 Apr 1852–4 Feb 1923 [70], New York NY; pneumonia). m. (1) Isabel Irving; (2) Lillian Dix. "Wm. H. Thompson, Veteran Actor, Dies; One of Best Known Players of Character Roles on American Stage a Victim of Pneumonia," *NYT,* 5 Feb 1923, 15:6. "William H. Thompson," *Variety,* 8 Feb 1923 (age 71; caught cold during the filming of an outdoor scene). AS, p. 1068. BHD, p. 317. IFN, p. 292.

Thompson, William H. [actor] (b. England, 1869–14 Feb 1929 [59?], New York NY; pneumonia). AS, p. 1068.

Thomson, Archibald [actor] (b. Elmira NY, 13 Apr 1901–22 Sep 1981 [80], New York NY). BHD1, p. 540.

Thomson, Fred[erick] **C**[lifton] [actor/photographer] (b. Pasadena CA, 26 Feb 1890–25 Dec 1928 [38], Los Angeles CA; tetanus and complications). m. Gail Dubois Jepson, 1913, Goldfield NV (d. Sep 1916); **Frances Marion**, Nov 1919, New York NY (d. 1973). Edgar M. Wyatt, *More Than a Cowboy; The Life and Films of Fred Thomson and Silver King* (Raleigh NC: Wyatt Classics, Inc., 1988). (FBO; Para.) "Fred Thomson," *Variety,* 2 Jan 1929. Edgar Wyatt, "Frederick Clifton Thomson III," *CI,* 276 (Jun 1998), 58:3 (grandson d. 5 May 1998 [49], Chapel Hill NC; apparent heart attack. His father was Dr. Fred Thomson, Jr.). AMD, p. 339. AS, p. 1068. BHD, p. 317. GK, pp. 938–46. IFN, p. 292. Katz, p. 1133 (began 1921). Truitt, p. 324. "Frances Marion Directs Hubby in Newest Film," *MPW,* 3 Dec 1921, 539. David A. Balch, "From Preacher to Movie Star," *MW,* 5 Apr 1924, 9. "Sign Fred Thomson," *MPW,* 5 Jul 1924, 47. "Injured Stars Better," *MPW,* 20 Sep 1924, 209. "Starts Work on 'Bandit's Baby,'" *MPW,* 18 Apr 1925, 715. "Fred Thomson," *MPW,* 16 May 1925, 344. "Fred Thomson," *MPW,* 31 Jul 1926, 2. Manfred B. Lee, "Fred Thomson; A Western Actor With a Sense of Humor and an Acetylene Intelligence," *Cinema Arts,* Oct 1926, 16–17. "Thomson Deal Hangs Fire," *MPW,* 29 Nov 1926, 4. Ruth M. Tildesley, "The Crusader of the Movies," *MPS,* 1 Mar 1927, 14–15, 33 ("Motion pictures are without exception the greatest single influence on the younger generation." Thomson served for three years as pastor of the First Presbyterian Chrch in Golffield NV. He joined the 143rd Field Artillery int he 40th Divison and was appointed chaplain. He previously attended Princeton. Pickford was godmother of the 143rd; cheering for her regiment in San Diego, she invited Thomson to her home where he met Frances Marion. He and Marion went to the war in Europe and were married in New York with Pickford and her mother as witnesses. Marion wrote and directed *The Love Light* and engaged Thomson for it.). "Fred Thomson," *MPW,* 16 Apr 1927, 647. "Fred Thomson Plans an EXceptioal Shot," *MPW,* 23 Jul 1927, 256. George A. Katchmer, "Fred Thomson; The Idol of the Young," *CI,* 110 (Aug 1984), 20–22. George A. Katchmer, "Fred Thomson Bits," *CI,* 112 (Sep 1984), 20. Edgar M. Wyatt, "Versatile Fred Thomson Was Genius at Photography," *CI,* 196 (Oct 1991), 52. R.E. Braff, "An Index to the Films of Fred Thomson," *CI,* 208 (Oct 1992), 44. Ed Wyatt, "Thomson Defied Desert Heat, Rattlesnakes in Motorcycle Dash," *CI,* 237 (Mar 1995), 22, 24.

Thomson, Kenneth [actor] (*né* Charles Kenneth Thomson, b. Pittsburgh PA, 7 Jan 1899–26 Jan 1967 [68], Los Angeles CA; emphysema and fibrosis). m. Alden Gay (d. 1979). "Kenneth Thomson," *NYT,* 27 Jan 1967, 45:3. "Kenneth Thomson, 68, Dies; Among Founders of Actors Union," *Variety,* 1 Feb 1967. AMD, p. 339. AS, p. 1068. BHD1, p. 540. FSS, p. 275. IFN, p. 292. Truitt, p. 324. "Signs with DeMille," *MPW,* 1 May 1926, 43. "Graduate of Stage," *MPW,* 25 Sep 1926, 239.

Thomson, Polly [actress] (b. Glasgow, Scotland, 1884–20 Mar 1960 [75?], Bridgeport CT). BHD, p. 317.

Thornburgh, Laura [scenarist]. No data found. AMD, p. 339. "Levey Appoints Chief Editor," *MPW,* 11 Dec 1920, 729.

Thornby, Robert T. [actor/director] (b. New York NY, 27 Mar 1888–6 Mar 1953 [64], Los Angeles Co. CA). (Universal; World.) AMD, p. 339. AS, p. 1068. BHD1, p. 541; BHD2, p. 261. IFN, p. 293. 1921 Directory, p. 276. Spehr, p. 170. "Robert Thornby Is Now William Fox DIrector," *MPW,* 8 Jun 1918, 1449. "Thornby to Direct May Allison," *MPW,* 14 Sep 1918, 1567. "R-C Signs Robert T. Thornby to Direct Six Features; Helped Put Carey Over," *MPW,* 25 Mar 1922, 360. "Thornby Signs with Christie," *MPW,* 31 Oct 1925, 728. "Engaged as Director," *MPW,* 14 Aug 1926, 3 (8 years as director and independent producer). "Thornby to Direct McCoy," *MPW,* 4 Sep 1926, 35.

Thorndike, Lucyle [actress] (b. Seattle WA, 1865–17 Dec 1935 [70], Los Angeles CA). AS, p. 1069 (Thorndyke). BHD, p. 317 (b. 1885). IFN, p. 293. Truitt, p. 325.

Thorndike, Russell (brother of **Sybil Thorndike**) [actor/writer] (*né* Arthur Russell Thorndike, b. Rochester, Kent, England, 6 Feb 1885–7 Nov 1972 [87], London, England). m. (2 sons, 3 daughters). (Stage debut, Theatre Royal, Cambridge, 1904.) "Russell Thorndike, Author, Dies; Actor Wrote the 'Dr. Syn' Novels [from 1915]," *NYT,* 9 Nov 1972, 50:3. "Russell Thorndike," *Variety,* 269, 15 Nov 1972, 79:3. AS, p. 1068. BHD1, p. 541. IFN, p. 293.

Thorndike, Sybil (sister of **Russell Thorndike**) [stage/film/TV actress] (b. Gainsborough, Lincolnshire, England, 24 Oct 1882–9 Jun 1976 [93], London, England; four days after a heart attack). m. **Lewis Casson**, 25 Dec 1908 (2 sons, 2 daughters; d. 1969). (First stage appearance: Oxford, 18 Jun 1904; London debut: 8 Feb 1908; film debut: *Moths and Rust,* 1921.) Albin Krebs, "Sybil Thorndike Is Dead; An Actress for 7 Decades," *NYT,* 10 Jun 1976, 1:1, 40:2 (made Dame Commander of the Order of the British Empire, 1931). "Dame Sybil Thorndike," *Variety,* 283, 16 Jun 1976, 76:1. AS, p. 1069. BHD1, p. 541. IFN, p. 293.

Thorne, Frank A., Sr. [actor] (b. Philadelphia PA, 12 Oct 1881–28 May 1953 [71], No. Hollywood CA). AS, p. 1069. BHD, p. 317; BHD2, p. 261. IFN, p. 293.

Thorne, John [stage/film actor] (b. 1880–28 Aug 1935 [55], Mercer PA). BHD1, p. 618 (d. 30 Aug). IFN, p. 293. "In the Picture Studios," *NYDM,* 14 Jul 1915, 27:1 (debuted in *The White Sister,* Essanay).

Thorne, Lizette [actress]. No data found. (Mustang.)

Thorne, Nellie [actress] (b. England, 1873–13 May 1960 [87?], Riverside CT). AS, p. 1069.

Thorne, Richard [actor] (b. 1905–31 Jan 1957 [51?], Los Angeles CA; heart attack). AS, p. 1069 (Dick Thorne). BHD, p. 317. IFN, p. 293 (Dick Thorne). Truitt, p. 325 (Dick Thorne).

Thorne, Robert [actor] (b. 18 Aug 1880–3 Jul 1965 [84], New York NY [Death Certificate Index No. 14093; M.E. Case No. 5770]; heart attack). "Robert Thorne," *NYT,* 6 Jul 1965, 33:2. "Robert Thorne," *Variety,* 14 Jul 1965. AS, p. 1069. BHD, p. 317. IFN, p. 293. Truitt, p. 325.

Thorne, William L. [actor] (b. Fresno CA, 14 Oct 1878–10 Mar 1948 [69], Fresno CA). AS, p. 1069 (d. Hollywood CA). BHD1, p. 541. IFN, p. 293.

Thornley, William H. [cinematographer] (b. Cincinnati OH, 1 Nov 1883–17 Jul 1956 [72], Los Angeles CA). BHD2, p. 261. FDY, p. 469.

Thornton, Edith [actress] (b. New York NY, 9 Jan 1896–13 Feb 1984 [88], Glendale CA). (Crystal.) m. **Charles Hutchison**, 1918 (d. 1949). AMD, p. 339. AS, p. 1069. BHD1, p. 618. "Edith Thornton, Unafraid," *MPW,* 15 May 1915, 1074. "Edith Thornton," *MPW,* 12 Apr 1924, 569. "Edith Thronton," *MPW,* 13 Sep 1924, 117. "Edith Thornton in N.Y.," *MPW,* 20 Sep 1924, 210. Billy Doyle, "Lost Players," *CI,* 142 (Apr 1987), C12–C13.

Thornton, James [vaudeville/burlesque/film/radio actor] (b. Liverpool, England, 1862?–27

Jul 1938 [76], Astoria, Queens NY; ill and paralyzed for several years. Buried at St. Raymond's Cemetery, Bronx NY). m. (1) singer Bonnie Cox; (2) Kathleen Barry. "James Thornton," *Variety*, 131, 3 Aug 1938, 54:1 (teamed with Charles Lawlor in vaudeville, the author of The Sidewalks of New York. When "vaudeville again hit bottom, Thornton had stepped out of the profession. It was not an altogether voluntary retirement, however, Thornton's predilection for liquor having a lot to do with it...."); "Jim Thornton Anedota," p. 44:4 (incarcerated in a sanitarium for a sobering-up process, his teeth were taken away by Alf T. Wilton, his agent-producer. "Latter heard nothing from Thornton for three days, then received a wire, 'Send me my teeth, I'm starving to death.'"). AMD, p. 339. "Forming Company in Cincinnati to Feature James Thornton," *MPW*, 23 Oct 1920, 1147.

Thornton, Richard [executive] (b. 1838?–21 Feb 1922 [83], Newcastle-upon-Tyne, Northunberland, England). "Richard Thornton," *Variety*, 3 Mar 1922. AS, p. 1069 (d. 15 Feb).

Thornton, Richard [actor] (b. 1873?–9 May 1936 [63], New York NY). "Richard Thornton," *Variety*, 13 May 1936. AS, p. 1069. BHD, p. 318. IFN, p. 291.

Thorp, Ruth (b. Hartford CT, 1890–1971 [81?]). BHD, p. 318.

Thorpe, Betty [actress]. No data found. (Southern Sun Corp.) "Spokane's First Picture," *NYDM*, 22 Jul 1914, 24:1 (*When Betty Marries* with Elvo Deffenbaugh).

Thorpe, Jim (son of actor William Thorpe, b. 22 Jan 1924) [actor/athlete] (descended from the Sac and Fox Indian tribes, *née* James Francis Thorpe and Wa-Tho-Huck ["Bright Path"], twin of Charles Thorpe [d. 1897], b. Prague OK, 28 May 1888–28 Mar 1953 [64], Lomita CA; heart attack). m. (1) Iva Miller, 1913; (2) Freeda Kirkpatrick, 1926; (3) Patricia Gladys Askew, 2 Jun 1945. (Appeared in *The Baseball Review of 1917*, Athletic Feature Films, 1917 as himself; film biography: *Jim Thorpe—All American*, WB, 1951.) "Jim Thorpe Is Dead on West Coast at 64," *NYT*, 29 Mar 1953, 1:1, 92:4. "Jim Thorpe," *Variety*, 1 Apr 1953. AS, p. 1069 (b. 1886). BHD1, p. 541 (b. 1886; d. LA CA). IFN, p. 293. J. Eugene Chrisman, "Out of the Ditch and into the Movies; Big Jim Thorpe, Greatest Athlete of All Time, Found Working as Laborer, Gets Chance as Movie Actor," *Movie Classic*, I, Sep 1931, 38. Gray Cutler, "Jim Thorpe: Native American Legend," *FIR*, Jul/Aug 1996, 4 *et passim* (b. Keokuk Falls OK; includes filmography).

Thorpe, Richard [director/scenarist] (*né* Rollo Smolt Thorpe, b. Hutchinson KS, 24 Feb 1896–1 May 1991 [95], Palm Springs CA). m. **Belva MacKay**. (MGM.) "Richard Thorpe, Film Director, 95," *NYT*, 4 May 1991, 10:5. "Richard Thorpe," *Variety*, 13 May 1991. AS, p. 1069. BHD, p. 318; BHD2, p. 261. FDY, p. 439. JS, p. 452 (worked in Italy in 1959–60). Katz, pp. 1133–34 (began 1921).

Thring, Frank, Sr. [director/producer/executive] (father of actor Frank Thring, Jr. [1926–1994]) (*né* Francis William Thring, b. Wenworth, Australia, 1883–1 Jul 1936 [53?], Melbourne, Australia). m. "Frank Thring Jr.," *Variety*, 16 Jan 1995, p. 100:4 (d. 29 Dec 1994). (Frank Thring, Sr., "headed up a successful Melbourne film studio, Eftee Productions, which made a number of feature films in the 1920s."). AS, p. 1069.

Thumb, Mrs. General Tom [actress] (aka Lavinia Warren and Adele Cox, b. Middlesboro MA, 1841–25 Nov 1919 [78?], Middlesboro MA). AS, p. 1069. BHD, p. 318.

Thumb, Tom [actor] (*né* Darius Adner Alder, b. 4 Jan 1842–24 Sep 1926 [84], Los Angeles CA; internal hemorrhage). AS, p. 1069 (b. 1938). BHD, p. 318.

Thurber, J[ames] **Kent** [actor/director] (b. 12 Aug 1894–26 May 1957 [62], St. Petersburg FL). AS, p. 1069. BHD2, p. 261 (b. 1892).

Thurman, Mary [actress: Sennett Bathing Beauty] (*née* Mary Christiansen, b. Richfield UT, 27 Apr 1894–22 Dec 1925 [31], New York NY, bronchopneumonia [Death Certificate No. 30722]). (Keystone; Goldwyn; Hampton; FP-L; Mayflower.) "Mary Thurman Dead; Motion Picture Actress to Be Buried at Old Home in Utah," *NYT*, 24 Dec 1925, 13:4 (age 25). "Mary Thurman," *Variety*, 30 Dec 1925 (age 30). AMD, p. 339. AS, p. 1069 (b. 1895). BHD, pp. 76–77; 318. IFN, p. 293 (age 25). MH, p. 139. Truitt, p. 325 (b. Richmond UT). WWS, p. 224. "Mary Thurman Enters Drama," *MPW*, 11 Jan 1919, 238. "Mary Thurman Painfully Burned When Incense Burner Exploded," *MPW*, 17 Apr 1920, 392. "Obituary," *MPW*, 9 Jan 1926, 125.

Thurn-Taxis, Alexis [director/producer] (*né* Alexis Prince von Thrun und Taxis, b. Austria, 1891–26 Jul 1979 [88?], Woodland Hills CA). AS, p. 1069.

Thursby, David [actor] (b. 28 Feb 1889–20 Apr 1977 [88], Los Angeles CA). AS, p. 1070.

Thurston, Charles E. [actor] (b. Oconto WI, 10 Aug 1868–4 Mar 1940 [71], Los Angeles CA). m. Pauline, 1935 (d. 1943). "Widow of Thurston Is Dead," *NYT*, 11 Feb 1943, 21:3 (twin of Mrs. Irene Martin; b. Chicago IL, d. 10 Feb 1943 [33], No. Adams MA). AS, p. 1070. BHD1, p. 541. IFN, p. 293. Truitt, p. 325. George Katchmer, "Remembering the Great Silents," *CI*, 204 (Jun 1992), 42.

Thurston, E. Temple [writer] (b. Cork, Ireland, 23 Sep 1879–19 Mar 1933 [53], London, England; influenza and pneumonia). "E. Temple Thurston," *Variety*, 4 Apr 1933. AS, p. 1070. BHD2, p. 261. SD, p. 1220.

Thurston, Harry [actor/scenarist] (b. London, England, 1874–2 Sep 1955 [81?], Red Bank NJ). AS, p. 1070. BHD2, p. 262.

Thurston, Howard [magician/illusionist] (b. Columbus OH, 20 Jul 1869–13 Apr 1936 [66], Miami Beach FL). m. 3 times. "Thurston Dies in Fla. at 66," *Variety*, 15 Apr 1936. AMD, p. 339. BHD, p. 318. "Howard Thurston Completes Expose of Fake Spiritualism," *MPW*, 21 Aug 1920, 988.

Thurston, Muriel [actress] (b. France, 1874–1 May 1943 [69?], Los Angeles CA). AS, p. 1070.

Tian, Han [director] (b. Changsha Xiangtan, China, 1898–1968 [70?], Changsha Xiangtran, China). AS, p. 1070.

Tichadel, Pierre [actor] (*né* Pierre Menvielle, b. Bordeaux, France, 28 Jun 1901–11 Dec 1944 [43], Paris, France). AS, p. 1070.

Tichenor, Edna [actress]. No data found. (*Fl.* 1923–27.)

Tichenor, Frank A. [producer] (b. Gethsemane KY, 1880–8 May 1950 [70?], Greenwich CT). BHD2, p. 262.

Tidblad, Inga [actress] (b. Stockholm, Sweden, 29 May 1901–12 Sep 1975 [74], Stockholm, Sweden). AS, p. 1070. BHD, p. 318. IFN, p. 293.

Tidmarsh, Ferdinand [actor] (b. Philadelphia PA, 1883–15 Nov 1922 [39?], Philadelphia PA). (Lubin.) AS, p. 1070. BHD, p. 318. IFN, p. 293.

Tiedtke, Jakob [stage/film actor] (*né* Karl Heinrich Wilhelm Tiedtke, b. Berlin, Germany, 23 Jun 1875–30 Jun 1960 [85], Berlin, Germany). *Sincerity of a Tired Liar* (1951). (Stage debut, 1899.) "Jakob Tiedtke," *Variety*, 219, 20 Jul 1960, 63:1. AS, p. 1070. BHD1, p. 542. IFN, p. 293.

Tierney, Florence [film editor] (b. 1901?–8 Nov 1931 [30], Los Angeles CA). "Tierney, Cutter, Dies," *Variety*, 17 Nov 1931 (cutter with Harold Lloyd for five years). BHD2, p. 262.

Tierney, Harry [composer/lyricist] (b. Perth Amboy NJ, 21 May 1890–22 Mar 1965 [74], New York NY; heart attack). (RKO.) "Harry Tierney," *Variety*, 24 Mar 1965. AS, p. 1070. ASCAP 66, p. 733 (b. 1891). BHD2, p. 262.

Tiesler, Hans [title writer]. No data found. FDY, p. 447.

Tietjen, Charles L[ester] [actor/director] (b. New York NY-d. 25 Dec 1938, New York NY). BHD, p. 318; BHD2, p. 262.

Tighe, George Francis [actor] (b. Boston MA, 7 Nov 1872 [MVRB, Vol. 243, p. 95]). *1916 Movie Directory* (b. 8 Oct 1875). (Appeared in *Child of the Sea*.)

Tighe, Harry [actor] (b. New Haven CT, 27 Jun 1884–10 Feb 1935 [50], Old Lynne CT). m. Marvel. "Harry Tighe," *Variety*, 27 Mar 1935. AS, p. 1070. BHD1, p. 542 (b. 1885). IFN, p. 293. Truitt, p. 325.

Tilbury, Zeffie [actress] (b. London, England, 20 Nov 1863–22 Jul 1950 [86], Los Angeles CA). m. (1) Arthur Lewis; (2) L.E. Woodthorpe (d. 1915). "Zeffie Tilbury," *Variety*, 2 Aug 1950 (d. 24 Aug; age 87). AS, p. 1070. BHD1, p. 542. IFN, p. 293. Truitt, p. 325.

Tilden, Milano C. [director] (b. Paris, France, 24 Apr 1878–30 Sep 1951 [73], New York NY). AS, p. 1070 (d. France). BHD2, p. 262.

Tilden, William T[atem], **II** [tennis player/actor] (b. Germantown PA, 10 Feb 1893–4 Jun 1953 [60], Los Angeles CA; heart attack). "Bill Tilden," *Variety*, 10 Jun 1953 (d. 5 Jun). AS, p. 1070. BHD1, p. 542. IFN, p. 293. Charles S. Gage, "Ciné-Sport-Ographs; What the Cinema Star Is Doing in Sports—'And Why,'" *Cinema Arts*, Sep 1927, 18.

Tilford, Walter Ford [technical director]. No data found. AMD, p. 339. "Walter Tilford Known as a Leading Technical Expert," *MPW*, 12 Jul 1924, insert.

Tilghman, William M[atthew] [actor] (b. Fort Dodge IA, 4 Jul 1854–1 Nov 1924 [70], Oklahoma City OK; murdered). AS, p. 1071. BHD, p. 318.

Tilley, Vesta, "The London Idol" [stage/film actress/singer] (*née* Matilda Ball, b. Worcester, England, 13 May 1864–16 Sep 1952 [88], London, England). m. Walter de Frece, 1890 (d. 1935). "Vesta Tilley [Lady de Frece] Dies; Vaudeville Star; 'London Idol' of Music Halls a Generation Ago

Captivated Audiences for 42 Years," *NYT,* 17 Sep 1952, 31:1 ("After her reputation was established she never departed from her male impersonations.... She never permitted publication of a photograph of herself in any but male attire.... Her retirement was marked by a farewell performance at the London Coliseum, where a testimonial signed by more than 1,000,000 persons was presented to her." Her husband was a music hall producer and a Member of Parliament.). "Vesta Tilley," *Variety,* 188, 24 Sep 1952, 63:1 (*née* Matilda Alice Powers). BHD, p. 318.

Tilton, Edwin Booth "E.B." (son of stage actor Edward Lafayette Tilton) [stage/film actor/director/playwright/scenarist] (b. Chicago IL, 15 Sep 1859–16 Jan 1926 [66], Los Angeles CA). m. Irene Grant. (Fox.) "Edwin Booth Tilton," *Variety,* 20 Jan 1926, 49:4 (age 60); 10 Feb 1926, 45:4 (died at 1640 N. Kenmore Avenue, Hollywood CA. His father and Edwin Booth were chums, "and 'E.B.' was named for the famous star."). AS, p. 1071. BHD, p. 318. IFN, p. 293. Truitt, p. 325 (b. 1860). George Katchmer, "Remembering the Great Silents," *CI,* 249 (Mar 1996), 47.

Timberg, Herman [actor/scenarist] (b. 1892–16 Apr 1952 [60?], New York NY). AS, p. 1071. BHD2, p. 262.

Timer, Julius E. [director]. No data found. AMD, p. 339. "Julius Timer Directing 'Motoy' Pictures," *MPW,* 21 Apr 1917, 435.

Timmons, Joseph [actor/stuntman] (b. 1896–29 May 1933 [37?], Los Angeles CA; auto accident). AS, p. 1071.

Tinchant, André [producer] (b. Paris, France, 16 Oct 1896). AS, p. 1071.

Tincher, Fay [stage/film actress] (b. Topeka KS, 17 Apr 1884–11 Oct 1983 [99], Brooklyn NY; heart attack in her sleep; interred at Silver Mount Cemetery, Staten Island NY). (Film debut: *The Battle of the Sexes,* Griffith; Komic Co, 1914–15; Fine Arts; Triangle; Christie, 1918–21; Universal.) AMD, p. 339. AS, p. 1071. BHD1, p. 542. KOM, p. 161. W.E. Wing, "On the Pacific Coast," *NYDM,* 6 Jan 1915, 23:2. "Fay Tincher's Anniversary," *MPW,* 23 Jan 1915, 499. "Fay Tincher Transformed," *MPW,* 27 Nov 1915, 1648. "Fay TIncher Becomes a 'World Star,'" *MPW,* 27 Apr 1918, 557. "Fay Tincher Leads Seattle Parade," *MPW,* 2 Aug 1919, 674. "Song Written for Fay Tincher," *MPW,* 30 Aug 1919, 1351 (*Dangerous Dan McGrew*). "Fay Tincher, Christie Star, Begins Long Trip," *MPW,* 29 Jan 1921, 550. "Signs Fay Tincher," *MPW,* 2 Dec 1922, 460. Billy H. Doyle and D.L. Nelson, "Lost Players," *CI,* 165 (Mar 1989), 33–34. Billy H. Doyle, "Lost Players," *CI,* 195 (Sep 1991), 20.

Tinling, James [director] (b. Seattle WA, 8 May 1898–14 May 1967 [69], Malibu CA). AMD, p. 340. AS, p. 1071 (d. LA CA). BHD2, p. 262. IFN, p. 294. "James Tinling," *MPW,* 13 Aug 1927, 455.

Tinney, Frank [stage/film actor] (*né* Aloysius Robert Tinney, b. Philadelphia PA, 29 Mar 1878–28 Nov 1940 [62], Northport, LI NY). m. Edna Davenport. "Frank Tinney, 53, Retired Comedian; Blackface Artist, Who Once Was Undertaker's Aide, Dies in Northport, L.I.; Served in World War; Made First Stage Appearance Here in 'Follies of 1910'—In Army During War," *NYT,* 29 Nov 1940, 21:3 (b. 1887). Jack Pulaski, "Frank Tinney Dies at 62; Show Biz Rated Him Most Underpaid Comic Star," *Variety,* 4 Dec 1940. AS, p. 1071. BHD, p. 318.

Tinsdale, Franklin M. [actor/director] (b. 1871–14 Feb 1947 [75?], Los Angeles CA). AS, p. 1071. BHD, p. 318; BHD2, p. 262. IFN, p. 294.

Tippert, William H. [scenarist]. No data found. AMD, p. 340. "William H. Tippert," *MPW,* 30 Oct 1915, 799.

Tippett, John D. [director]. No data found. AMD, p. 340. "Tippett Pleased with Universal City," *MPW,* 1 Jan 1916, 57.

Tisse, Edouard Cazimirovich [cinematographer] (b. Lepaja, Lithuania, 13 Apr 1897–18 Nov 1961 [64], Moscow, Russia). AS, p. 1072 (b. 1 Apr). BHD2, p. 262. FDY, p. 469. IFN, p. 294.

Tissier, Jean [actor] (b. Paris, France, 1 Apr 1896 [extrait de naissance no. 908]-31 Mar 1973 [76], Granville, France [extrait de décès no. 60/1973]). m. Louise Georgette Lalire (actress Georgette Tissier [1910–1959]). AS, p. 1072. BHD1, p. 542 (d. Paris, France).

Tissier, Marie [actress]. No data found. *Fl.* 1912 (Eclipse).

Tissot, Alice Claire Marie [actress] (b. Paris, France, 1 Jan 1890–5 May 1971 [81], Paris, France; cancer of the larnyx [extrait de décès no. 1179/1971]). AS, p. 1072. BHD1, p. 542. IFN, p. 294.

Titheradge, Dion (brother of **Madge Titheradge**) (b. Melbourne, Victoria, Australia, 30 Mar 1886–16 Nov 1934 [48], London, England). m. (1) Margaret A. Bolton; (2) Madge Stewart. AS, p. 1072 (b. 1889). BHD, p. 318; BHD2, p. 262. IFN, p. 294 (b. 1889).

Titheradge, Madge (sister of **Dion Titheradge**) [stage/film actress] (b. Melbourne, Australia, 2 Jul 1887–13 Nov 1961 [74], Fetcham, Surrey, England). m. (1) Charles Quartermaine; (2) Edgar Park (d. 1938). "Madge Titheradge of London Stage, 74," *NYT,* 15 Nov 1961, 43:3. AMD, p. 340. AS, p. 1072 (d. 14 Nov). BHD, p. 318. IFN, p. 294. "Madge Titheradge Is Popular in Second National Photoplay," *MPW,* 8 Jul 1922, 126.

Titmuss, Phyllis [actress] (b. London, England, 14 Jan 1900–6 Jan 1946 [45]). BHD, p. 318. IFN, p. 294 (b. 1901).

Titterington, Morris M. [actor] (d. Snyder PA, Jul 1928). BHD, p. 318.

Titus, Frederick [actor] (d. Feb 1918, Los Angeles CA). m. **Lydia Yeamans Titus** (d. 1929). BHD, p. 318.

Titus, Harold [writer]. No data found. AMD, p. 340. "Harold Titus, Fox Author, Began Writing Sioux Tales," *MPW,* 3 Jan 1920, 104.

Titus, Lydia Yeamans [actress] (*née* Lydia Yeamans, b. Australia, 1866?–29 Dec 1929 [63], Glendale CA, cerebral thrombosis). m. **Frederick Titus** (d. 1918). (Christie.) "Lydia Yeamans Titus," *Variety,* 1 Jan 1930. AMD, pp. 340, 372 (Lydia Yeamans). AS, pp. 1072 (b. 1866); 1174 (Yeamans Titus, Lydia). BHD1, p. 542 (b. at sea, 1866; d. LA CA). IFN, p. 294. Truitt, p. 326. "Lydia Yeamans Titus with Morosco," *MPW,* 11 Sep 1915, 1839. "Lydia Yeamans Member of Famous Family," *MPW,* 2 Mar 1918, 1229. "Lydia Yeamans Titus Makes First Appearance in a Short Subject," *MPW,* 23 Oct 1920, 1147. George Katchmer, "Remembering the Great Silents," *CI,* 239 (May 1995), 35–36.

Tobani, Theodore Moses, Sr. [composer] (b. Hamburg, Germany, 2 May 1855–12 Dec 1933 [78], Jackson Heights, LI NY [Death Certificate Index No. 7633]). "T.M. Tobani Dead; Popualr Composer; His 'Hearts and Flowers,' Written in Half an Hour in 1893, Sold in Thousands; Wrote Many Marches; Gavottes and Waltzes Among His 5,000 Selections—Prodigy at 5, He Was Violinist at 10," *NYT,* 13 Dec 1933, 23:3. "Theodore M. Tobani," *Variety,* 19 Dec 1933. AS, p. 1072.

Tobias, Charles (brother of **Harry Tobias**) [composer] (b. New York NY, 15 Aug 1897–7 Jul 1970 [72], Manhasset, LI NY; liver ailment). "Charles Tobias Is Dead at 72; Writer of Many Popular Songs," *NYT,* 8 Jul 1970, 43:2 (wrote *If I Had My Life to Live Over* and lyrics to Romberg's *Zing, Zing, Zoom, Zoom* and *Faithfully Yours*). "L. Wolfe Gilbert, 83, Chas. Tobias, 72; Both ASCAPERs with Top Catalogs," *Variety,* 15 Jul 1970 (wrote *Don't Sit Under the Apple Tree; We Did It Before and We Can Do It Again; The Old Lamplighter*). AS, p. 1072 (d. 7 Jun). BHD2, p. 262.

Tobias, Harry (brother of **Charles Tobias**) [composer] (b. New York NY, 1895?–15 Dec 1994 [99], St. Louis MO). "Harry Tobias, 99, Popular-Song Writer," *NYT,* 18 Dec 1994, I, 75:1 (wrote *I'll Keep the Lovelight Burning, It's a Lonesome Old Town, Miss You*). Wrote the title song for *Linda,* rel. 1 Apr 1929 (muscial score and sound effects). AS, p. 1072.

Tobias, Lester S. [scenarist] (b. Milwaukee WI, 1892–31 Aug 1968 [76?], North Hollywood CA). BHD2, p. 262.

Tobin, Frank [actor] (d. 20 Jul 1913, Omaha NB). BHD, p. 318.

Tobin, Genevieve [vaudeville/stage/film actress] (b. New York NY, 29 Nov 1903–31 Jul 1995 [93], Pasadena CA; cardiac arrest in her sleep). m. **William Keighley**, 1938 (d. 1984). (Universal; Paramount; RKO.) Last film: *Queen of Crime,* 1941.) "Genevieve Tobin, Actress, Dies at 93," *NYT,* 4 Aug 1995, A25:2. "Genevieve Tobin Keighley," *Variety,* 4 Sep 1995, 760:4. AMD, p. 340. AS, p. 1072 (b. 1901). BHD1, p. 543 (b. 1899; d. 21 Jul). Katz, p. 1137. "Genevieve Tobin in New Fox Film," *MPW,* 30 Jun 1923, 758.

Toch, Ernst [composer] (b. Vienna, Austria, 7 Dec 1887–1 Oct 1964 [76], Los Angeles CA). BHD2, p. 262.

Tod, Malcolm [stage/film actor] (b. Burton-on-Trent, England, 10 Mar 1897). AS, p. 1072. JS, p. 454 (in Italian silents in 1927–28; "Talkies cut short a not-too-brilliant career in movies.").

Todd, Arthur Lyle [cameraman] (b. New York NY, 1895?–28 Aug 1942 [47], Oceanside CA). (WB.) "Arthur Todd," *Variety,* 2 Sep 1942. AMD, p. 340. BHD2, p. 262. FDY, p. 469. "Todd Wins Gold Medal," *MPW,* 28 Aug 1920, 1193. "Arthur Todd," *MPW,* 27 Nov 1926, 209.

Todd, Harry [actor] (b. Allegheny PA, 13 Dec 1863–15 Feb 1935 [71], Glendale CA; heart attack). (Essanay.) m. Margaret Joslin. "Harry Todd," *Variety,* 27 Feb 1935. AMD, p. 340. AS, p. 1072 (d. 16 Feb). BHD1, p. 543. IFN, p. 294. Truitt, p. 326 (b. 1865). "Laughmakers Join Universal Company," *MPW,* 18 Mar 1916, 1833.

Todd, Lola [actress: Wampas Star, 1925] (b. New York NY, 14 May 1904–31 Jul 1995 [91], Los Angeles CA). BHD1, p. 618. George A. Katchmer, "Remembering the Great Silents," *CI,* 178 (Apr 1990), 58.

Todd, Ruth [title writer/scenarist]. No data found. FDY, pp. 439, 447.

Todd, Thelma, "Hot Toddy" or "The Ice

Cream Blonde" [actress] (*née* Alison Loyd, b. Lawrence MA, 29 Jul 1905–13? Dec 1935 [30], Santa Monica CA; found dead under mysterious circumstances). m. Pasquale "Pat" De Cicco, 18 Jul 1932, Prescott AZ—div. 3 Mar 1934 ("cruelty and incompatibility"). (Film debut: *Vamping Venus*.) Andy Edmonds, *Hot Toddy; The True Story of Hollywood's Most Sensational Murder* (NY: William Morrow and Company, Inc., 1989). "Denies Threatening Actress," *NYT*, 31 Oct 1935, 16:1 (Harry Schimanski, a janitor, sent her 3 letters. He was arrested and arraigned on $3,000 bail). "Thelma Todd Dead; Found in Garage; Actress, Discovered in Auto After 18 Hours, Was Monoxide Victim Surgeon Says; Friend's Story Differs; Actor's Wife Says Miss Todd Phoned Her Long After Hour of Death Set by Autopsy," *NYT*, 17 Dec 1935, 1:5, 4:3; "Actress Trained as a Teacher," 17 Dec 1935, 4:3 (in films 8 years); "Death Night Fears of Miss Todd Told; Chauffeur [Ernest O. Peters] Says She Had Him Drive at Breakneck Speed on Way from Party; Wanted to Avoid Gangs; Police Assert that She Had Tiff with Roland West, Her Partner in Cafe," 18 Dec 1935, 29:5; "Todd Death Sent to Grand Jurors; Inquest Verdict Leans to View of Accident but Asks for Further Inquiry; Actress Seen on Sunday; Estranged Wife [Jewel Carmen] of [Roland] West Says Star Was with a Man on Day After Supposed Demise," 19 Dec 1935, 8:1 (d. 15 Dec—"death appears to have been accidental"; "she had recently signed a film contract reputedly calling for $1,500 a week"); "Push Two Inquiries in the Todd Death; Police to Question West and Two Cafe Aides on Events of Sunday Morning; Waiter Reports Threat; Jury Foreman Hints Data on Murder—Thousands Pass Actress's Bier," 20 Dec 1935, 11:1 ("monoxide murder victim"?); "Todd Study Turns to Suicide Theory; Prosecutor Declares Evidence Indicates Actress Became Despondent at Party; Waiter [Alex Hounie] Receives 'Threat'; Four More Say They Saw Film Player Late Sunday, but Official Discounts It," 21 Dec 1935, 34:2; "Todd 'Death Walk' Traced for Clue; Woman Operative Climbs 270 Steps from Actress's Sidewalk Cafe to Garage; Slipper Marks Compared; Footwear More Scuffed than the Dead Woman's—De Cicco Is Expected on Coast Friday," 22 Dec 1935, 16:2; "Todd Jury Acts Today; Friends of Film Star Will Be Questioned Concerning Her Death," 23 Dec 1935, 9:1 (including Roland West, Pat De Cicco; Jewel Carmen and Mrs. Wallace Ford); "Miss Todd Linked to a 'Strange Man'; Store Owner Tells Grand Jury of Actress Phoning and Then Leaving Place with Escort; Quick Gas Action Shown; Detective Says Garage Tests Indicated Monoxide Had Fatal Effect in Two Minutes," 24 Dec 1935, 34:2 ("District Attorney Buron Fitts said tonight that Miss [Ida] Lupino and Miss [Margaret] Lindsay had informed him that Miss Todd told them of a 'marvelous romance' she was having with an unnamed San Francisco business man"); "ZaSu Pitts Called by Todd Case, Jury; Inquiry Turns to Report of a Luncheon Party Day Before Mysterious Death; Strange Escort Hinted; But Such a Gathering Is Denied—Head Waiter Says He Has Received New Threats," 25 Dec 1935, 44:5; "Reports Miss Todd Bruised on Throat; Prosecutor Will Question Surgeons but Says Any Marks Might Have Come Naturally; Hints Witnesses Erred; He Asserts Blonde Driving in Auto with Man Might Have Been Mistaken for Actress," 26 Dec 1935, 30:5; "New Todd Evidence Seen in Jury's Move; Inquirers Pay Unexpected Visit to Scene of Actress's Death in Los Angeles," 27 Dec 1935, 40:3 (De Cicco described as a "film colony Beau Brummel"; he left Smithtown, LI NY, for L.A. by plane on 26 Dec); "'Publicity Seekers' Confuse Todd Case; 'Hodge-Podge of Honest Evidence and Obvious Faking' Found by Prosecutor," 29 Dec 1935, 14:5; "Grand Jury Divides on Miss Todd's Death; Most of Them Favor Suicide Theory, but None Believes It Was Accidental," 4 Jan 1936, 34:3; "Thelma Todd Estate to Mother," 11 Jan 1936, 5:5 (in excess of $10,000 to Mrs. Alice Todd and $1 to De Cicco). "Thelma Todd Will Is Filed," 31 Jan 1936, 17:3 (will dated 19 Sep 1933). "Thelma Todd, 31, Dies, Monoxide Poisoning; No Mystery Angles," *Variety*, 18 Dec 1935 (d. 16 Dec, age 31). AMD, p. 340. AS, p. 1072 (d. 15 Dec; suicide by carbon monoxide). BHD1, p. 543 (d. 16 Dec, LA CA). FSS, p. 275. IFN, p. 294 (*née* Alison Loyd. Katz, p. 1138. Truitt, p. 326. "Three Little Girls from Paramount's School...," *Photoplay Magazine*, Jun 1926, 86. "Thelma Todd," *MPW*, 8 Jan 1927, 121. Charles Paton, "School Is Dismissed; And So Ends the Term of Paramount High," *MPC*, Jun 1927, 33, 70 (the graduates were Todd, Buddy Rogers, Mona Palma, Ivy Harris, Iris Gray, Jack Ludin, Josephine Dunn, Walter Goss, *et al.*). "Miss Todd Cast," *MPW*, 9 Jul 1927, 97. "Thelma Todd Injured," *MPW*, 12 Nov 1927, 19. Joyce A. Rogers, "Thelma Todd, No Dumb Blonde," *CI*, 118 (Apr 1985), 48–49 (b. 19 Jul). Eve Golden, "The Tragedy and Comedy of Thelma Todd," *CI*, 242 (Aug 1995), 20 *et passim*. R.E. Braff, "An Index to the Films of Thelma Todd," *CI*, 242 (Aug 1995), 24, 34. Patrick Jenning and Marshall Croddy, "The Mysteries of Thelma Todd [letter]," *CI*, 245 (Nov 1995), 6–7 (refutes Andy Edmonds' claim that Todd was murdered by Lucky Luciano). Frederick Santon, "Thelma Todd's Murder," *CI*, 246 (Dec 1995), 6 (alleges that Todd's killer confessed to Hal Roach, who withheld the information for years. Andy Edmonds, "'Hot Toddy' Response [letter]," *CI*, 248 (Feb 1996), 6. Richard W. Bann, "More on Thelma [letter]," *CI*, 248 (Feb 1996), 7, 10. John Patrick Feeney, "Focus on Thelma Todd's Life [letter]," *CI*, 253 (Jul 1996), 8. John Patrick Feeney, *Editor*, The Thelma Todd Society [newsletter], 4392 Bussey Road, Syracuse NY 13215.

Toddi [set decorator/director] (*né* Pietro S. Riverta). No data found. JS, p. 454 (in Italian silents from 1920).

Toelle, Carola [actress] (b. Berlin, Germany, 2 Apr 1893–28 Jan 1958 [64], Berlin, Germany). AS, p. 1073. Vittorio Martinelli, "Kino-Leiblinge," *Griffithiana*, 38/39 (Oct 1990), 35.

Tofano, Sergio [actor/director] (b. Rome, Italy, 20 Aug 1886). AS, p. 1073. JS, p. 455 (in Italian silents from 1916).

Toien, Paul J. [actor] (b. MA, 7 Dec 1915–26 Jan 1966 [50], Los Angeles CA). BHD1, p. 618.

Toland, Gregg [cinematographer] (b. Charleston IL, 29 May 1904–28 Sep 1948 [44], Los Angeles CA; coronary thrombosis). (Fox, 1919, as messenger.) m. (1) Mrs. Helen Barclay, 1934–45; (2) actress Virginia Thorpe. "Gregg Toland, 44, Camera Man, Dies; Pictorial Supervisor of Many Leading U.S. Films—He Began on Coast at 15," *NYT*, 29 Sep 1948, 30:2 (was to have filmed *Roseanna McCoy*). "Gregg Toland," *Variety*, 29 Sep 1948. AS, p. 1073. BHD2, p. 262. IFN, p. 294. Katz, pp. 1138–39.

Tolentino, Riccardo [director]. No data found. JS, p 456 (in Italian silents from 1915).

Toler, Hooper [actor] (b. Wichita KS, 1891–2 Jun 1922 [31?], Los Angeles CA; heart attack). AS, p. 1073. BHD, p. 319.

Toler, Sidney [stage/film actor/baritone] (b. Warrensburg MO, 28 Apr 1888–12 Feb 1947 [58], Los Angeles CA; bedridden for seven months with intestinal cancer). m. (1) Vivian (d. 1943); (2) Viva Tattersall, 1943. (Columbia Theatre Stock Co.; Broadway debut: *The Office Boy*, Victoria Theatre, 1903; film debut: *Madame X*, 1929.) "Sidney Toler Dies; Film Charlie Chan; Veteran Stage, Screen Star Played Chinese Detective Since 1939 [succeeded Warner Oland]—Had Been Playwright [*Ritzy*]," *NYT*, 13 Feb 1947, 23:1 ("In 1894 Mr. Toler joined the Corse Payton touring company and performed with it for four years. After becoming a great neighborhood attraction as a leading man with the Lee Avenue Academy in Brooklyn, he was invited by Julia Marlowe to join her dramatic company."). "Sidney Toler," *Variety*, 165, 19 Feb 1947, 54:1 (age 73. Toured with Julia Marlowe and Course Payton. As a playwright, he wrote *The Belle of Richmond, The Dancing Master*, and *The House on the Sands*, et al.). AS, p. 1073 (b. 1874; d. Beverly Hills CA). BHD1, p. 543 (b. 1874). IFN, p. 294. Charles P. Mitchell, "A Guide to Charlie Chan Films; Part Two: Sidney Toler at Fox," *CI*, 268 (Oct 1997), 20–22 (b. MO); Part III, *CI* (Nov 1997), 24–28/

Tollaire, August [actor] (b. Paris, France, 7 Mar 1866–15 Jan 1959 [92], Los Angeles Co. CA). (Paramount.) AS, p. 1073. BHD1, p. 543. IFN, p. 294.

Tolly, Frank [stuntman] (d. 26 Nov 1924, New York NY; accidentally killed during the filming of *The Great Circus Mystery*). AS, p. 1073. BHD, p. 319. IFN, p. 294.

Tolnaes, Gunnar [actor] (b. Cristiania, Norway, 7 Feb 1879–9 Nov 1940 [61], Oslo, Norway). BHD1, p. 618 (b. Oslo). IFN, p. 294.

Tolstoi, Countess (mother of **Ilya Tolstoi**) [actress] (*née* Sophie Behra, b. Russia, 1846–4 Nov 1919 [73?], Trasnaya Polyana, Russia). m. **Léon Tolstoi** (d. 1910; son, Ilya). AS, p. 1073. BHD, p. 319.

Tolstoi, Ilya (son of **Countess** and **Léon Tolstoi**) [scenarist/actor]. No data found. AMD, p. 340. FDY, p. 439. "Count Tolstoi to Appear in Rivoli Productions," *MPW*, 1 Feb 1919, 631. "Count Tolstoi Signed," *MPW*, 21 Aug 1926, 2. "Tolstoi's Son with Carewe," *MPW*, 2 Oct 1926, 284.

Tolstoi, Léon [actor] (father of **Ilya Tolstoi**) (b. Iasnaia, Russia, 9 Sep 1828–1910 [82?], Astapovo, Russia). m. Sophie Behra (**Countess Tolstoi**). AS, p. 1073.

Toluboff, Alexander [art director] (b. Lublin, Russia, 1882?–1 Jul 1940 [58], Bloomfield Hills MI). (MGM.) m. Theodora MacManus, 1935. "Alex Toluboff Dies; Wanger's Director; Had Helped Produce 200 Films—Was a Refugee from Russia," *NYT*, 2 Jul 1940, 21:4. "Alexander Toluboff," *Variety*, 3 Jul 1940. AS, p. 1073. BHD2, p. 262.

Tom, Konrad [actor/director] (b. Warsaw, Poland, 9 Apr 1887–1957 [70?], Los Angeles CA). AS, p. 1073.

Tomamoto, Thomas [actor] (*né* Tsunetaro Sugimoto) (b. Japan, 1879?–28 Sep 1924 [45], New York NY). "Thomas Tomamoto, Japanese Actor," *NYT*, 30 Sep 1934, 23:4. "Thomas Tomamoto," *Variety*, 1 Oct 1924. AS, p. 1073. BHD, p. 319. IFN, p. 294. Truitt, p. 326.

Tomarchio, Ludovico [actor/singer] (Catania, Italy, 6 Jan 1886–25 Jun 1947 [61], Los Angeles CA; arteriosclerosis). AS, p. 1073.

Tomatis, Giovanni [cinematographer] (b. Piozzo, Italy, 18 Apr 1871–24 Apr 1959 [88], Dogliani, Italy). JS, p. 457 (in Italian from 1910).

Tomick, Frank [actor/soundman] (b. 11 Sep 1894–29 Oct 1966 [72], Los Angeles Co. CA). "Frank Tomick," *Variety,* 23 Nov 1966. BHD1, p. 543.

Tonaka, Shoji [actor] (d. 19 Oct 1918, New York NY). BHD, p. 319.

Toncray, Kate V. [actress]. No data found. (Biograph, 1911; K&E.) George Katchmer, "Remembering the Great Silents," *CI,* 249 (Mar 1996), 47–48.

Tonge, H. Asheton (father of **Philip Tonge**) [actor] (b. 1872?–2 Apr 1927 [55], New York NY). AS, p. 1074 (d. Hollywood CA). BHD, p. 319. IFN, p. 295.

Tonge, Philip (son of **H. Asheton Tonge**) [actor] (*né* Philip Asheton Tonge, b. London, England, 26 Apr 1897–28 Jan 1959 [61], Los Angeles CA; after a brief abdominal malady). (Vitagraph.) "Philip Tonge," *Variety,* 4 Feb 1959. AS, p. 1074 (b. 1892). BHD1, p. 544 (b. 1892). IFN, p. 295. SD, pp. 1224–25 (b. 1892).

Tooker, William H. [stage/film actor] (b. New York NY, 2 Sep 1869–10 Oct 1936 [67], Los Angeles CA). (Life-Photo Co.) "William Tooker," *Variety,* 14 Oct 1936 (age 72). AMD, p. 340. BHD1, p. 544. IFN, p. 295. Truitt, p. 327. "William H. Tooker Cast for the Lead in 'Springtime,'" *MPW,* 24 Oct 1914, 476. "William Tooker," *NYDM,* 22 Sep 1915, 35:1 (with photo). "William H. Tooker," *MPW,* 9 Oct 1915, 260. "William H. Tooker with Bushman and Beverly Bayne," *MPW,* 1 Dec 1917, 1331. "In Two Pictures at Same Time," *MPW,* 25 Sep 1920, 513.

Toomey, Regis [actor] (b. Pittsburgh PA, 13 Aug 1898–12 Oct 1991 [93], Woodland Hills CA; heart attack). "Regis Toomey, Actor in Films, Dies at 93," *NYT,* 15 Oct 1991, D25:1. "Regis Toomey," *Variety,* 21 Oct 1991, p. 87. AS, p. 1074. BHD1, p. 544. Katz, p. 1140.

Toomey, W.C. [executive/general manager]. No data found. AMD, p. 340. "Toomey Joins Mirror Films," *MPW,* 13 Nov 1915, 1279.

Torá, Lia [actress] (b. Rio de Janeiro, Brazil). (Fox; WB.) Waldman, p. 282.

Tordesillas, Jesus [actor] (*né* Jesus Tordesillas Fernandez, b. Madrid, Spain, 28 Jan 1893–24 Mar 1973 [80], Madrid, Spain; heart attack). "Jesus Tordesilla," *Variety,* 270, 4 Apr 1973, 127:3 (in *Flor de España,* 1923). AS, p. 1074. BHD1, p. 544. IFN, p. 295.

Tornek, Anna [actress] (b. 1898–12 Aug 1985 [87?], Woodland Hills CA). AS, p. 1075. BHD1, p. 544.

Tornek, Jack [actor] (b. Russia, 2 Jan 1888–18 Feb 1974 [86], Los Angeles Co. CA). AS, p. 1075. BHD1, p. 544. IFN, p. 295.

Torney, Dadasaheb [director]producer] (*né* Ramchandra Gopal Torney, b. Poona, India, 13 Apr 1880). AS, p. 1075.

Torpe, Marie [actress] (b. 1904–28 Jul 1967 [63?], Woodland Hills CA). BHD, p. 319.

Torpey, Lester [actor] (b. 1899–25 Aug 1920 [21?], Weehawken NJ; car accident). AS, p. 1075. BHD, p. 319.

Torporkoff, N. [cinematographer]. No data found. FDY, p. 469.

Torrence, David (brother of **Ernest Torrence**) [actor] (b. Edinburgh, Scotland, 17 Jan 1864–26 Dec 1951 [87], Woodland Hills CA). AMD, p. 340. AS, p. 1075 (*né* Thoyson; d. Scotland). BHD1, p. 544. FFF, p. 168. IFN, p. 295. Katz, p. 1141, cites the following: *né* David Torrence Tayson, b. 1880–1972. MH, p. 140. "Torrence Forms New Sort of Club," *MPW,* 15 Jul 1922, 232 (the "Don't Quarrel Club"). George Katchmer, "David Torrence," *CI,* 214 (Apr 1993), 50.

Torrence, Ernest (brother of **David Torrence**) [actor] (*né* Ernest Thayson Torrence-Thomson, b. Edinburgh, Scotland, 26 Jun 1878–15 May 1933 [54], New York NY; complications after an operation [Death Certificate Index No. 11614]). m. Ilse Reamer. "Ernest Torrence, Film Actor, Dead; Succumbs in Hospital Here on the Eve of Premiere of His Final Motion Picture; Led in Character Roles; Since 'Tol'able David' He Had Created a Variety of Widely Admired Screen Portraits," *NYT,* 16 May 1933, 17:1. "Ernest Torrence," *Variety,* 16 May 1933. AMD, p. 340. AS, p. 1075 (*né* Thoyson). BHD1, p. 544. FFF, p. 47. FSS, p. 276. GK, pp. 536–64. IFN, p. 295. Katz, p. 1141. MH, p. 140. Slide, p. 166. Truitt, p. 327. Jane H. Lipman, "The Heavy; Ernest Torrence, the screen's most villainous villain tells his story," *Classic,* XVII, Jun 1923, 36–37, 77. "Ernest Torrence Spends a Busy Week End in New York," *MPW,* 16 Jun 1923, 562. Grace Greenwood, "The Ideal Home Life of Ernest Torrence," *MW,* 29 Mar 1924, 12–13, 41. Lois Wilson, "The Ernest Torrence I Know; The Story of a Villain Who Is a Hero to His Friends," *MW,* 7 Feb 1925, 14–15, 29–31. "Torrence Contract Renewed," *MPW,* 23 May 1925, 472. Robert Donaldson, "'I canna tak' the sixpence an' be true to m'sel'," So Ernest Torrence Goes In For Art," *MPC,* Jun 1927, 42, 81. R.E. Braff, "An Index to the Films of Ernest Torrence," *CI,* 203 (May 1992), 36–37. George Katchmer, "Remembering the Great Silents," *CI,* 229 (Jul 1994), 39.

Torres, Henry [actor/director] (b. Les Andelys, France, 17 Oct 1891 [extrait de naissance no. 120/1891]-4 Jan 1966 [74], Paris, France). AS, p. 1075.

Torres, Miguel Contretas [actor/director/producer] (b. Morelia, Michoacán, Mexico, 28 Sep 1899–5 Jun 1981 [81], Mexico City, Mexico; heart attack). Gabriel Ramirez, *Miguel Contreras Torres* (University of Guadalajara, Mexico, 1994; ISBN 968-895-466-7). AS, p. 1075 (b. Ciudad Hildalgo, Mexico, 16 Sep).

Torres, Ramirez [scenarist]. No data found. AMD, p. 340. "Torres to Summer in Los Angeles," *MPW,* 27 Jul 1918, 557. "Ramirez Torres Leaves Pathé Company," *MPW,* 22 Mar 1919, 1663.

Torres, Raquel [actress] (*née* Wilhelmina von Osterman, b. Hermosillo, Mexico, 11 Nov 1908–10 Aug 1987 [78], Malibu CA; heart attack). m. (1) Stephen Ames; (2) John Hall, 1959. "Raquel Torres," *NYT,* 13 Aug 1987, B8:6. "Raquel Torres," *Variety,* 19 Aug 1987 (*née* Paula Marie Osterman, d. Malibu CA, age 87). AS, p. 1075. BHD1, p. 544 (d. LA CA). Katz, p. 1142.

Torrey, Marian [actress] (aka Marianna de la Torre). No data found. AMD, p. 340. "Keystone Actress Changes Name [to Marian Torrey]," *MPW,* 19 Jan 1918, 367.

Toscane, Jean Elie [actor] (b. France, 2 Jun 1890–ca. 1960 [70?]). AS, p. 1076.

Toscano, Salvador [director] (*né* Salvador Toscano Barragán, b. Guadalajara, Jalisco, Mexico, 22 Mar 1872–14 Apr 1947 [75]). AS, p. 1076 (Salvator Toscano-Barragan, b. Zapotlan, Mexico, 24 Mar 1873-d. 13 Apr).

Tostary, Alfred [director] (b. Forst, Germany, 5 Jan 1872). AS, p. 1076.

Totheroh, Rolland (Rollie) H. [cinematographer] (b. San Francisco CA, 29 Nov 1890–18 Jun 1967 [76], Los Angeles CA). (Essanay, 1915; Keystone.) "Roland H. Totheroh," *Variety,* 28 Jun 1967. AMD, p. 340. AS, p. 1076. BHD2, p. 263. IFN, p. 295. Katz, p. 1142. "Grinds the Crank on Chaplin's Antics," *MPW,* 17 Aug 1918, 979.

Totheroh, Roy [cinematographer]. No data found. FDY, p. 469.

Totman, Llewellyn [scenarist] (b. MN, 3 Aug 1903–6 Oct 1977 [74], Los Angeles CA). AMD, p. 340. BHD2, p. 263 (Wellyn Totman). FDY, p. 439 (Wellyn Totman). "Totman Joins Mejador," *MPW,* 9 May 1925, 230.

Toto [actor] (*né* Antonio Furst de Curtis-Gagliardi Ducas Comeno di Bisanzio, b. Naples, Italy, 15 Feb 1898–15 Apr 1967 [69], Rome, Italy). AS, p. 1076.

Toto, the Clown (son of George Novello and Amalie Schoenberg, lion tamer) [contortionist/clown/film actor] (*né* Armando Novello, b. Geneva, Switzerland, 27 Oct 1888–15 Dec 1938 [50], Union Hospital, Bronx NY; stricken with appendicitis on 4 Dec; peritonitis set in; after operation on intestines. Burial in Beechwood Cemetery, New Rochelle NY). m. Hanny Frick (1 daughter). (Pathé.) "Toto, Famous Clown, Dies at 50; Fails to Recover from Operation; Born in Switzerland, He Came Here in 1914, Was for Years Favorite of Millions, Saved and Became Well to Do," *NYT,* 16 Dec 1938, 2:3 ("Toto was beloved of millions in the United States and Europe for his absurd pantomime and infectious grin. His only sound on stage was an occasional high cackle. ¶In 1917–1918 Toto worked as a screen comedian for Hal Roach. Then he went into vaudeville..."). "'Premature' Death Libel Suit Ended by Toto's Demise at 50," *Variety,* 133, 21 Dec 1938, 1:1 (sued the *New York Daily Mirror* for $50,000. "Paper had printed a feature story [by Hugo Roboz] in magazine section of its Sunday edition on Nov. 27 in which Toto was described as having died a pauper after being the highest paid clown...His estate may yet sue." Roboz died on 25 Nov.); "Armando (Toto) Novello," 47:1. AMD, p. 340. AS, p.1076. BHD1, p. 545 (*né* Arnold Novello). IFN, p. 295. "Toto at Rolin Studio in Los Angeles," *MPW,* 16 Jun 1917, 1806. "Clown Toto Is on the Job," *MPW,* 14 Jul 1917, 270:2. "Enter Toto, Comedian," *MPW,* 29 Dec 1917, 1926. "Toto Finishes New Comedy," *MPW,* 10 Aug 1918, 884.

Toto, Billie [actress] (b. 1904–24 Dec 1928 [24?], New York NY). BHD, p. 319. IFN, p. 295 (age 34).

Totten, Edyth [actress/scenarist/producer] (*née* Marguerite Edith Totten, b. New York NY, 1885?–12 Nov 1953 [68], Welfare Island, New York NY). m. Russell Moore Fanning, 1920, Bluepoint, LI NY—div. 1932. "Edyth Totten Dies; Play Producer, 68; Founder in '26 of Old President Theatre Had Staged Many Works—Wrote for Screen," *NYT,* 13 Nov 1953, 28:3. "Edyth Totten," *Variety,* 11 Nov 1953 (Mrs. Marguerite Edyth Totten Fanning). AMD, p. 340. AS, p. 1076. BHD, p. 319.

"Edyth Totten in Pictures," *MPW,* 5 Sep 1914, 1388.

Totten, Joseph Byron [playwright/scenarist/director/actor] (b. Brooklyn NY, 1876?–29 Apr 1946 [70], New York NY; heart attack). m. Leslie Bingham (d. 1945). (Essanay, 1908.) "Joe B. Totten; Theatrical Producer and Actor Was in Silent Films," *NYT,* 30 Apr 1946, 21:3. "Joseph Byron Totten," *Variety,* 1 May 1946. "Mrs. Joe Byron Totten; Actress, as Leslie Bingham, Had Played Leading Roles Here," *NYT,* 8 Feb 1945, 19:2 (b. Boston MA, 1883?–7 Feb 1945 [61], Adamston NJ). AMD, p. 340. AS, p. 1076. BHD, p. 319; BHD2, p. 263 (b. 1870). IFN, p. 295. "Essanay Travelers Back; Joseph Byron Totten's Traveling Company Returns to Chicago Studio," *NYDM,* 30 Oct 1915, 27:3. "Joseph Byron Totten," *MPW,* 6 Nov 1915, 1115.

Toulout, Jean Joseph Charles [actor] (b. Paris, France, 28 Sep 1887–18 Oct 1962 [75]. Paris, France [extrait de décès no. SN/10/1962]). AS, p. 1076. BHD1, p. 545. IFN, p. 295.

Tourel, Jennie [actress/singer] (*née* Jennie Davidson, b. Montreal, Canada, 26 Jun 1899–23 Nov 1973 [74], New York NY). AS, p. 1076.

Tourine, Victor Aleksandrovich [director] (b. St. Petersburg, Russia, 1895–1945 [50?], Moscow, Russia). AS, p. 1076.

Tourjansky, Victor [actor/director/scenarist] (*né* Vyachetslav K. Turzhanskiy, b. Kiev, Ukraine, Russia, 4 Mar 1891–13 Aug 1976 [85], Munich, Germany). m. Natalia Efimovna Kovanko (actress Nathalie Kovanko, 1899–1967). (MGM.) AMD, p. 341. AS, p. 1076 (*né* Victor Vyacheslav Turzhansky, b. Feodosia, Ukraine). BHD2, p. 263. IFN, p. 295. JS, p. 461 ("Began as an actor in Russia in 1912, and in 1914 began directing. Based in Germany and France from 1919." Made films in Italy from 1958 to 1963). Katz, p. 1143 (began acting in 1912; directing, 1914). Waldman, p. 284 (b. 1892). "Russian Directs Tim McCoy in 'Gallant Gringo,'" *MPW,* 11 Jun 1927, 422.

Tourneur, Andrée [actress]. No data found. AMD, p. 341. "Miss Tourneur Will Play in 'Phantom Bride,'" *MPW,* 17 Dec 1921, 794. George A. Katchmer, "Remembering the Great Silents," *CI,* 178 (Apr 1990), 58.

Tourneur, Jacques (son of **Maurice Tourneur**) [script clerk/film/TV actor/director] (*né* Jacques Thomas, b. Paris, France, 12 Nov 1904–19 Dec 1977 [73], Bergerec, France [extrait de décès no. 386]). (RKO; last film: *War Gods of the Deep,* 1965.) "Jacques Tourneur, Film Director, Dies; Expert in Horror Movies Was 73—Did 'I Walked with a Zombie,' 'Cat People' and 'Leopard Man,'" *NYT,* 24 Dec 1977, 22:4 (appeared in *Scaramouche,* 1923.). "Jacques Tourneur," *Variety,* 289, 28 Dec 1977, 62:3 (d. 22 Dec). AS, p. 1076. BHD, p. 319; BHD2, p. 263. IFN, p. 295.

Tourneur, Maurice (father of **Jacques Tourneur**) [director/producer] (*né* Maurice Thomas, b. Paris, France, 2 Feb 1873–4 Aug 1961 [88], Paris, France; car accident). m. Fernande Petit, 1904; **Louise Lagrange** (d. 1979). (Eclair, 1911; World; Paragon; Equitable; Paramount; MGM.) (Last film: *l' Impasse des Deux Anges,* 1948.) "Maurice Tourneur Dies at 85; Produced Silent-Film Classics," *NYT,* 5 Aug 1961, 17:4 (lost leg in 1952 after auto accident. "M. Tourneur brought to the silent motion picture screen a capacity for pictorial composition and for dramatic nuance that few directors possessed in a day of almost total dependence on cinematic clichés—brow smiting, breast beating and leering.") "Maurice Thomas Tourneur," *Variety,* 9 Aug 1961. AMD, p. 341. AS, p. 1076. BHD, p. 319; BHD2, p. 263. IFN, p. 295. Katz, pp. 1143–44. Spehr, p. 170. "Maurice Tourneur," *MPW,* 28 Nov 1914, 1242. "Maurice Tourneur," *NYDM,* 17 Mar 1915, 26:1. "Motion Pictures; 'A Gift from France,'" *NYDM,* 30 Jun 1915, 19:3 (age given as 38). Maurice Tourneur, "The Artistry of Motion Pictures," *MPW,* 21 Jul 1917, 378–79. "Maurice Tourneur," *MPW,* 23 Feb 1918, 1104. "Tourneur to Produce Independently," *MPW,* 13 Apr 1918, 224. "Twenty-Seven Features the Tourneur Record," *MPW,* 11 May 1918, 869. "War Influencing Against Long Pictures, Says Tourneur," *MPW,* 5 May 1918, 1166. "Tourneur Pays Respect to Star System," *MPW,* 22 Jun 1918, 1689. "Tourneur Believes War Is Reviving Melodrama," *MPW,* 29 Jun 1918, 1870. "Film Division Names Director Advisors," *MPW,* 20 Jul 1918, 363–64. "Tourneur Protests the Use of 'Photoplay' Promiscuously," *MPW,* 27 Jul 1918, 577. "Tourneur a Firm Believer in Element of Surprise," *MPW,* 31 Aug 1918, 1289. "Tourneur Selects Melodrama for Psychological Reasons," *MPW,* 7 Sep 1918, 1445. "'Dancing Excellent Training for Screen,' Says Tourneur," *MPW,* 2 Nov 1918, 611. "Maurice Tourneur to Make Pictures in California," *MPW,* 16 Nov 1918, 752. "Tourneur's Record for the Past Year," *MPW,* 4 Jan 1919, 109. "Maurice Tourneur a Pioneer in New Photoplay Movement," *MPW,* 8 Mar 1919, 1383. "Maurice Tourneur FInished His First California Film," *MPW,* 29 Mar 1919, 1832. "Tourneur Directs FIlm at Bottom of Ocean," *MPW,* 19 Apr 1919, 394. "Exhibitor Will Shape the Future of the Screen, Says Maurice Tourneur," *MPW,* 13 Mar 1920, 1820. "Tourneur Aids Government in Spreading Americanism Through the Picture Screen," *MPW,* 3 Apr 1920, 57. "Tourneur Will Go to Europe But Will Not Produce There," *MPW,* 3 Apr 1920, 62. "Not to Build Own Studio," *MPW,* 3 Jul 1920, 96. "Tourneur Ill with [ptomaine] Poisoning," *MPW,* 23 Oct 1920, 1134. "Close Deal with Tourneur," *MPW,* 7 Apr 1923, 613. "Tourneur, a Producer of Strong Imagination," *MPW,* 9 Jun 1923, 508. "Tourneur on His Fiftieth," *MPW,* 27 Oct 1923, 760 (*Jealous Husbands*). "Tourneur Sees Return of Shorter Features," *MPW,* 1 Dec 1923, 495. Maurice Tourneur, "Shorter Films and Less Production Costs Are Predicted for Next Year," *MPW,* 29 Dec 1923, 801. "Tourneur Signs with M-G-M; To Produce Verne Story," *MPW,* 20 Feb 1926, 711.

Tover, Leo[pold] [cinematographer] (b. New Haven CT, 6 Dec 1902–30 Dec 1964 [62], Los Angeles CA). (Fox; Paramount.) AS, p. 1077. BHD2, p. 263. FDY, p. 469. IFN, p. 295. Katz, p. 1144.

Towell, Sydney [executive] (b. 1896–9 Dec 1944 [48?], New York NY). BHD2, p. 263.

Tower, Halsey [actor] (b. Buffalo NY, 5 Oct 1889–24 Nov 1939 [50], Los Angeles CA). BHD, p. 319.

Towne, Charles Hanson [scenarist] (b. 1877–28 Feb 1949 [71?], New York NY). BHD, p. 319; BHD2, p. 263.

Towne, Elaine [scenarist]. No data found. FDY, p. 439.

Towne, Fennimore Cooper [vaudeville actor/writer] (b. 1892?–4 Dec 1917 [25], New York NY; septic poisoning from which he had been suffering for three months). "Fennimore Cooper Towne," *Variety,* XLIX, 11 Jan 1918, 20:1 (d. 4 Jan 1918). AMD, p. 341. "Obituary," *MPW,* 26 Jan 1918, 506.

Towne, Gene [title writer/scenarist/producer] (b. New York NY, 27 Mar 1904–17 Mar 1979 [74], Woodland Hills CA; heart attack). "Gene Towne," *Variety,* 28 Mar 1979. AS, p. 1077. BHD2, p. 263. FDY, p. 447. IFN, p. 295.

Townley, Jack [scenarist/director] (b. Kansas City MO, 3 Mar 1897–15 Oct 1960 [63], Los Angeles Co. CA). BHD, p. 319; BHD2, p. 263. FDY, p. 439. IFN, p. 295.

Townsend, Mrs. Anna "Grandma" [actress] (*née?*, b. Utica NY, 5 Jan 1845–11 Sep 1923 [78], Los Angeles CA). "Anna Townsend," *NYT,* 13 Sep 1923, 19:3 (age 79). "Anna Townsend," *Variety,* 13 Sep 1923. AS, p. 1077. BHD, p. 319. IFN, p. 295. Truitt, p. 327.

Townsend, David [art director] (b. 1892?–5 Aug 1935 [43], Sonora CA; car accident). (MGM.) "Art Director Killed," *Variety,* 7 Aug 1935. AS, p. 1077 (b. 1869). BHD2, p. 263.

Townsend, Genevieve [actress] (b. 1899–1 May 1927 [28?], Switzerland). BHD, p. 319.

Townsend, James [director] (b. 1869?–2 Feb 1935 [66], Los Angeles CA). "James Townsend," *Variety,* 27 Feb 1935.

Tracey, Thomas F. [actor/assistant director] (*né* Thomas W. Flynn, b. County Cork, Ireland, 1875?–27 Aug 1961 [86], New York NY [Death Certificate Index No. 18627]). "Thomas F. Tracey," *Variety,* 6 Sep 1961. AS, p. 1077 (b. 1880). BHD, p. 319 (b. 1880).

Tracy, Helen T. (mother of **Virginia Tracy**) (b. Jacksonville FL, 7 May 1850–5 Sep 1924 [74], Staten Island NY). (Paramount.) AS, p. 1077. BHD, p. 320. IFN, p. 296. SD, p. 1228.

Tracy, Louis [writer]. No data found. AMD, p. 341. "Louis Tracy to Write for Pathé," *MPW,* 27 May 1916, 1489.

Tracy, Virginia (daughter of **Helen Tracy**) [actress/author] (b. New York NY, 1874?–4 Mar 1946 [72], New York NY). "Virginia Tracy, 71, Actress and Author," *NYT,* 5 Mar 1946, 25:5 (age 71). "Virginia Tracy," *Variety,* 6 Mar 1946. AS, p. 1078.

Trader, George Henry [stage/film actor] (b. Sunderland, Durham, England, 1866?–12 Mar 1951 [85], Percy Williams Home, East Islip, LI NY). m. Gertrude Augarde. "George H. Trader, 85, Veteran of Theatre," *NYT,* 14 Mar 1951, 33:2 ("Mr. Trader's stage career was interrupted by roles in a few silent movies in Hollywood."). AS, p. 1078. BHD, p. 320 (b. 1865). IFN, p. 296. SD, p. 1228.

Trafton, Herbert (Curl) [actor: Keystone Cop] (b. 20 Jun 1893–1 Sep 1979 [86], San Diego CA). BHD, p. 320. IFN, p. 296.

Traggardh, Oliver [executive] (b. 1883–11 Jul 1943 [60?], Beverly Hills CA). BHD2, p. 263.

Trainor, Laura [actress]. No data found. AMD, p. 341. "Universal Engages Laura Trainor," *MPW,* 12 Jul 1919, 234.

Trainor, Leonard [actor] (b. Tahlequah OK, 24 Feb 1879–28 Jul 1940 [61], Los Angeles CA; heart attack). m. (2) Eva. "Leonard Trainor, Film Cowpuncher; Had Just Portrayed Will Rogers Role in Santa Monica Fete—Dies in Hollywood at 61; Born in Cherokee Strip; Marshal of Oklahoma Town as a Youth—Was 'Stand-In' for Humorist in Movies," *NYT,* 29 Jul 1940, 13:6 (began 1914; charter member of Chuck Wagon Riders, an association of old-time cow-punchers). AS, p. 1078. BHD1, p. 546 (d. Santa Monica CA). IFN, p. 298. Truitt, p. 328.

Tramel [actor] (*né* Antoine Félicien Martel, b. La Crau, France, 18 Apr 1880 [extrait de naissance no. 18]-11 Jan 1948 [67], Paris, France [extrait de décès no. 16/77/1948]). AS, p. 1078.

Trask, Wayland [actor] (b. New York NY, 16 Jul 1887–18 Nov 1918 [31], Los Angeles CA; influenza). "Wayland Trask," *Variety,* 22 Nov 1918 (no dates). AS, p. 1078. BHD, p. 320. IFN, p. 296. "Wayland Trask Dead; Broker Made Uphill Fight to Pay Claims After Failure," *NYT,* 29 Jan 1905, 7:6 (d. 28 Jan 1905, NY NY; pneumonia and Bright's disease; left a widow, two daughters and a son). Billy H. Doyle, "Lost Players," *CI,* 139 (Jan 1987), 55.

Traub, Joseph [title/film dialogue writer/scenarist] (b. New York NY, 12 Oct 1901–8 Nov 1936 [35], Los Angeles CA; found dead). (Columbia; Universal; WB.) "Joseph Traub," 124, *Variety,* 11 Nov 1936, 62:1 (registered at the Roosevelt Hotel on 1 Nov, from Hawaii. "Fact that the body was partly disrobed and a vial of sleeping tablets nearby caused the coroner to order an autopsy."). BHD2, p. 263. FDY, p. 447.

Trautmann, Ludwig [actor] (b. Dasebach an der Eisch, Germany, 22 Nov 1885–24 Jan 1957 [71], Berlin, Germany). AS, p. 1078. BHD, p. 320 (b. 1886). Vittorio Martinelli, "Kino-Lieblinge," *Griffithiana,* 38/39 (Oct 1990), 69 (began 1912).

Traver, Verna K. (mother of **Mary** and **Mildred Kornman**) [extra] (b. 1897?–20 May 1986 [89?], Santa Barbara CA). (Extra in Snub Pollard and Our Gang comedies of the '20s.) AS, p. 1078. BHD, p. 220 (Verna Kornman).

Travers, Ben [scenarist] (b. London, England, 12 Nov 1886–18 Dec 1980 [94], London, England). AS, p. 1078. BHD2, p. 264.

Travers, Henry [actor] (*né* Travers John Heagerty, b. Berwick-on-Tweed, England, 5 Mar 1874–18 Oct 1965 [95], Los Angeles CA). AS, p. 1078.

Travers, Nat [actor] (b. England, 1875–22 Dec 1958 [83?], London, England). AS, p. 1078.

Travers, Richard C. [actor] (*né* Richard Libb, b. Hudson Bay Trading Post, Northwest Territory, Canada, 15 Apr 1885–20 Apr 1935 [50], San Pedro CA; pneumonia). (Lubin; Essanay.) "Richard C. Travers," *Variety,* 1 May 1935. AMD, p. 341. AS, p. 1078 (d. 12 May). BHD1, p. 546. IFN, p. 296. MH, p. 140. Truitt, p. 328 (b. 1890). "New Stars with Essanay," *MPW,* 9 Aug 1913, 617. "Dick Travers Injured; Essanay Player Near Death as Result of Automobile Accident," *NYDM,* 10 Jun 1914, 24:4 (at the Indianapolis Speedway. "'Had be been exhaling, instead of inhaling,' said one of the surgeons, 'he would most certainly have been killed,'"). "Some Prominent Essanay Photoplayers," *MPW,* 11 Jul 1914, 234–35. "How I Became a Photoplayer," *Motion Picture Magazine,* Feb 1915, 114. "RIchard C. Travers," *MPW,* 8 May 1915, 887. "Among the Players," NYDM, 6 Nov 1915, 23:2 (filming *The Undertow* in Niles Center IL. He was to leap onto a car of a running train. The engineer wanted to watch the filming and leaned out of his window; his cap blew off and struck Travers in the face, momentarily blinding him. Travers missed the handle of the car and was hurled on the track, narrowly escaping being run over, although he suffered an 8-inch gash in his left arm, an injured kneecap, and broke several bones in his left hand."). "Richard C. Travers," *MPW,* 27 Nov 1915, 1641. "Richard Travers Returns to Screen," *MPW,* 10 Jan 1920, 218. George Katchmer, "Remembering the Great Silents," *CI,* 246 (Dec 1995), 49.

Travers, Vic[tor] [actor] (b. Bradford, England, 1886–26 May 1948 [62?], Los Angeles CA). AS, p. 1079.

Traversa, Alberto [director]. No data found. JS, p. 462 (in Italian silents from 1915).

Traverse, Jean [actress] (b. 1876–11 May 1947 [71?], Los Angeles CA). AS, p. 1079.

Traverse, Madlaine [actress] (aka Madeline or Madlaine Travers, *née* Madlaine Businsky, b. Cleveland OH, 1 Aug 1875–7 Jan 1964 [88], Cleveland OH). "Madlaine Traverse," *Variety,* 29 Jan 1964. (Fox.) AMD, p. 341. AS, p. 1079. BHD, p. 320. IFN, p. 296. 1921 Directory, p. 242 (b. Boston MA). Truitt, p. 328. "Madeline Travers in Pathé's 'Closing Net,'" *MPW,* 23 Oct 1915, 624. "Madeline Traverse," *MPW,* 8 Jan 1916, 224. "Madlaine Traverse, Star of Ivan," *MPW,* 26 Jan 1918, 541. "Madlaine Traverse Forming Company," *MPW,* 15 Jun 1918, 1581. "Madlaine Traverse Signs to Play in Excel Pictures," *MPW,* 12 Oct 1918, 239. "Miss Traverse's Injury Not Serious," *MPW,* 28 Jun 1919, 1956. "Madlaine Traverse," *MPW,* 19 Jul 1919, 360:1 ("One of the main attractions of the motion picture is the vicarious emotional experience that 'starved lives' draw from the story on the screen; and no actress is more gifted than is Miss Traverse in satisfying this intense human craving."). "Madlaine Traverse to Star in Series of Features for State Right RElease," *MPW,* 15 May 1920, 942. "Madlaine Traverse to Star in Big Special Production," *MPW,* 10 Jul 1920, 239. "Madlaine Traverse to Return to the Screen," *MPW,* 20 Nov 1920, 378. "Madlaine Traverse to Return to Screen in Her Own Films Made by the Trinity Company," *MPW,* 25 Dec 1920, 1028. "H.L. Smith Replies to Suit of Miss Traverse," *MPW,* 16 Apr 1921, 707. "Madlaine Traverse Denies Smith's Defense to Suit," *MPW,* 23 Apr 1921, 830. "Miss Traverse Charges $3,000 Salary Was Promised Her by Herbert L. Smith," *MPW,* 5 Nov 1921, 50. "Film Actress Sues Oil Man in Movies; Madlaine Traverse Seeks $225,000 from Herbert Lyon Smith for Picture Venture; Says He Broke Contract; Gave Up Five-Year Engagement with Fox Films, She Says, to Join Smith's Enterprise," *NYT,* 22 Jan 1924, 21:6 (Smith was to form the Madlaine Traverse Photoplay Corp., paying her $3,500 per week salary, $1,000 a week for expenses, and half the capital stock).

Travis, Charles William [actor] (b. 1861?–14 Aug 1917 [56], Brooklyn NY; pulmonary embolism). "Charles W. Travis," *Variety,* 17 Aug 1917. AMD, p. 342. AS, p. 1079. BHD, p. 320. IFN, p. 296. "Obituary," *MPW,* 1 Sep 1917, 1378 (age 52).

Travis, Don [actor] (b. Winfield KS, 17 Nov 1898–28 Jul 1970 [71], Newport Beach CA). BHD, p. 320.

Travis, Norton C. [cinematographer] (b. Brooklyn NY, 1881–24 May 1941 [60?], Los Angeles CA). BHD2, p. 264.

Treadwell, Laura B[utler] (actress] (b. 4 Jul 1879–22 Nov 1960 [81], Los Angeles CA). AS, p. 1079.

Treatt, Major C. Court [producer] (b. 1889–11 Jul 1952 [63?], Los Angeles CA). BHD2, p. 264.

Trebaol, Edouard [actor] (b. Hollywood CA-d. 2 Dec 1944, San Mateo Co. CA). AS, p. 1079. MH, p. 140.

Trebaol, Frençois [actor] (b. Los Angeles CA, 17 Jun 1910–30 Jan 1996 [86], Los Angeles CA). BHD1, p. 618.

Trebaol, Yves [actor] (b. Los Angeles CA, 1 Aug 1906–25 Feb 1974 [67], Venice CA). BHD1, p. 618.

Tree, Helen Maude *see* **Holt, Maude (Lady Tree)**

Tree, Herbert Beerbohm (half-brother of Max Beerbohm) [stage manager/film actor] (b. London, England, 17 Dec 1853–2 Jul 1917 [63], London, England). m. **Maud Holt** (d. 1937). Hesketh Pearson, *Beerbohm Tree: His Life and Laughter* (London, 1956). "Sir Herbert Tree Is Dead in London; Foremost English Actor Since Irving's Day Dies Suddenly in His 67th Year; His Roles of Forty Years; Manager of His Majesty's Strove in Shakespearean Productions to Attain Perfection for Art Alone," *NYT,* 3 Jul 1917, 9:3. "Sir Herbert Tree Dead," *Variety,* 6 Jul 1917. AMD, p. 342. AS, p. 1079 (b. Kensington, England). BHD, p. 320. GSS, pp. 385–88. IFN, p. 296. Waldman, p. 284 (b. 1852). J. Van Cartmell, "Film News from the Coast...," *NYDM,* 20 Nov 1915, 35:2 (to work at Triangle. "The sum to be paid the actor-knight is said to be one of the largest ever offered to a dramatic star, cash in excess of $100,000 being the remuneration agreed upon."). "Tree as Macbeth," *MPW,* 15 Jan 1916, 403. "Sir Herbert Leaves Los Angeles," *MPW,* 25 Mar 1916, 1988. "Sir Herbert Tree Returns to Los Angeles," *MPW,* 22 Jul 1916, 620. Edward Weitzel, "Sir Herbert Tree and the Screen," *MPW,* 21 Jul 1917, 430.

Tree, Viola [atress] (b. London, England, 17 Jul 1884–15 Nov 1938 [54], London, England; pleurisy). AS, p. 1079. BHD1, p. 546.

Treich, Léon Marie Joseph Eugène [scenarist/author] (b. Tulle, France, 17 Mar 1889 [extrait de naissance no. 112/1889]-13 Jun 1974 [85], Moisy-le-Sec, France). AS, p. 1079.

Tremayne, William A. [actor] (b. 1864?–2 Dec 1939 [75], Montreal, Canada). (Vitagraph.) "William A. Tremayne," *Variety,* 13 Dec 1939. AS, p. 1079.

Trenker, Luis [actor/scenarist/director] (*né* Alois Franz Trenker, b. Ortisei, Italy, 4 Oct 1893–13 Apr 1990 [96], Bolzano, Italy). AS, p. 1080 (b. St. Ulrich, Austria. 1892). BHD1, p. 547; BHD2, p. 264 (d. 12 Apr). JS, p. 462 (of German parents; started acting in 1920; in Italian silents from 1928 or earlier). Waldman, p. 285.

Trenor, Frank A. [stage/vaudeville actor/inventor] (b. Watervliet NY, 1876–4 Dec 1941 [65?], Watervliet NY). m. "Frank Trenor," *Variety,* 145, 10 Dec 1941, 54:1 ("...who because of his fine voice, was selected by Thomas A. Edison to aid in experimentations on the early phonograph."). BHD, p. 320.

Trent, Gordon *see* **Farnham, Joseph W[hite]**

Trent, Guy *see* **Trento, Guido**

Trent, Jack B. [actor] (*né* John Trent, b. TX, 24 Aug 1896–1 Aug 1961 [64]; Los Angeles CA; from injuries after falling off a horse). AS, p. 1080. BHD, p. 320. IFN, p. 296.

Trento, Guido [actor] (aka Guy Trent, b. Naples, Italy, 21 Jun 1892–31 Jul 1957 [65], San Francisco CA). AS, p. 1080 (b. 1900). BHD, p. 320. JS, p. 463 (in Italian silents from 1914; also in Hollywood).

Trenton, Pell [stage/film actor] (b. New York NY, ca. 1890). (Ira Hards stock company; Metro; Universal.) BHD, p. 320. "News of Stock Plays and Players; Pell Trenton," *NYDM,* 11 Nov 1914, 10:2. "Stock Notes," *NYDM,* 9 Dec 1914, 11:2 (in *The Marriage Game* at Mt. Vernon).

Treptow, Otto [actor] (b. Germany-d. 3 Mar 1924). BHD, p. 320.

Tresham, Mrs. Jennie [actress] (*née?,* b. 1881–18 Dec 1913 [32?], Portland OR). AS, p. 1080. BHD, p. 320.

Treskoff, Olga [stage producer/film actress] (*née* Olga Trachi, b. Glenlyon PA, 1902?–23 Apr 1938 [36], New York NY). "Olga Treskoff, 36, Producer of Plays; Associate of Russell Jannery in Stage Enterprises Dies at Her Home Here; An Early Movie Actress; Appeared in Many Pictures in Child Roles—Co-Producer of 'Vagabond King,'" *NYT,* 23 Apr 1938, 15:5 ("As a child she appeared in many of the early motion pictures."). "Olga Treskoff," *Variety,* 27 Apr 1938 ("She was for a time a player in the silent pictures"). AS, p. 1080. BHD, p. 320. IFN, p. 296. Truitt, p. 328.

Tressler, Otto [actor] (*né* Otto Karl August Mayer, b. Stuttgart, Germany, 13 Apr 1871–27 Apr 1965 [94], Vienna, Austria). AS, p. 1080.

Treumann, Wanda [actress] (b. Poland, 17 Nov 1887?). (Messter Film Co.) J.A. Fleitzer, "German Trade Notes," *MPW,* 15 Apr 1916, 431:2 (signed to co-star with Viggo Larsen to make 8 films a year for a number of years with Messter). Vittorio Martinelli, "Kino-Leiblinge," *Griffithiana,* 38/39 (Oct 1990), 36.

Trevelyan, Hilda [stage/film actress] (*née* Hilda Tucker, b. England, 4 Feb 1880–10 Nov 1959 [79], London, England). m. Sidney Blow. "Original Wendy [in *Peter Pan*] Dies at 79," *NYT,* 13 Nov 1959, 29:1. "Hilda Trevelyan," *Variety,* 18 Nov 1959, p. 87. BHD1, p. 547. IFN, p. 297.

Trevelyan, Una [actress] (b. Memphis TN, 1895–14 May 1948 [52], Los Angeles CA). (Goldwyn.) AS, p. 1080. BHD, p. 320. IFN, p. 297.

Treville, Georges [actor] (*né* Georges Troly, b. Paris, France, 28 Jul 1875–30 May 1944 [68], Wy-Dit-Joly-Village, France). AS, p. 1080.

Treville, Roger [actor] (*né* Roger Troly, b. Paris, France, 27 Nov 1902). AS, p. 1080.

Trevor, Anne [actress] (*née* Anne Trilnick, b. London, England, 1899–15 Jul 1970 [71?], England). AS, p. 1080. BHD1, p. 547. IFN, p. 297.

Trevor, Hugh [actor] (b. Yonkers NY, 28 Oct 1903–10 Nov 1933 [30], Los Angeles CA; complications after appendectomy). (Radio.) "Hugh Trevor," *Variety,* 14 Nov 1933. AMD, p. 342. AS, p. 1080 (d. 1973). BHD1, p. 547. IFN, p. 297. Truitt, p. 329. "Hugh Trevor," *MPW,* 10 Dec 1927, 48.

Trevor, Norman [stage/film actor] (*né* Norman Pritchard, b. Calcutta, India, 23 Jun 1877–31 Oct 1929 [52], Norwalk CA State Insane Hospital; brain malady). "Norman Trevor, Noted Actor, Dies; Star of Stage and Screen for Many Years Succumbs to Brain Malady in California; He Was Born in India; Once a Champion Athlete and Olympic Competitor—Began London Stage Career in 1907," *NYT,* 1 Nov 1929, 25:3 (In Apr 1928 his friend, H.B. Warner, filed an affidavit of insanity against him in Los Angeles; he had "delusions of wealth." Discharged from sanatorium in Aug 1928.). "Norman Trevor," *Variety,* 6 Nov 1929 (d. Patton CA, age 51). AMD, p. 342. AS, p. 1080 (d. Patton CA). BHD1, p. 547 (d. 30 Oct). IFN, p. 297. Truitt, p. 329. "Norman Trevor Signed by Ziegfeld; Films to Appear in Eight Pictures," *MPW,* 20 Nov 1920, 334. "Norman Trevor Signed," *MPW,* 11 Jul 1925, 190. "Norman Trevor Signs Big Contract with Paramount," *MPW,* 23 Jan 1926, 311.

Trevor, Olive [actress]. No data found. AMD, p. 342. "Olive Trevor Joins Gaumont," *MPW,* 26 Feb 1916, 1277.

Trevor, Spencer [actor] (b. Biarritz, France, 29 May 1875–22 May 1945 [69], London, England). AS, p. 1080.

Trewey, Félicien [actor/director] (*né* Félicien Trevey, b. Angouleme, France, 23 May 1848–2 Dec 1920 [72], Asnieres-sur-Seine, France). AS, p. 1080.

Treynor, Albert M. [scenarist] (b. 1884–24 Oct 1984 [100?], Jackson CA). BHD2, p. 264.

Tricerri, Lina [stage/film actress] (*née* Angiolina Tricerri, b. Bussoleno, Italy, 1894). m. **Sandra Ruffini** (d. 1954). JS, p. 463 (in Italian silents from 1916).

Trick, Martha [actress]. No data found. (Keystone.) AMD, p. 342. "Alice Davenport and Martha Trick, New Keystoners," *MPW,* 27 Oct 1917, 545.

Tricoli, Carlo [actor] (b. Italy, 2 Dec 1889–11 Apr 1966 [76], Los Angeles CA). AS, p. 1080.

Triller, Armand [actor] (b. Bucharest, Romania, 20 Mar 1883–12 Dec 1939 [56], CA). BHD1, p. 547. IFN, p. 297.

Trimble, George S[amuel] [stage/film actor] (b. New York NY, 10 Oct 1873?–23 Feb 1925 [51], Philadelphia PA; apoplexy). (Lubin; FP-L; Metro; World; Pathé.) "George S. Trimble," *NYT,* 25 Feb 1925, 19:2 (age 50). "George S. Trimble Drops Dead; Equity Official Stricken Monday with Apoplexy in Philly," *Variety,* 25 Feb 1925. AMD, p. 342. AS, p. 1081. BHD, p. 320 (b. Brooklyn NY, 1874). MSBB, p. 1028 (b. 1874). "George Samuel Trimble," *MPW,* 27 Mar 1915, 1939. "George Samuel Trimble," *MPW,* 7 Apr 1917, 100.

Trimble, Jeanette [actress]. No data found. AMD, p. 342. "Jeanette Trimble Rejoins Kleine-Cines Co.," *MPW,* 6 Sep 1913, 1073.

Trimble, Lawrence (Larry) [director/scenarist] (b. Robbinston ME, 15 Feb 1885–8 Feb 1954 [68], Woodland Hills CA). m. Marion Blackton (daughter of J. Stuart Blackton); opera singer Louise Trenton (daughter Janet). (Vitagraph.) "Lawrence Trimble Dies; Silent Film Director and Dog Trainer Succumbs on Coast," *NYT,* 10 Feb 1954, 29:1 (age 67). "Lawrence Trimble," *Variety,* 10 Feb 1954 (age 69). Kevin Brownlow, "Jan Zilliacus," *The Independent Review,* 1 Jun 1999, p. 6 (daughter Janet b. 18 Sep 1912-d. 2 May 1999, London). AMD, p. 342. AS, p. 1081. BHD, p. 320; BHD2, p. 264. FDY, p. 439. IFN, p. 297. Katz, pp. 1148–49. Slide, p. 153. "John Bunny in Merrie England," *MPW,* 20 Jul 1912, 252. "Several Vitagraph Artists Close," *MPW,* 29 Mar 1913, 1319. "Concerning Florence Turner," *MPW,* 6 Dec 1913, 1157. "American Players in England," *MPW,* 18 Jul 1914, 441. Lynde Denig, "Lawrence Trimble Brings Turner Films," *MPW,* 19 Aug 1916, 1223. "Larry Trimble a Goldwyn Director," *MPW,* 28 Jul 1917, 627. "Larry Trimble Petrova Director," *MPW,* 24 Nov 1917, 1157. "Larry Trimble VIsits Spokane," *MPW,* 6 Apr 1918, 82. "Power and Trimble Prepare for Work," *MPW,* 13 Apr 1918, 232. "Larry Trimble to Direct Zeena Keefe for Selznick," *MPW,* 10 Jan 1920, 294. Laurence Trimble, "Strongheart," *Classic,* Jul 1923, 20, 82, 84.

Trimmingham, Ernest [actor] (b. 1879–6 Feb 1942 [62?]). BHD, p. 320.

Trinchera, Paolo [director]. JS, p. 464 (in Italian silents from 1918).

Trivas, Victor [director] (b. St. Petersburg, Russia, 9 Jul 1894–12 Apr 1970 [75], New York NY). AS, p. 1081.

Troffey, Alexander [film editor] (b. 14 Jun 1895–11 Sep 1978 [83], Woodland Hills CA). (Universal.) "Alexander Troffee," *Variety,* 27 Sep 1978. BHD2, p. 264.

Troiano (or **Trojano), John** [actor]. No data found. (Vitagraph.)

Troland, L.T. [co-inventor of Technicolor] (b. 1889–27 May 1932 [43?], Pasadena CA; "s'est tué lors d'une chute dans un canyon"). AS, p. 1081.

Trop, J[ack] **D**[unne] [title writer/editor/producer/director/scenarist] (b. New York NY, 17 May 1900–17 May 1992 [92], Miami FL; respiratory infection). m. Sylvia. "J.D. Trop," *Variety,* 25 May 1992, p. 70. AS, p. 1081. BHD2, p. 264. FDY, p. 447.

Tropp, Oskar [actor/director] (b. Sweden, 1882–1934 [52?], Sweden). AS, p. 1081.

Trotsky, Léon [politician/extra] (*né* Lev Davydovich Bronstein, b. Yanovka, Ukraine, 8 Nov 1879–20 Aug 1940 [60], Mexico City, Mexico; assassinated; buried in Coyoacan, near Mexico City). m. (1) Alexandria Sokolovskaya (2 daughters); (2) Natalia Ivanova Sedova (never formally married; d. 23 Jan 1962, Corbell, France; son Leon, 1906–1937; son Sergei arrested by Soviets in 1935 and never heard from again). "Trotsky's Widow Dies in Paris at 79; Worked with Her Husband, a Leader of '17 Revolution," *NYT,* 24 Jan 1962, 33:1. AS, p. 1081 (b. 26 Oct; d. Coyoacan, Mexico). BHD, p. 321.

Trotta, VIncent [art director]. No data found. m. Rose Rispoli, 28 Feb 1924, Flushing NY. AMD, p. 342. "Begins Tenth Year as Art Department Head," *MPW,* 8 Dec 1923, 573. "Trotta to Wed," *MPW,* 1 Mar 1924, 28.

Troubetzkoy, Princess Youcca (granddaughter of W.C. Rives, senator from Virginia) [writer/scenarist] (*née* Amelie Rives, b. Richmond VA, 23 Aug 1863–15 Jun 1945 [81], Charlottesville VA). m. (1) John Armstrong Chanler, 14 Jun 1888, Castle Hill—div. 1895; (2) Prince Pierre Troubetzkoy, 18 Feb 1896, Castle Hill. "Amelie Rives Dies; Popular Novelist; Princess Troubetzkoy Scored Also as Playwright, Poet—Wrote 'Quick or the Dead?' [1888]," *NYT,* 17 Jun 1945, 26:3 (wrote *The Queerness of Celia* and *Firedamn* [1930]). "Amelie Rives," *Variety,* 20 Jun 1945. AS, p. 1082. BHD1, p. 548 (b. LA CA, 12 Dec 1905–22 Apr 1992 [86], Palm Beach FL). "Amelie Rives: An Impressionistic Interview; An Hour with the Author of 'The Quick or the Dead' and 'Selene' Before She Sailed for Europe Last Week; The First Sketch from Life in Seventeen Years—Not the Woman of 'The Quick or the Dead,' But a Happy Princess-o'-Dreams Who Holds the Secret of Eternal Youth—The Poet of Selene," *NYT,* 14 May 1905, III, 1. "Film Famous Authors; Vitagraph Company Prepares Novel Series for Authors' League Benefit," *NYDM,* 28 Jan 1914, 30:4.

Trouché, Adolphe [actor] (b. France). JS, p. 464 (in Italian silents only from 1917).

Trouncer, Cecil [actor] (b. Southport, England, 5 Apr 1898–15 Dec 1953 [55], Los Angeles CA). AS, p. 1082.

Troutman, Ivy [actress] (b. Long Branch NJ, 23 Sep 1883–12 Jan 1979 [95], Tinton Falls NJ). m. Waldo Peirce. (Mutual.) "Ivy Troutman," *Variety,* 17 Jan 1979. AMD, p. 342. AS, p. 1082. BHD, p. 321. SD, p. 1232. "Ivy Troutman," *MPW,* 11 Sep 1915, 1807.

Trouve, Roger Karl [actor] (b. France, 1881–4 May 1984 [103?], Paris, France). AS, p. 1082. BHD, p. 321.

Trow, William [actor] (b. IL, 19 Oct 1890–2 Sep 1973 [82], Los Angeles CA). AS, p. 1082. BHD, p. 321. IFN, p. 297.

Trowbridge, Charles [actor] (b. Vera Cruz, Mexico, 10 Jan 1882–30 Oct 1967 [85], Los Angeles CA). AS, p. 1082. BHD, p. 321. IFN, p. 297. Truitt, p. 329.

Truax, Maude [actress] (b. Chicago IL, 7 Nov 1884–6 Sep 1939 [54], Los Angeles CA). m. **Hugh Boswell** (d. 1964). "Maude Truax," *Variety,* 13 Sep 1939. AS, p. 1078 (Maude Traux); p. 1082. BHD1, p. 548. IFN, p. 297.

Truax, Sarah [stage/film actress] (b. Cincinnati OH, 12 Feb 1877–25 Apr 1958 [81], Seattle WA). m. Charles S. Albert. AMD, p. 342. BHD, p. 321. J. Van Cartmell, "Along the Pacific Coast," *NYDM,* 25 Aug 1915, 33:2 (to debut in an adaptation of Sir Gilbert Parker's *Jordan Is a Hard Road* for Fine Arts). "Trimble Engages Players for New Company," *MPW,* 25 May 1918, 1152.

True, Bessie [actress] (*née* Laurie Flateau, b. Anaconda MT, 1899?–9 Jul 1947 [48], New York NY). AS, p. 1082. BHD, p. 321. IFN, p. 297.

Truesdale, George Frederick [actor] (b. Montclair NJ, 1873?–3 May 1937 [64], New York NY [Death Certificate Index No. 11301]). "George Frederick Truesdell," *Variety,* 5 May 1937. AS, p. 1082. BHD, p. 321. IFN, p. 297.

Truesdale, Howard [actor] (b. Conneautville PA, 3 Jan 1861–8 Dec 1941 [80], Los Angeles CA; heart attack). AS, p. 1082 (b. Connellsville PA). BHD, p. 321; BHD1, p. 548. IFN, p. 297. George A. Katchmer, "Remembering the Great Silents," *CI,* 175 (Jan 1990), C9.

Truesdale, Mrs. Howard [vaudeville/film actress] (d. Sep 1910, Peekskill NY). "Mrs. Howard Truesdale," Variety, 1 Oct 1910, 12:1.

Truesdale, William [cinematographer]. No data found. FDY, p. 469.

Truesdell, Frederick C[harles] [stage/film actor] (b. Coldwater MI, 1874?–9 May 1929 [55], Quincy MI). m. Ethel Dovey. (Eclair; World; Pathé.) "Fred C. Truesdale," *Variety,* 15 May 1929, 67:4 (d. Chicago IL). AMD, p. 342. BHD, p. 321. IFN, p. 297. Spehr, p. 170 (b. 1870). *Photoplay Arts Portfolio* (b. Quincy MI). "Frederick Truesdell," *MPW,* 29 Jun 1918, 1823.

Truex, Ernest [stage/film/TV actor] (b. Kansas City MO, 19 Sep 1889–27 Jun 1973 [83], Fallbrook CA; heart attack). m. (1) Julia Mills; (2) Mary Jane Barrett; (3) actress Sylvia Field (d. 1998; 1 daughter, Sally). (FP-L; Paramount.) Louis Calta, "Ernest Truex, Actor in Films, Theater and TV, Is Dead at 83," *NYT,* 28 Jun 1973, 44:4. "Ernest Truex," *Variety,* 4 Jul 1973 (age 82). "Sally Field, Broadway and TV Actress, 97," *NYT,* 15 Aug 1998, D16. Doug Galloway, "Sally Field Truex," *Variety,* 31 Aug 1998, 107:4. AMD, p. 342. AS, p. 1082. BHD1, p. 348. FSS, p. 276. IFN, p. 297. Katz, p. 1150. MSBB, p. 1028. Spehr, p. 170. "Ernest Truex," *MPW,* 8 Apr 1916, 235. "Truex to Be 'Opposite' to Miss Shirley Mason," *MPW,* 8 Jun 1918, 1445. "Ernest Truex to Appear in Comedies with Mrs. Drew," *MPW,* 17 May 1919, 1040. "Truex Will Be Starred Individually in Comedies," *MPW,* 7 Jun 1919, 1486. "Truex Comedies Will Be Released by Famous Players," 20 Sep 1919, 1817. "Comedy Series Starring Ernest Truex to Be Distributed by Pathé Exchange," *MPW,* 15 Oct 1921, 760. "Truex with Fox," *MPW,* 9 Jun 1923, 522. "Truex, Noted Comedian[,] to Star In Fox Film," *MPW,* 30 Jun 1923, 756.

Trunnelle, Mabel [stage/film actress] (b. Dwight IL, 8 Nov 1879–29 Apr 1981 [101], Glendale CA). m. **Herbert Prior** (d. 1954). (Edison, 1907; Majestic; Vitagraph; Paramount; Asher.) AMD, p. 342. AS, p. 1082. BHD, pp. 80–81; 321. Katz, p. 1152. "Picture Personalities," *MPW,* 24 Sep 1910, 680. "Mabel Trunnelle, Playing Leads with the Edison Company," *MPS,* 29 Jan 1915, 25 (b. Chicago). "Mabel Trunnelle," *MPW,* 28 Aug 1915, 1481. "Mabel Trunnelle," *MPW,* 3 Feb 1917, 691. "Trunnelle Returns," *MPW,* 26 Aug 1922, 675. Billy H. Doyle, "Lost Players," *CI,* 158 (Aug 1988), 26.

Tryan, Cecyl [actress] (b. Saint-Julien, France, 7 Nov 1897). JS, p. 466 (in Italian silents from 1913).

Tryon, Glenn [actor/producer/director/scenarist] (b. Julietta ID, 14 Sep 1894–18 Apr 1970 [75], Orlando FL). m. Lillian Hall; (2) Jane Frazee (d. 1985). (Sennett.) AMD, p. 342. AS, p. 1083 (d. LA CA). BHD1, p. 549; BHD2, p. 265 (b. 1899). FSS, p. 277. IFN, p. 297 (1899–1970). Katz, p. 1152 (b. 1894; began 1924). "'U' Signs Glenn Tryon for Five Years," *MPW,* 9 Jul 1927, 99. "Glenn Tryon," *MPW,* 10 Sep 1927, 93.

Tschechowa, Olga [niece of Anton Chekhov] [actress/director/producer] (*née* Olga von Knipper-Dolling, b. Alexandropol, Russia, 26 Apr 1897–9 Mar 1980 [82], Munich, Germany). (Universal.) AS, p. 1083 (b. Alexandropol, Armenia). BHD1, p. 549 (b. Gyumri, Armenia). Waldman, p. 288 ("She made nearly 200 films in a career that spanned half a century, garnering the title 'Grande Dame of German film.'").

Tschernichin-Larsson, Jenny [actress] (*née* Jenny Tschernichin, b. Finland, 1867–15 Jun 1937 [70?], Stockholm, Sweden). AS, p. 1083.

Tsiang, H.T. [actor] (b. San Francisco CA, 1899?–16 Jul 1971 [72], Los Angeles CA). "H.T. Tsiang," *Variety,* 11 Aug 1971 (claimed to be nephew of Chiang Kai-Shek). AS, p. 1083. IFN, p. 298 (b. 1906).

Tsukamoto, Rynum K. [actor] (b. Japan, 1 Mar 1889–9 Aug 1974 [85], Los Angeles CA; auto accident). AS, p. 1083.

Tsukiyama, Kokichi [diretor/scenarist] (b. Osaka, Japan, 15 Dec 1885–26 Apr 1962 [76], Tokyo, Japan; stomach cancer). AS, p. 1083.

Tucherer, Eugene [actor/producer] (*né* Eugen Tascherez, b. Saryske Lecky, Czechoslovakia, 24 Sep 1899). AS, p. 1083. JS, p. 466 (in France from 1931, after years in Berlin; produced films in Italy from 1951–59).

Tuchock, Wanda [actress/director/scenarist] (b. Pueblo CO, 20 Mar 1898–10 Feb 1985 [86], Woodland Hills CA). m. actor/director George De Normand (d. 1976). "Wanda Tuchock," *Variety,* 20 Feb 1985. AS, p. 1083. BHD2, p. 265.

Tucker, Cy[ril] [actor] (b. England, 3 Jun 1890–4 Jul 1952 [62], Los Angeles CA). AS, p. 1084. BHD1, p. 549. IFN, p. 298.

Tucker, Ethel [actress] (d. 14 May 1926). BHD, p. 321. IFN, p. 298.

Tucker, George Loane [actor/director/producer] (b. Chicago IL, 12 Jun 1872–20 Jun 1921 [49], Los Angeles CA). m. **Elizabeth Risdon** (d. 1958). (Imp; Reliance-Majestic.) "George Loane Tucker," *NYT,* 22 Jun 1921, 15:3. "George Loane Tucker Dies; Producer of 'Miracle Man' Passes Away at 49, After Year's Illness," *Variety,* 24 Jun 1921. AMD, p. 342. AS, p. 1084. BHD, p. 321; BHD2, p. 265. IFN, p. 298. Katz, p. 1153. Spehr, p. 170. "George Tucker Succeeding in England," *MPW,* 19 Dec 1914, 1700. "George Tucker Coming to New York," *MPW,* 23 Dec 1916, 1783. "George Tucker in New York," *MPW,* 20 Jan 1917, 353. "Tucker to Direct Mabel Normand," *MPW,* 1 Dec 1917, 1306. "Tucker Finishes 'Cinderella Man,'" *MPW,* 22 Dec 1917, 1791. "Tucker to Be Goldwyn's Supervising Chief," *MPW,* 9 Feb 1918, 832. "Tucker Now Directing Anita Stewart," *MPW,* 17 Aug 1918, 993. "Tucker to Make Mayflowers," *MPW,* 14 Dec 1918, 1200. "Row Over 'Miracle Man'; Tucker Seeks Injunction Against Mayflower and Lasky's," *LA Times,* 9 Jan 1920, III, 4. "George Loane Tucker Asks Court for Injunction on 'Miracle Man,'" *MPW,* 17 Jan 1920, 384. "Tucker-Famous Players Case Is Argued in Court," *MPW,* 7 Feb 1920, 858. "George Loane Tucker Scores Temporary Success in Court," *MPW,* 6 Mar 1920, 1603. "Mayflower Attorney Denies Tucker Won Point in Court," *MPW,* 13 Mar 1920, 1758. "George Loane Tuicker Loses Again in Injunction Suit," *MPW,* 20 Mar 1920, 1998. "Tucker Recovering," *MPW,* 28 May 1921, 409. "Obituary," *MPW,* 2 Jul 1921, 31. "Honor Dead Producer," *MPW,* 16 Jul 1921, 311. "George Loane Tucker Leaves $22,000; Wid Gunning Shares in Picture Profits," *MPW,* 31 Dec 1921, 1074.

Tucker, Harland [actor] (*né* Harlan Tucker, b. OH, 8 Dec 1893–22 Mar 1949 [55], Los Angeles Co. CA; heart attack). m. **Marie Walcamp**, 1919, Japan (d. 1936). AMD, p. 343. AS, p. 1084. BHD1, p. 549. IFN, p. 298. "Marie Walcamp Weds Harland Tucker," *MPW,* 8 Nov 1919, 255.

Tucker, Jac [scenarist] (d. 8 Jun 1933, Long Meadow RI). BHD2, p. 265.

Tucker, John [actor] (b. 1860-Aug 1922 [62], New York NY). AMD, p. 343. BHD, p. 321. IFN, p. 298. "Jack Tucker Joins Lubin," *MPW,* 17 Apr 1915, 368.

Tucker, Lillian [stage/film actress]. No data found. (World.) AMD, p. 343. "Lillian Tucker," *MPW,* 21 Aug 1915, 1292. "Picture Actresses Want Club," *MPW,* 18 Sep 1915, 2003. "Miss Tucker on Stage," *NYDM,* 23 Oct 1915, 26:2 (to appear with Andrew Mack in *Charles O'Malley*).

Tucker, Lorenzo, "The Black Valentino" [actor] (b. Philadelphia PA, 27 Jun 1907–19 Aug 1986 [79], Los Angeles CA; cancer). m. Pauline Segura. Richard Grupen, *The Black Valentino: The Stage and Screen Career of Lorenzo Tucker* (Metuchen NJ: Scarecrow Press, 1988). "Lorenzo Tucker Dies; Stage and Screen Actor," *NYT,* 30 Aug 1986, A30:4. "Lorenzo Tucker," *Variety,* 27 Aug 1986. AS, p. 1084. BHD1, p. 549 (b. 1900).

Tucker, Richard [actor/title writer] (*né* Reuben Ticker, b. Brooklyn NY, 4 Jun 1884–7 Dec 1942 [58], Woodland Hills CA; heart attack). m.

Ruth Mitchell, 1924. (Edison, 1913.) "Richard Tucker," *NYT*, 9 Dec 1942, 27:3. "Richard Tucker," *Variety*, 16 Dec 1942 (d. 5 Dec, Hollywood CA). AMD, p. 343. AS, p. 1084 (d. 5 Dec). BHD1, p. 549 (b. 1883; d. 5 Dec). FDY, p. 447. FSS, p. 277. IFN, p. 298 (b. NY NY). Katz, p. 1153. Truitt, p. 329. "Richard Tucker," *MPW*, 31 Jul 1915, 828. "Unique California Wedding," *MPW*, 6 Dec 1924, 558.

Tuers, William H. [cameraman/actor] (b. New York NY, 1886?–8 Sep 1949 [63], Los Angeles CA). "William H. Tuers," *Variety*, 14 Sep 1949 (began 1916). AMD, p. 343. AS, p. 1084. BHD2, p. 265. FDY, p. 469. "Cameraman Just as Important as Star, Says Edward Hemmer, Landing Bill Tuers," *MPW*, 4 Sep 1920, 99.

Tugend, Harry [scenarist/director/producer/singer] (b. Brooklyn NY, 17 Feb 1897–11 Sep 1989 [92], Los Angeles CA). "Harry Tugend, Film Writer and Producer, 91," *NYT*, 19 Sep 1989, D25:1. "Harry Tugend," *Variety*, 27 Sep 1989 (age 91; helped to form Screen Writers Guild, 6 Apr 1933). AS, p. 1084. BHD2, p. 265 (b. 1898). Katz, pp. 1153–54.

Tully, Ethel [actress] (b. Brooklyn NY, 1898?–1 Oct 1968 [70], San Antonio TX). (Vitagraph, 1916.) "Mrs. Ethel Margaret Dunlap," *Variety*, 16 Oct 1968. AS, p. 1084. BHD, p. 321. IFN, p. 298. Truitt, p. 330.

Tully, Frank [acrobat/actor] (b. San Francisco CA, 1892–2 Dec 1924 [32?], San Bernardino CA; accident during filming). AS, p. 1084.

Tully, George F. [actor] (b. Co. Mayo, Ireland, 22 Nov 1876–2 Jul 1930 [53], London, England). m. actress Blanche Massey (d. 1929). (Stage debut: 1897.) "George Tully," *Variety*, C, 16 Jul 1930, 61:5. BHD, p. 321.

Tully, Jim [writer] (b. St. Mary's [Cleveland] OH, 3 Jun 1891–22 Jun 1947 [56], Los Angeles CA; heart attack). m. (2) Florence Bushnell; (3) Myrtle Zwetow. "Jim Tully, 56, Dies; Author, Once Hobo; Former Prizefighter, Circus Roustabout Wrote 'Beggars of Life' and 'Jarnegan,'" *NYT*, 23 Jun 1947, 23:3. "Jim Tully," *Variety*, 25 Jun 1947. AS, p. 1084. BHD2, p. 265. IFN, p. 298. Robert E. Hewes, "The Word Digger," *Classic*, Mar 1924, 62, 88.

Tully, May [actress/writer] (b. Victoria, B.C., 1884?–9 Mar 1924 [40], New York NY; nephritis). "May Tully," *NYT*, 11 Mar 1924, 19:2 (age 38). "May Tully," *Variety*, 12 Mar 1924. AS, p. 1084.

Tully, Richard Walton [writer] (b. Nevada City CA, 7 May 1877–31 Jan 1945 [67], New York NY). m. (1) Eleanor Gates—div. 1914; (2) Gladys C. Hanna, 1914. "Richard W. Tully, Dramatist, Is Dead; Author of 'Bird of Paradise,' Was the Victor in Notable Plagiarism Suit Here," *NYT*, 2 Feb 1945, 19:1. "Richard Walton Tully," *Variety*, 7 Feb 1945. AMD, p. 343. AS, p. 1084. BHD2, p. 265. SD, p. 1235. "Richard Walton Tully Tells More About His Independet Producing Organization," *MPW*, 16 Jul 1921, 296. "Tully to Picturize Novels and Stage Plays for First National," *MPW*, 3 Mar 1923, 40. "Tully's 'Bird of Paradise' Coming," *MPW*, 9 Jun 1923, 508. "Tully Makes Denial," *MPW*, 24 May 1924, 356.

Tully, Tom [actor] (*né* Thomas Lee Tully, b. Durango CO, 21 Aug 1896–27 Apr 1982 [85], Newport Beach CA). AS, p. 1084.

Tumiati, Gualtiero [actor] (b. Ferrara, Italy, 8 May 1876-ca. 1962 [86?]). AS, p. 1084.

Tummel[l], William F. [casting director/director] (b. Kansas City MO, 5 Mar 1892–16 Nov 1977 [85], Woodland Hills CA). BHD, p. 321; BHD2, p. 265.

Tunis, Fay [actress] (b. 1890?–4 Dec 1967 [77], Atlantic City NJ). "Fay Tunis," *Variety*, 20 Dec 1967 (in films with Theda Bara). AS, p. 1084. BHD, p. 321. IFN, p. 298. Truitt, p. 330.

Tunney, Gene [boxer/actor] (*né* James Joseph Tunney, b. New York NY, 25 May 1898–7 Nov 1978 [80], Greenwich CT; blood poisoning). AS, p. 1084. BHD1, p. 550. IFN, p. 298.

Tupper, Edith Sessions [scenarist]. No data found. FDY, p. 439.

Tupper, Katherine [actress] (b. 1882). AS, p. 1085.

Tupper, Tristram [scenarist] (b. 11 Sep 1886–30 Dec 1954 [68], Miles VA). BHD2, p. 265.

Turbett, Ben [singer/stage/film director] (b. Salem MA, 1874?–6 Mar 1936 [62?], Atlanta GA). (Edison, 1913.) AMD, p. 343. BHD, p. 321; BHD2, p. 265. "Alliance of Author and Director; A Rational Method Worked Out by the Edison Company on 'At the Rainbow's End' [released at *When Love Is King*]," *MPW*, 22 Jan 1916, 586.

Turin, Viktor [actor] (b. Leningrad, Russia, 1895–1945 [50?]). BHD, p. 321; BHD2, p. 265 (b. St. Petersburg, Russia).

Turk, Roy [lyricist] (b. New York NY, 20 Sep 1892–30 Nov 1934 [42], Los Angeles CA; pneumonia). "Roy Turk," *Variety*, 4 Dec 1934. AS, p. 1085. ASCAP 66, p. 743. BHD2, p. 265.

Turkin, V.K. [scenarist]. No data found. FDY, p. 439.

Turleigh, Veronica [actress] (b. Ballyhasky, Ireland, 14 Jan 1903–3 Sep 1971 [68], England). AS, p. 1085.

Turnbull, Hector (brother of **Margaret Turnbull**) [scenarist] (b. Arlington NJ, 11 Sep 1884–8 Apr 1934 [49], New Hope PA; heart attack). m. Blanche Lasky Goldwyn, 1919—d. 1931) (FP-L; Paramount.) "Hector Turnbull, Drama Critic, Dies; On Staff of New York Tribune 20 Years Ago—Victim of Heart Attack at 45; Movie Writer Since 1915; Associated with Brother-in-Law, Jesse L. Lasky—Author of 'The Cheat,' Film Classic," *NYT*, 9 Apr 1934, 17:3 (age 45). "Hector Turnbull," *Variety*, 10 Apr 1934. AMD, p. 343. AS, p. 1085 (b. 1899). BHD2, p. 265. "Turnbull Joins Lasky Staff," *MPW*, 15 May 1915, 1053. "Hector Turnbull Addresses Woman's Press Club," *MPW*, 17 Feb 1917, 1020. "The Roll of Honor," *MPW*, 21 Jul 1917, 433. "Hector Turnbull Goes to Europe for Conference," *MPW*, 11 Jun 1927, 425. "Turnbull Back from Europe After Survey," *MPW*, 20 Aug 1927, 511. "Turnbull Severs Paramount Bond; Goes to DeMille-Pathé," *MPW*, 1 Oct 1927, 289.

Turnbull, John [actor] (b. Dunbar, Scotland, 5 Nov 1880–23 Feb 1956 [75], London, England). AS, p. 1085.

Turnbull, Margaret (sister of **Hector Turnbull**) [scenarist] (b. Glasgow, Scotland, 1882–12 Jun 1942 [60?], Yarmouthport MA). "Miss M. Turnbull, Author, Scenarist; Her Plays 'Classmates' and 'Deadlock' Produced Here—Dies in Massachusetts; Began Film Work in 1916; Novels Depicted Bucks County Scene—Aunt of President of Rogers Peet Company," *NYT*, 13 Jun 1942, 15:6. "Margaret Turnbull," *Variety*, 17 Jun 1942 ("In 1916 and for some years thereafter she wrote scenarios for silent films in N.Y., Hollywood and London."). AMD, p. 343. AS, p. 1085 (b. Dunbar, Scotland). BHD2, p. 265. "Miss Turnbull's Book," *MPW*, 30 Nov 1918, 940 (*The Close-Up*, Harper's). "Margaret Turnbull to Write Continuities at Islington," *MPW*, 4 Sep 1920, 66. "WRiting Scenario," *MPW*, 12 May 1923, 174.

Turnbull, Roberto A. [cinematographer] (b. Sonora, Mexico, 1885). BHD2, p. 265.

Turnbull, Stanley [stage/vaudeville/film actor] (b. Whitby, Yorkshire, England, 1881?–8 May 1924 [43], London, England). (London stage debut: *His Borrowed Plumes*, Jul 1909.) "Stanley Turnbull," *Variety*, 28 May 1924, 35:5. BHD, p. 321. IFN, p. 298.

Turner, Alice [actress]. No data found. AMD, p. 343. "Little Alice Turner," *MPW*, 22 Apr 1916, 634.

Turner, Bowditch M. "Smoke" [actor] (b. Cumberland MD, 1878–12 Sep 1933 [55], Los Angeles CA). AS, p. 1086 (Smoke Turner). BHD, p. 322. IFN, p. 298 (b. VA).

Turner, D.H. [director] (b. New York NY, 12 Jan 1883). BHD, p. 322; BHD2, p. 265.

Turner, Doreen [actress] (b. Spokane WA, 10 Aug 1888). *Fl.* 1921–28. AS, p. 1085. George Katchmer, "Remembering the Great Silents," *CI*, 218 (Aug 1993), 41.

Turner, Eardley [actor] (d. 23 Jan 1929). BHD, p. 322.

Turner, Emanuel A. (brother of Josephine Meek) [actor] (b. 1884?–13 Dec 1941 [57], Los Angeles CA). "Emanuel Turner," *Variety*, 24 Dec 1941. AS, p. 1085. BHD, p. 322 and addendum (Emmuel Turner). IFN, p. 298.

Turner, Florence E., "The Vitagraph Girl" [actress/director/scenarist] (b. New York NY, 6 Jan 1885–28 Aug 1946 [61], Woodland Hills CA). (Vitagraph, 1906; Turner Films, Ltd.; MGM.) "Florence Turner, Top Film Star in '15," *NYT*, 30 Aug 1946, 18:3. "Florence Turner," *Variety*, 11 Sep 1946 (d. 29 Aug 1946, age 61). AMD, p. 343. AS, p. 1085. BHD1, p. 322; BHD2, p. 265 (b. 1887). FSS, p. 278. IFN, p. 298. Katz, p. 1154. MH, p. 140. Truitt, p. 330. WWS, p. 211. "Vitagraph Girl Feted," *MPW*, 23 Apr 1910, 644. "Picture Personalities," *MPW*, 23 Jul 1910, 187–88. F.H. Richardson, "A Vitagraph Girl Night," *MPW*, 31 Dec 1910, 1521. "Florence Turner in Notable Gallery," *MPW*, 14 Jan 1911, 73. Epes Winthrop Sargent, "Credit Where Credit Is Due," *MPW*, 14 Oct 1911, 106–07. "Miss Turner Goes to California," *MPW*, 9 Dec 1911, 810. "Florence Turner Appears in San Francisco," *MPW*, 30 Dec 1911, 1080. Louis Reeves Harrison, "Studio Saunterings," *MPW*, 17 Feb 1912, 557. "Miss Turner Gaining in Health," *MPW*, 2 Mar 1912, 770. "Florence Turner Gets Ovation in Portland," *MPW*, 30 Mar 1912, 1147. H.H. Hoffman, "Florence Turner Comes Back," *MPW*, 18 May 1912, 622. "Florence Turner Going to England; The Vitagraph Girl, First Real Photoplay Star, Will Produce Her Own Pictures in London," *MPW*, 22 Mar 1913, 1225. "Concerning Florence Turner," *MPW*, 6 Dec 1913, 1157. "American Players in England," *MPW*, 18 Jul 1914, 441. "Disclaimer as to Miss Turner's Return," *MPW*, 24 Oct 1914, 478. "Florence Turner in Impersonations," *MPW*, 13 Nov 1915, 1278–79. "Turner Pictures on Mutual Program," *MPW*, 1 Jul 1916, 98. Elizabeth Peltret, "The Return of Florence Turner," *MPC*, VII, Feb 1919, 28–29, 72–73. "Florence Turner in Universal Comedies," *MPW*, 19 Jul 1919, 339.

"Florence E. Turner in Radin Pictures," *MPW,* 27 Mar 1920, 2154. "Florence Turner Contracts to Appear Exclusively in Productions for Metro," *MPW,* 9 Oct 1920, 806. "Florence Turner Returns," *MPW,* 14 Mar 1925, 718. "To Shine Again," *MPW,* 18 Jul 1925, 350. "Florence E. Turner," *MPW,* 8 Aug 1925, 654. "Florence Turner Assigned Big Role in 'Padlocked,'" *MPW,* 6 Mar 1926, 32. "She Wins Role," *MPW,* 19 Mar 1927, 181. Peter Cowie, ed., *A Concise History of the Cinema* (NY: A.S. Barnes & Co., 1971), pp. 78–79 (discusses her English films).

Turner, Frank Delaney (Pops) [actor] (b. Boston MA, 1881?–27 Oct 1957 [76], Los Angeles Co. CA). AS, p. 1085. BHD, p. 322. IFN, p. 298.

Turner, Fred A. [actor] (b. NY, 12 Oct 1858–13 Feb 1923 [64]). AS, p. 1085 (b. Boston MA). BHD, p. 322. IFN, p. 298.

Turner, George [film/stage/TV actor] (*né* George Thirlwell, b. Findon Manor, England, 19 Feb 1902–27 Jul 1968 [66], New York NY; heart attack). "George Turner," *NYT,* 31 Jul 1968, 41:3. "George Turner," *Variety,* 251, 7 Aug 1968, 63:3. AS, p. 1085 (d. London, England). BHD1, p. 550.

Turner, George Kibbe [actor/author/scenarist] (b. 1869?–15 Feb 1952 [83], Miami FL). "George K. Turner," *Variety,* 20 Feb 1952. AS, p. 1085. BHD2, p. 266. IFN, p. 298.

Turner, John Hastings [scenarist] (b. London, England, 16 Dec 1892–29 Mar 1918 [25], Los Angeles CA). BHD2, p. 266.

Turner, K.M. [executive/inventor] (b. 1887?–15 Oct 1927 [40], Los Angeles CA). "K.M. Turner," *Variety,* 9 Nov 1927. AS, p. 1085.

Turner, Maidel [actress] (b. Sherman TX, 12 May 1888–12 Apr 1953 [64], Ocean Springs MS). "Maidel Turner," *NYT,* 14 Apr 1953, 27:5. "Maidel Turner," *Variety,* 15 Apr 1953 (Mrs. Maidel Turner Thomas). AS, p. 1085. BHD1, p. 550. IFN, p. 298 (age 72). Truitt, p. 330.

Turner, Martin [actor] (b. TX, 20 Dec 1882–14 May 1957 [74], Los Angeles Co. CA). AS, p. 1085. BHD1, p. 550. George Katchmer, "Remembering the Great Silents," *CI,* 215 (May 1993), 49.

Turner, Otis "Daddy" [actor/director /producer] (b. Fairfield IN, 29 Nov 1862–28 Mar 1918 [55], Los Angeles CA; heart attack). m. Etta French. (Universal.) "'Daddy' Turner Dead," *Variety,* 5 Apr 1918. AMD, p. 344. AS, p. 1086 (d. 3 Apr). BHD, p. 322; BHD2, p. 266. "Notes of the Trade," *MPW,* 5 Dec 1908, 453. "Otis Turner Joins Universal Western Co.," *MPW,* 31 Aug 1912, 889. "Otis Turner Takes Vacation," *MPW,* 12 Sep 1914, 1496. "Obituary," *MPW,* 20 Apr 1918, 377.

Turner, Raymond D. [actor] (b. NM, 28 Oct 1895–18 Aug 1981 [85], Los Angeles Co. CA). AS, p. 1086. BHD1, p. 550. Ragan 2, p. 1709. George A. Katchmer, "Forgotten Cowboys and Cowgirls—Part VIII," *CI,* 180 (Jun 1990), 53.

Turner, William H. [stage/film actor] (b. Ireland, 1861–27 Sep 1942 [80], Philadelphia PA; Edwin Forrest Home). (Lubin; Vitagraph; Hollywood.) m. Ann Vislaire. (Broadway debut: *Streets of New York,* 1883.) "William Turner, 81, 54 Years on Stage; Film Veteran, Seen with Ruth Chatterton, Tallulah Bankhead," *NYT,* 28 Sep 1942, 17:5 (age 81). "William H. Turner," *Variety,* 30 Sep 1942. AMD, p. 344. AS, p. 1086. BHD1, p. 550. IFN, p. 298. Truitt, p. 330. "William H. Turner," *MPW,* 2 May 1914, 659. "Turner Returns to Lubin," *MPW,* 30 Jan 1915, 692. George A. Katchmer, "Remembering the Great Silents," *CI,* 175 (Jan 1990), C9, 57.

Turpin, Ben [stage/film actor] (*né* Bernard R. Turpin, b. New Orleans LA, 19 Sep 1868?–1 Jul 1940 [71], Los Angeles CA; heart disease). m. (1) **Carrie** LeMieux, 1905, Chicago IL (d. 1925); (2) Babette Elizabeth Dietz, 8 Jul 1926, Beverly Hills CA. (Essanay, Chicago, 1907; Sennett.) "Ben Turpin Dead; Movie Comedian; Actor Who Won Fame in Silent Films, Once a Hobo, Stricken in Hollywood at 71; Was Not Born Cross-Eyed; Sight Impaired by Early 'Happy Hooligan' Role—Proud of His '108' Somersault," *NYT,* 2 Jul 1940, 21:5. "Ben Turpin," *Variety,* 3 Jul 1940 (age 71). AMD, p. 344. AS, p. 1086 (b. 1869). BHD1, p. 550 (b. 1869). FFF, p. 82. FSS, p. 278. GK, pp. 946–61. IFN, p. 298 (b. 1869). Katz, p. 1155. MH, p. 140 (b. 1874). Truitt, p. 330 (b. 17 Sep 1874). WWS, p. 192. "Life of a Moving Picture Comedian," *MPW,* 3 Apr 1909, 405. *MPW,* 4 Feb 1911, 253. "Ben Turpin Takes a Tumble," *MPW,* 23 Sep 1916, 1982–83. "Paramount Comedian Visits Chicago," *MPW,* 19 Apr 1919, 364. "Ben Turpin Signs Up with Sennett for Two Years More," *MPW,* 12 Jul 1919, 182. "Turpin Visits Chicago," *MPW,* 6 Aug 1921, 593. "Ben Turpin on Stage," *MPW,* 20 Aug 1921, 792. "Says Turpin Makes World Happier," *MPW,* 18 Aug 1923, 584. Dorothy Donnell, "Fortunate Misfortunes," *Classic,* Mar 1924, 12–14, 85 (others discussed are John Aasen, Tiny Ward, Bull Montana, Mast Comont, Sammy Brooks, and Dick Sutherland). "Mrs. Turpin Strangely Cured," *MW,* 5 Jul 1924, 21 (they visited St. Anne de Beauble, Canada; in St. Anne's Cathedral Mrs. Turpin knelt and prayed. "Arising, she declared to her husband that she had regained her hearing."). Dorothy Donnell, "The Lonely Clown; The Greatest Love Story of Hollywood," *MPC,* Jul 1925, 24–25, 80. "Turpin Weds Again," *MPW,* 24 Jul 1926, 4 (married Dietz). "As We Go to Press," *Pictures,* Aug 1926, 12, 14 (Turpin was to marry the first Mrs. Turpin's nurse). June Lee, "Dan Cupid's Bulletin Board," *Paris and Hollywood,* Sep 1926, 21 (engaged to Babette Dietz. "The little lady is a nurse in the hospital where Ben lay ill for many weeks." [They were already married.]). June Lee, "Dan Cupid's Bulletin Board," *Paris and Hollywood,* Oct 1926, 32 ("When Ben applied at the marriage bureau at Los Angeles for his license he wore black glasses which covered his famous crossed eyes and gave his correct surname Bernard. He would have passed unrecognized if he had not been forced to remove his glasses to sign the application.... His bride, Miss Babette Dietz, gave her ag as thirty-nine, while the joyous groom admitted that he was fifty-seven."). Daniel W. Horton, "Ben Turpin: Looking for Laughs," *CI,* 90 (Dec 1982), 16–17. Steve Rydzewski, "Turpin Facts [letter]," *CI,* 91 (Jan 1983), 59. Herb Gordon, "Ben Turpin: Here's Looking at You," *CI,* 97 (Jul 1983), 26 (b. 1874). George A. Katchmer, "Ben Turpin: The 5th Great Comedian," *CI,* 133 (Jul 1986), 28–30, 63. Richard E. Braff, "The Films of Ben Turpin," *CI,* 162 (Dec 1988), 11, 14; 163 (Jan 1989), 58. Barry Brown, "Ben Turpin, 1869–1940," *FIR,* Oct 1977, 467–84 (includes filmography). R.E. Braff, "Additional Film Credit for Ben Turpin," *CI,* 238 (Apr 1995), 42.

Turpin, Carrie [actress] (*née* Carrie LeMieux, b. Quebec, Canada, 1882–1 Oct 1925 [43?], Los Angeles CA; cerebral hemorrhage). m. **Ben Turpin** (d. 1940). AS, p. 1086. BHD, p. 322.

Tushock, Wanda [scenarist]. No data found. FDY, p. 439.

Tuttle, Frank W[right] [screenwriter/director] (b. New York NY, 6 Aug 1892–6 Jan 1963 [70], Los Angeles CA; heart attack). Wrote unpublished autobiography. (Paramount.) "Frank Tuttle," *Variety,* 16 Jan 1963. AMD, p. 344. AS, p. 1086. BHD2, p. 266. Katz, p. 1156. "Frank Tuttle Back," *MPW,* 25 Oct 1924, 680. "Tuttle SAils," *MPW,* 3 Apr 1926, 3.

Tweddell, Frank [actor] (b. Muree, India, 15 Mar 1895–20 Dec 1971 [76], New Haven CT). AS, p. 1086.

Twelvetrees, Helen [actress: Wampas Star, 1929] (*née* Helena E. Jurgens, b. Brooklyn NY, 8 Dec 1908 [Birth Certificate Index No. 39734]–13 Feb 1958 [49], Harrisburg [Olmstead Air Force Base] PA; accidental overdose of medicine). m. Clark Twelvetrees. "Helen Twelvetrees, Former Film Star," *NYT,* 14 Feb 1958, 23:1. "Helen Twelvetrees," *Variety,* 19 Feb 1958. AS, p. 1086 (b. 25 Dec). BHD1, p. 551 (b. 1909). IFN, p. 298. Katz, p. 1156. Truitt, pp. 330–31. Walter Ramsey, "Twelvetrees Is OKE; She Was Good as a Bad Girl But She's Willing to Change," *MPC,* May 1929, 40, 87, 89.

Twist, John Stuart [scenarist/producer] (b. Albany MO, 14 Jul 1898–11 Feb 1976 [77], Beverly Hills CA; heart attack). m. Eve. (FBO; RKO.) "John Twist," *Variety,* 18 Feb 1976 (AA for short, *La Cucaracha,* 1934). AS, p. 1086. BHD2, p. 266. IFN, p. 299.

Twist, Stanley H. [publicity manager for Selig Polyscope in Chicago]. No data found. (Universal.) AMD, p. 344. "Stanley Twist Leaves Selig," *MPW,* 11 Oct 1913, 142. "Twist Gives Gabfest," *MPW,* 8 Nov 1913, 615. "Twist Goes to Australia," *MPW,* 13 Dec 1913, 1262. "Stanley Twist Back from Australia," *MPW,* 13 Jun 1914, 1514. "Stanley H. Twist Convalescing," *NYDM,* 18 Nov 1914, 28:3 (from nervous breakdown).

Tyke, John [actor] (*né* Johnny Tyacke, b. OR, 20 Oct 1894–23 Feb 1940 [45], Los Angeles CA, Cowboy Row, near Columbia Studios; shot to death by Jerome [Blackjack] Ward). "Cowboys Shoot It Out," *Variety,* 28 Feb 1940. AS, p. 1086 (Tycke). BHD1, p. 551. IFN, p. 298.

Tykociner, Joseph T. [inventor] (b. Poland, 1878–12 Jun 1969 [91?], Urbana IL). AS, p. 1086.

Tyler, Dallas [actress] (b. 1883?–25 Jul 1953 [70], Philadelphia PA). m. Roy Fairchild; (2) Edward Bethel. "Dallas Tyler," *Variety,* 29 Jul 1953. AS, p. 1086. BHD, p. 322 (b. 1878).

Tyler, Fred C. [actor/director] (b. 1874?–3 May 1960 [86], Los Angeles CA). "Fred C. Tyler," *Variety,* 11 May 1960. AS, p. 1087. BHD2, p. 266.

Tyler, G. Vere [writer]. No data found. AMD, p. 344. "G. Vere Tyler," *MPW,* 8 Apr 1916, 286. "G. Vere Tyler Subject for Vivian Martin," *MPW,* 21 Oct 1916, 422. "G. Veere Tyler Writes Novel," *MPW,* 2 Dec 1916, 1340.

Tyler, Harry [actor] (b. New York NY, 13 Jun 1888–15 Sep 1961 [73], Los Angeles CA). AS, p. 1087.

Tyler, Odette [actress] (*née* Elizabeth Lee Kirkland, b. Savannah GA, 26 Sep 1869–8 Dec 1936 [67], Los Angeles CA). m. R.D. Shepherd. "Odette Tyler," *Variety,* 16 Dec 1936 (age 65). AS, p. 1087. BHD, p. 322. IFN, p. 299.

Tyler, Tom [actor] (*né* Vincent Markowski,

b. Port Henry [Witherbee?] NY, 9 Aug 1903–1 May 1954 [50], Hamtramck [Detroit] MI; heart attack). m. Jeanne Martel. (Began 1924; FBO; Syndicate; Monogram; Reliable; Victory; Columbia; RKO; Universal; Lippert; Allied Artists.) "Tom Tyler," *NYT,* 3 May 1954, 25:5 (*né* Vincent Marko). "Tom Tyler," *Variety,* 5 May 1954 (age 50). AMD, p. 344. AS, p. 1087. BHD1, p. 551. FSS, p. 279. GK, pp. 961–75. IFN, p. 299. Katz, p. 1157. Truitt, p. 331. "F.B.O. Announces Tom Tyler as 'Surprise' Western Star," *MPW,* 8 Aug 1925, 649 (*né* William Burns). "Tom Tyler Ill," *MPW,* 1 Jan 1927, 31. Dorothy Calhoun, "The Sucker Who Succeeded; Believe It or Not, Tom Tyler Learned Movie Acting by Mail," *MPC,* Jul 1928, 40, 76, 79 ("Before [Elinor Glyn and] two hundred extras Tom stripped to the waist—and got the part."). George A. Katchmer, "Tom Tyler; The Clean-Cut Hero," *CI,* 108 (Jun 1984), 23–24, 27. Mario De Marco, "Tom Tyler; The Strong, Silent Type," *CI,* 87 (Sep 1982), 59. John Cocchi, "The 2nd Feature; A History of the B Movies," *CI,* 145 (Jul 1987), 17. Nick C. Nicholls, "Tom Tyler," *CI,* 178 (Apr 1990), 20. George Katchmer, "Remembering the Great Silents," *CI,* 245 (Nov 1995), 45 (in *GWTW*).

Tynan, Brandon [actor] (b. Dublin, Ireland, 11 Apr 1875–19 Mar 1967 [91], New York NY [Death Certificate Index No. 5899]). m. (1) Caroline Whyte (d. 1918); **Lilly Cahill** (d. 1955). "Brandon Tynan, Actor, 91, Is Dead; Also Author of 7 Plays—Impersonated Belasco," *NYT,* 21 Mar 1967, 43:1. "Brandon Tynan," *Variety,* 22 Mar 1967 (in films in late 30's). AMD, p. 344. AS, p. 1087. BHD1, p. 551. IFN, p. 299. Truitt, p. 331. "Tynan Sues Crowley," *MPW,* 5 Nov 1921, 39.

Tynan, James J. [scenarist] (b. Philadelphia PA, 1890?–17 Aug 1934 [44], Los Angeles CA). "James Tynan," *Variety,* 21 Aug 1934. AS, p. 1087. BHD2, p. 266. FDY, p. 439.

Tynen, Thomas [actor/prison warden]. No data found. AMD, p. 344. "Warden Tynen in Selig Pictures," *MPW,* 7 Sep 1912, 982.

Tyrol, Jacques [director] (b. Italy, 5 May 1874–18 Oct 1961 [87], Los Angeles CA). BHD2, p. 266.

Tyroler, William X. [actor] (b. 1884–4 Jan 1959 [74?], Torrence CA). BHD, p. 322.

Tyrone, Madge [scenarist]. No data found. AMD, p. 344. "Madge Tyrone Joins Mayer," *MPW,* 10 Jul 1920, 238.

U

Uddenberg, Alice [actress] (b. Stockholm, Sweden, 1896). AS, p. 1089.

Ugarte y Pages, Eduardo [scenarist/director] (b. Spain, 1901–30 Dec 1955 [54], Mexico City, Mexico). AS, p. 1089 (b. 1908). Waldman, p. 290 (b. 1901-d. 1952).

Uher, Odon [director] (b. Hungary, 1897-d. Germany). AS, p. 1089.

Uhlig, Max E. [actor/technical director] (b. 1896?–28 May 1958 [62], North Tarrytown NY). m. Frances. "Max E. Uhlig," *NYT,* 29 May 1958, 27:4 ("appeared in silent movies with Pearl White, Rudolph Valentino and Mary Pickford"). AMD, p. 344. AS, p. 1089. BHD, p. 322. IFN, p. 299. Truitt, p. 331. "Uhlig Now with Metro," *MPW,* 11 Mar 1916, 1658.

Uleha, Vladimir [director/producer] (b. Vienna, Austria, 16 Jun 1888–3 Jul 1947 [59], Brno, Moravia, Czechoslovakia). AS, p. 1089 (d. Brum, Czechoslovakia). BHD2, p. 266.

Ulis, H. Jay [actor] (b. 1893?–15 Jan 1992 [98], Yountville CA; cardiac arrest in his sleep). m. Minerva Clark. "H. Jay Ulis," *Variety,* 27 Jan 1992, p. 67. AS, p. 1089.

Ullenger, Sepp [cinematographer]. No data found. FDY, p. 469.

Ullman, Edward G. [cameraman] (b. Natchez MS, 3 Jul 1867–9 Feb 1940 [72], Los Angeles CA). (Biograph, 1914; Universal.) "Edward Ullman," *Variety,* 21 Feb 1940 (age 70). BHD2, p. 266. FDY, p. 469. IFN, p. 299.

Ullman, I.W. [producer]. No data found. AMD, p. 344. "I.W. Ullman," *MPW,* 4 Apr 1908, 288.

Ullman, S. George [agent] (b. New York NY, 19 Sep 1863–1 Oct 1945 [82], Los Angeles CA). m. Beatrice. *Valentino As I Knew Him* (NY: Macy-Masius, 1926). "S. George Ullman," *Variety,* 8 Oct 1975 (managed Valentino). BHD2, p. 266 (d. 1975).

Ullmann, Arthur [director] (b. Germany, 29 Sep 1885). AS, p. 1089.

Ulman, Ethel [actress]. (Ince.) No data found.

Ulmer, Anna [actress] (b. 1853–28 Oct 1928 [75], Peak's Island ME). BHD, p. 322. IFN, p. 299.

Ulric, Lenore [stage/film actress] (*née* Lenore Ulrich, b. New Ulm MN, 21 Jul 1892–30 Dec 1970 [78], Orangeburg NY). m. **Sidney Blackmer,** 1928–39 (d. 1970). (Essanay [Chicago, 1911]; World.) "Lenore Ulric, Broadway Star of Belasco Era, Is Dead at 78; 'Tiger Rose' Fixed Actress in 'Femme Fatale' Pattern of Brilliant Career," *NYT,* 31 Dec 1970, 26:5. "Lenore Ulric," *Variety,* 6 Jan 1971. AMD, p. 344. AS, pp. 1089–90. BHD1, p. 552. FSS, p. 279. IFN, p. 299. Katz, p. 1159. Spehr, p. 170. Truitt, p. 331 (b. 1894). "Lenore Ulrich Under Morosco-Bosworth Banner," *MPW,* 15 May 1915, 1083. "Two Morosco Stars; William Desmond and Lenore Ulrich to Be Seen in Feature Films," *NYDM,* 19 May 1915, 32:1 (to debut in their stage play, *The Bird of Paradise.* Ulrich's age given as 19; discovered by Oliver Morosco, "[s]ome five years ago the little star was working in a dry-goods store.") "Lenore Ulrich Entertains the Press," *MPW,* 31 Jul 1915, 829. "Lenore Ulrich Signs with Knickerbocker," *MPW,* 7 Aug 1915, 984. "Lenore Ulrich Returns from Mexico," *MPW,* 8 Jan 1916, 249. "Farewell Party to Lenore Ulrich," *MPW,* 3 Jun 1916, 1668. "Lenore Ulric Is Signed for David Belasco's 'Tiger Rose' by Warners," *MPW,* 24 Mar 1923, 448.

Ulrich, Charles Kenmore [vaudeville sketch writer/playwright/novelist/publicist] (b. Cincinnati OH, 1859?–5 Jul 1941 [82], Long Island City NY; from injuries received in a recent fall). m. Carrie, 1883. (Pathé.) "Charles K. Ulrich," *Variety,* 143, 9 Jul 1941, 54:1 (developed the precursor of the modern press book). AMD, p. 345. "Ulrich's Latest Novel Out," *MPW,* 29 Jan 1921 544 (*The Wolf of Purple Canyon,* James A. McCann Co.).

Ulrich, Florence [actress]. No data found. AMD, p. 345. "Florence Ulrich to Play Lead in Cody Production," *MPW,* 27 Mar 1926, 263.

Umm, Kulthum [actress/singer] (*née* Umm Kulthum al Sayyid, b. Tamiyya-al-Zuhayra, Egypt, 30 Dec 1898–1975 [76?], Cairo, Egypt). AS, p. 1090.

Unda, Emilia [actress] (b. Riga, Latvia, 29 Jan 1879–7 Dec 1939 [61], Berlin, Germany). BHD1, p. 552.

Underhill, Harriette [scenarist] (b. Troy NY-d. 18 May 1928, New York NY). AS, p. 1090.

Underhill, John (or **Jack**) **G.** [actor/director] (b. New York NY, 26 Apr 1870–26 May 1941 [71], Los Angeles Co. CA). AS, p. 1090. BHD, p. 322; BHD2, p. 267. IFN, p. 299.

Underhill, William [cinematographer]. No data found. FDY, p. 469.

Underwood, Franklyn [stage/film actor/story editor] (b. Denver CO, 1877–22 Dec 1940 [63], Doctors Hospital, New York NY; after an abdominal operation). m. actress Frances Slosson. (Stage: Elitch's Gardens, Denver CO, 1904; general manager for Oliver Morosco; Central Play Co.) "Franklyn Underwood; Story Editor for 20th Century Fox Films [from 1930], Former Actor, Dies," *NYT,* 23 Dec 1940, 19:3. "Franklyn Underwood," *Variety,* 141, 25 Dec 1940, 54:1. BHD, p. 322 (Franklin Underwood). IFN, p. 299.

Underwood, Lawrence [actor/scenarist] (b. Albion IA, 1871–2 Feb 1939 [68], Los Angeles CA). AS, p. 1090. BHD, p. 322; BHD2, p. 267. IFN, p. 299. Truitt, p. 331.

Underwood, Loyal [actor] (b. Rockford IL, 6 Aug 1893–30 Sep 1966 [73], Los Angeles Co. CA). AS, p. 1090. BHD1, p. 552. IFN, p. 299.

Unger, Gladys B[uchanan] [playwright/scenarist] (b. San Francisco CA, 1885?–25 May 1940 [55], New York NY). m. Kai K. Ardaschir. (MGM; Paramount; TC-F.) "Gladys B. Unger, 55, Playwright, Dies; Adapter and Screen Writer Had First Play Produced in London in 1902; 'Nona' Was Shown Here; 'Ladies of Creation' and '$25 an Hour' Among Her Other Broadway Productions," *NYT,* 26 May 1940, 35:3. "Gladys B. Unger," *Variety,* 29 May 1940. AMD, p. 345. AS, p. 1090. BHD2, p. 267. FDY, p. 439. IFN, p. 299. "Joins Paramount," *MPW,* 28 Aug 1926, 3.

Unsell, Eve [actress/scenarist/writer] (b. Chicago IL, 1887?–6 Jul 1937 [50], Santa Monica CA). m. Lester Blankfield, 1 Mar 1911, NYC. (FP-L; Ince; 1st National; Fox; World, 1915; Universal; Paramount; Metro.) "Eve Unsell (Blankfield)," *Variety,* 14 Jul 1937. *The Cyclopedia of American Biography,* Supp. Ed., Vol. VII (1926), p. 476. AS, p. 1090. AMD, p. 345. AS, p. 1090. BHD2, p. 267. FDY, p. 439. "New Famous

Players Script Writer," *MPW*, 20 Dec 1913, 1427. "Eve Unsell Leaves Famous Players," *MPW*, 24 Apr 1915, 545. "Miss Eve Unsell with Lasky," *MPW*, 10 Jun 1916, 1894. Edward Weitzel, "Confessions of a Scenarist," *MPW*, 24 May 1919, 1169–70. "Eve Unsell Will Sail for England," *MPW*, 26 Jul 1919, 515. "Eve Unsell Turns the Spotlight on Foggy Projection in London," *MPW*, 13 Dec 1919, 798. Eve Unsell, "English Film Conditions Are Improved and Big Authors Interested in Screen," *MPW*, 2 Oct 1920, 612. "Eve Unsell Creates Scenario Service Bureau; Will Also Dispose of Film Rights to Books," *MPW*, 15 Jan 1921, 288. "Says Scenarios Must Be Made to Meet New Economic Needs of the Industry," MPW, 5 Mar 1921, 34. "Eve Unsell Heads Scenario Department of Robertson-Cole on the West Coast," *MPW*, 23 Jul 1921, 412.

Unterkircher, Hans [actor] (b. Germany, 22 Aug 1895-May 1971 [75]). BHD1, p. 552. IFN, p. 299.

Upcher, Peter [actor/composer] (b. Halesworth, England, 1892-Dec 1962 [70], London, England). (Began on stage, 1909.) "Peter Upcher," *Variety*, 229, 23 Jan 1963, 79:3 (composed *Song of Love and Friendship*). BHD, p. 323.

Updegraaf, Henry [actor] (b. 1889–29 Jul 1936 [47?], Los Angeles CA; heart attack). AS, p. 1090.

Upton, Lucille (sister of **Peggy Hopkins Joyce**) [actress]. No data found. AMD, p. 345. "Introducing—Miss Upton!," *MPW*, 1 Aug 1925, 556.

Uraneff, Vadim [actor] (b. St. Petersburg, Russia, 6 Feb 1895–5 Apr 1952 [57], Duarte CA). BHD1, p. 552.

Urban, Charles [inventor of Kinemacolor/director/producer] (b. Cleveland OH, 1870–29 Aug 1942 [72?], Brighton, England). AMD, p. 345. AS, p. 1090. BHD2, p. 267. Katz, p. 1179. WWVC, pp. 144–45 (b. 1867). Charles Urban, "The CInematograph in Science and Education [Part I]," *MPW*, 27 Jul 1907, 324; Part II, 3 Aug 1907, pp. 241–42; Part III, 10 Aug 1907, pp. 356–57; Part IV, 17 Aug 1907, pp. 372–73; Part V, 24 Aug 1907, pp. 388–89. "Urban Company in New Home," *MPW*, 23 May 1908, 457. "Kinemacolor," *MPW*, 18 Dec 1909, 873–74. "Men Who Made Kinemacolor Possible," *MPW*, 18 Dec 1909, 875. "The Kinemacolor Demonstration," *MPW*, 25 Dec 1909, 913–15. "Kinemacolor," *MPW*, 25 Dec 1909, 913–15. Burton H. Albee, "Impressions of Kinemacolor Films," *MPW*, 25 Dec 1909, 915–16. "The Kinemacolor Triumph in New York," *MPW*, 29 Jan 1910, 122. "Charles Urban Gives All His Time to Kinemacolor," *MPW*, 19 Feb 1910, 262. "Charles Urban in New York," *MPW*, 17 Sep 1910, 620–21. "The Father of Kinemacolor," *MPW*, 10 Feb 1912, 487–88. "Charles Urban Ill," *MPW*, 11 May 1912, 515. "Yankee Films Abroad," *MPW*, 10 May 1913, 573–74. Charles Urban, "'Instructive Pictures' to Be Backbone of Industry; Great Reserve Available," *MPW*, 27 Dec 1919, 1117–18. "Charles Urban's Ideas Are Made Effective in Russia," *MPW*, 17 Jul 1920, 362. "Urban His Own Editor," *MPW*, 21 Aug 1920, 1046. "Urban Shows to Trade the Spirograph, Educational and Home Picture Machine," *MPW*, 28 Aug 1920, 1151. Robert C. McElravy, "Many Scenes from Life and Nature Shown in Charles Urban's Classics," *MPW*, 2 Oct 1920, 619. "Charles Urban Says Showmen Should Give Picture Patrons Their Money's Worth," *MPW*, 6 Nov 1920, 101. "Charles Urban Buys Valuable Property for Home of His Two Screen Industries," *MPW*, 11 Dec 1920, 709. Charles Urban, "Urban Expects 1921 to See Fruition of His Plan for 'Home Made Movies,'" *MPW*, 25 Dec 1920, 1014. "Charles Urban Has Instructed Millions in His Twenty-Five Years as Film Man," *MPW*, 16 Jul 1921, 293. "'World' Always a Credit to Industry, Says Urban," *MPW*, 11 Mar 1922, 137. Arthur James, "Charles Urban and His Success," *MPW*, 11 Mar 1922, 190. Charles Urban, "Motion Picture of Today at Threshold of Greater Usefulness Than Ever Before," *MPW*, 11 Mar 1922, 190c.

Urban, Dorothy Karroll [actress] (b. 1869–29 Oct 1961 [92], Los Angeles CA). AS, p. 1090. BHD1, p. 552. IFN, p. 299.

Urban, Dorothy Karroll [actress] (b. 1869–29 Oct 1961 [92?], Los Angeles CA). AS, p. 1090.

Urban, Gretl *see* **Thurlow, Gretl Urban**

Urban, Joseph [set designer/director/general production manager of International Film Studio] (b. Vienna, Austria, 26 May 1872–10 Jul 1933 [61], New York NY). m. Mary Porter Beegle, Jan 1919. "Joseph Urban Dies; Versatile Artist; Won Fame as Architect, Stage Set Designer; Aided Opera and 'Follies'; Landscaped Gardens, Built Country Villas and Furnished Them—Long Celebrated in Europe," *NYT*, 11 Jul 1933, 17:1 ("furnished the scenic effects for many photoplays"). "Joseph Urban," *Variety*, 11 Jul 1933. AS, p. 1090. BHD2, p. 267.

Urban, Max [director/producer] (b. Prague, Czechoslovakia, 24 Aug 1882). AS, p. 1090.

Urbont, Harry [actor/musician] (b. Kipin, Russia, 1902–29 Sep 1987 [85?], New York NY). AS, p. 1091. BHD, p. 323.

Urecal, Minerva [actress] (*née* Minerva Holzer, b. Eureka CA, 22 Sep 1884–26 Feb 1966 [83], Glendale CA). AS, p. 1091.

Urie, John [cameraman/head of Crystal Motion Picture Co.] (b. Scotland, 1854?–16 May 1938 [84], Glen Ridge NJ). (Biograph; founded Crystal.) "John Urie, Pioneer in Motion Pictures; Associated with Edison in the Early Days of Films," *NYT*, 18 May 1938, 21:5. "John Urie," *Variety*, 25 May 1938 (retired in 1903). AS, p. 1091 (Urbie). BHD2, p. 267.

Urson, Frank B. [cameraman/director/producer] (nephew of E.J. Hite) (b. Chicago IL, 1887?–16 Aug 1928 [41], Indian Lake MI; drowned). "Frank Urson Drowns in Michigan Lake," *Variety*, 22 Aug 1928 (d. 17 Aug). AMD, p. 345. AS, p. 1091 (d. 17 Aug). BHD, p. 323; BHD2, p. 267 (d. Niles MI). IFN, p. 300. "Frank Urson Signed by Neilan; Will Direct 'Her Man' First," *MPW*, 8 Apr 1922, 623. "To Direct "Risky Business," *MPW*, 17 Apr 1926, 496.

Urueta, Chano [director] (b. Chihuahua, Mexico, 1890–1978 [88?], Mexico City, Mexico). AS, p. 1091.

Usell, Anna [actress] (*née* Anna Uzel, b. Brno, Moravia, 1903). m. director Otto Wilhelm Fischer (b. 1915). AS, p. 1091 (actress in German films).

Usher, Guy [actor] (b. Mason City IA, 9 Mar 1883–16 Jun 1944 [61], San Diego CA). AS, p. 1091.

Usher, Harry [actor] (b. 1887–28 Oct 1950 [63?], Los Angeles CA; heart attack). AS, p. 1091.

Uttal, Fred [actor/announcer] (b. New York NY, 1908?–28 Nov 1963 [55], New York NY). m. (3) Maurine Spindt. "Fred Uttal Dies; Radio Announcer; Pioneer Broadcaster on Air Since Early 1920's," *NYT*, 29 Nov 1963, 34:3 (He "got his start in show business at an early age. An uncle who had once been an actor had the boy's name placed on the preferred child-extra list at the movie studios then flourishing on Long Island. On weekends and during the summers the boy played in many of the mob scenes of the Marion Davies films." Appeared in *The Birth of a Nation*. Griffith fired him: "Young man, so far as I can see, you simply have no affinity for the pictures."). "Fred Uttal," *Variety*, 4 Dec 1963 ("As a youth he was extra in various Long Island studios. At one time he was a featured performer in D.W. Griffith's "Birth of a Nation.'"). AS, p. 1091. BHD, p. 323. IFN, p. 300. Truitt 3, p. 723 (b. 1905).

Uttenhoven, M. Harry [fencing coach]. No data found. AMD, p. 346. "World's Champion Fencer Joins Fairbanks Company," *MPW*, 23 Oct 1920, 1120.

Utterstrom, Johan [director] (b. Sweden, 16 May 1901). AS, p. 1091.

Uzzell, Corene [actress] (b. Houston TX, ca. 1890). AMD, p. 346. BHD, p. 323. "Corene Uzzell in Cast of 'Determination,'" *MPW*, 20 Nov 1920, 378.

V

Vaccaro, Frank A. [actor] (b. 1884–6 Jul 1948 [64], Derby CT). BHD, p. 323. IFN, p. 300.

Vachelle, Horace A. [scenarist] (b. Sydenham, England, 30 Oct 1861–10 Jan 1955 [93], Bath, England). BHD2, p. 267.

Vachet, Aloysius (Abbé) [actor] (*né* Claude-Louis de Gonzague Vachet, b. Buxy, France, 28 Jan 1896 [extrait de naissance no. SN/1896]-7 Aug 1958 [62], La Garenne-Colombes, France). AS, p. 1091.

Vachon, Jean [actor] (d. 2 Feb 1989). BHD1, p. 553.

Vail, Grace Wynden [publicist]. No data found. AMD, p. 346. "Grace Wynden Vail Is Now Publicist for American Cinema," *MPW*, 24 Apr 1920, 566.

Vajda, Ernest [playwright/scenarist] (*né* Erno Vajda, b. Papa, Hungary, 21 May 1887?–3

Apr 1954 [67], Woodland Hills CA; heart attack). m. Barbara. "Ernest Vajda, 67, Playwright, Dead; Author of Works Produced on Broadway [and in Europe] Also Wrote Many Movie Scripts," *NYT,* 4 Apr 1954, 88:3. "Ernest Vajda," *Variety,* 7 Apr 1954. AS, p. 1093 (b. Komaron, Hungary, 27 May 1889). BHD2, p. 268 (b. Komaron, 1886). FDY, p. 439 (Vadja). IFN, p. 300. Francis L. Perrett, "The Nation of the Happy Ending; So Ernest Vajda ("Pronounced Voya—no one knows why."). Describes America," *MPC,* May 1926, 43, 64.

Vajda, Ladislaus (father of Ladislao Vajda) [scenarist] (*né* Laszlo Vajda Weisz, b. Budapest, Hungary, ca. 1880–1933 [53?]). m. (son Ladislao, 1905–1965). AS, p. 1093. BHD2, p. 268.

Vaktangov, Evgeny Bagrationvich [actor/director] (b. Moscow, Russia, 2 Feb 1883–27 Mar 1922 [39], Moscow, Russia). AS, p. 1093.

Val, Adrio [scenarist] (*née* Henriette Sava-Giou). No data found. AMD, p. 346. "Here's New Film World, 'Photogenique,' Brought to America by Miss Sava-Giou," *MPW,* 12 Nov 1921, 189.

Val, Paul [director/producer] (b. 1888–23 Mar 1962 [74?], Los Angeles CA). AS, p. 1093. BHD2, p. 268.

Val del Omar, José [director] (b. Granada, Spain, 1904–4 Feb 1982 [77?], Madrid, Spain). AS, p. 1093.

Valbel, Henri (father of Marc Valbel, 1907–1960) [actor] (b. Paris, France, 19 May 1885–ca. 1948 [63?]). AS, p. 1094.

Valdemar, Tania [actress/dancer] (b. 1894–12 Nov 1955 [61?], New York NY). AS, p. 1094.

Valdez, Reina [actress]. No data found. AMD, p. 346. "Reina Valdez," *MPW,* 14 Mar 1914, 1395. "Reina Valdez Attains Ambition," *MPW,* 5 Jun 1915, 1619.

Vale, Louise [actress] (*nee?,* b. New York NY–d. 29 Oct 1918, Madison WI; influenza). m. **Edgar Jones,** 1914; **Travers Vale** (d. 1927). (K&E.) AMD, p. 346. AS, p. 1094 (d. 28 Oct). BHD, p. 323. IFN, p. 300. Billy H. Doyle, "Lost Players," *CI,* 139 (Jan 1987), 55. *MPS,* 20 Feb 1914, 21. "Louise Vale," *MPW,* 10 Jul 1915, 296. "Obituary," *MPW,* 16 Nov 1918, 730 (d. 28 Oct at home of mother).

Vale, Margaret [actress]. No data found. AMD, p. 346. "Margaret Vale in Pictures," *MPW,* 19 Dec 1914, 1698.

Vale, Travers [actor/director] (b. Liverpool, England, 31 Jan 1865–10 Jan 1927 [61], Los Angeles CA; cancer). m. **Louise** (d. 1918); Emmy Barbier, 10 Apr 1920, Hotel Biltmore, NY NY. (World.) "Travers Vale," *Variety,* 19 Jan 1927 (b. Australia; d. age 54). AS, p. 1094. AMD, p. 346. BHD, p. 323; BHD2, p. 268. IFN, p. 300. 1921 Directory, p. 276. Spehr, p. 170. "Biograph Directors," *MPW,* 10 Jul 1915, 243–44. "Travers Vale Breaks Arm," *MPW,* 1 Jun 1918, 1300. "Travers Vale in Film Advisory Board," *MPW,* 29 Jun 1918, 1854. "Film Division Names Director Advisors," *MPW,* 20 Jul 1918, 363–64. "Louise Vale Dies, Victim of Influenza," *MPW,* 16 Nov 1918, 730. "Wedding Is One of Many Attractions at Dinner-Dance of Directors' Association," *MPW,* 24 Apr 1920, 551.

Vale, Vola [stage/film actress] (aka Vola Smith until 1916, *née* Violet Irene Smith, b. Buffalo NY, 12 Feb 1897–17 Oct 1970 [73], Hawthorne CA; heart disease and diabetes). m. (1) **Albert Russell** (d. 1929); (2) **John W. Gorman,** 8 Dec 1926, Santa Ana CA; (3) Lawrence Carl McDougal, 21 Jan 1932. (K&E; Biograph, 1913; Lasky; Fox; Universal; Nestor; Victor; Imp; Paramount; Falcon; Pathé; Vitagraph; Metro; Republic.) AMD, p. 346. BHD1, p. 618. "Vola Smith Joins Universal," *MPW,* 13 May 1916, 1146. "Vola Vale," *MPW,* 11 Nov 1916, 835. "Vola Vale to Play Opposite Lytell," *MPW,* 3 Jan 1920, 100. "Now We Know It," *MPW,* 12 Feb 1927, 492 (m. Gorman). June Lee, "Dan Cupid's Bulletin Board," *Paris and Hollywood Screen Secrets Magazine,* May 1927, 53 (m. Gorman). George Katchmer, "Remembering the Great Silents," *CI,* 215 (May 1993), 49. Billy Doyle, "Lost Players: Vola Vale," *CI,* 296 (Feb 2000), 62.

Valedon, Lora [actress] (b. 1884–15 Sep 1946 [62?], Providence RI). AS, p. 1094.

Valente, Maria (mother of Catherine Valente, b. 1931) [actress] (*née* Maria Siri, b. Rome, Italy, 22 Dec 1897–29 Oct 1977 [79], Munich, Germany). AS, p. 1094.

Valenti, Osvaldo [actor] (b. Istanbul, Turkey, 17 Feb 1906–30 Apr 1945 [39], Milan, Italy; shot to death by Italian partisans along with fanatical Fascist actress Luisa Ferida). m. Fanny Musso. Romano Brancalini, *Celebri e dannati—Osvaldo Valenti e Luisa Ferida; storia e tragedia di due divi del regime* (Milan, Italy, Longanesi, 1985). JS, p. 470 (in German and Italian silents from 1927).

Valentin, Karl [actor/director] (*né* Valentin Ludwig Fey, b. Munich, Germany, 4 Jun 1882–9 Feb 1948 [65], Munich, Germany). AS, p. 1094.

Valentine, Elizabeth [actress] (b. New York NY, 16 Mar 1877–23 Jul 1971 [94], Los Angeles CA). AS, p. 1094.

Valentine, Grace [actress] (*née* Grace Sharrenberger, b. Springfield OH, 14 Feb 1884–12 Nov 1964 [80], New York NY [Death Certificate Index No. 23794]). m. **Wayne Nunn** (d. 1947). AMD, p. 346. AS, p. 1094. BHD, p. 323. IFN, p. 300 (age 80). SD, p. 1243. "Grace Valentine," *MPW,* 18 Nov 1916, 1028. "Grace Valentine to Star in Another Morosco Play," *MPW,* 14 Sep 1918, 1597.

Valentine, Joseph A. [cinematographer] (*né* Giuseppe Valentino, b. New York NY, 24 Jul 1900–18 May 1949 [45], Cheviot Hills CA; heart attack in his sleep). (Paragon [Ft. Lee NJ, 1918]; Fox; Universal.) "Joseph A. Valentine, 'Oscar' Camera Man," *NYT,* 20 May 1949, 27:4. "Joseph A. Valentine," *Variety,* 25 May 1949. AS, p. 1094. BHD2, p. 268 (b. 1903-d. LA CA). FDY, p. 469. IFN, p. 300 (b. 1903). Katz, p. 1181 (began 1920).

Valentine, Spencer [assistant business manager] (b. Lorain OH, 8 Jul 1886–16 Jun 1945 [58], Los Angeles CA). BHD2, p. 268.

Valentini, Vincent [scenarist] (b. 1896–15 Apr 1948 [52?], Baltimore MD). AS, p. 1094. BHD2, p. 268.

Valentino, Alberto (brother of **Rudolph Valentino**) [actor] (*né* Alberto Guglielmi di Valentina, b. Rome, Italy, 1892–4 Jun 1981 [89], Los Angeles CA). (Fox; MGM.) "Alberto G. Valentino," *Variety,* 17 Jun 1981 (to U.S. in 1926). AMD, p. 346. AS, p. 1094. BHD1, p. 553 (b. Castellaneta, Italy). "Valentino's Brother Has Face Reconstructed," *MPW,* 29 Oct 1927, 547.

Valentino, Rudolph (brother of **Alberto Valentino**) [dancer/actor] (*né* Rodolfo Alfonzo Rafaelo Pierre Filibert Guglielmi di Valentina d'Antonguolla, b. Castellaneta, Taranto, Italy, 6 May 1895–23 Aug 1926 [31], New York NY; poisoning from septic pneumonia). m. (1) **Jean Acker,** 5 Nov 1919, Hollywood CA–div. 4 Mar 1923 (d. 1978); (2) **Natacha Rambova,** 13 May 1922, Mexicali, Mexico, re-wed 14 Mar 1923, Crown Point IN–div. 19 Jan 1926, Paris (d. 1966). (Paramount.) *Daydreams* [poetry] (1923). S. George Ullman, *Valentino as I Knew Him* (NY: Macy-Masius, 1926). Irving Shulman, *Valentino* (NY: Trident Press, 1967). "Valentino Passes with No Kin at Side; Throngs in Street; Three Doctors and Two Nurses See 'Film's Greatest Lover' Die After Long Coma; Manager Weeps in Hall; Crowds Blocking Traffic, Held Back by Police Reserves, Rush to Funeral Church; Associates Pay Tributes; Actor Dead at 31 Left Little of Huge Earnings—Arrangements for Funeral Yet Unmade," *NYT,* 24 Aug 1926, 1:6, 3:2. "Movie World Pays Valentino Tribute; Will Hays Calls Actor's Death 'on Verge of Greater Things' a Great Loss; Pola Negri is Prostrated; Producers and Actors in Eulogies of Star's Talents and His Qualities as a Man," *NYT,* 24 Aug 1926, 3:1. "Valentino's Fame a Triumph of Youth; Actor Wanted to Be a Gardener and Went to California to Get Work on a Farm; Became 'The Sheik' at 26; Once Worked as Laborer in Central Park—Later Got Job Dancing at Maxim's and on Stage," *NYT,* 24 Aug 1926, 3:4. "Rudolph Valentino," *Variety,* 25 Aug 1926. AMD, p. 346. AS, p. 1094. BHD, p. 323. FFF, p. 94. IFN, p. 300. Katz, pp. 1181–82. MH, p. 140. Spehr, p. 172. Truitt, p. 332. "Jean Acker Weds Rodolpho Valentino," *MPW,* 22 Nov 1919, 435. "Valentino—Acker," *MPW,* 29 Nov 1919, 566. "Valentino and Cannon in Ibanez' 'Four Horsemen,'" *MPW,* 14 Aug 1920, 876. "Will Have Title Role in 'Sheik,'" *MPW,* 9 Jul 1921, 226. Herbert Howe, "Hitting the Hookah with Rudie," *MPC,* Dec 1921, 18–19, 72, 81. "Valentino Signs Paramount Contract; Lasky Names Notable Pictures Planned," *MPW,* 21 Jan 1922, 261. "Valentino in Benefit," *MPW,* 6 May 1922, 43. "Valentino to Marry," *MPW,* 20 May 1922, 344 (Rambova). "Rudolph Valentino Freed on the Charge of Bigamy," *MPW,* 17 Jun 1922, 614 (dismissed 5 Jun 1922). "Magazine Readers [of *Motion Picture Classic*] Demand Valentino as Cover Subject," *MPW,* 24 Jun 1922, 708. "Valentino Rebels," *MPW,* 9 Sep 1922, 110. Maude Cheatham, "The Darkest Hour," *Classic,* Oct 1922, 52, 87. "Valentino Loses Out," *MPW,* 14 Oct 1922, 552. "Legal Battle Goes On," *MPW,* 21 Oct 1922, 656. "Valentino Will Appeal; To Carry Famous Players' Case to Appellate Division—Can't Work for Months," *MW,* 28 Oct 1922, 10, 26. "Paramount Wins," *MPW,* 23 Dec 1922, 708. "Valentino Explains," *MPW,* 20 Jan 1923, 216. Rudolph Valentino, "What Is the Matter with the Movies?; Famous screen star declares 75 per cent of all pictures are insult to human intelligence—Is He Right or Wrong? Tell us what you think," *MW,* 16 Jun 1923, 3. "The Editor's Views," *MPW,* 28 Jul 1923, 285. "Ritz-Carlton Announces Valentino as Company's First Star," *MPW,* 28 Jul 1923, 289. "Valentino Wins in Court," *MPW,* 4 Aug 1923, 356. "Valentino Is Insured," *MPW,* 18 Aug 1923, 550. "Valentino Signs New Contract with Ritz; Ready for Production," *MPW,* 24 Nov 1923, 376. T. Howard Kelly, "Valentino Returns to America," *MW,* 8 Dec 1923, 4–5, 28. "J.D. Williams Says Whole World Wants Only Better Class Films," *MPW,* 22 Dec 1923, 689. "Valentino Does Two More for Famous—Then Joins Ritz," *MPW,* 5 Jan 1924, 29. "Suit Is Ended," *MPW,* 16 Feb1924, 542. Rudolph Valentino, "My Own Story of My Trip Abroad, Part I," *MW,* IV, 1 Mar 1924, 4–5, 27; Part II, 8

Mar 1924, 6–7, 29; Part III, 15 Mar 1924, 10–11, 28, 30; Part IV, 22 Mar 1924, 8–9, 22–26; Part V, 29 Mar 1924, 14–15, 45; Part VI, 5 Apr 1924, 10–11, 27–29; Part VII, 12 Apr 1924, 10–11, 28–29; Part VIII, 12 Apr 1924, 10–11, 28–29; Part IX, 19 Apr 1924, 10–11, 28; Part X, 26 Apr 1924, 10–11, 27–28; Part XI, 3 May 1924, 12–13, 25–26; Part XII, 10 May 1924, 12–13, 26; Part XIII, 17 May 1924, 14–15, 26; Part XIV, 24 May 1924, 12–13, 31; Part XV, 31 May 1924, 12–13, 30; Part XVI, 7 Jun 1924, 12–13, 31; Part XVII, 14 Jun 1924, 12–13, 30; Part XVIII, 21 Jun 1924, 10–11, 29–30; Part XIX, 28 Jun 1924, 14–15, 28; Part XX, 5 Jul 1924, 12–13, 28; Part XXI, 12 Jul 1924, 14–15; Part XXII, 19 Jul 1924, 13, 30; Part XXIII, 26 Jul 1924, 14, 30; Part XXIV, 2 Aug 1924, 15, 28; Part XXV, 9 Aug 1924, 9; Part XXVI, 16 Aug 1924, 17, 27. David A. Balch, "Valentino's First Day's Work in the Studio; Rudy returns to screen in Famous Players' Long Island Studio—Will act in and as *Monsieur Beaucaire*—Is supported by an all-star cast," *MW,* 14 Mar 1924, 4–5. "[Rodolph] Valentino a Buyer at Tapestry Sale; Pays $105 for 18th Century Moorish Scarf and $110 for a Velvet Coat; Day's Receipts Are $16,170...," *NYT,* 11 Apr 1924, 17:1 (No. 120, $105, was a drap d'or crimson scarf or runner in rose-crimson. Its ends woven in varied gold, blue, green and crimson stripes, 13 feet 8 inches long by 19 inches wide. No. 198, $110, was "a 17th-century Albanian gold-embroidered crimson velvet coat, with frontal panels of gold scrollings and the back with chevroned stripes in silver bordered in gold."). "Valentino Invests in Tolentino Art; Motion Picture Actor Buys Ancient Chest and Portraits at American Galleries Sale; Day's Total Is $37,215...," *NYT,* 24 Apr 1924, 17:1 (he bought a "15th century French Gothic carved walnut chest, the entire front a façade of cathedral windows with painted arches and elaborate Gothic tracery in carvo-relief. It is from the De Motte collection, Paris. He paid $475 for it." He also paid $640 for two portraits by Alonzo Sanchez-Coello, a Spanish painter. One was 'A Duke of Savoy,' the other, 'A Duchess of the House of Savoy,' both from the Saluzzo Castle of Verzuolo, Piedmont, Italy.). Dorothea B. Herzog, "Valentino Returns to Screen in Million Dollar Picture; '*Monsieur Beaucaure*, the popular young screen star's vehicle, in which he comes back to the silver screen after a two years' absence, has been produced with disregard of cost—Picture is one of the most lavish ever made," *MW,* 31 May 1924, 8–9. "[Harold] Lloyd and Valentino to Distribute Their Pictures Through Paramount," *MPW,* 11 Oct 1924, 472. "Valentino Returning," *MPW,* 8 Nov 1924, 122. "...Valentino Returns from Spain," *NYT,* 11 Nov 1924, 20:3 (on the *Leviathan,* with Jackie Coogan and Nita Naldi aboard. He had a small goatee beard, "which, he said, would be needed in the picture he is going to do in California, the scene of which is laid in Spain in the fourteenth century.") "Barbers Ban Valentino; Beard Brings Their Condemnation Upon Movie Star," *NYT,* 18 Nov 1924, 27:6 ("the convention of associated barbers [in Chicago] today [17 Nov] adopted a resolution that its members 'be pledged not to attend a showing of his photoplays as long as he remains bewhiskered.' They feared that the male population of America is very likely to be guided by Valentino to the extent of making whiskers fashionable again..."). "Valentino Back," *MPW,* 22 Nov 1924, 310. "Rudolph Valentino," *MPW,* 29 Nov 1924, 407. Gladys Hall and Adele Whitely Fletcher, "We Interview Valentino," *MW,* 13 Dec 1924, 10–12, 29. "Valentino Gold Medal to Best Performer," *MPW,* 3 Jan 1925, 22. L.B.N. Gnaedinger, "His Former Boarding-House Mistress Tells of Valentino as a Hall-Roonmer," *MW,* 14 Feb 1925, 4–5, 30. "Rudy—Williams Split Report Described as 'Nothing Startling,'" *MPW,* 14 Mar 1925, 140. "United Artists Signs Valentino Under Long-Term Film Contract," *MPW,* 21 Mar 1925, 241. "Valentino-United Artists Picture Starts Next Week," *MPW,* 25 Apr 1925, 804. "Rudolph Valentino Medal Awarded to John Barrymore," *MPW,* 2 May 1925, 72. "Wins Popularity Contest," *MPW,* 2 May 1925, 74. Lois Wilson, "The Rudolph Valentino I Know," *MW,* 27 Jun 1925, 9–10, 41. Jim Tully, "Men Wonder About the Adoring Eyes that Follow Valentino But Women Adore Him—and Say Why," *MPC,* Jun 1925, 16–17, 87. "Dinner with the Valentinos," *MM,* Oct 1925, 49, 105. Charles Edward Hastings, "Valentino," *MPW,* 21 Nov 1925, 208. Eugene V. Brewster, "Has Valentino Come Back?," *MPC,* Mar 1926, 42, 82. Don Ryan, "Has the Great Lover Become Just a Celebrity?," *MPC,* May 1926, 20–21, 69, 78. "Valentino in New York," *MPW,* 31 Jul 1926, 3. "Late Valentino Bulletin Says 'Recovery Probable,'" *MPW,* 28 Aug 1926, 1. "Rudolph Valentino [in memoriam page]," *Cinema Arts,* Sep 1926, 5. Paul Paige, "Close-Ups and Fade-Outs," *Paris and Hollywood,* Sep 1926, 91 (after his contract with United Artists expirred, he was to make three films for Feature Productions Co., headed by John W. Considine, general manager of the Joseph M. Schenck Co.). "Rodolpho Guglielmi," *MPW,* 4 Sep 1926, 7. "Obituary," *MPW,* 4 Sep 1926, 1–2. "'A Great Loss,' Says Will H. Hays," *MPW,* 4 Sep 1926, 2. "Tributes to Valentino," *MPW,* 4 Sep 1926, 2. "No Other Valentino Until—," *MPW,* 11 Sep 1926, 93. "Valentino to Rest in West; Tears Flow at N.Y. Funeral," *MPW,* 11 Sep 1926, 2. "Rest in Peace," *MPW,* 18 Sep 1926, 1. Joseph Jackson, "Things I Have Seen," *Paris and Hollywood,* Oct 1926, 33 ("Under his new contract with United Artists, Rudolph Valentino is receiving $6,500 a week and 25% of the profits from his pictures." Joseph M. Schenck holds his contract, "and he didn't give Rudy those terms out of sentiment. ¶When I [Jackson] was Rudy's publicity director he implored me to try to get the newspapers and the public to stop referring to him as the Sheik. He thought the name through general usage, had acquired an unsavory odor and he feared it would make him appear cheap. But now Rudy has gone back to the Sheik stuff deliberately with his latest picture, The Son of the Sheik. ¶Much water has flowed under the bridge, especially since Rudy and Natacha parted company."). "Hundreds Visit at Valentino's Old Home," *MPW,* 11 Dec 1926, 412. Samuel C. Peoples, "The Story of Rudolph Valentino: Out, Brief Candle!," *8mm Collector,* 14 (Spring, 1966), 6–7, 23–25. A.L. Woodridge, "When Rudy's Belongings Were Sold," *Picture Play Magazine,* Apr 1927, reprinted in *CI,* 121 (Jul 1985), 58–59. Eugene Vazzana, "Retrospective at the American Museum of the Moving Image Honors Valentino," *CI,* 199 (Jan 1992), 56 *et passim.* Edward Rothstein, "Clashing Keys for 'Valentino' and His Ambiguous Aspects," *NYT,* 17 Jan 1994, C11:4, C15:1 (review of the opera, *The Dream of Valentino*). Eve Golden, "The Greatest Star: Rudolph Valentino," *CI,* 239 (May 1995), C10–11, 33–34.

Valenzuela, Elena Sánchez [actress] (b. Mexico, F.D., 2 Mar 1900–30 Sep 1950 [50]).

Valerie, Gladys [actress] (b. New York NY, 1903). AS, p. 1095.

Valerie, Olive [actress] (b. 1893–27 Oct 1951 [58?], New York NY). BHD, p. 323.

Valerio, Albano [actor] (b. San Jose CA, 1888–2 Feb 1961 [72], Los Angeles CA). AS, p. 1095. BHD1, p. 554. IFN, p. 300. Truitt, p. 332.

Valetti, Rosa [actress] (*née* Rosa Vallentin, b. Berlin, Germany, 17 Mar 1878–10 Dec 1937 [59], Vienna, Austria). AS, p. 1095. BHD1, p. 554.

Valkyrien, Valda [stage/film dancer/actress] (*née* Adele Frede, b. Reykjavik, Iceland, 30 Sep 1895–22 Oct 1956 [61], Los Angeles CA). m. Baron Hrolf von Dewitz, 1914, Jersey City NJ—div. 1916; Robert Stuart Otto. (Great Northern [Denmark], 1912; Danish Biograph; Vitagraph; Thanhouser; World; Fox; Metro.) "Mrs. Albert K. Otto," *NYT,* 25 Oct 1956, 33:4 (age 59; known as Mrs. Adele Stuart Otto). "Valda Valkyrian," *Variety,* 31 Oct 1956. AMD, p. 347. AS, p. 1095 (b. Copenhagen, Denmark). BHD, p. 323 (b. Denmark). IFN, p. 300. MSBB, p. 1044 (b. 1897). Spehr, p. 172 (d. 1953). Truitt, p. 332 (d. 1953). "European Star Here; Horsley Signs Mlle. Volkyrien, Danish Player, for Centaur Comedy Programme," *NYDM,* 26 Aug 1914, 25:4 (20 years old). "European FIlm Star Joins Centaur," *MPW,* 29 Aug 1914, 1246. "Mlle. Valkyrien in 'The Valkyrien,'" *MPW,* 16 Oct 1915, 470. "Mlle. Valkyrien (The Baronness de Witz)," *NYDM,* 20 Nov 1915, 27:1 (married to director Baron Hrolp Dewitz. "Mlle. Valkyrien plays in only the best in her art. She is giving her youth, beauty and versatility as an actress and demands in return a setting which can only be furnished by the big picture producer and the capable director."). "Valda Valkyrien," *MPW,* 15 Apr 1916, 421. "Valda Valkyrien," *MPW,* 22 Jul 1916, 624. Richard Wallace, "Valkyrien, the Blonde Beautiful; The Swan-Maiden of the Sagas Lives on in ThIs Radiant Young Dane," *MPC,* Aug 1916, 13–15. "Valkyrien to Support Louise Huff," *MPW,* 29 Jun 1918, 1870. Hans J. Wollstein, "The Strange Case of Valda Valkyrien," *CI,* 259 (Jan 1997), 28–30 (*née* Adele Frede, b. 1894; renamed Valkyrien in 1914; includes filmography).

Valle, Federico [cinematographer] (b. Asti, Italy, 1880–25 Oct 1960 [80?], Santos Lugares, Argentina). AS, p. 1095. BHD2, p. 268.

Vallee, Marcel Alexandre Armand [actor] (b. Paris, France, 15 Jan 1880 [extrait de naissance no. 163/1880]–31 Oct 1957 [77], Fontaine-le-Port, France [extrait de décès no. 10/1957]). AS, p. 1095.

Vallee, Yvonne [actress] (*née* Marguerite Yvonne Vallee, b. Bordeaux, France, 21 Feb 1899–15 Jan 1996 [96], Vallauris, France [extrait de décès no. 61/1996]). m. **Maurice Chevalier**—div. (d. 1971). AS, p. 1095.

Vallejo, Enrique Juan [cameraman] (b. Mexico City, Mexico, 6 May 1882–2 May 1950 [67], Los Angeles CA; heart attack in his sleep). (Griffith; Chaplin; Sennett.) "Enrique J. Vallejo," *Variety,* 10 May 1950 (began 1910). AS, p. 1095. BHD2, p. 268 (d. 3 May).

Vallentin, Hermann [actor] (b. Berlin, Germany, 24 May 1872–18 Sep 1945 [73], Tel Aviv, Israel). AS, p. 1095 (b. 1870; d. 15 Oct). BHD1, p. 618. IFN, p. 300.

Valles, Fredrick [costumer] (b. England, 4 May 1886–12 Apr 1970 [83], Los Angeles CA). BHD2, p. 268.

Vallet, Harry [cinematographer]. No data found. FDY, p. 469.

Valli, Valli [actress] (b. Berlin, Germany, 11 Feb 1882–3 Nov 1927 [45], Hampstead, London, England). m. music publisher Louis Dreyfuss, Oct? 1917. (Film debut: *The High Road,* Metro, 1915.) "Valli Valli, Star of Operettas, Dies; Actress Succumbs at Her Home in Hampstead, Eng., After Four Months' Illness; Acted Leading Roles Here; Appeared in 'The Dollar Princess,' 'Kitty Grey' and 'Miss Millions'—Born in Berlin in 1882," *NYT,* 5 Nov 1927, 19:5 (last in U.S. in 1919). "Valli Valli's Death," *Variety,* 9 Nov 1927. AMD, p. 347. AS, p. 1095 (d. 4 Nov). BHD, p. 323. IFN, p. 300. "Valli Valli," *MPW,* 30 Oct 1915, 794. "Marriages," *Variety,* 19 Oct 1917, p. 9. Tollington Leigh, "Virginia Valli—Trhe Cameo Girl," *Cinema Arts,* Oct 1927, 18–19, 47.

Valli, Virginia [actress] (*née* Virginia Helen McSweeney, b. Chicago IL, 10 Jun 1898–24 Sep 1968 [70], Palm Springs CA). m. manager Demarest Lamson, 1926; **Charles Farrell** (d. 1990). "Virginia Valli," *Variety,* 2 Oct 1968. AMD, p. 347. AS, p. 1095 (b. 12 Jun). BHD1, p. 554. FFF, p. 167 (b. 1897). FSS, p. 280. IFN, p. 300. Katz, p. 1183 (b. 1895; began 1915). MH, p. 140 (b. 1902). Truitt, p. 332 (b. 19 Jan 1900). "Miss Valli a Dancer of Ability," *MPW,* 27 Oct 1917, 550. "Virginia Valli with Hope Hampton," *MPW,* 16 Oct 1920, 967. "Elaborate Plans for Virginia Valli," *MPW,* 4 Aug 1923, 419. "Virginia Valli's Rapid Rise," *MPW,* 10 Jan 1925, 167. "Playing with Men; Virginia Valli Reveals What She Has Learned About the Men Who Have Made Love to Her," *MPC,* May 1925, 32–33. "Virginia Valli Going Abroad," *MPW,* 18 Jul 1925, 357. June Lee, "Dan Cupid's Bulletin Board," *Paris and Hollywood,* Sep 1926, 95–96 (separated from Demmy Lamson); 2 (Oct 1926), 89 (divorced from Lamson. "She says that she supported him and that in return he abused her and horrible dictu occasionally he drank."). Richard Lamparski, "Virginia Valli," *Whatever Became of...* (NY: Crown Publishers, 1989), pp. 180–81.

Vallis, Robert [stage/film actor] (b. England, 1876–19 Dec 1932 [56], Brighton, England, "in poverty, after having eked out an existence as an unpaid car park attendant for the past five years."). "Robert Vallis," *Variety,* 100, 3 Jan 1933, 103:3 (He "is said to have given Roland [sic] Colman his first film part."). AS, p. 1095. BHD, p. 323. IFN, p. 300.

Vallois, Alain [actor] (b. Indianapolis IN, 12 Sep 1840–5 Jul 1907 [66], Los Angeles CA). AS, p. 1096.

Valluy, Julien Joseph ["pionnier du cinéma français"] (b. Lyon, France, 21 Dec 1872–23 Dec 1900 [28], Bizerte, Tunisia). AS, p. 1096.

Valori, Gino [director/scenarist] (b. Florence, Italy, 30 Apr 1890–28 May 1961 [71], Rome, Italy). AS, p. 1096.

Valpreux, Clémence [actress] (*née* Clémence Eugénie Boucher, b. Paris, France, 9 Feb 1895–20 Nov 1926 [31], Paris, France). AS, p. 1096.

Valroy, Jean [actor] (*né* Jean Baptiste Marius Mayan, b. Marseilles, France, 22 Mar 1890–26 Oct 1957 [67], Paris, France). AS, p. 1096.

Valsted, Myrtle Christine, "Miss Chicago" of 1927 [actress] (b. 12 Aug 1910–19 Sep 1928 [18], Los Angeles CA; appendicitis). "Myrtle Valsted," *Variety,* 26 Sep 1928. AS, p. 1096. BHD1, p. 618. IFN, p. 300. Truitt, p. 332.

Valvassura-Boetti, Teresa [actress] (*née* Teresa Boetti, b. Saluzzo, Italy, 1851–10 Mar 1930 [79?], Miltan, Italy). m. Ernesto Valvassura. JS, p. 474 (in Italian silents from 1916).

Van, Beatrice [actress/scenarist]. No data found. m. James Gruen. (American; Mutual). AMD, p. 347. FDY, p. 439. "New American Feature Players," *NYDM,* 28 Apr 1915, 24:1 (with C. Elliot Griffin). "Beatrice Van," *MPW,* 2 Oct 1915, 67. "Realism Singles Beatrice Van," *MPW,* LXV, 3 Nov 1923, 98:1 (began as an actress in 1912; in 1913 she sold her first story, *A Small Town Girl,* directed by Allan Dwan.). "Beatrice Van with F.B.O.," *MPW,* 17 May 1924, 276. "Beatrice Van to Write Featurettes for F.B.O.," *MPW,* 8 May 1926, 165. "Beatrice Van on Her Honeymoon," *MPW,* 8 Oct 1927, 354.

Van, Billy B. [stage/film actor] (b. Pottstown PA, 3 Aug 1878–16 Nov 1950 [72], Newport NH; heart attack). m. Grace Van Name (nom de stage, Grace Robinson)—div. 1913. "Billy B. Van," *Variety,* 22 Nov 1950. AS, p. 1096. ASCAP 66, p. 747 (b. 12 Aug 1857). BHD, p. 323. IFN, p. 300. Truitt, p. 332. "Divorced from Billy Van," *Variety,* 8 Aug 1913, p. 5 ("Chicago, Aug 6. Grace Van Name, wife of Billy Van, the minstrel, was granted a divorce here last week....").

Van, Gus [stage/film actor] (*né* August von Glahn, b. Brooklyn [Ridgewood] NY, 12 Aug 1887–13 Mar 1968 [80], Miami Beach FL; of injuries sustained when struck by car). m. twice. "Gus Van, Stage and Vaudeville Headliner, Dead; Teamed with Joe Schenck [Van & Schenck] in Hit Song and Comedy Act—Starred in 'Follies,'" *NYT,* 13 Mar 1968, 47. "Gus Van," *Variety,* 13 Mar 1968. AS, p. 1096. BHD1, p. 554 (d. 12 Mar). IFN, p. 301. Truitt, p. 333.

Van, Wally [actor/director] (*né* Wallace Van Nostrand, b. New Hyde Park NY, 27 Sep 1880–9 May 1974 [93], Englewood NJ). m. **Nitra Frazer** (d. 1979). AMD, p. 347. AS, p. 1096. BHD, p. 323; BHD2, p. 268 (b. 1885). IFN, p. 301 (b. 1885). 1921 Directory, p. 276. Slide, p. 154. "Wally Van Finishing New Serial Starring Earle Williams," *MPW,* 29 Apr 1916, 787. "Wally Van Leaves Vitagraph," *MPW,* 28 Oct 1916, 531. "Wally Van's First Picture," *MPW,* 4 Aug 1917, 818. "Wally Van to Direct for Rothapfel," *MPW,* 1 Mar 1919, 1194. "Wally Van Leaves New York for West with 'Challenge of Chance' Quickly Printed," *MPW,* 5 Jul 1919, 78.

Van Alstyne, Egbert A. [composer] (b. 1878–9 Jul 1951 [73?], Chicago IL). BHD2, p. 268.

Van Antwerp, Albert [actor] (b. Denver CO, 1898–30 Oct 1946 [48], Mendocino Co. CA). (Essanay.) BHD1, p. 554. IFN, p. 301. "New Essanay Player," *NYDM,* 18 Mar 1914, 30:3 (V.A. Van Antwerp).

Van Arsdale, Charles [director/production manager] (b. 1880–26 Jul 1957 [77?], Bloomfield NJ). AS, p. 1096. BHD2, p. 268.

Van Aucker, C[ecil] **K.** [actor] (b. Youngstown OH–d. 18 Feb 1938, Prescott AZ; tuberculosis). "C.K. Van Auker," *Variety,* 23 Feb 1938 (retired when sound came in). AS, p. 1096. BHD, p. 323. IFN, p. 301. Truitt, p. 333. George Katchmer, "C.K. Van Auker," *CI,* 204 (Jun 1992), 42.

Van Biene, Auguste [actor] (b. Holland, 16 May 1850–23 Jan 1913 [62], Brighton, England). BHD, p. 323.

Vanbrugh, Irene (sister of **Violet Vanbrugh**) [stage/film actress] (*née* Irene Barnes, b. Exeter, Devonshire, England, 2 Dec 1872–30 Nov 1949 [76], London, England). m. Dion Boucicault, Jr., 1901 (d. 1929). (Stage debut: *As You Like It,* Margate, 1888.) "Irene Vanbrugh, Actress, Is Dead; One of Britain's Outstanding Thespians for 50 Years, She Made Film Debut at 60 [in *Catherine the Great*]," *NYT,* 1 Dec 1949, 31:1. "Dame Irene Vanbrugh," *Variety,* 7 Dec 1949. AS, p. 1100. BHD1, p. 554. IFN, p. 301. Truitt, p. 333.

Vanbrugh, Violet (sister of **Irene Vanbrugh**) [stage/film actress] (*née* Violet Augusta Mary Barnes, b. Exeter, Devonshire, England, 11 Jun 1867–10 Nov 1942 [75], London, England). m. **Arthur Bourchier** (d. 1927). "Violet Vanbrugh, of British Stage; The Greatest Shakespearean Actress of Country Dies in London at Age of 75; Made Debut Here in 1889; Toured with Kendals—Last Theatrical Appearance Was in 'Merry Wives of Windsor,'" *NYT,* 12 Nov 1942, 25:3. "Violet Vanbrugh," *Variety,* 18 Nov 1942. AS, p. 1100. BHD1, p. 554 (d. 1982).

Van Buren, Amedee J. [producer/executive] (b. 1880–12 Nov 1938 [58?], Carmel NY). AMD, p. 347. BHD2, p. 268. Walkter K. Hill, "Showmanship-Plus Behind Drews," *MPW,* 18 Jan 1919, 319–20.

Van Buren, A[rchimedes] **H.** [actor/stage director] (b. Gloucester NJ, 9 Apr 1879–1 Aug 1965 [86], Los Angeles CA). m. Dorothy Bernard. (Lubin; Fox.) "A.H. Van Buren," *Variety,* 4 Aug 1965. AMD, p. 347. AS, p. 1096. BHD, p. 324; BHD2, p. 268. IFN, p. 301. SD, p. 1245 (Arthur H. Van Buren). "A.H. Van Buren," *MPW,* 2 Jan 1915, 82.

Van Buren, Mabel (mother of Kay Van Buren) [actress] (b. Chicago IL, 17 Jul 1878–4 Nov 1947 [69], Los Angeles CA; pneumonia). m. **Ernest C. Joy** (d. 1924); **James Gordon** (d. 1941). (Began 1914; DeMille.) "Mabel Van Buren," *Variety,* 12 Nov 1947. AMD, p. 347. AS, p. 1097. BHD1, p. 554. IFN, p. 301. Truitt, p. 333. "More Horsley Stars," *MPW,* 2 Oct 1915, 62. "Mabel Van Buren Engaged for Lasky Productions," *MPW,* 30 Sep 1916, 2118. "Mabel Van Buren," *MPW,* 10 Mar 1917, 1571. George Katchmer, "Remembering the Great Silents," *CI,* 242 (Aug 1995), 38.

Van Buren, Ned [cameraman] (b. Gouverneur NY, 27 Aug 1882–4 Apr 1969 [86], Los Angeles CA). AMD, p. 347. BHD2, p. 268. "Persons with DeLuxe Pictures," *MPW,* 5 Oct 1918, 73.

Vance, Clarice [actor] (b. Louisville KY, 14 Mar 1871–24 Aug 1961 [90], Napa CA). BHD, p. 324.

Vance, Louis Joseph [writer/scenarist] (b. Washington DC, 19 Sep 1879–16 Dec 1933 [54], New York NY; from inhalation of fumes from his clothing and arm chair apparently ignited by a smouldering cigarette when he fell asleep). m. Nance Elizabeth Hodges, 1898 (widow). "Vance, Author, Dies of Burns in Home; Writer of Adventure Stories Found in Blazing Arm Chair in 38th St. Apartment [at the Town House]; Dozed While Smoking; Robert W. Chambers, Also a Popular American Novelist, Succumbs in Hospital [age 68]," *NYT,* 17 Dec 1933, 1:4, 37:2. "Louis Joseph Vance," *Variety,* 19 Dec 1933 (age 43). AMD, p. 347. BHD2, p. 268 (b. 1890). FDY, p. 439. "Film Famous Authors; Vitagraph Company Prepares Novel Series for Authors' League Benefit," *NYDM,* 28 Jan 1914, 30:4. "Vance to Write New Universal Serial," *MPW,* 11 Jul 1914, 285. "Author Vance

Likes Picture Folk," *MPW,* 19 Sep 1914, 1650. "Vance Joins New Producing Combination [Ince]," *MPW,* 15 Jun 1918, 1559.

Vance, Mark W. [publicist]. No data found. AMD, p. 348. "Joins Publicity Staff," *MPW,* 15 Sep 1923, 235.

Vance, Virginia [actress] (*née* Dahlia Pears, b. 1902?–13 Oct 1942 [40], Los Angeles CA; heart attack). (Cameo Comedies.) AS, p. 1100. BHD1, p. 555. IFN, p. 301. Truitt, p. 333. Photo, *MW,* IV, 31 May 1924, 26.

Van Cortlandt, Jan [actor] (b. Holland, 1870–21 Jul 1928 [58], New York NY). AMD, p. 348. BHD, p. 324. IFN, p. 301 (age 68). "J. van Cortlandt," Blind, in Pictures," *MPW,* 17 Feb 1917, 1017. "Blind Actor in 'The Slacker,'" *MPW,* 7 Jul 1917, 106.

Van Court, De Witt [actor] (b. 1860–5 Oct 1937 [77?], Los Angeles CA). BHD, p. 324.

Vancura, Vladislav [director/scenarist] (b. Haje, Czechoslovakia, 1892–1942 [50?], Prague, Czechoslovakia; killed by Nazis). AS, p. 1100.

Van Daele, Edmond [actor] (*né* Edmond Jean Adolphe Minckwitz, b. Paris, France, 11 Aug 1884–12 Mar 1960 [75], Grez-Neuville, France). AS, p. 1097. Garth Pedler, "Sandra Milowanoff in 'Nene' (1924)," *CI,* 130 (Apr 1986), C3-C4.

Vandal, Marcel [director/producer] (b. Paris, France, 1 Mar 1882–1965 [83?], France). AMD, p. 348. AS, p. 1100. "Departure of Monsieur Vandal," *MPW,* 18 Feb 1911, 358.

van den Broek, John [cinematographer] (b. Rotterdam, Netherlands, 1895?–29 Jun 1918 [23], Schooner Head ME; drowned while filming *Woman,* 1918). *AFI Catalogue,* 1911–20, p. 1053. AMD, p. 348. AS, p. 1097. BHD2, p. 268 (d. Bar Harbor ME). "Obituary," *MPW,* 20 Jul 1918, 391.

Vanderbilt, Gertrude [stage/film actress] (b. 1899?–18 Feb 1960 [60], New York NY). m. (1) Joseph Pincus, 1917. "Gertrude Vanderbilt, 60, Dead; Former Ziegfeld Follies' Star," *NYT,* 19 Feb 1960, 27:1 (president of the Ziegfeld Alumni Association and of Show Folks, Inc.). "Gertrude Vanderbilt," *Variety,* 217, 24 Feb 1960, 111:1. AMD, p. 348. "Form Gertrude Vanderbilt Company," *MPW,* 31 May 1919, 1346.

Vanderbilt, William K. [executive]. No data found. AMD, p. 348. "William K. Vanderbilt Heads Film Company," *MPW,* 27 Jan 1917, 500.

Vandergrift, J. Monte [actor] (b. Pittsburgh PA, 12 Jan 1893–29 Jul 1939 [46], No. Hollywood CA; heart attack). AS, p. 1101.

van der Heyden, Jan [director] (b. Antwerp, Belgium, 10 Oct 1890–27 Mar 1961 [70]). AS, p. 1101. BHD2, p. 269.

Vanderveer, Ellinor [actress] (b. 5 Aug 1886–27 May 1976 [89], Loma Linda CA). (Roach; Sennett.) "Elinor, Vanderveer," *Variety,* 283, 9 Jun 1976, 77:4. AS, p. 1101. BHD1, p. 555. IFN, p. 301.

van der Veer, Willard [cameraman] (b. Brooklyn NY, 23 Aug 1894–16 Jun 1963 [68], Encino CA). AMD, p. 348. BHD2, p. 269. "Van der Veer Going to South America," *MPW,* 13 Jan 1917, 207. "Traveling Cameraman Get Thrills," *MPW,* 22 Sep 1917, 1832. "The Roll of Honor," *MPW,* 20 Oct 1917, 362.

Van Deusen, Cortland J. [director]. No data found. AMD, p. 348. "Van Deusen Internationalized," *MPW,* 27 May 1916, 1500.

Van Dommelen, Caroline [actress] (b. 1874–1957 [83?]). BHD, p. 324.

Van Dommelen, Jan [actor] (b. Amsterdam, Holland, 28 Apr 1878–26 Oct 1942 [64]). BHD1, p. 555.

Van Doren, Warren S. [studio manger] (b. 1867–5 May 1916 [49?], Bound Brook NJ). BHD2, p. 269.

Van Dorn, Mildred [actress] (b. New York NY, 10 Nov 1910). (*Fl.* 1929–31.) AS, p. 1097.

Van Duren, Ernest [actor/dancer] (b. Frane-d. 21 Jul 1930, Paris, France; overdose of barbituates). AS, p. 1097.

Van Dyke, Herbert [cinematographer] (b. 1895–24 Apr 1934 [39?], Los Angeles CA). BHD2, p. 269.

Van Dyke, Truman [actor] (b. Natchez MS, 15 Nov 1897–6 May 1984 [86], Los Angeles CA; heart attack). (Selig.) "Truman Van Dyke," *Variety,* 16 May 1984 ("His film career [was] brought to a halt by talking pictures due to his southern accent."). AS, p. 1098. BHD, p. 324.

Van Dyke, W.S. "Woody" [actor/scenarist/director/producer] (*né* Woodbridge Strong Van Dyke II, b. San Diego CA, 21 Mar 1889–5 Feb 1943 [53], Brentwood CA). m. Ruth Mannix. (Griffith, 1916; Essanay; MGM.) "W.S. Van Dyke Dies; Film Director, 53; Marine Corps Reserve Major Recently Had Completed 'Journey for Margaret'; Actor at Age of 7 Months; Produced 'Trader Horn,' 'Thin Man' and 'Naughty Marietta'—Once with D.W. Griffith," *NYT,* 6 Feb 1943, 13:1. "Director Van Dyke Dies After 6-Mo. Illness at 53," *Variety,* 10 Feb 1943. AMD, p. 348. AS, p. 1098. BHD, p. 324 (b. 1890); BHD2, p. 269 (b. 1887). FDY, p. 439. IFN, p. 301 (age 52). Katz, pp. 1184–85. "To Direct C.B.C. Series," *MPW,* 10 May 1924, 204. "Van Dyke Still with TIm McCoy," *MPW,* 23 Jul 1927, 257. John Roberts, "W.S. Van Dyke II," *CI,* 140 (Feb 1987), 15–16 (d. 6 Feb 1942). Henry R. Davis, "Additions & Deletions," *CI,* 141 (Mar 1987), 43.

Vane, Denton [stage/film actor] (b. Brooklyn NY, 1890?–17 Sep 1940 [50], Union Hill NJ; heart attack while walking on the street). (Selig; Kalem; Vitagraph, 1914.) "Denton Vane," *NYT,* 19 Sep 1940, 23:2 ("a former actor on the stage and silent screen"). AMD, p. 348. AS, p. 1101. BHD, p. 324 (b. 1886). IFN, p. 301. Truitt, p. 333. "Denton Vane," *MPW,* 10 Jun 1916, 1891.

Vane, Dorothy [actress] (b. England, 1871–4 Mar 1947 [75?]). BHD, p. 324.

Vane, Myrtle [actress] (b. 1870?–17 Feb 1932 [62], San Diego CA; paralytic stroke). m. Millar Bacon. "Myrtle Vane," *Variety,* 1 Mar 1932. AS, p. 1101. BHD1, p. 555 (b. 1868). IFN, p. 302. Ragan 2, p. 1742.

Vanel, Charles Marie [stage/film actor/director] (*né* Marie-Charles Vanel, b. Rennes, France, 21 Aug 1892–15 Apr 1989 [96], Cannes, France; heart attack [extrait de décès no. 466/1989]). m. Arlette Mauricette Bailly. "Charles Vanel, Stage and Screen Actor, 96," *NYT,* 16 Apr 1989, 36:3. Lenny Borger, "Charles Vanel, Esteemed Character Actor, Dead at 96; A Staple of 1930s Pix, His Career Spanned 75 Years. He Acted as Recently as 1987," *Variety,* 26 Apr 1989. AS, p. 1101. BHD1, p. 555 (d. 14 Apr). JS, p. 474. Katz, p. 1185 (began 1912). Waldman, p. 293.

Van Enger, Charles J. (brother of **Willard Van Enger**) [cameraman] (b. Port Jervis NJ, 29 Aug 1890–4 Jul 1980 [89], Woodland Hills CA). m. Gwendolyn. (Began 1911.) "Charles J. Van Enger," *Variety,* 16 Jul 1980. AS, p. 1098. BHD2, p. 269. FDY, p. 469.

Van Enger, Willard J. (brother of **Charles J. Van Enger**) [cameraman] (b. New York NY, 25 Oct 1901–22 Feb 1947 [45], Los Angeles CA). (WB.) "Willard Van Enger," *Variety,* 5 Mar 1947. AS, p. 1098. BHD2, p. 269.

Van Epps, John DeLacy [actor] (b. 1879–15 Sep 1960 [81?], Teaneck NJ). BHD, p. 324; BHD2, p. 269.

Van Every, Dale [scenarist/novelist] (b. MI, 23 Jul 1896–28 May 1976 [79], Santa Barbara CA). BHD2, p. 269.

Van Gasteren, Louis Augustaaf (father of director Louis Alphonse van Gasteren) [actor] (b. Rotterdam, Holland, 14 Nov 1887–9 Jul 1962 [74], Utrecht, Holland). AS, p. 1098.

Van Goitsenhoven, Louis [cameraman] (b. Brussels, Belgium, 1874–1942 [68?], France). AS, p. 1098.

Van Guysling, George E[dmund] [V.P. and General Manager, Biograph] (b. 1865?–24 Apr 1946 [81], Los Angeles CA; in sanitarium). "Edmund Van Guysling," *NYT,* 26 Apr 1946, 21:2 ("pioneer film camera man and former vice president and general manager of the old Biograph Film Company"). "George E. Van Guysling," *Variety,* 1 May 1946 ("credited with developing first practical motion picture camera in 1889"). AS, p. 1098.

Van Haden, Anders [actor/director/producer/scenarist] (b. New York NY, 1876–19 Jun 1936 [60?], Los Angeles CA; heart attack). AS, p. 1098. BHD1, p. 555; BHD2, p. 269.

Van Heusen, Dorothea [actress] (b. 1901–May 1989 [88?]). BHD, p. 324.

Van Horn, James "Jimmy" [actor] (b. SD, 24 Sep 1917–20 Apr 1966 [48], Los Angeles CA; internal hemorrhage). AS, p. 1099. BHD1, p. 555 (d. Pacoima CA). IFN, p. 301. Truitt, p. 333.

Van Horn, Maya [actress] (*née* Rose Menagé Challa, b. Amsterdam, Holland, 26 Dec 1896–8 Dec 1983 [86], Los Angeles CA). AS, p. 1099.

Vanin, Vasily Vasilyevich [actor/director] (b. Tambov, Ukraine, 13 Jan 1898–12 May 1951 [53], Moscow, Russia). AS, p. 1101.

Van Leer, Arnold [actor/pressagent] (b. London, England, 1894?–3 Jun 1975 [80], New England Medical Center, Boston MA). m. Follies girl Dorinda (son, Arnold, Jr., was killed in a car-train collision in 1972). "Arnold Van Leer," *Variety,* 279, 11 Jun 1975, 78:3 (extra in Chaplin films). AS, p. 1099. BHD, p. 324.

Van Loan, Charles E. [writer]. No data found. AMD, p. 348. "American Plans for Van Loan Series [*Buck Parvin*]," *MPW,* 25 Sep 1915, 2191.

Van Loan, H[arold] **H.** [publicist/scenarist/founder of the Stock Trend Service] (b. Athens NY, 1900?–7 Sep 1958 [58], W. Springfield MA). m. Marjorie O'Gorman (widow). "Harold H. Van Loan," *NYT,* 9 Sep 1958, 35:2 (does not cite film career). AMD, p. 348. BHD2, p. 269 (b. 1885). FDY, p. 439. "H.H. Van Loan," *MPW,* 6 Nov 1915, 1112. "Van Loan to Bradt," *MPW,* 11 Mar 1916, 1629. "H.H. Van Loan Leaves Universal," *MPW,* 21 Apr 1917, 416. "H.H. Van Loan, Screen Writer, Signs Contract with Universal," *MPW,* 16 Jan 1926, 236. "Van Loan Recovering," *MPW,* 14 Aug 1926, 5.

Van Loan, Philip [actor] (b. Amsterdam, Holland, 1884). BHD, p. 324.

Van Meter, Joseph [actor/director] (b. MO, 3 Aug 1876–22 Nov 1961 [85], Los Angeles CA). BHD2, p. 269.

Van Monkhoven, Désiré ["pionnier du cinéma belge"] (b. Gent, Belgium, 1834–25 Sep 1882 [48?], Belgium). AS, p. 1099.

Vann, Polly [actress] (*née* Polly Van Baley, b. Scranton PA, 29 Jul 1882–25 Aug 1952 [70], Los Angeles CA). AS, p. 1101. BHD1, p. 556.

Vann, W.T. [actor] (d. 15 Sep 1927). BHD, p. 324. IFN, p. 301.

Van Name, Elsie [actress/scenarist] (b. Staten Island NY, 1890?–4 Nov 1934 [44], Los Angeles CA). AS, p. 1099 (d. NY NY). BHD, p. 324; BHD2, p. 269. IFN, p. 301.

Van Ness, Frederick A. [publicist]. No data found. AMD, p. 348. "Van Ness Joins Goldwyn Pictures," *MPW,* 18 Aug 1917, 1076.

Van Pelt, Ernest [actor] (b. KS, 31 Mar 1883–1 Jul 1961 [78], Los Angeles CA). BHD1, p. 618; BHD2, p. 270.

Van Riel, Raimondo [actor] (b. Rome, Italy, 22 Jan 1881). m. actress Aidé Bongini, 1912 (b. 1887; stage name, Haydée), 1912. JS, p. 475 (in Italian silents from 1914).

Van Runkel, Sam [producer] (b. 1879–29 Nov 1951 [72?], Beverly Hills CA). AS, p. 1099.

Van (or **von**) **Schiller, Carl** [actor] (b. Columbus OH, 1891–15 Apr 1962 [70?], Los Angeles CA). m. **Ethel Brayton**. *Fl.* 1913. AS, p. 1100.

Van Sickle, Raymond [actor/playwright] (b. Frankfort IN, 1885?–10 Jul 1964 [79], Kobe, Japan; body found floating in Kobe harbor). (Fox.) (Stage debut: *The Fight,* NY NY, 1913, with Margaret Wycherly). "Raymond Van Sickle, Dramatist and Broadway Actor, 79, Dies," *NYT,* 11 Jul 1964, 25:1 ("screen writer for the Fox studio"). "Raymond Van Sickle," *Variety,* 22 Jul 1964. AS, p. 1100. BHD, p. 324; BHD2, p. 270.

Van Sloan, Edward Paul [actor] (b. San Francisco CA, 1 Nov 1881–8 Mar 1964 [82], San Francisco CA). (Last film: *Betty Co-Ed,* 1947; Universal.) "Edward Van Sloan," *Variety,* 8 Apr 1964. AS, p. 1100 (b. 1882-d. 6 Mar). BHD, p. 324 (b. 1882). IFN, p. 302. Blackie Seymour, "Edward Van Sloan: 'Nemesis of Evil,'" *CI,* 251 (May 1996), C-12-C13.

Van Tassell, Marie [actress] (b. Little Falls NY, 6 Apr 1873?–Jan 1946 [72], Oakland CA). (American.) AS, p. 1100 (b. 1874). BHD, p. 324 (b. 1874). IFN, p. 302.

Van Trees, James C[rawford] [cinematographer] (son of **Julia Crawford Ivers**) [cameraman] (*né* James Crawford Van Truys, b. CA, 13 Aug 1890–11 Apr 1973 [82], Los Angeles CA). m. June. "James C. Van Trees," *Variety,* 18 Apr 1973 (founder of the American Society of Cinematographers). AMD, p. 348. AS, p. 1100. BHD2, p. 270. FDY, p. 469. IFN, p. 302. "James C. Van Trees," *MPW,* 20 Nov 1926, 143.

Van Tress, Mabel [actress] (b. San Bernardino CA, 6 Oct 1872–16 Mar 1962 [89], Pasadena CA). AS, p. 1100 (d. LA CA). BHD, p. 324. IFN, p. 302.

Van Trump, Jessalyn [actress] (b. St. Johns OH, 16 Jan 1887–2 May 1939 [52], Los Angeles CA). (American.) "Jessalyn Van Trump," *Variety,* 10 May 1939 (age 44). AS, p. 1100. BHD, p. 324. BR, pp. 84–85. IFN, p. 302 (b. 1887). Truitt, p. 333 (b. 1885).

Van Tuyl, Helen Marr [actress] (b. IA, 4 Mar 1892–22 Aug 1964 [72], Los Angeles CA). AS, p. 1100.

Van Tuyle, Bert [actor/director] (b. NY, 11 Jan 1878–13 Jun 1951 [73], Los Angeles CA). AS, p. 1100. BHD2, p. 270.

Van Upp, Virginia [actress/scenarist/producer] (b. Chicago IL, 1902?–25 Mar 1970 [68], Los Angeles CA). (FBO; Paramount; Columbia.) "Virginia Van Upp," *Variety,* 15 Apr 1970. AS, p. 1100. BHD, p. 324; BHD2, p. 270. IFN, p. 302. Katz, p. 1187. Truitt, p. 334. "Miss Virginia Van Upp Is Student of Drama," *MPW,* 3 Nov 1923, 98:3 (age 22).

Van Vleck, William [actor] (b. San Antonio TX, 20 Jun 1886–19 May 1966 [79], Los Angeles Co. CA). BHD, p. 325. IFN, p. 302.

Vanzi, Pio [scenarist/director] (b. Florence, Italy, 9 Oct 1884–18 Oct 1957 [73], Palermo, Italy [extrait de décès no. N.2477–1/57]). AS, p. 1101. JS, p. 476 (in Italian silents from 1916).

Varconi, Victor [film/stage actor] (*né* Mihály Viktor Várkonyi, b. Kisvårda, Hungary, 31 Mar 1891–16 Jun 1976 [85], Santa Barbara CA; heart attack). m. light opera star Aronyosi Nusci, Budapest, Hungary, 1919. (Began 1913; Ufa; Paramount.) With Ed Honeck, *It's Not Enough to Be Hungarian* (Graphic Impressions, 1977). "Victor Varconi," *Variety,* 7 Jul 1976 (age 80). AMD, p. 348. AS, p. 1101. BHD1, p. 556. FSS, p. 280. IFN, p. 302. JS, p. 476 ("he was the first Hungarian movie star"; filmed in Germany, Austria, Italy and the U.S.A.). Katz, p. 1187 (began in Germany). Paul Paige, "Close-Ups and Fade-Outs," *Paris and Hollywood,* Sep 1926, 88–89 (married Nusci "with revolutions and counter-revolutions raging around them" in Budapest). "Varconi in Lead," *MPW,* 9 Jul 1927, 96. "Victor Varconi," *MPW,* 6 Aug 1927, 383. "Loses Accent, But Has to Recover It," *NY Journal,* 25 Jun 1936 ("Shed a tear for Victor Varconi. After studying in London for two years in an effort to lose his Hungarian accent and make a film 'comeback,' Varconi returned to Hollywood only to be cast in six consecutive foreign-accent roles.").

Vardannés, Emilio [actor/director] (aka Totò, *né* Émile Vardannès, b. Paris, France, 1868). (Itala [Turin]; Milano Film, 1912.) JS, p. 476 (in Italian silents from 1911).

Varden, Gladys [actress]. No data found. AMD, p. 348. "Gladys Varden," *MPW,* 20 Oct 1917, 392.

Varela, Nina [actress/singer] (*née* Alfonsina Varela Silva, b. Mexico City, Mexico, 16 Jan 1898–13 Feb 1982 [84], Los Angeles CA; cancer). AS, p. 1101.

Varennes, Jacques [actor] (*né* André Louis Henri Behue, b. Mantes-la-Jolie, France, 8 Nov 1894–6 Sep 1958 [63], Paris, France [extrait de décès no. 210/1958]). AS, p. 1101.

Varges, Ariel [cameramann]. No data found. AMD, p. 348. "Varges Is Official Photographer," *MPW,* 1 Jul 1916, 71.

Varian, Dorothy [artist]. No data found. AMD, p. 348. "Miss Varian Wins Fox Art Prizes," *MPW,* 27 Jan 1917, 524.

Varley, Beatrice [actress] (b. Manchester, England, 11 Jul 1896–4 Jul 1964 [67], England). AS, p. 1102.

Varna, Henri [actor] (*né* Henri Vantard, b. Marseilles, France, 1888–2 Apr 1969 [81?], Paris, France; heart attack). AS, p. 1102.

Varnel, Marcel [director] (b. Paris, France, 16 Oct 1894–13 Jul 1947 [52], London, England). AS, p. 1102. BHD2, p. 270.

Varney, Arthur [title writer]. No data found. FDY, p. 447.

Varvaro, Gloria [actress] (b. 1915–9 Apr 1976 [61?], New York NY). BHD1, p. 557.

Vas, Steven [scenarist] (b. Budapest, Hungray, 31 Oct 1894–2 Jun 1967 [72], New York NY; emphysema). AS, p. 1102. BHD2, p. 270.

Vaser, Ernesto (son of stage actor Pietro Vaser, d. 1898; brother of **Vittorio Vaser** and stage actor Ercole Vaser) [actor] (aka Fricot and Fringuelli, b. Turin, Italy, 31 Mar 1876 [extrait de naissance no. 895/1875]–23 Nov 1934 [58], Turin, Italy [extrait de décès no. 1732/1934]). (Ambrosio, 1909.) AS, p. 1102. BHD, p. 325. JS, pp. 477–78 (in Italian silents from 1905).

Vaser, Vittorio (son of **Ernesto Vaser**) [actor] (b. Turin, Italy, 12 Jun 1904–30 Oct 1963 [59], Rome, Italy). JS, p. 478 (in Italian silents in 1929).

Vass, Lulu [actress] (b. 1876–6 May 1952 [76?], Haverstraw NY). AS, p. 1102.

Vassallo, Orlando [director] (*né* Giovanni Orlando Vassalio, b. Italy, 1881–17 Jan 1960 [78?], Rome, Italy). AS, p. 1102. JS, p. 478 (in Italian silents from 1914).

Vassar, Queenie [actress] (b. Glasgow, Scotland, 28 Oct 1870–11 Sep 1960 [89], Los Angeles CA). AS, p. 1102.

Vaughan, Dorothy [actress] (b. St. Louis MO, 5 Nov 1889–15 Mar 1955 [65], Los Angeles CA; cerebral hemorrhage). AS, p. 1103.

Vaughan, William H. [assistant director] (b. Norfolk VA, 1869). BHD2, p. 270.

Vaughn, Adamae (sister of **Alberta Vaughn**) [actress: Wampas Star, 1927] (b. Ashland KY, 8 Nov 1905–11 Sep 1943 [37], Los Angeles CA). m. Mr. Hindman, May 1926—div. Sep 1926; rem. Nov 1927. AMD, p. 348. AS, p. 1103. BHD1, p. 557. IFN, p. 302. Truitt, p. 324. "Adamae Vaughn Signs," *MPW,* 20 Feb 1926, 713. James F. Taggart, "Rebuilding Noses for the Screen," *Paris and Hollywood Screen Secrets,* Oct 1927, 41–43 (photos on p. 42 show her before and after getting a rebuilt nose). "Adamae Vaughn to Remarry Hindman," *MPW,* 22 Oct 1927, 498.

Vaughn, Alberta (sister of **Adamae Vaughn**) [actress: Sennett Bathing Beauty/Wampas Star, 1924] (b. Ashland KY, 27 Jun 1904–26 Apr 1992 [87], Studio City CA). (Sennett; FBO; *The Telephone Girl* series; first feature, *Collegiate.*) AS, p. 1103 (b. 1907). BHD1, p. 557. FFF, p. 155. FSS, p. 281. MH, p. 140 (b. 1906). James M. Fidler, "The Pictures That Startled Hollywood; New and rare combination of art and photography coupled with the winsome charms of Miss Alberta Vaughn make blase Hollywooders sit up and take notice," *MW,* 3 May 1924, 15 [Persian artist John Oshanna used painting and photography to photograph Vaughn). Paula Gould, "Alberta Looks Into the Looking Glass; Alberta Vaughn looks at her screen self and refutes the contention that screen stars are vain and self-satisfied," *Cinema Arts,* Aug 1926, 19–45. Harry Carr, "Dining with George [O'Hara] and Alberta," *MPC,* Dec 1924, 34–35, 80. "Alberta Vaughn Signed for Leads by Schulberg," *MPW,* 13 Dec 1924, 654.

"Questions and Answers," *Photoplay*, Sep 1926, 91. Paula Gould, "Alberta Vaughn, Movie's Demurest Wise Cracker," *Paris and Hollywood*, Oct 1926, 47–48, 78 ("started in pictures three years ago when she was barely sixteen years old.... 'But tell the fans that I never, never chew gum off the set, unless, of course, I've eaten onions.'").

Vaughn, Evelyn [actress]. No data found. m. **Bert Lytell**—div. MO (d. 1954).

Vaughn, Patricia [actress] (b. Indianapolis IN, 10 Nov 1846–8 Jun 1911 [64], Los Angeles CA). AS, p. 1103.

Vaughn, Paula [actress] (b. Indianapolis IN, 26 May 1846–23 Apr 1905 [58], Los Angeles CA). AS, p. 1103.

Vaughn, Robert [actor] (b. St. Louis MO, 1877). AMD, p. 348. BHD, p. 325. "Robert Vaughn," *MPW*, 27 Jan 1917, 510.

Vaughn, Vivian (Gypsy Gould) [actress] (b. 1902–1 Feb 1966 [64], Los Angeles CA). (Edison.) "Gypsy Gould [Vivian Vaughn]," *Variety*, 9 Feb 1966. AS, p. 463 (Gypsy Gould). BHD1, p. 223 (Gypsy Gould). IFN, p. 302. Spehr, p. 172. Truitt, p. 324.

Vaultier, Georges [actor] (*né* Georges Wesbecher, b. Paris, France, 1885–26 Mar 1926 [41?], Paris, France). AS, p. 1103. BHD, p. 325.

Vautier, Elmira [actress] (*née* Armandine Elmire Vutier, b. Granchain, France, 28 Aug 1897–19 Apr 1954 [56], Livilliers, France [extraot de décès no. 4/CA23095/1954]). m. actor Jacques Eyser (Jacques Henri Louis Eysermann, b. 1912). AS, p. 1103. Rene de la Seine, "Moviettes from Gay Paree," *Paris and Hollywood Screen Secrets Magazine*, Aug 1927, 66 (Elmira Vautres, photo).

Vavasseur, Theodore [cinematographer] (d. Jul 1925, Messac, France). BHD2, p. 270.

Vaverka, Anton [actor] (b. Prague, Czechoslovakia-d. 2 Jul 1937, Prague, Czechoslovakia). (MGM.) AS, p. 1103. BHD1, p. 557. IFN, p. 302. Truitt, p. 334.

Vavitch, Michael [actor/singer] (*né* Mikhael Vavitch, b. Odessa, Russia, 1876–5 Oct 1930 [54], Los Angeles CA; heart attack in car). (Film debut: *The Swan*, Para.; MGM.) "Michael Vavitch Dies at Car's Wheel in L.A.," *Variety*, 8 Oct 1930. AS, p. 1103. BHD1, p. 557. IFN, p. 302.

Vecla, Emma [opera singer/actress] (*née* Adrienne Talmat, b. Oran, Algeria, Dec 1884). JS, p. 479 (in Italian silents from 1913; retired in Milan in 1929).

Vedder, William H. [actor] (b. OH, 9 Sep 1873–3 Mar 1961 [87], Los Angeles CA). AS, p. 1104.

Veeranna, G[ubbi] H. [actor/producer] (b. Gubbi, India, 1890). AS, p. 1104.

Vegeres, Joe [actor] (*né* Joseph Vegeres, b. Belgium, 1895–31 Mar 1977 [82?], Antwerp, Belgium). AS, p. 1104.

Veidt, Conrad [actor/director/producer] (b. Potsdam [Berlin], Germany, 22 Jan 1893–3 Apr 1943 [50], Los Angeles CA; heart attack while golfing). m. Lily. "Conrad Veidt Dies; Veteran Actor, 50; Stage and Screen Performer Stricken While Playing Golf on Course in Hollywood; Was Seen in 'Casablanca'; Born in Berlin, Later Became British Subject—Once Pupil of Max Reinhardt," *NYT*, 4 Apr 1943, 40:3. "Conrad Veidt," *Variety*, 7 Apr 1943. AMD, p. 348. AS, p. 1104. BHD1, p. 557. FSS, p. 281. IFN, p. 302. Katz, p. 1189 (began in Germany, 1917). Truitt, p. 334. Waldman, p. 293. "Veidt Arrives in Hollywood," *MPW*, 16 Oct 1926, 440. Charles Edward Hastings, "The Dreams of Conrad Veidt," *MPW*, 12 Feb 1927, 480, 484. Alexander Johns, "The True Story of the Emil Jannings Triangle," *Paris and Hollywood Screen Secrets Magazine*, May 1927, 34–37 (states that Jannings married Gussie Holl after Veidt divorced her). Charles Paton, "Conrad in Quest of His Art; The Star of 'Caligari' Pleads for the Universal Message of the Screen," *MPC*, Jul 1927, 48–49, 80. "Veidt's FIrst for U," *MPW*, 16 Jul 1927, 155. "German Star Makes First Location Trip," *MPW*, 30 Jul 1927, 334. Vittorio Martinelli, "Kino-Lieblinge," *Griffithiana*, 38/39 (Oct 1990), 70.

Veiller, Bayard [playwright/scenarist/director/producer] (b. Brooklyn NY, 2 Jan 1869–16 Jun 1943 [74], New York NY). m. (1) **Margaret Wycherly**, 1901 (d. 1956); (2) Martin Vale (pseudonym), 1922 (widow). *The Fun I've Had* (1941). "Bayard Veiller, Writer of Plays; Author of 'Within the Law' and 'Trial of Mary Dugan' Is Dead Here at 74; Wrote 'Thirteenth Chair'; Created Many Movie Scripts—Was Reporter on World, Managed Stock Company," *NYT*, 17 Jun 1943, 21:3. "$100 Wkly. for N.Y. Co., $50 for Each Road Unit Paid Veiller for 'Within,'" *Variety*, 23 Jun 1943. AMD, p. 349. AS, p. 1104. BHD2, p. 270. IFN, p. 303. SD, p. 1251. "Bayard Veiller Writes for Universal," *MPW*, 1 Mar 1919, 1206. "Bayard Veiller, Playwright, Decries Methods Pursued in Exploitation of Motion Pictures," *MPW*, 23 Aug 1919, 1126. "Bayard Veiller Writes for Ince," *MPW*, 17 Jan 1920, 397. "Veiller Signs with Metro," *MPW*, 6 Mar 1920, 1662. "Walter, Veiller and Smith, Prominent Dramatists, Turn Talents to Metro Screen," *MPW*, 24 Apr 1920, 557. Edward Weitzel, "Bayard Veiller Takes Part in Metro Two and Half Million Shopping Tour," *MPW*, 22 May 1920, 1061. "Bayard Veiller, Metro Production Chief, Sidetracks Traditions for Big Results," *MPW*, 10 Jul 1920, 220. "Name or Fame Counts Not at All with Bayard Veiller in Choosing Vehicles," *MPW*, 2 Oct 1920, 670. Bayard Veiller, "Films Cannot Do Without Good Titles; Some Day Pictures May Illustrate Text," *MPW*, 16 Oct 1920, 925. "Bayard Veiller in New York to Confer with Rowland and Purchase New Stories," *MPW*, 13 Nov 1920, 223. Sumner Smith, "Bayard Veiller Says Broadway 'Rep' of Stage Play Is Valueless to Pictures," *MPW*, 20 Nov 1920, 317. "Bayard Veiller Says Business of Picture Making Is Progressing to a Higher Plane," *MPW*, 12 Mar 1921, 189. "With Cosmopolitan," *MPW*, 20 Jan 1923, 218.

Vejar, Harry J. [actor] (b. Los Angeles CA, 24 Apr 1889–1 Mar 1968 [78], Los Angeles CA). AS, p. 1104 (b. 24 Aug). BHD1, p. 557 (d. Sawtelle CA). IFN, p. 303. Truitt, p. 334 (b. 1890).

Vekroff, Perry N. [actor/director/scenarist] (b. Alexandria, Egypt, 3 Jun 1880–4 Jan 1937 [56], Los Angeles CA; heart attack). (Metro.) AMD, p. 349. AS, p. 1104. BHD, p. 325; BHD2, p. 270. IFN, p. 303. "World Engages Vekroff to Direct Miss Castleton," *MPW*, 24 Aug 1918, 1138. "Vekroff to Direct 'Dust of Desire,'" *MPW*, 7 Jun 1919, 1505.

Velez, Elvira [actress] (*née* Alvira de Sales Velez Pereira, b. Lisbon, Portugal, 19 Nov 1892–8 Apr 1981 [88], Lisbon, Portugal). AS, p. 1104.

Velez, Lupe, "The Mexican Spitfire" [actress: Wampas Star, 1928] (*née* Maria Guadaloupe Velez de Villalobos, b. San Luis de Potosi, Mexico, 18 Jul 1908–14 Dec 1944 [36], Beverly Hills CA; suicide from overdose of sleeping tablets). m. Johnny Weissmuller [1904–84], 8 Oct 1933, Las Vegas NV—div. 15 Aug 1938, LA CA. Floyd Conner, *Lupe Velez and Her Lovers* (NY: Barricade Books, Inc., 1993. (Mexican shorts; American film debut: *What Women Did for Me*, Roach, Aug 1927; Griffith; first talkie: *The Gaucho*, 1927.) "Lupe Velez Suicide by Sleep Tablets; 'Tempestuous' Actress Was Depressed by Failure of Romance with French Actor [Harald Ramond]," *NYT*, 15 Dec 1944, 36:2; "Estate Put at $100,000 to $200,000," 36:3 (b. 1909). "Lupe Velez," *Variety*, 20 Dec 1944. AMD, p. 349. AS, p. 1104. BHD1, p. 558 (b. 1909). FSS, p. 282. HCH, p. 49. IFN, p. 303 (b. 1910). Katz, pp. 1189–90 (began 1926). Truitt, p. 335 (b. 1908). "Touch Luck, Indeed," *MPW*, 19 Mar 1927, 180. "Fairbanks' Lead in Comedy," *MPW*, 6 Aug 1927, 399. "Lupe Velez Sued by F.A. Woodyard," *MPW*, 12 Nov 1927, 19. Margaret Reid, "Goudal and Velez Fight to Draw; All of Jetta's Generalship Needed to Withstand Lupe's Tearing Attack," *MPC*, Dec 1928, 58, 78. Ruth Biery, "Don't You Dare Marry; Because Everyone's Said That to Gary Cooper and Lupe Velez, Is Why They Don't," *MPC*, Jul 1929, 22, 80. Nancy Pryor, "Lupe Velez' Own Story of Her Break with Gary Cooper," *Movie Classic*, I, Nov 1931, 60–61, 69. Eve Golden, "Mexican Spitfire: The Too-Brief Life of Lupe Velez," *CI*, 226 (Apr 1994), 34–36 (b. 1909).

Veloise, Harry [actor] (b. 1877–16 Jan 1936 [59], Oklahoma City OK). BHD, p. 325. IFN, p. 303.

Veness, Amy [actress] (b. Aldeburgh, England, 26 Feb 1876–22 Sep 1960 [84], Saltdean, Sussex, England). m. Basil Springer. "Amy Veness," *Variety*, 26 Oct 1960. AS, p. 1105. BHD1, p. 558. IFN, p. 303. Truitt, p. 335. *Winchester World Film Encyclopedia*, p. 123.

Veneziano, Carlo [writer] (b. Leporano, near Taranto, Italy, 12 Jun 1882–17 Jan 1950 [67], Milan, Italy). JS, p.479 (in Italian silents from 1913).

Veniat, Jeanne [actress] (b. Buenos Aires, Argentina, 1890). AS, p. 1105.

Venning, Una [actress] (b. Bedford, England, 12 Nov 1893–9 Mar 1985 [91]). BHD1, p. 558.

Venson, Florence [actress] (b. 1896–30 Oct 1964 [68?], Los Angeles CA). BHD1, p. 558.

Ventura, Marie [actress] (b. Bucharest, Rumania, 13 Jul 1890–1954 [64?], France). AS, p. 1105.

Venturini, Edward D. [director] (b. NJ, 27 Apr 1888–15 Jan 1960 [71], Los Angeles CA). BHD2, p. 270.

Venturini, Giordano [actor/producer] (b. Italy, 1906–15 Mar 1984 [78?], Rome, Italy). AMD, p. 349. AS, p. 1105. "Valentino Double?," *MPW*, 11 Dec 1926, 4.

Venuti, Joe [actor/composer] (*né* Giuseppe Venuti, b. Malgrate de Lecco, Italy, 16 Sep 1894–14 Nov 1978 [84], Seattle WA). AS, p. 1105.

Vercel, Roger [actor/scenarist] (*né* Roger Delphin Auguste Cretin, Le Mans, France, 8 Jan 1894 [extrit de naissance no. 28/1894]-26 Feb 1957 [63], Dinan, France). AS, p. 1105.

Verdet-Kleber, André [producer] (*né* Emile André Verdet-Kleber, b. Sorgues, France, 29 Aug 1899 [extrait de naissance no. 60/1899]). AS, p. 1105.

Verdi, Joe [actor] (*né* Joseph Verdi, 1885–27 Dec 1957 [72], New York NY). AS, p. 1105.

Vergani, Orio (brother of **Vera Vergani;** nephew of Vittorio Podrecca) [scenarist] (b. Milan, Italy, 6 Feb 1899–6 Apr 1960 [61], Milan, Italy). JS, p. 481 (in Italian silents from 1923).

Vergani, Vera (sister of **Orio Vergani**; niece of Vittorio Podrecca) [actress] (aka Vera Podrecca, b. Milan, Italy, 6 Feb 1894). AS, p. 1106 (b. 19 Feb). JS, p. 481 (in Italian silents from 1916).

Vergano, Aldo [scenarist/director] (b. Rome, Italy, 27 Aug 1891–21 Sep 1957 [65], Rome, Italy). AS, p. 1106 (b. 1894). BHD2, p. 271. JS, p. 481 (in Italian silents from 1929).

Verhalen, C.J. [publicist]. No data found. AMD, p. 349. "Verhalen with Paramount," *MPW,* 2 Sep 1916, 1518.

Verhylle, Armand [journalist/scenarist] (*né* Armand du Bouchet-Verhylle, b. Paris, France, 5 Apr 1881). AS, p. 1105.

Verina, Winifred [actress/ballet dancer]. No data found. AMD, p. 349. "Winifred Verina Wins Place in Pathé Serials," *MPW,* 25 Feb 1922, 817.

Verly, Michèle [actress] (*née* Michèle Armande Houillon, b. Paris, France, 19 Jul 1909–3 Mar 1952 [42], Nice, France). AS, p. 1105. BHD, p. 325 (b. 1911).

Vermilyea, Harold [stage/film actor] (b. New York NY, 10 Oct 1889–8 Jan 1958 [68], New York NY [Death Certificate Index No. 601; M.E. Case No. 262]). "Harold Vermilyea, Actor, Dies at 68; Appeared in 32 Plays on Broadway," *NYT,* 9 Jan 1958, 33:2. "Harold Vermilyea," *Variety,* 15 Jan 1958. AS, p. 1106. BHD1, p. 558. IFN, p. 303.

Vermoyal, Paul [actor] (b. France, 1888–14 Nov 1925 [37?], Neuilly-sur-Seine, France). "Deaths Abroad; Paul Vermoyal," *Variety,* 21 Oct 1925, 53:3. AS, p. 1106. BHD, p. 325. IFN, p. 303.

Verner, Charles [journalist/stage/film actor/writer] (*né* Charles Vernon?, b. Melbourne, Australia?, 1848–19 Mar 1926 [78], Boston MA; found dead in bed at the Hotel McAlpin). "Charles Verner," *Variety,* 24 Mar 1926, 47:4. BHD, p. 325.

Verneuil, Louis [scenarist] (*né* Louis Jacques Marie Collin du Bocage, b. Paris, France, 14 May 1893–3 Nov 1952 [59], Paris, France; suicide). AS, p. 1107. BHD2, p. 270.

Vernon, Agnes "Brownie" [actress]. No data found. (Nestor; Bluebird.) AMD, p. 349. "Turns Down Cupid for Thespis," *MPW,* 10 Apr 1915, 238. "Agnes Vernon in 'Big U' Company," *MPW,* 4 Sep 1915, 1651. "Agnes Vernon Drops Something," 21 Apr 1917, 434 (dropped Agnes in favor of Brownie). "Brownie Vernon," *MPW,* 19 May 1917, 1102. Edgar M. Wyatt, "Snowy Baker Galloped Across the Silver Screen Down Under," *CI,* 199 (Jan 1992), 34 (in the Australian films of Snowy Baker). George Katchmer, "Remembering the Great Silents," *CI,* 246 (Dec 1995), 49.

Vernon, Bobby (son of Harry Burns and **Dorothy Vernon**) [actor] (*né* Silvion des Jardiens, b. Chicago IL, 9 Mar 1897–28 Jun 1939 [42], Los Angeles CA; heart attack). m. Angie Repetto, 1918. (Universal; Triangle; Christie.) "Bobby Vernon, Actor of Silent Screen; Comedian Was Early Exponent of Slapstick Productions," *NYT,* 29 Jun 1939, 23:6. "Bobby Vernon," *Variety,* 5 Jul 1939. AMD, p. 349. AS, p. 1107. BHD1, p. 559. FFF, p. 218. IFN, p. 303 (age 42). Katz, p. 1191. MH, p. 141. WWS, p. 312. Truitt, p. 335 (b. 1897). 1921 Directory, p. 205 (b. 1897). "Vernon Playing with Christie," *MPW,* 22 Dec 1917, 1787. "Christie Signs Bobby Vernon to Continue in Comedy Roles," *MPW,* 8 May 1920, 848. "Stork Favors Stars," *MPW,* 3 Dec 1921, 566 (daughter b. 13 Nov 1921). "Bobby Vernon Luncheon," *MPW,* 2 May 1925, 28. "Insure Comedians," *MPW,* 13 Nov 1926, 4 (for $500,000). "Bobby Vernon," *MPW,* 29 Nov 1926, 275. Dorothy Lubou, "Grinding Out Grins; Bobby Vernon Cannot See Himself as an Artist," *MPC,* May 1929, 65, 82 (cites age as 33).

Vernon, Dorothy (mother of **Bobby Vernon**) [actress] (aka Dorothy Baird and Dorothy Burns, b. Germany, 11 Nov 1875–28 Oct 1970 [94], Granada Hills CA; heart attack). m. J.B. Irving (d. 1919); **John Christian** (d. 1950); **Harry Burns** (d. 1939). AS, p. 1107. BHD1, p. 559. IFN, p. 303. George Katchmer, "Remembering the Great Silents," *CI,* 215 (May 1993), 49; *CI,* 249 (Mar 1996), 48.

Vernon, G.L.P. [executive]. No data found. AMD, p. 349. George Blaisdell, "Mr. Vernon Goes Abroad," *MPW,* 28 Mar 1914, 1669. "G.L.P. Vernon in Big Deal," *MPW,* 11 Jul 1914, 273.

Vernon, Harry [scenarist] (b. 1880–11 Nov 1942 [62?], Woodland Hills CA). AS, p. 1107. BHD2, p. 271.

Vernon, Hedda [German actress]. No data found. Vittorio Martinelli, "Kino-Lieblinge," *Griffithiana,* 38/39 (Oct 1990), 37.

Vernon, Isabel [actress] (b. 1874?–21 Apr 1930 [56], New York NY). m. Henry Waterman. "Isabel Vernon," *Variety,* 30 Apr 1930. AS, p. 1107. BHD, p. 325. IFN, p. 303.

Vernon, Lou [actor/singer] (b. Australia, 1888–22 Dec 1971 [83?], Sydney, Australia). AS, p. 1107.

Vernon, Percy [actor] (b. Kettering, England, 29 Dec 1857–25 Dec 1926 [68], London, England). BHD, p. 325.

Vernon, Suzy [actress] (*née* Appollinie Paris, b. Perpignan, France, 26 Jun 1900–24 Jan 1997 [96], Mougins, France [extrait de décès no. 0027/1997]). (Joinville; 1st National.) AS, p. 1107 (b. 1901). BHD1, p. 618. Tulard, *Dictionnaire du cinema,* p. 941. Waldman, p. 296.

Vernot, Henry J. [scenarist/actor/director] (b. France, 1874–17 Jul 1928 [54?], New York NY). (Gaumont, 1910; Pathé; Eclectic.) "Gossip of the Studios; Henry Vernot," *NYDM,* 2 Sep 1914, 27:1. AMD, p. 349. BHD2, p. 271. "Henry J. Vernot," *MPW,* 15 Aug 1914, 971. "Vernot Becomes Gaumont Director," *MPW,* 25 Dec 1915, 2334.

Veronina, Vera [actress]. No data found. AMD, p. 349. "Russian Star in Paramount Group," *MPW,* 18 Dec 1926, 495.

Verschleiser, Ben [producer] (b. NY, 1888?–4 Apr 1936 [48], Los Angeles CA; after an operation). (Began 1920.) "Ben Verschleiser," *Variety,* 8 Apr 1936. AS, p. 1108. BHD2, p. 271.

Vertoz, Dziga [director] (*né* Denis Arkadievich Kaufman, b. Bialystok, Russia, 2 Jan 1896–12 Feb 1954 [58], Moscow, Russia; cancer). AS, p. 1108 (Vertov)). BHD2, p. 271.

Vespermann, Kurt [stage/film actor] (b. Kulmsee, West Prussia, 1 May 1887–13 Jul 1957 [70], Berlin, Germany; heart disease). m. actress Lia Elbenschuetz (son, Gert Vespermann, b. 24 Jul 1926). "Kurt Vespermann," *Variety,* 207, 24 Jul 1957, 79:2. AS, p. 1108. BHD1, p. 559 (b. Chelmza, Poland). IFN, p. 303.

Vessiliadou, Georgia [actress] (b. Greece, 1896–12 Feb 1980 [83?], Athens, Greece). AS, p. 1108.

Veyre, Gabriel Antoine [director] (aka Gabriel Vayre, b. Septème, near Lyons, France, 1 Feb 1871 [extrait de naissance no. 3]-13 January 1936 [64], Casablanca, Morocco). (Directed films in Mexico.) AS, p. 1108.

Vialar, Paul Marie Ernest [author/scenarist] (b. Saint-Denis, France, 18 Sep 1898 [extrait de naissance no. 1129]). AS, p. 1108.

Viarisio, Enrico Luigi Eugenio [actor] (b. Turin, Italy, 3 Dec 1897 [extrait de naissance no. 3091/2.1]-1 Nov 1967 [69], Rome, Italy). AS, p. 1108.

Vibart, Henry [actor] (b. Musselburgh, Scotland, 25 Dec 1863–1939 [76], England). AS, p. 1108. BHD1, p. 559. IFN, p. 303.

Vibert, François [actor] (*né* Henri François Pierre Vibert, b. Lyon, France, 7 Sep 1891 [extrait de naissance no. 453]-23 May 1978 [86], Montreuil, France). AS, p. 1108.

Vibert, Marcel Etienne [actor] (b. Paris, France, 2 Nov 1883 [extrait de naissance no. 3423]-11 Jun 1959 [75], Paris, France). AS, p. 1108.

Victor, Alexander F. [executive] (b. Bollnas, no. Sweden, 20 Jun 1878–30 Mar 1961 [82]). David H. Shepard, "The Victor Animatograph Company and the Genesis of Non-Theatrical Film, Part I," *CFC,* 50 (Spring, 1976), 8 *et passim* [operated in Davenport IA from April 1910 to May 1956]; II, 51 (Summer, 1976), 37–41. The papers of The Victor Animatograph Company are with the Manuscripts Librarian at the State University of Iowa.

Victor, Charles [actor] (*né* Charles Victor Harvey, b. Southport, England, 10 Feb 1896–23 Dec 1965 [69], London, England). AS, p. 1109.

Victor, Henry [actor] (b. London, England, 2 Oct 1892–15 May 1945 [52], Los Angeles CA). "Henry Victor," *Variety,* 23 May 1945 (age 53). AS, p. 1109. BHD1, p. 559. IFN, p. 303. Katz, p. 1193 (b. 1898; began in England). Truitt, p. 335 (b. 1898).

Victor Emmanuel III [actor] (b. Naples, Italy, 11 Nov 1869–28 Dec 1947 [78], Alexandria, Egypt). BHD, p. 325.

Victoria, Vesta (daughter of variety performer Joe Lawrence, who stood on his head, thus known as "the upside-down comedian") [music hall singing comedienne/film actress] (*née* Vesta Lawrence?, b. Leeds, Yorkshire, England, 26 Nov 1873–7 Apr 1951 [77], London, England). m. Herbert Terry, 1912 (son of Edward Terry)—div. 1926. "Vesta Victoria, 77, Variety Star, Dies; Vaudeville Headliner Here and in England Had Introduced Many Popular Songs," *NYT,* 8 Apr 1951, 92:1 ("In 1935, at the Motion Picture Club, 1569 Broadway, a group of older vaudeville performers, and other theatrical figures, gave a luncheon in Vesta Victoria's honor, at which many of the speeches discussed the sad subject of the popularity of vaudeville before motion pictures."). "Vesta Victoria," *Variety,* 182, 11 Apr 1951, 56:3 (acclaimed for singing *Daddy Wouldn't Buy Me a Bow Wow, Waiting at the Church, Poor John,* and *It's All Right in the Summer Time*). BHD1, p. 559.

Vidali, Emilia (daughter of **Enrico Vidali**; sister of Maria Gandini) [actress]. No data found. JS, p. 485 (in Italian silents from 1913).

Vidali, Enrico (father of **Emilia Vidali** and Maria Gandini) [director/actor] (*né* Gianni Enrico Vidali Novelli, b. 1869–3 Jul 1937 [67?], Rome, Italy). AS, p. 1109. JS, p. 485 (in Italian silents from 1908).

Vidor, Charles [director/scenarist] (b. Budapest, Hungary, 27 Jul 1900–4 Jun 1959 [58], Vienna, Austria; heart attack). m. Karen Morley, 1932–43; Doris Warner Leroy, 1945 (widow). (UFA; MGM.) "Charles Vidor, 58, Director, Is Dead; His Films Include 'The Swan,' 'Hans Christian Anderson'—Stricken in Vienna," *NYT,* 5 Jun 1959, 27:1 (began in Berlin studios; was to have directed *The Magic Flame*). "Vidor Rites Tomorrow," *NYT,* 10 Jun 1959, 37:3 (Jack Benny delivered the eulogy). "Charles Vidor," *Variety,* 10 Jun 1959. AS, p. 1109. BHD2, p. 271. IFN, p. 304. Katz, p. 1194.

Vidor, Florence [actress] (*née* Florence Arto [Cobb?], b. Houston TX, 23 Jul 1895–3 Nov 1977 [82], Pacific Palisades CA). m. **King Vidor**, 21 Sep 1915—div. 1925 (d. 1982; daughter Suzanne); Jascha Heifetz [*né* Keifetz], 1928—div. 1946 (Josepha and Robert). (Vitagraph; FP-L.) "Florence Vidor, 82, A Silent-Film Star, Is Dead on Coast," *NYT,* 6 Nov 1977, 44:1. "Florence Vidor," *Variety,* 9 Nov 1977. (Introduced to Hollywood by Corinne Griffith; Vitagraph; Paramount.) AMD, p. 349. AS, p. 1109. BHD1, p. 560. FFF, p. 92. FSS, p. 282. IFN, p. 304. Katz, p. 1194 (*née* Cobb; Arto from stepfather). MH, p. 141. "Pallas Engages Florence Vidor," *MPW,* 5 Aug 1916, 920. "Florence Vidor," *MPW,* 29 Dec 1917, 1933. Olive Carew, "Fame via Matrimony," *MPC,* Feb 1919, 41–42, 74. "Ince to Star Florence Vidor," *MPW,* 2 Oct 1920, 661. "Florence Vidor to Do Specials for the Associated Exhibitors," *MPW,* 28 May 1921, 417. "Florence Vidor Is Now a Star; Makes Her Debut in Associated Exhibitors' 'Woman, Wake Up,'" *MPW,* 11 Mar 1922, 167. "Florence Vidor Engaged by Warner," *MPW,* 13 Jan 1923, 174. Maude Cheatham, "A Lyric Poem," *Classic,* Apr 1923, 22–23, 84–85. "Florence Vidor," *MPW,* 12 Jul 1924, insert. "Florence Vidor Signed for Long Term Contract by Ince," *MPW,* 4 Oct 1924, 383. "Florence Vidor Signed," *MPW,* 24 Jan 1925, 371. Elisabeth Greer, "More Than a Lady," *MW,* 5 Sep 1925, 13–14. "Florence Vidor Now Starring for Paramount," *MPW,* 10 Apr 1926, 429. Alice L. Tildesley, "She Reached for the Moon and Got It!," *MPC,* Jul 1926, 32–33, 68 ("I believe Mr. Vidor and I were attracted to each other because we both loved pictures."). Paul Paige, "Close-Ups and Fade-Outs," *Paris and Hollywood,* Sep 1926, 89 (objected to a certain young leading man at Paramount; put into another production to be filmed in New York, to which she objected; and finally cast in a third film, "only to find that she had again drawn the leading man she dislikes."). "Illness Delays Film," *MPW,* 27 Nov 1926, 2. Dorothy Calhoun, "Haughty! Haughty!; Mr. and Mrs. Heifetz May Be Romantic But, Remember, They're Refined," *MPC,* Nov 1928, 26, 73, 79 (Hollywood is "[b]oastful, because at last a movie star has made a distinguished marriage and has chosen a man [Heifetz] whose fame is greater than her own. A home-town girl has made good.").

Vidor, King Wallis [actor/director/producer/scenarist] (*né* Charles King Wallis Vidor, b. Galveston TX, 8 Feb 1893–1 Nov 1982 [89], Paso Robles CA; heart attack). *A Tree Is a Tree* (New York: Harcourt, Brace and Co., 1952). m. **Florence** Cobb (Arto), 21 Sep 1915—div. 1925 (d. 1977); **Eleanor Boardman**, 8 Sep 1926, Beverly Hills home of Marion Davies—div. 1931 (d. 1991); Elizabeth Hill, Jul 1932. (Universal; MGM.) Peter B. Flint, "King Vidor, 88, Director of Films for More Than 40 Years, Is Dead," *NYT,* 2 Nov 1982, B8:1. Todd McCarthy, "King Vidor, 88, Film Pioneer, Dies at His California Ranch," *Variety,* 3 Nov 1982. AMD, p. 350. AS, p. 1109 ("dates prétendues par sa fille"). BHD1, p. 560; BHD2, p. 271 (b. 1894). FDY, p. 439. JS, p. 485 (b. 1893 into an immigrant Hungarian family; made *War and Peace,* Italy, 1956). Katz, pp. 1194–95. "King W. Vidor Directing Judge Brown Films," *MPW,* 23 Mar 1918, 1646. "Vidor Building Studio on Santa Monica Boulevard," *MPW,* 1 May 1920, 697. "Vidor to Be Represented in New York by E.C. Grainger," *MPW,* 21 Aug 1920, 988. "Japanese Censors' Opinions on Films Coincide with Those of King Vidor," *MPW,* 2 Oct 1920, 667. "King Vidor Says Screen Themes Will Not Be Dependent on Books and Plays," *MPW,* 6 Nov 1920, 100. "King Vidor Contracts to Release a Series of Special Productions Through Associated Producers," *MPW,* 26 Feb 1921, 1083. "Film Folk Purchase Homes," *MPW,* 14 May 1921, 179 (Selma Ave., LA CA). "Grainger Sues King Vidor Over Expenses of Office," *MPW,* 18 Jun 1921, 700 ($2,481). "GOlwyn Signs Vidor," *MPW,* 6 Jan 1923, 32. "Must Vitalize Screen Art, Vidor Tells N.Y. Critics," *MPW,* 28 Mar 1925, 385. "Vidor Renews with Metro," *MPW,* 18 Apr 1925, 705. "On the Set and Off," *MW,* 8 Aug 1925, 31, 40 (Florence Vidor got a divorce because her husband told her that "matrimony interfered with his career.... Mr. Vidor is seen frequently with Eleanor Boardman..."). "King Vidor Feted," *MPW,* 5 Dec 1925, 441. Covarrubias, "Distinguished Picture People," *MPW,* 6 Mar 1926, 16. Frederick James Smith, "Making 'The Big Parade,'" *MPC,* May 1926, 26, 71 ("It can be said with authority [and I am not quoting Vidor here] that few shreds of Stallings' original story outline remain in 'The Big Parade' as it stands in celluloid form."). "Trade Notes," *Paris and Hollywood,* Sep 1926, 44 (a careful director, "he seems to have been repaid for this care as he has never had a picture 'flop' yet."). "Vidor-Boardman," *MPW,* 25 Sep 1926, 1. S.M. Weller, "Without Benefit of Scripts; Scenarists Are Excess Baggage," *MPC,* Sep 1927, 23, 66. "These Title Changes," *MPW,* 10 Dec 1927, 10 (daughter Antonia born). Val Lewton, "'Hallelujah!'; About King Vidor's New Picture," *Screenland,* Jan 1929, 83.

Vie, Florence [actress] (b. 1876–12 Apr 1939 [62?]). BHD, p. 326.

Viera, Manuel Luis [director] (b. San Vicente, Madeira, 21 Jun 1885–1949 [64?], Portugal). AS, p. 1109.

Viertel, Berthold (son of scenarist Peter Viertel) [director/producer/scenarist] (b. Vienna, Austria, 28 Jun 1885–24 Sep 1953 [68], Vienna, Austria; heart attack). m. **Salka** (d. 1978). "Berthold Viertel Dies; Austrian Poet, Film Director Staged O'Neill in German," *NYT,* 26 Sep 1953, 17:4. "Berthold Viertel," *Variety,* 30 Sep 1953. AS, pp. 1109–10. BHD2, p. 271. FDY, p. 439. IFN, p. 304. Waldman, p. 297.

Viertel, Salka [actress/scenarist] (*née* Salomea Sara Steuermann, b. Sambor, Austria, 1889–20 Oct 1978 [89?], Klosters, Switzerland). m. **Berthold Viertel** (d. 1953). AS, p. 1110. BHD2, p. 271.

Vieuille, Roger [actor] (b. Baignes, France, 11 Feb 1883). AS, p. 1110.

Vigna, Grace [actress] (b. 1891–9 Dec 1926 [35?], Cincinnati OH). BHD, p. 326.

Vignola, Robert G. [actor/director] (b. Trivigno, Italy, 5 Aug 1882–25 Oct 1953 [71], Los Angeles CA). (Kalem; Selznick-Select.) "Robert G. Vignola, 71, Actor and Director," *NYT,* 26 Oct 1953, 21:5. "Robert G. Vignola," *Variety,* 28 Oct 1953. AMD, p. 350. AS, p. 1110. BHD, p. 326 (b. Albany NY); BHD2, p. 271. IFN, p. 304. Katz, pp. 1195–96. Lowrey, p. 182. Spehr, p. 172. Truitt, p. 336. "Robert Vignola, Famous Players Director," *MPW,* 22 Jan 1916, 584. "Vignola Renews Paramount Contract," *MPW,* 12 Jan 1918, 244. "Robert Vignola Joins Cosmopolitan," *MPW,* 15 Nov 1919, 337. "Although Twelve Years in the Industry Director Vignola Has Been with Only Three Firms," *MPW,* 26 Jun 1920, 1775 (Kalem, FP-L, Cosmopolitan). "Vignola Has Method to Lessen Subtitles; Brings Change in Continuity Technique," *MPW,* 17 Jul 1920, 352. "Vignola Visits Home Town [Albany NY] and Is Honored by Citizens," *MPW,* 17 Jul 1920, 353. "Vignola Says Showmen Should Give Credit to Work of Directors in Advertisements," *MPW,* 24 Jul 1920, 497. "VIgnola Receives Many Letters on His Defense of Director," *MPW,* 31 Jul 1920, p. 586 (*see* 24 Jul 1920 article). "Director Vignola Receives Offer from Japanese Firm," *MPW,* 7 Aug 1920, 738. "Frances Marion Gives Party to Director Robert G. Vignola," *MPW,* 21 Aug 1920, 1009. "Spanish Prince Compliments Director Robert G. Vignola," *MPW,* 18 Sep 1920, 342. Edward Weitzel, "Robert G. Vignola's Perfect Atmosphere and How He Failed of Its Proper Use," *MPW,* 2 Oct 1920, 617. "Director Vignola Says Chances Are Slim That Producers Will Move from Los Angeles," *MPW,* 9 Oct 1920, 784. "Vignola Says Picture Industry Is Aided by Appeal to Imagination of Public," *MPW,* 23 Oct 1920, 1123. "Exploitation Angle Is Necessary Element in Making Motion Pictrures, Says Vignola," *MPW,* 20 Nov 1920, 330. "Still Continuity, Vignola Invention, Is Newest Idea in Production of Good Stills," *MPW,* 11 Dec 1920, 757. Robert G. Vignola, "Public Criticism Is a Great Benefit to the Screen, Says Robert V. [sic] Vignola," *MPW,* 25 Dec 1920, 1018. "Vignola Says Star System Not on Decline Only Undergoing Change for the Better," *MPW,* 8 Jan 1921, 189. "Vignola and Companions Narrowly Escape Injury," *MPW,* 29 Jan 1921, 578. "Vignola Discusses Character Delinia-tion and the Director," *MPW,* 16 Apr 1921, 743. "Sons of Italy' Invites Vignola to Be Honorary Member of Society," *MPW,* 30 Jul 1921, 527. "Diplomacy Wins Declares Vignola," *MPW,* 13 Aug 1921, 718. "Vignola Has New Lighting System," *MPW,* 15 Oct 1921, 794. "Vignola Nominated for Hall of Fame," *MPW,* 10 Dec 1921, 686. Robert G. Vignola, "New Production Methods to Aid Directors to Realize True Psychology of Screen," *MPW,* 31 Dec 1921, 1050. "Vignola Gives His Views on Way to Destroy Censorship," *MPW,* 11 Mar 1922, 189. "Mrs. Vignola Dies," *MPW,* 16 Sep 1922 (mother, d. Labor Day 1922, Albany NY). "Vignola to Go Abroad," *MPW,* 14 Oct 1922, 567. "Making Some Films a Joy Says Vignola," *MPW,* 28 Oct 1922, 772. Robert G. Vignola, "Looking Backward—and Forward," *MPW,* 30 Dec 1922, 842. "Our Films Popular in Far East—Vignola," *MPW,* 17 Mar 1923, 360. "Vignola Visits Tomb," *MPW,* 14 Apr 1923, 718. "Marion Davies' Yachting Party Welcomes Vignola at Quarantine," *MPW,* 12 May 1923, 121 (Vignola's father died on the *Acquitania* on a world tour). "Vignola Back After Six Months' Vacation," *MPW,* 14 Jul

1923, 168. "Orientals Hugely Interested in Exhibition, Says Vignola," *MPW,* 6 Oct 1923, 480. "Vignola to Produce for Metro; Will Begin First Next Month," *MPW,* 12 Apr 1924, 543.

Vigny, Benno [author/scenarist] (*né* Benoit Philippe Weinfeld, b. Commercy, France, 28 Oct 1889 [extrait de naissance no. 134/1889]-31 Oct 1965 [76], Munich, Germany). AS, p. 1110.

Viguier, Francis [actor] (*né* Francis Marie Recco, b. Alger, Algeria, 26 Mar 1885–28 Jun 1946 [61], Paris, France). AS, p. 1110.

Viking, Vonceil [stunt woman/actress] (b. 1902–2 Dec 1929 [27?], Banning CA; car accident). AMD, p. 351. AS, p. 1110. BHD, p. 326. IFN, p. 304. Truitt, p. 336. "Vonceil Viking," *MPW,* 12 Nov 1927, 18. "'U' Stunt Girl in Spill," *MPW,* 19 Nov 1927, 11. "Vonceil Resumes," *MPW,* 26 Nov 1927, 8. "Vonceil Still Going," *MPW,* 10 Dec 1927, 14.

Vila, Sabra DeShon [actress] (b. Roxbury MA, 1850–20 Sep 1917 [67?], Brooklyn NY). AS, p. 1110. BHD, p. 326.

Vilches, Ernesto [stage manager/stage/film actor] (b. Tarragona, Spain, 6 Feb 1879–7 Dec 1954 [75], Barcelona, Spain; two days after having been struck by a taxi). (Film debut: *Aventuras de Pepín,* 1909; also in films 1919–20; later, in Spanish-language films for Fox; Paramount; Metro.) "Ernesto Vilches," *Variety,* 197, 22 Dec 1954, 63:1 (d. 8 Dec). AS, p. 1110 (d. 8 Dec). IFN, p. 304. Waldman, p. 299 (age 76).

Vildrac, Charles [author/scenarist] (*né* Charles Messager, b. Paris, France, 22 Nov 1882). AS, p. 1110.

Villareal, Julio [actor] (*né* Julio Villareal de Gonzaga, b. Lerida, Spain, 7 Dec 1888–4 Aug 1958 [69], Mexico City, Mexico). AS, p. 1111.

Villares, Jessie [actor] (d. Feb 1929). BHD, p. 326.

Villarías, Carlos [actor] (aka Carlos or Charles Villar, b. Cordoba, Spain, 7 Jul 1892). (Fox; last film: *Decameron Nights,* 1952.) AS, p. 1111. Waldman, p. 300.

Ville, Paul [actor] (*né* Marie Jean Baptiste Adolphe Paul Lacan, b. Paris, France, 18 Oct 1881–25 Dec 1977 [96], Paris, France). AS, p. 1111.

Villegas, Lucio [actor] (b. Lota, Chile, 25 Feb 1883–20 Jul 1968 [85], Los Angeles CA). AS, p. 1111.

Villiers, Mavis [actress] (b. Sydney, Australia, 18 Jan 1915-Mar 1976 [61]). BHD1, p. 560. IFN, p. 304.

Vina, Victor [actor] (*né* Victor Emmanuel Jules Vinatier, b. Saint-Maur-des-Fosses, France, 29 Aug 1885 [extrait de naissance no. SN/1885]-28 May 1961 [75], Paris, France). AS, p. 1111.

Vincenot, Louis [actor] (b. Hong Kong, China, 1 Sep 1883–25 Feb 1967 [83], England). AS, p. 1111.

Vincent, Clive [actor] (b. England-d. 11 Apr 1943). BHD, p. 326.

Vincent, James [stage/film actor/director/President, Motion Picture Directors Association, 1920] (b. Springfield MA, 19 Jul 1882–12 Jul 1957 [74], New York NY [Death Certificate Index No. 14700]). (Kalem; Cort Film Corp.; Pathé; Fox.) "James Vincent, 74, Director, Is Dead; Had Worked with Katharine Cornell, Theda Bara—Was Broadway, Stock Actor," *NYT,* 14 Jul 1957, 72:5. "James Vincent," *Variety,* 17 Jul 1957. AMD, p. 351. AS, p. 1111. BHD, p. 326; BHD2, p. 272. "Vincent Rejoins Kalem," *MPW,* 1 Feb 1913, 449. "James Vincent," *NYDM,* 25 May 1914, 28:4. "Briefs of Biography; A Director of the Younger Generation," *NYDM,* 9 Jun 1915, 36:1. "Jimmy Vincent Wears a Smile," *MPW,* 12 Jun 1915, 1782. "James Vincent," *MPW,* 19 Jun 1915, 1925. "James Vincent Directs 'The Hidden Hand' for Pathé," *MPW,* 1 Sep 1917, 1380. "James Vincent," *MPW,* 2 Mar 1918, 1233. "Film Division Names Director Advisors," *MPW,* 20 Jul 1918, 363–64. "James Vincent Returns to New York," *MPW,* 29 Nov 1919, 541.

Vincent, Mildred [actress]. No data found. (*Fl.* 1924–25.)

Vincent, Walter [executive] (b. Lake Geneva WI, 10 Aug 1868–10 May 1959 [90], New York NY). BHD2, p. 272.

Vincent-Brechignac, Francis (brother of **Jean** and **Hubert Vincent-Brechignac**) [producer] (b. Versailles, France, 1897–1947 [50?], France). AS, p. 1112.

Vincent-Brechignac, Hubert (brother of **Francis** and **Jean Vincent-Brechignac**) [producer] (*né* Pierre Hubert Vincent-Brechignac, b. Versailles, France, 13 May 1899 [extrait de naissance no. 402]-25 Aug 1955 [56], Versailles, France). AS, p. 1112.

Vincent-Brechignac, Jean Paul (brother of **Francis** and **Hubert Vincent-Brechignac**) [scenarist] (b. Versailles, France, 19 Jun 1901 [extrait de naissance no. 490]). AS, p. 1112.

Vinton, Horace [actor/scenarist/director/producer] (b. 1854?–26 Nov 1930 [76], New York NY). m. Eva Clayton. AMD, p. 351. AS, p. 1112 (d. Hollywood CA). BHD, p. 326. IFN, p. 304. "Director at Liberty," *MPW,* 31 Aug 1912, 883.

Violet, E.E. [actor] (*né* Emile Edouard Chane, b. Macon, France, 8 Dec 1880–4 Jan 1955 [74], Perpignan, France; suicide [extrait de décès no. 24/1955]). AS, p. 1112.

Viotti, Gino [actor] (*né* Luigi Viotti, b. Turin, Italy, 1875–14 Dec 1951 [76?], Rome, Italy). AS, p. 1112. BHD, p. 326. JS, p. 488 (in Italian silents from 1920).

Viragh-Flower, Albert [art director] (b. Budapest, Hungary, 1886–5 Feb 1922 [35?], New York NY). BHD2, p. 272.

Virginia, Harriet [title writer/scenarist]. No data found. FDY, pp. 439, 447.

Virginia, Violet [actress]. No data found. AMD, p. 351. "English Actress's Debut Here in 'Redeeming Sin,'" *MPW,* 6 Dec 1924, 555.

Visaroff, Michael S. [actor] (b. Russia, 18 Nov 1892–27 Feb 1951 [58], Los Angeles CA; pneumonia). (Paramount, 1924; RKO.) "Michael Visaroff," *Variety,* 7 Mar 1951. AS, p. 1112. BHD1, p. 561. IFN, p. 304. Truitt, p. 336.

Visaroff, Nina [actress] (b. Russia, 1888–14 Dec 1938 [50?], Beverly Hills CA). AS, p. 1112.

Visconti-Brignone, Lola (mother of Lilla Brignone [1913–1984]) [actress] (*née* Dolores Visconti, b. Rome, Italy, 24 Nov 1891–10 Jul 1924 [32], Turin, Italy). m. **Guido Brignone** (d. 1958). JS, p. 488 (in Italian silents from 1911; retired 1922).

Viskovsky, Vjatsjeslav Casimirovich [director/scenarist] (b. St. Petersburg, Russia, 1881–1933 [52?], Moscow, Russia). AS, p. 1113.

Vissieres, Charles Emile [actor] (b. Caen, France, 30 Oct 1880–13 Apr 1960 [79], Couilly-Pont-aux-Dames, France [extrait de décès no. 7/1960]). AS, p. 1113.

Vital, Geymond [stage/film/TV actor] (b. 1902). (MGM.) Waldman, p. 300.

Vitaliani, Italia (maternal cousin of **Eleonora Duse**) [actress] (b. Turin, Italy, 20 Aug 1866–6 Dec 1938 [72], Milan, Italy). m. actor/director Carlo Duse, Sr. (b. Udine, Italy, 5 Jan 1899). JS, p. 489 (in Italian silents from 1911).

Vitray, Georges [actor] (b. Paris, France, 29 Feb 1888–8 Sep 1960 [72], Paris, France). AS, p. 1113.

Vitrotti, Giovanni [cinematographer/director] (*né* Giuseppe Giovanni Bernardo Filippo Vitrotti, b. Turin, Italy, 1 May 1874 [extrait de naissance no. 1249/1874]-1 Dec 1966 [92], Rome, Italy). AS, p. 1113. BHD2, p. 272 (b. 1882). JS, p. 489 (b. 16 Nov 1882; in Italian silents from 1905; his filmography covers over seven columns).

Vitti, Achille [actor] (b. Zante, Ionian Islands, Italy, 22 Nov 1866). JS, p. 493 (in Italian silents from 1914).

Vivas, Eduardo [actor] (b. Spain, 1894–20 Aug 1957 [63?], Mexico City, Mexico). AS, p. 1113.

Vivian, Percival Seymour [actor] (b. England, 13 Mar 1890–15 Jan 1961 [70], Burbank CA). AS, p. 1113.

Vivian, Robert [stage/film actor] (b. London, England, 1859?–31 Jan 1944 [85], New York NY). (Stage debut: *The Bells,* London, 1886.) "Robert Vivian; Actor's Career Here and In Britain Covered 55 Years," *NYT,* 1 Feb 1944, 20:3 (age 83). "Robert Vivian," *Variety,* 2 Feb 1944. AS, p. 1113. BHD1, p. 561. IFN, p. 304.

Vivian, Ruth [actress] (b. England, 1883–24 Oct 1949 [66?], New York NY). AS, p. 1113.

Viviani, Raffaele [actor/playwright] (b. Castellammare di Stabia, Italy, 10 Jan 1888–22 Mar 1950 [62], Naples, Italy). JS, p. 494 (in Italian silents from 1908).

Vladimirsky, M. [cinematographer]. No data found. FDY, p. 469.

Vodnoy, Max [actor] (b. Russia, 1892–27 May 1939 [47?], New York NY; heart attack). AS, p. 1114.

Voegtlin, Arthur [producer] (father of assistant director Jack Voglin) (b. Chicago IL, 1857?–18 Jan 1948 [90], La Canada [Los Angeles] CA). m. Maude Caldwell, 1903 (d. 1942). "Arthur Voegtlin, Stage Producer, 90; Director at Hippodrome 14 Years Dies on Coast—Known for His Spectacular Shows," *NYT,* 20 Jan 1948, 23:3. "Arthur Voegtlin," *Variety,* 21 Jan 1948. BHD, p. 326.

Vogan, Emmett [actor] (*né* Charles Emmet Vogan, b. Cincinnati OH, 27 Sep 1893–13 Nov 1969 [76], Woodland Hills CA). AS, p. 1114.

Vogeding, Fredrik Wilhelm [actor] (b. Nymegue, Netherlands, 28 Mar 1887–18 Apr 1942 [55], Van Nuys CA; heart attack). m. **Florence Roberts** (d. 1927). "Fredrik Vogeding," *Variety,* 22 Apr 1942. AMD, p. 351. AS, p. 1114 (b. 1890). BHD1, p, 562 (b. Nijmegen, Netherlands). IFN, p. 304. Truitt, p. 336 (b. 1890). "Frederick Vogeding in Leading Role," *MPW,* 4 Sep 1920, 60.

Vogel, Franz [producer] (b. Germany, 1885–4 Oct 1956 [71?], Berlin, Germany). AS, p. 1114.

Vogel, Henry [actor/director] (b. 1865?–17 Jun 1925 [60], New York NY; heart attack). "Henry Vogel," *Variety,* 24 Jun 1925. AS, p. 1114 (d. 18 Jun). BHD, p. 326; BHD2, p. 272. IFN, p. 304. Truitt, p. 336.

Vogel, Paul C. [cinematographer] (b. New York NY, 22 Aug 1899–24 Nov 1975 [76], Woodland Hills CA). m. Gladys. (MGM.) "Paul Vogel," *Variety,* 3 Dec 1975 (age 75). AS, p. 1114. BHD2, p. 272. FDY, p. 469. Katz, p. 1198.

Vogel, William M. [executive] (b. Ruth MI, 1884–16 Jan 1945 [60?], Cross River NY). BHD2, p. 272.

Vogelsang, Georg [actor] (b. Germany, 15 May 1883–21 Dec 1952 [69], Schliersee, Germany). AS, p. 1114.

Voinoff, Anatole E. [actor] (b. Moscow, Russia, 1896?–9 Feb 1965 [69], New York NY [Death Certificate Index No. 3233; age 68]). m. Rosemary Bage (widow). "Anatole Voinoff, Matre d'Hotel at Russian Tea Room, Is Dead," *NYT,* 10 Feb 1965, 41:2 ("appeared in Russian character parts in silent films"). AS, p. 1114. BHD, p. 326. IFN, p. 305. Truitt, p. 336.

Vokes, Harry [vaudeville [Ward & Vokes]/film actor/singer] (b. 1865–17 Jun 1925 [60?], New York NY). (Gaumont, Flushing NY.) m. (1) Margaret Daly, 1893 (d. 1908); (2) Marie Francis, 1914 (2 sons, Harry and Thomas). "Harry Vokes," *Variety,* 21 Apr 1922, 19:3 (d. General Hospital, Lynn MA; from burns received in an explosion in the Beacon Oil Co. in Everett MA, where he had been employed for some time as a pump tender. Buried at Holy Cross Cemetery, Everett MA, on 17 Apr). AMD, p. 351. BHD, p. 326. IFN, p. 305. "Gossip of the Studios," *NYDM,* 13 Nov 1915, 33:1 (in vaudeville 31 years. In Casino Star comedies for Mutual; first, *Beauty in Distress.*). "Harry Vokes," *MPW,* 4 Dec 1915, 1813.

Vokes, May [stage/film actress] (b. 1882?–13 Sep 1957 [75], Stamford CT). m. Robert Lester (widower). "May Vokes, Acted in Theatre Here; Comedienne Who Appeared in Original 'Bat' Dies—Also Took Musical Roles," *NYT,* 14 Sep 1957, 19:6. "May Vokes," *Variety,* 18 Sep 1957. AS, p. 1114. BHD, p. 326. IFN, p. 305.

Volare, Lorna [child actress]. No data found. AMD, p. 351. "Baby Lorna Volare," *MPW,* 27 Jan 1917, 526.

Volkman, P[eter] **Thad** [actor/director] (d. 24 Dec 1922). m. Mae De Metz, 26 Feb 1913, Jacksonville FL. (Lubin; Metro; Fox.) *NYDM,* 12 Mar 1913, p. 28. "P. Thad Volkman a Location Expert," *MPW,* 15 Apr 1916, 471. "Obituary," *MPW,* 6 Jan 1923, 33.

Volkoff, Alexander [director/scenarist/actor] (*né* Aleksander A. Volkov, b. Moscow, Russia, 1885–22 May 1942 [57?], Rome, Italy). (Film debut, 1906.) AS, p. 1115. Garth Pedler, "Ivan Mosjoukine in 'Prince of Adventurers' (or 'Casanova') (1927)," *CI,* 222 (Dec 1993), C2, C4, C6, 57.

Voller-Buzzi, Mario [actor/director] (b. Turin, Italy, 6 Jul 1886–22 Feb 1966 [79], Turin, Italy). AS, p. 1115. JS, p. 495 (in Italian silents from 1909).

Vollmer, Lula [scenarist] (b. NC-2 May 1955, New York NY). AS, p. 1115 (Volmer). BHD2, p. 272.

Vollmoeller, Karl [author/scenarist] (b. 1879–17 Oct 1948 [69?], Los Angeles CA). AS, p. 1115. BHD2, p. 272.

Volnys, Jacques [actor] (d. May 1925, Paris, France). BHD, p. 326.

Volotskoy, Vladimir [actor] (b. St. Petersburg, Russia, 1853?–7 Nov 1927 [74], Los Angeles CA). "Vladimir Volotskoy," *Variety,* 16 Nov 1927. AS, p. 1115. BHD, p. 326. IFN, p. 305. Truitt, p. 336.

Volpe, Franco (twin brother of **Mario Volpe**) [director] (b. Naples, Italy, 18 Mar 1894). AS, p. 1115.

Volpe, Frederick B. [actor] (b. Liverpool, England, 31 Jul 1865–6 Mar 1932 [66], London, England). "Frederick Volpe," *Variety,* 106, 15 Mar 1932, 63:2 (d. 7 Mar, aged 60; "He never recovered from the shock of his wife's death."). AS, p. 1115. BHD1, p. 562. IFN, p. 305.

Volpe, Mario (twin brother of **Franco Volpe**) [director/scenarist] (b. Naples, 18 Mar 1894). AS, p. 1115. JS, p. 495 (in Italian silents form 1919).

Volterra, Léon [actor] (b. France, 1888–5 Jun 1949 [61?], France). AS, p. 1115.

Von Alten, Ferdinand [stage/film actor] (*né* Baron Ferdinand Freiherr von Lamezahn auf Altenhofen, b. Petrograd, Russia, 13 Apr 1885–17 Mar 1933 [47], Dessau, Germany; influenza). m. (2 children). "Ferdinand Von Alten," *Variety,* 110, 4 Apr 1933, 47:2. AS, p. 1115 (b. St. Petersburg, Russia, 23 Apr). BHD, p. 326. IFN, p. 305 (age 48).

Von Berne, Eva [actress] (*née* Eva Von Plentzner, b. Serbia, 9 Jul 1910). Mary Willis, "A Serbian Cinderella; Eva Von Berne's Hejira to Hollywood Argues that Fine Parts Are More than Coronets," *MPC,* Sep 1928, 63, 89 (discovered by Norma Shearer).

Von Block, Bela [actor/director/producer] (b. Moscow, Russia, 1889?–23 Mar 1962 [73], Culver City CA). (MGM.) "Bela von Block," *Variety,* 4 Apr 1962 ("film actor from 1924 to 1929"). AS, p. 1115 (b. Germany, 1888). BHD, p. 326; BHD2, p. 272. IFN, p. 305. Truitt, p. 337.

Von Blondel, Sacy [actress/poet] (*née* Sári Megyery, b. Blassagyarmat, Hungary, 28 Jul 1897–5 Feb 1983 [85], Paris, France). AS, p. 1115.

Von Bolvary, Geza [director/writer/actor] (*né* Geza Maria von Bolvary-Zahn, b. Budapest, Hungary, 27 Dec 1897–10 Aug 1961 [63], Altenbeuern, Germany; heart attack). AS, p. 1115 (b. 28 Dec). BHD, p. 326; BHD2, p. 272 (d. Munich, Germany). IFN, p. 305 (d. 11 Aug).

Von Bradow, Hans [actor] (b. Germany, 1872–7 Jun 1927 [55?], Los Angeles CA; heart attack due to alcoholism). AS, p. 1115.

Von Brincken, William [actor/director] (aka Roger Beckwith, *né* Wilhelm Vaughn, b. Flensburg, Germany, 27 May 1881–18 Jan 1946 [64], Los Angeles CA; ruptured artery). m. Milo Abercrombie. "Film Director Dies; Former German Spy [in 1915]," *NYT,* 20 Jan 1946, 42:3. "Wilhelm von Brincken," *Variety,* 30 Jan 1946. AS, p. 1115. BHD, p. 326; BHD2, p. 272. IFN, p. 305. Truitt, p. 337.

Von Cserepy, Arsen [director] (*né* Arzen Cserepy, b. Budapest, Hungary, 17 Jul 1881–1946 [65?], Budapest, Hungary). AS, p. 1116.

Von Diossy, Arthur [actor] (b. Austria, 1869–29 Sep 1940 [71?]). BHD1, p. 562. IFN, p. 305.

Von Eltz, Theodore [actor] (b. New Haven CT, 5 Nov 1893–6 Oct 1964 [70], Woodland Hills CA). "Theodor von Eltz, a Character Actor," *NYT,* 8 Oct 1964, 43:4 (d. 7 Oct). "Theodore von Eltz," *Variety,* 14 Oct 1964. AMD, p. 351. AS, p. 1116. BHD1, p. 562. FSS, p. 283. IFN, p. 305. Katz, p. 387 (began 1920). MH, p. 141. Truitt, p. 337. "Von Eltz with Metro," *MPW,* 13 Nov 1920, 219.

Von Esterhazy, Agnes [actress] (b. 21 Jan 1898–4 Apr 1956 [58], Munich, Germany). BHD1, p. 618.

Von Gerlach, Arthur [director] (b. Vienna, Austria, 1876–4 Aug 1925 [49?], Berlin, Germany). AS, p. 1116. BHD2, p. 272.

Von Goth, Rolf [actor] (b. South Africa, 5 Nov 1906–9 Nov 1981 [75]). BHD1, p. 562.

Von Harbou, C.F. [scenarist]. No data found. FDY, p. 439.

Von Harbou, Thea Gabriele [director/scenarist] (b. Berlin, Germany, 12 Dec 1888–1 Jul 1954 [65], Berlin, Germany). m. **Fritz Lang**, 1920—div. (d. 1976). AS, p. 1098 (Thea Van Harbou, b. Tauperlitz, Germany); p. 1116 (Von Harbou). BHD2, p. 272.

Von Hoffman, Carl [cameraman] (b. Riga, Latvia). "Lieut. Von Hoffman in Service," *Variety,* 7 Dec 1917, p. 49 (with the Signal Corps).

Von Hollay, Camilla [actress] (b. Budapest, Hungary, 7 Nov 1899–1967 [68?], Budapest, Hungary). BHD1, p. 618.

Von Kalterborn, Hans [actor] (b. Milwaukee WI, 9 Jul 1878–14 Jun 1965 [86], New York NY; heart attack). AS, p. 1116.

Von Korff, Heinrich [director] (b. Vienna, Austria, 5 Jun 1868). AS, p. 1116.

Von Ledebur, Leopold Ernst Gerhard Freiherr [actor] (b. Berlin, Germany, 18 May 1876–22 Aug 1955 [79], Wakendorf, Germany). AS, p. 1116.

Von Martens, Valerie [actress] (*née* Valerie Pajer Edle von Mayersberg, b. Lienz, Austria, 4 Nov 1894–7 Apr 1986 [91], Richen, Switzerland). AS, p. 1116.

Von Mayerling, Max [director] (b. Austria, 2 Sep 1885–12 May 1957 [71]). AS, p. 1116.

Von Meter, Harry L. [actor] (b. Malta Bend MO, 29 Mar 1871–2 Jun 1956 [85], Sawtelle CA). (Nestor; American.) AS, p. 1116 (d. LA CA). BHD1, p. 563. IFN, p. 301. Billy H. Doyle, "Lost Players," *CI,* 152 (Feb 1988), C13. George Katchmer, "Remembering the Great Silents," *CI,* 214 (Apr 1993), 50–51.

Von Meter, Joseph [actor] (b. MO, 3 Aug 1876–22 Nov 1961 [85], Los Angeles CA). AS, p. 1116. BHD, p. 324 (Vam Meter).

Von Meyerinck, Hubert Georg Werner Harald [actor] (b. Potsdam, Germany, 23 Aug 1896–13 May 1971 [74], Hamburg, Germany). AS, p. 1117 (appeared in over 250 films).

Von Meyerinck, Hubert Georg Werner Harald [actor] (b. Potsdam, Germany, 23 Aug 1896–13 May 1971 [74], Wankendorf, Germany; heart attack). "Hubert von Meyerinck," *Variety,* 26 May 1971 (d. Hamburg; began in films in Berlin, 1924). AS, p. 1117. BHD1, p. 563 (d. 14 Apr). IFN, p. 305 (d. 14 Apr). Truitt, p. 337.

Von Nagy, Kathe [actress] (*née* Ekatarina von Czizer Nagy, b. Satu Mar, Romania, 14 Apr 1904–20 Dec 1973 [69], Los Angeles CA; cancer). AS, p. 1117 (b. Szatmany Sutamare, Hungary 4

Apr-28 Dec). BHD1, p. 563. JS, p. 496 (b. Subotica, Hungary; appeared in *Rotaie*, Italy, 1929).

Vonnegut, Marjorie [actress] (b. Indianapolis IN, 1892–25 Oct 1936 [44?], New York NY). BHD, p. 326.

Von Ottinger, Leonora [stage/film actress]. No data found. AMD, p. 351. "A Recruit from the Legitimate," *MPW,* 1 Nov 1913, 499.

Von Perponcher, Friedrich Carl Albert Freddy Egon von Perponcher-Sedlnitzky [director/scenarist] (b. Demmin, Germany, 23 Aug 1896–28 Dec 1957 [61], Wiesbaden, Germany). AS, p. 1117. BHD2, p. 273.

Von Pugh-Winther, Carl [cameraman] (b. 1884–11 Apr 1954 [70?). AMD, p. 351. BHD2, p. 273 (Winthers Carl Von Pugh). "Balboa Cameraman Arrested as Spy," *MPW,* 19 Dec 1914, 1689.

Von Ritzau, Erik [actor] (b. Copenhagen, Denmark, 6 Jul 1877–28 Feb 1936 [58]). BHD, p. 327. IFN, p. 305.

Von Rottenthal, Imgard [actress]. No data found. AMD, p. 351. "Kalem Featuring Baroness," *MPW,* 3 Jul 1915, 42.

Von Rue, Greta [actress] (d. 2 Jun 1991, Los Angeles Co. CA). BHD1, p. 563.

Von Schiller, Carl (*né* Jerome Sheldon, b. Columbus OH, 13 Aug 1890–15 Apr 1962 [71], Los Angeles CA). AMD, p. 351. AS, p. 1100 (Carl Van Schiller). BHD1, p. 563. "Von Schiller's Admirers Increasing," *MPW,* 22 Jan 1916, 583.

Von Schlettow, Hans Adalbert [actor] (b. Frankfurt, Germany, 11 Jun 1888–30 Apr 1945 [56], Berlin, Germany). AS, p. 1117 (d. 11 Jun). BHD1, p. 563. IFN, p. 305.

Von Seyffertitz, Gustav [stage/film actor] (aka G. Butler Cloneblough, b. Vienna, Austria, 4 Aug 1863–25 Dec 1943 [80], Los Angeles CA). (Vitagraph.) "Gustav von Seyffertitz," *Variety,* 29 Dec 1943. AMD, p. 351. AS, p. 1117. BHD1, p. 563 (b. Tyrol, Austria). IFN, p. 305. Katz, p. 1044. Truitt, p. 337. "Well Known Actor Makes Screen Debut," *MPW,* 18 Aug 1917, 1096. "Seyffertitz to Remain with Famous Players," *MPW,* 25 May 1918, 1120. "Gustav von Seyffertitz," *MPW,* 8 Oct 1927, 359.

Von Stampfer, Simon Rutter [inventor of the Stroboscope] (b. Austria, 1792–1864 [72?], Austria). AS, p. 1117.

Von Sternberg, Josef [director/scenarist] (*né* Josef Sternberg, b. Vienna, Austria, 29 May 1894–22 Dec 1969 [75], Los Angeles CA; heart attack). m. **Riza Royce**, 1926; Meri. *Fun in a Chinese Laundry* (rpt. 1988; San Francisco: Mercury House, Inc., 1965). (World, Ft. Lee NJ; Paramount; UFA.) "Josef von Sternberg, Film Director, Is Dead," *NYT,* 23 Dec 1969, 31:1 (began as a film patcher ca. 1911). "Josef von Sternberg Dead at 75; 'Master' Shot Dietrich to Stardom," *Variety,* 24 Dec 1969 (*né* Jo Sternberg). AMD, p. 351. AS, p. 1117. BHD, p. 563; BHD2, p. 273. FDY, p. 439. IFN, p. 305. Katz, pp. 1090–91. Spehr, p. 172. Truitt, p. 337. Sumner Smith, "Von Sternberg! Who Is He?," *MPW,* 6 Dec 1924, 496–97. Le Roy Green, "The Talk of Hollywood," *MW,* 21 Feb 1925, 14–15, 30. June Lee, "Dan Cupid's Bulletin Board," *Paris and Hollywood,* Oct 1926, 85 (wed Royce). "Sternberg Assigned," *MPW,* 16 Apr 1927, 621. "Sternberg to Direct [Esther] Ralston," *MPW,* 25 Jun 1927, 570.

Von Stroheim, Erich, Jr. (son of **Erich von Stroheim, Sr.**, and **Valerie Germonprez**) [actor/assistant director] (b. Los Angeles CA, 25 Aug 1916–26 Oct 1968 [52], Woodland Hills CA; cancer). m. Mary (2 sons). (MGM.) "Von Stroheim Jr., Ex-Film Director," *NYT,* 29 Oct 1968, 47:3 (survived by wife, two sons, and a half-brother, Joseph von Stroheim). "Erich von Stroheim, Jr.," *Variety,* 252, 30 Oct 1968, 68:5 (1 half-brother). AS, p. 1117. BHD1, p. 563; BHD2, p. 273. IFN, p. 305.

Von Stroheim, Erich, Sr. (father of **Erich von Stroheim, Jr.**) [actor/director/scenarist] (*né* Eric Oswald Hans Carl Maria Stroheim von Nordenwald, b. Vienna, Austria, 22 Sep 1885–12 May 1957 [71], Maurepas, France; cancer [extrait de décès no. [6]. m. **Valerie Germonprez**, 1920 (d. 1988). *The Man You Loved to Hate* [video] (USA, 1979, 70 min.; director, Patrick Montgomery). Richard Koszarski, *The Man You Loved to Hate; Erich von Stroheim and Hollywood* (NY: Oxford University Press, 1983). (Griffith; Universal; MGM; Paramount.) "Von Stroheim, 71, Film Actor, Dies; Succumbs Near Paris After 6 Months' Illness—Made Last U.S. Movie 8 Years Ago," *NYT,* 12 May 1957, 31:1. "Erich von Stroheim," *Variety,* 15 May 1957. AMD, p. 351. AS, p. 1117. BHD1, p. 563; BHD2, p. 273. FDY, p. 439. FSS, p. 283. IFN, p. 305. JS, p. 496 (made films in Italy in 1953 and 1954). Katz, p. 1104–05. KOM, p. 162. Spehr, p. 172. Truitt, p. 337. "Von Stroheim Becomes Director," *MPW,* 12 Apr 1919, 231. "Stroheim Writes, Directs and Plays," *MPW,* 27 Sep 1919, 1961. "Von Stroheim in New York," *MPW,* 1 May 1920, 702. "Von Stroheim Tells Advertising Men of Days of Adversity Before Success Came," *MPW,* 22 May 1920, 1060. "Von Stroheim Back in Universal City," *MPW,* 5 Jun 1920, 1308. "Elks Fete Erich von Stroheim as Judge in Beauty Contest," *MPW,* 5 Jun 1920, 1344. "Von Stroheim Married," *MPW,* 6 Nov 1920, 55. "U Lets Three Drs. Go But Stroheim Works; Officials Say Lot Is Still Holding 15 Companies," *Variety,* 27 May 1921, p. 34:4 (Harry B. Harris, Jacques Jaccard, and Norman Dawn were let go. Stroheim "was to have finished 'Foolish Wives' May 14, but did not. He wanted to continue night shooting at Westlake Park. Executives stopped him. Later he wanted to go to San Diego, but this also was denied him and he was compelled to stay on the lot. He is due to finish this week."). Willis Goldbeck, "Von Stroheim, Man and Superman," *Classic,* Sep 1922, 18–19, 82–83. "A New von Stroheim," *MPW,* 30 Sep 1922, 355 (b. LA CA, Sep 1922). "Von Stroheim Will Direct for Goldwyn," *MPW,* 2 Dec 1922, 420. Jim Tully, "'The Man You Love to Hate'; A Phrase That Deserves Immortality," *Classic,* May 1924, 20–21, 77. "On the Set and Off," *MW,* 11 Jul 1925, 30 (filed petition for citizenship papers; came to U.S. in 1909). "Von Stroheim Will Direct Constance Talmadge Picture," *MPW,* 8 Aug 1925, 661. "Von Stroheim to Produce and Act in Series for Paramount," *MPW,* 21 Nov 1925, 230. Don Ryan, "Von, the Don Quixote of Pictures; The Director Who Is a Martyr to His Ideals of Realism," *MPC,* Mar 1926, 22–23, 68, 71. "Selected to Direct Ziegfeld Production," *MPW,* 21 Aug 1926, 1. "Stroheim Goes to Paramount Studio," *MPW,* 11 Dec 1926, 415. Don Juan, "So This Is Hollywood," *Paris and Hollywood Screen Secrets Magazine,* May 1927, 28–30 (finishing *The Wedding March*. In a brothel scene, he asked an "Ethiopian maiden" to kiss a jackass. "The dusky lily from Africa's iodine shores took one look at the jackass and exclaimed: 'I'se a perfick lady, Mister Vanstronheim, an' ah ain' kissin' no jackasses fo' the small check I'se gittin' fo' actin' in this pickshure!' Needless to add, this brunette that didn't prefer donkeys earned the five additional dollars she received for enacting the scene required of her." The scene will not be shown in America, but will be shipped with the European negative.). "Stroheim with Universal," *MPW,* 11 Jun 1927, 397. Tom Waller, "Erich von Stroheim Expresses Wish to Return to Griffith," *MPW,* 24 Sep 1927, 225. Dorothy Bay, "First the Artist Then the Human Being; That's Von," *MPC,* Dec 1927, 23, 72. Grace Wilcox, "Erich von Stroheim; The Man; He Breaks Everybody's Heart, Over and Over Again, then Apologizes. Tender, Human, Intelligent," *Screen Book,* Jul 1928, 70–75 ("He gets a kick out of shocking anaemic women and repressed men out of their smugness...Anything natural is entirely correct with him; only the artificial and affected are indecent.").

Von Suttner, Baroness Bertha [writer] (d. 21 Jun 1914). AMD, p. 352. "Lay Down Your Arms," *MPW,* 18 Jul 1914, 448 (posthumous article).

Von Tilzer, Albert [composer] (b. Indianapolis IN, 29 Mar 1878–1 Oct 1956 [78], Los Angeles CA). BHD2, p. 273.

Von Tilzer, Harry [composer] (b. Goshen IN, 8 Jul 1872–10 Jan 1946 [73], New York NY). BHD2, p. 273.

Von Twardowski, Hans H[einrich] [stage director/film/radio/TV actor/playwright] (b. Szczecin, Poland, 5 May 1898–19 Nov 1958 [60], 257 W. 55th Street, New York NY). (In *The Cabint of Dr. Caligari,* 1921; WB.) "Hans Heinrich von Twardowski Dead; Stage, Screen Actor Also Was Director," *NYT,* 20 Nov 1958, 35:1 ("Friends said yesterday that it was ironic that Mr. von Twardowski, a tall, blond handsome man of strongly anti-Nazi beliefs, frequently played German officers and Nazis in American screen melodramas."). "Hans Von Twardowski," *Variety,* 212, 26 Nov 1958, 79:1. AS, p. 1117. BHD1, p. 563. IFN, p. 305.

Von Walther, Hertha [actress] (b. Hildesheim, Germany, 12 Jun 1903–12 Apr 1987 [83], Munich, Germany). BHD1, p. 563.

Von Wangenheim, Gustav [actor/director/writer] (b. Wiesbaden, Germany, 18 Feb 1895–5 Aug 1975 [80], Munich, Germany). AS, p. 1117 (d. Berlin, Germany). BHD, p. 327; BHD2, p. 273. IFN, p. 305.

Von Winterstein, Eduard [stage/film actor] (né Eduard Klemens Franz Anna Freiherr von Wangenheim, b. Vienna, Austria, 1 Aug 1871–22 Jul 1961 [89], East Berlin, Germany). "Eduard Von Winterstein," *Variety,* 223, 2 Aug 1961, 103:1. AS, p. 1117. BHD1, p. 563. IFN, p. 305.

Von Wolowski, Curt [actor] (b. Berlin, Germany, 12 Jun 1897-Jun 1985 [88?], New York NY). BHD1, p. 563.

Von Wolzogen, Hans Freiherr [director/producer] (b. Berlin, Germany, 5 Jul 1888–20 May 1954 [65], Berlin, Germany). AS, p. 1117.

Voorhees, David "Slim" [actor] (b. 1890). AMD, p. 352. "The Roll of Honor," *MPW,* 4 Aug 1917, 807.

Vorhaus, Bernard [director/scenarist] (b. Germany, 1898-ca. 1941). AS, p. 1118. FDY, p. 439.

Vorkapich, Slavko [director/scenarist] (*né* Slavko Vorkapic, b. Dobrinijci, Serbia, 17 May 1892–20 Oct 1976 [84], Mijas, Spain). AS, p. 1118 (d. Mijas, Yugoslavia). BHD2, p. 273.

Voronica, Vera [actress] (b. Kiev, Ukrain, Russia, 1905). AS, p. 1118.

Vorzimer, Sidney [actor] (b. New York NY, 3 Oct 1896–16 Mar 1956 [59], Burbank CA). BHD1, p. 618.

Vosalik, Josef [actor] (b. Prague, Czechoslovakia, 11 Jul 1880). AS, p. 1118.

Vosburgh, Alfred *see* **Whitman, Gayne**

Vosburgh, Harold [actor] (b. Penetanguishene, Ontario, Canada, 1870?–17 Nov 1926 [56], New Orleans LA). "Harold Vosburgh Dead in New Orleans Hotel," *Variety,* 24 Nov 1926 (age 55). AMD, p. 352. AS, p. 1118. BHD, p. 327. IFN, p. 305. "A Royal Send Off," *MPW,* 24 Jun 1911, 1427.

Vosburgh, Jack [actor] (*né* Jack Vosper, b. Chicago IL, 3 Jul 1894–6 Apr 1954 [59], Los Angeles CA). AMD, p. 352. BHD, p. 327. "Jack Vosburgh Joins Mutual-American Company," *MPW,* 3 Feb 1917, 699.

Voshell, John M. "Jack," Sr. [assistant production manager/art director/actor] (b. Smyrna DE, 1883?–22 May 1952 [69], Los Angeles CA). "John M. 'Jack' Voshell, Sr.," *Variety,* 28 May 1952. AMD, p. 352. BHD2, p. 273. BHD, p. 327. "Voshell with Clara Kimball Young," *MPW,* 24 Nov 1917, 1157.

Voskovec, George [actor/scenarist] (*né* Jiri Washmann, b. Sazavabudy, Czechoslovakia, 19 Jun 1905–1 Jul 1981 [76], Pear Blossom CA). AS, p. 1118. BHD1, p. 564; BHD2, p. 273 (b. Sazava, Czechoslovakia).

Vosper, Frank O. [actor] (b. London, England, 15 Dec 1889–6 Mar 1937 [47], at sea). AS, p. 1118. BHD1, p. 564.

Vosper, John [actor] (b. Chicago IL, 3 Jul 1894–6 Apr 1954 [59], Los Angeles CA; heart attack). AS, p. 1118 (b. 1901). BHD1, p. 564.

Voss, Frank "Fatty" [actor] (b. IL, 12 Oct 1888–22 Apr 1917 [28], Los Angeles CA; heart ailment). m. (L-KO.) "Frank Voss, Comedian, Dead," *MPW,* 12 May 1917, 951. Cal York, "Plays and Players," *Photoplay,* Jul 1917, 111 (died recently, and "had just been married a few months. His home was in Chicago."). AMD, p. 352. AS, p. 1118. BHD, p. 327. IFN, p. 306. "L-KO Fun Makers," *MPW,* 20 Jan 1917, 382. "Obituary," *MPW,* 12 May 1917, 951.

Vosselli, Judith [actress]. No data found. (*Fl.* 1929–30.)

Votion, Jack [casting director/producer] (b. 1900?–16 Oct 1975 [75], Los Angeles CA). (Paramount; RKO.) "Jack Votion," *Variety,* 280, 29 Oct 1975, 78:5. AMD, p. 352. BHD2, p. 273. "Jack Votion," *MPW,* 12 Nov 1927, 22.

Vroom, Frederic William [actor] (b. Clement, Nova Scotia, Canada, 11 Nov 1857–24 Jun 1942 [84], Los Angeles CA; heart attack). AMD, p. 352. AS, p. 1118. BHD1, p. 564. IFN, p. 306. "Triangle Adds Two New Players," *MPW,* 17 Nov 1917, 1028.

Vuolo, Tito [actor] (b. Italy, 22 Mar 1893–14 Sep 1962 [69], Los Angeles CA; cancer). AS, p. 1119.

W

Wachner, Sophie [costumer]. No data found. AMD, p. 352. "Goldwyn Creates Costume Department at Culver City," *MPW,* 26 Jul 1919, 514.

Waddell, Walter [film editor] (b. 1887–8 Oct 1958 [71?], Los Angeles CA). BHD2, p. 273.

Waddington, Patrick [actor] (b. York, England, 19 Aug 1901–4 Feb 1987 [85], York, England). AS, p. 1121 (b. 1903). BHD1, p. 564.

Wade, Bessie [extra] (b. 1885?–19 Oct 1966 [81], Dallas TX). AS, p. 1121. BHD, p. 327. IFN, p. 306. Robert Donaldson, "Famous Extras," *MPC,* Feb 1927, 32–33 [photo], 68, 80.

Wade, Frank [set decorator] (b. 1906?–3 Jun 1969 [63], Sherman Oaks CA). m. Marian. "Frank Wade," *Variety,* 11 Jun 1969.

Wade, James [assistnt director] (b. 1895–15 Oct 1949 [54?], Los Angeles CA). BHD2, p. 273.

Wade, John Patrick [actor] (b. IN, 30 Jun 1876–13 Jul 1949 [73], Los Angeles CA). "John P. Wade," *Variety,* 20 Jul 1949. AS, p. 1121 (d. 14 Jul). BHD1, p. 564. IFN, p. 306.

Wadhams, Golden [actor] (b. 1869?–26 Jun 1929 [60], Los Angeles CA; heart ailment). AS, p. 1121. BHD, p. 328. IFN, p. 306. Truitt, p. 338.

Wadsworth, Henry, "The Perennial Juvenile" [stage/film actor/former president of the American Federation of Labor Film Council] (b. Maysville KY, 18 Jun 1902–5 Dec 1974 [72], New York NY). (Broadway debut: *Tommy,* 1927; Paramount; MGM.) "Henry Wadsworth, Stage, Film Actor," *NYT,* 7 Dec 1974, 32:6. "Henry Wadsworth," *Variety,* 11 Dec 1974. BHD1, p. 564. AS, p. 1121. IFN, p. 306.

Wadsworth, William [stage/film actor] (b. Boston MA, 7 Jun 1874–6 Jun 1950 [76], Jamaica, Queens NY). (Edison.) "W. Wadsworth, Actor, 77; Veteran Who Won Acclaim as Doctor in Golden's Play Dies," *NYT,* 7 Jun 1950, 29:2. "William Wadsworth," *Variety,* 14 Jun 1950. AMD, p. 352. AS, p. 1121. BHD, p. 328 (b. Pigeon Cover MA; d. Brooklyn NY). IFN, p. 306. SD. Truitt, p. 338. "Edison Touches Popular Chord," *MPW,* 3 Jan 1914, 28–29. "William Wadsworth in 'Cohen's Luck,'" *MPW,* 22 May 1915, 1248.

Wagar, Duane H. [stage/film executive/casting director for Vitagraph Picture Co., Santa Monica CA] (b. 1879–2 Sep 1933 [54?], Ocean Park CA). "Duane H. Wagar," *Variety,* 112, 12 Sep 1933, 63:1. BHD, p. 328.

Wagenseller, W[illiam] **H.** [actor] (b. 1879–25 Apr 1951 [72?], No. Hollywood CA). AS, p. 1121.

Waggner, George [actor/director/scenarist/producer/composer] (*né* George Waggoner, b. New York NY, 7 Sep 1894–11 Dec 1984 [90], Woodland Hills CA; heart attack in his sleep). m. Danny Shannon. "George Waggner," *Variety,* 12 Dec 1984. AS, p. 1121 (b. Philadelphia PA; d. 10 Dec). BHD, p. 328. Katz, p. 1200 (began 1920).

Wagner, Blake [cameraman/makeup artist] (*né* Blakeley Alan Wagner, b. 1893?–13 Jan 1957 [64], Woodland Hills CA). (Griffith; Sennett.) "Blakeley A. Wagner," *Variety,* 23 Jan 1957. BHD2, p. 273. FDY, p. 469.

Wagner, Elsa [actress] (*née* Elisabeth Karoline Auguste Wagner, b. Tallin, Estonia, 24 Jan 1881–17 Aug 1975 [94], Berlin, Germany). AS, p. 1121. BHD1, p. 564. IFN, p. 306.

Wagner, Emmett "Kid" [actor] (b. 30 Apr 1891–25 Apr 1977 [85], Woodland Hills CA). AS, p. 1121. BHD1, p. 564.

Wagner, Fred [film salesman] (b. 1875?–26 Nov 1940 [65], Sawtelle CA). "Fred Wagner," *Variety,* 4 Dec 1940.

Wagner, Fritz Arno [cameraman] (b. Schmiedefeld am Rennsteig, Germany, 5 Dec 1889–18 Aug 1958 [68], Gottingen, Germany; auto accident). AMD, p. 352. AS, p. 1121. BHD2, p. 273 (b. 1894). FDY, p. 469 (Arno Wagner and Fritz O. Wagner). IFN, p. 306. "A General for a Day," *MPW,* 4 Apr 1914, 46. "Wagner in Mexico," *MPW,* 18 Jul 1914, 440.

Wagner, Jack [cinematographer/scenarist] (b. San Ardo CA, 1891–12 Jul 1963 [72?], Los Angeles CA). BHD2, p. 273.

Wagner, Jack [actor] (b. OH, 5 Jan 1897–6 Feb 1965 [68], Los Angeles CA). "Jack Wagner," *Variety,* 17 Feb 1965. AS, p. 1121. BHD1, p. 565. IFN, p. 306.

Wagner, Leon [cameraman]. No data found. AMD, p. 352. "Leon Wagner a Photographic Sharp," *MPW,* 1 Aug 1914, 714.

Wagner, Max [actor] (b. Mexico City, Mexico, 28 Nov 1901–16 Nov 1975 [73], West Los Angeles CA; heart attack). AS, pp. 1121–22. BHD, p. 328. IFN, p. 306.

Wagner, Rob[ert] [scenarist/director] (b. Detroit MI?, 1873?–20 Jul 1942 [69], Santa Barbara CA; heart attack in the lounge of the Santa Barbara Hotel). (Began 1920; Paramount; Roach; Sennett.) *Film Folk* (1918). "Rob Wagner; Writer, Artist of Beverly Hills Edited Script Magazine," *NYT,* 21 Jul 1942, 19:5 (friend of Will Rogers and Charles Chaplin). AMD, p. 352. BHD2, p. 273. FDY, p. 439. Joseph McBride, *Frank Capra; The Catastrophe of Success* (NY: Simon & Schuster, 1992) (Capra's art teacher at Manual Arts High School). "Charles Ray Secures the First Scenario Written by Rob Wagner, Popular Author," *MPW,* 1 May 1920, 662. "To Be Paramount Director," *MPW,* 27 Jan 1923, 323. "Roach Signs Writer as Director," *MPW,* 6 Oct 1923, 514.

Wagner, Sidney [composer/cameraman] (b. 1900?–7 Jul 1947 [47], Los Angeles CA; heart attack). (Fox, 1917; MGM.) "Sidney Wagner," *Variety,* 9 Jul 1947. AS, p. 1122. BHD2, p. 274. FDY, p. 469.

Wagner, William [actor] (b. New York NY, 7 Nov 1883–11 Mar 1964 [80], Los Angeles CA). "William Wagner," *Variety,* 18 Mar 1964 (began 1930). AS, p. 1122. BHD1, p. 565. IFN, p. 306.

Wagowsky, Erich [producer] (d. Jun 1927). BHD2, p. 274.

Wague, Georges [actor] (*né* Georges Marie Valentin Waag, b. Paris, France, 14 Jan 1874–17 Apr 1965 [91], Menton, France). AS, p. 1122.

Wahbi, Youssef [actor/director/producer] (b. Cairo, Egypt, 14 Jul 1898–13 Oct 1982 [84], Cairo, Egypt). AS, p. 1122. BHD, p. 328; BHD2, p. 274.

Wainwright, Godfrey [actor] (b. Nova Scotia, Canada, 5 May 1883–19 May 1956 [73], Woodland Hills CA). AS, p. 1122 (d. Calabassas CA). BHD, p. 328. IFN, p. 306.

Wainwright, Marie [stage/film actress] (b. Philadelphia PA, 8 May 1853–17 Aug 1923 [70], Scranton PA). m. (1) Winston Henry Slaughter (d. 1882); (2) Franklyn Roberts (d. 1907); (3) Louis James. (Stage debut: Booth's Theatre, 17 May 1877.) "Marie Wainwright, Actress, Dies at 68; Once Famous Player Was Leading Woman for Barrett and Booth and Salvini," *NYT,* 19 Aug 1923, 26:4 (b. 1855); "Mass for Marie Wainwright"; 21 Aug 1923, 17:2 (at St. Peter's Cathedral; interred at Dunmere, near Scranton). "Marie Wainwright," *Variety,* 23 Aug 1923. AMD, p. 352. AS, p. 1122. BHD, p. 328. IFN, p. 306. SD. "Marie Wainwright of Famous Past in 'Polly with a Past,'" *MPW,* 21 Aug 1920, 1047.

Waite, James R. [vaudeville/film actor] (d. 9 Nov 1913, Home of Incurables, New York NY). m. Virginia Dower (1 five-year-old child). "James R. Waite," *Variety,* 14 Nov 1913, 23:2. BHD, p. 328.

Waite, Malcolm Ivan [actor] (b. Menominee WI, 7 May 1892–25 Apr 1949 [56], Van Nuys CA). AS, p. 1122. BHD1, p. 565. IFN, p. 306. George Katchmer, "Remembering the Great Silents," *CI,* 204 (Jun 1992), 42, 44.

Wakefield, Frances [actress] (b. 1891–26 Mar 1943 [51?], Batavia NY). BHD, p. 328.

Wakefield, Gilbert [scenarist] (b. Sandgate, England, 23 Apr 1892–4 Jul 1963 [71], London, England). BHD2, p. 274.

Wakefield, Hugh [actor/scenarist] (b. Wanstead, England, 10 Nov 1888–5 Dec 1971 [83], London, England). AS, p. 1122. BHD2, p. 274.

Walbrook, Anton (son of a Viennese circus clown) [stage/film actor] (*né* Adolph Wilhelm Anton Wohlbrück, b. Vienna, Austria, 19 Nov 1900–9 Aug 1967 [66], Starnberg, Germany; heart attack). "Anton Walbrook, Screen Actor in Britain and Germany, Is Dead; Appeared on London Stage in "Watch on the Rhine'—Fled Nazis in 1937," *NYT,* 10 Aug 1967, 37:3 ("In 1949, Mr. Walbrook refused to appear in a German film, "Dice of Fate," because the leading lady was La Baarova, onetime favorite actress of Goebbels, the Nazi propaganda chief. ¶He later said: 'I did not want to work with somebody who was so closely associated with the Nazis.'" He was visiting Hansl Burg, the widow of Hans Albers, when he died.). "Anton Walbrook," *Variety,* 16 Aug 1967, p. 63. AS, p. 1122 (b. 1896; d. Munich, Germany). BHD1, p. 565 (d. Munich). IFN, p. 306. Waldman, p. 303.

Walburn, Raymond [actor] (b. Plymouth IN, 9 Sep 1887–26 Jul 1969 [81], New York NY [Death Certificate Index No. 15525]). "Raymond Walburn," *Variety,* 30 Jul 1969. AS, p. 1122. BHD1, p. 565. IFN, p. 306. Katz, p. 1201. Truitt, p. 338. Ernest Corneau, "Raymond Walburn, 'The Lovable Rascal,'" *CFC,* 43 (Summer, 1974), 41.

Walcamp, Marie [stage/film actress] (b. Dennison OH, 27 Jul 1894–17 Nov 1936 [42], Los Angeles CA; suicide by gas). m. **Harland Tucker,** 1919, Tokyo, Japan (d. 1949). (Universal.) AMD, p. 352. AS, p. 1122. BHD, pp. 81–83; 328. BR, pp. 86–89 (b. 17 Jul). IFN, p. 306 (age 43). "Marie Walcamp," *MPW,* 6 Oct 1917, 60. "Marie Walcamp in Accident," *MPW,* 19 Apr 1919, 360. "Marie Walcamp Weds Harland Tucker," *MPW,* 8 Nov 1919, 255. "'Banzi, Miss Walcamp,' Says Japan," *MPW,* 20 Dec 1919, 952. "Signs Marie Walcamp," *MPW,* 2 Feb 1924, 373. "Marie Walcamp in F.B.O. Production," *MPW,* 23 Jul 1927, 260. Billy H. Doyle, "Lost Players," *CI,* 171 (Sep 1989), C2.

Walck, Ezra C. [actor] (d. Sep 1927). BHD, p. 328.

Walcott, Charles M[elton], **Jr.** [stage/film actor] (b. Boston MA, 1 Jul 1840–1 Jan 1921 [80], New York NY). m. Isabella Nickinson (d. 1906). "Charles M. Walcot," *Variety,* 7 Jan 1921. AS, p. 1122 (b. 1843). SD.

Walcott, Julia [actress] (b. 1845–25 May 1915 [70?], Chicago IL). BHD, p. 328.

Waldau, Gustav [actor] (*né* Gustav Theodore Clemens Robert Freiherr von Rummel, b. Piflas, Germany, 27 Feb 1871–25 May 1958 [87], Munich, Germany). AS, p. 1123.

Waldemar, Richard [actor/singer] (b. Austria, 1870–15 Jan 1947 [76?], Vienna, Austria). AS, p. 1123.

Walden, Harold [actor] (b. 1889–2 Dec 1955 [66]). "Harold Walden," *Variety,* 14 Dec 1955, p. 71. BHD, p. 328.

Walden, Harry [actor] (b. 22 Oct 1875–4 Jun 1921 [45]). "Harry Walden," *Variety,* 10 Jun 1921, p. 37. BHD, p. 328.

Waldman, Ernst Emil [director] (b. Hildesheim, Germany, 29 Jul 1880). AS, p. 1123.

Waldow, Ernst [actor] (*né* Ernst Hermann Adolf De Wolff, b. Berlin, Germany, 22 Aug 1893–5 Jun 1964 [70], Hamburg, Germany). AS, p. 1123.

Waldrige, Harold [stage/film actor] (b. New Orleans LA, 1900?–26 Jun 1957 [57], New York NY [Death Certificate Index No. 13587; age 57]). "Harold Waldrige, Stage-Movie Actor," *NYT,* 28 Jun 1957, 23:4 ("He once said if he were offered a character who might pass an intelligence test he would probably have to give up his stage career."). "Harold Waldrige," *Variety,* 3 Jul 1957. AS, p. 1122 (b. 1906). BHD1, p. 565 (b. 1905). IFN, p. 307 (age 50). Truitt, p. 339.

Waldron, Andrew V. [actor] (b. London, England, 20 Sep 1847–1 Mar 1932 [84]). AMD, p. 352. AS, p. 1123 (d. Hollywood CA). BHD, p. 328. IFN, p. 307. "'Stunt' Performer at Seventy-One," *MPW,* 5 Oct 1918, 96. George A. Katchmer, "Forgotten Cowboys and Cowgirls—Part X," *CI,* 182 (Aug 1990), 39.

Waldron, Charles D. [stage/film actor] (b. Waterford NY, 23 Dec 1874–4 Mar 1946 [71], Los Angeles CA). m. May. (NY stage debut: *The New South,* Murray Hill Theatre, 1898). "Charles Waldron, Noted Actor, Dies; Stage and Screen Veteran, 71, Played More than 400 Roles—Was in 'Deep Are Roots,'" *NYT,* 7 Mar 1946, 25:1. "Charles Waldron," *Variety,* 13 Mar 1946. AS, p. 1123. BHD1, p. 565 (b. 1877). IFN, p. 307 (b. 1877). Truitt, p. 339.

Waldron, Isabel (mother of John Emery, 1905–1964) [actress] (b. England, 1871–9 Jan 1950 [78?], Mamaroneck NY). AS, p. 1123.

Waldron, Jack [actor] (b. Brooklyn NY, 3 Feb 1893–21 Nov 1969 [76], New York NY; heart attack). AS, p. 1123. BHD1, p. 566.

Wales, Claude Henry (Buddy) [cinematographer] (b. Indianapolis IN-d. 11 Dec 1921, Los Angeles CA). BHD2, p. 274.

Wales, Ethel [actress] (b. Passaic NJ, 4 Apr 1878–15 Feb 1952 [73], Los Angeles CA). (MGM.) "Ethel Wales," *Variety,* 27 Feb 1952 (age 71). AMD, p. 353. AS, p. 1123 (b. NY NY). BHD1, p. 566. IFN, p. 307. Truitt, p. 339 (b. NY NY, 1881). "Selects Ethel Wales," *MPW,* 10 Oct 1925, 466. "Ethel Wales," *MPW,* 6 Aug 1927, 384.

Wales, Henry [scenarist] (b. Englewood NJ, 14 Jun 1888–29 Jan 1960 [71], Paris, France). BHD2, p. 274.

Wales, Wally *see* **Alderson, Floyd T.**

Walker, Allan [writer] (d. 2 Sep 1970, Orangeburg NY). "Allan Walker," *Variety,* 14 Oct 1970.

Walker, Mrs. Allan [actress] (*née?*). No data found. m. **Allan Walker** (d. 1970).

Walker, Antoinette [actress] (b. 1874–14 Jul 1970 [96?], Topsfield MA). BHD, p. 328.

Walker, Ben [actor] (b. 1859?–3 Jan 1924 [64], Everett MA). "Ben Walker," *Variety,* 10 Oct 1924. AS, p. 1123. BHD, p. 328.

Walker, Charles "Tex" (*né* Charles Herbert Walker, b. Altoona PA, 17 Oct 1866–21 Aug 1947 [80], Los Angeles CA; pneumonia). AS, p. 1124 (Tex Walker). BHD1, p. 566.

Walker, Charlotte (mother of Sara Haden) [stage/film actress] (*née* Charlotte Walker de Komlosy, b. Galveston TX, 29 Dec 1876?–23 Mar 1958 [81], Kerrville TX). m. (1) John B. Hayden (daughter Sara, 1897–1981); (2) **Eugene Walter** (d. 1941). (Lasky; McClure; Mutual; Fox.) "Charlotte Walker, Actress, Dies at 81; Star on Broadway in World War I Era," *NYT,* 26 Mar 1958, 37:1. "Charlotte Walker," *Variety,* 26 Mar 1958 (d. 24 Mar, age 80). AMD, p. 353. AS, p. 1123 (b. 1878). BHD1, p. 566 (b. 1878). FSS, p. 285. IFN, p. 307 (b. 1878). Katz, p. 1202 (b. 1878). MSBB, p. 1042 (b. 1878). SD. Truitt, p. 339 (b. 1878). "Charlotte Walker in Lasky-Belasco Photoplays," *MPW,* 13 Feb 1915, 993. "Charlotte Walker Joins Thanhouser," *MPW,* 21 Oct 1916, 406. Billy H. Doyle, "Lost Players," *CI,* 161 (Nov 1988), C19 (b. 1878).

Walker, Christy [actress] (*nee?,* b. 1898–29 Oct 1918 [20], New York NY; influenza). m. Capt. H.N. Walker. AMD, p. 353. AS, p. 1123. BHD, p. 328 (b. 1896). IFN, p. 307. "Obituary," *MPW,* 23 Nov 1918, 828 (d. 19 Nov).

Walker, David [actor/title writer] (d. 28 Jul 1976). BHD, p. 328. FDY, p. 447.

Walker, Earl [cameraman]. No data found. FDY, p. 471.

Walker, Edith Campbell [actress] (b. England-d. 8 Oct 1937, Sydney, Australia). "Dame Eadith C. Walker," *NYT,* 9 Oct 1937, 19:2. AS, p. 1123 (d. 1967).

Walker, Granville M. [scenarist/agent] (b. 1888–14 Apr 1945 [57?], Beverly Hills CA). BHD2, p. 274.

Walker, H[arley] **M. "Beanie"** [scenarist/title writer/President of Hal Roach Studios] (b.

Logan County OH, 27 Jun 1884?–23 Jun 1937 [53], Chicago IL; heart attack). m. dancer Virginia Grose. "H.M. Walker," *Variety*, 30 Jun 1937 (wrote for Harold Lloyd, 1916). AMD, p. 353. AS, p. 1124. BHD2, p. 274 (b. 1887). "Harold Lloyd's 'High and Dizzy' Heads Pathé Release List for July 11 Week," *MPW*, 17 Jul 1920, 361. "Walker Kept Busy," *MPW*, 8 Aug 1925, 649. "'Beany' Walker Is 'Daddy' of Title Writers," *MPW*, 5 Feb 1927, 433. "Walker Promoted,' *MPW*, 12 Mar 1927, 99. "Harley M. Walker, Hal Roach Aide, Visits New York," *MPW*, 9 Apr 1927, 536.

Walker, James John [politician/composer/lyricist (*Will You Love Me in December as You Do in May*)] (b. New York NY, 19 Jun 1881–18 Nov 1946 [65], New York NY; cerebral hemorrhage). m. (1) Janet Allen, 1912; (2) **Betty Compson**, 18 Apr 1933, Cannes, France—div. 15 Mar 1941, Key West FL (d. 1974). "Ex-Mayor Walker Succumbs at 65 to Clot on Brain; City Chief for Seven Years Kept Popularity After Resigning [on 1 Sep 1932] Under Seabury Charges; Father of State Boxing; Former Impartial Chairman of Garment Industry Had Been Senate Leader in Albany," *NYT*, 19 Nov 1946, 1:3, 21:2. Joe Laurie, Jr., "Jimmy Walker," *Variety*, 20 Nov 1946. AS, p. 1124. Ruth Biery, "Winning in a Walker; Hollywood Votes the Mayor of New York More Popular Than the Climate," *MPC*, Oct 1928, 21, 68.

Walker, Johnnie [stage/film actor/director/producer] (b. New York [Bronx?] NY, 7 Jan 1894–5 Dec 1949 [55], St. Albans, Queens, New York NY [Death Certificate Index No. 10351; buried at Pinelawn Military Cemetery. Farmingdale, LI NY]; coronary thrombosis). m. (1) Rena Parker—div.; (2) **Maude Wayne**, 7 Mar 1928, Ventura Mission, Ventura CA—div. Mar 1936 (d. 1983). Richard Woods, *Johnnie Walker; Silent Movies' Favorite Son* (Baldwin NY: Richard Woods, 1999). (Edison, 1915; Fox; Columbia.) "Johnny Walker," *Variety*, 7 Dec 1949. AMD, p. 353. AS, p. 1124. BHD1, p. 566; BHD2, p. 274 (Johnny Walker). FFF, p. 159. FSS, p. 285. IFN, p. 307. Katz, p. 1202. MH, p. 141. Truitt, p. 339 (b. 1896). "Walker Has Juvenile Lead in 'Impossible Catherine,'" *MPW*, 28 Jun 1919, 1954. "Jiohnnie Walker Signs Contract with R-C to Star in Pictures," *MPW*, 10 Jun 1922, 551. "Walker to Make Inedepndent Pictures," *MPW*, 2 Jun 1923, 403. "Walker Engaged by Emory Johnson," *MPW*, 14 Jul 1923, 170. "Johnnie Walker—the Showman's Star," *MPW*, 3 Nov 1923, 65. "Johnnie Walker's 1923 Successes," *MPW*, 3 Nov 1923, 66. "Johnnie Walker," *MPW*, 28 May 1927, 270. Walter Ramsey, "Still Going Strong; Johnnie Walker Has a Fine Future Behind Him—and a Finer One Ahead," *MPC*, Jul 1928, 55, 77 (discusses being typecast in boy-roles). Richard Woods, "Johnnie Walker: My Great Uncle," *CI*, 212 (Feb 1993), 12 *et passim* (with filmography). Richard Woods, "'Over the Hill' Put William Fox Over the Top," *CI*, 222 (Dec 1993), 26, 28, 55. Richard Woods, "*Old Ironsides*: Silent Sensation or Magnascopic Mistake?," *CI*, 239 (May 1995), 14–16.

Walker, Joseph Bailey [cinematographer] (b. Denver CO, 1892–1 Aug 1985 [92], Las Vegas NV). m. **Marjorie Warfield** (d. 1991). With Juanita Walker, *The Light on Her Face* (Hollywood: The ASC Press, 1984). "Joe Walker," *NYT*, 3 Aug 1985, 29:6. "Joseph Walker, Top Cameraman and Capra Regular, Dead at 92," *Variety*, 7 Aug 1985. AS, p. 1124. BHD2, p. 274. FDY, p. 471. Katz, pp. 1202–03.

Walker, June (mother of John Kerr) [stage/film actress] (b. New York NY, 14 Jun 1900–3 Feb 1966 [65], Sherman Oaks CA). (Essanay.) m. Geoffrey Kerr, 1926–43 (son John, b. 15 Nov 1931). "June Walker, 65, First Lorelei Lee; Broadway Star Dies—In '26 'Gentlemen Prefer Blondes,'" *NYT*, 5 Feb 1966, 29:3 (b. NY NY). "June Walker," *Variety*, 9 Feb 1966 (d. LA CA, age 61). AS, p. 1124. BHD1, p. 566 (b. Chicago IL. 1899). IFN, p. 307. Truitt, p. 339 (b. NY NY, 1904).

Walker, Laura [actress] (b. 1894–17 May 1951 [57?], New York NY). BHD1, p. 566.

Walker, Lewis [actor] (b. 1860?–1 Nov 1915 [55], Nottingham, England; double pneumonia). "Lewis Walker Dead," *Variety*, 5 Nov 1915. AS, p. 1124.

Walker, Lillian C., "The Dresden Doll" and "Dimples Walker" (sister of **Karin** Walker **Norman**) [stage/film actress] (*née* Lillian Wolke, b. Brooklyn NY, 21 Apr 1887–10 Oct 1975 [88], Trinidad, West Indies, Jamaica). (Vitagraph, 1911; Crest Productions; Lillian Walker Pictures Corp.) "Lillian Walker, 88, Silent-Movie Star," *NYT*, 8 Nov 1975, 30:5. "Lillian Walker," *Variety*, 12 Nov 1975. AMD, p. 353. AS, p. 1124. BHD1, p. 566. IFN, p. 307. Katz, p. 1203. MH, p. 141. MSBB, p. 1042. Slide, pp. 154–55. "Lillian Walker's Come-Back," *MPW*, 14 Mar 1914, 1386. "Lillian Walker," *MPW*, 15 Aug 1914, 962. "Mr. Zukor Hospital Fund Treasurer," *MPW*, 25 Sep 1915, 2186. "The Dresden Doll of the Movies," *MPC*, Apr 1916, 29. "Lillian Walker Meets with Serious Accident," *MPW*, 7 Oct 1916, 90. "Lillian Walker Leaves Vitagraph," *MPW*, 3 Feb 1917, 666. "Lillian Walker Has Not Renewed Vitagraph Contract," *MPW*, 17 Feb 1917, 1018. "Lillian Walker," *MPW*, 24 Feb 1917, 1183. "Lillian Walker, *MPW*, 17 Mar 1917, 1753. "Lillian Walker," *MPW*, 7 Apr 1917, 82. Ben H. Grimm, "Lillian Walker Wants Stories," *MPW*, 28 Jul 1917, 658. "Lillian Walker Signs with Ogden," *MPW*, 1 Sep 1917, 1393. "Lillian Walker Signs with Crest," *MPW*, 5 Jan 1918, 102. "Lillian Walker in Government Film," 9 Mar 1918, 1380. "Lillian Walker to Be Starred in Elght Productions," *MPW*, 10 Aug 1918, 866. "Lillian Walker Joins Ranks of Pathé Serial Players," *MPW*, 2 Aug 1919, 695. "Books Lillian Walker," *MPW*, 19 Mar 1921, 283. Julia Shawell, "How Lillian Walker, Star of Other Days, Paid for Hot Passion!," *New York Evening Graphic*, 3 Oct 1931, 1.

Walker, Martin [actor] (b. Harrow, England, 27 Jul 1901–18 Sep 1955 [54], London, England). AS, p. 1124.

Walker, Mildred, "Miss Pittsburgh" [actress]. No data found. (Began Mar 1927; film debut: bit in *The Night Bride*, Metropolitan; Gaiety Productions.) "Mildred Walker," *MPW*, 21 May 1927, 180. "Coming into Her Own; Mildred Walker," *MPW*, 23 Jul 1927, 239:4 (won a beauty contest in Pittsburgh and represented that city in the Atlantic City Pageant. To make ten 2-reel comedies with Billy Cinders for Victor Adamson, the first of which was *Trouble*.).

Walker, Nella [actress] (b. Chicago IL, 6 Mar 1886–22 Mar 1971 [85], Los Angeles CA; heart attack). AS, p. 1124. BHD1, p. 566. IFN, p. 307.

Walker, Norman [actor/director/producer] (b. Shaw, England, 28 Oct 1892–4 Nov 1963 [71], London, England). AS, p. 1124. BHD2, p. 274.

Walker, Raymond [composer] (*né* Warren Reynolds Walker, b. 29 Dec 1883–20 Jun 1960 [76], New York NY). "Ray Walker," *Variety*, 29 Jun 1960 (wrote *I'm the Messenger Boy in Demand; Oh What I Know About You; That Funny Bunny Hug*). ASCAP 66, p. 760. AS, p. 1124.

Walker, Robert Donald [stage/film actor] (b. Bethlehem PA, 18 Jun 1888–4 Mar 1954 [65], Los Angeles CA). (Kalem; Edison.) AMD, p. 353. AS, p. 1124. BHD1, p. 566. IFN, p. 307. "In the Picture Studios," *NYDM*, 8 Sep 1915, 36:4 (nephew of Robert Hilliard). "Robert Walker," *MPW*, 25 Sep 1915, 2192. "Robert Walker, Metro Player," *MPW*, 9 Dec 1916, 1499. George A. Katchmer, "Forgotten Cowboys and Cowgirls—Part XV," *CI*, 192 (Jun 1991), 42.

Walker, Stuart Armstrong [actor/director/author/producer] (b. Augusta KY, 4 Mar 1888–13 Mar 1941 [53], Beverly Hills CA; heart attack). (Paramount.) "Stuart Walker, 53, Producer, Is Dead; Paramount Films Executive Since 1936, Once Scenarist, Also Known as Playwright [*Five Flights Up*]; Began with Belasco at 21; Founder of the Portmanteau Theatre Was First to Stage Tarkington's 'Seventeen,'" *NYT*, 14 Mar 1941, 21:1. "Stuart Walker," *Variety*, 19 Mar 1941. AS, p. 1124. BHD2, p. 274. IFN, p. 307.

Walker, Syd [actor] (b. Manchester, England, 22 Mar 1887–13 Jan 1945 [57], Hove, England). AS, p. 1124 (b. Salford, England, 1866-d. London, England). BHD1, p. 567 (b. Salford, 1886). IFN, p. 307 (b. Salford, 1886).

Walker, Tex [actor] (*né* Charles Herbert Walker, b. Altoona PA, 17 Oct 1866–22 Aug 1947 [80], Los Angeles CA). AS, p. 1124.

Walker, Thomas (Whimsical) [actor] (b. Hull, England, 1850–5 Nov 1934 [84?], Gorleston, Norfolk, England). BHD, p. 329.

Walker, Vernon L. [cinematographer] (b. Detroit MI, 2 May 1894–14 Mar 1948 [53], Orange County CA). AS, p. 1124. BHD2, p. 274.

Walker, Waldo [assistant director] (b. Chicago IL, 1885–8 Sep 1961 [76?], Carmel NY). AMD, p. 353. BHD2, p. 274. "Waldo Walker Becomes Assistant Director," *MPW*, 8 Jan 1916, 223.

Walker, Wally [actor] (*né* Walter Walker, b. 1901–7 Aug 1975 [74], Woodland Hills CA). AS, p. 1125. BHD, p. 329. IFN, p. 307.

Walker, Walter [actor] (b. Trenton NJ?, 1864?–4 Dec 1947 [83], Honolulu HI). "Walter Walker," *NYT*, 5 Dec 1947, 26:2. AS, p. 1125 (b. 1916). BHD1, p. 567. IFN, p. 307.

Wall, David V. [stage/film actor] (b. Rochester NY, 1869–1 Jun 1938 [68], New York NY). m. Margaret. (Rex; FP-L; Pathé.) (Stage debut: Lyceum Theatre, Rochester NY.) "David V. Wall, Actor on Stage and Screen; Former Leading Man for Mary Pickford Dies Here at 68," *NYT*, 2 Jun 1938, 23:4 ("On the screen he acted character roles for Famous Players, Pathé and other companies."). "David V. Wall," *Variety*, 8 Jun 1938. AS, p. 1125 (b. Rochester NY). BHD, p. 329 (b. Coburg, Canada, 1870). IFN, p. 307. Truitt, p. 340.

Wall, Harry [scenarist] (b. Keighley, England, 6 Jun 1886–24 Jun 1966 [80], England). BHD2, p. 274.

Wall, Jean [actress] (*née* Jean Salomon Wallenstein, b. Paris, France, 31 Dec 1900 [extrait de naissance no. 20/23/1901]–24 Oct 1959 [58], Paris, France; heart attack). AS, p. 1125.

Wallace, Catherine [actress]. No data found. (*Fl.* 1924–28.)

Wallace, Charles Ray [film editor] (b. 1872?–15 Feb 1949 [77], Yonkers NY). "Charles Ray Wallace," *Variety,* 23 Feb 1949. AMD, p. 353. AS, p. 1125. "Wallace Is New Fox Film Editor," *MPW,* 27 Sep 1919, 1968.

Wallace, E.A. [cameraman]. No data found. AMD, p. 353. "A Camera Man in the Trenches," *MPW,* 20 Feb 1915, 1147.

Wallace, Edgar [actor/writer/scenarist] (*né* Richard Edgar Horatio Wallace, b. Ashburnham Grove, England, 1 Apr 1875–10 Feb 1932 [56], Beverly Hills CA; double pneumonia). m. (1) Ivy M. Caldecott; (2) Ethel Violet King. Autobiography, 1929. (RKO.) "Edgar Wallace, Noted Writer, Dies; Is Victim of Pneumonia at 56 in Hollywood Where He Was Writing for Movies; Was Author of 150 Books; His Detective Stories Sold 5,000,000 Yearly—Also Wrote 20 Plays and Countless Racing Articles," *NYT,* 11 Feb 1932, 21:1. "Edgar Wallace Dead; 200 Novels, 23 Plays in Amazing Career," *Variety,* 16 Feb 1932. AS, p. 1125. BHD1, p. 567; BHD2, p. 274 (b. Greenwich, England). FDY, p. 439. IFN, p. 308. Waldman, p. 304 (b. 1876; "His draft of *The Beast* became *King Kong* [1933].").

Wallace, Edna [actress] (b. San Francisco CA, 17 Jan 1874–14 Dec 1959 [85], New York NY). m. (1) **De Wolfe Hopper**—div. 1898 (d. 1935); (2) Albert O. Brown. "Edna Wallace Hopper," *Variety,* 16 Dec 1959 (toured with film of her facelift operation). AMD, p. 170. AS, p. 539 (Edna Wallace-Hopper); p. 1125 (b. 1882; d. 1957). BHD, p. 203. "Edna Wallace Hopper with Equitable," *MPW,* 22 Jan 1916, 613.

Wallace, Ethel Lee [actress] (b. Springfield MO, 1888?–7 Sep 1956 [68], Springfield MO). "Ethel Lee Wallace," *Variety,* 12 Sep 1956 ("vet musicomedy and silent film player" with Arbuckle and G.M. Anderson). AS, p. 1125. BHD, p. 329. IFN, p. 308. Truitt, p. 340.

Wallace, Frank R. [actor] (b. Fond du Lac WI, 1876?–29 Aug 1927 [51], Fon du Lac WI; suicide by shooting). "Frank R. Wallace," *Variety,* 7 Sep 1927. AS, p. 1125.

Wallace, George Stevenson (father of George Wallace, Jr., b. 25 Aug 1919) [actor/scenarist] (b. Aberdeen, Australia, 1894–3 Nov 1960 [66?], Sydney, Australia). AS, p. 1125.

Wallace, Grant [scenarist] (b. Hopkins MO, 1867–12 Aug 1954 [87?], Berkeley CA). BHD2, p. 274.

Wallace, Inez [actress/scenarist] (d. 28 Jun 1966, Cleveland OH). AS, p. 1125. BHD, p. 329; BHD2, p. 274. IFN, p. 308. Truitt, p. 340.

Wallace, Irene [actress]. No data found. (Victor; Selig; Universal.) AMD, p. 353. "Irene Wallace," *MPW,* 20 Sep 1913, 1270 ("an exponent of Hebraic parts"). "Irene Wallace," *MPW,* 13 Feb 1915, 1002. J. Van Cartmell, "...News from the Pacific Colony," *NYDM,* 8 Sep 1915, 32:3 ("Irene Wallace, the little ingenue with the Selig Company, has been granted a two weeks' lay-off to allow for an operation on her nose."). Emma-Lindsay Squier, "It's a Wild Life," *MPC,* Dec 1921, 36–37, 74.

Wallace, John [actor] (b. England, 24 Aug 1869–16 Jul 1946 [76], Los Angeles Co. CA). AS, p. 1125. BHD1, p. 567. IFN, p. 308.

Wallace, Lew [novelist] (b. Brookville, Franklin Couty, IN, 10 Apr 1827–15 Feb 1905 [77], Crawfordsville IN; ravages of a wasting disease). m. writer Susan A. Elston, 1852, Covington IN (d. 1907). AMD, p. 353. "General Lew Wallace Dies at Indiana Home; Author of 'Ben Hur' [1880] Expires After Long Illness; Won Fame in Many Ways; His Long Career as Lawyer, Soldier, Diplomat [former American Minister to Turkey], and Author—Was Nearly 78 Years Old," *NYT,* 16 Feb 1905, 9:3. "Lew Wallace Funeral Plans; Body to Be Viewed by Public To-day—Private Ceremony To-morrow," *NYT,* 17 Feb 1905, 9:5. "Gen. Lew Wallace's Funeral [Feb 18]; Crawfordville Suspended Business During the Simple Services," *NYT,* 19 Feb 1905, 7:2 ("Only the family and a few intimate friends attended." The choir sang *Face to Face.*). "Mrs. Lew Wallace Dead; Assisted Her Husband in His Work and Produced Books of Her Own," *NYT,* 3 Oct 1907, 9:4 (b. Crawfordsville IN, 25 Dec 1930. Wrote *The Patter of Little Feet* [poem], 1853. Son: Henry Lane.). "Lew Wallace's Heir Sues Klaw & Erlanger," *MPW,* 25 Sep 1915, 2178 (posthumous article).

Wallace, Maude Powers [actress] (b. 1893–23 Apr 1952 [59?], Los Angeles CA). AS, p. 1125.

Wallace, May [stage/comic opera/film actress] (b. 1880?–16 Sep 1928 [48], New York NY). m. **Tom Waters**, 1902 (d. 1953). "Mrs. Tom Waters (May Wallace)," *Variety,* 19 Sep 1928 (with Weber and Fields). "Another Team in Pictures," *MPW,* 20 Nov 1915, 1483:2.

Wallace, May [stage/film actress] (*née* May Maddox, b. Russiaville IN, 23 Aug 1877–11 Dec 1938 [61], Los Angeles CA; heart attack). m. Thomas W. Maddoxs. "May Wallace," *NYT,* 13 Dec 1938, 26:2 ("veteran motion picture and vaudeville actress"). AS, p. 1125. BHD1, p. 567. IFN, p. 308. Truitt, p. 340.

Wallace, Milton [actor] (b. 24 Sep 1887–16 Feb 1956 [68], Los Angeles CA). AS, p. 1125.

Wallace, Morgan [stage/film actor/writer] (b. Lompoc CA, 26 Jul 1881–12 Dec 1953 [72], Tarzana CA). m. Louise Chapman (d. 1962). "Morgan Wallace, Actor-Writer, 72; Former Stage and Film Player, Author of Broadway Comedy in 1929, Dies on Coast," *NYT,* 15 Dec 1953, 39:3 ("In Hollywood he played roles in silent and sound movies..."). "Morgan Wallace," *Variety,* 16 Dec 1953. AS, p. 1125. BHD1, p. 567. IFN, p. 308. Truitt, p. 340 (b. 1888).

Wallace, Nellie [actress] (b. Glasgow, Scotland, 18 Mar 1882–24 Nov 1948 [66], Bowdoinham ME). AS, p. 1125 (b. 1881; d. London, England). BHD1, p. 567 (d. London, England).

Wallace, Ramsey [stage/film actor]. No data found. (1st National.) "Ramsey Wallace a Star," *LA Times,* 28 Jan 1920, II, 11.

Wallace, Richard [director/producer] (*né* Clarence Richard Wallace, b. Sacramento CA, 26 Aug 1894–3 Nov 1951 [57], Los Angeles CA; heart attack). m. Mary Lewis. (Sennett; Paramount.) (Directorial debut: *McFadden's Flats,* 1927.) "Richard Wallace, Film Director, 57; Paramount Aide Who Handled Chevalier's First U.S. Movie Dies After Football Game," *NYT,* 5 Nov 1951, 31:5. "Richard Wallace," *Variety,* 7 Nov 1951. AMD, p. 353. AS, p. 1126 (d. 23 Oct). BHD2, p. 275. IFN, p. 308. Katz, p. 1204. "Richard Wallace May Join U.-A.," *MPW,* 23 Apr 1927, 714. "Richard Wallace Directs Five Big Successes in Year," *MPW,* 29 Oct 1927, 556. Herbert Cruikshank, "From Embalmy Days to Balmy; Before Becoming a Director, Richard Wallace Was in the Undertaking Game," *MPC,* Sep 1928, 33, 84.

Wallace, Thomas Henry [actor] (b. 1872?–18 Mar 1932 [60]). AS, p. 1126 (d. Hollywood CA). BHD, p. 329. IFN, p. 308.

Wallace, William [still photographer] (b. 1900?–22 Dec 1954 [54], Los Angeles CA). "William Wallace," *Variety,* 29 Dec 1954.

Wallack, Lester [actor/producer/writer]. No data found. AMD, p. 353. "Metro Gets Wallack Plays," *MPW,* 25 Sep 1915, 2192.

Wallen, Sigurd [actor/director] (b. Tierp, Sweden, 1 Sep 1884–20 Mar 1947 [62], Stockholm, Sweden). AS, p. 1126. BHD2, p. 275.

Wallentin, Claire [actress] (*née* Gräfin Metternich). m. Count Gisbert Wolff-Metternich. Vittorio Martinelli, "Kino-Lieblinge," *Griffithiana,* 38/39 (Oct 1990), 38.

Waller, Fred, Jr. [inventor of Cinerama] (b. Brooklyn NY, 1886–18 May 1954 [68?], Huntington NY). AMD, p. 354. AS, p. 1126. BHD2, p. 275. "Waller Invents Printing Machine," *MPW,* 3 Apr 1915, 82.

Waller, Lewis [stage/film actor] (*né* William Waller Lewis, b. Bilbao, Spain, 3 Nov 1860–1 Nov 1915 [55], Nottingham, England; double pneumonia). m. Florence West (d. 1912). (Stage debut: *Uncle Dick's Darling,* Toole's Theatre, London, Mar 1883). "Lewis Waller, Noted Romantic Actor, Dies; London Manager, Who Last Appeared Here in 'Beaucaire,' Expires of Pneumonia," *NYT,* 2 Nov 1915, 11:4. "Lewis Waller Dead," *Variety,* 5 Nov 1915 (came to America in 1911). AMD, p. 354. AS, p. 1126. BHD, p. 329 (d. London, England). IFN, p. 308. "Lewis Waller in Universal Picture," *MPW,* 8 Apr 1916, 267.

Waller, Tom [writer/publicist]. No data found. AMD, p. 354. "Waller Goes with Associated," *MPW,* 17 Oct 1925, 545.

Waller, Wallet [actor/producer] (b. 1882–19 Mar 1951 [68?]). BHD, p. 329; BHD2, p. 275.

Wallerstein, Pearl Avnet [actress] (b. 1895–2 Mar 1987 [91?], Burbank CA). BHD, p. 329.

Walling, Effie Bond [actress] (b. CA, 12 Apr 1879–9 Jun 1961 [82], Berkeley CA). AS, p. 1126. BHD, p. 329. IFN, p. 308. Truitt, p. 340.

Walling, Richard [actor] (b. New York NY, 6 Oct 1904–11 Dec 1983 [79], Burbank CA). AS, p. 1126. BHD1, p. 619.

Walling, Roy [actor] (b. OR, 1889–7 May 1964 [75], Stanfordville NY). BHD, p. 329. IFN, p. 308.

Walling, Will[iam] **R.** [actor] (b. Sacramento City IA, 2 Jun 1872–5 Mar 1932 [59], CA). (Fox.) AS, p. 1126 (*né* William Waller, b. OH, 1892). BHD1, p. 568. IFN, p. 308. George Katchmer, "Remembering the Great Silents," *CI* (Jun 1993), 49–50.

Wallis, Bertram [actor] (b. London, England, 22 Feb 1874–11 Apr 1952 [78]). AS, p. 1126 (d. London, England). BHD1, p. 568. IFN, p. 308.

Wallis, Hal B. [publicist/producer] (*né* Harold Brent Walinsky, b. Chicago IL, 14 Sep 1898–5 Oct 1986 [88], Rancho Mirage CA; complications from diabetes). m. **Louise Fazenda**, 24 Nov 1927 (d. 1962); Martha Hyer, 31 Dec 1966 (b. 10 Aug 1924). With Charles Higham, *Starmaker; The Autobiography of Hal Wallis* (New York: MacMillan Publishing Co., Inc., 1980). Tim Page, "Hal B. Wallis, Film Producer, Is Dead," *NYT,* 8

Oct 1986, D30:1. Todd McCarthy, "Hal Wallis, Studio Exec & Producer for Over 50 Years, Dies at 88," *Variety,* 15 Oct 1986. AMD, p. 354. AS, p. 1126. BHD2, p. 275. "Wedding March," *MPW,* 3 Dec 1927, 23. Frank Dolven, "Hal B. Wallis: The Golden-Arm Producer," *CI,* 220 (Oct 1993), C18-C19, 56 (b. 1899).

Wallock, Edwin N. [stage/film actor] (*né* Edward Wallock Wack, b. Council Bluffs IA, 6 Nov 1877–4 Feb 1951 [73], Los Angeles CA). (Selig; Universal.) BHD, p. 329 (Edwin L. Wallock). AS, p. 1126. IFN, p. 308. George Katchmer, "Remembering the Great Silents," *CI,* 247 (Jan 1996), 45.

Wallraven, J.H. [title writer]. No data found. FDY, p. 447.

Walls, Tom [actor/director] (b. Kingsthorpe, England, 18 Feb 1883–27 Nov 1949 [66], Edwell, England). AS, p. 1126. BHD2, p. 275.

Walpole, Hugh [Seymour] [novelist/scenarist] (b. Auckland, New Zealand, 13 Mar 1884–1 Jun 1941 [57], Brackenburn [near Keswick], England; heart attack). Bachelor. (First novel: *The Wooden Horse,* 1909.) "Sir Hugh Walpole Dies in England, 57; Noted Novelist Is Stricken at Home in Lake District, Scene of His 'Heiress' Series; Book a Year Since 1909; Son of Bishop, Former Tutor, Covered Wide Literary Field and Lectured Extensively," *NYT,* 2 Jun 1941, 17:1. "Hugh Walpole," *Variety,* 4 Jun 1941. AS, p. 1126. BHD2, p. 275. IFN, p. 308.

Walpole, Stanley [stage/film actor] (b. Melbourne, Australia, 1886). (Reliance; Eclair.) m. Ethel Phillips. AMD, p. 354. AS, p. 1126. BHD, p. 329. Photoplay Arts Portfolio. MSBB, p. 1030. 1921 Directory, p. 206 (b. 1886). "Stanley Walpole," *MPW,* 6 Jun 1914, 1418. "Stanley Walpole Versatile Player," *Motography,* 11 Jul 1914, 50. "Universal Signs Stanley Walpole," *MPW,* 11 Mar 1916, 1640.

Walsh, Billy [actor] (d. 16 Jun 1952, Brooklyn NY). (Keystone.) "Billy Walsh," *Variety,* 25 Jun 1952. AS, p. 1126. BHD, p. 329. Truitt, p. 341.

Walsh, Blanche [stage/vaudeville/film actress] (b. New York NY, 4 Jan 1873–31 Oct 1915 [42], Lakeside Hospital, Cleveland OH; nervous breakdown following an operation). m. (1) **Alfred D. Hickman,** 1896 (d. 1931); William H. Travers, 1906 (widower). (Stage debut: *Siberia,* 1888; NY debut: *Twelfth Night,* Tomkin's Fifth Avenue, 13 Dec 1889). "Blanche Walsh Dies After an Operation; Expires in a Cleveland Hospital to Which She Returned as Relapse Set In; Long Prominent on Stage; Actress Was Daughter of T.P. Walsh, Former Tombs Warden—Was Born in Mott Street," *NYT,* 1 Nov 1915, 11:5 (A.M. Palmer Stock Co.; Empire Theatre Stock Co., 1898). "Blanche Walsh's Funeral Today," *NYT,* 3 Nov 1915, 15:5. "Blanche Walsh," *Variety,* 5 Nov 1915. AMD, p. 354. AS, p. 1127. BHD, p. 329. IFN, p. 308. "Miss Walsh's Grip Did It; Dorothy Dorr's Thoat Has a Bad Attack of Stage Realism," *NYT,* 24 Feb 1905, 7:4 (in *The Woman in the Case* at the Herald Sq. Theatre, Dorr was injured because of "the violent manner in which Blanche Walsh, the star of the piece, choked her in the third act, resulting in an aggravated case of bruised tonsils.... On the opening night of the play at Rochester several weeks ago, Miss Walsh hit Miss Dorr's head so hard against the piano that Miss Dorr was knocked unconscious, and for a moment it looked as if there were to be no further continuation of the performance."). "Blanche Walsh in Pictures," *MPW,* 13 Jul 1912, 131. "Famous Players Engage Blanche Walsh," *MPW,* 22 Aug 1914, 1089. "Blanche Walsh Signs with Triumph," *MPW,* 14 Aug 1915, 1139. "Blanche Walsh Dead," *NYDM,* 6 Nov 1915, 9:2. "Obituary," *MPW,* 6 Nov 1915, 1143.

Walsh, Frank [actor] (*né* Miles Standish Marsh, b. 1860–18 Jul 1932 [72?], New York NY). AS, p. 1127 (d. 19 Jul). BHD, p. 329.

Walsh, George (brother of **Raoul Walsh**) [actor] (b. New York NY, 16 Mar 1889–13 Jun 1981 [92], Pomona CA; pneumonia). (Fox.) m. (1) **Seena Owen,** Feb 1916–24 (d. 1966). (Began 1915; Fox.) "George Walsh," *Variety,* 24 Jun 1981. AMD, p. 354. AS, p. 1127. BHD1, p. 568. FFF, p. 165 (b. 1892). FSS, p. 286. GK, pp. 976–85. Katz, p. 1205 (began 1914). MH, p. 141 (b. 1898). MSBB, p. 1030 (b. 1892). Spehr, p. 172 (b. 1892). "Two Stars United," *MPW,* 1 Jul 1916, 81 (married Owen). "George Walsh a Popular Favorite," *MPW,* 10 Aug 1918, 823. "The Walsh's Are Working Together," *MPW,* 17 Aug 1918, 997. "Victory Pictures Feature Brockwell, Mix and Walsh," *MPW,* 19 Jul 1919, 355. "George Walsh," *MPW,* 19 Jul 1919, 359. "Walsh on His Last Fox Film," *MPW,* 4 Sep 1920, 68. "Walsh WINs Contest," *MPW,* 16 Oct 1920, 986. "George Walsh to Head Company; His Style Is a Smile All the While," *MPW,* 23 Oct 1920, 1143. "Walsh with Circuit?," *MPW,* 2 Apr 1921, 480. "Goldwyn Signs Walsh," *MPW,* 3 Mar 1923, 33. "Goldwyn Renews Its Contract with Walsh," *MPW,* 18 Aug 1923, 582. Blake McVeigh, "Why I Am Not a 'Sport'; Popular young screen star who has gone abroad to play 'Ben Hur' tells why he prefers life of cloistered quietude to that of primrose path," *MW,* 29 Mar 1924, 24, 40. Louise Morgan, "What Evil Influence Wrecks the Happy Homes of Hollywood?," *MW,* 19 Apr 1924, 8–9, 28 (discusses separated couples). "I.E. Chadwick Signs George Walsh to Long Term Contract; Will Do Serial," *MPW,* 6 Dec 1924, 558. "Chadwick's Newest Star," *MPW,* 14 Feb 1925, 706. George A. Katchmer, "George Walsh, Athlete," *CI,* 106 (Apr 1984), 23–24, 46. Richard E. Braff, "An Index to the Films of George Walsh," *CI,* 180 (Jun 1990), 20, 37. R.E. Braff, "Additional Film Credits for George Walsh," *CI,* 238 (Apr 1995), 42.

Walsh, Joe [actor]. No data found. AMD, p. 354. "Joe Walsh to Play in Art Dramas," *MPW,* 16 Jun 1917, 1811.

Walsh, John [actor] (b. 1853–3 Jul 1914 [61?], New Britain CT). AS, p. 1127.

Walsh, Perry [actor] (b. Luon, England, 24 Apr 1888–19 Jan 1952 [63], London, England). AS, p. 1127.

Walsh, Phil [director]. No data found. AMD, p. 354. "Phil Walsh," *MPW,* 13 Nov 1915, 1279.

Walsh, Raoul A. (brother of **George Walsh**) [actor/director/producer/scenarist] (*né* Albert Edward Walsh, b. New York NY, 11 Mar 1887–31 Dec 1980 [93], Los Angeles CA; heart attack). m. (1) **Miriam Cooper,** Feb 1916, Hopi Indian Reservation near Albuquerque NM—div. 1927 (d. 1976); Lorraine Miller. *Each Man in His Own Time* (NY: Farrar, Strauss & Giroux, 1974). (Biograph, 1912; Pathé; Fox.) Peter B. Flint, "Raoul Walsh, Director, Dies at 93; His Action Films Reflected His Life," *NYT,* 2 Jan 1981, IV, 7:2. Todd McCarthy, "Raoul Walsh, 93, A Giant; Played John Wilkes Booth for Griffith—Directed 110 Features," *Variety,* 7 Jan 1981 (d. Hollywood). AMD, p. 354. AS, p. 1127 (d. Simi Valley CA). BHD1, p. 568; BHD2, p. 275 (b. 1889). FDY, p. 439. JS, p. 497 (worked in Italy in 1956 and 1960). Katz, p. 1206. Spehr, p. 172 (b. 1889). "Walsh an Adventurer," *Motography,* 4 Jul 1914, 18 (heavy leads for Reliance and Majestic). "Raoul Walsh Back to Coast," *MPW,* 19 Feb 1916, 1113. "Raoul A. Walsh to Direct Goerge Walsh," *MPW,* 22 Sep 1917, 1838. "Walsh Joins Goldwyn," *MPW,* 1 Dec 1917, 1301. "What Walsh Found in Goldwyn Studio," *MPW,* 5 Jan 1918, 57. "Walsh Talks About Casting," *MPW,* 12 Jan 1918, 57. "Waslk to Remain with Fox," *MPW,* 19 Jan 1918, 345. Hanford C. Judson, "A Modern Picture Director's Problems," *MPW,* 4 May 1918, 702. "Film Division Names Director Advisors," *MPW,* 20 Jul 1918, 363–64. "The Walsh's Are Working Together," *MPW,* 17 Aug 1918, 997. "His Beard Was Long and His Hair Hung Down, and the Girl of His Heart Was Coming to Town," *MPW,* 4 Oct 1919, 66. "Walsh to Occupy Municipal Studios in Long Island City Now Being Formed," *MPW,* 31 Jan 1920, 760. "Raoul A. Walsh to Make Special Stills for Use on Posters," *MPW,* 21 Aug 1920, 1055. "Raoul Walsh Asks Damages of $245,000, Charging Mayflower Violated Contract," *MPW,* 12 Mar 1921, 176. "To Probably Transfer Waslh-Mayflower Suit," *MPW,* 23 Apr 1921, 828. "Raoul A. Walsh Joins Goldwyn Directors," *MPW,* 20 May 1922, 308. David A. Balch, "Wanted: A Blonde [sic] Leading Man; Able young movie director who created 'The Thief of Bagdad' says screen is suffering from lack of new faces—Chance for blonde leading man," *MW,* 26 Apr 1924, 7, 30. "Raoul Walsh to Direct Gloria," *MPW,* 4 Jun 1927, 329 (in *Miss Sadie Thompson*). "Raoul Walsh Will Return to Fox," *MPW,* 24 Sep 1927, 223. "Raoul Walsh Plays and Directs," *MPW,* 17 Dec 1927, 27. Herbert Cruikshank, "He Envies His Actors; And Upon the Least Provocation Raoul Walsh Stops Directing and Joins Them," *MPC,* Jan 1929, 33, 79.

Walsh, Thomas B. [director]. No data found. AMD, p. 354. "Tom Walsh, Assistant Director," *MPW,* 8 May 1915, 920. "Walsh Gives Credit to Men Aiding in Making Next Picture," *MPW,* 23 Jul 1921, 425.

Walsh, Thomas H. [stage/film actor] (b. Chattanooga TN, 9 Jan 1863–25 Apr 1925 [62], New York NY; strangulation due to a goitre). (Broadway debut: *The Love Cure,* New Amsterdam, 1900.) "'Hell's Bells' Actor Dies; Thomas H. Walsh, Leading Man, Expires Suddenly of Heart Disease," *NYT,* 26 Apr 1925, II, 7:1. "Thomas H. Walsh," *Variety,* 29 Apr 1925. AS, p. 1127. BHD, p. 329. Truitt, p. 341.

Walsh, William C. [director] (b. 1882–7 Mar 1935 [53?], Los Angeles CA). BHD2, p. 275.

Walsh, William J. [actor] (b. 1869?–8 Nov 1921 [52], Mamaroneck NY; from gunshot wound of 6 Nov 1921). AMD, p. 354. AS, p. 1127. BHD, p. 329 (b. 1879). IFN, p. 308. "Obituary," *MPW,* 19 Nov 1921, 282 (accident at D.W. Griffith's Mamaroneck studio).

Walska, Ganna [opera singer/actress] (b. Poland, 24 Jun 1887–2 Mar 1984 [96], Santa Barbara CA). AMD, p. 354. BHD, p. 330. "Another Opera Singer Comes to Screen," *MPW,* 15 Jul 1916, 464 (lost her voice).

Waltemeyer, Jack K. [actor] (b. Salida CO, 10 Jun 1883–12 Jan 1959 [75], Los Angeles CA). BHD, p. 330.

Walter, Bruno [composer] (*né* Bruno Walter

Schlesinger, b. Berlin, Germany, 15 Sep 1876–17 Feb 1962 [85], Beverly Hills CA). AS, p. 1127.

Walter, Eugene [playwright/dialogue writer/scenarist] (b. Cleveland OH, 27 Nov 1874–26 Sep 1941 [66], Los Angeles CA). m. (1) **Charlotte Walker** (d. 1958); (2) Mary Kissel; (3) Mary Dorne. "Eugene Walter, Wrote Stage Hits; Author of 'Paid in Full,' 'The Easiest Way' and 'Trail of the Lonesome Pine' Dies at 64; A Hollywood Scenarist; Former Reporter Here and in the West Once Husband of Charlotte Walker, Actress," *NYT,* 27 Sep 1941, 17:4. AMD, p. 355. AS, p. 1127 (b. 1877). BHD, p. 330; BHD, p. 275. FDY, p. 447 (dialogue for *Mother Knows Best,* 1928) "Eugene Walter to Write for Screen," *MPW,* 26 Oct 1918, 525. "Eugene Walter Has Joined Goldwyn Studio Forces," *MPW,* 27 Sep 1919, 1986. "Eugene Walter Is Third Playwright to Join Metro's Staff of Eminent Authors," *MPW,* 3 Apr 1920, 129. "Walter, Veiller and Smith, Prominent Dramatists, Turn Talents to Metro Screen," *MPW,* 24 Apr 1920, 557.

Walter, J. Wallett [actor/director] (b. England, 1881–19 Mar 1951 [70?], England). AS, p. 1127.

Walter, Joseph [cinematographer]. No data found. FDY, p. 471 (may be Joseph Walker).

Walter, Vernon L. [cameraman] (b. 1895?–14 Mar 1948 [53], Balboa Island CA). (Sennett; Fox; Pathé; WB; Columbia.) "Vernon L. Walter," *Variety,* 17 Mar 1948. FDY, p. 471 (Vernon Walker).

Walter, Wilfrid [actor] (b. Ripon, England, 2 Mar 1882–9 Jul 1958 [76], Ashtead, England). AS, p. 1127.

Walter, Wilmer [stock/stage/film/radio actor] (b. Philadelphia PA, 1884–23 Aug 1941 [57], Mjt. Sinai Hospital, New York NY; after a fortnight's illness). "Wilmer Walter; Played David Harum 1,500 Times in Radio Sketch—Dies at 57," *NYT,* 25 Aug 1941, 15:1. "Wilmer Walter," *Variety,* 27 Aug 1941, p. 54. AS, p. 1127. BHD, p. 330. IFN, p. 308.

Walter, Wilmer [film/radio actor] (b. Philadelphia PA, 1884?–23 Aug 1941 [57], New York NY). "Wilmer Walter; Played David Harum 1,500 Times in Radio Sketch—Dies at 57," *NYT,* 25 Aug 1941, 15:1. "Wilmer Walter," *Variety,* 27 Aug 1941. AS, p. 1127. IFN, p. 308.

Walterlin, Oskar [actor/director] (b. Bale, Switzerland, 30 Jul 1895–4 Apr 1961 [65], Hamburg, Germany). AS, p. 1127.

Walters, Dorothy [actress] (b. 1877?–17 Apr 1934 [57], New York NY; bronchial pneumonia). "Dorothy Walters," *Variety,* 24 Apr 1934. AS, p. 1127. BHD, p. 330. IFN, p. 308 (age 56).

Walters, Easter [actress]. No data found. AMD, p. 355. "Breaking the Speed Laws Is Sport for Easter Walters," *MPW,* 19 Apr 1919, 413.

Walters, Frederick [technical director] (b. 1873?–5 Jun 1922 [49], Brooklyn NY). "Frederick Walters," *Variety,* 9 Jun 1922. AS, p.1127.

Walters, Mrs. George W. [actress] (b. England-d. 21 Feb 1916, New York NY). (Lubin.) AS, p. 1127. BHD, p. 330. IFN, p. 308. Photo, *MPSM,* Sep 1912, 10.

Walters, Hal [actor] (b. England, 29 Jan 1892–1940 [48?], London, England; bombardment of his city). AS, p. 1127.

Walters, John [actor] (b. Sylvia KS, 5 May 1884–23 Jan 1944 [59], Los Angeles CA). "Jack Walters," *Variety,* 2 Feb 1944. AS, p. 1127. BHD1, p. 569 (Jack Walters). IFN, p. 308. Truitt, p. 341 (Jack Walters). George Katchmer, "Remembering the Great Silents," *CI,* 204 (Jun 1992), 44.

Walters, Laura [actress] (b. 1894–10 Apr 1934 [40], Toledo OH). BHD, p. 330. IFN, p. 309.

Walters, Leo [extra] (b. Philadelphia PA, 10 Feb 1891–15 Feb 1958 [67?], Philadelphia PA). (Lubin.) AS, p. 1127 (d. 1959). BHD1, p. 619.

Walthall, Anna Mae (sister of **Henry B. Walthall**) [actress] (b. Shelby City AL, 3 Oct 1894–17 Apr 1950 [55], Van Nuys CA). "Anna Mae Eldridge," *Variety,* 26 Apr 1950. AS, p. 358 (Anna Mae Eldridge); p. 1128 (Anna Mae Walthall). IFN, p. 309 (Anna Mae Walthall). Truitt, p. 99.

Walthall, Henry B[razeale] (brother of **Anna Mae Walthall**) [stage/film actor] (b. on a plantation at Mallory Station on the Coosa River in Shelby County AL, 16 Mar 1878–17 Jun 1936 [58], Monrovia CA; tuberculosis peritonitis; interred in the Hollywood Cemetery). m. Isabelle Fenton (*née* O'Flanigan), 1907; **Mary Charleson,** 1917, IN (d. 1961). (Film debut: *The Convict's Sacrifice,* Biograph, 1909; Pathé; Reliance; Balboa; Griffith; Paralta; National; last film: *China Clipper,* 1936.) "Henry Walthall, Film Actor, Dead; Veteran of Early Cinema, 58, Made Reputation in 'The Birth of a Nation'; Entered Movies in 1909; Played in a Picture with Mary Pickford—Stricken After Finishing New Role," *NYT,* 18 Jun 1936, 23:3. "Henry B. Walthall," *Variety,* 24 Jun 1936 (age 56). AMD, p. 355. AS, p. 1128. BHD1, p. 569. FFF, p. 166. FSS, p. 286. IFN, p. 309. Katz, p. 1207. MH, p. 141. MSBB, p. 1030. Spehr, p. 172. Truitt, p. 341. WWS, p. 233. George Blaisdell, "At the Sign of the Flaming Arcs," *MPW,* 10 Jan 1914, 175. "Henry Walthall Joins Balboa," *MPW,* 12 Dec 1914, 1540. "Walthall in Mix-Up; Balboa Says He's Still Their Star—Woods Declares He's a Griffith Brilliant," *NYDM,* 10 Mar 19145, 24:2 (Walthall "prefers to make no statement for publication at this time."). "Latest on Walthall; Will Be with Griffith, Says 'Mirror' Correspondent [William E. Wing] on the Coast," *NYDM,* 17 Mar 1915, 24:1. "Walthall Still with Balboa," *MPW,* 27 Mar 1915,,1914f. "Walthall with Essanay," *MPW,* 5 Jun 1915, 1585. "Walthall at Essanay Studio," *MPW,* 26 Jun 1915, 2084. "Briefs of Biography," *NYDM,* 7 Jul 1915, 39:1 (left his father's farm in Shelby County AL to go on the stage. At the Players' Club in NYC in 1906, a producer asked him where Jim Kirkwood was. "I received a horrible shock when Mrs. Kirkwood told me he was playing in moving pictures. I determined to rescue him." Kirkwood grinned at this reaction, and introduced him to Griffith who wanted to use him on the spot. Walthall protested. 'Never mind what you want,' [Griffith] replied, 'get out into that ditch and get busy…' So my advent into this work was in a sewer."). Richard Willis, "'The Edison Booth of the Screen'; Henry B. Walthall Has Earned That Title for Himself, and Has But Few Competitors," *MPC,* Apr 1916, 55–56. "Walthall Takes Vacation," *MPW,* 6 May 1916, 963. "Walthall to Have His Own Company," *MPW,* 8 Sep 1917, 1544. "Walthall Announces Picture," *MPW,* 6 Oct 1917, 94. "Henry Walthall with Griffith," *MPW,* 25 May 1918, 1146. "Walthall Registers," *MPW,* 28 Sep 1918, 1862 (brother, Junius, d. 15 Jul 1918, Battle of the Marne). "Walthall Signs with National Film," *MPW,* 23 Nov 1918, 822. "Walthall to Appear in Six Pictures Made by Pioneer," *MPW,* 3 May 1919, 671. "Walthal Leaves National," *MPW,* 23 Aug 1919, 1120. "Walthall Returns to Screen in 'The Splendid Hazard,'" *MPW,* 3 Apr 1920, 128. "Walthall with Vitagraph," *MPW,* 23 Jul 1921, 413. "Henry B. Walthall Signed," *MPW,* 8 Nov 1924, 154. Dorothy Donnell, "'I Remember When—'; Henry Walthall Compares the Screen of the Old Days with the Films of 1925," *MPC,* Nov 1925, 40–41, 71. Irving Dillard, "Walthall, Henry Brazeal," *DAB,* Supp. 2 (1958), pp. 693–94. George A. Katchmer, "Remembering the Great Silents," *CI,* 163 (Jan 1989), 42–45. George Katchmer, "Remembering the Great Silents," *CI,* 252 (Jun 1996), 44, 46.

Walthall, Wallace [executive] (b. 1881–16 Jan 1971 [89?], Dallas TX). BHD2, p. 275.

Walther, Leon [actor] (b. Sorgues, France, 1880). AS, p. 1128.

Walther-Fein, Rudolf [director] (b. Berlin, Germany, 20 Nov 1876–1 May 1933 [56], Berlin, Germany; heart attack). AS, p. 1128. BHD2, p. 275.

Waltman, Claude Tynar [scenarist] (d. 6 Feb 1923, Los Angeles CA; suicide by asphyxiation). AS, p. 1128. BHD2, p. 275.

Walton, Charles [actor] (b. Sharpsburg PA, 1885?–18 Nov 1955 [70], New York NY). (Griffith.) "Charles Walton, 70, Actor and Manager," *NYT,* 21 Nov 1955, 29:4 (twin of James William Walton). "Charles Walton," *Variety,* 23 Nov 1955. AS, p. 1128. BHD, p. 330.

Walton, Edward L. [actor] (b. CA, 1845?–30 Apr 1925 [80], New York NY; pneumonia). "E.L. Walton, Old Actor; Dead at 80, He Leaves Note Requesting an Unostentatious Funeral ["Plain coffin, no flowers, no publicity]," *NYT,* 2 May 1925, 15:5. "Edward L. Walton," *Variety,* 6 May 1925. AS, p. 1128.

Walton, Florence [actress] (*née?,* b. Wilmington DE, 1890–7 Jan 1981 [90?], New York NY). m. **Maurice Walton**. AMD, p. 355. BHD, p. 330. "Maurice and Florence Walton with Famous Players," *MPW,* 22 Jul 1916, 622.

Walton, Frank [director] (b. 1868–18 Dec 1929 [61?], New York NY). BHD2, p. 275.

Walton, Fred [actor] (*né* Frederick Heming, b. Paisley, Scotland, 29 Aug 1866–27 Dec 1936 [70], Los Angeles CA). AS, p. 1128 (d. 28 Dec). BHD1, p. 569. IFN, p. 309. Truitt, p. 341 (b. England, 1865).

Walton, Gladys [film/stage actress] (b. Boston MA, 13 Apr 1903–15 Nov 1993 [90], Morro Bay CA; cancer). m. (1) Frank Liddell, 1921; (2) Henry M. Herbel, Jun 1923 (6 children; d. 1955); (3) ?. (Fox [Sunshine Comedies]; Universal; Rayart; Associated Exhibitors. Walton left films preferring family to fame.) "Gladys Walton Dead; Silent-Film Actress," *NYT,* 23 Nov 1993, B10:2 (age 90; ended career in 1925). AMD, p. 355. AS, p. 1128 (b. Nashville TN, 30 May 1896). BHD, p. 330. Finch, p. 284 (b. Nashville TN, 30 May 1896). MH, p. 141 (b. 1904). 1921 Directory, p. 243. "Gladys Walton Weds," *MPW,* 14 Jul 1923, 128 (m. Herbel). David A. Balch, "'I Want to Stay Married!,' Says Gladys Walton," *MW,* 24 May 1924, 7, 28. Alan Brock, "Gladys Walton," *CI,* 79 (Jan 1982), 52–53. Chapter 23, "Gladys Walton," *BS,* pp. 298–306 (includes filmography). Home estate: "Glad's Castle."

Walton, Henry E. [actor] (b. England). AMD, p. 355. Hugh Hoffman, "In the Catskills with Reliance," *MPW,* 24 Aug 1912, 751.

Walton, Maurice [actor]. No data found. m. **Florence** (d. 1981). AMD, p. 355. "Maurice and Florence Walton with Famous Players," *MPW,* 22 Jul 1916, 622.

Walz, F.E. [scenarist]. No data found. (Flying A Studios, Santa Barbara CA; American.) "New American Editor," *NYDM,* 4 Feb 1914, 42:1 (wrote *The Dream Child*).

Walz, Fred [music director] (b. 1874–10 Feb 1953 [78?], Los Angeles CA). BHD2, p. 275.

Wan, Madame Sul Te *see* **Sul-Te-Wan, Madame**

Wang, James [actor] (b. China, 1853–14 Apr 1935 [81?], Los Angeles CA). (*Fl.* 1924–35.) BHD1, p. 569.

Wangel, Hedwig [stage/film actress] (*née* Amelie Pauline Hedwig Simon, b. Berlin, Germany, 23 Sep 1875–12 Mar 1961 [85], Rendsburg, Germany). "Hedwig Wangel Is Dead; German Star Who Quit Stage for Salvation Army [1909] Was 86," *NYT,* 14 Mar 1961, 35:4 (returned to the stage in 1925 and made many films to earn more money for her social work. In such films as *Ohm Kreuger* [anti-British film] and *Rasputin* [Russo-German, 1929]). "Hedwig Wangel," *Variety,* 5 Apr 1961, p. 78. AS, p. 1128 (d. 5 Mar, Lobe, Germany). BHD1, p. 569. IFN, p. 309.

Wangemann, Richard [actor]. (Lubin). No data found.

Wanger, Walter F. [stage actor/producer] (*né* Walter Feuchtwanger, b. San Francisco CA, 11 Jul 1894–17 Nov 1968 [74], New York NY; heart attack). (FP-L, 1919.) m. (1) **Justine Johnstone,** 1919—div. 1938 (d. 1982); **Joan Bennett,** 1940 (d. 1990). *My Life with Cleopatra.* (Last film produced: *Cleopatra,* TC-F, 1963; MGM; Columbia; UA; Universal.) Vincent Canby, "Walter Wanger, Who Had a Long and Stormy Career as a Movie Producer in Hollywood, Dead at 74," *NYT,* 19 Nov 1968, 41:1 (on 22 Apr 1952, he was sentenced to serve four months at the Wayside Honor Farm, Castaic CA, for shooting Jennings Lang, talent agent, for trying to destroy his marriage to Benmett). "Wanger, 74, Dies; Money Showman Tho 'Erudite,'" *Variety,* 253, 20 Nov 1968, 5:2, 40 (d. 17 Nov). AMD, p. 355. AS, pp. 1128–29 (d. 16 Nov). BHD2, p. 275 (d. 18 Nov). IFN, p. 309 (d. 18 Nov). Edward Weitzel, "Says Walter Wanger, Production Head for Famous Players-Lasky Company—," *MPW,* 17? Jul 1920, 713:1 (presents himself as a man of ideals imbued with optimism). "Walter F. Wanger New General Manager of Production of Famous Players-Lasky," *MPW,* 13 Nov 1920, 236. "Wanger Re-engaged," *MPW,* 9 Aug 1924, 436.

Wango, S. [cinematographer]. No data found. FDY, p. 471.

Wanzer, Arthur G. [actor] (b. Chicago IL, 18 Mar 1880–15 Dec 1948 [68], Los Angeles CA; apoplexy). AS, p. 1129.

Waram, Percy C. [actor] (b. Kent, England, 1881–5 Oct 1961 [80?], Huntington NY). AS, p. 1129.

Ward, Abraham [actor] (b. 22 Oct 1848–5 Apr 1937 [88], Los Angeles CA). AS, p. 1129.

Ward, Albert [actor] (b. England, 1870–9 Dec 1956 [86?], England). AS, p. 1129. BHD, p. 330; BHD2, p. 275.

Ward, Beatrice [actress] (b. 1890?–11 Dec 1964 [74], Los Angeles CA). "Beatrice Ward," *Variety,* 16 Dec 1964 ("in silent pix"). AS, p. 1129. BHD1, p. 569. IFN, p. 309. Truitt, p. 341.

Ward, Carrie C. [actress] (*née* Carrie Clarke-Ward, b. Virginia City NV, 9 Jan 1862–6 Feb 1926 [64], Los Angeles CA). m. Sedley Brown. "Carrie Clarke-Ward," *Variety,* 10 Feb 1926. AS, p. 1129. BHD, p. 330. IFN, p. 309. Truitt, p. 342.

Ward, Chance E. [actor/assistant director] (aka Yancey Smith, *né* Chance Earle Smith, b. Dayton OH, 16 Sep 1877–2 Sep 1949 [71], West Hollywood CA). AS, p. 1129. BHD1, p. 569; BHD2, p. 276 (d. LA Co. CA). IFN, p. 309.

Ward, David [actor] (b. 1890?–31 Dec 1945 [55], Los Angeles CA). AS, p. 1129. BHD1, p. 369 (d. 1946). IFN, p. 309.

Ward, Edward [composer/conductor] (b. St. Louis MO, 8 Apr 1896–26 Sep 1971 [74], Los Angeles CA). (Universal; MGM.) "Edward Ward," *Variety,* 6 Oct 1971. AS, p. 1129 (b. 2 Apr). ASCAP 66, p. 764 (b. 2 Apr).

Ward, Fannie [stage/film actress] (*née* Fannie Buchanan, b. St. Louis MO, 22 Feb 1871?–27 Jan 1952 [80], New York NY; cerebral hemorrhage). m. (1) Joe "Diamond Joe" Lewis, 1900—div. 14 Jan 1913, London; **John W. "Jack" Dean,** 29 Dec 1915, NYC (d. 1950). (Film debut: *The Marriage of Kitty,* Paramount, 1915; Lasky; Pathé, 1918.) "Fannie Ward Dies; Perennial Flapper, Retired Actress Who Made a Career of Looking Youthful Succumbs After Stroke," *NYT,* 28 Jan 1952, 17:3; "Fannie Ward's Estate; Actress Left $40,000 but No Will Public Administrator Says," *NYT,* 5 Feb 1952, 23:8. "Fannie Ward," *Variety,* 30 Jan 1952. AMD, p. 355. AS, p. 1129 (b. 22 Jun 1872). BHD, p. 330 (b. 1872). FSS, p. 287. IFN, p. 309 (b. 1872). Spehr, p. 172 (b. 1872). Truitt, p. 342. "Fannie Ward Divorced; Does Not Defend Action of Divorce of Millionaire Husband," *NYDM,* 22 Jan 1913, 13:2 (stage actor John H. Donovan was named as correspondent). "Fannie Ward to Star for Lasky," *MPW,* 6 Mar 1915, 1455. "Fanny Ward Weds J.W. Dean," *NYDM,* 8 Jan 1916, p. 7. "Fannie Ward and Jack Dean Married," *MPW,* 15 Jan 1916, 402. "Fannie Ward," *MPW,* 17 Feb 1917, 1010. "Fannie Ward Resigns from Lasky Company," *MPW,* 7 Jul 1917, 101. "Fannie Ward Buys Bonds from President," *MPW,* 17 Nov 1917, 1025. "Fannie Ward Begins Her Work for Pathé," *MPW,* 1 Dec 1917, 1304. "May Produce Independently," *MPW,* 23 Nov 1918, 819. "Fannie Ward Effects Sold," *MPW,* 10 Sep 1921, 169. Rene de la Seine, "Filmettes from France; Sixty-Year-Old Flapper," *Paris and Hollywood Screen Secrets,* Oct 1927, 54 (said she was 60 years old and twice a grandmother). "Letters," *FIR,* Mar 1986, 190. Eve Golden, "Fannie Ward: The Youth Girl," *CI,* 256 (Oct 1996), 16–17 (b. 22 Jun 1872).

Ward, Fleming [stage/film actor] (b. Lock Haven PA, 28 Oct 1886–2 Aug 1962 [75], Bronx NY [Death Certificate Index No. 8364]). m. **Anna M. Pray** (d. 1971). "Fleming Ward, 95, Actor, Appeared in Broadway Hits," *NYT,* 3 Aug 1962, 23:4. "Fleming Ward," *Variety,* 8 Aug 1962. AS, p. 1129. BHD, p. 330. IFN, p. 309.

Ward, Fred [actor] (*né* Fred Swift, b. 1879?–15 Mar 1962 [83], Blackpool, England). "Fred Ward," *Variety,* 21 Mar 1962. AS, p. 1129.

Ward, Fred Israel [actor] (b. 1877?–6 Jul 1921 [44], Paris, France). "Fred Ward," *Variety,* 15 Jul 1921. AS, p. 1129.

Ward, Hap (father of Hap Ward, Jr., 1899–1940) (b. Philadelphia PA, 1862?–6 Jan 1944 [81], Philadelphia PA). m. Lucy Daly. "John O'-Donnell; Ex-Leader of the Philadelphia Democratic Group Dies at 81," *NYT,* 7 Jan 1944, 17:3. "Hap Ward," *Variety,* 12 Jan 1944 (d. 3 Jan 1944 [76], New York NY). AS, p. 1129 (b. Cameron PA, 1867-d. 3 Jan). BHD1, p. 570 (b. Cameron PA, 1867-d. 3 Jan).

Ward, Harry [actor] (*né* Angelo De Michele, b. 1890–16 Apr 1952 [62?], Los Angeles CA). AS, p. 1129.

Ward, Janet [actress] (b. 14 Apr 1896–25 Mar 1952 [55], Sauslito CA). AS, p. 1129.

Ward, Katherine Clare [actress] (*née?,* b. Bradford MA, 31 Mar 1871–14 Oct 1938 [67], Los Angeles CA). m. Charlie Ward. "Katherine Clare Ward," *Variety,* 19 Oct 1938. AS, p. 1129. BHD1, p. 570. IFN, p. 309 (Kathrin). Truitt, p. 342.

Ward, Leon [actor] (b. Parowan UT, 1906–28 May 1927 [21?], Los Angeles CA). AS, p. 1129. BHD, p. 330.

Ward, Lucille [actress] (b. Dayton OH, 25 Feb 1880–8 Aug 1952 [72], McLean Township, near Dayton OH). (American.) "Lucille Ward [Lucille Ward Smith]," *NYT,* 10 Aug 1952, 61:2 ("The 72-year-old actress had performed in early Hollywood silent films."). AS, p. 1129. BHD1, p. 570. IFN, p. 309. Truitt, p. 342.

Ward, May, "The Dresden China Doll" [vaudeville stage (May Ward and Her Eight Dresden Dolls)/film actress] (b. 1886?–5 Jul 1936 [50], Far Rockaway NY). m. Freeman Bernstein. (On stage since age 13; film debut: *A Continental Girl,* Continental Photo-Play Corp., Germantown PA, 1915.) "May Ward," *Variety,* 15 Jul 1936. AS, p. 1129. BHD, p. 330. "May Ward Deserts the Stage," *NYDM,* 11 Aug 1915, 22:1 (to debut in *The Continental Girl*).

Ward, Peggy [actress] (b. PA, 10 Feb 1879–8 Mar 1960 [81], Los Angeles CA). AS, p. 1130. BHD1, p. 570. IFN, p. 309.

Ward, Roscoe "Tiny" [actor] (b. 1893?–12 Sep 1956 [63], Los Angeles CA). (Paramount.) AS, p. 1130. BHD, p. 330. IFN, p. 309.

Ward, Sam [actor] (*né* George Herman Jacobs, b. 1889?–1 May 1952 [63], Sawtelle CA). (Roach.) "Sam Ward," *Variety,* 7 May 1952. AS, p. 1130. BHD, p. 330. IFN, p. 309. Truitt, p. 342.

Ward, Solly [actor] (b. New York NY, 11 Oct 1890–17 May 1942 [51], Los Angeles CA). m. Stella. (RKO.) "Solly Ward Dies; A Noted Comedian; Dialect Actor Played in 'Great Waltz,' 'Fabulous Invalid,'" *NYT,* 26 May 1942, 21:2. "Solly Ward," *Variety,* 20 May 1942. AS, p. 1130. BHD1, p. 570. IFN, p. 309. Truitt, p. 342.

Ward, Tom [director] (b. 1877–7 May 1956 [79?], New York NY). AS, p. 1130.

Ward, Vivian [actress] (b. 1848–19 Apr 1934 [86?], Los Angeles CA). AS, p. 1130.

Ward, Warwick Manson [actor/scenarist] (*né* Warwick Mannon, b. St. Ives, England, 3 Dec 1891–9 Dec 1967 [76], London, England). AS, p. 1130 (Warwick Mannon Ward). BHD1, p. 570; BHD2, p. 276. IFN, p. 309.

Warde, Ernest C. (son of **Frederick B. Warde**) [stage/film actor/director] (b. Liverpool, England, 1874?–9 Sep 1923 [49], Los Angeles CA; stomach ailment). "Ernest C. Warde," *Variety,* 13 and 20 Sep 1923. AMD, p. 355. AS, p. 1130. BHD, p. 331; BHD2, p. 276. IFN, p. 309. 1921 Directory, p. 277. Truitt, p. 342. "Thanhouser Again Raids 'Legit,'" *MPW,* 15 May 1915, 1084. "Ernest Warde to Direct for Thanhouser," *MPW,* 15 Jul 1916, 371. "Ernest Warde to Direct Keenan," *MPW,* 22 Dec 1917, 1818.

Warde, Frederick B[arkham] (father of **Ernest C. Warde**) [actor] (b. Warrington, Oxfordshire, England, 23 Feb 1851–7 Feb 1935 [83], Brooklyn NY; heart attack). m. Annie Edmondson, 1871 (d. 1923). (Stage debut: *Macbeth,* Lyceum Theatre, Sunderland, England, 4 Sep 1867; U.S. stage debut, 1874). *Fifty Years of Make Believe* (1920). "Frederick Warde, Noted Actor, Dead; On Stage 68 Years with Edwin Booth, Adelaide Neilson and Other Famous Stars; Author and Lecturer; Victim of Heart Disease at 84 Had Been in the Movies—Lived with Daughter in Brooklyn," *NYT,* 9 Feb 1935, 15:1 (began in Hollywood ca. 1922). "Frederick B. Warde," *Variety,* 12 Feb 1935. AMD, p. 355. AS, p. 1130. BHD, p. 331 (b. Deddington, England). IFN, p. 309. Truitt, p. 342 (b. 1872). "Frederick Warde with Thanhouser," *MPW,* 20 Nov 1915, 1468. "Frederick Warde Now with Thanhouser," *MPW,* 22 Apr 1916, 624:2 (signed a long-term contract. "This brings to the screen permanently the last of the old school of Booth and Barrett and McCullough."). "Frederick Warde," *MPW,* 26 May 1917, 1296. Frederick Warde, "The Legitimate Player in the Films," *MPW,* 21 Jul 1917, 400. "Frederick Warde Engaged by World Pictures," *MPW,* 13 Jul 1918, 215. Weinraub, Bernard, "Newfound film billed as oldest U.S. production," *Los Angeles Daily News,* 17 Sep 1996, pp. 1, 18 (*Richard III* [with Warde] may be the oldest complete American feature. It was filmed in Westchester County and City Island in the Bronx NY at a cost of $30,000. Only 5 features out of 12 made in 1912 survive, 3 of them complete. *See* interview with Warde, *Brooklyn Eagle,* Nov 1912).

Wardell, Geoffrey [actor] (b. York, England, 30 Jul 1900–9 Aug 1955 [55]). BHD1, p. 570.

Wardell, Harry [actor/scenarist] (b. New York NY, 8 Mar 1879–17 Sep 1948 [69], Los Angeles CA). AS, p. 1130. BHD2, p. 276.

Ware, Helen [stage/film actress] (*née* Helen Remer; mother's maiden name was Elinor Ware Remer) b. San Francisco CA, 15 Oct 1877–25 Jan 1939 [61], Carmel CA; throat infection). m. Frederic Burt (widower). (Stage debut: 1899.) "Helen Ware Dies; Actress 30 Years; Former Star of Successes on Stage Here—Leading Lady for Tellegen and Daly; Also Appeared in Films; Made Debut as Extra in Maude Adams's Production of 'The Little Minister,'" *NYT,* 26 Jan 1939, 21:1 ("She entered silent motion pictures, too, and continued to appear on the screen until well after the talkie revolution."). "Helen Ware," *Variety,* 1 Feb 1939. AMD, p. 355. AS, p. 1130. BHD1, p. 570. IFN, p. 310. Truitt, p. 342. "Miss Helen Ware with Cosmo Features," *MPW,* 17 Apr 1915, 371. "More for N.Y.M.P.; Helen Ware Added to List of Stars and Allan Dwan Signed to Produce," *NYDM,* 30 Jun 1915, 20:1. "Helen Ware Will Wear Fine Gowns," *MPW,* 11 Nov 1916, 883. "Helen Ware," *MPW,* 23 Dec 1916, 1811.

Ware, Walter [actor] (b. Boston MA, 1880?–3 Jan 1936 [56], Los Angeles CA). AS, p. 1130. BHD1, p. 571. IFN, p. 310. Truitt, p. 342.

Warfield, David [stage/film actor] (*né* David Wollfeld or Wohlfelt, b. San Francisco CA, 28 Nov 1866–27 Jun 1951 [84], New York NY [Death Certificate Index No. 13834]). m. Mary G. Brandt. "David Warfield, 84, Famous Actor, Dies; Star of 'The Auctioneer' and Three Other Hits Appeared on Stage Quarter of Century; Turned Down Film Offer; Discovered by David Belasco While Playing with Weber and Fields Troupe," *NYT,* 28 Jun 1951, 25:1. "David Warfield," *Variety,* 4 Jul 1951. AS, p. 1130 (listed as Arthur Warfield). Lowrey, p. 8. SD, p. 1279.

Warfield, Irene [actress] (b. 1896?–10 Apr 1961 [65], New York NY [Death Certificate Index No. 8505]). (Essanay.) AMD, p. 356. AS, p. 1130. BHD, p. 331. "Irene Warfield for 'Satan Sanderson,'" *MPW,* 2 Jan 1915, 57.

Warfield, Marjorie [actress] (*née* Marjorie Warfield Chase, b. Philadelphia PA, 2 Sep 1902–15 Apr 1991 [88], Los Angeles CA; pneumonia). m. **Joseph Bailey Walker** (d. 1985). "Marjorie Warfield," *Variety,* 22 Apr 1991. AS, p. 1130. BHD1, p. 571.

Waring, Mary W. [actress] (*née?,* b. 1891?–10 Jan 1964 [72], Washington DC). "Mary W. Waring, 72, Character Actress," *NYT,* 12 Jan 1964, 92:4. AS, p. 1131. BHD, p. 331. IFN, p. 310. Truitt, p. 342.

Warmington, Stanley J. [actor] (b. Hertfordshire, England, 16 Dec 1884–10 May 1941 [56], London, England). AS, p. 1131. BHD1, p. 571. IFN, p. 310.

Warner, Albert "Abe" (brother of **Harry, Jack** and **Sam Warner**) [executive] [*né* Abraham Warner, b. Poland, 23 Jul 1882?–26 Nov 1967 [84], Miami Beach FL). m. (1) d. 28 Oct 1918, pneumonia. "Albert Warner of Movies Dead; One of Four Brothers Who Founded Film Empire," *NYT,* 27 Nov 1967, 47:1. "Albert Warner, 84, Third Brother, Dies; Recall Amazing Vitaphone Boom," *Variety,* 29 Nov 1967. AMD, p. 356. AS, p. 1131 (b. 1884). BHD2, p. 276. IFN, p. 310. "Warners' Features," *MPW,* 6 Jul 1912, 51. "Warner Getting in Right," *MPW,* 21 Sep 1912, 1159. "Warner Back from Long Trip," *MPW,* 26 Apr 1913, 359. "Abe Warner Back," *MPW,* 1 Nov 1913, 479. "Abe Warner Back from Europe," *MPW,* 23 May 1914, 1098. "Abe Warner," *MPW,* 20 Mar 1915, 1767. "Abe Warner to 'Okeh' Crusader Contracts," *MPW,* 6 Jul 1918, 47. "Mrs. Abe Warner Dead," *MPW,* 9 Nov 1918, 653. "Warner Describes Full-Dress Comedies Starring Actor Met Wholly by Chance," *MPW,* 19 Jun 1920, 1603. "Abe Warner, Back from Coast[,] Looks to Biggest Year Yet," *MPW,* 20 Jan 1923, 258. "Warner Denies Combination with Lichtman-Mayer Organization," *MPW,* 28 Jul 1923, 315. "Production Work at Height; Sam Warner Visits Ill Brother [typhoid]," *MPW,* 6 Oct 1923, 479. "Warner Goes on Trip," *MPW,* 5 Jul 1924, 48. Jeffrey Blair, "Studio's Gift Saves Historic Theater from Wrecking Ball," *CI,* 253 (Jul 1996), 32 (Harry, Albert and Sam Warner got their start in 1906 in New Castle PA, 45 miles northwest of Pittsburgh).

Warner, Cecil [sic] ["actrice enfant américaine du cinéma muet"] (b. Los Angeles CA, 1901–22 May 1924 [23?], Los Angeles CA; suicide with an overdose of chloroform). AS, p. 1131.

Warner, Glen S. "Pop" [actor] (b. Springville NY, 5 Apr 1871–7 Sep 1954 [83], Los Angeles CA). AS, p. 1131.

Warner, H. B. (son of stage actor Charles Warner) [stage/film actor] (*né* Henry Byron Charles Stewart Warner-Lickford, b. St. John's Woods, London, England, 26 Oct 1875–21 Dec 1958 [83], Woodland Hills CA). m. Mrs. Fred R. Hamlin, 1907 (d. 1914); Marguerite Stanwood (**Rita Stanwood**), 3 May 1915, Chicago IL (d. 1961). (Stage debut: *The Streets of London,* 1883, Hanley, England; Triangle; Frohman.) "H.B. Warner, Acted in Films 42 Years," *NYT,* 23 Dec 1958, 2:6. AMD, p. 356. AS, p. 1131. BHD1, p. 571 (b. London, 1876). FSS, p. 287. GH, pp. 985–1001. IFN, p. 310 (b. 1875). Katz, p. 1209. MH, p. 141 (b. 1876). MSBB, p. 1030 (b. 1876). Truitt, p. 342. WWS, p. 92 (b. 1876). "Questions Answered," *NYDM,* 1 May 1912, p. 13. "'Billy Black' [a comedy-drama in 3 acts]; H.B. Warner, Under Contract with Frazee for Two Years, Star in Bradley Play," *NYDM,* 4 Feb 1914, 6:2. "H.B. Warner to Play for Lasky," *MPW,* 14 Mar 1914, 1366. "Two More Stars for Famous Players," *MPW,* 28 Mar 1914, 1692. "H.B. Warner a Suffrage Star; Adolph Zukor Permits Star of 'Lost Paradise' to Aid Suffrage Cause," *NYDM,* 9 Sep 1914, 24:4. "Warner Weds Miss Stanwood," *NYDM,* 12 May 1915, 7:2 ("To the marriage license clerk Mr. Warner said he was thirty-seven years old, while Miss Stanwood gave her age as twenty-six." Warner's first wife, formerly Mrs. Fred Hamlin, was killed in a car accident on Long Island in 1914.). "H.B. Warner a Selig Star," *MPW,* 21 Apr 1917, 428. "To Present Warner in a Series of Travel Stories," *MPW,* 15 Mar 1919, 1515. Barbara Beach, "Unto the Third and Fourth Generation; The Philosophy of H.B. Warner," *MPC,* Apr 1919, 22–23, 78. "Pathé to Release H.B. Warner Features; Star Plans Six Hampton Films Each Year," *MPW,* 12 Jun 1920, 1433. "H.B. Warner," *MPW,* 28 Nov 1925, 333. "Thalberg Signs H.B. Warner," *MPW,* 10 Apr 1926, 428. "Long Term DeMille Contract for Warner," *MPW,* 1 May 1926, 24. Logan Carlisle, "Warner: H.B.; The Warner Who Works Alone—Not One of the Brothers, but the Eminent Actor Who Works in Warner Pictures!," *Screenland,* Aug 1929, 72–73, 108–09. George A. Katchmer, "H.B. Warner; Man of Stage and Screen," *CI,* 139 (Jan 1987), 28–31, C15. "Index to the Films of H.B. Warner," *CI,* 140 (Feb 1987), 49–53. Henry R. Davis, "Additions & Deletions," *CI,* 141 (Mar 1987), 43. R.E. Braff, "Additional Film Credits for H.B. Warner," *CI,* 238 (Apr 1995), 42.

Warner, Harry M. (brother of **Albert, Jack** and **Sam Warner**) [executive] [b. Poland, 12 Dec 1881–25 Jul 1958 [76], Bel Air CA; cerebral occlusion). "Harry Warner of Films Is Dead; Cerebral Occlusion Is Fatal to Picture Studio Founder, Ill for Several Years," *NYT,* 26 Jul 1958, 15:3. "Emigrant Boy & Show Great Dies; Harry Warner's 'Political' Films of Both Wars, & Vitaphone, Memorable," *Variety,* 30 Jul 1958. AMD, p. 356. AS, p. 1131. BHD2, p. 276. IFN, p. 310. "Warners Celebrates Anniversary," *MPW,* 3 Oct 1914, 70. "Warner DIscusses Induiistry's Chief Need While Harry Rapf Forecasts Coming Winners," *MPW,* 31 Dec 1921, 1061. "Future of Motion Pictures Depends on Public's Attitude, Says Harry Warner," *MPW,* 18 Feb 1922, 712. Harry M. Warner, "Public Should Judge Worth of Pictures, Says Warner; Pays Tribute to Cinema," *MPW,* 25 Mar 1922, 357. "Who's Who in State Right Field: No. 2—Warner Brothers," *MPW,* 1 Apr 1922, 357. "Harry M. Warner on the Beautiful Press Book," *MPW,* 29 Apr 1922, 942. Harry M. Warner, "Warner Production Plans for Season of 1923," *MPW,* 23 Sep 1922, 274. "False Advertising Hurts Industry, Says Warner," *MPW,* 23 Sep 1922, 276. "Letters to Santa Claus," *MPW,* 30 Dec 1922, 833. "Imitations Ruinous, Says Harry Warner," *MPW,* 23 Jun 1923, 669. "Director Lubitsch Also Has an Eye for Business," *MPW,* 15 Sep 1923, 276. "Warners Will Not Quit Hays, But Will Demand Reforms, Harry Warner Says," *MPW,* 28 Feb 1925, 875–76. "Warners Will Paddle Own Canoe Says Harry M.

Warner," *MPW,* 28 Feb 1925, 880. "Harry M. Warner Coming," *MPW,* 7 Mar 1925, 90. "Harry M. Warner Urges Industry to Use Radio," *MPW,* 11 Apr 1925, 592. "Warner Bros. Buy Vitagraph; Acquire 50 Branches Throughout the World," *MPW,* 2 May 1925, 25–26. "Warner Bros. Will Retain Vitagraph Co. Trade Mark," *MPW,* 9 May 1925, 138. "Vitagraph Rejoins M.P.P.D.A.," *MPW,* 27 Jun 1925, 953. "Pay Visit to President," *MPW,* 7 Nov 1925, 52 (18 Oct 1925). "Writing a Chapter for the Warner Record," *MPW,* 5 Dec 1925, 418. "Warner's Plan Production in Great Britain," *MPW,* 13 Mar 1926, 2. Covarrubias, "Distinguished Picture People," *MPW,* 24 Apr 1926, 576. "Harry M. Warner Goes Abroad in August," *MPW,* 15 May 1926, 2. "Harry M. Warner in New York with Print of 'Don Juan'; Plans Elaborate Broadway Premiere," *MPW,* 5 Jun 1926, 473. "Harry M. Warner Recovers," *MPW,* 4 Dec 1926, 1 (from the grippe).

Warner, Irma [actress] (b. San Francisco CA, 12 Nov 1899–3 Aug 1982 [82], Los Angeles CA). BHD1, p. 619.

Warner, J.B. [actor] (b. NB, 1895–9 Nov 1924 [29]; tuberculosis). (Universal.) AS, p. 1131. IFN, p. 310.

Warner, Jack L[eonard] (brother of **Albert, Harry** and **Sam Warner**) [executive] (b. London, Ontario, Canada, 2 Aug 1892–9 Sep 1978 [86], Los Angeles CA; pulmonary edema). m. **Irma S. Rogell** (d. 1982; son, Jack, Jr., 1916–1995). With Dean Jennings, *My First Hundred Years in Hollywood* (New York: Random House, 1965). Bob Thomas, *Clown Prince of Hollywood; The Antic Life and Times of Jack L. Warner* (New York: McGraw-Hill Publishing Co., 1990). *NYT* [strike summary], 10 Sep 1978, 57:5 (has "Eichelbaum," mother's maiden name, as surname). "Jack L. Warner's Death Closes Out Pioneer Clan of 'Talkies,'" *Variety,* 13 Sep 1978. AMD, p. 356. AS, p. 1131. BHD1, p. 571; BHD2, p. 276. *Encyclopedia of Film and Television,* p. 356 (*né* Eichelbaum). IFN, p. 310. Katz, pp. 1209–10. Eddie Wheeler, "Pittsburgh," *MPW,* 15 Jun 1912, 1050 ("Lee Jack Warner" was manager of the Red Mill Theater in Wilkinsburg PA). "Jack L. Warner," *MPW,* 12 Dec 1914, 1526. "Warner's Features Has Many Branch Offices," *MPW,* 13 Jul 1912, 153. "Warners to Make Comedies for Famous Players-Lasky," *MPW,* 2 Aug 1919, 698. Jack L. Warner, "Jack Warner Points Out Weakness of Theatre Men in Selection of Pictures," *MPW,* 8 Jul 1922, 162. "A Wedding Anniversary," *MPW,* 1 Nov 1924, 28. "Jack Warner Arrives with Prints of Two Productions," *MPW,* 14 Feb 1925, 719. "Warners Building Own Radio Station to Boost Films," *MPW,* 21 Feb 1925, 769 (KWB, Hollywood, 4 Mar 1925). "On the Set and Off," *MW,* 25 Jul 1925, 44 (MGM sued Warner Bros. for $7300, "claimed as due under an uncompleted lease contract for the [directing] services of [E. Mason] Hopper." The writer called Warners' testimony "[p]robably one of the funniest monologues ever delivered in a Los Angeles courtroom..." Warner said that "Hopper refused to get down to business and direct [*Little Church Around the Corner*]." William Seiter was given the job. Kenneth Harlan also testified that Hopper objected to him because he was not "spiritual looking."). "Jack Warner to New York," *MPW,* 3 Jul 1926, 4. "Jack Warner in New York, " *MPW,* 10 Jul 1926, 4. Eve B. Bernstein, "Those Winning Warners; The Four Warner Brothers Have Written Their Own Arabian Nights on the Pages of Cinema History," *Cinema Arts,* Aug 1926, pp. 15, 44–45. "Jack L. Warner on Production," *MPW,* 2 Oct 1926, 286. "Jack Warner Returns to Coast; aves 1927–28 Production Path," *MPW,* 5 Mar 1927, 41. Scott Eyman, *The Speed of Sound: Hollywood and the Talkie Revolution 1926–1930* (Simon & Schuster, 1997).

Warner, James B. [actor] (b. NB, 1895–9 Nov 1924 [29?], Los Angeles CA). BHD, p. 331. Ragan 2, p. 1769.

Warner, Jethro [actor] (b. 1875?–12 Apr 1931 [56], New York NY). m. Estelle Floyd. "Jethro Warner," *Variety,* 15 Apr 1931. AS, p. 1131.

Warner, John [actor] (b. 1887?–24 Jul 1929 [42], Los Angeles CA; Bright's disease). "John Warner," *Variety,* 31 Jul 1929. AS, p. 1131. BHD1, p. 619. IFN, p. 310 (Jack Warner).

Warner, John E. [stage company manager] (d. 15 Aug 1924, Alameda CA). m. Daisy R. "John E. Warner," *Variety,* 20 Aug 1924. AS, p. 1131.

Warner, Samuel L. (brother of **Albert, Harry** and **Jack Warner**) [executive] (b. Baltimore MD, 10 Aug 1887–5 Oct 1927 [40], Los Angeles CA; pneumonia). m. **Lina Basquette**, 4 Jul 1925 (d. 1994). "Sam L. Warner Dies; Was Movie Pioneer; Succumbs to Pneumonia in Los Angeles at the Age of 40—Bought First Film at 16; AssociatedW:Th-Brothers [sic]; Their Corporation Became Leader in Production Field—Recently Acquired Vitaphone," *NYT,* 6 Oct 1927, 25:3. "Sam Warner," *Variety,* 12 Oct 1927. AMD, p. 357. AS, p. 1131. BHD2, p. 276. "Samuel L. Warner's New Venture," *MPW,* 5 Dec 1914, 1361. "Sam Warner in War Work," *MPW,* 9 Nov 1918, 679. "Production Work at Height; Sam Warner Visits Ill Brother," *MPW,* 6 Oct 1923, 479 (Abe ill with typhoid). Sumner Smith, "Vaudeville the One in Danger Not Vitaphone, Says Warner," *MPW,* 26 Mar 1927, 263–64. "Obituary," *MPW,* 8 Oct 1927, 336, 343. "Warner Gives Whole Estate to Relatives," *MPW,* 29 Oct 1927, 543.

Warren, C. Denier [actor/scenarist] (b. Chicago IL, 29 Jul 1889–27 Aug 1971 [82], Torquay, England). AS, p. 1131. BHD2, p. 276.

Warren, Dwight W. [cameraman] (b. Eagle Rock CA, 18 Jul 1888–14 Aug 1979 [91], North Hollywood CA). AMD, p. 357. BHD2, p. 276. "Dwight W. Warren," *MPW,* 25 Dec 1926, 573.

Warren, E. Alyn [actor] (*né* Fred Warren, b. Richmond VA, 2 Jun 1874–22 Jan 1940 [65], Los Angeles CA). "E. Alyn Warren," *NYT,* 24 Jan 1940, 21:3. AMD, p. 357. AS, p. 1131. BHD1, p. 571. IFN, p. 310. "The Actor Still Lives, But—," *MPW,* 25 Jul 1914, 588.

Warren, Eda [film editor] (b. Boston MA, 1904?–15 Jul 1980 [76], Woodland Hills CA). (Paramount; Fox; United Artists; Columbia.) "Eda Warren," *Variety,* 30 Jul 1980 (cut *Peter Pan* and *Hula*). BHD2, p. 276.

Warren, Edward [actor/director/producer] (b. Boston MA, 1857?–3 Apr 1930 [73], Los Angeles CA). (Solax, Ft. Lee NJ). "Edward Warren," *Variety,* 9 Apr 1930. AMD, p. 357. AS, p. 1131. BHD, p. 331; BHD2, p. 276. IFN, p. 310. 1921 Directory, p. 277. Truitt, p. 343. "Director Edward Warren Made It," *MPW,* 7 Jun 1913, 1034. "Edward Warren Leaves Solax," *MPW,* 16 Aug 1913, 725. "Edward Warren," *MPW,* 24 Oct 1914, 511. "Warren Joins Crystal," *MPW,* 7 Aug 1915, 1007. "Warren Directing Hilda Spong," *MPW,* 4 Sep 1915, 1624. "Edward Warren Starts Company," *MPW,* 24 Feb 1917, 1197. "Warren Explains 'Warafre of the Flesh,'" *MPW,* 14 Apr 1917, 293.

Warren Eleanor Stewart [actress] (b. Canada, 8 Jul 1892–6 Apr 1927 [34], Jamaica NY). AS, p. 1131. BHD, p. 331. IFN, p. 310.

Warren, Eliza [actress] (*née* Eliza Warren Sutton, b. 1864?–20 Jan 1935 [70], Cleveland OH). (Griffith.) "Eliza Warren," *Variety,* 6 Mar 1935. AS, p. 1131. BHD, p. 331. IFN, p. 310. Truitt, p. 343.

Warren, F.B. [executive]. No data found. AMD, p. 357. F.B. Warren, "Warren Describes Goldwyn Sellig Policty," *MPW,* 20 Jul 1918, 375–74. "Warren Joins Hodkinson Corporation," *MPW,* 5 Apr 1919, 48.

Warren, Forest [actor] (b. Los Angeles CA, 10 May 1841–26 Dec 1912 [71], Santa Monica CA). AS, p. 1132.

Warren, Fred H. [actor] (b. Rock Island NY, 16 Sep 1880–5 Dec 1940 [60], Los Angeles CA; perforation of a stomach ulcer). AS, p. 1132. BHD1, p. 571. IFN, p. 310. George A. Katchmer, "Remembering the Great Silents," *CI,* 184 (Oct 1990), 57–58.

Warren, Gene [actress/assistant director]. No data found. AMD, p. 357. "Gene Warren Is Made an Assistant Director," *MPW,* 26 Jul 1919, 521:2 (at the Ideal Studio, Hudson Heights NJ; with photo).

Warren, Giles R. [scenarist/director]. No data found. (Lubin; Imp; Selig; Majestic-Reliance.) AMD, p. 357. "Warren, Taylor and Leonard with Warners," *MPW,* 23 Aug 1913, 851. "Warren to Selig Coast Studio," *MPW,* 13 Feb 1915, 1145:2 (promoted and moved to the West Coast; succeeded by Lawrence Marston at the Chicago Selig studio). "Giles R. Warren," *NYDM,* 1 Sep 1915, 27:1. "Warren Joins World Scenario Force," *MPW,* 15 Jun 1918, 1578.

Warren, Herbert [scenarist/director/producer]. No data found. AMD, p. 357. "Arbuckle Scenario Editor Weds," *MPW,* 13 Oct 1917, 221. "Warren to Make Pictures," *MPW,* 21 Sep 1918, 1708–09.

Warren, Mary [actress] (b. New York NY, 21 Jan 1844–14 Sep 1928 [84], New York NY). (Universal.) AMD, p. 357. AS, p. 1132. "Mary Warren Featured for First Time," *MPW,* 2 Mar 1918, 1212.

Warren, Michael [actor] (b. Los Angeles CA, 13 Nov 1842–17 Jun 1922 [79], Los Angeles CA). AS, p. 1132.

Warren, Wilma [actress] (b. 1883–5 Jan 1925 [41?], Los Angeles CA). AS, p. 1132.

Warrender, Harold [actor] (b. London, England, 15 Nov 1903–6 May 1953 [49], Gerrards Crossing, England). AS, p. 1132. BHD1, p. 572.

Warrenrath, Reinald [actor]. No data found. AMD, p. 357. "Vitaphone Signs Jolson, Jessel and Warrenrath," *MPW,* 11 Sep 1926, 3.

Warrenton, Gilbert [cameraman] (b. 7 Mar 1894-Aug 1980 [86], CA). FDY, p. 471.

Warrenton, Lule [actress/director/producer] (b. Flint MI, 22 Jun 1862–14 May 1932 [69], Laguna Beach CA; complications from an operation). "Lule Warrenton," *Variety,* 24 May 1932. AMD, p. 357. AS, p. 1132. BHD, p. 331. IFN, p. 310. Truitt, p. 343. "Lule Warrenton; Clever Character Actress with the Universal Company," *MPS,* 27 Mar 1914, 27. "Lule Warrrenton Again Ill," *MPW,* 25 Mar 1916, 2019. "To Produce

Children's Pictures," *MPW,* 7 Oct 1916, 57–58. "Mrs. Warrenton Starts Children's Photoplays," *MPW,* 17 Feb 1917, 1030.

Warrington, Ann [actress] (*née* Mary L. Woods, b. Hillsboro WI, 26 Sep 1864–14 Nov 1934 [70], Philadelphia PA). "Ann Warrington," *Variety,* 20 Nov 1934. AS, p. 1132. BHD1, p. 572. IFN, p. 310.

Warrington, Charles [cinematographer] (b. 1877?–17 Aug 1926 [49], Los Angeles CA). (Fine Arts.) "Charles Warrington," *Variety,* 25 Aug 1926. BHD, p. 331; BHD2, p. 276.

Warters, William E. [actor] (b. New Bern NC, 1883–29 Aug 1953 [70], Los Angeles CA). BHD, p. 331. IFN, p. 310.

Warwick, James [scenarist] (b. England, 1894–15 Aug 1983 [89?], Briarcliff Manor NY). AS, p. 1132. BHD2, p. 277.

Warwick, John [actor] (*né* John McIntosh Beattle, b. Bellengen River, New So. Wales, Australia, 14 Jan 1905–10 Jan 1972 [66], Sydney, Australia; heart attack). "John Warwick," *Variety,* 2 Feb 1972. AS, p. 1132 (b. 4 Jan). BHD1, p. 572.

Warwick, Robert [stage/film/TV actor] (*né* Robert Taylor Bien, b. Sacramento CA, 9 Oct 1878–6 Jun 1964 [85], West Los Angeles CA; pulmonary embolism). m. (1) Arline Peck; (2) **Josephine Whittell** (d. 1961); **Stella** Lattimore (d. 1960). (Began on stage in *Glad of It,* 1903; World; Selznick; FP-L.) "Robert Warwick of Films and TV; Actor, Long a Leading Man on Broadway, Dies at 85," *NYT,* 7 Jun 1964, 86:4. "Robert Warwick," *Variety,* 10 Jun 1964. AMD, p. 357. AS, p. 1132. BHD1, p. 572. FSS, p. 288. IFN, p. 310. Katz, p. 1211. MH, p. 142. MSBB, p. 1030 (b. 1881). Spehr, p. 172. Truitt, p. 343. WWS, p. 38. "Robert Warwick," *MPW,* 10 Oct 1914, 199. "Robert Warwick Signs with World Film," *MPW,* 24 Oct 1914, 512. "Warwick Signs with World Film," *MPW,* 18 Sep 1915, 2000. "Warwick Will Have His Own Company," *MPW,* 18 Nov 1916, 995. "Robert Warwick," *MPW,* 27 Apr 1918, 518. "Warwick Back Gets First View of His Last Picture," *MPW,* 8 Jun 1918, 1457. "Robert Warwick Back from Europe," *MPW,* 15 Feb 1919, 873. Faith Service, "War and Women; Bob Warwick Discusses Battlefields and Femininity," *MPC,* May 1919, 24–25, 66. "Robert Warwick Is Signed by Famous Players-Lasky," *MPW,* 10 May 1919, 802. "Warwick Sues Famous Players Charging Breach of Contract," *MPW,* 22 May 1920, 1053. "Movie History in the Making Ten Years Ago," *Paris and Hollywood,* Oct 1926, 46 (he had been voted the most popular motion picture actor in Australia, beating out Francis X. Bushman and Dustin Farnum, who tied for second place). George A. Katchmer, "The Multi-Talented Entertainer, Robert Warwick," *CI,* 156 (Jun 1988), 17–20, C32.

Warwick, Robert, Sr. [actor/film editor/director] (b. England, 3 Apr 1868–3 Dec 1944 [76], Los Angeles CA). m. Bess. "Robert Warwick," *Variety,* 6 Dec 1944 (b. Sacramento CA; age 66). AS, p. 1132. BHD2, p. 277. IFN, p. 310.

Warwick, Stella Larrimore [stage/film actress] (*née* Stella Larrimore, b. 1905?–1 Dec 1960 [55?], Los Angeles CA). m. **Robert Warwick** (d. 1964). Truitt, p. 343 ("Lattimore"). "Stella Larrimore Dies; Actress Appeared on Stage Here in the Twenties," *NYT,* 2 Dec 1960, 29:1. AS, p. 1132.

Warwick, Virginia [actress]. No data found. (Metro.) AMD, P. 357. "Sennett Makes a Discovery," *MPW,* 14 Sep 1918, 1596. "Virginia Warwick Returns to Screen in Pathé Serial," *MPW,* 14 Nov 1925, 152. George A. Katchmer, "Forgotten Cowboys and Cowgirls—Part XIV," *CI,* 191 (May 1991), 24.

Wascher, Aribert Robert Ernst Wilhelm [actor] (b. Flensburg, Germany, 1 Dec 1895–14 Dec 1961 [66], Berlin, Germany). AS, p. 1133 (b. 14 Dec}. BHD1, p. 572.

Waschneck, Eric [director/producer/scenarist] (*né* Erich Johannes Washneck, b. Grimma, Germany, 29 Apr 1887–22 Sep 1970 [83], Berlin, Germany). AS, p. 1133. BHD2, p. 277. FDY, p. 439.

Washburn, Alice [actress] (b. Oshkosh WI, 12 Sep 1861–28 Nov 1929 [68], Oshkosh WI; heart attack). (Edison; Vitagraph; Kalem.) "Alice Washburn," *Variety,* 4 Dec 1929. AS, p. 1133 (d. 29 Nov). BHD, p. 331. IFN, p. 311. Truitt, p. 343. Alice Washburn, "The Recital," *Motion Picture Magazine,* Feb 1915, 97–98. Billy H. Doyle, "Lost Players," *CI,* 141 (Mar 1987), 31, C10, 45.

Washburn, Bryant [stage/film actor] (*né* Dwight Ludlow, b. Chicago IL, 28 Apr 1884?–30 Apr 1963 [79?], Woodland Hills CA; heart attack). m. Mabel Forest, 3 Jul 1914, Chicago IL. (Essanay, 1910; Paramount.) "Bryant Washburn, Silent-Movie Star," *NYT,* 3 May 1963, 32:2. "Bryant Washburn," *Variety,* 8 May 1963 (age 74). AMD, p. 358. AS, p. 1133 (b. 1889). BHD1, p. 572 (b. 1889). FFF, p. 226. FSS, p. 288. GK, pp. 1001–21. IFN, p. 311 (b. 1889). Katz, p. 1211. Lowrey, p. 186 (*né* Franklin Bryant Washburn). MH, p. 142 (b. 1889). MSBB, p. 1030. Truitt, pp. 343–44 (b. 1889). WWS, p. 16. "Some Prominent Essanay Photoplayers," *MPW,* 11 Jul 1914, 234–35. "Bryant Washburn's New Year Reception," *MPW,* 23 Jan 1915, 518. "Bryant Washburn," *MPW,* 11 Sep 1915, 1839. "Bryant Washburn," *MPW,* 13 Jan 1917, 234. Bryant Washburn, "Comedy Favored by War," *MPW,* 21 Jul 1917, 414. "Bryant Washburn Exonerated," *MPW,* 29 Sep 1917, 1983. "Washburn Temporarily Blinded," *MPW,* 29 Dec 1917, 1948. "Bryant Washburn Makes Pathé Debut In 'Twenty-One,'" *MPW,* 6 Apr 1918, 116. "Washburn and Paramount Sign Three-Year Contract," *MPW,* 29 Jun 1918, 1872. "Seven Players New to Artcraft-Paramount," *MPW,* 6 Jul 1918, 57. Edward Weitzel, "Travel Far to 'Get' Fifth Avenue," *MPW,* 19 Oct 1918, 359–60. Washburn Talks Briefly About His Present Work," *MPW,* 19 Oct 1918, 366–67. "Opposes Kipling; Washburn Doesn't Like English Author's Marriage Views," *LA Times,* 6 Feb 1920, II, p. 9 (Washburn objected to "Down in Gehenna or up to the throne/He travels the fastest who travels alone," Kipling's slap at matrimony. Washburn thought marriage gives a man something to work for, and that Kipling's opinions on marriage "aren't nearly as sound as those, which, for example, Theodore Roosevelt held."). "Washburn Gives Blood to Son," *MPW,* 17 Apr 1920, 421 (transfusion for Dwight Moody Washburn). "Bryant Washburn and Lee Ochs Combine; Plan Five Annual Independent Specials," *MPW,* 3 Jul 1920. Sumner Smith, "From Twenty To Five, with the Odds Favoring Bryant Washburn, Comedy Star," *MPW,* 17 Jul 1920, 355. "Bryant Washburn Returns from London; 'Bobbies' Helped Him Get Atmosphere," *MPW,* 20 Nov 1920, 358. "Bryant Washburn and Spyros Skouras Escape Death in Automobile Accident," *MPW,* 25 Jun 1921, 795. "Bryant Washburn Signed by C.B.C.," *MPW,* 27 Jan 1923, 368. "Bryant's Wife Picks 'Em," *MPW,* 17 Nov 1923, 318. "Plays Opposite Shirley Mason," *MPW,* 13 Dec 1924, 647. George A. Katchmer, "Who? Bryant Washburn," *CI,* 150 (Dec 1987), 23–25, 29, 61. Richard E. Braff, "The Films of Bryant Washburn," *CI,* 151 (Jan 1988), C34-C35, C37; 152 (Feb 1987), C18-C20, C29.

Washburn, Grace [actress]. No data found. AMD, p. 358. "Grace Washburn on Screen," *NYDM,* 17 Mar 1915, 21:3 (to appear in *When It Strikes Home,* Charles K. Harris Features Film Co.). "Grace Washburn in 'World Film,'" *MPW,* 27 Mar 1915, 1942.

Washburn, Hazel [actress] (b. Albany NY, 25 Oct 1898). AS, p. 1133. MH, p. 142.

Washburn, John H. [actor] (d. 11 Dec 1917, New York NY). AS, p. 1133. BHD, p. 331. IFN, p. 311.

Washington, Edgar "Blue" [actor] (b. Los Angeles CA, 12 Feb 1898–15 Sep 1970 [72], Los Angeles CA). AS, p. 1133. BHD1, p. 572. IFN, p. 311. Joseph McBride, *Frank Capra; The Catastrophe of Success* (NY: Simon & Schuster, 1992) (Capra's boyhood friend; in *The Birth of a Nation*), 35, 63.

Washington, Jesse [actor] (d. 4 Sep 1919, Newport RI, during filming of a fight scene). AMD, p. 358. AS, p. 1133. BHD, p. 331. IFN, p. 311. "Obituary," *MPW,* 27 Sep 1919, 1981.

Washington, Ned [lyricist] (b. Scranton PA, 15 Aug 1901–20 Dec 1976 [75], Beverly Hills CA). m. Patricia Page. "Ned Washington, Lyricist, Dead; Songs and Scores Won 3 Oscars," *NYT,* 22 Dec 1976, 32:5. "Ned Washington, Major Lyricist in H'wood, Dies at 75," *Variety,* 22 Dec 1976 (AA for *Pinocchio* [1940]; *High Noon* [1952]. Wrote *La Cucaracha; The Nearness of You; Stella by Starlight; My Foolish Heart; The High and the Mighty; Town Without Pity*). AS, p. 1133. BHD2, p. 277.

Waterhouse, Frank [actor] (b. 1876–7 Aug 1950 [74?], Los Angeles CA). AS, p. 1133.

Waterman, Ida [actress] (*née* Ida Shaw, b. 10 Mar 1852–22 May 1941 [89], Cincinnati OH). m. Joseph Francoeur (d. 1907); Fred Waterman. (Webb.) "Ida Waterman," *Variety,* 28 May 1941. AS, p. 1133. BHD, p. 331. IFN, p. 311. Truitt, p. 344.

Waters, Bessie [actress]. No data found. AMD, p. 358. "Wins Contest," *MPW,* 13 Aug 1921, 728.

Waters, Elsie [actress])b. London, England, 1894–14 Jun 1990 [96?], London, England). AS, p. 1133.

Waters, John S. [actor/director] (b. New York NY, 31 Oct 1893–5 May 1965 [71], Woodland Hills CA). (Biograph, 1910; Paramount; Metro.) "John S. Waters," *Variety,* 12 May 1965. AMD, p. 358. AS, pp. 1133–34. BHD2, p. 277. IFN, p. 311. "'Johnny' Waters to Assist Balshofer," *MPW,* 20 Oct 1917, 394. "'Johnnie' Waters Joins Colors," *MPW,* 22 Dec 1917, 1774. "Waters to Direct," *MPW,* 11 Jun 1927, 419.

Waters, Percy L[ee] [executive] (b. 1867?–31 Jan 1942 [74], New York NY). "Percival Lee Waters; President of Triangle Film Co., 1915–23, Dies Here at 74," *NYT,* 2 Feb 1942, 15:4 ("Mr. Waters had been one of the large preferred stockholders of the General Film Corporation."). "Percival Lee Waters," *Variety,* 145, 4 Feb 1942, 54:2 (President of Triangle from 1919). AMD, p. 358. "Percy L. Waters Screens 'Comeback,'" *MPW,* 24 May 1919, 1142.

Waters, Tom [minstrels/stage/film actor] (b.

1872–10 Jul 1953 [81?], Harrisburg PA). m. **May Wallace**, 1902 (d. 1928). (Mutual, Flushing, LI NY.) "Tom Waters," *NYT*, 12 Jul 1953, 65:3 (starred on stage in *The Pink Lady*. After retirement from the stage, he worked at the State Museum in Harrisburg.). "Tom Waters," *Variety*, 15 Jul 1953, p. 63. AMD, p. 358. BHD, p. 331. "Another Team in Pictures," *MPW*, 20 Nov 1915, 1483:2.

Waters, Mrs. Tom [actress] (b. 1880–16 Sep 1928 [48?], New York NY). BHD, p. 331.

Waters, William E. [actor] (b. New Bern NC, 1883–15 Sep 1953 [70?], Los Angeles CA). AS, p. 1134.

Watkins, Linda [stage/film actress] (b. Boston MA, 23 May 1908–31 Oct 1976 [68], Los Angeles CA). m. Gabriel L. Hess. "Linda Watkins," *Variety*, 3 Nov 1976. AS, p. 1134 (d. Santa Monica CA). BHD1, p. 573 (b. 1909; d. Santa Monica). SD, p. 1284.

Watson, Adele [actress] (b. MN, 31 Jan 1890–27 Mar 1933 [43], Los Angeles CA; double pneumonia). AS, p. 1134. BHD1, p. 573. IFN, p. 311. Truitt, p. 344.

Watson, Billy [director]. No data found. (Sennett.) AMD, p. 358. "Engages Watson," *MPW*, 31 Dec 1921, 1079.

Watson, Billy "Beef Trust" [stage/film actor] (aka Billy Buttons, *né* Isaac Levie, b. New York NY, 1867?–14 Jan 1945 [78], Asbury Park NJ). "Billy Watson, 78, Singer, Comedian; Star of His 'Beef Trust' for Many Years Dies—Scored on Burlesque Circuit," *NYT*, 15 Jan 1945, 19:5. "Billy Watson," *Variety*, 17 Jan 1945. AS, p. 1134. BHD, p. 331. IFN, p. 311.

Watson, Bobby [stage/vaudeville/film actor] (*né* Robert Watson Knucher, b. Springfield IL, 28 Nov 1887–22 May 1965 [77], Los Angeles CA). (Film debut: *That Royale Girl*, 1925; Griffith; RKO; Paramount; last film: *On the Double*, 1961.) "Bobby Watson," *Variety*, 2 Jun 1965. AS, p. 1134 (Robert Watson). BHD1, p. 573. IFN, p. 311. Katz, p. 1212. Truitt, p. 344. Charles P. Mitchell, "Der Fuehrer's Face: The Career of Bobby Watson," *CI*, 277 (Jul 1998), 26–28 (b. Evanston OH). Note: Not to be confused with child actor Bobby Watson.

Watson, Charles [production manager]. No data found. AMD, p. 358. "Charles Watson with Novagraph," *MPW*, 13 Sep 1919, 1666. "Charles Watson Recovers from Serious Injuries," *MPW*, 7 Feb 1920, 930.

Watson, Coy, Jr. (father of Bobs Watson and 8 other sibling actors) [actor] (*né* James Coy, Sr., b. 14 Apr 1890–23 May 1968 [78], Edendale CA). m. (Sennett; Vitagraph; Vitagraph; Fox.) "Coy Watson, Sr.," *Variety*, 29 May 1968 (began 1911.) AS, p. 1134 (d. 25 May). BHD1, p. 573. "Bobs Watson [film/TV actor/Methodist minister]; 1 of 9 child actor siblings, played Pee Wee in 'Boys Town,'" *PP-G*, 30 Jun 1999, B-6:1 (b. 1931–27 Jun 1999 [68], Laguna Beach CA; prostate cancer. Film debut: *Riding to Fame*, 1931; "The house I was raised in was about 600 feet from Mack Sennett's studios and offices [near] Echo Park....as a result of being so close to the studios, my dad started out renting horses for the silent movies for $2 a day.").

Watson, Harry, Jr. [actor]. No data found. AMD, p. 358. "Essanay Engages Harry Watson, Jr.," *MPW*, 4 Nov 1916, 723. "He Makes 'Em," *MPW*, 18 Nov 1916, 1036. "Watson in Films," *MPW*, 19 Jun 1926, 4.

Watson, Harry B., "Kid Duggan" [actor] (b. Philadelphia PA, Jun 1876–23 Sep 1930 [54], Monrovia CA). (Cosmopolitan [Hearst pictures].) "$10,000 Film Contract for Harry Watson, Jr.; Contract with Limit of Four Weeks for 'Little Old New York' [to play the pugilist]," *Variety*, 12 Jan 1923, 4:3 ("To complete the picture engagement Watson cancelled his vaudeville tour at Des Moines last week, having it placed back for four weeks..."). AS, p. 1134 (d. LA CA). BHD1, p. 573. IFN, p. 311.

Watson, Henrietta [actress] (b. Dundee, Scotland, 11 Mar 1873–29 Sep 1964 [91], London, England). BHD1, p. 574.

Watson, Joseph K. [scenarist] (b. Philadelphia PA, 12 Feb 1887–16 May 1942 [55], Los Angeles CA). AS, p. 1134. BHD2, p. 277.

Watson, Kitty [actress] (*née* Katherine Watson, b. 1886–3 Mar 1967 [80?], Buffalo NY). AS, p. 1134.

Watson, Lucile [stage/film actress] (b. Quebec, Canada, 27 May 1879–24 Jun 1962 [83], New York NY [Death Certificate Index No. 13757 (Lucile Shipman); age 82]). m. Louis E. Shipman (d. 1933); (2) **Rockcliffe Fellowes** (d. 1950). "Lucile Watson, Actress, Dead; Noted for Her Dowager Roles; Character Player, 83, Was in 50 Broadway Plays—Appeared in Movies," *NYT*, 25 Jun 1962, 29:2. "Lucile Watson," *Variety*, 27 Jun 1962. AS, p. 1134 (b. Ottawa, Canada). BHD1, p. 574. IFN, p. 311. Truitt, p. 345.

Watson, Margaret [actress] (b. 1875–31 Oct 1940 [65?]). BHD1, p. 574.

Watson, Minor [stage/film actor] (b. Marianna AR, 22 Dec 1889–28 Jul 1965 [75], Alton IL). m. Elinor Hewitt. "Minor Watson, 75, Character Actor; Veteran Performer in Films and on Stage Is Dead," *NYT*, 30 Jul 1965, 25:3. "Minor Watson," *Variety*, 4 Aug 1965. AS, p. 1134. BHD1, p. 574. IFN, p. 311. Truitt, p. 345.

Watson, Roy [actor] (b. Richmond VA, 1876?–7 Jun 1937 [61], Los Angeles CA). (Selig.) AS, p. 1134. BHD1, p. 574. IFN, p. 311. Truitt, p. 345. George A. Katchmer, "Forgotten Cowboys and Cowgirls—Part VIII," *CI*, 180 (Jun 1990), 53.

Watson, William (Sliding Billy) [actor] (d. 4 Jan 1939, New York NY). BHD, p. 332.

Watson, Wylie [actor] (*né* John Riley Watson, b. Scotland, 6 Feb 1889–3 May 1966 [77]). AS, p. 1135. BHD1, p. 574.

Watt, Allen M. [director] (b. PA, 1885–15 Sep 1944 [59?], Los Angeles CA). m. **Myrtle Gonzalez**, 1 Dec 1917 (d. 1918). (Universal.) AMD, p. 358. BHD2, p. 277. "Allen Watson Joins CHristie," *MPW*, 27 Dec 1919, 1175.

Watt, Charles [assistant director] (b. 1876–27 Feb 1959 [82?], Oxnard CA). BHD2, p. 277.

Watt, Nate C. [director] (b. Denver CO, 6 Apr 1887–26 May 1968 [81], Woodland Hills CA; emphysema). m. Jean Bachon. "Nate Watt," *Variety*, 29 May 1968. AMD, p. 358. AS, p. 1135. BHD2, p. 277 (b. 1889). IFN, p. 311. "Now Nate C. Watt Made Good When Opportunity Knocked," *MPW*, 9 Oct 1920, 1175.

Watters, George M[anker] [scenarist] (b. Rochester NY, 27 Apr 1892–14 Mar 1943 [50], Los Angeles CA). AS, p. 1135 (d. 4 Mar). BHD2, p. 277.

Watts, Charles [actor] (b. Clarksville TN–d. 13 Dec 1966, Nashville TN; cancer). "Charles Watts Is Dead; Character Actor in Films," *NYT*, 16 Dec 1966, 47:3. "Charles Watts," *Variety*, 4 Jan 1967. AS, p. 1135. IFN, p. 311. Ragan 2, p. 1779 (d. in his 60s).

Watts, Dodo [actress] (*née* Dorothy Margaret Watts, b. London, England, 27 Dec 1910–25 Dec 1990 [79], Teddington, England). AS, p. 1135. BHD1, p. 574.

Watts, George [actor] (b. Newark NJ, 17 Feb 1879–1 Jul 1942 [63], Los Angeles CA; massive heart attack). AS, p. 1135.

Watts, James A. [actor] (b. Australia, 1881–5 Oct 1961 [80?], London, England). "James A. Watts," *Variety*, 25 Oct 1961, p. 71. BHD, p. 332.

Watts, Peggy [actress] (b. 1906?–27 Apr 1966 [60], Hong Kong, China). m. Ridgeway Callow. "Peggy Callow," *Variety*, 4 May 1966. AS, p. 1135 (d. 27 Feb).

Waxman, Morris D. [actor] (b. 1876–10 Nov 1931 [55?]). "Morris D. Waxman," *Variety*, 17 Nov 1931, p. 63. BHD, p. 332.

Wayburn, Ned [vaudeville singer and "ragtime" piano-player/stage director/choreographer/director] (*né* Edward Claudius Wayburn, b. Pittsburgh PA, 30 Mar 1874–2 Sep 1942 [68], 90 Riverside Drive, New York NY; after illness of 8 months). m. (1) Agnes Saye; (2) Helene Davis; (3) Marguerite Kirby, 1916. (First NY stage appearance: *The Swell Miss Fitzwell*, 1897, with May Irwin; directed Ziegfeld Follies, 1916–19, 1922–23; ran a dancing school for 30 years.) "Ned Wayburn, 68, Dance Director; Aided in the Productions of Klaw and Erlanger, Shuberts and Florenz Ziegfeld; Stricken at Home Here; Ran Dancing School 37 Years and Staged 600 Works—Was Song Composer," *NYT*, 3 Sep 1942, 19:5 (Composed *Syncopated Sandy*, which sold over 1 million copies. Father of Ned Wayburn, Jr., from one of his earlier marriages. "He had been briefly associated with moving pictures in the early days of the films, but returned from Hollywood to New York with the conviction that substance was greater than shadows."). "Ned Wayburn," *Variety*, 9 Sep 1942, p. 46. AS, p. 1135 (d. Hollywood CA). BHD1, p. 574.

Wayman, H.P. [producer]. No data found. AMD, p. 358. "A New Kind of Weekly," *MPW*, 17 Jul 1915, 470.

Wayne, Gladys [actress]. No data found. AMD, p. 358. "Narrow Escape from Drowning," *MPW*, 10 Aug 1912, 532.

Wayne, John "Duke" (father of John Ethan [b. 1962] and Patrick Wayne [b. 1939]) [actor] (*né* Marion Robert [or Michael] Morrison, b. Winterset IA, 26 May 1907–11 Jun 1979 [72], Los Angeles CA; lung and stomach cancer). m. (1) Josephine Saenz, 1933–44; (2) Esperanza Bauer, 1946–53; (3) Pilar Weldy [Patette?], 1954. Aissa Wayne [daughter], *John Wayne, My Father* (NY: Random House, 1991); Richard D. McGhee, *John Wayne; Actor, Artist, Hero* (Jefferson NC: McFarland, 1990). Garry Willis, *John Wayne's America* (NY: Simon & Schuster, 1997). (AA, 1969) "John Wayne Dies of Cancer at 72; His Reel and Real Selves Akin," *Variety*, 13 Jun 1979. AS, p. 1135. BHD1, p. 575; BHD2, p. 277. JS, p. 498 (filmed in Italy, 1957). Katz, pp. 1213–14. Maureen Dowd, "The Duke Enshrined in Land of Corn," *NYT*, 27 Nov 1987, A26. Bob Hoover, "The myth is the message" [review of *John Wayne's America*], *Pittsburgh Post-Gazette*, 70, 13 Apr 1997, G10:2, G12.

Wayne, Justina [stage/film/radio actress]

(b. Oakland CA–d. 2 Dec 1951, Freeport, LI NY). (Universal; Republic.) "Justina Wayne, Actress 50 Years; Screen and Radio Performer Who Appeared in Broadway Hits Early in Century Dies," *NYT,* 3 Dec 1951, 31:6. "Justina Wayne," *Variety,* 5 Dec 1951. AS, p. 1135. BHD1, p. 575. IFN, p. 312.

Wayne, Mabel [actress/songwriter] (b. Brooklyn NY, 1892?–19 Jun 1978 [86], Glen Cove NY). "Mabel Wayne," *Variety,* 19 Jul 1978 (wrote *In a Little Spanish Town; Ramona; It Happened in Monterey*). AS, p. 1135. BHD2, p. 277.

Wayne, Marie [vaudeville: Deeley and Wayne/film actress] (b. Tokyo, Japan). No other data found. (Pathé.) AMD, p. 358. "Marie Wayne in Pictures," *NYDM,* 15 Sep 1915, 26:4. "Marie Wayne with Pathé," *MPW,* 2 Oct 1915, 81.

Wayne, Maude [actress] (b. Beatrice NB, 26 Mar 1895–10 Oct 1983 [88], Los Angeles CA). m. **Johnnie Walker** (d. 1949). (*Fl.* 1918–27; Keystone.) AMD, p. 358. BHD, p. 332. "Maud Wayne in Drama," *MPW,* 20 Apr 1918, 409. George Katchmer, "Remembering the Great Silents," *CI,* 240 (Jun 1995), 46.

Wayne, Richard [actor] (b. Beatrice NB, 16 Apr 1881–14 Mar 1958 [76], Los Angeles CA). AS, p. 1136 (d. 15 Mar). BHD1, p. 619. IFN, p. 312 (d. 15 Mar). Truitt, p. 345.

Wayne, Robert [actor] (b. Pittsburgh PA, 28 Oct 1864–26 Sep 1946 [81], Los Angeles CA). AS, p. 1136. BHD1, p. 575. IFN, p. 312.

Wead, Frank W. [scenarist] (b. 1894–15 Nov 1947 [53?], Santa Monica CA). AS, p. 1136. BHD2, p. 277.

Weadock, Louis [writer/scenarist] (b. Saginaw MI, 1880?–11 Feb 1942 [62], Los Angeles CA; fell or leapt from a hotel window). m. **Ouida Bergere** (d. 1974). "Louis Weadock," *Variety,* 18 Feb 1942. AMD, p. 359. AS, p. 1136. BHD2, p. 277. "Louis Weadock SIgns Up with Fairbanks Forces," *MPW,* 24 Jan 1920, 599.

Weatherby, Carleton [actor]. (Vitagraph.) No data found.

Weatherford, Tazwell [actor] (b. IN, 1889–22 Jul 1917 [28?], Los Angeles CA; suicide with poison). AS, p. 1136. BHD, p. 332.

Weathersby, Jennie [actress] (b. England, 10 Jul 1855–17 Mar 1931 [75], New York NY). BHD, p. 332.

Weatherwax, Paul J. [film editor] (b. MI, 8 Jul 1900–13 Sep 1960 [60], West Hollywood CA; apparent heart attack). (TC-F; Universal International; Columbia.) "Paul J. Weatherwax," *NYT,* 15 Sep 1960, 37:1 (AA for *The Naked City* [1948], and *Around the World in 80 Days* [1956]). "Paul J. Weatherwax," *Variety,* 21 Sep 1960. BHD2, p. 277.

Weatherwax, Walter S. [actor] (b. Fort Scott KS, 31 May 1867–19 Jan 1943 [75], Los Angeles Co. CA). (Universal.) AS, p. 1136. BHD, p. 332. IFN, p. 312.

Weaver, Harvey Cook]producer] (b. New York NY, 1880?–4 Nov 1943 [63], Los Angeles CA). m. Anna L. (Christie, 1918.) "Harvey Cook Weaver," *NYT,* 5 Nov 1943, 19:3 ("...old-time movie producer...officially credited with starting directors Frank Capra and W.H. Van Dyke on their successful careers."). AS, p. 1136 (Harry Weaver). BHD2, p. 277 (Harry Cook Weaver).

Weaver, Henry [actor] (b. Pittsburgh PA, 21 Jun 1858–9 May 1922 [63], Sea Bright NJ). BHD, p. 332.

Weaver, John V[an] **A**[lstyn] [playwright/scenarist] (b. Charlotte NC, 17 Jul 1893–14 Jun 1938 [44], Colorado Springs CO; tuberculosis). m. **Peggy Wood**, 1934 (d. 1978). (FP-L.) "John V.A. Weaver, Poet and Novelist; Also Playwright and Writer of Dialogue for Movies—Dies in West at 44; Former Book Reviewer; Verse Distinguished by Use of Idiom of Streets—Husband of Peggy Wood," *NYT,* 16 Jun 1938, 23:3. AS, p. 1136. BHD2, p. 277. FDY, p. 439.

Weaver, June "Elviry" [actress] (b. Chicago IL, 23 Jun 1891–27 Nov 1977 [86], Bakersfield CA). AS, p. 1136.

Weaver, Leon [actor/singer] (b. Ozark MO, 12 Aug 1882–27 May 1950 [67], Los Angeles CA). AS, p. 1136.

Webb, Austin [actor] (b. Guysville OH, 1879–8 Dec 1937 [58?], Los Angeles CA). AMD, p. 359. BHD, p. 332. "World Engages Austin Webb," *MPW,* 5 Jul 1919, 59.

Webb, Basil [actor]. No data found. AMD, p. 359. "Actor Seeks Damages for Eileen's Realism," *MPW,* 2 Jul 1927, 13.

Webb, Beth [actress] (b. 1897–25 Jul 1986 [89?], Studio City CA). BHD, p. 332.

Webb, Clifton [stage/film actor/dancer] (*né* Webb Parmelee Hollenbeck, b. Indianapolis IN, 19 Nov 1889–13 Oct 1966 [76], Beverly Hills CA; heart attack). Bachelor. "Clifton Webb, 72, Dies on Coast; Movies' Dignified Mr. Belvedere; Broadway Comedy Star Won Fame on Screen in Role of Babysitter," *NYT,* 14 Oct 1966, 40:1; 15 Oct 1966, 29:1 (repeated and corrected). "Clifton Webb," *Variety,* 19 Oct 1966. AMD, p. 359. AS, p. 1136. BHD1, p. 575. IFN, p. 312 (b. 1889). Katz, p. 1215. Truitt, p. 345 (b. 1889 or 1896). Frederick James Smith, "Vaudeville," *NYDM,* 25 Mar 1914, 21:2 ("Mae Murray and Clifton Webb made their dancing debut at the Palace.... Mr. Webb interfered with our view of Miss Murray at times, but otherwise he is forgettable." ¶"In the Barcarole, Miss Murray seems to interpret a sort of sliding down hill dance—with Mr. Webb in the silent role of the hill. Sometimes she leaped at the waiting Mr. Webb and then just slumped. A sort of Murray hill evolution, as it were. Anyway, makeup powder was distributed generously about Mr. Webb by the last twirl."). "Clifton Webb," *NYDM,* 2 Jun 1915, 17:4 (photo and quip: "Heading His Own Dancing Specialty in the Varieties."). "Webb Makes Screen Debut," *MPW,* 31 Jul 1920, 615 (*Polly with a Past*). I.E. Ward, "Clifton Webb (1893–1966)," *CI,* 111 (Sep 1984), 55–56 (includes filmography).

Webb, Fay [actress] (b. 1906?–18 Nov 1936 [30], Santa Monica CA; complications after an operation for appendicitis). (MGM.) "Fay Webb," *Variety,* 25 Nov 1936. AMD, p. 359. AS, p. 1136. BHD1, p. 575. IFN, p. 312. "High School Girl Signed by M-G-M," *MPW,* 9 Jul 1927, 98.

Webb, George [actor/director] (*né* George Webb Frey, b. Indianapolis IN, 3 Oct 1887–24 May 1943 [55], Los Angeles CA). (Universal.) m. **Esther Ralston** (d. 1994). AS, p. 1136. BHD1, p. 575; BHD2, p. 278. IFN, p. 312. Esther Ralston, *Some Day We'll Laugh; An Autobiography* (Metuchen NJ: Scarecrow Press, 1985), p. 64. George Katchmer, "Remembering the Great Silents," *CI,* 247 (Jan 1996), 45–46.

Webb, Harry [actor] (b. 1887–16 Jul 1984 [97?], Burbank CA). BHD, p. 332.

Webb, Harry S[amuel] [director] (b. 15 Oct 1892–4 Jul 1959 [66], Los Angeles CA; heart attack). "Harry Webb," *Variety,* 15 Jul 1959. AS, p. 1136 (b. 1898). BHD2, p. 278 (b. 1896). Birth data supplied by Grange B. McKinney, San Clemente CA.

Webb, Kenneth [actor/director/producer] (b. New York NY, 16 Oct 1892–5 Mar 1966 [73], Los Angeles CA). "Kenneth Webb," *Variety,* 23 Mar 1966. AMD, p. 359. AS, p. 1136. BHD2, p. 278. ASCAP 66, p. 772 (b. 1885). Lowrey, p. 188. 1921 Directory, p. 277. "Lasky Engages Three More Directors," *MPW,* 25 Jan 1919, 454. "Whitman Bennett Signs Kenneth Webb as Director," *MPW,* 7 Aug 1920, 722. "Completes Contract," *MPW,* 16 Sep 1922, 200. "Working on Pathé Film," *MPW,* 5 Jan 1924, 29. "Kenneth Webb to Direct," *MPW,* 22 Aug 1925, 844.

Webb, Millard [actor/scenarist/director/producer] (b. Clay City KY, 6 Dec 1893–21 Apr 1935 [41], Los Angeles CA; intestinal malady). m. actress Dorothy Wallace, LA CA; **Mary Eaton** (d. 1948). (Griffith; 1st National; WB.) "Millard Webb," *Variety,* 24 Apr 1935 (age 42). AMD, p. 359. AS, pp. 1136–37. BHD, p. 332; BHD2, p. 278. IFN, p. 312. Katz, p. 1216. Truitt, p. 346. "Fairbanks Adds Millard Webb to Producing Staff," *MPW,* 4 Aug 1917, 778. "On the Set and Off," *MW,* 28 Feb 1925, 34 ("Willard" Webb). "Webb Gets Contract," *MPW,* 20 Mar 1926, 173. "Webb Starts on Coogan Film," *MPW,* 31 Jul 1926, 278. "Webb to Direct 'U' Picture," *MPW,* 1 Oct 1927, 291. Herbert Cruikshank, "Just Good Enough to Be Bad; That's What Millard Webb Was as an Actor. And why He Turned Director," *MPC,* Aug 1929, 35, 82.

Webb, Robert D. [casting director] (b. Scottdale PA, 10 Oct 1901–26 Sep 1978 [76], Woodland Hills CA). AMD, p. 359. BHD2, p. 278. "Webb Heads Casting at Columbia Studios," *MPW,* 20 Mar 1926, 169.

Webb, Roy D. [assistant director/composer/music director] (b. New York NY, 3 Oct 1888–10 Dec 1982 [94], Santa Monica CA). AS, p. 1137 (b. 1898). BHD2, p. 278.

Webber, Christine [actress] (d. 8 Oct 1936, Los Angeles CA). BHD, p. 332.

Webber, Frederick [actor] (d. 21 Jul 1925, Cleveland OH). "Frederick Webber," *Variety,* 29 Jul 1925. AS, p. 1137. BHD, p. 332.

Webber, George F. [actor/cinematographer] (b. Kingston, Ontario, Canada 10 May 1876–29 Aug 1967 [91], New York NY [Death Certificate Index No. 31]). (Thanhouser; World; Biograph; Lubin; Gaumont; Pathé; Metro; Selig; Lasky; FP-L; Paramount.) "George Webber," *Variety,* 6 Sep 1967. AS, p. 1137. BHD2, p. 278. FDY, p. 471.

Weber, Joe [stage/film actor] (*né* Joseph Morris Weber, b. New York NY, 11 Aug 1867–10 May 1942 [74], Los Angeles CA). m. Lilian Friedman. "Service for Joe Weber," *NYT,* 12 May 1942, 19:6. "Joe Weber, at 74, Dies 9 Months After Lew Fields," *Variety,* 13 May 1942. AMD, p. 359. AS, p. 1137. BHD1, p. 575. IFN, p. 312. Katz, p. 1216. Truitt, p. 346 (*né* Morris Weber). "Weber & Fields in Pictures," *MPW,* 6 Sep 1913, 1051. "A Famous Team," *MPW,* 22 May 1915, 1239. "Weber and Fields Have Narrow Escape," *MPW,* 9 Oct 1915, 273. "Stars of 'Friendly Enemies' Plan Personal Appearances," *MPW,* 20 Dec 1924, 766. "Now Weber and Fields," *MPW,* 10 Jan 1925, 169.

Weber, Julia Taylor (daughter of **Mrs. May A. Taylor**) [actress]. No data found. (Lubin.)

Weber, L. Laurence [producer/founded Metro Pictures] (b. NY, 1871?–22 Feb 1940 [68], New York NY). m. (2) **Edith Hallor**—div. 1920 (d. 1971). "Lawrence Weber, Theatre Veteran; Producer, a Governor of New York League, Began Career with Circus When 13; He Dies of Heart Attack; Former Jockey and Promoter of Sports Events Staged Many Plays Here," *NYT,* 23 Feb 1940, 15:3 ("He had also been associated with the Warner Brothers in an early film enterprise."). "Larry Weber, Colorful Showman, Sports Promoter, Dies in N.Y. at 68," *Variety,* 28 Feb 1940. AMD, p. 359. AS, p. 1137. BHD2, p. 278. "Lawrence Weber Is with World Films," *MPW,* 16 Aug 1919, 974.

Weber, Lois [actress/director/scenarist] (b. Pittsburgh [Allegheny Co.] PA, 13 Jun 1881–13 Nov 1939 [58], Los Angeles CA). m. **Phillips Smalley**, 1905 (d. 1939); Harry Gantz, 1926. (Balboa, 1 Aug 1914; Rex; Universal; Paramount.) "Lois Weber, Director of Moving Pictures; Helped Anita Stewart and Other Stars to Win Success," *NYT,* 14 Nov 1939, 23:2 (age 56). "Lois Weber," *Variety,* 15 Nov 1939 (age 56). AMD, p. 359. AS, p. 1137. BHD, p. 332; BHD2, p. 278 (b. 1879). FDY, p. 439. IFN, p. 312. Katz, p. 1216. 1921 Directory, p. 277. "Ready to Resume," *MPW,* 12 Oct 1912, 129. "Lois Weber on Scripts," *MPW,* 19 Oct 1912, 241. "Lois Weber's Remarkable Record," *MPW,* 21 Feb 1914, 975. "The Smalleys Join Bosworth," *MPW,* 13 Jun 1914, 1550. "Bosworth's Rapid Rise; A Year and a Half of Progress Has Put Paramount Organization in Front Rank of Feature Producers," *NYDM,* 31 Mar 1915, 32:1 (Bosworth incorporated 8 Aug 1913, produced *The Sea Wolf;* Smalleys joined 1 Aug 1914). "Smalleys Back with Universal," *MPW,* 3 Apr 1915, 76. "Lois Weber Molds Artistic Surprises," *MPW,* 11 Mar 1916, 1668. "Lois Weber, Talks Shop," *MPW,* 27 May 1916, 1493. "Carl Laemmle Denies Lois Weber Rumors," *MPW,* 3 Mar 1917, 1366. "Lois Weber Starts Production," *MPW,* 30 Jun 1917, 2106. Arthur Denison, "A Dream in Realization," *MPW,* 21 Jul 1917, 417–18. "Lois Weber to Film 'K,'" *MPW,* 21 Jul 1917, 478. "Lois Weber Breaks Arm," *MPW,* 12 Oct 1918, 207 (on 18 Sep 1918, slipped in LA department store). "Lois Weber's Sister a Bride," *MPW,* 2 Nov 1918, 595 (Ethel Weber m. Louis Howland, 28 Sep 1918, Riverside CA). "Lois Weber to Direct Anita Stewart," *MPW,* 7 Dec 1918, 1056. "Broken Arm Causing Trouble," *MPW,* 8 Feb 1919, 754. "Lois Webers Arm," *MPW,* 12 Apr 1919, 218. "Lois Weber Signs with Famous Players-Lasky," *MPW,* 2 Aug 1919, 644. "Lois Weber Returns to Coast to Resume Work," *MPW,* 6 Sep 1919, 1458. "Lois Weber Buys Studio She Has Leased for Past Three Years," *MPW,* 2 Oct 1920, 635. "Film Folk Purchase Homes," *MPW,* 14 May 1921, 179 (1917 Ivar Ave., Hollywood). "Lois Weber Has Sailed for Long Tour of World," *MPW,* 1 Oct 1921, 535. "Lois Weber Sails for Europe: Plans Production of Big Films," *MPW,* 8 Oct 1921, 676. Pearl Malverne, "Romance Plus Common Sense," *Classic,* May 1923, 60, 82. "Lois Weber Engaged," *MPW,* 31 Jan 1925, 487. Don Juan, "So This Is Hollywood," *Paris and Hollywood,* Oct 1926, 18 (wed Gantz). "Assign Lois Weber to Direct Duncan Girls," *MPW,* 4 Dec 1926, 351. Josephine MacDowell, "Lois Weber Understands Girls; The only woman cinema director, although mature herself, can give lessons in grace, poise and charm to every girl who works under her," *Cinema Arts,* Jan 1927, 18, 38. "Lois Weber Signed by DeMille to Direct 'Angel of Broadway,'" *MPW,* 9 Jul 1927, 98. Ally Acker, "Lois Weber," *Ms. Magazine,* Feb 1988, pp. 66–67. Billy H. Doyle, "Lost Players," *CI,* 154 (Apr 1988), 54, 59. Anthony Slide, *Early Women Directors* (NY: A.S. Barnes and Co., 1977), pp. 34–51.

Weber, Rex [director] (*né* Frederick Webber, b. Lexington KY, 1889–9 Dec 1918 [29], Chicago IL; pneumonia after the flu). (Lubin; Vitagraph; Selig; Universal; Five A Studio.) "Rex Weber," *Variety,* 20 Dec 1918. AMD, p. 359. AS, p. 1137 (Webber, d. 8 Dec. BHD, p. 332; BHD2, p. 278. "Obituary," *MPW,* 21 Dec 1918, 1332 (b. Covington KY; age 30). Billy H. Doyle, "Lost Players," *CI,* 139 (Jan 1987), 55.

Webster, Ben[jamin] (father of actress/director/producer Margaret Webster) [stage/film actor] (b. London, England, 2 Jun 1864–26 Feb 1947 [82], Cedars of Lebanon Hospital, London, England; had had an operation on 14 Feb). m. **May Whitty**, 1892 (d. 1947). (Professional debut: *Clancarty,* St. James Theatre, 1887; film debut: *Enoch Arden,* with Whitty and Gertrude Lawrence.) "Ben Webster Dies; An Actor 50 Years; Husband of Dame May Whitty and Father of Margaret Had Started on Stage in 1887," *NYT,* 27 Feb 1947, 21:1 (he was the namesake of Benjamin Webster, an 18th-century actor/author, also his grandfather. His ancestors included Capt. John Frederick Webser, conductor of amusements at Bath in the 17th century). "Ben Webster," *Variety,* 5 Mar 1947, p. 62. AS, p. 1137. BHD1, p. 576 (d. LA CA). IFN, p. 312.

Webster, Dorothy Faire [writer]. No data found. AMD, p. 359. "Writer Joins Ince Press Staff," *MPW,* 21 Feb 1920, 1231.

Webster, George [vaudeville booker/executive] (b. 1868?–12 Oct 1926 [58], Chicago IL; heart attack). m. Jennie. "George Webster," *Variety,* 20 Oct 1926.

Webster, George H. [assistant director] (b. 1889–22 Nov 1949 [60?], Santa Monica CA). BHD2, p. 278.

Webster, H[arold] **T**[ucker] [animator] (b. 1885–22 Sep 1952 [67?], Stamford CT). AS, p. 1137.

Webster, Harry McRae [director]. No data found. m. **Lottie Briscoe**—div. in Chicago (d. 1950). AMD, p. 360. Lowrey, p. 192. "Webster Taken Ill Just as 'Reclaimed' Is Finished," *MPW,* 25 May 1918, 1174.

Webster, Lillian [actress] (d. 6 Jul 1920, Methodist Hospital, Los Angeles CA; complications after surgery). (National.) AMD, p. 360. AS, p. 1137. BHD, p. 332. IFN, p. 312. A.H. Giebler, "Los Angeles News Letter; Lillian Webster Dies," *MPW,* 24 Jul 1920, 447.

We-Chock-Be [actress] (d. 18 Dec 1937, Syracuse NY). m. **Jack Conway** (d. 1952). "We-Chock-Be," *Variety,* 12 Jan 1938.

Weed, Frank [actor]. No data found. AMD, p. 360. "Duncan Engages Weed," *MPW,* 24 Mar 1923, 456.

Weeks, Ada May (sister of **Marion Weeks**) [actress] (b. 8 Mar 1898–26 Apr 1978 [80], New York NY). AS, p. 1138.

Weeks, George W. [producer] (b. Ann Arbor MI, 21 Mar 1885–16 Nov 1953 [68], Los Angeles CA; heart attack). (Paramount; Monogram.) "George W. Weeks," *Variety,* 18 Nov 1953 ("Weeks entered the film industry in 1910 as supervisor of Kunsky Theatres in Michigan."). AS, p. 1138. BHD2, p. 278. IFN, p. 312.

Weeks, Marion (sister of **Ada May Weeks**) [actress] (b. 1887?–20 Apr 1968 [81], New York NY). m. Henri Barron. (Edison, 1912.) "Marion Weeks," *Variety,* 24 Apr 1968. AS, p. 1138. AS, p. 1138. BHD, p. 332. IFN, p. 312. Truitt, p. 346.

Weeks, Walter [actor/writer/director] (b. 1881–4 May 1961 [79], Hartford CT; heart attack in his sleep). Wife d. 20 Oct 1935. AS, p. 1138. BHD1, p. 576. IFN, p. 312.

Weel, Arne [director] (b. Arhus, Denmark, 15 Jan 1891–2 Oct 1975 [84], Frederiksborg, Denmark). AS, p. 1138. BHD2, p. 278.

Weems, Walter [actor/title writer/director/scenarist] (b. NC, 25 Jun 1886–2 Sep 1955 [69], Los Angeles CA). BHD1, p. 576. BHD2, p. 278. FDY, p. 447.

Weer, Helen *see* **Weir, Helen**

Wegener, Paul Hermann [actor/director/scenarist] (b. Bischdorf, Germany, 11 Dec 1874–13 Sep 1948 [73], Berlin, Germany). m. **Lyda Salmonova** (d. 1968). "Paul Wegener," *NYT,* 14 Sep 1948, 29:2. AS, p. 1138 (b. Jerrentowicz Arnoldsdorf, Germany). BHD1, p. 576; BHD2, p. 278. FDY, p. 439. IFN, p. 312. Katz, p. 1217 (began in Germany, 1913). Truitt, p. 346. "German Actors at the Front," *NYDM,* 4 Aug 1915, 5:3 (3,500 German actors "are fighting for their country," including Paul Wegner [sic], Ernest Multa and Otto Province).

Wehlen, Emily [stage/film actress] (b. Vienna, Austria, 1887). (Film debut: *When a Woman Loves,* Metro, 1915.) AMD, p. 360. BHD, p. 333 (b. Mannheim, Germany). MSBB, p. 1044. *The Strand Magazine,* Oct 1908. "New German Actress," *New York Telegraph,* 27 Mar 1909. "Comic Opera's Prettiest Girl," *Denver Times,* 18 Dec 1910. "And Still They Come; Metro Secures Services of More Stage Luminaries and Adds to Plays," *NYDM,* 30 Jun 1915, 24:1. "Ralph Herz with Metro," *MPW,* 3 Jul 1915, 69. "Emmy Wehlen in Screen Debut," *NYDM,* 4 Aug 1915, 23:1. Emmy Wehlen, "Bits About Screening," *Cleveland Leader,* 27 May 1917. Ethel Rosemon, "The Extra Girl Becomes a Newspaper Reporter," *MPC,* Jan 1919.

Wehn, Josephine (actress] (b. 1880–18 Jul 1939 [59?], Bronx NY). BHD, p. 333.

Weichert, Richard [director] (b. Berlin, Germany, 22 May 1880–15 Nov 1961 [81], Frankfurt am Main, Germany). BHD2, p. 278.

Weidman, Charles [actor] (b. 1902–15 Jul 1975 [73?]). BHD, p. 333.

Weigel, Paul [stage/film actor] (b. Halle, Saxony, Germany, 18 Feb 1867–25 May 1951 [84], Los Angeles Co. CA). AMD, p. 360. AS, p. 1138 (d. Germany). BHD1, p. 576. IFN, p. 312. "Cast Complete for Lloyd's FIrst Paramount Picture," *MPW,* 5 Sep 1925, 90. George Katchmer, "Remembering the Great Silents," *CI,* 247 (Jan 1996), 47.

Weight, F. Harmon [director] (b. Salt Lake City UT, 1 Jul 1887–15 Aug 1978 [91], Los Angeles CA). (FBO.) AMD, p. 360. AS, p. 1138. BHD2, p. 279 (Harmon F. Weight). IFN, p. 312. "Weight Directing 'Ragged Edge,'" *MPW,* 17 Feb 1923, 704. "Weight to Start Another," *MPW,* 7 Mar 1925, 76. "Weight Flinishes 'Viennese Lovers,'" *MPW,* 2 Jul 1927, 18. "Weight to Direct 'Midnight Madness,'" *MPW,* 10 Dec 1927, 21.

Weil, Harry [actor] (b. 1877?–23 Jan 1943

[65], Los Angeles CA). AS, p. 1138. BHD, p. 333. IFN, p. 313.

Weil, Jesse [publicist]. No data found. AMD, p. 360. "Weil with Artclass," *MPW,* 1 Nov 1924, 30.

Weil, Richard [publicist/title writer] (b. New York NY, 29 Oct 1893–16 Aug 1971 [77], Los Angeles CA). AMD, p. 360. BHD2, p. 279. FDY, p. 447. "Weil Rejoins Arrow," *MPW,* 14 Mar 1925, 175. "Richard Weil," *MPW,* 26 Mar 1927, 311. "Weil Leaves Rayart," *MPW,* 13 Aug 1927, 444.

Weil-Lorac, Roger ["pionnier du cinéma français"] (b. France, 1897–25 Aug 1983 [86?], France). AS, p. 1138.

Weill, Fernand Lucien Léon [producer] (b. Avesnes-sur-Meuse, France, 10 Mar 1884 [extrait de naissance no. 19]–14 Aug 1960 [76], Neuilly-sur-Marne, France). AS, p. 1138.

Weiman, Rita [scenarist] (b. Philadephia PA–d. 23 Jun 1954, Los Angeles CA; heart attack at the home of actress Mary Nash). m. playwright Maurice Marks, 1924 (d. ca. 1953). "Miss Rita Weiman, Was Playwright; Novelist of Twenties, Author of Articles and TV Stories Dies on Visit to Coast," *NYT,* 25 Jun 1954, 21:5. "RIta Weiman," *Variety,* 195, 30 Jun 1954, 63:1. AMD, p. 360. AS, p. 1138. BHD2, p. 279. "Rita Weiman Returns East," *MPW,* 31 Jul 1920, 566. "Rita Weiman to Write Script for DeMille Film," *MPW,* 9 Apr 1921, 593.

Weinberg, Gus [stage/film actor/playwright/composer] (b. Milwaukee WI, 1866?–11 Aug 1952 [86], Portland ME). "Gus Weinberg, Actor, Also Playwright, 86," *NYT,* 13 Aug 1952, 21:5 ("A silent screen movie actor, playwright and song-writer."). "Gus Weinberg," *Variety,* 20 Aug 1952 ("legit and silent screen actor"). AS, p. 1138. BHD, p. 333. IFN, p. 313. Truitt, p. 346.

Weingarten, Lawrence [publicist/actor/director/producer/President of SAG] (b. Chicago IL, 30 Dec 1898–5 Feb 1975 [76?], Los Angeles CA; leukemia). (Produced Biblical films in1921; Ince; 1st National; MGM, 1927.) "Lawrence Weingarten, 77, Dies; Produced 75 Movies for M-G-M," *NYT,* 9 Feb 1975, 48:1 (d. 6 Feb; Irving Thalberg Award, 1976). "Lawrence Weingarten," *Variety,* 12 Feb 1975, p. 94. AMD, p. 360. AS, p. 1139 (b. 1895). BHD, p. 333; BHD2, p. 279. "Weingarten with Coogan," *MPW,* 25 Aug 1923, 634.

Weir, Harry Graves [assistant director] (b. Berkeley CA, 1881). BHD2, p. 279.

Weir, Helen [actress] (b. Anderson IN, 1898?). (1st film: *A Barnyard Romeo;* Lubin.) AMD, p. 360 (Weer). AS, p. 1139. Photo, *NYDM,* 19 Feb 1916, 22. "Metro Engages Helen Weer," *MPW,* 24 Jul 1920, 441.

Weir, Hugh C. [writer] (b. Vergennes IL, 1885–16 Mar 1934 [49?], New York NY). AMD, p. 360. BHD2, p. 279. "Weir to Picturize Kalem Series," *MPW,* 1 Jan 1916, 66.

Weiser, Grethe [actress] (*née* Mathilde Ella Dorothea Margarethe Nowka, b. Hanover, Germany, 27 Feb 1903–2 Oct 1970 [67], Bad Tolz, Germany; auto accident). m. **Hermann Schwerin** (d. 1970). AS, p. 1139.

Weisfelft, Max J. [director/producer] (b. Milwaukee WI, 16 Oct 1889–8 Oct 1965 [75], Long Beach CA). BHD2, p. 279.

Weisker, Frederick E. [director] (b. Liverpool, England, 1878–15 Apr 1964 [86?], Liverpool, England). AS, p. 1139.

Weiss, Alfred [executive]. No data found. AMD, p. 360. "Weiss, Head of Artclass Pictures, Tells of Plans," *MPW,* 11 Nov 1922, 142.

Weiss, Carl [cinematographer]. No data found. FDY, p. 471.

Weiss, Louis [executive/general manager/producer] (b. 1889?–14 Dec 1963 [74], Beverly Hills CA). "Louis Weiss," *Variety,* 233, 25 Dec 1963, 47:1 (produced the first Tarzan film with Elmo Lincoln). AMD, p. 360. AS, p. 1139. BHD2, p. 279. "Daily Cartoon Have Tremendous Drawing Power, Says Louis Weiss," *MPW,* 5 May 1926, 245.

Weissburg, Edward [actor] (b. 1876–30 Aug 1950 [74?], Los Angeles CA; heart attack). AS, p. 1139.

Weisse, Hanni [actress] (b. Chemnitz, Germany, 16 Oct 1892–13 Dec 1967 [75], Bad Liebenzell/Saxony, Germany). AS, p. 1139. BHD1, p. 577. Vittorio Martinelli, "Kino-Lieblinge," *Griffithiana,* 38/39 (Oct 1990), 39.

Weitzenkorn, Louis [scenarist] (b. Wilkes- Barre PA, 1894–7 Feb 1943 [48?], Wilkes-Barre PA). BHD2, p. 279.

Weixler, Dorritt [actress] (b. 1894?–30 Nov 1918 [24?]; suicide). BHD, p. 333. Vittorio Martinelli, "Kino-Lieblinge," *Griffithiana,* 38/39 (Oct 1990), 40 (d. 1918).

Welch, Eddie [actor/scenarist] (b. 1893–24 Sep 1972 [79?], Los Angeles CA). BHD2, p. 279.

Welch, Eddie [actor/stuntman] (b. Columbus OH, 21 Apr 1894–15 Jan 1963 [68], Miami FL; diabetic coma). AS, p. 1140.

Welch, James [actor] (b. Liverpool, England, 6 Nov 1865–10 Apr 1917 [51], London, England). BHD, p. 333. IFN, p. 313.

Welch, James T. [actor] (b. New York NY, 14 Mar 1869–6 Apr 1949 [80], Los Angeles CA). AS, p. 1140. BHD1, p. 577. IFN, p. 313. Truitt, p. 346. George A. Katchmer, "Forgotten Cowboys and Cowgirls—Part X," *CI,* 182 (Aug 1990), 40–41.

Welch, Joe [actor] (*né* Joseph Wolinski, b. New York NY, 1869?–15 Jul 1918 [49], Groen's Farms CT; sanitarium, "hopeless paretic"). m. (1) Belle Gold—div. 1916. "Joe Welch, Comedian, Dead," *NYT,* 16 Jul 1918, 13:5. "Funeral of Joe Welch," *NYT,* 18 Jul 1918, 9:6 (buried in Washington Cemetery). "Joe Welch," *Variety,* 19 Jul 1918. AS, p. 1140 (b. 1889). BHD, p. 333.

Welch, Lew [actor] (b. 1885–22 Jun 1952 [67], Miami FL). BHD, p. 333. IFN, p. 313.

Welch, Niles [stage/film actor] (b. Hartford CT, 29 Jul 1888–21 Nov 1976 [88], Laguna Niguel CA). m. Dell Boone; Elaine Esher. (Vitagraph; Kalem; Metro; World; Universal.) "Niles Welch, Actor of Broadway and 20's and 30's Motion Pictures," *NYT,* 21 Dec 1976, 36:4. "Niles Welch," *Variety,* 22 Dec 1976. AMD, p. 360. AS, p. 1140. BHD1, p. 577. IFN, p. 313. MH, p. 142. WWS, p. 256. "Niles Welch," *MPW,* 9 Oct 1915, 263. "Metro Actor Injured," *MPW,* 25 Mar 1916, 1995. "Niles Welch to Support Frances Nelson," *MPW,* 30 Sep 1916, 2120. "Niles Welch, Juvenile Leads," *MPN,* 21 Oct 1916, 210. "Niles Welch," *MPW,* 16 Feb 1918, 961. "Niles Welch Asked to Visit Soldiers," *MPW,* 16 Mar 1918, 1496. "Welch Joins Famous Players-Lasky," *MPW,* 10 Aug 1918, 846. "Niles Welch Signs with Famous Players-Lasky," *MPW,* 17 Aug 1918, 999. "Three Stars Form Companies," *MPW,* 9 Aug 1919, 807. Billy Doyle, "Lost Players," *CI,* 162 (Dec 1988), 45.

Welch, Pauline [actress]. No data found. m. **Bud Fisher**. AMD, p. 360. "Paulie Welch with Metro," *MPW,* 30 Mar 1918, 1822. "Pauline Welch in Second Metro Play," *MPW,* 13 Apr 1918, 251.

Welch, Scott [actor/singer] (d. 19 Apr 1931, New York NY). "Scott Welch," *Variety,* 22 Apr 1931, p. 71. BHD, p. 333.

Welchman, Harry [actor/singer] (b. Barnstable, Devonshire, England, 24 Feb 1886–3 Jan 1966 [79], Penzance, England; coronary thrombosis). "Harry Welchman," *Variety,* 12 Jan 1966, p. 72. AS, p. 1140. BHD1, p. 577. IFN, p. 313.

Weldon, Francis (Bunny) [costumer/dance director/director] (b. Los Angeles CA, 14 Jun 1896–28 Oct 1959 [63], Santa Cruz CA). AS, p. 1140. BHD, p. 333; BHD2, p. 279.

Weldon, Jessie [actor] (b. Kleine Valley NY–d. 12 Aug 1925, Los Angeles CA). "Film Dwarf Dies," *Variety,* 30 Sep 1925 (was to have been tried for selling drugs, with two others, to narcotic agents). AS, p. 1140 (d. 29 Sep). BHD1, p. 619.

Weldon, Lillian [actress] (*née* Elizabeth Martin, b. 1869–22 Aug 1941 [72?], Los Angeles CA). AS, p. 1140.

Welford, Dallas (father of Nancy Welford [1904–1991]) [stage/film actor] (b. Liverpool, England, 23 May 1872–28 Sep 1946 [74], Santa Monica CA). m. Olive L. Leyton. (Edison.) AS, p. 1140. BHD, p. 333. IFN, p. 313. "Edison's New Comedian; Dallas Welford, Famous English Player, Now Seen in Edison Pictures," *NYDM,* 7 Apr 1915, 24:4.

Weller, Viola [actress] (b. Defiance OH). WWS, p. 179.

Wellesley, Charles [stage/film actor] (b. London, England, 17 Nov 1873–24 Jul 1946 [72], Amityville, LI NY [Brunswick Home]). m. Ina Rorke. (1st National; Universal.) "Charles Wellesley; Former Stage and Screen Actor Appeared with Olga Nethersole," *NYT,* 25 Jul 1946, 21:3. "Charles Wellesley," *Variety,* 31 Jul 1946. AS, p. 1140. BHD, p. 333 (b. Dublin, Ireland). IFN, p. 313. Truitt, p. 346.

Wellesley, Marie [actress] (d. 24 Sep 1927, Englewood NJ). "Marie Wellesley," *Variety,* 5 Oct 1927, p. 57. BHD, p. 333. IFN, p. 313.

Wellington, Babe [dancer/actor] (b. 1897?–28 Dec 1954 [57], New York NY). "Babe Wellington," *Variety,* 12 Jan 1955 (appeared with John Bunny). AS, p. 1040. BHD1, p. 619. IFN, p. 313. Truitt, p. 347.

Wellman, William Augustus (father of William Wellman, Jr., b. 20 Jan 1937) [actor/director/producer/scenarist] (b. Brookline MA, 29 Feb 1896–9 Dec 1975 [79], Brentwood, Los Angeles CA; leukemia). m. 5 times: **Helene Chadwick** (d. 1940); Marjorie Chapin; Dorothy Coonan; Marjorie Crawford, 22 Dec 1931. *A Short Time for Insanity; An Autobiography* (NY: Hawthorn Books, 1974); unpublished "Growing Old Disgracefully." (Paramount.) Albin Krebs, "William A. Wellman Dies; Directed Movie Classics," *NYT,* 11 Dec 1975, 48:1. "Deemed Hollywood 'Immortal,' Wm. A. Wellman Dies at 79," *Variety,* 17 Dec 1975 (d. Brentwood). AMD, p. 360. AS, p. 1141. BHD, p. 333; BHD2, p. 279. IFN, p. 313. Katz, pp. 1222–23. "Directs 'Dancing Days,'" *MPW,* 7 Nov 1925, 47. "To Direct Betty Bronson," *MPW,* 26 Dec 1925, 796. "William Wellman Gets New Contract," *MPW,* 21 Aug 1926, 467. "Wellman Resting," *MPW,* 11 Jun

1927, 432. "Wellman Returns," *MPW,* 25 Jun 1927, 595. William Wellman, Jr., "William A. Wellman; An Affectionate Portrait by His Son, William Wellman, Jr.," *FIR,* Jul/Aug 1991, pp. 232–37. John Andrew Gallagher, compiler, "Remembering William Wellman; A montage of memories on the occasion of the director's centennial," *FIR,* Jan/Feb 1997, pp. 46–53.

Wells, "Bombadier" Billy [gong striker for Rank Films] (*né* William Wells, b. London, England, 31 Aug 1887–11 Jun 1967 [79], London, England). AS, p. 1141. BHD1, p. 577. IFN, p. 313 (Bombadier Billy Wells).

Wells, Carolyn [scenarist] (d. 26 Mar 1942, New York NY). BHD2, p. 279.

Wells, Carveth [actor/producer] (b. 1886–16 Feb 1957 [70?], Los Angeles CA). BHD2, p. 279.

Wells, Charles B. [actor] (b. 1851?–14 Oct 1924 [73], Bayside, LI NY). "Charles B. Wells," *NYT,* 15 Oct 1924. "Charles B. Wells," *Variety,* 15 Oct 1924. AS, p. 1141. BHD, p. 333. IFN, p. 313.

Wells, Conrad *see* **Fried, Abe**

Wells, Deering [actor] (b. England, 1896–29 Sep 1961 [65?], London, England). AS, p. 1141.

Wells, H[erbert] **G**[eorge] (novelist/scenarist/historian/sociologist] (b. Bromley, Kent, England, 21 Sep 1866–13 Aug 1946 [79], Hanover Terrace, Regents Park, London, England). m. Amy Catherine Robbins (2 sons; d. 1927). "H.G. Wells Dead in London at 79; Forecast Atomic Age in 1914 Novel [in *The World Set Free* he predicted the atomic bomb]," *NYT,* 14 Aug 1946, 1:6, 25:2 ("To a friend who chided him about his inattentiveness in a conversation, the author said: 'Don't interrupt me. Can't you see I'm busy dying?" Wrote *The Time Machine,* 1895.). "H.G. Wells," *Variety,* 14 Aug 1946, p. 42. AS, p. 1141. BHD, p. 333; BHD2, p. 279.

Wells, Louis M. [actor] (b. Cincinnati OH, 5 Feb 1862–1 Jan 1923 [60]). (K&E; Universal.) m. Bessie Gilbert. AS, p. 1141. BHD, p. 333. IFN, p. 313. George M. Katchmer, "Remembering the Great Silents," *CI,* 246 (Dec 1995), 50.

Wells, Mai [actress] (b. San Francisco CA, 1862?–1 Aug 1941 [79], Los Angeles CA). (1st National.) "Mai Wells," *Variety,* 6 Aug 1941 ("in pictures for nearly 20 years"). AS, p. 1141. BHD, p. 333. IFN, p. 313. Truitt, p. 347.

Wells, Marie Edith [stage/film actress] (b. 1894?–2 Jul 1949 [55], Los Angeles CA; suicide with sleeping pills). (Film debut?: *The Builder of Bridges,* 1915.) "Marie Wells," *Variety,* 6 Jul 1949 ("stage and screen actress of the silent days"). AMD, p. 360. AS, p. 1141. BHD1, p. 578. IFN, p. 313. "Marie Edith Wells," *MPW,* 17 Apr 1915, 375. "Marie Edith Wells," *MPW,* 19 Aug 1916, 1257.

Wells, Raymond [actor/scenarist/director] (*né* Frank Wells Martin, b. Anna IL, 14 Oct 1880–9 Aug 1941 [60], Los Angeles Co. CA). (Griffith.) AMD, p. 360. AS, p. 1141. BHD1, p. 578; BHD2, p. 280. FDY, p. 439. IFN, p. 313. "Raymond Wells, Director, Universal," *MPN,* 21 Oct 1916, 227 (b. Dodge KS). "Director Wells Plans Benefit," *MPW,* 30 Mar 1918, 1800. T.S. daPonte, "Raymond Wells on Way to Mesopotamia to 'Shoot' Scenes for Sacred Films," *MPW,* 26 Nov 1921, 401. George Katchmer, "Remembering the Great Silents," *CI,* 249 (Mar 1996), 48.

Wells, Ted (Pawnee Bill, Jr.) [extra/actor/stuntman] (aka John Oscar Wells, *né* John Oscar Wells, b. Sweetwater TX, 11 Jul 1899?–7 Jul 1947 [47], Wickenburg AZ; heart attack). (Universal.) AS, p. 1141 (b. 1902). BHD1, p. 578 (b. Midland TX). Nick C. Nicholls, "Profiles; Ted Wells," *Westerns and Serials* #43 (1997), pp. 26, 28.

Wells, Wellington E. [manager] (b. Binghamton NY, 1866–29 Sep 1954 [88?], Binghamton NY). BHD2, p. 274.

Wells, William K. [actor/writer/scenarist] (b. New York NY, 1884?–17 Apr 1956 [72], New York NY). m. Eleanor Lewin. "William K. Wells, Writer of Stage Revues and 'Munchhausen' Radio Show, Is Dead," *NYT,* 18 Apr 1956, 31:3. "William K. Wells," *Variety,* 18 Apr 1956. AS, p. 1141. BHD, p. 333; BHD2, p. 280.

Welsh, Robert Emmett [publicist/title writer]. No data found. m. Cecilia M. Hickey, 27 Sep 1917. AMD, p. 360. FDY, p. 447. "Welsh Goes to Kalem," *MPW,* 13 Nov 1915, 1287. Epes Winthrop Sargent, "Welsh Writes a Book," *MPW,* 6 May 1916, 979. "Welsh—Hickey," *MPW,* 13 Oct 1917, 210. "Welsh Joins Associated as Advertising-Publicity Head," *MPW,* 10 Oct 1925, 462. "Robert Emmett Welsh with Universal," *MPW,* 29 May 1926, 1. "Robert Emmett Welsh," *MPW,* 26 Mar 1927, 311. "Laemmle Names Welsh Personal Representative," *MPW,* 22 Oct 1927, 481.

Welsh, William J[oseph] [actor] (aka William Welch, b. Philadelphia PA, 9 Feb 1870–16 Jul 1946 [76], Los Angeles CA). (Universal.) (Film debut: *Lady Audley's Secret,* 1912.) AMD, p. 361. AS, p. 1141. IFN, p. 313. "William Welch," *MPW,* 4 Nov 1916, 679. George Katchmer, "Remembering the Great Silents," *CI,* 217 (Jul 1993), 54.

Welsh, William J. [actor] (b. Philadelphia PA, 9 Feb 1870–16 Jul 1946 [76], Los Angeles CA). BHD, p. 334. IFN, p. 313.

Wenck, Eduard Herman Emanuel [actor] (b. Karlsruhe, Germany, 1 Jan 1894–17 May 1954 [60], Berlin, Germany; suicide because of an incurable heart condition). AS, p. 1141.

Wendelken, George T. [Our Gang comedies, as "Freckles": actor] (b. 1916?–3 Jan 1998 [81], Toms River NJ). m. (1 daughter, Ellen M. Dinneen; 2 sons, Gene G. and Donald B.). "George Wendelken, 'Our Gang' Actor, 81," *NYT,* 26 Jan 1998, A16.

Wendhausen, Fritz [director/scenarist] (b. Germany, 1891-Jan 1962 [71?], Germany). AS, p. 1141. BHD2, p. 280 (d. London, England). FDY, p. 439.

Wendt, Ernst Edwardus Amandus [director] (b. Danzig, Germany, 26 Oct 1876–12 Aug 1986 [109], Munich, Germany). AS, p. 1141.

Wenkhaus, Rolf [actor] (b. Germany, 9 Sep 1917–1942 [25?]). BHD, p. 334.

Wenman, Henry [actor] (b. Leeds, England, 7 Sep 1875–6 Nov 1953 [78]). BHD1, p. 578. IFN, p. 314.

Wenstrom, Harold [cameraman]. No data found. AMD, p. 361. FDY, p. 471. "Wenstrom Back with Metro," *MPW,* 28 Jun 1919, 1950.

Wentworth, Professor C. [scenarist] (d. 30 Dec 1913, New York NY). BHD2, p. 280.

Wentworth, Martha [actress] (*née* Verna Martha Wentworth, b. New York NY, 2 Jun 1889–8 Mar 1974 [84], Sherman Oaks CA). AS, p. 1142.

Wentworth, Stephen [actor] (b. England-d. 20 Mar 1935). BHD, p. 334.

Werbiseck, Gisela [actress] (*née* Gisela Werbezirk, b. Bratislava, Slovakia, 8 Apr 1875–15 Apr 1956 [81], Los Angeles CA). AS, p. 1142.

Werckmeister, Hans [director] (b. Berlin, Germany, 1879). AS, p. 1142.

Werker, Alfred L[ouis] [director] (b. Deadwood SD, 2 Dec 1896–28 Jul 1975 [78], Laguna Beach CA). AS, p. 1142 (d. LA CA). BHD2, p. 280. Katz, pp. 1223–24 (began 1917).

Werkmeister, Lotte [actress] (b. Berlin, Germany, 24 May 1886–15 Jul 1970 [84], Bergholz-Rehbrueck, Germany). "Lotte Werkmeister," *Variety,* 12 Aug 1970, p. 55. AS, p. 1142. BHD, p. 334. IFN, p. 314.

Werndorf, Oscar [art director] (b. Austria, 1886–6 Nov 1938 [52?], Wembley, England). BHD2, p. 280.

Werner, Alfred L. [director] (b. 1866?–20 Oct 1926 [60], Berlin, Germany). "Alfred Werner," *Variety,* 27 Oct 1926. AS, p. 1142.

Werner, David C. [casting director] (b. 30 Aug 1890–17 Aug 1941 [50], Los Angeles CA). BHD2, p. 280.

Werner, Elsie [scenarist]. No data found. FDY, p. 439.

Werner, Walter [actor] (*né* Walter Gotthard Werner, b. Gorlitz, Germany, 11 Apr 1883–9 Jan 1956 [72], Berlin, Germany; pneumonia). AS, p. 1142.

Werner-Kahle, Hugo [actor] (b. Aachen, Germany, 5 Aug 1882–1 May 1961 [78], Berlin, Germany). AS, p. 1142. BHD, p. 334. IFN, p. 314.

Wernicke, Otto Karl Robert [actor] (b. Osterode/Harz, Germany, 30 Sep 1893–7 Nov 1965 [72], Munich, Germany). AS, p. 1142. BHD1, p. 579. IFN, p. 314.

Wertz, Clarence P. [actor] (b. Bloomfield NJ, 3 Mar 1891–2 Dec 1935 [44], Los Angeles CA). AS, p. 1142. BHD1, p. 579. IFN, p. 314. Truitt, p. 347.

Wesner, A. Burt [actor] (b. 1866–3 Jan 1920 [53?], Boulder City CO). BHD, p. 334.

Wesner, Ella [stage/film actress: male impersonator] (b. 1841?–11 Nov 1917 [76], New York NY [Home for Incurables]). "Ella Wesner, Aged Actress, Dead," *NYT,* 12 Nov 1917, 13:6 ("Miss Wesner was one of the first women to win recognition as a male impersonator."). "Ella Wesner Lies in Man's Garb," *NYT,* 14 Nov 1917, 15:3 ("It was said that throughout her life Miss Wesner had preferred man's apparel.... Her first and only act, which she played in vaudeville throughout the country, was a male impersonation." Buried in Evergreen Cemetery.). "Ella Wesner," *Variety,* 16 Nov 1917. AS, p. 1142.

Wesselhoeft, Eleanor [actress] (*née* Elinor Wesselhoeft, b. Cambridge MA, 1883–9 Dec 1945 [62], Los Angeles CA). AS, p. 1142.

Wessell, Vivian [actress] (b. 1893-Oct 1965 [72?]). BHD, p. 334.

West, Arthur Pat [vaudeville/stage/film actor] (b. Paducah KY, 1889?–10 Apr 1944 [55], Van Nuys CA). m. Lucille. (Began ca. 1927.) "Arthur Pat West; Actor 30 Years Appeared in Stage Musicals and Films," *NYT,* 11 Apr 1944, 19:3. "Pat West," *Variety,* 12 Apr 1944. AS, p. 1143 (Pat West). BHD1, p. 580 (Pat West). IFN, p. 314.

West, Billie [actress] (b. KY, 5 Aug 1891–7

Jun 1967 [75], Plainfield NJ). m. **Frank Fisher Bennett** (d. 1967). AMD, p. 361. AS, p. 1143. BHD, p. 334. IFN, p. 314. "Robet Gray and 'Billy' West New Leads for American," *MPW,* 24 May 1913, 799. "Notes from the Studios," *MPW,* 14 Jun 1913, 1125 (with American).

West, Billy [actor] (*né* Roy William Weissberg, b. Russia, 22 Sep 1892–21 Jul 1975 [82], Los Angeles CA; heart attack). "Billy West," *Variety,* 30 Jul 1975. AMD, p. 361. AS, p. 1143. BHD1, p. 579. IFN, p. 314. Katz, p. 1225 (began 1916). MSBB, p. 1030. "Billy West Signs with New Company," *MPW,* 17 Feb 1917, 1038. "William B. West," *MPW,* 19 May 1917, 1119. "WIlliam B. West," *MPW,* 2 Jun 1917, 1453. "BIlly West Suits Dismissed," *MPW,* 30 Jun 1917, 2122. "Billy West's Waltzes Ready," *MPW,* 12 Jan 1918, 249. "Billy West to Write More Music," *MPW,* 19 Jan 1918, 361. "These Are the Men Who Have Made 'King-Bee,'" *MPW,* 9 Feb 1918, 837. "West Declines English Offer," *MPW,* 30 Mar 1918, 1838. "Billy West Writes a Scenario," *MPW,* 4 May 1918, 716. "Billy West Wins Suit Against Bull's Eye Company," *MPW,* 19 Jul 1919, 366. "Bull's Eye Denies West Has Won Suit," *MPW,* 2 Aug 1919, 698. "Billy West Has Signed a Contact o Make Two Reel Comics for the Joan Film Sales Company," *MPW,* 11 Sep 1920, 214. "Billy West Forms Company; Rayart to Distribute Product," *MPW,* 18 Jul 1925, 307. "Billy West Resumes," *Variety,* 106, 26 Apr 1932, 3:4 (made a comeback in talkers in *Competition;* next film to be *The Crooner,* both with WB).

West, Buster James [stage/film actor] (b. Philadelphia PA, 31 Mar 1901–18 Mar 1966 [64], Encino CA; brain tumor). m. Lucille Page (widow). "Buster West, 64, Is Dead; Broadway Comic Dancer," *NYT,* 20 Mar 1966, 86:6. "Buster West," *Variety,* 23 Mar 1966. BHD1, p. 579 (d. LA CA). IFN, p. 314. Truitt, p. 347.

West, Charles H. [actor] (b. Pittsburgh PA, 30 Nov 1885–10 Oct 1943 [57], Los Angeles CA). (Biograph, 1908; K&E; Fine Arts; Lasky; Selig.) AMD, p. 361. AS, p. 1143. BHD1, p. 579. IFN, p. 314. "Charles West, Leading Man, Selig," *MPN,* 21 Oct 1916, 220 (b. 1886). "Neilan Engages West," *MPW,* 17 Jan 1920, 433. "West Returns to Screen," *MPW,* 29 Aug 1925, 943.

West, Clare [costume designer]. No data found. (Began 1915.) AMD, p. 361. "Copied from Films," *MPW,* 3 Mar 1923, 33. Alice Tildesley, "A Creator of Personalities; Clare West, designer of screen costumes, reveals how she chooses the style that will fit the person for whom she is designing," *MW,* 24 May 1924, 11, 31. Adele Whitely Fletcher, "Tales Out of School," *MW,* 29 Nov 1924, 8–9, 27.

West, Claudine [scenarist] (b. Nottingham, England, 10 Jan 1890–11 Apr 1943 [53], Beverly Hills CA). AS, p. 1143 (b. London, England, 1883-d. 17 May). BHD2, p. 280.

West, De Jalma [actor] (b. Bowling Green KY). (K&E; Vitagraph; Pathé.)

West, Dorothy [actress]. (Biograph, 1909.) No data found.

West, Edna Rhys [actress] (b. Greenup KY, 1886–7 Feb 1963 [76?], Middletown NY). AS, p. 1143.

West, Ford [actor] (b. Dallas TX, 27 Mar 1873–3 Jan 1936 [62]). AS, p. 1143. BHD1, p. 579. IFN, p. 314.

West, George [actor] (b. 1890?–27 Oct 1963 [73], Glasgow, Scotland). "George West," *Variety,* 6 Nov 1963. AS, p. 1143. BHD, p. 334. IFN, p. 314.

West, Harry (or **Henry**) [actor] (b. 1867?–29 Jan 1936 [68], Norwalk CT). "Harry West," *Variety,* 5 Feb 1936. AS, p. 1143. BHD, p. 334. IFN, p. 314.

West, Henry St. Barbe [actor] (b. London, England, 7 Feb 1880–10 May 1935 [55]). BHD1, p. 579.

West, Isabelle [actress] (b. 1858?–21 Jul 1942 [84], Brentwood CA). AS, p. 1143. BHD, p. 334. IFN, p. 314.

West, Col. J.A. [actor] (b. 1841–10 Jul 1928 [87], Wilmington OH). BHD, p. 334. IFN, p. 314.

West, Josephine [actress]. No data found. AMD, p. 361. "Josephine West," *MPW,* 20 Feb 1915, 1149.

West, Katherine [actress] (aka Lillian Webster and Maxine Norton, b. 1883–26 Sep 1936 [53?], Los Angeles CA). AS, p. 1143.

West, Langdon (son of **William L. West**) [director] (b. Camden NJ, 1886). (Edison.) BHD2, p. 280.

West, Lillian Mildred [actress] (b. New York NY, 8 Feb 1890–23 Apr 1970 [80], Woodland Hills CA). BHD1, p. 579.

West, Madeline [actress]. No data found. m. **George M. Gebhardt** (d. 1919). (Pathé.) AMD, p. 361. "Madeline West," *MPW,* 16 Aug 1913, 732.

West, Madge [stage/film actress] (b. New York NY, 1892?–29 May 1985 [93], Memphis TN; cardiac arrest in her sleep). "Madge West, an Actress, 93; Made Theater Debut in 1897," *NYT,* 7 Jun 1965, D17:6. "Madge West," *Variety,* 5 Jun 1985. AS, p. 1143.

West, Neva [actress] (b. CA, 10 Sep 1883–5 Oct 1965 [82], Glendale CA). AS, p. 1143. BHD, p. 334.

West, Olive [actress] (*née* Althea Olive West, b. San Francisco CA, 18 Aug 1858?–29 May 1943 [85], Los Angeles CA). m. Willard Bowman. AS, p. 1143. BHD, p. 334. IFN, p. 314. *Who's Who in Music and Drama,* p. 321 (b. 1871).

West, Pat *see* **West, Arthur Pat**

West, Paul [Clarendon] [writer] (b. Boston MA, 26 Jan 1871–29 Oct 1918 [47], Paris, France; drowned in the Seine). m. Jane V. Corrigan. "Paul West," *Variety,* 1 Nov 1918 ("it is feared he made way with himself"). AMD, p. 361. AS, p. 1143. BHD2, p. 280. "Frank Woods Framing Up," *MPW,* 13 Dec 1913, 1282 (author of the *Bill* series for Mutual). "Scenario Department Again Expanded," *MPW,* 21 Oct 1916, 412. *Who's Who in Music and Drama,* p. 321.

West, Raymond B., "Boy Director" [director/producer] (b. Chicago IL, 11 Feb 1886–6 Sep 1923 [37], Los Angeles CA; cancer). (Ince.) "Raymond B. West," *Variety,* 20 Sep 1923 ("West lost his mind after a general breakdown a few years ago"). AMD, p. 361. AS, p. 1143. BHD2, p. 280 (d. 11 Sep). IFN, p. 315. Katz, p. 1225. "Raymond B. West," *MPW,* 28 Nov 1914, 1240. "Raymond B. West," *MPW,* 8 Apr 1916, 272. "Raymond B. West," *MPW,* 19 Aug 1916, 1225. "Raymond B. West Dean of Ince Directors," *MPW,* 19 May 1917, 1129 (b. Chicago IL). "Paralta Engages Raymond B. West," *MPW,* 6 Oct 1917, 92.

West, Roland [writer/director/producer] (b. Cleveland OH, 20 Feb 1885–31 Mar 1952 [67], Santa Monica CA; heart attack). m. **Jewel Carmen**, Dec 1918 (d. 1984); Lola Lane (d. 1981). (UA; TC-F.) "Roland West," *NYT,* 1 Apr 1952, 29:3 (age 65; produced *Alibi,* the first talkie for UA). "Roland West," *Variety,* 2 Apr 1952 (age 65). AMD, p. 361. AS, p. 1143. BHD2, p. 280. IFN, p. 315. Katz, pp. 1225–26 (b. 1887). "West Directing Own Play in Films," *MPW,* 1 Sep 1923, 60. "Roland West Productions to Release Through Truart," *MPW,* 19 Jan 1924, 198. "Celebrates 27th Year in Busiess," *MPW,* 2 Jul 1927, 19. Billy Doyle, "Jewel Carmen; Shaded in Scandal," *CI,* 287 (May 1999), C2-C3 (after the death of Thelma Todd, with which West was allegedly connected, Carmen divorced him).

West, Thomas, "Chinese Tommy" [actor] (b. Philadelphia PA, 1859?–28 Jul 1932 [73], Philadelphia PA). AS, p. 1143. BHD, p. 334. (Lubin.) "Thomas West," *Variety,* 2 Aug 1932. BHD, p. 334. IFN, p. 315. Ragan 2, p. 1796. Truitt, p. 347.

West, Tony [actor] (b. Chicago IL, 1866–25 Jun 1923 [56], Los Angeles CA). AS, p. 1143. BHD, p. 334. IFN, p. 315.

West, Will[ie] [actor] (b. England, 22 Sep 1867–5 Feb 1922 [54], London, England). BHD, p. 334. IFN, p. 315. SD, p. 1299.

West, William [actor] (b. ca. 1886–23 Sep 1918 [32?], New York NY; after a fall). AS, p. 1143. BHD, p. 334.

West, William B *see* **West, Billy**

West, William Herman [opera singer for ten years/stage/film actor] (b. Newport RI, 26 Jul 1860–20 Aug 1915 [55], Los Angeles CA). m. Roumelia G. Morris (d. 1891). (Kalem, 1910.) AMD, p. 361. AS, p. 1143 (d. Glendale CA). BHD, p. 334. IFN, p. 315 (d. 20 Aug). "William H. West," *MPW,* 17 Oct 1914, 340. "Wm. H. West Dies; Old Kalem Favorite Passes Away in California—Was Opera Singer," *NYDM,* 8 Sep 1915, 27:2. "Death of William H. West; Veteran Kalem Character Actor Expires Suddenly at His Home in Glendale, Near Los Angeles," *MPW,* 11 Sep 1915, 1839 (d. 30 Aug; "He was a gentleman as well as an actor of the old school—and a splendid type of each."). Billy H. Doyle, "Lost Players," *CI,* 157 (Jul 1988), 24.

West, William L. (father of **Langdon West**) [stage/film actor] (b. Wheeling WV, 1856–9 Dec 1915 [59], New York NY). (Kleine-Edison.) *In The Magic Skin.* AMD, p. 361. AS, p. 1143 (d. 15 Dec 1916). "A Study in Make-Up," *MPW,* 12 Jul 1913, 190. "West, Edison, Still Alive," *MPW,* 0 Oct 1915, 986. "William West, Edison, Dead," *MPW,* 25 Dec 1915, 2351 (age 62). "William West, Edison, Dead," *Motography,* 1 Jan 1916, 23 ("Mr. West was considered one of the best old men actors in the business and was loved both in the studio and on the screen for his gentleness and amiability.")

Westbrook, Georgia [actress] (b. 1886?–6 Dec 1921 [35?], New York NY). "Georgia Westbrook Swor," *Variety,* 9 Dec 1921. AS, p. 1143.

Westbrook, Virginia [actress] (b. 1844–28 Dec 1923 [79?], Eatontown NJ). BHD, p. 334.

Westcott, Netta [actress] (b. London, England, 1893–9 Aug 1953 [60]). AMD, p. 361. BHD1, p. 580. IFN, p. 315. "Netta Westcott to Be in 'Maytime,'" *MPW,* 21 Jul 1923, 243. "Miss Westcott Arrives," *MPW,* 4 Aug 1923, 421.

Westerberg, Fred [cinematographer]. No data found. FDY, p. 471.

Western, T.S. [actor/director] (b. 1884–8 Jun 1931 [47?], Philadelphia PA). AS, p. 1144 (d. Hollywood CA). BHD2, p. 280.

Westerton, Frank H. [actor] (b. London, England, 1871?–25 Aug 1923 [52?], New York NY). m. "Frank H. Westerton," *Variety,* 30 Aug 1923. AS, p. 1144. BHD, p. 334.

Westfall, Ralph R. [writer]. No data found. AMD, p. 361. "Westfall Writes Northwest Story," *MPW,* 2 Mar 1918, 1214.

Westfelt, Ragnar [director] (b. Goteborg, Sweden, 2 Feb 1888). AS, p. 1144.

Westford, Susan (sister of **Lillian Russell**) [actress]. No data found. "Kleine to Make More Comedies," *NYDM,* 20 Nov 1915, 25:3 (Westford "is another well-known photoplayer." She, Millicent Evans, and Eddie Boulden supported George Bickel of Bickel & Watson fame.).

Westley, John [actor] (*né* John Conroy, b. New York NY, 17 Nov 1878–26 Dec 1948 [70], Los Angeles CA). AS, p. 1144.

Westman, Theodore [actor/writer/director] (b. 1903?–22 Nov 1927 [24], New York NY). "Theodore Westman," *Variety,* 30 Nov 1957. AS, p. 1144. BHD, p. 334; BHD2, p. 281.

Westmore, Bud [actor] (*né* Hamilton Adolph Westmore, b. New York NY, 12 Oct 1840–13 Dec 1907 [67], New York NY; heart attack). AS, p. 1144.

Westmore, Dorothy [makeup artist]. No data found. m. **Arthur Stone**, Aug? 1927. (First National.) AMD, p. 361. "Dan Cupid Chalks Up Two Weddings," *MPW,* 3 Sep 1927, 23.

Westmore, Ernest H. (Ernie) (son of **George Westmore**, twin of **Percy Westmore**) [makeup artist] (b. Canterbury, England, 1903?–1 Feb 1967 [63], New York NY). m. (1) Veoda Snyder, 1922–29; **Ethlyne Claire**, 22 Feb 1930, West Hollywood CA—div. 1937 (d. 1996); Betty Harron. "Ernest Westmore, Film Makeup Man," *NYT,* 2 Feb 1967, 35:3.

Westmore, George [makeup artist] (father of **Percy** and **Ernest Westmore**) (b. Isle of Wight, England, 27 Jun 1879–12 Jul 1931 [52], Los Angeles CA); suicide by ingesting bichloride of mercury a week before). m. Ada Savage, 1901; (2) Anita Salazar. (Selig.) "George Westmore," *Variety,* 14 Jul 1931. BHD2, p. 281. Sue Laimans, "George Westmore: Movie Makeup Magic," *CI,* 203 (May 1992), 44.

Westmore, Percival H. (Percy) (son of **George Westmore**, twin of **Ernest H. Westmore**) [make-up artist/hair stylist] (b. Canterbury, England, 1905?–30 Sep 1970 [65], Los Angeles CA). "Perc Westmore," *Variety,* 7 Oct 1970. BHD1, p. 580; BHD2, p. 281. IFN, p. 315. Helen Carlisle, "How the Stars Manage Their Growing Bobbed Hair," *MM,* May 1926, 30–32, 76–77.

Westner, Lillian [actress] (*née* Katherine West, b. 1883–26 Sep 1936 [53?], Los Angeles CA; heart attack). AS, p. 1144.

Weston, Albert [actor] (d. Nov 1920). m. Nellie Lynch. "Albert Weston," *Variety,* 5 Nov 1920.

Weston, Cecil [actress] (*née* Cecil Balshofer, b. South Africa, 3 Sep 1889–7 Aug 1976 [86], Los Angeles CA). AS, p. 1144.

Weston, Charles [actor] (d. 1917). BHD, p. 334.

Weston, Garnet [scenarist] (b. Toronto, Ontario, Canada, 27 Jun 1890-Oct 1980 [90]). AMD, p. 361. BHD2, p. 281. FDY, p. 439. "Garnet Weston, Writer, Joins F.B.O. Staff," *MPW,* 1 Jan 1927, 37.

Weston, George [actor] (d. 7 Apr 1923, New York NY). AS, p. 1144. BHD, p. 334. Truitt, p. 348.

Weston, Joseph J. [actor] (b. New York NY, 22 Feb 1888–1 May 1972 [84], Los Angeles CA). AS, p. 1144 (d. 27 Apr). BHD1, p. 581.

Weston, Maggie [actress] (d. 3 Nov 1926, New York NY). m. James Connors. "Maggie Weston," *Variety,* 10 Nov 1926. AS, p. 1144. BHD, p. 335.

Weston, Mildred [actress]. No data found. (Essanay.)

Weston, Sammy [actor[(b. 1888–1 Feb 1951 [62?], Los Angeles CA). AS, p. 1144.

Weston, Willie [character comedian/dancer] (b. Brooklyn NY, 1883?–11 Nov 1919 [36], Marion NY). "'Willie' Weston, Dancer," *NYT,* 12 Nov 1919, 13:2 (age 35). "Willie Weston," *Variety,* 14 Nov 1919. AS, p. 1144.

Westover, Clyde C. [scenarist] (b. 1874?–6 Aug 1951 [77], Los Angeles CA). "Clyde Westover," *Variety,* 15 Aug 1951. AS, p. 1144. BHD2, p. 281 (b. 1877).

Westover, Winifred [actress] (b. San Francisco CA, 9 Nov 1899–18 Mar 1978 [78], Los Angeles CA). m. **William S. Hart**, 7 Dec 1921—div. 11 Feb 1927 (desertion), Reno NV (d. 1946; William Hart, Jr., b. 6 Sep 1922). (Fine Arts; American.) "Winifred Westover Hart," *NYT,* 22 Mar 1978, II, 25:3. "Winifred Westover," *Variety,* 29 Mar 1978. AMD, p. 362. AS, p. 1144 (d. 19 Mar). BHD1, p. 581. FSS, p. 289. IFN, p. 315. MH, p. 142. MSBB, p. 1042 (b. 1899). "Winifred Westover," *MPW,* 10 Mar 1917, 1571. "Home Robbed While Away," *MPW,* 15 Feb 1919, 882. "Winifred Westover in Fox Film," *MPW,* 29 May 1920, 1186. "Winifred Westover Due to Arrive Here on October 10," *MPW,* 16 Oct 1920, 966. Edward Weitzel, "Winifred Westover Went Over the Water to Join the Skandinavisk Filmcentrals," *MPW,* 13 Nov 1920, 185. "Signed for Lead," *MPW,* 12 Mar 1921, 175. "Winifred Westover Had Day Off to Visit Champion Jack Dempsey," *MPW,* 25 Jun 1921, 838. "Wm. S. Hart Marries Winifred Westover," *MPW,* 17 Dec 1921, 786. "Say Miss Westover's Marriage Can Get Publicity for Showmen," *MPW,* 18 Mar 1922, 264. Dorothy Donnell, "From Hollywood to You," *MPS,* 24 Feb 1925, 8 (at the Hart trial, she "sobbed that her husband had turned her out of his house when she was ill after 'taking her on his knee and telling her their marriage was a mistake.' Hart replied that "she wasn't so ill that she couldn't go shopping with her mother every day." As Hart left the witness box, he stopped and kissed his son, "while soft-hearted women in the audience wept sympathetically." Mrs. Hart sniffed and remarked, "that was the first time he had ever shown any interest in the kid." The judge "decided that the cause in the Hart contract keeping Mrs. Hart from the screen was illegal and she was informed she could go back into pictures, but must not call herself 'Mrs. William S. Hart.' She left the court weeping with joy and saying that she would be under contract in a few days." Hart said "he will appeal and that will keep his ex-wife from the films for at least two more years."). "On the Set and Off," *MW,* V, 16 May 1925, 34 (nervous breakdown). "Winifred Hart Goes to Coast to Start Work," *MPW,* 11 Jun 1927, 422. "Lot Talk," *Screenland,* Aug 1929, 4 (Westover gained 40 lbs. for her role in *Lummox*). George Katchmer, "Remembering the Great Silents," *CI,* 217 (Jul 1993), 55 (b. 1899) *see* **Hart, William S.**

Westrate, Edwin V. [scenarist] (b. Muscatine IA, 5 Jun 1894–26 Nov 1955 [61], Beverly Hills CA). AS, p. 1144. BHD2, p. 281.

Westwood, Martin F. [actor] (b. 1883?–19 Dec 1928 [45], Glendale CA; pneumonia). "Martin F. Westwood," *Variety,* 26 Dec 1928. AS, p. 1144. BHD, p. 335. IFN, p. 315. Truitt, p. 348.

Wetherall, Frances [actress] (b. Greenwich, Kent, England-d. 13 Nov 1923, London, England). BHD, p. 335.

Wetherall, M[amaduke] **A**[rundel] [actor/director/title writer/scenarist] (b. Leeds, England, 1884–25 Feb 1939 [54?], Johannesburg, South Africa). AS, p. 1144. BHD, p. 335; BHD2, p. 281. FDY, pp. 439 (Wetherell), 447. IFN, p. 315 (age 52).

Wetzel, Albert [cinematographer]. No data found. FDY, p. 471.

Weyers, Bruno [executive] (b. Brooklyn NY, 26 Aug 1870–16 Apr 1952 [81], Peapack-Gladstone NJ). BHD2, p. 281.

Weyher, Ruth Ellen [actress] (b. Nowinjasta, Poland, 28 May 1901-Jan 1983 [81]). AS, p. 1145 (b. 1902). BHD, p. 335.

Weymann, Frederic [cinematographer]. No data found. FDY, p. 471.

Whalen, J.P. [cinematographer]. No data found. FDY, p. 471.

Whalen, Michael [actor] (*né* Joseph Shovlin, b. Wilkes-Barre PA, 30 Jun 1902–14 Apr 1974 [71], Woodland Hills CA; bronchial pneumonia). "Michael Whalen," *Variety,* 14 Apr 1974 (age 72). AS, p. 1145. IFN, p. 315.

Wharton, Bessie E *see* **Emerick, Bessie**

Wharton, Leopold D. (brother of **Theodore Wharton**) [actor/scenarist/producer/director] (b. Manchester, England, 1870–1929 [59?]). (Wharton, Inc.; Pathé; Essanay.) AMD, p. 362. AS, p. 1145. BHD2, p. 281. Spehr, p. 174. Hugh Hoffman, "Wharton, Incorporated," *MPW,* 18 Apr 1914, 349. "Wharton Praises New York Police," *MPW,* 11 Jul 1914, 257. "Leopold D. Wharton," *MPW,* 16 Jan 1915, 378. "Pathé's 'Gold Rooster' Producers," *MPW,* 28 Aug 1915, 1485. "Wharton Doing General Producing," *MPW,* 22 Jan 1916, 570. Leopold Wharton, "New Art of the Motion Picture," *MPW,* 21 Jul 1917, 394. Neil G. Caward, "Screen Gossip," *Picture-Play Magazine,* Sep 1917, 108 (branching out into features from serials). "Leopold D. Wharton in Harness," *MPW,* 22 Dec 1917, 1790. "Mrs. Francis Wharton Dies," *MPW,* 9 Aug 1919, 840 (mother, d. 19 Jul 1919 [78], Bronxville NY sanitarium).

Wharton, Theodore (brother of **Leopold Wharton**) [director/producer] (b. Milwaukee WI, 12 Apr 1875–27 Nov 1931 [56], Los Angeles CA). (Wharton, Inc.; Essanay; Pathé.) "Theodore Wharton; Early Motion-Picture Director and Originator of Serials Dies," *NYT,* 29 Nov 1931, II, 8:2. "Theo. Wharton, Creator of Film Serials, Dies," *Variety,* 1 Dec 1931 (had studio in Ithaca NY, 1913). AMD, p. 362. AS, p. 1145 (b. NY NY). BHD2, p. 281. "Theodore Wharton's Big Job," *MPW,* 25 Oct 1913, 368. "Director Wharton Talks About 'Buffalo Bill' Series," *MPW,* 22 Nov 1913, 851. "Theodore Wharton Out of Essanay," *MPW,* 28 Feb 1914, 1097. Hugh Hoffman, "Wharton, Incorporated," *MPW,* 18 Apr 1914, 349. "Theo Wharton in Town," *MPW,* 10 Oct 1914, 171. "Theodore Wharton," *MPW,* 26 Jun 1915, 2103.

"Wharton Doing General Producing," *MPW,* 22 Jan 1916, 570. "Hearst Has No Interest in Whartons," *MPW,* 22 Apr 1916, 653. "WHarton Introduces New Film Trick," *MPW,* 26 Aug 1916, 1421. "Wharton Takes First Vacation in 11 Years," *MPW,* 2 Dec 1916, 1325. "Theodore Wharton Invents Idea," *MPW,* 9 Feb 1918, 836. "Mrs. Francis Wharton Dies," *MPW,* 9 Aug 1919, 840. Gene Fernett, "The Whartons Set Up at Ithaca," *CI,* 100 (Oct 1983), 43–45; Part II, 101 (Nov 1983), 47–51.

Wheat, Lawrence [actor] (b. Wheeling WV, 20 Oct 1876–7 Aug 1963 [86]; Los Angeles CA). AS, p. 1145. BHD1, p. 581. IFN, p. 315 (1876–1963). MH, p. 142.

Wheatcroft, Stanhope Nelson [actor] (b. New York NY, 11 May 1888–13 Feb 1966 [77], Woodland Hills CA; heart attack). AMD, p. 362. AS, p. 1145. BHD1, p. 581. IFN, p. 315. "Wheatcroft Rejoins Fox Forces," *MPW,* 9 Dec 1916, 1498.

Wheaton, Anna [stage/film actress] (b. 1896?–25 Dec 1961 [65], Pasadena CA). m. Walter T. Collins. "Anna Wheaton, 65, ex-Musical Actress," *NYT,* 27 Dec 1961, 27:4 (played Liza at age 8 in *Peter Pan,* with Maude Adams). "Anna Wheaton," *Variety,* 225, 3 Jan 1962, 63:1.

Wheaton, Edna [actress] (b. 1903?). m. Irving Stark, 8 Jun 1921 (age 23). AMD, p. 362. "Edna Wheaton Marries California Manufacturer," *MPW,* 18 Jun 1921, 720 (18 years old).

Wheeler, Bert [stage/film/TV actor] (*né* Albert Jerome Wheeler, b. Paterson NJ, 17 Apr 1895–18 Jan 1968 [72], New York NY; emphysema). m. (1) Betty—div. 1927; (2) Bernice Speer; (3) Sally Haines; (4) Patty Orr. Joe Cohen, "Bert Wheeler, Vaudeville Comic with Rubbery Face, Dead at 72; His Over 50-Year Career in Show Business Spanned Films, the Follies and TV," *NYT,* 19 Jan 1968, 44:2 (daughter died 2 weeks earlier). "Bert Wheeler, 73, Always a Pixie," *Variety,* 24 Jan 1968 (age 73). AS, p. 1145. BHD1, p. 581 (b. 7 Apr). IFN, p. 316. Katz, p. 1227. Truitt, p. 348. Chris Laube, "Wheeler and Woolsey; The Abbott and Costello of the Thirties," *CI,* 95 (May 1983), 8–9, 52. Linda Fitak, "Wheeler and Woolsey: Rediscovered—at Last," *CI,* 215 (May 1993), 36–37; Part II, 217 (Jul 1993), C22–C24; "Hook, Line and Sinker (RKO Pictures, 1930)," 221 (Nov 1993), 38, 40. Linda Fitak, "A Tribute to Bert Wheeler, 'The Perennial Pixie' on His 100th Anniversary," *CI,* 238 (Apr 1995), C12–13 (includes filmography).

Wheeler, Burritt Nash [actor] (b. IL, 25 Dec 1883–18 Jan 1968 [84], New York NY). AS, p. 1145.

Wheeler, DeWitt Clinton [maker of song slides/cameraman] (b. 1853?–21 Nov 1915 [62], New York NY; in an ambulance on the way to Fordham Hospital). m. "Veteran Picture Maker Dies," *NYDM,* 4 Dec 1915, 25:4. BHD2, p. 281 (b. 1862).

Wheeler, Jimmy [actor] (*né* Jimmy Wilson, b. Battersea, London, England, 16 Sep 1910–8 Oct 1973 [63], Brighton, England). "Jimmy Wheeler," *Variety,* 17 Oct 1973. AS, p. 1145 (d. 1970). IFN, p. 316.

Wheeler, Lucien C. "Jack" [film editor/scenarist] (b. Mechanicsville IA, 1877–23 Jul 1950 [73?], Los Angeles CA). AMD, p. 362. BHD2, p. 281. James S. McQuade, "Chicago Letter," *MPW,* 18 Dec 1915, 2180. "Selig-Tribune Auto Service," *MPW,* 22 Apr 1916, 625. "Selig-Tribune Goes After Mexican Stuff," *MPW,* 3 Jun 1916, 1716. "'Jack' Wheeler Off to London," *MPW,* 22 Jun 1918, 1719. "Lucien C. Wheeler Talks of His Duties," *MPW,* 31 Aug 1918, 1242.

Wheeler, Teresa (Cabaret Tess) [actress] (d. 26 Dec 1975, Los Angeles Co. CA). AS, p. 1145. BHD, p. 335.

Wheeler, William [cinematographer]. No data found. FDY, p. 471.

Wheelock, Charles C. [actor] (b. Boston MA, 1875?–25 May 1948 [73], Los Angeles CA). (Selig, 1914.) AS, p. 1145. BHD, p. 335. IFN, p. 316.

Whelan, Albert [actor] (b. Melbourne, Australia, 5 May 1875–19 Feb 1961 [84], London, England). AS, p. 1145. BHD1, p. 581.

Whelan, Hazel [actress] (d. 22 Jun 1937, East Orange NJ). BHD, p. 335.

Whelan, Leo M. [actor] (b. Bridgeport CT, 1876?–15 Oct 1952 [76?], Arlington NJ). AS, p. 1145. BHD, p. 335. Truitt, p. 348.

Whelan, Tim [actor/scenarist/director/producer] (b. Cannelton IN, 2 Nov 1893–12 Aug 1957 [63], Beverly Hills CA). m. Miriam. (Lloyd; MGM.) "Tim Whelan, Wrote and Directed Films," *NYT,* 13 Aug 1957, 27:2. AS, p. 1146. BHD, p. 335; BHD2, p. 282. FDY, p. 439. IFN, p. 316. Truitt, p. 348.

Whelar, Langois Mardi [actor] (b. France, 1898–17 Oct 1918 [20], France). AS, p. 1146. BHD, p. 335. IFN, p. 316.

Whiffen, Mrs. Thomas [stage/film actress] (*née* Blanche Galton, b. London, England, 12 Mar 1845–25 Nov 1936 [91], near Montvale VA). m. Thomas Whiffin, 1868. (Film debut: *Hearts and Flowers,* 1914.) "Mrs. Whiffen Dies in Virginia at 91; 'Grand Old Lady of American Stage' Played 400 Parts in 63 Years in Theatre; Toured in New Play at 83; Created Role of Buttercup Here—Appeared in New York Benefit in 1930," *NYT,* 27 Nov 1936, 21:1 (spelling of last name altered). "Mrs. Thomas Whiffen," *Variety,* 2 Dec 1936. AMD, p. 362. AS, p. 1146. BHD, p. 335. IFN, p. 316. Truitt, p. 348. "Mrs. THomas Whiffen," *MPW,* 14 Nov 1914, 934.

Whipper, Leigh [stage/film actor] (b. Charleston SC, 29 Oct 1876–26 Jul 1975 [98], New York NY [Death Certificate Index No. 12845]). m. Lillian Miles, 1904 (d. 1946). "Leigh Whipper," *Variety,* 30 Jul 1975 ("He was the first black member of Actors Equity"). AS, p. 1146. BHD1, p. 581. IFN, p. 316. Luther Hathcock, "Leigh Whipper: A Pioneer Who Crossed the Color Line," *CI,* 256 (Oct 1996), 30–31 (extra in Ft. Lee NJ; 1st black member of Actors Equity).

Whipple, Clara [actress/scenarist/direct descendant of a signer of the Declaration of Independence] (b. Pittsburgh PA?). m. **James L. Young, Jr.**, 10 Apr 1919, Riverside CA–separated 16 Jul 1921 (d. 1948). (Equitable.) AMD, p. 362. "Clara Whipple," *MPW,* 4 Sep 1915, 1657. "Picture Actresses Want Club," *MPW,* 18 Sep 1915, 2003. "How Clara Whipple Was 'Picked,'" *MPW,* 23 Oct 1915, 591. "Studio Gossip," *NYDM,* 20 Nov 1915, 34:4 (dieting by walking 15 miles each day). "In the Picture Studios," *NYDM,* 18 Dec 1915, 34:3 (returned "from a visit at her home in Pittsburg...her new film, *The Fourth Estate,* with Frank Sheridan, postponed until the spring.). "Clara Whipple in Ingenue Role," *MPW,* 22 Jan 1916, 612. "Clara Whipple in 'The Reapers,'" *MPW,* 19 Feb 1916, 1135. "James Young to Wed," *MPW,* 12 Apr 1919, 218. "Young—Whipple," *MPW,* 26 Apr 1919, 519. "Sued for Divorce," *MPW,* 20 Aug 1921, 793 (Whipple sued Young).

Whipple, U.K. [cameraman]. No data found. AMD, p. 362. "International News Reel Gets Complete Pictures of Rum War," *MPW,* 9 May 1925, 222.

Whistler, Edna [actress] (b. 1886–11 Jul 1934 [48], New York NY). "Edna Whistler," *Variety,* 17 Jul 1934. AMD, p. 362. AS, p. 1146. BHD, p. 335. IFN, p. 316. "Edna Whistler," *MPW,* 14 Apr 1917, 259. "Edna Whistler with Talmadge Co.," *MPW,* 21 Apr 1917, 409.

Whistler, Margaret [actress/costume designer at Columbia] (b. Louisville KY, 1886?–23 Aug 1939 [53?], Los Angeles CA). "Margaret Whistler," *Variety,* 30 Aug 1939. AS, p. 1146 (b. 1892). BHD, p. 335; BHD2, p. 282 (b. 1888). IFN, p. 316 (age 47).

Whitaker, Charles E. [scenarist/director] (b. Holyoke MA, 1876?–15 Oct 1921 [45], aboard ship). "Charles E. Whitaker Dies," *Variety,* 21 Oct 1921. "Obituary," *MPW,* 22 Oct 1921, 920 (b. SF CA; died on steamship *Admiral Dewey,* en route from SF to LA CA). AMD, p. 363. AS, p. 1146. BHD2, p. 282 (d. NY NY).

Whitaker, Charles "Slim" [actor] (*né* Charles Orbie Whitaker, b. Kansas City MO, 29 Jul 1893–27 Jun 1960 [66], Los Angeles CA; heart attack). AS, p. 1146. BHD, p. 335. IFN, p. 316.

Whitaker, Raymond [actor]. No data found. AMD, p. 363. "Raymond Whitaker Joins Universal," *MPW,* 5 Aug 1916, 925.

Whitbeck, Frank L. [actor/director] (b. Rochester NY, 1882–23 Dec 1963 [81?], Los Angeles CA). BHD2, p. 282.

Whitby, Arthur [actor] (b. Ottery St. Mary, England, 1869–29 Nov 1922 [53?], London, England). "Arthur Whitby," *Variety,* 8 Dec 1922, p. 2. BHD, p. 335.

Whitcomb, Barry [actor] (b. Australia, 1872?–25 Oct 1928 [56], New York NY). "Barry Whitcomb," *Variety,* 31 Oct 1928. AS, p. 1146. BHD, p. 335. IFN, p. 316.

Whitcomb, Daniel Frederick [scenarist] (b. Louisville KY, 1880–16 May 1944 [64?], Los Angeles CA). AMD, p. 363. BHD2, p. 282. "Whitcomb Again with Universal," *MPW,* 7 Oct 1916, 85. "Whitcomb Rejoins American's Forces," *MPW,* 26 Apr 1919, 523.

Whitcomb, Frank W. [actor] (b. 1873?–15 Feb 1933 [60], near Atlantic IA). "Frank W. Whitcomb," *Variety,* 7 Mar 1933. AS, p. 1146.

White, Alice [actress] (*née* Alva White, b. Paterson NJ, 28 Aug 1904–19 Feb 1983 [78], Los Angeles CA; apoplexy). m. **Sy Bartlett** (d. 1978); (2) Jack Roberts. "Alice White," *Variety,* 23 Feb 1983. AMD, p. 363. AS, p. 1146. BHD1, p. 582. FSS, p. 289. HCH, p. 57. Katz, p. 1228. "Alice White Has Meteoric Rise in Film," *MPW,* 7 Apr 1917, 547. "Alice White Signed," *MPW,* 2 Oct 1926, 281. Grant Harper, "Why, Alice! How Could You?; The White Girl Goes In for It—And Therein Lies a Story," *MPC,* May 1927, 54–55, 74, 83. Dorothy Manners, "Red-Headed Inside; So Alice White—Brunette by Birth and Blonde for Business—Says She Is," *MPC,* Aug 1929, 27, 81 ("I don't believe I would have ever gotten where I am if I had stayed a brunette."). Dorothy Manners, "Lessons in Love, VIII; Girls Should Neck, Says Alice White. But for Pleasure, Not Profit," *MPC,* Mar 1930, 38–39, 93.

White, Archibald [actor] (b. 1887–28 Sep 1924 [37?], Santa Rosa CA). BHD, p. 335.

White, Arthur [art director] (b. 1881–27 Sep 1924 [43?]). BHD2, p. 282.

White, Arthur [actor] (b. 1882-Jul 1957 [75?], Blackpool, England). BHD, p. 335.

White, Ben [cinematographer] (b. Hungary, 17 Feb 1903–7 Nov 1966 [63], Los Angeles CA). (DeMille; Jack White Comedies.) "Ben White," *Variety,* 16 Nov 1966 ("member of the White family of silent pix fame"). AS, p. 1146. BHD2, p. 282. FDY, p. 471.

White, Billy [actor] (*né* William A. Rattenberry, b. Sacramento CA, 26 Apr 1856–21 Apr 1933 [76], Los Angeles CA, heart attack). AS, p. 1146. BHD, p. 335. IFN, p. 316. Truitt, p. 348.

White, C.D. [production manager] (b. 16 Dec 1898–24 Nov 1935 [36], Los Angeles CA). BHD2, p. 282.

White, Carolina [actress/opera singer] (b. Boston MA, 23 May 1886–5 Oct 1961 [75], Rome, Italy). AMD, p. 363. AS, p. 1146. BHD, p. 335. IFN, p. 316. "Carolina White Plys Leads for Caruso," *MPW,* 3 Aug 1918, 685.

White, Chrissie [stage/film actress: The First British Film Star] (*née* Ada Constance White, b. Chiswick, England, 23 May 1895–18 Aug 1989 [93], London, England). m. actor/director **Henry Edwards** (d. 1952; 1 daughter, Henryetta). (Film debut: *For the Little Lady's Sake,* 1908; final film: *General John Regan,* 1933; Cecil M. Hepworth Studio.) Denis Gifford, "Chrissie White," *The Independent,* 22 Aug 1989, p. 24. "Chrissie White," *Variety,* 30 Aug 1989 (sge 94). AS, p. 1146 (b. 1896). BHD1, p. 582 (b. London; d. Chobham, England). "Ask the 'Picture Show,'" *Picture Show,* 5 Nov 1921, 22 (b. 1894).

White, Clayton [actor]. No data found. AMD, p. 363. "Clayton White Succumbs to Movies," *MPW,* 10 Apr 1920, 286.

White, Edward L. [cameraman]. No data found. AMD, p. 363. "Edward L. White Answers Call," *MPW,* 20 Jul 1918, 378.

White, Frances [actress] (b. Seattle WA, 1 Jan 1896–24 Feb 1969 [72], Los Angeles CA). m. Frank Fay; Clinton Donnelly. (Film debut: *The Warning,* Pathé, 1914.) "Frances White," *Variety,* 5 Mar 1969. AMD, p. 363. AS, p. 1146 (b. MO). BHD1, p. 582. IFN, p. 316. Truitt, p. 349. "Frances White Not Frances White," *MPW,* 20 Sep 1919, 1820 (*i.e.,* not the dancing partner of William Rock with the same name).

White, George [actor/director/producer] (*né* George Weitz, b. New York NY, 12 Mar 1890–11 Oct 1968 [78?], Los Angeles CA; leukemia). Bachelor. "George White, Showman, Dies; Produced Girl-Filled 'Scandals'; Staged Hit Revues in 1920's and Produced 3 Films of Show—Started as Dancer," *NYT,* 12 Oct 1968, 37:1. Joe Cohen, "George White Dies at 78, Big Supporter of Broadway Revues & Racetracks," *Variety,* 16 Oct 1968. AS, p. 1146. BHD1, p. 582; BHD2, p. 282 (b. Toronto, Ontario, Canada). Truitt, p. 349 (b. Toronto).

White, Glennwood [stage/film actor]. No data found. (Universal; Pathé; Biograph.) AMD, p. 363. "Dinner to Glenwood White," *MPW,* 29 Mar 1913, 1318. "Glen White with Kleine," *NYDM,* 28 Jul 1915, 24:1. "Glenwood White with Klein," *MPW,* 7 Aug 1915, 977.

White, Gordon S. [publicist] (b. St. Louis MO, 1893–15 Feb 1969 [75?], Providence RI). AMD, p. 363. BHD2, p. 282. "Gordon S. White," *MPW,* 26 Mar 1927, 311.

White, Grace Miller [writer]. No data found. AMD, p. 363. "Grame Miller White Likes Film Version of Her Tale," *MPW,* 14 Feb 1920, 1083.

White, Hugh [actor] (b. 1895–23 Jun 1938 [43?], Los Angeles CA; auto accident). AS, p. 1146.

White, J. Fisher [actor] (b . Clifton, Bristol, England, 1 May 1865–14 Jan 1945 [79], London, England). AS, p. 1146. BHD1, p. 582. IFN, p. 316.

White, J. Irving [actor] (b. 1865?–17 Apr 1944 [79], Los Angeles CA). AS, p. 1146. BHD1, p. 582. IFN, p. 316.

White, Jack [actor] (b. New York NY, 1893–13 Jul 1942 [49?], New York NY). AS, p. 1146.

White, Jack (brother of **Jules White**) [director] (*né* Jack Weiss, aka Preston Black, b. Budapest, Hungary, 2 Mar 1899–10 Apr 1984 [85], No. Hollywood CA). m. **Pauline Starke**, 1927, San Francisco CA (d. 1977); Toni, 1955. David N. Bruskin interviewer, *The White Brothers: Jack, Jules, & Sam White* (Metuchen NJ: The Directors Guild of America & Scarecrow Press, Inc., 1990). "Jack White," *Variety,* 18 Apr 1984. AMD, p. 363. AS, p. 1146. BHD, p. 336 (b. 1897); BHD2, p. 282. O&W, pp. 243–47 (b. Austria). "Educational Makes Big Comedy Contract; White, Hamilton and Adams Are Signed," *MPW,* 2 Apr 1921, 474. "Jack White Is Re-Engaged by Educational for Three Years," *MPW,* 26 May 1923, 338. "Busy Jack White Plans Great Year," *MPW,* 1 Sep 1923, 63. "Jack White in New York," *MPW,* 31 Jan 1925, 487. "Jack White Has Slogan," *MPW,* 12 Sep 1925, 190. "Starke—WHite Wed; Mary Astor Next," *MPW,* 10 Sep 1927, 89.

White, James H. [cameraman]. No data found. AMD, p. 363. Charles Edward Hastings, "A Cameraman Runs Into a War," *MPW,* 29 Jan 1927, 327.

White, Jules J. (brother of **Jack White**) [actor/director/producer] (*né* Jules J. Weiss, b. Budapest, Hungary, 17 Sep 1900–30 Apr 1985 [84], Van Nuys CA; Alzheimer's disease). m. (1) Margaret, 1922. "Jules J. White," *Variety,* 8 May 1985. AMD, p. 363. AS, p. 1147. BHD, p. 336; BHD2, p. 282. O&W, pp. 246–47. "White to Direct," *MPW,* 10 Jul 1926, 117.

White, Lasses [actor] (*né* Lee Roy White, b. Wills Point TX, 28 Aug 1888–16 Dec 1949 [61], Los Angeles CA). AS, p. 1147.

White, Lawrence [scenarist] (b. 1893–28 Apr 1928 [35?], Los Angeles CA). BHD2, p. 282.

White, Leo [actor] (*né* Leonard White, b. Graudenz, Germany, 10 Nov 1882–20 Sep 1948 [65], Glendale CA). (Essanay; "Swedie" comedies, 1914; Chaplin; FP-L; WB. In an estimated 2,000 films.) "Leo White, in Films for Many Years, 68," *NYT,* 22 Sep 1948, 32:3 (b. Manchester, England; age 68). "Leo White," *Variety,* 29 Sep 1948 (b. Manchester, England; age 68). AMD, p. 363. AS, p. 1147 (b. Manchester, England). BHD1, p. 582 (b. Grudziadz, Poland; d. LA CA). IFN, p. 316. Truitt, p. 349 (b. 1880). "Leo White," *MPW,* 19 May 1917, 1119. "Leo White Meets with Accident," *MPW,* 1 Mar 1919, 1239. Hal K. Wells, "Custard Pies to Chariots; Ever Since He Played the French Count in the Old Chaplin Comedies, Leo White Has Been Trying to Break Away from His Topper. Now He Has a Character Rôle in 'Ben-Hur,'" *MPC,* Mar 1926, 49, 76. George Katchmer, "Remembering the Great Silents," *CI,* 234 (Dec 1994), 41 (b. Manchester, England).

White, Madge [actress] (b. England, 28 Dec 1892–1978 [85], Isle of Wight). BHD, p. 336. Data contributed by Mrs. Janice Healy, Great Britain.

White, Marjorie [vaudevillian/actress] (b. Winnipeg, Canada, 22 Jul 1908–21 Aug 1935 [27], Los Angeles CA; auto accident). m. Eddie Tierney. "Marjorie White," *Variety,* 28 Aug 1935. AS, p. 1147. BHD1, p. 582. IFN, p. 316.

White, May [actress] (b. 1899–18 Oct 1979 [80?], Sarasota FL). BHD1, p. 619.

White, Merrill G. [film editor/director/producer/scenarist] (b. Valona CA, 13 Dec 1901–21 Mar 1959 [57], Los Angeles CA). (Sennett, 1924.) "Merrill G. White," *NYT,* 25 Mar 1959, 35:1. "Merrill G. White," *Variety,* 1 Apr 1959. BHD2, p. 282.

White, Myrle Wagner [opera singer/actress]. No data found. AMD, p. 363. "Mme. Myrle Wagner WHite in 'What Love Forgives,'" *MPW,* 5 Oct 1918, 66.

White, Olive C[eleste] **M**[oore] [actress] (b. Indianapolis IN, 1880?–19 Apr 1960 [80], Los Angeles CA). "Olive C.M. White," *Variety,* 27 Apr 1960. AS, p. 1147.

White, Pearl Fay [stage/film actress] (b. Greenridge IL, 4 Mar 1889–4 Aug 1938 [49], Neuilly-sur-Seine, Paris, France; cirrhosis of the liver [extrait de décès no. 575/1938]). m. (1) **Victor C. Sutherland**, 1907–14 (d. 1968); (2) **Wallace McCutcheon**, 1919–21 (d. 1928). *Just Me* (New York: George H. Doran Co., 1919). Manuel Weltman and Raymond Lee, *Pearl White: The Peerless Fearless Girl* (South Brunswick NJ: A.S. Barnes, 1969). (Powers, 1910; Pathé; last film, *Terror,* 1924.) "Pearl White Dead; ex-Star of Movies; Famous Actress in 'Perils of Pauline' and Other Silent Film Thrillers Was 49; Executed Daring Stunts; Saved Fortune and Retired to Paris in 1923—Spurned Offer for 'Comeback' Last Year," *NYT,* 5 Aug 1938, 17:1 (d. 5 Aug); "Father Says She Was 41" (b. Green Ridge MO, 1897). "Simple Funeral for Pearl White; Only Dozen Close Friends Are Present at Screen Star's Services in Paris; She Had Asked Privacy; Aged Priest to Whom Actress Once Gave Church and a Burial Plot, Officiates," *NYT,* 7 Aug 1938, 32:7. "Pioneer Cliffhanger, Pearl White, Dies in Paris, at Age of 49," *Variety,* 10 Aug 1938 (b. Green Ridge MO, 1897). AMD, p. 363. AS, p. 1147 (b. Greenridge MO, 1892). BHD, p. 336. IFN, p. 316. Katz, pp. 1228–29. MH, p. 142. MSBB, p. 1044 (b. MO). Spehr, p. 174. Truitt, p. 349. Vinson, pp. 648–49. "Picture Personalities," *MPW,* 3 Dec 1910, 1281. "Lives of the Players; Pearl White," *MPS,* I, 24 Jan 1913, 31. "Pearl White Visits Meriden," *MPW,* 19 Apr 1913, 269. "Pearl White to Tour Europe," *MPW,* 26 Jul 1913, 433. "Pearl White Injured; with Francis Carlyle Falls Flight of Stairs in Filming 'Pauline' Scene," *NYDM,* 6 May 1914, 28:4 (dislocated hip and facial lacerations. Carlyle carried White up a flight of stairs, wavered, lost his balance, and fell, with the camera still cranking). "No Pathe Stock; All But Three [White, Paul Panzer and CRane Wilbur] Players Let Out—Will Engage Actors as Pictures Are Put On," *NYDM,* 22 Jul 1914, 22:1 (Jersey City NJ company. Eclair had recently dropped its Eastern production). "Pearl White Thrown from Cab," *MPW,* 8 Aug 1914, 840. On cover of *NYDM,* 30 Dec 1914. "Pearl White," *MPW,* 23 Jan 1915, 499. "Pearl White Signs Again," *NYDM,* 6 Nov 1915, 33:1 (with Pathé for another year). Hector Ames, "The Champion Heroine of Movie Perils, Exploits, Plots and Conspiracies; Pearl White, the Girl with Ninety-Nine Lives, Has Been the Victim in 'The Perils of Pauline,' 'The Exploits of Elaine,' 'The Clutching Hand,' and 'The Iron Claw,' and Still Lives," *MPC,* Apr 1916, 50–52. "Pearl White in Press Stunt," *MPW,* 6 May 1916, 948. "J.A. Berst Rewards Pearl White," *MPW,* 2 Sep 1916, 1553. "Miss White To Have New Serial," *MPW,* 11 Nov 1916, 875. "Sarah Bernhardt Honors Pearl White," *MPW,* 10 Feb 1917, 864. Pearl White, "Thrills in Serial Making," *MPW,* 21 Jul 1917, 423–24. "Pearl White in Christy Army Poster," *MPW,* 21 Jul 1917, 462. Edward Weitzel, "Thrilling Rescue from Real Life," *MPW,* 12 Oct 1918, 245–46. "Pearl White Climbs Ladder for Lambs in War Drive," *MPW,* 30 Nov 1918, 930. "Pearl White To Push Coal Mining," *MPW,* 7 Dec 1918, 1062. Frederick James Smith, "A Pearl in the Rough," *MPC,* Jan 1919, 16–17, 72. "Pearl White at Actors Fund Benefit," *MPW,* 12 Apr 1919, 226. "Pearl White Wins Popularity Contest," *MPW,* 3 May 1919, 679. "Dedicates March to Pearl White," *MPW,* 10 May 1919, 822 (*Pretty Girls of the U.S.A.*). "Pearl White Wrutes a Book," *MPW,* 24 May 1919, 1164 (*My Struggle for Fame,* NY: Geo. H. Doran Co.). "Chambers' 'In Secret' Is Last Pearl White Serial," *MPW,* 9 Aug 1919, 849. "Pearl White WIthdraws as Candidate for Assembly," *MPW,* 30 Aug 1919, 1264. "Pearl White Sails for Europe; to Remain Abroad Six Weeks," *MPW,* 10 Apr 1920, 278. "Northern Children's Society Gives Pearl White Nugget," *MPW,* 10 Apr 1920, 290. "Pearl White Returning from France," *MPW,* 22 May 1920, 1053. "August to See Pearl White Debut as William Fox Star," *MPW,* 7 Aug 1920, 757. "Pearl White Wins British Film Popularity Contest," *MPW,* 9 Oct 1920, 810. "Pearl White Speeds in Aeroplane to Catch Vessel Leaving Bermuda and Eat Christmas Dinner at Home," *MPW,* 8 Jan 1921, 176. "Pearl White Gives Away 12,000 Toys," *MPW,* 2 Apr 1921, 505. "Pearl White, Serial Star, Signs a New Agreement with Pathé," *MPW,* 25 Feb 1922, 818. "Pearl White Soon to Be Again in Pathé Serial," *MPW,* 8 Apr 1922, 612. "Pearl White to Star in Film Made in France," *MPW,* 17 Nov 1923, 327. T. Howard Kelly, "Is Pearl White Deserting Films for Unknown Fiance?," *MW,* 8 Mar 1924, 5. "Pearl White Sued for Damages," *MW,* 29 Mar 1924, 32. Alma Talley, "The Pearl Her Director [Edward Jose] Knows," *MW,* 9 Aug 1924, 10–11, 26. Margaret Norris, "The Pearl White of 1926," *MPC,* Feb 1926, 57, 89 (in a London revue; made three pictures in France). Rene de la Seine, "Latest Gossip from Paris," *Paris and Hollywood,* Oct 1926, 44 (she went to France after a three months' tour of Egypt and Syria). Tom Dino, "The Heroine of the Cliffs," *8mm Collector,* 14 (Spring, 1966), 13. Eldon K. Everett, "A Postscript to Pearl White," *CFC,* 55 (Summer, 1977), 48–49, 56. George Katchmer, "Remembering the Great Silents," *CI,* 247 (Jan 1996), 44. Eve Golden, "Little White Lies: The Elusive Life of Pearl White," *CI,* 265 (Jul 1997), 26–30 (b. Greenridge MO; includes filmography).

White, Philip H. [film editor]. AMD, p. 364. "White to Edit Stone Productions," *MPW,* XL, 5 Apr 1919, 83. "Stage and Film News; Goes East on Contracts," *LA Times,* 25 Jan 1920, III, 13 (vice-president and general manager of Alkire Productions Co.).

White, Randall M. [publicist]. No data found. AMD, p. 364. "White Heads Selznick's Publicity and Advertising," *MPW,* 23 Oct 1920, 1122. "Where Randy Holds Forth with His Long Briar Cigarette Holder," *MPW,* 24 Apr 1926, 592.

White, Raymond [actor] (b. 1901–31 Jan 1934 [32?], Los Angeles CA). AS, p. 1147. BHD, p. 336. IFN, p. 316.

White, Robert L. [actor] (b. 1904?–26 Jul 1931 [27], near Stamford CT; drowned). "Robert L. White," *Variety,* 4 Aug 1931. AS, p. 1147.

White, Ruth Catherine [stage/film/TV actress] (b. Perth Amboy NJ, 24 Apr 1914–3 Dec 1969 [55], Perth Amboy NJ). Unmarried. "Ruth White, 55, of Stage and TV; Actress Who Won Emmy in 'Little Moon of Alban' Dies," *NYT,* 4 Dec 1969, 53:3. "Rites Today for Ruth White," *NYT,* 18 Dec 1969, 65:4. AS, p. 1147. BHD1, p. 582. IFN, p. 116.

White, Sam [stage/film/TV actor] (b. Providence RI, 28 May 1894–3 Mar 1960 [65], Beverly Hills CA). m. Eva Puck; Beatrice Curtis. "Sammy White, 65, Dies; Former Musical Comedy Star Acted in Films and on TV," *NYT,* 7 Mar 1960, 29:2 ("Clayton and White," blackface vaudevillists, ca. 1918–21). "Sammy White," *Variety,* 9 Mar 1960. AS, p. 1147. IFN, p. 316.

White, Tom [assistant director/executive] (b. Deal Island MD, 4 Jul 1892–2 Mar 1969 [76], England). AS, p. 1147. BHD2, p. 282.

White, William Allen [writer]. No data found. AMD, p. 364. "William Allen White Joins Film Colony," *MPW,* 27 Dec 1919, 1147.

White, William "Bill" [actor]. No data found. George Katchmer, "Remembering the Great Silents," *CI,* 249 (Mar 1996), 48.

White, William H. [stage/film/TV actor] (b. Weymouth MA, 1870?–7 Sep 1939 [69], New York NY). m. Ethel. "William H. White; Had Roles in Many Operettas and Musical Comedies," *NYT,* 9 Sep 1939, 17:6. "William H. White," *Variety,* 13 Sep 1939. AS, p. 1147.

Whiteford, John P. "Blackie" [actor] (b. New York NY, 27 Apr 1889–21 Mar 1962 [72], Los Angeles CA). AS, p. 1147.

Whitehead, John P. [actor] (b. 27 Apr 1873–21 Mar 1962 [88], Los Angeles CA). "John Whitehead," *NYT,* 24 Mar 1962, 25:2 (age 72). "John Whitehead," *Variety,* 4 Apr 1962 (age 89) (extra in *The Great Train Robbery;* "actor was one of oldest active thesps in the industry."). AS, p. 1147 (b. 1872). BHD1, p. 619 (b. 1889). IFN, p. 316 (b. 1889). Truitt, p. 349.

Whitelaw, Barrett [bit and extra actor] (b. Cape Girardeau MO, 25 May 1890–2 Oct 1947 [57], Los Angeles CA; cerebral hemorrhage). "Barrett Whitelaw," *Variety,* 8 Oct 1947 (age ca. 50). AS, p. 1147. BHD1, p. 583. IFN, p. 317. Robert Donaldson, "Famous Extras," *MPC,* Feb 1927, 32 [photo]-33, 68, 80.

Whitely, Tom [actor]. No data found. AMD, p. 364. "Tom Whitely Quits the Stage to Do Educational Comedies," *MPW,* 12 Nov 1927, 16.

Whiteman, Paul [orchestra leader/actor] (b. Denver CO, 28 Mar 1890–29 Dec 1967 [77], Doylestown PA; heart attack). m. (1) Nellie Stack, 1908; (2) (Miss) Jimmy Smith–div. 1922; (3) Mildred Vanderhoff [aka Wanda Hoff], 1922–31; (4) **Margaret Livingston**, 1931 (d. 1989). "Paul Whiteman, 'the Jazz King' of the Jazz Age, Is Dead at 77"; Alden Whitman, "Made Jazz Respectable," *NYT,* 30 Dec 1967, 1:5, 24:1. Abel Green, "Paul Whiteman, Misnomered 'King of Jazz,' Gave Dansapation Unique Status with 'Symphonic Syncopation,'" *Variety,* 10 Jan 1968. AS, p. 1147. BHD1, p. 583. IFN, p. 317. Truitt, p. 349. Alice Dyer, "Band Leader Marries Movie Star; Paul Whiteman Weds Margaret Livingston after Long-Distance Courtship Over 'Phone and Disproves Old Adage that Fat Men Are Not Great Lovers," *Movie Classic,* Nov 1931, 35.

Whiteside, Walker [stage/film actor] (b. Logansport IN, 16 Mar 1869–17 Aug 1942 [73], Hastings-on-Hudson NY). m. Leslie Wolstan McCord (widow), 1894? (Film debut: *The Melting Pot,* Cort Film Corp., 1915.) "Walker Whiteside, an Actor 47 Years; Starred Here in 'The Melting Pot,' 'Typhoon' and 'Mr. Wu'—Dies at His Home at 73; Was Noted Road Player; 'Master of Ballantrae' One of His Best—Last New York Performance Was in 1932," *NYT,* 18 Aug 1942, 21:5. "Walker Whiteside," *Variety,* 19 Aug 1942. "Mrs. W. Whiteside; Former Actress, 70; Wife of Noted Shakespearean Actor Led in Women's Groups," *NYT,* 5 Jan 1944, 17:2 (b. St. Louis MO, 1873?–3 Jan 1944 [70], Hastings-on-Hudson NY). AMD, p. 364. AS, p. 1147. BHD, p. 336. IFN, p. 317. Truitt, p. 349. "Whiteside to Make Patriotic Pictue," *MPW,* 22 Jun 1918, 1700.

Whitespear, Greg [actor] (b. OK, 18 Apr 1897–20 Feb 1956 [58?], Los Angeles Co. CA). BHD1, p. 583. IFN, p. 317.

Whiting, Dwight [general manager]. No data found. AMD, p. 364. "Rolin Company's Rise," *MPW,* 2 Jun 1917, 1426. "Rolin Official in New York," *MPW,* 24 Nov 1917, 1200. "Hal Roach Buys Whiting's Interest in Rolin," 4 May 1918, 681.

Whiting, Richard A. [songwriter] (b. Peoria IL, 12 Nov 1891–19 Feb 1938 [46], Beverly Hills CA; heart ailment). m. Eleanore Youngblood. (WB.) "Richard Whiting, Song Writer, Dies; Author of Many Hits as Well as Music for Broadway and Moving Picture Shows; Began as Player in Cafe; Wrote 'Mammy's Coal Black Rose,' 'Sing, Baby, Sing' and 'Japanese Sandman,'" *NYT,* 20 Feb 1938, II, 8:5. "Dick Whiting," *Variety,* 23 Feb 1938 ("he teamed up with Marshall 'Mickey' Neilan, later a film director, in a vaude singing act"). AS, p. 1147 (Dick Whiting); p. 1148 (Richard A. Whiting). BHD2, p. 282.

Whitlock, T. Lloyd [actor] (b. Springfield MO, 2 Jan 1891–8 Jan 1966 [75], Los Angeles CA). AMD, p. 364. AS, p. 1148. BHD1, p. 583. IFN, p. 317. "A Filmland Wedding," *MPW,* 13 Dec 1919, 821. "T. Lloyd Whitlock," *MPW,* 17 Sep 1927, 167. George A. Katchmer, "Remembering the Great Silents," *CI,* 183 (Sep 1990), 51.

Whitman, Alfred *see* **Whitman, Gayne**

Whitman, Ernest [actor] (b. Fort Smith AR, 21 Feb 1893–6 Aug 1954 [61], Los Angeles CA). AS, p. 1148.

Whitman, Estelle *see* **Allen, Estelle**

Whitman, Fred J. [stage/film actor] (b. Findlay OH, 6 Dec [or 15 Nov] 1887–11 Oct 1945 [57], South Pasadena CA). (Stage debut: 1904; Balboa, Nov 1913.) AS, p. 1148. BHD, p. 336. Jura, p. 104. Billy H. Doyle, "Lost Players," *CI,* 153 (Mar 1988), 54.

Whitman, Gayne [actor] (aka Alfred Vosburg[h] and Alfred Whitman) (b. Chicago IL, 19 Mar 1890–31 Aug 1958 [68], Los Angeles CA; heart attack). m. **Estelle Allen** (d. 1970). (WB.) "Gayne Whitman," *NYT,* 4 Sep 1958, 29:1 (Chandu the Magician on radio). "Gayne Whitman," *Variety,* 10 Sep 1958 (d. 3 Sep). AS, p. 1148. BHD1, p. 583. FSS, p. 290. IFN, p. 317. Truitt, p. 350. "Studio Gossip," *NYDM,* Jul 1914, 23 ("the arrival of a baby girl, born May 14, at Santa Monica, CA."). "Alfred Vosburg and Estelle Allen with Morosco," *MPW,* 14 Oct 1916, 217. "Vosburg Joins Ince Forces," *MPW,* 25 Nov 1916, 1174. Nell Shipman, *The Silent Screen and My Talking Heart* (Boise ID: Boise State University, 1988), pp. 54–56. George Katchmer, "Remembering the Great Silents," *CI,* 220 (Oct 1993), 41–42.

Whitman, Philip H. [director/scenarist] (b. New York NY, 1892–10 Jan 1935 [42], Los Angeles CA; heart attack). AS, p. 1148. BHD2, p. 282. "Pathé Author," *MPW,* 12 Mar 1927, 117.

Whitman, Philip H. "Slim" [writer]. No data found. AMD, p. 364. "Film Comedy's Grim Tragedy," *LA Times,* 6 Feb 1920, II, p. 1 (this may be the P.H. Whitman who was photographing a scene for a Fox film from an airplane when stuntman Earl Burgess plunged to his death on 5 Feb 1920).

Whitman, Velma Virginia [actress] (b. Richmond VA, ca. 1890). m. **Jack Roseleigh** (d. 1940). (Lubin.) AMD, p. 364. BHD, p. 336. "Velma Whitman; Leading Woman, Lubin Western Stock Co., Los Angeles," *MPW,* 18 Oct 1913, 269. "Velma Whitman," *MPW,* 30 May 1914, 1249. "In the Picture Studios," *NYDM,* 4 Dec 1915, 31:2.

Whitman, Walt [actor] (b. Lyon NY, 1859?–27 Mar 1928 [69], Santa Monica CA). "Walt Whitman," *Variety,* 4 Apr 1928. AS, p. 1148. BHD, p. 336. IFN, p. 317. MH, p. 142. Truitt, p. 350. George Katchmer, "Remembering the Great Silents," *CI,* 217 (Jul 1993), 54.

Whitmore, Virginia [scenarist]. No data found. AMD, p. 364. "American Adds to Its Scenario Force," *MPW,* 22 Mar 1913, 1203.

Whitney, Claire [stage/film actress] (b. New York NY, 6 May 1890–27 Aug 1969 [79], Sylmar CA). m. **John Sunderland**, Dec 1917; **Robert Emmett Keane** (d. 1981). (Began 1909; Biograph; Pathé; Rex; Fox; Solax; Select; CYK.) "Claire Whitney Keane," *Variety,* 3 Sep 1969. AMD, p. 364. AS, p. 1148 (d. LA CA). BHD1, p. 583 (d. LA CA). IFN, p. 317. MSBB, p. 1044. Spehr, p. 176. Truitt, p. 350 (d. Sylmar CA). "New Solax Leading Woman," *MPW,* 4 Oct 1913, 27 (22 years old; film debut cited as *Ben Bolt,* Solax, 1913). "Claire Whitney," *MPW,* 4 Apr 1914, 46. "Claire Whiteney Wins Cup," *MPW,* 27 Jun 1914, 1841. "Claire Whitney with Box Office," *MPW,* 10 Oct 1914, 206. "Fox Engages Claire Whitney," *MPW,* 5 Dec 1914, 1397. "Claire Whitney," *MPW,* 4 Aug 1917, 786. "Claire Whitney with Claire Kimball Young," *MPW,* 13 Oct 1917, 214. "Marriages," *Variety,* 21 Dec 1917, 9:4 ("Sunderland is a flight officer in the English aviation corps and came to America a couple of months ago on leave."). "'Shirley Kaye' Lovers Are Married," *MPW,* 5 Jan 1918, 58. "Claire Whitney," *MPW,* 16 Mar 1918, 1531. "Claire Whitney Featured in Schomer Photoplays," *MPW,* 7 Sep 1918, 1417. "Edward Jose Signs Claire Whitney," *MPW,* 19 Jul 1919, 385. "Claire Whitney Has Prominent Role in Wistaria's Melodrama 'Why Women Sin,'" *MPW,* 20 Mar 1920, 1951. "Tri-Star Signs Claire Whitney," *MPW,* 15 May 1920, 962. "Metro Gives Claire Whitney Part in New S-L Production," *MPW,* 15 May 1920, 971.

Whitney, Fred C. [producer] (b. 1865?–4 Jun 1930 [65], Los Angeles CA). "Fred C. Whitney," *Variety,* 11 Jun 1930. AS, p. 1148. BHD2, p. 283.

Whitney, Ralph [stuntman] (b. 1874?–14 Jun 1928 [54], Los Angeles CA; from injuries sustained in a fall during the filming of a western scene on the Universal lot). "Ralph Whitney," *Variety,* 20 Jun 1928. AS, p. 1148. BHD, p. 336. IFN, p. 317. Truitt, p. 350.

Whitney, Renee [actress] (b. 1908–1971 [63?]). BHD1, p. 583.

Whitson, Frank L. [actor] (b. New York NY, 22 Mar 1877–19 Mar 1946 [68], Los Angeles Co. CA). AS, p. 1148. BHD1, p. 584. IFN, p. 317. George Katchmer, "Remembering the Great Silents," *CI,* 204 (Jun 1992), 44.

Whitaker, Charles "Slim" [actor] (*né* Charles Orbie Whitaker, b. Kansas City MO, 29 Jul 1893–27 Jun 1960 [66], Los Angeles CA). BHD1, p. 619. IFN, p. 316.

Whittaker, Charles E[verand] [scenarist] (b. Dublin, Ireland, 31 May 1877–4 Jan 1953 [75], Woodland Hills CA). (MGM.) "Charles E. Whittaker," *Variety,* 14 Jan 1953 (d. 5 Jan). AMD, p. 364. AS, p. 1148. BHD2, p. 283. FDY, p. 439. IFN, p. 317. "Asks $4,500 for Four Sceenarios," *MPW,* 14 Feb 1920, 1060.

Whittaker, George [actor] (b. Wausau WI–d. Apr 1926, Logansport IN; blood poisoning). m. Emma Bunting. "George Whittaker," *Variety,* 21 Apr 1926. AS, p. 1148.

Whittaker, Raymond [actor] (b. Jackson MI, 1900?–21 Jun 1979 [79], Ormund Beach FL). "Ray Whittaker," *Variety,* 27 Jun 1979. AS, p. 1148.

Whittell, Josephine [actress] (b. AZ, 30 Nov 1883–1 Jun 1961 [77], Los Angeles CA). m. **Robert Warwick** (d. 1964). AMD, p. 365. AS, pp. 1148–49 (b. San Francisco CA). BHD1, p. 584. IFN, p. 317. Truitt, p. 350 (b. SF CA). "Josephine Whittell's Screen Bow in Alimony,'" *MPW,* 8 Dec 1917, 1519.

Whittier, Robert [actor]. No data found. AMD, p. 365. "Robert Whittier in Supreme Serial," *MPW,* 31 Jan 1920, 709.

Whittington, Margery [actress] (b. 1904–23 Oct 1957 [53], New York NY). AS, p. 1149 (d. LA CA). BHD1, p. 584. IFN, p. 317.

Whittle, W.E. [actor] (b. 1862–4 Jul 1924 [62?], Bloomfield NJ). BHD, p. 336.

Whitty, Dame May (father of actress/director/producer Margaret Webster) [stage/film actress] (b. Liverpool, England, 19 Jun 1865–29 May 1948 [82], Los Angeles CA; heart attack). m. **Ben Webster**, 1892 (d. 1947). (Stage debut: *Boccacio,* Comedy Theatre, 22 Apr 1882.) "Dame May Whitty Dies on Coast, 82; Character Actress on Stage and Screen Was Honored for Service in War," *NYT,* 30 May 1948, 34:1 (was to have been in the film *Julia Misbehaves,* but replaced by Lucille Watson). "Dame May Whitty," *Variety,* 2 Jun 1948, p. 55. AS, p. 1149 (b. 1864). BHD1, p. 584. IFN, p. 317.

Whitworth, Robert [actor] (b. England). No other data found. "In the Picture Studios," *NYDM,* 23 Oct 1915, 31:1 (to debut in Vitagraph's *Wasted Lives,* 3 reels, written by Ouida Bergere).

Whytal, Mrs. (Mary) Adelaide [actress] (b. New York NY, 8 Nov 1863–13 Jul 1946 [82], Los Angeles Co. CA). BHD, p. 336. IFN, p. 317.

Whytal, Russ [actor/writer] (b. Boston MA, 20 Jun 1860–24 Jan 1930 [69], New York NY). "Russ Whytal," *Variety,* 2 Jul 1930, p. 76. BHD, p. 337 (Whytall).

Whytock, Grant (brother of **Ora Carew**) [film editor] (b. Salt Lake City UT?, 18 Jun 1894–10 Nov 1981 [87], Los Angeles CA). m. **Leota** (d. 1972). "Grant Whytock," *Variety,* 18 Nov 1981. BHD2, p. 283.

Whytock, Leota [film editor] (*née?,* d. 13 Oct 1972, No Hollywood CA). m. **Grant Whytock** (d. 1981). "Leota Whytock," *Variety,* 25 Oct 1972.

Whytock, Ross D. [writer]. No data found. AMD, p. 365. "A Correction," *MPW,* 10 Jun 1916, 1910. "Whytock Author of Clark-Cornelius Detective Films," *MPW,* 3 Jun 1922, 490.

Wick, Bruno [actor] (b. Krefeld, Germany, 2 May 1892-Nov 1979 [87], Flushing NY). BHD1, p. 584.

Wickland, Larry [actor/director] (b. Kansas City MO, 28 Jun 1898–18 Apr 1938 [39], Los Angeles CA). (Paramount [Astoria NY]; Universal; DeMille; Mascot; Republic.) "Larry Wickland," *Variety,* 20 Apr 1938 ("cowboy actor in silents"). AS, p. 1149. BHD, p. 337; BHD2, p. 283 (d. 17 Apr). IFN, p. 317. Truitt, p. 350.

Wicks, John Daggett [actor] (b. Bay Shore NY, 17 May 1884–24 Jun 1935 [51], Culver City CA). AS, p. 1149.

Widdicombe, Wallace [actor] (b. England, 1869?–12 Jul 1969 [100], Somers NY). "Wallace Widdecombe," *Variety,* 23 Jul 1969. AS, p. 1149. BHD, p. 337.

Widen, Carl [cameraman] (b. Chester IL, 1872). m. Nelly Bell. (Kalem.) BHD2, p. 283. "Gossip of the Studios," *NYDM,* 8 Jul 1913, p. 23.

Widmann, Ellen [actress] (b. Biel, Switzerland, 15 Dec 1894–22 Oct 1985 [90], Kafferberg, Switzerland). AS, p. 1149.

Widom, Leonard "Bud" [actor] (b. 1917–18 Apr 1976 [59?], Los Angeles CA). BHD1, p. 584.

Wieck, Dorothea [actress] (*née* Doro Bertha Olavia Wieck, b. Davos, Switzerland, 12 Jan 1908–20 Feb 1986 [78], Berlin, Germany). AS, p. 1149 (d. 19 Feb). BHD1, p. 584.

Wieman, Mathias Carl Heinrich Franz [actor] (b. Osnabruck, Germany, 23 Jun 1902–3 Dec 1969 [67], Zurich, Switzerland; auto accident). "Mathias Wieman," *Variety,* 17 Dec 1969, p. 71. AS, p. 1149. BHD1, p. 584. IFN, p. 318.

Wiene, Conrad (brother of **Robert Wiene**) [director] (b. Sasku, Germany, 1879). AS, p. 1150.

Wiene, Robert (brother of **Conrad Wiene**) [actor/director/producer/scenarist] (b. Sasku, Germany, 15 Apr 1881–17 Jul 1938 [57], Paris, France; cancer). (Directed silents in Mexico.) AS, p. 1150 (b. Breslau, Poland). BHD2, p. 283.

Wifstrand, Naima [actress] (b. Stockholm, Sweden, 4 Sep 1890–30 Oct 1968 [78], Stockholm, Sweden). AS, p. 1150.

Wiggin, Con W. [actor] (d. 21 Nov 1917, Winnipeg, Manitoba, Canada; heart attack during the filming of *The Fatal Ring*). "Con W. Wiggin," *Variety,* 30 Nov 1917, p. 22. AS, p. 1150. BHD, p. 337 (Wirgin).

Wiggins, Lillian [actress] (b. Brooklyn NY). (Pathé.) "Gossip of the Studios," *NYDM,* 25 Feb 1914, 33:1. "Lillian Wiggins, Pathe Star[,] Now in St. Augustine, Fla. [photo only]," *NYDM,* 18 Mar 1914, 26:1.

Wight, George [scenarist/publicist]. No data found. AMD, p. 365. "New American Scenario Editor," *MPW,* 22 Jul 1916, 645.

Wilber, Robert [actor] (b. Louisville KY, 6 May 1896–21 Jun 1980 [84]). BHD1, p. 585.

Wilbert, George [actor]. No data found. AMD, p. 365. "Actor Hurt in Chest," *MPW,* 3 Oct 1914, 69.

Wilbur, Crane (nephew of **Tyrone Power, Sr.**) [stage/film actor/director/writer] (*né* Erwin Crane Wilbur, b. Athens NY, 17 Nov 1886–18 Oct 1973 [86], Toluca Lake CA; pulmonary embolism). m. (1) Edna Hermance; (2) Suzanne Cambert; (3) Beatrice Blinn; (4) actress Lenita Lane (d. 15 Mar 1995). (Pathé; Lubin; Horsley.) "Crane Wilbur, Film Actor, Writer and Director, Dies," *NYT,* 21 Oct 1973, 77:2. "Crane Wilbur," *Variety,* 24 Oct 1973 (d. No. Hollywood CA, age 83). AMD, p. 365. AS, p. 1150. BHD1, p. 585; BHD2, p. 283 (d. No. Hollywood CA). IFN, p. 318. Katz, pp. 1232–33 (began 1910). MSBB, p. 1030 (b. 1889). Spehr, p. 176 (b. 1889). 1921 Directory, p. 207 (b. 17 Nov 1889). "Crane Wilbur Not with Reliance," *MPW,* 14 Jun 1913, 1143. "No Pathe Stock; All But Three Players [Wilbur, Pearl White and Paul Panzer] Let Out—Will Engage Actors as Pictures Are Put On," *NYDM,* 22 Jul 1914, 22:1 (Jersey City NJ company. Eclair had recently dropped its Eastern production.). "Letter from Crane Wilbur," *NYDM,* 29 Jul 1914, 25:1 (Wilbur wrote that the song, *The Moving Picture Man,* was conceived by him based on his screen personality—and not on that of Paul Panzer [*see* Panzer, Paul, *NYDM,* 22 Jul 1914]. Wilbur had had the lyric and title copywrighted. "I admire Mr. Kraus's zeal in furthering the interests of the excellent actor he represents, but really I protest when he would help himself to the thunder of my guns before I have fired them."). "Crane Wilbur—Regular Fellow," *MPW,* 14 Nov 1914, 919–20. "Wilbur Leaves Pathe; Screen Star Has Several Offers, But Future Is Not Yet Decided," *NYDM,* Dec 1914, 24:1 ("...he leaves Pathe with the kindest of felings."). "Crane Wilbur Leaves Pathé," *MPW,* 12 Dec 1914, 1537. "Crane Wilbur on Tour," *MPW,* 19 Dec 1914, 1700. "Crane Wilbur Divorced," *Variety,* 12 Feb 1915, 21:4 (in court on 10 Feb, Mrs. Wilbur said her husband had trifled with her affections. A witness said he lived with another woman at 123 E. 34th St., calling her his wife. "Mrs. Wilbur got the divorce in about ten minutes."). "Crane Wilbur Joins Lubin," *NYDM,* 24 Feb 1915, 24:1 (after recent vaudeville tour). "Crane Wilbur Joins Lubin," *MPW,* 13 Mar 1915, 1620. "Horsley Signs New People," *MPW,* 11 Sep 1915, 1809. "Crane Wilbur on Art Dramas," *MPW,* 14 Jul 1917, 258. "Crane Wilbur," *MPW,* 1 Dec 1917, 1322. George Katchmer, "Remembering the Great Silents," *CI,* 252 (Jun 1996), 46.

Wilcox, Ella Wheeler [writer]. No data found. AMD, p. 365. "Authoress Won Over; Ella Wheeler Wilcox Likes 'The Price He Paid,' to Be Released by Warner's," *NYDM,* 25 Nov 1914, 24:2. "Metro Has Wilcox's Works," *MPW,* 27 Nov 1915, 1647.

Wilcox, Herbert [scenarist/director/producer] (*né* Graham Wilcox, b. Cork, Ireland, 19 Apr 1891–15 May 1977 [86], London, England). m. (1) Maude Bower; (2) Anna Neagle, Aug 1943 (d. 1986). (Began 1919.) Mary Breasted, "Herbert Wilcox, 85, Film Director, Dies; Briton Started Producing Movies in 1919—His Wife, Anna Neagle, Starred in Dozens of His Films," *NYT,* 16 May 1977, 33. "Film Pioneer Dies," *Brisbane Telegraph,* 16 May 197, reprinted in *CFC,* 58 (Spring 1978), X4 (age 85). AS, p. 1150 (b. 1892; d. Brighton, England). BHD2, p. 283. FDY, p. 439. IFN, p. 318.

Wilcox, Nina [author/scenarist] (b. 1885–11 Mar 1962 [77?], Cuernavaca, Mexico). AS, p. 1150.

Wilcox, Silas D. [actor] (b. OH, 8 Feb 1863–11 Feb 1945 [82], Los Angeles CA). AS, p. 1150. BHD, p. 337. IFN, p. 318.

Wilcox, Timothy [actor] (b. 15 Oct 1840–17 Nov 1909 [69], Los Angeles CA). AS, p. 1150.

Wilcox, Wilma [actress]. No data found. (Betzwood Film Co. [PA]; *Toonerville Trolley* series, Sep 1920–22). Joseph P. Eckhardt, "The Toonerville Trolley Films of the Betzwood Studio," *Griffithiana,* 53, May 1995, 24–33. Condensed from *Pennsylvania Heritage,* quarterly of the PA Historical and Museum Commission, XVIII, Summer 1992.

Wilcoxen, Henry [actor/producer] (*né* Harry Wilcoxon, b. Roseau, Dominica, West Indies, 3 Sep 1905–6 Mar 1984 [78], Burbank CA; cancer and congestive heart failure). m. **Joan Woodbury**, 1938—div. (d. 1989); (2) Heather Angel (1909–1986). "Henry Wilcoxon Dead at 78; Screen Actor and Producer," *NYT,* 8 Mar 1984, D22:6. "De Mille Associate Wilcoxon, 78, Dies," *Variety,* 14 Mar 1984. AS, p. 1150. BHD1, p. 585; BHD2, p. 283.

Wild, Anna [actress]. No data found. AMD, p. 365. "Frohman Engages Three Stars to Appear with Texas Guinan," *MPW,* 29 Mar 1919, 1786.

Wild, John P. [publicist] (b. Apponang RI–d. 2 May 1921, Venice CA). "Mr. John P. Wild," *Variety,* 20 May 1921. AMD, p. 365. AS, p. 1150. BHD, p. 337. "Wild Still with Gaumont," *MPW,* 4 Jul 1914, 79.

Wild, Wilma [actress]. No data found. (Betzwood Film Co. [PA]).

Wilde, Percival [scenarist] (b. 1887–19 Sep 1953 [66?], New York NY). (Universal; MGM.) AS, p. 1151.

Wilde, Ted [scenarist/director] (b. New York NY, 16 Dec 1890–17 Dec 1929 [39], Los Angeles CA; following paralytic stroke). (1st National.) "Ted Wilde," *Variety,* 25 Dec 1929 (gagman for Harold Lloyd; directed *Speedy* and *The Kid Brother.* Took sick while directing Charles Murray in *Playing the Market* [Eddie Small] at the Metropolitan studios). AMD, p. 365. AS, p. 1151 (b. 1878). BHD2, p. 283. IFN, p. 318. "Wilde Rejoins [Harold] Lloyd Staff," *MPW,* 11 Oct 1924, 509. "Wilde Co-Director," *MPW,* 12 Jun 1926, 8. "Ted Wilde," *MPW,* 7 May 1927, 19.

Wilder, Leslie Fiske [actor] (b. Brunswick GA, 1896?–26 Jul 1989 [93], Woodland Hills CA). "Leslie Fiske Wilder," *Variety,* 16 Aug 1989 (in films 1922–74). AS, p. 1151. BHD2, p. 283.

Wilder, Marshall P[inckney] [actor] (b. Geneva NY, 19 Sep 1859–10 Jan 1915 [55], St. Paul MN; heart ailment and pneumonia). (Vitagraph.) "Marshall Wilder, Famous Wit, Dead; Killed by Heart Attack While Ill with Pneumonia in St. Paul Hotel; Favorite of King Edward; Noted for His Optimism Despite Heavy Affliction—Long Career in Vaudeville—Made World Tour," *NYT,* 11 Jan 1915, 9:5. "Marshall P. Wilder," *Variety,* 16 Jan 1915 (age 56). AMD, p. 365. AS, p. 1151. BHD, p. 337. IFN, p. 318. Slide, p. 155 (b. 1860). "Marshall P. Wilder, a Photoplayer," *MPW,* 9 Dec 1911, 812. "Marshall P. Wilder," *MPW,* 4 Jan 1913, 30.

Wildhack, Robert [actor] (b. 1881–19 Jun 1940 [59?], Montrose CA; pulmonary embolism). AS, p. 1151.

Wiles, Mabel [actress] (b. TX, 25 Apr 1888–6 Jan 1964 [75], Los Angeles CA). BHD1, p. 619.

Wiley, Dwight M. [scenarist] (b. 1892–5 Apr 1949 [57?], Los Angeles CA). BHD2, p. 284.

Wiley, George H. [producer] (b. 1884–16 Jul 1940 [56?], Buffalo NY). BHD2, p. 284.

Wiley, Hugh [scenarist] (b. 1884–30 Dec 1968 [84?], Berkeley CA). AS, p. 1151. BHD2, p. 284.

Wiley, Jake [executive] (b. 1886–12 Nov 1956 [70?], New York NY). BHD2, p. 284.

Wiley, John A. [actor] (b. 1884?–30 Sep 1962 [78], San Antonio TX). AS, p. 1151. BHD, p. 337. IFN, p. 318. Truitt, p. 351.

Wiley, Harrison [art director] (b. 1898?–20 Jun 1935 [37], near Truinfo CA; plane crash?). (1st National; Columbia; Universal.) "Harrison Wiley," *Variety,* 3 Jul 1935 (killed along with Universal cameraman Charles Stumar).

Wiley, Hugh [writer] (b. 1884–30 Dec 1968 [84?], Berkeley CA; pneumonia and heart attack). AMD, p. 365. AS, p. 1151. "Hugh Wiley Affiliated with Marshall Neilan," *MPW,* 11 Jun 1921, 604.

Wiley, Wanda [actress]. No data found. AMD, p. 365. "Sign Wanda Wiley," *MPW,* 10 May 1924, 211. "Wanda Wiley Injured," *MPW,* 20 Sep 1924, 227. "Wanda Wiley Recovers," *MPW,* 4 Oct 1924, 416. "Plays Boy Part," *MPW,* 25 Oct 1924, 703. "Stern Signs Wanda Wiley," *MPW,* 15 Nov 1924, 256. "Julius and Abe Stern Pick Four Century Comedy Stars," *MPW,* 13 Dec 1924, 652. "Wanda Wiley Injured," *MPW,* 14 Mar 1925, 173. "Wanda Wiley on Way East," *MPW,* 30 May 1925, 528. "Wanda Wiley," *MPW,* 13 Jun 1925, 747. "Wanda Wiley," *MPW,* 13 Jun 1925, 796.

Wilhelm, Prins [director/scenarist] (b. Tullgarn Castle, Sweden, 17 Jun 1884–1965 [81?], Sweden,. AS, p. 1151.

Wilk, Jacob [publicist/executive] (*né* Jacob Wilk, b. England, 1886?–12 Nov 1956 [70], New York NY). m. Eva Zalk. (World.) "Jacob Wilk Dead; Movie Executive; Former Official of Warners Helped Bring Many Books to Stage and Screen," *NYT,* 13 Nov 1956, 37:1 (b. Minneapolis MN). "Jake Wilk Dies; Film Man with a Legit Yen," *Variety,* 14 Nov 1956. AMD, p. 365. BHD, p. 337. "Here and There," *NYDM,* 23 Oct 1915, 26:3 (resigned from World after 1 year, 3 months' service). "Resignation of Jacob Wilk," *MPW,* 6 Nov 1915, 1114.

Wilke, Hubert [actor/singer] (b. Stettin, Germany, 1855?–22 Oct 1940 [85], Yonkers NY). m. Frieda Stettmeyer (d. 1939). "Hubert Wilke, Acted with Lillian Russell; Retired Baritone, Also Leading Man for Marie Tempest, Dies," *NYT,* 23 Oct 1940, 23:5 (onstage in *The Tales of Hoffman* at Ring Theatre, 8 Dec 1881, when fire and collapsed ceiling killed 850 persons). "Hubert Wilke," *Variety,* 30 Oct 1940. AS, p. 1152. BHD, p. 337 (b. 1882).

Wilkerson, Guy [actor] (b. Whitewright TX, 21 Dec 1899–8 Jul 1971 [71], Los Angeles CA; cancer). AS, p. 1152 (b. Katy TX). BHD1, p. 585.

Wilkes, Lillian [actress] (b. 18 Apr 1892–16 Dec 1976 [84], Los Angeles CA). AS, p. 1152. BHD, p. 337.

Wilkes, Mattie ["colored prima donna"] (b. 1885?–9 Jul 1927 [42], Montclair NJ?; peritonitis). m. Ernest Hogan. "Mattie Wilkes," *Variety*, 13 Jul 1927. AS, p. 1152 (Nattie Wilkes). BHD, p. 337.

Wilkes, Winona [daughter of producer Tom Wilkes] [stage/film actress] (b. 1904–11 Jun 1926 [22], Seaside Hospital, Long Beach CA; following a Caesarian operation). m. Dudley Ayres (1 daughter). "Mrs. Dudley Ayres," *Variety*, 23 Jun 1926, p. 49:4. BHD, p. 337.

Wilkins, Charlotte [actress]. No data found. m. **Austin Oscar Huhn** (d. 1933). (Excelsior Feature Film Co.)

Wilkins, George H. [cameraman]. No data found. AMD, p. 365. "Cameraman Arrives from Arctics," *MPW*, 21 Oct 1916, 370.

Wilkinson, Mary [actress] (b. 1853?). "...Mary Wilkinson, who played the old woman in Betty Compson's 'The Little Minister' is seventy...," *Picture-Play Magazine*, Jun 1923, 94:2.

Wilky, L. Guy [cinematographer] (b. Phoenix AZ, 12 Oct 1888–25 Dec 1971 [83], Walnut Creek CA; heart attack). (American.) "Guy Wilky," *Variety*, 12 Jan 1972. BHD2, p. 284. FDY, p. 471.

Willa, Suzanne [actress] (b. Los Angeles CA, 1892–24 Mar 1951 [58], New York NY). AS, p. 1152. BHD1, p. 586. IFN, p. 318.

Willard, Amy [actress]. No data found. AMD, p. 365. "Amy Willard in Parmount Film," *MPW*, 12 Nov 1921, 210.

Willard, Mrs. Charles [actress] (*née?*, b. 1863–12 Jan 1945 [81?], New York NY). BHD, p. 337.

Willard, Edmund [actor] (b. Brighton, England, 19 Dec 1884–6 Oct 1956 [71], Kingston, England). AS, p. 1152 (d. Surrey, England). BHD1, p. 586.

Willard, Jess [heavyweight boxing champion/actor] (b. Pottawatamie Indian land KS, 29 Dec 1881–15 Dec 1968 [86], Los Angeles CA; cerebral hemorrhage). m. Hattie. (Universal.) "Jess Willard, Boxing Champion, Dies at 86; Giant Fighter Beat Johnson and Lost to Dempsey," *NYT*, 16 Dec 1968, 47:2 (Willard-Johnson fight filmed 5 Apr 1915, Havana, Cuba; had a "brief career in silent movies."). AMD, p. 365. AS, p. 1152. BHD1, p. 586. IFN, p. 318 (age 84). "Universal in Luck; Has Willard in 'The Fight Punch,' and Also in Animated Weekly," *NYDM*, 14 Apr 1915, 24:1 (title in article is *The Heart Punch*, 1 reel. Willard had just won a match.). "Willard Sues for $100,000," *NYDM*, 21 Apr 1915, 22:1 (vs. Universal for an accounting of the profits on *The Heart Punch*. Claimed he was to get 25% of the gross profits and that Universal sold the film to their own exchanges at deflated prices.). "Champion Jess Willard to Star in Big Production," *MPW*, 24 May 1919, 1146.

Willard, Jessie [actress] (b. England, 1857?–1 Mar 1929 [72], New York NY). "Jessie Willard," *Variety*, 6 Mar 1929. AS, p. 1152.

Willard, John [stage actor/scenarist/novelist] (b. San Francisco CA, 28 Nov 1885–30 Aug 1942 [56], Hollywood Hospital, Los Angeles CA; heart attack). "John Willard, 57, Playwright, Dead; Author of 'Cat and the Canary' Was Air Corp Captain in the Last War—Also an Actor; Wrote for the Screen; World Traveler Was Known Also for His Many Novels—Last Book on China," *NYT*, 1 Sep 1942, 20:2 (member of The Players and The Lambs). "John Willard," *Variety*, 2 Apr 1942, p. 62. AS, p. 1152. BHD1, p. 586 (d. 31 Aug). IFN, p. 318. "'[Adam] Souverguy' in Pictures," *Variety*, 23 Jan 1914, 5:4 (producer/scenarist for Universal).

Willard, Lee [actor]. No data found. (Began ca. 1913.) George Katchmer, "Remembering the Great Silents," *CI*, 252 (Jun 1996), 46.

Willat, C.A. "Doc" (brother of **Irvin V. Willat**; son-in-law of **William T. "Pop" Rock**) [producer] (*né* C.A. Willatowski, b. 23 Nov 1878–7 Aug 1937 [58], Los Angeles CA; lobar pneumonia). "C.A. Willat," *NYT*, 8 Aug 1937, II, 7:3. "C.A. Willat," *Variety*, 11 Aug 1937 (d. 6 Aug). AMD, p. 365. AS, p. 1152 (d. 6 Aug). BHD2, p. 284 (d. 6 Aug). Spehr, p. 176. "Willat Will Make Pictures," *MPW*, 27 Dec 1913, 1553. "'Doc' Willat Back from Boyhood Home," *MPW*, 7 Mar 1914, 1214.

Willat, Irvin V. (brother of **C.A. "Doc" Willat**) [title writer/actor/cinematographer/director] (*né* Irvin Willatowski, b. Stamford CT, 18 Nov 1890–17 Apr 1976 [85], Santa Monica CA). m. (1) **Billie Dove**, 27 Oct 1923, Santa Monica CA—div. Jul 1930 (d. 1997); (2) **Barbara Bedford** (d. 1981). "Irvin V. Willat," *Variety*, 28 Apr 1976. AMD, p. 365. AS, p. 1152. BHD, p. 337; BHD2, p. 284. IFN, p. 318. Lowrey, p. 196. 1921 Directory, p. 278. "Artistic Subtittles," *MPW*, 30 Dec 1916, 1966. "Lasky Engages Three More Directors," *MPW*, 25 Jan 1919, 454. "Irvin Willat Contracts to Produce Feature Pictures for Hodkinson," *MPW*, 14 Feb 1920, 1030. "Irvin V. Willat Promises Rural Drama from a New Angle in His 'Dabney Todd,'" *MPW*, 3 Jul 1920, 103. "Willat Injured," *MPW*, 25 Jun 1921, 807. "Irvin Willat to Direct Picture," *MPW*, 18 Mar 1922, 267. "Willat to Direct," *MPW*, 5 May 1923, 76. "Willat Ill; Ince to Succeed Him," *MPW*, 12 May 1923, 170. "Willat Adapts Talmadge Story," *MPW*, 28 Aug 1926, 528. "Willat Signed to Direct for Universal Now," *MPW*, 19 Feb 1927, 561. "Reynolds to Direct 'Show Boat'; Irvin Willat to Do 'The Big Gun,'" *MPW*, 12 Mar 1927, 108. "Irvin Willat," *MPW*, 23 Apr 1927, 716–17. "Billy Dove," *Variety*, 16 Feb 1998, 71:3 ("Willat, who had appeared in several Mary Pickford films before turning to directing, was paid $350,000 by [Howard] Hughes to divorce Dove, according to [Gail] Adelson [adopted daughter].").

Wille, Claire [artist]. No data found. AMD, p. 366. "Claire Wille Joins World Art Department," *MPW*, 15 Jun 1918, 1574.

Willemetz, Albert Lucien [scenarist/author] (b. Paris, France, 14 Feb 1887 [extrait de naissance no. 22/1964]-7 Oct 1964 [77], Marnes-la-Coquette, France). AS, p. 1152.

Willenz, Max [actor] (b. Vienna, Austria, 22 Sep 1888–10 Nov 1954 [66], Los Angeles CA). AS, p. 1152.

Willets, Gilson [scenarist] (b. Hempstead NY, 1869?–26 May 1922 [53], Los Angeles CA; stomach cancer). "Gilson Willets," *Variety*, 2 Jun 1922 ("was credited with having originated the picture serial"). AMD, p. 366. AS, p. 1152. BHD2, p. 284. IFN, p. 318. "Gilson Willets with Pathé," *MPW*, 22 Sep 1917, 1829. "Gilson Willets in New York," *MPW*, 22 Jun 1918, 1692. "Author of Serials Picturesque Figure," *MPW*, 10 Aug 1918, 818. "Only Best Screen Authors Will Survive, Says Gilson Willets, Talking Production," *MPW*, 25 Dec 1920, 1049. "Obituary," *MPW*, 10 Jun 1922, 540 (d. 25 May).

Willey, Leonard Louis [actor] (b. England, 15 Dec 1882–30 Jun 1964 [81], Los Angeles CA; arteriosclerosis). AS, p. 1152. IFN, p. 318.

William, Joseph (Ranger Bill) [actor] (b. 1878–12 Nov 1939 [61?]). AS, p. 1152. BHD, p. 337.

William, Warren [stage/film actor] (*né* Warren William Krech, b. Aitken MN, 2 Dec 1894–24 Sep 1948 [53], Encino CA; multiple myeloma and pneumonia). m. Helen Nelson. "Warren William, Movie Star, Dead; Detective in 'Lone Wolf' Series Appeared in Films 16 Years—Once Broadway Actor," *NYT*, 25 Sep 1948, 17:1. "Warren William," *Variety*, 29 Sep 1948. AS, p. 1152. BHD1, p. 586 (d. LA CA). IFN, p. 318. Katz, p. 1236. Truitt, p. 351 (b. 1895). Dan Van Neste, "Warren William: 'Lone Wolf,'" *CI*, 227 (May 1994), C12 *et passim* (b. 1896) (appeared in *The Town That God Forgot*, 1922, and *Plunder*, 1923).

Williams, Allen [cameraman]. No data found. FDY, p. 471 (Al Williams).

Williams, Arnold [actor] (b. 1875–1927 [52?]). BHD, p. 337. IFN, p. 319.

Williams, Barney [actor] (*né* Bernard A. Wilhelm, b. 1880–22 Sep 1948 [68?], Los Angeles CA). AS, p. 1153.

Williams, Ben [actor] (b. New York NY, 6 May 1842–3 Apr 1917 [74], New York NY). AS, p. 1153.

Williams, Ben Ames [scenarist] (b. 1889–4 Feb 1953 [63?], Brookline MA). AS, p. 1153.

Williams, Bert [actor] (*né* Egbert Austin Williams, b. New Providence, Nassau, British West Indies, 12 Nov 1874–4 Mar 1922 [47], New York NY; pneumonia). m. Lottie Cole. Mabel Rowland, *Bert Williams, Son of Laughter* (NY: The English Crafters, 1923); Eric Ledell Smith, *Bert Williams: A Biography of the Pioneer Black Comedian* (Jefferson NC: McFarland & Co., 1992). (Biograph; K&E.) Ben Hecht, "To Bert Williams," *Chicago Daily News*, 11 Mar 1922. "Bert Williams," *Variety*, 10 Mar 1922. AMD, p. 366. AS, p. 1153. BHD, p. 337. IFN, p. 319. Truitt, p. 351 (b. 1877). "Bert Williams in Biograph Comedies," *MPW*, 1 Jul 1916, 105. "Baker Slsigns Bert Williams to Star in Two-Reel Comdies," *MPW*, 17 Apr 1920, 375.

Williams, Bill [stuntman] (*né* Williams J. Williams, Jr., b. 1921?–13 Nov 1964 [43], Gallup NM; crushed by a wagon while filming a stunt for *The Hallelujah Trail*). m. Catherine. "Bill Williams, 43, Stuntman, Killed in Western Filming," *NYT*, 14 Nov 1964, 29:6. "Bill Williams," *Variety*, 18 Nov 1964. AS, p. 1153 (d. 14 Nov). IFN, p. 319.

Williams, Bransby [vaudeville/stage/film/TV actor] (*né* Eric Bransby Williams, b. London, England, 14 Aug 1870–3 Dec 1961 [91], London, England). "Bransby Williams, Character," *NYT*, 4 Deb 1961, 37:4 ("delighted audiences in many parts of the world with his stage impersonations of characters from Charles Dickens' works...Mr. Williams was credited with having introduced on the variety stage the method of making up for his characterizations in full view of the audience."). "Bransby Williams," *Variety*, 13 Dec 1961, p. 63:1. AS, p. 1153 (b. Hackney, England). BHD1, p. 586. IFN, p. 319 (b. Hackney, England).

Williams, C. Jay [actor/director/producer] (b. New York NY, 1858?–26 Jan 1945 [86], New York NY). (Vitagraph.) "C. Jay Williams; Veteran Stage Actor, 86, Had Supported Jeffries in Play," *NYT,* 27 Jan 1945, 11:4 ("He served for many years as a director of the Edison Vitagraph in the silent film days."). "C. Jay Williams," *Variety,* 31 Jan 1945. AMD, p. 366. AS, p. 1153. BHD, p. 337; bHD2, p. 284. IFN, p. 319. "Edison Touches Popular Chord," *MPW,* 3 Jan 1914, 28–29. "C. Jay Williams," *MPW,* 15 Aug 1914, 966. "C. Jay Williams Joins Vitagraph," *MPW,* 5 Dec 1914, 1366.

Williams, Charlie [extra] (b. AK). No data found. Robert Donaldson, "Famous Extras," *MPC,* Feb 1927, 32 [photo]-33, 68, 80.

Williams, Charles B. [actor/scenarist] (b. Albany NY, 27 Sep 1898–4 Jan 1958 [59], Los Angeles CA). (Paramount [Astoria NY]; Hollywood, 1934). "Charles B. Williams," *Variety,* 15 Jan 1958. AS, p. 1153 (d. 3 Jan). BHD1, p. 586; BHD2, p. 284. IFN, p. 319. Truitt, p. 351.

Williams, Clara [actress] (b. Seattle WA, 3 May 1888–8 May 1928 [40], Los Angeles CA). m. **Reginald C. Barker**, 1920 (d. 1945). (Lubin; Selig.) "Mrs. Clara Williams Barker," *Variety,* 16 May 1928. AMD, p. 366. AS, p. 1153. BHD, p. 337. IFN, p. 319. Truitt, p. 351. "Clara Williams," *MPN,* 20 Jul 1912, 21 ("the crack female rough rider of the Lubin Company"). "Clara Williams," *MPW,* 3 Aug 1912, 452. "Clara WIlliams," *MPW,* 18 Apr 1914, 349. "Clara Williams Joins Paralta," *MPW,* 6 Oct 1917, 67. "Director and Star Wed," *MPW,* 28 Feb 1920, 1480 (retired fom screen). "Mrs. Baker Ill," *MPW,* 18 Dec 19920, 901. Billy Doyle, "Lost Players," *CI,* 175 (Jan 1990), 38.

Williams, Cora, "The Girl with the Dimples" [actress] (b. Chelsea MA, 6 Dec 1870–1 Dec 1927 [56], Los Angeles CA; heart attack). (Edison.) "Cora Williams," *Variety,* 7 Dec 1927. AS, p. 1153. BHD, p. 337. IFN, p. 319. Truitt, p. 352.

Williams, Craig [stage/film actor] (b. Germany, 1877–5 Jul 1941 [63], Palace Hotel, 45th Street, New York NY; heart attack; buried in Kensico Cemetery NY). m. Beatrice. "Craig Williams, 64, an Actor, Dies Here; Seen Last in 'Madame Capet' with Eva La Gallienne [1938]," *NYT,* 6 Jul 1941, 27:4 (age 64; member of The Players and The Lambs). "Craig Williams," *Variety,* 9 Jul 1941, p. 54:2 (age 64; "A member of the Friars Club and the Actors Fund, he had also appeared briefly in pictures with Gloria Swanson and Bebe Daniels."). AS, p. 1153. BHD, p. 337. IFN, p. 319.

Williams, Cyrus J. [producer]. No data found. AMD, p. 366. "Pathé Contracts to Release Fifteen Two Reel Westerns with Tom Santschi," *MPW,* 4 Sep1920, 64.

Williams, Dow [actor] (b. 1875–15 Mar 1929 [54?], Idaho Falls ID). AS, p. 1153.

Williams, Earle R. (nephew of stage actor James Paget) [stage/film actor/director] (*né* Earle Rafael Williams, b. Sacramento CA, 28 Feb 1880–25 Apr 1927 [47], Los Angeles CA; bronchial pneumonia). m. Florine (or Florence) Walz (suicide, 1931). (Debut: *The Thumb Print,* Vitagraph, 1911.) "Earle Williams," *Variety,* 27 Apr 1927. AMD, p. 366. AS, p. 1153. BHD, p. 338; BHD2, p. 284. FFF, p. 247 (b. 1886). IFN, p. 319. Lowrey, p. 198. Katz, p. 1237. MH, p. 142. Slide, p. 155. Truitt, p. 352 (b. 1895). WWS, p. 60. "Earle Williams," *MPW,* 22 Aug 1914, 1077 . "William Earle Sues Earle Williams," *MPW,* 21 Jul 1917, 460. "James Young to Direct WIliams," *MPW,* 1 Jun 1918, 1299. Fritzi Remont, "Earle and His Ambitions," *MPC,* May 1919, 34–35, 69. "Obituary," *MPW,* 7 May 1927, 17. "Earle Williams Leaves Large Estate," *MPW,* 13 Aug 1927, 44. Dorothy Donnell, "Film Star's Widow Has Tragic End; Earle Williams Left Fortune to Pretty Florine Williams—Four Years Later, in Poverty and Despair, She Kills Self and Family [two children]," *Movie Classic,* Nov 1931, 40 (she squandered $300,000).

Williams, Elaine [actress] (d. 9 May 1947, Los Angeles CA). AS, p. 1153. BHD, p. 338. IFN, p. 319.

Williams, Emmett A. [cameraman] (b. 1893?–28 Apr 1916 [23], New Rochelle NY; septic poisoning following dental operation). (Thanhauser.) "Emmett A. Williams," *Variety,* 12 May 1916. AMD, p. 366. BHD2, p. 284. "Obituary," *MPW,* 13 May 1916, 1143.

Williams, Eric Bransby *see* **Williams, Bransby**

Williams, Estha [actress]. No data found. AMD, p. 366. "Estha WIlliams," *MPW,* 22 Aug 1914, 1087.

Williams, Florence [actress/executive director of Hollywood Studio Club from 1947–65] (d. 25 Mar 1968, Hollywood CA). (Lubin.) "Florence Williams," *Variety,* 3 Apr 1968. AS, p. 1153.

Williams, Frances [stage/TV/film actress/singer] (b. St. Paul MN, 1901?–27 Jan 1959 [57], New York NY). m. (5) Frank Lovejoy. "Frances Williams," *Variety,* 213, 4 Feb 1959, 79:1. AMD, p. 366. AS, p. 1153. IFN, p. 319. "Vitaphone Signs Frances Williams," *MPW,* 21 May 1927, 195.

Williams, Frank [actor]. No data found. AMD, p. 366. "Williams Signed by Character," *MPW,* 15 May 1920, 965.

Williams, Frank D. [cameraman] (b. Nashville MO). m. Mildred E. Hansen, 19 May 1917, NYC. AMD, p. 366. "Williams Cameraman for Arbuckle," *MPW,* 12 May 1917, 947. "Cameraman Williams an Old-Timer," *MPW,* 26 May 1917, 1295. "Cupid Gets 'Fatty' Arbuckle's Cameraman," *MPW,* 2 Jun 1917, 1445. "Metro Cameraman Has Submarine Tank," *MPW,* 28 Sep 1918, 1901. "Invention Shows Actor in Two Roles at Once," *MPW,* 21 Feb 1920, 1271.

Williams, Fred [actor] (d. 13 Jun 1916). "Fred Williams," *Variety,* 7 Jul 1916.

Williams, Fred G. [actor] (b. NY, 1849?–4 Aug 1924 [75], New York NY). Bachelor. "Colonel Fred Williams," *NYT,* 5 Aug 1924, 17:4. AS, p. 1154. BHD, p. 338 (d. Coney Island NY). IFN, p. 319.

Williams, Fred J. [actor/producer] (b. Chicago IL, 2 Jul 1874–29 May 1942 [67], Los Angeles CA). AS, p. 1154. BHD1, p. 587; BHD2, p. 284. IFN, p. 319. Truitt, p. 352.

Williams, George Albert [actor] (b. Kinnikinnic WI, 11 Aug 1854–21 Feb 1936 [81], Los Angeles CA). "George Williams," *Variety,* 26 Feb 1936 (age 82). AS, p. 1154. BHD, p. 338. IFN, p. 319 (age 82). Truitt, p. 352. Billy H. Doyle, "Lost Players," *CI,* 157 (Jul 1988), 24. George Katchmer, "George A. Williams," *CI,* 255 (Sep 1996), 36.

Williams, George B. [actor] (b. VT, 1866?–17 Nov 1931 [65], Santa Monica CA; killed in a car accident). AS, p. 1154. BHD, p. 338. IFN, p. 319. Truitt, p. 352.

Williams, George H. [technical director]. No data found. AMD, p. 366. "Universal Signs Williams of New York Hippodrome," *MPW,* 19 Jul 1919, 369.

Williams, Grace [actress] (b. New York NY). (Edison; Reliance; Biograph; Life Photo Film Co.) AMD, p. 366. "Grace Williams, Edison Leading Woman," *MPW,* 18 Dec 1915, 2189. "Grace Williams," *MPW,* 10 Jun 1916, 1895.

Williams, Guinn "Big Boy" [actor] (b. Decatur TX, 26 Apr 1899–6 Jun 1962 [63], Van Nuys CA; uremic poisoning). m. (1) Kathleen Collins; (2) Dorothy Patterson, Jan 1943. (Began in 1919.) "Guinn Williams, Actor, 63, Dies; Played in Many Western Films; Performer of Comic Roles Was Known as Big Boy—Expert Polo Player," *NYT,* 7 Jun 1962, 35:2 (age 63). "Guinn Williams," *Variety,* 13 Jun 1962. AMD, p. 366. AS, p. 1154. BHD1, p. 587. GK, pp. 1021–36. IFN, p. 319 (age 62). Katz, p. 1238. Truitt, p. 352. "Big Boy Williams Is Signed," *MPW,* LVI, 13 May 1922, 177. Herbert Cruikshank, "He's Through with Women; One Throwdown Was Enough for Big Boy Williams," *MPC,* May 1929, 63, 78. George A. Katchmer, "Guinn 'Big Boy' Williams," *CI,* 83 (May 1982), 30–31. George Katchmer, "Remembering the Great Silents," *CI,* 247 (Jan 1996), 44–45.

Williams, Gwen [actress] (d. 27 May 1962, Worthing, Sussex, England). BHD, p. 338.

Williams, Harcourt [actor] (b. Croydon, England, 30 Mar 1880–13 Dec 1957 [77], London, England). AS, p. 1154.

Williams, Harry H. [director/composer] (b. Fairbault MN, 29 Aug 1873?–15 May 1922 [48], Oakland CA; bronchitis-influenza). (Sennett; Fox.) "Harry H. Williams, Song Writer," *NYT,* 17 May 1922, 19:4 (wrote lyrics for *Tipperary; I'm Afraid to Go Home in the Dark; Cheyenne;* etc.). "Harry Williams," *Variety,* 19 May 1922. AS, p. 1154. ASCAP 66, pp. 791–92 (b. 1879). BHD2, p. 284 (b. 1879-d. 16 May). SD, p. 1317.

Williams, Hattie [vaudeville/stage/film actress] (b. Boston MA, 17 Mar 1870–17 Aug 1942 [72], Bronx NY). "Hattie Williams, 70; Starred in Comedies; Had Leading Roles in Musicals Until Retirement in 1915," *NYT,* 18 Aug 1942, 21:6. (Stage debut: chorus, *1492,* ca. 1864). "Hattie Williams," *Variety,* 19 Aug 1942, p. 46:2. AMD, p. 366. BHD, p. 338. IFN, p. 319. "Oliver Morosco's Latest Capture," *MPW,* 27 Nov 1915, 1644.

Williams, Hazel [actress: Sennett Bathing Beauty]. No data found.

Williams, Herg [actor] (*né* Herbert Schussler Billerbeck, b. Philadelphia PA, 1884–1 Oct 1936 [52?], Freeport NY). AS, p. 1154.

Williams, Horace [casting director] (b. Dallas TX, 1879). AMD, p. 367. BHD, p. 338. "Williams Has Animated Filing List," *MPW,* 29 Jun 1918, 1859. "Williams Returns to Metro," *MPW,* 3 Jan 1920, 114.

Williams, J[ames] **D**[ixon] [executive] (b. Credo WV, 1877?–28 Aug 1934 [57], New York NY; of a nervous breakdown following a complication of ailments, including two heart attacks). m. Ethel Hope. "James D. Williams," *Variety,* 115, 4 Sep 1934, 61:2 (organized Ritz-Carlton pictures). AMD, p. 367. BHD2, p. 284. "Rapid Rise of J.D. Williams in Australia," *MPW,* 23 Sep 1911, 880. "Williams Wires Farewell," *MPW,* 9 Dec 1911, 812. "A Kangaroo for Pictures," *MPW,* 20 Jul 1912, 245. "Williams No Longer with Hodkinson," *MPW,* 4

Jul 1914, 84. "Williams with World Film," *MPW,* 6 Mar 1915, 1428. "Pertinent Points by J.D. Williams," *MPW,* 1 Jan 1916, 87. "Williams Hits Out from Shoulder," *MPW,* 22 Feb 1919, 1009–10. J.D. Williams, "Williams Flays 'Single Pictures,'" *MPW,* 31 May 1919, 1317–18. J.D. Williams, "Growing Need for Exchange Executives," *MPW,* 8 Nov 1919, 247. "Williams of First National Proves Value of Trade Papers to Induustry," *MPW,* 13 Dec 1919, 792. J.D. Williams, "Monopoly Has Been Cut Down Twice; Now Faces Third and Final Battle," *MPW,* 27 Dec 1919, 1125. "New York News Is Small Town Stuff of Average Showman, Says Williams," *MPW,* 10 Jan 1920, 245. J.D. Williams, "Induistry Dividng into Two Factions, Declares Manager of FIrst National," *MPW,* 13 Mar 1920, 1763. J.D. Williams, "New Tests in Showmanship Are Imposed by New Era in Production of Pictures," *MPW,* 11 Sep 1920, 233. J.D. Williams, "J.D. Williams Says Year Has Been One of Accomplishment by First National," *MPW,* 25 Dec 1920, 1010. "Conbsolidatred System of Production Is Passing Away, Says J.D. Williams," *MPW,* 2 Apr 1921, 475. "J.D. Williams Represents Film Industry at President's Unemploymet Conference," *MPW,* 8 Oct 1921, 639. "J.D. Williams's Speech," *MPW,* 5 Nov 1921, 33. "'World' Honest, Unbiased, Fearless—J.D. Williams," *MPW,* 11 Mar 1922, 141. "Williams Resigns from First National; Rowland Appointed General Manager," *MPW,* 11 Nov 1922, 142. "Talks to Advertising Men," *MPW,* 24 Feb 1923, 764. "Club Dines Williams," *MPW,* 17 Mar 1923, 310. J.D. Williams, "Williams Denies Rumors," *MPW,* 14 Jul 1923, 133 (that Rittz-Carlton signed Harold Lloyd). "RItz-Carlton Announces Valentino as Company's First Star," *MPW,* 28 Jul 1923, 289. "J.D. Williams Says Whole World Wants Only Better Class Films," *MPW,* 22 Dec 1923, 689. "Inspired FIlm, Internationalized Will Fill Wants, Says Williams," *MPW,* 29 Dec 1923, 803. "Believes Faulty Distribution Will Cause Big Feature Shortage in Fall," *MPW,* 5 Apr 1924, 445. "J.D. WIlliams Has Not Signed Harold Lloyd," *MPW,* 12 Apr 1924, 539. "$500,000 Insurance," *MPW,* 9 Aug 1924, 439. "Rudy-Williams Split Report Described as 'Nothing Startling,'" *MPW,* 14 Mar 1925, 140. "J.D. Williams Here to Boost British FIlms," *MPW,* 30 Jan 1926, 1. Merritt Crawford, "From 'Balck Top' Days to the Roxy Theatre," *MPW,* 22 Jan 1927, 258, 306, 310.

Williams, Jeffrey [actor] (b. 1860?–27 Dec 1938 [78], Los Angeles CA; found dead). "Jeffrey Williams," *NYT,* 29 Dec 1938, 20:3. AS, p. 1154. BHD1, p. 587. IFN, p. 319. Truitt, p. 352.

Williams, John J. [actor] (b. Lynn MA, b. 1856–5 Oct 1918 [62], New York NY; influenza). "John J. Williams," *Variety,* 18 Oct 1918. AS, p. 1154. BHD, p. 338.

Williams, Josephine [stage/film actress] (b. Liverpool, England, 1855?–14 Jun 1937 [82], New York NY). "Josephine Williams, Character Actress; Appeared in 'Craig's Wife' and 'Royal Family' Among Many Productions—Dies at 82," *NYT,* 15 Jun 1937, 23:6. "Josephine Williams," *Variety,* 16 Jun 1937. AS, p. 1154. BHD, p. 338. IFN, p. 319.

Williams, Julia [actress] (b. 1878–7 Feb 1936 [57], New York NY). m. **Harry Scott Siggins** (d. 1928). (Pathé; Biograph.) "Julia Williams Siggins," *Variety,* 12 Feb 1936. AS, p. 1154. BHD, p. 338. IFN, p. 319. Truitt, p. 353.

Williams, Kathlyn, "The Selig Girl" [stage/film actress/producer] (b. Butte MT, 31 May 1884?–24 Sep 1960 [76?], Los Angeles CA; found dead, "apparently from natural causes"). m. (2) **Charles F. Eyton**, 1916–31 (d. 1941). (Began 1908; Biograph; Selig; Pallas-Morosco; Paramount.) "Kathlyn Williams," *NYT,* 25 Sep 1960, 86:4 (age 65). "Kathlyn Williams," *Variety,* 5 Oct 1960 (d. 23 Sep 1960, age 65). AMD, p. 367. AS, p. 1154 (b. 1888; d. 23 Sep). BHD1, p. 587 (b. 1888). BR, pp. 89–95. FSS, p. 290. IFN, p. 319 (age 72). Katz, pp. 1238–39 (began 1910). MH, p. 143. MSBB, p. 1044. Truitt, p. 353 (b. 1872 or 1888). "Miss Williams as 'Lady Bountiful,'" *MPW,* 21 Sep 1912, 1187. "Kathlyn Williams, Rival of Venus," *MPW,* 1 Mar 1913, 866 (145 lbs., 5 ft. 7 in., 38x24x41). "Kathlyn Williams to Produce Her Own Picture," *MPW,* 17 May 1913, 689. "Popular Players," *MPW,* 23 Aug 1913, 832. "Kathlyn Williams's New Play," *MPW,* 29 Nov 1913, 1017. Bertha H. Smith, "Interesting Westerners; A Nervy Movie Lady," *Sunset* (Jun 1914), 1323–25 (Williams was filming *The Adventures of Kathlyn* in an outdoor studio in Los Angeles for Selig. A leopard got loose and leaped into the enclosure where Williams stood. She saw it crouched for a spring. She hid her face nd it leaped on her while the camera clicked away; the keepers rushed in and beat the animal away. "A few scalp wounds, a wholesome distrust of all wild animals were the sum total of results for Miss Williams on that count. ¶'But I love them all' she declares enthusiastically." Another time, Williams was caught in a howdah during an elephant stampede, knocked out of it by a tree branch. "These are only a few of the reel and unreel adventures of Kathlyn, who was quite insulted a few years ago when a moving-picture concern made her an offer to go into photo-drama. You see, big things had been planned for her when she was a wee musical prodigy in Montana." She studied for the stage in New York and obtained a leading role with William Morris. "At the first chance she came back to the West she loves, acting in stock at Salt Lake City and Los Angeles. Then one day a 'movie' man hurt her pride. But just to see what the work was like she went to the studio and took a part, expecting to get about fifty cents for it. What she did get proved a sufficient apology for the wound to her pride, and she resigned from stock work then and there.") "Kathlyn Williams Honored," *MPW,* 12 Jun 1915, 1757. "Kathlyn Williams Honored by Soldiers," *MPW,* 21 Aug 1915, 1327. "Kathlyn Williams Joins Morosco," *MPW,* 26 Aug 1916, 1385. "Kathlyn Williams to Lecture," *MPW,* 14 Oct 1916, 252. "Kathlyn Williams Will Organize Own Company," *MPW,* 19 Apr 1919, 359. "Kathlyn Williams in Columbia's 'Sally,'" *MPW,* 9 Jul 1927, 98. Anthony Slide, *Idols of Silence* (NY: A.S. Barnes & Co., 1976), pp. 30–36. George Katchmer, "Remembering the Great Silents," *CI,* 242 (Aug 1995), 37–38. Eve Golden, "Kathlyn Williams: Girl of the Golden West," *CI,* 258 (Dec 1996), C6-C10 (includes filmography; lost a leg in a car accident on 29 Dec 1949).

Williams, Lawrence E. [actor] (b. PA, 24 May 1889–30 Mar 1956 [66], Los Angeles CA; heart attack). m. Helen Dickson. "Lawrence Williams," *Variety,* 4 Apr 1956 ("film actor for 25 years"). AS, p. 1154. BHD2, p. 285. IFN, p. 319.

Williams, L[awrence] **P**[aul] **"Bill"** [art director] (b. 10 Aug 1905–8 Oct 1996 [91], England). m. (1) actress Queenie Leonard, 1936; (2) Peggy Garratt (d. 1990). (Cricklewood Studios, late 20s; Elstree; worked on England's first talkie, *Wolves,* 1927; retired, 1949.) "L.P. Williams," *The London Times,* 12 Oct 1996, p. 21. BHD2, p. 285.

Williams, Lottie [actress] (b. Indianapolis IN, 20 Jan 1874–16 Nov 1962 [88], Los Angeles Co. CA). AS, p. 1154. BHD1, p. 587. IFN, p. 319.

Williams, Malcolm [stage/film actor] (b. Spring Valley MN, 16 Jul 1869–10 Jun 1937 [67], New York NY; heart attack). m. **Florence Reed**, 12 Nov 1915, Philadelphia PA (d. 1967). "Malcolm Williams, a Character Actor; Husband of Florence Reed Dies Here at 67—Played in Many Broadway Successes," *NYT,* 11 Jun 1937, 23:4 (in *The First Kiss,* Paramount, 1928). "Malcolm Williams," *Variety,* 16 Jun 1937. AMD, p. 367. AS, p. 1154. BHD, p. 338 (b. 1870). IFN, p. 319. Truitt, p. 353. "Famous Players Present Malcolm Williams," *MPW,* 11 Apr 1914, 187. "Florence Reed Marries," *NYDM,* 20 Nov 1915, 7:1 ("The couple are now playing a motion picture engagement.").

Williams, Margot [actress]. No data found. AMD, p. 367. "Margot Williams in MinA,"' *MPW,* 6 Nov 1915, 1160.

Williams, Marie [actress] (b. 1921–5 Jul 1967 [46?], Encino CA; heart attack). AS, p. 1155. BHD, p. 338.

Williams, Percy G[arnett] [stage/film actor] (b. Baltimore MD, 1857–21 Jul 1923 [66]), East Islip, LI NY; cirrhosis of the liver and heart disease). m. Ida. (Stage debut: Colonel Sinn's Theatre, Baltimore MD; Park Theatre, Brooklyn NY; Holliday St. Theatre Stock Co.) "Percy G. Williams, Long Ill, Dies at 66; Vaudeville Head Who Sold His Theatres to Keith for More than $5,000,000 [Apr 1912]; Began Career as Actor; Theatre Builder Brought Many Famous European Variety Stars to His Local Circuit," *NYT,* 22 Jul 1923, 24:5. "Services for Percy G. Williams," *NYT,* 25 Jul 1923, 11:6 (home estate: Pineacres, E. Islip, LI NY). AS, p. 1155. "Whole Town of Islip Turns Out for 'P.G.'s Services; Over 200 Journey from New York to Long Island—Vaudeville Manager's Remains Interred at Greenwood—Wilton Lackaye Makes Address," *Variety,* 26 Jul 1923.

Williams, Ralph V[aughan] [actor] (b. England, 1873–26 Aug 1958 [85?], London, England). AS, p. 1155.

Williams, Robert G. [actor] (b. Morgantown NC, 15 Sep 1897–3 Nov 1931 [34], Los Angeles CA; peritonitis). "Williams Dies in L.A. as Film Career Builds," *Variety,* 10 Nov 1931 (age 31). AS, p. 1155. BHD1, p. 588 (b. Morganton NC). IFN, p. 319 (b. 1899). Truitt, p. 353 (b. 1899).

Williams, Shirley [cinematographer]. No data found. FDY, p. 471.

Williams, Spencer [actor] (b. Vidalia LA, 14 Jul 1893–13 Dec 1969 [76], West Los Angeles LA; kidney infection). m. Eula. "Spencer Williams," *Variety,* 24 Dec 1969 (b. British West Indies). AS, p. 1155. BHD1, p. 588. IFN, p. 320. Truitt, p. 353.

Williams, Stanton (brother of Esther Williams) [child actor] (b. 1913–1929 [16]).

Williams, [Charles] Sumner [scenarist/industrialist] (b. San Francisco CA, 20 Jul 1889–22 May 1952 [62], Friendship ME)). m. Juliet Capers, 30 Apr 1924, Portsmouth NH. (Edison.) AMD, p. 367. "Alliance of Author and Director; A Rational Method Worked Out by the Edison Company on 'At the Rainbow's End,'" *MPW,* 22 Jan 1916, 586. "Williams, Charles Sumner," *The National Cyclopedia of American Biography,* 46 (1967), p. 559.

Williams, W. Emerson [singer] (b.

Centerville OH, 1882?–30 Oct 1940 [58], New York NY). m. Jane. "W. Emerson Williams," *NYT,* 1 Nov 1940, 25:1 ("one of the earliest singers for phonograph records"). "W. Emerson Williams," *Variety,* 6 Nov 1940 (pioneer radio and phonograph singer).

Williams, Walter [stage/film actor] (b. London, England, 15 Oct 1887–29 Oct 1940 [53], New York NY). "Walter Williams," *Variety,* 27 Nov 1940 (London musical comedy star). AS, p. 1155 (d. London, England). BHD, p. 338.

Williams, William A[lbert] [actor] (b. 1869–4 May 1942 [72], Los Angeles CA). AMD, p. 367. AS, p. 1155. BHD1, p. 588. IFN, p. 320. "Two Powers Players," *MPW,* 13 Apr 1912, 126.

Williams, Zack [actor] (b. LA, 6 Oct 1884–25 May 1958 [73], Los Angeles Co. CA). AS, p. 1155 (b. St. Louis LA). BHD1, p. 588. IFN, p. 320.

Williamson, Alan J. [actor/executive] (b. Kent, England, 3 Feb 1886–3 May 1952 [66], Sydney, New South Wales, Australia). BHD, p. 338; BHD2, p. 285.

Williamson, George M. [actor/producer] (b. 1885–23 May 1956 [71?], Denver CO). AMD, p. 367. BHD, p. 338; BHD2, p. 285. "Williamson Brothers to Make Films," *MPW,* 17 Feb 1917, 1013.

Williamson, James A. [actor/director/producer] (b. Howe, Scotland, 1855–1933 [78?]). AS, p. 1155. BHD, p. 338; BHD2, p. 285.

Williamson, James C. [actor/director/producer] (b. Mercer PA, 26 Aug 1845–6 Jul 1913 [67], Paris, France). BHD2, p. 285.

Williamson, John Ernest [actor/producer/executive] (b. Liverpool, England, 1881–15 Jul 1966 [85?], Nassau, Bahamas). m. Lilah Freeland, 1927 (d. 1992). (Submarine Film Corp., 1914; MGM.) (First film: *Thirty Leagues Under the Sea.*) Brian Taves, "A Pioneer Under the Sea: Library Restores Rare Film Footage," *Library of Congress Information Bulletin,* 55, 16 Sep 1996, 315–18.

Williamson, Melvin E. [director] (b. Memphis TN, 1900–15 Feb 1959 [58?], Scott Air Force Base IL). AS, p. 1155. BHD, p. 338; BHD2, p. 285.

Williamson, Robert (Bob) [actor] (b. Glasgow, Scotland, 1885–13 Mar 1949 [64], Brunswick Home, Amityville LI NY). "Robert Williamson," *NYT,* 15 Mar 1949, 27:3. AS, p. 1156. BHD, p. 338. IFN, p. 320. George A. Katchmer, "Forgotten Cowboys and Cowgirls—Part X," *CI,* 182 (Aug 1990), 41.

Williamson, Robin E. [actor/director] (b. Denver CO, 30 Jun 1889–21 Feb 1935 [45], Los Angeles CA; heart attack). (Sennett.) "Robin E. Williamson," *Variety,* 27 Feb 1935. AS, p. 1156 (d. 23 Feb). BHD, p. 338; BHD2, p. 285.

Willingham, Harry G. [actor] (b. 1881?–17 Nov 1943 [62], No. Hollywood CA; suicide with a gun to his head). AS, p. 1156 (Willinghan). BHD1, p. 588. IFN, p. 320. Truitt, p. 353.

Willis, Edwin B[ooth] [set decorator] (b. 1893?–26 Nov 1963 [70], Los Angeles CA; cancer). (Goldwyn, 1919; MGM.) "Edwin B. Willis," *Variety,* 4 Dec 1963 (AA for *Little Women,* MGM, 1949). AS, p. 1156 (b. 1898). BHD2, p. 285.

Willis, F. McGrew [scenarist] (aka Willis Woods, b. Pleasonton IA, 1890?–13 Oct 1957 [67], Menlo Park CA). m. **Viola Barry** (d. 1964). "F. McGrew Willis," *Variety,* 23 Oct 1957. AMD, p. 368. AS, p. 1156. BHD2, p. 285. FDY, p. 439. "F.N. Engages Willis," *MPW,* 9 Jun 1923, 515.

Willis, Hubert [actor] (b. Reading, Yorkshire, England-d. 29 Sep 1984, Suffolk, England). BHD, p. 339.

Willis, Leo [actor] (b. OK, 5 Jan 1890–10 Apr 1952 [62], Monterey Co. CA). (Metro.) AS, p. 1156 (d. LA CA). BHD1, p. 588. IFN, p. 320.

Willis, Leo [actor] (b. OK, 5 Jan 1890–10 Apr 1952 [62]). George Katchmer, "Leo Willis," *CI,* 255 (Sep 1996), 36–37.

Willis, Lloyd [executive] (b. Church Creek MD, 1878–12 Jun 1926 [48?], New York NY). BHD2, p. 285.

Willis, Louise [stage/film actress] (b. 1879?–2 Jan 1929 [49], Chicago IL; heart attack). m. Phil S. Greiner. "Louise Willis," *Variety,* 9 Jan 1929. AS, p. 1156. BHD, p. 339.

Willis, Paul [actor] (b. Chicago IL, 9 Apr 1900–3 Nov 1960 [60], West Hollywood CA). BHD1, p. 619.

Willis, Richard [writer/publicist/actor] (b. London, England, 15 Oct 1876–8 Apr 1945 [68], Los Angeles CA; cerebral hemorrhage). AMD, p. 368. AS, p. 1156. BHD1, p. 588; BHD2, p. 285. IFN, p. 320. "Richard Willis," *MPW,* 25 Jan 1913, 358.

Willoughby, Lewis/Louis [actor] (b. England, 10 Jul 1876–12 Sep 1968 [92], Clearwater FL). m. **Olga Petrova** (d. 1977). AMD, p. 368. AS, p. 1156. IFN, p. 320. "Willoughby to Support Miss Storey," *MPW,* 23 Mar 1918, 1682.

Willowbird, Chris [actor] (b. NM, 20 Feb 1887–16 Dec 1968 [81], Los Angeles CA). BHD1, p. 588.

Wills, Brember [actor] (*né* Brember Le Couteur, b. Reading, England, 1883–1 Dec 1948 [65?], England). AS, p. 1156.

Wills, Drusilla [stage/film actress] (b. London, England, 14 Nov 1884–6 Aug 1951 [66], London, England). "Drusilla Wills," *Variety,* 15 Aug 1951, p. 63:2. AS, p. 1156 (d. 11 Aug). BHD1, p. 589. IFN, p. 320.

Wills, Nat M. [actor] (*né* Louis McGrath Wills, b. Fredericksburg VA, 11 Jul 1873–9 Dec 1917 [44], Woodcliff NJ; accidental poisoning with carbon monoxide). AMD, p. 368. AS, p. 1156. BHD, p. 339. IFN, p. 320. "Nat Willis Becomes a Photo-Player," *MPW,* 22 Apr 1911, 874–75. "Nat Willis Will Soon Make His Debut," *MPW,* 1 Jul 1911, 1508.

Wills, Norma (mother of **Monte Collins, Jr.**) [actress]. No data found. m. **Monte Collins, Sr.** (d. 1951). Ragan 2, p. 1828.

Wills, Ross B. [singer/actor/scenarist] (b. 9 Dec 1844–14 Mar 1933 [88]). FDY, p. 439.

Wills, Walter [actor] (b. New York NY, 22 Aug 1881–18 Jan 1967 [85], Los Angeles CA). AS, p. 1156. BHD1, p. 589. IFN, p. 320. Truitt, p. 353.

Willson, Dixie [title writer/writer]. No data found. AMD, p. 368. "Girl to Title New Neilan Film," *MPW,* 30 Oct 1926, 548. "Dixie Willson Story Chosen For Filming," *MPW,* 8 Jan 1927, 118.

Wilmer-Brown, Maisie [actress] (b. 1892–13 Feb 1973 [80?], London, England). AS, p. 1156. BHD, p. 339.

Wilmont, Elaine [scenarist]. No data found. FDY, p. 439.

Wilsey, Jay C. (Buffalo Bill, Jr.) [actor] (b. Hillsdale MO, 6 Feb 1896–25 Oct 1961 [65], Los Angeles Co. CA). (Pathé; Action; Artclass; Arrow; Rayart; Universal; American; Columbia.) AS, p. 1157 (b. Hillsdale WY; d. Honolulu HI). BHD1, p. 589 (b. Hillsboro MO). IFN, p. 320. Katz, p. 180 (b. Cheyenne WY, 1902). Buck Rainey, *Wild West Stars Magazine,* 1977. Ed Wyatt, "Buffalo Bill, Jr.," *CI,* 147, Sep 1987, C20 (b. Hillsdale WY). George Katchmer, "Remembering the Great Silents," *CI,* 222 (Dec 1993), C16-C17 (b. Hillsdale WY, near Cheyenne).

Wilshin, Sunday [actress] (*née* Mary Aline Wilshin, b. Acton, England, 26 Feb 1905 [extrait de naissance no. 39/1905]-19 Mar 1991 [86], Broomfield, England [extrait de décès no. 145/1991]). AS, p. 1157. BHD1, p. 589.

Wilson, Al [cinematographer]. No data found (may be one below). FDY, p. 471.

Wilson, Al [actor] (b. KY-d. 5 Sep 1932, Cleveland OH). BHD1, p. 589. "Dares Death for New Record; Aviator Changes Planes Two Thousand Feet Above Earth," *LA Times,* 10 Jan 1920, II, 1 (may be another Wilson).

Wilson, Al [actor] (b. Harrisburg KY-d. 6 Mar 1936, New York NY). "Al Wilson," *Variety,* 121, 11 Mar 1936, 63:3. AS, p. 1157. IFN, p. 320.

Wilson, Al [vaudevillian/publicist/producer] (b. 1888?–20 Dec 1964 [76], Cleveland OH). m. Anna. (Paramount.) "Al Wilson," *Variety,* 237, 23 Dec 1964, 55:2. AS, p. 1157.

Wilson, Alice Lillian Houghton [actress] (aka Alice Rae, b. Offalan MO, 14 Jun 1887–12 May 1944 [56], Los Angeles CA). m. **Tod Browning,** 9 Jun 1917, New Rochelle NY (d. 1962). BHD, p. 339.

Wilson, Ben[jamin] **F**[ranklin] [actor/director/producer/writer] (b. Corning IA, 7 Jul 1876–25 Aug 1930 [54], Glendale CA; heart attack). m. Jessie. (Edison; Nestor.) "Benjamin F. Wilson," *Variety,* 3 Sep 1930 (b. Clinton IA). AMD, p. 368. AS, p. 1157 (b. Coming IA). BHD1, p. 589; BHD2, p. 285. FSS, p. 291. IFN, p. 320. Truitt, p. 353 (b. Clinton IA). WWS, p. 264. "New Edison Series; Will Feature Hanshew Detective Stories in Twelve Productions—Ben Wilson in Leading Role," *MPW,* 1 Nov 1913, 479 (b. Centerville IA). "Edison Touches Popular Chord," *MPW,* 3 Jan 1914, 28–29. "Ben Wilson, director; Is Also Author and Leading Man in the First Film He Produced," *NYDM,* 25 Feb 1914, 32:2 (in *When the Cartridges Failed,* with Wilson as scenarist/actor/director). "Ben Wilson; Director, Author, Leading Man," *MPW,* 28 Feb 1914, 1069. Thornton FIsher, "An Evening with Ben Wilson," *MPW,* 18 Apr 1914, 335. "Ben Wilson Builds Himself a House," *MPW,* 9 Oct 1915, 291. "Ben Wilson," *MPW,* 13 Jan 1917, 234. Neil G. Caward, "Screen Gossip," *Picture-Play Magazine,* Sep 1917, 108 (to make personal appearances at theaters by popular demand). "Ben Wilson in Another Accident," *MPW,* 22 Dec 1917, 1787. "Ben Wilson Re-Engaged by Universal," *MPW,* 12 Apr 1919, 216. "Ben Wilson to Release Ten Thru Grand-Asher," *MPW,* 10 Nov 1923, 249. Billy H. Doyle, "Lost Players," *CI,* 180, Jun 1990, 22–23.

Wilson, Bert [actor/photographer] (b. 1871–14 Oct 1956 [85?], Los Angeles Co. CA). (First feature: *Dolly's Vacation,* 1918.) BHD, p. 339 (Burton S. Wilson). George Katchmer, "Remembering the Great Silents," *CI,* 217 (Jul 1993), 56.

Wilson, Carey [scenarist/producer] (b. Philadelphia PA, 19 May 1889–1 Feb 1962 [72],

Los Angeles CA; stroke). m. **Carmelita Geraghty** (d. 1966). (Peerless, Ft. Lee NJ; Metro.) "Carey Wilson," *Variety*, 7 Feb 1962. AMD, p. 368. AS, p. 1157. BHD2, p. 286. FDY, p. 439. IFN, p. 320. "Wilson Is Made Associate Editor," *MPW*, 1 Apr 1922, 474. Carey Wilson, "Pearls from the Pacific, " *Classic*, Mar 1923, 61, 85. "Signs New Contract," *MPW*, 24 Mar 1923, 404. Tom Waller, "Carey Wilson," *MPW*, 14 May 1927, 94–95.

Wilson, Charles Cahill [actor] (b. New York NY, 29 Jul 1894–7 Jan 1948 [53], Los Angeles Co. CA; hemorrhage of the esophagus). AS, p. 1157. BHD1, p. 589. IFN, p. 320.

Wilson, Charles J., Jr. [scenarist]. No data found.

Wilson, Cherry [scenarist]. No data found. FDY, p. 439.

Wilson, Clarence H[ummell] [actor] (b. Cincinnati OH, 17 Nov 1876–5 Oct 1941 [64], Los Angeles CA). (Republic; Roach; MGM; Paramount.) "Clarence H. Wilson," *Variety*, 15 Oct 1941 (in silents ca. 1920). AS, p. 1157. BHD, p. 339. IFN, p. 320. Truitt, p. 354.

Wilson, Constance (sister of **Lois**, **Janice** and Roberta [aka Diana Kane] **Wilson**) [actress] (b. 1905–4 Jan 1968 [62?], Philadelphia PA). AMD, p. 368. "Constance Wilson Leading Woman," *MPW*, 14 Apr 1923, 773. Harry Carr, "The Hollywood Boulevardier Chats," *CLassic*, XVIII, Sep 1923, 60 (photo and quip; 1 film: *Fair Week*, 1924).

Wilson, Edna Mae [actress] (*née* Edna Bruns, b. 1880?–23 Jul 1960 [80], New York NY [Death Certificate Index No. 16024; M.E. Case No. 5922]). m. **Francis Wilson** (d. 1935). "Edna Wilson," *Variety*, 3 Aug 1960 ("one of the original Gibson Girls in early films"). AS, p. 1157. Truitt, p. 354.

Wilson, Edward L. [actor] (b. 1916–6 Feb 1975 [58?]). AS, p. 1157 (*né* Edmund Wilson, b. 8 May 1918). BHD1, p. 589.

Wilson, Elsie Jane [actress/director] (b. Australia, 7 Nov 1890–16 Jan 1965 [74], Los Angeles CA). m. **Rupert Julian** (d. 1943). AMD, p. 368. AS, p. 1157 (b. New Zealand). BHD, p. 339 (b. New Zealand). IFN, p. 320. "Elsie Wilson and Rupert Julian with Rex," *MPW*, 4 Jul 1914, 79. "Woman Director Dragged Through Street," *MPW*, 25 Jan 1919, 474–75.

Wilson, Francis [stage/film actor] (b. Philadelphia PA, 7 Feb 1854–7 Oct 1935 [81], New York NY). m. (1) Mira Barni (d. 1915); (2) **Edna** Bruns (d. 1960). (Sennett.) "Francis Wilson," *Variety*, 9 Oct 1935. AS, p. 1157. BHD, p. 339. IFN, p. 320. Truitt, p. 354. Cover, *NYDM*, 11 Aug 1915 (with Cyril Maude, Marie Tempest, and Graham Browne, all Frohman stage players).

Wilson, Frank H. [actor] (b. New York NY, 4 May 1886–16 Feb 1956 [70], Queens NY). "Frank H. Wilson," *Variety*, 22 Feb 1956. AS, p. 1157 (d. Bronx NY). IFN, p. 320.

Wilson, Frederick L. [actor] (d. 2 Oct 1920, London, England). BHD, p. 339.

Wilson, Harold "Hal" [actor/assistant director] (b. New York NY, 2 Oct 1861–22 May 1933 [71], Los Angeles CA; cerebral thrombosis). (Vitagraph.) "Hal Wilson," *Variety*, 30 May 1933. AMD, p. 368. AS, p. 1158. BHD1, p. 589. IFN, p. 320. Truitt, p. 354 (b. 1887). "Harold Wilson Leaves Vitagraph," *MPW*, 7 Dec 1912, 988 (one of the earliest players at Vitagraph). "Harold Wilson," *MPW*, 1 Aug 1914, 681. George Katchmer, "Remembering the Great Silents," *CI*, 252 (Jun 1996), 46, 48. (Note: If Harold Wilson is the same as Harry Wilson, husband of Maryon Aye, *see* entry for the latter, *LA Times*, 27 Feb 1920.)

Wilson, Mrs. Hal [actress]. No data found. m. **Harold Wilson** (d. 1933). "Mrs. Hal Wilson Injured," *MPW*, 26 Apr 1913, 363.

Wilson, Helene [actress] (b. 1888–29 Jul 1981 [93?], Woodland Hills CA). AS, p. 1158. BHD1, p. 589.

Wilson, Jack [actor] (b. San Francisco CA, 25 Dec 1876–Nov 1931 [56], New York NY; suicide by shooting). m. (1) Ada Lane (d. 1914); **Kitty Gordon** (d. 1974). "Jack Wilson Suicide While Callers Wait," *Variety*, 3 Nov 1931 (age 50). AS, p. 1158.

Wilson, James [cinematographer]. No data found. FDY, p. 471.

Wilson, Janice (sister of **Constance**, **Lois** and Roberta Wilson) [actress] (b. IL, 28 Oct 1900–5 Nov 1982 [82], Encino CA). BHD, p. 339. "Another Wilson Sister," *LA Times*, 25 Feb 1920, III, p. 4 ("Janis" Wilson to play in *The Pavillion on the Links*, produced by Maurice Tourneur).

Wilson, Jay [actor] (b. La Crosse WI, 1871?–27 Jul 1940 [69], New York NY). "Jay Wilson," *Variety*, 7 Aug 1940. AS, p. 1158. BHD1, p. 590.

Wilson, Jerome N. [publicist] (b. 1889?–3 Jun 1943 [54], New York NY). "Jerome Wilson," *Variety*, 9 Jun 1943. AMD, p. 368. AS, p. 1158. BHD2, p. 286 (d. 1 Jun). "Jerome Wilson a Universal Publicitor," *MPW*, 12 May 1917, 956.

Wilson, John Fleming [scenarist] (b. 1877–5 Mar 1922 [45?], Venice CA; from burns received when his dressing robe caught on fire from a small gas heater). "Fleming Wilson Dies," *Variety*, 17 Mar 1922, 46:4 (parents from Hemet CA). AMD, p. 368. BHD2, p. 286. "John Fleming WIlson Enters the Moving Picture Field," *MPW*, 16 Oct 1920, 985. "Jerome Fleming Wilson Has Signed with Ince," *MPW*, 1 Oct 1921, 560.

Wilson, Lois (sister of **Constance**, **Janice** and Roberta [aka Diana Kane] Wilson) [stage/film/TV actress: Wampas Star, 1922] (b. Pittsburgh PA, 28 Jun 1894–3 Mar 1988 [93?], Reno NV; pneumonia). (Began 1915; Universal.) "Lois Wilson, Actress of Stage, Television and Silent-Film Era," *NYT*, 10 Mar 1988, D22:4. "Lois Wilson," *Variety*, 16 Mar 1988. AMD, p. 368. AS, p. 1158. BHD1, p. 590. BR, pp. 227–32 (d. 1990). FFF, p. 48. FSS, p. 291. HCH, p. 85. Katz, p. 1241. MH, p. 143. 1921 Directory, p. 278. "Lois Wilson," SOS, pp. 246–72 (b. 28 Jun 1894). William M. Drew, *Speaking of Silents* (Vestal NY: Vestal Press, Ltd., 1989), pp. 246–72. "Beauty Contestant Gets Her Wish," *MPW*, 18 Sep 1915, 1976. "Lois Wilson," *MPW*, 26 Feb 1916, 1303. "Warren Kerrigan's New Leading Lady," *MPW*, 12 Aug 1916, 1105. "Lois Wilson Captivates Los Angeles Audience," *MPW*, 27 Oct 1917, 517. "Lois Wilson," *MPW*, 19 Jan 1918, 367. "Rainbow Veterans Honor Player," *MPW*, 24 Jul 1920, 487 (in "hometown," Birmingham AL). "Lois Wilson Engaged for Five Years to Play Leads in Paramount Pictures," *MPW*, 2 Oct 1920, 667. Gordon Gassoway, "Lois the Lovable; 'An afternoon chat with Lois Wilson is like keeping an appointment with a summer breeze,'" *Classic*, Sep 1922, 38–39, 75. Alma M. Talley, "Who Is the Girl on the Cover?; Meet Miss Lois Wilson, one of moviedom's loveliest and most charming women, and learn how she climbed the steep road of fame," *MW*, 5 Jan 1924, 17, 31. "Lois Wilson Loaned," *MPW*, 23 Feb 1924, 645. Gladys Hall, "Why Did They Choose Her?," *MW*, 2 Aug 1924, 4–5. "But Lois Shoots Craps!; Between Scenes, Some Stars May Prefer to Gossip, or Read, or Talk to Interviewers, or Solve Puzzles, or Snooze—Now Listen to Miss Wilson," *MPC*, May 1925, 20–21, 88. Joseph Faus, "The Girl of Today…Plays Fair and We Criticize Her," *MM*, I, Dec 1925, 23–24, 115. "Miss Wilson Leaves F.P.," *MPW*, 15 Jan 1927, 175. Ramon Romeo, "Reeling Down Broadway; Lois Prefers Sophistication," *Paris and Hollywood Screen Secrets Magazine*, May 1927, 63 (severed her connection with Famous Players-Lasky, where she had been for over ten years, "to get away from the namby-pamby parts of sweet damsels that has been her fate in the past." She was to appear on Broadway in *Broadway Nights* for Robert Kane, "to show off the fascinating new sophistication that she has acquired since coming to Broadway a little over a year ago."). "Columbia Pictures Signs Lois Wilson," *MPW*, 2 Jul 1927, 30. "Columbia Signs Lois Wilson for 5 Films," *MPW*, 24 Dec 1927, 12. Corinne Arkins, "Lois Wilson's Fad," *Screenland*, Dec 1927, 52, 78. Gladys Hall, "Confessions of the Stars VII; Lois Wilson Tells Her Untold Tale," *MPC*, Apr 1929, 20–21, 74–75. Murray Summers, "An Interview with Lois Wilson," *Filmograph*, I, No. 4 (1970), 2–10. Wilson's papers are housed at Kent State.

Wilson, Margery [actress/writer/director] (*née* Sara Barker Strayer, b. Gracey KY, 31 Oct 1896–21 Jan 1986 (89], Arcadia CA; heart attack in her sleep). *I Found My Way* (Philadelphia: Lippincott, 1956). "Margery Wilson," *NYT*, 5 Feb 1986, 5:5. "Margery Wilson," *Variety*, 5 Feb 1986 (d. Alhambra CA). AMD, p. 368. AS, p. 1158 (d. Alhambra CA). BHD, p. 339 (b. 1897). Anthony Slide, *Early Women Directors* (NY: A.S. Barnes and Co., 1977), pp. 62–72 (b. 1898). "Margery Wilson a Triangle Star," *MPW*, 14 Jul 1917, 269. "Margery Wilson Becomes Director," *MPW*, 3 Jul 1920, 93. George A. Katchmer, "Forgotten Cowboys and Cowgirls—Part XV," *CI*, 192 (Jun 1991), 56.

Wilson, Millard K[ent] [actor] (b. Louisville KY, 1890?–5 Oct 1933 [43], Long Beach CA; compound skull fracture received when his car collided with a truck). m. **Dorothy Wood**, 21 Aug 1925. (Universal; Paramount; Fox; Metro.) "Millard K. Wilson," *Variety*, 10 and 17 Oct 1933 (d. 9 Oct). AS, p. 1158 (Millard Kenneth Wilson, d. 9 Oct). BHD1, p. 590. IFN, p. 320.

Wilson, Mortimer [composer/conductor] (b. Chariton IA, 6 Aug 1876–27 Jan 1932 [55], New York NY). m. Hettie Lewis (d. 1948). "Mortimer Wilson," *Variety*, 2 Feb 1932. "Mrs. Mortimer Wilson," *NYT*, 19 Sep 1948, 76:6. ASCAP 66, p. 795. AS, p. 1158.

Wilson, Olivia McBride [actress] (b. Hemet CA, 5 Dec 1895–27 Aug 1976 [80]). BHD1, p. 619. IFN, p. 321 (Olivia Hodge Wilson).

Wilson, Robert E. [actor] (b. 1877?–1 Jul 1933 [56]). AMD, p. 368. IFN, p. 320 (Bobby Wilson). "Robert E. Wilson Joins Metro-Drew Staff," *MPW*, 10 Jun 1916, 1857. "The Roll of Honor," *MPW*, 4 Aug 1917, 807.

Wilson, Roberta [actress] (b. TX, 11 Jun 1905–2 Feb 1972 [66], Los Angeles CA; pulmonary embolism). "Roberta Wilson," *Variety*, 16 Feb 1972 (age 68). AS, p. 1158. BHD, p. 339. IFN, p. 321.

Wilson, Roy [actor] (b. 1902–25 Jun 1932 [30?], Dry Lake CA). BHD1, p. 590.

Wilson, Thomas H. [actor] (b. Helena MT, 27 Aug 1880–19 Feb 1965 [84], Woodland Hills CA). AS, p. 1159. BHD1, p. 590. IFN, p. 321. George Katchmer, "Remembering the Great Silents," *CI,* 149 (Mar 1996), 50.

Wilson, W. Cronin [playwright/stage/film actor] (b. 1877?–16 Feb 1934 [ca. 56], Charing Cross Hospital, London, England; double pneumonia). "W. Cronin Wilson," *Variety,* 113, 6 Mar 1934, 71:1. BHD1, p. 590.

Wilson, Walter M. [actor/stage director] (b. 1874?–13 Nov 1926 [52], New Haven CT). "Walter M. Wilson," *Variety,* 17 Nov 1926. AS, p. 1159.

Wilson, Wendell C. [actor] (b. 1889?–9 Jan 1927 [38?], Vancouver, B.C., Canada; pneumonia). AS, p. 1159. BHD, p. 340. Truitt, p. 354.

Wilson, William [actor] (*né* William Lisowski, b. 1898?–17 Oct 1926 [28], Saranac Lake NY). "William Wilson," *Variety,* 11 Mar 1936. AS, p. 1159.

Wilson, William F. [actor] (b. 1894?–10 May 1956 [62], Woodland Hills CA). AS, p. 1159. BHD1, p. 590. IFN, p. 321. Truitt, p. 354.

Wilson, William J. [director] (b. Scotland, 1874?–2 Mar 1936 [62], Cleveland OH). "William J.Wilson," *Variety,* 11 Mar 1936. AS.p. 1159 (Williams J. Wilson).

Wilton, Eric F. [actor] (b. London, England, 6 Nov 1882–23 Feb 1957 [74], Los Angeles Co. CA). AS, p. 1159 (d. England). BHD1, p. 590.

Wilton, Robb [actor] (b. Liverpool, England, 28 Aug 1881–1 May 1957 [75], London, England). BHD1, p. 590.

Wiltsie, Simeon [actor] (b. New York NY, 1853–12 Jan 1918 [64?], Englewood NJ). AS, p. 1159. BHD, p. 340.

Wiltsie, Simeon S. [actor] (b. New York NY, 1853–13 Jan 1918 [64?], Englewood NJ). AS, p. 1159.

Wiman, Dwight Deere [actor/producer] (b. Moline IL, 8 Aug 1895–20 Jan 1951 [55], Hudson NY; heart attack). m. (1) Dorothea Stephens—div. 1946. "Dwight D. Wiman, Producer, 55, Dies; Brought 56 Plays and Musicals to Broadway During Career—Sponsor of 'Country Girl,'" *NYT,* 21 Jan 1951, 76:3 (formed the Film Guild in 1920 with Osgood Perkins and Glenn Hunter, with studios at Astoria, LI NY; dissolved in 1924). "Dwight Deere Wiman," *Variety,* 24 Jan 1951 (Wiman joined his friend Frank Tuttle in New York at the Film Guild and "started writing film continuities, grinding cameras, and playing secondary villains, the way personnel was wont to do in those pioneer days"). AS, p. 1159. BHD, p. 340; BHD2, p. 287. Susan Elizabeth Brady, "The Young Adventurers," *Classic,* Apr 1923, 26–27 (discusses Film Guild members).

Wimer, Miguel [actor] (*né* Miguel Wimer Del Mar, b. Mexico, 4 Feb 1885–3 Mar 1941 [56], Mexico City, Mexico; auto accident). AS, p. 1159.

Wimperis, Arthur H. [author/actor/lyricist/scenarist] (b. London, England, 3 Dec 1874–14 Oct 1953 [78], Maidenhead, Berkshire, England). "Arthur Wimperis, British Scenarist; Dies in England at Age of 78—Adapted 'Mrs. Miniver' [AA] and 'Random Harvest' for Films," *NYT,* 15 Oct 1953, 33:3 (wrote *I'm So Merry and Gay* for *The Arcadians*). "Arthur H. Wimperus," *Variety,* 21 Oct 1953. AS, p. 1159. BHD, p. 1159; BHD2, p. 286. IFN, p. 321.

Winans, James [actor] (b. New York NY, 1900–21 Jun 1926 [26?], Los Angeles CA; auto accident). AS, p. 1159.

Winant, Forrest George [actor] (b. New York NY, 21 Feb 1888–30 Jan 1928 [39], Alameda CA). "Forest George Winant," *Variety,* 8 Feb 1928. AS, p. 1159. BHD, p. 340. IFN, p. 321 (age 36).

Winar, Ernst [actor/director/producer] (*né* Wilhelm Joseph Karl Eichoff, b. Leiden, Holland, 3 Sep 1894–28 Jun 1978 [83], Leiden, Holland). AS, p. 1159. BHD, p. 340; BHD2, p. 286.

Winchester, Tarleton [*Telegraph* editor/publicist]. No data found. (Pathé; Paramount.) AMD, p. 368. "Winchester with Paramount," *NYDM,* 14 Apr 1915, 24:4. "Winchester with Pathé," *MPW,* 27 May 1916, 1520. "Parsons to Give Whole TIme to Advertising," *MPW,* 6 Apr 1918, 71.

Wincott, Rosalie Avolo [actress] (b. 1873–3 Nov 1951 [78], Los Angeles CA). AS, p. 1159 (d. 12 Nov). BHD, p. 340. IFN, p. 321.

Windeck, Agnes [actress] (*née* Agnes Sophie Albertine Windel, b. Hamburg, Germany, 27 Mar 1888–28 Sep 1975 [87], Berlin, Germany). AS, p. 1159.

Windermere, Fred C. [actor/director] (b. Muscatine IA, 15 Apr 1892–18 Mar 1970 [77], Newport Beach CA). AMD, p. 369. BHD, p. 340; BHD2, p. 286. "Schulberg Signs Windemere [sic]," *MPW,* 27 Jun 1925, 1001.

Windheim, Marek [actor/singer] (b. Warsaw, Poland, 1895–1 Dec 1960 [65?], New York NY). AS, p. 1159.

Windom, Lawrence C. [actor/director/producer] (b. New York NY, 1876). (World; Pathé, Vitagraph). AMD, p. 369. AS, p. 1159. BHD2, p. 286. "Lawrence C. Windom Signs with World," *MPW,* 18 May 1918, 1003.

Window, Muriel [Ziegfeld Follies/film actress/singer] (*née* Muriel Turnley, d. 19 Sep 1965, Pompano Beach FL). "Muriel Window," *Variety,* 240, 29 Sep 1965, 63:3 (introduced *Till We Meet Again* and *I'm Forever Blowing Bubbles.* "The Muriel Cigar…reportedly was named after the former actress."). BHD, p. 340.

Windsor, Claire [extra/film/stage/TV actress: Wampas Star, 1922] (*née* Claire Viola Cronk, b. Cawker City KS, 14 Apr 1897–23 Oct 1972 [75], Los Angeles CA; heart attack). m. (1) David William Bowles (1 son, William Bowles, Jr.); (2) **Bert Lytell,** 14 May 1925, Juarez, Mexico—div. 1927 (d. 1954). (Goldwyn; MGM; Fox; last film: *How Doooo You Do?,* PRC, 1946.) "Claire Windsor, Actress, 74, Dead; Blonde Star of the Silent Screen for a Decade," *NYT,* 25 Oct 1972, 50:3 (*née* Clara Viola Cronk, age 74). "Claire Windsor," *Variety,* 1 Nov 1972 (b. Coffee City KS; no age). AMD, p. 369. AS, p. 1160. BHD1, p. 591 (b. 1895). FFF, p. 38 (b. 1898). FSS, p. 292. IFN, p. 321 (b. 1898). Katz, p. 1242. MH, p. 143 (b. 1898). "Claire Windsor," WBO2, pp. 186–87 (b. 1897). "Lost Two Days," *MPW,* 6 Aug 1921, 591 (horse riding accident; suffered head injury). "Goldwyn Signs Claire Windsor," *MPW,* 15 Jul 1922, 216. Regina Cannon, "Can a Prudish Girl Be Popular?," *MW,* 2 Jun 1923, 7, 29. Regina Cannon, "The Blonde Beauty of Pictures," *MW,* IV, 14 Jun 1924, 7. "Signs New Contract," *MPW,* 11 Jul 1925, 196. Katherine Albert, "Claire Windsor Talks of Herself; The Lovely Wife of Bert Lytell is an Ardent Advocate of Careers for Married Women," *Cinema Arts,* Dec 1926, 28–29. "Columbia Signs Three Stars of the First Magnitude," *MPW,* 30 Jul 1927, 331. "Claire Windsor Is Signed by Gotham," *MPW,* 6 Aug 1927, 397. June Lee, "Dan Cupid's Bulletin Board," *Paris and Hollywood Screen Secrets,* Oct 1927, 35 (to divorce Lytell. "Miss Windsor gained considerable notoriety for her mysterious disappearance in 1921 while riding in the hills back of Hollywood."). Ruth Biery, "The Forbidden Friendship; Even the Public Took Part in the Parting of Claire Windsor and Buddy Rogers," *MPC,* Nov 1928, 37, 80. Al Bohrer, "Claire Windsor: One Fan's Fond Remembrance," *CI,* 290 (Aug 1999), 20–23 (includes filmography).

Wing, Ah [actor] (b. 10 Nov 1905-Nov 1989 [84?], New York NY). BHD, p. 340 (b. China, 23 Jul 1851–27 Feb 1941 [89], Weimar CA). George Katchmer, "Remembering the Great Silents," *CI,* 215 (May 1993), 49, 52.

Wing, Maria A. [scenarist]. No data found. m. **William E. Wing** (d. 1947). Edward Azlant, "Screenwriting for the early silent film: forgotten pioneers, 1897–1911," *Film History,* 9 (1997), 244.

Wing, Paul R. (father of Toby Wing) [assistant director] (b. 1891–29 May 1957 [66?], Portsmouth VA; heart attack). m. (daughter Toby b. 15 Jul 1916). (AA winner.) AS, p. 1160 (Toby Wing, b. 14 Jul 1913). BHD2, p. 286.

Wing, Ward [actor/scenarist/director] (b. Springfield MO, 18 Feb 1893–4 Jun 1945 [52], Los Angeles CA). m. **Lori Bara,** Nov 1927 (d. 1965). AMD, p. 369. AS, p. 1160. BHD1, p. 591; BHD2, p. 286. IFN, p. 321 (b. Springfield MS). "Wedding March," *MPW,* 3 Dec 1927, 23.

Wing, William E. [writer/scenarist] (b. ME, 1870?–10 Mar 1947 [77], Los Angeles CA). m. **Maria A.** (Staff writer for *NYDM;* Biograph; Selig; Fine Arts; Vitagraph; National.) "William E. Wing," *Variety,* 19 Mar 1947. AMD, p. 369. AS, p. 1160. BHD2, p. 286. FDY, p. 439. "William E. Wing," *MPW,* 19 Sep 1914, 1628. "W.E. Wing; Writing Scripts for Selig," *NYDM,* 21 Oct 1914, 34:2 (photo only). W.E. Wing, "Along the Pacific Coast," *NYDM,* 30 Jun 1915, 22:2 (last weekly column for the *NYDM.* "Multiplying duties in photoplay and writing fields, to which has been added the editorship of *The Script,* have urged us out as correspondent to the daddy film publication of them all.").

Wingart, Earl W. [publicist]. No data found. AMD, p. 369. "Wingart Puclibity Director," *MPW,* 23 Apr 1927, 703.

Winge, Oscar [actor/director] (b. Malmo, Sweden, 1884–3 May 1951 [67?], Malmo, Sweden). AS, p. 1160.

Wingfield, H. Conway [stage/film actor] (b. Bray, near Dublin, Ireland, 1866?–9 Feb 1948 [81], New York NY). (Wm. L. Sherrill Feature Corp.) "Conway Wingfield, Actor for 50 Years," *NYT,* 10 Feb 1948, 23:4. "Conway Wingfield," *Variety,* 18 Feb 1948. BHD1, p. 591 (b. 1872). IFN, p. 321.

Winkler, Max [President of Belwin, Inc.] (b. Reiszka, Bucovina, Rumania, 1888?–5 Oct 1965 [77], Miami Beach FL). "Max Winkler, 77, founder and president of Belwin, Inc., music publishers, in Miami Beach, Oct. 5," *NYT,* 11 Oct 1965, 61:7. "Max Winkler," *Variety,* 13 Oct 1965 ("pioneer in the production of background music used in the early days of motion pictures.").

Winlock, Isabel [actress] (b. 1873–10 Oct 1953 [80?], New York NY). AS, p. 1160.

Winn, Godfrey [actor/writer] (b. Birmingham, Warwick, England, 15 Oct 1906–19 Jun 1971 [64], England). AS, p. 1160 (b. 1908). BHD1, p. 591. IFN, p. 321 (age 62).

Winninger, Charles J. [stage/film actor] (b. Athens WI, 26 May 1884–27 Jan 1969 [84], Palm Springs CA). m. **Blanche Ring** (d. 1961); (2) Gertrude Walke. (L-KO.) "Charles Winninger Dies at 84; Was Cap'n Andy of 'Show Boat'; Stage and Film Star Made Biggest Hit in Musical—Began Career at 6," *NYT,* 29 Jan 1969, 41:1. "Charles Winninger," *Variety,* 5 Feb 1969. AMD, p. 369. AS, p. 1160. BHD1, p. 591. FSS, p. 292. IFN, p. 321. Katz, p. 1243. Truitt, p. 355. "Charles J. Winninger," *MPW,* 26 Jun 1915, 2103.

Winogardoff, Anatol [actor] (b. Russia, 1891–27 Apr 1980 [89?], Canoga Park CA). AS, p. 1160.

Winscott, Bruce [actor] (*né* Charles Bruce Winston, b. 4 Mar 1879–27 Sep 1946 [67], onboard ship in the Atlantic). AS, p. 1160.

Winslow, Dick [actor] (aka Dick Winslow Johnson, *né* Richard W. Johnson, b. Jennings LA, 25 Mar 1915–7 Feb 1991 [75], Los Angeles CA; complications from diabetes). "Dick Winslow," *Variety,* Feb 1991. AS, p. 1160. BHD1, p. 591 (d. North Hollywood CA). Ragan 2, p. 1838.

Winslow, Herbert Hall [playwright/scenarist] (b. Keokuk IA, 23 Nov 1865–1 Jun 1930 [64], Hastings-on-Hudson NY). "Herbert Hall Winslow," *Variety,* 4 Jun 1930. AMD, p. 369. AS, p. 1160 (b. 25 Nov). BHD2, p. 286. "Herbert Hall Winslow," *MPW,* 30 Jan 1915, 679.

Winslow, Herbert Lippincott [actor] (b. 1895–1918 [23?]). BHD, p. 340.

Winston, Charles Bruce [actor/producer/scenic designer] (b. Liverpool, England, 4 Mar 1879–27 Sep 1946 [67], at sea, bound for New York NY). "Bruce Winston, 67, A British Comedian; Actor, Producer and Scenery Designer Dies Aboard Ship [the *John Ericsson*]—Once Weighed 347," *NYT,* 28 Sep 1946, 17:3 (appeared in *The Thief of Bagdad, Children of Dreams* and *The Private Life of Don Juan*). "Charles Bruce Winston," *Variety,* 2 Oct 1946 (began 1919). AS, p. 1161. BHD1, p. 591. IFN, p. 321.

Winston, Charles L. [publicist]. No data found. AMD, p. 369. "Winston with Sunbeam," *MPW,* 25 Nov 1916, 1144.

Winston, Laura [actress] (d. 10 Apr 1951, Los Angeles Co. CA). BHD, p. 340.

Winter, Charles R. [actor] (b. 1876–29 Jun 1952 [76?], Redondo Beach CA). AS, p. 1161.

Winter, Jessie (b. London, England, 1887–8 Aug 1971 [84?], London, England). BHD1, p. 591.

Winter, Laska [actress] (b. St. Louis MO, 28 Aug 1905–8 Aug 1980 [74], South Pasadena CA). AS, p. 1161. BHD1, p. 591 (d. Atladena CA). Ragan 2, p. 1839.

WInter, Louise [scenarist]. No data found. AMD, p. 369. "Louise Winter Joins Selznick Scenario Staff," *MPW,* 15 Nov 1919, 334.

Winter, Percy [director] (b. Toronto, Canada, 16 Nov 1861–4 May 1928 [66], Boonton NJ). AMD, p. 369. BHD, p. 340; BHD2, p. 287. "Percy Winter with Raver Film," *MPW,* 6 Nov 1915, 1128.

Winter, Winona [actress/singer] (b. Huntsville AL, 1891?–27 Apr 1940 [49], Los Angeles CA). m. Norman Sper. "Winona Winter," *Variety,* 1 May 1940. AS, p. 1161. BHD, p. 340 (b. 1888). IFN, p. 321.

Wintermeier, Fritz [actor]. (Essanay.) No data found.

Winters, Roland [actor] (*né* Roland Winternitz, b. Boston MA, 22 Nov 1904–22 Oct 1989 [84], Englewood NJ; pulmonary embolism). m. twice. (Film debut: *The Firebrand,* 1922; bit.) "Roland Winters, 84; Played Charlie Chan," *NYT,* 25 Oct 1989, D29:5. "Roland Winters," *Variety,* 1 Nov 1989, p. 85. AS, p. 1161 (b. Englewood MA).

Winters, Sally [scenarist]. No data found. FDY, p. 439.

Winterstein, Eduard von (son of actress Luise Dub; father of actor Gustav von Wangenheim) [actor] (*né* Eduard Klemens von Wangenheim, b. Vienna, Austria, 1 Aug 1871–22 Jul 1961 [89], Berlin, Germany). Vittorio Martinelli, "Kino-Lieblinge," *Griffithiana,* 38/39 (Oct 1990), 72.

Winther, Carl Pagh [cinematographer] (b. Denmark, 1884–11 Apr 1954 [70?], Los Angeles CA). BHD2, p. 287.

Winthrop, Barbara [actress] (b. 1890–5 Sep 1927 [37?], New York NY). BHD, p. 340.

Winthrop, Joy [actress] (*née* Josephine Williams, b. Philadelphia PA, 10 Oct 1864–1 Apr 1950 [85], Los Angeles CA). AS, p. 1161. BHD1, p. 591 (b. 1905). IFN, p. 321. Truitt, p. 355.

Winton, Jane, "The Green-Eyed Goddess of Hollywood" [stage/film actress/singer/writer] (b. Philadelphia PA, 10 Oct 1905–22 Sep 1959 [53], New York NY [Death Certificate Index No. 20713 (Jane Gottlieb); age 51]). m. **Charles Arthur Kenyon,** 1927 (d. 1961); Michael T. Gottlieb. (WB; Fox; 1st National; MGM.) "Jane Winton, 51, Actress, Singer; Movie Performer in 1920's Dies—Opera Soprano Was Also Writer (*Park Avenue Doctor,* 1951] and Painter," *NYT,* 23 Sep 1959, 35:6 (age 51). "Jane Winton," *Variety,* 30 Sep 1959 (age 51). AMD, p. 369. AS, p. 1161. BHD1, p. 591. FSS, p. 292. IFN, p. 321. Truitt, p. 355. "Has Part in 'Golden Bed,'" *MPW,* 20 Sep 1924, 199. "Jane Winton Signed to Contract by Warner Bros.," *MPW,* 6 Feb 1926, 544. Norma Johnstone, "Starring Lady Luck," *MPC,* Jun 1926, 43, 77. "Wedding Bliss Ousts Divorce in Film Mecca," *MPW,* 9 Jul 1927, 81. "Jane Winton," *MPW,* 30 Jul 1927, 319. June Lee, "Dan Cupid's Bulletin Board," *Paris and Hollywood Screen Secrets,* Oct 1927, 35–36 (married Kenyon).

Winwood, Estelle [stage/film actress] (*née* Estelle Goodwin, b. Lee, England, 24 Jan 1883–20 Jun 1984 [101], Woodland Hills CA; heart attack). (Film debut: *The House of Trent,* 1933). AS, p. 1161. BHD1, p. 592. Elizabeth Heinemann, "Estelle Winwood Says American Actresses 'Put It All Over' Their English Sisters," *Motion Picture Magazine,* Feb 1918, 54–55 ("...the English girl is taught to conceal everything she feels. What we in England are taught is 'breeding' is our greatest handicap as artistes...I am getting my courage up to have a test picture made. If I 'register' I shall do Moving Picture work as a vacation pastime this winter, and I shall continue to play Sweetie in 'A Successful Calamity,' which reopened at the Booth Theater in September." Evidently, she only registered in sound films.).

Wirth, Leo [actor] (b. New York NY, 7 Nov 1887). BHD, p. 340.

Wirth, Louise Daniel [actress]. No data found. AMD, p. 369. "Miss Wirth in Thanhouser Film," *MPW,* 3 Jun 1916, 1675.

Wise, Harry [actor] (b. New York NY, 1871?–26 Dec 1947 [76], New York NY). "Harry Wise," *Variety,* 31 Dec 1947. AS, p. 1162. BHD, p. 340. IFN, p. 322.

Wise, Jack [actor] (b. PA, 2 Jan 1888–7 Mar 1954 [66], Los Angeles CA). AS, p. 1162 (d. 6 Mar). BHD1, p. 592. IFN, p. 322.

Wise, Thomas A[lfred] [stage/film actor] (b. Faversham, Kent, England, 23 Mar 1865–21 Mar 1928 [63], New York NY; asthmatic stroke and heart attack). m. Gertrude Whitty. (Stage debut: Dixon CA, Apr 1883; Broadway, Bijou Theatre, *Lost in New York,* Jun 1888; World.) "Tom Wise, Actor for 40 Years, Dies; Shepherd of Lambs, Who Would Have Been 63 Tomorrow, Succumbs in Hotel Here; Noted for Falstaff Role; Got His Chance in Part When James K. Hackett Was Injured—Many Stage Folk Pay Tribute," *NYT,* 22 Mar 1928, 25:3). "Tom Wise," *Variety,* 28 Mar 1928. AS, p. 1162. BHD, p. 340. IFN, p. 322. Truitt, p. 355.

Withbeck, Frank [actor/director/scenarist] (b. Rochester NY, 1882–23 Dec 1963 [81?]). AS, p. 1162.

Withee, Mabel [stage/film actress] (b. Detroit MI, 1900?–3 Nov 1952 [52?], Bayside, LI NY). (Frohman Amusement Corp.) m. Larry Puck, 1928. "Miss Withee, Played in Musical Comedies," *NYT,* 4 Nov 1952, 29:2. "Mabel Withee," *Variety,* 5 Nov 1952 (does not cite films). AS, p. 1162. BHD, p. 340.

Withers, Charles [actor] (b. Louisville KY, 1889–10 Jul 1947 [58?], Bayside NY). AS, p. 1162.

Withers, Grant [actor] (*né* Granville G. Withers, b. Pueblo CO, 17 Jan 1904–27 Mar 1959 [55], No. Hollywood CA; suicide with sleeping pills). m. **Loretta Young** (d. 2000); Estelita Rodriguez (d. 1966). "Grant Withers Dies at Home, on Coast," *NYT,* 28 Mar 1959, 8:3 ("Please forgive me, my family, I was so unhappy."). "Grant Withers," *Variety,* 1 Apr 1959 (age 55). AMD, p. 369. AS, p. 1162 (b. 17 Jun). BHD1, p. 592. FSS, p. 293. IFN, p. 322 (b. 1905). Katz, p. 1245. Truitt, p. 355. "Withers Signed by F.B.O.," *MPW,* 6 Feb 1926, 546. "Grant Withers," *MPW,* 24 Apr 1926, 602.

Withers, Isabella Irene [actress] (b. Frankton IN, 20 Jan 1896–3 Sep 1968 [72], Los Angeles CA). AS, p. 1162. BHD1, p. 592. IFN, p. 322.

Withey, Chester "Chet" [actor/director/writer] (b. Park City UT, 8 Nov 1887–6 Oct 1939 [51], Los Angeles CA). m. Virginia Philley, 1915. (Selig; Ince; American Film Manufacturing Co.) AMD, p. 369. AS, p. 1162. BHD, p. 341' BHD2, p. 287. IFN, p. 322. KOM, pp. 162–63. 1921 Directory, p. 278. "Chet Withey Joins American Forces," *MPW,* 4 Jan 1913, 35. J. Van Cartmell, "Along the Pacific Coast," *NYDM,* 15 Sep 1915, 42:3 (married Philley). "We Have with Us To-Day," *MPW,* 8 May 1920, 802. "Chester Withey's Career a Successful One, First as an Actor, Then as a Scenario Writer and as a Director," *MPW,* 25 Dec 1920, 1027. Edward Weitzel, "Director Withey Starts 'Wedding Bells' and the Black Cat Starts a Hot Fight," *MPW,* 5 Feb 1921, 677. "Chester Withey to Direct," *MPW,* 23 May 1925, 472. "Hogan and Withey Added to F.B.O. Directorial Staff," *MPW,* 19 Dec 1925, 656.

Withfield, Walter W. [actor/singer/dentist] (b. 1887–13 Jan 1966 [78?], Cleveland OH). AS, p. 1162.

Witt, Wastl [actor] (b. Germany, 20 Jul 1882–21 Dec 1955 [73], Harlachinger, Germany). AS, p. 1162.

Wittels, Toni (b. Vienna, Austria, 10 Jul 1870–15 Aug 1930 [60], Munich, Germany). BHD, p. 341.

Witting, A[rthur] **E**[ugene] [actor] (b. Prairie du Chien MI, 21 Oct 1868–1 Feb 1941 [72], San Diego CA). m. **Mattie Davis** (d. 1945). AS, p. 1162 (d. LA CA). BHD, p. 341. IFN, p. 322.

Witting, Mattie Davis [actress] (*née* Mattie Davis, b. Palla IA, 9 Mar 1863–30 Jan 1945 [81], San Diego Co. CA). m. **A.E. Witting** (d. 1941). AS, p. 1162 (d. LA CA). BHD, p. 341. Ragan 2, p. 1843.

Witwer, Harry Charles [writer/director] (b. Athens PA, 1889–9 Aug 1929 [40?], Los Angeles CA). AMD, p. 369. AS, p. 1162. BHD, p. 341; BHD, p. 287. "Witwer to Write for Moran," *MPW,* 14 May 1921, 152. "Witwer Company to Aid Police on Field Day," *MPW,* 10 Sep 1921, 186. "Witwer to Film His Own Stories Which Fidelity Will Distribute," *MPW,* 1 Oct 1921, 552. "H.C. Witwer Helping to Direct," *MPW,* 2 Dec 1922, 423. "F.B.O. Signs Witwer," *MPW,* 3 Feb 1923, 436. "Signs F.B.O. Contract,," *MPW,* 9 Jun 1923, 458 (for 5 years). "Plans New Witwer Series for F.B.O.; Will Not Be Fight Plays," *MPW,* 1 Dec 1923, 505. "Honor for Witwer," *MPW,* 26 Jan 1924, 274.

Witzel, Erwin "Curley" [actor]. (Universal.) Ed Wyatt, "Real Cowboy Curley Witzel Made a Brief Splash as Western Star," *CI,* 202 (Apr 1992), C9.

Wix, Florence E. [actress] (b. England, 16 May 1883–23 Nov 1956 [73], Woodland Hills CA; cancer). AS, p. 1162. BHD1, p. 592. IFN, p. 322. Truitt, p. 356.

Wix, Jack [actor] (b. 1887–24 Jun 1935 [48?], Los Angeles CA; heart attack). AS, p. 1162.

Wodehouse, P[lenham] **G**[renville] [scenarist] (b. Guildford, England, 15 Oct 1881–14 Feb 1975 [93], Southampton NY). BHD2, p. 287.

Wogritsch, Max [actor] (b. Dresden, Germany, 1880). AS, p. 1163.

Wolbert, Dorothea [actress] (aka Ella Wolbert, b. Philadelphia PA, 12 Apr 1874–15 Sep 1958 [84], Los Angeles CA; arteriosclerosis). (Vitagraph.) AS, p. 1163. BHD1, p. 592. IFN, p. 322. Truitt, p. 356. George A. Katchmer, "Remembering the Great Silents," *CI,* 183 (Sep 1990), 54. George Katchmer, "Remembering the Great Silents," *CI,* 252 (Jun 1996), 48.

Wolbert, William [actor/director] (b. Petersburg VA, 1883–12 Dec 1918 [35?], Los Angeles CA; influenza and pneumonia). (Universal.) "William Wolbert," *Variety,* 20 Dec 1918. AMD, p. 369. AS, p. 1163. BHD, p. 341; BHD2, p. 287. "Wolbert to Produce Bluebirds," *MPW,* 6 Jul 1918, 79. Billy H. Doyle, "Lost Players," *CI,* 139 (Jan 1987), 55.

Wolcott, George [actor] (b. 1912?). AMD, p. 369. "Juvenile Actor Hurt by Elevator, Gets $60,000," *MPW,* 12 Mar 1921, 166 (from accident in Jul 1920; 9 years old).

Wolcott, Julia [actress] (b. 1845–25 May 1915 [70?], Chicago IL). BHD, p. 341.

Wolf, Barney [film editor] (b. 1894?–9 Oct 1938 [44], Los Angeles CA). (Fox; TC-F.) "Barney Wolf," *Variety,* 12 Oct 1938.

Wolf, Bill [actor] (b. New York NY, 14 Aug 1894–16 Feb 1975 [80], Los Angeles Co. CA). BHD, p. 341. IFN, p. 322.

Wolf, Edwin R. [actor] (b. 20 Jun 1893–22 Sep 1983 [90], Holmes NY). BHD1, p. 593.

Wolf, Friedrich [scenarist] (b. 23 Dec 1888–5 Oct 1953 [64], Berlin, Germany). AS, p. 1163. BHD2, p. 287.

Wolf, Rennold [writer/scenarist] (b. Ithaca NY, 4 Apr 1872–2 Jan 1922 [49], New York NY; apoplexy). m. (1) stage actress Hope Booth; (2) Harriet Raymond, 6 Jun 1912, Ridgewood NJ. "Rennold Wolf Dead; Dramatic Editor and Dramatist Dies After a Long Illness at 49," *NYT,* 3 Jan 1922, 17:3 (wrote *The Rainbow Girl; 1919 Follies*). "Rennold Wolf," *Variety,* 6 Jan 1922. BHD2, p. 287. "[Harriet Raymond] Asks Divorce from Playwright," *NYDM,* 3 Feb 1915, 7:3.

Wolfe, Jane [actress] (b. St. Petersburg PA, 21 Mar 1875–29 Mar 1958 [83], Glendale CA). (Began 1912.) AMD, p. 370. AS, p. 1163. BHD, p. 341. IFN, p. 322. Billy H. Doyle, "Lost Players," *CI*, 157 (Jul 1988), 24. "Miss Jane Wolfe," *MPW,* 17 Jan 1914, 269. George Katchmer, "Remembering the Great Silents,"*CI,* 254 (Aug 1996), 48.

Wolff, Carl Heinz [scenarist] (b. 1883–9 Dec 1942 [59?], Berlin, Germany). AS, p. 1163. BHD2, p. 287.

Wolff, Edgar Allen [title writer]. No data found. FDY, p. 447.

Wolff, Perry [actor] (d. Los Angeles CA, 4 May 1974). BHD1, p. 593.

Wolff, Dr. Willi [director] (b. Schonebeck, Germany, 16 Apr 1883–1947 [64?]). AS, p. 1163 (b. Schoeneberg, Germany). BHD2, p. 287.

Wolgast, Ad (b. Cadillac MI, 8 Jan 1888–14 Apr 1955 [67], Camarillo CA). BHD, p. 341.

Wolheim, Dan[iel] [actor] (b. New York NY, 8 Feb 1894-d. ca. 1939 [45?]. *Fl.* 1927–37. AS, p. 1163.

Wolheim, Louis R[obert] [actor] (b. New York NY or Germany, 28 Mar 1880–18 Feb 1931 [50], Los Angeles CA; stomach cancer). m. Ethel Dane. "Wolheim, 'Bad Man' of Movies, Is Dead; Excessive Dieting [weighed 200 lbs.] Hastens End, as Noted Screen and Stage Star Undergoes Operation; A Scholar in Private Life [spoke 4 foreign languages]; His Successes as Capt. Flagg in 'What Price Glory' Led to Many Film Triumphs—Was 49 Years Old," *NYT,* 19 Feb 1931, 23:1 (b. 1881; broke his nose 3 times playing football; last film: *Gentlemen's Fate,* MGM, 1931; had to abandon role in *The Front Page*—Adolph Menjou replaced him). "Louis Wolheim," *Variety,* 25 Feb 1931 (b. New York NY). AMD, p. 370. AS, p. 1163. BHD1, p. 593 (b. 1881). FSS, p. 293. IFN, p. 322 (b. NY). Katz, p. 1246. Truitt, p. 356. "Wolheim SIgns with Barrymore," *MPW,* 22 Oct 1927, 497. Frances Gilmore, "Hard-Boiled but Educated; Louis Wolheim Says a Mouthful About This Here Now Movie Busniess," *MPC,* Dec 1927, 25, 70.

Woloshin, Alex [actor] (b. Russia, 20 Apr 1886–23 Nov 1960 [74], Los Angeles Co., CA). BHD1, p. 593.

Wong, Anna May [film/stage/TV actress] (*née* Wong Liu Tsong ["Frosted Yellow Willow"], b. Los Angeles CA, 3 Jan 1905–3 Feb 1961 [56], Santa Monica CA; myocardial infarction; Laennec's cirrhosis, 10 years; cremated 9 Feb 1961, Chapel of the Pacific, Woodlawn Cemetery [Death Certificate State File No. 61–018716, State of CA Dept. of Public Heatlh; race listed as "Cauc.";]). Unmarried. "Anna May Wong Is Dead at 54; Actress Won Movie Fame in '24; Appeared with Fairbanks in 'Thief of Bagdad'—Made Several Films Abroad," *NYT,* 4 Feb 1961, 19:3. "Anna May Wong," *Variety,* 8 Feb 1961 (d. 2 Feb). AMD, p. 370. AS, p. 734 (May Wong, Anna, b.1907); p. 1164. BHD1, p. 593. FSS, p. 294. IFN, p. 322. JS, p. 501 (b. 1907; appeared in *Ombre bianche,* Italy, 1960). Katz, p. 1246. MH, p. 143. Truitt, p. 356 (b. 1907). Myrtle Gebhart, "Jazz Notes on Old China," *Picture-Play Magazine,* May 1923, 48–50, 102. Helen Carlisle, "A Chinese Puzzle," *MW,* IV, 30 Aug 1924, 9–10, 26. "Hollywooders Disband Over 'Draw' Credit; Detroit Week Brought Other Time, Also Bickering—$3,500 Weekly," *Variety,* 29 Apr 1925, 1:2, 54:2 (Bryant Washburn and his "Hollywooders" disbanded their act. "Anna May Wong is anticipating continuing as a single attraction in picture theatres."). "Starts on Big Fox Film," *MPW,* 5 Dec 1925, 439. Anna May Wong, "The True Life Story of a Chinese Girl [Part I]," *Pictures,* II, Aug 1926, 28–29, 106–08; Part II, Sep 1926, 34–35, 72, 74–75. Paul Paige, "Close-Ups and Fade-Outs," *Paris and Hollywood,* Oct 1926, 97 (pleaded in court for her younger brother, who was charged with illegally transporting firecrackers. He was found guilty, but the fine was suspended/). "Anna May Wong in Pathé Comedies," *MPW,* 2 Oct 1926, 291. "Anna May Wong in Gilda Gray's Picture," *MPW,* 20 Aug 1927, 533. "Anna May Wong, Family Sue for Death of Mother," 4 Feb 1931 [clipping] (brought suit for $50,000 damages against the driver of a car involved in an accident in Nov 1930 in which Toy Wong received fatal injuries). Audrey Rivers, "Anna May Wong Sorry She Cannot Be Kissed; Little Chinese Beauty Fated to Tragic Screen Life—Because Laws Forbid Happy Love Scenes Between Orientals and Whites," *Movie Classic,* Nov 1931, 39 (she received her first screen kiss from a Caucasian from John Langdon in *The Flame of Love.* A kiss from Jameson Thomas in *Piccadilly* was cut). "Anna May Wong, Oriental Star, Wants to Marry an American," *Wisconsin News,* Dec 1931. Garth Pedler, "Anna May Wong in 'Picadilly,'" *CI,* 167 (May 1989), 42, 44, 49. Philip Leibfried, "Anna May Wong's Silent Film Career," *The Silent Film Monthly,* III (Feb 1995), 1–2; filmography, 10–11. Buddy Barnett, "Anna May Wong: Hollywood's Orient Express," *Cult Movies,* No. 17, 1996, pp. 20–25. Barrie Roberts, "Anna May Wong: Daughter of the Orient," *CI,* 270 (Dec 1997), 20–24 (includes filmography. Began as an extra in *The Red Lantern.*) Newsletter: *The Shanghai Express,* I (Winter 1999), Mr. David R. Busch, PO Box 2668, St. Louis MO 63116-0668; <bigkahuna @pacificislander.com>.

Wong, Bessie [actress]. No data found. AMD, p. 370. "Bessie Wong Is a Newcomer in Motion Pictures," *MPW,* 29 Oct 1921, 1066.

Wong, Marion E. [producer]. No data found. AMD, p. 370. "Marion E. Wong, Chinese Film Producer," *MPW,* 7 Jul 1917, 63.

Wonn, Edward [actor] (b. 1872–5 Jan 1927 [54?], Baltimore MD). BHD, p. 341.

Wontner, Arthur [stage/film/TV actor] (b. London, England, 21 Jan 1875–10 Jul 1960 [85], Buckinghamshire, London, England). m. (1) Rose Pendennis (d. 1943); (2) Florence E. Lainchbury.

(Film debut: *The Bigamist,* 1915.) "Arthur Wontner, British Actor, 85; Player in 250 Stage Roles During 60 Years Dies—On U.S. Screen, TV," *NYT,* 12 Jul 1960, 35:2. AS, p. 1164. BHD1, p. 593. IFN, p. 322. Truitt, p. 356. William D. Lucas, "Arthur Wontner as Sherlock Holmes," *CI,* 95 (May 1983), 41.

Wood, Britt [actor] (b. TN, 27 Sep 1885–14 Apr 1965 [80], Los Angeles CA). m. Louise. "Britt Wood," *Variety,* 21 Apr 1965 (age 70). AS, p. 1164 (b. 1893). BHD1, p. 593 (b. 1893). IFN, p. 323 (b. 1893). Truitt, p. 356.

Wood, Clement [scenarist] (b. Tuscaloosa AL, 1 Sep 1888–26 Oct 1950 [62], Schenectady NY). BHD2, p. 288.

Wood, Dorothy [actress] (*née* Esther Dorothy Wood, b. IA, 20 Apr 1904). m. **Millard K. Wilson**, 21 Aug 1925. AMD, p. 370. BR, pp. 332–34. George A. Katchmer, "Remembering the Great Silents," *CI,* 178 (Apr 1990), 58. "Dorothy Wood New Lead in Comedies by Mermaid," *MPW,* 12 Feb 1921, 796. Data supplied by Grange B. McKinney, San Clemente CA.

Wood, Dorothy [actress] (d. 3 Feb 1919, Atlanta GA; pneumonia). AS, p. 1164.

Wood, Douglas [actor] (b. New York NY, 31 Oct 1880–13 Jan 1966 [85], Woodland Hills CA). AS, p. 1164. IFN, p. 323.

Wood, Ernest D. [actor] (b. Atchison KS, 17 Apr 1887–13 Jul 1942 [55], Los Angeles CA; heart attack). "Ernest D. Wood," *NYT,* 15 Jul 1942, 19:1. AS, p. 1164. BHD1, p. 594. IFN, p. 323. Truitt, p. 357.

Wood, Frank E. [scenarist] (b. 1860–1 May 1939 [79?]). BHD2, p. 288.

Wood, Franker [actor] (b. Stromsburg NB, 1883?–9 Nov 1931 [48], Farmingdale, LI NY; tuberculosis). m. Bunnee Wyde. "Franker Wood Victim of Sudden Seizure, Dies," *Variety,* 24 Nov 1931. AS, p. 1164 (d. 13 Nov). BHD1, p. 594 (d. NY NY). IFN, p. 323.

Wood, Freeman N. [actor] (b. Denver CO, 1 Jul 1896–19 Feb 1956 [59], Los Angeles CA). "Freeman N. Wood," *Variety,* 29 Feb 1956. AS, p. 1164. BHD1, p. 594. IFN, p. 323. Truitt, p. 357.

Wood, Baby Gloria (daughter of **Sam Wood**) [stage/film actress] (aka Katherine] T. Stevens, b. Brentwood, Los Angeles CA, 20 Jul 1919–13 Jun 1994 [74], Brentwood CA; lung cancer). m. Hugh Marlowe—div. 1967. (Broadway debut: *The Land Is Bright,* 1941.) "K.T. Stevens, 74, Actress and Unionist," *NYT,* 22 Jun 1994, A19:1. AS, p. 1033 (Katherine Stevens). BHD1, p. 521. Katz, p. 1092.

Wood, Grace [actress] (b. Fort Lyon MO, 1884?–30 May 1952 [68]). AS, p. 1164. BHD1, p. 594. IFN, p. 323.

Wood, Mrs. Henry [writer] (*née* Braddon). No data found. m. Henry Wood. AMD, p. 370. "Mrs. Henry Wood Wrote 'East Lynne,'" *MPW,* 24 Jul 1915, 671.

Wood, Leonard [scenarist] d. 27 Aug 1931, New York NY). BHD2, p. 288.

Wood, Marjorie [actress] (b. London, England, 5 Sep 1882–9 Nov 1955 [73], Los Angeles CA). "Marjorie Wood," *Variety,* 16 Nov 1955 (age 67). AS, p. 1165. BHD, p. 341. IFN, p. 323. SD, p. 1332 (b. 1887).

Wood, Peggy [stage/film/TV actress] (*née* Margaret Wood, b. Brooklyn NY, 9 Feb 1892–18 Mar 1978 [86], Stamford Hospital, Stamford CT; cerebral hemorrhage). m. (1) John Van Alstyn Weaver, 1934 (1 son, David; d. 1938); (2) William A. Wallling (d. 1973). *How Young You Look* (1941); *Arts and Flowers* (1953). Robert D. McFadden, "Peggy Wood, 86, Star in 'Mama' TV Series [1949–57]; Appeared in More than 70 Plays on Broadway in 60-Year Career," *NYT,* 19 Mar 1978, 38:3. "Service for Peggy Wood Monday," *NYT,* 5 Apr 1978, II, 2:1. "Peggy Wood," *Variety,* 22 Mar 1978. (AA nomination, supporting actress, *The Sound of Music,* TC-F, 1966.) AMD, p. 370. AS, p. 1165. BHD1, p. 594. IFN, p. 323. Katz, p. 1247. "Late Star of 'Maytime' Signs with Goldwyn Films," *MPW,* 21 Jun 1919, 1780.

Wood, Rose (grandmother of the **Bennett** sisters through her daughter Adrienne) [actress] (b. England, 1850?–7 Mar 1932 [82], Tenafly NJ). m. Lewis Morrison. "Rose Wood," *Variety,* 15 Mar 1932. BHD, p. 341. SD, p. 1332.

Wood, Sam (father of **Baby Gloria Wood** [K.T. Stevens]) [director/producer] (*né* Samuel Grosvenor Wood, b. Philadelphia PA, 10 Jul 1883–22 Sep 1949 [66], Los Angeles CA). m. (Paramount; MGM.) "Sam Wood Is Dead; Movie Director, 65; 39-Year Veteran in Industry Did 'Good-Bye, Mr. Chips' and 'For Whom the Bell Tolls,'" *NYT,* 23 Sep 1949, 23:1; "300 Attend Rites for Sam Wood," *NYT,* 25 Sep 1949, 92:7. "Sam Wood," *Variety,* 28 Sep 1949 (age 65). AMD, p. 370. AS, p. 1165 (b. 18 Jul). BHD, p. 341; BHD2, p. 288. IFN, p. 323. Katz, p. 1247. Truitt, p. 357 (b. 10 Jul 1883). "Sam Wood Made a Full Director," *MPW,* 4 Oct 1919, 115. "Wood Is Appointed Assistant Producer at F.B.O. Studios," *MPW,* 20 Nov 1926, 147. "Sam Wood Called 'The Busiest Man,'" *MPW,* 22 Jan 1927, 267. John Roberts, "Sam Wood, A No Nonsense Pro," *CI,* 167 (May 1989), 32, 59–60 (includes filmography).

Wood, Tommy (Fatty) [actor] (b. Eau Claire WI, May 1894–28 Dec 1932 [38], Minneapolis MN). BHD, p. 341. (*See* next entry.)

Wood, Thomas A. [actor] (b. Brainerd MN). AMD, p. 370. "Chaplin Signs Contract to Fit His Movie Trousers," *MPW,* 15 Mar 1919, 1480 (weighed 500 lbs.).

Woodbury, Joan [actress] (b. Los Angeles CA, 17 Dec 1915–22 Feb 1989 [73], Desert Hot Springs CA; respiratory complications). m. (1) **Henry Wilcoxen**, 1938 (d. 1984); (2) Roy Mitchell. AS, p. 1165. BR, pp. 460–62.

Woodford, John [actor] (b. Austin TX, 1862?–17 Apr 1927 [65], Saranac Lake NY). "John Woodford," *Variety,* 20 Apr 1927. AS, p. 1165. BHD, p. 341. IFN, p. 323. Truitt, p. 357.

Woodhouse, J.S. [scenarist]. No data found. FDY, p. 439.

Woodruff, Bert [actor] (*né* William Herbert Woodruff, b. Peoria IL, 29 Apr 1856–14 Jun 1934 [78], Los Angeles CA). (Pioneer.) AS, p. 1165. BHD1, p. 595. IFN, p. 323. Truitt, p. 357. George A. Katchmer, "Forgotten Cowboys and Cowgirls—Part XV," *CI,* 192 (Jun 1991), 56.

Woodruff, Edna [actress] (aka Edna Montague, b. 1874–16 Oct 1947 [73?], Los Angeles CA). AS, p. 1165.

Woodruff, Eleanor Stark, "The Ethel Barrymore of Motion Pictures" [stage/film actress] (b. Towanda PA, 12 Sep 1891–7 Oct 1980 [89], Princeton NJ; heart attack in her sleep). m. Dorsey Richardson, 4 Apr 1931 (d. 8 Nov 1961). (Pathé, 1912; Vitagraph, 2 Jan 1915; World, 1916.) AMD, p. 370. AS, p. 1165. BHD, p. 341. Spehr, p. 176. "Miss Eleanor Woodruff," *MPW,* 29 Nov 1913, 988. "Miss Woodruff Remains with Pathé," *MPW,* 3 Jan 1914, 61. "Eleanor Woodruff; Pathé's Popular Star, Appearing on This Week's Cover, Only Four Years on Stage," *NYDM,* 25 Feb 1914, 34:1 (b. 1892). "Eleanor Woodruff in Difficult Part," *MPW,* 17 Oct 1914, 320. "Miss Woodruff Helps Show Girls," *MPW,* 28 Nov 1914, 1213. "Eleanor Woodruff Off to the War," *MPW,* 5 Dec 1914, 1386. "Eleanor Woodruff with Vitagraph," *MPW,* 9 Jan 1915, 199. "Personal," *NYDM,* 2 Jun 1915, 5:2 (on cover). "Eleanor Woodruff," *MPW,* 15 Apr 1916, 451. "Eleanor Woodruff with Frohman," *MPW,* 22 Jul 1916, 646. Lester Sweyd, "What They Are Doing Now," *Motion Picture Magazine,* Feb 1918, 13 (played Otis Skinner's leading-lady in his "Mister Antonio.'"). Billy H. Doyle, "Lost Players," *CI,* 187 (Jan 1991), C4-C5 (b. 1892).

Woodruff, Eunice Elenor [actress] (b. 1910–15 Jul 1921 [11?], Los Angeles CA). BHD, p. 341.

Woodruff, Henry [stage/film actor] (b. Hartford CT, 1 Jun 1869–6 Oct 1916 [47], New York NY; Bright's disease). (Stage debut: Fourteenth St. Theatre, *H.M.S. Pinefore;* Ince.) "Henry Woodruff Dead; Actor Who Began His Career at 9 Dies of Bright's Disease," *NYT,* 7 Oct 1916, 11:4 (b. Jersey City NJ). "Henry Woodruff," *Variety,* 13 Oct 1916 (age 46). AS, p. 1165. BHD, p. 342. IFN, p. 323. "Henry Woodruff at Proctor's; To Become Leading Man of Fifth Avenue Stock Company," *NYT,* 12 Mar 1905, I, 9:2 (to make his initial appearance at Proctor's in *The Wife* during the week of 20 Mar, with Isabelle Evesson, Wallace Erskine, H. Dudley Hawley, Marion Berg, and Lilia Vane. He began as a chorus boy, age 9, with J.H. Haverly's *Juvenile Pinafore,* with Julia Marlowe, Annie Boswsell, and William Collier.). "Vaudeville," *NYT,* 19 Mar 1905, IV, 5:4 (Woodruff to appear with the acts of Eugene Cowles, Caine's pantomime dogs, Quigg and Nickerson, Caldera [juggler], and "the moving pictures will show the automobile races at Ormond Beach, Florida.").

Woodruff, Lorenzo F. [publicist]. No data found. AMD, p. 370. "Woodruff on Select's Exploitation Staff," *MPW,* 2 Aug 1919, 697.

Woods, Adelaide [actress] (d. Mar 1917). AMD, p. 370. BHD, p. 342. IFN, p. 323. "Pallas Pictures Engage Adelaide Woods," *MPW,* 3 Jun 1916, 1702.

Woods, Al [actor] (*né* Frederick Ludvig Dreeke, b. 1895?–3 Jun 1946 [51], Pasadena CA; heart attack). "Al Woods," *Variety,* 12 Jun 1946 ("actor in silent pictures"). AS, p. 1165. BHD, p. 342. IFN, p. 323.

Woods, Al H. [writer/producer/director] (*né* Aladore Herman, b. Hungary, 1870–24 Apr 1951 [81], New York NY). m. Louise Beaton. "A.H. Woods," *NYT,* 25 Apr 1951, 29:1 [page missing on microfilm]. "Al Woods, Producer of Hokey Hits and Flops, Dead at 81; Aided Stars," *Variety,* 25 Apr 1951. AMD, p. 370. "Pathé Gets Al H. Woods Play," *MPW,* 20 Nov 1915, 1467. "Al Woods Forms Picture Company," *MPW,* 24 Mar 1917, 1944. "Goldwyn Capital Now $20,000,000," *MPW,* 9 Aug 1919, 785.

Woods, Arthur (b. Boston MA, 29 Jan 1870–12 May 1942 [72], Washington DC; cerebral hemorrhage). m. Helen Morgan, 10 Jun 1916. "Arthur Woods, 72, Is Dead in Capital; Police Commissioner Here in 1914 to '18 Introduced New Methods of Enforcement; Air Colonel with A.E.F.;

Sociologist, Former Reporter, Taught Roosevelt at Groton—Wed Late J.P. Morgan Kin," *NYT,* 13 May 1942, 19:1.

Woods, Daddy [actor] (d. 1916). BHD, p. 342.

Woods, Ella [scenarist] (*née*, b. 1860?–3 Jul 1937 [77], Los Angeles CA). m. Frank Woods. "Ella Woods," *Variety,* 7 Jul 1937. AS, p. 1165. BHD2, p. 288.

Woods, Ernie [actor]. No data found. AMD, p. 370. "Sign with Sennett," *MPW,* 16 May 1925, 349.

Woods, Frank E[merson] **"Spec"** [journalist/scenarist/first president of the Photoplay Authors' League, 1914/director at Kinemacolor, 1912, and Reliance-Majestic/General Manager of the Fine Arts Studio] (b. Linesville PA, 1860?–1 May 1939 [79], Los Angeles CA). m. **Nancy Ellen Anderson**. (Wrote film reviews for *The Dramatic Mirror* using the pseudonynm of "Spectator"; Griffith, 1911; Ince; Sennett; FP-L; Kinemacolor; Imp; Universal; Mutual.) "Frank E. Woods, 79, Pioneer Scenarist; Associate of D.W. Griffith in the Biograph Company Is Dead in Hollywood," *NYT,* 2 May 1939, 23:2 (twin of Mrs. Carrie Woods Bush. Wrote one of the earliest film columns in *The Dramatic Mirror*). KOM, pp. 163–64. "Frank Woods," *Variety,* 3 May 1939. AMD, p. 370. AS, p. 1166. BHD2, p. 288. "Woods Leaves Mirror for Kinemacolor," *MPW,* 24 Aug 1912, 758. "Frank Woods Making Comedies," *MPW,* 10 May 1913, 586. P.M. Powell, "Doings at Los Angeles," *MPW,* 24 May 1913, 798. "Woods Back on Broadway," *MPW,* 14 Jun 1913, 1139. "Frank Woods Goes with Mutual," *MPW,* 8 Nov 1913, 618. "Frank Woods Framing Up," *MPW,* 13 Dec 1913, 1282. "Woods Heads Authors' League; Organization Progreessing Rapidly...," *NYDM,* 25 Mar 1914, 31:1. W.E. Wing, "Gleaned Along the Coast," *NYDM,* 3 Jun 1914, 25:4 (he "weighed but 1 1/2 pounds when born."). Frank E. Woods, "What Are We Coming To?," *MPW,* 18 Jul 1914, 442–43. "The Success of Frank Woods," *MPW,* 10 Jul 1915, 252. Frank Woods, "D.W. Griffith," *MPW,* 10 Jul 1915, 256. "Frank E. Woods Writes Four Features," *MPW,* 3 Mar 1917, 1358. "Frank E. Woods on Way East," *MPW,* 26 May 1917, 1284. Alfred A. Cohn, "The Empire Theater of the Screen; Fine Arts Studio [formerly Reliance-Majestic], an Artistic Temple, Classic Though Young, Which Has Just Passed into History," *Photoplay,* Jul 1917, 30–33, 136–37, 165 (this article chronicles the successful people who worked there. The last production was *Madam Bo-Peep,* with Seena Owen. Woods credited Griffith's participation with the studio's successes. "Whatever good has come out of Fine Arts originated with Mr. Griffith...Whenever Fine Arts has fallen below the standard, it has usually been because the Griffith teachings were not followed."). "Frank Wood Joins Famous Players-Lasky," *MPW,* 21 Jul 1917, 467. "Woods Engaged by Famous Players-Lasky," *MPW,* 28 Jul 1917, 625. "Frank E. Woods," *MPW,* 5 Apr 1919, 32 (incudes 1914–19 filmography). "Has Supervised 570 Film Productions," *MPW,* 26 Apr 1919, 520. "Improvement in Pictures Is Marked," *MPW,* 7 Jun 1919, 1498. "'Stick to Your Last,' Frank E. Woods Tells 'So-Called Producing Companies,'" *MPW,* 26 Jun 1920, 1733. "Frank E. Woods Resigns," *MPW,* 28 Oct 1922, 764 (as of 11 Nov 1922). "Frank E. Woods Quits FP-L to Produce Independent Pictures," *MPW,* 28 Oct 1922, 781. "Starts First Production," *MPW,* 23 Feb 1924, 634. "Woods with Hodkinson," *MPW,* 1 Mar 1924, 28. "Screen Must Have Own Authors, States Producer Frank Woods," *MPW,* 26 Apr 1924, 742. "Woods a Veteran Author-Director," *MPW,* 12 Jul 1924, insert. Edward Azlant, "Screenwriting for the early silent film: forgotten pioneers, 1897–1911," *Film History,* 9 (1997), 242–43 (covered movies in the *NYDM,* from 1908, under the byline "Spectator.").

Woods, Harry Lewis, Sr. [actor] (b. Cleveland OH, 5 May 1889–28 Dec 1968 [79], Los Angeles CA; uremic poisoning). AMD, p. 371. AS, p. 1166. BHD1, p. 595. IFN, p. 323. Katz, p. 1248. Truitt, p. 357. "Harry Woods," *MPW,* 15 Oct 1927, 431.

Woods, Jack [actor]. George Katchmer, "Remembering the Great Silents," *CI,* 204 (Jun 1992), 44, 56.

Woods, Joseph A. [actor] (b. New York NY, 1860?–13 Feb 1926 [66], New York NY; heart attack). "Joseph A. Woods," *Variety,* 24 Feb 1926. AS, p. 1166. BHD, p. 342. IFN, p. 323. Truitt, p. 358.

Woods, Lotta [title writer]. No data found. AMD, p. 371. FDY, p. 447. "Lotta Woods Signs," *MPW,* 25 Sep 1926, 4.

Woods, Nick, "N.S. Woods, The Boy Actor" [stage/film actor] (*né* Nicholas Schaber, b. Germany, 1857–21 Mar 1936 [78], New Rochelle NY). (Thanhouser.) "Nick Woods," *Variety,* 122, 25 Mar 1936, 62:2. AS, p. 1166. BHD, p. 342. IFN, p. 323.

Woods, Walter [title writer/scenarist/producer] (b. 1881?–7 Dec 1942 [61], Glendale CA). (Paramount.) "Walter Woods," *Variety,* 16 Dec 1942. AMD, p. 371. AS, p. 1166. BHD2, p. 288. FDY, pp. 439, 447. IFN, p. 323. "Woods Writes Story for Arbuckle," *MPW,* 4 Sep 1920, 60. "Woods Joins DeMille," *MPW,* 27 Nov 1926, 2. "James Cruze Joins P.D.C.-Pathé Unit; Walter Woods Also," *MPW,* 4 Jun 1927, 325.

Woodthorpe, Georgia [actress] (aunt of **James W. Horne**) (*née*?, b. CA, 11 Oct 1859–25 Aug 1927 [67], Glendale CA). "Georgia Woodthorpe," *Variety,* 31 Aug 1927 (Mrs. Georgia Woodthorpe Cooper Wallace; age 68). AS, p. 1166. BHD, p. 342. IFN, p. 323 (age 67). Truitt, p. 358.

Woodward, Mrs. Eugenie [stage/film actress] (*née* Eugenie Lindeman, b. Cincinnati OH, 1859?–29 Mar 1947 [88], White Plains NY). "Mrs. E. Woodward, Actress, Dies at 88; The Former Eugenie Lindeman Appeared with Ada Rehan, Sothern and Marlowe [in 1909]," *NYT,* 30 Mar 1947, 56:7. AS, p. 1166. BHD, p. 342. IFN, p. 323.

Woodward, Franc R.E. [publicist]. No data found. AMD, p. 371. "New Selig Publicity Manager," *MPW,* 11 Jul 1914, 233.

Woodward, H. Guy [actor] (b. Minneapolis MN, 1868?–20 Aug 1919 [51], Detroit MI; heart attack). "H. Guy Woodward," *Variety,* 29 Aug 1919. AS, p. 1166 (b. Detroit MI). BHD, p. 342. IFN, p. 323.

Woodward, Henry F. [actor] (b. Charleston WV, 11 Dec 1891). (Biograph; Universal; Monrovia; Lasky.) BHD, p. 342. MSBB, p. 1030.

Woodward, Jill [actress]. No data found. (Pathé.) George A. Katchmer, "Forgotten Cowboys and Cowgirls—Part V," *CI,* 177 (Mar 1990), C6.

Woodward, O.D. [producer] (b. 1866–9 Jan 1946 [79?], Culver City CA). AS, p. 1166.

Woody, John S[amuel] [producer/executive] (aka Jack Woody, b. St. Louis MO, 1890?–7 Apr 1929 [39], New York NY). (Real-Art Pictures; Associated Exhibitors, later absorbed by Pathé; Selznick Pictures; Fox Film Corp.) "John Samuel Woody," *Variety,* 24 Apr 1929, 60:1. AMD, p. 371. AS, p. 1166 (d. 24 Apr). BHD2, p. 288. John S. Woody, "Associated Exhibitors Pictures Are Based on Public Demand," *MPW,* 10 Nov 1923, 251. "Woody Scouts Alarm Talk; Doesn't Fear Buying Groups," *MPW,* 1 Nov 1924, 27. John S. Woody, "Associated Exhibitors Policy Involves Avoidance of Similarity in Productions," *MPW,* 8 Nov 1924, 164. "Associated Will Not Produce This Season, Woody Announces," *MPW,* 15 Nov 1924, 220. "Woody Explains Associated's Position in Selznick Matter," *MPW,* 6 Dec 1924, 509. "Associated Exhibitors Elects Woody; Radical Policy Changes Are Planned," *MPW,* 4 Apr 1925, 445. "Associated Exhibitors Guarantees Next Season's Product, Says Woody," *MPW,* 15 Aug 1925, 738. "John S. Woody Will Produce Bandit Film," *MPW,* 27 Feb 1926, 4 (re James and Youngers gangs).

Woolf, Charles M[oss] [manager/founder of General Film Distributors of England] (b. 1879–31 Dec 1942 [63?], London, England). m. (sons John and James, founders of Romulus Films). Tom Vallance, "Sir John Woolf," *The Independent Review,* 1 Jul 1999, p. 6 (b. London, 15 Mar 1913–28 Jun 1999, London).

Woolf, Edgar Allen [scenarist] (b. New York NY, 25 Apr 1891–9 Dec 1943 [52], Los Angeles CA). AS, p. 1166 (b. 1881). BHD2, p. 288.

Woolf, Mrs. Yetti [actress] (b. 1882–27 Nov 1965 [83?], Los Angeles CA). AS, p. 1167.

Woolfe, Harry Bruce [director] (b. London, England, 15 Jun 1880–1965 [85?], London, England). AS, p. 1167 (d. 1966). BHD2, p. 288 (b. 1888).

Woolnough, James [actor/ssistant director] (b. Cambridgeport MA, 1870–21 May 1937 [67?], Los Angeles CA). BHD, p. 342; BHD2, p. 288.

Woolrich, Cornell [writer/scenarist] (*né* William Irish, b. 1903?–1958 [55?]). AMD, p. 371. AS, p. 1167. "New Yorker Wins Prize," *MPW,* 7 May 1927, 12 (age 21).

Woolridge, Doris [actress] (b. San Francisco CA, 2 Apr 1890?–17 Jul 1921 [31], Los Angeles CA; after appendicitis operation). (Fox.) "Doris Wooldridge," *Variety,* 5 Aug 1921 (age 31). AS, p. 1167 (b. 1892). BHD, p. 342 (b. 1892). IFN, p. 324.

Woolsey, Robert [actor] (b. Oakland CA, 14 Aug 1889–31 Oct 1938 [49], Malibu Beach CA). AS, p. 1167.

Woolstenhulme, Charles [production manager] (b. 1892?–24 May 1960 [68], Glendale CA). (Universal; Fox; TC-F.) "Charles Woolstenhulme," *Variety,* 1 Jun 1960.

Wordsworth, William [actor] (b. 1873?–6 Jun 1950 [77], Queens NY). "William Wordsworth," *Variety,* 14 Jun 1950. AS, p. 1167.

Worlock, Frederic [actor] (b. London, England, 14 Dec 1886–1 Aug 1973 [86], Woodland Hills CA). AS, p. 1167. BHD1, p. 595.

Worms, Jean [actor] (*né* Gustave Jacques Jean Worms, b. Paris, France, 21 Feb 1884–17 Dec 1943 [59], Neuilly-sur-Seine, France). AS, p. 1167.

Worne, Howard B. (Duke) [actor/director/producer] (b. Philadelphia PA, 14 Dec

1888–13 Oct 1933 [44], Los Angeles CA). (Universal.) m. **Virginia Brown Faire** (d. 1980). "Howard B. Worne," *Variety,* 17 Oct 1933 (age 43). AMD, p. 371. AS, p. 1167 (d. 14 Oct). BHD, p. 342; BHD2, p. 289. IFN, p. 324. "Signs Vaudeville Star for Rayart Film," *MPW,* 31 Jul 1926, 278.

Worsley, Wallace, Jr. (son of **Wallace A. Worsley, Sr.**) [actor] (b. 27 Jun 1908–18 Jun 1991 [82], Los Angeles Co. CA). AMD, p. 371. BHD1, p. 619.

Worsley, Wallace A., Sr. (father of **Wallace Worsley, Jr.**) [actor/director] (b. Wappingers Falls NY, 8 Dec 1878–26 Mar 1944 [65], Los Angeles CA). m. **Julia Taylor** (d. 1976). "Wallace A. Worsley, Sr.," *Variety,* 29 Mar 1944 (age 66). AMD, p. 371. AS, p. 1167. BHD, p. 342; BHD2, p. 289. IFN, p. 324 (age 65). 1921 Directory, p. 278. "Worsley to Direct Rhea Mitchell," *MPW,* 6 Oct 1917, 94. "Three New Directors Are Signed by Goldwyn," *MPW,* 16 Aug 1919, 942. "Wallace Worsley Coming East to Direct Goldwyn Production," *MPW,* 19 Jun 1920, 1582. "Worsley Renews Contract," *MPW,* 1 Jan 1921, 77. "Worsley to Direct 'Notre Dame,'" *MPW,* 2 Dec 1922, 421.

Worth, Barbara [actress] (b. Cincinnati OH). (Universal.) AMD, p. 371. "Barbara Worth Signed in Universal Stock," *MPW,* 20 Mar 1926, 172. "Barbara's Role," *MPW,* 7 May 1927, 37. "Barbara Worth," *MPW,* 17 Sep 1927, 167. George A. Katchmer, "Forgotten Cowboys and Cowgirls—Part V," *CI,* 177 (Mar 1990), C6; "Update—Forgotten Cowboys/Girls," *CI,* 179 (May 1990), 44.

Worth, Bill [actor] (b. 1883–2 May 1951 [68?], Westwood Village CA; heart attack at 20th Century-Fox studios). AS, p. 1167.

Worth, Peggy [actress] (*née* Genevieve Wiggleworth, b. 1891?–23 Mar 1956 [65], New York NY). "Peggy Worth Is Dead; Comedienne of Early Movies Also Appeared on Stage," *NYT,* 25 Mar 1956, 92:8 (began in Hollywood at age 15). AS, p. 1167. BHD, p. 342. IFN, p. 324. Truitt, p. 358.

Worth, Thelma [actress]. No data found. AMD, p. 371. "Thelma Worth to Play Lead in Banks Comedies," *MPW,* 17 Dec 1921, 817.

Wortham, Robert [pioneer director] (b. 1881?–18 Mar 1928 [47], Brooklyn NY). "Robert Wortham," *Variety,* 21 Mar 1928. AS, p. 1167 (d. 23 Mar 1956, NYC). BHD2, p. 289.

Worthing, Helen Lee [stage/film actress] (b. Louisville KY, 31 Jan 1905–25 Aug 1948 [43], Los Angeles CA). m. (1) Charles Mac-Donald-div. 1922; (2) Dr. Eugene C. Nelson, 1927—annulled, 1933. "Helen Lee Worthing Dies; Former Ziegfeld Follies Beauty Stricken in Hollywood at 43," *NYT,* 27 Aug 1948, 21:6. "Ex-Follies Girl Left $16.18," *NYT,* 23 Sep 1948, 37:1 (her friends collected a fund for her burial). AMD, p. 371. AS, p. 1167. BHD, p. 342. IFN, p. 324. Truitt, p. 358. "Soon to Make Screen Debut," *MPW,* 13 Nov 1920, 216 (in *What's in a Name?*). "Sign Helen Lee Worthing," *MPW,* 4 Apr 1925, 480. "Sign Ziegfeld Girl," *MPW,* 26 Feb 1927, 633.

Worthington, William J. [actor/director/producer/President of Multicolor Film Co.] (b. Troy NY, 8 Apr 1872–9 Apr 1941 [69], Beverly Hills CA). (Universal.) "W.J. Worthington; Stage and Screen Actor Founded a Color-Film Company," *NYT,* 11 Apr 1941, 22:3 (began 1913 in Hollywood; in *Kid Boots; Cardinal Richelieu, The Keeper of the Bees, Can This Be Dixie?,* and *Battle of Greed*). "William Worthington," *Variety,* 16 Apr 1941. AS, p. 1167. BHD1, p. 596; BHD2, p. 289. IFN, p. 324. Truitt, p. 358. W.E. Wing, "Along the Pacific Coast," *NYDM,* 19 May 1915, 24:1 (made a Universal producer).

Worthington, William, Jr. [actor/script reader] (b. Baltimore MD, 1898?–9 Mar 1966 [68], New York NY [Death Certificate Index No. 5266]). "William Worthington, 68, a Play Reader and Actor," *NYT,* 10 Mar 1966, 33:3. "William Worthington," *Variety,* 30 Mar 1966. AS, p. 1167. IFN, p. 324.

Wortman, Don[ald A.] [actor (b. 1920–13 Jan 1981 [60?], San Bernardino CA; under mysterious circumstances). AS, p. 1167 (b. 1927). BHD1, p. 596.

Wortman, Frank "Huck" [contractor/builder of the sets for *Intolerance*]. No data found. m. "Here's the Chaldean Who Built Babylon," *Photoplay Magazine,* Feb 1917, 83.

Wray, John [stage/film actor/playwright] (*né* John Malloy, b. Philadelphia PA, 13 Feb 1887–5 Apr 1940 [53], Los Angeles CA). "John Wray Dies, 52; Character Actor; Went to Hollywood in 1929 for Role in 'All Quiet'—in 'Mr. Deeds Goes to Town'; On Stage Here for Years; Appeared in 'Hamlet,' 'Three Live Ghosts' and 'Cobra'—Co-Author of Play," *NYT,* 7 Apr 1940, 44:8 (this obituary confuses the two Wrays; cf. Henry R. Davis, "2 Wrays [letter]," *CI,* 139 [Jan 1987], C23). "John Griffith Wray," *Variety,* 10 Apr 1940 (actor/writer; d. Hollywood CA, age 52). AS, p. 1168 (b. 1888). BHD1, p. 596. IFN, p. 324 (b. 1887). Katz, p. 1249. Truitt, p. 358 (*né* John Griffith Wray).

Wray, John Griffith [director/producer] (*né* John Griffith Malloy, b. Minneapolis MN, 1896–15 Jul 1929 [33], Los Angeles CA; complications from an operation for appendicitis). m. (1) Virginia Brissac—div. 11 May 1928; (2) **Bradley King**, 7 Oct 1928, Riverside CA (d. 1929). "John G. Wray Dies, Director of Movies," *NYT,* 16 Jul 1929, 25:4. "John Griffith Wray," *Variety,* 17 Jul 1929, but *cf.* Henry R. Davis, "2 Wrays [letter]," *CI,* 139 (Jan 1987), C23. AMD, p. 371. AS, p. 1168. BHD2, p. 289. IFN, p. 324 (d. 12 Jul). "Films to Cause Only Surface Thoughts and Simple Emotions Are Wanted, Says John Griffith Wray," *MPW,* 11 Mar 1922, 167. Ruth Mabrey, "Movie Stars' Gossip Causes Most Scandal, Says Film Director; John Griffith Wray, who directed 'Anna Christie,' declares that stars themselves are responsible for public's opinion about movieland," *MW,* 17 May 1924, 11, 26. "Wray with Universal," *MPW,* 28 Feb 1925, 878. "Wray Resigns as Head of Universal City; Schrock Succeeds," *MPW,* 21 Mar 1925, 242 (ill health). "Borzage and Wray Added to List of Fox Directors," *MPW,* 25 Apr 1925, 802. "Wray Beats Schedule," *MPW,* 22 Aug 1925, 831. "John G. Wray Marries," *NYT,* 8 Oct 1928, 15.4.

Wren, P[ercival] **C**[hristopher] (actor] (b. England, 1885–1941 [56?], England). AS, p. 1167.

Wren, Sam [actor/director] (b. Brooklyn NY, 20 Mar 1896–15 Mar 1962 [65], Los Angeles CA). m. **Virginia Sale** (d. 1992). AS, p. 1168.

Wright, Cowley [stage/film actor] (b. Anerley, England, 6 Oct 1889–18 Jan 1923 [33], London, England; following an illness of three days). "Three Deaths in London; Cowley Wright, Kate Santley and George Carney's Wife," *Variety,* 25 Jan 1923, 2:5. BHD, p. 342.

Wright, Fanny [actress] (b. London, England, 1872–29 Dec 1954 [82]). BHD1, p. 596. IFN, p. 324.

Wright, Fred E. [director/producer/scenarist] (b. Catskill NY, 1868–5 Aug 1936 [68?], Los Angeles CA). AS, p. 1168. BHD2, p. 289.

Wright, Fred E., Jr. [stock/film actor/director] (b. Dover, Kent, England, 8 Mar 1871–12 Dec 1928 [57], New York NY). (Pathé; Essanay.) "Fred Wright," *Variety,* 2 Jan 1929. AMD, p. 372. AS, p. 1168. BHD, p. 342. IFN, p. 324. Truitt, p. 359. "Staging Essanay's Big Feature [*In the Palace of the King*]," *NYDM,* 29 Sep 1915, 32:3 (b. Troy NY. Director for 7 years.). "Fred E. Wright," *MPW,* 9 Oct 1915, 235. "Fred Wright Rejoins Pathé," *MPW,* 29 Dec 1917, 1950.

Wright, George A. [actor/director] (d. 14 Mar 1937, Norwalk CT). (Edison.) AMD, p. 372. BHD, p. 342. "George A. Wright," *MPW,* 8 May 1915, 902. "Wright to Direct Miss Nesbitt," *MPW,* 20 Nov 1915, 1470. "George A. Wright," *MPW,* 15 Jul 1916, 466.

Wright, George D. [cameraman/producer]. No data found. AMD, p. 372. "George D. Wright Has Made Remarkable Mexican Films," *MPW,* 15 Feb 1919, 890. "Portraying Mexico's Activities," *MPW,* 15 Feb 1919, 891.

Wright, Haidee (daughter of Frederick Wright; sister of **Huntley Wright**) [stage/film actress] (b. London, England, 13 Jan 1868–29 Jan 1943 [75], London, England). "Haidee Wright Dies; On Stage 65 Years; Appeared Here in 'The Royal Family' and 'Mariners' in 1927," *NYT,* 30 Jan 1943, 15:6. "Haidee Wright," *Variety,* 3 Feb 1943. AS, p. 1168. BHD1, p. 596. IFN, p. 324.

Wright, Harold Bell [novelist/scenarist] (b. Rome NY, 4 May 1872–24 May 1944 [72], La Jolla CA; bronchial pneumonia). m. (1) Frances E. Long, 1899–1920; (2) Mrs. Winifred Mary Potter Duncan (widow). *To My Sons* (1934). "Harold B. Wright, Novelist, 72, Dead; Preacher of the Ozarks Earned Huge Fortune as Author, Though Scorned by Critics ["purveyor of sweetness and light"]; Books Sold Millions; 'Winning of Barbara Worth' [1911] and 'Shepherd of the Hills' His Most Successful Works," *NYT,* 25 May 1944, 21:1. "Harold Bell Wright," *Variety,* 31 May 1944. AMD, p. 372. AS, p. 1168 (b. 1871). FDY, p. 439. Tom Waller, "Sol Lesser Gives Reasons for Publicizing Author as Star," *MPW,* 1 Nov 1924, 31. "Irving Lesser Discusses the Harold Bell Wright Books," *MPW,* 21 Mar 1925, 278. "Seven Wright Novels Reamin for Picturing by Principal," *MPW,* 25 Apr 1925, 813.

Wright, Henry Otho [actor] (b. 1892–7 Jun 1940 [48?], San Bernardino CA). AS, p. 1168.

Wright, Hugh E. [actor/dramatist/song writer/scenarist] (b. Cannes, France, 13 Apr 1879–12 Feb 1940 [60], Windsor, England). "Hugh E. Wright," *NYT,* 14 Feb 1940, 21:6 (age 59). "Hugh E. Wright," *Variety,* 21 Feb 1940. AS, p. 1168. BHD1, p. 596; BHD2, p. 289. IFN, p. 324. Truitt, p. 359.

Wright, Huntley (son of Frederick Wright; brother of **Haidee Wright**) [stage/film/radio/TV actor] (*né* Frederick Wright, b. London, England, 7 Aug 1869–10 Jul 1941 [71], Bangor, Wales; heart disease). (Professional stage debut: *Fate and Fortune,* Princess Theatre, London, 1891.) "Huntley Wright, British Actor, 71; Musical Comedy Player Who Appeared Here in '07 Dies—Brother of Haidee Wright, On Stage for 48 Years; Had Role Under Management of Frohman in London—Help Captaincy in World War," *NYT,* 12 Jul 1941, 13:3. "Huntley Wright," *Variety,* 143, 16 Jul 1941, 54:1. AS, p. 1168. BHD1, p. 596 (b. 1868). IFN, p. 324.

Wright, Joseph Charles [art director] (b. 1892–24 Feb 1985 [92], Oceanside CA). AS, p. 1168. BHD2, p. 289.

Wright, Mack V. [actor/director] (b. Princeton IN, 1895–14 Aug 1965 [69], Boulder City NV). (Universal.) "Mack V. Wright," *Variety,* 25 Aug 1965. AS, p. 1168. BHD1, p. 596; BHD2, p. 289. IFN, p. 324. George A. Katchmer, "Forgotten Cowboys and Cowgirls—Part V," *CI,* 177 (Mar 1990), C6.

Wright, Marie [actress] (b. England, 1862–1 May 1949 [87], London, England). BHD1, p. 596. IFN, p. 324.

Wright, Myrtle [scenarist] (b. 1884–27 Feb 1963 [78?], Hammond IN). AS, p. 1168. BHD2, p. 289.

Wright, Olive [actress]. No data found. (Edison.)

Wright, Tennant C. (Tenny) [director] (b. Brooklyn NY, 18 Nov 1885–13 Sep 1971 [85], Los Angeles CA). m. Marian. (WB.) "T.C. (Tenny) Wright," *Variety,* 30 Mar 1966 (age 86). AS, p. 1168. BHD, p. 342; BHD2, p. 289. IFN, p. 324.

Wright, Walter [actor] (b. Kansas City KS, 1895?–28 May 1936 [41], Honolulu HI). "Walter Wright," *Variety,* 10 Jun 1936. AS, p. 1168.

Wright, Watkins Eppes [writer]. No data found. AMD, p. 372. "Who Is Author of 'The Chalk Line,'" *MPW,* 4 Nov 1916, 719.

Wright, William H. [title writer/producer/VP and general manager of Kalem] (d. 5 May 1959, Lakeside Hospital, Cleveland OH). "William Wright," *NYT,* 7 May 1959, 33:5 (retired to Cleveland in 1942). "William Wright," *Variety,* 214, 13 May 1959, 79 (produced *From the Manger to the Cross*). AMD, p. 372. AS, p. 1169. BHD2, p. 289. WIlliam H. Wright, "Modern Business Tendencies," *MPW,* 2 Jan 1915, 58. William H. Wright, "Short Films the Best; So Says William H. Wright, of the Kalem Company, Who Believes in a Return to the Policy That Established the Film Industry," *NYDM,* 27 Jan 1915, 42:1 (obstinately argues that "[b]revity is the soul of a picture"; that transients who drop in to see a quick film for leisure want a short film; etc.). "Short Films the Best; 'The Trade Is Going to Extremes on Features,' Says William Wright, of Kalem, in Outlining Company's Plans," *NYDM,* 28 Jul 1915, 22:1 ("Where the service of an exhibitor has been made up entirely from the product of the old line concerns and care has been used in the operation of the house, business has continued on an even basis, and to-day that man, although operating a small theater, is still in the running and doing a good business.") Lynde Denig, "The Kalem Viewpoint," *MPW,* 7 Aug 1915, 1002. "'Exhibitors Skeptical,' Says Wright," *MPW,* 8 Apr 1916, 236. "Overproduction Not Feared," *MPW,* 21 Oct 1916, 394. "'Hazards of Helen' in Third Year," *MPW,* 11 Nov 1916, 869. "William Wright in Jacksonville," *MPW,* 30 Dec 1916, 1945. "Kalem's Achievements as Pioneer," *MPW,* 10 Mar 1917, 1504–05. "Wright to Write Titles for C.L. Chester Productions," *MPW,* 7 Aug 1920, 724. "Wright Praises 'World' and Tells of Early Days," *MPW,* 11 Mar 1922, 141.

Wright, William Lord [scenarist] (b. Bellefontaine OH, 1879?–15 Apr 1947 [68], Los Angeles CA). (Pathé; Universal.) "William L. Wright," *Variety,* 30 Apr 1947 (wrote "silent filmplays for Selig"). AS, p. 1169. BHD2, p. 289 (d. 21 Apr). "The Art of Writing Scenarios [review]," *MPW,* 25 Feb 1911, 419:1 (Bellefontaine OH: The Scenario Instruction Publishing Co.; $1. "*Poeta nascitur non fit:* The poet is born, not made. So we believe is the scenario writer...So we hope that Mr. Wright's book will encourage the aspirant who aspires to some reasonable hope of success, will discourage those who have no fitness for this form of work. There are too many of the latter kind in the moving picture field to-day.").

Wrigley, Dewey [composer/cameraman] (b. San Francisco CA, 1899?–20 Apr 1950 [51], Los Angeles CA; heart attack). (Paramount.) "Dewey Wrigley," *Variety,* 26 Apr 1950. AS, p. 1169. BHD2, p. 289. FDY, p. 471.

Wulf, Fred W. [actor] (d. 19 Nov 1947?, Los Angeles CA). AS, p. 1169.

Wulschleger, Henry [director/scenarist] (b. France-d. 1939, Paris, France). AS, p. 1169.

Wunderlee, Frank [actor] (b. St. Louis MO, 12 Mar 1875–11 Dec 1925 [50], New York NY; apoplexy). (Griffith.) "Frank Wunderlee," *Variety,* 16 Dec 1925. AS, p. 1169. BHD, p. 342. IFN, p. 325. Truitt, p. 359.

Wungfield, H. Conway [actor] (b. Bray, England, 1865–9 Feb 1948 [82?], New York NY). AS, p. 1169.

Wupperman, Frank *see* **Morgan, Frank**

Wurtzel, Sam (brother of **Sol M. Wurtzel**) [producer] (b. 1897?–12 Mar 1967 [70], Los Angeles CA). (Fox, 1917.) "Sam Wurtzel," *Variety,* 22 Mar 1967. AS, p. 1169.

Wurtzel, Sol M. (brother of **Sam Wurtzel**) [producer] (b. New York NY, 12 Sep 1881–9 Apr 1958 [76], Westwood CA). AS, p. 1169.

Wust, Ida [actress] (b. Frankfurt, Germany, 10 Oct 1884–2 Nov 1958 [74], Berlin, Germany). AS, p. 1169 (b. Wiesbaden, Germany). BHD1, p. 597. IFN, p. 325.

Wyatt, Eustace George William [actress] (b. Bath, England, 5 Mar 1882–25 Oct 1944 [62], Los Angeles CA). AS, p. 1169.

Wycherly, Margaret [stage/film actress] (*née* Margaret DeWolfe, b. London, England, 26 Oct 1881–6 Jun 1956 [74], New York NY [Death Certificate Index No. 12478, age 70]). m. **Bayard Veiller**, 1901 (d. 1943). "Miss Wycherly, Actress, Was 74," *NYT,* 7 Jun 1956, 31:5. "Margaret Wycherly," *Variety,* 13 Jun 1956. AMD, p. 372. AS, p. 1169. BHD1, p. 597. IFN, p. 325. Katz, p. 1250. Truitt, p. 359. "[William Butler] Yeats Plays Well Done; Margaret Wycherly's Special Matinee at Hudson Theatre," *NYT,* 22 Feb 1905, 7:3 (the three plays were *The Hour Glass; The Land of the Heart's Desire;* and *Cathleen Ni Houlihan.* In *The Hour Glass,* though Wycherly 'brought much sincerity to bear upon her portrayal of the fool, it cannot be said that she succeeded at any time in creating a complete illusion. Her efforts in this play were handicapped to an extent by the entirely uninspired playing of Caryll Gillin." ¶In *Cathleen Ni Houlihan* "...Miss Wycherly's playing, while generally competent, was also generally conventional and stereotyped."). "Margaret Wycherly," *MPW,* 23 Jan 1915, 500.

Wyckoff, Alvin [cameraman] (b. NY, 3 Jul 1877–30 Jul 1957 [80], Los Angeles CA). AMD, p. 372. BHD2, p. 290. FDY, p. 471. "Lasky Chiefs Working on Color Process," *MPW,* 9 Feb 1918, 832.

Wyckoff, Fred J. [actor] (b. 1873?–5 Feb 1914 [41], Lyons NY). "Fred Wyckoff Dead," *Variety,* 13 Feb 1914. AS, p. 1169 (listed under Alvin Wyckoff).

Wyler, William (distant cousin of **Carl Laemmle**) [director] (*né* Willi Wyler, b. Mulhouse, Framce, 1 Jul 1902 [extrait de naissance no. 1298]–27 Jul 1981 [79], Beverly Hills CA; heart attack). m. Margaret Sullavan, 1934–36 (d. 1960); (2) Margaret Tallichet (d. 1991). Axel Madsen, *William Wyler; The Authorized Biography* (NY: Crowell, 1973). (Universal.) "Wyler Is Dead at 79; Director Had Won 3 Academy Awards [in 1942, 1946, and 1959]," *NYT,* 29 Jul 1981, 1:1, 19:1. "William Wyler Is Dead at 79; From Two-Reelers to Three Oscars," *Variety,* 29 Jul 1981. AMD, p. 372. AS, p. 1170. BHD2, p. 290. JS, p. 501 (nephew of Carl Laemmle; finished *Ben-Hur,* Italy, 1959, when Sam Zimblist died). Katz, pp. 1250–51. "Willy Wyler Sails," *MPW,* 18 Oct 1924, 612 (assistant director on *Phantom of the Opera*). "Wyler Directing Acord," *MPW,* 20 Feb 1926, 715. "Wyler to Direct New Acord Film," *MPW,* 15 May 1926, 229. "Wyler Signs 'U' Contract," *MPW,* 11 Jun 1927, 422. Gene D. Phillips, "William Wyler Interview," *Focus on Film,* No. 24, Spring 1976, 5–10.

Wynard, Charles Edward [cameraman] (b. 1846-Dec 1929 [83?], New York NY). BHD2, p. 290.

Wynden-Vail, Grace [publicist]. "Grace Wyndn-Vail Paramount Publicist," *MPW,* 18 Nov 1916, 1023.

Wyndham, Charles [stage/film actor] (b. Liverpool, England, 23 Mar 1837–12 Jan 1919 [81], London, England). m. (1) Ella McFarlane (d. 1916); (2) Mary Moore (Mrs. James Albery), Mar 1916 (widow). (Stage debut: Olympic Theatre, NYC, Jan 1861; London, 1885.) "Charles Wyndham, Actor, Dies at 81; First Took to Stage in America and Served as Surgeon in Our Civil War; Knighted by King Edward; With His Criterion Company, He Made Many Tours—Last Seen Here at Empire in 1909," *NYT,* 13 Jan 1919, 11:3 (cites 1st wife as Emma Silberard, d. Jan 1916). "Sir Charles Wyndham," *Variety,* 17 Jan 1919. AS, p. 1170. BHD, p. 343. IFN, p. 325. "Sir CHarles Wyndham Hurt; Actor Knocked Down by Street Car—Couldn't Appear Last Night," *NYT,* 19 Jan 1905, 1:2 (was appearing in *The Case of Rebellious Susan* at the Lyceum Theatre. Struck down, went to the theater, where he collapsed—his arm and shoulder were painfully bruised. *Mrs. Gorringe's Necklace* was put on, with Frank Atherley in the star's place.).

Wyndham, Poppy [actress] (b. Simla, India, 1893–14 Mar 1928 [34], at sea). BHD, p. 343. IFN, p. 325.

Wynn, Bessie [actress] (b. 1876–8 Jul 1968 [92?], Towaco NJ). AS, p. 1170. BHD, p. 343.

Wynn, Doris [actress] (*née* Doris Rink, b. San Diego CA, 1910–14 Jul 1925 [15], Los Angeles CA; pneumonia). AS, p. 1170. BHD, p. 343. IFN, p. 325. Truitt, p. 359.

Wynn, Ed (father of Keenan Wynn; grandfather of Tracy Keenan Wynn, b. 28 Feb 1945) (*né* Isaiah Edwin Leopold, b. Philadelphia PA, 9 Nov 1886–19 Jun 1966 [79], Beverly Hills CA; cancer). m. (1) Hilda Keenan, 1914–37 (son Xavier Aloysius James Jeremiah Keenan Wynn, 1916–1986); (2) Frieda Mierse, 1937–39; (3) Dorothy Elizabeth Nesbitt, 1946–55. "Ed Wynn, 'the Perfect Fool,' Dies on Coast, at 79; Stage, Vaudeville, TV Star Was Radio's Fire Chief; Dramatic Triumphs Capped Comic's 64-Year Career," *NYT,* 20 Jun 1966, 1:2, 33:2. "Rites Thursday for Ed Wynn,"

NYT, 21 Jun 1966, 43:2 (to be cremated). "Ed Wynn Dies at 79; Career Spanned Musicomedy, Radio, H'wood and TV," *Variety,* 22 Jun 1966. AS, p. 1170. BHD1, p. 597. IFN, p. 325. Katz, p. 1252. Truitt, p. 359. Ramon Romeo, "Reeling Down Broadway; Musical Comedy Star in Films," *Paris and Hollywood Screen Secrets,* May 1927, 62 (filming *Rubber Heels*).

Wynn, Hugh [film editor] (b. 1889?–8 Jan 1936 [46], Culver City CA). "Hugh Wynn," *Variety,* 15 Jan 1936. BHD2, p. 290.

Wynn, Mary [actress] (*née* Phoebe Bassor). No data found. AMD, p. 372. "Miss Bassor Changes Name," *MPW,* 20 Nov 1920, 376. "A Rising Star," *MPW,* 22 Oct 1921, 932.

Wynne, Gladys [actress] (b. England, 1886–10 Nov 1964 [78?], Paris, France). AS, p. 1170.

Wynne, Gladys [actress] (*née* Gweldys Edith Wynne, b. 1886?–10 Nov 1964 [78], Paris, France). m. **Milton Sills**, 1910, London, England—div. 1925 (d. 1930). "Gladys Wynne Sills," *Variety,* 16 Dec 1964. AMD, p. 372. AS, p. 1170. BHD, p. 343. "Gladys Wynn," *MPW,* 24 Oct 1914, 506.

Wynne, Hugh [actor] (b. New York NY, 1866–10 Feb 1949 [82?], Huntington NY). BHD1, p. 597.

Wyre, Mrs. George E. [casting director]. No data found. m. George E. Wyre. AMD, p. 372. "Mrs. George E. Wyre, Casting Director for Metro," *MPW,* 16 Jun 1917, 1791.

X

Xeo, Tina [actress] (b. Sicily, Italy, 1897). JS, p. 502 (in Italian silents from 1916; retired in the 20s).

Xydias, Anthony J[ohn] [exhibitor/producer] (b. Tinos, Greece, 22 May 1879–27 Oct 1952 [73], Los Angeles CA). m. (2) Caroline Rawls, div. 1932; (3) Marine De Mos, ca. 1940, Ft. Worth TX (d. 23 Sep 1943); (4) Rose. Sophia Adamson [step-daughter], *God's Angels & Pearl's Roses* (El Monte CA: American International Publishing Co., 1982). "Anthony J. Xydias," *NYT,* 29 Oct 1952, 29:4. "Anthony J. Xydias," *Variety,* 5 Nov 1952. AS, p. 1171. BHD2, p. 290. "Exhibitor Xydias En Route to Greece; Will Also Visit Balkan States, Turkey and Egypt and Expects to Open Export Office on His Return," *MPW,* 26 Jul 1919, 521:1 (and to visit his father in Constantinople whom he had not seen in 26 years. Around 1914, Xydias fought censorship regulations in Houston TX, which required exhibitors to submit films daily in order to get a permit for their presentation. He tested the case by showing fims without a permit and was arrested. After the expenditure of $5,000 the case reached the Texas Supreme Court but it was decided against him. He then disposed of his Houston theaters and went to New Orleans...). Re divorce: *LA Times,* 2 Sep 1930; 6 Oct 1930. Edgar M. Wyatt, "Anthony J. Xydias," *CI,* 231 (Sep 1994), 28, 30.

Y

Yaconelli, Frank [musician/actor] (b. Palermo, Italy, 2 Oct 1898–19 Nov 1965 [67], Los Angeles CA; lung cancer). AS, p. 1173. BHD1, p. 598. IFN, p. 325. (Played mood music on sets of Junior Coghlan films; later became a comedian in western films).

Yamamoto, Kajiro [actor] (b. Japan, 15 Mar 1902–28 Sep 1974 [72], Tokyo, Japan; cirhossis of the liver). AS, p. 1173. BHD, p. 343.

Yanner, Joseph [actor] (b. 1879–12 Dec 1949 [70], Kansas City MO). BHD, p. 343. IFN, p. 325.

Yantis, Fanny [actress] (d. 19 Jul 1929, Glendale CA). BHD, p. 343. IFN, p. 325.

Yapp, Cecil [actor] (b. Montreal, Quebec, Canada, 4 Apr 1879–2 Feb 1959 [79], St. Paul MN). BHD, p. 343.

Yarbrough, Jean W. [director] (b. Marianna AR, 22 Aug 1900–2 Aug 1975 [74], Los Angeles CA). (Roach; Monogram; Universal.) AS, p. 1173. BHD2, p. 290. IFN, p. 325. Katz, p. 1254.

Yarde, Margaret [actress] (b. Dartmouth, Devonshire, England, 2 Apr 1878–11 Mar 1944 [65], London, England). AS, p. 1173. BHD1, p. 598. IFN, p. 325.

Yates, Herbert J. [founded Consolidated Film Industries/President, Republic Pictures Corp.] (b. Brooklyn NY, 24 Aug 1880–3 Feb 1966 [85], Sherman Oaks CA; cerebral thrombosis). m. (2) Vera Hruba Ralston, 1952 (widow). "Herbert J. Yates, 85, Moviemaker, Is Dead," *NYT,* 4 Feb 1966, 31:4 (b. England). "Herbert J. Yates," *Variety,* 9 Feb 1966 (d. 4 Feb) (in 1935 merged Liberty, Mascot, Monogram and Republic into Republic Pictures). AS, p. 1174 (d. 4 Feb). BHD2, p. 290. IFN, p. 326. Katz, p. 1254 (began 1910).

Yeamans, Lydia *see* **Titus, Lydia Yeamans**

Yearance, William [actor] (b. 1853–19 Dec 1917 [64?], Boston MA). BHD, p. 343.

Yearsley, Clarence L. [publicist] (b. Bracken County KY, 26 Jul 1877–27 Jun 1957 [79], Los Angeles CA). AMD, p. 372. BHD2, p. 290. "Yearsley Comes to First National," *MPW,* 20 Oct 1917, 368. Clarence L. Yearsley, "Great Values in 'Stunt' Publicity," *MPW,* 20 Jul 1918, 334. "Clarence L. Yearsley Talks on the Relation of Posters to Motion Picture Advertising," *MPW,* 6 Nov 1920, 26–27. "Yearsley with Williams," *MPW,* 28 Jun 1924, 789. "Clarence L. Yearsley," *MPW,* 26 Mar 1927, 311.

Yearsley, Ralph [actor] (b. London, England, 6 Oct 1896–4 Dec 1928 [31], Los Angeles CA; suicide). "Ralph Yearsley," *Variety,* 12 Dec 1928. AS, p. 1174. BHD1, p. 598. IFN, p. 326 (age 32). Truitt, p. 360.

Yellen, Jack [composer/lyricist/scenarist] (b. Poland, 6 Jul 1892–17 Apr 1991 [98], Springville NY). "Jack Yellen," *Variety,* 29 Apr 1991. AS, p. 1174. BHD2, p. 290.

Yeoman, George [actor] (b. 1869?–2 Nov 1936 [67], Los Angeles CA). "George Yeoman," *Variety,* 4 Nov 1936 ("Did bit parts in pictures for the past seven years"). AS, p. 1174.

Yezierska, Anzia [writer]. No data found. AMD, p. 372. "New Author Joins Goldwyn Company," *MPW,* 5 Feb 1921, 676.

Yma, Yvonne [actress] (*née* Yvonne adrienne Nez, b. Paris, France, 5 Mar 1887–11 Feb 1959 [71], Paris, France [extrait de décès no. SN/1959]). AS, p. 1174.

Yohe, May, "Madcap May" [opera/stage/film actress] (b. Bethlehem PA, 6 Apr 1869–28 Aug 1938 [69], Boston MA; heart disease). m. (1) Lord Francis Hope, 27 Nov 1894; (2) Putnam Bradlee Strong, 1902, Yokahama, Japan—div. 1910, Portland OR; (3) Capt. John A. Smuts, 1914. (Began on stage in 1879.) "May Yohe Dies in Boston at 69; Noted Actress of Generation Ago Once Possessed the Famous Hope Diamond [blue-white gem of 44 1/2 carats]; Wife of British Soldier; Capt. John A. Smuts Says She Was Ill Only a Day After a Heart Attack," *NYT,* 28 Aug 1938, 32:3 (she was permitted to wear the Hope Diamond only twice during her marriage). "May Yohe," *Variety,* 131, 31 Aug 1938, 62:1 ("Possessed of an insouciant personality and a decided flair for the theatre."). AS, p. 1175. BHD, p. 343.

Yokel, Alex [producer] (b. 1886–27 Nov 1947 [61?], Lawrence NY). BHD2, p. 290.

Yoltz, Greta *see* **Sedgwick, Eileen**

Yonnel, Jean [actor] (*né* Jon Schachman, b. Bucharest, Rumania, 8 Jul 1891–17 Aug 1968 [77], Beyenes, France [extrait de décès no. 9/1968]). AS, p. 1175.

Yorke, Alice [actress] (b. 1886–22 Oct 1938 [52?], Flushing NY). BHD, p. 343.

Yorke, Augustus [actor] (b. 1860–27 Dec 1939 [79?]). BHD, p. 343.

Yorke, Edith [actress] (*née* Edithe Byard, b. Croydon, England, 23 Dec 1867–28 Jul 1934 [66], Southgate CA). AS, p. 1175 (d. London). BHD1, p. 599 (b. Derby, England). IFN, p. 326.

Yorke, Oswald [stage/film actor] (*né* Oswald Harker, b. London, England, 24 Nov 1866–25 Jan 1943 [76], New York NY; lobar pneumonia). m. **Annie Russell** (d. 1936); Ruth Guiterman. (Stage debut, 1884; London debut: 26 Feb 1889.) "Oswald Yorke Dies; Had Large Roles Here and in Britain—Lately with Jane Cowl," *NYT,* 26 Jan 1943, 19:4. "Oswald Yorke," *Variety,* 27 Jan 1943. AS, p. 1175. BHD, p. 343. SD, p. 1346.

Yorkney, John Charles [stage/film actor] (b. Argentina, 1871?–20 Aug 1941 [70], Fort Lee NJ; heart attack). "John Charles Yorkney; Actor Who Appeared in Original Cast of 'Merry Widow' Dies at 70," *NYT,* 22 Aug 1941, 15:4 ("He had played also in the silent films in the days when Fort Lee was the filmmaking center."). AS, p. 1175. BHD, p. 343. IFN, p. 326. Truitt, p. 360.

Yorska, Madame [actress]. No data found. AMD, p. 373. "Mme. Yorska Arrives in Los Angeles," *MPW,* 24 Aug 1918, 1094. "Operation on Nose," *MPW,* 14 Dec 1918, 1195.

Yoshiwara, Tamaki [actor] (*né* Kyonosuke Yoshiwara, b. Japan, 17 May 1901–30 Nov 1979 [78], New York NY). "Kyonosuke Yoshiwara," *Variety,* 19 Dec 1979. AS, p. 1175. BHD1, p. 599. IFN, p. 326.

Yost, Dorothy (sister of **Robert M. Yost**) [title writer/scenarist] (b. St. Louis MO, 25 Apr 1889–10 Jun 1967 [78], Monrovia CA). m. **Dwight H. Cummins**, 1927 (d. 1985). AMD, p. 373. BHD2, p. 291. FDY, p. 447. "Cummins, Yost Wed Soon," *MPW,* 1 Oct 1927, 284 (to wed Dwight W. Cummins).

Yost, Herbert A[lms] [stage/film actor] (aka Barry O'Moore, b. Harrison OH, 1881?–24 Oct 1945 [64], New York NY [Death Certificate Index No. 22633]). m. Agnes Scott. (Biograph, 1909; Edison.) "Herbert A. Yost, 65, on Stage 48 Years," *NYT,* 25 Oct 1945, 21:4. "Herbert A. Yost," *Variety,* 31 Oct 1945 (d. 23 Oct 1945). AMD, p. 267. AS, p. 1175 (d. 23 Oct). BHD, p. 343 (d. 23 Oct). IFN, p. 326. SD. Truitt, p. 360. *See* Ramsaye, p. 511. "Edison Touches Popular Chord," *MPW,* 3 Jan 1914, 28–29. "Barry O'Moore Leaves Edison," *NYDM,* 15 Jul 1914, 22:3 (to vacation at his estate at Shandokin NY for a month).

Yost, Robert M. (brother of **Dorothy Yost**) [scenarist/publicist] (b. St. Louis MO, 7 Jul 1885–10 Apr 1967 [81], Los Angeles CA). BHD2, p. 291.

Youdine, Constantin [director] (b. Moscow, Russia, 1896–20 Mar 1957 [61?], Moscow, Russia). AS, p. 1175.

Young, Arthur [actor] (b. Bristol, Gloucestershire, England, 2 Sep 1898–24 Feb 1959 [60], London, England). m. Beatrice Kane. AS, p. 1175. BHD1, p. 599 (b. Bristol, England). IFN, p. 326. SD, p. 1346.

Young, Briant S. [producer] (b. Salt Lake City UT, 6 Oct 1871–31 May 1950 [78], Los Angeles Co. CA). BHD2, p. 291.

Young, Bull *see* **Young, John W. (Bull)**

Young, Clara Kimball (daughter of **Edward M. Kimball** and **Pauline Garrett**) [actress] (*née* Clara Kimball, b. Chicago IL, 6 Sep 1890–15 Oct 1960 [70], Woodland Hills CA). m. (1) **James Young, Jr.**, 1912—div. 8 Apr 1919 (1948); (2) **Harry Garson**, 1919 (d. 1938); (3) Arthur S. Fauman. (Vitagraph, 1909; Equitable [World], 1915; Selznick; Clara Kimball Young Film Company, 1916.) "Clara Kimball Young, Actress, Is Dead at 70; Star of Silent Motion Pictures Bowed in 1912; Advent of Talkies Terminated Career of Player Noted for Her Costume Roles," *NYT,* 16 Oct 1960, 88:2. "Clara Kimball Young," *Variety,* 19 Oct 1960. AMD, p. 373. AS, p. 609 (Clara Kimball); p. 1175 (Clara Young). BHD1, p. 599. FFF, p. 217 (b. 1893). Finch, p. 286 (b. 19 Feb 1882). FSS, p. 296. IFN, p. 326. Katz, p. 1256. Lowrey, p. 200. MH, p. 143 (b. 1893). MSBB, p. 1044. Slide, p. 155. Spehr, p. 176. Truitt, pp. 360–61. "Gossip of the Studios; Clara Kimball Young," *NYDM,* 29 Jul 1914, 23:1 (her mother, Pauline Grenier, born in Chicago IL, was a descendant of Lord and Lady de Becour. Her father.was a descendant of John Kemble [brother of Mary Siddons], who was buried in Westminster Abbey). "Clara Kimball Young," *MPW,* 3 Oct 1914, 41–42. "Reception to Clara Kimball Young," *MPW,* 20 Feb 1915, 1122. "Clara Kimball Young in the Forthcoming Equitable Revival of 'Trilby,'" *NYDM,* 1 Sep 1915, 25 (photo). "Clara Is a 'Crack Shot,'" *MPW,* 11 Sep 1915, 1853. "Clara Kimball Young, Film Star, Wins Grand Prize in Popularity Contest; Irene Meara [legitimate player] Her Closest Competitor; Sixty-Five Other Winners in Most Exciting Competition Yet Held; Ethel Jewitt Gets an Auto; Claude Golden, Second in 'Legitimate' Class, Awarded a Fine Maxwell Car; Another Goes to Fred Mace," *The [NY] Morning Telegraph,* 12 Dec 1915, 1:5 (Young, who received over a million votes, won a Haynes 6-passenger touring car. Of motion picture actors, Lena Viola Brown was third runner-up; W.S. Hart was 12th, and Pickford was 17th). "Realism in 'Camille,'" *MPW,* 18 Dec 1915, 2161. "Clara Kimball Young Back from Cuba," *MPW,* 18 Mar 1916, 1830. "Clara Kimball Young Declines Vaudeville Offers," *MPW,* 1 Apr 1916, 95. "Actress to Do Double Time," *MPW,* 8 Apr 1916, 265. "Studio for Clara Kimball Young," *MPW,* 17 Jun 1916, 2045. "Miss Young Goes on Vacation," *MPW,* 26 Jun 1915, 2240. "Clara Kimball Young for Chicago," *MPW,* 8 Jul 1916, 255. "Clara Kimball Young," *MPW,* 24 Feb 1917, 1183. "Clara Kimball Young Sues Selznick," *MPW,* 9 Jun 1917, 1580. "Selznick Would Enjoin Miss Young," *MPW,* 16 Jun 1917, 1761. "New Clara Kimball Young Company Announced," *MPW,* 7 Jul 1917, 66. "Miss Young Getting Ready to Produce," *MPW,* 14 Jul 1917, 250. "Miss Young Makes Answer to Selznick," *MPW,* 21 Jul 1917, 461. Margaret I. MacDonald, "Clara Kimball Young Discusses Picture Art," *MPW,* 21 Jul 1917, 461. "Miss Young Leases Thanhouser Studio," *MPW,* 4 Aug 1917, 804. "Clara Kimball Young Film Company Formed," *MPW,* 11 Aug 1917, 918. "Clara Kimball Young Bombards Soldeirs with Chocolate," *MPW,* 15 Sep 1917, 1668. "Clara Kimball Young," *MPW,* 15 Dec 1917, 1620. "Clara Kimball Young Going to Coast with Company," *MPW,* 30 Mar 1918, 1845. "Clara Kimball Young Likes the California Climate," *MPW,* 11 May 1918, 875. "Clara Kimball Young to Build Studio in Los Angeles," *MPW,* 29 Jun 1918, 1869. "Rocks Break Up Luncheon," *MPW,* 6 Jul 1918, 42. "Miss Young to Build in Pasadena," *MPW,* 13 Jul 1918, 191. "San Franciscans Greet Clara Kimball Young," *MPW,* 20 Jul 1918, 413. "Ovations Greet Clara Kimball Young," *MPW,* 3 Aug 1918, 690. "Many Subjects Slated for Miss Young," *MPW,* 10 Aug 1918, 817. S. Clark Patchin, "Clara Kimball Young Given Great Ovation," *MPW,* 10 Aug 1918, 872. Edward Weitzel, "Making 'Savage Woman' Savage," *MPW,* 7 Sep 1918, 1393. "Miss Young Back at Coast," *MPW,* 21 Sep 1918, 1722. "Clara Swears When Necessary," *MPW,* 2 Nov 1918, 596. "Both Sides 'Stand Pat' in Clara Kimball Young," *MPW,* 18 Jan 1919, 313. "Clara Kimball Young Moves from Sunset to Brunton," *MPW,* 8 Feb 1919, 798. "*Cheating Cheaters* [novelization]," *MPC,* Mar 1919, 39–42, 67, 81 (illustrated). "Clara Kimball Young Film Corporation Files Answer in Law Suit," *MPW,* 1 Mar 1919, 1234. "Stars' Cars Hit Boys," *MPW,* 22 Mar 1919, 1628. "Miss Young's Auto Knocks Down Boy," *MPW,* 22 Mar 1919, 1636 (7-year-old Laurence Conaway, Hollywood CA). "James Young to Wed," *MPW,* 12 Apr 1919, 519. "Equity Will Release Clara Kimball Young Films," *MPW,* 19 Jul 1919, 371. "Clara Kimball Young and Her Company Arrive in San Francisco for Fine Arts Film," *MPW,* 9 Aug 1919, 843. "Clara Kimball Young's Mother Dead in Los Angeles," *MPW,* 27 Dec 1919, 1108 (d. 12 Dec 1919; *née* Pauline Maddern). "Miss Young Creates Fashion Show for Display in 'Forbidden Woman,'" *MPW,* 14 Feb 1920, 1112. "Miss Young Heads Committee to Restore Old Missions; Is Background for Next Picture," *MPW,* 10 Apr 1920, 278. "Contest Proves Popularity of Clara Kimball Young in Films," *MPW,* 26 Jun 1920, 1767. "Fine Arts and Equity in Suit Over Young Pictures," *MPW,* 7 Aug 1920, 702. "Sues Clara Kimball Young for an Additional $50,000," *MPW,* 13 Nov 1920, 225. "Harriman National Bank Sues Clara Kimball Young," *MPW,* 20 Nov 1920, 374 (for $3,743.65). "Selznick Wins in Suit from Equity," *MPW,* 11 Dec 1920, 707. "Clara Kimball Young Relates Her Plans and Wishes All a Very Merry Christmas," *MPW,* 1 Jan 1921, 45. "Texas Cities Greet Clara Kimball Young; Crandall's Exploitation Most Effective," *MPW,* 5 Mar 1921, 72. "Clara Kimball Young's Triumphant Tour," *MPW,* 23 Jul 1921, 396. "Says New Stories Written for Screen Are Better Movie Stuff Than Filmed Novels," *MPW,* 29 Oct 1921, 1025. "Levy Sues Harry Garson and Clara Kimball Young," *MPW,* 29 Oct 1921, 1034. Maude Cheatham, "Time Flies—And Leaves No Trace," *Classic,* Mar 1923, 22–23. "*Cordelia the Magnificent* [review]," *MW,* 9 Jun 1923, 14 ("Miss Young is at the threshold of that period during which actresses play character roles or not at all."). "Popular Star Comes Back," *MPW,* 28 Feb 1925, 915. Henry R. Davis, "Clara Kimball Young; Was the Kind of a Beautiful Woman Who Has Little Practical Sense," *FIR,* Aug/Sep 1961, 419–25. Eldon K. Everett, "'Flora Fourflush' and Other Little Known Serials," *CI,* 88 (Oct 1982), 40–41. "Buck Rainey's Filmographies," *CI,* 161 (Nov 1988), 10, C13-C14; "Films of Clara Kimball Young, Part II," *CI,* 162 (Dec 1988), 53; Part III, *CI,* 163 (Jan 1989), 36–38. Eve Golden, "Clara Kimball Young: 'Dark Madonna' of the Early Silents," *CI,* 240 Jun 1995), 22, 24.

Young, Clarence Upson [scenarist] (b. MI, 14 Oct 1895–22 Jan 1969 [73], South Laguna CA). BHD2, p. 291.

Young, Clifton "Bonedust" [actor: child villain in Our Gang comedies] (aka Bobby Young, b. New York NY, 15 Sep 1917–10 Sep 1951 [33], Los Angeles CA). "Film Actor Dies in [Hotel] Room Fire," *NYT,* 11 Sep 1951, 33:4. AS, p. 1175. BHD1, p. 599. IFN, p. 326. Truitt, p. 361.

Young, Freddie [stuntman/cinematographer] (*né* frederick A. Young, b. London, England, 5 Oct 1902–1 Dec 1998 [96], London, England). m. (1) Marjorie, 1927 (d. 1963); (2) Joan. *Seventy Light Years; A Life in Movies,* Faber & Faber, 1999. (Gaumont; British and Dominions; stuntman in

Roy Roy, 1922, and *Triumph of the Rat*, 1926; AA for *Lawrence of Arabia*, 1962; *Dr. Zhivago*, 1965; and *Ryan's Daughter*, 1970). Sarah Lyall, "Freddie Young, 96, Cameraman for Hitchcock and David Lean," *NYT*, 5 Dec 1998, C16. AS, p. 1176. *The International Guardian*, 3 Dec 1998. Katz, p. 1256 (began in England, ca. 1917). Waldman, p. 312.

Young, Hal [cinematographer]. No data found. FDY, p. 471.

Young, Harold [actor] (b. 1900?–2 Feb 1959 [59]). IFN, p. 326.

Young, Howard Irving [writer/scenarist] (b. Jersey City NJ, 24 Apr 1893–24 Feb 1952 [58], Los Angeles CA; cancer). m. Kathleen Millay (d. 1943). "Howard Irving Young," *Variety*, 5 Mar 1952. AMD, p. 374. AS, p. 1176. IFN, p. 326. BHD2, p. 291 (b. 13 Nov). "Kathleen Millay, Sister of the Poet; Novelist, Writer of Verse and Fairy Tales Dies at 46 in Hospital Here; Had Worked in War Plant; Quit to Apply for the Wacs—Husband, Playwright H.I. Young, Is in England," *NYT*, 23 Sep 1943, 21:3 (*née* Kathleen Tolman, b. Union ME, 1897?–21 Sep 1943 [46], NY NY). "Howard Irving Young Joins Metro," *MPW*, 4 Mar 1916, 1485. "Another Youth at the Front," *MPW*, 2 Sep 1916, 1545. "Áoiung Goes to Officers' Training Camp," *MPW*, 16 Jun 1917, 1765. "Lieutenant Young Writes War Stories for World Film," *MPW*, 29 Jun 1918, 1865. "Howard Irving Young and C.D. Hobart Join Fox Scenario Staff," *MPW*, 23 Aug 1919, 1153. "William LeBaron Now Director-General of Cosmopolitan; Other Changes Made," *MPW*, 21 Jan 1922, 262. "Joins Theatre Magazine," *MPW*, 12 Jan 1924, 106. "Young a Playwright," *MPW*, 19 Jul 1924, 178.

Young, J. Arthur [stage/film/radio actor] (b. Chicago IL, b. 1880?–14 Sep 1943 [63], Kew Gardens, Queens NY). m. Marguerite Vandergrift. "J. Arthur Young, Character Actor; Player on Legitimate Stage for 45 Years Dies in Kew Gardens Home at 63; Had Film and Radio Roles; Seen on Boards Here in 'Ben Hur,' 'Night of January 16' and 'The Male Animal,'" *NYT*, 6 Sep 1943, 21:4. AS, p. 1176. BHD, p. 343. IFN, p. 326.

Young, Jack [actor] (*né* John Young, b. Toronto, Canada, 7 Oct 1894 [Birth certificate #042374, no. 3497]–28 Oct 1966 [72], Los Angeles CA). AS, p. 1176. IFN, p. 326.

Young, Jack R. [cinematographer] (b. 1896–1 Feb 1971 [74?], Los Angeles CA). BHD2, p. 291. FDY, p. 471.

Young, James L., Jr. (son of former MD senator James Young, Sr.) [actor/director/scenarist/producer] (b. Baltimore MD, 1 Jan 1872–9 Jun 1948 [76], New York NY). (Vitagraph, 1910; World.) m. (1) **Rida Johnson** (d. 1926); (2) **Clara Kimball Young**, 1910–19 (d. 1960); (3) **Clara Whipple**, 10 Apr 1919, Riverside CA–separated 16 Jul 1921; (4) Countess Julie de Valera, 1928. AMD, p. 374. AS, p. 1176 (b. 15 Mar 1876). BHD1, p. 619; BHD2, p. 291. Katz, p. 1257. 1921 Directory, p. 278. Ragan, p. 1870. Spehr, p. 178. "Misplaced Credit," *MPW*, 22 Jun 1912, 1113. "Vitagraph Notes," *MPW*, 22 Jun 1912, 1135 (appointed Vitagraph director). "James Young Writes," *MPW*, 8 Feb 1913, 588. "Young in Accident; Vitagraph Director's Auto Fatally Injures Boy Playing Recklessly in Street," *NYDM*, 8 Jul 1914, 22:3 (Young took the boy to a nearby drug store. A crowd threatened him. He left his card and number with a local resident. "I realize now that I should have immediately notified the police, but after seeing the boy, who did not seem to be badly injured, and with the incidental excitement, I failed to advise the authorities." The boy's skull was fractured.). "James Young Denies Running Away," *MPW*, 18 Jul 1914, 435. "He Spoke to Lord Roberts," *MPW*, 5 Dec 1914, 1391. "James Young Goes to Lasky," *MPW*, 5 Feb 1916, 785. "James Young Sues Selznick," *MPW*, 19 Feb 1916, 1103. "James Young to Direct Blanche Sweet," *MPW*, 29 Jul 1916, 781. "Jimmy Young to Direct Miss Barriscale," *MPW*, 9 Jun 1917, 1590. "Young to Direct Bessie Barriscale," *MPW*, 16 Jun 1917, 1761. "James Young to Direct [Earle] Williams," *MPW*, 1 Jun 1918, 1299. "James Young Engaged by Haworth," *MPW*, 22 Jun 1918, 1722. "Young Again Directs Williams," *MPW*, 8 Feb 1919, 750. "James Young to Wed," *MPW*, 12 Apr 1919, 218 (filed for divorce from CKY, Jun 1917; interlocutory decree granted 25 Mar 1918; final decree, 8 Apr 1919; m. 1912). "Young—Whipple," *MPW*, 26 Apr 1919, 519. "James Young Not with Vitagraph," *MPW*, 9 Aug 1919, 789. "James Young to Direct for Pathé First Rudyard Kipling Scenario; To Be Filmed at Brunton Studios," *MPW*, 26 Feb 1921, 1080 (*Without Benefit of Clergy*). Edward Weitzel, "An Ever-Ready Pathé Publicity Man; or Interviewing James Young by Proxy," *MPW*, 23 Apr 1921, 825. "Sued for Divorce," *MPW*, 20 Aug 1921, 793 (by Whipple). "James Young Lectures," *MPW*, 10 Jun 1922, 548 (on Hamlet at Univ. of CA). "Young Will Direct for First National," *MPW*, 27 Jan 1923, 384. "Able Directors Behind First National Pictures," *MPW*, 9 Jun 1923, 510. "James Young," *MPW*, 15 Jan 1927, 191.

Young, Joe [composer] (*né* Joseph Judewitz, b. New York NY, 4 Jul 1889–21 Apr 1939 [49], New York NY). m. Ruth Young. "Joe Young, Writer of Popular Songs; Lyricist Whose Verses Have Been Sung by Millions Is Dead Here at 50," *NYT*, 22 Apr 1939, 17:6 (d. 22 Apr; collaborated with Sam Lewis). "Joe Young Dies at 50; Wrote Top Seller of All Time [*Tuck Me Sleep in My Tucky Home* (sic)]—Prominent in ASCAP," *Variety*, 26 Apr 1939 (wrote *In a Little Spanish Town; Five Foot Two, Eyes of Blue*). AMD, p. 374. AS, p. 1176. ASCAP 66, pp. 809–10. AS, p. 1176. BHD2, p. 291. "Mack Sennett Gives Young a Chance," *MPW*, 21 Aug 1926, 489.

Young, John W. (Bull) [pugilist/actor] (d. 23 Aug 1913, Los Angeles CA; cerebral hemorrhage). "Pugilist Killed by Ring Knockout [by Jess Willard]; Accident in Vernon Starts Campaign to End Fighting in California," *NYT*, 24 Aug 1913, II, 1:4. "Majestic's 'Fighter' Dead," *MPW*, 17, 13 Sep 1913, 1163 (appeared in *One Round O'Brien Comes Back*, 1913). AS, p. 1175 (Bull Young). AMD, p. 373. BHD, p. 343. IFN, p. 326.

Young, Lon [publicist/title writer]. No data found. AMD, p. 374. FDY, p. 447. "Young Warner Publicity Head," *MPW*, 4 Nov 1922, 65. "Lon Young Resigns," *MPW*, 8 Nov 1924, 122. "Lon Young Not Candidate for Mayor of Indianapolis," *MPW*, 19 Nov 1927, 11.

Young, Loretta (sister of **Polly Ann** and Georgiana Young and **Sally Blane**) [film/TV actress: Wampas Star, 1929] (*née* Gretchen Michaela Young, b. Salt Lake City UT, 6 Jan 1913–12 Aug 2000 [87], Los Angeles CA, at the home of Georgiana and Ricardo Montalban; ovarian cancer). m. (1) **Grant Withers**, Yuma AZ, Jan 1930—annulled 1931 (d. 1959); (2) TV producer Thomas H.A. Lewis, 31 Jul 1940—div. (sons Christopher Paul, 1943, and Peter Chrles, 1945)—div. 1969; Jean Louis, 1994 (d. 1997; daughter with Clark Gable). Lena Williams, "Loretta Young, Glamorous Leading Lady of Film and Television, Dies at 87," *NYT*, 13 Aug 2000, 39. Stephanie Simon, "Loretta Young; Actress with beauty, wholesome image, romanticism," *PP-G*, 13 Aug 2000, E-5 ("Her cash-strapped mother allowed Gretchen and her sisters to act in 'the flickers' to raise extra money for the family. Little Gretchen made her debut at age 4 in 'The Only Way' as a child weeping on an operating table. She also appeared as an Arab child in Rudolph Valentino's 1921 classic 'The Shiek.' ...She set up a puritanical system to fine fellow actors who cursed on the set, but she held blazing love affairs with her leading men behind the scenes."). *The Things I Had to Learn* (1961); Morella & Epstein, *Loretta Young—An Extraordinary Life;* Judy Lewis [daughter], *Uncommon Knowledge* (NY: Pocket Books, 1994). (Film debut: *The Primrose Ring*, 1917; 1st National; Fox; Best Actress AA for *The Farmer's Daughter*, 1947; Emmy, *The Loretta Young Show*, 1955. This show premiered on NBC on 20 Sep 1953.) AS, p. 1176. Finch, p. 566 (b. 1911). FSS, p. 297. Katz, pp. 1257–58. Lena Williams, "Life Waltzes On," *NYT*, 30 Mar 1995, C1, C10. Kathleen Tracy, "Miracle of Prayer Reunites Loretta Young and Daughter; Insiders reveal secret of Clark Gable's love child," *Globe*, 42, 5 Sep 1995, 15 (as for confirmation from Young—"It is still her attitude that it's nobody's damn business except hers—and God's."). "Miss Loretta Young in the Desert; Another Smashing Entrance," *Palm Springs Life* (Dec 1995). Chris Doherty, "Loretta Young Tragedy," *Globe*, 47 (1 Aug 2000), pp. 6–9 (operated on for colon cancer on 3 Jul 2000).

Young, Lucile [actress] (b. 1892?–2 Aug 1934 [42], Los Angeles CA). (American.) AS, p. 1176. IFN, p. 326. Truitt, p. 361.

Young, Mrs. Martha Hamilton [stage/film actress] (*née?*, b. Norway). "Captain and Mrs. Young," *NYDM*, 27 Nov 1915, 30:4 ("Mrs. Young will be seen shortly in important roles with some of the big feature producers in the United States.").

Young, Marvin [child actor in silents/writer/producer] (b. 1903?–26 May 1993 [90], Los Angeles CA; cardiac arrest). "Marvin Young," *Variety*, 28 Jun 1993, 34:1. AS, p. 1176. BHD, p. 343.

Young, Mary L. [actress] (b. 1857?–13 Nov 1934 [77?], Los Angeles CA). AS, p. 1176. BHD, p. 343 (Mary H. Young). IFN, p. 326. Truitt, p. 361.

Young, Mary Marsden [actress] (b. New York NY, 21 Jun 1879–23 Jun 1971 [92], La Jolla CA). m. John Craig. "Mary Marsden Young," *Variety*, 30 Jun 1971. AS, p. 1176 (Mary Young). BHD1, p. 599 (b. 1880). IFN, p. 326.

Young, Noah [actor] (b. Nevada CO, 2 Feb 1887–18 Apr 1958 [71], Los Angeles Co. CA). AMD, p. 374. AS, p. 1176. BHD1, p. 599. IFN, p. 327. "Three Year Contract for Noah Young," *MPW*, 5 May 1923, 82. "Cast Complete for Lloyd's FIrst Paramount Picture," *MPW*, 5 Sep 1925, 90. George Katchmer, "Remembering the Great Silents," *CI*, 220 (Oct 1993), 42–43.

Young, Olive [actress] (b. St. Joseph MO, 21 Jun 1903?–4 Oct 1940 [37], Bayonne NJ; pneumonia). m. Dr. Alfred Lum. "Olive Young," *NYT*, 5 Oct 1940 ("...American-born former motion-picture actress whose parents were Chinese..."). "Olive Young," *Variety*, 16 Oct 1940. AS, p. 1176 (b. 1907). BHD1, p. 599.

Young, Polly Ann (sister of Georgiana and **Loretta Young** and **Sally Blane**) [actress] (b. Denver CO, 25 Oct 1908–14 Jan 1997 [88], Los Angeles CA). m. J. Carter Hermann. "Polly Ann Young [obituary]," *CI,* 262 (Apr 1997), 58. AMD, p. 374. AS, p. 1176. BHD1, p. 599. BR, pp. 462–64. Katz, p. 1257. "Polly Ann Young," *MPW,* 29 Jan 1927, 341.

Young, Rida Johnson [writer] (*née* Rida Johnson, b. Baltimore MD, 28 Feb 1875–8 May 1926 [51], Southfield Point, near Stamford CT). m. **James L. Young, Jr.** (d. 1948). "Rida Johnson Young, Playwright, Dies; Author of 'Brown of Harvard' Succumbs at Her Stamford Home After Long Illness; Was a Prolific Writer; 'Little Old New York,' 'Maytime' and 'Naughty Marietta' Among Her Best Known Works," *NYT,* 9 May 1926, II, 9:1. "Rida Johnson Young," *Variety,* 12 May 1926.

Young, Roland [stage/film actor] (b. London, England, 11 Nov 1887–5 Jun 1953 [65], New York NY). m. (1) Marjorie Kummer; (2) Dorothy Patience May (widow). "Roland Young Dies in Home Here at 65; Mr. Topper of Films Appeared Also in 'Ruggles of Red Gap' and in Many Stage Hits," *NYT,* 7 Jun 1953, 84:1. "Roland Young," *Variety,* 10 Jun 1953 (began 1929). AS, p. 1176. BHD1, p. 600. IFN, p. 327. Katz, p. 1258. Truitt, p. 361.

Young, Stark [scenarist] (b. Como MS, 1881–6 Jan 1963 [81?], Fairfield CT). BHD2, p. 291.

Young, Tammany [actor] (b. New York NY, 9 Sep 1886–26 Apr 1936 [49], Los Angeles CA; heart attack in his sleep). (FP-L.) "Tammany Young Dies in His Sleep, Aged 49," *Variety,* 29 Apr 1936. AS, p. 1177. BHD1, p. 600. IFN, p. 327. Truitt, p. 361.

Young, Tex "Shorty" [actor]. No data found. George Katchmer, "Forgotten Cowboys and Cowgirls—Part XIII," *CI,* 190 (Apr 1991), C8.

Young, Waldemar [title writer/scenarist] (grandson of Brigham Young) (b. Salt Lake City UT, 1 Jul 1878–30 Aug 1938 [60], Los Angeles CA; pneumonia). (MGM.) "Waldemar Young; Hollywood Film Scenarist Dies of Pneumonia," *NYT,* 31 Aug 1938, 15:3 (wrote *The Unholy Three* and *The Miracle Man*). "Waldemar Young," *Variety,* 7 Sep 1938. AMD, p. 374. AS, p. 1177. BHD2, p. 291. FDY, pp. 439, 447. IFN, p. 327. Katz, p. 1259 (began 1917). "Waldemar Young Engaged to Write Scenarios for Metro," *MPW,* 24 Jul 1920, 496. "Capable Scenario Writer Coming," *MPW,* 2 Oct 1920, 659. "Waldemar Young Signed for Paramount Scenario Staff," *MPW,* 9 Oct 1920, 780. "Young Joins Preferred," *MPW,* 2 Jun 1923, 381. "Writer for Preferred Helps Select Beauties for Screen," *MPW,* 18 Aug 1923, 580.

Young, Walter [actor] (b. 1878?–18 Apr 1957 [79], New York NY; pneumonia). "Walter Young," *NYT,* 20 Apr 1957, 17:1 (d. 19 Apr; in 19 films; actor for 50 years). (Fox; WB; Metro.) "Walter Young," *Variety,* 24 Apr 1957. AS, p. 1177. BHD, p. 344. IFN, p. 327.

Young Deer, James [actor] (b. Dakota City NB–d. 17 Apr 1946, New York NY). m. **Princess Red Wing** (d. 1974). (Bison; Pathé.) AMD, p. 374. AS, p. 1177 (m. Lillian St. Cyr). BHD, p. 147; 344. Spehr, p. 176. "James Young Deer," *MPW,* 6 May 1911, 999. "Young Deer Builds Mission," *MPW,* 29 Jun 1912, 1218 (made his 100th film). "Fined for Inhumane Realism," *MPW,* 26 Apr 1913, 367. "Youngdeer Back from France," *MPW,* 17 Jan 1920, 397.

Youngblood, Paul [art director] (b. MN, 27 Aug 1890–2 Oct 1956 [66], Woodland Hills CA). "Paul Youngblood," *Variety,* 17 Oct 1956. BHD2, p. 291.

Younge, Lucille K. [actress] (b. Lyons, France, 1892–2 Aug 1934 [42?], Los Angeles CA). AMD, p. 374. BHD1, p. 600. "Lucille K. Younge," *MPW,* 21 Feb 1914, 952. "Lucille Younge Engaged by American Company," *MPW,* 24 Feb 1917, 1198. "Lucille K. Younge with Paralta," *MPW,* 14 Jul 1917, 250.

Younger, A.P. [title writer/scenarist] (b. Sacramento CA, 28 Sep 1890–29 Nov 1931 [41], Los Angeles CA; possible suicide by shooting). (MGM.) "Younger Kills Self; Folks Say Accident," *Variety,* 1 Dec 1931. AMD, p. 374. AS, p. 1177. BHD2, p. 291. FDY, pp. 439, 447. "Younger's Stories for Wm. Haines," *MPW,* 19 Mar 1927, 191. "Younger Signs M-G-M COntract," *MPW,* 8 Oct 1927, 341.

Youngerman, Joseph [prop man/assistant director/executive director of DGA] (b. So. Chicago IL, 1906?–22 Nov 1995 [89], Los Angeles CA; after stroke). m. Molly. (Paramount, 1926.) Robert McG. Thomas, Jr., "Joseph Youngerman, 89, Aide to Directors on Film Backlots," *NYT,* 30 Nov 1995, B18:5. Ted Johnson, "Joseph Youngerman," *Variety,* 27 Nov 1995, 92:4. BHD2, p. 291.

Yowlachie, Chief [actor] (*né* Daniel Yowlachie/Daniel Simmons, b. Yakima Indian Reservation WA, 15 Aug 1891–7 Mar 1966 [74], Los Angeles CA; pneumonia). AS, p. 229 (listed under Chief Yowlachie). BHD1, p. 600 (b. Wakima WA). IFN, p. 327. George Katchmer, "Remembering the Great Silents," *CI,* 216 (Jun 1993), 50 (b. 1890).

Yule, Joe (father of Mickey Rooney) [actor] (Scotland, 30 Apr 1894–30 Mar 1950 [55], Los Angeles CA). m. (1) Nell Carter; (2) Leota. (MGM.) "Joe Yule, 55, Father of Mickey Rooney," *NYT,* 31 Mar 1950, 31:4 (age 55). "Joe Yule," *Variety,* 5 Apr 1950 (age 56). AS, p. 1177. IFN, p. 327.

Yurka, Blanche [stage/film actress] (*née* Blanche Jurka, b. St. Paul MN, 18 Jun 1887–6 Jun 1974 [86], New York NY; arteriosclerosis [Death Certificate Index No. 10385]). m. **Ian Keith** (d. 1960). AS, p. 1177. BHD1, p. 600. IFN, p. 327. "News of Stock Plays and Players," *NYDM,* 25 Nov 1914, 10:2.

Yvoneck [actor] (*né* Arthur Julian, b. 1873–23 Apr 1929 [56?], Paris, France). BHD, p. 344.

Yvonne, Mimi [actress] (b. 1908). No other data found. (Lubin; Photoplay Production Co.) AMD, p. 374. "'Littlest Rebel' Star in Danger," *NYDM,* 12 Aug 1914, 24:3 (stranded in Leipsic with her mother because of the war). "Mimi Yvonne a Star; Frank Tichenor to Present Child Actress in Forthcoming Feature," *NYDM,* 2 Sep 1914, 24:1. "Mimi Yvonne," *MPW,* 30 Oct 1915, 765. "Studio Gossip," *NYDM,* 6 Nov 1915, 37:2 (7½ years old).

Z

Zabelle, Flora [actress] (b. 1 Apr 1880?–7 Oct 1968 [88], New York NY [Death Certificate Index No. 20874]). m. **Raymond Hitchcock**, 1905 (d. 1929). "Flora Zabelle Hitchcock, ex-Actress and Designer," *NYT,* 8 Oct 1968, 47:2. "Flora Zabelle," *Variety,* 9 Oct 1968. AMD, p. 375. AS, p. 1179. BHD, p. 344. IFN, p. 327. SD, p. 1351. Truitt, p. 361. "Flora Zabelle with Famous Players," *MPW,* 16 Oct 1915, 421. Cover, *NYDM,* 6 Nov 1915 (with Roscoe Arbuckle and Raymond Hitchcock). "Flora Zabelle Supports Friend Mabel Normand," *MPW,* 14 Sep 1918, 1590.

Zaccaria, Gino [director]. JS, p. 502 (in Italian silents from 1912).

Zacconi, Ermete [actor] (*né* Ernesto Zacconi, b. Montecchio di Reggio Emilia, Italy, 14 Sep 1857–14 Oct 1948 [91], Reggio Emilia, Italy). *Ricordi e battaglie* (1946), autobiography. AMD, p. 375. AS, p. 1179 (d. Viareggio, Italy). BHD, p. 344 (d. Viareggio, Italy). JS, p. 502 (in Italian silents from 1912). "Italy's Irving Plays for Itala," *MPW,* 28 Dec 1912, 1274.

Zahler, Lee [actor/composer] (b. New York NY, 14 Aug 1893–21 Feb 1947 [53], Los Angeles CA). (Darmour studios; Columbia.) IFN, p. 327. "Lee Zahler," *Variety,* 26 Feb 1947. AS, p. 1179. BHD2, p. 292.

Zalibra, George C. [cinematographer] (b. Pittsburgh PA, 9 Feb 1887–17 Apr 1963 [76], Los Angeles CA).

Zambuto, Gero [director/actor/voice-overs] (*né* Calogero Lucrezio Zambuto, b. Grotte, Italy, 14 Apr 1887–11 Jan 1944 [56], Bassano del Grappa, Italy). m. actress Claudia Gaffino. AS, p. 1179 (b. Agrigento, Italy; d. Bassanodel Grappa, Italy). JS, p. 503 (in Italian silents from 1913).

Zamecnik, John S. [composer/conductor] (b. Cleveland OH, 14 May 1872–13 Jun 1953 [81], Los Angeles CA). "John S. Zamecnik," *NYT,* 14 Jun 1953, 85:2. "John S. Zamecnik," *Variety,* 17 Jun 1953. AS, p. 1179. BHD2, p. 292.

Zamkovoj, Lev Semjonovich [director] (b. Russia, 1886). AS, p. 1179.

Zampi, Mario [child actor/director/producer] (b. Sora, Italy, 1 Nov 1903–1 Dec 1963 [60], London, England). AS, p. 1179. BHD, p. 344 (b. Rome, Italy; d. 2 Dec); BHD2, p. 292 (b. Rome, 1 Nov 1903-d. 2 Dec). JS, p. 503 (in Great Britain from 1923; made films in Italy in 1953 and 1960).

Zandonai, Riccardo [composer] (b. Sacco-Trentino, Italy, 30 May 1861–5 Jun 1944 [83], Pesaro, Italy [extrait de décès no. 160/1944]). AS, p. 1179.

Zane, Bartine *see* **Burkett, Bartine**

Zanft, John [producer] (b. 1883–19 Nov 1960 [77?], New York NY). BHD2, p. 292.

Zangarini, Carlo [director]. JS, p. 504 (in Italian silents from 1917).

Zangenberg, Elnar [actor/director] (b. Germany, 1883–1918 [35?], Germany). AS, p. 1180.

Zangrilli, Orestes [cinematographer] (b. Italy, 11 Apr 1881–17 Aug 1965 [84], Los Angeles Co. CA). BHD2, p. 292.

Zannini, Giovanni [director]. m. **Lina Pellegrini.** JS, p. 504 (in Italian silents from 1915).

Zanuccoli, Umberto [actor] (b. 1882). JS, p. 504 (in Italian silents from 1914).

Zanuck, Darryl F[rancis] (father of Richard Darryl Zanuck) [actor/scenarist/executive/producer] (b. Wahoo NB, 5 Sep 1902–22 Dec 1979 [77], Palm Springs CA; pulmonary embolism and pneumonia). m. **Virginia Fox**, 24 Jan 1924 (d. 1982; daughters Darrylin and Susan; son, Richard D., b. Beverly Hills CA, 13 Dec 1934). Marlys J. Harris, *The Zanucks of Hollywood; The Dark Legacy of an American Dynasty* (NY: Crown Publishers, Inc., 1989). (WB; TC-F.) Janet Maslin, "Darryl F. Zanuck, Flamboyant Film Producer, Dead," *NYT,* 24 Dec 1979, 12:1; "Zanuck Services Are Scheduled for Thursday on the West Coast," *NYT,* 25 Dec 1979, 30:4. "Darryl F. Zanuck Dies at 77; Master-Showman & Scripter; Maker of Hits and History," *Variety,* 26 Dec 1979. AMD, p. 375. AS, p. 1180. BHD2, p. 292. FDY, p. 439. IFN, p. 327. Katz, p. 1261 (began 1910). "Zanuck Quits Scenario Job," *MPW,* 5 Feb 1927, 424. "Warner Studio Rumor Excites West Coast," *MPW,* 22 Oct 1927, 475.

Zanuck, Virginia F *see* **Fox, Virginia**

Zanussi, Lucia [actress] (b. Florence, Italy). JS, p. 504 (in U.S.A. and Italian silents from 1922).

Zany, King [actor] (*né* Charles W. Dill, b. OH, 11 Jun 1889–19 Feb 1939 [49], Mojave CA). AS, p. 1180. BHD, p. 344. IFN, p. 327. Truitt, p. 361.

Zarkhi, Alexander Grigorievich [director/producer/scenarist] (b. St. Petersburg, Russia, 18 Feb 1908–27 Jan 1997 [88], Moscow, Russia). "Alexander Zarkhi," *Variety,* 24 Feb 1997, 225:3 (buried 3 Feb, Novoderichy Cemetery, Moscow). Harris Lentz, III, "Alexander Zarkhi," *CI,* 266 (Aug 1997), 57 (b. 12 Apr). AS, p. 1180. BHD2, p. 292 (b. 12 Feb).

Zarkhi, Natan A. [title writer/scenarist] (b. Orcha, Beylorussia, 1900–18 Jul 1935 [35?], Moscow, Russia; instantly killed in a car accident). "N.A. Zarkhy," *Variety,* 119, 14 Aug 1935, 55:1 ("Zarkhy's age was not given by the Soviet press, but he was very young despite his high place amongst Soviet writers."). AS, p. 1180. FDY, p. 447.

Zbyszko, Stanbislaus [actor] (b. Poland, 1879–22 Sep 1967 [88?], St. Joseph MO). AS, p. 1180.

Zears, Marjorie [actress: Sennett Bathing Beauty] (*née* Marjorie Page, b. 1911?–9 Mar 1952 [41], Los Angeles CA; murdered). AS, p. 1181. BHD, p. 344. IFN, p. 327. Truitt, p. 361.

Zecca, Ferdinand [actor/director/producer] (b. Paris, France, 1864–26 Mar 1947 [83], Paris, France). AMD, p. 375. AS, p. 1181. BHD, p. 344; BHD2, p. 292. IFN, p. 327. "Ferdinand Zecca an Old Timer," *MPW,* 6 Apr 1918, 99. "Zecca Visiting Pacific Coast," *MPW,* 13 Jul 1918, 215. "Zecca and Franconi Return," *MPW,* 10 Aug 1918, 849.

Zech, Harry Alvin [director] (b. Lancaster PA, 1884–11 Dec 1944 [60?], Los Angeles CA). BHD2, p. 292.

Zegel, Ferdinand [actor] (b. NJ, 1 Jan 1895–16 Jun 1973 [78], Los Angeles CA). AS, p. 1181. BHD, p. 344. IFN, p. 327.

Zegfield, William K. [producer] (b. 1873–6 Jun 1927 [54?], Baltimore MD). AS, p. 1181.

Zeidler, Leatrice Joy *see* **Joy, Leatrice**

Zeidman, Bennie E. [publicist/producer] (b. PA, 4 Oct 1895–7 Aug 1970 [74], Woodland Hills CA). (Eaco Films.) "Bennie E. Zeidman," *Variety,* 12 Aug 1970. AMD, p. 375. AS, p. 1181. BHD2, p. 292. F.J.R., "With the Film Men," *NYDM,* 16 Sep 1914, 24:1 (includes photo). "Zeidman Begins Work with F-P-L," *MPW,* 2 Jul 1927, 17. "Zeidman to Edit Dix Pictures," *MPW,* 27 Aug 1927, 590.

Zelaya, Don Alfonso [actor/pianist] (b. Nicaragua, 6 Mar 1893–14 Dec 1951 [58], Los Angeles CA; heart attack). AS, p. 1181.

Zeliabuzsky, J.A. [cinematographer]. No data found. FDY, p. 471.

Zelliff, Seymour "Skipper" [actor] (b. NJ, 16 May 1886–17 Jan 1953 [66], Los Angelkes CA). AS, p. 1181 (b. NY NY). BHD, p. 344. IFN, p. 327.

Zellman, Tollie [stage/film actress] (b. Stockholm, Sweden, 31 Aug 1887–9 Oct 1964 [77], Stockholm, Sweden). (Stage debut, 1906; film debut: *The Judgment of the Society,* 1911.) "Tollie Zellman," *Variety,* 236, 21 Oct 1964, 79:2. AS, p. 1181. BHD1, p. 601. IFN, p. 327.

Zellner, Arthur J. [publicist/press agent/title writer/scenarist] (b. Memphis TN, 2 Dec 1893–9 Sep 1952 [58], Burbank CA). "Arthur J. Zellner," *NYT,* 10 Sep 1952, 29:6. "Arthur Zellner," *Variety,* 17 Sep 1952 (title writer "in the days of silent movies"). AMD, p. 375. BHD2, p. 293. "Zellner Is Head American Scenarist," *MPW,* 12 Jul 1919, 200. "Arthur Zellner En Route to New York to Write New Script," *MPW,* 27 Mar 1920, 2164. "Arthur Zellner to Write All Continuities for Bert Lytell," *MPW,* 2 Oct 1920, 672. "Arthur Zellner, Metro Script Writer, Will Soon Join Coast Scenario Staff," *MPW,* 26 Feb 1921, 1085.

Zelnik, Friedrich [actor/director/producer] (*né* Friedrich Zelnick, b. Czernowitz, Austria, 17 May 1885–29 Nov 1950 [65], London, England). AMD, p. 375. AS, p. 1181. BHD2, p. 293. "Zelnick Directs 10 F.N. Films in Berlin Featuring Lya Mara," *MPW,* 11 Jun 1927, 397, 403.

Zelwerowicz, Alexander [actor/director/producer] (*né* Alexander Gustav Zelwekowicz, b. Lublin, Poland, 2 Aug 1877–18 Jun 1955 [77], Warsaw, Poland). AS, p. 1181.

Zengerling, Alf Aloys [producer] (b. Heyerode, Germany, 21 Jan 1884–13 May 1961 [77], Berlin, Germany). AS, p. 1181. BHD2, p. 293.

Zerlett, Hans H. [director/scenarist] (b. Wiesbaden, Germany, 1892–1962 [70?], Germany). AS, p. 1181.

Zeyn, Willy [director] (b. Wandsbeck, Germany, 30 Jun 1876). AS, p. 1182.

Zhang, Shichuan [director] (b. Ningbo, China, 1889–1953 [64?], China). AS, p. 1182.

Zheng, Zhengqiu [director] (b. Chaozhou, China, 1885–1935 [50?], Shanghai, China). AS, p. 1182.

Ziegfeld, Florenz, Jr. (brother of **William K. Ziegfeld**) [producer] (b. Chicago IL, 21 Mar 1869–22 Jul 1932 [63], Los Angeles CA). m. **Anna Held**, 1901, Paris, France (d. 1918); **Billie Burke**, 11 Apr 1914, Hoboken NJ (d. 1970). AMD, p. 375. AS, p. 1182. BHD, p. 344. "Burke—Ziegfeld; Marriage Takes Place in Hoboken Apr 11 After Saturday Matinee," *NYDM,* 15 Apr 1914, 19:1. "A New Gloria in the Field," *MPW,* 11 Nov 1916, 873. "Ziegfeld Signs to Produce a Series of Paramount Pictures," *MPW,* 27 Jun 1925, 950.

Ziegfeld, William K. (brother of **Florenz Ziegfeld, Jr.**) [producer] (b. 1873?–6 Jun 1927 [54], Baltimore MD; after operation). "William K. Ziegfeld," *Variety,* 8 Jun 1927. AMD, p. 375. BHD2, p. 293. "Ziegfeld Films Corporation Formed," *MPW,* 18 Sep 1915, 1975. "Ziegfeld Starts for El Paso," *MPW,* 18 Aug 1917 1076. "Bartholomae Pays Tribute to Ziegfeld for Using Stage Players in Pictures," *MPW,* 25 Dec 1920, 1075.

Ziegfield, Zenaïde (daughter of Hugo Ziegfield) [actress] (b. 1903–17 Jan 1929 [25?], New York NY; pneumonia). AS, p. 1182.

Ziegler, Dorothy Louise [actress]. No data found. AMD, p. 375. "Dorothy Louise Ziegler," *MPW,* 27 Feb 1915, 1310.

Ziegler, Henry [scenarist]. No data found. FDY, p. 439.

Zierler, Samuel [executive] (b. Brooklyn NY, 5 Mar 1895-Oct 1964 [69]). AMD, p. 375. BHD2, p. 293. "Zierler Upholds Best Traditions of Independents in New Pictures," *MPW,* 5 Nov 1927, 29.

Zilke, Edna E. [actress]. m. **George A. Sowards** (d. 1975). (Pathé.) "Real Wild West Wedding," *Variety,* 24 Apr 1914, 19:3 (Zilke [a "picture cowgirl"] and Soward [sic] "were wed in open air here.... The guests rode horses and wore clothes of the plains.").

Zilzer, Max [actor] (b. Budapest, Hungary, 23 Nov 1868). BHD, p. 344.

Zilzer, Wolfgang [stage/film/TV actor] (*né* Paul Andor, b. Cincinnati OH, 20 Jan 1901–26 Jun 1991 [90], Berlin, Germany). "Wolfgang Zilzer," *Variety,* 12 Aug 1991. AS, p. 1182. BHD, p. 92. Ragan 2, p. 1878. In German films from at least 1915 (*Der Barbier von Filmersdorf*) and in U.S. films.

Zimbalist, Sam S. [producer/editor] (b. New York NY, 31 Mar 1901–4 Nov 1958 [57], Rome, Italy; heart attack). m. (1) Margaret C. Donovan, 1924—div. 1950; (2) Mary Taylor, 1952. (Metro, 1920; MGM.) "Sam Zimbalist, 57, Film-Maker, Dead; M-G-M Producer Is Stricken on 'Ben Hur' Set in Rome—Made 'Solomon's Mines,'" *NYT,* 5 Nov 1958, 39:1 (worked as office boy for Richard Rowland, president of the old Metro Co.). "Zimbalist of 'Quo Vadis' Dies at 57 on Eve of Winding M-G-M 'Ben Hur,'" *Variety,* 212, 12 Nov 1958. AS, p. 1182. IFN, p. 327. JS, p. 506 (died during the filming of *Ben-Hur*).

Zimina, Valentina [actress] (b. Russia, 1899?–3 Dec 1928 [29], Los Angeles CA; influenza). m. Elwood E. Hopkins. "Valentina Zimina," *Variety,* 5 Dec 1928 (Mrs. Elwood E. Hopkins). AS, p. 1183. BHD, p. 344 (b. Bordeaux, France). IFN, p. 328. Truitt, p. 362.

Zimlick, Celeste [actress] (*née* Celestine Zimlick, b. ca. 1902). Appeared in *A Restaurant Riot* (Universal/Rainbow, 1920), and *A Villain's Broken Heart* (Universal/Rainbow, 1920).

Zimmer, Bernard [author/scenarist] (b. Grandpre, France, 30 Apr 1891 [extrait de naissance no. SN/1891]-2 Jul 1964 [73], Paris, France). AS, p. 1183.

Zimmerly, Arline [actress: Sennett? Bathing Beauty] (d. 7 Mar 1923, Venice CA; murdered). "Bathing Beauty Shot," *Variety,* 8 Mar 1923 (Zimmerly, "one of the film bathing beauties, was found shot through the head in her apartment at Venice…"). AS, p. 1183. BHD, p. 344.

Zimmerman, Annie [scenarist] (b. 1901–11 Mar 1927 [26?], Los Angeles CA). AS, p. 1183. BHD2, p. 293.

Zinnemann, Fred (father of director Tim Zinnemann) [director/producer] (b. Vienna, Austria, 29 Apr 1907–14 Mar 1997 [89], London, England). m. **Renee Bartlett**, 1936 (d. 1997; 1 son). (Began as an assistant cameraman in Paris, 1927; Universal; MGM; AA for short *That Mothers Might Live;* AA for *From Here to Eternity,* 1952.) *Fred Zinnemann; A Life in the Movies,* 1992. "Fred Zinnemann, Director of Many Classics, Dies at 89," *NYT,* 15 Mar 1997, 31. Richard Natale and Timothy M. Gray, "Fred Zinnemann," *Variety,* 17 Mar 1998, 68:1 (directed 20 films). "Fred Zinnemann; Oscar-winning director, explored moral integrity," *Pittsburgh Post-Gazette,* 15 Mar 1997, C-3:5 ("He began studying law at the University of Vienna, but when he was 18 he saw two silent films, Erich von Stroheim's 'Greed' and King Vidor's 'Big Parade,' and knew he must make movies. ¶He studied filmmaking in Paris and was an assistant cameraman for several silent movies in Berlin." To Hollywood in 1929.). AS, p. 1183. BHD1, p. 601; BHD2, p. 293.

Zins, Sidney [actor] (b. Brooklyn NY, 1908–26 Nov 1986 [78?], Washington DC; cerebral hemorrhage). AS, p. 1183 ("pionnier di cinéma"). BHD1, p. 601.

Zintheo, Lucille [actress]. No data found. AMD, p. 375. "Two Prize Winners on Selznick Program," *MPW,* 11 Nov 1916, 857.

Zirato, Bruno [actor] (b. Italy, 28 Sep 1884–28 Nov 1972 [88], New York NY). BHD, p. 344.

Zittau, Friedrich [actor] (*né* Morislav Cikan, b. Czechoslovakia, 1896–1962 [66?], Czechoslovakia). AS, p. 1183.

Zorelli, Jeanine (sister of Georgette Letourneur) [actress] (*née* Delphine Jeanne Lucie Letourneur, b. Maisons-Alfort, France, 29 Aug 1880–21 Jul 1975 [94], Clamart, France [extrait de décès no. 541/427/1975]). AS, p. 1183.

Zorzi, Guglielmo [director/writer] (b. Bologna, Italy, 31 Jan 1879). JS, pp. 507–08 (born into a family of counts; in Italian silents from 1914).

Zuber, Byrdine Annette [actress] (b. IL, 18 Nov 1886–5 Sep 1968 [81], Glendale CA). AMD, p. 375. AS, p. 1184 (d. LA CA). BHD, p. 344. IFN, p. 328. "Byrdine Annette Zuber," *MPW,* 21 Jul 1917, 450. "Capital Star in Chicago," *MPW,* 29 Jan 1921, 576.

Zucca, Giuseppe [director/scenarist] (b. Messina, Italy, 1 May 1887–2 Dec 1949 [62], Rome, Italy). AS, p. 1184.

Zuker (or Zukor), Frank [cinematographer]. No data found. FDY, p. 471 (Frank Zucker).

Zukor ["sugar" in Hungarian], **Adolph** (father of Eugene Zukor) [executive] (b. Ricse, Hungary, 7 Jan 1873–10 Jun 1976 [103], Century City, Los Angeles CA). m. Lottie Kaufman (son, Eugene, b. Chicago IL, 25 Oct 1897-d. 21 Dec 1994 [97], Beverly Hills CA). *The Public Is Never Wrong; The Autobiography of Adolph Zukor* (NY: G.P. Putnam's Sons, 1953). (Famous Players; FP-L; Paramount.) Albin Krebs, "Adolph Zukor Is Dead at 103; Built Paramount Movie Empire," *NYT,* 11 Jun 1976, 1:1, D18:1. "Zukor, Master-Builder of Film Biz, Dies at 103," *Variety,* 16 Jun 1976. AMD, p. 375. AS, p. 1184. BHD2, p. 293. IFN, p. 328. Spehr, p. 178. George Blaisdell, "Adolf Zukor Talks of Famous Players," *MPW,* 11 Jan 1913, 136. "Famous Players Contemplates Educationals," *MPW,* 5 Apr 1913, 55. "Mildred Zukor's [daughter] Birthday Film," *MPW,* 12 Apr 1913, 166. "Adolph Zukor Returns from Abroad," *MPW,* 25 Oct 1913, 364. "Change in Famous Players Offices," *MPW,* 6 Dec 1913, 1157. "Adolph Zukor Leaves for Los Angeles," *MPW,* 7 Mar 1914, 1247. "Adolph Zukor Returns from Los Angeles," *MPW,* 11 Apr 1914, 193. "Feature Producers Affiliate," *MPW,* 30 May 1914, 1268–69. W. Stephen Bush, "New Blood in New Programs," *MPW,* 6 Jun 1914, 1394. Adolph Zukor, "Famous Players in Famous Plays," *MPW,* 11 Jul 1914, 186. "Famous Players Anniversary," *MPW,* 5 Sep 1914, 1384. Adolph Zukor, "American Features Supreme," *NYDM,* 27 Jan 1915, 40:1, 66:1. "First Move for Higher Prices," *MPW,* 13 Feb 1915, 966. "Anniversary for F.P.; Famous Players Organization Celebrates Third Birthday—A Review of Its Career," *NYDM,* 14 Apr 1915, 24:2 (formed FP-L on 12 Apr 1912 with Daniel Frohman and Edwin Porter). "Another Quality Triumph," *MPW,* 24 Apr 1915, 536. "Famous Players' President Speaks," *MPW,* 14 Aug 1915, 1166. "Fire Sweeps F.P. Studio [at W. 26th St., NYC on 11 Sep]; Loss Heavy in Blaze That Detroyds New York Plant—Officials Already Planning for Reorganization," *NYDM,* 15 Sep 1915, 25:2 (negatives destroyed: *The Twisting Road* [Mary Pickford]; *The Mummy and the Humming Bird* [Charles Cherry], *Zaza* [Pauline Frederick]; *Bella Donna* [Pauline Frederick]; and *The White Pearl* [Marie Doro]. Universal, Biograph, and Kessel and Baumann offered their studios. "The total insurance on studio is said to have been $50,000, as fire rates on film factories are excessively high." "Famous Players Quickly Recover from Disaster; Many Valuable Productions Found to Be Safe—Changes in Release Schedule Are Few," *NYDM,* 22 Sep 1915, 26:1 (negatives saved in the laboratory safe included *Zaza, The Prince and the Pauper* [Mary Pickford], *A Girl of Yesterday,* and 2/3 of *The White Pearl.* "The saving of the Mary Pickford subject which has recently been completed by Sidney Alcott, is a stroke of unusual fortune as the production is known to have cost over $75,000. Several hundreds of characters appear in many of the scenes." *The White Pearl,* scheduled to be released on 20 Sep, was moved back to 11 Oct; release of Charles Cherry in *The Mummy and the Hummingbird* was indefinitely postponed.). "Mr. Zukor Hospital Fund Treasurer," *MPW,* 25 Sep 1915, 2186. "Feature Films of the Week," *NYDM,* 23 Oct 1915, 28:4 (*The White Pearl* released 10 Oct). "Resume Work on 'Bella Donna,'" *NYDM,* 6 Nov 1915, 24:1. "'Bella Donna' Completed," *NYDM,* 13 Nov 1915, 25:4 (to be released by Paramount on 15 Nov). "Zukor Raps Sex Plays," *MPW,* 8 Jan 1916, 233. "Big Film Merger Underway," *MPW,* 13 May 1916, 1139. "Adolph Zukor Quit Furs for Films," *MPW,* 15 Jul 1916, 415. "Attacks the Open Booking System," *MPW,* 12 Aug 1916, 1088. "Another Combination of Picture Companies," *MPW,* 21 Oct 1916, 376. "Famous Players-Lasky Takes Over Paramount," *MPW,* 23 Dec 1916, 1778. "Famous Players Subsidiary Disbands," *MPW,* 3 Feb 1917, 672. "Films Cannot Stand Tax, Is Testimony," *MPW,* 10 Feb 1917, 823–24. Adolph Zukor, "Days of Worry Those of a Decade Ago," *MPW,* 10 Mar 1917, 1503–04. "A Million for General Advertising," *MPW,* 13 Oct 1917, 217. "Adolph Zukor Takes a Vacation," *MPW,* 24 Nov 1917, 1179. "The Grand of Pittsburgh Opened," *MPW,* 23 Mar 1918, 1635. "Zukor GIves Plan for Liberty Loan Drive," *MPW,* 6 Apr 1918, 59–61. "Adolph Zukor Moving Picture Day," *MPW,* 4 May 1918, 671. Adolph Zukor, "A Year's Budget," *MPW,* 6 Jul 1918, 52–53. "Sailors Send Thanks to Adolph Zukor," *MPW,* 20 Jul 1918, 379. "Zukor Will Aid Department of Labor," *MPW,* 24 Aug 1918, 1114. "Stars Come Through for Fourth Loan," *MPW,* 31 Aug 1918, 1231–32. "Fifty Stars Contribute to Loan," *MPW,* 7 Sep 1918, 1407. "One Billion for the Fourth Loan," *MPW,* 12 Oct 1918, 201–02. "Zukor Day Yields Over Half Million for Loan," *MPW,* 2 Nov 1918, 577. "Zukor Examines Chicago Conditions," *MPW,* 4 Jan 1919, 69. "Zukor at Coast Reports Conditions Are Improving," *MPW,* 1 Feb 1919, 630. "Zukor Says Star Series Plan Is Easy to Attack, Hard to Defend," *MPW,* 28 Jun 1919, 1918. "Mary Minter and Zukor Join Forces," *MPW,* 19 Jul 1919, 368. "'I Formed Realart to Make Every Picture with a Soul,' Says Zukor," *MPW,* 13 Dec 1919, 777. "Zukor Invites Theatre Managers to Hook Up with Famous Players-Lasky," *MPW,* 10 Jan 1920, 241. "Zukor—Loew," *MPW,* 17 Jan 1920, 400 (daughter Mildred Harriet m. Arthur Marcus Loew, 6 Jan 1920). "Famous Players-Lasky's Attitude Made Clear Through Adolph Zukor," *MPW,* 24 Jan 1920, 554. "Mildred Zukor Weds Arthur Loew Uniting Two Prominent Film Families," *MPW,* 24 Jan 1920, 578 (includes guest list). "Paramount-Artcraft Films to Aid Trade's Fight Against Censorship," *MPW,* 21 Feb 1920, 1206. Adolph Zukor, "2,200 Houses Now Playing Percentage, Declares Zukor, Just Before Sailing," *MPW,* 13 Mar 1920, 1762–62. "Adolph Zukor's Son Weds Kansas City School Teacher," *MPW,* 15 May 1920, 939 (Eugene J. Zukor m. Emma Dorothy Rush, 6 May 1920). Adolph Zukor, "Action of Exhibitors Themselves Forced Famous Players to Acquire Theatre Chain," *MPW,* 19 Jun 1920, 1568. Adolph Zukor, "Zukor in Formal Statement Declares He Will Take Up All Grievances of Exhibitors; Guarantees Full Justice," *MPW,* 31 Jul 1920, 565. "Famous Players and Theatre Owners Sign Agreement Which It Is Believed Marks Ending of Bitter Controversy," *MPW,* 21 Aug 1920, 987. "Letter from Theatre Owners to Mr. Zukor," *MPW,* 21 Aug 1920, 987. "Spirit of Equity and Conciliation Characterizes Discussions Between Cohen Committee and Zukor," *MPW,* 28 Aug 1920, 1141–42. "Big Features Will Soon Run Full Year on Broadway, Predicts Adolph Zukor," *MPW,* 4 Dec 1920, 574. Adolph Zukor, "Zukor, of Paramount, Says Future WIll Bring Year Long Moving Picture Ruins," *MPW,* 25 Dec 1920, 1008. "Adolph Zukor Is Re-elected Chairman of Producers' Division of N.A.M.P.I.," *MPW,* 4 Jun 1921, 502. "Zukor Proclaims His Principles, Promising to Correct All Evils," *MPW,* 2 Jul 1921, 26–27. "Acolph Zukor's Public Pledge," *MPW,* 2 Jul 1921, 29. "Sub-Committee and Zukor Confer Regarding Hartford-Black Controversy," *MPW,* 3

Sep 1921, 41–42. Adolph Zukor, "Producing and Exhibiting Overhead Must Be Reduced," *MPW,* 31 Dec 1921, 1051. "Zukor Favors Economy in Production Without Lessening Pictures' Quality," *MPW,* 4 Mar 1922, 43. "'World's' Policy Always Vigorous and Just—Zukor," *MPW,* 11 Mar 1922, 140. "Spanuth Denies Zukor Produced First Feature," *MPW,* 1 Apr 1922, 461. "Zukor to Deliver Addres by Radio," *MPW,* 8 Apr 1922, 615 (WJZ, Newark NJ). "Zukor's 'Quiet Day' Ends with a Fire as Hotel Is Threatened," *MPW,* 6 May 1922, 42. Adolph Zukor, "A New Milestone in the Progress of the Motion Picture Business," *MPW,* 20 May 1922, 269. "Zukor Scents Rival's Plot in Lasky Rumors," *MPW,* 21 Oct 1922, 657. "Executives Honor Zukor," *MPW,* 20 Jan 1923, 224. "Zukor Plans Big Conference to Consider Screen's Artistic Advance," *MPW,* 24 Feb 1923, 761. "Author's League to Assist Zukor in Holding World Congress on Picture Arts," *MPW,* 5 May 1923, 31. Robert E. Welsh, "An Open Letter—to Adolph Zukor," *MPW,* 23 Jun 1923, 634. Adolph Zukor, "A Development of the Needs of Today," *MPW,* 8 Sep 1923, 132. "Adolph Zukor Curtails Production; Cochrane and Rowland Prasie Move," *MPW,* 10 Nov 1923, 215. "Congratulates Laemmle," *MPW,* 26 Jan 1924, 290. John W. Vandercook, "The Man Who Stands Behind the Stars," *MW,* 6 Sep 1924, 10–11, 27–28. "Testimonial to Zukor," *MPW,* 22 Nov 1924, 304. "Adolph Zukor's $10,000 Prize Award Goes to Rafael Sabatini," *MPW,* 3 Jan 1925, 30. "New Faces Needed in Films, Zukor Tells Radio Audience," *MPW,* 24 Jan 1925, 324 (WOR Radio, 14 Jan 1925). "'Malicious Falsehood,' Comments Zukor on Lasky Rumor," *MPW,* 7 Nov 1925, 27. "Zukor Disclaims Intention of Hampering Film Progress," *MPW,* 14 Nov 1925, 114. "They Control Your Films!," *MPC,* Jan 1926, 26. Covarrubias, "Distinguished Picture People," *MPW,* 30 Jan 1926, 412. Sara Redway, "The Man with the Worst Job in the World; Besides All His Other Worries, Adolph Zukor Has to Deal with Temperamental Stars," *MPC,* Feb 1926, 27, 84. Gordon L. Edwards, "Adolph Zukor; The Amazing Career of a Master-Builder of the Motion Picture Industry," *Cinema Arts,* Sep 1926, 15–16, 48. "Famous to Change Name Because of Advertising," *MPW,* 19 Mar 1927, 162 (Paramount Famous Lasky Corp.). "Adolph Zukor Says:," *MPW,* 26 Mar 1927, 326. "Mr. and Mrs. Zukor Sail for Vacation," *MPW,* 2 Apr 1927, 463. "Berlin Cable," *MPW,* 7 May 1927, 11. "Mystery Pervades Zukor's Meetings with Big Germans," *MPW,* 14 May 1927, 87. Eleanore Wilson, "The Boy [Lindbergh] Who Said NO to Zukor," *MPC,* Sep 1927, 26, 83. "Employees Give Zukor an Ovation," *MPW,* 22 Oct 1927, 485. "Rumors All Wet," *MPW,* 3 Dec 1927, 7. Herbert G. Luft, "Remembering Adolph Zukor," *FIR,* Dec 1976, 595–98.

Zuro, Josiah. No data found.

Zweig, Stefan [scenarist] (b. 1881–23 Feb 1942 [60?], Petropolis, Brazil). BHD2, p. 293.

Zworykin, Vladimir Kosma [inventor] (b. Moturom, Russia, 30 Jul 1889–29 Jul 1982 [92], Princeton NJ). AS, p. 1185.